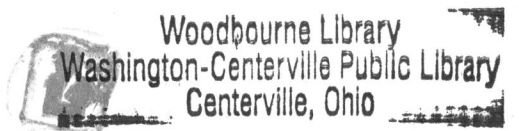

STAY UP-TO-DATE:
FREE 30-DAY TEST DRIVE!

Get Instant Updates, Free Research Requests,
Postage Refunds, Insider Information & More
FREE For 30 Days Using This Activation Link:

http://contactanycelebrity.com/join

You'll get INSTANT ACCESS to the Best Mailing Address,
Agent, Manager, Publicist, Production Company & Charitable Cause
For Over 67,000 Celebrities & Public Figures Worldwide!

You'll Get INSTANT ACCESS To All This & More:

Easy-To-Use, Fully-Searchable Online Database
67,000+ Celebrities & Public Figures Worldwide
Agent, Manager & Publicist Information
Celebrity Causes Database
Daily Real-Time Updates
Free Research Requests
Postage Refund Guarantee
Insider Interviews
Live Customer Service
Plus Much More!

Activate Your FREE 30-Day Test Drive:

http://contactanycelebrity.com.join

Look What People Are Saying:

"The range is amazing – this thing is HUGE!"
- CNN

"The solution to getting your products in celebrities' hands."
- Entrepreneur Magazine

"Recommended for all libraries."
- Library Journal

"The best resource and a great deal."
- Peter Shankman, HARO (Help A Reporter)

"This online directory and its helpful staff will
help you find any celebrity in the world."
- Timothy Ferriss, 'The 4-Hour Workweek'

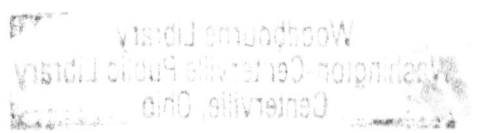

The Celebrity Black Book 2013: Over 67,000 Celebrity Addresses.

Mega Niche Media LLC
8721 Santa Monica Blvd. #431
West Hollywood, CA 90069-4507
310-388-6084 (Phone/Fax)
info@meganiche.com

Printed and bound in the United States of America.

Although the editor and publisher have made every effort to ensure the accuracy and completeness of the information contained in this book, we assume no responsibility for errors, inaccuracies, omissions or any inconsistency herein. Any slight of people, places or organizations is unintentional.

We can assume no responsibility for addresses that become outdated and cannot guarantee that a celebrity will personally or otherwise respond to his or her mail.

Please visit http://ContactAnyCelebrity.com for updates and new addresses.

ISBN: 978-1-60487-015-2

Edited by Contact Any Celebrity – http://ContactAnyCelebrity.com
Interior Layout by Data Management, Inc. – http://dbman.com

STAY UP-TO-DATE:
FREE 30-DAY TEST DRIVE!

Get Instant Updates, Free Research Requests,
Postage Refunds, Insider Information & More
FREE For 30 Days Using This Activation Link:

http://contactanycelebrity.com/join

You'll get INSTANT ACCESS to the Best Mailing Address,
Agent, Manager, Publicist, Production Company & Charitable Cause
For Over 67,000 Celebrities & Public Figures Worldwide!

BUZZ FOR THE CELEBRITY BLACK BOOK...

"The range is amazing – this thing is huge!"
- **CNN**

"I can do so much with this!"
- **Perez Hilton**

"This book is the solution to getting your products or services in celebrities' hands."
- **Entrepreneur Magazine**

"Of all the resources for celebrity addresses, this book is far and away the most useful."
- **Autograph Magazine**

"Similar titles do not boast as many entries. Recommended for all libraries."
- **Library Journal**

"A superb, quick and easy-to-use reference for professionals and fans alike."
- **Midwest Book Review**

"Priceless information that would otherwise take hours to research."
- **Curled Up with a Good Book**

"The time saved rather than Googling and cold-calling will pay for this book in the long run."
- **Absolute Write**

"Some of the best money you'll ever spend. Provides great publicity opportunities."
- **Paul Hartunian, Free Publicity Information Center**

"The most helpful book I have ever owned – worth every penny."
- **Jill Jackson, Syndicated Columnist, Jill Jackson's Hollywood**

"If you opt to pursue celebrities on your own, this is the place to get contact information."
- **Dan Kennedy, No B.S. Guide to Marketing to the Affluent**

STAY UP-TO-DATE:
FREE 30-DAY TEST DRIVE!

Get Instant Updates, Free Research Requests,
Postage Refunds, Insider Information & More
FREE For 30 Days Using This Activation Link:

http://contactanycelebrity.com/join

You'll get INSTANT ACCESS to the Best Mailing Address,
Agent, Manager, Publicist, Production Company & Charitable Cause
For Over 67,000 Celebrities & Public Figures Worldwide!

ABOUT THE EDITOR

Known as the 'King of Celebrity Contacts,' Jordan McAuley's http://ContactAnyCelebrity.com service helps charities and nonprofits; authors and writers; journalists and the media; and entrepreneurs and small businesses get in touch with celebrities worldwide for promotional and publicity use.

McAuley has been featured by the Associated Press, CNN, USA Today, Investor's Business Daily, Publisher's Weekly, Miami Herald, Village Voice, Writer's Digest, New York Daily News, Fox News, Star Magazine, Sirius/XM Satellite Radio, National Public Radio and more.

Jordan got his start as an intern in the publicity departments of CNN and Turner Entertainment in Atlanta. He also worked at a prominent modeling agency in South Beach, Miami; a film production company in Hollywood, California and a top talent agency in Beverly Hills.

He is featured in several best-selling books including Timothy Ferris' 'The 4-Hour Workweek,' Dan Kennedy's 'Marketing to the Affluent,' Dan Poynter's 'Book Publishing Encyclopedia,' John Kremer's '1001 Ways to Market Your Books' and Robin Blakely's 'PR Therapy.'

McAuley is also the author of 'Secrets to Contacting Celebrities: 101 Ways to Reach the Rich and Famous' 'Celebrity Leverage: Insider Secrets to Getting Celebrity Endorsements, Instant Credibility & Star-Powered Publicity' and 'The Lost Secrets of Fame & Fortune.'

Jordan is a member of the Public Relations Society of America, Association of Fundraising Professionals, GLAAD Media Circle, Independent Book Publishers Association, Information Marketing Association, Society of Professional Journalists and MediaBistro.

Follow him on Facebook and Twitter at:

http://twitter.com/ContactCelebs
http://facebook.com/ContactAnyCelebrity

Interested in getting your book, product or service in the hands of celebrities?

Visit Jordan McAuley's http://CelebrityPR.com

STAY UP-TO-DATE:
FREE 30-DAY TEST DRIVE!

Get Instant Updates, Free Research Requests,
Postage Refunds, Insider Information & More
FREE For 30 Days Using This Activation Link:

http://contactanycelebrity.com/join

You'll get INSTANT ACCESS to the Best Mailing Address,
Agent, Manager, Publicist, Production Company & Charitable Cause
For Over 67,000 Celebrities & Public Figures Worldwide

INTRODUCTION

Welcome to The Celebrity Black Book 2013!

Whether you're a fan, charity, nonprofit, entrepreneur, marketer, author, writer, journalist, publicist, or event planner, you're bound to find this book useful. Inside you'll discover the best mailing addresses for over 67,000 celebrities and public figures worldwide.

Everyone who is anyone is included: actors, musicians, politicians, world leaders, authors, artists, television hosts, even reality TV stars! The list goes on and on as you'll see once you start browsing the following pages.

The Celebrity Black Book is a staple for fans who want to request autographs, nonprofits who want to hold an autograph auction to raise money for their cause, businesses who want to get their products and services into celebrities' hands, authors who want to get celebrity endorsements for their books, and the media who want to get quotes and interviews.

There are so many uses, the possibilities are endless!

Of course, with over 67,000 celebrities who move and change representation on a daily basis, this book cannot possibly be 100% accurate. That's why you also get a FREE 30-Day Test Drive to our membership Web site and online database, http://ContactAnyCelebrity.com for updates!

Activate your FREE 30 Day Test Drive here: http://contactanycelebrity.com/join

You may be wondering how to write a fan letter, request an autograph, or get your product or service in the hands of celebrities. To find out, check out our other books:

- Secrets to Contacting Celebrities: 101 Ways to Reach the Rich & Famous
- Celebrity Leverage: Insider Secrets to Getting Celebrity Endorsements, Instant Credibility & Star-Powered Publicity
- The Lost Secrets of Fame & Fortune: How to Get – and Keep – Everything You Desire!

Enjoy your new Celebrity Black Book 2013, and let me know your success stories!

Reach for the stars,

Jordan McAuley, Founder
Contact Any Celebrity
8721 Santa Monica Blvd. #431
West Hollywood, CA 90069-4507
310-691-5466 (Phone)
jordan@contactanycelebrity.com
http://ContactAnyCelebrity.com

SEND A FREE CARD!

Tired of driving to the post office, waiting in lines, buying stamps, and handwriting cards to send to your favorite celebrities?

Well, you don't have to anymore!

Go to http://VIPcards.com and click on Send a Card to design a free card that will be printed and mailed in a real envelope with a real stamp the next business day!

Now you can quickly and easily send real cards from your computer to friends, family members, loved ones and celebrities!

If you decide to join Send Out Cards at http://VIPcards.com you'll be able to add advanced features like full-color photos, your own personalized handwriting font, and more!

You can also earn money as a Send Out Cards distributor. Visit the link above to watch a video and listen to an opportunity call.

Another option is to print postage from your computer with http://Stamps.com.

Enter promo code **C-48K4-W3W** when you sign up, and get a $100 offer that includes a digital scale and $45 in postage!

You'll be able to print U.S. and International stamps, plus exact postage so no more wasted stamps. And you'll never run out!

STAY UP-TO-DATE:
FREE 30-DAY TEST DRIVE!

Get Instant Updates, Free Research Requests,
Postage Refunds, Insider Information & More
FREE For 30 Days Using This Activation Link:

http://contactanycelebrity.com/join

You'll get INSTANT ACCESS to the Best Mailing Address,
Agent, Manager, Publicist, Production Company & Charitable Cause
For Over 67,000 Celebrities & Public Figures Worldwide

112 (Musician)
c/o Staff Member *Richard De La Font Agency*
3808 W South Park Blvd
Broken Arrow, OK 74011, USA

2 Chainz (Musician)
c/o Staff Member *Island Def Jam Group*
Worldwide Plaza
825 8th Ave Fl 28
New York, NY 10019, USA

311 (Music Group)
c/o Peter Raspler *Raspler Management*
946 N. Croft Ave
West Hollywood, CA 90069, USA

3 (Three) Doors Down (Music Group)
c/o Kim Estlund *Baker Winokur Ryder Public Relations (BWR-LA)*
9100 Wilshire Blvd
Suite 500, West Tower
Beverly Hills, CA 90212, USA

50 Cent (Actor, Musician)
c/o Keesha Johnson *Dan Klores Communications (NY)*
386 Park Ave S
10th Floor
New York, NY 10016, USA

A

A3 (Music Group)
c/o Staff Member *Paradigm (Monterey)*
404 W Franklin St
Monterey, CA 93940, USA

Aaker, Lee (Actor)
PO Box 3551
Big Bear Lake, CA 92315, USA

Aames, Willie (Actor)
c/o Staff Member *Jeff Ballard PR*
4814 N Lemona Ave
Sherman Oaks, CA 91403, USA

Aardsma, David (Athlete, Baseball Player)
6009 E TurQuoise Ave
Paradise Valley, AZ 85253-1234, USA

Aaron, Caroline (Actor)
Mindel/Donigan
9057-C Nemo St
W Hollywood, CA 90069, USA

Aaron, Hank (Athlete, Baseball Player)
Atlanta Braves
PO Box 4064
Attn: Sr Vice President
Atlanta, GA 30302-4064, USA

Aaron, Paul (Director)
c/o Staff Member *Elsboy Entertainment*
1581 N Crescent Heights Blvd
Los Angeles, CA 90046, USA

Aaron, Quinton (Actor)
Suzelle Enterprises
853 7th Ave #8D
New York, NY 10019, USA

Aaron, Tommy (Athlete, Golfer)
440 E Lake Dr
Gainesville, GA 30504, USA

Aase, Don (Athlete, Baseball Player)
5055 Via Ricardo
Yorba Linda, CA 92886-4526, USA

Abad, Andy (Athlete, Baseball Player)
1092 Chickasaw St
Jupiter, FL 33458-5610, USA

Abagnale, Frank (Business Person)
Abagnale & Associates
PO Box 701290
Tulsa, OK 74170, USA

Abair, Mindi (Musician)
c/o Bud Harner *Chapman Management*
14011 Ventura Blvd
Sherman Oaks 91423, USA

Abatantuono, Diego (Actor)
c/o Staff Member *Moviement*
Via P Cavallini 24
Rome 00193, ITALY

Abbado, Claudio (Conductor, Musician)
c/o Staff Member *Askonas Holt Ltd*
Lincoln House
300 High Holborn
London WC1V 7JH, UK

Abbatiello, Carmine (Horse Racer)
7 Whirlaway Rd
Manalapan, NJ 07726-9566, USA

Abbatiello, Tony (Horse Racer)
176 Stone Hill Rd
Colts Neck, NJ 07722-1730, USA

Abbe, Elfriede M (Artist)
Applewood
Manchester Center, VT 05255

Abbett, Robert (Artist)
P.O. Box 126
Bridgewater, CT 06752, USA

Abbey, Joe (Athlete, Football Player)
1814 S Bonnie Brae St
Denton, TX 76207, USA

Abbington, Amanda (Actor)
c/o Staff Member *Lip Service Casting Ltd*
60-66 Wardour St
London W1F 0TA, UK

Abbott, Christie (Actor)
c/o Marie Mathews *Marie Mathews Management*
8730 Sunset Blvd #200
Los Angeles, CA 90069, USA

Abbott, Diahnne (Actor)
460 W Ave 46
Los Angeles, CA 90065

Abbott, D Thomas (Business Person)
Salvin Corp
333 Ludlow St
Stamford, CT 06902, USA

Abbott, Glenn (Athlete, Baseball Player)
4413 Dawson Dr
North Little Rock, AR 72116-7037, USA

Abbott, Gregory (Musician)
Box 68
Bergenfield, NY 07621-0068, USA

Abbott, Jeff (Athlete, Baseball Player)
1095 Stonegate Dr
Roswell, GA 30075-2265, USA

Abbott, Jim (Athlete, Baseball Player, Olympic Athlete)
3449 Quiet Cv
Corona del Mar, CA 92625-1637, USA

Abbott, Josh (Musician)
c/o Joey Lee *WmE2 (WMA-TN)*
1600 Division St
Suite 300
Nashville, TN 37203, USA

Abbott, Kurt (Athlete, Baseball Player)
1704 NW Soruce Ridge Dr
Stuart, FL 34994-9528, USA

Abbott, Kyle (Athlete, Baseball Player)
332 Springfield Bnd
Argyle, TX 76226-6848, USA

Abbott, Matthew (Scientist)
2202 Gemini St Unit 1
Houston, TX 77058-2049, USA

Abbott, Norman (Director)
1520 San Ysidro Dr
Beverly Hills, CA 90210, USA

Abbott, Paul (Athlete, Baseball Player)
1809 Yermo Pl
Fullerton, CA 92833-1866, USA

Abbott, Preston S (Doctor)
1305 Namassin Rd
Alexandria, VA 22308

Abbott, Reg (Athlete, Hockey Player)
203-738 Sayward Hill Terr
Victoria, BC V8Y 3K1, CANADA

Abboud, A Robert (Business Person)
A Robert Abboud Co
960 Route 22
#212
Fox River Grove, IL 60021, USA

Abboud, Joseph M (Designer, Fashion Designer)
650 5th Ave #2700
New York, NY 10019, USA

Abdelkader, Justin (Athlete, Hockey Player)
1080 Edinborough Dr
Norton Shores, MI 49441-5371

Abdoo, Rose (Actor)
c/o Judy Orbach *Judy O Productions*
6136 Glen Holly
Hollywood, CA 90068, USA

Abdrashitov, Vadim Y (Director)
3D Frunzenskaya 8 #211
Moscow 119270, RUSSIA

Abdul, Paula (Actor, Musician, Reality TV Star)
c/o Michael Gagliardo *PMK/BNC Public Relations (PMK-NY)*
622 3rd Ave
8th Floor
New York, NY 10017, USA

Abdul-Aziz, Zaid (Athlete, Basketball Player)
Sunlight Inc
P.O. Box 75184
Seattle, WA 98175-0184, USA

Abdul-Jabbar, Kareem (Athlete, Basketball Player, Coach)
c/o Staff Member *Kareem Productions*
20434 S. Santa Fe Ave
Suite 194
Long Beach, CA 90810, USA

Abdul-Jabbar, Karim (Athlete, Football Player)
c/o Staff Member *Kareem Productions*
20434 S. Santa Fe Ave
Suite 194
Long Beach, CA 90810, USA

Abdullah, Khalid (Athlete, Football Player)
7634 Wexford Club Dr E
Jacksonville, FL 32256, USA

Abdullah, Rabih (Athlete, Football Player)
12810 Wallingford Dr
Tampa, FL 33624, USA

Abdullah, Rahim (Athlete, Football Player)
7634 Wexford Club Dr E
Jacksonville, FL 32256, USA

Abdulov, Aleksandr G (Actor)
Peschanaya Str 4 #3
Moscow 125252, RUSSIA

Abdul-Saboor, Mikal (Athlete, Football Player)
5465 Derby Chase Ct
Alpharetta, GA 30005, USA

Abdur-Rahim, Shareef (Athlete, Basketball Player)
c/o Staff Member *Atlanta Hawks*
1 CNN Center NW
Suite 405
Atlanta, GA 30303, USA

Abdus-Salaam, Sultan (Athlete, Football Player)
12715 Joust St
North Las Vegas, NV 89030, USA

Abeal, Marcelo "Bonny" (Actor)
Arenales 2756 1°
Apt B
Buenos Aires 1425, Argentina

Abed, Rodrigo (Actor)
c/o Gabriel Blanco *Gabriel Blanco Iglesias (Mexico)*
Rio Balsas 35-32
Colonia Cuauhtemoc
DF 06500, Mexico

Abel (DJ)
c/o Len Evans *Project Publicity*
312 West 53rd St
Suite 202
New York, NY 10019, USA

Abel, Gerry (Athlete, Hockey Player)
23570 Samoset Trl
Southfield, MI 48033-2820, USA

Abel, Jake (Actor)
c/o Cynthia Campos-Greenberg *Anthem Entertainment*
9595 Wilshire Blvd
Suite 900
Los Angeles, CA 90212-2509, USA

Abel, Jessica (Artist)
c/o Staff Member *Fantagraphics Books*
7563 Lake City Way
Seattle, WA 98115, USA

Abel, Joy (Bowler)
2440 187th St
Lansing, IL 60438-4102, USA

Abele, John (Misc)
PO Box 305
Shelburne, VT 05482-0305, USA

Abell, Bud (Athlete, Football Player)
919 E 25th Plz
Panama City, FL 32405, USA

Abell, Tim (Actor)
c/o Staff Member *Gold Levin Talent*
8424-A Santa Monica Blvd
Suite 706
Los Angeles, CA 90069, USA

Abelson, John (Biologist, Scientist)
112 Laidley St
San Francisco, CA 94131-2735, USA

Abelson, Robert P (Doctor)
1155 Whitney Ave
Hamden, CT 06517

Abendschan, Jack (Athlete, Football Player)
25 Wynrush Cir
Abilene, TX 79606-4363, USA

Abercrombie, John L (Musician)
Joel Chriss
300 Mercer St #3J
New York, NY 10003, USA

Abercrombie, Neil (Government Official)
1050 Ala Moana Blvd Ste D28
Honolulu, HI 96814, HAWAII

Abercrombie, Neil (Governor)
Governor, State of Hawaii
Executive Chambers, "State Capitol"
Honolulu, HI 96813, USA

Abercrombie, Neil (Congressman, Politician)
Prince Kuhio Federal Building
300 Ala Moana Blvd., Room 4-104
Honolulu, HI 96850, USA

Abercrombie, Reggie (Athlete, Baseball Player)
5920 Buxton Dr
Columbus, GA 31907-3635, USA

Abercrombie, Walter (Athlete, Coach, Football Coach, Football Player)
217 Westlane Cir
Woodway, TX 76712, USA

Abernathy, Brent (Athlete, Baseball Player, Olympic Athlete)
1787 Bridgeport Colony Ln
Fort Walton Beach, FL 32547-5711, USA

Abernathy, Frederick H (Engineer)
43 Islington Rd
Newton, MA 02166, USA

Abernathy, Robert (Athlete, Baseball Player)
2491 Walker Ln
Nashville, TN 37207, USA

Abernethy, Tom (Athlete, Basketball Player)
5268 Woodfield Dr N
Carmel, IN 46033-8794, USA

Abert, Donald B (Publisher)
Milwaukee Journal
333 W State St
Milwaukee, WI 53203

Abgrall, Dennis (Athlete, Hockey Player)
16607 S 12th Pl
Phoenix, AZ 85048-4703, USA

Abigail (Musician)
c/o Staff Member *Diva Central Inc*
7510 W Sunset Blvd Ste 1445
Los Angees, CA 90046, USA

Abiodun, Oyewole (Musician)
c/o Staff Member *Agency Group Ltd, The (UK)*
361-373 City Rd
London EC1V 1PQ, UK

Abir, Lili (Stylist)
Art Department
48 Greene St
4th Floor
New York, NY 10011, USA

Abizaid, John P (General)
Commander
US Central Command
MacDill Air Force Base, FL 33621, USA

Able, Forest (Athlete, Basketball Player)
11102 Mitchell Hill Rd
Fairdale, KY 40118-9425, USA

Able, Whitney (Actor)
c/o Lisa Gallant *Gallant Management*
1112 Montana Ave #454
Santa Monica, CA 90403, USA

Ableson, Andrew (Actor)
c/o Stephanie Blume *Imperium 7 Talent Agency*
5455 Wilshire Blvd
Suite 1706
Los Angeles, CA 90036, USA

Ablon, Ralph E (Business Person)
Ogden Corp
PO Box 2615
Fairfield, NJ 07004, USA

Ablow, Keith (Doctor)
c/o Greg Lipstone *WmE2 (WMA-LA)*
1 William Morris Pl
Beverly Hills, CA 90212, USA

Abner, Shawn (Athlete, Baseball Player)
1443 Olde Oak Ct
Mechanicsburg, PA 17050, USA

Abney Culberson, John (Congressman, Politician)
2352 Rayburn HOB
Washington, DC 20515, USA

Aboitiz, Gemina (Stylist)
c/o Staff Member *Cloutier Agency*
2632 La Cienega Ave
Los Angeles, CA 90034, USA

Aboulhosn, Hassan (Athlete, Football Player)
2703 Oaklawn Blvd
Hopewell, VA 23860, USA

Abourezk, James G (Politician)
1509 E Cedar Ln
Sioux Falls, SD 57103-4516, USA

Abragam, Anatole (Scientist)
33 Rue Croulebarbe
Paris 75013, FRANCE

Abraham, Clifton (Athlete, Football Player)
1413 Dutchman Creek Dr
Desoto, TX 75115, USA

Abraham, Donnie (Athlete, Football Player)
3038 Wentworth Way
Tarpon Springs, FL 34688, USA

Abraham, F Murray (Actor)
c/o Staff Member *Paradigm (LA)*
360 N Crescent Dr
North Bldg
Beverly Hills, CA 90210, USA

Abraham, John (Actor)
A1 418 Lower Parel
Mumbai 400013, INDIA

Abraham, John (Athlete, Football Player)
c/o Anthony J. Agnone *Eastern Athletic Services*
11350 McCormick Rd
Suite 800 - Executive Plaza
Hunt Valley, MD 21031, USA

Abraham, Nate (Athlete, Football Player)
3038 Wentworth Way
Tarpon Springs, FL 34688, USA

Abraham, Robert (Athlete, Football Player)
831 Canal St
Myrtle Beach, SC 29577, USA

Abraham, Spencer E (Politician)
Energy Dept
8016 Greenwich Woods Dr
Me Lean, VA 22102-1332, USA

Abrahamian, Emil (Cartoonist)
147 Woodleaf Dr
Winter Springs, FL 32708, USA

Abrahams, Jim S (Director)
c/o Staff Member *ICM Partners (ICM-LA)*
10250 Constellation Blvd Fl 7
Los Angeles, CA 90067, USA

Abrahams, Jon (Actor)
c/o Christian Donatelli *Schiff Company, The*
9465 Wilshire Blvd
Suite 480
Beverly Hills, CA 90212, USA

Abrahamse, Taylor (Musician)
Rockyz Kidz
146 Shuter St
Studio B
Toronto, ON M5A 1V9, Canada

Abrahamson, James A (Business Person, General)
3557 Havercamp Rd
Hibbig, MN 55746, USA

Abrahamson, James A (Astronaut)
20112 Marble Quarry Rd
Keedysville, MD 21756-1508, USA

Abrahamsson, Christer
Karlsarvet Varggropsvagen 1
Leksand 793 93, Sweden

Abrahamsson, Thommy (Athlete, Hockey Player)
Bjorkgatan 7
Kunghamm 45632, Sweden

Abram, Norm (Television Host)
PO Box 2284
So. Berrington, VT 05407

Abramovich, Roman (Business Person)
Chelsea Football Club
Stamford Bridge
Fulham Road
London SW6 1HS, UK

Abramowicz, Daniel (Danny) (Athlete, Football Player)
479 N Harlem Ave Apt 801
Oak Park, OH 60301, USA

Abramowicz, Sidney (Athlete, Football Player)
3340 Thomashire Ct
Marietta, GA 30066, USA

Abramowitz, Sid (Athlete, Football Player)
3341 Thomashire Ct
Marietta, GA 30066, USA

Abrams, Bobby (Athlete, Football Player)
1470 Pampas Dr
Montgomery, AL 36117, USA

Abrams, Casey (Musician)
c/o Simon Fuller *XIX Entertainment*
35-37 Parkgate Rd
32/33 Ransomes Dock
London SW11 4NP, UNITED KINGDOM (UK)

Abrams, Elliott (Politician)
10607 Dogwood Farm Ln
Great Falls, VA 22066-2937, USA

Abrams, JJ (Actor, Producer, Writer)
1582 Sorrento Dr
Pacific Palisades, CA 90272, USA

Abrams, Kevin (Athlete, Football Player)
1314 E Wilder Ave
Tampa, FL 33603, USA

Abrams, Robert (Politician)
531 Weaver St
Larchmont, NY 10538-1013, USA

Abramson, Leslie (Actor)
122-A E Foothill Blvd #4
Arcadia, CA 91006, USA

Abramson, Neil (Director, Writer)
c/o Staff Member *United Talent Agency (UTA)*
9336 Civic Center Dr
Beverly Hills, CA 90210, USA

Abrego, Johnny (Athlete, Baseball Player)
PO Box 681144
San Antonio, TX 78268-1144, USA

Abreu, Aldo (Musician)
Concert Artists Guild
850 7th Ave #1205
New York, NY 10019, USA

Abreu, Bobby (Athlete, Baseball Player)
5 Rockledge Ct
Marlton, NJ 08053, USA

Abreu, Irina (Actor)
c/o Staff Member *Televisa*
Blvd Adolfo Lopez Mateos 232
Colonia San Angel INN
DF CP 01060, MEXICO

Abreu, Winston
112 Bonnie Woods Dr
Greenville, SC 29605-5947, USA

Abrikosov, Alexei A (Nobel Prize Laureate)
804 Houston St
Lemont, IL 60439-4338, USA

Abril, Victoria (Actor)
c/o Stephane Zitzerman
1 Rue du Louvre
Paris 75001, FRANCE

Abroms, Edward M (Director)
EMA Enterprises
1866 Marlowe St
Thousand Oaks, CA 91360, USA

Abronzino, Umberto (Soccer Player)
1336 Seattle Ave
San Jose, CA 95125, USA

Abrue, Bobby (Athlete, Baseball Player)
c/o Staff Member *Los Angeles Dodgers (LA Dodgers)*
1000 Elysian Park Ave
Los Angeles, CA 90012, USA

Abrunhosa, Pedro (Musician)
Polygram Records
Worldwide Plaza
825 8th Ave
New York, NY 10019, USA

Abruzzo, Ray (Actor)
c/o Staff Member *Peter Strain & Associates Inc (LA)*
5455 Wilshire Blvd
Suite 1812
Los Angeles, CA 90036-4368, USA

Absher, Dick (Athlete, Football Player)
353 Tavistock Dr
Saint Augustine, FL 32095, USA

Abshire, David M (Diplomat)
Strategic/International Studies Center
1800 K St NW
Washington, DC 20006, USA

abtahi, omid (Actor)

Abul-Ragheb, Ali (Prime Minister)
Prime Minister's Office
PO Box 80
Amman 35215, JORDAN

Acaba, Joseph M (Astronaut)
2620 Loganberry Cir
Seabrook, TX 77586-1525, USA

Accardo, Jeremy (Athlete, Baseball Player)
1543 S Gibson St
Gilbert, AZ 85296-4290, USA

Accola, Candice (Actor)
c/o Katie Rhodes *Untitled Entertainment*
(LA)
350 S. Beverly Dr #200
Beverly Hills, CA 90212, USA

Accola, Paul (Skier)
Bolgenstr 17
Davos Platz 7270, SWITZERLAND

Acconci, Vito (Artist)
20 Jay St #215
Brooklyn, NY 11201, USA

AC/DC (Music Group, Musician)
c/o Christopher Dalston *Creative Artists*
Agency (CAA-LA)
2000 Ave Of The Stars
Los Angeles, CA 90067, USA

Ace, Buddy (Musician)
Rodgers Redding
1048 Tatnall St
Macon, GA 31201

Ace of Base (Music Group, Musician)
c/o John Orlando *Urbania Group*
(Sweden)
Box 3184
Stockholm 103 63, Stockholm

Acevedo, Hernan F (Scientist)
Allegheny-Singer Research Institute
320 E North Ave
Pittsburgh, PA 15212

Acevedo, Juan (Athlete, Baseball Player)
143 Madera Cir
Carpentersville, IL 60110-1110, USA

Acevedo, Kirk (Actor)
c/o Chris Schmidt *Paradigm (LA)*
360 N Crescent Dr
North Bldg
Beverly Hills, CA 90210, USA

Ache, Steve (Athlete, Football Player)
22 Lashley Estates Dr
Swansea, IL 62226, USA

Achebe, Chinua (Writer)
Bard College
Language & Literature Dept
PO Box 41
Annandale, NY 12504, USA

Achebe, Chinua (Writer)
University of Nigeria
PO Box 53 Nsukka
Anambra State, Nigeria, USA

Achica, George (Athlete, Football Player)
3165 Lone Bluff Way
San Jose, CA 95111, USA

Achtymichuk, Gene (Athlete, Hockey
Player)
305-9985 93 Ave
Fort Saskatchewan, AB T8L 1N5, Canada

Acid Test (Music Group)
83 Riverside Dr
New York, NY 10024, USA

Acker, Amy (Actor)
3721 Blue Canyon Dr
Studio City, CA 91604, USA

Acker, Bill (Athlete, Football Player)
1809 Walker Dr
Alice, TX 78332, USA

Acker, Jim (Athlete, Baseball Player)
Box AA
Freer, TX 78357-0214, USA

Acker, Joseph E (Doctor)
1307 Old Weisgarber Rd
Knoxville, TN 37909

Acker, Tom (Athlete, Baseball Player)
118 Gloucester Rd
Stuarts Draft, VA 24477-3328, USA

Ackeren, Robert V (Director)
Kurfurstendamm 132A
Berlin 10711, GERMANY

Acker-Macosko, Anna (Athlete, Golfer)
304 Earl Dr
Kerrville, TX 78028, USA

Ackerman, Doug (Horse Racer)
530 Lighthorse Cir
Aberdeen, NC 28315-3770, USA

Ackerman, Gary (Congressman,
Politician)
2111 Rayburn HOB
Washington, DC 20515, USA

Ackerman, Joshua (Actor)
c/o Joanna (Joanie) Burstein *Burstein*
Company, The
15304 Sunset Blvd
suite 208
Pacific Palisades, CA 90272, USA

Ackerman, Leslie (Actor)
5065 Calvin Ave
Tarzana, CA 91356, USA

Ackerman, Michael W (General)
Pentagon
HqUSA - Inspector General
Washington, DC 20310, USA

Ackerman, Rick (Athlete, Football Player)
995 N US Highway 30
Laramie, WY 82072, USA

Ackerman, Roger G (Business Person)
Coming Inc
Houghton Park
Coming, NY 14831, USA

Ackerman, Thomas E (Cinematographer)
1644 San Leandro Ln
Montecito, CA 93108, USA

Ackerman, Tom (Athlete, Football Player)
c/o Allain Roy *CMG Sports*
16476 Chesterfield Airport Road 2nd
Floor
Chesterfield, MO 63017, USA

Ackerman, William (Composer)
Drake Assoc
177 Woodland Ave
Westwood, NJ 07675, USA

Ackermann, Rosemarie (Athlete, Track
Athlete)
Str der Jugend 72
Cottbus 03050, GERMANY

Ackland, Joss (Actor)
c/o Staff Member *Jonathan Altaras Assoc*
Ltd
11 Garrick Street
Covent Garden
London WC2E 9AT, UNITED KINGDOM
(UK)

Ackles, Jensen (Actor)
134 Stonehaven Way
Los Angeles, CA 90049, USA

Ackroyd, David (Actor)
273 N Many Lakes Dr
Kalispell, MT 59901, USA

Ackroyd, Peter (Writer)
Anthony Shell Assoc
43 Doughty St
London WC1N 2LF, UNITED KINGDOM
(UK)

Acks, Ron (Athlete, Football Player)
563 Licklog Rdg
Hayesville, NC 28904, USA

Acomb, Doug (Athlete, Hockey Player)
18 Millstone Ct
Markham, ON L3R 7M4, Canada

Acorah, Derek (Actor)
PO Box 32
Ormskirk
Lancashire L40 9SN, UNITED KINGDOM

Acord, Lance (Cinematographer)
7069 Fernhill Dr
Malibu, CA 90265, USA

Acosta, Cy
Aug Ramirez 1420 Col
Gab Levva Culiacan
Sinaloa, Mexico, USA

Acosta, Eduardo (Ed) (Athlete, Baseball
Player)
22822 Boltana
Mission Viejo, CA 92691-1717, USA

Acovone, Jay (Actor)
c/o Richard Lewis *Geddes Agency, The*
8430 Santa Monica Blvd
Suite 200
Los Angeles, CA 90069, USA

Acre, Mark (Athlete, Baseball Player)
840 E Riviera Pl
Chandler, AZ 85249-6970, USA

Acres, Mark (Athlete, Basketball Player)
233 6th St
Manhattan Beach, CA 90266-5735, USA

Acrivos, Andreas (Scientist)
145 W 67th St
New York, NY 10023, USA

Acta, Manny (Athlete, Baseball Player,
Coach)
6427 Shoreline Dr
Saint Cloud, FL 34771-8786, USA

Acton, Bud (Athlete, Basketball Player)
P.O. Box 87
Empire, MI 49630-0087, USA

Acton, Keith (Athlete, Coach, Hockey
Player)
Toronto Maple Leafs
82 Mill St
Stouffville, ON L4A 1C6, Canada

Acton, Loren W (Astronaut)
PO Box 1857
Bozeman, MT 59771-1857, USA

Acton, Loren W Dr (Astronaut)
8490 Overlook Ln
Bozeman, MT 59715-7753, USA

Acuff, Amy (Athlete, Olympic Athlete,
Track Athlete)
4102 Bobwhite
Robstown, TX 78380-6060, USA

Acuna, Alicia (Correspondent)
c/o Staff Member *Fox News Channel (NY)*
1211 Ave of the Americas
Level C1
New York, NY 10036-8701, USA

Acuna, Jason (Actor)
1523 Manhattan Ave
Hermosa Beach, CA 90254, USA

Aczel, Janos D (Mathematician)
97 McCarron Crescent
Waterloo ON N2L 5M9, CANADA

Adade, Manohar (Actor, Bollywood)
199 Vellala Street
Purasawakkam
Chennai, TN 600 084, INDIA

Adair, Deborah (Actor)
c/o Staff Member *Cast Images*
2530 J St
Ste 330
Sacramento, CA 95816, USA

Adair, Rick
419 Winding Oak Dr
Woodruff, SC 29388-8015, USA

Adair, Tatum (Actor)
Mission Talent Agency
atten: Goro Hamasaki
10929 Vanowen Ste #138
North Hollywood, CA 91605, USA

Adam, Robert (Architect)
Winchester Design
9 Upper High St
Winchester
Hants S023 8UT, UNITED KINGDOM
(UK)

Adam, Russ (Athlete, Hockey Player)
69 Old Petty Harbour Rd
St. John's, NL A1G 1H6, Canada

Adam, Theo (Opera Singer)
Schillerstr 14
Dresden 01326, GERMANY

Adamchik, Ed (Athlete, Football Player)
234 Princeton Ave
Pittsburgh, PA 15229, USA

Adamek, Donna (Bowler)
25834 Webster Pl
Stevenson Ranch, CA 91381-1244, USA

Adamkus, Valdas (Politician, President)
President's Office
Gediminas 53
Vilnius 232026, LITHUANIA

Adamle, Mike (Sportscaster)
826 Lincoln St
Evanston, IL 60201-2405, USA

Adamowicz, Tony (Race Car Driver)
633 Skyview Lane
Costa Mesa, CA 92626, USA

Adams, Alvan (Athlete, Basketball Player)
5617 N Palo Cristi Rd
Paradise Valley, AZ 85253-7544, USA

Adams, Amy (Actor)
9030 Briarcrest Ln
Beverly Hills, CA 90210, USA

Adams, Bob (Athlete, Baseball Player)
31713 157th St E
Llano, CA 93544-1222, USA

Adams, Brent (Athlete, Football Player)
3615 Parkmont Ct
Norcross, GA 30092, USA

Adams, Brooke (Actor)
248 S Van Ness Ave
Los Angeles, CA 90004

Adams, Bryan (Musician)
c/o Bruce Allen *Bruce Allen Talent*
425 Carrall St
Suite 500
Vancouver, BC V6B 6E3, Canada

Adams, Bryan (Athlete, Hockey Player)
c/o Staff Member *Sports Personnel Services*
125 Lake St W
Suite 200
Wayzata, MN 55391, USA

Adams, Bud (Athlete, Football Executive, Football Player)
3218 Del Monte Dr
Houston, TX 77019-3218, USA

Adams, Charles (Athlete, Baseball Player)
6058 Puerto Dr
Rancho Murieta, CA 95683, USA

Adams, Charles J (Religious Leader)
Progressive National Baptist Convention
601 50th St NE
Washington, DC 20019

Adams, Craig (Athlete, Hockey Player)
8030 Sherwood Dr
Presto, PA 15142-1078, USA

Adams, Curtis (Athlete, Football Player)
258 W Towering Oaks Cir
Muskegon, MI 49442, us

Adams, Curtis (Athlete, Football Player)
258 W Towering Oaks Cir
Muskegon, MI 49442, USA

Adams, Danny (Athlete, Basketball Player)
7832 Surreywood Dr
North Bend, OH 45052, us

Adams, Dave (Athlete, Football Player)
2780 N La Cienega Dr
Tucson, AZ 85715, us

Adams, David (Dave) (Athlete, Football Player)
2780 N La Cienega Dr
Tucson, AZ 85715-3504, USA

Adams, Dick (Athlete, Baseball Player)
4650 Dulin Rd
Spc 136
Fallbrook, CA 92028-9362, USA

Adams, Doug (Athlete, Baseball Player)
1129 Harmony Cir NE
Janesville, WI 53545-2072, USA

Adams, Earnest (Athlete, Football Player)
1061 NW 25th Way
Fort Lauderdale, FL 33311, us

Adams, Earnest (Athlete, Football Player)
1061 NW 25th Way
Fort Lauderdale, FL 33311, USA

Adams, Evan (Actor)
c/o Staff Member *Characters Talent Agency, The (Vancouver)*
1505 W 2nd Ave
#200
Vancouver, BC V6H 3Y4, Canada

Adams, Flozell (Athlete, Football Player)
5201 Reflection Ct
Flower Mound, TX 75022, USA

Adams, Flozell (Football Player)
5201 Reflection Ct
Flower Mound, TX 75022, us

Adams, George (Athlete, Football Player)
2410 Damsel Katie Dr
Lewisville, TX 75056-5801, USA

Adams, George (Athlete, Basketball Player)
508 Watergate Cir
Gastonia, NC 28052-7718, USA

Adams, George (Football Player)
2410 Damsel Katie Dr
Lewisville, TX 75056, us

Adams, George R (Musician)
Joel Chriss
300 Mercer St #3J
New York, NY 10003

Adams, Gerard (Gerry) (Politician)
Sinn Fein/IRA
51/55 Falls Road
Belfast, Northern Ireland BT 12, USA

Adams, Glenn (Athlete, Baseball Player)
12333 E Tecumseh Rd
Norman, OK 73026-8640, USA

Adams, Greg (Athlete, Hockey Player)
19864 N 83rd Pl
Scottsdale, AZ 85255-3915, USA

Adams, Greg (Athlete, Hockey Player)
c/o Staff Member *Cowichan Valley Capitals*
2687 James St
Duncan, BC V9L 2X5, Canada

Adams, Hank (Athlete, Football Player)
53 4th St
California, PA 15419, USA

Adams, Henry
53 4th Street
California, PA 15419-1109, USA

Adams, Hunter Dr (Scientist)
Gesundheit Institute
PO Box 268
Hillsboro, WV 24946-0268, USA

Adams, Jane (Actor)
c/o Staff Member *Framework Entertainment (LA)*
9057 Nemo St
Suite C
West Hollywood, CA 90069, USA

Adams, Jeb Stuart (Actor)
1163 Calle Vista
Beverly Hills, CA 90210, USA

Adams, Joey Lauren (Actor)
c/o Staff Member *Caliber Media Company*
9229 W Sunset Blvd Ste 705
West Hollywood, CA 90069, USA

Adams, John (Athlete, Golfer)
4610 County Road 42200
Paris, TX 75462, USA

Adams, John (Athlete, Hockey Player)
109 Nottingham Crest
Thunder Bay, ON P7G 1B4, Canada

Adams, John C (Musician)
c/o Staff Member *Elektra Records*
75 Rockefeller Plaza
17th Floor
New York, NY 10019, USA

Adams, John H (Religious Leader)
African Methodist Church
1134 11th St
Washington, DC 20001

Adams, Julie (Actor)
2446 N. Commonwealth Ave
Los Angeles, CA 90027, USA

Adams, Julius (Athlete, Football Player)
2135 Jefferson Davis St
Macon, GA 31201, USA

Adams, Julius (Football Player)
2135 Jeff Davis St
Macon, GA 31201, us

Adams, Kevyn (Athlete, Hockey Player)
9172 Curry Ln
Clarence Center, NY 14032-9504, USA

Adams, Kevyn (Athlete, Hockey Player)
Buffalo Sabres 1 Seymour H Knox III Plz
Ste 1
Buffalo, NY 14203-3096

Adams, Linda
c/o Staff Member *Crews*
828 Clemont Dr
Atlanta, GA 30306, USA

Adams, Lindsey (Race Car Driver)
819 W. Arapho #24B-188
Richardson, TX 75080, USA

Adams, Lorraine (Journalist)
Washington Post - Editorial Dept
1150 15th St
Washington, DC 20071

Adams, Lynn (Athlete, Golfer)
2445 Brant St
Unit 207
San Diego, CA 92101, USA

Adams, Mary Kay (Actor)
Roe Enterprises
PO Box 2023
Fairfield, IA 52556, USA

Adams, Maud (Actor)
9420 Eden Dr
Beverly Hills, CA 90210, USA

Adams, Michael F (Educator)
University of Georgia
President's Office
Athens, GA 30602, USA

Adams, Michele (Stylist)
c/o Staff Member *Marnie Rose Agency*
37 Lower Shad
Pound Ridge, NY 10576, USA

Adams, Mike (Athlete, Baseball Player)
13205 Jo Ln NE
Albuquerque, NM 87111-7112, USA

Adams, Mike (Football Player)
228 Flinn St
Hutto, TX 78634, us

Adams, Mike (Athlete, Baseball Player)
800 Booty St
Sinton, TX 78387, USA

Adams, Mike (Athlete, Football Player)
228 Flinn St
Hutto, TX 78634, USA

Adams, Mike (Athlete, Football Player)
70 Graham Ave
Paterson, NJ 07524, USA

Adams, Neal (Producer)
Continuity Studios
15 W 39th Street Fl 9
New York, NY 10018, USA

Adams, Neile McQueen (Actor)
2323 Bowmont Dr.
Beverly Hills, CA 90210, USA

Adams, Noah (Correspondent)
National Public Radio
635 Massachusetts Ave NW
Washington, DC 20001, USA

Adams, Oleta (Music Group)
Engine Entertainment
209 10th Ave S Dr #429b
Nashville, TN 37203, USA

Adams, Pat (Artist)
370 Elm St
Bennington, VT 05201, USA

Adams, Patch (Doctor)
6855 Washington Blvd
Arlington, VA 22213, USA

Adams, Patrick (Actor)
c/o Andy Corren *Andy Corren Management*
Prefers to be contacted via email or telephone
CA, USA

Adams, Pete (Athlete, Football Player)
1443 Hygeia Ave
Encinitas, CA 92024, USA

Adams, Pete (Football Player)
1443 Hygeia Ave
Encinitas, CA 92024, us

Adams, Ranald T Jr (General)
1002 Emerald Dr
Alexandria, VA 22308, USA

Adams, Red (Athlete, Baseball Player)
6058 Puerto Dr
Rancho Murieta, CA 95683-9314, USA

Adams, Richard G (Writer)
Benwell's
26 Church St
Whitechurch
Hants RG28 7AR, UNITED KINGDOM (UK)

Adams, Robert (Photographer)
306 Lincoln St
Longmont, CO 80501-5346, USA

Adams, Russ (Athlete, Baseball Player)
7940 Scotch Meadows Dr
Laurinburg, NC 28352-2162, USA

Adams, Ryan (Music Group, Songwriter, Writer)
High Road
751 Bridgeway #300
Sausalito, CA 94965, USA

Adams, Sam (Athlete, Football Player)
8507 NE Juanita Dr
Kirkland, WA 98034, USA

Adams, Sam E (Athlete, Football Player)
12010 Holly Stone Dr
Houston, TX 77070, USA

Adams, Sandy (Congressman, Politician)
216 Cannon HOB
Washington, DC 20515, USA

Adams, Scott (Athlete, Football Player)
1171 Middlebrooks Rd
Watkinsville, GA 30677, USA

Adams, Scott (Cartoonist)
Harper Business Publishers
2751 Crellin Rd
Pleasanton, CA 94566-6914, USA

Adams, Scott (Football Player)
1171 Middlebrooks Rd
Watkinsville, GA 30677, us

Adams, Stan (Athlete, Football Player)
502 S Highland Dr
Cedar Hill, TX 75104, USA

Adams, Stefon (Athlete)
1734 Trotters Ln
Stone Mountain, GA 30087, USA

Adams, Stefon (Athlete, Football Player)
937 Bingham Ln
Stone Mountain, GA 30083, us

Adams, Sunrise (Adult Film Star)
c/o Staff Member *Vivid Entertainment*
3599 Cahuenga Blvd #400
Los Angeles, CA 90068, USA

Adams, Tag (Adult Film Star)
c/o Staff Member *Diva Central Inc*
7510 W Sunset Blvd Ste 1445
Los Angees, CA 90046, USA

Adams, Terry (Athlete, Baseball Player)
11315 Howells Ferry Rd
Semmes, AL 36575-6655, USA

Adams, Theo (Athlete, Football Player)
9555 Highland Park Dr
Roseville, CA 95678, USA

Adams, Tom (Athlete, Football Player)
20606 Crystal Springs Loop
Grand Rapids, MN 55744, USA

Adams, Tony (Athlete, Football Player)
14012 Juniper St
Overland Park, KS 66224, USA

Adams, Trace (Music Group)
Borman
1222 16th Ave S #23
Nashville, TN 37212, USA

Adams, Vashone (Athlete, Football Player)
2940 S Parker Ct
Aurora, CO 80014, USA

Adams, William J (Athlete, Football
Player)
12 Willowby Way
Lynnfield, MA 01940, USA

Adams, Willie (Athlete, Baseball Player)
11903 Kibbee Ave
La Mirada, CA 90638-1518, USA

Adams, Willie J (Athlete, Football Player)
2513 Forest Creek Dr
Fort Worth, TX 76123, USA

Adams, Willis (Athlete, Football Player)
7831 Quail Meadow Dr
Houston, TX 77071, USA

Adams, Yolanda (Music Group, Musician)
c/o Lynn Jeter *Lynn Jeter & Associates*
3699 Wilshire Blvd #850
Los Angeles, CA 90010, USA

Adams, Yolonda (Musician)
Elektra Records
75 Rockefeller Plaza
New York, NY 10019

Adams Jr, Robert McCornick (Misc)
PO Box ZZ
Basalt, CO 81621, USA

Adamson, Andrew (Director)
c/o Jeremy Zimmer *United Talent Agency
(UTA)*
9336 Civic Center Dr
Beverly Hills, CA 90210, USA

Adamson, James C Colonel (Astronaut)
25 Tradewind Cir
Fishersville, VA 22939-2141, USA

Adamson, Joel (Athlete, Baseball Player)
14832 S 46th Pl
Phoenix, AZ 85044-6872, USA

Adamson, Ken (Athlete, Football Player)
5061 Jardin Ln
Carmichael, CA 95608, USA

Adamson, Mike (Athlete, Baseball Player)
17610 Canterbury Dr
Monument, CO 80132-8310, USA

Adamson IV, Robert (Actor)
c/o Theo Swerissen *Theo Swerissen
Management*
Prefers to be contacted via telephone or
email
Los Angeles, CA, USA

Adamson Jr, Robert E (Admiral)
1709 Bohnhoff Court
Virginia Beach, VA 23454-2520, USA

Adar, Nir (Stylist)
c/o Celebrity Stylist *Zenobia Agency Inc*
PO Box 909
Groveland, CA 95321, USA

Addai, Joseph (Athlete, Football Player)
7521 Dubonnet Way
Indianapolis, IN 46278, USA

Addams, Abe (Athlete, Football Player)
477 Colesburg Rd
Elizabethtown, KY 42701, USA

Addams, Calpernia (Actor, Reality TV
Star)
c/o Staff Member *Deep Stealth
Productions*
5419 Hollywood Blvd #C-142
Hollywood, CA 90027, USA

Addeney, Herb (Athlete, Football Player)
1058 Tristram Cr
Mantua, NJ 08051, USA

Adderley, Herb (Athlete, Football Player)
1058 Tristram Cir
Mantua, NJ 08051, us

Addis, Bob (Athlete, Baseball Player)
7466 Hollycroft Ln
Mentor, OH 44060-5611, USA

Addison, Rafael (Athlete, Basketball
Player)
6 Bernadette Ct
East Hanover, NJ 07936-3425, USA

Addonizio, Kim (Writer)
3749 Park Boulevard Way
Oakland, CA 94610-2837, USA

Adduci, Jim (Athlete, Baseball Player)
9529 S Sawyer Ave
Evergreen Park, IL 60805-2343, USA

Adduono, Ray (Athlete, Hockey Player)
108A Spruce Crt
Thunder Bay, ON P7C 1X6, Canada

Adduono, Rick (Athlete, Hockey Player)
153 Donald St W
Thunder Bay, ON P7E 5X8, Canada

Addy, Mark (Actor)
c/o Staff Member *ID PR (LA)*
7060 Hollywood Blvd
8th Floor
Los Angeles, CA 90028, USA

Ade, King Sunny (Music Group)
Monterey International
200 W Superior #202
Chicago, IL 60610, USA

Adebayor, Emmanuel (Athlete, Soccer
Player)
c/o Staff Member *Manchester City FC*
City of Manchester Stadium
SportCity
Manchester M11 3FF, UK

Adedapo, Naima (Musician)
c/o Simon Fuller *XIX Entertainment*
35-37 Parkgate Rd
32/33 Ransomes Dock
London SW11 4NP, UNITED KINGDOM
(UK)

Adele (Musician)
c/o Jonathan Dickins *September
Management*
80/82 Chiswick High Rd
London W4 1SY, UK

Adelman, Jason (Actor)
19 Hitching Post Ln
Bell Canyon, CA 91307, USA

Adelman, Kenneth L (Government
Official)
Int'l Contemporary Studies Institute
4018 27th St N
Arlington, VA 22207, USA

Adelman, Rick (Athlete, Basketball Player,
Coach)
5109 Tangle Ln
Houston, TX 77056-2115, USA

Adelson, Sheldon (Misc)
27 Kittansett Loop
Henderson, NV 89052-6694, USA

Adelson, Sheldon (Business Person)
Venetian Resort Hotel Casino
3355 Las Vegas Blvd S
Las Vegas, NV 89109, USA

Adelstein, Paul (Actor)
2789 Westshire Dr
Los Angeles, CA 90068, USA

Adem (Music Group)
c/o Staff Member *Paradigm (Monterey)*
404 W Franklin St
Monterey, CA 93940, USA

Aderholt, Robert (Congressman,
Politician)
205 Fourth Ave NE
Suite 104
Cullman, AL 35055, USA

Adey, Christopher
137 Anson Road
Willesden Green NW2 4AH, UNITED
KINGDOM (UK)

Adeyamju, Victor (Athlete, Football
Player)
5375 S Maplewood Ave
Chicago, IL 60632, USA

Adeyanju, Victor (Athlete, Football Player)
5218 W Cavedale Dr
Phoenix, AZ 85083, us

Adickes, John M (Athlete, Football Player)
205 W Fair Oaks Pl
San Antonio, TX 78209, USA

Adickes, Mark (Athlete, Football Player)
6146 Bordley Dr
Houston, TX 77057, USA

Adie, Kate (Journalist)
c/o Staff Member *Peller Artistes Limited*
39 Princes Ave
London N3 2DA, UK

Adiga, Aravind (Writer)
c/o Staff Member *Penguin Group
(Australia)*
P.O. Box 701
Hawthorn VIC 3122, Australia

Adjani, Isabelle (Actor)
c/o Staff Member *ArtMedia*
20 avenue Rapp
Paris 75008, France

Adjodhia, Jules (Prime Minister)
Prime Minister's Office
Kleine Combeweg 1
Paramaribo, SURINAME

Adkins, Adele Laurie Blue (Adele)
(Musician)
c/o Staff Member *September Management*
80/82 Chiswick High Rd
London W4 1SY, UK

Adkins, Derrick (Athlete, Olympic
Athlete, Track Athlete)
909 Derrick Adkins Ln
W Hempstead, NY 11552-3915, USA

Adkins, James (Athlete, Baseball Player)
185 Cedar Ridge Ct
Coppell, TX 75019, USA

Adkins, Jim (Musician)
21 W Berridge Ln
Phoenix, AZ 85013, USA

Adkins, Jon (Athlete, Baseball Player)
5322 Fisher Bowen Branch Rd
Wayne, WV 25570-5946, USA

Adkins, Kevin (Athlete, Football Player)
209 Redwood Dr
Coppell, TX 75019, USA

Adkins, Margene (Athlete, Football Player)
2312 Donnyville Ct
Fort Worth, TX 76119, USA

Adkins, Sam (Athlete, Football Player)
15912 NE 160th St
Woodinville, WA 98072, USA

Adkins, Seth (Actor)
c/o Alisa Adler *Paradigm (LA)*
360 N Crescent Dr
North Bldg
Beverly Hills, CA 90210, USA

Adkins, Steve
16225 Sierra De Avila
Tampa, FL 33613-5222, USA

Adkins, Trace (Musician)
P.O. Box 121889
Nashville, TN 37212, USA

Adkisson, Perry L (Educator, Misc)
9211 Lake Forest Court N
College Station, TX 77845, USA

Adleman, Leonard (Scientist)
University of Southern California
Computer Math Dept
Los Angeles, CA 90089, USA

Adler, Andy (Sportscaster)
c/o Staff Member *WmE2 (WMA-LA)*
1 William Morris Pl
Beverly Hills, CA 90212, USA

Adler, Brian (Composer)
2316 Delaware Avenue
Suite #266
Buffalo, NY 14216-2687, USA

Adler, Charles (Actor)
c/o Luanne Salandy-Regis *Innovative
Artists (LA)*
1505 10th St
Santa Monica, CA 90401, USA

Adler, Cisco (Musician)
21653 Rambla Vis
Malibu, CA 90265, USA

Adler, Gilbert
2711 Bowmont Dr
Beverly Hills, CA 90210, USA

Adler, Jerry (Actor)
c/o Alisa Adler *Paradigm (LA)*
360 N Crescent Dr
North Bldg
Beverly Hills, CA 90210, USA

Adler, Lee (Artist)
Lime Kiln Farm
Climax, NY 12042, USA

Adler, Lou (Actor, Director, Producer)
21750/21756 Pacific Coast Hwy
Malibu, CA 90265, USA

Adler, Matt
PO Box 1866
Studio City, CA 91614, USA

Adler, Max (Actor)
c/o Brian Medavoy *Medavoy Management*
10203 Santa Monica Blvd
Suite 400
Los Angeles, CA 90067, USA

Adler, Stephen L (Physicist)
Institute for Advanced Study
Einstein Lane
Princeton, NJ 08540, USA

Adler, Steven (Music Group)
Adler's Appetite
P.O. Box 8074
Huntington Beach, CA 92615, USA

Adlesh, .Dave
9770 Avenida Monterey
Cypress, CA 90630-3446, USA

Adlesh, Dave (Athlete, Baseball Player)
9770 Avenida Monterey
Cypress, CA 90630-3446, USA

Adlon, Pamela (Actor, Voice Over Artist)
c/o Staff Member *Meghan Schumacher Management*
13351-D Riverside Dr #387
Sherman Oaks, CA 91423, USA

Adni, Daniel (Musician)
64A Menelik Road
London NW2 3RH, UNITED KINGDOM
(UK)

Adoboli, Koffi Eugene (Prime Minister)
Prime Minister's Office
BP 5618
Lome, TOGO

Adoor, Gopalkrishnan (Director)
Darsanam
Trivandrum, Kerala 695017, INDIA

Adorf, Mario (Actor)
Perlacher Str 28
Grunwald D-82031, GERMANY

Adoti, Rasaaq (Actor)
c/o Staff Member *Coast to Coast Talent Group*
3350 Barham Blvd
Los Angeles, CA 90068, USA

Adoti, Razaaq (Actor, Producer)
c/o Staff Member *Coast II Coast Entertainment*
8671 Wilshire Blvd Ste 500
Beverly Hills, CA 90211, USA

Adotta, Kip (Actor, Comedian)
PO Box 5734
Santa Rosa, CA 95402, USA

Adria, Ferran (Chef)
El Bulli
En Cala Montjoi Roses
Girona 17480, SPAIN

Adsit, Scott (Actor)
c/o Melanie Truhett *Messina Baker Entertainment*
955 Carrillo Dr
Suite 100
Los Angeles, CA 90048, USA

Adu, Helen Folasade (Sade) (Actor, Musician)
c/o Staff Member *RCA Records (UK)*
9 Derry St
London W8 5HY, UNITED KINGDOM
(UK)

Adu, Sade (Musician)
c/o Steven Manzano *RDWM America*
1158 26th St
Suite 564
Santa Monica, CA 90403, USA

Adubato, Richie (Basketball Coach, Coach)
290 Chiswell Pl
Lake Mary, FL 32746, USA

Adulyadey, King (King, Politician)
BhumibolVilla Chitralada
Bangkok, THAILAND

Adway, Dwayne (Actor)
c/o Mark Schumacher *Schumacher Management*
1122 San Vicente Blvd.
Santa Monica, CA 90402, USA

Adyrkhayeva, Svetlana D (Ballerina)
1 Smolensky Pereulor 9
#74
Moscow 121099, RUSSIA

Aebischer, David (Athlete, Hockey Player)
365 Jackson St
Denver, CO 80206, USA

Aedo, Daniela (Actor)
c/o Staff Member *Televisa*
Blvd Adolfo Lopez Mateos 232
Colonia San Angel INN
DF CP 01060, MEXICO

Aerosmith (Music Group)
c/o Irving Azoff *Azoff Music Management/ Front Line*
1100 Glendon Ave
Los Angeles, CA 90024, USA

Afanasiyev, Viktor M (Cosmonaut)
Potchta Kosmonavtov
Moskovskoi Oblasti
Syvisdny Goroduk 141160, RUSSIA

Afenir, Troy (Athlete, Baseball Player)
459 Old Via Rancho Dr
Escondido, CA 92029-7959, USA

Affeldt, Jeremy (Athlete, Baseball Player)
6211 E Mandalav Ln
Sookane, WA 99217-9339, USA

Affholter, Erik (Athlete, Football Player)
41734 N Maidstone Ct
Anthem, AZ 85086, us

Affholter, Erik (Athlete, Football Player)
40514 N Hawk Ridge Trl
Phoenix, AZ 85086, USA

Afflalo, Arron (Athlete, Basketball Player)
1221 Ocean Ave Apt 1603
Santa Monica, CA 90401-1049, USA

Affleck, Ben (Actor)
1700 San Remo Dr
Pacific Palisades, CA 90272, USA

Affleck, Bruce (Athlete, Hockey Player)
1847 Oxborough Ct
Chesterfield, MO 63017-8037, USA

Affleck, Bruce (Athlete, Hockey Player)
StLouis Blues 1401
Saint Louis, MO 63103-2700

Affleck, Casey (Actor, Producer, Writer)
2054 Laughlin Park Dr
Los Angeles, CA 90027, USA

Affleck, James G (Business Person)
American Cyanamid
5 Giralda Farms
Madison, NJ 07940, USA

Affleck, Ian K (Scientist)
3847 26th Ave W Upper
Vancouver, BC V6S 1P3, Canada

Afghan Raiders (Music Group)
c/o David Benveniste *Velvet Hammer*
9014 Melrose Ave
Los Angeles, CA 90069, USA

AFI (Music Group)
c/o Staff Member *Leave Home Booking*
1400 S. Foothill Dr
Suite 34
Salt Lake City, UT 84108, USA

Afinogenov, Maxim (Athlete, Hockey Player)
3700 S Ocean Blvd Apt 1502
Highland Beach, FL 33487-3376, USA

Afrika, Bambaataa (Artist, Musician)
KLB Productions
70A Greenwich Ave #441
New York, NY 10011, USA

Afrojack (DJ, Musician)
c/o Joel Zimmerman *WME (WMA-NY)*
1325 Ave of the Americas
New York, NY 10019, USA

Afroman (Artist, Music Group)
Crescent Moon
20 Music Square W
Nashville, TN 37203, USA

Aftermath (Music Group)
c/o Tom Workman *Starcrest Entertainment Corp*
4585 N River Rd E
Zanesville, OH 43701-8174, USA

Agajanian, Ben (Athlete, Football Player)
27950 Avenida Terrazo
Cathedral, CA 92234, us

Agajanian, Benjamin (Ben) (Athlete, Football Player)
4471 Farquhar Ave
Los Alamitos, CA 90720, USA

Aga Khan IV, Prince Karim (Religious Leader)
Aiglemont
Gouvieux 60270, FRANCE

Agam, Yaacov (Artist)
26 Rue Boulard
Paris 75014, FRANCE

Agarwal, Anu (Actor, Bollywood)
503 Godavari
Khan Pochkhawala Road Worli
Mumbai, MS 400025, INDIA

Agassi, Andre (Athlete, Olympic Athlete, Tennis Player)
8921 Andre Dr
Las Vegas, NV 89148, USA

Agatston, Arthur (Scientist)
1633 N View Dr
Miami Beach, FL 33140-4251, USA

Agbayani, Benny (Athlete, Baseball Player)
66-948 Kolu Pl
Waialua, HI 96791-9743, USA

Age, Louis (Athlete, Football Player)
7517 Park Ave
Houma, LA 70364, USA

Agee, Tommie (Athlete, Football Player)
1505 Blackhawk Dr
Opelika, AL 36801, USA

Agee, Tommie (Athlete, Football Player)
1505 Blackhawk Dr
Opelika, AL 36801, us

Agena, Keiko (Actor)
c/o Staff Member *Fenton Kritzer Entertainment*
8840 Wilshire Blvd Fl 3
Beverly Hills, CA 90211, USA

Ager, Nikita (Actor)
c/o Kim Byrd *Innovative Artists (LA)*
1505 10th St
Santa Monica, CA 90401, USA

Aghdashloo, Shohreh (Actor)
c/o Tamara Houston *Round Table Entertainment*
15301 Ventura Blvd
Suite 400, Bldg D
Sherman Oaks, CA 91403, USA

Agna, Tom (Actor, Producer, Writer)
c/o Lisa Harrison *WME (LA)*
9601 Wilshire Blvd Fl 3
Beverly Hills, CA 90210, USA

Agnello Jr, Carmine (Actor)
c/o Staff Member *Britto Agency PR*
234 W 56th St
Penthouse
New York, NY 10019, USA

Agnelo, Geraldo Majella Cardinal (Religious Leader)
Rue Martin Alfanso de Souza 270
Salvador, BA 40100-050, BRAZIL

Agnew, Harold M (Scientist)
322 Punta Baja Dr
Solana Beach, CA 92075-1720, USA

Agnew, Jim (Athlete, Hockey Player)
2747 Ancabide Ln
Missoula, MT 59803-2904, USA

Agnew, Ray (Athlete, Football Player)
2215 Cline St
Winston Salem, NC 27107, us

Agnew Jr, Ray (Athlete, Football Player)
2215 Cline St
Winston Salem, NC 27107, USA

Agnihotri, Atul (Actor, Bollywood)
Ashwini
Pali Mala Road Bandra
Mumbai, MS 400050, INDIA

Agnus, Michael (Business Person)
Whitbread PLC
Chiswell St
London EC1Y 4SD, UNITED KINGDOM
(UK)

Agoos, Jeff (Athlete, Soccer Player)
235 Pascack Road
Park Ridge, NJ 07656-1125, USA

Agostini, Didier (Actor)
Cineart
36 Rue de Ponthieu
Paris 75008, FRANCE

Agosto, Ben (Athlete, Figure Skater,
Olympic Athlete)
c/o Staff Member *Champions on Ice*
Tom Collins Enterprises Inc
3500 W 80th St
Minneapolis, MN 55431, USA

Agosto, Juan (Athlete, Baseball Player)
3815 65th St E
Bradenton, FL 34208-6613, USA

Agranoff, Bernard W (Biologist, Doctor)
1942 Boulder Dr
Ann Arbor, MI 48104, USA

Agre, Bernard Cardinal (Religious Leader)
Archeveche
Ave Jean-Paul II
Abidjan 01 BP 1287, IVORY COAST

Agre, Peter (Nobel Prize Laureate)
16 Chestnut Bluffs Ln
Durham, NC 27713-9163, USA

Agre, Peter (Nobel Prize Laureate)
7033 Lenleigh Road
Baltimore, MD 21212, USA

Agron, Dianna (Actor)
c/o Rick Yorn *LBI Entertainment*
2000 Avenue of the Stars
3rd Floor, North Tower
Los Angeles, CA 90067, USA

Agt, Andries A M Van (Prime Minister)
Europa House
9-15 Sambancho Chiyodaku
Tokyo 102, JAPAN

Aguayo, Albert (Scientist)
648 Av Belmont
Westmount, QC H3Y 2W2, Canada

Aguayo, Luis (Athlete, Baseball Player)
501 Calle Julio Andino
San Juan, PR 00924-2106, USA

Aguiar, Louie (Athlete, Football Player)
1411 Palmer Creek Dr
Columbia, IL 62236, USA

Aguila, Chris (Athlete, Baseball Player)
2011 Brittany Meadows Dr
Reno, NV 89521, USA

Aguilar, Pepe (Musician)
c/o Staff Member *Agency Group Ltd, The
(NY)*
142 West 57th St
6th Floor
New York, NY 10019, USA

Aguilera, Christina (Musician)
513 Doheny Rd
Beverly Hills, CA 90210, USA

Aguilera, Hellweg Max (Artist,
Photographer)
PO Box 289
White Plains, NY 10605-0289, USA

Aguilera, Richard W (Rick) (Athlete,
Baseball Player)
P O Box 174
Rancho Santa Fe, CA 92067-0174, USA

Aguirre, Beatriz (Actor)
c/o Staff Member *Televisa*
Blvd Adolfo Lopez Mateos 232
Colonia San Angel INN
DF CP 01060, MEXICO

Aguirre, Mark (Basketball Player,
Olympic Athlete)
10281 Highland Ct
Frisco, TX 75033-2415, USA

Agustoni, Gilberto Cardinal (Religious
Leader)
Piazzi della Citla Leorina 9
Rome 00193, ITALY

Agutter, Jenny (Actor)
c/o Staff Member *Marmont Management*
Langham House
308 Regent St
London W1B 3AT, UNITED KINGDOM
(UK)

Agyeman, Freema (Actor)
c/o Sarah Camlett *Independent Talent
Group (ITG-UK)*
Oxford House
76 Oxford St
London W1D 1BS, UK

Ahanotu, Chidi (Athlete, Football Player)
1000 S Harbour Island Blvd
Apt 2611
Tampa, FL 33602, USA

Ahanotu, Chidi (Athlete, Football Player)
301 W Platt St
Tampa, FL 33606-, us

Ahdout, Jonathan (Actor)
c/o Leonard Torgan *Collective*
8383 Wilshire Blvd
Suite 1050
Beverly Hills, CA 90211, USA

Aheam, Kevin (Athlete, Hockey Player)
174 Marlborough St
Boston, MA 02116, USA

Ahearn, Kevin (Athlete, Hockey Player,
Olympic Athlete)
174 Marlborough St
Boston, MA 02116-1822, USA

Ahearne, Pat (Athlete, Baseball Player)
246 Milam Ln
Bastrop, TX 78602-3108, USA

Ahem, Jim (Golfer)
314 E Wagon Wheel Dr
Phoenix, AZ 85020 4066, USA

Ahern, Bertie (Prime Minister)
Prime Minister's Office
Upper Merrion St
Dublin, IRELAND

Ahern, Cecelia (Writer)
c/o Staff Member *Bazar Forlag*
Hammarby Fabriksvag 25
Stockholm 12033, Sweden

Ahern, Fred (Athlete, Hockey Player)
807 E 5th St
Boston, MA 02127, USA

Ahern, Jim (Athlete, Golfer)
130 E Glendale Ave
Phoenix, AZ 85020, USA

Ahern, Neal (Producer)
c/o Staff Member *WmE2 (WMA-LA)*
1 William Morris Pl
Beverly Hills, CA 90212, USA

Ahith, Kumar (Actor)
8/10 Norton Apartment
I Floor Mandavelli
Chennai, TN 600 028, INDIA

Ahmed, Kazi Zafar (Prime Minister)
Jatiya Sangsad
Dhaka, BANGLADESH

Ahmed, Riz (Actor)
c/o Kate Bryden *Gordon and French*
12-13 Poland St
London W1F 8QB, UNITED KINGDOM
(UK)

Aho, Esko (Prime Minister)
Centre Party
Pursimiehenkatu 15
Helsinki 00150, FINLAND

Ahola, Peter (Athlete, Hockey Player)
Hiiralantie 11a
Espoo 02160, Finland

Ahrens, Chris (Athlete, Hockey Player)
1412 Linstock Dr
Holiday, FL 34690-6634, USA

Ahrens, Dave (Athlete, Football Player)
10224 Stillwell Dr
Avon, IN 46123, us

Ahrens, David (Dave) (Athlete, Football
Player)
5864 Manchester Ct
Pittsboro, IN 46167, USA

Ahrens, Lynn (Musician)
c/o Staff Member *Gersh (LA)*
9465 Wilshire Blvd
Suite 600
Beverly Hills, CA 90212, USA

Ahronovitch, Yuri
Stockholm Philharmonic
Hotorget 8
Stockholm, SWEDEN

Ahtisaari, Martti (Politician)
H E The President of Finland
Tasavallan Presidentin
Kanslia, Helsinki SF-00170, Finland

Ahtisaari, Martti (Nobel Prize Laureate)
Erottajankatu 11 A
Helsinki 00130, Finland

Ahuja, Shiney (Actor)
c/o Bunty Behl *Artist International
Management*
304-305 Oberoi Chambers II
B Wing Off New Link Road
Anderhi West, Mumbai 400053, India

Ah You, Junior (Athlete, Football Player)
55-690 Wahinepee St
Laie, NV 89129-7657, USA

Aida, Takefumi (Architect)
1-3-2 Okubo
Shinjukuku
Tokyo 169, JAPAN

Aiello, Anthony (Athlete, Football Player)
9 Taylor Ave
Norwalk, OH 44857, USA

Aiello, Danny (Actor, Director, Producer)
30 Chestnut Ridge Rd
Saddle River, NJ 07458, USA

Aiken, Blair (Race Car Driver)
4855 Highland Springs Rd.
Lakeport, CA 96453, USA

Aiken, Clay (Musician)
38 Topaz Jewel Ct
Durham, NC 27713, USA

Aiken, John (Athlete, Hockey Player)
18 Pinetree Rd
Billerica, MA 01821, USA

Aiken, Johnny (Athlete, Hockey Player)
18 Pine Tree Rd.
Billerica, MA 01821, USA

Alken, Liam (Actor)
c/o Ellen Gilbert *Abrams Artists Agency
(NY)*
275 Seventh Ave
26th Floor
New York, NY 10001, USA

Aiken, Linda H (Activist)
2209 Lombard St
Philadelphia, PA 19146, USA

Aiken, Sam (Athlete, Football Player)
103 New Bingham Ct
Cary, NC 27513, USA

Aiken, Sam (Athlete, Football Player)
9229 Dansforeshire Way
Wake Forest, NC 27587, us

Aikens, Carl (Athlete, Football Player)
931 W Arquilla Dr Apt 114
Glenwood, IL 60425, USA

Aikens, Carl (Athlete, Football Player)
931 W Arquilla Dr Apt 114s
Glenwood, IL 60425, s

Aikens, Curtis (Chef)
68 Baca Vista
Novato, CA 94947, USA

Aikens, Willie (Athlete, Baseball Player)
10206 Locust St
Kansas City, MO 64131-4214, USA

Aikman, Laura Holly (Actor)
551 Green Lanes
Palmers Green
London N13 3DR, UNITED KINGDOM
(UK)

Aikman, Troy (Athlete, Football Player,
Sportscaster)
4425 Highland Dr
Dallas, TX 75205, USA

Aikman-Smith, Valerie (Stylist)
2110 E Live Oak Dr
Los Angeles, CA 90068, USA

Ailes, Roger (Journalist)
218 Truman Dr
Cresskill, NJ 07626-1720, USA

Ailes, Roger E (Business Person)
c/o Staff Member *Fox News Channel (NY)*
1211 Ave of the Americas
Level C1
New York, NY 10036-8701, USA

Aimee, Anouk (Actor)
c/o Staff Member *ArtMedia*
20 avenue Rapp
Paris 75008, France

Aimi, Milton (Athlete, Soccer Player)
19927 Stonelodge Street
Katy, TX 77450-5201, USA

Ainge, Danny (Athlete, Baseball Player)
140 Wellesly Ave
Wellesly Hills, MA 02481-7209, USA

Ainge, Erik (Athlete, Football Player)
634 N.E.Kathleen Ct
Hillsboro, OR 97124-4029, USA

Ainsleigh, H Gordon (Athlete, Track
Athlete)
17119 Placer Hills Road
Meadow Vista, CA 95722, USA

Ainsworth, Kurt (Athlete, Baseball Player, Olympic Athlete)
15220 Memorial Tower Dr
Baton Rouge, LA 70810-0301, USA

Air, Donna (Model, Television Host)
c/o Staff Member *The Richard Stone Partnership*
2 Henrietta St
London WC2E 8PS, UK

Airborne Toxic Event, The (Music Group)
c/o Staff Member *Paradigm (Monterey)*
404 W Franklin St
Monterey, CA 93940, USA

Airpushers (Music Group)
c/o Staff Member *Paradigm (Monterey)*
404 W Franklin St
Monterey, CA 93940, USA

Air Supply (Music Group, Musician)
c/o Staff Member *Agency for the Performing Arts (APA-LA)*
405 S Beverly Dr
Suite 500
Beverly Hills, CA 90212-4425, USA

Air Traffic (Music Group, Musician)
c/o Staff Member *SuperVision Management Group*
Zeppelin Building
59-61 Farringdon Rd
London EC1M 3JB, UK

Al-Saud, Salman Sultan (Astronaut)
PO Box 18368
Riyadh 11415, SAUDI ARABIA

Aitay, Victor (Musician)
800 Deerfield Road
#203
Highland Park, IL 60035, USA

Aitch, Matt (Athlete, Basketball Player)
1525 Bentbrook Cir
Lansing, MI 48917-1402, USA

Aitken, Brad (Athlete, Hockey Player)
825 Royal Orchard Dr
Oshawa, ON L1K 1Z8, Canada

Aitken, Ellie Mae (Stylist)
c/o Staff Member *Fred Segal Beauty*
PO Box 5304
Beverly Hills, CA 90209, USA

Aitken, John (Artist)
University College
Slade Art School
London WC1E 6BT, UNITED KINGDOM (UK)

Aivazoff, Micah (Athlete, Hockey Player)
6916 Hammond St
Powell River, BC V8A 1R4, Canada

Aizenberg Selove, Fay (Physicist)
118 Cherry Lane
Wynnewood, PA 19096, USA

Aizley, Carrie (Actor)
c/o Staff Member *Much and House Public Relations*
8075 W 3rd St
Suite 500
Los Angeles, CA 90048, USA

Ajae, Franklyn (Comedian)
1312 S Orange Dr
Los Angeles, CA 90062, USA

Ajayrathnam (Actor)
78 Gajapathy Street
Shenoy Nagar
Chennai, TN 600 030, INDIA

Akaka, Daniel (Politician)
3656 Gunston Rd
Alexandria, VA 22302-2006, USA

Akaka, Daniel K. (Senator)
141 Hart Senate Office Building
Washington, DC 20510, USA

Akayev, Askar (President)
President's Office
Government House
Bishkek 720003, KYRGYZSTAN

Akbar, Hakim (Athlete, Football Player)
300 W Ocean Blvd Apt 6510
Long Beach, CA 90802, us

Akbar, Hakim (Athlete, Football Player)
29869 Vanderbilt St
Apt 4
Hayward, Ca 94544, USA

Akbar, Taufik (Astronaut)
Jalan Simp
Pahlawan III/24
Bandung 40124, INDONESIA

Akebono (Wrestler)
Azumazeki Stable
4-6-4 Higashi Komagala
Ryogoku
Tokyo, JAPAN

Akens, Jewel (Musician)
5228 Marburn Ave
Los Angeles, CA 90043, USA

Aker, Jack (Athlete, Baseball Player)
5911 E Bloomfield Rd
Scottsdale, AZ 85254-4338, USA

Akerlof, George A (Nobel Prize Laureate)
University of California
Berkeley 549 Evans
Hall# 3880
Berkeley, CA 94720-3181, USA

Akerlund, Jonas (Director)
c/o Staff Member *ICM Partners (ICM-LA)*
10250 Constellation Blvd Fl 7
Los Angeles, CA 90067, USA

Akerman, Malin (Actor)
2017 N Gramercy Pl
Los Angeles, CA 90068, USA

Akers, David (Athlete, Football Player)
16 Penhale Psge
Medford, NJ 08055, USA

Akers, Fred (Coach, Football Coach)
Purdue University
Athletic Dept
West Lafayette, IN 47907, USA

Akers, John F (Business Person)
PO Box 194
Pebble Beach, CA 93953, USA

Akers, Michelle (Athlete, Olympic Athlete, Soccer Player)
c/o Staff Member *US Soccer Federation*
1801 South Prairie Avenue
Chicago, IL 60616, USA

Akers, Thomas D Colonel (Astronaut)
HC 3 Box 35
Eminence, MO 65466-9504, USA

Akhtar, Farhan (Producer)
Excel Entertainment
205 Devroop Bldg, 36 Turner Rd
Opposite Tava Restaurant, Bandra West
Mumbai 400 050, India

Akhtar, Javed (Songwriter, Writer)
702 Sagar Samrat Green Field Road
Near Juhu P O Juhu
Bombay, MS 400 049, INDIA

Akihito (King)
Imperial Palace
1-1 Chiyoda
Chiyodaku
Tokyo 100, JAPAN

Akihito, Emperor (Politician)
Imperial Palace
1-1 Chiyoda-Chiyoda-Ku, Tokyo 100, Japan

Akihoto, EmperorThe Palace
1-1 ChiyodaChiyoda-Ku
Tokyo, JAPAN

Akil, Mara Brock (Producer, Writer)
c/o Andrea Nelson-Meigs *ICM Partners (ICM-LA)*
10250 Constellation Blvd Fl 7
Los Angeles, CA 90067, USA

Akil, Salim (Director)
c/o Staff Member *ICM Partners (ICM-LA)*
10250 Constellation Blvd Fl 7
Los Angeles, CA 90067, USA

Akili, Samaji (Athlete, Football Player)
10605 Caminito Cascara
San Diego, CA 92108, USA

Akin, Harold (Athlete, Football Player)
8216 NW 99th St
Oklahoma City, OK 73162, USA

Akin, Harold (Athlete, Football Player)
12608 Cobblestone Pkwy
Oklahoma, OK 73142, us

Akin, Henry (Athlete, Basketball Player)
18924 40th Pl NE
Lake Forest Park, WA 98155-2810, USA

Akin, W. Todd (Congressman, Politician)
117 Cannon HOB
Washington, DC 20515, USA

Akinnuoye-Agbaje, Adewale (Actor)
c/o Pamela Kohl *3 Arts Entertainment Inc*
9460 Wilshire Blvd
7th Floor
Beverly Hills, CA 90210, USA

Akins, Chris (Athlete, Football Player)
60 Gold Mine Springs Rd
Conway, AR 72032, USA

Akins, Chris (Athlete, Football Player)
11 McClure Acres Rd Apt 6
Conway, AR 72032, us

Akins, Rhett (Musician, Songwriter)
108 Cumberland Blue Trl
Hendersonville, TN 37075, USA

Akins, Sid (Athlete, Baseball Player, Olympic Athlete)
1655 W Sandtown Rd SW
Marietta, GA 30064-3744, USA

Akiu, Mike (Athlete, Football Player)
P.O. Box 1845
Kailua, HI 96734, USA

Akiu, Mike (Athlete, Football Player)
297 Kakahiaka St
Kailua, HI 96734, us

Akiyama, Kazuyoshi (Conductor)
Columbia Artists Mgmt Inc
165 W 57th St
New York, NY 10019, USA

Akiyama, Toyohiro (Astronaut, Journalist)
Tokyo Broadcasting Systems
3-6-5 Akasaka
Minaloku
Tokyo 107, JAPAN

Akiyoshi, Toshiko (Composer, Musician)
Berkeley Agency
2608 9th St
Berkeley, CA 94710, USA

Akon (Musician)
Konfidence Foundation
P.O. Box 190022
Atlanta, GA 31119-0022, USA

Akoshino (Royalty)
Imperial Palace
Tokyo, JAPAN

Akroyd, Dan (Actor, Musician, Producer, Writer)
c/o Fred Specktor *Creative Artists Agency (CAA-LA)*
2000 Ave Of The Stars
Los Angeles, CA 90067, USA

Aksyonov, Vassily P (Writer)
Random House
1745 Broadway
#B1
New York, NY 10019, USA

Aksyonov, Vladimir V (Cosmonaut)
Astrakhansky Per 5
Kv 100
Moscow 129010, RUSSIA

Alabama (Music Group)
c/o Coran Capshaw *Red Light Management (VA)*
PO Box 1467
Charlottesville, VA 22902, USA

Alagia, John (Producer)
c/o Sandy Robertson *Twenty First Republic Creative Management*
Prefers to be contact via telephone
CA, USA

Alagna, Roberto (Opera Singer)
Levon Sayan
2 Rue du Prieure
Nyon 1260, SWITZERLAND

Alaia, Azzeddine (Designer, Fashion Designer)
18 Rue de la Verrerie
Paris 75008, FRANCE

Alaigal, Selvakumar (Actor)
9A Pari St
Avvai Nagar Choolaimedu
Chennai, TN 600 094, INDIA

Alaimo, Doris (Stylist)
2560 Greencastle Ct
Oxnard, CA 93035, USA

Alaimo, Marc (Actor)
1936 Seminole Dr
Agoura Hills, CA 91301, USA

Alaina, Lauren (Musician)
c/o Simon Fuller *XIX Entertainment*
35-37 Parkgate Rd
32/33 Ransomes Dock
London SW11 4NP, UNITED KINGDOM (UK)

Alan, Buddy (Musician)
600 E Gilbert Dr
Tempe, AZ 85281, USA

Alan, Lori (Voice Over Artist)
9200 Sunset Blvd #1130
Los Angeles, CA 90069, USA

Alan, Reuber (Athlete, Football Player)
1202 Crosswind Dr
Murphy, TX 75094-4110, USA

Al and the Transamericans (Music Group)
c/o Staff Member *Paradigm (Monterey)*
404 W Franklin St
Monterey, CA 93940, USA

Alapa, Clifton (Athlete, Football Player)
3928 Country Light ST
Las Vegas, NV 89129-7657, USA

Alarcon, Arthur L (Judge)
US Court of Appeals
312 N Spring St
Los Angeles, CA 90012, USA

Alarie, Mark (Athlete, Basketball Player)
8514 Country Club Dr
Bethesda, MD 20817-4581, USA

Al-Assad, Bashar (Politician, President)
c/o Staff Member *Presidential Office (Syria)*
Muharreem Abu Rumanch
Al-Rashid Street
Damascas, Syria

Alatorre, Javier (Actor)
c/o Staff Member *TV Azteca*
Periferico Sur 4121
Colonia Fuentes del Pedregal
DF CP 14141, Mexico

al-Aziz, Abdullah Ibn Abdul (Prince)
Council of Ministers
Murabba
Riyadh 11121, SAUDI ARABIA

Alazraqui, Carlos (Actor)
4934 Cartwright Ave
Los Angeles, CA 91601, USA

Alba, Gibson (Athlete, Baseball Player)
87 E 17th St
Paterson, NJ 07524-1516, USA

Alba, Jessica (Actor)
1913 N Beverly Dr
Beverly Hills, CA 90210, USA

Albaladeio, Jonathan
12517 River Birch Dr
Riverview, FL 33569-8206, USA

Alban, Richard (Dick) (Athlete, Football Player)
306 Belpaire Ct
Newtown Square, PA 19073, USA

Albanese, Licia (Opera Singer)
Nathan Hale Dr
Wilson Point
South Norwalk, CT 06854, USA

Albarn, Damon (Musician, Songwriter, Writer)
CMO Mgmt
Ransomes Dock
35 Parkgale Road #32
London SW11 4NP, UNITED KINGDOM (UK)

Albaugh, Dennis (Misc)
1525 NE 36th St
Ankeny, IA 50021-6754, USA

Albea, Troy (Athlete, Football Player)
1070 L And N Rd
Lincolnton, GA 30817, USA

Albeck, Stan (Basketball Coach, Coach)
130 Tall Oak Dr
San Antonio, TX 78232, USA

Albee, Edward (Writer)
PO Box 697
Montauk, NY 11954-0503, USA

Albee, Edward F (Writer)
14 Harrison St
New York, NY 10013, USA

Albelin, Tommy (Athlete, Hockey Player)
Albany Devils 51S Pearl St Ste 14
Attn: Coaching Staff
Albany, NY 12207-1521, USA

Albelin, Tommy (Athlete, Coach, Hockey Player)
c/o Staff Member *New Jersey Devils*
Continental Arena
165 Mulberry St
Newark, NJ 07102-3611, USA

Alberghetti, Anna Maria (Actor, Musician)
10333 Chrysanthemum Lane
Los Angeles, CA 90077, USA

Alberghini, Tom (Athlete, Football Player)
8514 Hempstead Ave
Bethesda, MD 20817, USA

Alberoni, Sherry (Actor)
PO Box 161936
Altamonte Springs, FL 32716-1936, USA

Alberro, Jose
HC 2 Box4649
Sabana Hoyos, PR 00688-9405, USA

Albers, Hans (Business Person)
BASF AG
Carl-Bosch-Str 38
Ludwigshafen 78351, GERMANY

Albers, Kristi (Athlete, Golfer)
5872 Via Cuesta Dr
El Paso, TX 79912-6608, USA

Albers, Matthew James (Athlete, Baseball Player)
15 S Swanwick Pl
Tomball, TX 77375-4478, USA

Alberstein, Chara (Musician)
DL Media
PO Box 2728
Bala Cynwyd, PA 19004, USA

Albert, Calvin (Artist)
6525 Brandywine Dr S
Margate, FL 33063, USA

Albert, John G (General)
Albert Farms
RR2
Monroe, VA 24574, USA

Albert, Lewis (Athlete, Football Player)
3532 Macedonia Rd
Centreville, MS 39631-3634, USA

Albert, Marv (Sportscaster)
150 Columbus Ave PH 2A
New York, NY 10023-5972, USA

Albert, Marv (Sportscaster)
TNT-TV
Sports Department
1050 Techwood Dr
Atlanta, GA 30318, USA

Alberti, Micah (Actor)
c/o David Dean Portelli *David Dean Management*
6338 Wilshire Blvd
Los Angeles, CA 90048, USA

Albert II (King)
Koninklijk Palais
Rue de Brederode
Brussels 1000, BELGIUM

Alberto, Padre (Actor)
c/o Staff Member *Telemundo*
2470 West 8th Avenue
Hialeah, FL 33010, USA

Albert (Prince) (Royalty)
Palais de Monaco
Boite Postale 518
Monacode Cedex 98015, MONACO

Alberts, Andrew (Athlete, Hockey Player)
205 Mill St Apt 302
Excelsior, MN 55331-2105, USA

Alberts, Francis "Butch"
3063 Amberlea Ln
Baldwinsville, NY 13027-1613, USA

Alberts, Francis (Butch) (Athlete, Baseball Player)
3063 Amberlea Ln
Baldwinsville, NY 13027, USA

Alberts, Trev (Athlete, Football Player)
10430 E Hickory Ridge Dr
Rochelle, IL 61068, USA

Alberty, Robert (Scientist)
1573 Cambridge St Apt 655
Cambridge, MA 02138-4380, USA

Albinski, Gillian V (Stylist)
5927 Pepperhill Rd
Charlotte, NC 28212-4638, USA

Albita (Musician)
Estefan Enterprises
6205 SW 40th St
Miami, FL 33155, USA

Albom, Mitch (Writer)
25600 Franklin Park Dr
Franklin, MI 48025, USA

Alborn, Alan (Athlete, Olympic Athlete, Skier)
PO Box 109
Willow, AK 99688-0109, USA

Alborzian, Cameron (Model)
c/o Staff Member *Storm Model Management*
5 Jubilee Pl
1st Floor
London SW3 3TD, UNITED KINGDOM

Albrecht, A Chim (Wrestler)
Physique Promotions
9668 Moss Glen Ave
Fountain Valley, CA 92708, USA

Albrecht, Alex (Actor)
c/o Mieke Gotha *Agentur Gotha*
Elisabethstrasse 19
München 80796, Germany

Albrecht, Gerd
Mariedi Anders Artists
535 El Camino del Mar
San Francisco, CA 94121, USA

Albrecht, Karl (Business Person)
ALDI Corporate
1200 N Kirk Rd
Batavia, IL 60510, USA

Albrecht, Kate (Actor)
c/o Brad Petrigala *Brillstein Entertainment Partners*
9150 Wilshire Blvd #350
Beverly Hills, CA 90212, USA

Albrecht, Ted (Athlete, Football Player)
1205 Cherry St
Winnetka, IL 60093, USA

Albrecht, Ted (Athlete, Football Player)
1314 S West Fork Dr
Lake Forest, IL 60045, us

Albright, Ethan (Athlete, Football Player)
19181 Ferry Field Ter
Leesburg, VA 20176, USA

Albright, Ethan (Athlete, Football Player)
PO Box 38337
Greensboro, NC 27438, us

Albright, Gerald (Musician)
c/o Ron Moss *Chapman Management*
14011 Ventura Blvd
Sherman Oaks 91423, USA

Albright, Ira (Athlete, Football Player)
4019 Wind River Dr
Dallas, TX 75216, USA

Albright, Irene (Stylist)
Imelda's Closet
62 Cooper Square
#200
New York, NY 10003, USA

Albright, Lola (Actor)
4524 N Clybourne Ave #314
Burbank, CA 91505, USA

Albright, Madeleine (Politician)
1318 34th St NW
Washington, DC 20007-2801, USA

Albright, Tenley (Athlete, Figure Skater, Olympic Athlete)
70 Suffolk Rd
Chestnut Hills, MA 02467, USA

Albright, William (Bill) (Athlete, Football Player)
315 Bolands Private Dr
Shell Lake, WI 54871, USA

Albring, Werner (Scientist)
Sudhohe 9
Dresden D-01217, Germany

Albritton, Vince (Athlete, Football Player)
2801 Denton Tap Rd
Lewisville, TX 75067, us

Albuquerque, Lita (Artist)
305 Boyd St
Los Angeles, CA 90013, USA

Albury, Victor (Vic) (Athlete, Baseball Player)
2109 E Bougainvillea Ave
Tampa, FL 33612-7035, USA

Albus, Jim (Athlete, Golfer)
3972 Somerset Dr
Unit 1
Sarasota, FL 34242-1110, USA

Alcala, Santo (Athlete, Baseball Player)
Ramon Mota #18
San Pedro de Macoris, Dominican Republic, USA

Alcantara, Izzy (Athlete, Baseball Player)
4059 240th Pl SE
Issaquah, WA 98029, USA

Alcaraz, Luis (Athlete, Baseball Player)
679 Calle Chihuahua
Urb Venus Gdns Norte
San Juan, PR 00926-4614, USA

Alcorn, Gary (Athlete, Basketball Player)
2552 Trenton Ave
Clovis, CA 93619-4249, USA

Alcorn, Randy (Motivational Speaker, Writer)
Eternal Perspective Ministries
39085 Pioneer Blvd
Suite 206
Sandy, OR 97055, USA

Alcott, Amy S (Athlete, Golfer)
323 Amalfi Dr
Santa Monica, CA 90402, USA

Alda, Alan (Actor)
210 Olivers Cove Ln
Water Mill, NY 11976, USA

Alda, Rutanya (Actor)
c/o Hazel Shallon *Shallon Star Management*
14320 Ventura Blvd #624
Sherman Oaks, CA 91423, USA

Aldcorn, Gary (Athlete, Hockey Player)
24 Bendamere Cres
Markham, ON L3P 6Y2, CANADA

Aldean, Jason (Musician)
c/o Chris Parr *Spalding Entertainment*
1025 16th Ave S
#303
Nashville, TN 37212, USA

Alden, Bruce (Producer)
c/o Staff Member *Vision Art Management*
9465 Wilshire Blvd Ste 870
Beverly Hills, CA 90212, USA

Alden, Ginger (Actor, Model, Musician)
25 Rolling Hill Ct
Sag Harbor, NY 11963, USA

Alden Robinson, Phil (Director, Producer, Writer)
Writers Co-op
4000 Warner Blvd
Bldg 1
Burbank, CA 91522, USA

Alder, Berni (Scientist)
Lawrence Radiation Laboratory
PO Box 808
Livermore, CA 94551-0808, USA

Alderete, Loretta (Athlete, Golfer)
43750 Salpare Pl
Indio, CA 92203-2941, USA

Alderfer-Benner, Gertrude (Athlete, Baseball Player)
2191 County Line Rd
East Greenville, PA 18041-2700, USA

Aldering, Gregory (Scientist)
1300 Arlington Blvd
El Cerrito, CA 94530-2515, USA

Alderman, Darrell (Race Car Driver)
DA Construction Co
8130 Flemingsburg Rd
Morehead, KY 40351, USA

Alderman, Grady (Athlete, Football Player)
62 Elk Valley Way
Evergreen, CO 80439, us

Alderman, Grady (Athlete, Football Player)
1990 Elk Valley Dr
Evergreen, CO 80439, USA

Alderson, Kristen (Actor)
c/o Staff Member *One Life to Live*
56 West 66th St.
New York, NY 10023, USA

Alderson, Richard Sandy (Commentator)
305 E 85th St
Ph B
New York, NY 10028-4672, USA

Alderton, John (Athlete, Football Player)
12314 Williams Rd SE
Cumberland, MD 21502, USA

Aldisert, Ruggero J (Judge)
120 Cremona Dr
#0
Goleta, CA 93117, USA

Aldiss, Brian (Writer)
Woodlands, Foxcombe Road
Boars Hill
Oxfordshire, OX1 5DL, England

Aldiss, Brian W (Writer)
Hambledon
39 Saint Andrews Road
Old Headington
Oxford OX3 9DL, UNITED KINGDOM (UK)

Aldred, Scott (Athlete, Baseball Player)
13435 Lakebrook Dr
Fenton, MI 48430-8420, USA

Aldred, Sophie (Actor)
1 Duchess St
#1
London S1N 3EE, UNITED KINGDOM (UK)

Aldrete, Mike (Athlete, Baseball Player)
22160 Toro HIlls Dr
Salinas, CA 93908-1131, USA

Aldrich, Cole (Athlete, Basketball Player)
c/o Jeff Schwartz *Excel Sports Management*
9665 Wilshire Blvd #500
Los Angeles, CA 90212, USA

Aldrich, Jay (Athlete, Baseball Player)
9209 S 51st St
Franklin, WI 53132-9275, USA

Aldrich, John H (Politician, Scientist)
Duke University
Political Science Dept
Durham, NC 27708, USA

Aldridge, Allen (Athlete, Football Player)
1702 Mossback Cir
Fresno, TX 77545-, us

Aldridge, Cory (Athlete, Baseball Player)
417 Penrose Dr
Abilene, TX 79601-6228, USA

Aldridge, Donald O (General)
1004 Lincon Rd Ste 168
168
Bellevue, NE 68005-2341, USA

Aldridge, Edward C (General)
4308 Lorcom Ln
Arlington, VA 22207-3308, USA

Aldridge, Edward C (pete) Jr (Government Official)
Aerospace Corp
2350 E El Segundo Blvd
El Segundo, CA 90245, USA

Aldridge, Jerry (Athlete, Football Player)
297 Ellis
Jacksonville, TX 75766, USA

Aldridge, Jerry
307 Park Ln
Jacksonville, TX 75766, us

Aldridge, Keith (Athlete, Hockey Player)
80 Joslyn Rd
Lake Orion, MI 48362-2215, USA

Aldridge, Kevin (Athlete, Football Player)
2820 McKinnon St
Apt 3009
Dallas, TX 75201, USA

Aldridge, Kevin (Athlete, Football Player)
113 Sansovino
Ladera Ranch, CA 92694, us

Aldridge, Lamarcus (Athlete, Basketball Player)
23232 SW Stafford Hill Dr
West Linn, OR 97068-9615, USA

Aldridge, Melvin (Athlete, Football Player)
14618 Braden Dr E
Houston, TX 77047, USA

Aldridge, Sabrina (Actor)
c/o Allee Newhoff *Elite Model Management*
119 Washington Ave
Suite 501
Miami Beach, FL 33139, USA

Aldridge Jr, Allen (Athlete, Football Player)
2111 Hammerwood Dr
Missouri City, TX 77489, USA

Aldridge Sr, Allen (Athlete, Football Player)
2111 Hammerwood Dr
Missouri City, TX 77489, USA

Aldrin, Buzz (Astronaut)
10380 Wilshire Blvd. #703
Los Angeles, CA 90024, USA

Ale, Arnold (Athlete, Football Player)
308 E Desford St
Carson, CA 90745, USA

Aleaga, Ink (Athlete, Football Player)
14612 22nd Ave SW
Burien, WA 98166, USA

Aleandro, Norma (Actor)
Blanco Encalada 1150
Buenos Aires 1428, ARGENTINA

Alechinsky, Pierre (Artist)
2 Bis Rue Henri Barbusse
Bougival 78380, FRANCE

Alejandro, Kevin (Actor)
c/o Stewart Strunk *Main Title Entertainment*
8383 Wilshire Blvd
Suite 408
Los Angeles, CA 90211, USA

Alejo, Bob
3724A Portofino Way
Santa Barbara, CA 93105-4453, USA

Alekperov, Vagit (Business Person)
Lukoil
11, Sretensky Blvd
Moscow 101000, Russia

Aleksander, Grant (Actor)
66 Crow Hill Rd
Freehold, NJ 07728, USA

Aleksinas, Charles (Chuck) (Athlete, Basketball Player)
16 Litchfield St
Morris, CT 06763-1522, USA

Aleksiy II (Religious Leader)
Moscow Patriarchy
Chisty Per 5
Moscow 119034, RUSSIA

Aleno, Charles (Athlete, Baseball Player)
601 Marion Ct
Deland, FL 32720, USA

Alerlol, George (Nobel Prize Laureate)
University of California
Economics Dept
Berkeley, CA 94720, USA

Alesi, Jean (Race Car Driver)
HWA GmbH
Benzstr 8
Affalterbach 71563, GERMANY

Alessandri, Mary Beth (Stylist)
c/o Staff Member *Zenobia Agency Inc*
PO Box 909
Groveland, CA 95321, USA

Alessi, Raquel (Actor)
c/o Rhonda Price *Gersh (NY)*
41 Madison Ave
New York, NY 10010, USA

Alex (Actor)
2 Rajaji North Street
Pushpa Nagar Nungambakkam
Chennai, TN 600 034, India

Alex, Keith (Athlete, Football Player)
6985 Reno Cir
Beaumont, TX 77708-3594, USA

Alex, Keith (Athlete, Football Player)
9750 Windwater Dr Apt 128
Houston, TX 77075, us

Alexakis, Art (Musician)
Pinnacle Entertainment
30 Glenn St
White Plains, NY 10603, USA

Alexakos, Steve (Athlete, Football Player)
306 Linden St
Boise, ID 83706, USA

Alexakos, Steve (Athlete, Football Player)
22300 Hathaway Ave Unit A
Hayward, CA 94541, us

Alexander, A Lamar (Ex-Governor, Senator)
455 Dirksen Senate Office Building
Washington, DC 20510, USA

Alexander, Andrew (Producer)
9530 Cedarbrook Dr
Beverly Hills, CA 90210, USA

Alexander, Brent (Athlete, Football Player)
349 Remington Ave
Gallatin, TN 37066, USA

Alexander, Brooke (Actor)
c/o Staff Member *Abrams Artists Agency (LA)*
9200 Sunset Blvd
11th Floor
Los Angeles, CA 90069, USA

Alexander, Bruce (Athlete, Football Player)
508 Englewood Dr
Lufkin, TX 75901, USA

Alexander, Caroline (Writer)
c/o Staff Member *Random House Publicity (Toronto)*
1 Toronto St
Suite 300
Toronto, ON M5C 2V6, Canada

Alexander, Charles (Athlete, Football Player)
3711 Heritage Colony Dr
Missouri City, TX 77459, USA

Alexander, Christopher W J (Architect)
2701 Shasta Road
Berkeley, CA 94708, USA

Alexander, Claire (Athlete, Hockey Player)
11 Tammy Cir
St.Catherines, ON L2N 1R2, Canada

Alexander, Clifford L Jr (General, Politician)
412 A St SE
Washington, DC 20003-3807, USA

Alexander, Corey (Athlete, Basketball Player)
440 Alpha St
Waynesboro, VA 22980, USA

Alexander, Cory (Athlete, Basketball Player)
1226 Cardwell Rd
Crozier, VA 23039-2402, USA

Alexander, Dan (Athlete, Football Player)
58520 Saint Clement Ave
Plaquemine, LA 70764, USA

Alexander, Dan (Athlete, Football Player)
407 Knob Ct
Franklin, TN 37064, USA

Alexander, David (Athlete, Football Player)
11420 S Granite Pl
Tulsa, OK 74137, USA

Alexander, Denise (Actor)
270 N Canon Dr
#1919
Beverly Hills, CA 90210, USA

Alexander, Derrick (Athlete, Football Player)
1548 Lake Polo Dr
Odessa, FL 33556, USA

Alexander, Doyle
Los Angeles Dodgers
5416 Hunter Park Ct
Arlington, TX 76017-3557, USA

Alexander, Doyle (Athlete, Baseball Player)
5416 Hunter Park Ct
Arlington, TX 76017-3557, USA

Alexander, Eric (Musician)
Joel Chriss
300 Mercer St
#3J
New York, NY 10003, USA

Alexander, Eric
87 Franklin St Unit 204
Quincy, MA 02169, USA

Alexander, Erika (Actor)
c/o Staff Member Untitled Entertainment (LA)
350 S. Beverly Dr #200
Beverly Hills, CA 90212, USA

Alexander, Flex (Actor)
c/o Joel Zadak Principato/Young Management
9465 Wilshire Blvd
Suite 430
Beverly Hills, CA 90212, USA

Alexander, Gary (Athlete, Baseball Player)
5420 Senford Ave
Los Angeles, CA 90056-1029, USA

Alexander, Gerald (Athlete, Baseball Player)
307 Woodland Dr
Donaldsonville, LA 70346-9752, USA

Alexander, Gwen Cheeseman (Athlete, Hockey Player, Olympic Athlete)
502 Maury St
Lexington, VA 24450-2626, USA

Alexander, Harold (Athlete, Football Player)
590 J D Dr
Pickens, SC 29671, USA

Alexander, J (Reality TV Star, Television Host)
c/o Staff Member Bankable Productions
226 W 26th St
4th Floor
New York, NY 10001-6700, USA

Alexander, Jaimie (Actor)
c/o Randy James James/Levy/Jacobson Management Inc
3500 W Olive Ave
Suite 1470
Burbank, CA 91505, USA

Alexander, Jamie (Actor)
c/o Alicia Gelernt Alicia Gelernt
275 Madison Ave.
Floor 28
New York, NY 10016, USA

Alexander, Jane (Actor, Government Official)
William Morris Agency
1325 Ave of Americans
New York, NY 10019, USA

Alexander, Jason (Actor, Comedian, Producer)
355 S June St
Los Angeles, CA 90210, USA

Alexander, Jeff (Athlete, Football Player)
5283 Elkhart St
Denver, CO 80239, USA

Alexander, Jeff
5283 Elkhart St
Denver, CO 80239, USA

Alexander, John (Athlete, Football Player)
312 Lee Pl
Plainfield, NJ 07063, USA

Alexander, Jules (Musician)
Variety Artists
1924 Spring St
Paso Robles, CA 93446, USA

Alexander, Keith (Actor)
c/o Staff Member Cunningham Escott Slevin & Doherty (CESD-LA)
10635 Santa Monica Blvd
130
Los Angeles, CA 90025, USA

Alexander, Kenneth (Cartoonist)
1182 Glen Rd
Lafayette, CA 94549-3044, USA

Alexander, Kermit (Athlete, Football Player)
16651 Stallion Pl
Riverside, CA 92504, USA

Alexander, Khandi (Actor)
8262 Woodshill Tr
Los Angeles, CA 90069, USA

Alexander, Lamar (Politician)
565 Pennsylvania Ave
NW Apt 702, Washington DC, 20001-4936

Alexander, Lloyd (Writer)
c/o Staff Member Random House Publicity
1745 Broadway
New York, NY 10019, USA

Alexander, Manny (Athlete, Baseball Player)
3660 N Lake Dr
Apt 2664
Chicago, IL 60613, USA

Alexander, Matt (Athlete, Baseball Player)
2419 Stonewall St
Shreveport, LA 71103-3451, USA

alexander, maximillian (Actor)
c/o Staff Member Schumacher Management
1122 San Vicente Blvd.
Santa Monica, CA 90402, USA

Alexander, Mike
2700 N Hayden Rd Apt 1096
Scottsdale, AZ 85257, USA

Alexander, Millette (Actor)
157 Roseville Rd
Westport, CT 06880, USA

Alexander, Monty (Musician)
Bennett Morgan
1282 RR 376
Wappingers Falls, NY 12590, USA

Alexander, Narond
530 Winnepeg Dr
Colorado Springs, CO 80910, USA

Alexander, Newell (Actor)
5830 Morella Ave
N Hollywood, CA 91607, USA

Alexander, Patrise (Athlete, Football Player)
15035 Westpark Dr
Apt 514
Houston, TX 77082, USA

Alexander, P J
1004 Reap Ln
Lawrenceville, GA 30043, USA

Alexander, Ray (Athlete, Football Player)
1631 Royal Palm Dr
Edgewater, FL 32132-3213, USA

Alexander, Ray (Athlete, Football Player)
1631 Royal Palm Dr
Edgewater, FL 32132, USA

Alexander, R Minter (General)
824 Eden Court
Alexandria, VA 22308, USA

Alexander, Robert (Athlete, Football Player)
2312 S Walnut Dr
Saint Albans, WV 25177, USA

Alexander, Robert M (Misc)
14 Moor Park Mount
Leeds LS6 4BU, UNITED KINGDOM (UK)

Alexander, Robert M (General)
The Pentagon Deputy
Washington, DC 20301-0001, USA

Alexander, Roc (Athlete, Football Player)
22020 E Belleview Pl
Aurora, CO 80015, USA

Alexander, Rodney (Congressman, Politician)
316 Cannon HOB
Washington, DC 20515, USA

Alexander, Rogers (Athlete, Football Player)
8182 Rainwater Cir
Manassas, VA 20111, USA

Alexander, Sarah (Actor)
c/o Jane Brand Independent Talent Group (ITG-UK)
Oxford House
76 Oxford St
London W1D 1BS, UK

Alexander, Sasha (Actor, Producer)
2241 Chelan Dr
Los Angeles, CA 90068, USA

Alexander, Shasha (Actor, Producer)
c/o Steve Dontanville Circle of Confusion (NY)
8609 E Washington Blvd #8607
Culver City, CA 90232, USA

Alexander, Shaun (Athlete, Football Player)
c/o Ben Dogra CAA - St. Louis
222 S Central Ave
Suite 1008
St Louis, MO 63105, USA

Alexander, Stephen (Athlete, Football Player)
4700 Flint Ridge Cir
Norman, OK 73072, USA

Alexander, Susana (Actor)
c/o Staff Member TV Azteca
Periferico Sur 4121
Colonia Fuentes del Pedregal
DF CP 14141, Mexico

Alexander, Victor (Athlete, Basketball Player)
3450 Holy Trail Ln
Alpharetta, GA 30022-5943, USA

Alexander, Vincent (Athlete, Football Player)
622 W 30th Ave
Covington, LA 70433, USA

Alexander, Willie (Athlete, Football Player)
7219 Holder Forest Cir
Houston, TX 77088, USA

Alexander, Willie (Musician)
Tournmaline Music Group
894 Mayville Road
Bethel, PA 04217, USA

Alexander of Weedon, Robert S (Financier)
National Westminster Bank
41 Lothbury
London EC2P 2BP, UNITED KINGDOM (UK)

Alexander (Prince Yogoslavia) (Prince)
36 Park Lane
London W1Y 3LE, UNITED KINGDOM (UK)

Alexandre, Boniface (Judge, President)
President's Office
Palacio Nacional
Port-au-Prince, HAITI

Alexandrov, Alexander P (Cosmonaut)
Hovanskaya Ul 3
#27
Moscow 129515, RUSSIA

Alexeev, Nikita (Athlete, Hockey Player)
PO Box 3342
Riverview, FL 33578, USA

Alexie, Sherman (Writer)
PO Box 376
Wellpinit, WA 99040, USA

Alexis, Alton (Athlete, Football Player)
7020 Shadow Creek Ct
Fort Worth, TX 76162, USA

Alexis, Kim (Actor)
c/o Alexandria Alton *IMG*
304 Park Ave S Fl 12
New York, NY 10010, USA

Alexis, Kim (Athlete, Hockey Player)
982 Ponte Verda Blvd
Ponte Vedra Beach, FL 32082-4068, USA

Alfaro, Jason (Athlete, Baseball Player)
7409 Pensacola Ave
Fort Worth, TX 76116-7834, USA

Al Fayed, Mohammed
The Ritz Hotel Place Vendome
Paris, FRANCE

Alferov, Zhores (Nobel Prize Laureate)
Ioffe Physico-Technical Institute
26 Polyteknicheskaya
Saint Petersburg 194021, Russia

Alfieri, Janet (Cartoonist)
15 Bumpus road
Plymouth, MA 02360-3511, USA

Alflen, Ted (Athlete, Football Player)
960 NE 27th Ave
Pompano Beach, FL 33062, USA

Alfonseca, Antonio (Athlete, Baseball Player)
3020 SW 189th Ter
Miramar, FL 33029-5861, USA

Alfonsi, Sharyn (Correspondent)
c/o Staff Member *ABC News*
77 W 66th St
3rd Floor
New York, NY 10023, USA

Alfonso, Carlos (Athlete, Baseball Player, Coach)
1171 Royal Palm Dr
Naples, FL 34103-4849, USA

Alfonso, Kristian (Actor)
7577 Mulholland Dr
Los Angeles, CA 90046, USA

Alfonzo, Edgar (Athlete, Baseball Player)
3745 Marietta Way
Saint Cloud, FL 34772-8714, USA

Alfonzo, Edgardo (Athlete, Baseball Player)
8035 Spendthrift Ln
Port Saint Lucie, FL 34986, USA

Alford, Brian (Athlete, Football Player)
21011 Kenosha St
Oak Park, MI 48237, USA

Alford, Bruce
105 County Road 2965
Kopperl, TX 76652, USA

Alford, Darnell (Athlete, Football Player)
6874 Allen Cir Apt 13
Norcross, GA 30093, USA

Alford, Jay
150 Brittany Ct
Clifton, NJ 07013, USA

Alford, Lynwood (Athlete, Football Player)
355 Moon Clinton Rd Apt 2
Coraopolis, PA 15108, USA

Alford, Mike (Athlete, Football Player)
801 Valparaiso Blvd
Niceville, FL 32578, USA

Alford, Steve (Basketball Player, Olympic Athlete)
11600 Zinfandel Ave NE
Albuquerque, NM 87122-7104, USA

Alfredsson, Daniel (Athlete, Hockey Player)
c/o Staff Member *C A A Hockey*
822 11th Ave SW
Suite 204
Calgary, AB T2R 0E5, Canada

Alfredsson, Helen (Athlete, Golfer)
6043 Jamestown Park
Orlando, FL 32819-4435, USA

Algabid, Hamid (President)
National Assembly
Vice President's Office
Niamey, NIGER

Algate, Andrew (Scientist)
15507 Bay Green Ct
Houston, TX 77059-5815, USA

Al-Hoss, Selim (Prime Minister)
Premier's Office
Serail
Place de l'Eloile
Beirut, LEBANON

Al Hussein, HH King Abdullah (Royalty)
The Royal Hashemite Court
Amman, Jordan

Ali, Laila (Athlete, Boxer)
4801 Azucena Rd
Woodland Hills, CA 91364, USA

Ali, May May (Actor)
c/o Kristene Wallis *Wallis Agency*
210 N Pass Ave
Suite 205
Burbank, CA 915053989, USA

Ali, Muhammad (Athlete, Boxer)
Ali Farm
PO Box 187
Berrien Springs, MI 49103, USA

Ali, Somy (Actor, Bollywood)
208 Vindhyachal 22 Mount Mary Road
Bandra
Bombay, MS 400 050, INDIA

Ali, Tariq (Writer)
c/o Anthony Arnove *Roam Agency*
45 Main St
Suite 727
Brooklyn, NY 11201-1076

Ali, Tatyana (Actor)
c/o James Weir *Anderson Group Public Relations*
8060 Melrose Ave Fl 4
Los Angeles, CA 90046, USA

Alia, Alyssa (Stylist)
3 Edgewood Ct
North Caldwell, NJ 07006, USA

Alibar, Lucy (Writer)
c/o David Gersh *Gersh (LA)*
9465 Wilshire Blvd
Suite 600
Beverly Hills, CA 90212, USA

Alibaruho, Kwatsi (Scientist)
4504 Canyon Crest Dr
League City, TX 77573-3592, USA

Alicea, Luis (Athlete, Baseball Player)
2140 C Rd
Loxahatchee, FL 33470-3837, USA

Alicea, Wilmer (Baby Rasta) (Musician)
c/o Staff Member *Universal Music Publishing Group*
2440 Sepulveda Blvd
Suite 100
Los Angeles, CA 90064-1712, USA

Alice In Chains (Music Group)
c/o David Benveniste *Velvet Hammer*
9014 Melrose Ave
Los Angeles, CA 90069, USA

Alicia, Ana (Actor)
13555 Valley Vista Blvd
Sherman Oaks, CA 91423, USA

Alien Ant Farm (Music Group)
c/o David Gibson *New Ocean Media*
270 Doug Baker Blvd
Suite 700
Burmingham, AL 35242, USA

Aliens, The (Music Group)
c/o Staff Member *Paradigm (Monterey)*
404 W Franklin St
Monterey, CA 93940, USA

Alikhan, Anwar (Actor)
Parkavi Apartments Phase IV No 15-F 18
Mariamman Koil Street
West K K Nagar
Chennai, TN 600 078, INDIA

Ali Khan, Saif (Actor, Bollywood)
c/o Jai Khanna *Brillstein Entertainment Partners*
9150 Wilshire Blvd #350
Beverly Hills, CA 90212, USA

Alington, William H (Architect)
60 Homewood Crescent
Wellington, NEW ZEALAND

Alipate, Tuineau (Athlete, Football Player)
801 E 101st St
Minneapolis, MN 55420, USA

Alisha (Musician)
Famous Artists Agency
250 W 57th St
New York, NY 10107, USA

Alison, Jane (Writer)
FarrarStraus Giroux
19 Union Square W
New York, NY 10003, USA

Alito, Samuel A Jr (Judge)
US Court of Appeals
US Courthouse
50 Walnut St
Newark, NJ 07102, USA

Aliyev, Ilham (President)
President's Office
Baku 370066, AZERBAIJAN

Alkan, Erol (Musician)
c/o Joel Zimmerman *WME (WMA-NY)*
1325 Ave of the Americas
New York, NY 10019, USA

Al-Kharafi, Nasser (Business Person)
M A Kharafi Group Building
Shuwaikh Industrial Area
P.O. Box 886
Kuwait Safat 13009, Kuwait

Allaben, Maureen (Stylist)
6536 Jamestown Pl
Atlanta, GA 30084, USA

Allam, Roger (Actor)
Richard Stone Partnership
2 Henrietta St
London WC2E 8PS, UNITED KINGDOM

All American Rejects (Music Group, Musician)
c/o John Dehais *Pat's Management Company*
5900 Wilshire Blvd #1720
Los Angeles, CA 90036, USA

Allan, Gabrielle (Producer)
c/o Staff Member *United Talent Agency (UTA)*
9336 Civic Center Dr
Beverly Hills, CA 90210, USA

Allan, Gary (Musician)
114 Walnut Dr
Hendersonville, TN 37075, USA

Allan, Jed (Actor)
76470 Minaret Way
Palm Desert, CA 92211, USA

Allan, Nancy Mayer (Stylist)
c/o Staff Member *The Milton Agency (LA)*
6715 Hollywood Blvd
#204
Los Angeles, CA 90028, USA

Allan, Stephen D (Steve) (Golfer)
c/o Staff Member *Pro-Sport Management*
8355 E Hartford Dr
Suite 105
Scottsdale, AZ 85255-2533, USA

Allanson, Andy (Athlete, Baseball Player)
38713 Tierra Sub ida Ave
102
Palmdale, CA 93551-4562, USA

Allard, Beatrice (Athlete, Baseball Player)
1040 Ridgewood Dr
Lillian, AL 36549-5334, USA

Allard, Brian (Athlete, Baseball Player)
22102 N Perry Rd
Colbert, WA 99005-9488, USA

Allard, Brian (Athlete, Baseball Player)
22102 N Perry Rd
Colbert, WA 99005, USA

Allard, Wayne (Politician)
5328 Lighthouse Point Ct
Loveland, CO 80537-7915, USA

Allawi, Iyad (Prime Minister)
Prime Minister's Office
Karradat Mariam
Baghdad, IRAQ

Allbaugh, Joseph (Government Official)
Federal Emergency Management Agency
500 C St SW
Washington, DC 20472, USA

Allegre, Claude J (Misc)
Recherce/Technologie Institute
110 Rue Grenelle
Paris 75700, FRANCE

Allegre, Raul (Athlete, Football Player)
6500 Rain Creek Pkwy
Austin, TX 78759, USA

Allem, Fulton (Athlete, Golfer)
6876 Hidden Glade Pl
Sanford, FL 32771-6429, USA

Allen, Aleisha (Actor)
c/o Jan Jarrett *Jordan Gill & Dornbaum*
150 Fifth Ave
Suite 308
New York, NY 10011, USA

Allen, Andrew (Astronaut)
205 Highland Woods Dr
Safety Harbor, FL 34695-5437, USA

Allen, Andrew M Lt Colonel (Astronaut)
205 Highland Woods Dr
Safety Harbor, FL 34695-5437, USA

Allen, Anthony (Athlete, Football Player)
956 20th Ave
Seattle, WA 98122, USA

Allen, Bernie (Athlete, Baseball Player)
3725 Coventry Way
Carmel, IN 46033-3026, USA

Allen, Beth (Athlete, Golfer)
1602 Peacock Ave
Sunnyvale, CA 94087, USA

Allen, Betty (Opera Singer)
Harlem School of Arts
645 Saintt Nicholas Ave
New York, NY 10030, USA

Allen, Bob (Athlete, Baseball Player)
PO Box 677
Tatum, TX 75691-0677, USA

Allen, Bob (Athlete, Basketball Player)
117 Quarter Mile Way
Nicholasville, KY 40356-8220, USA

Allen, Bruce (Race Car Driver)
Reher Morrison Motorsports
1120 Enterprise Place
Arlington, TX 76001, USA

Allen, Bryan (Athlete, Hockey Player)
Octagon Sports Management
66 Slater St 23rd Fl
Attn Larry Kelly
Ottawa, ON K1P 5H1, Canada

Allen, Buddy (Athlete, Football Player)
3689 Westmoreland Dr
Mays Landing, NJ 08330, USA

Allen, Byron (Comedian)
1115 Calle Vista Dr
Beverly Hills, CA 90210, USA

Allen, Carl
1614 Hornsby Ave
Saint Louis, MO 63147, USA

Allen, Chad (Actor)
7326 Brightwater Oaks Dr
Tampa, FL 33625, USA

Allen, Chad (Athlete, Baseball Player, Olympic Athlete)
7152 Blackwood Dr
Dallas, TX 75231-5604, USA

Allen, Christa B. (Actor)
c/o Holly Williams *Williams Unlimited*
5010 Buffalo Ave
Sherman Oaks, CA 91423

Allen, Chuck
192 Victoria Loop
Port Townsend, WA 98368, USA

Allen, C Keith (Athlete, Hockey Player)
10000 Highland Ave
Long Beach Township, NJ 08008, USA

Allen, Clarence R (Scientist)
1763 Royal Oaks Dr #F306
Duarte, CA 91010-1987, USA

Allen, Dalva (Athlete, Football Player)
337 Daingerfield St
Pittsburg, TX 75686, USA

Allen, Damon (Athlete, Football Player)
Damon Allen Quarterback Academy
26-111 Zenway Blvd
Vaughan, ON L4H2Y7, Canada

Allen, Danielle Sherie (Actor)
c/o Staff Member *Privilege Talent Agency*
PO Box 260860
Encino, CA 91426-0860, USA

Allen, Debbie (Actor, Choreographer)
607 Marguerita Ave
Santa Monica, CA 90402, USA

Allen, Derek (Athlete, Football Player)
6206 Woodward Ln
Milton, FL 32570, USA

Allen, Dick (Athlete, Baseball Player)
983 Possum Hollow Rd
Wampum, PA 16157-2817, USA

Allen, Dick (Athlete, Baseball Player)
P.O. Box 254
Wampum, PA 16157, USA

Allen, Don (Athlete, Football Player)
17303 Kermier Rd
Hockley, TX 77447, USA

Allen, Doug (Athlete, Football Player)
10245 Collins Ave Apt 8A
Bal Harbour, FL 33154, USA

Allen, Doug (Artist)
c/o Staff Member *Fantagraphics Books*
7563 Lake City Way
Seattle, WA 98115, USA

Allen, Duane (Actor)
216 Spring Valley Rd
Hendersonville, TN 37075, USA

Allen, Dusty (Athlete, Baseball Player)
913 Estrella Vista St
Las Vegas, NV 89138-7578, USA

Allen, Earl (Athlete, Football Player)
8015 Duffield Ln
Houston, TX 77071, USA

Allen, Eddie (Athlete, Football Player)
3321 W Fisher St
Pensacola, FL 32505, USA

Allen, Egypt (Athlete, Football Player)
2115 Rubens Dr
Dallas, TX 75224, USA

Allen, Eric (Athlete, Football Player)
484 San Eliio St
San Diego, CA 92106, USA

Allen, Frances E (Scientist)
Finney Farm
Croton on Hudson, NY 10520, USA

Allen, George (Politician)
4296 Neitzey Pl
Alexandria, VA 22309-3069, USA

Allen, George F (Ex-Governor, Ex-Senator)
Young America's Foundation
F.M. Kirby Freedom Center
110 Eden St
Herndon, VA 20170, USA

Allen, Geri (Composer, Musician)
Clayton Ross Productions
307 Lake St
San Francisco, CA 94118, USA

Allen, Grady (Athlete, Football Player)
317 Circleview Dr N
Hurst, TX 76054, USA

Allen, Greg (Athlete, Football Player)
5006 Persimmon Hollow Rd
Milton, FL 32583, USA

Allen, Hank (Athlete, Baseball Player)
P.O. Box 4612
Upper Marlboro, MD 20775-0612, USA

Allen, Henry (Critic)
Washington Post
Editorial Dept 1150 15th St NW
Washington, DC 20071, USA

Allen, Herb (Business Person)
Allen & Co
711 5th Ave Fl 9
New York, NY 10022, USA

Allen, Jackie (Athlete, Football Player)
7152 Blackwood Dr
Dallas, TX 75231, USA

Allen, Jamie (Athlete, Baseball Player)
1920 E Belmont Dr
Tempe, AZ 85284-1719, USA

Allen, Jared (Athlete, Football Player)
c/o Ken Harris *Optimum Sports Management*
3225 S MacDill Ave
Suite 330
Tampa, FL 33629, USA

Allen, Jared (Athlete, Football Player)
c/o Denise White *EAG Sports Management*
12910 Agustin Pl
Playa Vista, CA 90094, USA

Allen, Jason (Athlete, Football Player)
2002 Edwards Ave
Muscle Shoals, AL 35661, USA

Allen, Jeff (Athlete, Football Player)
902 Warren Dr
Centerville, IN 47330, USA

Allen, Jerry (Athlete, Football Player)
14 Washington Valley Rd
Morristown, NJ 07960, USA

Allen, Jimmy (Athlete, Football Player)
13832 Iron Rock Pl
Victorville, CA 92395, USA

Allen, Joan (Actor)
c/o Simon Halls *Slate Public Relations*
9000 Sunset Blvd #915
West Hollywood, CA 90069, USA

Allen, Johnny (Race Car Driver)
301 Rockmont Rd
Greenville, SC 29615, USA

Allen, John R. (General)
ISAF Public Affairs Office
Media Operations Center, NATO
Headquarters
Blvd Leopold III
Brussels 1110, Belgium

Allen, Jonelle (Actor)
c/o Staff Member *Silver Massetti & Szatmary (SMS) Talent Inc*
8383 Wilshire Blvd
Suite 230
Beverly Hills, CA 90211, USA

Allen, Joseph P (Astronaut)
LBJ Sapce Center
c/o Astronaut Office
2101 NASA Rd 1
Houston, TX 77058, USA

Allen, Joseph P Dr (Astronaut)
4051 Mansion Dr NW
Washington, DC 20007-2135, USA

Allen, J Presson (Producer, Writer)
Lewis Allen Productions
1501 Broadway #1614
New York, NY 10036, USA

Allen, Karen (Actor)
Karen Allen Fiber Arts
8 Railroad St
Great Barrington, MA 01230, USA

Allen, Keegan (Actor)
c/o Konrad Leh *Creative Talent Group*
1900 Avenue of the Stars
Suite 2475
Los Angeles, CA 90067, USA

Allen, Keith
Philadelphia Flyers 3601 S Broad St Ste 2
Attn: Executive VP
Philadelphia, PA 19148-5297

Allen, Keith (Athlete, Hockey Player)
10000 Highland Ave
Long Beach Township, NJ 08008, USA

Allen, Kenderick (Athlete, Football Player)
5214 Lost Cove Ln
Spring, TX 77373, USA

Allen, Kevin (Athlete, Football Player)
2422 Hazelcrest Ln
Cincinnati, OH 45231, USA

Allen, Kevin (Director)
William Morris Agency
52/53 Poland Place
London W1F 7LX, UNITED KINGDOM (UK)

Allen, Kim (Athlete, Baseball Player)
2705 La Praix St
Highland, CA 92346-1928, USA

Allen, Kris (Musician)
c/o Staff Member *19 Entertainment*
33/32 Ransomes Dock
35-37 Parkgate Rd
London SW11 4NP, UK

Allen, Krista (Actor)
c/o Todd Eisner *Agency for the Performing Arts (APA-LA)*
405 S Beverly Dr
Suite 500
Beverly Hills, CA 90212-4425, USA

Allen, Larry C (Athlete, Football Player)
401 Kingswood Ln
Danville, CA 94506, USA

Allen, Leo (Writer)
c/o Staff Member *Saturday Night Live*
30 Rockefeller Plz Fl 17
New York, NY 10112, USA

Allen, Lily (Musician)
c/o Staff Member *Paradigm (Monterey)*
404 W Franklin St
Monterey, CA 93940, USA

Allen, Linwood (Stylist)
c/o Staff Member *Axis Models & Talent*
P.O. Box 367
Ringwood, NJ 07456-0367, USA

Allen, Lloyd (Athlete, Baseball Player)
2340 Castlewood Dr
Toledo, OH 43613-3923, USA

Allen, Loy Jr (Race Car Driver)
3197 Steamboat Ridge Road
Port Orange, FL 32128, USA

Allen, Lucius (Athlete, Basketball Player)
1915 Buckingham Rd
Los Angeles, CA 90016-1701, USA

Allen, Luke (Athlete, Baseball Player)
282 Cooper Rd
Social Circle, GA 30025-5119, USA

Allen, Marcus (Athlete, Football Player)
5301 Forecastle Ct
Carlsbad, CA 92008-3826, USA

Allen, Marty (Actor, Comedian)
c/o Staff Member *Lomar Productions*
5750 Wilshire Blvd #580
Los Angeles, CA 90036, USA

Allen, Marvin (Athlete, Football Player)
1806 Las Cruces Ln
Wichita Falls, TX 76306, USA

Allen, Maryon P (Ex-Senator, Politician)
1551 Creekstone Cir
Birmingham, AL 35243-2827, USA

Allen, Michael (Athlete, Football Player)
8839 NE 147th St
Kenmore, WA 98028, USA

Allen, Michael (Athlete, Golfer)
5827 E Anderson Dr
Scottsdale, AZ 85254-5941, USA

Allen, Mike (Athlete, Hockey Player)
P.O. Box 1416
International Falls, MN 56649, USA

Allen, Nancy (Activist, Actor)
weSPARK
13520 Ventura Blvd
Sherman Oaks, CA 91423, USA

Allen, Natalie (Correspondent)
Cable News Network
News Dept
1050 Techwood Dr NW
Atlanta, GA 30318, USA

Allen, Nate (Athlete, Football Player)
8239 Queen Ave N
Minneapolis, MN 55444, USA

Allen, Neil (Athlete, Baseball Player)
3619 Torrey Pines Blvd
Sarasota, FL 34238-2828, USA

Allen, Pam (Athlete, Golfer)
809 Delphinium Dr
Billings, MT 59102-3409, USA

Allen, Patrick (Athlete, Football Player)
427 20th Ave E
Seattle, WA 98112, USA

Allen, Paul (Business Person, Football Executive)
The Paul G Allen Family Foundation
505 5th Ave S #900
Seattle, WA 98104, USA

Allen, Rae (Actor)
c/o Staff Member *Kyle Fritz Management*
6325 Heather Dr
Los Angeles, CA 90068, USA

Allen, Randy (Athlete, Basketball Player)
10185 Nichols Lake Rd
Milton, FL 32583-9267, USA

Allen, Rax Jr (Music Group)
209 10th Ave #527
Nashville, TN 37203, USA

Allen, Ray (Actor, Athlete, Basketball Player)
86 Woodlawn Ave
Wellesley Hills, MA 02481-3129, USA

Allen, Rice (Athlete, Football Player)
4906 Laurel Hill Ct
Sugar Land, TX 77478-5424, USA

Allen, Richard (Actor)
89 Saltergate
Chesterfield S40 IUS, UNITED KINGDOM (UK)

Allen, Richard A (Richie) (Athlete, Baseball Player)
RR2
Possum Hollow Rd
Wampum, PA 16157, USA

Allen, Richard V (Government Official)
905 16th St NW
Washington, DC 20006, USA

Allen, Rick (Musician)
935 Camino Colibri
Calabasas, CA 91302, USA

Allen, Robert (Business Person, Writer)
Multiple Streams of Income
5072 North 300 W
Provo, UT 84604, USA

Allen, Rod (Athlete, Baseball Player)
3150 E Woodland Dr
Phoenix, AZ 85048-7702, USA

Allen, Ron (Athlete, Baseball Player)
917 Winona Dr
Youngstown, OH 44511-1404, USA

Allen, Rosalind (Actor)
c/o John Carrabino *John Carrabino Management*
5900 Wilshire Blvd Fl 4 #406
Los Angeles, CA 90036, USA

Allen, Sam (Athlete, Baseball Player)
2734 Gate House Rd
Apt 108
Norfolk, VA 23504-4057, USA

Allen, Scott (Athlete, Figure Skater, Olympic Athlete)
511 Knickerbocker Rd
W Sacramento, CA 95691-5848, USA

Allen, Sian Barbara (Actor, Writer)
1411 N Alberta St
Apt 7
Portland, OR 97217-3761, USA

Allen, Taje
1209 Valorie Ct
Cedar Park, TX 78613, USA

Allen, Taje (Athlete, Football Player)
1209 Valorie Ct
Cedar Park, TX 78613, USA

Allen, Ted (Chef, Television Host)
c/o Staff Member *WmE2 (WMA-LA)*
1 William Morris Pl
Beverly Hills, CA 90212, USA

Allen, Terry (Athlete, Football Player)
2729 Kelly Cove Dr
Buford, GA 30519, USA

Allen, Tessa (Actor)
c/o Staff Member *Bobby Ball Talent Agency*
4116 W Magnolia Blvd Ste 205
Burbank, CA 91505-2700, USA

Allen, Thomas B (Opera Singer)
I C M Artists
40 W 57th St
New York, NY 10019, USA

Allen, Tim (Actor, Comedian, Producer)
8430 Edwin Dr
Los Angeles, CA 90046, USA

Allen, Todd (Actor, Producer)
c/o David (Dave) Fleming *Mosaic Media Group*
9200 W. Sunset Blvd
10th Floor
Los Angeles, CA 90069, USA

Allen, Tony (Athlete, Basketball Player)
70 Kodiak Way Unit 2628
Waltham, MA 02451-0296, USA

Allen, Tremayne (Athlete, Football Player)
2910 Girvan Dr
Land 0 Lakes, FL 34638, USA

Allen, Will (Athlete, Football Player)
15 Fox Hill Ct
Wayne, NJ 07470, USA

Allen, Will (Athlete, Football Player)
2325 SW 105 Ter
Davie, FL 33324, USA

Allen, Will (Athlete, Football Player)
12721 Tar Flower Dr
Tampa, FL 33626, USA

Allen, Willard M (Doctor)
211 Key Haighway
Baltimore, MD 21230, USA

Allen, William (General)
PO Box 390879
Anza, CA 92539-0879, USA

Allen, William L (Editor)
National Geographic Magazine
17th & M NW
Washington, DC 20036, USA

Allen, Willie (Race Car Driver)
Modern Management
1625 Broadway #600
Nashville, TN 37203, USA

Allen, Woody (Actor, Comedian, Director, Writer)
118 E 70th St
New York, NY 10021, USA

Allen, Wyatt (Athlete, Olympic Athlete, Rower)
University of California
2227 Piedmont Ave
Attn: Men's Crew Coaching Staff
Berkeley, CA 94704, USA

Allenby, Robert (Athlete, Golfer)
105 Quayside Dr
Jupiter, Fl 33455, USA

Allende, Fernando (Actor)
c/o Staff Member *El Dorado Pictures*
725 Arizona Ave
Suite 100
Santa Monica, CA 90401, USA

Allende, Isabel (Writer)
92 Fernwood Dr
San Rafael, CA 94901-1533, USA

Allende, Isabel (Writer)
116 Caledonia St
Sausalito, CA 94965, USA

Allen Jr, Glenn (Race Car Driver)
7280 Jerry Dr.
Westchester, OH 45069, USA

Allen Jr, Rex (Musician)
Friends of Rex Allen Jr
PO Box 13436
Wichita, KS 67213, USA

Allen-Mullins, Doreen (Athlete, Baseball Player)
1104 Somonauk St
Sycamore, IL 60178, USA

Allenson, Gary (Athlete, Baseball Player)
711 SE 34th St
Cape Coral, FL 33904-4900, USA

Allensworth, Jermaine (Athlete, Baseball Player)
1824 Euclid Dr
Anderson, IN 46011-3937, USA

Allerman, Kurt (Athlete, Football Player)
2511 Blue Heron Dr
Hudson, OH 44236, USA

Allernnan, Kurt (Athlete, Football Player)
2511 Blue Heron Dr
Hudson, OH 44236, USA

Allert, Ty (Athlete, Football Player)
1504 County Road 308
Lexington, TX 78947-4113, USA

Allevi, Giovanni (Composer)
Via Arrigo Boito 9
Ascoli Piceno 63100, Italy

Alley, Alphonse (President)
Carre 181-182
BP 48
Cotonou, BENIN

Alley, Donald (Athlete, Football Player)
3258 Parade Cir W
Colorado Springs, CO 80917, USA

Alley, Gene (Athlete, Baseball Player)
10236 Steuben Dr
Glen Allen, VA 23060-3072, USA

Alley, Kirstie (Actor, Producer)
2600 Aberdeen Ave
Los Angeles, CA 90027, USA

Alley, Steve (Athlete, Hockey Player)
545 College Rd
Lake Forest, IL 60045-2319, USA

Alley Cats, The (Music Group, Musician)
c/o Staff Member *Harmony Artists*
8455 Beverly Blvd
Suite 400
Los Angeles, CA 90048, USA

All For One / All-4-One (Music Group)
c/o Staff Member *Performers of the World*
5657 Wilshire Blvd #280
Los Angeles, CA 90036, USA

Allfrey, Vincent G (Misc)
24 Winthrop Court
Tenafly, NJ 07670, USA

Allgaier, Justin (Race Car Driver)
c/o Staff Member *Penske Racing South*
200 Penske Way
Mooresville, NC 28115, USA

Allgood, Lonnie (Athlete, Football Player)
12 Drake Rd
Somerset, NJ 08873, USA

Allie, Gair (Athlete, Baseball Player)
11818 Button Willow Cv
San Antonio, TX 78213-1220, USA

Allietta, Bob
25 Robinson Rd
Falmouth, MA 02540-3840

Allimadi, E Otema (Prime Minister)
PO Box Gulu
Gulu District, UGANDA

Allinson, Michael (Actor)
112 Knollwood Dr
Larchmont, NY 10538, USA

Allione, Tsultrim (Religious Leader)
Tara Mandala Retreat Center
PO Box 3040
Pagosa Springs, CO 81147, USA

Allison, Aundrae (Athlete, Football Player)
2024 Summit Ridge Ln
Kannapolis, NC 28083

Allison, Bobby (Race Car Driver)
Box 3696
Mooresville, NC 28117-3696, USA

Allison, Dana (Athlete, Baseball Player)
322 Thomas Dr
Middleton, VA 22645-3992, USA

Allison, Dave (Athlete, Coach, Hockey Player)
c/o Staff Member *Iowa Stars*
833 5th Ave
Des Moines, IA 50309, USA

Allison, Donnie (Race Car Driver)
355 Quail Drive
Salisbury, NC 28147, USA

Allison, Glenn (Bowler)
1844 S Haster St Spc138
Anaheim, CA 92802-3750, USA

Allison, Henry (Hank) (Athlete, Football Player)
458 W Ellis Ave
Inglewood, CA 90302, USA

Allison, Herbert M (Business Person)
TIAA-CREF
730 3rd
New York, NY 10017, USA

Allison, Jason (Athlete, Hockey Player)
4965 16th Sideroad
Schomberg, ON LOG lTO, Canada

Allison, Jerry (Musician, Songwriter, Writer)
8455 New Bethal Road
Lyles, TN 37098, USA

Allison, Jim (Athlete, Football Player)
5706 Laramie Way
San Diego, CA 92120, USA

Allison, John A IV (Financier)
BB&T Corp
200 W 2nd St
Winston Salem, NC 27101, USA

Allison, Kate (Athlete, Golfer)
349 Canterbury Ln
Wyckoff, NJ 07481, USA

Allison, Mike (Athlete, Hockey Player)
P.O. Box 1416
International Falls, MN 56649-1416, USA

Allison, Mose J Jr (Composer, Musician)
82 Ballad Ct
Eastport, NY 11941, USA

Allison, Odis (Athlete, Basketball Player)
2945 20th St
San Pablo, CA 94806-2431, USA

Allison, Ray (Athlete, Hockey Player)
106 N Valleybrook Rd
Cherry Hill, NJ 08034, USA

Allison, Richard C (Judge)
24 Circle Dr
Manhasset, NY 11030, USA

Allison, Robert J Jr
Anadarko Petroleum Corp
1201 Lake Robbins Dr
Spring, TX 77380, USA

Allison, Stacy (Mountaineer)
6633 SE 29th Ave
Portland, OR 97202-8721, USA

Allison Jr, Graham T (Educator)
69 Pinhurst Road
Belmont, MA 02478, USA

Alliss, Peter (Sportscaster)
Int'l Mgmt Group
1 Erieview Plaza
1360 E 9th St #1300
Cleveland, OH 44114, USA

Alliston, Vaughn (Buddy) (Athlete, Football Player)
7493 Apple Yard Ln
Cordova, TN 38016, USA

Allman, Gregg (Musician)
706 Buckland Hall Rd
Richmond Hill, GA 31324, USA

Allman, Jamie Anne (Actor)
c/o Jordyn Palos *Persona PR*
8840 Wilshire Blvd
Suite 212
Beverly Hills, CA 90211, USA

Allman, Marshall (Actor)
c/o Nate Steadman *Gersh (LA)*
9465 Wilshire Blvd
Suite 600
Beverly Hills, CA 90212, USA

Allmendinger, AJ (Race Car Driver)
Richard Petty Motorsports
1120 Enterprise Pl
Arlington, TX 76001, USA

Allnutt, Robert (Scientist)
5415 Moorland Ln
Bethesda, MD 20814-1335, USA

Allor, Kristin
11940 Willow Ridge Dr
Willow Springs, IL 60480, USA

Allouache, Merzak (Director)
Cite des Asphodeles Bt D15
183 Ben Aknoun
Algiers, ALGERIA

Allport, Chris M (Actor)
1324 Pine St
Santa Monica, CA 90405, USA

Allport, Christopher (Actor)
c/o Staff Member *Pakula/King & Associates*
9229 Sunset Blvd
Suite 315
Los Angeles, CA 90069, USA

Allred, Beau (Athlete, Baseball Player)
2094 S Shannon Rd
Safford, AZ 85546-9344, USA

Allred, Brian (Athlete, Football Player)
16470 Ed Warfield Rd
Woodbine, MD 21797, USA

Allred, Gloria (Attorney, Lawyer)
6300 Wilshire Blvd Ste 1500
Los Angeles, CA 90048-5217, USA

Allred, Jason (Athlete, Golfer)
10239 E Salt Bush Dr
Scottsdale, AZ 85255, USA

Allred, John (Athlete, Football Player)
128 Avenida Cota
San Clemente, CA 92672, USA

All Saints (Music Group)
72 Chancellors Rd
London W6 9SG, UNITED KINGDOM (UK)

Allsopp, Kirstie (Actor)
c/o Staff Member *Arlington Enterprises Ltd*
1-3 Charlotte St
London W1P 1HD, UNITED KINGDOM (UK)

Allstar Weekend (Music Group, Musician)
c/o Staff Member *Hollywood Records*
500 S Buena Vista St
Burbank, CA 91521, USA

Allston, Aaron (Writer)
PO Box 564
Round Rock, TX 78680-0564, USA

Allsup, Mike (Music Group, Musician)
Mckenzie Accountancy
5171 Caliente St #134
Las Vegas, NV 89119, USA

Allsup, Tommy (Music Group)
Tophands Talent
P O Box 1547
Arlington, TX 76004, USA

All Time Low (Music Group)
Hopeless Records
PO Box 7495
Van Nuys, CA 91409, USA

Allums, Darrell (Athlete, Basketball Player)
3584 Brenton Ave
Apt B
Lynwood, CA 90262, USA

Al Maktum, Muhammad bin Raschid
Royal Palace
P.O.Box 899
Abu Dhabi, United Arabian Emirates

Al Maktum, Sheikh Muhammad bin Raschid (Government Official)
Royal Palace
P.O. Box 899
Abu Dhabi, United Arabian Emirates

Almanza, Armando (Athlete, Baseball Player)
1717 Villa Santos Cir
El Paso, TX 79935-3506, USA

Almanzar, Carlos (Athlete, Baseball Player)
c/o Staff Member *San Diego Padres*
100 Park Blvd
San Diego, CA 92101, USA

Almee, Anouk (Actor)
ICM France
37 Rue de Acacias
Paris 75017, FRANCE

Almen, Lowell G (Religious Leader)
Evangelical Lutheran Church
8765 W Higgins Road
Chicago, IL 60631, USA

Almirola, Aric (Race Car Driver)
1675 Coddle Creek Hwy
Mooresville, NC 38115, USA

Almodovar, Pedro (Director)
El Deseo SA
Ruiz Perello 25
Madrid 28028, SPAIN

Almon, Bill (Athlete, Baseball Player)
42 Channel Vw
Unit 4
Warwick, RI 02889-6544, USA

Almond, David (Writer)
c/o Staff Member *Doubleday/RandomHouse*
1745 Broadway
New York, NY 10019, USA

Almond, Marc (Musician)
105 Shed Row #B
Piermont, NY 10968-3001, USA

Almonte, Edwin (Athlete, Baseball Player)
3078 Clairmont Rd
NE Act 231
Atlanta, GA 30329-1659, USA

Almonte, Erick (Athlete, Baseball Player)
2150 Bayberry Dr
Pembroke Pines, FL 33024-3035, USA

Almonte, Hector (Athlete, Baseball Player)
16742 SW 12th St
Pembroke Pines, FL 33027-1408, USA

Almunia, Amann Joaquin (Government Official)
Piaza de las Cortes #9
4A Planta
Madrid 28014, SPAIN

Almy, Brook (Actor)
c/o Nyle Brenner *Brenner Management*
9171 Wilshire Blvd #441
Beverly Hills, CA 90210, USA

Al Nahyan, Mansour bin Zayed (Business Person)
First Gulf Bank
P.O. Box 6316
Abu Dhabi, United Arab Emirates

Al Nahyan, Sheikh Khalifa Bin Zayed (Royalty)
President's Office
Manhal Palace
Abu Dhabi, United Arab Emirates

Alois (Prince)
Schloss Vaduz
Vaduz 9490, LIECHTENSTEIN

Alomar, Roberto (Athlete, Baseball Player)
901 Palacio De Avila
Tamoa, FL 33613-5224, USA

Alomar Jr, Sandy (Athlete, Baseball Player)
1906 W Cortland St
Chicago, IL 60622-1037, USA

Alomar Sr, Sandy (Athlete, Baseball Player)
P.O. Box 367
Salinas, PR 00751-0367, USA

Alonsa, Alicia (Ballerina)
Calzada 510 Entre D & E
El Vedada, Havana CP 10400, CUBA

Alonso, Adrian (Actor)
c/o Staff Member *Featured Artists Agency*
1880 Century Park E #1402
Los Angeles, CA 90067, USA

Alonso, Alicia (Ballerina)
Calzada
510 Entre D & E
El Vedada
Havana, CP 10400, CUBA

Alonso, Anabel (Actor)
GRPC SL
Calles Fuencarral 17
Madrid 28004, SPAIN

Alonso, Daniella (Actor)
c/o Staff Member *Gersh (LA)*
9465 Wilshire Blvd
Suite 600
Beverly Hills, CA 90212, USA

Alonso, Fernando (Race Car Driver)
Villamiana, 67
Limanes 33199, SPAIN

Alonso, Laz (Actor)
c/o Ron West *Thruline Entertainment*
9250 Wilshire Blvd
Ground Fl
Beverly Hills, CA 90212, USA

Alonso, Maria Conchita (Actor, Musician)
9455 Eden Dr
Beverly Hills, CA 90210, USA

Alosio, Ryan (Actor)

Alou, Felipe (Athlete, Baseball Player)
6891 Cobia Cir
Boynton Beach, FL 33437-3639, USA

Alou, Jesus (Athlete, Baseball Player)
Apartado Postal 539/2
Lafaria
Santo Domingo, Dominican Republic,
USA

Alou, Moises (Athlete, Baseball Player)
13095 NW 13th St
Pembroke Pines, FL 33028-2711, USA

Alpay, David (Actor)
c/o Brian Wilkins *Kritzer Levine Wilkins
Entertainment (KLWG)*
11872 La Grange Ave
1st Floor
Los Angeles, CA 90025, USA

Alpert, Herb (Musician)
216 Notteargenta Rd
Pacific Palisades, CA 90272, USA

Alpert, Joseph S (Doctor)
3440 E Cathedral Rock Circle
Tucson, AZ 85718, USA

Alphand, Luc (Skier)
Chalet Le Balme Chantemarie
Sierra Chavalier 05330, FRANCE

Alpher, Ralph A (Physicist)
253 Ascot Lane
Schenectady, NY 12309, USA

Alphin, Big Kenny (Musician)
2325 Golf Club Ln
Nashville, TN 37215, USA

Alphin, Gerald (Athlete, Football Player)
4760 Lorient CT
Snellville, GA 30039-8721, USA

**Al Saud, HRH Crown Prince Emir Bandar
Ibn Sultan** (Royalty)
Council of Minister
Murabba, Riyadh 11121, Saudi Arabia

Al Saud, King Abdullah bin Abdul Aziz
(Royalty)
Council of Minister
Murabba, Riyadh 11121, Saudi Arabia

Alsbury, Mark (Aviator)
Scaled Composites LLC
1624 Flight Line
Mojave, CA 93501-1663, USA

Alsgaard, Thomas (Skier)
Cathinka Guldbergsveg 16
Holter 2034, NORWAY

Alsop, Marin (Musician)
c/o Staff Member *ICM Partners (ICM-LA)*
10250 Constellation Blvd Fl 7
Los Angeles, CA 90067, USA

Alsop, Will (Architect)
Bishop's Wharf
39-49 Parkgate Road
London SW11 4NP, UNITED KINGDOM
(UK)

Alston, Alyce Carolyn (Publisher)
The Reader's Digest Association, Inc.
Pleasantville, NY 10570, USA

Alston, Barbara (Music Group)
Superstars Unlimited
P O Box 371371
Las Vegas, NV 89137, USA

Alston, Dell (Athlete, Baseball Player)
101 Enchanted Hills Rd #103
Owings Mills, MD 21117-2793, USA

Alston, Garvin (Athlete, Baseball Player)
4705 E Thunderhill Pl
Phoenix, AZ 85044-4905, USA

Alston, Lyneal (Athlete, Football Player)
1318 Morning Sun Cir
Birmingham, AL 35242, USA

Alston, Mack (Athlete, Football Player)
5421 Echols Ave
Alexandria, VA 22311, USA

Alston, Rafer (Athlete, Basketball Player)
c/o Staff Member *Toronto Raptors*
400-40 Bay St
Toronto, Ontario M5J 2X2, Canada

Alstott, Mike (Athlete, Football Player)
Mike Alstott Family Foundation
PO Box 40055
St Petersburg, FL 33743-0055, USA

Alsup, Bill (Race Car Driver)
93 Rio Grande Drive
Durango, CO 81301, USA

Alt, Carol (Actor)
c/o Scott Hart *Scott Hart Entertainment*
14622 Ventura Blvd
#746
Sherman Oaks, CA 91403, USA

Alt, John M (Athlete, Football Player)
1 Scotch Pine Rd
Saint Paul, MN 55127, USA

Altamirano, Porfi (Athlete, Baseball
Player)
3676 SW 24th Ter
Miami, FL 33145-3041, USA

Altberg, Jonas Erik (Basshunter)
(Musician)
c/o Staff Member *Hackford Jones PR*
19 Nassau St
London W1W 7AF, UK

Altenberg, Wolfgang (General)
Birkenhof 44
Brenen-Saint-Magnus D-28759,
GERMANY

Alther, Lisa (Writer)
1086 Silver St
Hinesburg, VT 05461, USA

Althoff, James (Jim) (Athlete, Football
Player)
150 Red Top Dr Apt 302
Libertyville, IL 60048, USA

Altman, Chelsea (Actor)
c/o Matthew Sullivan *Sullivan Talent
Group*
305 W 105th St #3B
New York, NY 10025, USA

Altman, George (Athlete, Baseball Player)
915 Midpoint Dr
O Fallon, MO 63366-5906, USA

Altman, Jeff (Actor)
c/o Staff Member *Richard De La Font
Agency*
3808 W South Park Blvd
Broken Arrow, OK 74011, USA

Altman, Scott D (Astronaut)
3011 Harvest Hill Dr
Friendswood, TX 77546, USA

Altman, Scott D Cdr (Astronaut)
1247 33rd St NW
Washington, DC 20007-3228, USA

Altman, Sidney (Nobel Prize Laureate)
71 Blake Road
Hamden, CT 06S17-3404, USA

Altman, Stuart H (Educator)
11 Bakers Hill Road
Weston, MA 02493, USA

Altmeyer, Jeannine T (Opera Singer)
Im Muhlader
Herrliberg 8709, SWITZERLAND

Altmire, Jason (Congressman, Politician)
332 Cannon HOB
Washington, DC 20515, USA

Altobelli, Joe (Athlete, Baseball Player,
Coach)
10 Stowell Dr
Apt 3
Rochester, NY 14616-1889, USA

Altuna, Charlie (Stylist)
c/o Celebrity Stylist *Celestine - CA*
1666 20th St
#200-B
Santa Monica, CA 90404, USA

Alusik, George (Athlete, Baseball Player)
581 Garden Ave
Woodbridge, NJ 07095-3850, USA

Alva, Luigi (Opera Singer)
via Moscova 46/3
Mailand, Italy 20121

Alvarado, Allen (Actor)
c/o Scott Appel *Scott Appel Public
Relations*
13547 Ventura Blvd #203
Sherman Oaks, CA 91423, USA

Alvarado, Natividad (Naty) (Misc)
Equitable of Iowa
2700 N Main St
Santa Ana, CA 92705, USA

Alvarez, Clemente (Athlete, Baseball Player)
18711 NW 46th Ave
Miami Gardens, FL 33055-2655, USA

Alvarez, Gabe (Athlete, Baseball Player)
4401 La Madera Ave
El Monte, CA 91732-2009, USA

Alvarez, Isabel (Athlete, Baseball Player)
2402 Monmouth Ave
Fort Wayne, IN 46809-1732, USA

Alvarez, Jose (Athlete, Baseball Player)
210 Murphy Ln
Greenville, SC 29607-4934, USA

Alvarez, Juan (Athlete, Baseball Player)
10995 SW 107th Ave
Miami, FL 33176-3444, USA

Alvarez, Orlando (Athlete, Baseball
Player)
Cummunidad Dolores 37
Rio Grande, PR 00745, USA

Alvarez, Rogelio (Athlete, Baseball Player)
5010 NW 183rd St
Miami Gardens, FL 33055-2929, USA

Alvarez, Victor (Athlete, Baseball Player)
c/o Staff Member *Los Angeles Dodgers
(LA Dodgers)*
1000 Elysian Park Ave
Los Angeles, CA 90012, USA

Alvarez, Wilson (Athlete, Baseball Player)
State College Spikes
6927 Westchester Cir
Lakewood Ranch, FL 34202-2584, USA

Alvarez-Buylla, Arturo (Biologist)
Rockefeller University
Medical Center
1230 York Ave
New York, NY 10021, USA

Alvarez Martinez, Francisco Cardinal
(Religious Leader)
Arco de Palacio 3
Toledo 45002, SPAIN

Alvers, Steve (Athlete, Football Player)
9751 SW 115th Ave
Miami, FL 33176, USA

Alves, Camila (Model)
c/o *Stella Models*
Webgasse 1/12
Vienna 1060, AUSTRIA

Alves, Joe (Director)
4176 Rosario Road
Woodland Hills, CA 91364, USA

Alvim, Anna (Actor)
c/o Jean Fox *Fox-Albert Management*
88 Central Park W
New York, NY 10023, USA

Alvin, Dave (Musician, Songwriter,
Writer)
Mark Pucci
5000 Oak Bluff Court
Atlanta, GA 30350, USA

Alvina, Anicee (Actor)
41 Rue de l'Echese
Le Visinet 75008, FRANCE

Alvis, Max (Athlete, Baseball Player)
806 Hunterwood Dr
Jasper, TX 75951-2820, USA

Alvord, Steve (Athlete, Football Player)
3624 Westridge Pl
Bellingham, WA 98226, USA

Alward, Tom (Athlete, Football Player)
5051 Bensett Trl
Davison, MI 48423, USA

Alworth, Lance (Athlete, Football Player)
990 Highland Dr
Suite 300
Solana Beach, CA 92075, USA

Al-Yawer, Sheik Ghazi Mashal Ajll
(President)
President's Office
Al-Sijound Majalis
Karradat Mariam
Baghdad, IRAQ

Alyea, Brant (Athlete, Baseball Player)
3323 Manor Rd
Huntingdon Valley, PA 19006-4147, USA

Alyson, Jocelyn E (Musician)
c/o Staff Member *Diva Central Inc*
7510 W Sunset Blvd Ste 1445
Los Angees, CA 90046, USA

Alzne, Karl (Athlete, Hockey Player)
1301 N Troy St
Arlington, VA 22201-2521

alzner, karl (Athlete, Hockey Player)
1301 N Troy St
Arlington, VA 22201-2521, USA

al-Zubi, Mahmoud (Prime Minister)
Premier's Office
Damascas
SYRIA

Ama, Shola (Musician)
12 One Mgmt
Executive Suite
20 Damien St
London E1 2HX, UNITED KINGDOM
(UK)

Amaechi, John (Athlete, Basketball Player)
5747 E Aire Libre Ave
Scottsdale, AZ 85254-1206, USA

Amaker, Tommy (Athlete, Basketball Player, Coach)
University of Michigan
Athletic Dept
Ann Arbor, MI 48109, USA

Amalfitano, J Joseph (Joey) (Athlete, Baseball Player, Coach)
265 Bowstring Dr
Sedona, AZ 86336, USA

amalfitano, joe (Athlete, Baseball Player)
60 Sheath Dr
Sedona, AZ 86336-6510, USA

Amalou, J K (Director)
William Morris Agency
52/53 Poland Place
London W1F 7LX, UNITED KINGDOM
(UK)

Aman, Zeenat (Actor, Bollywood)
Neelam Apartments 3rd Floor
Mount Mary Road Bandra
Bombay, MS 400 050, INDIA

Amanar, Simona (Gymnast)
Gymnastic Federation
Str Vasile Conta 16
Budapest 70139, ROMANIA

Amandes, Tom (Actor)
2751 Pelham Pl
Los Angeles, CA 90068, USA

Amano, Eugene (Athlete, Football Player)
8354 Lochinver Park Ln
Brentwood, TN 37027, USA

Amanpour, Christiane (Correspondent, Journalist)
c/o Staff Member *CNN (Atlanta)*
One CNN Center
PO Box 105366
Atlanta, GA 30303, USA

Amante, Tony (Athlete, Hockey Player)
58 Turners Way
Norwell, MA 02061-2339, USA

Amara, Lucine (Opera Singer)
260 W End Ave
#7A
New York, NY 10023, USA

Amaral, Bob (Actor)
c/o Staff Member *Professional Artists Agency*
321 W 44th St #605
New York, NY 10036, USA

Amaral, Rich (Athlete, Baseball Player)
3122 Country Club Dr
Costa Mesa, CA 926263-2344, USA

Amarjargal, Rinchinnyamiyn (Prime Minister)
Prime Minister's Office
Ulan Bator, Great Hural 12, MONGOLIA

Amaro, Melanie (Musician)
6441 NW 24th Pl
Sunrise, FL 33313, USA

Amaro, Ruben (Commentator)
1063 Country Hills Rd
Yardley, PA 19067-6024, USA

Amaro Jr, Ruben (Athlete, Baseball Player)
Philadelphia Phillies
1063 Country Hills Rd
Yardley, PA 19067-6024, USA

Amaro Sr, Ruben (Athlete, Baseball Player)
4098 Cinnamon Way
Weston, FL 33331-3810, USA

Amash, Justin (Congressman, Politician)
114 Cannon HOB
Washington, DC 20515, USA

Amato, Bruno (Actor)
46354 Corte Cabral
Temecula, CA 92592, USA

Amato, Giuliano (Prime Minister)
Carmera dei Deputati
Piazza di Montecitorio
Rome 00186, ITALY

Amato, Joe (Race Car Driver)
Amato Racing
44 Tunkhannuck Ave
Exeter, PA 18643, USA

Amato, Ken (Athlete, Football Player)
641 Old Hickory Blvd
Unit 305
Brentwood, TN 37027, USA

Amato, Ken
641 Old Hickory Blvd Unit 305
Brentwood, TN 37027, USA

Amaya, Armando (Artist)
Lopex 137
Depto 1
Mexico City 06070 CP, MEXICO

Amays, Ashraf (Athlete, Basketball Player)
25030 Round Barn Rd
Plainfield, IL 60585-7490

Amazing Jonathan, The (Actor)
c/o Staff Member *ICM Partners (ICM-LA)*
10250 Constellation Blvd Fl 7
Los Angeles, CA 90067, USA

Amazing Rhythm Aces (Music Group)
c/o Staff Member *Fat City Artists*
1906 Chet Atkins Pl #502
Nashville, TN 37212, USA

Ambani, Anil (Business Person)
Reliance Capital
'H' Block 1st Floor
Dhirubhai Ambani Knowledge City, Navi
Mumbai 400 710, INDIA

Ambani, Mukesh (Business Person)
Reliance Industries Limited
Makers Chambers - IV
Nariman Point
Mumbai 400 021, India

Ambasz, Emilio (Architect)
43 E 63rd St
New York, NY 10065-7324, USA

Amber (Musician)
Artists & Audience Entertainment
PO Box 35
Pawling, NY 12564, USA

Ambres, Chip (Athlete, Baseball Player)
4460 Beale St
Beaumont, TX 77705-4705, USA

Ambro, Thomas L (Judge)
US Court of Appeals
Federal Building
844 N King St
Wilmington, DE 19801, USA

Ambros, Wolfgang (Musician)
c/o Staff Member *Sony Music
Entertainment Germany*
Neumarkter Str. 28
Muenchen 81673, Germany

Ambrose, Ashley (Athlete, Football Player)
2726 Eudora Trl
Duluth, GA 30097, USA

Ambrose, Lauren (Actor)
c/o Billy Lazarus *United Talent Agency (UTA)*
9336 Civic Center Dr
Beverly Hills, CA 90210, USA

Ambrose, Marcos (Race Car Driver)
Wood Bros Racing
7203 Caldwell Rd
Harrisburg, NC 29985-7580, USA

Ambrose, Richard (Dick) (Athlete, Football Player)
24049 Stonehedge Dr
Cleveland, OH 44145, USA

Ambrosio, Alessandra (Model)
c/o Staff Member *Elite Model Management (NY)*
404 Park Ave S Fl 9
New York, NY 10016, USA

Ambrosius, Marsha (Musician)
c/o Staff Member *WmE2 (WMA-LA)*
1 William Morris Pl
Beverly Hills, CA 90212, USA

Ambroziak, Peter (Athlete, Hockey Player)
PO Box 830
Ogdensburg, NY 13669-0830, USA

Ambuehl, Clindy (Actor)
Paul Kohner
9300 Wilshire Blvd
#555
Beverly Hills, CA 90212, USA

Ambulance Ltd (Music Group)
c/o Staff Member *Paradigm (Monterey)*
404 W Franklin St
Monterey, CA 93940, USA

Amedori, John Patrick (Actor)
4440 Elmer Ave
Studio City, CA 91602, USA

Ameling, Elly (Music Group, Musician)
Hubstein Artist Services
65 W 90th St
#13F
New York, NY 10024, USA

Amelio, Gilbert F (Business Person)
InterDigital
781 Third Ave
King of Prussia, PA 19406, USA

Amell, Stephen (Actor)
c/o Michael Garnett *Leverage Management*
3030 Pennsylvania Ave
Santa Monica, CA 90404, USA

Amelung, Ed (Athlete, Baseball Player)
16681 Cedar Cir
Fountain Valley, CA 92708-2310, USA

Amen, Irving (Artist)
PO Box 812365
Boca Raton, FL 33481-236S, USA

Amenabar, Alejandro (Director, Musician, Writer)
c/o Sunmin Park *Maxmedia*
1620 Broadway
Santa Monica, CA 90404, USA

Amend, Bill (Cartoonist)
620 w 51st St
Kansas City, MO 64112-2317, USA

Amendola, Tony (Actor)
c/o Staff Member *Beacon Talent Agency*
170 Apple Ridge Rd
Woodcliff, NJ 07677, USA

Ament, Jeff (Musician)
5702 S.W. Andover St
Seattle, WA 98116, USA

Amer, Nicolas (Actor)
14 Great Russell St
Flat 1
London WC1B 3NH, UK

America (Musician)
c/o Staff Member *WmE2 (WMA-LA)*
1 William Morris Pl
Beverly Hills, CA 90212, USA

American Gladiators (Reality TV Star)
MGM Television
10250 Constellation Blvd
Los Angeles, CA 90067, USA

Amerie (Musician)
c/o Len Nicholson *Feenix Rising Entertainment*
1360 Clifton Ave
Suite 318
Clifton, NJ 07012, USA

Amerson, Glenn (Athlete, Football Player)
4857 Mustang Rd
Brenham, TX 77833, USA

Ames, Aldrich (Government Official)
RN# 40087-083, USP Allenwood
P.O. Box 3000
White Deer, PA 17887, USA

Ames, Bruce N (Scientist)
1324 Spruce St
Berkeley, CA 94709-1435, USA

Ames, David (Athlete, Football Player)
7909 Alvarado Rd
Richmond, VA 23229, USA

Ames, Denise (Actor)
Studio Talent Group
1328 12th St
Santa Monica, CA 90401, USA

Ames, Ed (Actor, Musician)
c/o Staff Member *Paradise Artists*
P.O. Box 1821
Ojai, CA 93024-1821, USA

Ames, Frank Anthony (Musician)
1235 Potamac St NW
Washington, DC 20007, USA

Ames, Louise Bates (Scientist)
283 Edwards St
New Haven, CT 06511-3719, USA

Ames, Rachel (Actor)
Atkins Assoc
8040 Ventura Canyon Ave
Panorama City, CA 91402, USA

Ames, Trey (Actor)
TDA Enterprises
2082 Michelsen Dr #306
Irvine, CA 92612, USA

Amey, VInce (Athlete, Football Player)
4433 Callecita Ct
Union City, CA 94587, USA

Amezaga, Alfredo
12887 W Virginia Ave
Avondale, AZ 85392-7123, USA

Amick, Madchen (Actor)
c/o Kesha Williams Affirmative
Entertainment
425 N Robertson Blvd
Los Angeles, CA 90048, USA

Amiel, Jon (Director)
c/o Dave Brown Artist International
Management (LA)
9595 Wilshire Blvd Fl 9
Los Angeles, CA 90212, USA

Amiez, Sebastien (Skier)
Ave Chasse-Foret
Pralognan, FRANCE

Amigo Vallejo, Carlos Cardinal (Religious
Leader)
Archdiocese
Piaza Virgin de los Reyes S/N
Seville 41004, SPAIN

Amiina (Musician)
c/o Staff Member Paradigm (Monterey)
404 W Franklin St
Monterey, CA 93940, USA

Amini (Actor, Bollywood)
6 Parthasarathipuram
T Nagar
Chennai, TN 600017, INDIA

Amis, Martin (Journalist, Writer)
P F D
Drury House
34-43 Russell St
London WC2B 5HA, UNITED KINGDOM
(UK)

Amis, Suzy (Actor, Model)
Amis Construction Co
1647 Exchange Ave
Oklahoma City, OK 73108, USA

Amlong, Joe (Athlete, Olympic Athlete,
Rower)
2445 4th Ln SW
Vero Beach, FL 32962-3329, USA

Amlong, Thomas (Athlete)
166 Four Mile River Road
Old Lyme, CT 06371, USA

Ammaccapane, Danielle (Athlete, Golfer)
13214 N 13th St
Phoenix, AZ 85022-4936, USA

Ammaccapane, Dina (Athlete, Golfer)
4407 E Blanche Dr
Phoenix, AZ 85032-4881, USA

Ammachi (Religious Leader)
Amrita IInstitutions
Ettimadai
Coimbatore, Tamil Nadu 641105, INDIA

Amman, Dick (Athlete, Football Player)
2907 Lake Joanna Dr
Eustis, FL 32726, USA

Amman, Richard (Athlete, Football Player)
2907 Lake Joanna Dr
Eustis, FL 32726, USA

Ammann, Simon (Speed Skater)
Ski Verband
Worbstr 52
Muri 3074, SWITZERLAND

Amodeo, Mike (Athlete, Hockey Player)
556 Fralicks Beach Rd RR 5
Port Perry, ON L9L 1B6, Canada

Among the Oak & Asj (Music Group,
Musician)
c/o Staff Member MCT Management
520 8th Ave Rm 2205
New York, NY 10018, USA

Amons, Mary Schmidt (Reality TV Star)
c/o Staff Member Bravo (NY)
30 Rockefeller Plaza
New York, NY 10112, USA

Amonte, Tony (Athlete, Hockey Player,
Olympic Athlete)
58 Turners Way
Norwell, MA 02061-2339, USA

amor, Vicente (Athlete, Baseball Player)
13871 SW 52nd St
Miramar, FL 33027-5945, USA

Amor, Vincente (Athlete, Baseball Player)
13871 SW 52nd St
Miramar, FL 33027, USA

Amorosi, Vanessa (Musician)
Mar Jac Productions
PO Box 51
Caulfield South, VIC, AUSTRALIA

Amos, John (Actor)
c/o Belinda Foster AWJ Platinum PR
8200 Wilshire Blvd #200
Los Angeles, CA 90048, USA

Amos, Paul S (Business Person)
AFLAC Inc
1932 Wynnton Road
Columbus, GA 31999, USA

Amos, Tori (Musician)
114 S. Sewalls Point Rd
Sewalls Point, FL 34996, USA

Amos, Wally (Famous) (Misc)
P.O. Box 897
Kailua, HI 96734-0897, USA

Amoyal, Pierre A W (Musician)
Jacques Thelen
252 Rue de Faubourg Saint-Honore
Paris 75008, FRANCE

Amplas, John (Actor)
443 Meridian Dr
Pittsburgh, PA 15228, USA

Amram, David W III (Composer,
Musician)
Peekskill Hollow Farm
Peekskill Hollow Road
Putnam Valley, NY 10579, USA

Amrapurkar, Sadashiv (Actor, Bollywood,
Comedian)
A/201 Panchdhara Off Yari Road
Versova Andheri
Bombay, MS 400 058, INDIA

Amritraj, Vijay (Athlete, Tennis Player)
First Serve
10/5A 13th Ave
Harrington Rd
Chennai 00031, INDIA

Amsden, Ben (General)
Lexington Park
930 Hwy 466 #113
Lady Lake, FL 32159, USA

Amsler, Marty (Athlete, Football Player)
4009 Fairfax Rd
Evansville, IN 47710, USA

Amsterdam, Anthony G (Attorney,
Attorney General, Educator, General)
68 Middle Lane Highway
Southampton, NY 11968, USA

Amstrong, Otis (Athlete, Football Player)
7183 S Newport Way
Centennial, CO 80112, USA

Amstutz, Joe (Athlete, Football Player)
24840 Arrow Ct
Apt 29
Tehachapi, CA 93561, USA

Amte, Baba (Religious Leader)
Maharogi Sewa Samiti
Waora Anandwan
Dist Chandrapur, Maharashtra 442914,
INDIA

Amukamura, Prince (Football Player)
c/o Todd France France AllPro Athlete
Management
3500 Lenox Road, NE
Atlanta, GA 30326, USA

Amundsen, Norman (Athlete, Football
Player)
3901 Hemlock Dr
Valparaiso, IN 46383, USA

Amurri, Eva (Actor)
c/o JJ Harris One Talent Management
9220 Sunset Blvd
Los Angeles, CA 90069, USA

Amzallag, Manuela (Stylist)
c/o Staff Member Ennis
119 Braintree St
Boston, MA 02134, USA

Anagarano, Michael (Actor)
c/o Staff Member Coast to Coast Talent
Group
3350 Barham Blvd
Los Angeles, CA 90068, USA

Anagnostopoulos, Constantine E (Doctor)
3959 Mount Vernon Dr
Bloomfield Hills, MI 48301-3227, USA

Anahi (Actor)
c/o Staff Member Televisa
Blvd Adolfo Lopez Mateos 232
Colonia San Angel INN
DF CP 01060, MEXICO

Anakin, Douglas (Athlete)
PO Box 27
Windermere, BC V0B 2L, CANADA

Anand, Babu N (Actor)
1 A Officers Defence Colony St
Thomas Mount
Chennai, TN 600 097, INDIA

Anand, J N (Actor)
No 8 B N Reddy Road
T Nagar
Chennai, TN 600 017, INDIA

Anand, Sabita (Actor, Bollywood)
61 Sivan Koil Ist Cross Street
Kodambakkam
Chennai, TN 600024, INDIA

Anand, Tinnu (Actor, Bollywood,
Director, Filmmaker)
101 Lakshadeep Glmohar Cross Road No
4
JVPD Scheme
Bombay, MS 400 049, INDIA

Anand, Tinu (Actor, Bollywood, Director)
101 Lakshyadeep 4th X Road
Juhu Scheme
Mumbai, MS 400049, INDIA

Anand, Vijay (Actor, Bollywood, Director,
Filmmaker, Producer)
Ketnav 17 Union Park Pali Hill
Khar
Bombay, MS 400 052, INDIA

Ananiashvill, Nina G (Ballerina)
Bolshoi Theatre
1 Ploschad Sverdlove
Moscow 103009, RUSSIA

Anantha, Raaj (Actor)
25 2nd Cross Street
Lake Area
Chennai, TN 600 034, INDIA

Anapau, Kristina (Actor)
c/o Staff Member One Talent
Management
9220 Sunset Blvd
Los Angeles, CA 90069, USA

Anastacia (Musician)
2501 Bowmont Dr
Beverly Hills, CA 90210, USA

Anastasio, Trey (Musician)
40 Lawrence Ln
Palisades, NY 10964, USA

Anaya, Rudolfo (Writer)
5324 Canada Vista NW
Albuquerque, NM 87120, USA

Anaya, Toney (Politician)
Maldef
634 S Spring St
Los Angeles, CA 90014-3921, USA

Anaya, Toney (Ex-Governor)
Anaya Law Firm, P.A.
200 W DeVargas St
Santa Fe, NM 87501, USA

Anbusrinivas (Actor)
12 Ramanajum Street
Nungambakkam
Chennai, TN 600 034, INDIA

Ancheta, Bernie (Director, Writer)
c/o Staff Member Lenhoff & Lenhoff
830 Palm Ave
West Hollywood, CA 90069

Anchia, Juan-Ruiz (Cinematographer)
Stanford-Beckett-Skouras
1015 Gayley Ave
Los Angeles, CA 90024, USA

Ancker-Johnson, Betsy (Physicist)
222 Harbour Dr #311
Naples, FL 34103, USA

Ancona, Bill (Race Car Driver)
260 Nelson Wyatt Rd
Mansfield, TX 76083, USA

Andabaker, Rudy (Athlete, Football Player)
450 8th St
Donora, PA 15033, USA

Andere, Jacqueline (Actor)
c/o Staff Member *Televisa*
Blvd Adolfo Lopez Mateos 232
Colonia San Angel INN
DF CP 01060, MEXICO

Anderegg, Bob (Athlete, Basketball Player)
11708 E Onyx Ave
Scottsdale, AZ 85259-5017, USA

Anders, Andrea (Actor)
3615 Dixie Canyon Ave
Sherman Oaks, CA 91423, USA

Anders, Beth (Athlete, Hockey Player, Olympic Athlete)
9727 Bay Point Dr
Norfolk, VA 23518, USA

Anders, David (Actor)
c/o Kay Liberman *Liberman/Zerman Management*
252 N Larchmont Blvd
Suite 200
Los Angeles, CA 90004, USA

Anders, Kimble (Athlete, Football Player)
801 Landing Blvd
League City, TX 77573, USA

Anders, Sean (Director, Producer, Writer)
c/o John Elliott *Mosaic Media Group*
9200 W. Sunset Blvd
10th Floor
Los Angeles, CA 90069, USA

Anders, William A (Astronaut, General)
c/o Staff Member *NASA*
Johnson Space Center
2101 NASA Rd
Houston, TX 77058, USA

Anders, William A Maj Gen (Astronaut)
1156 Brighton Crest Dr
Bellingham, WA 98229-6905, USA

Andersen, Anthony (Actor)
1619 Broadway
#900
New York, NY 10019, USA

Andersen, Barbara (Actor)
PO Box 10118
Santa Fe, NM 87504, USA

Andersen, Elmer (Politician)
1483 Bussard Ct
Saint Paul, MN 55112-3628, USA

Andersen, Greta (Athlete, Olympic Athlete, Swimmer)
16222 Monterey Ln #264
Huntington Beach, CA 92649-2248, USA

Andersen, Hjalmar (Hjallis) (Speed Skater)
Velferden for Handelsflaten
Trondheimsvn 2
Oslo 5 0560, NORWAY

Andersen, Jason (Athlete, Football Player)
4530 W Lake Rd
Apt 410
Canandaigua, NY 14424, USA

Andersen, Larry (Athlete, Baseball Player)
120 Dickinson St Rear A
Philadelphia, PA 19147-6100, USA

Andersen, Linda (Yachtsman)
Aroysund
Torod 3135, NORWAY

Andersen, Mogens (Athlete, Football Player)
Strandagervej 28
Hellerup, Copenhagen 2900, Denmark

Andersen, Morten (Athlete, Football Player)
6501 Old Shadburn Ferry Rd
Buford, GA 30518, USA

Andersen, Reidar (Skier)
National Ski Hall of Fame
PO Box 191
Ishperning, MI 49849, USA

Andersen, Watts Teresa (Swimmer)
2582 Marsha Way
San Jose, CA 95125, USA

Andersion, Robert P (Athlete, Football Player)
244 Carmel Dr
Melbourne, FL 32940, USA

Anderson, Alfred (Athlete, Football Player)
2805 Chesterwood Ct
Mansfield, TX 76063, USA

Anderson, Allan (Athlete, Baseball Player)
1491 Lancaster Kirkersville Rd NW
Lancaster, OH 43130-8969, USA

Anderson, Anthony (Athlete, Football Player)
4001 Kennett Pike Ste 134
Wilmington, DE 19807, USA

Anderson, Anthony (Actor, Producer)
2509 Silver Ridge Ave
Los Angeles, CA 9039, USA

Anderson, Antonio (Athlete, Football Player)
463 Lexington Ave
Brooklyn, NY 11221, USA

Anderson, Aric (Athlete, Football Player)
16306 Rolling View Trl
Cypress, TX 77433, USA

Anderson, Aric (Athlete, Football Player)
528 Halifax Ln
Coppell, TX 75019, USA

Anderson, Audrey (Stylist)
c/o Staff Member *Koko Represents*
166 Geary St
#1007
San Francisco, CA 94108, USA

Anderson, Audrey Marie (Actor)
c/o Staff Member *Untitled Entertainment (NY)*
322 8th Ave #601
New York, NY 10001-6715, USA

Anderson, Bennie (Athlete, Football Player)
6450 Virginia Ave
Saint Louis, MO 63111, USA

Anderson, Bill (Athlete, Football Player)
6924 Lark Ln
Knoxville, TN 37919, USA

Anderson, Bill (Whispering) (Musician, Songwriter)
PO Box 81036
Phoenix, AZ 85069-1036, USA

Anderson, Bob (Athlete, Football Player)
244 Carmel Dr
Melbourne, FL 32940, USA

Anderson, Bob (Athlete, Baseball Player)
3140 E 89th St
Tulsa, OK 74137-3361, USA

Anderson, Bobby (Athlete, Football Player)
79125 Big Horn Trl
La Quinta, CA 92253, USA

Anderson, Bonnie (Stylist)
c/o Staff Member *Team*
423 W Broadway
4th Floor
Boston, MA 02127, USA

Anderson, Brad
13022 Wood Harbour Dr
Montgomery, TX 77356-8046, USA

Anderson, Brad (Director)
422 Santa Monica Court
Escondido, CA 92029, USA

Anderson, Brad (Athlete, Football Player)
13730 E Gary Rd
Scottsdale, AZ 85259-4644, USA

Anderson, Brad (Race Car Driver)
1240 S Cucamonga Ave
Ontario, CA 91761, USA

Anderson, Bradford (Actor)
c/o Staff Member *General Hospital*
4151 Prospect Ave
Hollywood, CA 90027, USA

Anderson, Brady (Athlete, Baseball Player)
32800 Pacific Coast Hwy
Malibu, CA 90265-2535, USA

Anderson, Brain (Athlete, Baseball Player)
W275N9303 Lake Five Rd
Hartland, WI 53029-9016, USA

Anderson, Brett (Musician)
c/o Staff Member *13 Artists (UK)*
11-14 Kensington St
Brighton BN1 4AJ, UK

Anderson, Brian (Commentator)
W275N9303 Lake Five Rd
Hartland, WI 53029-9016, USA

Anderson, Brian (Athlete, Baseball Player)
660 Saxony Blvd
St Petersburg, FL 33716-1284, USA

Anderson, Brian (Athlete, Baseball Player)
9553 N Corte Roca De Plata
Tucson, AZ 85704-8609, USA

Anderson, Bruce A (Athlete, Football Player)
910 NE Parkview Ct
Roseburg, OR 97470, USA

Anderson, Bud (Athlete, Baseball Player)
240 Twin Ln E
Wantagh, NY 11793-1963, USA

Anderson, Camille (Actor)
c/o Steven Neibert *Imperium 7 Talent Agency*
5455 Wilshire Blvd
Suite 1706
Los Angeles, CA 90036, USA

Anderson, CE (General)
1060 South ridge Dr
Auburn, CA 95603-5821, USA

Anderson, Chantelle (Athlete, Basketball Player)
Cleveland Rockers
Gund Arena
1 Center Ct
Cleveland, OH 44115, USA

Anderson, Charlie (Athlete, Football Player)
2323 Melrose Ave
Bossier City, LA 71111, USA

Anderson, Chris (Business Person, Writer)
The Long Tail
1165 Miller Ave
Berkeley, CA 94708, USA

Anderson, Christine (Psychic, Radio Personality)
Introspect...A Look Within
P.O. Box 8464
Minneapolis, MN 55104, USA

Anderson, Clayton (Astronaut)
2883 Carrera Ct
League City, TX 77573, USA

Anderson, Clifford (Athlete, Basketball Player)
2096A S John Russell Cir
Elkins Park, PA 19027, USA

Anderson, Courtney (Athlete, Football Player)
340 34th St
Richmond, CA 94805, USA

Anderson, Craig (Athlete, Baseball Player)
19217 SW 96th Loop
Dunnellon, FL 34432-4201, USA

Anderson, Craig (Athlete, Hockey Player)
2828 Carrington Dr
Dundee, FL 60118, USA

Anderson, Curtis (Athlete, Football Player)
967 Kemper Meadow Dr
Cincinnati, OH 45240, USA

Anderson, Dale (Athlete, Hockey Player)
2217 Haultain Ave
Saskatoon, SK S7J 1P7, Canada

Anderson, Dale (Athlete, Hockey Player)
2217 Av. Haultain
Saskatoon, Sask. S7J 1P7, CANADA

Anderson, Damien (Athlete, Football Player)
3563 S Cox Ct
Chandler, AZ 85248, USA

Anderson, Dan (Athlete, Basketball Player)
2230 SW Winchester Ave
Portland, OR 97225-4460, USA

Anderson, Dan (Athlete, Basketball Player)
100 3rd Ave s Unit 2002
Minneapolis, MN 55401-2716, USA

Anderson, Darren (Athlete, Football Player)
7328 Overland Park CT
West Chester, OH 45069, USA

Anderson, Daryl (Actor)
24136 Friar St
Woodland Hills, CA 91367, USA

Anderson, Dave (Commentator)
8 Inness Road
Tenafly, NJ 07670-2715, USA

Anderson, Dave (Athlete, Baseball Player)
Texas Rangers
PO Box 90111
Frisco, TX 75034, USA

Anderson, David (Athlete, Baseball Player)
207 Athletic Office Bldg
Memphis, TN 38152, USA

Anderson, Dennis (Race Car Driver)
Clear Channel Entertainment
495 N. Commons Dr
Suite 200
Aurora, IL 60504, USA

Anderson, Derek (Athlete, Basketball Player)
5562 Werburgh St
Charlotte, NC 28209-3693, USA

Anderson, Dick (Athlete, Football Player)
4603 Santa Maria St
Miami, FL 33146, USA

Anderson, Dion (Actor)
S D B Partners
1801 Ave of Stars
#902
Los Angeles, CA 90067, USA

Anderson, Don
California Institute OfTechnology
Geophysics
Pasadena, CA 91125-0001, USA

Anderson, Don (Athlete, Football Player)
10090 Beechdale St
Detroit, MI 48204, USA

Anderson, Don L (Misc)
669 Alameda St
#E
Altadena, CA 91001, USA

Anderson, Donny (Athlete, Football Player)
111 S St Joseph St
S Bend, IN 46601-1901, USA

Anderson, Drew (Athlete, Baseball Player)
209 GolfCt
Cold Spring, MN 56320-8749, USA

Anderson, Duwayne M (Scientist)
6119 139th Pl SE
Bellevue, WA 98006-4384, USA

Anderson, Dwain (Athlete, Baseball Player)
1807 Fallbrook Dr
Alamo, CA 94507-0410, USA

Anderson, Earl (Athlete, Hockey Player)
602 3rd Ave NE
Roseau, MN 56751-1809, USA

Anderson, Eddie Lee (Athlete, Football Player)
209 Shenandoah Trl
Warner Robins, GA 31088, USA

Anderson, Edward G (Ed) III (General)
Senior Representative
United Nations Military Committee
Washington, DC 20318, USA

Anderson, Eric (Athlete, Basketball Player)
12284 Whirlaway Dr
Noblesville, IN 46060-5536, USA

Anderson, Erich (Actor)
Paradigm Agency
10100 Santa Monica Blvd
#2500
Los Angeles, CA 90067, USA

Anderson, Erick (Athlete, Football Player)
2919 Attleboro Rd
Cleveland, OH 44120, USA

Anderson, Erika (Actor)
c/o Staff Member *Flick Commercials*
9057 Nemo St #A
W Hollywood, CA 90069, USA

Anderson, Erriestine I (Musician)
Thomas Cassidy
11761 E Speedway Blvd
Tucson, AZ 85748, USA

Anderson, Flipper (Athlete, Football Player)
190 Abbey Hill Rd
Suwanee, GA 30024, USA

Anderson, Fred (Athlete, Football Player)
11810 NE 48th Pl
Kirkland, WA 98033, USA

Anderson, Garret (Athlete, Baseball Player)
36 Boulder Vw
Irvine, CA 92603-0410, USA

Anderson, Gary (Athlete, Fisherman, Football Player)
265 Miskow Close
Canmore, Alberta T1W 3G7, Canada

Anderson, Gary W (Athlete, Football Player)
1 Ridgefield Ct
Little Rock, AR 72223, USA

Anderson, Gayle (Correspondent)
KTLA-TV
5800 Sunset Blvd
Los Angeles, CA 90028, USA

Anderson, Gerry (Director, Entertainer)
Gerry Anderson Magazine
332 Lytham Road
Blackpool FY4 1DW, UNITED KINGDOM (UK)

Anderson, Gillian (Actor)
c/o Justin Grey Stone *Untitled Entertainment (LA)*
350 S. Beverly Dr #200
Beverly Hills, CA 90212, USA

Anderson, Glenn (Athlete, Hockey Player)
42 W 69th St
Apt 2A
New York, NY 10023-5265, USA

Anderson, Hans Christian (Scientist)
Stanford University
Chemistry Dept
Stanford, CA 94305, USA

Anderson, Harry (Actor, Magician)
120 Flint St
Asheville, NC 28801, USA

Anderson, H George (Religious Leader)
Evangelical Lutheran Church
8765 W Higgins Road
Chicago, IL 60631, USA

Anderson, Ho Che (Artist)
c/o Staff Member *Fantagraphics Books*
7563 Lake City Way
Seattle, WA 98115, USA

Anderson, Howard A (Actor)
PO Box 2230
Los Angeles, CA 90028, USA

Anderson, Howard A Jr (Cinematographer)
c/o Staff Member *Howard Anderson Company*
5161 Lankershim Blvd
Hollywood, CA 91601, USA

Anderson, Ian (Musician, Songwriter, Writer)
43 Brook Green
London W6 7ER, UNITED KINGDOM (UK)

Anderson, Jamal (Athlete, Football Player)
10540 Montclair Way
Duluth, GA 30097, USA

Anderson, James (Cricketer)
c/o Staff Member *International Sports Management Ltd (ISM UK)*
Cherry Tree Farm
Cherry Tree Lane
Rostherne, Cheshire WA14 3RZ, UNITED KINGDOM

Anderson, James (Athlete, Football Player)
1544 Taylor Point Dr
Chesapeake, VA 23321, USA

Anderson, James F (Religious Leader)
12 Surf Ave
Ocean Grove, NJ 07756, USA

Anderson, James G (Misc)
Harvard Unviversity
Eatrh-Planetary Physics Center
Cambridge, MA 02138, USA

Anderson, James W (Doctor)
University of Kentucky
Medical Center
Endocrinology Dept
Lexington, KY 40506, USA

Anderson, Jamie (Actor)
c/o Craig Wyckoff *Wyckoff and Associates (LA)*
11350 Ventura Blvd
Suite 100
Studio City, CA 91604-3140, USA

Anderson, Janet (Athlete, Golfer)
4311 W Ardmore Rd
Laveen, AZ 85339-2112, USA

Anderson, Jason (Athlete, Baseball Player)
2022 Hidden Lake Dr Apt F
Stow, OH 44224-5321, USA

Anderson, J C (Athlete, Golfer)
1418 S 39th St
Quincy, IL 62305, USA

Anderson, Jeff (Actor, Director)
c/o Staff Member *Imperium 7 Talent Agency*
5455 Wilshire Blvd
Suite 1706
Los Angeles, CA 90036, USA

Anderson, Jesse (Athlete, Football Player)
4374 Redwood Cir
Jackson, MS 39212, USA

Anderson, Jim (Athlete, Baseball Player)
2111 Bennington Ct
Thousand Oaks, CA 91360-1977, USA

Anderson, Jimmy (Athlete, Hockey Player)
4H Castle Hill Rd
Agawam, MA 01001, USA

Anderson, Jimmy (Athlete, Baseball Player)
214 Pennington Blvd
Portsmouth, VA 23701-1226, USA

Anderson, Jo (Actor)
c/o Staff Member *Innovative Artists (LA)*
1505 10th St
Santa Monica, CA 90401, USA

Anderson, Joe (Actor)
c/o Lindy King *United Agents*
12-26 Lexington St
London W1F 0LE, UK

Anderson, John (Athlete, Hockey Player)
6751 N Sunset Blvd Ste 200
Glendale, AZ 85305-3124, USA

Anderson, John (Politician)
16609 W 133rd St
Olathe, KS 66062-1575, USA

Anderson, John (Musician)
671/673 Cordell Love Rd
Smithville, TN 37166, USA

Anderson, John (Athlete, Football Player)
14730 Crestwood Ct
Elm Grove, WI 53122, USA

Anderson, John B (Politician)
4120 48th St NW
Washington, DC 20016-2336, USA

Anderson, John B (Misc)
3300 NE 36th St
#1016
Fort Lauderdale, FL 33308, USA

Anderson, John Jr (Ex-Governor)
16609 W 133rd St
Olathe, KS 66062, USA

Anderson, Jon (Musician)
Sun Artists
9 Hillgate St
London W8 7SP, UNITED KINGDOM (UK)

Anderson, Josh (Athlete, Baseball Player)
3780 E Highway 452
Eubank, KY 42567-9731, USA

Anderson, June (Opera Singer)
Herbert Breslin
119 W 57th St
#1505
New York, NY 10019, USA

Anderson, Kalen (Athlete, Golfer)
c/o Jim Lehrman *SFX Golf*
36855 W Main St Ste 200
Purcellville, VA 20132, USA

Anderson, Keith (Musician)
c/o Staff Member *Fitzgerald-Hartley*
34 N Palms St
Suite 100
Ventura, CA 93001, USA

Anderson, Ken (Athlete, Football Player)
41 Sedge Fern Dr
Hilton Head Island, SC 29926, USA

Anderson, Kenny (Athlete, Basketball Player)
18145 SW 5th Ct
Pembroke Pines, FL 33029-4352, USA

Anderson, Kent (Athlete, Baseball Player)
925 E Twin Church Rd
Timmonsville, SC 29161-8528, USA

Anderson, Kevin (Actor)
c/o Staff Member *ICM Partners (ICM-LA)*
10250 Constellation Blvd Fl 7
Los Angeles, CA 90067, USA

Anderson, Kevin J (Writer)
Tom Doherty Associates, LLC
175 Fifth Ave
New York, NY 10010, USA

Anderson, Kim (Athlete, Basketball Player)
602 Somerset
Warrensburg, MO 64093, USA

Anderson, Kim S (Athlete, Football Player)
3500 W Manchester Blvd Unit 216
Inglewood, CA 90305, USA

Anderson, Larry (Athlete, Baseball Player)
1135 Saratoga Ave
GroverBeach, CA 93433-1723, USA

Anderson, Lars (Athlete, Baseball Player)
3948 Bannister Rd
Fair Oaks, CA 95628-6806, USA

Anderson, Laurie (Musician)
Maine Road
195 Chrystie St
#501F
New York, NY 10002, USA

Anderson, Lawrence A (Larry) (Athlete, Football Player)
3170 Blanchard Rd
Shreveport, LA 71103, USA

Anderson, Leonora (Aviator)
8015 Conservatory Dr
Sarasota, FL 34243-2952, USA

Anderson, Lloyd L (Astronaut)
1939 Live Oak Cemetery Rd
Killeen, TX 76542-5100, USA

Anderson, Loni (Actor)
14318 Valley Vista Blvd
Sherman Oaks, CA 91423, USA

Anderson, Louie (Actor, Comedian, Producer, Writer)
c/o Jackie Miller-Knobbe *Agency for the Performing Arts (APA-LA)*
405 S Beverly Dr
Suite 500
Beverly Hills, CA 90212-4425, USA

Anderson, Loule (Actor, Comedian)
8033 Sunset Blvd #605
West Hollywood, CA 90046, USA

Anderson, Lynn (Musician)
555 Piedmont
Taos, NM 87571, USA

Anderson, Marcus (General)
The Pentagon Inspector
Washington, DC 20330-0001, USA

Anderson, Marina (Actor)
c/o Nancy Harding *Powerhouse Talent*
P.O. Box 261939
Encino, CA 91426, USA

Anderson, Mark (Athlete, Football Player)
PO Box 27551
Tulsa, OK 74149, USA

Anderson, Marlon (Athlete, Baseball Player)
1603 Turning Leaf Ct
Sugar Land, TX 77479-6489, USA

Anderson, Marques (Athlete, Football Player)
213 W Gardner St
Long Beach, CA 90805, USA

Anderson, Mary (Actor)
1127 Norman Place
Los Angeles, CA 90049, USA

Anderson, Matt (Athlete, Golfer)
c/o Jim Lehrman *SFX Golf*
36855 W Main St Ste 200
Purcellville, VA 20132, USA

Anderson, Matt (Athlete, Baseball Player)
4115 Woodmont Park Ln
Louisville, KY 40245-8431, USA

Anderson, May (Model)
Jim Paris
c/o Lewis, Joffe & Company
10880 Wilshire Boulevard Suite 520
Los Angeles, CA 90024, USA

Anderson, Melissa Sue (Actor, Producer)
c/o Staff Member *Bret Adams Agency*
448 W 44th St
New York, NY 10036, USA

Anderson, Melody (Actor)
PO Box 350
New York, NY 10028, USA

Anderson, Melvin
2747 Sheridan Ave N
Minneapolis, MN 55411, USA

Anderson, Michael (Musician, Songwriter, Writer)
Brock Assoc
7106 Moores Ln
#200
Brentwood, TN 37027, USA

Anderson, Michael (Scientist)
University Of Colorado
Physics Dpt
Boulder, CO 80309-0001, USA

Anderson, Michael H (Physicist)
University of Colorado
Physics Dept
Boulder, CO 80309, USA

Anderson, Michael J (Director)
Paul Burford
52 Yorkminster Road
North York, ON M2P 1M3, CANADA

Anderson, Mike (Athlete, Coach, Football Player)
P.O. Box 12753
Chandler, AZ 85248, USA

Anderson, Mike (Athlete, Baseball Player)
407 Prairie Grass Ct
Hartland, WI 53029-8562, USA

Anderson, Mitchell (Actor)
MetroFresh
931 Monroe Dr #A106
Atlanta, GA 30308, USA

Anderson, Murray (Athlete, Hockey Player)
38 Head Ave
P.O. Box 38 Stn Main
The Pas, MB R9A 1K3, Canada

Anderson, Neal (Athlete, Football Player)
10626 SW 41st Pl
Gainesville, FL 32608, USA

Anderson, Neilson (Athlete, Basketball Player)
163 Harbor Isle Cir N
Memphis, TN 38103, USA

Anderson, Neil T. (Writer)
Freedom in Christ Ministries
9051 Executive Park Dr
Suite 503
Knoxville, TN 37923, USA

Anderson, Nick (Athlete, Basketball Player)
6672 Cherry Grove Cir
Orlando, FL 32809-6658, USA

Anderson, Nick (Cartoonist, Editor)
Courier Journal
Editorial Dept
525 W Broadway
Louisville, KY 40202, USA

Anderson, Nicole (Actor)
c/o Todd Justice *Justice & Ponder*
P.O. Box 480033
Los Angeles, CA 90048, USA

Anderson, Nikki (Stylist)
c/o Staff Member *Crews*
828 Clemont Dr
Atlanta, GA 30306, USA

Anderson, Ottis (Athlete, Football Player)
47 Duffield Dr
South Orange, NJ 07079, USA

Anderson, Ottis J (O J) (Athlete, Football Player)
P.O. Box 399
Orange, NJ 07051, USA

Anderson, Paige (Stylist)
c/o Staff Member *Independent Artists*
448 E Riverdale Ave
Orange, CA 92865, USA

Anderson, Pamela (Actor)
23445 Malibu Colony Rd
Malibu, CA 90265, USA

Anderson, Paul Thomas (Director, Writer)
4900 Casa Dr
Tarzana, CA 91356, USA

Anderson, Paul W S (Director)
c/o Ken Kamins *Key Creatives*
1800 N Highland Ave
Suite 500
Los Angeles, CA 90028, USA

Anderson, Perry (Athlete, Hockey Player)
4326 N 33rd St
Phoenix, AZ 85018, USA

Anderson, Philip W (Nobel Prize Laureate)
Princeton University
Physics Dept
Princeton, NJ 08544-0001, USA

Anderson, Ralph (Athlete, Football Player)
908 Hilltop Dr
Apt C
Irving, TX 75060, USA

Anderson, Randy (Race Car Driver)
Anderson Racing
1240 S Cucamonga Ave
Ontario, CA 91761, USA

Anderson, Rashard (Athlete, Football Player)
676 N First Ave
Forest, MS 39074, USA

Anderson, Ray (Musician)
James faith Entertainment
318 Wynne Lane
Port Jefferson, NY 11777, USA

Anderson, Reid B (Dancer, Director)
Stuttgart Ballet
Ober Schlossgarten 6
Stuttgart 70173, GERMANY

Anderson, Renee (Actor)
2818 Laurel Canyon Blvd
Los Angeles, CA 90046, USA

Anderson, Richard (Actor)
10120 Cielo Dr
Beverly Hills, CA 90210, USA

Anderson, Richard Dean (Actor)
28890 Selfridge Dr
Malibu, CA 90265, USA

Anderson, Richard (Dick) J (Athlete, Football Player)
206 Baker St
Lodi, OH 44254, USA

Anderson, Richard P (Dick) (Athlete, Football Player)
4603 Santa Maria St
Coral Gables, FL 33146, USA

Anderson, Richie (Athlete, Football Player)
6311 Meandering Woods Ct
Frederick, MD 21701, USA

Anderson, Rick (Athlete, Baseball Player)
3929 Benjamin Dr
Saint Paul, MN 55125-3396, USA

Anderson, Rick (Athlete, Baseball Player)
Minnesota Twins
1 Twins Way
minneapolis, MN 55403-1418, USA

Anderson, R Lanier III (Judge)
US Court of Appeals
56 Forsyth St NW
Atlanta, GA 30303, USA

Anderson, Robert (Writer)
William Morris Agency
1325 Avenue of the Americas
Bsmt 2
New York, NY 10019-6047, USA

Anderson, Ron (Athlete, Hockey Player)
4470 Meadowvale Dr
Niagara Falls, ON L2E 5W9, Canada

Anderson, Ron (Athlete, Hockey Player)
72 Woodside Close NW
Airdrie, AB T4B 2C7, Canada

Anderson, Ross (Journalist)
Seattle Times
Editorial Dept
1120 John St
Seattle, WA 98109-5321, USA

Anderson, Russ (Athlete, Hockey Player)
76 Fern Dr
Plantsville, CT 06479, USA

Anderson, Sam (Actor)
c/o Staff Member *TalentWorks (LA)*
3500 W Olive Ave
Suite 1400
Burbank, CA 91505, USA

Anderson, Scot (Writer)
c/o Staff Member *Premiere Speakers Bureau*
1000 Corporate Centre
Suite 120
Franklin, TN 37067, USA

Anderson, Scott (Athlete, Football Player)
2836 Queen Bee Ln
Saint Louis, MO 63129, USA

Anderson, Scott (Athlete, Baseball Player)
13061 Amber Pl
Lake Oswego, OR 97034-1524, USA

Anderson, Scott
13061 Amber Pl
Lake Oswego, OR 97034-1524, USA

Anderson, Scott (Athlete, Baseball Player)
13061 Amber Pl
Lake Oswego, OR 97034-1524, United States

Anderson, Scotty (Athlete, Football Player)
1405 Leon Dr
Jonesboro, LA 71251, USA

Anderson, Sean (Big Sean) (Musician)
c/o Staff Member *Island Def Jam Group*
Worldwide Plaza
825 8th Ave Fl 28
New York, NY 10019, USA

Anderson, Shandon (Athlete, Basketball Player)
63 Mangum St SW #5
Atlanta, GA 30313-1355, USA

Anderson, Shawn (Athlete, Hockey Player)
Hockey Specific Training
274 Boul Pincourt
Pincourt, QC J7V 9X9, Canada

Anderson, Shelly (Race Car Driver)
1240 S Cucamonga Ave
Ontario, CA 91761, USA

Anderson, Stephen H (Judge)
US Court of Appeals
Federal Building
125 S State St
Salt Lake City, UT 84138, USA

Anderson, Sterling (Writer)
c/o Abram Nalibotsky *Gersh (LA)*
9465 Wilshire Blvd
Suite 600
Beverly Hills, CA 90212, USA

Anderson, Stevie (Athlete, Football Player)
1405 Leon Dr
Jonesboro, LA 71251, USA

Anderson, Stuart (Athlete, Football Player)
100 Careys Ln
Cardinal, VA 23025, USA

Anderson, Sunny (Chef)
c/o Jonathan Rosen *WME (WMA-NY)*
1325 Ave of the Americas
New York, NY 10019, USA

Anderson, Susan (Psychic, Radio Personality)
Introspect...A Look Within
P.O. Box 8464
Minneapolis, MN 55408, USA

Anderson, Taz (Athlete, Football Player)
Taz Anderson Realty
2931 Paces Ferry Rd SE
Suite 150
Atlanta, GA 30339, USA

Anderson, Taz (Athlete, Football Player)
Taz Anderson Realty 2931 Paces Ferry Rd SE Ste 150
Atlanta, GA 30339, USA

Anderson, Terence (Politician)
668 Oak Tree Rd
Palisades, NY 10964-1532, USA

Anderson, Terence (Terry) (Journalist)
17 Sunlight Hill
Yonkers, NY 10704, USA

Anderson, Terry (Producer)
Pinewood Studios
Iverheath
Iver
Bucks SL0 0NH, UNITED KINGDOM (UK)

Anderson, Theodore W (Economist, Mathematician)
746 Santa Ynez St
Stanford, CA 94305, USA

Anderson, Tom (Business Person)
c/o MySpace, Inc
6060 Center Dr Ste 300
Los Angeles, CA 90045, USA

Anderson, Tom (Actor, Producer, Writer)
c/o Staff Member *Gersh (LA)*
9465 Wilshire Blvd
Suite 600
Beverly Hills, CA 90212, USA

Anderson, Tracy (Fitness Expert)
Tracy Anderson Studios
408 Greenwich St Fl 3
New York, NY 10013, USA

Anderson, Vickey Ray (Athlete, Football Player)
9308 S Harvey Ave
Oklahoma City, OK 73139, USA

Anderson, Warren M (Business Person)
270 Park Ave
New York, NY 10017, USA

Anderson, Wayne (Race Car Driver)
Liberty Racing
3086 Highway 301
Wildwood, FL 34785, USA

Anderson, Webster (War Hero)
3044 US Highway 321 N
Winnsboro, SC 29180, USA

Anderson, Wendell (Athlete, Hockey Player)
108 Chevy Chase Dr
Wayzata, MN 55391, USA

Anderson, Wes (Director, Writer)
c/o Leslee Dart *42West (NY)*
220 W 42nd St
12th Floor
New York, NY 10036, USA

Anderson, Wessell (Musician)
Fat City Artists
1906 Chet Atkins Place
#502
Nashville, TN 37212, USA

Anderson, Weston (Physicist)
Varian Assoc
611 Hansen Way
Palo Alto, CA 94304, USA

Anderson, W French (Scientist)
University Of Southern California
1510 San Pablo St
Attn Medical School
Los Angeles, CA 90033-5320, USA

Anderson, W French (Misc)
USC Medical School
144 E Lake View Terrace
Los Angeles, CA 90039, USA

Anderson, Wilford C (War Hero)
3585 Round Barn Blvd
Santa Rosa, CA 95403, USA

Anderson, William R (Misc)
10505 Miller Road
Oakton, VA 22124, USA

Anderson, Willie (Athlete, Football Player)
1490 Meadowcreek Ct
Atlanta, GA 30338, USA

Anderson, Willie (Athlete, Basketball Player)
Toronto Raptors
Air Canada Center
40 Bay St
Toronto, ON M5J 2N8, Canada

Anderson, W William (Athlete, Football Player)
6924 Lark Ln
Knoxville, TN 37919, USA

Anderson-Emmons, Aubrey (Actor)
c/o Carlyne Grager *Dramatic Artists Agency*
103 W. Alameda Ave
Suite 139
Burbank, CA 91502, USA

Anderson III, N Christian (Editor, Publisher)
Gazette Telegraph
30 S Prospect St
Colorado Springs, CO 80903, USA

Anderson-Sheriffs, Vivian (Athlete, Baseball Player)
2654 N 117th St
Wauwatosa, WI 53226-1124, USA

Andersson, Benny (Composer, Musician)
Mono Music
Sodra Brobaeken 41-A
Stockholm 111 49, SWEDEN

Andersson, Bibi (Actor)
Agents Associes Beaume
201 Faubourg Saint Honore
Paris 75008, FRANCE

Andersson, Erik (Athlete, Hockey Player)
Persilijav 9
Karlstad S-65351, Sweden

Andersson, Harriet (Actor)
Roslagsgatan 14/6
Stockholm 113 55, Sweden

Andersson, Henrik (Musician)
MOB Agency
6404 Wilshire Blvd
#505
Los Angeles, CA 90048, USA

Andersson, Kent-Erik (Athlete, Hockey Player)
Babordsg 11 7Tr
Karlstad S-65351, Sweden

Andersson, Mikael (Athlete, Hockey Player)
c/o Staff Member *Tampa Bay Lightning*
Ice Palace
401 Channelside Dr
Tampa, FL 33602, USA

Andersson, Peter (Athlete, Hockey Player)
Sultronvagen 35
Umea 904 35, Sweden

Andersson, Peter
Sultronvagen 35
Umea 904 35, Sweden

Anderszewski, Piotr (Conductor, Musician)
Virgin Classics Records
90 University Plaza
New York, NY 1000

Anderton, Sophie (Actor, Model)
c/o Staff Member *Premier Model Management*
40-42 Parker St
London WC2B 5PQ, UK

Andes, Karen (Misc)
G P Putnam's Sons
375 Hudson St
New York, NY 10014, USA

Andino, Robert (Athlete, Baseball Player)
645 Santa Clara Trl
Wellington, FL 33414-3921, USA

Ando, Hiromi (Stylist)
c/o Staff Member *Mercury Artists*
8460 Higuera St Fl 2
Culver City, CA 90232, USA

Ando, Tadao (Architect)
Tadao Ando Architect
5-23-2 Toyosaki
Kitaku, Osaka 531, JAPAN

Andov, Stojan (President)
Sobranje
11 Oktombri Blvd
Skopje 91000, MACEDONIA

Andrade, Fernanda (Actor)
c/o Robyn Holt *Genesis Entertainment Partners*
152 S Kilkea Blvd
Los Angeles, CA 90048, USA

Andrade, Sergio (Musician)
DreamWorks Records
9268 W 3rd St
Beverly Hills, CA 90210, USA

Andrade, William T (Billy) (Athlete, Golfer)
4439 E Brookhaven Dr NE
Atlanta, GA 30319, USA

Andrascik, Steve (Athlete, Hockey Player)
32 Early Ln
Annville, PA 17003-8623, USA

Andre, Carl (Artist)
689 Crown St
Brooklyn, NY 11213-5303, USA

Andre, Peter (Musician, Television Host)
55 Drury Ln
London 4217, UNITED KINGDOM

Andre 3000 (Artist, Musician)
4723 Jett Rd NW
Atlanta, GA 30327, USA

Andrea, Paul (Athlete, Hockey Player)
136 Regent St
North Sydney, NS B2A 2G5, Canada

Andreachuk, Randy_
17294 2 Ave
Surrey, BC V3S 9P9, Canada

Andreas, Dwayne O (Business Person)
181 Southmoreland Place
Decatur, IL 62521, USA

Andreas, G Allen (Business Person)
Archer-Daniels-Midland
4666 Faries Parkway
Decatur, IL 62526, USA

Andreasen, Nancy (Scientist)
506 Ashford Dr NE
Cedar Rapids, IA 52402-7321, USA

Andreasen, Nancy C (Doctor)
200 Hawkings Dr
Iowa City, IA 52242, USA

Andreason, Larry (Yachtsman)
10874 Kyle St
Los Alamitos, CA 90720, USA

Andre-Deshays, Claudie (Misc)
Hopital Cochin
Rhumatologie Dept
Paris 75000, FRANCE

Andreeff, Starr (Actor)
C N A Assoc
1875 Century Park East
#2250
Los Angeles, CA 90067, USA

Andreessen, Marc (Business Person, Designer)
23910 Malibu Rd
Malibu, CA 90265, USA

Andrei, Alessandro (Athlete, Track Athlete)
Via V Bellini 1
Scandicci, Firenze 50018, ITALY

Andreotti, Giulio (Government Official)
Piazza Montecitorio 13,1
Rome I-00186, Italy

Andress, Tuck (Musician)
Windham Hill Records
PO Box 5501
Beverly Hills, CA 90209, USA

Andress, Ursula (Actor)
1740 Clear View Dr
Beverly Hills, CA 90210, USA

Andretti, Jeff (Race Car Driver)
Andretti Racing Group
7615 Zionsville Rd
Indianapolis, IN 46268, USA

Andretti, John (Race Car Driver)
BAMR Racing
Box: 2010
Thomasville, NC 27360, USA

Andretti, Marco (Race Car Driver)
c/o John Caponigro *Sports Management
Network, Inc.*
1668 Telegraph Rd
Suite 200
Bloomfield Hills, MI 48302, USA

Andretti, Mario (Race Car Driver)
457 Rose Inn Ave
Nazareth, PA 18064, USA

Andretti, Michael (Athlete, Race Car
Driver)
471 Rose Inn Ave
Nazareth, PA 18064, USA

Andrew, C Robert (Rob) (Athlete, Misc)
Newcastle RFC
Newcastle-upon-Tyne NE3 2DT, UNITED
KINGDOM (UK)

Andrew, HRH (Prince)
Sunninghill Park
Windsor, England

Andrew, Kim (Athlete, Baseball Player)
10052 Densmore Ave
North Hills, CA 91343-1454, USA

Andrew, Phillip (Actor)
c/o Bonnie Liedtke *Principato/Young
Management*
9465 Wilshire Blvd
Suite 430
Beverly Hills, CA 90212, USA

Andrew, Prince (Prince, Royalty)
Buckingham Palace
London SW1A 1AA, UNITED KINGDOM
(UK)

Andrew, Troy (Athlete, Football Player)
James Crystal Radio Inc
206 Johnstone Ct
Durham, NC 27712, USA

Andrews, Al (Athlete, Football Player)
P.O. Box 82256
Atlanta, GA 30354, USA

Andrews, Al (Athlete, Boxer)
1119 River St
Rhinelander, WI 54501, USA

Andrews, Amy (Stylist)
2815 W Fargo
Chicago, IL 60645, USA

Andrews, Amy Leigh (Model)
PO Box 3184
Manhattan Beach, CA 90266, USA

Andrews, Andy (Actor, Comedian)
P.O. Box 17321
Nashville, TN 37217, USA

Andrews, Anthony (Actor)
13 Manor Place
Oxford, Oxon, UNITED KINGDOM (UK)

Andrews, Ariel (Race Car Driver)
PO Box 374
Newburgh, IN 47629, USA

Andrews, Billy (Athlete, Football Player)
PO Box 703 17164 Highway 10 E
Clinton, LA 70722, USA

Andrews, Clayton (Athlete, Baseball
Player)
1906 Westlev St
Safety Harbor, FL 34695-2147, USA

Andrews, Donna (Athlete, Golfer)
2301 Hawthorne Rd
Lynchburg, VA 24503-2903, USA

Andrews, Erin (Sportscaster)
c/o Alejandra Cristina *Ace PR*
4122 Sunnyslope Ave
Sherman Oaks, CA 91423, USA

Andrews, Fred (Athlete, Baseball Player)
PO Box 898
Wedowee, AL 36278-0898, USA

Andrews, Giuseppe (Actor)
PO Box 24561
Ventura, CA 93002, USA

Andrews, James (Doctor)
American Sports Medicine Institute
1313 13th St S
Birmingham, AL 35205, USA

Andrews, James E (Misc)
Presbyterian Church (USA)
100 Witherspoon St
Louisville, KY 40202, USA

Andrews, jeff (Baseball Player)
2613 NW 162nd Ter
Edmond, OK 73013-1257

Andrews, Jessica (Musician)
6535 Melinda Dr
Nashville, TN 37205, USA

Andrews, John (Athlete, Baseball Player)
9292 Gordon Ave
La Habra, CA 90631-2452, USA

Andrews, John H (Architect)
John Andrews Int'l
PO Box 7087
McMahon's Point, NSW 2060,
AUSTRALIA

Andrews, John M (Athlete, Football
Player)
7306 Summer Trail Dr
Sugar Land, TX 77479, USA

Andrews, John V (Athlete, Football Player)
7306 Summer Trail Dr
Sugar Land, TX 77479, USA

Andrews, Julie (Actor, Musician)
15 Cedar Haven Ln
N Haven, NY 11963, USA

Andrews, Ken (Musician)
c/o Staff Member *Paradigm (Monterey)*
404 W Franklin St
Monterey, CA 93940, USA

Andrews, Lee (Musician)
Mars Talent
27 L'Ambiance Court
Bardonia, NY 10954, USA

Andrews, Mark (Politician)
3354 165th Ave SE
Mapleton, ND 58059-9746, USA

Andrews, Mike (Athlete, Baseball Player)
5 Patriot Ln Unit 10
Geon^etown, MA 01833-2246, USA

Andrews, Mitch (Athlete, Football Player)
PO Box 672
Washington, LA 70589, USA

Andrews, Naveen (Actor)
c/o Renee Jennett *Renee Jennett
Management*
10028 Farragut Dr
Culver City, CA 90232, USA

Andrews, Patricia (Patti) (Musician)
9823 Aldea Ave
Northridge, CA 91325, USA

Andrews, Patty (Musician)
9823 Aldea Ave
Northridge, CA 91354, USA

Andrews, Rob (Athlete, Baseball Player)
1280 Mountbatten Ct
Concord, CA 94518-3927, USA

Andrews, Robert (Writer)
G P Putnam's Sons
375 Hudson St
New York, NY 10014, USA

Andrews, Robert E (Congressman,
Politician)
2265 Rayburn HOB
Washington, DC 20515, USA

Andrews, Robert F (Misc)
5879 Beulah Land
Lakeland, FL 33810, USA

Andrews, Russell (Actor)

Andrews, Shane (Athlete, Baseball Player)
1816 N Guadalupe St
Carlsbad, NM 88220-8813, USA

Andrews, Shawn (Actor)
c/o Laura Berwick *Hofflund/Polone*
9465 Wilshire Blvd #420
Beverly Hills, CA 90212, USA

Andrews, Shawn (Athlete, Football Player)
204 Deauville Pl
Little Rock, AR 72223, USA

Andrews, Stacy (Athlete, Football Player)
7 Deauville Cir
Little Rock, AR 72223, USA

Andrews, Stanley (General)
3205 Leslie Dr
Colorado Springs, CO 80909-1039, USA

Andrews, Theresa (Athlete, Olympic
Athlete, Swimmer)
2004 Homewood Rd
Annapolis, MD 21402, USA

Andrews, Thomas (Tom) (Athlete,
Football Player)
1918 Wickham Way
Louisville, KY 40223, USA

Andrews, Tina (Actor)
c/o Staff Member *Sharp & Associates
Public Relations*
8721 Sunset Blvd.
Suite 208
Los Angeles, CA 90069, USA

Andrews, William D (Athlete, Football
Player)
P.O. Box 703
Clinton, LA 70722, USA

Andrews, William L (Athlete, Football
Player)
3916 Toccoa Falls Dr
Duluth, GA 30097, USA

Andrews II, George E (Athlete, Football
Player)
10195 Overhill Dr
Santa Ana, CA 92705, USA

Andreychuk, Dave (Athlete, Hockey
Player)
401 Channelside
Tampa, FL 33607, USA

Andreychuk, Dave (Athlete, Hockey
Player)
107 Sable Park
East Amherst, NY 14051-2209, USA

Andrianarivo, Tantely (Prime Minister)
Prime Minister's Office
Mahazoarivo, Antananarivo,
MADAGASCAR

Andrie, George J (Athlete, Football Player)
26356 E Zeerip Dr
Drummond Island, MI 49726, USA

Andriessen, Louis (Composer)
Nonesuch Records
75 Rockefeller Plaza
New York, NY 10019, USA

Andrieu, Sebastien (Actor, Model)
c/o Staff Member *Creature Entertainment*
4111 Camero Ave
Los Angeles, CA 90027, USA

Androsky, Carol (Actor)
Henderson/Hogan
8285 W Sunset Blvd
#1
West Hollywood, CA 90046, USA

Andruff, Ron (Athlete, Hockey Player)
72 1/2 Irving Pl
Apt 1F
New York, NY 10003, USA

Andrulis, Greg (Coach, Football Coach)
Columbus Crew
2121 Velman Ave
Columbus, OH 43211, USA

Andrus, Cecil (Politician)
PO Box 852
Boise, ID 83701-0852, USA

Andrus, Lou (Athlete, Football Player)
739 W 550 S
Oren, UT 84058, USA

Andrus, Lou
Denver Broncos
739 W 550 S
Orem, UT 84058-6070, USA

Andrus, Sheldon (Athlete, Football Player)
210 Belle Meade Blvd
Thibodaux, LA 70301, USA

Andrusak, Greg (Athlete, Hockey Player)
5240 Hwy 3A
Nelson, BC V1L 6N6, Canada

Andruski, Frank (Athlete, Football Player)
303 W Cody Cir
Payson, AZ 85541-3173, United States

Andrusyshsyn, Zenon (Athlete, Football
Player)
2823 Lake Saxon Dr
Land O Lakes, FL 34639, USA

Andruzzi, Joe (Athlete, Football Player)
130 Brown Ave
Mansfield, MA 02048, USA

Anduiar, Joaauin (Baseball Player)
Ave L. Amiama Tio #47
San Pedro de Macoris Dominican
Rep_ublic, USA

Andujar, Joaquin (Athlete, Baseball Player)
Ave L, Amiama Tio #47
San Pedro de Macoris, Dominican Republic

Andy, Dorris (Athlete, Football Player)
12391 Ike White Rd
Conroe, TX 77303-3044, USA

Andy, Ekern (Athlete, Football Player)
2041 W Bradley Pl
Chicago, IL 60618, USA

Ane, Charles T (Charlie) III (Athlete, Football Player)
749 16th Ave
Honolulu, HI 96816, USA

Anemone (Actor)
82 rue Bonaparte
Paris 75006, France

Ang, Michelle (Actor)
c/o Karen Kay *Karen Kay Management*
P.O. Box 446
Auckland 1140, New Zealand

Ang, Stephen (Stylist)
37 W. 20th St.
Suite 603
New York, NY 10011, USA

Angarano, Michael (Actor)
23456 Dolorosa St
Woodland Hills, CA 91356, USA

Angel, Ashley Parker (Musician)
c/o Chuck James *ICM Partners (ICM-LA)*
10250 Constellation Blvd Fl 7
Los Angeles, CA 90067, USA

Angel, Criss (Magician, Musician)
1 Club Point Ct
Henderson, NV 89052, USA

Angel, Heather H (Photographer)
Highways
6 Vicarage Hill
Farnham, Surrey GU9 8HJ, UNITED KINGDOM (UK)

Angel, James R P (Astronomer)
University of Arizona
Steward Observatory
Tucson, AZ 85721, USA

Angel, Joe (Commentator)
209 S Temelec Cir
Sonoma, CA 95476-8329, USA

Angel, Roger (Scientist)
University Of Arizona
Steward
Tucson, AZ 85721-0001, USA

Angel, Ryland (Musician)
c/o Staff Member *Paradigm (Monterey)*
404 W Franklin St
Monterey, CA 93940, USA

Angel, Vanessa (Actor, Model)
8019 Woodrow Wilson Dr
Los Angeles, CA 90046, USA

Angeli, Donna Lee (Stylist)
234 E 52nd St
#2-D
New York, NY 10022, USA

Angelil, Rene (Actor, Writer)
c/o Staff Member *United Talent Agency (UTA)*
9336 Civic Center Dr
Beverly Hills, CA 90210, USA

Angelini, Florenzo Cardinal (Religious Leader)
Via Anneo Lucano 47
Rome 00136, ITALY

Angelini, Norm (Athlete, Baseball Player)
15063 E Chenango Pl
Aurora, CO 80015-2136, USA

Angell, Wayne D (Financier, Government Official)
Bear Steams Co
383 Madison Ave
New York, NY 10017, USA

Angelos, Peter (Commentator)
Baltimore Orioles
100 N Charles St
Baltimore, MD 21201-3804, USA

Angelou, Maya (Writer)
3240 Valley Rd.
Winston-Salem, NC 27106-2504, USA

Angels, Anaheim
Edison Field
2000 Gene Autry Way
Anaheim, CA 92806, USA

Angels & Airwaves (Music Group)
c/o Staff Member *Geffen Records*
9126 Sunset Blvd
West Hollywood, CA 90069, USA

Angelstad, Mel (Athlete, Hockey Player)
224-910 Main St RR 1
Humboldt, SK SOK 2Al, Canada

Angelycal Musical (Music Group)
c/o Staff Member *Sony Music Miami*
605 Lincoln Rd Fl 7
Miami Beach, FL 33139, USA

Angelyne (Actor, Artist, Model)
c/o Staff Member *Angelyne Management*
5670 Wilshire Boulevard Fl 22
Los Angeles, CA 90036, USA

Angerer, Paul (Composer)
Esteplatz 3/26
Vienna 1030, AUSTRIA

Angerer, Peter (Athlete)
Wagenau 2
Hammer 17326, GERMANY

Angle, Kurt (Athlete, Olympic Athlete, Wrestler)
227 Lakeview Dr
Coraopolis, PA 15108-9775, USA

Anglim, Philip (Actor)
2404 Grand Canal
Venice, CA 90291, USA

Anglin, Jennifer (Actor)
651 N Kilkea Dr
Los Angeles, CA 90048, USA

Angotti, Lou (Athlete, Hockey Player)
2850 NE 14th St Cswy
Apt 401B
Pompano Beach, FL 33062-3640, USA

Anguiano, Raul (Artist)
Anaxagoras 1326
Colonia Narvate
Mexico City 13 DF, MEXICO

Angullo, Richard (Athlete, Football Player)
3015 Val Verde Dr NE
Albuquerque, NM 87110, USA

Angullq, Richard
4801 W Libby St
Glendale, AZ 85308, USA

Angus & Julia Stone (Music Group, Musician)
c/o Dan Efram *The Muse Box - NY*
205 Lexington Ave
2nd Floor
New York, NY 10016, USA

Anhalt, Darrell (Athlete, Hockey Player)
4935-49th St
Hughenden, AB T0B 2EO, Canada

Anholt, Christien (Actor)
Covington International
4237 Morro Drvie
Woodland Hills, CA 91364, USA

Anholt, Darrell (Athlete, Hockey Player)
4935 49th St
Hughenden, AB T0B 2E0, Canada

Anikulap-Kuti, Femi (Musician, Songwriter, Writer)
MCA Records
70 Universal City Plaza
Universal City, CA 91608, USA

Animals, The (Music Group)
PO Box 1821
Ojai, CA 93024, USA

Anissina, Marina (Figure Skater)
c/o Staff Member *Champions on Ice*
Tom Collins Enterprises Inc
3500 W 80th St
Minneapolis, MN 55431, USA

Aniston, Jennifer (Actor)
901 Airole Way
Los Angeles, CA 90077, USA

Aniston, John (Actor)
PO Box 514
5520 Platt Ave
West Hills, CA 91307, USA

Anjali (Actor, Bollywood)
14 Ganapathi Colony
1 Street Gopalpuram
Chennai, TN 600006, INDIA

Anjali, Devi (Actor, Bollywood)
6 Bags Road
Raja Annamalai Puram
Chennai, TN 600028, INDIA

Anju (Actor, Bollywood)
37 Nagarathanammal Nagar
Janaki Nagar
Chennai, TN 600017, INDIA

Anka, Paul (Actor, Musician, Writer)
2674 Stafford Rd
Thousand Oaks, CA 91361, USA

Ankiel, Rick (Athlete, Baseball Player)
126 Sandpiper Cir
Jupiter, FL 33477-8433, USA

Ankrom, Scott (Athlete, Football Player)
1206 Harvest Cyn
San Antonio, TX 78258, USA

Anlyan, William G (Doctor)
Duke Medical Center
100 Seeley Mudd Building #109
Durham, NC 27710, USA

Annable, Dave (Actor)
1878 Greenfield Ave. #106
Los Angeles, CA 90025, USA

Annable, Odette (Actor)
1878 Greenfield Ave. #106
Los Angeles, CA 90025, USA

Annan, Kofi (Nobel Prize Laureate, Politician)
575 Main St
Apt 909
New York, NY 10044-0279, USA

Annand, Richard (General)
Springwell House
Whitesmocks
Durham, DH1 4ZL, England

Annaud, Jean-Jacques (Director)
Reperage
16 Rue Saint-Vincent
Paris 75018, FRANCE

Anne (Royalty)
Gatecombe Park
Gloucestershire, UNITED KINGDOM (UK)

Annenberg, Wallis (Publisher)
10273 Century Woods Dr
Los Angeles, CA 90067, USA

Anne of Bourbon-Palma (Royalty)
Villa Serena
77 Chemin Louis-Degallier
Versoix-Geneva 1290, SWITZERLAND

Annett, Chloe (Actor)
c/o Staff Member *Innovative Artists (LA)*
1505 10th St
Santa Monica, CA 90401, USA

Annett, Michael (Race Car Driver)
Germain Racing
218 Raceway Dr.
Mooresville, NC 28117, USA

Annis, Francesca (Actor)
c/o Staff Member *Independent Talent Group (ITG-UK)*
Oxford House
76 Oxford St
London W1D 1BS, UK

Anno, Sam (Athlete, Football Player)
12934 Ferndale Ave
Los Angeles, CA 90066, USA

Annu, Kapoor (Actor, Bollywood)
F-19 Flat No. 504 Green Crest Yamuna Nagar
Opp Parasrampuria Tower Andheri(W)
Mumbai, MS 400053, INDIA

Annunziata, Robert (Business Person)
Global Crossing Ltd
Wessex House
45 Reid St
Hamilton, HM 12, BERMUDA

Ansara, Edward (Actor)
Jack Scagnetti
5118 Vineland Ave #102
North Hollywood, CA 91601, USA

Ansara, Michael (Actor)
4624 Park Mirasol
Calabasas, CA 91302, USA

Ansari, Anousheh (Astronaut)
6101 W Plano Prkwy #210
Plano, Tx 75093, USA

Ansari, Aziz (Comedian)
c/o David (Dave) Becky *3 Arts Entertainment Inc*
9460 Wilshire Blvd
7th Floor
Beverly Hills, CA 90210, USA

Anschutz, Jody (Athlete, Golfer)
27307 N Palo Fierro Rd
Rio Verde, AZ 85263, USA

Anschutz, Philip F (Business Person)
c/o Staff Member *Anschutz Film Group*
1888 Century Park East 14th Fl
Century City, CA 90067, USA

Anschutz, Philip F. (Business Person)
Anschutz Company
555 17th St
Suite 2400
Denver, CO 80202-3941, USA

Anselmo, Philip (Musician)
Concrete Mgmt
361 W Broadway
#200
New York, NY 10013, USA

Anselmo, Tony (Animator, Voice Over Artist)
1953 N. Parish Pl
Burbank, CA 91504, USA

Ansley, Michael (Athlete, Basketball Player)
1809 Wood Violet Dr
Orlando, FL 32824-6411, USA

Anspach, Susan (Actor)
PO Box 5605
Santa Monica, CA 90409, USA

Anspaugh, David (Director, Producer)
c/o John Burnham *ICM Partners (ICM-LA)*
10250 Constellation Blvd Fl 7
Los Angeles, CA 90067, USA

Ant, Adam (Musician)
c/o Liam Collopy *Levine Communications Office*
9100 Wilshire Blvd
Suite 540, East Tower
Beverly Hills, CA 90212, USA

Antal, Nimrod (Director)
c/o Scott Greenberg *Creative Artists Agency (CAA-LA)*
2000 Ave Of The Stars
Los Angeles, CA 90067, USA

Antes, Horst (Artist)
Hohenbergstr 11
Karlsruhe (Wolfartsweier 76228, GERMANY

Anthony, Allyson (Stylist)
1980 15th St
San Francisco, CA 94114, USA

Anthony, Carl (Misc)
Harvard University
Kennedy Government School
Cambridge, MA 02138, USA

Anthony, Carmelo (Athlete, Basketball Player)
c/o Leon Rose *CAA - NJ*
4300 Haddenfield Rd
Suite 309
Pennsauken, NJ 08109, USA

Anthony, Charles (Athlete, Football Player)
38709 Farwell Dr
Fremont, CA 94536, USA

Anthony, Denman (Athlete, Football Player)
PO Box 2733
Spring, TX 77383, USA

Anthony, Edward (Athlete, Football Player)
3433 Mill Run Ln
Pfafftown, NC 27040, USA

Anthony, Eric (Athlete, Baseball Player)
42 Fosters Ct
Sugar Land, TX 77479-5866, USA

Anthony, Greg (Athlete, Basketball Player)
901 Wiggin Rd
Delray Beach, FL 33444-2851, USA

Anthony, Jasmine Jessica (Actor)
c/o Adam Griffin *Kritzer Levine Wilkins Entertainment (KLWG)*
11872 La Grange Ave
1st Floor
Los Angeles, CA 90025, USA

Anthony, Jason (Model)
c/o Staff Member *Boss Models*
80 8th Ave
New York, NY 10011-5126, USA

Anthony, Jeff (Stylist)
918 10th St
Wilmette, IL 60091, USA

Anthony, La La (La La Vazquez) (Actor)
c/o Christina Gualazzi *Collective*
8383 Wilshire Blvd
Suite 1050
Beverly Hills, CA 90211, USA

Anthony, Lysette (Actor)
46 Old Compton St
London WV 5PB, UNITED KINGDOM (UK)

Anthony, Marc (Actor, Musician, Songwriter)
25067 Jim Bridger Rd
Hidden Hills, CA 91302, USA

Anthony, Mark (Stylist)
c/o Staff Member *ESP (London)*
63 Charlotte St.
1st Floor
London W11 4PG, UK

Anthony, Michael (Musician)
Van Halen
10100 Santa Monica Blvd #1300
Los Angeles, CA 90067, USA

Anthony, Piers (Writer)
PO Box 2289
Inverness, FL 34451-2289

Anthony, Plers (Writer)
PO Box 2289
Inverness, FL 34451, USA

Anthony, Ray (Musician)
9288 Kinglet Dr
Los Angeles, CA 90069, USA

Anthony, Reidel (Athlete, Football Player)
P.O. Box 23
South Bay, FL 33493, USA

Anthony, Terry (Athlete, Football Player)
1200 Beville Rd
Apt 91
Daytona Beach, FL 32114, USA

Anthrax (Music Group)
c/o Dave Kirby *Agency Group Ltd, The (LA)*
1880 Century Park E
Suite 711
Los Angeles, CA 90067, USA

Anti, Michael (Athlete, Olympic Athlete, Shooter)
13383 Honey Run Way
Colorado Springs, CO 80921-2072, USA

Antin, Jonathan (Reality TV Star, Stylist)
Jonathan Salon
901 Westbourne Dr
West Hollywood, CA 90069, USA

Antin, Robin (Actor, Choreographer)
8819 Rosewood Ave
West Hollywood, CA 90048, USA

Antin, Steve (Actor, Writer)
c/o Doug MacLaren *ICM Partners (ICM-LA)*
10250 Constellation Blvd Fl 7
Los Angeles, CA 90067, USA

Antistia, Azlea (Adult Film Star)
29 Harley St
Suite B
London W1G 9QR, UK

Antoine, Daphne (Stylist)
2416 NE 10th St
Hallandale Beach, FL 33309, USA

Antoine, Lionel (Athlete, Football Player)
1455 Glencliff Dr
Dallas, TX 75217, USA

Antoine, Tamlin (Athlete, Football Player)
5452 New Grange Garth
Columbia, MD 21045, USA

Anton, Alan (Musician)
c/o Staff Member *Macklam Feldman Mgmt*
1505 W 2nd Ave
Suite 200
Vancouver BC V6H 3Y4, Canada

Anton, Craig (Actor)
c/o Staff Member *United Talent Agency (UTA)*
9336 Civic Center Dr
Beverly Hills, CA 90210, USA

Anton, Susan (Actor, Producer)
509 Pinnacle Heights Ln
Las Vegas, NV 89144, USA

Antonakakis, Dimitris (Architect)
Atelier 66
Emm Benaki 118
Athens 114-73, GREECE

Antonakakis, Suzana M (Architect)
Atelier 66
Emm Benaki 118
Athens 114-73, GREECE

Antonelli, Dominic A (Astronaut)
4106 Oak Blossom Court
Houston, TX 77059, USA

Antonelli, Dominic A Lt Cmdr (Astronaut)
4106 Oak Blossom Ct
Houston, TX 77059-3264, USA

Antonelli, Ennio Cardinal (Religious Leader)
Archdiocese
Piazza S Giovanni 3
Florence 50129, ITALY

Antonelli, Johnny (Athlete, Baseball Player)
18 Tobey Ct
Pittsford, NY 14534-1854, USA

Antonelli, Laura (Actor)
Pietrovalle
Via B Buozzi 51
Rome 00197, ITALY

Antonelli, matt (Baseball Player)
1 Antonelli Wa.y
Peabody, MA 01960-3772, USA

Antonetti, Chris (Commentator)
2994 Riviera Ln
Westlake, OH 44145-6845, USA

Antonetti, Lorenzo Cardinal (Religious Leader)
Patrimony of the Holy See
Palazzo Apostolico
Vatican City 00120

Antonio (Dancer)
Caslada 7
Madrid, SPAIN

Antonio, Banks
6211 Savannah Breeze Ct
Tampa, FL 33625, us

Antonio, Lou (Actor)
530 S Gaylord Dr
Burbank, CA 91505, USA

Antonio dos Santos R, Eanes (General, President)
Partido Renovador Democratico
Travessa do Falo 9
Lisbon 1200, Portugal

Antonovich, Mike (Athlete, Hockey Player)
PO Box 224
Coleraine, MN 55722-0224, USA

Antony and the Johnsons (Music Group, Musician)
c/o Staff Member *Alias Production*
22, Rue Douai
Paris F-75009, France

Antoski, Shawn (Athlete, Hockey Player)
285 Tannery Rd
RR 2
Madoc, ON K0K 2K0, Canada

Antoun (Khouri), Bishop (Religious Leader)
Antiochian Orthodox Christian Archdiocese
358 Mountain Rd
Englewood, NJ 07631, USA

Antropov, Nikolai (Athlete, Hockey Player)
Newport Sports Management
400-201 City Centre Dr
Attn Don Meehan
Mississauga, ON L5B 2T4, Canada

Antuofermo, Vito (Boxer)
16019 81st St
Howard Beach, NY 11414, USA

Anu, Christine (Musician)
Robert Bamham Mgmt
432 Tyagarah Road
Myocum, NSW 2481, AUSTRALIA

Anuja (Actor, Bollywood)
4-B Periyar Street Happee Home Apts
Gandhi Nagar Saligram
Chennai, TN 600093, INDIA

Anusha (Actor, Bollywood)
Flat Non 202 II Floor
167 Eldams Road
Chennai, TN 600018, INDIA

Anuszkiewicz, Richard J (Artist)
76 Chestnut St
Englewood, NJ 07631-3045, USA

Anwar, Gabrielle (Actor)
c/o Bradley Kramer *Kramer Management*
5699 Kanan Rd #275
Agoura Hills, CA 91301, USA

Anzulot, Cynthia (Athlete, Golfer)
21 Spring Creek Mnr
Hershey, PA 17033, USA

Aoki, Chieko N (Business Person)
Westin Hotels Co
Westin Building
777 Westchester Ave
White Plains, NY 10604, USA

Aoki, Devon (Actor)
2828 Benedict Canyon Dr
Beverly Hills, CA 90210, USA

Aoki, Isao (Athlete, Golfer)
I M G
1360 E 9th St
Suite 100
Cleveland, OH 44114, USA

Aoki, Rocky (Athlete, Business Person)
Benihana of Tokyo
8685 NW 53rd Terr
#201
Miami, FL 33166, USA

Aoki, Steve (DJ, Musician)
c/o Kirk Sommer *WME (LA)*
9601 Wilshire Blvd Fl 3
Beverly Hills, CA 90210, USA

Aoloo Sunshine (Music Group)
c/o Staff Member *Paradigm (Monterey)*
404 W Franklin St
Monterey, CA 93940, USA

Aouita, Said (Athlete, Track Athlete)
Abdejil Bencheikh
9 Rue Soivissi
Loubira
Rabat, MOROCCO

Apap, Gilles (Musician)
Columbia Artists Mgmt Inc
165 W 57th St
New York, NY 10019, USA

Aparicio, Luis (Athlete, Baseball Player)
Baltimore Orioles
Baltimore Orioles 333 W Camden St Attn:
Alumni Association
Baltimore, MD 21201-2496, USA

Apatow, Judd (Director, Producer, Writer)
239 N Bristol Ave
Los Angeles, CA 90049, USA

Apel, Katrin (Athlete)
Suedlung 9
Grafenroda 99330, GERMANY

Apice, Robert (Horse Racer)
69 Alissa Ter
Jackson, NJ 08527-3116, USA

Apke, Steve (Athlete, Football Player)
427 Kenmont Ave
Pittsburgh, PA 15228, USA

Apodaca, Bob (Athlete, Baseball Player)
Colorado Rockies 2001 Blake St Attn
Coaching Staff
denver, CO 80205-2000, USA

Apodaca, Jerry (Politician)
6223 Utah Ave NW
Washington, DC 20015-2431, USA

Apodaca, Raymond S (Jerry) (Ex-Governor)
1477 Miracerros Loop N
Santa Fe, NM 87505-4021, USA

Aponte Martinez, Luis Cardinal (Misc)
Arzobispado
Apatado S-1967
201 Calle San Jorge
Santurce, PR 00912, USA

Appel, Deena (Designer)
c/o Jon Furie *Montana Artists Agency*
9150 Wilshire Blvd Ste 100
Beverly Hills, CA 90212, USA

Appetite for Destruction (Music Group, Musician)

Appice, Carmine (Musician)
Long Distance Entertainment
568 SE Woodbright #234
Boynton Beach, FL 33435, USA

Appier, Kevin (Athlete, Baseball Player)
30743 VictoryRd
Paola, KS 66071-9477, USA

Apple, Fiona (Musician)
2212 Meade Pl
Venica, CA 90291, USA

Appleby, Shiri (Actor)
8743 Bonner Dr
West Hollywood, CA 90048, USA

Appleby, Stuart (Athlete, Golfer)
9724 Chestnut Ridge Dr
Windermere, FL 34786, USA

Applegate, Christina (Actor)
5402 Rincon Beach Park Dr
Ventura, CA 93001, USA

Applegate, Eddie (Actor)
20119 Marilla St
Chatsworth, CA 91311, USA

Applegate, Fred (Actor)
811 E Olive Ave
Burbank, CA 91501, USA

Applegate, Gideon (Athlete, Baseball Player)
7 Jenness Dr
South Newfane, VT 05351, USA

Applegate, Jodi (Correspondent)
WNYW
205 E 67th St
New York, NY 10021-6099, USA

Applen, Henry E (Misc)
Plant Guard Workers Union
25510 Kelly Road
Roseville, MI 48066, USA

Appleton, James R (Educator)
University of Redlands
President's Office
Redlands, CA 92373, USA

Appleton, Myra (Editor)
Cosmopolitan Magazine
Editorial Dept
224 W 57th St
New York, NY 10019, USA

Appleton, Steven R (Business Person)
Micron Technology
PO Box 6
Boise, ID 83707, USA

Applewhite, Major (Athlete, Football Player)
3911 Willow Bay Dr
Baton Rouge, LA 70809, USA

Appolonia (Kotero) (Actor)
c/o Staff Member *TalentWorks (LA)*
3500 W Olive Ave
Suite 1400
Burbank, CA 91505, USA

Apps, Syl (Athlete, Hockey Player)
36 Pennock Cres
Markham, ON L3R 3M4, Canada

Aprea, John (Actor)
727 N Martel Ave
Los Angeles, CA 90046, USA

April, Johnny (Musician)
c/o Staff Member *Mitch Schneider Organization (MSO)*
14724 Ventura Blvd #410
Sherman Oaks, CA 91403, USA

Apt, Jerome (Jay) (Astronaut)
4 Shadycourt Dr
Pittsburgh, PA 15232-2914, USA

Apted, Michael (Director)
12857 Via Grimaldi
Del Mar, CA 92014, USA

Apuna, Ben (Athlete, Football Player)
950 Lehua Ave
Apt 804
Pearl City, HI 96782, USA

Aqualung (Music Group)
c/o Staff Member *Paradigm (Monterey)*
404 W Franklin St
Monterey, CA 93940, USA

Aquarium Rescue Unit (Music Group, Musician)
c/o Staff Member *Skyline Music*
28 Union St
Whitefield, NH 03598, USA

Aquila, Chris
3955 Falline Water Dr
Reno, NV 89519-2143, USA

Aquilino, Thomas J Jr (Judge)
US Court of International Trade
1 Federal Plaza
New York, NY 10278, USA

Aquino, Amy (Actor)
c/o August Kammer *TalentWorks (LA)*
3500 W Olive Ave
Suite 1400
Burbank, CA 91505, USA

Aquino, Amy (Actor)
c/o Staff Member *Gersh (LA)*
9465 Wilshire Blvd
Suite 600
Beverly Hills, CA 90212, USA

Aquino, Corazon C (Politician)
119 de la Rosa Corner
Castro Street
Makati City, Manila, The Phillipines

Aquino, Luis (Athlete, Baseball Player)
17201 Collins Ave Apt 606
Apt 606
Sunny Isles Beach, FL 33160-3476, USA

Aquino III, Benigno (President)
Malacanang Palaces
J P Laurel St. Metro
Manila 100, Philippines

Arad, Avi (Producer)
29 Beverly Park Terr
Beverly Hills, CA 90210, USA

Aragaki-Van Horn, Kathy (Stylist)
7523 N Kenton
Skokie, IL 60076, USA

Aragall Garriga, Glacomo (Opera Singer)
Stafford Law Assoc
6 Barham Close
Weybridge
Surrey KT1 9PR, UNITED KINGDOM (UK)

Aragon, Art (Boxer)
19050 Wells Dr
Tarzana, CA 91356, USA

Aragon, Frank (Director)
c/o Reyna Trevino *Trevino Enterprises*
10 Universal City Plaza
20th Floor
Universal City, CA 91608, USA

Aragones, Sergio (Cartoonist)
PO Box 696
Ojai, CA 93024-0696, USA

Araguz, Leo (Athlete, Football Player)
3201 Araguz St
Harlingen, TX 78552, USA

Araiza, Francisco (Opera Singer)
Columbia Artists Mgmt Inc
165 W 57th St
New York, NY 10019, USA

Arakawa, Toyozo (Artist)
4-101 O-Hatacho
Tokyo, JAPAN

Araki, Gregg (Director)
c/o Brian Young *Untitled Entertainment (LA)*
350 S. Beverly Dr #200
Beverly Hills, CA 90212, USA

Arambulo, Angela (Stylist)
c/o Staff Member *Stockland Martel*
343 E 18th St
New York, NY 10003, USA

Aramburu, Juan Carlos Cardinal (Religious Leader)
Arzobispado
Suipacha 1034
Buenos Aires 1008, ARGENTINA

Arana, Facundo (Actor)
c/o Staff Member *Telefe - Argentina*
Pavon 2444 (C1248AAT)
Buenos Aires, ARGENTINA

Arana, Tomas (Actor)
c/o Kesha Williams *Affirmative Entertainment*
425 N Robertson Blvd
Los Angeles, CA 90048, USA

Arango, Juan Carlos (Actor)
c/o Gabriel Blanco *Gabriel Blanco Iglesias (Mexico)*
Rio Balsas 35-32
Colonia Cuauhtemoc
DF 06500, Mexico

Arapostathis, Evan (Athlete, Football Player)
5353 W Falls View Dr
San Diego, CA 92115, USA

Ararktsyan, Babken G (Government Official)
National Assembly
Marshal Bagzamyan Prosp 26
Yerevan 375019, ARMENIA

Arashi, Qadi Abdul Karim al
Constituent People's Assembly
Sana'a, Yemen

Arasmith, Lester (General)
2211 Devoe Dr
Lincoln, NE 68506-3122, USA

Arau, Alfonso (Director)
Productions AA
Privada Rafael Oliva 8
Coyoacan 04120, MEXICO

Arau, Fernando (Actor)
c/o Staff Member *Sanctuary Artist Management (UK)*
Sanctuary House
45-53 Sinclair Road
London W14 0NS, UNITED KINGDOM

Araujo, Serafim Fernandes de Cardinal
(Religious Leader)
Curia Metropolitana
Av Brasil 2079
Belo Horizonte, MG 30240-002, Brazil

Aravind, Ramesh (Actor, Bollywood)
F1 4th Block
Bajaj Apartments Nandanam Extn
Chennai, TN 600035, INDIA

Araya, Zeudy (Actor)
Carol Levi Co
Via Giuseppe Pisanelli
Rome 00196, ITALY

Arbaaz, Ali Khan (Actor, Bollywood)
602 Sea King Apts
Band Stand Bandra (W)
Mumbai, MS 400050, INDIA

Arbanas, Frederick V (Fred) (Athlete, Football Player)
3350 SW Hook Rd
Lees Summit, MO 64082, USA

Arber, Werner (Nobel Prize Laureate)
Biozentrun der Universitat
70 Klingelbergstr
Klingelbergstrasse
70 Department of Microbiology,
Basel CH-4056, SWITZERLAND

Arbour, Al (Athlete, Hockey Player)
2071 Harbour Links Dr
Longboat Key, FL 34228-4281, USA

Arbour, Al (Athlete, Hockey Player)
2071 Harbour Links Dr
Longboat Key, FL 34228, USA

Arbour, John (Athlete, Hockey Player)
125 Waterloo St
Fort Erie, ON L2A 3K1, Canada

Arbour, Louise (Government Official)
UN Human Rights Commision
1 United Nations Plaza
New York, NY 10017, USA

Arbour-Parrott, Beatrice (Athlete, Baseball Player)
691 Elm St
Somerset, MA 02726-4034, USA

Arbubakrr, Hasson (Athlete, Football Player)
76 Custer Ave
Newark, NJ 07112, USA

Arbuckle, Charles (Athlete, Football Player)
805 Oak Park Dr
Round Rock, TX 78681, USA

Arbulu Galliani, Guillermo (Prime Minister)
Prime Minister's Office
Urb Corpac
Calle 1 Oesta S/N
Lima 27, PERU

Arbus, Allan (Actor)
2208 N Beverly Glen Blvd
Los Angeles, CA 90077, USA

Arbus, Loreen (Producer)
8841 Appian Way
Los Angeles, CA 90046, USA

Arcade Fire (Music Group, Musician)
c/o Scott Rodger *Quest Management*
36 Warple Way
Unit 1D
London W3 0RG, UK

Arch, Lisa (Actor)
c/o Staff Member *The Paradise Group*
PO Box 69451
West Hollywood, CA 90069, USA

Archambault, Lee J (Astronaut)
4318 Sweet Cicely Court
Houston, TX 77059, USA

Archambault, Lee J Lt Colonel (Astronaut)
4318 Sweet Cicely Ct
Houston, TX 77059-3126, USA

Archambault, Yves (Athlete, Hockey Player)
Promotion Archie Sports Inc 7418 Av Baldwin
Aniou, QC HIK 3C8, Canada

Archambeau, Lester (Athlete, Football Player)
10520 Montclair Way
Duluth, GA 30097, USA

Archana (Actor, Bollywood)
8 North Cresent Road
T Nagar
Chennai, TN 600017, INDIA

Archer, Anne (Actor)
PO Box 57593
Sherman Oaks, CA 91403, USA

Archer, Beverly (Actor)
811 Adelaine Ave
S Pasadena, CA 91030, USA

Archer, Dan (Athlete, Football Player)
65 Sunnyside Ave
Mill Valley, CA 94941, USA

Archer, Dave (Artist)
1541 Buckhorn Rd
Roseburg, OR 97470-8461, USA

Archer, David (Athlete, Football Player)
3831 Upland Dr
Marietta, GA 30066, USA

Archer, Glenn L Jr (Judge)
US Court of Appeals
717 Madison Place NW
Washington, DC 20439, USA

Archer, Jeffrey (Actor, Writer)
c/o Staff Member *Curtis Brown Ltd*
Hay Market House
28-29 Hay Market
London SW1Y 4SP, UK

Archer, Jeffrey H (Writer)
93 Albert Embankment
London SE1, England

Archer, Jim (Athlete, Baseball Player)
1414 Oleander Dr
Tarpon Springs, FL 34689-2308, USA

Archer, John (Writer)
10901 176th Circle NE
#3601
Redmond, WA 98052, USA

Archer, Tasmin (Musician)
c/o Staff Member *Mushroom Music Publishing*
9 Dundas Ln
P.O. Box 158
Albert Park VIC 3206, Australia

Archer, Tommy (Race Car Driver)
Archer Motorsports
4415 Venture Ave
Duluth, MN 55811, USA

Archibaid, Nathaniel (Nate) (Athlete, Basketball Player)
2920 Holland Ave
Bronx, NY 10467, USA

Archibald, Dave (Athlete, Hockey Player)
6792 Henry St.
Chillwack, BC V2R 2W1, Canada

Archibald, Nate (Tiny) (Athlete, Basketball Player)
2920 Holland Ave
Bronx, NY 10467-8304, USA

Archibald, Nolan D (Business Person)
Black & Decker Corp
701 E Joppa Road
Towson, MD 21286, USA

Archie, Mike (Athlete, Football Player)
1178 Old Hickory Blvd
Brentwood, TN 37027, USA

Archipoeski, Ken (Musician)
PO Box 656507
Fresh Meadows, NY 11365, USA

Architecture in Helsinki (Music Group)
c/o Staff Member *Paradigm (Monterey)*
404 W Franklin St
Monterey, CA 93940, USA

Archuleta, Adam (Athlete, Football Player)
1237 W Galveston St
Chandler, AZ 85224, USA

Archuleta, David (Musician)
c/o Roger Widynowski *19 Entertainment - LA*
9000 W Sunset Blvd #1574
West Hollywood, CA 90069, USA

Arcia, Jose (Athlete, Baseball Player)
7325 NW 3rd St
Miami, FL 33126-4211, USA

Arcieri, Leila (Actor)
c/o Staff Member *Paradigm (LA)*
360 N Crescent Dr
North Bldg
Beverly Hills, CA 90210, USA

Arcineiga, Tomas A (Educator)
California State College
President's Office
Bakersfield, CA 9331, USA

Arctic Monkeys (Music Group)
c/o Staff Member *Paradigm (Monterey)*
404 W Franklin St
Monterey, CA 93940, USA

Arcuri, Mike (Congressman, Politician)
10 Broad St
Room 330
Utica, NY 13501, USA

Ard, Jim (Athlete, Baseball Player)
2325 Wayfarer Dr
Discovery Bay, CA 94505, USA

Ard, Johnny (Athlete, Baseball Player)
3815 Edinburg Cir
Valdosta, GA 31605, USA

Ard, William D (Bill) (Athlete, Football Player)
41 Vail Ln
Watchung, NJ 07069, USA

Ardalan, Nader (Architect)
KEO International Consultants
PO Box 3679
Safat 13037, KUWAIT

Ardant, Fanny (Actor)
c/o Staff Member *ArtMedia*
20 avenue Rapp
Paris 75008, France

Ardell, Dan (Athlete, Baseball Player)
554 Hazel Dr
Corona Del Mar, CA 92625-2535, USA

Ardell, Donald B (Doctor)
288 Beach Drive NE #11C
St Petersburg, FL 33701-3481, USA

Arden, Alicia (Actor)
c/o Vance Payton *Advance LA*
7904 Santa Monica Blvd
West Hollywood, CA 90046

Arden, Jann (Musician, Songwriter, Writer)
Macklam Feldman Mgmt
1505 W 2nd Ave
#200
Vancouver, BC V6H 3Y4, CANADA

Arden, John (Writer)
Cassarotto
60/66 Wardour St
London W1V 4ND, UNITED KINGDOM (UK)

Arden, Michael (Actor)
c/o Biff Liff *WME (WMA-NY)*
1325 Ave of the Americas
New York, NY 10019, USA

Arden, Toni (Musician)
1 N Golfview Rd #300
Lake Worth, FL 33460, USA

Arditi, Pierre (Actor)
c/o Staff Member *VMA*
20 Avenue Rapp
Paris 75007, France

Ardito, Doug (Musician)
7820 Caverna Dr
Los Angeles, CA 90068, USA

Ardito Barletta, Nicolas (President)
PO Box 7737
Panama City 9, PANAMA

Arditti, Irvine (Musician)
Lattidue Arts
109 Boul Saint-Joseph Quest
Montreal, PA H2T 2P7, CANADA

Ardizoia, Rinaldo (Athlete, Baseball Player)
130 Santa Rosa Ave
San Francisco, CA 94112-1930, USA

Ardizzone, Anthony (Tony) (Athlete, Football Player)
27 S Farview Ave
Paramus, NJ 07652, USA

Ardoin, Danny (Athlete, Baseball Player)
1524 Lee St
Ville Platte, LA 70586-6364, USA

Ardolino, Todd (Director)
c/o Staff Member *Creative Artists Agency (CAA-LA)*
2000 Ave Of The Stars
Los Angeles, CA 90067, USA

Ardolino, Tom (Musician)
Monterey International
200 W. Sunset Blvd.
#202
Chicago, IL 60610, USA

Aregood, Richards L (Journalist)
Philadelphia Daily News
Editorial Dept
400 N Broad St
Philadelphia, PA 19130, USA

Arellano, Stephanie (Actor)
c/o Ken Jacobson *Ken Jacobson Management*
Preferred to be contacted by phone or email
Los Angeles, CA 91367, USA

Arena, Tina (Musician)
Magnus Entertainment
5 Darley St
Neutral Bay, NSW 2089, AUSTRALIA

Arenas, Gilbert (Athlete, Basketball Player)
4550 Gable Dr
Encino, CA 91316, USA

Arenas, Joe (Athlete, Football Player)
780 W Bay Area Blvd
Apt 1215
Webster, TX 77598-4057, USA

Arenberg, Lee (Actor)
c/o Staff Member *Gage Group, The (LA)*
14724 Ventura Blvd
Suite 505
Sherman Oaks, CA 91403, USA

Arencibia, J P
770 Claug_hton Island Dr Apt 1104
Miami, FL 33131-2628, USA

Arend, Geoffrey (Actor)
c/o Jason Newman *Untitled Entertainment (LA)*
350 S. Beverly Dr #200
Beverly Hills, CA 90212, USA

Arend, Jeff (Race Car Driver)
888 De Anza Heights Dr
La Verne, CA 91750, USA

Arens, Moshe (Government Official)
Ministry of Defence
Rehov Kapian
Hakirya, Tel-Aviv 67695, ISRAEL

Arens, Moshe (Politician)
49 Hagderat
Savyon, Israel

Aresco, Joey (Actor)
Northern Exposure Talent Management Group
C/O Lisa King
2888 Birch St Unit #1
Vancouver V6H 2T6, CANADA

Areshenkoff, Ron (Athlete, Hockey Player)
329 12th Ave
Estevan, SK S4A 1E3, Canada

Aretsky, Ken (Business Person)
21 Club
21 W 52nd St
New York, NY 10019, USA

Arfons, Arthur E (Art) (Race Car Driver)
PO Box 1409
Saint Charles, MO 63302, USA

Argento, Asia (Actor)
Moviement
Via P Cavallini 24
Rome 00193, ITALY

Argento, Dario (Director)
ADC
Via Balemonti 2
Rome, ITALY

Argento, Dominick (Composer)
Universit of Minnesota
Music Dept
Ferguson Hall
Minneapolis, MN 55455, USA

Argenziano, Carmen (Actor)
824 S Bel Aire Dr
Burbank, CA 91501, USA

Argerich, Martha (Musician)
c/o Staff Member *Agence Artistique Jacques Thelen*
15 Avenue Montaigne
Paris 75008, France

Argota, Ashley (Actor)
c/o Monique Moss *Integrated PR*
8060 Melrose Ave
4th Floor
Los Angeles, CA 90046, USA

Argott, Don (Director, Producer)
c/o David Gersh *Gersh (LA)*
9465 Wilshire Blvd
Suite 600
Beverly Hills, CA 90212, USA

Argov, Sherry (Writer)
P.O. Box 91298
Los Angeles, CA 90009, USA

Arian, David (Misc)
International Longshoremen's Union
1188 Franklin St
San Francisco, CA 94109, USA

Arias, Alex (Athlete, Baseball Player)
37 Edmund Rd
West Park, FL 33023-5251, USA

Arias, George (Athlete, Baseball Player)
4343 W Tellurite Dr
Tucson, AZ 85745-4193, USA

Arias, Mariana (Actor)
c/o Staff Member *Telefe - Argentina*
Pavon 2444 (C1248AAT)
Buenos Aires, ARGENTINA

Arias, Moises (Actor)
c/o Matt Fletcher *Greene & Associates*
1901 Avenue Of The Stars Ste 130
Los Angeles, CA 90067, USA

Arias, Ricardo M (President)
Apdo 4549
Panama City, PANAMA

Arias, Rudy (Athlete, Baseball Player)
3911 NW 11th St
Miami, FL 33126-3614, USA

Arias, Silvana (Actor)
Diane Perez Entertainment
838 North Fairfax
Los Angeles, CA 90046, USA

Arias, Yancey (Actor)
c/o Chris Henze *Thruline Entertainment*
9250 Wilshire Blvd
Ground Fl
Beverly Hills, CA 90212, USA

Arie, India (Musician, Songwriter)
c/o Staff Member *Paradigm (Monterey)*
404 W Franklin St
Monterey, CA 93940, USA

Aries, Jacqueline Pinol (Actor)
c/o Tracy Quinn *Quinn Management*
17328 Ventura Blvd
Suite 416
Encino, CA 91316, USA

Ariey, Mike (Athlete, Football Player)
P.O. Box 708
Bakersfield, CA 93302, USA

Arigoni, Dulio (Misc)
Im Glockenacker 42
Zurich 8053, SWITZERLAND

Arima, Akito (Physicist)
Physical Research Institute
Hirosawa 2-1
Wakoshi, Saltarna 351-01, JAPAN

Arinze, Cardinal Francis (Religious Leader)
Pontifical Council for Inter-Religious Dialogue
Vatican City 00193

Arison, Micky (Misc)
9999 Collins Ave Apt 15G
Bal Harbour, FL 33154-1834, USA

Arison, M Micky (Business Person)
Camivai Corp
3655 NW 87th Ave
Miami, FL 33178, USA

Aristide, Jean-Bertrand (President)
President's Office
Palace du Gouvernement
Port-Au-Prince, HAITI

Ariyoshi, George R (Politician)
745 Fort Street Mall
Ste 500
Honolulu, HI 96813-3805, USA

Ariza, Trevor (Athlete, Basketball Player)
5848 Tampa Ave
Tarzana, CA 91356, USA

Arjona, Ricardo (Musician)

Arjona, Ricardo (Musician)
c/o Staff Member *Fenix Entertainment Group*
919 Fourth St
San Francisco, CA 94901, USA

Arjun (Actor)
B3-C Block
109 G N Chetty Road T Nagar
Chennai, TN 600 017, INDIA

Arkadius (Designer, Fashion Designer)
c/o Staff Member *Arkadius*
41 Brondesbury Road
London, England NW6 6BP, United Kingdom

Arkangel R-15 (Music Group)
c/o Staff Member *Sony Music Miami*
605 Lincoln Rd Fl 7
Miami Beach, FL 33139, USA

Arkhipov, Denis (Athlete, Hockey Player)
716 Sweet Cherry Ct
Nashville, TN 37215-6174, USA

Arkin, Adam (Actor)
3531 Coldwater Canyon Ave.
Los Angeles, CA 91604, USA

Arkin, Alan (Actor)
10 Camino Cielo Azul
Santa Fe, NM 87508, USA

Ark, The (Music Group)
c/o Staff Member *Paradigm (Monterey)*
404 W Franklin St
Monterey, CA 93940, USA

Arlauckas, Joe (Athlete, Basketball Player)
8 Brimley Mnr
Rochester, NY 14612-4414, USA

Arlich, Don (Athlete, Baseball Player)
7877 73rd St S
Cottage Grove, MN 55016-1919, USA

Arlin, Steve (Athlete, Baseball Player)
6819 Claremore Ave
San Diego, CA 92120-3125, USA

Arlovski, Andrei (Athlete, Boxer)
c/o Staff Member *John Lewis Entertainment Group*
3071 S Valley View
Las Vegas, NV 89102, USA

Arlt, Lynn (Stylist)
c/o Staff Member *Anyway Productions*
870 Avenue of the Americas
New York, NY 10001, USA

Arm, Mark (Musician)
Legends of 21st Century
7 Trinity Row
Florence, MA 01062, USA

Armacost, Michael H (Diplomat)
State Department
2201 C St NW
Washington, DC 20520, USA

Arman (Artist)
Arman Studios
430 Washington St
New York, NY 10013, USA

Armand, Arman
430 Washington St
New York, NY 10013-1721, USA

Armani, Giorgio (Designer, Fashion Designer)
Via Borgonuovo 11
Milan 20121, Italy

Armaou, Lindsay (Musician)
Clintons
55 Drury Lane
Covent Garden
London WC2B 5SQ, UNITED KINGDOM (UK)

Armas, Antonio R (Tony) (Athlete, Baseball Player)
Los Mercedes #37
P Piruto-Edo
Anzoatequi, VENEZUELA

Armas, Chris (Soccer Player)
Chicago Fire
980 N Michigan Ave
#1998
Chicago, IL 60611, USA

Armas, Marcos (Athlete, Baseball Player)
Calle Las Mercedes #37
Puerto Piritu, VENEZUELA

Armas, Tony (Athlete, Baseball Player)
c/o Staff Member *Washington Nationals*
1500 S Capitol St SE
Washington, DC 20003, USA

Armato, Ange (Athlete, Baseball Player)
5082 Valley Pines Dr
Rockford, IL 61109-3774, USA

Armatrading, Joan (Musician, Songwriter, Writer)
21 Ramilles St
London W1V 1DF, UNITED KINGDOM (UK)

Armbrister, Ed (Athlete, Baseball Player)
McQuay St
Box 2003
Nassau, Bahamas, WEST INDIES

Armdt-Proefrock, Ellen (Athlete, Baseball Player)
905 Alpine St
Brodhead, WI 53520, USA

Armenante, Jillian (Actor)
574 N Irving Blvd
Los Angeles, CA 90004, USA

Armendariz, Ramon
3952 Malaya Ct
Denver, CO 80249-8178, USA

Armisen, Fred (Actor, Comedian)
c/o Tim Sarkes *Brillstein Entertainment Partners*
9150 Wilshire Blvd #350
Beverly Hills, CA 90212, USA

Armitage, Alison (Actor, Model)
c/o Staff Member *Schiowitz Connor Ankrum Wolf*
1680 N Vine St
Suite 1016
Los Angeles, CA 90028, USA

Armitage, Karole (Choreographer, Dancer)
350 W 21st St
New York, NY 10011, USA

Armitage, Kenneth
22-A Avonmore Road
London, W14 8RR, England

Armitage, Richard (Actor)
c/o Duncan Millership *WME (LA)*
9601 Wilshire Blvd Fl 3
Beverly Hills, CA 90210, USA

Armor, James Majgen (Astronaut)
9120 Maria Ave
Great Falls, VA 22066-4008, USA

Armour, Jojuan (Athlete, Football Player)
1436 Rollins Rd
Toledo, OH 43612, USA

Armour, Justin (Athlete, Football Player)
765 Mays Hollow Ln
Encinitas, CA 92024-2734, USA

Armour, Justin (Athlete, Football Player)
8 Crystal Park Pl Unit B
Manitou Springs, CO 80829, us

Armour, Tommy (Athlete, Golfer)
3006 Woodside St #8017
Dallas, TX 75204-8538, USA

Arms, Russell (Actor, Musician)
312 Hillcrest Dr
Hamilton, IL 62341-1106, USA

Armstead, Jessie (Athlete, Football Player)
1316 Mill Stream Dr
Dallas, TX 75232, USA

Armstead, Ray (Athlete, Olympic Athlete, Track Athlete)
7953 Bloom Dr
St Louis, MO 63133-1109, USA

Armstrong, Adger (Athlete, Football Player)
6403 Paddington St
Houston, TX 77085, USA

Armstrong, A James (Misc)
Broadway Methodist Church
1100 W 42nd St
Indianapolis, IN 46208, USA

Armstrong, Alan (Actor)
Markham & Froggatt
Julian House
4 Windmill St
London W1P 1HF, UNITED KINGDOM (UK)

Armstrong, Antonio (Athlete, Football Player)
5314 Palmetto St
Houston, TX 77081, USA

Armstrong, Bess (Actor)
1518 N. Doheny Dr
West Hollywood, CA 90069, USA

Armstrong, Bill (Athlete, Hockey Player)
Century 21 420 York St
London, ON N6B lRl, Canada

Armstrong, Billie Joe (Musician, Songwriter)
93 Hampton Rd
Piedmont, CA 94611, USA

Armstrong, BJ (Athlete, Basketball Player)
SeS N Lake Shore Dr Apt 64e2
Chicago, IL 6e611-362S, USA

Armstrong, Brad (Adult Film Star)
c/o Staff Member *Vivid Entertainment*
3599 Cahuenga Blvd #400
Los Angeles, CA 90068, USA

Armstrong, Bruce (Athlete, Football Player)
12543 Brookwood Ct
Davie, FL 33330, USA

Armstrong, Charlotte (Athlete, Baseball Player)
5838 N 81st St
Scottsdale, AZ 85250, USA

Armstrong, Clay M (Scientist)
University of Pennsylvania
Medical School 3400 Spruce
Philadelphia, PA 19104, USA

Armstrong, Colby (Athlete, Hockey Player)
1597 Washington Pike #B14
Bridgeville, PA 15017, USA

Armstrong, Curtis (Actor)
3867 Shannon Rd
Los Angeles, CA 90027, USA

Armstrong, Darrell (Athlete, Basketball Player)
337 Broadmoor Way
McDonough, GA 3e253-429e, USA

Armstrong, Debbie (Athlete, Olympic Athlete, Skier)
681 Shekel Ln
Breckenridge, CO 80424-8931, USA

Armstrong, Derek (Athlete, Hockey Player)
9373 S Holland Way
Littleton, CO 80127-5934, USA

Armstrong, Dwight (Actor)
c/o Paul Greenstone *Paul Greenstone Entertainment*
3008 Sorrelwood Dr
San Ramon, CA 94582-5008, USA

Armstrong, George (Athlete, Hockey Player)
22 St Cuthberts Rd
East York, ON M4G 1 Vl, Canada

Armstrong, Gillian (Director)
Harry Linstead
500 Oxford St
Bondi Junction, NSW 2022, AUSTRALIA

Armstrong, Harvey (Athlete, Football Player)
2840 Olde Town Park Dr
Norcross, GA 30071, USA

Armstrong, Hilton (Athlete, Basketball Player)
c/o Jeff Schwartz *Excel Sports Management*
9665 Wilshire Blvd #500
Los Angeles, CA 90212, USA

Armstrong, Jack (Athlete, Baseball Player)
272 E River Park Dr
Jupiter, FL 33477-9381, USA

Armstrong, J D (Athlete, Football Player)
7906 W Meadow
Pass Cir
Wichita, KS 67205-1611

Armstrong, Jonas (Actor)
c/o Staff Member *Artists Rights Group (ARG)*
4 Great Portland St
London W1W 8PA, UNITED KINGDOM (UK)

Armstrong, Karen (Writer)
c/o Staff Member *Random House*
1540 Broadway
New York, NY 10036, USA

Armstrong, Kelley (Writer)
RR 4
Aylmer, ON N5H 2R3, CANADA

Armstrong, Kerry (Actor)
Barbara Leane Mgmt
261 Miller St
North Sydney, NSW 2060, AUSTRALIA

Armstrong, Lance (Athlete, Cycler, Olympic Athlete)
LiveStrong
2201 E. Sixth Street
Austin, TX 78702, USA

Armstrong, Malcolm (General)
21st Air Force
1907 E Arnold Ave Ofc
Trenton, NJ 08641-5612, USA

Armstrong, Matthew John (Actor)
c/o David Ginsberg *Insight*
1134 S Cloverdale Ave
Los Angeles, CA 90019, USA

Armstrong, Mike (Athlete, Baseball Player)
525 Ashbrook Ct
Athens, GA 30605-3985, USA

Armstrong, Neil (Athlete, Hockey Player)
607-1295 Sandy Lane
Sarnia, ON N7V 4KS, Canada

Armstrong, Neil (Referee)
1169 Sherwood Trail
Sarnia, ON N7V 2H3, CANADA

Armstrong, Neill (Athlete, Football Player)
312 Lakewood Dr
Roanoke, TX 76262, us

Armstrong, Otis (Athlete, Football Player)
9951 E Idaho Cir
Apt 202
Denver, CO 80247, USA

Armstrong, Otis (Athlete, Football Player)
7183 S Newport Way
Centennial, CO 80112, us

Armstrong, Quincy (Athlete, Football Player)
5801 E Fm 4
Grandview, TX 76050, USA

Armstrong, Robb (Cartoonist)
229 E 5th Ave
Conshohocken, PA 19428-1714, USA

Armstrong, Robert (Bob) (Athlete, Basketball Player)
6802 Packer Dr NE
Belmont, MI 493e6-924e, USA

Armstrong, Robin L (Scientist)
803-383 Ellis Park Rd
Toronto, ON M6S 5B2, Canada

Armstrong, Roger (Cartoonist)
21701 Rushford Dr
Lake Forest, CA 92630-6510, USA

Armstrong, Russell P (War Hero)
425 Bench Road
Fallen, NV 89406, USA

Armstrong, Samaire (Actor)
c/o Susan Calogerakis *Thruline Entertainment*
9250 Wilshire Blvd
Ground Fl
Beverly Hills, CA 90212, USA

Armstrong, Sheila A (Musician, Opera Singer)
Harvesters Tilford Road
Hindhead
Surrey GU26 6SQ, UNITED KINGDOM (UK)

Armstrong, Spence M (General)
9714 Bluedale St
Alexandria, VA 22308, USA

Armstrong, Tate (Athlete, Basketball Player)
14704 Westbury Rd
Rockville, MD 20853-1610, USA

Armstrong, Taylor (Reality TV Star)
1736 Family Crisis Center
2116 Arlington Ave #200
Los Angeles, CA 90018, USA

Armstrong, Thomas (Race Car Driver)
PacWest Racing Group
PO Box 1717
Bellevue, WA 98009, USA

Armstrong, Trace (Athlete, Football Player)
10191 Winding Ridge Rd
Saint Louis, MO 63124, USA

Armstrong, Trace (Athlete, Football Player)
8691 SW 28th Ln
Gainesville, FL 32608, us

Armstrong, Ty (Athlete, Golfer)
11529 Kensington Dr
Eden Prairie, MN 55347-4943, USA

Armstrong, Valorie (Actor)
Contemporary Artists
610 Santa Monica Blvd #202
Santa Monica, CA 90401, USA

Armstrong, Vaughn (Actor)
1903 Apex Ave
Los Angeles, CA 90039, USA

Armstrong, Wally (Athlete, Golfer)
Signature Sports Group
4150 Olson Memorial Hwy
Ste 110
Minneapolis, MN 55422-4804, USA

Armstrong, William (Writer)
6 Roland St
Newton Highlands, MA 02461-1920, USA

Armstrong, William L (Ex-Senator, Politician)
23 Sedgwick Dr
Englewood, CO 80113-4109, USA

Arnason, Chuck (Athlete, Hockey Player)
39 Grimston Rd
Winnipeg, MB R3T 3T2, Canada

Arnason, Tyler (Athlete, Hockey Player)
881 N La Salle Dr
Chicago, IL 60610, USA

Arnatt, John (Actor)
3 Warren Cottage Woodland Way
Surrey KT2 6NN, UK

Arnaud, Jean-Loup (Government Official)
55 Rue de Seine
Paris 75006, FRANCE

Arnault, Bernard (Business Person)
Moet Hennessy Louis Vuitton
30 Ave Hoche
Paris 75008, FRANCE

Arnaz, Lucie (Actor)
c/o Scott Stander *Scott Stander &
Associates*
13701 Riverside Dr
Suite 201
Sherman Oaks, CA 91423, USA

Arnaz Jr, Desi (Actor)
P.O. Box 60684
Boulder City, NV 89006, USA

Arndt, Denis (Actor)
c/o Suzanne DeWalt *Dewalt & Musik
Management*
623 N. Parish Place
Burbank, CA 91506, USA

Arndt, Larry (Athlete, Baseball Player)
5910 N Mina Vis
Tucson, AZ 85718-4128, USA

Arndt, Michael (Writer)
c/o Tom Strickler *WME (LA)*
9601 Wilshire Blvd Fl 3
Beverly Hills, CA 90210, USA

Arndt, Richard (Athlete, Football Player)
2130 Parkdale Dr
Kingwood, TX 77339, USA

Arneil, Richard A S (Composer)
Benhall Lodge
Benhall
Suffolk IP17 1DJ, UNITED KINGDOM
(UK)

Arnelle, Jesse (Athlete, Basketball Player)
400 Urbano Dr
San Francisco, CA 94127-2827, USA

Arnesen, Lasse (Athlete, Skier)
Fagerborggata 34
Oslo N-0360, Norway

Arnesen, Liv (Skier)
Yourexpidition 119 N 4th St #406
Minneapolis, MN 55401, USA

Arneson, Jim (Athlete, Football Player)
12649 South 71st St
Tempe, AZ 85284, USA

Arneson, Mark (Athlete, Football Player)
15902 Wetherburn Rd
Chesterfield, MO 63017, USA

Arnett, Angie (Stylist)
11403 NE 8th Ave
Biscayne Park, FL 33161, USA

Arnett, Jon (Athlete, Football Player)
200 Greenridge Dr Apt 715
Lake Oswego, OR 97035, us

Arnett, Jon D (Athlete, Football Player)
16869 65th Ave
Unit 330
Lake Oswego, OR 97035, USA

Arnett, Peter
Cnn News
820 1st St NESte 1000
Washington, DC 20002-8057, USA

Arnett, Peter (Journalist)
Cnn News
820 1st St NESte 1000
Washington, DC 20002-8057, USA

Arnett, Peter
Cnn News
820 1st St NESte 1000
Washington, DC 20002-8057, USA

Arnett, Peter (Journalist)
Cnn News
820 1st St NESte 1000
Washington, DC 20002-8057, USA

Arnett, Will (Actor)
c/o Peter Principato *Principato/Young
Management*
9465 Wilshire Blvd
Suite 430
Beverly Hills, CA 90212, USA

Arnette, Jay (Athlete, Basketball Player,
Olympic Athlete)
2 Hillside Ct
Austin, TX 78746-6436, USA

Arnette, Jeanetta (Actor)
466 N Harper Ave
Los Angeles, CA 90048, USA

Arnez J (Comedian)
c/o Staff Member *ICM Partners (ICM-LA)*
10250 Constellation Blvd Fl 7
Los Angeles, CA 90067, USA

Arngrim, Alison (Actor)
PO Box 98
Tujunga, CA 91043, USA

Arniel, Scott (Athlete, Hockey Player)
Columbus Blue Jackets
200 W Nationwide Blvd Unit 1
Columbus, OH 43215-2564, Canada

Arniel, Scott (Athlete, Hockey Player)
6 Edmond Muys Pl
Winnipeg, MB R3P 2Rl, Canada

Arning, Lisa (Actor)
c/o Julie Wolff *Morgan Agency, The*
1200 N Doheny Dr
Los Angeles, CA 90069-1723, USA

Arno, Ed
11220 72nd Dr
Flushing, NY 11375, USA

Arnold, Anna Bing (Philanthropist)
Anna Bing Arnold Foundation
9700 W Pico Blvd
Los Angeles, CA 90035, USA

Arnold, Ben (Musician)
Golden Guru
227 Pine St
Philadelphia, PA 19106, USA

Arnold, Ben (Race Car Driver)
309 Fair Oaks Dr.
Fairfield, AL 35064, USA

Arnold, Brian A (General)
Commander Space & Missile Systems
Center
Los Angeles Air Force Base, CA 90245,
USA

Arnold, Charles (Athlete, Baseball Player)
19537 Beaverland St
Detroit, MI 48219, USA

Arnold, Charlotte (Actor)
c/o Norbert Abrams *Noble Caplan
Abrams*
1260 Yonge St
2nd Floor
Toronto ON M4T 1W6, Canada

Arnold, Chris (Athlete, Baseball Player)
794 E 7th Ave
Denver, CO 80203-3820, USA

Arnold, David (Athlete, Football Player)
3079 Solar Dr NW
Warren, OH 44485, us

Arnold, David (Athlete, Football Player)
1615 Stanley St
New Britain, CT 06053, USA

Arnold, Debbie (Actor)
M Arnold Mgmt
12 Cambridge Park
Ease Twickenham
Middx TW1 2PF, UNITED KINGDOM
(UK)

Arnold, Dr Jennifer (Doctor, Reality TV
Star)
Texas Children's Hospital
6621 Fannin St
Houston, TX 77030, USA

Arnold, Eve (Photographer)
Magnum Photographic Agency
5 Old St
London EC1V 9HL, UNITED KINGDOM
(UK)

Arnold, Francis (Athlete, Football Player)
3312 W 80th St
Inglewood, CA 90305, USA

Arnold, Gary H (Critic)
5133 N 1st St
Arlington, VA 22203, USA

Arnold, Jackson D (General)
Cubic Corp
9333 Balboa Ave
San Diego, CA 92123-1589, USA

Arnold, Jahine (Athlete, Football Player)
4534 W Beachway Dr
Tampa, FL 33609, us

Arnold, Jahine (Athlete, Football Player)
10508 Greencrest Dr
Tampa, FL 33626, USA

Arnold, James E (Athlete, Football Player)
223 Boxwood Dr
Franklin, TN 37069, USA

Arnold, James R (Misc)
University of California
Chemistry Dept
Code 0524
La Jolla, CA 92093, USA

Arnold, Jamie (Athlete, Baseball Player)
17132 WTara Ln
Surprise, AZ 85388-1244, USA

Arnold, Jim (Athlete, Football Player)
223 Boxwood Dr
Franklin, TN 37069, us

Arnold, Kristine (Music Group)
Monty Hitchcock Mgmt
5101 Overton Rd
Nashville, TN 37220, USA

Arnold, Lenna (Athlete, Baseball Player)
4312 Dodge Ave
Fort Wayne, IN 46815, USA

Arnold, Louise (Athlete, Baseball Player)
52806 Brandel Ave
South Bend, IN 46635, USA

Arnold, Monica (Actor, Musician)
c/o Cara Lewis *Creative Artists Agency
(CAA-LA)*
1325 Ave of the Americas
New York, NY 10019, USA

Arnold, Murray (Athlete, Basketball
Player, Coach)
Western Kentucky University
Athletic Dept
Bowling Green, KY 42101, USA

Arnold, Pam (Stylist)
9767 S Gribble Rd
Canby, OR 97013-9363, USA

Arnold, Richard R (Astronaut)
16302 Heather Bend Ct
Houston, TX 77059-5579, USA

Arnold, Scott (Athlete, Baseball Player)
3282 Gondola Dr
Lexington, KY 40513-1083, USA

Arnold, Steven (General)
3rd US Army
Commander Ofc
Atlanta, GA 30330-0001, USA

Arnold, Stuart (Publisher)
Fortune Magazine
Rockefeller Center
New York, NY 10020, USA

Arnold, Tichina (Actor)
c/o Geoff Cheddy *Brillstein Entertainment
Partners*
9150 Wilshire Blvd #350
Beverly Hills, CA 90212, USA

Arnold, Tom (Actor, Comedian)
9958 Kip Dr
Beverly Hills, CA 90210, USA

Arnold, Tony (Athlete, Baseball Player)
Akron Aeros 300 S Main St Attn
Coaching Staff Akron, OH 44308-1204,
USA

Arnold, Walt (Athlete, Football Player)
8503 La Sala Grande NE
Albuquerque, NM 87111, USA

Arnoldi, Charles A (Artist)
721 Hampton Dr
Venice, CA 90291, USA

Arnold Jr, Harry L (Doctor, Writer)
250 Laurel St #301
San Francisco, CA 94118, USA

Arnott, Jason (Athlete, Hockey Player)
Newport Sports Management
400-201 City Centre Dr
Attn Wade Arnott
Mississauga, ON L5B 2T4, Canada

Arnoul, Francoise (Actor)
53 Rue Censier
Paris 75005, FRANCE

Arns, Paulo E Cardinal (Religious Leader)
Alvenida Higienopolos 890
CP 6778
Sao Paulo, SP 01064, BRAZIL

Arnsberg, Brad (Athlete, Baseball Player)
706 Chaffee Ct
Arlington, TX 76006-2001, USA

Arnsparger, Bill (Athlete, Football Coach,
Football Player)
18111 Colonnades Pl
San Diego, CA 92128, USA

Arnsparger, Bill (Athlete, Football Player)
1574 Pine Needles Ln
Lexington, KY 40513, us

Arnstein, Rolly (Music Group)
Bad Boy Entertainment
1540 Broadway #3000
New York, NY 10036, USA

Arntz, Jason (Athlete)
95A Finnegan Lane
Kendall Park, NJ 08824-1644, USA

Arnzen, Bob (Athlete, Basketball Player)
8 Grand Lake Dr
Fort Thomas, KY 41075-4100

Arnzen, Robert (Athlete, Basketball Player)
8 Grand Lake Dr
Fort Thomas, KY 41075

Arocha, Rene (Athlete, Baseball Player)
14652 SW 170th St
Miami, 33177-2040 33175-8001, USA

Aronofsky, Darren (Director)
c/o Karen Samfilippo *Image Management PR*
1810 14th St
Suite 205
Santa Monica, CA 90404, USA

Arons, Arnold B (Physicist)
10313 Lake Shord Blvd NE
Seattle, WA 98125, USA

Aronsohn, Lee (Writer)
14332 Roblar Pl
Sherman Oaks, CA 91423, USA

Aronson, David (Artist)
137 Brimstone Ln
Sudbury, MA 01776-3200, USA

Aronson, Doug (Athlete, Football Player)
36 Piermont Ter
Wayne, NJ 07470, us

Aronson, Judie (Actor)
11543 Laurelcrest Dr
Studio City, CA 91604, USA

Arora, Amrita (Actor, Bollywood)
c/o Bunty Bahl *Carving Dreams Entertainment*
304-305, Oberoi Chambers II
B Wing, Off New Link Road, Andheri West
Mumbai 400053, INDIA

Arp, Halton C (Scientist)
Max-Planck Labs Physics and Radiology Dept
Garching
Munich D-84518, Germany

Arpel, Adrien (Beauty Pageant Winner, Business Person)
Adrien Arpel Cosmetics
400 Hackensack Ave
Hackensack, NJ 07601, USA

Arpey, Gerard (Business Person)
AMR Corp
433 Amon Carter Blvd
Forth Worth, TX 76155, USA

Arpino, Gerald P (Choreographer)
City Center Joffrey Ballet
70 E Lake St #1300
Chicago, IL 60601, USA

Arquette, Alexis (Actor)
c/o Staff Member *Innovative Artists (LA)*
1505 10th St
Santa Monica, CA 90401, USA

Arquette, David (Actor, Director, Producer)
27460 Pacific Coast Hwy
Malibu, CA 90265, USA

Arquette, Patricia (Actor)
c/o Molly Madden *3 Arts Entertainment Inc*
9460 Wilshire Blvd
7th Floor
Beverly Hills, CA 90210, USA

Arquette, Rosanna (Actor)
c/o Laina Cohn *Laina Cohn Management*
15066 Sutton St
Sherman Oaks, CA 91403, USA

Arrants, Rod (Actor)
1173 Regent St
Alameda, CA 94501, USA

Arras, Maria Celeste (Actor)
c/o Staff Member *Telemundo*
2470 West 8th Avenue
Hialeah, FL 33010, USA

Arredondo, Rosa (Actor)
c/o Suzanne (Sue) Wohl *TalentWorks (LA)*
3500 W Olive Ave
Suite 1400
Burbank, CA 91505, USA

Arrieta, Jacob "Jake"
12320 Capitol Saddlery Trl
Austin, TX 78732-2373, USA

Arrigo, Gerry (Athlete, Baseball Player)
3740 Redthorne Dr
Amelia, OH 45102-1263, USA

Arrillaga, John (Misc)
500 Los Trances Rd
Portola Valley, CA 94028-8064, USA

Arrington, Buddy (Race Car Driver)
2820 Kings Mountain Rd
Martinsville, VA 24112, USA

Arrington, Jill (Sportscaster)
CBS-TV
Sports Dept 51 W 52nd St
New York, NY 10019, USA

Arrington, J J (Athlete, Football Player)
1599 E Beretta Pl
Chandler, AZ 85286, USA

Arrington, LaVar (Athlete, Football Player)
1514 Cedar Lane Farm Rd
Annapolis, MD 21409, USA

Arrington, Michael (Business Person, Internet Star)
3800 The Strand Apt 6
Manhattan Beach, CA 90266, USA

Arrington, Richard (Athlete, Football Player)
2585 King Cir SE
Conyers, GA 30013, USA

Arrington, Rick (Athlete, Football Player)
2585 King Cir SE
Conyers, GA 30013, us

Arriola, Dante (Director)
c/o Staff Member *MJZ*
2201 S Carmelina Ave
Los Angeles, CA 90064, USA

Arriota, Gus (Cartoonist)
P O Box 3275
Carmel, CA 93921, USA

Arrobio, Charles (Chuck) (Athlete, Football Player)
35 Essex St
Apt 5A
New York, NY 10002, USA

Arrobio, Chuck (Athlete, Football Player)
481 Linda Vista Ave
Pasadena, CA 91105, us

Arrojo, Luis (Athlete, Baseball Player)
5684 36th Ave N
Saint Petersburg, FL 33710, USA

Arrolo, Rolando (Athlete, Baseball Player)
5684 36th Ave N
Saint Petersburg, FL 33710-1914, USA

Arrovo, Fernando (Baseball Player)
5232 E Ingram St
Mesa, az 85205-3434, USA

Arrow, Kenneth J (Nobel Prize Laureate)
620 Sand Hill Rd
Apt 406C
Palo Alto, CA 94304-2093, USA

Arroyo, Bronson (Athlete, Baseball Player)
9256 Scarlette Oak Ave
Ft Meyers, FL 33967-5145, USA

Arroyo, Carlos (Athlete, Basketball Player)
1115 NW 126th Ct
Miami, FL 33182-2033, USA

Arroyo, Fernando (Athlete, Baseball Player)
5232 E Ingram St
Mesa, AZ 85205, USA

Arroyo, Jose (Writer)
c/o Staff Member *Kaplan Stahler Agency*
8383 Wilshire Blvd
Suite 923
Beverly Hills, CA 90211, USA

Arroyo, Luis (Athlete, Baseball Player)
P.O. Box 354
Penuelas, PR 00624-0354, USA

Arroyo, Martina (Opera Singer)
Berkshire Corsert Artists
20 Alfred Dr
Pittsfield, MA 01201, USA

Arroyo, Rudolph (Athlete, Baseball Player)
828 Sierra Vista Ave
Mountain View, CA 94043, USA

Arroyo, Rudy
28799 Seauoia Ct
Coarsegold, CA 93614-9161, USA

Arsenault, Kelly (Stylist)
c/o Staff Member *Judy Inc*
1 Yorkville Ave
Toronto ON M4W 1L1, Canada

Arsenault, pierre (Baseball Player)
17942 D'Amalfi St
Pierrefonds QC H9K 1M2 Canada, USA

Arsmstrong, Colby (Athlete, Hockey Player)
8030 Sherwood Dr
Presto, PA 15142-1078, USA

Arteage, Rosalia (President)
Vice President's Office
Gobiemo Palacio
Garcia Morena, Quito, ECUADOR

Arterburn, Elmer (Athlete, Football Player)
3819 29th St
Lubbock, TX 79410, USA

Arterburn, Stephen (Writer)
New Life Ministries
P.O. Box 1018
Laguna Beach, CA 92652, USA

Arterton, Gemma (Actor)
c/o Pippa Beng *Premier PR (UK)*
91 Berwick St
London W1F 0NE, UK

Artest, Ron (Athlete, Basketball Player)
5617 Ridge Park Dr
Loomis, CA 95650, USA

Arteta, Miguel (Director)
c/o David Lubliner *WmE2 (WMA-LA)*
1 William Morris Pl
Beverly Hills, CA 90212, USA

Arthur, Fred (Athlete, Hockey Player)
203-1408 Ernest Ave
London, ON N6E 3B2, Canada

Arthur, Fred Dr (Athlete, Hockey Player)
203-1408 Ernest Ave
London, ON NGE 3B2, Canada

Arthur, Joseph (Musician)
c/o Staff Member *Primary Talent International (UK)*
The Primary Building
10-11 Jockeys Fields
London WC1R 4BN, UK

Arthur, Maureen (Actor)
9171 Wilshire Blvd #530
Beverly Hills, CA 90210, USA

Arthur, Michelle (Actor)
c/o Steven Neibert *Imperium 7 Talent Agency*
5455 Wilshire Blvd
Suite 1706
Los Angeles, CA 90036, USA

Arthur, Mike (Athlete, Football Player)
10445 Sharondale Rd
Cincinnati, OH 45241, USA

Arthur, Mike (Athlete, Football Player)
11271 Terwilligers Valley Ln
Cincinnati, OH 45249, us

Arthur, Owen (Prime Minister)
Prime Minister's Office
Bay St
Saint Michael
Bridgetown, BARBADOS

Arthur, Perry (Athlete, Golfer)
7513 Zurich Dr
Plano, TX 75025, USA

Arthur, Rebeca (Actor)
Epstein-Wyckoff
280 S Beverly St #400
Beverly Hills, CA 90212, USA

Arthur, Stanley (General)
Department Of The Navy
Naval Operations
Washington, DC 20350-0001, USA

Arthurs, John (Athlete, Basketball Player)
1429 Henry Clay Ave
New Orleans, LA 70118-6059, USA

Arthurs, Paul (Bonehead) (Musician)
Ignition Mgmt
54 Linhope St
London NW1 6HL, UNITED KINGDOM (UK)

Artoe, Mike (Athlete, Football Player)
17 Canterbury Ct
Wilmette, IL 60091, USA

Art of Noise, The (Music Group)
PO Box 199
London W11 4AN, UNITED KINGDOM
(UK)

Artschwager, Richard E (Artist)
P O Box 12
Hudson, NY 12534, USA

Artsebarsky, Anatoli P (Cosmonaut)
Potchta Kosmonavtov
Moskovskoi Oblasti
Syvisdny Goroduk 141160, RUSSIA

Arturo, Lisa (Actor)
c/o Mitch Clem *Shadow Entertainment*
10 Universal City Plz
20th Floor
Universal City, CA 91608, USA

Artz, Mary Gail (Actor)
20501 Ventura Blvd #380
Woodland Hills, CA 91364, USA

Artzt, Alice J (Musician)
51 Hawthorne Ave
Princeton, NJ 08540-3803, USA

Artzt, Edwin L (Business Person)
3849 Hedgewood Dr
Lawrenceburg, IN 47025, USA

Arulmani (Actor)
15 Pookara Street
Saidapet
Chennai, TN 600 015, INDIA

Arum, Robert (Bob) (Boxer)
36 Gulf Stream Court
Las Vegas, NV 89113, USA

Arun, Ila (Actor, Bollywood)
401 Paradise Apartments
7th Road Santacruz East
Bombay, MS 400055, INDIA

Arvedson, Magnus (Athlete, Hockey
Player)
Edsgatevagen 145
Karlstad 655 92, Sweden

Arvesen, Nina (Actor)
412 Culver Blvd #9
Playa del Rey, CA 90293, USA

Arvie, Herman (Athlete, Football Player)
33844 Canterbury Rd
Solon, OH 44139, USA

Arvind, V (Actor)
1 65th Street 12th Avenue
Ashok Nagar
Chennai, TN 600 083, INDIA

Arvindasamy (Actor)
29A Muthiah Street
Cathedral Road
Chennai, TN 600 086, INDIA

Arvizu, Reginald (Musician)
27511 Hidden Trail Rd
Laguna Hills, CA 92653, USA

Arya (Actor)
c/o Staff Member *The Harbour Agency*
135 Forbes St
Woolloomooloo NSW 2011, Australia

Arzu Irigoyen, Alvaro E (President)
President's Office
Palacio Nacional
Guatemala City, GUATAMALA

Asad, Doug (Athlete, Football Player)
1701 Marquette Ct
Lake Forest, IL 60045, us

Asay, Chuck (Cartoonist)
Colorada Springs Gazette
303 S Prospect St
Colorado Springs, CO 80903, USA

Asbury, Kelly (Actor)
c/o Staff Member *Creative Artists Agency*
(CAA-LA)
2000 Ave Of The Stars
Los Angeles, CA 90067, USA

Asbury, Martin (Cartoonist)
Stoneworld
Pitch Green
Princes Risborough, Bucks HP27 9QG,
UNITED KINGDOM (UK)

Asbury, Richard (General)
1104 Kimberly Rd Unit 907
Bettendorf, IA 52722-4120, USA

Ascencio, Nelson (Actor)
c/o Heidi Rotbart *Heidi Rotbart
Management*
1810 Malcolm Ave.
Suite 207
Los Angeles, CA 90025, USA

Asch, Peter (Athlete, Water Polo Player)
1946 Green St
San Francisco, CA 94123-4811, USA

Aschbacher, Darrel (Athlete, Football
Player)
915 NE Wyoming Dr
Prineville, OR 97754, USA

Aschwege, David (Athlete, Baseball
Player)
3027 S 27th St
Lincoln, NE 68502, USA

Ash, Bob
1150 Patricia Ave
Brandon, MB R7A 7K7, Canada

Ash, Brandon (Race Car Driver)
Racing West
1772 Los Arboles #J-186
Thousand Oaks, CA 91362, USA

Ash, Brian (Producer, Writer)
c/o Simon Millar *Rumble Media*
1620 Broadway
Santa Monica, CA 90403, USA

Ash, Leslie (Actor)
c/o Michelle Milburn *International Artistes*
Holborn Hall - 4th Floor
London WC1V 7BD, UK

Ash, Ray (Athlete, Football Player)
3 Carriage Bay
Winnipeg, MB R2Y OM4, Canada

Asham, Arron (Athlete, Hockey Player)
4121 Murfield Cir
Presto, PA 15142-1070, CANADA

Ashanti (Musician)
23 St Andrews Ct
Old Westbury, NY 11568, USA

Ashbery, John L (Writer)
326 Belmont Ave
Buffalo, NY 14223-1550, USA

Ashbrook, Dana (Actor)
Rigberg Roberts Rugolo
1180 S Beverly Dr #601
Los Angeles, CA 90035, USA

Ashbrook, Daphne (Actor)
Innovative Artists
1505 10th St
Santa Monica, CA 90401, USA

Ashbrook, Stephen (Musician)
Green Room
2280 NW Thurman St
Portland, OR 97210, USA

Ashby, Alan (Athlete, Baseball Player)
12011 Cypress Creek Lakes Dr
Cypress, TX 77433-1872, USA

Ashby, Andy (Athlete, Baseball Player)
2 Osborne Dr
Pittston, PA 18640-3751, USA

Ashby, Jeffrey S (Astronaut)
NASA
Johnson Space Center 2101 NASA Road
Houston, TX 77058, USA

Ashby, Jeffrey S Captain
2834 W Nasa Rd # 1
Webster, TX 77598-6202, USA

Ashby, JeffreyS Captain (Astronaut)
2834 W Nasa Rd # 1
Webster, TX 77598-6202, USA

Ashby, Linden (Actor)
639 N Larchmont Blvd #207
Los Angeles, CA 90004, USA

Ashcroft, John (Politician)
5603 W Farm Road 54
Willard, MO 65781-8405, USA

Ashcroft, John D (Ex-Governor, Ex-
Senator)
The Ashcroft Group, LLC
1399 New York Ave, NW
Suite 950
Washington, DC 20005, USA

Ashcroft, Richard (Musician, Songwriter)
c/o Staff Member *Paradigm (NY)*
360 Park Ave S Fl 16
New York, NY 10010, USA

Ashdown, J J D (Paddy) (Government
Official)
Vane Cottage
Norton Sub Hamdon
Somerset TA14 6SG, UNITED KINGDOM
(UK)

Ashe, Chrstopher (Actor)
c/o Paul Greenstone *Paul Greenstone
Entertainment*
3008 Sorrelwood Dr
San Ramon, CA 94582-5008, USA

Ashenfelter III, Horace (Athlete, Track
Athlete)
100 Hawthome Ave
Glen Ridge, NJ 07028, USA

Asher, Barry (Bowler)
Professional Bowlers Assn
719 2nd Ave #701
Seattle, WA 98104, USA

Asher, Jamie (Athlete, Football Player)
6840 S Arlington Ave
Indianapolis, IN 46237, us

Asher, Jane (Actor)
24 Cale St
London SW3 3QU, UNITED KINGDOM
(UK)

Asher, Peter (Musician, Producer)
23446 Malibu Colony Rd
Malibu, CA 90265, USA

Asher, Phyllis (Stylist)
c/o Staff Member *Sydney Represents*
280 Mott St
New York, NY 10012, USA

Asher, Robert (Bob) (Athlete, Football
Player)
4800 S Chicago Beach Dr
Apt 612S
Chicago, IL 60615, USA

Asherson, Renee (Actor)
28 Elsworthy Road
London NW3, UNITED KINGDOM (UK)

Ashford, Mandy (Music Group)
Evolution Talent
1776 Broadway #1500
New York, NY 10019, USA

Ashford, Matthew (Actor)
404 S Bel Aire Dr
Burbank, CA 91501, USA

Ashford, Michelle (Producer, Writer)
c/o Staff Member *WmE2 (WMA-LA)*
1 William Morris Pl
Beverly Hills, CA 90212, USA

Ashford, Rob (Actor)
c/o Staff Member *Creative Artists Agency*
(CAA-LA)
2000 Ave Of The Stars
Los Angeles, CA 90067, USA

Ashford, Roslyn (Music Group)
Thomas Cassidy
11761 E Speedway Blvd
Tucson, AZ 85748, USA

Ashford, Tucker (Athlete, Baseball Player)
122 E Church Ave
Covington, TN 38019-2504, USA

Ashida, Jun (Designer, Fashion Designer)
1-3-3 Aobadai
Meguroku
Tokyo 153, JAPAN

Ashihara, Yoshinobu (Architect)
Ashihara Architects
31-15 Sakuragaokacho
Shibuyaku
Tokyo 150, JAPAN

Ashkenasi, Shmuel (Musician)
3800 N Lake Shore Dr
Chicago, IL 60613, USA

Ashkenazy, Vladimir D (Musician)
Savinka
Kappelistr 15
Meggen 6045, SWITZERLAND

Ashley, Billy (Athlete, Baseball Player)
2787 Autumn Ridge Dr
Thousand Oaks, CA 91362-4934, USA

Ashley, Elizabeth (Actor)
1223 North Ogden Dr
West Hollywood, CA 90046, USA

Ashley, Jennifer (Actor)
129 W Wilson #202
Costa Mesa, CA 92627, USA

Ashley, John (Athlete, Hockey Player,
Referee)
30 Yonge st.
Toronto, ON M5E 1XB, Canada

Ashley, Leon (Musician)
PO Box 567
Hendersonville, TN 37077, USA

Ashley, Mike (Race Car Driver)
Gotham City Racing
201 Old Country Rd. #101
Memville, NY 11747-2731, USA

Ashley, Walker (Athlete, Football Player)
4 Dwight St
Jersey City, NJ 07035, USA

Ashlund, Hilary (Stylist)
219 17th St
Wilmette, IL 60091, USA

Ashman, Duane (Athlete, Football Player)
2625 Antler Ct
Silver Spring, MD 20904, USA

Ashmore, Aaron (Actor)
KG Talent
55 1/2 Sumach Street
Toronto, ON M5A 3J6, Canada

Ashmore, Darryl (Athlete, Football Player)
8695 Thornbrook Terrace Pt
Boynton Beach, FL 33473, USA

Ashmore, Edward (General)
Ministry of Defense
Office of the Naval Secretary
London, SW1, England

Ashmore, Edward B (Admiral)
Naval Secretary
Victor Bldg
HM Naval Base
Portsmouth, Hants, UNITED KINGDOM
(UK)

Ashmore, Frank (Actor)
c/o Staff Member *Howard Talent West*
10657 Riverside Dr
Toluca Lake, CA 91602, USA

Ashmore, Shawn (Actor)
c/o Staff Member *KG Talent*
55 1/2 Sumach St
Toronto, Ontario M5A 3J6, Canada

Ashrawl, Hanan (Politician)
Higher Education Ministry
PO Box 17360
Jerusalem, West Bank, ISRAEL

Ashton, Brent (Athlete, Hockey Player)
311 Brabant Crest
Saskatoon, SK S7J 3Y9, Canada

Ashton, Dean (Actor)
c/o Staff Member *Laine Management*
Laine House
131 victoria road
Salford M6 8LF, UNITED KINGDOM

Ashton, John (Actor)
PO Box 272489
Ft Collins, CO 80527, USA

Ashton, Peter S (Scientist)
233 Herald Road
Carlisle, MA 01741, USA

Ashton, Susan (Music Group)
Bob Doyle Assoc
713 18th Ave S
Nashville, TN 37203, USA

Ashwell, Rachel (Business Person, Designer)
739 Superba Ave
Venice, CA 90291, USA

Ashworth, Frank (Athlete, Hockey Player)
5110 Hot Spring
Fairmont Hot Springs, BC V0B 1L0, Canada

Ashworth, Gerald (Gerry) (Athlete, Track Athlete)
PO Box 2
Ogunquit, ME 03907-2238, USA

Ashworth, Jeanne (Athlete, Olympic Athlete, Speed Skater)
PO Box 308
Wilmington, NY 12997-0308, USA

Ashworth, Landon (Actor)
c/o Staff Member *Snyder Management*
P.O. Box 5728
Beverly Hills, CA 90209, USA

Ashworth, Thomas (Athlete, Football Player)
7329 S Xanthia Way
Centennial, CO 80112, USA

Asia (Music Group)
%Michael Rosen
7715 Sunset Blvd 3rd Floor
Los Angeles, CA 90046, USA

Asian Dub Foundation (Music Group)
c/o Staff Member *Paradigm (Monterey)*
404 W Franklin St
Monterey, CA 93940, USA

As I Lay Dying (Music Group, Musician)
c/o Staff Member *Strong Management*
176-25 Union Turnpike
#405
Fresh Meadows, NY 11366, USA

Askea, Mike (Athlete, Football Player)
Front Gate Cir
Ooltewah, TN 37363, us

Askea, Mike (Athlete, Football Player)
P.O. Box 2391
ooltewah, TN 37363, USA

Askew, B J (Athlete, Football Player)
4216 Lantana Dr
Lebanon, OH 45036, USA

Askew, Desmond (Actor)
c/o Staff Member *Envision Entertainment*
8840 Wilshire Blvd
3rd Floor
Beverly Hills, CA 90211, USA

Askew, Luke (Actor)
3059 Green Canyon Rd
Fallbrook, CA 92028, USA

Askew, Matthias (Athlete, Football Player)
220 Greenup St
Covington, KY 41011, USA

Askew, Matthias (Athlete, Football Player)
3630 NW 6th St
Fort Lauderdale, FL 33311, us

Askew, Reubin (Politician)
PO Box 12487
Tallahassee, FL 32317-2487, USA

Askew, Reubin O (Ex-Governor)
255 Orange Ave.
Orlando, FL 32801, USA

Askey, Tom (Athlete, Hockey Player)
5732 S 6th St
Kalamazoo, MI 49009-9438, USA

Asking Alexandria (Music Group, Musician)
c/o Devin Timmons *The Artery Foundation*
PO Box 160451
Sacramento, CA 95816, USA

Askson, Bert (Athlete, Football Player)
7713 Charlesmont St
Houston, TX 77016, USA

Asleep At The Wheel
PO Box 463
Austin, TX 78767, USA

Aslyn (Musician)
c/o Staff Member *Paradigm (Monterey)*
404 W Franklin St
Monterey, CA 93940, USA

Asmonga, Don (Athlete, Basketball Player)
124 Naylor Dr
Belle Vernon, PA 15012-4729, USA

Asmundson, Freeman "Duke" (Athlete, Hockey Player)
22 Larter Cres
Winnipeg, MB R2P OT8, Canada

Asmussen, Cash (Horse Racer)
111 Devonshire Ct
Laredo, TX 78041-2659, USA

Asner, Ed (Actor)
11970 Montana Ave #210
Los Angeles, CA 90049, USA

Asner, Jules (Producer, Television Host)
c/o John Ferriter *Octagon Entertainment*
7th Floor
Beverly Hills, CA 90069, USA

Asomugha, Nnamdi (Athlete, Football Player)
1050 Armitage St
Alameda, CA 94502, USA

Asomugha, Nnamdi (Athlete, Football Player)
22632 Felbar Ave
Torrance, CA 90505, us

Aspen, Jennifer (Actor)
c/o Joel Stevens *Joel Stevens Entertainment*
5627 Allott Ave
Van Nuys, CA 91401, USA

Asphaug, Erik (Scientist)
1015 Laurel St
Santa Cruz, CA 95060-4237, USA

Aspromonte, Bob
Brooklyn Dodgers
1000 UPtown Park Blvd APt 241
Houston, TX 77056-3243, USA

Aspromonte, Ken (Athlete, Baseball Player, Coach)
2 Derham Parc St
Houston, TX 77024-5200, USA

Asrani (Actor, Bollywood)
B3 Beach House Apartments
Gandhigram Rd Juhu
Mumbai, MS 400049, INDIA

Assante, Armand (Actor)
c/o Michael Kaliski *Omniquest Entertainment (LA)*
1416 N La Brea Ave
Hollywood, CA 90028, USA

Asselstine, Brian (Athlete, Baseball Player)
1488 Country Ct
Santa Ynez, CA 93460-9754, USA

Asselstine, Ron (Athlete, Hockey Player)
338-224 Janefield Ave
Guelph, ON N1G 2L6, Canada

Assenmacher, Paul (Athlete, Baseball Player)
500 Covington Cv
Alpharetta, GA 30022-5574, USA

Assinger, Armin (Actor)
c/o Staff Member *ORF Enterprise*
Wurzburggasse 30
Wien A-1136, Austria

Assouline, Pierre (Writer)
78 Bd Flandrin
Paris 75116, France

Assuras, Thalia (Television Host)
c/o Staff Member *CBS News Productions*
524 W 57th St
8th Floor
New York, NY 10019, USA

Astacio, Pedro (Athlete, Baseball Player)
123 Blue Heron Dr
Greenwood Village, CO 80121-2162, USA

Astaire, Robyn (Horse Racer)
1155 San Ysidro Dr
Beverly Hills, CA 90210-2102, USA

As Tall as Lions (Music Group)
c/o Staff Member *Paradigm (Monterey)*
404 W Franklin St
Monterey, CA 93940, USA

Astanova, Lola (Musician)
c/o Gail Parenteau *Parenteau Guidance*
132 East 35th St #3J
New York, NY 10016, USA

Astin, John (Actor, Director)
3801 Canterbury Rd
Baltimore, MD 21218, USA

Astin, Mackenzie (Actor)
c/o Staff Member *WmE2 (WMA-LA)*
1 William Morris Pl
Beverly Hills, CA 90212, USA

Astin, Sean (Actor, Director, Producer)
24935 Normans Way
Calabasas, CA 91302, USA

Astin, Skylar (Actor)
c/o Mike Smith *Snax Memphis*
67 N. Cox St
Memphis, TN 38104, USA

Astley, Mark
PO Box 96061 RPO West Springs
RPO West Springs
Calgarv, AB T3H OL3, Canada

Astley, Rick (Musician)
Unit 4 Plato St
72-74 Saint Dionis Road
London SW6 4UT, UNITED KINGDOM
(UK)

Aston, Lottie (Athlete, Model)
PO Box 9272
Truckee, CA 96162, USA

Astor, Brooke (Misc)
Vincent Astor Foundations
405 Park Ave
New York, NY 10022, USA

Astrom, Hardy (Athlete, Hockey Player)
Bonasvagen 19B
Ornskoldsvik S-89072, Sweden

Astrom-Defina, Marianna (Stylist)
123 Union St
San Rafael, CA 94901, USA

Astroth, Joe (Athlete, Baseball Player)
6035 Verde Trl S Apt J310
Boca Raton, FL 33433-4435, USA

Asturaga, Nova (Government Official)
Permanent Mission of Nicaragua
820 2nd Ave #801
New York, NY 10017, USA

Asuma, Linda (Actor)
c/o JR Dibbs *Malaky International*
205 S. Beverly Dr
Suite 211
Beverly Hills, CA 90212, USA

Aswanikumar, G (Actor)
Plot 780 29th Street
T N H B Korattur
Chennai, TN 600 080, INDIA

Atack, Emily (Actor)
c/o Malcolm Browning *International Artistes*
Holborn Hall - 4th Floor
London WC1V 7BD, UK

Atari Teenage Riot (Music Group)
c/o Staff Member *Girlie Action*
243 W 30th St
12th Floor
New York, NY 10001, USA

Atcheynum, Blair
Battlefords North Stars
PO Box 1247
North Battleford, SK S9A 3K2, Canada

Atchison, Scott (Race Car Driver)
Day Enterprises Racing
1820 Barrington Dr
Keller, TX 76262-9004, USA

Atchley, Justin (Athlete, Baseball Player)
17958 Cove Ln
Mount Vernon, WA 98274-8126, USA

Aterciopelados (Musician)
c/o Staff Member *BMG*
1540 Broadway
New York, NY 10036, USA

Atessis, Bill (Athlete, Football Player)
P.O. Box 616
Phoenix, AZ 85001, USA

Atha, Dick (Athlete, Basketball Player)
PO Box 256 4e2 N Justus
Oxford, IN 47971-0256, USA

Atha, Richard (Athlete, Basketball Player)
P.O. Box 256
402 N. Justus
Oxford, IN 47971, USA

Athas, Pete (Athlete, Football Player)
1539 Mayo St
Hollywood, FL 33020-6514, USA

Atherton, Keith (Athlete, Baseball Player)
1014 Cobbs Creek Ln
Cobbs Creek, VA 23035-2137, USA

Atherton, William (Actor)
5102 San Feliciano Dr
Woodland Hills, CA 91364, USA

Athfield, Ian C (Architect)
105 Amritser St
Khandallah
Wellington, NEW ZEALAND

Athlete (Music Group)
c/o Staff Member *Paradigm (Monterey)*
404 W Franklin St
Monterey, CA 93940, USA

Athow, Kirk L (Misc)
2104 Crestview Court
Lafayette, IN 47905, USA

Atias, Moran (Actor)
c/o Evan Hainey *Untitled Entertainment (LA)*
350 S. Beverly Dr #200
Beverly Hills, CA 90212, USA

Atiyeh, Victor (Politician)
Victor Atiyeh Co
519 SW Park Ave Ste 205
Portland, OR 97205-3203, USA

Atkeson, Dale
Washington Redskins
4308 Crest Dr
Manhattan Beach, CA 90266-3082, USA

Atkin, Harvey (Actor)
527 S Curson St
Los Angeles, CA 90036, USA

Atkins, Bob (Athlete, Football Player)
15871 Misty Loch Ln
Houston, TX 77084, USA

Atkins, Christopher
6934 Bevis Ave
Van Nuys, CA 91405, USA

Atkins, Dave (Athlete, Football Player)
38140 Windy Hill Ln
Solon, OH 44139, USA

Atkins, Dave (Athlete, Football Player)
737 W Wildwood Dr
Phoenix, AZ 85045, us

Atkins, Doug (Athlete, Football Player)
5312 Sunset Rd
Knoxville, TN 37914, USA

Atkins, Doug (Athlete, Football Player)
PO Box 14007
Knoxville, TN 37914, us

Atkins, Eileen (Actor, Writer)
c/o Staff Member *ICM Partners (ICM-LA)*
10250 Constellation Blvd Fl 7
Los Angeles, CA 90067, USA

Atkins, Essence (Actor)
13047 Magnolia Blvd
Sherman Oaks, CA 91423, USA

Atkins, Garrett (Athlete, Baseball Player)
29 Blue Grass
Irvine, CA 92603-0412, USA

Atkins, Gene (Athlete, Football Player)
3515 Sunnyside Dr
Tallahassee, FL 32305, USA

Atkins, Gene (Athlete, Football Player)
204 SW 166th Ave
Pembroke Pines, FL 33027, us

Atkins, George (Athlete, Football Player)
3445 Polo Downs
Birmingham, AL 35226, USA

Atkins, Kelvin (Athlete, Football Player)
4978 Timber Ridge Trl
Ocoee, FL 34761, USA

Atkins, Kenneth "Chucky" (Athlete, Basketball Player)
229 S Ortman Dr
Orlando, FL 32811-4219, USA

Atkins, Larry (Athlete, Football Player)
1696 N Hughes Ave
Clovis, CA 93619, USA

Atkins, Rodney (Musician)
912 Holly Tree Gap Rd
Brentwood, TN 37027, USA

Atkins, Sharif (Actor)
c/o Christopher Wright *Christopher Wright Management*
3207 Winnie Dr
Los Angeles, CA 90068, USA

Atkins, Tom (Actor)
Paradigm Agency
10100 Santa Monica Blvd #2500
Los Angeles, CA 90067, USA

Atkins, Veronica (Business Person)
100 Park Avenue
Suite 1600
New York, New York 10017, USA

Atkinson, Al (Athlete, Football Player)
218 Wells Ln
Springfield, PA 19064, USA

Atkinson, Bill (Athlete, Baseball Player)
15 Argyle Cres
Chatham, ON N7L 4T7, CANADA

Atkinson, Frank (Athlete, Football Player)
7 Franciscan Rdg
Portola Valley, CA 94028, USA

Atkinson, George (Athlete, Football Player)
3570 Caldeira Dr
Livermore, CA 94550, USA

Atkinson, Jayne (Actor)
Innovative Atrists
1505 10th St
Santa Monica, CA 90401, USA

Atkinson, Jess (Athlete, Football Player)
2913 Southaven Dr
Annapolis, MD 21401, USA

Atkinson, Ray N (Business Person)
Guy F Atkinson Co
1001 Bayhill Dr
San Bruno, CA 94066, USA

Atkinson, Rick (Journalist)
Kansas City Times
1729 Grand Blvd
Attn Editorial Dept
Kansas City, MO 64108-1458, USA

Atkinson, Ron (Soccer Player)
Nottingham Forest
Pavillion Road
Bridgeford
Nottingham N62 5JF, UNITED KINGDOM (UK)

Atkinson, Rowan (Actor)
Oliver
Drury Ln
Theatre Royal
Catherine St WC2B 5JF, UK

Atkinson, Steve (Athlete, Hockey Player)

Atkisson, Sharyl (Correspondent)
Cable News Network
News Dept 1051 Techwood Dr NW
Atlanta, GA 30318, USA

Atkov, Oleg Y (Cosmonaut)
Potchta Kosmonavtov
Moskovskoi Oblasti
Syvisdny Gorroduk 141160, RUSSIA

Atogwe, Oshiomogho (Athlete, Football Player)
496 Speyer Pl
Saint Charles, MO 63303, USA

Atogwe, Oshiomogho (Athlete, Football Player)
43263 Parkers Ridge Dr
Leesburg, VA 20176, us

Atomic Kitten (Music Group)
c/o Staff Member *Concorde Intl Artists Ltd*
101 Shepherds Bush Rd
London W6 7LP, UNITED KINGDOM (UK)

Attal, Yvan (Actor, Director)
Artmedia
20 Ave Rapp
Paris 75007, FRANCE

Attanasio, Paul (Producer, Writer)
631 N Palm Dr
Beverly Hills, CA 90210, USA

Attardi, Michael (Athlete, Football Player)
11 Walada Ave
Port Monmouth, NJ 07758, USA

Attell, Dave (Actor, Comedian, Producer)
500 43rd St #35A
New York, NY 10036, USA

Attenborough, David F (Business Person, Writer)
5 Park Rd
Richmond, Surrey TW10 6NS, UK

Attenborough, Richard S (Actor, Director)
Old Farms
Beaver Lodge
Richmond Green, Surrey TW9 1NQ, UNITED KINGDOM (UK)

Atterton, Edward (Actor)
PFD
Drury House
34-43 Russell St
London WC2B 5HA, UNITED KINGDOM (UK)

Attlee, Frank III (Business Person)
Monsanto Co
800 N Lindbergh Blvd
Saint Louis, MO 63167, USA

Attles, Al (Athlete, Basketball Player, Coach)
195 Villanova Dr
Oakland, CA 94611-1108, USA

Attwell, Bob (Athlete, Hockey Player)
130 Rolling Hills Lane
Bolton, ON L7E 4E1, Canada

Attwell, Ron (Athlete, Hockey Player)
P.O. Box 292
Sundridge, ON P0A 1Z0, Canada

Atun, Hakki (Prime Minister)
Gov't Assembly
North Cyprus Republic
Via Mersin 10
Lefkosa, TURKEY

Atwater, Stephen D (Steve) (Athlete, Football Player)
2510 Sugarloaf Club Dr
Duluth, GA 30097, USA

Atwater Rhodes, Amelia (Writer)
c/o Staff Member *Random House Publicity*
1745 Broadway
New York, NY 10019, USA

Atwell, Alfred (Astronaut)
3253 Ennis Court
Las Vegas, NV 89121, USA

Atwell, Alfred Col (Aviator)
3253 Ennis Ct
Las Vegas, NV 89121-5761, USA

Atwood, Casey (Race Car Driver)
Day Enterprises Racing
107 Flat Ridge Rd
Goodlettsville, TN 37072, USA

Atwood, Harold L (Scientist)
602 Castlefield Ave
Toronto, ON M5N 1L8, Canada

Atwood, Jensen (Actor)
c/o Staff Member *Noah's Arc*
75 Charles Rowen House
Merlin Street
London WC1X 0EJ, UNITED KINGDOM

Atwood, Margaret E (Writer)
Oxford University Press
204-8 Sampson Mews
North York, ON M3C OHS, CANADA

Atwood, Susie (Sue) (Swimmer)
5624 E 2nd St
Long Beach, CA 90803, USA

Atzmon, Moshe
Marignanostr 12
Basel 4059, SWITZERLAND

Auber, Brigitte
56 rue Guy-Moquet
Paris F-75017, France

Auberjonois, Rene (Actor)
3629 Wonder View Dr
Los Angeles, CA 90068, USA

Aubert, KD (Actor)
c/o Scott Karp *Crystal Sky Pictures*
10203 Santa Monica Blvd
5th Floor
Los Angeles, CA 90067, USA

Aubin, Normand (Athlete, Hockey Player)
1287 rue des Berges
Sorel-Tracy, QC J3P 7X5, Canada

Aubin, Serge (Athlete, Hockey Player)
Box 105366
Atlanta, GA 30348, USA

Auboin, Jean A (Misc)
27 Ave des Baumettes
Nice 06000, FRANCE

Aubrey, Emlyn (Athlete, Golfer)
2013 Surrey Ln
Bossier City, LA 71111-5534, USA

Aubrey, James (Actor)
Van Gelder
18-21 Jermyn St #300
London SW1Y 6HP, UNITED KINGDOM
(UK)

Aubrey, Michael (Athlete, Baseball Player)
9622 Gardere Dr
Shreveport, LA 71115-4602, USA

Aubry, Cristina (Actor)
Carol Levi Co
Via Giuseppe Pisanelli
Rome 00196, ITALY

Aubry, Eugene E (Architect)
8021 Marina Isles Lane
Holmes Beach, FL 34217, USA

Aubry, Gabriel (Model)
c/o Staff Member *LW1*
7257 Beverly Blvd #200
Los Angeles, CA 90036, USA

Aubry, Pierre (Athlete, Hockey Player)
110 Rue Buisson
Trois-Rivieres, QC G8V 1K4, Canada

Aubry, Serge (Hockey Player)

Aubuchon, Remi (Producer)
c/o Staff Member *United Talent Agency
(UTA)*
9336 Civic Center Dr
Beverly Hills, CA 90210, USA

Auburn, David (Writer)
97 W Elmwood Ave
Clawson, MI 48017, USA

Aucoin, Adrian (Athlete, Hockey Player)
9820 E Thompson Peak Pkwy Unit 727
Scottsdale, AZ 85255-6657, USA

Aucoin, Derek (Athlete, Baseball Player)
233 W 77th St # 5E
New York, NY 10024-6809, USA

AuCoin, Les (Misc)
Bogle & Gates
601 13th St NW #370
Washington, DC 20005, USA

Aude, Rich (Athlete, Baseball Player)
4817 Natoma Ave
Woodland Hills, CA 91364-3416, USA

Audette, Donald (Athlete, Hockey Player)
15 rue de Chinon
Blainville, QC J7B 1Y2, Canada

Audick, Daniel (Athlete, Football Player)
13253 Sparren Ave
San Diego, CA 92129, USA

Audran, Stephane (Actor)
2F De Marthod
11 Rue Chanez 70016E, FRANCE

Auel, Jean M (Writer)
PO Box 8278
Portland, OR 97207, USA

Auel, Jean Marie (Writer)
PO Box 8278
Portland, OR 97207-8278, USA

Auer, Barbara (Actor)
Agentur Carola Studlar
Neurieder Str 1C
Planegg 82152, GERMANY

Auer, Joe (Athlete, Football Player)
1138 Washington Ave
Winter Park, FL 32789, USA

Auer, Scott (Athlete, Football Player)
2921 Burge Dr
Crown Point, IN 46307, USA

Auerbach, Frank (Artist)
Marlborough Fine Art Gallery
6 Albermarle St
London W1X 4BY, UNITED KINGDOM
(UK)

Auerbach, Rick (Athlete, Baseball Player)
2139 Stunt Rd
Calabasas, CA 1302-2358, USA

Auerbach, Stanley I (Misc)
3314 W End Ave #202
Nashville, TN 37203, USA

Auermann, Nadia (Model)
Elite Models
4 Rue de la Paiz
Paris 75002, FRANCE

Auermann, Nadja (Model)
c/o Staff Member *Models 1*
12 Macklin St
Covent Gardens
London WC2B 5SZ, UK

Aufderhaar, Grant C Dr (Scientist)
5510 Hamlet Hill Ct
Fairfax, VA 22030-7282, USA

AufDerMaur, Melissa (Music Group,
Musician)
Artist Group International
9560 Wilshire Blvd #400
Beverly Hills, CA 90212, USA

Auferio, Tony (Athlete, Baseball Player)
493 Indian Rd
Wavne, NJ 07470-4922, USA

Auge, Andrea (Stylist)
1065 E Prospect St
#103
Seattle, WA 98102, USA

Augenstein, Bryan (Athlete, Baseball
Player)
179 Cili)rona St
Sebastian, FL 32958-5607, USA

Auger, Brian (Music Group, Musician)
Earthtone
8306 Wilshire Blvd #981
Beverly Hills, CA 90211, USA

Auger, Claudine (Actor)
Artmedia
20 Ave Rapp
Paris 75007, FRANCE

Auger, Pierre V (Physicist)
12 Rue Emile Faguet
Paris 75014, FRANCE

Aughtman, Dowe (Athlete, Football
Player)
2 Buckhead Ln
Opelika, AL 36804, USA

Augmon, Stacey (Athlete, Basketball
Player)
2784 Botticelli Dr
Henderson, NV 89052-3108, USA

August, Bille (Director)
2800 Lyngby
DENMARK

August, Don (Athlete, Baseball Player,
Olympic Athlete)
N88W17812 Christman Rd
Menomonee Falls, WI 53051-2630, USA

August, John (Director, Musician,
Producer)
644 S June St
Los Angeles, CA 90005, USA

August, Pernilla (Actor)
Royal Dramatic Theater
Box 5037
Stockholm 102 41, SWEDEN

August, Steve (Athlete, Football Player)
7704 E 86th St
Tulsa, OK 74133, USA

Augusta, Kim (Athlete, Golfer)
16 Rachela Ct
East Providence, RI 02914-3063, USA

Augusta, Patrik (Athlete, Hockey Player)
c/o Staff Member *Phoenix Coyotes*
6751 N White Out Way
Suite 200
Glendale, AZ 85305, USA

Augustain, Ira (Actor)
c/o Staff Member *Diamond Artists*
9200 W Sunset Blvd #701
W Hollywood, CA 90069-3602, USA

Augustana (Musician)
c/o Staff Member *Paradigm (Monterey)*
404 W Franklin St
Monterey, CA 93940, USA

Augustine, Dave (Athlete, Baseball Player)
P.O. Box 1114
Saint Albans, WV 25177-1114, USA

Augustine, Jerry (Athlete, Baseball Player)
S74W13490 Courtland Ln
Muskego, WI 53150-3937, USA

Augustine, Norman R (Business Person)
*Review of U.S. Human Space Flight Plans
Committee*
NASA Headquarters
300 E St SW
Washington, DC 20024-3210, USA

Augustnyiak, Jerry (Music Group,
Musician)
Agency for Performing Arts
9200 Sunset Blvd #900
Los Angeles, CA 90069, USA

Augustus, Seimone (Athlete, Basketball
Player)
Matheny Sears Linkert & Long, LLP
3638 American River Dr
Sacramento, CA 95864, USA

Augustus, Sherman (Actor)
c/o Steven Jensen *Independent Group,
The*
6363 Wilshire Blvd
Suite 115
Los Angeles, CA 90048, USA

Augustyniak, Jerry (Musician)
c/o Staff Member *Agency for the
Performing Arts (APA-LA)*
405 S Beverly Dr
Suite 500
Beverly Hills, CA 90212-4425, USA

Augustyniak, Mike (Athlete, Football
Player)
10540 Castlebrook Dr
Jacksonville, FL 32257, USA

Augustyniak, Mike (Athlete, Football
Player)
244 Sweetbrier Branch Ln
Saint Johns, FL 32259, us

Auktyon (Music Group, Musician)
c/o Staff Member *Skyline Music*
28 Union St
Whitefield, NH 03598, USA

Aulby, Mike (Bowler)
1591 Springmill Ponds Cir
Carmel, IN 46032-8552, USA

Auld, Alex (Athlete, Hockey Player)
2205 Swallow Cres
Thunder Bay, ON P7C 4T9, Canada

Ault, Chris (Coach, Football Coach)
University of Nevada
Athletic Dept
Reno, NV 89557, USA

Ault, James M (Religious Leader)
1 Amoskegan Dr
Brunswick, ME 04011, USA

Aumann, Robert J (Nobel Prize Laureate)
Hebrew University of Jerusalem
Center for Rationality
Jerusalem 91904, Israel

Aumont, Michel (Actor)
c/o Staff Member *ArtMedia*
20 avenue Rapp
Paris 75008, France

Aunon, Serena Dr (Astronaut)
2536 Goldeneye Ln
League City, TX 77573-6434, USA

Auriemma, Frank (Horse Racer)
21 Jacob Rd
Plainview, NY 11803-6462, USA

Auriemma, Geno (Athlete, Basketball
Player, Coach)
180 Garth Rd
Manchester, CT 06040-5644, USA

Aurilia, Rich
5448 E Mariposa St
Phoenix, AZ 85018-3124, USA

Aurilla, Rich (Athlete, Baseball Player)
5448 E Mariposa St
Phoenix, AZ 85018, USA

Ausanio, Joe (Athlete, Baseball Player)
PO Box 213
Marlboro, NY 12542-0213, USA

Ausbie, Hubert (Athlete, Basketball Player)
902 Arthur Dr
Little Rock, AR 72204-1524, USA

Ausmus, Brad (Athlete, Baseball Player)
1644 Stratford Way
Del Mar, CA 92014-2444, USA

Ausoin, Derek (Athlete, Baseball Player)
233 W 77th St
Apt 5E
New York, NY 10024, USA

Aust, Abner (General)
PO Box 1875
Bartow, FL 33831-1875, USA

Aust, Dennis (Athlete, Baseball Player)
16252 Estuary Ct
Bokeelia, FL 33922-1535, USA

Auster, Paul (Director, Writer)
c/o Ron Bernstein ICM Partners (ICM-LA)
10250 Constellation Blvd Fl 7
Los Angeles, CA 90067, USA

Austin, Alana (Actor)
c/o Lena Roklin Luber Roklin Management
8530 Wilshire Blvd
6th Floor
Beverly Hills, CA 90211, USA

Austin, Andrea (Stylist)
c/o Staff Member Sally Bjornsen Represents
2008 3rd Ave
North Seattle, WA 98109, USA

Austin, A Woody (Athlete, Golfer)
10906 W Havenhurst St
Maize, KS 67101, USA

Austin, Bill (Athlete, Football Player)
9412 Shellfish Ct
Las Vegas, NV 89117, USA

Austin, Billy (Athlete, Football Player)
3435 Westheimer Rd
Apt 711
Houston, TX 77027, USA

Austin, Billy (Athlete, Football Player)
12723 Timbermeadow Dr
Houston, TX 77070, us

Austin, Charles (Athlete, Olympic Athlete, Track Athlete)
514 Duncan Dr
San Marcos, TX 78666, USA

Austin, Cliff (Athlete, Football Player)
1652 Valencia Rd
Decatur, GA 30032, USA

Austin, Cliff (Athlete, Football Player)
1278 Autumn Wood Trl
Sugar Hill, GA 30518, us

Austin, Coco Marie (Model, Reality TV Star)
31B Casta Ln
Edgewater, NJ 07020, USA

Austin, Dallas (Musician, Producer, Songwriter)
5335 Northside Dr NW
Atlanta, GA 30327, USA

Austin, Darlene (Musician, Songwriter)
PO Box 171143
Nashville, TN 37217-8143, USA

Austin, Darrell (Athlete, Football Player)
268 Austin Rd
Union, SC 29379, USA

Austin, Darrell (Athlete, Football Player)
720A S Duncan Byp
Union, SC 29379, us

Austin, Debbie (Athlete, Golfer)
6733 Bittersweet Ln
Orlando, FL 32819-4635, USA

Austin, Denise (Fitness Expert)
PrimeCare Systems, Inc
610 Thimble Shoals Blvd
Newport News, VA 23606, USA

Austin, Hise (Athlete, Football Player)
53 N Deerfoot Cir
Spring, TX 77380, USA

Austin, Ike (Athlete, Basketball Player)
1221 South 800 E
Salt Lake City, UT 84105-1207, USA

Austin, Isaac (Athlete, Basketball Player)
2451 Brickell Ave Apt 15J
Miami, FL 33129-2421, USA

Austin, Jake (Actor)
c/o Ryan Bartlett Paradigm (LA)
360 N Crescent Dr
North Bldg
Beverly Hills, CA 90210, USA

Austin, Jeff (Athlete, Baseball Player)
190 Rutherford Ave
Redwood City, CA 94061-3511, USA

Austin, Jeff (Musician)
c/o Staff Member Paradigm (Monterey)
404 W Franklin St
Monterey, CA 93940, USA

Austin, Jim (Athlete, Baseball Player)
20974 Rootstown Ter
Ashburn, VA 20147-4839, USA

Austin, John (Athlete, Basketball Player)
1330 Riggs St NW
Washington, DC 20009, USA

Austin, Johnny (Athlete, Basketball Player)
1330 Riggs St NW
Washington, DC 20009-4325, USA

Austin, Kent (Athlete, Football Player)
704 Legends Crest Dr
Franklin, TN 37069, USA

Austin, Miles (Athlete, Football Player)
4014 Travis St Unit C
Dallas, TX 75204, us

Austin, Miles (Athlete, Football Player)
c/o David Dunn Athletes First, LLC
9140 Irvine Center Dr
Irvine, CA 92618, USA

Austin, Ocie (Athlete, Football Player)
750 Macarthur Blvd
Apt 301
Oakland, CA 94610, USA

Austin, Oona (Stylist)
7681 Willow Glen Rd
Los Angeles, CA 90046, USA

Austin, Pat (Race Car Driver)
14823 47th Ave. E.
Tacoma, WA 98440, USA

Austin, Patti (Music Group)
3 Loudon Dr #8
Fishkill, NY 12524, USA

Austin, Reggie (Athlete, Football Player)
3339 Deerwood Ln
Rex, GA 30273, USA

Austin, Rick (Athlete, Baseball Player)
8107 Forest Parks Dr
Kansas City, MO 64152-3172, USA

Austin, Scott (Race Car Driver)
Meads Creek Rd
Painted Post, NY 14870, USA

Austin, Sherrie (Musician)
Splash Publications
1520 16th Ave N #2
Nashville, TN 37212, USA

Austin, Steve (Stone Cold) (Athlete, Wrestler)
906 Howard St
Marina del Rey, CA 90292, USA

Austin, Teri (Actor)
4245 Laurel Grove
Studio City, CA 91604, USA

Austin, Thomas (Athlete, Football Player)
500 Almer Rd
Apt 306
Burlingame, CA 94010, USA

Austin, Tracy (Athlete, Tennis Player)
5 Williamsburg Ln
Rolling Hills, CA 90274, USA

Austin, Walt (Race Car Driver)
Pro/Max Performance
5602 S. Tacoma Way
Tacoma, WA 98409, USA

Austin-Antelline, Charlotte (Actor)
3053 Valevista Trl
Los Angeles, CA 90068, USA

Austin Jr, M P (Business Person)
BMC Software
2101 City West Blvd
Houston, TX 77042, USA

Auston, Jim (Musician)
c/o Staff Member Curb Records (Nashville)
48 Music Sq E
Nashville, TN 37203, USA

Austregesilo de Athayde, Belarmino M (Journalist)
Rua Cosme Velho 599
Rio de Janeiro RJ, BRAZIL

Austria, Steve (Congressman, Politician)
439 Cannon HOB
Washington, DC 20515, USA

Austrian, Robert (Physicist)
Univ of Pennsylvania
Med Center 36 Hamilton Circle
Philadelphia, PA 19130, USA

Auteuil, Daniel (Actor)
Artmedia
20 Ave Rapp
Paris 75007, FRANCE

Auth, Tony (Cartoonist, Editor)
c/o Staff Member Universal Press Syndicate
1130 Walnut St
Kansas City, MO 64106-2109, USA

Autrey, Billy (Athlete, Football Player)
9810 Knoboak Dr
Houston, TX 77080, USA

Autry, Al
3108 Lennox Dr
El Dorado Hills, CA 95762-5662, USA

Autry, Alan (Actor)
c/o Staff Member David Shapira & Associates
193 N Robertson Blvd
Beverly Hills, CA 90211, USA

Autry, Albert (Al) (Athlete, Baseball Player)
3108 Lennox Dr
El Dorado Hills, CA 95762-5662, USA

Autry, Jim (Golfer, Misc)
Professional Golfer's Assn
P O Box 109601
Palm Beach Gardens, FL 33410, USA

Auyeung, Jin (Musician)
c/o Staff Member Virgin Records (NY)
150 5th Ave
New York, NY 10010, USA

Auzenne, Troy (Athlete, Football Player)
118 Oak Rd
Orinda, CA 94563, us

Auzenne, Troy (Athlete, Football Player)
1501 Bluff Ct
Diamond Bar, CA 91765, USA

Avala, Benny (Athlete, Baseball Player)
PO Box 222
Dorado, PR 00646-0222, USA

Avalon (Music Group)
PO Box 150867
Nashville, TN 37215, USA

Avalon, Frankie (Actor, Musician)
4303 Spring Forest Ln
Westlake Village, CA 91362, USA

Avant, Jason (Athlete, Football Player)
112 Villas Ct
Clementon, NJ 08021, us

Avant, Jason (Athlete, Football Player)
12136 S State St
Chicago, IL 60628, USA

Avants, Nick (Athlete, Baseball Player)
3914 Mount Carmel Rd
Bryant, AR 72022-6209, USA

Avari, Erick (Actor)
c/o Michael Greene Greene & Associates
1901 Avenue Of The Stars Ste 130
Los Angeles, CA 90067, USA

Avary, Roger (Director)
c/o Brian Siberell Creative Artists Agency (CAA-LA)
2000 Ave Of The Stars
Los Angeles, CA 90067, USA

Avdelsayed, Gabriel (Religious Leader)
Coptic Orthodox Curch
427 Westside Ave
Jersey City, NJ 07304, USA

Avdeyev, Sergei V (Cosmonaut)
Potchta Kosmonavtov
Moskovskoi Oblasti
Syvisdny Goroduk 141160, RUSSIA

Avedon, Gregg (Model)
PO Box 266401
Weston, FL 33326, USA

Avellan, Elizabeth (Producer)
c/o Staff Member ICM Partners (ICM-LA)
10250 Constellation Blvd Fl 7
Los Angeles, CA 90067, USA

Avellini, Bob (Athlete, Football Player)
1085 Flamingo Dr
Roselle, IL 60172, USA

Aven, Bruce (Athlete, Baseball Player)
4223 SW 141st Av
Davie, FL 33330-5724, USA

Avenged Sevenfold (Music Group)
c/o Staff Member *Warner Music Germany GmbH (WMI-Germany)*
Alter Wandrahm 14
Hamburg D - 20457, Germany

Avent, Anthony (Athlete, Basketball Player)
1166 Croton Rd
Flemington, NJ 08822-5607, USA

Averell, Tom (Athlete, Football Player)
100 Highland Pines Ct
Apt 32
Pittsburgh, PA 15237, USA

Averill Jr., Earl (Athlete, Baseball Player)
1806 19th Sr NE
Auburn, WA 98002-3465, USA

Averitt, William (Athlete, Basketball Player)
PO Box 802
Hopkinsville, KY 42241-0802, USA

Averre, Berton (Music Group, Musician)
17510 Posetano Road
Pacific Palisades, CA 90272, USA

Avery, Eric (Actor, Musician)
c/o Jeff Frasco *Creative Artists Agency (CAA-LA)*
2000 Ave Of The Stars
Los Angeles, CA 90067, USA

Avery, James (Actor)
3211 Waverly Dr
Los Angeles, CA 90027, USA

Avery, John (Athlete, Football Player)
1301 Kensington Pl Apt B
Asheville, NC 28803, us

Avery, John (Athlete, Football Player)
12 Ballantree Dr
Asheville, NC 28803, USA

Avery, Ken (Athlete, Football Player)
625 Indian Ridge Dr
Nashville, TN 37221, USA

Avery, Margaret (Actor)
2807 Pelham Pl
Los Angeles, CA 90068, USA

Avery, Rick (Actor)
4 Blades Inc
11991 Wood Ranch Rd
Granada Hills, CA 91344, USA

Avery, Sean (Athlete, Hockey Player)
c/o Staff Member *Los Angeles Kings*
1111 S. Figueroa St
Suite 3100
Los Angeles, CA 90015, USA

Avery, Shondrella (Actor)
c/o Vincent Cirrincione *Vincent Cirrincione Associates*
1516 N Fairfax Ave
Los Angeles, CA 90046, USA

Avery, Steve (Athlete, Baseball Player)
2 Gleneagles Ct
Dearborn, MI 48120-1165, USA

Avery, Steve (Athlete, Football Player)
2 Glenagles Ct
Dearborn, MI 48120, USA

Avery, Susan (Stylist)
6636 Mission Club Blvd
#305
Orlando, FL 32821, USA

Avery, Tom (Athlete, Mountaineer)
c/o Staff Member *WmE2 (WMA-LA)*
1 William Morris Pl
Beverly Hills, CA 90212, USA

Avery, Val (Actor)
84 Grove St #19
New York, NY 10014, USA

Avery, William J (Business Person)
Crown Cork & Seal
1 Crow Way
Philadelphia, PA 19154, USA

Aviance, Kevin (Musician)
Kevin Aviance World
115 E 57th St Fl 11
New York, NY 10022, USA

Avicii (DJ, Musician)
At Night Management

Avila, Alejandro (Actor)
c/o Staff Member *Televisa*
Blvd Adolfo Lopez Mateos 232
Colonia San Angel INN
DF CP 01060, MEXICO

Avila, Alex (Athlete, Baseball Player)
2163 Regency Hills Dr
Shelby Township, MI 48316-2055, USA

Avila, Mariana (Actor)
c/o Staff Member *Televisa*
Blvd Adolfo Lopez Mateos 232
Colonia San Angel INN
DF CP 01060, MEXICO

Avildsen, John (Director)
2423 Briarcrest Road
Beverly Hills, CA 90210, USA

Aviles, Mike (Athlete, Baseball Player)
49 Mayer Dr
Middletown 10940-3349, USA

Aviles, Ramon (Athlete, Baseball Player)
C19 Calle Juan Morell Campos
Jard De Monaco 1
Manati, PR 00674-6618, USA

Avinger, Clarence (Athlete, Football Player)
2021 Chardonnay Way
Birmingham, AL 35216, USA

Avital, Mili (Actor)
c/o Craig Shapiro *ICM Partners (ICM-LA)*
10250 Constellation Blvd Fl 7
Los Angeles, CA 90067, USA

Aviva (Actor)
4455 Los Feliz Blvd. #604
Los Angeles, CA 90027, USA

Avnet, Jon (Director, Producer)
20911/20929 Colina Dr
Topanga, CA 90290, USA

Avni, Aki
c/o Staff Member *Marshak/Zachary Company, The*
8840 Wilshire Blvd
1st Floor
Beverly Hills, CA 90210, USA

Avory, Mike (Musician)
Larry Page
29 Rushton Mews
London W11 1RB, UNITED KINGDOM (UK)

Avrault, joe (Athlete, Baseball Player)
2338 Vintage ST
Sarasota, FL 34240-8317, USA

Awalt, Rob (Athlete, Football Player)
5011 Highgrove Ct
Granite Bay, CA 95746, USA

Awasom, Adrian (Athlete, Football Player)
12330 Grove Meadow Dr
Stafford, TX 77477, USA

Awasom, Adrian (Athlete, Football Player)
5011 Highgrove Ct
Stafford, TX 77477, us

Awesome 3 (Music Group, Musician)
c/o Staff Member *Mission Control Artists Agency*
Unit 3 City Business Centre
St Olav's Court, Lower Road
London SE16 2XB, UNITED KINGDOM (UK)

Awrey, Donald W (Don) (Athlete, Hockey Player)
1015 Alaska Ave
Lehigh Acres, FL 33971, USA

Awtrey, Dennis (Athlete, Basketball Player)
3823e James Rd
Nehalem, OR 97131-9602, USA

Ax, Emmanuel (Music Group, Musician)
c/o Staff Member *Askonas Holt Ltd*
Lincoln House
300 High Holborn
London WC1V 7JH, UK

Axel, Richard (Nobel Prize Laureate)
435 Riverside Dr Apt 62
New York, NY 10025-7764, USA

Axelrod, Jack (Actor)
c/o Jennifer Lee Garland *Circle Talent Associates*
433 N Camden Dr #400
Beverly Hills, CA 90210, USA

Axelrod, Jonathan H (Biologist)
Salk Institute
10100 NTorrey Pines Road
La Jolla, CA 92037, USA

Axelsson, P. J. (Athlete, Hockey Player)
50 Fleet St.
#301
Boston, MA 02109-1129, USA

Axelsson, PJ (Athlete, Hockey Player)
121 Mt Vernon St
Boston, MA 02108, USA

Axford, John (Athlete, Baseball Player)
961rma Crt
Ancaster, ON L9G 1K7, Canada

Axley, Eric (Athlete, Golfer)
1700 Cottage Wood Way
Knoxville, TN 37919-8881, USA

Axum, Donna (Beauty Pageant Winner)
6312 Indian Creek Dr
Ft Worth, TX 76116, USA

Ayala, Alexis (Actor)
c/o Staff Member *Televisa*
Blvd Adolfo Lopez Mateos 232
Colonia San Angel INN
DF CP 01060, MEXICO

Ayala, Bobby (Athlete, Baseball Player)
11011 W Cottonwood Ln
Avondale, AZ 85392-4324, USA

Ayala, Fransisco J (Biologist, Misc)
2 Locke Court
Irvine, CA 92612, USA

Ayala, Paul (Boxer)
7524 Creek Meadow Dr
Fort Worth, TX 76123, USA

Ayanbadejo, Brendon (Athlete, Football Player)
2800 NE 30th St
Apt 2
Fort Lauderdale, FL 33306, USA

Ayanbadejo, Obafemi (Athlete, Football Player)
875 La Jolla Corona Ct
La Jolla, CA 92037, USA

Ayanbadejo, Obafemi (Athlete, Football Player)
301 W G St Unit 134
San Diego, CA 92101, us

Ayanna, Charlotte (Actor)
Industry Entertainment
955 Carillo Dr #300
Los Angeles, CA 90048, USA

Aybar, Erick (Athlete, Baseball Player)
1636 Orchard Dr Apt C
Placentia, CA 92870-5455, USA

Aybar, Manny (Athlete)
401 E Jefferson
Phoenix, AZ 85004

Aybar, Manuel (Athlete, Baseball Player)
3020 SW 189th Ter
Miramar, FL 33029, USA

Ayckbourn, Alan (Director, Writer)
M Ramsay
14A Goodwins Ct
Saint Martin's Lane
London WC2N 4LL, UNITED KINGDOM (UK)

Aycock, Alice (Artist)
62 Greene St Apt 4
New York, NY 10012-4346, USA

Aycock, H David (Business Person)
Nucor Corp
2100 Resford Road
Charlotte, NC 28211, USA

Aycock, Thomas (Misc)
2124 Glendale Ave
Texarkana, AR 71854-3564, USA

Aycox, Nicki (Actor)
c/o Jeb Brandon *Kritzer Levine Wilkins Entertainment (KLWG)*
11872 La Grange Ave
1st Floor
Los Angeles, CA 90025, USA

Aydelette, William (Athlete, Football Player)
115 Woodward Rd
Trussville, AL 35173, USA

Ayer, David (Producer, Writer)
Crave Films
3312 Sunset Blvd
Los Angeles, CA 90026, USA

Ayers, Chuck (Cartoonist)
Unversal Press Syndicate
4520 Main St
Kansas City, MO 64111, USA

Ayers, Dick (Cartoonist)
64 Beach St W
White Plains, NY 10604-2230, USA

Ayers, Randy (Athlete, Basketball Player, Coach)
Philadelphia 76ers
1st Union Center 3601 S Broad St
Philadelphia, PA 19148, USA

Ayers, Roy E Jr (Music Group, Musician)
Roy Ayers Ubiquity Inc
209 W 97th St
Apt 4D
New York, NY 10025, USA

Ayers, Sam (Actor)
c/o Staff Member *Bobby Ball Talent Agency*
4116 W Magnolia Blvd Ste 205
Burbank, CA 91505-2700, USA

Aykroyd, Dan (Actor, Comedian)
851 Paseo Miramar
Pacific Palisades, CA 90272, USA

Aylesworth, Reiko (Actor)
c/o Staff Member *Innovative Artists (LA)*
1505 10th St
Santa Monica, CA 90401, USA

Aylward, John (Actor)
c/o Staff Member *Mitchell K Stubbs & Assoc (MKS)*
8675 W. Washington Blvd
Suite 203
Culver City, CA 90232, USA

Aylwin Azocar, Patricio (President)
Teresa Salas 786
Providencia, Santiago, CHILE

Aynsley, Brock (Athlete, Football Player)
3893 Casorso Rd
Kelowna, BC V1W 4R7, Canada

Ayodele, Akin (Athlete, Football Player)
7105 David Ln
Colleyville, TX 76034, USA

Ayotte, Kelly (Senator)
188 Russell Senate Office Building
Washington, DC 20510, USA

Ayrault, Bob (Athlete, Baseball Player)
2395 S Arlington Ave
Reno, NV 89509-5671, USA

Ayrault, Joe (Athlete, Baseball Player)
Helena Brewers PO Box 6756
Attn: Managers Office
Helena, MT 59604-6756, USA

Ayre, Calvin (Business Person)
Bodog
Oficentro Ejecutivo Sabana Sur
Edificio 7, 5 Piso
San Jose 00000, Costa Rica

Ayres, Robert Temple (Artist)
1578 Masters Dr
Banning, CA 92220, USA

Ayres, Rosalind (Actor)
c/o Staff Member *Lou Coulson Agency*
37 Berwick St
1st Floor
London W1F 8RS, UNITED KINGDOM
(UK)

Ayres, Travis (Race Car Driver)
Ayres Motorsports
RR 1 Box 188
Granville Summi, PA 16926, USA

Ayres Kalish, Leah (Actor)
15718 Milbank St
Encino, CA 91436-1637, USA

Aytes, Rochelle (Actor)
c/o Ryan Daly *Zero Gravity Management*
1531 14th. St
Santa Monica, CA 90404, USA

Azad, Afshan (Actor)
c/o Staff Member *Gordon and French*
12-13 Poland St
London W1F 8QB, UNITED KINGDOM
(UK)

Azalea, Iggy (Musician)
c/o Simon Clarkson *WmE2 (WMA-UK)*
103 New Oxford St
London WC1A 1DD, UK

Azar, Steve (Music Group)
1116 Harpeth Ridge Rd
Franklin, TN 37069, USA

Azarenka, Victoria (Athlete, Tennis Player)
c/o John Tobias *Lagardere Unlimited - (D.C.)*
5335 Wisconsin Ave NW
Suite 850
Washington, DC 20015, USA

Azaria, Hank (Actor)
13544 Lucca Dr
Pacific Palisades, CA 90272, USA

Azcue, Jose (Joe) (Athlete, Baseball Player)
7609 W 115th St
Overland Park, KS 66210-2614, USA

Azelby, Joe (Athlete, Football Player)
14 Pierce Ave
Cresskill, NJ 07626, USA

Azimov, Yakhyo (Prime Minister)
Prime Minister's Office
Rudaki Prosp 42
Dushaube 743051, TAJIKISTAN

Azinger, Paul (Athlete, Golfer)
8910 21st Ave NW
Bradenton, FL 34209, USA

Aziz, Tariq (Prime Minister)
Prime Minister's Office
Karadat Mariam
Baghdad, IRAQ

Azizi, Anthony (Actor)
c/o Karen Embry *Sky Unlimited Arts*
7510 Sunset Blvd.
#554
Los Angeles, CA 90046, USA

Azlan, Muhibuddin Shah (King)
Sultan's Palace
Istana Bukit Serene
Kuala Lumpur, MALAYSIA

Azlynn, Valerie (Actor)
c/o Devon Jackson *Trademark Talent*
4758 Allott Avenue
Sherman Oaks, CA 91423-2403, USA

Azmi, Shabana (Actor, Bollywood)
702 Sagar Samrat
Greenfields Juhu
Mumbai, MS 400049, INDIA

Aznar, Jose Maria (Prime Minister)
Prime Minister's Office
Complejo de las Moncloa
Madrid 28071, SPAIN

Aznavour, Charles (Actor, Musician, Songwriter, Writer)
Agents Associes (AA)
210 rue du Faubourg st
Honore, PARIS, FRANCE

Azoff, Irving (Business Person)
244 Ladera Dr
Beverly Hills, CA 90210, USA

Azria, Max (Designer, Fashion Designer)
2761 Fruitland Ave
Vemon, CA 90058, USA

Azrieli, David (Architect)
The Azrieli Foundation
1010 St. Catherine St W
Suite 1200
Montreal, Quebec H3B 3S3, Canada

Azul Azul (Music Group)
c/o Staff Member *Sony Music Miami*
605 Lincoln Rd Fl 7
Miami Beach, FL 33139, USA

Azuma, Norio (Artist)
276 Riverside Dr
New York, NY 10025, USA

Azuma, Takamitsu (Architect)
Azuma Architects
3-6-1 Minami-Aoyama
Minatoku
Tokyo 107, JAPAN

Azumah, Jerry (Athlete, Football Player)
462 W Superior St
Chicago, IL 60610, USA

Azzara, Candice (Actor)

Azzaro, Chrissy (Designer, Fashion Designer)
c/o Staff Member *Perception Public Relations LLC*
3940 Laurel Canyon Blvd
Suite 169
Studio City, CA 91604, USA

Azzi, Jennifer (Athlete, Basketball Player, Olympic Athlete)
307 Lowell Ave
Mill Valley, CA 94941-3897, USA

B

B, Jon (Musician, Songwriter, Writer)
Devour Mgmt
6399 Wilshire Blvd
#426
Los Angeles, CA 90048, USA

B2K (Music Group)
c/o Staff Member *Pyramid Entertainment Group*
377 Rector Pl #21A
New York, NY 10280-1439, USA

B-52's (Music Group)
c/o Staff Member *Astralwerks Records*
150 Fifth Ave
4th Floor
New York, NY 10011, USA

Baab, Mike (Athlete, Football Player)
1705 Windlea Cir
Euless, TX 76040, USA

Baab, Mike (Athlete, Football Player)
PO Box 1808
Euless, TX 76039, us

Baack, Steve (Athlete, Football Player)
14370 SW Wilson Dr
Beaverton, OR 97008, us

Baack, Steve (Athlete, Football Player)
12322 SW Autumn View St
Portland, OR 97224, USA

Baas, David (Athlete, Football Player)
1701 Homestead Rd
Santa Clara, CA 95050, USA

Baas, David (Athlete, Football Player)
7004 Lacantera Cir
Lakewood Ranch, FL 34202, us

Baba, Enclik Abdul Ghafar Bin (Prime Minister)
Rural Development Ministry
Jalan Raja Laut
Kuala Lumpur 50606, MALAYSIA

Babando, Pete (Athlete, Hockey Player)
95 Main St
South Porcupine, ON PON 1HO, Canada

Babashoff, Jack (Athlete, Olympic Athlete, Swimmer)
17254 Santa Clara St
Fountain Valley, CA 92708-3337, USA

Babashoff, Shirley (Athlete, Olympic Athlete, Swimmer)
17254 Santa Clara St
Fountain Valley, CA 92708, USA

Babatunde, Obba (Actor)
Stone Manners
6500 Wilshire Blvd #550
Los Angeles, CA 90048, USA

Babb, Charlie (Athlete, Football Player)
371 Heron Ave
Naples, FL 34108, USA

Babb, Eugene (Gene) (Athlete, Football Player)
5110 W 9th Ave
Stillwater, OK 74074, USA

Babbar, Raj (Actor, Bollywood)
Nepathaya Plot 20
Gulmohar Road JVPD Scheme
Mumbai, MS 400049, INDIA

Babbit, Jamie (Director, Producer, Writer)
c/o Staff Member *Innovative Artists (LA)*
1505 10th St
Santa Monica, CA 90401, USA

Babbitt, Bruce E (Politician)
5169 Watson St NW
Washington, DC 20016-5330, USA

Babbs, Durrell (Tank) (Musician)
c/o Amy Malone *GIC Public Relations*
Prefers to be contacted via email or telephone
Los Angeles, CA 90069, USA

Babb-Sprague, Kristen (Swimmer)
4677 Pine Valley Dr
Stockton, CA 95219, USA

Babcock, Barbara (Actor)
PO Box 222271
Carmel, CA 93922, USA

Babcock, Bob (Athlete, Baseball Player)
7123 Fairway Dr
Butler, PA 16001-8597, USA

Babcock, Mike (Athlete, Hockey Player)
Detroit Red Wings
600 Civic Center Dr
Detroit, MI 48226-4419, USA

Babcock, Mike (Athlete, Coach, Hockey Player)
c/o Staff Member *Detroit Red Wings*
Joe Luis Arena
600 Civic Center Dr
Detroit, MI 48226, USA

Babcock, Tim M (Politician)
Ox Bow Ranch
PO Box 877
Helena, MT 59624-0877, USA

Babcock, Todd (Actor)
c/o Staff Member *Gage Group, The (LA)*
14724 Ventura Blvd
Suite 505
Sherman Oaks, CA 91403, USA

Babe, Warren (Athlete, Hockey Player)
15 Rocky Mtn Blvd W
Lethbridge, AB T1K 6V7, Canada

Babenco, Hector E (Director)
c/o Johnnie Planco *Parseghian Planco LLC*
322 8th Ave
Suite 601
New York, NY 10001, USA

Baber, Billy (Athlete, Football Player)
16292 S Chester St
Olathe, KS 22932, USA

Babers, Roderick (Athlete, Football Player)
11838 Murr Way
Houston, TX 77048, USA

Babic, Milos (Athlete, Basketball Player)
1500 Doris Dr
Cookeville, TN 38501-2026, USA

Babich, Bob (Athlete, Football Player)
4994 Mt Ashmun Dr
San Diego, CA 92111, USA

Babilonia, Tai (Athlete, Figure Skater, Olympic Athlete)
13889 Valley Vista Blvd
Sherman Oaks, CA 90423, USA

Babin, Jason (Athlete, Football Player)
2735 Peninsulas Dr
Missouri City, TX 77459, USA

Babin, Mitch (Athlete, Hockey Player)
519 Pleasant St
Apt 306
Leominster, MA 01453-6219, USA

Babin, Rex (Cartoonist, Editor)
Sacramento Bee
Editorial Dept 21st & Q Sts
Sacramento, CA 95852, USA

Babineaux, Jonathan (Athlete, Football Player)
2362 Strand Ave
Lawrenceville, GA 30043, USA

Babineaux, Jordan (Athlete, Football Player)
801 Dewalt Ave
Port Arthur, TX 77640, USA

Babinecz, John (Athlete, Football Player)
810 Trout Run Dr
Malvern, PA 19355, USA

Babitt, Shooty (Athlete, Baseball Player)
4912 Plaza Way
Richmond, CA 94804-4346, USA

Babka, Richard (Rink) (Athlete, Olympic Athlete)
2104 Lido Cir
Stockton, CA 95207-6016, USA

Babu, Ganesh (Actor)
No 1 Janaki Avenue
Abhiramapuram
Chennai, TN 600 028, INDIA

Baby, John (Athlete, Hockey Player)
252 Brebeut Ave
Sudbury, ON P3C 5H1, Canada

Baby, Peggy (Actor)
2219 Canyon Brook Lane
Newman, CA 95360, USA

Babych, Dave (Athlete, Hockey Player)
1315 Wellington Crest
Winnipeg, MB R3N 0A9, Canada

Babych, Wayne (Athlete, Hockey Player)
1315 Wellington Crest
Winnipeg, MB R3N 0A9, Canada

Baca, Edward (General)
US Army Headquarters the Pentagon
Washington, DC 20310-0001, USA

Baca, Jason Aaron (Race Car Driver)
17781 Cherokee Trail
Los Gatos, CA 95023, USA

Baca, Jimmy Santiago (Writer)
c/o Staff Member *Blue Flower Arts*
P.O. Box 1361
Millbrook, NY 12545, USA

Baca, Joe (Congressman, Politician)
2366 Rayburn HOB
Washington, DC 20515, USA

Baca, John P (General)
PO Box 154
Julian, CA 92036-0154, USA

Bacall, Lauren (Actor)
Dakota Hotel
1 W 72nd St
Apt 43
New York, NY 10023, USA

Bacasihua, Jason (Athlete, Hockey Player)
23411 Annapolis St
Dearborn Heights, MI 48125-2200, USA

Baccaglio, Marty (Athlete, Football Player)
15030 Montebello Rd
Cupertino, CA 95014, USA

Baccarin, Morena (Actor)
2979 Ingledale Terrace
Los Angeles, CA 90039, USA

Bach, Barbara (Actor)
918 N Hillcrest Rd
Beverly Hills, CA 90210, USA

Bach, Catherine (Actor)
15930 Woodvale Rd
Encino, CA 91436, USA

Bach, David (Writer)
c/o Jan Miller *Dupree Miller & Associates*
100 Highland Park Village
Suite 250
Dallas, TX 75205, USA

Bach, Emmanuelle (Actor)
Artmedia
20 Ave Rapp
Paris 75007, FRANCE

Bach, Jillian (Actor)
c/o Staff Member *Metropolitan (MTA)*
4526 Wilshire Blvd
Los Angeles, CA 90010, USA

Bach, John (Athlete, Basketball Player)
182 W Lake St Apt 21e6
Chicago, IL 60601-1126, USA

Bach, Pamela (Actor)
c/o Nelson Parks *ESI Network*
6310 San Vicente Blvd #340
Los Angeles, CA 90048, United States

Bach, Richard (Writer)
Dell Publishing
1540 Broadway
New York, NY 10036-4039, USA

Bach, Sebastian (Actor, Music Group)
99 Swimming River Rd
Lincroft, NJ 07738, USA

Bachan, Abhishek (Bollywood)
Pratiksha, 10th Rd
JVPD Scheme
Mumbai 400049, INDIA

Bachar, Carmit (Musician)
5778 Bucknell Ave
Valley Village, CA 91607, USA

Bacharach, Burt (Composer, Musician)
681 Amalfi Dr
Pacific Palisades, CA 90272, USA

Bachardy, Don (Writer)
145 Adelaide Dr
Santa Monica, CA 90402, USA

Bachchan, Abhishek (Actor, Bollywood)
c/o Simone Sheffield *Canyon Entertainment*
P.O. Box 256
Palm Springs, CA 92263, USA

Bachchan, Amitabh (Actor, Bollywood)
Pratiksha
10th Road Juhu Scheme
Mumbai, MS 400049, India

Bachchan, Jaya (Actor, Bollywood)
Pratiksha 10rh Road
JVPD Scheme
Mumbai, MS 400049, INDIA

Bachelart, Eric (Race Car Driver)
7326 W 88th Street
Indianapolis, IN 46278, USA

Bacher, Avron (Ali) (Cricketer, Misc)
United Cricket Board
PO Box 55009
Northlands 2116, SOUTH AFRICA

Bachleda-Curus, Alicja (Actor)
2966 Passmore Dr
Los Angeles, CA 90068, USA

Bachman, Jay (Athlete, Football Player)
4602 Delphene Cir
Louisville, KY 40241, USA

Bachman, Michelle (Congressman, Politician)
103 Cannon HOB
Washington, DC 20515, USA

Bachman, Randy (Music Group, Songwriter, Writer)
Entertainment Services
6400 Pleasant Park Dr
Chanhassen, MN 55317, USA

Bachman, Tal (Music Group, Musician, Songwriter, Writer)
Q Prime
729 7th Ave #1600
New York, NY 10019, USA

Bachman, Ted (Athlete, Football Player)
2890 Huntington Blvd
Apt 110
Fresno, CA 93721, USA

Bachmann, Maria (Music Group, Musician)
c/o Staff Member *Above the Line*
Goethestr 17
Munich D-80336, GERMANY

Bachmann, Michele (Congressman, Politician)
412 Cannon HOB
Washington, DC 20515, USA

Bachrach, Louis F Jr (Photographer)
Bachrach Inc
647 Boylston St #2
Boston, MA 02116, USA

Bachus, Spencer (Congressman, Politician)
2246 Rayburn HOB
Washington, DC 20515, USA

Bacic, Steve (Actor, Producer)
c/o Staff Member *Pipeline Productions*
25715 Haskell
Taylor, MI 48180, USA

Baciocco, Albert Juozas Cardinal (Admiral)
747 Pitt St
Mount Pleasant, SC 29464, USA

Backe, Brandon (Athlete, Baseball Player)
103 E Viejo Dr
Friendswood, TX 77546-5550, USA

Backe, John D (Business Person)
Backe Group
83 General Warren Blvd #100
Malvem, PA 19355, USA

Backer, Brian (Actor)
400 E. 56th St. #17E
New York, NY 10022, USA

Backes, David (Athlete, Hockey Player)
323 N Forsyth Blvd
Saint Louis, MO 63105-3617, USA

Backhaus, Robin (Athlete, Olympic Athlete, Swimmer)
PO Box 6271
Ocean View, HI 96737-6271, USA

Backis, Audrys Juozas Cardinal (Religious Leader)
Sventaragio 4
Vilnius, LITHUANIA

Backley, Stephen (Steve) (Athlete, Track Athlete)
Cambridge Harriers
56A-60 Glenhurst Ave
Bexley, Kent DA5 3QN, UNITED KINGDOM (UK)

Backlund, Bob (Athlete, Wrestler)
P.O. Box 973
Glastonbury, CT06033 USA

Backman, Jules (Economist, Writer)
59 Crane Road
Scarsdale, NY 10583, USA

Backman, Mike (Athlete, Hockey Player)
50 Pond Pl
Cos Cob, CT 06807-2220, USA

Backman, Wally (Athlete, Baseball Player)
Binghamton Mets PO Box 598
Attn: Managers Office
Binghamton, NY 13902-0598, USA

Backman, Walter W (Wally) (Athlete, Baseball Player)
241 SE Mercury Ln
Prineville, OR 97754-2803, USA

Backstreet Boys (Music Group)
c/o John Marx *WME (LA)*
9601 Wilshire Blvd Fl 3
Beverly Hills, CA 90210, USA

Backstrom, Niklas (Athlete, Hockey Player)
100 3rd AveS Unit 3604
Minneapolis, MN 55401-2732, USA

Backstrom, Ralph (Athlete, Hockey Player)
220 Habitat Circle
Windsor, CO 80550-6196, USA

Backus, Billy (Boxer)
308 N Main St
Canastota, NY 13032, USA

Backus, George E (Geophysicist, Physicist)
9362 La Jolla Farms Road
La Jolla, CA 92037, USA

Backus, Gus (Musician)
Lustig Talent
PO Box 770850
Orlando, FL 32877, USA

Backus, Jeff (Athlete, Football Player)
48075 Bellagio Ct
Northville, MI 48167, USA

Backus, John (Mathematician)
970 Garden Way
Ashland, OR 97520-3416, USA

Backus, Sharon (Coach)
University of California
Athletic Dept
Los Angeles, CA 90024, USA

Bacon, Edmund N (Architect)
1025 North 4th Street
Apt D
Philadelphia, PA 19123-1533, USA

Bacon, Henry (Athlete, Basketball Player)
10103 Grand Ave
Apt 218
Louisville, KY 40299-3145, USA

Bacon, Kelvin (Actor)
PO Box 668
Sharon, CT 06069, USA

Bacon, Kevin (Actor)
2800 Glendower Ave
Los Angeles, CA 90027, USA

Bacon, Michael (Actor)
12 Garnet Rd
Roxbury, CT 06783, USA

Bacon, Roger F (Admiral)
24285 Johnson Road NW
Poulsbo, WA 98370, USA

Bacon, Waine (Athlete, Football Player)
2900 McFarland Blvd E
Apt 516
Tuscaloosa, AL 35405, USA

Bacon Brothers, The (Music Group)
c/o Staff Member Paradigm (Monterey)
404 W Franklin St
Monterey, CA 93940, USA

Bacot, J Carter (Financier)
48 Porter Place
Montclair, NJ 07042, USA

Bacsik, Mike (Athlete, Baseball Player)
4014 Falcon Lake Dr
Arlington, TX 76016-4126, USA

Bacsik, Mike (Athlete, Baseball Player)
1126 N Clinton Ave
Dallas, TX 75208-3613, USA

Bacuicchi, Antonello (Misc)
Co-Regent's Office
Government Palace
San Marino 47031, SAN MARINO

Bada, Jeffrey (Misc)
Scripps Institute of Oceanography
Chemistry Dept
La Jolla, CA 92093, USA

Badalamenti, Angelo (Composer,
Musician)
11 Fidelian Way
Lincoln Park, NJ 07035, USA

Badalucco, Michael (Actor)
516 Highland Ave
#1A
Manhattan Beach, CA 90266, USA

Badar, Rich (Athlete, Football Player)
5877 Riceland Dr
Newburgh, IN 47630, USA

Badawi, Abdullah Ahamad (Prime
Minister)
Prime Minister's Office
Jalan Dato Onn
Kuala Lumpur 50502, MALAYSIA

Baddeley, Aaron (Athlete, Golfer)
8606 E Via Del Sol
Scottsdale, AZ 85255, USA

Baddiel, David (Actor, Writer)
c/o Staff Member Lip Service Casting Ltd
60-66 Wardour St
London W1F 0TA, UK

Baddoo, Agnes (Stylist)
c/o Staff Member Rex Agency, The
6311 Romaine St
Los Angeles, CA 90038, USA

Bade, Lance (Athlete, Olympic Athlete,
Shooter)
9491 Berry Ln
Colorado Springs, CO 80925-1320, USA

Badel, Sarah (Actor)
c/o Staff Member The Rights House (UK)
Drury House
34-43 Russell St
London WC2B 5HA, UK

Badelt, Klaus (Musician)
*c/o John Tempereau Soundtrack Music
Assoc*
1460 4th St
Suite 308
Santa Monica, CA 90401, USA

Badenhop, Burke (Athlete, Baseball
Player)
402 Berkshire Dr
Perrysburg, OH 43551-1281, USA

Bader, Beth (Athlete, Golfer)
713 S 7th St
Eldridge, IA 52748, USA

Bader, Diedrich (Actor)
131 N June St
Los Angeles, CA 90004, USA

Bader, Larry (Athlete, Hockey Player,
Olympic Athlete)
1413 Westwood Dr SW
Fairbault, MN 55021, USA

Baderinwa, Sade (Correspondent)
WABC-TV
7 Lincoln Sq
New York NY, 1003

Badger, Brad (Athlete, Football Player)
2552 Milleford Ct
Pleasanton, CA 94588, USA

Badgley, Mark (Fashion Designer)
c/o Staff Member Badgley Mischka
550 7th Ave
22nd Floor
New York, NY 10018, USA

Badgley, Penn (Actor)
c/o Doug Wald Anonymous Content (LA)
3531 Hayden Ave
Culver City, CA 90232, USA

Badham, John (Director)
Badham Company
344 Clerendon Road
Beverly Hills, CA 90210, USA

Badham, Mary (Actor)
3720 Whitehall Rd
Sandy Hook, VA 23153, USA

Badie, Mina (Actor)
c/o Staff Member Rugolo Entertainment
195 S Beverly Dr
Suite 400
Beverly Hills, CA 90212, USA

Badillo, Herman (Politician)
200 E 72nd St Apt 8K
New York, NY 10021-4539, USA

Badly Drawn Boy (Music Group)
c/o Staff Member Paradigm (Monterey)
404 W Franklin St
Monterey, CA 93940, USA

Badnarik, Michael (Politician)
Badnarik Campaign Headquarters
6633 Hwy 290 E
Austin, TX 78723, USA

Badu, Erykah (Musician, Songwriter)
Badu World, Inc.
P.O. Box 25092
Arlington, VT 22202, USA

Badura-Skoda, Paul (Composer, Musician)
Zuckerkandlgass 14
Vienna 1190, AUSTRIA

Bae, Doona (Actor)
c/o David Wirtschafter WME (LA)
9601 Wilshire Blvd Fl 3
Beverly Hills, CA 90210, USA

Baechtold, James (Jim) (Athlete,
Basketball Player)
225 W Irvine St
Richmond, KY 40475-2702, USA

Baeling, Becky (Musician)
c/o Staff Member Diva Central Inc
7510 W Sunset Blvd Ste 1445
Los Angees, CA 90046, USA

Baena, Marisa (Athlete, Golfer)
4036 Lantana Ln
Plano, TX 75093-7097, USA

Baer, Gordy (Bowler)
8577 Tullamore Dr
Tinley Park, IL 60487-4774, USA

Baer, Laurie (Stylist)
580 N Raymond Ave
Apt 2
Pasadena, CA 91103-4318, USA

Baer, Neal (Actor, Producer, Writer)
Wolf Films
100 UNiversal City Plaza
Bldg 2252
Universal City, CA 91608-1085, USA

Baer, Ralph (Inventor)
134 Mayflower Dr
Manchester, NH 03104-2819, USA

Baer, Robert J (Jacob) (General)
6213 Militia Court
Fairfax Station, VA 22039, USA

Baerga, Carlos (Athlete, Baseball Player)
P.O. Box 1667
Bayamon, PR 00960-1667, USA

Baer Jr, Max (Actor, Director, Producer)
3456 Pueblo Way
Las Vegas, NV 89169, USA

Baerwald, David (Musician)

Baez, Danys (Athlete, Baseball Player)
6190 SW 114th St
Miami, FL 33156-4953, USA

Baez, Eddie (DJ)
c/o Staff Member Diva Central Inc
7510 W Sunset Blvd Ste 1445
Los Angees, CA 90046, USA

Baez, Joan (Musician, Songwriter)
510 Whisky Hill Rd
Woodside, CA 94162, USA

Baez, Jose (Athlete, Baseball Player)
1028 E Jersey St
Apt 2
Elizabeth, NJ 07201, USA

Baez, Kevin
Long Island Ducks 3 Court House Dr
Attn: Managers Office
Central Islio, NY 11722-4605, USA

Baez, Kevin (Athlete, Baseball Player)
72 Hollywood Dr
Oakdale, NY 11769-1941, USA

Baeza, Braulio (Horse Racer)
1588 Rosalind Ave
Elmont, NY 11003-1821, USA

Baeza, Braulio (Jockey)
Janice Blake
214 South George St
Ranson, WV 25438, USA

Baeza, Paloma (Actor)
PFD
Drury House
34-43 Russell St
London WC2B 5HA, USA

Bafaro, Michael (Director, Writer)
c/o Staff Member Lenhoff & Lenhoff
830 Palm Ave
West Hollywood, CA 90069

Baffert, Bob (Horse Racer)
1419 Cambridge Rd
San Marino, CA 91108-1903, USA

Baffert, Bob (Misc)
Bob Baffert Horse Training
1050 S Prairie Ave
Inglewood, CA 90301, USA

Bagabandi, Ntsaagiyn (President)
President's Office
Great Hural
Ulan Bator, MONGOLIA

Bagach, Irene (Actor, Model)
Models One
12 Macklin St
Covent Garden
London WC2B 5SZ, UNITED KINGDOM

Bagdasarian Jr, Ross (Actor, Producer)
c/o Staff Member Bagdasarian Productions
1192 E Mountain Dr
Montecito, CA 93108

Bagge, Peter (Artist)
c/o Staff Member Fantagraphics Books
7563 Lake City Way
Seattle, WA 98115, USA

Baggetta, Vincent (Actor)
3928 Madelia Ave
Sherman Oaks, CA 91403, USA

Baggio, Roberto (Soccer Player)
Bologna FC
Via Casteldebole 10
Bologna 40132, ITALY

Bagian, James P (Astronaut)
21537 Holmbury Road
Northville, MI 48167, USA

Bagian, James P Dr (Astronaut)
21537 Holm bury Rd
Northville, MI 48167-1021, USA

Bagian, James P Dr
21537 Holm bury Rd
Northville, MI 48167-1021, USA

Bagley, John (Athlete, Basketball Player)
31W450 Circle Dr
Elgin, IL 60120-4784, USA

Bagley, Tom (Race Car Driver)
109 Walnut Drive
Shorewood, IL 60404, USA

Baglietto, Tara (Actor)
c/o Staff Member *Innovative Artists (NY)*
235 Park Ave S
7th Floor
New York, NY 10003, USA

Bagnal, Charles W (General)
Ratchford Assoc
221 W Springs Road
Columbia, SC 29223, USA

Bagwell, Jeffrey R (Jeff) (Athlete, Baseball Player)
405 Timberwilde Ln
Houston, TX 77024-6927, USA

Baham, Curtis (Athlete, Football Player)
5936 Oxford Pl
New Orleans, LA 70131, USA

Bahns, Maxine (Actor)
c/o Steven Jensen *Independent Group, The*
6363 Wilshire Blvd
Suite 115
Los Angeles, CA 90048, USA

Bahnsen, Ken (Athlete, Football Player)
671 N Masch Branch Rd
Denton, TX 76207, USA

Bahnsen, Stan (Athlete, Baseball Player)
3500 Blue Lake Dr
Apt 402
Pompano Beach, FL 33064-2026, USA

Bahouth, Peter (Misc)
Greenpeace
702 H St NW
Washington, DC 20001, USA

Bahr, Chris (Athlete, Football Player)
122 Kaywood Dr
Boalsburg, PA 16827, USA

Bahr, Egon (Government Official)
Ollenhauerster 1
Bonn 53113, GERMANY

Bahr, Matthew D (Matt) (Athlete, Football Player)
53 Parkridge Ln
Pittsburgh, PA 15228, USA

Bahr, Morton (Misc)
Communications Workers Union
501 3rd St NW
Washington, DC 20001, USA

Bahr, Sherry (Stylist)
c/o Staff Member *Arlene Wilson Management*
807 N Jefferson St
#200
Milwaukee, WI 53202, USA

Bahr, Walter (Athlete, Olympic Athlete, Soccer Player)
PO Box 312
Boalsburg, PA 16827-0312, USA

Bahrke, Shannon (Athlete, Olympic Athlete, Skier)
3556 Crestwood Dr
Salt Lake City, UT 84109-3206, USA

Bai, Pandari (Actor, Bollywood)
54 Pillayar Koil Street
Vadapalani
Chennai, TN 600026, INDIA

Bai, Yang (Actor)
978 Huashan Road
Shanghai 200050, CHINA

Bailar, Benjamin F (Educator, Government Official)
410 Walnut Road
Lake Forest, IL 60045, USA

Bailes, Margaret (Athlete, Olympic Athlete, Track Athlete)
11136 Vista Sorrento Pkwy #203
San Diego, CA 92130-7606, USA

Bailes, Scott (Athlete, Baseball Player)
5895 S Teters Ct
Springfield, MO 65804-7720, USA

Bailey, Ben (Actor, Television Host)
PO Box 113
Brookside, NJ 07926, USA

Bailey, Bob (Athlete, Hockey Player)
3190 W. 140th St.
Cleveland, OH 44111, USA

Bailey, Buddy (Athlete)
PO Box 590
Amherst, VA 24521-0590, USA

Bailey, Chris (Athlete, Hockey Player, Olympic Athlete)
13510 High Stone Cir
Pittsford, NY 14534, USA

Bailey, Claron (Athlete, Football Player)
7246 E Lakeview Ave
Mesa, AZ 85209, USA

Bailey, Cory (Athlete, Baseball Player)
10877 Paulton Rd
Pittsburg, IL 62974-1705, USA

Bailey, Cynthia (Model, Reality TV Star)
c/o Marcus Jackson *Caliber Models & Talent*
PO Box 79065
Atlanta, GA 30309, USA

Bailey, Damon (Athlete, Basketball Player)
723 Diamond Rd
Heltonville, IN 47436-8559, USA

Bailey, David (Athlete, Football Player)
1916 NE 29th St
Oklahoma City, OK 73111, USA

Bailey, David (Photographer)
Camera Eye Ltd
24-26 Brownlow Mews
London, WC1N 2LA, England

Bailey, David "Homer" (Athlete, Baseball Player)
4327 0 Quinn Branch Rd
La Grange, TX 78945-5695, USA

Bailey, Don (Athlete, Football Player)
14831 NW 7th Ave
Miami, FL 33168, USA

Bailey, Edwin (Athlete, Football Player)
3677 Cypress Point Dr
Augusta, GA 30907, USA

Bailey, Eion (Actor)
5601 Briarcliff Rd
Los Angeles, CA 90068, USA

Bailey, Elmer (Athlete, Football Player)
P.O. Box 551991
Opa Locka, FL 33055, USA

Bailey, F Lee (Attorney)
6231 Tidewater Island Cir
Ft Myers, FL 33908, USA

Bailey, Garnet "Ace" (Athlete, Hockey Player)

Bailey, GW (Actor)
22415 La Rochelle Dr
Santa Clarita, CA 91350, USA

Bailey, Harold (Athlete, Football Player)
22502 Prince George Ln
Katy, TX 77449, USA

Bailey, HB (Race Car Driver)
PO Box 450288
Houston, TX 77045, USA

Bailey, Howard (Athlete, Baseball Player)
11674 156th Ave
West Olive, MI 49460-9388, USA

Bailey, Jeff (Athlete, Baseball Player)
709 N 18th Ave
Kelso, WA 98626-5036, USA

Bailey, Jennifer (Stylist)
22606 Ironwood Rd
Lakeville, MN 55044, USA

Bailey, Jerry (Horse Racer)
9891 Winding Ridge Ln
Davie, FL 33324-7606, USA

Bailey, Jim (Athlete, Football Player)
5219 Stone Creek Ct
Lawrence, KS 66049, USA

Bailey, Jim (Athlete, Baseball Player)
250 Cade Rd
Ten Mile, TN 37880-2149, USA

Bailey, John (Cinematographer)
United Talent Agency
9560 Wilshire Blvd
#500
Beverly Hills, CA 90212, USA

Bailey, Karsten (Athlete, Football Player)
16 Salbide Ave
Newnan, GA 30263, USA

Bailey, Keith E (Business Person)
Williams Companies
1 One Williams Center
Tulsa, OK 74172, USA

Bailey, Leonard L (Doctor)
Loma Linda University Medical School
Loma Linda, CA 92350, USA

Bailey, Mark (Athlete, Football Player)
3229 Corniche Ln
Roseville, CA 95661, USA

Bailey, Mark (Athlete, Baseball Player)
32703 Waltham Xing
Fulshear, TX 77441-4203, USA

Bailey, Mark (Athlete, Baseball Player)
Tri-City Valleycats PO Box 694
Attn: Coaching Staff
Troy, NY 12181-0694, USA

Bailey, Maxwell C (General)
306 2nd St
Paris, KY 40361, USA

Bailey, Michael (Doctor)
Northwestern University
Psychology Dept
Evanston, IL 60208, USA

Bailey, Norman S (Opera Singer)
84 Warham Road
South Croydon, Surrey CR2 6LB, UNITED KINGDOM (UK)

Bailey, Otha (Athlete, Baseball Player)
937 6th Pl SW
Birmingham, AL 35211-1743, USA

Bailey, Palmer (Astronaut)
64710 Knob Hill Rd
Anchor Point, AK 99556-9160, USA

Bailey, Paul (Writer)
79 Davisville Road
London W12 9SH, UNITED KINGDOM (UK)

Bailey, Philip (Musician)
c/o Staff Member *Richard De La Font Agency*
3808 W South Park Blvd
Broken Arrow, OK 74011, USA

Bailey, Preston (Actor)
c/o Staff Member *Elements Entertainment*
312 W 5th St Apt 815
Los Angeles, CA 90013, USA

Bailey, Razzy (Musician, Songwriter, Writer)
Doc Sedelmeier
PO Box 62
Geneva, NE 68361, USA

Bailey, Robert M (Athlete, Football Player)
15325 SW 99th Ave
Miami, FL 33157, USA

Bailey, Roger (Athlete, Baseball Player)
1445 Forest Trails Dr
Castle Pines, CO 80108-8298, USA

Bailey, Roland (Champ) (Athlete, Football Player)
9071 E Mississippi Ave #28A
Denver, CO 80247, USA

Bailey, Scott (Actor)
c/o Staff Member *Stone Manners Salners Agency (LA)*
9911 W Pico Blvd Ste 1400
Los Angeles, CA 90035, USA

Bailey, Sean (Producer)
c/o Patrick Whitesell *WME (LA)*
9601 Wilshire Blvd Fl 3
Beverly Hills, CA 90210, USA

Bailey, Stacey (Athlete, Football Player)
3400 Lakewind Way
Alpharetta, GA 30005, USA

Bailey, Steve (Athlete, Baseball Player)
4600 Queen Anne Ave
Lorain, OH 44052-5648, USA

Bailey, Steven W (Reality TV Star)
c/o Scott Fedro *Lone Star Entertainment*
139 S Beverly Drive
Suite 314
Beverly Hills, CA 90212-3040, USA

Bailey, Teddy (Athlete, Football Player)
7825 Elbrook Ave
Cincinnati, OH 45237, USA

Bailey, Thomas H (Financier)
Janus Capital Corp
720 S Colorado Blvd
Suite 290A
Denver, CO 80246, USA

Bailey, Thurl (Athlete, Basketball Player)
10265 N 6960 West
Highland, UT 84003-9337, USA

Bailey, T Wayne (Activist, Politician)
Stetson University
Political Science Dept
Stetson, FL 32720, USA

Bailey, Victor (Athlete, Football Player)
1405 Oglethorpe Ave
Urbana, IL 61802, USA

Bailey, Welby (Buddy) (Athlete, Baseball Player)
PO Box 590
Amherst, VA 24521-0590, USA

Bailey II, Irving W (Business Person)
Providian Corp
400 W Market St
Louisville, KY 40202, USA

Bailey Rae, Corinne (Musician)
Running Media Group
14 Victoria Road
Douglas, Isle of Man IM2 4ER, BRITISH ISLES

Baillargeon, Joel (Athlete, Hockey Player)
165b Rue du Coutelier
Saint-Augustin-De-Desmaures, QC G3A 2J7, Canada

Bailon, Adrienne (Actor, Musician)
c/o Staff Member *FYI Public Relations*
174 5th Ave
Suite 404
New York, NY 10010, USA

Bailor, Bob (Athlete, Baseball Player)
1950 Swan Ln
Palm Harbor, FL 34683-6275, USA

Baily, Kirk (Actor)
c/o Staff Member *Independent Artists Agency*
9601 Wilshire Blvd.
Suite 750
Beverly Hills, CA 90210, USA

Bailyn, Bernard (Historian)
170 Clifton St
Belmont, MA 02478, USA

Bain, Barbara (Actor)
831 S Sunsmuir Ave
Los Angeles, CA 90036, USA

Bain, Conrad (Actor)
900 E Stanley Blvd
Livermore, CA 94550, USA

Bain, Rod (General)
2406 E 27th Ave
Anchorage, AK 99508-4137, USA

Bain, William E (Bill) (Athlete, Football Player)
27661 Paseo Barona
San Juan Capistrano, CA 92675, USA

Bainbridge, Merril (Musician, Songwriter, Writer)
001 Productions
PO Box 1760
Collingswood, VIC 3068, AUSTRALIA

Baines, Harold (Athlete, Baseball Player)
Chicago White Sox 333 W 35th St
Attn Coaching Staff
Chicago, IL 60616-3696, USA

Baines, Harold D (Athlete, Baseball Player)
9206 Martingham Dr
Saint Michaels, MD 21663-2222, USA

Baio, Scott (Actor)
20524 Chatsboro Dr
Woodland Hills, CA 91364, USA

Baiocchi, Hugh (Athlete, Golfer)
3656 Half Moon Dr
Orlando, FL 32812-3816, USA

Bair, Doug (Athlete, Baseball Player)
11545 Kemper Woods Dr
Cincinnati, OH 45249-1753, USA

Baird, Allard (Commentator)
1425 Brickell Ave
APt 62C
Miami, FL 33131-3424, USA

Baird, Bill (Athlete, Football Player)
6050 E Heaton Ave
Fresno, CA 93727, USA

Baird, Briny (Athlete, Golfer)
3340 SW Rivers End Way
Palm City, FL 34990, USA

Baird, Butch (Athlete, Golfer)
P.O. Box 2663
Carefree, AZ 85377-2663, USA

Baird, Diora (Actor)
c/o Lena Roklin *Luber Roklin Management*
8530 Wilshire Blvd
6th Floor
Beverly Hills, CA 90211, USA

Baird, James M (Religious Leader)
Presbyterian Church
PO Box 1428
Decatur, GA 30031, USA

baird, jenni (Actor)
c/o Michael P Levine *Levine Management*
9028 W Sunset Blvd #PH1
Los Angeles, CA 90069, USA

Baird, Ken (Athlete, Hockey Player)
Lot 4
Berry Bay
Snow Lake, MB R0B 1M0, Canada

Baird, Stuart (Director)
c/o Staff Member *Mirisch Agency*
8840 Wilshire Blvd
Suite 100
Beverly Hills, CA 90211, USA

Bairstow, Scott H (Actor)
c/o Andrea Pett-Joseph *Brillstein Entertainment Partners*
9150 Wilshire Blvd #350
Beverly Hills, CA 90212, USA

Baisden, Michael (Producer, Radio Personality, Writer)
Baisden Enterprises Inc
13901 Midway Rd
#102-274
Dallas, TX 75244, USa

Baisley, Jeff (Athlete, Baseball Player)
16222 Pebblebrook Dr
Tamoa, FL 33624-1072, USA

Baitz, Jon Robin (Producer)
c/o Simon Halls *Slate Public Relations*
9000 Sunset Blvd #915
West Hollywood, CA 90069, USA

Baiul, Oksana (Figure Skater)
c/o Phil Viardo *The Viardo Agency*
8484 Wilshire Blvd
Suite 220
Beverly Hills, CA 90211, USA

Baiyewe, Tunde (Musician)
c/o Staff Member *Kitchenware Management*
The Stables
St. Thomas Street
Newcastle Upon Tyne NE1 4LE, UK

Bajanowsky, Louis J (Architect)
Cambridge Seven Assoc
1050 Massachusetts Ave
Cambridge, MA 02138, USA

Bajardi, Lane (Television Host)
c/o Staff Member *Bloomberg Television*
731 Lexington Ave
New York, NY 10022, USA

Bajcsy, Ruzena (Engineer)
University of California
Electrical Engineering Dept
Berkeley, CA 94720, USA

Bajema, Billy (Athlete, Football Player)
2605 SW 120th St
Oklahoma City, OK 73170, USA

Bajenaru, Jeff (Athlete, Baseball Player)
3717 E Megan St
Gilbert, AZ 85295-4818, USA

Bajpai, Manoj (Actor, Bollywood)
304 Victoria Shastrinagar
Lokhandwala Complex Andheri(W)
Mumbai, MS 4000593, INDIA

Bakalyan, Richard (Actor)
1070 S Bedford St
Los Angeles, CA 90035, USA

Bakanic, Laddie (Athlete, Gymnast, Olympic Athlete)
7 David Ter
White Plains, NY 10603-3516, USA

Bakatin, Vadim V (Government Official)
Kotelnicheskaya Nab 17
Moscow 103240, RUSSIA

Bakay, Nick (Actor)
1437 Bluebird Ave
West Hollywood, CA 90069, USA

Bakenhaster, Dave (Athlete, Baseball Player)
3710 Rome Corners Rd
Galena, OH 43021-9490, USA

Baker, Al (Athlete, Football Player)
2784 Trinity Ct
Avon, OH 44011, USA

Baker, Anita (Actor, Musician, Songwriter)
2 Dodge Pl
Grosse Pointe, MI 482300, USA

Baker, Art (Athlete, Football Player)
24 Quail Hollow Rd # B
Mashpee, MA 02649, us

Baker, Art (Athlete, Football Player)
247 Main St
Buzzards Bay, MA 02532, USA

Baker, Becky Ann
484 W. 43rd St. #31H
New York, NY 10036, USA

Baker, Bill (Athlete, Hockey Player, Olympic Athlete)
5638 Ojibwa Rd
Brainerd, MN 56401-7017, USA

Baker, Blanche (Actor)
2501 Palisade Ave #B2
Bronx, NY 10463, USA

Baker, Brad (Race Car Driver)
565 Brick Church Park Dr.
Nashville, TN 37207-3219, USA

Baker, Brenda (Actor)
Agency for Performing Arts
9200 Sunset Blvd #900
Los Angeles, CA 90069, USA

Baker, Buddy (Race Car Driver)
4860 Moonlite Bay Dr
Sherrills Ford, NC 28673, USA

Baker, Carroll (Actor)
Abrams Artists
9200 Sunset Blvd
#1125
Los Angeles, CA 90069, USA

Baker, Charles (Actor)
c/o Linda McAlister *Linda McAlister Talent*
100 Oak Ln
Waxahachie, TX 75167-8412, USA

Baker, Charles (Charlie) (Athlete, Football Player)
P.O. Box 112593
Carrollton, TX 75011, USA

Baker, Christine (Stylist)
c/o Celebrity Stylist *Artists by Timothy Priano (NY)*
15 Watts St
6th Floor
New York, NY 10013, USA

Baker, Chuck (Athlete, Baseball Player)
3035 Mescalero Dr
Lake Havasu City, AZ 86404-9605, USA

Baker, Colin (Actor)
Evans & Reiss
100 Fawe Park Road
London SW15 2EA, UNITED KINGDOM (UK)

Baker, Danny (Radio Personality)
c/o Staff Member *Noel Gay Artists*
19 Denmark St
London WC2H 8NA, United Kingdom

Baker, Dave (Athlete, Baseball Player)
1207 N 6th St Apt 7
Indianola, IA 50125-4747, USA

Baker, Diane (Actor)
2733 Outpost Dr
Los Angeles, CA 90068, USA

Baker, Donald K (Cinematographer)
11789 Lakeshore N
Auburn, CA 95602, USA

Baker, Doug (Athlete, Baseball Player)
116 Woodthrush Ln
Fallbrook, CA 92028-4149, USA

Baker, Dusty (Athlete, Baseball Player)
Cincinnati Reds 100 Joe Nuxhall Way
Attn Managers Office
Cincinnati, OH 45202-4109, USA

Baker, Dylan (Actor)
484 W 43rd St #31H
New York, NY 10036, USA

Baker, Earl P Jr (War Hero)
10100 Cypress Cove Dr
Fort Myers, FL 33908, USA

Baker, Edward (Athlete, Football Player)
74 Page Hill Rd
Far Hills, NJ 07931, USA

Baker, Edward Dr
74 Page Hill Rd
Far Hills, NJ 07931, us

Baker, Ellen Dr (Astronaut)
2207 Garden Stream Ct
Houston, TX 77062-3650, USA

Baker, Ellen Shulman (Astronaut)
2207 Garden Stream Court
Houston, TX 77062, USA

Baker, Frank
PO Box 3066
Meridian, MS 39303-3066, USA

Baker, Ginger (Musician)
Twist Mgmt
4230 Del Rey Ave
#621
Marina Del Rey, CA 90292, USA

Baker, Graham (Director)
10 Buckingham St
London WC2, UNITED KINGDOM (UK)

Baker, Homer (General)
8112 S Los Feliz Dr
Tempe, AZ 85284-1711, USA

Baker, Jack (Athlete, Baseball Player)
5513 Hunters Hill Rd
Irondale, AL 35210-3011, USA

Baker, James A (Bubba) (Athlete, Football Player)
2784 Trinity Ct
Avon, OH 44011, USA

Baker, Jamie (Athlete, Hockey Player)
San Jose Sharks
525 W Santa Clara St
SanJose, CA 95113-1500

Baker, Jamie (Athlete, Hockey Player)
18590 Farragut Ln
Los Gatos, CA 95030-3045, USA

Baker, Janet A (Musician, Opera Singer)
Transart Ltd
8 Bristol Gardens
London W9 2JG, UNITED KINGDOM (UK)

Baker, Jason (Athlete, Football Player)
505 E 6th St
Unit 707
Charlotte, NC 28202, USA

Baker, Jeff Baker (Athlete, Baseball Player)
4747 Timber Ridge Dr
Dumfries, VA 22025-1081, USA

Baker, Jerry (Athlete, Football Player)
7780 W 38th Ave
Apt 305
Wheat Ridge, CO 80033, USA

Baker, Joe Don (Actor)
23339 Hatteras St
Woodland Hills, CA 91367, USA

Baker, John (Athlete, Baseball Player)
623 Alamatos Dr
Danville, CA 94526-2710, USA

Baker, Johnnie B (Dusty) (Athlete, Baseball Player, Coach)
9090 Stockhorse Ln
Granite Bay, CA 95746-7165, USA

Baker, Johnny (Athlete, Football Player)
466 Jan Kelly Ln
Houston, TX 77024, us

Baker, John W (Athlete, Football Player)
72 Oak Village Blvd S
Homosassa, FL 34446, USA

Baker, Kathy (Actor)
c/o Rebecca (Becca) Kovacik *Hofflund/Polone*
9465 Wilshire Blvd #420
Beverly Hills, CA 90212, USA

Baker, Keith (Athlete, Football Player)
3203 S Marsalis Ave
Dallas, TX 75216, USA

Baker, Ken (Journalist)
1155 7th Pl
Hermosa Beach, CA 90254, USA

Baker, Kendall L (Educator)
University of North Dakota
Lehr Memorial 201A
525 S Main Street
Ada, OH 45810, USA

Baker, Kitana (Actor)
c/o Jason Newman *Untitled Entertainment (LA)*
350 S. Beverly Dr #200
Beverly Hills, CA 90212, USA

Baker, Laurie (Athlete, Hockey Player, Olympic Athlete)
85 Monsen Rd
Concord, MA 01742, USA

Baker, Leslie David (Actor)
13952 Hartsook St
Sherman Oaks, CA 91423, USA

Baker, Lewis (Musician)
Joe Terry Mgmt
PO Box 1017
Turnersville, NJ 08012, USA

Baker, Loris (Athlete, Football Player)
1009 Brentwood Pl
Fircrest, WA 98466, USA

Baker, Michael A Captain (Astronaut)
18138 Lakeside Ln
Houston, TX 77058-4331, USA

Baker, Michael A (Mike) (Astronaut)
NASA
Johnson Space Center
2101 NASA Road
Houston, TX 77058, USA

Baker, Michael Andrew (Actor)
c/o David Chandler Secor *Daniel Hoff Agency*
5455 Wilshire Blvd
Suite 1100
Los Angeles, CA 90036, USA

Baker, Myron (Athlete, Football Player)
297 Peart Rd
Alexandria, LA 71302, USA

Baker, Paul T (Misc)
1000 Escalon Ave
#A3005
Sunnyvale, CA 94085, USA

Baker, Rae (Actor)
c/o Staff Member *Marmont Management*
Langham House
308 Regent St
London W1B 3AT, UNITED KINGDOM (UK)

Baker, Ralph (Athlete, Football Player)
36 Sunshine Cir
Lewistown, PA 17044, USA

Baker, Randy (Race Car Driver)
Speed Tech
4333 S Motorsport
Concord, NC 2802Z, USA

Baker, Ray (Actor)
11749 Chenault St
Los Angeles, CA 90049, USA

Baker, Rick (Stylist)
c/o Staff Member *Cinovation Studios*
6527 San Fernando Rd
Glendale, CA 91201, USA

Baker, Robby (Musician)
Management Trust
219 Dufferin St #309B
Toronto, ON M5K 3J1, CANADA

Baker, Robert (Actor)
c/o Amanda Glazer *Kohner Agency, The*
9300 Wilshire Blvd
Suite 555
Beverly Hills, CA 90212, USA

Baker, Robert (Attorney, Attorney General, General)
Baker Silberberg Keener
2850 Ocean Park Blvd
Santa Monica, CA 90405, USA

Baker, Ron (Athlete, Football Player)
1119 S Main St
Stillwater, OK 74074, USA

Baker, Roy Ward (Director)
c/o Staff Member *Directors Guild Of Great Britain*
4 Windmill St
London W1T 2HZ, UK

Baker, Russell (Journalist)
202 W Market St
Leesburg, VA 20176-2709, USA

Baker, Scott (Athlete, Baseball Player)
327 Lingering Ln
Henderson, NV 89012-3262, USA

Baker, Scott (Athlete, Baseball Player)
340 Johns Bluff Cir
Shreveport, LA 71106-4733, USA

Baker, Scott Thompson (Actor)
17651 Sidwell
Granada Hills, CA 91344, USA

Baker, Shaun (Actor)
c/o Staff Member *Brady, Brannon & Rich Talent*
5670 Wilshire Blvd.
Suite 820
Los Angeles, CA 90036, USA

Baker, Simon (Actor)
425 23rd S
Santa Monica, CA 90402, USA

Baker, Stephen (Athlete, Football Player)
280 Water St
Perth Amboy, NJ 08861, USA

Baker, Steve (Athlete, Hockey Player)
2431 E Cheryl Dr
Phoenix, AZ 85028-4316, USA

Baker, Steve (Athlete, Baseball Player)
27527 Easy Acres Dr
Eugene, OR 97405-4500, USA

Baker, Terry (Athlete, Football Player, Heisman Trophy Winner)
3208 SW Fairmount Blvd
Portland, OR 97239, USA

Baker, Tim
PO Box 2177
Edwards, CO 81632, us

Baker, Tom (Actor, Writer)
c/o Edward Hill *Edward Hill Management*
Dolphin House
2-5 Manchester Street
London BN2 1TF, United Kingdom

Baker, Tony (Athlete, Football Player)
3847 Eagleston Ct
High Point, NC 27265, us

Baker, Vin (Athlete, Basketball Player)
P.O. Box 179
Old Saybrook, CT 06475-0179, USA

Baker, Wayne (Athlete, Football Player)
626 Cedar Cliff Rd
Waco, KY 40385, USA

Baker, William O (Misc)
AT&T Bell Lucent Laboratory
600 Mountain Ave
New Providence, NJ 07974, USA

Baker, W Thane (Athlete, Track Athlete)
6704 Saint John Court
Granbury, TX 76049, USA

Baker-Finch, Ian (Athlete, Golfer)
849 Harbour Isle Pl
West Palm Beach, FL 33410, USA

Baker III, James A (Politician)
Baker And Botts
1299 Pennsylvania Ave
NW Ste 1200
Washington, DC 20004-2408, USA

Baker Jr, Howard H (Politician)
US Embassy
PO Box 8
Huntsville, TN 37756-0008, USA

Baker Jr, Leslie M (Business Person, Financier)
Marsh & McLennan Companies
1166 Avenue of the Americas
New York, NY 10036, USA

Bakhtair, Rudi (Correspondent)
Cable News Network
News Dept
1050 Techwood Dr NW
Atlanta, GA 30318, USA

Bakhtiar, Jim (Athlete, Football Player)
PO Box 863
Charles Town, WV 25414-0863, USA

Bakke, Brenda (Actor)
c/o Staff Member *House of Representatives, The*
1434 6th St
Suite 1
Santa Monica, CA 90401, USA

Bakkedahl, Dan (Actor)
c/o Christie Smith *Mosaic Media Group*
9200 W. Sunset Blvd
10th Floor
Los Angeles, CA 90069, USA

Bakken, James L (Jim) (Athlete, Football Player)
230 Glen Hollow Rd
Madison, WI 53705, USA

Bakken, Jill (Athlete, Bobsledder, Olympic Athlete)
23701 3rd Pl W
Bothell, WA 98021-8694, USA

Bakker, James O (Jim) (Religious Leader)
123 E End Road
Branson, MO 65616, USA

Bako, Brigitte (Actor)
8329 Anthony Cir
Los Angeles, CA 90046, USA

Bako, Paul (Athlete, Baseball Player)
500 Princeton Woods Loo^
Lafayette, LA 70508-6672, USA

Bakovic, Pete (Athlete, Hockey Player)
7991 S 47th St
Franklin, WI 53132-8468, USA

Bakshi, Ralph (Cartoonist)
PO Box 2858
Silver City, NM 88062-2858, USA

Bakula, Scott (Actor)
2540 Outpost Dr
Los Angeles, CA 90068, USA

Bala, Chris (Athlete, Hockey Player)
271 Beacon Dr
Phoenixville, PA 19460-2046, USA

Balaban, Bob (Director, Producer)
310 Highland Terr
Bridgehampton, NY 11932, USA

Balaban, Liane (Actor)
c/o Ralph Zimmerman *Great North Artists
Management Inc (Canada)*
350 Duponte
Toronto, Ontario M5R 1V9, Canada

Baladmenti, Angelo (Composer)
4146 Lankershim Blvd
#401
North Hollywood, CA 91602, USA

Balambika (Actor, Bollywood)
3 Indira Gandhi Street
Chennai, TN 600093, INDIA

Balandin, Aleksandr N (Cosmonaut)
Potcha Kosmonavtov
Moskovskoi Oblasti
Syvisdny Goroduk 141160, RUSSIA

Balas, Mike
8807 Bluehaw Meadow Ln
Katy, TX 77494-0479, USA

Balaski, Belinda (Actor)
731 N. Laurel Ave
Los Angeles, CA 90046, USA

Balassa, Sandor (Composer)
18 Sumegvar Str
Budapest 1118, HUNGARY

Balasubramaniyam, S P (Actor, Musician)
16 Kamdar Nagar
Nungambakkam
Chennai, TN 600 034, INDIA

Balaz, John (Athlete, Baseball Player)
2916 Worden St
San Diego, CA 92110-5708, USA

Balazs, Andre (Business Person)
Andre Balazs Properties
The Puck Bldg
295 Lafayette St Fl 7
New York, NY 10012, USA

Balboa, Marcelo (Soccer Player)
13139 Hedda Dr
Cerritos, CA 90703, USA

Balboni, Steve (Athlete, Baseball Player)
117 Burlington Rd
New Providence, NJ 07974-2709, USA

Balcazar, Javier Hernández (Athlete,
Soccer Player)
c/o Staff Member *Manchester United PLC*
Sir Matt Busby Way
Old Trafford
Manchester M160RA, UNITED
KINGDOM

Balcer, Rene (Producer, Writer)
c/o Adam Berkowitz *Creative Artists
Agency (CAA-LA)*
2000 Ave Of The Stars
Los Angeles, CA 90067, USA

Baldacci, David (Writer)
c/o Aaron Priest *Aaron M. Priest Literary
Agency*
708 3rd Ave
23rd FL
New York, NY 10017, USA

Baldacci, John (Politician)
192 State St
Augusta, ME 04330-6406, USA

Baldacci, Lou (Athlete, Football Player)
983 Coral Dr
Pebble Beach, CA 93953, USA

Baldachino, Gerald (Horse Racer)
208 Sweetmans Ln
Millstone Township, NJ 08535-8110, USA

Baldassin, Mike (Athlete, Football Player)
7914 Interlaaken Dr SW
Lakewood, WA 98498, USA

Baldavin, Barbara (Actor)
228 17th St
Manhattan Beach, CA 90266, USA

Baldelli, Rocco (Athlete, Baseball Player)
5301 Gulf Blvd Unit 610
St Pete Beach, FL 33706-2307, USA

Balderis, Helmut (Athlete, Hockey Player)
Latvian Ice Hockey Federation
Raunas Iela 23
Riga LV-1039, Latvia

Balderson, Dick (Commentator)
1676 Raybrad Dr
Cordova, TN 38016-6038, USA

Balderstone, James S (Business Person)
115 Mont Albert Road
Canterbuy, VIC 3126, AUSTRALIA

Baldeschwieler, John D (Misc)
PO Box 50065
Pasadena, CA 91115, USA

Baldessari, John (Artist)
626 Vernon Ave
Venice, CA 90291-2737, USA

Balding, Rebecca (Actor)
2001 Winnetka Place
Woodland Hills, CA 91364, USA

Baldinger, Brian (Athlete, Football Player,
Sportscaster)
21 S Elmwood Rd
Marlton, NJ 08053, USA

Baldinger, Gary (Athlete, Football Player)
114 Adam Rd
Massapequa, NY 11758, USA

Baldinger, Rich (Athlete, Football Player)
5401 Phelps Rd
Kansas City, MO 64136, USA

Baldischwiler, Karl (Athlete, Football
Player)
3033 N Willow Dr
Newcastle, OK 73065, USA

Baldissin, Mike (Athlete, Football Player)
13834 Bandix Rd SE
Olalla, WA 98359, USA

Baldock, Bobby R (Judge)
US Court of Appeals
PO Box 2388
Roswell, NM 88202, USA

Baldoni, Justin (Actor)
c/o Adam Griffin *Kritzer Levine Wilkins
Entertainment (KLWG)*
11872 La Grange Ave
1st Floor
Los Angeles, CA 90025, USA

Baldrige, Leticia (Writer)
Letitia Baldrige Enterprises Inc
2339 Massachussetts Ave NW
Washington, DC 20008, USA

Baldry, Long John (Musician)
Macklam Feidman Mgmt
1505 W 2nd Ave #200
Vancouver, BC V6H 3Y4, CANADA

Baldschun, Jack (Athlete, Baseball Player)
311 Erie Rd
Green Bav, WI 54311-7706, USA

Baldschun, Jack E (Athlete, Baseball
Player)
311 Erie Rd
Green Bay, WI 54311, USA

Baldwin, Adam (Actor)
c/o Abe Hoch *A Management*
9107 Wilshire Blvd.
Suite 650
Beverly Hills, CA 90210, USA

Baldwin, Alec (Actor)
335 Town Ln
Amagansett, NY 11930, USA

Baldwin, Bobby (Misc)
16 Vintage Valley Dr
Las Vegas, NV 89141-6060, USA

Baldwin, Daniel (Actor)
c/o John McGalliard *Chaotik*
6446 Santa Monica Blvd
Los Angeles, CA 90036, USA

Baldwin, Dave (Athlete, Baseball Player)
P.O. Box 190
Yachats, OR 97498-0190, USA

Baldwin, Don (Athlete, Football Player)
3624 Wind Chime Ln
Saint Charles, MO 63301-7405, USA

Baldwin, Doug (Athlete, Hockey Player)
180 Cook Ave
Gimli, MB R0C 1B0, Canada

Baldwin, Howard (Producer)
c/o Staff Member *Baldwin Entertainment*
9200 Sunset Blvd
Suite 550
West Hollywood, CA 90069, USA

Baldwin, Jack (Race Car Driver)
4748 Balmoral Way NE
Marietta, GA 30068, USA

Baldwin, Jack E (Misc)
Oxford University
Dyson Perrins Lab
S Park Rd
Oxford OX1 3QY, UNITED KINGDOM
(UK)

Baldwin, James (Athlete, Baseball Player)
18 Monteith Pl
Pinehurst, NC 28374-8542, USA

Baldwin, Jeff (Athlete, Baseball Player)
70 Goodwill Rd
Huntington, WV 25704-8820, USA

Baldwin, Jerry (Business Person)
1400 Park Ave
Emeryville, CA 94608-3520, USA

Baldwin, John A (Jack) Jr (General)
1371 Millersville Road
Millersville, MD 21108, USA

Baldwin, John W (Historian)
Johns Hopkins University
History Dept
Baltimore, MD 21218, USA

Baldwin, Jonathan (Football Player)
c/o Ken Zuckerman *Priority Sports &
Entertainment - (LA)*
15233 Ventura Blvd
Suite 718
Sherman Oaks, CA 91403, USA

Baldwin, Judy (Actor)
c/o Larry Metzger *Grant Savic Kopaloff &
Associates*
6399 Wilshire Blvd #414
Los Angeles, CA 90048, USA

Baldwin, Keith M (Athlete, Football
Player)
124 Leonardville Rd
Belford, NJ 07718, USA

Baldwin, Margaret (Writer)
PO Box 1106
Williams Bay, WI 53191, USA

Baldwin, Matisha (Actor)
c/o Marianne Golan *Marianne Golan
Management*
6528 W. 6th St
Los Angeles, CA 90048-4716, USA

Baldwin, Randy (Athlete, Football Player)
862 S 9th St
Griffin, GA 30224, USA

Baldwin, Reggie (Athlete, Baseball Player)
763 S Liebold St
Detroit, MI 48217-1219, USA

Baldwin, Rick (Athlete, Baseball Player)
2601 Stoneridge Dr
Modesto, CA 95355-3454, USA

Baldwin, Robert E (Economist)
125 Nautilus Dr
Madison, WI 53705, USA

Baldwin, Stephen (Actor)
71 Old Mountain Rd
S Nyack, NY 10960, USA

Baldwin, Tammy (Congressman,
Politician)
2446 Rayburn HOB
Washington, DC 20515, USA

Baldwin, William (Editor)
Forbes Magazine
Editorial Dept
60 5th Ave
New York, NY 10011, USA

Baldwin, William (Billy) (Actor)
c/o Daniel (Danny) Sussman *Brillstein
Entertainment Partners*
9150 Wilshire Blvd #350
Beverly Hills, CA 90212, USA

Bale, Christian (Actor)
150 Mabery Rd
Santa Monica, CA 90402, USA

Bale, John (Athlete, Baseball Player)
9017 Roberts Rd
Odessa, FL 32556-1947, USA

Bales, Lee (Athlete, Baseball Player)
7422 Greatwood Lake Dr
Sugar Land, TX 77479-6302, USA

Bales, Michael (Athlete, Hockey Player)
470 Brunswick Ave
Toronto, ON M5R 2Z5, Canada

Bales, Mike
470 Brunswick Ave
Toronto, ON M5R 2Z5, Canada

Bales, Steve (Scientist)
17 Hart Ln
Sewell, NJ 08080-9734, USA

Balester, Collin (Athlete, Baseball Player)
18892 Carolyn Ln
Huntington Beach, CA 92646-1911, USA

Balfour, Earl (Athlete, Hockey Player)
71 Beasley Cres
Cambridge, ON N1T 1P5, Canada

Balfour, Eric (Actor)
c/o Brian Medavoy *Medavoy
Management*
10203 Santa Monica Blvd
Suite 400
Los Angeles, CA 90067, USA

Balfour, Grant (Athlete, Baseball Player)
2678 N McMullen Booth Rd
Clearwater, FL 33761-4409, USA

Balgimbayev, Nurlan (Prime Minister)
Dom Pravieelstva
Pl im Vl Lenina
Astana 148008, KAZAKHSTAN

Baliani, Marco (Actor)
Carol Levi Co
Via Giuseppe Pisanelli
Rome 00196, ITALY

Baliles, Gerald L (Politician)
Riverfront Plaza East Tower
951 E Byrd St
Richmond, VA 23219-4040, USA

Balin, Marty (Musician)
12413 Stillwater Terr Dr
Tampa, FL 33618, USA

Balitran, Celine (Model)
c/o Staff Member *Ford Models (NY)*
238 E 4th St
New York, NY 10009, USA

Balk, Fairuza (Actor)
Rigberg Roberts Rugolo
1180 S Beverly Dr
#601
Los Angeles, CA 90035, USA

Balkenende, Jan-Peter (Prime Minister)
Premier's Office
Binnenhof 20
Postbus 20001
EA Hague, NETHERLANDS

Balkenhol, Klaus (Athlete)
Narzissenweg 11A
Hilden 40723, GERMANY

Ball, Alan (Producer)
7443 Woodrow Wilson Dr
Los Angeles, CA 90046, USA

Ball, Blake (Athlete, Hockey Player)

Ball, Dave (Athlete, Football Player)
9234 Carrisbrook Ln
Brentwood, TN 37027, us

Ball, Dave (Athlete, Football Player)
1020 Hillview Dr
Dixon, CA 95620, USA

Ball, David (Musician)
Buddy Lee
38 Music Square E
#300
Nashville, TN 37203, USA

Ball, Edward (Writer)
Farrar Straus Giroux
19 Union Square W
New York, NY 10003, USA

Ball, Eric C (Athlete, Football Player)
10614 Margate Ter
Cincinnati, OH 45241, USA

Ball, Ian (Musician)
c/o Staff Member *Paradigm (Monterey)*
404 W Franklin St
Monterey, CA 93940, USA

Ball, Jason (Athlete, Football Player)
325 S Jessie Doe
Durham, NH 03824, USA

Ball, Jason
22 Coe Dr
Durham, NH 03824, us

Ball, Jeff (Athlete, Baseball Player)
1166 6th Ave APt 9C
Vero Beach, FL 32960-5960, USA

Ball, Jerry L (Athlete, Football Player)
3311 Meadowside Dr
Sugar Land, TX 77478, USA

Ball, Larry (Athlete, Football Player)
8830 SW 57th St
Cooper City, FL 33328, USA

Ball, Marcia (Musician)
P.O. Box 2629
Austin, TX 78768, USA

Ball, Michael A (Actor, Musician)
PO Box 2073
Colchester, Essex CO4 3WS, UNITED
KINGDOM (UK)

Ball, Robert (Athlete, Football Player)
35 Summit Rd
Clifton, NJ 07012, USA

Ball, Sam (Athlete, Football Player)
1220 Glenshield Way
Henderson, KY 42420, USA

Ball, Sam (Actor)
c/o Robert Stein *Robert Stein Management*
PO Box 3797
Beverly Hills, CA 90212, USA

Ball, Taylor (Actor)
c/o Shannon Barr *Shannon Barr Public
Relations*
1600 Rosecrans Ave
Media Center Bldg. 7, 4th Floor
Manhattan Beach, CA 90266-3708, USA

Ball, Terry (Athlete, Hockey Player)
4502 Torrington Ave
Parma, OH 44134-2163, USA

Ball, William (General)
Department of the Navy
Washington, DC 20330-0001, USA

Balladur, Edouard (Politician)
5 Rue Jean Formige
Paris F-75015, FRANCE

Ballantine, Sara (Actor)
Talent Group
5670 Wilshire Blvd #820
Los Angeles, CA 90036, USA

Ballantyne (Designer, Fashion Designer)
c/o Staff Member *Ballantyne*
4-6 Savile Road
London, England W1S 3PD, United
Kingdom

Ballard, Carroll (Director)
P.O. Box 556
Saint Helena, CA 94574, USA

Ballard, Del Jr (Bowler)
Ebonite International
PO Box 746
Hopkinsville, KY 42241, USA

Ballard, Donald E (General)
PO Box 34593
Kansas City, MO 64116-0993, USA

Ballard, Florence (Musician)
c/o Staff Member *Diva Central Inc*
7510 W Sunset Blvd Ste 1445
Los Angees, CA 90046, USA

Ballard, Glen (Musician, Songwriter)
911 N Beverly Dr
Beverly Hills, CA 90210, USA

Ballard, Greg (Athlete, Basketball Player)
100 Arborcrest Ct
Tyrone, GA 30290-1555, USA

Ballard, Howard (Athlete, Football Player)
P.O. Box 584
Ashland, AL 36251, USA

Ballard, Jeff (Athlete, Baseball Player)
4828 Rimrock Rd
Billings, MT 59106-1317, USA

Ballard, J G (Writer)
36 Old Charlton Rd
Shepperton, Middlesex England, USA

Ballard, Jim (Athlete, Football Player)
1215 Stone Crossing St NE
Canton, OH 44721, us

Ballard, Kaye (Actor)
PO Box 922
Rancho Mirage, CA 92270, USA

Ballard, Keith (Athlete, Hockey Player)
2336 River Pointe Cir
Minneapolis, MN 55411-4414, USA

Ballard, Quinton (Athlete, Football Player)
4005 Saint Patrick Dr
Greensboro, NC 27406, USA

Ballard, Robert
Woods Hole Oceanographic Institute
86 Water St
Woods Hole, MA 02543-1052, USA

Ballard, Robert (Scientist)
Woods Hole Oceanographic Institute
86 Water St
Woods Hole, MA 02543-1052, USA

Ballard, Robert D (Oceanographer)
Institute for Exploration
55 Coogan Blvd
Mystic, CT 06355, USA

Ballas, Mark (Dancer, Reality TV Star)
c/o Jessica Cohen *JCPR*
9903 Santa Monica Blvd
Suite 983
Beverly Hills, CA 90212, USA

Ballatore, Antonio (Stylist)
c/o Celebrity Stylist *Creative Exchange
Agency*
53 Gansevoort St
3rd Floor
New York, NY 10014, USA

Baller, Jay (Athlete, Baseball Player)
303 Spring Valley Rd
Reading, PA 19605-2747, USA

Ballerini, Edoardo (Actor)
3350 Atwater Ave
Los Angeles, CA 90039, USA

Ballesteros, Roberto (Actor)
c/o Staff Member *Televisa*
Blvd Adolfo Lopez Mateos 232
Colonia San Angel INN
DF CP 01060, MEXICO

Ballestros, Anderson (Actor)
c/o J R Heermans *LatinActors*
920 Leavenworth St #302
San Francisco, CA 94109

Balley, Otha (Athlete, Baseball Player)
937 6th Pl SW
Birmingham, AL 35211, USA

Ballhaus, Florian M (Cinematographer)
115 Berkeley Place
Brooklyn, NY 11217, USA

Ballhaus, Michael (Cinematographer)
11 Elm Place
Rye, NY 10580, USA

Ballina, Frank (Athlete, Baseball Player)
PO Box 54
Freeport, PA 16229-0054, USA

Ballingall, Chris (Athlete, Baseball Player)
52879 25th St
Mattawan, MI 49071-8803, USA

Ballinger, Mark (Athlete, Baseball Player)
1212 SW 5th Ave
Okeechobee, FL 34974-5014, USA

Ballmer, Steve (Business Person)
Microsoft Corp
1 Microsoft Way
Redmond, WA 98052, USA

Ballon, Adrienne (Actor)
c/o Staff Member *ICM Partners (ICM-LA)*
10250 Constellation Blvd Fl 7
Los Angeles, CA 90067, USA

Ballou, Mark (Actor)
c/o Staff Member *Imperium 7 Talent
Agency*
5455 Wilshire Blvd
Suite 1706
Los Angeles, CA 90036, USA

Ballou, Tyson (Model)
c/o Staff Member *IMG*
304 Park Ave S Fl 12
New York, NY 10010, USA

Balmaseda, Liz (Journalist)
Miami Herald
Editorial Dept
1 Herald Plaza
Miami, FL 33132, USA

Balmer, Earl (Race Car Driver)
8115 No. Skyline Dr.
Floyd's Knob, IN 47119, USA

Balmer, Jean-Francois (Actor, Director)
c/o Staff Member *ArtMedia*
20 avenue Rapp
Paris 75008, France

Balmilero, Kimee (Actor)
c/o Staff Member *Rogers Orion Talent
Agency*
13731Ventura Blvd.
Suite D
Sherman Oaks, CA 91423, USA

Balon, Dave (Athlete, Hockey Player)
D. 5-29-2007
USA

Balotelli, Mario (Athlete, Soccer Player)
c/o Staff Member *Manchester City FC*
City of Manchester Stadium
SportCity
Manchester M11 3FF, UK

Balraaj, Anand (Actor, Bollywood)
72/1 AV Villa, Kakori Camp
Aram Nagar, Seven Bungalows Versova
Andheri
Mumbai, MS 400058, INDIA

Balsam, Talia (Actor)
c/o Sue Leibman *Barking Dog Entertainment*
609 Greenwich St
6th Floor
New York, NY 10014, USA

Balsamo, Tony (Athlete, Baseball Player)
15 Doral Ln
Bay Shore, NY 11706-8840, USA

Balsley, Darren (Athlete, Baseball Player, Coach)
1200 Harper Pl
Knoxville, TN 37922-5560, USA

Balsley, Phil (Musician)
1409 N Augusta St
Staunton, VA 24401, USA

Baltes, Jameson (Actor)
Hervey/Grimes
PO Box 64249
Los Angeles, CA 90064, USA

Baltica, Kremerata (Musician)
c/o Staff Member *ICM Partners (ICM-LA)*
10250 Constellation Blvd Fl 7
Los Angeles, CA 90067, USA

Baltimore, Bryon (Athlete, Hockey Player)
McCauig Desrochers Ltd
2401-10088 102 Ave NW
Edmonton, AB T5J 2Z1, Canada

Baltimore, David (Nobel Prize Laureate)
1255 S Grand Ave
Pasadena, CA 91105-2835, USA

Baltray, Charies (Astronomer)
Yale University
Astronomy Dept
New Haven, CT 06520, USA

Baltron, Donna (Actor)
C N A Assoc
1925 Century Park East
#750
Los Angeles, CA 90067, USA

Baltsa, Agnes (Opera Singer)
Manuela Kursidem
Wasagasse 12/1/3
Vienna 1090, AUSTRIA

Baltz, Lewis (Photographer)
11693 San Vincente Blvd #527
Los Angeles, CA 90049-5105, USA

Baluik, Stan (Athlete, Hockey Player)
809 8th Terrace
Palm Beach Gardens, FL 33418, USA

Balukas, Jean (Billiards Player)
9818 4th Ave
Brooklyn, NY 11209, USA

Balul, Oksana (Figure Skater)
Bob Young
PO Box 988
Niantic, CT 06357, USA

Bama, James (Artist)
P.O. Box 148
Wapiti, WY 82450, USA

Bama, Jim (Artist)
PO Box 148
Wapiti, WY 82450, USA

Bamber, Jamie
c/o Alan Siegel *Alan Siegel Entertainment*
345 N Maple Dr
Suite 375
Beverly Hills, CA 90210, USA

Bamford, Maria (Actor)
c/o Bob Read *ReBar Management*
10061 Riverside Drive
#722
Toluca Lake, CA 91602

Bana, Eric (Actor, Comedian)
c/o Lauren Bergman *Lauren Bergman Management*
37 Browns Road, Main Ridge
Victoria 3928, Australia

Banach, Ed (Athlete, Olympic Athlete, Wrestler)
2128 Country Club Blvd
Ames, IA 50014, USA

Banach, Lou (Athlete, Olympic Athlete, Wrestler)
1828 Tallgrass Cir
Waukesha, WI 53188-2661, USA

Banachowski, Andy (Athlete, Coach, Volleyball Player)
University of California
Athletic Dept - J.D. Morgan Center
P.O. Box 24044
Los Angeles, CA 90024, USA

Banaszak, John A (Athlete, Football Player)
420 Robinhood Ln
Canonsburg, PA 15317, USA

Banaszak, Pete (Athlete, Football Player)
1021 Inverness Dr
Saint Augustine, FL 32092, USA

Banaszek, Cas (Athlete, Football Player)
1018 Cohen Ct
Petaluma, CA 94952, USA

Banaszek, Nancy Koutek (Stylist)
5448 N Lakewood Ave
Chicago, IL 60640, USA

Banaszynski, Jacqui (Journalist)
Saint Paul Pioneer Press
Editorial Dept
345 Cedar St
Saint Paul, MN 55101, USA

Banbury, F H Frith (Director)
18 Park Saint James
Prince Albert Road
London NW8 7LE, UNITED KINGDOM (UK)

Bancroft, Cameron (Actor)
c/o Staff Member *Gersh (LA)*
9465 Wilshire Blvd
Suite 600
Beverly Hills, CA 90212, USA

Bancroft, George M Dr (Scientist)
University of Western Ontario
1151 Richmond St
Attn: Chemistry Dept
London, ON N6A 3K7, Canada

Band, Richard H (Composer)
24053 Bessemer St
Woodland Hills, CA 91367, USA

Banda El Limon, Arrolladora (Music Group)
c/o Staff Member *Sony Music Miami*
605 Lincoln Rd Fl 7
Miami Beach, FL 33139, USA

Banda Imperio (Music Group, Musician)
c/o Staff Member *Morena Music*
5021 Columbus Ave
Sherman Oaks, CA 91403, USA

Banda Pachuco (Music Group)
c/o Staff Member *Sony Music Miami*
605 Lincoln Rd Fl 7
Miami Beach, FL 33139, USA

Banderas, Antonio (Actor, Director, Musician, Producer)
c/o Robin Baum *Slate Public Relations*
9000 Sunset Blvd #915
West Hollywood, CA 90069, USA

B. Anderholf, Robert (Congressman, Politician)
2264 Rayburn HOB
Washington, DC 20515, USA

Bandholz, Antonio (Misc)
Sohnholm 92
Westerholz 24977, GERMANY

Bandiera, Bob (Bobby) (Musician)
29C Court B
Bricktown, NJ 08724, USA

Bando, Chris (Athlete, Baseball Player)
5811 S Mack Ave
Gilbert, AZ 85298-8709, USA

Bando, Chris (Athlete, Baseball Player)
Washington Wild Things 1 Washington Federal Way
Attn M:maeers Office
Washington, PA 15301, USA

Bando, Salvatore L (Sal) (Athlete, Baseball Player)
W308N6225 Shore Acres Rd
Hartland, WI 53029-8723, USA

Band of Bees, A (Music Group)
c/o Staff Member *Paradigm (Monterey)*
404 W Franklin St
Monterey, CA 93940, USA

Band of Skulls (Music Group, Musician)
c/o Staff Member *Vagrant Records*
2118 Wilshire Blvd.
#361
Santa Monica, CA 90403, USA

Bandura, Jeff (Athlete, Hockey Player)
27257 32B Ave
Aldergrove, BC V4W 3H8, Canada

Bandy, Don (Athlete, Football Player)
215 E Calvin St
Taft, CA 93268, USA

Bandy, Moe (Musician, Songwriter)
2577 US 160
Reeds Spring, MO 65737, USA

Bane (Music Group, Musician)
c/o Mike Pike *Kenmore Agency, The*
59 Park St
2nd Floor
Beverly, MA 01915, USA

Bane, Eddie (Athlete, Baseball Player)
1132 Los Campaneros
San Marcos, CA 92078-5225, USA

Banes, Lisa (Actor)
c/o Tim Angle *Buchwald/Fortitude (LA)*
6500 Wilshire Blvd
Suite 2200
Los Angeles, CA 90048, USA

Baney, Dick (Athlete, Baseball Player)
2231 Northup Dr
Tustin, CA 92782-1028, USA

Banfield, Ashleigh (Correspondent)
c/o Staff Member *NBC Universal (NY)*
30 Rockefeller Plaza
New York, NY 10112, USA

Banfield, Tony (Athlete, Football Player)
1102 Myrtlewood Dr
Friendswood, TX 77546, us

Bang, Molly (Writer)
43 Drumlin Road
Falmouth, MA 02540-2505, USA

Bangash, Ali Haider Khan (General)
PO Hangu, Tensil Hangu
Distt Kohat
Mohallah, Khan Bari, Pakistan

Bangemann, Martin (Government Official)
European Commission
200 Rue de la Loi
Brussels 1049, BELGIUM

Bangerter, Norman (Politician)
9947 Congressional Way
South Jordan, UT 84095-3304, USA

Bangles, The (Music Group)
c/o Staff Member *Agency Group Ltd, The (UK)*
361-373 City Rd
London EC1V 1PQ, UK

Bang Lime (Music Group)
c/o Staff Member *Paradigm (Monterey)*
404 W Franklin St
Monterey, CA 93940, USA

Banham, Frank (Athlete, Hockey Player)
139 W Grayling Ln
Suffield, CT 06078-1960, USA

Banhart, Bobby (Reality TV Star)
c/o Elizabeth Much *Much and House Public Relations*
8075 W 3rd St
Suite 500
Los Angeles, CA 90048, USA

Bani, John (President)
President's Office
Port Vila, VANUATU

Banister, Jeff (Athlete, Baseball Player)
5228 Hidden Brook Ln
League City, TX 77573-5783, USA

Banister, Jeff
Pittsburgh Pirates PO Box 7000
Attn Coaching Staff
Pittsburgh, PA 1 'i717-00'IR, USA

Bank, Frank (Actor)
PO Box 902
N Palm Springs, CA 92258, USA

Bank, Melissa (Producer, Writer)
c/o Sylvie Rabineau *Rabineau Wachter and Sanford Literary Agency*
522 Wilshire Boulevard Suite L
Santa Monica, CA 90401, USA

Bank, Raymond (General)
254 Embassy Ct
Columbus, OH 43230-2517, USA

Bank, Raymond
254 Embassy Ct
Columbus, OH 43230-2517, USA

Banke, Paul (Boxer)
1926 Bobolink Way
Pomona, CA 91767, USA

Banker, Ted (Athlete, Football Player)
1862 Park Ave
East Meadow, NY 11554, USA

Bankhead, Scott (Athlete, Baseball Player, Olympic Athlete)
1236 Idlewood Dr
Asheboro, NC 27205-4119, USA

Banks, Brian (Stylist)
c/o Staff Member *Rex Agency, The*
6311 Romaine St
Los Angeles, CA 90038, USA

Banks, Brian (Athlete, Baseball Player)
2232 E 900 S
Salt Lake City, UT 84108-1404, USA

Banks, Brianna (Adult Film Star)
c/o Staff Member *Atlas Multimedia Inc*
9005 Eton Ave Ste C
Canoga Park, CA 91304-1743, USA

Banks, Carl (Athlete, Football Player)
7 Glenview Dr
Warren, NJ 07059, USA

Banks, Chip (Athlete, Football Player)
55 Fair Haven Way SE
Smyrna, GA 30080, USA

Banks, Chris (Athlete, Football Player)
712 Franklin Ave
Lexington, MO 64067, us

Banks, Chuck (Athlete, Football Player)
3705 Valley Hill Dr
Randallstown, MD 21133, USA

Banks, Darren (Athlete, Hockey Player)
11 Millington Rd
Pleasant Ridge, MI 48069-1108, USA

Banks, David (Actor)
Shane Collins Assoc
2-5 Stedham Pl
Bloomsbury
London WC1A 1BU, ENGLAND

Banks, Dennis (Misc)
General Delivery
Oglala, SD 57764, USA

Banks, Elizabeth (Actor)
11635 Canton Pl
Studio City, CA 91604, USA

Banks, Ernie (Athlete, Baseball Player)
27 N Wacker Dr #466
Chicago, CA 60606-2800, USA

Banks, Estes (Athlete, Football Player)
640 Gooseberry Dr Unit 703
Longmont, CO 80503, us

Banks, Fred (Athlete, Football Player)
P.O. Box 1571
Mableton, GA 30126, USA

Banks, Gene (Athlete, Basketball Player)
Bluefield State College
Athletic Dept
219 Rock St
Bluefield, WV 24701, USA

Banks, Gene (Athlete, Basketball Player)
1210 Sloan St
Greensboro, NC 2740-3442, USA

Banks, Gordon (Athlete, Football Player)
2644 E Trinity Mills Rd
Carrollton, TX 75006, USA

Banks, Jonathan (Actor)
29734 Harvester Rd
Malibu, CA 90265, USA

Banks, Josh (Athlete, Baseball Player)
489 Old Orchard Cir
Millersville, MD 21108-2010, USA

Banks, Lloyd (Musician)
c/o Staff Member *Money Management*
22 Noel Street
London W1f 8GS, United Kingdom

Banks, Lynne Reid (Writer)
Avon Books
1350 Avenue of the Americas
New York, NY 10019-4702, USA

Banks, Mike (Athlete, Football Player)
1615 1 Ave
Boone, IA 50036, us

Banks, Morwenna (Actor, Writer)
c/o Staff Member *ICM Partners (ICM-LA)*
10250 Constellation Blvd Fl 7
Los Angeles, CA 90067, USA

Banks, Robert (Athlete, Football Player)
2412 Laguard Dr
Hampton, VA 23661, USA

Banks, Russell (Writer)
Princeton University
English Debt
Princeton, NJ 08544, USA

Banks, Skeeter (Athlete, Baseball Player)
3810 Castlewood Rd
Richmond, VA 23234, USA

Banks, Steven (Actor, Comedian)
Gersh Agency
232 N Canon Dr
Beverly Hills, CA 90210, USA

Banks, Steven Gary (Producer, Writer)
c/o Staff Member *Evolution Entertainment (LA)*
901 N Highland Ave
Los Angeles, CA 90038, USA

Banks, Ted (Coach)
Riverside Community College
Athletic Dept
Riverside, CA 92506, USA

Banks, Tom (Athlete, Football Player)
358 Wisteria St
Fairhope, AL 36532, USA

Banks, Tony (Athlete, Football Player)
735 Laguna
Irving, TX 75039-3218, USA

Banks, Tyra (Actor, Model, Producer)
c/o Staff Member *Bankable Productions*
226 W 26th St
4th Floor
New York, NY 10001-6700, USA

Banks, Walker (Athlete, Basketball Player)
3207 Brentwood Dr
Champaign, IL 61821-3482, USA

Banks, William
709 Albany Ave
Augusta, GA 30901, us

Banks, Willie (Athlete, Baseball Player)
3443 Corte Sonrisa
Carlsbad, CA 92009-9341, USA

Bankston, Michael (Athlete, Football Player)
938 Kingwood Dr
Apt 220
Humble, TX 77339, USA

Bankston, Michael (Athlete, Football Player)
182 N Burberry Park Cir
Spring, TX 77382, us

Bankston, Warren (Athlete, Football Player)
4201 Bordeaux Dr
Kenner, LA 70065, USA

Bankston, Wes
3900 Valdez Ct
Plano, TX 75074-7941, USA

Bannan, Justin (Athlete, Football Player)
561 Mockingbird Dr Belgrade MT 59714-8139
Belgrade, MT 59714, us

Bannatyne, Duncan
Bannatyne Fitness Ltd
Powerhouse, Haughton Rd
Attn: Kim Crowther
Darlington DL1 1ST, UK

Banner, David (Actor, Musician, Producer)
c/o Peter Schwartz *Agency Group Ltd, The (NY)*
142 West 57th St
6th Floor
New York, NY 10019, USA

Bannerman, Bill (Director, Producer)
Mirisch Agency
c/o Lawrence Mirisch
1875 Century Park E Ste 2025
Los Angeles, CA 90067, USA

Bannerman, Isabella (Cartoonist)
41 South Drive
Hastings-on-Hudson, NY 10706, USA

Bannerman, Murray (Athlete, Hockey Player)
826 Raintree Dr
Naperville, IL 60540, USA

Bannister, Alan (Athlete, Baseball Player)
6349 N 78th St
Unit 129
Scottsdale, AZ 85250-4771, USA

Bannister, Alan (Athlete, Baseball Player)
405 48th St NW
Bradenton, FL 34209, USA

Bannister, Brian (Athlete, Baseball Player)
6701 E Caballo Dr
Paradise Valley, AZ 85253-2706, USA

Bannister, Floyd (Athlete, Baseball Player)
6701 E Caballo Dr
Paradise Valley, AZ 85253-2706, USA

Bannister, Ken (Athlete, Basketball Player)
2322 Broadgreen Dr
Missouri City, TX 77489-5002, USA

Bannister, Reggie (Actor, Musician)
Magic Inc
4450 California Place
Box 315
Long Beach, CA 90807, USA

Bannister, Roger G (Athlete, Scientist, Track Athlete)
21 Bardwell Rd
Oxford OX2 6SV, UK

Bannon, Bruce (Athlete, Football Player)
5845 Hickory Hollow Ln
Doylestown, PA 18902, USA

Bannon, Jack (Actor)
6470 E Sunnyside Rd
Coeur D Alene, ID 83814-9503, USA

Bannon, Shaun (Musician)
Artist Group International
9560 Wilshire Blvd #400
Beverly Hills, CA 90212, USA

Banois, Vincent J (Athlete, Football Player)
24256J Tamarack Trl
Southfield, MI 48075, USA

Banowsky, William S (Business Person, Educator)
Gaylord Broadcasting Co
PO Box 25125
Oklahoma City, OK 73125, USA

Banta, Brad (Athlete, Football Player)
2069 Linwood Cir
Soddy Daisy, TN 37379, USA

Banta, Brad (Athlete, Football Player)
1100 Smith Ave Birmingham MI 48009-2031
Birmingham, MI 48009, us

Banta-Cain, Tully (Athlete, Football Player)
111 Ruest Rd North Attleboro MA 02760-6610
North Attleboro, MA 02760, us

Bantle, Jeffrey (Scientist)
17 Amesbury Parke
Medford, NJ 08055-3359, USA

Bantock, Nick (Writer)
Chronicle Books
85 2nd St
San Francisco, CA 94105, USA

Bantom, Michael (Basketball Player, Olympic Athlete)
418 Egret Ln
Secaucus, NJ 07094-2219, USA

Bantom, Mike (Athlete, Basketball Player)
418 Egret Ln
Secaucus, NJ 07094-2219, USA

Bantu, Inanna M (Stylist)
10945 Burbank Blvd
#173
North Hollywood, CA 91601, USA

Banuchandar (Actor)
26 B N Reddy Road
Chennai, TN 600 017, INDIA

Banx, Brooke (Model)
8491 Sunset Blvd #285
W Hollywood, CA 90069, USA

Bao, Joseph Y (Doctor)
17436 Terry Lyn Lane
Cerritos, CA 90703, USA

Bapitha (Actor, Bollywood)
7 Ayyappan Nagar 2nd Street
Cinmaya Nagar
Chennai, TN 600111, INDIA

Baptist, Travis (Athlete, Baseball Player)
12269 Deersong Dr
Jacksonville, FL 32218-9038, USA

Baptista, Juan Alfonso (Actor)
c/o Gabriel Blanco *Gabriel Blanco Iglesias (Mexico)*
Rio Balsas 35-32
Colonia Cuauhtemoc
DF 06500, Mexico

Baptiste, Baron (Athlete)
c/o Staff Member *St Martins Press*
Publicity Dept
175 5th Ave
New York, NY 10010, USA

Baquero, Ivana (Actor)
c/o Tom Drumm *The Safran Company*
8748 Holloway Dr
Los Angeles, CA 90069, USA

Bar, Olaf (Opera Singer)
Organisation of Int'l Artistique
16 Ave FD Roosevelt
Paris 75008, FRANCE

Barahona, Ralph (Athlete, Hockey Player)
4608 Bellflower Blvd
Lakewood, CA 90713, USA

Barajas, Rod (Athlete, Baseball Player)
723 Avocado Pl
Del Mar, CA 92014-3943, USA

Barak, Ehud (Politician)
Israel Labor Party
16 Hayarkon St
Tel-Aviv 63571, ISRAEL

Baraka, Imiri (Writer)
State University Of New York
Dept of African Studies
Stony Brook, NY 11794-0001, USA

Baranova, Anastasia (Actor)
c/o Staff Member *Gersh (LA)*
9465 Wilshire Blvd
Suite 600
Beverly Hills, CA 90212, USA

Baranski, Christine (Actor)
316 Woodcreek Rd
Bethlehem, CT 06751, USA

Barany, Istvan (Swimmer)
I Attila Utca 87
Budapest 01012, HUNGARY

Barash, Brandon (Actor)
c/o Martin Berneman *Precision Entertainment*
6338 Wilshire Blvd
Los Angeles, CA 90048, USA

Baratta, Adam (Actor)
c/o Gary Raskin *Raskin Peter Rubin & Simon*
1801 Century Park E
Suite 2300
Los Angeles, CA 90067, USA

Barbacid, Mariano (Misc)
CNIO
Melchor Fernandez Almagro 3
Madrid 28029, SPAIN

Barbara, Kingsolver E (Writer)
c/o Staff Member *HarperCollins Publishers*
10 East 53rd St
c/o Author mail, 7th Floor
New York, NY 10022, USA

Barbarin, Phillipe X I Cardinal (Religious Leader)
Archdiocese
1 Place de Fouriere
Lyon Cedex 05 69321, FRANCE

Barbaro, Gary W (Athlete, Football Player)
1000 Giuffrias Ave
Metairie, LA 70001, USA

Barbat, Roxanne (Director, Producer, Writer)
c/o Staff Member *Fantastic Films*
3854 Clayton Ave
Los Angeles, CA 90027, USA

Barbeau, Adrienne (Actor, Musician)
3851 Avenida Del Sol
Studio City, CA 91604, USA

Barber, Aaron (Athlete, Basketball Player)
2830 Fillmore St NE
Minneapolis, MN 55418, USA

Barber, Andrea (Actor)
1391 Beechwood Dr
Brea, CA 92821, USA

Barber, Ava (Musician)
1508 N Courtney Oan Ln
Knoxville, TN 37938, USA

Barber, Bill (Athlete, Hockey Player)
105 Harmon Drive
Blackwood, NJ 08012-5198, USA

Barber, Bob (Athlete, Football Player)
PO Box 552 Shreveport LA 71162-0552
Shreveport, LA 71162, us

Barber, Brian (Athlete, Baseball Player)
347 Blue Stone Cir
Winter Garden, FL 34787-5231, USA

Barber, Chris (Musician)
Cromwell Mgmt
45 High St
Huntington
Cambridgeshire PE29 3TE, UNITED KINGDOM (UK)

Barber, Christopher E (Athlete, Football Player)
2621 Monaco Cove Cir
Orlando, FL 32825, USA

Barber, Don (Athlete, Hockey Player)
1275 Park Ave
Washington, PA 15301, USA

Barber, Gary (Producer)
6114 Camino De La Costa
La Jolla, CA 90237, USA

Barber, Glynis (Actor)
11-12 Dover St
Mayfair
London W1S 4LJ, UK

Barber, John (Athlete, Basketball Player)
1554 Mahan St
Orangeburg, SC 29118-3546, USA

Barber, Kurt (Athlete, Football Player)
400 E Main St
Frankfort, KY 40601-2334, USA

Barber, Kurt (Athlete, Football Player)
6850 Silver Eagle Ave Las Vegas NV 89122-8387
Vegas, NV 89122, us

Barber, Marion (Athlete, Football Player)
PO Box 46106
Minneapolis, MN 55446, USA

Barber, Michael (Athlete, Football Player)
3020 Prosperity Church Rd
Suite 1
Charlotte, NC 28269, USA

Barber, Mike (Athlete, Football Player)
PO Box 2424
Desoto, TX 75123, USA

Barber, Miller (Athlete, Golfer)
8215 N 54th St
Paradise Valley, AZ 85253, USA

Barber, Paul (Actor, Producer, Writer)
c/o Staff Member *Paradigm (LA)*
360 N Crescent Dr
North Bldg
Beverly Hills, CA 90210, USA

Barber, Ronde (Athlete, Football Player)
17119 Journeys End Dr
Odessa, FL 33556, USA

Barber, Rudy (Athlete, Football Player)
1411 NW 175th St
Miami, FL 33169, USA

Barber, Shawn (Athlete, Football Player)
20035 Canterbury Dr
Stilwell, KS 66085, USA

Barber, Steve (Athlete, Baseball Player)
902 San Eduardo Ave
Henderson, NV 89002-8900, USA

Barber, Stewart C (Stew) (Athlete, Football Player)
2138 Country Manor Dr
Mount Pleasant, SC 29466, USA

Barber, Tiki (Athlete, Football Player, Sportscaster)
c/o Mark Lepselter *Maxx Sports & Entertainment*
546 Fifth Ave Fl 6
New York, NY 10036, USA

Barber, William (Cinematographer)
2509 White Chapel Place
Thousand Oaks, CA 91362, USA

Barbera, Catrina (Stylist)
4431 133rd Ave SE
Bellevue, WA 98006, USA

Barberie, Bret (Athlete, Baseball Player)
11607 Bos St
Cerritos, CA 90703-6744, USA

Barberie, Jillian (Actor, Television Host)
19413 Bilmoor Pl
Tarzana, CA 91356, USA

Barberio, Nicholas (Stylist)
c/o Staff Member *AFG Management*
Pier 62
Chelsea Piers #203
New York, NY 10011, USA

Barberos, Alessandro (Business Person)
Fiat Spa
Corso G Marconi 10/20
Turin 10125, ITALY

Barbi, Shane (Model)
c/o Jeffery LeBeau *Peacock & LeBeau*
3741 E 4th St
Long Beach, CA 90814, CA

Barbi, Sia (Model)
c/o Jeffery LeBeau *Peacock & LeBeau*
3741 E 4th St
Long Beach, CA 90814, CA

Barbieri, Anastasia (Stylist)
c/o Staff Member *Art Partner*
145 Hudson St
2nd Floor
New York, NY 10013, USA

Barbieri, Gato (Musician)
Central Entertainment Services
123 Hardvard Ave
Staten Island, NY 10301, USA

Barbieri, Jim (Athlete, Baseball Player)
13619 E 5th Ave
Spokane Valley, WA 99216-0600, USA

Barbon, Roberto (Athlete, Baseball Player)
Gabukun Dencho-2-Chome 6-Ban 460
Nishinomiya City
Hyogok, JAPAN

Barbosa, Derek Keith (Chino XL) (Musician)
c/o Staff Member *Universal Music Publishing Group (Latin)*
420 Lincoln Rd
Suite 200
Miami Beach, FL 33139, USA

Barbosa, Leandro (Athlete, Basketball Player)
3ee1 NW 4th Ter
Apt 175
Pompano Beach, FL 33064-3165, USA

Barbot, Ivan (Lawyer)
4 Rue Marguerite
Paris 75017, FRANCE

Barbour, Benny (Athlete, Football Player)
661 Barbour Rd
Smithfield, NC 27577-5579, USA

Barbour, Haley R (Politician)
648 Dogwood Dr
Yazoo City, MS 39194-8205, USA

Barbour, Ian (Physicist, Scientist)
Carleton College
Theology Dept
Northfield, MN 55057, USA

Barbour, John (Actor, Comedian, Writer)
54 Pine Isle Court
Henderson, NV 89074, USA

Barbree, Jay (Journalist)
9320 S Tropical Trl
Merritt Island, FL 32952-6821, USA

Barbutti, Pete (Musician)
Thomas Cassidy
11761 E Speedway Blvd
Tucson, AZ 85748, USA

Barcelo, Lorenzo (Athlete, Baseball Player)
1520 N Blacklawn Ave
Tucson, AZ 85745-3356, USA

Barcelo, Rich (Athlete, Basketball Player)
5195 N Spring View Dr
Tucson, AZ 85749, USA

Barcelona, Custo (Designer, Fashion Designer)
c/o Staff Member *Custo Barcelona*
2 Michael Road
1927 Bldg, North Entrance
London, England SW6 2AD, United Kingdom

Barch, Krys (Athlete, Hockey Player)
2601 Aye. of the Stars
Frisco, TC 77034

Barch, Krystofer (Athlete, Hockey Player)
1589 Foard Dr
Frisco, TX 75034-1828, USA

Barclay, Dave (Actor)
c/o Staff Member *Coolwaters Productions*
10061 Riverside Dr.
Box 531
Toluca Lake, CA 91602, USA

Barclay, Paris (Actor)
c/o Steve Lovett *Lovett Management*
1327 Brinkley Ave
Los Angeles, CA 90049, USA

Bard, Allen J (Misc)
6202 Mountainclimb Dr
Austin, TX 78731, USA

Bard, Daniel
205 Clermont Dr
Madison, MS 39110-4526, USA

Bard, Josh (Athlete, Baseball Player)
2139 Beechnut Pl
Castle Rock, CO 80108-7827, USA

Bardem, Javier E (Actor, Producer)
c/o Kelly Bush *ID PR (LA)*
7060 Hollywood Blvd
8th Floor
Los Angeles, CA 90028, USA

Barden, Brian (Athlete, Baseball Player)
6018 N 133rd Dr
Litchfield Park, AZ 85340-7311, USA

Bardo, Cori (Stylist)
c/o Staff Member *Rex Agency, The*
6311 Romaine St
Los Angeles, CA 90038, USA

Bardole, Kirk (Stylist)
c/o Staff Member *Blink Management*
421 Washington Ave
#202
Miami Beach, FL 33139, USA

Bardot, Brigitte (Actor)
La Madrague
St. Tropez F-83990, France

Bare, Bobby (Musician)
112 Galway Lake S
Hendersonville, TN 37075, USA

Barefoot, Ken (Athlete, Football Player)
1204 Lawrence Grey Dr
Virginia Beach, VA 23455, USA

Bareikis, Arija (Actor)
c/o Rhonda Price *Gersh (NY)*
41 Madison Ave
New York, NY 10010, USA

Bareikis, Arlia (Actor)
360 W 23rd St
New York, NY 10011, USA

Bareilles, Sara (Musician)
2312 Penmar Ave
Venice, CA 90291, USA

Barenaked Ladies (Music Group)
c/o Shaw Saltzberg *SL Feldman &
Associates (Vancouver)*
200-1505 West 2nd Ave
Vancouver BC V6H 3Y4, CANADA

Barenboim, Daniel (Conductor, Musician)
29 Rue de la Coulouvreeniere
Geneva 1206, SWITZERLAND

Baretto, Ray (Musician)
Creative Music Consultants
181 Christle St #300
New York, NY 10002, USA

Barfield, Amanda (Actor)
Snyder Management
6409 Primrose Ave Ste 7
Los Angeles, CA 90068, USA

Barfield, Jesse L (Athlete, Baseball Player)
5814 Spanish Moss Ct
Spring, TX 77379-6482, USA

Barfield, John (Athlete, Baseball Player)
2107 Hobson Ave
Hot Springs National Park, AR 71913,
USA

Barfield, Josh (Athlete, Baseball Player)
18082 N 93rd Pl
Scottsdale, AZ 85255-6055, USA

Barfield, Ron (Race Car Driver)
PO Box 6495
Florence, SC 29502, USA

Barfod, Hakon (Yachtsman)
Jon Ostensensy 15
Nesbru 1360, NORWAY

Bargar, Greg (Athlete, Baseball Player)
902 Felbar Ave
Torrance, CA 90503, USA

Barger, Ralph (Sonny) (Actor)
c/o Staff Member *HarperCollins Publishers*
10 East 53rd St
c/o Author mail, 7th Floor
New York, NY 10022, USA

Bargnani, Andrea (Athlete, Basketball
Player)
c/o Leon Rose *CAA - NJ*
2000 Ave Of The Stars
Los Angeles, CA 90067, USA

Barhorst, Barney (Athlete, Basketball
Player)
8004 River Bay Dr E
Indianapolis, IN 46240, USA

Barinholtz, Ike (Comedian)
c/o Jai Khanna *Brillstein Entertainment
Partners*
9150 Wilshire Blvd #350
Beverly Hills, CA 90212, USA

Barisich, Carl J (Athlete, Football Player)
10747 McGregor Dr
Columbia, MD 21044-4956, USA

Barjatya, Sooraj (Bollywood, Director,
Producer)
Bhana 1st Floor
422 Veer Sawarkar Road Prabhadevi
Dadar
Mumbai, MS 400025, INDIA

Bar-Josef, Ofer (Archaeologist)
Harvard University
Archaeology Dept
Cambridge, MA 02138, USA

Bark, Brian (Athlete, Baseball Player)
12308 Silver Cup Ct
Reisterstown, MD 21136-6481, USA

Barkauskas, Antanas S (President)
Akmenu 71
Vilnus, LITHUANIA

Barker, Bob
The DJ&T Foundation
200 N Larchmont Blvd
Suite 3
Los Angeles, CA 90004, USA

Barker, Bryan (Athlete, Football Player)
1225 Selva Marina Cir
Atlantic Beach, FL 32233, USA

Barker, Clive (Writer)
9332 Readcrest Dr
Beverly Hills, CA 90210-2533, USA

Barker, Clyde F (Doctor)
3 Coopertown Road
Haverford, PA 19041, USA

Barker, David J P (Biologist)
Manor Farm
East Dean near Salisbury
Wilts SP5 1HB, UNITED KINGDOM (UK)

Barker, Ed (Athlete, Football Player)
12002 Clover Creek Dr SW
Lakewood, WA 98499, USA

Barker, Glen (Athlete, Baseball Player)
363 2nd Ave
Albany, NY 12209-1924, USA

Barker, Jay (Athlete, Football Player, Talk
Show Host)
11 Elm St
Mountain Brook, AL 35213, USA

Barker, Jordan (Actor)
c/o Staff Member *Select Artists Ltd (CA-
Westside Office)*
1138 12th Street
Suite 1
Santa Monica, CA 90403, USA

Barker, Kevin (Athlete, Baseball Player)
PO Box 96
Mendota, VA 24270-0096, USA

Barker, Len (Athlete, Baseball Player)
10690 Locust Grove Dr
Chardon, OH 44024-8870, USA

Barker, Leo (Athlete, Football Player)
520 Grove Park Pl
Roswell, GA 30075, USA

Barker, Leo
25 Via Lucena San
San Clemente, CA 92673, USA

Barker, Lois (Athlete, Baseball Player)
195 W Main St
Apt 6
Chester, NJ 07930-2451, USA

Barker, Nigel (Photographer)
c/o Staff Member *WmE2 (WMA-LA)*
1 William Morris Pl
Beverly Hills, CA 90212, USA

Barker, Pat (Writer)
Gillion Aitken
29 Fernshaw Road
London SW10 0TG, UNITED KINGDOM
(UK)

Barker, Ray (Athlete, Baseball Player)
303 Greenbriar Rd
Martinsburg, WV 25401-2827, USA

Barker, Rich (Athlete, Baseball Player)
17 Landers Rd
Stoneham, MA 02180-1409, USA

Barker, Richard A (Religious Leader)
Orthodox Presbyterian Church
PO Box P
Willow Grove, PA 19090, USA

Barker, Roy (Athlete, Football Player)
23 Saint Marks Cir
Islandia, NY 11749, USA

Barker, Sean (Athlete, Baseball Player)
2454 C St
Bakersfield, CA 93301-2716, USA

Barker, Sue (Athlete, Tennis Player)
c/o Staff Member *BBC Artist Mail*
PO Box 1116
Belfast BT2 7AJ, United Kingdom

Barker, Tom (Actor)
London Mgmt
2-4 Noel St
London W1V 3RB, UNITED KINGDOM
(UK)

Barker, Travis (Musician)
2371 Buckingham Ln
Los Angeles, CA 90077, USA

Barker-Lequia, Joan (Athlete, Baseball
Player)
3236 34th St SW
Grandville, MI 49418, USA

Barkett, Andy (Athlete, Baseball Player)
1016 Willa Lake Cir
Oviedo, Fl 32765-6445, USA

Barkin, Ellen (Actor)
c/o Stephen Huvane *Slate Public
Relations*
9000 Sunset Blvd #915
West Hollywood, CA 90069, USA

Barkley, Brian (Athlete, Baseball Player)
9208 Spring Ridge Cir
Woodway, TX 76712-8764, USA

Barkley, Charles (Athlete, Basketball
Player, Olympic Athlete)
7615 E Vaquero Dr
Scottsdale, AZ 85258-2100, USA

Barkley, Dean M (Politician)
1300 West Medicine Lake Drive
Apt 101
Minneapolis, MN 55441-4854, USA

Barkley, Doug (Athlete, Hockey Player)
583 63rd Ave.
Calgary, AB T3E 7N4, Canada

Barkley, Iran (Boxer)
2645 3rd Ave
Bronx, NY 10451, USA

Barkley, Jeff (Athlete, Baseball Player)
264 3rd Ave NE
Hickory, NC 28601-5016, USA

Barkman, Tyler Jane (Janie) (Swimmer)
Princeton University
Athletic Dept
Princeton, NJ 08544, USA

Barksdale, James (Jim) (Business Person)
Time Warner Inc.
One Time Warner Center
New York, NY 10019-8016, USA

Barksdale, Lance (Athlete, Baseball
Player)
4507 Pine Lake Dr
Terry, MS 39170-8741, USA

Barksdale, LaQuanda (Athlete, Basketball
Player)
San Antonio Silver Stars
1 SBC Center
San Antonio, TX 78219, USA

Barksdale, Rhesa H (Judge)
US Court of Appeals
245 E Capitol St
Jackson, MS 39201, USA

Barkum, Jerome P (Athlete, Football
Player)
2720 Palmer Dr
Apt J5
Gulfport, MS 39507, USA

Barletta, Joseph (Publisher)
TV Guide Magazine
100 Matsonford Road
Radnor, PA 19080, USA

Barletta, Lou (Congressman, Politician)
510 Cannon HOB
Washington, DC 20515, USA

Barlow, Bob (Athlete, Hockey Player)
4912 Westket Rd.
Victoria, BC V8Y 1Y5, Canada

Barlow, Corey (Athlete, Football Player)
1009 Narrows Point Dr
Birmingham, AL 35242, USA

Barlow, Craig (Athlete, Golfer)
231 W Horizon Ridge Pkwy #1515
Henderson, NV 89012-5427, USA

Barlow, Elizabeth J (Betty) (Stylist)
11 Eagleview Dr
Newton Square, PA 19073, USA

Barlow, Gary (Musician, Songwriter)
c/o Staff Member *WmE2 (WMA-UK)*
103 New Oxford St
London WC1A 1DD, UK

Barlow, Kevan (Athlete)
c/o Doug Hendrickson *Octagon Football*
832 Sansome St.
1st Floor
San Francisco, CA 94111, USA

Barlow, Mike (Athlete, Baseball Player)
4524 Francis Rd
Cazenovia, NY 13035-8470, USA

Barlow, Perry (Cartoonist)
New Yorker Magazine
Editorial Dept
4 Times Square
New York, NY 10036, USA

Barlow, Reggie (Athlete, Football Player)
8311 Timber Trace Ln
Pike Road, AL 36064, USA

BarlowGirl (Music Group, Musician)
c/o Greg Oliver *Greg Oliver Agency*
1710 Gen. George Patton Dr
#104
Brentwood, TN 37027, USA

Barmes, Bruce (Athlete, Baseball Player)
509 McDonald Ave
Charlotte, NC 28203-5321, USA

Barmes, Cllnt (Athlete, Baseball Player)
113 Mallard Ct
Mead, CO 80542-8802, USA

Barmore, Leon (Athlete, Basketball Player)
1100 Brookhaven Ave
Ruston, LA 71270-8505, USA

Barnaby, Matthew (Athlete, Hockey Player)
134 King Anthony Way
Getzville, NY 14068, USA

Barndt, Tom (Athlete, Football Player)
11041 Romola St
Las Vegas, NV 89141, USA

Barnes, Ben (Actor)
c/o Lena Roklin *Luber Roklin Management*
8530 Wilshire Blvd
6th Floor
Beverly Hills, CA 90211, USA

Barnes, Benny J (Athlete, Football Player)
5003 Fleming Ave
Richmond, CA 94804, USA

Barnes, Billy Ray (Athlete, Football Player)
501 W Ryder Ave
Landis, NC 28088, USA

Barnes, Brandon (Athlete, Football Player)
912 Westview Dr
Sikeston, MO 63801, USA

Barnes, Brian (Athlete, Baseball Player)
860 River Cove Dr
Dacula, GA 30019-2090, USA

Barnes, Bruce (Athlete, Football Player)
7129 Alexandria Pl
Stockton, CA 95207, USA

Barnes, Christopher Daniel (Actor)
3824 Fairway Ave
Studio City, CA 91604, USA

Barnes, Darian (Athlete, Football Player)
805 Lowell Ave
Toms River, NJ 08753, USA

Barnes, Erich (Athlete, Football Player)
712 Warburton Ave
Yonkers, NY 10701, USA

Barnes, Ernest E (Athlete, Football Player)
4435 Camellia Ave
North Hollywood, CA 91602, USA

Barnes, Frank (Athlete, Baseball Player)
1508 Brazil St
Greenville, MS 38701-2622, USA

Barnes, Frank S (Engineer)
University of Colorado
Engineering Dept
Boulder, CO 80309, USA

Barnes, Gary (Athlete, Football Player)
172 Falling Springs Rd
Central, SC 29630, USA

Barnes, Jeff (Athlete, Football Player)
10738 Versailles Blvd
Clermont, FL 34711, USA

Barnes, Jhane (Designer, Fashion Designer)
Jhane Barnes Inc
140 W 57th St #5B
New York, NY 10019-3326, USA

Barnes, Jimmy (Musician)
Harbour Agency
135 Forbes St
Wooloomooloo, NSW 2011, AUSTRALIA

Barnes, Joanna (Actor)
P.O. Box 1103
Gualala, CA 95445-1103, USA

Barnes, Joe (Race Car Driver)
Barnes Racing
200 Neil Thompson Rd.
Lackawaxen, PA 18435, USA

Barnes, John (Athlete, Baseball Player)
1455 Godell St
Templeton, CA 93465-9424, USA

Barnes, Johnnie (Athlete, Football Player)
212 Charlemagne Dr
Suffolk, VA 23435, USA

Barnes, Julian P (Writer)
P F D Drury House
34-43 Russell St
London WC2B 5HA, UNITED KINGDOM (UK)

Barnes, Khalif (Athlete, Football Player)
7967 Monterey Bay Dr
Jacksonville, FL 32256, USA

Barnes, Kim (Writer)
c/o Staff Member *Knopf Publishing Group*
1745 Broadway
New York, NY 10019, USA

Barnes, Larry (Athlete, Baseball Player)
11906 Crockett Ct
Bakersfield, CA 93312-5710, USA

Barnes, Larry (Athlete, Football Player)
2202 Belle Chase Cir
Tampa, FL 33634, USA

Barnes, Larry (Athlete, Football Player)
410 Navajo Ave
Simla, CO 80835, USA

Barnes, Linda (Writer)
56 Seaver St
Brookline, MA 02445-5749, USA

Barnes, Lute (Athlete, Baseball Player)
35911 Donny Cir
Palm Desert, CA 92211-2657, USA

Barnes, Marlon (Athlete, Football Player)
7092 W Autumn Gold Ct
Tucson, AZ 85743, USA

Barnes, Matt (Athlete, Basketball Player)
c/o Aaron Goodwin *Goodwin Sports Management*
Prefers to be contacted via email or telephone
Seattle, WA, USA

Barnes, Mike H (Athlete, Football Player)
205 Cindy St S
Keller, TX 76248, USA

Barnes, Mike J (Athlete, Football Player)
27474 Plank Rd
Guys Mills, PA 16327, USA

Barnes, Norm (Athlete, Hockey Player)
17 Meadow Crossing
Simsbury, CT 06070, USA

Barnes, Pat (Athlete, Football Player)
5 Willowglade
Trabuco Canyon, CA 92679, USA

Barnes, Pricilla (Actor)
c/o Staff Member *GVA Talent Agency Inc*
8981 Sunset Blvd.
Suite 101
Los Angeles, CA 90069, USA

Barnes, Priscilla (Actor)
3109 Buckingham Rd
Glendale, CA 91206, USA

Barnes, Rashidi (Athlete, Football Player)
8748 Kentshire Way
Sacramento, CA 95828, USA

Barnes, Reggie (Athlete, Football Player)
3110 Merrimac Ct
Southlake, TX 76092, USA

Barnes, Rich (Athlete, Baseball Player)
2845 Wilderness Rd
West Palm Beach, FL 33409-2030, USA

Barnes, Rick (Athlete, Basketball Player)
Texas University
Athletic Dept
Austin, TX 78713, USA

Barnes, Robert H (Psychic)
Texas Tech University
Medical School
PO Box 4349
Lubbock, TX 79409, USA

Barnes, Rod (Athlete, Basketball Player)
Mississippi State University
Athletic Dept
Mississippi State, MS 39762, USA

Barnes, Rodrigo (Athlete, Football Player)
4310 Gram Ln
Waco, TX 76705, USA

Barnes, Roger (Actor)
3 Cardiff Ct
Whitby, ON L1N 5N8, Canada

Barnes, Ron (Athlete, Baseball Player)
5304 Macdonald Ave
El Cerrito, CA 94583-5100, USA

Barnes, Skeeter (Athlete, Baseball Player)
11544 Winding Wood Dr
Indianapolis, IN 46235-9731, USA

Barnes, Stu (Athlete, Hockey Player)
5069 Royal Creek Ln
Plano, TX 75093, USA

Barnes, Stu (Athlete, Hockey Player)
Dallas Stars
2601 Avenue of the Stars Ste 100
Attn: Hockey Operations Dept
Frisco, TX 75034-9016, USA

Barnes, Tomur (Athlete, Football Player)
520 Flying Dutchman St
Crosby, TX 77532-5218, USA

Barnes, Wallace (Business Person)
Barnes Group
123 Main St
Bristol, CT 06010, USA

Barnes, William (Athlete, Baseball Player)
19792 Ardmore St
Detroit, MI 48235, USA

Barnes Jr, Roosevelt (Athlete, Football Player)
3128 Covington Manor Rd
Fort Wayne, IN 46814, USA

Barnes-McCoy, Joyce (Athlete, Baseball Player)
1313 E 19th Ave
Hutchinson, KS 67502-5061, USA

Barnet, Lisa (Stylist)
Lisa Barnet
Prefers to be contact via telephone or email
Los Angeles, CA 90069, USA

Barnett, Charlie (Actor)
c/o Carl Rumbaugh *Simmons & Scott Entertainment*
4110 W. Burbank Blvd.
Burbank, CA 91505, USA

Barnett, Dave (Commentator)
606 Witt Rd
Little Elm, TX 75068-5811, USA

Barnett, Dean (Athlete, Football Player)
8 Cozy Glen Cir
Henderson, NV 89074, USA

Barnett, Dick (Athlete, Basketball Player)
1227 Pine Ridge
Bushkill, PA 18324, USA

Barnett, Douglas (Athlete, Football Player)
651 Park Ln
Billings, MT 59102, USA

Barnett, Doyle (Writer)
c/o Staff Member *New World Library*
14 Pamaron Way
Novato, CA 94949, USA

Barnett, Fred (Athlete, Football Player)
P.O. Box 604
Bala Cynwyd, PA 19004, USA

Barnett, Gary (Coach, Football Coach)
Colorado University
Athletic Dept
Boulder, CO 80309, USA

Barnett, Jim (Athlete, Basketball Player)
7 Kittiwake Rd
Orinda, CA 94563-1716, USA

Barnett, Jonathan (Architect)
225 S Bonsall St
Philadelphia, PA 19103-5507, USA

Barnett, Larry (Athlete, Baseball Player)
6298 Hughes Rd
Prospect, OH 43342-9602, USA

Barnett, Mandy (Musician)
320 Old Hickory Blvd #1911
Nashville, TN 37209, USA

Barnett, Mike (Athlete, Baseball Player)
465 Bramblewood Ln
Knoxville, TN 37922-4371, USA

Barnett, Nate (Athlete, Basketball Player)
71e N Jefferson St
Wilmington, DE 19801-1412, USA

Barnett, Nick (Athlete, Football Player)
3496 Country Winds Ct
Green Bay, WI 54311, USA

Barnett, Oliver (Athlete, Football Player)
1133 Autumn Ridge Dr
Lexington, KY 40509, USA

Barnett, Pam (Athlete, Golfer)
4908 E Rancho Tierra Dr
Cave Creek, AZ 85331, USA

Barnett, Sloan (Correspondent, Writer)
c/o Staff Member *Simon & Schuster*
1230 Avenue of the Americas
New York, NY 10020, USA

Barnett, Steven (Steve) (Athlete, Football Player)
308 Romae Ct
Danville, CA 94526, USA

Barnett, Walter (Stylist)
c/o Celebrity Stylist *Photogenics Media*
8549 Higuera St
Building B
Culver City, CA 90232, USA

Barnette, Curtis H (Business Person)
Bethlehem Steel
1170 8th Ave
Bethlehem, PA 18016, USA

Barney, Darwin (Athlete, Baseball Player)
20467 SW Skiver St
Beaverton, OR 97007-5815, USA

Barney, Edith (Athlete, Baseball Player)
329 Blackburn Blvd
Venice, FL 34287, USA

Barney, Matthew (Artist, Entertainer)
Barbara Gladstone Gallery
515 W 24th St
New York, NY 10011

Barney, Tamra (Reality TV Star)
c/o Pamela Hicks *Hicks and Associates*
Prefers to be contacted via email or telephone
Los Angeles, CA 90069, USA

Barney Jr, Lemuel J (Lem) (Athlete, Football Player)
775 Kentbrook Dr
Commerce Township, MI 48382, USA

Barnhardt, Tom (Athlete, Football Player)
503 Park St
China Grove, NC 28023, USA

Barnhart, Vic (Athlete, Baseball Player)
13102 Unger Rd
Hagerstown, MD 21742-1428, USA

Barnhill, Herbert (Athlete, Baseball Player)
Jacksonville Red Caps
3712 Owen Ave
Jacksonville, FL 32208, USA

Barnhill, John (Athlete, Basketball Player)
28511 Lomo Dr
Rancho Palos Verdes, CA 90275-3137, USA

Barnhill, Norton (Athlete, Basketball Player)
1718 Park Terrace Ln
Winston Salem, NC 27127-4794, USA

Barnhill, Scott (Model)
c/o Staff Member *IMG*
304 Park Ave S Fl 12
New York, NY 10010, USA

Barnowski, Ed (Athlete, Baseball Player)
2380 Lake Lucy Rd
Chanhassen, MN 55317-7561, USA

Barnum, Harvey C (General)
12008 Walnut Branch Rd
Reston, VA 20194-5617

Barnum, HC Barney (War Hero)
12008 Walnut Branch Rd
Herndon, VA 20194, USA

Barnwell, Chris (Athlete, Baseball Player)
PO Box 600070
Jacksonville, FL 32260-0070, USA

Barnwell, Malcolm (Athlete, Football Player)
4045 Gullah Ave Apt 103 North
Charleston, SC 29405, USA

Barnwell, Ysaye (Musician)
Sweet Honey Agency
PO Box 600099
Newtonville, MA 02460, USA

Barocco, Rocco (Designer, Fashion Designer)
Via Occhio Marion
Capri/Napoli 80773, ITALY

Baron, Caroline (Producer)
c/o Paul Hook *ICM Partners (ICM-LA)*
10250 Constellation Blvd Fl 7
Los Angeles, CA 90067, USA

Baron, Crespo Enrique (Government Official)
European Parliament
97/113 Rue Velliard
Brussels 1040, BELGIUM

Baron, Jimmy (Athlete, Baseball Player)
7402 Conner Ln
Edwardsville, IL 62025-4668, USA

Baron, Joanne (Actor)
940 N Tigertail Rd
Los Angeles, A 90049, USA

Baron, Martin D (Editor)
Boston Globe
Editorial Dept
135 WT Morrissey Blvd
Dorchester, MA 02125, USA

Baron, Murray (Athlete, Hockey Player)
23723 N. Scottsdale Rd.
#D-3
Scottsdale, AZ 85255, USA

Baron, Natalia (Actor)
c/o Tiffany Kuzon *Evolution Entertainment (LA)*
901 N Highland Ave
Los Angeles, CA 90038, USA

Barone, Anita (Actor)
17628 McCormick St
Encino, CA 91316, USA

Barone, Daniel (Athlete, Baseball Player)
120 Joes Ln
Hollister, CA 95023-6353, USA

Barone, Dick (Athlete, Baseball Player)
1481 McDonald Cir
Shasta Lake, CA 95023-6743, USA

Baron-Reid, Colette Baron-Reid (Writer)
c/o Staff Member *Hay House, Inc*
P.O. Box 5100
Carlsbad, CA 92018-5100, USA

Barr, Bob (Business Person, Politician)
Office of Bob Barr
4401 Northside Parkway #100
Atlanta, GA 30327, USA

Barr, Brenda (Stylist)
c/o Staff Member *Illusions Management*
129 W 27th St
Penthouse
New York, NY 10001, USA

Barr, Cynthia (Athlete, Olympic Athlete, Swimmer)
3995 Aiken Rd
Pensacola, FL 32503-3301, USA

Barr, Dave (Athlete, Hockey Player)
c/o Staff Member *Guelph Storm Hockey Club*
55 Wyndham St N
Guelph, ON N1H 7T8, Canada

Barr, Dave (Golfer)
Duncan MacKenzie
10620 Southdale Rd
Richmond, BC V7A 2W7, CANADA

Barr, Doug (Actor)
PO Box 63
Rutherford, CA 94573, USA

Barr, Jim (Athlete, Baseball Player)
6335 Oak Hill Dr
Granite Bay, CA 5746-8908, USA

Barr, Julia (Actor)
c/o Robert Attermann *Abrams Artists Agency (LA)*
9200 Sunset Blvd
11th Floor
Los Angeles, CA 90069, USA

Barr, Matt (Actor)
c/o Matt Luber *Luber Roklin Management*
8530 Wilshire Blvd
6th Floor
Beverly Hills, CA 90211, USA

Barr, Mike (Athlete, Basketball Player)
350 38th St NW
Canton, OH 44709-1523, USA

Barr, Nevada (Writer)
G P Putnam's Sons
375 Hudson St
New York, NY 10014, USA

Barr, Office of Bob (Ex-Congressman, Politician)
900 Circle 75 Pkwy SE
Suite 1280
Atlanta, GA 30339-6016, USA

Barr, Roseanne (Actor, Comedian, Producer)
47-4567 Honokaa Waipio Rd
Honokaa, HI 96727, USA

Barr, Steve (Athlete, Baseball Player)
470 Village Cir SW
Winter Haven, FL 33880-1668, USA

Barr, William (Politician)
1 Stamford Forum
Stamford, CT 06901-3516, USA

Barragan, Cuno (Athlete, Baseball Player)
1824 Saint Ann Ct
Carmichael, CA 95608, USA

Barranca, German (Athlete, Baseball Player)
199 Kreidler Ave
York, PA 17402, USA

Barrasso, John (Senator)
307 Dirksen Senate Office Building
Washington, DC 20510, USA

Barrasso, Tom (Athlete, Hockey Player)
Carolina Hurricanes 1400 Edwards Mill Rd
Attn Coaching Staff
Raleigh, NC 27607-3624, USA

Barrasso, Tom (Athlete, Hockey Player)
12820 Rosalie St
Raleigh, NC 27614-7970, USA

Barratt, Michael R (Astronaut)
2102 Pleasant Palm Circle
League City, TX 77573, USA

Barratt, Michael R Dr (Astronaut)
2102 Pleasant Palm Cir
League City, TX 77573-6670, USA

Barrault, Doug (Athlete, Hockey Player)
1305 Pine Dr
Golden, BC V0A 1H1, CANADA

Barrault, Marie-Christine (Actor)
Cineart
36 Rue de Ponthlieu
Paris 75008, FRANCE

Barraza, Adriana (Actor)
c/o Craig Shapiro *ICM Partners (ICM-LA)*
10250 Constellation Blvd Fl 7
Los Angeles, CA 90067, USA

Barraza, Maria (Actor)
c/o Staff Member *TV Caracol*
Calle 76 #11 - 35
Piso 10AA
Bogota DC 26484, COLOMBIA

Barre, Raymond (Prime Minister)
4-6 Ave Emile-Acollas
Paris 75007, FRANCE

Barrese, Sasha (Actor)
c/o Erik Kritzer *Kritzer Levine Wilkins Entertainment (KLWG)*
11872 La Grange Ave
1st Floor
Los Angeles, CA 90025, USA

Barre-Sinoussi, Francoise (Nobel Prize Laureate)
Institut Pasteur
25 rue du Docteur Roux
RetroviralInfections Unit
Paris Cedex 75724, France

Barreto, Alexandra (Actor)
c/o Robert Marsala *Wishlab*
2225-A Hyperion Ave
Los Angeles, CA 90027, USA

Barreto, Bruno (Director)
c/o Martin Spencer *Creative Artists Agency (CAA-LA)*
2000 Ave Of The Stars
Los Angeles, CA 90067, USA

Barrett, Alice (Actor)
Alliance Talent
9171 Wilshire Blvd #441
Beverly Hills, CA 90210, USA

Barrett, Bo (Actor)
c/o Staff Member *Badass Haircut Productions*
2718 Lakewood Ave
Los Angeles, CA 90039, USA

Barrett, Bob (Athlete, Football Player)
610 54th Ave W
Bradenton, FL 34210, USA

Barrett, Brendan Ryan (Actor)
c/o Carol Elsner *Gage Group, The (LA)*
14724 Ventura Blvd
Suite 505
Sherman Oaks, CA 91403, USA

Barrett, Brendon Ryan (Actor)
9255 Sunset Bvd
#1010
West Hollywood, CA 90069, USA

Barrett, Colleen (Business Person)
Southwest Airlines
PO Box 36611
2702 Love Field Dr
Dallas, TX 75235, USA

Barrett, Craig R (Business Person)
Intel Corp
2200 Mission College Blvd
Santa Clara, CA 95054, USA

Barrett, Danny
University At Buffalo
104 Stadium Complex Attn Football
Couching Staff
Buffalo, NY 14260-5100, USA

Barrett, David (Athlete, Football Player)
1423 E Rose St
Blytheville, AR 72315, USA

Barrett, Ernie (Athlete, Basketball Player)
2105 Grand Ridge Ct
Manhattan, KS 66503-8695, USA

Barrett, Fred (Athlete, Hockey Player)
3016 Leitrim Rd
Gloucester, ON K1T 3V9, Canada

Barrett, Jacinda (Actor)
c/o Joan Green *Joan Green Management*
1836 Courtney Terr
Los Angeles, CA 90046, USA

Barrett, James E (Judge)
US Court of Appeals
2120 Capitol Ave
Cheyenne, WY 82001, USA

Barrett, Jean (Athlete, Football Player)
7494 S Sleepy Hollow Dr
Tulsa, OK 74136, USA

Barrett, John (Athlete, Hockey Player)
4570 Bank St
Gloucester, ON KlT 3W6, Canada

Barrett, Kelli (Actor)
c/o Emily Gerson Saines *Brookside Artists Management (NY)*
250 W 57th St
Suite 2303
New York, NY 10107, USA

Barrett, Malcolm (Actor)
c/o Craig Dorfman *Frontline Management*
5670 Wilshire Blvd.
Suite 1370
Los Angeles, CA 90036, USA

Barrett, Mario (Actor, Musician)
c/o Tammy Brook *FYI Public Relations*
174 5th Ave
Suite 404
New York, NY 10010, USA

Barrett, Martin G (Marty) (Athlete, Baseball Player)
3552 Ridge Meadow St
Las Vegas, NV 89135-7811, USA

Barrett, Michael (Athlete, Baseball Player)
Career Sports Management 600 Galleria
Pkwy SE Ste 1900
Atlanta, GA 30339-5990, USA

Barrett, Stanton (Race Car Driver)
Sky Motorsports
1055 Gateway Dr.
Mooresville, NC 28115, USA

Barrett, Stephen (Activist, Doctor)
PO Boc 1747
Allentown, PA 18105, USA

Barrett, Ted (Athlete, Baseball Player)
4380 E Sundance Ct
Gilbert, AZ 87116-3205, USA

Barrett, Thomas J (Admiral)
Vice Commandant US Court Guard
2100 2nd St SW
Washington, DC 20593, USA

Barrett, Tim (Athlete, Baseball Player)
5588 Jandel Dr
Aurora, IN 47001, USA

Barrett, Tom (Athlete, Baseball Player)
5306 W Jupiter Way
Chandler, AZ 85226-8622, USA

Barrett, Wade (Soccer Player)
Fredrikstad Fotballklubb Sport ASA
Mads Stangs gate 20
Fredrikstad N-1610, NORWAY

Barrett, William (Misc)
34 Harwood Ave
Sleepy Hollow, NY 10591, USA

Barrichello, Rubens (Race Car Driver)
c/o Staff Member *Jaguar Racing Ltd*
Bradbourne Drive
Tilbrook
Milton Keynes MK7 8BJ, United Kingdom

Barrie, Barbara (Actor)
c/o Staff Member *Innovative Artists (LA)*
1505 10th St
Santa Monica, CA 90401, USA

Barrie, Chris (Actor, Comedian)
International Creative Mgmt
76 Oxford St
London W1N 0AX, UNITED KINGDOM
(UK)

Barrie, Doug (Athlete, Hockey Player)
12130 46 St NW
Edmonton, AB T5W 2W4, Canada

Barrie, Len (Athlete, Hockey Player)
Bear Mountain Gold Club
208-2800 Bryn Maur Rd
Victoria, BC V9B 3T4, Canada

Barrie, Sebastian (Athlete, Football Player)
502 Heritage Meadows Rd
Pleasant Hill, CA 94523, USA

Barrile, Anthony (Actor)
Alliance Talent
9171 Wilshire Blvd #441
Beverly Hills, CA 90210, USA

Barrileaux, James (Misc)
Dryden Flight Research Center
PO Box 273
Edwards, CA 93523, USA

Barrilleaux, James (Aviator)
18471 Norlene Way
Grass Valley, CA 95949-7386, USA

Barrino, Fantasia (Musician)
5500 Bevington Pl
Charlotte, NC 28277, USA

Barrios, Jose (Athlete, Baseball Player)
6484 SW 25th St
Miami, FL 33155-2958, USA

Barris, Chuck (Television Host)
80 Washington Spring Rd
Palisades, NY 10964, USA

Barris, George (Designer, Misc)
Barris Kustom Industries
10811 Riverside Drive
North Hollywood, CA 91602, USA

Barritt, Randi (Stylist)
315 W 23rd St
#6-D
New York, NY 10011, USA

Barriw, Barbara (Actor)
15 W 72nd St
#2A
New York, NY 10023, USA

Barron, Alex (Athlete, Football Player)
630 Emerson Rd
Apt 206
Saint Louis, MO 63141, USA

Barron, Alex
630 Emerson Rd Apt 206
Saint Louis, MO 63141, USA

Barron, Alex (Race Car Driver)
Dan Gurney's Racing
2334 S. Broadway
Santa Ana, CA 92707, USA

Barron, Chris (Music Group, Musician)
c/o Staff Member *Skyline Music*
28 Union St
Whitefield, NH 03598, USA

Barron, Dana (Actor)
c/o Kevin Turner *Coast to Coast Talent Group*
3350 Barham Blvd
Los Angeles, CA 90068, USA

Barron, Doug (Athlete, Golfer)
5080 Peg Ln
Memphis, TN 38117-2147, USA

Barron, Kenneth (Kenny) (Composer, Musician)
Joel Chriss
300 Mercer St
#3J
New York, NY 10003, USA

Barron, Lynn (Stylist)
c/o Staff Member *Rex Agency, The*
6311 Romaine St
Los Angeles, CA 90038, USA

Barron, Mark (Athlete, Baseball Player)
110 N Randolph Ave
Clarksville, IN 47129-2633, USA

Barron, Tony (Athlete, Baseball Player)
16014 123rd Ave Ct E
Puyallup, WA 98374-9649, USA

Barros, Dana (Athlete, Basketball Player)
67 Fairfield Cir
Norwood, MA 02062-5564, USA

Barrow, Barbara (Athlete, Golfer)
11427 Mayapple Way
San Diego, CA 92131, USA

Barrow, Dean (Prime Minister)
Office Of The Prime Minister
Sir Edney Cain Building
Belmopan, Belize

Barrow, Geoff (Musician)
Fruit
Saga Center
326 Kensal Road
London W10 5BZ, UNITED KINGDOM
(UK)

Barrow, John (Athlete, Football Player)
4111 Bay Shore Dr
Missouri City, TX 77459-1829, USA

Barrow, Michael (Athlete, Football Player)
1115 S Alhambra Cir Coral
Gables, FL 33146, USA

Barrowman, John (Actor)
c/o Staff Member *Gavin Barker Assoc*
2D Wimpole St
London W1G 0EB, UK

Barrowman, Mike (Swimmer)
706 N Wamer St
Bay City, MI 48706, USA

Barrows, Scott (Athlete, Football Player)
3600 Kern Rd
Lake Orion, MI 48360, USA

Barrows, Sydney Biddle (Misc)
210 W 70th St Apt 209
New York, NY 10023-4363, USA

Barrs, Jay (Athlete, Olympic Athlete, Shooter)
646 Kings Peak Cv
Draper, UT 84020-7922, USA

Barrueco, Manuel (Musician)
Columbia Artists Mgmt Inc
165 W 57th St
New York, NY 10019, USA

Barry, A L (Religious Leader)
Lutheran Church Missouri Synod
1333 S Kirkwood Road
Saint Louis, MO 63122, USA

Barry, Allan (Athlete, Football Player)
3760 Edgeview Dr
Pasadena, CA 91107, USA

Barry, Brent (Athlete, Basketball Player)
617 Grandview Pl
San Antonio, TX 78209, USA

Barry, Daniel T (Dan) (Astronaut)
46 Ashton Lane
South Hadley, MA 01075, USA

Barry, Daniel T Dr (Astronaut)
46 Ashton Ln
South Hadley, MA 01075-2143, USA

Barry, Dave (Journalist, Writer)
Miami Herald
Editorial Dept
1 Herald Plaza
Miami, FL 33132, USA

Barry, Ed (Athlete, Hockey Player)
61 Pleasant St
Needham, MA 02492, USA

Barry, Jeff (Athlete, Baseball Player)
322 N Barneburg Rd
Medford, OR 97504-6683, USA

Barry, Jeff (Composer)
BMI
8730 Sunset Blvd #300W
Los Angeles, CA 90069, USA

Barry, Jon (Athlete, Basketball Player)
3325 Piedmont Rd NE
Atlanta, GA 30305-1889, USA

Barry, Kevin (Athlete, Baseball Player)
72 Burlington Path Rd
Cream Ridge, NJ 08514-1601, USA

Barry, Len (Musician)
Cape Entertainment
1161 NW 76th Ave
Plantation, FL 33322, USA

Barry, Lynda (Cartoonist)
PO Box 447
Footville, WI 53537, USA

Barry, Marion S (Politician)
161 Raleigh St SE
Washington, DC 20032, USA

Barry, Max (Writer)
c/o Staff Member *Scribe Publications Pty Ltd*
595 Drummond St
Carlton North Vic 3054, Australia

Barry, Odell (Athlete, Football Player)
2561 Ranch Reserve Rdg
Denver, CO 80234, USA

Barry, Patricia (Actor)
12742 Highwood St
Los Angeles, CA 90049, USA

Barry, Paul (Athlete, Football Player)
409 Kingswood Dr
El Paso, TX 79932, USA

Barry, Pauline (Stylist)
Pauline Barry
Prefers to be contacted
via telephone or email
San Francisco, CA, USA

Barry, Randy (Reality TV Star)
c/o Michael Martin *MM Agency*
3937 Nobel Drive
San Diego, CA 92122, USA

Barry, Raymond J (Actor)
c/o Bob McGowan *McGowan Management*
8733 W Sunset Blvd
Suite 103
West Hollywood, CA 90069, USA

Barry, Rich (Athlete, Baseball Player)
12020 Hoffman St
Apt K
Studio City, CA 91604-4760, USA

Barry, Rick (Athlete, Basketball Player)
5240 Broadmoor Bluffs Dr
Colorado Springs, CO 80906-7912, USA

Barry, Rod (Adult Film Star)
c/o Staff Member *Diva Central Inc*
7510 W Sunset Blvd Ste 1445
Los Angees, CA 90046, USA

Barry, Scott (Athlete, Baseball Player)
148 Lukesport Dr
Quincy, MI 49082-9596, USA

Barry, Seymour (Sy) (Artist, Cartoonist)
225 Fairfield Dr E
Holbrook, NY 11741, USA

Barry, Todd (Comedian)
c/o David (Dave) Becky *3 Arts Entertainment Inc*
9460 Wilshire Blvd
7th Floor
Beverly Hills, CA 90210, USA

Barry III, Richard F D (Rick) (Athlete, Basketball Player)
KNBR Radio
55 Hawthorne #1100
San Francisco, CA 94106, USA

Barrymore, Drew (Actor, Producer)
1270 Pepper Ln
Montecito, CA 93108, USA

Barrymore, Rhonda (Stylist)
c/o Staff Member *Help Me Rhonda*
541 10th St NW #294
Atlanta, GA 30318, USA

Barsh, Gregory S (Doctor)
Stanford University
Medical Center
Pediatrics Dept
Stanford, CA 94305, USA

Barsotti, Charles (Cartoonist)
419 E 55th St
Kansas City, MO 64110, USA

Bart, Peter (Writer)
c/o Daniel Strone *Trident Media Group LLC*
41 Madison Ave
36th Floor
New York, NY 10010, USA

Bart, Roger (Actor)
c/o Michael Baum *Impression Entertainment*
9229 W Sunset Blvd #700
West Hollywood, CA 90069, USA

Bartecko, Lubos (Athlete, Hockey Player)
121 Windy Acres Estates Dr
Ballwin, MO 63021, USA

Bartee, Kimera (Athlete, Baseball Player)
State College Spikes 112 Medlar Field at
Lubrano Park 'Attn: Managers Office
University Park, PA 16802, USA

Bartee, William (Athlete, Football Player)
17 Talaquah Blvd
Ormond Beach, FL 32174, USA

Bartek, Steve (Musician)
c/o Staff Member *Kraft-Engel Management*
15233 Ventura Blvd
Suite 200
Sherman Oaks, CA 91403, USA

Bartel, Robin (Athlete, Hockey Player)
210 Forsyth Crt
Saskatoon, SK S7N 4H2, Canada

Bartels, Wolfgang (Skier)
Womdihof Hintersee
Ransau 83486, GERMANY

Barth, Robert (Religious Leader)
Churches of Christ in Christian Union
Po Box 30
Circleville, OH 43113, USA

Bartha, Justin (Actor, Producer)
8599 Wonderland Ave
Los Angeles, CA 90046, USA

Barthmaier, Jimmy (Athlete, Baseball Player)
5005 Waters Edge Trl
Roswell, GA 30075-8237, USA

Bartholomay, William C (Commentator)
180 E Pearson St
Apt 3307
Chicago, IL 60611-6730, USA

Bartholomew, Brent (Athlete, Football Player)
809 N Lake Pleasant Rd
Apopka, FL 32712, USA

Bartholomew, Jean (Athlete, Golfer)
411 Capistrano Dr
Palm Beach Gardens, FL 33410, USA

Bartholomew, Ken (Athlete, Olympic Athlete, Speed Skater)
17574 Sunray Cir SW
Prior Lake, MN 55372, USA

Bartholomew, Logan (Actor)
c/o Beverly Strong *Strong Management*
9350 Wilshire Blvd
#224
Beverly Hills, CA 90212, USA

Bartilson, Lynsey (Actor)
c/o Staff Member *Talent Company, The*
P.O. Box 4227
Burbank, CA 91503, USA

Bartirome, Tony (Athlete, Baseball Player)
1104 Palma Sola Blvd
Bradenton, FL 34209, USA

Bartiromo, Maria (Correspondent)
c/o Staff Member *CNBC (DC)*
400 N Capitol St NW Ste 850
Washington, DC 20001, USA

Bartkowski, Steven J (Steve) (Athlete, Football Player)
10745 Bell Rd
Duluth, GA 30097, USA

Bartle, Cheryl (Actor)
8281 Melrose #200
Los Angeles, CA 90046, USA

Bartles, Carl Bartles (Athlete, Football Player)
405 E 4th St
Kannapolis, NC 28083-3606, United States

Bartles, Edward (Athlete, Basketball Player)
105 Hemlock Dr
Killingworth, CT 06419, USA

Bartlett, Bonnie (Actor, Musician)
12805 Hortense St
Studio City, CA 91604, USA

Bartlett, Doug (Athlete, Football Player)
9133 26th St
Brookfield, IL 60513, USA

Bartlett, Erinn (Actor)
c/o Randy James *James/Levy/Jacobson Management Inc*
3500 W Olive Ave
Suite 1470
Burbank, CA 91505, USA

Bartlett, Jason (Athlete, Baseball Player)
15476 Artesian Spring Rd
San Diego, CA 92127-5736, USA

Bartlett, Jennifer L (Artist)
Paula Cooper Gallery
534 W 21st St
New York, NY 10011, USA

Bartlett, Jim (Athlete, Hockey Player)
8718 Chadwick Dr
Tampa, FL 33635, USA

Bartlett, Murray (Actor)
c/o Rosanne Quezada *Paradigm (LA)*
360 N Crescent Dr
North Bldg
Beverly Hills, CA 90210, USA

Bartlett, Neil (Misc)
6 Oak Dr
Orinda, CA 94563, USA

Bartlett, Robin (Actor)
2202 Pearl St
Santa Monica, CA 90405, USA

Bartlett, Thomas A (Educator)
1209 SW 6th St
#904
Portland, OR 97204, USA

Bartletti, Don (Journalist)
Los Angeles Times
Editorial Dept
202 W 1st St
Los Angeles, CA 90012, USA

Bartlett O'Reilly, Alison (Actor)
c/o Carolyn Anthony *Anthony & Associates*
P.O. Box 910
New York, NY 10108

Bartley, Boyd (Athlete, Baseball Player)
7500 Noreast Dr
North Richland Hills, TX 76180-6736, USA

Bartley, Ephesians (Athlete, Football Player)
3552 Kittery Dr
Snellville, GA 30039, USA

Bartmann, Bill (Business Person)
8556 E 101st St
Suite C
Tulsa, OK 74133-7036, USA

Bartoe, John-David F (Astronaut)
2724 Lighthouse Dr
Houston, TX 77058, USA

Bartoletti, Bruno (Conductor)
Chicago Lyric Opera
20 N Wacker Dr
Chicago, IL 60606, USA

Bartoletti, Louis (Athlete, Golfer)
1450 Longlea Ter
Wellington, FL 33414, USA

Bartoli, Cecilia (Musician)
Decca Music Group Limited
8 St James's Square
London SW1Y 4JU, UNITED KINGDOM

Bartolome, Victor (Athlete, Basketball Player)
1025A Rinconada Rd
Santa Barbara, CA 93101-1424, USA

Barton, Austin (Artist)
100 N Lake
Joseph, OR 97846, USA

Barton, Bob (Athlete, Baseball Player)
37193 Stardust Way
Murrieta, CA 92563-5076, USA

Barton, Brian (Athlete, Baseball Player)
1217 W 76th St
Los Angeles, CA 90044-2411, USA

Barton, Daric (Athlete, Baseball Player)
958 Naples Dr
Corona, CA 92882-6350, USA

Barton, Dorie (Actor)
c/o Daniel Spilo *Industry Entertainment Partners*
955 S Carrillo Dr
Suite 300
Los Angeles, CA 90048, USA

Barton, Eric (Athlete, Football Player)
23 Hayes Hill Dr
Northport, NY 11768, USA

Barton, Glenys (Artist)
Angela Flowers Gallery
199-205 Richmond Road
London E8 3NJ, UNITED KINGDOM (UK)

Barton, Greg (Athlete, Kayaker, Olympic Athlete)
Epic Kayaks Inc
645 Marina Dr
Charleston, SC 29492-7626, USA

Barton, Greg (Athlete, Football Player)
13965 SW Barlow Ct
Beaverton, OR 97008, USA

Barton, Harris S (Athlete, Football Player)
334 Lincoln Ave
Palo Alto, CA 94301, USA

Barton, Jim (Athlete, Football Player)
2126 Taylor Ln
Newark, OH 43055, USA

Barton, Joe (Congressman, Politician)
2109 Rayburn HOB
Washington, DC 20515, USA

Barton, Katie (Stylist)
c/o Kristy Charroin *Straub Collaborative Inc*
2503 N Albina
Portland, OR 97227, USA

Barton, Lou Ann (Musician)
2010 Kinney Ave
Austin, TX 78704, USA

Barton, Mischa (Actor)
2670 Bowmont Dr
Beverly Hills, CA 90210, USA

Barton, Peter (Actor)
10417 Eastbourne Ave #3
Los Angeles, CA 90024, USA

Barton, Rachel (Musician)
I C M Artists
40 W 57th St
New York, NY 10019, USA

Barton, Shawn (Athlete, Baseball Player)
1009 Helm Ln
Reading, PA 19605-3313, USA

Bartosh, Cliff (Athlete, Baseball Player)
939 Fairlawn Dr
Duncanville, TX 75116-3003, USA

Bartosik, Alison (Swimmer)
c/o Staff Member *Premier Management Group (PMG Sports)*
115 Crescent Commons Dr Ste 250
Cary, NC 27518, USA

Bartovic, Milan (Athlete, Hockey Player)
141 Bennington Hills Ct
West Henrietta, NY 14586, USA

Bartrum, Mike (Athlete, Football Player)
43375 Carlton Pl
Pomeroy, OH 45769, USA

Bartucelli, Jean-Louis (Actor)
9 rue Benard
Paris F-75014, France

Bartulis, Oskars (Athlete, Hockey Player)
45 Wimbledon Way
Marlton, NJ 08053-2087, USA

Bartz, Carol A (Business Person)
Autodesk Inc
111 McInnis Parkway
San Rafael, CA 94903, USA

Bartz, Gary L (Composer, Musician)
Joel Chriss
300 Mercer St #3J
New York, NY 10003, USA

Bartz, Randall (Athlete, Olympic Athlete, Speed Skater)
3820 Baker Rd
Hopkins, MN 55419-5359, USA

Baruch, Lisa (Stylist)
c/o Staff Member *Ford Models (Chicago)*
311 W Superior St
Chicago, IL 60654, USA

Baruchel, Jay (Actor)
c/o Willie Mercer *Thruline Entertainment*
9250 Wilshire Blvd
Ground Fl
Beverly Hills, CA 90212, USA

Baryshnikov, Mikhail (Actor, Dancer)
12 Lawrence Ln
Palisades, NY 10964, USA

Barzilauskas, Carl (Athlete, Football Player)
4444 Lower Schooner Rd
Nashville, IN 47448, USA

Barzilla, Phil (Athlete, Baseball Player)
3310 Crvstal Creek Dr
SugarLand, TX 77478-4045, USA

Basak, Chris (Athlete, Baseball Player)
1371 N Mohawk St
Chicago, IL 60610-1713, USA

Basana, Fred (Athlete, Baseball Player)
222 Diamond Oaks Rd
Roseville, CA 85678, USA

Basañez, Sergio (Actor)
c/o Staff Member *TV Azteca*
Periferico Sur 4121
Colonia Fuentes del Pedregal
DF CP 14141, Mexico

Basaraba, Gary (Actor)
26 Rue Albus
Toulouse 31300, FRANCE

Basch, Harry (Actor)
920 1/2 S Serrano Ave
Los Angeles, CA 90006, USA

Basche, David (Actor)
c/o Mark Rousso *New Wave Entertainment (LA)*
2660 W Olive Blvd
Burbank, CA 91505, USA

Basche, David Alan (Actor)
c/o Brad Mendelsohn *New Wave Entertainment (LA)*
2660 W Olive Blvd
Burbank, CA 91505, USA

Baschnagel, Brian D (Athlete, Football Player)
1824 Ridgewood Ln W
Glenview, IL 60025, USA

Basco, Dante (Actor)
Don Buchwald
6500 Wilshire Blvd #2200
Los Angeles, CA 90048, USA

Basco, Derek (Actor)
c/o Staff Member *GVA Talent Agency Inc*
8981 Sunset Blvd.
Suite 101
Los Angeles, CA 90069, USA

Basco, Dion (Actor)
Schiowitz/Clay/Rose
1680 N Vine St #1016
Los Angeles, CA 90028, USA

Bash, Dana (Correspondent, Television Host)
5003 Belt Rd NW
Washington, DC 20016, USA

Bashir, Idrees (Athlete, Football Player)
5579 Mountain View Pass
Stone Mountain, GA 30087, USA

Bashir, Idrees
5579 Mountain View Pass Stone
Mountain, GA 30087, USA

Bashir, Martin (Correspondent, Journalist, Television Host)
c/o Staff Member *John Miles Organisation*
Cadbury Camp Lane
Clapton in Gordano
Bristol BS20 7SB, United Kingdom

Bashkirov, Dmitri A (Musician)
25 Martirez Oblatos
Pozuelo
Madrid, SPAIN

Bashoff, Blake (Actor)
c/o Marni Rosenzweig *Abrams Artists Agency (LA)*
9200 Sunset Blvd
11th Floor
Los Angeles, CA 90069, USA

Basia (Music Group)
c/o Staff Member *Creative Artists Agency (CAA-LA)*
2000 Ave Of The Stars
Los Angeles, CA 90067, USA

Basil, Toni (Musician)
830 S Ridgeley Dr
Los Angeles, CA 90036, USA

Basinger, Kim (Actor)
4833 Don Juan Pl
Woodland Hills, CA 91364, USA

Basinski, Ed (Athlete, Baseball Player)
8530 SW Curry Dr
Unit B
Wilsonville, OR 97070, USA

Basinski, Eddie (Athlete, Baseball Player)
4110 SE Jackson S
Portland, OR 97222-5936, USA

Baska, Richard (Rick) (Athlete, Football Player)
176 Josephine Ct Central
Point, OR 97502, USA

Basralian, Stephanie (Stylist)
Prefers to be contacted
via telephone or email

Bass, Anthony (Athlete, Football Player)
120 Ridgewood Frst
Saint Albans, WV 25177, USA

Bass, Bob (Athlete, Basketball Player, Coach)
2266 Deerfield Dr
Fort Mill, SC 29715, USA

Bass, Brian (Athlete, Baseball Player)
423 Seminole Dr
Montgome.rv, AL 36117-3905, USA

Bass, Doug (Actor)
c/o Jana Marimpietri *Mosaic Media Group*
9200 W. Sunset Blvd
10th Floor
Los Angeles, CA 90069, USA

Bass, Fontella (Music Group, Musician)
c/o Staff Member *Nonesuch Records*
75 Rockefeller Plz Fl 8
New York, NY 10019, USA

Bass, George F (Archaeologist)
1600 Dominik Dr
College Station, TX 77840, USA

Bass, Glenn (Athlete, Football Player)
4185 Diplomacy Cir
Tallahassee, FL 32308, USA

Bass, Jules (Director, Musician, Producer, Writer)
c/o Staff Member *Rankin/Bass Productions*
24 West 55th Street
New York, NY 10019, USA

Bass, Karen (Congressman, Politician)
405 Cannon HOB
Washington, DC 20515, USA

Bass, Kevin (Athlete, Baseball Player)
3630 Maranatha Dr
Sugar Land, TX 77479-9665, USA

Bass, Lance (Musician)
252 7th Ave #10J
New York, NY 10001, USA

Bass, Michael T (Athlete, Football Player)
4703 NW 36th St
Gainesville, FL 32605, USA

Bass, Mike (Athlete, Football Player)
4703 NW 36th St
Gainesville, FL 32605, USA

Bass, Norm (Athlete, Baseball Player)
156 E 70th St
Los Angeles, CA 90003-2102, USA

Bass, Norm (Athlete, Football Player)
156 E 70th St Los
Angeles, CA 90003, USA

Bass, Randy (Athlete, Baseball Player)
2709 SW Coombs Rd
Lawton, OK 73505-0809, USA

Bass, Ronald (Writer)
c/o Staff Member *Creative Artists Agency (CAA-LA)*
2000 Ave Of The Stars
Los Angeles, CA 90067, USA

Bass, Ronald (Ron) (Actor, Producer, Writer)
c/o Staff Member *Writers Co-Op*
4000 Warner Blvd
Bldg 1
Burbank, CA 91522, USA

Bass, Sid (Business Person)
4824 Crestline Rd
Ft Worth, TX 76107, USA

Bassen, Bob (Athlete, Coach, Hockey Player)
1742 Coldstone Dr
Frisco, TX 75034, USA

Bassett, Angela (Actor)
4710 Hillard Ave
La Canada Flintridge, CA 91011, USA

Bassett, Brian (Cartoonist, Editor)
Seattle Times
Editorial Dept 1120 John St
Seattle, WA 98109, USA

Bassett, Leslie R (Composer, Musician)
5433 Ashmoore Ln
Flowery Branch, GA 30542-2777, USA

Bassett, Tim (Athlete, Basketball Player)
1143 Dorsey Pl
Plainfield, NJ 07062-2207, USA

Bassey, Dame Shirley (Musician)
24 Avenue Princess Grace
Monte Carlo 1200, Monaco

Bassey, Jennifer (Actor)
12 E 86th St
#1728
New York, NY 10028, USA

Bassham, Lanny (Athlete, Olympic Athlete, Shooter)
2112 Bellanca Ct
Flower Mound, TX 75028-8360, USA

Bassingthwaighte, Natalie (Actor)
c/o Staff Member *Mark Byrne Management*
1/2 Cooper St
Double Bay
Sydney, NSW 2028, Australia

Basslitz, Georg (Artist)
Schloss Demeberg
Holle 31188, GERMANY

Bassman, Herman (Red) (Athlete, Football Player)
910 Sunset Ave
Petersburg, VA 23805, USA

Basso, Gabriel (Actor)
c/o David Eisenberg *Protege Entertainment*
710 E. Angeleno Ave
Burbank, CA 91501, USA

Bast, William (Producer)
6691 Whitley Ter
Los Angeles, CA 90068, USA

Bastedo, Alexandra (Actor)
Charlesworth
68 Old Brompton Rd #280
London SW7 3LQ, UNITED KINGDOM
(UK)

Bastel, Emily (Athlete, Golfer)
5377 County Highway 430
Upper Sandusky, OH 43351, USA

Baston, Maceo (Athlete, Basketball Player)
PO Box 4846
Troy, MI 48099-4846, USA

Basu, Bipasha (Actor)
c/o Simone Sheffield *Canyon
Entertainment*
P.O. Box 256
Palm Springs, CA 92263, USA

Baswell, Jack (Athlete, Baseball Player)
9629 Bella Dr
Daphne, AL 36526-6271, USA

Batali, Dean (Writer)
c/o Michael Van Dyck *Genesis*
360 N Crescent Dr
Beverly Hills, CA 90210-6820, USA

Batali, Mario (Chef, Television Host)
Otto Enoteca Pizzeria
1 5th Ave
New York, NY 10003, USA

Batalla, Rick (Actor)
c/o Staff Member *Halpern Management*
P.O. Box 5042
Santa Monica, CA 90409-5042, USA

Batch, Baron (Athlete, Football Player)
c/o Jordan Woy *Willis and Woy
Management*
3030 Olive St #520
Dallas, TX 75219, USA

Batch, Charlie (Athlete, Football Player)
1844 Willow Oak Dr
Wexford, PA 15090, USA

Batchelder, Joseph (Athlete, Olympic
Athlete, Sailor)
29 Meadowbank Rd
Billerica, MA 01821-4315, USA

Batchelor, Rich (Athlete, Baseball Player)
1004 Pineneedle Rd
Hartsville, SC 29550-8452, USA

Bateman, Brian (Athlete, Golfer)
2910 River Oaks Dr
Monroe, LA 71201-2028, USA

Bateman, Jason (Actor)
8828 Wonderland Park Ave
Los Angeles, CA 90046, USA

Bateman, Justine (Actor)
7445 Woodrow Wilson Dr
Los Angeles, CA 90046, USA

Bateman, Marv (Athlete, Football Player)
1189 E Pinion St
Washington, UT 84780, USA

Bates, Alfred (Athlete, Track Athlete)
4215 Skymont D
Belmont, CA 94002, USA

Bates, Bill (Athlete, Football Player)
1252 Neck Rd Ponte
Vedra Beach, FL 32082, USA

Bates, Billy Ray (Athlete, Basketball
Player)
340 Eastbrook Rd
Ridgewood, NJ 07450, USA

Bates, Charles C (Oceanographer)
501 South La Posada Circle
Apt 388
Green Valley, AZ 85614-5109, USA

Bates, Dick (Athlete, Baseball Player)
5859 W Cielo Grande
Glendale, AZ 85310-3631, USA

Bates, Dwayne (Athlete, Football Player)
555 W Madison St
Apt 2901
Chicago, IL 60661, USA

Bates, Emma (Actor)
c/o Marianne Golan *Marianne Golan
Management*
6528 W. 6th St
Los Angeles, CA 90048-4716, USA

Bates, Jason (Athlete, Baseball Player)
4775 Silver Pine Dr
Castle Rock, CO 80108-7833, USA

Bates, Kathy (Actor)
243 S Muirfield Rd
Los Angeles, CA 90004, USA

Bates, Mario (Athlete, Football Player)
PO Box 5832
Scottsdale, AZ 85261, USA

Bates, Michael (Athlete, Football Player)
1239 W Keuhne Ct
Tucson, AZ 85755, USA

Bates, Pat (Athlete, Golfer)
215 Ward Cir
Suite 200
Brentwood, TN 37027, USA

Bates, Patrick J (Athlete, Football Player)
2745 N Collins St
Apt 11123
Arlington, TX 76006, USA

Bates, Robert T (Misc)
Railroad Signalman Brotherhood
601 W Golf Road
Mount Prospect, IL 60056, USA

Bates, Shawn (Athlete, Hockey Player)
35 Bradshaw St
Medford, MA 02155, USA

Bates, Ted (Athlete, Football Player)
4036 Paige St
Los Angeles, CA 90031, USA

Bates, Tyler (Composer, Musician)
11733 Valleycrest Rd
Studio City, CA 91064, USA

Bat for Lashes (Music Group)
c/o Staff Member *Red Light Management
(LA)*
8439 W Sunset Blvd
Suite 2
Los Angeles, CA 90069, USA

Bathe, Bill (Athlete, Baseball Player)
5378 N Ridge Spring Pl
Tucson, AZ 85749-7106, USA

Bathe, Frank (Athlete, Hockey Player)
2 Meadowood Dr
Scarborough, ME 04074, USA

Bathe, Ryan Michelle (Actor)
c/o Nick Campbell *Commonwealth Talent
Group*
PO Box 36514
Los Angeles, CA 90036, USA

Bathgate, Andy (Athlete, Hockey Player)
43 Brentwood Dr
Brampton, ON L6T 1R1, Canada

Bathgate, Frank (Athlete, Hockey Player)
602-330 Mill St S
Brampton, ON L6Y 3V3, Canada

Batikis, Annastasia (Athlete, Baseball
Player)
1023 Crab Tree Ln
Racine, WI 53406-4109, USA

Batinkoff, Randall (Actor)
1330 4th St
Santa Monica, CA 90401, USA

Batista, Cardinal Giovanni (Religious
Leader)
Palazzo Delle Congregazioni
Piazza Pio XII #10
Roma I-00193, ITALY

Batista, Dave (Wrestler)
Demon Wrestling Inc
2020 Penn Ave NW #179
Washington, DC 20006, USA

Batista, Eike (Business Person)
EBX
Praia Do Flamengo, 66, 10º Andar
Flamengo
Rio De Janerio, RJ 22210-903, Brazil

Batista, Tony (Athlete)
333 W Camden St
Baltimore, MD 21201

Batiste, Kevin (Athlete, Baseball Player)
2501 Westridge St Apt 255
Houston, TX 77054-1519, USA

Batiste, Kim (Athlete, Baseball Player)
16163 Aikens Rd
Prairieville, LA 70769-4903, USA

Batiste, Michael (Athlete, Football Player)
2720 Edmonds St
Beaumont, TX 77705, USA

Batiuk, Thomas M (Tom) (Cartoonist)
Universal Press Syndicate
4520 Main St
Kansas City, MO 64111, USA

Batra, Pooja (Actor, Bollywood)
403H Gokul Vihar II
Thakur Complex Kandivli (E)
Mumbai, MS 400068, INDIA

Batt, Bryan (Actor)
c/o Marc Chancer *Origin Talent Agency*
4705 Laurel Canyon #306
Studio City, CA 91607, USA

Battaglia, Bates (Athlete, Hockey Player)
832 Graham St
Raleigh, NC 27605-1125, USA

Battaglia, Marco (Athlete, Football Player)
15832 79th St
Howard Beach, NY 11414, USA

Battaglia, Matt (Actor)
c/o Stewart Strunk *Main Title
Entertainment*
8383 Wilshire Blvd
Suite 408
Los Angeles, CA 90211, USA

Battaglia, Rik (Actor)
Viale Montegrappa 10
Colle Verde Guidonia
Rome 00012, ITALY

Battelle, Ann (Athlete, Olympic Athlete,
Skier)
1355 Walton Creek Rd
Steamboat Springs, CO 80487-1702, USA

Batten, Kim (Athlete, Olympic Athlete,
Track Athlete)
24107 Plantation Dr NE
Atlanta, GA 30324, USA

Batten, Pat (Athlete, Football Player)
9403 E 64th Ter
Raytown, MO 64133, USA

Batterman, Barbara Jo (Misc)
9171 Placer Bullion Ave
Las Vegas, NV 89178-6200, USA

Battie, Demetrius "Tony" (Athlete,
Basketball Player)
11264 Bridge House Rd
Windermere, FL 34786-5405

Battie, Demetrius (Tony) (Athlete,
Basketball Player)
11264 Bridge House Rd
Windermere, FL 34786, USA

Battier, Shane (Athlete, Basketball Player)
490 Bruin Lake Rd
Gregory, MI 48137-9648, USA

Battifarano, AJ (Stylist)
230 W 76th St
#10-G
New York, NY 10023, USA

Battista, Bobbie
c/o Staff Member *Atamira*
3400 Peachtree Rd #300
Atlanta, GA 30326, USA

Battle, Allen (Athlete, Baseball Player)
106 Donette Loop
Daphne, AL 36526-7764, USA

Battle, Arnaz (Athlete, Football Player)
1091 Broadmoore Ln
Prosper, TX 75078, USA

Battle, Greg (Athlete, Football Player)
1217 W Saltstage Dr
Phoenix, AZ 85045-0735, USA

Battle, Howard (Athlete, Baseball Player)
238 Romana Ave SE
Albuquerque, NM 87102-5039, USA

Battle, James (Athlete, Football Player)
5 Oasis Ct
St Albert, AB T8N 6X2, Canada

Battle, John (Athlete, Basketball Player)
234 Chadmore Ln
Tyrone, GA 30290-1573, USA

Battle, Julian (Athlete, Football Player)
196 Monterey Way
West Palm Beach, FL 33411, USA

Battle, Kenny (Athlete, Basketball Player)
Northwest Sports and Entertainment Inc
835 W Warner Rd
Suite 101-445
Gilbert, AZ 85233, USA

Battle, Lois (Writer)
Viking Press
375 Hudson St
New York, NY 10014, USA

Battle, Mike (Athlete, Football Player)
P.O. Box 1156
Amherst, VA 24521, USA

Battle, Ralph (Athlete, Football Player)
184 Timber Oak Rd
Huntsville, AL 35806, USA

Battle, Terry (Athlete, Football Player)
7049 N 7th Ave
Phoenix, AZ 85021, USA

Battles, Ainslev (Athlete, Football Player)
1237 Misty Valley Ct
Lawrenceville, GA 30045, USA

Battles, Ainsley (Athlete, Football Player)
2859 Yellow Pine Dr
Jacksonville, FL 32277, USA

Battles, Zoe (Stylist)
c/o Staff Member *LA Rep*
8312 Utica Dr
Los Angeles, CA 90046, USA

Batton, Chris (Athlete, Baseball Player)
29806 Yorkton Rd
Mirrueta, CA 92563-4748, USA

Batton, Dave (Athlete, Basketball Player)
6506 Bayonne Dr
Spring, TX 77389-3607, USA

Batts, Lloyd (Athlete, Basketball Player)
500 S Denton Ave
Glenwood, IL 60425-2137, USA

Batts, Matt (Athlete, Baseball Player)
17927 Silver Creek Ct
Baton Rouge, LA 70810-8918, USA

Batts, Warren L (Business Person)
Premark International
3600 W Lake Ave
Glenview, IL 60025, USA

Baty, Greg (Athlete, Football Player)
4 King St
Redwood City, CA 94062, USA

Bauchau, Patrick (Actor)
1941 Lookout Dr
Agoura, CA 91301, USA

Baucus, Max (Senator)
511 Hart Senate Office Bldg
Washington, DC 20510, USA

Baudin, Belinda (Horse Racer, Olympic Athlete)
15939 NW 162nd Terr
Williston, FL 32696, USA

Baudry, Patrick
305 Ave Mairie
Eaunas 31600, FRANCE

Bauer, Alice (Athlete, Golfer)
LPGA Pioneer
77165 Avenida Arteaga
La Quinta, CA 92253-2552, USA

Bauer, Belinda (Actor)
c/o Staff Member *The Rights House (UK)*
Drury House
34-43 Russell St
London WC2B 5HA, UK

Bauer, Chris (Actor)
c/o Peg Donegan *Framework Entertainment (LA)*
9057 Nemo St
Suite C
West Hollywood, CA 90069, USA

Bauer, Donna (Business Person)
The Note Buyer
11006 Reading Rd Ste 201
Cincinnati, OH 45241, USA

Bauer, Hank (Athlete, Football Player)
11150 Alejo Pl
San Diego, CA 92124, USA

Bauer, Jaime Lyn (Actor)
4212 Carmellia Ave
Studio City, CA 91604, USA

Bauer, Jamie Lyn (Actor)
4213 Camellia Ave
Studio City, CA 91604, USA

Bauer, Kristen (Actor)
c/o Arthur Toretsky *Paradigm (LA)*
360 N Crescent Dr
North Bldg
Beverly Hills, CA 90210, USA

Bauer, Kristin (Actor)
c/o Sheree Cohen *Kohner Agency, The*
9300 Wilshire Blvd
Suite 555
Beverly Hills, CA 90212, USA

Bauer, Linda Susan (Actor)
2476 Glendale Cir
Smyrna, GA 30080, USA

Bauer, Peter (Publisher)
People Magazine
Time-Life Building
Rockefeller Center
New York, NY 10020, USA

Bauer, Rick (Athlete, Baseball Player)
6643 W Limelight Dr
Boise, ID 83714-6109, USA

Bauer, Steven (Actor)
c/o Staff Member *Innovative Artists (LA)*
1505 10th St
Santa Monica, CA 90401, USA

Bauer, William J (Judge)
US Court of Appeals
111 N Canal St
Chicago, IL 60606, USA

Bauer van Straten, Kristin (Actor)
c/o Ben Levine *Kritzer Levine Wilkins Entertainment (KLWG)*
11872 La Grange Ave
1st Floor
Los Angeles, CA 90025, USA

Baugh, Gavin (Athlete, Baseball Player)
3605 Pasadena Dr
San Mateo, CA 94403, USA

Baugh, Laura (Athlete, Golfer)
5225 Timberview Ter
Orlando, FL 32819-3924, USA

Baugh, Sammy (Athlete, Football Coach, Football Player)
General Delivery
Rotan, TX 79546, USA

Baugh, Tom (Athlete, Football Player)
14716 S Bynum Rd
Lone Jack, MO 64070, USA

Baughan, Maxie C (Athlete, Coach, Football Player)
3355 Lawndale Rd
Reisterstown, MD 21136, USA

Baughman, J Ross (Journalist, Misc, Photographer)
203 S Payne St
Alexandria, VA 22314, USA

Baughman, Justin (Athlete, Baseball Player)
4052 NE 21st Ave
Portland, OR 97212-1433, USA

Baum, Herbert M (Business Person)
Quarker State Corp
700 Milam St
Houston, TX 77002, USA

Baum, John (Athlete, Basketball Player)
8216 Fenton Rd
Glenside, PA 19038-7144, USA

Baum, Justine (Stylist)
11 Cushing Dr
Mill Valley, CA 94941-1060, USA

Baum, Rich (Stylist)
8562 Gunner Way
Fair Oaks, CA 95628, USA

Bauman, Jon (Bowzer) (Musician)
3168 Oakshire Dr
Los Angeles, CA 90068-1743, USA

Bauman, Rashad (Athlete, Football Player)
14724 SE Loren Ln
Portland, OR 97267, USA

Baumann, Charlie
5434 Sago Palm Ct
Orlando, FL 32819, USA

Baumann, Frank M (Athlete, Baseball Player)
7712 Sunray Ln
Saint Louis, MO 63123-1938, USA

Baumann, Herbert K W (Composer)
Franziskaserster 16 #1419
Munich 81669, GERMANY

Baumann, Kenny (Actor)
c/o Michael Valeo *Valeo Entertainment*
8265 Sunset Blvd
Suite 103
Los Angeles, CA 90046, USA

Baumbach, Noah (Actor)
c/o Brad Gross *Brad Gross Agency, The*
161 S Arden Blvd
Los Angeles, CA 90004, USA

Baumgardner, Larry (Athlete, Football Player)
1125 Loma Ave
Coronado, CA 92118, USA

Baumgarten, Ross (Athlete, Baseball Player)
1020 Bluff Rd
Glencoe, IL 60022-1152, USA

Baumgartner, Brian (Actor)
3896 Franklin Ave
Los Angeles, CA 90027, USA

Baumgartner, Bruce (Athlete, Motivational Speaker, Olympic Athlete, Wrestler)
12765 Forrest Drive
Edinboro, PA 16412, USA

Baumgartner, John (Athlete, Baseball Player)
1215 Oxford Ct
Birmingham, AL 35242-4676, USA

Baumgartner, Ken (Athlete, Hockey Player)
39 Court St
Apt 1
Newton, MA 02458-1372, USA

Baumgartner, Mary (Athlete, Baseball Player)
60 Lane
440 Jimmerson Lk
Fremont, IN 46737-9634, USA

Baumgartner, Mike (Athlete, Hockey Player)
39998 290th St
Roseau, MN 56751-8321, USA

Baumgartner, Steve (Athlete, Football Player)
144 Brookside Dr
Mandeville, LA 70471, USA

Baumgartner, William (Doctor)
Johns Hopkins Hospital
600 N Wolfe St
Baltimore, MD 21287, USA

Baumhower, Robert G (Bob) (Athlete, Football Player)
21201 Ayrshire Ln
Fairhope, AL 36532, USA

Baumler, Hans-Jurgen (Actor)
18 chemin du Casteller
Le Rouret F-06650, France

Baun, Bob (Athlete, Hockey Player)
35 Pittman Cres
Ajax, ON L1S 3G4, CANADA

Baun, Bobby (Athlete, Hockey Player)
576 Stonebridge Lane
Pickering, ON L1W 3B3, CANADA

Bause, Inka (Musician)
PF 08 03 04
Berlin 10003, Germany

Bauta, Ed (Athlete, Baseball Player)
3792 Long Grove Ln
Port Orange, FL 32129-8617, USA

Baute, Joseph A (Business Person)
Nashua Corp
11 Trafalgar Square #200
Nashua, NH 03063, USA

Bautin, Sergei (Athlete, Hockey Player)
19715 W 100th Ter
Lenexa, KS 66220-8306, USA

Bautista, Danny (Athlete, Baseball Player)
901 E Van Buren St
Apt 1063
Phoenix, AZ 85006, USA

Bautista, David (Athlete, Wrestler)
c/o Staff Member *World Wrestling Entertainment (WWE)*
Titan Towers
1241 E Main St
Stamford, CT 06905-3857, USA

Bautista, Franciso Javier Jr (Frankie J) (Musician)
c/o Staff Member *BMG*
1540 Broadway
New York, NY 10036, USA

Bautista, Jose (Athlete, Baseball Player)
100 Shockoe Slip Fl 4
Richmond, VA 23219-4100, USA

Bavaro, David (Athlete, Football Player)
55 Ash St
Apt 14
Danvers, MA 01923, USA

Bavaro, Mark (Athlete, Football Player)
17 Long Hill
Boxford, MA 01921, USA

Bavasi, Peter (Commentator)
1001 Genter St Unit 3G
La Jolla, CA 92037-5531, USA

Bawel, Edward (Athlete, Football Player)
1169 2nd Ave
Jasper, IN 47546, USA

Bax, Kylie (Actor, Model)
8309 Kirkwood Dr
Los Angeles, CA 90046, USA

Baxendale, Helen (Actor)
c/o Staff Member *Yakety Yak*
8-A Bloomsbury Sq
London WC1A 2NE, UNITED KINGDOM (UK)

Baxes, Mike (Athlete, Baseball Player)
303 Wickham Dr
Mill Valley, CA 94941-3443, USA

Baxley, Rob (Athlete, Football Player)
39 Oak Creek Dr
Yorkville, IL 60560, USA

Baxter, Fred (Athlete, Football Player)
P.O. Box 14
Brundidge, AL 36010, USA

Baxter, James (Animator)
Dream Works SKG
100 University City Plaza
University City, CA 91608, USA

Baxter, Jeff (Skunk) (Music Group,
Musician)
Monterey Peninsula Artists
509 Hartnell St
Monterey, CA 93940, USA

Baxter, Lea-Anne (Stylist)
c/o Staff Member *Judy Inc*
1 Yorkville Ave
Toronto ON M4W 1L1, Canada

Baxter, Lloyd (Athlete, Football Player)
2500 Homedale Dr
Austin, TX 78704, USA

Baxter, Meredith (Actor)
14186 Alisal Ln
Santa Monica, CA 90402, USA

Baxter, Paul (Athlete, Hockey Player)
1610 Saint John St
Wichita Falls, TX 76302-3315, USA

Baxter, Stephen (Writer)
Tom Doherty Associates, LLC
175 Fifth Ave
New York, NY 10010, USA

Baxter-Johnson, Patricia (Athlete, Golfer)
111 Byrn Mawr Dr
Lake Worth, FL 33460, USA

Bay, Jason (Athlete, Baseball Player)
c/o Joe Urbon *Creative Artists Agency
(CAA-NY)*
162 Fifth Ave
6th Floor
New York, NY 10010, USA

Bay, Michael (Actor, Director, Producer)
13244 Chalon Rd
Los Angeles, CA 90049, USA

Bay, Susan (Actor)
801 Stone Canyon Road
Los Angeles, CA 90077, USA

Bay, Willow
1050 Techwood Dr
Atlanta, GA 30318

Bay City Rollers (Music Group)
297-101 Kinderkamack Road
Oradell, NJ 07649, USA

Baye, Nathalie (Actor)
Théâtre De L'Atelier
1 Place Charles Dullin
Paris F-75 018, France

Bayer, Samuel (Director)
c/o Doreen Wilcox Little *Anonymous
Content (LA)*
3531 Hayden Ave
Culver City, CA 90232, USA

Bayle, Silvia (Actor)
c/o Staff Member *Telefe - Argentina*
Pavon 2444 (C1248AAT)
Buenos Aires, ARGENTINA

Bayless, Jerryd (Athlete, Basketball Player)
c/o Jeff Schwartz *Excel Sports
Management*
9665 Wilshire Blvd #500
Los Angeles, CA 90212, USA

Bayless, Martin (Athlete, Football Player)
757 Ernroe Dr
Dayton, OH 45408, USA

Bayless, Rick (Athlete, Football Player)
885 Dawn Ave
Shoreview, MN 55126, USA

Baylis, Jerald (Athlete, Football Player)
PO Box 33921
Portland, OR 97292-3291, USA

Bayliss, Jonah (Athlete, Baseball Player)
41 Front St
Williamstown, MA 01267-2403, USA

Bayliss, Rachel (Musician)
Somerset Park Farm
Congelton Chelshire, UK

Baylon, Noah (Writer)
c/o James (Jamie) Feldman *Lichter
Grossman Nichols Adler & Goodman*
9200 Sunset Blvd
Suite 1200
Los Angeles, CA 90069-3507, USA

Baylor, Don (Athlete, Baseball Player,
Coach)
Arizona Diamondbacks PO Box 2095
Attn: Coaching Staff
PhnPnix, AZ 85001-2095, USA

Baylor, Elgin (Athlete, Basketball Player)
2480 Briarcrest Rd
Beverly Hills, CA 90210-1820, USA

Baylor, John (Athlete, Football Player)
7436 Freeport Ln
Apt A
Indianapolis, IN 46214, USA

Baylor, Raymond (Athlete, Football
Player)
5302 Heathercrest St
Houston, TX 77045, USA

Baylor, Tim (Athlete, Football Player)
1302 Douglas Ave
Minneapolis, MN 55403, USA

Bayne, Howard (Athlete, Basketball
Player)
11840 Yarnell Rd
Knoxville, TN 37932, USA

Bayne, Trevor (Race Car Driver)
Wood Bros Racing
7291 Caldwell Rd
Harrisburg, NC 28075, USA

Baynes, Michelle (Race Car Driver)
Bayshore Communications
2839 Ogletown Rd.
Newark, DE 19713, USA

Baynham, Craig (Athlete, Football Player)
1 7th St
Apt 1102
Augusta, GA 30901, USA

Bayo, Maria (Opera Singer)
Opera et Concert
Maxifilianstr 22
Munich 80539, GERMANY

Bayona, Alvaro (Actor)
c/o Gabriel Blanco *Gabriel Blanco
Iglesias (Mexico)*
Rio Balsas 35-32
Colonia Cuauhtemoc
DF 06500, Mexico

Bayona, Juan Antonio (Director,
Producer, Writer)
c/o Robert Newman *WME (LA)*
9601 Wilshire Blvd Fl 3
Beverly Hills, CA 90210, USA

Bays, Brandon (Motivational Speaker)
The Journey Seminars LTD
P.O. Box 2
Cowbridge CF71 7WN, United Kingdom

Baz, Farouk El- (Geophysicist, Physicist)
Boston University
Remot Sensing Center
Boston, MA 02215, USA

Baze, Winiford (Athlete, Football Player)
5317 New Copeland Rd
Apt 119
Tyler, TX 75703-3964, USA

Bazell, Robert J (Correspondent)
NBC-TV News Dept
4001 Nebraska Ave NW
Washington, DC 20016, USA

Bazemore, Whit (Race Car Driver)
50 Gasoline Alley #H
Indianapolis, IN 46222, USA

Bazer, Fuller W (Scientist)
8600 Creekview Court
College Station, TX 77845, USA

BB Mak (Music Group)
c/o Staff Member *Hollywood Records*
500 S Buena Vista St
Burbank, CA 91521, USA

BBMAK (Musician)
P.O. Box 22580
London W86YR, UK

Beach, Adam (Actor)
c/o Daniel Spilo *Industry Entertainment
Partners*
955 S Carrillo Dr
Suite 300
Los Angeles, CA 90048, USA

Beach, Bill (Bowler)
435 Koehler Dr
Sharpsville, PA 16150, USA

Beach, Ed (Athlete, Football Player)
938 Sedgewick Ave
Scotch Plains, NJ 07076, USA

Beach, Gary (Actor)
62 W 62nd St
#6F
New York, NY 10023, USA

Beach, Michael (Actor)
4434 Moorpark Way #107
Toluca Lake, CA 91602, USA

Beach, Pat (Athlete, Football Player)
2523 W Beach Rd
Oak Harbor, WA 98277, USA

Beach, Roger C (Business Person)
Unocal Corp
2141 Rosecrans Ave
El Segundo, CA 90245, USA

Beach, Sanjay (Athlete, Football Player)
2989 Riveria Ln
Westlake, OH 44145-6844, USA

Beach, Walter
2010 Winthrop Way
Macungie, PA 18062, USA

Beacham, Stephanie (Actor)
c/o Staff Member *The Rights House (UK)*
Drury House
34-43 Russell St
London WC2B 5HA, UK

Beacher, Jeff (Producer, Television Host)
5777 W Century Blvd #1600
Los Angeles, CA 90045, USA

Beach House (Music Group)
c/o Frank Nieto *Sub Pop*
2013 Fourth Ave Fl 3
Seattle, WA 98121, USA

Beachy, Brandon (Athlete, Baseball
Player)
339 Caswyck Tree
Alpharetta, GA 30022-2693, USA

Beachy, Roger N (Scientist)
526 W Polo Dr
Saint Louis, MO 63105, USA

Beadle, Carol (Stylist)
c/o Staff Member *Rex Agency, The*
6311 Romaine St
Los Angeles, CA 90038, USA

Beagle, Ronald G (Ron) (Athlete, Football
Player)
3830 San Ysidro Way
Sacramento, CA 95864, USA

Beahan, Kate (Actor)
c/o Suzan Bymel *Management 360*
9111 Wilshire Blvd
Beverly Hills, CA 90210, USA

Beal, Damien (Athlete, Baseball Player)
12836 Stanwyck Cir
Tampa, FL 33626-4465, USA

Beal, Jack (Artist)
80 Epps Road
Oneonta, NY 13820, USA

Beal, Jeff (Composer)
c/o Staff Member *Gorfaine/Schwartz
Agency Inc*
4111 W Alameda Ave
Suite 509
Burbank, CA 91505, USA

Beal, Jeremy (Athlete, Football Player)
3709 Furneaux Ln
Carrollton, TX 75007, USA

Beal, Norm (Athlete, Football Player)
21246 Jade St
Rocky Mount, MO 65072, USA

Beale, Betty (Writer)
2926 Garfield St NW
Washington, DC 20008, USA

Beale, Simon Russell (Actor)
c/o Tony Lipp *Anonymous Content (LA)*
3531 Hayden Ave
Culver City, CA 90232, USA

Beall, Bob (Athlete, Baseball Player)
513 NE Birchwood Rd
Hillsboro, OR 97124-3374, USA

Bealor, Bruce (Athlete, Football Player)
6010 Blue Ridge Dr
Apt F
Highlands Ranch, CO 80130-3617, USA

Beals, Jennifer (Actor)
c/o David Lust *Rogers & Cowan PR (LA)*
9171 Wilshire Blvd
Suite 441
Beverly Hills, CA 90210, USA

Beals, Shawn (Athlete, Football Player)
250 Edward Ave
Pittsburg, CA 94565, USA

Beals, Vaughn L Jr (Business Person)
Harley-Davidson Inc
3700 W Juneau Ave
Milwaukee, WI 53208, USA

Beam, C Arien (Judge)
US Court of Appeals
Federal Building
100 Centennial Mall N
Lincoln, NE 68508, USA

Beam, T J (Athlete, Baseball Player)
8505 E Pepper Tree Ln
Scottsdale, AZ 85250-491, USA

Beaman, Lee Anne (Actor)
Cavaleri Assoc
178 S Victory Blvd
#205
Burbank, CA 91502, USA

Beamer, Frank (Coach, Football Coach)
Virginia Polytechnic Institute
Athletic Dept
Blacksburg, VA 24061, USA

Beamer, Lisa (Writer)
The Todd M Beamer Foundation
P.O. Box 32
Cranbury, NJ 08512

Beamon, Autry (Athlete, Football Player)
2664 Lakeview Dr
Shakopee, MN 55379, USA

Beamon, Bob (Athlete, Hockey Player,
Olympic Athlete)
20533 Biscayne Blvd #113
Miami, FL 33180-1529, USA

Beamon, Clifford "Trey" (Athlete, Baseball
Player)
2125 Highwood St
Mesauite, TX 75181-1727, USA

Beamon, Trey (Athlete, Baseball Player)
9730 Whitehurst Dr
Apt 51
Dallas, TX 75243, USA

Beamon Jr, Charlie (Athlete, Baseball
Player)
355 W Grant Line Rd Apt 212
Tracy, CA 95376-2579, USA

Beamon Sr, Charlie (Athlete, Baseball
Player)
1717 Woodland Ave
Apt 313
Palo Alto, CA 94303, USA

Bean, Alan L (Astronaut)
9173 Briar Forest Dr
Houston, TX 77024-7222, USA

Bean, Andy (Athlete, Golfer)
2912 Grasslands Dr
Lakeland, FL 33803, USA

Bean, Bill (Athlete, Baseball Player)
520 Brickell Key Dr
Miami, FL 33131-2441, USA

Bean, Bubba (Athlete, Football Player)
1117 Todd Trl
College Station, TX 77845, USA

Bean, Colter (Athlete, Baseball Player)
2116 Shades Crest Rd
Vestavia, AL 35216-1534, USA

Bean, Dawn Pawson (Swimmer)
11902 Red Hill Ave
Santa Ana, CA 92705, USA

Bean, Dexter (Race Car Driver)
Black Cat Racing
304 Performance Dr.
Mooresville, NC 28115, USA

Bean, Earnest (Athlete, Football Player)
1117 Todd Trl
College Station, TX 77845, USA

Bean, Ed (Athlete, Baseball Player)
'827 3rd Ct SE
Winter Haven, FL 33880-4417, USA

Bean, Henry (Director)
c/o Staff Member *Fuller Films*
625 Santa Clara Ave
Venice, CA 90291, USA

Bean, Noah (Actor)
c/o Nick Campbell *Commonwealth Talent
Group*
PO Box 36514
Los Angeles, CA 90036, USA

Bean, Orson (Actor, Comedian)
444 Caroll Canal
Venice, CA 90291, USA

Bean, Robert (Athlete, Football Player)
4197 Summit Crossing Dr
Decatur, GA 30034, USA

Bean, Sean (Actor)
1 Daleham Mews Camden
London NW3 5DB, UNITED KINGDOM

Bean, Shoshana (Actor, Musician)
c/o Tim Marshal *Bauman Redanty &
Shaul Agency*
5757 Wilshire Blvd
Suite 473
Beverly Hills, CA 90212, USA

Beane, Billy (Athlete, Baseball Player)
Oakland Athletics 7000 Coliseum Way
Ste 3
Attn: General Manager
Oakland, CA 94621-1992, USA

Beane, Billy (Commentator)
33 Brightwood Ln E
Danville, CA 94506-1926, USA

Bear, Greg
c/o Vince Gerardis *Grok! Studio*
Prefers to be contacted via email or
telephone
Los Angeles, CA, USA

Beard, Al (Athlete, Basketball Player)
1201 Orange St Apt 201
Fort Valley, GA 31030-3427, USA

Beard, Alana (Athlete, Basketball Player)
Washington Mystics
MCI Center
601 F St NW
Washington, DC 20004, USA

Beard, Alfred "Butch" (Athlete, Basketball
Player)
gee Palisade Ave Apt 6E
Fort Lee, NJ 07024-4137, USA

Beard, Alfred (Butch) (Athlete, Basketball
Player, Coach)
3834 Berleigh Hill Ct
Burtonsville, MD 20866, USA

Beard, Amanda (Athlete, Olympic Athlete,
Swimmer)
4609 W Saguaro Cliffs Dr
Tucson, AZ 85745-8840, USA

Beard, Beverly (Stylist)
c/o Staff Member *Crews*
828 Clemont Dr
Atlanta, GA 30306, USA

Beard, Dave (Athlete, Baseball Player)
5325 Derby Chase Ct
Alpharetta, GA 30005-7883, USA

Beard, Ed (Athlete, Football Player)
4861 Strand Dr
Virginia Beach, VA 23462, USA

Beard, Frank (Athlete, Golfer)
70 Rocio Ct
Palm Desert, CA 92260, USA

Beard, Frank (Musician)
918 Pitts Rd
Richmond, TX 77406, USA

Beard, Mike (Athlete, Baseball Player)
90 Elcano Dr
Hot Springs Village, AR 71909-7833, USA

Beard, Tom (Athlete, Football Player)
164 Gale Rd
Mason, MI 48854, USA

Beardsley, Marni (Stylist)
852 NW Albemarle Ter
Portland, OR 97210-3117, USA

Beare, Gary (Athlete, Baseball Player)
17666 Tatia Ct
San Diego, CA 92128-2082, USA

Bearse, Amanda (Actor)
629 Elmwood Dr NE
Atlanta, GA 30306, USA

Bearse, Kevin (Athlete, Baseball Player)
656 Saint Andrews Pl
Manalapan, NJ 07726-9551, USA

Beart, Emmanuelle (Actor)
c/o Staff Member *Agence Artistique
Adequat*
108 rue Reaumur
Paris 75002, France

Beart, Guy (Musician, Songwriter, Writer)
Editions Temporel
2 Rue du Marquis de Mores
Garches 92380, FRANCE

Beasley, Aaron (Athlete, Football Player)
1635 Braid Hills Dr
Pasadena, MD 21122, USA

Beasley, Allyce (Actor)
SBV
145 S Fairfax Ave
#310
Los Angeles, CA 90036, USA

Beasley, Alyce (Actor)
c/o Staff Member *TalentWorks (LA)*
3500 W Olive Ave
Suite 1400
Burbank, CA 91505, USA

Beasley, Bruce M (Artist)
322 Lewis St
Oakland, CA 94607, USA

Beasley, Charles (Athlete, Basketball
Player)
6308 Winton St
Dallas, TX 75214-2645, USA

Beasley, Chris (Athlete, Baseball Player)
1013 W Cooley Dr
Gilbert, AZ 85233-2540, USA

Beasley, Derrick (Athlete, Football Player)
141 North St
Andover, MA 01810, USA

Beasley, Fred (Athlete, Football Player)
P.O. Box 210931
Montgomery, AL 36121, USA

Beasley, John
W3848 Turtle Patch Rd
Pine River, WI 54965, USA

Beasley, John (Athlete, Basketball Player)
113 Oak Acres Dr W
Malakoff, TX 75148-3163, USA

Beasley, John (Actor)
c/o Staff Member *Bauman Redanty &
Shaul Agency*
5757 Wilshire Blvd
Suite 473
Beverly Hills, CA 90212, USA

Beasley, Lew (Athlete, Baseball Player)
24653 Newtown Rd
Bowling Green, VA 22427-2725, USA

Beasley, Michael (Athlete, Basketball
Player)
c/o Jeff Schwartz *Excel Sports
Management*
9665 Wilshire Blvd #500
Los Angeles, CA 90212, USA

Beasley, Terry (Athlete, Football Player)
4052 Wellington Way
Moody, AL 35004, USA

Beasley, Tom (Athlete, Football Player)
RR 1 Box 185
Hiltons, VA 24258, USA

Beasley, Tony (Athlete, Baseball Player)
4490 CCC Rd
Ruther Glen, VA 22546-2701, USA

Beastie Boys (Music Group)
c/o John Silva *SAM*
722 Seward St
Los Angeles, CA 90038, USA

Beathard, Pete (Athlete, Football Player)
3770 Drake St
Houston, TX 77005, USA

Beaton, Frank (Athlete, Hockey Player)
3327 Chapel Hills Pkwy
Fultondale, AL 35068-1596, USA

Beatrix, HM Queen (Royalty)
Kabinet Van De Koningin
Korte Vijverberg 3
The Hague 2513 AB, The Netherlands

Beattie, Jim (Athlete, Baseball Player)
P.O. Box 231
Quechee, VT 05059-0231, USA

Beattie, Joseph (Actor)
Ken McReddie Associates
36 - 40 Glasshouse St
London W1B 5DL, UNITED KINGDOM

Beattle, Ann (Writer)
Janklow & Nesbit
445 Park Ave
#1300
New York, NY 10022, USA

Beattle, Bob (Skier)
210 Aabc
#N
Aspen, CO 81611, USA

Beattle, Bruce (Cartoonist)
Daytona Beach News-Journal
Editorial Dept
901 6th St
Daytona Beach, FL 32117, USA

Beatty, Blaine (Athlete, Baseball Player)
867 Kolodzey Rd
Victoria, TX 77905-2520, USA

Beatty, Blaine (Athlete, Baseball Player)
Frederick Keys 21 Stadium Dr
Attn: Coaching Staff
Frederick, MD 21703-6553, USA

Beatty, Charles (Athlete, Football Player)
P.O. Box 2634
Waxahachie, TX 75168, USA

Beatty, Chuck
300 Oldham St
Waxahachie, TX 75165, USA

Beatty, Jim (Athlete, Olympic Athlete,
Track Athlete)
1516 Larochelle Ln
Charlotte, NC 28226-6888, USA

Beatty, Ned (Actor)
32608 Montgomery Dr
Springville, CA 93265, USA

Beatty, Warren (Actor, Director,
Producer)
12431 Mulholland Dr
Beverly Hills, CA 90210, USA

Beaty, Zelmo (Athlete, Basketball Player)
2808 120th Ave NE
Bellevue, WA 98005-1515, USA

Beatz, Swizz (Musician, Producer)
c/o Keith Estabrook *Estabrook Group LLC*
2 5th Ave #3S
New York, NY 10011-8834, US

Beau Brummels, The (Music Group,
Musician)
P.O. Box 53664
C/O Jeff Hubbard
Indianapolis, IN 46253, USA

Beauchamp, Al (Athlete, Football Player)
533 Pinegate Rd
Peachtree City, GA 30269, USA

Beauchamp, Joe (Athlete, Football Player)
10525 Vista Sorrento
Pkwy Ste 110
San Diego, CA 92121, USA

Beauchamp, Rolando (Stylist)
c/o Staff Member *Independent NY*
15 E 30th St #401
New York, NY 10016, USA

Beauchemin, Francois (Athlete, Hockey
Player)
Jandec Inc
803-3080 Le Carrefour Blvd
Attn Robert Sauve
Laval, QC H7T 2R5, Canada

Beaudin, Norm (Athlete, Hockey Player)
8625 Stone Harbour Loop
Bradenton, FL 34212-6322, USA

Beaudoin, Doug (Athlete, Football Player)
15143 Springview St
Tampa, FL 33624, USA

Beaudoin, Jocelyne (Stylist)
c/o Celebrity Stylist *Jean Gabriel Kauss/
JGK*
161 Avenue of the Americas
13th Floor
New York, NY 10013, USA

Beaufait, Mark (Athlete, Hockey Player,
Olympic Athlete)
5454 Longwood Ct SE
Ada, MI 49301-7755, USA

Beauford, Carter (Musician)
3000 Lonesome Mountain Rd
Charlottesville, VA 22911, USA

Beaufoy, Simon (Director, Producer,
Writer)
c/o Staff Member *The Rod Hall agency*
6th Floor Fairgate House
78 New Oxford Street
London WC1A 1HB, United Kingdom

Beaule, Alain (Athlete, Hockey Player)
230 154e Rue
Saint-Georges, QC G5Y 7L8, Canada

Beaumon, Sterling (Actor)
c/o Staff Member *Stevenson Talent
Management*
22838 Epsilon St
Woodland Hills, CA 91364, USA

Beaumont, Jimmy (Musician)
2002 Duquesne Ave
McKeesport, PA 15132, USA

Beaumont, Thomas (Actor)
c/o Staff Member *Scott Stander &
Associates*
13701 Riverside Dr
Suite 201
Sherman Oaks, CA 91423, USA

Beaupre, Don (Athlete, Hockey Player)
5020 Scriver Rd.
Minneapolis, MN 55436-1158, USA

Beauregard, DJ Paul (DJ, Musician)
5073 Topeka Dr
Tarzana, CA 91356, USA

Beauregard, Robin (Athlete, Olympic
Athlete, Water Polo Player)
467 Midvale Ave
Los Angeles, CA 90024-6707, USA

Beauregard, Stephane (Athlete, Hockey
Player)
BMO Nesbitt Burns
991 Boul du Semina ire N
St-Jean-Sur-Richelieu, QC J3A IKl, Canada

Beauvais, Garcelle (Actor)
4030 Stansbury Ave
Sherman Oaks, CA 91423, USA

Beaver, Jim (Actor)
4213 Gentry Ave
Studio City, CA 91604, USA

Beaver, Joe (Rodeo Rider)
Po Box 1595
Huntsville, TN 77342, USA

Beaver, Terry (Actor)
Paradigm Agency
10100 Santa Monica Blvd #2500
Los Angeles, CA 90067, USA

Beavers, Aubrey (Athlete, Football Player)
PO Box 321474
Houston, TX 77221, USA

Beavers, Scott (Athlete, Football Player)
4030 Pittman Rd
College Park, GA 30349, USA

Beban, Gary (Athlete, Football Player)
20 Timber Ln
Northbrook, IL 60062, USA

Bebout, Nick (Athlete, Football Player)
1719 E Park Ave
Riverton, WY 82501, USA

Becerra, Xavier (Congressman, Politician)
1226 Longworth HOB
Washington, DC 20515, USA

Bech, Brett (Athlete, Football Player)
206 Lairds Dr
Coppell, TX 75019, USA

Bech, Debra (Actor)
Minnesota Public Radio
480 Cedar St
St Paul, MN 55101-2230, USA

Becht, Anthony (Athlete, Football Player)
1122 Oxbridge Dr
Lutz, FL 33549, USA

Bechtel, Riley P (Business Person)
Bechtel Group
50 beale St
San Francisco, CA 94105, USA

Bechtel, Stephen D Jr (Business Person)
Bechtel Group
50 beale St
San Francisco, CA 94105, USA

Beck, Aaron T (Doctor)
3600 Market St #700
Philadelphia, PA 19104, USA

Beck, Barry (Athlete, Hockey Player)
c/o Staff Member *Osoyoos Storm*
2 Kildeer Pl
Osoyoos, BC V0H 1V5, Canada

Beck, Braden (Athlete, Football Player)
691 Milverton Rd
Los Altos, CA 94022, USA

Beck, Byron (Athlete, Basketball Player)
1909 S Williams St
Kennewick, WA 99338-1820, USA

Beck, Chip (Athlete, Golfer)
11 Pembroke Dr
Lake Forrest, IL 60045, USA

Beck, Corey (Athlete, Basketball Player)
9444 Austin Dr
Olive Branch, MS 38654-7647, USA

Beck, Ernie (Athlete, Basketball Player)
1523 Brierwood Rd
Havertown, PA 19083-2910, USA

Beck, Glenn (Radio Personality,
Television Host)
2208 Vaquero Estates Blvd
Westlake, TX 76262, USA

Beck, Jeff (Musician)
c/o Staff Member *Creative Artists Agency
(CAA-LA)*
2000 Ave Of The Stars
Los Angeles, CA 90067, USA

Beck, John (Athlete, Football Player)
17172 Glen Aspen Dr
San Diego, CA 92127, USA

Beck, Jordan (Athlete, Football Player)
560 Wycombe Ct
Windsor, CO 80550, USA

Beck, Kimberly (Actor)
941 Kagawa St
Pacific Palisades, CA 90272, USA

Beck, Laurie Jean (Stylist)
81 Mallard Dr
Avon, CT 06001, USA

Beck, Maria (Actor)
c/o Staff Member *Shamon Freitas Talent
Agency*
3916 Oregon St
San Diego, CA 92104, USA

Beck, Martha (Writer)
18011 N 14th Pl
Phoenix, AZ 85022-7201, USA

Beck, Martin (Actor)
c/o Dale Garrick *Dale Garrick
International Agency*
1017 N La Cienega Blvd #109
Los Angeles, CA 90069, USA

Beck, Mat (Cinematographer)
621 Via de la Paz
Pacific Palisades, CA 90272, USA

Beck, Michael (Actor)
c/o Staff Member *Paradigm (LA)*
360 N Crescent Dr
North Bldg
Beverly Hills, CA 90210, USA

Beck, Rich (Athlete, Baseball Player)
8218 N Sumter Ct
Spokane, WA 99208-5749, USA

Beck, Robin (Musician)
Cavaricci & White
156 W 56th St #1803
New York, NY 10019, USA

Beck, Tom (Athlete, Football Player)
806 Saddlewood Dr
Glen Ellyn, IL 60137, USA

Beckel, Bob (Misc)
c/o Staff Member *HarperCollins Publishers*
10 East 53rd St
c/o Author mail, 7th Floor
New York, NY 10022, USA

Beckel, Heather (Writer)
Milkshake Media
4203 Guadalupe
Austin, TX 78751, USA

Beckel, Robert D (General)
New Mexico Military Institute
Superintendent's Office
Roswell, NM 88201, USA

Beckenbauer, Franz (Soccer Player)
Postfach 90 04 51
München 81504, Germany

Becker, Arthur (Athlete, Basketball Player)
1879 E Brentup Dr
Tempe, AZ 85283-4275, USA

Becker, Beth (Stylist)
c/o Staff Member *Blink Management*
421 Washington Ave
#202
Miami Beach, FL 33139, USA

Becker, Boris (Athlete, Tennis Player)
c/o Staff Member *IMG (Cleveland)*
1360 E 9th St
Suite 100
Cleveland, OH 44114, USA

Becker, Donna (Athlete, Baseball Player)
5316 40th Ave
Kenosha, WI 53144-2707, USA

Becker, Doug (Athlete, Football Player)
6716 Lincoln Ave
Evansville, IN 47715, USA

Becker, Edward R (Judge)
US Court of Appeals
US Couthouse
601 Market St
Philadelphia, PA 19106, USA

Becker, Gary S (Nobel Prize Laureate)
1308 E 58th St
Chicago, IL 60637, USA

Becker, George (Misc)
United Steelworkers of America
5 Gateway Center
Pittsburgh, PA 15222, USA

Becker, Gerry (Actor)
c/o Oliver Mossi *Paradigm (LA)*
360 N Crescent Dr
North Bldg
Beverly Hills, CA 90210, USA

Becker, Gretchen (Actor)
Acme Talent
4727 Wilshire Blvd
#333
Los Angeles, CA 90010, USA

Becker, Harold (Director, Producer)
c/o Jack Gilardi *ICM Partners (ICM-LA)*
10250 Constellation Blvd Fl 7
Los Angeles, CA 90067, USA

Becker, Isaura (Actor)
c/o Staff Member *Televisa*
Blvd Adolfo Lopez Mateos 232
Colonia San Angel INN
DF CP 01060, MEXICO

Becker, Kuno (Actor)
c/o Ivan De Paz *DePaz Management*
2011 N Vermont Ave.
Los Angeles, CA 90027, USA

Becker, Kurt (Athlete, Football Player)
49W412 Scott Rd
Big Rock, IL 60511, USA

Becker, Kurt
49W412 Scott Rd
Big Rock, IL 60511, USA

Becker, Margaret (Musician)
Sparrow Communications
101 Winners Circle
Brentwood, TN 37027, USA

Becker, Quinn H (Doctor, General)
2111 Peninsula Drive
San Antonio, TX 78239-3077, USA

Becker, Rich (Athlete, Baseball Player)
210 Mary Senica Ct
La Salle, IL 61301-9676, USA

Becker, Rob (Actor, Comedian)
c/o Staff Member *WmE2 (WMA-LA)*
1 William Morris Pl
Beverly Hills, CA 90212, USA

Becker, Robert J (Misc)
2200 S Ocean Ln
Apt 1905
Fort Lauderdale, FL 33316-3832, USA

Becker, Thomas (Athlete)
Hagedomweg 6A
Solingen 42697, GERMANY

Becker, Tony (Actor)
Howard Talent West
c/o Bonnie Howard
10657 Riverside Dr
Toluca Lake, CA 91602, USA

Becker, Walt (Director)
c/o Matt Luber *Luber Roklin Management*
8530 Wilshire Blvd
6th Floor
Beverly Hills, CA 90211, USA

Becker, Walter (Musician)
543 Hana Hwy
Paia, HI 96779, USA

Beckert, Glenn (Athlete, Baseball Player)
1953 Arkansas Ave
Englewood, FL 34224-5505, USA

Becket, MacDonald G (Architect)
Becket Group
2501 Colorado Blvd
Santa Monica, CA 90404, USA

Beckett, Bob (Athlete, Hockey Player)
38 Fonthill Blvd
Markham, ON L3R 1V7, Canada

Beckett, Josh (Athlete, Baseball Player)
1 Avery St
Apt 20B
Boston, MA 02111-1025, USA

Beckett, Robbie (Athlete, Baseball Player)
15625 Harry Lind Rd
Elgin, TX 78621-3824, USA

Beckett, Rogers (Athlete, Football Player)
635 Gaelic Ct
Apopka, FL 32712, USA

Beckett, Wendy (Sister)
BBC-TV
Center Wood Ln
London, ENGLAND W12 7R3

Beckett, William (Musician)
c/o Staff Member *Fueled By Ramen*
PO Box 1803
Tampa, FL 33601, USA

Beckford, Roxanne (Actor)
9255 Sunset Blvd
#401
Los Angeles, CA 90069, USA

Beckford, Tyson (Actor, Model)
Bethann Entertainment
388 Second Avenue #223
New York, NY 10010, USA

Beckham, Brice (Actor)
6561 Espanita St
Long Beach, CA 90815

Beckham, David (Athlete, Soccer Player)
1105 San Ysidro Dr
Beverly Hills, CAq 90210, USA

Beckham, Gordon (Athlete, Baseball Player)
8 Habersham Park NW
Atlanta, GA 30305-2856, USA

Beckham, Victoria (Actor, Musician)
1105 San Ysidro Dr
Beverly Hills, CA 90210, USA

Beckinsale, Kate (Actor)
c/o Geyer Kosinski *Media Talent Group*
9200 Sunset Blvd
Suite 550
Los Angeles, CA 90069, USA

Becklean, William (Athlete, Olympic Athlete, Rower)
254 Fairhaven Mill Rd
Concord, MA 01742-4404, USA

Beckless, Ian (Athlete, Football Player)
4915 Andros Dr
Tampa, FL 33629, USA

Beckley, Gerry (Music Group, Musician)
Agency for Performing Arts
9200 Sunset Blvd #900
Los Angeles, CA 90069, USA

Beckman, Cameron (Athlete, Golfer)
923 Campanile
San Antonio, TX 78734, USA

Beckman, Ed (Athlete, Football Player)
4295 18th St NE
Naples, FL 34120, USA

Beckman, Stefan (Stylist)
c/o Staff Member *Exposure NY*
177 Prince St
5th Floor
New York, NY 10012, USA

Beckman, Thomas (Athlete, Football Player)
3672 Cedar Shake Dr
Rochester Hills, MI 48309, USA

Beckman, Tom (Athlete, Football Player)
3672 Cedar Shake Dr
Rochester Hills, MI 48309, USA

Beckman, Witt (Athlete, Football Player)
568 Peachtree Pkwy
Cumming, GA 30041-7403, United States

Beckum, Travis (Athlete, Football Player)
c/o Roosevelt Barnes *Maximum Sports Management*
6435 W Jefferson Blvd
#197
Fort Wayne, IN 46804, USA

Beckwith, Alan (Actor)
3928 Carpenter Ave
Studio City, CA 91604, USA

Beckwith, Darry (Athlete, Football Player)
c/o Jimmy Sexton *CAA (Memphis)*
1100 Ridgeway Loop Rd
5th Floor
Memphis, TN 38120, USA

Beckwith, Joe (Athlete, Baseball Player)
859 Anna brook Dr
Auburn, AL 36830-7531, USA

Becquer, Julio (Athlete, Baseball Player)
2461 Kyje Ave N
Minneapolis, MN 55422-3626, USA

Becton, C W (Religious Leader)
United Pentacostal Free Will Baptist Church
8855 Dunn Rd
Hazelwood, MO 63042, USA

Becton, Julius W Jr (Educator, General)
Prairie View A & M University
President's Office
Prairie View, TX 77446, USA

Bedard, Irene (Actor)
Don Buchwald
6500 Wilshire Blvd #2200
Los Angeles, CA 90048, USA

Bedard, James A (Athlete, Hockey Player)
c/o Staff Member *Detroit Red Wings*
Joe Luis Arena
600 Civic Center Dr
Detroit, MI 48226, USA

Bedard, James L (Athlete, Hockey Player)
317 Crawford Ave E
Melfort, SK S0E 1A0, Canada

Bedard, Jim (Athlete, Hockey Player)
Detroit Red Wings 600 Civic Center Dr
Attn Coaching Staff
Detroit, MI 48226-4419, USA

Bedard, Jim (Athlete, Hockey Player)
139 Marine Dr
Windsor, ON N8N 3Z3, Canada

Bedard, Myriam (Athlete)
3329 Pinecourt
Neufchatel, QC G2B 2E4, CANADA

Bedard, Patrick (Race Car Driver)
1462 Indian Pass Road
Port Saint Jo, FL 32456, USA

Bedelia, Bonnie (Actor)
c/o Nevin Dolcefino *Innovative Artists (LA)*
1505 10th St
Santa Monica, CA 90401, USA

Bedell, Bob (Athlete, Basketball Player)
3107 Kipling Way
Louisvillie, KY 40205-3005, USA

Bedell, Brad (Athlete, Football Player)
545 N Altura Rd
Arcadia, CA 91007, USA

Bedell, Howie (Athlete, Baseball Player)
1187 Crestwood Dr
Pottstown, PA 19464-2931, USA

Bedford, Brian (Actor)
Arts Management Group
1133 Broadway #1025
New York, NY 10010, USA

Bedford, Steuart J R
Harrison/Parrott
12 Penzance Place
London W11 4PA, UNITED KINGDOM (UK)

Bedford, Vance (Athlete, Football Player)
141 Treslyn Way
Louisville, KY 40245, USA

Bedi, Kabir (Actor, Bollywood)
B4 Beach House Apt
Gandhigram Road
Mumbai, MS 400054, INDIA

Bedingfield, Daniel (Musician)
Island Def Jam Music Group, The
825 Eighth Avenue
New York, NY 10019

Bedingfield, Natasha (Musician)
2035 De Mille Dr
Los Angeles, CA 90027, USA

Bednarik, Charles P (Chuck) (Athlete, Football Player)
6379 Winding Rd
Coopersburg, PA 18036, USA

Bednarski, John (Athlete, Hockey Player)
1005 Windfaire Pl
Roswell, GA 30076-3310, USA

Bedore, Thomas (Athlete, Football Player)
211 73rd St
Niagara Falls, NY 14304, USA

Bedore, Tom (Athlete, Football Player)
9 Catherine Ave
Latrobe, PA 15650, USA

Bedrosian, Steve (Athlete, Baseball Player)
3915 Gordon Rd
Senoia, GA 30276-3041, USA

Bedsole, Harold (Hal) (Athlete, Football Player)
78661 Rainswept Way
Palm Desert, CA 92211, USA

Bee, Samantha (Actor, Comedian, Producer, Writer)
c/o Brian Stern *Stern Entertainment Group (Brillstein Entertainment Partners)*
14 E 38th St
7th Floor
New York, NY 10016, USA

Beeba, Mike (Governor)
State Capitol
Room 250
Little Rock, AR 72201, USA

Beebe, Dion (Cinematographer)
International Creative Mgmt
8942 Wilshire Blvd #219
Beverly Hills, CA 90211, USA

Beebe, Don (Athlete, Football Player)
1246 Verona Ridge Dr
Aurora, IL 60506, USA

Beeby, Thomas H (Architect)
Hammond Beeby Babka
440 N Wells St
Chicago, IL 60610, USA

Beech, Matt (Athlete, Baseball Player)
516 Sheffield Dr
Richardson, TX 75081-5610, USA

Beecham, Earl (Athlete, Football Player)
11 Terrace Cir Apt 1E
Great Neck, NY 11021, USA

Beechen, Adam (Writer)
c/o Staff Member *Natural Talent Inc*
3331 Ocean Park Blvd #203
Santa Monica, CA 90405, USA

Beechler, Donnie (Race Car Driver)
1605 Arlington Chase
Sherman, IL 62684, USA

Beecroft, David
1231 N Vista St
West Hollywood, CA 90046, USA

Beede, Frank (Athlete, Football Player)
1645 Somerset Pl
Antioch, CA 94509, USA

Bee Gees, The (Music Group)
c/o Staff Member *United Talent Agency (UTA)*
9336 Civic Center Dr
Beverly Hills, CA 90210, USA

Beekley, Bruce (Athlete, Football Player)
1351 Eaton Ave
San Carlos, CA 94070, USA

Beem, Rich (Athlete, Golfer)
104 Bella Cima Dr
Austin, TX 78734, USA

Beeman, Greg (Actor, Director, Producer, Writer)
c/o Jay Sures *United Talent Agency (UTA)*
9336 Civic Center Dr
Beverly Hills, CA 90210, USA

Beene, Andy (Athlete, Baseball Player)
113 Forest Brook St
Red Oak, TX 75154-6028, USA

Beene, Fred (Athlete, Baseball Player)
P.O. Box 143
Oakhurst, TX 77359-0143, USA

Beer, A M (Editor)
Spectator
Editorial Dept
44 Frid St
Hamilton, ON L8N 3G3, CANADA

Beer, Tom (Athlete, Football Player)
292 Changebridge Rd
Apt 3
Pine Brook, NJ 07058, USA

Beering, Steven C (Educator)
Purdue University
President's Office
West Lafayette, IN 47907, USA

Beers, Bob (Athlete, Hockey Player)
97 Blake Rd
Lexington, MA 02420-3212, USA

Beers, Bob (Athlete, Hockey Player)
Boston Bruins
100 Legends Way Ste 250
Attn: Broadcast Dept
Boston, MA 02114-1389, USA

Beers, Ed (Athlete, Hockey Player)
5-11442 Best St
Maple Ridge, BC V2X 7C7, Canada

Beers, Gary (Musician)
8 Hayes St
#1
Neutral Bay, NSW 20891, USA

Beesley, Max (Actor)
c/o Beth Holden-Garland *Untitled Entertainment (LA)*
350 S. Beverly Dr #200
Beverly Hills, CA 90212, USA

Beeson, Paul B (Doctor, Physicist)
7 Riverwoods Dr #F125
Exeter, NH 03833, USA

Beeson, Terry (Athlete, Football Player)
1302 Hibbard St
Coffeyville, KS 67337, USA

Bega, Leslie (Actor)
31 1/2 Buccaneer Ave
MDR, CA 90292, USA

Bega, Lou (Musician)
c/o Staff Member *Unicade Music*
Truderingerstrasse 259
Munchen 81821, Germany

Begala, Paul (Commentator, Television Host)
1581 Highland Glen Pl
McLean, VA 22101, USA

Begay, Notah (Athlete, Golfer)
3620 Vista Del Sur St NW
Albuquerque, NM 87120-1583, USA

Begert, William J (General)
Commander Pacific Air Force
Hickam Air Force Base, HI 96853, USA

Begg, Varyl (Admiral)
Copyhold Cottage Chilbotton
Stockbridge
Hants, UNITED KINGDOM (UK)

Beggs, James M (Government Official, Misc)
1177 N Great Southwest Parkway
Grand Prairie, TX 75050, USA

Beghe, Jason (Actor)
3800 Decker Edison Rd
Malibu, CA 90265, USA

Beghe, Renato (Judge)
US Tax Court
400 2nt St NW
Washington, DC 20217, USA

Begich, Mark
111 Russell Senate Office Building
Washington4, DC 20510, USA

Begler, Michael (Producer)
c/o Staff Member *WmE2 (WMA-LA)*
1 William Morris Pl
Beverly Hills, CA 90212, USA

Begley Jr, Ed (Actor, Director)
3850 Mound View Ave
Studio City, CA 91604, USA

Beglin, Elizabeth (Athlete, Hockey Player, Olympic Athlete)
2070 Silver Maple Trl
N Liberty, IA 52317-4765, USA

Begovich, Mike (Actor)
c/o Beverly Strong *Strong Management*
3532 Hayden Ave
Culver City, CA 90232, USA

Behagen, Ron (Athlete, Basketball Player)
1101 Juniper St NE
Apt 401
Atlanta, GA 30309-7655, USA

Behar, Joy (Actor)
205 W 89th St #9H
New York, NY 10024, USA

Beharie, Nicole (Actor)
c/o Andrew Rogers *ICM Partners (ICM-LA)*
10250 Constellation Blvd Fl 7
Los Angeles, CA 90067, USA

Behe, Michael (Writer)
Lehigh University
Biochemistry Dept
Bethlehem, PA 18015, USA

Behl, Mohnish (Actor, Bollywood)
Sagar Sangeet 30th Floor
Opp Colaba Post Office
Bombay, MS 400 005, INDIA

Behle, Jochen (Skier)
Sonnenhof 1
Willingen 34508, GERMANY

Behm, Donald (Athlete, Olympic Athlete, Wrestler)
1398 Compton Ct
E Lansing, MI 48823-2386, USA

Behm, Forrest E (Athlete, Football Player)
3 Briarcliff Dr
Coming, NY 14830, USA

Behney, Mel (Athlete, Baseball Player)
2800 Woodshire Dr
Arlington, TX 76016-1553, USA

Behning, Mark (Athlete, Football Player)
2224 Woodbrook St
Denton, TX 76205, USA

Behnke, Elmer (Athlete, Basketball Player)
3412 Ivy Chase Cir
Birmingham, AL 35226-2276, USA

Behnken, Robert L (Astronaut)
43708 Dejay St
Lancaster, CA 93536, USA

Behr, Aaron (Actor)
c/o Staff Member *Acme Talent & Literary (LA)*
1400 Atlantic Ave
Suite 274
Long Beach, CA 90814, USA

Behr, Daniel (Politician)
C/O Deutscher Bundestag
Platz Der Republik, 1
Berlin D-11011, Germany

Behr, Jason (Actor)
c/o Robert Stein *Robert Stein Management*
PO Box 3797
Beverly Hills, CA 90212, USA

Behrend, Marc (Athlete, Hockey Player, Olympic Athlete)
1808 Savannah Way
Waunakee, WI 53597-2307, USA

Behrendt, Greg (Actor, Writer)
c/o Staff Member *Simon & Schuster*
1230 Avenue of the Americas
New York, NY 10020, USA

Behrendt, Greg (Comedian, Radio Personality)
The Greg Behrendt Show
9336 W Washington Blvd
Culver City, CA 90232, USA

Behrens, Sam (Actor)
530 Bryant Drive
Canoga Park, CA 91304, USA

Behrman, Dave (Athlete, Football Player)
10187 25 1/2 Mile Rd
Albion, MI 49224, USA

Behrs, Beth (Actor)
c/o Chuck Binder *Binder & Associates*
1465 Lindacrest Dr
Beverly Hills, CA 90210, USA

Beier, Thomas (Athlete, Football Player)
5055 Hammock Lake Dr
Coral Gables, FL 33156, USA

Beilina, Nina (Musician)
400 W 43rd St #7D
New York, NY 10036, USA

Beimel, Joe (Athlete, Baseball Player)
4723 Boone Mountain Rd
Kersey, PA 15846-2109, USA

Beinfest, Larry (Commentator)
13700 Mustang Trl
Southwest Ranches, FL 33330-3610, USA

Beirne, Jim (Athlete, Football Player)
2 Cedar Chase Pl
Spring, TX 77381, USA

Beirne, Kevin (Athlete, Baseball Player)
2 Cedar Chase Pl
Spring, TX 77381-3030, USA

Beisel, Monty (Athlete, Football Player)
16557 Goldenrod Pl
Encino, CA 91436, USA

Beisler, Randy (Athlete, Football Player)
306 Ramona St
Palo Alto, CA 94301, USA

Bejo, Berenice (Actor)
c/o Chris Harris *Actual Management Company*
7 Great Russell St
London WC1B 3NH, UK

Bekar, Derek (Athlete, Hockey Player)
29 Windjammer Rdg
Laconia, NH 03246-1841, USA

Belafonte, Harry (Actor, Musician)
2112 Broadway #4A/4B
New York, NY 10023, USA

Belafonte, Shari (Actor, Musician)
530 Bryant Dr
Canoga Park, CA 91304, USA

Belaga, Julie (Activist, Financier)
Connecticut League of Conservative Voters
553 Farmington Ave
Suite 201
Hartford, CT 06105, USA

Beland, Jessi Ann Gravel (Model)
c/o Staff Member *Models 1*
12 Macklin St
Covent Gardens
London WC2B 5SZ, UK

Belanger, Eric (Athlete, Hockey Player)
957 7th St
Hermosa Beach, CA 90254-4824, USA

Belanger, Ken (Athlete, Hockey Player)
KBX Hockey School
143-A Great Northern Rd
Suite 133
Sault Ste Marie, ON P6B 4Y9, Canada

Belanova (Music Group, Musician)

Belanova (Music Group, Musician)
c/o Staff Member *APA Talent and Literary Agency*
9200 Sunset Blvd
#900
Los Angeles, CA 90069, USA

Belbin, Tanith (Figure Skater)
c/o Staff Member *Champions on Ice*
Tom Collins Enterprises Inc
3500 W 80th St
Minneapolis, MN 55431, USA

Bel Biv Devoe (Music Group, Musician)
8942 Wilshire Blvd
Beverly Hills, CA 90211, USA

Belcher, Kevin (Athlete, Baseball Player)
2957 Silvercrest Ln
Grapevine, TX 76021-2423, USA

Belcher, Tim (Athlete, Baseball Player)
P.O. Box 153
Sparta, OH 43350-0153, USA

Belchlavek, Jiri (Conductor)
Czechoslovakia Philharmonic
Alsovo Nabr 12
Prague 11001, CZECH REPUBLIC

Belden, Bob (Athlete, Football Player)
6701 Militia Hill St NW
Canton, OH 44718, USA

Belew, Adrian (Musician)
Umbrella Artists Mgmt
2612 Erie Ave
Cincinnati, OH 45208, USA

Belew, Adrian (Musician)
2004 Hidden Ridge Ct
Mt Juliet, TN 37122, USA

Belfi, Jordan (Actor)
c/o Mark Schumacher *Schumacher Management*
1122 San Vicente Blvd.
Santa Monica, CA 90402, USA

Belford, Christine (Actor)
116 Inlet Ct
Hampstead, NC 28443, USA

Belfour, Ed (Athlete, Hockey Player)
544 Studebaker Rd
Whitewright, TX 75491-7288, USA

Belhumeur, Michel (Athlete, Hockey Player)
58 Little Falls Ln
Rockville, VA 23146-2123, USA

Belichick, Bill (Athlete, Football Coach, Football Player)
PO Box 715
Foxboro, MA 02035, USA

Belichik, William S (Bill) (Coach, Football Coach)
New England Patriots
Gillette Stadium RR1
60 Washington
Foxboro, MA 02035, USA

Belin, Gaspard D (Attorney, Attorney General, General)
4 Willard St
Cambridge, MA 02138, USA

Belinda, Stan (Athlete, Baseball Player)
4208 Reservoir Cir
Alexandria, PA 16611, USA

Belisle, Danny (Athlete, Hockey Player)
3967 Glen Oaks Manor Dr
Sarasota, FL 34232-1045, USA

Belisle, Matt (Athlete, Baseball Player)
4009 Sierra Dr
Austin, TX 78731-3913, USA

Belitz, Todd (Athlete, Baseball Player)
17901 N Colton Ct
Colbert, WA 99005-9174, USA

Beliveau, Jean (Athlete, Hockey Player)
c/o Staff Member *Montreal Canadiens*
1275 Rue Saint-Antoine O
Montreal, QB H3C 5L2, Canada

Belk, Bill (Athlete, Football Player)
12 Ricemill Fry
Columbia, SC 29229, USA

Belk, Tim (Athlete, Baseball Player)
14714 Carolcrest Dr
Houston, TX 77079-6408, USA

Belka, Marek (Prime Minister)
Ul Ursad Rady Ministrow
Ul Wiejska 4/8
Warsaw 00-583, POLAND

Belknap, Anna (Actor)
c/o Steve Stone *Cornerstone Talent Agency*
37 W 20th St
New York, NY 10011, USA

Bell, Albert (Athlete, Football Player)
16222 Hunsaker Ave
Paramount, CA 90723-4762, USA

Bell, Anthony (Athlete, Football Player)
1564 Fitzgerald Dr
Pinole, CA 94564, USA

Bell, Art (Business Person)
c/o Staff Member *Court TV*
600 Third Ave Fl 2
New York, NY 10016, USA

Bell, Bill (Athlete, Football Player)
1601 Walnut St
Apt 611
Kansas City, MO 64108, USA

Bell, Bill (Athlete, Baseball Player)
3401 Urbandale Ave
Des Moines, IA 50310-4006, USA

Bell, Billy Ray (Athlete, Football Player)
4006 Mossy Grove Ct
Humble, TX 77346, USA

Bell, Bob (Athlete, Football Player)
700 Lower State Rd #128G
N Wales, PA 19454-2109, USA

Bell, Brad (Athlete, Golfer)
6255 Oakridge Way
Sacramento, CA 95831, USA

Bell, Brian (Musician)
3611 Sapphire Dr
Encino, CA 91436, USA

Bell, Bruce (Athlete, Hockey Player)
101 Canyon Close W
Lethbridge, AB TlK 6W5, Canada

Bell, Buddy (Athlete, Baseball Player)
Chicago White Sox 333 W 35th St
Attn Director of Player Development
Chicago, IL 60616-3696

Bell, Buddy (Athlete, Baseball Player, Coach)
420 E Ohio St APt 40E
Chicago, IL 60611-4672, USA

Bell, Byron (Athlete, Basketball Player)
1141 Williams St
Lake Geneva, WI 53147, USA

Bell, Carl (Musician)
10690 Fairfield Ave
Las Vegas, NV 89183, USA

Bell, Carlos (Athlete, Football Player)
14411 Hartshill Dr
Houston, TX 77044, USA

Bell, Catherine (Actor)
c/o Daniel (Danny) Sussman *Brillstein Entertainment Partners*
9150 Wilshire Blvd #350
Beverly Hills, CA 90212, USA

Bell, C Gordon (Scientist)
Microsoft Corp
1 Microsoft Way
Redmond, WA 98052, USA

Bell, Charles (Business Person)
McDonald's Corp
1 McDonald's Plaza
1 Kroc Dr
Oak Brook, IL 60523, USA

Bell, Coby (Actor)
5534 E Oleta St
Long Beach, CA 90815, USA

Bell, Coleman (Athlete, Football Player)
3236 Gianna Way
Land 0 Lakes, FL 34638, USA

Bell, David (Athlete, Baseball Player)
420 E Ohio St Apt 40E
Chicago, IL 60611-4672, USA

Bell, Dennis (Athlete, Basketball Player)
111 Springfield Pike
Cincinnati, OH 45215-4263, USA

Bell, Derek (Athlete, Baseball Player)
3404 Pine Top Dr
Valrico, FL 33594-7618, USA

Bell, Drake (Actor)
3356 Ley Dr
Los Angeles, CA 90027, USA

Bell, Drew Tyler (Actor, Director, Producer, Writer)
c/o Beverly Strong *Strong Management*
3532 Hayden Ave
Culver City, CA 90232, USA

Bell, Eddie (Athlete, Football Player)
4529 Tacoma Ter
Fort Worth, TX 76123, USA

Bell, Eddie A (Actor)
4529 Tacoma Terrace
Forth Worth, TX 76123-4005, USA

Bell, Emma (Actor)
c/o Scott Wexler *Brillstein Entertainment Partners*
9150 Wilshire Blvd #350
Beverly Hills, CA 90212, USA

Bell, Eric (Athlete, Baseball Player)
1140 S 124th St
Chandler, AZ 85286-1121, USA

Bell, Fifi (Stylist)
c/o Celebrity Stylist *Oliver Piro Inc*
725 Riverside Dr Apt 3A
New York, NY 10031, USA

Bell, Gary (Athlete, Baseball Player)
2107 Oak Ranch
San Antonio, TX 78259-1819, USA

Bell, Gerard (Athlete, Football Player)
1347 Deerbourne Dr
Zephyrhills, FL 33543, USA

Bell, Glen (Business Person)
Bell Charitable Foundation
P.O. Box 642
Rancho Santa Fe, CA 92067-0642, USA

Bell, Gordon (Athlete, Football Player)
205 Le Moyne Pkwy
Oak Park, IL 60302, USA

Bell, Grantis (Athlete, Football Player)
3049 La Mirage Dr
Lauderhill, FL 33319, USA

Bell, Greg (Athlete, Track Athlete)
831 W Miami Ave
Logansport, IN 46947-2543, USA

Bell, Greg (Athlete, Football Player)
5662 Calle Real
Goleta, CA 93117, USA

Bell, Harry (Athlete, Hockey Player)
7711 N. Invergordon Rd.
Paradise Valley, AZ 85253, USA

Bell, Heath (Athlete, Baseball Player)
7437 Los Brazos
San Diego, CA 92127-3852, USA

Bell, Hilari (Writer)
PO Box 877
Chestertown, MD 21620, USA

Bell, Jacob (Athlete, Football Player)
511 S Warson Rd
Saint Louis, MO 63124, USA

Bell, Jaime (Actor)
c/o Staff Member *WME (LA)*
9601 Wilshire Blvd Fl 3
Beverly Hills, CA 90210, USA

Bell, James D (Diplomat)
154 Zinfandel Circle
Scotts Valley, CA 95066, USA

Bell, Jamie (Actor)
c/o Brian Swardstrom *WME (LA)*
9601 Wilshire Blvd Fl 3
Beverly Hills, CA 90210, USA

Bell, Janice (Stylist)
915 W Gunnison
Chicago, IL 60640, USA

Bell, Jason (Athlete, Football Player)
3387 N Studebaker Rd
Long Beach, CA 90808, USA

Bell, Jay (Athlete, Baseball Player)
3217 E Piro St
Phoenix, AZ 85044-3618, USA

Bell, Jerry (Athlete, Football Player)
1347 Deerbourne Dr
Zephyrhills, FL 33543, USA

Bell, Jerry (Athlete, Baseball Player)
631 Audrey Rd
Mount Juliet, TN 37122-3844, USA

Bell, John (Musician)
Brown Cat Inc
400 Foundry St
Athens, GA 30601, USA

Bell, John Anthony (Actor, Director)
Bell Shakespeare Co
88 George St
Level 1
Rocks, NSW 200, AUSTRALIA

Bell, Jorge A M (George) (Athlete, Baseball Player)
Lamiama #14
Bell 2nd Planto
San Pedro de Macoris, Dominican Republic

Bell, Joshua (Musician)
24 E 22nd St #7
New York, NY 10010, USA

Bell, Ken (Athlete, Football Player)
8335 Fairmount Dr Unit 9-106 Denver
CO 80247-1137
Denver, CO 80247, us

Bell, Kendrell (Athlete, Football Player)
400 W Peachtree St NW
Unit 1211
Atlanta, GA 30308-3547, USA

Bell, Kendrell (Athlete, Football Player)
1270 Caroline St NE Ste D120 Atlanta GA
30307-2758
Atlanta, GA 30307, us

Bell, Kerwin (Athlete, Football Player)
525 3rd Street N
Apt 508
Jacksonville Beach, FL 32250, USA

Bell, Kerwin (Athlete, Football Player)
1822 Waterbury Ln Fleming Island FL
32003-7749
Fleming Island, FL 32003, us

Bell, Kevin (Athlete, Football Player)
5780 Phyllis Ln
Beaumont, TX 77713, USA

Bell, Kevin (Athlete, Baseball Player)
621 Sue St
Little Chute, WI 54140-2424, USA

Bell, Kristen (Actor)
c/o Emily Gerson Saines *Brookside Artists
Management (NY)*
250 W 57th St
Suite 2303
New York, NY 10107, USA

Bell, Lake (Actor)
c/o Joanna (Joanie) Burstein *Burstein
Company, The*
15304 Sunset Blvd
suite 208
Pacific Palisades, CA 90272, USA

Bell, Larry S (Artist)
PO Box 4101
Taos, NM 87571, USA

Bell, Lauralee (Actor)
c/o Brenda Feldman *Feldman PR*
13636 Ventura Blvd
#440
Sherman Oaks, CA 91423, USA

Bell, Lynette (Swimmer)
149 Henry St
Merwether NSW 22, Australia

Bell, Madison Smartt (Writer)
Random House
1745 Broadway
#B1
New York, NY 10019, USA

Bell, Marcus (Athlete, Football Player)
678 S School Bus Rd
Eagar, AZ 85925, USA

Bell, Mark E (Athlete, Football Player)
2701 Wild Rose St
Wichita, KS 67205, USA

Bell, Marshall (Actor)
IFA Talent Agency
8730 Sunset Blvd #490
Los Angeles, CA 90069, USA

Bell, Michael (Actor)
4906 Encino Ave
Encino, CA 91316, USA

Bell, Michelle (Athlete, Golfer)
18895 Pond Cypress Ct
Jupiter, FL 33458, USA

Bell, Mike (Athlete, Baseball Player)
5125 Piney Grove Dr
Cumming, GA 30040-9673, USA

Bell, Mike (Race Car Driver)
American Motorcycle Assn
13515 Yarmouth Dr
Pickerington, OH 43147, USA

Bell, Mike J (Athlete, Football Player)
7405 Lakewood Cir
Wichita, KS 67205, USA

Bell, Mikw (Athlete)
244 W Goldfinch Way
Chandler, AZ 85286, USA

Bell, Myron (Athlete, Football Player)
3027 Crawford Ave Gastonia NC 28052-
6076
Gastonia, NC 28052, USA

Bell, Nick (Athlete, Football Player)
1641 Minorca Dr Costa
Mesa, CA 92626, USA

Bell, Peggy (Athlete, Golfer)
400 Grove Rd
Southern Pines, NC 28387, USA

Bell, Raja (Athlete, Basketball Player)
22 E Cactus601 NE 36th St
Apt 1812 Wren Dr
Miami, FL 33137-3968, USA

Bell, Richard T (Athlete, Football Player)
12106 City View Ln SE
Chatfield, MN 55923, USA

Bell, Ricky (Athlete, Football Player)
c/o Staff Member *Sosincere Entertainment*
2054 Nostrand Ave Apt 4F
Brooklyn, NY 11210, USA

Bell, Rini (Actor)
c/o Sherry Marsh *Marsh Entertainment*
12444 Ventura Blvd #203
Studio City, CA 91604, USA

Bell, Rob (Athlete, Baseball Player)
28 Blossom Hill Dr
Marlboro, NY 12542-6000, USA

Bell, Robert (Musician)
c/o Staff Member *J Bird Entertainment
Agency*
4905 S Atlantic Ave
Daytona Beach, FL 32127, USA

Bell, Robert F (Athlete, Football Player)
7415 N 12th St
Melrose Park, PA 19027, USA

Bell, Roxanne (Stylist)
c/o Staff Member *Maximum Talent*
1873 S Bellaire St
Suite 915
Denver, CO 80222-4356, USA

Bell, Sam (Coach)
2310 E Woodstock Place
Bloomington, IN 47401, USA

Bell, Sean (Actor)
c/o Daniel Sladek *Daniel Sladek
Entertainment Corporation*
8306 Wilshire Blvd #510
Beverly Hills, CA 90212, USA

Bell, Tatum (Athlete, Football Player)
18754 E Powers Dr
Aurora, CO 80015, us

Bell, Terry (Athlete; Baseball Player)
8352 Normandy Creek Dr
Dayton, OH 45458-3284, USA

Bell, Tobin (Actor)
c/o Alan Saffron *Saffron Management*
9171 Wilshire Blvd #441
Beverly Hills, CA 90210, USA

Bell, Tom (Actor)
Shepherd & Ford
13 Randor Walk
London SW3 4BP, UNITED KINGDOM
(uk)

Bell, Tom (Stylist)
c/o Staff Member *Jed Root Inc*
61-A Walker St
New York, NY 10013, USA

Bell, Tommy (Astronaut)
205 S Redondo Ave
Manhattan Beach, CA 90266, USA

Bell, Townsend (Race Car Driver)
524 15th Street
Santa Monica, CA 90402, USA

Bell, Wally (Athlete, Baseball Player)
1675 W Western Reserve Rd
Unit 3F
Youngstown, OH 44515-4220, USA

Bell, W Kamau (Comedian, Television
Host)
c/o Keri Smith Esguia *Whitesmith
Entertainment*
Prefers to be contact via email or
telephone
Los Angeles, CA 90069, USA

Bell, Yeremiah (Athlete, Football Player)
1886 Sirius Ln
Weston, FL 33327-, us

Bell, Zoe (Actor)
c/o Todd Diener *Collective*
8383 Wilshire Blvd
Suite 1050
Beverly Hills, CA 90211, USA

Bella, Ivan (Cosmonaut)
Potchta Kosmonavtov
Moskovskoi Oblasti
Syvisdny Goroduk 141160, RUSSIA

Bella, John (Athlete, Baseball Player)
409 N Cypress Dr
Apt 7
Jupiter, FL 33469, USA

bella, John "Zeke"
24 Taylor Dr
Cos Cob, CT 06807-2314, USA

Bella, Rachael (Actor)
c/o Leonard Torgan *Collective*
8383 Wilshire Blvd
Suite 1050
Beverly Hills, CA 90211, USA

Bellamy, Bill (Actor, Comedian)
17219 Benner Pl
Encino, CA 91316, USA

Bellamy, Carol (Misc)
United Nations Children's Fund
3 United Nations Plaza
New York, NY 10017, USA

Bellamy, David J (Writer)
Mill House Bedbum
Bishop Auckland
County Durham DL13 3NN, UNITED
KINGDOM (UK)

Bellamy, Ned (Actor)
c/o Laina Cohn *Laina Cohn Management*
15066 Sutton St
Sherman Oaks, CA 91403, USA

Bellamy, Walt (Athlete, Basketball Player,
Olympic Athlete)
P.O. Box 42751
Atlanta, GA 30311-0751, USA

Belland, Neil (Athlete, Hockey Player)
868 Renaissance Dr
Oshawa, ON L1J 8K9, Canada

Bellani, Adrian (Actor)
8004 Woodrow Wilson Dr
Los Angeles, CA 90046, USA

Bell Calloway, Vanessa (Actor)
c/o Staff Member *Nine Yards
Entertainment*
8530 Wilshire Blvd Fl 5
Beverly Hills, CA 90211, USA

Belle, Albert (Athlete, Baseball Player)
9299 E Marioosa Grande Dr
Scottsdale, AZ 85255-3789, USA

Belle, Camilla (Actor)
c/o Brad Cafarelli *PMK/BNC - LA*
8687 Melrose Ave
8th Floor
West Hollywood, CA 90069, USA

Belle, Regina (Musician)
Green Light
PO Box 3172
Beverly Hills, CA 90212, USA

Belleci, Tory (Special Effects Designer)
Mythbusters
1268 Missouri Street
San Francisco, CA 94107, USA

Bellecourt, Vernon (Activist)
American Indian Vovement
1209 4th St SE
Minneapolis, MN 55414, USA

Bellefeuille, Blake (Athlete, Hockey
Player)
1 Angelica Ln
Southborough, MA 01772-1339, USA

Beller, Kathleen (Actor)
PO Box 806
Half Moon Bay, CA 94019, USA

Bellflower, Nellie (Actor, Producer)
c/o Staff Member *Keylight Entertainment
Group*
425 Park Ave S #19D
New York, NY 10016-8019, USA

Bellhorn, Mark (Athlete, Baseball Player)
19550 N Grayhawk Dr
Unit 1083
Scottsdale, AZ 85255-3993, USA

Bellhorn, Mark (Athlete, Basketball
Player)
1447 Palomino Way
Oviedo, FL 32765, USA

Belliard, Rafael (Athlete, Baseball Player)
10846 King Bay Dr
Boca Raton, FL 33498-4548, USA

Belliard, Ronnie (Athlete, Baseball Player)
2999 NW 96th St
Miami, FL 33147-2337, USA

Bellinger, Clay (Athlete, Baseball Player)
1390 E Horseshoe Dr
Chandler, AZ 85249-4761, USA

Bellinger, Rodney (Athlete, Football
Player)
6721 SW 48th Ter
Miami, FL 33155, USA

Bellingham, Lynda (Actor)
c/o Staff Member *Yakety Yak*
8-A Bloomsbury Sq
London WC1A 2NE, UNITED KINGDOM
(UK)

Bellingham, Norman (Athlete, Kayaker, Olympic Athlete)
1825 Cantwell Grv
Colorado Springs, CO 80906-6911, USA

Bellini, Mario (Architect)
Architecture Center
66 Portland Place
London W1, UNITED KINGDOM (UK)

Bellino, Alexis (Reality TV Star)

Bellino, Dan (Athlete, Baseball Player)
1456 Trailwood Dr
Crystal Lake, IL 60014-1966, USA

Bellino, Joe (Athlete, Football Player)
45 Hayden Ln
Bedford, MA 01730, USA

Bellisario, Donald P (Actor, Director, Producer, Writer)
3301 Oakdell Rd
Studio City, CA 91604, USA

Bellisario, Troian (Actor)
c/o Matthew Lesher *Insight*
1134 S Cloverdale Ave
Los Angeles, CA 90019, USA

Bell-Lundy, Sandra (Cartoonist)
255 Northwood Dr
Welland ON L3C 6V1, Canada

Bellman, Gina (Actor)
c/o Matthew Lesher *Insight*
1134 S Cloverdale Ave
Los Angeles, CA 90019, USA

Bellman-Balchunas, Lois (Athlete, Baseball Player)
1008 Southport Ave
Lisle, IL 60532-1346, USA

Bello, Maria (Actor)
800 Marco Pl
Venice, CA 90291, USA

Belloir, Rob (Athlete, Baseball Player)
PO Box 2933
Savannah, GA 31402-2933, USA

Bellorin, Edwin
44523 Fenhold St
Lancaster, CA 93535-3420, USA

Bellotti, Mike (Coach, Football Coach)
University of Oregon
Athletic Dept
Eugen, OR 97403, USA

Bellovin, Steven M (Scientist)
AT & T Research Labs
180 Park Ave
PO Box 971
Florham Park, NJ 07932, USA

Bellows, Brian (Athlete, Hockey Player)
5205 Mirror Lakes Dr
Minneapolis, MN 55436-2050, USA

Bellows, Gil (Actor)
c/o Emily Gerson Saines *Brookside Artists Management (NY)*
250 W 57th St
Suite 2303
New York, NY 10107, USA

Bellucci, Monica (Actor, Model)
c/o Laurent Gregoire *Agence Artistique Adequat*
108 rue Reaumur
Paris 75002, France

Bellugi, Piero
50027 Strada In Chianti
Florence ITALY

Bellwood, Pamela (Actor)
1696 San Leandro Ln
Santa Barbara, Ca 93108, USA

Bell X1 (Music Group)
c/o Staff Member *Paradigm (Monterey)*
404 W Franklin St
Monterey, CA 93940, USA

Belm, Michaela (Model)
Agentur Talents
Ohmstr 5
Munich 80802, GERMANY

Belmares, Roland (DJ)
c/o Staff Member *Diva Central Inc*
7510 W Sunset Blvd Ste 1445
Los Angees, CA 90046, USA

Belmondo, Jean-Paul (Actor)
9 Rue des Saint Peres
Paris 75007, FRANCE

Belo, Carlos Filipe Ximenes (Nobel Prize Laureate, Religious Leader)
Catholic Bishop Dili
EAST TIMOR

Belote, Melissa (Athlete, Olympic Athlete, Swimmer)
1504 E Coronado Dr
Tempe, AZ 85282-5763, USA

Belousova, Ludmila (Figure Skater)
Chalet Hubel
Grindelwald 3818, SWITZERLAND

Belov, Sergei (Athlete, Basketball Player)
Basketball Hall of Fame
1000 Hall of Fame Ave
Ste 100
Springfield, MA 01105-2545, USA

Below, Duane
4330 Eaglehurst Rd
Sylvania, OH 43560-3411, USA

Belser, Ceaser (Athlete, Football Player)
317 Cooper Dr
Hurst, TX 76053, USA

Belser, Jason (Athlete, Football Player)
20474 Middlebury St
Ashburn, VA 20147, USA

Belton, Horace (Athlete, Football Player)
2047 General Lee Ave
Baton Rouge, LA 70870-6325

Beltrami, Marco (Composer)
c/o Staff Member *Greenspan Artist Management*
8760 W Sunset Blvd
West Hollywood, CA 90069, USA

Beltran, Carlos (Athlete, Baseball Player)
18 Paseo Alcala
Urb Hacienda Hermanas Mena
Manati, PR 00674-5766, USA

Beltran, Rigo (Athlete, Baseball Player)
3950 Laurelwood Ln
Dekray Beach, FL 33445-3503, USA

Beltran, Robert (Actor)
2210 Talmadge St
Los Angeles, CA 90027, USA

Beltre, Adrian (Athlete, Baseball Player)
340 Old Ranch Rd
Bradbury, CA 91008, USA

Belushi, James (Jim) (Actor)
12323 12th Helena Dr
Los Angeles, CA 90049, USA

Belvin, Art (Athlete, Football Player)
6506 Centre Place Cir
Spring, TX 77379, USA

Belzer, Richard (Actor, Comedian)
60 Riverside Dr #14C/D
New York, NY 10024, USA

Beman, Deane R (Athlete, Golfer)
Golf HOF
255 Deer Haven Dr
Ponte Vedra Beach, FL 32082-2108, USA

Bemhard (Prince)
Soestdijk Palace
Baarn, NETHERLANDS

Bemiller, Al (Athlete, Football Player)
Buffalo Bills
5002 Armor Rd
Orchard Park, NY 14127-4401, USA

Bemis, Cliff (Actor)
Beartooth Productions
11271 Ventura Blvd
PMB 366
Studio City, CA 91604, USA

Bemvenuti, Luciana (Athlete, Golfer)
3673 Wickford Ln
Duluth, GA 30096, USA

Benackova, Gabriela (Opera Singer)
Oper et Concert
Maximilianstr 22
Munich 80539, GERMANY

Benade Leo, Edward (General)
417 Pine Ridge Road
#A
Carthage, NC 28327, USA

Ben Ali, Zine al-Abidine (General)
President's Office
Palais Presidentiel
Tunis, TUNISIA

Benami, Didi (Musician)
c/o Simon Fuller *XIX Entertainment*
35-37 Parkgate Rd
32/33 Ransomes Dock
London SW11 4NP, UNITED KINGDOM (UK)

Benanti, Laura (Actor)
c/o Staff Member *Creative Artists Agency (CAA-LA)*
2000 Ave Of The Stars
Los Angeles, CA 90067, USA

Benard, Marvin (Athlete, Baseball Player)
30405 S 903 PR SE
Kennewick, WA 99338-7346, USA

Benard, Maurice (Actor)
c/o Staff Member *Stone Manners Salners Agency (LA)*
9911 W Pico Blvd Ste 1400
Los Angeles, CA 90035, USA

Benassi, Benny (Musician)
c/o Staff Member *Mission Control Artists Agency*
Unit 3 City Business Centre
St Olav's Court, Lower Road
London SE16 2XB, UNITED KINGDOM (UK)

Benatar, Pat (Musician, Songwriter)
0 Hana Hwy
Hana, HI 96713, USA

Benavides, Fortunato P (Pete) (Judge)
US Court of Appeals
903 San Jacinto Blvd
Austin, TX 78701, USA

Benavides, Freddie (Athlete, Baseball Player)
3007 Wincrest Cir
Laredo, TX 78045-8149, USA

Benavides, Osvaldo (Actor)
c/o Staff Member *Televisa*
Blvd Adolfo Lopez Mateos 232
Colonia San Angel INN
DF CP 01060, MEXICO

Benben, Brian (Actor)
c/o Erwin More *Paradigm (LA)*
360 N Crescent Dr
North Bldg
Beverly Hills, CA 90210, USA

Bench, Johnny (Athlete, Baseball Player)
3899 Ridgedale Dr
Cincinnati, OH 45247-6946, USA

Benchoff, Dennis L (Den) (General)
380 Arbor Road
Lancaster, PA 17601, USA

Bendekovits, Joe (Athlete, Baseball Player)
9410 N Newport Ave
Tampa, FL 33612-7724, USA

Bender, Carey (Athlete, Football Player)
716 Delta Downs Dr
Cary, NC 27519, USA

Bender, Gary N (Sportscaster)
TNT-TV
Sports Dept
1050 Techwood Dr NW
Atlanta, GA 30318, USA

Bender, Jack (Director)
13055 Evanston St
Los Angeles, CA 90049, USA

Bender, Thomas (Historian)
54 Washington Mews
New York, NY 10003, USA

Bender, Wes (Athlete, Football Player)
114 Skyline Dr
Burbank, CA 91501, USA

Bendix, Simone (Actor)
Joy Jameson
2/19 Plaza
535 Kings Road
London SW10 0SZ, UNITED KINGDOM (UK)

Bendlin, Kurt (Athlete, Track Athlete)
DLV
Asfelder Str 27
Leverkusen 64289, GERMANY

Bendre, Sonali (Actor, Bollywood)
A/203 43 Paradise Apts
Swami Samarth Nagar 1st Cross Lane
Andheri(W)
Mumbai, MS 400053, INDIA

Bendross, Jesse (Athlete, Football Player)
5226 SW 22nd St
Hollywood, FL 33023, USA

Bene, Bill (Athlete, Baseball Player)
1063 Bella Vista Ave
San Gabriel, CA 91775-2548, USA

Benedek, George B (Physicist)
Massachusetts Institute of Technology
Physics Dept
Cambridge, MA 02139, USA

Benedek, Joana (Actor)
c/o Staff Member *Televisa*
Blvd Adolfo Lopez Mateos 232
Colonia San Angel INN
DF CP 01060, MEXICO

Benedeti, Paulo (Actor)
1560 nw 13th Ave
Boca Raton, Fl 33486, USA

Benedict, Bruce (Athlete, Baseball Player)
335 Quiet Water Ln
Atlanta, GA 30350-3724, USA

Benedict, Dirk (Actor, Director, Writer)
c/o Staff Member *Acme Talent & Literary
(LA)*
1400 Atlantic Ave
Suite 274
Long Beach, CA 90814, USA

Benedict, Manson (Engineer)
410 East Las Olas Blvd
Fort Lauderdale, FL 33301-2210, USA

Benedict, Robert Patrick (Actor)
c/o Charles Silver *Silver Massetti &
Szatmary (SMS) Talent Inc*
8383 Wilshire Blvd
Suite 230
Beverly Hills, CA 90211, USA

Benedicto, Lourdes (Actor)
6223 Enfield Ave
Encino, CA 91316, USA

Benedict XVI, Pope (Religious Leader)
Apostolic Palace
Vatican City 00120, ITALY

Benefield, Daved (Athlete, Football
Player)
420 N Rodeo Dr
Apt 15281
Beverly Hills, CA 90210, USA

Benepe, Jim (Athlete, Golfer)
1955 1/2 Frackelton St
Sheridan, WY 82801-2526, USA

Benes, Alan (Athlete, Baseball Player)
754 Kraffel Ln
Chesterfield, MO 63017-8057, USA

Benes, Andy (Athlete, Baseball Player,
Olympic Athlete)
1127 Highland Pointe Dr
St Louis, MO 63131-1420, USA

Benet, Eric (Actor, Musician)
5358 Oak Park Ave
Encino, CA 91316, USA

Benet, Kiki (Stylist)
c/o Staff Member *Rex Agency, The*
6311 Romaine St
Los Angeles, CA 90038, USA

Benetton, Giuliana (Business Person)
Benetton Group SpA
Via Minelli
Ponzano Treviso 31050, ITALY

Benetton, Lucianno (Business Person)
Benetton Group
Villa Minelli
Ponzano
Treviso 31050, Italy

Benetton, Luciano (Business Person)
Benetton Group SpA
Via Minelli
Ponzano Treviso 31050, ITALY

Benfatti, Lou (Athlete, Football Player)
29 Colonial Oaks Dr
Ridge, NJ 07438, USA

Benflis, Ali (Prime Minister)
Prime Minister's Office
Palais du Gouvernement
Algiers, ALGERIA

Benford, Gregory (Writer)
c/o Staff Member *Little, Brown Book
Group*
100 Victoria Embankment
London EC4Y 0DY, UK

Bengis, Fred (Athlete, Baseball Player)
546 Quail Ct
Longs, SC 29568, USA

Benglis, Lynda (Artist)
222 Bowery St
New York, NY 10012, USA

Bengston, Billy Al (Artist)
805 Hampton Dr
Venice, CA 90291, USA

Bengston, Michelle (Olympic Athlete)
General Delivery
West Glacier, MT 59936-9999, USA

Bengtson, Michelle (Stylist)
2220 W Mission Lane
#2259
Phoenix, AZ 85021, USA

Benhima, Mohamed (Prime Minister)
Km 5.5
Route des Zaers
Rabat, MOROCCO

Benigni, Roberto (Actor, Director)
Melampo Cinematografica
Via Ludovisi, 35
Rome IT-00187, Italy

Benignl, Roberto (Actor, Director)
Via Traversa 44
Vergaglio
Provinz di Prato, ITALY

Bening, Annette (Actor)
12431 Mulholland Dr
Beverly Hills, CA 90210, USA

Benioff, David (Producer, Writer)
c/o Guymon Casady *Management 360*
9111 Wilshire Blvd
Beverly Hills, CA 90210, USA

Beniquez, Juan (Athlete, Baseball Player)
Villa Carolina
87-12 Calle 99A
Carolina, PR 00985-4127, USA

Benirschke, Rolf J (Athlete, Football
Player)
4326 Vista De La Tierra
Del Mar, CA 92014, USA

Benish, Dan (Athlete, Football Player)
318 Creek Manor Way
Suwanee, GA 30024, USA

Benishek, Dan (Congressman, Politician)
514 Cannon HOB
Washington, DC 20515, USA

Benitez, Armando (Athlete, Baseball
Player)
2205 Warwick Way Ste 200
Marriottsville, MD 21104-1632, USA

Benitez, Elsa (Model)
c/o Staff Member *M Fashion Model
Management*
Via Monte Rosa, 80
Milan 20149, Italy

Benitez, Jellybean (Musician)
Jellybean Recordings
235 Park Ave
New York, NY 10003, USA

Benitez, Wilfred (Athlete, Boxer)
Wilfred Benitez Foundation, NFP
P.O. Box 2338
Temecula, CA 92593, USA

Benitez, Yamil (Athlete, Baseball Player)
Calle 13 Bo
918 Caperra Terrace
San Juan, PR 00921, USA

Benitz, Max (Actor)
c/o Michael Baum *Impression
Entertainment*
9229 W Sunset Blvd #700
West Hollywood, CA 90069, USA

Benjamin, Benoit (Athlete, Basketball
Player)
28 Morning Grn
San Antonio, TX 78257-2602, USA

Benjamin, Guy (Athlete, Football Player)
91-443 Ewa Beach Rd Apt B
Ewa Beach, HI 96706, USA

Benjamin, Jill (Actor)
c/o Staff Member *Principato/Young
Management*
9465 Wilshire Blvd
Suite 430
Beverly Hills, CA 90212, USA

Benjamin, Mike (Athlete, Baseball Player)
25608 S 182 Pl
Queen Creek, AZ 85142-8188, USA

Benjamin, Richard (Actor, Director)
c/o Staff Member *Gersh (LA)*
9465 Wilshire Blvd
Suite 600
Beverly Hills, CA 90212, USA

Benjamin, Ryan (Athlete, Football Player)
8332 Boyce Ct
New Port Richey, FL 34654, USA

Benjamin, Stephen (Athlete, Yachtsman)
P.O. Box 399
Norwalk, CT 06856-0399, USA

Benjamin, Steve (Athlete, Olympic
Athlete, Sailor)
PO Box 399
Norwalk, CT 06856-0399, USA

Benjamin, Tony (Athlete, Football Player)
7448 E Leland Cir
Mesa, AZ 85207, us

Benkovic, Stephen J (Misc)
771 Teaberry Lane
State College, PA 16803, USA

Benmosche, Robert H (Business Person)
Metropolitan Life Insurance
1 Madison Ave
New York, NY 10010, USA

Benn, Anthony N W (Tony) (Government
Official)
House of Commons
Westminster
London SW1A 0AA, UNITED KINGDOM
(UK)

Benn, Nigel (Boxer)
Matchroom Boxing
10 Western Road
Romford Essex RM1 3JT, UNITED
KINGDOM

Benner, Dyne (Stylist)
311 E 60th St
New York, NY 10022, USA

Benners, Fred (Athlete, Football Player)
5211 Shadywood Ln
Dallas, TX 75209, USA

Bennet, Michael F. (Senator)
458 Russell Senate Office Building
Washington, DC 20510, USA

Bennett, Adam (Athlete, Hockey Player)
3on3 Hockey
2193 Dunwin Dr
Mississauga, ON L5L 1X2, Canada

Bennett, A L (Athlete, Basketball Player)
523 N Willow Pl
Jenks, OK 74037, USA

Bennett, Antoine
5011 SW 173rd Ave
Miramar, FL 33029, us

Bennett, Barry (Athlete, Football Player)
22047 Ginseng Rd
Long Prairie, MN 56347, USA

Bennett, Bennett (Actor)
c/o Paul Young *Principato/Young
Management*
9465 Wilshire Blvd
Suite 430
Beverly Hills, CA 90212, USA

Bennett, Bill (DJ)
c/o Staff Member *Diva Central Inc*
7510 W Sunset Blvd Ste 1445
Los Angees, CA 90046, USA

Bennett, Bill (Athlete, Hockey Player)
14 Glen Ave
Cranston, RI 02905, USA

Bennett, Bob (Musician, Songwriter,
Writer)
c/o Vicki Jennette *The Benjamin Artist
Agency*
PO Box 92348
Nashville, TN 37209, USA

Bennett, Bob (Athlete, Olympic Athlete,
Swimmer)
70 Rivo Alto Canal
Long Beach, CA 90803-4047, USA

Bennett, Brad (Race Car Driver)
PO Box 16759
Stamford, CT 06905, USA

Bennett, Brandon (Athlete, Football
Player)
308 Daybrook Ct
Greenville, Sc 29605, us

Bennett, Brooke (Athlete, Olympic
Athlete, Swimmer)
2585 Rowe Road
Milford, MI 48380, USA

Bennett, Bruce (Athlete, Football Player)
8620 NW 13th St Lot 391
Gainesville, FL 32653-6325

Bennett, Carl (Athlete, Basketball Player)
2834 Little River Run
Fort Wayne, IN 46804-2573, USA

Bennett, Charles A (Athlete, Football
Player)
18311 Tomlinson Dr
Lutz, FL 33549, USA

Bennett, Clay (Cartoonist)
Christian Science Monitor
Editorial Dept
1 Norway St
Boston, MA 02115, USA

Bennett, Cornelius (Athlete, Football
Player)
818 S 7th Ave
Hollywood, FL 33019, us

Bennett, Curt (Athlete, Hockey Player)
260 Awapuhi Pl
Wailuku, HI 96793-2117, USA

Bennett, Darren (Athlete, Football Player)
3347 Corte Del Cruce
Carlsbad, CA 92009, USA

Bennett, Dave (Athlete, Baseball Player)
101 S Fairchild St
Yreka, CA 96097-2263, USA

Bennett, Donnell (Athlete, Football Player)
129 NW 16th Ave Pompano
Beach, FL 33069, USA

Bennett, Drew (Athlete, Football Player)
2335 Hyde St # 1 San
Francisco, CA 94109, us

Bennett, Edgar (Athlete, Football Player)
1880 Horsehoe Ln
De Pere, WI 54115, USA

Bennett, Elmer (Athlete, Basketball Player)
2820 Avenue of the Woods
Louisville, KY 40241-6232, USA

Bennett, Erik (Athlete, Baseball Player)
PO Box 4108 Attn Coaching Staff
salt LakP Citv, UT 84110-4108, USA

Bennett, Fran (Actor)
749 N Lafayette Park Place
Los Angeles, CA 90026, USA

Bennett, Gary (Athlete, Baseball Player)
14905 Creekside Path
Libertville, IL 60048-1104, USA

Bennett, Haley (Actor)
c/o Mimi DiTrani *Schiff Company, The*
9465 Wilshire Blvd
Suite 480
Beverly Hills, CA 90212, USA

Bennett, Harvey (Athlete, Hockey Player)
1096 Warwick Neck Ave
Warwick, RI 02889-6815, USA

Bennett, Hywel (Actor)
Gavin Barker
45 S Molton St
London W1Y 3RD, UNITED KINGDOM
(UK)

Bennett, Jeff (Athlete, Baseball Player)
408 Five Oaks Blvd
Lebanon, TN 37087-1321, USA

Bennett, Jimmy (Actor)
c/o Jason Newman *Untitled Entertainment (LA)*
350 S. Beverly Dr #200
Beverly Hills, CA 90212, USA

Bennett, Joe C (Educator)
4101 Altamont Road
Birmingham, AL 35213, USA

Bennett, Joel (Athlete, Baseball Player)
401 Riley Rd
Windsor, NY 13865-1043, USA

Bennett, John
5151 Collins Ave Apt 426
Miami Beach, FL 33140-2714, USA

Bennett, Jonathan (Actor)
c/o Staff Member *Amplitude Entertainment*
8033 Sunset Blvd #823
Los Angeles, CA 90046

Bennett, Leeman (Athlete, Football Coach, Football Player)
PO Box 9269 Fleming
Island, FL 32006, USA

Bennett, Michael (Athlete, Football Player)
17110 Journeys End Dr
Odessa, FL 33556, USA

Bennett, Monte (Athlete, Football Player)
2075 Avenue U
Sterling, KS 67579, USA

Bennett, Nelson (Skier)
807 S 20th Ave
Yakima, WA 98902, USA

Bennett, Nigel (Actor)
c/o Larry Goldhar *Characters Talent Agency (Toronto)*
8 Elm St
2nd Floor
Toronto, ON M5G 1G7, CANADA

Bennett, Paris (Musician)

Bennett, Richard Rodney (Composer)
Novello Co
8-9 Firth St
London W1V 5TZ, UNITED KINGDOM
(UK)

Bennett, Rick (Athlete, Hockey Player)
55 Evergreen Ave
Clifton Park, NY 12065-4032, USA

Bennett, Robert R (Business Person)
Home Shopping Network
2501 118th Ave N
Saint Petersburg, FL 33716, USA

Bennett, Robert S (Attorney, Attorney General, General)
1840 24th St NW
Washington, DC 20008, USA

Bennett, Roy (Athlete, Football Player)
4850 Pine Hill Ct W Stone
Stone Mountain, GA 30088, USA

Bennett, Sean (Athlete, Football Player)
12163 E State Road 62
Saint Meinrad, IN 47577, USA

Bennett, Shayne (Athlete, Baseball Player)
346 Franklin Pl
Plainfield, NJ 07060-2548, USA

Bennett, Tony (Musician)
130 W 57th St #9D
New York, NY 10019, USA

Bennett, Tony (Athlete, Basketball Player)
3408 Cesford Grange
Keswick, VA 22947-9126, USA

Bennett, Tracie (Actor)
Annette Stone
9 Newburgh St
London W1V 1LA, UNITED KINGDOM
(UK)

Bennett, Wendell (Athlete, Hockey Player)
726 Maryland Dr
Vista, CA 92083-3333, USA

Bennett, William (Athlete, Hockey Player)
75 Tucker Ave
Cranston, RI 02905-3314, USA

Bennett, William J. (Politician, Radio Personality, Secretary)
1901 N Moore St
Suite 201B
Arlington, VA 22209, USA

Bennett, Winston (Athlete, Basketball Player)
54 Barrington Cir
Paducah, KY 42003-8895, USA

Bennett, Woody (Athlete, Football Player)
7175 Via Leonardo Lake
Worth, FL 33467, us

Bennie, Dan (Musician)
22121 Cleveland St
Dearborn, MI 48124, USA

Benning, Brian (Athlete, Hockey Player)
Interstate Batteries
11216 156 St NW
Edmonton, AB T5M 1Y3, Canada

Benning, Jim (Athlete, Hockey Player)
P.O. Box 1264
Sherwood, OR 97140-1264, USA

Benning, Jim (Athlete, Hockey Player)
Boston Bruins
100 Legends Way Ste 250
Attn: Asst General Manager
Boston, MA 02114-1389, USA

Benning, Norm (Race Car Driver)
3359 Babcock Blvd.
Pittsburgh, PA 15237, USA

Bennington, Chester (Musician)
2959 E Bonanza Rd
Gilbert, AZ 85297, USA

Benny, Joan (Actor)
1131 Coldwater Canyon
Beverly Hills, CA 90210, USA

Benoit, David (Musician)
Fitzgerald-Hartley
34 N Palm St
#100
Ventura, CA 93001, USA

Benoit, Morgan (Actor)
c/o Staff Member *Bluestone Entertainment*
9000 Sunset Blvd
Suite 700
Los Angeles, CA 90069, USA

Benrubi, Abraham (Actor)
c/o Erik Kritzer *Kritzer Levine Wilkins Entertainment (KLWG)*
11872 La Grange Ave
1st Floor
Los Angeles, CA 90025, USA

Bensimon, Kelly Killoren (Model, Reality TV Star, Writer)
c/o Staff Member *Bravo (NY)*
30 Rockefeller Plaza
New York, NY 10112, USA

Benson, Amber (Actor)
c/o Staff Member *United Talent Agency (UTA)*
9336 Civic Center Dr
Beverly Hills, CA 90210, USA

Benson, Andrew A (Misc)
6044 Folsom Dr
La Jolla, CA 92037, USA

Benson, Anna (Model)
6025 Sandy Springs Cir #313
Atlanta, GA 30328, USA

Benson, Ashley (Actor)
1610 N Kings Rd
West Hollywood, CA 90069, USA

Benson, Brad (Athlete, Football Player)
840 Amwell Rd
Rd Hillsborough, NJ 08844, USA

Benson, Brendan (Musician)
1504 Woodmont Blvd
Nashville, TN 37215, USA

Benson, Cedric (Athlete, Football Player)
6307 W Courtyard Dr
Austin, TX 78731, USA

Benson, Charles (Athlete, Football Player)
1514 Hanover Ln
Van Alstyne, TX 75495, USA

Benson, Cliff (Athlete, Football Player)
PO Box 821957
Vancouver, WA 98682, USA

Benson, Darren (Athlete, Football Player)
P.O. Box 742614
Dallas, TX 75374, USA

Benson, Doug (Comedian)
c/o Staff Member *OmniPop Talent Group*
10700 Ventura Blvd.
2nd Floor
Studio Clty, CA 91604, USA

Benson, George (Actor, Musician)
6132 E Foothill Dr N.
Paradise Valley, AZ 85253, USA

Benson, George (Race Car Driver)
16700 State Highway
96 Unit 16
Klamath River, CA 96050, USA

Benson, Harry (Photographer)
181 E 73rd St
#18A
New York, NY 10021, USA

Benson, Herbert (Doctor)
Mind/Body Medical Institute
Beth Israel Hospital
Brookline, MA 02146, USA

Benson, Jodi (Voice Over Artist)
c/o Staff Member *Innovative Artists (LA)*
1505 10th St
Santa Monica, CA 90401, USA

Benson, Joyce (Athlete, Golfer)
5310 Papaya Cir
Harlingen, TX 78552, USA

Benson, Kent (Athlete, Basketball Player)
3921 W Maybury Mall
Apt 12
Bloomington, IN 47403-3738, USA

Benson, Kris (Athlete, Baseball Player, Olympic Athlete)
2140 Vicki Ln
Cumming, GA 30041-6556, USA

Benson, Robby (Actor)
c/o Staff Member *Creative Artists Agency (CAA-LA)*
2000 Ave Of The Stars
Los Angeles, CA 90067, USA

Benson, Steve (Cartoonist)
Arizona Republic
Editorial Dept
200 E Van Buren St
Phoenix, AZ 85004, USA

Benson, Sydney W (Misc)
1110 N Bundy Dr
Los Angeles, CA 90049, USA

Benson, Thomas (Athlete, Football Player)
P.O. Box 701341
Dallas, TX 75370, USA

Benson, Troy (Athlete, Football Player)
1038 Victoria Pl
Gibsonia, PA 15044, USA

Benson, Vern (Athlete, Baseball Player, Coach)
1040 De Lara Cir
Granite Quarry, NC 28146-8850, USA

Benson-Landes, Wendy (Actor)
1236 N.= Doheny Dr
West Hollywood, CA 90069, USA

Bent, Lyriq (Actor)
c/o Staff Member *Stone Manners Salners Agency (LA)*
9911 W Pico Blvd Ste 1400
Los Angeles, CA 90035, USA

Bentham, Lee (Race Car Driver)
Forsythe Racing Inc
1111 Willis Ave
Wheeling, IL 60090-5815, USA

Bentley, Albert (Athlete, Football Player)
13631 Eagle Ridge Dr Apt 234 Fort
Myers, FL 33912, USA

Bentley, Dierks (Musician)
4410 Granny White Pike
Nashville, TN 37204, USA

Bentley, Eric (Writer)
194 Riverside Dr
New York, NY 10025, USA

Bentley, Kevin (Athlete, Football Player)
3001 Murworth Dr Unit 904
Houston, TX 77025, us

Bentley, Lecharles (Athlete, Football Player)
1177 Windsor Ave
Broadview Heights, OH 44147, USA

Bentley, Ray (Athlete, Football Player, Sportscaster)
4050 Redbush Dr SW
Grandville, MI 49418, USA

Bentley, Robert (Governor)
Office of the Governor
11 S Union St
Montgomery, AL 36130, USA

Bentley, Scott (Athlete, Football Player)
7756 S Trenton Ct
Centennial, CO 80112, us

Bentley, Stacey (Misc)
PO Box 26
Santa Monica, CA 90406, USA

Bentley, Wes (Actor)
c/o Kevin Morris *Morris, Yorn, Barnes, Levine, Krintzman, Rubenstein and Kohner*
2000 Ave of the Stars
3rd Floor, North Tower
Los Angeles, CA 90067, USA

Benton, Andrew K (Educator)
Pepperdine University
President's Office
Malibu, CA 90263, USA

Benton, Barbi (Actor, Model)
840 N Starwood Dr
Aspen, CO 81611, USA

Benton, Brad (Adult Film Star)
c/o Staff Member *Diva Central Inc*
7510 W Sunset Blvd Ste 1445
Los Angees, CA 90046, USA

Benton, Butch (Athlete, Baseball Player)
12314 SE 60th Ave
Belleview, FL 34420-5200, USA

Benton, Fletcher (Artist)
250 Dore St
San Francisco, CA 94103, USA

Benton, Robert (Writer)
SRJ Inc
930 3rd Ave Fl 26
New York, NY 10022, USA

Bentrim, Jeff (Athlete, Football Player)
303 10A St NW Calgary
Canada, AB T2N, us

Bentsen, William (Athlete, Sailor)
N1946 Birches Dr
Lake Geneva, WI 53147-4119, USA

Bentz, Chad (Athlete, Baseball Player)
78 Skyline Dr
West Rutland, VT 05777-9808, USA

Benvenuti, Giovanni (Nino) (Boxer)
FPI Viaie Tiziano 70
Rome 00196, ITALY

Benvenuti, Leo (Director, Producer, Writer)
c/o John Elliott *Mosaic Media Group*
9200 W. Sunset Blvd
10th Floor
Los Angeles, CA 90069, USA

Ben-Victor, Paul (Actor)
c/o Michael Garnett *Leverage Management*
3030 Pennsylvania Ave
Santa Monica, CA 90404, USA

Benymon, Chico (Actor)
c/o Staff Member *Gersh (LA)*
9465 Wilshire Blvd
Suite 600
Beverly Hills, CA 90212, USA

Benz, Amy (Athlete, Golfer)
85133 Shinnecock Hills Dr
Fernandina Beach, FL 32034, USA

Benz, Julia (Actor)
Innovative Artists
1505 10th St
Santa Monica, CA 90401, USA

Benz, Julie (Actor)
9031 Ashcroft Ave
West Hollywood, CA 90048, USA

Benz, Larry (Athlete, Football Player)
1526 Brummel St
Evanston, IL 60202, USA

Benz, Nikki (Adult Film Star)
Nikki Benz, Inc.
15030 Ventura Blvd
Suite 19654
Sherman Oaks, CA 91403, USA

Benz, Sepp (Athlete)
Kiefernweg 37
Zurich 8057, SWITZERLAND

Benza, AJ (Actor)
5670 Wilshire Blvd
#400W
Los Angeles, CA 90036, USA

Benzali, Daniel (Actor)
c/o Staff Member *WME (LA)*
9601 Wilshire Blvd Fl 3
Beverly Hills, CA 90210, USA

Benzelock, Jim (Athlete, Hockey Player)
626 Greene Ave
Winnipeg, MB R2K OM6, Canada

Benzi, Roberto
12 Villa Sainte Foy
Neuilly-sur-Seine 92200, FRANCE

Benzinger, Todd (Athlete, Baseball Player)
1047 Shore Point Ct
Loveland, OH 45140-6970, USA

Beotti, Valentina (Actor)
Carol Levi Co
Via Giuseppe Pisanelli
Rome 00196, ITALY

Beracasa, Fabiola
Circa Inc
415 Madison Ave 19th Fl
New York, NY 10017, USA

Berard, Bryan (Athlete, Hockey Player, Olympic Athlete)
160 Bleecker Street
Apt 5BW
New York, NY 10012-0128, USA

Berardino, Dick
37 Emmeline Ave
Waltham, MA 02452-7935, USA

Berblinger, Jeff (Athlete, Baseball Player)
102 Swanee Dr
Goddard, KS 67052-9420, USA

Bercaw, John E (Misc)
California Institute of Technology
Chemistry Dept
Pasadena, CA 91125, USA

Berce, Gene (Athlete, Basketball Player)
1119 Hawthorne Pl
Apt G
Pewaukee, WI 53072-6576, USA

Bercich, Bob (Athlete, Football Player)
19017 Edward Pkwy
Mokena, IL 60448, USA

Bercich, Pete (Athlete, Football Player)
17448 Honeysuckle Ave
Lakeville, MN 55044, USA

Bercu, Michaela (Actor, Model)
c/o Staff Member *Elite Model Management (NY)*
404 Park Ave S Fl 9
New York, NY 10016, USA

Berdahl, Robert M (Educator)
University of California
Chancellor's Office
Berkeley, CA 94720, USA

Berdy, Sean (Actor)
18685-101 Main St
#331
Huntington Beach, CA 92648, USA

Berdych, Thomas (Athlete, Tennis Player)
c/o Staff Member *ATP Tour*
201 ATP Tour Blvd
Ponte Vedra Beach, FL 32082-3211, USA

Bere, Jason (Athlete, Baseball Player)
40 Berrington Pl
North Andover, MA 01845-2152, USA

Berehowsky, Drake (Athlete, Hockey Player)
20455 N 95th St
Scottsdale, AZ 85255-6629, USA

Berenblum, Isaac (Doctor)
Weizmann Institute of Science
Pathology Dept
Rehovot, ISRAEL

Berendt, John (Writer)
c/o Suzanne Gluck *WME (WMA-NY)*
1325 Ave of the Americas
New York, NY 10019, USA

Berendzen, Richard E (Educator)
1300 Crystal Dr
Arlington, VA 22202, USA

Berenger, Tom (Actor)
65/67/70 Camp Saint Mary Rd
Okatie, SC 29909, USA

Berenguer, Juan (Athlete, Baseball Player)
8616 Alisa Ct
Chanhassen, MN 55317-9373, USA

Berens, Ricky (Athlete, Swimmer)
1 Olympic Plaza
Colorado Springs, CO 80909-5770, USA

Berenson, Ken (Red) (Athlete, Coach, Hockey Player)
3555 Daleview Dr
Ann Arbor, MI 48105-9686, USA

Berenyi, bruce (Baseball Player)
10 Pine Grove Rd
Exeter, NH 03833-4718, USA

Berenyl, Bruce (Athlete, Baseball Player)
P.O. Box 133
Sherwood, OH 43556, USA

Berenzweig, Andrew (Athlete, Hockey Player)
4603 Brookside Rd
Ottawa Hills, OH 43615-2207, USA

Beresford, Bruce (Director)
c/o Steve Kenis *Steve Kenis & Company*
Royalty House
72-74 Dean St
London W1D 3SG, UK

Beresford, Meg (Activist)
Wiston Lodge
Wiston
Biggar ML12 6HT, SCOTLAND

Bereson, Karin (Stylist)
c/o Celebrity Stylists *Utopia*
12 West End Ave.
2nd Fl.
New York, NY 10023, USA

Berezan, Perry (Athlete, Hockey Player)
43 Mount Cascade Close SE
Calgary, AB T2Z 2K4, Canada

Berezhnaya, Yelena (Figure Skater)
Ice House Skating Rink
111 Midtown Bridge Approach
Hackensack, NJ 07601, USA

Berezin, Sergei (Athlete, Hockey Player)
1645 SW 4th Ave
Boca Raton, FL 33432-7232, USA

Berezovsky, Boris V (Musician)
IMG Artists
3 Burlington Lane
Chiswick
London W4 2TH, UNITED KINGDOM (UK)

Berezovy, Anatoli N (Cosmonaut)
Potchia Kosmonavtov
Moskovskoi Oblasti
Syvisdny Goroduk 141160, RUSSIA

Berfield, Justin (Actor, Director, Producer)
2337 Abbot Kinney Blvd
Venice, CA 90291, USA

Berg, Aki (Athlete, Hockey Player)
7400 Metro Blvd
Suite 280
Minneapolis, MN 55439, USA

Berg, Aki-Petteri (Athlete, Hockey Player)
1751 Pinnacle Dr
Suite 1500
McLean, VA 22102, USA

Berg, Bill (Athlete, Hockey Player)
c/o Staff Member *The NHL Network*
9 Channel Nine Ct
Toronto, ON M1S 4B5, Canada

Berg, Dave (Athlete, Baseball Player)
Jamestown Jammers PO Box 638 Attn
Jamestown, NV 14702-063&, USA

Berg, Dave (Baseball Player)
1917 Stonecastle Dr
Keller, TX 76262-4912, USA

Berg, Eric (Stylist)
c/o Staff Member *Rex Agency, The*
6311 Romaine St
Los Angeles, CA 90038, USA

Berg, justin (Baseball Player)
N3628 Heights Dr
Bryant, WI 54418-9563, USA

Berg, Kevin (Business Person)
c/o Staff Member *CBS Paramount Network Television*
CBS Studios
4024 Radford Ave
Studio City, CA 91604, USA

Berg, Laura (Athlete, Olympic Athlete, Softball Player)
USA Softball
2801 NE 50th St
Oklahoma, OK 73111-7203, USA

Berg, Matraca (Musician)
Joe's Garage
4405 Belmont Park Terr
Nashville, TN 37215, USA

Berg, Paul (Nobel Prize Laureate)
Stanford University
Medical School
Beckman Center
Stanford, CA 94305, USA

Berg, Peter (Actor)
c/o Staff Member *Film 44*
12233 W Olympic Blvd #352
Los Angeles, CA 90064, USA

Berg, Rick (Congressman, Politician)
323 Cannon HOB
Washington, DC 20515, USA

Berg, Steve (Actor)
c/o Ilan Breil *Mosaic Media Group*
9200 W. Sunset Blvd
10th Floor
Los Angeles, CA 90069, USA

Berg, Yehuda (Religious Leader)
Kabbalah Center International
1066 S La Cienega Blvd
Los Angeles, CA 90035, USA

Berganio, David Jr (Athlete, Golfer)
17811 Lahey St
Granada Hills, CA 91344-4030, USA

Berganza, Teresa (Opera Singer)
La Rossinlana Archanda 5
28200 San Lorenzo del Escorial
Madrid, SPAIN

Berge, Francine (Actor)
Cineart
36 Rue de Ponthiew
Paris 75008, FRANCE

Berge, Ole M (Misc)
Maintenance of Way Brotherhood
12050 Woodward Ave
Detroit, MI 48203, USA

Berge, Pierre V G (Business Person)
Yves Saint Laurent SA
5 Ave Marceau
Paris 75116, FRANCE

Bergen, Candice (Actor)
540 Picacho Ln
Montecito, CA 93108, USA

Bergen, Danny (Actor)
c/o Staff Member *Paul Lane Entertainment*
468 N Camden Dr.
Beverly Hills, CA 90210, USA

Bergen, Gary (Athlete, Basketball Player)
1386 Graham Cir
Erie, CO 80516-3617, USA

Bergen, Polly (Actor, Musician, Producer, Writer)
Jan McCormack
1746 S Britain Rd
Southbury, CT 06488, USA

Berger, Brandon (Athlete, Baseball Player)
2276 Dixie
Ft Mitchell, KY 41017-2949, USA

Berger, Gerhard (Race Car Driver)
Berger Motorsport
Postfach 1121
Vaduz 9490, AUSTRIA

Berger, Helmut (Actor)
Viale Parioli 50
Rome 00197, ITALY

Berger, Isaac (Athlete, Olympic Athlete, Weightlifter)
206 E 31st St
Apt 8A
New York, NY 10016-6357, USA

Berger, John (Writer)
Quincy
Mieussy
Taninges 74440, FRANCE

Berger, Lee (Actor)
57 Fellows Dr
Brentwood, NH 03833, USA

Berger, Mike (Athlete, Hockey Player)
9915 Tudor Ct
Fishers, IN 46037-9458, USA

Berger, Ronald (Athlete, Football Player)
6000 Lagorce Dr
Miami Beach, FL 33140, USA

Berger, Senta (Actor)
Sentana Films
Gebsattelstr 30
Munich 81541, GERMANY

Berger, Sy (Commentator)
36 Whitehall Rd
Rockville Centre, NY 11570-3244, USA

Berger, Thomas L (Writer)
PO Box 11
Palisades, NY 10964, USA

Berger-Brown, Barbara (Athlete, Baseball Player)
1321 S Finley Rd Apt 109
Lombard, IL 60148-4355, USA

Berger-Knebl, Joan (Athlete, Baseball Player)
8 Lochmeath Way
Dover, DE 19904-6447, USA

Bergeron, J C (Athlete, Hockey Player)
c/o Staff Member *Reebok / CCM*
3400 Raymond-Lasnier St
Montreal, QC H4R 3L3, Canada

Bergeron, Marc-Andre (Athlete, Hockey Player)
Paraphe Sports Management
190 Rue Fusey
2nd Paul Corbeil
Trois-Rivieres, QC G8T 2V8, Canada

Bergeron, Michel (Athlete, Coach, Hockey Player)
T Q S
612 Rue Saint-Jacques
Montreal, QC H3C 1C8, CANADA

Bergeron, Patrice (Athlete, Hockey Player)
c/o Staff Member *Boston Bruins*
TD Banknorth Garden
100 Legends Way, Suite 250
Boston, MA 02114, USA

Bergeron, Peter (Athlete, Baseball Player)
3495 Manatee Dr SE
Saint Petersburg, FL 33705-4144, USA

Bergeron, Tom (Actor, Producer)
24856 Paseo Del Rancho
Calabasas, CA 91302, USA

Bergeron, Yves (Athlete, Hockey Player)
1035 Clearwater Ave
Bathurst, NB E2A 4H5, Canada

Berger-Taylor, Norma (Athlete, Baseball Player)
529 N Blerman Ave
Villa Park, IL 60181-1437, USA

Bergeson, Eric (Athlete, Football Player)
2579 Sherwood Dr
Salt Lake City, UT 84108, USA

Bergeson, James (Athlete, Olympic Athlete, Water Polo Player)
7 Promontory
Trabuco Canyon, CA 92679-3811, USA

Bergeson, Pat (Musician)
3614 Central Ave
Nashville, TN 37205, USA

Bergevin, Marc (Athlete, Hockey Player)
404 Canterbury Ct
Hinsdale, IL 60521-2826, USA

Bergevin, Marc (Athlete, Hockey Player)
Chicago Blackhawks
1901 W Madison St
Attn Assistant G M
Chicago, IL 60612-2459, USA

Bergey, Bruce (Athlete, Football Player)
7700 SW River Rd
Hillsboro, OR 97123, USA

Bergey, John (Inventor)
1807 Mayflower Circle
Lancaster, PA 17603-6039, USA

Bergey, William E (Bill) (Athlete, Football Player)
2 Hickory Ln
Chadds Ford, PA 19317, USA

Berggren, Jenny (Musician)
Basic Music Mgmt
Norrtullsgatan 51
Stockholm 113 45, SWEDEN

Berggren, Jonas (Musician)
Basic Music Mgmt
Norrtullsgatan 51
Stockholm 11345, SWEDEN

Berggren, Malin (Musician)
Basic Music Mgmt
Norrtullsgatan 51
Stockholm 11345, SWEDEN

Berggren, Thommy (Actor)
Swedish Film Institute
PO Box 27126
Stockholm 102 52, SWEDEN

Bergh, Kate (Stylist)
Prefers to be contacted
via telephone

Bergh, Larry (Athlete, Basketball Player)
7020 Peoto Ln
Crossville, TN 38572-4501, USA

Berghman, Carl (Race Car Driver)
134 Bay State Rd
Rehobeth, 02769 MA, USA

Bergi, Emily (Actor)
Innovative Artists
1505 10th St
Santa Monica, CA 90401, USA

Bergin, Michael (Actor, Model)
15347 Sutton St
Sherman Oaks, CA 91403, USA

Bergin, Patrick (Actor)
Hyler Mgmt
25 Sea Colony Dr
Santa Monica, CA 90405, USA

Bergkamp, Dennis (Soccer Player)
Arsenal FC
Arsenal Stadium
Avenell Road
London N5 1BU, UNITED KINGDOM (UK)

Bergl, Emily (Actor)
c/o Craig Shapiro *ICM Partners (ICM-LA)*
10250 Constellation Blvd Fl 7
Los Angeles, CA 90067, USA

Bergland, Robert S (Bob) (Politician, Secretary)
1104 7th Ave SE
Roseau, MN 56751, USA

Bergland, Tim (Athlete, Hockey Player)
721 Labree Ave N
Thief River Falls, MN 56701-1632, USA

Berglind (Icey) (Television Host)
c/o Staff Member *E! Entertainment Television (LA)*
5750 Wilshire Blvd
Los Angeles, CA 90036, USA

Bergloff, Bob (Athlete, Hockey Player)
10200 Harriet Ave S
Minneapolis, MN 55420-5233, USA

Berglund, Art (Athlete, Hockey Player)
3749 Blue Merion Ct
Colorado Sjll'ings, CO 80906-4444, USA

Berglund, Bo (Athlete, Hockey Player)
c/o Staff Member *Buffalo Sabres*
1 Seymour H KNox III Plz
Suite 1
Buffalo, NY 14203, USA

Bergman, Alan (Musician)
714 N Maple Dr
Beverly Hills, CA 90210, USA

Bergman, Andrew C (Director, Writer)
c/o Robert (Bob) Bookman *Creative Artists Agency (CAA-LA)*
2000 Ave Of The Stars
Los Angeles, CA 90067, USA

Bergman, Arnfinn (Skier)
Nils Collett Vogtsv 58
Oslo 7 0765, NORWAY

Bergman, Bridget (Stylist)
Prefers to be contacted
via telephone or email

Bergman, Dave (Athlete, Baseball Player)
PO Box 380135
clintnn township, MI 48038-0060, USA

Bergman, Dusty (Athlete, Baseball Player)
1549 Koontz Ln
Carson City, NV 89701-6504, USA

Bergman, Jaime
c/o Holly Shelton *Precision Entertainment*
6338 Wilshire Blvd
Los Angeles, CA 90048, USA

Bergman, Jamie (Actor, Model)
c/o Staff Member *Special Artists Agency*
9465 Wilshire Blvd #820
Beverly Hills, CA 90212, USA

Bergman, Marilyn K (Musician)
714 N Maple Dr
Beverly Hills, CA 90210, USA

Bergman, Martin (Producer)
641 Lexington Ave
New York, NY 10022, USA

Bergman, Peter (Actor)
4799 White Oak Ave
Encino, CA 91316, USA

Bergman, Robert G (Misc)
501 Coventry Road
Kensington, CA 94707, USA

Bergman, Rushka (Stylist)
c/o Staff Member *Katy Barker Agency Inc*
6606 10th Ave Apt 3R
Brooklyn, NY 11219, USA

Bergman, Sean (Athlete, Baseball Player)
14421 Scott Rd
Bryan, OH 43506-9624, USA

Bergman, Thommie (Athlete, Hockey Player)
c/o Staff Member *Toronto Maple Leafs*
Air Canada Centre
400-40 Bay St
Toronto, ON M5J 2X2, Canada

Bergmann, Erma (Athlete, Baseball Player, Commentator)
6613 Morganford Rd
Saint Louis, MO 63116-2835, USA

Bergmann, Jay (Athlete, Baseball Player)
13 Abilene Ln
Manalapan, NJ 07726, USA

Bergmann, S
3620 Gatlin Dr
Rockledge, Fl 32955-6049, USA

Bergoglio, Jose Mario Cardinal (Religious Leader)
Arzobispado
Rivadavia 415
Buenos Aires 1002, ARGENTINA

Bergomi, Giuseppe (Athlete, Football Player)
via Trento 1
Settala (MI) I-20090, Italy

Bergonzi, Caroline (Stylist)
c/o Staff Member *Jean Jacques Visual Representation*
7118 Upper River Rd
Prospect, KY 40059, USA

Bergoust, Eric (Athlete, Olympic Athlete, Skier)
1430 Shadow Ln
Missoula, MT 59803-3405, USA

Bergquist, Curt (Doctor)
Allergon AB
Valinge 2090
Angelhoim 262 92, SWEDEN

Bergstein, Eleanor (Director, Producer, Writer)
c/o Staff Member *Creative Artists Agency (CAA-LA)*
2000 Ave Of The Stars
Los Angeles, CA 90067, USA

Bergsten, C Fred (Economist)
4106 Sleepy Hollow Road
Annandale, VA 22003, USA

Berhendt, Greg (Actor, Comedian)
c/o Staff Member *Avalon Management*
4A Exmoor St
London W10 6BD, UK

Beristain, Gabriel L (Cinematographer)
United Talent Agency
9560 Wilshire Blvd
#500
Beverly Hills, CA 90212, USA

Berkeley, Michael F (Composer)
Rogers Coleridge White
20 Powis Mews
London W11 1JN, UNITED KINGDOM (UK)

Berkeley, Xander (Actor, Producer)
2946 N Beachwood Dr
Los Angeles, CA 90068, USA

Berken, Jason
1303 Grasswoods Ct
De Pere, WI 54115-7613, USA

Berkhoel, Adam (Athlete, Hockey Player)
1744 Manning AveS
Saint Paul, MN 55129-9251, USA

Berkley, Elizabeth (Actor, Producer)
c/o Adam Griffin *Kritzer Levine Wilkins Entertainment (KLWG)*
11872 La Grange Ave
1st Floor
Los Angeles, CA 90025, USA

Berkley, Shelley (Congressman, Politician)
405.Cannon HOB
Washington, DC 20515, USA

Berkman, Lance (Athlete, Baseball Player)
5 Farnham Park Dr
Houston, TX 77024-7501, USA

Berkner, Laurie (Musician)
Po Box 250774
Columbia University Station
New York, NY 10025, USA

Berkoff, David (Swimmer)
Harvard University
Athletic Dept
Cambridge, MA 02138, USA

Berkowitz, Bob (Entertainer)
CNBC-TV
2200 Fletcher Ave
Fort Lee, NJ 07024, USA

Berkus, Nate (Designer, Television Host)
406 N Wood St
Chicago, IL 60622-6260, USA

Berlanti, Greg (Producer)
8713 Sunset Plaza Terr
West Hollywood, CA 90069, USA

Berlin, Clay (Publisher)
2935 Franciscan Way
Carmel, CA 93923, USA

Berlin, Eddie (Athlete, Football Player)
604 44th St
Des Moines, IA 50312, USA

Berlin, Mike (Bowler)
12 Coventry Lane
Muscatine, IA 52761-5659, USA

Berlin, Steve (Musician)
c/o Staff Member *Paradigm (Monterey)*
404 W Franklin St
Monterey, CA 93940, USA

Berliner, Alain (Director)
United Talent Agency
9560 Wilshire Blvd #500
Beverly Hills, CA 90212, USA

Berlinger, Warren (Actor)
10642 Arnet Pl
Chatsworth, CA 91311, USA

Berlinsky, Dmitri (Musician)
35 W 64th St #7F
New York, NY 10023, USA

Berlioux, Daniel (Actor)
Cineart
36 Rue de Ponthieu
Paris 75008, FRANCE

Berlusconi, Silvio (Politician, Prime Minister)
Palazzo Grazioli
Via Del Plebiscito 102
Rome I-00186, Italy

Berman, Andy (Actor)
c/o Staff Member *Gersh (LA)*
9465 Wilshire Blvd
Suite 600
Beverly Hills, CA 90212, USA

Berman, Benica (Stylist)
399 E 72nd St
#11-F
New York, NY 10021, USA

Berman, Boris (Musician)
Columbia Artists Mgmt Inc
165 W 57th St
New York, NY 10019, USA

Berman, Chris (Commentator)
31 Peach Tree Ct
Cheshire, CT 06410, USA

Berman, David (Musician)
2406 Canyon Dr
Los Angeles, CA 90068, USA

Berman, Jennifer (Doctor)
University of California
Women's Sexual Health Center
Los Angeles, CA 90024, USA

Berman, Josh (Producer)
c/o Staff Member *Creative Artists Agency (CAA-LA)*
2000 Ave Of The Stars
Los Angeles, CA 90067, USA

Berman, Julie (Actor)
c/o Nicole Nassar *Nicole Nassar PR*
1111 10th St
Suite 104
Santa Monica, CA 90403, USA

Berman, Laura (Doctor)
University of California
Women's Sexual Health Center
Los Angeles, CA 90024, USA

Berman, Lazar N (Musician)
12 Nicola Ln
Nesconset, NY 11767, USA

Berman, Shari Springer (Director)
c/o Staff Member *Creative Artists Agency (CAA-LA)*
2000 Ave Of The Stars
Los Angeles, CA 90067, USA

Berman, Shelley (Actor, Comedian)
268 Bell Canyon Rd
Bell Canyon, CA 91307, USA

Bermudez, Carolina (Musician)
c/o Staff Member *Buchwald/Fortitude (LA)*
6500 Wilshire Blvd
Suite 2200
Los Angeles, CA 90048, USA

Bermudez, Gustavo (Actor)
c/o Staff Member *Telefe - Argentina*
Pavon 2444 (C1248AAT)
Buenos Aires, ARGENTINA

Bermudez, Joe (DJ)
c/o Staff Member *Diva Central Inc*
7510 W Sunset Blvd Ste 1445
Los Angees, CA 90046, USA

Bern, Howard A (Biologist)
1010 Shattuck Ave
Berkeley, CA 94707, USA

Bernal, Gael Garcia (Actor)
c/o Staff Member *Canana Films*
Jose Maria Tornel #14
Colonia San Miguel Chapultepec
Mexico City 11850, MEXICO

Bernanke, Ben (Business Person, Economist)
12 Richmond Dr
Skillman, NJ 08558, USA

Bernard, Betsy (Business Person)
American Telephone & Telegraph Corp
32 Ave of Americas
New York, NY 10013, USA

Bernard, Carlos (Actor)
8901 Wonderland Ave
Los Angeles, CA 90046, USA

Bernard, Claire M A (Musician)
53 Rue Rabelais
Lyon 69003, FRANCE

Bernard, Crystal (Actor, Musician, Songwriter, Writer)
PO Box 202
Montrose, CA 91021, USA

Bernard, Dwight (Athlete, Baseball Player)
5120 N Norwich Ln
Belle Rive, IL 62810-2703, USA

Bernard, Ed (Actor)
PO Box 7965
Northridge, CA 91327, USA

Bernard, Henry (Architect)
44 Av D'llena
Paris 75116, FRANCE

Bernard, James (Race Car Driver)
PO Box 758
McHenry, MD 21541, USA

Bernard, Robyn (Actor)
The Bernard Bookstore
P.O. Box 202
Montrose, CA 91021-0202, USA

Bernardi, Barry (Producer)
c/o Staff Member *Gersh (LA)*
9465 Wilshire Blvd
Suite 600
Beverly Hills, CA 90212, USA

Bernardi, Frank (Athlete, Football Player)
P.O. Box 1015
Broomfield, CO 80038, USA

Bernazard, Tony (Athlete, Baseball Player)
D25 Calle Santa Ana Urb Santa Elvira
Caguas, PR 00725-3418, USA

Berner, Robert A (Misc)
15 Hickory Hill Road
North Haven, CT 06473, USA

Bernero, Adam (Athlete, Baseball Player)
11 Columbus Dr
Savannah, GA 31405-4101, USA

Bernero, Ed (Writer)
c/o Jeffrey Jacobs *Creative Artists Agency
(CAA-LA)*
2000 Ave Of The Stars
Los Angeles, CA 90067, USA

Berners-Lee, Timothy J (Scientist)
Massachusetts Institute of Technology
Computer Sci Lab
Cambridge, MA 01742-4804, USA

Bernet, Ed (Athlete, Football Player)
7967 Caruth Ct
Dallas, TX 75225, USA

Bernet, Lee (Athlete, Football Player)
4689 Stoddart Ln
Saint Paul, MN 55127, USA

Berney, Bob (President)
c/o Staff Member *Newmarket Films*
597 5th Ave Fl 7
New York, NY 10017, USA

Bernhard, Ruth (Photographer)
1826 Loyola Dr
Burlingame, CA 94010-5749, USA

Bernhard, Sandra (Actor, Comedian,
Musician)
11233 Blix St
N Hollywood, CA 91602, USA

Bernhardt, Carlos
Calle Duverge 196 San Pedro De Macoris
Dominican Reoublic, USA

Bernhardt, Daniel (Actor)
6500 Wilshire Blvd #2200
Los Angeles, CA 90048, USA

Bernhardt, Juan (Athlete, Baseball Player)
Eduardo Brito 13
San Pedro de Macoris, Dominican
Republic

Bernhardt, Kevin (Writer)
c/o Luke Rivett *Anonymous Content (LA)*
3531 Hayden Ave
Culver City, CA 90232, USA

Bernhardt, Roger (Athlete, Football
Player)
P.O. Box 4631
Lawrence, KS 66046, USA

Bernhardt, Tim (Athlete, Hockey Player)
RR 1
Schomberg, ON L0G 1T0, Canada

Bernheimer, Martin (Musician)
17350 Sunset Blvd
#702C
Pacific Palisades, CA 90272, USA

Bernice Johnson, Eddie (Congressman,
Politician)
2468 Rayburn HOB
Washington, DC 20515, USA

Bernich, Ken (Athlete, Football Player)
504 Woodland Park Cir
Mary Esther, FL 32569, USA

Bernier, Jean (Athlete, Hockey Player)
2350 Rue du Couvent-De-Lorette
St-Hyacinthe, QC J2T 4R3, Canada

Bernier, Serge (Athlete, Hockey Player)
534 Rue Elisabeth
Rimouski, QC G5L 3M9, Canada

Bernier, Sylvie (Race Car Driver)
Olympic Assn
Cite du Harve
Montreal QC H3C 3R4, CANADA

Berning, Susie (Athlete, Golfer)
80413 Portobello Dr
Indio, CA 92201, USA

Berns, Rick (Athlete, Football Player)
127 Merry Trl San
Antonio, TX 78232, USA

Bernsen, Corbin (Actor)
11955 Addison St
Valley Village, CA 91607, USA

Bernstein, Assaf (Director)
c/o Brad Kaplan *Evolution Entertainment
(LA)*
901 N Highland Ave
Los Angeles, CA 90038, USA

Bernstein, Besil (Misc)
90 Farquhar Road
Dulwich SE19 1LT, UNITED KINGDOM
(UK)

Bernstein, Bonnie (Television Host)
c/o Staff Member *CBS Television*
51 W 52nd St
New York, NY 10019, USA

Bernstein, Carl (Journalist, Writer)
9 Salt Meadow Ln
Sag Harbor, NY 11963, USA

Bernstein, Charles (Composer, Musician)
c/o John Tempereau *Soundtrack Music
Assoc*
1460 4th St
Suite 308
Santa Monica, CA 90401, USA

Bernstein, Fred (Stylist)
c/o Staff Member *Artists by Timothy
Priano (CA)*
8447 Wilshire Blvd
#301
Beverly Hills, CA 90211, USA

Bernstein, Josh (Television Host)
c/o Jim Ornstein *WME (WMA-NY)*
1325 Ave of the Americas
New York, NY 10019, USA

Bernstein, Kenny (Race Car Driver)
King Racing
26231 Dimension Dr
Lake Forest, CA 92630, USA

Bernstine, Rod (Athlete, Football Player)
6675 S Robertsdale Way
Aurora, CO 80016, USA

Bernthal, Jon (Actor)
3028 Stanford Ave
Marina del Ray, CA 90292, USA

Berov, Lyuben (Prime Minister)
Rights & Freedom Movement
Tzarigradsko Shosse 47/1
Sofia 1408, BULGARIA

Berra, Dale (Athlete, Baseball Player)
164 Eagle Rock Wav
Montclair, NJ 07042-1623, USA

Berra, Steve (Skateboarder)
3716 Clayton Ave
Los Angeles, CA 90027, USA

Berra, Tim (Athlete, Football Player)
23 Wilson Ter
West Caldwell, NJ 07006, USA

Berra, Yogi (Athlete, Baseball Player,
Coach)
The Yogi Berra Museum
8 Quarry Rd
Little Falls, NJ 07424-2161, USA

Berresford, Josh (Actor)
Auz & Associates PR
PO Box 601
Homewood, IL 60430

Berresford, Susan V (Misc)
Ford Foundation
320 E 43rd St
New York, NY 10017, USA

Berri, Claude (Director, Producer)
Renn Espace d'Art Contemporain
7 Rue de Lille
Paris 75007, FRANCE

Berrian, Bernard (Athlete, Football Player)
7209 Tokay Cir
Winton, CA 95388, USA

Berridge, Elizabeth (Actor)
Judy Schoen
606 N Larchmont Blvd
#309
Los Angeles, CA 90004, USA

Berridge, Michael J (Biologist)
13 Home Close
Histon
Cambridge CB4 4JL, UNITED KINGDOM
(UK)

Berrier, Max (Race Car Driver)
6262 N.N.C. Hwy 109
High Point, NC 27265, USA

Berrigan, Daniel (Politician)
220 W 98th St
#11L
New York, NY 10012-3110, USA

Berroa, Geronimo (Athlete, Baseball
Player)
3681 Broadwav Act 23
New York, NY 10031-1539, USA

Berruti, Livio (Activist)
Via Avigliana 45
Torino 10138, ITALY

Berry, Adam (Composer, Musician)
c/o Staff Member *Greenspan Artist
Management*
8760 W Sunset Blvd
West Hollywood, CA 90069, USA

Berry, Bert (Athlete, Football Player)
1402 E Coral Cove Dr
Gilbert, AZ 85234, USA

Berry, Bill (Musician)
1661 Old Farmington Rd
Watkinsville, GA 30677, USA

Berry, Bill (Baseball Player)
Negro Baseball Leagues
2231 Dickinson St
Philadelphia, PA 19146-4204, USA

Berry, Bob (Athlete, Football Player)
1351 Wilson Dr
Gardnerville, NV 89410, USA

Berry, Brad (Athlete, Hockey Player)
Columbus Blue Jackets
200 W Nationwide Blvd Unit 1
Attn Coaching Staff
Columbus, OH 43215-2564, USA

Berry, Brad (Athlete, Hockey Player)
PO Box 5182
Grand Forks, ND 58206-5182, USA

Berry, Chuck (Musician, Songwriter)
Berry Park
691 Buckner Rd
Wentzville, MO 63385, USA

Berry, David (Actor)
5903 Winton St
Dallas, TX 75206, USA

Berry, Ed (Athlete, Football Player)
4215 Skymont Dr
Belmont, CA 94002, USA

Berry, Eric (Athlete, Football Player)
c/o Chad Speck *Allegiant Athletic Agency*
35 Market Sq
Suite 201
Knoxville, TN 37902, USA

Berry, Fred (Athlete, Hockey Player)
1330 Jaclyn Dr
Brookfield, WI 53045-4452, USA

Berry, Glen (Actor)
c/o Staff Member *The Rights House (UK)*
Drury House
34-43 Russell St
London WC2B 5HA, UK

Berry, Halle (Actor, Model)
c/o Vincent Cirrincione *Vincent
Cirrincione Associates*
1516 N Fairfax Ave
Los Angeles, CA 90046, USA

Berry, Jadagrace (Actor)
c/o Monique Moss *Integrated PR*
8060 Melrose Ave
4th Floor
Los Angeles, CA 90046, USA

Berry, Jennifer (Beauty Pageant Winner)
c/o Staff Member *The Miss America
Organization*
Two Miss America Way #1000
Atlantic City, NJ 08401, USA

Berry, Jim (Artist, Cartoonist)
United Feature Syndicate
PO Box 5610
Cincinnati, OH 45201, USA

Berry, John (Musician)
2162 Elder Mill Rd
Watkinsville, CA 90677, USA

Berry, Joy (Writer)
c/o Staff Member *Trident Media Group
LLC*
41 Madison Ave
36th Floor
New York, NY 10010, USA

Berry, Ken (Athlete, Hockey Player)
14112 Marine Dr
White Rock, BC V4B 1A7, Canada

Berry, Ken (Athlete, Baseball Player)
1131 SW Camden Ln
Topeka, KS 66604-1980, USA

Berry, Ken (Actor)
13911 Fenton Ave
Sylmar, CA 91342, USA

Berry, Kevin (Swimmer)
28 George St
Manly, NSW 2295, AUSTRALIA

Berry, Latin (Athlete, Football Player)
925 Prater Rd
Sulphur, LA 70663, USA

Berry, Mark (Athlete, Baseball Player)
5201 Keene Dr
Plant Citv, Fl 33566-9798, USA

Berry, Michael J (Misc)
PO Box 1421
Pebble Beach, CA 93953, USA

Berry, Neil (Athlete, Baseball Player)
407 Inkster Ave
Kalamazoo, MI 49001-4220, USA

Berry, Ray (Athlete, Football Player)
12 Winged Foot Cir W
Abilene, TX 79606, USA

Berry, Raymond E (Athlete, Football Coach, Football Player)
1110 SE Broad St
Murfreesboro, TN 37130, USA

Berry, Reggie (Athlete, Football Player)
1803 E Ocean Blvd
Unit 402
Long Beach, CA 90802, USA

Berry, Robert V (Bob) (Athlete, Coach, Hockey Player)
640 3rd St
Hermosa Beach, CA 90254, USA

Berry, Royce (Athlete, Football Player)
PO Box 909
Comfort, TX 78013, USA

Berry, R Stephen (Misc)
5317 S University Ave
Chicago, IL 60615, USA

Berry, Sean (Athlete, Baseball Player)
307 Susannah Ln
Paso Robles, CA 93446-7114, USA

Berry, Vincent (Actor)
Academy Kids Mgmt
4942 Vineland Ave #103
North Hollywood, CA 91601, USA

Berry, Walter (Athlete, Basketball Player)
5206 Village Ct
Union City, GA 30291-5146, USA

Berry, Wendell E (Writer)
River Road
Port Royal, KY 40058, USA

Berryhill, Damon (Athlete, Baseball Player)
11 Springbrook Rd
Laguna Niguel, CA 92677-5719, USA

Berryman, Michael (Actor)
P.O. Box 697
Clearlake, CA 95422-0697, USA

Bersia, John (Journalist)
Orlando Sentinel
Editorial Dept
633 N Orange Ave
Orlando, FL 32801, USA

Bertelmann, Fred (Actor, Musician)
Am Hohenberg 9
Berg/Starnberger D-82335, Germany

Bertelsen, Jim (Athlete, Football Player)
2001 Days End Rd
Wimberley, TX 78676, USA

Bertelson, Richard (Civil Rights Activist, General)
7655 Century Pl
Chanhassen, MN 55317-4418, USA

Berteotti, Missy (Athlete, Golfer)
3065 Annandale Dr
Presto, PA 15142, USA

Berthiaume, Daniel (Athlete, Hockey Player)
P.O. Box 673
Hardy, VA 24101-0673, USA

Berthiaume-Wicken, Elizabeth (Baseball Player)
52 E 20th Ave
Vancouver, BC V5V 1L6, CANADA

Berthold, Helmut (Misc)
Meyerstr 21
Hamburg 21075, GERMANY

Berti, Joel (Actor)
c/o Melissa Hirschenson *Innovative Artists (LA)*
1505 10th St
Santa Monica, CA 90401, USA

Bertie, Diego (Musician)
c/o Gabriel Blanco *Gabriel Blanco Iglesias (Mexico)*
Rio Balsas 35-32
Colonia Cuauhtemoc
DF 06500, Mexico

Bertil (Prince)
Hert Av Halland
Kungl Slottet
Stockholm 1130, SWEDEN

Bertinelli, Valerie (Actor)
3496 Berry Dr
Studio City, CA 91064, USA

Bertini, Catherine (Misc)
United Nations
1 United Nations Plaza
New York, NY 10017, USA

Bertolucci, Bernardo (Actor)
Via Della Lungara 3
Rome 00165, ITALY

Bertolucci, Irene (Stylist)
2514 Prairie Ave
#2-B
Evanston, IL 60201, USA

Bertone, Cardinal Tarcisio (Religious Leader)
Palazzo Del S Uffizio LI
Rome 00193, ITALY

Bertotti, Mike (Athlete, Baseball Player)
14 Juoiter Rd
Highland Mls, NY 10930-2916, USA

Bertram, Laura (Actor)
c/o Staff Member *Lucas Talent Inc*
100 W. Pender St
Sun Tower, 7th Floor
Vancouver, BC V6B 1R8, Canada

Bertsch, Jackie (Athlete, Golfer)
8215 E Bronco Trl
Scottsdale, AZ 85255, USA

Bertuca, Tony (Athlete, Football Player)
2014 N Newcastle Ave
Chicago, IL 60707, USA

Bertuzzi, Todd (Athlete, Hockey Player)
900 Deer Ridge Ct
Kitchener, ON N2P 2L3, Canada

Berube, Craig (Athlete, Hockey Player)
Philadelphia Flyers
3601 S Broad St Ste 2
Attn Coaching Staff
Philadelphia, PA 19148-5297, USA

Berube, Craig (Athlete, Hockey Player)
1341 Durham Rd
New Hope, PA 18938-9479, USA

Berumen, Andres (Athlete, Baseball Player)
P.O. Box 1436
Banning, CA 92220-0010, USA

Berzon, Marsha S (Judge)
US Court of Appeals
Court Building
95 7th St
San Francisco, CA 94103, USA

Besana, Fred (Baseball Player)
Baltimore Orioles
222 Diamond Oaks Rd
Roseville, CA 95678-1007, USA

Beschorner-Baskovich, Mary (Baseball Player)
211 Sandy Ln
Piano, IL 60545-2054, USA

Besedin, Vladimir (Figure Skater)
c/o Staff Member *Champions on Ice*
Tom Collins Enterprises Inc
3500 W 80th St
Minneapolis, MN 55431, USA

Beshear, Steve (Governor)
700 Capitol Ave
Suite 100
Frankfort, KY 40601, USA

Beshore, Del (Athlete, Basketball Player)
1404 Cobblestone Ln
Pomona, CA 91767-3562, USA

Bess, Daniel (Actor)
c/o Raelle Koota *Anonymous Content (LA)*
3531 Hayden Ave
Culver City, CA 90232, USA

Bess, Rufus (Athlete, Football Player)
8685 Magnolia Trl
Apt 214
Eden Prairie, MN 55344, USA

Bessey, Joe
c/o Joe Bessey Motorsport
PO Box 525
Scarborough, ME 04070 - 0525, USA

Bessillieu, Donald A (Don) (Athlete, Football Player)
4787 Gardiner Dr
Columbus, GA 31907, USA

Bessmertnova, Natalia (Ballerina)
Sretenskii Blvd 6/1
#9
Moscow 101000, RUSSIA

Bessmertnykh, Aleksandr (Government Official)
Yelizarova Str 10
Moscow 103064, RUSSIA

Besson, Luc (Director, Producer, Writer)
1415 Devlin Dr
West Hollywood, CA 90069, USA

Best, Art (Athlete, Football Player)
420 Lockville Rd
Pickerington, OH 43147, USA

Best, Grady (Stylist)
309 E 108th St
#2-H
New York, NY 10029, USA

Best, Greg (Athlete, Football Player)
2859 Darlington Rd
Beaver Falls, PA 15010, USA

Best, Jahvid (Athlete, Football Player)
c/o Tony Fleming *Impact Sports - LA*
11331 Ventura Blvd Ste 1A
Studio City, CA 91604, USA

Best, John O (Soccer Player)
1065 Lomita Ave
Harbor City, CA 90710, USA

Best, Karl (Athlete, Baseball Player)
P.O. Box 1790
Snohomish, WA 98291-1790, USA

Best, Kevin (Artist)
27 Dartford Rd
Thornleigh 2120, Australia

Best, Pete (Musician)
8 Hymans Green
W Derby
Liverpool 12, UNITED KINGDOM (UK)

Best, Travis (Athlete, Basketball Player)
703 Bradley Rd
Springfield, MA 01109-1424, USA

Bestar, Maria (Musician)
c/o Staff Member *Sony Music Miami*
605 Lincoln Rd Fl 7
Miami Beach, FL 33139, USA

Bester, Allan (Athlete, Hockey Player)
12527 Crayford Ave
Orlando, FL 32837-8536, USA

Bestwick, Arnie (Race Car Driver)
10643 Court Rd.
Morrison, IL 61270, USA

Bestwicke, Martine (Actor)
Goldey Co
1156 S Carmelia Ave #B
Los Angeles, CA 90049, USA

Beswick, Jim (Athlete, Baseball Player)
6911 Buckhorn Dr
Columbus, GA 31904, USA

Beswicke, Martine (Actor)
Goldey Co
1156 S Carmelina Ave
#8
Los Angeles, CA 90049, USA

Betancourt, Jeff (Director)
c/o Staff Member *Broder Webb Chervin Silbermann Agency, The (BWCS)*
10250 Constellation Blvd
Los Angeles, CA 90067-6200, USA

Betancourt, Rafael
6857 Valhalla Way
Windermere, FL 34786-5627, USA

Betancourt, Yuniesky (Athlete, Baseball Player)
9500 SW 146th St
Miami, FL 33176-7871, USA

Betancurt, Natalia (Actor)
c/o Staff Member *TV Caracol*
Calle 76 #11 - 35
Piso 10AA
Bogota DC 26484, COLOMBIA

Bethea, Antoine (Athlete, Football Player)
3588 Windward Way
Carmel, IN 46032, us

Bethea, Bill (Athlete, Baseball Player)
166 Penny ln
Georgetown, TX 78633-2016, USA

Bethea, Ellen (Actor)
Independent Artists
505 8th Avenue Ste 2208
New York, NY 10018, USA

Bethea, Elvin L (Athlete, Football Player)
16211 Leslie Ln
Missouri City, TX 77489, USA

Bethel, Wilson (Actor)
c/o Ryan Daly *Zero Gravity Management*
1531 14th. St
Santa Monica, CA 90404, USA

Bethell, Tabrett (Actor)
c/o El Erdmane *RGM Artist Group*
64-76 Kippax St
Level 2, Suite 202 & 206
Surry Hills, NSW 2010, Australia

Beth Hart Band (Music Group, Musician)
c/o Staff Member *WME (LA)*
9601 Wilshire Blvd Fl 3
Beverly Hills, CA 90210, USA

Bethke, Jim (Athlete, Baseball Player)
4305 N Jarboe Ct
Kansas City, MO 64116-4655, USA

Bethune, Bobby (Athlete, Football Player)
P.O. Box 692
Leeds, AL 35094, USA

Bethune, George (Athlete, Football Player)
2817 Gas Light Ln W
Mobile, AL 36695, USA

Bethune, Patricia (Actor)
c/o Peter Himberger *Impact Artists Group LLC*
42 Hamilton Ter
New York, NY 10031, USA

Bets, Maxim (Athlete, Hockey Player)
5566 Candlelight Dr
La Jolla, CA 92037-7711, USA

Betsill, Roscoe (Stylist)
270 Park Ave. So. #11D
New York, NY 10010, USA

Bettany, Paul (Actor)
288 West St #8E/8W
New York, NY 10013, USA

Bettencourt, Liliane (Business Person)
L'Oreal
18 Rue Delabordere
Neuilly-sur-Seine F-92 200, France

Bettendorf, Jeff (Athlete, Baseball Player)
10349 SE Nicole Loop
Happy Valley, OR 97086-6881, USA

Bettenhausen, Gary (Race Car Driver)
2741 Chesterfield Dr.
Bellendori, IA 52722, USA

Betters, Doug L (Athlete, Football Player)
77 Better Way
Whitefish, MT 59937, USA

Betterson, Doug (Athlete, Football Player)
2442 46th St
Pennsauken, NJ 08110, USA

Betterson, James (Athlete, Football Player)
234 Allen Ln
Mullica, NJ 08062, USA

Bettiga, Mike (Athlete, Football Player)
1165 Vista Dr
Fortuna, CA 95540, USA

Bettis, Angela (Actor)
c/o Ryan Revel *Benderspink*
5870 W Jefferson Blvd
Studio E
Los Angeles, CA 90016, USA

Bettis, Jerome (Actor, Athlete)
c/o Lou Oppenheim *Headline Media Management*
888 7th Ave #503
New York, NY 10106, USA

Bettis, Jerome (Athlete, Football Player)
1651 Randall Mill Pl
NW Atlanta, GA 30327, USA

Bettis, Tom (Athlete, Football Coach, Football Player)
3523 N Peach Hollow Cir
Pearland, TX 77584, USA

Bettman, Gary (Athlete, Hockey Player)
23 Baldwin Rd
Saddle River, NJ 07458-3203, USA

Bettman, Gary B (Misc)
National Hockey League
1251 Ave of Americas
New York, NY 10020, USA

Bettridge, Ed (Athlete, Football Player)
200 Seaward Way
Avon Lake, OH 44012, USA

Betts, Austin W (General)
8003 N Hollow
Unit 204
San Antonio, TX 78240-2360, USA

Betts, Dickie (Musician)
FreeFalls
PO Box 604
Chagrin Falls, OH 44022, USA

Betts, Erik (Actor)
9068 Hayvenhurst Ave
North Hills, CA 91343, USA

Betts, Jack (Actor)
c/o Jon Simmons *Simmons & Scott Entertainment*
4110 W. Burbank Blvd.
Burbank, CA 91505, USA

Betts, Katherine (Editor)
Harper's Bazaar
Editorial Dept
1770 Broadway
New York, NY 10019, USA

Betts, Ladell (Athlete, Football Player)
42515 Regal Wood Dr
Ashburn, VA 20148, USA

Betts, Richard (Dickey) (Musician)
325 Palmetto Ave
Osprey, FL 34229, USA

Beuchel, Ted (Musician)
Variety Artists
1924 Spring St
Paso Robles, CA 93446, USA

Beueriein, Stephen T (Steve) (Athlete, Football Player)
15624 McCullers Ct
Charlotte, NC 28277, USA

Beuerlein, Steve (Athlete, Football Player)
6 Roshelle Ln Ladera
Ranch, CA 92694, USA

Beukeboom, Jeff (Athlete, Hockey Player)
Sudbury Wolves
240 Elgin St
Attn: Coaching Staff
Sudbury, ON P3E 3N6, Canada

Beukeboom, Jeff (Athlete, Hockey Player)
c/o Staff Member *Lindsay Muskies*
Lindsay Recreation Complex
Lindsay, ON K9V 4S3, Canada

Beutler, Bruce (Nobel Prize Laureate)
10358 Wateridge Cir Unit 318
San Diego, CA 92121-5717, USA

Beutler, Ernest (Doctor)
2707 Costebelle Dr
La Jolla, CA 92037, USA

Beutler, Tom (Athlete, Football Player)
7218 Longwater Dr
Maumee, OH 43537, USA

Bevacqua, Kurt (Athlete, Baseball Player)
7668 El Camino Real Ste 104-435
Carlsbad, CA 92009-7932, USA

Bevan, Tim (Actor, Producer)
c/o Staff Member *Working Title Films*
9720 Wilshire Blvd Fl4
Beverly Hills, CA 90212, USA

Bevan, Timothy H (Financier)
Barclay's Bank
54 Lombard St
London EC3P 3AH, UNITED KINGDOM (UK)

Beverley, Frankie (Musician)
115 Cherokee Rose Lane
Fairburn, GA 30213, USA

Beverley, Nick (Athlete, Coach, Hockey Player)
c/o Staff Member *Nashville Predators*
501 Broadway
Nashville, TN 37203, USA

Beverley Sisters (Actor, Music Group)
Adam Nolan
80 Highcroft Ave Bispham
Blackpool, Lancashire FY20BW, UNITED KINGDOM

Beverlin, Jason (Athlete, Baseball Player)
1128 Old Shire Way
Statesboro, GA 30461, USA

Beverly, David (Athlete, Football Player)
15 Wood Cove Dr
Spring, TX 77381, USA

Beverly, Don (Race Car Driver)
1801 Coxendale Rd.
Chester, VA 23831, USA

Beverly, Ed (Athlete, Football Player)
13051 Golansville Rd
Ruther Glen, VA 22546, USA

Beverly, Eric (Athlete, Football Player)
P.O. Box 492433
Lawrenceville, GA 30049, USA

Beverly, Randy (Athlete, Football Player)
P.O. Box 425
Westbury, NY 11590, USA

Bevil, Brian (Athlete, Baseball Player)
20103 Oakwood Ct
Humble, TX 77338-2500, USA

Bevill, Lisa (Musician)
Jeff Roberts
206 Bluebird Dr
Goodlettsville, TN 37072, USA

Bevington, Terry (Athlete, Baseball Player, Coach)
2600 Halle Pkw_y
Collierville, TN 38017-8888, USA

Bevis, Muriel (Baseball Player)
538 Idlewood Dr
Mount Juliet, TN 37122-2118, USA

Bey, Andy (Musician)
Megaforce Entertainment
PO Box 779
New Hope, PA 18938, USA

Bey, Richard (Entertainer)
445 Park Ave #1000
New York, NY 10022, USA

Bey, Turhan (Actor)
Paradisgasse Ave 47
Vienna, XIX 1190, AUSTRIA

Beyer, Andy (Sportscaster)
4237 Lenore Ln NW
Washington, DC 20008-3835, USA

Beyer, Brad (Actor)
c/o Jeff Hunter *WME (WMA-NY)*
1325 Ave of the Americas
New York, NY 10019, USA

Beyer, Troy (Actor)
14333 Greenleaf St
Sherman Oaks, CA 91423, USA

Beyer, William (Civil Rights Activist, General)
24 Elm St
Danville, PA 17821-8530, USA

Beymer, Richard (Actor)
1818 N Fuller Ave
Los Angeles, CA 90046, USA

Beynon, Tom (Athlete, Football Player)
441 Winchester Dr
Waterloo, ON N2T 1H6, Canada

Bezic, Sandra (Figure Skater, Sportscaster)
c/o Staff Member *NBC Sports (NY)*
30 Rockefeller Plaza
New York, NY 10112, USA

Bezos, Jeff (Business Person, Misc)
Amazon Inc
1200 12th Ave S
#1200
Seattle, WA 98144, USA

Bezucha, Tom (Director)
c/o Simon Halls *Slate Public Relations*
9000 Sunset Blvd #915
West Hollywood, CA 90069, USA

Bhagwati, Jagdish N (Economist)
Columbia University
Economics Dept
New York, NY 10027, USA

Bhagyashree (Actor, Bollywood)
96/B Hirak Society
SV Rd Vile Parle
Mumbai, MS 400056, INDIA

Bhakta, Raj (Business Person)
238 50th St
New York, NY 10022, USA

Bhan Bhagta Gurung (War Hero)
Victoria Cross Assn
Old Admiralty Building
London SW1A 2BL, UNITED KINGDOM (UK)

Bhandary Ram, Subadar (Civil Rights Activist, General)
Viii and Po Auhar
The Ghumarwin, Bombay 50, INDIA

Bhanu, Prakash (Bharathan) (Actor)
12/2 Circular Road United India Colony
Kodambakkam
Chennai, TN 600 024, INDIA

Bhanupriya (Actor, Bollywood)
4 1st Cross Street
Vijayaraghava Road
Chennai, TN 600017, INDIA

Bhardwaj, Mohini (Athlete, Gymnast, Olympic Athlete)
53 Juergens Ave
Cincinnati, OH 45220-1227, USA

Bhaskar, Sanjeev (Actor)
c/o Staff Member *BBC Artist Mail*
PO Box 1116
Belfast BT2 7AJ, United Kingdom

Bhatnagar, Deepti (Actor, Bollywood)
42 Ashok Apts
Gandhigram Road Juhu
Mumbai, MS 400049, INDIA

Bhatnagar, Dipti (Actor, Bollywood)
42 Ashoka Apts
Gandhigram Rd Juhu
Mumbai, MS 400049, INDIA

Bhatt, Brinda (Actor)
c/o Staff Member *Innovative Artists (LA)*
1505 10th St
Santa Monica, CA 90401, USA

Bhatt, Mahesh (Bollywood, Director, Filmmaker)
205 Silver Beach Apartments
Near Sun-N-Sand Hotel Juhu
Bombay, MS 400049, INDIA

Bhatt, Mukesh (Bollywood, Director, Filmmaker, Producer)
10 Shubh Jeevan Co-op Society
JVPD Scheme
Bombay, MS 400 049, INDIA

Bhattacharya, Basu (Actor, Bollywood, Director)
36 Carter Road Bandra
Mumbai, MS 400050, INDIA

Bhave, Ashwini (Actor, Bollywood)
A-9 Green View
Suburban Soc Shiv Shrushti
Mumbai, MS 400024, INDIA

Bhavsar, Raj (Athlete, Gymnast)
Pan American Plaza, Suite 300
201 South Capitol Avenue
Indianapolis, IN 46225

Bhumibol, Adulyadej (King)
Royal Residence
Chirtalad a Villa
Bangkok, THAILAND

Biafra, Jello (Musician)
c/o Staff Member *Simon & Schuster*
1230 Avenue of the Americas
New York, NY 10020, USA

Biagiotti, Laura (Designer, Fashion Designer)
Studio Biagiotti
Via Borgopesco 19
Milan 20121, ITALY

Biakabutuka, Tshimanga (Tim) (Athlete, Football Player)
110 Sonnys Way
Fort Mill, SC 29708, USA

Bialas, Dave (Baseball Player)
14080 N Bayshore Dr
Madeira Beach, FL 33708-2211, USA

Bialik, Mayim (Actor)
c/o Tiffany Kuzon *Evolution Entertainment (LA)*
901 N Highland Ave
Los Angeles, CA 90038, USA

Bialorucki, Larry (Athlete, Baseball Player)
5511 Armada Dr
Toledo, OH 43623-1709, USA

Bialosuknia, Wesley (Athlete, Basketball Player)
29 Bayberry Dr
Bristol, CT 06010-7604, USA

Bialowas, Dwight (Athlete, Hockey Player)
15616 Park Terrace Dr
Eden Prairie, MN 55346-2429, USA

Bialowas, Frank (Athlete, Hockey Player)
1640 New Brooklyn Rd
Williamstown, NJ 08094-3717, USA

Bianca, Viva (Actor)
c/o Matt Andrews *Marquee Management*
The Gatehouse
188 Oxford St Studio B
Paddington NSW 2021, Australia

Biancalana, Buddy (Athlete, Baseball Player)
1204 Lakeview Dr
Fairfield, IA 52556-9670, USA

Bianchi, Al (Athlete, Baseball Player, Basketball Coach, Basketball Player, Coach)
4350 N 40th St
Phoenix, AZ 85018-4105, USA

Bianchi, Rosa Maria (Actor)
c/o Staff Member *Televisa*
Blvd Adolfo Lopez Mateos 232
Colonia San Angel INN
DF CP 01060, MEXICO

Bianchin, Wayne (Athlete, Hockey Player)
2091 Wellington Rd E
Nanaimo, BC V9S 5V2, Canada

Bianchl, Alfred (Al) (Athlete, Basketball Player, Coach)
Miami Heat
American Airlines Arena
601 Biscayne Blvd
Miami, FL 33132, USA

Bianco, Tom (Athlete, Baseball Player)
12 Knolltop Dr
Nesconset, NY 11767, USA

Bianco, tommy
12 Knolltop Dr
Nesconset, NY 11767-2222, USA

Biasucci, Dean (Athlete, Football Player)
3484 Sandy Beach Dr
Canandaigua, NY 14424, USA

Bibb, John (Writer)
Nashville Tennessean
Editorial Dept
1100 Broadway
Nashville, TN 37203, USA

Bibb, Laslie (Actor)
9615 Brighton Way
#300
Beverly Hills, CA 90210, USA

Bibb, Leslie (Actor)
c/o John Carrabino *John Carrabino Management*
5900 Wilshire Blvd Fl 4 #406
Los Angeles, CA 90036, USA

Bibby, Henry (Athlete, Basketball Player)
Memphis Grizzlies
191 Beale St
Memphis, TN 38103-3715, USA

Bibby, Mike (Athlete, Basketball Player)
c/o David Falk *F.A.M.E*
Prefers to be contacted via telephone
Washington, DC, USA

Bible, Jon (Athlete, Baseball Player)
11254 Pinehurst Dr
Austin, TX 78747-1432, USA

Biccum, Del (Horse Racer)
RR 23 Box 27
Montague, NJ 07827, USA

Bice, Bo (Musician)
115 Gloryland Ln
Antioch, TN 37013, USA

Bichette, Dante (Athlete, Baseball Player)
1830 Gipson Green Ln
Winter Park, FL 32789, USA

Bichir, Demian (Actor)
c/o Sekka Scher *Sekka Scher Management*
Prefers to be contacted via telephone
New York, NY 10012, USA

Bickerstaff, Bernard T (Bernie) (Coach)
Charlotte Bobcats
129 W Trade St
#700
Charlotte, NC 28202, USA

Bickett, Duane (Athlete, Football Player)
508 Van Dyke Ave
Del Mar, CA 92014, USA

Bickford, Valerie (Actor)
c/o Staff Member *The Learning Channel (TLC)*
10100 Santa Monica Blvd
Suite 1500
Los Angeles, CA 90067, USA

Bickle, Dick (Race Car Driver)
9l6-A Bambi Dr.
Destin, FL 32541, USA

Bickle, Mike (Religious Leader)
International House of Prayer
3535 E. Red Bridge Rd
Kansas City, MO 64137, USA

Bickle, Jr., Rich (Race Car Driver)
Ballew Motorsports
802-A Performance Rd.
Mooresville, NC 28117, USA

Bicknell, Charlie (Athlete, Baseball Player)
304 E Summit St
Livingston, MT 59047-2126, USA

Bicks, Jenny (Producer)
9003 St Ives Dr
West Hollywood, CA 90069, USA

Bidart, Frank (Writer)
Wellesley College
English Dept
106 Central St
Wellesley, MA 02481, USA

Biddle, Dennis "Bose" (Athlete, Baseball Player)
9418 N Green Bay Rd Apt 241
Milwaukee, WI 53209-1070, USA

Biddle, Dennis (Bose) (Athlete, Baseball Player)
9418 N Green Bay Rd
Apt 241
Milwaukee, WI 53209, USA

Biddle, Martin (Archaeologist)
19 Hamilton Road
Oxford OX2 7OY, UNITED KINGDOM (UK)

Biddle, Melvin E (General, War Hero)
918 Essex Dr
Anderson, IN 45177-9423, USA

Biddle, Rocky (Athlete, Baseball Player)
2031 E Rancho Culebra Dr
Covina, CA 91724-3331, USA

Biden, Jill (Misc)
1600 Pennsylvania Avenue NW
Washington, DC 20500, USA

Biden, Joe (Ex-Senator, Politician, Vice President)
Office Of The Vice President
The White House
1600 Pennsylvania Avenue NW
Washington, DC 20500, USA

Biden, Joseph (Politician)
PO Box 3817
Wilmington, DE 19807-0817, USA

Bidner, Todd (Athlete, Hockey Player)
434 Oozloffsky
Petrolia, ON N0N 1R0, Canada

Bidwell, Charles E (Misc)
5835 S Kimbark Ave
Chicago, IL 60637, USA

Bidwell, Josh (Athlete, Football Player)
1380 West 40th Ave
Eugene, OR 97405, USA

Bieber, Justin (Musician)
c/o Scooter Braun *Island Def Jam Group*
Worldwide Plaza
825 8th Ave Fl 28
New York, NY 10019, USA

Bieber, Nita (Actor)
PO Box 1889
Avalon, CA 90704, USA

Bieber, Owen F (Misc)
United Auto Workers Union
8000 E Jefferson Ave
Detroit, MI 48214, USA

Biebl-Prelevic, Heidi (Skier)
Haus Olympia
Oberstaufen 87534, GERMANY

Biedenbach, Edward (Athlete, Basketball Player)
92 Kimberly Ave
Asheville, NC 28804-3607, USA

Biederman, Charles J (Artist)
5840 Collischan Road
Red Wing, MN 55066, USA

Biedermann, Jeanette (Actor)
Postfach 121004
Berlin 10599, Germany

Biedermann, Leo (Athlete, Football Player)
11640 Evergreen Creek Ln
Las Vegas, NV 89135, USA

Biegler, David W (Business Person)
Texas Utilities Co
Energy Plaza
1601 Bryan St
Dallas, TX 75201, USA

Biehn, Michael (Actor)
11220 Valley Spring Ln
N Hollywood, CA 91602, USA

Bieka, Silverstre Siale (Prime Minister)
Prime Minister's Office
Malabo, EQUATORIAL GUINEA

Biekert, Gregory (Athlete, Football Player)
2360 Fish Creek Pl
Danville, CA 94506, USA

Biel, Jessica (Actor)
338 S Anita Ave
Los Angeles, CA 90049, USA

Bielecki, J Krzysztof (Prime Minister)
Urzad Rady Ministrow
Al Ujazdowskie 9
Warsaw 00-918, POLAND

Bielecki, Mike (Athlete, Baseball Player)
1505 Habersham Pl
Crownsville, MD 21032-2230, USA

Bielke, Don (Athlete, Basketball Player)
3768 Corte Cancion
Thousand Oaks, CA 91360-7017, USA

Biellmann, Denise (Figure Skater)
Im Brachli 25
Zurich 8053, SWITZERLAND

Bielski, Dick (Athlete, Football Player)
27 Malibu Ct
Towson, MD 21204, USA

Bienen, Andy (Writer)
c/o Staff Member *United Talent Agency (UTA)*
9336 Civic Center Dr
Beverly Hills, CA 90210, USA

Bieniemy, Eric (Athlete, Football Player)
3314 Fox Trl Dr NW
Prior Lake, MN 55372, USA

Bierbrodt, Nick (Athlete, Baseball Player)
1200 White Hawk Ranch Dr
Boulder, CO 80303-1668, USA

Biercevicz, Greg (Baseball Player)
21 Mead Farm Rd
Seymour, CT 06483-2453, USA

Bierko, Craig (Actor, Musician)
c/o Jill Littman *Impression Entertainment*
9229 W Sunset Blvd #700
West Hollywood, CA 90069, USA

Biermann, Kroy (Athlete, Football Player)
c/o Staff Member *Atlanta Falcons*
4400 Falcon Pkwy
Flowery Branch, GA 30542, USA

Bies, Don (Athlete, Golfer)
1262 NW Blakely Ct
Seattle, WA 98177-4340, USA

Bieser, Steve (Athlete, Baseball Player)
11770 Royal Oak Ct
Sainte Genevieve, MO 63670-8690, USA

Bieshu, Mariya L (Opera Singer)
24 Pushkin Str
Chisinau 2012, MOLDOVA

Bies Susan, Schmidt (Government Official)
Federal Reserve Board
20th St & Constitution Ave
Washington, DC 20551, USA

Bietila, Walter (Skier)
General Delivery
Iron Mountain, MI 49801, USA

Biffen, John (Government Official)
Tanat House
Llanyblodwel Oswestry
Shropshire SY10 8NQ, UNITED KINGDOM (UK)

Biffi, Giacomo Cardinal (Religious Leader)
Archdiocese of Bologna
Via Altabella 6
Bologna 40126, ITALY

Biffle, Greg (Race Car Driver)
c/o Staff Member *Roush Fenway Racing Team*
4600 Roush Pl
Concord, NC 28027, USA

Biffle, Jerome (Athlete, Track Athlete)
3205 Monaco Parkway
Denver, CO 80207, USA

Big & Rich (Music Group)
c/o Keith Miller *WmE2 (WMA-TN)*
1600 Division St
Suite 300
Nashville, TN 37203, USA

Big Bad Voodoo Daddy (Music Group, Musician)
c/o Staff Member *Vanguard Records*
2700 Pennsylvania Ave
Santa Monica, CA 90404, USA

Bigbie, Larry (Athlete, Baseball Player)
140 Timber Point Ct
Valparaiso, IN 46385-9312, USA

Big Dismal (Music Group)
c/o Staff Member *Wind-up Records*
72 Madison Ave Fl 8
New York, NY 10016, USA

Bigelow, Kathryn (Director, Producer, Writer)
3201 Coldwater Canyon Ln
Beverly Hills, CA 90210, USA

Bigelow, Tom (Race Car Driver)
Rt. 1
Box 158A
Winchester, IN 47394, USA

Biggerstaff, Sean (Actor)
c/o Jeff Morrone *Jeff Morrone Entertainment*
9350 Wilshire Blvd
Suite 224
Beverly Hills, CA 90212, USA

Biggert, Judy (Congressman, Politician)
2113 Rayburn HOB
Washington, DC 20515, USA

Biggins, Al-Mela (Reality TV Star)
c/o Staff Member *Trading Spouses*
Rocket Science Laboratories
3151 Cahuenga Blvd W #300
Los Angeles, CA 90068, USA

Biggio, Craig (Athlete, Baseball Player)
6520 Belmont St
Houston, TX 77005-3804, USA

Bigglo, Craig A (Baseball Player)
6520 Belmont St
Houston, TX 77005, USA

Biggs, Don (Athlete, Hockey Player)
10050 Somerset Dr
Loveland, OH 45140-1863, USA

Biggs, Jason (Actor)
8515 Hollywood Blvd
West Hollywood, CA 90069, USA

Biggs, John H (Business Person)
240 E 47th St
#47D
New York, NY 10017, USA

Biggs, Peter M
Willows
London Road
Saint Ives, Huntingdon Cam PE17 4ES, UNITED KINGDOM (UK)

Biggs-Dawson, Roxann (Actor)
Innovative Artists
1505 10th St
Santa Monica, CA 90401, USA

Biggs-Dawson, Rozann
c/o Staff Member *Innovative Artists (LA)*
1505 10th St
Santa Monica, CA 90401, USA

Bigley, Thomas J (Admiral, General)
1329 Carpers Ferry Way
Vienna, VA 22182, USA

Bignell, Larry (Athlete, Hockey Player)
51279 Range Road 223
Sherwood Park, AB T8C 1H2, Canada

Bignotti, George (Race Car Driver)
9413 Steeplehill Dr
Las Vegas, NV 89117, USA

Big Preach (Musician)
c/o Staff Member *UGF Entertainment Inc*
3105 S MLK Jr Blvd #313
Lansing, MI 48910, USA

Big Tigger (Television Host)
c/o Staff Member *Britto Agency PR*
234 W 56th St
Penthouse
New York, NY 10019, USA

Big Time Rush (Music Group)
c/o Pearl Servat *PMK/BNC Public Relations (PMK-LA)*
8687 Melrose Ave Fl 8
West Hollywood, CA 90069, USA

Big Tymers (Music Group)
c/o Staff Member *ICM Partners (ICM-LA)*
10250 Constellation Blvd Fl 7
Los Angeles, CA 90067, USA

Biil Young, C.W (Congressman, Politician)
2407 Rayburn HOB
Washington, DC 20515, USA

Biittner, Larry (Athlete, Baseball Player)
915 3rd Ave NW
Pocahontas, IA 50574-1413, USA

Bikel, Theodore (Actor)
94 Honey Hill Rd
Wilton, CT 06897, USA

Bila, Lucie (Actor, Musician)
Theate Ta Fantastika
Karlova UI 8
Prague 1 110 00, CZECH REPUBLIC

Bilardello, Dann (Athlete, Baseball Player)
299 Bank St Attn
batavia, NV 14020-1615, USA

Bilderback, Nicole (Actor)
c/o Jeff Morrone *Jeff Morrone Entertainment*
9350 Wilshire Blvd
Suite 224
Beverly Hills, CA 90212, USA

Bildt, Carl (Prime Minister)
Svenges Riksdag
Stockholm 10012, SWEDEN

Bileck, Pamela (Athlete, Gymnast, Olympic Athlete)
2475 Redbud Ct
San Jose, CA 95128-4226, USA

Biletnikoff, Frederick (Fred) (Athlete, Football Player)
1736 Avondale Dr
Roseville, CA 95747, USA

Bilheimer, Robert S (Religious Leader)
15256 Knightwood Road
Cold Spring, MN 56320, USA

Bill, Dunstan (Athlete, Football Player)
PO Box 514
Rancho Mirage, CA 92270-0514, USA

Bill, Tony (Actor, Director, Producer)
Barnstorm Films
73 Market St
Venice, CA 90291, USA

Billard, Lani (Actor)
c/o Staff Member *Insight Production Company LTD*
489 King St W
Suite 401
Toronto, Ontario M5V 1K4, Canada

Billick, Brian (Athlete, Football Coach, Football Player)
12500 Ivy Mill Rd
Reisterstown, MD 21136, USA

Billie (Musician)
CIA
Concorde House
101 Sherpherds Bush Road
London W6 7LP, UNITED KINGDOM (UK)

Billingham, Jack (Athlete, Baseball Player)
625 Faulkner Street
New Smyrna Beach, FL 32168-6421, USA

Billings, Dick (Athlete, Baseball Player)
1917 Creek Wood Dr
Arlington, TX 76006-6611, USA

Billings, Earl (Actor)
c/o Staff Member *Stone Manners Salners Agency (LA)*
9911 W Pico Blvd Ste 1400
Los Angeles, CA 90035, USA

Billings, Marland P (Misc)
Westside Road
RFD
North Conway, NH 03860, USA

Billingslea, Beau (Actor)
6025 Sepulveda Blvd
#201
Van Nuys, CA 91411, USA

Billingslea, Shavonda (Reality TV Star)
c/o Michael Martin *MM Agency*
3937 Nobel Drive
San Diego, CA 92122, USA

Billingsley, Brent (Athlete, Baseball Player)
16112 Medlar Ln
Chino Hills, CA 91709-3625, USA

Billingsley, Chad (Athlete, Baseball Player)
1434 Monarch Dr
Lemoore, CA 93245-1786, USA

Billingsley, John (Athlete, Baseball Player)
3614 N 24th Pl
Milwaukee, WI 53206, USA

Billingsley, John (Actor)
8480 Hillside Ave
Los Angeles, CA 90069, USA

Billingsley, Peter (Director)
6225 Winans Dr
Los Angeles, CA 90068, USA

Billingsley, Ray (Cartoonist)
c/o Staff Member *King Features Syndication*
300 W 57th St
15th Floor
New York, NY 10019-5238, USA

Billingsley, Ron (Athlete, Football Player)
P.O. Box 2455
Gadsden, AL 35903, USA

Billingsley, Sam (Baseball Player)
Memphis Red Sox
1426 W State St
Milwaukee, WI 53233-1249, USA

Billington, Craig (Athlete, Hockey Player)
3254 Elk View Dr
Evergreen, CO 80439-7972, USA

Billington, Craig (Athlete, Hockey Player)
c/o Staff Member *Colorado Avalanche*
Pepsi Center
1000 Chopper Cir
Denver, CO 80204, USA

Billington, David P (Engineer)
45 Hodge Road
Princeton, NJ 08540, USA

Billington, James (Misc)
1520 Highwood Dr
Mclean, VA 22101-5800, USA

Billington, Kevin (Director)
33 Courtnell St
London W2 5BU, UNITED KINGDOM
(UK)

Billmeyer, mick (Baseball Player)
616 Palm Beach Dr
Hagerstown, MD 21740-5749, USA

Billups, Chauncey (Athlete, Basketball Player)
c/o Andy Miller *ASM Sports*
920 Undercliff Ave.
Edgewater, NJ 07020, USA

Billups, Terry (Athlete, Football Player)
1801 E 12th St
Apt 1721
Cleveland, OH 44114, USA

Bill Wyman's Rhythm Kings (Music Group, Musician)
c/o Staff Member *Concerted Efforts*
P.O. Box 440326
Somerville, MA 02144, USA

Billy Talent (Music Group)
Nettwerk Productions
1650 West 2nd Ave
Vancouver V6J 4R3, CANADA

Billy Vera and the Beaters (Music Group)
c/o Troy Blakely *Agency for the Performing Arts (APA-LA)*
405 S Beverly Dr
Suite 500
Beverly Hills, CA 90212-4425, USA

Bilodeau, Gilles (Athlete, Hockey Player)
D. 8-12-2008
USA

Bilodeau, Jean-Luc (Actor)
c/o Allan Grifka *Alchemy Entertainment*
7024 Melrose Ave
Suite 420
Los Angeles, CA 90038, USA

Bilodeau, Yvon (Athlete, Hockey Player)
GD
Clyde, AB TOG OPO, Canada

Bilson, Bruce (Director)
Downwind Enterprices
12505 Sarah St
Studio City, CA 91604, USA

Bilson, Malcolm (Musician)
132 N Sunset Dr
Ithaca, NY 14850, USA

Bilson, Rachel (Actor)
c/o Jason Weinberg *Untitled Entertainment (LA)*
350 S. Beverly Dr #200
Beverly Hills, CA 90212, USA

bin Abdul-Aziz, Sheikh Sulaiman Al-Rajhi (Business Person)
Al Rajhi Bank
P.O. Box 22330
Riyadh 11495, Saudi Arabia

Binder, John (Religious Leader)
North American Baptist Conference
1S210 Summit
Oakbrook Terrace, IL 60181, USA

Binder, Mike (Actor, Director, Writer)
c/o Jason Hodes *WME (WMA-NY)*
1325 Ave of the Americas
New York, NY 10019, USA

Binder, Steve (Director)
c/o Staff Member *Freeman, Heinecke and Sutton*
8961 Sunset Blvd
Los Angeles, CA 90069, USA

Binder, Theodor (Physicist)
Taos Canyon
Taos, NM 87571, USA

Bindler, Robb (Director, Writer)
c/o Susan Weaving *WME (WMA-NY)*
1325 Ave of the Americas
New York, NY 10019, USA

Bindu (Actor, Bollywood)
C1-2 Eden Hall Opp Lotus Cinema
Worli
Mumbai, MS 400018, INDIA

Bindugosh (Actor, Bollywood)
76A 1st Cross Street
Ventatesa Nagar
Chennai, TN 600093, INDIA

Bing, Dave (Athlete, Basketball Player)
29555 Woodhaven Ln
Southfield, MI 48076-5281, USA

Bing, Jonathan
c/o Daniel Strone *Trident Media Group LLC*
41 Madison Ave
36th Floor
New York, NY 10010, USA

Bingaman, Jeff (Politician)
5028 Overlook Rd NW
Washington, DC 20016-1912, USA

Bingaman, Jeff (Senator)
703 Hart Senate Office Bldg.
Washington, DC 20510, USA

Bingham, Craig (Athlete, Football Player)
179 Black Oak Dr
Pittsburgh, PA 15220, USA

Bingham, Gregory R (Greg) (Athlete, Football Player)
3710 W Valley Dr
Missouri City, TX 77459, USA

Bingham, Guy (Athlete, Football Player)
9214 Keegan Trl
Missoula, MT 59808, USA

Bingham, Ryan (Musician)
c/o Jenna Adler *Creative Artists Agency (CAA-LA)*
2000 Ave Of The Stars
Los Angeles, CA 90067, USA

Bingham, Traci (Actor, Model)
c/o Gloria Kisel *Trendy P.R.*
264 S LaCienega Blvd.
Suite 968
Beverly Hills, CA 90211, USA

Bingle, Lara (Model)
c/o Staff Member *TCN Nine Publicity*
TCN Nine Publicity
Willoughby, NSW 2068, Australia

Binkley, Gregg (Actor)
c/o Staff Member *Schachter Entertainment*
1157 S Beverly Dr Fl 2
Los Angeles, CA 90035, USA

Binkley, Leslie J (Les) (Athlete, Hockey Player)
RR 3
Main Station
Hanover, ON N4N 3B9, Canada

Binmore, Kenneth G (Economist)
Newsmills
Whitebrooks
Monmouth, Gwent NP5 4TY, UNITED KINGDOM (UK)

Binn, Dave (Athlete, Football Player)
2005 Loring St
San Diego, CA 92109, USA

Binnicker, James (Civil Rights Activist, General)
2037 Grayson Dr
Navarre, FL 32566-3026, USA

Binnie, William B (Astronaut)
3039 Erica Ave
Rosamond, CA 93560-6776, USA

Binnig, Gerd K (Nobel Prize Laureate)
IBM Research Laboratory
Saumerstr 4
Ruschlikon 8803, SWITZERLAND

Binns, Malcolm (Musician)
233 Court Road
Orpington, Kent BR6 9BY, UNITED KINGDOM (UK)

Binoche, Juliette (Actor)
c/o Jason Weinberg *Untitled Entertainment (LA)*
350 S. Beverly Dr #200
Beverly Hills, CA 90212, USA

Binotto, John (Athlete, Football Player)
277 E McMurray Rd
Canonsburg, PA 15317, USA

bin Talal, Al-Waleed (Royalty)
P.O. Box 1
Riyadh 11321, SAUDI ARABIA

Bintley, David (Choreographer)
Royal Ballet
Covent Garden
Bow St
London WC2E 9DD, UNITED KINGDOM (UK)

Binyon, Conrad (Actor)
17805 Margate
Encino, CA 91316, USA

Biodrowski, Denny (Athlete, Football Player)
2305 Grizzly Run Ln
Euless, TX 76039-6073, USA

Biondi, Frank J Jr (Business Person)
Seagram Co
1430 Peel St
Monstreal, QC H3A 1S9, CANADA

Biondi, Matt (Athlete, Oceanographer, Swimmer)
PO Box 731
Kamuela, HI 96743-0731, USA

Birch, L Charles (Misc)
5A/73 Yarranabbe Road
Darling Point, NSW 2027, AUSTRALIA

Birch, Stanley F Jr (Judge)
US Court of Appeals
56 Forsyth St NW
Atlanta, GA 30303, USA

Birch, Thora (Actor)
c/o Jack Birch *Keep the Peace Productions*
PO Box 691576
West Hollywood, CA 90069, USA

Birchard, Bruce (Religious Leader)
Friends General Conference
1216 Arch St
Philadelphia, PA 19107, USA

Birck, Michael J (Business Person)
Tellabs Inc
1415 W Diehl Road
Naperville, IL 60563, USA

Bird, Antonia (Director)
International Creative Mgmt
76 Oxford St
London W1N 0AX, UNITED KINGDOM (UK)

Bird, Brad (Director, Writer)
170 San Geronimo Valley Dr
Woodacre, CA 94973, USA

Bird, Cory (Athlete, Football Player)
4618 Harding Hwy
Mays Landing, NJ 08330, USA

Bird, Doug (Athlete, Baseball Player)
11821 Lady Anne Cir
Cape Coral, FL 33991-7548, USA

Bird, Forrest M (Inventor)
212 N Cerritos Dr
Palm Springs, CA 92262-6538, USA

Bird, Jerry Lee (Athlete, Basketball Player)
1114 Scenic View Hts
Corbin, KY 40701-2156, USA

Bird, Larry (Athlete, Basketball Player, Olympic Athlete)
308 Neapolitan Way
Naples, FL 34103, USA

Bird, Lester B (Prime Minister)
Prime Minister's Office
Factory Road
Saint John's, ANTIGUA

Bird, R Byron (Engineer)
University of Wisconsin
Chemical Engineering Dept
Madison, WI 53706, USA

Bird, Rodger (Athlete, Football Player)
215 S Elm St
Henderson, KY 42420, USA

Bird, Sue (Athlete, Basketball Player)
c/o Dan Levy *Wasserman Media Group*
10960 Wilshire Blvd
Suite 2200
Los Angeles, CA 90024, USA

Bird, Thora (Actor)
Old Loft 21 Leinster Mews
Lancaster Gate
London W2, UNITED KINGDOM (UK)

Birdman (Musician)
70 Palm Ave
Miami Beach, FL 33139, USA

Bird-Phillips, Nalda (Baseball Player)
2033 Honeydew Ln NW
Kennesaw, GA 30152-5852, USA

Birdsell, Lilli (Actor)
c/o John Crosby *Crosby/Spilo Management*
1310 N Spaulding Ave
Los Angeles, CA 90046, USA

Birdsong, Carl (Athlete, Football Player)
1807 Clubview Dr
Amarillo, TX 79124, USA

Birdsong, Cindy (Musician)
c/o Staff Member *Diva Central Inc*
7510 W Sunset Blvd Ste 1445
Los Angees, CA 90046, USA

Birdsong, Mary (Actor, Writer)
c/o Stacy Abrams *Abrams Entertainment*
5225 Wilshire Blvd #515
Suite 515
Los Angeles, CA 90036, USA

Birdsong, Otis (Athlete, Basketball Player)
P.O. Box 316
Little Rock, AR 72203-0316, USA

Bires, Kally (Race Car Driver)
Black Cat Racing
304 Performance Dr
Mooresville, NC 28115, USA

Bires, Kelly (Race Car Driver)
JTG Racing
304 Performance Dr.
Mooresville, NC 28115, USA

Birk, Matt (Athlete, Football Player)
620 Hidden Creek Trl
Saint Paul, MN 55118, USA

Birk, Roger E (Business Person)
Federal National Mortgage Assn
3900 Wilconsin Ave NW
Washington, DC 20016, USA

Birkavs, Valdis (Prime Minister)
Foreign Affairs Ministry
Brivbas Blvd 36
Riga 1395, LATVIA

Birkbeck, Mike (Athlete, Baseball Player)
1705 W Hill Dr
Orrville, OH 44667-1331, USA

Birkell, Lauren (Actor)
c/o Tiffany Kuzon *Evolution Entertainment (LA)*
901 N Highland Ave
Los Angeles, CA 90038, USA

Birkerts, Gunnar (Architect)
Gunnar Birkets Assoc
28105 Greenfield Road
Southfield, MI 48076, USA

Birkett, Zoe (Musician)
Palace Theatre
Shaftesbury Ave
London W1V 8AY, UK

Birkhead, Larry
P O Box 99800
Emeryville, California 94662, USA

Birkin, David (Actor)
c/o Scott Zimmerman *Evolution Entertainment (LA)*
901 N Highland Ave
Los Angeles, CA 90038, USA

Birkin, Jane (Actor)
Cineart
36 Rue de Ponthieu
Paris 75008, FRANCE

Birkins, Kurt (Athlete, Baseball Player)
24106 Vanowen St
West Hills, CA 91307-2932, USA

Birman, Len (Actor)
Michael Mann talent
617 S Olive St
#311
Los Angeles, CA 90014, USA

Birmingham, Stephen (Writer)
Brandt & Brandt
1501 Broadway
New York, NY 10036, USA

Birnes, William J. (Writer)
c/o Staff Member *Simon & Schuster*
1230 Avenue of the Americas
New York, NY 10020, USA

Birney, David (Actor)
20 Ocean Park Blvd
#118
Santa Monica, CA 90405, USA

Birney, Earle (Writer)
1204-130 Carlton St
Toronto, ON M5A 4K3, CANADA

Birney, Frank (Actor)
c/o Staff Member *Bauman Redanty & Shaul Agency*
5757 Wilshire Blvd
Suite 473
Beverly Hills, CA 90212, USA

Birns, Jack (Photographer)
2021 Castilian Dr
Los Angeles, CA 90068-2608, USA

Biron, Martin (Athlete, Hockey Player)
Sport Prospects Inc
93 Whippoorwill Rd
Armonk, NY 10504-1108, USA

Biron, Mathieu (Athlete, Hockey Player)
5723 NW 199th Dr
Coral Springs, FL 33076, USA

Birren, James E (Misc)
University of California
Borun Gerontology Center
Los Angeles, CA 90024, USA

Birrer, Babe (Athlete, Baseball Player)
9705 The Maples
Clarence, NY 14031-1594, USA

Birthistle, Eva (Actor)
c/o Staff Member *WME (LA)*
9601 Wilshire Blvd Fl 3
Beverly Hills, CA 90210, USA

Birtsas, Tim (Athlete, Baseball Player)
43 Robertson Ct
Clarkston, MI 48346-1547, USA

Birturk, Ricia (Stylist)
12 Queen Ave
South Minneapolis, MN 55405, USA

Birtwistle, Harrison (Composer)
Allied Artists
42 Montpelier Square
London SW7 1JZ, UNITED KINGDOM (UK)

Biscaha, Joe (Athlete, Football Player)
700 N Delaware Ave
Apt 3
Beach Haven, NJ 08008, USA

Bischoff, Eric (Athlete, Wrestler)
35011 N Sunset Trail
Cave Creek, AZ 85331, USA

Bisciotti, Steve (Business Person, Football Executive)
511 Point Field Dr
Millersville, MD 21108-2052, USA

Bisenius, Joe (Athlete, Baseball Player)
4212 Village Green Ct
Sioux City, IA 51106-3635, USA

Bishe, Kerry (Actor)
c/o Staff Member *Brookside Artists Management (NY)*
250 W 57th St
Suite 2303
New York, NY 10107, USA

Bishil, Summer (Actor)
c/o Brian Swardstrom *WME (LA)*
9601 Wilshire Blvd Fl 3
Beverly Hills, CA 90210, USA

Bishop, Ben (Athlete, Hockey Player)
11 Huntleigh Trails Lane
S1. Louis, MO 63131-4801, USA

Bishop, Elvin (Musician)
DeLeon Artists
4031 Panama Court
Piedmont, CA 94611, USA

Bishop, Greg (Athlete, Football Player)
P.O. Box 2263
Lodi, CA 95241, USA

Bishop, Harold (Athlete, Football Player)
4113 Woodland Hills Dr
Tuscaloosa, AL 35405, USA

Bishop, J Michael (Nobel Prize Laureate)
University of California
Hooper Foundation
San Francisco, CA 94143-0001, USA

Bishop, Keith (Athlete, Football Player)
P.O. Box 133111
Spring, TX 77393, USA

Bishop, Kelly (Actor)
c/o Robert Attermann *Abrams Artists Agency (LA)*
9200 Sunset Blvd
11th Floor
Los Angeles, CA 90069, USA

Bishop, Kevin (Actor)
c/o Staff Member *Gavin Barker Assoc*
2D Wimpole St
London W1G 0EB, UK

Bishop, Michael (Athlete, Football Player)
113 Philpot St
Willis, TX 77378, USA

Bishop, Rob (Congressman, Politician)
123 Cannon HOB
Washington, DC 20515, USA

Bishop, Sonny (Athlete, Football Player)
22843 Hale Rd
Land O Lakes, FL 34639, USA

Bisplinghoff, Raymond L (Engineer)
Tyco Laboratories
273 Corporate Dr
#100
Portsmouth, NH 03801, USA

Bissell, Charles O (Cartoonist, Editor)
1006 Tower Place
Nashville, TN 37204, USA

Bissell, Charles P (Phil) (Cartoonist)
Cartoon Corner
4 Cross Hill Circle
Forestdale, MA 01966-1262, USA

Bissell, Jean G (Judge)
US Court of Appeals
717 Madison Place NW
Washington, DC 20439, USA

Bissell, Mina J (Physicist)
Lawrence Berkeley Laboratory
1 Cyclotron Road
Berkeley, CA 94720, USA

Bisset, Jacqueline (Actor)
1815 Benedict Canyon
Beverly Hills, CA 90210, USA

Bissett, Josie (Actor)
1020 91st Ave NE
Bellevue, WA 98004, USA

Bissett, Tom (Athlete, Hockey Player)
3620 Arbor Chase Ct NE Apt 11
Grand Rapids, MI 49525-9453, United States

Bissinger, Buzz (Writer)
c/o *Houghton Mifflin Company Trade Division*
Adult Editorial 8th Fl
222 Berkeley St
Boston, MA 02116-3764, USA

Bisson, Yannick (Actor)
c/o Jamie Levitt *Lauren Levitt & Associates Inc*
1525 W 8th St 3rd Fl
Vancouver V6J 1T5, British Columbia

Bista, Kirti Nidhi (Prime Minister)
Gyaneshawor
Kathmandu, NEPAL

Bisutti, Kylie (Model)
c/o Anne Watkins *Lizzie Grubman Public Relations*
270 Lafayette St
Suite 504
New York, NY 10012, USA

Bitker, Joe (Athlete, Baseball Player)
39 Blackstone Ct
Chico, CA 95928-9428, USA

Bittan, Roy (Musician)
28929 Boniface Dr
Malibu, CA 90265, USA

Bitterlich, Don (Athlete, Football Player)
101 Medinah Dr
Blue Bell, PA 19422, USA

Bitterman, Shem (Writer)
6616 Colgate Ave
Los Angeles, CA 90048, USA

Bittiger, Jeff (Athlete, Baseball Player)
RR 5 Box 5348
Saylorsburg, PA 18353-9206, USA

Bittinger, Ned (Designer)
16 Camino De Vecinos
Santa Fe, NM 87507-7901, USA

Bittle, Ryan (Actor)
1345 Paseo Isabella
San Dimas, CA 91773, USA

Bittner, Armin (Skier)
Rauchbergstr 30
Izell 83334, GERMANY

Bittner, Jayne (Baseball Player)
15536 Northville Forest Dr Apt U250
Plymouth, MI 48170-4901, USA

Bittner, Jaynne (Athlete, Baseball Player, Commentator)
15535 Northville Forest Dr Apt 250
Plymouth, MI 48170-4947, USA

Bittner, Lauren (Actor)
c/o Jill McGrath *The Group Entertainment*
275 Seventh Ave
26th Floor
New York, NY 10001, USA

Bivens, Heidi (Stylist)
61 Carmine St
#2C
New York, NY 10014, USA

Bixler, Brian (Athlete, Baseball Player)
3525 Teakwood Ln
Plano, TX 75075-1783, USA

Biya, Paul (President)
Palais Presidentiel
Rue de L'Exploration
Yaounde, CAMEROON REPUBLIC

Bizkit, Limp (Music Group)
c/o Joanne Wiles *ICM Partners (ICM-LA)*
10250 Constellation Blvd Fl 7
Los Angeles, CA 90067, USA

Bizzy, Bone (Actor, Artist, Composer, Musician)
c/o Mary Bowlin *7th Sign Records*
145 Baker Street
Marion, OH 43302, USA

Bjarni V, Tryggvason (Astronaut)
Space Agency
Canadian Space Agency 6767 Rte de L'Aeroport Attn: Astronaut Office
Saint Hubert, QC J3Y 8Y9, CANADA

Bjedov-Gabrilo, Djurdjica (Swimmer)
Brace Santini 33
5800 Split
Serbia & Montenegro, SERBIA & MONTENEGRO

B. Jones, Walter (Congressman, Politician)
2333 Raybarn HOB
Washington, DC 20515, USA

Bjorge, Jamie (Actor)
10061 Riverside Dr
Box 113
Toluca Lake, CA 91602

Bjork (Musician)
39 Woods Rd
Palisades, NY 10964, USA

Bjorklund, Anders (Doctor)
University of Lund
Neurology Dept
Lund, SWEDEN

Bjorkman, George (Athlete, Baseball Player)
3525 Teakwood Ln
Plano, TX 75075, USA

Bjorkman, Jonas (Tennis Player)
Octagon
1751 Pinnacle Dr
#1500
McLean, VA 22102, USA

Bjorkman, Olle E (Biologist)
3040 Greer Road
Palo Alto, CA 94303, USA

Bjorkman, Reuben (Athlete, Hockey Player, Olympic Athlete)
504 Lake St NW
Warroad, MN 56763, USA

Bjorlin, Nadia (Actor)
13156 Hartsook St
Sherman Oaks, CA 91423, USA

Bjornson, Eric (Athlete, Football Player)
40 Orchard Rd
Orinda, CA 94563, USA

Bjugstad, Scott (Athlete, Hockey Player, Olympic Athlete)
2874 Lisbon Ave N
Lake Elmo, MN 55042-8554, USA

Blab, Uwe (Athlete, Basketball Player)
5993 Mount Gainor
Wimberley, TX 78676-4278, USA

Blachnik, Gabriele (Designer, Fashion Designer)
Blachnik Gabriele KG
Marstallstr 8
Munich 80539, GERMANY

Black, Alex (Actor)
c/o Staff Member *Innovative Artists (LA)*
1505 10th St
Santa Monica, CA 90401, USA

Black, Avion (Athlete, Football Player)
7140 Park Glen Dr
Fairview, TN 37062, USA

Black, Barbara A (Attorney, Attorney General, Educator, General)
Columbia University
Law School
435 W 116th St
New York, NY 10027, USA

Black, Bibi (Musician)
Columbia Artists Mgmt Inc
165 W 57th St
New York, NY 10019, USA

Black, BiBi (Musician)
c/o Staff Member *EMI Music Group (NY)*
150 Fifth Avenue
New York, NY 10011, USA

Black, Bill (Baseball Player)
Detroit Tigers
264 Braeshire Dr
Ballwin, MO 63021-5659, USA

Black, Brantley (Actor)
c/o Taylor Jacobs *Cinema Talent Agency*
468 N Camden Dr #200
Beverly Hills, CA 90210, USA

Black, Bud (Athlete, Baseball Player)
PO Box 2133
Rancho Santa Fe, CA 92067-2133, USA

Black, Bud (Athlete, Baseball Player)
San Diego Padres PO Box 122000
San Dielm, CA 92112-2000, USA

Black, Carole (Business Person)
c/o Staff Member *Lifetime Entertainment Services*
309 W 49th St
New York, NY 10019, USA

Black, Cathie (Business Person, Writer)
c/o Staff Member *Hearst Magazines*
959 8th Ave
Sutie 100
New York, NY 10019, USA

Black, Cilla (Actor, Musician)
c/o Nick Fiveash *The Works PR*
11 Marshalsea Rd
London SE1 1EN, UK

Black, Claudia (Actor)
907 S Ogden Dr
Los Angeles, CA 90036, USA

Black, Clint (Actor, Musician)
141 Chickering Meadows
Nashville, TN 37215, USA

Black, Conrad (Business Person, Publisher)
26 Park Lane Cir
Toronto, ON M3B 1Z7, CANADA

Black, David (Producer, Writer)
c/o Johnnie Planco *Parseghian Planco LLC*
322 8th Ave
Suite 601
New York, NY 10001, USA

Black, Debbie (Stylist)
c/o Staff Member *Directions USA*
3717-C W Market St
Greensboro, NC 27403, USA

Black, Diane (Congressman, Politician)
1531 Longworth HOB
Washington, DC 20515, USA

Black, Dustin Lance (Producer, Writer)
1618 N Fairfax Ave
Los Angeles, CA 90046, USA

Black, Holly (Writer)
Ten Pleasant Ct
Amherst, MA 07764, USA

Black, Jack (Actor, Comedian, Musician)
4900 Los Feliz Blvd
Los Angeles, CA 90027, USA

Black, James (Athlete, Hockey Player)
235 Callingwood Pl NW
Edmonton, AB T5T 2C6, Canada

Black, Jay (Musician)
c/o Staff Member *Charles Rapp Enterprises Inc*
88 Pine St
New York, NY 10005, USA

Black, Karen (Actor, Director, Producer, Writer)
c/o Brian McCabe *Venture IAB*
3211 Cahuenga Blvd W Ste 104
Los Angeles, CA 90068, USA

Black, Leon (Misc)
750 Park Ave Apt 11-A
New York, NY 10021-4252, USA

Black, Leonard (Athlete, Football Player)
2705 Preston Woods Ln
Apt 12
Fayetteville, NC 28304, USA

Black, Lewis (Actor, Comedian)
c/o Staff Member *Agency for the Performing Arts (APA-LA)*
405 S Beverly Dr
Suite 500
Beverly Hills, CA 90212-4425, USA

Black, Lisa Hartman (Actor)
141 Chickering Meadows
Nashville, TN 37215, USA

Black, Lucas (Actor)
c/o Staff Member *Agency for the Performing Arts (APA-LA)*
405 S Beverly Dr
Suite 500
Beverly Hills, CA 90212-4425, USA

Black, Marina (Actor)
c/o Matt Schwartz *Christopher Wright Management*
3207 Winnie Dr
Los Angeles, CA 90068, USA

Black, Mary (Musician)
International Music Network
278 S Main St
#400
Gloucester, MA 01930, USA

Black, Michael Ian (Actor, Architect)
United Talent Agency
9560 Wilshire Blvd
#500
Beverly Hills, CA 90212, USA

Black, Mike (Athlete, Football Player)
5690 Stonekirk Pl NW
Acworth, GA 30101, USA

Black, Mike D (Athlete, Football Player)
609 Grider Dr
Roseville, CA 95678, USA

Black, Milt (Athlete, Hockey Player)
41 Willow Glen Dr
Kanata, ON K2M 1K9, Canada

Black, Pippa (Actor)
c/o Kimberlin Dalehite *Magnolia Entertainment (LA)*
9595 Wilshire Blvd
Suite 601
Beverly Hills, CA 90212, USA

Black, Rebecca (Musician)
c/o Debra Baum *DB Entertainment Group*
8033 Sunset Blvd #1062
Los Angeles, CA 90046, USA

Black, Ronnie (Athlete, Golfer)
5118 N Ocean Ave
Tucson, AZ 85704-2545, USA

Black, Shane (Writer)
104 Fremont Pl
Los Angeles, CA 90005, USA

Black, Stan (Athlete, Football Player)
470 Johnstone St
Madison, MS 39110, USA

Black, Tim (Athlete, Football Player)
10520 Kilo Rd
Clarendon, TX 79226, USA

Black, Todd (Producer)
c/o Staff Member *ICM Partners (ICM-LA)*
10250 Constellation Blvd Fl 7
Los Angeles, CA 90067, USA

Black 47 (Music Group, Musician)
c/o Staff Member *Skyline Music*
28 Union St
Whitefield, NH 03598, USA

Blackabv, Ethan (Athlete, Baseball Player)
2308 E Orangewood Ave
Phoenix, AZ 85020-4730, USA

Blackaby, Ethan (Athlete, Baseball Player)
2308 E Orangewood Ave
Phoenix, AZ 85020, USA

Black Box Recorder (Music Group)
c/o Staff Member *Paradigm (Monterey)*
404 W Franklin St
Monterey, CA 93940, USA

Blackburn, Al (Astronaut)
1300 Woodside Dr
Me Lean, VA 22102-1529, USA

Blackburn, Bob (Athlete, Hockey Player)
141 Robert St
P.O. Box 1761
New Liskeard, ON P0J 1P0, Canada

Blackburn, Chase (Athlete, Football Player)
562 Wagonwheel Ln
Marysville, OH 43040, USA

Blackburn, Dan (Athlete, Hockey Player)
12 Carey Dr
Bedford, NY 10506, USA

Blackburn, Don (Athlete, Hockey Player)
637 S Owl Dr
Sarasota, FL 34236-1907, USA

Blackburn, Elizabeth (Nobel Prize Laureate)
Department Of Biochemistry And Biophysics
University Of California San Francisco
600 16th Street, GH-5312F, Box 2200
San Francisco, CA 94158-2517, USA

Blackburn, Greta (Actor)
Dade/Schultz
6442 Coldwater Canyon Ave
#206
Valley Green, CA 91606, USA

Blackburn, Marsha (Congressman, Politician)
217 Cannon HOB
Washington, DC 20515, USA

Blackburn, Tyler (Actor)
c/o Jason Carter *Society Entertainment*
10 Universal City Plaza
20th Floor
Universal City, CA 91608, USA

Blackburn, Woody (Athlete, Golfer)
P.O. Box 215
Orange Park, FL 32067-0215, USA

Black Crowes (Music Group)
c/o Staff Member *Paradigm (Monterey)*
404 W Franklin St
Monterey, CA 93940, USA

Black Eyed Peas, The (Music Group, Musician)
c/o David Sonenberg *DAS Communications*
83 Riverside Dr
New York, NY 10024, USA

Blackiston, Caroline (Actor)
Caroline Dawson
125 Gloucester Road
London SW7 4IE, UNITED KINGDOM (UK)

Black Keys, The (Music Group)
c/o John Peets *Q Prime South*
131 South 11th St
Nashville, TN 37206, USA

Blackledge, Todd A (Athlete, Football Player, Sportscaster)
2711 Glenmont Dr NW
Canton, OH 44708, USA

Blacklev, Travis (Athlete, Baseball Player)
8510 E 29th St N ARt 1517
Wichita, KS 67226-2254, USA

Blackman, Don (Athlete, Football Player)
48 Shire Dr S
East Amherst, NY 14051, USA

Blackman, Honor (Actor)
c/o Staff Member *Natasha Stevenson Mgmt*
Studio 7C Clapham North Arts Centre
Voltaire Rd
London SW4 6DH, UK

Blackman, Ken (Athlete, Football Player)
529 33rd Ave N
Clinton, IA 52732, USA

Blackman, Robert (Athlete, Football Player)
111 Glenwood Dr
Van Vleck, TX 77482, USA

Blackman, Robert R Jr (General)
Commanding General
III Expeditionary Force Okinawa
FPO, AP 96602, USA

Blackman, Rolando (Athlete, Basketball Player, Olympic Athlete)
8223 Santa Clara Dr
Dallas, TX 75218-4449, USA

Blackmar, Phil (Athlete, Golfer)
4420 Janssen Dr
Corpus Christi, TX 78411-2817, USA

Blackmon, Don (Athlete, Football Player)
4340 Lansfaire Ter
Suwanee, GA 30024, USA

Blackmon, Harold (Athlete, Football Player)
6937 S Crandon Ave Apt 4E
Chicago, IL 60649, USA

Blackmon, Robert (Athlete, Football Player)
70 Glenwood N Van
Vieck, TX 77482, USA

Blackmon, Roosevelt (Athlete, Football Player)
PO Box 1347 Belle
Glade, FL 33430, USA

Blackmon, Will (Athlete, Football Player)
37 Portalon Ct Ladera
Ranch, CA 92694, USA

Blackmon, Will (Athlete, Football Player)
c/o Eugene Parker *Maximum Sports Management*
6435 W Jefferson Blvd
#197
Fort Wayne, IN 46804, USA

Blackmore, Billie (Stylist)
220 E. 18th St.
New York, NY 10003, USA

Blackmore, Ritchie (Musician)
Blackmore Productions
P.O. Box 735
Nesconset, NY 11767, USA

Blackmore, Stephanie (Actor)
1265 Leona Dr
Beverly Hills, CA 90210, USA

Blacknall, Hubert (Athlete, Baseball Player)
46 Avenue A
Freehold, NJ 07728, USA

Black Sabbath (Music Group)
c/o Rob Light *Creative Artists Agency (CAA-LA)*
2000 Ave Of The Stars
Los Angeles, CA 90067, USA

Blackshear, Jeff (Athlete, Football Player)
9229 Christo Ct
Owings Mills, MD 21117, USA

Blackthorne, Paul (Actor)
2136 Mayview Dr
Los Angeles, CA 90027, USA

Black Veil Brides (Music Group)
c/o Ash Avildsen *The Pantheon Agency*
14930 Ventura Blvd.
Suite 340
Sherman Oaks, CA 91403, USA

Blackwelder, Myra (Athlete, Golfer)
2009 Hill Gail Way
Versailles, KY 40383-9132, USA

Blackwell, Alois (Athlete, Football Player)
2450 Louisiana St
Ste 400
Houston, TX 77006, USA

Blackwell, Chris (Business Person, Musician)
6 Hadley Gardens
C F Blackwell
London W4 4NX, UNITED KINGDOM

Blackwell, Harolyn (Opera Singer)
Columbia Artists Mgmt Inc
165 W 57th St
New York, NY 10019, USA

Blackwell, Nathaniel (Athlete, Basketball Player)
1926 S 22nd St
Philadelphia, PA 19145-2724, USA

Blackwell, Tim (Athlete, Baseball Player)
8854 Whiteport Ln
San Diego, CA 92119-2135, USA

Blackwell, Will (Athlete, Football Player)
6450 Dougherty Rd
Apt 336
Dublin, CA 94568, USA

Blackwell, Will (Athlete, Football Player)
6168 Seneca Cir
Discovery Bay, CA 94505-2632, USA

Blackwell, Willie (Athlete, Football Player)
152 Glenmore Ln
McDonough, GA 30253, USA

Blackwood, Glenn (Athlete, Football Player)
3480 Ambassador Dr
Wellington, FL 33414, USA

Blackwood, Lyle (Athlete, Football Player)
18020 Windtop Ln
Dallas, TX 75287, USA

Blackwood, Nina (Entertainer)
c/o Danny Sheridan *Marquee Management*
The Gatehouse
188 Oxford St Studio B
Paddington NSW 2021, Australia

Blackwood, Sarah (Musician)
Primary Talent Int'l
2-12 Petonville Road
London N1 9PL, UNITED KINGDOM (UK)

Blackwood, Vas (Actor)
c/o David Ginsberg *Insight*
1134 S Cloverdale Ave
Los Angeles, CA 90019, USA

Blacque, Taurean (Actor)
5049 Rock Springs Road
Lithonia, GA 30038, USA

Bladd, Stephen Jo (Musician)
Nick Ben-Meir
652 N Doheny Dr
Los Angeles, CA 90069, USA

Blade, Brian (Musician)
Ted Kurland
173 Brighton Ave
Boston, MA 02134, USA

Blade, Willie (Athlete, Football Player)
331 Cobblestone Rd
Auburn, GA 30011, USA

Blades, Bennie (Athlete, Football Player)
3409 NW 14th Ct Fort
Lauderdale, FL 33311, USA

Blades, Brian K (Athlete, Football Player)
1900 SW 70th Ter
Plantation, FL 33317, USA

Blades, Jack (Musician)
2000/2200 Warrington Rd
Santa Rosa, CA 95404, USA

Blades, Ruben (Actor, Composer)
Instituto Panameño De Turismo
Apartado 4421
Centro De Convenciones Atlapa
Vía Israel, San Francisco, Republic Of Panamá

Blados, Brian (Athlete, Football Player)
7087 Clawson Ridge Ct
Liberty Twp, OH 45011, USA

Bladt, Rick (Athlete, Baseball Player)
525 Maole St
Mount Angel, OR 97362-9616, USA

Blagojevich, Rod (Politician)
2934 W Sunnyside Ave
Chicago, IL 60625, USA

Blaha, John E (Astronaut)
18219 Indian Row
San Antonio, TX 78259, USA

Blaha, John E Colonel (Astronaut)
346 Whitestone Dr
Spring Branch, TX 78070-6046, USA

Blahak, Joseph (Athlete, Football Player)
4040 N 21st St
Lincoln, NE 68521, USA

Blahnik, Manolo (Designer, Fashion Designer)
49-51 Old Church St
London SW3 5BS, UNITED KINGDOM (UK)

Blahoski, Alana (Athlete, Hockey Player, Olympic Athlete)
60 E 9th St
Apt 315
New York, NY 10003-6400, USA

Blaine, David (Magician)
354 Broadway #1B
New York, NY 10013, USA

Blaine, Ed (Athlete, Football Player)
4 E Clarkson Rd
Columbia, MO 65203, USA

Blair, Anthony C L (Tony) (Politician, Prime Minister)
Office of Tony Blair
P.O. Box 60519
London W2 7JU, UK

Blair, Charles (Athlete, Hockey Player)
869 Niagara Pky
Fort Erie, ON L2A 5M4, Canada

Blair, Dennis (Athlete, Baseball Player)
1706 Aurora Dr
Richardson, TX 75081-2115, USA

Blair, George (Athlete, Football Player)
1233 Karen Dr
Laurel, MS 39440, USA

Blair, Isla (Actor)
Mayer & Eden
Grafton House
2/3 Golden House
London W1R 3AD, UNITED KINGDOM (UK)

Blair, Jayson (Actor)
c/o Todd Justice *Justice & Ponder*
P.O. Box 480033
Los Angeles, CA 90048, USA

Blair, Ken (Athlete, Football Player)
1837 NE 51st St
Oklahoma City, OK 73111, USA

Blair, Kimberly (Actor)
c/o John Elliott *Mosaic Media Group*
9200 W. Sunset Blvd
10th Floor
Los Angeles, CA 90069, USA

Blair, Linda (Actor)
The Linda Blair WorldHeart Foundation
10061 Riverside Dr
#1003
Toluca Lake, CA 91602, USA

Blair, Lionel (Dancer)
68 Old Brompton Road #200
London, England SW7 3LQ, United Kingdom

Blair, Matt (Athlete, Football Player)
16725 43rd Ave N
Minneapolis, MN 55446, USA

Blair, Maybelle (Athlete, Baseball Player, Commentator)
39220 Palm Greens Pkwy
Palm Desert, CA 92260-1362, USA

Blair, Natalie (Actor)
c/o Staff Member *RGM Artist Group*
64-76 Kippax St
Level 2, Suite 202 & 206
Surry Hills, NSW 2010, Australia

Blair, Paul (Athlete, Baseball Player)
4177 Lotus Cir
Ellicott City, MD 21043-4874, USA

Blair, Paul (Athlete, Football Player)
4325 the Ranch Rd
Edmond, OK 73034, USA

Blair, Selma (Actor)
c/o Cari Ross *Balance Public Relations*
375 Greenwich St
Suite 512
New York, NY 10013, USA

Blair, Stanley (Athlete, Football Player)
901 Deer Run N
Pine Bluff, AR 71603, USA

Blair, William (Director)
c/o Staff Member *New Star Entertainment*
PO Box 84172
San Diego, CA 92138, USA

Blair, William (Athlete, Baseball Player)
1411 E Red Bird Ln
Dallas, TX 75241-2111, USA

Blair, William Draper Jr (Attorney, Attorney General, Diplomat, General)
435 East 52nd Street
#6B
New York, NY 10022-6445, USA

Blair, Willie (Athlete, Baseball Player)
Fort Wayne Tincaps 1301
Fort wayne, IN 46802-3343, USA

Blair-Cruikshank, Bonnie (Athlete, Olympic Athlete, Speed Skater)
1223 Aspen Court
Delafield, WI 53018-1300, USA

Blais, Madeleine H (Journalist)
Miami Herald
Editorial Dept
1 Herald Plaza
Miami, FL 33132, USA

Blais, Richard (Chef, Reality TV Star)
c/o Staff Member *Creative Artists Agency (CAA-LA)*
2000 Ave Of The Stars
Los Angeles, CA 90067, USA

Blaisdell, Mike (Athlete, Hockey Player)
458 Nicholl Ave
Regina Beach, SK S0G 4C0, Canada

Blaise, Kerlin (Athlete, Football Player)
37026 Aspen Dr
Farmington Hills, MI 48335, USA

Blake, Andre (Actor)
c/o Staff Member *Kerin-Goldberg Associates*
155 E 55th St #5D
New York, NY 10022, USA

Blake, Asha (Correspondent)
NBC-TV
News Dept
30 Rockefeller Plaza
New York, NY 10112, USA

Blake, Casey (Athlete, Baseball Player)
8224 150th Ave
Indianola, IA 50125, USA

Blake, David (DJ Quik) (Musician)
c/o Linda Jones *The Mass Appeal*
3940 Laurel Canyon Blvd
Unit 447
Studio City, CA 91604, USA

Blake, Geoffrey (Writer)
416 Sherman Canal
Venice, CA 90291, USA

Blake, George R (Editor)
Cincinnati Enquirer
Editorial Dept
617 Vine St
Cincinnati, OH 45202, USA

Blake, Hamish (Radio Personality, Talk Show Host)
2DayFM Studios
Level 15
50 Goulburn St
Sydney, NSW 2000, Australia

Blake, James (Athlete, Tennis Player)
16223 Sierra de Avila
Tampa, FL 33613, USA

Blake, Jason (Athlete, Olympic Athlete)
11322 S Lake Eunice Rd
Detroit Lakes, MN 56501, USA

Blake, Jay Don (Athlete, Golfer)
2859 Calle Del Sol
Saint George, UT 84790-7968, USA

Blake, Jeff (Athlete, Football Player)
1 Novacare Way
Philadelphia, PA 19145, USA

Blake, Jim (Race Car Driver)
Wild Side Racing
107 Highway 198 E.
Tylertown, MS 29667, USA

Blake, John C (Artist)
Oz Voorburgwal 131
Amsterdam 1012 ER, NETHERLANDS

Blake, Josh (Actor)
c/o Staff Member *Pakula/King & Associates*
9229 Sunset Blvd
Suite 315
Los Angeles, CA 90069, USA

Blake, Julian W (Bud) (Cartoonist)
PO Box 146
Damariscotta, ME 04543, USA

Blake, Kayla (Actor)
c/o Todd Diener *Collective*
8383 Wilshire Blvd
Suite 1050
Beverly Hills, CA 90211, USA

Blake, Marcia (Writer)
c/o Staff Member *Creative Artists Agency (CAA-LA)*
2000 Ave Of The Stars
Los Angeles, CA 90067, USA

Blake, Norman (Musician)
Scott O'Malley Assoc
433 E Cucharras St
Colorado Springs, CO 80903, USA

Blake, Peter (Architect)
1377 Walnut Street
Newton Highlands, MA 02461-1851, USA

Blake, Peter T (Artist)
Waddington Galleries
11 Cork St
London W1X 1PD, UNITED KINGDOM (UK)

Blake, Quentin (Artist, Philanthropist)
The Roald Dahl Foundation
92 High Street
Great Missenden
Buckinghamshire HP16 0AN, United Kingdom

Blake, Ricky (Athlete, Football Player)
13 Harper Dr
Fayetteville, TN 37334, USA

Blake, Rob (Athlete, Hockey Player)
C A A Sports
2000 Avenue of the Stars Fl 3
Los Angeles, CA 90067-4704, USA

Blake, Rockwell (Opera Singer)
1 Onondaga Lane
Plattsburgh, NY 12901, USA

Blake, Stephanie (Actor)
First Artists
1631 N Bristol St
#820
Santa Ana, CA 92706, USA

Blake, Steve (Athlete, Basketball Player)
3479 Cascade Ter
West Linn, OR 97068-9271, USA

Blake, Susan (Correspondent)
News Center 4
1001 Van Ness Ave
San Francisco, CA 94109, USA

Blake, Tchad (Musician)
Monterey International
200 W Superior
#202
Chicago, IL 60610, USA

Blake, Teresa (Actor)
Stone Manners
6500 Wilshore Blvd
#550
Los Angeles, CA 90048, USA

Blake, Theo (Adult Film Star)
c/o Staff Member *Diva Central Inc*
7510 W Sunset Blvd Ste 1445
Los Angees, CA 90046, USA

Blake, Tom (Athlete, Football Player)
2017 Tullis Dr
Middletown, OH 45042, USA

Blake, Victoria (Actor)
23801 Calabasas Rd
Suite 2023
Calabasas, CA 91302-1558, USA

Blakeley, Ronee (Actor, Musician)
8033 Sunset Blvd
#693
West Hollywood, CA 90046, USA

Blakely, Rachel (Actor)
c/o Staff Member *Morrissey Management*
77 Glebe Point Road
Sydney NSW 2037, AUSTRALIA

Blakely, Sara (Business Person)
Spanx Inc.
3391 Peachtree Rd
Suite 105
Atlanta, GA 30326, USA

Blakely, Susan (Actor, Model)
c/o Kim Dorr *Defining Artists Agency*
10 Universal City Plaza
Suite 2000
Universal City, CA 91608, USA

Blakemore, Colin B (Doctor)
University Laboratory of Physiology
Parks Road
Oxford OX1 3PT, UNITED KINGDOM (UK)

Blakemore, Michael (Actor, Director, Writer)
18 Upper Park Rd
London NW3 2UP, UNITED KINGDOM (UK)

Blakemore, Sean (Actor)
c/o Steven Jang *SDB Partners Inc*
1801 Ave of the Stars
Suite 902
Los Angeles, CA 90067, USA

Blaker, Clay (Musician, Songwriter, Writer)
Texas Sounds Entertainment
2317 Pecan
Dickinson, TX 77539, USA

Blakey, G Robert (Lawyer)
1341 Wayne St N
South Bend, IN 46615-1047, USA

Blakey, Marion (Government Official)
Federal Aviation Agency
800 Independence Ave SW
Washington, DC 20591, USA

Blalack, Robert (Cinematographer)
12251 Huston St
North Hollywood, CA 91607, USA

Blalock, Hank (Athlete, Baseball Player)
1541 Black Walnut Dr
San Marcos, CA 92078-7985, USA

Blalock, Jane (Athlete, Golfer)
197 8th St
Suite 300
Charlestown, MA 02129, USA

Blalock, Jolene (Actor)
7651 Willow Glen Rd
Los Angeles, CA 90046, USA

Blamire, Larry (Actor, Director, Writer)
10878 Bloomfield St
Toluca Lake, CA 91602, USA

Blanc, Georges (Chef)
Le Mere Blanc
Vonnas, Ain 01540, FRANCE

Blanc, Jennifer (Actor)
c/o Melanie Sharp *Sharp Talent*
117 N Orlando Ave
Los Angeles, CA 90048, USA

Blanc, Michel (Actor)
c/o Dominique Besnehard *ArtMedia*
20 avenue Rapp
Paris 75008, France

Blanc, Raymond R A (Chef)
Le Manoir
Church Road
Great Milton, Oxford OX44 7PD, UNITED KINGDOM (UK)

Blancas, Homero (Athlete, Golfer)
6826 Queensclub Dr
Houston, TX 77069, USA

Blanchard, Cary (Athlete, Football Player)
7208 NW 131st St
Oklahoma City, OK 73142, USA

Blanchard, George S (General)
9160 Belvoir Woods Parkway
Fort Belvoir, VA 22060-2703, USA

Blanchard, James H (Financier)
Synovus Financial Corp
901 Front Ave
PO Box 120
Columbus, GA 31902, USA

Blanchard, James J (Diplomat, Ex-Governor)
Council Of American Ambassadors
888 17th St, NW
Suite 306
Washington, DC 20006-3312, USA

Blanchard, John A (Business Person)
Delux Corp
3680 Victoria St N
Shoreview, MN 55126, USA

Blanchard, Ken (Business Person, Writer)
The Ken Blanchard Companies
125 State Place
Escondido, CA 92029, USA

Blanchard, Nina (Misc)
3610 Wrightwood Dr
Studio City, CA 91604, USA

Blanchard, Rachel (Actor)
c/o Christian Donatelli *Schiff Company, The*
9465 Wilshire Blvd
Suite 480
Beverly Hills, CA 90212, USA

Blanchard, Tammy (Actor)
c/o Carol Bodie *ICM Partners (ICM-LA)*
10250 Constellation Blvd Fl 7
Los Angeles, CA 90067, USA

Blanchard, Terence (Composer, Musician)
BMI
8730 Sunset Blvd
#300W
Los Angeles, CA 90069, USA

Blanchard, Tim (Religious Leader)
Conservative Baptist Assn
1501 W Mineral Ave
#B
Littleton, CO 80120, USA

Blanchard, Tom (Athlete, Football Player)
217 Independence Dr
Grants Pass, OR 97527, USA

Blanchett, Cate (Actor)
4 N Parade
Hunters Hill, NSW 2110, AUSTRALIA

Blanco, Gil (Athlete, Baseball Player)
18403 N 16th Pl
Phoenix, AZ 85022-1355, USA

Blanco, Henry (Athlete, Baseball Player)
5510 N 132nd Dr
Litchfield Park, AZ 85340-8328, USA

Blanco, Kathleen (Politician)
702 Myrtle Pl
Lafayette, LA 70506-3457, USA

Blanco-Cervantes, Raul (President)
Apdo 918
San Jose, COSTA RICA

Bland, Anthony (Tony) (Athlete, Football Player)
20429 Walnut Grove Ln
Tampa, FL 33647, USA

Bland, Bobby Blue (Musician)
c/o Staff Member *Wenig-LaMonica Associates*
580 White Plains Rd
Suite 130
Tarrytown, NY 10591, USA

Bland, Carl (Athlete, Football Player)
1985 Crossbridge Ct
Saint Charles, MO 63303, USA

Bland, John (Athlete, Golfer)
P.O. Box 451436
Westlake, OH 44145-0638, USA

Bland, Nate (Athlete, Baseball Player)
1504 Oxmoor Rd
Birmingham, AL 35209-3908, USA

Bland, Tom (Athlete, Football Player)
66 S Winter Park Dr
Casselberry, FL 32707-4409, USA

Blandford, Roger D (Astronomer)
California Institute of Technology
Astrophysics Dept
Pasadena, CA 91125, USA

Blandi, Oscar (Business Person)
Oscar Blandi Salon
746 Madison Avenue
New York, NY 10065, USA

Blandon, Roberto (Actor)
c/o Staff Member *TV Azteca*
Periferico Sur 4121
Colonia Fuentes del Pedregal
DF CP 14141, Mexico

Blaney, Dave (Race Car Driver)
Bill Davis Racing
211 N. Emily Ct.
High Point, NC 27265-7667, USA

Blaney, George (Athlete, Basketball Player)
1633 Main St
Glastonbury, CT 06033-3133, USA

Blank, Arthur (Business Person, Football Executive)
1080 W Paces Ferry Rd NW
Atlanta, GA 30327-2600, USA

Blank, Barbie (Actor, Wrestler)
1157 Ovington Rd S
Jacksonville, FL 32216, USA

Blank, Matt (Athlete, Baseball Player)
5226 Overridge Dr
Arlington, TX 76017-1211, USA

Blankenship, Greg (Athlete, Football Player)
2067 La Con Ct
Apt 1
Campbell, CA 95008, USA

Blankenship, Kevin (Athlete, Baseball Player)
5014 Regency Dr
Rocklin, CA 95677-4420, USA

Blankenship, Lance (Athlete, Baseball Player)
340 Kimberwicke Ct
Alamo, CA 94507-2703, USA

Blankers-Koen, Fanny (Athlete, Track Athlete)
Olympic Committe
Surinamestraat 33
La Harve 2585, NETHERLANDS

Blankley, Anthony (Tony) (Correspondent)
Edelman
International Square
1875 Eye St, NW Suite 900
Washington, DC 20006, USA

Blanks, Billy (Actor, Athlete)
c/o Staff Member *WmE2 (WMA-LA)*
1 William Morris Pl
Beverly Hills, CA 90212, USA

Blanks, Jamie (Composer, Director, Editor)
c/o Simon Millar *Rumble Media*
1620 Broadway
Santa Monica, CA 90403, USA

Blanks, Larvell (Athlete, Baseball Player)
PO Box 562
Del Rio, TX 78841-0562, USA

Blanks, Sid (Athlete, Football Player)
4402 Warm Springs Rd
Houston, TX 77035, USA

Blanton, Dain (Athlete, Olympic Athlete, Volleyball Player)
1615 Stoner Ave
Apt 3
Los Angeles, CA 90025-7340, USA

Blanton, Jerry (Athlete, Football Player)
1942 Calumet Ave
Toledo, OH 43607, USA

Blanton, Joe (Athlete, Baseball Player)
636 Farragut Ave
Haddonfield, NJ 08033-3834, USA

Blaqk Audio (Music Group)
c/o Staff Member *Silva Artist Management (SAM)*
722 Seward St
Los Angeles, CA 90038, USA

Blarikfield, Mark (Actor)
Artists Group
10 100 Santa Monica Blvd
#2490
Los Angeles, CA 90067, USA

B. Larson, John (Congressman, Politician)
1501 Longworth HOB
Washington, DC 20515, USA

Blasberg, Erica (Athlete, Golfer)
2280 Treemont Pl
Apt 206
Corona, CA 92879, USA

Blasco, Chuck (Musician)
Media Promotion Enterprises
423 6th Ave
Hurlington, WV 25701, USA

Blasdel, Wendy (Stylist)
c/o Staff Member *Edible Style*
1358 Ruberta Ave
Glendale, CA 91201, USA

Blaser, Cory (Athlete, Baseball Player)
10528 Ross Pl
Broomfield, CO 80021-3549, USA

Blashford-Snell, John N (Misc)
Exploration Society
Motcome
Shaftesbury
Dorset SP7 9PB, UNITED KINGDOM (UK)

Blasi, Rosa (Actor)
c/o Evan Hainey *Untitled Entertainment (LA)*
350 S. Beverly Dr #200
Beverly Hills, CA 90212, USA

Blasingame, Wade (Athlete, Baseball Player)
5207 Riverhill Rd NE
Marietta, GA 30068, USA

Blass, (Steve) (Athlete, Baseball Player)
PO Box 7000
Pittsburgh, PA 15212-0038, USA

Blasucci, Dick (Producer)
c/o Staff Member *Kaplan Stahler Agency*
8383 Wilshire Blvd
Suite 923
Beverly Hills, CA 90211, USA

Blatche, Andray (Athlete, Basketball Player)
914 Jennings Mill Dr
Bowie, MD 20721-6223, USA

Blateric, Steve (Athlete, Baseball Player)
2855 S Monaco Pkwy
Apt 2-304
Denver, CO 80222-7191, USA

Blatny, Zdenek (Athlete, Hockey Player)
c/o Staff Member *International Sports Advisors*
878 Ridge View Way
Franklin Lakes, NJ 07417, USA

Blatt, Melanie (Musician)
c/o Staff Member *Concorde Intl Artists Ltd*
101 Shepherds Bush Rd
London W6 7LP, UNITED KINGDOM (UK)

Blatter, Joseph (Sepp) (Football Executive)
Federation Int'l Football Assn
PO Box 85
Zurich 8030, SWITZERLAND

Blatty, William Peter (Writer)
7018 Longwood Dr
Bethesda, MD 20817, USA

Blatz, Kelly (Actor)
c/o Lena Roklin *Luber Roklin Management*
8530 Wilshire Blvd
6th Floor
Beverly Hills, CA 90211, USA

Blau, Daniel (Artist)
Belgradstr 26
Munich 80796, GERMANY

Blauser, Jeff (Athlete, Baseball Player)
6080 Carlisle Ln
All:>_haretta, GA 30022-6279, USA

Blavatnik, Leonard (Business Person)
128 Porchuck Rd
Greenwich, CT 06831, USA

Blaylock, Anthony (Athlete, Football Player)
604 Glen Iris Dr NE
Atlanta, GA 30308, USA

Blaylock, Bob (Athlete, Baseball Player)
472933 E 1122 Rd
Muldrow, OK 74948, USA

Blaylock, Caroline (Athlete, Golfer)
232 Hennon Dr NW
Rome, GA 30165, USA

Blaylock, Daren "Mookie" (Athlete, Basketball Player)
7601 Belmount Rd
Rowlett, TX 75089-7479, USA

Blaylock, Daron (Athlete, Basketball Player)
1017 Gresham Rd
Zebulon, GA 30295, USA

Blaylock, Derrick (Athlete, Football Player)
1471 Edgewater Rd
Crown Point, IN 46307, USA

Blaylock, Gary (Athlete, Baseball Player)
PO Box 241
Maiden, MO 63863-0241, USA

Blazejowski, Carol (Athlete, Basketball Player, Olympic Athlete)
126 Walnut St
Nutley, NJ 07110-2851, USA

Blazelowski, Carol A (Athlete, Basketball Player)
New York Liberty
Madison Square Garden
2 Penn Plaza
New York, NY 10121, USA

Blazer, Phil (Athlete, Football Player)
16 Tranquil Ave
Greenville, SC 29615, USA

Blazier, Ron (Athlete, Baseball Player)
610 N 9th St
Bellwood, PA 16617-1524, USA

Blazitz, Micael (Athlete, Football Player)
27100 Bunert Rd
Warren, MI 48088, USA

Bleak, David B (War Hero)
355 Louise Dr
Arco, ID 83213, USA

Bleaney, Brebis (Physicist)
Garford House
Garford Road
Oxford OX1 3PU, UNITED KINGDOM (UK)

Bledel, Alexis (Actor, Model)
c/o Paul Brown *New Wave Entertainment (LA)*
2660 W Olive Blvd
Burbank, CA 91505, USA

Bledsoe, Curtis (Athlete, Football Player)
1012 Red Oak Pl
Chula Vista, CA 91910, USA

Bledsoe, Drew (Athlete, Football Player)
845 Delrey Rd
Whitefish, MT 59937, USA

Bledsoe, Tempestt (Actor)
c/o Staff Member *GVA Talent Agency Inc*
8981 Sunset Blvd.
Suite 101
Los Angeles, CA 90069, USA

Bleek (Cox), Memphis (Malik) (Artist, Musician)
Green Light Talent Agency
PO Box 3172
Beverly Hills, CA 90212, USA

Bleeth, Yasmine (Actor)
308 N Sycamore Ave #202
Los Angeles, CA 90036, USA

Blegen, Judith (Opera Singer)
91 Central Park West
#1B
New York, NY 10023, USA

Bleick, Tom (Athlete, Football Player)
P.O. Box 187
Talladega, AL 35161, USA

Bleier, Robert P (Rocky) (Athlete, Football Player)
929 Osage Rd
Pittsburg, PA 15243, USA

Bleiler, Gretchen (Athlete, Olympic Athlete, Speed Skater)
USOC Headquarters
PO Box 5774
Snowmass Village, CO 81615-5774, USA

Blerk, Zac (Athlete, Hockey Player)
Team Shutout Goalie School
7044 Baskerville Run
Attn Manager of Player Development
Mississauga, ON L5W 1A2, Canada

Blesse, Frederick (Civil Rights Activist, General)
370 Oak Haven Dr
Melbourne, FL 32940-1818, USA

Blessed, Brian (Actor)
Associated International Mgmt
5 Denmark St
London WC2H 8LP, UNITED KINGDOM (UK)

Blessen, Karen A (Journalist)
Karen Blessen Illustration
6327 Vickery Blvd
Dallas, TX 75214, USA

Blessing, Jack (Actor)
c/o Marianne Golan *Marianne Golan Management*
6528 W. 6th St
Los Angeles, CA 90048-4716, USA

Blessitt, Ike (Athlete, Baseball Player)
19712 Anglin St
Detroit, MI 48234-1469, USA

Blethen, Frank A (Publisher)
Seattle Times Publisher's Office
1120 John St
Seatle, WA 98109, USA

Blethyn, Brenda A (Actor)
61-63 Portobello Road
London W1N OAX, UNITED KINGDOM (UK)

Bleu, Corbin (Actor)
309 N Naomi St
Burbank, CA 91505, USA

Blevins, Michael (Actor)
13 W 100th St #2C
New York, NY 10025, USA

Blewett III, John (Race Car Driver)
John Blewett Motorsports
246 Herbertsville Rd
Howell, NJ 07731, USA

Bley, Carla B (Composer, Musician)
Watt Works
PO Box 67
Willow, NY 12495, USA

Bley, Paul (Composer, Musician)
Legacy Records
550 Madison Ave
#1700
New York, NY 10022, USA

Blick, Richard (Dick) (Athlete, Swimmer)
1602 N Nye Ave
Fremont, NE 68025-3328, USA

Blier, Bertrand (Director)
11 Rue Margueritte
Paris 75017, FRANCE

Blige, Mary J (Musician)
119 E Saddle River Rd
Saddle River, NJ 07458, USA

Bligen, Dennis (Athlete, Football Player)
P.O. Box 101
West Hempstead, NY 11552, USA

Blim, Richard D (Doctor)
304 W 172nd St
Belton, MO 64012, USA

Blind Boys of Alabama, The (Music Group, Musician)
c/o Eric (Ricky) McKinnie
192 Warren St. SE
Atlanta, GA 30317, USA

Blinder, Alan S (Financier, Government Official)
Princeton University
Economics Dept
Princeton, NJ 08544, USA

Blink 182 (Music Group)
c/o Karen Wiessen *Universal Music Group*
1755 Broadway
New York, NY 10019, USA

Blinka, Stan (Athlete, Football Player)
3304 Carriage Cir
Export, PA 15632, USA

Blinks, Susan (Athlete, Horse Racer, Olympic Athlete)
362 Vista Del Rey Dr
Encinitas, CA 92024-3651, USA

Bliss, Boti Anne (Actor)
Chase/Goldberg Management
3400 San Marino #A
Los Angeles, CA 90006

Bliss, Caroline (Actor)
c/o Staff Member *The Rights House (UK)*
Drury House
34-43 Russell St
London WC2B 5HA, UK

Bliss, Mike (Race Car Driver)
195 Jones Rd.
Spartanberg, SC 29307, USA

Blitt, Ricky (Writer)
c/o Nick Reed *ICM Partners (ICM-LA)*
10250 Constellation Blvd Fl 7
Los Angeles, CA 90067, USA

Blittner, Larry (Baseball Player)
Washington Senators
915 3rd Ave NW
Pocahontas, IA 50574-1413, USA

Blitz, Andy (Writer)
c/o Staff Member *3 Arts Entertainment Inc*
9460 Wilshire Blvd
7th Floor
Beverly Hills, CA 90210, USA

Blitzer, Wolf (Correspondent, Television Host)
8929 Holly Leaf Ln
Bethesda, MD 20817, USA

Blobel, Gunter K J (Nobel Prize Laureate)
Rockefeller University
Cell Biology Dept
1230 York Ave
New York, NY 10065, USA

Bloch, Erich (Engineer, Scientist)
National Science Foundation
1800 C St NW
Washington, DC 20550, USA

Bloch, Henry W (Business Person)
H & R Block Inc
4410 Main St
Kansas City, MO 64111, USA

Bloch, Phillip (Stylist, Television Host)
c/o Chantal Cloutier *Cloutier Agency*
2632 La Cienega Ave
Los Angeles, CA 90034, USA

Blochwitz, Hans-Peter (Opera Singer)
18 Allison Ave
Staten Island, NY 10306, USA

Block, Francesca Lia (Writer)
c/o Angela Cheng Caplan *Cheng Caplan Co*
1680 N Vine St #808
Hollywood, CA 90028, USA

Block, Hunt (Actor)
Box 462
Green's Farms, CT 06436-0462, USA

Block, John (Athlete, Basketball Player)
Point Loma Nazarene College
1069 Santa Barbara St
San Diego, CA 92107-4160, USA

Block, John R (Politician, Secretary)
National Wholesale Grocers Assn
201 Park Washington
Falls Church, VA 22046, USA

Block, Ken (Athlete, Hockey Player)
4901 Windrift Way
Carmel, IN 46033-9510, USA

Block, Lawrence (Writer)
299 W 12th St #12D
New York, NY 10014, USA

Block, Ned J (Misc)
29 Washington Square
New York, NY 10011, USA

Block, Ron (Musician)
2065 Carters Creek
Pike Franklin, TN 37064, USA

Blocker, Dirk (Actor)
5063 La Ramada Dr
Santa Barbara, CA 93111, USA

Blocker, Terry (Athlete, Baseball Player)
745 Guide Post Ln
Stone Mountain, GA 30088-1943, USA

Blocker, Terry (Athlete, Baseball Player)
745 Guide Post Ln
Stone Mountain, GA 30088, USA

Bloedorn, Greg (Athlete, Football Player)
816 N Catherine Ave
La Grange Park, IL 60526, USA

Bloemberg, Jeff (Athlete, Hockey Player)
170 Diagonal Rd
Wingham, ON N0G 1W0, Canada

Bloembergen, Nicolaas (Nobel Prize Laureate)
13835 E Langtry Ln
Tucson, AZ 85747-9637, USA

Bloemstedt, Herbert T
Kunstleragentur Raab & Bohm
Plankengasse 7
Vienna 1010, AUSTRIA

Blomberg, Ron (Athlete, Baseball Player)
11660 Mountain Laurel Dr
Roswell, GA 30075-1329, USA

Blombergen, Nicolaas (Nobel Prize Laureate)
13835 W Langtree Lane
Tucson, AZ 85747, USA

Blomdahl, Ben (Athlete, Baseball Player)
9 Emmy Ln
Ladera Ranch, CA 92694-1521, USA

Blomgren, Jim (Race Car Driver)
1206 S.
13th Ave.
Yakima, WA 98902, USA

Blomgren, Michael (Actor)
c/o Staff Member *Select Artists Ltd* (CA-Westside Office)
1138 12th Street
Suite 1
Santa Monica, CA 90403, USA

Blomquist, Rich (Actor)
c/o Staff Member *Creative Artists Agency (CAA-LA)*
2000 Ave Of The Stars
Los Angeles, CA 90067, USA

Blomqvist, Timo (Athlete, Hockey Player)
HIFK Helsinki Ligaforeningen HIFK rd
Mantytie 23
Helsinki SF-00270, Finland

Blomsten, Arto (Athlete, Hockey Player)
c/o Staff Member *Canal + Television*
Teleluddsvagen 7
Stockholm S-11584, Sweden

Blonde streak (Music Group)
c/o John Elias *Three Twins Entertainment, Inc*
PO Box 210
Staten Island, NY 10310, USA

Blondie (Musician)
c/o Staff Member *10th Street Entertainment (NY)*
38 W 21st St
Suite 300
New York, NY 10010, USA

Blong, Jenni (Actor)
c/o Susan Smith *Susan Smith Company, The*
1344 N Wetherly Dr
Los Angeles, CA 90069-1817, USA

Blonsky, Nikki (Actor)
c/o Teal Cannaday *Rogers & Cowan PR (LA)*
Pacific Design Center
8687 Melrose Ave, 7th Floor
West Hollywood, CA 90069, USA

Blood, Edward J (Skier)
2 Beech Hill
Durham, NH 03824, USA

Blood, Peter (Horse Racer)
290 SE 5th Ave
Pompano Beach, FL 33060-8024, USA

Bloodgood, Moon (Actor)
1238 S Holt Ave #4
Los Angeles, CA 90035, USA

Bloodworth-Thomason, Linda (Producer, Writer)
Richland Wunsch Agency
9220 W Sunset Blvd #311
West Hollywood, CA 90069, USA

Bloom, Alfred H (Educator)
Swarthmore College
President's Office
Swarthmore, PA 19081, USA

Bloom, Anne (Actor)
Abrams Artists
9200 Sunset Blvd #1125
Los Angeles, CA 90069, USA

Bloom, Brian (Actor)
16760 Escalon Dr
Encino, CA 91436, USA

Bloom, Claire (Actor)
c/o Staff Member *Conway van Gelder*
8-12 Broadwick St
London W1F 8HW, UK

Bloom, Floyd E (Physicist)
628 Pacific View Dr
San Diego, CA 92109, USA

Bloom, Jeremy (Athlete, Olympic Athlete, Sportscaster)
c/o Staff Member *Maxx Sports & Entertainment*
546 Fifth Ave Fl 6
New York, NY 10036, USA

Bloom, Lisa (Attorney, Commentator)
The Bloom Firm
22130 Clarendon St
Woodland Hills, CA 91367, USA

Bloom, Luka (Music Group)
Mattie Fox Mgmt
Derryneel Ballinalee
Longford, IRELAND

Bloom, Mike (Athlete, Hockey Player)
3214 Marina Circle
Marina, CA 93933, USA

Bloom, Orlando (Actor)
c/o Robin Baum *Slate Public Relations*
9000 Sunset Blvd #915
West Hollywood, CA 90069, USA

Bloom, Samantha (Actor)
c/o Paul Lyon-Maris *Independent Talent Group (ITG-UK)*
Oxford House
76 Oxford St
London W1D 1BS, UK

Bloom, Ursula (Writer)
Newton House Walls Dr Ravenglass
Cumbria, UNITED KINGDOM (UK)

Bloom, Verna (Actor)
327 E 82nd St
New York, NY 10028, USA

Bloomauist, Willie (Athlete, Baseball Player)
7026 E Blue Sky Dr
Scottsdale, AZ 85266-7S18, USA

Bloomberg, Michael (Politician)
Mayor's Office
City Hall
New York, NY 10075-0101, USA

Bloomfield, Jack (Athlete, Baseball Player)
1310 W Iris Ave
McAllen, TX 78501-3995, USA

Bloomfield, Michael J (Mike) (Astronaut)
14302 Autumn Canyon Terrace
Houston, TX 77062, USA

Bloomfield, Sara (Director, Misc)
Holocaust Memorial Museum
100 Wallenberg Place SW
Washington, DC 20024, USA

Bloomfield, Willie (Athlete, Baseball Player)
3145 NE Magnolia St
Issaquah, WA 98029, USA

Bloomquist, Scott (Race Car Driver)
219 Brooks Rd.
Mooresburg, TN 3i811, USA

Bloor, James E (Stylist)
117 W 15th St
#1-FE
New York, NY 10011, USA

Blosser, Greg (Athlete, Baseball Player)
5525 47th Ct E
Bradenton, FL 34203-5655, USA

Blount, Alvin (Athlete, Football Player)
1943 Lakeshore Overlook
Cir NW
Kennesaw, GA 30152, USA

Blount, Corie (Athlete, Basketball Player)
5427 Kyles Ln
Liberty Township, OH 45044-9462, USA

Blount, Eric (Athlete, Football Player)
1388 Institute Rd
Kinston, NC 28504, USA

Blount, Jeb (Athlete, Football Player)
1212 Daffodil Ln
Longview, TX 75604, USA

Blount, John E (Athlete, Football Player)
1212 Daffodil Ln
Longview, TX 75604, USA

Blount, Mark (Athlete, Basketball Player)
5723 High Flyer Rd S
Palm Beach Gardens, FL 33418-7745, USA

Blount, Mel (Athlete, Football Player)
6 Mel Blount Dr
Claysville, PA 15323, USA

Blount, Melvin C (Mel) (Athlete, Football Executive, Football Player)
6 Mel Blount Dr
Claysville, PA 15323, USA

Blount, Winton M III (Business Person)
Blount Inc
4909 SE Internationl Way
Portland, OR 97222, USA

Blout, Elkan R (Misc)
1010 Memorial Dr #12A
Cambridge, MA 02138, USA

Blow, Kurtis (Music Group)
Entertainment Artists
2409 21st Ave #100
Nashville, TN 37212, USA

Blowers, Mike (Athlete, Baseball Player)
Seattle Mariners PO Box 4100
seattle, WA 98194-0100, USA

Blu, D K (Musician)
c/o Mike Rosen *Working Artists Agency*
13525 Ventura Blvd
Sherman Oaks, CA

Blucas, Marc (Actor)
c/o Sandra Chang *Anonymous Content (LA)*
955 S Carrillo Dr
Suite 300
Los Angeles, CA 90048, USA

Blue (Musician)
c/o Staff Member *Concorde Intl Artists Ltd*
101 Shepherds Bush Rd
London W6 7LP, UNITED KINGDOM (UK)

Blue, Callum (Actor)
c/o Staff Member *Untitled Entertainment (LA)*
350 S. Beverly Dr #200
Beverly Hills, CA 90212, USA

Blue, Janice (Stylist)
1708 Rosewood
Houston, TX 77004, USA

Blue, John (Athlete, Hockey Player)
2301 Half Moon Ln
Costa Mesa, CA 92627, USA

Blue, Luther (Athlete, Football Player)
6952 Ravines Cir
West Bloomfield, MI 48322, USA

Blue, Sam (Race Car Driver)
Blue Racing
1400 W. 6th St.
Red Wing, MN 55066, USA

Blue, Vida (Athlete, Baseball Player)
P.O. Box 1449
Pleasanton, CA 94566-0349, USA

Blues Traveler (Music Group)
c/o Keith Sarkisian *WME (LA)*
9601 Wilshire Blvd Fl 3
Beverly Hills, CA 90210, USA

Bluford, Guion (Astronaut)
PO Box 549
N Olmstead, OH 44070, USA

Bluhm, Kay (Athlete)
Bahnorstr 104
Potsdam 14480, GERMANY

Blum, Arlene (Mountaineer)
University of California
Biochemistry Dept
Berkeley, CA 94720, USA

Blum, Geoff (Athlete, Baseball Player)
7 Calle An^^:elitos
San Clemente, CA 92673-6911, USA

Blum, H Steven (General)
Chief National Guard Bureau
HqUSA Pentagon
Washington, DC 20310, USA

Blum, John (Athlete, Coach, Hockey Player)
416 Marlborough St
Boston, MA 02115, USA

Blum, Stephanie (Comedian)
c/o Staff Member *Buchwald/Fortitude (LA)*
6500 Wilshire Blvd
Suite 2200
Los Angeles, CA 90048, USA

Blum, Steve (Actor)
c/o Staff Member *Arlene Thornton & Associates*
12711 Ventura Blvd
Suite 490
Studio City, CA 91604, USA

Blum, Walter (Horse Racer)
5710 NW 65th Way
Tamarac, FL 33321-5778, USA

Bluma, Jaime (Athlete, Baseball Player)
15219 Reeds St
Overland Park, KS 66223-3241, USA

Blumas, Trevor (Actor)
c/o Staff Member *Premier Artists Management Ltd*
1502 Stoneybrook Cresc
London ON N5X 1C5, CANADA

Blume, Bernard (Athlete, Basketball Player)
29248 SE Powell Valley Rd
Gresham, OR 97080-9040, USA

Blume, Judy (Writer)
JB Props Inc
C/o Tashmoo Productions 244 Fifth Ave
11th Fl
New York, NY 10023-7667, USA

Blume, Martin (Physicist)
Brookhaven National Laboratory
2 Center St
Upton, NY 11973, USA

Blumenauer, Earl (Congressman, Politician)
1502 Longworth HOB
Washington, DC 20515, USA

Blumenthal, Richard (Senator)
702 Hart Senate Office Bldg.
Washington, DC 20510, USA

Blumenthal, W Michael (Financier, Misc, Secretary)
227 Ridgeview Road
Princeton, NJ 08540, USA

Blundell, Mark (Race Car Driver)
4001 Methanol Lane
Indianpolis, IN 46268, USA

Blundell, Pamela (Designer, Fashion Designer)
Copperwheat Blundell
14 Cheshire St
London E2 6EH, UNITED KINGDOM (UK)

Blundin, Matt (Athlete, Football Player)
731 Milmont Ave
Swarthmore, PA 19081, USA

Blunstone, Colin (Music Group)
Barry Collins
21A Cliftown Southend-on-Sea
Sussex SS1 1AB, UNITED KINGDOM (UK)

Blunt, Emily (Actor)
1250 Foothill Rd
Ojai, CA 93023, USA

Blunt, James (Musician)
c/o Todd Interland *Twenty-First Artists Ltd (UK)*
1 Blythe Rd
London W14 OHG, UK

Blunt, Matt (Ex-Governor)
The Ashcroft Group, LLC
1399 New York Avenue, N.W.
Suite 950
Washington, DC 20005, USA

Blunt, Roy (Senator)
260 Russell Senate Office Building
Washington, DC 20510, USA

Blur (Music Group)
c/o Staff Member *United Talent Agency (UTA)*
9336 Civic Center Dr
Beverly Hills, CA 90210, USA

Blurth, Ray (Bowler)
569 Beauford Dr
Saint Louis, MO 63122, USA

Blush (Music Group, Musician)
c/o Staff Member *Mitch Schneider Organization (MSO)*
14724 Ventura Blvd #410
Sherman Oaks, CA 91403, USA

Bluth, Don (Cartoonist)
10121 E Shangri La Rd
Scottsdale, AZ 85260-6302, USA

Bluth, Ray (Bowler)
569 Beauford Dr
Saint Louis, MO 63122-1413, USA

BLVD (Music Group, Musician)
c/o Staff Member *Skyline Music*
28 Union St
Whitefield, NH 03598, USA

Bly, Dre (Athlete, Football Player)
4312 Topsail Lndg
Chesapeake, VA 23321, USA

Bly, Dre' (Athlete, Football Player)
4312 Topsail Landing
Chesapeake, VA 23321, USA

Bly, Robert (Bob) (Athlete, Hockey Player)
7588 Av Henri-Julien
Montreal, QC H2R 2B5, Canada

Blyleven, Bert (Athlete, Baseball Player)
Minnesota Twins 1 Twins Way
Minneaoolis, MN 55403-1418, USA

Blyth, Ann (Actor, Music Group)
Box 9754
Rancho Santa Fe, CA 92067, USA

Blyth, Chay (Misc, Yachtsman)
Inmans House 12 London Road Sheet Petersfield
Hamps GU31 4BE, UNITED KINGDOM (UK)

Blythe, Jamie (Reality TV Star)
c/o Michael (Mike) Esterman
Esterman.Com, LLC
Prefers to be contacted via email
MD, USA

B. Maloney, Carolyn (Congressman, Politician)
2332 Rayburn HOB
Washington, DC 20515, USA

B. McKinley, David (Congressman, Politician)
313 Cannon HOB
Washington, DC 20515, USA

B. Nugent, Richard (Congressman, Politician)
1517 Longworth HOB
Washington, DC 20515, USA

Boal, Mark (Writer)
c/o Staff Member *Creative Artists Agency (CAA-LA)*
2000 Ave Of The Stars
Los Angeles, CA 90067, USA

Board, Dwaine (Athlete, Football Player)
651 Arlington Rd
Redwood City, CA 94062, USA

Boat, Billy (Race Car Driver)
23045 N.
15th Ave
Phoenix, AZ 85027, USA

Boath, Freddie (Actor)
c/o Staff Member *Sasha Leslie Management*
34 Pember Rd
London NW10 5LS, UNITED KINGDOM

Boatman, Michael (Actor)
1432 Sunnycrest Dr
Fullerton, CA 92835, USA

Boatwright, Bon (Athlete, Football Player)
1801 E Main St
Henderson, TX 75652, USA

Boatwright, Ron (Athlete, Football Player)
1801 E Main St
Henderson, TX 75652, USA

Bob, Tim (Music Group, Musician)
c/o Staff Member *ArtistDirect*
9046 Lindblade St
Culver City, CA 90232, USA

Bobby Chacon, Bobby Chacon (Boxer)
Main Street III Gym
Huntington Hotel
752 S Main St
Las Vegas, CA 90014, USA

Bobek, Nicole (Figure Skater)
19220 Seaview Road #100
Jupiter, FL 33469, USA

Bober, Chris (Athlete, Football Player)
605 N 264th St
Waterloo, NE 68069, USA

Bobko, Karol J (Astronaut)
32 Mansion Ct
Menio Park, CA 94025-6658, USA

Bobo, DJ (Music Group)
Postfach
Wauwil 6242, SWITZERLAND

Bobo, Jonah (Actor)
c/o Ellen Gilbert *Abrams Artists Agency (LA)*
9200 Sunset Blvd
11th Floor
Los Angeles, CA 90069, USA

Bocachica, Hiram (Athlete, Baseball Player)
PO Box 364952
SanJuan, PR 00936-4952, USA

Bocanegra, Carlos (Athlete, Soccer Player)
c/o Lyle York *Proactive Sports Management USA*
3233 M St NW
Washington, DC 20007, USA

Boccabella, John (Athlete, Baseball Player)
1035 Lea Dr
San Rafael, CA 94903-3747, USA

Bocelli, Andrea (Music Group, Musician)
Vittoria Apuana
Forte dei Marmi 55042, ITALY

Bochco, Steven (Producer, Writer)
3970 Archdale Rd
Encino, CA 91436, USA

Bochefort, Dave (Athlete, Hockey Player)
7035 83 St NW
Edmonton, AB T6C 2Y1, Canada

Bochenski, Brandon (Athlete, Hockey Player)
10590 Kumquat St NW
Apt 3
Minneapolis, MN 55448, USA

Bochner, Hart (Actor)
1746 Correa Way
Los Angeles, CA 90049, USA

Bochte, Bruce (Athlete, Baseball Player)
80 Centurv Ln
Petaluma, CA 94952-1218, USA

Bochtler, Doug (Athlete, Baseball Player)
PO Box 483
Yakima, WA 98907-0483, USA

Bochy, Bruce (Athlete, Baseball Player, Coach)
24 Willie Mays Plz
san fransisco, CA 94107-2199, USA

Bock, Charles (Writer)
c/o Staff Member *The Rights House (UK)*
Drury House
34-43 Russell St
London WC2B 5HA, UK

Bock, Charles Col
PO Box 4197
Incline Village, NV 89450-4197, USA

Bock, Charles Jr (Misc)
P O Box 4197
Incline Village, NV 89450, USA

Bock, Edward J (Athlete, Business Person, Football Player)
2232 Clifton Forge Dr
Saint Louis, MO 63131, USA

Bock, Jerrold L (Jerry) (Composer)
145 Wellington Ave
New Rochelle, NY 10804, USA

Bock, Joe (Athlete, Football Player)
12 Heron Way N
Fairport, NY 14450, USA

Bock, John (Athlete, Football Player)
7394 NW 114th Ter
Parkland, FL 33076, USA

Bock, Joseph (Athlete, Football Player)
319 East Elm St
Eact Rochester, NY 14445, USA

Bockhorn, Arlen (Athlete, Basketball Player)
3540 Big Tree Rd
Bellbrook, OH 45305-1971, USA

Bockus, Randy (Athlete, Baseball Player)
560 Helena Dr
Tallmadge, OH 44278-2667, USA

Bockwoldt, Colby (Athlete, Football Player)
1630 E 2450 S Unit 220
Saint George, UT 84790, USA

Bocock, Brian (Baseball Player)
140 Cantermill Ln
Mount Crawford, VA 22841-2355, USA

Bocuse, Paul (Business Person, Misc)
40 Rue de la Plage
Collonges-au-Mont d'Or 69660, FRANCE

Bodden, Alonzo (Actor, Comedian)
c/o Staff Member *Rozon/Mercer Management*
9250 Wilshire Blvd #100
Beverly Hills, CA 90212-3343, USA

Bodden, Leigh (Athlete, Football Player)
14409 Woodmore
Oaks Ct
Bowie, MD 20721, USA

Boddicker, Michael J (Mike) (Athlete, Basketball Player)
11324 W 121st Terr
Overland Park, KS 66213, USA

Boddicker, Mike (Athlete, Baseball Player)
11324 W 121st Ter
Overland Park, KS 66213-1978, USA

Boddie, Tony (Athlete, Football Player)
330 Golden Pond St
Port Orchard, WA 98366, USA

Boddy, Gregg (Athlete, Hockey Player)
2271 Sorrento Dr
Coquitlam, BC V3K 6P4, Canada

Bode, John R (War Hero)
1100 Warm Sands Dr SE
Albuquerque, NM 87123, USA

Bode, Ken (Correspondent, Educator)
Northwestern University
Journalism School
Evanston, IL 60206, USA

Boden, Lynn (Athlete, Football Player)
7103 N 146th St
Bennington, NE 68007, USA

Boden, Margaret A (Misc)
Brighton University
Cognitive Science School
Brighton BN1 9QH, UNITED KINGDOM (UK)

Bodenheimer, George W. (Business Person)
c/o Staff Member *ESPN (Main)*
ESPN Plaza
935 Middle St
Bristol, CT 06010-1001, USA

Bodett, Tom (Entertainer, Writer)
P.O. Box 268
Putney, VT 05346-0268, USA

Bodger, Doug (Athlete, Hockey Player)
Eddy's Hockey Shop
2827 James St
Duncan, BC V9L 2X9, Canada

Bodine, Brett (Race Car Driver)
304 Performance Rd
Mooresville, NC 28115, USA

Bodine, Eric (Race Car Driver)
Billy Hill Vineyards
6843 Georgetown Taylor Memori.al Dr
Hammondsport, NY 14840, USA

Bodine, Geoff (Athlete, Race Car Driver)
Geoff Bodine Fan Club
3672 Joslin Way
Melbourne, FL 32904, USA

Bodine, Geoffrey (Race Car Driver)
Gunselman Motorsports
208 Rolling Hills Rd.
Mooresville, NC 28117, USA

Bodine, Todd (Race Car Driver)
120 Harris Farm Dr
Mooresville, NC 28115-5768, USA

Bodine, Vance (Race Car Driver)
11881 Vance Davis Dr.
Charlotte, NC 28269, USA

Bodison, Wolfgang (Actor)
c/o Amy Macnow *Envoy Entertainment*
2637 Centinela Ave #8
Santa Monica, CA 90405, USA

Bodmer, Walter F (Misc, Scientist)
Oxford University
Hertford College
Oxford OX1 3BW, UNITED KINGDOM
(UK)

Bodrov, Sergei (Director)
c/o Steve Rabineau *United Talent Agency (UTA)*
9336 Civic Center Dr
Beverly Hills, CA 90210, USA

Boe, Eric A Major
4219 Roaring Rapids Dr
Houston, TX 77059-5530, USA

Boede, Marvin J (Misc)
Plumbing & Pipe Fitting Union
901 Massachusetts Ave NW
Washington, DC 20001, USA

Boedeker, Bill (Athlete, Football Player)
1632 Thistle Ln
Fort Wayne, IN 46825, USA

Boeheim, Jim (Athlete, Basketball Player, Coach)
702 Tiffany Cir
Fayetteville, NY 13066, USA

Boehm, Gottfried K (Architect, Historian)
Sevogelplatz 1
Basel 4052, SWITZERLAND

Boehm, Ron (Athlete, Hockey Player)
235 Simons Rd NW
Calgary, AB T2K 2X4, Canada

Boehmer, Len (Athlete, Baseball Player)
206 Townview Ct
Wentzville, MO 63385-2925, USA

Boehne, Edward G (Financier)
Federal Reserve Bank
Independance Mall 100 N 6th St
Philadelphia, PA 19106, USA

Boehner, John (Congressman, Politician)
1011 Longworth HOB
Washington, DC 20515, USA

Boehringer, Brian (Athlete, Baseball Player)
10 Sunset Dr
Fenton, MO 63026-4959, USA

Boehrs, Jessica (Actor)
Jondral Kunstlermanagement
Am Kliepesch 13a 50859
Cologne, Germany

Boeke, Jim (Athlete, Football Player)
18914 San Blas St
Fountain Valley, CA 92708, USA

Boen, Earl (Actor)
3015 Kalakaua Ave
Honolulu, HI 96815, USA

Boerigter, Marc (Athlete, Football Player)
220 W 2nd St
Apt 2324
Kansas City, MO 64105, USA

Boerner, Jacqueline (Speed Skater)
Bemhard-Bastlein-Str 55
Berlin 10367, USA

Boerwinkle, Tom (Athlete, Basketball Player)
8524 Walredon Ave
Burr Ridge, IL 60527-8344, USA

Boeschenstein, William W (Business Person)
10617 Cardiff Road
Perrysburg, OH 43551, USA

Boese, Lawrence (General)
11th Air Force 5800 G St Ofc
Elmendorf Afb, AK 99506, USA

Boesel, Raul (Athlete, Race Car Driver)
230 Island Dr.
Miami, FL 33149-2412, USA

Boesen, Dannis L (Astronaut)
6613 Sandra Ave NE
Albuquerque, NM 87109, USA

Boesen, Dennis (Astronaut)
6613 Sandra Ave NE
Albuquerque, NM 87109-3639, USA

Boever, Joe (Athlete, Baseball Player)
416 Savannah Way
Franklin, TN 37067-2630, USA

Boff, Leonardo G D (Misc)
Pr M Leao 12/204 Alto Vale Encantado
Rio de Janeiro 20531-350, BRAZIL

Boffill, Angela (Music Group)
1385 York Ave #6B
New York, NY 10021, USA

Bofill, Ricardo (Architect)
Taller de Arguitectura
14 Ave de la Indurstria
Barcelona 08960, SPAIN

Bofinger, Heinz (Architect)
Beibricher Allee 49
Wiesbaden 65187, GERMANY

Bogans, Keith (Athlete, Basketball Player)
8345 Lake Burden Cir
Windermere, FL 34786-5322, USA

Bogar, Tim (Athlete, Baseball Player)
4 Yawkey Way
boston, MA 05512-3496, USA

Bogart, Andrea (Actor)
c/o Staff Member *Kazarian Spencer Ruskin & Assoc.*
11969 Ventura Blvd
3rd Floor
Studio City, CA 91604, USA

Bogdanovich, Peter (Director)
c/o Staff Member *Media Talent Group*
9200 Sunset Blvd
Suite 550
Los Angeles, CA 90069, USA

Bogeberg, J B (Misc)
Bandana Mgmt
11 Elvaston Place #300
London SW7 5QC, UNITED KINGDOM
(UK)

Bogener, Terry (Athlete, Baseball Player)
411 E McCabe Ave
Palmyra, MO 63461-2012, USA

Boggs, Bill (Journalist)
400 Central Park W Apt 18H
New York, NY 10025-5856, USA

Boggs, Brandon (Athlete, Baseball Player)
209 Riversgate Dr
Aot 41
Atlanta, GA 30339-2975, USA

Boggs, Haskell (Cinematographer)
3710 Goodland Ave
Studio City, CA 91604, USA

Boggs, Mitchell Boggs (Athlete, Baseball Player)
901 W Walnut Ave
Dalton, GA 30720-3952, USA

Boggs, Tommy (Athlete, Baseball Player)
1450 Long Mdw
Salado, TX 76571-5367, USA

Boggs, Wade (Athlete, Baseball Player)
6006 Windham Pl
Tampa, FL 33647-1149, USA

Bogguss, Suzy (Musician, Songwriter)
707 Sneed Rd W
Franklin, TN 37069, USA

Bogle, John C (Financier)
612 Shipton Lane
Bryn Mawr, PA 19010, USA

Bogle, Warren (Athlete, Baseball Player)
3400 Gulf Shore Blvd
N Aot M8
Naples, FL 34103-3609, USA

Bogle, Warren (Athlete, Baseball Player)
11605 SW 103rd Ave
Miami, FL 33176, USA

Boglioli, Wendy (Athlete, Olympic Athlete, Swimmer)
2014
210th Cir NE
Sammamish, WA 98074-4210, USA

Bogner, Willy (Designer, Fashion Designer)
Bogner Film GmbH
Saint-Veit-Str 4
Munich 81673, GERMANY

Bogosian, Eric (Actor, Artist)
100 Hudson St #3D
New York, NY 10013, USA

BOGRAKOS, Steve (Athlete, Football Player)
9051 E Chenango Ave
Greenwood Village, CO 80111-1320,
USA

Bogues, Muggsy (Athlete, Basketball Player)
527 E 83rd St
Apt 2W
New York, NY 10028, USA

Bogues, Tyrone "Muggsy" (Athlete, Basketball Player)
2318 Houston Branch Rd
Charlotte, NC 28270-0795, USA

Boguniecki, Eric (Athlete, Hockey Player)
58 Hine St
West Haven, CT 06516, USA

Bogusevic, Brian (Athlete, Baseball Player)
12623 S 69th Ct Aot 3
Palos Heights, IL 60463-1746, USA

Bogush, Elizabeth (Actor)
c/o Craig Shapiro *ICM Partners (ICM-LA)*
10250 Constellation Blvd Fl 7
Los Angeles, CA 90067, USA

Bohan, Marc (Designer, Fashion Designer)
35 Rue du Bourg a Mont
Chatillon Sur Seine 21400, FRANCE

Bohanon, Brian (Athlete, Baseball Player)
243 W Thorn Way
Houston, TX 77015-2069, USA

Bohay, Heidi (Actor)
5004 Sanlo Pl
Woodland Hills, CA 91364, USA

Bohbot, Daniel (Designer)
Hale Bob
2140 E 25th St
C/O Marc Springer
Vernon, CA 90058, USA

Bohem, Les (Producer, Writer)
c/o Staff Member *United Talent Agency (UTA)*
9336 Civic Center Dr
Beverly Hills, CA 90210, USA

Bohigas, Guardiola Oriol (Architect)
Calle Calvert 71
Barcelona 21, SPAIN

Bohling, Dewey (Athlete, Football Player)
5705 Cambria Rd NW
Albuquerque, NM 87120, USA

Bohlinger, Rob (Athlete, Football Player)
12650 69th Ave N
Maple Grove, MN 55369, USA

Bohlke, Sanders (Musician)
c/o Staff Member *Paradigm (Monterey)*
404 W Franklin St
Monterey, CA 93940, USA

Bohlmann, Ralph A (Religious Leader)
Lutheran Church Missouri Synod
1333 S Kirkwood Road
Saint Louis, MO 63122, USA

Bohm-Vitense, Erika
12503 Greenwood Ave N Apt E104
Seattle, WA 98133-8069, USA

Bohn, Jason (Athlete, Golfer)
161 Graves Rd
Acworth, GA 30101-6117, USA

Bohn, Parker III (Bowler)
25 Pitney Lane
Jackson, NJ 08527, USA

Bohn, Stephanie (Stylist)
c/o Staff Member *Clutts Agency, The*
1400 Turtle Creek Blvd
#171
Dallas, TX 75207, USA

Bohn, T J (Athlete, Baseball Player)
PO Box 332
Millerstown, PA 17062-0332, USA

Bohne, Petra (Stylist)
c/o Staff Member *Stephanie Louise Inc*
17 Little West 12th St
#205-C
New York, NY 10014, USA

Bohner, Otto A (Aviator)
Barbarossastrasse 28
Annweiler am Trifels, D-76855 Germany,
USA

Bohnet, John (Athlete, Baseball Player)
224 Panorama Dr
Benicia, CA 94510-1523, USA

Bohr, Aage N (Nobel Prize Laureate)
Strangade 34 1-Sal
Copenhagen 1401, DENMARK

Bohrer, Thomas (Athlete, Olympic
Athlete, Rower)
77 Crest St
Concord, MA 01742-3006, USA

Bohringer, Romane (Actor)
c/o Staff Member *Agence Artistique
Adequat*
108 rue Reaumur
Paris 75002, France

Boi, Big (Artist, Music Group, Musician)
180 Parkwood Ln
Fayetteville, GA 30215, USA

Boikov, Alexandre (Athlete, Hockey
Player)
2138 Charleys Creek Rd
Culloden, WV 25510, USA

Boileau, Linda (Cartoonist, Editor)
Frankfort State Journal
Editorial Dept 321 W Main St
Frankfort, KY 40601, USA

Boiman, Rocky (Athlete, Football Player)
9583 Dick Rd
Harrison, OH 45030, USA

Boimistruck, Fred (Athlete, Hockey
Player)
20 Cedar Ave
P.O. Box 92
Hornepayne, ON P0M 1Z0, Canada

Boiovic, Novo (Athlete, Football Player)
22097 Worcester Dr
Novi, MI 48374, USA

Boireau, Michael (Athlete, Football
Player)
1729 SW 101st Way
Miramar, FL 33025, USA

Boisclair, Bruce (Athlete, Baseball Player)
5423 Spanish Oak Ln
Unit D
Oak Park, CA 91377-3728, USA

Boisson, Christine (Actor)
Artmedia
21 Ave Rapp
Paris 75007, FRANCE

Boisvert, Gilles (Athlete, Hockey Player)
10213 Grenside Dr
Cockeysville, MD 21030, USA

Boitano, Brian (Athlete, Figure Skater,
Olympic Athlete)
Brian Boitano Enterprises
1072 Inverness Way
Sunnyvale, CA 94087-4921, USA

Boitano, Danny (Athlete, Baseball Player)
15400 Winchester Blvd
Apt 43
Los Gatos, CA 95030-2346, USA

Boivin, Leo J (Athlete, Hockey Player)
P.O. Box 406
Prescott, ON K0E 1T0, Canada

Bok, Arthur (Athlete, Football Player)
3280 Early Rd
Dayton, OH 45415, USA

Bok, Bart J (Astronomer, Educator)
200 N Sierra Vista Dr
Tucson, AZ 85719, USA

Bok, Chip (Cartoonist, Editor)
709 Castle Blvd
Akron, OH 44313, USA

Bok, Derek C (Educator)
Harvard University
Kennedy Government School
Cambridge, MA 02138, USA

Bok, Sissela (Misc)
75 Cambridge Parkway #610
Cambridge, MA 02142, USA

Bokadia, K C (Bollywood, Director,
Filmmaker, Producer)
A12 Neha Apartments Juhu Tara Road
Juhu
Bombay, MS 400 049, INDIA

Bokamper, Kim (Athlete, Football Player)
301 NW 127th Ave
Plantation, FL 33325, USA

Bokelmann, Dick (Athlete, Baseball
Player)
629 N Belmont Ave
Arlington Heights, IL 60004-5601, USA

Bolaños, Enrique (President)
President's Office
Casa de Gobierno #2398
Managua, Nicaragua

Bolcom, William E (Composer)
3080 Whitmore Lake Road
Ann Arbor, MI 48105, USA

Bolden, Charles F Jr (Astronaut, General)
14111 Lake Scene Trl
Houston, TX 77059-4406, USA

Bolden, Juran (Athlete, Football Player)
1606 Deep Well Ct
Valrico, FL 33594, USA

Bolden, Rickey (Athlete, Football Player)
301 High Pointe Dr
Lagrange, GA 30240, USA

Boldin, Anquan (Athlete, Football Player)
16225 Bridlewood Cr
Delray Beach, FL 33445-6675, USA

Boldirev, Ivan (Athlete, Hockey Player)
2003 Woodmere Dr E
Valparaiso, IN 46383, USA

Boldon, Ato (Athlete, Track Athlete)
PO Box 3703
Santa Cruz, Trinidad, TRINIDAD &
TOBAGO

Bolduc, Dan (Athlete, Hockey Player,
Olympic Athlete)
27 Daisy Ln
Sidney, ME 04330-1809, USA

Bolek, Ken (Athlete, Baseball Player)
4816 1st Avenue Dr NW
Bradenton, FL 34209-2861, USA

Boles, Carl (Athlete, Baseball Player)
5618 Pine Bay Dr
Tampa, FL 33625-4025, USA

Boles, John E (Athlete, Baseball Player,
Coach)
7901 Timberlake Dr
West Melbourne, FL 32904-2151, USA

Boley, Michael (Athlete, Football Player)
2934 Misty Rock Cv
Dacula, GA 30019, USA

Boleyn, Brook (Stylist)
c/o Staff Member *Campbell Agency, The*
3838 Oak Lawn Ave
Suite 900
Dallas, TX 75219-4510, USA

Bolger, Bill (Athlete, Basketball Player)
525 Ahlstrand Rd
Glen Ellyn, IL 60137-6926, USA

Bolger, Emma (Actor)
c/o Abby Bluestone *Innovative Artists (LA)*
1505 10th St
Santa Monica, CA 90401, USA

Bolger, Gary (Race Car Driver)
3632 Washington
Lansing, MI 60438, USA

Bolger, James B (Jim) (Prime Minister)
New Zealand Embassy
37 Observatory Circle NW
Washington, DC 20008, USA

Bolger, Jim (Athlete, Baseball Player)
5524 Sidney Rd
Cincinnati, OH 45238, USA

Bolger, Sarah (Actor)
c/o Hylda Queally *Creative Artists Agency
(CAA-LA)*
2000 Ave Of The Stars
Los Angeles, CA 90067, USA

Bolick, Frank (Athlete, Baseball Player)
381 Virginia Ln
Kulpmont, PA 17834-2024, USA

Bolin, Bobby D (Athlete, Baseball Player)
100 Medinah Dr
Easley, SC 29642-3126, USA

Bolin, Treva (Athlete, Football Player)
PO Box 281
New Waverly, TX 77358, USA

Bolkiah, Hassanal (Royalty)
Office Of The Sultan
Istana Nurul Iman
Bandar Seri, Begawan BA1000, Brunei

Bolkiah, Mu'izuddin Waddaulah (Misc)
Istana Darul Hana, Brunei Darussalam

Bolkovac, Nick (Athlete, Football Player)
1418 Humbolt Ave
Youngstown, OH 44502, USA

Bolleau, Linda (Cartoonist, Editor)
Frankfort State Journal
Editorial Dept 321 W Main St
Frankfort, KY 40601, USA

Bollen, Roger (Cartoonist)
Tribune Media Services
435 N Michigan Ave #1500
Chicago, IL 60611, USA

Boller, Kyle (Athlete, Football Player)
14945 Via La Senda
Del Mar, CA 92014, USA

Bolles, Richard N (Writer)
10 Stirling Dr
Danville, CA 94526-2921, USA

Bollettieri, Nick (Coach, Tennis Player)
Nick Bollettieri Tennis Academy
5500 34th St W
Bradenton, FL 34210, USA

Bolli, Justin (Athlete, Golfer)
3309 Buckhead Forest Mews NE
Atlanta, GA 30305, USA

Bolliger, Beat (Stylist)
c/o Staff Member *Art Partner*
145 Hudson St
2nd Floor
New York, NY 10013, USA

Bolling, Claude (Composer, Music Group)
20 Ave de Lorrainne
Garches, FRANCE

Bolling, Eric (Television Host)
c/o Staff Member *Fox News Channel (NY)*
1211 Ave of the Americas
Level C1
New York, NY 10036-8701, USA

Bolling, Frank (Athlete, Baseball Player)
171 Fenwick Rd
Mobile, AL 36608-1743, USA

Bolling, Milt (Athlete, Baseball Player)
4009 Old Shell Road
Apt E11
Mobile, AL 36608-2038, USA

Bolling, Tiffany (Actor)
116 S Burris Ave
Compton, CA 90221, USA

Bollinger, Brian (Athlete, Football Player)
763 Malibu Ln
Indialantic, FL 32903, USA

Bollinger, Brooks (Athlete, Football
Player)
3549 Birchpond Rd
St. Paul, MN 55122, USA

Bollinger, Danielle (Musician)
c/o Len Evans *Project Publicity*
312 West 53rd St
Suite 202
New York, NY 10019, USA

Bollinger, Lee C (Educator)
Columbia University
President's Office
New York, NY 10027, USA

Bollman, Ryan (Actor)
c/o Staff Member *Lichtman/Salners
Company*
12216 Moorpark St
Studio City, CA 91604, USA

Bollo, Greg (Athlete, Baseball Player)
4105 7th St
Wvandotte, MI 48192-7109, USA

Bologna, Joseph (Actor, Director, Writer)
613 N Arden Dr
Beverly Hills, CA 90210, USA

Bolonchuk, Larry (Athlete, Hockey Player)
385 Woodlawn St
Winnipeg, MB R3J 2J2, Canada

Bolstorff, Douglas (Athlete, Basketball
Player)
1553 Skyline Ct
Saint Paul, MN 55121-1148, USA

Bolt, Jackson (Actor)
c/o Jack Scagnetti *Jack Scagnetti Agency*
5118 Vineland Ave
North Hollywood, CA 91601, USA

Bolt, Jeremy (Producer)
c/o Ken Kamins *Key Creatives*
1800 N Highland Ave
Suite 500
Los Angeles, CA 90028, USA

Bolt, Mae (Athlete, Bowler)
1516 Robinhood Lane
La Grange Park, IL 60526-1129, USA

Bolt, Tommy (Athlete, Golfer)
8 Whispering Winds Trace
Cherokee Village, AR 72529, USA

Bolt, Usain (Athlete)
c/o Grainne O'Dea *Pace Sports Management*
6 The Causeway
Teddington, Middlesex TW11 oHE, UK

Bolten, Joshua (Government Official)
Office of Management/Budget
Executive Office Building
Washington, DC 20503, USA

Bolton, Michael (Musician, Songwriter)
27/31 Kings Hwy
N Westport, CT 06880, USA

Bolton, Rodney (Athlete, Baseball Player)
2195 Ooltewah Ringgold Rd
Ooltewah, TN 37363-9392, USA

Bolton, Ron (Athlete, Football Player)
408 Maiden Ln
Chesapeake, VA 23325, USA

Bolton, Scott (Athlete, Football Player)
1635 Ashmoor Dr E
Mobile, AL 36695, USA

Bolton, Tom (Athlete, Baseball Player)
2288 Rolling Hills Dr
Nolensville, TN 37135-9483, USA

Bolton-Holifield, Ruthie (Athlete, Basketball Player)
Sacramento Monarchs
Arco Arena
1 Sports Pkwy
Sacramento, CA 95834, USA

Boltz, Ray (Musician)
c/o Staff Member *Ray Boltz Music*
P.O. Box 175
Albany, IN 47320, USA

Bolyard, John (General)
1200 E 3rd St
Panama City, FL 32401-3742, USA

Bolzan, Scott (Athlete, Football Player)
2074 E Linda Ln
Gilbert, AZ 85234, USA

Bomback, Mark (Athlete, Baseball Player)
2482 Riverside Ave
Somerset, MA 02726-5149, USA

Bombard, Marc (Athlete, Baseball Player)
8612 Barkwood Pl
Tampa, FL 33615-1501, USA

Bombardir, Brad (Athlete, Hockey Player)
Minnesota Wild
317 Washington St
Player Development
Saint Paul, MN 55102-1667, USA

Bomer, Matthew (Actor)
444 S Rossmore Ave
Los Angeles, CA 90020, USA

Bonaduce, Danny (Actor, Musician, Producer)
4039 Cromwell Ave
Los Angeles, CA 90027, USA

Bonaly, Surya (Figure Skater)
c/o Staff Member *Champions on Ice*
Tom Collins Enterprises Inc
3500 W 80th St
Minneapolis, MN 55431, USA

Bonamassa, Joe (Musician)
c/o Andrew Lanoie *WME (LA)*
9601 Wilshire Blvd Fl 3
Beverly Hills, CA 90210, USA

Bonamy, James (Musician)
Hallmark Direction
15 Music Square West
Nashville, TN 37203, USA

Bonanno, Louis (Louie) (Actor)
P.O. Box 583
Laguna Beach, CA 92652, USA

Bonar, Dan (Athlete, Hockey Player)
361 Mandeville St
Winnipeg, MB R3J 2G8, Canada

Bonazzi, Noemi (Stylist)
c/o Staff Member *Marek & Associates Inc*
508 W 26th St
#12-C
New York, NY 10001, USA

Bond, Alan (Business Person, Yachtsman)
89 Watkins Road
Dalkeith, WA 6069, AUSTRALIA

Bond, Christopher S (Kit) (Ex-Governor, Ex-Senator, Politician)
14 Jefferson Rd.
Mexico, MO 65265-3732, USA

Bond, Edward (Writer)
Orchard Way
Great Wilbraham, Cambridge CB1 5KA, UNITED KINGDOM (UK)

Bond, H Julian (Activist)
54435 41st Place NW
Washington, DC 20015-2911, USA

Bond, J Max Jr (Architect)
Davis Broder Assoc
100 E 42nd St
New York, NY 10017, USA

Bond, Larry (Writer)
c/o Robert Gottlieb *Trident Media Group LLC*
41 Madison Ave
36th Floor
New York, NY 10010, USA

Bond, Phillip (Phil) (Athlete, Basketball Player)
208 Northwestern Pkwy
Louisville, KY 40212-2732, USA

Bond, Samantha (Actor)
Conway Van Gelder Robinson
18-21 Jermyn St
London SW1Y 6NB, UNITED KINGDOM (UK)

Bond, Samatha (Actor)
c/o Staff Member *Innovative Artists (LA)*
1505 10th St
Santa Monica, CA 90401, USA

Bond, Victoria A (Composer)
Roanoke Symphony
541 Luck Ave SW #200
Roanoke, VA 24016, USA

Bond, Walter (Athlete, Basketball Player)
P.O. Box 87
Hamel, MN 55340-0087, USA

Bondar, Roberta L (Astronaut)
Space Agency
P O Box 7014 Station V
Vanier, ON K1L8E2, CANADA

Bonderman, Jeremy (Athlete, Baseball Player)
=
10 Ridgeview Dr
Pasco, WA 99301-8808, USA

Bondevik, Kjell Magne (Prime Minister)
Statsministerens Kontor
Postboks 8001 Dep
Oslo 0030, Norway

Bondi, Hermann (Mathematician)
61 Mill Lane
Impington, Cambridgeshire CB4 4XN, UNITED KINGDOM (UK)

Bondra, Peter (Athlete, Hockey Player)
372 Carriage Park Way
Annapolis, MD 21401-7709, USA

Bonds, Barry (Athlete, Baseball Player)
44 Beverly Park Cir.
Beverly Hills, CA 90210-1565, USA

Bonds, Gary U S (Music Group)
Entity Communications
875 Ave of Americas #1908
New York, NY 10001, USA

Bondurant, Bob (Race Car Driver)
Firebird Racing School
20,000 S. Maricopa Rd
Box 5023
Chandler, AZ 85226, USA

Bondy, A.A. (Musician)
c/o Ken Weinstein *Big Hassle Media*
40 Exchange Pl #1900
New York, NY 10005, USA

Boneham, Rupert (Reality TV Star)
c/o Staff Member *Abrams Artists Agency (NY)*
275 Seventh Ave
26th Floor
New York, NY 10001, USA

Bonehman, Rupert (Actor)
c/o Staff Member *Ruth Webb Enterprises*
10580 Des Moines Ave
Northridge, CA 91326, USA

Bonell, Carlos A (Composer, Music Group)
Upbeat Mgmt
Sutton Business Centre
Wallington, Surrey SM6 7AH, UNITED KINGDOM (UK)

Bonelli, Ernest (Athlete, Football Player)
1200 E Peppertree Ln
Apt 602
Sarasota, FL 34242, USA

Bonerz, Peter (Actor, Comedian, Director)
3637 Lowry Road
Los Angeles, CA 90027, USA

Bones, Ricky (Athlete, Baseball Player)
908 NW lOOth Ave
Pembroke Pines, FL 33024-4371, USA

Bonet, Lisa (Actor)
1551 Will Geer Rd
Topanga, CA 90290, USA

Bonet, Pep (Architect)
C/Pujades 62
Barcelona 08005, SPAIN

Boneta, Diego (Actor)
c/o Lena Roklin *Luber Roklin Management*
8530 Wilshire Blvd
6th Floor
Beverly Hills, CA 90211, USA

Bone Thugs-N-Harmony (Music Group)
c/o Staff Member *Sony Music Entertainment*
555 Madison Avenue
New York, NY 10022-3211, USA

Bong, Jung (Baseball Player)
Atlanta Braves
2917 Asteria Pointe
Duluth, GA 30097-5221, USA

Bongiovi, Tony (Producer)
Bongiovi Acoustics
649 SW Whitmore Dr
Port St Lucie, FL 34984, USA

Bongo, Albert-Bernard Omar (President)
President's Office
Blvd de Independence
Libreville BP 546, GABON

Bonham, Bill (Athlete, Baseball Player)
2135 Holly Ln
Solvang, CA 93463-2207, USA

Bonham, Jason (Musician)
10324 El Caballo Ct
Delray Beach, FL 33446, USA

Bonham, Ron (Athlete, Basketball Player)
8020 S County Road 700 E
Selma, IN 47383-9621, USA

Bonham, Shane (Athlete, Football Player)
3431 Ardennes Dr
Maryville, TN 37801, USA

Bonham, Tracy (Music Group, Songwriter)
c/o Staff Member *Paradigm (Monterey)*
404 W Franklin St
Monterey, CA 93940, USA

Bonham Carter, Helena (Actor)
c/o Shelley Browning *Magnolia Entertainment (LA)*
9595 Wilshire Blvd
Suite 601
Beverly Hills, CA 90212, USA

Bonifant, J Evan (Actor)
c/o Staff Member *Pacific Artists Management*
1285 W Broadway
Suite 685
Vancouver, BC V6H 3X8, Canada

Bonikowski, Joe (Athlete, Baseball Player)
6701 Old Reid Rd
Charlotte, NC 28210-4622, USA

Bonilla, Hector (Actor)
c/o Staff Member *TV Azteca*
Periferico Sur 4121
Colonia Fuentes del Pedregal
DF CP 14141, Mexico

Bonilla, Juan (Athlete, Baseball Player)
2902 Orchidcrest Dr
Crestview, FL 32539-8528, USA

Bonilla, Roberto M A (Bobby) (Athlete, Baseball Player)
1774 Meadowood St
Sarasota, FL 34231-3014, USA

Bonin, Brian (Athlete, Hockey Player)
2279 8th St
Saint Paul, MN 55110-2869, USA

Bonin, Celeste Beryl (Athlete, Wrestler)
c/o Staff Member *World Wrestling Entertainment (WWE)*
Titan Towers
1241 E Main St
Stamford, CT 06905-3857, USA

Bonin, Gordie (Race Car Driver)
12471 Stanford St
Los Angeles, CA 90066, USA

Bonin, Greg (Athlete, Baseball Player)
509 Boulder Creek Pkwy
Lafayette, LA 70508-1717, USA

Bonin, Marcel (Athlete, Hockey Player)
225-230 Rue du Juge-Guibault
Saint-Charles-Borromee, QC J6E 9B4, Canada

Bonine, Eddie (Athlete, Baseball Player)
5809 W Plum Rd
Phoenix, AZ 85083-9346, USA

Bonington, Christian J S (Mountaineer)
Badger Hill Nether Row Hesket
Newmarket
Cumbria, UNITED KINGDON (UK)

Boniol, Chris (Athlete, Football Player)
5309 Townsend Dr
Flower Mound, TX 75028, USA

Bonjour, Daniel (Actor)
c/o Staff Member *Tinoco Management*
8033 Sunset Blvd
Suite 573
West Hollywood, CA 90046, USA

Bon Jovi, Jon (Actor, Composer, Musician, Songwriter)
583 Broadway #PH
New York, NY 10012, USA

Bonk, John (Athlete, Football Player)
54 Audubon St S
Stoney Creek, ON L8J 1J7, Canada

Bonk, Radek (Athlete, Hockey Player)
137 Allenhurst Cir
Franklin, TN 37067-7272, USA

Bonnaire, Sandrine (Actor)
36 rue de Ponthieu
Paris, FRANCE F-75008

Bonnell, Barry (Athlete, Baseball Player)
2102 179th Ct NE
Redmond, WA 98052-6064, USA

Bonner, Anthony (Athlete, Basketball Player)
5854 Elmbank Ave
Saint Louis, MO 63120-1116, USA

Bonner, Bobby (Athlete, Baseball Player)
990 Manitou Rd
Hilton, NY 14468-9390, USA

Bonner, Frank (Actor)
Stone Manners
6500 Wilshire Blvd #550
Los Angeles, CA 90048, USA

Bonner, Jo (Congressman, Politician)
2236 Rayburn HOB
Washington, DC 20515, USA

Bonner, John T (Biologist)
52 Patton Ave #A
Princeton, NJ 08540, USA

Bonner, Melvin (Athlete, Football Player)
2500 Fairway Dr Apt 102
Alvin, TX 77511, USA

Bonner, Steven (General)
6043 Sunset Dr
Guymon, OK 73942-5803, USA

Bonness, Rik (Athlete, Football Player)
18914 Boyle Cir
Elkhorn, NE 68022, USA

Bonneville, Hugh (Actor)
c/o Staff Member *Paradigm (LA)*
360 N Crescent Dr
North Bldg
Beverly Hills, CA 90210, USA

Bonney, Barbara (Opera Singer)
Gunnarsbyn
Edane 671 94, SWEDEN

Bono (Musician, Songwriter)
145 Central Park W #27E/#28E
New York, NY 10024, USA

Bono, Chaz (Actor, Musician, Writer)
c/o Howard Bragman *Fifteen Minutes (LA)*
8436 W 3rd St
Suite 650
Los Angeles, CA 90048, USA

Bono, Mary (Politician)
Mary Bono
1555 South Palm Canyon Drive
Suite D105
Palm Springs, CA 92264, USA

Bono, Steven C (Steve) (Athlete, Football Player)
1100 Hamilton Ave
Palo Alto, CA 94301, USA

Bonoff, Karla (Musician, Songwriter)
2122 E Valley Road
Santa Barbara, CA 93108, USA

Bono Mack, Mary (Congressman, Politician)
104 Cannon HOB
Washington, DC 20515, USA

Bonsall, Joe (Musician)
100 Surrey Hill Pt
Hendersonville, TN 37075, USA

Bonsalle, George (Athlete, Basketball Player)
11804 Del Rey Ave NE
Albuquerque, NM 87122-2417, USA

Bonser, Boof (Athlete, Baseball Player)
9251 126th Ave
Largo, FL 33773-1247, USA

Bonsignore, Jason (Athlete, Hockey Player)
2152 Edgemere Dr
Rochester, NY 14612-1102, USA

Bontemps, Ron (Athlete, Basketball Player, Olympic Athlete)
133 S Illinois Ave
Morton, IL 61550-2683, USA

Bonvicini, Joan (Athlete, Basketball Player, Coach)
University of Arizona
McKale Memorial Center
Atheletic Dept
Tucson, AZ 85721, USA

Bonvie, Dennis (Athlete, Hockey Player)
54 Grandville Dr
Kingston, PA 18704-1251, USA

Bonynge, Richard A
Chale Monet Rte de Sonloup
Les Avants, 1833 SWITZERLAND

Boo, Jim (Athlete, Hockey Player)
416 4th St S
Stillwater, MN 55082-4912, USA

Boo, Katherine (Journalist)
Washington Post
Editorial Dept 1150 15th St NW
Washington, DC 20071, USA

Book, Asher (Actor)
c/o Bryan Leder *Management 101*
11271 Ventura Blvd
#102
Studio City, CA 91604, USA

Booka Shade (Music Group)
c/o Joel Zimmerman *WME (WMA-NY)*
1325 Ave of the Americas
New York, NY 10019, USA

Booker, Buddy (Athlete, Baseball Player)
P.O. Box 59
Brookneal, VA 24528-0059, USA

Booker, Butch (Athlete, Basketball Player)
305 Barker Ave
Lansdowne, PA 19050-1215, USA

Booker, Chris (Correspondent)
c/o Staff Member *Entertainment Tonight (ET)*
4024 Radford Ave.
Studio City, CA 91604, USA

Booker, Chris (Athlete, Baseball Player)
2052 Perryville Rd
Monroeville, AL 36460-6852, USA

Booker, Greg (Athlete, Baseball Player)
1535 Charleigh Ct
Elon, NC 27244-9770, USA

Booker, Marty (Athlete, Football Player)
19920 NW 8th St
Pembroke Pines, FL 33029, USA

Booker, Rod (Athlete, Baseball Player)
526 W Altadena Dr
Altadena, CA 91001-4204, USA

Booker, Vaughn (Athlete, Football Player)
56 E Mitchell Ave
Cincinnati, OH 45217, USA

Booko, Daniel (Actor)
c/o Glenn Hughes III *Gem Entertainment Group*
10701 Wilshire Blvd.
Ste. 1202
Los Angeles, CA 90024, USA

Bookwalter, JR (Director)
PO Box 6573
Akron, OH 44312, USA

Boom, Benn (Actor)
c/o Staff Member *WmE2 (WMA-LA)*
1 William Morris Pl
Beverly Hills, CA 90212, USA

Boomer, Linwood (Producer, Writer)
c/o Philip Raskind *WME (LA)*
9601 Wilshire Blvd Fl 3
Beverly Hills, CA 90210, USA

Boon, David C (Cricketer)
Durham Cricket Club
Chester-le-Street
County Durham DH3 3QR, UNITED KINGDOM (UK)

Boone, Aaron (Athlete, Baseball Player)
19860 N 97th St
Scottsdale, AZ 85255-6682, USA

Boone, Alfonso (Athlete, Football Player)
14290 W Lyle Ct
Libertyville, IL 60048, USA

Boone, Bob (Athlete, Baseball Player)
1432 Misty Sea Way
San Marcos, CA 92078-1010, USA

Boone, Bret (Athlete, Baseball Player)
6383 Calle Ponte Bella
Rancho Santa Fe, CA 92091-0288, USA

Boone, Danny (Athlete, Baseball Player)
320 Minnesota Ave
El Cajon, CA 92020-6118, USA

Boone, Debby (Actor, Musician)
4334 Kester Ave
Sherman Oaks, CA 91403, USA

Boone, Greg (Athlete, Football Player)
10426 Hunters Haven Blvd
Riverview, FL 33578

Boone, James (Athlete, Football Player)
2529 Butler Bay Dr N
Windermere, FL 34786, USA

Boone, Jim (Athlete, Football Player)
2529 Butler Bay Dr N
Windermere, FL 34786, USA

Boone, Lesley (Actor)
12523 Landale St
Studio City, CA 91604, USA

Boone, Pat (Actor, Musician)
904 N Beverly Dr
Beverly Hills, CA 90210, USA

Boone, Randy (Actor)
1611 Bluffside Dr #130
Fayetteville, NC 28312, USA

Boone, Ron (Athlete, Basketball Player)
2200 s 100 E
Salt Lake City, UT 84106-1836, USA

Boone, Steve (Music Group, Musician)
Pipeline Artists Mgmt
620 16th Ave S
Hopkins, MN 55343, USA

Booras, Steve (Athlete, Football Player)
1441 Parkhill Dr
Billings, MT 59102-3147, USA

Boorem, Mika (Actor)
129 N Lincoln St
Burbank, CA 91506, USA

Boorman, Charley (Actor, Producer, Writer)
c/o Lindy King *United Agents*
12-26 Lexington St
London W1F OLE, UK

Boorman, John (Director)
Merlin Films
16 Upper Pembroke St
Dublin 2, IRELAND

Booros, James (Athlete, Golfer)
2615 W Pennsylvania St
Allentown, PA 18104-2921, USA

Boortz, Neal (Radio Personality)
1601 W Peachtree St
Atlanta, GA 30309, USA

Boose, Dorian (Athlete, Football Player)
1630 NE Valley Rd
Apt K102t Ct
Pullman, WA 99163, USA

Boosler, Elayne (Actor, Comedian)
11061 Wrightwood Ln
Studio City, CA 91604, USA

Bootcheck, Chris (Athlete, Baseball Player)
6105 Lakeaires Dr
Cumming, GA 30040-1109, USA

Booth, Adrian (Actor)
3922 Glenridge Dr
Sherman Oaks, CA 91423, USA

Booth, Brad (Athlete, Football Player)
2201 W 229th Pl
Torrance, CA 90501, USA

Booth, Calvin (Athlete, Basketball Player)
6001 E Horseshoe Rd
Paradise Valley, AZ 85253-8125, USA

Booth, Clarence (Athlete, Football Player)
33 Cor Dale Ct
Lafayette, IN 47904, USA

Booth, Connie (Actor)
Kate Feast
Primrose Hill Studios
Fitzroy Rd
London NW1 8TR, UNITED KINGDOM
(UK)

Booth, David (Athlete, Hockey Player)
Octagon Sports Management
5110 Crystal Creek Ln
Washington, MI 48094-4238, USA

Booth, Douglas
c/o Kate Staddon *Curtis Brown Group*
Haymarket House
28 - 29 Haymarket
London SW1Y 4SP, UNITED KINGDOM

Booth, George (Cartoonist)
P O Box 1539
Stony Brook, NY 11790-0830, USA

Booth, Kellee (Athlete, Golfer)
4804 Goldeneyes Ln
McKinney, TX 75070, USA

Booth, Kristin (Actor)
c/o Vicki McCarty *Covington International*
4237 Morro Dr
Woodland Hills, CA 91364, USA

Booth, Lindy (Actor)
c/o Christopher Wright *Christopher Wright Management*
3207 Winnie Dr
Los Angeles, CA 90068, USA

Boothe, Kevin (Athlete, Football Player)
12100 NW 18th St
Plantation, FL 33323, USA

Boothe, Powers (Actor)
23629 Long Valley Rd
Hidden Hills, CA 91302, USA

Boothie, Powers (Actor)
23629 Long Valley Rd
Hidden Hills, CA 91302, USA

Boothroyd, Betty (Government Official)
House of Commons
Westminster
London SW1A 0AA, UNITED KINGDOM
(UK)

Booty, John (Athlete, Football Player)
1408 Flatwood Ct
Crofton, MD 21114, USA

Booty, Josh (Athlete, Baseball Player)
6248 N Windermere Dr
Shreveport, LA 71129-3423, USA

Booty, Josh (Athlete, Football Player)
6248 N Windermere Dr
Shreveport, LA 71129, USA

Boozer, Carlos (Athlete, Basketball Player)
c/o Rob Pelinka *Landmark Sports Agency*
10990 Wilshire Blvd
Suite 1000
Los Angeles, CA 90024, USA

Boozer, Emerson (Athlete, Football Player)
25 Windham Pl
Huntington Station, NY 11746, USA

Boozman, John
320 Hart Senate Office Building
Washington, DC 20510, USA

Bopp, Thomas (Scientist)
4138 W Barbara Ave
Phoenix, AZ 85051-3650, USA

Borbon, Julio (Athlete, Baseball Player)
522 Vinings Oaks Run
Mableton, GA 30126-7239, USA

Borchard, Joe (Athlete, Baseball Player)
791 E lemon Dr
Camarillo, CA 93010-2339, USA

Borchardt, Jon (Athlete, Football Player)
18815 201st Ave NE
Woodinville, WA 98077, USA

Borchelt, Earl (Athlete, Olympic Athlete, Rower)
7 Blueberry Ln
Sterling, MA 01564-2143, USA

Borcherds, Richard E (Mathematician)
University of California
Mathematics Dept
Berkeley, CA 94720, USA

Borcky, Dennis (Athlete, Football Player)
18 Weathervane Rd
Aston, PA 19014, USA

Bordano, Chris (Athlete, Football Player)
2788 Morning Moon
New Braunfels, TX 78132, USA

Bordeleau, Christian (Athlete, Hockey Player)
1242 Rue Rabelais
Repentigny, QC J5V 3R7, Canada

Bordeleau, J P (Athlete, Hockey Player)
94 Lakemist Crt
Dartmouth, NS B3A 4Z1, Canada

Bordeleau, Paulin (Athlete, Hockey Player)
281a Rue Principale
La Sarre, QC J9Z 1Z1, Canada

Bordelon, Ben (Athlete, Football Player)
PO Box 250
Lockport, LA 70374, USA

Bordelon, Kenneth (Athlete, Football Player)
1224 Octavia St
New Orleans, LA 70115, USA

Borden, Amanda (Gymnast)
Cincinnati Gymnastics Acadamy
3536 Woodridge Blvd
Fairfield, OH 45014, USA

Borden, Lynn (Actor)
Associated Artists
6399 Wilshire Blvd #211
Los Angeles, CA 90048, USA

Borden, Robert (Producer)
c/o Staff Member *United Talent Agency (UTA)*
9336 Civic Center Dr
Beverly Hills, CA 90210, USA

Borden, Scott (Actor)
c/o Staff Member *Progressive Artists Agency*
1041 N Formosa Ave
West Hollywood, CA 90046, USA

Borden, Steve (Sting) (Wrestler)
16654 Soledad Canyon Rd #315
Canyon Country, CA 91387-3025, USA

Border, Allan R (Cricketer)
Cricket Board
90 Jolimont St
Jolimont VIC 3002, AUSTRATIA

Borders, Nate (Athlete, Football Player)
950 Franklin St
Winchester, VA 22601, USA

Borders, Pat (Athlete, Baseball Player, Olympic Athlete)
2650 Burns Ave
Lake Wales, FL 33898-7947, USA

Bordi, Rich (Athlete, Baseball Player)
1133 Hailev Ct
Rohnert Park, CA 94928-1875, USA

Bordick, Mike (Athlete, Baseball Player)
1302 Locust Ave
Towson, MD 21204-6619, USA

Bordley, Bill (Athlete, Baseball Player)
39 Moccasin Ln
Rolling Hills Estate, CA 90274-2506, USA

Boreanaz, David (Actor)
5739 Penland Rd
Hidden Hills, CA 91302-2443, USA

Borel, Calvin (Jockey)
16502 Briston Avon Ln
Louisville, KY 40245-4280, USA

Boren, Dan (Congressman, Politician)
2447 Rayburn HOB
Washington, DC 20515, USA

Boren, David L (Ex-Governor, Ex-Senator)
University of Oklahoma
President's Office, Evans Hall, Room 101
660 Parrington Oval
Norman, OK 73019, USA

Boren, Matt (Actor)
c/o Steven Jensen *Independent Group, The*
6363 Wilshire Blvd
Suite 115
Los Angeles, CA 90048, USA

Borg, Bjorn R (Tennis Player)
International Management Group
Pier House Chiswick
London W4M 3NN, UNITED KINGDOM
(UK)

Borg, Kim (Opera Singer)
Osterbrogade 158
Copenhagen 2100, DENMARK

Borg-Aplin, Lorraine (Baseball Player)
3611 Laverne Cir N Apt 2
Baxter, MN 56425-5908, USA

Borgeson, Don (Athlete, Hockey Player)
2211 Highway 49 W
Ashland City, TN 37015, USA

Borghi, Frank (Soccer Player)
4123 Poepping St
Saint Louis, MO 63123, USA

Borgman, James A (Jim) (Cartoonist, Editor)
c/o Staff Member *King Features Syndication*
300 W 57th St
15th Floor
New York, NY 10019-5238, USA

Borgmann, Glenn (Athlete, Baseball Player)
16 Lundy Ter
Butler, NJ 07405-1926, USA

Borgnine, Ernest (Actor)
3055 Lake Glen Dr
Beverly Hills, CA 90210, USA

Borgognone, Dirk (Athlete, Football Player)
7148 Voyage Dr
Sparks, NV 89436, USA

Boris, Angel (Actor)
c/o Staff Member *Acme Talent & Literary (LA)*
1400 Atlantic Ave
Suite 274
Long Beach, CA 90814, USA

Boris, Paul (Athlete, Baseball Player)
28 Sunnyside Ln
Hillsborough, NJ 08844-4738, USA

Boris, Ruthanna (Ballerina, Choreographer)
6510 Gladys Avenue
El Cerrito, CA 94530-2210, USA

Bork, Erik (Producer, Writer)
c/o Staff Member *Creative Artists Agency (CAA-LA)*
2000 Ave Of The Stars
Los Angeles, CA 90067, USA

Bork, Frank (Athlete, Baseball Player)
8488 Dunsinane Dr
Dublin, OH 43017-9420, USA

Bork, George (Athlete, Football Player)
7316 Conventry Dr S
Spring Grove, IL 60081, USA

Borkh, Inge (Opera Singer)
Haus Weitblick
Wienacht 9405, SWITZERLAND

Borkowski, Bob (Athlete, Baseball Player)
1031 Gerhard St
Dayton, OH 45404-2052, USA

Borkowski, David (Dave) (Athlete, Baseball Player)
2124 Mcintosh Dr
Holland, OH 43528-7930, USA

Borland, Toby (Athlete, Baseball Player)
8642 Quitman Hwy
Quitman, LA 71268-1282, USA

Borland, Tom (Athlete, Baseball Player)
624 W Cherokee Ave
Stillwater, OK 74075-1405, USA

Borland, Wes (Musician)
8464 Brier Dr
Los Angeles, CA 90046, USA

Borlaug, Norman E (Nobel Prize Laureate)
P O Box 6-641
Mexico City DF SP 06600, MEXICO

Borle, Christian (Actor)
c/o Peter Kiernan *Management 360*
9111 Wilshire Blvd
Beverly Hills, CA 90210, USA

Borlenghi, Matthew (Actor)
3200 Coldwater Canyon Ave
Studio City, CA 91604, USA

Borman, Frank (Astronaut, Business Person)
P.O. Box 64
Bighorn, MT 59010-0064, USA

Born, Ruth (Athlete, Baseball Player, Commentator)
4205 Meridian Woods Drive
Valparaiso, IN 46385-7014, USA

Bornheimer, Kyle (Actor, Comedian)
3427 Ben Lomond Pl
Los Angeles, CA 90027, USA

Bornstein, Jonathan (Athlete, Soccer Player)
c/o Lyle York *Proactive Sports Management* USA
3233 M St NW
Washington, DC 20007, USA

Borntrager, Mary Christner (Writer)
c/o Staff Member *Herald Press*
616 Walnut Ave
Scottsdale, PA 15683, USA

Borodina, Olga V (Opera Singer)
Lies Askonas
6 Henrietta St
London WC2E 8LA, UNITED KINGDON (UK)

Boron, Kathrin (Athlete)
Potsdamer RG
An Der Pirschheide
Potsdam 14471, GERMANY

Boros, Guy (Athlete, Golfer)
2900 NE 40th St
Ft Lauderdale, FL 33308-5743, USA

Boross, Peter (Prime Minister)
Kossouth Lajos Ter 1-3
Budapest 1055, HUNGARY

Borotsik, Jack (Athlete, Hockey Player)
Lakeview Road
Onanole, MB ROJ 1NO, Canada

Borowski, Joe (Athlete, Baseball Player)
13782 E Gail Rd
Scottsdale, AZ 85259-4642, USA

Borrego, Jesse (Actor)
c/o Kay Liberman *Liberman/Zerman Management*
252 N Larchmont Blvd
Suite 200
Los Angeles, CA 90004, USA

Borrero, Alejandra (Actor)
c/o Gabriel Blanco *Gabriel Blanco Iglesias (Mexico)*
Rio Balsas 35-32
Colonia Cuauhtemoc
DF 06500, Mexico

Borresen, Richard (Athlete, Football Player)
2291 Jefferson St
East Meadow, NY 11554, USA

Borris, Angel (Actor)
c/o Lara Rosenstock *Lara Rosenstock Management*
8371 Blackburn Ave #1
Los Angeles, CA 90048, USA

Borsato, Luciano (Athlete, Hockey Player)
200-4 Tortoise Crt
Brampton, ON L6P 0A1, Canada

Borsavage, Ike (Athlete, Basketball Player)
219 Doris Ave
Southampton, PA 18966-2771, USA

Borschevsky, Nikolai (Athlete, Hockey Player)
3 Geranium Crt
Richmond Hill, ON L4C 7M7, Canada

Borschman, Laurie (Athlete, Hockey Player)
27 Delamere Dr
Stittsville, ON K2S 1G7, Canada

Borst, Plet (Misc)
Meentweg 87
Bussum 1406 KE, NETHERLANDS

Borstein, Alex (Actor)
c/o Brandon Liebman *WME (LA)*
9601 Wilshire Blvd Fl 3
Beverly Hills, CA 90210, USA

Borth, Michelle (Actor)
c/o Mark Rousso *New Wave Entertainment (LA)*
2660 W Olive Blvd
Burbank, CA 91505, USA

Bortnick, Ethan (Actor, Musician)
c/o Michael Katcher *Creative Artists Agency (CAA-LA)*
2000 Ave Of The Stars
Los Angeles, CA 90067, USA

Borton, Della (D B) (Writer)
Ohio Wesleyan University
Dept of English
Delaware, OH 43015, USA

Bortz, Mark (Athlete, Football Player)
PO Box 3504
Quincy, IL 62305, USA

Boryla, Mike (Athlete, Football Player)
6092 Blue Terrace Cir
Castle Rock, CO 80108, USA

Boryla, Vince (Athlete, Basketball Player, Olympic Athlete)
5577 S Emporia Cir
Greenwood Village, CO 80111-3543, USA

Borysenko, Joan (Doctor, Writer)
Mind-Body Health Sciences Inc
393 Dixon Rd
Boulder, CO 80302, USA

Borzov, Valeri F (Athlete, Track Athlete)
Sport & Youth Ministry
Esplanadna St 42
Kiev 23 252023, UKRAINE

Bosa, John (Athlete, Football Player)
2400 Magnolia Dr
North Miami, FL 33181, USA

Bosarge, Wade (Athlete, Football Player)
8366 Via Rosa
Orlando, FL 32836, USA

Bosch, Don (Athlete, Baseball Player)
14446 N State Highway 3
Fort Jones, CA 96032-9773, USA

Bosch, Francisco (Actor)
Re.Animator Management
c/o Suzanne Gielgud
Victoria House 125 Queens Rd
Brighton BN1 3WB, UNOTED KINGDOM

Boschetti, Ryan (Athlete, Football Player)
120 23rd Ave
San Mateo, CA 94403, USA

Boschman, Ed (Religious Leader)
Mennonite Brethren Churches General Conference
P O Box 347
Newton, KS 67114, USA

Boschman, Laurie (Athlete, Hockey Player)
27 Delamere Dr
Stittsville, ON K2S 1G7, Canada

Bosco, Philip (Actor)
Judy Schoen
606 N Larchmont Blvd #309
Los Angeles, CA 90004, USA

Bose, Amar G (Inventor)
Bose Corp Mountain
Framington, MA 01778-3208, USA

Bose, Bimal K (Engineer)
215 Ski Mountain Road
Gatlinburg, TN 37738, USA

Bose, Eleanora (Model)
I M G Models
304 Park Ave S #1200
New York, NY 10010, USA

Bose, Miguel (Actor, Music Group, Songwriter, Writer)
RLM Producciones
Puerto Santa Maria 65
Madrid 28043, SPAIN

Bose, Rahul (Actor, Writer)
APM - Alpita Patel

BoselII, Tony (Athlete, Football Player)
6 Glendenning Ln
Houston, TX 77024, USA

Boselli, Tony (Athlete, Football Player)
356 San Juan Dr
Pante Vedra Beach, FL 32082, USA

Bosetti, Rick (Athlete, Baseball Player)
1471 Arroyo Manor Dr
Redding, CA 96003-9215, USA

Bosh, Chris (Athlete, Basketball Player)
6396 N Bay Rd
Miami Beach, FL 33141, USA

Boshard, Lisa (Stylist)
4574 Wellington St
Holladay, UT 84117, USA

Bosio, Chris (Athlete, Baseball Player)
Lawrence University
417 Hidden Ridges Way
Attn: Baseball Office
Combined locks, WI 54113-1337, USA

Boskie, Shawn (Athlete, Baseball Player)
10220 N 55th St
Paradise Valley, AZ 85253-1168, USA

Boskin, Michael J (Government Official)
Stanford University
Hoover Instution
Stanford, CA 94305, USA

Bosley, Thad (Athlete, Baseball Player)
20660 Stevens Creek Blvd
Cupertino, CA 95014-2120, USA

Bosman, Dick (Athlete, Baseball Player)
3511 Landmark Trl
Palm Harbor, FL 34684-5015, USA

Boso, Casper (Athlete, Football Player)
8811 Calumet Dr
Indianapolis, IN 46236, USA

Bossard, Andre (Judge, Lawyer, Misc)
228 Rue de la Convention
Paris 75015, FRANCE

Bosseler, Don J (Athlete, Football Player)
7782 SW 54th Ave
Miami, FL 33143, USA

Bosson, Barbara (Actor)
742 Milwood Ave
Venice, CA 90291, USA

Bossy, Michael (Mike) (Athlete, Hockey Player)
New York Islanders
1255 Hempstead Tpke Attn VP, Corporate Partnerships
Uniondale, NY 11553-1200, Canada

Bostelle, Tom (Artist)
Aeolian Palace Gallery
P O Box 8
Pocopson, PA 19366, USA

Bostic, Jeff (Athlete, Football Player)
8250 Royal Saint Georges Ln
Duluth, GA 30097, USA

Bostic, Jim (Athlete, Basketball Player)
111 Valentine Ln
Apt 2D
Yonkers, NY 10705-3426, USA

Bostic, Joe (Athlete, Football Player)
3507 Bromley Wood Ln
Greensboro, NC 27410, USA

Bostic, John (Athlete, Football Player)
611 Canaveral Ave
Titusville, FL 32796, USA

Bostic, Keith (Athlete, Football Player)
2419 Duchess Way
Stafford, TX 77477, USA

Boston (Music Group, Musician)
c/o Staff Member *Agency for the Performing Arts (APA-LA)*
405 S Beverly Dr
Suite 500
Beverly Hills, CA 90212-4425, USA

Boston, Daryl (Athlete, Baseball Player)
3136 Northchester Pl
lithonia, GA 30038-2292, USA

Boston, David (Athlete, Football Player)
5580 SW 104th Ter
Cooper City, FL 92130, USA

Boston, Lawrence (Athlete, Basketball Player)
6362 Holiday Hill Ct
Bedord, OH 44146-3159, USA

Boston, McKinley (Athlete, Football Player)
1986 Coyote Ridge Dr
Las Cruces, NM 88011, us

Boston, McKinley (Athlete, Football Player)
1986 Coyote Ridge Dr
Las Cruces, NM 88011, USA

Boston, Rachel (Actor)
c/o Vera Mihailovich *Forward Entertainment*
9255 Sunset Blvd
Suite 805
Los Angeles, CA 90069, USA

Boston, Ralph (Athlete, Olympic Athlete)
3301 Woodbine Ave
Knoxville, TN 37914-4448, USA

Bostridge, Ian (Musician)
c/o Staff Member *ICM Partners (ICM-LA)*
10250 Constellation Blvd Fl 7
Los Angeles, CA 90067, USA

Bostrom, Zachary (Actor)
Kazarian/Spencer
11365 Ventura Blvd #100
Box 7403
Studio City, CA 91604

Bostwick, Barry (Actor, Musician)
c/o Staff Member *Vanguard Management Group*
8060 Melrose Ave
4th Floor
Los Angeles, CA 90046, USA

Bostwick, Dunbar (Race Car Driver)
1623 Dewey Ave
Pompano Beach, FL 33060, USA

Bostwick, Jackson
Shazam!
PO Box 1452
Mt. Juliet, TN 37121, USA

Boswell, Ken (Athlete, Baseball Player)
1103 live Oak Dr
Marble Falls, TX 78654-7258, USA

Boswell, Thomas M (Writer)
Washington Post
Sports Dept 1150 15th St NW
Washington, DC 20071, USA

Boswell, Tom (Athlete, Basketball Player)
341 N Anton Dr
Montgomery, AL 36105-2112, USA

Bosworth, Brian (Actor, Athlete, Football Player)
4400 Arlen Ct
Plano, TX 75093, USA

Bosworth, Kate (Actor)
2633 La Cuesta Dr
Los Angeles, CA 90046, USA

Bosworth, Lauren (Lo) (Reality TV Star)
c/o Nicole Perez-Krueger *PMK/BNC Public Relations (PMK-LA)*
8687 Melrose Ave Fl 8
West Hollywood, CA 90069, USA

Botchan, Ron (Athlete, Football Player)
55 Toscana Way E
Rancho Mirage, CA 92270, USA

Boteach, Rabbi Shmuley (Activist, Writer)
c/o Robert Gottlieb *Trident Media Group LLC*
41 Madison Ave
36th Floor
New York, NY 10010, USA

Botehho, Joao (Director)
Assicuacai de Realizadores
Rua de Palmeira 7 R/C
Lisbon 1200, PORTUGAL

Botelho, Derek (Athlete, Baseball Player)
1819 Orchard St
Burlington, IA 52601-6136, USA

Botero, Fernando (Artist)
2 Rue Honore Labarde
Principaute De Monaco 98 000, Monaco

Botes, Liz (Stylist)
c/o Staff Member *Legend Inc*
8855 Hollywood Blvd
Los Angeles, CA 90069, USA

Botha, Francois (Frans) (Boxer)
White Buffalo
P O Box 3982
Clearwater, FL 33767, USA

Botha, Pieter W (President)
Die Anker
Wildemess, 6560 SOUTH AFRICA

Botha, Roelof F (Government Official)
P O Box 16176
Pretoria North 0116, SOUTH AFRICA

Botham, Ian T (Athlete, Cricketer)
c/o Staff Member *Mission Sports Management*
11 Nortfields Prospect
London SW18 1PE, UK

Bothwell, Tim (Athlete, Coach, Hockey Player)
14 Billings Ct
Burlington, VT 05408-1104, USA

Botkin, Kirk (Athlete, Football Player)
7210 Shadow Brk
Texarkana, TX 75503, USA

Botsford, Beth (Athlete, Olympic Athlete, Swimmer)
2210 River Bend Court
White Hall, MD 21161-9214, USA

Botsford, Sara (Actor)
Kordek Agency
8490 W Sunset Blvd #403
West Hollywood, CA 90069, USA

Bott, Raoul (Mathematician)
1 Richdale Ave #9
Cambridge, MA 02140, USA

Botta, Mario (Architect)
Via Ciani 16
Lugano 6904, SWITZERLAND

Bottalico, Ricky (Athlete, Baseball Player)
10 Rocamora Rd
Rocky Hill, CT 06067-2069, USA

Bottcher, Martin (Composer)
Postfach 96
Brusino Arsizio CH-6827, Switzerland

Bottenfield, Kent (Athlete, Baseball Player)
12168 142nd Ct N
West Palm Beach, Fl 33418-7901, USA

Botterill, Jason (Athlete, Hockey Player)
2359 Railroad St #3602
Pittsburgh, PA 15222, USA

Botti, Chris (Musician)
c/o Bobby Colomby *The Colomby Group*
2110 Main St
Suite 302
Santa Monica, CA 90405, USA

Botting, Ralph (Athlete, Baseball Player)
7 Somerset
Trabuco Canyon, CA 92679-3701, USA

Bottom, Joe (Swimmer)
PO Box 3840
Chico, CA 95927, USA

Bottom, Joseph (Athlete, Olympic Athlete, Swimmer)
374 Spanish Garden Dr
Chico, CA 95928-8869, USA

Bottomley, Virginia (Government Official)
House of Commons
Westminster
London SW1A 0AA, UNITED KINGDOM (UK)

Bottoms, Joseph (Actor)
c/o Belle Zwerdling *B and B Management*
1041 N Formosa Ave
West Hollywood, CA 90046, USA

Bottoms, Timothy (Actor)
532 Hot Springs Rd
Montecito, CA 93108, USA

Bottrell, David Dean (Actor, Writer)
c/o Alan Gasmer *Alan Gasmer Management Company*
10877 Wilshire Blvd.
Suite 603
Los Angeles, CA 90024, USA

Botts, Jason (Athlete, Baseball Player)
405 Peachtree Ln
Paso Robles, CA 93446-2869, USA

Botts, Mike (Athlete, Football Player)
PO Box 247 105 S Market St
Elizabethville, PA 17023-0247, USA

Botz, Bob (Athlete, Baseball Player)
14229 Desert Fire Ct
Horizon City, TX 79928-6422, USA

Boublil, Alain A (Songwriter, Writer)
Cameron Mackintosh Ltd
1 Bedford Square
London WC1B 3RA, UNITED KINGDOM (UK)

Boucha, Henry (Athlete, Hockey Player, Olympic Athlete)
7200 Biglerville Cir
Anchorage, AK 99507-2885, USA

Bouchard, Dan (Athlete, Hockey Player)
3111 Hillsdale Ct SE
Marietta, GA 30067, USA

Bouchard, Daniel (Athlete, Hockey Player)
3111 Hillsdale Ct SE
Marietta, GA 30067-5431, USA

Bouchard, Joel (Athlete, Hockey Player)
Club de Hockey Junior de Montreal
1410 Stanley St Suite 602 Attn Coaching Staff Montreal
Attn Coaching Staff Montreal, QC H3A 1P8, Canada

Bouchard, Ken (Race Car Driver)
PO Box 60
Thompson, CT 06277, USA

Bouchard, Marc (Producer)
c/o Staff Member *Cirque du Soleil Inc*
8400 2e Avenue
Montreal QB H1Z 4M6, CANADA

Bouchard, Pierre (Athlete, Hockey Player)
208 Marie-Victorian
Vercheres, QC J0L 2R0, Canada

Bouchard, Pierre-Marc (Athlete, Hockey Player)
9950 Wellington Ln
Woodbury, MN 55125-8459, USA

Bouchard, Ron (Race Car Driver)
300 Lonenburg St.
Fitchburg, MA 01420, USA

Bouchee, Ed (Athlete, Baseball Player)
1621 E Tremaine Ave
Gilbert, AZ 85234-8140, USA

Bouchee, Ed
Philadelphia Phillies
1621 E Tremaine Ave
Gilbert, AZ 85234-8140, USA

Boucher, Brian (Athlete, Hockey Player)
3009 Allansford Ln
Raleigh, NC 27613-5468, USA

Boucher, Denis (Athlete, Baseball Player)
201-644 36e Av
Lachine, Quebec H8T 3M1, Canada

Boucher, Gaetan (Speed Skater)
Center Sportif
3850 Edger
Saint Hubert, QC J4T 368, CANADA

Boucher, Guy (Athlete, Hockey Player)
3505 Holland Dr
Brandon, FL 33511-8172, USA

Boucher, Guy (Athlete, Hockey Player)
Tampa Bay Lightning
401 Channelside Dr
Attn Coaching Staff
Tampa, FL 33602-5400, USA

Boucher, Philippe (Athlete, Hockey Player)
533 Rue Tessier
Rimouski, QC G5L 4L8, Canada

Boucher, Philippe (Athlete, Hockey Player)
Rimouski Oceanic Hockey Club
CP 816 Succ A Attn: General Manager
Rimouski, QC G5L 7C9, Canada

Boucher, Pierre (Photographer)
L'Ermitage 7th Ave Massoul
Faremountiers
Coulomiers 77120, FRANCE

Boucher, Savannah (Actor)
H W A Talent
3500 W Olive Ave #1400
Burbank, CA 91505, USA

Bouchez, Elodie (Actor)
c/o Scott Zimmerman *Evolution Entertainment (LA)*
901 N Highland Ave
Los Angeles, CA 90038, USA

Bouck, Brittany Paige (Actor)
c/o Henry Penner *Penner PR*
8225 Santa Monica Blvd
West Hollywood, CA 90046

Boudart, Michel (Engineer, Misc)
512 Gerona Road
Stanford, CA 94305, USA

Boudia, David (Athlete, Olympic Athlete)
USA Diving Inc
Pan American Plaza #430
201 South Capitol Ave
Indianapolis, IN 46225, USA

Boudin, Michael (Judge)
US Appeals Court
McCormack Federal Building
Boston, MA 02109, USA

Boudreau, Bruce (Athlete, Hockey Player)
PO Box 59727
Potomac, MD 20859-9727, USA

Boudreau, Bruce (Athlete, Hockey Player)
627 N Glebe Rd Ste 850
Attn: Coaching Staff
Arlington, VA 22203-2144, United States

Boudrias, Andre (Athlete, Hockey Player)
1008-4300 Place des Cageux
Laval, QC H7W 4Z3, Canada

Bouffard, Danielle (Actor)

Bouffard, Danielle (Actor)
c/o Staff Member *King Talent*
303-228 E 4th Ave
Vancouver V5T-1G5, CANADA

Bouggess, Lee (Athlete, Football Player)
171 Villa Knoll Ct
Sicklerville, NJ 08081, USA

Boughner, Barry (Athlete, Hockey Player)
52 Locke Ave
St Thomas, ON N5P 3X7, Canada

Boughner, Bob (Athlete, Hockey Player)
c/o Staff Member *Windsor Spitfires*
334 Wyandotte St E
Windsor, ON N9A 3H6, Canada

Boujenah, Michel (Actor)
c/o Staff Member *ArtMedia*
20 avenue Rapp
Paris 75008, France

Boukadakis, Joey (Director, Producer, Writer)
c/o Michael Lasker *Mosaic Media Group*
9200 W. Sunset Blvd
10th Floor
Los Angeles, CA 90069, USA

Bouklas, Penelope (Stylist)
32-34 36th St
Long Island City, NY 11106, USA

Boulanger, Pierre (Actor)
c/o Paul Nelson *Mosaic Media Group*
9200 W. Sunset Blvd
10th Floor
Los Angeles, CA 90069, USA

Bouldin, Carl (Athlete, Baseball Player)
42 Fairwav Dr
Southgate, KY 41071-3024, USA

Boulerice, Jesse (Athlete, Hockey Player)
502 Oak Island Dr
Cary, NC 27513-2236, USA

Boulez, Pierre (Composer, Conductor)
IRCAM
1 Place Igor Stravinsky
Paris 75004, FRANCE

Boullion, Jean-Christophe (Race Car Driver)
Pescarolo
40 bis rue fabert
Paris F-75007, France

Boulos, Frenchy (Soccer Player)
20 Elvin St
Staten Island, NY 10314, USA

Boulter, Roy (Actor, Producer, Writer)
c/o Peter MacFarlane *MacFarlane Chard Associates*
33 ercy St
London W1T 2DF, UK

Boulton, Eric (Athlete, Hockey Player)
1867 Misty Woods Dr
Duluth, GA 30097-8108, USA

Boulud, Daniel (Chef)
Daniel Restaurant
60 E 65th St
New York, NY 10021, USA

Boulware, Michael (Athlete, Football Player)
c/o Eugene Parker *Maximum Sports Management*
6435 W Jefferson Blvd #197
Fort Wayne, IN 46804, USA

Boulware, Peter (Athlete, Football Player)
305 Leaning Tree Rd
Columbia, SC 29223, USA

Bouman, Todd (Athlete, Football Player)
3070 Dartmouth Dr
Excelsior, MN 55331, USA

Bouquet, Carole (Actor, Model)
Agents Associes Beaume
201 Faubourg Saint Honore
Paris 75008, FRANCE

Bourbeau, Allen (Athlete, Hockey Player, Olympic Athlete)
2210 Robinswood Road
Titusville, FL 32780-4513, USA

Bourbonnais, Claude (Race Car Driver)
122 S. Southgate
Chandler, AZ 85226, USA

Bourbonnais, Rick (Athlete, Hockey Player)
643 E Parkway Ct
Boise, ID 83706, USA

Bourbonnals, Rick (Athlete, Hockey Player)
643 E Parkway Ct
Boise, ID 83706-6526, USA

Bource, Ludovic (Composer)
c/o Staff Member *First Artists Management*
4764 Park Granada
Suite 210
Calabasas, CA 91302, USA

Bourdain, Anthony (Chef, Television Host)
c/o Kimberly Witherspoon *Inkwell Management*
521 Fifth Ave
New York, NY 10175, USA

Bourdeaux, Brandy (Actor)
c/o Staff Member *Coralie Jr Theatrical Agency*
907 S Victory Blvd
Burbank, CA 91502-2430, USA

Bourdeaux, Michael (Religious Leader)
Keston College
Heathfield Road Keston
Kent BR2 6BA, UNITED KINGDOM (UK)

Bourdian, Anthony (Chef)
Food Network
1180 Ave of Americas #1200
New York, NY 10036, USA

Boures, Emil (Athlete, Football Player)
426 W Swissvale Ave
Pittsburgh, PA 15218, USA

Bourgeois, Charles (Athlete, Hockey Player)
P.O. Box 1481
Stn Main
Moncton, NB E1C 8T6, Canada

Bourgeois, Charlie (Athlete, Hockey Player)
PO Box 1481 Stn Main
Moncton, NB E1C 8T6, Canada

Bourgeois, Jason (Athlete, Baseball Player)
16755 Ella Blvd
Ant 178
Houston, TX 77090-4211, USA

Bourgeois, Lawrence (Scientist)
137 Paradise Point Dr
Boerne, TX 78006-9437, USA

Bourgeois, Steve (Athlete, Baseball Player)
P.O. Box 143
Paulina, LA 70763-0143, USA

Bourgignon, Serge (Director)
18 Rue de General-Malterre
Paris 75016, FRANCE

Bourgoin, Louise (Actor)
c/o Jessica Kovacevic *WME (LA)*
9601 Wilshire Blvd Fl 3
Beverly Hills, CA 90210, USA

Bourjos, Chris (Athlete, Baseball Player)
10345 E Dreyfus Ave
Scottsdale, AZ 85260-9006, USA

Bourjos, Peter
3872 E Melinda Dr
Phoenix, AZ 85050-4999, USA

Bourn, Michael (Athlete, Baseball Player)
24604 Belvon Vallev ln
Porter, TX 77365-5743, USA

Bourne, Bob (Athlete, Hockey Player)
Bob Bourne Realty
1-1890 Cooper Rd
Kelowna, BC V1Y 8B7, Canada

Bourne, JR (Actor)
c/o John Elliott *Mosaic Media Group*
9200 W. Sunset Blvd
10th Floor
Los Angeles, CA 90069, USA

Bourne, Martin (Stylist)
c/o Staff Member *Judy Casey Inc*
114 E 13th St
New York, NY 10003, USA

Bourne, Shae-Lynn (Figure Skater)
Connecticut Skating Center
300 Alumni Road
Newington, CT 06111, USA

Bournigal, Rafael (Athlete, Baseball Player)
230 Canterwood ln
Mulberry, FL 33860-7637, USA

Bournissen, Chantal (Skier)
1983 Evolene
SWITZERLAND

Bourque, Pat (Athlete, Baseball Player)
2001 N Chiomunk Ct
Flagstaff, AZ 86004-7587, USA

Bourque, Phil (Athlete, Hockey Player)
5117 Yale Dr
Aliquippa, PA 15001-4949, USA

Bourque, Phil (Athlete, Hockey Player)
Pittsburgh Penguins
66 Mario Lemieux Pl Ste 2
Attn: Broadcast Dept
Pittsburgh, PA 15219-3504, USA

Bourque, Pierre (Misc)
Hotel de Ville
275 Rue Notre Dame Est
Montreal, QC H2Y 1C6, CANADA

Bourque, Raymond J (Athlete, Hockey Player)
Tresca Restaurant
233 Hanover St
Boston, MA 02113-2310, USA

Bourque, Rene (Athlete, Hockey Player)
9110 93
Lac la Biche, AB TOA 2CO, Canada

Bourret, Caprice (Actor)
c/o Nadja Koglin *Richard Schwartz Management*
2934-1/2 Beverly Glen Cir #107
Los Angeles, CA 90077, USA

Boushka, Dick (Athlete, Basketball Player, Olympic Athlete)
9844 Cypresswood Dr #209
Houston, TX 77070-3822, USA

Bouteflika, Abdul Aziz (President)
President's Office
Al-Mouradia
Algiers, Algeria

Boutette, Pat (Athlete, Hockey Player)
The Doctors House Restaurant
21 Nashville Road
Kleinburg, ON L0J 1C0, Canada

Boutiette, K C (Athlete, Olympic Athlete, Speed Skater)
1911 E 72nd St
Tacoma, WA 98404-5408, USA

Boutilier, Paul (Athlete, Hockey Player)
79 Lakemist Crt
Dartmouth, NS B3A 4Z1, Canada

Bouton, Jim (Athlete, Baseball Player)
PO Box 909
North Egremont, MA 01230-0909, USA

Boutros-Ghali, Boutros (Politician)
Inter'l Francophonie Org
2 Ave El Nil
Giza, Cairo 75007, Egypt

Boutte, Denise (Actor)
c/o Charles Newman *Newman-Thomas Management*
8306 Wilshire Blvd #996
Beverly Hills, CA 90211, USA

Boutte, Marc (Athlete, Football Player)
906 Derby Ln
Missouri City, TX 77489, us

Boutwell, Thomas (Athlete, Football Player)
32353 Oaken Wood St
Denham Springs, LA 70726, USA

Boutwell, Tommy (Athlete, Football Player)
32353 Oaken Wood St
Denham Springs, LA 70726, us

Bouvet, Didier (Skier)
Bouvet-Sports
Abondance 74360, FRANCE

Bouvia, Gloria (Bowler)
2827 SW Corbeth Ln
Troutdale, OR 97060-3137, USA

Bouwmeester, Jay (Athlete, Hockey Player)
McQuaig Desrochers LLP
28 Greenoch Cres NW
Attn Bryon Baltimore
Edmonton, AB TGL 1B4, Canada

Bouyer, Willie (Athlete, Football Player)
6560 Chesterbrook Dr
Elk Grove, CA 95758, USA

Bouza, Matt (Athlete, Football Player)
1042 Via Nueva
Lafayette, CA 94549, USA

Bouzeos, Phil (Athlete, Football Player)
10 Pembroke Ln
Oak Brook, IL 60523, USA

Bova, Raoul (Actor)
c/o Alan Siegel *Alan Siegel Entertainment*
345 N Maple Dr
Suite 375
Beverly Hills, CA 90210, USA

Bovee, Mike (Athlete, Baseball Player)
11405 Affinity Ct
Unit 236
San Diego, CA 92131-2718, USA

Boven, Don (Athlete, Basketball Player)
4434 Garth Rd
Charlottesville, VA 22901-5103, USA

Bovey, Terry (Athlete, Baseball Player)
7700 E Speedway Blvd Apt 206
Tucson, AZ 85710-1619, usa

Bowa, Lawrence R (Larry) (Athlete, Baseball Player, Coach)
302 Overlook Ln
Conshohocken, PA 19428-2634, USA

Bowab, John (Actor)
2598 Green Valley
Los Angeles, CA 90046, USA

Bowdell III, Gordon (Athlete, Football Player)
14615 Harrison Ave
Allen Park, MI 48101, USA

Bowden, Craig (Athlete, Golfer)
4651 S Amber Dr
Bloomington, IN 47401-8359, USA

Bowden, James (Commentator)
172 Capitol Island Rd
Southport, ME 04576-3241, USA

Bowden, Joe (Athlete, Football Player)
7026 Thistlewood Park Ct
Katy, TX 77494, us

Bowden, Katrina (Actor)
c/o William Choi *Management 360*
9111 Wilshire Blvd
Beverly Hills, CA 90210, USA

Bowden, Mark (Director, Writer)
c/o Ron Bernstein *ICM Partners (ICM-LA)*
10250 Constellation Blvd Fl 7
Los Angeles, CA 90067, USA

Bowden, Michael (Athlete, Baseball
Player)
596 Sudbury Cir
Oswego, IL 60543-7147

Bowden, Robert (Bobby) (Athlete, Coach,
Football Coach, Football Player)
2813 Shamrock St
Tallahassee, FL 32309, USA

Bowden, Terry (Coach, Football Coach,
Sportscaster)
ABC-TV
Sports Dept 77 W 66th St
New York, NY 10023, USA

Bowden, Tommy (Coach, Football Coach)
Clemson University
Athletic Dept
Clemson, SC 29364, USA

Bowdler, William G (Diplomat)
State Department
2201 C St NW
Washington, DC 20520, USA

Bowe, David (Actor)
Karg/Weissenbach
329 N Wetherly Dr #101
Beverly Hills, CA 90211, USA

Bowe, Dwayne (Athlete, Football Player)
2520 NE Bitter Creek Ct
Lees Summit, MO 64086, us

Bowe, Riddick L (Boxer)
714 Ahmer Dr
Fort Washington, MD 20744, USA

Bowe, Rosemarie (Actor)
321 St Pierre Rd
Los Angeles, CA 90077, USA

Bowen, Andrea (Actor)
12327 Landale St
Studio City, CA 91604, USA

Bowen, Bruce (Athlete, Basketball Player)
1810 Settler Ct
San Antonio, TX 78258-4764, USA

Bowen, Heather (Stylist)
5120 SW Richardson Dr
Portland, OR 97201, USA

Bowen, Jason (Athlete, Hockey Player)
4900 W 14th Ave
Kennewick, WA 99338, USA

Bowen, Jimmy (Music Group, Musician)
PO Box 454
Lebanon, TN 37088, USA

Bowen, Julie (Actor)
3253 Oakdell Rd
Studio City, CA 91604, USA

Bowen, Michael (Actor)
Diverse Talent Agency
1875 Century Park East #2250
Los Angeles, CA 90067, USA

Bowen, Nanci (Athlete, Golfer)
193 Tucker Rd
Macon, GA 31210, USA

Bowen, Otis R (Politician)
27912B Rd
Bremen, IN 46506-9047, USA

Bowen, Pamela (Actor)
c/o Staff Member *Henderson Hogan
Agency (LA)*
8929 Wilshire Blvd
Suite 312
Beverly Hills, CA 90211, USA

Bowen, Rob (Athlete, Baseball Player)
389 Knight Dr
Elliiay, GA 30540-4381, USA

Bowen, Ryan (Athlete, Baseball Player)
3702 Frankford Rd
Apt 18203
Dallas, TX 75287-7811, USA

Bowen, Sam (Athlete, Baseball Player)
8219 Victory Trl
Brentwood, TN 37027-7374, USA

Bowen, Stephen G Cdr (Astronaut)
508 Oak Dr
Friendswood, TX 77546-5531, USA

Bowen, Wade (Musician)
c/o Joey Lee *WmE2 (WMA-TN)*
1600 Division St
Suite 300
Nashville, TN 37203, USA

Bowen, William G (Educator, Misc)
Andrew Mellon Foundation
140 E 62nd St
New York, NY 10021, USA

Bowens, Tim (Athlete, Football Player)
P.O. Box 93
Okolona, MS 38860, USA

Bowens, Tom (Athlete, Basketball Player)
304 Martin Luther King St
Okolona, MS 38860-1330, USA

Bower, Antoinette (Actor)
1529 N Beverly Glen Blvd
Los Angeles, CA 90077, USA

Bower, Jaime Campbell (Actor)
c/o Simon Beresford *Dalzell & Beresford
Ltd*
26 Astwood Mews
London SW7 4DE, UNITED KINGDOM
(UK)

Bower, Johnny (Athlete, Hockey Player)
3937 Parkgate Dr
Mississauga, ON L5N 7B4, Canada

Bower, Michael (Actor)
c/o Dora Whitaker *Whitaker Agency, The*
4924 Vineland Avenue
N Hollywood, CA 91601, USA

Bower, Robert W (Inventor)
University of California
8722 Sail port Dr
Huntington Beach, CA 92646-2640, USA

Bowers, Brent (Athlete, Baseball Player)
19257 Manchester Dr
Mokena, IL 60448-7747, USA

Bowers, Cedrick
10336 NW 28th Pl
Gainesville, FL 32606-8666, USA

Bowers, Chris (Actor)
c/o Staff Member *Gersh (LA)*
9465 Wilshire Blvd
Suite 600
Beverly Hills, CA 90212, USA

Bowers, Dane (Actor, Musician)
Penshurst Place
90-92 SouthBridge Rd
Croydon, Surrey CRO 1AF, UNITED
KINGDOM

Bowers, John (Football Player, Misc)
International Longshoremen's Assn
198 Woodland Dr
Pulaski, PA 16143, USA

Bowers, John W (Religious Leader)
Foursquare Gospel Int'l Church
1100 Glendale Blvd
Los Angeles, CA 90026, USA

Bowers, Sam (Athlete, Football Player)
11211 John F Kennedy Dr #311
Hagerstown, MD 21742-6768, USA

Bowers, Scotty (Writer)
c/o Staff Member *Grove / Atlantic, Inc*
841 Broadway
4th Floor
New York, NY 10003, USA

Bowers, Shane (Athlete, Baseball Player)
535 S Rancho Alegre Dr
Covina, CA 91724-3325, USA

Bowers, William (Athlete, Football Player)
43295 Lacovia Dr
Indio, CA 92201, USA

Bowersox, Crystal (Musician)
c/o Simon Fuller *XIX Entertainment*
35-37 Parkgate Rd
32/33 Ransomes Dock
London SW11 4NP, UNITED KINGDOM
(UK)

Bowersox, Kenneth D (Astronaut)
16907 Soaring Forest Dr
Houston, TX 77059, USA

Bowersox, Kenneth D Captain (Astronaut)
16907 Soaring Forest Dr
Houston, TX 77059-4003, USA

Bowes, Margie (Musician)
1502 Brentwood Pt
Brentwood, TN 37087, USA

Bowes, William (General)
12108 Polo Dr
Fairfax, VA 22033-4017, USA

Bowick, Tony (Athlete, Football Player)
PO Box 234
Slocomb, AL 36375

Bowick, Vantonio (Athlete, Football
Player)
P.O. Box 234
Slocomb, AL 36375, USA

Bowie, David (Actor, Musician)
285 Lafayette St #7DE
New York, NY 10012, USA

Bowie, Heather (Athlete, Golfer)
3017 Elm River Dr
Ft Worth, TX 76116, USA

Bowie, Jim (Athlete, Baseball Player)
1241 Swan Lake Dr
Fairfield, CA 94533-8137, USA

Bowie, John Ross (Actor, Comedian)
976 Sanborn Ave
Los Angeles, CA 90029, USA

Bowie, Larry D (Athlete, Football Player)
739 Echo Shores Ct
Saint Paul, MN 55115, USA

Bowie, Larry G (Athlete, Football Player)
260 Clarence St
Saint Paul, MN 55106, USA

Bowie, Micah (Athlete, Baseball Player)
2039 Small Town Dr
New Braunfels, TX 78130-9063, USA

Bowie, Sam (Athlete, Basketball Player,
Olympic Athlete)
PO Box 306
Lexington, KY 40588-0306, USA

Bowker, Albert H (Educator)
1523 New Hampshire Ave NW
Washington, DC 20036, USA

Bowker, Gordon (Business Person, Writer)
c/o Staff Member *Little, Brown Book
Group*
100 Victoria Embankment
London EC4Y 0DY, UK

Bowker, John
3912 Cayente Way
Sacramento, CA 95864-2938, USA

Bowker, Judi (Actor)
66 Berkeley House 5 Hay Hill
London W1X 7LH, UNITED KINGDOM
(UK)

Bowlby, April (Actor)
740 N Kings Rd #106
Los Angeles, CA 90069, USA

Bowler, Grant (Actor)
c/o Beth Holden-Garland *Untitled
Entertainment (LA)*
350 S. Beverly Dr #200
Beverly Hills, CA 90212, USA

Bowles, Brian (Athlete, Baseball Player)
1535 Steinhart Ave
Redondo Beach, CA 90278-2745, USA

Bowles, Charlie (Athlete, Golfer)
42009 Cherry Hill Rd
Novi, MI 48375, USA

Bowles, Crandall C (Business Person)
Springs Industries
205 N White St
Fort Mill, SC 29715, USA

Bowles, Erskine B (Politician)
6725 Old Providence Road
Charlotte, NC 28226-7735, USA

Bowles, Lauren (Actor)
c/o Staff Member *Main Title Entertainment*
8383 Wilshire Blvd
Suite 408
Los Angeles, CA 90211, USA

Bowles, Peter (Actor)
c/o Staff Member *Conway van Gelder*
8-12 Broadwick St
London W1F 8HW, UK

Bowlin, Weldon (Hoss) (Athlete, Baseball
Player)
P.O. Box 1026
Livingston, AL 35470-1026, USA

Bowling, Andy (Athlete, Football Player)
7421 Straightstone Rd
Long Island, VA 24569, USA

Bowling, Orbie (Athlete, Basketball
Player)
10179 Frank Rd
Collierville, TN 38017-3623, USA

Bowling, Steve (Athlete, Baseball Player)
524 E 117th St S
Jenks, OK 74037-3618, USA

Bowling for Soup (Music Group)
c/o Staff Member *Agency Group Ltd, The (UK)*
361-373 City Rd
London EC1V 1PQ, UK

Bowman, Bob
8340 Riesling Wav
San Jose, CA 95135-1435, USA

Bowman, Elizabeth (Athlete, Golfer)
82 Davidson St
Chula Vista, CA 91910-3002, USA

Bowman, Ernie (Athlete, Baseball Player)
123 Carter Dr
Apt 8
Johnson City, TN 37601-2973, USA

Bowman, Harry W (Business Person)
Outboard Marine
P O Box 410
Waukegan, IL 60079, USA

Bowman, Jim (Athlete, Football Player)
12 Stony Field Rd
Norton, MA 02766, USA

Bowman, Joshua (Actor)
c/o Eric Kranzler *Management 360*
9111 Wilshire Blvd
Beverly Hills, CA 90210, USA

Bowman, Ken (Athlete, Football Player)
13664 N Placita
Montanas, De, USA

Bowman, Kirk (Athlete, Hockey Player)
740 Point Pelee Dr
740 Point Pelee Dr
RR 1 STN MAIN
Leamington, ON N8H 3V4, Canada

Bowman, Pasco M II (Judge)
US Court of Appeals
US Courthouse 811 Grand Ave
Kansas City, MO 64106, USA

Bowman, Scotty (Athlete, Coach, Hockey Player)
5760 Midnight Pass Rd #104D
Sarasota, FL 34242-3022, CANADA

Bown, Chuck (Race Car Driver)
2503 Wedge Pl.
Asheboro, NC 27205, USA

Bown, Jim (Race Car Driver)
5045 Old NC 49
Asheboro, NC 27203, USA

Bownass, Rick (Athlete, Hockey Player)
Vancouver Canucks
800 Griffiths Way
Attn: Coaching Staff
Vancouver, BC VGB 6G1, Canada

Bownes, Fabien (Athlete, Football Player)
8127 149th Pl NE
Unit B112
Redmond, WA 98052, USA

Bowness, Rick (Athlete, Hockey Player)
10 Shadowstone Ln
Lawrence Township, NJ 08648-1027, USA

Bowser, Charles (Athlete, Football Player)
1188 Dovetai
Virginia Beach, VA 23464, us

Bowsfield, Ted (Athlete, Baseball Player)
980 Briar Rose Ln
Nipomo, CA 93444-8989, USA

Bowyer, Clint (Race Car Driver)
Richard Childress Racing
425 Industrial Dr.
Welcome, NC 27374, USA

Bowyer, William (Artist)
12 Cleveland Ave Chiswick
London W4 1SN, UNITED KINGDOM (UK)

Bowyer Jr, Walter (Athlete, Football Player)
203 Main St N
Bethlehem, CT 06751, USA

Boxberger, Loa (Politician)
P O Box 708
Russell, KS 67665-0708, USA

Boxer, Barbara (Politician)
136 Yale Dr
Rancho Mirage, CA 92270-3677, USA

Boxerbaum, David (Actor)
c/o Staff Member *Agency for the Performing Arts (APA-Nashville)*
3017 Poston Ave
Nashville, TN 37203

Boxleitner, Bruce (Actor)
18600 Ringling St
Tarzana, CA 91356, USA

Boxx, Gillian (Athlete, Olympic Athlete, Softball Player)
15111 Chelsea Dr
San Jose, CA 95124-2704, USA

Boxx, Shannon (Athlete, Olympic Athlete, Soccer Player)
1454 Monterey Blvd
Apt 102
Hermosa Beach, CA 90254-3642, USA

Boy, Soulja (Musician)
c/o Michael Becker *Imprint Entertainment*
100 Universal City Plaza
Bungalow #7152
Universal City, CA 91608, USA

Boyar, Lombardo (Actor)
Greene & Associates
526 North Larchmont Blvd
#201
Los Angeles, CA 90004

Boyarsky, Jerry (Athlete, Football Player)
RR 1 Box 357
Olyphant, PA 18447, USA

Boyce, Charles (Cartoonist)
563 Shorely Dr Apt 101
Barrington, IL 60010-3313, USA

Boyce, Kim (Music Group)
200 Nathan Dr
Hollister, MO 65672, USA

Boycott, Geoffrey (Cricketer)
Cricket Club
Headingley Cricket Ground Leeds
Yorks LS6 3BY, UNITED KINGDOM (UK)

Boyd, Alan S (Misc, Secretary)
437 5th Avenue S
Apt 3D
Edmonds, WA 98020-3460, USA

Boyd, Billy (Actor)
c/o Sarah Jackson *Seven Summits Pictures & Management*
8906 W Olympic Blvd
Ground Floor
Beverly Hills, CA 90211, USA

Boyd, Bobby (Athlete, Football Player)
2105 Lansdowne Dr
Garland, TX 75040, us

Boyd, Brandon (Musician)
515 Marguerita Ave
Santa Monica, CA 90402, USA

Boyd, Brent (Athlete, Football Player)
948 N Coast Highway 101
Apt 185
Encinitas, CA 92024, USA

Boyd, Carrie Griffin (Stylist)
c/o Staff Member *Fifty8 Artists*
58 W Huron St
Chicago, IL 60610, USA

Boyd, Cayden (Actor)
c/o Ellen Drantch-Billet *EDB Management*
1953 Barry Ave
Los Angeles, CA 90025-5381, USA

Boyd, Cletis L (Clete) (Baseball Player)
2034 20th Avenue Parkway
Indian Rocks Beach, FL 33785, USA

Boyd, Danny (Athlete, Football Player)
4167 Day Bridge Pl
Ellenton, FL 34222, us

Boyd, Davis (Oil Can) (Athlete, Baseball Player)
PO Box 8058
Meridian, MS 39303-8058, USA

Boyd, Dennis (Athlete, Baseball Player)
45 Swan St
East Providence, RI 02914-2406, USA

Boyd, Elmo (Athlete, Football Player)
219 S Short St
Troy, OH 45373, USA

Boyd, Fred (Athlete, Basketball Player)
10915 Open Trail Rd
Bakersfield, CA 93311-2892, USA

Boyd, Gary (Athlete, Baseball Player)
15308 Haas Ave
Gardena, CA 90249, USA

Boyd, Greg (Baseball Player)
9 Inez Way
Stafford, VA 22554-5515, USA

Boyd, Greg P (Athlete, Football Player)
4021 N 59th St
Phoenix, AZ 85018, USA

Boyd, Herbert W (Inventor, Misc)
P O Box 7318
Rancho Santa Fe, CA 92067, USA

Boyd, James (Athlete, Football Player)
3355 Sweetwater Rd Apt 10204
Lawrenceville, GA 30044, USA

Boyd, Jason (Athlete, Baseball Player)
7962 State Route 140
Edwardsville, IL 62025-6110, USA

Boyd, Jenna (Actor)
c/o Ellen Drantch-Billet *EDB Management*
1953 Barry Ave
Los Angeles, CA 90025-5381, USA

Boyd, Johnny (Race Car Driver)
7635 N. Gearhart
Fresno, CA 93120-2548, USA

Boyd, Lance (Stylist)
c/o Staff Member *Art House Management*
1548 16th St
Santa Monica, CA 90404, USA

Boyd, Lavell (Athlete, Football Player)
4421 Charlotte Ann Dr
Louisville, KY 40216, us

Boyd, Lynda (Actor)
c/o Michael Greene *Greene & Associates*
1901 Avenue Of The Stars Ste 130
Los Angeles, CA 90067, USA

Boyd, Malcolm (Religious Leader, Writer)
Saint Augustine-by-Sea Episcpal Church
1227 4th St
Santa Monica, CA 90401, USA

Boyd, Malik (Athlete, Football Player)
5815 Fairway Manor Ln
Spring, TX 77373-, USA

Boyd, Paul D (Nobel Prize Laureate)
1033 Somera Road
Los Angeles, CA 90077, USA

Boyd, Randy (Athlete, Hockey Player)
1769 Blackwillow Dr.
Marietta, GA 30066-1954, USA

Boyd, Richard A (Misc)
Fraternal Order of Police
2100 Gardiner Lane
Louisville, KY 40205, USA

Boyd, Robert (Athlete, Golfer)
828 Robert E Lee Dr
Wilmington, NC 28412-7138, USA

Boyd, Stanley Col (Aviator)
2800 Ringgold Ct
Woodbridge, VA 22192-1212, USA

Boyd, Stephen (Athlete, Football Player)
1268 Marginal Rd
Atlantic Beach, NY 11509, USA

Boyd, Stuart Briggen (Aviator)
6805 S 2125 E
Ogden, UT 84405-9830, USA

Boyd, Tommie (Athlete, Football Player)
46824 Amberwood Dr
Shelby Township, MI 48317, us

Boyens, Philippa (Writer)
c/o Nick Reed *ICM Partners (ICM-LA)*
10250 Constellation Blvd Fl 7
Los Angeles, CA 90067, USA

Boyer, Blaine (Athlete, Baseball Player)
4825 Bellingham Dr
Marietta, GA 30062-6412, USA

Boyer, Brant (Athlete, Football Player)
1683 Old Lake Ln
Kaysville, UT 84037, USA

Boyer, Cloyd (Athlete, Baseball Player)
14528 County Road 210
Jasper, MO 64755-7226, USA

Boyer, Mark (Athlete, Football Player)
21942 Kaneohe Ln
Huntington Beach, CA 92646, USA

Boyer, Paul (Nobel Prize Laureate)
1033 Somera Rd
Los Angeles, CA 90077-2625, USA

Boyer, Verdi (Athlete, Football Player)
300 N Lake
Suite 930
Pasadena, CA 91101, USA

Boyer, Wally (Athlete, Hockey Player)
400 Manly St.
Midland, ON L4R 3E3, Canada

Boyes, Brad (Athlete, Hockey Player)
11711 Fawnridge Dr.
St. Louis, MO 63131-4235, USA

Boyett, Lon (Athlete, Football Player)
902 W Newgrove St
Lancaster, CA 93534, USA

Boyette, Garland (Athlete, Football Player)
4003 E Valley Dr
Missouri City, TX 77459, USA

Boy Hits Car (Music Group)
c/o Staff Member *Wind-up Records*
72 Madison Ave Fl 8
New York, NY 10016, USA

Boykin, Deral (Athlete, Football Player)
3972 Lake Run Blvd
Kent, OH 44224, USA

Boykin, Gerda (Athlete, Golfer)
3019 Colonnade Ct NW
Albuquerque, NM 87107, USA

Boykin, William G (General)
DepUndersecretary Intelligence
Defense Dept Pentagon
Washington, DC 20301, USA

Boykins, Earl
7572 Sanctuary Cir
Brecksville, OH 44141-3195, USA

Boyko, Darren (Athlete, Hockey Player)
1341 Wolseley Ave
Winnipeg, MB R3G 1H8, Canada

Boylan, Barbara (Dancer)
7945 S Eudora Cir
Centennial, CO 80122, USA

Boylan, Dean (Athlete, Hockey Player)
300 2nd Ave Unit 3169
Needham Heights, MA 02494-2959, USA

Boylan, Eileen (Actor)
c/o Staff Member *Stone Manners Salners Agency (LA)*
9911 W Pico Blvd Ste 1400
Los Angeles, CA 90035, USA

Boylan, Jeanne
c/o Staff Member *WmE2 (WMA-LA)*
1 William Morris Pl
Beverly Hills, CA 90212, USA

Boylan, Jim (Athlete, Football Player)
13155 Portofino Dr
Del Mar, CA 92014, USA

Boyland, Dorian (Athlete, Baseball Player)
548 Setting Sun Dr
Winter Garden, FL 34787-5933, USA

Boyle, Brian (Athlete, Hockey Player)
The Orr Hockey Group
PO Box 290836
Charlestown, MA 02129-0215, USA

Boyle, Clune Charlotte (Swimmer)
50 Brown's Grove Box 31
Scottsville, NY 14546, USA

Boyle, Dan (Athlete, Hockey Player)
18232 Daves Ave
Monte Sereno, CA 95030-3112, USA

Boyle, Danny (Director)
c/o Robert Newman *WME (LA)*
9601 Wilshire Blvd Fl 3
Beverly Hills, CA 90210, USA

Boyle, Jim (Athlete, Football Player)
920 Beechmeadow Ln
Cincinnati, OH 45238, USA

Boyle, Lara Flynn (Actor)
c/o Gina Rugolo-Judd *Rugolo Entertainment*
195 S Beverly Dr
Suite 400
Beverly Hills, CA 90212, USA

Boyle, Lisa (Actor, Model)
7336 Santa Monica Blvd
#776
W Hollywood, CA 90046, USA

Boyle, Susan (Musician, Reality TV Star)
5 Riddoch Hill View
Blackburn
Bathgate EH47 7LZ, UK

Boyle, T Coraghessan (Writer)
University of Southern California
English Dept
Los Angeles, CA 90089, USA

Boyne, Walter (Writer)
10833 Margate Rd
Silver Spring, MD 20901-1615, USA

Boynes, Winford (Athlete, Basketball Player)
8979 Haflinger Way
Elk Grove, CA 95757-3262, USA

Boynton, George (Athlete, Football Player)
917 Sartain Dr
Andrews, TX 79714, USA

Boynton, John (Athlete, Football Player)
PO Box 468
Pikeville, TN 37367, USA

Boynton, Nick (Athlete, Hockey Player)
3326 N Valencia Ln
Phoenix, AZ 85018-6611, USA

Boynton, Robert M (Doctor, Misc)
6632 Grulla St
Carlsbad, CA 92009-5315, USA

Boynton, Sandra (Artist, Writer)
c/o Staff Member *Simon & Schuster*
1230 Avenue of the Americas
New York, NY 10020, USA

Boys, Trevor (Race Car Driver)
Boys Will Be Boys Racing
610 Performance Rd .
Mooresville, NC 28115, USA

Boysaw, Gregory (Athlete, Football Player)
P.O. Box 501762
Indianapolis, IN 46250, USA

boysetsfire (Music Group)
c/o Staff Member *Wind-up Records*
72 Madison Ave Fl 8
New York, NY 10016, USA

Boys Like Girls (Music Group)
c/o Staff Member *Primary Talent International (UK)*
The Primary Building
10-11 Jockeys Fields
London WC1R 4BN, UK

Boyz II Men (Music Group)
c/o Joann Mignano *Krupp Kommunications*
59 West 19th St Fl 4 #4C
New York, NY 10011, USA

Bozak, Tyler (Athlete, Hockey Player)
Newport Sports Management
400-201 City Centre Dr
Attn Wade Arnott
Mississauga, ON L5B 2T4, Canada

Bozarth, Marci (Athlete, Golfer)
30417 Briarcliff Dr
Georgetown, TX 78628, USA

Boze, Marshall (Athlete, Baseball Player)
13139 Windv Lea Ln
Huntersville, NC 28078-2230, USA

Bozek, Steve (Athlete, Hockey Player)
8410 E Whispering Wind Dr
Scottsdale, AZ 85255-2863, USA

Bozilovic, Ivana (Actor)
c/o Jon Orlando *WNWN Media*
348 S. Hauser Blvd #PH414
Los Angeles, CA 90036, USA

Boznic, Josip Cardinal (Religious Leader)
Zagreb Archdiocese
Kaptol 31 PP 553
Zagreb Hrvatska 10001, CROATIA

Bozo, Laura (Actor)
c/o Staff Member *Telemundo*
2470 West 8th Avenue
Hialeah, FL 33010, USA

Bozza, Anthony (Writer)
c/o Richard Abate *3 Arts Entertainment - NY*
49 West 27th St.
5th Floor
New York, NY 10001, USA

BR5-49 (Music Group, Musician)
c/o Staff Member *Creative Artists Agency (CAA-TN)*
3310 West End Ave
5th Floor
Nashville, TN 37203, USA

Braase, Ordell (Athlete, Football Player)
204 3rd St W
Apt 201
Bradenton, FL 34205, USA

Brabham, Daniel (Athlete, Football Player)
16378 Pailette St
Prairieville, LA 70769, USA

Brabham, John A (Jack) (Race Car Driver)
5 Ruxley Lane Ewell
Surrey KT19 0JB, UNITED KINGDOM (UK)

Brabham, Sir Jack (Race Car Driver)
Suite 404 Bag No 1
Robina Town Centre, Queenstown 4230, Australia

Bracco, Lorraine (Actor)
460 Butter Ln
Bridgehampton, NY 11932, USA

Brace, William F (Geophysicist, Misc, Physicist)
49 Liberty St
Concord, MA 01742, USA

Bracelin, Greg (Athlete, Football Player)
5465 Calumet Ave
La Jolia, CA 92037, USA

Bracewell, Ronald N (Engineer)
836 Santa Fe Ave
Stanford, CA 94305, USA

Bracey, Luke (Actor)
c/o Mark Morrissey *Mark Morrissey and Associates*
16 Princess Ave
Rosebery
Sydney NSW 2018, Australia

Bracher, Karl D (Historian, Misc, Politician)
Unversitat Bonn
Stationsweg 17
Bonn 53127, GERMANY

Bracht, Stephanie (Athlete, Golfer)
2004 Delancey Dr
Norman, OK 73071-3872, USA

Brack, Kenny (Race Car Driver)
Team Rahal
4601 Lyman Dr
Hillard, OH 43026, USA

Brack, Reginald K Jr (Publisher)
12 Huntzinger Dr
Greenwich, CT 06831, USA

Bracken, Don (Athlete, Football Player)
15950 W Diamond St
Goodyear, AZ 85338, USA

Brackenbury, Curt (Athlete, Hockey Player)
W378N5861 Valley Rd
Oconomowoc, WI 53066-2246, USA

Brackens, Tony (Athlete, Football Player)
193 Private Road 407
Fairfield, TX 75840, USA

Brackensick, Deandre (Musician)
c/o Staff Member *19 Entertainment - LA*
9000 W Sunset Blvd #1574
West Hollywood, CA 90069, USA

Brackett, Gary (Athlete, Football Player)
7808 Parkdale Dr
Zionsville, IN 46077, us

Brackett, Griffin (Model)
860 NE 73rd St
Miami, FL 33138-5228

Brackett, M L (Athlete, Football Player)
1216 Monte Vista Dr
Gadsden, AL 35904, USA

Brackins, Charles (Athlete, Football Player)
200 Hallow Tre Ln
Apt 1907
Houston, TX 77090-2815, USA

Bradberry, Allyson (Stylist)
c/o Staff Member *Arlene Wilson Management*
807 N Jefferson St
#200
Milwaukee, WI 53202, USA

Bradberry, Gary (Race Car Driver)
c/o *Tri Star Motorsports*
6006 Ball Park Rd
Thomasville, NC 27360, USA

Bradbury, Allyson (Stylist)
c/o Staff Member *Directions USA*
3717-C W Market St
Greensboro, NC 27403, USA

Bradbury, Gary (Race Car Driver)
Hoover Motorsports
10705 Bringle Perry Rd
Salisbury, NC 28146, USA

Bradbury, Janette Lane (Actor)
10817 King St
Toluca Lake, CA 91602, USA

Bradbury, Norris (Scientist)
1069 Camino Manana
Santa Fe, NM 87501-1088, USA

Braddock, Paige (Cartoonist)
7596 Bodega Ave
Sebastopol, CA 95472-3654, USA

Braddy, Johanna (Actor)
c/o Julian Rosenberg *Tower 10 Entertainment*
412 S. Willaman Dr #507
Los Angeles, CA 90048, USA

Brademas, John (Educator)
New York University
Presindent's Emeritus Office
New York, NY 10012, USA

Braden, Dallas
1459 W Walnut St
Stockton, CA 95203-1527, USA

Braden, Jeannine (Stylist)
c/o Staff Member *Luxe*
6442 Santa Monica Blvd
#200-B
Los Angeles, CA 90038, USA

Braden, Vic (Coach, Tennis Player)
22000 Trabuco Canyon Road
Trabuco Canyon, CA 92678, USA

Bradey, Don (Athlete, Baseball Player)
330 Council Bluff Pkwy
Murfreesboro, TN 37127-8317, USA

Bradford, Barbara Taylor (Writer)
450 Park Ave Bsmt
New York, NY 10022-2630, USA

Bradford, Buddy (Athlete, Baseball Player)
6440 Springpark Ave
Los Angeles, CA 90056-2222, USA

Bradford, Chad (Athlete, Baseball Player)
218 Trace Cir
Raymond, MS 39154-9555, USA

Bradford, Corey (Athlete, Football Player)
13002 Highway 955 E
Ethel, LA 70730, us

Bradford, Jesse (Actor)
2101 Loma Vista Pl
Los Angeles, CA 90039, USA

Bradford, Paul (Athlete, Football Player)
2239 Pulgas Ave
Palo Alto, CA 94303, USA

Bradford, Richard (Actor)
2511 Canyon Dr
Los Angeles, CA 90068, USA

Bradford, Ronnie (Athlete, Football Player)
965 Allen Lake Ln
Suwanee, GA 30024, USA

Bradford, Sam (Athlete, Football Player)
c/o Tom Condon *CAA - St. Louis*
222 S Central Ave
Suite 1008
St Louis, MO 63105, USA

Bradford, William (Business Person)
Halliburton Co
Lincoln Plaza 500 N Akard St
Dallas, TX 75201, USA

Bradfute, Byron (Athlete, Football Player)
939 Moonglow Ave
New Braunfels, TX 78130, USA

Bradlee, Benjamin C (Journalist)
3014 N St NW
Washington, DC 20007-3404, USA

Bradley, Alonzo (Athlete, Basketball Player)
1713 Briaroaks Dr
Flower Mound, TX 75e28-3482, USA

Bradley, Bert (Athlete, Baseball Player)
6039 Old State Rd
Mattoon, IL 61938-8815, USA

Bradley, Bill (Basketball Player, Olympic Athlete, Politician)
Betty Sue Flowers
200 Central Park S #15-B
New York, NY 10019-1443, USA

Bradley, Bob (Coach, Soccer Player)
Chicago Fire
980 N Michigan Ave #1998
Chicago, IL 60611, USA

Bradley, Brian (Athlete, Hockey Player)
6417 E MacLaurin Dr
Tampa, FL 33647-1171, USA

Bradley, Bruce (Athlete, Misc)
262 Saint Joseph Ave
Long Beach, CA 90803, USA

Bradley, Carlos (Athlete, Football Player)
1316 E Cliveden St
Philadelphia, PA 19119, USA

Bradley, Charles (Athlete, Basketball Player)
10310 Mountshire Cir
Highlands Ranch, CO 80126-7502, USA

Bradley, Christopher (Actor)
c/o Staff Member *Ford/Robert Black Agency*
4032 N Miller Rd
Suite 104
Scottsdale, AZ 85251, USA

Bradley, Dick (Cartoonist, Misc)
10176 Corporate Square Dr #200
Saint Louis, MO 63132, USA

Bradley, Doug (Actor)
c/o Elaine Murphy *Elaine Murphy Associates*
50 High St
Suite 1
London E11 2RJ, UK

Bradley, Dudley (Athlete, Basketball Player)
9830 Clanford Rd
Randallstown, MD 21133-25e8, USA

Bradley, Ed (Athlete, Football Player)
206 Mossy Oak Dr
Winston Salem, NC 27127, us

Bradley, Frank (Baseball Player)
Kansas City Monarchs
PO Box 516
Benton, LA 71006-0516, USA

Bradley, Gordon (Coach, Soccer Player)
14300 Bakerwood Place
Haymarket, VA 20169, USA

Bradley, Henry (Athlete, Football Player)
42927 Corte Siero
Temecula, CA 92592, us

Bradley, Kathleen (Actor)
Kazarian/Spencer
11365 Ventura Blvd #100
Studio City, CA 91604, USA

Bradley, Luther (Athlete, Football Player)
19575 Stratford Rd
Detroit, MI 48221, USA

Bradley, Mark (Athlete, Baseball Player)
1605 S Nebraska St
Pine Bluff, AR 71601, USA

Bradley, Michael (Athlete, Basketball Player)
6150 Blackjack Ct N
Punta Gorda, FL 33982, USA

Bradley, Michael (Mike) (Athlete, Golfer)
17914 Burnt Oak Ln
Lithia, FL 33547-4802, USA

Bradley, Milton (Athlete, Baseball Player)
5359 Oak Park Ave
Encino, CA 91316-2627, USA

Bradley, Myron (Athlete, Olympic Athlete, Water Polo Player)
262 Saint Joseph Ave
Long Beach, CA 90803-1720, USA

Bradley, Otha (Athlete, Football Player)
P.O. Box 59071
Los Angeles, CA 90059, USA

Bradley, Phil (Athlete, Baseball Player)
6950 Seminole Ct
Columbia, MO 65203-9669, USA

Bradley, Rebecca (Athlete, Golfer)
14443 W Lee Shore Dr
Willis, TX 77318-7407, USA

Bradley, Robert A (Physicist)
2465 S Downing St
Denver, CO 80210, USA

Bradley, Ryan (Athlete, Baseball Player)
3454 Alder Pl
Chino Hills, CA 91709-2005, USA

Bradley, Scott (Athlete, Baseball Player)
43 Chicory Ln
Pennington, NJ 08534-1926, USA

Bradley, Shawn (Athlete, Basketball Player)
6e6 Sunny Flowers Ln
Salt Lake City, UT 841e7-5411, USA

Bradley, Tom (Athlete, Baseball Player)
4104 Woodberry St
University Park, MD 20782-1169, USA

Bradley Jr, Harold (Athlete, Football Player)
1302 Asbury Ave
Evanston, IL 60201, USA

Bradshaw (Wrestler)
139 Denny Ln
Athens, TX 75751

Bradshaw, Craig (Athlete, Football Player)
9481 Carson Dr
Lantana, TX 76226, us

Bradshaw, James A (Athlete, Football Player)
449 Tresham Rd
Gahanna, OH 43230, USA

Bradshaw, Jim (Athlete, Football Player)
5653 Eagle Harbor Dr
Westerville, OH 43081, us

Bradshaw, John (Actor, Director, Writer)
c/o Victoria Wisdom *Wisdom Literary*
287 S. Robertson Blvd
Suite 258
Beverly Hills, CA 90211, USA

Bradshaw, Morris (Athlete, Football Player)
82 Steuben Bay
Alameda, CA 94502, USA

Bradshaw, Terry (Athlete, Football Player, Sportscaster)
5912 Eagle Mountain Dr
Argyle, TX 76226, USA

Brady, Beau (Actor)
c/o Darren Gray *Darren Gray Management*
2 Marston Ln
Portsmouth
Hampshire PO3 5TW, UK

Brady, Brian (Athlete, Baseball Player)
920 W 23rd St
Odessa, TX 79763-2504, USA

Brady, Charles E (Astronaut)
92 Red Wing Lane
Eastsound, WA 98245-8517, USA

Brady, Doug (Athlete, Baseball Player)
5878 Iron Bridge Rd
Chatham, IL 62629-8014, USA

Brady, Ed (Athlete, Football Player)
5755 White Path Ln
Hamilton, OH 45011, USA

Brady, James (Politician)
Handgun Control 1225 I St NW Ste 1100
Washington, DC 20005-3991, USA

Brady, Jeff (Athlete, Football Player)
1506 NW 37th Pl
Cape Coral, FL 33993, USA

Brady, Jim (Athlete, Baseball Player)
1072 Meadow View Ln
Saint Augustine, FL 32092-1055, USA

Brady, Kevin (Congressman, Politician)
301 Cannon HOB
Washington, DC 20515, USA

Brady, Kyle (Athlete, Football Player)
2221 Alicia Ln
Atlantic Beach, FL 32233, USA

Brady, Neil (Athlete, Hockey Player)
Anipet Animal Supplies
125-4300 26 St NE
Attn: Warehouse Manager
Calgary, AB T1Y 7H7, Canada

Brady, Nicholas F (Politician)
Darby Overseas Investments
PO Box 1410W
Easton, MD 21601-8927, USA

Brady, Orla (Actor)
19534 Bowers Dr
Topanga, CA 90290, USA

Brady, Pat (Cartoonist)
United Feature Syndicate
200 Madison Ave
New York, NY 10016, USA

Brady, Patrick (Athlete, Football Player)
8990 Lombardi Rd
Reno, NV 89511, USA

Brady, Patrick H (General)
10419 Felsblock Ln
New Braunfels, TX 78132-4317, USA

Brady, Ray (Correspondent)
CBS-TV
News Dept 524 W 57th St
New York, NY 10019, USA

Brady, Rickey
609 Holly Dr
Edmond, OK 73034, us

Brady, Robert (Congressman, Politician)
102 Cannon HOB
Washington, DC 20515, USA

Brady, Roscoe O (Misc)
6026 Valerian Lane
Rockville, MD 20852, USA

Brady, Sarah (Activist)
Handgun Control
1225 I St NW #1100
Washington, DC 20005, USA

Brady, Tina (Stylist)
Stewart Talent
58 W. Huron
Chicago, IL 60610, USA

Brady, Tom (Athlete, Football Player)
12780 Chalon Rd
Los Angeles, CA 90049, USA

Brady, Wayne (Actor, Comedian, Musician, Producer)
14888 Valley Vista Blvd
Sherman Oaks, CA 91403, USA

Braeden, Eric (Actor)
13723 Romany Dr
Pacific Palisades, CA 90272, USA

Braff, Zach (Actor, Writer)
8816 Lookout Mountain Ave
Los Angeles, CA 90046, USA

Braga, Alice (Actor)
c/o Will Ward *ROAR (LA)*
9701 Wilshire Blvd
8th Floor
Los Angeles, CA 90212, USA

Braga, Brannon (Writer)
c/o Staff Member *WME (LA)*
9601 Wilshire Blvd Fl 3
Beverly Hills, CA 90210, USA

Braga, Sonia (Actor)
149 Avenue C #2R
New York, NY 10009, USA

Bragg, Billy (Musician)
Sincere Mgmt
6 Bravington Road
#6
London W9 3AH, UNITED KINGDOM (UK)

Bragg, Darrell B (Misc)
University of British Columbia
Vancouver BC V6T 2AZ, CANADA

Bragg, Darren (Athlete, Baseball Player)
163 Patriot Rd
Southbury, CT 06488-1274, USA

Bragg, Don (Athlete, Olympic Athlete, Track Athlete)
965 Oak St
Clayton, CA 94517-1313, USA

Bragg, Melvyn (Writer)
12 Hampstead Hill Gardens
London NW3 2PL, UNITED KINGDOM (UK)

Bragg, Mike (Athlete, Football Player)
807 5 6th St
Saint Charles, MO 63301, USA

Bragg, Rick (Journalist)
New York Times 229 W 43rd St
New York, NY 10036-3913, USA

Braggs, Byron (Athlete, Football Player)
19469 Mill Dam Pl
Leesburg, VA 20176, USA

Braggs, Glenn (Athlete, Baseball Player)
28369 Falcon Crest Dr
Canyon Country, CA 91351-5016, USA

Braggs, Stephen (Athlete, Football Player)
4110 Pickfair St
Houston, TX 77026-, USA

Bragnalo, Rick (Athlete, Hockey Player)
515 Christine St E
Thunder Bay, ON P7E 4P3, Canada

Bragonier, Dennis (Athlete, Football Player)
P.O. Box 1206
Roseville, CA 95678, USA

Braham, Rich (Athlete, Football Player)
19 Miramichi Trl
Morgantown, WV 26508, USA

Brahaney, Thomas F (Tom) (Athlete, Football Player)
1602 W Cuthbert Ave
Midland, TX 79701, USA

Brainard, Don (Horse Racer)
880 Banks Rd
Coconut Creek, FL 33063-4621, USA

Brainin, Nobert (Musician)
19 Prowse Ave
Busbey Heath
Herts WD2 1JS, UNITED KINGDOM (UK)

Brainville, Ives (Actor)
34 Cours de Vincennes
Paris F-75012, France

Brakes, The (Music Group)
c/o Staff Member *Paradigm (Monterey)*
404 W Franklin St
Monterey, CA 93940, USA

Bramall of Busfield, Edwin N W (Misc)
House of Lords
Westminster
London SW1A 0PW, UNITED KINGDOM (UK)

Braman, Norman (Business Person, Football Executive)
1 Indian Creek Dr
Indian Creek Village, FL 33154, USA

Bramhall, Mark (Actor)
c/o Alexandra Karrys *Divine Management*
3822 Latrobe St
Los Angeles, CA 90031

Bramhill, Gina (Actor)
c/o Staff Member *ICM*
76 Oxford St
London W1D 1BS, UK

Bramlet, Casey (Athlete, Football Player)
801 15th St
Wheatland, WY 82201, US

Bramlett, John (Athlete, Football Player)
159 Cotton Ridge Cv S
Cordova, TN 38018, USA

Brammell, Abby (Actor)
c/o Robert (Rob) Gomez *Precision Entertainment*
6338 Wilshire Blvd
Los Angeles, CA 90048, USA

Brammer, Mark (Athlete, Football Player)
1680 Amherst St
Buffalo, NY 14214, USA

Branagh, Kenneth (Actor, Director)
c/o Judy Hofflund *Hofflund/Polone*
9465 Wilshire Blvd #420
Beverly Hills, CA 90212, USA

Branca, John G (Attorney, Attorney General, General)
Ziffren Brittenham Branca
1801 Century Park West
Los Angeles, CA 90067, USA

Branca, Ralph (Athlete, Baseball Player)
99 Biltmore Ave
Rye, NY 10580-1837, USA

Brancaccio, David
2100 Crystal Dr
Arlington, Virginia 22202, USA

Brancati, Paula (Actor)
AMI Artists Management
c/o Shari Quallenburg
464 King St E
Toronto, ON M5A 1L7, CANADA

Brancato, George (Athlete, Football Player)
25 Nancy Ave
Nepean, ON K2H 8L3 Canada, USA

Brancato, John D (JD) (Producer, Writer)
c/o Staff Member *Broder Webb Chervin Silbermann Agency, The (BWCS)*
10250 Constellation Blvd
Los Angeles, CA 90067-6200, USA

Brancato Jr, Lillo (Actor)
c/o Craig Shapiro *ICM Partners (ICM-LA)*
10250 Constellation Blvd Fl 7
Los Angeles, CA 90067, USA

Branch, Adrian (Athlete, Basketball Player)
803 Grand Provincial Ave
Matthews, NC 28105-1833, USA

Branch, Clifford (Cliff) (Athlete, Coach, Football Coach, Football Player)
2071 Stonefield Ln
Santa Rosa, CA 95403, USA

Branch, Colin (Athlete, Football Player)
121 Three Greens Dr
Huntersville, NC 28078, us

Branch, Deion (Athlete, Football Player)
13382 W Sherbern Dr
Carmel, IN 46032, us

Branch, Harvey (Athlete, Baseball Player)
4995 Jolly Dr
Memphis, TN 38109-7123, USA

Branch, Michelle (Musician, Songwriter)
4415 Forsythe Pl
Nashville, TN 37205, USA

Branch, Reggie (Athlete, Football Player)
515 San Lanta Cir
Sanford, FL 32771, USA

Branch, Roy (Athlete, Baseball Player)
5322 Terry Ave
Saint Louis, MO 63120-2021, USA

Branch, Vanessa (Actor)
c/o Staff Member *3 Arts Entertainment Inc*
9460 Wilshire Blvd
7th Floor
Beverly Hills, CA 90210, USA

Branch, William B (Writer)
53 Cortlandt Ave
New Rochelle, NY 10801, USA

Branco, Antonio (Stylist)
c/o Celebrity Stylist *Bryan Bantry*
900 Broadway Ste 400
New York, NY 10003, USA

Brand, Colette (Skier)
Rigistr 24
Baar 6340, SWITZERLAND

Brand, Daniel (Dan) (Wrestler)
4321 Bridgeview Dr
Oakland, CA 94602, USA

Brand, Elton (Athlete, Basketball Player)
942 S Mansfield Ave
Los Angeles, CA 90036, USA

Brand, Glen (Athlete, Olympic Athlete, Wrestler)
PO Box 6069
Omaha, NE 68106-0069, USA

Brand, Jolene (Actor)
G.S. Prod
8321 Beverly Blvd
Los Angeles, CA 90048, USA

Brand, Joshua (Producer)
c/o Staff Member *WmE2 (WMA-LA)*
1 William Morris Pl
Beverly Hills, CA 90212, USA

Brand, Julie (Athlete, Golfer)
6 Emerald Way
Ocala, FL 34472-2333, USA

Brand, Myles (Educator)
Indiana University
President's Office
Bloomington, IN 47405, USA

Brand, Neville (Actor)
c/o Staff Member *ICM Partners (ICM-LA)*
10250 Constellation Blvd Fl 7
Los Angeles, CA 90067, USA

Brand, Oscar (Musician, Songwriter, Writer)
Gypsy Hill Music
141 Baker Hill Road
Great Neck, NY 11023, USA

Brand, Robert (Designer)
508 W End Ave
New York, NY 10024, USA

Brand, Ron (Athlete, Baseball Player)
4421 Staten Island Dr
Plano, TX 75024-3867, USA

Brand, Russell (Actor, Comedian)
1868 N Doheny Dr
West Hollywood, CA 90069, USA

Brand, Simon (Director)
5513 Tuxedo Terr
Los Angeles, CA 90068, USA

Brand, Steven (Actor)
c/o Brian Medavoy *Medavoy Management*
10203 Santa Monica Blvd
Suite 400
Los Angeles, CA 90067, USA

Brand, Vance D (Astronaut)
NASA Dryden Flight Center
21825 Hidden Canyon Dr
Tehachapi, CA 93561-9528, USA

Brandauer, Klaus Maria (Actor)
Novapool Gmbh
Paul Lincke Ufer 42-43
Berlin 10999, GERMANY

Brandenburg, Dan" (Athlete, Football Player)
1028 Dewitt Ave
Encinitas, CA 92024-, us

Brandenburg, Mark (Athlete, Baseball Player)
152 Cottonwood Dr
Coppell, TX 75019-2511, USA

Brandenstein, Daniel C (Astronaut)
12802 Tri-City Beach Road
Baytown, TX 77520, USA

Brandenstein, Daniel C Captain (Astronaut)
15203 Greenleaf Ln
Houston, TX 77062-3672, USA

Brandes, John (Athlete, Football Player)
905 Ashland Ct
Mansfield, TX 76063, USA

Brandi (Model)
Next Model Mgmt
23 Watts St
New York, NY 10013, USA

Brandler, Shellylyn (Actor)
c/o Simon Millar *Rumble Media*
1620 Broadway
Santa Monica, CA 90403, USA

Brandon, Barbara (Cartoonist)
Universal Press Syndicate
4520 Main St
Kansas City, MO 64111, USA

Brandon, Clark (Actor)
Jennings Assoc
28035 Dorothy Dr
#210A
Agoura, CA 91301, USA

Brandon, Darrell (Athlete, Baseball Player)
590 White Cliff Dr
Plymouth, MA 02360-1483, USA

Brandon, David (Athlete, Football Player)
218 Crystal Downs Way
Suwanee, GA 30024, us

Brandon, Jay (Writer)
PO Box 6764
San Antonio, TX 78209-0764, USA

Brandon, Jeb (Actor)
c/o Staff Member *WME (LA)*
9601 Wilshire Blvd Fl 3
Beverly Hills, CA 90210, USA

Brandon, John (Actor)
Coast to Coast Talent
3350 Barham Blvd
Los Angeles, CA 90068, USA

Brandon, Michael (Athlete, Football Player)
910 E Green St
Perry, FL 32347, USA

Brandon, Michael (Actor)
c/o Joel Dean *TalentWorks (LA)*
3500 W Olive Ave
Suite 1400
Burbank, CA 91505, USA

Brandon, Sam (Athlete, Football Player)
10827 County Road 148
Flint, TX 75762, us

Brandon, Terrell (Athlete, Basketball Player)
3310 NE Shaver St
Portland, OR 97212-1860, USA

Brands, Terry (Athlete, Olympic Athlete, Wrestler)
3744 Lacina Dr SW
Iowa City, IA 52240-8620, USA

Brands, Tom (Wrestler)
4494 Taft Ave SE
Lowa City, IA 52240, USA

Brands, X (Actor)
17171 Roscoe Blvd
#104
Northridge, CA 91325, USA

Brandt, Betsy (Actor)
2415 Green View Pl
Los Angeles, CA 90046, USA

Brandt, David" (Athlete, Football Player)
2214 Christine Ct SE
Grand Rapids, MI 49546-, us

Brandt, Hank (Actor)
Contemporary Artists
610 Santa Monica Blvd
#202
Santa Monica, CA 90401, USA

Brandt, Jackie (Athlete, Baseball Player)
602 Eastwood Ln
Leesburg, FL 34748-8777, USA

Brandt, Jim (Athlete, Football Player)
714 Zumbro Dr NW
Rochester, MN 55901, USA

Brandt, Jon (Musician)
Monterey Peninsula Artists
509 Hartnell St
Monterey, CA 93940, USA

Brandt, Kyle (Actor, Producer, Reality TV Star)
2317 N Parish Pl
Burbank, CA 91504, USA

Brandt, Paul (Musician)
c/o Staff Member *WmE2 (WMA-LA)*
1 William Morris Pl
Beverly Hills, CA 90212, USA

Brandt, Stella (Stylist)
c/o Staff Member *Anyway Productions*
870 Avenue of the Americas
New York, NY 10001, USA

Brandt, Victor (Actor)
H David Moss
733 Seward St
#PH
Los Angeles, CA 90038, USA

Branduardi, Angelo (Musician)
c/o Faustini Srl.
Via Veneto, 18
Pontoglio I-25 037, Italy

Brandy, J C (Actor)
Henderson/Hogan
8285 W Sunset Blvd
#1
West Hollywood, CA 90046, USA

Brandywine, Marcia (Correspondent)
743 Huntley Dr
Los Angeles, CA 90069, USA

B. Rangel, Charles (Congressman, Politician)
2354 Rayburn HOB
Washington, DC 20515, USA

Brannagh, Brigid (Actor)
c/o Adam Levine *Levine Okwu Erickson Management*
9601 Wilshire Blvd
3rd Floor
Beverly Hills, CA 90210, USA

Brannan, Charles F (Secretary)
3131 E Alameda Ave
Denver, CO 80209, USA

Brannan, Solomon (Athlete, Football Player)
2500 Cascade Rd SW
Atlanta, GA 30311, USA

Brannon, Ronald (Religious Leader)
Wesleyan Church
PO Box 50434
Indianapolis, IN 46250, USA

Branscomb, Lewis (Scientist)
Harvard University 1737 Cambridge St
Attn Physics Dept
Cambridge, MA 02138-3016, USA

Branshaw, David (Athlete, Golfer)
1617 Renaissance Way
Tampa, FL 33602, USA

Branson, Brad (Athlete, Basketball Player)
7419 Cortes Dr
Houston, TX 77083-3617, USA

Branson, Jeff (Athlete, Baseball Player)
10749 Spokane Ct
Union, KY 41091-7160, USA

Branson, Jeff (Athlete, Baseball Player)
Indianapolis Indians 501 W Maryland St
Attn Coaching Staff
Indianapolis, IN 46225-1041, USA

Branson, Jeff Branson (Actor)
c/o Robert Attermann *Abrams Artists Agency (LA)*
9200 Sunset Blvd
11th Floor
Los Angeles, CA 90069, USA

Branson, Jesse (Athlete, Basketball Player)
309 Forest Dr
Graham, NC 27253-4405, USA

Branson, Laura (Stylist)
c/o Staff Member *Judy Inc*
1 Yorkville Ave
Toronto ON M4W 1L1, Canada

Branson, Richard (Business Person)
Virgin Group
120 Campden Hill Rd
London W8 7AR, UNITED KINGDOM (UK)

Branstad, Terry (Politician)
E Grand Ave
Des Moines, IA 50319, USA

Brant, Marshall (Athlete, Baseball Player)
604 Scotland Dr
Santa Rosa, CA 95409-4419, USA

Brant, Tim (Sportscaster)
ABC-TV
Sports Dept
77 W 66th St
New York, NY 10023, USA

Brantley, Betsy (Actor)
c/o Staff Member *Mitchell K Stubbs & Assoc (MKS)*
8675 W. Washington Blvd
Suite 203
Culver City, CA 90232, USA

Brantley, Chris (Athlete, Football Player)
257 Hamilton Rd
Teaneck, NJ 07666, USA

Brantley, Cliff (Athlete, Baseball Player)
90 Grandview Ave
Staten Island, NY 10303-2000, USA

Brantley, Jeff (Athlete, Baseball Player)
104 Cherry Laurel Cv
Ridgeland, MS 39157-8643, USA

Brantley, Jeff (Athlete, Baseball Player)
Cincinnati Reds 100 Joe Nuxhall Way
Attn Broadcast Dept
Cincinnati, OH 45202-4109, USA

Brantley, John (Athlete, Football Player)
328 Jefferson Rd
Bishop, GA 30621, USA

Brantley, Michael (Athlete, Baseball Player)
Double Diamond Sports Management
7640 NW 79th Ave
Apt L8
Tamarac, FL 33321-2868, USA

Brantley, Mickey (Athlete, Baseball Player)
3095 SW Boxwood Cir
Port Saint Lucie, FL 34953-6971, USA

Brantley, Ollie (Athlete, Baseball Player)
215 S Alabama St
Marianna, AR 72360, USA

Brantley, Rick (Musician)
c/o Staff Member *Paradigm (Monterey)*
404 W Franklin St
Monterey, CA 93940, USA

Brantley, Scot (Athlete, Football Player)
11309 Galleria Dr
Tampa, FL 33618, USA

Branton, Gene (Athlete, Football Player)
7008 Hazelhurst Ct
Tampa, FL 33615, USA

Branyan, Russell (Athlete, Baseball Player)
3301 Running Springs Ct
Franklin, TN 37064-6257, USA

Brar, Karan (Actor)
c/o Jordyn Palos *Persona PR*
8840 Wilshire Blvd
Suite 212
Beverly Hills, CA 90211, USA

Brasar, Per-Olov (Athlete, Hockey Player)
Heden Lisshedsvagen 19
Leksand S-79329, Sweden

Brasco, Jim (Athlete, Basketball Player)
225 W Neck Rd
Huntington, NY 11743-2458, USA

Brashares, Ann (Writer)
c/o Jennifer Rudolph Walsh *WME (WMA-NY)*
1325 Ave of the Americas
New York, NY 10019, USA

Brashear, Carl (Misc)
3 Stuttaford Drive
Sandston, VA 23150-1434, USA

Braslow, Paul (Artist)
118 Saint Thomas Way
Belvedere Tiburon, CA 94920-1032, USA

Brassette, Amy (Actor)
c/o Marv Dauer *Marv Dauer Management*
11661 San Vicente Blvd
Suite 104
Los Angeles, CA 90049, USA

Brasseur, Claude (Actor)
Artmedia
20 Ave Rapp
Paris 75007, FRANCE

Brassfield, Darin (Race Car Driver)
541 Division St.
Campbel, CA 95008, USA

Brathwaite, Nicholas (Prime Minister)
House of Representatives
Saint George's, GRENADA

Bratkowski, Edmund R (Zeke) (Athlete, Coach, Football Player)
224 Anchors Lake Dr N
Santa Rosa Beach, FL 32459, USA

Bratt, Benjamin (Actor)
c/o Staff Member *Dontanville/Frattaroli (D/F)*
270 Lafayette St
Suite 402
New York, NY 10012, USA

Bratton, Creed (Musician)
Thomas Cassidy
11761 E Speedway Blvd
Tucson, AZ 85748, USA

Bratton, Jason (Athlete, Football Player)
1104 Regal Oak Dr
Longview, TX 75604, USA

Bratton, Joseph K (General)
5902 Blakeford Drive
Windermere, FL 34786-5601, USA

Bratton, William J (Lawyer)
5683 Holly Oak Dr
Los Angeles, CA 90068, USA

Bratz, Mike (Athlete, Basketball Player)
7503 Tillman Hill Rd
Colleyville, TX 76034-6929, USA

Bratzke, Chad (Athlete, Football Player)
10850 Ruby Ct
Carmel, IN 46032, USA

Brauer, Arik (Artist)
Academy of Fine Arts
Schillerplatz 3
Vienna 1010, AUSTRIA

Braugher, Andre (Actor)
393 Charlton Ave
S Orange, NJ 07079, USA

Brauman, John (Misc)
849 Tolman Dr
Palo ALto, CA 94305, USA

Braun, Allen (Scientist)
National Institute on Deafness
9000 Rockville Pike
Bethesda, MD 20892, USA

Braun, Carol Moseley (Politician)
1229 E 56th St
Chicago, IL 60637-1616, USA

Braun, Colin (Race Car Driver)
c/o Staff Member *Roush Fenway Racing Team*
4600 Roush Pl
Concord, NC 28027, USA

Braun, Nicholas (Actor)
c/o Staff Member *Levine Okwu Erickson Management*
6363 Wilshire Blvd
Suite 300
Los Angeles, CA 90048, USA

Braun, Pinkas (Actor, Director)
Unterdorf
8261
Hemishofen/SH, SWITZERLAND

Braun, Richard L (War Hero)
1912 Whittle Wood Road
Williamsburg, VA 23185, USA

Braun, Rick (Musician)
c/o Staff Member *APA Talent And Literary Agency (NY)*
45 W 45th St Ste 804
New York, NY 10036, USA

Braun, Ryan (Athlete, Baseball Player)
3769 Puerco Canyon Rd
Malibu, CA 90265, USA

Braun, Scooter (Business Person, Producer)
9066 St. Ives Dr
West Hollywood, CA 90069, USA

Braun, Steve (Actor)
c/o Tiffany Kuzon *Evolution Entertainment (LA)*
901 N Highland Ave
Los Angeles, CA 90038, USA

Braun, Steve (Athlete, Baseball Player)
108 Gainsboro Rd
Lawrence Township, NJ 08648-3916, USA

Braun, Tamara (Actor)
c/o Brianne Castillo-Huang *Schiff Company, The*
9465 Wilshire Blvd
Suite 480
Beverly Hills, CA 90212, USA

Braun, Wendy (Actor)
c/o Staff Member *House of Representatives, The*
1434 6th St
Suite 1
Santa Monica, CA 90401, USA

Braunduardi, Angelo (Musician)
Faustini Srl.
Via Veneto, 18
Pontoglio I-25 037, Italy

Braunwald, Eugene (Physicist)
Partners Healthcare
800 Boylston St
Boston, MA 02199, USA

Braver, Rita (Correspondent)
CBS-TV
News Dept
2020 M St NW
Washington, DC 20036, USA

Braverman, Bart (Actor)
c/o Staff Member *Henriksen Talent Management*
13024 Hesby St
Sherman Oaks, CA 91423, USA

Braverman, Chuck (Director, Producer)
Braverman Productions Inc
3000 Olympic Blvd
Santa Monica, CA 90404, USA

Bravo, Alex (Athlete, Football Player)
2316 Pine Ave
Manhattan Beach, CA 90266, USA

Bravo, Duncan (Actor)
3401 Oak Glen Dr
Los Angeles, CA 90068, USA

Braxton, Anthony (Composer)
Berkeley Agency
2608 9th St
Berkeley, CA 94710, USA

Braxton, David (Athlete, Football Player)
26898 Primrose Ln
Westlake, OH 44145, USA

Braxton, Tamar (Actor)
5697 Hoback Glen Rd
Hidden Hills, CA 91302, USA

Braxton, Toni (Musician, Songwriter)
10120 Empyrean Way #202
Los Angeles, CA 90067, USA

Braxton, Trina (Musician, Reality TV Star)
c/o Staff Member *Primary Wave Talent Management*
116 E 16th St
9th Floor
New York, NY 10003, USA

Braxton, Tyrone S (Athlete, Football Player)
455 Keamey St
Denver, CO 80220, USA

Braxton III, Hezekiah (Athlete, Football Player)
12715 Norwood Ln
Fort Washington, MD 20744, USA

Bray, Charles (Athlete, Football Player)
1321 Millersport Hwy
Amherst, NY 14221-2900, USA

Bray, Deanne (Actor)
c/o Sid Craig *Craig Management*
2240 Miramonte Circle East
Unit C
Palm Springs, CA 92264-5734, USA

Bray, Kevin (Actor, Director, Producer)
c/o Simon Millar *Rumble Media*
1620 Broadway
Santa Monica, CA 90403, USA

Brayton, Tyler (Athlete, Football Player)
6023 Ascot Dr
Oakland, CA 94611, USA

Brazadskas, Algirdas (President)
Tumiskiu 30
Vilnius 2016, LITHUANIA

Brazell, Craig (Athlete, Baseball Player)
8512 Rockbridge Cir
Montgomery, AL 36116-8807, USA

Brazelton, Dewon (Athlete, Baseball Player)
107 Scenic Dr
Tullahoma, TN 37388-5422, USA

Brazelton, T Berry (Doctor)
23 Hawthorn St
Cambridge, MA 02138, USA

Brazen, Randi
10138 Main St
Bellevue, WA 98039, USA

Braziel, Larry (Athlete, Football Player)
831 Netherland Dr
Arlington, TX 76017, USA

Brazier, Garry (Race Car Driver)
Stanton Racing
100 Memorial Dr.
Nicholsville, KY 40356, USA

Brazil, Jeff (Journalist)
Orlando Sentinel
Editorial Dept
633 N Orange Ave
Orlando, FL 32801, USA

Brazil, John R (Educator)
Bradley University
President's Office
Peoria, IL 61625, USA

Brazile Jr, Robert L (Athlete, Football Player)
813 Fielder Ave
Mobile, AL 36612, USA

Brazill, Mark (Producer)
10428 Valley Spring Ln
Toluca Lake, CA 91602, USA

Brazoban, Yhency (Athlete, Baseball Player)
13609 N 20th St
Tampa, FL 33613-4324, USA

Brazzell, Chris (Athlete, Football Player)
1205 Las Palmas Cir
Alice, TX 78332, USA

Brea, Leslie (Athlete, Baseball Player)
222 N 153rd Ave
Goodvear, AZ 85338-2966, USA

Bready, Richard L (Business Person)
166 President Ave
Providence, RI 02906, USA

Breaker, Daniel (Actor)
c/o Brian Liebman *Liebman Entertainment*
25 E 21st St #PH
New York, NY 10011-8503, USA

Breaking Benjamin (Music Group)
c/o Staff Member *Hollywood Records*
500 S Buena Vista St
Burbank, CA 91521, USA

Breaking Point (Music Group)
c/o Staff Member *Wind-up Records*
72 Madison Ave Fl 8
New York, NY 10016, USA

B-Real (Artist, Musician)
17116 Labrador St
Northridge, CA 91325, USA

Bream, Julian (Musician)
Hazard Chase
Richmond House
16-20 Regent St
Cambridge CB2 1DB, UNITED KINGDOM (UK)

Bream, Sid (Athlete, Baseball Player)
115 Sabie Run
Zelienople, PA 16063-3141, USA

Breathed, Berkeley (Cartoonist)
Washington Post Writers Group
1150 15th St NW
Washington, DC 20071, USA

Breathwaite, Edward (Writer)
University of West Indies
History Dept
Mona
Kingston 7, JAMAICA

Breaux, Don (Athlete, Football Player)
19027 Southport Dr
Cornelius, NC 28031, USA

Breaux, John (Politician)
25860 Royal Oak Road
Royal Oak, MD 21662, USA

Breaux, Tim (Athlete, Basketball Player)
845 Augusta Dr Apt E75
Apt E75
Houston, TX 77e57-2e29, USA

Breazeale, Jim (Athlete, Baseball Player)
790 County Road 297
Bay City, TX 77414-3644, USA

Breck, Jonathan (Actor)
c/o Staff Member *Vanguard Management Group*
8060 Melrose Ave
4th Floor
Los Angeles, CA 90046, USA

Breckenridge, Alex (Actor)
c/o Staff Member *Kritzer Levine Wilkins Entertainment (KLWG)*
11872 La Grange Ave
1st Floor
Los Angeles, CA 90025, USA

Breckenridge, Laura (Actor)
c/o Glenn Rigberg *HYPHENATE*
9701 Wilshire Blvd.
10th floor
Beverly Hills, CA 90212, USA

Brecker, Randy (Musician)
Tropix International
163 3rd Ave
#206
New York, NY 10003, USA

Bredahl, Charlotte (Athlete, Horse Racer, Olympic Athlete)
PO Box 318
Solvang, CA 93464-0318, USA

Brede, Brent (Athlete, Baseball Player)
1891 J Rock Rd
Trenton, IL 62293-2924, USA

Breder, Charles M (Misc)
6275 Manasola Key Road
Englewood, FL 34223, USA

Bredesen, Philip (Politician)
1724 Chickering Rd
Nashville, TN 37215-4908, USA

Breding, Ed (Athlete, Football Player)
126 NW Pritchard
Harlowton, MT 59036, USA

Bredsen, Espen (Skier)
Hellerud Gardsvei 18
Oslo 0671, NORWAY

Breech, Jim (Athlete, Football Player)
3189 Princeton Rd
#266
Hamilton, OH 45011, USA

Breeden, Danny (Athlete, Baseball Player)
5111 B Ave
Loxley, AL 36551-4537, USA

Breeden, Hal (Athlete, Baseball Player)
665 Middle Rd S
Leesburg, GA 31763-3442, USA

Breeden, Joe (Athlete, Baseball Player)
1305 Bonaventure Dr
Melbourne, FL 32940-1904, USA

Breeden, Louis (Athlete, Football Player)
11264 Grooms Rd
Apt E
Cincinnati, OH 45242, USA

Breeden, Richard C (Government Official)
Coopers & Lybrand
1800 M St NW
Washington, DC 20036, USA

Breedlove, Craig (Race Car Driver)
200 N. Front St.
Rio Vista, CA 94571-1420, USA

Breedlove, Leory (Athlete, Baseball Player)
1910 N 16th St
Orange, TX 77630, USA

Breedlove, Rod (Athlete, Football Player)
1664 Carlyle Dr
Apt H
Crofton, MD 21114, USA

Breen, Adrian (Athlete, Football Player)
6899 Longview Dr
Hamilton, OH 45011, USA

Breen, Bobby (Actor)
10550 NW 71st Pl
Tamarac, FL 33321, USA

Breen, Edward D (Business Person)
Tyco International
273 Corporate Dr
#100
Portsmouth, NH 03801, USA

Breen, Gene (Athlete, Football Player)
1018 Henley Downs Pl
Lake Mary, FL 32746-1972, USA

Breen, George (Athlete, Olympic Athlete, Swimmer)
425 Pepper Mill Court
Sewell, NJ 08080-2963, USA

Breen, John G (Business Person)
18800 N Park Blvd
Shaker Heights, OH 44122, USA

Breen, Monica (Producer, Writer)
c/o Ilan Breil Mosaic Media Group
9200 W. Sunset Blvd
10th Floor
Los Angeles, CA 90069, USA

Breen, Patrick (Actor)
Gersh Agency
232 N Canon Dr
Beverly Hills, CA 90210, USA

Breen, Shelley (Musician)
8106 Patrice Dr
Brentwood, TN 37027, USA

Breen, Stephen (Steve) (Cartoonist)
San Diego Union-Telegram
PO Box 120191
San Diego, CA 92112, USA

Breer, Murle (Athlete, Golfer)
7008 Sand Rd
Savannah, GA 31410, USA

Brees, Drew (Athlete, Football Player)
576 Audubon St
New Orleans, LA 70118, USA

Bregel, Jeff (Athlete, Football Player)
15431 Tulsa St
Spc 33
Mission Hills, CA 91345, USA

Bregman, Buddy (Actor)
c/o Staff Member Paul Lane Entertainment
468 N Camden Dr.
Beverly Hills, CA 90210, USA

Bregman, Martin (Producer)
Martin Bregman Productions
240 E 39th St
New York, NY 10016, USA

Bregman, Tracey (Actor)
6275 Zumirez Dr
Malibu, CA 90265, USA

Brehaut, Jeff (Athlete, Golfer)
1085 Leonello Ave
Los Altos, CA 94024-4914, USA

Breidenbach, Warren (Doctor)
Jewish Hospital
Surgery Dept
217 E Chestnut
Louisville, KY 40202, USA

Breiman, Valerie (Director)
c/o Staff Member Industry Entertainment Partners
955 S Carrillo Dr
Suite 300
Los Angeles, CA 90048, USA

Breining, Fred (Athlete, Baseball Player)
2120 Ticonderoga Dr
San Mateo, CA 94402-4045, USA

Breitenbach, Ken (Athlete, Hockey Player)
8 Greenvale Crt
SS 1
Fonthill, ON L0S 1E1, Canada

Breitenstein, Robert (Athlete, Football Player)
4215 WE 95th St
Tulsa, OK 74137-2311, USA

Breitenstien, Robert (Athlete, Football Player)
8524 S Winston Ave
Tulsa, OK 74137, USA

Breitmayer, Peter (Actor)
2582 Lake View Ave
Los Angeles, CA 90039, USA

Breitner, Paul (Athlete, Soccer Player)
Eichendorfstrasse 10
Sauerlach, GERMANY 82054

Breitschwerdt, Werner (Business Person)
Daimler-Benz AG
Mercedesstr 136
Stuttgart 70322, GERMANY

Breland, Mark (Athlete, Boxer)
P.O. Box 980
Denmark, SC 29042-0980, USA

Bremer, Dick (Commentator)
15910 56th St NE
Saint Michael, MN 55376-3201, USA

Bremmer, Paul L (Politician, Writer)
c/o Staff Member Simon & Schuster
1230 Avenue of the Americas
New York, NY 10020, USA

Bremmer, Rory
c/o Staff Member BBC Artist Mail
PO Box 1116
Belfast BT2 7AJ, United Kingdom

Bremner, Ewen (Actor)
International Creative Mgmt
76 Oxford St
London W1N 0AX, UNITED KINGDOM (UK)

Bren, Donald (Business Person, Philanthropist)
Donald Bren School of Environmental Science & Management
2400 Bren Hall
University of California
Santa Barbara, CA 93106-5131, USA

B. Renacci, James (Congressman, Politician)
130 Cannon HOB
Washington, DC 20515, USA

Brenan, Gerald (Writer)
Alhaurin El Grande
Malaga, SPAIN

Brendel, Alfred (Musician)
Vanguard/Omega Classics
27 W 72nd St
New York, NY 10023, USA

Brendel, Wolfgang (Opera Singer)
Manuela Kursiden
Wasagasse 12/1/3
Vienna 1090, AUSTRIA

Brenden, Hallgeir (Skier)
2417 Torberget
NORWAY

Brendi, Pavel (Athlete, Hockey Player)
1400 Edwards Mill Rd
Raleigh, NC 27607, USA

Brendon, Nicholas (Actor)
Platform
2666 N Beachwood Dr
Los Angeles, CA 90068, USA

Breneman, Curtis E (Scientist)
47 Farrell Rd
Troy, NY 12180-9533, USA

Brenly, Bob (Athlete, Basketball Player)
Chicago Cubs 1060 W Addison St Ste 1
Attn: Broadcast Dept
Chicago, IL 60613-4398, USA

Brenly, Bob (Athlete, Baseball Player, Coach)
9726 E Laurel Ln
Scottsdale, AZ 85260-5959, USA

Brennaman, Marty (Commentator)
Cincinnati Reds
2363 Heather Hill Blvd N
Cincinnati, OH 45244-2666, USA

Brennaman, Thom (Commentator)
738 Park Avenue
Terrace Park, OH 45174-1021, USA

Brennan, Brian (Athlete, Football Player)
2961 Edgewood Rd
Cleveland, OH 44124, USA

Brennan, Christine (Writer)
Washington Post
Sports Dept
1150 15th Ave NW
Washington, DC 20071, USA

Brennan, Dan (Athlete, Hockey Player)
1912 108 Ave
Dawson Creek, BC V1G 2T8, Canada

Brennan, Edward A (Business Person)
AMR Corp
433 Amon Carter Blvd
Fort Worth, TX 76155, USA

Brennan, Eileen (Actor)
c/o Jessica Moresco Unified Management
4231 National Ave
Burbank, CA 91505, USA

Brennan, Joseph E (Politician)
104 Frances St
Portland, ME 04102-2512, USA

Brennan, Kevin (Actor, Comedian)
United Talent Agency
9560 Wilshire Blvd
#500
Beverly Hills, CA 90212, USA

Brennan, Maire (Musician, Songwriter, Writer)
Soho Agency
55 Fulham High St
London SW6 3JJ, UNITED KINGDOM (UK)

Brennan, Margaret (Anchor)
c/o Staff Member CNBC (DC)
400 N Capitol St NW Ste 850
Washington, DC 20001, USA

Brennan, Melissa (Actor)
6520 Platt Ave
#634
W Hills, CA 91307, USA

Brennan, Mike (Athlete, Football Player)
33660 Fox Rd
Easton, MD 21601, USA

Brennan, Neal (Actor, Comedian)
c/o Gregory McKnight Creative Artists Agency (CAA-LA)
2000 Ave Of The Stars
Los Angeles, CA 90067, USA

Brennan, Pete (Athlete, Basketball Player)
1ee6 Oak Tree Dr
Chapel Hill, NC 27517-4075, USA

Brennan, Rich (Athlete, Hockey Player)
14 Reflection Way
South Yarmouth, MA 02664-2045, USA

Brennan, Terrance P (Terry) (Athlete, Coach, Football Player)
1731 Wildberry Dr
#C
Glenview, IL 60025, USA

Brennan, Tom (Athlete, Baseball Player)
8204 Millbank Dr
Orland Park, IL 60462-1726, USA

Brennan, William (Athlete, Baseball Player)
802 Cottage Hill Dr
Macon, GA 31210-7628, USA

Brenneman, Amy (Actor, Producer)
17145 Rancho St
Encino, CA 91316, USA

Brenneman, John (Athlete, Hockey Player)
247 Radley Rd
Mississauga, ON L5G 2R6, Canada

Brenner, David (Actor, Comedian)
3749 Amber Lantern Cir
Las Vegas, NV 89147, USA

Brenner, Dori (Actor)
210 W 101st St #15C
New York, NY 10025, USA

Brenner, Hoby (Athlete, Football Player)
40 Calle Ameno
San Clemente, CA 92672, USA

Brenner, Lisa (Actor)
7729 Sunset Blvd
Los Angeles, CA 90046, USA

Brenner, Sydney (Nobel Prize Laureate)
Salk Institute
The Molecular Science Institute 2168
Shattuck Ave Ste 200
Berkeley, CA 94704-1321, USA

Brenner, Teddy (Boxer)
24 W 55th St
#9C
New York, NY 10019, USA

Bresee, Bobbie (Actor)
8282 Hollywood Blvd
Hollywood, CA 90069, USA

Breslawsky, Marc C (Business Person)
Pitney Bowes Inc
1 Elmcroft Road
Stamford, CT 06926, USA

Breslin, Abigail (Actor)
c/o Beth Cannon *Envision Entertainment*
8840 Wilshire Blvd
3rd Floor
Beverly Hills, CA 90211, USA

Breslin, Jimmy (Journalist)
Newsday
Editorial Dept
235 Pinelawn Road
Melville, NY 11747, USA

Breslin, Spencer (Actor)
c/o Beth Cannon *Envision Entertainment*
8840 Wilshire Blvd
3rd Floor
Beverly Hills, CA 90211, USA

Breslow, Craig (Athlete, Baseball Player)
26 Finchwood Dr
Trumbull, CT 06611-4040, USA

Breslow, Lester (Physicist)
10926 Verano Road
Los Angeles, CA 90077, USA

Breslow, Ronald C (Misc)
295 Three Mile Harbor Road
East Hampton, NY 11937, USA

Bresnik, Randolph J Major (Astronaut)
14119 Lake Scene Trl
Houston, TX 77059-4406, USA

Bress, Eric (Director, Producer, Writer)
c/o Tobin Babst *Kaplan/Perrone
Entertainment*
9560 Wilshire Blvd Fl 5
Beverly Hills, CA 90212, USA

Bressoud, Eddie (Athlete, Baseball Player)
515 Marble Canyon Ln
San Ramon, CA 94582-4830, USA

Brest, Martin (Director, Producer)
c/o John Burnham *ICM Partners (ICM-LA)*
10250 Constellation Blvd Fl 7
Los Angeles, CA 90067, USA

Bretche, Fred
3330 Chimney Rock Ln
Sedona, AZ 86336-3020, USA

Bretherton, Billy (Reality TV Star)
Vexcon Inc.
Animal And Pest Control
1201 Linton Rd
Benton, LA 71006, USA

Bretos, Max (Athlete, Soccer Player)
c/o Staff Member *Maxx Sports &
Entertainment*
546 Fifth Ave Fl 6
New York, NY 10036, USA

Brett, George (Athlete, Baseball Player)
Kansas City Royals PO Box 419969
Attn Vice President - BB Operations
Kansas City, MO 64141-6969, USA

Brett, George (Athlete, Baseball Player)
6528 Seneca Rd
Mission Hills, KS 66208-1718, USA

Brett, Jonathan (Actor)
Agency for Performing Arts
9200 Sunset Blvd
#900
Los Angeles, CA 90069, USA

Brettschneider, Carl (Athlete, Football
Player)
4649 Bird View Ct
Las Vegas, NV 89129, USA

Breuer, Grit (Athlete, Track Athlete)
Konrad-Adenauer-Str 16
Garbsen 30823, GERMANY

Breuer, Jim (Comedian)
c/o Staff Member *Agency for the
Performing Arts (APA-LA)*
405 S Beverly Dr
Suite 500
Beverly Hills, CA 90212-4425, USA

Breuer, Randy (Athlete, Basketball Player)
10481 Misty Morning Ln
Eden Prairie, MN 55347-5023, USA

Breunig, Robert P (Bob) (Athlete, Football
Player)
9215 Westview Cir
Dallas, TX 75231, USA

Brevak, Bob (Race Car Driver)
Brevak Racing
206 Performance Rd.
Mooresville, NC 28115, USA

Brew, Dorian (Athlete, Football Player)
1948 Lunenburg Dr
Saint Peters, MO 63376-8168, USA

Brewer, Albert P (Politician)
Samford University 800 Lakeshore Dr
Birmingham, AL 35229-0002, USA

Brewer, Billy (Athlete, Baseball Player)
7405 Woodway Dr
Woodway, TX 76712-6153, USA

Brewer, Carl (Athlete, Hockey Player)
Caledon Village Ontario Provincial Police
18473 Hurontario St
Caledon Village, ON L7K 0X8, Canada

Brewer, Chris (Athlete, Football Player)
6703 St Augustine Rd #116
Jacksonville, FL 32217-2859, USA

Brewer, Craig (Director, Producer)
c/o Brad Gross *Brad Gross Agency, The*
161 S Arden Blvd
Los Angeles, CA 90004, USA

Brewer, Derek Stanley (Educator)
Emmanuel College
English Dept
Cambridge CB2 3AP, UNITED
KINGDOM (UK)

Brewer, Dewell (Athlete, Football Player)
4804 Bloomfield Dr
Memphis, TN 38125-3356, USA

Brewer, Donald (Musician)
Lustig Talent
PO Box 770850
Orlando, FL 32877, USA

Brewer, Eric (Athlete, Hockey Player)
7396 Stratford Ave
Saint Louis, MO 63130-4137, USA

Brewer, Jamison (Athlete, Basketball
Player)
1322 Wind Castle Trl
Indianapolis, IN 46280-2723, USA

Brewer, Jan (Governor)
Governor of Arizona
1700 West Washington
Phoenix, AZ 85007, USA

Brewer, Jim (Athlete, Basketball Player,
Olympic Athlete)
1814 S 23rd Ave
Maywood, IL 60153-2810, USA

Brewer, Mike (Athlete, Baseball Player)
40 Amherst Ave
Menlo Park, CA 94025-3802, USA

Brewer, Richard G (Scientist)
IBM Almaden Research Center 650 Harry
Rd
SanJose, CA 95120-6099, USA

Brewer, Rod (Athlete, Baseball Player)
2105 Carpathian Dr
Apopka, FL 32712-4711, USA

Brewer, Sean (Athlete, Football Player)
9232 Grangehill Dr
Riverside, CA 92508-9329, USA

Brewer, Tom (Athlete, Baseball Player)
409 State Rd
Cheraw, SC 29520-1621, USA

Brewer, Tony (Athlete, Baseball Player)
659 Wildwood Ln
Palo Alto, CA 94303-3117, USA

Brewer, Tony
Los Angeles Dodgers
839 Golden Poppy St
Las Vegas, NV 89110-2858, USA

Brewington, Jamie (Athlete, Baseball
Player)
3370 S Roger Ct
Chandler, AZ 85286-2481, USA

Brewster, Darrel "Pete" (Athlete, Football
Player)
PO Box 183
Peculiar, MO 64078-0183, USA

Brewster, Jordana (Actor)
1326 N. Wetherly Dr
West Hollywood, CA 90069, USA

Brewster, Kithe (Stylist)
c/o Staff Member *Creative Exchange
Agency*
53 Gansevoort St
3rd Floor
New York, NY 10014, USA

Brewster, Paget (Actor)
4978 Cromwell Ave
Los Angeles, CA 90027, USA

Brewster, Pete (Athlete, Football Player)
P.O. Box 183
Peculiar, MO 64078, USA

Brewton, Maia (Actor)
525 W 49th St
New York, NY 10019, USA

Brey, Mike (Coach)
Notre Dame University
Athletic Dept
Notre Dame, IN 46556, USA

Breyer, Stephen G (Attorney)
US Supreme Court
United States Supreme Court 11st St NE
Washington, DC 20543-0002, USA

Brezec, Primoz (Athlete, Basketball
Player)
10030 Hazelview Dr
Charlotte, NC 28277-2948, USA

Brezina, Bobby (Athlete, Football Player)
1204 Pine Hollow Dr
Friendswood, TX 77546-4634, USA

Brezina, Greg (Athlete, Football Player)
155 Tillinghast Trce
Newnan, GA 30265-6000, USA

Brezina, Thomas (Writer)
ORF
Wurzburggasse 30
Wien 1136, Austria

Brezis, Haim (Mathematician)
18 Rue de la Glaciere
Paris Cedex 13 75640, FRANCE

Brezner, Larry (Producer)
c/o Larry Brezner *Morra Brezner Steinberg
& Tenenbaum (MBST) Entertainment*
345 N Maple Dr
Suite 200
Beverly Hills, CA 90210, USA

'Brian, Demarco (Athlete, Football Player)
4364 Tomahawk Ln
Vermilion, OH 44089, USA

Brian, Frank (Athlete, Basketball Player)
23757 Brian Rd
Zachary, LA 7e791-6231, USA

Brian duffy, colonel (Astronaut)
Lockheed Martin Space Systems 2625 Bay
Area Blvd Attn V Pres Altair Luna
Houston, TX 77058-1523, USA

Brice, Alan (Athlete, Baseball Player)
6726 71st St E
Bradenton, FL 34203-7173, USA

Brice, Alundis (Athlete, Football Player)
928 N Egypt Cir
Brookhaven, MS 39601-3556, USA

Brice, Lee (Musician)
c/o Joey Lee *WmE2 (WMA-TN)*
1600 Division St
Suite 300
Nashville, TN 37203, USA

Brice, Pierre (Actor)
c/o Staff Member *Thomas Claasen*
Bismarkstr 22
Itzehoe D-25524, Germany

Brice, Will (Athlete, Football Player)
1139 Craig Ave
Lancaster, SC 29720-8227, USA

Brice, William J (Artist)
427 Beloit St
Los Angeles, CA 90049, USA

Bricekel, James R (General)
4798 Hanging Moss Lane
Sarasota, FL 34238, USA

Bricekell, Beth (Director)
PO Box 119
Paron, AR 72122, USA

Bricekell, Edie (Musician, Songwriter,
Writer)
88 Central Park West
New York, NY 10023, USA

Brickell, Beth (Actor)
3001 N Grant St
Little Rock, AR 72207-2819, USA

Brickell, Edie (Musician)
88 Central Park W
New York, NY 10023, USA

Bricker, Neal S (Physicist)
4240 Piedmont Mesa Road
Claremont, CA 91711, USA

Brickhouse, Smith N (Religious Leader)
Church of Christ
PO Box 472
Independence, MO 64051, USA

Brickley, Andy (Athlete, Hockey Player)
Boston Bruins
100 Legends Way Ste 250
Attn: Broadcast Dept
Boston, MA 02114-1389, United States

Brickley, Andy (Athlete, Hockey Player)
5 Mill River Lane
Hingham, MA 02043-3455, USA

Bricklin, Daniel S (Designer)
Trellix Corp
300 Bahr Ave
Concord, MA 01742, USA

Brickman, Jim (Composer, Musician,
Producer)
c/o Staff Member *ICM Partners (ICM-LA)*
10250 Constellation Blvd Fl 7
Los Angeles, CA 90067, USA

Brickman, Paul (Director)
4116 Holly Knoll Dr
Los Angeles, CA 90027, USA

Brickowski, Frank (Athlete, Basketball
Player)
589 7th St
Lake Oswego, OR 97034-2906, USA

Briclges, Roy D Maj Gen (Astronaut)
113 William Barksdale
Williamsburg, VA 23185-8211, USA

Bricusse, Leslie (Composer, Musician)
8730 Sunset Blvd #300W
Los Angeles, CA 90069, USA

Bridgeforth, William (Athlete, Baseball
Player)
4766 Drakes Branch Road
Nashville, TN 37218-1436, USA

Bridgeman, Ulysses (Athlete, Basketball
Player)
16e4 Cherokee Rd
Apt 5
Lousville, KY 40205-1349, USA

Bridgers, Sean (Actor)
c/o Darris Hatch *Daris Hatch
Management*
10027 Rossbury Pl
Los Angeles, CA 90064-4825, USA

Bridges, Alan J S (Director)
28 High St
Shepperton
Middx TW7 9AW, UNITED KINGDOM
(UK)

Bridges, Angelica (Actor, Model)
c/o Marv Dauer *Marv Dauer Management*
11661 San Vicente Blvd
Suite 104
Los Angeles, CA 90049, USA

Bridges, Beau (Actor)
5525 Jed Smith Rd
Hidden Hills, CA 91302, USA

Bridges, Bill (Athlete, Basketball Player)
2322 44rd St
Santa Monica, CA 90405-2102, USA

Bridges, Jeff (Actor, Producer)
985 Hot Springs Rd
Montecito, CA 93108, USA

Bridges, Jeremy (Athlete, Football Player)
16213 S 31st Way
Phoenix, AZ 85048-7727, USA

Bridges, Jordan (Actor)
c/o Myrna Jacoby *MJ Management*
130 W 57th St
Suite 11A
New York, NY 10019, USA

Bridges, Krista (Actor)
c/o JJ Harris *One Talent Management*
9220 Sunset Blvd
Los Angeles, CA 90069, USA

Bridges, Rocky (Athlete, Baseball Player)
1128 W Shane Dr
Coeur D Alene, ID 83815-9788, USA

Bridges, Todd (Actor)
16002 Nordhoff St
North Hills, CA 91423, USA

Bridges Jr, Roy D (Astronaut, General)
113 William Barksdale
Williamsburg, VA 23185-8211, USA

Bridgewater, Brad (Athlete, Olympic
Athlete, Swimmer)
3630 Lincoln Dr
Frisco, TX 75034-6366, USA

Bridgewater, Dee Dee (Musician)
B H Hopper Mgmt
Elvirastr 25
Munich 80636, GERMANY

Bridgman, Mel (Athlete, Hockey Player)
221 Concord St # 17
El Segundo, CA 90245-3799, USA

Bridgmohan, Shaun (Horse Racer)
4541 NW 5th St
Plantation, FL 33317-2132, USA

Bridwell, Norman (Artist)
PO Box 869
Edgartown, MA 02539-0869, USA

Brie, Alison (Actor)
c/o Scott Fish *Vital Management Group
(VMG)*
5405 Wilshire Blvd #200
Los Angeles, CA 90036, USA

Brief Smile, A (Music Group)
c/o Staff Member *Paradigm (Monterey)*
404 W Franklin St
Monterey, CA 93940, USA

Briehl, Tom (Athlete, Football Player)
7752 N Via De La Montana
Scottsdale, AZ 85258-3320, USA

Briem, Anita (Actor)
c/o Steve Cohen *United Talent Agency
(UTA)*
9336 Civic Center Dr
Beverly Hills, CA 90210, USA

Brien, Doug (Athlete, Football Player)
55 Cambrian Ave
Piedmont, CA 94611-3606, USA

Brier, Kathy (Actor, Musician)
c/o Judy Katz *Judy Katz PR*
250 W 57th St
Suite 1818
New York, NY 10107, USA

Briere, Daniel (Athlete, Hockey Player)
17 S Hinchman Ave
Haddonfield, NJ 08033-3714, USA

Brierley, Ronald A (Business Person)
Guinness Peat Group
21-26 Garlick Hill
London EC4 2AU, UNITED KINGDOM
(UK)

Briers, Richard (Actor, Comedian)
c/o Christian Hodell *Hamilton Hodell Ltd*
66-68 Margaret St Fl 5
London W1W 8SR, UK

Brigance, O J (Athlete, Football Player)
14 Woodfield Ct
Reisterstown, MD 21136-4639, USA

Brigati, Eddie (Musician, Songwriter,
Writer)
Dassinger Creative
32 Ardsley Road
#201
Montclair, NJ 07042, USA

Briggs, Dan (Athlete, Baseball Player)
8270 Rookery Way_
Westerville, OH 43082-8236, USA

Briggs, Danny (Athlete, Golfer)
3730 Ravens Trace Ln
Franklin, TN 37064-4710, USA

Briggs, Edward S (Admiral)
3648 Lago Sereno
Esxondido, CA 92029, USA

Briggs, Greg (Athlete, Football Player)
11115 Harvest Dale Ave
Houston, TX 77065-3338, USA

Briggs, John (Johnny) (Athlete, Baseball
Player)
238 Wall Ave
Paterson, NJ 07504-1016, USA

Briggs, Johnny T (Athlete, Baseball Player)
216 Tom Bell Rd Spc 133
Murphys, CA 95247-9552, USA

Briggs, Kathy (Stylist)
c/o Staff Member *Zenobia Agency Inc*
PO Box 909
Groveland, CA 95321, USA

Briggs, Lance (Athlete, Football Player)
225 NE Mizner Blvd Ste 685
Boca Raton, FL 33432-4080, USA

Briggs, Raymond R (Cartoonist, Writer)
Weston
Underhill Lane
Westmeston near Hassocks
Sussex, UNITED KINGDOM (UK)

Briggs, Robert W (Biologist)
480 Rale St
Palo Alto, CA 94301, USA

Briggs, Wilma (Athlete, Baseball Player,
Commentator)
111 Summit Ave
Wakefield, RI 02879-2228, USA

Briggs of Lewes, Asa (Historian)
Caprons Keere St
Lewes
Sussex, UNITED KINGDOM (UK)

Brigham, Jeremy (Athlete, Football Player)
1141 Catalina Dr
Livermore, CA 94550-5928, USA

Bright, Cameron (Actor)
c/o Stephanie Comer *United Talent
Agency (UTA)*
9336 Civic Center Dr
Beverly Hills, CA 90210, USA

Bright, Greg
PO Box 41761
Arlington, VA 22204-8761, USA

Bright, Jason (Race Car Driver)
29103 Arnold Dr.
Sonoma, CA 95476, USA

Bright, Kevin (Director, Producer)
12903 Chalon Rd
Los Angeles, CA 90049, USA

Bright, Leon (Athlete, Football Player)
1183 Dutton Ave
Deland, FL 32720-5011, USA

Bright, Myron H (Judge)
655 1st Ave N
#340
Fargo, ND 58102, USA

Brightbill, Susan (Actor, Writer)
c/o Michael Lasker *Mosaic Media Group*
9200 W. Sunset Blvd
10th Floor
Los Angeles, CA 90069, USA

Brightman, Sarah (Musician)
2505 Bowmont Dr
Beverly Hills, CA 90210, USA

Brigman, D J (Athlete, Golfer)
8304 Calle Soquelle NE
Albuquerque, NM 87113, USA

Briley, Greg (Athlete, Baseball Player)
2170 Sunnybrook Rd
Greenville, NC 27834-1164, USA

Briley, John (Writer)
c/o Jack Gilardi *ICM Partners (ICM-LA)*
10250 Constellation Blvd Fl 7
Los Angeles, CA 90067, USA

Brill, Charlie (Actor)
3635 Wrightwood Dr
Studio City, CA 91604, USA

Brill, Francesca (Actor)
Kate Feast Primrose Hill Studios
Fitzroy Road
London NW1 8TR, UNITED KINGDOM
(UK)

Brill, Winston J (Misc)
12529 237th Way NE
Redmond, WA 98053, USA

Brill, Yvonne C (Inventor)
914 Route 518
Skillman, NJ 08558-2616, USA

Brillant, Dany (Actor, Musician)
c/o Laurent Gregoire *Agence Artistique
Adequat*
108 rue Reaumur
Paris 75002, France

Brilley, Greg (Athlete, Baseball Player)
2170 Sunnyprook Rd
Greenville, NC 27834-1164, usa

Brilz, Darrick (Athlete, Football Player)
794 Riverwatch Dr
Crescent Springs, KY 41017-5389, USA

Brim, James (Athlete, Football Player)
4310 Alderny Pl
High Point, NC 27265-9277, USA

Brimacombe, Keith (Scientist)
2825 13th Ave W
Vancouver, BC V6K 2T6, Canada

Brimanis, Aris (Athlete, Hockey Player)
12909 Badger Ln
Anchorage, AK 99516-3034, USA

Brimley, Wilford (Actor)
240 Greybull Ave
Greybull, WY 82426, USA

Brimmer, Andrew F (Economist,
Government Official)
Brimmer Co
4400 MacArthur Blvd NW
Washington, DC 20007, USA

Brin, Sergey (Business Person, Engineer,
Producer)
c/o Staff Member *Google Inc*
1600 Ampitheatre Pkwy
Mountain View, CA 94043, USA

Brind'amour, Rod (Athlete, Hockey
Player)
Carolina Hurricanes
1400 Edwards Mill Rd Attn Coaching Staff
Raleigh, NC 27607-3624, USA

Brind'amour, Rod (Athlete, Hockey
Player)
12304 Birchfalls Dr
Raleigh, NC 27614-7900, USA

Brindley, Doug (Athlete, Hockey Player)
Caledon Village Ontario Provincial Police
18473 Hurontario St
Caledon Village, ON L7K OX8, Canada

Brinegar, Claude (Politician)
2444 Sharon Oaks Dr
Menlo Park, CA 94025-6829, USA

Bring, Murray H (Business Person)
Altria Group
120 Park Ave
New York, NY 10017, USA

Brink, Andre P (Writer)
University of Cape Town
English Dept
Rondebosch 7700, SOUTH AFRICA

Brink, Brad (Athlete, Baseball Player)
2628 Surrey Ave
Modesto, CA 95355-4668, USA

Brink, Frank Jr (Physicist)
Pine Run
#E1 Ferry & Iron Roads
Doylestown, PA 18901, USA

Brink, Larry (Athlete, Football Player)
13310 Tierra Heights Rd13310 Tierra
Heights Rd13310 Tierra Heights Rd
Redding, CA 96003-7489, USA

Brink, R Alexander (Misc)
8301 Old Sauk Road
#326
Middleton, WI 53562, USA

Brinker, Bob (Business Person, Radio
Personality)
AdPad Inc
5226 E Wagoner Rd
Scottsdale, AZ 85254-7636

Brinker, Christopher (Producer)
c/o David Krintzman *Morris, Yorn,
Barnes, Levine, Krintzman, Rubenstein
and Kohner*
2000 Ave of the Stars
3rd Floor, North Tower
Los Angeles, CA 90067, USA

Brinker, Nancy (Business Person)
*The Susan G. Komen Breast Cancer
Foundation, Inc*
5005 LBJ Freeway
Suite 250
Dallas, TX 75244

Brinkley, Christie (Model)
121 Brick Kiln Rd
Sag Harbor, NY 11963, USA

Brinkman, Chuck (Athlete, Baseball
Player)
126 Country Club Rd
Bryan, OH 43506-9136, USA

Brinkman, Joe (Athlete, Baseball Player)
10551 NW 70th St
Chiefland, FL 32626-5042, USA

Brinkman, John A (Historian)
1321 56th St
#4
Chicago, IL 60637, USA

Brinkman, William F (Physicist)
20 Constitution Hill W
Princeton, NJ 08540, USA

Brinkmann, Robert S (Cinematographer)
Murtha Agency
c/o Ann Murtha
4240 Promenade Way Ste 232
Marina Del Rey, CA 90292, USA

Brino, Lorenzo (Actor)
c/o Wendy Wilke *Media Partners*
636 Acanto St.
Suite 207
Bel Air, CA 90049, USA

Brino, Nikolas (Actor)
c/o Wendy Wilke *Media Partners*
636 Acanto St.
Suite 207
Bel Air, CA 90049, USA

Brino, Zachary (Actor)
c/o Wendy Wilke *Media Partners*
636 Acanto St.
Suite 207
Bel Air, CA 90049, USA

Brinson, Dana (Athlete, Football Player)
1100 Clark St
Valdosta, GA 31601-3744, USA

Brinson, Larry (Athlete, Football Player)
4614 Rainbow Run
Sugar Land, TX 77479-2039, USA

Brinster, Ralph L (Biologist)
University of Pennsylvania
Veterinary Medicine School
Philadelphia, PA 19104, USA

Brintz, Lisa (Stylist)
c/o Staff Member *Brintz & Associates*
16 Irving St
Newton, MA 02459, USA

Brion, Francoise (Actor)
c/o Staff Member *Cineart*
36 Rue de Ponthieu
Paris F-75008, France

Brion, John (Composer, Musician)
c/o Staff Member *Kraft-Engel Management*
15233 Ventura Blvd
Suite 200
Sherman Oaks, CA 91403, USA

Brisbin, David (Actor)
c/o Geneva Bray *GVA Talent Agency Inc*
8981 Sunset Blvd.
Suite 101
Los Angeles, CA 90069, USA

Brisby, Vincent (Athlete, Football Player)
12612 Waterside Way
Houston, TX 77041-6635, USA

Brisco, Jack (Wrestler)
19018 Blake Road
Odessa, FL 33556, USA

Brisco, Marlin (Athlete, Football Player)
379 Newport Ave
Apt 107
Long Beach, CA 90814, USA

Brisco, Valerie (Athlete, Track Athlete)
USA Track & Field
4341 Starlight Dr
Indianapolis, IN 46239, USA

Briscoe, Brent (Actor)
c/o Robert Enriquez *Red Baron
Management*
1600 Rosecrans Ave
Bldg 7 Fl 4
Long Beach, CA 90266, USA

Briscoe, John (Athlete, Baseball Player)
6815 Casa Loma Ave
Dallas, TX 75214-4003, USA

Briscoe, Marlin (Athlete, Football Player)
675 Coronado Ave
Long Beach, CA 90814-1439, USA

Briscoe, Mary Beck (Judge)
US Appeals Court
4839 W 15th St
Lawrence, KS 66049, USA

Briscoe, Ryan (Race Car Driver)
108 Hickory Hill Road
Mooresville, NC 28117, USA

Brisebois, Danielle (Musician, Producer)
1034 Garfield Ave
Venice, CA 90291, USA

Brisebois, Patrice (Athlete, Hockey Player)
4723 Castle Cir
Broomfield, CO 80023-4079, USA

Brissie, Leland V (Lou) (Athlete, Baseball
Player)
1908 White Pine Dr
North Augusta, SC 29841-2147, USA

Brisson, Elzear (Horse Racer)
PO Box 228
New Kent, VA 23124-0228, USA

Brisson, Lance (Actor)
4570 Noeline Way
Encino, CA 91436, USA

Brister, Walter A (Bubby) III (Athlete,
Football Player)
139 Fontainbleau Dr
Mandeville, LA 70471-6434, USA

Bristol, Dave (Athlete, Baseball Player,
Coach)
1748 Fairview Rd
Andrews, NC 28901-7426, USA

Bristor, John (Athlete, Football Player)
70 Rinehart Ln
Waynesburg, PA 15370, USA

Bristow, Allan (Athlete, Basketball Player)
510 Sand Hill Ct
Marco Island, FL 34145-5859, USA

Bristow, Allan M (Athlete, Basketball
Player, Coach)
P.O. Box 635
Gloucester Point, VA 23062, USA

Britain, Radie (Composer)
PO Box 17
Smithville, IN 47458, USA

Brito, Jorge (Athlete, Baseball Player)
9348 Snake Rd
Athens, AL 35611-8031, USA

Brito, Michelle (Athlete, Tennis Player)
Tenis De Portugal
Rua Actor Chaby Pinheiro, 7 - A
Linda-A-Velha 2795 - 060, Portugal

Brito, Tilson (Athlete, Baseball Player)
6809 Fishers Farm Ln
Unit F1
Charlotte, NC 28277-0334, USA

Britt, Charley (Athlete, Football Player)
128 Savannah Pointe
North Augusta, SC 29841-3586, USA1

Britt, Chris (Cartoonist)
State Journal-Register
Editorial Dept
1 Copley Plaza
Springfield, IL 62701, USA

Britt, James (Athlete, Football Player)
PO Box 371202
Decatur, GA 30037, USA

Britt, Jessie (Athlete, Football Player)
4003 Coltrain Rd
Greensboro, NC 27455, USA

Britt, May (Actor)
5059 Enfield Ave
Encino, CA 91316, USA

Britt, Tyrone (Athlete, Basketball Player)
4631 Germantown Ave
Philadelphia, PA 19144-3010, USA

Britt, Wayman (Athlete, Basketball Player)
973 Paradise Lake Dr SE
Grand Rapids, MI 49546-3828, USA

Brittain, Michael (Mike) (Athlete,
Basketball Player)
2101 Sunset Point Rd
Apt 602
Clearwater, FL 33765-1277, USA

Brittany, Morgan (Actor, Model)
3434 Cornell Road
Agoura Hills, CA 91301, USA

Britten, Roy J (Misc)
Kerckhoff Marine Laboratory
101 Dahlia Ave Ave
Corona del Mar, CA 92625, USA

Brittenham, Harry (Attorney, Attorney General, General)
Ziffren Brittenham Branca
1801 Century Park West
Los Angeles, CA 90067, USA

Brittenum, John (Athlete, Football Player)
P.O. Box 3773
Fayetteville, AR 72702, USA

Britton, Benjamin (Inventor)
University of Cincinnati
Fine Arts Dept
Cincinnati, OH 45221, USA

Britton, Bill (Athlete, Golfer)
41 Allen St
Rumson, NJ 07760, USA

Britton, Chris (Athlete, Baseball Player)
7481 NW 11th Ct
Plantation, FL 33313-5913, USA

Britton, Christopher (Actor)
c/o Staff Member *Red Management*
Box 3
415 West Esplanade
North Vancouver, BC V7M 1A6, Canada

Britton, Connie (Actor)
c/o Greg Clark *Untitled Entertainment (LA)*
350 S. Beverly Dr #200
Beverly Hills, CA 90212, USA

Britton, Dave (Athlete, Basketball Player)
6321 Old Ox Rd
Dallas, TX 75241-2733, USA

Britton, Jim (Athlete, Baseball Player)
825 Forestwalk Dr
Suwanee, GA 30024-4243, USA

Britton, Tony (Actor)
International Creative Mgmt
76 Oxford St
London W1N 0AX, UNITED KINGDOM (UK)

Britton, Zach (Athlete, Baseball Player)
101 Heritage Ln
Weatherford, TX 76087-4422, USA

Britts, Sam (Athlete, Football Player)
10 Kingsbrook Ln
Saint Louis, MO 63132-3006, USA

Britz, Greg (Athlete, Hockey Player)
245 Ocean Ave
Marblehead, MA 01945-3700, USA

Britz, Jerilyn (Athlete, Golfer)
415 E Lincoln St
Apt 7
Luverne, MN 56156, USA

Brizzolara, Tony (Athlete, Baseball Player)
1638 Princess Cir NE
Atlanta, GA 30345-4160, USA

Broad, Eli (Business Person)
Eli and Edythe Broad Foundation
10900 Wilshire Blvd Fl 12
Los Angeles, CA 90024, USA

Broadbent, Jim (Actor)
c/o Staff Member *Independent Talent Group (ITG-UK)*
Oxford House
76 Oxford St
London W1D 1BS, UK

Broadbent, John Edward (Government Official)
1386 Nicola
#30
Vancouver BC V6G 2G2, CANADA

Broaddus, J Alfred Jr (Financier)
Federal Reserve Bank
PO Box 27622
Richmond, VA 23261, USA

Broadhead, James L (Business Person)
FPL Group
700 Universe Blvd
Juno Beach, FL 33408, USA

Broadnax, Jerry (Athlete, Football Player)
429 Weaver St
Cedar Hill, TX 75104-9074, USA

Broadway, Lance (Athlete, Baseball Player)
4106 Greenwood Way_
Mansfield, TX 76063-5562, USA

Brobeck, John R (Physicist)
224 Vassar Ave
Swarthmore, PA 19081, USA

Broberg, Gus (Athlete, Basketball Player)
208 El Pueblo Way
Palm Beach, FL 33480, USA

Broberg, Pete (Athlete, Baseball Player)
220 Monterey Rd
Palm Beach, FL 33480-3228, USA

Brocail, Doug (Athlete, Baseball Player)
8011 Meadow Vista Dr
Missouri City, TX 77459-5734, USA

Broccoli, Barbara (Producer)
709 N. Hillcrest Rd
Beverly Hills, CA 90210, USA

Broches, Aron (Attorney, Attorney General, General)
44 Pond St
Wakefield, RI 02879, USA

Brochtrup, William (Bill) (Actor)
S D B Partners
1801 Ave of Stars
#902
Los Angeles, CA 90067, USA

Brochu, Stephane (Athlete, Hockey Player)
6029 Evergreen Ln
Grand Blanc, MI 48439, USA

Brock, Chris (Athlete, Baseball Player)
7684 Markham Bend Pl
Sanford, FL 32771-8107, USA

Brock, Clyde (Athlete, Football Player)
5592 Yorkshire Pl
Lake Oswego, OR 97035-3382, USA

Brock, Dieter (Athlete, Football Player)
436 Cambrian Ridge Trl
Pelham, AL 35124-4832, USA

Brock, Greg (Athlete, Baseball Player)
3727 Valley Oak Dr
Loveland, CO 80538-8930, USA

Brock, Lou (Athlete, Baseball Player)
9716 Bonhomme Estates Dr
Saint Louis, MO 63132-4102, USA

Brock, Matt (Athlete, Football Player)
3105 SW 98th Ave
Portland, OR 97225-2924, USA

Brock, Pete (Athlete, Football Player)
111 Main St
Topsfield, MA 01983-1420, USA

Brock, Raheem (Athlete, Football Player)
1017 Serpentine Ln
Wyncote, PA 19095-1616, USA

Brock, Stanley J (Stan) (Athlete, Football Player)
2555 SW 81st Ave
Portland, OR 97225-3839, USA

Brock, Stevie (Actor)
c/o Johnny Wright *Wright Entertainment & Sports Productions*
9452 Thurloe Pl
Orlando, FL 32827, USA

Brock, Tarrik (Athlete, Baseball Player)
8111 Fairchild Ave
Winnetka, CA 91306-2012, USA

Brock, Willie (Athlete, Football Player)
3732 NE 70th Ave
Portland, OR 97213-5141, USA

Brockermeyer, Blake (Athlete, Football Player)
413 Crestwood Dr
Fort Worth, TX 76107-1079, USA

Brockert, Richard C (Misc)
United Telegraph Workers
701 E Gude Dr
Rockville, MD 20850, USA

Brock III, William E (Bill) (Politician)
16 Revell St
Annapolis, MD 21401-2611, USA

Brockington, John (Athlete, Football Player)
The Guardian 311 Camino Del Rio N Ste 1150
Suite1500
San Diego, CA 92108, USA

Brock Jr, Lou (Athlete, Football Player)
1015 Sandstone Dr
Saint Louis, MO 63146, USA

Brocklander, Fred (Athlete, Baseball Player)
317 Eagles Landing Ct
Apt K
Odenton, MD 21113, USA

Brockovich, Erin (Writer)
29365 Castlehill Dr
Agoura Hills, CA 91301, USA

Broden, Connie (Athlete, Hockey Player)
88 Valecrest Dr
Etobicoke, ON M9A 4P6, Canada

Broder, Samuel (Misc)
IVAX Corp
4400 Biscayne Blvd
Miami, FL 33137, USA

Broderick, Beth (Actor)
Innovative Artists
1505 10th St
Santa Monica, CA 90401, USA

Broderick, Ken (Athlete, Hockey Player)
5142 Citation Rd
Niagara Falls, ON L2H 3H7, Canada

Broderick, Len (Athlete, Hockey Player)
216 Inverness Way
Easley, SC 29642, USA

Broderick, Matthew (Actor)
P.O. Box 10459
Burbank, CA 91510-0459, USA

Broderson, Morris (Artist)
5707 Costello Ave
Valley Glen, CA 91401, USA

Brodeur, Martin (Athlete, Hockey Player)
100 Mountain Ave
West Orange, NJ 07052, USA

Brodeur, Richard (Athlete, Hockey Player)
5007 Angus Dr
Vancouver, BC V6M 3M6, Canada

Brodie, H Keith H (Misc)
63 Beverly Dr
Durham, NC 27707, USA

Brodie, John (Athlete, Football Player, Golfer)
49350 Avenida Fernando
La Quinta, CA 92253, USA

Brodie, Kevin (Actor)
3925 Big Oak Dr #5
Studio City, CA 91604-3800, USA

Brodowski, Dick (Athlete, Baseball Player)
120 Pine St
Manchester, MA 01944-1022, USA

Brodsky, Julian A (Business Person)
Comcast Corp
1500 Market St
Philadelphia, PA 19102, USA

Brody, Adam (Actor)
1539 N. Laurel Ave. #305
Los Angeles, CA 90046, USA

Brody, Adrien (Actor)
737 Stone Barn Rd
Cleveland, NY 13042, USA

Brody, Jon Lee (Actor)
c/o Terry Cohen *Cohen Entertainment*
964 Hancock Ave
Suite 305
West Hollywood, CA 90069, USA

Brody, Kenneth D (Financier)
Taconic Capital Advisors
450 Park Avenue
9th Floor
New York, NY 10022, USA

Brody, Lane (Music Group)
Black Stallion Country Productions
PO Box 368
Tujunga, CA 91043, USA

Broecker, Wallace S (Geophysicist, Misc, Physicist)
Lamont-Doherty Earth Observatory
P O Box 1000
Palisades, NY 10964, USA

Broelsch, Christopher E (Doctor, Misc)
University of Chicago
Medical Center Surgery Dept Box 259
Chicago, IL 60690, USA

Brogan, James (Athlete, Basketball Player)
6631 Hollycrest Ct
San Diego, CA 92121-4137, USA

Brogdon, Cindy (Athlete, Basketball Player, Olympic Athlete)
4162 Anson Trl
Suwanee, GA 30024-6753, USA

Broglio, Ernie (Athlete, Baseball Player)
2838 Via Carmen
San Jose, CA 95124-1442, USA

Brogna, Rico (Athlete, Baseball Player)
2 Gate Post Ln
Woodbury, CT 06798-2136, USA

Brohamer, Jack (Athlete, Baseball Player)
39017 Narcissus Dr
Palm Desert, CA 92211-1882, USA

Brohawn, Troy (Athlete, Baseball Player)
1619 Taylors Island Rd
Woolford, MD 21677-1328, USA

Brohm, Jeff (Athlete, Football Player)
3820 Balmoral Dr
Champaign, IL 61822-8117, USA

Brokaw, Gary (Athlete, Basketball Player)
6614 Augustine Way
Charlotte, NC 28270-0891, USA

Brokaw, Tom (Journalist)
c/o Sara Perkowski *NBC Nightly News*
30 Rockefeller Plz #300S
New York, NY 10112, USA

Broken Lizard (Comedian)
c/o Staff Member *United Talent Agency (UTA)*
9336 Civic Center Dr
Beverly Hills, CA 90210, USA

Brolin, James (Actor)
c/o Jeff Wald *Jeff Wald Entertainment*
3000 W Olympic Blvd
Bldg 2 #1400
Santa Monica, CA 90404, USA

Brolin, Josh (Actor)
8200 Dover Canyon Rd
Paso Robles, CA 93446, USA

Brolly, Shane (Actor)
1416 Havenhurst Dr. #3C
West Hollywood, CA 90046, USA

Bromberg, David (Musician)
c/o Staff Member *Agency Group Ltd, The (LA)*
1880 Century Park E
Suite 711
Los Angeles, CA 90067, USA

Bromell, Loranzo (Athlete, Football Player)
18 Forest View Rd
Cumberland, VA 23040-2508, USA

Bromley, D Allan (Government Official, Physicist)
3102 23rd Street
Lubbock, YX 79410-2123, USA

Bromley, Gary (Athlete, Hockey Player)
1130 Munro St
Victoria, BC V9A 5P1, Canada

Bromstad, David (Designer)
c/o Ken Slotnick *WME (WMA-NY)*
1325 Ave of the Americas
New York, NY 10019, USA

Bron, Eleanor (Actor)
c/o Rebecca Blond *Rebecca Blond Associates*
69a Kings Rd
London SW3 4NX, UNITED KINGDOM

Bronars, Edward J (General)
3354 Rose Lane
Falls Church, VA 22042, USA

Bronfman, Charles (Commentator)
501 N Lake Way
Palm Beach, FL 33480-3520, USA

Bronfman, Yefin (Musician)
I C M Artists
40 W 57th St
New York, NY 10019, USA

Bronkey, Jeff (Athlete, Baseball Player)
622 Sunny Brook Dr
Edmond, OK 73034-4224, USA

Bronleewe, Matt (Musician)
Flood Burnstead McCready McCarthy
1700 Hayes St
#304
Nashville, TN 37203, USA

Bronson, Ben (Athlete, Football Player)
13333 West Rd Apt 1717
Houston, TX 77041-6153, USA

Bronson, John
1104 NE 19th St
Cape Coral, FL 33909-5363, USA

Bronson, Oswald P Sr (Educator)
Bethune-Cookman College
President's Office
Daytona Beach, FL 32114, USA

Bronson, Po (Writer)
Random House
1745 Broadway
#B1
New York, NY 10019, USA

Bronson, Zack (Athlete, Football Player)
5735 Jackie Ln
Beaumont, TX 77713-9261, USA

Bronstad, Jim (Athlete, Baseball Player)
63 One Main Pl
Benbrook, TX 76126-4224, USA

Bronstein, Elizabeth (Producer)
c/o Staff Member *Creative Artists Agency (CAA-LA)*
2000 Ave Of The Stars
Los Angeles, CA 90067, USA

Brook, Apple (Actor)
c/o Staff Member *Grays Management & Associates*
Panther House
38 Mount Pleasant
London WC1X 0AP, UK

Brook, Holly (Musician)
c/o Staff Member *Paradigm (Monterey)*
404 W Franklin St
Monterey, CA 93940, USA

Brook, Jayne (Actor)
c/o Leslie Siebert *Gersh (LA)*
9465 Wilshire Blvd
Suite 600
Beverly Hills, CA 90212, USA

Brook, Kelly (Actor)
c/o Joan Hyler *Hyler Management*
20 Ocean Park Blvd
Suite 25
Santa Monica, CA 90405, USA

Brook, Peter S P (Director)
CICT
13 Blvd de Rochechouart
Paris 75009, FRANCE

Brooke, Allison (Music Group, Songwriter, Writer)
2-K/EMI Records
6920 Sunset Blvd
Los Angeles, CA 90028, USA

Brooke, Bob (Athlete, Hockey Player, Olympic Athlete)
15496 Stanbury Curve
Eden Prairie, MN 55347-2433, USA

Brooke, Edward (Politician)
NLIHC
808 Brickell Key Dr Apt 3204
Miami, FL 33131-2692, USA

Brooke, Jonatha (Musician, Songwriter, Writer)
Brooke
1255 5th Ave Apt 7j
New York, NY 10029, USA

Brooke, Paul (Actor)
c/o Staff Member *Caroline Dawson Assoc.*
125 Gloucester Rd
2nd Floor
London SW7 4TE, UK

Brookens, Ike (Athlete, Baseball Player)
1053 Brookens Rd
Fayetteville, PA 17222-9314, USA

Brookens, Tom (Athlete, Baseball Player)
488 Black Gap Rd
Fayetteville, PA 17222-9717, USA

Brooker, Gary (Musician, Songwriter, Writer)
5 Cranley Gardens
London SW7, UNITED KINGDOM (UK)

Brooker, Tommy (Athlete, Football Player)
306 Woodbridge Dr
Tuscaloosa, AL 35406-1923, USA

Brookes, Harvey (Physicist)
Harvard University
Aiken Computation Laboratory
Cambridge, MA 02138, USA

Brookes, Peter (Cartoonist)
London Times
Editorial Dept
1 Pennington St
London E98 1S5, UNITED KINGDOM (UK)

Brooke-Taylor, Tim (Actor, Comedian)
Jill Foster Ltd
3 Lonsdale Road
London SW13 9ED, UNITED KINGDOM (UK)

Brookhart, Maurice S (Misc)
University of North Carolina
Chemistry Dept
Chapel Hill, NC 27514, USA

Brooking, Keith (Athlete, Football Player)
883 Lenox Ct NE
Atlanta, GA 30324-2982, USA

Brookins, Clarence (Athlete, Basketball Player)
8266 Fayette St
Philadelphia, PA 191S0-2002, USA

Brookins, Gary (Cartoonist)
Richmond Newspapers
Editorial Dept
PO Box 85333
Richmond, VA 23293, USA

Brookins, Jason (Athlete, Football Player)
523 N Wade St Apt C
Mexico, MO 65265-1880, USA

Brookner, Anita (Writer)
68 Elm Park Gardens
#6
London SW10 9PB, UNITED KINGDOM (UK)

Brooks, Aaron (Athlete, Football Player)
1005 Middle Quarter Ct
Henrico, VA 23238-5920, USA

Brooks, Albert (Actor, Director, Writer)
3051 Antelo View Dr
Los Angeles, CA 90077, USA

Brooks, Alex (Athlete, Hockey Player)
423 Glenmeadow Dr
Ballwin, MO 63011-3466, USA

Brooks, Amanda (Actor)
c/o Staff Member *Nine Yards Entertainment*
8530 Wilshire Blvd Fl 5
Beverly Hills, CA 90211, USA

Brooks, Angelle (Actor)
c/o Staff Member *Pakula/King & Associates*
9229 Sunset Blvd
Suite 315
Los Angeles, CA 90069, USA

Brooks, Avery (Actor)
360 Christopher Dr
Princeton, NJ 08540, USA

Brooks, Barrett (Athlete, Football Player)
11 Berkshire Dr
Voorhees, NJ 08043-3448, USA

Brooks, Bill (Athlete, Football Player)
1088 Laurelwood
Carmel, IN 46032, USA

Brooks, Bobby D (Athlete, Football Player)
7416 Red Osier Rd
Dallas, TX 75249-1349, USA

Brooks, Bucky (Athlete, Football Player)
5124 Casland Dr
Raleigh, NC 27604, USA

Brooks, Chet (Athlete, Football Player)
655 Shadyway Dr
Dallas, TX 75232, USA

Brooks, Conrad (Actor)
P.O. Box 264
Inwood, WV 25428-0264, USA

Brooks, Danny (Musician)
American Promotions
2011 Ferry Ave
#U19
Camden, NJ 08104, USA

Brooks, David Allen (David A) (Actor)
c/o Staff Member *Candy Entertainment Management*
8981 West Sunset Blvd #310
Hollywood, CA 90069, USA

Brooks, Derrick (Athlete, Football Player)
Derrick Brooks Charities 10014 N Dale Mabry Hwy Ste 101
Tamna, FL 33618-4426, USA

Brooks, Donnie (Musician)
Al Lampkin Entertainment
1817 W Verdugo Ave
Burbank, CA 91506, USA

Brooks, Ed (Athlete, Golfer)
6604 Augusta Rd
Fort Worth, TX 76132-4564, USA

Brooks, E R (Business Person)
Central & South West Corp
1616 Woodall Rogers Freeway
Dallas, TX 75202, USA

Brooks, Ethan (Athlete, Football Player)
8 Gatewood
Avon, CT 06001, USA

Brooks, Frederick P Jr (Mathematician, Scientist)
413 Granville Road
Chapel Hill, NC 27514, USA

Brooks, Garth (Actor, Musician, Producer, Songwriter)
20955 S. 4092nd Rd
Claremore, OK 74019, USA

Brooks, Geraldine (Writer)
c/o Staff Member *Viking Press*
375 Hudson St
New York, NY 10014, USA

Brooks, Golden (Actor)
7230 Pacific View Dr
Los Angeles, CA 90068, USA

Brooks, Greg (Athlete, Football Player)
3041 Alex Kornman Blvd
Harvey, LA 70058-2012, USA

Brooks, Harvey (Scientist)
35 N Great Rd
Lincoln, MA 01773-1305, USA

Brooks, Heather (Stylist)
c/o Staff Member *Fifty8 Artists*
58 W Huron St
Chicago, IL 60610, USA

Brooks, Herb (Athlete)
180 Birchwood Ave
St Paul, MN 55110-1612

Brooks, Hubert (Hubie) (Athlete, Baseball
Player)
15001 Olive St
Hesperia, CA 92345-3306, USA

Brooks, Jamal (Athlete, Football Player)
8 Chestnut Bluffs Ct
Greensboro, NC 27407-6376, USA

Brooks, James (Athlete, Football Player)
2876 Sycamore Creek Dr
Independence, KY 41051-8410, USA

Brooks, James (General)
2257 Mandeville Canyon Rd
Los Angeles, CA 90049-1826, USA

Brooks, James L (Actor, Director,
Producer)
1716 Westridge Rd
Los Angeles, CA 90049, USA

Brooks, Jason (Actor)
c/o Staff Member *Commonwealth Talent
Group*
PO Box 36514
Los Angeles, CA 90036, USA

Brooks, Jerry (Athlete, Baseball Player)
15152 Mountain View Ln
Frisco, TX 75035-6882, USA

Brooks, Jimmie (Athlete, Football Player)
4505 Cherry Forest Cir
Louisville, KY 40245-2124

Brooks, Joel (Actor)
c/o Martin Gage *Gage Group, The (LA)*
14724 Ventura Blvd
Suite 505
Sherman Oaks, CA 91403, USA

Brooks, John E (Educator)
College of Holy Cross
President's Office
Worcester, MA 01610, USA

Brooks, Jon (Athlete, Football Player)
104 Carver St
Saluda, SC 29138, USA

Brooks, Karen (Musician)
5408 Clear View Lane
Waterford, WI 53185, USA

Brooks, Kevin (Athlete, Football Player)
11620 Audelia Rd Apt 614
Dallas, TX 75243-5683, USA

Brooks, Kimberly A (Actor)
c/o Kevin Turner *Coast to Coast Talent
Group*
3350 Barham Blvd
Los Angeles, CA 90068, USA

Brooks, Kix (Musician, Songwriter)
Brooks & Dunn
PO Box 120669
Nashville, TN 37212, USA

Brooks, Lala (Misc)
Superstars Unlimited
PO Box 371371
Las Vegas, NV 89137, USA

Brooks, Larry (Athlete, Football Player)
Virginia State University PO Box 9058
Attn: Football Coaching Staff
Petersburu, VA 23806-0001, USA

Brooks, Lee (Athlete, Football Player)
4206 Bamford Dr
Austin, TX 78731, USA

Brooks, Macey (Athlete, Football Player)
693 Manhattan Cir
Oswego, IL 60543-9802, USA

Brooks, Mark (Athlete, Golfer)
4215 Pershing Ave
Fort Worth, TX 76107-4314, USA

Brooks, Mehcad (Actor)
c/o David (Dave) Fleming *Mosaic Media
Group*
9200 W. Sunset Blvd
10th Floor
Los Angeles, CA 90069, USA

Brooks, Mel (Actor, Director)
c/o Staff Member *BrooksFilms Ltd / Culver
Studios*
9336 W Washington Blvd
Culver City, CA 90232

Brooks, Meredith (Musician)
2591 Leicester Dr
Los Angeles, CA 90046, USA

Brooks, Michael (Athlete, Football Player)
30 Pine Tree Dr
Honey Brook, PA 19344, USA

Brooks, Michael (Athlete, Basketball
Player, Olympic Athlete)
495 Bethany St
San Diego, CA 92114-5539, USA

Brooks, Michael (Athlete, Football Player)
5002 Weatherstone Dr
Greensboro, NC 27406, USA

Brooks, Mike (Athlete, Football Player)
716 2nd Ave
Ruston, LA 71270-6066, USA

Brooks, Nate (Athlete, Boxer, Olympic
Athlete)
21274 Ellacott Pkwy
Apt M208
Cleveland, OH 44128-6600, USA

Brooks, Nathan (Boxer)
3139 Albion Road
Cleveland, OH 44120, USA

Brooks, Reggie (Athlete, Football Player)
1701 Portage Ave
South Bend, IN 46616-1919, USA

Brooks, Reggie (Athlete, Football Player)
1701 Portage Ave
South Bend, IN 46616, USA

Brooks, Rich (Athlete, Coach, Football
Coach, Football Player)
700 Delaney Woods
Nicholasville, KY 40356-8781, USA

Brooks, Richard (Actor)
333 Washington Blvd
#102
Marina del Rey, CA 90292, USA

Brooks, Robert (Athlete, Football Player)
8611 N 17th Pl
Phoenix, AZ 85020, USA

Brooks, Ross (Athlete, Hockey Player)
196 Old River Rd
Apt 215
Lincoln, RI 02865, USA

Brooks, Steve (Athlete, Football Player)
3403 36th St
Lubbock, TX 79413-2233, USA

Brooks, Terry (Writer)
Del Rey Books
1540 Broadway
New York, NY 10036, USA

Brooks, Tony (Athlete, Football Player)
19626 Northrop St
Cassopolis, MI 49031, USA

Brooks & Dunn (Music Group, Musician)
c/o Rick Shipp *WmE2 (WMA-TN)*
1600 Division St
Suite 300
Nashville, TN 37203, USA

Brooks Jr, Cliff (Athlete, Football Player)
12023 Briar Forest Dr
Houston, TX 77077, USA

Brooks Jr., Mo (Congressman, Politician)
1641 Longworth HOB
Washington, DC 20515, USA

Brophy, Jay (Athlete, Football Player)
2117 Prestwick Dr
Uniontown, OH 44685-8847, USA

Brophy, John (Athlete, Hockey Player)
141 Carpenter Ln
Harrisonburg, VA 22801-9777, USA

Brophy, Kevin (Actor)
15010 Hamlin St
Van Nuys, CA 91411, USA

Brophy, Nancy (Athlete, Golfer)
141 Carpenter Ln
Harrisonburg, VA 22801, USA

Brophy, Theodore F (Business Person)
60 Arch St
Greenwich, CT 06830, USA

Brorby, Wade (Judge)
US Court of Appeals
2120 Capitol Ave
Cheyenne, WY 82001, USA

Broshears, Robert (Artist)
Robert Broshears Studio
8020 NW Holly Road
Bremerton, WA 98312, USA

Brosius, Scott D (Athlete, Baseball Player)
Linfield College
900 SE Baker St
HHPA Complex, Mail Code A440
McMinnville, OR 97128-fiRq4, USA

Broski, David C (Educator)
University of Illinois
President's Office
Chicago, IL 60607, USA

Brosnan, Jim (Athlete, Baseball Player)
7742 Churchill St
Morton Grove, IL 60053-1805, USA

Brosnan, Pierce (Actor, Producer)
31112 Broad Beach Rd
Malibu, CA 90265, USA

Bross, Terry (Athlete, Baseball Player)
7952 E Camino Real
Scottsdale, AZ 85255-6136, USA

Brossart, Willie (Athlete, Hockey Player)
9318 Susquehanna Trl
Ashland, VA 23005, USA

Brosseau, Frank (Athlete, Baseball Player)
41 Island Rd
Saint Paul, MN 55127-2635, USA

Brostek, Bern (Athlete, Football Player)
PO Box 44552
Kamuela, HI 96743-4552, USA

Broten, Aaron (Athlete, Hockey Player)
307 3rd Ave.
Roseau, SE 56751, USA

Broten, Neal (Athlete, Hockey Player,
Olympic Athlete)
N8216 690th St
River Falls, WI 54022-4535, USA

Broten, Paul (Athlete, Hockey Player)
2971 Jordan Ct
Saint Paul, MN 55125, USA

Brothers, Bellamy, The (Musician)
c/o Staff Member *Agency for the
Performing Arts (APA-LA)*
405 S Beverly Dr
Suite 500
Beverly Hills, CA 90212-4425, USA

Brothers, Dr Joyce (Scientist)
c/o Monique Moss *Integrated PR*
9025 Wilshire Blvd
Suite 400
Beverly Hills, CA 90211, USA

Brotherton, John (Actor)
c/o Gabrielle Krengel *Domain Talent*
9229 Sunset Boulevard
Suite 710
Los Angeles, CA 90069, USA

Brotherton, Michael (Race Car Driver)
1317 Summertime Trails
Lewisville, TX 75067, USA

Brotman, Jeffrey (Business Person)
Costco Wholesale Corp
999 Lake Dr
Issaquah, WA 98027, USA

Brough, Randi (Actor)
11684 Ventura Blvd
#476
Studio City, CA 91604, USA

Brough Clapp, A Louise (Tennis Player)
1808 Voluntary Rd
Vista, CA 92083, USA

Broughton, Bruce (Composer)
c/o Staff Member *Evolution Music
Partners*
1680 N. Vine St.
Hollywood, CA 90028, USA

Broughton, Luther (Athlete, Football
Player)
PO Box 371
Huger, SC 29450, USA

Broughton, Willie (Athlete, Football
Player)
1724 Lacy Ln
Mesquite, TX 75181, USA

Brouhard, Mark (Athlete, Baseball Player)
6289 Jackie Ave
Woodland Hills, CA 91367-1424, USA

Broussard, Ben (Athlete, Baseball Player)
2067 Cedar Breaks Rd
Georgetown, TX 78633-8200, USA

Broussard, Fred (Athlete, Football Player)
2856 FM 1011 Rd
Liberty, TX 77575-7430, USA

Broussard, Marc (Musician)
c/o Staff Member *Paradigm (Monterey)*
404 W Franklin St
Monterey, CA 93940, USA

Broussard, Rebecca (Actor)
413 Howland Canal
Venice, CA 90291, USA

Broussard, Steve (Athlete, Football Player)
113 Waterland Way
Frederick, MD 21702-4094, USA

Broussard, Susan (Stylist)
63 Starview Way
San Francisco, CA 94131

Brouwenstyn, Gerada (Actor)
Bachplein 3
Amsterdam NL-1077 GH, The
Netherlands

Brouwenstyn, Gerarda (Opera Singer)
3 Bachpiein
Armsterdam, NETHERLANDS

Brow, Scott (Athlete, Baseball Player)
1194 W Remington Dr
Chandler, AZ 85286-6385, USA

Browder, Ben (Actor)
551 Live Oak Circle Dr
Calabasas, CA 91302, USA

Browder, Felix E (Mathematician)
4 Foulet Dr
Princeton, NJ 08540-7638, USA

Brower, Bob (Athlete, Baseball Player)
2703 North Van Buren St
Hutchinson, KS 67502-2017, USA

Brower, James (Jim) (Athlete, Baseball
Player)
Kane County Cougars 34W002 Cherry Ln
Attn Coaching Staff
Geneva, IL 60134-4104, USA

Brower, Jordan
9100 Wilshire Blvd #503E
Beverly Hills, CA 90212

Brower, Jordan Lloyd (Actor)
c/o Beverly Strong *Strong Management*
3532 Hayden Ave
Culver City, CA 90232, USA

Brower, Laurie (Athlete, Golfer)
6407 Peoria Ave
Lubbock, TX 79413, USA

Brown, Aaron (Correspondent)
c/o Staff Member *NS Bienstock Inc*
250 W 57th St
Suite 333
New York, NY 10107, USA

Brown, Aaron C (Athlete, Football Player)
3922 W Robson St
Tampa, FL 33614-2636, USA

Brown, A B (Athlete, Football Player)
224 Wesley St
Salem, NJ 08079, USA

Brown, Adrian (Baseball Player)
Pittsburgh Pirates
604 Pike St
McComb, MS 39648-2250, USA

Brown, Alison (Musician, Songwriter,
Writer)
SRO Artists
6629 University Ave
#206
Middleton, WI 53562, USA

Brown, Allen (Athlete, Football Player)
454 Highway 569
Ferriday, LA 71334-4445, USA

Brown, Alton (Chef, Television Host)
441 Church St NE
Marietta, GA 30060, USA

Brown, Alton (Athlete, Baseball Player)
253 Consul Ave
Virginia Beach, VA 23462-3511, USA

Brown, Andre (Athlete, Football Player)
11245 S Emerald Ave
Chicago, IL 60628, USA

Brown, Andrew
561 Placid Run Rd
Orange Citv, FL 32763-6626, USA

Brown, Andy (Athlete, Hockey Player)
6243 s 125 w
Trafalgar, IN 46181-8799, USA

Brown, Anthony (Athlete, Football Player)
42561 Cavalier Ct
Canton, MI 48187-2375, USA

Brown, Antonio (Athlete, Football Player)
c/o Drew Rosenhaus *Rosenhaus Sports
Representation*
6400 Allison Road
Miami Beach, FL 33141, USA

Brown, Antron (Race Car Driver)
45 Waln Rd
Trenton, NJ 08620, USA

Brown, Arnie (Athlete, Hockey Player)
General Delivery
Woodview, ON K0L 3E0, Canada

Brown, Arnold (Athlete, Football Player)
8763 Stephens Church Rd
Wilmington, NC 28411-7985, USA

Brown, Arthur E Jr (General)
35 Fairway Winds Place
Hilton Head Island, SC 29928, USA

Brown, Ashley Nicole (Actor)
Hervey/Grimes
PO Box 64249
Los Angeles, CA 90064, USA

Brown, Bailey (Judge)
US Court of Appeals
Federal Building
167 N Main St
Memphis, TN 38103, USA

Brown, Bill (Commentator)
15910 Knolls Lodge Dr
Houston, TX 77095-1664, USA

Brown, Bill (Athlete, Football Player)
9365 Libby Ln
Eden Prairie, MN 55347-4282, USA

Brown, Billy Aaron (Actor)
c/o Staff Member *Stone Manners Salners
Agency (LA)*
9911 W Pico Blvd Ste 1400
Los Angeles, CA 90035, USA

Brown, Billy Ray (Athlete, Golfer)
4110 Woodlake Ln
Missouri City, TX 77459-4330, USA

Brown, Blair (Actor)
18 E 53rd St
#140
New York, NY 10022, USA

Brown, Bob (Athlete, Football Player)
PO Box 211081
Saint Louis, MO 63121-9081, USA

Brown, Bob (Athlete, Basketball Player)
7 Charleston St S
Sugar Land, TX 77478-3656, USA

Brown, Bobby (Athlete, Baseball Player)
700 Pleasant Ridge Ct
Chesapeake, VA 23322-2747, USA

Brown, Bobby (Athlete, Baseball Player)
4100 Clarke Ave
Fort Worth, TX 76107-2407, USA

Brown, Bobby (Actor, Dancer, Musician,
Producer, Songwriter)
c/o Staff Member *WmE2 (WMA-LA)*
1 William Morris Pl
Beverly Hills, CA 90212, USA

Brown, Booker (Athlete, Football Player)
3354 Arthur Ave
Mojave, CA 93501-1304, USA

Brown, Boyd (Athlete, Football Player)
1610 167th Ave NE
Bellevue, WA 98008-2909, USA

Brown, Brant (Athlete, Baseball Player)
Frisco Roughriders 7300 Rough Riders Trl
Attn: Coaching Staff
Frisco, TX 75034-9088, USA

Brown, Brianna (Actor)
c/o Gladys Gonzalez *John Carrabino
Management*
5900 Wilshire Blvd Fl 4 #406
Los Angeles, CA 90036, USA

Brown, Bruce (Photographer)
15550 Calle Real
Gaviota, CA 93117, USA

Brown, Bryan (Actor)
c/o Staff Member *Steve Himber
Entertainment*
211 S Beverly Dr #601
Beverly Hills, CA 90212, USA

Brown, Campbell (Correspondent)
c/o Staff Member *CNN (Atlanta)*
One CNN Center
PO Box 105366
Atlanta, GA 30303, USA

Brown, Candace (Actor)
c/o Judy Orbach *Judy O Productions*
6136 Glen Holly
Hollywood, CA 90068, USA

Brown, Carlos (Athlete, Football Player)
1106 E Newhall Dr
Fresno, CA 93720, USA

Brown, Cedric (Athlete, Football Player)
9005 Salsbury ln Apt 11
Oklahoma City, OK 73132-2050, USA

Brown, Cedrick (Athlete, Football Player)
74 Arbor Meadow Dr
Sicklerville, NJ 08081-1754, USA

Brown, C Edward (Eddie) (Athlete,
Football Player)
3465 Commodore Pt
Knoxville, TN 37922, USA

Brown, Chad (Athlete, Football Player)
10287 Dowling Way
Highlands Ranch, CO 80126-4769, USA

Brown, Chad (Actor)
c/o Staff Member *Sterling/Winters
Company, The*
10877 Wilshire Blvd.
15th Floor
Los Angeles, CA 90024, USA

Brown, Charles (Athlete, Football Player)
2942 River Rd
Johns Island, SC 29455, USA

Brown, Charles E (Athlete, Football
Player)
7317 S Merrill Ave
Chicago, IL 60649, USA

Brown, Charlie (Athlete, Hockey Player,
Olympic Athlete)
4677 Parkridge Dr
Saint Paul, MN 55123-2130, USA

Brown, Charlie (Athlete, Football Player)
7317 5 Merrill Ave
Chicago, IL 60649-3208, USA

Brown, Charlie (Athlete, Football Player)
5243 Wabada Ave
Saint Louis, MO 63113-1121, USA

Brown, Charlie (Athlete, Football Player)
3113 Cherry Valley Cir
Fairfield, CA 94534-7510, USA

Brown, Charlie R (Athlete, Football
Player)
5226 Washington Pl
Saint Louis, MO 63108, USA

Brown, Chris (Athlete, Football Player)
7161 Cypress Dr
Westerville, OH 43082, USA

Brown, Chris (Musician)
2738 Rinconia Dr
Los Angeles, CA 90068, USA

Brown, Chris (Athlete, Football Player)
251 Riverbend Dr
Franklin, TN 37064-5518, USA

Brown, Chuck (Race Car Driver)
5082 Old North Carolina Hwy. 49
Asheboro, NC 27203, USA

Brown, Chucky (Athlete, Basketball
Player)
102 Balsamwood Ct
Cary, NC 27513-3456, USA

Brown, Cindy (Athlete, Basketball Player)
2 Championship Dr
Auburn Hills, MI 48326, USA

Brown, Clancy (Actor)
3141 Oakdell Lane
Studio City, CA 91604, USA

Brown, Clay (Athlete, Football Player)
PO Box 904
Eagar, AZ 85925-0904, USA

Brown, Cleophus (Athlete, Baseball
Player)
3912 Sharon Church Rd
Pinson, AL 35126-2660, USA

Brown, Clifford (Athlete, Baseball Player)
5104 N 37th St
Tampa, FL 33610-6421, USA

Brown, Cornell (Athlete, Football Player)
1600 Sangloe Pl
Lynchburg, VA 24502-1822, USA

Brown, Corrine (Congressman, Politician)
2336 Rayburn HOB
Washington, DC 20515, USA

Brown, Corwin (Athlete, Football Player)
613 Primrose Ln
Matteson, IL 60443-1762, USA

Brown, Courtney (Athlete, Football Player)
1133 Schurlknight Rd
Saint Stephen, SC 29479-3617, USA

Brown, Curt (Athlete, Baseball Player)
8331 Sawpine Rd
Delray Beach, FL 33446-9796, USA

Brown, Curtis (Athlete, Football Player)
7370 San Diego Ave Apt 1
Saint Louis, MO 63121-2259, USA

Brown, Curtis (Athlete, Baseball Player)
3200 Cloudview Dr
Sacramento, CA 95833-2700, USA

Brown, Curtis (Athlete, Hockey Player)
467 Carroll St
Sunnyvale, CA 94086-6204, USA

Brown, Curtis L Colonel (Astronaut)
19500 E Highway 6
Alvin, TX 77511-7458, USA

Brown, Curtis L Jr (Astronaut)
204 Starrwood
Hudson, WI 54016, USA

Brown, Dale (Writer)
c/o Robert Gottlieb *Trident Media Group LLC*
41 Madison Ave
36th Floor
New York, NY 10010, USA

Brown, Dale D (Coach, Sportscaster)
ESPN-TV
Sports Dept ESPN Plaza
935 Middle St
Bristol, CT 06010, USA

Brown, Dan (Writer)
c/o Staff Member *Doubleday/RandomHouse*
1745 Broadway
New York, NY 10019, USA

Brown, Daniel G (General)
Deputy CinC
US Transportation Command
Scott Air Force Base, IL 62225, USA

Brown, Dante (Athlete, Football Player)
c/o Liza Anderson *Anderson Group Public Relations*
8060 Melrose Ave Fl 4
Los Angeles, CA 90046, USA

Brown, Daren (Athlete, Baseball Player)
Tacoma Rainiers 2502 S Tyler St Attn:
Managers Office
Tacoma, WA 98405-1051, USA

Brown, Darrell (Athlete, Baseball Player)
Detroit Tigers
2808 Northampton Pl
Oklahoma City, OK 73120-3010, USA

Brown, Darryl (Stylist)
c/o Staff Member *Ken Barboza Associates*
115 W 30th St Rm 203
New York, NY 10001, USA

Brown, Dave
216 Watchung Frk
Westfield, NJ 07090-3814, USA

Brown, Dave (Athlete, Hockey Player)
c/o Staff Member *Philadelphia Flyers*
First Union Spectrum
3601 S Broad St, Suite 2
Philadelphia, PA 19148, USA

Brown, David P (Athlete)
345 Willow Springs Drive
Talent, OR 97540-9682, USA

Brown, Dee (Athlete, Football Player)
3278 Margellina Dr
Charlotte, NC 28210-4086, USA

Brown, Dee (Athlete, Baseball Player)
2626 Balmoral Ct
Kissimmee, FL 34744-8442, USA

Brown, Dee (Athlete, Basketball Player)
575 Birnamwood Dr
Suwanee, GA 30024-7577, USA

Brown, Denise (Misc)
PO Box 3777
Monarch Bay, CA 92629, USA

Brown, Derek
1283 Carrizo St NW
Los Lunas, NM 87031-6938, USA

Brown, Derek (Athlete, Football Player)
13 Four Leaf Mnr
Rexford, NY 12148, USA

Brown, Dermal (Baseball Player)
Kansas City Royals
2626 Balmoral Ct
Kissimmee, FL 34744-8442, USA

Brown, Don (Athlete, Football Player)
5167 SW 129th Ter
Miramar, FL 33027-5837, USA

Brown, Donald C (Athlete, Football Player)
2797 Union Ave
San Jose, CA 95124, USA

Brown, Donald David (Biologist)
6511 Abbey View Way
Baltimore, MD 21212-1373, USA

Brown, Dorian (Actor)
c/o Staff Member *McKeon-Myones Management*
3500 Olive Ave
Suite 770
Burbank, CA 91505, USA

Brown, Doug (Athlete, Hockey Player)
3188 Bradway Blvd
Bloomfield Hills, MI 48301, USA

Brown, Dustin (Athlete, Hockey Player)
226 Bundy Rd
Ithaca, NY 14850, USA

Brown, Eddie (Athlete, Football Player)
8400 SW 133rd Avenue Rd Apt 214
Miami, FL 33183-4543, USA

Brown, Elton
1955 W Yosemite Dr
Chandler, AZ 85248-4897, USA

Brown, Emil (Athlete, Baseball Player)
17804 Paxton Ave
Lansing, IL 60438-1520, USA

Brown, Eric (Athlete, Football Player)
2226 Drake Falls Dr
Pearland, TX 77584-1760, USA

Brown, Errol (Musician)
c/o Staff Member *International Artistes*
Holborn Hall - 4th Floor
London WC1V 7BD, UK

Brown, Faith (Actor)
Million Dollar Music Co
12 Praed Mews
London W2 1QY, UNITED KINGDOM (UK)

Brown, Foxy (Musician)
c/o Lee Daniels *Lee Daniels Entertainment*
315 W 36th St Fl 10
New York, NY 10037, USA

Brown, Fred (Athlete, Football Player)
1050 Riverbend Club Dr SE
Atlanta, GA 30339-2805, USA

Brown, Fred (Athlete, Basketball Player, Coach)
3696 72nd Pl SE
Mercer Island, WA 98040-3353, USA

Brown, Fred R (Athlete, Football Player)
4128 Rigel Ave
Lompoc, CA 93436, USA

Brown, Gary (Athlete, Football Player)
5 Crystal Ln
Brentwood, NY 11717, USA

Brown, Gary (Athlete, Football Player)
35401 Saddle Crk
Avon, OH 44011-4917, USA

Brown, Gates (Athlete, Baseball Player)
17206 Santa Barbara Dr
Detroit, MI 48221-2525, USA

Brown, George (Athlete, Basketball Player)
24652 Santa Barbara St
Southfield, MI 48075-2526, USA

Brown, Georg Stanford (Actor)
2565 Greenvalley Rd
Los Angeles, CA 90046, USA

Brown, Gilbert (Athlete, Football Player)
49374 Sherwood Ct
Belleville, MI 48111-8844, USA

Brown, Gordie (Comedian)
c/o Staff Member *WmE2 (WMA-LA)*
1 William Morris Pl
Beverly Hills, CA 90212, USA

Brown, Greg (Athlete, Football Player)
1016 Hartley Ct
Sicklerville, NJ 08081, USA

Brown, Greg (Athlete, Hockey Player)
43 Ladds Way
Scituate, MA 02066, USA

Brown, Guy (Athlete, Football Player)
2233 Forest Hollow Park
Dallas, TX 75228-7826, USA

Brown, Hal (Athlete, Baseball Player)
4216 Henderson Rd
Greensboro, NC 27410-4305, USA

Brown, Harold (Politician)
Strategic/International Studies Center
Strategic Study Center1800 K St NW
Washington, DC 20006-2230, USA

Brown, Henry (Actor)
1101 E Pike St
#300
Seattle, WA 98122, USA

Brown, Henry (Athlete, Baseball Player)
4075 N 61st St
Milwaukee, WI 53216-1210, USA

Brown, Henry W (War Hero)
2825 Carter Road
Unit 117
Sumter, SC 29150-1733, USA

Brown, Heritage Doris (Athlete, Track Athlete)
Seattle Pacific College
Athletic Dept
Seattle, WA 98119, USA

Brown, Hubie (Basketball Coach, Coach)
120 Foxridge Rd NW
Atlanta, GA 30327-4310, USA

Brown, Hyman (Engineer)
Colorado State University
Civil Engineering Dept
Fort Collins, CO 80523, USA

Brown, Ivory Lee (Athlete, Football Player)
9811 Dale Crest Dr Apt 1026
Dallas, TX 75220, USA

Brown, Jackie (Athlete, Baseball Player)
7337 E 136 Rd
Holdenville, OK 74848-6012, USA

Brown, James (Sportscaster)
Fox-TV
Sports Dept
205 W 67th St
New York, NY 10021, USA

Brown, James (Athlete, Football Player)
3723 SW 49th Pl
Fort Lauderdale, FL 33312-8231, USA

Brown, James (Musician)
c/o Rob Heller *WME (LA)*
9601 Wilshire Blvd Fl 3
Beverly Hills, CA 90210, USA

Brown, James R (General)
18286 Buccaneer Terrace
Leesburg, VA 20176-8479, USA

Brown, Jamie (Athlete, Football Player)
25023 Riding Center Dr
Chantilly, VA 20152-6039, USA

Brown, Jamie (Athlete, Baseball Player)
4050 Bailey Acres Cir
Meridian, MS 39305-9263, USA

Brown, Jamie (Actor)
c/o Melisa Spamer *Domain Talent*
9229 Sunset Boulevard
Suite 710
Los Angeles, CA 90069, USA

Brown, Jammal (Athlete, Football Player)
2223 NE 36th Street
Lawton, OK 73507, USA

Brown, Janice Lee (Aviator)
12240 Backdrop Ct
Bakersfield, CA 93306-9717, USA

Brown, Jarvis (Athlete, Baseball Player)
1537 Teal Dr
Lawrenceville, GA 30043-3296, USA

Brown, Jason (Athlete, Football Player)
8810 Gilly Way
Randallstown, MD 21133-5300, USA

Brown, Jay W Jr (Financier)
MBIA Inc
113 King St
Armonk, NY 10504, USA

Brown, J B (Athlete, Football Player)
12520 Woodsong Ln
Bowie, MD 20721-4224, USA

Brown, J Cristopher (Cris) (Baseball Player)
5015 Brighton Ave
Los Angeles, CA 90062, USA

Brown, Jeff (Athlete, Hockey Player)
800 Tara Oaks Dr
Chesterfield, MO 63005, USA

Brown, Jeremy (Athlete, Baseball Player)
704 Cobb St
Birmingham, AL 35209-6515, USA

Brown, Jerry (Politician)
288 3rd St Unit 506
Oakland, CA 94607-4571, USA

Brown, J Glen (Horse Racer)
US Trotting Association 750 Michigan
Ave
Columbus, OH 43215-1191, USA

Brown, J Gordon (Government Official)
House of Commons
Westminister
London SW1A 0AA, UNITED KINGDOM
(UK)

Brown, Jim (Athlete, Football Player)
1851 Sunset Plaza Dr
West Hollywood, CA 90069, USA

Brown, Jim Ed (Musician)
5930 Cloverland Dr
Brentwood, TN 37027, USA

Brown, John (Athlete, Basketball Player)
1329 N Florissant Rd
Saint Louis, MO 63135, USA

Brown, John (Athlete, Football Player)
101 Gadshill Pl
Pittsburgh, PA 15237-2341, USA

Brown, Johnny (Actor)
2732 Woodhaven Dr
Los Angeles, CA 90068, USA

Brown, Jonathan Daniel (Actor)
c/o Shawna Kornberg *Creative Artists
Agency (CAA-LA)*
2000 Ave Of The Stars
Los Angeles, CA 90067, USA

Brown, Jophrey (Athlete, Baseball Player)
3008 W 81st St
Inglewood, CA 90305, USA

Brown, Judge Joe (Judge)
P.O. Box 949
Los Angeles, CA 90078, USA

Brown, Julie (Downtown) (Entertainer)
3351 Berry Dr
Studio City, CA 91604, USA

Brown, Junior (Musician)
c/o Staff Member *Paradigm (Monterey)*
404 W Franklin St
Monterey, CA 93940, USA

Brown, Kaci (Musician)
c/o Staff Member *Interscope Records (LA)
- Main*
2220 Colorado Ave
Santa Monica, CA 90404, USA

Brown, Kale (Actor)
c/o Staff Member *Gage Group, The (LA)*
14724 Ventura Blvd
Suite 505
Sherman Oaks, CA 91403, USA

Brown, Katie (Designer, Television Host)
c/o Staff Member *Style Network*
5750 Wilshire Blvd
Los Angeles, CA 90036, USA

Brown, Kedrick (Athlete, Basketball
Player)
151 Merrimac St
#1
Boston, MA 02114, USA

Brown, Keith (Athlete, Baseball Player)
139 Lakeshore Dr
Old Hickorv, TN 37138-1110, USA

Brown, Keith (Athlete, Hockey Player)
4615 Sloan Rdg
Cumming, GA 30028, USA

Brown, Ken (Athlete, Football Player)
14811 Valleyheart Dr
Sherman Oaks, CA 91403-1602, USA

Brown, Ken (Athlete, Football Player)
1952 S Magnolia St Apt 3T
Denver, CO 80224-2208, USA

Brown, Ken (Athlete, Hockey Player)
2708 Checker Dr
Cedar Park, TX 78613-1640, USA

Brown, Ken J (Athlete, Football Player)
2004 Miramar Blvd
Oklahoma City, OK 73111, USA

Brown, Kenneth J (Misc)
Graphic Communications Int'l Union
1900 L St NW
Washington, DC 20036, USA

Brown, Kevin (Athlete, Baseball Player)
105 Browns Rdg
Macon, GA 31210-8614, USA

Brown, Kevin (Athlete, Baseball Player)
20 McKilt Ct
Sacramento, CA 95835-1334, USA

Brown, Kevin (Athlete, Baseball Player)
9201 Ryan Ct
Evansville, IN 47712-5410, USA

Brown, Kevin (Race Car Driver)
Jokers Wild Racing
99 S. 1000 West
Clearfield, UT 84015, USA

Brown, Kimberlin Ann (Actor)
c/o Staff Member *Pakula/King &
Associates*
9229 Sunset Blvd
Suite 315
Los Angeles, CA 90069, USA

Brown, Kimberly J (Actor)
c/o Diane Brown *Gemstone Talent*
27943 Seco Canyon Rd #212
Santa Clarita, CA 91350, USA

Brown, Koffee (Musician)
Red Entertainment Group
481 Eight Ave
#1750
New York, NY 10001

Brown, Kris (Athlete, Football Player)
9715 Rockbrook Rd
Omaha, NE 68124-1928, USA

Brown, Kwame
8713 Sagekirk Ct
Charlotte, NC 28278-9040, USA

Brown, Kwarne (Athlete, Basketball
Player)
601 F St NW
Washington, DC 20004, USA

Brown, Lacey (Musician)
c/o Staff Member *19 Entertainment*
33/32 Ransomes Dock
35-37 Parkgate Rd
London SW11 4NP, UK

Brown, Larry (Athlete, Hockey Player)
21 Landing Dr
Dobbs Ferry, NY 10522, USA

Brown, Larry (Athlete, Hockey Player)
5781 Eucalyptus Dr
Garden Valley, CA 95633, USA

Brown, Larry (Athlete, Football Player)
1377 Glencoe Ave
Pittsburgh, PA 15205, USA

Brown, Larry (Basketball Coach,
Basketball Player, Coach, Olympic
Athlete)
1030 Green Valley Rd
Bryn Mawr, PA 19010-1912, USA

Brown, Larry (Athlete, Football Player)
12004 Piney Glen Ln
Potomac, MD 20854, USA

Brown, Larry (Athlete, Baseball Player)
13158 La Mirada Cir
Wellington, FL 33414-3997, USA

Brown, Lee P (Government Official)
Mayor's Office
City Hall
901 Bagby St #300
Houston, TX 77002, USA

Brown, Leon (Athlete, Baseball Player)
7537 S La Rosa Dr
Tempe, AZ 85283-4627, USA

Brown, Leonard (Baseball Player)
Homestead Grays
4411 19th St NE
Wahington, DC 20018-3305, USA

Brown, Les (Motivational Speaker)
PO Box 806217
Chicago, IL 60680, USA

Brown, Levi (Athlete, Football Player)
2065 E Champagne Pl
Chandler, AZ 85249-3530, USA

Brown, Lomas (Athlete, Football Player)
5049 Elizabeth Lake Rd
Waterford, MI 48327-2741, USA

Brown, Louis (Business Person)
Street Smart Systems
4426-B Hugh Howell Rd Ste 200
Tucker, GA 30084, USA

Brown, Mack (Coach)
University of Texas
Athletic Dept
Austin, TX 78712, USA

Brown, Marc (Writer)
PO Box 873
W Tisbury, MA 02575-0873, USA

Brown, Mark (Athlete, Football Player)
27615W 81st Way
Davie, FL 33328, USA

Brown, Mark (Athlete, Baseball Player)
108 NE 1st Street Ter
Blue Springs, MO 64014-2814, USA

Brown, Mark N (Astronaut)
80 Earlsgate Road
Dayton, OH 45440, USA

Brown, Mark N Colonel (Astronaut)
M T C Technologies Inc 4032 Linden Ave
Attn Presidents Office
Dayton, OH 45432-3006, USA

Brown, Marty (Athlete, Baseball Player)
Las Vegas Sls 850 Las Vegas Blvd N Attn
Managers Office
Las Vegas, NV 89101-2062, USA

Brown, Matt (Director)
c/o James Adams *Schreck Rose Dapello
Adams & Hurwitz*
1790 Broadway
20th Floor
New York, NY 10019, USA

Brown, Matthew (Athlete, Baseball
Player)
11259 N Cutlass St
Hayden, ID 83835-8654, USA

Brown, Max (Actor)
c/o Lena Roklin *Luber Roklin
Management*
8530 Wilshire Blvd
6th Floor
Beverly Hills, CA 90211, USA

Brown, Melanie (Dancer, Musician)
2132 Mount Olympus Dr
Los Angeles, CA 90046, USA

Brown, Michael S (Nobel Prize Laureate)
5719 Redwood Lane
Dallas, TX 75209-2421, USA

Brown, Mike (Athlete, Baseball Player)
710 95th Ave N
Naples, FL 34108-2457, USA

Brown, Mike (Astronomer)
California Institute of Technology
Astronomy Dept
Pasadena, CA 91125, USA

Brown, Mike (Athlete, Baseball Player)
2904 E Minton St
Mesa, AZ 85213-1697, USA

Brown, Mike (Coach)
c/o Staff Member *Cleveland Cavaliers*
1 Center Ct
Cleveland, OH 44115, USA

Brown, Milford (Athlete, Football Player)
6282 Chamar Cir
Kannapolis, NC 28081-7726, USA

Brown, Myron (Athlete, Basketball Player)
3025 Timbercreek Dr
McKrees Rocks, PA 15136-1509, USA

Brown, Na (Athlete, Football Player)
PO Box 853
Fletcher, NC 28732-0853, USA

Brown, Norman (Musician)
c/o Staff Member *APA Talent And Literary
Agency (NY)*
45 W 45th St Ste 804
New York, NY 10036, USA

Brown, Norman W (Business Person)
Foote Cone Belding
101 E Erie St
Chicago, IL 60611, USA

Brown, Norris (Athlete, Football Player)
320 Pinehaven St Ext
Laurens, SC 29360, USA

Brown, Olivia (Actor)

Brown, Ollie (Athlete, Baseball Player)
8462 Country Club Dr
Buena Park, CA 90621-1421, USA

Brown, Orlando (Actor)
c/o Sharyn Berg *Sharyn Talent
Management*
P.O. Box 18033
Encino, CA 91416, USA

Brown, Oscar (Athlete, Baseball Player)
19113 Gunlock Ave
Carson, CA 90746-2825, USA

Brown, Owsley II (Business Person)
Brown-Forman Corp
850 Dixie Highway
Louisville, KY 40210, USA

Brown, Patricia (Athlete, Baseball Player,
Commentator)
1100 Governors Dr Apt 26
Winthrop, MA 02152-3254, USA

Brown, Patrick (Misc)
Stanford University
Medical School
Biochemistry Dept
Stanford, CA 94305, USA

Brown, Paul (Athlete, Baseball Player)
3617 Highway 75
Holdenville, OK 74848-9421, USA

Brown, Paul (Musician)
c/o Staff Member *Verve Music Group*
1755 Broadway Fl3
New York, NY 10019, USA

Brown, Peter (Actor)
5328 Alhama Dr
Woodland Hills, CA 91364, USA

Brown, Philip (Actor)
c/o Staff Member *Independent Artists Agency*
9601 Wilshire Blvd.
Suite 750
Beverly Hills, CA 90210, USA

Brown, P J (Athlete, Basketball Player)
2142 Hampshire Dr
Slidell, LA 70461-5065, USA

Brown, Preston (Athlete, Football Player)
6804 Jones Valley Dr SE
Huntsville, AL 35802, USA

Brown, Ralph (Athlete, Football Player)
9395 Old Post Dr
Rancho Cucamonga, CA 91730, USA

Brown, Randy (Baseball Player)
California Angels
PO Box 326
Plymouth, FL 32768-0326, USA

Brown, Ray (Athlete, Football Player)
Buffalo Bills 1 Bills Dr Attn Coaching Staff
Orchard Park, NY 14127-2296, USA

Brown, Ray (Athlete, Football Player)
1225 Stanfield Point Rd
Gautier, MS 39553-3204, USA

Brown, Ray (Athlete, Football Player)
4936 Lake Fjord Pass
Marietta, GA 30068-1639, USA

Brown, Raymond (Athlete, Football Player)
4936 Lake Fjord Pass
Marietta, GA 30068, USA

Brown, Reb (Actor)
c/o Staff Member *Gyst Management*
9107 Wilshire Blvd
Suite 450
Beverly Hills, CA 90210, USA

Brown, Reggie (Athlete, Football Player)
560 Dutch Valley Rd NE Apt 302
Atlanta, GA 30324-5363, USA

Brown, Reggie (Athlete, Football Player)
2242 NW 93rd Ter
Miami, FL 33147-3068, USA

Brown, Reggie D (Athlete, Football Player)
17025 Tortoise St
Round Rock, TX 78664-8600, USA

Brown, Reggie V (Athlete, Football Player)
1325 Oxford Ln
Union, NJ 07083, USA

Brown, R Hanbury (Astronomer)
White Cottage
Penton Mewsey
Andover Hants SP11 0RQ, UNITED KINGDOM (UK)

Brown, Ricardo (Kurupt) (Actor, Composer, Musician)
c/o Stephen Barnes *Morris, Yorn, Barnes, Levine, Krintzman, Rubenstein and Kohner*
2000 Ave of the Stars
3rd Floor, North Tower
Los Angeles, CA 90067, USA

Brown, Richard (Athlete, Football Player)
5652 Alfred Ave
Westminster, CA 92683, USA

Brown, Richard E (Tex) III (General)
Deputy CofS for Personnel
HqUSAF Pentagon
Washington, DC 20330, USA

Brown, Rita Mae (Actor, Writer)
American Artists Inc
PO Box 4671
Charlottesville, VA 22905, USA

Brown, Rob (Athlete, Hockey Player)
5204 84th St
Edmonton, AB T6E 5N8, Canada

Brown, Rob (Athlete, Hockey Player)
Edmonton Oilers
11230 110 St NW Dept
Attn Broadcasting Dept
Edmonton, AB T5G 3H7, Canada

Brown, Rob (Actor)
c/o Gabrielle (Gaby) Morgerman *WME (LA)*
9601 Wilshire Blvd Fl 3
Beverly Hills, CA 90210, USA

Brown, Robert (Athlete, Football Player)
8624 Oak Chase Cir
Fairfax Station, VA 22039-3328, USA

Brown, Robert (Athlete, Football Player)
P.O. Box 3
Merigold, MS 38759, USA

Brown, Robert Curtis (Actor)
2401 Pier Ave
Santa Monica, CA 90405, USA

Brown, Robert D (Business Person)
Milacron Inc
2090 Florence Ave
Cincinnati, OH 45206, USA

Brown, Robert S (Bob) (Athlete, Football Player)
1200 Lakeshore Ave Apt 25G
Oakland, CA 94606-1689, USA

Brown, Roger (Athlete, Football Player)
9 N Point Dr
Portsmouth, VA 23703, USA

Brown, Ron (Athlete, Football Player)
2212 Radcourt Dr
Hacienda Heights, CA 91745-5716, USA

Brown, Ronnie (Athlete, Football Player)
10751 Hawks Vista St
Plantation, FL 33324-8210, USA

Brown, Roosevelt (Athlete, Baseball Player)
308 Newitt Vick Dr
Vicksburg, MS 39183-8741, USA

Brown, Roosevelt (Athlete)
6551 Thea Lane
Apt S17
Columbus, GA 31907-0822

Brown, Ruben (Athlete, Football Player)
170 Fox Meadow Ln
Orchard Park, NY 14127, USA

Brown, Rush (Athlete, Football Player)
2425 Cartertown Rd
Clinton, NC 28328, USA

Brown, Samantha (Actor)
c/o Erika Martineau *Brooks Group*
15 W 37th St Fl 16
New York, NY 10008, USA

Brown, Samuel M (Athlete, Football Player)
25 Franklin Creek Rd N
Savannah, GA 31411, USA

Brown, Sandra (Writer)
1306 W Abram St
Arlington, TX 76013-1703, USA

Brown, Sara (Actor)
Media Artists Group
6300 Wilshire Blvd
#1470
Los Angeles, CA 90048, USA

Brown, Sarah (Actor)
c/o Staff Member *McKeon-Myones Management*
3500 Olive Ave
Suite 770
Burbank, CA 91505, USA

Brown, Scott (Athlete, Baseball Player)
1238 Alton Pierce Rd
Dequincy, LA 70633-4501, USA

Brown, Scott P. (Senator)
359 Dirksen Senate Office Building
Washington, DC 20510, USA

Brown, Selwyn (Athlete, Football Player)
3533 Inverrary Blvd W
Lauderhill, FL 33319-7114, USA

Brown, Shane (Athlete, Basketball Player, Coach)
Ohio Valley University
Athletic Dept
1 Campus View Dr
Vienna, WV 26105, USA

Brown, Shay (Athlete, Misc)
World Skating League
499 Erin Dr
Knoxville, TN 37919, USA

Brown, Sheldon (Athlete, Football Player)
2616 Stonetrace Dr
Rock Hill, SC 29730, USA

Brown, Sherrod (Senator)
713 Hart Senate Office Bldg
Washington, DC 20510, USA

Brown, Sonny (Athlete, Football Player)
825 Shadow Wood Dr
Edmond, OK 73034, USA

Brown, Stan (Athlete, Football Player)
P.O. Box 533
Benicia, CA 94510, USA

Brown, Stan (Athlete, Basketball Player)
2201 Tremont St
Philadelphia, PA 19115, USA

Brown, Steve (Athlete, Baseball Player)
9626 Cecilwood Dr
Santee, CA 92071-1428, USA

Brown, Steve (Athlete, Football Player)
2207 Osage St
Saint Louis, MO 63118, USA

Brown, Susan (Actor)
11931 Addison St
N Hollywood, CA 91607, USA

Brown, Tarrick (Baseball Player)
Chicago Cubs
18631 Collins St Apt 33
Tarzana, CA 91356-2178, USA

Brown, Ted (Athlete, Football Player)
7320 130th St W
Saint Paul, MN 55124, USA

Brown, Terry (Athlete, Football Player)
605 W Apache St
Marlow, OK 73055, USA

Brown, T Graham (Musician)
8437 Rolling Hills Dr
Nashville, TN 37221, USA

Brown, Theotis (Athlete, Football Player)
9604 W 121st Ter
Overland Park, KS 66213, USA

Brown, Thomas M (Athlete, Football Player)
6024 Approach Rd
Sarasota, FL 34238, USA

Brown, Thomas W (Athlete, Football Player)
201 High Point Dr
Waco, TX 76705, USA

Brown, Thomas Wilson (Actor)
c/o Staff Member *SDB Partners Inc*
1801 Ave of the Stars
Suite 902
Los Angeles, CA 90067, USA

Brown, Tim (Athlete, Football Player, Heisman Trophy Winner)
1107 W Pleasant Run Rd
Desoto, TX 75115-7402, USA

Brown, Timmy (Athlete, Football Player)
505 S Farrell Dr Unit E28
Palm Springs, CA 92264, USA

Brown, Tina (Talk Show Host, Writer)
c/o Staff Member *Topic A With Tina Brown*
CNBC
900 Sylvan Ave
Englewood Cliffs, NJ 07632, USA

Brown, Tom (Athlete, Baseball Player)
27981 Nanticoke Rd
Salisbury, MD 21801-1645, USA

Brown, Tom (Athlete, Baseball Player)
600 Valencia Rd
Venice, FL 34285-2538, USA

Brown, Tom (Athlete, Football Player)
10143 Deer Run
Brecksville, OH 44141, USA

Brown, Tommy (Athlete, Baseball Player)
8119 Shady Pl
Brentwood, TN 37027, USA

Brown, Tom W (Athlete, Football Player)
201 High Point Dr
Waco, TX 76705, USA

Brown, Tony (Athlete, Football Player)
11629 Garrick Ave
Sylmar, CA 91342, USA

Brown, Tracy (Ballerina)
c/o Staff Member *Royal Ballet*
Covent Garden
Bow St
London WC2E 9DD, UK

Brown, Travis (Athlete, Football Player)
6556 W Melinda Ln
Glendale, AZ 85308, USA

Brown, Trisha (Choreographer, Dancer)
Trisha Brown Dance Co
211 W 61st St
New York, NY 10023, USA

Brown, Troy (Athlete, Football Player)
124 Pine Hvn
Barnwell, SC 29812, USA

Brown, Troy (Athlete, Football Player)
3 Edgewater Dr
Norton, MA 02766, USA

Brown, Tyree (Actor)
c/o Nicole Jolley *Amsel, Eisenstadt & Frazier Talent Agency (AEF)*
5055 Wilshire Blvd
Suite 860
Los Angeles, CA 90036-6108, USA

Brown, Vincent (Athlete, Football Player)
PO Box 71268
Henrico, VA 23255, USA

Brown, Wayne (Athlete, Hockey Player)
50 Montgomerry Blvd
Belleville, ON K8N 1H9, Canada

Brown, W Earl (Actor)
c/o Staff Member *WME (LA)*
9601 Wilshire Blvd Fl 3
Beverly Hills, CA 90210, USA

Brown, Wes (Actor)
c/o Stacy Abrams *Abrams Entertainment*
5225 Wilshire Blvd #515
Suite 515
Los Angeles, CA 90036, USA

Brown, Wilbert (Athlete, Football Player)
1707 Dominic Ln
Houston, TX 77049, USA

Brown, William D (Bill) (Athlete, Coach, Football Player)
514 Northdale Blvd
Minneapolis, MN 55448, USA

Brown, William F (Willie) (Athlete, Coach, Football Player)
27138 Lillegard Ct
Tracy, CA 95304, USA

Brown, William S (Horse Racer)
US Trotting Association 750 Michigan Ave
Columbus, OH 43215-1191, USA

Brown, Willie (Baseball Player)
3430 John Hancock Dr
Tallahassee, FL 32312-1536, USA

Brown, Winston (Baseball Player)
12144 SW 50th St
Cooper City, FL 33330-4476, USA

Brown, Woody (Actor)
11844 Otsego St
Valley Village, CA 91607-3223, USA

Brown, Wren (Actor)
1861 Wellington Rd
Los Angeles, CA 90019, USA

Brownback, Sam (Politician)
1 SW Cedar Crest Rd
Topeka, KS 66606-2275, USA

Browne, Anthony (Writer)
c/o Staff Member *Random House Publicity (Toronto)*
1 Toronto St
Suite 300
Toronto, ON M5C 2V6, Canada

Browne, Byron (Athlete, Baseball Player)
9708 W Riverside Ave
Tolleson, AZ 85353, USA

Browne, Chris (Cartoonist)
c/o Staff Member *King Features Syndication*
300 W 57th St
15th Floor
New York, NY 10019-5238, USA

Browne, E John P (Business Person)
BP Exploration Co
1 Finsbury Circus
London EC2M 7BA, UNITED KINGDOM (UK)

Browne, Gordie (Athlete, Football Player)
1001 Lakeridge Ct
Colleyville, TX 76034, USA

Browne, Gordon (Athlete, Football Player)
25 Harbourside Rd
North Quincy, MA 02171, USA

Browne, Jackson (Musician, Songwriter)
181 S. Alta Vista Blvd
Los Angeles, CA 90036, USA

Browne, Jerry (Athlete, Baseball Player)
Hagerstown Suns
274 Memorial Blvd E
Attn: Coaching Staff
Hagerstown, MD 21740, USA

Browne, Kale (Actor)
c/o Staff Member *Gage Group, The (LA)*
14724 Ventura Blvd
Suite 505
Sherman Oaks, CA 91403, USA

Browne, Leslie (Actor, Ballerina)
2025 Broadway
#6F
New York, NY 10023, USA

Browne, Less (Athlete, Football Player)
19 Amblecote PL
Hamilton, ON L8W 3E9, Canada

Browne, Olin (Athlete, Golfer)
9562 SE Sandpine Ln
Hobe Sound, FL 33455, USA

Browne, Secor D (Engineer, Government Official)
2101 L St NW
#207
Washington, DC 20037, USA

Browne, Sylvia (Psychic, Writer)
Sylvia Browne Corporation
1700 Winchester Blvd
Suite 100
Campbell, CA 95008, USA

Browne, Victor (Actor)
c/o Lara Rosenstock *Lara Rosenstock Management*
8371 Blackburn Ave #1
Los Angeles, CA 90048, USA

Browne, Zachary (Actor)
c/o Staff Member *Iris Burton Agency*
10100 Santa Monica Blvd Ste 1300
Los Angeles, CA 90067, USA

Browner, Jim (Athlete, Football Player)
6265 Crest Forest Ct E
Clarkston, MI 48348, USA

Browner, Joey (Athlete, Football Player)
2017 Pin Oak Dr
Saint Paul, MN 55122, USA

Browner, Joey (Athlete, Football Player)
P.O. Box 571
Pierz, MN 56364, USA

Browner, Keith (Athlete, Football Player)
5017 Chesley Ave
Los Angeles, CA 90043, USA

Browner, Ross (Athlete, Football Player)
7900 Inidian Springs Dr
Nashville, TN 37221, USA

Brown-Findlay, Jessica (Actor)
c/o Duncan Millership *WME (LA)*
9601 Wilshire Blvd Fl 3
Beverly Hills, CA 90210, USA

Browning, Cal (Athlete, Baseball Player)
111 N Eagle Dr
Ruidoso, NM 88345, USA

Browning, Dave (Athlete, Football Player)
10117 S Lambs Ln
Mica, WA 99023, USA

Browning, Dominique (Writer)
c/o Staff Member *Curtis Brown Group*
Haymarket House
28 - 29 Haymarket
London SW1Y 4SP, UNITED KINGDOM

Browning, Edmond L (Religious Leader)
5164 Imai Road
Hood River, OR 97031, USA

Browning, Emily Jane (Actor)
c/o Michael D Aglion *Signpost*
250 S Beverly Dr
Suite 201
Beverly Hills, CA 90212, USA

Browning, James R (Judge)
US Court of Appeals
Court Building 95 7th St
San Fransisco, CA 94103, USA

Browning, Kurt (Figure Skater)
Int'l Management Group
175 Bloor St E #400
Toronto, ON M4W 3R8, CANADA

Browning, Logan (Actor)
c/o Ken Jacobson *Ken Jacobson Management*
Preferred to be contacted by phone or email
Los Angeles, CA 91367, USA

Browning, Ricou (Actor)
5221 SW 196th Lane
Southwest Ranches, FL 33332, USA

Browning, Ryan (Actor)
United Talent Agency
9560 Wilshire Blvd #500
Beverly Hills, CA 90212, USA

Browning, Thomas L (Tom) (Athlete, Baseball Player)
3094 Friars Ln
Edgewood, KY 41017, USA

Brown Jr, Larry (Athlete, Football Player)
5603 Sycamore Dr
Colleyville, TX 76034, USA

Brownlee, Claude (Athlete, Football Player)
2711 Hood St
Columbus, GA 31906, USA

Brownlow, Kevin (Producer)
Photoplay Productions
21 Princess Road
London NW1, UNITED KINGDOM (UK)

Brown-Miller, Lisa (Athlete, Hockey Player, Olympic Athlete)
US Olympic Committee
1 Olympic Plz Bldg 4E
Colorado Springs, CO 80909-5760, USA

Brownmiller, Susan (Activist)
61 Jane St
New York, NY 10014, USA

Brownschidle, Jack (Athlete, Hockey Player)
35 Hidden Pines Ct
East Amherst, NY 14051, USA

Brownson, Mark (Athlete, Baseball Player)
13992 Aster Ave
Wellington, FL 33414, USA

Brownstein, Carrie (Music Group, Musician)
Legends of 21st Century
7 Trinity Row
Florence, MA 01062, USA

Brownstein, Michael L (Publisher)
Ladies Home Journal
125 Park Ave
New York, NY 10017, USA

Broxton, Jonathan (Athlete, Baseball Player)
4751 Rocky Creek Church Rd
Waynesboro, GA 30380, USA

Broyles, Frank F (Coach, Football Player, Sportscaster)
517 E Lafayette St
Fayetteville, AR 72701, USA

Brozer, Kim (Athlete, Golfer)
2700 N 16th St
Beaumont, TX 77703, USA

Bruant, Joel (Chef)
Joel Restaurant 5-6-24 Minami Aoyama
Kyodo Building Minato-ku
Tokyo, Japan

Brubaker, Bruce (Athlete, Baseball Player)
Champion Ford
140 Southtown Blvd
Owensboro, KY 42303, USA

Brubaker, Jeff (Athlete, Hockey Player)
1827 Oak Ridge Rd
Unit A
Oak Ridge, NC 27310-9865, USA

Brubeck, Dave (Musician)
221 Millstone Rd
Wilton, CT 06897

Brubeck, William H (Government Official)
7 Linden St
Cambridge, MA 02138, USA

Bruce, Aundray (Athlete, Football Player)
1730 Wentworth Dr
Montgomery, AL 36106, USA

Bruce, Bob (Athlete, Baseball Player)
633 Mission Cir
Irving, TX 75063, USA

Bruce, Bruce (Comedian)
c/o Staff Member *Agency for the Performing Arts (APA-LA)*
405 S Beverly Dr
Suite 500
Beverly Hills, CA 90212-4425, USA

Bruce, Christopher (Choreographer)
Rambert Dance Co
94 Chiswick High Road
London W4 1SH, UNITED KINGDOM (UK)

Bruce, David (Athlete, Hockey Player)
975 Grand Blvd
Bellingham, WA 98229-2776, USA

Bruce, Earle (Athlete, Football Player)
5988 Roundstone Pl
Dublin, OH 43016, USA

Bruce, Ed
1022 16th Ave S
Nashville, TN 37212, USA

Bruce, Elia (Athlete, Football Player)
1110 Hudson St Apt 4N
Hoboken, NJ 07030, USA

Bruce, George (Writer)
c/o Staff Member *Counterpoint*
2117 4th St
Suite D
Berkeley, CA 94710, USA

Bruce, Isaac (Athlete, Football Player)
333 Las Olas Way Apt 2606
Fort Lauderdale, FL 33301, USA

Bruce, Jack (Music Group, Songwriter,
Writer)
International Creative Mgmt
40 W 57th St #1800
New York, NY 10019, USA

Bruce, Richard Francis (Editor)
Mirisch Agency
1801 Century Park East
#1801
Los Angeles, CA 90067, USA

Bruce, Robert V (Historian)
606 13th Avenue SE
Olympia, WA 98501-2313, USA

Bruce, Thomas (Tom) (Swimmer)
122 Seaterrace Way
Aptos, CA 95003, USA

Bruce, Tom (Athlete, Swimmer)
USOC Alumni Relations
1750 E. Boulder St
Colorado Springs, CO 80909-5793, USA

Bruckheimer, Jerry (Director, Producer)
c/o Staff Member *Jerry Bruckheimer Films
/ Television*
1631 10th St
Santa Monica, CA 90404, USA

Bruckner, Agnes (Actor)
c/o Rich Hueners *Paradigm (LA)*
360 N Crescent Dr
North Bldg
Beverly Hills, CA 90210, USA

Bruckner, Amy (Actor)
c/o Susan Curtis *Curtis Talent
Management*
9607 Arby Dr
Beverly Hills, CA 90210, USA

Bruckner, Greg (Athlete, Golfer)
3906 E Potter Dr
Phoenix, AZ 85050-4837, USA

Bruckner, Les (Athlete, Football Player)
1325 Valley View Rd
Apt 307
Glendale, CA 91202, USA

Brudzinski, Robert L (Bob) (Athlete,
Football Player)
1057 Lido Ct
Weston, FL 33326, USA

Brue, Bob (Athlete, Golfer)
4316 N Sheffield Ave
Milwaukee, WI 53211-1432, USA

Brueckman, Charlie (Athlete, Football
Player)
7439 Plott Rd
Charlotte, NC 28215, USA

Brueckner, Keith A (Scientist)
7723 Ludington Pl
La Jolla, CA 92037-3806, USA

Bruel, Patrick (Music Group)
Artmedia
20 Ave Rapp
Paris 75007, FRANCE

Bruen, John D (Business Person, General)
6104 Greenlawn Court
Springfield, VA 22152, USA

Bruener, Mark (Athlete, Football Player)
26 Commanders Pl
Missouri City, TX 77459, USA

Bruening, Justin (Actor)
c/o Marnie Sparer *Innovative Artists (LA)*
1505 10th St
Santa Monica, CA 90401, USA

Bruestle, Martin (Director)

Bruett, J T (Athlete, Baseball Player)
1437 Woods Creek Dr
Delano, MN 55328, USA

Bruggink, Eric G (Judge)
US Claims Court
717 Madison Place NW
Washington, DC 20439, USA

Bruguera, Sergi (Tennis Player)
C'Escipion 42
Barcelona 08023, SPAIN

Bruhert, Mike (Athlete, Baseball Player)
907 Center Dr
Franklin Square, NY 11010, USA

Bruhin, John (Athlete, Football Player)
6960 Taylors View Ln
Knoxville, TN 37921, USA

Bruhl, Daniel (Actor)
c/o Katrina Bayonas *Kuranda
Management*
Santo Angel, 84
Madrid 28043, Spain

Brumback, Charles T (Publisher)
435 N Michigan Ave
Floor 7
Chicago, IL 60611-4027, USA

Brumbaugh, Cliff (Athlete, Baseball
Player)
216 Moore Ave
New Castle, DE 19720, USA

Brumbly, Charlie (Actor)
c/o Staff Member *DDO Artist Agency (LA)*
6725 W Sunset Blvd
Suite 230
Los Angeles, CA 90028-7163, USA

Brumel, Valeryi (Actor)
Louknetzkaya Nab 8
Moscow, Russia

Brumfield, Jackson (Athlete, Football
Player)
25644 Highway 25
Franklinton, LA 70438, USA

Brumfield, Jacob D (Athlete, Baseball
Player)
7970 Creekstone Way
Riverdale, GA 30274, USA

Brumfield, Scott (Athlete, Football Player)
1150 E 900 S
Spanish Fprl, UT 84660, USA

Brumfield-White, Dolly (Athlete, Baseball
Player, Commentator)
1604 Millcreek Dr
Arkadelphia, AR 71923-3024, USA

Brumfield-White, Dolores (Baseball
Player)
1604 Millcreek Dr
Arkadelphia, AR 71923-3024, USA

Brumley, Duff (Athlete, Baseball Player)
230 Cg Earnest Rd NW
Charleston, TN 37310, USA

Brumley, Mike (Athlete, Baseball Player)
1020 Western Trl
Keller, TX 76248-4924, USA

Brumley, Robert L (Athlete, Football
Player)
256 E Sunset Rd
San Antonio, TX 78209-2760, USA

Brumm, Donald D (Don) (Athlete,
Football Player)
511 County Road 442
New Franklin, MO 65274, USA

Brumme, Margo (Stylist)
c/o Staff Member *Zenobia Agency Inc*
PO Box 909
Groveland, CA 95321, USA

Brummer, Glenn (Athlete, Baseball
Player)
1830 Dalton Dr
Belleville, IL 62226, USA

Brummer, Renate (Astronaut)
NOAA/FSL
325 Broadway
Boulder, CO 80305, USA

Brummett, Greg (Athlete, Baseball Player)
605 W 10th St
Concordia, KS 66901, USA

Brumwell, Murray (Athlete, Hockey
Player)
727 Tabriz Dr
Billings, MT 59105-2809, USA

Brunansky, Thomas A (Tom) (Athlete,
Baseball Player)
13411 Summit Cir
Poway, CA 92064, USA

Brundage, Dewey (Athlete, Football
Player)
220 S 400 West
Orem, UT 84058-5358, USA

Brundage, Howard D (Publisher)
RR 2 Box 332-47
Old Lyme, CT 06371, USA

Brundage, Jennifer (Athlete, Olympic
Athlete, Softball Player)
4487 Augusta Ct
Ann Arbor, MI 48108-9789, USA

Brundige, Bill (Athlete, Football Player)
2050 Roanoke St
Christiansburg, VA 24073, USA

Brundtland, Gro Harlem (Politician)
Storting
Oslo, Norway

Brundy, Stan (Athlete, Basketball Player)
4644 Stephen Girard Ave
New Orleans, LA 70126-4756, USA

Brune, Jesse (Actor)
c/o Cat Josell *Synergy Management*
15233 Ventura Blvd
Suite 707
Sherman Oaks, CA 91403, USA

Brunell, Mark (Athlete, Football Player)
876 Rock Mesa Pt
Castle Rock, CO 80108-7435, USA

Brunelli, Sam (Athlete, Football Player)
1080 Wisconsin Ave NW
Apt 104
Washington, DC 20007, USA

Bruner, Jack (Athlete, Football Player)
701 Lewiston Street
Cottonwood, ID 83522, USA

Bruner, Jerome S (Misc)
200 Mercer St
New York, NY 10012, USA

Bruner, Michael L (Mike) (Athlete,
Olympic Athlete, Swimmer)
339 Garcia Ave
Half Moon Bay, CA 94019-1886, USA

Brunet, Andree Joly (Figure Skater)
2805 Boyne City Road
Boyne City, MI 49712, USA

Brunet, Bob (Athlete, Football Player)
25011 La Highway 1032
Denham Springs, LA 70726, USA

Brunetta, Mario (Athlete, Hockey Player)
3874 de l'Hetriere St
Saint-Augustin-De-Desmaures, QC G3A
2X1, Canada

Brunette, Andrew (Athlete, Hockey
Player)
2392 Morgan Ave N
Stillwater, MN 55082-1967, USA

Brunette, Justin (Athlete, Baseball Player)
11 Atherton
Irvine, CA 92620, USA

Brunettes, The (Music Group)
c/o Staff Member *Paradigm (Monterey)*
404 W Franklin St
Monterey, CA 93940, USA

Brunetti, Melvin T (Judge)
US Court of Appeals
40 W Liberty St
Reno, NV 89501, USA

Brunetti, Wayne H (Business Person)
New Century Energies
1225 17th St
Denver, CO 80202, USA

Bruney, Brian (Athlete, Baseball Player)
c/o Staff Member *Gaylord Sports
Management*
13845 N Northsight Blvd
Suite 200
Scottsdale, AZ 85260, USA

Bruney, Fred (Athlete, Football Coach,
Football Player)
800 Mountain Creek Trce NW
Atlanta, GA 30328, USA

Brungardt, Kurt
c/o Daniel Strone *Trident Media Group
LLC*
41 Madison Ave
36th Floor
New York, NY 10010, USA

Bruni-Sarkozy, Carla (First Lady, Model,
Musician)
Palais De L'Elysée
55 Rue Du Faubourg Saint-Honoré
Paris F-75008, France

Brunkhorst, Brian (Athlete, Basketball
Player)
6182 Brumder Dr
Hartland, WI 53029-3145, USA

Brunner, J Terrance (Misc)
Better Government Assn
230 N Michigan Ave
Chicago, IL 60601, USA

Bruno, Billi (Actor)
c/o Dana Edrick Fletcher *Coast to Coast Talent Group*
3350 Barham Blvd
Los Angeles, CA 90068, USA

Bruno, Chris (Actor)
3678 Alta Mesa Dr
Studio City, CA 91604, USA

Bruno, Corbucci (Actor)
Via dei Colli della Farnesina
#144
Rome I-00194, Italy

Bruno, Dylan (Actor)
1481 W. Paseo Del Mar
San Pedro, CA 90731, USA

Bruno, Frank (Athlete, Boxer)
Little Billington
Leighton Buzzard
Bedfordshire LU7 9BS, UK

Bruno, Franklin R (Frank) (Boxer)
P O Box 2266 Brentwood
Essex CM15 0AQ, UNITED KINGDOM (UK)

Bruno, Tom (Athlete, Baseball Player)
316 Ft Sully Trl
Pierre, SD 57501, USA

Bruns, George (Athlete, Basketball Player)
16 E Poplar St
Floral Park, NY 11001-3145, USA

Brunsberg, Ario (Athlete, Baseball Player)
883 104th Ln NW
Minneapolis, MN 55433, USA

Brunson, Doyle (Poker Player)
c/o Staff Member *Poker Royalty, LLC*
10789 W. Twain Ave.
Suite 200
Las Vegas, NV 89135, USA

Brunson, Larry (Athlete, Football Player)
6104 E Peakview Pl
Centennial, CO 80111, USA

Brunson, Will (Athlete, Baseball Player)
13119 Rudys Way
Streetman, TX 75859, USA

Brunt, Maureen (Athlete, Olympic Athlete)
430 Silver Lake Dr
Portage, WI 53901-1340, USA

Bruntlett, Eric (Athlete, Baseball Player)
1106 Marconi St
Apt A
Houston, TX 77019, USA

Brupbacher, Ross (Athlete, Football Player)
200 Pembroke Ln
Lafayette, LA 70508, USA

Bruschi, Tedy (Athlete, Football Player)
31 Jeffrey Dr
North Attleboro, MA 02760, USA

Bruske, Jim (Athlete, Baseball Player)
5242 North Quail Run Pl
Paradise Valley, AZ 85253, USA

Bruskin, Grisha (Artist)
236 W 26th St #705
New York, NY 10001, USA

Bruson, Renato (Opera Singer)
Columbia Artists Mgmt Inc
165 W 57th St
New York, NY 10019, USA

Brusstar, Warren (Athlete, Baseball Player)
3320 Redwood Rd
Napa, CA 94558, USA

Brustein, Robert S (Critic, Educator, Producer)
Harvard University
Loeb Drama Center 64 Brattle St
Cambridge, MA 02138, USA

Brutcher, Len (Baseball Player)
4510 Hallam Hill Ln
Lakeland, FL 33813-1808, USA

Bruton, John G (Prime Minister)
Qomelstown
Dunboyne, County Meath, IRELAND

Bry, Ellen (Actor)
Media Artists Group
6300 Wilshire Blvd #1470
Los Angeles, CA 90048, USA

Bryan, Alan (Archaeologist)
University of Alberta
Archaeology Dept
Edmonton, AB T6G 2J8, CANADA

Bryan, Ashley (Writer)
General Delivery
Islesford, ME 04646-9999, USA

Bryan, Billy (Athlete, Baseball Player)
3001 Hickory Ln
Opelika, AL 36801, USA

Bryan, Billy (Athlete, Baseball Player)
3408 Creekwood Dr
Tuscaloosa, AL 35453, USA

Bryan, Billy (Athlete, Football Player)
3408 Creekwood Dr
Vestavia, AL 35243, USA

Bryan, Bob (Athlete, Tennis Player)
3931 Fawnmist Dr
Wesley Chapel, FL 33544, USA

Bryan, David (Musician)
45 Phalanx Rd
Colts Neck, NJ 07722, USA

Bryan, Dora (Actor)
11 Marine Parade Brighton
Sussex, UNITED KINGDOM (UK)

Bryan, Jimmy (Race Car Driver)
Box 194
Nov, MI 48376-0194, USA

Bryan, Luke (Musician)
373 Childe Harolds Cir
Brentwood, TN 37027, USA

Bryan, Mark (Musician)
816 Stone Point Rd
Awendaw, SC 29429, USA

Bryan, Mary (Athlete, Golfer)
1735 Golf Garden Way
Apopka, FL 32712, USA

Bryan, Mike (Athlete, Tennis Player)
3931 Fawnmist Dr
Wesley Chapel, FL 33544, USA

Bryan, Richard (Politician)
269 Russell
Washington, DC 20510-0001, USA

Bryan, Sabrina (Actor, Dancer)
c/o Staff Member *Puravida Enterprises*
2480 Corinth Ave
Suite 3
Los Angele, CA 90064, USA

Bryan, Steve (Athlete, Football Player)
33659 E 147th St S
Coweta, OK 74429, USA

Bryan, Walter (Athlete, Football Player)
757 Kenwood Dr
Albene, TX 79601, USA

Bryan, Zachery Ty (Actor)
c/o Samantha Crisp *Kohner Agency, The*
9300 Wilshire Blvd
Suite 555
Beverly Hills, CA 90212, USA

Bryant, Anita (Beauty Pageant Winner, Musician)
2377 NW 206th St
Edmond, OK 73012, USA

Bryant, Anthony (Athlete, Football Player)
1136 County Road 16
Newbern, AL 36765, USA

Bryant, Antonio (Athlete, Football Player)
c/o Staff Member *All Pro Sports and Entertainment*
36 Steele St
Suite 100
Denver, CO 80206, USA

Bryant, Bart (Athlete, Golfer)
1233 Lake Whitney Dr
Windermere, FL 34786, USA

Bryant, Bill (Athlete, Football Player)
3516 Dewberry Dr
Shreveport, LA 71118, USA

Bryant, Bobby (Athlete, Football Player)
509 Nottingham Rd
Columbia, SC 29210, USA

Bryant, Bonnie (Athlete, Golfer)
2427 Wasabinang St
Hastings, MI 49058, USA

Bryant, Brad (Golfer)
3407 Bridgefield Dr
Lakeland, FL 33803-5914, USA

Bryant, Brad (Athlete, Golfer)
3407 Bridgefield Dr
Lakeland, FL 33803, USA

Bryant, Clark Rosalyn (Athlete, Track Athlete)
3901 Somerset Dr
Los Angeles, CA 90008, USA

Bryant, Darrell (Race Car Driver)
171 Brenda Dr.
Thomasville, NC 27360, USA

Bryant, Derek (Athlete, Baseball Player)
1047 Redwood Dr
Lexington, KY 40511, USA

Bryant, Dez (Athlete, Football Player)
c/o Eugene Parker *Maximum Sports Management*
6435 W Jefferson Blvd
#197
Fort Wayne, IN 46804, USA

Bryant, Domingo (Athlete, Football Player)
19703 Campfield Dr
Katy, TX 77449, USA

Bryant, Don (Athlete, Baseball Player)
1844 Swiss Oaks St
Saint Johns, FL 32259, USA

Bryant, Edward (Junior) (Athlete, Football Player)
2906 South 102nd St
Omaha, NE 68124, USA

Bryant, Emmette (Athlete, Basketball Player)
P.O. Box 6229
Chicago, IL 60680-6229, USA

Bryant, Fernando (Athlete, Football Player)
1740 Hudson Bridge Rd
Stockbridge, GA 30281, USA

Bryant, Gray (Editor)
34 Horatio St
New York, NY 10014, USA

Bryant, Gyude (President)
President's Office
Executive Mansion Capitol Hill
Monrovia, LIBERIA

Bryant, Hubie (Athlete, Football Player)
4804 Branch Rd
Roanoke, VA 24014, USA

Bryant, Jeff (Athlete, Football Player)
P.O. Box 362240
Decatur, GA 30036, USA

Bryant, Joe (Athlete, Basketball Player)
1835 N 72nd St
Philadelphia, PA 19151-2311, USA

Bryant, Joshua (Actor)
216 Paseo Del Pueblo Norte #M
Taos, NM 87571, USA

Bryant, Joy (Actor)
c/o Brian Young *Untitled Entertainment (LA)*
350 S. Beverly Dr #200
Beverly Hills, CA 90212, USA

Bryant, Kevin (Athlete, Football Player)
701 East Church St
Tarboro, NC 27885, USA

Bryant, Kobe (Athlete, Basketball Player)
c/o Rob Pelinka *Landmark Sports Agency*
10990 Wilshire Blvd
Suite 1000
Los Angeles, CA 90024, USA

Bryant, Lucas (Actor)
c/o Perry Zimel *Oscars Abrams Zimel & Associates, Inc. (OAZ)*
438 Queen St E
Toronto ON M5A 1T4, CANADA

Bryant, Maeion (Stylist)
c/o Staff Member *Mirror Image Cosmetic Studio*
1708 Whitehead Rd
Baltimore, MD 21207

Bryant, Mark (Athlete, Basketball Player)
3300 Everett Dr
Edmond, OK 73013-7443, USA

Bryant, Ralph (Athlete, Baseball Player)
367 Spruill Bridge Rd
Temple, GA 30179, USA

Bryant, Ron (Baseball Player)
San Francisco Giants
90 Oak St #1
Westerly, RI 02891-1737, USA

Bryant, Ronald Ray (Baby Bash) (Actor, Musician, Producer)
c/o Staff Member *Sony Music International*
550 Madison Ave
New York, NY 10022-3211, USA

Bryant, Steve (Athlete, Football Player)
12618 Laleu Ln
Houston, TX 77071, USA

Bryant, Taman (Athlete, Football Player)
2742 Bryant St
Vineland, NJ 08361, USA

Bryant, Todd (Actor)
9150 Wilshire Blvd #175
Beverly Hills, CA 90212, USA

Bryant, Tony (Athlete, Football Player)
2351 Sombrero Blvd
Marathon, FL 33050, USA

Bryant, Trent (Athlete, Football Player)
4801 S Tiemey Dr
Independence, MO 64055, USA

Bryant, Walter (Athlete, Football Player)
509 Nottingham Rd
Columbia, SC 29210, USA

Bryant, Waymond (Athlete, Football
Player)
2440 Covington Dr
Flower Mound, TX 75028, USA

Bryant, Wendell (Athlete, Football Player)
P.O. Box 888
Phoenix, AZ 85001, USA

Bryars, R Gavin (Composer)
Bolton-Quinn Ltd
8 Pottery Lane
London W11 4LZ, UNITED KINGDOM
(UK)

Bryden, T R (Athlete, Baseball Player)
1021 9th St
Clarkston, WA 99403, USA

Brye, Steve (Athlete, Baseball Player)
621 S Spring St
Apt 603
Los Angeles, CA 90014, USA

Brylin, Sergei (Athlete, Hockey Player)
32 Robert Dr.
Short Hills, NJ 07078-1507, USA

Bryson, Bill (Writer)
*c/o Staff Member Random House
Publicity*
1745 Broadway
New York, NY 10019, USA

Bryson, David (Musician)
299 Panoramic Way
Berkeley, CA 94704, USA

Bryson, Peabo (Music Group, Musician,
Songwriter, Writer)
Agency for the Performing Arts
9200 Sunset Blvd #900
Los Angeles, CA 90069, USA

Bryson, Peabo (Musician)
*c/o Staff Member Agency for the
Performing Arts (APA-LA)*
405 S Beverly Dr
Suite 500
Beverly Hills, CA 90212-4425, USA

Bryson, Shawn (Athlete, Football Player)
418 Heatherstone Dr
Franklin, NC 28734, USA

Bryson, William C (Judge)
US Appeals Court
717 Madison Place NW
Washington, DC 20439, USA

Bryzgalov, Ilya (Athlete, Hockey Player)
4092 Santa Anita Ln
Yorba Linda, CA 92886-7014, USA

Brzeska, Magdalena (Gymnast)
Vitesse Karcher GmbH
Porschestr 6
Fellbach 70736, GERMANY

Brzezinski, Mika (Talk Show Host)
MSNBC
30 Rockefeller Plaza
New York, NY 10112, USA

Brzezinski, Zbigniew (Politician)
1061 Spring Hill Rd
McLean, VA 22102, USA

B. Schiff, Adam (Congressman, Politician)
2411 Rayburn HOB
Washington, DC 20515, USA

B-Side Players (Music Group, Musician)
c/o Staff Member Skyline Music
28 Union St
Whitefield, NH 03598, USA

Buacharern, Tym (Stylist)
*c/o Staff Member Karlee Artist
Management*
2658 Griffith Park Blvd
#171
Los Angeles, CA 90039, USA

Buanne, Patrizio (Musician)
PO Box 293
Tadworth KT20 5SX, UNITED KINGDOM

Buatta, Mario (Designer)
120 E 80th St
New York, NY 10021, USA

Bubas, Vic (Athlete, Basketball Player,
Coach)
133 Robert E Lee Ln
Bluffton, SC 29909, USA

Bubela, Jaime (Athlete, Baseball Player)
14927 Royal Birkdale St
Houston, TX 77095, USA

Bubka, Sergie N (Athlete, Track Athlete)
Andresi Kulikowski
Vasavagen 13
Solna 171 39, SWEDEN

Bubka, Surgei N (Athlete, Track Athlete)
Andresi Kulikowski
Vasavagen 13
Solna 171 39, SWEDEN

Bubla, Jiri (Athlete, Hockey Player)
405-1050 Bowron Crt
North Vancouver, BC V7H 2X7, Canada

Buble, Michael (Musician)
1638 Blue Jay Way
West Hollywood, CA 90069, USA

Bubna, P F (Religious Leader)
Christian & Missionary Alliance
P O Box 3500
Colorado Springs, CO 80935, USA

Bucatinsky, Dan (Actor, Producer, Writer)
c/o Staff Member WME (LA)
9601 Wilshire Blvd Fl 3
Beverly Hills, CA 90210, USA

Buccellati, Giorgio (Misc)
University of California
Near Eastern Languages Dept
Los Angeles, CA 90024, USA

Buccellato, Benedetta (Actor)
Carlo Levi Co
Via Giuseppe Pisanelli
Rome 00196, ITALY

Bucci, George (Athlete, Basketball Player)
15 Peter Ave
Newburgh, NY 12550, USA

Bucha, Paul W (General)
Medal of Honor Society
139 Main St
Ridgefield, CT 06877-4932, USA

Buchan, William E (Athlete, Olympic
Athlete, Sailor)
21107 SE 5th St
Sammamish, WA 98074, USA

Buchanan, Bill (Athlete, Baseball Player)
94 Twill Valley Dr
Saint Peters, MO 63376-6566, USA

Buchanan, Bob (Athlete, Baseball Player)
2035 Bever Ave SE
Cedar Rapids, IA 52403, USA

Buchanan, Brian (Athlete, Baseball Player)
8600 El Mirasol Ct
Fort Myers, FL 33967, USA

Buchanan, Charles (Athlete, Football
Player)
1715 Windover Dr
Nashville, TN 37218, USA

Buchanan, Edna (Writer)
156 5th Ave Ste 625
New York, NY 10010-7002, USA

Buchanan, Ian (Actor, Model)
Gold Marshak Liedtke
3500 W Olive Ave #1400
Burbank, CA 91505, USA

Buchanan, Isobel (Opera Singer)
Marks Mgmt
14 New Burlington St
London W1X 1FF, UNITED KINGDOM
(UK)

Buchanan, James M (Nobel Prize
Laureate)
George Mason University
PO BoxG
Blacksburg, VA 24063-1021, USA

Buchanan, Jeff (Athlete, Hockey Player)
Wealth Management
1404 E Chocolate Ave
Hershey, PA 17033-1118, USA

Buchanan, Jensen (Actor)
Paradigm Agency
10100 Santa Monica Blvd #2500
Los Angeles, CA 90067, USA

Buchanan, Ken (Boxer)
45 Marmion Road Greenfaulds
Cumbemaul G67 4AN, SCOTLAND

Buchanan, Pat (Politician)
1017 Savile Ln
McLean, VA 22101, USA

Buchanan, Phillip (Athlete, Football
Player)
6185 Meadowview Cir
Fort Myers, FL 33916, USA

Buchanan, Ray (Athlete, Football Player)
2888 Major Ridge Trl
Duluth, GA 30097, USA

Buchanan, Richard (Athlete, Football
Player)
216 Brookwood Ln W
Bolingbrook, IL 60440, USA

Buchanan, Robert S (Astronaut)
3 Lariat Lane
Rolling Hills, CA 90274, USA

Buchanan, RobertS Col (Aviator)
3 Lariat Ln
Rolling Hills Estates, CA 90274-4119,
USA

Buchanan, Ron (Athlete, Hockey Player)
156 Sierra Blanca Trl
Ruidoso, NM 88345-7140, USA

Buchanan, Tim (Athlete, Football Player)
888 Magnolia Ave
Apt 1
Pasadana, CA 91106, USA

Buchanan, Tom (Reality TV Star)
3130 Valley Rd
Saltville, VA 24370

Buchanan, Vern (Congressman, Politician)
221 Cannon HOB
Washington, DC 20515, USA

Buchanan, Willie J (Athlete, Football
Player)
2742 Mesa Dr
Oceanside, CA 92054, USA

Buchanon, Willie (Athlete, Football
Player)
2742 Mesa Dr
Oceanside, CA 92054, USA

Buchberger, Kelly (Athlete, Hockey
Player)
c/o Staff Member Springfield Falcons
45 Falcons Way
Springfield, MA 01103, USA

Buchbinder, Rudolf (Music Group,
Musician)
Columbia Artists Mgmt Inc
165 W 57th St
New York, NY 10019, USA

Buchek, Jerry (Athlete, Baseball Player)
815 NW Flagler Ave
Apt 303
Stuart, FL 34994-1158, USA

Buchel, Lloyd M (Misc)
16296 Rostrata Hill
Poway, CA 92064, USA

Buchel, Marco (Skier)
Ramschwagweg 55
Balzers 9496, SWITZERLAND

Buchheim, Lothar-Gunther (Writer)
Johann-Biersack-Str 23
Feldafing 82340, GERMANY

Buchholz, Christopher (Actor)
c/o Staff Member TNA The New Agency
Viale Parioli 41
Roma I-00197, Italy

Buchholz, Clay (Athlete, Baseball Player)
630 King Oaks St
Lumberton, TX 77657, USA

Buchholz, Taylor (Athlete, Baseball
Player)
321 Southcroft Rd
Springfield, PA 19064, USA

Buchko, Steve (Athlete, Football Player)
460 Sinclair St
Winnipeg, MB R2X 1Y1, Canada

Buchli, James F Colonel (Astronaut)
14761A Innerarity Point Rd
Pensacola, FL 32507-8452, USA

Buchli, James F (Jim) (Astronaut)
1602 Fairoaks St
Seabrook, TX 77586, USA

Buchwald, Art (Misc, Writer)
4327 Hawthorne St NW #W
Washington, DC 20016, USA

Buck, Craig (Athlete, Olympic Athlete, Volleyball Player)
2208 Moline Ave
Pueblo, CO 81003-3810, USA

Buck, Detlev (Director)
Agentur Sigrid Narjes
Goethestr 17
Munich 80336, GERMANY

Buck, Joe (Commentator, Television Host)
18 Upper Warson Rd
St Louis, MO 63124, USA

Buck, John E (Artist)
11229 Cottonwood Road
Bozeman, MT 59718, USA

Buck, Linda B. (Nobel Prize Laureate)
Fred Hutchinson Cancer Research Center
14295 Sherwood Rd NW
Seattle, WA 98177-3956, USA

Buck, Mike E (Athlete, Football Player)
321 Fox Den Ct
Destin, FL 32541, USA

Buck, Peter (Musician)
2033 2nd Ave. #2003
Seattle, WA 98121, USA

Buck, Robert T Jr (Director, Misc)
Brooklyn Museum
200 Eastern Parkway
Brooklyn, NY 11238, USA

Buck, Samantha (Actor)
c/o Elise Konialian *Untitled Entertainment (NY)*
322 8th Ave #601
New York, NY 10001-6715, USA

Buck, Scott (Producer)
c/o Ann Blanchard *Creative Artists Agency (CAA-LA)*
9200 W. Sunset Blvd
10th Floor
Los Angeles, CA 90069, USA

Buckbee, Ed (Scientist)
47 Revere Way
Huntsville, AL 35801-2847, USA

Buckcherry (Music Group, Musician)
c/o Staff Member *10th Street Entertainment (NY)*
38 W 21st St
Suite 300
New York, NY 10010, USA

Buckels, Gary (Athlete, Baseball Player)
3510 E Longridge Dr
Orange, CA 92867, USA

Buckey, Don (Athlete, Football Player)
8809 Audley Cir
Raleigh, NC 27615, USA

Buckey, Jay C Dr (Astronaut)
1 Sargent St
Hanover, NH 03755-1912, USA

Buckey, Jay C Jr (Astronaut)
14 Valley Road
Hanover, NH 03755, USA

Buckhalter, Joe (Athlete, Basketball Player)
3900 Rose Hill Ave
Apt 201A
Cincinnati, OH 45229-1467, USA

Buckingham, Gregory (Greg) (Swimmer)
338 Ridge Road
San Carlos, NH 94070, USA

Buckingham, Jane (Television Host)
c/o Staff Member *Style Network*
5750 Wilshire Blvd
Los Angeles, CA 90036, USA

Buckingham, Lindsay (Musician)
299 N Saltair Ave
Los Angeles, CA 90049-2912, USA

Buckingham, Lindsey (Musician)
299 N. Saltair Ave
Los Angeles, CA 90049, USA

Buckingham, Marcus (Business Person, Writer)
Simon & Schuster/Pocket/Summit
1230 Ave of Americas
New York, NY 10020, USA

Buckinghams, The (Music Group)
Paradise Artists
PO Box 1821
Ojai, CA 93024-1821, USA

Buckland, Jonny (Musician)
21 Astor Pl. #6C
New York, NY 10033, USA

Buckles, Bradley (Government Official, Misc)
Alcohol Tobacco Firearms Agency
650 Massachusetts NW
Washington, DC 20001, USA

Bucklew, Neil S (Educator)
West Virginia University
President's Office
Morgantown, WV 26506, USA

Buckley, A J (Actor)
Innovative Artists
1505 10th St
Santa Monica, CA 90401, USA

Buckley, Barry (Athlete, Football Player)
26 Forest Notch
Cohasset, MA 02025, USA

Buckley, Betty (Actor, Director, Musician)
233 Russell Bend Rd
Weatherford, TX 76088, USA

Buckley, Carol (Misc)
Elephant Sanctuary
P O Box 393
Hohenwald, TN 38462, USA

Buckley, Curtis (Athlete, Football Player)
2208 Cantura Dr
Mesquite, TX 75181, USA

Buckley, D Terrell (Athlete, Football Player)
11111 Pinelodge Trl
Davie, FL 33328, USA

Buckley, James L (Politician)
PO Box 597
Sharon, CT 06069-0597, USA

Buckley, Jean (Athlete, Baseball Player, Commentator)
143 Monarch Dr
Fortuna, CA 95540-3451, USA

Buckley, Kathy (Actor)
c/o Staff Member *GVA Talent Agency Inc*
8981 Sunset Blvd.
Suite 101
Los Angeles, CA 90069, USA

Buckley, Kevin (Athlete, Baseball Player)
34 Calvin St
Braintree, MA 02184, USA

Buckley, Marcus W (Athlete, Football Player)
7100 Monterey Dr
Forth Worth, TX 76112, USA

Buckley, Mike (Race Car Driver)
Buckley Racing
424 Hollister Drive
Ann Arbor, MI 48103, USA

Buckley, Richard E (Conductor)
310 W 55th St #1K
New York, NY 10019, USA

Buckley, Robert (Actor)
c/o Gary Mantoosh *Baker Winokur Ryder Public Relations (BWR-LA)*
9100 Wilshire Blvd
Suite 500, West Tower
Beverly Hills, CA 90212, USA

Buckley, Roy (Bowler)
6900 Lee Rd
Westerville, OH 43081-9556, USA

Buckley, Travis (Baseball Player)
10020 England Dr
Overland Park, KS 66212-4138, USA

Buckman, James E (Business Person)
Cendant Corp
9 W 57th St
New York, NY 10019, USA

Buckman, Tara (Actor)
4525 Coldwater Canyon #2
Studio City, CA 91604, USA

Buckman, Tom (Athlete, Football Player)
212 Foxford Dr
Keller, TX 76248-2532, USA

Buckner, Betty (Actor)
10643 Riverside Dr
Toluca Lake, CA 91602, USA

Buckner, Bill (Athlete, Baseball Player)
4405 E Wild Horse Ln
Boise, ID 83712, USA

Buckner, Brentson (Athlete, Football Player)
423 Leary Ct
Columbus, GA 31907, USA

Buckner, Cindy (Stylist)
4347 Valley Spring Dr
Westlake Village, CA 91362, USA

Buckner, Cleveland (Athlete, Basketball Player)
19227 S Grandee Ave
Carson, CA 90746, USA

Buckner, Greg (Athlete, Baseball Player)
4129 Catawba Ave
Newburgh, NY 12550-8812, USA

Buckner, Pam (Bowler)
645 Utah St
Reno, NV 89506-8979, USA

Buckner, Quinn (Athlete, Basketball Player, Olympic Athlete)
857 Valencia Blvd
Irving, TX 75039-3057, USA

Buckner, Shelley (Actor)
c/o Staff Member *Cunningham Escott Slevin & Doherty (CESD-LA)*
10635 Santa Monica Blvd
130
Los Angeles, CA 90025, USA

Bucknor, C B (Athlete, Baseball Player)
46 Midwood St
Brooklyn, NY 11225-5004, USA

Bucknum, Jeff (Race Car Driver)
2428 Frederick Lane
Lake Havasuaty, AZ 86404, USA

Buckson, David P (Politician)
2710 Rismen Ct
Kissimmee, FL 34743-5370, USA

Bucshon, Larry (Congressman, Politician)
1123 Longworth HOB
Washington, DC 20515, USA

Bucyk, John (Athlete, Hockey Player)
c/o Staff Member *Boston Bruins*
TD Banknorth Garden
100 Legends Way, Suite 250
Boston, MA 02114, USA

Bucyk, Randy (Athlete, Hockey Player)
23 Glenwood Cres
St. Albert, AB T8N IXS, Canada

Buczkowski, Bob (Athlete, Football Player)
4515 Northern Pike
Monroeville, PA 12146, USA

Budaj, Peter (Athlete, Hockey Player)
1271 Buffalo Ridge Rd
Castle Pines, CO 80108-8192, USA

Budarin, Nikolai M (Cosmonaut)
Potchta Kosmonavtov
Moskovskoi Oblasti
Syvisdny Goroduk 141160, RUSSIA

Budaska, Mark (Athlete, Baseball Player)
15025 W Buttonwood Dr
Sun City West, AZ 85375, USA

Budd, Boyce (Athlete, Olympic Athlete, Rower)
PO Box 203
160 Geiger Rd
Erwinna, PA 18920-0203, USA

Budd, David (Athlete, Basketball Player)
40 N Woodland Ave
Woodbury, NJ 08096, USA

Budd, Frank (Athlete, Football Player, Track Athlete)
138 Dorchester Rd
Mount Laurel, NJ 08054, USA

Budd, Harold (Composer, Misc)
Opal/Warner Bros Records
6834 Camrose Dr
Los Angeles, CA 90068, USA

Budd, Julie (Actor, Music Group)
Julie Budd Productions
163 Amsterdam Ave #224
New York, NY 10023, USA

Budd, Pieterse Zola (Athlete, Track Athlete)
General Delivery
Bloemfontein, SOUTH AFRICA

Budde, Brad E (Athlete, Football Player)
5121 W 159th Ter
Stilwell, KS 66085, USA

Budde, Ed (Athlete, Football Player)
5121 W 159th Ter
Stillwell, KS 66085, USA

Budde, Jordan (Producer, Writer)
c/o Ann Blanchard *Creative Artists Agency (CAA-LA)*
9200 W. Sunset Blvd
10th Floor
Los Angeles, CA 90069, USA

Budde, Ryan (Athlete, Baseball Player)
3109 N Peebly Dr
Oklahoma City, OK 73110, USA

Budden, Joe (Actor)
c/o Staff Member *ICM Partners (ICM-LA)*
10250 Constellation Blvd Fl 7
Los Angeles, CA 90067, USA

Buddie, Mike (Athlete, Baseball Player)
157 Scottsdale Dr
Advance, NC 27006, USA

Budd-Pieterse, Zola (Athlete, Track Athlete)
c/o Staff Member *British Olympic Association*
1 Wandsworth Plain
London SW18 1EH, UK

Buddy, Brandon (Actor)
c/o Jon Simmons *Simmons & Scott Entertainment*
4110 W. Burbank Blvd.
Burbank, CA 91505, USA

Budig, Gene (Commentator)
5 Sandwedge Ln
Isle of Palms, SC 29451-2820, USA

Budig, Rebecca (Actor)
3156 Lindo St
Los Angeles, CA 90068, USA

Budka, Frank (Athlete, Football Player)
2637 SW Abel St
Port Saint Lucie, FL 34953, USA

Budko, Walter (Athlete, Basketball Player)
2525 Pot Spring Rd
Unit L703
Lutherville Timonium, MD 21093-2852, USA

Budness, Bill (Athlete, Football Player)
401 Huckle Hill Rd
Bernardston, MA 01337, USA

Budnick, Neil G (Financier)
MBIA Inc
113 King's St
Armonk, NY 10504, USA

Budrewicz, Tom (Athlete, Football Player)
13 Olde Farms Rd
Boxford, MA 01921, USA

Budzinski, Mark (Athlete, Baseball Player)
4919 Packard Rd
Glen Allen, VA 23060, USA

Bueche, Wendell F (Business Person)
IMC Global
2100 Sanders Road
Northbrook, IL 60062, USA

Buechele, Steve (Athlete, Baseball Player)
2600 Royal Glen Dr
Arlington, TX 76012, USA

Buechler, John Carl (Director)
12031 Vose St #19-21
North Hollywod, CA 91605, USA

Buechler, Jud (Athlete, Basketball Player)
1515 West Ln
Delmar, CA 92014-4137, USA

Buechrle, James (Baseball Player)
Chicago White Sox
Comiskey Park 333 W 35th St
Chicago, IL 60616, USA

Buehler, George (Athlete, Football Player)
63 Tara Rd
Orinda, CA 94563, USA

Buehler, Jud (Athlete, Basketball Player)
4576 South Ln
Del Mar, CA 92014, USA

Buehrle, Mark (Athlete, Baseball Player)
5653 N Ridge Ave
Chicago, IL 60660, USA

Buell, Bebe (Actor)
c/o Ivan Bart *IMG Models (NY)*
304 Park Ave S
12th Floor
New York, NY 10010, USA

Buenning, Dan
N2351 Ashley Ct
Waupaca, WI 54981, us

Bueno, Maria (Tennis Player)
Rua Consolagao 3414 #10 Edificio Agustus
Sao Paulo 1001, BRAZIL

Buer, Aaron (Actor)
c/o Staff Member *RPM Talent Agency*
741 N Cahuenga Blvd
Suite 101
Los Angeles, CA 90038, USA

Buerge, Aaron (Reality TV Star)
c/o Staff Member *Maximum Talent*
1873 S Bellaire St
Suite 915
Denver, CO 80222-4356, USA

Buerger, Martin J (Misc)
Weston Road
Lincoln, MA 01773, USA

Buerkle, Ann Marie (Congressman, Politician)
1630 Longworth HOB
Washington, DC 20515, USA

Buerkle, Dick (Athlete, Olympic Athlete, Track Athlete)
3086 Dale Dr NE
Atlanta, GA 30305-2776, USA

Buetow, Bart (Athlete, Football Player)
4152 Kipling St
Wheat Ridge, CO 80033, USA

Buetow, Brad (Athlete, Hockey Player)
1419 Alamo Ave
Colorado Springs, CO 80907-7301, USA

Buffenbarger, R Thomas (Misc)
International Machinists Assn
9000 Machinists Place
Upper Marlboro, MD 20772, USA

Buffett, Howard Graham (Business Person)
407 Southmoreland Pl
Decatur, IL 62521, USA

Buffett, Jimmy (Composer, Songwriter)
424-A Fleming St
Key West, FL 33040, USA

Buffett, Peter (Musician)
c/o Staff Member *Paradigm (Monterey)*
404 W Franklin St
Monterey, CA 93940, USA

Buffett, Warren (Business Person)
Berkshire Hathaway
1440 Kiewit Plaza
Omaha, NE 68131, USA

Buffkins, Archie Lee (Misc)
Kennedy Center
Executive Suite
Washington, DC 20566, USA

Buffone, Douglas J (Doug) (Athlete, Football Player)
1272 W Lexington St
Chicago, IL 60607, USA

Bufi, Ylli (Prime Minister)
Privatization Ministry
Keshilli i Ministrave
Tirana, ALBANIA

Bufman, Zev (Producer)
520 Brickett Key Dr #612
Miami, FL 33131, USA

Buford, Damon J (Athlete, Baseball Player)
791 E Birchwood Pl
Chandler, AZ 85249, USA

Buford, Don (Athlete, Baseball Player)
15412 Valley Vista Blvd
Sherman Oaks, CA 91403, USA

Buford, Maury (Athlete, Football Player)
2901 Sweet Briar St
Grapevine, TX 76051, USA

Bugai, Lynne (Stylist)
746 N McCadden Pl
Los Angeles, CA 90038, USA

Bugel, Joe (Athlete, Football Coach, Football Player)
15517 E Cactus Dr
Fountain Hills, AZ 85268, USA

Bugenhagen, Gary (Athlete, Football Player)
4337 Henneberry Rd
Manlius, NY 13104, USA

Buggs, Danny
190 Austin Oaks Dr
Ellenwood, GA 30294, us

Buggs, Dany (Athlete, Football Player)
3186 Evans Mill Rd
Lithonia, GA 30038, USA

Buggs, Wamon (Athlete, Football Player)
5700 Sonoma Tr
Antioch, TN 37013, USA

Buggy, Regina (Athlete, Hockey Player)
550 N Limekin Pike
Chalfont, PA 18914, USA

Bugliosi, Vincent (Writer)
663 Arbor St
Pasadena, CA 91105-1519, USA

Bugner, Joe (Boxer)
22 Buckingham St
Surrey Hills, NSW 2010, AUSTRALIA

Buhari, Muhammadu (General, President)
GRA
Daura
Katsina State, NIGERIA

Buhl, Robbie (Race Car Driver)
24530 Hilliard Boulevard
Westlake, OH 44145, USA

Buhner, Jay (Athlete, Baseball Player)
David and Kay Buhner
2014 Sandy Coast Cir
League City, TX 77573, USA

Buhrmaster, Robert C (Business Person)
Jostens Inc
3601 Minnesota Dr #400
Bloomington, MN 55435, USA

Buice, Dewayne (Athlete, Baseball Player)
P.O. Box 5185
Incline Village, NV 89450, USA

Buie, Drew (Athlete, Football Player)
2815 Eland Dr
Winston Salem, NC 27127, USA

Buitenhuis, Penelope (Director, Writer)
c/o Carl Lieberman *Characters Talent Agency, The (Vancouver)*
1505 W 2nd Ave
#200
Vancouver, BC V6H 3Y4, Canada

Bujnoch, Glenn (Athlete, Football Player)
7598 Fairwayglen Dr
Cincinnati, OH 45248, USA

Bujold, Genevieve (Actor)
Blake Agency
1327 Ocean Parkway #J
Santa Monica, CA 90401, USA

Bukich, Rudy (Athlete, Football Player)
12764 Via Terceto
San Diego, CA 92130-, USA

Buktenica, Raymond (Actor)
Special Artists Agency
345 N Maple Dr #302
Beverly Hills, CA 90210, USA

Bukvich, Ryan (Athlete, Baseball Player)
200 Apple Blossom Cir
Brandon, MS 39047, USA

Bulaich, Norman B (Norm) (Athlete, Football Player)
421 Linndale Ct
Hurst, TX 76054, USA

Bulatovic, Momir (President)
Vlada Savezne Republike
Lenina 2
Belgrade 11070, SERBIA & MONTENEGRO

Bulger, Jason (Athlete, Baseball Player)
1898 Harbour Oaks Dr
Snellville, GA 30078, USA

Bulger, Marc (Athlete, Football Player)
c/o Tom Condon *CAA - St. Louis*
222 S Central Ave
Suite 1008
St Louis, MO 63105, USA

Bulifant, Joyce (Actor)
James/Levy/Jacobson
3500 W Olive Ave #1470
Burbank, CA 91505, USA

Buljung, Erich (Athlete, Olympic Athlete, Shooter)
7570 Stampede Dr
Colorado Springs, CO 80920-3715, USA

Bull, John S (Astronaut)
PO Box 1106
S Lake Tahoe, CA 96156, USA

Bull, Richard (Actor)
750 N Rush St
Apt 1903
Chicago, IL 60611-2581, USA

Bull, Ronald D (Ronnie) (Athlete, Football Player)
15 Redspire Ct
Bolingbrook, IL 60490, USA

Bull, Scott (Athlete, Football Player)
11446 Mountain Spring Dr
Fayetteville, AR 72701, USA

Bullard, Courtland (Athlete, Football Player)
22200 SW 113th Ct
Miami, FL 33170-, us

Bullard, Kendricke (Athlete, Football Player)
PO Box 2330
North Little Rock, AR 72115, US

Bullard, Matt (Athlete, Basketball Player)
10 Balmoral Pl
Spring, TX 77382-1343, USA

Bullard, Mike (Athlete, Hockey Player)
1170 Shillington Ave
Ottawa, ON K1Z 7Z4, Canada

Bullet, Scott (Athlete, Baseball Player)
218 Vicky Bullett St
Martinsburg, WV 25404, USA

Bulling, Terry (Bud) (Athlete, Baseball Player)
203 Laurelhurst Dr
Newport, WA 99156, USA

Bullinger, Jim (Athlete, Baseball Player)
2504 Elise Ave
Metairie, LA 70003, USA

Bullinger, Kirk (Athlete, Baseball Player)
3608 David Dr
Metairie, LA 70003, USA

Bullington, Bryan (Athlete, Baseball Player)
20116 Oakwood Dr
Mokena, IL 60448, USA

Bullins, Ed (Writer)
425 Lafayette St
New York, NY 10003, USA

Bullitt, John C (Attorney, Attorney General, General, Government Official)
Shearman Sterling
53 Wall St
New York, NY 10005, USA

Bullmann, Maik (Wrestler)
AC Bavaria Goldbach
Postfach 1112
Goldbach 63769, GERMANY

Bulloch, Jeremy (Actor)
Fett Photos
10 Birchwood Rd
London SW17 9BQ, UNITED KINGDOM (UK)

Bullock, Bruce (Athlete, Hockey Player)
5226 Redbird Rd
Phoenix, AZ 85083, USA

Bullock, Eric (Athlete, Baseball Player)
17503 Harwick Ct
Carson, CA 90746, USA

Bullock, Jim J (Actor)
612 Lighthouse Ave #200
Pacific Grove, CA 93950, USA

Bullock, Jim J (Actor)
c/o Staff Member *Bohemia Group*
1680 Vine St Ste 216
Los Angeles, CA 90028, USA

Bullock, J R (Business Person)
Laidlaw Inc
3221 N Service Road
Burlington, ON L7R 3Y8, CANADA

Bullock, Sandra (Actor, Producer)
1225 Angelo Dr
Beverly Hills, CA 90210, USA

Bullock, Theodore H (Biologist)
University of California
Neurosciences Dept
La Jolla, CA 92093, USA

Bullock, Vicki (Athlete, Basketball Player)
Charlotte Sting
100 Hive Dr
Charlotte, NC 28217, USA

Bullocks, Amos (Athlete, Football Player)
17209 Dobson Ave
South Holland, IL 60473, USA

Bullough, Hank (Athlete, Football Player)
4439 Copperhill Dr
Okemos, MI 48864, USA

Bulluck, Keith (Athlete, Football Player)
874 Nialta Ln
Bentwood, TN 37027, USA

Bulriss, Mark P (Business Person)
Great Lakes Chemical
9025 River Road #400
Indianapolis, IN 46240, USA

Bum, Kim (Actor)
c/o Staff Member *Glory Entertainment*
1-25-5-3F Higashi Azabu
Minatoku
Tokyo 106-0044, Japan

Bumbeck, David (Artist)
Drew Lane RD 3
Middleburry, VT 05753, USA

Bumbry, Alonzo B (Al) (Athlete, Baseball Player)
28 Tremblant Ct
Lutherville Timonium, MD 21093, USA

Bumbry, Grace (Opera Singer)
Opera et Concert
Maximilianstr 22
Munich 80539, GERMANY

Bumgarner, Wayne (Actor)
P.O. Box 208
Clairmont, NC 28610, USA

Bump, Nate (Athlete, Baseball Player)
274 Caravello Dr
Jupiter, FL 33458, USA

Bumpas, Dick (Athlete, Football Player)
3612 Bellaire Dr N
Fort Worth, TX 76109-2115, USA

Bumpers, Dale (Politician)
Arent Fox
12723 Hunters Field Rd
Little Rock, AR 72211-2248, USA

Bunce, Gregory (Athlete, Basketball Player)
1710 Redwood Way
Upland, CA 91784-1767, USA

Bunce, Larry (Attorney, Basketball Player)
1000 Vintage Ln
Apt 338
Mount Vernon, WA 98273-5532, USA

Bunch, Ashli (Athlete, Golfer)
1629 Country Club Dr
Morristown, TN 37814, USA

Bunch, Jarrod (Athlete, Football Player)
1580 Hemlock Dr
Ashtabula, OH 44004, USA

Bunch, Melvin (Athlete, Baseball Player)
782 Horseshoe Loop
Texarkana, TX 75501, USA

Bunch, Sidney (Athlete, Baseball Player)
3285 Towne Village Rd
Antioch, TN 37013, USA

Bund, Karlheinz (Business Person)
Huyssenallee 82-84
Essen Ruhr 45128, GERMANY

Bundchen, Gisele (Model)
12780 Chalon Rd
Los Angeles, CA 90049, USA

Bundren, Jim (Athlete, Football Player)
359 Capstone Ln
Spartanburg, SC 29301, us

Bundy, Brooke (Actor)
833 N Martel Ave
Los Angeles, CA 90046, USA

Bundy, Laura Bell (Actor, Musician)
c/o Tom Storms *Sanctuary Artist Management (TN)*
54 Music Square East
Suite 300
Nashville, TN 37203, USA

Bungee, Suzanne (Stylist)
c/o Staff Member *Arlene Wilson Management*
807 N Jefferson St
#200
Milwaukee, WI 53202, USA

Bunim, Mary-Ellis (Producer)
c/o Staff Member *Bunim/Murray Productions Inc*
6007 Sepulveda Blvd
Van Nuys, CA 91411, USA

Bunker, Wallace E (Wally) (Athlete, Baseball Player)
330 Coosaw Way
Unit 38
Ridgeland, SC 29936, USA

Bunkowsky-Scherbak, Barb (Athlete, Golfer)
8725 Marlamoor Ln
West Palm Beach, FL 33412-1614, USA

Bunnell, John (Actor, Television Host)
c/o Greg Horangic *WME (LA)*
9601 Wilshire Blvd Fl 3
Beverly Hills, CA 90210, USA

Bunnett, Joseph F (Misc)
608 Arroyo Seca
Santa Cruz, CA 95060, USA

Bunnetta, Bill (Bowler)
1176 E San Bruno Ave
Fresno, CA 93710, USA

Bunning, James P D (Jim) (Politician)
4 Fairway Dr
Southgate, KY 41071-3022, USA

Bunny, Lady (Comedian, DJ)
c/o Staff Member *Diva Central Inc*
7510 W Sunset Blvd Ste 1445
Los Angees, CA 90046, USA

Bunt, Dick (Actor)
11 Irving Pl
Greenlawn, NY 11740, USA

Bunt, Richard (Athlete, Basketball Player)
38 Lawrence Ave
Danbury, CT 06810-5181, USA

Bunting, Eve (Writer)
Harper Collins Publishers
1512 Rose Villa St
Pasadena, CA 91106-3525, USA

Bunting, John (Athlete, Football Player)
134 Soundview Dr
Hampstead, NC 28443, USA

Bunting, William (Athlete, Basketball Player)
11000 Pacer Ct
Raleigh, NC 27614-9604, USA

Bunton, Emma (Music Group, Musician)
c/o Jeff Frasco *Creative Artists Agency (CAA-LA)*
2000 Ave Of The Stars
Los Angeles, CA 90067, USA

Bunyan, John (Athlete, Football Player)
92 Radburn Rd
Glen Rock, NJ 07452, USA

Bunz, Dan (Athlete, Football Player)
4230 Rocklin Rd
Apt 2
Rocklin, CA 95677, USA

Buoniconti, Nicholas A (Nick) (Athlete, Business Person, Football Player)
445 Grand Bay Dr
Apt 803
Key Biscayne, FL 33149, USA

Buono, Cara (Actor)
c/o Joanna (Joanie) Burstein *Burstein Company, The*
15304 Sunset Blvd
suite 208
Pacific Palisades, CA 90272, USA

Buono, Carla (Actor)
25 Sea Colony Dr
Santa Monica, CA 90405-5321, USA

Buraas, Hans-Peter (Skier)
Norges Skiforbund
Postboks 3853
Ulleval Hageby, Oslo 0805, NORWAY

Burakovsky, Robert (Athlete, Hockey Player)
John Lundvallsgatan 40
Bunkeflostrand S-21831, Sweden

Burba, Dave (Athlete, Baseball Player)
378 N Shore Ln
Gilbert, AZ 85233, USA

Burba, Edwin H Jr (General)
256 Montrose Dr
McDonough, GA 30253, USA

Burbach, Bill (Athlete, Baseball Player)
147 Shenandoah Dr
Johnson City, TN 37601, USA

Burbage, Cornell (Athlete, Football Player)
1309 Copper Run Blvd
Lexington, KY 40514-, us

Burbank, Daniel C Cdr (Astronaut)
364 Route 6A
Yarmouth Port, MA 02675-1820, USA

Burbank, Daniel C (Dan) (Astronaut)
3210 Water Elm Way
Houston, TX 77059, USA

Burbano, Mindy (Actor)
12 Fairway Pt
Newport Coast, CA 92657, USA

Burbidge, E Margaret P (Scientist)
University of California
2320 Calle Corta
La Jolla, CA 92093-3030, USA

Burbules, Peter G (General)
8287 Chestnut Point Lane
Hayes, VA 23072-3835, USA

Burch, Elliot (Race Car Driver)
402 Corey Lane
Middletown, RI 02842, USA

Burch, Jerry (Athlete, Football Player)
1501 Plantation Dr
Simpsonville, SC 29681, USA

Burch, Rick (Musician)
3302 E. Mitchell Dr
Phoenix, AZ 85018, USA

Burch, Tory
Tory Burch
11 W 19th St
7th Floor
New York, NY 10011, USA

Burchart, Larry (Athlete, Baseball Player)
5310 E 94th St
Tulsa, OK 74137, USA

Burchfiel, Burrell C (Geophysicist, Misc, Physicist)
9 Robinson Park
Winchester, MA 01890, USA

Burchfield, Don (Athlete, Football Player)
26450 Summer Greens Dr
Bonita Springs, FL 34135, USA

Burchuladze, Paata (Opera Singer)
Raab & Bohm
Piankengasse 7
Vienna 1010, AUSTRIA

Burckhalter, Joseph H (Inventor)
705 Valley Brook Road
Wilmington, NC 28412, USA

Burd, Steven A (Business Person)
Safeway Inc
5918 Stoneridge Mall Road
Pleasanton, CA 94588, USA

Burda, Bob (Athlete, Baseball Player)
5285 S Roanoke
Mesa, AZ 85206-2129, USA

Burden, Ross (Chef)
c/o Staff Member *Roseman Organisation, The*
51 Queen Anne St
London W1G 9HS, UK

Burden, Ticky (Athlete, Basketball Player)
4332 Grove Ave
Apt C
Winston Salem, NC 27105-2837, USA

Burden, William A M (Diplomat, Financier)
820 5th Ave
New York, NY 10021, USA

Burden, Willie (Athlete, Football Player)
112 Olde Towne Dr N
Fort Worth, TX 30458-1673, USA

Burdick, Clinton (General)
1134 26th St Apt 4
Santa Monica, CA 90403-4626, USA

Burditt, Joyce (Producer, Writer)
c/o Staff Member *WME (LA)*
9601 Wilshire Blvd Fl 3
Beverly Hills, CA 90210, USA

Burdon, Eric (Music Group, Songwriter, Writer)
Lustig Talent
PO Box 770850
Orlando, FL 32877, USA

Bure, Paval
V100 N. Renfrew St.
Vancouver BC V5K 3N7, CANADA

Bure, Pavel (Athlete, Hockey Player)
7632 Fisher Island Drive
Fisher Island, FL 33109, USA

Bure, Valeri (Athlete, Hockey Player)
10371 Golden Eagle Ct
Plantation, FL 33324, USA

Bureau, Marc (Athlete, Hockey Player)
Ecole de Power Skating Julie Robitaille
3950 12e Av
Shawinigan-Sud, QC G9P 4T6, G9P 4T6

Burega, Bill (Athlete, Hockey Player)
122 Farmstead Crt
Kingston, ON K7P 3H9, Canada

Bureker-Stopper, Geraldine (Baseball Player)
2006 SE 41st Ave
Portland, OR 97214-5966, USA

Buress, Hannibal (Actor, Comedian)
c/o David (Dave) Becky *3 Arts Entertainment Inc*
9460 Wilshire Blvd
7th Floor
Beverly Hills, CA 90210, USA

Burfeindt, Betty (Athlete, Golfer)
70 San Simeon Pl
Rancho Mirage, CA 92270, USA

Burford, Christopher W (Chris) (Athlete, Football Player)
1215 Broken Feather Ct
Reno, NV 89511, USA

Burg, Bob (Writer)
Burg Communications Inc
3607 Fairway Dr N
Jupiter, FL 33477-9525, USA

Burg, Mark (Producer)
14050 Aubrey Rd
Beverly Hills, CA 90210, USA

Burgee, John H (Architect)
Perelanda Farm Skunks Misery Road
Millerton, NY 12546, USA

Burger, Michael (Actor)
c/o Staff Member *Richard De La Font Agency*
3808 W South Park Blvd
Broken Arrow, OK 74011, USA

Burger, Neil (Director)
c/o Staff Member *WME (LA)*
9601 Wilshire Blvd Fl 3
Beverly Hills, CA 90210, USA

Burgere, Andre
67 quai d'Orsay
Paris F-75007, FRANCE

Burgess, Adrian (Mountaineer)
324 G Street
Anderson, SC 29625-2147, USA

Burgess, Annie (Athlete)
601 F Street NW
Washington, DC 20004

Burgess, Bobby (Actor)
11684 Ventura Blvd.
#691
Studio City, CA 91604, USA

Burgess, Christian
33 Gastein Rd
London W6 8LT, ENGLAND

Burgess, Don (Cinematographer)
Gersh Agency
232 N Canon Dr
Beverly Hills, CA 90210, USA

Burgess, Mitchell (Writer)
c/o Staff Member *Broder Webb Chervin Silbermann Agency, The (BWCS)*
10250 Constellation Blvd
Los Angeles, CA 90067-6200, USA

Burgess, Neil (Engineer)
201 E 5th St #2200
Cincinnati, OH 45202, USA

Burgess, Ronnie (Athlete, Football Player)
303 Brandymill Blvd
Myrtle Beach, SC 29588, USA

Burgess, Tom (Athlete, Football Player)
1399 Maryland Rd
Phelps, NY 14532-9508, USA

Burgess, Tony (Misc)
US Geological Survey
119 National Center
Reston, VA 22092, USA

Burgess, Warren D (Religious Leader)
Reformed Church in America
475 Riverside Dr
New York, NY 10115, USA

Burghardt, Raymond F (Diplomat)
US Embassy
7 Lang Ha St
Ba Dinh
Hanoi, VIETNAM

Burghardt, Walter J (Misc)
19 I St NW
Washington, DC 20001, USA

Burghoff, Gary (Actor)
1271 Nunneley Rd
Paradise, CA 95969, USA

Burgi, Richard (Actor)
124 Sunset Terrace
Laguna Beach, CA 92651, USA

Burgin, C David (Editor)
Oakland Tribune
Editorial Dept
409 13th St
Oakland, CA 94612, USA

Burgio, Danielle (Actor)
c/o Carl Scott *Simmons & Scott Entertainment*
4110 W. Burbank Blvd.
Burbank, CA 91505, USA

Burgmeier, Ted (Athlete, Football Player)
861 Scenic Hts
East Dubuque, IL 61025, USA

Burgmeler, Tom (Athlete, Baseball Player)
13118 Walmer St
Leawood, KS 66209, USA

Burham, Daniel (Business Person)
Raytheon Co
870 Winter St
Waltham, MA 02451, USA

Burham, James B (Financier)
Mellon Bank
1 Mellon Bank Center
#0400
Pittsburgh, PA 15258, USA

Burhoe, Ralph Wendell (Misc)
Montgornery Place
5550 S South Shore Dr #715
Chicago, IL 60637, USA

Burish, Adam (Athlete, Hockey Player)
635 N Dearborn St Apt 2802
Chicago, IL 60654-6795, USA

Burk, Mack (Athlete, Baseball Player)
5710 Glen Pines Dr
Houston, TX 77069, USA

Burk, Scott (Athlete, Football Player)
1330 Castlepoint Cir
Castle Pines, CO 80108, USA

Burka, Vern (Athlete, Football Player)
580 Riviera Cir
Nipomo, CA 93444, USA

Burkart, Phil (Race Car Driver)
114 Oriskany Blvd
Yorkville, NY 13495, USA

Burke, Bernard F (Physicist)
10 Bloomfield St
Lexington, MA 02421, USA

Burke, Billy (Actor)
4180 Crisp Canyon Rd
Sherman Oaks, CA 91403, USA

Burke, Brooke (Actor, Model)
2221 Ocean Ave #302
Santa Monica, CA 90405, USA

Burke, Cheryl (Dancer, Reality TV Star)
3520 Multiview Dr
Los Angeles, CA 90068, USA

Burke, Chris (Actor)
426 S Orange Grove Ave
Los Angeles, CA 90036, USA

Burke, Chris (Athlete, Baseball Player)
15415 Crystal Springs Way
Louisville, KY 40245, USA

Burke, Clement (Clem) (Musician)
Shore Fire Media
32 Court St
#1600
Brooklyn, NY 11201, USA

Burke, David (Writer)
c/o Jamie Mandelbaum *Jackoway Tyerman Wertheimer Austen Mandelbaum Morris & Klein*
1925 Century Park E
22nd Floor
Los Angeles, CA 90067, USA

Burke, Delta (Actor)
4270 Farmdale Ave
Studio City, CA 91604, USA

Burke, Ed (Actor)
285 E Main St
Los Gatos, CA 95030, USA

Burke, Edward (Athlete, Olympic Athlete)
16717 La Mirada Rd
Los Gatos, CA 95030-4118, USA

Burke, Ernest (Athlete, Baseball Player)
9451 Common Brook Road
Apt 302
Owings Mills, MD 21620-1681, USA

Burke, Hederman Lynn (Swimmer)
26 White Oak Tree Road
Syosset, NY 11791, USA

Burke, James (Correspondent)
Henley House
Terrace Bames
London SW13 0NP, UNITED KINGDOM (UK)

Burke, James D (Director)
Saint Louis Art Museum
Forest Park
Saint Louis, MO 63110, USA

Burke, James Lee (Writer)
c/o Staff Member *Random House Publicity (Toronto)*
1 Toronto St
Suite 300
Toronto, ON M5C 2V6, Canada

Burke, James Lee (Writer)
Boubleday Press
1540 Broadway
New York, NY 10036, USA

Burke, Joe (Athlete, Football Player)
7 Maplewood St
Albany, NY 12208, USA

Burke, John (Athlete, Football Player)
612 Valley Rd
Bride, NJ 08730, USA

Burke, John (Athlete, Baseball Player)
3490 Westbrook Ln
Littleton, CO 80129, USA

Burke, Joseph C (Educator)
Rockefeller Institute
411 State St
Albany, NY 12203, USA

Burke, Kathy (Actor)
Stephen Halton Mgmt
83 Shepperton Road
London N1 3DF, UNITED KINGDOM
(UK)

Burke, Kelly H (General)
Stafford Burke Hecker
1006 Cameron St
Alexandria, VA 22314, USA

Burke, Leo (Athlete, Baseball Player)
12916 Woodburn Dr
Hagerstown, MD 21742, USA

Burke, Mark (Athlete, Football Player)
10 Maple Shade Dr
Marietta, OH 45750, US

Burke, Michael Reilly (Actor)
c/o Staff Member *Paradigm (LA)*
360 N Crescent Dr
North Bldg
Beverly Hills, CA 90210, USA

Burke, Mike (Athlete, Football Player)
720 Deodara Pl
Dixon, CA 95620, USA

Burke, Patrick (Athlete, Golfer)
24 Saint Georges Ct
Trabuco Canyon, CA 92679, USA

Burke, Philip (Artist)
L.B. Madison Fine Art
335 Buffalo Ave
Niagara Falls, NY 14303, USA

Burke, Randall (Athlete, Football Player)
3420 Chestnut Hill Ln
Lexington, KY 40509, USA

Burke, Randy (Athlete, Football Player)
3420 Chestnut Hill Ln
Lexington, KY 40509, US

Burke, Robert John (Actor)

Burke, Sarah (Reality TV Star)
c/o Michael (Mike) Esterman
Esterman.Com, LLC
Prefers to be contacted via email
MD, USA

Burke, Sean (Athlete, Hockey Player)
9016 N 60th St
Paradise Valley, AZ 85253-1718, USA

Burke, Sean (Athlete, Hockey Player)
7701 N. Calle Caballeros
Paradise, AZ 85253, USA

Burke, Shawn (Athlete, Hockey Player)
7701 N Calle Caballeros
Paradise Valley, AZ 85253, USA

Burke, Soloman (Musician)
c/o Staff Member *Coalition Management*
Devonshire House
12 Barley Mow Passage
London W4 4PH, UK

Burke, Steve (Athlete, Football Player)
RR 3 Box 553-F
Austin, TX 78754, USA

Burke, Steve (Athlete, Baseball Player)
1812 Amber Leaf Way
Lodi, CA 95242, USA

Burke, Tim (Athlete, Baseball Player)
5016 S Nelson St
Apt D
Littleton, CO 80127, USA

Burke Sr, Jack (Athlete, Golfer)
5602 Glen Pines Dr
Houston, TX 77069, USA

Burket, Harriet (Editor)
700 John Ringling Blvd
Sarasota, FL 34236, USA

Burkett, Chris (Athlete, Football Player)
296 Dover Ln
Madison, MS 39110, USA

Burkett, Jackie (Athlete, Football Player)
895 Santa Rosa Blvd
Apt 709
Fort Walton Beach, FL 32548, USA

Burkett, John D (Athlete, Baseball Player)
1404 Laurel Ln
Southlake, TX 76092, USA

Burkhalter, Correll (Athlete, Football
Player)
221 Robert Owens Rd
Mount Olive, MS 39119, USA

Burkhalter, Edward A Jr (Admiral)
4128 Fort Washington Place
Alexandria, VA 22304, USA

Burkhard, Jolanda (Stylist)
441 E 12th St
#4-A
New York, NY 10009, USA

Burkhardt, Francois (Architect)
3 Rue de Venise
Paris F-75004, FRANCE

Burkhardt, Lisa (Sportscaster)
Madison Square Garden Network
4 Pennsylvania Plaza
New York, NY 10001, USA

Burkhart, Morgan (Athlete, Baseball
Player)
105 Turtle Rock Ct
Saint Charles, MO 63304-7679, USA

Burkholder, JoAnn (Physicist)
North Carolina State University
Botany Dept
Raleigh, NC 27695, USA

Burkholder, Max (Actor)
c/o Emily Urbani *Osbrink Talent Agency*
4343 Lankershim Blvd
Suite 100
Universal City, CA 91602, USA

Burkholder, Owen E (Religious Leader)
421 S 2nd St
#600
Elkhart, IN 46516, USA

Burkl, Fred A (Misc)
United Retail Workers Union
9865 W Roosevelt Road
Westchester, IL 60154, USA

Burkle, Ron (Business Person)
2607 Glendower Ave
Los Angeles, CA 90027, USA

Burkley, Dennis (Actor)
5145 Costello Ave
Sherman Oaks, CA 91423, USA

Burkman, Roger (Athlete, Basketball
Player)
3242 Beals Branch Dr
Dallas, TX 75237-0861, USA

Burkovich, Shirley (Athlete, Baseball
Player, Commentator)
67430 Ovante Rd
Cathedral City, CA 92234-8402, USA

Burks, Arthur W (Mathematician)
3445 Vintage Valley Road
Ann Arbor, MI 48105, USA

Burks, Audra (Athlete, Golfer)
584 Brantley Terrace Way
Unit 205
Altamonte Springs, FL 32714, USA

Burks, Ellis R (Athlete, Baseball Player)
115 South Ln
Chagrin Falls, OH 44022-1145, USA

Burks, Randy (Athlete, Football Player)
300 Moyer Dr
Broken Bow, OK 74728, USA

Burks, Shawn (Athlete, Football Player)
5752 Nottaway Dr
Baton Rouge, LA 70820, USA

Burks, Steve (Athlete, Football Player)
2568 Mount Tabor Rd
Cabot, AR 72023, USA

Burleson, Dyrol (Athlete, Olympic
Athlete, Track Athlete)
12024 S Shadow Hills Ct SE
Turner, OR 97392-9353, USA

Burleson, Richard P (Rick) (Athlete,
Baseball Player)
241 E Country Hills Dr
La Habra, CA 90631-7623, USA

Burleson, Tom (Athlete, Basketball Player,
Olympic Athlete)
P.O. Box 861
Newland, NC 28657-0861, USA

Burley, Gary (Athlete, Football Player)
514 Bristol Ln
Birmingham, AL 35226, USA

Burley, Nichola
c/o Michael Duff *Troika*
74 Clerkenwell Rd
3rd Floor
London EC1M 5QA, United Kingdom

Burlinson, Tom (Actor)
c/o Staff Member *June Cann Management*
73 Jersey Rd
Woollahra 2025, AUSTRALIA

Burman, George (Athlete, Football Player)
1646 James St
Syracuse, NY 13203, USA

Burn, Scott (Writer)
c/o Staff Member *Creative Artists Agency
(CAA-LA)*
2000 Ave Of The Stars
Los Angeles, CA 90067, USA

Burnell, Jocelyn Bell (Scientist)
Bell Open University
Bell Open University Physics Dept
Milton Keynes MK7 GAA, UNITED
KINGDOM (UK)

Burner, David L (Business Person)
B F Goodrich Co
3 Coliseum Centre
2550 W Tyvola Road
Charlotte, NC 28205, USA

Burnes, Karen (Correspondent)
CBS-TV
News Dept
51 W 52nd St
New York, NY 10019, USA

Burnett, A J (Athlete, Baseball Player)
15208 Jarrettsville Pike
Monkton, MD 21111-2423, USA

Burnett, Bobby (Athlete, Football Player)
5321 Gould Cir
Castle Rock, CO 80109, USA

Burnett, Carol (Actor, Comedian)
10580 Wilshire Blvd. #44
Los Angeles, CA 90024, USA

Burnett, Chester (Athlete, Football Player)
2610 Ivanhoe St
Denver, CO 80207, USA

Burnett, David (Stylist)
c/o Staff Member *Agency, The*
1800 Avenue of The Stars
Suite 1114
Los Angeles, CA 90067

Burnett, Erin (Correspondent)
c/o Staff Member *CNBC (DC)*
400 N Capitol St NW Ste 850
Washington, DC 20001, USA

Burnett, Howard J (Educator)
Washington & Jefferson College
President's Office
Washington, PA 15301, USA

Burnett, James E (Government Official)
Transportations Safety Board
800 Independence Ave SW
Washington, DC 20594, USA

Burnett, Kelly (Athlete, Hockey Player)
206-202 Walter Havill Dr
Halifax, NS B3N 3M4, Canada

Burnett, Mark (Producer)
27540 Pacific Coast Hwy
Malibu, CA 90265, USA

Burnett, Molly (Actor)
c/o Shepard Smith *Archetype*
1608 Argyle Ave
Los Angeles, CA 90028, USA

Burnett, Nancy (Director)
Nancy Burnett Productions
32 Watson St
Unadilla, NY 13849-0735, USA

Burnett, Sean (Athlete, Baseball Player)
14016 Aster Ave
Wellington, FL 33414-2145, USA

Burnett, T-Bone (Musician, Producer,
Songwriter)
c/o Staff Member *Paradigm (Monterey)*
404 W Franklin St
Monterey, CA 93940, USA

Burnett, Webbie D (Athlete, Football
Player)
5305 San Antonio Ave
Apt 128
Orlando, FL 32839, USA

Burnette, Dave (Athlete, Football Player)
4201 Senator St
Texarkana, AR 72854, USA

Burnette, Olivia (Actor)
c/o Staff Member *RPM Talent Agency*
741 N Cahuenga Blvd
Suite 101
Los Angeles, CA 90038, USA

Burnette, Reggie (Athlete, Football Player)
7803 Chasewood Dr
Missouri City, TX 77489, USA

Burnette, Rocky (Musician)
1900 Ave of Stars
#2530
Los Angeles, CA 90067, USA

Burnette, Thomas N Jr (General)
Deputy Cinc
US Joint Forces Command
Norfolk, VA 23551, USA

Burnine, Hank (Athlete, Football Player)
709 W Rieck Rd
Tyler, TX 75703, USA

Burning, Spear (Musician)
13034 231st St
Springfield Gardens, NY 11413, USA

Burnitz, Jeromv (Athlete, Baseball Player)
PO Box 676032
Rancho Santa, CA 2067-6032, USA

Burnitz, Jeromy (Athlete, Baseball Player)
18520 Old Coach Dr
Poway, CA 92064, USA

Burnley, Benjamin (Musician)

Burnley, James H IV (Politician)
Shaw Pittman Potts Trowbridge
9401 Mount Vernon Cir
Alexandria, VA 22309-3221, USA

Burns, Annie (Musician, Songwriter, Writer)
Drake Assoc
177 Woodland Ave
Westwood, NJ 07675, USA

Burns, Bob (Musician)
12512 Fraser Ave
Granada Hills, CA 91344-4416, USA

Burns, Bob (Athlete, Golfer)
12512 Fraser Ave
Granada Hills, CA 91344, USA

Burns, Brent
63 Ellenwood Ave
Los Gatos, CA 95030-5220, USA

Burns, Brian Major (General)
4601 N Via Entrada Apt 1056
Tucson, AZ 85718-5871, USA

Burns, Britt (Athlete, Baseball Player)
2315 Cactus Finch
Katy, TX 77494-5872, USA

Burns, Brooke (Actor, Model)
4320 Mariota Ave
Toluca Lake, CA 91602, USA

Burns, Charles (Artist)
c/o Staff Member *Fantagraphics Books*
7563 Lake City Way
Seattle, WA 98115, USA

Burns, Charlie (Athlete, Hockey Player)
7 Fawn Dr
Wallingford, CT 06492, USA

Burns, Charlie (Athlete, Hockey Player)
7 Fawn Dr
Wallingford, CT 06492-3307, USA

Burns, Christian (Musician)
Day Time
Crown House
225 Kensington High St
London W8 8SA, UNITED KINGDOM
(UK)

Burns, Conrad (Politician)
PO Box 51293
Billings, MT 59105-1293, USA

Burns, David (Athlete, Basketball Player)
2623 Bainbridge Dr
Dallas, TX 75237-2801, USA

Burns, Edward (Actor, Director)
c/o JoAnne Colonna *Brillstein Entertainment Partners*
9150 Wilshire Blvd #350
Beverly Hills, CA 90212, USA

Burns, Eileen (Actor)
4000 W 43rd St.
New York, NY 10036, USA

Burns, Evers (Athlete, Basketball Player)
7216 Lost Spring Ct
Lanham, MD 20706-3834, USA

Burns, George (Athlete, Basketball Player)
16 E Poplar St
Flower Park, NY 11001, USA

Burns, George (Athlete, Golfer)
10459 Prestwick Rd
Boynton Beach, FL 33436-4418, USA

Burns, Heather (Actor)
c/o Courtney Kivowitz *Schiff Company, The*
9465 Wilshire Blvd
Suite 480
Beverly Hills, CA 90212, USA

Burns, James (Athlete, Basketball Player)
2706 Lincoln St
Evanston, IL 60201-2043, USA

Burns, James MacGregor (Historian, Scientist)
High Mowing
Bee Hill Road
Williamstown, MA 01267, USA

Burns, Jason (Athlete, Football Player)
8923 S Marshfield Ave
Chicago, IL 60620, USA

Burns, Jeannie (Musician, Songwriter, Writer)
Drake Assoc
177 Woodland Ave
Westwood, NJ 07675, USA

Burns, Jere (Actor)
c/o Staff Member *ICM Partners (ICM-LA)*
10250 Constellation Blvd Fl 7
Los Angeles, CA 90067, USA

Burns, Jere II (Actor)
Binder
1465 Lindacrest Dr
Beverly Hills, CA 90210, USA

Burns, Jerry (Athlete, Football Coach, Football Player)
9520 Viking Dr.
Eden Prairie, MN 55344

Burns, Jim (Writer)
c/o Staff Member *Da Capo Press*
Eleven Cambridge Center
Cambridge, MA 02142, USA

Burns, Keith (Athlete, Football Player)
7991 S Kittredge Way
Englewood, CO 80112, USA

Burns, Ken (Photographer)
c/o Staff Member *Florentine Films*
59 Maple Grove Rd
PO Box 613
Walpole, NH 03608, USA

Burns, Kenneth L (Ken) (Director)
Florentine Films
Maple Grove Road
Walpole, NH 03608, USA

Burns, Lamont (Athlete, Football Player)
104 Northwood St
Greensboro, NC 27417, USA

Burns, M Anthony (Business Person)
Ryder System Inc
3600 NW 82nd Ave
Miami, FL 33166, USA

Burns, Marie (Musician, Songwriter, Writer)
Drake Assoc
177 Woodland Ave
Westwood, NJ 07675, USA

Burns, Marilyn (Writer)
Marilyn Burns Educational Associates 150
Gate 5 Rd # 101
Sausalito, CA 94965-1404, USA

Burns, Marilyn (Actor)
12951 Briar Forest Dr #926
Houston, TX 77077, USA

Burns, Megan (Actor)
c/o Kathryn Fleming *The Rights House (UK)*
Drury House
34-43 Russell St
London WC2B 5HA, UK

Burns, Michael (Business Person)
8365 Sunset View Dr
West Hollywood, CA 90069, USA

Burns, Mike (Athlete, Football Player)
540 Stege Ave
Richmond, CA 94804, USA

Burns, Pat (Coach)
New Jersey Devils
Continental Arena
50 RR 120 N
East Rutherford, NJ 07073, USA

Burns, Patty (Stylist)
c/o Staff Member *Ennis*
119 Braintree St
Boston, MA 02134, USA

Burns, Pete
c/o LIVING
160 Great Portland Street
London, not applicable W1W 5QA,
United Kingdom

Burns, Regan (Actor)
c/o Bruce Smith *OmniPop Talent Group*
10700 Ventura Blvd.
2nd Floor
Studio Clty, CA 91604, USA

Burns, Robert H (Misc)
1015 University Bay Dr
Madison, WI 53705, USA

Burns, Robin (Athlete, Hockey Player)
186 Sherwood Rd
Beaconsfield, QC H9W 2G8, Canada

Burns, Steven (Actor)
c/o Staff Member *Davis Spylios Management*
244 West 54th Street #707
New York, NY 10019

Burns, Todd (Athlete, Baseball Player)
P.O. Box 111
Princeton, AL 35766-0111, USA

Burnside, Pete (Athlete, Baseball Player)
1945 Chestnut Ave
Wilmette, IL 60091-1569, USA

Burnside, Sheldon (Athlete, Baseball Player)
7519 Wynford Cir
Montgomery, AL 36117-7483, USA

Burnstein, Nanette (Director, Producer)
c/o Scott Greenberg *Creative Artists Agency (CAA-LA)*
2000 Ave Of The Stars
Los Angeles, CA 90067, USA

Burpo, George (Athlete, Baseball Player)
8981 E Palms Park Dr
Tucson, AZ 85715-5644, USA

Burr, Bill (Comedian)
c/o Staff Member *WmE2 (WMA-LA)*
1 William Morris Pl
Beverly Hills, CA 90212, USA

Burr, Gary (Musician)
51 Park Crescent Cir
Nashville, TN 37215, USA

Burr, Richard (Senator)
217 Russell Senate Office Building
Washington, DC 20510, USA

Burr, Shawn (Athlete, Hockey Player)
1615 River Rd
Saint Clair, MI 48079, USA

Burr, Shawn (Athlete, Hockey Player)
1615 River Rd
Saint Clair, MI 48079-3552, USA

Burrell, Garland L Jr (Judge)
US District Court
5011 St
Sacramento, CA 95814, USA

Burrell, George R (Athlete, Football Player)
129 W Upsal St
Philadelphia, PA 19119, USA

Burrell, John (Athlete, Football Player)
376 Park Lake Dr
Mead, OK 73449-6352, USA

Burrell, Kenneth E (Kenny) (Composer, Musician)
Tropix International
163 3rd Ave
#143
New York, NY 10003, USA

Burrell, Kenny (Musician)
c/o Staff Member *Concord Music Group, Inc*
900 N. Rohlwing Road
Itasca, IL 60143, USA

Burrell, Leroy (Athlete, Track Athlete)
University of Houston
Athletic Dept
Houston, TX 77023, USA

Burrell, Orville (Shaggy) (Musician)
c/o Staff Member *Big Yard Music Group*
P.O. Box 1060
Valley Stream, NY 11580, USA

Burrell, Pat (Athlete, Baseball Player)
P.O. Box 1770
Boulder Creek, CA 95006-1770, USA

Burrell, Scott (Athlete, Basketball Player)
331 Evergreen Ave
Hamden, CT 06518-2745, USA

Burrell, Ty (Actor)
9900 Culver Blvd #PHD
Culver City, CA 90232, USA

Burres, Brian (Athlete, Baseball Player)
533 SW Edgefield Meadows Ave
Troutdale, OR 98122-8505, USA

Burress, Hedy (Actor)
c/o David Lillard *IFA Talent Agency*
8730 Sunset Blvd
Suite 490
Los Angeles, CA 90069, USA

Burress, Plaxico (Athlete, Football Player)
47 Huntington Terrace
Totowa, NJ 07512, USA

Burridge, Randy (Athlete, Hockey Player)
1915 Magnolia Dr.
Henderson, NV 89014-4539, USA

Burridge, Randy (Athlete, Hockey Player)
1696 Navarre Ln
Henderson, NV 89014-7517, USA

Burright, Larrv
1239 E Palm Dr
Glendora, CA 91741-2347, USA

Burright, Larry (Athlete, Baseball Player)
1239 E Palm Dr
Glendora, CA 91741, USA

Burris, Jeffrey L (Jeff) (Athlete, Football Player)
77 Reynolds St
Rock Hill, SC 29730, USA

Burris, Rav (Athlete, Baseball Player)
Erie Sea Wolves 110 E lOth St
Attn Coaching Staff Erie, PA 16501-1256, USA

Burris, Ray (Athlete, Baseball Player)
2708 Golden Creek Ln
Apt 1208
Arlington, TX 76006, USA

Burriss, Bo (Athlete, Football Player)
818 Pinemont Dr
Apt 38
Houston, TX 77018, USA

Burrough, Junior (Athlete, Basketball Player)
6950 Fernwood Dr
Apt A
Charlotte, NC 28211-7210, USA

Burrough, Kenneth O (Ken) (Athlete, Football Player)
7979 Westheimer Rd
Houston, TX 77063, USA

Burroughs, Augusten (Writer)
c/o Christopher Schelling *Ralph Vicinanza, Ltd.*
303 W 18th St
New York, NY 10011, USA

Burroughs, Jeffrey A (Jeff) (Athlete, Baseball Player)
6155 Laguna Ct
Long Beach, CA 90803-4812, USA

Burroughs, Sean (Athlete, Baseball Player, Olympic Athlete)
6155 Laguna Ct
Long Beach, CA 90803-4812, USA

Burroughs, William S (Musician)
PO Box 147
Lawrence, KS 66044, USA

Burrow, Bob (Athlete, Basketball Player)
2228 Oakbranch Cir
Franklin, TN 37064-7407, USA

Burrow, Curtis (Athlete, Football Player)
51 W Cadron Ridge Rd
Greenbrier, AR 72058, USA

Burrow, Jim (Athlete, Football Player)
7961 Floyd Dr
The Plains, OH 45780-1403, USA

Burrow, Ken (Athlete, Football Player)
5371 Dunwoody Club Creek
Atlanta, GA 30360, USA

Burrow, Robert (Athlete, Basketball Player)
2228 Oakbranch Cir
Franklin, TN 37064, USA

Burrowes, Norma E (Opera Singer)
56 Rochester Road
London NW1 9JG, UNITED KINGDOM (UK)

Burrows, Darren E (Actor)
c/o Deborah Miller *Shelter Entertainment*
9454 Wilshire Blvd.
Suite 715
Beverly Hills, CA 90212, USA

Burrows, Dave (Athlete, Hockey Player)
RR 1 Stn Main Site 3x4
Parry Sound, ON P2A 2W7, CANADA

Burrows, Edwin G (Writer)
Oxford University Press
198 Madison Ave
New York, NY 10016, USA

Burrows, Eva (Religious Leader)
102 Domain Park
193 Domain Road
South Yarra, VIC 3141, AUSTRALIA

Burrows, Irv (Aviator)
1824 Nettlecreek Dr
Saint Louis, MO 63131-1506, USA

Burrows, Irv
1824 Nettlecreek Dr
Saint Louis, MO 63131-1506, USA

Burrows, James (Director)
5555 Melrose Ave. D Bldg. 228
Los Angeles, CA 90038, USA

Burrows, J Stuart (Opera Singer)
Nirvana
35 Saint Fagans Dr Saint Fagans
Cardiff, Wales CF5 6EF, UNITED KINGDOM (UK)

Burrows, Saffron (Actor)
c/o Staff Member *Premier Model Management*
40-42 Parker St
London WC2B 5PQ, UK

Burrows, Terrv (Athlete, Baseball Player)
7019 Burgandy Dr
Lake Charles, LA 70605-0252, USA

Burrows, Terry (Athlete, Baseball Player)
7019 Burgandy Dr
Lake Charles, LA 70605, USA

Burrus, William (Misc)
American Postal Workers Union
1300 L St NW
Washington, DC 20005, USA

Burruss, Kandi (Musician, Reality TV Star)
3499 Prince George St
Atlanta, GA 30344, USA

Bursch, Daniel W (Astronaut)
13-05 Buena Vista Ave
Pacific Grove, CA 93950-5505, USA

Bursch, Daniel w captain (Astronaut)
1305 Buena Vista Ave
Pacific Grove, CA 93950-5505, USA

Burshnick, Anthony J (General)
7715 Carrleigh Parkway
Springfield, VA 22152, USA

Burson, Jim (Athlete, Football Player)
351 Heath Rd
Dawsonville, GA 30534, USA

Burstyn, Ellen (Actor)
P.O. Box 217
Palisades, NY 10964, USA

Burt, Adam (Athlete, Hockey Player)
34 Smull Ave
Caldwell, NJ 07006, USA

Burt, Jim (Athlete, Football Player)
10 River Farms Ln
Saddle River, NJ 07458, USA

Burtnett, Wellington (Athlete, Hockey Player)
1703 Poullot Pl
Wilmington, MA 01887, USA

Burton, Albert (Athlete, Football Player)
339 S Martin Luther King Blvd
Daytona Beach, FL 32114, USA

Burton, Amanda (Actor)
c/o Staff Member *Independent Talent Group (ITG-UK)*
Oxford House
76 Oxford St
London W1D 1BS, UK

Burton, Brandie (Athlete, Golfer)
27102 Pleasant Hill Dr
Highland, CA 92346-7214, USA

Burton, Brian (Danger Mouse) (Musician)
960 W Avenue 37
Los Angeles, CA 90065, USA

Burton, Cummy (Athlete, Hockey Player)
419 John St
Sudbury, ON P3E 1R4, Canada

Burton, Dan (Congressman, Politician)
2308 Raybunn HOB
Washington, DC 20515, USA

Burton, Ed (Actor)
660 W Hile Rd
North Shores, MI 49441, USA

Burton, Edward (Athlete, Basketball Player)
660 W Hile Rd
Norton Shores, MI 48234-1392, USA

Burton, Ellis (Athlete, Baseball Player)
15621 Beach Blvd
Spc 7
Westminster, CA 92683-7120, USA

Burton, Gary (Musician)
Berklee College of Music
1140 Boylston St
Boston, MA 02215, USA

Burton, Glenn W (Misc)
PO Box 472
Clayton, GA 30525-0012, USA

Burton, Hilarie (Actor)
4176 Farmdale Ave
Studio City, CA 91604, USA

Burton, Jake (Skier)
Burton Snowboards
80 Industrial Parkway
Burlington, VT 05401, USA

Burton, James (Musician)
James Burton Foundation
714 Elvis Presley Ave
Shreveport, LA 71101, USA

Burton, James (Athlete, Football Player)
458 W Altadena Dr
Altadena, CA 91001, USA

Burton, Jared
PO Box 506
Westminster, SC 29693-0506, USA

Burton, Jeff (Race Car Driver)
15555 Huntersville-Concord Rd
Huntersville, NC 28078, USA

Burton, Jim (Athlete, Baseball Player)
6540 Shaftesbury Rd
Charlotte, NC 28270, USA

Burton, Kate (Actor, Musician)
c/o Larry Taube *Principal Entertainment (LA)*
1964 Westwood Blvd #400
Los Angeles, CA 90025, USA

Burton, Lance (Magician)
Monte Carlo Hotel
3770 S Las Vegas Blvd
Las Vegas, NV 89109, USA

Burton, Lawrence (Athlete, Football Player)
41 San Gabriel
Rancho Santa Margari, CA 92688, USA

Burton, Leonard (Athlete, Football Player)
7728 Evening Shade Cv
Memphis, TN 38125, USA

Burton, LeVar (Actor)
13251 Stoneridge Pl
Sherman Oaks, CA 91423, USA

Burton, Mike (Athlete, Olympic Athlete, Swimmer)
1119 N 31st St
Billings, MT 59101-0132, USA

Burton, Nelson (Athlete, Hockey Player)
128 Collington Ct
Arnold, MD 21012, USA

Burton, Nelson Jr (Bowler)
9359 SW Eagles Landing
Stuart, FL 34997, USA

Burton, Norman (Actor)
3641 Meadville Dr
Sherman Oaks, CA 91403, USA

Burton, Robert G (Publisher)
World Color Press
101 Park Ave
New York, NY 10178, USA

Burton, Shane (Athlete, Football Player)
PO Box 522
Hewitt Road
Catawba, NC 28609, USA

Burton, Steve (Actor)
6 Canyon Peak
Newport Coast, CA 92657, USA

Burton, Tim (Director, Producer)
Tim Burton Productions
8033 Sunset Blvd #7500
W Hollywood, CA 90046, USA

Burton, Tony (Actor)
3500 W Olive Ave #1400
Burbank, CA 91505, USA

Burton, Ward (Race Car Driver)
The Ward Burton Wildlife Foundation
PO Box 519
Halifax, VA 24558, USA

Burton, Warren
c/o Steven Neibert *Imperium 7 Talent Agency*
5455 Wilshire Blvd
Suite 1706
Los Angeles, CA 90036, USA

The Celebrity Black Book 2013

Burton, Willie (Athlete, Basketball Player)
18900 Fleming St
Detroit, MI 48234-1392, USA

Burton Jr, John (Actor)
12711 Ventura Blvd Ste 490
Studio City, CA 91604, USA

Burton-Woody, Patty (Baseball Player)
918 N Walnut St
Steele, MO 63877-1316, USA

Burtt, Dennis (Athlete, Baseball Player)
135 W Stadium Dr
Stockton, CA 95204, USA

Burtt, Steve (Athlete, Basketball Player)
200 W 143rd St
Apt 12D
New York, NY 10030-1527, USA

Burwell, Barbara (Actor)
1100 Millstone Rd
Wayzata, MN 55391, USA

Burwell, Carter (Composer)
Body Studio
105 Hudson Street
New York, NY 10013, USA

Burwell, Dick (Athlete, Baseball Player)
7424 N San Manuel Rd
Scottsdale, AZ 85258, USA

Bury, Pol (Artist)
12 Vallee da la Taupe-Perdreauville
Mantes-La-Jolie 78200, FRANCE

Busbv, Mike
20251 N 75th Ave APt 2006
Glendale, AZ 85308-7911, USA

Busby, Aretha (Stylist)
c/o Staff Member *Ford Models (Chicago)*
311 W Superior St
Chicago, IL 60654, USA

Busby, Mike (Athlete, Baseball Player)
27399 N 84th Gln
Peoria, AZ 85383, USA

Busby, Steve (Athlete, Baseball Player)
2701 Brittany Ln
Grapevine, TX 76051-4302, USA

Busby, Wayne (Athlete, Baseball Player)
287 S Tampa Ave
Orlando, FL 32805, USA

Buscemi, Steve (Actor, Director)
c/o Staff Member *Olive Productions*
161 Ave Of The Americas
11th Floor
New York, NY 10013, USA

Busch, Adam (Actor)
c/o Ryan Revel *Benderspink*
5870 W Jefferson Blvd
Studio E
Los Angeles, CA 90016, USA

Busch, August A III (Business Person)
Anheuser-Busch Cos
1 Busch Place
Saint Louis, MO 63118, USA

Busch, Charles (Actor, Writer)
c/o Jeff Melnick *Eighth Square Entertainment*
606 N Larchmont #307
Los Angeles, CA 90004, USA

Busch, Kurt (Race Car Driver)
Kurt Busch Inc
151 Lugnut Ln
Mooresville, NC 28117, USA

Busch, Kyle (Race Car Driver)
151 Fox Hunt Dr
Mooresville, NC 28117, USA

Busch, Mike (Athlete, Baseball Player)
103 E 1st Ave
Donahue, IA 50075-0007, USA

Buscher, Brian (Athlete, Baseball Player)
876 Burnside Dr
Columbia, SC 29209-2505, USA

Buschhorn, Don (Athlete, Baseball Player)
17804 E 26th St S
Independence, MO 64057-1350, USA

Buse, Don (Athlete, Basketball Player)
7300 W State Rd 64
Huntingburg, IN 47542-9781, USA

Busemann, Frank (Athlete, Track Athlete)
Borkumstr 13A
Recklinghausen 45665, GERMANY

Buser, Martin (Race Car Driver)
PO Box 520997
Big Lake, AK 99652, USA

Busey, Gary (Actor)
18424 Coastline Dr
Malibu, CA 90265, USA

Busey, Jake (Actor)
642 Skyline Dr
Ventura, CA 93003, USA

Busfield, Timothy (Actor)
50265 Courtland Rd
Clarksburgh, CA 95612, USA

Bush (Music Group)
535 Kings Rd. The Plaza
London, England SW1 OOS, UNITED KINGDOM

Bush, Barbara P (Politician)
9 N West Oak Dr
Houston, TX 77056-2119, USA

Bush, Billy (Television Host)
4161 High Valley Rd
Encino, CA 91436, USA

Bush, Blair (Athlete, Football Player)
1223 Spring St
Apt 601
Seattle, WA 98104, USA

Bush, Dave (Musician)
CMO Mgmt
Ransomes Dock
35-37 Parkgate Road
London SW11 4NP, UNITED KINGDOM (UK)

Bush, David (Athlete, Baseball Player)
518 Delancy Cir
Devon, PA 19333, USA

Bush, Dick
8 Grande Parade #16 Plymouth
Devon PL1 3DF, ENGLAND

Bush, Frank (Athlete, Football Player)
1126 West Armstrong Way
Chandler, AZ 85266, USA

Bush, George (Ex-President, President)
The Office of George Bush
10000 Memorial Dr
Suite 900
Houston, TX 77024, USA

Bush, George W (Ex-President, Politician)
Office Of George W. Bush
P.O. Box 259000
Dallas, TX 75225, USA

Bush, Homer (Athlete, Baseball Player)
1402 Exeter Ct
Southlake, TX 76092-4219, USA

Bush, Jeb (Governor) (Politician)
629 Altara Ave
Coral Gables, FL 33146-1303, USA

Bush, Jenna (Writer)
1345 S Charles St
Baltimore, MD 21230, USA

Bush, Jim (Coach)
5106 Bounty Lane
Culver City, CA 90230, USA

Bush, Kate (Musician, Songwriter, Writer)
c/o Staff Member *Jukes Productions Ltd*
P.O. Box 13995
London W9 2FL, UK

Bush, Kristian (Musician)
Sugarland
917 Stratford Rd
Avondale Estates, GA 30002, USA

Bush, Laura (First Lady, Politician)
Office Of George W. Bush
P.O. Box 259000
Dallas, TX 75225, USA

Bush, Lauren (Model)
c/o Staff Member *Elite Model Management (NY)*
404 Park Ave S Fl 9
New York, NY 10016, USA

Bush, Randv (Athlete, Baseball Player)
1000 Chestnut Ct
Slidell, LA 70458-5486, USA

Bush, Randy (Athlete, Baseball Player)
7713 E McKinley St
Scottsdale, AZ 85257, USA

Bush, Rebeccah (Actor)
c/o Staff Member *Cunningham Escott Slevin & Doherty (CESD-LA)*
10635 Santa Monica Blvd
130
Los Angeles, CA 90025, USA

Bush, Reggie (Football Player)
1501 Viewsite Terrace
West Hollywood, CA 90069, USA

Bush, Sophia (Actor)
c/o Joan Green *Joan Green Management*
1836 Courtney Terr
Los Angeles, CA 90046, USA

Bush, Walter L (Misc)
5200 Malibu Dr
Minneapolis, MN 55436, USA

Bush, William Green (Actor)
Gold Marshak Liedtke
3500 W Olive Ave
#1400
Burbank, CA 91505, USA

Bushbeck, Chuck (Athlete, Football Player)
2806 Angus Rd
Philadelphia, PA 19114-3414, USA

Bushell, Matt (Actor)
c/o Sandra Joseph *SLJ Management*
833 N Edinburgh Ave Ph 11
Los Angeles, CA 90046, USA

Bushing, Chris (Athlete, Baseball Player)
12830 NW 21st St
Pembroke Pines, FL 33028-2534, USA

Bushinsky, Joseph M (Jay) (Correspondent)
Rehov Hatsafon 5
Savyon 56540, ISRAEL

Bush, Jr., Walter L (Athlete, Hockey Player)
5200 Malibu Dr
Minneapolis, MN 55436, USA

Bushland, Raymond C (Misc)
200 Concord Plaza Dr
San Antonio, TX 78216, USA

Bushnell, Bill (Director)
2751 Pelham Place
Los Angeles, CA 90068, USA

Bushnell, Candace (Producer, Writer)
253 Tophet Rd
Roxbury, CT 06783, USA

Bushy, Ronald (Ron) (Musician)
Entertainment Services Int'l
6400 Pleasant Park Dr
Chanhassen, MN 55317, USA

Busick, Steve (Athlete, Football Player)
6246 W Long Dr
Littleton, CO 80123, USA

Busino, Orlando (Cartoonist)
12 Shadblow Hill Road
Ridgefield, CT 06877-5221, USA

Buskas, Rod (Athlete, Hockey Player)
182 Wentworth Dr
Henderson, NV 89074, USA

Buskey, Mike (Athlete, Baseball Player)
117 Cedar Woods Trl
Canton, GA 30114, USA

Buskey., Mike (Athlete, Baseball Player)
117 Cedar Woods Trl
Canton, GA 30114-7769, USA

Busniuk, Mike (Athlete, Hockey Player)
420 Sycamore Pl
Thunder Bay, ON P7C 1W9, Canada

Busniuk, Ron (Athlete, Hockey Player)
540 Laurentian Dr
Thunder Bay, ON P7C 5J8, Canada

Buss, Jerry (Athlete, Basketball Player)
42 Gulf Stream Ct
McKees Rocks, PA 15136-1509, USA

Busse, Ray (Athlete, Baseball Player)
4265 Lemon St
Cocoa, FL 32926, USA

Bussell, Darcey A (Ballerina)
155 New King's Road
London SW6 4SJ, UNITED KINGDOM (UK)

Bussell, Gerry (Athlete, Football Player)
2922 Justin Ct
Orange Park, FL 32065, USA

Bussey, Barney (Athlete, Football Player)
5059 Park Ridge Ct
West Chester, OH 45069, USA

Bussey, Dexter (Athlete, Football Player)
2565 Bloomfield Xing
Bloomfield Hills, MI 48304, US

Bustamante, Carlos (Scientist)
University of California
Howard Hughes Medical Institute
Berkeley, CA 94720, USA

Busted (Music Group)
c/o Staff Member *Helter Skelter (UK)*
535 Kings Rd
The Plaza
London SW10 0SZ, UNITED KINGDOM
(UK)

Buster, Dolly (Adult Film Star)
Am Schornacker 66
Wesel D-46485, Germany

Buster, John E (Misc)
Harbor-UCLA Medical Center
PO Box 2910
Torrance, CA 90509, USA

Bustion, Dave (Athlete, Basketball Player)
706 Tarrant Ct
Gadsden, AL 35901, USA

Butala, Tony (Musician)
PO Box 151
McKees Rocks, PA 15136, USA

Butcher, Clyde (Photographer)
52388 Tamiami Trail E
Chokoloskee, FL 34138, USA

Butcher, Donnie (Athlete, Basketball Player)
1725 Burns Rd
Milford, MI 48381-1215, USA

Butcher, Garth (Athlete, Hockey Player)
1524 Maple Ln
Bellingham, WA 98229, USA

Butcher, Jade (Athlete, Football Player)
9730 N Moon Rd
Gosport, IN 47433-9517

Butcher, Jim (Writer)
c/o *St. Martin's Press*
ATTN: PUBLICITY DEPT
175 Fifth Avenue
New York, NY 10010, USA

Butcher, John (Athlete, Baseball Player)
820 Woodridge Dr S
Chaska, MN 55318, USA

Butcher, Mike (Athlete, Baseball Player)
324 33rd Ave
East Moline, IL 61244-3124, USA

Butcher, Paul (Athlete, Football Player)
c/o Mitchell Gossett *Cunningham Escott Slevin & Doherty (CESD-LA)*
9560 Wilshire Blvd Fl 5
Beverly Hills, CA 90212, USA

Butcher, Rodney (Athlete, Golfer)
7333 Hideaway Trl
New Port Richey, FL 34655-4006, USA

Butcher-Marsh, Mary (Athlete, Baseball Player, Commentator)
PO Box 563
Lovelock, NV 89419-0563, USA

Butera, Sal (Athlete, Baseball Player)
324 Tersas Ct
Lake Mary, FL 32746-5143, USA

Buthelezi, Chief Mangosuthu G (Politician)
Home Affairs Ministry
Private Bag x741
Pretoria 0001, SOUTH AFRICA

Buthelezi, Minister Mangosuthu (Politician)
Parliament of the Republic of South Africa
Parliament St
Cape Town 8000, South Africa

Butkus, Richard J (Dick) (Actor, Athlete, Football Player)
c/o Richard Lewis *Geddes Agency, The*
8430 Santa Monica Blvd
Suite 200
Los Angeles, CA 90069, USA

Butler, Adam (Athlete, Baseball Player)
815 Providence Rd
Towson, MD 32746-5143, USA

Butler, Austin (Actor)
c/o Doug Wald *Anonymous Content (LA)*
3531 Hayden Ave
Culver City, CA 90232, USA

Butler, Bernard (Musician)
Interceptor Enterprises
98 White Lion St
London N1 9PF, UNITED KINGDOM
(UK)

Butler, Bill (Athlete, Baseball Player)
3173 E Long Cir S
Centennial, CO 80122, USA

Butler, Bill C (Cinematographer)
1097 Aviation Blvd
Hermosa Beach, CA 90254, USA

Butler, Bob (Athlete, Football Player)
120 Holly Hills Dr
Mount Sterling, KY 40353, USA

Butler, Bobby (Athlete, Hockey Player)
c/o John and Wendy Butler 56 Ethier Cir
Marlborough, MA 01752-7211, USA

Butler, Brent (Athlete, Baseball Player)
10441 Scotland Farm Rd
Laurinburg, NC 28352-7977, USA

Butler, Brett (Actor, Comedian)
c/o Staff Member *TalentWorks (LA)*
3500 W Olive Ave
Suite 1400
Burbank, CA 91505, USA

Butler, Brett M (Athlete, Baseball Player)
4488 E Thomas Rd
Unit 2012
Phoenix, AZ 85255-6092, USA

Butler, Caron (Athlete, Basketball Player)
3808 Millard Way
Fairfax, VA 22033-2753, USA

Butler, Cecil (Athlete, Baseball Player)
263 Hickory Gap Trl
Dallas, GA 30157-5353, USA

Butler, Charles (Athlete, Basketball Player)
453 Arbor Cir
Youngstown, OH 44505 -1915, USA

Butler, Charles W (Athlete, Football Player)
5496 Celestial Dr
Atwater, CA 95301, USA

Butler, Chuck (Athlete, Football Player)
5496N Celestial Dr
Atwater, CA 95301, US

Butler, Conrad (Actor)
Paradigm Agency
10100 Santa Monica Blvd
#2500
Los Angeles, CA 90067, USA

Butler, Dan (Actor)
c/o Staff Member *ATA Management*
12 Desbrosses St
New York, NY 10013, USA

Butler, David (Actor)
c/o Staff Member *The Rights House (UK)*
Drury House
34-43 Russell St
London WC2B 5HA, UK

Butler, Dean (Actor)
1310 Westholme Ave
Los Angeles, CA 90024, USA

Butler, Donald (Athlete, Football Player)
c/o Roosevelt Barnes *Maximum Sports Management*
6435 W Jefferson Blvd
#197
Fort Wayne, IN 46804, USA

Butler, Elbert (Athlete, Basketball Player)
153 Willow Ave
Rochester, NY 14609-1244, USA

Butler, Gary (Athlete, Football Player)
6660 S Piney Creek Cir
Centennial, CO 80016, USA

Butler, Gary C (Athlete, Football Player)
Automatic Data Processing
212 Oak Hollow St
Conroe, TX 77301, USA

Butler, George L (General)
Peter Kiewit & Sons
11122 William Plaza
Omaha, NE 68144, USA

Butler, Gerard (Actor)
4828 Glencairn Rd
Los Angeles, CA 90027, USA

Butler, Greg (Athlete, Basketball Player)
216 Beverly Rd
Scarsdale, NY 10583-1514, USA

Butler, Jack (Athlete, Football Player)
510 E 11th Ave
Homestead, PA 15120, USA

Butler, James (Athlete, Football Player)
3181 Spring St
Atlanta, GA 30349, USA

Butler, Jerametrius
1717 High Valley Ln
Cedar Hill, TX 75104, US

Butler, Jerry (Athlete, Hockey Player)
City of Winnipeg 83-30 Fort St Attn: Plan Examination Dept
Winnipeg, MB R3C 4X7, Canada

Butler, Jerry (Iceman) (Musician, Songwriter, Writer)
c/o Jeremy Plager *Creative Artists Agency (CAA-LA)*
2000 Ave Of The Stars
Los Angeles, CA 90067, USA

Butler, Jerry O (Athlete, Football Player)
17117 Shaker Blvd
Cleveland, OH 44120, USA

Butler, Jim "Cannonball" (Athlete, Football Player)
1261 Cahaba Dr SW
Atlanta, GA 30311, US

Butler, Joe (Musician)
Pipeline Artists Mgmt
620 16th Ave S
Hopkins, MN 55343, USA

Butler, John (Musician)
c/o Staff Member *Paradigm (Monterey)*
404 W Franklin St
Monterey, CA 93940, USA

Butler, Jonathan (Musician)
294 Bell Canyon Rd
Bell Canyon, CA 91307, USA

Butler, Keith (Athlete, Football Player)
805 Cavan Dr
Cranberry Twp, PA 16066, USA

Butler, Kerry (Actor)
c/o Erica Tuchman *One Entertainment (NY)*
12 W 57th St
Penthouse
New York, NY 10019, USA

Butler, Kevin (Athlete, Football Player)
3256 Bagley Psge
Duluth, GA 30097, USA

Butler, LeRoy (Athlete, Football Player)
4119 Westloop Ln
Jacksonville, FL 32277, USA

Butler, Lucy (Actor)
c/o Judy Orbach *Judy O Productions*
6136 Glen Holly
Hollywood, CA 90068, USA

Butler, Martin (Composer)
Princeton University
Music Dept
Princeton, NJ 08544, USA

Butler, Michael (Athlete, Football Player)
3107 Magalene Forest Ct
Tampa, FL 33618, USA

Butler, Mike (Athlete, Basketball Player)
3107 Magdalene Forest Ct
Tampa, FL 33618, USA

Butler, Mitchell (Athlete, Basketball Player)
1468 Paseo De Oro
Pacific Palisades, CA 90272-1961, USA

Butler, Paul (Astronomer)
University of California
Astronomy Dept
Berkeley, CA 94720, USA

Butler, Rasual
1463 SW 161st Ave
Pembroke Pines, FL 33027-5139, USA

Butler, Ray (Athlete, Football Player)
9700 Leawood Blvd
Apt 1307
Houston, TX 77099, USA

Butler, Robert (Director)
650 Club View Dr
Los Angeles, CA 90024, USA

Butler, Robert (Athlete, Football Player)
5567 Naylor Ct
Norcross, GA 30092, USA

Butler, Robert Olen (Writer)
1009 Concord Road
#230
Tallahassee, FL 32308, USA

Butler, Robert olen (Writer)
3909 Reserve Dr Apt 1611
Tallahassee, FL 32311-1284, USA

Butler, Samuel C (Attorney, Attorney General, General)
Cravath Swain Moore
825 8th Ave
New York, NY 10019, USA

Butler, Skip (Athlete, Football Player)
1311 Spyglass Dr
Mansfield, TX 76063-4023, USA

Butler, Steve (Race Car Driver)
1820 S Buckeye Street
Kokomo, IN 46902, USA

Butler, Terence (Geezer) (Musician)
2109 San Ysidro Dr
Beverly Hills, CA 90210

Butler, Tom (Athlete, Bobsledder,
Olympic Athlete)
4950 Buchanan Pl
Sarasota, FL 34231-8509, USA

Butler, William D (Athlete, Football
Player)
200 E Liberty St
Berlin, WI 54923, USA

Butler, William E (Athlete, Football
Player)
3030 Cherry Hi
Manhattan, KS 66503, USA

Butler, William E (Business Person)
Eaton Corp
Eaton Center
1111 Superior Ave
Cleveland, OH 44114, USA

Butler, Yancy (Actor)
c/o Peg Donegan *Framework
Entertainment (LA)*
9057 Nemo St
Suite C
West Hollywood, CA 90069, USA

Butler Billy, Billy (Athlete, Baseball
Player)
2007 Kansas City Royals
7724 E Santa Catalina Dr, Scottsdale AZ,
USA

Butler-Henderson, Vicki (Actor)
c/o Staff Member *Princess Productions*
Newcombe House
45 Notting Hill Gate
London W11 3LQ, UNITED KINGDOM

Butor, Michael (Writer)
A L'Ecart
Lucinges
Bonne 74380, FRANCE

Butsayev, Vyacheslav (Athlete, Hockey
Player)
17555 Collins Ave Apt 1704
Sunny Isles Beach, FL 33160-2888, USA

Butsko, Harry (Athlete, Football Player)
4 Milo Cir
Duncannon, PA 17020, USA

Butt, Yondani
Gurtman & Murtha
450 Fashion Ave
#603
New York, NY 10123, USA

Buttafuoco, Joey (Actor)
10835 DeSoto Ave
Chatsworth, CA 91311, USA

Buttafuoco, Mary Jo

Buttelmann, Henry (General)
3117 Highland Falls Dr
Las Vegas, NV 89134-7423, USA

Butterfield, Alexander P (Government
Official)
3410 Brookwood Dr
Fairfax, VA 22030, USA

Butterfield, Asa (Actor)
c/o Liz Mahoney *ID Public Relations
(ID-LA)*
7060 Hollywood Blvd
8th Floor
Los Angeles, CA 90028, USA

Butterfield, Betty (Comedian)
c/o Staff Member *Diva Central Inc*
7510 W Sunset Blvd Ste 1445
Los Angees, CA 90046, USA

Butterfield, Brian
PO Box 1538
Standish, ME 04084-1538, USA

Butterfield, Deborah K (Artist)
11229 Cottonwood Road
Bozeman, MT 59718, USA

Butterfield, G. K. (Congressman,
Politician)
2305 Rayburn HOB
Washington, DC 20515, USA

Butterfield, Jack (Misc)
55 Pineridge Drive
Westfield, MA 08085, USA

Butterfly Boucher (Music Group)
c/o Staff Member *Paradigm (Monterey)*
404 W Franklin St
Monterey, CA 93940, USA

Butters, Bill (Athlete, Hockey Player)
12579 Europa Ave N
Saint Paul, MN 55110-5957, USA

Butters, Tom (Athlete, Baseball Player)
4 Turnberry Ct
Durham, NC 27712, USA

Butters, Torn (Athlete, Baseball Player)
4 Turn berry Ct
Durham, NC 27712-9465, USA

Butterworth, Dean (Musician)
4310 Canoga Dr
Woodland Hills, CA 91364, USA

Butthole Surfers, The (Music Group,
Musician)
c/o Staff Member *Mute Records*
1 Albion Pl
London W6 0QT, UK

Buttke, Nathan (Race Car Driver)
Mark III Motorsports
211 Greenwich Rd
Charlotte, NC 28211, USA

Buttle, Gregory E (Greg) (Athlete,
Football Player)
5 Hollacher Dr
Northport, NY 11768, USA

Button, Dick (Athlete, Figure Skater,
Olympic Athlete)
Candid Productions
765 Park Ave
#6B
New York, NY 10021-4271, USA

Butts, Earl (Actor)
2741 N Salisbury St
#2116
West Lafayette, IN 47906-1499, USA

Butts, James (Athlete, Track Athlete)
16950 Belforest Dr
Carson, CA 90746, USA

Butts, Marion (Athlete, Football Player)
4600 Lacosta Dr
Albany, GA 31721, US

Butts, Robert (Athlete, Football Player)
108 Circle Dr
Flushing, OH 43977, USA

Butz, David E (Dave) (Athlete, Football
Player)
2324 Esther Ave
Saint Louis, MO 63139, USA

Butzer, Hans E (Architect)
University of Oklahoma
Architecture Division
Gould Hall
Norman, OK 73019, USA

Butzner, John D Jr (Judge)
US Court of Appeals
PO Box 2188
Richmond, VA 23218, USA

Buxton, Sarah (Actor)
1416 Havenhurst Dr. #3C
West Hollywood, CA 90046, USA

Buyers, William (Scientist)
Atomic Energy of Canada Ltd2251
Speakman Dr
Mississauga, ON L5K 1B2, Canada

Buynak, Gordie (Athlete, Hockey Player)
11512 Douglas Lake Rd
Pellston, MI 49769-9105, USA

Buzek, Jerzy (Prime Minister)
Kancelaria Prezesa Ministrow
Al Ujazdowskie
1/3
Warsaw 00-583, POLAND

Buzin, Rich (Athlete, Football Player)
23004 Mastick Rd
Apt 216
North Olmstead, OH 44070, USA

Buzolin, Mariah (Actor)
c/o Staff Member *Leslie Allan-Rice
Management*
1007 Maybrook Dr
Beverly Hills, CA 90210, USA

Buzzi, Ruth (Actor, Comedian)
1321 Saint Albans Rd.
Southlake, TX 76092, USA

B. West, Allen (Congressman, Politician)
1708 Longworth HOB
Washington, DC 20515, USA

B*Witched (Music Group)
c/o Staff Member *Concorde Intl Artists Ltd*
101 Shepherds Bush Rd
London W6 7LP, UNITED KINGDOM
(UK)

Byars, Betsy C (Writer)
401 Rudder Ridge
Seneca, SC 29678-2035, USA

Byars, Keith (Athlete, Football Player)
3657 NW 5th Ter
Boca Raton, FL 33431-, US

Byas, Rick (Athlete, Football Player)
19925 Greenwald Dr
Southfield, MI 48075, US

Byce, John (Athlete, Hockey Player)
9701 Hill Creek Dr
Verona, QI 53593, USA

Bychkov, Semyon
Buffalo Symphony Orchestra
71 Symphony Circle
Buffalo, NY 14201, USA

Bye, Karyn (Athlete, Hockey Player,
Olympic Athlete)
322 Gandy Dancer Cir
Hudson, WI 54016-8186, USA

Bye, Kermit E (Judge)
US Court of Appeals
657 2nd Ave N
Fargo, ND 58102, USA

Byers, Clinton (Athlete, Basketball Player)
4257 Leewood Rd
Stow, OH 44224, USA

Byers, Ken (Athlete, Football Player)
4650 Willow Hills Ln
Cincinnati, OH 45243, USA

Byers, Lyndon (Athlete, Hockey Player)
8 Lindbergh Rd
20 Guest St, Suite 300
Framingham, MA 01702-2334, USA

Byers, Mike (Athlete, Hockey Player)
2743 Victoria Park Ave
Scarborough, ON MlT 1A8, Canada

Byers, Nina (Physicist)
University of California
Physics Dept
Los Angeles, CA 90024, USA

Byers, Randell (Randy) (Athlete, Baseball
Player)
31 Waldens Dr
Bridgeton, NJ 08302-4424, USA

Byers, Scott (Athlete, Football Player)
6060 Buckingham Pkwy Apt 314
Culver City, CA 90230, USA

Byers, Steve (Actor)
c/o Robyn Friedman *Artist Management
Inc*
464 King St E
Toronto ON M5A 1L7, CANADA

Byers, Walter (Athlete, Basketball Player)
25707 Aiken Switch Rd
Emmett, KS 66422, USA

Byfuglien, Dustin (Athlete, Hockey Player)
33626 State Highway 11
Roseau, MN 56751-8107, USA

Bykovsky, Valeri F (Cosmonaut)
Potchta Kosmonavtov
Moskovskoi Oblasti
Syvisdny Goroduk 141160, RUSSIA

Bylsma, Dan (Athlete, Hockey Player)
401 Avonworth Heights Dr
Pittsburgh, PA 15237-1260, USA

Bylsma, Dan (Athlete, Hockey Player)
Pittsburgh Penguins 66 Mario Lemieux Pl
Ste 2
Pittsburgh, PA 15219-3504, USA

Byman, Bob (Athlete, Golfer)
9325 Eagle Ridge Dr
Las Vegas, NV 89134, USA

Byner, Earnest A (Athlete, Football Player)
1016 Sattui Ct
Franklin, TN 37064, USA

Byner, John (Actor)
American Mgmt
19948 Mayall St
Chatsworth, CA 91311, USA

Bynes, Amanda (Actor, Comedian)
25571 Prado De Las Bellotas
Calabasas, CA 91302, USA

Bynoe, Peter C B (Misc)
Denver Nuggets
Pepsi Center
1000 Chopper Circle
Denver, CO 80204, USA

Bynum, Andrew (Athlete, Basketball Player)
c/o Philip Button *WME (LA)*
9601 Wilshire Blvd Fl 3
Beverly Hills, CA 90210, USA

Bynum, Freddie (Athlete, Baseball Player)
2987 Pope Farm Rd
Stantonsburg, NC 227883-8556, USA

Bynum, Juanita (Actor, Motivational Speaker)
c/o Staff Member *Just Borne Mega Entertainment*
P.O. Box 668
Snellville, GA 30078, USA

Bynum, Mike (Athlete, Baseball Player)
4576 Junction Dr
Middleburg, FL 77056-6943, USA

Bynum, Will (Athlete, Basketball Player)
c/o Brad Ames *Priority Sports & Entertainment - (LA)*
15233 Ventura Blvd
Suite 718
Sherman Oaks, CA 91403, USA

Byrd, Benjamin F Jr (Doctor)
4220 Hardling Pike
#380
Nashville, TN 37205, USA

Byrd, Boris (Athlete, Football Player)
1376 Richpond Rockfield Rd
Bowling Green, KY 42101, USA

Byrd, Dan (Actor)
2450 Rinconia Dr
Los Angeles, CA 90068, USA

Byrd, Darryl (Athlete, Football Player)
138 Mission Dr
Palo Alto, CA 94303, USA

Byrd, Dennis (Athlete, Football Player)
10757 E 350 Rd
Talala, OK 74080, USA

Byrd, Dominique (Athlete, Football Player)
c/o Eugene Parker *Maximum Sports Management*
6435 W Jefferson Blvd
#197
Fort Wayne, IN 46804, USA

Byrd, Donald (Musician)
DL Media
PO Box 2728
Bala Cynwyd, PA 19004, USA

Byrd, Eugene (Actor)
c/o Steve Caserta *Sanders Armstrong Caserta*
2120 Colorado Blvd
Suite 120
Santa Monica, CA 90404, USA

Byrd, George (Athlete, Football Player)
23 Wayside Rd
Westborough, MA 01581, USA

Byrd, Gill (Athlete, Football Player)
5347 Notting Hill Rd
Gurnee, IL 60031, US

Byrd, Harry F Jr (Politician)
Rockingham Publishing Co
2 N kent St
Winchester, VA 22601-5038, USA

Byrd, Isaac (Athlete, Football Player)
5712 Astra Ave
Saint Louis, MO 63147, USA

Byrd, Israel (Athlete, Football Player)
5712 Astra Ave
Saint Louis, MO 63147, USA

Byrd, Jairus (Athlete, Football Player)
c/o Eugene Parker *Maximum Sports Management*
6435 W Jefferson Blvd
#197
Fort Wayne, IN 46804, USA

Byrd, Jeff (Athlete, Baseball Player)
39376 Opalocka Rd
Boulevard, CA 91905-9682, USA

Byrd, Jim (Athlete, Baseball Player)
511 NW Woodridge Dr
Lawton, OK 73507-2265, USA

Byrd, Jonathan (Athlete, Golfer)
110 Meadow Bark
Saint Simons Island, GA 31522, USA

Byrd, Marion
2002 Philadelohia Phillies
Chicago, IL 60657-3013, USA

Byrd, Marlon (Athlete, Baseball Player)
3620 Hamilton Key
West Palm Beach, FL 33411, USA

Byrd, McArthur (Athlete, Football Player)
10291 Sheldon Rd
Elk Grove, CA 95624, USA

Byrd, Paul (Athlete, Baseball Player)
29254 Grande Ct
Westlake, OH 30004-0977, USA

Byrd, Richard (Athlete, Football Player)
2230 Haley Rd
Terry, MS 39170, USA

Byrd, Robin (Adult Film Star)
Robin Byrd Show
P.O. Box 305
Lenox Hill Station
New York, NY 10021, USA

Byrd, Tom (Actor)
United Talent Agency
14011 Ventura Blvd
#213
Sherman Oaks, CA 91423, USA

Byrd, Tracy (Musician)
4695 Monticello St
Beaumont, TX 77706, USA

Byrd, Vivkey L (Stylist)
PO Box 8
Rock Falls, IL 61071, USA

Byrdak, Tim (Athlete, Baseball Player)
16721 W Seneca Dr
Lockport, IL 60441-4269, USA

Byrds, The (Music Group, Musician)
P.O. Box 1222
Pleasanton, CA 94566, USA

Byrne, Brendan T (Politician)
Carella Byrne
5 Becker Farm Rd
Roseland, NJ 07068, USA

Byrne, Chris (Actor)
c/o Staff Member *Kazarian Spencer Ruskin & Assoc.*
11969 Ventura Blvd
3rd Floor
Studio City, CA 91604, USA

Byrne, David (Musician, Songwriter)
231 10th Ave #PH1
New York, NY 10011, USA

Byrne, Gabriel (Actor)
211 Elizabeth St #2N
New York, NY 10012, USA

Byrne, Garry (Publisher)
Variety Inc
5700 Wilshire Blvd
Los Angeles, CA 90036, USA

Byrne, John (Cartoonist)
DC Cornics
1700 Broadway
#700
New York, NY 10019, USA

Byrne, Josh (Actor)
Hervey/Grimes
PO Box 64249
Los Angeles, CA 90064, USA

Byrne, Martha
c/o Staff Member *Innovative Artists (LA)*
1505 10th St
Santa Monica, CA 90401, USA

Byrne, Michael (Actor)
Conway Van Gelder Robinson
18-21 Jermyn St
London SW1Y 6NB, UNITED KINGDOM (UK)

Byrne, Nicky (Musician)
c/o Staff Member *Solo Agency Ltd (UK)*
55 Fulham High St
2nd Floor
London SW6 3JJ, United Kingdom

Byrne, Rhonda (Writer)
c/o Staff Member *Simon & Schuster*
1230 Avenue of the Americas
New York, NY 10020, USA

Byrne, Rose (Actor)
c/o Robyn Gardiner *RGM Artist Group*
64-76 Kippax St
Level 2, Suite 202 & 206
Surry Hills, NSW 2010, Australia

Byrne, Steve (Musician)
c/o Staff Member *Paradigm (Monterey)*
404 W Franklin St
Monterey, CA 93940, USA

Byrne, Thomas J (Tommy) (Athlete, Baseball Player)
1108 Fairway Villas Dr
Wake Forest, NC 27587, USA

Byrnes, Edd (Actor)
PO Box 1623
Beverly Hills, CA 90213, USA

Byrnes, Eric (Athlete, Baseball Player)
c/o Staff Member *WmE2 (WMA-LA)*
1 William Morris Pl
Beverly Hills, CA 90212, USA

Byrnes, Eric (Athlete, Baseball Player)
24404 N 61st Dr
Glendale, AZ 94019-8002, USA

Byrnes, Jim (Actor)
c/o Staff Member *Characters Talent Agency, The (Vancouver)*
1505 W 2nd Ave
#200
Vancouver, BC V6H 3Y4, Canada

Byrnes, Kevin P (General)
Assistant Vice Chief of Staff
HqUSA
Pentagon
Washington, DC 20310, USA

Byrnes, Marty (Athlete, Basketball Player)
8739 3rd Ave
Pleasent Prairie, WI 53158-4709, USA

Byron, Kari
Mythbusters Beyond Productions
1268 Missouri Street
San Francisco, CA 94107, USA

Byrorn, Don (Musician)
Hans Wendl Productions
2220 California St
Berkeley, CA 94703, USA

Byrorn, Monty (Musician, Songwriter, Writer)
Gurley Co
1204B Cedar Lane
Nashville, TN 37212, USA

Byrum, Carl (Athlete, Football Player)
209 Castlewood Dr
Buffalo, NY 14227, us

Byrum, Curt (Athlete, Golfer)
12441 N 86th St
Scottsdale, AZ 85260-5343, USA

Byrum, John W (Director)
7435 Woodrow Wilson Dr
Los Angeles, CA 90046, USA

Byrum, Tom (Athlete, Golfer)
70 Sierra Oaks Dr
Sugar Land, TX 77479, USA

Bystrom, Marty (Athlete, Baseball Player)
P.O. Box 89
Geigertown, PA 19087-3058, USA

Byung-Hun, Lee
c/o Larry Galper *Creative Artists Agency (CAA-LA)*
2000 Ave Of The Stars
Los Angeles, CA 90067, USA

Bywater, William H (Misc)
International Electronic Workers
1126 16th St NW
Washington, DC 20036, USA

Bzdelik, Jeff (Coach)
Denver Nuggets
Pepsi Center
1000 Chopper Circle
Denver, CO 80204, USA

c, Peter (Athlete, Hockey Player)
V. Storgatan 10
Jonkoping S-55315, Sweden

Caan, James (Actor, Director)
2791 Hutton Dr
Beverly Hills, CA 90210, USA

Caan, James (Business Person)
Hamilton Bradshaw
18 Hanover Sq
London W1S 1HX, UK

Caan, Scott (Actor)
2049 Oakstone Way
Los Angeles, CA 90046, USA

Caballe, Monserrat (Opera Singer)
Avenida Madronos 27
Madrid E-28043, Spain

Caballe, Montserrat (Opera Singer)
Opera Carlos Caballe
Via Augusta 59
Barcelona 08006, SPAIN

Caballero, Celestino (Athlete, Boxer)
c/o Jody Kohn *Talent Without Borders*
Prefers to be contacted by telephone
Las Vegas, NV 89145, USA

Caballero, Ralph (Putsy) (Athlete,
Baseball Player)
1120 Shirley Dr
Matairie, LA 70001, USA

Cabana, Robert D (Astronaut)
18315 Cape Bahamas Lane
Houston, TX 77058, USA

cabana, Robert d colonel (Astronaut)
1626 Manor Dr
Cocoa, FL 32922-6922, USA

Cabas (Musician)
c/o Staff Member *Creative Artists Agency
(CAA-LA)*
2000 Ave Of The Stars
Los Angeles, CA 90067, USA

Cabas, Victor n briggen (General)
31021 Marne Dr
Rancho Palos Verdes, CA 90275-5613,
USA

Cabel, Barney (Athlete, Basketball Player)
1134 S Main St
Hampstead, MD 21074, USA

Cabell, Enos M (Athlete, Baseball Player)
4103 Frost Lake Ct
Missouri City, TX 77459-2304, USA

Cabibbo, Nicola (Physicist)
ENEA
Viale Regina Margherita 125
Rome 00198, ITALY

Cable, Barney (Athlete, Basketball Player)
1134 S Main St
Hampstead, MD 21074-2255, USA

Cable, Candace (Athlete, Olympic
Athlete)
PO Box 8264
Truckee, CA 96162-8264, USA

Cable, Tom (Athlete, Football Player)
Oakland Raiders 1220 Harbor Bay Pkwy
Alameda, a CA 94502-, us

Cable Guy, The, Larry (Comedian)
c/o J P Williams *Parallel Entertainment*
9420 Wilshire Blvd #250
Beverly Hills, CA 90212, USA

Cabot, Louis W (Business Person)
Brookings Institution
1775 Massachusetts Ave NW
Washington, DC 20036, USA

Cabot, Meg (Writer)
PO Box 4904
Key West, FL 33041, USA

Cabral, Brian (Athlete, Football Player)
5008 Ellsworth Pl
Boulder, CO 80303, USA

Cabral, Sam A (Misc)
Police Associations International Union
1421 Prince St
Alexandria, VA 22314, USA

Cabranes, Jose A (Judge)
US District Court
141 Church St
New Haven, CT 06510, USA

Cabrera, John (Actor)
c/o Adam Griffin *Kritzer Levine Wilkins
Entertainment (KLWG)*
11872 La Grange Ave
1st Floor
Los Angeles, CA 90025, USA

Cabrera, Jolbert (Baseball Player)
c/o Staff Member *Los Angeles Dodgers
(LA Dodgers)*
1000 Elysian Park Ave
Los Angeles, CA 90012, USA

Cabrera, Melky (Athlete, Baseball Player)
7912 River Rd
North Bergen, NJ 07047, USA

Cabrera, Miguel (Athlete, Baseball Player)
3255 NE 184th St
Apt 12101
North Miami Beach, FL 48009-1275, USA

Cabrera, Orlando (Athlete, Baseball
Player)
9248 Scarlette Oak Ave
Fort Myers, FL 33967-5145, USA

Cabrera, Ryan (Musician)
c/o Staff Member *CEG Talent*
251 W. 39th St
7th Floor
New York, NY 10011, USA

Cabrera, Santiago (Actor)
c/o Suzan Bymel *Management 360*
9111 Wilshire Blvd
Beverly Hills, CA 90210, USA

Caccialanza, Lorenzo (Actor)
Ambrosio/Mortimer
P O Box 16758
Beverly Hills, CA 90209, USA

Cacciavillan, Agnostino Cardinal
(Religious Leader)
Patrimony of Holy See
Palazzo Apostolico
Vatican City 00120, VATICAN CITY

Cacek, Craig (Athlete, Baseball Player)
909 6th St
Apt 3
Santa Monica, CA 90403-2700, USA

Caceres, Edgar (Athlete, Baseball Player)
2575 51st St
Sarasota, FL 34203-7905, USA

Caceres, Kurt (Actor)
c/o Kathy Atkinson *Washington Square
Arts (LA)*
1041 N Formosa Ave
The Lot Writers Bldg, Room 305
West Hollywood, CA 90046, USA

Cackowski, Liz (Actor, Comedian)
c/o Staff Member *Creative Artists Agency
(CAA-LA)*
2000 Ave Of The Stars
Los Angeles, CA 90067, USA

Cada, Joseph (Misc)
11134 Speedway Dr
Shelby Township, MI 48317-3546, USA

Cadaret, Greg (Athlete, Baseball Player)
22636 Bridlewood Ln
Palo Cedro, CA 96073-9567, USA

Cadbury, Adrian (Business Person)
Bank of England
Threadneedle St
London EC2R 8AH, UNITED KINGDOM
(UK)

Caddell, Patrick (Politician)
p
1048 Dominion Dr
Hanahan, SC 29410-2408, USA

Cade, Eddie (Athlete, Football Player)
501 W 4th St
Eloy, AZ 85231, USA

Cade, Michael (Actor)

Cade, Mossy (Athlete, Football Player)
400 W Pasadena Ave Apt 19
Phoenix, AZ 85013-, USA

Cadell, Ava (Actor, Model)
c/o Rick Hersh *Celebrity Consultants LLC*
3340 Ocean Park Blvd
Suite 1030
Santa Monica, CA 90405, USA

Cadell, Dr. Ava (Adult Film Star)
Loveology University
9000 W Sunset Blvd
Suite 1115
Los Angeles, CA 90069-5811, USA

Cadigan, Dave (Athlete, Football Player)
14416 Katie Rd
Phoenix, MD 21131, USA

Cadile, Jim (Athlete, Football Player)
1738 Spring St
Medford, OR 97504, USA

Cadogan, William J (Business Person)
ADC Communications
PO Box 1101
Minneapolis, MN 55440, USA

Cadorette, Mary (Actor)
114 W Granby Rd
Granby, CT 06035, USA

Cadrez, Glenn (Athlete, Football Player)
1294 Mariposa Rd
Carlsbad, CA 92011, USA

Cady, Sherry (Scientist)
Portland State University
Geology Dept
Portland, OR 97207, USA

Caesar, Shirley (Music Group)
Shirley Caesar Outreach Ministries
3310 Croasdaile Dr #902
Durham, NC 27705, USA

Caesar, Sid (Actor, Comedian)
c/o Staff Member *Cunningham Escott
Slevin & Doherty (CESD-LA)*
10635 Santa Monica Blvd
130
Los Angeles, CA 90025, USA

Caesars, The (Music Group)
c/o Staff Member *Paradigm (Monterey)*
404 W Franklin St
Monterey, CA 93940, USA

Cafagna-Tesoro, Ashley (Actor)
c/o Staff Member *Tesoro Entertainment*
205D N Stephanie St No115
Henderson, NV 89074, USA

Cafferata, Hector A jr (General)
1807 Plum Lane
Venice, FL 34293-2040, USA

Cafferty, Jack (Commentator)
41 Vincent Rd
Cedar Grove, NJ 07009, USA

Caffery, Terry (Athlete, Hockey Player)
2743 Victoria Park Ave
Scarborough, ON M1T 1A8, Canada

Caffey, Charlotte (Musician)
4827 Glencairn Rd
Los Angeles, CA 90027, USA

Caffey, Jason (Athlete, Basketball Player)
PO Box 131
Roswell, GA 30075-0131, USA

Caffrey, Bob (Athlete, Baseball Player,
Olympic Athlete)
2305 Sunnyside Ave
Burlington, IA 52601-2537, USA

Cagatay, Mustafa (Prime Minister)
60 Cumhuriyet Caddesi
Kyrenia, Cyprus

Cage, Byron (Musician)
c/o Staff Member *Verity Gospel Music
Group*
550 Madison Ave
Room 2356
New York; NY 10022, USA

Cage, Michael (Athlete, Basketball Player)
21163 Newport Coast
Dr
Newport Coast, CA 92657-1123, USA

Cage, Nicolas (Actor)
898 Francisco St
San Francisco, CA 94109, USA

Cage, Wavne (Athlete, Baseball Player)
1305 Davis Blvd
Ruston, LA 71270-6405, usa

Cage, Wayne (Athlete, Baseball Player)
1305 Davis Blvd
Ruston, LA 71270, USA

Cagle, Buddy (Race Car Driver)
11713 E 118th Street N
Collinsville, OK 74021, USA

Cagle, Chris (Musician)
c/o Scott McGhee *McGhee Entertainment*
8730 Sunset Blvd
Suite 175
Los Angeles, CA 90069, USA

Cagle, J Douglas (Business Person)
Cagle's Inc
2000 Hills Ave NW
Atlanta, GA 30318, USA

Cagle, Jim (Athlete, Football Player)
745 Sharpshooters Ridge NW
Marietta, GA 30064, USA

Cagle, Johnny (Athlete, Football Player)
1645 Citation Dr
Aiken, SC 29803, USA

cagle, Myrtle k (Aviator)
RR 3 Lake Tobesofkee
Lizella, GA 31052, USA

Cagle, Yvonne D (Astronaut)
c/o Staff Member *NASA*
Johnson Space Center
2101 NASA Rd
Houston, TX 77058, USA

Caglini, Umperto (Actor)
via Don Crocetti #3
Fabriano (Ancona) I-60044, Italy

Cahan, Larry (Athlete, Hockey Player)
PO Box 249
Bala, ON POC IAO, Canada

Cahill, Dave (Athlete, Football Player)
11 Kara E
Irvine, CA 92620, us

Cahill, Eddie (Actor)
c/o David Seltzer *Management 360*
9111 Wilshire Blvd
Beverly Hills, CA 90210, USA

Cahill, Erin (Actor)
c/o Cary Anderson *Simmons & Scott Entertainment*
4110 W. Burbank Blvd.
Burbank, CA 91505, USA

Cahill, James (Actor)
31 Chambers St
#311
New York, NY 10007, USA

Cahill, Jason (Producer)
2316 Nottingham Ave
Los Angeles, CA 90027, USA

Cahill, Katja (Stylist)
c/o Staff Member *Photogenics Media*
8549 Higuera St
Building B
Culver Clty, CA 90232, USA

Cahill, Laura (Writer)
c/o Staff Member *Broder Webb Chervin Silbermann Agency, The (BWCS)*
10250 Constellation Blvd
Los Angeles, CA 90067-6200, USA

Cahill, Leo (Athlete, Football Player)
161A Nelson St
Sarnia, ON N7T757, Canada

Cahill, Mike (Director, Writer)
c/o George Heller *Apostle Management*
9465 Wilshire Blvd
Suite 430
Beverly Hills, CA 90212, USA

Cahill, Teresa M (Opera Singer)
65 Leyland Road
London SE12 8DW, UNITED KINGDOM (UK)

Cahill, Thomas (Writer)
Doubleday Press
1540 Broadway
New York, NY 10036, USA

Cahill, Trevor (Athlete, Baseball Player)
286 Juaneno Ave
Oceanside, CA 92057-4515, usa

Cahill, William (Bill) (Athlete, Football Player)
24328 Crystal Lake Way
Woodinville, WA 98077, USA

Cahn, John W (Misc)
2032 43rd Avenue E
Apt 18
Seattle, WA 98112-2764, USA

Cahoon, Todd (Actor)
c/o Laura Pallas *Pallas Management*
5301 Bellaire Ave
Valley Vilage, CA 91607, US

Cahouet, Frank V (Financier)
Mellon Bank Corp
1 Mellon Bank Center 500 Grant St
Pittsburgh, PA 15219, USA

Caifanes (Music Group)
c/o Staff Member *BMG*
1540 Broadway
New York, NY 10036, USA

Caillat, Colbie (Musician)
31803 Saddletree Dr
Westlake Village, CA 91361, USA

Cain, Betty Ann (Actor)
19379 Arkay Ct
Sonoma, CA 95476, USA

Cain, Carl (Athlete, Basketball Player, Olympic Athlete)
3045 Sun Valley Dr
Pickerington, OH 43147-9090, USA

Cain, Carl (Athlete, Basketball Player)
3045 Sun Valley Dr
Pickerington, OH 43147-9090, USA

Cain, Dean (Actor)
24630 Blue Dane Ln
Malibu, CA 90265, USA

Cain, Joe (Athlete, Football Player)
1219 W Piru St
Compton, CA 90222-, us

Cain, John Paul (Athlete, Golfer)
1404 Avondale St
Sweetwater, TX 79556-2614, USA

Cain, Jonathan (Musician)
311 Granny White Pike
Brentwood, TN 37027, USA

Cain, Leroy (Scientist)
4218 Island Hills Dr
Houston, TX 77059-5538, USA

Cain, Les (Athlete, Baseball Player)
31 Cutting Ct
Richmond, CA 94804-4217, USA

Cain, Lorenzo (Athlete, Baseball Player)
3680 Lindley Cir
Powder Sorings, GA 30127-2702, USA

Cain, Lynn (Athlete, Football Player)
P.O. Box 90881
Los Angeles, CA 90009-0881, USA

Cain, Matt (Athlete, Baseball Player)
2005 San Francisco Giants
Mesa, AZ 85207-4462, USA

Cain, Mick (Actor)
7800 Beverly Blvd
#3371
Los Angeles, CA 90036, USA

Cain, Scott (Race Car Driver)
6059 West Ashlan
Fresno, CA 93722, USA

Caine, Michael (Actor)
c/o Duncan Heath *Independent Talent Group (ITG-UK)*
Oxford House
76 Oxford St
London W1D 1BS, UK

Caio, Francesco (Business Person)
Ing C Olivetti Co
Via G Jervos 77
Ivrea/Truin 10015, USA

Cairns, Eric (Athlete, Hockey Player)
1291 Treeland St
Burlington, ON L7R 3TS, Canada

Cairns, Hugh J F (Biologist)
Holly Grove House
Wilcote
Shipping Norton
Oxon OX7 3EA, UNITED KINGDOM (UK)

Cairns, Leah (Actor)
Armada Partners
c/o David M Rudy
815 Moraga Drive
Los angeles, CA 90045, USA

Cairo, Miguel (Athlete, Baseball Player)
209 Highland Woods Dr
Safety Harbor, FL 34695-5437, USA

Calabrese, Gerry (Athlete, Basketball Player)
351 Esplanade Pl
Cliffside Park, NJ 07010-2708, USA

Calabresi, Guido (Judge)
US Appeals Court
157 Church St
New Haven, CT 06510, USA

Calabro, Deborah (Stylist)
c/o Staff Member *Team*
423 W Broadway
4th Floor
Boston, MA 02127, USA

Calabro, Thomas (Actor)
4318 Ben Ave
Studio City, CA 91604, USA

Calacurcio-Thomas, Aldine (Athlete, Baseball Player, Commentator)
5438 Nottingham Dr
Loves Park, IL 61111-3605, USA

Calatrava, Santiago (Architect, Engineer)
Santiago Calatrava SA
Hoschgasse 5
Zurich 8008, SWITZERLAND

Calaway, Mark (The Undertaker) (Athlete, Wrestler)
Calahart Crossroads, LLC
3722 Eagle Spirit Ct
Fort Collins, CO 80528, USA

Calcagni, Ron (Athlete, Football Player)
340 Savannah Park Cir
Conway, NY AR, 72034-7277

Calcavecchia, Mark (Athlete, Golfer)
354 W Riverside Dr
Jupiter, FL 33469-2950, USA

Calder, David (Actor)
1 Winterwell Rd
London SW2 5TB, UK

Calder, Eric (Athlete, Hockey Player)
259 Stanley Dr
Waterloo, ON N2L 1H9, Canada

Calder, Kyle (Athlete, Hockey Player)
726 Monterey Blvd
Hermosa Beach, CA 90254-4549, USA

Calder, Nigel (Writer)
8 The Chase, Furnace Green
Crawley W. Sussex RH10 6HW, UK

Calderon, Leticia (Actor)
c/o Staff Member *Televisa*
Blvd Adolfo Lopez Mateos 232
Colonia San Angel INN
DF CP 01060, MEXICO

Calderon, Sila Maria (Ex-Governor)
LA Fortaleza
P.O. Box 9020082
San Juan, PR 00902, USA

Calderon, Wilmer (Actor)
c/o Lena Roklin *Luber Roklin Management*
8530 Wilshire Blvd
6th Floor
Beverly Hills, CA 90211, USA

Calderon Fournier, Rafael A (President)
Partido Unidad Social Cristiana
San Jose, COSTA RICA

Caldicott, Helen (Activist, Doctor)
Physicians for Responsibility
4423 Lehigh Road #337
College Park, MD 20740, USA

Caldwell, Adrian (Athlete, Basketball Player)
10990 West Rd
Apt 311
Houston, TX 77064-5496, USA

Caldwell, Alan (Athlete, Football Player)
1370 Kerner Rd
Kernersville, NC 27284, USA

Caldwell, Bobby (Musician, Songwriter, Writer)
Public Relations Partners
12702 Landale St
Studio City, CA 91604, USA

Caldwell, Cynthia (Stylist)
PO Box 953
Northampton, MA 01061, USA

Caldwell, Darryl (Athlete, Football Player)
4604 Malinta Ln
Chattanooga, TN 37416, USA

Caldwell, Gail (Journalist)
c/o Staff Member *Zachary Shuster Harmsworth*
535 Boylston St
11th Floor
Boston, MA 02116, USA

Caldwell, Jim (Athlete, Basketball Player)
705 Freedom Lane
Roswell, GA 30075-7911, USA

Caldwell, Joe (Athlete, Basketball Player, Olympic Athlete)
15 E Pebble Beach Dr
Tempe, AZ 85282-5127, USA

Caldwell, John (Cartoonist)
c/o Staff Member *King Features Syndication*
300 W 57th St
15th Floor
New York, NY 10019-5238, USA

Caldwell, Kimberly (Musician, Reality TV Star)
c/o Anthony Cordova *Story Road Entertainment*
809 South Bundy Drive #209
Los Angeles, CA 90049, USA

Caldwell, Matt (Musician)
c/o Staff Member *Paradigm (Monterey)*
404 W Franklin St
Monterey, CA 93940, USA

Caldwell, Mike (Athlete, Baseball Player)
1645 Brook Run Dr
Raleigh, NC 27614, USA

Caldwell, Mike (Athlete, Football Player)
646 Robertsville Rd
Oak Ridge, TN 37830, USA

Caldwell, Mike T (Athlete, Football Player)
41621 N Bent Creek Ct
Phoenix, AZ 85086, USA

Caldwell, Philip (Business Person)
Smith Barney Shearson
200 Vesey St
New York, NY 10285, USA

Caldwell, Ralph W (Football Player)
4054 Charlene Dr
Los Angeles, CA 90043, us

Caldwell, Ralph W (Athlete, Football Player)
4054 Charlene Dr
Los Angeles, CA 90043, USA

Caldwell, Ravin (Athlete, Football Player)
4415 Johnson St
Fort Smith, AR 72904, USA

Caldwell, Scott (Athlete, Football Player)
1037 Tuskegee St
Grand Prairie, TX 75051, USA

Caldwell, Tracy e dr (Astronaut)
827 Timber Cove Dr
Seabrook, TX 77586-4617, USA

Caldwell, Travis (Actor)
c/o Ellen Meyer *Ellen Meyer Management*
8899 Beverly Blvd
Suite 612
West Hollywood, CA 90048, USA

Caldwell, William A (Editor)
Vineyard Gazette
Editorial Dept S Summer St
Edgartown, MA 02539, USA

Caldwell, Zoe (Actor)
Whitehead-Stevens
1501 Broadway
New York, NY 10036, USA

Cale, J J (Music Group, Musician)
Rosebud Agency
P O Box 170429
San Fransisco, CA 94117, USA

Cale, John (Music Group, Musician)
Firebrand Mgmt
12 Rickett St
West Brompton
London SW6 1RU, UNITED KINGDOM
(UK)

Cale, Paula (Actor)
2518 Canyon Dr
Los Angeles, CA 90068, USA

Cale, Puala (Actor)
Gersh Agency
232 N Canon Dr
Beverly Hills, CA 90210, USA

Caleb, Jamie (Athlete, Football Player)
8889 Brandywine Rd
Northfield, OH 44067, USA

Calero, Enriaue (Athlete, Baseball Player)
21465 65th Sts
1465 65th St, Emervville CA, 94608-1062

Calero, Kiko (Athlete, Baseball Player)
18 Danson Dr
Saint Peters, MO 63376, USA

Caley, Don (Athlete, Hockey Player)
7127 E Aloe Vera Dr
Scottsdale, AZ 85266, USA

Calfa, Don (Actor)
Richard Sundel
1910 Holmby Ave
#1
Los Angeles, CA 90025, USA

Calfa, Marian (Prime Minister)
Calfa Pravni Kancelar Premyslovska 28
Prague 3 130 00, USA

Calhoun, Bill (Athlete, Basketball Player)
3740 El Cerro View Cir
Reno, NV 89509-5610, USA

Calhoun, Corky (Misc, Yachtsman)
Surfer Magazine
P O Box 1028
Dana Point, CA 92629, USA

Calhoun, David (Athlete, Basketball
Player)
17912 Lafayette Drive
Olney, MD 20832-2129, USA

Calhoun, Donald C (Don) (Athlete,
Football Player)
PO Box 49104
Wichita, KS 67201-9104, USA

Calhoun, Jeff (Athlete, Baseball Player)
10002 Springwood Forest Dr
Houston, TX 77080, USA

Calhoun, Jim (Athlete, Basketball Player,
Coach)
P.O. Box 379
Pomfret Center, CT 06259-0379, USA

Calhoun, Monica (Actor)
Innovative Artists
1505 10th St
Santa Monica, CA 90401, USA

Cali, Carmen (Athlete, Baseball Player)
5751 Copper Leaf Ln
Naples, FL 34116-6713, USA

Cali, Joseph (Actor)
25630 Edenwild Road
Monte Nido, CA 91302, USA

Calico, Tyrone (Athlete, Football Player)
3028 Brookview Forest Dr
Nashville, TN 37211, USA

Caliendo, Frank (Actor)
12808 Halkirk St
Studio City, CA 91604, USA

Califano, Joseph A Jr (Politician)
Casa at Columbia
42 Morningside DrS
Westport, CT 06880-5413, USA

Califano Jr, Joseph A (Government
Official)
Casa At Columbia
633 3rd Ave
#1900
New York, NY 10017, USA

Caligiuri, Fred (Athlete, Baseball Player)
100 Baker St
Rimersburg, PA 16248-4324, USA

Calip, Brad
5325 E 92nd St
Tulsa OK 74137-4004, OK
74137-4004 74137-4004, USA

Calip, Demetrius (Athlete, Basketball
Player)
7321 Lennox Ave Unit
G5
Van Nuys, CA 91405-6262, USA

Calipari, John (Basketball Coach, Coach)
1732 Richmond Rd
Lexington, KY 40502-1622, USA

Calis, Natasha (Actor)
c/o Jill Littman *Impression Entertainment*
9229 W Sunset Blvd #700
West Hollywood, CA 90069, USA

Calkins, Buzz (Race Car Driver)
1630 Chicago Av
#904
Evanston, IL 60201-4589, USA

Call, Anthony (Actor)
Michael Thomas Agency
134 E 10th St
New York, NY 10021, USA

Call, Brandon (Actor)
5918 Van Nuys Blvd
Van Nuys, CA 91401, USA

Call, Jack
PO Box 361
Churchvill, MD 21028-0361, USA

Call, Jack (Athlete, Football Player)
PO Box 361
Churchville, MD 21028, USA

Call, Kevin (Athlete, Football Player)
839 Carey Rd
Carmel, IN 46033-9324, USA

Call, Kevin (Athlete, Football Player)
839 Carey Rd
Carmel, IN 46033, USA

Callaghan-Maxwell, Margaret (Athlete,
Baseball Player, Commentator)
5-250 15th Ave E
Vancouver, BC VST 2P9, Canada

Callahan, Bill (Athlete, Coach, Football
Coach, Football Player)
405 Christinas Ct
Cranberry Township, PA 16066, USA

Callahan, John (Actor)
Levin Representatives
2402 4th St #6
Santa Monica, CA 90405, USA

Callan, Cecile (Actor)
SMZ
8730 Sunset Blvd #480
Los Angeles, CA 90069, USA

Callan, K (Actor)
4957 Matilija Ave
Sherman Oaks, CA 91423, USA

Callan, Michael (Actor)
1651 Camden Ave #3
Los Angeles, CA 90025, USA

Calland, Lee (Athlete, Football Player)
6624 Windwood Cir
Douglasville, GA 30135, USA

Callander, Drew (Athlete, Hockey Player)
11 Edenwold Cres
Regina, SK S4R 8A6, Canada

Callander, Jock (Athlete, Hockey Player)
Lake Erie Monsters 1 Center Ice
Cleveland, OH 44115-4004, USA

Callaway, Howard H (Bo) (Government
Official)
Callaway Gardens
Pine Mountain, GA 31822, USA

Callaway, Liz (Actor, Artist, Voice Over
Artist)
c/o Staff Member *Gage Group, The (NY)*
450 7th Ave
Suite 1809
New York, NY 10123, USA

Callaway, Mickey (Athlete, Baseball
Player)
8061 Stonewyck Rd
Germantown, TN 38138-2351, USA

Callaway, Paul Smith (Music Group,
Musician)
Washington Cathedral
Mount Saint Alban
Washington, DC 20016, USA

Calle 13 (Music Group, Musician)
c/o Staff Member *Sony Music Miami*
605 Lincoln Rd Fl 7
Miami Beach, FL 33139, USA

Callen, Bryan (Actor, Musician)
2320 Glyndon Ave
Venice, CA 90291, USA

Callen, Jones Gloria (Swimmer)
1508 Chafton Road
Charleston, WV 25314, USA

Callender, Jock (Athlete, Hockey Player)
388 Lear Rd
Avon Lake, OH 44012, USA

Callery, Sean (Composer, Musician)
c/o Staff Member *Gorfaine/Schwartz
Agency Inc*
4111 W Alameda Ave
Suite 509
Burbank, CA 91505, USA

Callicutt, Ken (Athlete, Football Player)
969 Suchava Dr
White Lake, MI 48386, USA

Callier, Frances (Comedian)
c/o Staff Member *Gekis Management*
4217 Verdugo View Dr
Los Angeles, CA 90065-4317, USA

Callies, Sarah Wayne (Actor)
c/o Alissa Vradenburg *Untitled
Entertainment (LA)*
350 S. Beverly Dr #200
Beverly Hills, CA 90212, USA

Callighen, Brett (Athlete, Hockey Player)
PO Box 249
Bala, ON POC IAO, Canada

Calling, The (Music Group)
c/o Staff Member *WmE2 (WMA-LA)*
1 William Morris Pl
Beverly Hills, CA 90212, USA

Callis, James (Actor, Director)
c/o Alan Siegel *Alan Siegel Entertainment*
345 N Maple Dr
Suite 375
Beverly Hills, CA 90210, USA

Callner, Marty (Director, Producer)
c/o David Steinberg *Morra Brezner
Steinberg & Tenenbaum (MBST)
Entertainment*
345 N Maple Dr
Suite 200
Beverly Hills, CA 90210, USA

Callow, Simon (Actor)
Marina Martin
12/13 Poland St
London WlV 3DE, UNITED KINGDOM
(UK)

Calloway, AJ (Television Host)
c/o Michael (Mike) Esterman
Esterman.Com, LLC
Prefers to be contacted via email
MD, USA

Calloway, Chris (Athlete, Football Player)
1277 Ponti Mews NW
Atlanta, GA 30318-4179, USA

Calloway, Ernie (Athlete, Football Player)
4027 Lenox Blvd
Orlando, FL 32811, USA

Calloway, Ron (Athlete, Baseball Player)
3868 Las Colinas Dr
Las Cruces, NM 88012-0693, USA

Callum, Keith Rennie (Actor)
c/o Staff Member *Elizabeth Hodgson
Management Group*
1688 Cypress St
Suite 405
Vancouver, BC V6J 5J1, Canada

Calmus, Dick (Athlete, Baseball Player)
3823 S 28th West Ave
Tulsa, OK 74107-5452, USA

Calmus, Rocky (Athlete, Football Player)
4131 Trinity Rd
Franklin, TN 37067, USA

Calne, Roy Y (Doctor)
Addenbrooke's Hospital
Hills Road
Cambridge CB2 2QQ, UNITED
KINGDOM (UK)

Calombaris, George (Chef)
The Press Club
72 Flinders St
Melbourne, Vic 3000, Australia

Caltabiano, Tom (Comedian)
c/o Staff Member *United Talent Agency (UTA)*
9336 Civic Center Dr
Beverly Hills, CA 90210, USA

Calvaer, Andre J (Engineer)
Blvd Louis Mettewie 270
Molenbeek-Saint-Jean 1080, BELGIUM

Calvert, Ken (Congressman, Politician)
2269 Rayburn HOB
Washington, DC 20515, USA

Calvert, Mark (Athlete, Baseball Player)
908 W Waco St
Broken Arrow, OK 74011-2819, USA

Calvert, Patricia (Writer)
c/o Staff Member *Simon & Schuster*
1230 Avenue of the Americas
New York, NY 10020, USA

Calvert, Rita (Stylist)
1518 Circle Dr
Annapolis, MD 21401, USA

Calvet, Jacques (Financier)
31 Ave Victor Hugo
Paris 75116, FRANCE

Calvin, John (Actor)
2503 Ware Road
Austin, TX 78741, USA

Calvin, Mack (Basketball Player)
930 Figueroa Ter
Apt 602
Los Angeles, CA 90012, USA

Calvin, Thomas (Athlete, Football Player)
2712 McTavish Ave SW
Decatur, AL 35603, USA

Calvin, Tom (Athlete, Football Player)
2712 McTavish Ave SW
Decatur, AL 35603, USA

Calvin, William H (Biologist)
University of Washington
Neurobiology Dept
Seattle, WA 98195, USA

Calvo, Paul M (Ex-Governor)
115 Chalen Sando Papa
Hagatna, GU 96910, USA

Calvo-Sotelo, Bustelo Leopoldo (Prime Minister)
Buho 1 Somosaguas
Madrid, SPAIN

Calzaghe, Joe (Boxer)
51 Caerbryn Pentwynmawar
Newbridge Gwent
South Wales, UNITED KINGDOM

Camacho, Ernie (Athlete, Baseball Player)
746 Saint Regis Way
Salinas, CA 93905-1642, USA

Camacho, Joe (Athlete, Baseball Player)
48 Massasoit Ave
Act 3-R
Fairhaven, MA 02719-3266, USA

Camarda, Charles J (Astronaut)
2386 Sabal Park Lane
League City, TX 77573, USA

Camarda, charles j dr (Astronaut)
2386 Saba I Park Ln
League City 77573-0777, USA

Camareno, Joe (Actor)
c/o Staff Member *Conana Caroll & Associates*
6117 Rhodes Ave
N Hollywood, CA 91606, Uninted States

Camarillo, Greg (Athlete, Football Player)
PO Box 712827
San Diego, CA 92171, USA

Camarillo, Rich (Athlete, Football Player)
1941 E Clubhouse Dr
Phoenix, AZ 85048, USA

Camastra, Danielle (Actor)
c/o Staff Member *Henderson Hogan Agency (LA)*
8929 Wilshire Blvd
Suite 312
Beverly Hills, CA 90211, USA

Cambal, Dennis (Athlete, Football Player)
24 Hedge Row
West Yarmouth, MA 02673, USA

Cambre, Ronald C (Business Person)
Newmont Mining
9903 W Laurel Place
Littleton, CO 80127, USA

Cambria, Fred (Athlete, Baseball Player)
12 Iris Ct
Northport, NY 11768-3207, USA

Camby, Marcus (Athlete, Basketball Player)
6725 Fite Rd
Pearland, TX 77584-1089, USA

Camden, John (Business Person)
RMC Group
Coldgarbour Lane
Thorpe
Egham, Surrey TW20 8TD, UNITED KINGDOM (UK)

Camdessus, Michel J (Financier)
International Monetary Fund
700 19th St NW
Washington, DC 20431, USA

Camelia-Romer, Susanne (Prime Minister)
Primier's Office
Fort Amsterdam 17
Willemstad, NETHERLANDS ANTILLES

Cameron, Al (Athlete, Hockey Player)
1225 Ormsby Lane NW
Edmonton, AB TST 6R2, Canada

Cameron, Al (Athlete, Hockey Player)
1225 Ormsby Ln NW
Edmonton, AB T5T 6R2, Canada

Cameron, Austin (Race Car Driver)
10 New Bridge Parkway
Asheville, NC 28804, USA

Cameron, Bob (Athlete, Football Player)
349 Clare Ave
Winnipeg, MB R3L1S2, Canada

Cameron, Candance (Actor)
Barbara Camaron Assoc
8369 Sausalito Ave #A
Canoga Park, CA 91304, USA

Cameron, Dallas (Athlete, Football Player)
Hialeah-Miami Lakes High School
7977 W 12th Ave
Hialeah, FL 33014, USA

Cameron, Dave (Athlete, Coach, Hockey Player)
c/o Staff Member *Mississauga St Michaels Majors*
5500 Rose Cherry Pl
Mississauga, ON L4Z 4B6, Canada

Cameron, David (Designer, Fashion Designer)
Schauspielschule Krauss
Weihburggasse 19
Vienna 1010, AUSTRIA

Cameron, Dean (Actor)
Landmark Artists Mgmt
4116 W Magnolia Ave
Burbank, CA 91505, USA

Cameron, Don R (Educator, Misc)
National Education Association
1201 16th St NW
Washington, DC 20036, USA

Cameron, Duncan (Music Group, Musician)
Sawyer Brown Inc
5200 Old Harding Road
Franklin, TN 37064, USA

Cameron, Dwayne (Actor)
c/o Scott Karp *Crystal Sky Pictures*
10203 Santa Monica Blvd
5th Floor
Los Angeles, CA 90067, USA

Cameron, Glenn S (Athlete, Football Player)
8082 Steeplechase Dr
Palm Beach Gardens, FL 33418, USA

Cameron, James (Director, Producer)
26818 Hot Springs Pl
Calabasas, CA 91301, USA

Cameron, John (Composer)
Chester Music & Novello
8-9 Firth St
London W1D 3JB, UK

Cameron, Julia (Writer)
c/o Staff Member *HarperCollins Publishers*
10 East 53rd St
c/o Author mail, 7th Floor
New York, NY 10022, USA

Cameron, Kenneth D (Astronaut)
Austvagen 13
Vastra Frotunda 42676, SWEDEN

Cameron, Kenneth d colonel (Astronaut)
11333 Gulf Beach Hwy
Pensacola, FL 32507-9100, USA

Cameron, Kevin (Athlete, Baseball Player)
26435 S Ivy Ln
Channahon, IL 60410-3341, USA

Cameron, Kirk (Actor)
29091 Wagon Rd
Agoura, CA 91301, USA

Cameron, Laura (Actor)
8383 Wilshire Blvd
#954
Beverly Hills, CA 90211, USA

Cameron, Mat (Music Group, Musician)
Susan Silver Mgmt
6523 California Ave SW #348
Seattle, WA 98136, USA

Cameron, Matt (Musician)
10910 Algonquin Rd
Woodway, WA 98020, USA

Cameron, Mechelle (Swimmer)
Box 2 Site 1SS3
Calgary, AL T3C 3N9, CANADA

Cameron, Mike (Athlete, Baseball Player)
615 ChamQions Dr
McDonough, GA 30253-4284, USA

Cameron, Paul (Athlete, Football Player)
29457 Georgetown Ln
Temecula, CA 92591-1896, USA

Cameron, Paul (Athlete, Football Player)
29457 Georgetown Ln
Temecula, CA 92591, USA

Cameron, Rhona (Actor)
c/o Staff Member *Jeremy Hicks Associates*
114-115 Tottenham Court Rd
London W1T 5AH, UK

Cameron, Scotty (Golfer)
Acushnet Company
c/o Gordon Sanborn
333 Bridge St
Fairhaven, MA 02719, USA

Cameron, Warren (Horse Racer)
PO Box 1306
De Leon Springs, FL 32130-1306

Cameron, W Bruce (Writer)
c/o Scott Miller *Trident Media Group LLC*
41 Madison Ave
36th Floor
New York, NY 10010, USA

Cameron-Bure, Candace (Actor)
10371 Golden Eagle Ct
Plantation, FL 33324, USA

Camerota, Brett (Athlete, Olympic Athlete, Skier)
3118 Elk Run Dr
Park City, UT 84098-5300, USA

Camerota, Eric (Athlete, Olympic Athlete, Skier)
3118 Elk Run Dr
Park City, UT 84098-5300, USA

Camiletti, Rob (Actor)
643 N. La Cienega Blvd.
Los Angeles, CA 90048, USA

Camille (Stylist)
c/o Staff Member *Campbell Agency, The*
3838 Oak Lawn Ave
Suite 900
Dallas, TX 75219-4510, USA

Camilleri, Louis C (Business Person)
Altria Group
120 Park Ave
New York, NY 10017, USA

Camilleri, Terry (Actor)
c/o Christopher Mario Parker *Access LA Talent Management*
2850 Ocean Park Bl
Suite 215
Santa Monica, CA 90405, USA

Camilli, Doug (Athlete, Baseball Player)
4245 61st Ave
Vero Beach, FL 32967-8807, USA

Camilli, Lou (Athlete, Baseball Player)
1314 Sigma Chi Rd NE
Albuquerque, NM 87106, USA

Camilo, Michael (Musician)
Joel Chriss
300 Mercer St
#3J
New York, NY 10003, USA

Camilo, Michel (Music Group, Musician)
Redondo Music
590 W End Ave #6
New York, NY 10024, USA

Caminito, Jerry (Race Car Driver)
Blue Thunder Racing
P O Box 1486
Jackson, NJ 08527, USA

Cammack, Eric (Athlete, Baseball Player)
605 Remington Dr
Bridge City, TX 77611-2234, USA

Cammalleri, Mike (Athlete, Hockey Player)
Pulver Sports
479 Bedford Park Ave
Attn tan Pulver
Toronto, ON M5M 1K2, Canada

Cammermeyer, Margarethe (General)
4632 S. Tompkins Rd.
Langley, WA 98260-9695, USA

Cammuso, Frank (Cartoonist)
Syracuse Post-Standard PO Box 4915
Syracuse, NY 13221-4915, USA

Camoy, Martin (Economist)
Stanford University
Economic Studies Center
Stanford, CA 94305, USA

Camp, Anna (Actor)
c/o Robert Glennon *Authentic Talent and Literary Management*
45 Main St
Suite 1004
Brooklyn, NY 11201, USA

Camp, Colleen (Actor)
473 N Tigertail Rd
Los Angeles, CA 90049, USA

Camp, Dave (Congressman, Politician)
341 Cannon HOB
Washington, DC 20515, USA

Camp, Greg (Composer, Musician)
c/o Staff Member *Creative Artists Agency (CAA-LA)*
2000 Ave Of The Stars
Los Angeles, CA 90067, USA

Camp, Jeremy (Musician)
c/o Staff Member *BEC Recordings*
P.O. Box 12698
Seattle, WA 98111, USA

Camp, John (Journalist)
Saint Paul Pioneer Press
Editorial Dept 345 Cedar St
Saint Paul, MN 55101, USA

Camp, Rick (Athlete, Baseball Player)
F P C Montgomery ID # 11973-021
Maxwell Air Force Base
Montgomery, AL 36112, USA

Camp, Steve (Music Group)
Third Coast Artists
2021 21st Ave S #220
Nashville, TN 37212, USA

Campanale, David (General)
14445 S Placita Asidera
Sahuarita, AZ 85629-6634, USA

Campanella, Joseph (Actor)
4196 Colfax Ave
Studio City, CA 91604-2165, USA

Campaneris, Bert (Athlete, Baseball Player)
P.O. Box 5096
Scottsdale, AZ 85261, USA

Campanis, Jim (Athlete, Baseball Player)
17082 Cascades Ave
Yorba Linda, CA 92886, USA

Campau, Thomas E (Cinematographer)
2000 S Hammond Lake Dr
West Bloomfield, MI 90212, USA

Campbell, A Kim (Prime Minister)
Harvard University
Kennedy School of Government
Cambridge, MA 02138, USA

Campbell, Alan (Actor)
Gersh Agency
41 Madison Ave #3300
New York, NY 10010, USA

Campbell, Allan McCulloch (Biologist)
947 Mears Court
Stanford, CA 94305, USA

Campbell, Bek David (Beck) (Musician)
c/o John Silva *SAM*
722 Seward St
Los Angeles, CA 90038, USA

Campbell, Ben Nighthorse (Politician)
PO Box 639
Ignacio, CO 81137-0639, USA

Campbell, Bill (Athlete, Baseball Player)
133 S Hale St
Palatine, IL 60067, USA

Campbell, Billy (Actor)
c/o Sean Fay *Kritzer Levine Wilkins Entertainment (KLWG)*
11872 La Grange Ave
1st Floor
Los Angeles, CA 90025, USA

Campbell, Brian (Athlete, Hockey Player)
Octagon Sports Management
66 Slater St 23rd Fl
Attn Larry Kelly
Ottawa, ON K1P 5H1, Canada

Campbell, Bruce (Actor, Director, Producer)
735 Roca St
Ashland, OR 97520, USA

Campbell, Bryan (Athlete, Hockey Player)
10895 Tamoron Ln
Boca Raton, FL 33498, USA

Campbell, Carter (Athlete, Football Player)
24834 Winterberry Ln
Plainfield, IL 60585, USA

Campbell, Chad (Athlete, Golfer)
200 Glade Rd
Colleyville, TX 76034, USA

Campbell, Cheryl (Actor)
Michael Whitehall
125 Gloucester Road
London SW7 4TE, UNITED KINGDOM (UK)

Campbell, Christa (Actor)
c/o Staff Member *Origin Talent Agency*
4705 Laurel Canyon #306
Studio City, CA 91607, USA

Campbell, Christian (Actor)
12533 Woodgreen
Los Angeles, CA 90066, USA

Campbell, Colin (Soupy) (Athlete, Coach, Hockey Player)
c/o Staff Member *National Hockey League (NHL)*
50 Bay St
11th Floor
Toronto, ON M5J 2X8, Canada

Campbell, Dan (Athlete, Football Player)
PO Box 977
Meridian, TX 76665-0977, USA

Campbell, Dan (Athlete, Football Player)
PO Box 977
Meridian, TX 76665, USA

Campbell, Darren (Athlete, Track Athlete)
1 Wandsworth Plain
London SW18 1EH, UK

Campbell, Dave (Athlete, Baseball Player)
726 N Dundee Dr
Post Falls, ID 83854, USA

Campbell, Dave (Athlete, Baseball Player)
878 Amidon St
Deltona, FL 32725, USA

Campbell, Dick (Athlete, Football Player)
2557 Nicolet Dr
Green Bay, WI 54311-7225, USA

Campbell, Dick (Athlete, Football Player)
2557 Nicolet Dr
Green Bay, WI 54311, USA

Campbell, Dick (Athlete, Football Player)
PO Box 198
Jensen Beach, FL 34958, USA

Campbell, Earl (Athlete, Football Player)
The Tyler Rose
701 W 11th St
Austin, TX 78701, USA

Campbell, Elden (Athlete, Basketball Player)
17252 Hawthome Blvd
#493
Torrance, CA 90504-1032, USA

Campbell, Gaetana (Actor)
1620 Richmond Cir #105
Joliet, IL 60435, USA

Campbell, Garry (Producer, Writer)
c/o Staff Member *Creative Artists Agency (CAA-LA)*
2000 Ave Of The Stars
Los Angeles, CA 90067, USA

Campbell, Gary (Athlete, Football Player)
PO Box 775353
Steamboat Springs, CO 80477-5353, USA

Campbell, Gary (Athlete, Football Player)
P.O. Box 775353
Steamboat Springs, CO 80477, USA

Campbell, Gene (Athlete, Hockey Player)
1554 Wilshire Dr NE
Rochester, MN 55906, USA

Campbell, Glen (Musician)
6324 Cavalleri Rd
Malibu, CA 90265, USA

Campbell, Gregory (Athlete, Hockey Player)
RR 2
Tillsonburg, ON N4G 4G7, Canada

Campbell, Helen Hannah (Athlete, Baseball Player)
17077 San Mateo St
Fountain Valley, CA 92708, USA

Campbell, Isobel (Music Group, Musician)
Legends of 21st Century
7 Trinity Row
Florence, MA 01062, USA

Campbell, Jack (Politician)
PO Box 2208
Santa Fe, NM 87504-2208, USA

Campbell, James (Jim) (Athlete, Baseball Player)
209 W Seven Pines St
Lamar, SC 29069, USA

Campbell, Jeff (Athlete, Football Player)
2601 Berenson Ln
Austin, TX 78746-1963, USA

Campbell, Jeff (Athlete, Football Player)
2601 Berenson Ln
Austin, TX 78746, USA

Campbell, Jeff (Baseball Player)
Homestead Grays
4194 San Miguel Ave
San Diego, CA 92113-1842, USA

Campbell, Jennifer Lynn (Actor)
11871 Dubarry Dr
Carmel, IN 46033-8259, USA

Campbell, Jesse (Athlete, Football Player)
, 1608 32nd Ave
Gulfport, MS 39501, USA

Campbell, Jessica (Actor)
Somers Teitelbaum David
8840 Wilshire Blvd
#200
Beverly Hills, CA 90211, USA

Campbell, Jim (Horse Racer)
31 Mill Pond Rd
Jackson, NJ 08527-4888, USA

Campbell, Jim (Athlete, Hockey Player)
32 Lemp Rd
Saint Louis, MO 63122-6947, USA

Campbell, Jim (Athlete, Baseball Player)
1924 Knollwood Ln
Los Altos, CA 94024, USA

Campbell, Jim (Athlete, Baseball Player)
1671 6th St
Oroville, CA 95965, USA

Campbell, Joe (Athlete, Baseball Player)
330 Legends Ct
Bowling Green, KY 42103, USA

Campbell, John (Horse Racer)
John D Campbell Stable
823 Allison Dr
River Vale, NJ 07675-6602, USA

Campbell, John (Congressman, Politician)
1507 Longworth HOB
Washington, DC 20515, USA

Campbell, John W
12908 Welcome Ln
Burnsville, MN 55337-3626, USA

Campbell, John W (Athlete, Football Player)
12908 Welcome Ln
Burnsville, MN 55337, USA

Campbell, Joshua (Actor)
c/o Staff Member *Select Artists Ltd (CA-Westside Office)*
1138 12th Street
Suite 1
Santa Monica, CA 90403, USA

Campbell, Julia (Actor)
Innovative Artists
1505 10th St
Santa Monica, CA 90401, USA

Campbell, Kevin (Athlete, Baseball Player)
207 Ridout Dr
Des Arc, AR 72040, USA

Campbell, Kim (Politician)
Canadian Consulate
Canadian Consulate 550 S Hope St Ste 900
Los Angeles, CA 90071-2654, USA

Campbell, Lamar (Athlete, Football Player)
2511 W 7th St
Chester, PA 19013, USA

Campbell, Larry Joe (Actor)
30306 Diamonte Ln
Palos Verdes, CA 90275, USA

Campbell, L Arthur (Misc, Scientist)
Rockefeller University
Medical center
1230 York Ave
New York, NY 10021, USA

Campbell, Leslie (Stylist)
4 Coco Pl
Pacific Palisades, CA 90272, USA

Campbell, Lewis B (Business Person)
Textron Inc
40 Westminster St
Providence, RI 02903, USA

Campbell, Luther (Musician)
7180 Oakmont Dr
Hialeah, FL 33015, USA

Campbell, Lynn (Stylist)
c/o Staff Member *Montana Artists Agency*
9150 Wilshire Blvd Ste 100
Beverly Hills, CA 90212, USA

Campbell, Marion (Athlete, Football Coach, Football Player)
351 Marsh Point Cir
Saint Augustine, FL 32080, USA

Campbell, Mark (Athlete, Football Player)
8303 SW 64th Pl
Gainesville, FL 32608, USA

Campbell, Martin (Director)
International Creative Mgmt
8942 Wilshire Blvd #219
Beverly Hills, CA 90211, USA

Campbell, Matt (Athlete, Football Player)
9 Timberidge Dr
North Augusta, SC 29860, USA

Campbell, Matthew (Matt) (Athlete, Football Player)
9 Timberidge Dr
North Augusta, SC 29860, USA

Campbell, Michael (Athlete, Golfer)
c/o Adrian Mitchell *IMG (UK)*
McCormack House, Hogarth Business Park
Burlington Lane
Chiswick London W4 2TH, UNITED KINGDOM (UK)

Campbell, Mike (Athlete, Football Player)
383 Inverness Dr
Winston Salem, NC 27107-6030, USA

Campbell, Mike (Athlete, Baseball Player)
4500 36th Avenue SW
Apt 12
Seattle, WA 98126, USA

Campbell, Mike (Athlete, Football Player)
383 Inverness Dr
Winston Salem, NC 27107, USA

Campbell, Mike (Musician)
19950 Redwing St
Woodland Hills, CA 91364, USA

Campbell, Milt (Athlete, Football Player)
3805 Reservoir Dr
Gainesville, GA 30507, USA

Campbell, Naomi (Actor, Model, Music Group)
c/o Vanessa Pereira *Artists Independent Management (LA)*
825 Nowita Pl
Venice, CA 90291, USA

Campbell, Nell (Actor)
246 W 14th St
New York, NY 10011, USA

Campbell, Nell (Actor)
Andrew Taylor Management
P.O. Box 709
Broadway NSW 2007, Australia

Campbell, Neve (Actor)
c/o Arlene Forster *Forster Entertainment*
12533 Woodgreen St
Los Angeles, CA 90066, USA

Campbell, Nicholas (Actor)
1206 N Orange Grove
West Hollywood, CA 90046, USA

Campbell, Pamela (Stylist)
c/o Staff Member *Artist Untied (LA)*
845 S Mansfield Ave
#1
Los Angeles, CA 90036, USA

Campbell, Patrick J (Misc)
Carpenter & Joiners Union
101 Constitution Ave NW
Washington, DC 20001, USA

Campbell, Paul (Actor)
c/o Staff Member *ROAR (LA)*
9701 Wilshire Blvd
8th Floor
Los Angeles, CA 90212, USA

Campbell, Rich (Athlete, Football Player)
3176 Leeds Rd
Columbus, OH 43221-2625, USA

Campbell, Rich (Athlete, Football Player)
3176 Leeds Rd
Columbus, OH 43221, USA

Campbell, Robert (Architect, Critic)
54 Antrim St
Cambridge, MA 02139, USA

Campbell, Robert H (Business Person)
Sunoco Inc
10 Penn Center 1801 Market St
Philadelphia, PA 19103, USA

Campbell, Ron (Athlete, Baseball Player)
1104 Sweetbriar Ave NW
Cleveland, TN 37311, USA

Campbell, Scott (Athlete, Football Player)
123 Oak Ln
Hershey, PA 17033-1748, USA

Campbell, Scott (Athlete, Football Player)
123 Oak Ln
Hershey, PA 17033, USA

Campbell, Scott Michael (Actor)
c/o Danielle Allman-Del *D2 Management*
141 S. Barrington Ave
Los Angeles, CA 90049, USA

Campbell, Sonny (Athlete, Football Player)
6250 N Desert Willow Dr
Tucson, AZ 85743-8701, USA

Campbell, Sonny (Athlete, Football Player)
6250 N Desert Willow Dr
Tucson, AZ 85743, USA

Campbell, Stacy Dean (Musician)
1105-C 16th Ave Sq
Nashville, TN 37212, USA

Campbell, Tevin (Musician)
c/o Staff Member *Universal Attractions*
135 W 26th St
12 Floor
New York, NY 10001, USA

Campbell, Tony (Athlete, Basketball Player)
1445 Teaneck Road
Teaneck, NJ 07666-3627, USA

Campbell, Vivian (Musician)
2621 N Vermont Ave
Los Angeles, CA 90027, USA

Campbell, William J (General)
3267 Alex Findlay Place
Sarasota, FL 34240, USA

Campbell, William Ltgen (Aviator)
Burdeshaw Associates Inc 4701 Sangamore Rd Ste N100 Attn Air Force Programs
Bethesda, MD 20816-2500, USA

Campbell, Woodrow (Athlete, Football Player)
9122 Weymouth Dr
Houston, TX 77031, USA

Campbell, Woody (Athlete, Football Player)
9122 Weymouth Dr
Houston, TX 77031-3034, USA

Campbell Bower, Jamie (Actor)
c/o Warren Zavala *WME (LA)*
9601 Wilshire Blvd Fl 3
Beverly Hills, CA 90210, USA

Campbell-Hannah, Helen (Athlete, Baseball Player, Commentator)
17077 San Mateo St
Fountain Valley, CA 92708-7645, USA

Campbell-Martin, Tisha (Actor)
22401 S Summit Ridge Cir
Chatsworth, CA 91311, USA

Campeau, Rychard (Athlete, Hockey Player)
301 Rue Georges-Phaneuf
Saint-Jean-Sur-Richelieu, QC J3B 1J9, Canada

Campedelli, Dominic (Athlete, Hockey Player)
732 Jerusalem Rd
Cohasset, MA 02025, USA

Campen, James (Athlete, Football Player)
2789 Ichabod Ln
Green Bay, WI 54313, USA

Campese, David I (Athlete, Misc)
D C Management Group
870 Pacific Highway #4
Gordon, NSW 2072, AUSTRALIA

Campfield, Billy (Athlete, Football Player)
930 Glenmore Way Apt K
Westerville, OH 43082, USA

Campfield, William (Billy) (Athlete, Football Player)
532 Radcliff Dr
Westerville, OH 43082, USA

Campion, Jane (Director)
c/o Kate Richter *HLA Management*
PO Box 1536
Strawberry Hills 2012, AUSTRALIA

Campisi, Sal (Athlete, Baseball Player)
644 77th Ave
St Pete Beach, FL 33706, USA

Campo, Dave (Coach, Football Coach)
Celveland Browns
76 Lou Groza Blvd
Berea, OH 44017, USA

Campos, Angel (Athlete, Baseball Player)
6305 W Velvet Senna
Dr Tucson, AZ 85757-7518, USA

Campos, Arsenio (Actor)
c/o Staff Member *Televisa*
Blvd Adolfo Lopez Mateos 232
Colonia San Angel INN
DF CP 01060, MEXICO

Campos, Bruno (Actor)
SDB Partners
1801 Ave of Stars
#902
Los Angeles, CA 90067, USA

Campos, Jorge (Soccer Player)
Federacion de Futbol Assn
Col Juarez
Mexico City 6, DF CP 06600, MEXICO

Cam'ron (Musician)
c/o Staff Member *ICM Partners (ICM-LA)*
10250 Constellation Blvd Fl 7
Los Angeles, CA 90067, USA

Canada, Larry (Athlete, Football Player)
17691 Sarah Ln
Country Club Hills, IL 60478-4995, USA

Canada, Larry (Athlete, Football Player)
17691 Sarah Ln
Country Club Hills Ln, IL 60478, USA

Canada, Ron (Actor)
c/o Christopher Wright *Christopher Wright Management*
3207 Winnie Dr
Los Angeles, CA 90068, USA

Canadas, Esther (Actor, Model)
Wilhelmina Models
300 Park Ave S #200
New York, NY 10010, USA

Canadian Brass (Music Group)
c/o Darcy Gregoire *Agency Group Ltd, The (Canada)*
2 Berkeley Street
Suite 202
Toronto M5A 4J5, Canada

Canadian Tenors, The (Music Group, Musician)
c/o Jeffrey Latimer *Jeffrey Latimer Entertainment*
280 Jarvis St
Suite 301
Toronto, ON M5B 2C5, Canada

Canady, James (Jim) (Athlete, Football Player)
303 Sunset Dr
Burnet, TX 78611, USA

Canagata, Bill (Baseball Player)
Indianapolis Clowns
25 W 132nd St Apt 10R
New York, NY 10037-3205, USA

Canale, George (Athlete, Baseball Player)
7333 Old Mill Rd
Roanoke, VA 24018, USA

Canalis, Elisabetta (Actor, Model)
c/o Staff Member *Corsa Agency, The*
11704 Wilshire Blvd #204
Los Angeles, CA 90025, USA

Canals-Barrera, Maria (Actor)
c/o Jason Newman *Untitled Entertainment (LA)*
350 S. Beverly Dr #200
Beverly Hills, CA 90212, USA

Canary, David (Actor)
110 Belden Hill Rd
Wilton, CT 06897, USA

Candaele, Casey (Athlete, Baseball Player)
251 Broad St
San Luis Obispo, CA 93405, USA

Candelari, Richard
3812 Conough Ln
Las Vegas, NV 89129-2707, USA

Candelaria, John (Athlete, Baseball Player)
319 N Monongahela Ave
Glassport, PA 15045, USA

Candeloro, Philippe (Figure Skater)
Federation des Sports de Glace
35 Rue Felicien David
Paris 75016, FRANCE

Candeloro, Philippe (Figure Skater)
42 rue de Louvre
Paris F-75001, FRANCE

Candills, Georges (Architect)
17 Rue Campagne-Premiere
Paris 75014, FRANCE

Candiotti, Thomas C (Tom) (Athlete, Baseball Player)
6061 E Jenan Dr
Scottsdale, AZ 85254, USA

Candlebox (Music Group)
c/o Staff Member *Maverick Recording Co (LA)*
3300 Warner Blvd
Burbank, CA 91505-4632, USA

Caneira, John (Athlete, Baseball Player)
18 Spruce Dr
Naugatuck, CT 06770, USA

Canela, Jencarlos (Actor)
c/o Oswaldo Pisfil *NCM Productions*
10770 NW 66 Th Street Suite 512
Miami, FL 33178, USA

Canella, Guldo (Architect)
Via Revere 7
Milan 20123, ITALY

Canellas, Natalia (Stylist)
c/o Celebrity Stylists *Utopia*
12 West End Ave.
2nd Fl.
New York, NY 10023, USA

Canerday, Natalie (Actor)
c/o Staff Member *The Agency Inc*
802 W 8th St
Little Rock, AR 72201, USA

Canet, Guillaume (Actor, Director, Writer)
c/o Robert Newman *WME (LA)*
9601 Wilshire Blvd Fl 3
Beverly Hills, CA 90210, USA

Canete, Ariel (Athlete, Golfer)
Advantage International
1751 Pinnacle Dr
Suite 1500
Mc Lean, VA 22102-3833, USA

Canfield, Jack (Business Person, Writer)
The Jack Canfield Companies
PO Box 30880
Santa Barbara, CA 93130, USA

Canfield, Mary Grace (Actor)
Shelly & Pierce
13775A Mono Way
#220
Sonora, CA 95370, USA

Canfield, Paul (Physicist)
Iowa State University
Physics Dept
Arnes, IA 50011, USA

Canfield, William L (Bill) (Cartoonist, Editor)
Star Ledger
Editorial Dept ! Star Ledger Plaza
Newark, NJ 07102, USA

Cangelosi, John (Athlete, Baseball Player)
10914 Caribou Ln
Orland Park, IL 60467, USA

Cangemi, Joseph P (Misc)
1409 Mount Ayr Circle
Bowling Green, KY 42103, USA

Canidate, Trung (Athlete, Football Player)
1707 W Clarendon Ave
Phoenix, AZ 85015, USA

Canipe, David (Athlete, Golfer)
505 Oakwood Ave
New Smyrna Beach, FL 32169, USA

Canizales, Gaby (Boxer)
2205 Saint Maria Ave
Laredo, TX 78040, USA

Canizaro, Jay (Athlete, Baseball Player)
19523 Piney Lake Dr
Spring, TX 77388, USA

Canley, Sheldon (Athlete, Football Player)
264 Altair Ave
Lompoc, CA 93436, USA

Cannatella, Trishelle (Reality TV Star)
c/o Staff Member *Bunim/Murray Productions Inc*
6007 Sepulveda Blvd
Van Nuys, CA 91411, USA

Cannava, Anthony (Tony) (Athlete, Football Player)
26 Royal St
Medford, MA 02155, USA

Cannavale, Bobby (Actor)
c/o Peg Donegan *Framework Entertainment (LA)*
9057 Nemo St
Suite C
West Hollywood, CA 90069, USA

Cannavino, Joe (Athlete, Football Player)
346 Claymore Blvd
Cleveland, OH 44143-1730, USA

Canned Heat (Music Group, Musician)
P.O. Box 3773
San Rafael, CA 94912, USA

Cannida, James (Athlete, Football Player)
4504 Harmony Pl
Rohnert Park, CA 94928, USA

Canning, Doug
700 Brookside Rd
Maitland, FL 32751-5170, USA

Canning, Lisa (Actor, Correspondent)
880 Hilldale Ave #12
West Hollywood, CA 90069, USA

Canning, Sara (Actor)
c/o Laura Myones *McKeon-Myones Management*
3500 Olive Ave
Suite 770
Burbank, CA 91505, USA

Cannizaro, Andy (Athlete, Baseball Player)
968 Nancy St
Mandeville, LA 70448, USA

Cannizzaro, Chris (Athlete, Baseball Player)
13597 Grain Ln
San Diego, CA 92129, USA

Cannon (Stylist)
c/o Staff Member *Oliver Piro Inc*
725 Riverside Dr Apt 3A
New York, NY 10031, USA

Cannon, Ace (Musician)
American Mgmt
19948 Mayall St
Chatsworth, CA 91311, USA

Cannon, Billy (Athlete, Football Player)
8851 Sage Hill Rd
Saint Francisville, LA 70775-7168, USA

Cannon, Billy (Athlete, Football Player)
8857 Sage Hill Rd
Saint Francisville, LA 70775-7168, USA

Cannon, Billy (Athlete, Football Player, Heisman Trophy Winner)
8857 Sage Hill Rd
Saint Francisville, LA 70775, USA

Cannon, Carey (Actor)
c/o Staff Member *Geddes Agency, The*
8430 Santa Monica Blvd
Suite 200
Los Angeles, CA 90069, USA

Cannon, Danny (Producer)
c/o Staff Member *Creative Artists Agency (CAA-LA)*
2000 Ave Of The Stars
Los Angeles, CA 90067, USA

Cannon, Don (Producer)
Cannon Music Enterprise
P. O. Box 360055
Decatur, GA 30036, USA

Cannon, Dyan (Actor)
1100 Alta Loma Rd #808
West Hollywood, CA 90069, USA

Cannon, Freddy (Musician)
18641 Cassandra St
Tarzana, CA 91356, USA

Cannon, Glenn (Actor)
University of Hawaii at Manoa
2500 Campus Rd
C/O Cinematic and Digital Arts
Honolulu, HI 96822, USA

Cannon, Harold (Actor)
c/o Staff Member *Select Artists Ltd (CA-Valley Office)*
PO Box 4359
Burbank, CA 91503, USA

Cannon, Joe (Soccer Player)
c/o Staff Member *Colorado Rapids Soccer Club*
Pepsi Center
1000 Chopper Circle
Denver, CO 80204-5805, USA

Cannon, Joe (J J) (Athlete, Baseball Player)
3017 Cedarwood Village Ln
Pensacola, FL 32514, USA

Cannon, John (Athlete, Football Player)
2911 W Bay Vista Ave
Tampa, FL 33611, USA

Cannon, Katherine (Actor)
1310 Westholme Ave
Los Angeles, CA 90024, USA

Cannon, Larry (Athlete, Basketball Player)
12661 Kelly Sands Way #113
Ft Myers, FL 33908, USA

Cannon, Mark (Athlete, Football Player)
2604 Riveroaks Dr
Arlington, TX 76006, USA

Cannon, Nick (Actor, Producer)
3130 Antelo Rd
Los Angeles, CA 90077, USA

Cano, Christi (Athlete, Golfer)
834 Alametos
San Antonio, TX 78212, USA

Cano, Martin (Stylist)
c/o Staff Member *Crews*
828 Clemont Dr
Atlanta, GA 30306, USA

Cano, Roberto (Actor)
c/o Staff Member *TV Caracol*
Calle 76 #11 - 35
Piso 10AA
Bogota DC 26484, COLOMBIA

Cano, Robinson (Athlete, Baseball Player)
c/o Team Member *New York Yankees*
Yankee Stadium
161st St & River Ave
Bronx, NY 10451, USA

Canonero, Milena (Designer)
c/o Paul Hook *ICM Partners (ICM-LA)*
10250 Constellation Blvd Fl 7
Los Angeles, CA 90067, USA

Canova, Diana (Actor)
Grand View Management
578 Washington Blvd Ste 688
Marina Del Rey, CA 90292, USA

Canseco, Jose (Athlete, Baseball Player, Reality TV Star)
c/o Susan Haber *Haber Entertainment*
434 S Canon Dr
Suite 204
Beverly Hills, CA 90212, USA

Canseco, Ozzie (Athlete, Baseball Player)
10833 Wilshire Blvd
Apt 525
Los Angeles, CA 90024, USA

Cansino, Athena (Actor)
c/o Victor (Viktor) Kruglov *Victor Kruglov Talent Management*
7461 Beverly Blvd Ste 403
Los Angeles, CA 90036, USA

Cantafio, Jim (Actor)
c/o Laura Lichen *Laura Lichen Management*
P.O. Box 33051
Granada Hills, CA 91394, USA

Cantaline, Anita (Bowler)
31455 Pinto Dr
Warren, MI 48093-7624, USA

Cantano, Mark (Athlete, Football Player)
9036 Walton St
Inidanapolis, IN 46231, USA

Cantey, Charisie (Sportscaster)
ABC-TV
Sports Dept 77 W 66th St
New York, NY 10023, USA

Cantillo, Jose Pablo (Actor)
c/o Staff Member *New Wave Entertainment (LA)*
2660 W Olive Blvd
Burbank, CA 91505, USA

Canton, Denio (Baseball Player)
New York Cubans
1330 NW 5th St Apt 5
Miami, FL 33125-4734, USA

Canton, Joanna (Actor)
c/o Staff Member *Liberman/Zerman Management*
252 N Larchmont Blvd
Suite 200
Los Angeles, CA 90004, USA

Cantona, Eric (Actor)
French Federation de Football
60 Bis Ave D'Ilena
Paris 75783, France

Cantone, Mario (Actor)
c/o Rhonda Price *Gersh (NY)*
41 Madison Ave
New York, NY 10010, USA

Cantone, Vic (Cartoonist, Editor)
238 Blackpool Court
Ridge, NY 11961, USA

Cantoni, Giulio L (Biologist, Misc)
6938 Blaisdell Road
Bathesda, MD 20817, USA

Cantor, Andres (Sportscaster)
c/o Staff Member *WmE2 (WMA-LA)*
1 William Morris Pl
Beverly Hills, CA 90212, USA

Cantor, Charles R (Biologist)
11 Bay Street Road
Boston, MA 02116, USA

Cantor, Eric (Congressman, Politician)
303 Cannon HOB
Washington, DC 20515, USA

Cantoral, Itati (Actor)
c/o Gabriel Blanco *Gabriel Blanco Iglesias (Mexico)*
Rio Balsas 35-32
Colonia Cuauhtemoc
DF 06500, Mexico

Cantrell, Barry (Athlete, Football Player)
142 Underwood Dr
Palatka, FL 32177, USA

Cantrell, Bill (Race Car Driver)
PO Box 194
Novi, MI 48376-0194, USA

Cantrell, Blu (Music Group)
c/o Michael (Mike) Esterman *Esterman.Com, LLC*
Prefers to be contacted via email
MD, USA

Cantrell, Jerry (Musician)
c/o Michael Moses *Baker Winokur Ryder Public Relations (BWR-LA)*
9100 Wilshire Blvd
Suite 500, West Tower
Beverly Hills, CA 90212, USA

Cantrell, Lana (Musician)
300 E 71st St
New York, NY 10021, USA

Cantu, Jorge (Athlete, Baseball Player)
5009 S 24th St
McAllen, TX 78503, USA

Cantuniar, Sonia (Stylist)
c/o Staff Member *Artist Untied (LA)*
845 S Mansfield Ave
#1
Los Angeles, CA 90036, USA

Cantwell, Maria (Politician)
904 7th AveS
Edmonds, WA 98020-4014, USA

Canty, Chris (Athlete, Football Player)
26 Berkery Pl
Alpine, NJ 07620, USA

Canup, Robin (Astronomer)
Southwest Reasearch Institute
1050 Walnut St #400
Boulder, CO 80302, USA

Canyon, George (Musician)
c/o Staff Member *Paradigm (Monterey)*
404 W Franklin St
Monterey, CA 93940, USA

Cap, Kelly (Athlete, Golfer)
3023 Alcazar Pl
Apt 208
Palm Beach Gardens, FL 33410, USA

Capa, Cornell (Photographer)
275 5th Ave
New York, NY 10016, USA

Capalbo, Carmen C (Director, Producer)
500 2nd Ave
New York, NY 10016, USA

Caparulo, John (Comedian)
c/o Staff Member *Brillstein Entertainment Partners*
9150 Wilshire Blvd #350
Beverly Hills, CA 90212, USA

Capasso, Federico (Physicist)
Lucent Technologies
Bell Labs 600 Mountain Ave
New Providence, NJ 07974, USA

Capecchi, Mario R (Nobel Prize Laureate)
1172 South Bonneville Drive
Salt Lake City, UT 84108-2052, USA

Capece, Bill (Athlete, Football Player)
867 Hill Roost Rd
Tallahassee, FL 32312, USA

Capel, John (Athlete, Track Athlete)

Capel, Mike (Athlete, Baseball Player)
3901 Northshore Dr
Montgomery, TX 77356, USA

Capellas, Michael (Business Person)
MCI
500 Clinton Center Dr
Clinton, MS 39056, USA

Capellino, Ally (Designer, Fashion Designer)
N1R Metropolitan Wharf
Wapping Wall
London E1 9SS, UNITED KINGDOM (UK)

Capers, Dom (Athlete, Coach, Football Coach, Football Player)
814 Hilltop Dr
Walpole, MA 02081-4412, USA

Capers, Wayne (Athlete, Football Player)
28 Greenlawn Dr
Pittsburgh, PA 15220, USA

Caperton, Gaston (Ex-Governor)
The College Board
PO Box 1386
Charleston, WV 25325-1386, USA

Capilla, Doug (Athlete, Baseball Player)
642 Nello Dr
Apt 1
Campbell, CA 95008, USA

Capilla, Perez Joaquin (Misc)
Torres de Mixcoac
Lomas de Platerce
Mexico City 19, DF, MEXICO

Capitain, Jenny (Stylist)
c/o Staff Member *AFG Management*
Pier 62
Chelsea Piers #203
New York, NY 10011, USA

Caplan, Arthur L (Biologist, Misc)
University of Pennsylvania
Biomedical Ethics Center
Philadelphia, PA 19104, USA

Caplan, Lizzy (Actor)
c/o Ryan Revel *Benderspink*
5870 W Jefferson Blvd
Studio E
Los Angeles, CA 90016, USA

Capleton (Musician)
c/o Staff Member *Agency Group Ltd, The (NY)*
142 West 57th St
6th Floor
New York, NY 10019, USA

Caplin, Mortimer M (Government Official)
5610 Wisconsin Ave NW
#18E
Bethesda, MD 20815, USA

Capodice, John (Actor)
c/o Staff Member *Sharp Talent*
117 N Orlando Ave
Los Angeles, CA 90048, USA

Capon, Edwin G (Religious Leader)
Swedenborgian Church
11 Highland Ave
Newtonville, MA 02460, USA

Capone, Warren (Athlete, Football Player)
1076 W Tom Stokes Ct
Baton Rouge, LA 70810-3194, USA

Caponera, John (Actor, Comedian)
Messina Baker Entertainment
955 Carillo Dr
#100
Los Angeles, CA 90048, USA

Caponetto, Megan (Stylist)
c/o Staff Member *Mel Bryant Management*
611 Broadway #623
New York, NY 10012

Caponi, Donna M (Athlete, Golfer)
2731 Silver River Trl
Orlando, FL 32828, USA

Caponigro, Paul (Photographer)
135 S 6th Ave
Tucson, AZ 85701-2007, USA

Capp, Dick (Athlete, Football Player)
PO Box 2193
Cary, NC 27512-2193, USA

Cappadona, Robert (Bob) (Athlete, Football Player)
25 Summer St
Watertown, MA 02472, USA

Cappelletti, Gino (Athlete, Football Player)
19 Louis Dr
Wellesley Hills, MA 02481-1164, USA

Cappelletti, John (Athlete, Football Player, Heisman Trophy Winner)
23791 Brant Ln
Laguna Niguel, CA 92677-1341, USA

Cappelman, Bill (Athlete, Football Player)
1506 Sydney Ln
Lynn Haven, FL 32444-2928, USA

Cappleman, William (Bill) (Athlete, Football Player)
1506 Sydney Ln
Lynn Haven, FL 32444, USA

Cappos, Connie (Stylist)
c/o Staff Member *LA Rep*
8312 Utica Dr
Los Angeles, CA 90046, USA

Capps, Lois (Congressman, Politician)
2231 Rayburn HOB
Washington, DC 20515, USA

Capps, Matt (Athlete, Baseball Player)
6348 S Summers Cir
Douglasville, GA 30135, USA

Capps, Ron (Race Car Driver)
Copenhagen Racing
1232 Distribution Way
Vista, CA 92083, USA

Capps, Thomas E (Business Person)
Dominion Resources
120 Tredegar St
Richmond, VA 23219, USA

Cappuzzello, George (Athlete, Baseball Player)
2024 Stillwood Pl
Windermere, FL 34786, USA

Capra, Buzz (Athlete, Baseball Player)
15039 W Keswick Pl
Lockport, IL 60441, USA

Capra, Francis (Actor)

Capra, Nick (Athlete, Baseball Player)
300 Town Park Rd
Norman, OK 73072, USA

Capri, Ahna (Actor)
16547 Vanowen St
Apt 209
Van Nuys, CA 91406-4710, USA

Capri, Mark (Actor)
The Blithe Spirit
The Shubert Theatre
225 West 44th St
New York, NY 10036, USA

Capria, Carl (Athlete, Football Player)
9003 Nautical Watch Dr
Indianapolis, IN 46236-9035, USA

Capriati, Jennifer (Athlete, Olympic Athlete, Tennis Player)
5326 Foxhunt Dr
Wesley Chapel, FL 33543-4245, USA

Caprice (Model, Music Group, Songwriter, Writer)
Mission Control
Business Center Lower Road
London SE16 2XB, UNITED KINGDOM (UK)

Caprice, Frank (Athlete, Hockey Player)
536 Lake Louise Cir Unit 202
Naples, FL 34110-7020, USA

Capshaw, Jessica (Actor)
c/o Raj Raghavan *Creative Artists Agency (CAA-LA)*
2000 Ave Of The Stars
Los Angeles, CA 90067, USA

Capshaw, Kate (Actor)
c/o Kevin Huvane *Creative Artists Agency (CAA-LA)*
2000 Ave Of The Stars
Los Angeles, CA 90067, USA

Captain, Raj (Actor)
951 Munuswamy Salai
K K Nagar
Chennai, TN 600 078, INDIA

Capuano, Chris (Athlete, Baseball Player)
19550 N Grayhawk Dr
Unit 1112
Scottsdale, AZ 85255, USA

Capuano, Dave (Athlete, Hockey Player)
145 Capuano Way
Cranston, RI 02920, USA

Capuano, Jack (Athlete, Coach, Hockey Player)
c/o Staff Member *Bridgeport Sound Tigers*
600 Main St
Suite 1
Bridgeport, CT 06604, USA

Capucill, Terese (Dancer)
Martha Graham dance Center
440 Lafayette St
New York, NY 10003, USA

Caputo, Theresa (Psychic, Reality TV Star)
PO Box 490
Hicksville, NY 11802, USA

Capuzzi, Jim (Athlete, Football Player)
10538 Rancho Carmel Dr
San Diego, CA 92128-3627, USA

Cara, Irene (Actor, Musician)
2160 Moon Shadow Rd
New Port Richey, FL 34655, USA

Carafoli, John F (Stylist)
106 Lexington Ave
New York, NY 10016, USA

Carafotes, Paul (Actor)
8033 Sunset Blvd #3554
West Hollywood, CA 90046, USA

Caraluzzi, Joseph (Horse Racer)
44 Greenwood Dr
Freehold, NJ 07728-4005

Caraman, Alina (Stylist)
c/o Staff Member *Judy Inc*
1 Yorkville Ave
Toronto ON M4W 1L1, Canada

Caramanlis, Costas (Prime Minister)
Premier's Office
17 Stissichoros St
King George V Ave
Athens, GREECE

Carano, Gina (Crush) (Athlete, Wrestler)
c/o Scott Karp *Crystal Sky Pictures*
10203 Santa Monica Blvd
5th Floor
Los Angeles, CA 90067, USA

Carano, Glenn (Athlete, Football Player)
2551 E Lake Ridge Shrs
Reno, NV 89519-5, USA

Carapella, Alfred (Al) (Athlete, Football Player)
10 Woodlot Rd
Eastchester, NY 10709, USA

Carasco, Joe (King) (Music Group)
Texas Sounds
2317 Pecan
Dickinson, TX 77539, USA

Caravello, Joe (Athlete, Football Player)
633 W Palm Ave
El Segundo, CA 90245, USA

Caray, Chip (Commentator)
1302 Azalea Ln
Maitland, FL 32751-6404, USA

Carbajal, Michael (Athlete, Boxer, Olympic Athlete)
P.O. Box 510
Phoenix, AZ 85001-0510, USA

Carberry, Deirdre (Ballerina)
American Ballet Theater
890 Broadway
New York, NY 10003, USA

Carbo, Bernie (Athlete, Baseball Player)
6352 Woodside Dr S
Theodore, AL 36582, USA

Carbonara, David (Composer, Musician)
c/o Staff Member *Gorfaine/Schwartz Agency Inc*
4111 W Alameda Ave
Suite 509
Burbank, CA 91505, USA

Carbonaro, Michael (Actor)
c/o Staff Member *Grapevine Public Relations*
5237 N Cahuenga Blvd #2
N Hollywood, CA 91601, USA

Carbone, Frank (Horse Racer)
6004 Dickens Ct
Norristown, PA 19403-1373, USA

Carbonell, Nestor (Actor)
128 S Larchmont Blvd
Los Angeles, CA 90004, USA

Carbonneau, Guy (Athlete, Coach, Hockey Player)
c/o Staff Member *Montreal Canadiens*
1275 Rue Saint-Antoine O
Montreal, QB H3C 5L2, Canada

Carcaterra, Lorenzo (Producer, Writer)
c/o Staff Member *Pitt Group, The*
9465 Wilshire Blvd
Suite 420
Beverly Hills, CA 90212, USA

Carcieri, Donald (Politician)
PO Box 701
Saunderstown, RI 02874-0701, USA

Card, Andrew (Politician)
White House
8405 Spring Crk
College Station, TX 77845-4608, USA

Card, Michael (Music Group, Musician)
1143 Dora Whitley Road
Franklin, TN 37064, USA

Card, Orson Scott (Writer)
401 Willoughby Blvd
Greensboro, NC 27408-3135, USA

Cardamone, Richard J (Judge)
US Court of Appeals
10 Broad St
Utica, NY 13501, USA

Cardellini, Linda (Actor)
214 Raymundo Dr
Woodside, CA 94062, USA

Carden, Joan M (Opera Singer)
Jennifer Eddy
596 Saint Kilda Road #11
Melbourne, VIC 3004, AUSTRALIA

Cardenal, Jose D (Athlete, Baseball Player)
118 Bridgewater Ct
Bradenton, FL 34212, USA

Cardenas, Leo (Athlete, Baseball Player)
5412 Ravenna St
Cincinnati, OH 45227, USA

Cardenas, Robert L Briggen (Aviator)
6143 Madra Ave
San Diego, CA 92120-3905, USA

Cardich, Augusto (Archaeologist)
University of La Plata
Archaeology Dept
La Plata, ARGENTINA

Cardiff, Jack (Cinematographer)
32 Woodland Rise
London N10, UNITED KINGDOM (UK)

Cardigans, The (Music Group)
c/o Staff Member *International Talent Booking (ITB - UK)*
27A Floral St Fl 3
Covent Garden
London WC2E 9, UNITED KINGDOM

Cardille, Lori (Actor)
c/o Tracey Goldblum *Abrams Artists Agency (NY)*
275 Seventh Ave
26th Floor
New York, NY 10001, USA

Cardin, Benjamin L. (Senator)
509 Hart Senate Office Building
Washington, DC 20510, USA

Cardin, Claude (Athlete, Hockey Player)
13 Rue Boucher
Sorel-Tracy, QC J3P 1E7, Canada

Cardin, Pierre (Designer, Fashion Designer)
59 Rue du Foubourg-St-Honore
Paris 75008, FRANCE

Cardinahl, Jessika (Actor)
Galerie Am Arkonaplatz
Wolliner Str. 11
Berlin D-10435, Germany

Cardinal, Brian (Athlete, Basketball Player)
1680 Lane 105
Lake James
Angola, IN 46703-8533, USA

Cardinal, Conrad (Athlete, Baseball Player)
162 E hunter Ln
Central, UT 84722, USA

Cardinal, Douglas J (Architect)
7011A Manchester Blvd #315
Alexandria, VA 22310, USA

Cardinal, Randy (Baseball Player)
Houston Colt 45's
3810 W Verde Way
North Las Vegas, NV 89031-4812, USA

Cardinale, Claudia (Actor)
Via Flaminia Km 77
Prima Porta
Rome 00188, ITALY

Cardinalem, Lindsey (Musician)

Cardona, Manolo (Actor)
c/o Nina Shaw *Del Shaw Moonves Tanaka Finkelstein & Lezcano*
2120 Colorado Blvd
Suite 200
Santa Monica, CA 90404, USA

Cardone, Vivien (Actor)
c/o Staff Member *Persona Management*
40 E 9th St #11J
Suite 11J
New York, NY 10003, USA

Cardos, John Bud (Director)
P.O. Box 7430
Burbank, CA 91505, USA

Cardosa, Patricia (Director)
c/o Staff Member *ICM Partners (ICM-LA)*
10250 Constellation Blvd Fl 7
Los Angeles, CA 90067, USA

Cardoso, Fernando (Ex-President, Politician)
Instituto Fernando Henrique Cardoso
Rua Formosa, 367
6º andar, Centro
San Paulo 01049-000, Brazil

Cardoso, Patricia (Director)
c/o Rosalie Swedlin *Anonymous Content (LA)*
3531 Hayden Ave
Culver City, CA 90232, USA

Cardoza, Dennis (Congressman, Politician)
2437 Rayburn HOB
Washington, DC 20515, USA

Care, Peter (Cinematographer, Director, Writer)
Bob Industries
1313 5th Street
Santa Monica, CA 90401, USA

Carell, Steve (Actor)
4310 Arcola Ave
Toluca Lake, CA 91602, USA

Carelli, Rick (Race Car Driver)
Chesrow Auto Group
2009 Market St.
Denver, CO 80205, USA

Carenard, Brian (Saigon) (Musician)
Abandoned Nation Ent. Inc.
86-110 Orchard St.
2nd Floor
Hackensack, NJ 07601, USA

Caretto-Brown, Patty (Swimmer)
16079 Mesquite Circle
Santa Ana, CA 92708, USA

Carew, Drew (Actor, Comedian)
Messina Baker Entertainment
955 Carillo Dr #100
Los Angeles, CA 90048, USA

Carew, Rod (Athlete, Baseball Player)
4271 Vale St
Irvine, CA 92604-2208, USA

Carey, Clare (Actor)
1025 Nowita Pl
Venice, CA 90291, USA

Carey, Danny (Musician)
2174 Canyon Dr
Los Angeles, CA 90068, USA

Carey, Drew (Actor, Comedian)
7680 Mulholland Dr
Los Angeles, CA 90046, USA

Carey, Duane G (Astronaut)
5938 Instone Cir
Colorado Springs, CO 80922-1716, USA

Carey, Duane G Lt Colonel (Astronaut)
5938 Instone Cir
Colorado Springs, CO 80922-1716, USA

Carey, Ezekiel (Music Group)
509 E Ridge Crest Blvd #A
Ridge Crest, CA 93555, USA

Carey, George (Religious Leader)
University of Gloucestershire
Chancellors Office
Cheltenham GL50 2RH, UNITED
KINGDOM

Carey, Jim (Athlete, Hockey Player)
5351 Hunt Club Way
Sarasota, FL 34238-4011, USA

Carey, Marey (Adult Film Star)
c/o Pure Play Media
19800 Nordhoff Pl
Chatsworth, CA 91311, USA

Carey, Mariah (Musician, Songwriter)
3130 Angelo Rd
Los Angeles, CA 90077, USA

Carey, Mary (Adult Film Star, Reality TV
Star)

Carey, Matthew Thomas (Actor)
c/o Abby Bluestone Innovative Artists (LA)
1505 10th St
Santa Monica, CA 90401, USA

Carey, Michelle (Actor)
H David Moss
733 Seward St
#PH
Los Angeles, CA 90038, USA

Carey, Paul (Athlete, Baseball Player)
5334 Olive Ave
Sarasota, FL 34231, USA

Carey, Peter (Writer)
International Creative Mgmt
40 W 57th St #1800
New York, NY 10019, USA

Carey, Rick (Athlete, Swimmer)
119 Rockland Ave.
Larchmont, NY 10538, USA

Carey, Tony (Musician)
BMG Postfach 800149
Munich D-81601, Germany

Carey, Vernon (Athlete, Football Player)
16875 Stratford Ct
Southwest Ranches, FL 33331-1362, USA

Carey Jr, Harry (Actor)
P O Box 1388
Goleta, CA 93116, USA

Cargo, David F (Politician)
6422 Concordia Road NE
Albuquerque, NM 87111-1228, USA

Carhart, Timothy (Actor)
29228 Circle Dr
Agoura Hills, CA 91301, USA

Carides, Gia (Actor)
Robyn Gardiner Mgmt
397 Riley St
Surrey Hills, NSW 2010, AUSTRALIA

Caridis, Miltiades (Conductor)
Himmelhofgasse 10
Vienna 1130, AUSTRIA

Carillo, Mary (Sportscaster)
822 Boylston St #203
Chestnut Hill, PA 02467, USA

Carimi, Gabe (Football Player)
c/o Gary Uberstine Premier Sports
Management
1401 Ocean Ave
Suite 302
Santa Monica, CA 90401, USA

Cariou, Len (Actor)
c/o Clifford Stevens Paradigm (NY)
360 Park Ave S Fl 16
New York, NY 10010, USA

Carithers, William Jr (Scientist)
Fermi Net Acceleration Lab
D-Zero Collaboration
PO Box 500
Batavia, IL 60510-5011, USA

Carius, Otto (War Hero)
Tiger-Apotheke
Hauptstr. 77
Herschweiler-Pettersheim 66909,
GERMANY

Carkner, Terry (Athlete, Hockey Player)
4 Remington Ln
Malvern, PA 19355, USA

Carl, Harland (Athlete, Football Player)
1419 N Douglas St
Appleton, WI 54914, USA

Carl, Jann (Television Host)
704 Magnolia Ave
Pasadena, CA 91106, USA

Carle, Eric (Artist)
PO Box 485
Northampton, MA 01060, USA

Carlei, Carlo (Director, Writer)
c/o Staff Member Creative Artists Agency
(CAA-LA)
2000 Ave Of The Stars
Los Angeles, CA 90067, USA

Carles Gordo, Ricardo M Cardinal
(Religious Leader)
Carrer del Bisbe 5
Barcelona 08002, SPAIN

Carlesimo, PJ (Basketball Coach, Coach,
Sportscaster)
1429 Willard Avenue West
Seattle, WA 98119, USA

Carlestrom, John E (Astronomer)
University of Chicago
Astronomy Dept 5640 S Ellis Ave
Chicago, IL 60637, USA

Carleton, Wayne (Athlete, Hockey Player)
9846 Hwy 26 East
RR 2 LCD Collingwood
collingwood, ON L9Y 3Z1, Canada

Carlile, Brandi (Musician)
25647 SE 179th St
Maple Valley, WA 98038, USA

Carlile, Forbes (Coach, Swimmer)
16 Cross St
Ryde, NSW 2112, AUSTRALIA

Carlin, Brian (Athlete, Hockey Player)
103 Mt Norquay Pk SE
Calgary, AB T2Z 2R3, Canada

Carlin, John (Politician)
1208 Wyndham Heights Drive
Manhattan, KS 66503-8676, USA

Carlin, Thomas R (Publisher)
Saint Paul Pioneer Press
Publisher's Office
345 Cdear
Saint Paul, MN 55101, USA

Carlin, Vidal (Athlete, Football Player)
930 Palm Ave Apt 417
West Hollywood, CA 90069-4080, USA

Carling, William D C (Athlete, Misc,
Sportscaster)
Insights Ltd
22 Suffolk St
London SW1Y 4HG, UNITED KINGDOM
(UK)

Carlino, Lewis John (Director, Writer)
991 Oakmont Dr
Los Angeles, CA 90049, USA

Carlisie, Rick (Basketball Player)
Boston Celtics
RR 4
Ogdensburg, NY 13669, USA

Carlisle, Belinda (Musician, Songwriter)
c/o Carlos Keyes Red Entertainment
Agency
505 8th Ave
Suite 1004
New York, NY 10018, USA

Carlisle, Cooper (Athlete, Football Player)
2032 Sorrelwood Ct
San Ramon, CA 94582, USA

Carlisle, James B (Ex-Governor)
POB W1644
Saint John's, Antigua

Carlisle, Jennifer (Stylist)
c/o Staff Member Celestine - CA
1666 20th St
#200-B
Santa Monica, CA 90404, USA

Carlisle, Jodi (Actor, Comedian)
c/o Staff Member ICM Partners (ICM-LA)
10250 Constellation Blvd Fl 7
Los Angeles, CA 90067, USA

Carlisle, Mary (Actor)
517 N Rodeo Dr
Beverly Hills, CA 90210, USA

Carlisle, Rick (Athlete, Basketball Coach,
Basketball Player, Coach)
3925 Greenbrier Dr
Dallas, TX 75225-5405, USA

Carlos, Bun (Musician)
6951 Belvidere Rd
Caledonia, IL 61011, USA

Carlos, Emmons (Athlete, Football Player)
435 Verdi Ln
Atlanta, GA 30350, USA

Carlos, Francisco (Cisco) (Athlete,
Baseball Player)
6027 N 7th St
Phoenix, AZ 85014, USA

Carlos, John (Athlete, Olympic Athlete,
Track Athlete)
68640 Tortuga Rd
Cathedral City, CA 92234-3874, USA

Carlos, Jordan (Comedian)
c/o Scott Metzger Paradigm (NY)
360 Park Ave S Fl 16
New York, NY 10010, USA

Carlos, Roberto (Musician)
c/o Jorge Pinos WmE2 (WMA-LA)
1 William Morris Pl
Beverly Hills, CA 90212, USA

Carlos I, Juan (King)
Palacio de la Zarzuela
Madrid 28671, SPAIN

Carlos Moco, Marcolino Jose (Prime
Minister)
Movimento Popular de Libertacao de
Angola
Luanda, ANGOLA

Carlot, Maxime (Prime Minister)
P O Box 698
Port Vila, VANUATU

Carlson, Amy (Actor)
c/o Darris Hatch Daris Hatch
Management
10027 Rossbury Pl
Los Angeles, CA 90064-4825, USA

Carlson, Arne H (Ex-Governor)
95 N Marion Ct
#136
Punta Gorda, FL 33950, USA

Carlson, Brendyn "Tyce" (Race Car
Driver)
13436 Lorenzo Boulevard
Carmel, IN 46074, USA

Carlson, Bruce (General)
The Pentagon Department ()_fAir Global
Pow
Washington, DC 20330-0001, USA

Carlson, Cody (Athlete, Football Player)
3417 Foothill Ter
Austin, TX 78731, USA

Carlson, Dale (Race Car Driver)
Mike Johnson Racing
1931 E. 4th St.
Olympia, WA 98506, USA

Carlson, Dan (Athlete, Baseball Player)
Mobile Baybears 755 Boiling Brothers
Blvd
Attn: Coaching Staff
Mobile, AL 36606-2505, USA

Carlson, Dan (Athlete, Baseball Player)
334 N Wickford Cir
Shreveport, LA 71115-2935, USA

Carlson, Dudley L (Admiral)
Navy League
2300 Wilson Blvd
Arlington, VA 22201, USA

Carlson, Gretchen (Television Host)
c/o Staff Member Fox News Channel (NY)
1211 Ave of the Americas
Level C1
New York, NY 10036-8701, USA

Carlson, Jack (Athlete, Hockey Player)
18259 Embers Ave
Farmington, MN 55024-9259, USA

Carlson, Jack W (Misc)
American Assn of Retired Persons
1901 K St NW
Washington, DC 20006, USA

Carlson, Jeff (Athlete, Hockey Player)
2935 Princeton Ct
Muskegon, MI 49441-3764, USA

Carlson, Jeff (Athlete, Football Player)
3542 Ballastone Dr
Land O Lakes, FL 34638, USA

Carlson, Jesse (Athlete, Baseball Player)
1461 Willard Ave
Apt C
Newington, CT 06111-4545, USA

Carlson, John (Athlete, Football Player)
323 E 5th St
Litchfield, MN 55355-1801, USA

Carlson, John (Athlete, Golfer)
c/o Jim Lehrman *SFX Golf*
36855 W Main St Ste 200
Purcellville, VA 20132, USA

Carlson, Karen (Actor)
3700 Ventura Canyon Ave
Sherman Oaks, CA 91423, USA

Carlson, Katrina (Actor)
c/o Staff Member *Sara Bennett Agency*
6404 Hollywood Blvd #316
Los Angeles, CA 90028, USA

Carlson, K C (Cartoonist)
DC Comics
1700 Broadway
New York, NY 10019, USA

Carlson, Kelly (Actor)
c/o Margot Klar *Cunningham Escott Slevin & Doherty (CESD-LA)*
10635 Santa Monica Blvd
130
Los Angeles, CA 90025, USA

Carlson, Kent (Athlete, Hockey Player)
58 Branch Tpke Unit 103
Concord, NH 03301-5779, USA

Carlson, Mark (Athlete, Baseball Player)
359 Tall Oak Trl
Tarpon Springs, FL 34688-7711, USA

Carlson, Paulette (Music Group)
Mark Sonder Music
Fisk Building 250 W 57th St #1830
New York, NY 10107, USA

Carlson, Richard (Writer)
Pennsylvania State Univ
613 Moore Bldg
University Park, PA 16802

Carlson, Robert j (General)
3000 39th Ave Apt 307
Columbus, NE 68601-2244

Carlson, Steve (Race Car Driver)
539 Brickel Rd
W Salem, WI 54669, USA

Carlson, Steve (Athlete, Hockey Player)
PO Box 3476
Rancho Cordova, CA 95741-3476, USA

Carlson, Stuart (Cartoonist)
Universal Press Syndicate
4520 Main St
Kansas City, MO 64111, USA

Carlson, Tucker (Television Host)

Carlson, Vanessa (Musician)
c/o Kurt Steffek *Razor & Tie*
P.O. Box 585
Cooper Station, NY 10276, USA

Carlson, Veronica (Actor)
7844 Kavanagh Court
Sarasota, FL 34240, USA

Carlsson, Arvid (Nobel Prize Laureate)
Gotheburg University
University of Goteborg Medicinaregatan 7, Box 431 Pharmacology Dept Goteborg
Gotheburg S-40530, SWEDEN

Carlsson, Ingvar G (Prime Minister)
Riksdagen
Stockholm 100 12, SWEDEN

Carlton, Carl (Musician)
Randolph Enterprises
Oakland
Inkster, MI 48141, USA

Carlton, Larry (Musician)
c/o Staff Member *Paradigm (Monterey)*
404 W Franklin St
Monterey, CA 93940, USA

Carlton, Steve (Athlete, Baseball Player)
555 S Camino Del Rio
Suite B2
Durango, CO 81303-6852, USA

Carlton, Vanessa (Musician)
182 Lafayette St #5TH
New York, NY 10013, USA

Carlton, Venessa (Music Group)
Peter Malkin Mgmt
410 Park Ave #420
New York, NY 10022, USA

Carlton, Wray (Athlete, Football Player)
29 Pine Ter
Orchard Park, NY 14127, USA

Carlucci, Dave (Athlete, Baseball Player)
580 Pond St
Franklin, MA 02038-2710, USA

Carlucci, Frank (Politician)
Carlyle Group
Carlyle Group Inc 1001 Pennsylvania Ave NW Ste 220
Washington, DC 20004-2525, USA

Carlucci, Frank C
1001 Pennsylvania Ave NW
Washington, DC 20004-2506, USA

Carl XVI, Gustaf (King)
Kungliga Slottet
Slottsbacken
Stockholm 111 30, SWEDEN

Carlyle, Buddy (Athlete, Baseball Player)
205 Ash mere Ct
Tyrone, GA 30290-2845, USA

Carlyle, Joan H (Opera Singer)
Laundry Cottage Hammer
North Wales SY13 4QX, UNITED KINGDOM (UK)

Carlyle, Randy (Athlete, Coach, Hockey Player)
180 S Lakeview Ave
Anaheim, CA 92807 -3606, USA

Carlyle, Randy (Athlete, Hockey Player)
Anaheim Ducks 2695 E Katella Ave
Attn Coaching Staff
Anaheim, CA 92806-5904, USA

Carlyle, Robert (Actor)
c/o Jon Rubinstein *Authentic Talent and Literary Management*
45 Main St
Suite 1004
Brooklyn, NY 11201, USA

Carmack, Chris (Actor)
c/o Theodore B Gekis *Gekis Management*
4217 Verdugo View Dr
Los Angeles, CA 90065-4317, USA

Carman, Don (Athlete, Baseball Player)
555 Murex Dr
Naples, FL 34102-5141, USA

Carman, Gregory W (Judge)
US Court of International Trade
1 Federal Plaza
New York, NY 10278, USA

Carman, Jon (Athlete, Football Player)
13 Nautilus Dr
Barnegat, NJ 08005-1302, USA

Carman, Patrick (Writer)
1247 Studebaker Drive
Walla Walla, WA 99362-8845, USA

Carmazzi, Giovanni (Athlete, Football Player)
9401 Cook Riolo Rd
Roseville, CA 95747-9221, USA

Carmel, duke (Athlete, Baseball Player)
10 Pheasant Valley Dr
Coram, NY 11727-2320, USA

Carmen, Eric (Musician, Songwriter)
2155 Woodstock Rd
Gates Mills, OH 44040, USA

Carmen, Jeanne (Actor, Model)
Brandon James
P O Box 11812
Newport Beach, CA 92658, USA

Carmen, Julie (Actor)

Carmichael, Al (Athlete, Football Player)
72525 Desert Flower Dr
Palm Desert, CA 92260-6269, USA

Carmichael, Dan (General)
2764 Elm Ave
Columbus, OH 43209-1836, USA

Carmichael, Greg (Musician)
Monterey International
200 W Superior #202
Chicago, IL 60610, USA

Carmichael, Harold (Athlete, Football Player)
38 Birch Ln
Glassboro, NJ 08028, USA

Carmichael, Jesse (Musician)
8062 Woodrow Wilson Dr
Los Angeles, CA 90046, USA

Carmichael, Paul (Athlete, Football Player)
550 Orange Ave Unit 335
Long Beach, CA 90802, USA

Carmichael, Ricky (Motorcycle Racer)
American Honda Motor Co Inc
Motorcycle Sports 100-4C-3B
1919 Torrance Blvd
Torrance, CA 90501, USA

Carmindy (Stylist, Television Host)
Jay at Kramer + Kramer
156 5th Ave Rm 420
New York, NY 10010, USA

Carmine, Michael (Cinematographer)
3615 West Dr
Douglaston, NY 11363, USA

Carmine, Robert (Musician)
c/o Staff Member *Geffen Records*
9126 Sunset Blvd
West Hollywood, CA 90069, USA

Carmody, Steve (Athlete, Football Player)
P.O. Box 119
Jackson, MS 39205, USA

Carmona, Richard Dr (Misc)
5800 Arlington Ave Apt 9K
Bronx, NY 10471-1412, USA

Carmona, Richard H (Government Official, Misc, Physicist)
Surgeon General's Office
200 Independence Ave SW
Washington, DC 20201, USA

Carn, Jean (Musician)
P.O. Box 27641
Philadelphia, PA 19150, USA

Carnahan, Joe (Director)
7715 Southcliff Dr
Fair Oaks, CA 95628, USA

Carnahan, Russ (Congressman, Politician)
1710 Longworth HOB
Washington, DC 20515, USA

Carne, Jean (Music Group)
Walt Reeder Productions
P O Box 27641
Philadelphia, PA 19118, USA

Carne, Judy (Actor, Comedian)
2 Horatio St #10N
New York, NY 10014, USA

Carnegie, Dale (Business Person)
Dale Carnegie & Associates, Inc
290 Motor Pkwy
Hauppauge, NY 11788, USA

Carnelly, Ray (Athlete, Football Player)
4650 Collier St
Apt 135
Beaumont, TX 77706-6999, USA

Carner, Joanne (Athlete, Golfer)
3030 S Ocean Blvd
Apt 325
Palm Beach, FL 33480-6610, USA

Carnes, Kim (Musician, Songwriter)
1829 Tyne Blvd
Nashville, TN 37215, USA

Carnes, Ryan (Actor)
c/o Jon Simmons *Simmons & Scott Entertainment*
4110 W. Burbank Blvd.
Burbank, CA 91505, USA

Carnesale, Albert (Educator)
University of California
Chancellor's Office
Los Angeles, CA 90024, USA

Carnesecca, Lou (Basketball Coach, Coach)
18247 Midland Pkwy
Jamaica, NY 11432-1535, USA

Carnett, Eddie (Athlete, Baseball Player)
RR 1 Box 20C
Ringling, OK 73456-9701, USA

Carnevale, Mark (Athlete, Golfer)
24 Loggerhead Ln
Ponte Vedra Beach, FL 32082-2581, USA

Carney, John (Athlete, Football Player)
2950 Wishbone Way
Encinitas, CA 92024, USA

Carney, Keith (Athlete, Hockey Player, Olympic Athlete)
8701 N 55th Pl
Paradise Valley, AZ 85253-2107, USA

Carney, Lester (Athlete, Olympic Athlete, Track Athlete)
986 Winton Ave
986 Winton Ave, OH 44320-2846, USA

Carney, Reeve (Musician)
c/o Staff Member *Paradigm (Monterey)*
404 W Franklin St
Monterey, CA 93940, USA

Carney, Thomas P (General)
9806 Kirktree Court
Fairfax, VA 22032, USA

Carns, Michael P C (Mike) (General)
966 Coral Dr
Pebble Beach, CA 93953, USA

Caro, Anthony A (Artist, Misc)
111 Frognal Hampstead
London NW3, UNITED KINGDOM (UK)

Caro, Niki (Director, Writer)
c/o Sophy Holodnik *ICM Partners (ICM-LA)*
10250 Constellation Blvd Fl 7
Los Angeles, CA 90067, USA

Caro, Robert A (Writer)
Robert A Caro Assoc
250 W 57th St
New York, NY 10107, USA

Carolan, Brett (Athlete, Football Player)
3218 43rd Ave W
Seattle, WA 98199-2437, USA

Caroline, James C (J C) (Athlete, Football Player)
2501 Stanford Dr
Champaign, IL 61820, USA

Caroline, Princess (Misc)
80 Ave Foch
Paris F-7501, France

Carolla, Adam (Radio Personality, Talk Show Host)
3052 Lake Hollywood Dr
Los Angeles, CA 90068, USA

Carollo, Joe (Athlete, Football Player)
4634 Meyer Way
Carmichael, CA 95608, USA

Carolyn, Avelino (Stylist)
c/o Staff Member *CL Avelino & Associates*
152-1 Singingwood St
Orange, CA 92869, USA

Caron, Alain (Athlete, Hockey Player)
6426 Moorings Point Cir Unit 201
Lakewood Ranch, FL 34202-1204, USA

Caron, Jacques (Athlete, Hockey Player)
6426 Moorings Point Cir Unit 201
Lakewood Ranch, FL 34202-1204

Caron, Jacques (Athlete, Hockey Player)
New Jersey Devils 165 Mulberry St
Attn Special Assignment Coach
Newark, NJ 07102-3607, USA

Caron, Jason (Athlete, Golfer)
150 Silo Ridge Ln
Vilas, NC 28692, USA

Caron, Leslie (Actor, Dancer)
c/o Staff Member *The Rights House (UK)*
Drury House
34-43 Russell St
London WC2B 5HA, UK

Caron, Roger (Athlete, Football Player)
10 Main St
Cheshire, CT 06410-2403, USA

Carothers, Robert L (Educator)
University of Rhode Island
President's Office
Kingston, RI 02881, USA

Carothers, Veronica (Actor)
535 N Heatherstone Dr
Orange, CA 92869, USA

Carpendale, Howard (Actor, Composer)
200 Admiral's Cove Blvd.
Jupiter, FL 33477, USA

Carpenetr, M scott cdr (Astronaut)
PO Box 3161
Vail, CO 81658-3161, USA

Carpenter, Andrew (Athlete, Baseball Player)
1894 SW Mistv_brook Dr
Grants Pass, OR 97527-6441, USA

Carpenter, Bob
205 S Princeton Ave
Arlington Heights, IL 60005-1666, USA

Carpenter, Bob (Bobby) (Athlete, Hockey Player)
P.O. Box 451
Alton Bay, NH 03810, USA

Carpenter, Bobby (Athlete, Football Player)
2396 Andover Rd
Columbus, OH 43221-3744, USA

Carpenter, Brian (Athlete, Football Player)
22018 Auction Barn Dr
Ashburn, VA 20148-4110, USA

Carpenter, Bubba (Athlete, Baseball Player)
4601 Saddlebrook Ave
Springdale, AR 72762-0503, USA

Carpenter, Carleton (Actor)
RR 2 Chardavoyne Road
Warwick, NY 10990, USA

Carpenter, Chad (Athlete, Football Player)
21311 S 187th Way
Queen Creek, AZ 85142-3668, USA

Carpenter, Charisma (Actor, Model)
c/o John Carrabino *John Carrabino Management*
5900 Wilshire Blvd Fl 4 #406
Los Angeles, CA 90036, USA

Carpenter, Chris (Athlete, Baseball Player)
809 S Warson Rd
Saint Louis, MO 63124-1258, USA

Carpenter, Cris (Athlete, Baseball Player)
1484 Heritage Pl
Gainesville, GA 30501-1249, USA

Carpenter, Dave (Cartoonist)
PO Box 520
Emmetsburg, IA 50536-0520, USA

Carpenter, Ed (Race Car Driver)
Vision Racing
6803 Coffman Rd.
Indianapolis, IN 46268, USA

Carpenter, George (War Hero)
1010 Green Hill Drive
Paris, TN 38242-5226, USA

Carpenter, James (Football Player)
c/o Ken Zuckerman *Priority Sports & Entertainment - (LA)*
15233 Ventura Blvd
Suite 718
Sherman Oaks, CA 91403, USA

Carpenter, Jennifer (Actor)
c/o Stephanie Ritz *WME (LA)*
9601 Wilshire Blvd Fl 3
Beverly Hills, CA 90210, USA

Carpenter, John (Director)
8532 Hollywood Blvd
West Hollywood, CA 90069, USA

Carpenter, John M (Opera Singer)
Maurel Enterprises
225 W 34th St #1012
New York, NY 10122, USA

Carpenter, Keion (Athlete, Football Player)
2009 Shin Ct
Buford, GA 30519-6808, USA

Carpenter, Kip (Athlete, Olympic Athlete, Speed Skater)
W375S10897 Prairie Lane
Eagle, WI 53119-1742, USA

Carpenter, Liz (Activist)
116 Skyline Dr
Austin, TX 78746, USA

Carpenter, Marj C (Religious Leader)
Presbyterian Church USA
100 Witherspoon St
Louisville, KY 40202, USA

Carpenter, Mary Chapin (Musician)
6734 Plank Rd
Charlottesville, VA 22903, USA

Carpenter, M Scott (Astronaut)
PO Box 3161
Vail, CO 81658, USA

Carpenter, Patrick (Race Car Driver)
Team Players
2015 Peel
#500
Montreal, PQ H3A 1T8, CANADA

Carpenter, Richard (Musician, Songwriter, Writer)
960 Country Valley Road
Westlake Village, CA 91362, USA

Carpenter, Rob (Athlete, Football Player)
1601 Wheeling Rd NE
Lancaster, OH 43130, USA

Carpenter, Rob (Athlete, Football Player)
1601 Wheeling Rd NE
Lancaster, OH 43130-8706, USA

Carpenter, Ron (Athlete, Football Player)
1181 Chersonese Round
Mount Pleasant, SC 29464, USA

Carpenter, Ron (Athlete, Football Player)
1500 Wade Haven Ct
McKinney, TX 75071, USA

Carpenter, Russell P (Cinematographer)
Gersh Agency
232 N Canon Dr
Beverly Hills, CA 90210, USA

Carpenter, Teresa (Journalist)
Village Voice
Editorial Dept
36 Cooper Square
New York, NY 10003, USA

Carpenter, William S (Bill) Jr (Athlete, Football Player)
P.O. Box 4067
Whitefish, MT 59937, USA

Carpenter, W M (Business Person)
Bausch & Lomb
1 Bausch & Lomb Place
Rochester, NY 14604, USA

Carpenter-Phinney, Connie (Athlete, Cycler, Olympic Athlete)
470 Juniper Ave
Boulder, CO 80304-1716, USA

Carper, Thomas R. (Politician)
600 W Matson Run Pkwy
Washington, DC 19802-1911, USA

Carpin, Frank (Athlete, Baseball Player)
4014 Park Ave
Richmond, VA 23221-1120, USA

Carpinello, James (Actor)
3721 Blue Canyon Dr
Studio City, CA 91604, USA

Carpitella, John J III (Stylist)
1816 Adams Way
Jamison, PA 18929, USA

Carr, Alan (Actor, Writer)
c/o Staff Member *Off The Kerb Productions*
Hammer House, 3rd Fl
113-117 Wardour St
London W1F 0UN, UK

Carr, Antoine (Athlete, Basketball Player)
5724 Croyden Cir
Wichita, KS 67220-3119, USA

Carr, Austin (Athlete, Basketball Player)
4547 Saint Germain Blvd
Cleveland, OH 44128, USA

Carr, Catherine (Cathy) (Swimmer)
409 10th St
Davis, CA 95616, USA

Carr, Charmian (Actor)
P.O. Box 260584
Encino, CA 91426-0584, USA

Carr, Chuck (Athlete, Baseball Player)
4101 NW Expressway
Apt 16178
Oklahoma City, OK 73116, USA

Carr, Darleen (Actor)
Abrams Artists
9200 Sunset Blvd #1125
Los Angeles, CA 90069, USA

Carr, David (Athlete, Football Player)
c/o Jeff Sperbeck *The Novo Agency*
2121 N. Califorña Blvd
Suite 1025
Walnut Creek, CA 94596, USA

Carr, Edwin (Athlete, Football Player)
1908 Scott Rd
Oreland, PA 19075, USA

Carr, Fred (Athlete, Football Player)
6274 S 17th Pl
Phoenix, AZ 85042, USA

Carr, Gene (Athlete, Hockey Player)
P.O. Box 57258
Sherman Oaks, CA 91413, USA

Carr, Gerald (Astronaut)
49 Maple St.
Apt 123
Manchester Center, VT 05255-4485, USA

Carr, Gerald P Colonel (Astronaut)
49 Maple St Apt 123
Manchester Center, VT 05255-4485, USA

Carr, Gregg (Athlete, Football Player)
4314 Kennesaw Dr
Birmingham, AL 35213, USA

Carr, Henry (Athlete, Football Player)
3653 Summerwind Cir
Bradenton, FL 34209, USA

Carr, Henry (Athlete, Olympic Athlete, Track Athlete)
3653 Summerwind Cir
Bradenton, FL 34209-5807, USA

Carr, James H (Athlete, Football Player)
13718 Indigo Ln
Fishers, IN 46038, USA

Carr, Jane (Actor)
6200 Mount Angelus Dr
Los Angeles, CA 90042, USA

Carr, Kenneth (General)
38 Atlantic Ave
Groton, CT 06340-8801, USA

Carr, Kenny (Athlete, Basketball Player,
Olympic Athlete)
1210 W Adams Blvd
Apt 106
Los Angeles, CA 90007-7700, USA

Carr, Levert (Athlete, Football Player)
169 Brookwood Ln W
Bolingbrook, IL 60440, USA

Carr, Lloyd (Coach)
University of Michigan
Athletic Dept
Ann Arbor, MI 48109, USA

Carr, Lydell (Athlete, Football Player)
2217 Harrisburg Ln
Plano, TX 75025, USA

Carr, Michael L (M L) (Athlete, Basketball
Player, Coach)
168 Beaver Road
Weston, MA 02493, USA

Carr, M L (Basketball Player)
St Louis Spirits
168 Beaver Rd
Weston, MA 02493-1036, USA

Carr, M L (Athlete, Basketball Player)
168 Beaver Rd
Weston, MA 02493-1036, USA

Carr, M L
168 Beaver Rd
Weston, MA 02493-1036, United States

Carr, Nathaniel (Athlete, Olympic
Athlete, Wrestler)
9401 Foxburrow Way
Dayton, OH 45458-9623, USA

Carr, Roger D (Athlete, Football Player)
101 Green Forest Dr
Monroe, LA 71203, USA

Carr, Steve (Director, Producer)
c/o Nicole Chabot *Re: Group*
8687 Melrose Ave
8th Floor
West Hollywood, CA 90069, USA

Carr, Vikki (Actor, Musician)
Po Box 780968
San Antonio, TX 78278, USA

Carrabba, Chris (Musician)
323 NW 9th Terr
Boca Raton, FL 33486, USA

Carrack, Paul (Musician, Songwriter,
Writer)
Firstars Mgmt
14724 Ventura Blvd
#PH
Sherman Oaks, CA 91403, USA

Carradine, Ever (Actor)
c/o Lainie Sorkin Becky *Management 360*
9111 Wilshire Blvd
Beverly Hills, CA 90210, USA

Carradine, Keith (Actor, Musician,
Songwriter)
10895 Willowcrest Pl
Studio City, CA 91604, USA

Carradine, Robert (Actor, Director,
Producer)
c/o Staff Member *Marshak/Zachary
Company, The*
8840 Wilshire Blvd
1st Floor
Beverly Hills, CA 90210, USA

Carragher, Jamie (Soccer Player)
The FA
25 Soho Square
London W1D 4FA, UNITED KINGDOM

Carrasco, D J (Athlete, Baseball Player)
1216 W 18th St
Safford, AZ 85546-3564, USA

Carre, Isabelle (Actor)
c/o Staff Member *Agence Intertalent*
5 Rue Gay Lusac
Paris 75008, France

Carreira, Tony (Composer, Musician)
Rua Helena Felix N 30 4 Esq
Palhais, Charneca Da Caparica 2820-595,
Portugal

Carreker, Alphonso (Athlete, Football
Player)
5599 Asheforde Ln
Marietta, GA 30068, USA

Carrelas, Gina (Stylist)
c/o Staff Member *Help Me Rhonda*
541 10th St NW #294
Atlanta, GA 30318, USA

Carrell, Duane (Athlete, Football Player)
6525 Willow Springs Rd
Springfield, IL 62712, USA

Carrell, John (Athlete, Football Player)
2303 Cliffs Edge Dr
Austin, TX 78733, USA

Carreno, J Manuel (Ballerina)
Royal Ballet
Covent Garden
Bow St
London WC2E 9DD, USA

Carreon, Mark (Athlete, Baseball Player)
413 Ashland Crk
Victoria, TX 77901-3687, USA

Carrera, Asia (Adult Film Star)
c/o Staff Member *Atlas Multimedia Inc*
9005 Eton Ave Ste C
Canoga Park, CA 91304-1743, USA

Carrera, Barbara (Actor)
9191 Burton Way
Beverly Hills, CA 90210, USA

Carrera, Carlos (Director)
c/o Staff Member *Creative Artists Agency
(CAA-LA)*
2000 Ave Of The Stars
Los Angeles, CA 90067, USA

Carreras, Jose (Opera Singer)
c/o Darcy Gregoire *Agency Group Ltd,
The (Canada)*
2 Berkeley Street
Suite 202
Toronto M5A 4J5, Canada

Carrere, Tia (Actor, Model, Producer)
21051 Saddle Peak Rd
Topanga, CA 90290, USA

Carretto, Joseph A
2006 Stillwater Dr
Friendswood, TX 77546-7851, USA

Carretto, Joseph A Jr (Astronaut)
4534 E 85th St
Tulsa, OK 74137, USA

Carrey, Jim (Actor, Comedian)
615 N Tigertail Rd
Los Angeles, CA 90049, USA

Carrick, Michael (Soccer Player)
The FA
25 Soho Square
London W1D 4FA, UNITED KINGDOM

Carrier, Darel (Athlete, Basketball Player)
4224 Glasgow Road
Oakland, KY 42159-6836, USA

Carrier, George F (Mathematician)
PO Box 5039
Wayland, MA 01778-6039, USA

Carrier, Mark A (Athlete, Football Player)
4115 Highland Park Cir
Lutz, FL 33558, USA

Carriere, Jean P J (Writer)
Les Broussanes Domessargues
Ledignan 30350, FRANCE

carriere, Larry (Athlete, Hockey Player)
94 Dawnbrook Ln
Buffalo, NY 14221-4932, USA

Carriere, Mathieu (Actor)
Agentur Schafer
Friesenstr 53
Cologne 50670, GERMANY

Carrigan, Sam (Athlete, Baseball Player)
607 Sunrise Ave
Alamogordo, NM 88310, USA

Carril, Pete (Athlete, Basketball Player,
Coach)
372 Carter Rd
Princeton, NJ 08540-7422, USA

Carrillo, Cesar (Athlete, Baseball Player)
2716 W 47th St # 1
Chicago, IL 60632-1931, USA

Carrillo, Elpidia (Actor)
Bresler Kelly Assoc
11500 W Olympic Blvd
#510
Los Angeles, CA 90064, USA

Carrillo, Erick (Actor)
c/o Staff Member *Three Moons
Entertainment Inc*
7040-F W Sunset Blvd #206
Los Angeles, CA 90028, USA

Carrillo, Yadhira (Actor)
c/o Staff Member *Televisa*
Blvd Adolfo Lopez Mateos 232
Colonia San Angel INN
DF CP 01060, MEXICO

Carrington, Alan (Misc)
46 Lakewood Road
Chandler's Ford
Hants SO53 1EX, UNITED KINGDOM
(UK)

Carrington, Alex (Athlete, Football Player)
c/o Roosevelt Barnes *Maximum Sports
Management*
6435 W Jefferson Blvd
#197
Fort Wayne, IN 46804, USA

Carrington, Bob (Athlete, Basketball
Player)
P.O. Box 131301
Carlsbad, CA 92013-1301, USA

Carrington, Chuck (Actor)
c/o Kate Edwards *Grand View
Management*
578 Washington Blvd #688
Marina del Rey, CA 90292, USA

Carrington, Darren (Athlete, Football
Player)
14097 Montfort Ct
San Diego, CA 92128, USA

Carrington, Debbie Lee (Actor)
Jonis
8147 Tunney Ave
Reseda, CA 91335, USA

Carrington, Paul (Attorney, Educator)
Duke University
Law School
Durham, NC 27708, USA

Carrington, Peter A R (Government
Official)
Manor House
Bledlow near Aylesbury
Bucks HP17 9PE, UNITED KINGDOM
(UK)

Carrithers, Don (Athlete, Baseball Player)
9367 Sunny Glade Ct
Elk Grove, CA 95758-4208, USA

Carr of Hadley, L Robert (Government
Official)
14 North Court
Great Peter St
London SW1 3LL, UNITED KINGDOM
(UK)

Carroll, Ahmad (Athlete, Football Player)
1389 Pollard Dr SW
Atlanta, GA 30311, USA

Carroll, Billy (Athlete, Hockey Player)
Carroll Home Improvements
239 Station St
Ajax, ON L1S 1S3, Canada

Carroll, Brett (Athlete, Baseball Player)
Florida Marlins 2267 NW 199th St
Miami Gardens, FL 33056-^664, USA

Carroll, Brian (Buckethead) (Musician)
915-C West Foothill Blvd
Suite 545
Claremont, CA 91711, USA

Carroll, Bruce (Musician, Songwriter,
Writer)
William Morris Agency
2100 W End Ave #1000
Nashville, TN 37203, USA

Carroll, Clay P (Athlete, Baseball Player)
12475 Burrouehs Ln
Soddv Daisv, TN 37379-9119, USA

Carroll, Diahann (Actor, Musician)
9255 Doheny Rd. #1705
West Hollywood, CA 90069, USA

Carroll, James (Athlete, Football Player)
13880 Stirling Rd
Southwest Ranches, FL 33330, USA

Carroll, Jamey (Athlete, Baseball Player)
3492 Siderwheel Dr
Rockledge, FL 32955-6031, USA

Carroll, Jay (Athlete, Football Player)
117 Homedale Rd
Hopkins, MN 55343, USA

Carroll, Jim (Athlete, Football Player)
13880 Stirling Rd
Southwest Ranches, FL 33330, USA

Carroll, Joe (Athlete, Football Player)
4541 Fairfield St
Pittsburgh, PA 15201, USA

Carroll, Joe Barry (Athlete, Basketball Player)
5220 Cascade Rd SW
Atlanta, GA 30331-7358, USA

Carroll, Julian (Politician)
413 Shelby St
Frankfort, KY 40601-2821, USA

Carroll, Kent J (Admiral)
Country Club of North Carolina
1600 Morganton Road
#30X
Pinehurst, NC 28374, USA

Carroll, Leo (Athlete, Football Player)
34448 Agua Dulce Canyon Rd
Santa Clarita, CA 91390, USA

Carroll, Lester (Les) (Cartoonist)
1715 Ivyhill Loop N
Columbus, OH 43229, USA

Carroll, Madeline (Actor)
c/o Susan Curtis *Curtis Talent Management*
9607 Arby Dr
Beverly Hills, CA 90210, USA

Carroll, Matt (Athlete, Basketball Player)
300 West Fifth Street
Unit 604
Charlotte, NC 28202, USA

Carroll, Pat (Actor)
c/o Gabrielle Allabashi *Ellis Talent Group*
4705 Laurel Canyon Blvd
Suite 300
Valley Village, CA 91607, USA

Carroll, Pete (Athlete, Football Player)
0 Openbrand Rd
Rolling Hills, CA 90274, USA

Carroll, Rocky (Actor)
c/o Erik Kritzer *Kritzer Levine Wilkins Entertainment (KLWG)*
11872 La Grange Ave
1st Floor
Los Angeles, CA 90025, USA

Carroll, Ron (Ronnie) (Athlete, Football Player)
3320 La Vista Ave
Bay City, TX 77414-2793, USA

Carroll, Sonny (Athlete, Baseball Player)
3311 Lawson St
Richmond, VA 23224, USA

Carroll, Tom (Athlete, Baseball Player)
38572 Pheasant Hill Ln
Hamilton, VA 20158-3302, USA

Carroll, Tom (Tommy) (Athlete, Baseball Player)
304 Sonnet Ct
Peachtree City, GA 30269-3357, USA

Carroll, Wesley (Athlete, Football Player)
11740 SW 102nd St
Miami, FL 33186, USA

Carroll, Willard (Director, Producer, Writer)
c/o Staff Member *Hyperion Pictures*
111 N Maryland Ave #300
Glendale, CA 91206, USA

Carrozzi, Chris (Athlete, Hockey Player)
101 Marketta St. NW
#1900
Atlanta 30303

Carruth, Paul (Athlete, Football Player)
373 Brentwood Ave
Trussville, AL 35173, USA

Carruth, Rae (Athlete, Football Player)
12653 Tucker Crossing Ln
Charlotte, NC 28273, USA

Carruthers, Dwight (Athlete, Hockey Player)
9513 W Nelson Dr
Nine Mile Falls, WA 99026-9620, USA

Carruthers, Garrey E (Politician)
1 Mansion Dr
Santa Fe, NM 88011, USA

Carruthers, James H (Red) (Skier)
8 Malone Ave
Garnerville, NY 10923, USA

Carruthers, Peter (Athlete, Figure Skater, Olympic Athlete)
239 Via Monterey
Newbury Park, CA 91320-6824, USA

Carsey, Marcia L P (Producer)
Carsey-Warner Productions
4024 Radford Ave
Building 3
Studio City, CA 91604, USA

Carsey, Marcy (Producer)
c/o Staff Member *Carsey-Werner-Mandabach*
16027 Ventura Blvd
6th Floor
Encino, CA 91436, USA

Carson, Andre (Congressman, Politician)
425 Cannon HOB
Washington, DC 20515, USA

Carson, Benjamin S (Doctor)
Johns Hopkins University
Medical Center
Baltimore, MD 21218, USA

Carson, Carlos A (Athlete, Football Player)
4747 W 150th Ter
Overland Park, KS 66224-3410, USA

Carson, Charlotte (Stylist)
c/o Staff Member *Judy Inc*
1 Yorkville Ave
Toronto ON M4W 1L1, Canada

Carson, Crystal (Actor)
6725 McLennan Ave
Van Nuys, CA 91406, USA

Carson, David (Director)
c/o Chris Simonian *Creative Artists Agency (CAA-LA)*
2000 Ave Of The Stars
Los Angeles, CA 90067, USA

Carson, Harold (Athlete, Football Player)
Harry Carson Inc
P.O. Box 852
Westwood, NJ 07675, USA

Carson, Hunter (Actor)
c/o Staff Member *Elkins Entertainment*
8306 Wilshire Blvd
Suite 438
Beverly Hills, CA 90211, USA

Carson, James (Jimmy) (Athlete, Hockey Player)
1154 Ridgeway Dr
Rochester, MI 48307-1771, USA

Carson, Jeff (Musician)
1104 Hunting Creek Road
Franklin, TN 37069-4754, USA

Carson, Leonardo (Athlete, Football Player)
9728 Windy Hollow Dr
Irving, TX 75063

Carson, Lindsay (Athlete, Hockey Player)
5050 40th Street
NE, Calgary T3J 4P8, Canada

Carson, Lisa Nicole (Actor)
c/o Scott Zimmerman *Evolution Entertainment (LA)*
901 N Highland Ave
Los Angeles, CA 90038, USA

Carson, Malcolm (Athlete, Football Player)
P.O. Box 11847
Birmingham, AL 35202, USA

Carson, Matt (Athlete, Baseball Player)
33352 Madera De Playa
Temecula, CA 92592-9289, USA

Carson, Rachelle (Actor)
c/o Staff Member *JC Robbins Management*
113 S Kilkea Dr
Los Angeles, CA 90048, USA

Carson, T C
1505 10th St
Santa Monica, CA 90401, USA

Carson, William H (Willie) (Jockey)
Minster House
Bamsley
Cirencester, Glos, UNITED KINGDOM (UK)

Carsten, Peter
Photography & Film
Meilenberger Str. 1
Icking-Dorfen G-82057, Germany

Carstens, Jordan (Athlete, Football Player)
2487 140th St
Bagley, IA 50026, USA

Carswell, Diana L (Stylist)
PO Box 7996
McLean, VA 22106, USA

Carswell, Dwayne (Athlete, Football Player)
8202 Abbeyfield Dr
Jacksonville, FL 32277, USA

Carswell, Robert (Athlete, Football Player)
5906 Heritage Walk
Lithonia, GA 30058, USA

Cartagena, Victoria (Actor)
c/o Larry Taube *Principal Entertainment (LA)*
1964 Westwood Blvd #400
Los Angeles, CA 90025, USA

Carter, Aaron (Actor, Musician)
c/o Jane Carter *Spectra Management*
9300 Overseas Hwy
Marathon, FL 33050

Carter, Alex (Actor)
c/o Richard Caplan *Noble Caplan Abrams*
1260 Yonge St
2nd Floor
Toronto, ON M4T 1W6, Canada

Carter, Allen (Athlete, Football Player)
13133 Le Parc
Unit 609
Chino Hills, CA 91709, USA

Carter, Amy (Misc)
1 Woodland Dr.
Plains, GA 31780, USA

Carter, Andy (Athlete, Baseball Player)
106 Montgomery Ave
Glenside, PA 19038-8228, USA

Carter, Anson (Athlete, Hockey Player)
820 Haven Oaks Ct NE
Atlanta, GA 30342-4348, USA

Carter, Anthony (Athlete, Football Player)
4314 Danielson Dr
Lake Worth, FL 33467, USA

Carter, Anthony (Athlete, Basketball Player)
15250 E Caley Ave
Centennial, CO 80016-1058, USA

Carter, Antonio (Athlete, Football Player)
7839 Maple Grove Dr
Lewis Center, OH 43035, USA

Carter, Bernard (Athlete, Football Player)
261 Pinestraw Cir
Altamonte Springs, FL 32714, USA

Carter, Beth (Stylist)
c/o Staff Member *Karlee Artist Management*
2658 Griffith Park Blvd
#171
Los Angeles, CA 90039, USA

Carter, Betsy (Musician)
7561 Brush Lake Road
North Lewisburg, OH 43060

Carter, Billy (Athlete, Hockey Player)
28 Dale St RR 3
Ingleside, ON K0C lM0, Canada

Carter, Carl (Athlete, Football Player)
3256 Centennial Rd
Fort Worth, TX 76119, USA

Carter, Carl (Athlete, Football Player)
7568 Kings Trl
Fort Worth, TX 76133, USA

Carter, Cheryl (Actor)
CunninghamEscottDipene
10635 Santa Monica Blvd
#130
Los Angeles, CA 90025, USA

Carter, Chris (Athlete, Football Player)
606 American Falls Dr
Rio Vista, CA 94571-2205, USA

Carter, Chris (Producer)
566 Picacho Ln
Montecito, CA 93108, USA

Carter, Clarence (Athlete, Basketball Player)
300 Love St SW
Atlanta, GA 30315-1048, USA

Carter, Clarence (Musician)
Rodgers Redding
1048 Tatnall St
Macon, GA 31201, USA

Carter, Cris (Athlete, Football Player)
2493 NW 46th St
Boca Raton, FL 33431, USA

Carter, Darren (Comedian)
c/o Staff Member *WmE2 (WMA-LA)*
1 William Morris Pl
Beverly Hills, CA 90212, USA

Carter, David (Athlete, Football Player)
2401 Long Reach Dr
Sugar Land, TX 77478, USA

Carter, Deana (Musician, Songwriter)
7708 Waring Ave.
Los Angeles, CA 90046, USA

Carter, Deanna (Actor, Musician)
c/o John Huie *Creative Artists Agency*
(CAA-TN)
3310 West End Ave
5th Floor
Nashville, TN 37203, USA

Carter, Dexter A (Athlete, Football Player)
13715 Richmond Park Dr N
Unit 1205
Jacksonville, FL 32224, USA

Carter, Dr Jay (Writer)
PO Box 6048
Wyomissing, PA 19610, USA

Carter, Duane (Pancho) (Race Car Driver)
32 Forest
Brownsburg, IN 46112, USA

Carter, Dyshod (Athlete, Football Player)
916 W Carter Rd
Phoenix, AZ 85041, USA

Carter, Finn (Actor)
c/o Craig Dorfman *Frontline Management*
5670 Wilshire Blvd.
Suite 1370
Los Angeles, CA 90036, USA

Carter, Frank (Misc)
Glass Molders Pottery Plastics Union
608 E Baltimore Pike
Media, PA 19063, USA

Carter, Fred (Athlete, Basketball Player)
2617 Dekalb Pike
Norristown, PA 19401-1838, USA

Carter, Frederick J (Fred) (Baseball
Player, Coach)
5070 Parkside Ave
#3500
Philadelphia, PA 19131, USA

Carter, Gerald (Athlete, Football Player)
3917 Cheshire Ct
Byran, TX 77802, USA

Carter, Graydon (Editor)
Vanity Fair Magazine
Editorial Dept.
350 Madison Ave.
New York, NY 10017, USA

Carter, Herbert E (Biologist, Educator)
2401 Cerrada de Promesa
Tucson, AZ 85718, USA

Carter, Hodding (Journalist)
1643 Brickell Ave Apt 3604
Miami, FL 33129-1297, USA

Carter, Hodding III (Government Official)
c/o Staff Member *Random House
Publicity (Toronto)*
1 Toronto St
Suite 300
Toronto, ON M5C 2V6, Canada

Carter, Howard (Athlete, Basketball
Player)
8026 Jefferson Hwy
Apt 112
Baton Rouge, LA 70809-1661, USA

Carter, Jack (Actor, Comedian)
1023 Chevy Chase Dr
Beverly Hills, CA 90210, USA

Carter, Jake (Athlete, Basketball Player)
4632 Country Creek Dr
Apt 1220
Dallas, TX 75236-1253, USA

Carter, Jay (Musician)
Brothers Mgmt
141 Dunbar Ave
Fords, NJ 08863, USA

Carter, Jeff (Athlete, Baseball Player)
4625 River Overlook Dr
Valrico, FL 33596-7878, USA

Carter, Jim (Athlete, Golfer)
12575 N 130th Way
Scottsdale, AZ 85259-3542, USA

Carter, Jim (Athlete, Football Player)
1500 Morning Glory Ln
Wausau, WI 54401, USA

Carter, Jimmy (Nobel Prize Laureate)
The Carter Center_453 Freedom Pkwy NE
Atlanta, GA 30307-1406, USA

Carter, Jodie (Athlete, Football Player)
5921 Timberview Rd
Little Rock, AR 72204, USA

Carter, Joe (Athlete, Baseball Player)
3000 W 117th St
Leawood, KS 66211-2923, USA

Carter, John (Athlete, Hockey Player)
27 Country Ln
Sharon, MA 02067-2339, USA

Carter, John (Musician)
Resort Attractions
2375 E Tropicana Ave
#304
Las Vegas, NV 89119, USA

Carter, John Mack (Editor)
Good Housekeeping Magazine
Editorial Dept
959 8th Ave
New York, NY 10019, USA

Carter, Kent (Athlete, Football Player)
18657 Klum Pl
Rowland Heights, CA 91748, USA

Carter, Kevin (Athlete, Football Player)
1070 Vaughn Crest Ct
Franklin, TN 37069, USA

Carter, Kevin (Athlete, Football Player)
17111 Journeys End Dr
Odessa, FL 33556-2442, USA

Carter, Ki-Jana (Athlete, Football Player)
1293 NW 121st Ave
Plantation, FL 33323, USA

Carter, Lance (Athlete, Baseball Player)
13805 18th Pl E
Bradenton, FL 34212, USA

Carter, Larry (Athlete, Baseball Player)
4305 Wilmette Dr
Denton, TX 76208, USA

Carter, Louis (Athlete, Football Player)
8209 Swamp Rose Pl
Laurel, MD 20724, USA

Carter, Louis (Athlete, Football Player)
8209 Swamp Rose Pl
Laurel, MD 20724-1963, USA

Carter, Lyle (Athlete, Hockey Player)
13 Hamilton Ave
Brookfield, NS B0N 1C0, Canada

Carter, Lynda (Actor)
9200 Harrington Dr
Potomac, MD 20854, USA

Carter, Marshall N (Financier)
State Street Corp
225 Franklin St
Boston, MA 02110, USA

Carter, Marty (Athlete, Football Player)
1397 Waterford Green Dr
Marietta GA 30068-2927,
GA 30068-2927, USA

Carter, Mel (Musician)
Cape Entertainment
1161 NW 76th Ave
Plantation, FL 33322, USA

Carter, Michael (Actor)
London Mgmt
2-4 Noel St
London W1V 3RB, UNITED KINGDOM
(UK)

Carter, Michael D (Athlete, Football
Player)
901 Red Oak Creek Dr
Red Oak, TX 75154, USA

Carter, Michael D (Athlete, Football
Player)
901 Red Oak Creek Dr
Red Oak, TX 75154-3615, USA

Carter, Mike (Baseball Player)
Atlanta Braves
12215 Magnolia Crescent Dr Apt D
Roswell, GA 30075-5568, USA

Carter, Mike (Athlete, Football Player)
10705 CeleoLn
San Jose, CA 95127, USA

Carter, M L (Athlete, Football Player)
PO Box 1971
Seaside, CA 93955, USA

Carter, M L (Athlete, Football Player)
1765 Napa St
Seaside, CA 93955-4018, USA

Carter, Nathan (Actor)
c/o Norbert Abrams *Noble Caplan
Abrams*
1260 Yonge St
2nd Floor
Toronto ON M4T 1W6, Canada

Carter, Nick (Musician, Songwriter)
1577 Championship Blvd
Franklin, TN 37064, USA

Carter, Pat (Athlete, Football Player)
11321 Cambray Creek Loop
Riverview, FL 33579, USA

Carter, Paula (Bowler)
10331 SW 102nd Ave
Miami, FL 33176-3507, USA

Carter, Perry (Athlete, Football Player)
15719 Sweeny Park Ln
Houston, TX 77084, USA

Carter, Powell F Jr (General)
699 Fillmore St
Harpers Ferry, WV 25425, USA

Carter, Quinton (Athlete, Football Player)
3922 Crooked Oak St
North Las Vegas, NV 89032

Carter, Rachel (Aviator)
P.O. Box 1663
Julian, CA 92036-1663, USA

Carter, Rodney (Athlete, Football Player)
4490 Jasmine Dr
Bethlehem, PA 18020, USA

Carter, Ronald L (Ron) (Composer,
Musician)
Bridge Agency
35 Clark St
#A5
Brooklyn, NY 11201, USA

Carter, Rosalynn (First Lady, Politician)
Carter Center
The Carter Center 453 Freedom Pkwy NE
Atlanta, GA 30307-1406, USA

Carter, Rosana (Opera Singer)
Angel Records
150 5th Ave
New York, NY 10011, USA

Carter, Rubin (Athlete, Coach, Football
Player)
1793 Vineyard Way
Tallahassee, FL 32317-7915, USA

Carter, Rubin (Hurricane) (Boxer)
*Assoc in Defense of the Wrongly
Convicted*
85 King St E #318
Toronto, ON M5C 1G3, CANADA

Carter, Rublin (Athlete, Football Player)
1793 Vineyard Way
Tallahassee, FL 32317, USA

Carter, Russell (Athlete, Football Player)
216 Lilac Ln
Douglassville, PA 19518, USA

Carter, Sarah (Actor)
c/o Darren Goldberg *Global Creative*
1051 Cole Ave # B
Los Angeles, CA 90038, USA

Carter, Stephen L (Attorney, Attorney
General, General, Writer)
Yale University
Law School
New Haven, CT 06520, USA

Carter, Steve (Athlete, Baseball Player)
13006 Innisbrook Dr
Beltsville, MD 20705-1196, USA

Carter, Terry (Actor)
244 Madison Ave
#332
New York, NY 10016, USA

Carter, Thomas (Director)
140 N Tigertail Rd
Los Angeles, CA 90049, USA

Carter, Tim (Athlete, Football Player)
4860 26th Ct S
Saint Petersburg, FL 33712, USA

Carter, Tom (Athlete, Golfer)
3787 County Line Rd
Quakertown, PA 18951-2085, USA

Carter, Tom (Athlete, Football Player)
4548 Bristol Ln
Cincinnati, OH 45229, USA

Carter, Tony (Athlete, Football Player)
7839 Maple Grove Dr
Lewis Center, OH 43035, USA

Carter, Travis (Race Car Driver)
Carter Motorsports
2668 Peachtree Rd.
Statesville, NC 28625-8252, USA

Carter, Vince (Athlete, Basketball Player)
PO Box 9596
Daytona Beach, FL 32120, USA

Carter, Virgil (Athlete, Football Player)
PO Box 9
Helendale, CA 92342, USA

Carter III, W Hodding (Government
Official)
214 N Columbus
Alexandria, VA 22314, USA

Carteris, Gabrielle (Actor)
4019 Longridge Ave
Sherman Oaks, CA 91423, USA

Carter Jr, James E (Jimmy) (Ex-President, Nobel Prize Laureate, Politician, President)
Carter Presidential Center
1 Copenhill Ave. NE
Atlanta, GA 30307, USA

Carter's Chord (Music Group)
c/o Staff Member *Paradigm (Monterey)*
404 W Franklin St
Monterey, CA 93940, USA

Carthen, Jason (Athlete, Football Player)
10310 Townley Ct
Aurora, OH 44202, USA

Carthon, Maurice (Athlete, Football Player)
4515 Walnut St
Kansas City, MO 64111, USA

Carthy, Eliza (Musician)
c/o Staff Member *Agency Group Ltd, The (NY)*
142 West 57th St
6th Floor
New York, NY 10019, USA

Cartier, Jean-Yves (Athlete, Hockey Player)
815 Bel-Air St
Montreal, QC H4C 2K4, Canada

Cartwright, Angela (Actor)
4330 Bakman Ave
N Hollywood, CA 91602, USA

Cartwright, Bill (Athlete, Basketball Player)
1839 Wedgewood Ct
Lake Forest, IL 60045-3705, USA

Cartwright, Catherine (Athlete, Golfer)
28382 Tasca Dr
Bonita Springs, FL 34135, USA

Cartwright, James F (General)
Director Structure Resources Assessment
HqUSMC Navy Station
Washington, DC 20380, USA

Cartwright, Nancy (Actor)
The Nancy Show
9420 Reseda Blvd #572
Northridge, CA 91324, USA

Cartwright, Rock (Athlete, Football Player)
231 Interstate 45 N
Apt 21115
Conroe, TX 77304, USA

Cartwright, Ryan (Actor)
c/o Susan Calogerakis *Thruline Entertainment*
9250 Wilshire Blvd
Ground Fl
Beverly Hills, CA 90212, USA

Cartwright, Veronica (Actor)
c/o Mitch Clem *Shadow Entertainment*
10 Universal City Plz
20th Floor
Universal City, CA 91608, USA

Carty, Jay (Athlete, Basketball Player)
5425 Lower Honoapiilani Rd
Lahaina, HI 96761-8766, USA

Carty, Johndale (Athlete, Football Player)
PO Box 552076
Opa Locka, FL 33055, USA

Carty, Rico (Athlete, Baseball Player)
5 Ens Enriquillo
San Pedro de Macoris, Dominican Republic

Caruana, Patrick P (Sat) (General)
1922 Havemeyer Lane
Redondo Beach, CA 90278, USA

Caruana, Peter R (Politician)
Chief Minister's Office
10/3 Irish Town
GIBRALTAR

Caruso, Ann S (Stylist)
69 5th Ave
#10-A
New York, NY 10003, USA

Caruso, David (Actor)
4134 Murietta Ave
Sherman Oaks, CA 91423, USA

Caruso, D.J. (Director)
c/o Geyer Kosinski *Media Talent Group*
9200 Sunset Blvd
Suite 550
Los Angeles, CA 90069, USA

Caruso, Mike (Athlete, Baseball Player)
900 N Ocean Blvd
Apt E
Pompano Beach, FL 33062-4045, USA

Carver, Brent (Actor, Musician)
Live Entertainment
1500 Broadway
#902
New York, NY 10036, USA

Carver, Dale (Athlete, Football Player)
1745 Golfview Dr
Titusville, FL 32780, USA

Carver, Dana (Actor, Comedian)
775 E Blithedale Ave SE
#501
Mill Valley, CA 94941, USA

Carver, Johnny (Musician)
House of Talent
9 Lucy Lane
Sherwood, AR 72120, USA

Carver, Melvin (Mel) (Athlete, Football Player)
10840 Breaking Rocks Dr
Lithia, FL 33547, USA

Carver, Randall (Actor)
Tyler Kjar
5144 Vineland Ave
North Hollywood, CA 91601, USA

Carver, Richard (War Hero)
Wood End House
Wickham near Fareham
Hants, England P017 7JZ, UK

Carver, Richard
Wood End House
Wickham near Fareham
Hants, England P017 7JZ, UK

Carver, Richard
Wood End House
Wickham near Fareham
Hants, England P017 7JZ, United Kingdom

Carver, Shante (Athlete, Football Player)
2834 S Extension Rd Unit 2033
Mesa, AZ 85210, USA

Carveth-Dunn, Betty (Athlete, Baseball Player, Commentator)
11531 77th Avenue
Edmonton, AB T6G 0M2, CANADA

Carvey, Dana (Actor)
1 Roosevelt Ave
Mill Valley, CA 94941, USA

Carvilie, C James Jr (Politician)
209 Pennsylvania Ave SE
#800
Washington, DC 20003, USA

Carville, James (Television Host)
424 S Washington St
Alexandria, VA 22314-3630, USA

Carville, James (Journalist)
1711 Palmer Ave
New Orleans, LA 70118-6115, USA

Cary, Chuck (Athlete, Baseball Player)
1016 Stephen Dr
Niceville, FL 32578-2330, USA

Cary, Diane (Baby Peggy) Serra (Actor)
712 5th Ave
Gustine, CA 95322, USA

Cary, Duane G (Astronaut)
5938 Instone Circle
Colorado Springs, CO 80922-1716, USA

Cary, W Sterling (Religious Leader)
2344 Vardon Lane
Flossmoor, IL 60422-1363, USA

Cary Brothers (Music Group)
c/o Staff Member *Paradigm (Monterey)*
404 W Franklin St
Monterey, CA 93940, USA

casa, Joseh
11134 Speedway Dr
Shelby Township, MI 48317-3546, USA

Casablancas, Julian (Musician, Songwriter)
c/o Staff Member *Wiz Kid Management*
123 East 7th St
New York, NY 10009, USA

Casadesus, Jean-Claude (Conductor)
23 Blvd de la Liberte
Lille 59800, FRANCE

Casados, Eloy (Actor)
c/o Michelle Gordon *Michelle Gordon & Assoc*
260 S Beverly Dr
Beverly Hills, CA 90212, USA

Casados, Rene (Actor)
c/o Staff Member *Televisa*
Blvd Adolfo Lopez Mateos 232
Colonia San Angel INN
DF CP 01060, MEXICO

Casady, Jack (Musician)
Ron Rainey Mgmt
315 S Beverly Dr
#407
Beverly Hills, CA 90212, USA

Casale, Gerald (Musician)
7960 Fareholm Dr
Los Angeles, CA 90046, USA

Casale, Jerry (Athlete, Baseball Player)
600 County Ave
Apt 408
Secaucus, NJ 07094-2610, USA

Casali, Kim (Cartoonist)
Times-Mirror Syndicate
Times-Mirror Square
Los Angeles, CA 90053, USA

Casals, Rosemary (Rosie) (Tennis Player)
Sportswoman Inc
PO Box 537
Sausalito, CA 94966, USA

Casals, Rosemary (Rosie) (Athlete, Tennis Player)
c/o Staff Member *International Tennis Hall Of Fame*
194 Bellevue Ave
Newport, RI 02840, USA

Casanega, Ken (Athlete, Football Player)
37405 Westridge Ave
Palm Desert, CA 92211, USA

Casanova, Paul (Athlete, Baseball Player)
5370 NW 183rd St
Miami Gardens, FL 33055-2304, USA

Casanova, Raul (Athlete, Baseball Player)
1441 Ortiz Ave
Fort Myers, FL 3905-4903, USA

Casanova, Thomas H (Tommy) (Athlete, Football Player)
345 Casanova Rd
Crowley, LA 70526, USA

Casares, Ricardo (Rick) (Athlete, Football Player)
4107 Starfish Ln
Tampa, FL 33615, USA

Casbarian, John (Architect)
Taft Architects
2370 Rice Blvd
#112
Houston, TX 77005, USA

Cascada (Musician)
Blue Art Event GmbH
c/o Frank Ehrlich
Varlar 41
D- 48720, Rosendahl, GERMANY

Cascadden, Chad (Athlete, Football Player)
2611 Winsor Dr
Eau Claire, WI 54703, USA

Cascio, Frank (Writer)
c/o Staff Member *HarperCollins Publishers*
10 East 53rd St
c/o Author mail, 7th Floor
New York, NY 10022, USA

Case, John (Writer)
Random House
1745 Broadway
#B1
New York, NY 10019, USA

Case, J Scott (Athlete, Football Player)
4930 Price Dr
Suwanee, GA 30024, USA

Case, Ronald (Ron) (Athlete, Football Player)
6960 Driskell Cir
Cumming, GA 30041, USA

Case, Sharon (Actor)
265 S Linden Dr
Beverly Hills, CA 90212, USA

Case, Steve (Business Person)
700 Chain Bridge Rd
McLean, VA 22101, USA

Case, Stoney (Athlete, Football Player)
1813 E 49th St
Odessa, TX 79762, USA

case, Walter (Horse Racer)
8795 Crow Dr
Macedonia, OH 44056-1647, USA

Case Jr, Walter (Race Car Driver)
142 Summer St.
Lisbon Falls, ME 04252-9732, USA

Casel, Nitanju Bolade (Musician)
Sweet Honey Agency
PO Box 600099
Newtonville, MA 02460, USA

Casella, Max (Actor)
c/o Marcia Hurwitz *Innovative Artists (LA)*
1505 10th St
Santa Monica, CA 90401, USA

Casely-Hayford, Joe (Designer, Fashion Designer)
c/o Staff Member *Joe Casely-Hayford*
128 Shoreditch High Street
London, England E1 6JE, United Kingdom

Casey, Bernie (Athlete, Football Player)
6145 Flight Ave
Los Angeles, CA 90056, USA

Casey, Brent (Stylist)
4312 1st Ave
South Minneapolis, MN 55409, USA

Casey, Dillon (Actor)
c/o Tim Taylor *Luber Roklin Management*
8530 Wilshire Blvd
6th Floor
Beverly Hills, CA 90211, USA

Casey, Harry Wayne (Musician)
7530 Loch Ness Dr
Miami Lakes, FL 33014, USA

Casey, John D (Writer)
University of Virginia
English Dept
Charlottesville, VA 22903, USA

Casey, Jon (Athlete, Hockey Player)
651 Bluffs View Ct
Eureka, MO 63025-3727, USA

Casey, Kent (Stylist)
c/o Staff Member *Rex Agency, The*
6311 Romaine St
Los Angeles, CA 90038, USA

Casey, Lawrence P. (Actor)
4139 Vanette Pl.
Studio City, CA 91604, USA

Casey, Lee
Paul Kohner Agency Inc
9300 Wilshire Blvd #555
Beverly Hills, CA 90212

casey, Maurice (General)
7017 Union Mill Rd
Clifton, VA 20124-1122, USA

Casey, Maurice F (General)
7017 Union Mill Road
Clinton, VA 20124, USA

Casey, Paddy (Musician)
c/o Staff Member *Helter Skelter (UK)*
535 Kings Rd
The Plaza
London SW10 0SZ, UNITED KINGDOM (UK)

Casey, Paul (Athlete, Golfer)
29167 N 108st St
Scottsdale, AZ 85262, USA

Casey, Peter (Director)
Jim Preminger Agency
450 N Roxbury Dr
#1050
Beverly Hills, CA 90210, USA

Casey, Sean (Athlete, Baseball Player)
Major League Basebal Network 40 Hartz Way Ste 10
Attn: On Air Personality
Secaucus, NJ 07094-7403, USA

Casey, Sean (Athlete, Baseball Player)
271 Trotwood Dr
Pittsburgh, PA 15241-2244, USA

Casey Jr, Robert P. (Senator)
393 Russell Senate Office Building
Washington, DC 20510, USA

Cash, Antoine (Athlete, Football Player)
14441 Mirabelle Vista Cir
Tampa, FL 33626, USA

Cash, Cornelius (Athlete, Basketball Player)
1661 Miami Chapel Road
Dayton, OH 45417-4527, USA

Cash, Dave (Athlete, Baseball Player)
16308 Birkdale Dr
Odessa, FL 33556-2802, USA

Cash, Keith (Athlete, Football Player)
1600 NW 54th Terr
Kansas City, MO 64118, USA

Cash, Kerry (Athlete, Football Player)
1414 Gator Creek Dr
Cedar Park, TX 78613, USA

Cash, Kevin (Athlete, Baseball Player)
14607 Mirabelle Vista Cir
Tampa, FL 33626-3347, USA

Cash, Pat (Tennis Player)
281 Clarence St
Sydney NSW 2000, AUSTRALIA

Cash, Rick (Athlete, Football Player)
203 E Benton St
Savannah, MO 64485, USA

Cash, Rosanne (Musician, Songwriter)
c/o Mike Leahy *Concerted Efforts*
P.O. Box 440326
Somerville, MA 02144, USA

Cash, Roseanne (Musician)
1309 Boscobel St
Nashville, TN 37206, USA

Cash, Sam (Athlete, Basketball Player)
25825 Karisa Circle
Moreno Valley, CA 92551-1968, USA

Cash, Swin (Basketball Player)
Detroit Shock
Palace
2 Championship Dr
Auburn Hills, MI 48326, USA

Cash, Tommy (Musician, Songwriter, Writer)
PO Box 1230
Hendersonville, TN 37077, USA

Cashen, Frank (Commentator)
28894 Jasper Ln
Easton, MD 21601-8317, USA

Cashen, Frank (Athlete, Baseball Player)
7600 Mahogany Run
Port St Lucie, FL 34986, USA

Cashion, Red (Athlete, Football Player)
P.O. Box 3889
Bryan, TX 77805, USA

Cashman, Brian (Commentator)
40 Peach Hill Rd
Darien, CT 06820-2821, USA

Cashman, Capt John (Aviator)
Boeing Commercial Airplane
Group PO Box 3707
Seattle, WA 98124-2207, USA

Cashman, John (Horse Racer)
PO Box 11889
Group PO Box 3707
Lexington, KY 40578-1889, United States

Cashman, John Jr (Misc)
PO Box 11889
Lexington, KY 40578, USA

Cashman, Terry (Musician)
15 Engle St
Englewood, NJ 07631, USA

Cashman, Wayne (Athlete, Hockey Player)
5150 NW 80th Avenue Rd
Ocala, FL 34482-2028, USA

Cashner, Andrew (Athlete, Baseball Player)
104 Lyndsey Dr
Montgomery, TX 77316-6824, USA

Casian, Larry (Athlete, Baseball Player)
1939 Popcorn St NW
Salem, OR 97304-2841, USA

Casiavska, Vera (Gymnast)
SVS Sparta Prague
Korunovacni 29
Prague 7, CZECH REPUBLIC

Casida, John E (Misc)
1570 La Vereda Road
Berleley, CA 94708, USA

Casillas, Tony (Athlete, Football Player)
6201 Bay Valley Ct
Flower Mound, TX 75022, USA

Casiraghi, Pierlulgi (Soccer Player)
Lazio Rorna
Via Novaro 32
Rome 00197, ITALY

Caskey, Craig (Athlete, Baseball Player)
17422 Palomino Dr
Bothell, WA 98012-6419, USA

Caskey, C Thomas (Biologist, Scientist)
Baylor College of Medicine
Molecular Genetics Dept
Houston, TX 77030, USA

Casnoff, Philip (Actor)
216 S Plymouth Blvd
Los Angeles, CA 90004, USA

Cason, Aveion (Athlete, Football Player)
4416 Ashbury ln
Mansfield, TX 76063, USA

Cason, James (Jim) (Athlete, Football Player)
1002 King Arthur Dr Apt 116
Apt 29
Harlingen, TX 78550, USA

Caspar, Donald L D (Physicist)
2605 Lotus Drive
Tallahassee, FL 32312-3009, USA

Caspary, Tina (Actor)
11350 Ventura Blvd #206
Studio City, CA 91604, USA

Casper, Billy (Athlete, Golfer)
2561 Stonebury Loop Rd
Springville, UT 84663, USA

Casper, Colonel John H (Astronaut)
4414 Village Corner Dr
Houston, TX 77059-4025, USA

Casper, David J (Dave) (Athlete, Football Player)
1525 Alamo Way
Alamo, CA 94507, USA

Casper, Gerhard (Attorney, Educator)
Stanford University
Law School
Abbott Way
Stanford, CT 94305, USA

Casper, John H (Astronaut)
4414 Village Corner Dr
Houston, TX 77059, USA

Casper, Robert (Actor)
CunninghamEscottDipene
10635 Santa Monica Blvd #130
Los Angeles, CA 90025, USA

Caspersson, Tobjorn O (Doctor)
Emanuel Birkes Vag 2
Ronninge 14400, SWEDEN

Cass, Christopher (Actor)
Halpern Assoc
PO Box 5597
Santa Monica, CA 90409, USA

Cassaday, Leann (Athlete, Golfer)
542 Orpheus Ave
Encinitas, CA 92024, USA

Cassady, Craig (Athlete, Football Player)
3647 Lakestone Cir
Columbus, OH 43026, USA

Cassady, Howard (Hopalong) (Athlete, Football Player, Heisman Trophy Winner)
Talis Sports Management
PO Box 7828
Columbus, OH 43207-0828, USA

Cassar, Jon (Producer)
c/o Jeff Benson *Paradigm (LA)*
360 N Crescent Dr
North Bldg
Beverly Hills, CA 90210, USA

Cassara, Frank (Athlete, Football Player)
9113 Brookshire Ave
Downey, CA 90240, USA

Cassata, Rick (Athlete, Football Player)
133 Burch Ave
Buffalo, NY 14210-2638, USA

Cassatt, Chris (Cartoonist)
616 Evans Ct
Basalt, CO 81621-8300, USA

Cassaveters, Nick (Actor, Director)
22223 Buena Ventura St
Woodland Hills, CA 91364, USA

Cassavetes, Nick (Actor, Director, Writer)
2067 Hercules Dr
Los Angeles, CA 90046, USA

Cassel, Jack (Athlete, Baseball Player)
19427 Superior St
Northridge, CA 91324-1646, USA

Cassel, Matt (Athlete, Football Player)
150 Street of Dreams
Village Of Loch Lloyd, MO 64012, USA

Cassel, Seymour (Actor)
c/o Harry Abrams *Abrams Artists Agency (LA)*
9200 Sunset Blvd
11th Floor
Los Angeles, CA 90069, USA

Cassel, Vincent (Actor)
c/o Staff Member *United Talent Agency (UTA)*
9336 Civic Center Dr
Beverly Hills, CA 90210, USA

Cassell, Sam (Athlete, Basketball Player)
5205 N Charles St
Baltmore, MD 21210-2042, USA

Cassels, A James H (Misc)
Hamble End Higham Road
Barrow Bury Saint Edmunds
Suffolk, UNITED KINGDOM (UK)

Cassels, Andrew (Athlete, Hockey Player)
8614 Tartan Fields Dr
Dublin, OH 43017-8908, USA

Cassels, James (General)
Hamble End Higham Road, Barrow
Bury St Edmunds Suffolk, ENGLAND, UK

Casserino, Lt Col Frank J (Misc)
2407 Willow Geln Drive
Colorado Springs, CO 80920-1200, USA

Casserta, Bettina (Stylist)
c/o Staff Member *Ford Models (Chicago)*
311 W Superior St
Chicago, IL 60654, USA

Cassese, Tom (Athlete, Football Player)
80 Van Buren St
Port Jefferson Stati, NY 11776, USA

Casseus, Gabriel (Actor)
c/o Dan Baron *Agency for the Performing Arts (APA-LA)*
405 S Beverly Dr
Suite 500
Beverly Hills, CA 90212-4425, USA

Cassevah, Bobby (Athlete, Baseball Player)
11095 Chippewa Way
Pensacola, FL 32534-9755, USA

Cassidy (Musician)
c/o Staff Member *J Records (Division of BMG Entertainment)*
745 Fifth Ave 6th Fl
New York, NY 10151, USA

Cassidy, Bill (Congressman, Politician)
1535 Longworth HOB
Washington, DC 20515, USA

Cassidy, Bruce (Athlete, Coach, Hockey Player)
c/o Staff Member *Kingston Frontenacs*
P.O. Box 665
Stn Main
Kingston, ON K7L 4X1, Canada

Cassidy, Bruce
50 Park Row W Apt 217
Providence, RI 02903-1144, usa

Cassidy, Christopher (Astronaut)
1207 Spring Cress Ln
Seabrook, TX 77586-4721, USA

Cassidy, David (Actor, Musician, Producer)
DBC, INC.
1536 W. 25th St.
PMB: 233
San Pedro, CA 90732-4402, USA

Cassidy, Edward I Cardinal (Religious Leader)
Council for Christian Unity
Piazza del S Uffizio 11
Rome 00193, ITALY

Cassidy, Elaine (Actor)
c/o Staff Member *ICM Partners (ICM-LA)*
10250 Constellation Blvd Fl 7
Los Angeles, CA 90067, USA

Cassidy, Joanna (Actor)
c/o Bette Smith *Bette Smith Management*
499 N Canon Dr
Beverly Hills, CA 90210, USA

Cassidy, Katie (Actor)
c/o Doreen Wilcox Little *Anonymous Content (LA)*
3531 Hayden Ave
Culver City, CA 90232, USA

Cassidy, Michael (Actor)
c/o Vic Ramos *Vic Ramos Management*
337 E. 13th St
Suite 6
New York, NY 10003, USA

Cassidy, Patrick (Actor)
Innovative Artists
1505 10th St
Santa Monica, CA 90401, USA

Cassidy, Ron (Athlete, Football Player)
2214 W 171st St
Torrance, CA 90504, USA

Cassidy, Ron (Athlete, Football Player)
2214 W 171st St
Torrance, CA 90504

Cassidy, Scott (Athlete, Baseball Player)
1006 4th St
Liverpool, NY 13088-4407, USA

Cassidy, Shaun (Actor, Musician)
24924 Jim Bridger Rd
Hidden Hills, CA 91302, USA

Cassivi, Frederic (Athlete, Hockey Player)
7521 Clover Lee Blvd
Harrisburg, PA 17112-8945, USA

Cassolato, Tony (Athlete, Hockey Player)
576 Camino El Dorado
Encinitas, CA 92024-3820, USA

Casson, Mel (Cartoonist)
c/o Staff Member *King Features Syndication*
300 W 57th St
15th Floor
New York, NY 10019-5238, USA

Cast, Edward
4 Bankside Dr Thames Ditton
Surrey, ENGLAND KT7 0AQ, ENGLAND

Cast, PC (Writer)
c/o Sean T. Daily *Hotchkiss & Associates*
611 Broadway
#741
New York, NY 10012, USA

Cast, Tricia (Actor)
1346 Pond Creek Rd
Ashland City, TN 37015, USA

Casta, Laetitia (Actor)
c/o Staff Member *ArtMedia*
20 avenue Rapp
Paris 75008, France

Castaldi, Debbie (Stylist)
Prefers to be contacted
via telephone or email
Los Angeles, CA 90069, USA

Castaneda, Jorge A (Government Official)
Anillo Perferico Sur 3180 #1120
Jardines del Pedregal 01900, MEXICO

Castaneda, Pedro (Actor)
c/o Maggie Woods *Online Talent Group*
Prefers to be contacted via email or telephone
Los Angeles, CA 90069, USA

Castel, Nico (Opera Singer)
RPA Mgmt
4 Adelaide Lane
Washingtonville, NY 10992, USA

Castellaneta, Dan (Actor, Musician, Voice Over Artist)
1520 Amalfi Dr
Pacific Palisades, CA 90272, USA

Castellano, Pedro (Athlete, Baseball Player)
Parcela 63 #63-6
Cabudare Lara, Venezuela

Castellini, Clateo (Business Person)
Becton Dickinson Co
1 Becton Dr
Franklin Lakes, NJ 07417, USA

Castellini, Robert (Commentator)
2180 Grandin Rd
Cincinnati, OH 45208-3306, USA

Castelluccio, Frederico (Actor)
c/o Robyn Ziegler *Robyn Ziegler Management*
30 Irving Pl
6th Floor
New York, NY 10003, USA

Caster, Rich (Athlete, Football Player)
41 Lincoln Ct
Rockville Centre, NY 11570, USA

Castete, Jesse (Athlete, Football Player)
302 W Lee St
Sulphur, LA 70663, USA

Castiglia, James (Athlete, Football Player)
5301 Westbard Cir
Apt 313
Bethesda, MD 20816, USA

Castiglione, Joe (Commentator)
Boston Red Sox
100 Kling Phillips Pathe
Marshfield, MA 02050-5714, USA

Castilla, Vinny (Athlete, Baseball Player)
Colorado Rockies 2001 Blake St
Attn Coaching Staff
Denver, CO 80205-2000, USA

Castilla, Vinny (Athlete, Baseball Player)
7680 Polo Ridge Dr
Littleton, CO 80128-2502, USA

Castille, Jeremiah (Athlete, Football Player)
2904 Kirkcaldy Ln
Birmingham, AL 35242, USA

Castillio, Susie (Actor, Beauty Pageant Winner)
c/o Gordon Gilbertson *Gilbertson Management*
1334 3rd St Promenade #201
Santa Monica, CA 90401, USA

Castillo, Alberto (Athlete, Baseball Player)
13600 Coco Palm Ct
Bakersfield, CA 93314-6662, USA

Castillo, Alberto (Athlete, Baseball Player)
400 SW Lakota Ave
Port Saint Lucie, FL 34953-3029, USA

Castillo, Bobby (Athlete, Baseball Player)
JD Legends Promotions
10808 Foothill Blvd #160-454
Rancho Cucamonga, CA 91730-3889, USA

Castillo, Carmen (Athlete, Baseball Player)
344 Prospect Ave
Apt 6A
Hackensack, NJ 07601-2603, USA

Castillo, Frank (Athlete, Baseball Player)
498 N Alder St
Gilbert, AZ 85233-4422, USA

Castillo, Joey (Musician)
1456 Angelus Ave
Los Angeles, CA 90026, USA

Castillo, Luis (Athlete, Baseball Player)
10782 Hawks Vista St
Plantation, FL 33324-8212, USA

Castillo, Luis (Athlete, Football Player)
14165 Augusta Ct
Poway, CA 92064

Castillo, Manny (Athlete, Baseball Player)
Bowling Green Hot Rods 300 8th Ave
Attn: Coaching Staff
Bowling Green, KY 42101-2115, USA

Castillo, Marty (Athlete, Baseball Player)
589 Palisade Dr
Brunswick, GA 31523-8208, USA

Castillo, Patricio (Actor)
c/o Staff Member *Televisa*
Blvd Adolfo Lopez Mateos 232
Colonia San Angel INN
DF CP 01060, MEXICO

Castillo, Rafael (De La Ghetto) (Musician)
c/o Staff Member *Baby Records Corp*
Ave. Galicia R104
Villa Venacia, Vistamar Marina
Carolina, PR 00983, USA

Castillo, Tony (Athlete, Baseball Player)
6402 Silverwood Dr
Huntington Beach, CA 92647-3366, USA

Castillo, Vinicio (Athlete, Baseball Player)
c/o Staff Member *Atlanta Braves*
755 Hank Aaron Dr SW
Atlanta, GA 30315, USA

Castillo Lara, Rosalio Jose Cardinal (Religious Leader)
Palazzo del Governatorato
00120, VATICAN CITY

Casting Crowns (Music Group, Musician)
c/o Stacey Jannette *Proper Management*
P.O. Box 150867
Nashville, TN 37215, USA

Castino, John (Athlete, Baseball Player)
6290 Bluestern Rd S
Hamel, MN 55340-4546, USA

Castle, Don (Athlete, Baseball Player)
560 Country Club Dr
Senatobia, MS 38668-6317, USA

Castle, Eric (Athlete, Football Player)
41984 Cut Off Dr
Lebanon, OR 97355, USA

Castle, John (Actor)
Larry Dalzell
91 Regent St
London W1R 7TB, UNITED KINGDOM (UK)

Castle, Michael (Congressman, Ex-Governor)
300 S New St
Dover, DE 19904-6726, USA

Castle, Nick (Actor, Director, Writer)
PO Box 92136
Pasadena, CA 91109, USA

Castle-Hughes, Keisha (Actor)
c/o Jennifer Rawlings *Principato/Young Management*
9601 Wilshire Blvd Fl 3
Beverly Hills, CA 90210, USA

Castleman, Albert W Jr (Misc)
425 Hillcrest Ave
State College, PA 16803, USA

Castleman, E Riva (Misc)
Museum of Modern Art
11 W 53rd St
New York, NY 10019, USA

Castleman, Foster (Athlete, Baseball
Player)
8250 Graves Rd
Cincinnati, OH 45243-3633, USA

Castle of Blackbum, Barbara A
(Government Official)
House of Lords
Westminster
London SW1A 0PW, UNITED KINGDOM
(UK)

Castles, Neil (Race Car Driver)
1525 Stoneyridge Dr.
Charlotte, NC 27214, USA

Casto, Kory (Athlete, Baseball Player)
14820 SW Village Ln
Beaverton, OR 97007-3631, USA

Castonzo, Anthony (Football Player)
c/o Ben Dogra *CAA - St. Louis*
222 S Central Ave
Suite 1008
St Louis, MO 63105, USA

Castor, Chris (Athlete, Football Player)
206 Connors Cir
Cary, NC 27511, USA

Castor, Kathy (Congressman, Politician)
137 Cannon HOB
Washington, DC 20515, USA

Castrillon Hoyos, Dario Cardinal
(Religious Leader)
Arzobispado
Calle 33 N 21-18
Bucaramanga
Santander, COLOMBIA

Castro, Bill (Athlete, Baseball Player)
5217 West Harvard Dr
Franklin, WI 53132-8192, USA

Castro, Cristian (Musician)
c/o Staff Member *BMG*
1540 Broadway
New York, NY 10036, USA

Castro, Daniela (Actor)
c/o Staff Member *Televisa*
Blvd Adolfo Lopez Mateos 232
Colonia San Angel INN
DF CP 01060, MEXICO

Castro, David (Actor)
c/o Staff Member *Persona Management*
40 E 9th St #11J
Suite 11J
New York, NY 10003, USA

Castro, Jason (Musician)
c/o Staff Member *Atlantic Recording
Corporation*
1290 Avenue of the Americas
New York, NY 10104, USA

Castro, Juan (Athlete, Baseball Player)
7324 W Artie Ave
Peoria, AZ 85383-3291, USA

Castro, Ramon (Athlete, Baseball Player)
1230 Windway Cir
Kissimmee, FL 34744-2552, USA

Castro, Raquel (Actor)
c/o Staff Member *WME (LA)*
9601 Wilshire Blvd Fl 3
Beverly Hills, CA 90210, USA

Castro, Raul (Diplomat, Ex-Governor)
429 W Crawford St
Nogales, AZ 85621-2507, USA

Castroneves, Helio (Race Car Driver)
325 Seven Isles Dr
Ft Lauderdale, FL 33301, USA

Castronuova, Cara (Actor, Reality TV Star)
c/o Seth Greenky *Green Key Mgmt (NY)*
251 W 89th St
Suite 4-A
New York, NY 10024, USA

Castro Ruz, Fidel (President)
Palacio del Gobierno
Plaza de Revolucion
Havana, CUBA

Castro Ruz, Raul (Prime Minister)
First Vice President's Office
Plaza de la Revolucion
Havana, CUBA

Caswell, Dean (General)
2309 Village Way Dr
Austin, TX 78745-2741, USA

Catalanotto, Frank (Athlete, Baseball
Player)
Frank Catalanotto Foundation
PO Box 236
Saint James, NY 11780-0236, USA

Catalino, Ken (Cartoonist, Editor)
Creators Syndicate
5777 W Century Blvd #700
Los Angeles, CA 90045, USA

Catalona, William J (Misc)
Washington University
Medical School
Urology Division
Saint Louis, MO 63110, USA

Catan, Pete (Athlete, Football Player)
1261 Blakely St
Woodstock, IL 60098-3631, USA

Catanho, Alcides (Athlete, Football Player)
931 Pennington St
Apt 1
Elizabeth, NJ 07202, USA

Catanzaro, Tony (Dancer)
3496 NW 7th St
Miami, FL 33125, USA

Catchings, Harvey (Athlete, Basketball
Player)
17406 Edenwalk
Spring, TX 77379-8513, USA

Catchings, Tamika (Athlete)
125 S Pennsylvania St
Indianapolis, IN 46024

Catchings, Tamika (Basketball Player)
Indiana Fever
Conseco Fieldhouse
125 S Pennsylvania
Indianapolis, IN 46204, USA

Catchings, Toney (Athlete, Football
Player)
6213 Zoellners Pl
Hamilton, OH 45011

Cate, Troy (Athlete, Baseball Player)
32499 Via Destello
Temecula, CA 92592-3961, USA

Cater, Danny (Athlete, Baseball Player)
Unlimited Autographs 7028 W Waters Av
Ave# 229 Re: Danny Cater
Tamoa, FL 33634-2292, USA

Cater, Greg (Athlete, Football Player)
19 Warwick Way SE
Rome, GA 30161, USA

Cates, Challen (Actor)
179 S Hudson Ave
Los Angeles, CA 90004, USA

Cates, Dariene (Actor)
13340 FM 740
Forney, TX 75126, USA

Cates, Georgina (Actor)
118 S Kilkea Dr
Los Angeles, CA 90048, USA

Cates, Phoebe (Actor)
1636 3rd Avenue
#309
New York, NY 10128, USA

Cathcard, Patti (Musician)
Windham Hill Records
PO Box 5501
Beverly Hills, CA 90209, USA

Cathcart, Sam (Athlete, Football Player)
370 Las Alturas Rd
Santa Barbara, CA 93103, USA

Cather, Mike (Athlete, Baseball Player)
12215 Magnolia Crescent Dr
Roswell, GA 30075-5568, USA

Catherwood, Mike (Radio Personality,
Reality TV Star)
c/o Staff Member *Core Entertainment*
14742 Ventura Blvd
Penthouse
Sherman Oaks, CA 91403, USA

Catledge, Terry (Athlete, Basketball
Player)
170 Hall St
Houston, MS 38851-1605, USA

Catlett, Elizabeth (Artist)
PO Box AP694
Cuernovaca, Mexico 62000, USA

Catlett, Mary Jo (Actor)
4375 Farmdale Ave
Studio City, CA 91604, USA

Catlett, Sid (Athlete, Basketball Player)
3110 Scottish Ave
Suitland, MD 20746-3136, USA

Cato, Keefe (Athlete, Baseball Player)
98 Maryton Rd
White Plains, NY 10603-2016, USA

Cato, Kelvin (Athlete, Basketball Player)
13607 Winter Creek Court
Houston, TX 77077-1550, USA

Cato, Robert Milton (Prime Minister)
PO Box 138
Ratho Mill
SAINT VINCENT & GRENADINES

Caton, Jack Joseph (General)
17230 Citronia St
Northridge, CA 91325, USA

Caton Jones, Michael (Director)
c/o Staff Member *WmE2 (WMA-LA)*
1 William Morris Pl
Beverly Hills, CA 90212, USA

Catrow, David (Cartoonist, Editor)
Springfield News-Sun
Editorial Dept
202 N Limestone St
Springfield, OH 45503, USA

Cattage, Bobby (Athlete, Basketball
Player)
4838 US Highway 29 South
Auburn, AL 36830-8184, USA

Cattaneo, Peter (Director)
International Creative Mgmt
76 Oxford St
London W1N OAX, UNITED KINGDOM
(UK)

Cattermole, Paul (Actor)
Eden Lifestyle
4 Flitcroft Street
London WC2H 8D, United Kingdom

Catto, Henry E Jr (Diplomat)
110 E Crockett St
San Antonio, TX 78205, USA

Cattrall, Kim (Actor)
89 Gerard Dr E
Hampton, NY 11937-4701, USA

Caubere, Philippe (Actor)
La Comédie Nouvelle
23 Avenue Philippe-Auguste
Paris F-75011, France

Caudill, Bill (Athlete, Baseball Player)
11605 NE 41st St
Kirkland, WA 98033-8742, USA

Caudill, Daniel (Stylist)
c/o Staff Member *Celestine - CA*
1666 20th St
#200-B
Santa Monica, CA 90404, USA

Cauduro, Eugenia (Actor)
c/o Staff Member *Televisa*
Blvd Adolfo Lopez Mateos 232
Colonia San Angel INN
DF CP 01060, MEXICO

Cauffiel, Jessica (Actor)
c/o Michael Greene *Greene & Associates*
1901 Avenue Of The Stars Ste 130
Los Angeles, CA 90067, USA

Caufield, Jay (Athlete, Hockey Player)
106 Quail Hollow Ln
Wexford, PA 15090-7596, USA

Caulfield, Emma (Actor)
c/o Ellen Drantch-Billet *EDB Management*
1953 Barry Ave
Los Angeles, CA 90025-5381, USA

Caulfield, Lore (Designer, Fashion
Designer)
2228 Cotner Ave
Los Angeles, CA 90064, USA

Caulfield, Maxwell (Actor)
5252 Lennox Ave5252 Lennox Ave
Sherman Oaks, CA 91401, USA

Caulkins, Tracy (Athlete, Olympic Athlete,
Swimmer)
511 Oman St.
Nashville, TN 37203-1234, USA

Causey, Kevin (Athlete, Baseball Player)
5719 Hereld Green Dr
Chesterfield, VA 23832-4048, USA

Causey, Wayne (Athlete, Baseball Player)
2905 Paynter Dr
Ruston, LA 71270-5242, USA

Causwell, Duane (Athlete, Basketball
Player)
3 Pierce Drive
Stony Point, NY 10980-3701, USA

Causwell, Duane (Athlete, Baseball Player)
3 Pierce Dr
Stony Point, NY 10980-3701

Cauterize (Music Group)
c/o Staff Member *Wind-up Records*
72 Madison Ave Fl 8
New York, NY 10016, USA

Cauthen, Stephen M (Steve) (Misc)
Cauthen Ranch
RFD Boone County
167 S Main St
Walton, KY 41094, USA

Cauthen, Steve (Horse Racer)
15541 Porter Rd
Verona, KY 41092-9205, USA

Cauthen, Steve (Athlete, Jockey)
167 S. Main St.
Walton, KY 41094-1139, USA

Cavadini, Catherine (Cathy) (Actor)
c/o Staff Member *ICM Partners (ICM-LA)*
10250 Constellation Blvd Fl 7
Los Angeles, CA 90067, USA

Cavaiani, Jon R (War Hero)
10956 Green St Unit 230
Columbia, CA 95310-9742, USA

Cavalera, Max (Musician)
Variety Artists
1924 Spring St
Paso Robles, CA 93446, USA

Cavaleri, Ray (Producer)
c/o Staff Member *Cavaleri & Associates*
178 S Victory Blvd
Suite 205
Burbank, CA 91502, USA

Cavaliere, Felix (Composer, Musician)
Primo Productions
PO Box 253
Audubon, NJ 08106, USA

Cavallari, Kristin (Actor, Reality TV Star)
c/o Susan Calogerakis *Thruline Entertainment*
9250 Wilshire Blvd
Ground Fl
Beverly Hills, CA 90212, USA

Cavalli, Carmen (Athlete, Football Player)
6221 Madison Ct
Bensalem, PA 19020, USA

Cavalli, Constanza (Actor)
c/o Gabriel Blanco *Gabriel Blanco Iglesias (Mexico)*
Rio Balsas 35-32
Colonia Cuauhtemoc
DF 06500, Mexico

Cavalli, Roberto (Designer, Fashion Designer)
Via del Cantone 29
Osmannoro Sesto Florentino
Firenze 50019, ITALY

Cavallini, Gino (Athlete, Hockey Player)
6614 Clayton Rd
Unit 315
Saint Louis, MO 63117-1602, USA

Cavallini, Paul (Athlete, Hockey Player)
7201 Kingsbury Blvd
Saint Louis, MO 63130-4139, USA

Cavanagh, Megan (Actor)
c/o Staff Member *Framework Entertainment (LA)*
9057 Nemo St
Suite C
West Hollywood, CA 90069, USA

Cavanagh, Tom (Actor)
c/o Daniel Pancotto *Circle of Confusion (LA)*
8607 Washington Blvd
Culver City, CA 90232, USA

Cavanaugh, Christine (Actor)
Allman
342 S Cochran Ave
#30
Los Angeles, CA 90036, USA

Cavanaugh, Joe (Athlete, Hockey Player)
25 Nathaniel Greene Dr
East Greenwich, RI 02818-2019, USA

Cavanaugh, Matt (Athlete, Football Player)
644 Robinwood Dr Apt C
Pittsburgh, PA 15216, USA

Cavanaugh, Matthew A (Matt) (Athlete, Football Player)
8 Barstad Ct
Lutherville Timonium, MD 21093, USA

Cavanaugh, Michael (Actor)
Ambrosio/Mortimer
165 W 46th St
New York, NY 10036, USA

Cavanaugh, Page (Musician)
9420 Reseda Blvd
Northridge, CA 91324-2932, USA

Cavaretta, Philip J (Phil) (Athlete, Baseball Player, Coach)
4637 Kellogg Dr SW
Lilburn, GA 30047, USA

Cavazos, Andy (Athlete, Baseball Player)
244 E Bernard St
Clute, TX 77531-4609, USA

Cavazos, Lauro (Politician)
173 Annursnac Hill Rd
Concord, MA 01742-5402, USA

Cavazos, Lauro F (Secretary)
173 Annursnac Hill Road
Concord, MA 01742, USA

Cavazos, Lumi (Actor)
Visionary Entertainment
8265 W Sunset Blvd
#203
West Hollywood, CA 90046, USA

Cave, Jessie (Actor)
c/o Dallas Smith *United Agents*
12-26 Lexington St
London W1F OLE, UK

Cave, Nick (Musician, Songwriter, Writer)
Billions Corp
833 W Chicago Ave
#101
Chicago, IL 60622, USA

Caven, Ingrid (Actor)
Green Ufos
Parque Pisa
C/Exposición, 8, 1° izq
Mairena del Aljarafe 41927, Spain

Cavenall, Ron (Athlete, Basketball Player)
P.O. Box 450983
Houston, TX 77245-0983, USA

Caveness, Ronnie (Athlete, Football Player)
17 Brookridge Cv
Little Rock, AR 72205, USA

Caver, James (Athlete, Football Player)
10722 Mersington Ave
Kansas City, MO 64137, USA

Caver, Quinton (Athlete, Football Player)
PO Box 335
China, TX 77613, USA

Caverly, Kristen (Athlete, Olympic Athlete, Swimmer)
9 Puerto Caravaca
San Clemente, CA 92672-6054, USA

Cavett, Dick (Actor, Writer)
181 Deforest Rd
Montauk, NY 11954, USA

Cavic, Milorad (Mike) (Swimmer)
Cal Bears Athletics
Swimming
Haas Pavilion #4422
Berkeley, CA 94720-4422, USA

Caviezel, James (Actor)
4491 Valley Spring Dr
Thousand Oaks, CA 91362, USA

Cavil, Kwame (Athlete, Football Player)
2005 Dan Rowe St
Waco, TX 76704, USA

Cavill, Henry (Actor)
c/o Jennifer Allen *Viewpoint Inc*
8820 Wilshire Blvd.
Suite 220
Beverly Hills, CA 90211, USA

Cavness, Grady (Athlete, Football Player)
7007 Roberson Rd
Missouri City, TX 77489, USA

Cavuto, Neil (Television Host)
55 Prentice Ln
Mendham, NY 07945, USA

Cawley, Tucker (Actor)
c/o Adam Berkowitz *Creative Artists Agency (CAA-LA)*
2000 Ave Of The Stars
Los Angeles, CA 90067, USA

Cawley, Warren (Rex) (Athlete, Track Athlete)
1655 San Rafael Dr
Corona, CA 92882, USA

Caylor, Lowell (Athlete, Football Player)
403 Woodway Dr
Greer, SC 29651, USA

Cayne, Candis (Actor, Model)
c/o Nikki Weiss *Nikki Weiss & Co.*
754 N. La Jolla Ave
Los Angeles, CA 90046, USA

C. Burgess, Michael (Congressman, Politician)
2241 Rayburn HOB
Washington, DC 20515, USA

C. Carney Jr., John (Congressman, Politician)
1429 Longworth HOB
Washington, DC 20515, USA

Ceasar, Andrew (Stylist)
c/o Staff Member *The Montgomery Group*
210 W 29th St
#6
New York, NY 10001, USA

Ceaser, Curtis (Athlete, Football Player)
4805 Corley St
Beaumont, TX 77707, USA

Ceballos, Cedric (Athlete, Basketball Player)
3068 FM 1252 West
Kilgore, TX 75662-4830, USA

Ceberano, Kate (Musician)
Richard East Productions
Kildean Lane
Winchelsea, VIC 3241, AUSTRALIA

Ceccacci, Anthony (Scientist)
3246 Mossy Elm Ct
Houston, TX 77059-3228, USA

Ceccato, Aldo (Conductor)
Chaunt da Crusch
Zuoz 7524, SWITZERLAND

Cece (Stylist)
c/o Staff Member *Maximum Talent*
1873 S Bellaire St
Suite 915
Denver, CO 80222-4356, USA

Cech, Thomas (Nobel Prize Laureate)
PO Box 215
Boulder, CO 80309-0001, USA

Cechmanek, Roman (Athlete, Hockey Player)
1111 S Figueroa St
Los Angeles, CA 90015, USA

Cecil, Brett (Athlete, Baseball Player)
2989 Estancia Pl
Clearwater, FL 33761-2646, USA

Cecil, Chuck (Radio Personality)
KJazz 88.1 FM
2008 Waterstone Dr
Franklin, TN 37069, USA

Cedano, Roger (Athlete, Baseball Player)
9325 Byron Ave
Surfside, FL 33154, USA

Cedar, Larry (Actor)
12949 Hartsook St
Sherman Oaks, CA 91423, USA

Cedarstrom, Gary (Athlete, Baseball Player)
1610 18th St SE
Minot, ND 58701, USA

Cedeno, Cesar (Athlete, Baseball Player)
9919 Sagedowne Ln
Houston, TX 77089-4309, USA

Cedeno, Matt (Actor)
c/o Ryan Daly *Zero Gravity Management*
1531 14th. St
Santa Monica, CA 90404, USA

Cedeno, Roger (Athlete, Baseball Player)
9325 Byron Ave
Surfside, FL 33154-2437, USA

Cederstrom, Gary (Athlete, Baseball Player)
755 Whidbey St
Melbourne, FL 32904-7484, USA

Cedras, Raoul (General)
Continental Riande Hotel
Panama City, PANAMA

Cedric The Entertainer (Actor, Comedian, Producer)
22720 LaQuilla Dr
Chatsworth, CA 91311, USA

Cefalo, Jimmy (Athlete, Football Player)
6675 Roxbury Ln
Miami Beach, FL 33141, USA

Ceglarski, Leonard (Len) (Athlete, Hockey Player, Olympic Athlete)
61 Lantern Ln
Duxbury, MA 02332-4915, USA

Ceika, Alex (Athlete, Golfer)
11589 Caldiot Dr
Las Vegas, NV 89138, USA

Cejka, Alex (Athlete, Golfer)
11589 Caldicot Dr
Las Vegas, NV 89138, USA

Cejudo, Henry (Athlete, Olympic Athlete, Wrestler)
Novuss Media
9943 E Bell Rd
Scottsdale, AZ 85260, USA

Celant, Gerwano (Misc)
Solomon Guggenheim Museum
1971 5th Ave
New York, NY 10128, USA

Celaya, Adolfo (War Hero)
977 Schulman St
Santa Clara, CA 95050, USA

Celeda (Musician)
c/o Staff Member *Diva Central Inc*
7510 W Sunset Blvd Ste 1445
Los Angees, CA 90046, USA

Celek, Brent (Athlete, Football Player)
2150 Verona Dr Apt 68
Philadelphia, PA 19145, us

Celestand, John (Athlete, Basketball Player, Sportscaster)
c/o Staff Member *Maxx Sports & Entertainment*
546 Fifth Ave Fl 6
New York, NY 10036, USA

Celeste, Richard
720 Crestfield Grv
Colorado Springs, CO 80906-1228, USA

Celestin, Oliver (Athlete, Football Player)
PO Box 6963
New Orleans, LA 70174, USA

Celi, AJ (Reality TV Star)
Playhouse Nightclub
6506 Hollywood Blvd
Los Angeles, CA 90028, USA

Celi, Ari (Actor)
c/o Staff Member *Silver Massetti & Szatmary (SMS) Talent Inc*
8383 Wilshire Blvd
Suite 230
Beverly Hills, CA 90211, USA

Cellini, Cristina (Stylist)
c/o Staff Member *Artists by Timothy Priano (CA)*
8447 Wilshire Blvd
#301
Beverly Hills, CA 90211, USA

Cellins, Art (Basketball Player)
Atlanta Hawks
4915 NW 15th Ct
Miami, FL 33142-4122, USA

Cellucci, A Paul (Diplomat, Ex-Governor)
McCarter & English, LLP
265 Franklin St
Boston, MA 02110, USA

Celmins, Vija (Artist)
49 Crosby St
New York, NY 10012, USA

Celotto, Mario (Athlete, Football Player)
47 Evirel Pl
Oakland, CA 94611, USA

Celtic Woman (Music Group, Musician)
c/o Staff Member *WME (LA)*
9601 Wilshire Blvd Fl 3
Beverly Hills, CA 90210, USA

Ce Marco, Cardinal (Religious Leader)
S Marco 318
Venice 30124, ITALY

Cena, John (Actor, Wrestler)
2326 Camp Indianhead Rd
Land O'Lakes, FL 34639, USA

Cenci, John (Athlete, Football Player)
942 Rita Dr
Pittsburgh, PA 15221, USA

Cenker, Robert J (Astronaut)
GORCA Inc
155 Hickory Corner Road
East Windsor, NJ 08520-2417, USA

Cennamo, Ralph (Misc)
Leather Plastics & Novelty Workers Union
265 W 14th St
New York, NY 10011, USA

Centers, Larry (Athlete, Football Player)
5023 Stagecoach Way
Southlake, TX 76092-9519, USA

Cepeda, Angie (Actor)
c/o Katrina Bayonas *Kuranda Management*
Santo Angel, 84
Madrid 28043, Spain

Cepeda, Orlando (Athlete, Baseball Player)
2305 Palmer Ct
Fairfield, CA 94534-7550, USA

Cepicky, Matt (Athlete, Baseball Player)
7 Upper Bluffs View Ct
Eureka, MO 63025-3724, USA

Cepicky, Scott (Athlete, Baseball Player, Olympic Athlete)
1606 Harrison Way
Spring Hill, TN 37174-2669, USA

Cera, Michael (Actor)
c/o William Mercer *Thruline Entertainment*
9250 Wilshire Blvd
Ground Fl
Beverly Hills, CA 90212, USA

Cerami, Anthony (Misc)
Ram Island Dr
Shelter Island, NY 11964, USA

Cerbone, Jason (Actor)
c/o Vera Mihailovich *Forward Entertainment*
9255 Sunset Blvd
Suite 805
Los Angeles, CA 90069, USA

Cerbone, John (Race Car Driver)
168 Fordham St.
City Island, NY 10464, USA

Cerda, Jaime (Athlete, Baseball Player)
2707 Northhill St
Selma, CA 93662-4313, USA

Ceresine, Ray (Athlete, Hockey Player)
13282 Ocean Vista Rd
San Diego, CA 92130-1862, USA

Ceresino, Gordy (Athlete, Football Player)
P.O. Box 675515
Rancho Santa Fe, CA 92067, USA

Cerezo, Arevalo M Vincio (President)
Partido Democracia Cristiana
Avda Elena 20-66
Guatemala City, GUATEMALA

Cerf, Vinton (Inventor)
1435 Woodhurst Blvd
Mclean, VA 22102-2234, USA

Cerf, Vinton G (Scientist)
3614 Camelot Dr
Annandale, VA 22003, USA

Cerha, Friedrich (Composer, Conductor)
Doblinger Music
Dorotheergasse 10
PO Box 882
Vienna 1011, AUSTRIA

Cerlan, Paul G (General)
3524 Old Course Lane
Valrico, FL 33594, USA

Cernadas, Segundo (Actor)
c/o Staff Member *Telefe - Argentina*
Pavon 2444 (C1248AAT)
Buenos Aires, ARGENTINA

Cernan, Eugene (Astronaut)
11310 Innisfree St
Houston, TX 77024-6748, USA

Cernan, Eugene A. (Astronaut)
c/o Staff Member *St Martins Press*
Publicity Dept
175 5th Ave
New York, NY 10010, USA

Cerne, Joseph (Joe) (Athlete, Football Player)
536 Valley West Ct
West Des Moines, IA 50265, USA

Cernik, Frantisek (Athlete, Hockey Player)
HC Vitkovice Steel CEZ
Arena Ruska 3077/135
Ostraka-Zabreh PSC 702 00, Czech Republic

Cerny, Jobe (Artist, Voice Over Artist)
259 Hazel Ave
Highland Park, IL 60035-3359

Ceron, Laura (Actor)
2338 Holly Dr
Los Angeles, CA 90068, USA

Cerone, Rick (Athlete, Baseball Player)
34 Winding Way
West Paterson, NJ 07424-2669, USA

Cerqua, Marq (Athlete, Football Player)
18800 NE 29th Ave Apt 1122
Miami, FL 33180, USA

Cerrone, Rick (Athlete)
100 Old Palisade Road
Fort Lee, NJ 07024-7027

Cerruda, Ron (Golfer)
c/o Staff Member *Pro Golfers Association (PGA) Tour*
112 TPC Blvd
Ponte Vedra Beach, FL 32082, USA

Cerruti, Nino (Designer, Fashion Designer)
3 Place de la Madeleine
Paris 75008, FRANCE

Certo, Tish (Athlete, Golfer)
151 Buffalo Ave
Suite 211
Niagara Falls, NY 14303, USA

Cerv, Bob (Athlete, Baseball Player)
805 N 22nd St
Apt 1A
Blair, NE 68008-1195, USA

Cervantes, Gary (Actor)
2240 Mardel Ave
Whittier, CA 90601, USA

Cervelli, Francisco (Athlete, Baseball Player)
c/o Team Member *New York Yankees*
Yankee Stadium
161st St & River Ave
Bronx, NY 10451, USA

Cervenak, Mike (Athlete, Baseball Player)
27199 Carol Ln
New Boston, MI 48164-9636, USA

Cervenka, Exene (Musician)
Performers of the World
8901 Melrose Ave
#200
West Hollywood, CA 90069, USA

Cerveris, Michael (Musician)
c/o Erica Tarin *ID Public Relations (ID-LA)*
7060 Hollywood Blvd
8th Floor
Los Angeles, CA 90028, USA

Cervl, Alfred N (Al) (Basketball Player)
177 Dunrovin Lane
Rochester, NY 14618, USA

Cervl, Valentina (Actor)
Artmedia
20 Ave Rapp
Paris 75007, FRANCE

Cesaire, Aime Ferdinand (Writer)
La Mairie
Fort-de-France
Martinique 97200, WEST INDIES

Cesaire, Jacques (Athlete, Football Player)
13388 Greenstone Ct
San Diego, CA 92131, USA

Cesare, Billy (Athlete, Football Player)
1655 Hendry Isles Blvd
Clewiston, FL 33440, USA

Cestaro, Alexander (Athlete, Football Player)
289 Devoe Ave
Yonkers, NY 10705, USA

Cester, Chris (Musician)
2010 Holly Hill Terr
Los Angeles, CA 90068, USA

Cetara, Peter (Musician)
c/o Staff Member *MPI Talent Agency*
1801 Avenue of the Stars
Suite 1420
Los Angeles, CA 90067, USA

Cetera, Peter (Musician, Songwriter)
691 Spruce Ave
Ketchum, ID 83340, USA

Cetlinski, Matthew (Matt) (Swimmer)
13121 SE 93rd Terrace Road
Summerfield, FL 34491, USA

Ceulemans, Raymond
Mister 100
Grote Markt 28
Lier BE-2500, BELGIUM

Cey, Ron (Athlete, Baseball Player)
22714 Creole Rd
Woodland Hills, CA 91364, USA

Chabat, Alain (Actor, Producer)
Chez Wam
18, blvd Montmartre
Paris 75009, France

Chaber, Madelyn J (Attorney, Attorney General, General)
101 California St
San Francisco, CA 94111, USA

Chabert, Lacey (Actor)
c/o Aaron Ray Collective
8383 Wilshire Blvd
Suite 1050
Beverly Hills, CA 90211, USA

Chablis, Lady (Entertainer)
1015 Mohawk Dr
W Columbia, SC 29169, USA

Chabon, Michael (Writer)
c/o Staff Member United Talent Agency (UTA)
9336 Civic Center Dr
Beverly Hills, CA 90210, USA

Chabot, Frederic (Athlete, Hockey Player)
Edmonton Oilers
11230 110 St
Attn Coaching Staff Edmonton
NW, AB TSG 3H7, Canada

Chabot, Herbert L (Judge)
US Tax Court
400 2nd St NW
Washington, DC 20217, USA

Chabot, John (Athlete, Coach, Hockey Player)
c/o Staff Member New York Islanders
1535 Old Country Rd
Plainview, NY 11803, USA

Chabot, Steve (Congressman, Politician)
2351 Rayburn HOB
Washington, DC 20515, USa

Chabraja, Nicholas D (Business Person)
General Dynamics
3190 Fairview Park Dr
Falls Church, VA 22042, USA

Chabria, Renee (Director)
c/o Staff Member Management 360
9111 Wilshire Blvd
Beverly Hills, CA 90210, USA

Chace, William E (Educator)
Emory University
President's Office
Atlanta, GA 30322, USA

Chacon, Alex Pineda (Soccer Player)
Los Angeles Galaxy
1010 Rose Bowl Dr
Pasadena, CA 91103, USA

Chacon, Shawn (Athlete, Baseball Player)
7610 W 19th Street Rd
Greeley, CO 80634, USA

Chacurian, Chico (Soccer Player)
96 Stratford Road
Stratford, CT 06615, USA

Chadha, Gurinder (Director)
c/o Staff Member ICM Partners (ICM-LA)
10250 Constellation Blvd Fl 7
Los Angeles, CA 90067, USA

Chadirji, Rifat Kamil (Architect)
28 Troy Court
Kensington High St
London W8, UNITED KINGDOM (UK)

Chadli, Bendjedid (President)
Palace Emir Abedelkader
Algiers, ALGERIA

Chadwick, Bill (Athlete, Hockey Player)
7 Country Club Dr.
Box 789
Cutchoque, NY 11935, USA

Chadwick, Ed (Athlete, Hockey Player)
12 Bowen Rd
Fort Erie, ON L2A 2Y4, Canada

Chadwick, Jeff (Athlete, Football Player)
23062 Village Dr
Apt A
Lake Forest, CA 92630, USA

Chadwick, J Leslie (Les) (Musician)
Barry Collins
21A Cliftown Road
Southend-on-Sea
Essex SS1 1AB, UNITED KINGDOM (UK)

Chadwick, June (Actor)
Contemporary Artists
610 Santa Monica Blvd
#202
Santa Monica, CA 90401, USA

Chadwick, Ray (Athlete, Baseball Player)
607 Gattis St
Durham, NC 27701, USA

Chadwick, William L (Bill) (Misc)
PO Box 501
Country Club Dr
Cutchogue, NY 11935, USA

Chafee, Lincoln (Governor, Politician)
22 Beachwood Dr
East Greenwich, RI 02818-4733, USA

Chafer, Derek (Actor)
Ugly Enterprises Ltd
Tigris House
256 Edgware Rd
London W2 1DS, UK

Chafetz, Sidney (Artist)
Ohio State University
Art Dept
Columbus, OH 43210, USA

Chaffee, Don (Director)
7020 La Presa Dr
Los Angeles, CA 90068, USA

Chaffee, Susan (Suzy) (Athlete, Olympic Athlete, Skier)
55 Roadrunner Rd
Sedona, AZ 86336-5204, USA

Chaffetz, Jason (Congressman, Politician)
1032 Longworth HOB
Washington, DC 20515, USA

Chaffey, Pat (Athlete, Football Player)
10415 SW Gardner Ct
Tualatin, OR 97062, USA

Chafin, Bryan (Actor)
c/o Heather Collier Collier Talent Agency
2313 Lake Austin Blvd
Suite 103
Austin, TX 78703, USA

Chagall, Rachel (Actor)
251 S. Van Ness Ave
Los Angeles, CA 90004, USA

Chagnon, Marcel (Musician)
6535 Melinda Dr
Nashville, TN 37205, USA

Chaiken, Ilene (Producer, Writer)
2614 Reppert Ct
Los Angeles, CA 90046, USA

Chaikin, Carly (Actor)
c/o Andrew Rogers ICM Partners (ICM-LA)
10250 Constellation Blvd Fl 7
Los Angeles, CA 90067, USA

Chailly, Riccardo (Conductor)
Royal Concertgebrew
Jacob Obrechtstraat 51
Armsterdam, 1071 KJ 41, HOLLAND

Chairmen of the Board (Musician)
c/o Staff Member The Willis Blume Agency
P.O. Box 509
Orangeburg, SC 29116-0509, USA

Chakiris, George (Actor, Dancer, Musician)
c/o Elisabeth Simpson Agence Elisabeth Simpson
62 Boulevard Du Montparnasse
Paris 75015, FRANCE

Chakraborty, Pramod (Bollywood, Director, Filmmaker, Producer)
Natraj Studios 194 M V Road
Andheri (E)
Bombay, MS 400 069, INDIA

Chakravarthi, Vinu (Actor, Bollywood)
63 Apusali Street
Chennai, TN 600093, INDIA

Chakravarthy, Dheephan (Actor)
Auroammaa 5/17 Royal Villa 4th Main Road Extn
Kottur Gardens
Chennai, TN 600 085, INDIA

Chalayan, Hussein (Designer, Fashion Designer)
71 Endell Road
London WC2 9AJ, UNITED KINGDOM (UK)

Chalenski, Mike (Athlete, Football Player)
225 S Michigan Ave
Kenilworth, NJ 07033, USA

Chalfie, Martin (Nobel Prize Laureate)
15 Claremont Ave
New York, NY 10027-6809, USA

Chalfont, A G (Arthur) (Government Official)
House of Lords
Westminster
London SW1A 0PW, UNITED KINGDOM (UK)

Chalk, Dave (Athlete, Baseball Player)
137 Cross Timbers Trl
Coppell, TX 75019, USA

Chalke, Sarah (Actor)
3903 Ethel Ave
Studio City, CA 91604, USA

Chalker, Will (Model)
c/o Staff Member New York Model Management
596 Broadway #701
New York, NY 10012, USA

Challis, Christopher (Cinematographer)
BSC Office
c/o Frances Russell
P.O. Box 2587, Winsor Rd
Gerrards Cross SL9 7WZ, UK

Chalmers, Judith (Actor)
23 Eyot Gardens
London W10 5AT, UK

Chalmers, Thea (Stylist)
2459 Mar East
Tiburon, CA 94920, USA

Chaloner, William G (Misc)
20 Parke Road
London SW13 9NG, UNITED KINGDOM (UK)

Chambaret, Catherine (Stylist)
5015 W 8th St
Los Angeles, CA 90005, USA

Chamberlain, Bill (Athlete, Basketball Player)
10111 Daniel Dweane
Dr
Charlotte, NC 27502, 28214-2709

Chamberlain, Byron (Athlete, Football Player)
PO Box 326
Montclair, CA 91763, USA

Chamberlain, Craig (Athlete, Baseball Player)
11292 Los Alamitos Blvd
Los Alamitos, CA 90720, USA

Chamberlain, Dan (Athlete, Football Player)
6356 Puerto Dr
Rancho Murieta, CA 95683, USA

Chamberlain, Jimmy (Actor, Musician)
c/o Staff Member WmE2 (WMA-LA)
1 William Morris Pl
Beverly Hills, CA 90212, USA

Chamberlain, Joba (Athlete, Baseball Player)
c/o Team Member New York Yankees
Yankee Stadium
161st St & River Ave
Bronx, NY 10451, USA

Chamberlain, John A (Artist)
Ten Coconut Inc
PO Box 3022
Shelter Island Heights, NY 11965-3022, USA

Chamberlain, Joseph W (Astronomer)
Rice University
Space Physics & Astronomy Dept
Houston, TX 77001, USA

Chamberlain, Owen (Nobel Prize Laureate)
882 Santa Barbara Road
Berkeley, CA 94707, USA

Chamberlain, Richard (Actor)
3040 S Kihei Rd
Kihei, HI 96753, USA

Chamberlain, Wes (Athlete, Baseball Player)
P.O. Box 1358
Homewood, IL 60430, USA

Chambers, Al (Athlete, Baseball Player)
1303 N 14th St
Harrisburg, PA 17103, USA

Chambers, Anne Cox (Business Person, Diplomat)
Cox Enterprises
1440 Lake Hearn Dr NE
Atlanta, GA 30319, USA

Chambers, Christina (Athlete, Football Player)
c/o Lena Roklin Luber Roklin Management
8530 Wilshire Blvd
6th Floor
Beverly Hills, CA 90211, USA

Chambers, Emma (Actor)
c/o Staff Member *Conway van Gelder*
8-12 Broadwick St
London W1F 8HW, UK

Chambers, Erin (Actor)
c/o Ted Schachter *Schachter Entertainment*
1157 S Beverly Dr Fl 2
Los Angeles, CA 90035, USA

Chambers, Faune (Actor)
c/o Mara Santino *Luber Roklin Management*
8530 Wilshire Blvd
6th Floor
Beverly Hills, CA 90211, USA

Chambers, Faune (Actor)
c/o Staff Member *Luber Roklin Management*
8530 Wilshire Blvd
6th Floor
Beverly Hills, CA 90211, USA

Chambers, Jerry (Athlete, Basketball Player)
4135 Don Diablo Drive
Los Angeles, CA 90008-4305, USA

Chambers, Justin (Actor)
c/o Sandra Chang *Anonymous Content (LA)*
955 S Carrillo Dr
Suite 300
Los Angeles, CA 90048, USA

Chambers, Kasey (Musician)
c/o Staff Member *Paradigm (Monterey)*
404 W Franklin St
Monterey, CA 93940, USA

Chambers, Kirk (Athlete, Football Player)
1294 Lakeview Dr
Provo, UT 84604, USA

Chambers, Lester (Musician)
Lustig Talent
PO Box 770850
Orlando, FL 32877, USA

Chambers, Lucinda (Stylist)
c/o Staff Member *Art Partner*
145 Hudson St
2nd Floor
New York, NY 10013, USA

Chambers, Munro (Actor)
c/o Paul Young *Principato/Young Management*
9465 Wilshire Blvd
Suite 430
Beverly Hills, CA 90212, USA

Chambers, Shawn (Athlete, Hockey Player)
9999 Wood Rdg
Peggout Lakes, MN 56472-4873, USA

Chambers, Tom (Athlete, Basketball Player)
7437 East Via Dona Road
Scottsdale, AZ 85266-2154, USA

Chambers, Wallace (Wally) (Athlete, Football Player)
1838 Joslin St
Saginaw, MI 48602, USA

Chambers, Willie (Musician)
Noga Mgmt
PO Box 1428
Studio City, CA 91614, USA

Chamblee, Al (Athlete, Football Player)
845 Garrow Rd
Newport News, VA 23608, USA

Chamblee, Brandel (Athlete, Golfer)
10800 E Cactus Rd
Unit 32
Scottsdale, AZ 85259-2505, USA

Chamblee, Jim (Athlete, Baseball Player)
1408 Broadway St
Denton, TX 76201, USA

Chambliss, Chris (Athlete, Baseball Player)
12755 Wyngate Trl
Alpharetta, GA 30005, USA

Chambliss, Saxby (Senator)
416 Russell Senate Office Building
Washington, DC 20510, USA

Chambliss, Saxby (Politician)
27 Cherokee Rd
Moultrie, GA 31768-6541, USA

Chambon, Pierre H (Misc)
Institute Genetique Moleculaire/Cellulaire
BP 163
Illkirch 67404, FRANCE

Chamitoff, Gregory E Dr (Astronaut)
2742 Dunsmere Ct
Pearland, TX 77584-9273, USA

Champagne, Andre (Athlete, Hockey Player)
6936 E 75th St
Tulsa, OK 74133, USA

Champine, Robert (Aviator)
205 Tipton Rd
Newport News, VA 23606-3663, USA

Champion, Billy (Athlete, Baseball Player)
240 Triple H Farm Rd
Inman, SC 29349, USA

Champion, Mike (Athlete, Baseball Player)
28952 Modjeska Canyon Rd
Silverado, CA 92676, USA

Champion, Will (Musician)
Nettwerk Mgmt
1650 W 2nd Ave
Vancouver, BC V6J 4R3, CANADA

Champlin, Charles (Critic)
2169 Linda Flora Dr
Los Angeles, CA 90077, USA

Champnella, Eric (Actor, Director, Writer)
c/o Paul Nelson *Mosaic Media Group*
9200 W. Sunset Blvd
10th Floor
Los Angeles, CA 90069, USA

Champoux, Bob (Athlete, Hockey Player)
8861 Centaurus Way
San Diego, CA 92126-1916, USA

Chan, Ernie (Cartoonist)
4131 Vale Ave
Oakland, CA 94619-2223, USA

Chan, Jackie (Actor, Producer)
c/o Philip Button *WME (LA)*
9601 Wilshire Blvd Fl 3
Beverly Hills, CA 90210, USA

Chan, Johnny (Misc)
c/o Mark Karowe
Box 3247
Manhattan Beach, CA 90266, USA

Chan, Jullus (Prime Minister)
PO Box 6030
Boroto
PAPUA NEW GUINEA

Chan, Michael Paul (Actor)
13888 Valley Vista Blvd
Sherman Oaks, CA 91423, USA

Chan, Sy (Misc)
Premier's Office
Phnom-Penh
PEOPLE'S REPUBLIC OF KAMPUCHEA

Chance, Bob (Athlete, Baseball Player)
2258 Oakridge Dr
Charleston, WV 25311, USA

Chance, Bobbie Shaw (Actor)
Expressions Unlimited
13317 Ventura Blvd
Studio G
Sherman Oaks, CA 91423, USA

Chance, Dean (Athlete, Baseball Player)
9505 W Smithville Western Rd
Wooster, OH 44691, USA

Chance, Greyson (Musician)
c/o Guy Oseary *Untitled Entertainment (LA)*
350 S. Beverly Dr #200
Beverly Hills, CA 90212, USA

Chance, Larry (Musician)
Brothers Mgmt
141 Dunbar Ave
Fords, NJ 08863, USA

Chancellor, Chris (Athlete, Football Player)
c/o Jordan Woy *Willis and Woy Management*
3030 Olive St #520
Dallas, TX 75219, USA

Chancellor, Justin (Musician)
19805 Valley View Dr
Topanga, CA 90290, USA

Chancellor, Van (Coach)
Houston Cornets
2 Greenway Plaza
#400
Houston, TX 77046, USA

Chancey, Robert (Athlete, Football Player)
PO Box 212
Coosada, AL 36020, USA

Chanchez, Hosea (Actor)
c/o Glenn Rigberg *Inphenate*
9701 Wilshire Blvd.
10th Floor
Beverly Hills, CA 90212, USA

Chandler, Al (Athlete, Football Player)
P.O. Box 21733
Oklahoma City, OK 73156, USA

Chandler, Ben (Congressman, Politician)
1504 Longworth HOB
Washington, DC 20515, USA

Chandler, Christopher M (Chris) (Athlete, Football Player)
1625 Lugano Ln
Del Mar, CA 92014, USA

Chandler, Gene (Athlete, Football Player)
550 Southmoor Cir
Stockbridge, GA 30281, USA

Chandler, Jeff (Boxer)
6242 Horner St
Philadelphia, PA 19144, USA

Chandler, Karl (Athlete, Football Player)
5 Plymouth Rd
Newtown Square, PA 19073, USA

Chandler, Kim (Stylist)
c/o Staff Member *Jam Arts, Inc*
154 W 57th St
New York, NY 10019, USA

Chandler, Kyle (Actor)
222068 Topanga School Rd
Topanga, CA 90290, USA

Chandler, Mark (Stylist)
c/o Staff Member *Art Department*
48 Greene St
4th Floor
New York, NY 10013, USA

Chandler, Michael Ltcolonel (General)
3525 Wild Eagle Run
Oviedo, FL 32766-8131, USA

Chandler, Michael "Mike" (Race Car Driver)
61883 Bunker Hill Court
Bend, OR 97702, USA

Chandler, Thornton (Athlete, Football Player)
8646 Guinevere St
Houston, TX 77029, USA

Chandler, Tom (Athlete, Football Player)
16310 Axis Trl
San Antonio, TX 78232-2804, USA

Chandler, Tyson (Athlete, Basketball Player)
21731 Ventura Blvd
Ste 300
Woodland, CA 91364-1851, USA

Chandler, Wesley S (Wes) (Athlete, Football Player)
207 Howard St
New Smyrna Beach, FL 32168, USA

Chandler, Wilson (Athlete, Basketball Player)
c/o Chris Luchey *CGL Sports*
885 Woodstock Rd
Suite 430-303
Roswell, GA 30075, USA

Chando, Alexandra (Actor)
c/o Elise Koseff *J Mitchell Management*
440 Park Ave S
New York, NY 10016, USA

Chandoha, Walter (Photographer)
SO Spring Hill Rd
Annandale, NJ 08801-3505, USA

Chandola, Walter (Photographer)
50 Spring Hill Road
Annandale, NJ 08801, USA

Chandra, Asha (Actor, Bollywood)
C6/6 Sangeeta Apartments
Juhu Santacruz
Mumbai, MS 400049, INDIA

Chandran, S S (Actor)
34A Asumpon Muthuramalingum Street
Rajaji Colony
Chennai, TN 600 092, INDIA

Chandran, Sudha (Actor, Bollywood)
4, Mahant Road Extension 6141250
Vile Parkel (E)
Mumbai, MS 400057, INDIA

Chandran, T K S (Actor)
D25 Amutham Colony
South Boag Road
Chennai, TN 600 017, INDIA

Chandrasekar (Actor)
34 Senthil Nagar Main Road Chinna Porur
Near Valasaravakkam
Chennai, TN 600 116, INDIA

Chandrasekhar, Bhagwat S (Cricketer)
571 31st Cross
4th Block Jayanagar
Bangalore 56011, INDIA

Chandrasekhar, Jay (Comedian)
c/o Staff Member *United Talent Agency*
(UTA)
9336 Civic Center Dr
Beverly Hills, CA 90210, USA

Chanel, Tally (Actor, Model)
Don Gerler
3349 Cahuenga Blvd W
#1
Los Angeles, CA 90068, USA

Chaney, Darrel (Athlete, Baseball Player)
906 Woodbrier
Sautee Nacoochee, GA 30571, USA

Chaney, Don (Athlete, Basketball Player)
20711 Park Pine Drive
Katy, TX 77450-2811, USA

Chaney, John (Athlete, Basketball Player)
1639 Sharp Road
Baton Rouge, LA 70815-4879, USA

Chaney, John (Coach)
Temple University
Athletic Dept
Philadelphia, PA 19122, USA

Chang, Christina (Actor)
c/o Myrna Jacoby *MJ Management*
130 W 57th St
Suite 11A
New York, NY 10019, USA

Chang, Chun-hsiung (Prime Minister)
Premier's Office
1 Chunghsiao East Road
Section 1
Taipei, TAIWAN

Chang, Dr Thomas (Scientist)
3665 Rue Fenelon
Montreal, QC H2A 1M9, Canada

Chang, Irene (Stylist)
501 Arguello Blvd
#302
San Francisco, CA 94118, USA

Chang, Michael (Athlete, Tennis Player)
Chang Family Foundation
28562 Oso Pkwy #D343
Rancho Santa Margarita, CA 92688, USA

Chang, Sarah (Musician)
I C M Artists
40 W 57th St
New York, NY 10019, USA

Chang-Diaz, Franklin R (Astronaut)
1110 Pine Ci
Seabrook, TX 77586-4709, USA

Chang-Diaz, Franklin R (Astronaut)
NASA
Johnson Space Center
2101 NASA Road
Houston, TX 77058, USA

Changeux, Jean-Pierre G (Biologist)
47 Rue du Four
Paris 75006, FRANCE

Channing, Carol (Actor, Musician)
Channing-Kullijian Foundation
101 First St #443
Los Altos, CA 94022, USA

Channing, Stockard (Actor)
8044 Woodrow Wilson Dr
Los Angeles, CA 90046, USA

Chant, Charlie (Athlete, Baseball Player)
930 Starlight Ct
Banning, CA 92220-1710, USA

Chantels, The (Music Group)
c/o Staff Member *Creative Entertainment*
Associates Inc
6 Esterbrook Lane
Cherry Hill, NJ 08003-4002, USA

Chanticleer (Musician)
c/o Staff Member *ICM Partners (ICM-LA)*
10250 Constellation Blvd Fl 7
Los Angeles, CA 90067, USA

Chantos, Heather (Stylist)
c/o Staff Member *Workgroup (Hollywood)*
8491 Sunset Blvd
#368
West Hollywood, CA 90069, USA

Chantres, Carlos (Baseball Player)
67 Amherst St
Nashua, NH 03064-2561

Chao, Elaine (Politician)
2318 Dundee Rd
Louisville, KY 40205-2070, USA

Chao, Elaine L (Secretary)
Labor Department
200 Constitution Ave NW
Washington, DC 21210, USA

Chao, Rosalind (Actor)
305 15th St
Santa Monica, CA 90402, USA

Chao, Vic (Actor)
c/o Staff Member *Osbrink Talent Agency*
4343 Lankershim Blvd
Suite 100
Universal City, CA 91602, USA

Chapdelaine, Rene (Athlete, Hockey
Player)
662 S Division Rd
Petoskey, MI 49770-8218, USA

Chapin, Darrin (Athlete, Baseball Player)
328 Portage Easterly Rd
Cortland, OH 44410, USA

Chapin, Doug (Actor, Producer)
Doug Chapin Management
1100 Alta Loma Rd
Suite 605
West Hollywood, CA 90069, USA

Chapin, Dwight L (Government Official,
Publisher)
San Francisco Examiner
110 5th St
San Francisco, CA 94103, USA

Chapin, Lauren (Actor)
11940 Reedy Creek Dr
#207
Orlando, FL 32836, USA

Chapin, Schuyler G (Misc)
650 Park Ave
New York, NY 10021, USA

Chapin, Tom (Musician, Songwriter,
Writer)
57 Piermont Place
Piermont, NY 10968, USA

Chaplin, Alexander (Actor)
c/o Tammy Rosen *Sanders Armstrong*
Caserta
425 N Robertson Blvd
Los Angeles, CA 90048, USA

Chaplin, Ben (Actor)
c/o Simon Halls *Slate Public Relations*
9000 Sunset Blvd #915
West Hollywood, CA 90069, USA

Chaplin, Geraldine (Actor, Writer)
c/o Staff Member *WmE2 (WMA-LA)*
1 William Morris Pl
Beverly Hills, CA 90212, USA

Chaplin, Greg (Athlete, Baseball Player)
12426 Glenfield Avenue
Tampa, FL 33626-2606, USA

Chaplin, Josephine (Actor)
Association Chaplin
58 Rue Jean Jacques Rousseau
Paris F-70001, France

Chaplin, Kiera (Actor, Producer)
c/o Staff Member *Creative Artists Agency*
(CAA-LA)
2000 Ave Of The Stars
Los Angeles, CA 90067, USA

Chaplynsky, Renata (Stylist)
c/o Staff Member *Faucher Artists*
636 Broadway #1218
New York, NY 10012, USA

Chapman, Al (Race Car Driver)
RD #1
Box 212
Atoens, PA 18810, USA

Chapman, Alvah H Jr (Publisher)
Grove Harbour
1690 S Bayshore Lane
#10A
Miami, FL 33133, USA

Chapman, Beth Nielsen (Reality TV Star)
Sussman Assoc
1383 Queen Emma St
Honolulu, HI 96813, USA

Chapman, Blair (Athlete, Hockey Player)
2068 Redcoach Rd
Allison Park, PA 15101-3231, USA

Chapman, Brian (Athlete, Hockey Player)
32 Deer Run Rd
Agawam, MA 01001-3669, USA

Chapman, Bruce K (Government Official)
Discovery Institute
1201 3rd Ave #4000
Seattle, WA 98101, USA

Chapman, Clarence (Athlete, Football
Player)
14820 Parkside St
Detroit, MI 48238, USA

Chapman, David S (Athlete, Football
Player)
789 N Main St
New Martinsville, WV 26155, USA

Chapman, Doug (Athlete, Football Player)
6215 Chesterfield Meadows Dr
Chesterfield, VA 23832, USA

Chapman, Dr Philip K (Astronaut)
11460 E Helm Dr
Scottsdale, AZ 85255-1885, USA

Chapman, Duane (Dog) (Actor, Reality
TV Star)
c/o Alan Nevins *Renaissance Literary &*
Talent
P.O. Box 17379
Beverly Hills, CA 90209, USA

Chapman, E T (General)
Victoria Cross Society
Old Admiralty Building
London, England SW1A 2BE, UK

Chapman, Gary (Musician)
8382 Collins Rd
Nashville, TN 37221, USA

Chapman, Georgina (Designer)
Marchesa
601 W 26th St
Suite 1425
New York, NY 10001, USA

Chapman, Gil (Athlete, Football Player)
771 Cranford Ave
Westfield, NJ 07090, USA

Chapman, Johnny (Race Car Driver)
Douglas & Sons Racing
1025 W. Chipley Ford Rd.
Statesville, NC 28625, USA

Chapman, Judith (Actor)
11670 Sunset Blvd
#312
Los Angeles, CA 90049, USA

Chapman, Kelvin (Athlete, Baseball
Player)
9301 Laughlin Way
Redwood Valley, CA 95470, USA

Chapman, Kevin (Actor)
c/o Ellen Meyer *Ellen Meyer Management*
8899 Beverly Blvd
Suite 612
West Hollywood, CA 90048, USA

Chapman, Lamar (Athlete, Football
Player)
18513 N Whitedove Ln
Cleveland, OH 44130, USA

Chapman, Lanei (Actor)
c/o Judy Page *Mitchell K Stubbs & Assoc*
(MKS)
8675 W. Washington Blvd
Suite 203
Culver City, CA 90232, USA

Chapman, Leland (Actor, Reality TV Star)
c/o Staff Member *Dog the Bounty Hunter*
235 E 45th St
New York, NY 10017, USA

Chapman, Mark David (Misc)
#81 A 3860 Box 149
Attica Corr. Facility
Attica, NY 14011, USA

Chapman, Mark Lindsay (Actor)
c/o Michael Zanuck *Michael Zanuck*
Agency
28035 Dorothy Drive
Suite 120
Agoura Hills, CA 91301, USA

Chapman, Michael J (Cinematographer,
Director)
501 S Beverly Dr
#300
Beverly Hills, CA 90212, USA

Chapman, Mike (Athlete, Football Player)
8731 Avator Cir
Boerne, TX 78015, USA

Chapman, Nicki (Actor)
c/o Staff Member *Arlington Enterprises Ltd*
1-3 Charlotte St
London W1P 1HD, UNITED KINGDOM
(UK)

Chapman, Paul (Actor)
The Spotlight
7 Leicester Pl
London WC2H 7RJ, UK

Chapman, Rex (Athlete, Basketball Player)
6014 East Jenan Drive
Scottsdale, AZ 85254-4907, USA

Chapman, Robert F (Judge)
PO Box 253
Linville, NC 28646, USA

Chapman, Steven Curtis (Musician, Songwriter)
Sparrow Records
PO Box 5010
Brentwood, TN 37024, USA

Chapman, Thomas F (Business Person)
Equifax Inc
1550 Peachtree St NE
Atlanta, GA 30309, USA

Chapman, Tracy (Musician, Songwriter)
2700 Purissima Creek Rd
Half Moon Bay, CA 94019, USA

Chapman, Travis (Athlete, Baseball Player)
5215 Hickson Rd
Jacksonville, FL 32207, USA

Chapman, Wayne (Athlete, Basketball Player)
3593 Salisbury Drive
Lexington, KY 40510-9742, USA

Chapman, Wes (Ballerina)
American Ballet Theater
890 Broadway
New York, NY 10003, USA

Chapot, Frank (Athlete, Horse Racer, Olympic Athlete)
1075 Opie Rd
Branchburg, NJ 08853-4163, USA

Chapoy, Pati (Actor)
c/o Staff Member *TV Azteca*
Periferico Sur 4121
Colonia Fuentes del Pedregal
DF CP 14141, Mexico

Chappas, Harry (Athlete, Baseball Player)
22 SE 1st Ave
Dania, FL 33004, USA

Chappell, Crystal (Actor)
235 Newport Avenue
Grover Beach, CA 93433-1512, USA

Chappell, Fred D (Writer)
305 Kensington Road
Greensboro, NC 27403, USA

Chappell, Gregory S (Greg) (Athlete, Cricketer)
Cricket Australia Centre of Excellence
60 Jolimont St
Jolimont, VIC 5006, Australia

Chappell, Len (Athlete, Basketball Player)
7624 Chestnut Lane
Waterford, WI 53185-1707, USA

Chappelle, Dave (Actor, Comedian, Producer)
3420 Grinnell Rd
Yellow Springs, OH 45387, USA

Chappelle, Emmett (Inventor)
2502 Allendale Rd
Baltimore, MD 21216-2106, USA

Chapple, Dave (Athlete, Football Player)
5 Kara E
Irvine, CA 92620, USA

Chapuisat, Stephane (Soccer Player)
Borussia Dortmund Soccer Club
Strobeialle
Dortmund 44139, GERMANY

Chapura, Richard (Dick) (Athlete, Football Player)
7853 Saddle Creek Trl
Sarasota, FL 34241, USA

Chara, Zdeno (Athlete, Hockey Player)
343 Commercial St
Unit 211-213
Boston, MA 02109-1245, USA

Charan, Raaj N (Actor)
Shri Renuka Mandir 154
Vasudevan Nagar Jaffarkhanpet
Chennai, TN 600 095, INDIA

Charboneau, Joe (Athlete, Baseball Player)
33020 Leafy Mill Ln
North Ridgeville, OH 44039, USA

Charbonneau, Patricia (Actor)
749 1/2 N Lafayette Park Place
Los Angeles, CA 90026, USA

Charbonneau, Stephane (Athlete, Hockey Player)
1 Wilderness Dr
Voorhees, NJ 08043-3415, USA

Charbonnier, CArole (Athlete, Golfer)
19 Carolina Ave
West Orange, NJ 07052, USA

Charen, Mona (Writer)
c/o Staff Member *HarperCollins Publishers*
10 East 53rd St
c/o Author mail, 7th Floor
New York, NY 10022, USA

Charland, Colin (Baseball Player)
Fleer
5303 Alta Vista Ln
Arlington, TX 76017-1735, USA

Charlap, Bill (Musician)
Abby Hoffer
223 1/2 E 48th St
New York, NY 10017, USA

Charlebois, Bob (Athlete, Hockey Player)
318 Duncairn Ave
Ottawa, ON K1Z 7G9, Canada

Charles, Bob (Athlete, Golfer)
5329 Sea Biscuit Rd
Palm Beach Gardens, FL 33418-7818, USA

Charles, Caroline (Designer, Fashion Designer)
56/57 Beauchamp Place
London SW3, UNITED KINGDOM (UK)

Charles, Craig (Actor)
PFD
Drury House
34-43 Russell St
London WC2B 5HA, UNITED KINGDOM (UK)

Charles, Daedra (Athlete, Basketball Player, Olympic Athlete)
Los Angeles Sparks
26730 Joy Rd
Apt 3
Redford, MI 48239-1939, USA

Charles, Ed (Athlete, Baseball Player)
57 Park Ter E
Apt B58
New York, NY 10034, USA

Charles, Frank (Athlete, Baseball Player)
114 Garden Ct
Buffalo, NY 14226, USA

Charles, Gaius (Actor)
c/o Stephen Hirsh *Gersh (LA)*
9465 Wilshire Blvd
Suite 600
Beverly Hills, CA 90212, USA

Charles, John (Athlete, Football Player)
5644 Westheimer Rd
Apt 164
Houston, TX 77056, USA

Charles, Josh (Actor)
c/o Stephanie Ritz *WME (LA)*
9601 Wilshire Blvd Fl 3
Beverly Hills, CA 90210, USA

Charles, Ken (Athlete, Basketball Player)
621 Putnam Avenue
Brooklyn, NY 11221-1601, USA

Charles, Max (Actor)
c/o Margot Menzel *Evolution Entertainment (LA)*
901 N Highland Ave
Los Angeles, CA 90038, USA

Charles M Brig Gen, Duke (Astronaut)
PO Box 310345
New Braunfels, TX 78131-0345, USA

Charleson, Leslie (Actor)
4851 Cromwell Ave
Los Angeles, CA 90027, USA

Charlesworth, James H (Misc)
Princeton Theological Seminary
Theology Dept
Princeton, NJ 08540, USA

Charlesworth, Todd (Athlete, Hockey Player)
914 N Brookside Dr
Muskegon, MI 49441, USA

Charlie, Diamond
7300 SW 69th Ct
Miami, FL 33143, USA

Charlie, Dupre (Athlete, Football Player)
407 Bay St N
Texas City, TX 77590-6427, USA

Charlton, Clifford (Athlete, Football Player)
3708 Carrington Pl
Tallahassee, FL 32303, USA

Charlton, Norm (Athlete, Baseball Player)
312 Estes Dr
Rockport, TX 78382, USA

Charlton, Robert (Bobby) (Soccer Player)
Garthollerton
Cleford Road
Ollerton near Knutsford, Cheshire,
UNITED KINGDOM (UK)

Charm City Devils (Music Group, Musician)
c/o Staff Member *10th Street Entertainment (NY)*
38 W 21st St
Suite 300
New York, NY 10010, USA

Charmila (Actor, Bollywood)
27/1 Habibullah Road
T Nagar
Chennai, TN 600017, INDIA

Charmoli, Tony (Choreographer, Director)
1271 Sunset Plaza Dr
Los Angeles, CA 90069, USA

Charney, Jordan (Actor)
c/o Staff Member *Leading Artists*
145 W 45th St
Suite 1000
New York, NY 10036, USA

Charney, Kim (Actor)
4811 Seashore Dr
Newport Beach, CA 92663, USA

Charo (Musician)
1801 Lexington Rd
Beverly Hills, CA 90210, USA

Charren, Peggy (Activist)
Action for Children's Television
PO Box 383090
Cambridge, MA 02238, USA

Charron, Guy (Athlete, Hockey Player)
80 Country Village
Cir NE, Calgary T3K 6E2, Canada

Charron, Guy
Kamloops Blazers
300 Lorne St
Attn: Coaching Staff Kamlooos, BC V2C
1W3, Canada

Charron, Paul R (Business Person)
Liz Claiborne Inc
1441 Broadway
New York, NY 10018, USA

Chartier, Dave (Athlete, Hockey Player)
SW 13-19-28 W
Binscarth, MB R0J 0G0, Canada

Chartoff, Melanie (Actor)
Artists Agency
1180 S Beverly Dr
#301
Los Angeles, CA 90035, USA

Chartoff, Robert (Producer)
PO Box 3628
Granada Hills, CA 91394, USA

Charton, Pete (Athlete, Baseball Player)
27 Vincinda Ln
Harriman, TN 37748, USA

Chartraw, Rick (Athlete, Hockey Player)
600 Chaparral Rd
Sierra Madre, CA 91024-1115, USA

Charuhasan (Actor)
37 Maharani Chinnamani Road
Chennai, TN 600 018, INDIA

Charvet, David (Actor)
3551 Cross Creek Rd
Malibu, CA 90265, USA

Charyk, Joseph V (Business Person)
790 Andrews Ave
#A302
Delray Beach, FL 33483, USA

Chase, Alison (Director)
Pilolobus Dance Theater
PO Box 388
Washington Depot, CT 06794, USA

Chase, Alston (Writer)
c/o Deborah Clarke Grosvenor *The Bohrman Agency*
8899 Beverly Blvd #811
Los Angeles, CA 90048, USA

Chase, Bailey (Actor)
c/o Staff Member *McKeon-Myones Management*
3500 Olive Ave
Suite 770
Burbank, CA 91505, USA

Chase, Barrie (Actor, Dancer)
446 Carrol Canal
Venice, CA 90291, USA

Chase, Chevy (Actor, Comedian, Producer)
PO Box 257
Bedford, NY 10506, USA

Chase, Daveigh (Actor)
c/o Bonnie Liedtke *Principato/Young Management*
9465 Wilshire Blvd
Suite 430
Beverly Hills, CA 90212, USA

Chase, David (Producer)
c/o Staff Member *United Talent Agency (UTA)*
9336 Civic Center Dr
Beverly Hills, CA 90210, USA

Chase, Hayley (Actor)
c/o Staff Member *Bobby Ball Talent Agency*
4116 W Magnolia Blvd Ste 205
Burbank, CA 91505-2700, USA

Chase, John (Athlete, Hockey Player)
170 Broadway
Apt 609
New York, NY 10038, USA

Chase, Jonathan (Actor)
c/o Tracy Steinsapir *Main Title Entertainment*
8383 Wilshire Blvd
Suite 408
Los Angeles, CA 90211, USA

Chase, Kelly (Athlete, Hockey Player)
16476 Horseshoe Ridge Rd
Chesterfield, MO 63005-4422, USA

Chase, Kristen (Writer)
c/o Staff Member *Adams Media Corporation*
57 Littlefield St
Avon, MA 02322, USA

Chase, Leah (Chef, Writer)
c/o Staff Member *Pelican Publishing Company*
1000 Burmaster St
Gretna, LA 70053-2246, USA

Chase, Lorraine (Actor)
c/o Staff Member *Peter Charlesworth & Assoc*
68 Old Brompton Rd
London SW7 3LQ, UK

Chase, Peggy (Stylist)
c/o Staff Member *Team*
423 W Broadway
4th Floor
Boston, MA 02127, USA

Chase, Sylvia B (Correspondent)
ABC-TV
News Dept
77 W 66th St
New York, NJ 10023, USA

Chasez, JC (Musician)
2304 Sunset Plz Dr
Los Angeles, CA 90069, UASA

Chass, Murray (Commentator)
22-20 Radburn Rd
Fair Lawn, NJ 07410-4524, USA

Chassey, Steve (Race Car Driver)
2409 Corsican Circle
Westfield, IN 46074, USA

Chast, Roz (Comedian)
New Yorker Magazine
Editorial Dept
4 Times Square
New York, NY 10036, USA

Chastain, Brandi (Athlete, Olympic Athlete, Soccer Player)
1661 University Way
San Jose, CA 95126-1555, USA

Chastain, Jessica (Actor)
c/o Paul Nelson *Mosaic Media Group*
9200 W. Sunset Blvd
10th Floor
Los Angeles, CA 90069, USA

Chastel, Andre (Writer)
30 Rue de Lubeck
Paris 75116, FRANCE

Chatham, Matt (Athlete, Football Player)
2502 Old Bridge Ln
Bellingham, NY 02019, USA

Chatham, Russell (Artist)
General Delivery
Deep Creek
Livingston, MT 59047, USA

Chatham, Wes (Actor)
c/o Robert Stein *Robert Stein Management*
PO Box 3797
Beverly Hills, CA 90212, USA

Chatman, Charles (Baseball Player)
Detroit Clowns
2024 Clarksdale Ave
Memphis, TN 38108-1313, USA

Chatman, Jesse (Athlete, Football Player)
c/o Eugene Parker *Maximum Sports Management*
6435 W Jefferson Blvd
#197
Fort Wayne, IN 46804, USA

Chatterjee, Moushumi (Actor, Bollywood)
Nibbana annexe 1st Floor
Pali Hill Bandra
Bombay, MS 400 050, INDIA

Chatterji, Basu (Actor, Bollywood, Director, Filmmaker)
Violete Villa 1st Floor West Avenue
Santacruz
Mumbai, MS 400054, INDIA

Chatwin, Justin (Actor)
c/o Theresa Peters *United Talent Agency (UTA)*
9336 Civic Center Dr
Beverly Hills, CA 90210, USA

Chau, François (Actor)

Chaudhry, Mahima (Actor, Bollywood)
D/5 4th Floor Silver View Versova
Andheri
Mumbai, MS 400061, INDIA

Chauvez, Patric (Stylist)
c/o Staff Member *Fifty8 Artists*
58 W Huron St
Chicago, IL 60610, USA

Chauvin, Yves (Nobel Prize Laureate)
Institut Francaise Du Pétrol
1&4 Avenue De Bois-Préau
Rueil-Malmaison F-92852, France

Chauvire, Yvette (Ballerina)
21 Place du Commerce
Paris 75015, FRANCE

Chavarria, Ossie (Athlete, Baseball Player)
3707 Cardiff St
Burnaby, BC V5G 2H1, Canada

Chaves, Richard J (Actor)
c/o Staff Member *Media Artists Group (NY)*
140 E 46th St #PHC
New York, NY 10017, USA

Chavez, Anthony (Athlete, Baseball Player)
10569 S Varner Dr
Vail, AZ 85641, USA

Chavez, Eric (Athlete, Baseball Player)
6635 N 66th Pl
Paradise Valley, AZ 85253, USA

Chavez, Hugo (President)
Palacio de Miraflores
Avenida Urdaneta
Caracas 1010, Venezuela

Chavez, Jorge (Horse Racer)
106 John St
Garden City, NY 11530-3006, USA

Chavez, Julio Cesar (Athlete, Boxer)
c/o Staff Member *Boxing Hall of Fame*
1 Hall Of Fame Dr.
Canastota, NY 13032, USA

Chavez, Linda (Correspondent)
c/o Staff Member *Fox News Channel (NY)*
1211 Ave of the Americas
Level C1
New York, NY 10036-8701, USA

Chavez, Marga (Actor)
c/o Staff Member *Select Artists Ltd (CA-Valley Office)*
PO Box 4359
Burbank, CA 91503, USA

Chavira, Ricardo (Actor)
3151 Glencrest Dr
Glendale, CA 91208, USA

Chavous, Barney L (Athlete, Coach, Football Coach, Football Player)
601 Chavous Rd
Aiken, SC 29803, USA

Chavous, Corey (Athlete, Football Player)
1218 S Main St
Saint Charles, MO 63301, USA

Chawla, Juhi (Actor, Bollywood)
153 Oxford Tower Yamuna Nagar
Oshiwara Complex Andheri (W)
Mumbai, MS 400058, INDIA

Chayanne (Actor, Musician)
4600 N Bay Rd
Miami Beach, FL 33140, USA

Chazov, Yevgeny I (Doctor)
Cardiology Research Center
Cherepkovskaya UI 15-A
Moscow 121552, RUSSIA

Cheadle, Don (Actor)
534 Dryad Rd
Santa Monica, CA 90402, USA

Cheaney, Calbert N (Athlete, Basketball Player)
110 Bow Ln
Indianpolis, IN 46220-1024, USA

Cheatham, Ernie (Athlete, Football Player)
400 Ashton St
Pittsburgh, PA 15207, USA

Cheatham, Maree (Actor)
Yvette Schumer
8787 Shoreham Dr
West Hollywood, CA 90069, USA

Check, Lude (Athlete, Hockey Player)
516-100 Grant Carman Dr
Nepean, ON K2E 8B8, Canada

Checker, Chubby (Musician, Songwriter, Writer)
Twisted Booking
c/o Mary Parisi
320 Fayette St Fl 2
Conshohocken, PA 19428, USA

Checo, Robinson (Baseball Player)
Boston Red Sox
Romulo Bentan Cul #04
Santiago, DOMINICAN REPUBLIC

Cheechoo, Jonathan (Athlete, Hockey Player)
707 Iris Gardens Ct
San Jose, CA 95125-1642, USA

Cheek, John (Opera Singer)
ICM Artists
40 W 57th St
New York, NY 10019, USA

Cheek, Louis (Athlete, Football Player)
545 Woelke Rd
Seguin, TX 78155, USA

Cheek, Molly (Actor)
c/o Staff Member *Pakula/King & Associates*
9229 Sunset Blvd
Suite 315
Los Angeles, CA 90069, USA

Cheeks, Judy (Musician)
50 New Bond St.
London W1S 1RD, UK

Cheeks, Maurica E (Mo) (Athlete, Basketball Player, Coach)
7325 SW Childs Road
Portland, OR 97224, USA

Cheeks, Maurice (Athlete, Basketball Player)
301 NE 4th St
Oklahma City, OK 73104-2225, USA

Cheena, Manager (Actor)
No 8 Vivekanandapuram Ist Street
West Mambalam
Chennai, TN 600 033, INDIA

Cheeseborough, Chandra (Athlete, Olympic Athlete, Track Athlete)
104 W Harbor
Hendersonville, TN 37075-3556, USA

Cheesman, Barry (Athlete, Golfer)
2901 Theresa Ln
Sarasota, FL 34239, USA

Cheetwood, Derk (Actor)
12925 Valleyheart Dr
Studio City, CA 91604, USA

Cheever, Eddie (Race Car Driver)
8227 Northwest Blvd
Ste 300
Indianapolis, IN 46278, USA

Cheever, Michael (Athlete, Football Player)
2638 Weddington Pl NE
Marietta, GA 30068, USA

Cheevers, Gary (Athlete, Hockey Player)
2 Jakobek Way
Merrimac, MA 01860-1017, USA

Cheevers, Gerry (Athlete, Hockey Player)
106 Appleton St
North Andover, MA 01845-3138, USA

Chekamauskas, Vitautas (Architect)
State Arts Academy
Maironio 6
Vilnius 2600, LITHUANIA

Chelberg, Robert D (General)
Cubic Applications
Patch Community
Unit 30400 Box R65
APO, AE 09128, USA

Chelf, Donald(Don) (Athlete, Football Player)
7329 Bottle Brush Dr
Spring Hill, FL 34606-7023, USA

Cheli, Giovanni Cardinal (Religious Leader)
Pastoral Care of Migrants Council
Piazza Calisto 16
Rome 00153, ITALY

Cheli, Lt Colonel Maurizio (Astronaut)
Alenia Spazio Spa
Officio Piloti
Caselle Stud, Torino 1-10072, Italy

Cheli, Maurizio (Astronaut)
c/o Staff Member *NASA*
Johnson Space Center
2101 NASA Rd
Houston, TX 77058, USA

Cheli-Merchez, Marianne (Astronaut)
132 Rue Van Aliard
Bruxelles 1180, BELGIUM

Chelios, Chris (Athlete, Hockey Player, Olympic Athlete)
28026 Sea Lane Dr
Malibu, CA 90265, USA

Chellgren, Paul W (Business Person)
Ashland Inc
PO Box 391
Covington, KY 41015, USA

Chelsom, Peter (Actor)
c/o Staff Member *Principato/Young Management*
9465 Wilshire Blvd
Suite 430
Beverly Hills, CA 90212, USA

Chemical Brothers (Music Group)
c/o Staff Member *Target Concerts GmbH*
Müllerstrasse 42
München 80469, GERMANY

Chen, Bruce (Athlete, Baseball Player)
114 Dutchfork Creek Trl
Irmo, SC 29063, USA

Chen, Camille (Actor)
c/o Scott Zimmerman *Evolution Entertainment (LA)*
901 N Highland Ave
Los Angeles, CA 90038, USA

Chen, Da (Writer)
c/o Staff Member *Writers and Artists Group Intl (NY)*
360 Park Ave #16
New York, NY 10022-5909, USA

Chen, Edith (Musician)
Columbia Artists Mgmt Inc
165 W 57th St
New York, NY 10019, USA

Chen, Guang Biao (Business Person)
Jiangsu Huangpu Investment
Nanjing
Jiangsu Province, China

Chen, Irvin S Y (Scientist)
University of California
Med Center
Hematology Dept
Los Angeles, CA 90024, USA

Chen, Joan (Actor, Director)
2601 Filbert St
San Francisco, CA 94123, USA

Chen, Joie (Correspondent)
Cable News Network
News Dept
1050 Techwood Dr NW
Atlanta, GA 30318, USA

Chen, Julie (Reality TV Star, Television Host)
c/o Staff Member *CBS News*
Viacom Inc
524 W 57th St
New York, NY 10019, USA

Chen, Kaige (Director)
International Creative Mgmt
8942 Wilshire Blvd
#219
Beverly Hills, CA 90211, USA

Chen, Lincoln C (Doctor)
302 Dean Road
Brookline, MA, USA

Chen, Lu (Figure Skater)
Skating Assn
54 Baishiqiao Road
Haidian District
Beijing 10044, CHINA

Chen, Lynn (Actor)
c/o Staff Member *ICM Partners (ICM-LA)*
10250 Constellation Blvd Fl 7
Los Angeles, CA 90067, USA

Chen, Robert (Musician)
Columbia Artists Mgmt Inc
165 W 57th St
New York, NY 10019, USA

Chen, Shui-bian (President)
President's Office
Chieshshou Hall
Chung-King Road
Taipei 100, TAIWAN

Chen, Steve S (Engineer)
Chen Systems Corp
1414 W Hamilton Ave
Eau Claire, WI 54701, USA

Chen, Xieyang
Shanghai Symphony Orchestra
105 Hunan Road
Shanghai 200031, CHINA

Chen, Yi (Composer)
University of Missouri
Music Dept
Kansas City, MO 64110, USA

Chen, Zuohuang (Conductor)
Wichita Symphony Orchestra
Concert Hall
225 W Douglas St
Wichita, KS 67202, USA

Chenault, Kenneth (Business Person)
1044 Brick Kiln Rd
Sar Harbor, NY 11963, USA

Chenery, Penny (Misc)
20 Roberts Lane
Saratoga Springs, NY 12866, USA

Cheney, Dick (Ex-Vice President, Politician)
American Enterprise Institute
1150 17th St Nw
Washington, DC 20036, USA

Cheney, Lynne V (Government Official)
American Enterprise Institute
1150 17th St NW
Washington, DC 20036, USA

Cheney, Richard B (President, Secretary, Vice President)
6613 Madison Dr
McLean, VA 22101, USA

Cheng, Olivia (Actor)
c/o Elena Kirschner *Lucas Talent Inc*
100 W. Pender St
Sun Tower, 7th Floor
Vancouver, BC V6B 1R8, Canada

Cheng, Pei-pei (Actor)
c/o Andrew Ooi *Echelon Talent Management*
3674 Oxford St
Vancouver BC V5K 1P3, Canada

Chenier, Phil (Athlete, Basketball Player)
907 Mount Holly Street
Baltimore, MD 21229, USA

Chenier, Phil
7410 Hindon Cir
Unit 301
Windsor Mill, MD 21244-5620, USA

Chennault, Anna (Business Person)
TAC International
Chennault Building
1049 30th St NW
Washington, DC 20007, USA

Chennault, Anna Chan (General)
Chennault Building 1049 30th St NW
Washington, DC 20007-3823, USA

Chenoweth, Kristin (Actor, Musician)
200 Riverside Blvd #309
New York, NY 10069, USA

Cher (Actor, Director, Musician, Producer)
125 Vista Pl.
Venice, CA 90291, USA

Chereau, Patrice (Director)
Nanterre-Amandiers
7 Ave Pablo Picasso
Nanterre 9200, FRANCE

Cherestal, Jean-Marie (Prime Minister)
Prime Minister's Office
Palais Ministeres
Port-au-Prince, HAITI

Cherington, Ben (Commentator)
338 Commercial St
Apt 401
Boston, MA 02109-1128, USA

Chermayeff, Peter (Architect)
Chermayeff, Sollogub And Poole Inc
51 Melcher St Fl 9
Boston, MA 10010, USA

Chernin, Peter (Business Person)
News Corp
1211 Ave of the Americas
New York, NY 10036, USA

Chernobrovkina, Tatyana A (Ballerina)
Moscow Musical Theater
B Dimitrovka Str 17
Moscow 103009, RUSSIA

Chernoff, Mike (Athlete, Hockey Player)
864 Algoma Ave
Moose Jaw, SK S6H 3Z3, Canada

Chernomaz, Rich (Athlete, Hockey Player)
6041 Sierra Way
Nanaimo, BC V9V 1R8, Canada

Chernov, Vladimir K (Opera Singer)
Columbia Artists Mgmt Inc
165 W 57th St
New York, NY 10019, USA

Chernow, Ron (Writer)
63 Joralemon St
Brooklyn, NY 11201, USA

Chernus, Michael (Actor)
c/o Jill Kaplan *Principal Entertainment (NY)*
130 W 42nd St
Suite 614
New York, NY 10036, USA

Cherrelle (Musician)
c/o Staff Member *Associated Booking Corp*
PO Box 2055
New York, NY 10021-0051, USA

Cherri, Agustina (Actor)
c/o Staff Member *Telefe - Argentina*
Pavon 2444 (C1248AAT)
Buenos Aires, ARGENTINA

Cherry, Deron (Athlete, Football Player)
13800 S Pebblebrook Ln
Greenwood, MO 64034-8216, USA

Cherry, Dick (Athlete, Hockey Player)
Box 346
RR 1
Bath, ON K0H 1G0, Canada

Cherry, Dick (Athlete, Hockey Player)
PO Box 346 RR 1
Bath, ON KOH IGO, Canada

Cherry, Don S (Athlete, Coach, Hockey Player)
CBC TV
P.O. Box 500, STN A, 5H100
Attn: Hockey Night in Canada
Toronto, ON M5W IEG, Canada

Cherry, D Richard (Stylist)
Richard Cherry Design
220 Renaissance Pkwy #1109
Atlanta, GA 30308, USA

Cherry, Fred V (War Hero)
720 Dale Dr
Silver Springs, MD 20910, USA

Cherry, Jeirod (Athlete, Football Player)
993 Mimosa Dr
Macedonia, OH 44056-2391, USA

Cherry, Je'rod (Athlete, Football Player)
993 Mimosa Dr
Macedonia, OH 44056, USA

Cherry, Joann (Stylist)
14513 Chateau Lane
Burnsville, MN 55306, USA

Cherry, Jonathan (Actor)
c/o Jim Sheasgreen *Look Management*
1529 W 6th Ave #110
Vancouver V6J 1R, CANADA

Cherry, Marc (Producer, Writer)
4261 Hazeltine Ave
Sherman Oaks, CA 91423, USA

Cherry, Mike (Athlete, Football Player)
4106 Central Pl
Texarkana, AR 71854, USA

Cherry, Nena (Musician)
c/o Staff Member *Paradigm (Monterey)*
404 W Franklin St
Monterey, CA 93940, USA

Cherry, Neneh (Musician)
PO Box 1622
London NW10 5TF, UNITED KINGDOM
(UK)

Cherry, Raphel (Athlete, Football Player)
1102 Church St
Jacksonville, AR 72076-5410, USA

Cherry, Rocky (Athlete, Baseball Player)
5624 Gleneagles Dr
Plano, TX 75093, USA

Cherry Poppin' Daddies (Music Group,
Musician)
c/o Jim Lenz *Paradise Artists*
P.O. Box 1821
Ojai, CA 93024-1821, USA

Chertoff, Michael (Attorney, Attorney
General, General, Government Official)
Justice Department
10th St & Constitution Ave NW
Washington, DC 20530, USA

Chertok, Jack (Producer)
515 Ocean Ave
#305
Santa Monica, CA 90402, USA

Cherundolo, Charles (Chuck) (Athlete,
Football Player)
4230 Simms Rd
Lakeland, FL 33810, USA

Chervyakov, Denis (Athlete, Hockey
Player)
21051 Roaming Shores Ter
Ashburn, VA 20147-3208, USA

Chesley, Al (Athlete, Football Player)
2604 32nd St SE
Washington, DC 20020, USA

Chesney, Kenny (Musician)
414 Lake Valley Dr
Franklin, TN 37069, USA

Chesnutt, Mark (Musician)
2454 S Pine Island Rd
Beaumont, TX 77713, USA

Chesson 3rd, Wes (Athlete, Football
Player)
1028 Marlowe Rd
Raleigh, NC 27609-6962, USA

Chester, Colby (Actor)
Talent Group
5670 Wilshire Blvd #820
Los Angeles, CA 90036, USA

Chester, Larry (Athlete, Football Player)
6359 Celtic Dr SW
Atlanta, GA 30331, USA

Chester, Raymond (Athlete, Football
Player)
4722 Grass Valley Rd
Oakland, CA 94605, USA

Chestnut, Cyrus (Musician)
Avenue Management Group
250 W 57th St #407
New York, NY 10019, USA

Chestnut, Mary Boykin (Educator)
Sweet Briar College
President's Office
Sweet Briar, VA 24595, USA

Chestnut, Morris (Actor)
11551 Jerry St
Cerritos, CA 90703, USA

Chetry, Kiran (Anchor)
c/o Staff Member *CNN (NY)*
1 Time Warner Center
New York, NY 10019, USA

Chetti, Joseph(Joe) (Athlete, Football
Player)
7 Baur St
West Babylon, NY 11704, USA

Chetwynd, Lionel (Producer, Writer)
c/o Bruce Vinokour *Creative Artists
Agency (CAA-LA)*
2000 Ave Of The Stars
Los Angeles, CA 90067, USA

Cheung, Maggie (Actor)
c/o Ted Schachter *Schachter
Entertainment*
1157 S Beverly Dr Fl 2
Los Angeles, CA 90035, USA

Cheung, Tim (Animator)
c/o Staff Member *DreamWorks SKG*
1000 Flower St
Glendale, CA 91201, USA

Chevalier, Franck (Stylist)
c/o Staff Member *Photogenics Media*
8549 Higuera St
Building B
Culver City, CA 90232, USA

Chevalier, Tracy (Writer)
EP Dutton
375 Hudson St
New York, NY 10014, USA

Chevelle (Music Group)
c/o Staff Member *Creative Artists Agency
(CAA-LA)*
2000 Ave Of The Stars
Los Angeles, CA 90067, USA

Chevrier, Alain (Athlete, Hockey Player)
6857 Rain Forest Dr
Boca Raton, FL 33434, USA

Chevrier, Alain (Athlete, Hockey Player)
5138 Greenwich Preserve Ct
Boynton Beach, FL 33436-5802, USA

Chew, Geoffrey F (Physicist)
10 Maybeck Twin Dr
Berkeley, CA 94708, USA

Chew, Gloria Ann (Actor)
351 N El Dorado St
San Mateo, CA 94401, USA

Chew Jr, Sam
8075 W 3rd St #303
Los Angeles, CA 90048, USA

Cheylov, Milan (Director)
c/o Bill Douglass *Paradigm (LA)*
360 N Crescent Dr
North Bldg
Beverly Hills, CA 90210, USA

Cheyne, Lori (Stylist)
c/o Staff Member *Creative Talent
Columbus*
5864 Nike Dr
Hilliard, OH 43026, USA

Cheyunski, Jim (Athlete, Football Player)
821 W Locust St
Seaford, DE 19973-2122, USA

Chi, Haotian (General)
National Defense Ministry
Jingshanqiq Jie
Beijing, CHINA

Chia, Sandro (Artist)
Castello Romitorio
Montalcino, Siena, ITALY

Chiacchia, Darren (Athlete, Horse Racer,
Olympic Athlete)
PO Box 278
East Aurora, NY 14052-0278, USA

Chiadel, Dana (Athlete)
5302 Flanders Ave
Kensington, MD 20895, USA

Chiamparino, Scott (Athlete, Baseball
Player)
179 Ortega Ave
Mountain View, CA 94040-1439, USA

Chianese, Dominic (Actor)
c/o Brian Liebman *Liebman Entertainment*
25 E 21st St #PH
New York, NY 10011-8503, USA

Chiao, Dr Leroy (Astronaut)
J._429 Bissonnet St Ste 4^6
Houston, TX 77005-1451, USA

Chiara, Maria (Opera Singer)
Columbia Artists Mgmt Inc
165 W 57th St
New York, NY 10019, USA

Chiarello, Michael (Chef)
Napastyle
360 Industrial Ct #A
Benicia, CA 94510-1138, USA

Chiasson, Scott (Athlete, Baseball Player)
3660 N Lake Rd
Erieville, NY 13061, USA

Chiaverini, Darrin (Athlete, Football
Player)
11442 Springwood Ct
Riverside, CA 92505-5120, USA

Chicago (Music Group)
c/o Howard Rose *Howard Rose Agency
Ltd, The*
9460 Wilshire Blvd #310
Beverly Hills, CA 90210, USA

Chick, Travis (Athlete, Baseball Player)
2201 Villa Dr
Tyler, TX 75703, USA

Chickillo, Anthony (Tony) (Athlete,
Football Player)
6920 Spanish Moss Cir
Tampa, FL 33625-6556, USA

Chiechi, Carolyn P (Judge)
US Tax Court
400 2nd St NW
Washington, DC 20217, USA

Chieftans, The (Music Group)
c/o Staff Member *ICM Partners (ICM-LA)*
10250 Constellation Blvd Fl 7
Los Angeles, CA 90067, USA

Chiesa, Fabrizio (Producer)
c/o Matt Leipzig *Original Artists (LA)*
9465 Wilshire Blvd Ste 870
Beverly Hills, CA 90212, USA

Chievous, Derrick (Athlete, Basketball
Player)
2300 Cherry Ridge Lane
Columbia, MO 65203-5744, USA

Chiffer, Floyd (Athlete, Baseball Player)
4325 Levelside Ave
Lakewood, CA 90712, USA

Chiffons, The (Music Group, Musician)
c/o Staff Member *Lustig Talent Enterprises
Inc*
PO Box 770850
Orlando, FL 32877, USA

Chihara, Charles S (Misc)
567 Cragmont Ave
Berkeley, CA 94708, USA

Chihara, Paul (Composer)
3815 W Olive Ave
#202
Burbank, CA 91505, USA

Chihuly, Dale P (Artist)
Chihuly Inc
1111 NW 50th St
Seattle, WA 98107, USA

Chikezie (Musician)

Chikezie, Caroline (Actor)
c/o Jane Lehrer *Jane Lehrer Associates*
100A Chalk Farm Road
London NW1 8EH, UNITED KINGDOM

Chiklis, Michael (Actor, Director,
Producer)
4310 Sutton Pl
Sherman Oaks, CA 91403, USA

Chilcutt, Pete
9054 High Flight Ct
Fair Oaks, CA 95628-4188

Child, Desmond (Musician)
509 Tuckaway Ct
Nashville, TN 37205, USA

Child, Jane (Musician)
2031 Holly Hill Terr
Los Angeles, CA 90068, USA

Childers, Ambyr (Actor)
c/o Laura Myones *McKeon-Myones
Management*
3500 Olive Ave
Suite 770
Burbank, CA 91505, USA

Childers, Ernest (War Hero)
13681 S 308th East Ave
Coweta, OK 74429, USA

Childers, Jason (Athlete, Baseball Player)
417 Aumond Rd
Augusta, GA 30909, USA

Childers, Matt (Athlete, Baseball Player)
417 Aumond Rd
Augusta, GA 30909, USA

Childress, Josh (Athlete, Basketball Player)
1433 Cherokee Trl
Lawrenceville, GA 30043-5807, USA

Childress, Kallie Flynn (Actor)
c/o TJ Stein *Stein Entertainment Group*
1351 N Crescent Heights Blvd #312
West Hollywood, CA 90046, USA

Childress, Randolph (Athlete, Basketball
Player)
9900 Nicol Ct W
Bowie, MD 20721-2960

Childress, Raymond C (Ray) Jr (Athlete,
Football Player)
639 Shady Hollow St
Houston, TX 77056, USA

Childress, Richard (Race Car Driver)
Childress Racing
9543 Hampton Rd.
Lexington, NC 27295-9780, USA

Childress, Rocky (Athlete, Baseball Player)
5 Meadow Glen Ct
Santa Rosa, CA 95404, USA

Childs, Billy (Musician)
Integrity Talent
PO Box 961
Burlington, MA 01803, USA

Childs, Brevard S (Misc)
508 Amity Road
Bethany, CT 06524, USA

Childs, Charissa (Athlete, Golfer)
25 Green Springs Cir
Columbia, SC 29223, USA

Childs, Chris (Athlete, Basketball Player)
10830 Willow Meadow
Cir
Alpharetta, GA 30022-6516, USA

Childs, Clarence (Athlete, Football Player)
1652 Lawrence Cir
Daytona Beach, FL 32117-3942, USA

Childs, David M (Architect)
Skidmore Owings Merrill
14 Wall St
New York, NY 10005, USA

Childs, Henry (Athlete, Football Player)
8304 Allman Rd
Lenexa, KS 66219, USA

Chiles, Adrian (Actor)
The One Show
BBC Television Centre
Wood Ln
London W12 7RJ, UK

Chiles, Henry G (Hank) Jr (Admiral)
6436 Pima St
Alexandra, VA 22312, USA

Chiles, Linden (Actor)
2521 Skyline Dr
Topanga, CA 90290, USA

Chiles, Lois (Actor)
c/o Staff Member *Abrams Artists Agency
(LA)*
9200 Sunset Blvd
11th Floor
Los Angeles, CA 90069, USA

Chiles, Rich (Athlete, Baseball Player)
18147 Mallard St
Woodland, CA 95695, USA

Chilies, Lois (Actor)
c/o Staff Member *Abrams Artists Agency
(LA)*
9200 Sunset Blvd
11th Floor
Los Angeles, CA 90069, USA

Chi-Lites, The (Music Group)
c/o Staff Member *Universal Attractions*
135 W 26th St
12 Floor
New York, NY 10001, USA

Chillar, Brandon (Athlete, Football Player)
1030 Iris Ct
Carlsbad, CA 92011, USA

Chillemi, Connie (Athlete, Golfer)
2701 NE 10th St
Apt 705
Ocala, FL 34470-5689, USA

Chilstrom, Ken (Aviator)
9120 Belvoir Woods
Pkwy Apt 211
Fort Belvoir, VA 22060-2723, USA

Chilstrom, Ken (Misc)
9120 Belvoir Woods Pkwy
Apt 211
Fort Belvoir, VA 22060-2723, USA

Chilton, Gene (Athlete, Football Player)
45828 US Highway 69 N
Jacksonville, TX 75766-8749, USA

Chilton, General Kevin P (General)
2555 Talleson Ct
Colorado Springs, CO 80919-4874, USA

Chilton, Kevin P (Astronaut)
16 Custer Drive
Offutt Air Force Base, NE 68113-1018,
USA

Chimera, Jason (Athlete, Hockey Player)
2468 Club Road
Columbus, OH 43221:40Q7, USA

Chimes, Terry
Chimes Chiropractic Ltd
21-25 York Rd
Ilford, Essex IG3 8BJ, UK

Chiminello, Bianca (Actor)
c/o Staff Member *Matt Sherman
Management*
7510 W Sunset Blvd
Suite 1413
Los Angeles, CA 90046, USA

Chin, Tsai (Actor)
c/o Donald Spradlin *Essential Talent
Management*
6399 Wilshire Blvd
Suite 401
Los Angeles, CA 90048, USA

Chinlund, Nick (Actor)
c/o Gordon Gilbertson *Gilbertson
Management*
1334 3rd St Promenade #201
Santa Monica, CA 90401, USA

Chinn, Jerry (Stylist)
5622 Corson Ave South
Seattle, WA 98108, USA

Chinn, Simon (Cinematographer,
Producer, Writer)
c/o Paul Stevens *Independent Talent
Group (ITG-UK)*
Oxford House
76 Oxford St
London W1D 1BS, UK

Chinnick, Rick (Athlete, Hockey Player)
55 Gregory Dr E
Chatham, ON N7L 2R5, Canada

Chinny, Jayanth (Actor)
67 1st Main Road
R A Puram
Chennai, TN 600 028, INDIA

Chino, Chino
440 E 23rd St Act 1508
Hialeah, FL 33013-3941, usa

Chiodo, Andy (Athlete, Hockey Player)
17 Fairhaven Dr
Etobicoke, ON M9P 2P8, Canada

Chiodos (Music Group, Musician)
c/o Staff Member *Equal Vision Records*
P.O. Box 38202
Albany, NY 12203-8202, USA

Chipchase, Jack (Athlete, Hockey Player)
143 Andrew St
Exeter, ON N0M 1S1, Canada

Chipperfield, Ron (Athlete, Hockey
Player)
Optima World Sports
Box 248
Wilcox, SK S0G 5E0, Canada

Chiranjeevi (Actor, Bollywood)
No. 4 Porur Somasundaram Street T
Nagar
Chennai, TN 600017, INDIA

Chishholm-Carrillo, Linda (Athlete,
Volleyball Player)
17213 Vose St
Van Nuys, CA 91406, USA

Chisholm, Art (Athlete, Hockey Player)
9 Jefferson Ct
Woburn, MA 01801-4326, USA

Chisholm, Ashleigh (Actor)
c/o Staff Member *Nickelodeon UK*
PO Box 6425
LONDON W1A 6UR, UNITED
KINGDOM

Chisholm, Melanie (Musician)
c/o Nancy Phillips *45 Management Ltd*
13 Tottenham Mews
London W1T 4AG, UK

Chism, Tom (Athlete, Baseball Player)
532 W Brookhaven Rd
Apt F1
Brookhaven, PA 19015, USA

Chissano, Joaquim A (President)
President's Office
Avda Julius Nyerere 2000
Maputo, MOZAMBIQUE

Chistov, Stanislav (Athlete, Hockey
Player)
Puckagency LLC
555 Pleasantville Rd Ste 210N
Attn Jay Grossman
Briarcliff Manor, NY 10510-1900, USA

Chistov, Stanislaw (Athlete, Hockey
Player)
c/o Jay Grossman *PuckAgency LLC*
555 Pleasantville Rd
North Building, Suite 210
Briarcliff Manor, NY 10510, USA

Chitalada, Sot (Boxer)
Home Express Co
242/19 Moo 10
Sukhumvit Road
Cholburi 20210, THAILAND

Chitren, Steve (Athlete, Baseball Player)
10417 Smokemont Ct
Las Vegas, NV 89129, USA

Chittister, Joan D (Misc)
Saint Scholastica Priory
335 E 9th St
Erie, PA 16503, USA

Chittum, Nelson (Athlete, Baseball Player)
616 Bonita Pkwy
Hendersonville, TN 37075-4632, USA

Chitty, Dennis (Scientist)
1602-5775 Hampton Pl
Vancouver, BC V6T 2G6, Canada

Chitwood Jr, Joey (Race Car Driver)
Chicagoland Speedway
4410 W. Aliva St.
Tamp, FL 33614-7639, USA

Chiu, Dr Raymond (Scientist)
3815 Rue des Cypres
Brossard, QC J4Z OE5, Canada

Chiu Wai, Tony Leung (Actor)
c/o Staff Member *WME (LA)*
9601 Wilshire Blvd Fl 3
Beverly Hills, CA 90210, USA

Chivers, Warren (Skier)
Vermont Academy
Saxtons River, WI 05154, USA

Chlebek, Ed (Athlete, Football Player)
6160 Waxmyrtle Way
Naples, FL 34109-5940, USA

Chlumsky, Anna (Actor)
c/o Cory Richman *Liebman Entertainment*
25 E 21st St #PH
New York, NY 10011-8503, USA

Chlupsa, Bob (Athlete, Baseball Player)
55 Willow St
Garden City, NY 11530-6316, USA

Chmerkovskiy, Maksim (Choreographer,
Dancer)
c/o Susan Madore *Guttman Associates*
118 S Beverly Dr
Suite 201
Beverly Hills, CA 90212, USA

Chmura, Mark W (Athlete, Football
Player)
S18 W28948 Price Ct
Waukesha, WI 53188, USA

Cho (Actor)
26-A Raja Annamataipuram
2nd Main Road
Chennai, TN 600 028, INDIA

Cho, Alfred Y (Inventor)
1 Beniamin Franklin
Dr Apt 43
Sarasota, FL 34236-1236, USA

Cho, Alfred Y (Engineer)
AT & T Bell Lucent Laboratory
600 Mountain Ave
New Providence, NJ 07974, USA

Cho, Catherine (Musician)
Columbia Artists Mgmt Inc
165 W 57th St
New York, NY 10019, USA

Cho, Frank (Cartoonist)
Creators Syndicate
5777 W Century Blvd #700
Los Angeles, CA 90045, USA

Cho, Fujio (Business Person)
Toyota Motor Corp
1 Toyotacho
Toyota City, Aicji Prefecture 471, JAPAN

Cho, Henry (Actor, Comedian, Writer)
c/o Alex Murray *McDonald-Murray
Management*
11846 Ventura Blvd Ste 202
Studio City, CA 91604, USA

Cho, John (Actor)
2152 Panorama Terr
Los Angeles, CA 90039, USA

Cho, Margaret (Actor, Comedian)
1875 Oakwood Ave
Glendale, CA 91208, USA

Cho, Paul (Misc)
Full Gospel Central Church
Yoida Plaza
Seoul, SOUTH KOREA

Cho, Smith (Actor)
c/o Amy Guenther *Gateway Management Company Inc*
860 Via De La Paz
Suite F10
Pacific Palisades, CA 90272, USA

Choate, Don (Athlete, Baseball Player)
9506 Maryann Dr
Fairview Heights, IL 62208-1625, USA

Choate, Jerry D (Business Person)
Allstate Insurance
Allstate Plaza
2775 Sanders Road
Northbrook, IL 60062, USA

Choate, Putt (Athlete, Football Player)
9800 Rockbrook Dr
Dallas, TX 75220, USA

Choate, Randy (Athlete, Baseball Player)
316 Leon Pl
Devis, CA 95616-0236, USA

Chobot, Jessica (Correspondent)
IGN Entertainment
625 2nd St
3rd Floor
San Francisco, CA 94107, USA

Chodor, Allan (Bowler)
30729 Whaleboat Pl
Agoura Hills, CA 91301-1949

Chodorow, Marvin (Engineer, Physicist)
6151 Forty Oaks Ln
Paradise, CA 95969-3079, USA

Choi, Edmund (Composer, Musician)
c/o Anita Greenspan *Greenspan Artist Management*
8760 W Sunset Blvd
West Hollywood, CA 90069, USA

Choi, Hee Seop (Athlete, Baseball Player)
14310 SE 29th Cir
Vancouver, WA 98683-7691, USA

Choi, Jane (Stylist)
c/o Staff Member *Montana Artists Agency*
9150 Wilshire Blvd Ste 100
Beverly Hills, CA 90212, USA

Choi, Kathy (Athlete, Golfer)
7912 Beachpoint Cir
Apt 18
Huntington Beach, CA 92648, USA

Choi, Kenneth (Actor)
c/o Gail Abbott *Gail Abbott Management*
3019 Hollycrest Dr
Los Angeles, CA 90068, USA

Choi, KJ (Athlete, Golfer)
1360 E 9th St
Cleveland, OH 44114-1737, USA

Choi, Yun (Actor)
c/o Staff Member *Select Artists Ltd (CA-Westside Office)*
1138 12th Street
Suite 1
Santa Monica, CA 90403, USA

Chojnowska-Liskiewicz, Krystyna (Yachtsman)
Ul Norblina 29 m 50
Gdansk, Oliwa 80 304, POLAND

Chokachi, David (Actor)
1036 S Ridgeley Dr
Los Angeles, CA 90019, USA

Chokkalinga, Bhavadhar (Actor)
10 Thiruvalluvar Street
M G R Nagar
Chennai, TN 600 078, INDIA

Cholodenko, Lisa (Director, Editor, Producer, Writer)
c/o Bart Walker *ICM Partners (ICM-LA)*
555 W 25th St
4th Floor
New York, NY 10001, USA

Choma, John (Athlete, Football Player)
1544 Carol Ave
Burlingame, CA 94010, USA

Chomet, Sylvain (Director, Writer)
c/o Robert Newman *WME (LA)*
9601 Wilshire Blvd Fl 3
Beverly Hills, CA 90210, USA

Chomsky, A Noam (Linguist)
15 Suzanne Road
Lexington, MA 02420-1831, USA

Chomsky, Marvin J (Director)
15200 W Sunset Blvd #209
Pacific Palisades, CA 90272-3621

Chon, Justin (Actor)
c/o Staff Member *Abrams Artists Agency (LA)*
9200 Sunset Blvd
11th Floor
Los Angeles, CA 90069, USA

Chonacas, Katie (Actor, Model)
c/o Jordyn Palos *Persona PR*
8840 Wilshire Blvd
Suite 212
Beverly Hills, CA 90211, USA

Chones, Jim (Athlete, Basketball Player)
26400 George Zeiger
Dr Apt 305
Beachwood, OH 44122-7511, USA

Chong, Rae Dawn (Actor)
c/o David Fox *Myman Abell Fineman Fox Greenspan Light*
11601 Wilshire Blvd
Suite 2200
Los Angeles, CA 90025, USA

Chong, Tommy (Actor, Comedian)
1625 Casale Rd
Pacific Palisades, CA 90272, USA

Chopra, B R (Bollywood, Director)
B R House Juhu Tara Road
Santacruz
Mumbai, MS 400049, INDIA

Chopra, Daniel (Athlete, Golfer)
9838 Laurel Valley Dr
Windermere, FL 34786, USA

Chopra, Deepak (Doctor, Writer)
c/o Robert Gottlieb *Trident Media Group LLC*
41 Madison Ave
36th Floor
New York, NY 10010, USA

Chopra, Prem (Actor, Bollywood)
144A Nibbana Pali Hill
Bandra
Bombay, MS 400 050, INDIA

Chopra, Priyanka (Actor)
Rajesh Chopra
1826 Amar Nath Bldg #2
Bhagirath Palace
Delhi 110006, INDIA

Chopra, Ravi (Bollywood, Director, Filmmaker, Producer)
B R House
Juhu Tara Road Santacruz
Bombay, MS 400 049, INDIA

Chopra, Uday (Actor)
c/o Staff Member *Yash Raj Films Private Ltd (India)*
17 Vkas Park
Jalpankhi Society, Juhu
Mumbai 400 049, India

Chopra, Vidhu Vinod (Bollywood, Director, Filmmaker, Producer)
Bhagtani Krishang, RH1
Plot 16C, Dattatray Road
Santacruz (West), Mumbai 400054, INDIA

Chorske, Tom (Athlete, Hockey Player)
23 Cooper Cir
Minneapolis, MN 55436-1316, USA

Chorvat, Scarlett (Actor)
1727 N Crescent Heights Blvd
West Hollywood, CA 90069, USA

Chorzempa, Daniel W (Misc)
Kunstleragentur Raab & Bohm
Plankengasse 7
Vienna 1010, AUSTRIA

Chou, Collin (Actor)
c/o Tim Kwok *Convergence Entertainment*
9150 Wilshire Blvd
Suite 247
Beverly Hills, CA 90212, USA

Chou, Jay (Musician)
c/o Staff Member *BMG*
1540 Broadway
New York, NY 10036, USA

Choudhury, Sarita (Actor)
c/o Kathy Atkinson *Washington Square Arts (LA)*
1041 N Formosa Ave
The Lot Writers Bldg, Room 305
West Hollywood, CA 90046, USA

Chouinard, Bobby (Athlete, Baseball Player)
6024 S Paris Pl
Englewood, CO 80111-4152, USA

Chouinard, Guy (Athlete, Hockey Player)
Quebec Remparts Laval University Peps
Rm 1564
Ste-Foy, QC G1K 7P4, Canada

Chouinard, Josee (Figure Skater)
c/o Staff Member *IMG (Canada)*
175 Bloor St E
S Tower #400
Toronto M4W 3R8, CANADA

Chouinard, Marie (Choreographer, Dancer)
Compagnie Chouinard
3981 Boul Saint-Laurent
Montreal, PQ H2W 1Y5, CANADA

Choureau, Etchika (Actor)
9 rue du Docteur Blanche
Paris F-75016, France

Chow, Amy (Athlete, Gymnast, Olympic Athlete)
West Valley Gym
1190 Dell Ave
#1
Campbell, CA 95008, USA

Chow, China (Actor)
c/o Andy Stabile *Creative Artists Agency (CAA-LA)*
2000 Ave Of The Stars
Los Angeles, CA 90067, USA

Chow, Gregory C (Economist)
30 Hardy Dr
Princeton, NJ 08540, USA

Chow, Raymond (Producer)
c/o Staff Member *Golden Harvest Entertainment*
The Peninsula Office Tower
18 Middle Road 16/F Tsim Sha Tsui
Kowloon, Hong Kong

Chow, Stephen (Actor, Director, Writer)
Star Overseas
Rm 1201-1204 Sea Bird House
22-28 Wyndham Street
Hong Kong, China

Chow, Steven (Actor)
c/o Alan Grodin *Weissman Wolff Bergman Coleman Silverman Holmes*
9665 Wilshire Blvd
9th Floor
Beverly Hills, CA 90212, USA

Chrebet, Wayne (Athlete, Football Player)
147 Heulitt Rd
Colts Neck, NJ 07722-1427, USA

Chretien, Jean (Prime Minister)
Prime Minister's Office
House of Commons
PO Box 1103
Ottawa, ON KlA OA6, CANADA

Chretien, Jean-Loup (Astronaut, General)
Astronautes Direction
2 Place Maurice Quentin
Paris 75029, FRANCE

Chretien, Jean-Loup Brig Gen (Astronaut)
2092 N Pointe Alexis Dr
Dr Apt 43
Tarpon Springs, FL 34689-2048, USA

Chriqui, Emmanuelle (Actor)
c/o Emily Gerson Saines *Brookside Artists Management (NY)*
250 W 57th St
Suite 2303
New York, NY 10107, USA

Chris, Chris (Athlete, Hockey Player)
287 Brantwood Park Rd
Brantford, ON N3P 1H6, Canada

Chris, Mike (Athlete, Baseball Player)
31257 Corte Alhambra
Temecula, CA 92592-5420, USA

Chrisley, Neil (Athlete, Baseball Player)
280 Myrtle Green Dr
Apt B
Conway, SC 29526-9040, USA

Christ, Chad (Actor)
c/o Brian Liebman *Liebman Entertainment*
25 E 21st St #PH
New York, NY 10011-8503, USA

Christ, Dorothy (Athlete, Baseball Player, Commentator)
120 E Battell St Apt 108
Mishawaka, IN 46545-6660, USA

Christ, Fred (Athlete, Basketball Player)
514 Banyan Way
Melbourne Beach, FL 32951-2102, USA

Christensen, Anne (Stylist)
c/o Staff Member *Art + Commerce*
531 W 25th St # 4
New York, NY 10001, USA

Christensen, Bruce (Athlete, Baseball Player)
P.O. Box 178
Moroni, UT 84646-0178, USA

Christensen, Erika (Actor)
c/o Staff Member *Brillstein Entertainment Partners*
9150 Wilshire Blvd #350
Beverly Hills, CA 90212, USA

Christensen, Hayden (Actor)
11210 Briarcliff Ln
Studio City, CA 91604, USA

Christensen, Helena (Model)
c/o Lene Seested *Panorama Agency*
Ryesgade 103B
CopenHagen DK-2100, Denmark

Christensen, John (Athlete, Baseball Player)
2931 Yuma Dr
Lake Havasu City, AZ 86406-8568, USA

Christensen, Kai (Architect)
100 Vester Voldgade
Copenhagen V 1552, DENMARK

Christensen, McKay (Athlete, Baseball Player)
2720 W Shady Hollow Ln
Lehi, UT 84043-5713, USA

Christensen, Todd (Athlete, Football Player)
991 Sunburst Ln
Alpine, UT 84004, USA

Christensen Jr, Erik (Athlete, Football Player)
308 Sentinel Ln
Newark DE, DE 19702-8504, USA

Christenson, Gary (Athlete, Baseball Player)
436 E Tremaine Ave
Gilbert, AZ 85234-4624, USA

Christenson, Larry (Athlete, Baseball Player)
1465 Le Boutillier Rd
Malvern, PA 19355-8741, USA

Christenson, Ryan (Athlete, Baseball Player)
100 Lismore Ct
Tyrone, GA 30290-2549, USA

Christenson, Ryan (Athlete, Baseball Player)
4021 Canario St
Unit 136
Carlsbad, CA 92008, USA

Christian, Andrew (Designer, Fashion Designer)
Andrew Christian Clothing
325 West Cerritos Ave
Glendale, CA 91204, USA

Christian, Ash (Actor, Director, Writer)
c/o Simon Millar *Rumble Media*
1620 Broadway
Santa Monica, CA 90403, USA

Christian, Bob (Athlete, Football Player)
9450 Lincolnwood Dr
Evanston, IL 60203-1114, USA

Christian, Christina (Actor, Musician)
c/o Allee Newhoff *Elite Model Management*
119 Washington Ave
Suite 501
Miami Beach, FL 33139, USA

Christian, Claudia (Actor)
c/o Staff Member *Abrams Artists Agency (LA)*
9200 Sunset Blvd
11th Floor
Los Angeles, CA 90069, USA

Christian, David W (Dave) (Athlete, Hockey Player, Olympic Athlete)
Christian Brothers Hockey Company
513 Queens Ct
Moorhead, MN 56560-6777, USA

Christian, Eddie (Baseball Player)
1126 NE Lija Loop
Portland, OR 97211-1318, USA

Christian, Gabrielle (Actor)
c/o Robert Haas *Innovative Artists (LA)*
1505 10th St
Santa Monica, CA 90401, USA

Christian, Gordon (Athlete, Hockey Player)
604 Lake St NW
Warroad, MN 56763, USA

Christian, Jeff (Athlete, Hockey Player)
2000 SE Manor Pl
Blue Springs, MO 64014-3823, USA

Christian, Richard (Actor)
c/o Staff Member *Select Artists Ltd (CA-Westside Office)*
1138 12th Street
Suite 1
Santa Monica, CA 90403, USA

Christian, Shawn (Actor)
543 N Fuller Ave
Los Angeles, CA 90036, USA

Christian, William (Bill) (Athlete, Hockey Player, Olympic Athlete)
502 Carrol St NW
Warroad, MN 56763, USA

Christian Dior (Designer, Fashion Designer)
St-Anna-Platz 2
Munich 80538, Germany

Christian-Jacque (Director, Writer)
42 Bis Rue de paris
Boulogne, Billancourt 92100, FRANCE

Christians, F Wilhelm (Financier)
Kobigsallee 51
Dusseldorf, GERMANY

Christiansen, Clay (Athlete, Baseball Player)
7227 Eby Ave
Overland Park, KS 66204-1638, USA

Christiansen, Helena (Actor)
62 Blvd Sebastopol
Paris 75003, FRANCE

Christiansen, Jason (Athlete, Baseball Player)
3428 E Jasmine Cir
Mesa, AZ 85213-3245, USA

Christiansen, Keith (Athlete, Hockey Player, Olympic Athlete)
1023 Timberline Ln
Duluth, MN 55811-4451, USA

Christiansen, Robert S (Bob) (Athlete, Football Player)
5228 G St
Sacramento, CA 95819-3217, USA

Christianson, Bob (Musician)
c/o Mike Rosen *Working Artists Agency*
13525 Ventura Blvd
Sherman Oaks, CA

Christie, Chris (Governor)
Office of the Governor
P.O. Box 001
Trenton, NJ 08625, USA

Christie, Doug (Athlete, Basketball Player)
14150 NE 20th St
Bellevue, WA 98007-3700, USA

Christie, George
65 Fix Way
Ventura, CA 93001, USA

Christie, Julianna (Actor)
252 N Larchmont Blvd. #200
Los Angeles, CA 90004, USA

Christie, Julianne (Actor)
252 N Larchmont Blvd
#200
Los Angeles, CA 90004, USA

Christie, Julie (Actor, Model)
c/o Renee Missel *Renee Missel Management*
846 South Wooster
Los Angeles, CA 90035, USA

Christie, Linford (Athlete, Track Athlete)
Nuff Respect
107 Sherland Road
Twickenham
Middx TW9 4HB, UNITED KINGDOM (UK)

Christie, Lou (Musician)
c/o Staff Member *Dick Fox Entertainment*
1650 Broadway
New York, NY 10019, USA

Christie, Mike (Athlete, Hockey Player)
6093 S Krameria St
Centennial, CO 80111-4273, USA

Christie, Ryan (Athlete, Hockey Player)
Christie's Dairy 4819 Union St
Beamsville, ON L0R 1B4, Canada

Christie, Steve (Athlete, Football Player)
6150 Gulfport Blvd S #102
Gulfport, FL 33707-3101, USA

Christie, Tony (Musician)
c/o Staff Member *Chris Davis Management Ltd.*
Tenbury House
36 Teme St, Tenbury Wells
Worcestershire WR15 8AA, UK

Christie, Warren (Actor)
c/o Trina Allen *Play Management*
807 Powell St
Suite 220
Vancouver V6A 1H7, CANADA

Christie, William (Musician)
Les Arts Florissants
2 Rue de Saint-Petersbourg
Paris 75008, FRANCE

Christine, Andrew (Andy) (Cartoonist)
c/o Staff Member *King Features Syndication*
300 W 57th St
15th Floor
New York, NY 10019-5238, USA

Christine, Zola (Stylist)
c/o Staff Member *Dossier*
556 S Fair Oaks
#431
Pasadena, CA 91105, USA

Christlieb, Peter (Pete) (Musician)
Thomas Cassidy
11761 E Speedway Blvd
Tucson, AZ 85748, USA

Christman, Tim (Athlete, Baseball Player)
213 Duns bach Ferry Rd
Cohoes, NY 12047-4900, USA

Christmas, Steve (Athlete, Baseball Player)
600 Bentley St
Oviedo, FL 32765-8169, USA

Christoff, Steve (Athlete, Hockey Player, Olympic Athlete)
542 Fairview Ave S
Saint Paul, MN 55116-1466, USA

Christofferson, Debra (Actor)
5658 Lemp Ave
N Hollywood, CA 91601, USA

Christo (Javacheff) (Artist)
48 Howard St
New York, NY 10013, USA

Christon, Shameka (Athlete, Basketball Player)
c/o Staff Member *New York Liberty*
2 Penn Plz Fl 14
New York, NY 10121, USA

Christopher, Dennis (Actor)
BR&S
5757 Wilshire Blvd
#473
Los Angeles, CA 90036, USA

Christopher, Gerald (Actor)
11900 Goshen Ave
#203
Los Angeles, CA 90049, USA

Christopher, Gerard
11900 Goshen Ave. #203
Los Angeles, CA 90049-6380, USA

Christopher, Gretchen (Musician)
509 E Ridgecrest Blvd
#1A
Ridgecrest, CA 93555, USA

Christopher, Herb (Athlete, Football Player)
PO Box 554
Redan, GA 30074-0554, USA

Christopher, Joe (Athlete, Baseball Player)
Chris Potter Sports 9722
Owings Mills, MD 71117-6341, USA

Christopher, Matt (Writer)
c/o Dale Christopher
PO Box 2511
Wilton, NY 12831, USA

Christopher, Mike (Athlete, Baseball Player)
8707 Courthouse Rd
Church Road, VA 23833-2712, USA

Christopher, Patrick (Athlete, Basketball Player)
c/o Sam Goldfelder *Excel Sports Management*
9665 Wilshire Blvd #500
Los Angeles, CA 90212, USA

Christopher, Ted (Race Car Driver)
Marsh Racing
81 Mile Creek Rd
Old Lyme, CT 06371, USA

Christopher, Thom (Actor)
Ambrosio/Mortimer
PO Box 16758
Beverly Hills, CA 90209, USA

Christopher, Tyler (Actor)
11523 Duque Dr
Studio City, CA 91604, USA

Christopher, William (Actor)
c/o Wes Stevens *Vox*
6420 Wilshire Blvd Ste 1080
Los Angeles, CA 90048, USA

Christopherson, James (Jim) (Athlete,
Football Player)
526 Queens Ct
Moorhead, MN 56560, USA

Christy, Barrett (Athlete, Olympic Athlete,
Snowboarder)
131 Lois Ln
Sequim, WA 98382, USA

Christy, Brenda (Stylist)
c/o Staff Member *Maximum Talent*
1873 S Bellaire St
Suite 915
Denver, CO 80222-4356, USA

Christy, Earl (Athlete, Football Player)
10825 S Prairie Ave
Chicago, IL 60628-3620, USA

Christy, George
170 N. Carmelina Ave.
Los Angeles, CA 90049

Christy, Greg (Athlete, Football Player)
3 Concord St
Natrona Heights, PA 15065-9732, USA

Christy, James W (Scientist)
7285 Golden Eagle Dr
Flagstaff, AZ 86004-3254, USA

Christy, Jeff (Athlete, Football Player)
138 Horseshoe Dr
Freeport, PA 16229, USA

Chryplewicz, Pete (Athlete, Football
Player)
11473 Claymont Cir
Windermere, FL 34786, USA

Chrysostom, Bishop (Religious Leader)
Serbian Orthodox Church
St Sava Monastery
PO Box 519
Libertville, IL 60048, USA

Chryssa (Artist)
565 Broadway
Soho
New York, NY 10012, USA

Chrystal, Bob (Athlete, Hockey Player)
231 Rita St
Winnipeg, MB R3J 2Y3, Canada

Chu, Anna (Stylist)
c/o Staff Member *Artists by Timothy
Priano (CA)*
8447 Wilshire Blvd
#301
Beverly Hills, CA 90211, USA

Chu, Judy (Congressman, Politician)
1520 Longworth HOB
Washington, DC 20515, USA

Chu, Julie (Athlete, Hockey Player,
Olympic Athlete)
145 Primrose Ln
Fairfield, CT 06825-2309, USA

Chu, Paul C W (Physicist)
University of Houston
Center for Superconductivity
Houston, TX 77204, USA

Chu, Steven (Nobel Prize Laureate)
4820 Drummond Ave
Chevy Chase, MD 20815-5429, USA

Chubais, Anatoly B (Government Official)
United Power Grids
Kitaigorodsky Proyezd 7
Moscow 103074, RUSSIA

Chubin, Steve (Athlete, Basketball Player)
2324 S Gray Dr
Lakewood, CO 80227-3954, USA

Chuck, Chuck (Athlete, Football Player)
268 Babbitt Rd Apt M5
Bedford Hills, NY 10507-2123, USA

Chuck, D (Musician)
Richard Walters
1800 Argyle Ave
#408
Los Angeles, CA 90028, USA

Chuck, Wendy (Designer)
c/o Heather Parker *Innovative Artists (LA)*
1505 10th St
Santa Monica, CA 90401, USA

Chuck Wagon Gang
4408 Buffalo Ln
Joshua, TX 76058

Chukwurah, Patrick (Athlete, Football
Player)
6757 Camino Rio
Irving, TX 75039-3064

Chulack, Christopher (Director, Producer,
Writer)
c/o Staff Member *Creative Artists Agency
(CAA-LA)*
2000 Ave Of The Stars
Los Angeles, CA 90067, USA

Chulk, Vinnie (Athlete, Baseball Player)
7580 SW 162nd St
Palmetto Bay, FL 33157-3822, USA

Chum, Chuck
733 Trevino Drive
Lady Lake, FL 32159-5575, USA

Chung, Alexa (Musician)
c/o Staff Member *Liz Matthews PR*
83 Charlotte Street
London W1T 4PR, United Kingdom

Chung, Connie (Correspondent, Journalist)
1 W 72nd St Apt 4
New York, NY 10023-3414, USA

Chung, Doo Ri (Designer)
c/o Meghan Wood *KCD Worldwide Inc*
450 W 15th St
Suite 604
New York, NY 10011, USA

Chung, Eugene (Athlete, Football Player)
109 Surrey Ln
Ponte Vedra Beach, FL 32082, USA

Chung, Jamie (Actor)
c/o Ben Levine *Kritzer Levine Wilkins
Entertainment (KLWG)*
11872 La Grange Ave
1st Floor
Los Angeles, CA 90025, USA

Chung, Mark (Soccer Player)
Columbus Crew
2121 Velman Ave
Columbus, OH 43211, USA

Chung, Myung-Whun (Musician)
Hans Ulrich Schmid
Postfach 1617
Hanover 30016, GERMANY

Chupack, Cindy
c/o Daniel Strone *Trident Media Group
LLC*
41 Madison Ave
36th Floor
New York, NY 10010, USA

Church, Charlotte (Musician)
7 Dials Cambridge Bridge
Covent Garden
London WC2H 9HU, UNITED
KINGDOM (UK)

Church, Eric (Musician)
714 Farrell Rd
Nashville, TN 37220, USA

Church, Ryan (Athlete, Baseball Player)
3500 Thurloe Dr
Rockledge, FL 32955-6066, USA

Church, Sam (Misc)
United Mine Workers of America
8315 Lee Highway
#500
Fairfax, VA 22031, USA

Churches, Brady J (Business Person)
Consolidated Stores
1105 N Market St
Wilmington, DE 19801, USA

Churchill, Caryl (Writer)
Cassarotto
60/66 Wardour St
London W1V 4ND, UNITED KINGDOM
(UK)

Churchman, Ricky (Athlete, Football
Player)
445 Cherry Blossom Loop
Richland, WA 99352-7851, USA

Churla, Shane (Athlete, Hockey Player)
31826 Scotch Pine Dr
Bigfork, MT 59911-8275, USA

Churla, Steve (Athlete, Hockey Player)
19299 E. Shore Route
Bigfork, MT 55911, USA

Churn, Chuck (Athlete, Baseball Player)
733 Trevino Dr
Lady Lake, FL 32159-5575, USA

Chute, Robert M (Biologist, Songwriter,
Writer)
10 Richards Drive
Brunswick, ME 04011-3209, USA

Chuy, Don (Athlete, Football Player)
11690 Oxnard St
North Hollywood, CA 91606, USA

Chvatal, Cynthia (Producer)
c/o Staff Member *United Talent Agency
(UTA)*
9336 Civic Center Dr
Beverly Hills, CA 90210, USA

Chwast, Seymour (Artist)
Push Pin Group
55 E 9th St #1G
New York, NY 10003, USA

Chychrun, Jeff (Athlete, Hockey Player)
6423 NW 32nd Way
Boca Raton, FL 33496-3396, USA

Chynoweth, Dean (Athlete, Hockey
Player)
131 Shawnee Rise SW
Calgary, AB T2Y 2S3, CANADA

Chyzowski, Dave (Athlete, Hockey Player)
c/o Staff Member *Kamloops Blazers*
300 Lorne St
Kamloops, BC V2C 1W3, Canada

Ciaffa, Chris
627 N. Las Palmas Ave.
Los Angeles, CA 90004

Cialini, Julie (Artist, Model)
PO Box 55536
Valencia, CA 91385, USA

Ciampi, Carlo A (Prime Minister)
President's Office
Palazzo del Quirinale
Rome 00187, ITALY

Ciampi, Joe (Coach)
Auburn University
Athletic Dept
Auburn, AL 36831, USA

Ciampl, Joe (Coach)
Aubuin University
Athletic Dept
Auburn, AL 36831, USA

Cianfrocco, Archi (Athlete, Baseball
Player)
12424 Addax Ct
San Diego, CA 92129-4141, USA

Ciara (Musician)
c/o Patti Webster *W&W PR*
476 Union Ave
2nd Floor
Middlesex, NJ 08846, USA

Ciaramello, Benny (Actor)
c/o Scott Zimmerman *Evolution
Entertainment (LA)*
901 N Highland Ave
Los Angeles, CA 90038, USA

Ciardi, Mark (Athlete, Baseball Player)
21 Mitchell Ave
Piscataway, NJ 08854-5560, USA

Cias, Darryl (Athlete, Baseball Player)
12330 Lithuania Dr
Granada Hills, CA 91344-1637, USA

Ciavaglia, Peter (Athlete, Hockey Player,
Olympic Athlete)
1137 Carrie Ct
Rochester Hills, MI 48309-3766, USA

Cibak, Martin (Athlete, Hockey Player)
Nabrezie Dr Aurela Stodolu
1799/66
Liptovsky, Mikulas 03101, Slovakia

Cibrian, Eddie (Actor)
4434 Moorpark Way #103
Toluca Lake, CA 91602, USA

Cibulkova, Dominika (Athlete, Tennis
Player)
WTA
1 Progress Plz #1500
St Peterburgh, FL 33701, USA

Ciccarelli, Dino (Athlete, Hockey Player)
37934 Lakeshore Dr
Harrison Township, MI 48045-2853, USA

Ciccarelli, Dino (Athlete, Hockey Player)
1872 Clarence St.
Rome 1-00123, ITALY

Ciccio, Robbin (Stylist)
423 Washington St
Winchester, MA 01890, USA

Ciccippio, Joseph
2107 3rd St.
Norristown, PA 19401

Ciccolella, Jude (Actor)
705 N Screenland Dr
Burbank, CA 91505, USA

Ciccolella, Mike (Athlete, Football Player)
8145 Station House Rd
Dayton, OH 45458-2931, USA

Ciccone, Christopher (Designer)
Bernhardt Design/Pacific Design Center
8687 Melrose Ave
Space B230
West Hollywood, CA 90069

Ciccone, Enrico (Athlete, Hockey Player)
c/o Staff Member *Sports Prospects Inc*
77 Rue de Bleury
Rosemere, QC J7A 4L9, Canada

Cicerone, Aldo (Musician)
Gerhild Baron Mgmt
Dombacher Str 41/III/3
Vienna 1170, AUSTRIA

Cicerone, Ralph J (Scientist)
University of California
Earth Science Dept
Rowland Hall
Irvine, CA 92717, USA

Cichocki, Chris (Athlete, Hockey Player)
3955 Pine Lake Cir
Stockton, CA 95219-2021, USA

Cichowski, Gene (Chick) (Athlete, Football Player)
3903 Oak Ave
Northbrook, IL 60062, USA

Cichowski, Tom (Athlete, Football Player)
443 N Hill Rd
Kalispell, MT 59901-8107, USA

Cichy, Joe J (Athlete, Football Player)
1220 N Mandan St
Bismarck, ND 58501-2608, USA

Cid, Celeste (Actor)
c/o Staff Member *Telefe - Argentina*
Pavon 2444 (C1248AAT)
Buenos Aires, ARGENTINA

Cidre, Cynthia (Producer, Writer)
c/o Ann Blanchard *Creative Artists Agency (CAA-LA)*
2000 Ave Of The Stars
Los Angeles, CA 90067, USA

Ciechanover, Aaron (Nobel Prize Laureate)
Technion Israel Inst. Of Technology
Technion 1 Efron Street
PO Box 9697
Haifa 31096, Israel

Cienfuegos, Mauricio (Soccer Player)
Los Angeles Galaxy
1010 Rose Bowl Dr
Pasadena, CA 91103, USA

Ciger, Zdeno (Athlete, Hockey Player)
Hotel 21 Nerudova 8
Bratislava 82104, Slovakia

Cigliuti, Natalia (Actor)
c/o Felicia Sager *Sager Management*
260 S Beverly Dr
Suite 205
Beverly Hills, CA 90212, USA

Cihocki, Al (Athlete, Baseball Player)
43 Cochise Cir
Medford, NJ 08055-9769, USA

Cihocki, Al (Athlete, Baseball Player)
43 Cochise Cir
Medford, NJ 08055, USA

Ciller, Tansu (Prime Minister)
True Path Party
Selanik Cod 40
Kizilay, Ankara, TURKEY

Cilmi, Gabriella (Musician)
c/o David (Dave) Chumbley *Primary Talent International (UK)*
The Primary Building
10-11 Jockeys Fields
London WC1R 4BN, UK

Cimarro, Mario (Actor)
c/o Arlene Forster *Forster Entertainment*
12533 Woodgreen St
Los Angeles, CA 90066, USA

Cimber, Matt (Director, Producer, Writer)
Cimero Enterprises
3620 Beverly Glenn Blvd
#1A
Sherman Oaks, CA 91423, USA

Cimellaro, Tony (Athlete, Coach, Hockey Player)
c/o Staff Member *Kingston Frontenacs*
P.O. Box 665
Stn Main
Kingston, ON K7L 4X1, Canada

Cimetta, Rob (Athlete, Hockey Player)
Cimetta Properties
207-834 Yonge St
Toronto, ON M4W 2HI, Canada

Cimino, Michael (Director)
9015 Alto Cedro
Beverly Hills, CA 90210, USA

Cimino, Pete (Athlete, Baseball Player)
14 Fillmore St
Bristol, PA 19007-5415, USA

Cimmo, Leonardo (Actor)
Michael Hartig Agency
156 5th Ave #820
New York, NY 10010, USA

Cimorelli, Frank (Athlete, Baseball Player)
2448 N 112th St
Milwaukee, WI 53226-1210, USA

Cincotti, Peter (Musician)
c/o Staff Member *WME (LA)*
9601 Wilshire Blvd Fl 3
Beverly Hills, CA 90210, USA

Cinderella (Music Group, Musician)
Tom Keifer
6129 S Riverbend Dr
Nashville, TN 37221, USA

Cindric, Ann (Baseball Player)
210 Greenside Ave Apt 4
Canonsburg, PA 15317-3862, USA

Cindrich, Joe (Athlete, Football Player)
1310 Trinity Dr
Menlo Park, CA 94025-6680, USA

Cindrich, Ralph (Athlete, Football Player)
151 Fort Pitt Blvd Apt 1501
Pittsburgh, PA 15222-1572, USA

Cinematic Sunrise (Music Group, Musician)
c/o Staff Member *Equal Vision Records*
P.O. Box 38202
Albany, NY 12203-8202, USA

Cineson All-Stars (Music Group)
c/o Staff Member *Paradigm (Monterey)*
404 W Franklin St
Monterey, CA 93940, USA

Cink, Stewart (Athlete, Golfer)
2195 Lockett Ct
Duluth, GA 30097, USA

Cinninger, Jake (Musician)
19350 State Line Rd
South Bend, IN 46637, USA

Cintron, Alex (Athlete, Baseball Player)
HC 2 Box 8575
Yabucoa, PR 00767-9599, USA

Cioffi, Charles (Actor)
Paradigm Agency
10100 Santa Monica Blvd
#2500
Los Angeles, CA 90067, USA

Ciokey, Janna (Actor)
J Michael Bloom
9255 Sunset Blvd
#710
Los Angeles, CA 90069, USA

Cipa, Larry (Athlete, Football Player)
250 Torrent Ct
Rochester Hills, MI 48307, USA

Cipriani, Frank (Athlete, Baseball Player)
14 Oakhill Dr
Buffalo, NY 14224-4214, USA

Cipriani Thorne, Juan Luis Cardinal (Religious Leader)
Arzobispado
Plaza de Armas S/N
Apartado 1512
Lima 100, PERU

Circa Survive (Music Group)
c/o Brian Schechter *Riot Squad Management*
335 Cortlandt St
2nd Floor
Belleville, NJ 07109, USA

Circi, Cristian (Architect)
Cirici Arquitecte
Carrer de Pujades 63 2-N
Barcelona 08005, SPAIN

Cirella, Joe (Athlete, Hockey Player)
Teranet 600-1 Adelaide St E
Toronto, ON M5C 2V9, Canada

Ciriani, Henri (Architect)
61 Rue Pascal
Paris 75013, FRANCE

Cirillo, Jeff (Athlete, Baseball Player)
P.O. Box 233
Medina, WA 98039-0233, USA

Cirrincione, Vincent (Producer)
Vincent Cirrincione Associates
1516 N Fairfax Ave
Los Angeles, CA 90046, USA

Cisco, Galen (Athlete, Baseball Player)
604 Elmwood Ln
Celina, OH 45822-2966, USA

Cishek, Steven (Athlete, Baseball Player)
4 Clearwater Dr
East Falmouth, MA 02536-4768, USA

Cisneros, Evelyn (Ballerina)
San Francisco Ballet
455 Franklin St
San Francisco, CA 94102, USA

Cisneros, Evelyo (Ballerina)
San Francisco Ballet
455 Franklin St
San Francisco, CA 94102, USA

Cisneros, Henry (Politician)
2002 W Houston St
San Antonio, TX 78207-3419, USA

Cisneros, Henry G (Secretary)
2002 W Houslon St
San Antonio, TX 78207, USA

Cisowski, Steve (Athlete, Football Player)
1090 3rd St
Gilroy, CA 95020, USA

Citarella, Ralph (Athlete, Baseball Player)
29 E Sherman Ave
Colonia, NJ 07067-1412, USA

Citro, Ralph (Boxer)
32 N Black Horse Pike
Blackwood, NJ 08012, USA

Citron, Martin (Biologist)
Amgen Co
152A 226 Amgen Center
Thousand Oaks, CA 91320, USA

Citron, Ralph (Boxer)
32 N Black Horse Pike
Blackwood, NJ 08012, USA

Citterio, Antonio (Architect)
Antonio Citterio Partners
Via Cerva 4
Milan 20122, ITALY

Citti, Christine (Actor)
Artmedia
20 Ave Rapp
Paris 75007, FRANCE

City High (Music Group)
c/o Staff Member *WmE2 (WMA-LA)*
1 William Morris Pl
Beverly Hills, CA 90212, USA

Ciufo, Leonard (Athlete, Football Player)
3300 Pagent Ct
Thousand Oaks, CA 91360-2837

Civiletti, Benjamin (Politician)
5900 Old Ocean
Blvd Apt B3
Boynton Beach, FL 33435-6228, USA

Civiletti, Benjamin R (Attorney, Attorney General, General)
14 Meadow Road
Baltimore, MD 21212, USA

C. Johnson Jr., Henry (Congressman, Politician)
1427 Longworth HOB
Washington, DC 20515, USA

CK, Louis (Actor, Comedian)
c/o David (Dave) Becky *3 Arts Entertainment Inc*
9460 Wilshire Blvd
7th Floor
Beverly Hills, CA 90210, USA

Claar, Brian (Athlete, Golfer)
27 Bentgrass Pl
Spring, TX 77381, USA

Clabo, Neal (Athlete, Football Player)
1100 Beaverton Rd
Knoxville, TN 37919, USA

Clabo, Neil (Athlete, Football Player)
1100 Beaverton Rd Apt 1
Knoxville, TN 37919-7089, USA

Clabo, Tyson (Athlete, Football Player)
c/o Chad Speck *Allegiant Athletic Agency*
35 Market Sq
Suite 201
Knoxville, TN 37902, USA

Clack, Darryl (Athlete, Football Player)
3891 S Halsted Dr
Chandler, AZ 85286-2612, USA

Clackson, Kim (Athlete, Hockey Player)
342 Thomas Rd
Canonsburg, PA 15317-3534, USA

Claes, Willy (Government Official)
Berkenlaan 23
Hasselt 3500, BELGIUM

Claffey, Norine (Stylist)
4455 N Hamilton
Chicago, IL 60625, USA

Claflin, Sam (Actor)
c/o Staff Member *Independent Talent Group (ITG-UK)*
Oxford House
76 Oxford St
London W1D 1BS, UK

Claggett, Anthony (Athlete, Baseball Player)
123 Arezzo Ct
Palm Desert, CA 92211-0715, USA

Claiborne, Chris (Athlete, Football Player)
Premier Sports Management
1000 N Green Valley Pkwy
Ste 440-128
Henderson, NV 89074, USA

Claiborne, Craig
30 Park Place
E. Hampton, NY 11937-2407

Claire, Fred (Commentator)
1458 Rutherford Dr
Pasadena, CA 91103-2773, USA

Clairmont, Patsy (Writer)
Milk n Honey Inc
PO Box 36
Brighton, MI 48116, USA

Claitt, Rickey (Athlete, Football Player)
5830 Grand Canyon Dr
Orlando, FL 32810, USA

Clampett, Bobby (Athlete, Golfer)
5722 Belmont Valley Ct
Raleigh, NC 27612-6464, USA

Clampi, Cario A (President, Prime Minister)
President's Office
Palazzo del Quirinale
Rome 00187, ITALY

Clampi, Joe (Coach)
Auburn University
Athletic Dept
Auburn, AL 36831, USA

Clancy, Edward B Cardinal (Religious Leader)
Sydney Archdiocese
Polding House 276 Pitt St
Sydney, NSW 2000, AUSTRALIA

Clancy, Jack (Athlete, Football Player)
Landmark Graphics AS PO Box 200
Stavanger, N-Norway 4065

Clancy, Jim (Athlete, Baseball Player)
2598 Gary Cir # 502
Dunedin, FL 34698-1789, USA

Clancy, Sam (Athlete, Football Player)
1308 Crest Ln
Oakdale, PA 15071, USA

Clancy, Sean (Athlete, Football Player)
211 Bal Cross Dr
Bal Harbour, FL 33154, USA

Clancy, Terry (Athlete, Hockey Player)
65 Golfdale Rd
Toronto, ON M4N 2B5, Canada

Clancy, Tom (Writer)
2901 Boston St
Apt 407
Baltimore, MD 21224-4889, USA

Clancy Brothers
177 Woodland Ave
Westwood, NJ 07675, US

Clanton, Jimmy (Musician)
4425 Kingwood Dr
Kingwood, TX 77339, USA

Clapinski, Chris (Athlete, Baseball Player)
83328 Wagon Rd
Indio, CA 92203-2837, USA

Clapp, Gordon (Actor)
Paul Kohner
9300 Wilshire Blvd
#555
Beverly Hills, CA 90212, USA

Clapp, Nicholas R (Producer)
P.O. Box 1019
Borrego Springs, CA 90004-1019, USA

Clapp, Stubby (Athlete, Baseball Player)
140 P Haynes Ln
Savannah, TN 38372-3517, USA

Clapp, Thomas (Athlete, Football Player)
804 Live Oak St
Metairie, LA 70005, USA

Clapton, Eric (Musician)
c/o Kristin Foster *PMK/BNC Public Relations (PMK-NY)*
622 3rd Ave
8th Floor
New York, NY 10017, USA

Clap Your Hands Say Yeah (Music Group)
c/o Staff Member *Paradigm (Monterey)*
404 W Franklin St
Monterey, CA 93940, USA

Clardy, Jon C (Misc)
Cornell University
Chemistry Dept
Ithaca, NY 14853, USA

Clarence, Ellis (Athlete, Football Player)
5849 Leisure South Dr SE
Grand Rapids, MI 49548, USA

Clarey, Doug (Athlete, Baseball Player)
2116 Hillhurst Ave
Los Angeles, CA 90027-2004, USA

Claridge, Dennis (Athlete, Football Player)
2621 Calvert St
Lincoln, NE 68502, USA

Clarin, Hans Joachim
Zellerhornstr. 75
Aschau, GERMANY D-83229

Clarizio, Louis (Athlete, Baseball Player)
133 Lela Ln
Shaumburg, IL 60193, USA

Clark, Al (Athlete, Baseball Player)
1185 SW 5th Ave
Boca Raton, FL 33432, USA

Clark, Alan (Musician)
Damage Mgmt
16 Lambton Place
London W11 2SH, UNITED KINGDOM (UK)

Clark, Annie (Actor)
c/o Norbert Abrams *Noble Caplan Abrams*
1260 Yonge St
2nd Floor
Toronto ON M4T 1W6, Canada

Clark, Anthony (Actor, Comedian)
7110 Senalda Rd
Los Angeles, CA 90068, USA

Clark, Archie (Athlete, Basketball Player)
4268 10th Street
Ecorse, MI 48229-1219, USA

Clark, Bernard (Athlete, Football Player)
306 York Dale Dr
Ruskin, FL 33570, USA

Clark, Blake (Actor, Writer)
c/o Adrienne McWhorter *Abrams Artists Agency (LA)*
9200 Sunset Blvd
11th Floor
Los Angeles, CA 90069, USA

Clark, Bob (Correspondent)
ABC-TV
News Dept
5010 Creston St
Hyattsville, MD 20781, USA

Clark, Bobby (Athlete, Baseball Player)
1030 Perrisito St
Perris, CA 92570-2345, USA

Clark, Brady (Athlete, Baseball Player)
19275 Green Lakes Loop
Bend, OR 97702-1171, USA

Clark, Bret (Athlete, Football Player)
815 Manes Ct
Lincoln, NE 68505, USA

Clark, Brett (Athlete, Hockey Player)
9708 Sunset Hill Dr
Lone Tree, CO 80130-3952, USA

Clark, Brian (Athlete, Football Player)
811 Woodland Forest Dr
Waxhaw, NC 28173, USA

Clark, Bruce (Athlete, Football Player)
3150 Shellers Bnd
State College, PA 16801, USA

Clark, Bryan (Baseball Player)
Seattle Mariners
508 Clark St
Madera, CA 93638-1662, USA

Clark, Bryan (Athlete, Football Player)
1482 Lochridge Rd
Bloomfield Hills, MI 48302, USA

Clark, Candy (Actor)
13935 Hatteras St
Van Nuys, CA 91401, USA

Clark, Carol Higgins (Writer)
300 E 56th St
New York, NY 10022, USA

Clark, Cecelia (Stylist)
8036 Hampton Arbor Circle
Chesterfield, VA 23832, USA

Clark, Chris (Athlete, Hockey Player)
160 Pine Tree Ln
South Windsor, CT 06074-3219, USA

Clark, Corinne (Athlete, Baseball Player)
7224 Hawthorn Avenue NE
Albuquerque, NM 87113-2084, USA

Clark, Dallas (Athlete, Football Player)
2995 Belle Maison Dr
Zionsville, IN 46077, USA

Clark, Daniel (Actor)
c/o Staff Member *Schachter Entertainment*
1157 S Beverly Dr Fl 2
Los Angeles, CA 90035, USA

Clark, Danny (Athlete, Football Player)
213 Seneca Trl
Bloomingdale, IL 60108, USA

Clark, Dave (Athlete, Baseball Player)
4842 Mayfield Rd W
Collierville, TN 38017-3309, USA

Clark, Derrick (Athlete, Football Player)
430 Sunset Dr
Apt 2
Orlando, FL 32805, USA

Clark, Desmond (Athlete, Football Player)
2190 Shadow Creek Ct
Vernon Hills, IL 60061

Clark, Doran
6399 Wilshire Blvd. #414
Los Angeles, XA 90048

Clark, Doug (Athlete, Baseball Player)
106 Piedmont St
Springfield, MA 01104-2042, USA

Clark, Dwight (Athlete, Football Player)
1801 Pinewood Cir
Charlotte, NC 28211, USA

Clark, Earl (Swimmer)
1145 NE 126th St
#4
North Miami, FL 33161, USA

Clark, Eugenie (Biologist)
1255 N Gulfstream Ave
#503
Sarasota, FL 34236, USA

Clark, Gail (Athlete, Football Player)
PO Box 335
Bellefontaine, OH 43311, USA

Clark, Gene (Musician)
Artists International Mgmt
9850 Sandaltoot Road
#458
Boca Raton, FL 33428, USA

Clark, General Wesley (General)
1 Crestmont Dr
Little Rock, AR 72227-2203, USA

Clark, George W (Physicist)
Massachusetts Institute of Technology
Physics Dept
Cambridge, MA 02139, USA

Clark, Glen (Athlete, Baseball Player)
5605 Marblehead Dr
Dallas, TX 75232-2356, USA

Clark, Gordie (Athlete, Hockey Player)
1 Stratham Green
Stratham, NH 03885-2341, USA

Clark, Gordie
New York Rangers
2 Penn Plz Fl 22 Attn Dir
Player Personnel, New York
NY 10121-2299, USA

Clark, Guy (Musician, Songwriter)
102 Stoneway Close
Nashville, TN 37209, USA

Clark, Harry (Athlete, Football Player)
1121 Patton Dr
Morgantown, WV 26505, USA

Clark, Helen (Prime Minister)
Prime Minister's Office
Parliament Buildings
Wellington, NEW ZELAND

Clark, Hilary (Stylist)
c/o Staff Member *Ennis*
119 Braintree St
Boston, MA 02134, USA

Clark, Howie (Athlete, Baseball Player)
14204 439th Ave SE
North Bend, WA 98045-9209, USA

Clark, Jack (Athlete, Baseball Player)
6541 Scottsdale Way
Frisco, TX 75034-4015, USA

Clark, James (Jim) (Business Person)
My CFO.com
111 West Monroe
P.O. Box 755
Chicago, IL 60690, USA

Clark, Jerald (Athlete, Baseball Player)
12325 Crisscross Ln
San Diego, CA 92129-3766, USA

Clark, Jermaine (Athlete, Baseball Player)
2 Ute Ct
San Ramon, CA 94583-2455, USA

Clark, Jessie (Athlete, Football Player)
7611 S 9th Way
Phoenix, AZ 85042, USA

Clark, Jim (Athlete, Baseball Player)
659 S Indian Hill Blvd Apt C
Claremont, CA 91711-5486, USA

Clark, Joe (Prime Minister)
1300-707 7 Ave SW
Calgary, AB T2P 3H6, CANADA

Clark, Joe
PO Box 96848
Washington, DC 20090-6848

Clark, Joe (Educator)
Essex County Detention Center
208 Essex Ave
Newark, NJ 07103, USA

Clark, Kelly (Athlete, Skier)
178 Route 100
West Dover, VT 05356-0725, USA

Clark, Kelvin (Athlete, Football Player)
3812 Evesham Dr
Plano, TX 75025, USA

Clark, Kenneth B (Psychic)
PO Box 126
Hastings-on-Hudson, NY 10706, USA

Clark, Keon (Basketball Player)
Utah Jazz Delta Center
301 W South Temple
Salt Lake Clty, VT 84101, USA

Clark, Kevin (Athlete, Football Player)
3962 South Chase Way
Denver, CO 80235, USA

Clark, Kevin Alexander (Actor)
c/o Anne Geddes *Geddes Agency, The*
8430 Santa Monica Blvd
Suite 200
Los Angeles, CA 90069, USA

Clark, Larry (Filmmaker)
c/o Staff Member *ICM Partners (ICM-LA)*
10250 Constellation Blvd Fl 7
Los Angeles, CA 90067, USA

Clark, Laurel B (Doctor)
1731 Sunset Blvd
Houston, TX 77005-1713, USA

Clark, Lawrence (General)
728 Calle Vallarta
San Clemente, CA 92673-3070, USA

Clark, Leroy (Athlete, Football Player)
5458 Osprey Dr
Houston, TX 77048, USA

Clark, L Hill (Business Person)
Crane Co
100 Stamford Place
Stamford, CT 06902, USA

Clark, Louis S (Athlete, Football Player)
6149 Kissengen
Springs Ct
Jacksonville, FL 32258, USA

Clark, Marcia (Lawyer)
5457 Hobson Ct
Calabasas, CA 91302, USA

Clark, Mario (Athlete, Football Player)
8155 Bangor Ave
Apt 695
Hesperia, CA 92345, USA

Clark, Mark (Athlete, Baseball Player)
18262 E Cr 520N
Kilbourne, IL 62655-6628, USA

Clark, Mary Ellen (Athlete, Diver, Olympic Athlete)
117 Blue Hills Rd
Amherst, MA 01002-2221, USA

Clark, Mary Higgins (Writer)
MHC-Clark
15 Werimus Brook Rd
Saddle River, NJ 07458, USA

Clark, Mary Higgins (Writer)
210 Central ParkS
New York, NY 10019-1428, USA

Clark, Matt (Actor)
1199 Park Ave
#15D
New York, NY 10128, USA

Clark, Mel (Baseball Player)
Philadelphia Phillies
RR 1 Box 97
West Columbia, WV 25287-9721, USA

Clark, Micheal (Choreographer, Dancer)
Barbican Centre
Silk St
London EC2Y 8DS, UNITED KINGDOM

Clark, Mystro (Actor, Comedian)
c/o Staff Member *ICM Partners (ICM-LA)*
10250 Constellation Blvd Fl 7
Los Angeles, CA 90067, USA

Clark, Perry (Coach)
Miami University
Athletic Dept
Coral Gables, FL 33124, USA

Clark, Peter B (Publisher)
7675 La Jolla Blvd
#203
La Jolla, CA 92037, USA

Clark, Petula (Musician)
5415 Collins Ave #PHF
Miami Beach, FL 33140, USA

Clark, Phil (Athlete, Baseball Player)
112 Hicks Rd
Dawson, GA 39842, USA

Clark, Phil (Athlete, Baseball Player)
112 Hicks Rd
Dawson, GA 39842-4002, USA

Clark, Phil (Athlete, Football Player)
PO Box 3021
Barrington, IL 60011, USA

Clark, Ramsey (Politician)
37 W 12th St Apt 2B
New York, NY 10011-8503, USA

Clark, Richard (Ex-Senator, Politician)
4424 Edmunds St NW #1070
Washington, DC 20007-1117, USA

Clark, Rickey (Athlete, Baseball Player)
8953 Emerald Waters Ct
Las Vegas, NV 89147-6501, USA

Clark, Robert (General)
9224 Forest Haven Dr
Alexandria, VA 22309-32--03, USA

Clark, Robert C (Artist)
34 Monterey Court
Manhattan Beach, CA 90266, USA

Clark, Ron (Athlete, Baseball Player)
700 Starkey Rd
Apt 511
Largo, FL 33771-2344, USA

Clark, Roy (Musician)
Roy Clark Productions
3225 S Norwood Ave
Tulsa, OK 74135, USA

Clark, Ryan (Athlete, Football Player)
1236 Camarta Dr
Pittsburgh, PA 15227, USA

Clark, Sedric (Athlete, Football Player)
7819 Chasewood Dr
Missouri City, TX 77489, USA

Clark, Spencer Treat (Actor)
c/o Michael Greenwald *Buchwald/Fortitude (LA)*
6500 Wilshire Blvd
Suite 2200
Los Angeles, CA 90048, USA

Clark, Stephen E (Steve) (Swimmer)
29 Martling Road
San Anselmo, CA 94960, USA

Clark, Susan (Actor)
7943 Woodrow Wilson Dr
Los Angeles, CA 90046, USA

Clark, Terry (Athlete, Baseball Player)
1607 E Tam O Shanter St
Ontario, CA 91761-6356, USA

Clark, Tim (Athlete, Golfer)
22400 N 97th St
Scottsdale, AZ 85255, USA

Clark, Tony (Athlete, Baseball Player)
14125 N 65th Ave
Glendale, AZ 85306-3757, USA

Clark, Vernon E (Admiral)
Chief of Naval Operations
HqUSN Pentagon
Washington, DC 20350, USA

Clark, Vinnie (Athlete, Football Player)
1120 Virescent Ct
Cincinnati, OH 45224, USA

Clark, Wayne (Athlete, Football Player)
14241 Lambeth Way
Tustin, CA 92780-2230, USA

Clark, Wendel (Athlete, Hockey Player)
c/o Staff Member *Toronto Maple Leafs*
Air Canada Centre
400-40 Bay St
Toronto, ON M5J 2X2, Canada

Clark, Wendel (Athlete, Hockey Player)
14922 Bathurst St
King City, ON L7B 1K5, Canada

Clark, Wesley K (Wes) (General)
Stephens Group
111 Center St
Little Rock, AR 72201, USA

Clark, W G (Architect)
Clark & Menefee Architects
4048 E Main St
Charlottesville, VA 22902, USA

Clark, Will (Athlete, Baseball Player, Olympic Athlete)
18555 Saint Andrews Ct E
Prairieville, LA 70769-3248, USA

Clark, Will (Adult Film Star)
c/o Staff Member *Diva Central Inc*
7510 W Sunset Blvd Ste 1445
Los Angees, CA 90046, USA

Clark, William P (Politician, Secretary)
1031 Pine St
Paso Robles, CA 93446-2537, USA

Clark, W Ramsey (General)
37 W 12th St #2B
New York, NY 10011, USA

Clark-Cole, Dorinda (Musician)
c/o Staff Member *Gospocentric*
421 E Beach Ave
Inglewood, GA 90302, USA

Clark-Diggs, Joetta (Athlete, Olympic Athlete, Track Athlete)
1856 Clarence Dr
Hellertown, PA 18055-2701, USA

Clarke, Allan (Music Group, Musician)
Hill Farm Hackleton
Northantshire NN7 2DH, UNITED KINGDOM (UK)

Clarke, Angela (Actor)
3930 Weeping Willow Dr
Moorpark, CA 93021-2842, USA

Clarke, Bob (Cartoonist)
7480 Rivershore Dr
Seaford, DE 19973-4328, USA

Clarke, Bobby (Athlete, Hockey Player)
Philadelphia Flyers
3601S Broad St Ste 2
Philadelphia, PA 19148-5297, USA

Clarke, Brian Patrick (Actor)
c/o Staff Member *Orange Grove Group, The*
12178 Ventura Blvd #205
Studio City, CA 91604, USA

Clarke, Darren (Athlete, Golfer)
c/o Andrew "Chubby" Chandler
International Sports Management Ltd (ISM UK)
Cherry Tree Farm
Cherry Tree Lane
Rostherne, Cheshire WA14 3RZ, UNITED KINGDOM

Clarke, Elis E I (President)
16 Frederick St
Port of Spain, TRINADAD & TOBAGO

Clarke, Emilia (Actor)
c/o Michael Hallett *Emptage Hallett*
14 Rathbone Pl
London W1T 1HT, UNITED KINGDOM (UK)

Clarke, Emily (Actor)
c/o Darren Goldberg *Global Creative*
1051 Cole Ave # B
Los Angeles, CA 90038, USA

Clarke, Emmy (Actor)
c/o Darren Goldberg *Global Creative*
1051 Cole Ave # B
Los Angeles, CA 90038, USA

Clarke, Frank (Athlete, Football Player)
6016 Pine Ridge Blvd
McKinney, TX 75070-9518, USA

Clarke, Gary (Actor, Writer)
1113 Heep Run
Buda, TX 78610-5091, USA

Clarke, Gilby (Music Group, Musician)
Sammy Boyd Entertainment
212 Allen Ave
Allenhurst, NJ 07711, USA

Clarke, Gilmore D (Architect)
480 Park Ave
New York, NY 10022, USA

Clarke, Hagood (Athlete, Football Player)
2500 NE 37th Dr
Fort Lauderdale, FL 33308, USA

Clarke, Hansen (Congressman, Politician)
1319 Longworth HOB
Washington, DC 20515, USA

Clarke, Horace (Athlete, Baseball Player)
P.O. Box 891
Frederiksted, VI 00841-0891, USA

Clarke, John (Actor)
Days of Our Lives Show
KNBC-TV 3000W Alameda Ave
Burbank, CA 91523, USA

Clarke, Kate (Actor)
1470 Angelus Ave
Los Angeles, CA 90026, USA

Clarke, Ken (Athlete, Football Player)
7610 WillouLhby Ct
Alpharetta, GA 30005, USA

Clarke, Kenneth H (Government Official)
House of Commons
Westminster
London SW1A 0AA, UNITED KINGDOM
(UK)

Clarke, Lenny (Actor)
c/o Staff Member *Paradigm (LA)*
360 N Crescent Dr
North Bldg
Beverly Hills, CA 90210, USA

Clarke, Martha (Choreographer, Dancer)
Sheldon Soffer Mgmt
130 W 56th St
New York, NY 10019, USA

Clarke, Melinda (Actor)
4935 Morse Ave
Sherman Oaks, CA 91423, USA

Clarke, Michael (Music Group, Musician)
Artists International Mgmt
9850 Sandalfoot Blvd #458
Boca Raton, FL 33428, USA

Clarke, Noah
4683 Oberle Ct
La Verne, CA 91750-2126

Clarke, Noel (Actor, Director, Writer)
c/o Staff Member *Liz Matthews PR*
83 Charlotte Street
London W1T 4PR, United Kingdom

Clarke, Richard (Lawyer)
National Security Council
1600 Pennsylvania Ave NW
Washington, DC 20500, USA

Clarke, Robert L (Government Official)
Bracewell & Patterson
711 Louisiana St #2900
Houston, TX 77002, USA

Clarke, Ronald (Ron) (Athlete, Track Athlete)
1 Bay St
Brighton, VIC 3186, USA

Clarke, Sarah (Actor)
c/o Staff Member *Levine Management*
9028 W Sunset Blvd #PH1
Los Angeles, CA 90069, USA

Clarke, Stan (Athlete, Baseball Player)
5333 Sanders Dr
Toledo, OH 43615-6860, USA

Clarke, Stanley (Musician)
880 Greenleaf Canyon Rd
Topanga, CA 90290, USA

Clarke, Susanna (Writer)
Tom Doherty Associates, LLC
175 Fifth Ave
New York, NY 10010, USA

Clarke, Thomas E (Business Person)
Nice Inc
1 Bowerman Dr
Beaverton, OR 97005, USA

Clark II, Michael (Athlete, Golfer)
4007 Pintail Cir
Rocky Face, GA 30740, USA

Clark-Sheard, Karen (Musician)
c/o Staff Member *Elektra Records*
75 Rockefeller Plaza
17th Floor
New York, NY 10019, USA

Clarkson, Adrienne (Ex-Governor)
12A Admiral Rd
Ottawa, ON M5R 2L5, Canada

Clarkson, Jeremy (Television Host)
c/o Staff Member *XS Promotions*
57 Fonthill Rd
Aberdeen AB11 6UQ, UNITED
KINGDOM (UK)

Clarkson, Kelly (Musician, Songwriter)
900 20th Ave S #1214
Nashville, TN 37212, USA

Clarkson, Patricia (Actor)
c/o Tony Lipp *Anonymous Content (LA)*
3531 Hayden Ave
Culver City, CA 90232, USA

Clary, Julian (Actor)
PO Box 976
Swindon
 SN5 7HN, UNITED KINGDOM

Clary, Marty (Athlete, Baseball Player)
205 Yorktown Ct
Easley, SC 29642-9042, USA

Clary, Robert (Actor)
10001 Sun Dial Ln
Beverly Hills, CA 90210, USA

Clasby, Bob (Athlete, Football Player)
8180 E Shea Blvd Unit 1090
Scottsdale, AZ 85260, USA

Clash, Kevin (Artist, Voice Over Artist)
c/o Staff Member *Sesame Workshop*
One Lincoln Plaza
New York, NY 10023, USA

Clash, The
268 Camden Rd.
London, ENGLAND NW1

Clatney, Paul (Athlete, Football Player)
302-190 Manitoba St
Toronto, ON M8Y 3Y8, Canada

C. LaTourette, Steven (Congressman, Politician)
2371 Rayburn HOB
Washington, DC 20515, USA

Clatworthy, Robert (Artist, Misc)
Moelfre Cynghordy
Landovery Dyfed
Wales SA20 0UW, UNITED KINGDOM
(UK)

Clatyon, Barry (Artist, Voice Over Artist)
Talking Heads
88-90 Crawford St
London W1H 2BS, UNITED KINGDOM
(UK)

Claudel, Aurelie (Model)
c/o Staff Member *IMG*
304 Park Ave S Fl 12
New York, NY 10010, USA

Claudel, Philippe (Director, Writer)
c/o Staff Member *ArtMedia*
20 avenue Rapp
Paris 75008, France

Clauser, Francis H (Educator, Engineer)
4072 Chevy Chase
Flintridge, CA 91011, USA

Clauss, Jared (Athlete, Football Player)
215 S 82nd St
West Des Moines, IA 50266-8524, USA

Claussen, Brandon (Athlete, Baseball Player)
4114 124th St
Lubbock, TX 79423-8905, USA

Clavier, Christian (Actor)
Agents Associes Beaume
201 Faubourg Saint Honore
Paris 75008, FRANCE

Clawhammer
Box 1519
Nijnegen, NETHERLANDS 6501 BM

Clawson, John (Athlete, Basketball Player, Olympic Athlete)
30 Eagle Lake Pl
Unit 31
San Ramon, CA 94582-4858, USA

Claxton, Craig (Speedy) (Athlete, Basketball Player)
Golden State Warriors
57 Hichcock Ln
Old Westbury, NY 11568-1403, USA

Claxton, Paul (Athlete, Golfer)
P.O. Box 485
Claxton, GA 30417, USA

Clay, Andrew (Actor, Comedian)
Artist Group International
9560 Wilshire Blvd #400
Beverly Hills, CA 90212, USA

Clay, Andrew Dice (Comedian)
121 Stonewood Ct
Las Vegas, NV 89107, USA

Clay, Bryan (Athlete, Olympic Athlete)
c/o Staff Member *USA Track & Field*
132 E Washington St
Suite 800
Indianapolis, IN 46204, USA

Clay, Danny (Athlete, Baseball Player)
5434 Ravine Bluff Ct
Columbus, OH 43231-3157, USA

Clay, Hayward (Athlete, Football Player)
PO Box 234
Snyder, TX 79550, USA

Clay, John (Athlete, Football Player)
1441 S 10th St
Saint Louis, MO 63104-3724, USA

Clay, Ken (Athlete, Baseball Player)
4523 60th Street Ct W
Bradenton, FL 34210-2729, USA

Clay, Nicholas
15 Golden Sq. #315
London, ENGLAND W1R 3AG

Clay, Walter (Athlete, Football Player)
2827 Arlington Ave
Pueblo, CO 81003, USA

Clay, Willie (Athlete, Football Player)
1460 Hawthorne St
Pittsburgh, PA 15201-2025, USA

Clayborn, Adrian (Football Player)
c/o Blake Baratz *The Institute for Athletes*
3600 Minnesota Dr
#550
Edina, MN 55435, USA

Clayborn, Raymond D (Ray) (Athlete, Football Player)
20610 Aspen Canyon Dr
Katy, TX 77450, USA

Claybrooks, Devon (Athlete, Football Player)
725 Auburn Pl
Martinsville, VA 24112, USA

Clayderman, Richard (Musician)
Denis Vaughan Management
P O Box 28286
London N21 3WT, UNITED KINGDOM
(UK)

Claydon, Phil (Director)
c/o Jason Burns *United Talent Agency (UTA)*
9336 Civic Center Dr
Beverly Hills, CA 90210, USA

Clayman, Ralph V (Doctor, Misc)
Bames Hospital
Surgery Dept
416 S Kingshighway Blvd
Saint Louis, MO 63110, USA

Claypool, James (Athlete, Hockey Player)
302 Paine Farm Rd
Duluth, MN 55804-2632, USA

Claypool, Les (Musician)
3909 Heather Ln
Sebastopol, CA 95472, USA

Clayson, Jane (Correspondent)
c/o Staff Member *CBS Television*
51 W 52nd St
New York, NY 10019, USA

Clayton, Adam (Music Group, Musician)
Principle Mgmt
30-32 Sir John Rogersons Quay
Dublin @, IRELAND

Clayton, Amber (Actor)
c/o Steve Glick *Glick Agency*
1321 7th St
Suite 203
Santa Monica, CA 90401, USA

Clayton, Donald D (Misc)
Clemson University
Physic/Astrophysics Dept
Clemson, SC 29634, USA

Clayton, Harvey (Athlete, Football Player)
15303 SW 143rd St
Miami, FL 33196, USA

Clayton, Mark (Athlete, Football Player)
16426 Canyon Chase Dr
Houston, TX 77095, USA

Clayton, Mark (Athlete, Football Player)
9407 Manor Forge Way
Owings Mills, MD 21117, USA

Clayton, Michael (Athlete, Football Player)
8501 Kentucky Derby Dr
Odessa, FL 33556-2446, USA

Clayton, Ralph (Athlete, Football Player)
6356 Selkirk St
Detroit, MI 48221, USA

Clayton, Robert N (Geophysicist, Misc, Physicist)
5201 S Comell Ave
Chicago, IL 60615, USA

Clayton, Royce (Athlete, Baseball Player)
6035 Debutts Terr
Malibu, CA 90265, USA

Clayton, Thomas David (Music Group, Musician)
Music Avenue Inc
43 Washington St
Groveland, MA 01834, USA

Cleamons, Jim (Athlete, Basketball Player)
29 Sausalito Cir W
Manhattan Beach, CA 90266-7234, USA

Clear, Mark (Athlete, Baseball Player)
15654 S Rene St
Olathe, KS 66062-4676, USA

Clearwater, Keith (Athlete, Golfer)
1077 E Bretonwoods Ln
Orem, UT 84097-8200, USA

Clearwater, Ray (Athlete, Hockey Player)
98 George St
East Haven, CT 06512-4726, USA

Cleary, Beverly (Writer)
William Morrow And Co
1350 Avenue of the Americas
New York, NY 10019-4702, USA

Cleary, Danielle (Stylist)
c/o Staff Member *Mark Edward Inc*
325 W 8th St
#1011
New York, NY 10018, USA

Cleary, Jon Stephen (Writer)
HarperCollins
23 Ryde Road
Pymble, NSW 2073, AUSTRALIA

Cleary, Robert (Bob) (Athlete, Hockey Player, Olympic Athlete)
680 South Ave
Unit 8
Weston, MA 02493-1192, USA

Cleary, Thomas (Writer)
c/o Staff Member *Random House*
1540 Broadway
New York, NY 10036, USA

Cleary, William J (Bill) Jr (Athlete, Hockey Player, Olympic Athlete)
27 Kingwood Rd
Auburndale, MA 02466-1013, USA

Cleave, Dr Mary L (Astronaut)
596 Pinewood Dr
Annaoolis, MD 21401-7113, USA

Cleave, Mary L (Astronaut)
NASA
Earth Science Office
Code AS Room 7R86
Washington, DC 20546, USA

Cleaver, Alan (Designer, Fashion Designer)
Via Vallone 11
Monte Conero
Sirolo, ITALY

Cleaver, Emanuel (Congressman, Politician)
1433 Longworth HOB
Washington, DC 20515, USA

Cledwyn of Penrhos (Government Official)
Penmorfa Trearddur
Holyhead Gwynedd
Wales, UNITED KINGDOM (UK)

Cleeland, Cam (Athlete, Football Player)
23160 Lanyard Ln
Mount Vernon, WA 98274, USA

Cleese, John (Actor, Comedian, Writer)
c/o Tony Lipp *Anonymous Content (LA)*
3531 Hayden Ave
Culver City, CA 90232, USA

Cleese, John (Writer)
David Williamson 15 Hazlebury Road
London, England SW6 2LX, UK

Clef (Music Group, Musician)
DAS Communications
83 Riverside Dr
New York, NY 10024, USA

Clegg, Johnny (Music Group, Musician)
c/o Staff Member *Monterey International (Chicago)*
200 W Superior
Suite 202
Chicago, IL 60610, USA

Cleghorne, Ellen (Actor, Comedian)
c/o Frederick Levy *Management 101*
11271 Ventura Blvd
#102
Studio City, CA 91604, USA

Cleland, Max (Ex-Senator, Politician)
2460 Peachtree Rd NW Apt 1406
Atlanta, GA 30305-4158, USA

Clemens, Barry (Athlete, Basketball Player)
3111 Clinton Avenue
Cleveland, OH 44113-2973, USA

Clemens, Donella (Religious Leader)
Monnonite Church
722 N Main St
Newton, KS 67114, USA

Clemens, Doug (Athlete, Baseball Player)
4799 Lower Mountain Rd
New Hope, PA 18938-9454, USA

Clemens, Robert (Bob) (Athlete, Football Player)
2007 Poole Dr NW Ste D
Huntsville, AL 35810-4900, USA

Clemens, Roger (Athlete, Baseball Player)
11535 Quail Hollow Ln
Houston, TX 77024-6508, USA

Clemenson, Christian (Actor)
2666 La Cuesta Dr
Los Angeles, CA 90046, USA

Clement, Anthony (Athlete, Football Player)
141 Navajo Ln
Opelousas, LA 70570-0324, USA

Clement, Aurore (Actor)
Artmedia
20 Ave Rapp
Paris 75007, FRANCE

Clement, Bill (Athlete, Hockey Player)
Philadelphia Flyers
3601 S Broad St Ste 2
Philadelphia, PA 19148-5297, USA

Clement, Jeff (Athlete, Baseball Player)
1318 NE 29th St
Marshalltown, IA 50021, USA

Clement, Jemaine (Actor, Writer)
c/o Jason Heyman *Creative Artists Agency (CAA-LA)*
2000 Ave Of The Stars
Los Angeles, CA 90067, USA

Clement, Matt (Athlete, Baseball Player)
143 Milt Miller Rd
Renfrew, PA 16053-9613, USA

Clement, Skip (Athlete, Football Player)
620 Tennis Club Dr Apt 106
Fort Lauderdale, FL 33311, USA

Clemente, Carmine D (Misc, Physicist)
11737 Bellagio Road
Los Angeles, CA 90049, USA

Clemente, Fransesco (Artist)
684 Broadway
New York, NY 10012, USA

Clement F, Haynsworth Jr (Judge)
111 Boxwood Lane
Greenville, SC 29601, USA

Clements, Dick (Director, Producer, Writer)
c/o Bruce Kaufman *ICM Partners (ICM-LA)*
10250 Constellation Blvd Fl 7
Los Angeles, CA 90067, USA

Clements, John A (Misc, Physicist)
University of California
Cardiovascular Institute
San Fransisco, CA 94143, USA

Clements, Kim (Writer)
c/o Staff Member *Creative Artists Agency (CAA-LA)*
2000 Ave Of The Stars
Los Angeles, CA 90067, USA

Clements, Lennie (Athlete, Golfer)
PO Box 182197
Coronado, CA 92178-2197, USA

Clements, Nate (Athlete, Football Player)
1 Bills Dr
Orchard Park, NY 14127, USA

Clements, Pat (Athlete, Baseball Player)
166 Lazy S Ln
Chico, CA 95928-9112, USA

Clements, Ronald (Director, Producer, Writer)
c/o Staff Member *Creative Artists Agency (CAA-LA)*
2000 Ave Of The Stars
Los Angeles, CA 90067, USA

Clements, Suzanne (Designer, Fashion Designer)
Clements Ribeiro Ltd
48 S Molton St
London W1X 1HE, UNITED KINGDOM (UK)

Clements, Tom (Athlete, Football Player)
101 Cherry St Unit 216
Green Bay, WI 54301-4247, USA

Clements, Vincent (Vin) (Athlete, Football Player)
62 Chatham Rd
Berlin, CT 06037, USA

Clemmensen, Scott (Athlete, Hockey Player)
Edge Sports Management
26 Autumn Ridge Rd
Pound Ridge, NY 10576-1400, USA

Clemmer, Ronnie (Producer)
c/o Staff Member *Longbow Productions*
PO Box 240
Van Nuys, CA 91408-0240, USA

Clemmons, Ruth (Stylist)
9549 Windy Knoll Dr
Dallas, TX 75243, USA

Clemons, Charlie (Athlete, Football Player)
1973 Bertha Ct
Hampton, GA 30228-4006, USA

Clemons, Chris (Athlete, Baseball Player)
521 Karen Dr
Robinson, TX 76706-5122, USA

Clemons, Craig (Athlete, Football Player)
1517 D Ave NE
Cedar Rapids, IA 52402-5148, USA

Clemons, Duane (Athlete, Football Player)
30181 W 231st St
Spring Hill, KS 66083-6019, USA

Clendenen, Mike (Athlete, Football Player)
1987 Denver Broncos
Dana Point, CA 92629-3837, USA

Clendenin, Robert (Bob) (Actor)
2343 N Reese Pl
Burbank, CA 91504, USA

Clennon, David (Actor)
2309 27th St
Santa Monica, CA 90405, USA

Clerico, Christian (Business Person, Misc)
Lido-Normandie
116 Bis Ave des Champs Elyees
Paris 75008, FRANCE

Clervoy, Jean-Francois (Astronaut)
NASA
EAC Postfach 90 26 96
Koln, Germany D-51127, USA

Cleveland, Charles (General)
3603 Thomas Ave
Montgomery, 36111-2013 AL, USA

Cleveland, Paul M (Diplomat)
808 Crooked Crow Lane
Great Falls, VA 22066-2409, USA

Cleveland, Reggie (Athlete, Baseball Player)
202 Creekview Drive
Anna, TX 75409-3577, USA

Clevenger, Raymond C III (Judge)
US Court of Appeals
717 Madison Place NW
Washington, DC 20439, USA

Clevenger, Tex (Athlete, Baseball Player)
31727 Country Club Dr
Porterville, CA 93257-9610, USA

Clevlen, Brent (Athlete, Baseball Player)
14100 Averv Ranch Blvd Unit 1703
Austin, TX 78717-4012, USA

Clexton, Edward W Jr (Admiral)
1000 Bobolink Dr
Virginia Beach, VA 23451, USA

Cliburn, Stan (Athlete, Baseball Player)
Sioux City Explorers 3400
c;ioull Ciru, IA 51106, USA

Cliburn, Stew (Athlete, Baseball Player)
425 William Dr
Pleasant View, TN 37146-7910, USA

Cliburn, Van (Musician)
PO Box 470219
Fort Worth, TX 76147, USA

Cliche, Karen (Actor)
c/o Sandy Martinez *Martinez Creative Management*
7012 St Laurent Blvd
Suite 200
Montreal, QC H2S 3E2, Canada

Click, Shannan (Model)
1672 Mountcrest Ave
West Hollywood, CA 90069, USA

Cliff, Jimmy (Music Group, Songwriter, Writer)
51 Lady Musgrave Rd
Kingston, JAMAICA

Clifford, Chris (Athlete, Hockey Player)
600 Compass Crt
Kingston, ON K7M 8V9, Canada

Clifford, Linda (Music Group)
c/o Staff Member *Diva Central Inc*
7510 W Sunset Blvd Ste 1445
Los Angees, CA 90046, USA

Clifford, Lt Colonel Michael R (Astronaut)
4327 N Pine Brook Wav
Houston, TX 77059-3038, USA

Clifford, M Richard (Rich) (Astronaut)
3700 Bay Area Blvd
Houston, TX 77058, USA

Clift, Eleanor
1750 Pennsylvania Ave NW #1220
Washington, DC 20006

Clift, William B III (Photographer)
P O Box 6035
Santa Fe, NM 87502, USA

Clifton, Chad (Athlete, Football Player)
346 Heidelberg Ct
Green Bay, WI 54302, USA

Clifton, Greg (Athlete, Football Player)
2717 Botany St
Charlotte, NC 28216, USA

Clifton, Kyle (Athlete, Football Player)
777 S Point Ct
Aledo, TX 76008, USA

Clijsters, Kim (Athlete, Tennis Player)
2120 Baileys Corner Rd
Wall Township, NJ 07719, USA

Cliks, The (Music Group)
c/o Staff Member *Paradigm (Monterey)*
404 W Franklin St
Monterey, CA 93940, USA

Climie, Ron (Athlete, Hockey Player)
5 Ackland St
Stoney Creek, ON L8J 1H5, Canada

Cline, Bruce (Athlete, Hockey Player)
8-890 Rue St Pierre
Drummondville, QC J2C 3X3, Canada

Cline, Jackie (Athlete, Football Player)
5935 High Forest Dr
Mc Calla, AL 35111, USA

Cline, Martin J (Educator, Misc)
University of California
Med Center Hematology Dept
Los Angeles, CA 90024, USA

Cline, Richard (Cartoonist)
New Yorker Magazine
Editorial Dept
4 Times Square
New York, NY 10036, USA

Cline, Ty (Athlete, Baseball Player)
37 Wappoo Creek Pl
Charleston, SC 29412-2121, USA

Clines, Gene (Athlete, Baseball Player)
5303 9th Avenue Dr W
Bradenton, FL 34209-4205, USA

Cline Sr, Tony (Athlete, Football Player)
59 Chestnut Pl
Danville, CA 94506, USA

Clinkscale, F Dextor (Athlete, Football Player)
206 Machaux Dr
Greenville, SC 29605-3156, USA

Clinkscales, Joey (Athlete, Football Player)
10207 Shrewsbury Run W
Collierville, TN 38017-8304, USA

Clinkscales, Sherard (Baseball Player)
7314 N Layman Ave
Indianapolis, IN 46250-2634, USA

Clinton, Bill (Ex-President, Politician)
The Office Of President William J. Clinton
77 Water St
New York, NY 10005, USA

Clinton, Chelsea
15 Old House Ln
Chappaqua, NY 10514, USA

Clinton, George (Musician, Songwriter)
c/o Vasi Vangelos *First Artists Management*
4764 Park Granada
Suite 210
Calabasas, CA 91302, USA

Clinton, Hillary Rodham (Ex-First Lady, Ex-Senator, First Lady, Government Official, Politician)
U.S. Department of State
3067 Whitehaven St NW
Washington, DC 20008-3620, USA

Clinton, Kate (Comedian)
230 West End Avenue
#10C
New York, New York 10023, USA

Clinton-Davis of Hackney, Stanley C (Government Official)
House of Lords
Westminster
London SW1A 0PW, UNITED KINGDOM (UK)

Clippard, Tyler (Athlete, Baseball Player)
2160 Chianti Pl Unit 118
Palm Harbor, FL 34683-7736, USA

Clippingdale, Steve (Athlete, Hockey Player)
5560 Swordfern Pl
North Vancouver, BC V7R 4T1, Canada

Clique Girlz (Music Group, Musician)
c/o Staff Member *Clique Entertainment Productions*
11 Forest View Ct
Egg Harbor Township, NJ 08234, USA

Clisters, Kim (Tennis Player)
Assn of Tennis Professionals
200 Tournament Road
Ponte Vedra Beach, FL 32082, USA

Clive, John
4 Court Lodge Chelsea
London, ENGLAND SW3 AJA

Cloepfil, Brad (Architect)
Allied Works Architecture
910 NW Hoyt St #200
Portland, OR 97209, USA

Clohessy, Robert (Actor)
Don Buchwald
6500 Wilshire Blvd #2200
Los Angeles, CA 90048, USA

Cloke, Kristen (Actor)
c/o Staff Member *Mitchell K Stubbs & Assoc (MKS)*
8675 W. Washington Blvd
Suite 203
Culver City, CA 90232, USA

Cloninger, Tony (Athlete, Baseball Player)
PO Box 1500
Denver, NC 28037-1500, USA

Clontz, Brad (Athlete, Baseball Player)
735 Eider Down Ct
Alpharetta, GA 30022-6198, USA

Clooney, George (Actor, Producer)
c/o Staff Member *Smoke House Productions*
12001 Ventura Pl
Suite 200
Studio City, CA 91604, USA

Clooney, Nick (Writer)
American University
School Of Communication, Room 330A
4400 Massachusetts Avenue NW
Washington, DC 20016, USA

Close, Bill (Basketball Player)
555 Byron St #409
Palo Alto, CA 94301, USA

Close, Chuck (Artist)
20 Bond St Frnt A
New York, NY 10012-2689, USA

Close, Eric (Actor)
4243 Saugus Ave
Sherman Oaks, CA 91403, USA

Close, Glenn (Actor)
136 Succabone Rd
Bedford Hills, NY 10507, USA

Close, Joshua (Actor)

Closser, J D (Athlete, Baseball Player)
2202_U._32nd Ave
Alexandria, IN .Jl0602-4679, USA

Closter, Al (Athlete, Baseball Player)
4103 Hickory Rd
Richmond, VA 23235, USA

Closure In Moscow (Music Group, Musician)
c/o Andrew Cook *Run Artist Management*
5753 Cobblestone Dr.
Rocklin, CA 95765, USA

Clotet, Lluis (Architect)
Studio PER
Caspe 151
Barcelona 08013, SPAIN

Clotworthy, Bob (Athlete, Olympic Athlete, Swimmer)
2301 Moss Rose Ln
Fort Collins, CO 80526-2178, USA

Cloud, Mike (Athlete, Football Player)
5126 Miller Ave
Dallas, TX 75206-6419, USA

Cloude, Ken (Athlete, Baseball Player)
8126 Del Haven Rd
Dundalk, MD 21222, USA

Clough, Gerald W (Educator)
Georgia Institute of Techonlogy
President's Office
Atlanta, GA 30332, USA

Clougherty, Pat (Athlete, Baseball Player)
3160 Arden Drive
Saint Paul, MN 55129-7782, USA

Clough Jr, Ray W (Engineer)
19800 SW Touchmark Way
Apt 280
Bend, OR 97702-3405, USA

Clouston, Cory
Brandon Wheat Kings
2-1175 18th St
Brandon, MB R7A 7C5, Canada

Cloutier, Dan (Athlete, Hockey Player)
Vaughan Vipers
9201 Islington Ave
Goaltending Coach
Woodbridge, ON L4L 1A7, CANADA

Cloutier, Jacques (Athlete, Hockey Player)
12172 Triple Crown Dr
Parker, CO 80134-7747, USA

Cloutier, Real (Athlete, Hockey Player)
1798 Rue de la Petite-Oasis
Quebec, QC G3E 1K7, Canada

Cloutier, Roland
783 Boivin St RR 3
Vai-D'or, QC J9P OB9, Canada

Clovers, The
Rt. 1 Box 56
Belvidere, NC 27CA919

Clowe, Ryane
356 Santana Row Apt 303
San Jose, CA 95128-2046

Clower, Lee (Stylist)
c/o Staff Member *Sarah Laird Inc*
12 Charles Ln
New York, NY 10014, USA

Clowes, Dan (Artist)
c/o Staff Member *Fantagraphics Books*
7563 Lake City Way
Seattle, WA 98115, USA

Clowes, Daniel (Writer)
Fantagraphics
7563 Lake City Way NE
Seattle, WA 98115, USA

Clune, Don (Athlete, Football Player)
322 N Orange St
Media, PA 19063, USA

Clunes, Martin (Actor)
c/o Samira Higham *Independent Talent Group (ITG-UK)*
Oxford House
76 Oxford St
London W1D 1BS, UK

Clunie, Michelle Renee (Actor)
c/o Bernard Kira *Vanguard Management Group*
8060 Melrose Ave
4th Floor
Los Angeles, CA 90046, USA

Clutch (Music Group, Musician)
c/o Paul Ryan *Agency Group Ltd, The (UK)*
361-373 City Rd
London EC1V 1PQ, UK

Clutterbuck, Bryan (Athlete, Baseball Player)
2320 Parkwood Ave
Ann Arbor, MI 48104, USA

Clwson, John (Basketball Player)
Oakland Oaks
33 San Ysidro Ct
Danville, CA 94526-1545, USA

Clyde, Ben (Basketball Player)
Bosten Celtics
8356 A Street Apt
#1
Saint Petersburg, FL 33701, USA

Clyde, David (Athlete, Baseball Player)
7806 Pinehurst Shadows Dr
Humble, TX 77346-1511, USA

Clymer, Ben (Athlete, Hockey Player)
7040 Mill Creek Ln
Excelsior, MN 55331-5706, USA

Clyne, Nikki (Actor)
c/o David Miner *3 Arts Entertainment Inc*
9460 Wilshire Blvd
7th Floor
Beverly Hills, CA 90210, USA

CM Punk (Athlete, Wrestler)
1456 N Milwaukee Ave
Chicago, IL 60622, USA

Coachman, Alice (Athlete, Olympic
Athlete, Track Athlete)
*Alice Coachman Track & Field
Foundation*
PO Box 936
Akron, OH 44372, USA

Coachman, Bobby (Baseball Player)
California Angels
PO Box 44
Cottonwood, AL 36320-0044, USA

Coachman, Pete (Athlete, Baseball Player)
8795 S County 55 Rd
Cottonwood, AL 36320, USA

Coad, Barbara (Stylist)
7825 Castle Lane
Indianapolis, IN 46256, USA

Coady, Richard (Rich) (Athlete, Football
Player)
17106 Spanky Pl
Dallas, TX 75248, USA

Coakley, Dexter (Athlete, Football Player)
1304 Sunset Ridge Cir
Cedar Hill, TX 75104-4541, USA

Coalter, Gary (Athlete, Hockey Player)
Lot 23 Concession 6 RR 1
South River, ON P0A 1X0, Canada

Coan, Bert (Athlete, Football Player)
14517 N US Highway 59
Nacogdoches, TX 75965-9004, USA

Coan, Gil (Athlete, Baseball Player)
P.O. Box 668
Brevard, NC 28712, USA

Coase, Ronald H (Nobel Prize Laureate)
University of Chicago
University Of Chicago Law School
1111 E 60th St
Chicago, IL 60637-2786, USA

Coasters, The (Music Group, Musician)
2756 N. Green Valley Parkway #449
Las Vegas, NV 89014-2100, USA

Coates, Ben (Athlete, Football Player)
1740 Deer Creek Dr Ste 1
Xenia, OH 45385-8069, USA

Coates, Brian (Athlete, Hockey Player)
PO Box 213
Roland, MB ROG lTD, Canada

Coates, Jim (Athlete, Baseball Player)
1098 Oak Hill Rd
Lancaster, VA 22503, USA

Coates, Kim (Actor)
1769 La Paz Rd
Altadena, CA 91001, USA

Coates, Phyllis (Actor)
PO Box 1969
Boyes Hot Springs, CA 95416, USA

Coates, Ray (Athlete, Football Player)
6219 Louis XIV St
New Orleans, LA 70124-3024, USA

Coates, Sherrod (Athlete, Football Player)
12233 Silveroak Ln
Charlotte, NC 28277, USA

Coates, Steve (Athlete, Hockey Player)
Philadelphia Flyers
3601 S Broad St Ste 2
Philadelphia, PA 19148-5297

Coates, Steve (Athlete, Hockey Player)
102 Stoney Creek Dr
Egg Harbor Township, NJ 08234-7559,
USA

Coats, Dan (Ex-Senator)
1700 Pennsylvania Ave NW
Washington, DC 20006, USA

Coats, Daniel (Senator)
United States Senate SR-493
Washington, DC 20510, USA

Coats, Daniel (Athlete, Football Player)
419 S 380 W
Tooele, UT 84074-2958, USA

Coats, Kristi (Athlete, Golfer)
185 Wildwood Trl
Petal, MS 39465-2681, USA

Coats, Michael L (Astronaut)
3203 Acorn Wood Way
Houston, TX 77059-3175, USA

Coats, Michael L Captain (Astronaut)
3203 Acorn Wood Wav
Houston, TX 77059-3175, USA

Cobb, Capt Jerrie (Aviator)
The Jerrie Cobb Foundation
19834 Lions Gate Ct
Humble, TX 77338-1924, USA

Cobb, Charles (Athlete, Football Player)
6075 N Forkner Ave
Fresno, CA 93711, USA

Cobb, David (Politician)
c/o Staff Member *The Green Party of the
United States*
PO Box 57065
Washington, DC 20037, USA

Cobb, Garry (Athlete, Football Player)
1258 Chanticleer
Cherry Hill, NJ 08003, USA

Cobb, Henry N (Architect)
Pei Cobb Freed Partners
88 Pine St
New York, NY 10005, USA

Cobb, Jewel Plummer (Scientist)
California state University At Fullerton
PO Box 3480
Fullerton, CA 92834, USA

Cobb, Julie (Actor)
S D B Partners
1801 Ave of the Stars #902
Los Angeles, CA 90067, USA

Cobb, Keith Hamilton (Actor)
c/o Steven Jensen *Direct Management
Group*
6363 Wilshire Blvd
Suite 115
Los Angeles, CA 90048, USA

Cobb, Marvin (Athlete, Football Player)
655 S Flower St
Unit 290
Los Angeles, CA 90017, USA

Cobb, Mike
969 Pacific Ave Apt C
Hoffman Estates, IL 60169-4725, USA

Cobb, Reggie (Athlete, Football Player)
13315 Orchard Harvest Dr
Richmond, TX 77407-3219, USA

Cobb, Trevor (Athlete, Football Player)
2001 Bering Dr
Apt 2H
Houston, TX 77057, USA

Cobbin, James (Athlete, Baseball Player)
389 Redondo Rd
Youngstown, OH 44504-1451, USA

Cobbs, Bill (Actor, Producer)
c/o Staff Member *Forster Entertainment*
12533 Woodgreen St
Los Angeles, CA 90066, USA

Cobbs, Cedric (Athlete, Football Player)
4710 Fairlee Dr
Little Rock, AR 72209, USA

Cobert, Bob (Composer)
B M I
8730 Sunset Blvd #300
Los Angeles, CA 90069, USA

Cobham, William C (Billy) (Music Group,
Musician)
Joel Chriss
300 Mercer St #3J
New York, NY 10003, USA

Coble, Drew (Athlete, Baseball Player)
205 80th Ave N
Myrtle Beach, SC 29572-4339, USA

Coble, Howard (Congressman, Politician)
2188 Rayburn HOB
Washington, DC 20515, USA

Coblenz, Walter (Director, Producer)
4310 Cahuenga Blvd #401
Toluca Lake, CA 91602, USA

Cobos, Jesus Lopez (Conductor)
Cincinnati Symphony
1241 Elm St
Cincinnati, OH 45202, USA

Cobra Starship (Music Group)
c/o Jonathan Daniel *Crush Management*
60-62 E 11th St
7th Floor
New York, NY 10003, USA

Cobum, Cindy C (Bowler)
Ladies Professional Bowling Tour
7200 Harrison Ave #7171
Rockford, IL 61112, USA

Cobum, Doris (Bowler)
130 Dalton Dr
Buffalo, NY 14223, USA

Coburn, Braydon (Athlete, Hockey Player)
c/o Gerry Johansson *The Sports
Corporation*
2735 Toronto Dominion Tower
10088-102 Ave
Edmonton ABc T5J 2Z1, CANADA

Coburn, Doris (Bowler)
130 Dalton Dr
Buffalo, NY 14223-2221, USA

Coburn, John G (General)
Commanding General Army Material
Command
Alexandra, VA 22333, USA

Coburn, Tom (Senator)
172 Russell Senate Office Bldg.
Washington, DC 20510, USA

Cocanower, James S (Jaime) (Athlete,
Baseball Player)
10777 Gram B Cir
Lowell, AR 72745, USA

Coccioletti, Philip (Actor)
c/o Carmen Lavia *Fifi Oscard Agency*
110 W 40th St
Suite 1601
New York, NY 10018, USA

Cochereau, Pierre (Musician)
15 Bis des Ursins
Paris 75004, FRANCE

Cochran, Anita L (Astronomer)
University of Texas
Astronomy Dept
Austin, TX 78712, USA

Cochran, Antonio (Athlete, Football
Player)
8433 Manchester Hwy
Woodland, GA 31836-2038, USA

Cochran, Barbara (Athlete, Olympic
Athlete, Skier)
213 Brown Hill W
Starksboro, VT 05487-7283, USA

Cochran, John (Athlete, Football Player)
1249 Driftwood Dr
De Pere, WI 54115, USA

Cochran, John (Correspondent)
ABC-TV
News Dept 5010 Creston St
Hyattsville, MD 20781, USA

Cochran, Leslie H (Educator)
Youngstown State University
President's Office
Youngstown, OH 44555, USA

Cochran, Robert (Producer, Writer)
c/o Staff Member *Agency for the
Performing Arts (APA-LA)*
405 S Beverly Dr
Suite 500
Beverly Hills, CA 90212-4425, USA

Cochran, Russ (Athlete, Golfer)
3 Circle Lake Dr
Paducah, KY 42001-9753, USA

Cochran, Shannon (Actor)
Stubbs
1450 S Robertson Blvd
Los Angeles, CA 90035, USA

Cochran, Thad (Senator)
113 Dirksen Senate Office Building
Washington, DC 20510-2402, USA

Cochran, Thad (Politician)
218 Maryland Ave NE
Washington, DC 20002-5704, USA

Cochrane, Dave (Athlete, Baseball Player)
11 Muirfield
Trabuco Canyon, CA 92679, USA

Cochrane, Glen (Athlete, Hockey Player)
405 Collett Rd
Kelowna, BC VlW 1K6, Canada

Cochrane, Rory (Actor)
c/o Beth Holden-Garland *Untitled Entertainment (LA)*
350 S. Beverly Dr #200
Beverly Hills, CA 90212, USA

Cockburn, Anna (Stylist)
c/o Staff Member *Management & Production/MAP Inc*
48 St Marks Pl
4th Floor
New York, NY 10003, USA

Cockburn, Bruce (Musician)
c/o Staff Member *Agency Group Ltd, The (NY)*
142 West 57th St
6th Floor
New York, NY 10019, USA

Cocker, Jarvis (Musician, Songwriter)
c/o Staff Member *Paradigm (Monterey)*
404 W Franklin St
Monterey, CA 93940, USA

Cocker, Joe (Musician)
43401/43405/43409 Cottonwood Creek Rd
Crawford, CO 81415, USA

Cockerill, Franklin (Biologist, Misc)
Mayo Clinic
Microbiology Dept 200 1st St SW
Rochester, MN 55905, USA

Cockerill, Kay (Athlete, Golfer)
1345 Arroyo Ave
San Carlos, CA 94070-3912, USA

Cockrell, Alan (Athlete, Baseball Player)
306 Millstream Ter
Colorado Springs, CO 80904, USA

Cockrell, Gene (Athlete, Football Player)
8652 County Road 21
Pampa, TX 79065-1313, USA

Cockrell, Kenneth D (Astronaut)
2300 Richmond Ave Apt 350
Houston, TX 77098-3265, USA

Cockroft, Donald L (Don) (Athlete, Football Player)
2418 Dunkeith Dr NW
Canton, OH 44708, USA

Cockroft, Sherman (Athlete, Football Player)
2504 Christopher Ln
Costa Mesa, CA 92626, USA

Cocks, Burling (Race Car Driver)
PO Box 512
Unionville, PA 19375-0512, USA

Cocozza, Elizabeth (Stylist)
c/o Staff Member *Loox Agency*
12 Desbrosses St
New York, NY 10013, USA

Cocroft, Sherman
2504 Christopher Ln
Costa Mesa, CA 92626-6750, USA

Code, Arthur D (Astronomer)
University of Wisconsin
WUPPE Project Astronomy Dept
Madison, WI 53706, USA

Code, Merl (Athlete, Football Player)
100 Rearden Dr
Greenville, SC 29605-3261, USA

Coder, Ron (Athlete, Football Player)
25 N Bryant Ave
Pittsburgh, PA 15202, USA

Coder, Ron (Athlete, Football Player)
25 N Bryant Ave
Pittsburgh, PA 15202-3346, USA

Codey, Lawrence R (Business Person)
Public Service Enterprise
80 Park Plaza PO Box 1171
Newark, NJ 07101, USA

Codiroli, Chris (Athlete, Baseball Player)
2700 Hillcrest Dr
Cameron Park, CA 95682, USA

Codling, Samantha (Stylist)
c/o Staff Member *Sydney Represents*
280 Mott St
New York, NY 10012, USA

Codrescu, Andrei (Writer)
Louisiana State University
English Dept
Baton Rauga, LA 70803, USA

Coduri, Camille (Actor)
International Creative Mgmt
76 Oxford St
London W1N 0AX, UNITED KINGDOM (UK)

Cody, Bill (Athlete, Football Player)
209 Orleans Dr
Fairhope, AL 36532, USA

Cody, Commander (Musician)
Skyline Music
Old Cherry Mountain Road
Jefferson, NH 03583, USA

Cody, Dan (Athlete, Football Player)
104 W 17th St
Ada, OK 74820-7612, USA

Cody, Diablo (Writer)
8024 Mulholland Dr
Los Angeles, CA 90046, USA

Coe, Barry (Actor)
PO Box 100
Sun Valley, ID 83353-0100

Coe, David Allan (Musician)
129 Caldwell Dr
Hendersonville, TN 37075, USA

Coe, George (Actor)
c/o Martin Gage *Gage Group, The (LA)*
14724 Ventura Blvd
Suite 505
Sherman Oaks, CA 91403, USA

Coe, Sabastian N (Athlete, Track Athlete)
Starswood High Barn Road
Effingham
Surrey KT24 5PW, UNITED KINGDOM (UK)

Coe, Sebastian (Athlete, Politician)
London 2012
One Churchill Place
Canary Wharf
London E14 5LN, UK

Coe, Sue (Artist)
527 W 26th St
New York, NY 10001, USA

Coe-Jones, Dawn (Athlete, Golfer)
17319 Emerald Chase Dr
Tampa, FL 33647-3516, USA

Coelen, Chris (Director, Producer, Writer)

Coelho, Paulo (Writer)
Instituto Paulo Coelho
Henrique Pechman
Av Copacabana 1133 salas 601 / 602
Rio de Janeiro 22070-010, BRAZIL

Coelho, Susie (Actor)
1347 Rossomyne Ave
Glendale, CA 91207, USA

Coen, Ethan (Director, Writer)
c/o Jim Berkus *United Talent Agency (UTA)*
9336 Civic Center Dr
Beverly Hills, CA 90210, USA

Coen, Joel (Director, Writer)
23 Rafael Ave
Bolinas, CA 94924, USA

Coetzee, Gerrie (Boxer)
22 Sydney Road
Ravenswood, Boksburg 1460, SOUTH AFRICA

Coetzee, John M (Nobel Prize Laureate)
P O Box 92
Rondebosch, Cape Province 7700, SOUTH AFRICA

Coetzer, Amanda (Tennis Player)
Octagon
1751 Pinnacle Dr #1500
Mclean, VA 22102, USA

Cofer, J Michael (Mike) (Athlete, Football Player)
2688 Hollowvale Ln
Henderson, NV 89052-2846, USA

Cofer, Mike (Athlete, Football Player)
2688 Hollowvale Ln
Henderson, NV 89052-2846, USA

Cofer, Mike (Race Car Driver)
Racing West
1772 Los Arboles
#J-186
Thousand Oaks, CA 91362, USA

Cofer, Mike (Athlete, Football Player)
110 Bridgestone Cv
1983 Detroit Lions, GA 30215-8159, USA

Coffee, Claire (Actor)
c/o Liza Anderson *Anderson Group Public Relations*
8060 Melrose Ave Fl 4
Los Angeles, CA 90046, USA

Coffee, Coena (Stylist)
7815 Queens Ct
Downers Grove, IL 60516, USA

Coffey, Don (Athlete, Football Player)
231 Redfield Dr
Jackson, TN 38305, USA

Coffey, John L (Judge)
US Court Appeals
US Courthouse 517 E Wisconsin Ave
Milwaukee, WI 53202, USA

Coffey, Junior L (Athlete, Football Player)
17228 32nd Ave S
Apt E-12
Seatac, WA 98188, USA

Coffey, Kellie (Musician)
c/o Staff Member *WmE2 (WMA-TN)*
1600 Division St
Suite 300
Nashville, TN 37203, USA

Coffey, Ken (Athlete, Football Player)
3322 Medinah Ct
Sugar Land, TX 77479, USA

Coffey, Paul
633 Hawthorne St.
Birmingham, MI 48009-1650

Coffey, Paul D (Athlete, Hockey Player)
Paul Coffey's Bolton Toyota
13050 Albion-Vaughan Rd.
Bolton, ON L7E 1S7, Canada

Coffey, Richard (Athlete, Basketball Player)
4624 Flag Ave N
Minneapolis, MN 55428-4741, USA

Coffey, Scott
143 Wadsworth Ave
Santa Monica, CA 90405

Coffey, Tabatha (Reality TV Star, Stylist)
c/o Staff Member *Bravo (NY)*
30 Rockefeller Plaza
New York, NY 10112, USA

Coffey, Todd (Athlete, Baseball Player)
109 Colonel Hampton Ct
Rutherfordton, NC 28139, USA

Coffield, Kelly (Actor)
c/o Staff Member *Innovative Artists (NY)*
235 Park Ave S
7th Floor
New York, NY 10003, USA

Coffield, Randy (Athlete, Football Player)
7110 Lake Basin Rd
Tallahassee, FL 32312, USA

Coffin, Edmund (Tad) (Horse Racer)
General Delivery
Strafford, VT 05072, USA

Coffin, Fredrick (Actor)
Susan Smith
121 A N San Vicente Blvd
Beverly Hills, CA 90211, USA

Coffin, Jeff (Musician)
816 Kendall Dr
Nashville, TN 37029, USA

Coffman, Kevin (Athlete, Baseball Player)
313 Kelly Dr
Victoria, TX 77904, USA

Coffman, Mike (Congressman, Politician)
1222 Longworth HOB
Washington, DC 20515, USA

Coffman, Paul (Athlete, Football Player)
14103 E 195th St
Peculiar, MO 64078, USA

Coffman, Vance D (Business Person)
Lockheed Martin Corp
6801 Rockledge Dr
Bethesda, MD 20817, USA

Cofield, Fred (Athlete, Basketball Player)
833 Frederick Street
St, Ypsilanti 48197-5270, USA

Cofield, Tim (Athlete, Football Player)
312 NE Warrington Ct
Lees Summit, MO 64064, USA

Coflin, Hugh (Athlete, Hockey Player)
244 Murphy Dr W
Delta, BC V4M 3P2, Canada

Cogan, Kevin (Race Car Driver)
205 Rocky Point Rd
Palos Verdes Estates, CA 90274, USA

Cogan, Tony (Athlete, Baseball Player)
151 Pine Point Dr
Highland Park, IL 60035, USA

Cogdill, Gail (Athlete, Football Player)
12922 E 36th Ave
Spokane Valley, WA 99206, USA

Coggin, David (Athlete, Baseball Player)
861 Emerson St
Upland, CA 91784, USA

Coggins, Rich (Athlete, Baseball Player)
4095 Fruit St
Spc 219
La Verne, CA 91750, USA

Coghill, George (Athlete, Football Player)
307 Chancellor Pl
Fredericksburg, VA 22401, USA

Coghlan, Eamon (Athlete, Track Athlete)
Int'l Mgmt Group
1 Erieview Plaza
1360 E 9th St #1300
Cleveland, OH 44114, USA

Coghlan, Frank Junior
12522 Argyle Ave
Los Alamitos, CA 90720

Coghlan, Frank (Junior) Jr (Actor)
28506 Ray Court
Saugus, CA 91350, USA

Cogliano, Andrew (Athlete, Hockey Player)
c/o Staff Member *Edmonton Oilers*
11230 110 St NW
GM, AB T5G 3H7, Canada

Cohan, Chris (Basketball Player, Misc)
Goldan State Warriors
1001 Broadway
Oakland, CA 94607, USA

Cohan, Lauren (Actor)
c/o Staff Member *Liberman/Zerman Management*
252 N Larchmont Blvd
Suite 200
Los Angeles, CA 90004, USA

Cohan, Robert P (Choreographer)
The Place 17 Dukes Road
London WC1H 9AB, UNITED KINGDOM (UK)

Cohen, Aaron (Astronaut, Misc)
1310 Essex Green
College Station, TX 77845, USA

Cohen, Adam (Writer)
c/o Staff Member *Penguin Press HC*
375 Hudson St
New York, NY 10014, USA

Cohen, Andy (Business Person, Television Host)
Watch What Happens Live
325 Hudson St
Suite 101
New York, NY 10013, USA

Cohen, Avishai (Music Group, Musician)
Ron Moss Mgmt
2635 Griffith Park Blvd
Los Angeles, CA 90039, USA

Cohen, Ben (Business Person)
Ben & Jerry's
30 Community Dr.
South Burlington, VT 05403, USA

Cohen, Ben (Inventor)
394 Willow Brook Ln
Williston, VT 05495-7076, USA

Cohen, Bruce (Actor, Producer)
c/o Staff Member *Jinks/Cohen Company*
4000 Warner Blvd
Bldg 138
Burbank, CA 91522, USA

Cohen, Etan (Director, Producer, Writer)
c/o Jimmy Miller *Mosaic Media Group*
9200 W. Sunset Blvd
10th Floor
Los Angeles, CA 90069, USA

Cohen, Gary (Commentator)
136 Haviland Rd
Ridgefield, CT 06877-2822, USA

Cohen, Hy (Athlete, Baseball Player)
35734 Donny Cir
Palm Desert, CA 92211, USA

Cohen, John (Musician, Photographer)
Deborah Bell Photographs
511 W 25th St
Room 73
New York, NY 10001, USA

Cohen, Larry (Director)
2111 Coldwater Canyon
Beverly Hills, CA 90210, USA

Cohen, Leonard (Musician)
954 Venango Ave
Los Angeles, CA 90029, USA

Cohen, Linda (Musician)
c/o Staff Member *Greenspan Artist Management*
8760 W Sunset Blvd
West Hollywood, CA 90069, USA

Cohen, Lyor (Producer)
75 Rockefeller Plaza
New York, NY 10019, USA

Cohen, Marshall H (Astronomer)
California Institute of Technology
Astronomy Dept
Pasadena, CA 91125, USA

Cohen, Marvin L (Physicist)
10 Forest Lane
Berkeley, CA 94708, USA

Cohen, Mary Ann (Judge)
US Tax Court
400 2nd St NW
Washington, DC 20217, USA

Cohen, Matt (Actor)
c/o Sharon Lane *Lane Management Group*
13017 Woodbridge St
Studio City, CA 91604, USA

Cohen, Michael (Race Car Driver)
Cohen Motorsports
1210 S 56th Ave
Hollywood, FL 33023, USA

Cohen, Morris (Engineer)
72 River Park St
Needham Heights, MA 02494-2643, USA

Cohen, Paul J (Mathematician)
755 Santa Ynez St
Stanford, CA 94305, USA

Cohen, Richard M (Journalist, Writer)
c/o Staff Member *The New Press*
38 Greene St Fl 4
New York, NY 10013, USA

Cohen, Rob (Director)
United Talent Agency
9560 Wilshire Blvd #500
Berverly Hills, CA 90212, USA

Cohen, Sacha Baron (Actor, Producer)
7640 Mulholland Dr
Los Angeles, CA 90046, USA

Cohen, Sarah (Journalist)
Washington Post
Editorial Dept 1150 15th St NW
Washington, DC 20071, USA

Cohen, Sasha (Figure Skater)
c/o Staff Member *Champions on Ice*
Tom Collins Enterprises Inc
3500 W 80th St
Minneapolis, MN 55431, USA

Cohen, Scott (Actor)
c/o Heather Reynolds *One Entertainment (NY)*
12 W 57th St
Penthouse
New York, NY 10019, USA

Cohen, Seymour S (Biologist, Misc)
10 Carrot Hill Road
Woods Hole, MA 02543, USA

Cohen, Sheldon S (Government Official)
5518 Trent St
Chevy Chase, MD 20815, USA

Cohen, Stanley (Nobel Prize Laureate)
Vanderbilt University
Vanderbilt University 607 Biochem
Lh Medica Deot 607
Nashville, TN 37232-0001, USA

Cohen, Stanley N (Biologist, Misc)
Stanford University
Medical Center Genetics Dept
Stanford, CA 94305, USA

Cohen, Steve (Actor)
c/o Staff Member *WmE2 (WMA-LA)*
1 William Morris Pl
Beverly Hills, CA 90212, USA

Cohen, Steve (Business Person)
SAC Capital Advisors
72 Cummings Ave
Stamford, CT 06902, USA

Cohen, Steve (Congressman, Politician)
1005 Longworth HOB
Washington, DC 20515, USA

Cohen, Steven A (Business Person)
S.A.C. Capital Advisors
72 Cummings Point Rd
Stamford, CT 06902, USA

Cohen, Susan (Stylist)
c/o Staff Member *Judy Inc*
1 Yorkville Ave
Toronto ON M4W 1L1, Canada

Cohen, William (Politician)
The Cohen Group 500
Eight Street NW Ste 200
Washington, DC 20004, us

Cohen-Tannoudji, Claude K (Nobel Prize Laureate)
Laboratoire Kastler-Brossel 24 rue Ljomond
Ecole Normale Superieure
Paris F-75231, FRANCE

Cohn, Al (Bowler)
85 Odyssey Dr
Tinley Park, IL 60477-4853, USA

Cohn, Alfred (Al) (Athlete, Bowler)
85 Odyssey Dr
Tinley Park, IL 60477-4853, USA

Cohn, Bobette (Stylist)
c/o Staff Member *Solo Artists*
2148 Federal Ave
Los Angeles, CA 90025, USA

Cohn, Ethan (Actor)
c/o Darren Goldberg *Global Creative*
1051 Cole Ave # B
Los Angeles, CA 90038, USA

Cohn, Gary (Journalist)
Balitmore Sun
Editorial Dept 501 N Calvert St
Baltimore, MD 21202, USA

Cohn, Marc (Musician)
c/o Staff Member *The Agency Group*
Vastergatan 23
Malmo 211 21, Sweden

Cohn, Mildred (Biologist, Misc, Physicist)
226 W Rittenhouse Square
Philadelphia, PA 19103, USA

Cohn, Mindy (Actor)
Osbrink Talent Agency
4343 Lankershim Blvd #100
Universal City, CA 91602, USA

Cohoon Friedman, Patti (Actor)
11630 Dona Teresa Dr
Studio City, CA 91604, USA

Coia, Arthur A (Misc)
Laborers' International Uinon
905 16th St NW
Washington, DC 20006, USA

Coifman, Ronald R (Scientist)
11 Hickory Road
North Haven, CT 06473, USA

Coil, Austin (Race Car Driver)
John Force Racing
22722 Old Canal Rd
Yorba Linda, CA 92887, USA

Coiro, Rhys (Actor)
2233 Baxter St
Los Angeles, CA 90039, USA

Cojocaru, Steven (Correspondent)
c/o Staff Member *Entertainment Tonight (ET)*
4024 Radford Ave.
Studio City, CA 91604, USA

Coke, Phil (Athlete, Baseball Player)
c/o Team Member *New York Yankees*
Yankee Stadium
161st St & River Ave
Bronx, NY 10451, USA

Coker, Larry (Coach, Football Coach)
Miami University
Athletic Dept
Coral Gables, FL 33124, USA

Cokes, Curtis (Boxer)
618 Calcutta Dr
Dallas, TX 75241, USA

Cola, Angelo (Athlete, Football Player)
11 McDermott Pl
Brigantine, NJ 08203, USA

Colalucci, Gianluigi (Artist, Misc)
Office of Restoration
Vatican City 00120, VATICAN CITY

Colangelo, Jerry (Commentator)
70 E Country Club Dr
Phoenix, AZ 85014-5435, USA

Colangelo, Mike (Athlete, Baseball Player)
5751 Fincastle Dr
Manassas, VA 20112, USA

Colantoni, Enrico (Actor)
11931 Hesby St
Valley Village, CA 91607, USA

Colasanti, Robert (Horse Racer)
4 Duke Pass
Colts Neck, NJ 07722-1761, USA

Colavito, Rocky (Athlete, Baseball Player)
656 Scenic Dr
Bernville, PA 19506, USA

Colavito, Steve (Athlete, Football Player)
57 Fairview Ct
Nanuet, NY 10954, USA

Colbern, Mike (Athlete, Baseball Player)
5120 E Tano St
Phoenix, AZ 85044-4121, USA

Colbert, Craig (Athlete, Baseball Player)
6635 SE 42nd Ave
Portland, OR 97206, USA

Colbert, Darrell (Athlete, Football Player)
6514 River Bluff Dr
Houston, TX 77085, USA

Colbert, Jim (Athlete, Golfer)
118 Wanish Pl
Palm Desert, CA 92260-7316, USA

Colbert, Keary (Athlete, Football Player)
580 Lantana St Apt 80
Camarillo, CA 93010-6107, USA

Colbert, Nate (Athlete, Baseball Player)
2756 N Green Valley Pkwy
Henderson, NV 89014, USA

Colbert, Rondy (Athlete, Football Player)
5622 Cedarburg Dr
Houston, TX 77048-1821, USA

Colbert, Stephen (Actor, Producer, Writer)
2211 Ion Ave
Sullivans Island, SC 29482, USA

Colbert, Steve (Actor, Talk Show Host, Writer)
The Colbert Report
513 W 54th St
New York, New York 10019, USA

Colbert, Vince (Athlete, Baseball Player)
18071 Blandford Rd
Cleveland, OH 44121, USA

Colborn, James W (Jim) (Athlete, Baseball Player)
2932 Solimar Beach Dr
Ventura, CA 93001, USA

Colborn, Richard (Musician)
Legends of 21st Century
7 Trinity Row
Florence, MA 01062, USA

Colbrunn, Greg (Athlete, Baseball Player)
3196 Pignatelli Cres
Mount Pleasant, SC 29466, USA

Colby, Angel (Actor)
Hobsons International
62 Chiswick High Rd
London W4 1SY, UK

Colby, Terry (Stylist)
900 Heritage Pl
Decatur, GAA 30033, USA

Colchico, Dan (Athlete, Football Player)
5160 Paul Scarlet Dr
Concord, CA 94521, USA

Coldplay (Music Group)
c/o Estelle Wilkinson *Propaganda Management*
Clearwater Yard
35 Iverness St
London NW1 7HB, UK

Cold War Kids (Music Group)
c/o Staff Member *Paradigm (Monterey)*
404 W Franklin St
Monterey, CA 93940, USA

Cole, Alex (Athlete, Baseball Player)
6545 N Stevens Hollow Dr
Chesterfield, VA 23832, USA

Cole, Anne (Designer, Fashion Designer)
Cole of California
6040 Bandini Blvd
Los Angeles, CA 90040, USA

Cole, Artemas (Cartoonist)
15 Regency Manor #15-8
Rutland, VT 05701-5310, USA

Cole, Ashley (Athlete, Soccer Player)
c/o Staff Member *Chelsea Football Club*
Stamford Bridge
Fulham Road
London SW6 1HS, UNITED KINGDOM

Cole, Bob (Sportscaster)
Molstar Communications
250 Bloor St E #805
Toronto, ON M4W 1E6, CANADA

Cole, Bobby (Athlete, Golfer)
204 W 2nd Ave
Windermere, FL 34786, USA

Cole, Bradley (Actor)
c/o Staff Member *The Rights House (UK)*
Drury House
34-43 Russell St
London WC2B 5HA, UK

Cole, Cecil (Baseball Player)
Newark Eagles
201 N 12th St
Connellsville, PA 15425-2422, USA

Cole, Cheryl (Musician)
1322 N Detroit St #12
Los Angeles, CA 90046, USA

Cole, Chris (Athlete, Football Player)
6642 Hudnall Rd
Orange, TX 77632, USA

Cole, Christina (Actor)
c/o Lorrie Bartlett *ICM Partners (ICM-LA)*
10250 Constellation Blvd Fl 7
Los Angeles, CA 90067, USA

Cole, Colin (Athlete, Football Player)

Cole, Danton (Athlete, Hockey Player)
7180 Wapiti Way
Saline, MI 48176-9176, USA

Cole, Dick (Athlete, Baseball Player)
3149 Madeira Ave
Costa Mesa, CA 92626, USA

Cole, Emerson (Athlete, Football Player)
1661 Indiana Ave
Toledo, OH 43607-3966, USA

Cole, Erik (Athlete, Hockey Player, Olympic Athlete)
Sports Consulting Group
65 Monroe Ave Ste D
Pittsford, NY 14534-1318, USA

Cole, Eunice (Misc)
American Nurses Assn
2420 Pershing Road
Kansas City, MO 64108, USA

Cole, Ford (Athlete, Football Player)
PO Box 3218
Olympic Valley, CA 96146, USA

Cole, Fred (Athlete, Football Player)
10 Tuscan Rd
Livingston, NJ 07039, USA

Cole, Freddy (Music Group)
Producers Inc
11806 N 56th St
Tampa, FL 33617, USA

Cole, Gary (Actor)
3855 Berry Dr
Studio City, CA 91604, USA

Cole, George (Actor)
Joy Jameson Ltd
2-19 The Plaza
535 Kings Road
London SW10 0SZ, UNITED KINGDOM (UK)

Cole, Holly (Musician)
Alert Music
41 Britain St
#305
Toronto, ON M5A 1R7, CANADA

Cole, Jermaine (J Cole) (Musician)
c/o Cameron Mitchell *ICM Partners (ICM-LA)*
10250 Constellation Blvd Fl 7
Los Angeles, CA 90067, USA

Cole, Joanna (Writer)
c/o Staff Member *Scholastic Entertainment*
557 Broadway
New York, NY 10012, USA

Cole, John (Cartoonist)
Durham Herald-Sun
2828 Pickett Road
Durham, NC 27705, USA

Cole, Julie Dawn (Actor)
Barry Burnett
31 Coventry St
London W1V 8AS, UNITED KINGDOM (UK)

Cole, Kenneth (Scientist)
2404 Loring St
San Diego, CA 92109-2347, USA

Cole, Kenneth (Designer)
Kenneth Cole Productions Inc
601 West 50th St
New York, NY 10019, USA

Cole, Keyshia (Musician)
3710 Milton Park Dr
Alpharetta, GA 30022, USA

Cole, Kimberly Lynn (Actor)
36 Longview Court
Montgomery, AL 36108, USA

Cole, Kyla (Adult Film Star)
Adrian Daskalov
Nabrezi SPB 446
Ostrava 70800, CZECH REPUBLIC

Cole, Larry R (Athlete, Football Player)
400 Country Pl
Colleyville, TX 76034, USA

Cole, Lily (Actor, Model)
c/o Staff Member *Storm Model Management*
5 Jubilee Pl
1st Floor
London SW3 3TD, UNITED KINGDOM

Cole, Linzy (Athlete, Football Player)
7700 Creekbend Dr Apt 18
Houston, TX 77071, USA

Cole, Lloyd (Musician)
Supervision Mgmt
109B Regents Park Road
London NW1 8UR, UNITED KINGDOM (UK)

Cole, Michael (Actor)
5121 Varna Ave
Sherman Oaks, CA 91423, USA

Cole, Natalie (Actor, Musician)
10445 Wilshire Blvd #1004/#1005
Los Angeles, CA 90024, USA

Cole, Nigel (Director, Writer)
c/o Rosalie Swedlin *Anonymous Content (LA)*
3531 Hayden Ave
Culver City, CA 90232, USA

Cole, Olivia (Actor)
Century Artists
PO Box 59747
Santa Barbara, CA 93150, USA

Cole, Paula (Musician)
675 Hale St #D
Beverly, MA 01915, USA

Cole, P K
32522 Bowman Knoll
Westlake Village, CA 91362, USA

Cole, Richard (General)
48 Blaschke Rd
Comfort, TX 78013-3013, USA

Cole, Robin (Athlete, Football Player)
9 Brook Ln
Eighty Four, PA 15330, USA

Cole, Stu (Athlete, Baseball Player)
6527 Willow Gate Ln
Charlotte, NC 28215, USA

Cole, Taylor (Actor)
c/o Joanna (Joanie) Burstein *Burstein Company, The*
15304 Sunset Blvd
suite 208
Pacific Palisades, CA 90272, USA

Cole, Tina (Actor)
Junior League of Sacramento
778 University Ave
Sacramento, CA 95825, USA

Cole, Tom (Congressman, Politician)
2458 Rayburn HOB
Washington, DC 20515, USA

Cole, Victor (Athlete, Baseball Player)
138 Estonallie Rd
Mercer, TN 38392, USA

Colella, Richard (Rick) (Swimmer)
217 19th Place
Kirkland, WA 98033, USA

Coleman, Andre (Athlete, Football Player)
2955 Megan Cir
Youngstown, OH 44505-4384, USA

Coleman, Ben (Athlete, Basketball Player)
206 Mallard Dr
Shakopee, MN 55379-9375, USA

Coleman, Casey (Athlete, Football Player)
11901 Northumberland Dr
Tampa, FL 33626-1327

Coleman, Catherine G (Cady) (Astronaut)
30 Frank Williams Rd
Shelburne Falls, MA 01370-9724, USA

Coleman, Catherine G Lt Colonel (Astronaut)
30 Frank Williams Rd
Shelburne Falls, MA 01370-9724, USA

Coleman, Chris (Athlete, Football Player)
2425 Evans St SW
Lenoir, NC 28645-6358, USA

Coleman, Cosey (Athlete, Football Player)
11901 Northumberland Dr
Tampa, FL 33626, USA

Coleman, Dabney (Actor)
360 N Kenter Ave
Los Angeles, CA 90049, USA

Coleman, Daniel J (Publisher)
Popular Mechanics Magazine
224 W 57th St
New York, NY 10019, USA

Coleman, Derrick D (Basketball Player)
Philadelphia 76ers
1st Union Center
3601 S Broad St
Philadelphia, PA 19148, USA

Coleman, Don E (Athlete, Football Player)
424 McPherson Ave
Lansing, MI 48915, USA

Coleman, E C (Basketball Player)
Houston Rockets
370 E Harmon Ave
Las Vegas, NV 89109-7003, USA

Coleman, Eric (Athlete, Football Player)
2933 Elm St
Denver, CO 80207-2658, USA

Coleman, George E (Musician)
63 E 9th St
New York, NY 10003, USA

Coleman, Greg (Athlete, Football Player)
2313 River Pointe Cir
Minneapolis, MN 55411-4279, USA

Coleman, Harry (Athlete, Football Player)
c/o Tony Paige *Perennial Sports and Entertainment*
1455 Pennsylvania Ave NW
Suite 225
Washington, DC 20004, USA

Coleman, Jack (Actor)
3816 Goodland Ave
Studio City, CA 91604, USA

Coleman, Jermaine (Maino) (Musician)
c/o Staff Member *Atlantic Records (NY)*
1290 Ave of the Americas
New York, NY 10104

Coleman, Jerry (Commentator)
1004 Havenhurst Dr
La Jolla, CA 92037-6803, USA

Coleman, Karon (Athlete, Football Player)
19503 E 58th Ave
Aurora, CO 80019-2014, USA

Coleman, Kelly (Athlete, Basketball Player)
P.O. Box 204
Wayland, KY 41666, USA

Coleman, Kenyon (Athlete, Football Player)
35723 Stock St
Murrieta, CA 92562-4467, USA

Coleman, Leonard (Commentator)
519 S Maple Ave
Basking Ridge, NJ 07920-1318, USA

Coleman, Leonard (Athlete, Football Player)
125 NE 13th Ave
Boynton Beach, FL 33435-3124, USA

Coleman, Lincoln (Athlete, Football Player)
PO Box 496
Seguin, TX 78156, USA

Coleman, Marco (Athlete, Football Player)
105 Monarch Ct
Saint Augustine, FL 32095, USA

Coleman, Marco D (Athlete, Football Player)
11036 Turnbridge Dr
Jacksonville, FL 32256, USA

Coleman, Marcus (Athlete, Football Player)
1736 Mapleleaf Dr
Wylie, TX 75098-8166, USA

Coleman, Mark (Athlete, Wrestler)
Dream Stage Entertainment
6535 Wilshire Blvd #208
Los Angeles, CA 90048, USA

Coleman, Mary Sue (Educator)
University of Michigan
President's Office
Ann Arbor, MI 48109, USA

Coleman, Michael (Mike) (Athlete, Baseball Player)
1053 Mallow Dr
Madison, TN 37115, USA

Coleman, Monique (Actor)
c/o Gina Sorial *Rogers & Cowan PR (LA)*
Pacific Design Center
8687 Melrose Ave, 7th Floor
West Hollywood, CA 90069, USA

Coleman, Monte (Athlete, Football Player)
4700 S Beech St
Pine Bluff, AR 71603, USA

Coleman, Norm (Politician)
909 Osceola Ave
Saint Paul, MN 55105-3209, USA

Coleman, Norris (Athlete, Basketball Player)
445 Monument Road
Apt 1007
Jacksonville, FL 32225, USA

Coleman, Norris (Athlete, Basketball Player)
445 Monument Rd
Apt 1007
Jacksonville, FL 32225-6456, USA

Coleman, Oliver (Actor)
c/o Troy Zien *3 Arts Entertainment Inc*
9460 Wilshire Blvd
7th Floor
Beverly Hills, CA 90210, USA

Coleman, Ornette (Composer, Musician)
Monterey International
200 W Superior
#202
Chicago, IL 60610, USA

Coleman, Paul (Athlete, Baseball Player)
2704 Brentwood Dr
Tyler, TX 75701-5902, USA

Coleman, Roderick (Rod) (Athlete, Football Player)
6735 Great Water Dr
Flowery Branch, GA 30542-6639, USA

Coleman, Ronnie (Athlete, Football Player)
16039 Williwaw Dr
Houston, TX 77083, USA

Coleman, Sidney (Athlete, Football Player)
8034 King Rd
Meridian, MS 39305-9261, USA

Coleman, Sidney R (Physicist)
1 Richdale Ave
#12
Cambridge, MA 02140, USA

Coleman, Signy (Actor)
9200 Sunset Blvd
#625
Los Angeles, CA 90069, USA

Coleman, Steve (Athlete, Football Player)
81 W Johnson St
Philadelphia, PA 19144, USA

Coleman, Vincent M (Vince) (Athlete, Baseball Player)
12936 N 137th St
Scottsdale, AZ 85259, USA

Coleman, Walter (Baseball Player)
New York Yankees
HC 1 Box 236
New Russia, NY 12964-9705, USA

Coleman, William (Politician, Secretary)
O'Melveny & Myers
O'Melveny And Myers LLP
1625 I St NW
Washington, DC 20006-4061, USA

Coleman, Zendaya
c/o Jessie Greene *Monster Talent Management*
6333 W 3rd St
Suite 912
Los Angeles, CA 90036, USA

Coleman Jr, Leonard (Baseball Player)
283 3rd St
Beach Haven, NJ 08008-1857, USA

Coles, Bimbo (Athlete, Basketball Player)
203 E Washington St
Lewisburg, WV 24901-1423, USA

Coles, Darnell (Athlete, Baseball Player)
306 Signature Ter
Safety Harbor, FL 34695, USA

Coles, Janet (Athlete, Golfer)
1452 Floribunda Ave
Apt 202
Burlingame, CA 94010, USA

Coles, Kim (Actor, Comedian)
9000 Cynthia St
#403
West Hollywood, CA 90069, USA

Coles, Laveranues (Athlete, Football Player)
87 Coles Ct
Saint Johns, FL 32259-8898, USA

Coles, Robert M (Psychic)
Harvard University
Health Services
75 Mount Auburn St
Cambridge, MA 02138, USA

Colescott, Warrington W (Artist)
RR1
Hollandale, WI 53544, USA

Coletta, Chris (Athlete, Baseball Player)
206 SW 45th St
Cape Coral, FL 33914, USA

Coley, Daryl (Musician)
Daryl Coley Ministries
417 E Regent St
Inglewood, CA 90301, USA

Coley, James (Athlete, Football Player)
111 Pebble Park Rd
Starr, SC 29684, USA

Coley, John Ford (Musician, Songwriter, Writer)
Earthtone
8306 Wilshire Blvd
#981
Beverly Hills, CA 90211, USA

Colfer, Chris (Actor)
8207 Mannix Dr
Los Angeles, CA 90046, USA

Colgate, Stirling A (Physicist)
422 Estante Way
Los Alamos, NM 87544, USA

Colgrass, Michael C (Composer)
583 Palmerston Ave
Toronto, ON M6G 2P6, CANADA

Colicchio, Tom (Chef, Television Host)
Craft
43 East 19th Street
New York, NY 10003, USA

Colier, Jason (Basketball Player)
Houston Rockets
19318 Kristen Pine Dr
Humble, TX 77346-2084, USA

Colin, Charlie (Musician)
Jon Landau
80 Main St
Greenwich, CT 06830, USA

Colin, Margaret (Actor)
41 Bradford Ave
Montclair, NJ 07043, USA

Colinet, Stalin (Athlete, Football Player)
3 Mohawk Dr
Framingham, MA 01701, USA

C'Oliveira, Damon (Actor)
c/o Staff Member *LeFeaver Talent Management Ltd*
2 College St #202
Toronto ON M5G 1K3, CANADA

Coll, Stephen W (Journalist)
Washington Post
Editorial Dept
1150 15th St NW
Washington, DC 20071, USA

Colladay, Martin G (General)
409 Dowding Court
Bellevue, NE 68005, USA

Collard, Jean-Philippe (Musician)
Boite Postal 210
Paris Cedex 09 75426, USA

Collective Soul (Music Group)
c/o Jordan Feldstein *Career Artist Management*
203-207 W. Hastings St
Vancouver, BC V6B 1H7, Canada

Colledge, Daryn
11815 S Montezuma Ct
Phoenix, AZ 85044-3442, USA

Collee, John (Writer)
c/o Alex Lerner *Kaplan/Perrone Entertainment*
9744 Wilshire Blvd
Suite 300
Beverly Hills, CA 90212, USA

Collen, Phil (Music Group, Musician)
26971 Highwood Cir
Laguna Hills, CA 92653, USA

Collet, Christopher
8730 Sunset Blvd. #480
Los Angeles, CA 90069

Collett, Elmer (Athlete, Football Player)
PO Box 522 10 Avenida
Farralone Stinson Beach, CA 94970-0522, USA

Collette, Toni (Actor)
848 N Las Palmas Ave
Los Angeles, CA 90038, USA

Colletti, Roseanne (Correspondent)
WNBC-TV
30 Rockefeller Plaza
7th Floor
New York, NY 10112, USA

Colletti, Stephen (Reality TV Star)
14635 Hawes St
Whittier, CA 90604, USA

Collett-Serra, Jaume (Director)
1662 Marmont Ave
Los Angeles, CA 90069, USA

Colley, Dana (Musician)
Creative Performance Group
48 Laight St
New York, NY 10013, USA

Colley, Ed (Artist, Cartoonist)
11 Blaisdell Terr
Ipswich, MA 01938-1706, USA

Colley, Kenneth (Actor)
Kenneth McReddie
91 Regent St
London W1R 7TB, UNITED KINGDOM
(UK)

Colley, Michael C (Admiral)
444 Magnolia Dr
Gulf Shores, AL 36542, USA

Colley, Tom (Athlete, Hockey Player)
71 Dillon Dr
Collingwood, ON L9Y 4S4, Canada

Colley-Lee, Myrna (Designer)
Mississippi State University Libraries
395 Hardy Road
P.O. Box 5408
Mississippi State, MS 39762-5408

Collie, Bruce (Athlete, Football Player)
9595 Ranch Road 12 Ste 13
Wimberley, TX 78676-5248, USA

Collie, Mark (Actor, Musician, Songwriter,
Writer)
7426 Huntwick Trl
Nashville, TN 37221-5411, USA

Collier, Don
PO Box 1269
Benson, AZ 85602

Collier, James (Athlete, Football Player)
922 Bromley Dr
Baton Rouge, LA 70808, USA

Collier, Jim (Athlete, Football Player)
1670 Terral Island Rd
Farmerville, LA 71241-4013, USA

Collier, Lesley F (Ballerina)
c/o Staff Member *Royal Ballet*
Covent Garden
Bow St
London WC2E 9DD, UK

Collier, Lou (Athlete, Baseball Player)
5140 S Hyde Park Blvd Apt 17B
Chicago, IL 60615-4266, USA

Collier, Mark (Actor)
c/o John Crosby *Crosby/Spilo
Management*
1310 N Spaulding Ave
Los Angeles, CA 90046, USA

Collier, Mike (Athlete, Football Player)
528 W Church St Apt B
Hagerstown, MD 21740, USA

Collier, Steve (Athlete, Football Player)
3473 S King Dr
Chicago, IL 60616, USA

Collier, Timothy (Tim) (Athlete, Football
Player)
3116 50th St
Dallas, TX 75216, USA

Collingwood, Chris (Musician, Songwriter,
Writer)
MOB Agency
6404 Wilshire Blvd
#505
Los Angeles, CA 90048, USA

Collins, Alfred (Sonny) (Athlete, Football
Player)
2455 Cedar Canyon Ct SE
Marietta, GA 30067, USA

Collins, Art (Athlete, Basketball Player)
1812 NW 55th Ter
Miami, FL 33142-3044, USA

Collins, Arthur D Jr (Business Person)
Medtronic Inc
7000 Central Ave NE
Minneapolis, MN 55432, USA

Collins, Bill (Athlete, Hockey Player)
5000 Town Center
Apt 505
Southfield, MI 48075-1112, USA

Collins, Billy (Writer)
PO Box 2487
Winter Park, FL 32790-2487, USA

Collins, Blake Jeremy
4942 Vineland Ave. #200
No. Hollywood, CA 91601

Collins, Bobby (Athlete, Football Player)
1100 Indian Trail Lilburn Rd Apt 1024
Norcross, GA 30093-4581, USA

Collins, Bootsy (Musician)
817 Barg Salt Run Rd
Cincinnati, OH 45244, USA

Collins, Brett W (Athlete, Football Player)
21275 NW Rock Creek Blvd
Portland, OR 97229, USA

Collins, Bud (Sportscaster)
822 Boylston St
#203
Chestnut Hill, MA 02467, USA

Collins, C F (Athlete, Football Player)
10065 Garden St
Livonia, MI 48150, USA

Collins, Clarence
4912 Soaring Springs Ave
Las Vegas, NV 89131-2639, USA

Collins, Clifton (Actor)
12933 Bloomfield St
Studio City, CA 91604, USA

Collins, David S (Dave) (Athlete, Baseball
Player)
92 Lauretta Mae Dr Unit A
Lebanon, OH 45036-2652, USA

Collins, Donald E (Don) (Athlete, Baseball
Player)
127 Deerwood Trl
Sharpsburg, GA 30277-2002, USA

Collins, Douglas (Doug) (Athlete,
Basketball Player, Coach, Sportscaster)
10040 East Happy Valley Road
Unit 617
Scottsdale, AZ 85255-2355, USA

Collins, Dr Francis S (Scientist)
National Human Genome Research
Institute 31 Center Dr MS 2152
Bethesda, MD 20892-0001, USA

Collins, Duane E (Business Person)
Parker Hannifin Corp
6035 Parkland Blvd
Cleveland, OH 44124, USA

Collins, Dwight (Athlete, Football Player)
821 12th St
Beaver Falls, PA 15010, USA

Collins, Eileen M (Astronaut)
2024 Pebble Beach Dr
League City, TX 77573, USA

Collins, Francis S (Misc)
*National Human Genome Research
Institute*
31 Center St
Bethesda, MD 20892, USA

Collins, Gary (Actor)
2751 Hutton Dr
Beverly Hills, CA 90210, USA

Collins, Gary (Athlete, Hockey Player)
1908-1320 Islington Ave
Etobicoke, ON M9A 5C6, Canada

Collins, Gary J (Athlete, Football Player)
221 Lamp Post Ln
Hershey, PA 17033, USA

Collins, George (Athlete, Football Player)
2043 Northside Rd
Perry, GA 31069, USA

Collins, Glen L (Athlete, Football Player)
17 Autumn Park
Jackson, MS 39202, USA

Collins, Jack (Actor)
Contemporary Artists
610 Santa Monica Blvd
#202
Santa Monica, CA 90401, USA

Collins, Jackie (Writer)
10624 Wellworth Ave
Los Angeles, CA 90024-5012, USA

Collins, Jarron (Athlete, Basketball Player)
11173 Cashmere St
Los Angeles, CA 90049-3233, USA

Collins, Jason (Basketball Player)
13120 Constable Ave
Granada Hills, CA 91344, USA

Collins, Javiar (Athlete, Football Player)
2503 S Pennsylvania St
Denver, CO 80210-5722, USA

Collins, Jerome (Athlete, Football Player)
25540 Soya Ln
Warrenville, IL 60555, USA

Collins, Jerry (Athlete, Football Player)
405 Monterey Ave
Annapolis, MD 21401-1329, USA

Collins, Jessica
c/o Rick Ax *Gold Coast Management*
438 S Venice Blvd Apt 5
Venice, CA 90291, USA

Collins, Jim (Athlete, Football Player)
2140 E Oceanfront
Newport Beach, CA 92661-1525, USA

Collins, Joan (Actor)
9255 Doheny Rd #2501
West Hollywood, CA 90069, USA

Collins, Joely (Actor)
c/o Staff Member *TalentWorks (LA)*
3500 W Olive Ave
Suite 1400
Burbank, CA 91505, USA

Collins, Judy (Musician, Songwriter,
Writer)
Rocky Mountains Production
P.O. Box 1296
Cathedral Station, NY 10025, USA

Collins, Kate (Actor)
1410 York Ave
#4D
New York, NY 10021, USA

Collins, Kerry (Athlete, Football Player)
3 Spyglass Hill
Brentwood, TN 37027, USA

Collins, Kevin (Athlete, Baseball Player)
9121 Point Charity Dr
Pigeon, MI 48755-9624, USA

Collins, Lauren (Actor)
c/o Steven Kavovit *Thruline Entertainment*
9250 Wilshire Blvd
Ground Fl
Beverly Hills, CA 90212, USA

Collins, Lewis
22 Westbere Rd
London, ENGLAND NW2 3SR

Collins, Lily (Actor)
c/o Will Ward *ROAR (LA)*
9701 Wilshire Blvd
8th Floor
Los Angeles, CA 90212, USA

Collins, Lynn (Actor)
c/o Nick Frenkel *3 Arts Entertainment Inc*
9460 Wilshire Blvd
7th Floor
Beverly Hills, CA 90210, USA

Collins, Mark (Athlete, Football Player)
2x Champ Sports PO Box 23056
Overland Park, KS 66283-0056, USA

Collins, Martha (Educator, Ex-Governor,
Politician)
921 Taborlake Ct
Lexington, KY 40502-3032, USA

Collins, Marva (Educator)
Westside Preparatory School
8035 S Honore St
Chicago, IL 60620, USA

Collins, Michael (Astronaut)
c/o Staff Member *Farrar, Straus and
Giroux*
18 W 18th St
New York, NY 10011-4607, USA

Collins, Michael Brig Gen (Astronaut)
272 Polynesia Ct
Marco Island, FL 34145-3826, USA

Collins, Misha (Actor)
c/o Brian Wilkins *Kritzer Levine Wilkins
Entertainment (KLWG)*
11872 La Grange Ave
1st Floor
Los Angeles, CA 90025, USA

Collins, Mo (Actor)
c/o Nicole Cataldo *Diverse Talent Group*
9911 W Pico Blvd Ste 340W
Los Angeles, CA 90035, USA

Collins, Patrick (Actor)
c/o Staff Member *Tisherman Gilbert
Motley Drozdoski Talent Agency (TGMD)*
6767 Forest Lawn Dr
Suite 101
Los Angeles, CA 90068, USA

Collins, Paul (Athlete, Football Player)
1441 Bayshore Dr
Kemah, TX 77565, USA

Collins, Paul (Athlete, Football Player)
4370 Chamberlain Dr
Bloomfield Hills, MI 48301-3741, USA

Collins, Pauline (Actor)
c/o Sarah Camlett *Independent Talent Group (ITG-UK)*
Oxford House
76 Oxford St
London W1D 1BS, UK

Collins, Phil (Musician, Songwriter)
Phil Collins Ltd
25 Ives St
London SW3 2ND, UK

Collins, Roosevelt (Athlete, Football Player)
3600 Holly St
Dension, TX 75020, USA

Collins, Samuel C (Engineer)
P.O. Box 441937
Fort Washington, MD 20749-1937, USA

Collins, Shane (Athlete, Football Player)
PO Box 11090
Bozeman, MT 59719, USA

Collins, Shanna (Actor)
c/o Stephanie Simon *Untitled Entertainment (LA)*
350 S. Beverly Dr #200
Beverly Hills, CA 90212, USA

Collins, Shawn (Athlete, Football Player)
2744 Preece St
San Diego, CA 92111, USA

Collins, Shawn (Athlete, Football Player)
PO Box 711933
San Diego, CA 92171-1933, USA

Collins, Stephen (Actor)
12960 Brentwood Terr
Los Angeles, CA 90049, USA

Collins, Susan (Senator)
413 Dirksen Senate Office Building
Washington, DC 20510, USA

Collins, Suzanne (Writer)
c/o Rosemary B. Stimola *Stimola Literary Studio*
306 Chase Ct
Edgewater, NJ 07020, USA

Collins, Suzanne (Actor)
c/o Tracey Bell *Red Door Actors Management*
21/22 Great Castle St
London W1 G0HZ, UK

Collins, Terry (Athlete, Baseball Player, Coach)
New York Mets 12301 Roosevelt Ave
Attn: Managers Office
Flushine, NY 11368-1629, USA

Collins, Terry L (Misc)
PO Box 508
Okemos, MI 48805, USA

Collins, Thomas H (Admiral)
Commandant US Coast Guard
2100 2nd St SW
Washington, DC 20593, USA

Collins, Todd
1279 Collins Rd
New Market, TN 37820-3837, USA

Collins, Todd F (Athlete, Football Player)
1279 Collins Rd
New Market, TN 37820, USA

Collins, Todd S (Athlete, Football Player)
26 Cambridge Cir
Victor, NY 14564, USA

Collins, Tony (Athlete, Football Player)
10709 N Preserve Way Apt 203
Miramar, FL 33025-6553, USA

Collinsworth, Cris (Athlete, Football Player, Sportscaster)
31 Crow Hill Rd
Fort Thomas, KY 41075-1801, USA

Collis, Shannon (Actor)
c/o Meredith Fine *Coast to Coast Talent Group*
3350 Barham Blvd
Los Angeles, CA 90068, USA

Collison, Darren (Athlete, Basketball Player)
c/o Bill Duffy *BDA Sports Management (BDA-CA)*
700 Ygnacio Valley Rd
Suite 330
Walnut Creek, CA 94596, USA

Collison, Nick (Athlete, Basketball Player)
Seattle SuperSonics
16 Comstock St
Seattle, WA 98109-3211, USA

Collman, James P (Misc)
794 Tolman Dr
Stanford, CA 94305, USA

Collyard, Bob (Athlete, Hockey Player)
5300 Knox Ave N
Minneapolis, MN 55430-3058, USA

Colman, Booth (Actor)
2160 Century Park E
#603
Los Angeles, CA 90067, USA

Colman, Wayne (Athlete, Football Player)
604 N Somerset Ave
Ventnor City, NJ 08406, USA

Colmenares, Grecia (Actor)
c/o Staff Member *Telefe - Argentina*
Pavon 2444 (C1248AAT)
Buenos Aires, ARGENTINA

Colmes, Alan (Correspondent)
c/o Staff Member *Hannity & Colmes*
1211 Ave of the Americas
New York, NY 10036-8701, USA

Colo, Don (Athlete, Football Player)
7355 E Claremont St
Scottsdale, AZ 85250, USA

Coloma, Marcus (Actor)
c/o Paul Rosicker *Gersh (LA)*
9465 Wilshire Blvd
Suite 600
Beverly Hills, CA 90212, USA

Colombini, Aldo (Director, Producer)
PO BOx 829
Newbury Park, CA 91319-0829, USA

Colombo, Emilio (Prime Minister)
Via Aurelia
Rome 239, ITALY

Colombo, Marc (Athlete, Football Player)
1250 Biltmore Dr
Southlake, TX 76092-3462, USA

Colomby, Bobby
1423 Holmby Ave.
Los Angeles, CA 90024

Colomby, Scott (Actor)
Borinstein Oreck Bogart
3172 Dona Susana Dr
Studio City, CA 91604, USA

Colon, Bartolo (Athlete, Baseball Player)
14 Federal St # 1
Passaic, NJ 07055-3209, USA

Colon, Harry (Athlete, Football Player)
12102 Red Rust Ln
Charlotte, NC 28277-3679, USA

Colon, Mercedes (Actor)
c/o Jay Schachter *Mavrick Artists Agency*
6100 Wilshire Blvd
Suite 550
Los Angeles, CA 90048, USA

Colon, Miriam (Actor)
51 W 52nd St
New York, NY 10019, USA

Colorito, Tony (Athlete, Football Player)
17805 SW Cicero Ct
Beaverton, OR 97007-9036, USA

Color Me Badd (Music Group, Musician)
P.O. Box 552113
Carol City, FL 33055-0113, USA

Colpaert, Dick (Athlete, Baseball Player)
47412 Eldon Dr
Shelby Township, MI 48317-2912, USA

Colquitt, Craig (Athlete, Football Player)
1905 Pitts Field Ln
Knoxville, TN 37922-6197, USA

Colquitt, Dustin (Athlete, Football Player)
1905 Pitts Field Ln
Knoxville, TN 37922-6197, USA

Colquitt, Jimmy (Athlete, Football Player)
11722 Hardin Valley Rd
Knoxville, TN 37932-2319, USA

Colson, Elizabeth F (Misc)
University of California
Anthropology Dept
Berkeley, CA 94720, USA

Colson, Loyd A (Athlete, Baseball Player)
309 E Sycamore St
Hollis, OK 73550-1233, USA

Colson, William (Bill) (Editor)
Sports Illustrated
Editorial Dept
Time-Life Building
New York, NY 10020, USA

Colston, Tim (Athlete, Football Player)
6804 N 47th St
Tampa, FL 33610-1808, USA

Colt, Marshall (Actor)
1150 Anchorage Lane
Unit 612
San Diego, CA 92106-4356, USA

Colter, Jessie (Musician)
Shout Factory
2042-A Armacost Ave
Los Angeles, CA 90025, USA

Colter, Steve (Athlete, Basketball Player)
802 East Mountain Sage Dr
Phoenix, AZ 85048-4428, USA

Colton, Frank B (Inventor)
6402 N 27th St
Phoenix, AZ 85016, USA

Colton, Graham (Musician)
c/o Staff Member *Red Light Management (LA)*
8439 W Sunset Blvd
Suite 2
Los Angeles, CA 90069, USA

Colton, Lawrence R (Larry) (Athlete, Baseball Player)
3027 NE 68th Ave
Portland, OR 97213-5215, USA

Colton, Michael (Writer)
c/o Tony Etz *Creative Artists Agency (CAA-LA)*
2000 Ave Of The Stars
Los Angeles, CA 90067, USA

Coltraine, Robbie (Actor)
19 Sydney Mews
London SW3 6HL, United Kingdom

Coltrane, Chi
5955 Tuxedo Terrace
Los Angeles, CA 90068

Coltrane, Robbie (Actor)
Caroline Dawson & Associates
125 Gloucester Road
2nd Fl
London SW7 4TE, UNITED KINGDOM

Coluccio, Bob (Athlete, Baseball Player)
369 Flower St
Costa Mesa, CA 92627-2352, USA

Columbu, Franco (Misc)
2265 Westwood Blvd
#A
Los Angeles, CA 90064, USA

Columbus, Chris (Director, Producer)
c/o Simon Halls *Slate Public Relations*
9000 Sunset Blvd #915
West Hollywood, CA 90069, USA

Columbus, Chris (Writer)
290W End Ave
New York, NY 10023-8106, USA

Columbus, Christopher J (Chris) (Director, Writer)
Leavensden Studios
PO Box 3000
Leavesden WD2 7LT, UNITED KINGDOM (UK)

Colunga, Fernando (Actor)
c/o Staff Member *Crossover Agency*
801 SW 3rd Ave
Suite 302
Miami, FL 33130, USA

Colussy, Dan A (Business Person)
20 Saint Thomas Dr
West Palm Beach, FL 33418, USA

Colville, Alex (Artist)
7Lynwood Dr
Wolfville, NS B0P 1XO, Canada

Colvin, James (Jim) (Athlete, Football Player)
4583 S Deer Poppy Cir
Saint George, UT 84790-4722, USA

Colvin, John O (Judge)
US Tax Court
400 2nd St NW
Washington, DC 20217, USA

Colvin, Roosevelt (Athlete, Football Player)
12170 Annette Ln
Fishers, IN 46037-8197, USA

Colvin, Shawn (Musician, Songwriter)
615 Pressler St
Austin, TX 78703, USA

Colvin, Tyler (Athlete, Baseball Player)
4335 E Fox Cir
Mesa, AZ 85205-5104, USA

Colwell, John A (Physicist)
American Diabetes Assn
1701 N Beauregard St
Alexandria, VA 22311, USA

Colwell, Rita R (Biologist, Misc)
5110 River Hill Road
Bethesda, MD 20816, USA

Colwill, Les (Athlete, Hockey Player)
714 20 St N
Lethbridge, AB T1H 3N6, Canada

Colyar, Michael (Actor, Comedian)
Mysterie Talent Management
1301 S Ogden Dr
Los Angeles, CA 90019, USA

Colyer, Steve (Athlete, Baseball Player)
205 S Saint Jacques St
Florissant, MO 63031-6950, USA

Colzie, Jim (Athlete, Baseball Player)
3140 Day Ave
Miami, FL 33133, USA

Comaneci, Nadia (Gymnast)
4421 Hidden Hill Road
Norman, OK 73072, USA

Combe, Geoff (Athlete, Baseball Player)
743 Tudor Cir
Thousand Oaks, CA 91360-5246, USA

Combes, Willard W (Cartoonist)
1266 Oakridge Dr
Cleveland, OH 44121, USA

Combichrist (Music Group, Musician)
c/o Staff Member *Metropolis Records*
P.O. Box 974
Media, PA 19063, USA

Combs, Chris (Athlete, Football Player)
3435 Cromwell Rd
Durham, NC 27705-5408, USA

Combs, Glenn (Athlete, Basketball Player)
3627 Dogwood Ln SW
Roanoke, VA 24015-4503, USA

Combs, Holly Marie (Actor, Producer, Writer)
223 Saddlebow Rd
Bell Canyon, CA 91307, USA

Combs, Jeffrey (Actor)
c/o Leland LaBarre *Bleu, An Entertainment Company*
5225 Wilshire Blvd
Suite 701
Los Angeles, CA 90036, USA

Combs, Leroy (Athlete, Basketball Player)
1631 Glenn Bo Dr
Norman, OK 73071-2813, USA

Combs, Patrick D (Pat) (Athlete, Baseball Player)
203 Timber Lake Way
Southlake, TX 76092-7217, USA

Combs, Rodney (Race Car Driver)
201 Old Country Rd.
#101
Memville, NY 11747-2731, USA

Combs, Sean (Musician, Producer)
2 Star Island Dr
Miami Beach, FL 33139, USA

Comden, Danny (Director)
c/o Ruthanne Secunda *United Talent Agency (UTA)*
9336 Civic Center Dr
Beverly Hills, CA 90210, USA

Comeau, Andy (Actor)
c/o Staff Member *Rugolo Entertainment*
195 S Beverly Dr
Suite 400
Beverly Hills, CA 90212, USA

Comeau, Rey (Athlete, Hockey Player)
4 Rue de Cernay
Lorraine, QC J6Z 2Z1, Canada

Comeaux, Darren (Athlete, Football Player)
15677 W Glen rosa Ave
Goodyear, AZ 85395-7758, USA

Comeaux, John (Athlete, Basketball Player)
P.O. Box 327
Carencro, LA 70520-0327, USA

Comegys, Dallas (Athlete, Basketball Player)
4330 Wanye Avenue
Philadelphia, PA 19140-1745, USA

Comella, Greg (Athlete, Football Player)
90 Fairbanks Ave
Wellesley Hills, MA 02481-5256, USA

Comer, Anjanette (Actor)
Dade/Schultz
6442 Coldwater Canyon Ave
#206
Valley Green, CA 91606, USA

Comer, Francis (Philanthropist)
The Comer Foundation
939 West North Avenue
Suite 850
Chicago, illinois 60642, USA

Comer, James P (Psychic)
Yale University
Child Study Center
230 S Frontage Road
New Haven, CT 06519, USA

Comer, Steve (Athlete, Baseball Player)
4131 Dynasty Dr
Minnetonka, MN 55345-1812, USA

Comer, Wayne (Athlete, Baseball Player)
145 Marcus St
Shenandoah, VA 22849-3917, USA

Comess, Aaron (Musician)
DAS Communications
83 Riverside Dr
New York, NY 10024, USA

Comfort, Brad
PO Box 715
Mercer Island, WA 98040

Comi, Paul (Actor)
2395 Ridgeway Road
San Marino, CA 91108, USA

Comiskey, Chuck (Athlete, Football Player)
2502 Convent Ave
Pascagoula, MS 39567, USA

Comissiona, Sergiu (Conductor)
Helsinki Philharmonic
Karamzininkatu 4
Helsinki 00100, FINLAND

Command, Jim (Athlete, Baseball Player)
2136 Cranbrook Dr NE
Grand Rapids, MI 49505-5721, USA

Commerford, Tim (Musician)
5908 Zumirez Dr
Malibu, CA 90265, USA

Commiskey, Chuck
2502 Convent Ave
Pascagoula, MS 39567-4517, USA

Commodore, Mike (Athlete, Hockey Player)
Newport Sports Management
400-201 City Centre Dr
Attn Wade Arnott
Mississauga, ON L5B 2T4, Canada

Commodores, The (Music Group, Musician)
1920 Benson Ave.
St. Paul, MN 55116, USA

Common (Musician)
c/o Staci Wolfe *Polaris PR*
8135 W 4th St
2nd Floor
Los Angeles, CA 90048, USA

Compagnonl, Deborah (Skier)
Via Frodonfo 3
Santa Catarina Valfurna 2303, ITALY

Compaore, Blaise (President)
President's Office
Boile Postale 7031
Ouagadougou, BURKINA FASO

Complete Stone Roses, The (Music Group)
c/o Ross Morrison *Primary Talent International (UK)*
The Primary Building
10-11 Jockeys Fields
London WC1R 4BN, UK

Compte, Maurice (Actor)
c/o British Reece *PMK/BNC Public Relations (PMK-LA)*
8687 Melrose Ave Fl 8
West Hollywood, CA 90069, USA

Compton, Ann Woodruff (Correspondent)
ABC-TV
News Dept
5010 Creston St
Hyattsville, MD 20781, USA

Compton, Clint (Athlete, Baseball Player)
77 Glen St Aj:>t 1
Augusta, ME 04330-3916, USA

Compton, Denis C S (Cricketer)
Sunday Express
245 Blackfriars Road
London SE1 9UX, UNITED KINGDOM (UK)

Compton, Dick (Athlete, Football Player)
3408 Briarcliff Ct S
Irving, TX 75062, USA

Compton, Forrest (Actor)
245 E 72nd St
New York, NY 10021, USA

Compton, John G M (Prime Minister)
PO Box 149
Castries, SAINT LUCIA

Compton, Mike (Athlete, Baseball Player)
8624 Leighton Dr
Tampa, FL 33614-1723, USA

Compton, Ogden (Athlete, Football Player)
13918 Preston Valley Pb
Dallas, TX 75240-4769, USA

Compton, Richard (Actor)
Agency for Performing Arts
9200 Sunset Blvd
#900
Los Angeles, CA 90069, USA

Compton, Stacy (Race Car Driver)
Team St
286 Brown's Hill Rd.
Locust, NC 28047, USA

Compton-Rock, Malaak (Philanthropist)
The Angel Rock Project
Box #996
Tenafly, NJ 07670, USA

Comrie, Mike (Athlete, Hockey Player)
10800 Wilshire Blvd Apt 1703
Los Angeles, CA 90024-4217, USA

Comrie, Paul (Athlete, Business Person, Hockey Player)
The Brick Group Income Fund
16930 114 Ave NW
Attn: Office of the President
Edmonton, AB T5M 3S2, Canada

Comstock, Keith (Athlete, Baseball Player)
9615 E Desert Trl
Scottsdale, AZ 85260-4624, USA

Conacher, Brian (Athlete, Hockey Player)
202-500 Avenue Rd
Toronto, ON M4V 2J6, Canada

Conacher, Jim (Athlete, Hockey Player)
422-980 Lynn Valley Rd
North Vancouver, BC V7J 3V7, Canada

Conacher, Pat (Athlete, Hockey Player)
PO Box 104 Stn Main
Regina, SK S4P 2Z5, Canada

Conacher, Pete (Athlete, Hockey Player)
3 Conifer Dr
Etobicoke, ON M9C 1X3, Canada

Conant, Kenneth J (Archaeologist)
3 Carlton Village
#T105
Bedford, MA 01730, USA

Conant, Sean (Actor)
c/o Staff Member *Rising Picture*
PO Box 2
North Hampton, NH 03862, USA

Conatser, Clint (Athlete, Baseball Player)
26701 Quail Crk Apt 191
Laguna Hills, CA 92656-3010, USA

Conatsor, Clint (Athlete, Baseball Player)
26701 Quail Crk
Apt 191
Laguna Hills, CA 92656, USA

Conaty, William (Bill) (Athlete, Football Player)
203 Country Club Dr
Moorestown, NJ 08057, USA

Conaway, Christi
334 Huntley
Los Angeles, CA 90048-1919

Conaway, Cristi (Actor)
443 14th Street
San Monica, CA 90402-2131, USA

Conaway, K. Michael (Congressman, Politician)
2430 Rayburn HOB
Washington, DC 20515, USA

Concepcion, David I (Davey) (Athlete, Baseball Player)
Urbanizacion el Castano
Botalon 5-D
Maracay, Venezuela, Venezuela

Concepcion, Onix (Athlete, Baseball Player)
1486 Steeplechase Ln
Deltona, FL 32725-4752, USA

Concha, Billy (Actor)
P.O. Box 1129
Hermosa Beach, CA 90254, USA

Concina, Tommaso (Stylist)
c/o Staff Member *Stockland Martel*
343 E 18th St
New York, NY 10003, USA

Concrete Blonde (Music Group)
Concrete Blonde Touring Company Inc
16830 Ventura Blvd Ste 501
Encino, CA 91436, USA

Concretes, The (Music Group)
c/o Staff Member *Paradigm (Monterey)*
404 W Franklin St
Monterey, CA 93940, USA

Conde, Ninel (Actor)
c/o Gabriel Blanco *Gabriel Blanco*
Iglesias (Mexico)
Rio Balsas 35-32
Colonia Cuauhtemoc
DF 06500, Mexico

Conde, Ramon (Athlete, Baseball Player)
P.O. Box 57
Juana Diaz, PR 00795-0057, USA

Condit, Garth (Stylist)
c/o Staff Member *Artists by Timothy*
Priano (NY)
15 Watts St
6th Floor
New York, NY 10013, USA

Condit, Philip M (Business Person)
Boeing Co
PO Box 3707
Seattle, WA 98124, USA

Condon, Bill (Director, Writer)
c/o Adam Shulman *Anonymous Content*
(LA)
3531 Hayden Ave
Culver City, CA 90232, USA

Condon, Jill (Producer, Writer)
c/o Staff Member *United Talent Agency*
(UTA)
9336 Civic Center Dr
Beverly Hills, CA 90210, USA

Condon, Paul (Lawyer)
Metropolitan Police
New Scotland Yard Broadway
London SW1H 0BG, UNITED KINGDOM
(UK)

Condon, Tom (Athlete, Football Player)
c/o Staff Member *CAA Sports (LA)*
2000 Avenue of the Stars
Los Angeles, CA 90067, USA

Condra, Julie (Actor)
c/o Staff Member *Gold Coast*
Management
438 S Venice Blvd Apt 5
Venice, CA 90291, USA

Condredge, Holloway (Athlete, Football Player)
8137 Faircrest Ln
Knoxville, TN 37919, USA

Condren, Glen (Athlete, Football Player)
8557 N 175th East Ave
Owasso, OK 74055-5638, USA

Condren, Steve (Horse Racer)
36-130 Robert St
Milton, ON L9T 6E3, Canada

Condrey, Clay (Athlete, Baseball Player)
412 N 8th St
Navasota, TX 77868-2927, USA

Condron, Christopher M (Financier)
Melton Financial Corp
Mellon Bank Center
500 Grant St
Pittsburgh, PA 15258, USA

Cone, David B (Athlete, Baseball Player)
303 E 83rd St
Apt 6A
New York, NY 10028-4316, USA

Cone, Fred (Athlete, Football Player)
PO Box 1819
Blairsville, GA 30514-1819, USA

Confederate Railroad (Music Group)
The Bobby Roberts Company Inc
PO Box 1547
Goodlettsville, TN 37070-1547, USA

Conforti, Gino (Actor)
Orange Gove Group
12178 Ventura Blvd
#205
Studio City, CA 91604, USA

Congdon, Jeff (Athlete, Basketball Player)
13712 S 500 E
Drapper, UT 84020-8926, USA

Congemi, John (Athlete, Football Player)
1015 Trailmore Ln
Weston, FL 33326-2820

Conger, Harry M (Business Person)
Homestake Mining Co
650 California St
San Francisco, CA 94108, USA

Coniar, Larry (Athlete, Football Player)
PO Box 5133
Evanston, IL 60204-5133, USA

Conigliaro, Billy (Athlete, Baseball Player)
501 Cabot St
Unit 2
Beverly, MA 01915-2580, USA

Conine, Jeff (Athlete, Baseball Player)
3166 Inverness
Weston, FL 33332-1816, USA

Conjar, Larry (Athlete, Football Player)
542 Sheridan Rd
Evanston, IL 60202, USA

Conkey, Margaret (Archaeologist)
University of California
Archaeological Research Facility
Berkeley, CA 94720, USA

Conklin, Cary (Athlete, Football Player)
4695 Savannah Ln
Boise, ID 83714-7424, USA

Conklin, Ty (Athlete, Hockey Player)
K 0 Sports
501 S Cherry St Ste 580
Attn Kurt Overhardt
Denver, CO 80246-1327, USA

Conlan, Shane P (Athlete, Football Player)
521 East Dr
Sewickley, PA 15143-1114, USA

Conlee, John (Musician)
John Conlee Enterprises
38 Music Square East
#117
Nashville, TN 37203, USA

Conley, Bob (Athlete, Baseball Player)
16A Canton Dr
Whiting, NJ 08759-1977, USA

Conley, Clare D (Editor)
Hemlock Farms
Hawley, PA 18428, USA

Conley, Darby (Cartoonist)
c/o Staff Member *United Press Media*
200 Madison Ave
New York, NY 10016, USA

Conley, D Eugene (Gene) (Athlete, Basketball Player)
2105 Grafton Ave
Clermont, FL 34711-5241, USA

Conley, Earl Thomas (Musician, Songwriter)
657 Baker Road
Smyrna, TN 37167, USA

Conley, Gene (Athlete, Baseball Player)
400 Foxboro Blvd
Apt 3102
Foxboro, MA 02035-3803, USA

Conley, Jack (Actor)
c/o Julia Buchwald *Buchwald/Fortitude*
(LA)
6500 Wilshire Blvd
Suite 2200
Los Angeles, CA 90048, USA

Conley, Jill
10332 Christine Pl
Chatsworth, CA 91311

Conley, Joe (Actor)
78806 Gorham Ln
Palm Desert, CA 92211, USA

Conley, Larry (Athlete, Basketball Player)
5422 Forest Springs Drive
Atlanta, GA 30338-3606, USA

Conley, Michael (Mike) (Athlete, Track Athlete)
University of Arkansas
Athletic Dept
Fayetteville, AR 72701, USA

COnley, Mike (Athlete, Basketball Player)
3496 Windgarden Cove
Memphis, TN 38125-1732, USA

Conley, Steve (Athlete, Football Player)
1745 N Independence Pl
Fayetteville, AR 72704-5789, USA

Conlin, Chris (Athlete, Football Player)
4864 Tropicana Ave
Cooper City, FL 33330, USA

Conlin, Edward (Athlete, Basketball Player)
153 North Mountain Avenue
Montclair, NJ 07042-2347, USA

Conlin, Michaela (Actor)
2818 Effie St
Los Angeles, CA 90026, USA

Conlon, James J
Shuman Assoc
120 W 58th St
#8D
New York, NY 10019, USA

Conlon, Marty (Athlete, Basketball Player)
180 Woodbine Dr
East Hampton, NY 11937-1747, USA

Conn, Didi (Actor, Musician)
19 Ludlow Ln
Palisades, NY 10964, USA

Conn, Richard (Dick) (Athlete, Football Player)
144 Sugarmill Ln
Moore, SC 29369, USA

Conn, Terri (Actor)
1268 E 14th St
Brooklyn, NY 11230, USA

Connally, Fritz (Athlete, Baseball Player)
615 Portofino Dr
Arlington, TX 76012, USA

Connally, Fritzie (Athlete, Baseball Player)
615 Portofino Dr
Arlington, TX 76012-2700, USA

Conneff, Kevin (Musician)
Macklam Feldman Mgmt
1505 W 2nd Ave
#200
Vancouver, BC V6H 3Y4, CANADA

Connell, Albert (Athlete, Football Player)
2320 Cherrybrook Ln Apt 279
Pasadena, TX 77502-4194, USA

Connell, Chad (Actor)
c/o Marc Hamou *Thruline Entertainment*
9250 Wilshire Blvd
Ground Fl
Beverly Hills, CA 90212, USA

Connell, Desmond Cardinal (Religious Leader)
Archbishop's House
Drumcondra
Dublin 9, IRELAND

Connell, Evan S Jr (Writer)
Fort Macy 13
320 Artist Road
Santa Fe, NM 87501, USA

Connell, Jane
905 West End Ave.
New York, NY 10025

Connell, Thurman C (Financier)
Federal Home Loan Bank
907 Walnut St
Des Moines, IA 50309, USA

Connelly, Jennifer (Actor)
288 West St #8E/8W
New York, NY 10013, USA

Connelly, Lynn (Athlete, Golfer)
40 W Elm St
Apt 3L
Greenwich, CT 06830, USA

Connelly, Michael (Writer)
52 Ladoga Ave
Tampa, FL 33606, USA

Connelly, Mike (Athlete, Football Player)
9352 Creel Creek Dr
Dallas, TX 75228-4132, USA

Connelly, Steve (Athlete, Baseball Player)
1863 Litchfield Ave
Long Beach, CA 90815-3037, USA

Connelly, Wayne (Athlete, Hockey Player)
Site 2 Box 61
RR 2
Swastika, ON P0K 1T0, Canada

Conner, Bart (Athlete, Gymnast, Olympic Athlete)
4421 Hidden Hill Rd
Norman, OK 73072-2899, USA

Conner, Chris (Actor)
c/o Staff Member *Nine Yards Entertainment*
8530 Wilshire Blvd Fl 5
Beverly Hills, CA 90211, USA

Conner, Darion (Athlete, Football Player)
9553 Prairie Point Rd
Macon, MS 39341, USA

Conner, Dennis (Athlete, Olympic Athlete, Sailor)
Dennis Conner SportsDennis Conner Sports
2525 Shelter Island Dr Ste E
San Diego, CA 92106-3161, USA

Conner, Frank (Golfer)
c/o Staff Member *Pro Golfers Association (PGA) Tour*
112 TPC Blvd
Ponte Vedra Beach, FL 32082, USA

Conner, Jimmy Dan (Athlete, Basketball Player)
5009 Old Federal Road
Louisville, KY 40207, USA

Conner, Jimmy Dan (Athlete, Basketball Player)
Kentucky Colonels
5009 Old Federal Rd
Louisville, KY 40207-1200, USA

Conner, Lester (Athlete, Basketball Player)
13836 Coldwater Drive
Carmel, IN 46032-8562, USA

Conners, Dan (Athlete, Football Player)
1895 Partridge Dr
San Luis Obispo, CA 93405-6321, USA

Connery, Jason (Actor)
6235 Holly Mont Dr
Los Angeles, CA 90068, USA

Connery, Sean (Actor)
Lyford Cay
P.O. Box N-7776
Nassau, The Bahamas

Connery, Vincent L (Misc)
National Treasury Employees Union
1730 K St NW
Washington, DC 20006, USA

Connes, Alain (Mathematician)
Leon Motchane I'HES
35 Route Chartres
Bures-sur-Yvette 91440, FRANCE

Conney, Terry (Athlete, Baseball Player)
3205 Filbert Ave
Clovis, CA 93611, USA

Connick Jr, Harry (Actor, Musician)
671 West Rd
New Canaan, CT 06840, USA

Conniff, Cal (Skier)
157 Pleasantview Ave
Longrneadow, MA 01106, USA

Connolly, Billy (Actor, Musician, Producer, Writer)
c/o Gene Parseghian *Parseghian Planco LLC*
322 8th Ave
Suite 601
New York, NY 10001, USA

Connolly, Dee (Stylist)
c/o Staff Member *Judy Inc*
1 Yorkville Ave
Toronto ON M4W 1L1, Canada

Connolly, Kevin (Actor)
9256 Thrush Way
West Hollywood, CA 90069, USA

Connolly, Kristen (Actor)
525 Rialto Ave
Venice, CA 90291, USA

Connolly, Olga Fikotova (Athlete, Track Athlete)
514 Huntington St
Huntington Beach, CA 92648-4929, USA

Connolly, Ted (Athlete, Football Player)
1805 N Carson St Unit 86
Carson City, NV 89701-1216, USA

Connolly, Tim (Athlete, Hockey Player)
772 Forest Ave
Buffalo, NY 14209-1042, USA

Connor, Cam (Athlete, Hockey Player)
2716 118 St NW
Edmonton, AB T6J 3P6, Canada

Connor, Chris (Musician)
Maxine Harvard Unlimited
7942 W Bell Road
#C5
Glendale, AZ 85308, USA

Connor, Christopher M (Business Person)
Sherwin-Williams Co
101 W Prospect Ave
Clveland, OH 44115, USA

Connor, Joseph E (Business Person, Government Official)
Under-Secretary General's Office
United Nations
UN Plaza
New York, NY 10021, USA

Connor, Mark (Athlete, Baseball Player)
7312 Wheatfield Pl
Knoxville, TN 37919-7201, USA

Connor, Patrick
3 Spring Bank
New Mills nr. Stockport, ENGLAND SK12 4AS

Connor, Ralph (Misc)
9866 Highwood Court
Sun City, AZ 85373, USA

Connor, Richard L (Publisher)
Fort Worth Star-Telegram
400 W 7th St
Fort Worth, TX 76102, USA

Connor, Sarah (Musician)
Postfach 3053
Hannover 30030, GERMANY

Connor, Shannon (Model)
4 Rockage Rd
Warren, NJ 07059

Connors, Bill (Billy) (Athlete, Baseball Player)
3329 Enterprise Rd E
Safety Harbor, FL 34695-5307, USA

Connors, Carol (Musician, Songwriter)
1709 Ferrari Dr
Beverly Hills, CA 90210, USA

Connors, Jimmy (Tennis Player)
1962 E Valley Rd
Santa Barbara, CA 93108-1428, USA

Connors, Mike (Actor, Producer)
4810 Louise Ave
Encino, CA 91316, USA

Connors, Patrick (Athlete, Baseball Player)
1075 Maricopa Dr
Oshkosh, WI 54904-8116, USA

Connot, Scott (Athlete, Football Player)
1726 Torrey Pines Dr
Brookings, SD 57006-5498, USA

Connway, Craig (Business Person)
PeopleSoft Inc
4460 Hacienda Dr
Pleasanton, CA 94588, USA

Conombo, Joseph I (Prime Minister)
2003 Ave de la Liberte
BP 613
Dadoya, Ouagadougou, BURKINA FASO

Conover, Lloyd H (Inventor)
5200 Brittany Drive South
Apt 304
Saint Petersburg, FL 33 715-1523, USA

Conover, Scott (Athlete, Football Player, Sportscaster)
28 Windsor Ter Apt B
Freehold, NJ 07728-3240, USA

Conoway, Christi
PO Box 46515
Los Angeles, CA 90046

Conrad, Barnaby
3530 Pine Valley Dr.
Sarasota, FL 34239

Conrad, Bobby Joe (Athlete, Football Player)
140 County Road 3270
Clifton, TX 76634-4678, USA

Conrad, Brooks (Athlete, Baseball Player)
3964 E Wateka Ct
Gilbert, AZ 85297-9497, USA

Conrad, Chris (Athlete, Football Player)
984 Orangewood Dr
Brea, CA 92821-2514, USA

Conrad, David (Actor)
c/o Staff Member *Gersh (LA)*
9465 Wilshire Blvd
Suite 600
Beverly Hills, CA 90212, USA

Conrad, Eve Burch
23388 Mulholland Dr.
Woodland Hills, CA 91364

Conrad, Kent (Politician, Senator)
530 Hart Senate Office Building
Washington, DC 20003-1340, USA

Conrad, Kimberly
10236 Charing Cross Rd
Los Angeles, CA 90077

Conrad, Lauren (Actor, Reality TV Star)
325 N Oakhurst Dr #PH3
Beverly Hills, CA 90210, USA

Conrad, Robert (Actor)
3800 Weatherly Cir
Westlake Village, CA 91361, USA

Conrad, Shane
9255 Sunset Blvd. #620
Los Angeles, CA 90069

Conradt, Jody (Athlete, Basketball Player, Coach)
9614 Leaning Rock Circle
Austin, TX 78730-2725, USA

Conran, Jasper A T (Designer, Fashion Designer)
Jasper Conran Ltd
2 Munden St
London W14 0RH, UNITED KINGDOM (UK)

Conran, Philip J (War Hero)
4706 Calle Reina
Santa Barbara, CA 93110, USA

Conran, Terence O (Designer)
22 SHad Thames
London SE1 2YU, UNITED KINGDOM (UK)

Conroy, Christopher (Athlete, Baseball Player)
307 E Main St
North Adams, MA 01247-4427, USA

Conroy, Craig (Athlete, Hockey Player, Olympic Athlete)
P.O. Box 549
Henderson Harbor, NY 13651-0549, USA

Conroy, Frances (Actor)
c/o Staff Member *ICM Partners (ICM-LA)*
10250 Constellation Blvd Fl 7
Los Angeles, CA 90067, USA

Conroy, Jeff (Producer)
Original Productions
308 W Verdugo Ave
Burbank, CA 91502, USA

Conroy, Kevin (Actor)
c/o Staff Member *Imperium 7 Talent Agency*
5455 Wilshire Blvd
Suite 1706
Los Angeles, CA 90036, USA

Conroy, Pat (Writer)
c/o Marly Rusoff *Marly Rusoff & Associates Inc*
PO Box 524
Bronxville, NY 10708, USA

Conroy, Tim (Athlete, Baseball Player)
109 Moonlight Dr
Monroeville, PA 15146-2028, USA

Conroy, Zack (Actor)
c/o Danielle Quinoa *Innovative Artists (NY)*
235 Park Ave S
7th Floor
New York, NY 10003, USA

Considine, John (Actor)
16 1/2 Red Coal Lane
Greenwich, CT 06830, USA

Considine, Paddy (Actor, Writer)
c/o Staff Member *Creative Artists Agency (CAA-LA)*
2000 Ave Of The Stars
Los Angeles, CA 90067, USA

Considine, Tim (Actor)
3708 Mountain View Ave
Los Angeles, CA 90066, USA

Conspirator (Music Group)
c/o Staff Member *Paradigm (Monterey)*
404 W Franklin St
Monterey, CA 93940, USA

Constantin, Charles (Athlete, Hockey Player)
1277 Av de Meriel
Quebec, QC G1S 3H8, Canada

Constantin, Michel
17 blvd. Bartole Beauvallon
St. Maxime, FRANCE 83120

Constantine, Kevin
5928 Jenny Lind Ct.
San Jose, CA 95120

Constantine, Michael (Actor)
1604 Bern St
Reading, PA 19604, USA

Constantine II (King)
4 Linnell Dr
Hampstead Way
London NW11, UNITED KINGDOM (UK)

Consuelos, Mark (Actor)
c/o Brian Liebman *Liebman Entertainment*
25 E 21st St #PH
New York, NY 10011-8503, USA

Conte, Dino
2325 Fox Hills Dr
Los Angeles, CA 49006, USA

Conte, Lansana (President)
President's Office
Conakry, GUINEA

Conte, Lou (Choreographer)
Hubbard Street Dance Co
1147 W Jackson Blvd
Chicago, IL 60607, USA

Contella, Dina (Scientist)
2704 Porto Bianco Ln
League City, TX 77573-2370, USA

Conti, Al
Box 701
Portsmouth, RI 02871

Conti, Bill (Composer, Musician)
117 Fremont Place W
Los Angeles, CA 90005, USA

Conti, Guy (Athlete, Baseball Player)
448 53rd Sq
Vero Beach, FL 32968-1021, USA

Conti, Jason (Athlete, Baseball Player)
740 N April Dr
Chandler, AZ 85226-1632, USA

Conti, Tom (Actor)
Chatto & Linnit
Prince of Wales Coventry St
London W1V 7FE, UNITED
KINGDOM(UK)

Contini, Joe (Athlete, Hockey Player)
302 Domville
Arthur, ON N0G 1A0, Canada

Contino, Dick (Music Group, Musician)
3355 Nahatan Way
Las Vegas, NV 89109, USA

Contner, James A (Cinematographer)
4532 Murietta Ave
Apt 105
Sherman Oaks, CA 91423-5430, USA

Contorakes, Maria (Stylist)
7160 SW 47th St
Miami, FL 33155, USA

Contostavlos, Tulisa (Model)
c/o Staff Member *Cole Kitchenn Personal Management*
212 Strand
London WC2R 1AP, USA

Contoulis, John (Athlete, Football Player)
404 Champion Cir
Throop, PA 18512-1451, USA

Contours, The
1161 NW 76th Ave.
Ft. Lauderdale, FL 33322

Contreras, Jose (Athlete, Baseball Player)
8501 Lithia Pinecrest Rd
Lithia, FL 33547, USA

Contreras, Nardi (Athlete, Baseball Player)
5052 Lurgan Rd Land 0
Lakes, FL 34638-7653, USA

Contz, Bill (Athlete, Football Player)
106 Grace Dr
Cranberry Twp, PA 16066, USA

Converse, Frank (Actor)
c/o Phil Sutfin *ICM Partners (ICM-LA)*
10250 Constellation Blvd Fl 7
Los Angeles, CA 90067, USA

Converse, Jim (Athlete, Baseball Player)
11865 Cobble Brook Dr
Rancho Cordova, CA 95742-8008, USA

Converse-Roberts, William (Actor)
Innovative Artists
1505 10th St
Santa Monica, CA 90401, USA

Convery, Brandon (Athlete, Hockey Player)
PO Box 2556
Manhattan Beach, CA 90267-2556, USA

Conway, Billy (Music Group, Musician)
Creative Performance Group
48 Laight St
New York, NY 10013, USA

Conway, Brett (Athlete, Football Player)
630 Virginia Ave NE
Atlanta, GA 30306-3629, USA

Conway, Curtis (Athlete, Football Player)
4801 Azucena Rd
Woodland Hills, CA 91364, USA

Conway, Gary (Actor)
2035 Mandeville Canyon Rd
Los Angeles, CA 90049, USA

Conway, James (General)
Commanding General I Marine
Expeditionary Force
Camp Pendleton, CA 92055, USA

Conway, James (Race Car Driver)
420 Fair Hill Dr.
#1
Elkton, MD 21921-2573, USA

Conway, James L (Director, Producer, Writer)
c/o Andrea Simon *Andrea Simon Entertainment*
4230 Woodman Avenue
Sherman Oaks, CA 91423, USA

Conway, James T General (General)
5740 N Carlin Springs Rd
Arlington, VA 22203-1204, USA

Conway, Jill K (Historian)
65 Commonwealth Ave #8B
Boston, MA 02116, USA

Conway, John W (Business Person)
Crown Cork & Seal
1 Crown Way
Philadelphia, PA 19154, USA

Conway, Kevin (Actor)
25 CenturyPark W
New York, NY 10023, USA

Conway, Tim (Actor, Comedian)
4425 Haskell Ave
Encino, CA 91436, USA

Conwell, Angell (Actor)
c/o Staff Member *Evolution Entertainment (LA)*
901 N Highland Ave
Los Angeles, CA 90038, USA

Conwell, Easther M (Physicist)
800 Philips Road
Webster, NY 14580, USA

Conwell, Ernie (Athlete, Football Player)
5301 McGavock Rd
Brentwood, TN 37027-5185, USA

Conwell, Joseph (Joe) (Athlete, Football Player)
1301 Stoney River Dr
Ambler, PA 19002-1159, USA

Conwell, Tommy (Music Group, Musician)
Brothers Mgmt
141 Dunbar Ave
Fords, NJ 08863, USA

Conyers Jr., John (Congressman, Politician)
2426 Rayburn HOB
Washington, DC 20515, USA

Coobar, Abdulmegid (Prime Minister)
Asadu El-Furat St 29
Garden City
Tripoli, LIBYA

Cooder, Ry (Composer, Musician)
326 Entrada Dr
Santa Monica, CA 90402, USA

Coody, Charles (Athlete, Golfer)
1555 Oldham Ln
Abliene, TX 79602-4143, USA

Coogan, Dodie
PO Box 413
Palm Springs, CA 92263

Coogan, Keith (Actor)
c/o Drew Elliot *Universal Media Artists*
8255 W Sunset Blvd
Los Angeles, CA 90046, USA

Coogan, Richard
5805 Whitsett Ave. #103
No. Hollywood, CA 91607

Coogan, Steve (Actor, Producer, Writer)
Baby Cow Productions
77 Oxford Street
London W1D 2ES, United Kingdom

Cook, Aaron (Athlete, Baseball Player)
18716 W 56th Dr
Golden, CO 80403-2351, USA

Cook, AJ (Actor)
643 6th St
Hermosa Beach, CA 90254, USA

Cook, Andrea Joy (A.J.) (Actor)
c/o Jeff Morrone *Jeff Morrone Entertainment*
9350 Wilshire Blvd
Suite 224
Beverly Hills, CA 90212, USA

Cook, Andy (Athlete, Baseball Player)
3312 Central Ave
Memphis, TN 38111-4402, USA

Cook, Ann T
5412 Riverhills Dr
Temple Terrace, FL 33617, USA

Cook, Ann Turner (Misc)
12401 N 22nd St Apt E501
Tampa, FL 33612-4625, USA

Cook, Anthony (Athlete, Football Player)
111 Elm St
Salisbury, NC 28144-6115, USA

Cook, Barbara (Actor, Musician)
c/o Staff Member *Cunningham Escott Slevin & Doherty (CESD-LA)*
10635 Santa Monica Blvd
130
Los Angeles, CA 90025, USA

Cook, Becket (Stylist)
c/o Staff Member *Celestine - CA*
1666 20th St
#200-B
Santa Monica, CA 90404, USA

Cook, Bert (Athlete, Basketball Player)
2571 West 5725 South
Roy, UT 84067-1326, USA

Cook, Bob (Athlete, Football Player)
100 Sioux Ct
Hendersonville, TN 37075, USA

Cook, Carole (Actor, Comedian)
8829 Ashcroft Ave
Los Angeles, CA 90048, USA

Cook, Cliff (Athlete, Baseball Player)
605 E Williamsburg Mnr
Arlington, TX 76014-1145, USA

Cook, Daequan (Basketball Player)
c/o Staff Member *Miami Heat*
1 SE 3rd Avenue
Suite 2300
Miami, FL 33131, USA

Cook, Dane (Actor)
1561 Viewsite Dr
West Hollywood, CA 90069, USA

Cook, Darwin (Athlete, Basketball Player)
1840 W Avenue J12
Apt 103
Lancaster, CA 93534-4642, USA

Cook, David (Musician)
3170 Durand Dr
Los Angeles, CA 90068, USA

Cook, Dennis (Athlete, Baseball Player)
3413 Serene Hills Ct
Austin, TX 78738-1230, USA

Cook, Doris (Athlete, Baseball Player, Commentator)
1059 Airport Rd
Muskegon, MI 49441-5101, USA

Cook, Edward J (Athlete, Football Player)
902 Briarwood Ct
Sewell, NJ 08080, USA

Cook, Fielder
180 Central Park So
New York, NY 10019

Cook, Fred (Athlete, Football Player)
4402 Market St
Pascagoula, MS 39567-2224, USA

Cook, Glen (Athlete, Baseball Player)
424 Scarlet Sage Dr
League City, TX 77573-6426, USA

Cook, Jameel (Athlete, Football Player)
PO Box 131647
Houston, TX 77219-1647, USA

Cook, Jason (Actor)
c/o Katie Mason *Luber Roklin Management*
8530 Wilshire Blvd
6th Floor
Beverly Hills, CA 90211, USA

Cook, Jeff (Music Group, Musician)
P O Box 35967
Fort Payne, AL 35967, USA

Cook, Jeff (Athlete, Basketball Player)
4908 East Doubletree Ranch Road
Paradise Valley, AZ 85253-1556, USA

Cook, Jerry (Race Car Driver)
117 Palmetto Drive
Mooresville, NC 28117, USA

Cook, John (Athlete, Golfer)
9742 Green Island Cv
Windermere, FL 34786, USA

Cook, Judy (Bowler)
Ladies Professional Bowling Tour
7200 Harrison Ave #7171
Rockford, IL 61112, USA

Cook, Katie (Television Host)
1201 Kenwood Dr
Nashville, TN 37216, USA

Cook, Kristy Lee (Musician)
c/o Marty Rendleman *Rendleman Management Group, Inc.*
P. O. Box 670366
Dallas, TX 75367, USA

Cook, Kyle (Musician)
626 Calverton Ln
Brentwood, TN 37027, USA

Cook, Leigh
9560 Wilshire Blvd. #516
Beverly Hills, CA 90212

Cook, Marv (Athlete, Football Player)
425 Butternut Ln
Iowa City, IA 52246-2782, USA

Cook, Mike (Athlete, Baseball Player)
216 Harlech Way
Charleston, SC 29414-6876, USA

Cook, Paul (Music Group, Musician)
Solo Agency
55 Fulham High St
London SW6 3JJ, UNITED
KINGDOM(UK)

Cook, Paul M (Business Person)
SRI International
333 Ravenswood Ave
Mento Park, CA 94025, USA

Cook, Peter F C (Architect)
54 Compayne Gardens
London NW6 3RY, UNITED
KINGDOM(UK)

Cook, Rachael Leigh (Actor)
1270 Sunset Plaza Dr
West Hollywood, CA 90069, USA

Cook, Rachel Leigh (Actor, Producer)
c/o Staff Member *James/Levy/Jacobson Management Inc*
3500 W Olive Ave
Suite 1470
Burbank, CA 91505, USA

Cook, Rashard (Athlete, Football Player)
517 Ocean Breeze Way
Chula Vista, CA 91914-2022, USA

Cook, Richard (Scientist)
Jet Propulsion Laboratory
4800 Oak Grove Dr
Pasadena, CA 91109, USA

Cook, Robert (Opera Singer)
Quavers 53 Friars Ave
Fiem Barnet
London N2O OXG, UNITED
KINGDOM(UK)

Cook, Robert (Athlete, Baseball Player)
179 Royal Farm E
Blacklick, OH 43004, USA

Cook, Robert F (Robin) (Government Official)
House of Commons
Westminster
London SW1A 0AA, UNITED
KINGDOM(UK)

Cook, Robin (Writer)
16 Louisburg Sq
Boston, MA 02108-1203, USA

Cook, Robin (Writer)
4601 Gulf Shore Blvd #P4
Naples, FL 33940, USA

Cook, Ron (Athlete, Baseball Player)
1918 Franklin Dr
Longview, TX 75601-4111, USA

Cook, Sandra (Stylist)
829 Carolina St
San Francisco, CA 94107, USA

Cook, Stanton R (Publisher)
224 Raleigh Road
Kenitworth, IL 60043, USA

Cook, Steve (Bowler)
1209 Devonshire Court
Roseville, CA 95661, USA

Cook, Terry (Race Car Driver)
177 Knob Hill Rd
Mooresville, NC 28117, USA

Cook, Thomas A (Writer)
Bantam Books
1540 Broadway
New York, NY 10036, USA

Cook, Timothy (Business Person)
1428 W Hood Ave
Chicago, IL 60660-1805, USA

Cook, Toi (Athlete, Football Player)
5064 Llano Dr
Woodland Hills, CA 91364-3029, USA

Cooke, Amelia (Actor)
c/o Darren Goldberg *Global Creative*
1051 Cole Ave # B
Los Angeles, CA 90038, USA

Cooke, Christian (Actor)
c/o Olivia Homan *United Agents*
12-26 Lexington St
London W1F OLE, UK

Cooke, David (Athlete, Basketball Player)
P.O. Box 270591
San Diego, CA 92198-2591, USA

Cooke, Ed (Athlete, Football Player)
2093 Wake Forest St
Virginia Beach, VA 23451-1421, USA

Cooke, Howard F H (Ex-Governor)
20 Peter Pan Ave
Montego Bay, Saint James, Jamaica

Cooke, Janis (Journalist)
Washington Post
1150 15th St NW
Washington, DC 20017, USA

Cooke, Joe (Athlete, Football Player)
2550 E River Rd
Unit 3101
Tucson, AZ 85718-9504, USA

Cooke, John P (Misc)
290 Branchville Road
Ridgefield, CT 06877, USA

Cooke, Josh (Actor)
7516 Woodrow Wilson Dr
Los Angeles, CA 90046, USA

Cooke, Steve (Athlete, Baseball Player)
9791 Jefferson Pkwy Apt A3
Englewood, CO 80112-5962, USA

Cooke, William (Bill) (Athlete, Football Player)
1851 Hillside Rd
Fairfield, CT 06824, USA

Cooks, Johnie (Athlete, Football Player)
2416 Sun Creek Rd
Starkville, MS 39759-8475, USA

Cooks, Kerry (Athlete, Football Player)
5358 Lismore Ln
Fitchburg, WI 53711-7680, USA

Cooks, Rayford (Athlete, Football Player)
1839 Nomas St
Dallas, TX 75212-3806, USA

Cooksey, Danny
9300 Wilshire Blvd. #410
Beverly Hills, CA 90212

Cooksey, Dave (Religious Leader)
Brethren Church
524 College Ave
Ashland, OH 44805, USA

Cooksey, Patty (Athlete)
c/o*Churchill Downs*
Race Office
700 Central Avenue
Lousiville, KY 40208

Cookson, Brent (Athlete, Baseball Player)
1232 Manzanita Dr
Santa Paula, CA 93060-1239, USA

Cookson, Peter
30 Norfolk Rd.
Southfield, MA 01259

Coolbaugh, Scott (Athlete, Baseball Player)
6708 Carriage Ln
Colleyville, TX 76034-5771, USA

Cool Breeze
PO Box 470642
San Francisco, CA 94147-0642

Cooley, Chris (Athlete, Football Player)
PO Box 144
Hamilton, VA 20159-0144, USA

Cooley, Denton (Scientist)
3014 Del Monte Dr
3014 Del Monte Dr, Houston TX, USA

Cooley, Denton (Doctor, Misc)
3014 Del Monte Dr
Houston, TX 77019, USA

Cooley, Ryan (Actor)
c/o Norbert Abrams *Noble Caplan Abrams*
1260 Yonge St
2nd Floor
Toronto ON M4T 1W6, Canada

Cooley, Tonya (Reality TV Star)
c/o Staff Member *Bunim/Murray Productions Inc*
6007 Sepulveda Blvd
Van Nuys, CA 91411, USA

Cooleyb, Chelsea (Beauty Pageant Winner)
c/o Staff Member *Miss Universe Organization, The*
1370 Ave of the Americas Fl 16
New York, NY 10019, USA

Coolidge, Charles H (General)
1054 Balmoral Dr
Signal Mountain, TN 37377-2904, USA

Coolidge, Charles H (War Hero)
1054 Balmoral Dr
Signal Mountain, TN 37377, USA

Coolidge, Charles H Jr (General)
Vice CinC Air Force Material Command
Wright-Patterson Air Force Base,
OH 45433, USA

Coolidge, Harold J (Misc)
38 Standley St
Beverly, MA 01915, USA

Coolidge, Jennifer (Actor)
2071 Grace Ave
Los Angeles, CA 90068, USA

Coolidge, Martha (Director)
760 N La Cienega Blvd
Los Angeles, CA 90069, USA

Coolidge, Rita (Musician)
560 Hilbert Dr
Fallbrook, CA 92028, USA

Coolio (Actor, Musician)
c/o Chris Johnston-Davies *Intrigue Management*
25 Spinney Way
Needingworth
Cambridgeshire PE27 4SR, United
Kingdom

Cool kids (Music Group, Musician)
c/o Cara Lewis *Creative Artists Agency (CAA-LA)*
1325 Ave of the Americas
New York, NY 10019, USA

Coombe, George W (Attorney, Attorney General, General)
Graham & James
1Maritime Plaza
San Fransisco, CA 94111, USA

Coombs, Danny (Athlete, Baseball Player)
14130 Cleobrook Dr
Houston, TX 77070-3744, USA

Coombs, Pat
5 Wendela Ct Harrow-On-The-Hill
Middlesex, ENGLAND, ENGLAND

Coombs, Philip H (Economist)
617 W Main St
Chester, CT 06412, USA

Coombs, Torrance (Actor)
c/o Danielle Allman-Del *D2 Management*
141 S. Barrington Ave
Los Angeles, CA 90049, USA

Coombs-Mueller, Carol (Actor)
5200 Irvine Blvd
Space 364
Irvine, CA 92620, USA

Coomer, Ron (Athlete, Baseball Player)
7021 Howard Ln
Eden Prairie, MN 55346-3053, USA

Coon, Christopher (Senator)
127A Russell Senate Office Building
Washington, DC 20510, USA

Coonce, Ricky (Music Group, Musician)
Thomas Cassidy
11761 E Speedway Blvd
Tucson, AZ 85748, USA

Cooney, Gerry (Boxer)
370 North
Fanwood, NJ 07023, USA

Cooney, Joan Ganz (Educator, Misc, Television Host)
Children's TV Workshop
1 Lincoln Plaza
New York, NY 10023, USA

Cooney, Mark (Athlete, Football Player)
8005 Flower Ct
Arvada, CO 80005, USA

Coonts, Stephen (Writer)
116 W 14th St Apt 8S
New York, NY 10011-7315, USA

Coonts, Stephen (Writer)
40 Upland Rd
Colorado Springs, CO 80906

Cooooinger, Rocky (Athlete, Baseball Player)
7208 Alto Rev Ave
El Paso, TX 79912-2100

Cooper, Adrian (Athlete, Football Player)
3120 Saint Paul St
Denver, CO 80205-4840, USA

Cooper, Alexander (Architect)
Cooper Robertson & Partners
311 W 43rd St
New York, NY 10036, USA

Cooper, Alice (Musician, Songwriter)
4135 E Keim Dr
Paradise Valley, AZ 85253, USA

Cooper, Amy Levin (Editor)
60 Sutton Place S #16C
New York, NY 10022, USA

Cooper, Anderson (Correspondent, Journalist, Television Host)
84 W 3rd St
New York, NY 10012, USA

Cooper, Artis (Athlete, Basketball Player)
5013 Millstone Way
Granite Bay, CA 95746-6126, USA

Cooper, Ashley
194 Bellevue Ave.
Newport, RI 02840-3515

Cooper, Bert (Athlete, Football Player)
3152 Aldon Ave
Las Vegas, NV 89121-5610, USA

Cooper, Bill (Athlete, Football Player)
16056 Greenwood Rd
Monte Sereno, CA 95030-3018, USA

Cooper, Bonnie (Athlete, Baseball Player, Commentator)
PO Box 26 119 Sampson Street
Tremont, IL 61568-0026, USA

Cooper, Bradley (Actor)
733 Brooktree Rd
Pacific Palisades, CA 90272, USA

Cooper, Brian (Athlete, Baseball Player)
San Jose Giants
PO Box 21727
san jose, CA 95151-1727, USA

Cooper, Brian (Athlete, Baseball Player)
346 W Ada Ave
Glendora, CA 91741-4248, USA

Cooper, Camille (Basketball Player)
New York Liberty
Madison Square Garden
2 Penn Plaza
New York, NY 10121, USA

Cooper, Carl (Athlete, Golfer)
4823 Scenic Woods Trl
Kingwood, TX 77345-2323, USA

Cooper, Cathy (Stylist)
c/o Staff Member *Mercury Artists*
8460 Higuera St Fl 2
Culver City, CA 90232, USA

Cooper, Cecil (Athlete, Baseball Player)
7208 Alto Rev Ave
El Paso, TX 79912-2100, U S A

Cooper, Cecil (Athlete, Baseball Player)
24802 Boulder Lakes Ct
Katy, TX 77494-3900, USA

Cooper, Charles (Actor)
c/o Joel Kleinman *Baier/Kleinman International*
3575 Cahuenga Blvd W #500
Los Angeles, CA 90068, USA

Cooper, Charles (General)
3410 Barger Dr
Falls Church, VA 22044-1201, USA

Cooper, Charles G (General)
3410 Barger Dr
Falls Church, VA 22044, USA

Cooper, Chris (Actor)
19 Jones River Dr
Kingston, MA 02364, USA

Cooper, Christin (Athlete, Olympic Athlete, Skier)
1001 E Hyman Ave
Aspen, CO 81611-2612, USA

Cooper, Daniel Admiral (General)
Navy, Marine And Coast
Guard 6251 Old Dominion Dr# Op
Me Lean, VA 22101-4827, USA

Cooper, Daniel L (Admiral)
121 Leisure Court
Wyomissing, PA 19610, USA

Cooper, Darin (Actor)
c/o Marianne Golan *Marianne Golan Management*
6528 W. 6th St
Los Angeles, CA 90048-4716, USA

Cooper, Dave (Artist)
c/o Staff Member *Fantagraphics Books*
7563 Lake City Way
Seattle, WA 98115, USA

Cooper, Dominic (Actor)
c/o Joel Lubin *Creative Artists Agency (CAA-LA)*
2000 Ave Of The Stars
Los Angeles, CA 90067, USA

Cooper, Don (Athlete, Baseball Player)
2109 Willowmet Dr
Brentwood, TN 37027, USA

Cooper, Don (Athlete, Baseball Player)
2320 Arborfield Ln
Sarasota, FL 34235-1807, USA

Cooper, Duane (Athlete, Basketball Player)
13813 Ocana Avenue
Bellflower, CA 90706-2528, USA

Cooper, Earl (Athlete, Football Player)
2224 E Highway 21
Lincoln, TX 78948, USA

Cooper, Eric (Athlete, Baseball Player)
5404 Longview Ct
Unit 4
Johnston, IA 50131, USA

Cooper, Gary (Athlete, Baseball Player)
1136 Birch Cir
Alpine, UT 84004-1212, USA

Cooper, Gary (Baseball Player)
Atlanta Braves
402 E Victory Dr
Savannah, GA 31405-2254, USA

Cooper, George (Athlete, Football Player)
1230 Bowstring Rd
Monument, CO 80132-8599, USA

Cooper, Hal (Director)
2651 Hutton Dr
Beverly Hills, CA 90210, USA

Cooper, Imogen (Music Group, Musician)
Van Walsum Mgmt
4 Addison Bridge Place
London W14 8XP, UNITED KINGDOM(UK)

Cooper, Jeanne (Actor)
8401 Edwin Dr
Los Angeles, CA 90046, USA

Cooper, Jilly (Writer)
c/o Staff Member *Transworld Publishers*
20 Vauxhall Bridge Road
London SW1V 2SA, UK

Cooper, Jim (Congressman, Politician)
1536 Longworth HOB
Washington, DC 20515, USA

Cooper, Jim (Athlete, Football Player)
12910 Low Meadow Ct
Charlotte, NC 28277-4030, USA

Cooper, Joel D (Doctor)
Washington University
Medical School Surgery Dept
Saint Louis, MO 63110, USA

Cooper, John M (Misc)
182 Western Way
Princeton, NJ 08540, USA

Cooper, Lattie F (Educator)
Arizona State University
President's Office
Tempe, AZ 85287, USA

Cooper, Leon N (Nobel Prize Laureate)
49 Intervale Rd
Providence, RI 02906-4843, USA

Cooper, Lester I (Producer)
45 Morningside Dr S
Westport, CT 06880, USA

Cooper, Louis (Athlete, Football Player)
200 Gregg Ave
Marion, SC 29571, USA

Cooper, Marcus Ramone (Pleasure P) (Musician)
c/o Staff Member *Atlantic Records (NY)*
1290 Ave of the Americas
New York, NY 10104

Cooper, Marilyn (Actor)
Gage Group
315 W 57th St
#4H
New York, NY 10019, USA

Cooper, Mark S (Athlete, Football Player)
6598 S Telluride St
Aurora, CO 80016, USA

Cooper, Matthew T (General)
9326 Fairfax St
Alexandria, VA 22309, USA

Cooper, Minor J (Biologist)
1901 Austin Ave
Ann Arbor, MI 48104, USA

Cooper, Oliver (Actor)
c/o Matthew DelPiano *Creative Artists Agency (CAA-LA)*
2000 Ave Of The Stars
Los Angeles, CA 90067, USA

Cooper, Paula (Misc)
Paula Cooper Gallery
534 W 21st St
New York, NY 10011, USA

Cooper, Scott (Athlete, Baseball Player)
7 Fairways Cir
Apt F
Saint Charles, MO 63303-3353, USA

Cooper, Scott (Actor)
c/o Leland LaBarre *Bleu, An Entertainment Company*
5225 Wilshire Blvd
Suite 701
Los Angeles, CA 90036, USA

Cooper, Stephen (Business Person)
Enron Corp
1400 Smith St
Houston, TX 77002, USA

Cooper, Wayne (Athlete, Basketball Player)
5013 Millstone Way
Granite Bay, CA 95746-6126, USA

Cooper, Wayne (Artist)
P.O. Box 106
Depew, OK 74028-0106, USA

Cooper, Wima Lee (Musician)
c/o Staff Member *Charles Rapp Enterprises Inc*
88 Pine St
New York, NY 10005, USA

Cooperfield, David (Misc)
c/o Staci Wolfe *Polaris PR*
8135 W 4th St
2nd Floor
Los Angeles, CA 90048, USA

Cooperwheat, Lee (Designer, Fashion Designer)
Cooperwheat Blundell
14 Cheshire St
London E2 6EH, UNITED KINGDOM (UK)

Coors, William K (Business Person)
Adolph Coors Co
1221 Ford St
Golden, CO 80401, USA

Coover, Robert (Writer)
Brown University
Linden Press
49 George St
Providence, RI 02912, USA

Copa, Tom (Athlete, Basketball Player)
10068 Circleview Dr
Austin, TX 78733-6302, USA

Cope, Amber (Race Car Driver)
PO Box 44337
Tacoma, WA 98444, USA

Cope, Derrike (Race Car Driver)
CLR Racing
103 Turnerlair Ct.
Mooresville, NC 28117-5655, USA

Cope, Jonathan (Dancer)
Royal Ballet
Covent Garden
Bow St
London WC2E 9DD, UNITED KINGDOM (UK)

Cope, Julian (Musician, Songwriter, Writer)
International Talent Group
729 7th Ave
#1600
New York, NY 10019, USA

Cope, Kenneth
61-63 Kent House 87 Regent St.
London, ENGLAND W1R 7HF

Cope, Mike (Race Car Driver)
60th St. North
Clearwater, FL 34620, USA

Copeland, Adam (Edge) (Wrestler)
c/o Kerry Rodgerson *World Wrestling Entertainment (WWE)*
Titan Towers
1241 E Main St
Stamford, CT 06905-3857, USA

Copeland, Al (Business Person, Race Car Driver)
5001 Folse Dr
Metairie, LA 70006, USA

Copeland, Cyrus
c/o Daniel Strone *Trident Media Group LLC*
41 Madison Ave
36th Floor
New York, NY 10010, USA

Copeland, Danny (Athlete, Football Player)
186 Old Newton Rd
Pelham, GA 31779, USA

Copeland, Hollis (Athlete, Basketball Player)
257 Upland Avenue
Ewing, NJ 08638-2331, USA

Copeland, Horace (Athlete, Football Player)
4195 Blakemore Pl
Spring Hill, FL 34609, USA

Copeland, Joan (Actor)
88 Central Park West
New York, NY 10023, USA

Copeland, John (Athlete, Football Player)
4226 Maxwell Dr
Mason, OH 45040, USA

Copeland, Kenneth (Misc)
Kenneth Copeland Ministries
PO Box 2908
Fort Worth, TX 76113, USA

Copeland, Kristina (Actor)
Collingwood Management
1572 W 4th Ave 2nd Fl
Vancouver, BC V6J1L7, CANADA

Copeland, Lanard (Athlete, Basketball Player)
4115 Pierce Road
Atlanta, GA 30349-3648, USA

Copeland, Miles (Musician)
1830 N Sierra Bonita Ave
Los Angeles, CA 90046, USA

Copeland, Stewart (Composer, Musician)
2420 Arbutus Dr
Los Angeles, CA 90049, USA

Copeland Jr., Zane (Lil Zane) (Musician)
c/o Elayne Rivers *Toonzworld Management*
P.O. Box 759
New York, NY 10116, USA

Copley, Jeff E
687 State Hwy 194
Kimper, KY 41539, USA

Copley, Sharlto (Actor)
c/o Phillip d'Amecourt *WME (LA)*
9601 Wilshire Blvd Fl 3
Beverly Hills, CA 90210, USA

Copley, Teri (Actor, Model)
13351 Riverside Dr
#D513
Sherman Oaks, CA 91423, USA

Copon, Michael (Actor)
c/o Lena Roklin *Luber Roklin Management*
8530 Wilshire Blvd
6th Floor
Beverly Hills, CA 90211, USA

Copp, D Harold (Misc)
4755 Belmont Ave
Vancouver, BC V6T 1A8, CANADA

Copp, D Harold Dr (Scientist)
4755 Belmont Ave
Vancouver, BC V6T IAS, Canada

Coppenbarger, Ron (Athlete, Football Player)
7890 James Island Trl
Jacksonville, FL 32256, USA

Coppens, Gus (Athlete, Football Player)
2413 Deerpark Dr
Fullerton, CA 92835, USA

Coppens, Yves (Misc)
4 Rue du Pont-aux-Choux
Paris 75003, FRANCE

Copperfield, David (Magician)
111675 Glowing Sunset Ln
Las Vegas, NV 89135, USA

Copping, Allen A (Educator)
Louisiana State University System
President's Office
Baton Rouge, LA 70808, USA

Coppinger, Rocky (Athlete, Baseball Player)
7208 Alto Rey Ave
El Paso, TX 79912, USA

Coppo, Paul (Athlete, Hockey Player)
3458 Solitude Rd
De Pere, WI 54115, USA

Coppola, Alicia (Actor)
12109 Hillslope St
Studio City, CA 91604, USA

Coppola, Chris (Actor)
c/o Staff Member *IMG (LA)*
717 N Alta Vista Blvd
Los Angeles, CA 90046, USA

Coppola, Francis Ford (Director)
c/o Staff Member *American Zoetrope*
916 Kearny St
San Francisco, CA 94133, USA

Coppola, Roman (Director)
6740 Milner Rd
Los Angeles, CA 90068, USA

Coppola, Sofia (Actor, Director, Writer)
46 Morton St
New York, NY 10014, USA

Coppolla, Alicia (Actor)
c/o Jeff Witjas *Agency for the Performing Arts (APA-LA)*
405 S Beverly Dr
Suite 500
Beverly Hills, CA 90212-4425, USA

CopQO, Paul (Athlete, Hockey Player)
3458 Solitude Rd
De Pere, WI 54115-8617, USA

Coquillette, Trace (Athlete, Baseball Player)
5200 Mississippi Bar Dr
Orangevale, CA 95662-5717, USA

Cora, Alex (Athlete, Baseball Player)
F12 Calle 14
Caguas, PR 00727-6935, USA

Cora, Cat (Chef)
c/o Erika Martineau *Brooks Group*
15 W 37th St Fl 16
New York, NY 10008, USA

Cora, Joey (Athlete, Baseball Player)
17734 SW 47th St
Miramar, FL 33029-5050, USA

Cora, Joey (Athlete, Baseball Player)
Florida Marlins
2267 NW 199th St
Miami Gardens, FL 33056-2664, USA

Cora, Jose M (Joey) (Athlete, Baseball Player)
F12 Calle 14
Villa Nueva
Caguas, PR 00725, USA

Corabi, John (Musician)
c/o Staff Member *Union Entertainment Group*
1323 Newbury Rd
Suite 104
Thousand Oaks, CA 91320, USA

Coraci, Frank (Director)
9738 Arby Dr
Beverly Hills, CA 90210, USA

Coral, The (Music Group)
c/o Staff Member *Paradigm (Monterey)*
404 W Franklin St
Monterey, CA 93940, USA

Corazzini, Carl (Athlete, Hockey Player)
583 Winter St
Framingham, MA 01702-5634, USA

Corbet, Brady (Actor)
c/o Brian Young *Untitled Entertainment (LA)*
350 S. Beverly Dr #200
Beverly Hills, CA 90212, USA

Corbet, Rene (Athlete, Hockey Player)
68 Aspen Stone Way SW
Calgary, AB T3H OH5, Canada

Corbett, Doug (Athlete, Baseball Player)
75083 Edwards Rd
Yulee, FL 32097-2660, USA

Corbett, Gretchen (Actor)
6932 N Vincent Ave
Portland, OR 97217, USA

Corbett, Holly (Stylist)
c/o Staff Member *Bernstein & Andriulli*
58 W 40th St
New York, NY 10018, USA

Corbett, James (Athlete, Football Player)
2723 Marlo Way
Lakeside Park, KY 41017, USA

Corbett, John (Actor)
5323 Baseline Ave
Santa Ynez, CA 93460, USA

Corbett, Luke R (Business Person)
Kerr-McGee Corp
Kerr-McGee Center
Oklahoma City, OK 73125, USA

Corbett, Michael (Actor)
2665 Chart Place
Los Angeles, CA 90046, USA

Corbett, Mike (Athlete, Football Player)
P.O. Box 2809
Oakhurst, CA 93644-2809, USA

Corbett, Ronnie (Actor, Comedian)
International Artistes
235 Regent St
London W1R 8AX, UNITED KINGDOM (UK)

Corbett, Sherman (Athlete, Baseball Player)
7031 Washita Way
San Antonio, TX 78256-2310, USA

Corbett, Steve (Athlete, Football Player)
3 Wake Robin Rd
Sudbury, MA 01776, USA

Corbett, Tom (Governor, Politician)
Governor's Office
225 Main Capitol Building
Harrisburg, PA 17120, USA

Corbin, Archie (Athlete, Baseball Player)
7525 Tram Rd
Beaumont, TX 77713-8723, USA

Corbin, Barry (Actor)
2113 Greta Lane
Fort Worth, TX 76120, USA

Corbin, Ray (Athlete, Baseball Player)
65 Moore St
Franklin, NC 28734-9307, USA

Corbin, Tyrone (Athlete, Basketball Player)
652 Edgewood Dr
North Salt Lake, UT 84054-2640, USA

Corbin, Tyrone (Basketball Player)
New York Knicks
Madison Square Garden
2 Penn Plaza
New York, NY 10121, USA

Corbo, Vincent J (Business Person)
Hercules Inc
Hercules Plaza
1313 N Market St
Wilmington, DE 19894, USA

Corbucci, Bruno
via dei Colli della Farnesia 144
Rome, ITALY

Corbus, William (Athlete, Football Player)
1100 Union St
Apt 1100
San Francisco, CA 94109, USA

Corchiani, Chris (Athlete, Basketball Player)
1106 Harvey Street
Raleigh, NC 27608-2205, USA

Corcoran, Barbara (Business Person)
226 W 26th St 8th Fl
New York, NY 10001, USA

Corcoran, Donna (Actor)
22408 Canaina Ct
Chatsworth, CA 91311, USA

Corcoran, Kevin (Actor)
8617 Balcom Ave
Northridge, CA 91325, USA

Corcoran, Norm (Athlete, Hockey Player)
20 Nickerson Ave
St Catharines, ON L2N 3M4, Canada

Corcoran, Roy (Athlete, Baseball Player)
PO Box 173
Slaughter, LA 70777-0173, USA

Corcoran, Tim (Athlete, Baseball Player)
4349 Friar Cir
La Verne, CA 91750-2718, USA

Corcoran, Tim (Athlete, Baseball Player)
PO Box 173
Slaughter, LA 70777-0173, USA

Cord, Alex (Actor)
c/o Staff Member *Coast to Coast Talent Group*
3350 Barham Blvd
Los Angeles, CA 90068, USA

Cordalis, Costa
Rippoldsauer Str. 32
Freudenstadt, GERMANY D-72250

Corday, Barbara (Business Person)
2011 Cummings Dr
Los Angeles, CA 90027, USA

Corday, Mara (Actor)
25932 Mendoza Dr
Valencia, CA 91355, USA

Corddry, Nate (Actor)
c/o Jill McGrath *The Group Entertainment*
275 Seventh Ave
26th Floor
New York, NY 10001, USA

Corddry, Rob (Actor)
3813 Evans St
Los Angeles, CA 90027, USA

Corder, Roger (Inventor)
Queen Mary Medical School
Turner St
London E1 2AD, UNITED KINGDOM
(UK)

Cordero, Angel (Horse Racer)
4 Osborne Ln
Greenvale, NY 11548-1141, USA

Cordero, Angelo
PO Box 90
Jamaica, NY 11411

Cordero, Angel T Jr (Jockey)
New York Racing Assn
PO Box 170090
Ozone Park, NY 11417, USA

Cordero, Chad (Athlete, Baseball Player)
2825 Live Oak Ave
Fullerton, CA 92835-2237, USA

Cordero, Francisco (Athlete, Baseball Player)
4125 Oak Tree Ct
Loveland, OH 45140-1077, USA

Cordero, Joaquin (Actor)
c/o Staff Member *Televisa*
Blvd Adolfo Lopez Mateos 232
Colonia San Angel INN
DF CP 01060, MEXICO

Cordero, Wilfredo N (Wil) (Baseball Player)
Montreal Expos
25844 Kensington Dr
Westlake, OH 44145-1472, USA

Cordes-Elliott, Gloria (Athlete, Baseball Player, Commentator)
86 Malone Ave
Staten Island, NY 10306-4110, USA

Cordes-Elliott, Gloria (Baseball Player)
86 Malone Ave
Staten Island, NY 10306-4110, USA

Cordileone, Lou (Athlete, Football Player)
5312 Mark Ct
Agoura Hills, CA 91301, USA

Cordova, France (Scientist)
University Of California-Riverside
900 Aver Un Attn
Riverside, CA 92521-0001, USA

Cordova, Francisco (Athlete, Baseball Player)
c/o Staff Member *San Diego Padres*
100 Park Blvd
San Diego, CA 92101, USA

Cordova, Jorge (Athlete, Football Player)
10800 Scripps Ranch Blvd #108
San Diego, CA 92131-6012, USA

Cordova, Marty (Athlete, Baseball Player)
47 Club Vista Dr
Henderson, NV 89052-0804, USA

Cordovez, Zegers Diego (Educator, Government Official)
Foreign Affairs Ministry
Avda 10 Agosta y Carrion
Quito, ECUADOR

Corduner, Allan (Actor)
c/o Staff Member *Conway van Gelder*
8-12 Broadwick St
London W1F 8HW, UK

Corea, Chick (Composer, Musician)
Chick Corea Productions
10400 Samoa Ave
Tujunga, CA 91042, USA

Corella, Angel
890 Broadway
New York, NY 10003-1218

Corev, Brvan (Athlete, Baseball Player)
7829 E Riverdale Cir
Mesa, AZ 85207-0804, USA

Corey, Bryan (Athlete, Baseball Player)
7829 E Riverdale Cir
Mesa, AZ 85207-0804, USA

Corey, Elias J (Nobel Prize Laureate)
20 Avon Hill St
Cambridge, MA 02140-3608, USA

Corey, Irwin (Professor) (Actor, Comedian)
c/o Richard Corey *Worlds Foremost Management*
165 W 21 Street
New York, NY 10011, USA

Corey, Jill (Musician)
64 Division Ave
Lavittown, NY 11756, USA

Corey, Mark (Athlete, Baseball Player)
9321 Cornell Cir
Littleton, CO 80130-4143, USA

Corey, Mark (Athlete, Baseball Player)
P.O. Box 113
Austin, PA 16720-0113, USA

Corey, Walt (Athlete, Football Player)
26007 Timber Meadows Dr
Lees Summit, MO 64086, USA

Corgan, Billy (Musician, Songwriter)
1249 Sheridan Rd
Highland Park, IL 60035, USA

Cori, Carl T (Business Person)
Sigma-Aldrich Corp
3050 Spruce St
Saint Louis, MO 63103, USA

Cori, Yarckin (Musician)
GreeneHouse Management, Inc
PO Box 151234
Altamonte Springs, FL 32715-1234, USA

Corigliano, John P (Composer)
365 W End Ave
New York, NY 10024, USA

Corker, Bob (Senator)
Dirksen Senate Office Building SD-185
Washington, DC 20510, USA

Corker, John (Athlete, Football Player)
825 Martin Luther King Jr Blvd
Baltimore, MD 21201, USA

Corkins, Mike (Athlete, Baseball Player)
3760 Chemehuevi Blvd
Lake Havasu City, AZ 80130-4143, USA

Corkum, Bob (Athlete, Hockey Player)
165 Scotland Rd
Newbury, MA 01951, USA

Corley, Al (Actor)
Code Entertainment
9229 Sunset Blvd #615
Los Angeles, CA 90069, USA

Corley, Annie (Actor)
c/o Renee Jennett *Renee Jennett Management*
5757 Wilshire Blvd #473
Los Angeles, CA 90036, USA

Corley, Anthony (Athlete, Football Player)
7465 Rodin Ct
Sun Valley, NV 89433, USA

Corley, Kathy (Stylist)
4705 Hazelwood Circle
Nashville, TN 37220, USA

Corley, Ray (Athlete, Basketball Player)
590 Elwood Road
East Northport, NY 11731-5629, USA

Corley, W Gene (Engineer)
Construction Tech Labs
5400 Old Orchard Road
Skokie, IL 60077-1030, USA

Corman, Avery (Writer)
International Creative Mgmt
40 W 57th St
#1800
New York, NY 10019, USA

Corman, Roger (Actor, Director, Producer)
2501 La Mesa Dr
Santa Monica, CA 90402, USA

Cormier, Joe (Athlete, Football Player)
9110 La Salle Ave
Los Angeles, CA 90047, USA

Cormier, Lance (Athlete, Baseball Player)
3630 Windv Rdg
Tuscaloosa, AL 35406-3671, USA

Cormier, Rheal (Athlete, Baseball Player)
2640 Cody Cir
Park City, UT 84098-6281, USA

Corn, Laura (Writer)
c/o Staff Member *Literary Group International*
14 Penn Plaza
Suite 925
New York, NY 10122, USA

Corneille (Artist)
Society of Independent Artists
Cours la Reine
Paris 75008, FRANCE

Corneisen, Rufus (Religious Leader)
415 S Chester Road
Swarthmore, PA 19081, USA

Cornejo, Mardie (Athlete, Baseball Player)
321 E 3rd St
Wellington, KS 67152-2706, USA

Cornejo, Nate (Athlete, Baseball Player)
1600 N B St
Wellington, KS 67152-4405, USA

Cornelison, Jerry (Athlete, Football Player)
12713 Cedar St
Leawood, KS 66209, USA

Cornelius, Charles (Athlete, Football Player)
8865 Okeechobee Blvd
Apt 306
West Palm Beach, FL 33411, USA

Cornelius, Helen (Musician, Songwriter, Writer)
PO Box 121089
Nashville, TN 37212, USA

Cornelius, James (Business Person)
Guidant Corp
111 Monument Circle
Indianapolis, IN 46204, USA

Cornelius, Jemalle (Athlete, Football Player)
c/o Chad Speck *Allegiant Athletic Agency*
35 Market Sq
Suite 201
Knoxville, TN 37902, USA

Cornelius, Kathy (Athlete, Golfer)
5744 W Del Rio St
Chandler, AZ 85226, USA

Cornelius, Reid (Athlete, Baseball Player)
10117 Hunt Club Ln
Palm Beach Gardens, FL 33418-4568, USA

Cornell, Chris (Musician)
2791 Ellison Dr
Beverly Hills, CA 90210, USA

Cornell, Eric A (Nobel Prize Laureate)
University of Colorado
University Of Colorado Campus# 440
Boulder, CO 80309-0001, USA

Cornell, Harry M Jr (Business Person)
leggett & Platt Inc
1 Leggett Road
Carthage, MO 64836, USA

Cornell, Jeff (Athlete, Baseball Player)
1644 SW Jeffrey Cir
Lees Summit, MO 64081-4115, USA

Cornell, Lydia (Actor)
269 S Beverly Dr
Beverly Hills, CA 90212, USA

Cornell, Robert (Bo) (Athlete, Football Player)
2605 239th Ave SE
Sammamish, WA 98075, USA

Cornett, Betty Jane (Athlete, Baseball Player)
99 Corbett Court
Apt 410
Pittsburgh, PA 15237-3030, USA

Cornett, Brad (Athlete, Baseball Player)
1704 N Avenue I
Lamesa, TX 79331-3140, USA

Cornett, Leanza (Actor)
c/o Staff Member *WME (LA)*
9601 Wilshire Blvd Fl 3
Beverly Hills, CA 90210, USA

Cornfeld, Stuart (Producer)
1543 Marmont Ave
West Hollywood, CA 90069, USA

Cornforth, John W (Nobel Prize Laureate)
Saxon Down, Cuilfail Lewes
East Sussex, England BN7 2BE, UK

Cornforth, Mark (Athlete, Hockey Player)
11 Indian Spring Rd
Milton, MA 02186, USA

Cornish, Abbie (Actor)
c/o Hylda Queally *Creative Artists Agency (CAA-LA)*
2000 Ave Of The Stars
Los Angeles, CA 90067, USA

Cornish, Frank (Athlete, Football Player)
406 20th St
Apt 29
Gretna, LA 70053, USA

Cornish, Nick (Actor)
c/o Robert Stein *Robert Stein Management*
PO Box 3797
Beverly Hills, CA 90212, USA

Cornthwaite, Robert (Actor)
23388 Mulholland Dr
#12
Woodland Hills, CA 91364, USA

Cornutt, Terry (Athlete, Baseball Player)
179 W Hazel St
Roseburg, OR 97471-2211, USA

Cornwell, Fred (Athlete, Football Player)
2107 Windward Ln
Newport Beach, CA 92660, USA

Cornwell, Johnny (Musician)
Overland Productions
156 W 56th St
#500
New York, NY 10019, USA

Cornwell, Patricia (Actor, Producer, Writer)
c/o Staff Member *Simon & Schuster*
1230 Avenue of the Americas
New York, NY 10020, USA

Cornyn, John (Politician)
1348 S Carolina Ave SE
Washington, DC 20003-2371, USA

Cornyn, John (Senator)
517 Hart Senate Office Bldg.
Washington, DC 20510, USA

Corolla, Adam (Actor, Producer, Writer)
c/o Staff Member *Dixon Talent Agency*
375 Greenwich St
5th Floor
New York, NY 10013, USA

Corona, Catherine (Stylist)
c/o Staff Member *Maximum Talent*
1873 S Bellaire St
Suite 915
Denver, CO 80222-4356, USA

Coronado, Bob (Athlete, Football Player)
1539 Sereno Dr
Vallejo, CA 94589, USA

Corone, Antoni (Actor)
c/o Bonni Allen *Allen - O'leary*
1138 Twelfth St.
Suite 1
Santa Monica, CA 90403, USA

Coronel, Felipe (Immortal Technique) (Musician)
c/o Staff Member *Viper Records*
230 Mott St
New York, NY 10012, USA

Corr, Andrea (Musician)
c/o Staff Member *Luber Roklin Management*
8530 Wilshire Blvd
6th Floor
Beverly Hills, CA 90211, USA

Corr, Caroline (Music Group)
John Hughes
6 Martello Terr Sandycove
Dunlaoughaire
Dublin, IRELAND

Corr, Edwin G (Diplomat)
1617 Jenkins Ave
Norman, OK 73072, USA

Corr, Jim (Music Group)
John Hughes
6 Martello Terr Sandycove
Dunlaoughaire
Dublin, IRELAND

Corr, Ryan (Actor)
c/o Staff Member *Nickelodeon UK*
PO Box 6425
LONDON W1A 6UR, UNITED KINGDOM

Corr, Sharon (Music Group, Musician)
c/o Staff Member *Solo Agency Ltd (UK)*
55 Fulham High St
2nd Floor
London SW6 3JJ, United Kingdom

Corrado, Fred (Business Person)
Great A & P Tea Co
2 Paragon Dr
Montvale, NJ 07645, USA

Corrado, Gabriel (Actor)
c/o Staff Member *Telefe - Argentina*
Pavon 2444 (C1248AAT)
Buenos Aires, ARGENTINA

Corral, Frank (Athlete, Football Player)
Riverside Municipal Building
3900 Main St
Attn Graffiti Control Coordinator
Riverside, CA 92522, USA

Corrales, Pat (Athlete, Baseball Player, Coach)
2 W Wesley Rd NW Aot 18
Atlanta, GA 30305-3500, USA

Correa, Charles M (Architect)
Sonmarg Napean Sea Road
Bombay 40006, INDIA

Correa, Ed (Athlete, Baseball Player)
A2 Calle Milagros Cabezas
Urb Carolina Alta
Carolina, PR 00987-7101, USA

Correal, Charles (Athlete, Football Player)
110 Springbrooke Dr
Venetia, PA 15367, USA

Correale, Pete (Musician)
c/o Staff Member *Monterey International (Chicago)*
200 W Superior
Suite 202
Chicago, IL 60610, USA

Correia, Kevin (Athlete, Baseball Player)
San Francisco Giants
1200 Crestview Dr
Cardiff B'l The Sea, CA 92007-1400, USA

Correia, Rod (Athlete, Baseball Player)
82 Perrwille Rd
Rehoboth, MA 02769-1808, USA

Correll, Alston D (Pete) (Business Person)
Georgia-Pacific Corp
133 Peachtree St NE
Atlanta, GA 30303, USA

Correll, Vic (Athlete, Baseball Player)
119 Kentucky Downs
Perry, GA 31069-8514, USA

Corrente, Michael (Actor, Director, Producer)
c/o David Greenblatt *Greenlit*
1800 N Highland Ave
Suite 500
Los Angeles, CA 90028, USA

Correnti, John D (Business Person)
Nucor Corp
2100 Rexford Road
Charlotte, NC 28211, USA

Corretja, Alex (Tennis Player)
Assn of Tennis Professionals
200 Tournament Road
Ponte Vedra Beach, FL 32082, USA

Corri, Andrienne (Actor)
c/o Staff Member *Rolf Kruger Management*
205 Chudleigh R
London SE4 1EG, UNITED KINGDOM (UK)

Corridon-Mortell, Marie (Swimmer)
13 Heritage Village #A
Southbury, CT 06488, USA

Corrie, Emily (Actor)
c/o Kathryn Fleming *The Rights House (UK)*
Drury House
34-43 Russell St
London WC2B 5HA, UK

Corrigal, Jim (Athlete, Football Player)
560 Deerwood Dr
Tallmadge, OH 44278-2008, USA

Corrigan, E Gerald (Financier, Government Official)
Goldman Sanchs Co
85 Broad St
New York, NY 10004, USA

Corrigan, Kevin (Actor)
220 W. Broadway #310
New York, NY 10013, USA

Corrigan, Mike (Athlete, Hockey Player)
21 Birchwood Rd
Enfield, CT 06082, USA

Corrigan, Patrick (Cartoonist, Editor)
Toronto Star
Editorial Dept 1 Yonge St
Toronto, ON M5E 1E5, CANADA

Corrigan, Robert A (Educator)
San Fransisco State University
President's Office
San Fransisco, CA 94123, USA

Corrigan, Wilfred J (Business Person)
LSI Logic
1621 Barber Lane
Milpitas, CA 95035, USA

Corrigan-Maguire, Mairead (Nobel Prize Laureate)
Peace People
Peace People Community_
224 Lisburn Road
Belfast BT9 6GE, NORTHERN IRELAND

Corrinet, Chris
25 Overland Rd
Greenfield, MA 01301-1127, USA

Corrington, Kip (Athlete, Football Player)
6407 Olympic Ct
Greensboro, NC 27410, USA

Corripio Ahumada, Ernesto Cardinal (Religious Leader)
Apotinar Nieto 40 Col Tetlameyer
Mexico City 04730, MEXICO

Corriveau, Yvon (Athlete, Hockey Player)
396 Willard Ave
Apt A2
Newington, CT 06111, USA

Corrock-Luby, Susan (Athlete, Olympic Athlete, Skier)
3809 S Geiger Blvd
Apt 603
Spokane, WA 9922, USA

Corroface, Georges
1 rue Guenegaud
Paris, FRANCE F-75006

Corry, Megan (Actor)
c/o Staff Member *Mary Anne Claro Talent Agency*
1513 W Passyunk Ave
Philadelphia, PA 19145, USA

Corsaro, Frank A (Director)
33 Riverside Dr
New York, NY 10023, USA

Corsi, Jim (Athlete, Baseball Player)
48 Eastview Rd
Hookinton, MA 01748-1853, USA

Corsi, Jim (Athlete, Hockey Player)
785 Rue Maugue
L'lle-Bizard, QC H9C 2T7, Canada

Corsi, Richard (Race Car Driver)
Cormac Motorsports
7954 S. Castle Bay St.
Tucson, AZ 85747, USA

Corso, John A (Cinematographer)
241 W 13th St #21
New York, NY 10011, USA

Corson, Keith D (Business Person)
Coachmen Industries
P O Box 3300
Elkhart, IN 46515, USA

Corson, Shayne (Athlete, Hockey Player)
Tappo Restaurant and Wine Bar
55 Mill St
Bldg 3
Toronto, ON N5A 3C4, Canada

Cort, Barry (Athlete, Baseball Player)
1812 E Okaloosa Ave
Tampa, FL 33604-2032, USA

Cort, Bud (Actor)
c/o Staff Member *Don Buchwald & Associates Inc (NY)*
10 E 44th St
New York, NY 10017

Cortazar, Esteban (Designer, Fashion Designer)
Esteban Cortazar Inc
11 1 NE 1st St
9th Fl
Miami, FL 33132, USA

Cortes, Ron (Journalist)
Philadelphia Inquirer
Editorial Dept 400 N Broad St
Philadelphia, PA 19130, USA

Cortese, Dan (Actor)
28873 Via Venezia
Malibu, CA 90265, USA

Cortese, Genevieve (Actor)
c/o Joanna (Joanie) Burstein *Burstein Company, The*
15304 Sunset Blvd
suite 208
Pacific Palisades, CA 90272, USA

Cortese, Joe (Actor)
100 S Hayworth Ave
Apt 201
Los Angeles, CA 90048-3658, USA

Cortese, Valentina (Actor)
Pretta S Erasmo 6
Milan 20121, ITALY

Cortez, Alfonso (Actor)
CunninghamEscottDipene
10635 Santa Monica Blvd #130
Los Angeles, CA 90025, USA

Corti, Jesse (Voice Over Artist)
5250 Vista Lejana Ln
La Canada Flintridge, CA 91011, USA

Cortina, George (Stylist)
c/o Celebrity Stylists *Lighthouse Artists Management*
110 Greene St
#1102
New York, NY 10012, USA

Cortright, Edgar M Jr (Astronaut, Engineer, Misc)
9701 Calvin St
Northbridge, CA 91324, USA

Corver, Clayton (Athlete, Football Player)
1401 8th St SE
Orange City, IA 51041-7463

Corvino, Anthony (Athlete, Football Player)
P.O. Box 57
North Haven, CT 06473, USA

Corvo (Musician)
c/o Staff Member *Sony Music Miami*
605 Lincoln Rd Fl 7
Miami Beach, FL 33139, USA

Corvo, Joe (Athlete, Hockey Player)
943 Wenonan
Oak Park, IL 60304, USA

Corwin, Jeff (Actor)
c/o Staff Member *WmE2 (WMA-LA)*
1 William Morris Pl
Beverly Hills, CA 90212, USA

Corwin, Lola (Reality TV Star)
c/o Cindy Osbrink *Osbrink Talent Agency*
4343 Lankershim Blvd
Suite 100
Universal City, CA 91602, USA

Corwin, Sinead (Stylist)
c/o Staff Member *Sydney Represents*
280 Mott St
New York, NY 10012, USA

Coryatt, Quentin J (Athlete, Football Player)
611 Cannon Ln
Sugar Land, TX 77479, USA

Coryell, Larry (Music Group, Musician)
Tedd Kurland
173 Brighton Ave
Boston, MA 02134, USA

Corzine, Dave (Athlete, Basketball Player)
1161 West Hunting Drive
Palatine, IL 60067-6673, USA

Corzine, Jon (Politician)
PO Box 1276
Hoboken, NJ 07030-1276, USA

Corzine, Lester (Athlete, Football Player)
38423 Nasturtium Way
Palm Desert, CA 92211-5075, USA

Cosbie, Doug (Athlete, Football Player)
4241 Val Verde Rd
Loomis, CA 95650-9474, USA

Cosby, Bill (Actor, Comedian)
P.O. Box 808
Greenfield, MA 01301, USA

Cosby, Rita (Television Host)

Coscarelli, Don (Director, Producer, Writer)
c/o Staff Member *Starway International*
12021 Wilshire Blvd #661
Los Angeles, CA 90025, USA

Coscina, Dennis (Athlete, Golfer)
211 Main St
East Windsor, CT 06088-9518, USA

Cose, Ellis (Activist)
Harper Collins Publisher
10 E 53rd St
New York, NY 10022, USA

Cosentino, Frank (Athlete, Football Player)
PO Box 316
Eganville, ON K0J 1T0, Canada

Cosey, Ray (Athlete, Baseball Player)
139 Byxbee St
San Francisco, CA 94132-2602, USA

Cosgrave, Liam (Prime Minister)
Beachperk Templeogue County
Dublin, IRELAND

Cosgrove, Daniel (Actor)
c/o Staff Member *James/Levy/Jacobson Management Inc*
3500 W Olive Ave
Suite 1470
Burbank, CA 91505, USA

Cosgrove, Mike (Athlete, Baseball Player)
8813 W Corrine Dr
Peoria, AZ 85381-8166, USA

Cosgrove, Miranda (Actor)
c/o Jillian Fowkes *ID Public Relations (ID-LA)*
7060 Hollywood Blvd
8th Floor
Los Angeles, CA 90028, USA

Cosic, Dobrica (President)
Sciences/Arts Academy
Knez Mikallove 35
Belgrade, SERBIA-MONTENEGRO

Cosiga, Fransesco (President)
Palazzo Giustiniani
Via Della Dogana Vecchia 29
Rome 00186, ITALY

Coslet, Bruce N (Athlete, Coach, Football Coach, Football Player)
1778 Ivy Pointe Ct
Naples, FL 34109, USA

Cosman, Jim (Athlete, Baseball Player)
299 Northgate Trce
Roswell, GA 30075-2329, USA

Cosmovici, Cristiano B (Astronaut)
Istituto Fisica Spazio Interplanetario
CP 27
Frascati 00044, ITALY

Cosner, Don (Athlete, Football Player)
141 NW Carter Farms Ct
Bremerton, WA 98310, USA

Cosper, Kina (Music Group)
Green Light Talent Agency
P O Box 3172
Beverly Hills, CA 90212, USA

Cosso, Pierre
13 rue Madeleine Michelis
Neuilly, FRANCE 92200

Cossotto, Fiorenza (Opera Singer)
IUMA
Via E Filiberto 125
Rome 00185, ITALY

Costa, David J (Dave) (Athlete, Football Player)
40 Halili Ln
Apt 4M
Kihei, HI 96753, USA

Costa, Don
7920 Sunset Blvd. #300
Los Angeles, CA 90069

Costa, Gal (Music Group)
Bridge Agency
35 Clark St #A5
Brooklyn Heights, NY 11201, USA

Costa, Jim (Congressman, Politician)
1314 Longworth HOB
Washington, DC 20515, USA

Costa, Mary (Musician, Opera Singer)
3340 Kingston Pike #1
Knoxville, TN 37919, USA

Costa, Nikka (Musician)
14313 Greenleaf St
Sherman Oaks, CA 91423, USA

Costa, Paul (Athlete, Football Player)
8017 Kristina Ln
North Richland Hills, TX 76180, USA

Costa, Shane (Athlete, Baseball Player)
127 E Arlen Ave
Visalia, CA 93277-7691, USA

Costabile, David (Actor)
c/o Craig Gartner *Gartner/Green Entertainment*
5225 Wilshite Blvd #1200
Los Angeles, CA 90036, USA

Costa-Gavras (Director, Producer, Writer)
c/o Bertrand de Labbey *ArtMedia*
20 avenue Rapp
Paris 75008, France

Costanza, John (Race Car Driver)
Demand Flow Racing
6625 S. Galena St.
Englewood, CO 80112, USA

Costanzo, Paulo (Actor)
United Talent Agency
9560 Wilshire Blvd #500
Beverly Hills, CA 90212, USA

Costanzo, Robert (Actor)
832 Masselin Ave
Los Angeles, CA 90036, USA

Costas, Bob (Commentator)
16380 Paddock Ln
Weston, FL 33326, USA

Costas, Carlos
Entenze 332-334 Atico 2a
Barcelona, SPAIN E-08029

Coste, Chris (Athlete, Baseball Player)
3774 Polk St S
Fargo, ND 58104-7595, USA

Costello, Brad (Athlete, Football Player)
9 Stout Rd
Princeton, NJ 08540, USA

Costello, Elvis (Musician, Songwriter)
c/o Rebecca Shapiro *Shore Fire Media*
32 Court St
16th Floor
Brooklyn, NY 11201, USA

Costello, John (Athlete, Baseball Player)
16614 Willow Glen Dr
Grover, MO 63040-1750, USA

Costello, Mariclare (Actor)
Borinstein Oreck Bogart
3172 Dona Susana Dr
Studio City, CA 91604, USA

Costello, Mark (Writer)
Fordham Univesity
Law School
New York, NY 10458, USA

Costello, Murray (Athlete, Hockey Player)
105 Kenilworth St
Ottawa, ON K1Y 3Y8, Canada

Costello, Patty (Bowler)
715 S Crystal Lake Dr
Orlando, FL 32803-6906, USA

Costello, Rich (Athlete, Hockey Player)
242 Monarch Bay Dr
Dana Point, CA 92629, USA

Costello, Sean (Actor, Producer)
c/o Staff Member *Concerted Efforts*
P.O. Box 440326
Somerville, MA 02144, USA

Costello, Sue (Actor)
United Talent Agency
9560 Wilshire Blvd #500
Beverly Hills, CA 90212, USA

Costello, Thomas (Tom) (Athlete, Football Player)
P.O. Box 299
Rocky Point, NY 11778, USA

Costello, Vince (Athlete, Football Player)
12300 Perry St
Overland Park, KS 66213, USA

Costelloe, Paul (Designer, Fashion Designer)
Moygashel Mills
Dungannon BT71 7PB, NORTHERN IRELAND

Coster, Nicolas (Actor)
c/o Staff Member *Momentum Talent and Literary Agency*
9401 Wilshire Blvd
Suite 501
Beverly Hills, CA 90212, USA

Coster, Ritchie (Actor)
c/o Glenn Daniels *Glenn Daniels Arts Management*
56 Warren St #5E
New York, NY 10007, USA

Coster Waldau, Nikolaj (Actor)
c/o Jill Littman *Impression Entertainment*
9229 W Sunset Blvd #700
West Hollywood, CA 90069, USA

Costin, Simon (Stylist)
c/o Staff Member *Camilla Lowther Managment (CLM Represents)*
30-32 Ericsson Pl
New York, NY 10013, USA

Costle, Douglas M (Educator, Government Official)
Harvard University
Public Health School
Cambridge, MA 02138, USA

Costner, Kevin (Actor, Director)
3270 Beach Club Rd
Carpinteria, CA 93013, USA

Costo, Tim (Athlete, Baseball Player)
3107 Pintail Ln
Signal Mountain, TN 37377-1439, USA

Cota, Chad (Athlete, Football Player)
216 Island Pointe Dr
Medford, OR 97504, USA

Cota, Humberto (Baseball Player)
c/o Staff Member *Pittsburgh Pirates*
PNC Park
115 Federal Street
Pittsburgh, PA 15212, USA

Cotchery, Jerricho (Athlete, Football Player)
79 Carriage Ln
Plainview, NY 11803, USA

Cotchett, Joseph W (Attorney, Attorney General, General)
840 Malcolm Road
Burlingame, CA 94010, USA

Cote, Alain (Athlete, Hockey Player)
1352 Rue Gabrielle-Roy
Quebec, QC G1Y 3K3, Canada

Cote, David (Business Person)
TRW Inc
1900 Richmond Road
Cleveland, OH 44124, USA

Cote, Del (Horse Racer)
292 Route 539
Cream Ridge, NJ 08514-1516, USA

Cote, Ray (Athlete, Hockey Player)
5802 E Leland St
Mesa, AZ 85215-2716, CANADA

Cote, Riley (Athlete, Hockey Player)
1485 Kearsley Rd
Sicklerville, NJ 08081-5215, USA

Cote, Sylvain (Athlete, Hockey Player)
1432 Wild Cranberry Ct
Crownsville, MD 21032-2039, USA

Cotham, Frank (Cartoonist)
7763 Sunny Trail Dr
Memphis, TN 38135-0418, USA

Cothran, Jeff (Athlete, Football Player)
5671 Oakview Ter
Liberty Township, OH 45011, USA

Cothren, Paige (Athlete, Football Player)
1332 Highway 15 S
Woodland, MS 39776, USA

Cotillard, Marion (Actor)
c/o Mara Buxbaum *ID PR (LA)*
7060 Hollywood Blvd
8th Floor
Los Angeles, CA 90028, USA

Cotler, Kami (Actor)
7425 Arizona Ave
Los Angeles, CA 90045, USA

Cotlow, Lewis N (Misc)
132 Lakeshore Dr
North Palm Beach, FL 33408, USA

Cotney, Mark (Athlete, Football Player)
4809 Cheval Blvd
Lutz, FL 33558, USA

Cotorna, D (Actor)
c/o Jeff Golenberg *Collective*
8383 Wilshire Blvd
Suite 1050
Beverly Hills, CA 90211, USA

Cotrona, DJ (Actor)
c/o Aron Giannini *Collective*
8383 Wilshire Blvd
Suite 1050
Beverly Hills, CA 90211, USA

Cotroneo, Vince (Commentator)
4455 E Palmdale Ln
Gilbert, AZ 85298-4024, USA

Cotrubas, Ileana (Opera Singer)
Royal Opera House
Convent Garden Bow St
London WC2, UNITED KINGDOM(UK)

Cottee, Kay (Yachtsman)
Showcase Productions
113 Willoughby Road
Crows Nest, NSW 2065, AUSTRALIA

Cotten, Carole (Stylist)
c/o Staff Member *Zenobia Agency Inc*
PO Box 909
Groveland, CA 95321, USA

Cotterill, Harriet (Stylist)
c/o Staff Member *ESP (London)*
63 Charlotte St.
1st Floor
London W11 4PG, UK

Cottet, Mia (Actor)
c/o David Sweeney *Sweeney Management*
6253 Hollywood Blvd
Suite 201
Los Angeles, CA 90028, USA

Cotti, Flavio (President)
Christian Democratic Party
Klaraweg 6
Bem 3001, SWITZERLAND

Cottier, Chuck (Athlete, Baseball Player, Coach)
7129 Lake Ballinger Way
Edmonds, WA 98026-8545, USA

Cottier, George Cardinal (Religious Leader)
Convento Santa Sabina
Piazza Pierro d'Illiria
Rome 00193, ITALY

Cottingham, Robert (Artist)
P O Box 604 Blackman Road
Newtown, CT 06470, USA

Cottle, Tameka (Tiny) (Musician)
Major P Productions LLC
325 Edgewood Ave SE
Atlanta, GA 30312, USA

Cotto, Delilah (Actor)
c/o Ivan De Paz *DePaz Management*
2011 N Vermont Ave.
Los Angeles, CA 90027, USA

Cotto, Henry (Athlete, Baseball Player)
1141 W Thomas Rd
Phoenix, AZ 85013-4206, USA

Cotto, Miguel (Athlete, Boxer)
c/o Staff Member *Top Rank Inc.*
3908 Howard Hughes Pkwy
#580
Las Vegas, NV 89109, USA

Cotton, Barney (Athlete, Football Player)
2402 Sundown Dr
Ames, IA 50014, USA

Cotton, Blaine (Actor)
Jack Scagnetti Talent
5118 Vineland Ave #102
North Hollywood, CA 91601, USA

Cotton, Craig (Athlete, Football Player)
5617 Moraga Ct
Bakersfield, CA 93308, USA

Cotton, Fearne (Actor)
c/o Staff Member *Rabbit Vocal Management*
27 Poland St
3rd Floor
London W1F 8QW, UK

Cotton, Frank A (Misc)
Twaycliffe Ranch RR 2 Box 230
Bryan, TX 77808, USA

Cotton, James (Musician)
James Cotton Mgmt
235 W Eugene St #G 10
Chicago, IL 60614, USA

Cotton, John (Athlete, Basketball Player)
11426 Country Road 4 South
Alamosa, CO 81101-9630, USA

Cotton, Joseph F (Misc)
20 Linda Vista Ave
Atherton, CA 94027, USA

cotton, Joseph FCol (Aviator)
20 Linda Vista Ave
Atherton, CA 94027-5429, USA

Cotton, Josie (Music Group)
2794 Hume Road
Malibu, CA 90265, USA

Cotton, Marcus (Athlete, Football Player)
484 Lake Park Ave
Apt 280
Oakland, CA 94610, USA

Cotton, Maxwell Perry (Actor)
c/o Matt Fletcher *Greene & Associates*
1901 Avenue Of The Stars Ste 130
Los Angeles, CA 90067, USA

Cotton, Robin (Doctor)
20271 Goldenrod Lane #120
Germantown, MD 20876-4964, USA

Cottrell, Dana (Athlete, Football Player)
1 Driftwood Ln
North Billerica, MA 01862, USA

Cottrell, Ted (Athlete, Football Player)
135 Spring Meadow Dr
Apt 5
Buffalo, NY 14221, USA

Cottrell, William (Bill) (Athlete, Football Player)
39675 Patterson Ln
Solon, OH 44139, USA

Cottringer, Tom (Athlete, Hockey Player)
6 Fernwood Terr
Weiland, ON L3C 2R8, Canada

Cotts, Neal (Athlete, Baseball Player)
939 N Winchester Ave
Aot 1
Chicago, IL 60622-4167, USA

Couch, Chris (Athlete, Golfer)
307 Johns Creek Pkwy
Saint Augustine, FL 32092-5064, USA

Couch, Tim (Athlete, Football Player)
2110 N Ocean Blvd
Apt 28-D
Fort Lauderdale, FL 33305, USA

Couchee, Mike (Athlete, Baseball Player)
3060 N Ridgecrest
Unit 155
Mesa, AZ 85207-1080, USA

Coughlan, Marisa (Actor)
c/o Paul Nelson *Mosaic Media Group*
9200 W. Sunset Blvd
10th Floor
Los Angeles, CA 90069, USA

Coughlin, Bernard J (Educator)
Gonzaga University
Chancellor's Office
Spokane, WA 99258, USA

Coughlin, John (Race Car Driver)
Jeg's High Performance Racing
751 E. 11th Ave.
Columbu, OH 43211, USA

Coughlin, Kevin
1090 N. Euclid Ave.
Sarasota, FL 34237

Coughlin, Mike (Race Car Driver)
Jeg's High Performance Racing
751 E. 11th Ave.
Columbu, OH 43211, USA

Coughlin, Natalie (Athlete, Olympic Athlete, Swimmer)
4139 Coralee Ln
Lafayette, CA 94549-3356, USA

Coughlin, Tom (Coach, Football Coach)
New York Giants
Giants Stadium
East Rutherford, NJ 07073, USA

Coughlin, Troy (Race Car Driver)
Jeg's High Performance Racing
751 E. 11th Ave.
Columbu, OH 43211, USA

Coughlin, Jr., Jeg (Race Car Driver)
Jeg's High Performance Racing
751 E. 11th Ave.
Columbu, OH 43211, USA

Coughran, John (Athlete, Basketball Player)
5476 Morningside Drive
San Jose, CA 95138-2244, USA

Coughtry, Marlan (Athlete, Baseball Player)
5504 NE 55th St
Vancouver, WA 98661-2168, USA

Coulier, Dave (Actor)
4754 Lindley Ave
Encino, CA 91316, USA

Coulson, Catherine E (Actor)
1115 Terra Ave
Ashland, OR 97520, USA

Coulson, Christian (Actor)
c/o Staff Member *Artists Rights Group (ARG)*
4 Great Portland St
London W1W 8PA, UNITED KINGDOM (UK)

Coulter, Allen (Director)
c/o Paul Alan Smith *ICM Partners (ICM-LA)*
10250 Constellation Blvd Fl 7
Los Angeles, CA 90067, USA

Coulter, Ann (Writer)
242 Seabreeze Ave
Palm Beach, FL 33480, USA

Coulter, Art
500 Spanish Fort Blvd. #203
Spanish Fort, AL 36527-5998

Coulter, Brian (Music Group, Musician)
Ashley Talent
2002 Hogback Road #20
Ann Arbor, MI 48105, USA

Coulter, Catherine (Writer)
PO Box 17
Mill Valley, CA 94942-0017, USA

Coulter, Cher (Stylist)
c/o Staff Member *Luxe*
6442 Santa Monica Blvd
#200-B
Los Angeles, CA 90038, USA

Coulter, Chip (Athlete, Baseball Player)
718 Trenton St
Toronto, OH 43964-1269, USA

Coulter, Michael (Cinematographer)
35 Carlton Mansions Randolph Ave
London W9 1NP, UNITED
KINGDOM(UK)

Coulter, Phil (Music Group)
87th Street Ltd
24 Upper Mount St
Dublin, IRELAND

Coulthard, David (Race Car Driver)
Martin Brundle
Kings Lynn
Tottenhill
Norfolk PE32 0PX, UNITED KINGDOM
(UK)

Council, Keith (Athlete, Football Player)
4418 Lenox Blvd
Orlando, FL 32811, USA

Counsell, Craig (Athlete, Baseball Player)
992 E Circle Dr
Milwaukee, WI 53217-5361, USA

Counting Crows (Music Group)
c/o Gary Gersh *The Artists Organization*
212 Marine St
Suite 307
Santa Monica, CA 90045, USA

Counts, Mel (Athlete, Basketball Player,
Olympic Athlete)
1581 Matheny Rd NE
Gervais, OR 97026-8762, USA

Coupe, Eliza (Actor)
c/o Rhett Usry *ID Public Relations
(ID-NY)*
150 W 30th St
19th Floor
New York, NY 10001, USA

Coupland, Douglas (Writer)
c/o Michael Siegel *Michael Siegel &
Assoc*
8330 W 3rd
Los Angeles, CA 90048, USA

Couples, Fred (Athlete, Golfer)
127 S Carmelina Ave
Los Angeles, CA 90049, USA

Courant, Ernest D (Physicist)
40 W 72nd St Apt 41
New York, NY 10023-4192, USA

Couric, Katie (Journalist, Television Host)
677/697 Deep Hollow Rd
Washington, NY 12545, USA

Courier, Jim (Athlete, Olympic Athlete,
Tennis Player)
9533 Blandford Road
Orlando, FL 32827-7008, USA

Cournoyer, Yvan (Athlete, Hockey Player)
c/o Staff Member *Montreal Canadiens*
1275 Rue Saint-Antoine O
Montreal, QB H3C 5L2, Canada

Courreges, Andre (Designer, Fashion
Designer)
27 Rue Delabordere
Neuilly-Sur-Seine 92, FRANCE

Court, Alyson (Actor)
c/o Staff Member *Newton-Landry
Management*
19 Isabella St
Toronto ON M4Y 1M7, Canada

Courtemanche, Michael (Actor)
c/o Staff Member *Encore Management*
6300 Avenue du Parc bur406
Montreal, QB H2V 4H8, CANADA

Courtenay, Ed (Athlete, Hockey Player)
1422 Whispering Oaks Trl
Mount Pleasant, SC 29466-8584, USA

Courtenay, Tom (Actor)
Jonathan Altaras
13 Shorts Gardens
London WC2H 9AT, UNITED
KINGDOM(UK)

Courtin, Steve (Athlete, Basketball Player)
1109 Grinnell Road
Wilmington, DE 19803-5125, USA

Courtland, Jerome
1837 Westleigh Dr.
Glenview, IL 60025-7611

Courtnall, Geoff (Athlete, Hockey Player)
1270 Dallas Rd
Victoria, BC V8V 1C4, Canada

Courtnall, Russ (Athlete, Hockey Player)
c/o Staff Member *Victoria Atom B Hockey*
3651 Shelbourne St
Victoria, BC V8P 4H1, Canada

Courtney, Jai (Actor)
c/o Sam Maydew *Collective*
8383 Wilshire Blvd
Suite 1050
Beverly Hills, CA 90211, USA

Courtney, Joe (Congressman, Politician)
215 Cannon HOB
Washington, DC 20515, USA

Courtney, Joel (Actor)
c/o Bonnie Liedtke *Principato/Young
Management*
9465 Wilshire Blvd
Suite 430
Beverly Hills, CA 90212, USA

Courtney, Patricia (Baseball Player)
8 Eagle Loop Ln
Freedom, NH 03836-5311, USA

Courtney, Stephanie (Actor)
c/o Naomi Odenkirk *Odenkirk Provissiero
Entertainment*
Raleigh Studios
650 N. Bronson Ave, Bldg. B145
Los Angeles, CA 90004, USA

Courtney, Thomas W (Tom) (Athlete,
Olympic Athlete, Track Athlete)
336 Edgemere Way E
Naples, FL 34105-7151, USA

Courtright, John (Athlete, Baseball Player)
316 S Roosevelt Ave
Columbus, OH 43209-1829, USA

Court Yard Hounds (Music Group,
Musician)
c/o Staff Member *Columbia Records UK*
Bedford House
69-79 Fulham High St
London SW6 3JW, United Kingdom

Courville, Larry (Athlete, Hockey Player)
c/o Staff Member *Reading Royals*
700 Penn St
Reading, PA 19602-1107, USA

Courville, Vince (Athlete, Football Player)
5123 Avenue R
Galveston, TX 77551, USA

Coury, Dick (Athlete, Football Player)
4553 Campus Ave
Apt 6
San Diego, CA 92116-1162, USA

Coury, Steve (Athlete, Football Player)
6003 Newcastle Dr
Lake Oswego, OR 97035-8757, USA

Cousin, Terry (Athlete, Football Player)
4061 Blossom Hill Dr
Matthews, NC 28104, USA

Cousineau, Tom (Athlete, Football Player)
910 Eaton Ave
Akron, OH 44303, USA

Cousino, Brad (Athlete, Football Player)
8778 Kenwood Rd
Cincinnati, OH 45242, USA

Cousins, Christopher (Actor)
c/o Deborah Miller *Shelter Entertainment*
9454 Wilshire Blvd.
Suite 715
Beverly Hills, CA 90212, USA

Cousins, Derryl (Athlete, Baseball Player)
78136 Desert Mountain Cir
Bermuda Dunes, CA 92203, USA

Cousins, Jomo (Athlete, Football Player)
12425 Bramfield Dr
Riverview, FL 33579, USA

Cousins, Ralph W (Admiral)
Leconfield House Curzon St
London W1Y 8JR, UNITED
KINGDOM(UK)

Cousins, Robin (Figure Skater)
Billy Marsh
174-8 N Gower St
London NW1 2NB, UNITED
KINGDOM(UK)

Coustas, Mary (Actor)
c/o Nanette Fox *Nanette Fox Artist
Representation & Development*
P.O. Box 138
Fitzroy, Victoria 3065, Australia

Cousteau, Jean-Michel (Oceanographer)
Ocean Futures Society
325 Chapala St
Santa Barbara, CA 93101, USA

Cousteau, Jean-Michel (Scientist)
7 rue d'Amiral d'Estraing Paris
France, F 75116, USA

Cousy, Robert J (Bob) (Athlete, Basketball
Player)
427 Salisbury Street
Worcester, MA 01609-1266, USA

Coutlangus, Jon (Athlete, Baseball Player)
428 Starbridge Ct
Pleasant Hill, CA 94523-4723, USA

Coutteure, Ronny
28 rue Basfroi
Paris, FRANCE 75011

Coutu, Rich (Athlete, Hockey Player)
22 Rue Florian-Paiement
Salaberry-De-Valleyfield, QC J6S 5Z9,
Canada

Couture, Randy (Athlete, Wrestler)
c/o Brett Norensberg *Gersh (LA)*
9465 Wilshire Blvd
Suite 600
Beverly Hills, CA 90212, USA

Covay, Don (Music Group, Songwriter,
Writer)
Rawstock
P O Box 110002
Cambria Heights, NY 11411, USA

Covelli, Coco Crisp (Athlete, Baseball
Player)
508 Judy Dr
Redondo Beach, CA 90277-3830, USA

Coverdale, David (Musician)
757 Champagne Rd
Incline Village, NV 89451, USA

Cover Girls
141 Dunbar Ave.
Fords, NJ 08863

Coverly, Dave (Cartoonist, Editor)
Bloomington Herald-Times
Editorial Dept 1900 Walnut
Bloomington, IN 47401, USA

Covert, Allen (Actor, Comedian)
6963 Los Tilos Rd
Los Angeles, CA 90068, USA

Covert, James (Jimbo) (Athlete, Football
Player)
2647 Nelson Ct
Weston, FL 33332, USA

Covey, Richard 0 Colonel (Astronaut)
1155 High Lake Vw
Colorado Springs, CO 80906-8717, USA

Covey, Richard O (Astronaut)
1155 High Lake View
Colorado Springs, CO 80906, USA

Covic, Nebojsa (Prime Minister)
Prime Minister's Office
Nemanjina 11
Belgrade 11000, SERBIA

Coville, Bruce
PO Box 6110
Syracuse, NY 13217

Covington, John (Athlete, Football Player)
10901 Valley Forge Cir
Carmel, IN 46032, USA

Covington, Scott (Athlete, Football Player)
7444 W 81st St
Los Angeles, CA 90045, USA

Covington, Tony (Athlete, Football Player)
11160 C1 South Lakes Dr
Reston, VA 20191, USA

Covington, Warren (Music Group)
1627 Open Field Loop
Brandon, FL 33510, USA

Cowan, Billy (Athlete, Baseball Player)
1539 Via Coronel
Palos Verdes Estates, CA 90274-1941,
USA

Cowan, Dr. Connell (Writer)
c/o Staff Member *Reece Halsey North*
98 Main St
#704
Tiburon, CA 94920, USA

Cowan, Elliot (Actor)
c/o Laura Berwick *Hofflund/Polone*
9465 Wilshire Blvd #420
Beverly Hills, CA 90212, USA

Cowan, Lawrence (Larry) (Athlete,
Football Player)
1456 McCluer Rd
Jackson, MS 39212, USA

Cowan, Liz (Stylist)
c/o Staff Member *Photogenics Media*
8549 Higuera St
Building B
Culver Clty, CA 90232, USA

Cowan, Ralph Wolfe (Artist)
243 29th St
West Palm Beach, FL 33407, USA

Coward, Herbert (Actor)
1399 Worley Cove Rd
Canton, NC 28716, USA

Cowart, Sam (Athlete, Football Player)
11110 Fallgate Point Ct
Jacksonville, FL 32256, USA

Cowboy Junkies
c/o Staff Member *Paradigm (Monterey)*
404 W Franklin St
Monterey, CA 93940, USA

Cowboy Mouth (Music Group, Musician)
c/o Konrad Leh *Creative Talent Group*
1900 Avenue of the Stars
Suite 2475
Los Angeles, CA 90067, USA

Cowell, Simon (Business Person, Judge,
Reality TV Star)
717 N Palm Dr
Beverly Hills, CA 90210, USA

Cowen, Robert E (Judge)
US Court of Appeals
Judicial Complex
402 E State St
Trenton, NJ 08608, USA

Cowen, Scott (Educator)
Tulane University
President's Office
New Orleans, LA 70118, USA

Cowen, Wilson (Judge)
US Court of Appeals
717 Madison Place NW
Washington, DC 20439, USA

Cowen, Zelman (Attorney, Attorney
General, Educator, General)
4 Treasury Place
East Melbourne, VIC 3002, AUSTRALIA

Cowens, Dave (Athlete, Basketball Player)
132 Deep Cv
Raymond, ME 04071-6523, USA

Cowher, Bill (Athlete, Football Coach,
Football Player)
1225 Briar Patch Ln
Raleigh, NC 27615, USA

Cowhill, William J (Admiral)
9428 Vernon Drive
Great Falls, VA 22066-2227, USA

Cowick, Bruce (Athlete, Hockey Player)
2953 Cressida Crest
Victoria, BC V9B 5W7, Canada

Cowie, Colin (Entertainer)
568 Broadway Sue 705
New York, NY 10012, USA

Cowie, Lennox L (Astronomer, Scientist)
University of Hawaii
University Of Hawaii 2600 Campus Rd
Attn Astronomy Dept
Honolulu, HI 96822-2224, USA

Cowie, Rob
7501 E Phantom Way
Scottsdale, AZ 85255-4619, USA

Cowley, Joe (Athlete, Baseball Player)
904 Andover Grn
Lexington, KY 40509-2929, USA

Cowley, Wayne (Athlete, Hockey Player)
Bottom Line Restaurant 700-22 Front St
W Toronto, ON M5J 2W5, Canada

Cowlings, Al (Athlete, Football Player)
P.O. Box 1064
Pacific Palisades, CA 90272, USA

Cowper, Nicola (Actor)
Brunskill Mgmt
169 Queens Gate #A8
London SW7 5EH, UNITED
KINGDOM(UK)

Cowper, Stephen C (Steve) (Ex-Governor)
2301 McGregor Ct
Vienna, VA 22182, USA

Cowper, Steve (Politician)
PO Box A
Juneau, AK 99811, USA

Cowsill, Susan (Musician)
c/o Valerie Turner Polishook *V Public
Relations LLC*
PO Box 341810
Bethesda, MD 20827, USA

Cox, Alex (Actor, Director)
United Talent Agency
9560 Wilshire Blvd #500
Beverly Hills, CA 90212, USA

Cox, Billy (Athlete, Football Player)
5192 Marsh Field Ln
Sarasota, FL 34235, USA

Cox, Bobby (Commentator)
c/o Staff Member *Atlanta Braves*
755 Hank Aaron Dr SW
Atlanta, GA 30315, USA

Cox, Brian (Scientist)
Apollo's Children Ltd
P.O. Box 67130
London SW11 9ET, UK

Cox, Brian (Actor)
Conway Van Gelder Robinson
18-21 Jermyn St
London SW1Y 6NB, UNITED KINGDOM
(UK)

Cox, Bryan (Athlete, Football Player)
3040 Peachtree Rd NW
Unit 1206
Atlanta, GA 30305, USA

Cox, Casey (Athlete, Baseball Player)
2840 La Concha Dr
Clearwater, FL 33762-2203, USA

Cox, Charles C (Government Official)
Lexecon Inc
332 S Michigan Ave
Chicago, IL 60604, USA

Cox, Charlie (Actor)
c/o Nick Frenkel *3 Arts Entertainment Inc*
9460 Wilshire Blvd
7th Floor
Beverly Hills, CA 90210, USA

Cox, Chris (Musician)
c/o Staff Member *Diva Central Inc*
7510 W Sunset Blvd Ste 1445
Los Angees, CA 90046, USA

Cox, Christina (Actor)
Rysher Entertainment
3400 Riverside Dr #600
Burbank, CA 91505, USA

Cox, C Jay (Director, Producer, Writer)
c/o Scott Zimmerman *Evolution
Entertainment (LA)*
901 N Highland Ave
Los Angeles, CA 90038, USA

Cox, Courteney (Actor)
9255 Doheny Rd #2505
West Hollywood, CA 90069, USA

Cox, Danny (Athlete, Baseball Player)
306 Feagin Mill Rd
Warner Robins, GA 31088-6208, USA

Cox, Danny (Motivational Speaker,
Writer)
17381 Bonner Dr
Tustin, TX 92780, USA

Cox, Darron (Athlete, Baseball Player)
13681 Stuart St
Broomfield, CO 80023-5527, USA

Cox, David R (Doctor, Misc)
Stanford University
Human Genome Center
Stanford, CA 94305, USA

Cox, Deborah (Musician, Songwriter)
8348 NW 62nd Pl
Parkland, FL 33067, USA

Cox, Emmett R (Judge)
US Court of Appeals
113 St Joseph St
Mobile, AL 36602, USA

Cox, Frederick W (Fred) (Athlete, Football
Player)
401 E River St
Monticello, MN 55362, USA

Cox, G David (Religious Leader)
Church of God
P O Box 2420
Anderson, IN 46018, USA

Cox, Harvey G Jr (Educator, Misc)
Harvard University
Divinity School
Cambridge, MA 02140, USA

Cox, Jeff (Athlete, Baseball Player)
2727 E Vanderhoof Dr
West Covina, CA 91791-2247, USA

Cox, Jennifer Elise (Actor)
c/o Lisa DiSante-Frank *DiSante Frank &
Company*
10061 Riverside Dr #377
Toluca Lake, CA 91602, USA

Cox, Jim (Athlete, Baseball Player)
8370 E Charter Oak Rd
Scottsdale, AZ 85260-5256, USA

Cox, John (Athlete, Football Player)
5192 Marsh Field Ln
Sarasota, FL 34235, USA

Cox, Johnny (Athlete, Basketball Player,
Coach)
849 North Main Street
Hazard, KY 41701-1345, USA

Cox, Joshua (Actor)
7185 Pacific View Dr
Los Angeles, CA 90068, USA

Cox, Kris (Athlete, Golfer)
5350 Richard Ave
Dallas, TX 75206-6712, USA

Cox, Larry (Athlete, Football Player)
10326 Catlett Ln
La Porte, TX 77571, USA

Cox, Lynne (Swimmer)
Advanced Sport Research
4141 Ball Road #142
Cypress, CA 90630, USA

Cox, Mark (Tennis Player)
Oaks Astead Woods
Astead
Surrey KT21 2ER, UNITED
KINGDOM(UK)

Cox, Nathalie (Actor)
c/o Chuck James *ICM Partners (ICM-LA)*
10250 Constellation Blvd Fl 7
Los Angeles, CA 90067, USA

Cox, Nikki (Actor)
737 El Medio Ave
Pacific Palisades, CA 90272, USA

Cox, Paul (Director)
Illumination Films
1 Victoria Ave
Albert Park, VIC 3208, AUSTRALIA

Cox, Philip S (Architect)
Cox Richardson Architects
469 Kent St
Sydney, NSW 2000, AUSTRALIA

Cox, Ralph (Athlete, Hockey Player)
1 Harborside Dr
Apt 200S
East Boston, MA 02128, USA

Cox, Richard
9200 Sunset Blvd. #900
Los Angeles, CA 90069

Cox, Richard Ian
8730 Sunset Blvd. #480
Los Angeles, CA 90069

Cox, Robert G (Business Person,
Financier)
Federal Trust Corporation
312 West First St
Sanford, FL 32771, USA

Cox, Ronny (Actor)
13948 Magnolia Blvd
Sherman Oaks, CA 91423, USA

Cox, Stephen J (Artist)
154 Barnsbury Road
Islington
London N1 0ER, UNITED KINGDOM
(UK)

Cox, Steve (Athlete, Football Player)
1001 E Lakeshore Dr
Jonesboro, AR 72401, USA

Cox, Steve (Athlete, Baseball Player)
22678 Avenue 188
Strathmore, CA 93267-9680, USA

Cox, Ted (Athlete, Baseball Player)
3990 E Seward Rd
Guthrie, OK 73044-9854, USA

Cox, Terry (Athlete, Baseball Player)
707 N Broadwav St
Aot 302
Pittsbure:, KS 66762-3942, USA

Cox, Thomas (Race Car Driver)
2321 Race Track Rd
Sophia, NC 27350, USA

Cox, Tom (Athlete, Football Player)
2121 S Mill Ave
Apt 231
Tempe, AZ 85282, USA

Cox, Tony (Actor)
c/o Staff Member *New Wave Entertainment (LA)*
2660 W Olive Blvd
Burbank, CA 91505, USA

Cox, Torrie (Athlete, Football Player)
42 NW 92nd St
Miami Shores, FL 33150, USA

Cox, Veanne (Actor)
c/o Nyle Brenner *Brenner Management*
Prefers to be contacted via telephone or email
CA, USA

Cox, Vera
345 N. Maple Dr. #397
Beverly Hills, CA 90210

Cox, Warren J (Architect)
Hartman Cox Architects
3111 N St NW
Washington, DC 20007-3420, USA

Coxe, Craig (Athlete, Hockey Player)
W3059 Oak St
Saint Ignace, MI 49781-9849, USA

Coyle, Eric (Athlete, Football Player)
397 County Road 26
Longmont, CO 80504, USA

Coyle, Nadine (Actor, Musician)
c/o Julie Colbert *WME (LA)*
9601 Wilshire Blvd Fl 3
Beverly Hills, CA 90210, USA

Coyle, Ross (Athlete, Football Player)
P.O. Box 68
Blanchard, OK 73010, USA

Coyne, Colleen (Athlete, Hockey Player, Olympic Athlete)
79 Cedar St
Amesbury, MA 01913-1821, USA

Coyne, Dale (Race Car Driver)
13627 Sharp Drive
Plainfield, IL 60544, USA

Coyne, Wayne (Musician)
1715 NW 13th St
Oklahoma City, OK 73106, USA

Coyote, Peter (Actor)
774 Marin Dr
Mill Valley, CA 94941, USA

Cozler, Jimmy (Musician, Songwriter, Writer)
J Racords
745 5th Ave
#600
New York, NY 10151, USA

Cozzarelli, Nicholas R (Biologist)
University of California
Biology Dept
Berkeley, CA 94720, USA

C. Peters, Gary (Congressman, Politician)
1609 Longworth HOB
Washington, DC 20515, USA

C. Peterson, Collin (Congressman, Politician)
2211 Rayburn HOB
Washington, DC 20515, USA

Crabb, Claude (Athlete, Football Player)
49851 Wayne St
Indio, CA 92201, USA

Crabb, Joey (Athlete, Hockey Player)
9100 Granite Pl
Anchorage, AK 99507-3947, USA

Crabbe, Cullen (Actor)
9437 N 122nd Pl
Scottsdale, AZ 85259, USA

Crable, Bob (Athlete, Football Player)
564 Miami Trace Ct
Loveland, OH 45140, USA

Crabtree, Eric (Athlete, Football Player)
3342 Arapahoe St
Denver, CO 80205, USA

Crabtree, Michael (Athlete, Football Player)
c/o Eugene Parker *Maximum Sports Management*
6435 W Jefferson Blvd
#197
Fort Wayne, IN 46804, USA

Crabtree, Teresa (Stylist)
c/o Staff Member *Crews*
828 Clemont Dr
Atlanta, GA 30306, USA

Crabtree, Tim (Athlete, Baseball Player)
1503 Kingswood Ln
Colleyville, TX 76034-5580, USA

Craddock, Bantz (General)
Commander
US Southern Command Miami
APO, AA 34001, USA

Craddock, Billy (Crash) (Musician, Songwriter, Writer)
3007 Old Martinsville Road
Greensboro, NC 27455, USA

Craddock, Billy Crash
PO Box 428
Portland, TN 37148-0428

Cradle, Rickey (Athlete, Baseball Player)
1311 Dry Gap Pike
Knoxville, TN 37918-9785, USA

Cradle Of Filth (Music Group, Musician)
c/o Staff Member *In Phase Management*
P O Box 756A
Surbiton KT6 6YZ, UK

Craft, Chris
14919 Village Elm St.
Houston, TX 77062

Craft, Jason (Athlete, Football Player)
11688 Amistad Ct
Jacksonville, FL 32256, USA

Craft, Sammi (Actor)
c/o Staff Member *Paradigm (LA)*
360 N Crescent Dr
North Bldg
Beverly Hills, CA 90210, USA

Craft, Terry (Athlete, Baseball Player)
16 Sheldon Ave
Castle Rock, CO 80104, USA

Crafter, Jane (Athlete, Golfer)
317 W Almeria Rd
Phoenix, AZ 85003-1140, USA

Crafts, Hannah (Writer)
c/o Staff Member *Creative Artists Agency (CAA-LA)*
2000 Ave Of The Stars
Los Angeles, CA 90067, USA

Cragg, Anthony D (Tony) (Artist)
Adolt-Vorwerk-Str 24
Wuppertal 42287, GERMANY

Craggs, George (Soccer Player)
6223 6th Ave NW
Seattle, WA 98107, USA

Craig, Adam Jamal (Actor)
c/o Christopher Rockwell *Global Creative*
1051 Cole Ave # B
Los Angeles, CA 90038, USA

Craig, Daniel (Actor)
68 Regent's Park Rd
Camden Town, Greater London GNW1 8, UNITED KINGDOM (UK)

Craig, Demeyune (Athlete, Football Player)
5102 31st Ave
Valley, AL 36854, USA

Craig, Elijah (Actor)
Agency for Performing Arts
9200 Sunset Blvd
#900
Los Angeles, CA 90069, USA

Craig, Jenny (Business Person, Doctor)
5973 Rancho Diegueno
Solana Beach, CA 92067, USA

Craig, Jim (Athlete, Hockey Player, Olympic Athlete)
29907 County Road 3
Merrifield, MN 56465-4402, USA

Craig, Larry (Politician)
8935 W Cornwall Dr
Boise, ID 83704-4310, USA

Craig, Michael (Actor)
Chatto & Linnit
Prince of Wales
Coventry St
London W1V 7FE, UNITED KINGDOM (UK)

Craig, Mike (Athlete, Hockey Player)
29907 County Road 3
Merrifield, MN 56465-4402, USA

Craig, Neal (Athlete, Football Player)
2231 Crane Ave
Cincinnati, OH 45207, USA

Craig, Paco (Athlete, Football Player)
23458 Marguerite Cir
Moreno Valley, CA 92557, USA

Craig, Pete (Athlete, Baseball Player)
5915 Carmel Ln
Raleigh, NC 27609-3953, USA

Craig, Richard (Inventor)
Pacific Northwest National Laboratory
902 Battelle Blvd
Richland, WA 99352, USA

Craig, Rod (Athlete, Baseball Player)
1200 E Kay St #C
Compton, CA 90221-1573, USA

Craig, Roger (Athlete, Football Player)
271 Vista Verde Way
Portola Valley, CA 94028, USA

Craig, Roger (Athlete, Baseball Player, Coach)
PO Box 2174
Borrego Springs, CA 92004-2174, USA

Craig, Wendy
29 Roehampton Gate
London, ENGLAND SW15 5JR

Craig, William (Bill) (Swimmer)
PO Box 629
Newport Beach, CA 92661, USA

Craig, Yvonne (Actor)
YC/MC Ltd
PO Box 827
Pacifc Palisades, CA 90272, USA

Craighead, John (Athlete, Hockey Player)
JC's Extreme Hockey
2595 Barnet Hwy
Coquitlam, BC V3E 1K9, Canada

Craighead, John J (Misc)
5125 Orchard Ave
Missoula, MT 59803, USA

Craig of Radley, David B (Misc)
House of Lords
Westminster
London SW1A 0PW, UNITED KINGDOM (UK)

craigwell, dale
Beyond The Pond Hockey
467 Meadow St
Oshawa, ON L1L 1B9, Canada

Crain, Jesse (Athlete, Baseball Player)
20702 Hartford Way
Lakeville, MN 55044-4438, USA

Crain, Keith E (Publisher)
Crain Communications
1400 Woodbridge Ave
Detroit, MI 48207, USA

Crain, Rance (Publisher)
Crain Communications
360 N Michigan Ave
Chicago, IL 60601, USA

Crain, William (Director)
Contemporary Artists
610 Santa Monica Blvd
#202
Santa Monica, CA 90401, USA

Crais, Robert (Writer)
1647 Blue Jay Way
West Hollywood, CA 90069, USA

Cram, Jerry (Athlete, Baseball Player)
Salem-Keizer Volcanoes PO Box 20936
Attn: Coaching Staff
Keizer, OR Q97307-0936, USA

Cram, Jerry (Athlete, Baseball Player)
33015 Victoria Brooke Ln
Lake Elsinore, CA 92530-5467, USA

Cram, Stephen (Steve) (Athlete, Track Athlete)
General Delivery
Jarrow, UNITED KINGDOM (UK)

Cramer, Douglas
738 Sarbonne Rd.
Los Angeles, CA 90077

Cramer, Grant (Actor)
Richard Sindell
1910 Holmby Ave
#1
Los Angeles, CA 90025, USA

Cramer, James (Television Host)
c/o Staff Member *CNBC*
900 Sylvan Ave
Englewood Cliffs, NJ 07632, USA

Cramer, Peggy (Athlete, Baseball Player, Commentator)
1160 E Old Andrew Johnson Hwy
Talbott, TN 37877-3103, USA

Cramer, Richard Ben (Journalist, Writer)
Philadelphia Inquirer 400 N Broad St Attn
Editorial Dept
Philadelphia, PA 19130-4099, USA

Cramps, The (Music Group)
c/o Stormy Shepherd *Leave Home Booking*
1400 S. Foothill Dr
Suite 34
Salt Lake City, UT 84108, USA

Crampton, Barbara (Actor)
Stone Manners
6500 Wilshire Blvd
#550
Los Angeles, CA 90048, USA

Crampton, Bruce (Athlete, Golfer)
225 Winter Crest Ln
Severna Park, MD 21146-3104, USA

Cramton, Roger C (Attorney, Attorney General, General)
49 Highgate Circle
Ithaca, NY 14850, USA

Cranberries, The (Music Group)
c/o Staff Member *Creative Artists Agency (CAA-LA)*
2000 Ave Of The Stars
Los Angeles, CA 90067, USA

Crandall, Bruce (Admiral)
PO Box 736
Manchester, WA 98353-0736, USA

Crandall, Del (Athlete, Baseball Player, Coach)
1355 Clear Lake Pl
Brea, CA 92821-2807, USA

Crane, Ben (Athlete, Golfer)
2223 Cedar Elm Ter
Westlake, TX 76262-9028, USA

Crane, Brian (Cartoonist)
PO Box 51771
Sparks, NV 89435-1771, USA

Crane, Caprice (Actor, Writer)
c/o Brad Petrigala *Brillstein Entertainment Partners*
9150 Wilshire Blvd #350
Beverly Hills, CA 90212, USA

Crane, David (Director, Producer, Writer)
c/o Staff Member *Bright Kauffman Crane Productions*
4000 Warner Blvd
Bldg 160 #750
Burbank, CA 91522

Crane, Gary (Athlete, Football Player)
6 Greystone
Bentonville, AR 72712-4098, USA

Crane, Horace R (Physicist)
66 Cavanaugh Lake Rd
Chelsea, MI 48118, USA

Crane, John (Writer)
c/o Staff Member *Agency for the Performing Arts (APA-LA)*
405 S Beverly Dr
Suite 500
Beverly Hills, CA 90212-4425, USA

Crane, Kenneth G (Director)
6627 Linderhurst Ave
Los Angeles, CA 90048, USA

Crane, Paul (Athlete, Football Player)
12 N Monterey St
Mobile, AL 36604, USA

Crane, Tony (Actor)
Abrams Artists
9200 Sunset Blvd
#1125
Los Angeles, CA 90069, USA

Cranston, Bryan (Actor)
4109 Greenbush Ave
Sherman Oaks, CA 91423, USA

Cranston, Toller (Figure Skater)
Int'l Management Grp
1st Clair Ave E
#700
Toronto, ON M4T 2V7, CANADA

Crapo, Michael (Politician)
3212nd St SE
Washington, DC 20003-1902, USA

Crapo, Mike (Senator)
239 Dirksen Senate Building
Washington, DC 20510, USA

Crashley, Bart (Athlete, Hockey Player)
90 Goacher Rd RR 1
Campbellford, ON K0L 1L0, Canada

Crash Test Dummies (Music Group, Musician)
c/o Sandy Rogers *Deep Fried Records*
1146 Lakeshore Rd
PO Box 195
Selkirk, ON N0A 1P0, Canada

Cravaack, Chip (Congressman, Politician)
508 Cannon HOB
Washington, DC 20515, USA

Craven, Bill (Athlete, Football Player)
4363 N Buckhead Dr NE
Atlanta, GA 30342, USA

Craven, Gemma (Actor)
c/o Jonathan Arun *Jonathan Arun*
Studio 9
33 Stanary St.
London SE11 4AA, UK

Craven, Matt (Actor)
6108 Dorcas Pl
Los Angeles, CA 90068, USA

Craven, Murray (Athlete, Hockey Player)
2802 Rest Haven Dr
Whitefish, MT 59937-8015, USA

Craven, Ricky (Race Car Driver)
PO Box 472
Concord, NC 28027, 28028

Craven, Wes (Director)
2419 Solar Dr
Los Angeles, CA 90046, USA

Cravens, Greg (Cartoonist)
312 N Mclean Blvd
Memphis, TN 38112-5341, USA

Craver, Aaron (Athlete, Football Player)
821 W Maple St
Compton, CA 90220, USA

Crawford, Bill Dr (Athlete, Football Player)
701 Redwood Dr
Qualicum Beach, BC V9K 2J2, Canada

Crawford, Bob (Athlete, Hockey Player)
6 Progress Dr
Cromwell, CT 06416-1055, USA

Crawford, Brad (Athlete, Football Player)
RR2
Winamac, IL 46996, USA

Crawford, Bryce L Jr (Misc)
3220 Lake Johanna Blvd
#58
Saint Paul, MN 55112, USA

Crawford, Carl (Athlete, Baseball Player)
12515 Silverglen Estates Dr
Houston, TX 77014-2843, USA

Crawford, Carlos (Athlete, Baseball Player)
1605 Martin Luther Kine: Ave E
Bradenton, FL 34208-2801, USA

Crawford, Chace (Actor)
c/o Eric Podwall *Podwall Entertainment*
710 N Orlando Ave
Loft 203
Los Angeles, CA 90069, USA

Crawford, Cheyne (Actor)
c/o Amy Slomovits *Evolution Entertainment (LA)*
9320 Wilshire Blvd
Suite 202
Beverly Hills, CA 90212, USA

Crawford, Christina (Writer)
7 Springs Farm Sanders Road
Tensed, ID 83870-9615, USA

Crawford, Cindy (Actor, Model)
33246 Pacific Coast Hwy
Malibu, CA 90265, USA

Crawford, Clayne (Actor)
c/o Alex Cole *Elevate Entertainment*
10100 Santa Monica Blvd.
Suite 300
Los Angeles, CA 90067, USA

Crawford, Ed (Athlete, Football Player)
204 Country Club Rd
Oxford, MS 38655, USA

Crawford, Eric (Congressman, Politician)
1408 Longworth HOB
Washington, DC 20515, USA

Crawford, Fred (Athlete, Basketball Player)
24 West Lawn Drive
Teaneck, NJ 07666-5612, USA

Crawford, Hilton (Athlete, Football Player)
262 Hagen St
Buffalo, NY 14215, USA

Crawford, Jamal (Basketball Player)
Chicago Bulls United Center
1901 W Madison St
Chicago, IL 60612, USA

Crawford, Jennifer (Stylist)
c/o Staff Member *Sydney Represents*
280 Mott St
New York, NY 10012, USA

Crawford, Jerry (Athlete, Baseball Player)
111 9th St E
Saint Petersburg, FL 33715, USA

Crawford, Jim (Athlete, Baseball Player)
4370 E Gemini Pl
Chandler, AZ 85249-5829, USA

Crawford, Joan (Athlete, Basketball Player)
4728 S Harvard Ave
Apt 22
Tulsa, OK 74135-3045, USA

Crawford, Joe (Athlete, Baseball Player)
5428 US Highway 50
Hillsboro, OH 45133-7533, USA

Crawford, Johnny (Actor, Musician)
2440 El Cantento Dr
Los Angeles, CA 90068, USA

Crawford, Keith (Athlete, Football Player)
RR 5 Box 5008
Palestine, TX 75801, USA

Crawford, Kirsty (Musician)
c/o Zoe Sobol *Rocket Music & Management*
7 Albert Studios
London SW11 4QD, UK

Crawford, Lou (Athlete, Hockey Player)
50 New Gower St
St. John's, NL A1C 1J3, Canada

Crawford, Marc (Athlete, Coach, Hockey Player)
c/o Staff Member *Los Angeles Kings*
1111 S. Figueroa St
Suite 3100
Los Angeles, CA 90015, USA

Crawford, Michael (Actor, Musician)
c/o Steve Levine *ICM Partners (ICM-LA)*
10250 Constellation Blvd Fl 7
Los Angeles, CA 90067, USA

Crawford, Missy Neville (Stylist)
c/o Staff Member *Elite Model Management/Atlanta*
1708 Peachtree St NW
#210
Atlanta, GA 30309, USA

Crawford, Paxton (Athlete, Baseball Player)
PO Box 345
Plumerville, AR 72127-0345, USA

Crawford, Rachael (Actor)
c/o Staff Member *Coast to Coast Talent Group*
3350 Barham Blvd
Los Angeles, CA 90068, USA

Crawford, Randy (Musician)
911 Park St SW
Grand Rapids, MI 49504, USA

Crawford, Steve (Athlete, Baseball Player)
6122 E 480
Salina, OK 74365-2496, USA

Crawford, Vernon (Athlete, Football Player)
2001 Gemini St
Apt 1305
Houston, TX 77058-2062, USA

Crawford, William J (War Hero)
28520 Country Road 14
Rocky Ford, CO 81067, USA

Crawford-Indri, Marisa (Stylist)
c/o Staff Member *Tricia Joyce Inc*
79 Chambers St
2nd Floor
New York, NY 10007, USA

Crawley, Pauline (Baseball Player)
68670 Raposa Rd
Cathedral City, CA 92234-8148, USA

Cray, Robert (Musician)
Rosebud Agency
PO Box 170429
San Francisco, CA 94117, USA

Craybas, Jill (Athlete, Tennis Player)
2603 Delaware St
Huntington Beach, CA 92648, USA

Craymer, Judy (Producer)
Winter Garden Theater
1634 Broadway
New York, NY 10019, USA

Crayton, Patrick (Athlete, Football Player)
2301 Silver Table Dr
Lewisville, TX 75056-5679, USA

Crazy Mohan (Actor)
5 Chokkalingam Street
Mandavelli
Chennai, TN 600 028, INDIA

Creamer, Paula (Athlete, Golfer)
4812 Alexandra Garden Ct
Windermere, FL 34786, USA

Creamer, Robert W (Commentator)
180 E Hartsdale Ave
Apt 2E
Hartsdale, NY 10530-3540, USA

Creamer, Roger W (Writer)
180 E Hartsdale Ave #2E
Hartsdale, NY 10530, USA

Creamer, Timothy J (Astronaut)
5103 Carefree Dr
League City, TX 77573, USA

Creamer, Timothy J Lt Colonel
(Astronaut)
5103 Carefree Dr
League City, TX 77573-3195, USA

Crear, Mark (Athlete, Olympic Athlete, Track Athlete)
Octagon
9420 Reseda Blvd Ste 600
Northridge, CA 91324-2932, USA

Creavalle, Laura (Misc)
Club Creavalle
230 Danforth Ave
Toronto ON M4K 1N4, CANADA

Creber, William (Misc)
1800 N Highland Ave
Suite 717
Los Angeles, CA 90028, USA

Crecion, Gabe (Athlete, Football Player)
4800 Coyote Wells Cir
Westlake Village, CA 91362-4712, USA

Crede, Joe (Athlete, Baseball Player)
42 Dry Creek Trl
Linn, MO 65051-2617, USA

Creech, Bob (Athlete, Football Player)
1905 Windsor Dr
Mesquite, TX 75181-2358, USA

Creech, Sharon (Writer)
Harper Collins 10 E 53rd St Frnt 1
New York, NY 10022-5069, USA

Creech, Wilbur L (General)
20 Quail Run Road
Henderson, NV 89014, USA

Creed, Clifford Ann (Athlete, Golfer)
240 N Rosemont Dr
Sulphur, LA 70665, USA

Creek, Doug (Athlete, Baseball Player)
12440 Oakview Ct
Newbur^, MD 20664-2209, USA

Creel, Donna (Stylist)
1188 Meadows Rd
Luthersville, GA 30251, USA

Creel, Gavin (Actor)
c/o Amy Brownstein *Brownstein & Associates Inc*
630 9th Ave #209
New York, NY 10036, USA

Creel, Keith (Athlete, Baseball Player)
527 Trail Ridge Dr
Duncanville, TX 75116-2433, USA

Creel, Monica (Actor)
c/o Mike Eistenstadt *Amsel, Eisenstadt & Frazier Talent Agency (AEF)*
5055 Wilshire Blvd
Suite 860
Los Angeles, CA 90036-6108, USA

Cregar, Bill (Athlete, Football Player)
22 Locust Ct
Spring Lake, NJ 07762-2109, USA

Creighton, Adam (Athlete, Hockey Player)
Boston Bruins
Scouting Dept
100 Legends Way #250
Boston, MA 02114-1389, USA

creighton, fred
8151 Stallion Way
Sacramento, CA 95830-9334

Creighton, Jim (Athlete, Basketball Player)
5297 South Geneva Street
Englewood, CO 80111-6210, USA

Creighton, Joanne V (Educator)
Mount Holyoke College
President's Office
South Hadley, MA 01075, USA

Creighton, John D (Publisher)
Toronto Sun
333 King St E
Toronto, ON M5A 3X5, CANADA

Creighton, John O (Astronaut)
2111 SW 174th St
Burien, WA 98166, USA

Creighton, John O Captain (Astronaut)
2111 SW 174th St
Burien, WA 98166-3259, USA

Creighton Sr, Dave (Athlete, Hockey Player)
5202 Spectacular Bid Dr
Wesley Chapel, FL 33544-1576, USA

Creme, Lol (Musician)
Heronden Hall
Tenferden
Kent, UNITED KINGDOM (UK)

Cremins, Bobby (Coach)
150 Bobby John Road
Atlanta, GA 30332, USA

Crenkovski, Branko (Prime Minister)
Prime Minister's Office
Dame Grueva 6
Skopje 9100, MACEDONIA

Crennel, Carl (Athlete, Football Player)
1501 Dupont St
Conway, PA 15027-1329, USA

Crennel, Romeo (Athlete, Football Coach, Football Player)
80 Cayman Pl
Palm Beach Gardens, FL 33418-8096, USA

Crenshaw, Ander (Congressman, Politician)
440 Cannon HOB
Washington, DC 20515, USA

Crenshaw, Ben (Athlete, Golfer)
P.O. Box 50568
Austin, TX 78763, USA

Crenshaw, Marshall (Musician)
c/o Staff Member *MCT Management*
520 8th Ave Rm 2205
New York, NY 10018, USA

Crenshaw, Willis (Athlete, Football Player)
22 Carly Rd
Woodstock, NY 12498-2524, USA

Creole, Kid (Musician)
Ron Rainey Mgmt
315 S Beverly Dr
#407
Beverly Hills, CA 90212, USA

Creskoff, Rebecca (Actor)
c/o Steven Levy *Framework Entertainment (LA)*
9057 Nemo St
Suite C
West Hollywood, CA 90069, USA

Crespin, Regine (Opera Singer)
Musicaglotz
3 Ave Frochet
Paris 75009, FRANCE

Crespino, Robert (Athlete, Football Player)
109 Heatherdown Rd
Decatur, GA 30030-3817, USA

Crespo, Elvis (Musician)
c/o Staff Member *Sony Music Miami*
605 Lincoln Rd Fl 7
Miami Beach, FL 33139, USA

Crespo, Felipe (Athlete, Baseball Player)
C2 Calle 6 Urb Santa Juana 2
Caguas, PR 00725-2019, USA

Cresse, Mark (Athlete, Baseball Player)
3222 Clav St
Newoort Beach, CA 92663-4207, USA

Cressend, Jack (Athlete, Baseball Player)
2409 W Ranch Dr
Friendswood, TX 77546-5579, USA

Cressman, Dave (Athlete, Hockey Player)
University of Waterloo
200 University Ave W
Attn: Hockey Program
Waterloo, ON N2L 3G1, Canada

cressman, glen
5757 Lake Murray Blvd Apt 13
La Mesa, CA 91942-2216

Cresson, Edith (Prime Minister)
Mairie
Chatellerault Cedex 86018, FRANCE

Cressy, Jr., Dale (Race Car Driver)
1336 Paralllount Parkway
Batavia, IL 60510, USA

Creswell, Smiley (Athlete, Football Player)
1 Academy Way
Monroe, WA 98272, USA

Cretler, Jean-Luc (Skier)
153 Ave du Marechal Lereic
BP 20
Bourq Saint Maurice 73700, FRANCE

Creutz, Edward C (Physicist)
PO Box 2757
Rancho Santa, CA 92067, USA

Crevalle, Laura
PO Box 557
Old Orchard Beach, ME 04064

Crew, Amanda (Actor)
c/o Vickie Petronio *Play Management*
807 Powell St
Suite 220
Vancouver V6A 1H7, CANADA

Crew-Cuts, The
29 Cedar St
Creskill, NJ 07626

Crewdson, John M (Journalist)
Chicago Tribune 435 N Michigan Ave Ste 200 Attn Editorial Dept
Chicago, IL 60611-4024, USA

Crews, Albert (Astronaut)
444 Sllja terway Dr
Satellite Beach, FL 32937-3834, USA

Crews, David P (Biologist)
University of Texas
Zoology Dept
Austin, TX 78712, USA

Crews, Gina (Reality TV Star)
10211 W State Rd 235
Alachua, FL 32615, USA

Crews, Philip (Misc)
University of California
Chemistry Dept
Santa Cruz, CA 99504, USA

Crews, Terry (Actor)
16 Stillman Ln
Greenwich, CT 06831, USA

Crewson, Wendy (Actor)
438 Queen St E
Toronto, ON M5A 1T4, CANADA

Crha, Jiri (Athlete, Hockey Player)
16390 Braeburn Ridge Trl
Delray Beach, FL 33446-9508, USA

Crha, Jiri (Athlete, Hockey Player)
8023 Laurel Ridge Ct
Delray Beach, FL 33446, USA

Crialese, Emanuele (Director)
c/o Staff Member *WME (LA)*
9601 Wilshire Blvd Fl 3
Beverly Hills, CA 90210, USA

Cribbins, Barnard (Actor)
Hamm Court
Weybridge, Surrey, UNITED KINGDOM (UK)

Cribbs, Joe S (Athlete, Football Player)
5333 Creekside Loop
Birmingham, AL 35244-3985, USA

Cribbs, Joshua (Athlete, Football Player)
9333 W Hampton Dr
North Royalton, OH 44133-2884, USA

Cricket Team, Australian (Cricketer)
60 Jolimont St
Jolimont, Victoria 3002, Australia

Cricketts, The
3322 West End Ave. #520
Nashville, TN 37203

Crickhowell of Pont Esgob, Nicholas E
(Politician)
4 Henning St
London SW11 3DR, UNITED KINGDOM (UK)

Crider, Melissa (Actor)
c/o Daniel Spilo *Industry Entertainment Partners*
955 S Carrillo Dr
Suite 300
Los Angeles, CA 90048, USA

Crider, Melissa (Actor)
Paradigm Agency
10100 Santa Monica Blvd
#2500
Los Angeles, CA 90067, USA

Crier, Catherine (Correspondent, Television Host)
Catherine Crier Live
Courtroom Television Network
600 3rd Ave
New York, NY 10016-1901, USA

Crier, Catherine (Journalist)
Cnn 190 Marietta St NW Ste 280
Atlanta, GA 30303-2713, USA

Crile, Susan (Artist)
168 W 86th St
New York, NY 10024, USA

Crim, Chuck (Athlete, Baseball Player)
50039 Golden Horse Dr
Oakhurst, CA 93644-9497, USA

Crim, Chuck (Athlete, Baseball Player)
Chattanooga Lookouts PO Box 11002
Attn: Coaching Staff
Chattanooga, TN ^7401-7001, USA

Crimian, Jack (Athlete, Baseball Player)
3012 Green St
Claymont, DE 19703-2026, USA

Cripe, Dave (Athlete, Baseball Player)
1835 Montara Way
San Jacinto, CA 92583-5832, USA

Crippen, Robert L (Astronaut)
781 Harbour Isle Place
West Palm Beach, FL 33410, USA

Crippen, Robert L Captain (Astronaut)
781 Harbour Isle Pl
West Palm Beach, FL 33410-4408, USA

Crippen, Susie (Stylist)
c/o Staff Member *Exclusive Artists Mgmt*
7700 Sunset Blvd
#205
Los Angeles, CA 90046, USA

Criqui, Don (Sportscaster)
CBS-TV
Sports Dept
51 W 52nd St
New York, NY 10019, USA

Criscione, Dave (Athlete, Baseball Player)
87 Hamlet St
Fredonia, NY 14063-2143, USA

Crisman, Joel (Athlete, Football Player)
8823 Creekside Way Apt 1836
Highlands Ranch, CO 80129-1593, USA

Crisman, Joel (Athlete, Football Player)
8823 Creekside Way
Apt 1836
Littleton, CO 80129, USA

Crisostomo, Manny (Journalist, Photographer)
Pacific Daily News
PO Box DN
Hagatna, GU 96932, USA

Crisp, Coco (Athlete, Baseball Player)
508 Judy Dr
Redondo Beach, CA 90277, USA

crisp, terry (Athlete, Hockey Player)
Nashville Predators
501 Broadway
Nashville, TN 37203-3980

Crisp, Terry A (Athlete, Coach, Hockey Player)
805 Cherry Laurel Ct
Nashville, TN 37215-6173, USA

Crispin, Anne C (Writer)
Tom Doherty Associates, LLC
175 Fifth Avenue
New York, NY 10010, USA

Criss, Charles (Athlete, Basketball Player)
4310 Melanie Lane
Atlanta, GA 30349-2849, USA

Criss, Darren (Actor)
c/o Ricky Rollins *Schumacher Management*
1122 San Vicente Blvd.
Santa Monica, CA 90402, USA

Criss, Peter (Musician)
2111 Friar Ct
Wall Township, NJ 07719, USA

Crist, Charlie (Attorney)
Charlie Crist for Governor
P.O. Box 311
Tallahassee, FL 32302-0311, USA

Crist, Chuck (Athlete, Football Player)
P.O. Box 369
Greenhurst, NY 14742, USA

Crist, George B (General)
CBS-TV
News Dept
51 W 52nd St
New York, NY 10019, USA

Cristal, Linda ((Actor)
9129 Hazen Drive
Beverly Hills, CA 90210, USA

Cristofer, Michael (Writer)
Lovett 9830 Wilshire Blvd
Beverly Hills, CA 90212-1804, USA

Cristofer, Michael (Director, Writer)
c/o Geyer Kosinski *Media Talent Group*
9200 Sunset Blvd
Suite 550
Los Angeles, CA 90069, USA

Cristol, Stanley J (Misc)
1638 West 3rd Avenue
Durango, CO 81301-4912, USA

Criswell, Jeff (Athlete, Football Player)
1101 Walnut St
Kansas City, MO 64106, USA

Criswell, Ray
2216 Jones Rd
Jacksonville, FL 32220-1210, USA

Critchfield, Charles L (Physicist)
PO Box 993
Los Alamos, NM 87544, USA

Critchfield, Russell (Athlete, Basketball Player)
7 Patches Drive
Chico, CA 95928-4353, USA

Crite, Winston (Athlete, Basketball Player)
8812 Heely Court
Bakersfield, CA 93311-1923, USA

Critelli, Michael (Business Person)
Pitney Bowes Inc
1 Elmcroft Road
Stamford, CT 06926, USA

Criter, Ken (Athlete, Football Player)
PO Box 441343
Aurora, CO 80044-1343, USA

Criter, Ken (Athlete, Football Player)
P.O. Box 441343
Aurora, CO 80044, USA

Crittenden, Ray
8915 Garden Gate Dr
Fairfax, VA 22031-1475, USA

Crittenden, Ray (Athlete, Football Player)
8915 Garden Gate Dr
Fairfax, VA 22031, USA

Crivello, Anthony (Actor)
c/o Neil Bagg *Buchwald/Fortitude (LA)*
6500 Wilshire Blvd
Suite 2200
Los Angeles, CA 90048, USA

Croce, A J
1027 Meade Ave
San Diego, CA 92116, USA

Croce, Pat (Basketball Player, Business Person, Sportscaster)
c/o Staff Member *WmE2 (WMA-LA)*
1 William Morris Pl
Beverly Hills, CA 90212, USA

Crocicchia, James (Athlete, Football Player)
11 Lanesboro Rd
Ladera Ranch, CA 92694, USA

Crocicchia, Jim (Athlete, Football Player)
2867 Calle Heraldo
San Clemente, CA 92673-3536, USA

Crocker, Chris (Actor, Reality TV Star)
44 Blue Productions
4040 Vineland Ave Ste 105
Studio City, CA 91604, USA

Crocker, Dillard (Athlete, Basketball Player)
5601 Holiday Park Blvd
North Port, FL 34287-2615, USA

Crocker, Erin (Race Car Driver)
Evernham Motors
320 Aviation Dr
Statesville, NC 28677, USA

Crocker, Ian (Athlete, Olympic Athlete, Swimmer)
8901 Ovalla Dr
Austin, TX 78749-5100

Crocker, Mary Lou (Athlete, Golfer)
1403 Sutton Dr
Carrollton, TX 75006, USA

Crockett, Bobby (Athlete, Football Player)
PO Box 26
Harriet, AR 72639-0026, USA

Crockett, Bobby (Athlete, Football Player)
P.O. Box 26
Harriet, AR 72639, USA

Crockett, Gibson (Cartoonist)
4713 Great Oak Road
Rockville, MD 20853, USA

Crockett, Ivory (World Record Holder)
812 N Elm Ave
Saint Louis, MO 63119-1721, USA

Crockett, Monte (Athlete, Football Player)
2696 Halleck Dr
Columbus, OH 43209, USA

Crockett, Ray (Athlete, Football Player)
361 S White Chapel Blvd
Southlake, TX 76092-7312, USA

Crockett, Willis (Athlete, Football Player)
493 Bojo Ella Dr
Douglas, GA 31533, USA

Crockett, Zack (Athlete, Football Player)
6136 NW 120th Ter
Coral Springs, FL 33076, USA

Croel, Mike (Athlete, Football Player)
8305 Lookout Mountain Ave
Los Angeles, CA 90046, USA

Croft, Don (Athlete, Football Player)
511 Larry Dr
Irving, TX 75060-2847, USA

Croft, Dwayne (Opera Singer)
Columbia Artists Mgmt Inc
165 W 57th St
New York, NY 10019, USA

Croftcheck, Don (Athlete, Football Player)
120 Mine Street
Allison, PA 15413, USA

Crofts, Dash (Musician, Songwriter, Writer)
Nationwide Entertainment
2756 N Green Valley Parkway
Henderson, NV 89014, USA

Croghan, Emma-Kate (Director)
Hilary Linstead
500 Oxford St
Bondi Junction, NSW 2022, AUSTRALIA

Croker, Stephen B (Steve) (General)
2 Byford Court
Chestertown, MD 21620, USA

Croll, Jimmy (Misc)
Thoroughbred Racing Assn
420 Fair Hill Dr
#1
Elkton, MD 21921, USA

Cromartie, Warren (Athlete, Baseball Player)
c/o Staff Member *Montreal Expos*
4549 Avenue Pierre de Coubertin
Montreal
Quebec H1V 3N7, CANADA

Crombeen, Mike (Athlete, Hockey Player)
817 Foxcroft Blvd
Newmarket, ON L3X 1M8, Canada

Crombie, Ed (Race Car Driver)
10 Davoren
Clearwater, BC VOE INO, Canada

Crombie, Jonathan (Actor)
Sullivan Entertainment
111 Davenport Road
Toronto, ON M5R 3R3, CANADA

Crombie, Robert B (Astronaut)
20632 Queens Park Ln
Huntington Beach, CA 92646-6018, USA

Cromer, D T (Athlete, Baseball Player)
134 Ridge Top Rd
Lexington, SC 29072-7130, USA

Cromer, Tripp (Athlete, Baseball Player)
32 W Tombee Ln
Columbia, SC 29209-0844, USA

Cromwell, James (Actor)
c/o Nancy Seltzer *Nancy Seltzer & Associates*
6220 Del Valle Drive
Los Angeles, CA 90048, USA

Cromwell, Nolan (Athlete, Coach, Football Coach, Football Player)
2624 140th Ave NE
Bellevue, WA 98005, USA

Cron, Chris (Athlete, Baseball Player)
14879 S 43rd Pl
Phoenix, AZ 85044-6788, USA

Cron, Chris (Athlete, Baseball Player)
Erie Sea Wolves 110 E lOth St
Attn: Managers Office
Erie, PA 16501-1256, USA

Cronan, Pete (Athlete, Football Player)
13 Saddle Hill Rd
Hopkinton, MA 01748-1151, USA

Cronan, Pete (Athlete, Football Player)
13 Saddle Hill Rd
Hopkinton, MA 01748, USA

Cronbach, Lee J (Educator)
2614 Oregon St
Union City, CA 94587, USA

Crone, Ray (Athlete, Baseball Player)
508 Panorama
Waxahachie, TX 75165-5919, USA

Cronenberg, David (Actor)
c/o Renee Tab *Sentient*
881 Alma Real Dr
317
Los Angeles, CA 90272, USA

Cronenweth, Regina
5410 Wilshire Blvd. #227
Los Angeles, CA 90036

Cronin, Eugene (Athlete, Football Player)
2445 37th Ave
Sacramento, CA 95822, USA

Cronin, James W (Nobel Prize Laureate)
175 N Harbor Dr Apt 4902
Chicago, IL 60601-7892, USA

Cronin, Kevin (Musician)
1547 Pathfinder Ave
Westlake Village, CA 91362, USA

Cronin, Mark (Producer)
1015 Oak Grove Ave
San Marino, CA 91108, USA

Cronin, Rachel (Actor)
c/o Lisa King *King Talent*
303-228 E 4th Ave
Vancouver V5T-1G5, CANADA

Cronin, Shawn (Athlete, Hockey Player)
4163 SE Oakland St
Stuart, FL 34997-5415, USA

Cronkite, Kathy (Actor)
PO Box 5261
Austin, TX 78763, USA

Cronnenberg, David (Director)
Toronto Antenna
244 DuPont St #200
Toronto, ON M5R 1V7, CANADA

Cronyn, Christopher (Producer)
c/o Staff Member *Lichter Grossman
Nichols Adler & Goodman*
9200 Sunset Blvd
Suite 1200
Los Angeles, CA 90069-3507, USA

Cronyn, Susan Cooper (Producer, Writer)
c/o Ron Bernstein *ICM Partners (ICM-LA)*
10250 Constellation Blvd Fl 7
Los Angeles, CA 90067, USA

Crook, Edward Jr (Boxer)
4512 Moline Ave
Columbus, GA 31907, USA

Crook, Lorianne (Musician)
1111 Wilson Pike
Brentwood, TN 37027, USA

Crook & Chase
3201 Dickerson Pike
Nashville, TN 37207-2905

Crooke, Edward A (Business Person)
Constellation Energy Group
39 W Lexington St
Baltimore, MD 21201, USA

Croom, Corey (Athlete, Football Player)
414 Lawrence St
Sandusky, OH 44870, USA

Croom, Sylvester (Athlete, Coach,
Football Player)
3909 12th St NE
Tuscaloosa, AL 35404, USA

Crooms, Chris (Athlete, Football Player)
810 Landon Springs Ln
Spring, TX 77373-8461, USA

Crooms, Chris (Athlete, Football Player)
1522 Beaumont St
Baytown, TX 77520, USA

Cropper, Marshall (Athlete, Football
Player)
2932 Fort Baker Dr SE
Washington, DC 20020, USA

Cropper, Steve (Musician)
819 Tyne Blvd
Nashville, TN 37220, USA

Crosbie, Annette
c/o Staff Member *Independent Talent
Group (ITG-UK)*
Oxford House
76 Oxford St
London W1D 1BS, UK

Crosbie, John C (Politician)
235 Water St
Saint John's NF A1C 5L3, CANADA

Crosby, Alfred W (Historian)
2506 Bowman Ave
Austin, TX 78703, USA

Crosby, Bobby (Athlete, Baseball Player)
11463 Anticost Way
Cypress, CA 90630-5429, USA

Crosby, Bubba (Athlete, Baseball Player)
4309 Jane St
Bellaire, TX 77401-4605, USA

Crosby, Caitlin (Musician)
c/o Gerry Cagle *Crysis Management*
8424 Santa Monica Blvd
West Hollywood, CA 90069, USA

Crosby, Cathy Lee (Actor)
CLC Productions
1223 Wilshire Blvd
#404
Santa Monica, CA 90403, USA

Crosby, Cleveland
2703 Sandal Walk
Pearland, TX 77584-3365, USA

Crosby, Cleveland (Athlete, Football
Player)
2703 Sandal Walk
Pearland, TX 77584-3365, USA

Crosby, David (Musician)
1876 Sky Dr
Santa Ynez, CA 93460, USA

Crosby, Denise (Actor, Model)
935 Embury St
Pacific Palisades, CA 90272, USA

Crosby, Ed (Athlete, Baseball Player)
6952 Brightwood Ln
Apt 9
Garden Grove, CA 92845-2976, USA

Crosby, Elaine (Athlete, Golfer)
2580 Meadowbrook Ln
Jackson, MI 49201-7702, USA

Crosby, J Ted (Admiral)
21966 Dolores St Apt 255
Castro Valley, CA 94546-6964, USA

Crosby, Kathryn
Box 85
Genda, NV 89411

Crosby, Kathryn Grant (Actor)
PO Box 85
Genoa, NV 89411, USA

Crosby, Ken (Athlete, Baseball Player)
P.O. Box 680306
Park City, UT 84068-0306, USA

Crosby, Lucinda (Actor)
4942 Vineland Ave
#200
North Hollywood, CA 91601, USA

Crosby, Mark
3500 W. Olive Ave. #1400
Burbank, CA 91505

Crosby, Mary
3500 W. Olive Ave. #1400
Burbank, CA 91505

Crosby, Mason (Athlete, Football Player)
2050 S Point Rd
Green Bay, WI 54313-5445, USA

Crosby, Norm (Actor, Comedian)
c/o Staff Member *WmE2 (WMA-LA)*
1 William Morris Pl
Beverly Hills, CA 90212, USA

Crosby, Paul (Musician)
Helter Skelter
Plaza
535 Kings Road
London SW10 0S, UNITED KINGDOM
(UK)

Crosby, Phil (Athlete, Football Player)
14614 Waterside Dr
Charlotte, NC 28278-7355, USA

Crosby, Sidney (Athlete, Hockey Player)
c/o J P Barry *C A A Hockey*
822 11th Ave SW
Suite 204
Calgary, AB T2R 0E5, Canada

Crosby, Steve (Athlete, Football Player)
San Diego Chargers PO Box 609609
San Diego, CA 92160-9609, USA

Crosby, Steve (Athlete, Coach, Football
Coach, Football Player)
Vanderbilt University
2201 W End Ave
Attn: Football Coaching Staff
Nashville, TN 37235, USA

Croshere, Austin (Athlete, Basketball
Player)
11721 Sea Star Dr
Indianapolis, IN 46256-9438, USA

Cross, Ben (Actor)
c/o Jeff Goldberg *Jeff Goldberg
Management*
817 Monte Leon Dr
Beverly Hills, CA 90210, USA

Cross, Billy (Athlete, Football Player)
PO Box 103
Canadian, TX 79014-0103, USA

Cross, Burton (Politician)
8 Lonsdale Rd
Farmingdale, ME 04344, USA

Cross, Christopher (Musician, Songwriter)
1708 W. 29th St
Austin, TX 78703, USA

Cross, Cory (Athlete, Hockey Player)
2963 W Bayshore Ct
Tampa, FL 33611, USA

Cross, David (Actor, Comedian)
c/o Tim Sarkes *Brillstein Entertainment
Partners*
9150 Wilshire Blvd #350
Beverly Hills, CA 90212, USA

Cross, Howard
79 Poplar Dr
Paramus, NJ 07652-1357, USA

Cross, Howard (Athlete, Football Player)
79 Poplar Dr
Paramus, NJ 07652, USA

Cross, Irv (Athlete, Football Player,
Sportscaster)
2196 Marison Rd
Saint Paul, MN 55113, USA

Cross, Iry
2196 Marion Rd
Saint Paul, MN 55113-3824, USA

Cross, Jeff (Athlete, Football Player)
8045 SW 100th St
Miami, FL 33156-2523, USA

Cross, Jeff (Athlete, Basketball Player)
5 Patterson Cir
Exeter, NH 03833-6542, USA

Cross, Jeff (Athlete, Football Player)
2715 Walkers Way
Weston, FL 33331, USA

Cross, Joseph (Actor)
Innovative Artists
1505 10th St
Santa Monica, CA 90401, USA

Cross, Justin (Athlete, Football Player)
10 Longwood Dr
Hampton, NH 03842-1122, USA

Cross, Justin (Athlete, Football Player)
10 Longwood Dr
Hampton, NH 03842, USA

Cross, Kendall (Athlete, Olympic Athlete,
Wrestler)
2209 Kings Pass
Rockwall, TX 75032-5921

Cross, Marcia (Actor)
870 5th Ave
Los Angeles, CA 90005, USA

Cross, Randall L (Randy) (Athlete,
Football Player, Sportscaster)
155 Travertine Trl
Alpharetta, GA 30022, USA

Cross, Roger (Actor)
c/o Staff Member *Silver Massetti &
Szatmary (SMS) Talent Inc*
8383 Wilshire Blvd
Suite 230
Beverly Hills, CA 90211, USA

Cross, Russell (Basketball Player)
Elmhurst College
Athletic Dept
190 S Prospect Ave
Elmhurst, IL 60126, USA

Cross, Terry M (Admiral)
Commander US Coast Guard Pacific
Coast Guard Island
Alameda, CA 94501, USA

Crossan, Dave (Athlete, Football Player)
3590 Round Bottom Rd
Cincinnati, OH 45244-3026, USA

Crosse, Liris (Actor, Model)
c/o Staff Member *Cinematic Management*
249 1/2 E 13th St
New York, NY 10003, USA

Crossley, Charlotte (Actor, Musician)
Stone Manners Agency
6500 Wilshire Blvd #550
Los Angeles, CA 90048, USA

Crossley-Holland, Kevin (Writer)
c/o Staff Member *Random House Publicity (Toronto)*
1 Toronto St
Suite 300
Toronto, ON M5C 2V6, Canada

Crossman, Doug (Athlete, Hockey Player)
PO Box 634
Somers Point, NJ 08244, USA

Crosswhite, Leon (Athlete, Football Player)
1955 E 120th St Rear
Cleveland, OH 44106-1907, USA

Croston, Dave (Athlete, Football Player)
400 Homestead Ln
Sergeant Bluff, IA 51054-3512, USA

Croteau, Gary (Athlete, Hockey Player)
8380 E. Hinsdale Ave.
Centennial, CO 80112-1905, USA

Crotty, Jim (Athlete, Football Player)
215 5 195th St
Des Moines, WA 98148-2137, USA

Crotty, John (Athlete, Basketball Player)
685 Destacada Ave
Miami, FL 33156-8001, USA

Crouch, Andrae (Musician, Songwriter)
20265 Wells Dr
Woodland Hills, CA 91364, USA

Crouch, Eric (Athlete, Football Player, Heisman Trophy Winner)
1505 N 138th St
Omaha, NE 68154-3888, USA

Crouch, Lindsay (Actor)
15115 1/2 Sunset Blvd
#A
Pacific Palisades, CA 90272, USA

Crouch, Matthew (Producer)
3556 Multiview Dr
Los Angeles, CA 90068, USA

Crouch, Paul (Misc)
Trinity Broadcasting Network
PO Box A
Santa Ana, CA 92711, USA

Crouch, Robbie (Race Car Driver)
106 Pierremount Ave
New Britain, CT 06053, USA

Crouch, Roger K (Astronaut)
120 6th St NE
Washington, DC 20002-8307, USA

Crouch, Sandra (Musician, Songwriter, Writer)
Sparrow Communications Group
101 Winners Circle
Brentwood, TN 37027, USA

Crouch, William T (Bill) (Journalist, Photographer)
5660 Valley Oaks Court
Placerville, CA 95667-9363, USA

Crouch, Zach (Athlete, Baseball Player)
9418 San Paulo Cir
Elk Grove, CA 95624-2126, USA

Croucher, Juan
45 Cayuse Lane
Rancho Palos Verdes, CA 90274

Crouse, Lindsay (Actor)
263 Monte Grigio Dr
Pacific Palisades, CA 90272, USA

Croushore, Rich (Athlete, Baseball Player)
3110 Bastogne Way
Benton, AR 72019-2943, USA

Croushore, Rick (Athlete, Baseball Player)
4001 Tanglewilde St
Apt 101
Houston, TX 77063, USA

Crouthamel, Jake (Athlete, Football Player)
385 Elliott Rd
Centerville, MA 02632, USA

Crouther, Lance (Actor, Producer, Writer)
c/o Ari Greenburg *WME (LA)*
9601 Wilshire Blvd Fl 3
Beverly Hills, CA 90210, USA

Crow, Al (Athlete, Football Player)
6191 Occoquan Forest Dr
Manassas, VA 20112, USA

Crow, Bill (Athlete, Basketball Player)
21300 River Road
15
Perris, CA 92570-8390, USA

Crow, Dean (Athlete, Baseball Player)
11507 Wickchester Ln
Houston, TX 77043-4521, USA

Crow, Don (Athlete, Baseball Player)
1023 E Lincoln Ave
Nampa, ID 83686-5321, USA

Crow, F Trammell (Business Person)
Trammell Crow Co
Trammell Crow Center
2001 Ross Ave
Dallas, TX 75201, USA

Crow, Harian R (Business Person)
Trammell Crow Co
Trammell Crow Center
2001 Ross Ave
Dallas, TX 75201, USA

Crow, John David (Athlete, Coach, Football Coach, Football Player, Heisman Trophy Winner)
5004 Augusta Cir
College Station, TX 77845, USA

Crow, Lindon (Athlete, Football Player)
2869 Riachuelo
San Clemente, CA 92673, USA

Crow, Mark (Athlete, Basketball Player)
501 West Bay Street
Jacksonville, FL 32202-4428, USA

Crow, Martin D (Cricketer)
PO Box 109302
New Market
Auckland, NEW ZEALAND

Crow, Rachel (Actor, Musician)
c/o Christian Carino *Creative Artists Agency (CAA-LA)*
2000 Ave Of The Stars
Los Angeles, CA 90067, USA

Crow, Sheryl (Musician, Songwriter)
1900 N Vista St
Los Angeles, CA 90046, USA

Crow, Wayne (Athlete, Football Player)
16561 Fawn St
Truckee, CA 96161, USA

Crowded House, 3 Mitchell Rd
Rose Bay
Sydney, AUSTRALIA NSW 2929, AUSTRALIA

Crowder, Bruce (Athlete, Hockey Player)
7 Kyle Dr
Nashua, NH 03062-4539, USA

Crowder, Channing (Athlete, Football Player)
8921 Southern Orchard Rd N
Davie, FL 33328, USA

Crowder, Corey (Athlete, Basketball Player)
725 Ballard Bridge Road
Carrollton, GA 30117-9104, USA

Crowder, Keith (Athlete, Hockey Player)
P.O. Box 95
Stn Main
Essex, ON N8M 2Y1, Canada

Crowder, Randy (Athlete, Football Player)
803 Strawberry Ln
Brandon, FL 33511, USA

Crowder, Troy (Athlete, Hockey Player)
Adventure North Hockey
103 Panache North Shore Rd
Whitefish, ON P0M 3E0, Canada

Crowe, Cameron (Director, Writer)
1016 Amalfi Dr
Pacific Palisades, CA 90272, USA

Crowe, James (J.D.) (Musician)
JD Crowe Festival
201 South Lexington Avenue
Wilmore, KY 40390, USA

Crowe, Martin (Cricketer)
Marylebone Cricket Club
Lord's Cricket Ground
London NW8 8QN, UK

Crowe, Mia (Actor, Model)
Mia Crowe Official Fan Club
7336 Santa Monica Blvd #633
West Hollywood, CA 90046, USA

Crowe, Pat (Horse Racer)
202-100 Millside Dr
Milton, ON L9T 5E2, USA

Crowe, Phil (Athlete, Hockey Player)
1409 Pintail Ct
Windsor, CO 80550-6144, USA

Crowe, Russell (Actor)
P.O.Box 5062
Sth Turramurra, N.S.W 2074, AUSTRALIA

Crowe, Sara
13 Shorts Garden
London, ENGLAND WC2H 9AT

Crowe, Tonya (Actor)
6502 Hayes Dr
Los Angeles, CA 90048, USA

Crowe, William J Jr (Admiral, Diplomat)
Global Options
1615 L St NW
#300
Washington, DC 20036, USA

Crowell, Angelo (Athlete, Football Player)
5309 Dockery Dr
Charlotte, NC 28209-3668, USA

Crowell, Craven H Jr (Government Official)
Tennessee Valley Authority
400 W Summit Hill Dr
Knoxville, TN 37902, USA

Crowell, Germane (Athlete, Football Player)
200 Luzelle Dr
Winston Salem, NC 27103, USA

Crowell, Jim (Athlete, Baseball Player)
4003 Sleighbell Ln
Valparaiso, IN 46383-1943, USA

Crowell, John C (Misc)
300 Hot Springs Road
Montecito, CA 93108, USA

Crowell, Rodney (Musician)
c/o David Whitehead *Maine Road Management*
195 Chrystie St
Suite 901F
New York, NY 10002, USA

Crowley, Ben (Actor)
c/o Staff Member *Kass & Stokes Management*
9229 Sunset Blvd
Suite 504
Los Angeles, CA 90069, USA

Crowley, Candy (Correspondent)
5709 Ridgefield Rd
Bethesda, MD 20816, USA

Crowley, Joseph (Congressman, Politician)
2404 Rayburn HOB
Washington, DC 20515, USA

Crowley, Joseph N (Educator)
University of Nevada
President's Office
Reno, NV 89557, USA

Crowley, Kevin (Actor)
c/o Lorraine Berglund *Lorraine Berglund Management*
11537 Hesby St.
North Hollywood, CA 91601, USA

Crowley, Monica (Television Host)

Crowley, Pat (Actor)
551 Perrugia Way
Los Angeles, CA 90077, USA

Crowley, Paul (Athlete, Hockey Player)
Canadian Hockey Enterprises
727 Lansdowne St W
Peterborough, ON K9J 1Z2, Canada

Crowley, Ted (Athlete, Hockey Player)
248 Seaward Bnd Apt 53-2
Teaticket, MA 02536-5843, USA

Crowley, Terry (Athlete, Baseball Player)
18405 Ensor Farm Ct
Parkton, MD 21120-9685, USA

Crowley, Terry (Athlete, Baseball Player)
Baltimore Orioles 333 W Camden St
Attn: Coaching Staff
Baltimore, MD 21201-2496, USA

Crown, David A (Misc)
3344 Twin Lakes Lane
Sanibel, FL 33957, USA

Crown, Lester (Business Person)
Henry Crown & Co
222 N. LaSalle St
Chicago, IL 60601

Crowson, Richard (Cartoonist, Editor)
Wichita Eagle-Beacon
Editorial Dept
825 E Douglas Ave
Wichita, KS 67202, USA

Crowton, Gary (Coach, Football Coach)
Brigham Young University
Athletic Dept
Provo, UT 84602, USA

Croyle, Brodie (Athlete, Football Player)
105 Apple Blossom Dr
Brandon, MS 39047-7443, USA

Croyle, Philip (Athlete, Football Player)
5883 Treetop Ct
San Jose, CA 95123, USA

Crozier, Eric (Athlete, Baseball Player)
3142 Clermont Rd
Columbus, OH 43227-1833, USA

Crozier, Joseph R (Joe) (Athlete, Coach, Hockey Player)
299 Randwood Dr
Buffalo, NY 14221-1444, USA

Crudale, Mike (Athlete, Baseball Player)
2319 Tree Creek Pl
Danville, CA 94506-2065, USA

Crudup, Billy (Actor)
c/o Jimmy Darmody *Creative Artists Agency (CAA-LA)*
2000 Ave Of The Stars
Los Angeles, CA 90067, USA

Cruickshank, John (Admiral)
34 Frogston Road W
Edinburgh, EH10 7AJ Scotland, USA

Cruikshank, Dave (Athlete, Olympic Athlete, Speed Skater)
1223 Aspen Ct
Delafield, WI 53018-1300, USA

Cruikshank, Lucas (Actor)
c/o Evan Weiss *Collective*
8383 Wilshire Blvd
Suite 1050
Beverly Hills, CA 90211, USA

Cruikshank, Thomas H (Business Person)
5949 Sherry Lane
#1035
Dallas, TX 75225, USA

Cruise, Asia (Musician)
c/o Staff Member *11-16 Entertainment*
11048 La Maida
Suite 9
North Hollywood, CA 91601, USA

Cruise, Earl (Horse Racer)
151 Liberty St Apt 16
Little Ferry, NJ 07643-1790, USA

Cruise, Jimmy (Horse Racer)
34431 Windley Cir
Eustis, FL 32736-7265, USA

Cruise, Tom (Actor, Director, Producer)
c/o Amanda Lundberg *42West (NY)*
220 W 42nd St
12th Floor
New York, NY 10036, USA

Cruisie, Jennifer (Writer)
c/o *Argh Ink LLC*
285 5th Ave #470
Brooklyn, NY 11215, USA

Crum, E Denzel (Denny) (Athlete, Basketball Player, Coach)
6901 Routt Rd
Louisville, KY 40299-5243, USA

Crumb, George H (Composer)
240 Kirk Lane
Media, PA 19063, USA

Crumb, Robert (Artist, Cartoonist)
c/o Staff Member *Fantagraphics Books*
7563 Lake City Way
Seattle, WA 98115, USA

Crumb, Robert (R) (Cartoonist)
20 Rue du Pont Vieux
Sauve 30610, FRANCE

Crumley Jr, James R (Religious Leader)
108 Castle Church Road
Chapin, SC 29036-7853, USA

Crump, Diane (Horse Racer)
PO Box 297
Linden, VA 22642-0297, USA

Crump, Dwayne (Athlete, Football Player)
35708 Marciel Ave
Madera, CA 93636-8414, USA

Crump, Harry (Athlete, Football Player)
9601 Collins Ave PH 201
Bal Harbour, FL 33154, USA

Crumpler, Alge (Athlete, Football Player)
2155 Enclave Mill Dr
Dacula, GA 30019-3290, USA

Crumpler, Carlester (Athlete, Football Player)
4355 River Gate Ln Unit B
Little River, SC 29566-6833, USA

Crusan, Doug (Athlete, Football Player)
6263 Hanover Ct
Fishers, IN 46038-1799, USA

Crutcher, Chris
3405 E. Marion Ct.
Spokane, WA 99223-7215

Crutcher, Lawrence M (Publisher)
Book-of-the-Month Club
Rockefeller Center
New York, NY 10020, USA

Crutchfield, Dwayne (Athlete, Football Player)
6936 Rebecca Dr
Niagara Falls, NY 14304, USA

Crutchfield, Edward E (Financier)
First Union Corp
1 First union Center
Charlotte, NC 28288, USA

Crutzen, Paul J (Nobel Prize Laureate)
max Planck Chemistry Institut Jon-Joachim Becher Weg 27
Mainz 55128, GERMANY

Cruyff, Johan (Coach, Soccer Player)
Koninklijke Nederlandse Voetbalbond
Postbus 515
Zeist, AM 3700, NETHERLANDS

Cruz, Alexis (Actor)
c/o Staff Member *Abrams Artists Agency (LA)*
9200 Sunset Blvd
11th Floor
Los Angeles, CA 90069, USA

Cruz, Cirilio (Baseball Player)
St Louis Cardinals
E8 Calle H
Arroyo, PR 00714-2236, USA

Cruz, Deivi (Baseball Player)
Detroit Tigers
611 Woodward Ave
Detroit, MI 48226-3408, USA

Cruz, Hector (Athlete, Baseball Player)
1646 N Monticello Ave
Chicago, IL 60647-4719, USA

Cruz, Henry (Athlete, Baseball Player)
Los Angeles Dodgers
PO Box 70012
Fajardo, PR 00738-7012, USA

Cruz, Ivan (Athlete, Baseball Player)
3874 Bright Leaf Ct
Jacksonville, FL 32246-7660, USA

Cruz, Jacob (Athlete, Baseball Player)
Yakima Bears PO Box 483
Attn: Coaching Staff
Yakima, WA 98907-0483, USA

Cruz, Jacob (Athlete, Baseball Player)
1582 W Commerce Ave
Gilbert, AZ 85233-4103, USA

Cruz, Juan (Athlete, Baseball Player)
c/o Staff Member *Chicago Cubs*
Wrigley Field
1060 West Addison Street
Chicago, IL 60613, USA

Cruz, Julio (Athlete, Baseball Player)
6599 170th Pl SE
Bellevue, WA 98006-6012, USA

Cruz, Mike (DJ)
c/o Staff Member *Diva Central Inc*
7510 W Sunset Blvd Ste 1445
Los Angees, CA 90046, USA

Cruz, Monica (Actor)
c/o Antonio Rubial *Kuranda Management*
Santo Angel, 84
Madrid 28043, Spain

Cruz, Nelson (Athlete, Baseball Player)
2021 Stone Canyon Ct
Arlington, TX 76012-5762, USA

Cruz, Penelope (Actor, Model)
9578 Hidden Valley Rd
Beverly Hills, CA 90210, USA

Cruz, Raymond
8383 Wilshire Blvd. #954
Beverly Hills, CA 90211

Cruz, Smith Martin (Writer)
Random House
1745 Broadway
#B1
New York, NY 10019, USA

Cruz, Taio (Musician)
c/o Staff Member *Energon Entertainment*
276 5th Ave
Suite 712
New York, NY 10001, USA

Cruz, Tommy (Athlete, Baseball Player)
High Desert Mavericks 12000 Stadium Rd
Attn Coaching Staff
Adelanto, CA 92301-3400, USA

Cruz, Tommy (Athlete, Baseball Player)
E8 Calle H
Arroyo, PR 00714-2236, USA

Cruz, Valerie (Actor)
c/o Staff Member *Innovative Artists (LA)*
1505 10th St
Santa Monica, CA 90401, USA

Cruz, Victor (Athlete, Football Player)
c/o Malik Hafeez Shareef *Dimensional Sports, Inc.*
3148 Circle Drive SW
Roanoke, VA 24018, USA

Cruz, Wilson
Latin Hollywood Films
153 San Vicente Blvd #2-G
Santa Monica, CA 90402, USA

Cruz Jr, Jose (Athlete, Baseball Player)
8475 SW 53rd Ave
Miami, FL 77584-1566, USA

Cruz-Romo, Gilda (Opera Singer)
1315 Lockhill-Selma Road
San Antonio, TX 78213, USA

Cruz Sr, Jose D (Athlete, Baseball Player)
2309 Delta Bridge Dr
Pearland, TX 77584-1566, USA

Crvenkovski, Branko (President)
President's Office
Skopje, MACEDONIA

Cryder, Robert (Athlete, Football Player)
17411 NE 129th St
Redmond, WA 98052-1323, USA

Crye, John B (Actor, Producer, Writer)
c/o Staff Member *Fewdio*
13348 Reedley St
Panorama City, CA 91402, USA

Cryer, Gretchen (Actor, Songwriter, Writer)
885 W End Ave
New York, NY 10025, USA

Cryer, Jon (Actor)
4702 Klump Ave
N Hollywood, CA 90068, USA

Cryer, Suzanne (Actor)
c/o Chris Schmidt *Paradigm (LA)*
360 N Crescent Dr
North Bldg
Beverly Hills, CA 90210, USA

Cryner, Bobby
PO Box 2147
Hendersonville, TN

Crystal, Billy (Actor, Comedian)
860 Chatauqua Blvd
Pacific Palisades, CA 90272, USA

Crystal, McClory (Stylist)
c/o Staff Member *ESP (London)*
63 Charlotte St.
1st Floor
London W11 4PG, UK

Crystals (Music Group)
27-L Ambiance Ct
Bardonia, NY 10954-1421, USA

Crystat, Ronald G (Biologist)
435 E 70th St
#34B
New York, NY 10021, USA

C. Scott, Robert (Congressman, Politician)
1201 Longworth HOB
Washington, DC 20515, USA

Csikszentmihalyi, Mihaly (Misc)
5848 S University Ave
Chicago, IL 60637, USA

Csokas, Marton (Actor)
c/o George Freeman *WME (LA)*
9601 Wilshire Blvd Fl 3
Beverly Hills, CA 90210, USA

Csonka, Lawrence R (Larry) (Athlete, Football Player)
Zonk Productions PO Box 39
Oak Hill, FL 32759, USA

Csupo, Gabor (Animator, Director, Producer)
12835 Mulholland Dr
Beverly Hills, CA 90210, USA

Ctvrtlik, Bob (Athlete, Olympic Athlete, Volleyball Player)
5525 E Seaside Walk #B
Long Beach, CA 90803, USA

Cua, Rick (Musician)
1086 Rip Steele Road
Columbia, TN 38401-7745, USA

Cuaron, Alfonso (Director)
Esperanto Filmoj
443 Greenwich St 5th Fl
New York, NY 10013, USA

Cuban, Mark (Business Person)
5424 Deloache Ave
Dallas, TX 75220, USA

Cuban, Mark (Actor, Director)
2929 Entertainment
9100 Wilshire Blvd
Ste 500 W
Beverly Hills, CA 90212, USA

Cubbage, Mike (Athlete, Baseball Player, Coach)
3349 Carroll Creek Rd
Keswick, VA 22947-9156, USA

Cube, Ice (Actor, Director, Musician)
4615 Petit Ave
Encino, CA 91436, USA

Cubillan, Darwin (Athlete, Baseball Player)
11505 Clumbet Ln
Lehigh Acres, FL 33971-3748, USA

Cubitt, David (Actor)
c/o Shelley Browning *Magnolia Entertainment (LA)*
9595 Wilshire Blvd
Suite 601
Beverly Hills, CA 90212, USA

Cuccurullo, Waren (Musician)
DD Productions
93A Westbourne Park Villas
London W2 5ED, UNITED KINGDOM (UK)

Cuche, Didier (Skier)
Les Bugnenets
Le Paquier 2058, SWITZERLAND

Cucinotta, Maria Grazia (Actor)
Cucchini Mgmt
Lundolevere del Melini 10
Rome 00192, ITALY

Cuckney, John G (Financier)
1 Comhill
London EC3V 3QR, UNITED KINGDOM (UK)

Cudahy, Richard D (Judge)
US Court of Appeals
219 S Dearborn St
Chicago, IL 60604, USA

Cuddie, Steve (Athlete, Hockey Player)
18 Hill Country Dr
Gormley, ON L0H 1G0, Canada

Cuddle, Steve (Athlete, Hockey Player)
24 Dodie St
Aurora, ON L4G 2L2, Canada

Cuddy, Jim (Musician)
c/o Staff Member *Agency Group Ltd, The (NY)*
142 West 57th St
6th Floor
New York, NY 10019, USA

Cuddyer, Michael (Athlete, Baseball Player)
10240 Washingtonia Palm Way
Apt 2024
Fort Myers, FL 33966-6915, USA

Cudi, Kid (Musician)
c/o Drew Elliot *Universal Media Artists*
8255 W Sunset Blvd
Los Angeles, CA 90046, USA

Cudlitz, Michael (Actor)
4221 Allott Ave
Sherman Oaks, CA 91423, USA

Cudmore, Daniel (Actor)
c/o Murray Gibson *Characters Talent Agency, The (Vancouver)*
1505 W 2nd Ave
#200
Vancouver, BC V6H 3Y4, Canada

Cuellar, Bobby (Athlete, Baseball Player)
Rochester Red Wings 1 Morrie Silver Way
Attn Coaching Staff
Rochester, NY 14608-1754, USA

Cuellar, Bobby (Athlete, Baseball Player)
705 E 6th St
Alice, TX 78332-4651, USA

Cueller, Henry (Congressman, Politician)
2463 Rayburn HOB
Washington, DC 20515, USA

Cueto, Al (Athlete, Basketball Player)
5714 Riviera Drive
Coral Gables, FL 33146-2751, USA

Culbertson, FrankL Captain (Astronaut)
15500 Meherrin Dr
Centreville, VA 20120-3733, USA

Culbertson Jr, Frank L (Astronaut)
15500 Meherrin Dr
Centreville, VA 20120-3733, USA

Culbreath, Jim (Athlete, Football Player)
212 Elder Ave
Lansdowne, PA 19050, USA

Culbreath, Joshua (Josh) (Athlete, Track Athlete)
Central State University
Athletic Dept
Wilberforce, OH 45384, USA

Culbreth, Feildin (Athlete, Baseball Player)
224 Claiborne Ct
Spartanburg, SC 29301, USA

Culhane, Jim (Athlete, Hockey Player)
Western Michigan University
8547 HathawayRd
Kalamazoo, MI 49009-6999, USA

Culkin, Kieran (Actor)
c/o Emily Gerson Saines *Brookside Artists Management (NY)*
250 W 57th St
Suite 2303
New York, NY 10107, USA

Culkin, Macaulay (Actor)
c/o Emily Gerson Saines *Brookside Artists Management (NY)*
250 W 57th St
Suite 2303
New York, NY 10107, USA

Culkin, Rory (Actor)
c/o Emily Gerson Saines *Brookside Artists Management (NY)*
250 W 57th St
Suite 2303
New York, NY 10107, USA

Cullars, Willie (Athlete, Football Player)
1034 Garfield Ave
Kansas City, KS 66104, USA

Cullen, Barry (Athlete, Hockey Player)
Cullen Motors
905 Woodlawn Rd W
Guelph, ON N1K 8B7, Canada

Cullen, Betsy (Athlete, Golfer)
4144 Greystone Way
Apt 707
Sugar Land, TX 77479, USA

Cullen, Brett (Actor)
2229 Glyndon Ave
Venice, CA 90291, USA

Cullen, Brian (Athlete, Hockey Player)
Brian Cullen Motors
386 Ontario St
St Catharines, ON L2R 5L8, Canada

Cullen, Jack (Athlete, Baseball Player)
164 Alexander Ave
Nutley, NJ 07110-1002, USA

Cullen, John (Athlete, Hockey Player)
1002 Legacy Hills Dr
McDonough, GA 30253-8824, USA

Cullen, Kimberly (Actor)
8916 Ashcroft Ave
West Hollywood, CA 90048, USA

Cullen, Matt (Athlete, Hockey Player)
5109 2nd StE
West Fargo, ND 58078-8211, USA

Cullen, Peter (Actor, Voice Over Artist)
c/o Staff Member *Tisherman Gilbert Motley Drozdoski Talent Agency (TGMD)*
6767 Forest Lawn Dr
Suite 101
Los Angeles, CA 90068, USA

Cullen, Ray (Athlete, Hockey Player)
20 Sydenham Dr
RR 2
Ilderton, ON N0M 2A0, Canada

Cullen, Sean M
10100 Santa Monica Blvd #2500
Los Angeles, CA 90067, USA

Cullen, Tim (Athlete, Baseball Player)
159 W G St
Benicia, CA 94510-3114, USA

Cullens, E Van (Business Person)
Harris Corp
1025 W NASA Blvd
Melbourne, FL 32919, USA

Culler, Glen (Scientist)
Culler Scientific Systems Corp
100 Burns Place
Goleta, CA 93117, USA

Cullerton, William (Admiral)
189 Briarwood Loop
Oak Brook, IL 60523-8714, USA

Culligan, Joe (Writer)
Research Investigative Services
650 NE 126th St
North Miami, FL 33161, USA

Cullimore, Jassen (Athlete, Hockey Player)
5509 S Washington St
Hinsdale, IL 60521-4965, USA

Cullinan, Edward H (Architect)
Wharf
1 Baldwin Terrace
London N1 7RU, UNITED KINGDOM (UK)

Cullity, Dave (Athlete, Football Player)
5420 Jarman St
Colorado Springs, CO 80906-8210, USA

Cullocks, Josh (Athlete, Football Player)
5511 Eastover Dr S
New Orleans, LA 70128-3658, USA

Cullum, Jamie (Musician)
c/o Martin Kirkup *Direct Management Group*
947 N La Cienega Blvd
Suite G
Los Angeles, CA 90069, USA

Cullum, Kaitlin (Actor)
c/o Norma Robbins *Abrams Artists Agency (LA)*
9200 Sunset Blvd
11th Floor
Los Angeles, CA 90069, USA

Cullum, Kimberly
8916 Ashcroft Ave.
Los Angeles, CA 90046

Cullum, Mark E (Cartoonist, Editor)
5401 Forest Acres Dr
Nashville, TN 37220, USA

Culp, Curley (Athlete, Football Player)
16811 Gravesend Rd
Pflugerville, TX 78660-1830, USA

Culp, Jason (Actor, Voice Over Artist)
c/o Staff Member *Random House Publicity (Toronto)*
1 Toronto St
Suite 300
Toronto, ON M5C 2V6, Canada

Culp, Ray (Athlete, Baseball Player)
7400 Waterline Rd
Austin, TX 78731-2055, USA

Culp, Stephen (Actor)
c/o Miriam Milgrom *Miriam Milgrom Management*
100 Garden City Plz
Garden City, NY 11530, USA

Culp, Steven (Actor)
1680 Las Lunas St
Pasadena, CA 91106, USA

Culpepper, Brad (Athlete, Football Player)
136 W Davis Blvd
Tampa, FL 33606, USA

Culpepper, Daunte (Athlete, Football Player)
16730 Berkshire Ct
Southwest Ranches, FL 33331-1331, USA

Culpepper, Ed (Athlete, Football Player)
811 Bluewater Dr
Sun City Center, FL 33573-6245, USA

Culpepper, Robert E (Athlete, Football Player)
1535 45th Ave E
Ellenton, FL 34222, USA

Cult, The
c/o Staff Member *Immortal Entertainment*
11965 Venice Blvd #204
Los Angeles, CA 90034-1063, USA

Cult Jam
PO Box 284
Brooklyn, NY 11203

Culture Beat
Schleiermacher Str. 2
Darmstadt, GERMANY D-64283

Culver, Curt S (Financier)
MGIC Investment Corp
250 E Killbourn Ave
Milwaukee, WI 53202, USA

Culver, George (Athlete, Baseball Player)
5409 Rustic Canyon St
Bakersfield, CA 93306-7315, USA

Culver, John C (Ex-Senator, Politician)
5409 Spangler Ave
Bethesda, MD 20816-1847, USA

Culver, Michael
77 Beak St.
London, ENGLAND W1F 9ST

Culver, Molly (Actor)
4537 Finley Ave
Los Angeles, CA 90027, USA

Cumberbatch, Benedict (Actor)
c/o Billy Lazarus *United Talent Agency (UTA)*
9336 Civic Center Dr
Beverly Hills, CA 90210, USA

Cumberland, John (Athlete, Baseball Player)
1771 Muddy Creek Rd
Dandridge, TN 37725-6674, USA

Cumberland Gap
159 Madison Ave. #2G
New York, NY 10016

Cumby, George E (Athlete, Football Player)
12090 Cross Fence Trl
Tyler, TX 75706-4239, USA

Cumming, Alan (Actor, Musician)
c/o Danielle Thomas *Untitled Entertainment (LA)*
350 S. Beverly Dr #200
Beverly Hills, CA 90212, USA

Cummings, Burton (Musician, Songwriter)
3758 Woodcliff Rd
Sherman Oaks, CA 91403, USA

Cummings, Dave
4130 La Village Dr. #107
La Jolla, CA 92037

Cummings, Donald (Admiral)
6577 Monte Vista Dr
San Bernardino, CA 92404-5525, USA

Cummings, Ed (Athlete, Football Player)
237 Schearbrook Ln
Stevensville, MT 59870-6405, USA

Cummings, Erin (Actor)
c/o Nate Bryson *Paradigm (LA)*
360 N Crescent Dr
North Bldg
Beverly Hills, CA 90210, USA

Cummings, Jim (Voice Over Artist)
29482 Malibu View Ct
Agoura Hills, CA 91301, USA

Cummings, Joe (Athlete, Football Player)
4034 Oshaughnessy St
Missoula, MT 59808-5659, USA

Cummings, John (Athlete, Baseball Player)
21 Park Paseo
Laguna Niguel, CA 92677-5317, USA

Cummings, Midre (Athlete, Baseball Player)
19525 Morden Blush Dr
Lutz, FL 33558-9084, USA

Cummings, Pat (Athlete, Basketball Player)
9024 Symmes Knoll Court
Loveland, OH 45140-9330, USA

Cummings, Quinn (Actor)
3870 Glenfeliz Blvd
Los Angeles, CA 90039, USA

Cummings, Ralph W (Misc)
106 Darcy Drive
Clarksville, VA 23927-3524, USA

Cummings, Steve (Athlete, Baseball Player)
11010 Sagecrest Ln
Houston, TX 77089-3904, USA

Cummings, Terry (Athlete, Basketball Player)
2400 Parkland Dr NE Unit 108
Atlanta, GA 30324-3592, USA

Cummings, Terry (Athlete, Basketball Player)
12820 West Golden Lane
San Antonio, TX 78249, USA

Cummings, Whitney (Actor)
3633 Bellfield Way
Studio City, CA 91604, USA

Cummins, Barry (Athlete, Hockey Player)
155 Marsden St
Kimberley, BC V1A 1G8, Canada

Cummins, Gregory Scott (Actor)
Schiowitz/Clay/Rose
1680 N Vine St
#1016
Los Angeles, CA 90028, USA

cummins, jim (Athlete, Hockey Player)
25640 Kinyon
Taylor, MI 48180-3281, USA

Cummins, Peggy (Actor)
17 Greenacres Dr
Otterborune Winchester SO212HE,
UNITED KINGDOM (UK)

Cumpsty, Michael (Actor)
c/o Staff Member *Innovative Artists (LA)*
1505 10th St
Santa Monica, CA 90401, USA

Cundall, Teri (Stylist)
222 Alexander Ave
San Rafael, CA 94901, USA

Cundey, Dean R (Cinematographer)
344 Georgian Road
La Canada, CA 91011, USA

Cundieff, Rusty (Actor)
c/o Norman Aladjem *Levity Entertainment Group*
360 N Crescent Dr
North Bldg
Beverly Hills, CA 90210, USA

Cundiff, Billy (Athlete, Football Player)
4488 E Thomas Rd Unit 2046
Phoenix, AZ 85018-7632, USA

Cunnane, Will (Athlete, Baseball Player)
123 Sleeoy Hollow Ln
Congers, NY 10920-1515, USA

Cunneyworth, Randy (Athlete, Coach, Hockey Player)
c/o Staff Member *Rochester Americans*
1 War Memorial Sq
Suite 228
Rochester, NY 14614, USA

cunneyworth, randy (Athlete, Hockey Player)
Montreal Canadiens
1275 Rue Saint-Antoine 0
Montreal, QC H3C 5L2, Canada

Cunniff, Jill (Musician)
Metropolitan Entertainment
2 Penn Plaza
#2600
New York, NY 10121, USA

Cunniff, John (Athlete, Hockey Player)

Cunningham, Bennie L (Athlete, Football Player)
P.O. Box 1086
Seneca, SC 29679, USA

Cunningham, Bill (Radio Personality)
8044 Montgomery Rd #650
Cincinnati, OH 45236, USA

Cunningham, Bill (Musician)
Horizon Mgmt
PO Box 8770
Endwell, NY 13762, USA

Cunningham, Brian (Race Car Driver)
PTG Racing
441 Victory Rd
Winchester, VA 22602, USA

Cunningham, Carl (Athlete, Football Player)
4471 Saddleworth Cir
Orlando, FL 32826, USA

Cunningham, Colin (Actor)
c/o Jordyn Palos *Persona PR*
8840 Wilshire Blvd
Suite 212
Beverly Hills, CA 90211, USA

Cunningham, Dick (Athlete, Football Player)
100 Rosewood Ct
Peachtree City, GA 30269-2237, USA

Cunningham, Dick (Athlete, Basketball Player)
5349 Desoto Pkwy
Sarasota, FL 34234-3076, USA

Cunningham, Doug (Athlete, Football Player)
5060 Harling Pl
Jackson, MS 39211, USA

Cunningham, Ed (Athlete, Football Player)
4154 Vinton Ave
Culver City, CA 90232-3420, USA

Cunningham, Gunther (Athlete, Coach, Football Coach, Football Player)
2250 E Hammond Lake Dr
Bloomfield Hills, MI 48302-0131, USA

Cunningham, Jay (Athlete, Football Player)
3617 Farland Rd
Cleveland, OH 44118-3016, USA

Cunningham, Jeffrey M (Publisher)
Forbes Magazine
60 5th Ave
New York, NY 10011, USA

Cunningham, Jennifer (Stylist)
c/o Staff Member *Rex Agency, The*
6311 Romaine St
Los Angeles, CA 90038, USA

Cunningham, Joe (Athlete, Baseball Player)
RR 1 Box 80A
Koshkonong, MO 65692-9526, USA

Cunningham, Katherine (Actor)
c/o Jean-Pierre (JP) Henraux *Henraux Management*
Prefers to be contacted by telephone
CA, USA

Cunningham, Kristan (Actor, Television Host)
c/o Cat Josell *Synergy Management*
15233 Ventura Blvd
Suite 707
Sherman Oaks, CA 91403, USA

Cunningham, Lee (Stylist)
2501 Commonwealth Ave
Los Angeles, CA 90027, USA

Cunningham, Leon (Athlete, Football Player)
5484 Brookwood Dr SW
Mableton, GA 30126-2028, USA

Cunningham, Liam (Actor)
Marina Martin
12/13 Poland St
London W1V 3DE, UNITED KINGDOM (UK)

Cunningham, Michael (Writer)
Farrar Straus Giroux
19 Union Square W
New York, NY 10003, USA

Cunningham, Randall (Admiral)
8651 anrol ave
San Diego, CA 92123-3430, USA

Cunningham, Randall (Athlete, Football Player)
9367 Jeremy Blaine Ct
Las Vegas, NV 89139-8358, USA

Cunningham, Richard (Athlete, Football Player)
100 Rosewood Ct
Peachtree City, GA 30269, USA

Cunningham, Richie (Athlete, Football Player)
610 Cheyenne Dr
Houma, LA 70360, USA

Cunningham, Sam (Athlete, Football Player)
9316 5 4th Ave
Inglewood, CA 90305, USA

Cunningham, Sean (Director, Producer)
4420 Hayvenhurst Ave
Encino, CA 91436, USA

Cunningham, T J (Athlete, Football Player)
11640 E Walsh Pl
Aurora, CO 80012, USA

Cunningham, Walter (Astronaut)
AVD
PO Box 604
Glenn Dale, MD 20769, USA

Cunningham, Walter Colonel (Astronaut)
1707 Post Oak Blvd Ste 263
Houston, 77056-3801 TX, USA

Cunningham, William J (Billy) (Athlete, Basketball Player, Coach)
Cunningham's Court Restaurant
31 Front Street
#33
Conshohocken, PA 19428-2867, USA

Cuoco, Kaley (Actor)
14717 Sutton St
Sherman Oaks, CA 91403, USA

Cuomo, Andrew (Politician)
717 5th Ave
New York, NY 10022-8101, USA

Cuomo, Andrew M (Governor)
Governor of New York State
NYS State Capitol Building
Albany, NY 12224, USA

Cuomo, Christopher (Chris)
(Correspondent)
c/o Staff Member *Primetime*
147 Columbus Ave
New York, NY 10023, USA

Cuomo, Jerome J (Inventor)
IBM T J Watson Research Center
PO Box 218
Yorktown Heights, NY 10598, USA

Cuomo, Mario (Ex-Governor)
Willkie, Farr & Gallagher LLP
787 Seventh Ave
New York, NY 10019, USA

Cuomo, Mario (Politician)
50 Sutton Pl S Apt 11G
New York, NY 10022-4130, USA

Cuomo, Rivers (Musician)
1027 Chelsea Ave
Santa Monica, CA 90403, USA

Cuozzo, Gary S (Athlete, Football Player)
911 Middletown Lincroft Rd
Middletown, NJ 07748-3109, USA

Cupp, James N (War Hero)
4904 Aspen Hill Road
Rockville, MD 20853-3710, USA

Cura, Francesco (Actor)
c/o Staff Member *Origin Talent Agency*
4705 Laurel Canyon #306
Studio City, CA 91607, USA

Cura, Jose (Opera Singer)
Columbia Artists Mgmt Inc
165 W 57th St
New York, NY 10019, USA

Curatola, Vincent (Actor)
26 Possum Trail
Upper Saddle River, NJ 07458, USA

Curb, Michael (Mike) (Business Person, Composer)
3907 W Alameda Ave
#2
Burbank, CA 91505, USA

Curb, Mike
3907 W. Alameda Ave
Burbank, CA 91505

Curbeam, Robert L Cdr (Astronaut)
13727 Briaridge Ct
Highland, MD 20777-9539, USA

Curbeam, Robert L Jr (Astronaut)
15806 Virginia Fern Way
Houston, TX 77059, USA

Curci, Francis (Athlete, Football Player)
14707 Croydon Pl
Tampa, FL 33618, USA

Curcillo, Anthony (Athlete, Football Player)
23887 Corte Emerado
Murrieta, CA 92562-3539, USA

Curcio, Michael (Athlete, Football Player)
165 Lincoln Ave
Hightstown, NJ 08520-4117, USA

Curd, Francis (Athlete, Football Player)
14707 Croydon Pl
Tampa, FL 33618-2160, USA

Cure, Robert (Athlete, Football Player)
145 Main St
Los Altos, CA 94022, USA

Cure, The (Music Group)
c/o Rick Roskin *Creative Artists Agency (CAA-LA)*
2000 Ave Of The Stars
Los Angeles, CA 90067, USA

Cureton, Earl (Athlete, Basketball Player)
7306 Balsam Court
West Bloomfield, MI 48322-2821, USA

Cureton, Thomas K (Misc)
501 E Washington
Urbana, IL 61801, USA

Cureton, Will (Athlete, Football Player)
1999 McKinney Ave Apt 1408
Dallas, TX 75201-1713, USA

Curfman, Shannon (Musician)
Monterey International
200 W Superior
#202
Chicago, IL 60610, USA

Curie-Good, Louise
1317 Delresto Dr.
Beverly Hills, CA 90210

Curl, Carolyn (Skier)
Robert U Curt
405 N Westridge Dr
Idaho Falls, ID 83402, USA

Curl, Robert F Jr (Nobel Prize Laureate)
1824 Bolsover St
Houston, TX 77005-1728, USA

Curlander, Paul J (Business Person)
Lexmark International
740 W New Circle Road
Lexington, KY 40550, USA

Curler, James (Business Person)
Bernis Co
222 S 9th St
Minneapolis, MN 55402, USA

Curley, Bill (Athlete, Basketball Player)
377 Autumn Avenue
Duxbury, MA 02332-4614, USA

Curley, Edwin M (Misc)
2645 Pin Oak Dr
Ann Arbor, MI 48103, USA

Curley, John J (Publisher)
Gannett Co
1100 Wilson Blvd
Arlington, VA 22209, USA

Curley, Marianne (Writer)
43 Nariah Cres
Toormina NSW 2452, AUSTRALIA

Curley, Walter J P Jr (Diplomat, Financier)
885 3rd Ave
#1200
New York, NY 10022, USA

Curnen, Monique (Actor)
c/o Sheree Cohen *Kohner Agency, The*
9300 Wilshire Blvd
Suite 555
Beverly Hills, CA 90212, USA

Curnin, Thomas F (Attorney, Attorney General, General)
Cahill Gordon Reindel
80 Pine St
New York, NY 10005, USA

Curran, Brian (Athlete, Hockey Player)
3600 Vanrick Dr
Attn: Director of Hockey Operations
Kalamazoo, MI 49001, USA

Curran, Brian (Athlete, Coach, Hockey Player)
c/o Staff Member *Quad City Mallards*
1509 3rd Avenue A
Moline, IL 61265, USA

Curran, Charles E (Misc)
Southern Methodist University
Dallas Hall
Dallas, TX 75275, USA

Curran, Kevin (Tennis Player)
5808 Back Court
Austin, TX 78731, USA

Curran, Mike (Athlete, Hockey Player, Olympic Athlete)
7615 Lanewood Ln N
Osseo, MN 55311-2608, USA

Curran, Pat (Athlete, Football Player)
1525 Glenwood Dr
San Diego, CA 92103-4732, USA

Curran, Tony (Actor)
c/o Tammy Rosen *Sanders Armstrong Caserta*
425 N Robertson Blvd
Los Angeles, CA 90048, USA

Currence, Lafayette (Athlete, Baseball Player)
113 Rock Springs Way
Rock Hill, SC 29730, USA

Currey, Francis S (War Hero)
106 Catfish Landing Circle
Bonneau, SC 29431, USA

Currey, Francis S (General)
PO Box 515
Selkirk, Ny 12158-0515, USA

Currie, Bill (Athlete, Baseball Player)
242 Lakeside Dr SW
Arlington, GA 39813-2345, USA

Currie, Brian (Writer)
c/o David Krintzman *Morris, Yorn, Barnes, Levine, Krintzman, Rubenstein and Kohner*
2000 Ave of the Stars
3rd Floor, North Tower
Los Angeles, CA 90067, USA

Currie, Cherie (Musician)
Cherie Currie's Chainsaw Art Gallery
8511 Hanna Ave
West Hills, CA 91304, USA

Currie, Daniel (Dan) (Athlete, Football Player)
6650 W Flamingo Rd Apt 152
Las Vegas, NV 89103-2144, USA

Currie, Gordon (Actor)
c/o Jennifer Goldhar *Characters Talent Agency (Toronto)*
8 Elm St
2nd Floor
Toronto, ON M5G 1G7, CANADA

Currie, Louise (Actor)
1317 Delresto Dr
Beverly Hills, CA 90210, USA

Currie, Malcolm R (Business Person)
Hughes Aircraft Co
PO Box 956
El Segundo, CA 90245, USA

Currie, Nancy J (Astronaut)
1863 Bending Stream Dr
League City, TX 77573-3699, USA

Currie, Nancy Jane Colonel (Astronaut)
6601 Pearson Rd
Santa Fe, TX 77517-3290, USA

Currie, Sondra (Actor)
3951 Longridge Ave
Sherman Oaks, CA 91423, USA

Currie, Tony (Athlete, Hockey Player)
2600-2 Bloor St W
Toronto, ON M4W 3E2, Canada

Currier, William(Bill) (Athlete, Football Player)
8661 Monticello Rd
Columbia, SC 29203-9706, USA

Currin, James A (Athlete, Football Player)
11770 Thayer Ln
Cincinnati, OH 45249, USA

Currington, Billy (Music Group, Musician)
c/o Staff Member *WmE2 (WMA-TN)*
1600 Division St
Suite 300
Nashville, TN 37203, USA

Curris, Constantine W (Educator)
Clemson University
President's Office
Sikes Hall
Clemson, SC 29634, USA

Curry, Adrianne (Model, Reality TV Star)
1600 Monterey Blvd
Hermosa Beach, CA 90254, USA

Curry, Alana (Actor)
PO Box 1852
Burbank, CA 91507-1852, USA

Curry, Ann (Television Host)
c/o Staff Member *Dateline NBC*
NBC News
30 Rockefeller Plz
New York, NY 10112, USA

Curry, Bill (Athlete, Coach, Football Coach, Football Player)
2660 Peachtree Rd NW Apt 27H
Atlanta, GA 30305, USA

Curry, Buddy (Athlete, Football Player)
4407 Trestle Way
Buford, GA 30518, USA

Curry, Chad (Stylist)
c/o Staff Member *Seaminx Artist Management*
2806 Greenville Ave
#B
Dallas, TX 75206, USA

Curry, Craig (Athlete, Football Player)
3210 Amber Forest Dr
Houston, TX 77068, USA

Curry, Dell (Athlete, Basketball Player)
1615 Rutledge Ave
Charlotte, NC 28211-2752, USA

Curry, Demarcus (Athlete, Football Player)
765 Forest Crossing Dr SW
Atlanta, GA 30331-7387, USA

Curry, Denise (Athlete, Basketball Player, Coach)
21 Maple Dr
Aliso Viejo, CA 92656-4273, USA

Curry, Don (Athlete, Boxer, Olympic Athlete)
2509 McKenzie St
Fort Worth, TX 76105, USA

Curry, Don (DC) (Actor, Comedian)
c/o Tony Spires *Full Circle Entertainment*
6320 Canoga Ave
Suite 1550
Woodland Hills, CA 91367, USA

Curry, Dwen (Stylist)
c/o Staff Member *Dawn to Dusk Image Agency*
8306 Wilshire Blvd
#412
Beverly Hills, CA 30211, USA

Curry, Eddy (Athlete, Basketball Player)
17 Magnolia Drive
Purchase, NY 10577-1137, USA

Curry, Eric F (Athlete, Football Player)
PO Box 17321
Jacksonville, FL 32245-7321, USA

Curry, Lucy (Stylist)
c/o Staff Member *Tricia Joyce Inc*
79 Chambers St
2nd Floor
New York, NY 10007, USA

Curry, Mark (Actor)
12540 Kling St
Studio City, CA 91604, USA

Curry, Mike (Athlete, Basketball Player)
2880 Wells Drive
Augusta, GA 30906-5373, USA

Curry, Ronald (Athlete, Football Player)
1881 Brawley School Rd
Mooresville, NC 28117-7084, USA

Curry, Roy (Athlete, Football Player)
9045 S Paxton Ave
Chicago, IL 60617, USA

Curry, Stephen (Actor)
c/o Robyn Gardiner *RGM Artist Group*
64-76 Kippax St
Level 2, Suite 202 & 206
Surry Hills, NSW 2010, Australia

Curry, Steve (Athlete, Baseball Player)
10725 Obee Rd
Whitehouse, OH 43571-9250, USA

Curry, Tim (Actor)
c/o Jonathan Howard *Innovative Artists (LA)*
1505 10th St
Santa Monica, CA 90401, USA

Curtale, Tony (Athlete, Hockey Player)
11351 Balcones Dr
Frisco, TX 75033-7379, USA

Curtin, David S (Journalist)
Colorado Springs Gazette Telegraph
30 S Prospect
Colorado Springs, CO 80903, USA

Curtin, Jane (Actor)
181 Mudge Pond Rd
Sharon, CT 06069, USA

Curtin, John J Jr (Attorney, Attorney General, General)
Bingham Dana Gould
150 Federal St
#3500
Boston, MA 02110, USA

Curtin, Valerie
15622 Meadowgate Rd.
Encino, CA 91316

Curtis, Ben (Actor)
c/o Staff Member *Abrams Artists Agency (NY)*
275 Seventh Ave
26th Floor
New York, NY 10001, USA

Curtis, Ben (Athlete, Golfer)
8959 Bevington Ln
Orlando, FL 32837, USA

Curtis, Bonnie (Producer)
c/o Staff Member *Mockingbird Pictures, LLC*
2312 Lorenzo Dr
Los Angeles, CA 90068, USA

Curtis, Chad (Athlete, Baseball Player)
621 Eagle Point Rd
Lake Odessa, MI 48849-9445, USA

Curtis, Cliff (Actor)
c/o Joseph (Joe) Rice *Abrams Artists Agency (LA)*
9200 Sunset Blvd
11th Floor
Los Angeles, CA 90069, USA

Curtis, Cuneo Ann E (Athlete, Olympic Athlete, Swimmer)
35 Golden Hinde Blvd
San Rafael, CA 94903-3816, USA

Curtis, Don (Wrestler)
920 Middleton Rd
Jacksonville, FL 32211, USA

Curtis, Isaac F (Athlete, Football Player)
711 Clinton Springs Ave
Cincinnati, OH 45229, USA

Curtis, Jack (Athlete, Baseball Player)
4949 Ike Starnes Rd
Granite Falls, NC 28630-8631, USA

Curtis, Jamie Lee (Actor)
122/126 Barlow Rd
Ketchum, ID 83340, USA

Curtis, J Michael (Mike) (Athlete, Football Player)
5101 River Rd Apt 1803
Bethesda, MD 20816-1574, USA

Curtis, John (Athlete, Baseball Player)
1800 Roundhill Rd
Apt 1207
Charleston, WV 25314-1559, USA

Curtis, John (Athlete, Baseball Player)
Huntsville Stars 3125 Leeman Ferry Rd SW
Attn Coaching Staff
Huntsville, AL 35801-5331, USA

Curtis, Kelly (Actor)
651 N. Kilkea Dr
Los Angeles, CA 90048, USA

Curtis, Kenneth (Politician)
1211 Southport Dr
Sarasota, FL 34242-1716, USA

Curtis, Kenneth M (Ex-Governor)
Curtis Thaxter
1 Canal Plaza
Suite 1000
Portland, ME 04112, USA

Curtis, King (Baseball Player)
St Louis Cardinals
2538 Beechwood Dr
Vineland, NJ 08361-2932, USA

Curtis, Liane (Actor)
12556 Everglade St
Los Angeles, CA 90066, USA

Curtis, Paul (Athlete, Hockey Player)
PO Box 6325
Abilene, TX 79608-6325, USA

Curtis, Richard (Writer)
c/o Staff Member *The Rights House (UK)*
Drury House
34-43 Russell St
London WC2B 5HA, UK

Curtis, Robin (Actor)
1147 Beverly Hill Dr
Cincinnati, OH 45208, USA

Curtis, Scott (Athlete, Football Player)
31661 Prairie Dunes Ct
Evergreen, CO 80439-5902, USA

Curtis, Todd (Actor)
2046 14th St
#10
Santa Monica, CA 90405, USA

Curtis, Tom (Athlete, Football Player)
5433 NW 94th Doral Pl
Doral, FL 33178, USA

Curtis, Travis (Athlete, Football Player)
9905 Sorrel Ave
Potomac, MD 20854-4703, USA

Curtola, Bobby (Musician)
ESP Productions
720 Spadina Ave
#PH2
Toronto, ON M5S 2T9, CANADA

Cusack, Ann (Actor)
Innovative Artists
1505 10th St
Santa Monica, CA 90401, USA

Cusack, Joan (Actor, Comedian)
60 E Cedar St
Chicago, IL 60611, USA

Cusack, John (Actor)
24460 Malibu Rd
Malibu, CA 90265, USA

Cusack, Sinead (Actor)
Markham & Froggatt Julian House
4 Windmill St.
London W1P 1HF, UNITED KINGDOM (UK)

Cuschieri, Paul (Writer)
c/o Naren Desai *Brillstein Entertainment Partners*
9150 Wilshire Blvd #350
Beverly Hills, CA 90212, USA

Cuse, Carlton (Producer)
c/o Staff Member *WmE2 (WMA-LA)*
1 William Morris Pl
Beverly Hills, CA 90212, USA

Cushenan, Ian (Athlete, Hockey Player)
4014 Dryden Dr
North Olmsted, OH 44070-1928, USA

Cushing, Matt (Athlete, Football Player)
5752 Lyman Ave
Downers Grove, IL 60516-1401, USA

Cushman, David W (Misc)
20 Lake Shore Dr
Princeton Junction, NJ 08550, USA

Cushman, Karen (Writer)
17804 Thorsen Rd SW
Vashon, WA 98070-4502, USA

Cusick, Henry Ian (Actor)
c/o Abi Harris *Ken McReddie Ltd*
11 Connaught Pl
London W2 2ET, UNITED KINGDOM

Cusick, Pete (Athlete, Football Player)
807 Esplanade
Redondo Beach, CA 90277-4734, USA

Cussler, Clive (Writer)
13835 N Tatum Blvd #9-421
Phoenix, AZ 85032, USA

cusson, jean
265 Claude Ave
Dorval, QC H9S 3B1, Canada

Cust, Jack (Athlete, Baseball Player)
9 Club House Dr
Whitehouse Station, NJ 08889-3366, USA

Cutcliffe, David (Coach, Football Coach)
University of Mississippi
Athletic Dept
University, MS 38677, USA

Cute Is What We Aim For (Music Group)
Fueled By Ramen
PO Box 1803
Tampa, FL 33601, USA

Cuthbert, Elisha (Actor)
1531 Marmont Ave
Los Angeles, CA 90069, USA

Cuthbert, Randy (Athlete, Football Player)
PO Box 101
Perkasie, PA 18944, USA

Cuthbeth, Elizabeth (Betty) (Athlete, Track Athlete)
4/7 Karara Close
Halls Head
Mandurah, WA 6210, AUSTRALIA

Cutler, Alexander M (Business Person)
Eaton Corp
Eaton Center
1111 Superior Ave
Cleveland, OH 44114, USA

Cutler, Bruce (Attorney, Attorney General, General)
41 Madison Ave
New York, NY 10010, USA

Cutler, Dave (Athlete, Football Player)
4980 Cordova Bay Rd
Victoria, BC V8Y2K2, Canada

Cutler, Jay (Athlete)
c/o Brad Marks *Apoko Group*
1550 17th St
Santa Monica, CA 90404-3402, USA

Cutler, Jay (Athlete, Football Player)
c/o Bus Cook *Bus Cook Sports, Inc*
1 Willow Bend Dr
Hattiesburg, MS 39402, USA

Cutler, RJ (Director, Producer)
c/o Rowena Arguelles *Creative Artists Agency (CAA-LA)*
2000 Ave Of The Stars
Los Angeles, CA 90067, USA

Cutler, Walter L (Diplomat)
Meridian International Center
1630 Crescent Place NW
Washington, DC 20009, USA

Cutliffe, Molly (Actor)
Herney/Grimes
PO Box 64249
Los Angeles, CA 90064, USA

Cutrone, Kelly (Business Person, Reality TV Star)
People's Revolution Inc
62 Grand Street
New York, NY 10013, USA

Cutrufello, Mary (Musician, Songwriter, Writer)
Joe's Garage
4405 Belmont Park Terrace
Nashville, TN 37215, USA

Cutsinger, Gary (Athlete, Football Player)
600 Mountain Dew Rd
Horseshoe Bay, TX 78657-6341, USA

Cutter, Kiki (Skier)
PO Box 1317
Carbondale, CO 81623, USA

Cutter, Lise (Actor)
PO Box 2665
Sag Harbor, NY 11963, USA

Cutter, Slade D (Athlete, Football Player)
9214 River Cresent Dr
Annapolis, MD 21401, USA

Cutts, Don (Athlete, Hockey Player)
222 15th St NW
Main Floor
Calgary, AB T2N 2A7, CANADA

Cuviello, Peter M (General)
Director
Defence Information Systems Agency
Alington, VA 22204, USA

Cuwinski, Kevin (Race Car Driver)
Brevak Racing
206 Performance Rd
Mooresville, NC 28115, USA

Cuyler, Milt (Athlete, Baseball Player)
962 Lamar Rd
Macon, GA 31210-7109, USA

Cuzzi, Phil (Athlete, Baseball Player)
32 Mapes Ave
Nutley, NJ 07110, USA

Cwiklinski, Stanley (Athlete, Olympic Athlete)
2840 Maple Street
San Diego, CA 92140-4940, USA

C. Woolsey, Lynn (Congressman, Politician)
2263 Rayburn HOB
Washington, DC 20515, USA

Cymphonique (Dancer, Musician)
c/o Ben Press *Buchwald/Fortitude (LA)*
6500 Wilshire Blvd
Suite 2200
Los Angeles, CA 90048, USA

C. Young, Todd (Congressman, Politician)
1721 Longworth HOB
Washington, DC 20515, USA

Cypher, John
9229 Sunset Blvd. #315
Los Angeles, CA 90069

Cypher, Jon (Actor)
498 Manzanita Ave
Ventura, CA 93001, USA

Cyphers, Charles (Actor)
8567 E American Dream Way
Sierra Vista, CA 85650, USA

Cypress, Tawny
c/o Staff Member *Abrams Artists Agency (NY)*
275 Seventh Ave
26th Floor
New York, NY 10001, USA

Cypress Hill (Music Group)
c/o David Benveniste *Velvet Hammer*
9014 Melrose Ave
Los Angeles, CA 90069, USA

Cyr, Conrad K (Judge)
US Courts of Appeals
PO Box 635
Bangor, ME 04402, USA

Cyr, Denis (Athlete, Hockey Player)
9816 N Townsend Dr
Peoria, IL 61615-1388, USA

Cyrus, Billy Ray (Musician, Songwriter)
10313 Woodbridge St
Toluca Lake, CA 91602, USA

Cyrus, Brandi (Actor)
c/o Staff Member *United Talent Agency (UTA)*
9336 Civic Center Dr
Beverly Hills, CA 90210, USA

Cyrus, Miley (Actor, Musician)
11524 Amanda Dr
Studio City, CA 91604, USA

Cywinski, Kevin (Race Car Driver)
709 Performance Rd.
Mooresville, NC 28115, USA

Czajkowski, Jim (Athlete, Baseball Player)
1648 Rivergate Dr
Sevierville, TN 37862-9321, USA

Czajkowski, Jim (Athlete, Baseball Player)
Vancouver Canadians 4601 Ontario St
Attn Coaching Staff
Vancouver, BC V5V 3H4, Canada

Czapsky, Stefan (Cinematographer)
RR 3 Box 278
Unadilla, NY 13849, USA

Czemy, Henry (Actor)
438 Queen St E
Toronto, ON M5A 1T4, CANADA

Czerny, Henry (Actor)
c/o Perry Zimel *Oscars Abrams Zimel & Associates, Inc. (OAZ)*
438 Queen St E
Toronto ON M5A 1T4, CANADA

Czrongursky, Jan (Prime Minister)
Prime Minister's Office
Nam Slobody 1
Bratislava 81370, SLOVAKIA

Czuchry, Matt (Actor)
c/o Jeff Golenberg *Collective*
8383 Wilshire Blvd
Suite 1050
Beverly Hills, CA 90211, USA

Czyz, Bobby (Boxer)
110 Pennsylvania Ave
Flemington, NJ 08822, USA

D, Deezer (Actor)
c/o Staff Member *Acme Talent & Literary (LA)*
1400 Atlantic Ave
Suite 274
Long Beach, CA 90814, USA

D, Mike (Musician)
7126 Fernhill Dr
Malibu, CA 90265, USA

D-12 (Musician)
Evolution Talent Agency
1776 Broadway
15th Floor
New York, NY 10019

D12 (Music Group)
c/o Staff Member *WME (WMA-NY)*
1325 Ave of the Americas
New York, NY 10019, USA

Daal, Omar (Athlete, Baseball Player)
3859 E Bellerive Dr
Queen Creek, AZ 85142-3233, USA

Daanen, Jerome (Athlete, Football Player)
1011 S Erie St
De Pere, WI 54115, USA

D'Abaldo, Chris (Musician)
Helter Skelter Plaza
535 Kings Road
London SW10 0S, UNITED KINGDOM (UK)

Da Band (Music Group)
c/o Staff Member *Bad Boy Worldwide Entertainment*
1440 Broadway
16th Floor
New York, NY 10018, USA

Daberko, David A (Financier)
National City Corp
National City Center
1900 E 9th St
Cleveland, OH 44114, USA

Dabich, Mike (Athlete, Basketball Player)
PO Box 236
Hudson, WY 82515-0236, USA

Dabney, Carlton (Athlete, Football Player)
2522 Northumberland Ave
Richmond, VA 23220, USA

D'Abo, Maryam (Actor)
Artist Independent
32 Tavistock St
London WC2E 7PB, UNITED KINGDOM (UK)

D'Abo, Olivia (Actor)
3480 Berry Dr
Studio City, CA 91604, USA

Da Brat (Musician)
c/o Staff Member *WmE2 (WMA-LA)*
1 William Morris Pl
Beverly Hills, CA 90212, USA

Dacascos, Mark (Actor)
1479 Aldercreek Pl
Westlake Village, CA 91362, USA

dackell, andreas (Athlete, Hockey Player)
Tegnervagan 1
Gavle 822 67, Sweden

Dacquisto, John (Athlete, Baseball Player)
32010 N 20th Ln
Phoenix, AZ 85085-7081, USA

D'Acquisto, John F (Athlete, Baseball Player)
1441 Santa Lucia Rd #615
Chula Vista, CA 91913-3600, USA

Dacruz Policarpo, Jose Cardinal (Religious Leader)
Curia Patriarcal
Camo dos Martires da Patria 45
Lisbon 1150, PORTUGAL

Dacus, Don (Actor)
8455 Fountain Ave
#512
Los Angeles, CA 90069, USA

Daddario, Alex (Actor)
c/o Jerry Shandrew *Shandrew Public Relations*
1050 S Stanley Ave
Los Angeles, CA 90019-6634, USA

Daddario, Alexandra (Actor)
c/o Donnalyn Carfi *Harvest Talent Management*
P.O. Box 279
Jefferson Valley, NY 10535, USA

Dade, Paul (Athlete, Baseball Player)
5212 66th Street Ct W
University Place, WA 98467-3337, USA

Dadswell, Doug (Athlete, Hockey Player)
54-10030 Oakmoor Way SW
Calgary, AB T2V 4S8, Canada

Daehlie, Bjorn (Skier)
Cathinka Guldbergs Veg 64
Holler 2034, NORWAY

Daetweiler, Louella (Baseball Player)
415 S Poplar Ave
Brea, CA 92821-6650, USA

Dafoe, Byron (Athlete, Hockey Player)
6620 Lakeshore Rd
Kelowna, BC V1W 4J5, Canada

Dafoe, Willem (Actor)
c/o Frank Frattaroli *Circle of Confusion (NY)*
270 Lafayette St
Suite 402
New York, NY 10012, USA

Daft, Douglas (Business Person)
Coca Cola Co
1 Coca Cola Plaza
310 North Ave NW
Atlanta, GA 30313, USA

Daft, Kevin (Athlete, Football Player)
6033 Old Quarry Loop
Oakland, CA 94605-3375, USA

Daggett, Jensen (Actor)
682 Palisades Dr
Pacific Palisades, CA 90272, USA

Daggett, Timothy (Tim) (Gymnast)
134 Country Club Dr
East Longmeadow, MA 01028, USA

Daghe, Noelle (Athlete, Golfer)
1300 Tamarac St
Denver, CO 80220, USA

D'agnillo, Ann (Stylist)
c/o Staff Member *Axis Models & Talent*
P.O. Box 367
Ringwood, NJ 07456-0367, USA

D'Agosto, Nicholas (Nick) (Actor)
c/o Faras Rabadi *Emerald Talent Group*
10 Universal City Plaza
20th Floor
Universal City, CA 91608, USA

Dagres, Angie (Athlete, Baseball Player)
P.O. Box 27
Rowley, MA 01969-0027, USA

Dagworthy Prew, Wendy A (Designer, Fashion Designer)
18 Melrose Terrace
London W6, UNITED KINGDOM (UK)

Dahl, Ariene (Actor)
Dahlmark Productions
PO Box 116
Sparkill, NY 10976, USA

Dahl, Arlene (Actor)
PO Box 116
Sparkill, NY 10976, USA

Dahl, Bob (Athlete, Football Player)
363 Elliotts Hill Ln
Lexington, VA 24450, USA

Dahl, Christopher (Educator)
State University of New York College
President's Office
Genesco, NY 14454, USA

Dahl, Craig (Athlete, Football Player)
62503 Shorewood Ln
Madison Lake, MN 56063-4434, USA

Dahl, John (Director, Writer)
c/o Jason Spitz WME (LA)
9601 Wilshire Blvd Fl 3
Beverly Hills, CA 90210, USA

Dahl, Kevin (Athlete, Hockey Player)
4000 Astoria Way
Avon, OH 44011-3426, USA

Dahl, Lawrence F (Misc)
4817 Woodburn Dr
Madison, WI 53711, USA

Dahl, Perry (General)
4232 Brentwood Park Cir
Tampa, FL 33624-1308, USA

Dahl, Sophie (Actor, Model)
c/o Staff Member Special Artists Agency
9465 Wilshire Blvd #820
Beverly Hills, CA 90212, USA

Dahlen, Ulf (Athlete, Hockey Player)
2500 Victory Ave.
Dallas, TX 75219, USA

Dahler, Ed (Athlete, Basketball Player)
511 East Tremont Street
Hillsboro, IL 62049-1801, USA

Dahlin, Kjell (Athlete, Hockey Player)
Sidvallsgatan 5
Karlstad 654 65, Sweden

Dahllof, Eva (Athlete, Golfer)
419 Glen Crest Dr
Moore, SC 29369, USA

Dahlquist, Chris (Athlete, Hockey Player)
10859 Purdey Rd
Eden Prairie, MN 55347-5236, USA

Dahm, Jaclyn (Actor)
c/o Amy Godsick Candy Entertainment
Management
8981 West Sunset Blvd #310
Hollywood, CA 90069, USA

Dahrendorf, Ralf Gustav
Postfach 5560
Konstanz, GERMANY D-78434

Dai, Ailian (Choreographer, Dancer)
Hua Qiao Gong Yu #2-16
Hua Yuan Cun
Hai Dian, Beijing 100044, CHINA

Dai, Sijie (Writer)
c/o Staff Member Knopf Publishing Group
1745 Broadway
New York, NY 10019, USA

Dai, Weili (Misc)
Marvell Semiconductor Inc 5488 Marvell
Ln Attn: Executive V P- Communications
Business Group
Santa Clara, CA 95054-3606, USA

Daiches, David (Writer)
22 Belgrave Crescent
Edinburgh EH4 3AL, SCOTLAND

Daigle, Alain (Athlete, Hockey Player)
3510 Rue de Bordeaux
Trois-Rivieres, QC G8Y 3P7, Canada

Daigle, Alexander (Athlete, Hockey
Player)
3510 Rue Bordeaux
Trois-Rivieres-Quest, QC G8Y 3P7,
Canada

Daigle, Casey (Athlete, Baseball Player)
2607 Wpa Rd
Sulphur, LA 70663-9408, USA

Daigneau, Maurice (Athlete, Football
Player)
32 Redmond Ave
Buffalo, NY 14216-1511, USA

Daigneault, J J (Athlete, Coach, Hockey
Player)
c/o Staff Member Hartford Wolf Pack
196 Trumbull St
Floor 3
Hartford, CT 06103, USA

Daigneault, Rejean (Horse Racer)
95 Hildreth Pl
Yonkers, NY 10704-2220, USA

Dailey, Bill (Athlete, Baseball Player)
5019 Meadow Way
Dublin, VA 24084, USA

Dailey, Bob (Athlete, Hockey Player)
249 Harrison Ave
Elkins Park, PA 19027-2731

Dailey, Dianne (Athlete, Golfer)
4220 Stonehenge Ln
Lakeland, FL 33813, USA

Dailey, Peter H (Diplomat)
State Department
2201 C St NW
Washington, DC 20520, USA

Daily, Bill (Actor)
1331 Park Ave SW
#802
Albuquerque, NM 87104, USA

Daily, EG (Actor, Musician, Voice Over
Artist)
2324 Jupiter Dr
Los Angeles, CA 90046, USA

Daily, Gretchen (Misc)
Stanford University
Ecology Dept
Stanford, CA 94305, USA

Daily, Parker (Religious Leader)
Baptist Bible Fellowship International
PO Box 191
Springfield, MO 65801, USA

Daingerfield, Michael (Actor)
c/o Staff Member Kirk Talent Agencies Inc
70 East 2nd. Ave
Suite 301
Vancouver, BC V5T 1B1, Canada

Dainton, Frederick S (Misc)
Fieldside
Water Eaton Lane
Kidlington, Oxford OX5 2PR, UNITED
KINGDOM (UK)

Daio, Norberto J D C A (Prime Minister)
Prime Minister's Office
CP 38
Sao Tome, SAO TOME & PRINCIPE

Daisey, Gene (Horse Racer)
5335 Havasu Ct
Lake Worth, FL 33467-5533, USA

Dajani, Nadia (Actor)
22 Perry St #3C/D
New York, NY 10014, USA

Daland, Peter (Coach)
PO Box 2443
Aquebogue, NY 11931, USA

Dalbavie, Andre (Composer)
Van Walsum Mgmt
4 Addison Bridge Place
London W14 8XP, UNITED KINGDOM
(UK)

Dalberto, Michel (Musician)
13 Blvd Henri Plumof
Vevey 1800, SWITZERLAND

Daldry, Stephen (Director)
Royal Court Theater
Sloane Square
London SW1, UNITED KINGDOM (UK)

Dale, Alan (Actor)
c/o Dan Baron Agency for the Performing
Arts (APA-LA)
405 S Beverly Dr
Suite 500
Beverly Hills, CA 90212-4425, USA

Dale, Bruce (Photographer)
National Geographic Magazine 1145 17th
St NW
Washington, DC 20036-4707, USA

Dale, Carl (Athlete, Baseball Player)
3358 Oak Trl
Cookeville, TN 38501, USA

Dale, Carroll
9332 Coeburn Mountain Rd
Wise, VA 24293-5946, USA

Dale, Carroll W (Athlete, Football Player)
1 College Ave
Wise, VA 24293, USA

Dale, Dick (Actor)
PO Box 1713
Twentyninepalms, CA 92277, USA

Dale, James Badge (Actor)
c/o Myrna Jacoby MJ Management
130 W 57th St
Suite 11A
New York, NY 10019, USA

Dale, Jerry (Athlete, Baseball Player)
2112 Middlewood Dr
Maryville, TN 37803, USA

Dale, Jim (Actor)
Mark Sendroff
230 W 56th St
#63B
New York, NY 10019, USA

Dale, William B (Economist, Government
Official)
9707 Old Georgetown Road
Apt 2201
Bethesda, MD 20814-1755, USA

Dale & Grace (Music Group)
Sea Cruise Productions
PO Box 1875
Gretna, LA 70054-1875, USA

D'Alema, Massima (Prime Minister)
Prime Minister's Office
Piazza Colomma 370
Rome 00187, ITALY

Dalembert, Samuel (Athlete, Basketball
Player)
899 NE Orchid Bav Dr
Boca Raton, FL 33487-1751, USA

Dalena, Pete (Athlete, Baseball Player)
4951 N Thorne Ave
Fresno, CA 93704-2935, USA

D'Aleo, Angelo (Musician)
Paramount Entertainment
PO Box 12
Far Hills, NJ 07931, USA

Dalesandro, Mark (Athlete, Baseball
Player)
1908 Arbor Fields Dr
Plainfield, IL 60586-5729, USA

Dale Scott, Cynthia (Actor)
c/o Derek Maki Coolwaters Productions
10061 Riverside Dr.
Box 531
Toluca Lake, CA 91602, USA

D'Alesio, Tracy (Stylist)
55 Beverly Rd NE
Atlanta, GA 30309, USA

Dales-Schuman, Stacey (Basketball Player)
Washington Mystics
MCI Center
601 F St NW
Washington, DC 20004, USA

D'Alessio, Diana (Golfer)
6955 Nunn Rd
Lakeland, FL 33813-3821, USA

D'Alessio, Diana (Athlete, Golfer)
6955 Nunn Rd
Lakeland, FL 33813, USA

Daley, Bill (Athlete, Baseball Player)
SBC Communications
5824 Hansen Rd
Minneapolis, MN 55436-2402, USA

Daley, Bud (Athlete, Baseball Player)
922 Moose Dr
Riverton, WY 82501-2537, USA

Daley, Joe (Athlete, Hockey Player)
Joe Daley's Cards
666 St James St
Winnipeg, MB R3G 3J6, Canada

Daley, John (Golfer)
c/o Staff Member Pro Golfers Assoc of
America (PGA)
112 TPC Blvd
Ponte Vedra Beach, FL 32082-3077, USA

Daley, John (Golfer)
10015 E Mountain View Rd
Apt 2126
Scottsdale, AZ 85258, USA

Daley, John Francis (Actor)
c/o Staff Member The Management
Company
2030 Pinehurst Road
Los Angeles, CA 90068, USA

Daley, Margaret (Stylist)
3054 Braemar Dr
Santa Barbara, CA 93109-1006, USA

Daley, Matt (Athlete, Baseball Player)
173 Kildare Rd
Garden City, NY 11530-1120, USA

Daley, Patrick (Athlete, Hockey Player)
118 Mount Olive Dr
Toronto, ON M9V 2E2, Canada

Daley, Pete (Athlete, Baseball Player)
4019 Calle Mira Monte
Newbury Park, CA 91320-1932, USA

Daley, Richard M (Politician)
Mayor's Office
City Hall
121 N LaSalle St
Chicago, IL 60602, USA

Daley, Rosle (Chef, Writer)
Harpo Productions
110 N Carpenter St
Chicago, IL 60607, USA

Dalgarno, Alexander (Astronomer)
27 Robinson St
Cambridge, MA 02138, USA

Dalgarno, Brad (Athlete, Hockey Player)
1146 Fairfield Pl
Oakville, ON L6M 2L9, Canada

Dalgilsh, Kenneth M (Kenny) (Coach, Soccer Player)
c/o Staff Member *Liverpool Football Club*
69/71 Anfield Road
Liverpool L4 0TQ, UNITED KINGDOM

Dalheimer, Patrick (Musician)
Freedman & Smith
350 W End Ave
#1
New York, NY 10024, USA

Dalhousie, Simon R (Government Official)
Brechin Castle
Brechin DD9 6SH, SCOTLAND

Dali, Tracy (Actor, Model)
PO Box 69541
Los Angeles, CA 90069, USA

Dalian, Susan (Actor)
c/o Staff Member *GVA Talent Agency Inc*
8981 Sunset Blvd.
Suite 101
Los Angeles, CA 90069, USA

Dalie, Beatrice (Actor)
Artmedia
20 Ave Rapp
Paris 75007, FRANCE

Dalio, Raymond
40 Glenwood Dr
Greenwich, CT 06830-7015, USA

Dalis, Irene (Opera Singer)
1731 Cherry Grove Dr
San Jose, CA 95125, USA

Dalkas, Nicole (Athlete, Golfer)
288 Green Mountain Dr
Palm Desert, CA 92211-3246, USA

Dalkowski, Steve (Baseball Player)
Walnut Hill Care Center 55 Grand St
New Britain, CT 06052-2021, USA

Dall, Bobby (Musician)
160 Ocean Oaks Dr
Indialantic, FL 32903, USA

Dallafior, Ken (Athlete, Football Player)
188 Four Seasons Dr
Lake Orion, MI 48360-2645, USA

Dallas, Joshua (Actor)
c/o John Carrabino *John Carrabino Management*
5900 Wilshire Blvd Fl 4 #406
Los Angeles, CA 90036, USA

Dallas, Matt (Actor)
c/o Katie Rhodes *Untitled Entertainment (LA)*
350 S. Beverly Dr #200
Beverly Hills, CA 90212, USA

Dallas Cowboys Cheerleaders
1 Cowboys Parkway
Irving, TX 75063-4727

Dallenbach Jr., Wally (Race Car Driver)
2561 Frying Pan Road
Basalt, CO 81621, USA

Dallimore, Brian (Athlete, Baseball Player)
10531 Haywood Dr
Las Vegas, NV 89135-2850, USA

Dallman, Kevin
6710 Domenic Cres
Niagara Falls, ON L2J 4L5, Canada

Dallman, Marty (Athlete, Hockey Player)
3843 Main St
Niagara Falls, ON L2G 6B4, Canada

Dallman, Rod
769 Branion Dr
Prince Albert, SK S6V 2S4, Canada

Dallyn, Stacy (Stylist)
c/o Staff Member *Celestine - CA*
1666 20th St
#200-B
Santa Monica, CA 90404, USA

Dalm, Jan
DALM
Dv de Merwedestraat
HI Ambacht
GB 3341, Netherlands

Dalmacci, Ricardo (Actor)
c/o Gabriel Blanco *Gabriel Blanco Iglesias (Mexico)*
Rio Balsas 35-32
Colonia Cuauhtemoc
DF 06500, Mexico

Dalmas, Yannick (Race Car Driver)
Rue Raimus
83330 Le Beaunet
FRANCE

Dalrymple, Clay (Athlete, Baseball Player)
28248 Mateer Rd
Gold Beach, OR 97444-9618, USA

Dalrymple, Gary B (Misc)
1847 NW Hillcrest Dr
Corvallis, OR 97330, USA

Dalrymple, Jack (Governor)
Office of Governor
600 E Boulevard Ave
Bismarck, ND 58505-0100, USA

Dalton, Audrey (Actor)
22461 Labrusca
Mission Viejo, CA 92692, USA

Dalton, James (General)
61 Misty Acres Rd
Rolling Hills Estates, CA 90274-5749, USA

Dalton, James E (General)
61 Misty Acres Road
Rolling Hills Estate, CA 90274, USA

Dalton, Kristin (Actor)
c/o Bob McGowan *McGowan Management*
8733 W Sunset Blvd
Suite 103
West Hollywood, CA 90069, USA

Dalton, Lacy J (Musician)
820 Cartwright Road
Reno, NV 89521, USA

Dalton, Lional (Athlete, Football Player)
9858 Clint Moore Rd Ste 128
Boca Raton, FL 33496, USA

Dalton, Mike (Athlete, Baseball Player)
42410 Palm Ave
Fremont, CA 94539-4729, USA

Dalton, Nic (Musician)
c/o Staff Member *Agency Group Ltd, The (NY)*
142 West 57th St
6th Floor
New York, NY 10019, USA

Dalton, Nicole (Actor)
c/o Staff Member *Commonwealth Talent Group*
PO Box 36514
Los Angeles, CA 90036, USA

Dalton, Oakley (Athlete, Football Player)
3647 Highway 131
Washburn, TN 37888-4015, USA

Dalton, Timothy (Actor)
8322 Marmont Ln
West Hollywood, CA 90069, USA

Daltrey, Roger (Actor, Musician)
Holmhurst Manor Farm
Burwash
East Sussex, UK

Daltry, Roger (Actor, Musician)
Conway Van Gelder Robinson
18-21 Jermyn St
London SW1Y 6NB, UNITED KINGDOM (UK)

Daluiso, Brad (Athlete, Football Player)
13258 Glencliff Way
San Diego, CA 92130, USA

Daly, Carson (Television Host)
101/111 Ocean Way
Santa Monica, CA 90402, USA

Daly, Derek (Race Car Driver)
18300 Deshane Avenue
Noblesville, IN 46060, USA

Daly, John (Athlete, Golfer)
c/o John Mascatello *SFX World Sports Management*
11921 Freedom Dr
Suite 1180
Reston, VA 20190, USA

Daly, Rad (Actor)
c/o Staff Member *Brady Brannon & Rich*
5670 Wilshire Blvd
Suite 820
Los Angeles, CA 90036, USA

Daly, Robert (Baseball Player)
Los Angeles Dodgers
10779 Bellagio Rd
Los Angeles, CA 90077-3731, USA

Daly, Tess (Television Host)
c/o Staff Member *John Noel Management*
10A Belmont St
Floor 2
London NW1 8HH, UNITED KINGDOM (UK)

Daly, Tim (Actor, Producer)
212 Marine St #203
Santa Monica, CA 90405, USA

Daly, Tyne (Actor)
1617 N Sierra Bonita Ave
Los Angeles, CA 90046, USA

Daly-Donofrio, Heather (Athlete, Golfer)
414 Long Cove Ct
Apt 212
Ormond Beach, FL 32174-9290, USA

Dam, Kenneth W (Attorney, Attorney General, General, Government Official)
University of Chicago
Law School
1111 E 60st St
Chicago, IL 60637, USA

Damadian, Raymond V (Inventor)
FONAR Corp
110 Marcus Dr
Melville, NY 11747-4292, USA

Damageplan (Music Group)
2706 Monterrey
Arlington, TX 76015, USA

Damanchiah, Godfrey (Actor, Comedian)
c/o Brian Stern *Stern Entertainment Group (Brillstein Entertainment Partners)*
1 William Morris Pl
Beverly Hills, CA 90212, USA

Damas, Bertila (Actor)
PO Box 17193
Beverly Hills, CA 90209, USA

Damasio, Antonio R (Doctor)
University of Iowa Hospital
Neurology Dept
Iowa City, IA 52242, USA

Damaska, Jack (Athlete, Baseball Player)
252 Blackhawk Rd
Beaver Falls, PA 15010-1404, USA

D'Amato, Lisa (Musician)
c/o Staff Member *Brendan Vaughn*
Prefers to be contact via telephone or email
Los Angeles, CA 90069, USA

D'Amato, Mike (Athlete, Football Player)
7 Lansing Ln
East Northport, NY 11731, USA

DaMatta, Cristiano (Race Car Driver)
Newman-Haas Racing
500 Tower Pkwy
Lincolnshire, IL 60069, USA

D'Amboise, Jacques (Choreographer, Dancer)
National Dance Institute
594 Broadway
#805
New York, NY 10012, USA

D'Ambrosio, Dominick (Misc)
Allied Industrial Workers Union
3520 W Oklahoma Ave
Milwaukee, WI 53215, USA

Dames, Romi (Actor)
c/o Nicole Walter *Metro Public Relations*
6525 W Sunset Blvd
6th Floor
Hollywood, CA 90028, USA

Dameshek, David (Actor, Writer)
c/o Staff Member *Creative Artists Agency (CAA-LA)*
2000 Ave Of The Stars
Los Angeles, CA 90067, USA

Damian, Alexa (Actor)
c/o Staff Member *Televisa*
Blvd Adolfo Lopez Mateos 232
Colonia San Angel INN
DF CP 01060, MEXICO

Damian, Michael (Actor, Musician)
Gold Marshak Liedtke
3500 W Olive Ave
#1400
Burbank, CA 91505, USA

Damiani, Damiano (Director)
Via Delle Terme Deciane 2
Rome 00153, ITALY

D'Amico, Jeff (Athlete, Baseball Player)
30 Evelyn Ct
Oldsmar, FL 34677-2322, USA

Damico, Jeff (Athlete, Baseball Player)
2223 Muirfield Way
Oldsmar, FL 34677, USA

Damico, Jeff (Athlete, Baseball Player)
9567 NE Northtown Loop
Bainbridge Island, WA 98110-3532, USA

D'Amico, William D (Athlete)
30 Greenwood St
Lake Placid, NY 12946, USA

Damkroger, Maury (Athlete, Football Player)
1722 S 166th Cir
Omaha, NE 68130, USA

Dammerman, Dennis D (Business Person)
General Electric Co
3135 Easton Tumpike
Fairfield, CT 06828, USA

Damon, Grey (Actor)
c/o Toni Benson Third Hill Entertainment
195 S Beverly Dr
Suite 400
Beverly Hills, CA 90212, USA

Damon, Johnny (Athlete, Baseball Player)
PO Box 8540
Stockton, CA 95208-0540, USA

Damon, Mark (Actor)
2781 Benedict Canyon Dr
Beverly Hills, CA 90210, USA

Damon, Matt (Actor)
1401 San Remo Dr
Pacific Palisades, CA 90272, USA

Damon, Stuart (Actor)
387 N Van Ness Ave
Los Angeles, CA 90004, USA

Damon, Una (Actor)
c/o Suzanne DeWalt Dewalt & Musik Management
623 N. Parish Place
Burbank, CA 91506, USA

Damone, Vic (Actor, Musician)
200 Via Bellaria
Palm Beach, FL 33480

Damore, John (Athlete, Football Player)
627 Citadel Dr
Westmont, IL 60559, USA

D'Amour, Marc
70 Jacobs Creek Dr
Hershey, PA 17033-8918

Damphousse, Vincent (Athlete, Hockey Player)
c/o Staff Member NHL Players Association
1700-20 Bay St
Toronto, ON M5J 2R8, Canada

Dampier, Erick (Athlete, Basketball Player)
18724 Wainsborough Ln
Dallas, TX 75287-5525, USA

Dampier, Louie (Athlete, Basketball Player)
2808 New Moody Lane
La Grange, KY 40031-9453, USA

Dampler, Erick (Basketball Player)
2635 Sea View Parkway
Alameda, CA 94502, USA

Dampler, Louie (Basketball Player)
Dampler Ditributing
2808 New Moody Lane
La Grange, KY 40031, USA

Damron, Robert (Athlete, Golfer)
6001 Masters Blvd
Orlando, FL 32819-4303, USA

Damus, Mike (Actor)
c/o Staff Member United Talent Agency (UTA)
9336 Civic Center Dr
Beverly Hills, CA 90210, USA

Dan, Dercher (Athlete, Football Player)
3448 W 131st St
Leawood, KS 66209, USA

Dan, Judith (Stylist)
2751 Monte Mar Terrace
Los Angeles, CA 90064, USA

Dan, Reeder (Athlete, Football Player)
703 Southwood Rd
Hockessin, DE 19707-1040, USA

Dan, Rice (Athlete, Football Player)
247 Bramblebush Rd
Stoughton, MA 02072-3096, USA

Dana, Bill (Actor, Comedian)
c/o Staff Member Amsel, Eisenstadt & Frazier Talent Agency (AEF)
5055 Wilshire Blvd
Suite 860
Los Angeles, CA 90036-6108, USA

Dana, Bill
15805 W Vale Dr
Goodyear, AZ 85395-8760, USA

Dana, Justin (Actor)
13111 Ventura Blvd
#102
Studio City, CA 91604, USA

Danare, Malcolm (Actor)
c/o Monique Moss Integrated PR
8060 Melrose Ave
4th Floor
Los Angeles, CA 90046, USA

Danby, Gordon T (Inventor)
126 Sound Road
Wading River, NY 11792, USA

Danby, John (Athlete, Hockey Player)
20 Jb Dr
Marstons Mills, MA 02648-1521, USA

Dance, Bill (Fisherman)
Bill Dance's Fishing
PO Box 198
Brownsville, TN 38012, USA

Dance, Charies (Actor)
7812 Forsythe St
Sunland, CA 91040, USA

Dance, Charles (Actor)
c/o Susan Smith Susan Smith Company, The
1344 N Wetherly Dr
Los Angeles, CA 90069-1817, USA

Dancer, Donald (Horse Racer)
30 Amherst Rd
Marlboro, NJ 07746-1557, USA

Dancer, Harold (General)
343 Monmouth Rd
Freehold, NJ 07728-7939, USA

Dancer, James (Horse Racer)
102 Ricemill Cir Apt 1
Sunset Beach, Nc 28468-4479, USA

Dancer, Rachel (Horse Racer)
4051 NE 31st Ave
Lighthouse Point, FL 33064-8436, USA

Dancer, Ronald (Horse Racer)
PO Box 235
New Egypt, NJ 08533-0235, USA

Dancer, Stanley F (Race Car Driver)
1300 S Ocean Blvd
Pompano Beach, FL 33062, USA

Dancy, Bill (Athlete, Baseball Player)
2225 Hemerick Pl
Clearwater, FL 33765-2228, USA

Dancy, Hugh (Actor)
42 Wooster St #4SO
New York, NY 10013, USA

Dancy, John (Correspondent)
Harvard University
Kennedy Government School
Cambridge, MA 02138, USA

Dandenault, Mathieu (Athlete, Hockey Player)
2615 Dorchester Rd
Birmingham, MI 48009, USA

Dando, Evan (Musician)
c/o Staff Member Good Cop Public Relations
425 W 13th St #502
New York, NY 10014, USA

Dandridge, Bob (Athlete, Basketball Player)
1708 Saint Denis Avenue
Norfolk, VA 23509-1004, USA

Dandy Warholds, The (Music Group)
c/o Staff Member Tsunami Entertainment
2525 Hyperion Ave
Los Angeles, CA 90027, USA

Dandy Warhols (Music Group)
c/o Staff Member Tsunami Entertainment
2525 Hyperion Ave
Los Angeles, CA 90027, USA

Dane, Alexandra (Actor)
Rolf Kruger Mgmt
205 Chudliegh Road
London SE4 1EG, UNITED KINGDOM (UK)

Dane, Eric (Actor)
2101 N Beverly Dr
Beverly Hills, CA 90210, USA

Dane, Lloyd (Race Car Driver)
4165 Amarillo Drive SW
Concord, NC 28027, USA

Dane, Paul (Misc)
12105 Ambassador Dr
#515
Colarado Springs, CO 80921, USA

Danehe, Dick (Athlete, Football Player)
23871 Willows Dr Apt 378
Laguna Hills, CA 92653-1951, USA

Daneker, Pat (Athlete, Baseball Player)
107 Van Buren Rd
Voorhees, NJ 08043-2464, USA

Danelli, Dino (Musician)
Rascals Cassidy
11761 Speedway Blvd
Tucson, AZ 85748, USA

Danelo, Joe (Athlete, Football Player)
3601 Roxbury St
San Pedro, CA 90731, USA

Danenhauer, Bill (Athlete, Football Player)
10 Kirkby Cir
Bella Vista, AR 72715, USA

Danenhauer, Eldon (Athlete, Football Player)
1030 SW Exmoor Ln
Topeka, KS 66604, USA

Danes, Claire (Actor)
42 Wooster St #4SO
New York, NY 10013, USA

Daneyko, Ken (Athlete, Hockey Player)
11 Combs Hollow Rd
Mendham, NJ 07945, USA

Daney_ko, Ken (Athlete, Hockey Player)
10 Mahogany_ Way
Randolph, NJ 07869-3734

Danforth, Douglas D (Athlete, Baseball Player, Business Person)
8787 Bay Colony Drive
Apt 1002
Naples, FL 34108-0784, USA

Danforth, Fred (Artist)
PO Box 828
Middlebury, VT 05753, USA

Danforth, John (Politician)
HC 1 Box 91
Newburg, MO 65550, USA

Danforth, John C (Jack) (Ex-Senator)
US Permanent Mission
United Nations
799 UN Plaza
New York, NY 10017, USA

D'Angelo (Musician, Songwriter, Writer)
c/o Staff Member WmE2 (WMA-LA)
1 William Morris Pl
Beverly Hills, CA 90212, USA

D'Angelo, Beverly (Actor)
7708 Woodrow Wilson Dr
Los Angeles, CA 90046, USA

D'Angelo, Josephine (Athlete, Baseball Player, Commentator)
6141 W Higgins Ave Apt 5A
Chicago, IL 60630-1853, USA

D'Angio, Giulio J (Misc)
Children's Hospital
34th & Civic Center Blvd
Philadelphia, PA 19104, USA

Daniel, Brittany (Actor)
c/o Glenn Rigberg HYPHENATE
9701 Wilshire Blvd.
10th floor
Beverly Hills, CA 90212, USA

Daniel, Elizabeth A (Beth) (Athlete, Golfer)
219 Palm Trl
Delray Beach, FL 33483, USA

Daniel, Eugene (Athlete, Football Player)
PO Box 80345
Baton Rouge, LA 70898-0345, USA

Daniel, Kenny (Athlete, Football Player)
2911 Center Ave
Richmond, CA 94804, USA

Daniel, Robert (Athlete, Football Player)
9860 Scyene Rd
Apt 518
Dallas, TX 75227, USA

Daniel, Willie (Athlete, Football Player)
1711 Oktoc Rd
Starkville, MS 39759, USA

Daniel, Willie (Athlete, Football Player)
508 S Jackson St
Starkville, MS 39759-3352, USA

Danielpour, Richard (Composer)
Sony Classics Records
2100 Colorado Ave
Santa Monica, CA 90404, USA

Daniels, Anthony (Actor)
c/o Fifi Oscard *Fifi Oscard Agency*
110 W 40th St
Suite 1601
New York, NY 10018, USA

Daniels, Antonio (Basketball Player)
Seatle SuperSonics
351 Elliot Ave W
#500
Seattle, WA 98119, USA

Daniels, Bennie (Athlete, Baseball Player)
938 W 156th St
Compton, CA 90220-3504, USA

Daniels, Charlie (Musician, Songwriter, Writer)
16225/16832/16836/16850/17060 Central Pike
Lebanon, TN 37090, USA

Daniels, Cheryl (Bowler)
6574 Crest Top Dr
West Bloomfield, MI 48322, USA

Daniels, Clem (Athlete, Football Player)
8683 Mountain Blvd
Oakland, CA 94605, USA

Daniels, Dexter (Athlete, Football Player)
518 E Magnolia St
Valdosta, GA 31601, USA

Daniels, Erin (Actor)
10171 Valley Spring Ln
Toluca Lake, CA 91602, USA

Daniels, Fred (Athlete, Baseball Player)
P.O. Box 6208
Statesville, NC 28687-6208, USA

Daniels, Greg (Actor)
c/o Howard Klein *3 Arts Entertainment Inc*
9460 Wilshire Blvd
7th Floor
Beverly Hills, CA 90210, USA

Daniels, Jack (Athlete, Baseball Player)
811 S Lombard Ave
Evansville, IN 47714-0428, USA

Daniels, Jeff (Athlete, Hockey Player)
108 Delaplane Ct
Morrisville, NC 27560, USA

Daniels, Jeff (Actor)
701 Glazier Rd
Chelsea, MI 48118, USA

Daniels, Jenna (Athlete, Golfer)
85140 Amagansett Dr
Fernandina Beach, FL 32034, USA

Daniels, Jerome (Athlete, Football Player)
311 Park Ave
Bloomfield, CT 06002-3103, USA

Daniels, Jon (Commentator)
602 Aberdeen Way
Southlake, TX 76092-9553, USA

Daniels, Jon (Athlete, Baseball Player)
602 Aberdeen Way
Southlake, TX 76092-9553, USA

Daniels, Kal (Athlete, Baseball Player)
100 Echo Ln
Warner Robins, GA 31088-7458, USA

Daniels, Kevin (Actor)
c/o Staff Member *Insight*
1134 S Cloverdale Ave
Los Angeles, CA 90019, USA

Daniels, Kimbi
9159 Cranberry St
Anchorage, AK 99502-5575

Daniels, Lee (Director, Producer)
c/o Christina Bazdekis *ICM Partners (ICM-LA)*
555 W 25th St
4th Floor
New York, NY 10001, USA

Daniels, Leshun (Athlete, Football Player)
593 Magnolia St
Dekalb, IL 60115, USA

Daniels, Marquis
c/o Staff Member *Dallas Mavericks*
2500 Victory Ave
Dallas, TX 75219, USA

Daniels, Marquis (Athlete, Basketball Player)
2501 Sutton Place Dr S
Carmel, IN 46032-8694, USA

Daniels, Melvin (Mel) (Athlete, Basketball Player)
19789 Centennial Road
Sheridan, IN 46069-9789, USA

Daniels, Mitch (Governor)
Office of the Governor
Statehouse
Indianapolis, IN 46204-2797, USA

Daniels, Owen
5425 Inwood Dr
Houston, TX 77056-4215, USA

Daniels, Owen (Athlete, Football Player)
5333 Elm St
Houston, TX 77081, USA

Daniels, Phillip (Athlete, Football Player)
1703 N Pebble Beach Way
Vernon Hills, IL 60061, USA

Daniels, Scott (Athlete, Hockey Player)
36 Deer Run
Southwick, MA 01077-9523, USA

Daniels, Spencer (Actor)
c/o Staff Member *Stone Manners Salners Agency (LA)*
9911 W Pico Blvd Ste 1400
Los Angeles, CA 90035, USA

Daniels, Susan (Athlete, Golfer)
251 N Lake Blvd
Tahoe City, CA 96145, USA

Daniels, Travis (Athlete, Football Player)
4665 SW 75th Way
Unit 104
Davie, FL 33314, USA

Daniels, William (Actor)
12805 Hortense St
Studio City, CA 91604, USA

Daniels, William B (Physicist)
283 Dallam Road
Newark, DE 19711, USA

Danielsen, Egil (Athlete, Track Athlete)
Roreks Gate 9
Hamar 2300, NORWAY

Danielson, Gary D (Athlete, Football Player)
10112 Magnolia Bnd
Bonita Springs, FL 34135, USA

Danielsson, Bengt F (Misc)
Box 558
Papette, TAHITI

Daniloff, Nicholas (Journalist)
PO Box 892
Chester, VT 05143, USA

Danity Kane (Music Group)
c/o Tammy Brook *FYI Public Relations*
174 5th Ave
Suite 404
New York, NY 10010, USA

Danks, John (Athlete, Baseball Player)
702 Oaklands Dr
Round Rock, TX 78681-4029, USA

Danley, Kerwin (Athlete, Baseball Player)
3769 E Libra Pl
Chandler, AZ 85249, USA

Danmeier, Rick (Athlete, Football Player)
4917 Ridge Rd
Minneapolis, MN 55436, USA

Danneels, Godfried Cardinal (Religious Leader)
Aartsbisdom
Wollemarkt 15
Mechelen 2800, BELGIUM

Danner, Blythe (Actor)
1 5th Ave #17B-C
New York, NY 10003, USA

Danner, Christian (Misc)
JAS Engineering
Viale Europa
72 Strada Bn 1
Cusago 20090, ITALY

Danning, Sybil (Actor, Model)
8578 Walnut Dr
Los Angeles, CA 90046, USA

Danny & The Juniors (Music Group)
PO Box 279
Williamstown, NJ 08094-0279

Dano, Paul Franklin (Actor)
c/o Sandra Chang *Anonymous Content (LA)*
955 S Carrillo Dr
Suite 300
Los Angeles, CA 90048, USA

Dansby, Karlos (Athlete, Football Player)
16850 Stratford Ct
Southwest Ranches, FL 33331-1359, USA

Danson, Ted (Actor)
656 Moreno Ave
Los Angeles, CA 90049, USA

Dante, Joe (Director)
c/o Staff Member *Gersh (LA)*
9465 Wilshire Blvd
Suite 600
Beverly Hills, CA 90212, USA

Dante, Michael (Actor)
71372 Biskra Rd
Rancho Mirage, CA 92270, USA

Dante, Peter (Actor)
5815 Ramirez Canyon Rd
Malibu, CA 90265, USA

Dante Bichette, Alphonse (Baseball Player)
2298 Robin Rd
Orlando, FL 32814-6548, USA

Dantine, Nikki (Actor)
707 North Palm Dr
Beverly Hills, CA 90210, USA

Dantley, Adrian (Athlete, Basketball Player, Olympic Athlete)
9 Barn Ridge Court
Silver Spring, MD 20906-1105, USA

Danto, Arthur C (Misc)
Columbia University
Philosophy Dept
New York, NY 10024, USA

Danton, Mike (Athlete, Hockey Player)
Fort Dix F C I
P.O. Box 1000 #10096-111
Fort Dix, NJ 08640, USA

Dantoni, Mike (Athlete, Basketball Player)
9 Hunter Ln
Rye, NY 10580-1614, USA

Dantzig, George B (Scientist)
2509 Tamalpais Ave
El Cerrito, CA 94530-1561, USA

Danz, Shirley (Athlete, Baseball Player, Commentator)
330 Greystone Dr.
Hendersonville, NC 28792-9173, USA

Danza, Tony (Actor)
11911 Ashdale Ln
Studio City, CA 91604, USA

Danzig
PO Box 884563
San Francisco, CA 94188

Danzig, Frederick P (Editor)
Advertising Age
Editorial Dept
220 E 42nd St
New York, NY 10017, USA

Danziger, Cory (Actor)
c/o Staff Member *Iris Burton Agency*
10100 Santa Monica Blvd Ste 1300
Los Angeles, CA 90067, USA

Danziger, Jeff (Cartoonist, Editor)
RFD
Plainfield, VT 05667, USA

Dao, Chloe (Fashion Designer)
Lot 8 Boutique
6127 Kirby Dr
Houston, TX 77005, USA

Daoud, Ignace Moussa I Cardinal (Religious Leader)
Palazzo del Bramante
Via della Conciliazione 34
Rome 00193, ITALY

Daoust, Dan (Athlete, Hockey Player)
55 John Stiver Crest
Markham, ON L3R 9B6, Canada

Dapin, Marti (Stylist)
3748 N Sawyer Ave
Chicago, IL 60618, USA

Dapkus-Wolf, Eleanor (Baseball Player)
9150 Mallard Cv
Saint John, IN 48373-9019, USA

Dapolito, Deborah (Stylist)
3731 Folsom St
San Francisco, CA 94110, USA

Dapper, Marco (Actor, Model)
c/o Steve Himber *Steve Himber Entertainment*
211 S Beverly Dr #601
Beverly Hills, CA 90212, USA

Dara, Olu (Actor)
c/o Staff Member *Monterey International (Chicago)*
200 W Superior
Suite 202
Chicago, IL 60610, USA

D'Arabian, Melissa (Chef)
c/o Josh Bider *WME (WMA-NY)*
1325 Ave of the Americas
New York, NY 10019, USA

Darabont, Frank (Director)
4474 Dundee Dr
Los Angeles, CA 90027, USA

D'Arbanville, Patti (Actor)
c/o Staff Member *Moskowit Agency*
10440 Queens Blvd #15V
Forest Hills, NY 11375, USA

Darbo, Patrka (Musician)
346 N Avon St
Burbank, CA 91505, USA

Darboven, Hanne (Artist)
Am Burgberg 26
Hamburg 21079, GERMANY

Darby, Chartric (Athlete, Football Player)
14335 Simonds Rd NE Apt A302
Kirkland, WA 98034-9277, USA

Darby, Craig (Athlete, Hockey Player)
40 Vista Dr
Saratoga Springs, NY 12866-8772

Darby, Kim (Actor)
4255 Laurel Grove Ave
Studio City, CA 91604, USA

Darby, Matt (Athlete, Football Player)
501 Sagecreek Ct
Winter Springs, FL 32708-2731, USA

D'Arby, Terence Trent (Musician)
c/o Staff Member *Creative Artists Agency (CAA-LA)*
2000 Ave Of The Stars
Los Angeles, CA 90067, USA

D'Arby, Terence Trent (Sananda Maitreya) (Musician)
Sananda Records
Sempione 38
Milan 20154, Italy

Darc, Mireille (Actor)
Agents Associes Beaume
201 Faubourg Saint Honore
Paris 75008, FRANCE

D'Arcangelo, Ildebrando (Opera Singer)
Lies Askonas
6 Henrietta St
London WC2E 8LA, UNITED KINGDOM (UK)

Darcey, Pete (Athlete, Basketball Player)
17600 North Anderson Road
Arcadia, OK 73007-7113, USA

Darche, Jean-Philippe (Athlete, Football Player)
9507 W 160th Ter
Stilwell, KS 66085, USA

Darcum, Max (Skier)
PO Box 189
Dillon, CO 80435, USA

D'Arcy (Musician)
Cohen Brothers Mgmt
500 Molino St
#104
Los Angeles, CA 90013, USA

Darcy, Dame (Artist)
c/o Staff Member *Fantagraphics Books*
7563 Lake City Way
Seattle, WA 98115, USA

D'Arcy, James (Actor)
c/o Joel Lubin *Creative Artists Agency (CAA-LA)*
2000 Ave Of The Stars
Los Angeles, CA 90067, USA

D'Arcy, Margaretta (Writer)
Cassarotto
60/66 Wardour St
London W1V 4ND, UNITED KINGDOM (UK)

Darcy, Pat (Athlete, Baseball Player)
515 S Columbus Blvd
Tucson, AZ 85711-4753, USA

D'Arcy James, Brian (Actor)
c/o JB Roberts *Thruline Entertainment*
9250 Wilshire Blvd
Ground Fl
Beverly Hills, CA 90212, USA

Dar Dar, Kirby (Athlete, Football Player)
P.O. Box 2872
Syracuse, NY 13220, USA

Darden, Christopher (Attorney)
19150 Allandale Dr
Tarzana, CA 91356, USA

Darden, Ollie
319 Boynton Bay Cir
Boynton Beach, FL 33435-2568, USA

Darden, Thom (Athlete, Football Player)
637 20th Ave SW
Cedar Rapids, IA 52404, USA

Daredevil (Music Group)
c/o Staff Member *Wind-up Records*
72 Madison Ave Fl 8
New York, NY 10016, USA

Darego, Agbani (Model)
c/o Staff Member *Miss World Ltd*
21 Golden Sq
London W1R 3PA, UNITED KINGDOM (UK)

Darehshori, Nader F (Publisher)
Houghton Mifflin Co
222 Berkeley St
Boston, MA 02116, USA

Darensbourg, Vic (Athlete, Baseball Player)
4151 Abernethy Forest Pl
Las Vegas, NV 89141, USA

Darensbourg., Vic
4151 Abernethy Forest Pl
Las Veg_as, NV 89141-4336, USA

Dareus, Marcell (Football Player)
c/o Todd France *France AllPro Athlete Management*
3500 Lenox Road, NE
Atlanta, GA 30326, USA

Darish, Frank (Horse Racer)
11 March Ln
Westbury, NY 11590-6301, USA

Darius, Donovin (Athlete, Football Player)
1357 Lawrence Rd
Danville, CA 94506-4735, USA

Dark, Al (Athlete, Baseball Player, Coach)
103 Cranberry Way
Easley, SC 29642-3200, USA

Dark, Mike (Athlete, Hockey Player)
741 Wellington St
Sarina, ON N7T 1J3, Canada

Darkins, Chris (Athlete, Football Player)
10903 Shawnbrook Dr
Houston, TX 77071, USA

Dark Star Orchestra (Music Group)
PO Box 1282
Evanston, IL 60202, USA

Darling, Chuck (Athlete, Basketball Player, Olympic Athlete)
8066 S Krameria Way
Centennial, CO 80112-3040, USA

Darling, Devard (Athlete, Football Player)
11410 Via Fontana Ct
Richmond, TX 77406-4598, USA

Darling, Gary (Athlete, Baseball Player)
16422 S 36th Pl
Phoenix, AZ 85048, USA

Darling, Jean (Actor)
294 S Circular Rd
Dublin 8, IRELAND

Darling, Jennifer (Actor)
13351 Riverside Dr
#427
Sherman Oaks, CA 91423, USA

Darling, Joan (Actor)
PO Box 6700
Tesuque, NM 87574, USA

Darling, Ron (Athlete, Baseball Player)
c/o Staff Member *SportsNet New York*
75 Rockefeller Plz
New York, NY 10019, USA

Darmaatmadja, Julius Riyadi Cardinal (Religious Leader)
Keuskupan Agung
Jl Katedral 7
Jakarta 10710, INDONESIA

Darnell, Erik (Race Car Driver)
Darmer Motorsports Ltd
3627 Washington St.
Park City, IL 60085, USA

Darnell, James E Jr (Biologist)
Rockefeller University
Medical Center
1230 York Ave
New York, NY 10021, USA

Darnell, Mike (Producer)
24962 Lorenzo Ct
Calabasas, CA 91302, USA

Darnton, Robert C (Historian)
6 McCosh Circle
Princeton, NJ 08540, USA

Darr, Mike
1461 Maplebrook Ln
Corona, CA 92881-0704, USA

Darragh, Dan (Athlete, Football Player)
201 Sewickley Ridge Ct
Sewickley, PA 15143, USA

Darren, James (Actor, Musician)
PO Box 1088
Beverly Hills, CA 90213, USA

Darrian, Raquel (Adult Film Star)
49 Eaton Ct
Manhasset, NY 11030

Darrieux, Danielle (Actor)
Nicole Cann
1 Rue Alfred de Vigny
Paris 75008, FRANCE

Darrow, Barry (Athlete, Football Player)
2406 Chief Victor Camp Rd
Victor, MT 59875, USA

Dart, Iris Rainer (Writer)
938 Coral Dr
Pebble Beach, CA 93953, USA

Darwin, Bobby (Athlete, Baseball Player)
6516 Pleasant Hill Cir
Corona, CA 92880-3015, USA

Darwin, Danny (Athlete, Baseball Player)
11131 Lakecrest Dr
Sanger, TX 76266-3446, USA

Darwin, Jeff (Athlete, Baseball Player)
1010 W Russell Ave
Bonham, TX 75418-2332, USA

Darwin, Matt (Athlete, Football Player)
414 Love Bird Ln
Murphy, TX 75094-3263, USA

Darwitz, Natalie (Athlete, Hockey Player, Olympic Athlete)
c/o Staff Member *US Olympic Committee*
Alumni Relations
1750 E Boulder St
Colorado Springs, CO 80909-5793, USA

Das, Alisha (Actor)
19583 Bowers Dr
Topanga, CA 90290, USA

Das, Nandita (Actor)
c/o Aude Powell *Brunskill Management*
Suite 8A
169 Queen's Gate
London SW7 5HE, United Kingdom

Dascascos, Marc (Actor)
PO Box 1549
Studio City, CA 91614, USA

Dascenzo, Doug (Athlete, Baseball Player)
111 Eastgate Rd
Uniontown, PA 15401-5615, USA

Daschle, Thomas (Politician)
1020 N Jay St Apt 212
Aberdeen, SD 57401-2478, USA

D'Ascoli, Bernard (Musician)
Clarion/Seven Muses
47 Whitehall Park
London N19 3TW, UNITED KINGDOM (UK)

Dash, Damon (Actor, Director, Producer, Writer)
c/o Staff Member *Fortitude*
8619 Washington Blvd
Culver City, CA 90232, USA

Dash, Julie (Actor, Director, Producer, Writer)
c/o Kimber Wheeler *TalentWorks (LA)*
3500 W Olive Ave
Suite 1400
Burbank, CA 91505, USA

Dash, Leon O Jr (Journalist)
Washington Post
Editorial Dept
1150 15th Ave NW
Washington, DC 20071, USA

Dash, Sam
110 Newlands
Chevy Chase, MD 20015

Dash, Stacey (Actor)
c/o Staff Member *Bleu, An Entertainment Company*
5225 Wilshire Blvd
Suite 701
Los Angeles, CA 90036, USA

Dashboard Confessional (Music Group, Musician)
c/o Richard Egan *Hard 8 Management*
1100 Glendon Ave
Suite 1100
Los Angeles, CA 90024, USA

da Silva, Luiz Inacio Lula (Politician)
Partido Dos Trabalhadores
Setor Comercial Sul - Quadra 2
Bloco C - Nº 256
Edifício Toufic, Brasília DF, CEP: 70302-,
Brazil

Daskalakis, Cleon (Athlete, Hockey
Player)
752 Main St
Boxford, MA 01921-1127, USA

Dassier, Uwe (Swimmer)
Stolze-Schrey-Str 6
Wilday 15745, GREECE

Dastmalchi, Hamid (Misc)
4759 Sunset Heights Ct
San Diego, CA 92130-1302, USA

Dater, Judy L (Photographer)
2430 5th St Ste J
Berkeley, CA 94710-2452, USA

Datsyuk, Pavel (Athlete, Hockey Player)
3166 Rosedale St
Ann Arbor, MI 48108-1884, USA

Dattilo, Bryan (Actor)
12217 Emelita St
Valley Village, CA 91607, USA

Dattilo, Kristin (Actor)
c/o Jim Hess *Hess Entertainment*
360 N Crescent Dr
North Bldg
Beverly Hills, CA 90210, USA

Datz, Jeff (Athlete, Baseball Player)
4775 Elen Ct
Shingle SPrings, CA 95682-9519, USA

Daubach, Brian (Athlete, Baseball Player)
2709 Timberline Dr
Belleville, IL 62226-4933, USA

Daubechies, Ingrid C (Mathematician)
Princeton University
Mathematics Dept
Princeton, NJ 08544, USA

Dauben, William G (Misc)
20 Eagle Hill
Kensington, CA 94707, USA

Dauer, Rich (Athlete, Baseball Player)
10546 Gravmont Ln Unit A
Highlands Ranch, CO 80126-6719, USA

Daugaard, Dennis (Governor, Politician)
Office of the Governor
500 E Capitol Ave
Pierre, SD 57501, USA

Daugheity, Jim (Photographer)
94 Biscayne Dr
San Rafael, CA 94901-1561, USA

Daugherty, Brad (Misc)
1613 Cimarron Crest St
Las Vegas, NV 89144-1101, USA

Daugherty, Bradley L (Brad) (Athlete,
Basketball Player)
62 Willow Farm Rd
Fairview, NC 28730, USA

Daugherty, Doc (Athlete, Baseball Player)
314 Summers Dr
Lancaster, PA 17601-5884, USA

Daugherty, Jack (Athlete, Baseball Player)
20360 N 95th Pl
Scottsdale, AZ 85255-6646, USA

Daugherty, Martha Craig (Judge)
US Court of Appeals
701 Broadway
Nashville, TN 37203, USA

Daughtry, Chris (Musician)
8482/8486/8488 Haw River Rd
Oak Ridge, NC 27310, USA

Dauline, Marie (Musician)
Todo Mundo
PO Box 652
Cooper Station
New York, NY 10276, USA

Daulton, Darren (Athlete, Baseball Player)
211 N 3rd St
Arkansas City, KS 67005-2452, USA

Dauplaise, Norman (Jockey)
29 W 36th St
#1000
New York, NY 10018, USA

Dausset, Jean (Nobel Prize Laureate)
9 rue de Villersexel
Paris, F F-75007 France, USA

Dausset, Jean B G (Nobel Prize Laureate)
9 Rue de Villersexel
Paris 75007, FRANCE

Davalillo, Vic (Athlete, Baseball Player)
Calle Trujillo 7
Mariperez Q V
Caracas, Venezuela

Davalos, Alexa (Actor)
c/o Staff Member *Anonymous Content*
(LA)
3531 Hayden Ave
Culver City, CA 90232, USA

Davalos, Elyssa
2934 1/2 Beverly Glen Circle #53
Los Angeles, CA 90077

Davalos, Richard (Actor)
23388 Mulholland Sr
#28
Woodland Hills, CA 91364-2733, USA

Davanon, Jeff (Athlete, Baseball Player)
2811 Piedmont Ave
Los Alamitos, CA 90720-4244, USA

Davanon, Jerry (Athlete, Baseball Player)
350 Grevoine W
Montgomery, TX 77356-8192, USA

Dave, Al (Athlete, Football Player)
5173 Waring Rd
Apt 441
San Diego, CA 92120, USA

Dave, Al
5173 Waring Rd #441
San Diego, CA 92120-2705, USA

Dave Matthews Band (Music Group)
c/o Coran Capshaw *Red Light
Management (VA)*
PO Box 1467
Charlottesville, VA 22902, USA

Davenport, Adell (Baseball Player)
Topps
1764 Belt Line Rd Apt 155
Garland, TX 75044-6824, USA

Davenport, A Nigel (Actor)
5 Ann's Close
Kinnerton Street
London SW1, UNITED KINGDOM (UK)

Davenport, Charles (Athlete, Football
Player)
206 Wapiti Dr
Spring Lake, NC 28390-1530, USA

Davenport, Jack (Actor)
c/o Lorraine Hamilton *Hamilton Hodell
Ltd*
66-68 Margaret St Fl 5
London W1W 8SR, UK

Davenport, Jim (Athlete, Baseball Player,
Coach)
1016 Hewitt Dr
San Carlos, CA 94070-3601, USA

Davenport, Joe (Athlete, Baseball Player)
10102 Wy_cliffe St
Santee, CA 92071-1176, USA

Davenport, Lindsay (Athlete, Olympic
Athlete, Tennis Player)
704 Emerald Bay
Laguna Beach, CA 92651, USA

Davenport, Lindsey (Tennis Player)
PO Box 10179
Newport Beach, CA 92658, USA

Davenport, Madison (Actor)
c/o Erik Kritzer *Kritzer Levine Wilkins
Entertainment (KLWG)*
11872 La Grange Ave
1st Floor
Los Angeles, CA 90025, USA

Davenport, Naieh
792 SW 106th Ave
Pembroke Pines, FL 33025-6911, USA

Davenport, Najeh (Athlete, Football
Player)
1225 NW 103rd Ln
Miami, FL 33147, USA

Davenport, Nigel (Actor)
Green & Underwood
2 Conduit St
London W1R9TG, UNITED KINGDOM
(UK)

Davenport, Ron
6 School Lane
Sandys

Davenport Cabinet (Musician)
c/o Blaze James *Black Sheep Fellowship*
6255 Sunset Blvd
Suite 910
Los Angeles, CA 90028, USA

Davenport Jr, Guy M (Writer)
621 Sayre Ave
Lexington, KY 40508, USA

Davenport Jr, Wilbur B (Engineer)
1120 Skyline Dr
Medford, OR 97504, USA

Davey, Don (Athlete, Football Player)
1525 Beach Ave
Atlantic Beach, FL 32233-5735, USA

Davey, Mike (Athlete, Baseball Player)
902 W Melinda Ln
Spokane, WA 99203-1363, USA

Davey, Rohan (Athlete, Football Player)
24696 Plank Rd
Slaughter, LA 70777-9703, USA

Davey, Tom (Athlete, Baseball Player)
13125 Andover Dr
Plymouth, MI 48170-8208, USA

Davi, Robert (Actor)
10044 Calvin Ave
Northridge, CA 91324, USA

Daviau, Allen (Cinematographer)
2249 Bronson Hill Dr
Los Angeles, CA 90068, USA

Daviault, Ray (Athlete, Baseball Player)
2864 Ch des Pins RR 1
Notre-Dame-De-La-Merci, QC J0T 2A0,
Canada

Davich, Jacob (Actor)
c/o Brad Schenck *Paradigm (LA)*
360 N Crescent Dr
North Bldg
Beverly Hills, CA 90210, USA

Davich, Marty (Composer)
530 S Greenwood Lane
Pasadena, CA 91107, USA

David, Andre (Athlete, Baseball Player)
17341 W Banff Ln
Surprise, AZ 85388-7712, USA

David, Charlie (Actor)
CTM International
205-309 W Cordova St
Vancouver BC V6B 1E5, Canada

David, Craig (Musician)
c/o Cara Lewis *Creative Artists Agency
(CAA-LA)*
1325 Ave of the Americas
New York, NY 10019, USA

David, Duke (Politician)
240 Garden Ave
Mandeville, LA 70471-2910, USA

David, George A L (Business Person)
United Technologies Corp
United Technologies Building
Hartford, CT 06101, USA

David, John R (Misc)
Harvard Public Health School
665 Huntington Ave
Boston, MA 02115, USA

David, Keith (Actor)
c/o Josh Silver *Silver Mine Entertainment*
6705 Sunset Blvd.
Hollywood, CA 90028, USA

David, Larry (Actor, Producer, Writer)
212 Vance St
Pacific Palisades, CA 90272, USA

David, Laurie (Activist)
Lightray Productions
2934 1/2 Beverly Glen Circle
Los Angeles, CA 90077, USA

David, Mack
1575 Toledo Circle
Palm Springs, CA 92262

David, Mohato (Prince)
Royal Palace
PO Box 524
Maseru, LESOTHO

David, Peter (Actor)
PO Box 239
Bayport, NY 11705, USA

David, Peter (Writer)
PO Box 239
Bayport, NY 11705-0239, USA

David, Richie (Athlete, Football Player)
3712 NE 110th St
Vancouver, WA 98686-3991, USA

David, Silvana (Stylist)
c/o Staff Member *Rex Agency, The*
6311 Romaine St
Los Angeles, CA 90038, USA

David, Stan (Athlete, Football Player)
502 Baja Cir
Denver City, TX 79323, USA

David, Stan (Athlete, Football Player)
502 Baja Cir
Denver City, TX 79323-3747, USA

David, Yuval (Actor, Musician)
c/o Stanzi Stokes *Trio Entertainment Group*
16060 Ventura Blvd. #105-349
Encino, CA 91436, USA

David Bossert, David Bossert (Director, Producer)
c/o Staff Member *Walt Disney Television Animation*
500 S Buena Vista St
Burbank, CA 91521

David Crowder Band (Musician)
c/o Staff Member *Third Coast Artists Agency*
2021 21st Ave S
Suite 220
Nashville, TN 37212, USA

David Jr, Edward E (Engineer)
EED Inc
PO Box 435
Bedminster, NJ 07921, USA

Davidoff, Dov (Actor)
c/o Stephanie Davis *Wet Dog Entertainment*
9460 Wilshire Blvd
7th Floor
Beverly Hills, CA 90210, USA

Davidovich, Bella (Musician)
c/o Staff Member *Columbia Artists Mgmt Inc*
1790 Broadway Fl 6
New York, NY 10019-1412, USA

Davidovich, Lolita (Actor)
15200 Friends St
Pacific Palisades, CA 90272, USA

Davidovsky, Mario (Composer)
Harvard University
Music Dept
Cambridge, MA 02138, USA

Davids, Hollace (Producer)
c/o Staff Member *Universal Pictures*
100 Universal City Plz
Universal City, CA 91608, USA

Davidson, Adam (Actor)
c/o Andrea Simon *Andrea Simon Entertainment*
4230 Woodman Avenue
Sherman Oaks, CA 91423, USA

Davidson, Amy (Actor)
4435 Colfax Ave #112
N Hollywood, CA 91602, USA

Davidson, Bob (Athlete, Baseball Player)
91 Deerwood Dr
Littleton, CO 80127, USA

Davidson, Bob (Athlete, Baseball Player)
1420 Bruton Parish Way
Fairfield, OH 45014-4536, USA

Davidson, Bruce O (Misc)
RR 842
Unionville, PA 19375, USA

Davidson, Cleatus (Athlete, Baseball Player)
112 Lincoln Ave
Dundee, FL 33838-4394, USA

Davidson, Cotton (Athlete, Football Player)
435 Old Osage Rd
Gatesville, TX 76528, USA

Davidson, Diane Mott (Writer)
c/o Author Mail *Bantam-Dell Publishing (NY)*
1745 Broadway
New York, NY 10019, USA

Davidson, Doug (Actor)
295 Toro Canyon Rd
Carpinteria, CA 93013, USA

Davidson, Eileen (Actor)
11300 West Olympic Blvd
#610
Los Angeles, CA 90064, USA

Davidson, Ernest R (Scientist)
18514 36th Avenue W
Apt A
Lynnwood, WA 98037-7623, USA

Davidson, Gary L (Athlete, Hockey Player)
245 Fischer Ave Ste D1
Costa Mesa, CA 92626-4539, USA

Davidson, George A Jr (Business Person)
Consolidated Natural Gas
625 Liberty Ave
Pittsburgh, PA 15222, USA

Davidson, Gordon (Director, Producer)
Center Theatre Group
Mark Taper Forum
135 N Grand Ave
Los Angeles, CA 90012, USA

Davidson, Jeff (Athlete, Football Player)
10036 Gristmill Rdg
Eden Prairie, MN 55347-4759, USA

Davidson, Jeff (Motivational Speaker)
Breathing Space Institute
2417 Honeysuckle Road
Chapel Hill, NC 27514, USA

Davidson, Jeremy (Actor)
c/o Matthew Lesher *Insight*
1134 S Cloverdale Ave
Los Angeles, CA 90019, USA

Davidson, Jim (Actor)
c/o Staff Member *International Artistes*
Holborn Hall - 4th Floor
London WC1V 7BD, UK

Davidson, John (Athlete, Hockey Player)
c/o Josh Pultz *Douglas Gorman Rothacker & Wilhelm Inc*
1501 Broadway
Suite 703
New York, NY 10036, USA

Davidson, John (Athlete, Hockey Player)
6 Briarbrook Trl
Saint Louis, MO 63131-3947, USA

Davidson, Ken (Athlete, Football Player)
1922 Thompson Crossing Dr
Richmond, TX 77406-6707, USA

Davidson, Mark (Athlete, Baseball Player)
996 Old Mountain Rd
Statesville, NC 28677-2082, USA

Davidson, Matthew (Athlete, Golfer)
3 Westminster Pl
Cranbury, NJ 08512, USA

Davidson, Owen (Athlete, Tennis Player)
39 N Lakemist Harbour Pl
Spring, TX 77381-3344, USA

Davidson, Ralph P (Publisher)
494 Harbor Road
Southport, CT 06890, USA

Davidson, Ronald (Scientist)
Princeton University Plasma Physics Lab
Princeton, NJ 08544-0001, USA

Davidson, Ronald C (Physicist)
Princeton University
Plasma Physics Laboratory
Princeton, NJ 08544, USA

Davidson, Satch (Athlete, Baseball Player)
2400 Westheimer Rd
Apt 209W
Houston, TX 77098, USA

Davidson, Tommy (Actor, Comedian)
3800 Weslin Ave
Sherman Oaks, CA 91423, USA

Davidtz, Embeth (Actor)
345 S Chadbourne Ave
Los Angeles, CA 90049, USA

Davie, Alan (Artist)
Gamels Studio
Rush Green
Hertford SG13 7SB, UNITED KINGDOM (UK)

Davie, Donald A (Writer)
4 High St
Silverton
Exeter EX5 4JB, UNITED KINGDOM (UK)

Davie, Jerry (Athlete, Baseball Player)
2800 US Highway 17 92 W Ofc
Haines City, FL 33844-7375, USA

Davies, Dave (Musician)
Larry Page
29 Ruston Mews
London W11 1RB, UNITED KINGDOM (UK)

Davies, Dennis Russell
Am Wichelshof 24
Bonn 53111, GERMANY

Davies, Gail (Musician)
246 Cherokee Road
Nashville, TN 37205, USA

Davies, Geralnt Wyn (Actor)
Oscars Abrams Zimel
438 Queen St W
Toronto, ON M5A 1T4, CANADA

Davies, Jeremy (Actor)
United Talent Agency
9560 Wilshire Blvd
#500
Beverly Hills, CA 90212, USA

Davies, Kyle (Athlete, Baseball Player)
5436 Glenridge Vw NE
Atlanta, GA 30342-1737, USA

Davies, Lane (Actor)
PO Box 20531
Thousand Oaks, CA 91358, USA

Davies, Laura (Athlete, Golfer)
I M G
1360 E 9th St
Suite 100
Cleveland, OH 44114, USA

Davies, Linda (Writer)
Calle Once 286
La Molona
Lima, PERU

Davies, Matt (Artist, Cartoonist, Editor)
Journal News
Editorial Dept
One Gannett Dr
White Plains, NY 10604, USA

Davies, Mike (Architect)
Rogers Partnership
Thames Wharf
Rainville Road
London N6 94A, UNITED KINGDOM (UK)

Davies, Paul C W (Mathematician, Physicist)
PO Box 389
Burnside, SA 5066, AUSTRALIA

Davies, Peter (Misc)
Albert Einstein Medical College
Biochemistry Dept
Bronx, NY 10461, USA

Davies, Peter Maxwell (Composer)
Judy Arnold
50 Hogarth Road
London SW5 OPU, UNITED KINGDOM (UK)

Davies, Russel T (Writer)
c/o Lisa Harrison *WME (LA)*
9601 Wilshire Blvd Fl 3
Beverly Hills, CA 90210, USA

Davies, Ryland (Opera Singer)
71 Fairmile Lane
Cobham
Surrey KT11 2DG, UNITED KINGDOM (UK)

Davies, Tamara (Actor)
c/o Staff Member *Bauman Redanty & Shaul Agency*
5757 Wilshire Blvd
Suite 473
Beverly Hills, CA 90212, USA

Davies, Terence (Director)
c/o Tony Peake *Peake Associates*
14 Grafton Crescent
London NW1 8SL, UK

Davies, Warrick (Actor)
International Creative Mgmt
76 Oxford St
London W1N 0AX, UNITED KINGDOM (UK)

Davies, Wyn (Actor)
c/o Staff Member *Screen Actors Guild (SAG-LA)*
5757 Wilshire Blvd
Los Angeles, CA 90036, USA

Davis, A Dano (Business Person)
Winn-Dixie Stores
5050 Edgewood Court
Jacksonville, FL 32254, USA

Davis, Alecia (Actor)
c/o Jonathan Clements *Nashville Agency*
501 Metroplex Dr
Suite 116
Nashville, TN 37222, USA

Davis, Alvin (Athlete, Baseball Player)
7983 Arma101osa Dr
Riverside, CA 92S08-8713, USA

Davis, Andra (Athlete, Football Player)
21230 Greenfield Pl
Strongsville, OH 44149, USA

Davis, Andra (Athlete, Football Player)
5839 Pinehurst Ct
Lake View, NY 14085-9719, USA

Davis, Andre (Athlete, Football Player)
11407 Jutland Rd
Houston, TX 77048, USA

Davis, Andre (Athlete, Football Player)
11407 Jutland Rd
Houston, TX 77048-2631, USA

Davis, Andrew (Director)
c/o Laurence Becsey *Intellectual Property Group (IPG)*
9200 Sunset Blvd #820
Los Angeles, CA 90069, USA

Davis, Andrew (Misc)
14500 Fiske Drive
Silver Spring, MD 20906-1737, USA

Davis, Andy (Athlete, Football Player)
14500 Fiske Dr
Silver Spring, MD 20906, USA

Davis, Angela (Politician)
10463 Royal Oak Rd
Oakland, CA 94605-5041, USA

Davis, Angela Y (Activist, Educator, Politician)
Speakout
PO Box 99096
Emeryville, CA 94662, USA

Davis, Ann B (Actor)
23315 Eagle Gap Rd
San Antonio, TX 78255, USA

Davis, Anthony (Athlete, Football Player)
A D 28 Development Inc 29 Firwood
Irvine, CA 92604-4632, USA

Davis, Anthony (Composer, Musician)
Andriolo Communications
115 E 9th St
New York, NY 10003, USA

Davis, Anthony (Athlete, Football Player)
8500 W 131st Ter Apt 1834
Overland Park, KS 66213-5157, USA

Davis, Antone (Athlete, Football Player)
2252 Red Bud Road
Sevierville, TN 37876, USA

Davis, Antonio (Athlete, Basketball Player)
21 Buford Village Walk
Buford, GA 30518-8840, USA

Davis, Ardie A (Writer)
c/o Staff Member *Harvard Common Press, The*
535 Albany St
Boston, MA 02118, USA

Davis, Aree (Actor)
c/o Myrna Lieberman *Myrna Lieberman Management*
3001 Hollyridge Drive
Hollywood, CA 90068, USA

Davis, Arthur (Athlete, Football Player)
8260 SW Woodbridge Ct
Wilsonville, OR 97070-7458, USA

Davis, Bard (Basketball Player)
Los Angeles Lakers
2703 Ridge Top Ln
Arlington, TX 76006-2729, USA

Davis, Baron (Athlete, Basketball Player)
c/o Staff Member *BDA Sports Management (BDA-CA)*
700 Ygnacio Valley Rd
Suite 330
Walnut Creek, CA 94596, USA

Davis, Barrie (Misc)
307 Nostalgia Ln
Zebulon, NC 27597-6875, USA

Davis, Barry (Athlete, Olympic Athlete, Wrestler)
417 N High Point Rd
Madison, WI 53717-1849, USA

Davis, Ben (Athlete, Football Player)
1144 Brandon Rd
Cleveland, OH 44112-3632, USA

Davis, Ben (Athlete, Baseball Player)
416 Homestead Dr
West Chester, PA 19382, USA

Davis, Bennie L (General)
101 Golden Road
Georgetown, TX 78628, USA

Davis, Bill (Race Car Driver)
11 N. Robbins St.
Thomasville, NC 27360-8970, USA

Davis, Bill (Athlete, Baseball Player)
6638 Knox AveS
Minneapolis, MN 55423-2161, USA

Davis, Billy (Athlete, Football Player)
5813 Tautoga Dr
El Paso, TX 79924, USA

Davis, Bob (Athlete, Baseball Player)
PO Box 198
Locust Grove, OK 74352-0198, USA

Davis, Brad (Athlete, Basketball Player)
2703 Ridge Top Lane
Arlington, TX 76006-2729, USA

Davis, Brian (Athlete, Football Player)
9874 Red Sumac Pl
Parker, CO 80138-7868, USA

Davis, Brian (Athlete, Golfer)
10545 Down Lakeview Cir
Windermere, FL 34786-7911, USA

Davis, Brianne (Actor)
c/o Staff Member *Art Work Entertainment*
5900 Wilshire Blvd #2150
Los Angeles, CA 90036, USA

Davis, Brock (Athlete, Baseball Player)
23759 Heliotrope Way
Moreno Valley, CA 92557-2858, USA

Davis, Buddy (Athlete, Basketball Player, Olympic Athlete)
6582 FM 841
Lufkin, TX 75901-4633, USA

Davis, Butch (Athlete, Baseball Player)
1108 Brucemont Dr
Garner, NC 27529-4505, USA

Davis, Carlos (Stylist)
c/o Staff Member *Mel Bryant Management*
611 Broadway #623
New York, NY 10012

Davis, Carole (Actor)
c/o Judy Orbach *Judy O Productions*
6136 Glen Holly
Hollywood, CA 90068, USA

Davis, Charles (Athlete, Basketball Player)
615 Main St
Nashville, TN 37206-3603, USA

Davis, Charles (Actor)
c/o Anthony Embry *AE Entertainment Public Relations*
124 Evening Shade Dr
Charleston, SC 29414, USA

Davis, Charles "Chili (Athlete, Baseball Player)
4625 Lake Washington Blvd SE
Bellevue, WA 98006-2625, USA

Davis, Charles (Chili) (Athlete, Baseball Player)
c/o Team Member *San Francisco Giants*
SBC Park
24 Willie Mays Plaza
San Francisco, CA 94107, USA

Davis, Charles D (Athlete, Football Player)
8935 Aspen Eadow Dr
Houston, TX 77071, USA

Davis, Charles M (Athlete, Football Player)
2391 Crescent Park Dr
Houston, TX 77077-6756, USA

Davis, Charlie (Athlete, Basketball Player)
302 Heather Ridge Court
Greensboro, NC 27455-8360, USA

Davis, Chip (Musician)
c/o Staff Member *Brokaw Company, The*
9255 Sunset Blvd
Suite 804
Los Angeles, CA 90069, USA

Davis, Chris (Baseball Player)
1310 Blueridge Pkwy
Longview, TX 75605-1912, United States

Davis, Christine (Writer)
Lighthearted Press Inc
P.O. Box 90125
Portland, OR 97290, USA

Davis, Christopher (Chris) W (Athlete, Football Player)
P.O. Box 5000
Ogdensburg, NY 13669-5000, USA

Davis, Clarence (Athlete, Football Player)
171 Longleaf St
Pickerington, OH 43147-7940, USA

Davis, Clifton (Actor)
c/o Staff Member *Agency for the Performing Arts (APA-LA)*
405 S Beverly Dr
Suite 500
Beverly Hills, CA 90212-4425, USA

Davis, Clive (Business Person, Producer)
29 Col Sheldon Ln
Pound Ridge, NY 10576, USA

Davis, Colin R
Alison Glaster
39 Huntingdon St
London N1 1BP, UNITED KINGDOM (UK)

Davis, Dale (Athlete, Basketball Player)
2000 Westwood Cir SE
Smyrna, GA 30080-5851, USA

Davis, Dale (Baseball Player)
Indiana Pacers
7945 Beaumont Green PL
Indianapolis, NC 27455-8360, USA

Davis, Dana (Actor)
10752 Hortense St #3
N Hollywood, CA 91602, USA

Davis, Daniel (Actor)
350 Dalkeith Ave
Los Angeles, CA 90049, USA

Davis, David Brion (Historian, Writer)
783 Lambert Road
Orange, CT 06477, USA

Davis, David (Dave) (Bowler)
DeStasio
710 Shore Road
Spring Lake Heights, NJ 07762, USA

Davis, DeRay (Actor)
c/o April Lim *Global Artists Agency*
6253 Hollywood Blvd
Suite 508
Los Angeles, CA 90028, USA

Davis, Dexter (Athlete, Football Player)
5054 Vermack Rd
Atlanta, GA 30338-4627, USA

Davis, Dick (Athlete, Football Player)
1626 N 137th St
Omaha, NE 68154-3826, USA

Davis, Dick (Athlete, Baseball Player)
11091 Sultan St
Moreno Valley, CA 92557-4917, USA

Davis, Dick (Athlete, Football Player)
1626 N 137th St
Omaha, NE 68154, USA

Davis, Domanick (Athlete, Football Player)
1023 Johnson Rd
Breaux Bridge, LA 70517-7018, USA

Davis, Donald (Athlete, Football Player)
739 E 48th St
Los Angeles, CA 90011, USA

Davis, Don H Jr (Business Person)
Rockwell International
777 E Wisconsin Ave
#1400
Milwaukee, WI 53202, USA

Davis, Dorsett (Athlete, Football Player)
605 Rosemary Rd
Cleveland, MS 38732-2048, USA

Davis, Doug (Athlete, Baseball Player)
279 Whites Church Rd
Bloomsburg, PA 17815-7156, USA

Davis, Doug (Athlete, Baseball Player)
26125 N 116th St Unit 7
Scottsdale, AZ 85255-8721, USA

Davis, Dwight (Athlete, Basketball Player)
PO Box 324
Newfields, NH 03856-0324, USA

Davis, Ed (Athlete, Basketball Player)
36750 US Highway 19 North
#26-3437
Palm Harbor, FL 34684-1239, USA

Davis, Elizabeth (Musician)
Rave Booking
PO Box 310780
Jamaica, NY 11431, USA

Davis, Elliot M (Cinematographer)
1328 Arch St
Berkeley, CA 94708, USA

Davis, Eric (Athlete, Baseball Player)
5334 Collingwood Cir
Calabasas, CA 91302, USA

Davis, Eric W (Athlete, Football Player)
3737 Coyote Cyn
Soquel, CA 95073-3034, USA

Davis, Frenchie (Musician)
c/o Belinda Foster *AWJ Platinum PR*
8200 Wilshire Blvd #200
Los Angeles, CA 90048, USA

Davis, Gary (Athlete, Football Player)
10750 San Marcos Rd
Atascadero, CA 93422-2126, USA

Davis, Geena (Actor)
15432 Albright St
Pacific Palisades, CA 90272, USA

Davis, Geoff (Congressman, Politician)
1119 Longworth HOB
Washington, DC 20515, USA

Davis, George (Athlete, Baseball Player)
3092 Kimball Ave
Memphis, TN 38114, USA

Davis, Georgia (Stylist)
c/o Staff Member *Loox Agency*
12 Desbrosses St
New York, NY 10013, USA

Davis, Gerry (Athlete, Baseball Player)
2440 Stroebe Island Dr
Appleton, WI 54914, USA

Davis, Glenn
31 Cascade Rd
Columbus, GA 31904-2806, USA

Davis, Gray (Ex-Governor)
State Capitol Building
Sacramento, CA 95814, USA

Davis, Gray (Politician)
10430 Wilshire Blvd A^t 605
Los Angeles, CA 90024-4653, USA

Davis, Greg (Athlete, Football Player)
PO Box 925
Ouray, CO 81427-0925, USA

Davis, Harper (Athlete, Football Player)
1224 Springdale Dr
Jackson, MS 39211-3130, USA

Davis, Harrison (Athlete, Football Player)
6409 Lesser Dr
Greeley, CO 80634-9595, USA

Davis, Harry (Athlete, Basketball Player)
1966 East 75th Street
Cleveland, OH 44103-4125, USA

Davis, Hope (Actor)
152 Jermain Ave
Sag Harbor, NY 11963, USA

Davis, Hubert (Athlete, Basketball Player)
204 Lancaster Dr
Chapel Hill, NC 27517-3429, USA

Davis, Jack (Athlete, Football Player)
305 Crest Ct
Poteau, OK 74953-2128, USA

Davis, Jacke (Athlete, Baseball Player)
6806 Castle Pines Ct
Tyler, TX 75703-5890, USA

Davis, James (Athlete, Football Player)
5701 S St Andrews Pl
Los Angeles, CA 90062-2649, USA

Davis, James (Cartoonist)
5440 E Country Rd 450 N
Albany, IN 47320-9728, USA

Davis, James (Basketball Player)
Rochesster Royals
44 Van Ter
Sparkill, NY 10976-1406, USA

Davis, James B (General)
3600 Wimber Blvd
Palm Harbor, FL 34685, USA

Davis, James O (Doctor)
546 Warren Avenue
Saint Luis, MO 63130-4154, USA

Davis, Jason (Athlete, Baseball Player)
474 Leatha Ln NW
Cleveland, TN 37312-6522, USA

Davis, Jay (Athlete, Golfer)
2152 S State St
Springfield, IL 62704, USA

Davis, Jeff (Actor)
c/o Staff Member *United Talent Agency (UTA)*
9336 Civic Center Dr
Beverly Hills, CA 90210, USA

Davis, Jeff (Athlete, Football Player)
106 Sycamore Dr
Clemson, SC 29631-2071, USA

Davis, Jerome (Athlete, Football Player)
515 N 4th St
Palatka, FL 32177, USA

Davis, Jerry (Baseball Player)
San Diego Padres
72 Theresa St
Trenton, NJ 08618-1531, USA

Davis, Jesse (Musician)
Concord Records
100 N Crescent Dr
#275
Beverly Hills, CA 90210, USA

Davis, Jill A (Writer)
Random House
1745 Broadway
#B1
New York, NY 10019, USA

Davis, Jimmy (Athlete, Football Player)
616 Briar Patch Ter
Waxhaw, NC 28173-6822, USA

Davis, J J (Baseball Player)
7302 Forrest Rader Dr
Mint Hill, NC 28227-9830, USA

Davis, J J (Athlete, Baseball Player)
7302 Forrest Rader Dr
Charlotte, NC 28227, USA

Davis, Jody (Athlete, Baseball Player)
5631 N 79th St Unit 4
Scottsdale, AZ 85250-6546, USA

Davis, Joel (Athlete, Baseball Player)
609 Matterhorn Rd
Jacksonville, FL 32216-9166, USA

Davis, John (Athlete, Baseball Player)
76871 Castle Ct
Palm Desert, CA 92211-7100, USA

Davis, John (Actor, Composer, Director, Producer)
c/o Staff Member *Davis Entertainment*
150 S Barrington Pl
Los Angeles, CA 90049, USA

Davis, John (Athlete, Football Player)
901 Forest Pond Dr
Marietta, GA 30068-4420, USA

Davis, Johnny (Athlete, Basketball Player, Coach)
28 S Kaufman Stone Way
Biltmore Lake, NC 28715-7722, USA

Davis, Johnny (Athlete, Football Player)
PO Box 550
Edgewater, NJ 07020-0550, USA

Davis, Jonathan (Musician)
5253 Horizon Dr
Malibu, CA 90265, USA

Davis, Josie (Actor)
CunninghamEscottDipene
10635 Santa Monica Blvd
#130
Los Angeles, CA 90025, USA

Davis, Judy (Actor)
c/o Ann Churchill-Brown *Shanahan Management*
Level 3 Berman House
Surry Hills 2010, AUSTRALIA

Davis, Kane (Athlete, Baseball Player)
1558 Noble Rdg
Reedy, WV 25270-9540, USA

Davis, Kara (Adult Film Star)
PO Box 9465
Newport Beach, CA 92058, USA

Davis, Keith B (Athlete, Football Player)
1343 Marvin Gdns
Lancaster, TX 75134-1684, USA

Davis, Kenneth E (Athlete, Football Player)
1224 Brooklawn Dr
Arlington, TX 76018, USA

Davis, Kim (Athlete, Hockey Player)
14 Shorecrest Dr
Winnipeg, MB R3P 1N2, Canada

Davis, Kristin (Actor, Producer)
2242 Jeffersonia Way
Los Angeles, CA 90049, USA

Davis, Kyle (Athlete, Football Player)
104 Futurity Ln
Weatherford, TX 76087-4606, USA

Davis, Lance (Athlete, Baseball Player)
5845 Old Berkley Rd
Auburndale, FL 33823-8361, USA

Davis, L Edward (Religious Leader)
Evangelical Presbyterian Church
26049 Five Mile Road
Detroit, MI 48239, USA

Davis, Lee (Athlete, Basketball Player)
5024 Fieldgreen Crossing
Apt B2
Stone Mountain, GA 30088-3103, USA

Davis, Lee (Director)
Gersh Agency
232 N Canon Dr
Beverly Hills, CA 90210, USA

Davis, Leonard (Athlete, Football Player)
5105 Monterey Dr
Frisco, TX 75034-4081, USA

Davis, Linda (Musician)
PO Box 767
Hermitage, TN 37076, USA

Davis, Lorenzo (Athlete, Football Player)
149 Vista Luna Dr
Davie, FL 33325-6929, USA

Davis, Lucy (Actor, Director)
512 N Gower St
Los Angeles, CA 90004, USA

Davis, Mac (Actor, Musician, Songwriter)
346 N Tigertail Rd
Los Angeles, CA 90049, USA

Davis, Mark (Athlete, Baseball Player)
8867 E Sierra Pinta Dr
Scottsdale, AZ 85255-9174, USA

Davis, Mark A (Athlete, Basketball Player)
108 Government Circle
A
Thibodaux, LA 70301-6615, USA

Davis, Mark G (Basketball Player)
Milwaukee Bucks
3120 Aarion Dr
Chesapeake, VA 23323-2600, USA

Davis, Mark M (Biologist, Misc)
Stanford University
Medical Center
Microbiology Dept
Stanford, CA 94305, USA

Davis, Mark W (Athlete, Baseball Player)
8867 E Sierra Pinta Dr
Scottsdale, AZ 85255-9174, USA

Davis, Martha (Musician)
Paradise Artists
108 E Matilija St
Ojai, CA 93023, USA

Davis, Marv (Butch) (Athlete, Football Player)
700 Ponce De Leon Ave
Clewiston, FL 33440, USA

Davis, Mary (Athlete, Football Player)
700 Ponce De Leon Ave
Clewiston, FL 33440-2413, USA

Davis, Matthew (Actor)
1958 Glencoe Way
Los Angeles, CA 90068, USA

Davis, Melvyn (Athlete, Basketball Player)
P.O. Box 29
Suffern, NY 10901-0029, USA

Davis, Michael (Athlete, Basketball Player)
110 West Clay Road
Richmond, VA 23220-3913, USA

Davis, Michael A (Athlete, Football Player)
4913 W 11th Street Rd Unit 7
Greeley, CO 80634-1908, USA

Davis, Michael L (Athlete, Football Player)
P.O. Box 614
Beaver Falls, PA 91405, USA

Davis, Mike (Athlete, Baseball Player)
c/o Staff Member *Oakland Athletics*
7000 Coliseum Way
Oakland, CA 94621, USA

Davis, Mike (Athlete, Football Player)
37039 N 109th St
Scottsdale, AZ 85262-3582, USA

Davis, Mike (Athlete, Basketball Player)
100 West 92nd Street
Apt 29E
New York, NY 10025-7546, USA

Davis, Milton (Composer)
c/o Staff Member *Windswept (LA)*
9320 Wilshire Blvd #200
Beverly Hills, CA 90212, USA

Davis, Monti (Athlete, Basketball Player)
328 Tod Lane
Youngstown, OH 44504-1403, USA

Davis, Musiello
Janette200 Windemere Way
Naples, FL 33999-8125

Davis, N Jan (Astronaut)
4105 Cumberland Pass
Apt 814
Forth Worth, TX 76116-0753, USA

Davis, Odie (Athlete, Baseball Player)
7314 Hidden His N
San Antonio, TX 78244-1504, USA

Davis, Oliver (Athlete, Football Player)
1527 Evanston Ct
Marietta, GA 30062-2148, USA

Davis, Paige (Television Host)
c/o Staff Member *WmE2 (WMA-LA)*
1 William Morris Pl
Beverly Hills, CA 90212, USA

Davis, Paschall (Athlete, Football Player)
937 Plumeria Dr
Arlington, TX 76002-2402, USA

Davis, Patti (Actor, Writer)
6947 N Gleneagles Pl
Tucson, AZ 85718, UISA

Davis, Paul (Athlete, Football Player)
227 Oval Park Pl
Chapel Hill, NC 27517-8116, USA

Davis, Phyllis (Actor)
29330 SE Hillyard Drive
#D14
Boring, OR 97009, USA

Davis, Preston (Athlete, Football Player)
1282 W 100th Pl
Northglenn, CO 80260-6208, USA

Davis, Raiai (Athlete, Baseball Player)
9 Pear Grv
East Lyme, CT 06333-1177, USA

Davis, Ralph (Athlete, Basketball Player)
2624 South Kathwood Circle
Cincinnati, OH 45236-1026, USA

Davis, Rennie (Politician)
Birth of a New Nation
905 S Gilpin St
Denver, CO 80209, USA

Davis, Reuben (Athlete, Football Player)
7105 Kepley Rd
Chapel Hill, NC 27517-8792, USA

Davis, Richard (Musician)
SRO Artists
6629 University Ave
#206
Middleton, WI 53562, USA

Davis, Ricky (Athlete, Basketball Player)
c/o Jeff Schwartz *Excel Sports Management*
9665 Wilshire Blvd #500
Los Angeles, CA 90212, USA

Davis, Ricky (Athlete, Football Player)
5715 Whirlaway Rd
Palm Beach Gardens, FL 33418-7739, USA

Davis, Robbie (Horse Racer)
756 Stone Church Rd
Middle Grove, NY 12850-1131, USA

Davis, Roger (Actor)
Janette Anderson Talent Agency
9682 Via Torino
Burbank, CA 91504, USA

Davis, Roger (Athlete, Football Player)
27950 Belcourt Rd
Cleveland, OH 44124-5614, USA

Davis, Ron (Athlete, Basketball Player)
11748 N 90th Pl
Scottsdale, AZ 85260-6841, USA

Davis, Ronald (Ron) (Athlete, Football Player)
4717 Pompton Ln
Chester, VA 23831-4335, USA

Davis, Ronald (Ron) (Artist)
PO Box 293
Arroyo Hondo, NM 87513, USA

Davis, Ross (Athlete, Baseball Player)
8042 Highway 71
Garwood, TX 77442-4158, USA

Davis, Russ (Athlete, Baseball Player)
3351 Crescent Dr
Bessemer, AL 35023-2919, USA

Davis, Russell (Athlete, Football Player)
605 Jones Ferry Rd
Carrboro, NC 27510-2106, USA

Davis, Russell (Athlete, Football Player)
1208 Tanbark Ln E
Jackson, MI 49203, USA

Davis, Russell A (Athlete, Football Player)
4236 Crosswood Dr
Burtonsville, MD 20866, USA

Davis, Russell C (General)
Chief National Guard Bureau
HqUSAF
Pentagon
Washington, DC 20310, USA

Davis, Russell S (Russ) (Baseball Player)
3351 Crescent Dr
Hueytown, AL 35023, USA

Davis, Ruth (Athlete, Baseball Player, Commentator)
1917 Park Ave
Cheyenne, WY 82007-3395, USA

Davis, Sam (Athlete, Football Player)
423 Edgemont St
Mt Washington, PA 15211-2405, USA

Davis, Sammy (Athlete, Football Player)
4020 Murphy Canyon Rd
San Deigo, CA 92123, USA

Davis, Sammy L (General)
2995 Straight Line Rd
Freedom, IN 47431-7292, USA

Davis, Sammy L (War Hero)
3376 N 100th St
Flat Rock, IL 62427, USA

Davis, Spencer
PO Box 1821
Ojai, CA 93024

Davis, Stephen (Athlete, Football Player)
16 Dunleith Ct
Irmo, SC 29063, USA

Davis, Stephen H (Engineer, Mathematician)
2735 Simpson St
Evanston, IL 60201, USA

Davis, Steve (Misc)
Matchroom Snooker Ltd
10 Western Road
Romford
Essex RM1 3JT, UNITED KINGDOM (UK)

Davis, Steve (Athlete, Baseball Player)
601186th St
Lubbock, TX 79424-6708, USA

Davis, Steve (Athlete, Football Player)
356 E 29th St
Buena Vista, VA 24416-1204, USA

Davis, Steve (Athlete, Baseball Player)
6011 86th St
Lubbock, TX 79424, USA

Davis, Storm (Athlete, Baseball Player)
8469 Mizner Cir E
Jacksonville, FL 32217, USA

Davis, Storm George (Baseball Player)
7931 Dawsons Creek Dr
Jacksonville, FL 32222-4905, USA

Davis, Susan (Congressman, Politician)
1526 Longworth HOB
Washington, DC 20515, USA

Davis, Tamra (Director)
7126 Fernhill Dr
Malibu, CA 90265, USA

Davis, Ted (Athlete, Football Player)
5401 Riverbend Dr
Knoxville, TN 37919-8953, USA

Davis, Terrell (Athlete, Football Player)
Boss Hogg LLC 39252 Winchester Rd Ste 107-290
Murrieta, CA 92563-3509, USA

Davis, Terry (Athlete, Basketball Player)
2933 Kenmore Road
Richmond, VA 23225-1429, USA

Davis, Tim (Athlete, Baseball Player)
16161 NW Lakeside Ln
Bristol, FL 32321-3932, USA

Davis, Todd (Actor)
245 S Keystone St
Burbank, CA 91506, USA

Davis, Tommy (Athlete, Baseball Player)
JD Legends Promotions
Chris Potter Sports 9722
Owin11s Mills, MD 21117- 6341, USA

Davis, Tracy (Stylist)
c/o Staff Member *Help Me Rhonda*
541 10th St NW #294
Atlanta, GA 30318, USA

Davis, Travis (Athlete, Football Player)
3253 Aqueous Ln
Indianapolis, IN 46214-4131, USA

Davis, Trench (Athlete, Baseball Player)
306 40th Street Cir W
Palmetto, FL 34221-9516, USA

Davis, Troy (Athlete, Football Player)
11861 SW 190th St
Miami, FL 33177-3940, USA

Davis, Truman A (Misc)
Congress of Industrial Unions
303 Ridge St
Alton, IL 62002, USA

Davis, Vernon (Athlete, Football Player)
c/o Todd France *France AllPro Athlete Management*
3500 Lenox Road, NE
Atlanta, GA 30326, USA

Davis, Vicki (Actor)
c/o Staff Member *Innovative Artists (LA)*
1505 10th St
Santa Monica, CA 90401, USA

Davis, Viola (Actor)
17755 Arvida Dr
Granada Hills, CA 91344, USA

Davis, Wade (Athlete, Baseball Player)
PO Box46
Marlboro, NY 12542-0046, USA

Davis, Wade (Writer)
c/o Staff Member *Simon & Schuster*
1230 Avenue of the Americas
New York, NY 10020, USA

Davis, Walter (Athlete, Basketball Player, Olympic Athlete)
5200 E Donald Ave
Apt A
Denver, CO 80222-5539, USA

Davis, Warren (Athlete, Basketball Player)
44429 Oriole Dr Unit 1e1
Fort Mill, sc 29707-5400, USA

Davis, Warwick (Actor)
c/o Staff Member *Willow Personal Management*
151 Main St
Yaxley
Peterborough PE7 3LD, UK

Davis, Wendell (Athlete, Football Player)
180 Rinconada Ave
Palo Alto, CA 94301-3725, USA

Davis, Wendell (Athlete, Football Player)
10850 Green Mountain Cir Unit 117
Columbia, MD 21044-2300, USA

Davis, Wendell (Athlete, Football Player)
180 Rinconada Ave
Palo Alto, CA 94301-3725, USA

Davis, W Eugene (Judge)
US Court of Appeals
556 Jefferson St
Lafayette, LA 70501, USA

Davis, William (Actor)
c/o Staff Member *Lucas Talent Inc*
100 W. Pender St
Sun Tower, 7th Floor
Vancouver, BC V6B 1R8, Canada

Davis, William D (Willie) (Athlete, Football Player)
7352 Vista Del Mar Ln
Playa Del Rey, CA 90293-7650, USA

Davis, William E (Business Person)
Niagara Mohawk Holdings
300 Erie Blvd W
Syracuse, NY 13202, USA

Davis, William G (Government Official)
Tory Tory DesLauries
Aetna Tower
#3000
Toronto, ON M5K 1N2, CANADA

Davis, William L (Business Person)
R R Donnelley & Sons
77 W Wacker Dr
Chicago, IL 60601, USA

Davison, Beverly C (Religious Leader)
American Baptist Churches
PO Box 851
Valley Forge, PA 19482, USA

Davison, Bruce (Actor)
3708 Whitespeak Dr
Sherman Oaks, CA 91403, USA

Davison, Fred C (Educator)
1 7th St #502
Augusta, GA 30901, USA

Davison, Michelle
1830 Grace Ave. #7
Los Angeles, CA 90028

Davison, Mike (Athlete, Baseball Player)
578 Prospect St NE
Hutchinson, MN 55350-1715, USA

Davison, Peter (Actor)
'Legally Blonde', Savoy Theatre
The Strand
London WC2R 0ET, UK

Davison, Sam (Religious Leader)
International Baptist Bible Fellowship
720 E Kearnet St
Springfield, MO 65803, USA

Davison, Scott (Athlete, Baseball Player)
4507 Sharynne Ln
Torrance, CA 90505-3454, USA

Davis-Wrightsil, Clarissa (Basketball Player)
Phoenix Mercury
American West Arena
201 E Jefferson St
Phoenix, AZ 85004, USA

Davitian, Ken (Actor)
c/o Tess Finkle *Metro Public Relations*
6525 W Sunset Blvd
6th Floor
Hollywood, CA 90028, USA

Davkin, Tony (Athlete, Football Player)
5204 Cross Ridge Cir
Woodstock, GA 30188-4381, USA

Davoli, Andrew (Actor)
c/o Greg Clark *Untitled Entertainment (LA)*
350 S. Beverly Dr #200
Beverly Hills, CA 90212, USA

Daw, Jeff (Athlete, Hockey Player)
609 Rollstone Rd
Fitchburg, MA 01420-6104

Dawber, Pam (Actor)
564 N Cliffwood Ave
Los Angeles, CA 90049, USA

Dawe, Jason (Athlete, Hockey Player)
9077 Drayton Ln
Fort Mill, SC 29707-6484, USA

Dawes, Dominique (Athlete, Gymnast, Olympic Athlete)
1611 Hugo Cir
Silver Spring, MD 20906-5921, USA

Dawes, Joseph (Cartoonist)
20 Church Court
Closter, NJ 07624-2803, USA

Dawkins, Brian (Athlete, Football Player)
10010 Tavistock Rd
Orlando, FL 32827, USA

Dawkins, C Richard (Biologist)
Oxford University
Museum Parks Road
Oxford OX1 3PW, UNITED KINGDOM (UK)

Dawkins, Dale (Athlete, Football Player)
390 Concord Dr
Bozeman, MT 59715-7100, USA

Dawkins, Dale (Athlete, Football Player)
388 Woodman Dr
Belgrade, MT 58714, USA

Dawkins, Darryl (Athlete, Basketball Player)
1708 Glacier Court
Allentown, PA 18104-1710, USA

Dawkins, Joe (Athlete, Football Player)
9200 S Harvard Blvd
Los Angeles, CA 90047, USA

Dawkins, Joe (Athlete, Football Player)
4235 Ensenada Dr
Woodland Hills, CA 91364-5403, USA

Dawkins, Johnny (Athlete, Basketball Player)
601A Olmsted Rd
Stanford, CA 94305-7498, USA

Dawkins, Johnny (Basketball Player)
San Antonio Spurs
2604 Vintage Hill Ct
Durham, NC 27712-9492, USA

Dawkins, Paul (Athlete, Basketball Player)
2728 North Hampton Drive
Grand Prairie, TX 75052-4201, USA

Dawkins, Pete (Business Person, Football Player, General, Heisman Trophy Winner, Politician)
PO Box 218
Rumson, NJ 07760-0218, USA

Dawkins, Sean (Athlete, Football Player)
826 Weichert Dr
Morgan Hill, CA 95037-3785, USA

Dawkins, Travis (Athlete, Baseball Player, Olympic Athlete)
1290 Calhoun Rd
Greenwood, SC 29649, USA

Dawley, Bill (Athlete, Baseball Player)
2919 Twin Fountains Dr
Houston, TX 77068-3750, USA

Dawley, Joey (Athlete, Baseball Player)
27951 Cactus Ave
Unit A
Moreno Valley, CA 92555-3609, USA

Dawley, Joseph W (Joe) (Artist)
13 Wholly St
Cranford, NJ 07016, USA

Dawsey, Lawrence (Athlete, Football Player)
4341 Cheval Blvd
Lutz, FL 33558-5328, USA

Dawson, Andre (Athlete, Baseball Player)
Andre Dawson Foundation
PO Box 431339
Miami, FL 33243-1339, USA

Dawson, Anthony
Via Riccione 6 Fregene
Fiumicino RM, ITALY 00050

Dawson, Ashley Taylor (Actor)
c/o Staff Member *Blackburn Sachs Associates*
88-90 Crawford St
London W1H 2BS, UNITED KINGDOM (UK)

Dawson, Buck (Swimmer)
Swimming Hall of Fame
1 Hall of Fame Dr
Fort Lauderdale, FL 33316, USA

Dawson, Dale (Athlete, Football Player)
1710 E Oak Knoll Cir
Davie, FL 33324-6424, USA

Dawson, Dermontti (Athlete, Football Player)
PO Box 712481
San Diego, CA 92171-2481, USA

Dawson, Douglas A (Doug) (Athlete, Football Player)
Dawson Financial Services
1 Riverway
Suite 900
Houston, TX 77056-1906, USA

Dawson, Jajuan (Athlete, Football Player)
2302 Sun Shadow Ln
Spring, TX 77386-1871, USA

Dawson, Jajuan (Athlete, Football Player)
2302 Sun Shadow Ln
Spring, TX 77386, USA

Dawson, J Cutler Jr (Admiral)
Commander
Striking Fleet Atlantic/2nd Fleet
FPO, AE 08506, USA

Dawson, Jim (Athlete, Basketball Player)
61 Glendale Avenue
Rye, NY 10580-1547, USA

Dawson, Keyunta (Athlete, Football Player)
8417 Codesa Way
Indianapolis, IN 46278-5067, USA

Dawson, Kim (Actor, Producer, Writer)
c/o Staff Member *Skydog Productions*
1000 Universal Studios Plaza
Bldg 22A
Orlando, FL 32819, USA

Dawson, Lake (Athlete, Football Player)
33228 37th Pl SW
Federal Way, WA 98023-2959, USA

Dawson, Lake (Athlete, Football Player)
33228 37th Pl SW
Federal Way, WA 98023, USA

Dawson, Len (Athlete, Football Player)
1025 W 59th Ter
Kansas City, MO 64113-1335, USA

Dawson, Leonard R (Lenny) (Athlete, Football Player, Sportscaster)
4950 Central St
Apt 606
Kansas City, MO 64112-2588, USA

Dawson, Marco (Athlete, Golfer)
3053 Shoal Creek Village Dr
Lakeland, FL 33803-5425, USA

Dawson, Phil (Athlete, Football Player)
13321 Coleto Creek Trl
Austin, TX 78732-2070, USA

Dawson, Phil (Athlete, Football Player)
1770 Arlington Rd
Westlake, OH 44145, USA

Dawson, Rhett (Athlete, Football Player)
1717 W 6th St
Suite 260
Austin, TX 78703, USA

Dawson, Rosario (Actor)
544 E 13th St #1B
New York, NY 10009, USA

Dawson, Roxann (Actor)
227 Bell Canyon Rd
Bell Canyon, CA 91307, USA

Dawson, Shane (Actor)
c/o Staff Member *3 Arts Entertainment Inc*
9460 Wilshire Blvd
7th Floor
Beverly Hills, CA 90210, USA

Day, Bill (Cartoonist)
Memphis Commercial-Appeal
Editorial Dept
495 Union Ave
Memphis, TN 38103, USA

Day, Boots (Athlete, Baseball Player)
1154 Vespasian Way
Chesterfield, MO 63017-3016, USA

Day, Charlie (Actor)
c/o Nick Frenkel *3 Arts Entertainment Inc*
9460 Wilshire Blvd
7th Floor
Beverly Hills, CA 90210, USA

Day, Chon (Cartoonist)
127 Main St
Ashaway, RI 02804, USA

Day, Dewon (Athlete, Baseball Player)
1935 Marshall Pl
Jackson, MS 39213-4450, USA

Day, Doris (Actor)
6730 Carmel Valley Rd
Carmel, CA 93923, USA

Day, Felicia (Actor)
c/o Ari Greenburg *WME (LA)*
9601 Wilshire Blvd Fl 3
Beverly Hills, CA 90210, USA

Day, Gail (Publisher)
Plaboy Magazine
680 N Lake Shore Dr
Chicago, IL 60611, USA

Day, George E (War Hero)
23 Bayshore Dr
Shalimar, FL 32579, USA

Day, George E (General)
32 Beal Pkwv SW Fort
Walton Beach, FL 32548-5391, USA

Day, Glen (Athlete, Golfer)
25 Valley Estates Ct
Little Rock, AR 72212, USA

Day, Howie (Musician)
c/o Staff Member *Paradigm (Monterey)*
404 W Franklin St
Monterey, CA 93940, USA

Day, Inaya (Musician)
c/o Staff Member *Diva Central Inc*
7510 W Sunset Blvd Ste 1445
Los Angees, CA 90046, USA

Day, Jason (Actor)
c/o Julio Caro *Caro Entertainment*
3221 Hutchison Ave #H
Los Angeles, CA 90034, USA

Day, Jennifer
PO Box 120479
Nashville, TN 37212

Day, Joanne (Stylist)
5039 Foothills Rd
Apt G
Lake Oswego, OR 97034-4107, USA

Day, Joe (Athlete, Hockey Player)
805 Shoreline Rd
Lake Barrington, IL 60010-3878, USA

Day, Julian (Business Person)
KMART
PO Box 8073
Royal Oak, MI 48068-8073, USA

Day, Mark
Day Enterprises Racing
107 Flat Ridge Rd
Goodlettsville, TN 37072, USA

Day, Mary (Misc)
Washington Ballet
3515 Wisconsin Ave NW
Washington, DC 20016, USA

Day, Matt (Actor)
Robyn Gardiner Mgmt
397 Riley St
Surrey Hills, NSW 2010, AUSTRALIA

Day, Morris (Musician)
805 Hampton Bluff Dr
Alpharetta, GA 30004, USA

Day, Pat (Horse Racer)
14703 Isleworth Ct
Louisville, KY 40245-5256, USA

Day, Peter R (Scientist)
8200 Tarsier Ave
New Port Richey, FL 34653-6559, USA

Day, Robert (Actor, Director)
8832 Ferncliff Avenue N.E.
Bainbridge Island, WA 98110, USA

Day, Sandra (Stylist)
100 Tackaberry Rd
Lafayette, LA 70503, USA

Day, Terry (Athlete, Football Player)
PO Box 85
Pickens, MS 39146-0085, USA

Day, Terry (Athlete, Football Player)
P.O. Box 85
Pickens, MS 39146, USA

Day, Thomas B (Educator)
San Diego State University
President's Office
San Diego, CA 92182, USA

Day, Zach (Athlete, Baseball Player)
9663 Lupine Dr
Cincinnati, OH 45241-3693, USA

Dayan, Isaac (Actor)
c/o Staff Member *TV Caracol*
Calle 76 #11 - 35
Piso 10AA
Bogota DC 26484, COLOMBIA

Daye, Darren (Athlete, Basketball Player)
17 Elderberry
Irvine, CA 92603-3703, USA

Dayett, Brian (Athlete, Baseball Player)
276 Phillips Dr
Winchester, TN 37398-4268, USA

Day-George, Lynda (Actor)
10310 Riverside Dr
#104
Toluca Lake, CA 91602, USA

Daykin, Anthony (Athlete, Football Player)
5204 Cross Ridge Cir
Woodstock, GA 30188, USA

Day-Lewis, Daniel (Actor)
232 Tophet Rd
Roxbury, CT 06783, USA

Dayley, Ken (Athlete, Baseball Player)
1300 Windgate Way Ct
Chesterfield, MO 63005-4497, USA

Dayne, Ron (Athlete, Football Player, Heisman Trophy Winner)
2135 Regent St
Madison, WI 53726-3941, USA

Dayne, Taylor (Actor, Musician)
15541 Huston St
Encino, CA 91436, USA

Days, Drews S III (Educator, Government Official)
Yale University
Law School
New Haven, CT 06520, USA

Dayton, Jonathan (Director)
505 Radcliffe Ave
Pacific Palisades, CA 90272, USA

Dayton, June (Actor)
Abrams Artists
9200 Sunset Blvd
#1125
Los Angeles, CA 90069, USA

Dayton, Mark (Politician)
330 Maryland Ave NE
Washington, DC 20002-5712, USA

Daze, Eric (Athlete, Hockey Player)
606 S Washington St
Hinsdale, IL 60521-4439, USA

Daze, Skylar (Adult Film Star)
PO Box 89222
Tampa, FL 33689, USA

D. Bishop Jr., Sanford (Congressman, Politician)

D. Clarke, Yvette (Congressman, Politician)
1029 Longworth HOB
Washington, DC 20515, USA

dc Talk (Music Group, Musician)
c/o Staff Member *True Artist Management*
227 3rd Ave
North Franklin, TN 37064, USa

D. Dicks, Norman (Congressman, Politician)
2467 Rayburn HOB
Washington, DC 20515, USA

D. Dingell Jr., John (Congressman, Politician)
2328 Rayburn HOB
Washington, DC 20515, USA

Dea, Bill (Athlete, Hockey Player)
2636 W Bartlett Way
Queen Creek, AZ 85142-6611, USA

Deacon, Brian
85 Gladstone Rd.
London, ENGLAND SW19

Deacon, John (Musician)
The Mill Mill Lane
367 Windsor Highway
New Windsor, NY 12553, USA

Deacon, Richard (Artist)
Lisson Gallery
67 Lisson St
London NW1 5DA, UNITED KINGDOM (UK)

Deacon, Terrence (Misc)
Harvard University
Neuroanatomy Dept
Cambridge, MA 02138, USA

Dead Can Dance (Music Group)
c/o Staff Member *WmE2 (WMA-LA)*
1 William Morris Pl
Beverly Hills, CA 90212, USA

Dead marsh, Adam (Athlete, Hockey Player)
Colorado Avalanche
1000 Chopper Cir
Denver, CO 80204-5805

Deadmarsh, Adam (Athlete, Hockey Player, Olympic Athlete)
519 Backcountry Ln Highlands
Highlands Ranch, CO 80126-5633, USA

Deadmarsh, Butch (Athlete, Hockey Player)
282 Diamond Dr SE
Calgary, AB T2J 7E2, Canada

deadmau5 (Music Group)
c/o Todd Jacobs *WME (LA)*
9601 Wilshire Blvd Fl 3
Beverly Hills, CA 90210, USA

Deadsy (Music Group)

Dead, The (Music Group)
c/o Staff Member *Paradigm (Monterey)*
404 W Franklin St
Monterey, CA 93940, USA

DeAgostini, Doris (Skier)
6780 Airolo
SWITZERLAND

Deakin, Paul (Musician)
AristoMedia
1620 16th Ave S
Nashville, TN 37212, USA

Deakins, Roger (Cinematographer)
International Creative Mgmt
8942 Wilshire Blvd
#219
Beverly Hills, CA 90212, USA

Deal, Cot (Athlete, Baseball Player)
9009 N May Ave
Apt 164
Oklahoma City, OK 73120-4464, USA

Deal, Ellis (Athlete, Baseball Player)
9009 North May Avenue
Apt 164
Oklahoma City, OK 73120-4464, USA

Deal, Kelley (Musician)
Wire & Twine
P.O. Box 520
Oxford, OH 45056, USA

Deal, Kim (Musician)
c/o Dan Brooks *Key Music Group (Canada)*
227 King St E
Hamilton, Ontario L8N 1B6, Canada

Deal, Lance (Athlete, Olympic Athlete)
4715 Fox Hollow Rd
Eugene, OR 97405-5302, USA

Deal, Nathan (Governor)
The Office of the Governor
State of Georgia
203 State Capitol
Atlanta, GA 30334, USA

de Almeida, Joaquim (Actor)
c/o Estelle Lasher *Principal Entertainment (NY)*
1964 Westwood Blvd
Suite 400
Los Angeles, CA 90025, USA

DeAlmeida, Joaquin
2372 Veteran Ave. #102
Los Angeles, CA 90064

Dean, Barry (Athlete, Hockey Player)
315 Marsh
Maple Creek, SK S0N 1N0, Canada

Dean, Billy (Musician)
c/o Staff Member *Billy Dean Music Group*
P.O. Box 150889
Nashville, TN 37215-0889, USA

Dean, Christopher (Dancer)
124 Ladies Mile Road
Brighton
East Sussex BN1 8TE, UNITED KINGDOM (UK)

Dean, Debby (Stylist)
c/o Celebrity Stylists *Christine Willes Artists Mgmt, Inc.*
11906 Lawler St
Los Angeles, CA 90066, USA

Dean, Eddie (Actor, Musician)
32161 Sailview Lane
Westlake Village, CA 91361, USA

Dean, Fred
3911 Whitchurch Dr
Houston, TX 77066-4535, USA

Dean, Fred (Athlete, Football Player)
3911 Whitchurch Dr
Houston, TX 77066-4535, USA

Dean, Fred (Athlete, Football Player)
3911 Whitchurch Dr
Houston, TX 77066, USA

Dean, Fred (Athlete, Football Player)
2411 Highway 3061
Ruston, LA 71270, USA

Dean, Hazel
7 Kentish Town Rd.
London, ENGLAND NW1 8N4

Dean, Howard (Politician)
325 S Cove Rd
Burlington, VT 05401-5447, USA

Dean, Ira (Musician)
Graham Agency
6999 East Highway 80
Odessa, TX 79762, USA

Dean, John (Politician)
9496 Rembert Lane
Beverly Hills, CA 90210-1720, USA

Dean, John G (Diplomat)
29 Blvd Jules Sandeau
Paris 75116, FRANCE

Dean, Kevin (Athlete, Hockey Player)
c/o Staff Member *Lowell Devils*
300 Martin Luther King Jr Way
Lowell, MA 01852, USA

Dean, Kiley (Musician)
c/o Staff Member *Interscope Records (LA) - Main*
2220 Colorado Ave
Santa Monica, CA 90404, USA

Dean, Laura (Choreographer, Composer)
Dean Dance & Music Foundation
552 Broadway
#400
New York, NY 10012, USA

Dean, Loren (Actor)
c/o Amy Guenther *Gateway Management Company Inc*
860 Via De La Paz
Suite F10
Pacific Palisades, CA 90272, USA

Dean, Mark E (Inventor)
9 Sarahs Way
Bethel, CT 06801-2949, USA

Dean, Randy (Athlete, Football Player)
1310 E Bay Point Rd
Milwaukee, WI 53217-1405, USA

Dean, Randy (Athlete, Football Player)
1310 E Bay Point Rd
Milwaukee, WI 53217, USA

Dean, Stafford R (Opera Singer)
I C M Artists
40 W 57th St
New York, NY 10019, USA

Dean, Ted (Athlete, Football Player)
16474 W Lava Dr
Surprise, AZ 85374, USA

Dean, Tina (Stylist)
c/o Staff Member *Arlene Wilson Management*
807 N Jefferson St
#200
Milwaukee, WI 53202, USA

Dean, Tommy (Athlete, Baseball Player)
PO Box 1014
Luka, MS 38852-6014, USA

Dean, Vernon (Athlete, Football Player)
2223 Fall Meadow Dr
Missouri City, TX 77459, USA

DeAnda, Paula (Musician)
c/o Staff Member *RCA Label Group UK*
9 Derry St
London W8 5HY, UK

Deane, William Patrick (General)
Government House
Canberra, ACT 26000, AUSTRALIA

DeAngelis, Barbara (Writer)
c/o Staff Member *St Martins Press*
Publicity Dept
175 5th Ave
New York, NY 10010, USA

DeAngelis, Beverly (Psychic)
505 S Beverly Dr #1017
Beverly Hills, CA 90212, USA

Deangelis, Billy (Athlete, Basketball Player)
14 Pickering Drive
Trenton, NJ 08691-2332, USA

De Angelis, Rosemary
817 West End Ave.
New York, NY 10025

De Aragon, Maria (Actor)
c/o Staff Member *Coolwaters Productions*
10061 Riverside Dr.
Box 531
Toluca Lake, CA 91602, USA

de Aragow, Maria
1159 Tenth Ave.
San Diego, CA 92101

Dear and the Headlights (Music Group, Musician)
c/o Brigitte Wright *Brigitte Wright Management*
1674 Broadway
3rd Floor
New York, NY 10019, USA

Dearden, James (Director)
International Creative Mgmt
8942 Wilshire Blvd
#219
Beverly Hills, CA 90211, USA

Deardorff, Jeff (Athlete, Baseball Player)
16823 Rockwell Heights Ln
Clermont, FL 34711, USA

Deardurff-Schmidt, Deena (Swimmer)
742 Murray Dr
El Cajon, CA 92020, USA

De Armas, Ana (Actor)
c/o Liz Dalling *Special Artists Agency*
9465 Wilshire Blvd #820
Beverly Hills, CA 90212, USA

de Armas, Roly (Baseball Player)
2650 Countryside Blvd Apt B102
Clearwate, FL 33761-3604, USA

DeArmond, Frank (Astronaut)
3086 Ravencrest Circle
Prescott, AZ 86303-5790, USA

Deas, Justin (Actor)
41 Bradford Ave
Montclair, NJ 07043, USA

D'Eath, Tom (Athlete, Misc)
P.O. Box 350437
Grand Island, FL 32735-0437, USA

Deavenport, Earnest Jr (Business Person)
Eastman Chemical Co
100 N Eastman Road
Kingsport, TN 37660, USA

Deaver, Jeffrey (Writer)
Pocket Star Books
1230 Ave of Americas
New York, NY 10020, USA

Deaver, Michael K (Government Official)
Deaver Assoc
1025 Thomas Jefferson St NW
Washington, DC 20007, USA

Deb, Debbie (Musician)
c/o Staff Member *Green Light Talent Agency*
P.O. Box 3172
Beverly Hills, CA 90212, USA

DeBarge, Eldra (El) (Musician)
c/o Staff Member *Geffen Records*
9126 Sunset Blvd
West Hollywood, CA 90069, USA

DeBarge, Kristinia (Musician)
c/o Staff Member *Edmonds Entertainment*
1635 N Cahuenga Blvd Fl 5
Los Angles, CA 90028, USA

Debarr, Denny (Athlete, Baseball Player)
33843 Juliet Cir
Fremont, CA 94555-3452, USA

De Becker, Gain (Commentator)
5064 Lemona Ave
Sherman Oaks, CA 91403, USA

DeBell, Kristine (Actor)
c/o Ted Elston *Karma Talent Management*
453 S. Rexford Dr.
Beverly Hills, CA 90212, USA

DeBellevue, Charles B (General)
916 Huntsman Road
Edmond, OK 73003-3520, USA

De Bello, James (Actor, Musician)
c/o Craig Shapiro *ICM Partners (ICM-LA)*
10250 Constellation Blvd Fl 7
Los Angeles, CA 90067, USA

DeBello, James (Actor)
c/o Craig Shapiro *ICM Partners (ICM-LA)*
10250 Constellation Blvd Fl 7
Los Angeles, CA 90067, USA

Debenedet, Nelson (Athlete, Hockey Player)
38142 N Vista Dr
Livonia, MI 48152-1066, USA

De Benning, Burr (Actor)
4235 Kingfisher Road
Calabasas, CA 91302, USA

DeBenning, Burr (Actor)
4235 Kingfisher Road
Colabasas, CA 91302, USA

DeBerg, Steve (Athlete, Coach, Football Player)
17920 Simms Rd
Odessa, FL 33556, USA

De Blanc, Jefferson J (Misc)
321 Saint Martin Street
Saint Martinville, LA 70582, USA

Deblois, Lucien (Athlete, Hockey Player)
c/o Staff Member *Vancouver Canucks*
800 Griffiths Way
Vancouver V6B 6G1, Canada

Debney, John (Composer, Musician)
2906 Olney Pl
Burbank, CA 91504, USA

DeBoer, Harm E (Business Person)
Russell Corp
755 Lee St
Alexander City, AL 35010, USA

DeBoer, Nicole (Actor)
c/o Jeff Witjas *Agency for the Performing Arts (APA-LA)*
405 S Beverly Dr
Suite 500
Beverly Hills, CA 90212-4425, USA

Deboer, Peter (Athlete, Hockey Player)
New Jersey Devils
165 Mulberry St
Newark, NJ 07102-3607

DeBoer, Rick (Actor)
Pacific Artists
510 W Hastings St
#1404
Vancouver, BC V6B 1L8, CANADA

Debol, Dave (Athlete, Hockey Player)
288 Clark St Apt 7
Saline, MI 48176-1247, USA

DeBold, Adolfo J (Doctor, Physicist)
Ottawa Civic Hospital
1053 Carling Ave
Ottawa, ON K1Y 4E9, CANADA

De Bont, Jan (Director, Producer)
c/o Martin Bauer *Bauer Company, The*
9720 Wilshire Blvd Mezzanine
Beverly Hills, CA 90212, USA

DeBorchgrave, Arnaud (Editor)
2141 Wyoming Ave NW
Washington, DC 20008, USA

DeBorda, Dorothy (Actor)
PO Box 2723
Livermore, CA 94551, USA

DeBranges, Louis (Mathematician)
Purdue University
Mathematics Dept
West Lafayette, IN 47907, USA

Debre, Michael (Prime Minister)
20 Rue Jacob
Paris 75006, FRANCE

De Bruijn, Inge (Athlete, Olympic Athlete, Swimmer)
Top voor Talent
Van Ostadestraat 368-2
Amsterdam 1074 XA, NETHERLANDS

DeBrunhoff, Laurent (Writer)
527 W 26th St
New York, NY 10001-5503, USA

Debrusk, Louie (Athlete, Hockey Player)
Edmonton Oilers
11230 110 St NW Dept
Edmonton, AB T5G 3H7, Canada

DeBurgh, Chris (Musician, Songwriter, Writer)
Kenny Thomson Mgmt
754 Fulham Road
London, SW6 5SW, UNITED KINGDOM (UK)

Debus, Jon (Baseball Player, Basketball Coach)
4875 26th St
Vera Beach, FL 32966-2017, USA

Debus, Kim (Stylist)
c/o Celebrity Stylist *Jam Arts, Inc*
154 W 57th St
New York, NY 10019, USA

Deby, Idriss (General, President)
President's Office
N'Djamena
CHAS

De Caestecker, Iain (Actor)
c/o Sandra Chang *Anonymous Content (LA)*
3531 Hayden Ave
Culver City, CA 90232, USA

Decambra-Kelley, Lillian (Athlete, Baseball Player, Commentator)
250 South St
Somerset, MA 02726-5616, USA

DeCamilli, Pietro V (Biologist)
Yale University
Medical School
Cell Biology Dept
New Haven, CT 06512, USA

DeCarava, Roy (Photographer)
81 Halsey St
Brooklyn, NY 11216, USA

DeCarl, Nancy
4615 Winnetka
Woodland Hills, CA 91364

Decarlo, Arthur (Athlete, Football Player)
9030 Manordale Ln
Ellicott City, MD 21042, USA

DeCarlo, Mark (Actor, Television Host)
3292 Carse Dr
Los Angeles, CA 90068, USA

DeCasabianca, Carnille (Actor)
Artmedia
20 Ave Rapp
Paris 75007, FRANCE

DeCastelia, F Robert (Athlete, Track Athlete)
Australian Institute of Sport
PO Box 176
Belconnen, ACT 2616, AUSTRALIA

Deccio, Joan (Stylist)
PO Box 442
Vashon Island, WA 98070, USA

DeCesare, Carmella (Actor, Model)
c/o Staff Member *Playboy Enterprises Inc*
680 North Lake Shore Drive
Chicago, IL 60611, USA

Decinces, Doug (Athlete, Baseball Player)
124 Riviera Way
Laguna Beach, CA 92651-1012, USA

Deck, Inspectah (Musician)
A&E Entertainment
13280 NE Freeway #F328
Houston, TX 77040, USA

Decker, Brooklyn (Actor)
c/o Chris Kiely *Marilyn Model Management*
32 Union Square East #PH
New York, NY 10003, USA

Decker, Franz-Paul (Conductor)
Herbert Barrett
266 W 37th St
#2000
New York, NY 10018, USA

Decker, Lori (Stylist)
4912 Midmoor Rd
Monona, WI 53716, USA

Decker, Marty (Athlete, Baseball Player)
1630 Youngs Ln
Yuba City, CA 95991-1925, USA

Decker, Scott (Business Person)
HEALTHvision
6330 Commerce Drive
Suite 100
Irving, TX 75063, USA

Decker, Steve (Athlete, Baseball Player)
1024 Laurelridge St NE
Keizer, OR 97303-7208, USA

Decker, Susan (Business Person)
33 Old Coach Rd
Napa, CA 94558, USA

Deckers, Daphne (Actor)
Nagtzaan
Hoge Naardenweg 44
Hilversum, AG 1217, NETHERLANDS

DeConcini, Dennis (Politician)
6014 Chesterbrook Rd
McLean, VA 22101-3210, USA

de Cordova, Fred (Actor, Director, Producer)
1875 Carla Ridge
Beverly Hills, CA 90210

Decosmo, Joe (Stylist)
253 Saxton Rd
Mansfield, OH 44907, USA

DeCosta, Roger (Race Car Driver)
MC Sports
1919 Torrance Blvd.
Torrance, CA 90501, USA

DeCosta, Sara (Athlete, Hockey Player, Olympic Athlete)
200 Cowesett Green Dr
Warwick, RI 02886, USA

DeCoster, Roger (Race Car Driver)
MC Sports
1919 Torrance Blvd
Torrance, CA 90501, USA

Decter, Midge (Writer)
120 East 81st St
New York, NY 10028, USA

De De, Dorsey (Athlete, Football Player)
6522 Southern Trace Dr
Leeds, AL 35094-6605, USA

de Dios, Silvia (Actor)
c/o Staff Member *TV Caracol*
Calle 76 #11 - 35
Piso 10AA
Bogota DC 26484, COLOMBIA

Dedkov, Anatoli I (Cosmonaut)
Potchta Kosmonavtov
Moskovskoi Oblasti
Syvisdny, Goroduk 141160, RUSSIA

Dedler, Karin
Hohenegg 21
Dietmannsried, GERMANY D-87463

Dedmon, Jeff (Athlete, Baseball Player)
21102 Broadwell Ave
Torrance, CA 90502-1636, USA

Dedrick, Jim (Athlete, Baseball Player)
2929 NW Kennedy Ct
Portland, OR 97229-8099, USA

De Duve, Christian (Nobel Prize Laureate)
80 Central Park West
New York, NY 10023-5204, USA

Dee, Donald (Athlete, Basketball Player, Olympic Athlete)
7924 North Pennsylvania Avenue
Kansas City, MO 64118-1416, USA

Dee, Donnie (Athlete, Football Player)
633 Rolling Hills Rd
Vista, CA 92081, USA

Dee, Francine (Adult Film Star)
Extreme Models
PO Box 472170
Reseda, CA 91337, USA

Dee, Joey (Musician)
Horizon Mgmt
PO Box 8770
Endwell, NY 13762, USA

Dee, Ruby (Actor)
Emmalyn II
P.O. Box 1318
New Rochelle, NY 10802, USA

Dee, Sally (Athlete, Golfer)
3508 W Barcelona St
Tampa, FL 33629-7010, USA

Dee, Toni (Fitness Expert)
Toni Dee Fitness
PO Box 834
Corta Madera, CA 94976, USA

Deeb, Gary (Critic)
Chicago Sun-Times
Editorial Dept
401 N Wabash Ave
Chicago, IL 60611, USA

Deedes of Aldington, William F (Government Official)
New Hayters
Aldington, Kent TN25 7DT, UNITED KINGDOM (UK)

Deedle, Nelson
PO Box 5358
Scottsdale, AZ 85261

Deegan, Bill (Athlete, Baseball Player)
8392 77th Ave
Seminole, FL 33777-4413, USA

Deeley, Cat (Actor)
1619 Tower Grove Dr
Beverly Hills, CA 90210, USA

Dee-Lite (Musician)
428 Cedar Street NW
Washington, DC 20012, USA

Deemer, Audrey (Athlete, Baseball Player, Commentator)
241 NeffSt
Powhatan Point, OH 43942-1328, USA

Deen, James (Actor, Adult Film Star)
5009 Cerrillos Dr
Woodland Hills, CA 91364, USA

Deen, Paula (Chef)
818 Wilmington Island Rd
Savannah, GA 31410, USA

Deependra Bir, Bikaram Shah Dev (Prince)
Narayanhiti Royal Palace
Durbeg Marg
Kathmandu, NEPAL

Deep Purple (Music Group)
c/o Staff Member *Agency Group Ltd, The (UK)*
361-373 City Rd
London EC1V 1PQ, UK

Deer, Ada E (Government Official)
2537 Mutchler Road
Fitchburg, WI 53711, USA

Deer, Rob (Athlete, Baseball Player)
22217 N 78th St
Scottsdale, AZ 85255-4011, USA

Deering, John (Cartoonist)
6701 Westover Dr
Little Rock, AR 72207, USA

Deery, Tom
49 Yale Sq
Morton, PA 19070-1923, USA

Dees, Archie (Athlete, Basketball Player)
4405 North Hillview Drive
Bloomington, IN 47408-9770, USA

Dees, Bowen C (Scientist)
29059 Meadow Glen Way W
Escondido, CA 92026, USA

Dees, Charlie (Athlete, Baseball Player)
1064 Allison Woods Ct
Lawrenceville, GA 30043-5383, USA

Dees, Morris (Civil Rights Activist, Lawyer)
Southern Poverty Law Center
PO Box 548
Montgomery, AL 36101, USA

Dees, Morris S Jr (Activist)
Southern Poverty Law Center
PO Box 548
Montgomery, AL 36101, USA

Dees, Rick (Actor, Entertainer, Musician, Radio Personality)
Dees Entertainment
3601 West Olive Avenue
#675
Burbank, CA 91505, USA

Deese, Derrick (Athlete, Football Player)
P.O. Box 3356
Cerritos, CA 90703, USA

De Eugenia, Coco (Actor)
c/o Nancy Harding *Powerhouse Talent*
P.O. Box 261939
Encino, CA 91426, USA

Deezen, Eddie (Actor)
c/o Staff Member *Coolwaters Productions*
10061 Riverside Dr.
Box 531
Toluca Lake, CA 91602, USA

DeFanti, Tom (Inventor)
University of Illinois
Electronic Visualization Labe
Chicago, IL 60607, USA

Default (Music Group)
c/o Staff Member *Agency Group Ltd, The (NY)*
142 West 57th St
6th Floor
New York, NY 10019, USA

Defauw, Brad (Athlete, Hockey Player)
Jane And Russell Defauw
13030 Florida Ct.
St. Paul, MN 55124-7943, USA

Defazio, Dean (Athlete, Hockey Player)
2475 Logan Ave
Oakville, ON L6H 6P3, Canada

DeFazio, Peter (Congressman, Politician)
2134 Rayburn HOB
Washington, DC 20515, USA

Defebo, Brian (Race Car Driver)
Magic Motorsports
122 E. Front St.
Berwick, PA 18603, USA

Defee, Lois (Dancer, Model)
223 Wink Rd
Oak Grove, LA 71236, USA

DeFelitta, Raymond (Director, Writer)
c/o Gary Ungar *Exile Entertainment*
732 El Medio Ave
Pacific Palisades, CA 90272, USA

DeFer, Kaylee (Actor)
c/o Staff Member *Abrams Artists Agency (LA)*
9200 Sunset Blvd
11th Floor
Los Angeles, CA 90069, USA

de Ferran, Gil (Race Car Driver)
Penske Racing
13400 Outer Rd. W.
Detrott, MI 48239, USA

DeFigueiredo, Rul J P (Engineer)
University of California
Intelligent Sensors/Systems Lab
Irvine, CA 92717, USA

De Filipis, Antonio (Stylist)
c/o Staff Member *Blink Management*
421 Washington Ave
#202
Miami Beach, FL 33139, USA

DeFina, Barbara (Producer)
Columbia University
School of Arts
513 Dodge Hall, Mail Code 1808, 2960 Broadway
New York, NY 10027, USA

Def Leppard (Music Group)
c/o Rod MacSween *International Talent Booking*
74A Charlotte St
London W1T 4QJ, UNITED KINGDOM (UK)

DeFleur, Lois B (Educator)
State University of New York
President's Office
Binghamton, NY 13902, USA

Deford, Frank (Sportscaster)
PO Box 1109
Greens Farms, CT 06838-1109, USA

DeForest, Roy (Artist)
PO Box 47
Port Costa, CA 94569, USA

DeForrest, Jeff (Sportscaster)
2249 SE 8th Ct
Pompano Beach, FL 33062-6727, USA

Defrancesco, Dona (Stylist)
c/o Staff Member *That's a Wrap*
PO Box 693
Shrewsbury, MA 01545, USA

DeFrancesco, Tony (Basketball Coach)
7159 E Quince St
Mesa, AZ 85207-1841, USA

DeFrancisco, Joseph E (Joe) (General)
7754 Chars Lane
Springfield, VA 22153, USA

DeFranco, Buddy (Musician)
22525 Coral Avenue
Panama City, FL 32413, USA

DeFrank, Joe (Horse Racer)
PO Box 655
Lake Pleasant, NY 12108-0655, USA

DeFrantz, Anita (Misc)
US Olympic Committee
1 Olympia Plaza
Colorado Springs, CO 80909, USA

DeFreitas, Eric (Bowler)
175 W 12th St
New York, NY 10011-8275, USA

Deftones (Music Group)
c/o David Benveniste *Velvet Hammer*
9014 Melrose Ave
Los Angeles, CA 90069, USA

Deganhardt, Johannes J Cardinal
(Religious Leader)
Erzbischofliches Generalvikariat
Domplatz 3
Paderborn 33098, GERMANY

DeGarmo, Diana (Musician)
c/o Erica Bines *Headline Talent*
PO Box 131518
Staten Island, NY 10313, USA

DeGaspa, Philippe (Publisher)
Canadian Living Magazine
50 Holly St
Toronto, ON M4S 3B3, CANADA

Degen, Bruce (Writer)
62 Castle Meadow Rd
Newtown, CT 06470-2502, USA

DeGeneres, Betty (Activist, Writer)
c/o Staff Member *HarperCollins Publishers*
10 East 53rd St
c/o Author mail, 7th Floor
New York, NY 10022, USA

DeGeneres, Ellen (Actor, Comedian, Talk
Show Host)
The Ellen DeGeneres Show
Time Telepictures Television
3500 W Olive Ave, Suite 1000
Burbank, CA 91505, USA

DeGennes, Pierre-Gilles (Nobel Prize
Laureate)
11 Place Marcelin-Berthelot
Paris 75005, FRANCE

Deger, Vicky (Stylist)
c/o Staff Member *Rex Agency, The*
6311 Romaine St
Los Angeles, CA 90038, USA

Degerick, Mike (Athlete, Baseball Player)
2702 Lake Osborne Dr
Lake Worth, FL 33461-5665, USA

DeGette, Diana (Congressman, Politician)
2335 Rayburn HOB
Washington, DC 20515, USA

Degg, Jakki (Actor, Model)
Neon Management
34 Clare Ln
London N13DB, UNITED KINGDOM

DeGioia, John (Educator)
Georgetown University
President's Office
Washington, DC 20057, USA

DeGiorgi, Salvatore Cardinal (Religious
Leader)
Curia Archivescovile
Corso Vittorio Emanuele 461
Palermo 90134, ITALY

DeGivenchy, Hubert (Designer, Fashion
Designer)
Givenchy
3 Avenue George V
Paris 75008, France

Degler, Carl N (Historian, Writer)
907 Mears Court
Stanford, CA 94305, USA

Degnan, John J (Business Person)
Chubb Corp
15 Mountain View Road
Warren, NJ 07059, USA

De Gouw, Jessica (Actor)
c/o Theresa Huska *RGM Artist Group*
64-76 Kippax St
Level 2, Suite 202 & 206
Surry Hills, NSW 2010, Australia

Degraffenreid, Allen (Athlete, Football
Player)
3823 E Thunderheart Trl
Gilbert, AZ 85297, USA

DeGrate, Tony (Athlete, Football Player)
203 Newport Landing Pl
Round Rock, TX 78665, USA

**DeGrate Jr, Donald Earle (DeVante
Swing)** (Musician)
c/o Staff Member *De Swing Mob Inc /
EMI April Music Inc*
c/o EMI Music Publishing
810 7th Avenue
New York, NY 10019, USA

DeGraw, Gavin (Musician)
330 N 13th Ave
Hollywood, FL 33019, USA

Degray, Dale (Athlete, Hockey Player)
c/o Staff Member *Owen Sound Attack*
P.O. Box 1420
Stn Main
Owen Sound, ON N4K 6T5, Canada

de Gruiin, Inge
PO Box 302
Arnhem, NETHERLANDS 6800 AH

Degruttola, Raffaello
c/o Lorraine Berglund *Lorraine Berglund
Management*
11537 Hesby St.
North Hollywood, CA 91601, USA

Deguise, Michel (Athlete, Hockey Player)
380 Rue Moge
Sorel-Tracy, QC J3P 7A6, Canada

Dehaan, Dane (Actor)
c/o Courtney Kivowitz *Schiff Company,
The*
9465 Wilshire Blvd
Suite 480
Beverly Hills, CA 90212, USA

Dehaan, Kory (Athlete, Baseball Player)
19040 E Superstition Dr
Queen Creek, AZ 85242, USA

DeHaan, Richard W (Religious Leader)
3000 Kraft Ave SE
Grand Rapids, MI 49512, USA

Dehaene, Jean-Luc (Prime Minister)
Berkendallaan 52
Vilvoorde 1800, BELGIUM

Dehart, Rick (Athlete, Baseball Player)
811 NE Wabash Ave
Topeka, KS 66616, USA

DeHaven, Gloria (Actor)
9232 Sunnyfield Drive
Las Vegas, NV 89134-6348, USA

DeHaven, Penny
Box 83
Brentwood, TN 37027

de Havilland, Olivia (Actor)
3 Rue Benouville
Paris 75016, FRANCE

De Heer, Rolf (Director, Producer, Writer)
c/o Staff Member *Vertigo Productions Pty
Ltd*
3 Butler Dr
Hendon SA 5014, AUSTRALIA

Dehere, Terry (Athlete, Basketball Player)
120 Wayne Street
Jersey City, NJ 07302-3406, USA

Dehmelt, Hans G (Nobel Prize Laureate)
1600 43rd Ave E
Seattle, WA 98112, USA

Deidel, Jim (Athlete, Baseball Player)
14312 Wright Way
Broomfield, CO 80023, USA

Deidrick, Casey (Actor)
c/o Jon Simmons *Simmons & Scott
Entertainment*
4110 W. Burbank Blvd.
Burbank, CA 91505, USA

Deighton, Len
10 Iron Bridge House Bridge Approach
London, ENGLAND NW1 8BD

Deighton, Leonard C (Len) (Writer)
Fairymount Blackrock
Dundalk
County Louth, IRELAND

Deisenhofer, Johann (Nobel Prize
Laureate)
3860 Echo Brook lane
Dallas, TX 75229-5221, USA

Deitch, Donna (Director)
International Creative Mgmt
8942 Wilshire Blvd
#219
Beverly Hills, CA 90211, USA

Deja (Musician)
c/o Anthony Embry *AE Entertainment
Public Relations*
124 Evening Shade Dr
Charleston, SC 29414, USA

Deja, Andreas (Animator)
3494 Berry Dr
Studio City, CA 91604, USA

DeJager, Cornelis (Astronomer)
Zonnenburg 1
Utrecht, NL 352, NETHERLANDS

Deja Vu
1 Touchstone Lane Chard
Somerset, ENGLAND TA20 1RF

Dejdel, Jim (Baseball Player)
New York Yankees
14312 Wright Way
Broomfield, CO 80020-4045, USA

Dejesus, David (Athlete, Baseball Player)
2009 Burnham Pl
Wheaton, IL 60189-8155, USA

Dejesus, Ivan (Athlete, Baseball Player)
14608 Velleux Dr
Orlando, FL 32837-5467, USA

Dejesus, Jose (Athlete, Baseball Player)
Kansas City Royals
PO Box 9960
Cidra, PR 00739-8960, USA

De Jesus, Wanda (Actor)
c/o Bob McGowan *McGowan
Management*
8733 W Sunset Blvd
Suite 103
West Hollywood, CA 90069, USA

Dejohn, Mark (Athlete, Baseball Player)
24 New Hampshire Dr
Apt 1C
New Britain, CT 06052-1166, USA

DeJohnette, Jack (Composer)
Silver Hollow Road
Willow, NY 11201, USA

DeJong, jordan (Baseball Player)
5305 Via Cartagena
Yorba Linda, CA 92886-4561, USA

De Jong, Michael
c/o Staff Member *Mark Edward Inc*
325 W 8th St
#1011
New York, NY 10018, USA

DeJong, Pierre (Misc)
Laerence Livermore Laboratory
7000 East St
Livermore, CA 94550, USA

de Jongh, John (Governor, Politician)
Government House
21-22 Kongens Gade
Charlote Amalie
St Thomas, VI

DeJordy, Denis E (Athlete, Hockey Player)
472 Chemin Des Patriotes
St-Charles-Sur-Richelieu, QC J0H 2G0,
Canada

DeJoria, John Paul (Business Person)
Paul Mitchell Systems
26455 Golden Valley Road
Santa Clarita, CA 91350-2621, USA

Dejurnett, Charles (Athlete, Football
Player)
1355 Heritage Ct
Escondido, CA 92027, USA

DeKay, Tim (Actor)
4649 Willowcrest Ave
Toluca Lake, CA 91602, USA

DeKierk, Albert (Composer)
Crayenesterlaan
Haarlem 22, NETHERLANDS

DeKierk, Frederik (Nobel Prize Laureate)
Private Bag X999
CapeTown 8000, South Africa

DeKieweit, Cornelis W (Historian)
22 Berkeley St
Rochester, NY 14607, USA

Dekker, Fred (Director)
9818 Easton Dr
Beverly Hills, CA 90210, USA

Dekker, Thomas (Actor, Director)
c/o Mimi DiTrani *Schiff Company, The*
9465 Wilshire Blvd
Suite 480
Beverly Hills, CA 90212, USA

DeLaBilliere, Peter (General)
Robert Fleming Holdings
25 Copthall Ave
London EC2R 7DR, UNITED KINGDOM
(UK)

Delacote, Jacques
Dr Hilbert Maximilianstr 22
Munich 80539, GERMANY

De La Cruz, David (Stylist)
c/o Staff Member *Illusions Management*
129 W 27th St
Penthouse
New York, NY 10001, USA

de la Cruz, Melissa (Writer)
c/o Richard Abate *3 Arts Entertainment -
NY*
49 West 27th St.
5th Floor
New York, NY 10001, USA

DeLaCruz, Rosie (Model)
Willhelmina Models
300 Park Ave S
#200
New York, NY 10010, USA

De La Cruz, Veronica (Television Host)
c/o Staff Member *CNN (Atlanta)*
One CNN Center
PO Box 105366
Atlanta, GA 30303, USA

De La Fuente, Cristian (Actor, Producer, Writer)
Efetres

DeLaFuente, Joel (Actor)
LMRK
130 W 42nd St
#1906
New York, NY 10036, USA

de la Fuente, Marian (Actor)
c/o Staff Member *Telemundo*
2470 West 8th Avenue
Hialeah, FL 33010, USA

De La Garza, Alana (Actor)
10570 Valley Spring Ln
Toluca Lake, CA 91602, USA

Delahoussaye, Eddie (Horse Racer)
1024 4th Ave
Arcadia, CA 91006-4218, USA

Delahoussaye, Ryan (Musician)
Ashley Talent
2002 Hogback Road
#20
Ann Arbor, MI 48105, USA

De La Hoya, Oscar (Athlete, Boxer)
c/o Richard Schaefer *Golden Boy Promotions*
626 Wilshire Blvd #350
Los Angeles, CA 90017, USA

De La Hoz, Mike (Athlete, Baseball Player)
P.O. Box 441233
Miami, FL 33144-1233, USA

De la Huerta, Paz (Actor)
c/o Katie Rhodes *Untitled Entertainment (LA)*
350 S. Beverly Dr #200
Beverly Hills, CA 90212, USA

Delain, Moneca (Actor)
c/o Staff Member *Pacific Artists Management*
1285 W Broadway
Suite 685
Vancouver, BC V6H 3X8, Canada

Delaire, Suzy
46 rue de Varenne
Paris, FRANCE 75007

De La Maza, Roland (Athlete, Baseball Player)
28533 Silverking Trl
Santa Clarita, CA 91390-5248, USA

DeLamielleure, Joseph M (Joe) (Athlete, Football Player)
7818 Ridgeloch Pl
Charlotte, NC 28226, USA

Del Amitri (Music Group, Songwriter, Writer)
c/o Scott Clayton *Creative Artists Agency (CAA-TN)*
3310 West End Ave
5th Floor
Nashville, TN 37203, USA

DeLancie, John (Actor)
1313 Brunswick Ave
South Pasadena, CA 91030, USA

Delaney, Don (Basketball Coach, Coach)
25 High Point Lane
Willoughby, OH 44094, USA

Delaney, Jeff (Athlete, Football Player)
215 Village Green Dr
Canonsburg, PA 15317, USA

Delaney, Kim (Actor, Model)
711 Walden Dr
Beverly Hills, CA 90210, USA

Delaney, Pat
PO Box 273
Tamworth, NH 03886

Delaney, Shelagh (Writer)
Tess Sayle
11 Jubilee Place
London SW3 3TE, UNITED KINGDOM (UK)

Delaney, Tracie (Stylist)
c/o Staff Member *Judy Inc*
1 Yorkville Ave
Toronto ON M4W 1L1, Canada

Delano, Diane (Actor)
Gold Marshak Liedtke
3500 W Olive Ave
#1400
Burbank, CA 91505, USA

Delano, Michael (Actor)
c/o Cody Garden *McCarty Agency*
2600 West Olive Avenue
5th Floor
Burbank, CA 91505, USA

Delano, Robert B (Misc)
American Farm Bureau Federation
225 W Tuuhy Ave
Park Ridge, IL 60068, USA

Delany, Dana (Actor)
2522 Beverly Ave
Santa Monica, CA 90405, USA

DeLap, Tony (Artist)
225 Jasmine St
Corona del Mar, CA 92625, USA

DeLaPuente, Raygada Oscar (Prime Minister)
Prime Minister's Office
Urb Corpac
Calle 1 Oeste
Lima, S/N, PERU

Del Arco, Jonathan (Actor)
c/o Kyle Fritz *Kyle Fritz Management*
6325 Heather Dr
Los Angeles, CA 90068, USA

DelArco, Jonathan (Actor)
Michael Slessinger
8730 Sunset Blvd
#220W
Los Angeles, CA 90069, USA

de la Reguera, Ana (Actor)
c/o Will Ward *ROAR (LA)*
9701 Wilshire Blvd
8th Floor
Los Angeles, CA 90212, USA

De La Renta, Oscar (Fashion Designer)
550 Seventh Ave Fl 8
New York, NY 10018, USA

DeLaria, Lea (Actor)
c/o Diana Doussant *TalentWorks (LA)*
3500 W Olive Ave
Suite 1400
Burbank, CA 91505, USA

DeLaRocha, Zack (Musician)
GAS Entertainment
8935 Lindblade St
Culver City, CA 90232, USA

DeLaRosa, Evelyn (Opera Singer)
Dorothy Cone Artists
150 W 55th St
New York, NY 10019, USA

De La Rosa, Jo (Actor)
c/o Jack Ketsoyan *EMC / Bowery*
8145 Santa Monica Blvd
Suite 200
West Hollywood, CA 90046, USA

DeLaRosa, Yvonne (Actor)
c/o Staff Member *Heidi Rotbart Management*
1810 Malcolm Ave.
Suite 207
Los Angeles, CA 90025, USA

Delasin, Dorothy (Athlete, Golfer)
20 Longview Dr
Daly City, CA 94015, USA

De La Soul (Music Group)
2697 Heath Avenue
Bronx, NY 10463, USA

De Lassus, Christine (Stylist)
c/o Staff Member *Michele Filomeno New York LLC*
515 Greenwich St Ste 503
New York, NY 10013, USA

Delate, Joseph (Stylist)
c/o Staff Member *Bernstein & Andriulli*
58 W 40th St
New York, NY 10018, USA

DeLatour, David (Actor)
c/o Staff Member *Kass & Stokes Management*
9229 Sunset Blvd
Suite 504
Los Angeles, CA 90069, USA

De La Tour, Frances (Actor)
c/o Carl Scott *Simmons & Scott Entertainment*
4110 W. Burbank Blvd.
Burbank, CA 91505, USA

De Laurentiis, Giada (Chef)
418 Mt Holyoke Ave
Pacific Palisades, CA 90272, USA

De Laurentiis, Raffaella (Actor, Producer)
Rafaella Productions
100 Universal City Plaza
Bungalow 5162
Universal City, CA 91608-1085, USA

Delavan, Burt (Athlete, Football Player)
1161 Jacob Ln
Carmichael, CA 95608-6202, USA

Delay, Tom (Ex-Congressman, Politician)
242 Cannon HOB
Washington, DC 20515, USA

Delays Delirium (Music Group)
c/o Staff Member *Paradigm (Monterey)*
404 W Franklin St
Monterey, CA 93940, USA

Del Bello, Jack (Athlete, Football Player)
391 Belfast Ter
Sebastian, FL 32958, USA

del Boca, Andrea (Actor)
c/o Staff Member *Telefe - Argentina*
Pavon 2444 (C1248AAT)
Buenos Aires, ARGENTINA

Delcarmen, Manny (Athlete, Baseball Player)
68 Surrey LN
East Bridgewater, MA 02333-3110, USA

del Castillo, Eric (Actor)
c/o Staff Member *Televisa*
Blvd Adolfo Lopez Mateos 232
Colonia San Angel INN
DF CP 01060, MEXICO

Del Castillo, Kate (Actor)
c/o Jack Ketsoyan *EMC / Bowery*
8145 Santa Monica Blvd
Suite 200
West Hollywood, CA 90046, USA

Del Castillo-Kinney, Ysora (Athlete, Baseball Player, Commentator)
1555 W 44th Pl Apt 216C
Hialeah, FL 33012-7837, USA

deLeeuw, Rob (Actor)
5075 Trail Canyon Dr
Mira Loma, CA 91752, USA

DeLeeuw, Ton (Composer)
Costerusiaan 4
Hilversum, NETHERLANDS

Delehanty, Hugh (Editor)
AARP Publications
Editorial Dept
601 E St NW
Washington, DC 20049, USA

DeLeo, Dean (Musician)
Q Prime
729 7th Ave
#1600
New York, NY 10019, USA

DeLeo, Robert (Composer)
2225 Via Cerritos
Palos Verdes Estates, CA 90274, USA

Deleon, Jose (Athlete, Baseball Player)
Pittsburgh Pirates
348 Herbert St
Perth Amboy, NJ 08861-3708, USA

de Leon, Miguel (Actor)
c/o Staff Member *Televisa*
Blvd Adolfo Lopez Mateos 232
Colonia San Angel INN
DF CP 01060, MEXICO

Deleone, Tom (Athlete, Football Player)
P.O. Box 681472
Park City, UT 84068, USA

de Lesseps, LuAnn (Reality TV Star)
c/o Staff Member *Bravo (NY)*
30 Rockefeller Plaza
New York, NY 10112, USA

Delfino, Carlos Francisco (Basketball Player)
Detroit Pistons
Palace
2 Championship Dr
Auburn Hills, MI 48326, USA

Delfino, Majandra (Actor)
c/o Bradley Frank *Platform Public Relations*
2666 N Beachwood Dr
Los Angeles, CA 90068, USA

Delfino, Marieh (Actor)
c/o Amanda Glazer *Kohner Agency, The*
9300 Wilshire Blvd
Suite 555
Beverly Hills, CA 90212, USA

Delfs, Andreas (Conductor)
Saint Paul Chamber Orchestra
408 Saint Peter St
Saint Paul, MN 55102, USA

Delgado, Carlos (Athlete, Baseball Player)
9 Repto Ramos Bo Borinquen
Aguadilla, PR 00603-5944, USA

Delgado, Chiquinquira (Actor)
c/o Gabriel Blanco *Gabriel Blanco Iglesias (Mexico)*
Rio Balsas 35-32
Colonia Cuauhtemoc
DF 06500, Mexico

Delgado, Felix Avila (Cuban Link)
(Musician)
c/o Staff Member *Mob Records*
Unit 2A Queens Studios
21 Salusbury Rd
London NW6 6RG, USA

Delgado, Frankie (Actor)
c/o Eric Podwall *Podwall Entertainment*
710 N Orlando Ave
Loft 203
Los Angeles, CA 90069, USA

Delgado, Issac (Musician)
Ralph Mercado Mgmt
568 Broadway
#806
New York, NY 10012, USA

Delgado, Jose Maria Gil Roble (Politician)
97-113 Rue Belliard
Brussels 1047, Belgium

Del Gaizo, Jim (Athlete, Football Player)
9581 NW 13th St
Plantation, FL 33322, USA

Del Greco, Al (Athlete, Football Player)
1012 Little Turtle Cir
Birmingham, AL 35242, USA

Del Greco, Bobby (Athlete, Baseball
Player)
625 Southview Dr
Pittsburgh, PA 15226-2540, USA

Delguidice, Matt (Athlete, Hockey Player)
25 Church St
North Branford, CT 06471-1418, USA

Delhaven, Robert M (War Hero)
3716 Terrace View Dr
Encino, CA 91436, USA

Delhi, Ganesh (Actor)
No12 62nd Street
Ashok Nagar
Chennai, TN 600 083, INDIA

Delhomme, Jake (Athlete, Football Player)
2896 Rocky Ridge Dr
Westlake, OH 44145, USA

Delhoyo, George (Actor)
c/o Staff Member *TalentWorks (LA)*
3500 W Olive Ave
Suite 1400
Burbank, CA 91505, USA

D'Elia, Chris (Actor, Writer)
c/o Stephanie Davis *Wet Dog
Entertainment*
9460 Wilshire Blvd
7th Floor
Beverly Hills, CA 90210, USA

D'Elia, Federico (Actor)
c/o Staff Member *Telefe - Argentina*
Pavon 2444 (C1248AAT)
Buenos Aires, ARGENTINA

Delia, Joseph (Athlete, Football Player)
P.O. Box 19654
Irvine, CA 92623, USA

Deligne, Pierre R (Mathematician)
Institute for Advanced Study
Math School
Einstein Dr
Princeton, NJ 08540, USA

Delilah (Radio Personality)
Radio Delilah Media Group
15260 Ventura Blvd #400
Sherman Oaks, CA 91403, USA

DeLillo, Don (Writer)
57 Rossmore Ave
Bronxville, NY 10708, USA

DeLine, Donald (Producer)
120 N Hudson Ave
Los Angeles, CA 90004, USA

Delinsky, Barbara (Writer)
c/o Staff Member *Simon & Schuster*
1230 Avenue of the Americas
New York, NY 10020, USA

de Lint, Derek (Actor)
c/o Vanessa Henneman *Features Creative
Managment*
76a Entrepotdok
Amsterdam 1018 AD, NETHERLANDS

Delisle, Jim (Athlete, Football Player)
S34W32228 Journeys Way
Waukesha, WI 53189, USA

Delizia, Cara (Actor)
6238 De Longpre Ave
Hollywood, CA 90028

Delk, Joan (Athlete, Golfer)
830 Forest Path Ln
Alpharetta, GA 30022-6468, USA

Delk, Tony (Athlete, Basketball Player)
1843 Glenhill Drive
Lexington, KY 40502-2817, USA

Dell, Donald (Athlete, Tennis Player)
Lagardere Unlimited
5335 Wisconsin Ave, NW
Suite 850
Washington, DC 20015, USA

Dell, Michael (Misc)
Dell Inc
3400 Toro Canyon Rd
Austin, TX 78746-1502, USA

Dell'Abate, Gary (Producer)
2 Old Farm Ln
Old Greenwich, CT 06870, USA

Dellaero, Jason (Athlete, Baseball Player)
3240 Chapel Creek Cir
Wesley Chapel, FL 33544-7700, USA

Del La Hoya, Daisy (Actor, Model, Reality
TV Star)
c/o Michael (Mike) Esterman
Esterman.Com, LLC
Prefers to be contacted via email
MD, USA

Dellanos, Myrka (Actor)
c/o Staff Member *Univision*
605 3rd St. Fl12
New York, NY 10158, USA

Dellenbach, Jeff (Athlete, Football Player)
1002 Pine Branch Dr
Weston, FL 33326, USA

Delli Colli, Tomino
Via Pietro Micheli 78
Rome, ITALY I-00197

Dellinger, Bill (Athlete, Olympic Athlete,
Track Athlete)
1993 Fircrest Dr
Eugene, OR 97403-3112, USA

Dellinger, Dustin (Dusty) (Athlete,
Baseball Player)
5203 Grindstone Ln
Granite Falls, NC 28602-5533, USA

Dellinger, Walter (Educator)
Duke University
Law School
Durham, NC 27706, USA

DelloJolo, Norman (Composer)
PO Box 154
East Hampton, NY 11937, USA

Dellucci, David (Athlete, Baseball Player)
5512 Summer Lake Dr
Baton Rouge, LA 70817-4313, USA

Del Negro, Matthew (Actor)
c/o Adam Lazarus *Bauman Redanty &
Shaul Agency*
5757 Wilshire Blvd
Suite 473
Beverly Hills, CA 90212, USA

Del Negro, Vinny (Athlete, Basketball
Player)
7320 N 71st St
Paradise Valley, AZ 85253-3616, USA

Delo, Ken (Actor)
161 Avondale Drive
#93-8
Branson, MO 65616, USA

Delock, Ike (Athlete, Baseball Player)
433 Cypress Way E
Naples, FL 34110-1107, USA

Delon, Alain (Actor)
Alain Delon International
7 Rue Des Battoirs
Genève CH-1 205, Switzerland

Delon, Anthony (Actor)
Intertalent
5 Rue Clement-Marot
Paris 75008, FRANCE

Delon, Nathalie
3 Quai Malaquais
Paris, FRANCE 75006

Delong, Greg (Athlete, Football Player)
4960 Shady Maple Ln
Winston Salem, NC 27106, USA

DeLong, Keith A (Athlete, Football Player)
1850 Greywell Rd
Knoxville, TN 37922, USA

DeLong, Michael P (General)
Deputy Commander
US Central Command
MacDill Air Force Base, FL 33621, USA

Delong, Nate (Athlete, Basketball Player)
P.O. Box 485
Hayward, WI 54843-0485, USA

DeLonge, Thomas Matthew (Music
Group, Musician)
c/o Staff Member *Geffen Records*
9126 Sunset Blvd
West Hollywood, CA 90069, USA

DeLonge, Tom (Actor, Musician)
18433 Via Candela Rancho
Santa Fe, CA 92091, USA

De Longis, Anthony
PO Box 323
Burbank, CA 91503-0323

DeLongis, Anthony (Actor)
PO Box 2445
Canyon Country, CA 91386, USA

Deloplaine, Jack (Athlete, Football Player)
215 Montana St
Pittsburgh, PA 15214, USA

Delora, Jennifer (Actor)
Gilla Roos
9744 Wilshire Blvd
#203
Beverly Hills, CA 90212, USA

Delorenzi, Ray (Athlete, Hockey Player)
184 Lantern back Island Dr
Satellite Beach, FL 32937-4703, USA

DeLorenzo, Michael (Actor)
c/o Staff Member *Shelter Entertainment*
9454 Wilshire Blvd.
Suite 715
Beverly Hills, CA 90212, USA

Delorme, Daniele
16 rue de Marignan
Paris, FRANCE 75008

Delorme, Gilbert (Athlete, Hockey Player)
Le Rocket de Montreal
195 Boul Sir-Wilfrid-Laurier
Saint-Basile-Le-Grand, QC J3N 1R1,
Canada

Delorme, Ron (Athlete, Hockey Player)
94 Ravine Dr
Port Moody, BC V3H 4T8, Canada

Delors, Jacques L J (Government Official)
19 Blvd de Bercy
Paris 75012, FRANCE

De Los Santos, Valerio (Athlete, Baseball
Player)
9838 N 119th Pl
Scottsdale, AZ 85259-5069, USA

Delparte, Guy (Athlete, Hockey Player)
173 Sandy Hill Rd
South Portland, ME 04106, USA

Del Piero, Alessandro (Soccer Player)
Juventus FC
Piazza Crimea 7
Turin 10131, ITALY

Delpino, Robert L (Athlete, Football
Player)
9569 Calle Del Casa
Riverside, CA 92503, USA

Del Pino, Robin (Stylist)
233 E 77th St
#16
New York, NY 10021, USA

Delpy, Julie (Actor)
534 Westmount Dr
West Hollywood, CA 90048, USA

Del Regil, Estrellita
PO Box 2004
Beverly Hills, CA 90213

Del Rey, Lana (Musician)
c/o Ed Millett *Connected Artists*
1-5 Exchange Court
Maiden Ln Covent Garden
London WC2R0JU, UNITED KINGDOM

del Rincon, Fernando (Actor)
c/o Staff Member *Univision*
605 3rd St. Fl12
New York, NY 10158, USA

Del Rio, Jack (Athlete, Football Coach, Football Player)
1605 Beach Ave
Atlantic Beach, FL 32233, USA

Del Rio, Rebekah (Musician)
2280 Grass Valley Hwy #138
Auburn, CA 90213, USA

Del Rubio, Millie
PO Box 6923
San Pedro, CA 90734-6923

Delsing, Jay (Athlete, Golfer)
1833 Aston Way
Chesterfield, MO 63005-4579, USA

del Solar, Fernando (Actor)
c/o Staff Member *TV Azteca*
Periferico Sur 4121
Colonia Fuentes del Pedregal
DF CP 14141, Mexico

Delson, Brad (Musician)
12097 Summit Cir
Beverly Hills, CA 90210, USA

Delta Spirit (Music Group)
c/o Staff Member *Paradigm (Monterey)*
404 W Franklin St
Monterey, CA 93940, USA

Del Toro, Benicio (Actor)
1511/1515 Malcolm Ave
Los Angeles, CA 90024, USA

Del Toro, Guillermo (Director, Writer)
5970 Kingham Ct
Agoura Hills, CA 91301, USA

DelTredici, David (Composer)
463 West St
#G121
New York, NY 10014, USA

Deluca, Annette (Athlete, Golfer)
7 Turtle Creek Dr
Apt D
Jupiter, FL 33469-1530, USA

Deluca, Fred (Misc)
1924 Sunrise Key Blvd
Fort Lauderdale, FL 33304-3818, USA

DeLuca, Mike (Producer)
Michael De Luca Productions
10202 W Washington Blvd
Astaire Bldg Ste 3028
Culver City, CA 90232, USA

Deluca, Silvana (Stylist)
c/o Staff Member *Ford Models (Chicago)*
311 W Superior St
Chicago, IL 60654, USA

DeLucas, Lawrence J (Astronaut)
909 19th St S
Birmingham, AL 35205, USA

Delucas, Lawrence J Dr (Astronaut)
90819th St S
Birmingham, AL 35205-3704, USA

Delucca, Jerry (Athlete, Football Player)
27 Pulaski St
Peabody, MA 01960, USA

DeLucchi, Michele (Architect)
Via Cenisio 40
Milan 20154, ITALY

DeLucia, Paco (Musician)
International Music Network
278 S Main St
#400
Gloucester, MA 01930, USA

Delucia, Rich (Athlete, Baseball Player)
4 Rick Rd
Reading, PA 19607-9704, USA

Delugg, Milton (Musician)
2740 Claray Drive
Los Angeles, CA 90024, USA

DeLuise, David (Actor)
1225 N Olive Dr
Los Angeles, CA 90069, USA

Deluise, Michael (Actor)
1186 Corsica Dr
Pacific Palisades, CA 90272, USA

Deluise, Peter (Actor, Director, Producer)
c/o Lee Dinstman *Agency for the Performing Arts (APA-LA)*
405 S Beverly Dr
Suite 500
Beverly Hills, CA 90212-4425, USA

Delvecchio, Alexander P (Alex) (Athlete, Hockey Player)
Pen Pro
2602 Stood leigh Dr
Rochester Hills, MI 48309-2836, USA

DelVecchio, Paul (DJ Pauly D) (Reality TV Star)
c/o Amanda Ruisi *AKR Public Relations*
Prefers to be contacted via email or telephone
New York, NY, USA

Del-Vikings, The (Music Group)
PO Box 770850
Orlando, FL 32877, USA

Demaestri, Joe (Athlete, Baseball Player)
50 Fairway Dr
Novato, CA 94949-5904, USA

DeMaiziere, Lothar (Prime Minister)
Am Kupfergraben 6/6A
Berlin 10117, GERMANY

Demao, Al (Athlete, Football Player)
16206 Atlantis Dr
Bowie, MD 20716, USA

Demar, Enoch (Athlete, Football Player)
1579 Olympian Cir SW
Atlanta, GA 30310, USA

Demarchelier, Patrick (Photographer)
162 W 21st St
New York, NY 10011-3244, USA

Demarco, Ab (Athlete, Hockey Player)
211 Regal Rd
North Bay, ON P1B 8G4, Canada

Demarco, Bob (Athlete, Football Player)
13055 Midfield Ter
Saint Louis, MO 63146-6053, USA

DeMarco, Guido (President)
President's Office
Palace
Valletta, MALTA

DeMarco, Jean (Artist)
Cervaro
Prov-Frosinore 03044, ITALY

Demarco, Robert (Bob) (Athlete, Football Player)
13055 Midfield Ter
Saint Louis, MO 63146, USA

DeMarco, Tony (Boxer)
PO Box 53664
Indianapolis, IN 46253, USA

DeMarcus, Jay (Musician)
24 Inveraray
Nashville, TN 37215, USA

Demarest, Arthur A (Archaeologist)
Vanderbilt University
Anthropology Dept
Nashville, TN 37235, USA

Demarie, John (Athlete, Football Player)
2019 Choupique Rd
Sulphur, LA 70663, USA

Demars, Billy (Athlete, Baseball Player)
770 Island Way
Apt 305
Clearwater, FL 33767-1824, USA

Demars, Bruce (Admiral)
41 Manters Point Road
Plymouth, MA 02360, USA

Demartino, Ricci (Stylist)
c/o Staff Member *Cloutier Agency*
2632 La Cienega Ave
Los Angeles, CA 90034, USA

de Matteo, Drea (Actor)
8803 Appian Way
Los Angeles, CA 90046, USA

Dembo, Fennis (Athlete, Basketball Player)
430 North Pine Street
San Antonio, TX 78202-2850, USA

DeMedeiros, Maria (Actor, Director, Writer)
c/o Staff Member *Alsira García-Maroto Talent Agency*
Calle De Los Invencibles 8
Bajo
Madrid 28019, Spain

Demel, Sam (Athlete, Baseball Player)
18650 N 120th Pl
Scottsdale, AZ 85259, USA

DeMenezes, Fradique (President)
President's Office
Pargo do Povo
Sao Tome, SAO TOME & PRINCIPE

DeMent, Iris (Songwriter, Writer)
c/o Staff Member *Paradigm (Monterey)*
404 W Franklin St
Monterey, CA 93940, USA

DeMent, Jack (Misc)
Oregon Health Care Center
11325 NE Weidler St
#44
Portland, OR 97220, USA

Dement, Kenneth (Athlete, Football Player)
8 Bel Air Dr
Sikeston, MO 63801-1916, USA

Dementieva, Elena (Tennis Player)
c/o Staff Member *Octagon (VA)*
1751 Pinnacle Dr #1500
McLean, VA 22102, USA

DeMerchant, Paul (Religious Leader)
Missionary Church
PO Box 9127
Fort Wayne, IN 46899, USA

Demerit, John (Athlete, Baseball Player)
550 W Walters St
Port Washington, WI 53074-1430, USA

DeMerritt, Marty (Athlete, Baseball Player)
7511 Creekridge Ln
Citrus Heights, CA 95610-3273, USA

Demery, Larry (Athlete, Baseball Player)
10627 Kurt St
Svlmar, CA 91342-6838, USA

Demeter, Don (Athlete, Baseball Player)
6240 S Country Club Dr
Oklahoma City, OK 73159-1844, USA

Demeter, Steve (Athlete, Baseball Player)
6032 Ravine Blvd
Cleveland, OH 44134-3047, USA

Demetral, Chris (Actor)
c/o Jamie Gold *JMG Management*
18000 Coastline Dr #8
Malibu, CA 90265, USA

Demetriadis, Phoklon (Cartoonist)
3rd September St 174
Athens, GREECE

Demetrios (Religious Leader)
Greek Orthodox Church
89 E 79th St
#19
New York, NY 10021, USA

Demeulemeester, Ann (Designer, Fashion Designer)
c/o Staff Member *Ann Demeulemeester*
6 Rue Milne Edwards
Paris 75017, France

Demic, Larry (Athlete, Basketball Player)
680 South Lassen Court
Anaheim, CA 92804-3123, USA

DeMille, Nelson (Writer)
61 Hilton Ave
#23
Garden City, NY 11530-2813, USA

Demin, Lev S (Cosmonaut)
Potchta Kosmonavtov
Moskovskol Oblasti
Syvisdny Goroduk 141160, RUSSIA

Deming, Peter (Cinematographer)
Sandra Marsh Mgmt
9150 Wilshire Blvd
#220
Beverly Hills, CA 90212, USA

DeMita, L Ciriaco (Prime Minister)
Partito Democrazia Cristiana
Piazza de Gesu 46
Rome 00186, ITALY

Demme, Jonathan (Director, Producer, Writer)
15 Castle Heights Ave
Nyack, NY 10960, USA

Demmings, Pancho (Actor)
c/o Judy Orbach *Judy O Productions*
6136 Glen Holly
Hollywood, CA 90068, USA

de Mol, John (Producer)
c/o Staff Member *WmE2 (WMA-LA)*
1 William Morris Pl
Beverly Hills, CA 90212, USA

Demola, Don (Athlete, Baseball Player)
352 Village Dr
Hauppauge, NY 11788-3225, USA

de Molina, Raul (Actor)
c/o Staff Member *Univision*
605 3rd St. Fl12
New York, NY 10158, USA

Demong, Bill (Athlete, Olympic Athlete, Skier)
1607 Pheasant Way
Park City, UT 84098-5417, USA

Demon Hunter (Music Group)
c/o Staff Member *Agency Group Ltd, The (NY)*
142 West 57th St
6th Floor
New York, NY 10019, USA

DeMont, Rick (Athlete, Swimmer)
P.O. Box 1453
Waianae, HI 96792-6453, USA

DeMontebello, Philippe L (Misc)
Metropolitan Museum of Art
82nd St & 5th Ave
New York, NY 10028, USA

DeMornay, Rebecca (Actor)
2179 Castilian Dr
Los Angeles, CA 90068, USA

Demory, Joe (Athlete, Football Player)

Demoss, Bob (Athlete, Football Player)
117 Knox Dr
West Lafayette, IN 47906, USA

Demoss, Darcy (Actor)
7732 Chandelle Pl
Los Angeles, CA 90046, USA

Demps, Will (Athlete)
c/o Staff Member *EAG Sports Management*
12910 Agustin Pl
Playa Vista, CA 90094, USA

Dempsey, Cedric (Misc)
National Collegiate Athletic Assn
70 W Washington St
Indianapolis, IN 46204, USA

Dempsey, George (Athlete, Basketball Player)
6945 Cedar Avenue
Pennsauken, NJ 08109-2713, USA

Dempsey, Mark (Athlete, Baseball Player)
673 W Martindale Rd
Englewood, OH 45322-3043, USA

Dempsey, Michael (Actor)
c/o Vincent Cirrincione *Vincent Cirrincione Associates*
1516 N Fairfax Ave
Los Angeles, CA 90046, USA

Dempsey, Nathan (Athlete, Hockey Player)
c/o Art Breeze *Pro-Rep Entertainment Consulting*
113-276 Midpark Way SE
Calgary, AB T2X 1J6, Canada

Dempsey, Pat (Baseball Player)
10116 Oro Vista Ave
Sunland, CA 91040-3238, USA

Dempsey, Patrick (Actor)
29715 Cuthbert Rd
Malibu, CA 90265, USA

Dempsey, Rick (Athlete, Baseball Player)
1673 Crown Ridge Ct
Westlake VIllage, CA 91362-4731, USA

Dempsey, Robert (Scientist)
11622 Mighty Redwood Dr
Houston, TX 77059-5589, USA

Dempsey, Tanya (Actor)
c/o Dino May *Dino May Management*
6362 Hollywood Blvd #422
Hollywood, CA 90028-6323, USA

Dempsey, Thomas (Tom) (Athlete, Football Player)
541 Juluis Ave
New Orleans, LA 70121, USA

Dempster, Ryan (Athlete, Baseball Player)
3537 N Greenview Ave
Chicago, IL 60657-1317, USA

Demsetz, Harold (Economist)
University of California
Economics Dept
Los Angeles, CA 90024, USA

Demsey, Todd (Athlete, Golfer)
8140 E Arroyo Seco Rd
Scottsdale, AZ 85266, USA

DeMunn, Jeffrey (Actor)
c/o Staff Member *Gersh (LA)*
9465 Wilshire Blvd
Suite 600
Beverly Hills, CA 90212, USA

De Munn, Jeffrey (Jeff) (Actor)
c/o Larry Taube *Principal Entertainment (LA)*
1964 Westwood Blvd #400
Los Angeles, CA 90025, USA

DeMuron, Pierre (Architect)
Herzog & De Meuron Architekten
Rheinschanze 6
Basel 4056, SWITZERLAND

Demus, Jorg (Musician)
LYRA
Doblinger Hauptstr 77-A/10
Vienna 1190, AUSTRIA

Demus, Lashinda (Athlete, Track Athlete)
c/o Staff Member *Pure Perception PR*
10535 Rose Ave
#2
Los Angeles, CA 90034, USA

Demuth, Dana (Athlete, Baseball Player)
1156 W Wagner Dr
Gilbert, AZ 85233-7980, USA

Demuth, Richard H (Attorney, Attorney General, Financier, General)
7 Eliot Road
Lexington, MA 02421-5649, USA

Den, Tagayasu (Choreographer)
Ondekoza
Koda Performing Arts Co
Sado Island, JAPAN

Denard, Michael (Dancer)
Paris Opera Ballet
Place de l'Opera
Paris 75009, FRANCE

Denberg, Lori Beth (Actor)
c/o Staff Member *Acme Talent & Literary (LA)*
1400 Atlantic Ave
Suite 274
Long Beach, CA 90814, USA

Denbo, Gary (Athlete, Baseball Player)
27740 Water Ash Dr
Wesley Chapel, FL 33544-8752, USA

Denby-Ashe, Daniela (Actor)

Dench, Judi (Actor)
c/o Gene Parseghian *Parseghian Planco LLC*
322 8th Ave
Suite 601
New York, NY 10001, USA

Dencik, David (Actor)
c/o Alissa Feldman *Magnolia Entertainment (LA)*
9595 Wilshire Blvd
Suite 601
Beverly Hills, CA 90212, USA

Denebeim, Amy (Stylist)
c/o Staff Member *Artist Untied (LA)*
845 S Mansfield Ave
#1
Los Angeles, CA 90036, USA

Denehy, Bill (Athlete, Baseball Player)
5008 Eastwinds Dr
Orlando, FL 32819-3518, USA

Denes, Agnes C (Artist)
595 Broadway
New York, NY 10012, USA

Deneuve, Catherine (Actor)
c/o Claire Blondel *ArtMedia*
20 avenue Rapp
Paris 75008, France

Deng, Luol (Athlete, Basketball Player)
3280 Sunset Trl
Northbrook, IL 60062-6332, USA

Denham, Jeff (Congressman, Politician)
1605 Longworth HOB
Washington, DC 20515, USA

Denhardt, David T (Biologist)
Rutgers University
Nelson Biological Laboratories
Piscataway, NJ 08855, USA

Den Herder, Vern W (Athlete, Football Player)
2342 Riviera Rd
Sioux Center, IA 51250, USA

Denicourt, Marianne (Actor)
Artmedia
20 Ave Rapp
Paris 75007, FRANCE

De Niro, Robert (Actor)
242 Old Montauk Hwy
Montauk, NY 11954, USA

Denis, Louis (Athlete, Hockey Player)
412-1450 First St E
Cornwall, ON K6H 6H2, Canada

Denis, Marc (Athlete, Hockey Player)
Montreal Canadiens
1275 Rue Saint-Antoine 0
Montreal, QC H3C SL2, Canada

Denisof, Alexis (Actor)
c/o Nancy Gates *United Talent Agency (UTA)*
9336 Civic Center Dr
Beverly Hills, CA 90210, USA

Denison, Anthony (Actor)
10100 Santa Monica Blvd
#1060
Los Angeles, CA 90067, USA

Denisov, Edison V (Composer)
Studentcheskaia 44/28
#35
Moscow 121165, RUSSIA

Denisse, Francois-Jean (Astronomer)
48 Rue Monsieur Le Prince
Paris 75006, FRANCE

Denisyuk, Yuri N (Engineer)
Vavilov Optical Institute
12 Burzhevaya
Saint Petersburg 199034, RUSSIA

Denker, Travis (Athlete, Baseball Player)
845 Palmetto Pl
Brea, CA 92821-4127, USA

Denkinger, Don (Athlete, Baseball Player)
3505 Kingswood Pl
Waterloo, IA 50701-4537, USA

Denman, Brian (Athlete, Baseball Player)
16 Cindy Dr
Buffalo, NY 14221-3002, USA

Denman, David (Actor)
c/o Rebecca (Becca) Kovacik *Hofflund/Polone*
9465 Wilshire Blvd #420
Beverly Hills, CA 90212, USA

Denman, Tony (Actor)
c/o Beverly Strong *Strong Management*
3532 Hayden Ave
Culver City, CA 90232, USA

Dennard, Kenny (Athlete, Basketball Player)
6641 Westchester Avenue
Houston, TX 77005-3755, USA

Dennard, Mark (Athlete, Football Player)
4990 Afton Oaks Dr
College Station, TX 77845, USA

Dennard, Preston (Athlete, Football Player)
4545 Green Ave NW
Albuquerque, NM 87114, USA

Dennard, Robert (Inventor)
2054 Quaker Ridge Rd
Croton On Hudson, NY 10520-3514, USA

Dennehy, Brian (Actor)
141 Joy Rd
Woodstock, CT 06281, USA

Dennehy, Kathleen (Actor)
Susan Nathe
8281 Melrose Ave
#200
Los Angeles, CA 90046, USA

Dennen, Barry (Actor, Musician)
6923 Camrose Dr
Los Angeles, CA 90068, USA

Dennen, Brett (Musician)
c/o Michael McDonald *Mick Management*
35 Washington St
Brooklyn, NY 11201, USA

Denneriein, Barbara (Musician)
Tsingtauer Str 66
Munich 81827, GERMANY

Dennert-Hill, Pauline (Athlete, Baseball Player, Commentator)
415 Clinton St
Owosso, MI 48867-2718, USA

Dennett, Daniel C (Misc)
20 Ironwood Road
North Andover, MA 01845, USA

Denney, Kyle (Athlete, Baseball Player)
P.O. Box 300
Prague, OK 74864-0300, USA

Denney, Mike (Athlete, Football Player)
6419 Oakley St
Philadelphia, PA 19111, USA

Denney, Ryan (Athlete, Football Player)
351 Silver Cir
Alpine, UT 84004, USA

Denning, Blaine (Athlete, Basketball Player)
1283 NW Bentley Circle
Port Saint Lucie, FL 34986-1834, USA

Denning, Hazel M (Writer)
Llewellyn Worldwide
PO Box 64383
St Paul, MN 55164-0383

Denning, Jon (Race Car Driver)
Dobbs Motorsports
23 Springfield Ave
Springfield, NJ 07081, USA

Dennings, Kat (Actor)
c/o Nicole King *Management 360*
9111 Wilshire Blvd
Beverly Hills, CA 90210, USA

Dennis, Cathy (Musician)
19 Music
Ransomes Gate #32
35-37 Parkgate
London SW11 4NP, UNITED KINGDOM
(UK)

Dennis, Clark (Athlete, Golfer)
4117 Sarita Dr
Fort Worth, TX 76109-4743, USA

Dennis, Donna F (Artist)
131 Duane St
New York, NY 10013, USA

Dennis, Gabrielle (Actor)
c/o Staff Member *JC Robbins Management*
113 S Kilkea Dr
Los Angeles, CA 90048, USA

Dennis, Guy (Athlete, Football Player)
PO Box 2500
Hawthorne, FL 32640, USA

Dennis, Jim (Race Car Driver)
1810 Little Masters Corner Road
Harrington, DE 19952, USA

Dennis, Lisl (Photographer)
3101 Old Pecos Trl
Unit 698
Santa Fe, NM 87505-9548, USA

Dennis, Marc (Athlete, Hockey Player)
16336 Bumiston Drive
Tampa, FL 33647-2763, USA

Dennis, Mark (Athlete, Football Player)
52 Cambridge Ln
Lincolnshire, IL 60069, USA

Dennis, Mark (Athlete, Football Player)
52 Cambridge Ln
Lincolnshire, IL 60069-3101, USA

Dennis, Mike (Athlete, Football Player)
332 Long Cove Dr
Madison, MS 39110, USA

Dennis, Mike (Athlete, Football Player)
332 Long Cove Dr
Madison, MS 39110-9183, USA

Dennis, Mike (Musician)
American Promotions
2011 Ferry Ave
#U19
Camden, NJ 08104, USA

Dennis, Norm (Athlete, Hockey Player)
1531 Highway 3-B
Fruitvale, BC V0G 1L0, Canada

Dennis, Pamela (Designer, Fashion Designer)
c/o Jerry Shandrew *Shandrew Public Relations*
1050 S Stanley Ave
Los Angeles, CA 90019-6634, USA

Dennis, Pat (Athlete, Football Player)
600 S MacArthur Blvd Apt 2821
Coppell, TX 75019-6733, USA

Dennison, Bonnie (Actor)
c/o Staff Member *Terrific Talent Associates*
419 Park Ave #1009
New York, NY 10016, USA

Dennison, Doug (Athlete, Football Player)
2309 Daybreak Trl
Plano, TX 75093, USA

Dennison, Glenn (Athlete, Football Player)
1104 Tucker Ln
Ashton, MD 20861, USA

Dennison, Rick (Athlete, Football Player)
12322 Overcup Dr
Houston, TX 77024, USA

Denny, Christopher (Musician)
c/o Staff Member *Paradigm (Monterey)*
404 W Franklin St
Monterey, CA 93940, USA

Denny, Dorothy (Actor)
15707 La Verida Dr
Victorville, CA 92395-3413, USA

Denny, Floyd W Jr (Misc)
1 Carolina Meadows
#308
Chapel Hill, NC 27517, USA

Denny, John (Athlete, Baseball Player)
13750 W Colonial Dr Ste 350
Winter Garden, FL 34787-6148, USA

Denny, Robyn (Artist)
20/30 Wilds Rents
#4B
London SE14QG, UNITED KINGDOM
(UK)

Denny, Simone (Musician)
c/o Staff Member *Diva Central Inc*
7510 W Sunset Blvd Ste 1445
Los Angees, CA 90046, USA

Denorfia, Chris (Athlete, Baseball Player)
8 Hawks Nest Dr
Southampton, CT 06489-1372, USA

DenOuden, Wilerninintie (Willy)
(Swimmer)
Goudsewagenstraat 23B
Rotterdam, HOLLAND

Densham, Gary (Race Car Driver)
Densham Racing
16661 Grand St.
Bellflower, CA 90701, USA

Densham, Pen (Director)
International Creative Mgmt
8942 Wilshire Blvd
#219
Beverly Hills, CA 90211, USA

Densmore, Elizabeth (Actor)
c/o Sharon Lane *Lane Management Group*
13017 Woodbridge St
Studio City, CA 91604, USA

Densmore, John (Musician)
49 Haldeman Rd
Santa Monica, CA 90402, USA

Denson, Al (Athlete, Football Player)
6019 Bart Rd
Jacksonville, FL 32209, USA

Denson, Autry (Athlete, Football Player)
1025 S Beach St Apt 30
Daytona Beach, FL 32114, USA

Denson, Drew (Athlete, Baseball Player)
1718 Avonlea Ave
Cincinnati, OH 45237-6110, USA

Denson, Keith (Athlete, Football Player)
28024 Eagle Peak Ave
Canyon Country, CA 91387, USA

Denson, Moses (Athlete, Football Player)
14005 Drake Dr
Rockville, MD 20853, USA

Dent, Bucky (Athlete, Baseball Player, Coach)
8895 Indian River Run
Boynton Beach, FL 33472-2445, USA

Dent, Burnell (Athlete, Football Player)
2904 Essex Ave
La Place, LA 70068, USA

Dent, Catherine (Actor)
3330 Appleton St
Los Angeles, CA 90039, USA

Dent, Frederick (Politician)
221 Montgornery St
Spartanburg, SC 29302-3443, USA

Dent, Jim (Athlete, Golfer)
P.O. Box 290656
Tampa, FL 33687-0656, USA

Dent, Richard L (Athlete, Coach, Football Coach, Football Player)
4453 RFD
Long Grove, IL 60047, USA

Dent, Robert (Bob) (Athlete, Football Player)
6669 Embarcadero Dr
Apt 7
Stockton, CA 95219, USA

Dent, Russell E (Bucky) (Athlete, Baseball Player)
Bucky Dent Baseball School
490 Dotterel Rd
Delray Beach, FL 33444, USA

Dent, Taylor (Athlete, Tennis Player)
7143 Hawks Harbor Cir
Bradenton, FL 34207, USA

Denton, Derek A (Physicist)
816 Irring Road
Toorak, VIC 3142, AUSTRALIA

Denton, James (Actor)
1620 Lamego Dr
Glendale, CA 91207, USA

Denton, Jeremiah (Politician)
531 Thomas Bransby
Williamsburg, VA 23185-8245, USA

Denton, Judy (Writer)
400 Main St S
Atwater, MN 56209, USA

Denton, Kelly (Race Car Driver)
Henderson Motosports
566 E. Main St.
Abington, VA 24210, USA

Denton, Mona (Baseball Player)
1880 S Newton St
Denver, CO 80219-4503, USA

Denton, Randy (Athlete, Basketball Player)
515 Sunnybrook Road
Raleigh, NC 27610-2850, USA

Denton, Sandi (Pepa) (Musician)
Famous Artists Agency
250 W 57th St
New York, NY 10107, USA

Denton, Sandra (Pepa) (Musician)
570/580 Johnson Ave
Aspen, CO 81611, USA

Denvir, John (Athlete, Football Player)
23250 Walker Basin Rd
Caliente, CA 93518, USA

Denzongapa, Danny (Actor, Bollywood)
Dzongrilla 11th Road
Juhu
Mumbai, MS, INDIA

Deol, Bobby (Actor, Bollywood)
Plot No 22, 11th Road
JVPD Scheme Juhu
Mumbai, MS 400049, INDIA

Deol, Dharmendra (Actor, Bollywood)
Plot No 22 11th Rd
Juhu
Mumbai, MS 400049, INDIA

Deol, Sunny (Actor, Bollywood)
Plot No 22
11th Road JVPD Scheme
Mumbai, MS 400026, INDIA

DeOre, Bill (Cartoonist)
Dallas News
Editorial Dept
Communications Center
Dallas, TX 75265, USA

Deossie, Steve (Athlete, Football Player)
835 Chestnut St
North Andover, MA 01845, USA

de Pablo, Cote (Actor)
c/o Catherine Olim *PMK/BNC Public Relations (PMK-LA)*
8687 Melrose Ave Fl 8
West Hollywood, CA 90069, USA

De Palma, Brian (Director)
302 Marguerita Ave
Santa Monica, CA 90402, USA

Depalo, Jim (Baseball Player)
TCMA
4727 7th Ave SW
Naples, FL 34119-4039, USA

DePalva, James (Actor)
PO Box 11152
Greenwich, CT 06831, USA

DePaola, Tomie (Actor, Writer)
c/o Staff Member *Penguin Putnam Books for Young Readers*
345 Hudson Street
New York, NY 10014

Depardieu, Gerard (Actor)
c/o Amanda Bross *Finch & Partners - Paris*
Top Floor
29-37 Heddon St
London W1B 4BR, UNITED KINGDOM

Depardon, Raymond (Photographer)
18 Bis Rue Henri Barbusse
Paris 75005, FRANCE

Departure, Themm (Music Group)
c/o Staff Member *Paradigm (Monterey)*
404 W Franklin St
Monterey, CA 93940, USA

Depaso, Tom (Athlete, Football Player)
2108 Polo Pointe Dr
Vienna, VA 22181, USA

de Passe, Suzanne (Producer)
9701 Oak Pass Rd
Beverly Hills, CA 90210, USA

Depastino, Joe (Athlete, Baseball Player)
12853 Sheringham Way
Sarasota, FL 34240-8762, USA

De Paul, Lynsey
21A Clifftown Rd
Southend-on-Sea Essex, ENGLAND SSl
1AB

Depaula, Sean (Athlete, Baseball Player)
2 Thomas St
Derry, NH 03038-2988, USA

DePavia, James
PO Box 11152
Greenwich, CT 06831

Depeche Mode (Music Group)
c/o Jonathan Kessler *Baron, Inc*
235 S Westgate Ave
Los Angeles, CA 90049, USA

DePeyer, Gervase
Porto Vecchio 109
1250 S Washington St
Alexandria, VA 22314, USA

Deply, Julie (Actor)
c/o Glenn Rigberg *HYPHENATE*
9701 Wilshire Blvd.
10th floor
Beverly Hills, CA 90212, USA

Depodesta, Paul (Commentator)
2775 Costebelle Dr
La Jolla, CA 92037-3518, USA

DePortzamparc, Christian (Architect)
Architecte DPLG
1 Rue de L'Aude
Paris 75014, FRANCE

DePoyster, Jerry D (Athlete, Football Player)
P.O. Box 3029
Rock Springs, WY 82902, USA

Depp, Johnny (Actor, Director)
1480 N Sweetzer Ave
West Hollywood, CA 90069, USA

Depre, Joe (Athlete, Basketball Player)
59 Oneida Street
Rochester, NY 14621-4027, USA

DePree, Hopwood (Actor)
c/o Staff Member *ROAR (LA)*
9701 Wilshire Blvd
8th Floor
Los Angeles, CA 90212, USA

DePreist, James A (Conductor)
Konsert AB
Kungsgatan 32
Stockholm 11135, SWEDEN

DePrume, Cathryn (Actor)
c/o Staff Member *Flick Commercials*
9057 Nemo St #A
W Hollywood, CA 90069, USA

Dequenne, Emilie (Actor)
c/o Daniele Gain *Cineart*
36 Rue de Ponthieu
Paris F-75008, France

Dequenne, Emilie (Cartoonist)
Houston Post
Editorial Dept
4888 Loop Cantral Dr #390
Houston, TX 77081, USA

de Ravin, Emilie (Actor)
c/o Darren Goldberg *Global Creative*
1051 Cole Ave # B
Los Angeles, CA 90038, USA

Derbez, Eugenio (Producer, Writer)
c/o Susan Weaving *WME (WMA-NY)*
1325 Ave of the Americas
New York, NY 10019, USA

Derbez, Silvia (Actor)
c/o Staff Member *Televisa*
Blvd Adolfo Lopez Mateos 232
Colonia San Angel INN
DF CP 01060, MEXICO

Derby, Dean (Athlete, Football Player)
1682 Corkrum Rd
Walla Walla, WA 99362, USA

Derbyshire, Andrew G (Architect)
4 Sunnyfield
Hatfield
Herts AL9 5DX, UNITED KINGDOM (UK)

Derek, Bo (Actor, Model)
P.O. Box 1940
Santa Ynez, CA 93460, USA

Dereuck, Colleen (Athlete)
4172 Saint Croix St
Boulder, CO 80301, USA

Dergan, Lisa (Actor, Model, Television Host)
c/o Jon Orlando *WNWN Media*
348 S. Hauser Blvd #PH414
Los Angeles, CA 90036, USA

Derhak, Rob (Musician)
45 Hadlock Rd
Falmouth, ME 04105, USA

Deriso, Walter M Jr (Financier)
Synovus Financial Corp
901 Front Ave
PO Box 120
Columbus, GA 31902, USA

Derlago, Bill (Athlete, Hockey Player)
Seven View Chrysler
2685 Highway 7
Concord, ON L4K 1V8, Canada

Derline, Rodney (Athlete, Basketball Player)
12612 SE 215th Street
Kent, WA 98031-2287, USA

Dern, Bruce (Actor)
P.O. Box 1581
Santa Monica, CA 90406, USA

Dern, Laura (Actor)
2314 La Mesa Dr
Santa Monica, CA 90402, USA

Dernesch, Helga (Opera Singer)
Neutorgasse 2/22
Vienna 1013, AUSTRIA

Dernier, Bob (Athlete, Baseball Player)
1242 SW Arbormill Ter
Lees Summit, MO 64082-4165, USA

Deroo, Brian (Athlete, Football Player)
49224 Escalante St
Indio, CA 92201, USA

Derosa, Mark (Athlete, Baseball Player)
878 Crescent River Pass
Suwanee, GA 30024-1761, USA

DeRosa, William (Misc)
Columbia Artists Mgmt Inc
165 W 57th St
New York, NY 10019, USA

DeRosier, David (Physicist)
27 Chesterfield Road
Newton, MA 02465, USA

Derosier, Michael (Musician)
Borman Entertainment
1250 6th St
#401
Santa Monica, CA 90401, USA

De Rosnay, Tatiana (Writer)
c/o Staff Member *Bazar Forlag*
Hammarby Fabriksvag 25
Stockholm 12033, Sweden

De Rossi, Portia (Actor)
c/o Megan Moss Pachon *ID Public Relations (ID-LA)*
7060 Hollywood Blvd
8th Floor
Los Angeles, CA 90028, USA

de Rothschild, David (Producer)
Adventure Ecology
Zetland House
5/25 Scrutton St
London EC2A 4HJ, UK

Derow, Peter A (Publisher)
PO Box 534
Bedford, NY 10506, USA

Derr, Kenneth T (Business Person)
Chevron Corp
6001 Bollinger Canyon Road
San Ramon, CA 94583, USA

Derrick, Edward (Athlete, Baseball Player)
P.O. Box 158473
Nashville, TN 37215, USA

Derricks, Cleavant (Actor)
480 Burano Court
Agoura Hills, CA 91377, USA

Derrickson, Scott (Director)
2026 W Mountain St
Glendale, CA 91201, USA

D'Errico, Donna (Actor, Model)
4356 Hillview Dr
Malibu, CA 90265, USA

Derringer, Rick (Musician)
c/o Steve Peck *Fantasma Productions Inc*
854 Conniston Road
West Palm Beach, FL 33405-2131, USA

Derrington, Bob (Race Car Driver)
1704 Aspen Lane
Searbook, TX 77586, USA

Derrington, Jim (Athlete, Baseball Player)
711 Sandlewood Ave
La Habra, CA 90631-7248, USA

Derry, Kathy (Physicist)
PO Box 1656
Laguna Beach, CA 92652, USA

Derryberry, Debi (Actor)
P.O. Box 2726
Toluca Lake, CA 91610-0726, USA

Dersch, Hans (Swimmer)
7217 E 55th Place
Tulsa, OK 74145, USA

Dershowitz, Alan (Attorney)
1563 Massachusetts Ave
Cambridge, MA 02138-2903, USA

DeRulo, Jason (Musician)
c/o John Marx *WME (LA)*
9601 Wilshire Blvd Fl 3
Beverly Hills, CA 90210, USA

Dervan, Peter B (Misc)
California Institute of Technology
Chemistry Dept
Pasadena, CA 91125, USA

Derwin, Mark (Actor)
4034 Lamarr Ave
Culver City, CA 90232, USA

Desai, Anita (Writer)
Deborah Rogers Ltd
20 Powis Mews
London W11 1JN, UNITED KINGDOM (UK)

Desai, Anoop (Musician)

Desai, Ketan (Bollywood, Director, Producer)
3C Swapnalok Jagmohandas Marg
Bombay, MS 400 026, INDIA

Desailly, Marcel (Soccer Player)
FC Chelsea Stamford Bridge
Fulham Road
London SW6 1HS, UNITED KINGDOM (UK)

Desalvo, Matt (Athlete, Baseball Player)
10 Village Gate Blvd
Delaware, OH 43015-8844, USA

deSando, Anthony
PO Box 5617
Beverly Hills, CA 90210

deSantis, Guiseppe
Fiano Romano Via del Commercio 1
Rome, ITALY I-00154

DeSantis, Jaclyn (Actor)
c/o Sarah Fargo *Paradigm (NY)*
360 Park Ave S Fl 16
New York, NY 10010, USA

deSantis, Luigi
Via della Villa di Lucina 72
Rome, ITALY I-00145

Desanto, Tom (Producer)
c/o Renee Kurtz *Creative Artists Agency (CAA-LA)*
1 William Morris Pl
Beverly Hills, CA 90212, USA

Des Barres, Michael (Actor)
c/o Pam Ellis *Ellis Talent Group*
4705 Laurel Canyon Blvd
Suite 300
Valley Village, CA 91607, USA

Descalso, Daniel (Athlete, Baseball Player)
1937 Eaton Ave
San Carlos, CA 94070-4740, USA

Descendants, The
4230 Del Rey Avenue #621
Marina del Rey, CA 90292, USA

Deschaine, Dick (Athlete, Football Player)
205 Cavil Way
De Pere, WI 54115, USA

Deschanel, Caleb (Cinematographer)
Dark Light Pictures
812 N Highland Ave
Los Angeles, CA 90038, USA

Deschanel, Emily (Actor)
c/o Lainie Sorkin Becky *Management 360*
9111 Wilshire Blvd
Beverly Hills, CA 90210, USA

Deschanel, Mary Jo (Actor)
844 Chautauqua Blvd
Pacific Palisades, CA 90272, USA

Deschanel, Zooey (Actor)
c/o Sarah Jackson *Seven Summits Pictures & Management*
8906 W Olympic Blvd
Ground Floor
Beverly Hills, CA 90211, USA

Descher, Sandra (Actor)
4544 Arcola Ave
North Hollywood, CA 91602, USA

Descombes-Dinehart, Nancy (Baseball Player)
59607 County Road 11
Elkhart, IN 46517-9178, USA

DesCombes Lesko, Jeneane (Baseball Player)
4401 145th Ave NE
Apt J5
Bellevue, WA 98007-3160, USA

Descombes-Lesko, Jeneane (Athlete, Baseball Player, Commentator)
11227 NE 109th Ln Apt L108
Kirkland, WA 98033-5029, USA

Desert, Alex (Actor)
2572 Verbena Dr
Los Angeles, CA 90068, USA

deSeve, Peter (Artist)
25 Park Pl
Brooklyn, NY 11217, USA

Desfor, Max (Photographer)
15115 Interlachen Dr
Apt 1018
Silver Spring, MD 20906-5644, USA

Deshaies, Jim (Baseball Player)
151 N TID'ior Point Dr
spring, TX 77382-1240, USA

Deshales, Jim (Athlete, Baseball Player)
151 N Taylor Point Dr
Spring, TX 77382, USA

DeShannon, Jackie (Musician)
606 N Arden Dr
Beverly Hills, CA 90210, USA

DeShields, Delino L (Athlete, Baseball Player)
3399 Kiveton Ct
Norcross, GA 30092-3374, USA

Desiderio, Robert (Actor)
1475 Sierra Vista Dr
Aspen, CO 81611, USA

Desilva, John (Athlete, Baseball Player)
32750 Airport Rd
Fort Bragg, CA 95437-9514, USA

de Silva, Jorge (Actor)
c/o Staff Member *Televisa*
Blvd Adolfo Lopez Mateos 232
Colonia San Angel INN
DF CP 01060, MEXICO

DeSimone, Livio D (Desi) (Business Person)
Minnesota Mining & Manufacturing
3M Center
Saint Paul, MN 55144, USA

Desjardins, Eric (Athlete, Hockey Player)
9 Woodglen Ln
Voorhees, NJ 08043, USA

Desjardins, Gerry (Athlete, Hockey Player)
252 Suffolk Pl
London, ON N6G 3S4, Canada

Des Jardins, Richard (Stylist)
140 7th Ave
#2-F
New York, NY 10011, USA

DesJarlais, Scott (Congressman, Politician)
413 Cannon HOB
Washington, DC 20515, USA

Deskins, Donald (Athlete, Football Player)
3240 Pittsview Dr
Ann Arbor, MI 48108, USA

Deskur, Andrzej Maria Cardinal (Religious Leader)
Palazzo S Carlo
 00120, VATICAN CITY

Deslauriers, Jacques (Athlete, Hockey Player)
8874 Sainte-Claire St
Montreal, QC H1L 1Y8, Canada

Deslongchamps, Pierre (Misc)
1884 Rue des Orioles
Laval, QC H7L 5T8, CANADA

Desman, Shawn (Musician)
c/o Staff Member *BMG*
1540 Broadway
New York, NY 10036, USA

Desmond, Ian
8023 36th Street Cir E
Sarasota, FL 34243-6309

Desmormeaux, Kent (Jockey)
Desmormeaux Racing Stable
385 W Huntington Dr
Arcadia, CA 91007, USA

Desormeaux, Kent (Horse Racer)
c/o Staff Member *Jockeys Guild*
103 Wind Haven Dr
Suite 200
Nicholasville, KY 40356, USA

De Souza, Steven (Producer, Writer)
c/o Alan Gasmer *Alan Gasmer Management Company*
10877 Wilshire Blvd.
Suite 603
Los Angeles, CA 90024, USA

Despadovich, Nada
6500 Wilshire Blvd #2200
Los Angeles, CA 90048, USA

Despotopoulos, Johannes (Jan) (Architect)
Anapiron Polemou 7
Athens 11521, GREECE

Des'ree (Musician)
Solo Agency
55 Fulham High St
London SW6 3JJ, UNITED KINGDOM (UK)

Dess, Darrell (Athlete, Football Player)
224 Summer Ave
New Castle, PA 16105, USA

Dessay, Natalie (Opera Singer)
Herbert Breslin
119 W 57th St
#1505
New York, NY 10019, USA

Dessens, Elmer (Athlete, Baseball Player)
5542 E Estrid Ave
Scottsdale, AZ 85254-2973, USA

Destiny's Child (Music Group)
c/o Matthew Knowles *Music World Entertainment*
1384 Broadway #2200
New York, NY 10018, USA

Destrade, Orestes (Athlete, Baseball Player)
10653 Garda Dr
Trinity, FL 34655-7051, USA

Destri, Jimmy (Misc)
Shore Fire Media
32 Court St
#1600
Brooklyn, NY 11201, USA

Desurvive, Emmanuel (Engineer)
Alcatel Submarine Networks
Villarceaux Centre
Nozay 91625, FRANCE

Desutter, Wayne (Athlete, Football Player)
4450 Antietam Creek Trl
Leesburg, FL 34748, USA

De Swert, Nico (Stylist)
c/o Staff Member *Bernstein & Andriulli*
58 W 40th St
New York, NY 10018, USA

DeTar, Dean E (War Hero)
7785 Portwood Road
Azle, TZ 76020, USA

De Teliga, Louise (Stylist)
c/o Staff Member *LA Rep*
8312 Utica Dr
Los Angeles, CA 90046, USA

Deters, Harold (Athlete, Football Player)
1602 Woods Creek Dr
Garner, NC 27529, USA

DeThe, Guy Blaudin (Biologist)
14 Rue Le Regrattier
Paris 75004, FRANCE

Detherage, Bob (Athlete, Baseball Player)
322 Turf Ln
Carl Junction, MO 64834-9575, USA

Detmer, Amanda (Actor)
c/o John Carrabino *John Carrabino Management*
5900 Wilshire Blvd Fl 4 #406
Los Angeles, CA 90036, USA

Detmer, Koy (Athlete, Football Player)
2906 Spring Bend St
San Antonio, TX 78209, USA

Detmer, Ty (Athlete, Football Player, Heisman Trophy Winner)
142 Lakota Pass
Austin, TX 78738-6563, USA

Detmers, Maruschka (Actor)
c/o Staff Member *Agence Alvares Correa*
34, Rue Jouffroy D'Abbans
Paris 75017, France

Detorie, Rick (Cartoonist)
Creators Syndicate
5777 W Century Blvd
#700
Los Angeles, CA 90045, USA

Detroit, Marcella (Musician, Songwriter, Writer)
MCM Mgmt
40 Langham St
#300
London W1N 5RG, UNITED KINGDOM (UK)

Dettlaff, Bill (Athlete, Golfer)
133 Clearlake Dr
Ponte Vedra Beach, FL 32082-2178, USA

Dettmer, John (Athlete, Baseball Player)
549 Hickory View Ln
Ballwin, MO 63011-1500, USA

Dettore, Tom (Athlete, Baseball Player)
1120 McEwen Ave
Canonsburg, PA 15317-1928, USA

Detweiler, David K (Physicist)
Waverty Heights
1400 Waverty Road #A212
Gladwyne, PA 19035, USA

Detweiler, Ducky (Athlete, Baseball Player)
312 Holt St
Federalsburg, MD 21632-1403, USA

Detweiler, Robert C (Educator)
1450 Ellis Ave
Cambria, CA 93428, USA

Detwiler, Chuck (Athlete, Football Player)
79898 Viento Dr
La Quinta, CA 92253, USA

Detwiler, Ross (Baseball Player)
359 Brown Swiss Cir
Duncansville, PA 16635-8061, USA

Deukmejian, C George (Ex-Governor)
5366 E Broadway
Long Beach, CA 90803, USA

Deukmejian, George (Politician)
5366 East Broadway
Long Beach, CA 90803-3549, USA

Deutch, Howard (Director)
International Creative Mgmt
8942 Wilshire Blvd
#219
Beverly Hills, CA 90211, USA

Deutch, Howie (Actor, Director, Producer, Writer)
c/o Daniel J Talbot *ICM Partners (ICM-LA)*
10250 Constellation Blvd Fl 7
Los Angeles, CA 90067, USA

Deutch, John (Politician)
51 Clifton St
Belmont, MA 02478-3353, USA

Deutekom, Cristina (Opera Singer)
Lancasterdreet 41
Dronten, TG 8251, HOLLAND

Deutsch, Dave (Athlete, Basketball Player)
315 Fairmount Road
Long Valley, NJ 07853-3012, USA

Deutsch, Donny (Television Host)
Open City Films
122 Hudson St 5th Fl
New York, NY 10013, USA

Deutsch, Liz (Stylist)
184 W 4th St
#8
New York, NY 10014, USA

Deutsch, Patti (Actor)
1811 San Ysidro Dr
Beverly Hills, CA 90210, USA

Dev, Mukul (Actor, Bollywood)
Karan Apts 5th Floor
Yari Road Versova
Mumbai, MS 40061, INDIA

Deva, Prabhu (Actor, Choreographer, Comedian, Dancer, Musician)
68 T T K Road
Alwarpet
Chennai, TN 600 018, INDIA

DeValeria, Dennis (Sportscaster)
213 Hillendale Road
Pittsburgh, PA 15237-1803, USA

Devane, William (Actor)
c/o Deborah Miller *Shelter Entertainment*
9454 Wilshire Blvd.
Suite 715
Beverly Hills, CA 90212, USA

Devarez, Cesar (Athlete, Baseball Player)
35 Arden St Apt B
New York, NY 10040-1318, USA

DeVarona, Donna (Athlete, Olympic Athlete, Swimmer)
TWI
3 Avon Ln
Greenwich, CT 06830-3926, USA

de Vasconcelos, Tasha (Actor)
c/o Samira Higham *Independent Talent Group (ITG-UK)*
Oxford House
76 Oxford St
London W1D 1BS, UK

DeVasquez, Devin (Model)
3165 Dona Christina Pl
Studio City, CA 91604, USA

Devaty, Susan (Stylist)
423 Pennsylvania Ave
#4
San Francisco, CA 94107, USA

Devaughn, Dennis (Athlete, Football Player)
2416 Clear Field Dr
Plano, TX 75025, USA

DeVaughn, Raheem (Actor, Musician)
c/o Eva Arthur *Universal Attractions*
135 W 26th St
12 Floor
New York, NY 10001, USA

Devault, Calvin (Actor)
c/o John Frazier *Amsel, Eisenstadt & Frazier Talent Agency (AEF)*
5055 Wilshire Blvd
Suite 860
Los Angeles, CA 90036-6108, USA

Devayani (Actor, Bollywood)
51 Indira Gandhi Street
Saligramam
Chennai, TN 600093, INDIA

Devellano, Jim (Athlete, Hockey Player)
300 Riverfront Dr Apt 23G
Detroit, MI 48226-4584

Devenzio, Dick (Athlete, Basketball Player)
1116 Home Place
Matthews, NC 28105-6891, USA

Dever, Kaitlyn (Actor)
c/o Matt Sherman *Matt Sherman Management*
7510 W Sunset Blvd
Suite 1413
Los Angeles, CA 90046, USA

Dever, Seamus (Actor)
622 N Crescent Heights Blvd
Los Angeles, CA 90048, USA

Deveraux, Jude (Writer)
Pocket Books
1230 Ave of Americas
New York, NY 10020, USA

Devereaux, Boyd (Athlete, Hockey Player)
10766 E Palm Ridge Dr
Scottsdale, AZ 85255, USA

Devereaux, Mike (Athlete, Baseball Player)
2236 W Doublegrove St
West Covina, CA 91790-5607, USA

Devers, Gail (Athlete, Olympic Athlete, Track Athlete)
2825 Victoria Park Dr
Duluth, GA 30519-4171, USA

Devgan, Ajay (Actor, Bollywood)
c/o Bunty Bahl *Carving Dreams Entertainment*
304-305, Oberoi Chambers II
B Wing, Off New Link Road, Andheri West
Mumbai 400053, INDIA

DeVicenzo, Roberto (Golfer)
Nonl Lann
5025 Veloz Ave
Tarzana, CA 91356, USA

Devicq, Paula (Actor, Model)
c/o Joanne Horowitz *Joanne Horowitz Management*
9350 Wilshire Blvd #224
Beverly Hills, CA 90212, USA

Deville, CC (Musician)
c/o Michael (Mike) Esterman
Esterman.Com, LLC
Prefers to be contacted via email
MD, USA

Deville, Michael (Director)
36 Rue Reinhardt
Boulogne 92100, FRANCE

Devine, Adrian (Athlete, Baseball Player)
271 Timber Laurel Ln
Lawrenceville, GA 30043-6504, USA

Devine, Harold (Boxer)
595 Wyckoff Ave
Wyckoff, NJ 07481, USA

Devine, Joey (Athlete, Baseball Player)
932 Chattooga Tree
Suwanee, GA 30024-7672, USA

Devine, Loretta (Actor)
3829 Crestway Pl
Los Angeles, CA 90043, USA

DeVink, Lodewijk J R (Business Person)
Warner-Lambert Co
201 Tabor Road
Morris Plains, NJ 07950, USA

Devisree (Actor, Bollywood)
1 Bharathi Apts
Bharathi Nagar 3rd Street T Nagar
Chennai, TN 600017, INDIA

DeVita, Vincent T Jr (Misc)
Yale Comprehensive Cancer Center
333 Cedar St
New Haven, CT 06510, USA

DeVito, Danny (Actor, Comedian, Director)
1028 Ridgedale Dr
Beverly Hills, CA 90210, USA

Devito, Louie (Athlete, Snowboarder)
c/o Len Evans *Project Publicity*
312 West 53rd St
Suite 202
New York, NY 10019, USA

Devitt, John (Swimmer)
46 Beacon Ave
Beacon Hill, NSW 2100, AUSTRALIA

DeVitto, Torrey (Actor)
c/o Matthew Lesher *Insight*
1134 S Cloverdale Ave
Los Angeles, CA 90019, USA

Devliegher, Charles (Chuck) (Athlete, Football Player)
27307 N 89th Ave
Peoria, AZ 85383, USA

Devlin, Barry (Director, Writer)

Devlin, Bruce (Athlete, Golfer)
3601 Foot Hills Dr
Weatherford, TX 76087-2239, USA

Devlin, Chris (Athlete, Football Player)
100 Meadow Lark Ln
Boalsburg, PA 16827, USA

Devlin, Dean (Actor, Director, Producer)
Electric Entertainment
1438 North Gower St #24
Los Angeles, CA 90028, USA

Devlin, Joseph (Athlete, Football Player)
3715 Schintzius Rd
Eden, NY 14057, USA

Devlin, Mike (Athlete, Football Player)
48 Shore Rd
Mount Sinai, NY 11766, USA

Devlin, Robert M (Business Person)
American General Corp
2929 Allen Parkway
Houston, TX 77019, USA

Devlins, The (Music Group)
c/o Staff Member *Paradigm (Monterey)*
404 W Franklin St
Monterey, CA 93940, USA

Devo (Music Group, Musician)
c/o Ian Fintak *Agency Group Ltd, The (LA)*
1880 Century Park E
Suite 711
Los Angeles, CA 90067, USA

De Voe, Ronald (Musician)
c/o Michael (Mike) Esterman
Esterman.Com, LLC
Prefers to be contacted via email
MD, USA

DeVoe, Ronnie (Musician)
3540 Hicks Rd SW
Marietta, GA 30060, USA

Devol, George (Inventor)
990 Ridgefield Rd
Wilton, CT 06897-1005, USA

Devon (Adult Film Star)
c/o Staff Member *Atlas Entertainment*
6100 Wilshire Blvd #1170
Los Angeles, CA 90048, USA

Devon, Dayna (Actor, Television Host)
545 S Plymouth Blvd
Los Angeles, CA 900210, USA

Devore, Doug (Athlete, Baseball Player)
5247 Willow Grove Pl S
Dublin, OH 43017-2116, USA

Devorski, Paul (Athlete, Hockey Player)
6292 Farmers Ln
Harrisburg, PA 17111-7066

DeVos, Richard (Business Person)
1720 S Ocean Blvd
Lantana, FL 33462, USA

Devries, Greg (Athlete, Hockey Player)
25 Colonel Winstead Dr
Brentwood, TN 37027-8937, USA

Devries, Jared (Athlete, Football Player)
15342 Lambert Dr
Clear Lake, IA 50428, USA

Devries, Jed (Athlete, Football Player)
2433 W 1425 S
Syracuse, UT 84075, USA

De Vries, Peter
170 Cross Highway
Westport, CT 06880

DeVries, William C (Scientist)
7 Snowmound Court
Rockville, MD 20850-2850, USA

deVry, William (Actor)
3268 Bennett Dr
Los Angeles, CA 90068, USA

DeWaart, Edo (Conductor)
Essenlaan 68
Rotterdam 3016, NETHERLANDS

Dewan, Jenna (Actor)
c/o Courtney Knittel *Patricola Lust PR*
9171 Wilshire Blvd
Suite 441
Beverly Hills, CA 90210, USA

Dewar, Faber (Designer)
c/o Staff Member *Trading Spaces*
The Learning Channel
7700 Wisconsin Ave
Bethesda, MD 20814, USA

Dewar, Jane E (Editor)
Legion Magazine
359 Kent St
#504
Ottawa, ON K2P 0R6, CANADA

Dewar, Susan (Cartoonist)
Universal Press Syndicate
4520 Main St
Kansas City, MO 64111, USA

Deward, Scott (Race Car Driver)
479 Bay Rd
Easton, MA 02375, USA

Dewberry, Michelle (Reality TV Star)
Taylor Herring
11 Westway Centre
69 St Marks Road
London W10 6JG, UNITED KINGDOM

Dewese, Mohandas (Kool mo Dee) (Actor)
c/o Staff Member *Identity Talent Agency (ID)*
9107 Wilshire Blvd
Suite 500
Beverly Hills, CA 90210, USA

DeWet, Shaun (Model)
c/o Staff Member *Elite Model Management (NY)*
404 Park Ave S Fl 9
New York, NY 10016, USA

Dewey, Duane E (General)
RR 1 Box 494
Irons, MI 49644, USA

Dewey, Mark (Athlete, Baseball Player)
28150 Rivermont Dr
Meadowview, VA 24361-2822, USA

Dewey, Tommy (Actor)
c/o Paul Brown *New Wave Entertainment*
(LA)
2660 W Olive Blvd
Burbank, CA 91505, USA

DeWilde, Edy (Director)
Stedelijk Museum
Amsterdam, NETHERLANDS

Dewillis, Jeff (Athlete, Baseball Player)
8918 Wind Side Dr
Houston, TX 77040-3460, USA

Dewine, Mike (Politician)
336 Phillips St
Yellow Springs, OH 45387-1724, USA

DeWinne, Frank (Cosmonaut)
349 Squadron
Vilegbaiss
Kleine Brogel
Peer, 10W TAC 3990, BELGIUM

De Winne, Frank Major (Astronaut)
European Astronaut Centre Linder Hohe
Potsfach 90 60 96 Koln
 D-51142, Germany

Dewitt, Blake (Athlete, Baseball Player)
212 Holmes Dr
Sikeston, MO 63801-4907, USA

DeWitt, Bryce S (Physicist)
University of Texas
Physics Dept
Austin, TX 78712, USA

DeWitt, Doug (Boxer)
2035 Central Ave
Yonkers, NY 10710, USA

DeWitt, Joyce (Actor)
c/o Staff Member *JG Business*
Management Inc
PO Box 7309
Santa Monica, CA 90406-7309, USA

Dewitt, Matt (Athlete, Baseball Player)
7704 Bird of Paradise Ct
Las Vegas, NV 89123-0450, USA

DeWitt, Rosemarie (Actor)
c/o Troy Nankin *Wishlab*
2225-A Hyperion Ave
Los Angeles, CA 90027, USA

Dewitt, William 0 (Commentator)
5825 Drewry Farm Ln
Cincinnati, OH 45243-3441, USA

Dewitt, William O (Baseball Player)
St Louis Cardinals
5825 Drewry Farm Ln
Cincinnati, OH 45243-3441, USA

DeWitt, Willie (Boxer)
605 N Water St
Bumet, TX 78611, USA

DeWitt-Morette, Cecile (Physicist)
2411 Vista Lane
Austin, TX 78703, USA

DeWolfe, Chris (Business Person)
624 N Hillcrest Rd
Beverly Hills, CA 90210, USA

Dews, Bobby (Athlete, Baseball Player)
423 S Audubon Dr
Albany, GA 31707-3005, USA

Dews, Peter B (Psychic)
280 Newtonville Avenue
Apt 221
Newtonville, MA 02460-2098, USA

DeWulf, Noureen (Actor)
c/o Tiffany Kuzon *Evolution Entertainment*
(LA)
901 N Highland Ave
Los Angeles, CA 90038, USA

DeWyze, Lee (Musician)
c/o Simon Fuller *XIX Entertainment*
35-37 Parkgate Rd
32/33 Ransomes Dock
London SW11 4NP, UNITED KINGDOM
(UK)

Dexter, Dex (Stylist)
1133 Broadway #529
New York, NY 10010, USA

Dexter, Mary (Director)
Hank Tani
14542 Delaware Dr
Moorpark, CA 93021, USA

Dexter, Pete (Writer)
c/o Author Mail *Doubleday*
1745 Broadway
New York, NY 10019, USA

Dexter, Peter W (Writer)
Sacramento Bee
Editorial Dept
21st & Q Sts
Sacramento, CA 95852, USA

Dey, Susan (Actor)
210 E 73rd St #4D
New York, NY 10021, USA

Deyette, Alison (Stylist)
c/o Staff Member *Gabler Group*
7 E 14th St
#1627
New York, NY 10003, USA

Deyn, Agyness (Actor)
c/o Danie Streisand *WME (WMA-NY)*
1325 Ave of the Americas
New York, NY 10019, USA

DeYoung, Cliff (Actor)
481 Savona Way
Oak Park, CA 91377, USA

DeYoung, Dennis (Musician)
12/13 Ambriance Dr
Burr Ridge, IL 60527, USA

Dezelan, Frank (Athlete, Baseball Player)
7423 Lighthouse Pt
Pittsburgh, PA 15221, USA

Dezhurov, Vladimir N (Cosmonaut)
Potchta Kosmonavtov
Moskovskoi Obtasti
Syvisdny Goroduk 141160, RUSSIA

Dhabhara, Firdaus S (Scientist)
Rockefeller University
Neurology Dept
1230 York Ave
New York, NY 10021, USA

Dhamu (Actor)
84 Pycrofts Road 36 ADK Mansion
Triplicane
Chennai, TN 600 005, INDIA

Dhanapal (Actor)
8 A G Block
Pallaku Maa Nagar Luz
Chennai, TN 600 004, INDIA

Dhanoa, Guddu (Actor)
8A My Little Home
10th Road JVPD Scheme
Bombay, MS 400 049, INDIA

Dharmasakti, Sanya (Prime Minister)
15 Saukhumvit Road
Soi 41
Bangkok, THAILAND

D'Harnoncourt, Anne (Director)
Philadelphia Museum of Art
25th & Franklin Parkway
Philadelphia, PA 19101, USA

Dhavernas, Caroline (Actor)
c/o Marla Farrell *WKT Public Relations -*
NY
584 Broadway
Suite 310
New York, NY 10012, USA

Dhawan, David (Director, Filmmaker)
A-15 Sagar Darshan
Carter Road Khar
Mumbai, MS 400052, INDIA

D. Hinchey, Maurice (Congressman,
Politician)
2431 Rayburn HOB
Washington, DC 20515, USA

Dhoni, Mahendra Singh (Athlete,
Cricketer)
c/o Staff Member *IMG (UK)*
McCormack House, Hogarth Business
Park
Burlington Lane
Chiswick London W4 2TH, UNITED
KINGDOM (UK)

Dhue, Laurie (Anchor)
c/o Staff Member *Fox News Channel (NY)*
1211 Ave of the Americas
Level C1
New York, NY 10036-8701, USA

Diachuk, Ed (Athlete, Hockey Player)
6010 50 St
Vegreville, AB T9C 1H4, Canada

Diallo, Mmadou (Soccer Player)
New England Revolution
CMGI Field
1 Patriot Place
Foxboro, MA 02035, USA

Diamantopoulos, Chris (Actor)
c/o Van Johnson *Van Johnson Company*
350 S. Beverly Dr.
Suite 200
Beverly Hills, CA 90212, USA

Diamini, Barnabas S (Prime Minister)
Prime Minister's Office
PO Box 395
Mbabane, SWAZILAND

Diamond, Abel J (Architect)
Diamond Schmitz Co
2 Berkeley St
#600
Toronto, ON M5A 2W3, CANADA

Diamond, Bobby
5309 Comercio Way
Woodland Hills, CA 91364

Diamond, Charles (Athlete, Football
Player)
7300 SW 69th Ct
Miami, FL 33143, USA

Diamond, Chris (Race Car Driver)
J&L Racing
5171 Icard Ridge Rd
Hickory, NC 28601, USA

Diamond, Diane (Television Host)
c/o Staff Member *Court TV*
600 Third Ave Fl 2
New York, NY 10016, USA

Diamond, Dustin (Actor)
124 Grandview Dr
Port Washington, WI 53074, USA

Diamond, Jared (Scientist)
1043 Stone Canyon Rd
Los Angeles, CA 90077-2915, USA

Diamond, Joel (Producer)
Joel Diamond Entertainment
3940 Laurel Canyon Blvd Suite 441
Studio City, CA 91604, USA

Diamond, Marian C (Misc)
2583 Virginia St
Berkeley, CA 94709, USA

Diamond, Michael (Mike D) (Musician)
GAS Entertainment
8935 Lindblade St
Culver City, CA 90232, USA

Diamond, Michael T (DJ)
c/o Staff Member *Diva Central Inc*
7510 W Sunset Blvd Ste 1445
Los Angees, CA 90046, USA

Diamond, Neil (Musician)
PO Box 3357
Los Angeles, CA 90028, USA

Diamond, Peter A (Nobel Prize Laureate)
15 Franklin Rd
Lexington, MA 02420-3517, USA

Diamond, Reed (Actor)
c/o David Weise *David Weise and*
Associates
16000 Ventura Blvd
Suite 600
Encino, CA 91436-2753, USA

Diamond, Seymour (Doctor)
Diamond Headache Clinic
467 W Deming Place
#500
Chicago, IL 60614, USA

Diamond, Thomas (Athlete, Baseball
Player)
310 Edgewood Ln
La Place, LA 70068-8964, USA

Diamond Rio (Music Group)
c/o Staff Member *WmE2 (WMA-TN)*
1600 Division St
Suite 300
Nashville, TN 37203, USA

Diamonds, The (Music Group)
561 Keystone Avenue #224
Reno, NV 89503, USA

Diamont, Don (Actor)
Craig Mgmt
125 S Sycamore Ave
Los Angeles, CA 90036, USA

Diana, Rich (Athlete, Football Player)
2 Munson Dr
Unit 7
Wallingford, CT 06492, USA

Dias, Ivan Cardinal (Religious Leader)
Archbishop's House
21 Nathalal Parekh Marg
Mumbai, MS 400001, INDIA

Dias Dos Santos, Fernando da Piedade
(Prime Minister)
Prime Minister's Office
Council of Ministers
Luanda, ANGOLA

Diaw, Boris (Athlete, Basketball Player)
8632 N Via La Serena
Paradise Valley, AZ 85253-2130, USA

Diaz, Aaron (Actor)

Diaz, Arnold (Correspondent)
c/o Staff Member *Shame on You !*
WCBS-TV
524 West 57th St
New York, NY 10019, USA

Diaz, Cameron (Actor)
9552 Hidden Valley Rd
Beverly Hills, CA 90210, USA

Diaz, Carlos (Athlete, Baseball Player)
45-236 Ka Hanahou Cir
Kaneohe, HI 96744-3009, USA

Diaz, Carlos (Athlete, Baseball Player)
3037 Homestead Oaks Dr
Clearwater, FL 33759-1626, USA

Diaz, David (Athlete, Boxer)
c/o Staff Member *Top Rank Inc.*
3908 Howard Hughes Pkwy
#580
Las Vegas, NV 89109, USA

Diaz, Einar (Athlete, Baseball Player)
4315 70th Ave E
Ellenton, FL 34222-7329, USA

Diaz, Guillermo (Actor)
c/o Meghan Schumacher *Meghan
Schumacher Management*
13351-D Riverside Dr #387
Sherman Oaks, CA 91423, USA

Diaz, Helga (Actor)
c/o Gabriel Blanco *Gabriel Blanco
Iglesias (Mexico)*
Rio Balsas 35-32
Colonia Cuauhtemoc
DF 06500, Mexico

Diaz, Izzy (Actor)
c/o Scott Zimmerman *Evolution
Entertainment (LA)*
901 N Highland Ave
Los Angeles, CA 90038, USA

Diaz, Jorge (Athlete, Football Player)
9282 123rd Ave
Largo, FL 33773, USA

Diaz, Laura (Golfer)
c/o Staff Member *Ladies Pro Golf
Association (LPGA)*
100 International Golf Dr
Daytona Beach, FL 32124-1092, USA

Diaz, Lazaro (Athlete, Baseball Player)
13557 Meadow Bay Loop
Orlando, FL 32824-5082, USA

Diaz, Manny (Politician)
Mayor's Office
3500 Pan American Dr
Miami, FL 33133, USA

Diaz, Mario (Athlete, Baseball Player)
90 Calle Menta
Gurabo, PR 00778-9655, USA

Diaz, Matt (Athlete, Baseball Player)
1147 Interlochen Blvd
Winter Haven, FL 33884-3707, USA

Diaz, Mike (Athlete, Baseball Player)
225 Hillside Dr
Pacifica, CA 94044-3032, USA

Diaz, Robison (Actor)
c/o Staff Member *TV Caracol*
Calle 76 #11 - 35
Piso 10AA
Bogota DC 26484, COLOMBIA

Diaz, Rocsi (Actor)
c/o Daniel Ryan Kinney *Artist and Brand
Management - NY*
250 Hudson St
2nd Floor
New York, NY 10013, USA

Diaz Balart, Jose (Actor)
c/o Staff Member *Telemundo*
2470 West 8th Avenue
Hialeah, FL 33010, USA

Diaz-Balart, Jose (Correspondent)
CBS-TV
News Dept
51 W 52nd St
New York, NY 10013, USA

Diaz-Balart, Mario (Congressman,
Politician)
436 Cannon HOB
Washington, DC 20515, USA

Diaz-Infante, David (Athlete, Football
Player)
24723 E Park Crescent Dr
Aurora, CO 80016, USA

Diaz-Rahi, Yamila (Model)
Next Model Mgmt
23 Watts St
New York, NY 10013, USA

Dibble, Dorne (Athlete, Football Player)
18601 Jamestown Cir
Northville, MI 48167, USA

Dibble, Rob (Athlete, Baseball Player)
30020 Trail Creek Dr
Agoura Hills, CA 91301-4041, USA

Dibel, John C (Business Person)
Meade Instruments Corp
6001 Oak Canyon
Irvine, CA 92618, USA

DiBeliglojoso, Lodovico B (Architect)
Studio Architetti BBPR
2 Via Dei Chiostri
Milan 20121, ITALY

Dibernardo, Rick (Athlete, Football
Player)
31942 Via Oso
Trabuco Canyon, CA 92679, USA

DiBiaggio, John A (Educator)
Tufts University
President's Office
Medford, MA 02155, USA

DiBlasio, Raul (Musician)
Esterfan Enterprises
420 Jefferson Ave
Miami Beach, FL 33139, USA

Diblassio, Raul (Musician)
c/o Staff Member *BMG*
1540 Broadway
New York, NY 10036, USA

DiBona, Craig (Cinematographer)
333 E 66th St
#7O
New York, NY 10021, USA

di Bonaventura, Lorenzo (Producer)
332 N Tigertail Rd
Los Angeles, CA 90049, USA

Dibos, Alicia (Athlete, Golfer)
1465 E Putnam Ave
Apt 112E
Old Greenwich, CT 06870-1330, USA

Dibra, Bash
c/o Daniel Strone *Trident Media Group
LLC*
41 Madison Ave
36th Floor
New York, NY 10010, USA

DiCamillo, Brandon (Actor)
c/o Staff Member *Stoic Management*
947 Trinity Ln
King Of Prussia, PA 19406, USA

Dicamillo, Gary T (Business Person)
1001 Saint Georges Road
Baltimore, MD 21210, USA

DiCaprio, Leonardo (Actor)
9045/9051 Oriole Way
West Hollywood, CA 90069, USA

Dichter, Misha (Musician)
Columbia Artists Mgmt Inc
165 W 57th St
New York, NY 10019, USA

Dicillo, Tom (Cinematographer, Director,
Writer)
c/o Jennifer Levine *Untitled Entertainment
(LA)*
350 S. Beverly Dr #200
Beverly Hills, CA 90212, USA

Di Cione, Sevy (Actor)
c/o Cindy Sheffield *The Sheffield Agency*
14020 NW Passage
Suite 104
Marina Del Rey, CA 90292, USA

Dick, Andy (Actor, Comedian)
c/o Michael Green *Collective*
8383 Wilshire Blvd
Suite 1050
Beverly Hills, CA 90211, USA

Dick, Degen (Athlete, Football Player)
15871 Springdale St
Huntington Beach, CA 92649

Dick, Douglas (Actor)
604 S Gretna Green Way
Los Angeles, CA 90049, USA

Dick, Ed (Baseball Player)
TCMA
501 Washington Ave
Ocean Springs, MS 39564-4631, USA

Dickau, Dan (Basketball Player)
Atlanta Hawks
190 Marietta St SW
Atlanta, GA 30303, USA

Dickel, Dan (Athlete, Football Player)
832 Normandy Dr
Iowa City, IA 52246, USA

Dicken, Paul (Athlete, Baseball Player)
2775 NW 49th Ave
Unit 205, Ocala FL, 34482-6213

Dickens, Jimmy (Musician)
5010 W Concord Road
Brentwood, TN 37027, USA

Dickens, Kim (Actor)
c/o Stephen Hirsh *Gersh (LA)*
9465 Wilshire Blvd
Suite 600
Beverly Hills, CA 90212, USA

Dickenson, Herb (Athlete, Hockey Player)
6 McCarthy Cres 55 3
Angus, ON LOM 1B3, Canada

Dicker, Cintia (Model)
c/o Staff Member *Nova Models Munich*
Siegesstrasse 3
Munich 80802, Germany

Dickerson, Dan (Baseball Player)
7950 Brookwood Dr
Clarkston, MI 48348-4471, USA

Dickerson, Eric (Athlete, Football Player,
Sportscaster)
26815 Mulholland Hwy
Calabsas, CA 91302, USA

Dickerson, Ernest R (Director)
c/o Staff Member *Chasen & Company*
8899 Beverly Blvd
Suite 405
Los Angeles, CA 90048, USA

Dickerson, Henry (Athlete, Basketball
Player)
3204 Skybrook Lane
Durham, NC 27703-5979, USA

Dickerson, John (Athlete, Baseball Player)
1702 26th St N
Columbus, MS 39701, USA

Dickerson, Kenneth (Athlete, Football
Player)
2406 Alabama Ave
Tuskegee Institute, AL 36088, USA

Dickerson, Marty (Athlete, Golfer)
4225 Luzon Way
Sarasota, FL 34241, USA

Dickerson, Sam (Athlete, Football Player)
551 Waddell Way
Modesto, CA 95357-1477, USA

Dickerson, Sandra (Actor)
Howes & Prior
Berkeley House
Hay Hill
London W1X 7LH, UNITED KINGDOM
(UK)

Dickey, Boh A (Business Person)
SAFECO Corp
SAFECO Plaza
Seattle, WA 98185, USA

Dickey, Charlie (Athlete, Football Player)
1992 Farm Cir
Sandy, UT 84093, USA

Dickey, Curtis (Athlete, Football Player)
702 Glenview Dr
Mansfield, TX 76063, USA

Dickey, Lucinda (Actor)
517 James Cir
Royal Oak, MI 48067, USA

Dickey, Lynn (Athlete, Football Player)
9220 Pawnee Ln
Leawood, KS 66206, USA

Dickey, R A (Athlete, Baseball Player)
701 Cantrell Ave
Nashville, TN 37215-1022, USA

Dickey, Richard (Athlete, Basketball
Player)
1109 Red Maple Drive
Plymouth, IN 46563-3697, USA

Dickey, Wallace (Athlete, Football Player)
220 E Montana Dr
Shiner, TX 77984, USA

Dickinson, Angie (Actor)
1715 Carla Ridge
Beverly Hills, CA 90210, USA

Dickinson, Bruce (Musician)
c/o Staff Member *Agency Group Ltd, The (UK)*
361-373 City Rd
London EC1V 1PQ, UK

Dickinson, David (Actor)
Bargain Hunt
PO Box 229
Bristol BS99 7JN, ENGLAND

Dickinson, Gary (Bowler)
501 Wade Martin Road
Edmond, OK 73034-6716, USA

Dickinson, Janice (Model, Reality TV Star)
c/o Brad Taylor *Big Machine Media*
780 3rd Ave
15th Floor
New York, NY 10017, USA

Dickinson, Judy (Athlete, Golfer)
18277 SE Heritage Dr
Jupiter, FL 33469-1439, USA

Dickinson, Parnell (Athlete, Football Player)
1646 Wallace Rd
Lutz, FL 33549, USA

Dickinson, Richard (Athlete, Football Player)
P.O. Box 166
New Augusta, MS 39462, USA

Dickinson, Steve (Cartoonist)
c/o Staff Member *King Features Syndication*
300 W 57th St
15th Floor
New York, NY 10019-5238, USA

Dickman, James B (Journalist)
1471 Peach Creek Dr
Splendora, TX 77372, USA

Dickman, Jay (Photographer)
4450 Sumac Ln
Littleton, CO 80123-2743, USA

Dickson, Bob (Athlete, Golfer)
140 Woodlands Creek Dr
Pointe Vedra Beach, FL 32082, USA

Dickson, Bruce (Bad) (Race Car Driver)
1370 Bridge Rd
West Chester, PA 19382, USA

Dickson, Chris (Yachtsman)
Int'l Mgmt Group
1 Erieview Plaza
1360 E 9th St #1300
Cleveland, OH 44114, USA

Dickson, Clarence (Lawyer)
Police Department
Metro Justice
1351 NW 12th St
Miami, FL 33125, USA

Dickson, Jason (Athlete, Baseball Player)
15 Edison St
St Margarets, NB E1N 5B4, Canada

Dickson, Jennifer (Artist, Photographer)
20 Osborne Ave
Ottawa, ON K1S 4Z9, CANADA

Dickson, Jim (Athlete, Baseball Player)
685 Franklin Ave
Astoria, OR 97103-4615, USA

Dickson, John (Athlete, Basketball Player)
4646 Wynmeade Park NE
Marietta, GA 30067-4098, USA

Dickson, Lance (Athlete, Baseball Player)
4615 N Placita Roca Blanca
Tucson, AZ 85718-7476, USA

Dickson, Neil (Actor)
c/o Lorraine Berglund *Lorraine Berglund Management*
11537 Hesby St.
North Hollywood, CA 91601, USA

Dickson, Ngila (Designer)
c/o Staff Member *Sandra Marsh Management*
9150 Wilshire Blvd #220
Beverly Hills, CA 90212, USA

Dicus, Charles (Chuck) (Athlete, Football Player)
7 Valley Club Cir
Little Rock, AR 72212, USA

Didier, Bob (Athlete, Baseball Player)
1819 N Lynch
Mesa, AZ 85207-3179, USA

Didier, Clint (Athlete, Football Player)
5015 S Regal St Apt L3089
Spokane, WA 99223-7975, USA

Didion, Joan (Writer)
8955 Beverly Blvd
West Hollywood, CA 90048-2423, USA

Didion, John (Athlete, Football Player)
48 Elk Ridge Ln
Naselle, WA 98638, USA

Dido (Musician, Songwriter)
c/o Staff Member *Paradigm (NY)*
360 Park Ave S Fl 16
New York, NY 10010, USA

Diduck, Gerald (Athlete, Hockey Player)
3303 Drexel Dr
Dallas, TX 75205-2914

Die Antwoord (Music Group)
c/o Joel Zimmerman *WME (WMA-NY)*
1325 Ave of the Americas
New York, NY 10019, USA

Diebel, Nelson (Athlete, Olympic Athlete, Swimmer)
401 Webb Rd
Newark, DE 19711-2652, USA

Diebold, John (Business Person)
Diebold Group
PO Box 515
Bedford Hills, NY 10507, USA

Diehl, David (Athlete, Football Player)
116 Liberty Ridge Trl
Totowa, NJ 07512, USA

Diehl, Digby (Journalist)
788 South Lake Avenue
Pasadena, CA 91106, USA

Diehl, Digby R (Journalist)
788 S Lake Ave
Pasadena, CA 91106, USA

Diehl, John (Actor)
c/o Sandi Dudek *Paradigm (LA)*
360 N Crescent Dr
North Bldg
Beverly Hills, CA 90210, USA

Diehl, John A (Athlete, Football Player)
900 S Henry St
Williamsburg, VA 23185, USA

Dieken, Doug H (Athlete, Football Player)
29876 Lake Rd
Bay Village, OH 44140, USA

Diem, Ryan (Athlete, Football Player)
11522 Willow Ridge Dr
Zionsville, IN 46077, USA

Diemecke, Enrique Arturo (Conductor)
Herbert Barrett
266 W 37th St
#2000
New York, NY 10018, USA

Diener, Robert (Business Person)
9 Indian Creek Dr
Indian Creek Village, FL 33154, USA

Diener, Theodor O (Misc)
PO Box 272
11711 Battersea Dr
Beltsville, MD 20705, USA

Diener, Travis (Athlete, Basketball Player)
1007 Springs Rd
Fond Du Lac, WI 54935-7613, USA

Dienhart, Mark (Athlete, Football Player)
1944 Bayard Ave
Saint Paul, MN 55116, USA

Dierassi, Carl (Inventor)
2325 Bear Gulch Road
Redwood City, CA 94062, USA

Dierassi, Issac (Doctor)
2034 Delancey Place
Philadelphia, PA 19103, USA

Diercks, Justin (Race Car Driver)
c/o Steve Diercks
1030 E. 4th St.
Davenport, IA 52807, USA

Dierdof, Daniel L (Dan) (Athlete, Football Player, Sportscaster)
13302 Buckland Hall Rd
Saint Louis, MO 63131, USA

Dierdorf, Dan (Athlete, Football Player)
13302 Buckland Hall Road
Saint Louis, MO 63131, USA

Diering, Chuck (Athlete, Baseball Player)
1 Nob Hill Dr
Saint Louis, MO 63138-1400, USA

Dierker, Larry (Athlete, Baseball Player, Coach)
8318 N Tahoe Dr
Jersey Village, TX 77040-1258, USA

Dierker, Robert R (General)
Deputy Commander Pacific Fleet
Camp H M Smith
Honolulu, HI 96861, USA

Dierking, Connie (Athlete, Basketball Player)
5730 Windridge Vw
Cincinnati, OH 45243-2981, USA

Dierking, Scott (Athlete, Football Player)
1862 Wingate Ln
Wheaton, IL 60189, USA

Dierkop, Charles (Actor)
c/o Staff Member *The Actors Studio*
8341 DeLongpre Ave.
West Hollywood, CA 90069, USA

Diesel (Music Group)
c/o Staff Member *The Harbour Agency*
135 Forbes St
Woolloomooloo NSW 2011, Australia

Diesel, Vin (Actor, Director, Producer)
2222 Sunset Crest Dr
West Hollywood, CA 90069, USA

Dieselboy (DJ, Musician)
c/o Joel Zimmerman *WME (WMA-NY)*
1325 Ave of the Americas
New York, NY 10019, USA

Dieterich, Chris (Athlete, Football Player)
804 Edisto River Rd
Myrtle Beach, SC 29588, USA

Dietrich, Dena (Actor)
c/o Staff Member *Bauman Redanty & Shaul Agency*
5757 Wilshire Blvd
Suite 473
Beverly Hills, CA 90212, USA

Dietrich, Don (Athlete, Hockey Player)
310 Finlay Ave E
Deloraine, MB R0M 0M0, Canada

Dietrich, Jan (Aviator)
Debra Dolch Services 167 SPark St
Attn Deb Fox
San Francisco, CA 94107-1808, USA

Dietrich, William A (Bill) (Journalist)
Seattle Times Fairview Avenue NAnd John Street
Attn: Editorial Dept
Seattle, WA 98111, USA

Dietrick, Coby (Athlete, Basketball Player)
644 Patterson Avenue
San Antonio, TX 78209-5655, USA

Dietzel, Roy (Athlete, Baseball Player)
8421 Coulwood Oak Ln
Charlotte, NC 28214-1165, USA

Difelice, Mark (Athlete, Baseball Player)
324 Rittenhouse Cir
Havertown, PA 19083-2117, USA

Difelice, Mike (Athlete, Baseball Player)
3980 Mimosa Pl
Palm Harbor, FL 34685-3674, USA

Diffie, Joe (Musician)
9435 Weatherly Dr
Brentwood, TN 37027, USA

Diffie, Whitfield (Inventor)
288 Eleanor Dr
Woodside, CA 94062-1116, USA

Difrient, Niels (Designer)
General Delivery
Ridgefield, CT 06877, USA

DiFranco, Ani (Musician, Songwriter)
189 Bidwell Pkwy
Buffalo, NY 14222, USA

Digby, Marie (Musician)
c/o Staff Member *Nettwerk Management (LA)*
1545 Wilcox Ace
Suite 200
Los Angeles, CA 90028, USA

DiGenova, Joseph E (Lawyer)
DiGenova & Toensing
901 15th St NW
#430
Washington, DC 20005, USA

Diggins, Ben (Athlete, Baseball Player)
4804 E Merrell St
Phoenix, AZ 85018-7876, USA

Diggs, Nail (Athlete, Football Player)
2006 Connonade Dr
Waxhaw, NC 28173, USA

Diggs, Shelton (Athlete, Football Player)
261 Washington Ave
Apt 3R
New Rochelle, NY 10801, USA

Diggs, Taye (Actor)
3121 Oakdell Ln
Studio City, CA 91604, USA

Digiacomo, Curt (Athlete, Football Player)
830 Ida Ave
Solana Beach, CA 92075, USA

Digible Planets (Music Group)
345 North Maple Drive #123
Beverly Hills, CA 90210, USA

Digitalism (Music Group)
c/o Staff Member *Girlie Action*
243 W 30th St
12th Floor
New York, NY 10001, USA

DiGregorio, Ernie (Athlete, Basketball Player)
60 Chestnut Avenue
Narragansett, RI 02882-6113, USA

Dilauro, Jack (Athlete, Baseball Player)
102 Sea Oats Dr
Panama City Beach, FL 32413-2763, USA

Dilba (Musician)
United Stage Production
PO Box 11029
Stockholm 10061, SWEDEN

Dildarian, Steve (Voice Over Artist)
2481 N Edgemont St
Los Angeles, CA 90027, USA

Dilfer, Trent F (Athlete, Football Player)
15288 Quito Rd
Saratoga, CA 95070, USA

Dilger, Ken (Athlete, Football Player)
10403 Windemere
Carmel, IN 46032, USA

Dilip (Actor)
74 Baskara Colony
Virugambakkam
Chennai, TN 600 092, INDIA

Dill, Craig (Athlete, Basketball Player)
10200 Thomas Woods Road
Saginaw, MI 48609-9512, USA

Dill, Laddie John (Artist)
1625 Electric Ave
Venice, CA 90291, USA

Dill, Terry (Athlete, Golfer)
7003 Western Oaks Blvd
Austin, TX 78749, USA

Dillahunt, Garret (Actor)
1077 E Santa Anita Ave
Burbank, CA 91501, USA

Dillam, Bradford (Actor)
770 Hot Springs Rd
Santa Barbara, CA 93108, USA

Dillane, Stephen (Actor)
Michelle Braidman
10/11 Lower John St
#300
London W1R 3PE, UNITED KINGDOM
(UK)

Dillard, Alex (Business Person)
Dillard's Inc
1600 Cantrell Road
Little Rock, AR 72201, USA

Dillard, Annie (Writer)
Russell Volkering
50 W 29th St
New York, NY 10001, USA

Dillard, Don (Athlete, Baseball Player)
45 Bream Ln
Waterloo, SC 29384-4868, USA

Dillard, Gordon (Athlete, Baseball Player)
840 Via Manzana
Aromas, CA 95004-9026, USA

Dillard, Harrison H. (Athlete, Olympic
Athlete, Track Athlete)
3842 E 147th St
Cleveland, OH 44128, USA

Dillard, Mickey (Athlete, Basketball
Player)
224 SW 11th Avenue
Dania, FL 33004-3515, USA

Dillard, Phillip (Athlete, Football Player)
c/o Roosevelt Barnes *Maximum Sports
Management*
6435 W Jefferson Blvd
#197
Fort Wayne, IN 46804, USA

Dillard, Rodney (Actor, Musician)
Superior Communications Co. Talent
c/o Randy Campbell
340 So Columbus Blvd
Tucson, AZ 85711-4l38, USA

Dillard, Stacey (Athlete, Football Player)
3188 County Road 4220
Annona, TX 75550, USA

Dillard, Steve (Athlete, Baseball Player)
154 Drive 841
Saltillo, MS 38866-9362, USA

Dillard, Tim (Athlete, Baseball Player)
2682 Avery Park Dr
Nashville, TN 37211-7182, USA

Dillard, Victoria (Actor)
25 Chittenden Ave #3C
New York, NY 10033, USA

Dillard, W Harrison (Athlete, Olympic
Athlete, Track Athlete)
485 Pierson Dr
Cleveland, OH 44143-2775, USA

Dillard, William T Jr (Business Person)
Dillard's Inc
1600 Cantrell Road
Little Rock, AR 72201, USA

Dille, Bob (Athlete, Basketball Player)
200 Albi Road
Apt 3
Naples, FL 34112-6108, USA

Dillehay, Thomas (Tom) (Misc)
University of Kentucky
Anthropology Dept
Lexington, KY 40506, USA

Dilleita, Dilleita Mohamed (Prime
Minister)
Prime Minister's Office
PO Box 2086
Djibouti, DJIBOUTI

Diller, Barry (Business Person)
IAC/InterActive Corp
555 W 18th St
New York, NY 10011, USA

Dillion, Wayne (Athlete, Hockey Player)
Hockey Development Centre of Ontario
301-1185 Eglinton Ave E
North York, ON M3C 3C6, Canada

Dillman, Bill (Athlete, Baseball Player)
P.O. Box 5167
Winter Park, FL 32793-5167, USA

Dillman, Bradford (Actor)
770 Hot Springs Road
Santa Barbara, CA 93103, USA

Dillman, Brooke (Actor)
1632 S Point View St
Los Angles, CA 90035, USA

Dillon, Austin (Race Car Driver)
Childress Racing
236 Industrial Dr
Welcom, NC 27374, USA

Dillon, Bobby (Athlete, Football Player)
1289 Morgan Dr
Temple, TX 76502, USA

Dillon, Corey (Athlete, Football Player)
26535 Alsace Dr
Calabasas, CA 91302, USA

Dillon, David B (Business Person)
Kroger Co
1014 Vince St
Cincinnati, OH 45202, USA

Dillon, Denny (Actor, Comedian)
International Creative Mgmt
8942 Wilshire Blvd
#219
Beverly Hills, CA 90211, USA

Dillon, Joe (Athlete, Baseball Player)
1220 Islemere Dr
Rockwall, TX 75087-2412, USA

Dillon, Kevin (Actor)
1259 S Stanley Ave
Los Angeles, CA 90019, USA

Dillon, Matt (Actor, Director)
35 W 81st St #88BCD
New York, NY 10024, USA

Dillon, Melinda (Actor)
4065 Michael Ave
Los Angeles, CA 90066, USA

Dillon, Mike (Race Car Driver)
PO Box 30414
Winston-Salem, NC 27130, USA

Dillon, Steve (Athlete, Baseball Player)
511 Wateredge Ave
Baldwin, NY 11510-3728, USA

Dillon, Wayne (Athlete, Hockey Player)
312-3 Concorde Gate
Toronto, ON M3C 3N7, Canada

Dilmancheff, Babe (Athlete, Football
Player)
3917 Edgehill Dr
Los Angeles, CA 90008, USA

Dilone, Miguel (Athlete, Baseball Player)
Calle El Sol #190
Santiago, Dominican Republic

Dils, Steve (Athlete, Football Player)
10285 Midway Ave
Alpharetta, GA 30022, USA

Dilts, Bucky (Athlete, Football Player)
240 McCaslin Blvd # 101
Louisville, CO 80027, USA

Dilts, Douglas (Athlete, Football Player)
1231 Defoor Ct NW
Atlanta, GA 30318, USA

Dilweg, Anthony (Athlete, Football Player)
5310 S Alston Ave
Suite 210
Durham, NC 27713, USA

DiMaggio, John (Actor)
c/o Paul Rosicker *Gersh (LA)*
9465 Wilshire Blvd
Suite 600
Beverly Hills, CA 90212, USA

Dimaio, Rob (Athlete, Hockey Player)
c/o Staff Member *Dallas Stars*
2601 Avenue of the Stars
Suite 100
Frisco, TX 75034-9016, USA

DiMarco, Chris (Athlete, Golfer)
3545 Rice Lake Loop
Longwood, FL 32779, USA

Dimas, Trent (Gymnast)
Gold Cup Gymnastics School
6009 Carmel Ave NE
Albuquerque, NM 87113, USA

Dimbleby, David (Correspondent,
Journalist)
14 King St
Richmond
Surrey TW9 1NF, UNITED KINGDOM
(UK)

DiMeo, Paul (Actor, Reality TV Star)
c/o Staff Member *Extreme Makeover:
Home Edition*
Endemol Entertainment USA
9225 Sunset Blvd #1100
Los Angeles, CA 90069, USA

Di Meola, Al (Musician)
c/o Staff Member *Entourage Talent
Associates*
133 West 25th St
New York, NY 10001, USA

Dimichele, Frank (Athlete, Baseball
Player)
119 Clemens Cir
Norristown, PA 19403-3087, USA

Dimitrakos, Niko (Athlete, Hockey Player)
149 Timber Ct
Wood Dale, IL 60191-1356

Dimitriades, Alex (Actor)
c/o Staff Member *Shanahan Management*
Level 3 Berman House
Surry Hills 2010, AUSTRALIA

Dimitrova, Ghena (Opera Singer)
I C M Artists
40 W 57th St
New York, NY 10019, USA

Dimma, Suzanne (Stylist)
c/o Staff Member *Judy Inc*
1 Yorkville Ave
Toronto ON M4W 1L1, Canada

Dimmel, Mike (Athlete, Baseball Player)
526 Country Ln
Coppell, TX 75019-5129, USA

Dimmick, Thomas (Athlete, Football
Player)
204 Broadmoor Blvd
Lafayette, LA 70503, USA

Dimon, James (Jamie) (Business Person)
J P Morgan Chase
270 Park Ave
New York, NY 10017, USA

Di Montezemolo, Luca (Business Person,
Race Car Driver)
c/o Staff Member *Jaguar Racing Ltd*
Bradbourne Drive
Tilbrook
Milton Keynes MK7 8BJ, United Kingdom

Dimple (Actor, Bollywood)
The Gallop Broad Acres Stud Farm
Avan Hali Estate
Bangalore, KA, INDIA

Dimry, Charles (Athlete, Football Player)
3530 Calle Palmito
Carlsbad, CA 92009, USA

DiMucci, Dion
1650 Broadway #503
New York, NY 10019

Dimuro, Mike (Athlete, Baseball Player)
22594 E Peakview Pl
Aurora, CO 80016-3148, USA

Dimuro, Ray (Athlete, Baseball Player)
9625 N 33rd St
Phoenix, AZ 85028-4919, USA

Dinapoli, Gennaro (Athlete, Football Player)
10 White Oak Farm Rd
Newtown, CT 06470, USA

diNapoli, Marc
8 rue de Georges-de-Porto-Riche
Paris, FRANCE F-75014

DiNardo, Gerry (Coach, Football Coach)
Indiana University
Athletic Dept
Bloomington, IN 47405, USA

Dinardo, Lenny (Athlete, Baseball Player)
23015 NW 227th Dr
High Springs, FL 32643-9031, USA

Dindal, Mark (Director)
c/o Peter Nichols *Lichter Grossman Nichols Adler & Goodman*
9200 Sunset Blvd
Suite 1200
Los Angeles, CA 90069-3507, USA

Dine, James (Artist)
Pace Gallery
32 E 57th St
New York, NY 10022, USA

Dineen, Bill (Athlete, Hockey Player)
18 Fairwood Dr
Queensbury, NY 12804-2175

Dineen, gord (Athlete, Hockey Player)
Toronto Marlies
100 Princes Blvd
Toronto, ON M6K 3C3, Canada

Dineen, Gord (Athlete, Hockey Player)
51 Fitzgerald Rd
Queensbury, NY 12804-1344

Dineen, Kenny (Athlete, Baseball Player)
112 S Ranch St
Santa Maria, CA 93454, USA

Dineen, Kerry
2155 Arrowhead Dr
Santa Maria, CA 93455-5762, USA

Dineen, Kevin (Athlete, Hockey Player)
149 Birdsall Rd
Queensbury, NY 12804-1384

Dineen, Kevin (Athlete, Hockey Player)
Florida Panthers
1 Panther Pkwy
Sunrise, FL 33323-5315

Dineen, Peter (Athlete, Hockey Player)
65 Birch Rd
Lake George, NY 12804-1384

Dineen, William P (Bill) (Coach)
Saint Louis Blues
Sawis Center
1401 Clark Ave
Saint Louis, MO 63103, USA

Dinerstein, James (Artist)
Salander-O'Reilly Gallery
20 E 79th St
New York, NY 10021, USA

Dingle, Adrian (Athlete, Football Player)
3228 W Canyon Ave
San Diego, CA 92123, USA

Dingle, Mike (Athlete, Football Player)
512 Menlo Dr
Columbia, SC 29210, USA

Dingman, Chris (Athlete, Hockey Player)
9220 Pine Island Ct
Tampa, FL 33647-2301

Dingman, Craig (Athlete, Baseball Player)
3573 Del Sienno St
Wichita, KS 67203-4349, USA

Dini, Paul (Actor, Producer, Writer)
c/o Staff Member *United Talent Agency (UTA)*
9336 Civic Center Dr
Beverly Hills, CA 90210, USA

Dinkel, Tom (Athlete, Football Player)
4883 Dartmouth Dr
Burlington, KY 41005, USA

Dinkelman, Brian (Athlete, Baseball Player)
20 Edgewood Lane N
Centralia, IL 62801, USA

Dinkeloo, John (Architect)
Roche & Dinkeloo
20 Davis St
Hamden, CT 06517, USA

Dinkins, Byron (Athlete, Basketball Player)
10326 Tallent Lane
Huntersville, NC 28078-5903, USA

Dinkins, Darnell (Athlete, Football Player)
9006 Pembroke Ct
Pittsburgh, PA 15237, USA

Dinkins, Howard (Athlete, Football Player)
5980 Covered Creek Ln
Jacksonville, FL 32277, USA

Dinklage, Peter (Actor)
c/o David Ginsberg *Insight*
1134 S Cloverdale Ave
Los Angeles, CA 90019, USA

Dinnel, Harry (Athlete, Basketball Player)
1427 El Nido Drive
Fallbrook, CA 92028, USA

Dinner, Michael (Director)
c/o Staff Member *Creative Artists Agency (CAA-LA)*
2000 Ave Of The Stars
Los Angeles, CA 90067, USA

Dinnigan, Collette (Designer, Fashion Designer)
22-24 Hutchinson St
Surry Hills
Sydney, NSW 2010, AUSTRALIA

Dinwiddle, Ryan (Athlete, Football Player)
2931 S Zach Pl
Boise, ID 83706-6807

Diogu, Ike
2052 W Lagoon Rd
Pleasanton, CA 94566-3576, USA

DioGuardi, Kara (Musician, Reality TV Star, Songwriter)
11400 Sunshine Terr
Studio City, CA 91604, USA

Dion (Musician)
3099 NW 63rd St
Boca Raton, FL 33496, USA

Dion, Celine (Actor, Musician)
215 S Beach Rd
Hobe Sound, FL 33455, USA

Dion, Colleen (Actor)
Abrams Artists
9200 Sunset Blvd
#1125
Los Angeles, CA 90069, USA

Dion, Connie (Athlete, Hockey Player)
333 Rue Saint-Edmond
Asbestos, QC J1T 2A6, Canada

Dion, Michel (Athlete, Hockey Player)
33 Mulrain Way
Bluffton, SC 29910-6530, USA

Dion, Terry (Athlete, Football Player)
106 E Libby Rd
Shelton, WA 98584, USA

Dionisi, Stefano (Actor)
Carol Levi Co
Via Giuseppe Pisanelli
Rome 00196, ITALY

Dionne, Gilbert (Athlete, Hockey Player)
196 Bender Ave
Tavistock, ON N0B 2R0, Canada

Dionne, Joseph L (Business Person, Publisher)
McGraw-Hill Inc
1221 Ave of Americas
New York, NY 10020, USA

Dionne, Marcel E (Athlete, Hockey Player)
Marcel Dionne Inc
PO Box 2596
Niagara Falls, NY 14302-2596

Diop, DeSagana (Athlete, Basketball Player)
4300 Haddonfield Rd Ste 309
Pennsauken, NJ 08109-3376, USA

Diop, Majhemout (President)
210 HCM Guediawaye
Dakar, SENEGAL

Diorio, Nick (Soccer Player)
273 Clark St
Lemoyne, PA 17043, USA

Diorio, Ron (Athlete, Baseball Player)
2 White Oak Ln
Waterbury, CT 06705-1835, USA

Di Pasquale, James (Composer, Musician)
c/o Staff Member *Gorfaine/Schwartz Agency Inc*
4111 W Alameda Ave
Suite 509
Burbank, CA 91505, USA

Dipierro, Ramon (Athlete, Football Player)
1750 Brownstone Blvd
Apt H
Toledo, OH 43614, USA

Dipietro, Rick (Athlete, Hockey Player, Olympic Athlete)
Pulver Sports
479 Bedford Park Ave
Attn I an Pulver
Toronto, ON M5M 1K2, Canada

Dipietro, Rocky (Athlete, Football Player)
1 Logan St
St Catharines, ON L2N 286, Canada

Dipino, Frank (Athlete, Baseball Player)
5479 Pebble Beach Dr
Camillus, NY 13031-8651, USA

Diplo (DJ, Musician)
c/o Tom Windish *The Windish Agency*
1658 N Milwaukee Ave
#211
Chicago, IL 60647, USA

Dipoto, Jerry (Commentator)
15130 E Camelview Dr
Fountain Hills, AZ 85268-6405, USA

DiPreta, Tony (Cartoonist)
North American Syndicate
235 E 45th St
New York, NY 10017, USA

DiPrete, Edward D (Politician)
555 Wilbur Ave
Cranston, RI 02921-1435, USA

Di Prima, Denise (Stylist)
c/o Staff Member *L'Agence*
5901-C Peachtree Dunwoody Rd
#60
Atlanta, GA 30328, USA

Dirda, Michael (Journalist)
Washington Post
Editorial Dept
1150 15th St NW
Washington, DC 20071, USA

Dirden, Johnnie (Athlete, Football Player)
1403 S Ulster St
Denver, CO 80231, USA

Director, Kim (Actor)
c/o Rachel Sheedy *Don Buchwald & Associates Inc (NY)*
10 E 44th St
New York, NY 10017

Direnzo, Daniel (Dan) (Athlete, Football Player)
P.O. Box 958
Albrightsville, PA 18210, USA

Direnzo, Fred (Athlete, Football Player)
5 Togno St
Netcong, NJ 07857, USA

Diresta, John (Actor, Comedian)
c/o Ruthanne Secunda *United Talent Agency (UTA)*
9336 Civic Center Dr
Beverly Hills, CA 90210, USA

Dirie, Waris (Activist, Model)
London Mgmt
2-4 Noel Street
London W1V 3RB, UNITED KINGDOM (UK)

Dirk, Robert (Athlete, Hockey Player)
Okanagan Hockey School
201-853 Eckhardt Ave W
Penticton, BC V2A 9C4, Canada

Dirks, Andy
11516 E Trail West Rd
Burrton, KS 67020-8810, USA

Dirnt, Mike (Musician)
3457 Bonnie Hill Dr
Los Angeles, CA 90068, USA

Dirt Band, The
PO Box 1915
Aspen, CO 81611

Dirty Pretty Things (Music Group)
c/o Staff Member *Paradigm (Monterey)*
404 W Franklin St
Monterey, CA 93940, USA

DiSalvatore, Jon
1742 Main St
South Windsor, CT 06074-1042

Di Salvo, Danielle (Stylist)
3243 Harrison St
San Francisco, CA 94110, USA

Disarcina, Gary (Athlete, Baseball Player)
141 Martingale Ln
Plymouth, MA 02360-3275, USA

Dischinger, Terry (Athlete, Basketball Player, Olympic Athlete)
1730 Oak Ave
Northbrook, IL 60062-5428, USA

Disco, Shanthi (Actor, Bollywood)
19 Habibullah Road
T Nagar
Chennai, TN 600017, INDIA

Disco Biscuits, The (Music Group)
c/o Staff Member *Red Light Management (LA)*
8439 W Sunset Blvd
Suite 2
Los Angeles, CA 90069, USA

Disel, Vin (Actor, Director)
c/o Stacy Boniello *Firm, The*
2049 Century Park E #2550
Los Angeles, CA 90067, USA

Dishman, Chris E (Athlete, Football Player)
1561 Raymond Rd
Garland, NE 68360, USA

Dishman, Cris (Athlete, Football Player)
5019 Mariposa Cir
Fresno, TX 77545, USA

Dishman, Glenn (Athlete, Baseball Player)
5400 Fairway Dr
San Jose, CA 95127-1609, USA

Dishy, Bob (Actor)
20 E 9th St
New York, NY 10003, USA

Disi, Ursula (Skier)
Krumme Gasse 10A
Ruhpolding 83324, GERMANY

Disi, Uschi (Misc)
Unterer Plattenberg 6
Flossenberg 92696, GERMANY

Disney, Anthea (Editor)
News Corporation
1211 Avenue of Americas 8th Fl
New York, NY 10036, USA

Disney, Bill (Athlete, Olympic Athlete, Speed Skater)
1610 Kirk Dr Lake
Havasu City, AZ 86404-2449

Disney, William (Speed Skater)
1610 Kirk Dr
Lake Havasu City, AZ 86404, USA

DiSpirito, Rocco (Chef, Reality TV Star)
60 E Randolph St #3203
Chicago, IL 60601, USA

Distefano, Benny (Athlete, Baseball Player)
9911 Murray Lndg
Missouri City, TX 77459-6417, USA

Distel, Sascha
20 rue de Fosses-Saint-Jacques
Paris F-75005, FRANCE

Distler, Natalie (Actor)
c/o Cynthia Booth *Global Artists Agency*
6253 Hollywood Blvd
Suite 508
Los Angeles, CA 90028, USA

Disturbed (Music Group, Musician)
c/o Silda Palerm *Warner Bros Records (NY)*
75 Rockefeller Center
New York, NY 10019, USA

DiSuvero, Mark (Artist)
PO Box 2218
Astoria, NY 11102, USA

Ditka, Mike (Athlete, Coach, Football Coach, Football Player)
161 E Chicago Ave
Apt 39F
Chicago, IL 60611, USA

Ditmar, Arthur J (Art) (Athlete, Baseball Player)
6687 Wisteria Dr
Myrtle Beach, SC 29588-6481, USA

Dittemore, Ronald (Scientist)
5385 Shoshone Cir
Ogden, UT 84403-4654, USA

Dittmer, Andreas (Athlete)
Fischerbank 5
Neubrandenburg 17033, GERMANY

Dittmer, Edward C (Scientist)
702 Old Mescalero Road
Tularosa, NM 88352, USA

Dittmer, Jack (Athlete, Baseball Player)
P.O. Box 98
Elkader, IA 52043, USA

Dittmer, Jack
PO Box 98
Elkader, IA 52043-0098

Ditto, Beth (Musician)
c/o Marc Gerald *Agency Group Ltd, The (LA)*
1880 Century Park E
Suite 711
Los Angeles, CA 90067, USA

Dityatin, Aleksandr N (Gymnast)
Nevski Prosp 18
#25
Saint Petersburg, RUSSIA

Ditz, Nancy (Athlete, Track Athlete)
524 Moore Road
Woodside, CA 94062, USA

Diulio, Albert J (Educator)
Marquette University
President's Office
Milwaukee, WI 53233, USA

Diva, Amanda (Television Host)
c/o Michael (Mike) Esterman
Esterman.Com, LLC
Prefers to be contacted via email
MD, USA

Divac, Vlade (Athlete, Basketball Player)
c/o Marc Fleisher *Entersport-World HQ*
128 Heather Dr
New Canaan, CT 06840, USA

DiVello, Adam (Producer)
1235 N Kenter Ave
Los Angeles, CA 90049, USA

Divina, Luz (DJ)
c/o Len Evans *Project Publicity*
312 West 53rd St
Suite 202
New York, NY 10019, USA

Divine, Gary W (Misc)
National Federation of Federal Employees
1016 16th St
Washington, DC 20038, USA

Divine Comedy, The (Music Group)
c/o Staff Member *Paradigm (Monterey)*
404 W Franklin St
Monterey, CA 93940, USA

Divins, Charles (Actor)
c/o Staff Member *Innovative Artists (LA)*
1505 10th St
Santa Monica, CA 90401, USA

Divis, Reinhard (Athlete, Hockey Player)
Unterer Hubertusweg 5
Thuringen 6712, Austriil

Divoff, Andrew (Actor)
c/o Staff Member *Marshak/Zachary Company, The*
8840 Wilshire Blvd
1st Floor
Beverly Hills, CA 90210, USA

Diwakar, R R (Writer)
Sri Arvind Krupa
233 Sadashiv Nagar
Bangalore, Karnataka 560006, INDIA

Dix, Drew D (General)
2910 Country Club Dr
Pueblo, CO 81008-1201, USA

Dixie Chicks (Music Group)
c/o Simon Renshaw *Strategics Artist Management*
1100 Glendon Ave #1000
Los Angeles, CA 90024, USA

Dixie Cups, The (Music Group)
2535 Noble Street
North Las Vegas, NV 89030, USA

Dixieland Rhythm Kings, The
PO Box 12403
Atlanta, GA 30355

Dixit, Madhuri (Actor, Bollywood)
Rocky Mountain CV Surgeons PC
C/O Dr. Shriram Madhav Nene
1390 S Potomac St, Suite 120
Aurora, CO 80012, USA

Dixon, Al (Athlete, Football Player)
386 Somerset St
Apt 1
North Plainfield, NJ 07060, USA

Dixon, Alan J (Politician)
7606 Foley Dr
Belleville, IL 62223-2322, USA

Dixon, Alesha (Musician)
c/o Staff Member *Independent Talent Group (ITG-UK)*
Oxford House
76 Oxford St
London W1D 1BS, UK

Dixon, Becky (Sportscaster)
ABC-TV
Sports Dept
77 W 66th St
New York, NY 10023, USA

Dixon, Cal (Athlete, Football Player)
179 Las Palmas
Merritt Island, FL 32953, USA

Dixon, Cathy (Stylist)
c/o Celebrity Stylist *Jed Root Inc*
61-A Walker St
New York, NY 10013, USA

Dixon, Colton (Musician)
c/o Staff Member *19 Entertainment - LA*
9000 W Sunset Blvd #1574
West Hollywood, CA 90069, USA

Dixon, Craig (Athlete, Olympic Athlete, Track Athlete)
10630 Wellworth Ave
Los Angeles, CA 90024, USA

Dixon, David (Athlete, Football Player)
4795 W 131 1/2 St
Savage, MN 55378, USA

Dixon, D Jeremy (Architect)
41 Shelton St
London WC2H 9HJ, UNITED KINGDOM (UK)

Dixon, Donna (Actor)
7708 Woodrow Wilson Dr
Los Angeles, CA 90046, USA

Dixon, Dwayne (Athlete, Football Player)
78 Westfield Pl
Athens, OH 45701, USA

Dixon, Floyd (Musician)
Folklore Prod
1671 Appian Way
Santa Monica, CA 90401, USA

Dixon, Gerald (Athlete, Football Player)
1315 Big Rock Ct
Fort Mill, SC 29708, USA

Dixon, Juan (Basketball Player)
Washington Wizards
MCI Centre
601 F St NW
Washington, DC 20004, USA

Dixon, Ken (Athlete, Baseball Player)
4317 Highview Ave
Baltimore, MD 21229-5303, USA

Dixon, Larry (Race Car Driver)
Don Prudhomme Racing
1232 Distribution Way
Vista, CA 92083, USA

Dixon, Leslie (Director, Producer, Writer)
c/o Todd Feldman *Creative Artists Agency (CAA-LA)*
2000 Ave Of The Stars
Los Angeles, CA 90067, USA

Dixon, Mark (Athlete, Football Player)
4016 Ivy Ln
Kitty Hawk, NC 27949, USA

Dixon, Randolph C (Randy) (Athlete, Football Player)
9910 Summerlakes Dr
Carmel, IN 46032, USA

Dixon, Robert (General)
5100 John D Ryan Blvd
Apt 2206
San Antonio, TX 78245-3513, USA

Dixon, Rodney (Rod) (Athlete, Track Athlete)
22 Entrican Ave
Remuera
Auckland 5, NEW ZEALAND

Dixon, Ronnie (Athlete, Football Player)
1440 W Kemper Rd Apt 510
Cincinnati, OH 45240, USA

Dixon, Scott (Race Car Driver)
Target Chip Ganassi Racing
7161 Zionville Rd.
Indianapolis, IN 46250, USA

Dixon, Steve (Athlete, Baseball Player)
6510 Hollow Tree Rd
Louisville, KY 40228-1336, USA

Dixon, Tamecka (Basketball Player)
Los Angeles Sparks
Staples Center
1111 S Figueroa St
Los Angeles, CA 90015, USA

Dixon, Thomas F (Engineer)
1761 Cuba Island Lane
Hayes, VA 23072, USA

Dixon, Tom (Athlete, Baseball Player)
540 W Graves Ave
Orange City, FL 32763-5170, USA

Dixon, Tony (Athlete, Football Player)
1521 Riverchase Trl
Birmingham, AL 35244, USA

Dixon, Zachary (Athlete, Football Player)
19365 Hottinger Cir
Germantown, MD 20874, USA

Dizon, Jesse
PO Box 572105
Tarzana, CA 91357-2105, USA

Djalili, Omid (Actor)
c/o Brian Stern *Stern Entertainment Group
(Brillstein Entertainment Partners)*
1 William Morris Pl
Beverly Hills, CA 90212, USA

DJ Ashba (Musician)
Ashba Media
700 San Vicente
Suite G410
West Hollywood, CA 90069, USA

Djerassi, Carl (Inventor)
2325 Bear Gulch Rd
Redwood City, CA 94062-4405, USA

DJ Jazzy Jeff (Actor, Musician)
A Touched of Jazz
444 N 3rd Street
Philadelphia, PA 19123, USA

DJ Mendez (Musician)
c/o Leopoldo Mendez *Macabro Records*
Bolidenvagen 10
Johanneshov 121 63, SWEDEN

Djodjov Pejoski, Marjan (Designer,
Fashion Designer)
c/o Staff Member *Marjan Djodjov Pejoski*
75 Garden Flat
Warwick Avenue
London, England W1Y 1DH, United
Kingdom

Djokovic, Novak (Athlete, Tennis Player)
c/o Staff Member *Family Sport*
Futog
Novi Sad 21000, Serbia

Djoussouf, Abbass (Prime Minister)
Prime Minister's Office
Moroni, BP 421, COMOROS

Djukanovic, Milo (President)
Executive Council
Bul Lenjina 2
Novi Belgrad 11075, SERBIA &
MONTENEGRO

Dlouhy, Lukas (Athlete, Tennis Player)
c/o Staff Member *ATP Tour*
201 ATP Tour Blvd
Ponte Vedra Beach, FL 32082-3211, USA

D. Lucas, Frank (Congressman, Politician)
2311 Rayburn HOB
Washington, DC 20515, USA

Dlugach, Brent
9847 Laurel Hollow Cir
Germantown, TN 38139-6967, USA

D'Lyn, Shae (Actor)
c/o Miles Levy *James/Levy/Jacobson
Management Inc*
3500 W Olive Ave
Suite 1470
Burbank, CA 91505, USA

Dmitriev, Artur (Figure Skater)
Russian Skating Federation
Luchneksaia Nab 8
Moscow 119871, RUSSIA

Doak, Gary (Athlete, Hockey Player)
117 Hill St Apt 505
Stoneham, MA 02180-3756, USA

Do Amaral, Diogo F (Government
Official)
Ave Fontes Perelra de Melo 35
#13A
Lisbon 1050, PORTUGAL

Doan, Charles A (Doctor)
4935 Oletangy Blvd
Columbus, OH 43214, USA

Doan, Shane (Athlete, Hockey Player)
9820 E Thompson Peak Pkwy #728
Scottsdale, AZ 85255-6657, CANADA

Doar, John (Lawyer)
9 E 63rd St
New York, NY 10021, USA

Dobbek, Dan (Athlete, Baseball Player)
4042 SE Yamhill St
Portland, OR 97214-4445, USA

Dobbin, Brian (Athlete, Hockey Player)
5075 Shiloh Line
Petrolia, ON N0N 1R0, Canada

Dobbin, Edmund J (Educator)
Villanova University
President's Office
Villanova, PA 19085, USA

Dobbins, Herb (Athlete, Football Player)
10 Keating Pt
Saint Albert, AB T8N 5W8, Canada

Dobbins, Oliver (Athlete, Football Player)
11126 Piscataway Rd
Clinton, MD 20735, USA

Dobbs, Greg (Athlete, Baseball Player)
2255 Richey Dr
La Canada Flintridge, CA 91011-1350,
USA

Dobbs, Leka (Stylist)
c/o Staff Member *Koko Represents*
166 Geary St
#1007
San Francisco, CA 94108, USA

Dobbs, Lou (Television Host)
7112 Eagle Ter
West Palm Beach, FL 33412, USA

Dobbs, Mattiwilda (Opera Singer)
1101 S Arlington Ridge Road
Arlington, VA 22202, USA

Dobek, Bob (Athlete, Hockey Player,
Olympic Athlete)
3813 Observation Pl
Escondido, CA 92025-7933, USA

Dobek, Michelle (Athlete, Golfer)
292 Chicopee St
Chicopee, MA 01013-1744, USA

Dobie, Alan
Pontus Molash
Kent CT4 8HW, ENGLAND

Dobkin, Alix (Musician)
P.O. Box 761
Woodstock, New York 12498, USA

Dobkin, David (Director)
H S I Productions
3630 Eastham Dr
Culver City, CA 90232, USA

Dobkin, Lawrence
1787 Old Ranch Rd
Los Angeles, CA 90049, USA

Dobkins, Carl Jr (Musician)
7640 Cheviot Road
#212
Cincinnati, OH 45247, USA

Dobler, Conrad F (Athlete, Football
Player)
12600 Fairway Rd
Leawood, KS 66209, USA

Dobler, David (Religious Leader)
Presbyterian Church USA
100 Witherspoon St
Louisville, KY 40202, USA

Dobo, Kata (Actor)
c/o Sara Ramaker *Paradigm (LA)*
360 N Crescent Dr
North Bldg
Beverly Hills, CA 90210, USA

Dobrev, Nina (Actor)
c/o Norbert Abrams *Noble Caplan
Abrams*
1260 Yonge St
2nd Floor
Toronto ON M4T 1W6, Canada

Dobslow, Bill (Musician)
945 Handlebar Road
Mishawaka, IN 46544, USA

Dobson, Chuck (Athlete, Baseball Player)
4208 Locust St
Kansas City, MO 64110-1017, USA

Dobson, Dominic (Race Car Driver)
2719 63rd Avenue SE
Mercer Island, WA 98040, USA

Dobson, Fefe (Musician)
c/o Staff Member *Island Records*
825 Eighth Ave
New York, NY 10019, USA

Dobson, Helen (Athlete, Golfer)
7638 Eagle Creek Dr
Sarasota, FL 34243-4613, USA

Dobson, James C (Religious Leader)
Focus on the Family
8605 Explorer Dr
Colorado Springs, CO 80920, USA

Dobson, Kevin (Actor)
12527 Sarah St
Studio City, CA 91604, USA

Dobson, Peter (Actor)
1351 N Crescent Heights Blvd
#318
West Hollywood, CA 90046, USA

Dockery, Derrick (Athlete, Football
Player)
7102 Jack Franzen Dr
Garland, TX 75043, USA

Dockery, John (Athlete, Football Player)
17 Garden Pl
Brooklyn, NY 11201, USA

Dockett, Darnell (Athlete, Football Player)
6815 Sand Cherry Way
Clinton, MD 20735, USA

Dockson, Robert R (Financier)
1301 Collingwood Place
Los Angeles, CA 90069, USA

Dockstader, Frederick J (Misc)
165 W 66th St
New York, NY 10022, USA

Docter, Mary (Athlete, Olympic Athlete,
Speed Skater)
3400 S Russell Rd
New Berlin, WI 53151-4637, USA

Docter, Pete (Actor, Director, Writer)
c/o Staff Member *Pixar Animation Studios*
1200 Park Avenue
Emeryville, CA 94608, USA

Doctorow, Cory (Internet Star)
Box 306 456-458
Strand, London WC2R0DZ, UNITED
KINGDOM

Doctorow, E L (Writer)
c/o Ron Bernstein *ICM Partners (ICM-LA)*
10250 Constellation Blvd Fl 7
Los Angeles, CA 90067, USA

Doda, Carol (Actor, Dancer)
PO Box 387
Fremont, CA 94537, USA

Dodd, Alice (Model)
574 N Irving Blvd
Los Angeles, CA 90004, USA

Dodd, Christopher (Politician)
87th St NE
Washington, DC 20002-6022, USA

Dodd, Deryl (Musician, Songwriter,
Writer)
823 Mgmt
PO Box 186
Waring, TX 78074, USA

Dodd, Jamie (Actor)
c/o Staff Member *Nikki Bond
Management*
Aspect Court
47 Park Square East
Leeds LS1 2NL, United Kingdom

Dodd, Maurice (Cartoonist)
Daily Mirror
Editorial Dept
1 Canada Square
London E14 5AP, UNITED KINGDOM
(UK)

Dodd, Michael T (Mike) (Athlete,
Volleyball Player)
AVP Pro Beach Volleyball Tour
960 Knox Street
Suite A
Torrance, CA 90502, USA

Dodd, Patty D (Athlete, Volleyball Player)
Fonz
1017 Manhattan Ave
Manhattan Beach, CA 90266, USA

Dodd, Robert (Athlete, Baseball Player)
3467 Overhill Dr
Frisco, TX 75033-1112, USA

Dodd, Tom (Athlete, Baseball Player)
3735 NE Shaver St
Portland, OR 97212-1871, USA

Dodds, Megan (Actor)
c/o Ron West *Thruline Entertainment*
9250 Wilshire Blvd
Ground Fl
Beverly Hills, CA 90212, USA

Dodds, Trevor (Athlete, Golfer)
9730 Plummer St
Houston, TX 77029-4230, USA

Dodge, Brooks (Skier)
PO Box C
Jackson, NH 03846, USA

Dodge, Dedrick (Athlete, Football Player)
1109 Bowlin Dr
Locust Grove, GA 30248, USA

Dodge, GeaHrey (Publisher)
Money Magazine
Time-Life Building
New York, NY 10020, USA

Dodge, Geoffrey (Publisher)
Money Magazine
Time-Life Building
New York, NY 10020, USA

Dodge, Julie (Stylist)
c/o Staff Member *Koko Represents*
166 Geary St
#1007
San Francisco, CA 94108, USA

Dodge, Kirk (Athlete, Football Player)
27382 Pinavete
Mission Viejo, CA 92691, USA

Dodrill, Dale (Athlete, Football Player)
2579 S Independence St
Lakewood, CO 80227, USA

Dodson, Pat (Athlete, Baseball Player)
1034 Hillside Rd
Grove, OK 74344-3514, USA

Dodson, Quintin (Reality TV Star)
4571 Haskell Ave
Encino, CA 91436, USA

Dodson, Richard (Athlete, Football Player)
P.O. Box 81302
Phoenix, AZ 85069, USA

Doe, Cathy Jeneen (Actor)

Doelling, Fred (Athlete, Football Player)
60 South St
Valparaiso, IN 46383, USA

Doerfling, B J (Stylist)
4045 Liberty Canyon Rd
Agoura Hills, CA 91301, USA

Doerger, Jerome (Athlete, Football Player)
8309 Ridgevalley Ct
Cincinnati, OH 45247, USA

Doering, Chris (Athlete, Football Player)
3843 SW 92nd Ter
Gainesville, FL 32608, USA

Doering, Jason (Athlete, Football Player)
24 Milford St
Apt 1
Boston, MA 02118, USA

Doerr, Robert P (Bobby) (Athlete, Baseball Player)
94449 Territorial Hwy
Junction City, OR 97448-9326, USA

Doerre-Heinig, Katrin (Athlete, Track Athlete)
Westring 53
Erbach 6471, GERMANY

Dogg, Snoop (Actor, Artist, Musician)
c/o Daniel Weiner *Paradigm (Monterey)*
9100 Wilshire Blvd
Suite 500, West Tower
Beverly Hills, CA 90212, USA

Doggett, Lloyd (Congressman, Politician)
201 Cannon HOB
Washington, DC 20515, USA

Dogins, Kevin (Athlete, Football Player)
8861 Cameron Crest Dr
Tampa, FL 33626, USA

Dog Pschology Center (Misc)
P.O. Box 54069
Los Angeles, CA 90054-0069, USA

Dog Star (Music Group)
1900 Avenue of the Stars #1040
Los Angeles, CA 90067, USA

Dohan, Meital (Actor, Musician)
c/o Cory Richman *Liebman Entertainment*
25 E 21st St #PH
New York, NY 10011-8503, USA

Doherty, James (Horse Racer)
9 Jane St
East Rutherford, NJ 07073-1420, USA

Doherty, John (Athlete, Baseball Player)
109 Wakefield St
Reading, MA 01867-1854, USA

Doherty, Peter (Musician)
c/o Staff Member *Bucks Music Group*
Onward House
11 Uxbridge Street
London W8 7TQ, United Kingdom

Doherty, Peter (Nobel Prize Laureate)
262 Danny Thomas Pl
Memphis, TN 38105-3678, USA

Doherty, Shannen (Actor)
3626 Malibu Country Dr
Malibu, CA 90265, USA

Dohery, Peter C (Nobel Prize Laureate)
172 Kimbrough Place #506
Memphis, TN 38104, USA

Dohm, Gaby (Actor)
Omnis Agentur
Wiedenmayerstr 11
Munich 80538, GERMANY

Dohmann, Scott (Athlete, Baseball Player)
3222 W Paxton Ave
Tampa, FL 33611-3920, USA

Dohring, Jason (Actor)
c/o Joel Stevens *Joel Stevens Entertainment*
5627 Allott Ave
Van Nuys, CA 91401, USA

Dohrmann, Angela (Actor)
Innovative Artists
1505 10th St
Santa Monica, CA 90401, USA

Dohrmann, George (Journalist)
Saint Paul Pioneer Press
Editorial Dept
345 Cedar St
Saint Paul, MN 55101, USA

Doi, Takako (Government Official)
Daini Giinkaikan
2-1-2 Nagatacho
Chiyodaku
Tokyo, JAPAN

Doi, Takao (Astronaut)
NASDA
Tsukuba Space Ctr
2-1-2 Sengern
Tukubashi, Ibaraki, JAPAN

Doi, Takao Dr (Astronaut)
NASDA, Tsukuba Space Center 2-1-1, Sengen
Tukuba-shi Ibaraka 305, Japan

Doig, Jason (Athlete, Hockey Player)
2153 Broderick Ave
Duarte, CA 91010-3508, USA

Doig, Lex (Actor)
Andromeda Productions
8651 Eastlake Drive
Vancouver, BC V5A 4T7

Doig, Lexa (Actor)
c/o Adam Levine *Levine Okwu Erickson Management*
9601 Wilshire Blvd
3rd Floor
Beverly Hills, CA 90210, USA

Doig, Steve (Athlete, Football Player)
P.O. Box 206
North Reading, MA 01864, USA

Dokey, Merritt (Horse Racer)
439 Yerkes St
Northville, MI 48167-1683, USA

Dokish, Wanita (Athlete, Baseball Player, Commentator)
403 Todd Farm Rd
Belle Vernon, PA 15012-3869, USA

Dokken, Don (Musician)
Agency for Performing Arts
9200 Sunset Blvd
#900
Los Angeles, CA 90069, USA

Doktor, Martin (Athlete)
Canoe Prosport Sezemice
Slinecni 627
Sezemice 533 04, CZECH REPUBLIC

Dolan, Chuck (Business Person)
330 Cove Neck Rd
Oyster Bay, NY 11771, USA

Dolan, Don (Actor)
14228 Emelita St
Van Nuys, CA 91401, USA

Dolan, Ellen (Actor)
Don Buchwald
10 E 44th St
New York, NY 10017, USA

Dolan, Lawrence J (Commentator)
16 Windward Way
Chagrin Falls, OH 44023-6705, USA

Dolan, Louise A (Physicist)
University of North Carolina
Physics Dept
Chapel Hill, NC 27599, USA

Dolan, Michael P (Government Official)
Internal Revenue Service
1111 Constitution Ave NW
Washington, DC 20224, USA

Dolan, Tom (Athlete, Olympic Athlete, Swimmer)
12 S Manchester St
Arlington, VA 22204-1075

Dolbin, Jack (Athlete, Football Player)
1775 Howard Ave
Pottsville, PA 17901, USA

Dolby, Raymond M (Ray) (Engineer, Inventor)
Dolby Laboratories
100 Potrero Ave
San Francisco, CA 94103, USA

Dolby, Thomas (Musician, Songwriter, Writer)
Inteinational Talent Group
729 7th Ave
#1600
New York, NY 10019, USA

Dolce (Musician)
c/o Staff Member *Diva Central Inc*
7510 W Sunset Blvd Ste 1445
Los Angees, CA 90046, USA

Dolce, Domenico (Designer, Fashion Designer)
Dolce & Gabbana
Via Santa Cecilia 7
Milan 20122, ITALY

Dolci, Danilo (Activist, Writer)
Centro Iniziative Studl
Largo Scalia 5
Partinico/Palermo
Sicily, ITALY

Dold, R Bruce (Journalist)
501 N Park Road
#HSE
La Grange Park, IL 60526, USA

Dole, Bob (Politician)
The Atlantic Building
950 F St NW Fl 10
Washington, DC 20004, USA

Dole, Elizabeth H (Politician)
c/o Staff Member *WmE2 (WMA-LA)*
1 William Morris Pl
Beverly Hills, CA 90212, USA

Dole, Vincent P (Misc, Scientist)
Rockefeller University
1230 York Ave
New York, NY 10021, USA

Doleac, Michael (Athlete, Basketball Player)
1155 Old Rail Ln
Park City, UT 84098-6640, USA

Doleman, Christopher J (Chris) (Athlete, Football Player)
1025 Leadenhall St
Alpharetta, GA 30022, USA

Dolenz, Ami (Actor)
1860 Bel Air Road
Los Angeles, CA 90077, USA

Dolenz, Micky (Actor, Musician)
22 Baymare Rd
Bell Canyon, CA 91307, USA

Dolfini, Monica (Stylist)
c/o Staff Member *Camilla Lowther Managment (CLM Represents)*
30-32 Ericsson Pl
New York, NY 10013, USA

D'Oliveira, Luisa (Actor)
c/o Staff Member *Levine Okwu Erickson Management*
6363 Wilshire Blvd
Suite 300
Los Angeles, CA 90048, USA

Dollansky, Craig (Race Car Driver)
Craig Dollansky Racing
28223 Lake Diann Rd
Zimmerman, MN 55398, USA

Dollar, Aubrey (Actor)
c/o Rhonda Price *Gersh (NY)*
41 Madison Ave
New York, NY 10010, USA

Dollar, Linda (Coach)
Southwest Missouri State University
Athletic Dept
Springfield, MO 65804, USA

Dollard, Christopher Edward (Actor)
Gold Marshak Liedtke
3500 W Olive Ave
#1400
Burbank, CA 91505, USA

Dollas, Bobby (Athlete, Hockey Player)
c/o Staff Member *Contact Image*
185 rue du Seminaire
Montreal, QC H3C 2A3, Canada

Dollens, Ronald (Business Person)
Guidant Corp
111 Monument Circle
Indianapolis, IN 46204, USA

Dolley, Jason (Actor)
c/o Nils Larsen *Principato/Young
Management*
312 W 5th St Apt 815
Los Angeles, CA 90013, USA

Dollfus, Audouin (Scientist)
Observatoire de Paris
Attn: Director's Office
Meudon F-92190, France

Dolmayan, John (Musician)
Velvet Hammer
9911 W pico Blvd
#350
Los Angeles, CA 90035, USA

Dologuele, Anicet Georges (Prime
Minister)
Prime Minister's Office
Bangui, CENTRAL AFRICAN REPUBLIC

Doman, Brandon (Athlete, Football
Player)
4616 Pheasant Ridge Trl
Lehi, UT 84043, USA

Doman, John (Actor)
c/o Staff Member *Peter Strain &
Associates Inc (LA)*
5455 Wilshire Blvd
Suite 1812
Los Angeles, CA 90036-4368, USA

Domar, Evsey D (Economist)
264 Heath's Bridge Road
Concord, MA 01742, USA

Dombasle, Arielle (Actor)
Agence Intertalent
5 Rue Clemet Marot
Paris 75008, FRANCE

Dombroski, Paul (Athlete, Football Player)
19122 Beckett Dr
Odessa, FL 33556, USA

Dombrowski, Dave (Commentator)
Detroit Tigers
345 Woodridge Rd
Bloomfield Hills, MI 48304-3468, USA

Dombrowski, James M (Jim) (Athlete,
Football Player)
220 Evangeline Dr
Mandeville, LA 70471, USA

Domenichelli, Hnat (Athlete, Hockey
Player)
1500 Mansell Rd
Alpharetta, GA 30009-4709, USA

Domenici, Pete (Politician)
120 3rd St NE
Washington, DC 20002-7320, USA

Domi, Tie (Athlete, Hockey Player)
1-7357 Woodbine Ave
Suite 415
Markham, ON L3R 6L3, Canada

Domi, Tim (Athlete, Hockey Player)
46 Florence St
Ottawa, ON K2P 0W7, Canada

Dominczyk, Dagmara (Actor)
c/o Bill Butler *Industry Entertainment
Partners*
955 S Carrillo Dr
Suite 300
Los Angeles, CA 90048, USA

Dominczyk, Marika (Actor)
c/o Sally Ware *Gersh (NY)*
41 Madison Ave
New York, NY 10010, USA

Domingo, Placido (Musician, Opera
Singer)
Zaungergasse 1-3
Tur 16
Vienna 1030, AUSTRIA

Dominguez, Fernandez Adolfo (Designer,
Fashion Designer)
Polingono Industrial Calle 4
San Ciprian de Vinas, Ourense 32901,
SPAIN

Dominguez, Mario (Race Car Driver)
Herdez Racing
57A Gasoline Alley
Indianapolis, IN 46222, USA

Dominguez, Matt (Athlete, Football
Player)
4804 Counts Cv
Austin, TX 78749, USA

Dominic, Rhodes (Athlete, Football
Player)
6411 Canyon Lake Dr
Dallas, TX 75249-3021, USA

Dominik, Andrew (Director, Writer)
c/o Spencer Baumgarten *Creative Artists
Agency (CAA-LA)*
2000 Ave Of The Stars
Los Angeles, CA 90067, USA

Dominique, Andy (Athlete, Baseball
Player)
2016 Lamego Way
El Dorado Hills, CA 95762-7557, USA

Dominis, John (Photographer)
252 W 102nd St
Apt 4
New York, NY 10025-4967, USA

Domino, Fats (Musician)
9 Wedgewood Ct
Harvey, LA 70058, USA

Dominy, Charles E (Chuck) (General)
300 Fox Mill Road
Oakton, VA 22124, USA

Domres, Martin F (Marty) (Athlete,
Football Player)
Deutsche Bank
1 South St
Suite 2400
Baltimore, MD 21202, USA

Do Muoi (Politician)
Chairman's Office
Council of Ministers
Hanoi, VIETNAM

Donahue, Aichie G (War Hero)
2402 Lary Lake Dr
Harlingen, TX 78550, USA

Donahue, Archie G (War Hero)
2402 Lazy Lake Dr
Harlingen, TX 78550, USA

Donahue, Debrah E (Stylist)
873 Broadway
#302
New York, NY 10003, USA

Donahue, Elinor (Actor)
78533 Sunrise Mountain View
Palm Desert, CA 92211, USA

Donahue, Heather (Actor)
Rigberg Roberts Rugolo
118D S Bevedy Dr
#601
Los Aneles, CA 90035, USA

Donahue, Kenneth (Misc)
245 S Westgate Ave
Los Angeles, CA 90049, USA

Donahue, Mitch (Athlete, Football Player)
2220 Beloit Dr
Billings, MT 59102, USA

Donahue, Phil (Talk Show Host)
120/122 Beachside Ave
Westport, CT 06880, USA

Donahue, Terry (Athlete, Baseball Player,
Commentator)
215 N 3rd Ave
Saint Charles, IL 60174-2005, USA

Donahue, Thomas R (Misc)
American Federation of Labor
815 l6th St NW
Washington, DC 20006, USA

Donald, Kirkland H (Admiral)
Commander Submarine Command
Atlantic
7958 Blandy Road
Norfolk, VA 23511, USA

Donald, Luke (Athlete, Golfer)
8 Bristol Rd
Northfield, IL 60093, USA

Donald, Mike (Athlete, Golfer)
2400 NW 65th Way
Hollywood, FL 33024-4046, USA

Donaldson, Colby (Actor, Reality TV Star)
c/o Nicole David *WME (LA)*
9601 Wilshire Blvd Fl 3
Beverly Hills, CA 90210, USA

Donaldson, Holly (Stylist)
c/o Staff Member *Team*
423 W Broadway
4th Floor
Boston, MA 02127, USA

Donaldson, James (Athlete, Basketball
Player)
2843 34th Avenue West
Seattle, WA 98199-2602, USA

Donaldson, Jeff (Athlete, Football Player)
4529 Stover St
Fort Collins, CO 80525, USA

Donaldson, John (Athlete, Football Player)
3913 Yates Ct
Charlotte, NC 28215, USA

Donaldson, John (Athlete, Baseball Player)
3913 Yates Ct
Charlotte, NC 28215-3955, USA

Donaldson, Ray (Athlete, Football Player)
3128 Crestwell Dr
Indianapolis, IN 46268, USA

Donaldson, Roger (Director, Producer,
Writer)
c/o Martin Spencer *Creative Artists
Agency (CAA-LA)*
2000 Ave Of The Stars
Los Angeles, CA 90067, USA

Donaldson, Sam (Journalist)
1211 Crest Ln
Me Lean, VA 22101-1837, USA

Donaldson, Samuel (Sam)
(Correspondent)
1125 Crest Lane
McLean, VA 22101, USA

Donaldson, Simon K (Mathematician)
Bristol University
Mathematics Dept
Bristol BS8 1TH, UNITED KINGDOM
(UK)

Donan, Holland R (Athlete, Football
Player)
212 Valley View
Pompton Plains, NJ 07444, USA

Do Nascimento, Alexandre Cardinal
(Religious Leader)
Arcebispado
CP 87
Luanda 1230 C, ANGOLA

Donat, Peter (Actor)
PO Box 441
Wolfville, NS B0P 1X0, CANADA

Donatelli, Clark (Athlete, Hockey Player)
1101 Curtis Corner Rd
Wakefield, RI 02879-1470

Donatelli, Don (Athlete, Football Player)
54846 Seneca Lake Rd
Quaker City, OH 43773, USA

Donath, Helen (Opera Singer)
Bergstr 5
Wedemark 30900, GERMANY

Donato, Ted (Athlete, Hockey Player,
Olympic Athlete)
34 Whitcomb Rd
Scituate, MA 02066-1123

Donckers, William (Athlete, Football
Player)
13708 SE 141st St
Renton, WA 98059, USA

Done, Kenneth S (Ken) (Artist, Misc)
28 Hopetoun Ave
Mosman, NSW 2088, AUSTRALIA

Donegan, Dan (Musician)
c/o Staff Member *Mitch Schneider
Organization (MSO)*
14724 Ventura Blvd #410
Sherman Oaks, CA 91403, USA

Donella, Chad E (Actor)
c/o Staff Member *TalentWorks (LA)*
3500 W Olive Ave
Suite 1400
Burbank, CA 91505, USA

Donelly, Tanya (Music Group, Songwriter,
Writer)
Helter Skelter
Plaza 535 Kings Road
London SW10 0S, UNITED KINGDOM
(UK)

Donen, Stanley (Director)
c/o Staff Member *La Grange Group, The*
11828 La Grange Ave
Los Angeles, CA 90025, USA

Dong Ghua, Li
rue des O'Euches 10
Moutier 1 CP 359 274, SWITZERLAND

Doniger, Wendy (Historian, Misc)
1319 E 55th St
Chicago, IL 60615, USA

Donlan, Yolande (Actor)
11 Mellina Place
London NW8, UNITED KINGDOM (UK)

Donlavey, Junie (Race Car Driver)
5011 Old Midlothian Pike
Richmorid, VA 23224, USA

Donleavy, James Patrick (J P) (Writer)
Levington Park Mullingar
County Westmeath, IRELAND

Donley, Doug (Athlete, Football Player)
8005 Pullam Cir
Plano, TX 75024, USA

Donlon, Roger H C (General)
2101 Wilson Ave
Leavenworth, KS 66048-4634, USA

Donnahoo, Roger (Athlete, Football Player)
20 Rock Brook Cv
Rossville, GA 30741, USA

Donnalley, Kevin (Athlete, Football Player)
8910 Dove Stand Ln
Charlotte, NC 28226, USA

Donnalley, Rick (Athlete, Football Player)
1796 Danforth Dr
Marietta, GA 30062, USA

Donnan, Jim (Coach, Football Coach)
University of Georgia
Athletic Dept
Athens, GA 30602, USA

Donnellan, Declan (Director)
Cheek by Jowl Theatre Co
Aveline St
London SW11 5DQ, UNITED KINGDOM (UK)

Donnelley, James R (Business Person)
R R Donnelley & Sons
77 W Wacker Dr
Chicago, IL 60601, USA

Donnelly, Andrew (Actor)
c/o Ruthanne Secunda *United Talent Agency (UTA)*
9336 Civic Center Dr
Beverly Hills, CA 90210, USA

Donnelly, Brendan (Athlete, Baseball Player)
2815 E Arrowhead Trl
Gilbert, AZ 85297-5270, USA

Donnelly, Declan (Actor, Television Host)
c/o Staff Member *Rabbit Vocal Management*
27 Poland St
3rd Floor
London W1F 8QW, UK

Donnelly, George (Athlete, Football Player)
2S530 Beechwood Rd
Glen Ellyn, IL 60137-6955, USA

Donnelly, Gord (Athlete, Coach, Hockey Player)
c/o Staff Member *Hockey Montreal International*
4612 Royal Ave
Montreal, QC H4A 2M8, Canada

Donnelly, Joe
1530 Longworth HOB
Washington, DC 20515, USA

Donnelly, Mike (Athlete, Hockey Player)
18429 Stoneridge Ct
Northville, MI 48168-8571, USA

Donnelly, Rich (Athlete, Baseball Player)
101 Bryden Rd
Steubenville, OH 43953-3429, USA

Donnelly, Rick (Athlete, Football Player)
10408 Buck Brush Rd
Cheyenne, WY 82009, USA

Donnelly, Russell J (Physicist)
2175 Olive St
Eugene, OR 97405, USA

Donnels, Chris (Athlete, Baseball Player)
5 Stone Pne
Aliso Vieio, CA 92656-2131, USA

Donner, Jom J (Director)
Pohjoisranta 12
Helsinki 17 00170, FINLAND

Donner, Jorn
Pohjoisranta 12
Helsinki SF-00170, FINLAND

Donner, Lauren Shuler (Producer)
c/o Staff Member *Donners' Company, The*
9465 Wilshire Blvd #420
Beverly Hills, CA 90212, USA

Donner, Richard (Director)
8688 Hollywood Blvd
West Hollywood, CA 90069, USA

Donnie, Elder (Athlete, Football Player)
16613 Norwood Dr
Tampa, FL 33624, USA

Donnovan, Elisa (Actor)
SMS Talent
8730 Sunset Blvd #440
Los Angeles, CA 90069, USA

Donoahoe, John (Business Person)
10 Palmer Ln
Portola Valley, CA 94028, USA

D'Onofrio, Mark (Athlete, Football Player)
295 Harmon Ave
Fort Lee, NJ 07024, USA

D'Onofrio, Vincent (Actor, Producer)
c/o Sam Maydew *Collective*
8383 Wilshire Blvd
Suite 1050
Beverly Hills, CA 90211, USA

Donohoe, Amanda (Actor)
Markham & Froggatt
Julian House
4 Windmill Street
London W1P 1HF, UNITED KINGDOM (UK)

Donohoe, Michael (Athlete, Football Player)
505 Juneberry Rd
Riverwoods, IL 60015, USA

Donohoe, Peter (Music Group, Musician)
82 Hampton Lane Solihull
West Midlands B91 2RS, UNITED KINGDOM (UK)

Donohue, Jim (Athlete, Baseball Player)
16 Huntleigh Downs
Saint Louis, MO 63131-3416, USA

Donohue, Leon (Athlete, Football Player)
1904 Bechelli Ln
Redding, CA 96002, USA

Donohue, Terry
11918 Laurelwood
Studio City, CA 91604

Donohue, Timothy (Business Person)
Nextel Communications
2001 Edmund Halley Dr
Reston, VA 20191, USA

Donohue, Tom (Athlete, Baseball Player)
249 Liberty Ave
Westbury, NY 11590-2135, USA

Donoso, Jose (Writer)
Calceite
Province of Teruel, SPAIN

Donovan (Music Group, Songwriter, Writer)
P O Box 1119
London SW9 9JW, UNITED KINGDOM (UK)

Donovan, Alan B (Educator)
State University of New York College
President's Office
Oneonta, NY 13820, USA

Donovan, Anne (Athlete, Basketball Player, Olympic Athlete)
138 Ridge Rd
Nutley, NJ 07110-2137, USA

Donovan, Billy (Athlete, Basketball Player)
8515 SW 31st Avenue
Gainesville, FL 32608-2725, USA

Donovan, Brian (Journalist)
Newsday
Editorial Dept 235 Pinelawn Road
Melville, NY 11747, USA

Donovan, Elisa (Actor)
c/o Staff Member *Seven Summits Pictures & Management*
8906 W Olympic Blvd
Ground Floor
Beverly Hills, CA 90211, USA

Donovan, Francis R (Frank) (Admiral)
9216 Dellwood Dr
Vienna, VA 22180, USA

Donovan, Harry (Athlete, Basketball Player)
8303 Bayonet Point Court
Apt C
Fredericksburg, VA 22407-2125, USA

Donovan, Jason S (Actor, Music Group)
Richard East Productions
PO Box 342
South Yarra, VIC 3141, AUSTRALIA

Donovan, Jeffrey (Actor)
21042 Entrada Rd
Topanga, CA 90290, USA

Donovan, Landon (Athlete, Soccer Player)
Los Angeles Galaxy
18400 Avalon Blvd Ste 200
Carson, CA 90746, USA

Donovan, Martin (Actor)
c/o Gene Parseghian *Parseghian Planco LLC*
322 8th Ave
Suite 601
New York, NY 10001, USA

Donovan, Pat (Athlete, Football Player)
113 S Prairiesmoke Cir
Whitefish, MT 59937, USA

Donovan, Raymond J (Politician)
1600 Paterson Park Rd
Secaucus, NJ 07094-4019, USA

Donovan, Shean (Athlete, Hockey Player)
11 Mountain Rd
Lexington, MA 02420, USA

Donovan, Tate (Actor)
654 Ashland Ave
Santa Monica, CA 90405, USA

Donovan Jr, Arthur J (Art) (Athlete, Football Player)
8300 Alston Road
Towson, MD 21204, USA

Donovan (Leich)
PO Box 106
Rochdale OL16 4HW, ENGLAND

Donowho, Ryan (Actor)
c/o Staff Member *Brookside Artists Management (NY)*
250 W 57th St
Suite 2303
New York, NY 10107, USA

Doobie Brothers (Music Group)
c/o Staff Member *Paradigm (Monterey)*
404 W Franklin St
Monterey, CA 93940, USA

Doocy, Steve (Television Host)
c/o Staff Member *Fox News Channel (NY)*
1211 Ave of the Americas
Level C1
New York, NY 10036-8701, USA

Doody, Alison (Actor)
Julian Belfarge
46 Albermarle St
London W1X 4PP, UNITED KINGDOM (UK)

Doolan, Wendy (Athlete, Golfer)
3353 Turnberry Dr
Lakeland, FL 33803-5460, USA

Dooley, Paul (Actor)
4420 N Clybourn Ave
Burbank, CA 91505, USA

Dooley, Taylor (Actor)
c/o Heather Reynolds *One Entertainment (NY)*
12 W 57th St
Penthouse
New York, NY 10019, USA

Dooley, Thomas (Athlete, Soccer Player)
55 San Simeon
Laguna Niguel, CA 92677, USA

Dooley, Vince
PO Box 1472
Athens, GA 30603

Dooley, Vincent J (Vince) (Athlete, Coach, Football Coach, Football Player)
University of Georgia
P.O. Box 1472
Athletic Dept
Athens, GA 30603, USA

Dooling, Keyon (Athlete, Basketball Player)
Los Angeles Clippers
6001 N Ocean Dr
Apt 302
Hollywood, FL 33019-4616, USA

Doolittle, Eliza (Musician)
c/o James Whitting *Coda Music Agency -
UK*
229 Shoreditch High St
London E1 6PJ, UK

Doolittle, Melinda (Musician, Reality TV
Star)
1524 Braden Cir
Franklin, TN 37067, USA

Doom, Ryan (Actor)
c/o Katie Rhodes *Untitled Entertainment
(LA)*
350 S. Beverly Dr #200
Beverly Hills, CA 90212, USA

Doornink, Dan (Athlete, Football Player)
402 S 12th Ave
Yakima, WA 98902, USA

Dopazo, Cecilia (Actor)
c/o Staff Member *Telefe - Argentina*
Pavon 2444 (C1248AAT)
Buenos Aires, ARGENTINA

Dope, Edsel (Musician)
c/o Bob Ringe *Survival Management*
30765 Pacific Coast Hwy
#325
Malibu, CA 90265, USA

Dopson, John (Athlete, Baseball Player)
3337 Old Gamber Rd
Finksburg, MD 21048-2223, USA

Dora Brown, Kathryne (Actor)
1617 N. Sierra Bonita Ave
Los Angeles, CA 90046, USA

Doran, Bill (Athlete, Baseball Player)
5720 Grand Legacy Dr
Maineville, OH 45039-7757, USA

Doran, Walter F (Admiral)
Chairman Joint Chiefs of Staff Pentagon
Washington, DC 20318, USA

Dorazio, Joyce (Stylist)
c/o Staff Member *Ennis*
119 Braintree St
Boston, MA 02134, USA

Dore, Andre (Athlete, Hockey Player)
73 Betsys Ln
New Canaan, CT 06840-5202, USA

Dore, Daniel (Athlete, Hockey Player)
c/o Staff Member *Boston Bruins*
TD Banknorth Garden
100 Legends Way, Suite 250
Boston, MA 02114, USA

Dore, Jimmy (Comedian)
c/o Staff Member *OmniPop Talent Group*
10700 Ventura Blvd.
2nd Floor
Studio City, CA 91604, USA

Dore, Patricia (Actor)
Cineart
36 Rue de Ponthieu
Paris 75008, FRANCE

Dore, Ronald Philip (Educator)
157 Surrenden Road Brighton
East Sussex BN1 6ZA, UNITED
KINGDOM (UK)

Doremus, David (Actor)
41516 25th St W
Palmdale, CA 93551, USA

Dorensky, Sergey L (Music Group,
Musician)
Bryusov Per 8/10 #75
Moscow 103009, RUSSIA

Dorey, Jim (Athlete, Hockey Player)
105 Aaron Pl
Amherstview, ON K7N 2A1, Canada

Dorff, Stephen (Actor)
31 Round up Ln
Bell Canyon, CA 91307, USA

Dorfman, Ariel (Writer)
Duke University
International Studies Center
2122 Campus Dr
Durham, NC 27706, USA

Dorfman, David (Actor)
c/o Wendi Green *Paradigm (LA)*
360 N Crescent Dr
North Bldg
Beverly Hills, CA 90210, USA

Dorfmeister, Michaela (Skier)
Quellensteig
Neusiedl 2763, AUSTRIA

Dorgan, Byron (Politician)
1702 Esquire Ln
Me Lean, VA 22101-4754, USA

Dorin, Francoise (Actor, Writer)
Artmedia
20 Ave Rapp
Paris 75007, FRANCE

Dorio, Gabriella (Athlete, Track Athlete)
Federation of Light Athletics
Viale Tialano 70
Rome 00196, ITALY

Dorion, Dan (Athlete, Hockey Player)
10910 Queens Blvd #12H
Forest Hill, NY 11375, USA

Dority, Douglas R (Misc)
*United Food & Commercial Workers
Union*
1775 K St NW
Washington, DC 20006, USA

Dormann, Dana (Athlete, Golfer)
4887 Arlene Pl
Pleasanton, CA 94566-7824, USA

Dormeker, Jerry (Race Car Driver)
Bad Moon Rising
2243 Ravenna St.
Hudson, OH 44236, USA

Dormer, Natalie (Actor)
c/o Staff Member *Artists Rights Group
(ARG)*
4 Great Portland St
London W1W 8PA, UNITED KINGDOM
(UK)

Dorn, Michael (Actor)
c/o Nicolas Bernheim *Seven Summits
Pictures & Management*
8906 W Olympic Blvd
Ground Floor
Beverly Hills, CA 90211, USA

Dornan, Robert (Politician)
8623 Beaver Pond Ln
Fairfax Station, VA 22039-2725, USA

Dornbrook, Thom (Athlete, Football
Player)
5918 Emerald Lakes Dr
Medina, OH 44256, USA

Dorney, Keith R (Athlete, Football Player)
2450 Blucher Valley Rd
Sebastopol, CA 95472, USA

Dornhoefer, Gary (Athlete, Hockey
Player)
267 Chestnut Neck Rd
Port Republic, NJ 08241-9701

Dornseif, Dave (Athlete, Hockey Player)
3989 E Phillips Cir
Centennial, CO 80122-3647, USA

Doro & Warlock
Postfach 87 21
Dusseldorf D-40086, GERMANY

Doronina, Tatyana (Actor)
Gorky Arts Theater
22 Tverskoi Blvd
Moscow 119146, RUSSIA

Dorough, Howie (Musician)
PO Box 110697
Palm Day, FL 32911, USA

Dorrell, Karl (Coach, Football Coach)
University of California
Athletic Dept
Los Angeles, CA 90024, USA

Dorris, Andrew (Athlete, Football Player)
RR 22 Box 549
Conroe, TX 77303, USA

Dorris, Derek (Athlete, Football Player)
4504 Adobe Dr
Fort Worth, TX 76123-1825, USA

Dorroh, Jefferson D (War Hero)
24603 12th Ave S
Des Moines, WA 98198, USA

D'Orsay, Brooke (Actor)
c/o Chris Fenton *H2F Entertainment*
644 N Cherokee Ave
Los Angeles, CA 90004, USA

Dorsch, Hank (Athlete, Football Player)
801 Shannon Rd
Reegina, SK S4S 5K1, Canada

Dorsch, Travis (Athlete, Football Player)
PO Box 2086
West Lafayette, IN 47996-2086, USA

Dorsen, Norman (Attorney, Attorney
General, General)
New York University
Law School 40 Washington Square S
New York, NY 10012, USA

Dorsett, Brian (Athlete, Baseball Player)
700 Dobbs Glen St
Terre Haute, IN 47803-2480, USA

Dorsett, Tony (Athlete, Football Player,
Heisman Trophy Winner)
5990 Haley Way
Frisco, TX 75034, USA

Dorsett Jr, Anthony (Athlete, Football
Player)
3817 Bowser Ave Apt C
Dallas, TX 75219-4385, USA

Dorsey, Christopher (BG) (Musician)
c/o Staff Member *Sosincere Entertainment*
2054 Nostrand Ave Apt 4F
Brooklyn, NY 11210, USA

Dorsey, Eric (Athlete, Football Player)
5 London Ct
Teaneck, NJ 07666, USA

Dorsey, Jack (Business Person)
Twitter, Inc
795 Folsom St.
San Francisco, CA 94107, USA

Dorsey, Jacky (Athlete, Basketball Player)
1231 South Teal Estates Circle
Fresno, TX 77545-8652, USA

Dorsey, Jim (Athlete, Baseball Player)
335 Elm St
Seekonk, MA 02771-1724, USA

Dorsey, John (Athlete, Football Player)
425 Arrowhead Dr
Green Bay, WI 54301-2635, USA

Dorsey, Ken (Athlete, Football Player)
7108 Presidio Gin
Lakewood Ranch, FL 34202, USA

Dorsey, Kerris (Actor)
c/o DebraLynn Findon *Discover Inc
Management*
11425 Moorpark St
Studio City, CA 91602, USA

Dorsey, Nate (Athlete, Football Player)
5023 S 87th St
Tampa, FL 33619, USA

Dorsey, Ron (Athlete, Basketball Player)
3925 Mallard Way
Cumming, GA 30028-4862, USA

Dorsey Brothers Orchestra (Music Group,
Musician)
P.O. Box 643176
Vero Beach, FL 32964-3176, USA

Dorta, Melvin (Athlete, Baseball Player)
1351 Cambridge Ct
Palmyra, PA 17078-9351, USA

Doshi, Balkkrishna V (Architect)
Sangath Thaltej Road
Ahmedbad, GJ 380 054, INDIA

Dosien, Mila (Stylist)
c/o Staff Member *Maximum Talent*
1873 S Bellaire St
Suite 915
Denver, CO 80222-4356, USA

Doss, Desmond T (War Hero)
372 Valley Creek Road
Piedmont, AL 36272-7969, USA

Doss, Murphy (Actor)
52 Hospital Road
Saidapet
Chennai, TN 600 015, INDIA

Dos Santos, Alexandre J M Cardinal
(Religious Leader)
Paco Arquiepiscopal
Avenida Eduardo Mondlane
CP Maputo 1448, MOZAMBIQUE

Dossey, M.D., Larry (Doctor, Writer)
c/o Author Mail *Bantam-Dell Publishing
(NY)*
1745 Broadway
New York, NY 10019, USA

Doster, David (Athlete, Baseball Player)
4123 Sugarhill Run
New Haven, IN 46774-2736, USA

Dosunmu, Andrew (Stylist)
c/o Staff Member *Art Department*
48 Greene St
4th Floor
New York, NY 10013, USA

Dotel, Octavio (Athlete, Baseball Player)
382 Oakland Rd
Lawrenceville, GA 30044-3726, USA

Dotolo, Laura (Stylist)
c/o Staff Member *Art House Management*
1548 16th St
Santa Monica, CA 90404, USA

Dotrice, Roy (Actor)
Lord
6 Meadow Lane Leasingham
Sleaford
Linconshire NG34 8LL, UNITED
KINGDOM (UK)

Dotson, Al (Athlete, Football Player)
Coyues 24 Las Playas
Acapulco 39390, Mexico

Dotson, Dewayne (Athlete, Football
Player)
P.O. Box 425
White House, TN 37188, USA

Dotson, Earl (Athlete, Football Player)
1112 Azalea Dr
Longview, TX 75601, USA

Dotson, Richard E (Rich) (Athlete,
Baseball Player)
7 Colonel Watson Dr
New Richmond, OH 45157-9002, USA

Dotson, Santana (Athlete, Football Player)
P.O. Box 79134
Houston, TX 77279-9134, USA

Dotter, Bobby (Race Car Driver)
MPH Racing
118 Stutt Road
Mooresville, NC 28117, USA

Dotter, Gary (Athlete, Baseball Player)
7413 Ravenswood Rd
Granbury, TX 76049-4742, USA

Dotter, Robert (Race Car Driver)
3632 N. Pacific Ave.
Chicago, IL 60634-2012, USA

Dottley, John (Athlete, Football Player)
1438 Wisteria Dr
Vicksburg, MS 39180, USA

Doty, Paul M (Biologist, Misc)
4 Kirland Place
Cambridge, MA 02138, USA

Douaihy, Saliba (Artist)
Vining Road
Windham, NY 12496, USA

Doubleday, Nelson (Commentator)
New York Mets
84 Gomez Rd
Hobe Sound, FL 33455-2330, USA

Doucet, Michael (Music Group, Musician)
Rosebud Agency
P O Box 170429
San Fransisco, CA 94117, USA

Doucett, Linda (Actor, Model)
c/o Caron Feldman *Feldman Management*
10642 Santa Monica Blvd #205
Los Angeles, CA 90025, USA

Doucette, Paul (Musician)
8071 Woodrow Wilson Dr
Los Angeles, CA 90046, USA

Doug, Doug E (Musician)
4024 Radford Avenue #3
Studio City, CA 91604, USA

Dougan, Angel Serafin Seriche (Prime
Minister)
Prime Minister's Office
Malabo, EQUATORIAL GUINEA

Doughboys (Musician)
Box 5559 Station B
Montreal, QC PQ H3P 4P1, Canada

Dougherty, Dennis A (Misc)
1817 Bushnell Ave
South Pasadena, CA 91030, USA

Dougherty, Ed (Athlete, Golfer)
448 SW Fairway Vis
Port Saint Lucie, FL 34986-2131, USA

Dougherty, Jim (Athlete, Baseball Player)
102 Pinnacle Ct
Kitty Hawk, NC 27949-5911, USA

Dougherty, Joseph (Joe) (Director,
Producer, Writer)
c/o Ken Freimann *WmE2 (WMA-LA)*
1 William Morris Pl
Beverly Hills, CA 90212, USA

Dougherty, Richard (Athlete, Hockey
Player, Olympic Athlete)
1501 W Paulson Rd
Green Bay, WI 54313-6025, USA

DOugherty, RObert (Scientist)
864 Flint Rdg
Newport, KY 41076-7112, USA

Dougherty, William A Jr (Admiral)
1505 Colonial Court
Arlington, VA 22209, USA

Doughty, Glenn (Athlete, Football Player)
1825 Seven Pines Dr
St Louis, MO 63801-1916, USA

Doughty, Kenny (Actor)
c/o Alan Siegel *Alan Siegel Entertainment*
345 N Maple Dr
Suite 375
Beverly Hills, CA 90210, USA

Douglas, Aaron (Actor)
c/o Russ Mortensen *Pacific Artists
Management*
1285 W Broadway
Suite 685
Vancouver, BC V6H 3X8, Canada

Douglas, Anslem (Composer, Entertainer)
JW Records
2833 Church Ave
Brooklyn, NY 11226, USA

Douglas, Barry (Music Group, Musician)
I C M Artists
40 W 57th St
New York, NY 10019, USA

Douglas, Bobby (Coach, Wrestler)
Iowa State University
Athletic Dept
Ames, IA 50011, USA

Douglas, Carl (Attorney)
6611 Shenandoah Avenue
Los Angeles, CA 90056-2115, USA

Douglas, Carol (Music Group)
Famous Artists Agency
250 W 57th St
New York, NY 10107, USA

Douglas, Cathleen (Lawyer)
815 Connecticut Ave NW
Washington, DC 20006, USA

Douglas, Charles (Whammy) (Athlete,
Baseball Player)
1711 Catherine Lake Rd
Jacksonville, NC 28540-8755, USA

Douglas, David (Athlete, Football Player)
605 Snowshill Way
Maryville, TN 37803, USA

Douglas, Denzil L (Prime Minister)
Premier's Office
Government Building
Basseterre, SAINT KITTS & NEVIS

Douglas, Diana (Actor)
c/o Staff Member *Bauman Redanty &
Shaul Agency*
5757 Wilshire Blvd
Suite 473
Beverly Hills, CA 90212, USA

Douglas, Donna (Actor)
619 S Gretna Green Way
Los Angeles, CA 90049, USA

Douglas, Gabby (Athlete, Gymnast,
Olympic Athlete)
Chow's Gymnastics
2210 Park Dr
West Demoines, IA 50265, USA

Douglas, Hugh (Athlete, Football Player)
5 Pen nbrook Ln
Glen Mills, PA 19342, USA

Douglas, Ileana (Actor)
c/o Staff Member *Baumgarten
Management*
11925 Wilshire Blvd
Suite 310
Los Angeles, CA 90025, USA

Douglas, Illeana (Actor, Director,
Producer)
1419 N Ogden Dr
Los Angeles, CA 90046, USA

Douglas, James (Buster) (Athlete, Boxer)
PO Box 342
Johnstown, OH 43031, USA

Douglas, Jay (Athlete, Football Player)
2909 Laurel Cherry Way
The Woodlands, TX 77380, USA

Douglas, Jerry (Actor)
739 Rodney Dr
Nashville, TN 37205, USA

Douglas, Jordy (Athlete, Hockey Player)
Courts Financial Group
200-1215 Henderson Hwy
Winnipeg, MB R2G 1L8, Canada

Douglas, Katie (Basketball Player)
Connecticut Sun
Mohegan Sun Arena
Uncasville, CT 06382, USA

Douglas, Kirk (Actor, Producer)
805 N Rexford Dr
Beverly Hills, CA 90210, USA

Douglas, Kyan (Stylist, Television Host)
c/o Michael Flutie *MFO*
17 Little West 12th St
Studio 333
New York, NY 10014, USA

Douglas, Leon (Athlete, Basketball Player)
P.O. Box 58
Leighton, AL 35646-0058, USA

Douglas, Merrill (Athlete, Football Player)
2185 E 3970 S
Salt Lake City, UT 84124, USA

Douglas, Michael (Actor, Director,
Producer)
541 Guard Hill Rd
Bedford, NY 10506, USA

Douglas, Nik (Writer)
c/o Staff Member *Simon & Schuster*
1230 Avenue of the Americas
New York, NY 10020, USA

Douglas, Santiago (Actor)
c/o Charlton Blackburne *A Management*
9107 Wilshire Blvd.
Suite 650
Beverly Hills, CA 90210, USA

Douglas, Sarah (Actor)
c/o Staff Member *Vic Murray Talent*
185 A Latchmere Rd
London SW11 2JZ, UK

Douglas, Sherman (Athlete, Basketball
Player)
1330 West Ave
Apt 1107
Miami Beach, FL 33139-0905, USA

Douglass, Bobby (Athlete, Football Player)
151 E Laurel Ave Apt 203
Lake Forest, IL 60045, USA

Douglass, Dale (Athlete, Golfer)
6601 E San Miguel Ave
Paradise Valley, AZ 85253-5983, USA

Douglass, Maurice (Athlete, Football
Player)
1021 Sunset Dr
Englewood, OH 45322, USA

Douglass, Mike (Athlete, Football Player)
1725 Porterfield Pl
El Cajon, CA 92019, USA

Douglass, Robyn (Actor)
407 S. Dearborn St #1675
Chicago, IL 60606, USA

Douglass, Sean (Athlete, Baseball Player)
43956 Johns Ct
Lancaster, CA 93536-8213, USA

Doumit, Ryan (Athlete, Baseball Player)
17716 E Apollo Rd
Spokane Valley, WA 99016-5068, USA

Doumit, Sam (Actor)
c/o Staff Member *Baker Winokur Ryder
Public Relations (BWR-LA)*
9100 Wilshire Blvd
Suite 500, West Tower
Beverly Hills, CA 90212, USA

Dourda, Abu Zaid Umar (Prime Minister)
Prime Minister's Office
Bab el Aziziya Barracks
Tripoli, LIBYA

Dourdan, Gary (Actor)
4151 Moore St
Los Angeles, CA 90066, USA

Dourif, Brad (Actor)
173 Macdaniel Rd
Bearsville, NY 12409, USA

Douris, Peter (Athlete, Hockey Player)
P.O. Box 488
York Beach, ME 03910-0488, USA

Douse, Joseph (Athlete, Baseball Player)
16722 Fenmore St
Detroit, MI 48235, USA

Douthitt, Earl (Athlete, Football Player)
8100 Central Ave
Apt 211
Cleveland, OH 44104, USA

Dove, Dennis (Athlete, Baseball Player)
144 Kirk Ln
Ocilla, GA 31774-3725, USA

Dove, Eddie (Athlete, Football Player)
1750 Poppy Ave
Menlo Park, CA 94025, USA

Dove, Rita F (Writer)
1757 Lambs Road
Charlottesville, VA 22901-8911, USA

Dove, Ronnie (Music Group)
c/o Staff Member *Time Machine*
2109 S. Wilbur Ave
Walla Walla, WA 99362, USA

Doves (Music Group)
c/o Staff Member *Paradigm (Monterey)*
404 W Franklin St
Monterey, CA 93940, USA

Dovolani, Tony (Choreographer, Dancer)
c/o Tej Bhatia Herring *Rogers & Cowan PR (LA)*
Pacific Design Center
8687 Melrose Ave, 7th Floor
West Hollywood, CA 90069, USA

Dow, Ellen (Actor)
20327 Oxnard St
Woodland Hills, CA 91367, USA

Dow, Harley (Athlete, Football Player)
73531 Cabazon Peak Dr
Palm Desert, CA 92260, USA

Dow, Peggy (Actor)
2121 South Yorkstown Ave
Tulsa, OK 74114, USA

Dow, Tony (Actor)
1731 Gunnison Dr
Topanga, CA 90290, USA

Dowd, Jim (Athlete, Hockey Player)
708 New Jersey Ave
Point Pleasant Beach, NJ 08742-2970, USA

Dowd, Maureen (Editor)
c/o Staff Member *The New York Times Company*
229 W 43rd St
New York, NY 10036, USA

Dowdell, Marcus (Athlete, Football Player)
16 Charleston Park Dr
Houston, TX 77025, USA

Dowdle, Walter R (Biologist, Misc)
1708 Mason Mill Road
Atlanta, GA 30329, USA

Dowdy, Adam (Athlete, Baseball Player)
909 E Chestnut St
Pontiac, IL 85248-4137, USA

Dowdy, Steven (Misc, Scientist)
Howard Hughes Medical Institute
Washington Univesity
Saint Louis, MO 63110, USA

Dowell, Anthony J (Ballerina)
c/o Staff Member *Royal Ballet*
Covent Garden
Bow St
London WC2E 9DD, UK

Dowell, Jake
2014 Rice Ct
Eau Claire, WI 54701-7977

Dowell, Ken (Athlete, Baseball Player)
5221 Helen Way
Sacramento, CA 95822-2868, USA

Dower, John W (Writer)
Massachusetts Institute of Technology
History Dept
Cambridge, MA 02139, USA

Dowhower, Rod (Athlete, Football Coach, Football Player)
5 Fairway Ct
Dahlonega, GA 30533, USA

Dowie, Bruce (Athlete, Hockey Player)
3277 Star Lane
Burlington, ON L7M 5A4, Canada

Dowle, David (Music Group, Musician)
Int'l Talent Booking
27A Floral St #300
London WC2E 9DQ, UNITED KINGDOM (UK)

Dowler, Boyd H (Athlete, Football Player)
3013 Grove View Ct
Dacula, GA 30019, USA

Dowling, Brian (Athlete, Football Player)
114 Arboretum Way
Burlington, MA 01803, USA

Dowling, Dave (Athlete, Baseball Player)
173 Whelan Way
Manteca, CA 95336-5945, USA

Dowling, John E (Biologist, Misc)
135 Charles St
Boston, MA 02114, USA

Dowling, Peter (Director)
3608 Avenida Del Sol
Studio City, CA 91604, USA

Dowling, Robert J (Editor, Publisher)
Hollywood Reporter
5055 Wilshire Blvd
Los Angeles, CA 90036, USA

Dowling, Timothy (Actor)
c/o Staff Member *WME (LA)*
9601 Wilshire Blvd Fl 3
Beverly Hills, CA 90210, USA

Dowling, Vincent (Director, Writer)
322 East River Road
Huntington, MA 01050, USA

Down, Lesley-Anne (Actor)
6525 Paseo Canyon Dr
Malibu, CA 91604, USA

Down, Leslie-Anne (Actor)
6252 Paseo Canyon Dr
Malibu, CA 90265, USA

Down, Rick (Athlete, Baseball Player)
10908 Salford Dr
Las Veeas, NV 89144-4498, USA

Down, Sarah (Cartoonist)
Playboy Magazine
Reader Services 680 N Lake Shore Dr
Chicago, IL 60611, USA

Downes, Edward (Opera Singer)
Royal Opera House
Covent Garden
London WC2E 9DD, UNITED KINGDOM (UK)

Downes, Robin Atkin (Actor)
c/o Staff Member *Gordon Agency*
260 S Beverly Drive #308
Beverly Hills, CA 90212, USA

Downey, Bill (Athlete, Basketball Player)
1035 South Moorings Drive
Arlington Heights, IL 60005-3217, USA

Downey, James (Writer)
c/o Staff Member *3 Arts Entertainment Inc*
9460 Wilshire Blvd
7th Floor
Beverly Hills, CA 90210, USA

Downey, Jim (Writer)
c/o Staff Member *3 Arts Entertainment Inc*
9460 Wilshire Blvd
7th Floor
Beverly Hills, CA 90210, USA

Downey, Robert J (Director)
55 W 900 S
Salt Lake City, UT 84101, USA

Downey, Roma (Actor)
23422 Malibu Colony Rd
Malibu, CA 90265, USA

Downey Jr, Robert (Actor)
30228 Morning View Dr
Malibu, CA 90265, USA

Downie, Leonard Jr (Editor)
Washington Post
Editorial Dept 1150 15th St NW
Washington, DC 20071, USA

Downing, Al (Athlete, Baseball Player)
25343 Silver Asoen
Wav Ant 735
Valencia, CA 91381-0698, USA

Downing, Alphonso E (Al) (Athlete, Baseball Player)
25343 Silver Aspen Way
Apt 735
Valencia, CA 91381, USA

Downing, Brian J (Athlete, Baseball Player)
8095 County Road 135
Celina, TX 75009-2539, USA

Downing, George (Misc, Yachtsman)
Get Wet!
3021 Waialee Ave
Honolulu, HI 96816, USA

Downing, Jim (Race Car Driver)
5096 Peachtree Rd.
Atlanta, GA 30341, USA

Downing, Kathryn (Publisher)
Mypotential.com
2821 Main St
Santa Monica, CA 90405, USA

Downing, Sara (Actor)
c/o Steven Siebert *Lighthouse Entertainment*
9220 W Sunset Blvd Ste 200
West Hollywood, CA 90069, USA

Downing, Steve (Athlete, Basketball Player)
6433 Lakeside Woods Cir
Indianapolis, IN 46278-1663, USA

Downing, Vern (Bowler)
523 Napa St
Rodeo, CA 94572-1512, USA

Downing, Walt (Athlete, Football Player)
1141 Durham Cir NW
Massillon, OH 44646, USA

Downs, Dave (Athlete, Baseball Player)
925 E 1050 N
Bountiful, UT 84010-2620, USA

Downs, Gary (Athlete, Football Player)
3953 Balleycastle Ct
Duluth, GA 30097, USA

Downs, Hugh (Correspondent, Journalist)
7993 N Ridgeview Dr
Paradise Valley, AZ 85253-3088, USA

Downs, Jonathan (Writer)
Centre for Fortean Zoology
Myrtle Cottage
Woolfardisworthy
Bideford, North Devon EX39 5QR, UK

Downs, Kelly (Athlete, Baseball Player)
6459 Willow Creek Rd
Morgan, UT 84050-6746, USA

Downs, Lila (Musician)
c/o Bill Traut *Open Door Management*
865 Via de la Paz
Suite 365
Pacific Palisades, CA 90272, USA

Downs, Matt (Athlete, Baseball Player)
448 Cruise Ave
Centreville, AL 35042-6653, USA

Downs, Michael (Athlete, Football Player)
1405 Knob Hill Dr
Desoto, TX 75115, USA

Downs, Nicholas (Actor)
c/o Andrew Stawiarski *ADS Management*
269 S. Beverly Dr #441
Beverly Hills, CA 90212, USA

Downs, Robert (Athlete, Football Player)
28024 High Vista Dr
Escondido, CA 92026, USA

Downs, Scott (Athlete, Baseball Player)
6814 Barbrook Rd
Louisville, KY 40258-2668, USA

Dowson, Philip M (Architect)
Royal Academy of the Arts
Piccadilly
London W1V 0DS, UNITED KINGDOM (UK)

Doyen De Montaillou, Jean (Stylist)
c/o Staff Member *Halley Resources*
37 W 20th St
#603
New York, NY 10011, USA

Doyle, Allen (Athlete, Golfer)
512 Riverside Dr
Lagrange, GA 30240-9633, USA

Doyle, Brian (Athlete, Baseball Player)
P.O. Box 9156
Winter Haven, FL 33883-9156, USA

Doyle, Christopher (Cinematographer)
c/o Staff Member *ICM Partners (ICM-LA)*
10250 Constellation Blvd Fl 7
Los Angeles, CA 90067, USA

Doyle, Dennis (Race Car Driver)
DRG Motorsports
37 Meghan Blvd.
Plymouth, CT 06782, USA

Doyle, Denny (Athlete, Baseball Player)
P.O. Box 9156
Winter Haven, FL 33883-9156, USA

Doyle, James (Politician)
2001 Hawks Ridge Dr
Verona, WI 53593-9195, USA

Doyle, Jeff (Athlete, Baseball Player)
830 SE Bayshore Cir
Corvallis, OR 97333-3206, USA

Doyle, Patrick (Composer)
Air-Edel
18 Rodmarton St
London W1H 3FW, UNITED KINGDOM (UK)

Doyle, Paul (Athlete, Baseball Player)
19361 Brookhurst St
Snc 15
Huntington Beach, CA 92646-2949, USA

Doyle, Roddy (Writer)
Secker & Warburg
38A West Road Bromsgrove
Worc B60 2NQ, UNITED KINGDOM (UK)

Doyle, Shawn (Actor)
3744 San Rafael Ave
Los Angeles, CA 90065, USA

Doyle & Debbie Show, The (Music Group)
c/o Staff Member *Paradigm (Monterey)*
404 W Franklin St
Monterey, CA 93940, USA

Doyle-Childress, Cartha (Athlete, Baseball Player, Commentator)
1516 Carowinds Cir
Maryville, TN 37803-7704, USA

Doyle Kennedy, Maria (Actor)
c/o Ruth Young *United Agents*
12-26 Lexington St
London W1F OLE, UK

Doyne, Cory (Athlete, Baseball Player)
20228 County Line Rd
Lutz, FL 33558-5074, USA

Doyon, Mario (Athlete, Hockey Player)
12530 Windsor Dr
Carmel, IN 46033-3148

Dozier, D J (Athlete, Baseball Player)
5821 N Cherokee Cluster
Vireinia Beach, VA 23462-3214, USA

Dozier, James L (General)
2150 Channel Way
North Fort Myers, FL 33917, USA

Dozier, Jan Davis Dr (Astronaut)
4105 Cumberland Pass
Apt 814
Fort Worth, TX 76116-0753, USA

Dozier, Terry (Athlete, Basketball Player)
521 Sparkleberry Ln
Columbia, SC 29229-8609, USA

Dozier, Tom (Athlete, Baseball Player)
1231 Willow Ave
Apt D7
Hercules, CA 94547-1200, USA

Drabble, Margaret (Writer)
P F D
Drury House 34-43 Russell St
London WC2B 5HA, UNITED KINGDOM
(UK)

Drabek, Doug (Athlete, Baseball Player)
15 Ivy Pond Ln
Spring, TX 77381, USA

Drabek, Kyle (Athlete, Baseball Player)
18 Cokeberrv St
Spring, TX 77380-1885, USA

Drabinsky, Garth H (Producer)
Livent Inc
165 Avenue Road #600
Toronto, ON M5R 3S4, CANADA

Draffen, Willis (Music Group)
16103 Vista Del Mar Dr
Houston, TX 77083, USA

Draft, Chris (Athlete, Football Player)
970 E Oak St
Anaheim, CA 92805, USA

Dragila, Stacy (Athlete, Olympic Athlete, Track Athlete)
988 Wind Cave Pl
Chula Vista, CA 91914-3613, USA

Draglia, Stacy (Athlete, Track Athlete)
1112 E Monte Cristo Ave
Phoenix, AZ 85022, USA

Drago, Billy (Actor)
3800 Burham Blvd #303
Los Angeles, CA 90068, USA

Drago, Richard A (Dick) (Athlete, Baseball Player)
4703 Belle Chase Cir
Tampa, FL 33634-4256, USA

Dragon
122 McEvoy Street
Alexandria, NSW 2015, AUSTRALIA

Dragon, Daryl (Musician)
4225 W Latham Cir
Prescott, AZ 86305, USA

Drahman, Brian (Athlete, Baseball Player)
9984 Nob Hill Ln
Sunrise, FL 33351-4671, USA

Drahos, Nick (Athlete, Football Player)
3158 State Route 90
Aurora, NY 13026, USA

Drai, Victor (Producer)
10527 Bellagio Road
Beverly Hills, CA 90210, USA

Draiman, Dave (Musician)
c/o Staff Member *Mitch Schneider
Organization (MSO)*
14724 Ventura Blvd #410
Sherman Oaks, CA 91403, USA

Drake (Actor, Musician)
5841 Round Meadow Rd
Hidden Hills, CA 91302, USA

Drake, Bebe (Actor)
c/o Staff Member *Baron Entertainment*
13848 Ventura Blvd
Suite A
Sherman Oaks, CA 91423-3654

Drake, Betsy (Actor)
10850 Wilshire Blvd #575
Los Angeles, CA 90024, USA

Drake, Dallas (Athlete, Hockey Player)
11472 E Cedar Bay Trl
Traverse City, MI 49684-6841

Drake, Frank D (Astronomer)
University of California
Lick Observatory
Santa Cruz, CA 9064, USA

Drake, Jeremy (Astronomer)
*Harvard-Smithsonian Center for
Astrophysics*
Cambridge, MA 02138, USA

Drake, Jerry (Athlete, Football Player)
2857 Regal Cir
Apt E
Birmingham, AL 35216, USA

Drake, Jerry (Athlete, Football Player)
1893 Colonnade Rd
Cleveland, OH 44112, USA

Drake, Jessica (Adult Film Star)
c/o Staff Member *Wicked Pictures*
9040 Eton Ave
Canoga Park, CA 91304, USA

Drake, Judith (Actor)
20th Century Artists
4605 Lankershim Blvd #305
North Hollywood, CA 91602, USA

Drake, Juel D (Misc)
Iron Workers Union
1750 New York Ave NW
Washington, DC 20006, USA

Drake, Larry (Actor)
15260 Ventura Blvd #2100
Sherman Oaks, CA 91403, USA

Drake, Robert (Athlete, Baseball Player)
5409 Barrett Cir
Buena Park, CA 85215-7755, USA

Drake, Solly (Athlete, Baseball Player)
1732 S Corning St
Los Angeles, CA 90035-4302, USA

Drakeford, Tyronne (Athlete, Football Player)
7153 Comrie Ct
Warrenton, VA 20187, USA

Drane, Dwight (Athlete, Football Player)
200 NW 107th Ave
Plantation, FL 33324, USA

Dransfeldt, Kelly (Athlete, Baseball Player)
2011 Prairie Rose Dr
Morris, IL 60450-6851, USA

Draper, Charla (Stylist)
5422 S Ingleside Ave
Chicago, IL 60615, USA

Draper, Courtnee
c/o Steve Simon *Landis-Simon
Productions Talent Management*
625 E. Thousand Oaks Blvd #279
Thousand Oaks, CA 91362, USA

Draper, Denny (Athlete, Football Player)
11105 Baker Creek Rd
McMinnville, OR L2N 286 Canada, USA

Draper, E Lynn Jr (Business Person)
American Electric Power
1 Riverside Plaza
Columbus, OH 43215, USA

Draper, Kris (Athlete, Hockey Player)
3418 Westchester Rd
Bloomfield Hills, MI 48304-2573

Draper, Mike (Athlete, Baseball Player)
7608 NW 18th St
Act 105
Mareate, FL 33063-3143, USA

Draper, Polly (Actor)
3856 Berry Dr
Studio City, CA 91604, USA

Draper, Tim (Athlete, Hockey Player)
76 Blackstone Ave
Binghamton, NY 13903, USA

Draper, Tom
76 Blackstone Ave
Binghamton, NY 13903-1328

Draper, William H III (Financier)
91 Tallwood Court
Atherton, CA 94027, USA

Dratch, Rachel (Actor, Comedian)
c/o Tucker Voorhees *Principato/Young
Management*
9465 Wilshire Blvd
Suite 430
Beverly Hills, CA 90212, USA

Draughon, Harold (Scientist)
3502 Emerald Falls Ct
Houston, TX 77059-3770, USA

Dravecky, David F (Dave) (Athlete, Baseball Player)
9154 Viaeeio Way
Highlands Ranch, Co 80126-3613, USA

Draven, Jamie (Actor)
c/o Staff Member *Independent Talent
Group (ITG-UK)*
Oxford House
76 Oxford St
London W1D 1BS, UK

Draves, Victoria (Vickie) (Athlete, Swimmer)
23842 Shady Tree Circle
Laguna Niguel, CA 92677, USA

Drayton, Charlie (Music Group, Musician)
Direct Mangement Group
947 N La Cienega Blvd #2
Los Angeles, CA 90069, USA

Drayton, Troy (Athlete, Football Player)
10707 NW 49th Mnr
Coral Springs, FL 33076, USA

Drdek, John (Writer)
c/o Will Ward *ROAR (LA)*
9701 Wilshire Blvd
8th Floor
Los Angeles, CA 90212, USA

Dr Demento (Entertainer)
6102 Pimenta Ave
Lakewood, CA 90712, USA

Dr Dog (Musician)
c/o Staff Member *Paradigm (Monterey)*
404 W Franklin St
Monterey, CA 93940, USA

Dr Dre (Actor, Musician)
Beats By Dr. Dre
7251 W Lake Mead Blvd
Las Vegas, NV 89128, USA

Dream (Music Group)

Dream So Real
PO Box 8061
Athens, GA 30603

Dreamstreet (Music Group)
c/o Staff Member *Adonis Productions*
175 Skillman St
Brooklyn, NY 11205, USA

Dream Warriors
1505 W 2nd Ave #200
Vancouver, BC V6H 3Y4, Canada

Drechsler, Dave (Athlete, Football Player)
1135 Arabian Farms Rd
Clover, SC 29710, USA

Drechsler, Heike (Athlete, Track Athlete)
LAC Chemnitz
Reichenhainer Str 154
Chmnitz 09135, GERMANY

Dreckman, Bruce (Athlete, Baseball Player)
110 N Maple St
Marcus, IA 51035-7175, USA

Drees, Tom (Athlete, Baseball Player)
18638 Bearoath Trl
Eden Prairie, MN 55347-3459, USA

Dreesen, Tom (Actor, Comedian)
14538 Benefit Street #301
Sherman Oaks, CA 91403, USA

Dreifort, Darren (Athlete, Baseball Player, Olympic Athlete)
463 Wynola St
Pacific Palisades, CA 90272-4243, USA

Dreifuss, Ruth (President)
Federal Chancellery
Bundeshaus-W
Bundesgasse
Beme 3033, SWITZERLAND

Dreiling, Greg (Athlete, Basketball Player)
5952 Willowross Way
Plano, TX 75093-4776, USA

Dreilling, Greg (Athlete, Basketball Player)
5952 Willowross Way
Plano, TX 75093, USA

Drell, Persis (Physicist)
Stanford University
Linear Accelerator Center
Stanford, CA 94305, USA

Drell, Sidney (Scientist)
620 Sand Hill Road
Apt 420D
Palo Alto, CA 94304-2075, USA

Drescher, Fran (Actor)
19734 Pacific Coast Hwy
Malibu, CA 90265, USA

Drese, Ryan (Athlete, Baseball Player)
2201 Bear Lake Dr
Euless, TX 76039-6058, USA

Dressel, Chris (Athlete, Football Player)
410 Whiskey Hill Rd
Woodside, CA 94062, USA

Dresselhaus, Mildred (Scientist)
147 Jason St
Arlington, MA 02476-8033, USA

Dresselhaus, Mildred S (Engineer, Physicist)
Energy Department
1000 Independence Ave SW
Washington, DC 20585, USA

Dressendorfer, Kirk (Athlete, Baseball Player)
1004 Oaklands Dr
Round Rock, TX 78681-4033, USA

Dressler, Alan (Scientist)
Carnegie Observatory 813 Santa Barbara St
Pasadena, CA 91101-1232, USA

Dressler, Doug (Athlete, Football Player)
118 Frostwood Dr
Westwood, CA 96137, USA

Dressler, Rob (Athlete, Baseball Player)
2037 17th Ave
Forest Grove, OR 97116-2709, USA

Drew, B Alvin (Astronaut)
2814 Lighthouse Dr
Houston, TX 77058, USA

Drew, B Alvin Lt Colonel (Astronaut)
2814 Lighthouse Dr
Houston, TX 77058-4320, USA

Drew, Cameron (Athlete, Baseball Player)
31 Highbridge Rd
Trenton, NJ 08620-9632, USA

Drew, David Jonathan (J D) (Athlete, Baseball Player)
5006 Old US 41 N
Hahira, GA 31632-4405, USA

Drew, Elizabeth H (Publisher)
Avon/William Morrow
1350 Ave of Americas
New York, NY 10019, USA

Drew, Heather (Athlete, Golfer)
78160 Desert Mountain Cir
Bermuda Dunes, CA 92203-8151, USA

Drew, JD (Athlete, Baseball Player)
c/o Scott Boras *Boras Corporation*
18 Corporate Plaza
Newport Beach, CA 92660, USA

Drew, John (Athlete, Basketball Player)
2303 W Tidwell Rd #3404
Houston, TX 77091, USA

Drew, Larry (Athlete, Basketball Player)
4942 Densmore Avenue
Encino, CA 91436-1538, USA

Drew, Sarah (Actor)
233 Spencer St
Glendale, CA 91202, USA

Drew, Stephen (Athlete, Baseball Player)
4254 Oak Forest Dr
Valdosta, GA 31602-0838, USA

Drew, Tim (Athlete, Baseball Player)
5006 Old Us 41 N
Hahira, GA 31632-4405, USA

Drew, Urban (General)
451 Neptune Ave
Encinitas, CA 92024-2016, USA

Drewiske, Davis (Athlete, Hockey Player)
3327 Humboldt AveS# B
Minneapolis, MN 55408-3331

Drewrey, Willie (Athlete, Football Player)
2714 Cheryl Ct
Missouri City, TX 77459, USA

Drexler, Clyde (Athlete, Basketball Player, Olympic Athlete)
4045 Piping Rock Lane
Houston, TX 77027-3916, USA

Drexler, Clyde (Basketball Player, Coach)
Dade/Schultz
6442 Coldwater Canyon Ave #206
North Hollywood, CA 91606, USA

Dreyer, Pamela (Athlete, Hockey Player, Olympic Athlete)
111 E 88th St Apt 4A
New York, NY 10128-1158, USA

Dreyer, Steve (Athlete, Baseball Player)
6018 Greywood Cir
Johnston, IA 50131-1687, USA

Dreyfus, George (Composer)
3 Grace St
Camberwell, VIC 3124, AUSTRALIA

Dreyfuss, Richard (Actor, Producer)
P.O. Box 10459
Burbank, CA 91510, USA

Drickamer, Harry G (Engineer)
1174 Old Racebrook Rd
Woodbridge, CT 06525-1811, USA

Driedger, Florence G (Activist)
3833 Montaigne St
Regina, SK S4S 3J6, CANADA

Drier, David (Congressman, Politician)
233 Cannon HOB
Washington, DC 20515, USA

Drier, Moosey (Actor)
3501 Camino de la Cumbre
Sherman Oaks, CA 91423, USA

Drier, Moosie (Actor, Director)
3501 Camino De La Cumbre
Sherman Oaks, CA 91423, USA

Driessen, Dan (Athlete, Baseball Player)
208 Mitchellville Rd
Hilton Head Island, SC 29926-2820, USA

Driest, Burkhard
Alter Militarring 8
Koln 50933, GERMANY

Drills, David (Athlete, Cycler, Olympic Athlete)
3736 Brookside Rd
Ottawa Hills, OH 43606-2614

Drinan, Robert F (Educator, Misc)
Georgetown University
1507 Isherwood St NE #1
Washington, DC 20002, USA

Drinfeld, Vladimir (Mathematician)
Steklov Mathematics Institute
42 Vavilova
ESP-1 Moscow 117966, RUSSIA

Drinkard, Bobby Jon (Reality TV Star)
c/o Staff Member *Mark Burnett Productions*
640 N Sepulveda Blvd
Los Angeles, CA 90049, USA

Drinkwater, Carol (Writer)
c/o Ken McReddie *Ken McReddie Ltd*
11 Connaught Pl
London W2 2ET, UNITED KINGDOM

Drinkwater-Simmons, Maxine (Athlete, Baseball Player, Commentator)
18 Belmont Ave
Camden, ME 04843-2028, USA

Driscoll, Daniel (General)
10 Arbor St
West Yarmouth, MA 02673-3304, USA

Driscoll, Edward "Terry" (Athlete, Basketball Player)
101 Tayloe Cir
Williamsburg, VA 23185-8248, USA

Driscoll, Edward (Terry) (Athlete, Basketball Player)
William & Mary University
Athletics Department
P.O. Box 399
Williamsburg, VA 23187, USA

Driscoll, Jean (Athlete, Motivational Speaker, Olympic Athlete)
Pat Fettig
8142 Traverse Ct
Cincinnati, OH 45242, USA

Driscoll, Jim (Athlete, Baseball Player)
8050 E Indian School Rd
Scottsdale, AZ 85251, USA

Driscoll, John (Actor)
c/o Staff Member *Talented Managers*
65 West 90th StSte 7D
NYC, NY 10024, USA

Driscoll, Peter (Athlete, Hockey Player)
422 N Cypress Dr
Apt B
Jupiter, FL 33469, USA

Driscoll, Peter (Athlete, Hockey Player)
14839 Senator Way
Carmel, IN 46032-5128, USA

Driscoll, William (General)
1244 Via Mil Cumbres
Solana Beach, CA 92075-1727, USA

Driskill, Travis (Athlete, Baseball Player)
800 Blue Spring Cir
Round Rock, TX 78681-4047, USA

Driver, Adam (Actor)
c/o Randi Goldstein *Gersh (NY)*
41 Madison Ave
New York, NY 10010, USA

Driver, Bruce (Athlete, Hockey Player)
21A Crest Ter
Montville, NJ 07045-9370

Driver, Donald (Athlete, Football Player)
1501 Noble Way
Flower Mound, TX 75022, USA

Driver, Minnie (Actor)
2569 Creston Dr
Los Angeles, CA 90068, USA

Driver, William J (Government Official)
215 W Columbia St
Falls Church, VA 22046, USA

D'Rivera, Paquito
Charismic Productions
2704 Mozart Place NW
Washington, DC 20009, USA

Dr John (Musician)
53 Millstone Brook Rd
Southampton, NY 11968, USA

Drnovsek, Janez (Prime Minister)
Prime Minister's Office
Gregorcicova St 20
Ljubljana 61000, SLOVENIA

Drobny, Jaroslav (Actor)
23 Kenilworth Court
Lower Richmond Road
London SW15 1EW, United Kingdom

Drogba, Didier (Athlete, Soccer Player)
c/o Staff Member *IMG Artists Worldwide (UK)*
The Light Box
111 Power Road
London W4 5PY, United Kingdom

Drolet, Claude (Horse Racer)
156 Greeley Lake Rd
Greeley, PA 18425-9765, USA

Drolet, Jean (Horse Racer)
1 White Rd
Airmont, NY 10901-7108, USA

Drollinger, Ralph (Athlete, Basketball Player)
22831 Market Street
Newhall, CA 91321-3605, USA

Droppa, Ivan (Athlete, Hockey Player)
Palucanska 632/89
Liptovsky Mikulas 031 01, Slovakia

Drosdick, John G (Business Person)
Sunoco Inc
10 Penn Center 1801 Market St
Philadelphia, PA 19103, USA

Drougas, Tom (Athlete, Football Player)
P.O. Box 1596
Sun Valley, ID 83353, USA

Droughns, Reuben (Athlete, Football Player)
5955 S Elkhart Ct
Centennial, CO 80016, USA

Drouin, Jude (Athlete, Hockey Player)
44479 Maltese Falcon Sq
Ashburn, VA 20147-3886

Droulez, Veronique (Stylist)
c/o Celebrity Stylists *Area 51, Inc.*
104 W. 14th St
New York, NY 10011, USA

Drowning Pool (Music Group)
c/o Staff Member *10th Street Entertainment (NY)*
38 W 21st St
Suite 300
New York, NY 10010, USA

Drozdov, Darren (Athlete, Football Player)

Drozdova, Margarita S (Ballerina)
Stanislavsky Musical Theater
Pushkinskaya Str 17
Moscow, RUSSIA

Druce, John (Athlete, Hockey Player)
Freedom 55 Financial 405-360 George St N
Peterborough, ON K9H 7E7, Canada

Druck, Mirchea (Prime Minister)
Str 31 August 123 #7
Kishinev 277012, MOLDOVA

Druckenmiller, Jim (Athlete, Football Player)
2351 E Aragon Blvd
Unit 6
Sunrise, FL 33313, USA

Drucker, Eugene (Music Group, Musician)
I M G Artists
3 Burlington Lane
Chiswick
London W4 2TH, UNITED KINGDOM (UK)

Drucker, Mort (Cartoonist)
Famous Artists Agency
250 W 57th St
New York, NY 10107, USA

Drudge, Matt (Internet Star, Journalist)
106 2nd Rivo Alto Terr
Miami Beach, FL 33139, USA

Drugg, Herb (Race Car Driver)
PO Box 916
Troy, NH 03465, USA

Dru Hill (Music Group)
c/o Staff Member *WME (LA)*
9601 Wilshire Blvd Fl 3
Beverly Hills, CA 90210, USA

Druken, Harold (Athlete, Hockey Player)
16 Shaw Dr
Wayland, MA 01778-3214, USA

Druker, Brian J (Misc)
Oregon Health Science University
Cancer Research Center
Portland, OR 97201, USA

Drulia, Stan (Athlete, Hockey Player)
3939 Essex Pl
Fort Gratiot, MI 48059, USA

Drummond, Alice (Actor)
351 E 50th St
New York, NY 10003, USA

Drummond, Jonathan (Jon) (Athlete, Track Athlete)
P.O. Box 982
Arlington, TX 86004-0982, USA

Drummond, Roscoe (Writer)
6637 MacLean Dr Olde Dominion Square
McLean, VA 22101, USA

Drummond, Ryan (Actor)
c/o Staff Member *Bobby Ball Talent Agency*
4116 W Magnolia Blvd Ste 205
Burbank, CA 91505-2700, USA

Drummond, Tim (Athlete, Baseball Player)
102 Haldane Ct
La Plata, MD 20646-4308, USA

Drungo, Elbert (Athlete, Football Player)
216 Lake Chateau Dr
Hermitage, TN 37076, USA

Drury, Chris (Athlete, Hockey Player, Olympic Athlete)
25 Central Park W Apt 27J
New York, NY 10023-7200, USA

Drury, James (Actor)
12126 Osage Park Dr
Houston, TX 77065, USA

Drury, Ted (Athlete, Hockey Player)
28 Cottage Pl
Trumbull, CT 06611, USA

Drury, Ted (Athlete, Hockey Player)
2507 Greenwood Ave.
Wilmette, MI 60091-1303, USA

Druschel, Rick (Athlete, Football Player)
724 Cochran Dr
Greensburg, PA 15601, USA

Drut, Guy J (Athlete, Track Athlete)
Maine
Coulommiers 77120, FRANCE

Dry, Tim (Actor)
c/o Staff Member *Coolwaters Productions*
10061 Riverside Dr.
Box 531
Toluca Lake, CA 91602, USA

Dryburgh, Stuart (Cinematographer)
Sandra Marsh Mgmt
9150 Wilshire Blvd #220
Beverly Hills, CA 90212, USA

Dryden, Dave (Athlete, Hockey Player)
2257 All Saints Cres
Oakville, ON L6J 5N1, Canada

Dryden, Kenneth (Ken) (Athlete, Hockey Player)
House of Commons
58 Poplar Plains Rd
Toronto, ON M4V 2M8, Canada

Dryer, Fred (Actor, Athlete, Football Player)
10421 Windtree Dr
Los Angeles, CA 90077, USA

Dryke, Matthew (Athlete, Olympic Athlete, Shooter)
292 Dryke Rd
Sequim, WA 98382-7221, USA

Drynan, Jeanie (Actor)
c/o Staff Member *Essential Talent Management*
6399 Wilshire Blvd
Suite 401
Los Angeles, CA 90048, USA

Drysdale, Cliff (Sportscaster, Tennis Player)
Landfall
1801 Eastwood Road #F
Wilmington, NC 28403, USA

Drzewiecki, Ron (Athlete, Football Player)
5977 S 34th St
Milwaukee, WI 53221, USA

D. Schakowsky, Janice (Congressman, Politician)
2367 Rayburn HOB
Washington, DC 20515, USA

D'Souza, Lawrence (Bollywood, Director, Filmmaker, Producer)
302B Red Rose New Link Road
Versova Andheri
Bombay, MS 400 058, INDIA

DSquared2 (Fashion Designer)
DSquared2
220 West 19th Street
11th Floor
New York, NY 10011, USA

Duany, Andres (Architect)
Duany & Plater-Zaberk Architects
1023 SW 25th Ave
Miami, FL 33135, USA

DuArt, Louise (Religious Leader, Television Host)
c/o Staff Member *Living the Life*
Christian Broadcasting Network
977 Centerville Tpke
Virginia Beach, VA 23463, USA

Duarte, Marci (Stylist)
c/o Staff Member *Team*
423 W Broadway
4th Floor
Boston, MA 02127, USA

Dubbels, Britta (Model)
c/o Staff Member *Ford Models (NY)*
238 E 4th St
New York, NY 10009, USA

Dubble, Curtis (Religious Leader)
Church of Brethren
1451 Dundee Ave
Elgin, IL 60120, USA

Dube, Gilles (Athlete, Hockey Player)
606-800 Rue de Vimy
Sherbrooke, QC J1J 2N7, Canada

Dube, Joseph (Joe) (Athlete, Wrestler)
8821 Eaton Ave
Jacksonville, FL 32211, USA

Dube, Lucky (Musician)
Fast Lane Int'l
4856 Haygood Road
#200
Virginia Beach, VA 23455, USA

Dube, Norm (Athlete, Hockey Player)
1590 Rue John-Griffith
Sherbrooke, QC J1J 4L4, Canada

Dubee, Rich (Athlete, Baseball Player)
8517 Eaele Preserve Way
Sarasota, FL 34241-8505, USA

Dubenion, Elbert (Athlete, Football Player)
610 E Walnut St
Westerville, OH 43081, USA

Duberman, Justin (Athlete, Hockey Player)
4 E 4th St
Hinsdale, IL 60521-4460

Dubia, John A (General)
10095 Cover Place
Fairfax, VA 22030-2494, USA

Dubielewicz, Wade (Athlete, Hockey Player)
132 Wintergreen Ave
Hamden, CT 06514-3346

Dubinbaum, Gail (Opera Singer)
Metropolitan Opera Assn
Lincoln Center Plaza
New York, NY 10023, USA

Dubinsky, Brandon (Athlete, Hockey Player)
10110 Salix Cir
Anchorage, AK 99507, USA

Dubinsky, Steve (Athlete, Hockey Player)
939 Central Ave
Highland Park, IL 60060035-3249, USA

Dublinski, James L (Athlete, Football Player)
723 S 900 E
Salt Lake City, UT 84102, USA

Dublinski, Tom (Athlete, Football Player)
15918 E El Lago Blvd
Fountain Hills, AZ 85268, USA

Dubois, Allison
P.O.Box 7497
Phoenix, Arizona 85011-7497, USA

Dubois, Brian (Athlete, Baseball Player)
3 Soartan Pl
Sorinefield, IL 62703-4715, USA

Dubois, Janet (Actor)
c/o Staff Member *Cunningham Escott Slevin & Doherty (CESD-LA)*
10635 Santa Monica Blvd
130
Los Angeles, CA 90025, USA

Dubois, Jason (Athlete, Baseball Player)
2204 Lord Seaton Cir
Virginia Beach, VA 23454-2923, USA

DuBois, Marta (Actor)
Three Moons Entertainment
5441 East Beverly Blvd #G
Los Angeles, CA 90022, USA

Dubois, Phil (Athlete, Football Player)
405 Speedway Ave
Missoula, MT 59802, USA

Dubose, Brian (Baseball Player)
Ted Williams
15336 Oakfield St
Detroit, MI 48227-1532, USA

Dubose, Eric (Athlete, Baseball Player)
326 County Road 8
Gilbertown, AL 36908-2211, USA

DuBose, G Thomas (Misc)
United Transportation Union
14600 Detroit Ave
Cleveland, OH 44107, USA

DuBose, James (Director, Producer)
c/o Toni Thompson *Toni Thompson PR*
Accepts Calls Only
Los Angeles, CA 90001, USA

Dubose, Jimmy (Athlete, Football Player)
11420 Walker Rd
Thonotosassa, FL 33592, USA

Dubzinski, Walt (Athlete, Football Player)
158 Lovewell St
Gardner, MA 01440, USA

Ducasse, Alain (Chef)
Groupe Alain Ducasse
Hotel de Paris Louis XV Restaurant
Monte Carlo, Monaco, USA

Ducey, Rob (Athlete, Baseball Player)
699 Richmond Close
Tarpon Springs, FL 34688-8423, USA

Duchesnay, Isamelle (Dancer)
Im Steinach 30
Oberstdorf 87561, GERMANY

Duchesnay, Paul (Figure Skater)
Bundesleistungszentrum
Rossbichstr 2-6
Oberstdorf 87561, GERMANY

Duchesne, Steve (Athlete, Hockey Player)
2104 Cedar Elm Ter
Westlake, TX 76262-9025, USA

Duchovny, David (Actor, Producer)
170 E 78th St #124C
New York, NY 10075, USA

Duchscherer, Justin (Athlete, Baseball Player)
3405 E Birchwood Pl
Chandler, AZ 85249-4564, USA

DuCille, Michel (Journalist, Photographer)
9571 Pine Meadow Lane
Burke, VA 22015, USA

Duckett, Forey (Athlete, Football Player)
7518 Winona Ave N
Seattle, WA 98103, USA

Duckett, Mahlon (Athlete, Baseball
Player)
5325 Old York Rd
Apt 611
Philadelphia, PA 19141-2952, USA

Duckett, Richard (Athlete, Basketball
Player)
10 Wyckham Rd
Spring Lake, NJ 07762-2255, USA

Duckett, TJ (Athlete, Football Player)
c/o Joel Segal *Lagardere Unlimited - NY*
845 UN Plaza
New York, NY 10017, USA

Ducksworth, Sheila (Producer)
c/o Staff Member *Creative Artists Agency
(CAA-LA)*
2000 Ave Of The Stars
Los Angeles, CA 90067, USA

Duckworth, Brandon (Athlete, Baseball
Player)
4460 W 6095 S
Salt Lake City, UT 84118-5289, USA

Duckworth, Henry E (Scientist)
403-99 Wellington Cres
Winnipeg, MB R3M OA2, Canada

Duckworth, Jim (Athlete, Baseball Player)
3736 Ferrero Way
Redding, CA 96001-0180, USA

Duckworth, Tyler (Reality TV Star)
c/o Len Evans *Project Publicity*
312 West 53rd St
Suite 202
New York, NY 10019, USA

Ducsmal, Agnieszka
Polish Radio Orchestra
Al Marchinkowskiego 3
Pozna 61-745, POLAND

Duda, Mark (Athlete, Football Player)
1707 Cherry St
Scranton, PA 18505, USA

Dudamel, Gustavo (Conductor)
c/o Jordi Martin Mont *Van Walsum
Management*
The Tower Building
11 York Rd
London SE1 7NX, UK

Dudek, Anne (Actor)
c/o Sandra Chang *Anonymous Content
(LA)*
955 S Carrillo Dr
Suite 300
Los Angeles, CA 90048, USA

Dudek, Joseph A (Joe) (Athlete, Football
Player)
31 Ryan Rd
Auburn, NH 03032, USA

Dudek, Mitch (Athlete, Football Player)
1241 Forest Ave
Wilmette, IL 60091, USA

Duden, H Richard (Dick) Jr (Athlete,
Football Player)
11 Old Station Rd
Severna Park, MD 21146, USA

Duderstadt, James J (Educator,
Government Official)
National Science Foundation
1800 G St NW
Washington, DC 20006, USA

Dudikoff, Michael (Actor)
11 Santa Bella Rd
Rolling Hills Estates, CA 90274, USA

Dudley, Brian (Athlete, Football Player)
6319 London Ave
Rancho Cucamonga, CA 91737, USA

Dudley, Charles (Athlete, Basketball
Player)
4032 42nd Avenue South
Seattle, WA 98118-1121, USA

Dudley, Chris (Athlete, Basketball Player)
1150 Fairway Road
Lake Oswego, OR 97034-2818, USA

Dudley, Debra
Box 40
Bonnieville, KY 42713

Dudley, James (Baseball Player)
Baltimore Elite Giants
607 Delafield Pl NW
Wahington, DC 20011-4054, USA

Dudley, Jaquelin (Biologist, Misc)
University of Texas
Microbiology Dept
Austin, TX 78712, USA

Dudley, Rick (Athlete, Coach, Hockey
Player, Misc)
5150 Oakhill Dr
Lewiston, NY 14092, USA

dudley, Rick (Athlete, Hockey Player)
5150 Oakhill Dr
Lewiston, NY 14092-1857

Dudley, Rickey (Athlete, Football Player)
4529 Mahogany Ln
Lewisville, TX 75077, USA

Duell, Chad (Actor)
c/o Earl Shank *Earl Shank Management*
520 North Kings Rd
Suite 316
West Hollywood, CA 90048, USA

Duenkel, Ginny (Athlete, Olympic
Athlete, Swimmer)
2132 NE 17th Ter Fl 5
Wilton Manors, FL 33305-2414, USA

Duenkel Fuldner, Virginia (Swimmer)
2132 NE 17th Terrace #500
Wilton Manors, FL 33305, USA

Duensing, Brian Duensing (Athlete,
Baseball Player)
524 S 198th St
Elkhorn, NE 68022-6457, USA

Duerod, Terry (Athlete, Basketball Player)
6S42 Chirrewa St
Westland, MI 48185-2807, USA

Dues, Hal (Athlete, Baseball Player)
3932 Amanda Dr
Dickinson, TX 77539-6405, USA

Dueto Voces del Rancho (Musician)
c/o Staff Member *Sony Music Miami*
605 Lincoln Rd Fl 7
Miami Beach, FL 33139, USA

Dufek, Don (Athlete, Football Player)
570 S Maple Rd
Ann Arbor, MI 48103, USA

Dufek, Joe (Athlete, Football Player)
17015 N 7th St
Suite 1
Phoenix, AZ 85022, USA

Duff, Haylie (Actor, Musician)
4440 Sancola Ave
Toluca Lake, CA 91602, USA

Duff, Hilary (Actor, Musician)
12092 Summit Cir
Beverly Hills, CA 90210, USA

Duff, Jamal (Athlete, Football Player)
P.O. Box 20058
Long Beach, CA 90801, USA

Duff, John (Athlete, Football Player)
P.O. Box 20058
Long Beach, CA 90801, USA

Duff, John B (Educator)
Columbia College
President's Office
Chicago, IL 60605, USA

Duff, John E (Artist, Misc)
7 Doyers St
New York, NY 10013, USA

Duff, Matt (Athlete, Baseball Player)
Major League Bowhunter
500 N Highway 18
Chandler, OK 74834, USA

Duff, T Richard (Dick) (Athlete, Hockey
Player)
4-7 Elmwood Ave S
Mississauga, ON L5G 3J6, Canada

Duffalo, Jim (Athlete, Baseball Player)
1505 Savannah St
Mesquite, TX 75149-8715, USA

Duffell, Peter
29 Roehampton Gate
London, ENGLAND SW15 5JR

Duffie, John (Athlete, Baseball Player)
177 Lakeside Circle
Douglas, GA 31535-6627, USA

Duffield, David (Business Person)
PeopleSoft Inc
4460 Hacienda Dr
Pleasanton, CA 94588, USA

Duffner, Mark (Coach, Football Coach)
University of Maryland
Athletic Dept
College Park, MD 20740, USA

Duffus, Parris (Athlete, Hockey Player)
8609 Timbermill Pl
Fort Wayne, IN 46804-3411, USA

Duffy, Aimee Anne (DUFFY) (Musician)
c/o Staff Member *Island Records*
825 Eighth Ave
New York, NY 10019, USA

Duffy, Brian (Astronaut)
14805 Pristine Drive
Colorado Springs, CO 80921-3549, USA

Duffy, Brian (Cartoonist, Editor)
Des Moines Regester
Editorial Dept P O Box 957
Des Moines, IA 50304, USA

Duffy, Chris (Athlete, Baseball Player)
23212 N 70th Ln
Glendale, AZ 85310-5864, USA

Duffy, Dorothy (Actor)
PFD
Drury House
34-43 Russell St
London WC2B 5HA, UNITED KINGDOM
(UK)

Duffy, Frank (Athlete, Baseball Player)
1740 E Silver St
Tucson, AZ 85719-3152, USA

Duffy, James (Business Person)
Saint Paul Companies
385 Washington St
Saint Paul, MN 55102, USA

Duffy, James (General)
1147 W 162nd St
Gardena, CA 90247-4421, USA

Duffy, JC (Cartoonist)
Universal Press Syndicate
4520 Main St
Kansas City, MO 64111, USA

Duffy, John (Composer)
Meet the Composer
2112 Broadway
New York, NY 10023, USA

Duffy, Julia (Actor)
540 Live Oak Circle Dr
Calabasas, CA 91302, USA

Duffy, Karen (Actor, Model)
c/o Staff Member *Rebel Entertainment
Partners*
5700 Wilshire Blvd
Suite 456
Los Angeles, CA 90036, USA

Duffy, Keith (Music Group)
Carol Assoc-War Mgmt
Bushy Park Road 57 Meadowgate
Dublin, IRELAND

Duffy, Matthew (DJ)
c/o Len Evans *Project Publicity*
312 West 53rd St
Suite 202
New York, NY 10019, USA

Duffy, Patrick (Actor, Director, Producer)
2026 Palisades Dr
Pacific Palisades, CA 90272, USA

Duffy, Roger (Athlete, Football Player)
6509 Lutz Ave NW
Massillon, OH 44646, USA

Duffy, Troy (Actor, Director, Writer)
c/o David Krintzman *Morris, Yorn,
Barnes, Levine, Krintzman, Rubenstein
and Kohner*
2000 Ave of the Stars
3rd Floor, North Tower
Los Angeles, CA 90067, USA

Dufner, Jason (Athlete, Golfer)
c/o Clarke Jones *IMG (Cleveland)*
1360 E 9th St
Suite 100
Cleveland, OH 44114, USA

Dufour, Luc (Athlete, Hockey Player)
334 Rue Des Champs-Elysees
Chicoutimi, QC G7H 2V8, Canada

Dufresne, Donald (Athlete, Coach,
Hockey Player)
c/o Staff Member *Rimouski Oceanic
Hockey Club*
CP 816 Succ A
Rimouski, QC G5L 7C9, Canada

Dugan, Dennis (Actor, Director)
4505 Woodley Ave
Encino, CA 91436, USA

Dugan, Fred (Athlete, Football Player)
1827 Tamiami Trl N
Nokomis, FL 34275, USA

Dugan, Jeff (Athlete, Football Player)
13701 Ashcroft Rd
Savage, MN 55378, USA

Dugan, Michael J (General, Misc)
National Multiple Sclerosis Society
733 3rd Ave
New York, NY 10017, USA

Dugans, Ron (Athlete, Football Player)
1549 Coleman St
Tallahassee, FL 32310, USA

Duggan, Catherine (Athlete, Golfer)
5923 Marilyn Dr
Knoxville, TN 37914, USA

Duggan, Jim (Athlete, Football Player)
1328 Hornsby Cir
Lugoff, SC 29078, USA

Duggan, Jim (Athlete, Wrestler)
1328 Hornsby Circle
Lugoff, SC 29078-9722, USA

Duggar, Michelle (Reality TV Star)
548 Arbor Acres Ave
Springdale, AR 72762, USA

Dugger, John S (Artist)
410 Evelyn Ave
Apt 201
Albany, CA 94706-1358, USA

Dugiud, Matthew (Stylist)
c/o Staff Member *Exclusive Artists Mgmt*
7700 Sunset Blvd
#205
Los Angeles, CA 90046, USA

Duguary, Ron (Actor, Athlete, Hockey Player)
982 Porte Vedra Blvd
Porta Vedra Beach, FL 32082, USA

Duguay, Ron (Athlete, Hockey Player)
982 Ponte Verda Blvd
Ponte Vedra Beach, FL 32082-4068, USA

Duhamel, Josh (Actor)
1310 N Kenter Ave
Los Angeles, CA 90049, USA

Duhe, Adam J (A J) Jr (Athlete, Football Player)
379 Coconut Cir
Weston, FL 33326, USA

Duhe, John M Jr (Judge)
US Court of Appeals
556 Jefferson St
Lafayette, LA 70501, USA

Duhon, Josh (Actor)
c/o Abby Bluestone *Innovative Artists (LA)*
1505 10th St
Santa Monica, CA 90401, USA

Duhon, Robert (Bobby) (Athlete, Football Player)
4384 Whitewater Creek Rd NW
Atlanta, GA 30327, USA

Duich, Steve (Athlete, Football Player)
P.O. Box 2
Descanso, CA 91916, USA

Dujardin, Jean (Actor)
c/o Bryna Rifkin *ID PR (LA)*
7060 Hollywood Blvd
8th Floor
Los Angeles, CA 90028, USA

Dukakis, Kitty
85 Perry St
Brookline, MA 02146

Dukakis, Michael (Ex-Governor)
Northeastern University
85 Perry St
Brookline, MA 02446-6935, USA

Dukakis, Olympia (Actor)
684 Broadway #6E
New York, NY 10012, USA

Duke, Annie (Poker Player)
c/o Glen Clarkson *Synergy Management*
15233 Ventura Blvd
Suite 707
Sherman Oaks, CA 91403, USA

Duke, Bill (Director)
Duke Media
7510 Sunset Blvd #523
Los Angeles, CA 90046, USA

Duke, Charles
PO Box 310345
New Braunfels, TX 78130

Duke, Charles M Jr (Astronaut, General)
280 Lakeview Blvd
New Braunfels, TX 78130, USA

Duke, Clark (Actor)
c/o Andy Corren *Andy Corren Management*
1545 26th St
Suite 200
Santa Monica, CA 90404, USA

Duke, George (Musician)
1970 Outpost Cir
Los Angeles, CA 90068, USA

Duke, Ken (Athlete, Golfer)
3612 SW Rivers End Way
Palm City, FL 34990, USA

Duke, Norm (Bowler)
10836 Country Road 561A
Clermont, FL 34711, USA

Duke, Patty (Actor)
2865 N Sugar Pines Dr
Coeur D'Alene, ID 83815, USA

Duke, Randolph (Fashion Designer)
c/o Diana Bianchini *Di Moda Public Relations*
9713 Santa Monica Blvd
Suite 220
Beverly Hills, CA 90210, USA

Duke, Robin (Actor)
c/o Staff Member *Oscars Abrams Zimel & Associates*
438 Queen St. E
Toronto ON M5A 1T4, Canada

Duke, Zach (Athlete, Baseball Player)
221 Harper Ct
Keller, TX 76248-3022, USA

Dukes, Elijah (Athlete, Baseball Player)
2430 Cedar Trace Cir # B
Tampa, FL 33613-5628, USA

Dukes, Jamie (Athlete, Football Player)
2452 Stone Manor Dr
Buford, GA 30519, USA

Dukes, Jan (Athlete, Baseball Player)
959 Helena Dr
Sunnyvale, CA 94087-4126, USA

Dukes, Michael (Athlete, Football Player)
115 N 23rd St
Nederland, TX 77627-5909, USA

Dukes, The (Music Group)
11 Chartfield Square
London, England SW15, United Kingdom

Dukes, Tom (Athlete, Baseball Player)
325 Monte Vista Rd
Arcadia, CA 91007-6147, USA

Dukes of Dixieland, The
PO Box 56757
New Orleans, Los Angeles 70156-6757

Duke Special
c/o Staff Member *Paradigm (Monterey)*
404 W Franklin St
Monterey, CA 93940, USA

Duke Spirit, The (Music Group)
c/o Staff Member *Paradigm (Monterey)*
404 W Franklin St
Monterey, CA 93940, USA

Dukochitz, Jonathan (Actor, Musician)
c/o Staff Member *Innovative Artists (LA)*
1505 10th St
Santa Monica, CA 90401, USA

Dulany, Caitlin (Actor)
Gersh Agency
232 N Canon Dr
Beverly Hills, CA 90210, USA

Duley, Ed (Athlete, Football Player)
5219 N Casa Blanca Dr
Paradise Valley, AZ 85253, USA

Dulgan, John (Director)
54A Tite St
London SW3 4JA, UNITED KINGDOM (UK)

Dulhalde, Eduardo (President)
Casa de Gobierno
Balcarce 50
Buenos Aires 1064, ARGENTINA

Duliba, Bob (Athlete, Baseball Player)
327 Philadelphia Ave
West Pittston, PA 18643-2146, USA

Dullea, Keir (Actor)
c/o Staff Member *Bret Adams Agency*
448 W 44th St
New York, NY 10036, USA

Dulles, Avery R Cardinal (Misc)
Fordham University
Jesuit Community
Bronx, NY 10458, USA

Dulli, Greg (Musician)
3211 Hamilton Way
Los Angeles, CA 90026, USA

Dumais, Justin (Athlete, Diver, Olympic Athlete)
2301 N Millbend Dr
Spring, TX 77380-1360, USA

Dumais, Troy (Athlete, Diver, Olympic Athlete)
2301 N Millbend Dr
Spring, TX 77380-1360, USA

Dumars III, Joe (Athlete, Basketball Player)
3499 Franklin Road
Bloomfield Hills, MI 48302-0960, USA

Dumas, Marlene (Artist)
Tolstraat 94 HS
Amsterdam 1073 BE, The Netherlands

Dumas, Michel (Athlete, Hockey Player)
c/o Staff Member *Chicago Blackhawks*
1901 W Madison St
Chicago, IL 60612, USA

Dumas, Mike (Athlete, Football Player)
6735 Alden Nash Ave SE
Alto, MI 49302, USA

Dumas, Tony (Athlete, Basketball Player)
674 Jay Court
San Marcos, CA 92069-7393, USA

Dumatrait, Phil (Athlete, Baseball Player)
1412 Stub Oak Ave
Bakersfield, CA 93307-6917, USA

Dumbauld, Jonathan (Athlete, Football Player)
1530 E Sagebrush Ct
Gilbert, AZ 85296, USA

Dumelie, Larry (Athlete, Football Player)
3619 4th Line Rd
Osgoode, ON K0A 2W0, Canada

Dumervil, Elvis (Athlete, Football Player)
1717 N Bayshore Dr Apt A-2641
Miami, FL 33132, USA

Dumler, Doug (Athlete, Football Player)
1526 Peterson St
Fort Collins, CO 80524, USA

Dummar, Melvin
Dummar's Restaurant
Gabbs, NV 89409

Dummett, Michael A E (Misc)
54 Park Town
Oxford OX2 6SJ, UNITED KINGDOM (UK)

Dummit, Dennis (Athlete, Football Player)
111 Via Di Roma Walk
Long Beach, CA 90803-4156, USA

Dumont, J P (Athlete, Hockey Player)
1512 Kimberleigh Ct
Franklin, TN 37069-7226, USA

Dumont, Sky (Actor)
ZBF Agentur
Leopoldstr 19
Munich 80802, GERMANY

Dumont, Tom (Musician)
326 Glendora Ave
Laguna Beach, CA 90803, USA

Dumoulin, Dan (Athlete, Baseball Player)
202 Nancy Dr
Kokomo, IN 46901-5907, USA

Dumpson, William "Showboat" (Athlete, Baseball Player)
555 Ellis Ave
Orangeburg, SC 29115-5021, USA

Dunagan, Donnie (Actor)
422 S Bishop St
San Angelo, TX 76901, USA

Dunagin, Ralph (Cartoonist)
North American Syndicate
235 E 45th St
New York, NY 10017, USA

Dunaway, Craig (Athlete, Football Player)
1000 Westchester Way
Birmingham, MI 48009, USA

Dunaway, Faye (Actor)
901 N Spaulding Ave
West Hollywood, CA 90046, USA

Dunaway, James E (Athlete, Football Player)
170 Mount Carmel Church Rd
Sandy Hook, MS 39478, USA

Dunbar, Bonnie J (Astronaut)
2200 Todville Road
Seabrook, TX 77586, USA

Dunbar, Dale (Athlete, Hockey Player)
41 Nahant Ave
Winthrop, MA 02152-1514, USA

Dunbar, Dr. bonnie j (Astronaut)
2200 Todville Rd
Seabrook, TX 77586-3005, USA

Dunbar, Huey (Musician)
c/o Staff Member *Sony Music Miami*
605 Lincoln Rd Fl 7
Miami Beach, FL 33139, USA

Dunbar, Matt (Athlete, Baseball Player)
6328 County Donegal Ct
Charlotte, NC 28277-9652, USA

Dunbar, Rockmond (Actor)
5260 Medina Rd
Woodland Hills, CA 91364, USA

Dunbar, Vaughn (Athlete, Football Player)
1085 Greatwood Mnr
Alpharetta, GA 30005, USA

Duncan, Allison (Race Car Driver)
McNally Racing
8636 Antelope North Rd.
Antelope, CA 95843, USA

Duncan, Andy (Basketball Player)
Rochester Royals
608 Berry Pl
Marion, VA 24354-4168, USA

Duncan, Angus (Actor)
Thomas Jennings
28035 Dorothy Dr #210A
Agoura, CA 90301, USA

Duncan, Arthur (Dancer)
Greg Purcott Productions
P.O. Box 276005
Boca Raton, FL 33427, USA

Duncan, Brian (Athlete, Football Player)
739 Elm St
Graham, TX 76450, USA

Duncan, Charles K (Admiral)
813 1st St
Coronado, CA 92118, USA

Duncan, Charles W Jr (Politician, Secretary)
2 Briarwood Ct
Houston, TX 77019-5802, USA

Duncan, Chris (Athlete, Baseball Player)
626 Eaglesridge Dr
Ballwin, MO 63021-2020, USA

Duncan, Courtney (Athlete, Baseball Player)
121 Adalene Ln
Madison, AL 35757-8423, USA

Duncan, Curtis (Athlete, Football Player)
4915 Glen Hollow St
Sugar Land, TX 77479, USA

Duncan, Dan (Business Person)
Enterprise Products Partners L.P
1100 Louisiana St
Houston, TX 77002, USA

Duncan, Dave (Athlete, Baseball Player)
205 Hunters Glenn
Ln
Kimberling City, MO 65686-9862, USA

Duncan, David Douglas (Journalist, Photographer)
Castellaras
Mouans-Sartoux F-06370, FRANCE

Duncan, Dennis (Athlete, Baseball Player)
7650 N Zack Rd
Columbia, MO 65202-9240, USA

Duncan, Donna (Race Car Driver)
Mike Murphy Racing
PO Box 3936
Portsmouth, VA 23701, USA

Duncan, Iain (Athlete, Hockey Player)
1956 W Alexis Rd
Apt 406
Toledo, OH 43613, USA

Duncan, Jamie (Athlete, Football Player)
217 Remi Dr
New Castle, DE 19720, USA

Duncan, Jeff (Congressman, Politician)
116 Cannon HOB
Washington, DC 20515, USA

Duncan, Jeff (Athlete, Baseball Player)
825 Lincoln Ln
Frankfort, IL 60423-1087, USA

Duncan, Ken (Athlete, Football Player)
4 Christina Ave
Camarillo, CA 93012, USA

Duncan, Iain (Athlete, Hockey Player)
453 Cedarwood Rd
Avon Lake, OH 44012-3141, USA

Duncan, Leslie (Speedy) (Athlete, Football Player)
1607 Porter Way
Stockton, CA 95207, USA

Duncan, Lindsay (Actor)
Ken McReddie
91 Regent St
London W1R 7TB, UNITED KINGDOM (UK)

Duncan, Mariano (Athlete, Baseball Player)
11142 NW 71st Ter
Doral, FL 33178-3789, USA

Duncan, Melvin (Athlete, Baseball Player)
P.O. Box 980407
470 Bedford Dr
Ypsitanta, MI 48198-0407, USA

Duncan, Meredith (Athlete, Golfer)
244 Arthur Ave
Shreveport, LA 71105, USA

Duncan, Mike (Race Car Driver)
PO Box 21235
Bakersfield, CA 93390, USA

Duncan, Patrick S (Director, Producer, Writer)
c/o David Kanter *Anonymous Content (LA)*
3531 Hayden Ave
Culver City, CA 90232, USA

Duncan, Robert (Astronomer, Misc, Physicist)
University of Texas
Astronomy Dept
Austin, TX 78712, USA

Duncan, Robert (General)
1511 Ryder Cup Blvd
Marion, IL 62959-5221, USA

Duncan, Sandy (Actor)
15222 De Pauw St
Pacific Palisades, CA 90272, USA

duncan, Shelley (Athlete, Baseball Player)
6547 N Turnberrv Dr
Tucson, AZ 85718-2600, USA

Duncan, Speedy (Athlete, Football Player)
1607 Porter Way
Stockton, CA 95207, USA

Duncan, Tim (Athlete, Basketball Player)
21321 Babcock Rd
Lot 3
San Antonio, TX 78255, USA

Duncan, Todd (Motivational Speaker, Writer)
The Duncan Group
3760 Peachtree Crest Dr
Suite A
Duluth, GA 30097, USa

Duncanson, Craig (Athlete, Hockey Player)
Laurentian University
935 Ramsey Lake Dr
Attn: Hockey Program
Sudbury, ON P3E 2C6, Canada

Dundas, Jason (Reality TV Star)
c/o Michelle Elliot
PO Box 128
Surry Hills NSW 2010, AUSTRALIA

Dundas, Rocky (Athlete, Hockey Player)
14 Nantucket Dr
Richmond Hill, ON L4E 3V1, Canada

Dunderstadt, James (Educator)
University of Michigan
President's Office
Ann Arbor, MI 48109, USA

Dunegan, Jim (Athlete, Baseball Player)
20246 180th St
New London, IA 52645-8555, USA

Dungan, Fred (General)
427 Camino San Clemente
San Clemente, CA 92672-3707, USA

Dungey, Merrin (Actor)
2906 Nichols Canyon Rd
Los Angeles, CA 90046, USA

Dungian, Matt
CanWest Global Communications
3100 Canwest Global place
Attn: Road Grill Show
Winnipeg, MB R3B 3L7 Canada, USA

Dungy, Tony (Athlete, Coach, Football Coach, Football Player)
16604 Villalenda De Avila
Tampa, FL 33613, USA

Dunham, Archie W (Business Person)
ConocoPhilips Inc
600 N Dairy Ashford
Houston, TX 77079, USA

Dunham, Chip (Cartoonist)
Universal Press Syndicate
4520 Main St
Kansas City, MO 64111, USA

Dunham, Duane R (Business Person)
Bethlehem Steel Corp
1170 8th Ave
Bethlehem, PA 18016, USA

Dunham, Jeff (Comedian)
c/o Judy Brown-Marmel *Levity Entertainment Group*
6701 Center Drive West
Suite 1111
Los Angles, CA 90045, USA

Dunham, John L (Business Person)
May Department Stores
611 Olive St
Saint Louis, MO 63101, USA

Dunham, Lena (Actor, Writer)
c/o Jenny Maryasis *United Talent Agency (UTA)*
9336 Civic Center Dr
Beverly Hills, CA 90210, USA

Dunham, Michael (Mike) (Athlete, Hockey Player, Olympic Athlete)
39 Garfield Rd
Concord, MA 01742-4930, USA

Dunham, Mike
New York Islanders
1255 Hempstead Tpke
Attn Coaching Staff
Uniondale, NY 11553-1200, USA

Dunigan, Matt (Athlete, Football Player)
CanWest Global Communications
3100 CanWest Global
Place Attn: Road Grill Show
Winnipeg, MB R3B 3L7, Canada

Dunitz, Jack D (Misc)
Obere Heslibachstr 77
Kusnacht 8700, SWITZERLAND

Dunkie, Nancy (Basketball Player)
University of California
Campus Police
Berkeley, CA 94720, USA

Dunkle, Nancy (Athlete, Basketball Player, Olympic Athlete)
1350 Lorawood St
La Habra, CA 90631-7405, USA

Dunlap, Alexander W (Astronaut)
721 Parkside Dr
Woodstock, GA 30188-6057, USA

Dunlap, Carla (Gymnast, Misc)
Diamond
732 Irvington Ave
Maplewood, NJ 07040, USA

Dunlap, Grant (Athlete, Baseball Player)
1431 Alga Ct
Vista, CA 92081-5016, USA

Dunlap, Page (Athlete, Golfer)
8728 Misty Creek Dr
Sarasota, FL 34241-9561, USA

Dunlap, Robert H (War Hero)
P O Box 584
Monmouth, IL 61462, USA

Dunlap, Scott (Athlete, Golfer)
104 Summerour Vale
Duluth, GA 30097-2464, USA

Dunlea, Jennifer (Stylist)
c/o Staff Member *Team*
423 W Broadway
4th Floor
Boston, MA 02127, USA

Dunleavy, Mary (Opera Singer)
c/o Staff Member *Columbia Artists Mgmt Inc*
1790 Broadway Fl 6
New York, NY 10019-1412, USA

Dunleavy, Michael J (Mike) (Athlete, Basketball Player, Coach)
127 S Carmelina Ave
Los Angeles, CA 90049, USA

Dunleavy, Mike (Athlete, Basketball Player)
Golden State Warriors
127 S Carmelina Ave
Los Angeles, CA 90049-3901, USA

Dunleavy Jr, Mike (Athlete, Basketball Player)
127 S Carmelina Ave.
Los Angeles, CA 90049, USA

Dunleavy Sr, Mike (Athlete, Basketball Player, Coach)
c/o Warren LeGarie *Warren LeGarie Sports Management*
1108 Masonic Ave
San Francisco, CA 94117, USA

Dunlop, Andy (Music Group, Musician)
Wildlife Entertainment
21 Heathmans Road
London SW6 4TJ, UNITED KINGDOM (UK)

Dunlop, Blake (Athlete, Hockey Player)
8112 Maryland Ave
Saint Louis, MO 63105-3700, USA

dunlop, Harry
5605 Laguna Quail Way
Elk Grove, CA 95758-5710, USA

Dunn, Adam (Athlete, Baseball Player)
11 Netherfield Way
Spring, TX 77382-1730, USA

Dunn, Alan (Athlete, Baseball Player)
8536 Glenfield Dr
Baton Rouge, LA 70809-5214, USA

Dunn, Andrew W (Cinematographer)
525 Broadway #250
Santa Monica, CA 90401, USA

Dunn, Annie (Stylist)
c/o Staff Member *The Milton Agency (LA)*
6715 Hollywood Blvd
#204
Los Angeles, CA 90028, USA

Dunn, Colton (Actor)
c/o Joel Zadak *Principato/Young Management*
9465 Wilshire Blvd
Suite 430
Beverly Hills, CA 90212, USA

Dunn, Dave (Athlete, Hockey Player)
1433 Hamilton St
Regina, SK S4R 7V4, Canada

Dunn, Douglas (Writer)
c/o Staff Member *The Rights House (UK)*
Drury House
34-43 Russell St
London WC2B 5HA, UK

Dunn, Gary (Athlete, Football Player)
243 Navajo St
Tavernier, FL 33070, USA

Dunn, Gertie (Baseball Player)
PO Box 88
Chadds Ford, PA 19317-0088, USA

Dunn, Gregory (Publisher)
Redbook Magazine
224 W 57th St
New York, NY 10019, USA

Dunn, Halbert L (Mathematician)
3637 Edelmar Terrace
Silver Spring, MD 20906, USA

Dunn, Holly (Actor, Musician)
Holly Dunn Enterprises
PO Box 2525
Hendersonville, TN 37077, USA

Dunn, Jim (Race Car Driver)
840 Kallin Ave
Long Beach, CA 90815-5004, USA

Dunn, Keldrick (K.D.) (Athlete, Football Player)
1640 Township Ter
McDonough, GA 30252, USA

Dunn, Kevin (Actor)
321 E Grandview Ave
Sierra Madre, CA 91024, USA

Dunn, Mignon (Opera Singer)
Warden Assoc
5626 Deer Run Road
Doylestown, PA 18901, USA

Dunn, Mike (Race Car Driver)
Team Mopar
PO Box 128
Wrightsville, PA 17368, USA

Dunn, Moira (Athlete, Golfer)
15803 Bridgewater Ln
Tampa, FL 33624-1044, USA

Dunn, Nora (Actor, Comedian)
c/o Steven Siebert *Lighthouse Entertainment*
9220 W Sunset Blvd Ste 200
West Hollywood, CA 90069, USA

Dunn, Patricia (Tricia) (Athlete, Hockey Player, Olympic Athlete)
4 Huson Ave
Derry, NH 03038, USA

Dunn, Perry Lee (Athlete, Football Player)
64 Glenway Pl
Brandon, MS 39042, USA

Dunn, Richie (Athlete, Hockey Player)
12229 Clarence Center Rd
Akron, NY 14001-9334, USA

Dunn, Ron (Athlete, Baseball Player)
1161 Husted Ave
San Jose, CA 95125-3633, USA

Dunn, Ronnie (Musician, Songwriter)
PO Box 120669
Nashville, TN 37212, USA

Dunn, Sarah Jayne (Actor)
RDF Management
c/o Michael Ford
3-6 Kenrick Place
London W1U 6HD, UNITED KINGDOM

Dunn, Scott (Athlete, Baseball Player)
1331 Arizona Ash St
San Antonio, TX 78232-3409, USA

Dunn, Shannon (Stylist)
c/o Staff Member *Zenobia Agency Inc*
PO Box 909
Groveland, CA 95321, USA

Dunn, Steve (Athlete, Baseball Player)
484 Broadmoor Dr
Maryville, TN 37803-6575, USA

Dunn, Susan (Opera Singer)
1212 Lancaster
Champaign, IL 61821, USA

Dunn, Todd (Athlete, Baseball Player)
12030 London Lake Dr W
Jacksonville, FL 32258-3317, USA

Dunn, T R (Athlete, Basketball Player)
1014 19th Street SW
Birmingham, AL 35211-3623, USA

Dunn, Warrick (Athlete, Football Player)
6016 Beacon Shores St
Tampa, FL 33616-1317, USA

Dunn, Winfield (Governor, Politician)
Harpeth Consulting LLC 3100 West End Ave Ste 710
Nashville, TN 37203-5801, USA

Dunne, Griffin (Actor, Director)
26 E 10th St #1011F
New York, NY 10003, USA

Dunne, Mike (Athlete, Baseball Player, Olympic Athlete)
5115 W Ancient Oak Dr
Peoria, IL 61615-2247, USA

Dunne, Robin (Actor)
c/o Chris Fenton *H2F Entertainment*
644 N Cherokee Ave
Los Angeles, CA 90004, USA

Dunne, Roisin (Music Group, Musician)
Rave Booking
P O Box 310780
Jamaica, NY 11431, USA

Dunnigan, Frank J (Publisher)
1500 Palisade Ave
Fort Lee, NJ 07024, USA

Dunnigan, T Kevin (Business Person)
Thomas & Betts Corp
8155 Thomas & Betts Blvd
Memphis, TN 38125, USA

Dunning, Debbe (Actor, Model)
1373 Crest Rd
Del Mar, CA 92014, USA

Dunning, Steve (Athlete, Baseball Player)
35 Prairie
Irvine, CA 92618-8840, USA

Dunphry, Jessica (Actor)
c/o Staff Member *Station3*
1051 Cole Av
Culver City, CA 90038, USA

Dunphy, Jessica (Actor)

Dunphy, Marv (Athlete, Coach, Volleyball Player)
33370 Decker School Rd
Malibu, CA 90265, USA

Dunphy, T J Dermot (Business Person)
Sealed Air Corp
Park 80 Plaza E
Saddle Park, NJ 07663, USA

Dunsmore, Barrie (Correspondent)
ABC-TV
News Dept
5010 Creston St
Hyattsville, MD 20781, USA

Dunst, Kirsten (Actor)
10056 Toluca Lake Ave
Toluca Lake, CA 91602, USA

Dunst, Kristen (Actor)
8916 Ashcroft Ave
West Hollywood, CA 90048, USA

Dunstan, William (Athlete, Football Player)
P.O. Box 514
Rancho Mirage, CA 92270, USA

Dunston, Shawon D (Athlete, Baseball Player)
957 Corte Del Sol
Fremont, CA 94539-4925, USA

Dunton, Gary C (Financier)
MBIA Inc
113 King St
Armonk, NY 10504, USA

Dunwoody, Catherine (Stylist)
c/o Staff Member *Celestine - CA*
1666 20th St
#200-B
Santa Monica, CA 90404, USA

Dunwoody, Richard (Jockey, Race Car Driver)
14 Saint Maur Road Fulham
London SW6 4DP, UNITED KINGDOM (UK)

Dunwoody, Todd (Athlete, Baseball Player)
4212 S Monolith Ct
West Lafayette, IN 47906-5670, USA

Dunye, Cheryl (Actor, Director, Producer, Writer)
c/o Staff Member *Broder Webb Chervin Silbermann Agency, The (BWCS)*
10250 Constellation Blvd
Los Angeles, CA 90067-6200, USA

Duos, Deena (Adult Film Star)
3661 S Maryland Pkwy #31
PMB 285
Las Vegas, NV 89109, USA

Dupard, Reggie (Athlete, Football Player)
1316 Green Hills Ct
Duncanville, TX 75137, USA

Duper, Mark (Athlete, Football Player)
1905 Banks Rd
Margate, FL 33063-7713, USA

Dupere, Denis (Athlete, Hockey Player)
Tournament Embroidery
26 Lorraine Ave
Kitchener, ON N2B 2M8, Canada

Duplan, Mane (Stylist)
c/o Celebrity Stylist *Frame Representatives*
275 West St
New York, NY 10013, USA

Duplass, Mark (Director, Producer)
3636 Amesbury Rd
Los Angeles, CA 90027, USA

DuPlessis, Christian (Opera Singer)
Performing Arts
1 Hinde St
London W1M 5RH, UNITED KINGDOM (UK)

Dupont, Andre (Athlete, Hockey Player)
905 Rue Guilbert
Trois-Rivieres, QC G8T 5V5, Canada

Dupont, Claire (Stylist)
c/o Staff Member *Leyla Basakinci Inc*
681 Lexington Ave
5th Floor
New York, NY 10022, USA

Dupont, Jacques (Politician)
Minister of State's Office
Boite Postale 522
Monaco-Cedex 98015, MONACO

Dupont, Jerry (Athlete, Hockey Player)
216 Rosemar Gdns
Richmond Hill, ON L4C 3Z9, Canada

Dupont, Norman (Athlete, Hockey Player)
3289 Rue Alfred-De Musset
Laval, QC H7P 0A7, Canada

Dupont, Normand
3289 Rue Alfred-De Musset
Laval, QC H7P OA7, Canada

DuPont, Pierre (Ex-Governor, Politician)
National Center For Policy Analysis
Richards, Layton And Finger Pa PO Box 551 920 N King St Wilmington
Washington, DE 19899-0551, USA

DuPont, Pierre S IV (Ex-Governor)
National Center For Policy Analysis
601 Pennsylvania Avenue, NW
Suite 900, South Building
Washington, DC 20004, USA

Dupont, Tiffany (Actor)
c/o Leonard Torgan *Collective*
8383 Wilshire Blvd
Suite 1050
Beverly Hills, CA 90211, USA

Dupre, Ashley Alexandra (Model)
c/o David Kokakis *The Foundry Media Group*
598 Broadway
3rd Floor
New York, NY 10012, USA

Dupre, Isabel (Stylist)
c/o Staff Member *Bryan Bantry*
900 Broadway Ste 400
New York, NY 10003, USA

Dupree, Billy Joe (Athlete, Football Player)
2512 Springhill Dr
McKinney, TX 75070-6137, USA

Dupree, Donald (Don) (Athlete)
3 Center St
Saranac Lake, NY 12983, USA

Dupree, Marcus (Athlete, Football Player)
274 Davis St
Philadelphia, MS 39350, USA

Dupree, Mike (Athlete, Baseball Player)
2358 E Richmond Ave
Fresno, CA 93720-0438, USA

Dupree, Myron (Athlete, Football Player)
1553 Tadlock Ave
Rocky Mount, NC 27801, USA

Du Prez, John (Composer)
c/o Staff Member *WME (LA)*
9601 Wilshire Blvd Fl 3
Beverly Hills, CA 90210, USA

Dupri, Jermaine (Musician)
1240 Mt Paran Rd NW
Atlanta, GA 30327, USA

Dupuis, Bob (Athlete, Hockey Player)
446 Algonquin Ave
North Bay, ON P1B 4W5, Canada

Dupuis, Roy (Actor)
Agence Premier Role Inc
3451 Hotel de Ville
Montreal
Quebec, Canada H2X 3B5

Duque, Bernardo (Musician)
c/o Gabriel Blanco *Gabriel Blanco Iglesias (Mexico)*
Rio Balsas 35-32
Colonia Cuauhtemoc
DF 06500, Mexico

Duque, Pedro (Astronaut)
ESTEC Postbus 299
Noordwijk, NL 2200, Netherlands

Duquette, Dan (Commentator)
112 W Acton Rd
Stow, MA 01775-2141, USA

Durack, David T (Physicist)
815 West Knox Street
Durham, NC 27701-1645, USA

Duran, Clarence (Athlete, Football Player)
201 W 54th St
Los Angeles, CA 90037-3803, USA

Duran, Dan (Athlete, Baseball Player)
493 Maxine Ct
Sunnyvale, CA 94086-6338, USA

Duran, German
1101 Colina Vista Ln
Crowley, TX 76036-9156, USA

Duran, Micki (Actor)
c/o Staff Member *DDO Artist Agency (LA)*
6725 W Sunset Blvd
Suite 230
Los Angeles, CA 90028-7163, USA

Duran, Roberto (Boxer)
Nuevo Reperto El Carmen
PANAMA

Durance, Erica (Actor)
c/o Jeff Palffy *PMG Management*
8826 Burton Way
Beverly Hills, CA 90211, USA

Durand, Kevin (Actor)
2608 Hargrave Dr
Los Angeles, CA 90068, USA

Duran Duran (Music Group)
c/o Staff Member *DD Productions*
93A Westbourne Park Villas
London W2 5ED, UNITED KINGDOM (UK)

Durant, Graham J (Inventor)
Cambridge NeuroScience
333 Boston Providence Tumpike
Norwood, MA 02062, USA

Durant, Joe (Athlete, Golfer)
8451 Sunshine Hill Rd
Molino, FL 32577-4168, USA

Durant, Justin (Athlete, Football Player)
7818 Mount Ranier Dr
Jacksonville, FL 32256-2998, USA

Durant, Kevin (Athlete, Basketball Player)
c/o Aaron Goodwin *Goodwin Sports Management*
Prefers to be contacted via email or telephone
Seattle, WA, USA

Durant, Mike (Athlete, Baseball Player)
9437 Caoe Wrath Dr
Dublin, OH 43017-7624, USA

Durante, Viviana P (Ballerina)
20 Bristol Gardens Little Venice
London W9, UNITED KINGDOM (UK)

Durao Barroso, Jose Manuel (Prime Minister)
Prime Minister's Office
Rua du Imprensa a Estrela 8
Lisbon 1300, PORTUGAL

Durazo, Erubiel (Athlete, Baseball Player)
3800 S Cantabria Cir
Unit 1079
Chandler, AZ 85248-4250, USA

Durbano, Steve (Athlete, Hockey Player)

Durbin, Chad (Athlete, Baseball Player)
17918 Jefferson Ridge Dr
Baton Rouge, LA 70817-9535, USA

Durbin, Deanna (Actor, Music Group)
BP 3315
Paris Cedex 03 75123, FRANCE

Durbin, James (Musician)
c/o Simon Fuller *XIX Entertainment*
35-37 Parkgate Rd
32/33 Ransomes Dock
London SW11 4NP, UNITED KINGDOM (UK)

Durbin, J D (Athlete, Baseball Player)
1913 E Pinto Dr
Gilbert, AZ 85296-3214, USA

Durbin, Mike (Bowler)
Professional Bowlers Assn
1042 Wilshire Dr
Roanoke, TX 76262-5446, USA

Durbin, Richard (Politician, Senator)
1525 S Bates Ave
Springfield, IL 62704-3347, USA

Durcal, Rocio (Musician)
c/o Staff Member *BMG*
1540 Broadway
New York, NY 10036, USA

Duren, Clarence (Athlete, Football Player)
201 W 54th St
Los Angeles, CA 90037-3803, USA

Duren, John (Athlete, Basketball Player)
1107 1st Street NW
Washington, DC 20001-1304, USA

Duren, Steven (Musician)
35316 Mulholland Hwy
Malibu, CA 90265, USA

Durenberger, David (Politician, Senator)
University Of StThomas 1000 Lasalle Ave
Attn NatIlnst of Healt
Minneapolis, MN 55403-2005, USA

Durfee, Peter (Athlete, Baseball Player)
54 Lobelia Ct
Chico, CA 95973-8507, USA

Durham, Don (Athlete, Baseball Player)
2627 Pennington Bend Rd
Nashville, TN 37214-1107, USA

Durham, Hugh (Basketball Player, Coach)
Jacksonville University
Athletic Dept
Jacksonville, FL 32211, USA

Durham, Jarrett (Athlete, Basketball Player)
18 McKelvey Avenue
Pittsburgh, PA 15218-1454, USA

Durham, Joe (Athlete, Baseball Player)
9715 Mendoza Rd
Randallstown, MD 21133-2530, USA

Durham, Leon (Athlete, Baseball Player)
1553 Williamson Dr
Cincinnati, OH 45240-1549 .., USA

Durham, Ray (Sugar Ray) (Athlete, Baseball Player)
199 Lake Rd
Stanley, NC 28164-2312, USA

Duris, Slava (Athlete, Hockey Player)
1-92 Walmer Rd
Toronto, ON M5R 2X7, Canada

Duritz, Adam (Musician, Songwriter)
52 Cooper Sq #5B
New York, NY 10003, USA

Durkee, Charlie (Athlete, Football Player)
1210 Danbury Dr
Mansfield, TX 76063-3809, USA

Durkin, Clare (Model)
c/o Staff Member *Ford Models (NY)*
238 E 4th St
New York, NY 10009, USA

Durkin, John A (Ex-Senator)
60 Lenz St
Manchester, NH 03102, USA

Durko, Sandy (Athlete, Football Player)
2020 Paseo Del Mar
Palos Verdes Estates, CA 90274, USA

Durkota, Jeff (Athlete, Football Player)
1020 Lititz Ave
Lancaster, PA 17602-1921, USA

Durnbaugh, Bobby (Athlete, Baseball Player)
1638 N Central Dr
Beavercreek, OH 45432-2118, USA

Durocher, Jayson (Athlete, Baseball Player)
3997 E Robin Ln
Phoenix, AZ 85050-5416, USA

Durr, Francoise
195 rue de Lourmel
Paris, FRANCE F-75015

Durr, Jason (Actor)
536 N Gower St
Los Angeles, CA 90004, USA

Durrance, Samuel T (Astronaut, Astronomer)
770 Kerry Downs Circle
Melbourne, FL 32940, USA

Durrance, Samuel T Dr (Astronaut, Scientist)
770 Kerry Downs Cir
Melbourne, FL 32940-1774, USA

Durrant, Devin (Athlete, Basketball Player)
6239 Pineview Rd
Dallas, TX 75248-3933, USA

Durr Browning, Francoise (Tennis Player)
195 Rue de Lourmel
Paris, 75015, FRANCE

Durringer, Annemarie
Hawelgasse 17
Vienna, AUSTRIA 1180

Durrington, Trent (Athlete, Baseball Player)
499 N Canon Dr
Apt 400
Beverly Hills, CA 90210-4887, USA

Durslag, Melvin
PO Box 559
Salisbury, NC 28144

Durst, Fred (Musician)
c/o Joanne Wiles *ICM Partners (ICM-LA)*
10250 Constellation Blvd Fl 7
Los Angeles, CA 90067, USA

Durst, Will (Actor, Comedian)
Entertainment Alliance
P O Box 5734
Santa Rosa, CA 95402, USA

Dusan, Gene (Athlete, Baseball Player)
2241 SE Pilatus Ln
Bend, OR 97702-2498, USA

Dusay, Debra (Actor)
Susan Nathe
8281 Melrose Ave #200
Los Angeles, CA 90046, USA

Dusay, Mari (Actor)
320 W 66th St
New York, NY 10023, USA

Dusay, Marj (Actor)
Susan Nathe
8281 Melrose Ave #200
Los Angeles, CA 90046, USA

Dusbabek, Mark (Athlete, Football Player)
11452 Dona Dorotea Dr
Studio City, CA 91604, USA

Dusek, Brad (Athlete, Football Player)
The 4th Quarter Ranch 8311 Fm 2086
Temple, TX 76501, USA

Dusenberry, Ann (Actor)
1615 San Leandro Lane
Montecito, CA 93108, USA

Duser, Carl (Athlete, Baseball Player)
3021 Cornwall Rd
Bethlehem, PA 18017-3313, USA

Dushku, Eliza (Actor, Producer)
2548 Laurel Pass
Los Angeles, CA 90046, USA

Dushku, Nate (Actor)
c/o Matt Schwartz *Christopher Wright Management*
6100 Wilshire Blvd #1170
Los Angeles, CA 90048, USA

Dusick, Ryan (Musician)
5181 Franklin Ave
Los Angeles, CA 90027, USA

Dusk, Matt (Musician)
c/o Garry Kief *Stiletto Entertainment*
8295 S La Cienega Blvd
Inglewood, CA 90301-1521, USA

Dussault, Jean H (Misc)
Laval Medical Center
2705 Blvd Laurier
Sainte Foy, PQ G1V 4G2, CANADA

Dussault, Jean H Dr (Scientist)
26 Ch du Hameau Stoneham-Et
Tewkesbury, QC G3C 1X4, Canada

Dussault, Nancy (Actor)
c/o Staff Member *The Artists Group Ltd (LA)*
3345 Wilshire Blvd #915
Los Angeles, CA 90010, USA

Dussault, Normand (Athlete, Hockey Player)
552 Rue Papineau
Sherbrooke, ON J1E 1X8, Canada

Dussault, Rebecca (Athlete, Olympic Athlete, Skier)
313 N Taylor St
Gunnison, CO 81230-2135

Dustal, Bob (Athlete, Baseball Player)
625 Marian Ln
Lakeland, FL 33813-1412, USA

Dustrude-Roberson, Beverly (Baseball Player)
2422 Lobelia Dr
Oxnard, CA 93036-6260, USA

Dutch, Deborah (Actor)
850 N Kings Road #100
West Hollywood, CA 90069, USA

du Tertre, Celine (Actor)
c/o Staff Member *Harvest Talent Management*
P.O. Box 279
Jefferson Valley, NY 10535, USA

Dutilleux, Henri (Composer)
12 Rue Saint Louis-en-l'sle
Paris 75004, FRANCE

Dutoit, Charles E
Montreal Symphony
85 Sainte Catherine St W
Montreal, QC H2X 3P4, CANADA

Du Toit, Elize (Actor)
c/o Vanessa Pereira *Artists Independent Management (LA)*
825 Nowita Pl
Venice, CA 90291, USA

Dutt, Hank (Music Group, Musician)
Kronos Quartet
1235 9th Ave
San Fransisco, CA 94122, USA

Dutt, Sanjay (Actor, Bollywood)
58 Smt Nargis Dutt Road
Pali Hill Bandra(W)
Mumbai, MS 400050, INDIA

Dutta, Divya (Actor, Bollywood)
C-17 Nehru Nagar
Kishore Kumar Gangulay Marg Juhu Tara Road
Mumbai, MS 400049, INDIA

Dutta, Lara (Beauty Pageant Winner)
c/o Staff Member *Globosport Mumbai Pvt Ltd*
Prime Plaza, 5th Flr, 501, 38 S.V. Rd
Santacruz (W).
Mumbai 400 054, India

Dutta, Tanushree (Actor, Bollywood)
c/o Bunty Bahl *Carving Dreams Entertainment*
304-305, Oberoi Chambers II
B Wing, Off New Link Road, Andheri West
Mumbai 400053, INDIA

Dutton, Charles S (Actor)
2790 W Marriottsville Rd
Marriottsville, MD 21104, USA

Dutton, James P Major (Astronaut)
1604 Mossy Stone Dr
Friendswood, TX 77546-5576, USA

Dutton, John O (Athlete, Football Player)
5706 Moss Creek Trl
Dallas, TX 75252, USA

Dutton, Lawrence (Music Group, Musician)
I M G Artists
3 Burlington Lane Chiswick
London W4 2TH, UNITED KINGDOM (UK)

Dutton, Simon (Actor)
Marmont Management
Langham House 302/8 Regent St
London W1R 5AL, UNITED KINGDOM (UK)

Duva, Lou (Boxer, Misc)
Main Events
811 Totowa Road #100
Totowa, NJ 07512, USA

Duval, David (Athlete, Golfer)
1000 E Oxford Ln
Englewood, CO 80113-4857, USA

Duval, Dennis (Athlete, Basketball Player)
8105 Verbeck Drive
Manlius, NY 13104-9306, USA

Duval, Helen (Bowler)
PO Box 2071
Oakland, CA 94604-2071, USA

Duval, James (Actor)
c/o Ryan Revel *Benderspink*
5870 W Jefferson Blvd
Studio E
Los Angeles, CA 90016, USA

Duval, Juliette (Actor)
Cineart
36 Rue de Ponthieu
Paris 75008, FRANCE

Duval, Mike (Athlete, Baseball Player)
2743 Nature Pointe Loop
Fort Myers, FL 33905-2468, USA

Duvall, Brad (Baseball Player)
Bowman
438 Sycamore Trl
Woodstock, GA 30189-7423, USA

Duvall, Carol (Television Host)
c/o Staff Member *HGTV/Home & Garden Television*
9721 Sherrill Blvd
Knoxville, TN 37932, USA

DuVall, Clea (Actor)
4504 Lennox Ave
Sherman Oaks, CA 91423, USA

Duvall, Jed (Correspondent)
ABC-TV
News Dept 5010 Creston St
Hyattsville, MD 20781, USA

Duvall, Robert (Actor)
P.O. Box 520
The Plains, VA 20198-0520, USA

Duvall, Sammy (Skier)
P O Box 871
Windermere, FL 34786, USA

Duvall, Shelley (Actor)
8545 Ranch Rd
1623
Blanco, TX 78606, USA

Duvall-Hero, Camille (Skier)
P O Box 871
Windermere, FL 34786, USA

Duvignaud, Jean (Writer)
28 Rue Saint-Leonard
La Rochelle 1700, FRANCE

Duvillard, Henri (Skier)
Le Monte d'Arbois
Megere 74120, FRANCE

Duwelius, Richard L (Rich) (Athlete, Olympic Athlete, Volleyball Player)
266 Stoddards Wharf Rd
Gales Ferry, CT 06335, USA

Duwez, Pol E (Physicist)
1535 Oakdale St
Pasadena, CA 91106, USA

Dvorak, Radek (Athlete, Hockey Player)
10342 Lexington Estates Blvd
Boca Raton, FL 33428, USA

Dvorak, Richard (Rick) (Athlete, Football Player)
13587 SE 230 Rd
Spearville, KS 67876, USA

Dvorovenko, Irina (Ballerina)
Amirican Ballet Theatre
890 Broadway
New York, NY 10003, USA

Dvorsky, Peter (Opera Singer)
Bradianska Ulica 11
Bratislave SK-811 08, SLOVAKIA

Dwight, Edward Captain (Astronaut)
Ed Dwight Studio Gallery 3824 Dahlia S
Denver, CO 80207-1020, USA

Dwight, Edward Jr (Astronaut)
4022 Montview Blvd
Denver, CO 80207, USA

Dwight, Tim (Athlete, Football Player)
26164 Indigo Dr
Park Rapids, MN 56470, USA

Dworaczyk, Hope (Model)
c/o Liza Anderson *Anderson Group Public Relations*
8060 Melrose Ave Fl 4
Los Angeles, CA 90046, USA

Dwork, Melvin (Designer)
Melvin Dwork Inc
196 Ave of Americas
New York, NY 10013, USA

Dworkin, Martin (Biologist, Misc)
2123 Hoyt Ave W
Saint Paul, MN 55108, USA

Dworkins, Lenny (Len) (Cartoonist)
2906 Wilmette Ave
Wilmette, IL 60091, USA

Dworsky, Daniel L (Dan) (Architect, Athlete, Football Player)
9225 Nightingale Dr
Los Angeles, CA 990069-1117, USA

Dwyer, Bil (Comedian, Game Show Host)
c/o Staff Member *OmniPop Talent Group*
10700 Ventura Blvd.
2nd Floor
Studio Clty, CA 91604, USA

Dwyer, Clark (Race Car Driver)
3935 Elisa Ct.
Colorado Springs, CO 80904, USA

Dwyer, Gordie
P E I Rocket 46 Kensington Rd
Attn Coaching Staff
Charlottetown, PE ClA 5H7, Canada

Dwyer, Jim (Athlete, Baseball Player)
825 Hancock Bridge Pkwy
Cope Coral, FL 33990-1235, USA

Dwyer, Karyn (Actor)
Oscars Abrams Zimel
438 Queen St E
Toronto, ON M5A 1T4, CANADA

Dwyer, Mary (Athlete, Golfer)
460 Sunningdale Dr
Rancho Mirage, CA 92270, USA

Dyal, Mike (Athlete, Football Player)
609 Rock Creek Loop
Kerrville, TX 78028-2097, USA

Dybdahl, Thomas (Musician)
c/o Staff Member *Paradigm (Monterey)*
404 W Franklin St
Monterey, CA 93940, USA

Dybzinski, Jerry (Athlete, Baseball Player)
1626 Haywood Pl
Fort Collins, CO 80526-2289, USA

Dychtwald, Ken (Doctor, Misc)
Age Wave Inc
1900 Powell St
Emeryville, CA 94608, USA

Dyck, Ed (Athlete, Hockey Player)
59 Templeby Cres NE
Calgary, AB T1Y 5G3, Canada

Dye, Cameron (Actor)
13035 Woodbridge St
Studio City, CA 91604, USA

Dye, Dale (Actor)
16129 Tupper St
N Hills, CA 91343, USA

Dye, Ian (Composer, Musician)
c/o Staff Member *Gorfaine/Schwartz Agency Inc*
4111 W Alameda Ave
Suite 509
Burbank, CA 91505, USA

Dye, Jermaine (Athlete, Baseball Player)
6655 N 66th Pl
Paradise Valley, AZ 85253-4340, USA

Dye, Lee (Architect, Golfer)
Dye Designs
5500 E Yale Ave
Denver, CO 80222, USA

Dye, Nancy Schrom (Educator)
Oberlin College
President's Office
Oberlin, OH 44074, USA

Dye, Paul (Scientist)
2306 Butler Dr
Friendswood, TX 77546-5518, USA

Dyer, Danny (Actor)
c/o Staff Member *ICM Partners (ICM-LA)*
10250 Constellation Blvd Fl 7
Los Angeles, CA 90067, USA

Dyer, David W (Judge)
US Court of Appeals
300 NE 1st Ave
Miami, FL 33132, USA

Dyer, Duffy (Athlete, Baseball Player)
742 W Las Palmaritas Dr
Phoenix, AZ 85021-5545, USA

Dyer, Ellen (Stylist)
c/o Staff Member *Dyer Circumstances*
1406 Lisbon St
Miami, FL 33134, USA

Dyer, Hector (Athlete, Track Athlete)
1620 E Chapman #214
Fullerton, CA 92831, USA

Dyer, Henry (Athlete, Football Player)
23464 Reames Rd
Zachary, LA 70791, USA

Dyer, Joseph W Jr (Athlete, Football Player)
46 Windy Way
Alexander City, AL 35010-9407, USA

Dyer, Mike (Athlete, Baseball Player)
22392 Manacor
Mission Viejo, CA 92692-1188, USA

Dyer, Wayne (Writer)
c/o Staff Member *Hay House, Inc*
P.O. Box 5100
Carlsbad, CA 92018-5100, USA

Dyk, Timothy B (Judge)
US Court of Appeals
717 Madison Place NW
Washington, DC 20439, USA

Dyke, Charles W (General, Misc)
International Technical/Trade Assoc
1330 Connecticut NW
Washington, DC 20036, USA

Dykema, Craig (Athlete, Basketball Player)
10525 Destino Street
Bellflower, CA 90706-7125, USA

Dykes, Donald
47408 N Cherry St
Hammond, LA 70401-7233, USA

Dykes, Hart Lee (Athlete, Football Player)
30 Dorothea Ln
Sugar Land, TX 77479, USA

Dykes, Keilen (Athlete, Football Player)
36572 W Bilbao St
Maricopa, AZ 85138-5360, USA

Dykes, Sean (Athlete, Football Player)
7186 Copperfield Cir
Lake Worth, FL 33467-7129, USA

Dykes Bower, John (Music Group, Musician)
4Z Artillery Mansions Westminster
London SW1, UNITED KINGDOM (UK)

Dykhoff, Radhames (Baseball Player)
Baltimore Orioles
105 Angelfish Ln
Jupiter, FL 33477 7227, USA

Dykinga, Jack (Journalist, Photographer)
1519 East Tascal Loop
Tucson, AZ 85737-8570, USA

Dykstra, John (Animator, Artist, Cinematographer)
15060 Encanto Drive
Sherman Oaks, CA 91403, USA

Dykstra, Lenny (Athlete, Baseball Player)
1072 Newbern Ct
Westlake Village, CA 91361, USA

Dylan, Bob (Composer, Musician, Songwriter)
29400 Bluewater Rd
Malibu, CA 90265, USA

Dylan, Jakob (Musician)
6225 Zumirez Dr
Malibu, CA 90265, USA

Dylan, Jesse (Director)
2741 Woodstock Rd
Los Angeles, CA 90046, USA

Dyrdek, Rob (Actor, Athlete, Skateboarder)
8283 Skyline Dr
Los Angeles, CA 90046, USA

Dyroen-Lancer, Rebekah (Athlete, Olympic Athlete, Swimmer)
31101 Via Madera
San Juan Capistrano, CA 92675-2830, USA

Dysart, Richard (Actor)
654 Copeland Court
Santa Monica, CA 90405, USA

Dyson, Andre (Athlete, Football Player)
3367 N Shoreline Cir
Layton, UT 84040, USA

Dyson, Freeman J (Scientist)
105 Battle Road Circle
Princeton, NJ 08540, USA

Dyson, Kevin (Athlete, Football Player)
905 Calib Dr
Franklin, TN 37067, USA

Dyson, Michael Eric (Writer)
DePaul University
English Dept
Chicago, IL 60604, USA

Dystel, Oscar (Publisher)
Springs Purchase Hills Dr
Purchase, NY 10577, USA

Dzau, Victor (Misc, Scientist)
Stanford University Hospital
Cardiovascular Medicine Div
Stanford, CA 94305, USA

Dzeliwe (Misc)
Royal Palace
Mbabane, SWAZILAND

Dzhanibekov, Vladimir A (Astronaut, General, Misc)
Potchta Kosmonavtov
Moskovskoi Oblasti
Syvisdny Goroduk 141160, RUSSIA

Dzhanibelkov, Vladimir
Potchka Kosmon 141 160 Svyosdny Gorodok
Moscow, RUSSIA

Dziedzic, Joe (Athlete, Hockey Player)
2195 Marion Rd
Apt 102
Saint Paul, MN 55113-3805, USA

Dziedzic, Stanley (Athlete, Olympic Athlete, Wrestler)
835 Hedgegate Ct
Roswell, GA 30075-2281, USA

Dziena, Alexis (Actor)
c/o Adam Schweitzer *ICM Partners (ICM-NY)*
730 Fifth Ave
New York, NY 10019, USA

Dzienny, Gracie (Actor)
c/o Cameron Curtis *Curtis Talent Management*
9607 Arby Dr
Beverly Hills, CA 90210, USA

Dziura, Jennifer (Comedian)
316 W 39th St #3W
New York, NY 10018-1420, USA

Dzundza, George (Actor)
c/o Glenn Robbins *Raw Talent Management*
545 Veterans Ave
Los Angeles, CA 90024, USA

Dzurlnda, Mikulas (Prime Minister)
Prime Minister's Office
Nam Slobody 1
Bratislava 1 81370, SLOVAKIA

E 40 (Music Group)
BME Recordings
2144 Hills Ave D-2
Atlanta, GA 30318, USA

Eaben, Bill (Athlete, Basketball Player)
12254 Colliers Reserve Drive
Naples, FL 34110-0910, USA

Eackles, Ledell (Athlete, Basketball Player)
9134 Elmgrove Garden Drive
Baton Rouge, LA 70807-4307, USA

Eade, George J (General)
1131 Sunnyside Dr
Healdsburg, CA 95448, USA

Eads, Ora W (Religious Leader)
Christian Congregation
804 W
Hemlock St
La Follette, TN 37766, USA

Eads III, George Coleman (Actor)
c/o Alan Iezman *Shelter Entertainment*
9454 Wilshire Blvd.
Suite 715
Beverly Hills, CA 90212, USA

Eagan, James (Writer)
c/o Greg Cavic *Creative Artists Agency (CAA-LA)*
2000 Ave Of The Stars
Los Angeles, CA 90067, USA

Eagle, Ian (Sportscaster)
CBS-TV
Sports Dept
51 W 52nd St
New York, NY 10019, USA

Eaglen, Jane (Musician, Opera Singer)
c/o Staff Member *Columbia Artists Mgmt Inc*
1790 Broadway Fl 6
New York, NY 10019-1412, USA

Eagles, Mike (Athlete, Hockey Player)
Saint Thomas University 51 Dineen Drive
Attn: Hockey Coaching Staff
Fredericton, NB E3B 5G3, Canada

Eagleson, Alan (Athlete, Hockey Player)
53 Georgian Manor Dr
Collingwood, ON L9Y 3Zl, Canada

Eagles, The (Music Group)
c/o Irving Azoff *Azoff Music Management/ Front Line*
1100 Glendon Ave
Los Angeles, CA 90024, USA

Eagleton, Thomas (Ex-Senator)
1 Mercantile Center
St. Louis, MO 63101, USA

Eagleton, Thomas F (Ex-Senator)
1 Firstar Center
Saint Louis, MO 63101, USA

Eagling, Wayne J (Choreographer, Dancer)
Postbus 16486
1001 RN
Amsterdam, Netherlands

Eakes, Bobbie (Actor)
c/o Staff Member *WmE2 (WMA-LA)*
1 William Morris Pl
Beverly Hills, CA 90212, USA

Eakin, Bruce
7685 Persian Ct
Orlando, FL 32819-4629, USA

Eakin, Richard R (Educator)
East Carolina University
Chancellor's Office
Greenville, NC 27858, USA

Eakin, Thomas C (Business Person)
245 Sandover Dr
Aurora, OH 44202-8774, USA

Eakins, Dallas (Athlete, Hockey Player)
21579 N 81st St
Scottsdale, AZ 85255-6477, USA

Eakins, Dallas (Athlete, Hockey Player)
Toronto Marlies 100 Princes Blvd
Attn Coaching Staff
Toronto, ON M6K 3C3, Canada

Eakins, Gretchen (Actor)
Mattie Management
c/o Mattie Semradek
1438 N Gower St Bldg 34 2nd Fl
Los Angeles, CA 90027, USA

Eakins, Jim (Athlete, Basketball Player)
2575 Little Cottonwood Road
Sandy, UT 84092-3469, USA

Eaks, RW (Athlete, Golfer)
9359 E Windrose Dr
Scottsdale, AZ 85260-4595, USA

Ealey, Chuck (Athlete, Football Player)
37 Links Lane
Brampton, ON L6Y 5H2, Canada

Ealy, Michael (Actor)
c/o Darryl Taja *Epidemic Pictures*
1635 N Cahuenga Blvd
5th Floor
Hollywood, CA 90028, USA

Earl, Acie (Athlete, Basketball Player)
301 S Iowa St
Solon, IA 52333-9428, USA

Earl, Anthony (Politician)
2810 Arbor Dr Unit B
Madison, WI 53711-1809, USA

Earl, Denny (Athlete, Football Player)
3600 Ozark Acres Dr
Bentonville, AR 72712, USA

Earl, Glenn (Athlete, Football Player)
838 N Doheny Dr Apt 1207
West Hollywood, CA 90069-4851, USA

Earl, Robbie
8314 Holy Cross Pl
Los Angeles, CA 90045-2633, USA

Earl, Robin D (Athlete, Football Player)
439 Ferndale Ct
Buffalo Grove, IL 60089-1730, USA

Earl, Roger (Musician)
Lustig Talent
PO Box 770850
Orlando, FL 32877, USA

Earl, Scott (Athlete, Baseball Player)
8102 Salt Fork Way
Indianapolis, IN 46256-1679, USA

Earle, Ed (Athlete, Basketball Player)
1940 Burton Lane
Park Ridge, IL 60068-1572, USA

Earle, Steve (Actor, Musician)
c/o Danny Goldberg *Gold Village Entertainment*
37 W 17th St
Suite 7W
New York, NY 10011, USA

Earle, Sylvia Alice (Oceanographer)
12812 Skyline Blvd
Oakland, CA 94619, USA

Earles, Jason (Actor)
c/o Dede Binder-Goldsmith *Defining Artists Agency*
10 Universal City Plaza
Suite 2000
Universal City, CA 91608, USA

Earley, Anthony F Jr (Business Person)
Detroit Edison
2000 2nd Ave
Detroit, MI 48226, USA

Earley, Bill (Athlete, Baseball Player)
112 Carruthers Pond Dr
Cincinnati, OH 45246-3854, USA

Earley, Liz (Athlete, Golfer)
24 Morton Dr
Buffalo, NY 14226-3338, USA

Earley, Michael M (Business Person)
Triton Group
550 W C St
San Diego, CA 92101, USA

Earley, Quinn (Athlete, Football Player)
P.O. Box 675752
Rancho Santa Fe, CA 92607, USA

Early, David (Actor)
P.O. Box 154
Homestead, PA 15120, USA

Early, Gerald L (Writer)
Washington University
English Dept
Saint Louis, MO 63130, USA

Early, Quinn (Athlete, Football Player)
5770 Aster Meadows Pl
San Diego, CA 92130-6907, USA

Earnhardt, Dale Jr. (Race Car Driver)
4400 Papa Joe Hendrick Blvd.
Charlotte, NC 28226, USA

Earnhardt, Jeffrey (Race Car Driver)
c/o Staff Member *Rick Ware Racing*
111 Sunrise Center Dr
Thomasville, NC 27360-4928, USA

Earnhardt, Kelley (Race Car Driver)
Dale Earnhardt Inc
1675 Coddle Creek Hwy
Mooresville, NC 28115, USA

Earnhardt, Kerry (Race Car Driver)
Kerry Earnhardt Fan Club
1675 Coddle Creek Hwy
Mooresville, NC 28115, USA

Earnhardt Jr, Dale (Race Car Driver)
955 Shinnville Rd.
Mooresville, NC 28115-9829, USA

Earnie, Rhone (Athlete, Football Player)
3603 Potomac Ave
Texarkana, TX 75503-3519, USA

Earon, Blaine (Athlete, Football Player)
6640 Lake Run Dr
Flowery Branch, GA 30542, USA

Earp, Mildred (Athlete, Baseball Player, Commentator)
217 Dolly
West Fork, AR 72774-9109, USA

Earth Wind & Fire (Music Group)
c/o Damien Smith *Azoff Music Management/Front Line*
1100 Glendon Ave
Los Angeles, CA 90024, USA

Easler, Mike (Athlete, Baseball Player)
3121 Kookaburra Way
North Las Vegas, NV 89084-2310, USA

Easley, Bill (Musician)
Hot Jazz Mgmt
328 W 43rd St
#4FW
New York, NY 10036, USA

Easley, Damion (Athlete, Baseball Player)
6420 W Line Dr
Glendale, AZ 85310-5751, USA

Easley, Kenny (Athlete, Football Player)
3906 Kegagie Dr
Norfolk, VA 23518, USA

Easley, Logan (Athlete, Baseball Player)
753 W Cagney Dr
Meridian, ID 83646-5299, USA

Easley, Michael (Politician)
216 River Dr
Southport, NC 28461-4108, USA

Easmon, Ricky (Athlete, Football Player)
6605 N Rivera Manor Dr
Apt A4
Tampa, FL 33604, USA

Eason, Eric (Actor, Director, Writer)
c/o Simon Millar *Rumble Media*
1620 Broadway
Santa Monica, CA 90403, USA

Eason, Tony (Athlete, Football Player)
P.O. Box 340
Walnut Grove, CA 95690, USA

East, Clyde (General)
6643 Maplegrove St
Oak Park, PA 91377-1315, USA

East, Jeff (Actor)
c/o Vaughn Hart *Vaughn Hart & Associates*
12304 Santa Monica Blvd
Suite 111
Los Angeles, CA 90025-2586, USA

East, Ron (Athlete, Football Player)
PO Box 2228
Anacortes, WA 98221-8106, USA

East 17
Box 153 Stanmore
Middlesex, ENGLAND HA7 2HF

Easterbrook, Frank (Judge)
US Court of Appeals
111 N Canal St
Building 6
Chicago, IL 60606, USA

Easterbrook, Leslie (Actor)
, CA

Easterbrrok, Frank H (Judge)
US Court of Appeals
111 N Canal St, Building 6
Chicago, IL 60606, USA

Easterday, Deanna (Stylist)
c/o Staff Member *Help Me Rhonda*
541 10th St NW #294
Atlanta, GA 30318, USA

Easterly, David E (Business Person)
Cox Enterprises
1400 Lake Heam Dr NE
Atlanta, GA 30319, USA

Easterly, Dick (Athlete, Football Player)
206 S Gardenia Ave
Tampa, FL 33609-2506, USA

Easterly, Jamie (Athlete, Baseball Player)
1306 Plantation Dr
Crockett, TX 75835-2314, USA

Easterly, Richard (Athlete, Football Player)
206 S Gardenia Ave
Tampa, FL 33609, USA

Eastern Conference Champions (Music Group)
c/o Staff Member *Paradigm (Monterey)*
404 W Franklin St
Monterey, CA 93940, USA

Eastgate, Peter
c/o Staff Member *Poker Royalty, LLC*
10789 W. Twain Ave.
Suite 200
Las Vegas, NV 89135, USA

Eastham, Dean E (Physicist)
281 Bloomingbank Road
Riverside, IL 60456, USA

Eastin, Steve (Actor)
c/o Staff Member *Agency for the Performing Arts (APA-LA)*
405 S Beverly Dr
Suite 500
Beverly Hills, CA 90212-4425, USA

Eastman, John (Attorney, Attorney General, General)
Eastman & Eastman
39 W 54th St
New York, NY 10019, USA

Eastman, Kevin (Cartoonist)
1932 Coldwater Canyon Dr
Beverly Hills, CA 90210-1731, USA

Eastman, Madeline (Musician)
Prince/SF Productions
1450 Southgate Ave
#206
Daly City, CA 94015, USA

Eastman, Marilyn (Actor)
Hardman-Eastman Studios
138 Hawthome St
Pittsburgh, PA 15218, USA

Eastman, Rodney (Actor)
c/o Justin Evans *The Independent Group*
6363 Wilshire Blvd
Suite 115
Los Angeles, CA 90048, USA

Easton, Michael (Actor)
c/o Danielle Allman-Del *D2 Management*
141 S. Barrington Ave
Los Angeles, CA 90049, USA

Easton, Micheal (Actor)
c/o Danielle Allman-Del *D2 Management*
141 S. Barrington Ave
Los Angeles, CA 90049, USA

Easton, Millard E (Bill) (Coach)
1704 NW Weatherstone Dr
Blue Springs, MO 64051, USA

Easton, Robert
Paul Kohner
9300 Wilshire Blvd
#555
Beverly Hills, CA 90212, USA

Easton, Sheena (Musician)
Emmis Mgmt
18136 Califa St
Tarzana, CA 91356, USA

Eastwick, Rawly (Athlete, Baseball Player)
10 River Meadow Dr
West Newbury, MA 01985-1400, USA

Eastwick-Field, Elizabeth (Architect)
Low Farm Low Road
Denham Eye
Suffolk IP21 5ET, UNITED KINGDOM

Eastwood, Alison (Actor, Model)
c/o Bob McGowan *McGowan Management*
8733 W Sunset Blvd
Suite 103
West Hollywood, CA 90069, USA

Eastwood, Bob (Athlete, Golfer)
P.O. Box 14769
Haltom City, TX 76117-0769, USA

Eastwood, Clint (Actor, Producer)
Malpaso Productions
4000 Warner Blvd
Bldg 81
Burbank, CA 91522, USA

Eastwood, Dina (Correspondent, Reality TV Star)
California Museum
1020 O St
Sacramento, CA 95814, USA

Eastwood, Kyle (Composer)
c/o Staff Member *Gorfaine/Schwartz Agency Inc*
4111 W Alameda Ave
Suite 509
Burbank, CA 91505, USA

Eastwood, Mike (Athlete, Hockey Player)
Sports Radio 1200 - The Team
87 George St
Attn: Hockey Broadcast Dept
Ottawa, ON KlN 9H7, Canada

Easum, Donald B (Diplomat)
801 W End Ave
#3A
New York, NY 10025, USA

Easy, Omar (Athlete, Football Player)
102 Fernwood Ct
State College, PA 16803-1661, USA

Eathorne, A J (Athlete, Golfer)
23023 N 25th Pl
Phoenix, AZ 85024-7567, USA

Eaton, Adam (Athlete, Baseball Player)
17404 NE 126th Pl
Redmond, WA 98052-2296, USA

Eaton, Andrew (Producer)
c/o Staff Member *Revolution Films*
9A Dallington St
London EC1V 0BQ, UNITED KINGDOM
(UK)

Eaton, Brando (Actor)
c/o Staff Member *Art Work Entertainment*
5900 Wilshire Blvd #2150
Los Angeles, CA 90036, USA

Eaton, Chad (Athlete, Football Player)
1285 SE Sun nymead Way
Pullman, WA 99163-5475, USA

Eaton, Craig (Athlete, Baseball Player)
3307 Baltusrol Ln
Lake Worth, FL 33467-1301, USA

Eaton, Dan L (Doctor)
Genentech Inc
460 Point San Bruno Blvd
South San Francisco, CA 94080, USA

Eaton, Don (Babtunde) (Composer,
Musician)
Agency Group Ltd
370 City Road
London EC1V 2QA, UNITED KINGDOM

Eaton, John C (Composer)
4585 N Hartstrait Road
Bloomington, IN 47404, USA

Eaton, Mark (Basketball Player)
Utah Jazz
2104 Dayton Ave NE
Renton, WA 98056-2719, USA

Eaton, Mark (Athlete, Hockey Player)
28 Hathaway Ln
Manhasset, NY 11030-4120, USA

Eaton, Mark (Athlete, Basketball Player)
P.O. Box 982108
Park City, UT 84098-2108, USA

Eaton, Meredith (Actor)
c/o Staff Member *Bresler Kelly &
Associates*
11500 W Olympic Blvd
Suite 510
Los Angeles, CA 90064, USA

Eaton, Scott (Athlete, Football Player)
3950 W Lake Sammamish Pkwy SE
Bellevue, WA 98008, USA

Eaton, Shirley (Actor)
Guild House
Upper Saint Martin's Lane
London WC2H PEG, UNITED KINGDOM

Eaton, Tracey (Athlete, Football Player)
P.O. Box 881
Preston, WA 98050, USA

Eaton, Vic (Athlete, Football Player)
610 Brockton Ln N
Minneapolis, MN 55447, USA

Eatough, Jeff (Athlete, Hockey Player)
2050 Insley Rd
Mississauga, ON L4Y 1P9, Canada

Eave, Gary (Athlete, Baseball Player)
1601 King Ave
Bastrop, LA 71220-4957, USA

Eaves, Jerry (Athlete, Basketball Player)
10 Perch Place
Greensboro, NC 27455-3437, USA

Eaves, Mike (Athlete, Hockey Player)
27 Quail Ridge Dr
Madison, WI 53717, USA

Eaves, Murray (Athlete, Hockey Player)
Shattuck-St Mary's School
3610 Archer Ln N
Minneapolis, MN 55446-2685, USA

Eaves, Patrick (Athlete, Hockey Player)
3615 Culver Trl
Fairbault, MN 55021-7769, USA

Ebadi, Shirin (Nobel Prize Laureate)
University of Tehran
Enghelab Ave & 16 Azar St
Tehran, IRAN

Ebanks, Selita (Actor, Model)
c/o Staff Member *Full Picture* (NY)
915 Broadway
20th Floor
New York, NY 10010, USA

Ebashi, Setsuro (Physicist)
17-503 Nahaizumi Myodaiji
Okazaki 444, JAPAN

Ebben, Bill (Basketball Player)
Detroit Pistons
12254 Colliers Reserve Dr
Naples, FL 34110-0910, USA

Ebebole, Christine (Actor)
c/o Barry McPherson *Agency for the
Performing Arts (APA-LA)*
405 S Beverly Dr
Suite 500
Beverly Hills, CA 90212-4425, USA

Ebel, David M (Judge)
US Court of Appeals
US Courthouse
1929 Stout St
Denver, CO 80294, USA

Ebel, Dino (Athlete, Baseball Player)
c/o Staff Member *Los Angeles Dodgers
(LA Dodgers)*
1000 Elysian Park Ave
Los Angeles, CA 90012, USA

Eben, Petr (Composer)
Hamsikova 19
Prague 150 00 Prague 5, CZECH
REPUBLIC

Eber, Richard (Athlete, Football Player)
13 Stoney Pt
Laguna Niguel, CA 92677, USA

Eber, Rick (Athlete, Football Player)
13 Stoney Pt
Laguna Niguel, CA 92677-1000, USA

Eberhard, Al (Athlete, Basketball Player)
203 West Parkway Drive
Columbia, MO 65203-3450, USA

Eberhart, Ralph E (Ed) (General)
Commander
US Northen Command
Peterson Air Force Base, CO 80914, USA

Eberharter, Stefan (Athlete, Skier)
Dorfstr 21
6272 Stumm
AUSTRIA

Eberle, Jordan (Athlete, Hockey Player)
c/o Craig Oster *Newport Sports
Management*
201 City Centre Dr
Suite 400
Mississauga, ON L58 2T4, Canada

Eberle, Markus (Skier)
Unterwestweg 27
Rieztem 87567, GERMANY

Eberle, William D (Business Person)
13 Garland Road
Concord, MO 01742, USA

Ebersole, Christine (Actor)
c/o Barry McPherson *Agency for the
Performing Arts (APA-LA)*
405 S Beverly Dr
Suite 500
Beverly Hills, CA 90212-4425, USA

Ebersole, Dick (Business Person)
174 West St #54
Litchfield, CT 06759, USA

Ebersole, Drew (Actor)
c/o Staff Member *House of
Representatives, The*
1434 6th St
Suite 1
Santa Monica, CA 90401, USA

Ebersole, John (Athlete, Football Player)
1470 Village Sq
Mount Pleasant, SC 29464, USA

Ebert, Derrin (Athlete, Baseball Player)
13785 W Acapulco Ln
Surprise, AZ 85379-8303, USA

Ebert, Peter (Musician)
Col di Mura
06010 Lippiano, ITALY

Ebert, Robert D (Physicist)
16 Brewster Road
Wayland, MA 01778, USA

Ebert, Roger (Journalist)
Ephraim & Associates P.C.
PO Box 146366
Chicago, IL 60614-6300, USA

Ebertharter, Stefan (Skier)
Dorfstr 21
6272 Stumm
Austria

Ebi, Ndudi (Basketball Player)
Minnesota Timberwolves
Target Center
600 1st Ave N
Minneapolis, MN 55403, USA

Ebrahim, Vincent (Actor)
c/o Staff Member *BBC Artist Mail*
PO Box 1116
Belfast BT2 7AJ, United Kingdom

Ebron, Roy (Athlete, Basketball Player)
7100 Virgillian Street
New Orleans, LA 70126-2633, USA

Ebsen, Bonnie (Actor)
PO Box 356
Agoura, CA 91376, USA

E. Capuano, Michael (Congressman,
Politician)
1414 Longworth HOB
Washington, DC 20515, USA

Eccleston, Christopher (Actor)
c/o Larry Taube *Principal Entertainment
(LA)*
1964 Westwood Blvd #400
Los Angeles, CA 90025, USA

Ecclestone, Bernie (Race Car Driver)
26 Chelsea Square
London, England SW3 6LQ, UK

Ecclestone, Timothy J (Tim) (Athlete,
Hockey Player)
10095 Fairway Village Dr
Roswell, GA 30076-3718, USA

Ecclestone Stunt, Petra (Model)
594 Mapleton Dr
Los Angeles, CA 90024, USA

Ecevit, Bulent (Prime Minister)
Or-An Sehri 69/5
Ankara, TURKEY

Echevarria, Angel (Athlete, Baseball
Player)
23830 231st PL SE
Maple Valley, WA 98038-5257, USA

Echeverria Alvarez, Luis (President)
Magnolia 131
San Jeronimo Lidice
Magdalena Contreras, CP 10200,
MEXICO

Echikunwoke, Megalyn (Actor)
c/o Ira Belgrade *Ira Belgrade Management*
5850E W Third St
Los Angeles, CA 90036, USA

Echivard, Katia Zimninsky (Stylist)
c/o Staff Member *Zenobia Agency Inc*
PO Box 909
Groveland, CA 95321, USA

Echols, Terry (Athlete, Football Player)
6123 Sissonville Dr
Charleston, WV 25312, USA

Eck, Keith (Athlete, Football Player)
7426 Solano St
Carlsbad, CA 92009, USA

Eckenstahler, Eric (Athlete, Baseball
Player)
24250 W Alpine Ct
Lake Villa, IL 60046-8637, USA

Eckersley, Dennis (Athlete, Baseball
Player)
6 Macy Ln
Ipswich, MA 01938-1185, USA

Eckert, Robert (Business Person)
Mattel Inc
333 Continental Ave
El Segundo, CA 90245, USA

Eckert, Shari (Actor)
PO Box 5761
Sherman Oaks, CA 91413, USA

Eckhart, Aaron (Actor, Producer)
c/o Staci Wolfe *Polaris PR*
8135 W 4th St
2nd Floor
Los Angeles, CA 90048, USA

Eckholdt, Steven (Actor)
137 N Larchmont Blvd
#138
Los Angeles, CA 90004, USA

Eckhouse, James (Actor, Director)
c/o Tracy Steinsapir *Main Title Entertainment*
8383 Wilshire Blvd
Suite 408
Los Angeles, CA 90211, USA

Ecko, Marc (Fashion Designer, Producer)
c/o David Schiff *The Schiff Company*
9107 Wilshire Blvd #600
Beverly Hills, CA 90210-5519, USA

Eckstein, Ashley (Drane)
c/o Kathy Carter *Axiom Management (LA)*
1875 Century Park E #H3600
Los Angeles, CA 90067, USA

Eckstein, David (Athlete, Baseball Player)
1917 Lake Markham Preserve Tril
Sanford, FL 32771-8103, USA

Eckstein, Rick
103 Aldean Dr
Sanford, FL 32771-3612, USA

Eckwood, Jerry (Athlete, Football Player)
496 Pickett Rd
Memphis, TN 38109, USA

E. Clyburn, James (Congressman, Politician)
2135 Rayburn HOB
Washington, DC 20515, USA

Eco, Umberto (Tennis Player)
Piazza Castello 13
Milan, ITALY 20121, ITALY

E. Connolly, Gerald (Congressman, Politician)
424 Cannon HOB
Washington, DC 20515, USA

Econoline Crush
1505 N. 2nd Ave. #200
Vancouver, CANADA BC V6H 3Y4

E. Cummings, Elijah (Congressman, Politician)
2235 Rayburn HO.B
Washington, DC 20515, USA

Ed, Reynolds (Athlete, Football Player)
173 Moyer Rd
Stoneville, NC 27048-8462, USA

Edberg, Rolf (Athlete, Hockey Player)
Helmerdalsve 4
Farst S-12352, Sweden

Edberg, Stefan (Athlete, Tennis Player)
International Tennis Hall Of Fame
194 Bellevue Ave
Newport, RI 02840, USA

Eddie, Patrick (Basketball Player)
New York Knicks
4424 N 76th St
Apt 3
Milwaukee, WI 53218-5336, USA

Eddie X (DJ)
c/o Staff Member *Diva Central Inc*
7510 W Sunset Blvd Ste 1445
Los Angees, CA 90046, USA

Eddings, Doug (Athlete, Baseball Player)
1405 5th St
Las Cruces, NM 88007-8981, USA

Eddings, Floyd (Athlete, Football Player)
988 S Brampton Ave
Rialto, CA 92376-7833, USA

Eddy, Chris (Athlete, Baseball Player)
47 Winterbury Cir
Wilmington, DE 19808-1429, USA

Eddy, Don (Athlete, Baseball Player)
421 1st St N
Rockwell, IA 50469-1002, USA

Eddy, Duane (Musician)
1083 Cedarview Ln
Franklin, TN 37067, USA

Eddy, Nicholas M (Nick) (Athlete, Football Player)
2225 London Cir
Modesto, CA 95356, USA

Eddy, Sonya (Actor)
c/o Staff Member *Marshak/Zachary Company, The*
8840 Wilshire Blvd
1st Floor
Beverly Hills, CA 90210, USA

Eddy, Steve (Athlete, Baseball Player)
4491 W Folley Pl
Chandler, AZ 85226-4746, USA

Edelen, Chris (Scientist)
15802 Longvale Dr
Houston, TX 77059-5232, USA

Edelen, Joe (Athlete, Baseball Player)
P.O. Box 38
Washington, OK 73093-0038, USA

Edelin, Kent (Athlete, Basketball Player)
10950 Clara Barton Drive
Fairfax Station, VA 22039-1431, USA

Edell, Marc Z (Attorney, Attorney General, General)
Budd Larner Gross
150 John F Kennedy Parkway
#1000
Short Hills, NJ 07078, USA

Edelman, Brad M (Athlete, Football Player)
Brad Edelman Photography 537 Bienville St
New Orleans, LA 70130-2206, USA

Edelman, Gerald M (Nobel Prize Laureate)
Scripps Research Institute
Scripps Research Institute 10550 N Torrey Pines Rd
La Jolla, CA 92037-1000, USA

Edelman, Isidore S (Biologist)
464 Riverside Dr
New York, NY 10027, USA

Edelman, John (Athlete, Baseball Player)
922 Monte Vista Dr
West Chester, PA 19380-6030, USA

Edelman, Marian Wright (Politician)
Children's Defense Fund 122 C St NW
Washington, DC 20001-2109, USA

Edelman, Marian Wright (Business Person)
Children's Defense Fund
25 E St NW
Washington, DC 20001, USA

Edelman, Pawel (Cinematographer)
c/o Staff Member *ICM Partners (ICM-LA)*
10250 Constellation Blvd Fl 7
Los Angeles, CA 90067, USA

Edelman, Randy (Composer, Musician)
c/o Staff Member *Gorfaine/Schwartz Agency Inc*
4111 W Alameda Ave
Suite 509
Burbank, CA 91505, USA

Edelstein, Jean (Artist)
48 Brooks Ave
Venice, CA 90291, USA

Edelstein, Lisa (Actor)
c/o Cynthia Campos-Greenberg *Anthem Entertainment*
9595 Wilshire Blvd
Suite 900
Los Angeles, CA 90212-2509, USA

Edelstein, Michael (Producer)
c/o Staff Member *Industry Entertainment Partners*
955 S Carrillo Dr
Suite 300
Los Angeles, CA 90048, USA

Edelstein, Victor (Designer, Fashion Designer)
3 Stanhope Mews West
London SW7 5RB, UNITED KINGDOM (UK)

Eden, Barbara (Actor)
9816 Denbigh Dr
Beverly Hills, CA 90210, USA

Eden, Harry (Actor)
c/o Peter McGrath *Affirmative Entertainment*
425 N Robertson Blvd
Los Angeles, CA 90048, USA

Eden, Mike (Athlete, Baseball Player)
11531 Forest Hills Dr
Tampa, FL 33612-5121, USA

Eden, Richard (Actor)
The Agency
1800 Ave of the Stars
#400
Los Angeles, CA 90067, USA

Eden, Sondi (Echo) (Race Car Driver)
Eden Racing
1962 Crescent Dr.
Crawfordsville, IN 47933, USA

Edenfield, Ken (Athlete, Baseball Player)
4627 Avlesburv Dr
Knoxville, TN 37918-7049, USA

Edens, Billy (General)
5705 Queen Aire Ln
Ch(Ittanooga, TN 37415-7024, USA

Edens, Tom (Athlete, Baseball Player)
2033 Quailridge Ct
Clarkston, WA 99403-1787, USA

Edens, Wesley (Misc)
271 Central Park W Apt 4E
New York, NY 10024-3020, USA

Eder, Elfriede
Rain 12
Leogang, AUSTRIA 5771

Eder, Linda (Actor)
c/o Staff Member *Agency Group Ltd, The (LA)*
1880 Century Park E
Suite 711
Los Angeles, CA 90067, USA

Eder, Richard G (Journalist)
Los Angeles Times
Editorial Dept
202 W 1st ST
Los Angeles, CA 90012, USA

Edestrand, Darryl (Athlete, Hockey Player)
391 Beechwood Ave
London, ON N6J 3J9, Canada

E. Deutch, Theodore (Congressman, Politician)
1024 Longworth HOB
Washington, DC 20515, USA

Edgar, David
917 NE 16th Ave. #13
Ft. Lauderdale, FL 33304

Edgar, David (Dave) (Swimmer)
2633 Middle River Dr
#3
Fort Lauderdale, FL 33306, USA

Edgar, James (Politician)
University Of Illinois 1007 W Nevada St
Attn Institute of Government
Urbana, IL 61801-3812, USA

Edgar, Jim (Ex-Governor)
1007 W. Nevada
MC 037
Urbana, IL 61801, USA

Edgar, Robert W (Religious Leader)
National Council of Churches
475 Riverside Dr #1880
New York, NY 10115, USA

Edge (Musician)
Regine Moylet
145A Ladbroke Grove
London W10 6HJ, UNITED KINGDOM (UK)

Edge, Butch (Athlete, Baseball Player)
63553 Gold Spur Way
Bend, OR 97701-9182, USA

Edge, Claude (Butch) Edge (Athlete, Baseball Player)
63553 Gold Spur Way
Bend, OR 97701-9182, USA

Edge, Mitzi (Athlete, Golfer)
118 Kings Chapel Rd
Augusta, GA 30907-4002, USA

Edge, Shayne (Athlete, Football Player)
350 SW Legacy Gin
Lake City, FL 32025, USA

Edgerson, Booker (Athlete, Football Player)
68 Union Common
Buffalo, NY 14221, USA

Edgerton, Bill (Athlete, Baseball Player)
9700 Fairway Dr
Foley, AL 36535-9334, USA

Edgerton, Joel (Actor)
c/o Ann Churchill-Brown *Shanahan Management*
Level 3 Berman House
Surry Hills 2010, AUSTRALIA

Edgley, Gigi (Actor)
Forster - Delaney Management
12533 Woodgreen St
Los Angeles, CA 90066, USA

Edgley, Gigi
Forster - Delaney Management
12533 Woodgreen St
Los Angeles, CA 90066, USA

Edinger, Paul (Athlete, Football Player)
2313 York Pl
Lakeland, FL 33810, USA

Edlen, Bengt (Physicist)
University of Lund
Physics Dept
Lund, SWEDEN

Edler, Dave (Athlete, Baseball Player)
1504 S 34th Ave
Yakima, WA 98902-4808, USA

Edler, Inge G (Doctor)
University Hospital
Cadiology Dept
Lund, SWEDEN

Edler, Lee
1725 K St. NW #1202
Washington, DC 20006

Edlund, David J (Inventor)
Northwest Power Systems
PO Box 5339
Bend, OR 97708, USA

Edlund, Richard P (Cinematographer)
2710 Wilshire Blvd
Santa Monica, CA 90403, USA

Edmonds, James P (Jim) (Athlete, Baseball Player)
25 Boulder Vw
Irvine, CA 92603-0409, USA

Edmonds, Kenneth (Babyface) (Musician, Producer)
15030 Ventura Blvd #710
Sherman Oaks, CA 91403, USA

Edmonds, Louis
250 W. 57th St. #2317
New York, NY 10107

Edmonds, Tracey E (Producer)
c/o Staff Member *Edmonds Entertainment*
1635 N Cahuenga Blvd Fl 5
Los Angles, CA 90028, USA

Edmondson, Brian (Athlete, Baseball Player)
304 Ridgeview Trce
Canton, GA 30114-7000, USA

Edmondson, James L (Judge)
US Court of Appeals
56 Forsyth St NW
Atlanta, GA 30303, USA

Edmund-Davies, Herbert E (Judge)
5 Gray's Inn Square
London WC1R 5EU, UNITED KINGDOM (UK)

Edmunds, Dave (Musician, Songwriter, Writer)
Entertainment Services
Main Street Plaza 1000
#303
Voorhees, NJ 08043, USA

Edmunds, Ferrell (Athlete, Football Player)
PO Box 414
Blairs, VA 24527-0414, USA

Edmunds, Randall (Athlete, Football Player)
2307 Amity Woodlawn Rd
Lincolnton, GA 30817, USA

Edmunds, Randy (Athlete, Football Player)
2307 Amity Woodlawn Rd
Lincolnton, GA 30817-1910, USA

Edmundson, Gary (Athlete, Hockey Player)
Silvercrest Western Homes Corp
299 N Smith Ave
Corona, CA 92880-1741, USA

Edna, Dame (Actor, Comedian)
c/o Staff Member *PBJ Management*
7 Soho Street
London W1D 3DQ, United Kingdom

Edner, Ashley (Actor)
c/o Nicole Cataldo *Diverse Talent Group*
9911 W Pico Blvd Ste 340W
Los Angeles, CA 90035, USA

Edner, Bobby (Actor)
c/o Kendall Park *JLA Talent Agency*
9151 Sunset Blvd.
West Hollywood, CA 90069, USA

Edney, Leon A (Bud) (Admiral)
1037 Encino Row
Coronado, CA 92118, USA

Edney, Tyus (Athlete, Basketball Player)
1800 South Floyd Court
La Habra, CA 90631-2058, USA

Edson, Hilary (Actor)
400 S Beverly Road
#216
Beverly Hills, CA 90212, USA

Edson, James (Actor)
c/o Staff Member *Synergy Talent*
13251 Ventura Blvd
Studio City, CA 91604, USA

Eduardo dos Santos, Jose (President)
President's Office
Palacio do Povo
Luanda, ANGOLA

Edur, Tom (Athlete, Hockey Player)
Puhanga 77
Tallinn 10316, Estonia

Edward (Prince)
Bagshot
Bagshot Park
Surrey, ENGLAND GU19 5PN, UNITED KINGDOM

Edward, John (Psychic, Television Host)
c/o Jill Fritzo *PMK/BNC Public Relations (PMK-NY)*
622 3rd Ave
8th Floor
New York, NY 10017, USA

Edwards, Al (Athlete, Football Player)
3225 Arkansas Ave
Kenner, LA 70065-3612, USA

Edwards, Anthony (Actor, Producer)
c/o Steve Lovett *Lovett Management*
1327 Brinkley Ave
Los Angeles, CA 90049, USA

Edwards, Antonio (Athlete, Football Player)
716 2nd St NW
Moultrie, GA 31768, USA

Edwards, Antuan (Athlete, Football Player)
8108 Connestee Dr
McKinney, TX 75070, USA

Edwards, Barbara (Actor, Model)
Hansen
7767 Hollywood Blvd
#202
Los Angeles, CA 90046, USA

Edwards, Bill (Athlete, Basketball Player)
6670 Linzie Court
Franklin, OH 4S005-5373, USA

Edwards, Brad (Athlete, Football Player)
202 Southwood Dr
Columbia, SC 29205, USA

Edwards, Braylon (Athlete, Football Player)
2266 Attard
Birmingham, MI 48009-6814, USA

Edwards, Carl (Race Car Driver)
Roush/Fenway Racing
4600 Roush Pl.
Concord, NC 28027, USA

Edwards, Cid (Athlete, Football Player)
5343 Adobe Falls Rd
San Diego, CA 92120, USA

Edwards, Danny (Athlete, Golfer)
8361 E Evans Rd
Suite 106
Scottsdale, AZ 85260, USA

Edwards, Dave (Athlete, Baseball Player)
7356 Walling Cir
Dallas, TX 75231-7332, USA

Edwards, David (Athlete, Golfer)
5 Champion Pl
Stillwater, OK 74074-1065, USA

Edwards, Dennis (Musician, Opera Singer, Songwriter, Writer)
Green Light Talent Agency
PO Box 3172
Beverly Hills, CA 90212, USA

Edwards, Doc (Athlete, Baseball Player, Coach)
3706 Driftwood Dr
San Angelo, TX 76904-5972, USA

Edwards, Don (Athlete, Hockey Player)
c/o Staff Member *Saginaw Spirit*
P.O. Box 6157
Saqinaw, MI 48608, USA

Edwards, Don (Music Group, Musician, Songwriter, Writer)
Scott O'Malley Assoc
433 S Cuchamas St
Colorado Springs, CO 80903, USA

Edwards, Doug (Athlete, Basketball Player)
3001 Brookville Dr
Manhattan, KS 66502-8434, USA

Edwards, Dwan (Athlete, Football Player)
42 Woodthrush Trl
Orchard Park, NY 14127-3071, USA

Edwards, Earl (Athlete, Football Player)
1534 W Saint Thomas Dr
Gilbert, AZ 85233, USA

Edwards, Eddie (Athlete, Football Player)
533 SW 61st Ter
Margate, FL 33068-1717, USA

Edwards, Edwin (Politician)
2225 Edinburgh Ave
Baton Rouge, LA 70808-3920, USA

Edwards, Eric (Cinematographer)
2865 Highway 139
Monroe, LA 71203-8558, USA

Edwards, Gail
651 N. Kilkea Dr.
Los Angeles, CA 90048-2213

Edwards, Gareth (Soccer Player)
211 West Rd
Nottage
Porthcawl, Mid-Clamorgan CF363RT, WALES

Edwards, Gary (Athlete, Hockey Player)
6818 Pecan Ave
Moorpark, CA 93021-1661, USA

Edwards, Geoff
249 Main
Ilderton, CANADA Ont. N0M 2

Edwards, Glen (Athlete, Football Player)
4115 31st St S
St Petersburg, FL 33712, USA

Edwards, Harry (Activist, Educator)
University of California
Sociology Dept
Berkeley, CA 94720, USA

Edwards, Harry T (Judge)
US Court of Appeals
333 Constitution Ave NW
Washington, DC 20001, USA

Edwards, Herm (Athlete, Football Coach, Football Player)
1627 Highland St
Seaside, CA 93955-4511, USA

Edwards, James (Athlete, Basketball Player)
22750 Civic Center Dr Apt B4
Southfield, MI 48033-7149, USA

Edwards, James B (Ex-Governor, Politician)
100 Venning St
Mount Pleasant, SC 29464-5323, USA

Edwards, Jay (Athlete, Basketball Player)
121 North Washington Street
Apt 506
Marion, IN 46952-2865, USA

Edwards, Jennifer (Actor)
4123 Saint Clair
Studio City, CA 91604, USA

Edwards, Jesse E (Doctor)
211 2nd Street NW
Apt 1911
Rochester, MN 55901-3101, USA

Edwards, Joe F Cdr (Astronaut)
24051 Hunters Trail Ln
Aldie, VA 20105-2760, USA

Edwards, Joe F Jr (Astronaut)
Enron Broadband Services
P.O. Box 1188
Houston, TX 77251, USA

Edwards, Joel (Athlete, Golfer)
280 Benson Ln
Coppell, TX 75019-4548, USA

Edwards, John (Musician)
Buddy Allen Mgmt
3750 Hudson Manor Terr #3AE
Bronx, NY 10463, USA

Edwards, John (Politician)
1201 Old Greensboro Rd
Chapel Hill, NC 27516-5224, USA

Edwards, Johnny (Athlete, Baseball Player)
2511 E Blue Lake Dr
Magnolia, TX 77354-4827, USA

Edwards, Jonathan (Athlete, Track Athlete)
MTC
10 Kendall Place
London, England W1H3AH, United Kingdom

Edwards, Jonathan (Music Group, Songwriter, Writer)
Northern Lights
437 Live Oak Loop NE
Albuquerque, NM 87122, USA

Edwards, Kalimba (Athlete, Football Player)
6140 Sibling Pine Dr
Durham, NC 27705, USA

Edwards, Kalimba (Athlete)
c/o Staff Member *Detroit Lions*
222 Republic Dr
Allen Park, MI 48101, USA

Edwards, Kelvin (Athlete, Football Player)
1716 Brookarbor Ct
Arlington, TX 76018, USA

Edwards, Kevin (Athlete, Basketball Player)
821 Reilly Lane
Lake Forest, IL 60045-4915, USA

Edwards, Lena F (Physicist)
821 Woodland Dr
Lakewood, NJ 08701, USA

Edwards, Luke (Actor)
Ensemble Entertainment
10474 Santa Monica Blvd #380
Los Angeles, CA 90025, USA

Edwards, Marc (Athlete, Football Player)
6426 Autumn Crest Ct
Westerville, OH 43082, USA

Edwards, Mario (Athlete, Football Player)
PO Box 216
Prosper, TX 75078-0216, USA

Edwards, Marshall (Baseball Player)
5059 Quail Run Rd Apt 75
Riverside, CA 92507-6485, USA

Edwards, Marv (Athlete, Hockey Player)
3277 1st Ave
Lot 40
Mims, FL 32754, USA

Edwards, Mike (Athlete, Baseball Player)
11370 Moreno Beach Dr
Moreno Valley, CA 92555-5240, USA

Edwards, Mike (Athlete, Baseball Player)
502 Sharon Ave
Mechanicsburg, PA 17055-6630, USA

Edwards, Paddi
1800 Avenue of the Stars #400
Los Angeles, CA 90067

Edwards, Paul A. (Producer)
c/o Geoffrey Brandt *Course Management*
15159 Greenleaf St
Sherman Oaks, CA 91403, USA

Edwards, Randy (Athlete, Football Player)
1369 Mountain Park Dr NW
Kennesaw, GA 30152, USA

Edwards, R Lavell (Coach, Football Coach, Football Player)
Brighan Young University
2161 N 1400 E
Provo, UT 84604-2104, USA

Edwards, Robert (Athlete, Football Player)
931 Knight Rd
Tennille, GA 31089, USA

Edwards, Robert A (Bob) (Correspondent)
National Public Radio
News Dept
635 Massachusetts NW
Washington, DC 20001, USA

Edwards, Robert G (Nobel Prize Laureate)
Duck End Farm
Dry Drayton
Cambridge, England CB38DB, United Kingdom

Edwards, Robert J (Editor)
Williamscot House
near Banbury
England Oxon OX17 1AE, UNITED KINGDOM

Edwards, Sian (Conductor)
70 Twisden Road
London, England NW5 1DN, UNITED KINGDOM

Edwards, Stacy (Actor)
Paradigm Agency
10 100 Santa Monica Blvd
#2500
Los Angeles, CA 90067, USA

Edwards, Stephanie (Actor)
c/o Staff Member *Tisherman Gilbert Motley Drozdoski Talent Agency (TGMD)*
6767 Forest Lawn Dr
Suite 101
Los Angeles, CA 90068, USA

Edwards, Steve (Composer)
3980 Royal Oak Place
Encino, CA 91436, USA

Edwards, Teresa (Athlete, Basketball Player, Olympic Athlete)
2501 Oak Quarters SE
Smyrna, GA 30080-8292, USA

Edwards, Theodore "Blue" (Athlete, Basketball Player)
11945 Maria Ester Ct
Charlotte, NC 28277-2303, USA

Edwards, Theodore (Blue) (Athlete, Basketball Player)
10914 Lee Manor Ln
Charlotte, NC 28277, USA

Edwards, Tommy Lee (Cartoonist)
DC Comics
1700 Broadway
New York, NY 10019, USA

Edwards, Tonya (Basketball Player)
Phoenix Mercury
American West Arena
201 E Jefferson St
Phoenix, AZ 85004, USA

Edwards, Troy (Athlete, Football Player)
6835 Foghorn Ln
Grand Prairie, TX 75054-7276, USA

Edwards, Wayne (Athlete, Baseball Player)
9738 Aqueduct Ave
North Hills, CA 91343-2035, USA

Edwards, Williams (Monk) (Athlete, Football Player)
3518 Teakwood Dr
Pearland, TX 77584, USA

Edwards III, Dixon (Athlete, Football Player)
8959 Zodiac Dr
Cincinnati, OH 45231-4168, USA

Edwards Jr, Charles C (Publisher)
Des Moines Register & Tribune
715 Locust St
Des Moines, IA 50309, USA

Eenhoorn, Robert (Athlete, Baseball Player)
Zermilieplaats 15 3068J
Rotterdam, Netherlands, USA

Efron, Zac (Actor)
c/o Jason Barrett *Alchemy Entertainment*
7024 Melrose Ave
Suite 420
Los Angeles, CA 90038, USA

Egan, Christopher (Actor)
c/o Sandra Chang *Anonymous Content (LA)*
3531 Hayden Ave
Culver City, CA 90232, USA

Egan, Dick (Athlete, Baseball Player)
709 Carnoustie Ct
Garland, TX 75044-5054, USA

Egan, Edward M Cardinal (Religious Leader)
Archdiocese of New York
1011 1st St
New York, NY 10022, USA

Egan, Jennifer (Writer)
Doubleday Press
1540 Broadway
New York, NY 10036, USA

Egan, John (Johnny) (Athlete, Basketball Player)
2124 Nantucket Drive
Apt B
Houston, TX 77057-2906, USA

Egan, John L (Business Person)
130 Wilton Road
London, England SW1V 1LQ, UNITED KINGDOM

Egan, Kian (Musician)
c/o Staff Member *Solo Agency Ltd (UK)*
55 Fulham High St
2nd Floor
London SW6 3JJ, United Kingdom

Egan, Peter (Actor)
James Sharkey
21 Golden Square
London, England W1R 3PA, UNITED KINGDOM

Egan, Richard J (Business Person)
ECM Corp
35 Parkwood Dr
Hopkinton, MA 01748, USA

Egan, Susan (Actor)
13801 Ventura Blvd
Sherman Oaks, CA 91423, USA

Egan, Tom (Athlete, Baseball Player)
184 E Myrna Ln
Tempe, AZ 85284-3118, USA

Egbert, Dave (Television Host)
P.O. Box 484
Big Sur, CA 93920-0484, USA

Egdahl, Richard H (Doctor)
505 Tremont St #704
Boston, MA 02116-6353, USA

Ege, Julie (Actor)
Guild House
Upper Saint Martins
London, England WC2H 9EG, UNITED KINGDOM

Eger, David (Athlete, Golfer)
501 Marsh Cove Ln
Ponte Vedra Beach, FL 32082-1660, USA

Egers, Jack (Athlete, Hockey Player)
1-24 Zinkann Cres RR 1
Wellesley, ON N0B 2T0, Canada

Egerszegi, Kristina
Feszti A. u 4
Budapest, HUNGARY 1032

Egerszegi, Krisztina (Swimmer)
Budapest Spartacus
Koer Utca 1/A
1103 Budapest, HUNGARY

Eggar, Robin (Writer)
c/o Staff Member *Simon & Schuster*
1230 Avenue of the Americas
New York, NY 10020, USA

Eggar, Samantha (Actor)
5005 Varna Ave
Sherman Oaks, CA 91423, USA

Eggby, David (Cinematographer)
c/o Ann Murtha *Murtha Agency*
1025 Colorado Ave
Suite B
Santa Monica, CA 902401, USA

Eggeling, Dale (Athlete, Golfer)
8918 Magnolia Chase Cir
Tampa, FL 33647-2219, USA

Eggers, Dave (Writer)
Simon & Schuster
1230 Ave of Americas
New York, NY 10020, USA

Eggers, Doug (Athlete, Football Player)
12803 Cedarbrook Ln
Laurel, MD 20708, USA

Eggert, Nicole (Actor)
c/o David Weintraub *DWE Talent*
Prefers to be contacted via telephone
CA, USA

Eggert, Robert J (Economist)
1195 S Bates Rd
Cottonwood, AZ 86326-5415, USA

Eggerth, Marta
Park Dr. No.
Rye, NY 10580

Egglesfield, Colin (Actor)
c/o Colton Gramm *Brillstein Entertainment Partners*
9150 Wilshire Blvd #350
Beverly Hills, CA 90212, USA

Eggleston, William (Photographer)
Robert Miller Gallery
526 W 26th St
#10A
New York, NY 10001, USA

Eggleton, Arthur C (Government Official)
National Defence Ministry
101 Colonel By Dr
Ottawa ON K1A OK2, CANADA

Eggold, Ryan (Actor)
c/o Andy Corren *Andy Corren Management*
1545 26th St
Suite 200
Santa Monica, CA 90404, USA

Egielski, Richard
525 B St. #1900
San Diego, CA 92101

Egloff, Bruce (Athlete, Baseball Player)
3136 S Emporia Ct
Denver, CO 80231-4739, USA

Egloff, Ron (Athlete, Football Player)
975 Lincoln St
#5G-NT
Denver, CO 80203, USA

Egnew, Danielle (Musician)
Danielle Egnew Spiritual Advisory
15030 Ventura Blvd Suite 843
Sherman Oaks, CA 91403, USA

Egoyan, Atom (Actor)
Ego Film Artiosts
80 Niagara St
Toronto ON M5V 1C5, CANADA

Ehle, Jennifer (Actor)
c/o Staff Member *ICM Partners (ICM-LA)*
10250 Constellation Blvd Fl 7
Los Angeles, CA 90067, USA

Ehlers, Beth (Actor)
c/o Staff Member *Stone Manners Salners Agency (LA)*
9911 W Pico Blvd Ste 1400
Los Angeles, CA 90035, USA

Ehlers, Edwin (Athlete, Basketball Player)
PO Box 303
Notre Dame, IN 46556-0303, USA

Ehlers, Tom (Athlete, Football Player)
13898 Layton Rd
Mishawaka, IN 46544, USA

Ehlers, Walter D (General)
8382 Valley View
Buena Park, CA 90620-2738, USA

Ehlo, Craig (Athlete, Basketball Player)
3323 East 77th Avenue
Spokane, WA 99223-1943, USA

Ehrbar, Nicole (Stylist)
c/o Staff Member *Cartier (LA)*
370 N Rodeo Dr
Beverly Hills, CA 90210, USA

Ehrenfeld, Lauren (Stylist)
c/o Staff Member *Celestine - CA*
1666 20th St
#200-B
Santa Monica, CA 90404, USA

Ehrenreich, Alden (Actor)
c/o JoAnne Colonna *Brillstein Entertainment Partners*
9150 Wilshire Blvd #350
Beverly Hills, CA 90212, USA

Ehret, Gloria (Athlete, Golfer)
3335 Royal Ln
Dallas, TX 75229, USA

Ehrhoff, Christian (Athlete, Hockey Player)
4517 Carlyle Ct
Santa Clara, CA 95054-3917, USA

Ehrlich, Paul R (Biologist)
Stanford University
Biological Sciences Dept
Stanford, CA 94305, USA

Ehrlich, Robert (Politician)
110 State Cir
Annapolis, MD 21401-1924, USA

Ehrlich, S Paul Jr (Physicist)
1132 Seaspray Ave
Delray Beach, FL 33483, USA

Ehrman, Bart D (Writer)
The Department of Religious Studies
125 Saunders Hall, CB# 3225
University of North Carolina at Chapel Hill
Chapel Hill, NC 27599-3225, USA

Ehrmann, Joe (Athlete, Football Player)
5 Elmhurst Rd
Baltimore, MD 21210, USA

Eiber, Janet
9300 Wilshire Blvd. #410
Beverly Hills, CA 90212

Eichelberger, Charles B (General)
California Microwave
124 Sweetwater Oaks
Peachtree City, GA 30269, USA

Eichelberger, Dave (Athlete, Golfer)
1947 Judd Hillside Rd
Honolulu, HI 96822, USA

Eichelberger, Juan (Athlete, Baseball Player)
14674 Silverset St
Poway, CA 92064-6408, USA

Eichhorn, Lisa (Actor)
c/o Staff Member *Conway van Gelder*
8-12 Broadwick St
London W1F 8HW, UK

Eichhorn, Mark (Athlete, Baseball Player)
147 Norma Ct
Aptos, CA 95003-9789, USA

Eichhorst, Richard (Athlete, Basketball Player)
2701 Sheridan Road
Saint Louis, MO 63125-4168, USA

Eichorn, Lisa
1501 Broadway #2600
New York, NY 10036

Eick, Dick (Producer, Writer)
Dick Eick Productions
100 Universal City Plaza
Bldg 2372A, Suite E
Universal City, CA 91608, USA

Eidem, Erik (Actor, Producer)
c/o Scott Zimmerman *Evolution Entertainment (LA)*
901 N Highland Ave
Los Angeles, CA 90038, USA

Eidson, Jim (Athlete, Football Player)
3116 Purdue Ave
Dallas, TX 75225, USA

Eifrid, Jim (Athlete, Football Player)
2710 Tyler Ave
Fort Wayne, IN 46808, USA

Eigeman, Chris (Actor)
c/o Thomas Cushing *Innovative Artists (LA)*
1505 10th St
Santa Monica, CA 90401, USA

Eigen, Manfred (Nobel Prize Laureate)
Georg-Dehio-Weg 14
Gottingen-Nikolausburg D-37075, Germany

Eigenberg, David (Actor)
c/o Sheree Cohen *Kohner Agency, The*
9300 Wilshire Blvd
Suite 555
Beverly Hills, CA 90212, USA

Eighth Wonder
50 Lisson St Unit 1B
London, ENGLAND NW1 5DF

Eigsti, Roger H (Business Person)
SAFECO Corp
SAFECO Plaza
Seattle, WA 98185, USA

Eikenberry, Jill (Actor)
c/o Wes Stevens *Vox*
6420 Wilshire Blvd Ste 1080
Los Angeles, CA 90048, USA

Eikenes, Adele (Opera Singer)
Van Walsum Mgmt
4 Addison Bridge Place
London, England W14 8XP, UNITED KINGDOM

Eiland, Dave (Athlete, Baseball Player)
2824 Blue Springs Pl
Wesley Chapel, FL 33544-8746, USA

Eilbacher, Cynthia
PO Box 8920
Universal City, CA 91608

Eilbacher, Lisa (Actor)
4600 Petit Ave
Encino, CA 91436, USA

Eilber, Janet (Actor, Dancer)
Martha Graham Dance Center Of Contemporary Dance
344 East 59th St
New York, NY 10022, USA

Eilers, Dave (Athlete, Baseball Player)
602 Perkins Ln
Brenham, TX 77833-4394, USA

Eilers, Pat (Athlete, Football Player)
177 De Windt Rd
Winnetka, IL 60093, USA

Eilts, Hermann F (Diplomat)
67 Cleveland Road
Wellesley, MA 02481, USA

Einertson, Darrell (Athlete, Baseball Player)
221 Hawthorne Dr
Norwalk, IA 50211-9665, USA

Einziger, Mike (Musician)
c/o Staff Member *ArtistDirect*
9046 Lindblade St
Culver City, CA 90232, USA

Eischeid, Mike (Athlete, Football Player)
306 Auburn St
West Union, IA 52175, USA

Eischen, Joey (Athlete, Baseball Player)
Asheville Tourists
30 Buchanan Pl
Asheville, NC JRR01-4243, USA

Eischen, Joey (Athlete, Baseball Player)
16912 Hawkridge Rd
Lithia, FL 33547-5809, USA

Eisele, Eileen (Stylist)
c/o Staff Member *Ennis*
119 Braintree St
Boston, MA 02134, USA

Eisen, Hal (Actor)
c/o Staff Member *Caldwell Jeffery*
943 Queen St E Fl 2
Toronto ON M4M 1J6, CANADA

Eisen, Herman N (Doctor)
9 Homestead St
Waban, MA 02468, USA

Eisen, Thelma (Athlete, Baseball Player, Commentator)
396 Pintoresca Dr
Pacific Palisades, CA 90272-3318, USA

Eisen, Tripp (Music Group)
Andy Gould Mgmt
9100 Wilshire Blvd #400W
Beverly Hills, CA 90212, USA

Eisenberg, Jesse (Actor)
c/o Jennifer Allen *Viewpoint Inc*
8820 Wilshire Blvd.
Suite 220
Beverly Hills, CA 90211, USA

Eisenberg, Lee B (Editor)
Edison Project
3286 N Park Blvd
Alcoa, TN 37701, USA

Eisenberg, Melvin A (Attorney, Attorney General, Educator, General)
1197 Keeler Ave
Berkeley, CA 94708, USA

Eisenberg, Warren (Business Person)
Bed Bath & Beyond
650 Liberty Ave
Union, NJ 07083, USA

Eisenhauer, Lawrence (Larry) (Athlete, Football Player)
Pro Action
2 Winter St
Suite 402B
Waltham, MA 02451, USA

Eisenhauer, Stephen S (Steve) (Athlete, Football Player)
105 Abbey Rd
Winchester, VA 22602, USA

Eisenhooth, John (Athlete, Football Player)
25602 Conde Ln
Watertown, NY 13601, USA

Eisenhower, David (Politician)
255 Foxall Ln
Berwyn, PA 19312-1843, USA

Eisenhower, John (Politician)
27318 Morris Rd.
Trappe, MD 21673-1915

Eisenhower, Julie Nixon
Foxall Lane
Berwyn, PA 19312

Eisenhower, Susan
1050 17th St. NW #600
Washington, DC 20030

Eisenhut, Neil
951 Westview Way
West Kelowna, BC VlZ 3Y9, Canada

Eisenman, Peter D (Architect)
Eisenman Architects
40 W 25th St
New York, NY 10010-2707, USA

Eisenmann, Ike
6556 Blucher Ave.
Van Nuys, CA 91406

Eisenmann, Ike (Actor)
6556 Blucher Ave
Van Nuys, CA 91406, USA

Eisenreich, Jim (Athlete, Baseball Player)
11 Emerald Shore Dr
Blue Springs, MO 64015-9658, USA

Eisenstein, Michael (Music Group)
Little Big Man
155 Ave of Americas #700
New York, NY 10013, USA

Eisler, Lloyd
211-800 Montarville
Boucherville, CANADA PQ JYB 125

Eisley, Howard (Athlete, Basketball Player)
20250 Rodeo Court
Southfield, MI 48075-1285, USA

Eisley, India (Actor)
c/o Todd Justice *Justice & Ponder*
P.O. Box 480033
Los Angeles, CA 90048, USA

Eisman, Hy (Cartoonist)
99 Boulevard
Glen Rock, NJ 07452, USA

Eisner, Breck (Director)
c/o Gregory McKnight *Creative Artists Agency (CAA-LA)*
2000 Ave Of The Stars
Los Angeles, CA 90067, USA

Eisner, Michael (Business Person)
The Tornante Company
9401 Wilshire Blvd #760
Beverly Hills, CA 90212, USA

E. Issa, Darrell (Congressman, Politician)
2347 Rayburn HOB
Washington, DC 20515, USA

Eitan, Raphael (Admiral, General)
Tsomet Party
Knesset, Tel-Aviv, ISRAEL

Eitzel, Mark (Music Group, Songwriter, Writer)
Legends of 21st Century
7 Trinity Row
Florence, MA 01062, USA

Eizenstat, Stuart E (Diplomat, Government Official)
9107 Briety Road
Chevy Chase, MD 20815, USA

Ejiofor, Chiwetel (Actor)
c/o Christina Papadopoulos *Baker Winokur Ryder Public Relations BWR (BWR-NY)*
292 Madison Ave
12th Floor
New York, NY 10017, USA

Ejogo, Carmen (Actor)
c/o Erica Tarin *ID Public Relations (ID-LA)*
7060 Hollywood Blvd
8th Floor
Los Angeles, CA 90028, USA

Ek, Daniel
Spotify
76 9th Ave
Suite 1110, 11th Floor
New York, NY 10011, USA

Ekberg, Anita (Actor)
Via Aspro N2
Cerzano de Roma
Roma 00045, ITALY

Ekberg, Ulf (Musician)
Basic Music Mgmt
Norrtullsgatan 52
Stockholm 113 45, SWEDEN

Eker, T Harv (Business Person)
True Power International Limited
300 N Commercial
Be, WA 98227-5008

E. Kildee, Dale (Congressman, Politician)
2107 Rayburn HOB
Washington, DC 20515, USA

Ekland, Britt (Actor)
1888 N Crescent Heights Blvd
Los Angeles, CA 90069, USA

Eklund, A Sigvard (Scientist)
Krapfenwaldgasse 48
Vienna 1190, AUSTRIA

Eklund, Brian
66 Blossom Rd
Braintree, MA 02184-3806, USA

Eklund, Greg (Music Group)
Pinnacle Entertainment
30 Glenn St
White Plains, NY 10603, USA

Eklund, Pelle (Athlete, Hockey Player)
c/o Staff Member *San Jose Sharks*
525 W Santa Clara St
San Jose, CA 95113, USA

Ekstran, Garner (Athlete, Football Player)
10867 Samish Beach Ln
Bow, WA 98232-9405

Ekstrom, Mike (Athlete, Baseball Player)
10065 SE Bristol Loop
Happv Vallev, OR 97086-3239, USA

Ektaa (Actor, Bollywood)
Sagar Sangeet
Opp. Colaba Post Office
Mumbai, MS 400005, INDIA

Ekuban, Ebenezer (Athlete, Football Player)
5391 Moonlight Way
Parker, CO 80134, USA

El, Antwaan Randle (Athlete, Football Player)
c/o Fletcher Smith *Blueprint Sports Group*
221 W. Jefferson Ave
Naperville, IL 60540, USA

Elam, Jason (Athlete, Football Player)
PO Box 1425
Soldotna, AK 99669, USA

Elander, Diane (Stylist)
552 Las Casas Ave
Pacific Palisades, CA 90272, USA

Elarton, Scott (Athlete, Baseball Player)
13501 County Road 33
Karval, CO 80823, USA

E. Latta, Robert (Congressman, Politician)
1323 Longworth HOB
Washington, DC 20515, USA

Elavarasan (Actor)
7 Mahalinga Road
Chennai, TN 600 034, INDIA

Elba, Idris (DJ Big Driis) (Actor)
c/o Rupert Fowler *ID Public Relations*
Pall Mall Deposit 124-128 Barlby Rd
Unit 27A
London W10 6BL, UK

El Bambino, Tito (Musician)
c/o Staff Member *EMI Music Publishing (Latin America)*
1688 Meridian Ave
Suite 900
Miami Beach, FL 33139, USA

ElBaradei, Mohamed (Nobel Prize Laureate)
IAEA, Intern. Atomenergiebehörde
Vienna International Centre
Wagramer Str. 5
Wien A-1400, Austria

Elbaradel, Mohamed (Government Official)
International Atomic Energy Agency
Wagramserstr
Vienna 1400, AUSTRIA

Elbert I, Rutan (Aviator)
6383 E Dewey Cir
Coeur D Alene, ID 83814-7918, USA

Eldard, Ron (Actor)
c/o William Choi *Management 360*
9111 Wilshire Blvd
Beverly Hills, CA 90210, USA

Eldebrink, Anders
Batsmansgrand 4
Mariefred 64730, Sweden

Elder, Christian (Race Car Driver)
Atkins Motorsports
222 Raceway Dr
Mooresville, NC 28115, USA

Elder, Dave (Athlete, Baseball Player)
2642 High St SW
Conyers, GA 30094-6843, USA

Elder, George (Athlete, Baseball Player)
423 Amethyst Dr
Fruita, CO 81521-8813, USA

Elder, Larry (Actor)
c/o Ari Emanuel *WME (LA)*
9601 Wilshire Blvd Fl 3
Beverly Hills, CA 90210, USA

Elder, Lee E (Athlete, Golfer)
1440 S Ocean Blvd
Apt 3C
Pompano Beach, FL 33062-7368, USA

Elder, Mark P
Natinal Opera
London Coliseum
London WC2N 4ES, UNITED KINGDOM (UK)

Elder, Ray (Race Car Driver)
15252 S Cherry
Caruthers, CA 93609, USA

Elders, Joycelyn (Scientist)
810 Marcia Cv
Little Rock, AR 72206-4755, USA

Elders, M Jocelyn (Doctor, Government Official)
University of Arkansas Medical School
Pediatrics Dept
Little Rock, AR 72205, USA

Eldred, Brad (Athlete, Baseball Player)
4182 SW Saint Lucie Ln
Palm City, FL 34990-3830, USA

Eldred, Cal (Athlete, Baseball Player)
1893 Horn Rd
Mount Vernon, IA 52314-9517, USA

Eldredge, Allison (Music Group)
C M Artists
40 W 25th St
New York, NY 10019, USA

Eldredge, Todd (Athlete, Olympic Athlete, Speed Skater)
20030 Buttermere Ct
Estero, FL 33928-7724, USA

Electra, Carmen (Actor, Model)
c/o Stephanie Simon *Untitled Entertainment (LA)*
350 S. Beverly Dr #200
Beverly Hills, CA 90212, USA

Electrik Red (Music Group, Musician)
c/o Staff Member *Island Def Jam Group*
Worldwide Plaza
825 8th Ave Fl 28
New York, NY 10019, USA

Elegant, Robert S (Writer)
Manor House
Middle Green near Langley
Bucks SL3 6BS, UNITED KINGDOM (UK)

Eleniak, Erika (Actor, Model)
c/o Danielle Bilodeau *Kirk Talent Agencies Inc*
70 East 2nd. Ave
Suite 301
Vancouver, BC V5T 1B1, Canada

El Fadil, Siddig (Actor)
Paramount
5555 Melose Ave
Los Angeles, CA 90038, USA

Elfman, Bodhi (Actor)
c/o Staff Member *Stone Manners Salners Agency (LA)*
9911 W Pico Blvd Ste 1400
Los Angeles, CA 90035, USA

Elfman, Danny (Composer, Musical Director, Musician)
c/o Richard Kraft *Kraft-Engel Management*
15233 Ventura Blvd
Suite 200
Sherman Oaks, CA 91403, USA

Elfman, Jenna (Actor, Model, Producer)
c/o David McIlvain *Brillstein Entertainment Partners*
9150 Wilshire Blvd #350
Beverly Hills, CA 90212, USA

Elfont, Harry (Director, Writer)
c/o Staff Member *WmE2 (WMA-LA)*
1 William Morris Pl
Beverly Hills, CA 90212, USA

Elgaard, Ray (Athlete, Football Player)
9529 Cloudcroft Ave
Las Vegas, NV 89134-6231, United States

Elgart, Larry
2065 Gulf of Mexico Dr.
Longboat Key, FL 34228

Elgart, Larry J (Music Group)
2065 Gulf of Mexico Dr
Longboat Key, FL 34228, USA

Elgen, Manfred (Nobel Prize Laureate)
Georg-Dehio-Weg 4
37075 Gottingen, Germany

Elia, Bruce (Athlete, Football Player)
7 Grant Ave
Grant, MI 49327, USA

Elia, Lee (Athlete, Baseball Player)
11613 Innfields Dr
Odessa, FL 33556-5407, USA

Elias, Eliane (Composer, Director, Music Group, Musical Director, Musician)
Bennett Morgan
1282 RR 376
Wappingers Falls, NY 12590, USA

Elias, Jonathan (Composer, Musician)
c/o Staff Member *Gorfaine/Schwartz Agency Inc*
4111 W Alameda Ave
Suite 509
Burbank, CA 91505, USA

Elias, Keith (Athlete, Football Player)
4507 Norma Pl
Toms River, NJ 08755, USA

Elias, Patrick (Composer)
1005 Smith Manor Blvd #98
West Orange, NJ 07052, USA

Elias, Patrik (Athlete, Hockey Player)
1005 Smith Manor Blvd
West Orange, NJ 07052-4227, USA

Elias, Rosalind (Opera Singer)
Rober Lombardo
Harkness Plaza 61 W 62nd St #6F
New York, NY 10023, USA

Elich, Matt (Athlete, Hockey Player)
276 McKinley Ave
Grosse Pointe Farms, MI 48236-3614, USA

Elie, Mario (Athlete, Basketball Player)
1 Mott Lane
Houston, TX 77024-7315, USA

Eliel, Ernest L (Misc)
345 Carolina Meadows Villa
Chapell Hill, NC 27517, USA

Eliff, Tom (Religious Leader)
Southern Baptist Convention
901 Commerce St #750
Nashville, TN 37203, USA

Elik, Bo (Athlete, Hockey Player)
1-668 Dean Ave
Oshawa, ON L1H 3E9, Canada

Elinson, Jack (Scientist)
655 Pomander Walk Avenue
Teeneck, NJ 07666-1673, USA

Eliopulos, Jim (Athlete, Football Player)
2500 Macero St
Roseville, CA 95747, USA

Eliot, Alison
2 Ironsides #18
Marina del Rey, CA 90292

Eliot, Darren (Athlete, Hockey Player)
1100 Grayton St
Grosse Pointe Park, MI 48230-1427, USA

Eliot, Jan (Cartoonist)
P O Box 50032
Eugene, OR 97405, USA

Eliot, Sharon (Stylist)
2600 Netherland Ave
#2105
Riverdale, NY 10463, USA

Elise, Christine (Actor, Writer)
c/o Mara Santino *Luber Roklin Management*
8530 Wilshire Blvd
6th Floor
Beverly Hills, CA 90211, USA

Elise, Kimberly (Actor)
c/o Evan Hainey *Untitled Entertainment (LA)*
350 S. Beverly Dr #200
Beverly Hills, CA 90212, USA

Elisha, Walter Y (Business Person)
Springs Industries
205 N White St
Fort Mill, SC 29715, USA

Eli Young Band (Music Group)
c/o Staff Member *Paradigm (Monterey)*
404 W Franklin St
Monterey, CA 93940, USA

Elizabeth, Princess
1526 N. Beverly Dr.
Beverly Hills, CA 90210

Elizabeth, Shannon (Actor, Producer)
c/o Wes Stevens *Vox*
6420 Wilshire Blvd Ste 1080
Los Angeles, CA 90048, USA

Elizondo, Hector (Actor)
c/o Nina Nisenholtz *N2N Entertainment*
1230 Montana Ave
Suite 203
Santa Monica, CA 90403, USA

Elk, Jim (Actor)
Dade/Schultz
6442 Coldwater Canyon Ave #206
Valley Green, CA 91606, USA

Elkes, Joel (Doctor, Psychic)
University of Louisville
Psychiatry/Behavioral Sci Dept
Louisville, KY 40292, USA

Elkind, Mortimer M (Physicist)
16925 Hierba Dr
San Diego, CA 92128, USA

Elkington, Steve (Athlete, Golfer)
7010 Kelsey Rae Ct
Houston, TX 77069-1102, USA

Elkins, Corey (Athlete, Hockey Player)
2668 Silverside Rd
Waterford, MI 48328-1762, USA

Elkins, Larry
111 S. St. Joseph St.
South Bend, IN 46601-1901

Elkins, Larry (Athlete, Football Player)
4407 McArthur Cir
Brownwood, TX 76801, USA

Elkins, Lawrence C (Larry) (Athlete, Football Player)
1 Keats Avenue Norden
Rochdale, Lancestershire OL12 7PZ, UK

Elkins, Mike (Athlete, Football Player)
743 Drifting Wind Run
Dripping Springs, TX 78620, USA

Ell, Erica (Stylist)
c/o Staff Member *Team*
423 W Broadway
4th Floor
Boston, MA 02127, USA

Ellacott, Ken (Athlete, Hockey Player)
131 Crawford Cres
Cambridge, ON NIT 1X6, Canada

Ellard, Henry A (Athlete, Football Player)
29 Knob Hill Dr
Summit, NJ 07901, USA

Ellenbogen, Bill (Athlete, Football Player)
777 Pelham Rd
Apt 2G
New Rochelle, NY 10805, USA

Ellenstein, Robert (Actor)
5212 Sepulveda Blvd #23F
Culver City, CA 90230, USA

Eller, Carl (Athlete, Football Player, Misc)
Carl Eller Foundation 8014
Highway 55 Ste 241
Golden Valley, MN 55427, USA

Ellerbee, Linda (Journalist)
LRB Services Inc
c/o Lori Seidner
96 Morton Street
New York, NY 10014, USA

Ellerson, Gary (Athlete, Football Player)
S86W18643 Sue Marie Ln
Muskego, WI 53150, USA

Ellett, Dave (Athlete, Hockey Player)
36611 N 51st St
Cave Creek, AZ 85331-8820, USA

Elliman, Donald M Jr (Publisher)
Sports Illustrated Magazine
Rockefeller Center
New York, NY 10020, USA

Ellin, Doug (Actor, Director, Producer, Writer)
c/o Stephen (Steve) Levinson *Leverage Management*
3030 Pennsylvania Ave
Santa Monica, CA 90404, USA

Elling, Kurt (Music Group, Musician)
c/o Ted Kurland *Ted Kurland Associates*
173 Brighton Ave
Boston, MA 02134, USA

Ellingsen, Bruce (Athlete, Baseball Player)
5873 Daneland St
Lakewood, CA 90713-1830, USA

Ellingson, Evan (Actor)
c/o Staff Member *Reel Talent Management*
P.O. Box 491035
Los Angeles, CA 90049, USA

Elliot, Ernie (Race Car Driver)
PO Box 476
Dawsonville, GA 30534-0476, USA

Elliot, Larry (Athlete, Baseball Player)
13010 Caminito Bracho
San Diego, CA 92128-1808, USA

Elliot, Lin (Athlete, Football Player)
540 Lost Hunters Cyn
China Spring, TX 76633, USA

Elliot, Ross
5702 Graves Ave.
Encino, CA 91316

Elliot, Stephan
Box 452
Paddington, AUSTRALIA NSW 2021

Elliot, Tony (Athlete, Football Player)
45907 Riverwoods Dr
Macomb, MI 48044, USA

Elliott, Abby (Actor, Comedian)
c/o Tom Demko *Bauer Company, The*
9465 Wilshire Blvd
Suite 420
Beverly Hills, CA 90212, USA

Elliott, Alecia (Actor, Music Group)
PO Box 3075
Muscle Shoals, AL 35662, USA

Elliott, Alison (Actor)
2 Ironsides #18
Marina del Rey, CA 90292, USA

Elliott, Allison
1505 10th St.
Santa Monica, CA 90401

Elliott, Bill (Race Car Driver)
Bill Elliott Racing
200 Woodhaven Lane
Ball Ground, GA 30107-3109, USA

Elliott, Brennan (Actor)
c/o Christopher Wright *Christopher Wright Management*
3207 Winnie Dr
Los Angeles, CA 90068, USA

Elliott, Brook (Actor)
c/o Nancy Curtis *Harden-Curtis Associates*
850 7th Ave
Suite 903
New York, NY 10019, USA

Elliott, Brooke (Actor)
c/o Jonathan Howard *Innovative Artists (LA)*
1505 10th St
Santa Monica, CA 90401, USA

Elliott, Chalmers (Bump) (Coach, Football Coach, Football Player)
University of Iowa
Athletic Dept
Iowa City, IA 52242, USA

Elliott, Chris (Actor, Comedian)
c/o Tom Demko *Bauer Company, The*
9720 Wilshire Blvd Mezzanine
Beverly Hills, CA 90212, USA

Elliott, David James (Actor)
c/o Bob McGowan *McGowan Management*
8733 W Sunset Blvd
Suite 103
West Hollywood, CA 90069, USA

Elliott, Dennis (Music Group)
Hard to Handle Mgmt
16501 Ventura Blvd #602
Encino, CA 91436, USA

Elliott, DJ (Actor)
c/o Evan Silverberg *Silverberg Management Group (SMG)*
PO Box 572559
Tarzana, CA 91357-2559, USA

Elliott, Donnie (Athlete, Baseball Player)
1206 Bayou Vista Dr
Deer Park, TX 77536-6902, USA

Elliott, Gordon (Chef, Producer)
c/o Staff Member *Follow Productions*
589 Eighth Ave
12th Floor
New York, NY 10011, USA

Elliott, Harry (Athlete, Baseball Player)
9608 Los Coches Rd
Lakeside, CA 92040-4240, USA

Elliott, Herbert (Herb) (Athlete, Track Athlete)
Athletics Australia
431 St Kilda Rd
#22
Melbourne, VIC 3004, AUSTRALIA

Elliott, Joe (Musician)
c/o Rod MacSween *International Talent Booking*
74A Charlotte St
London W1T 4QJ, UNITED KINGDOM (UK)

Elliott, John (Athlete, Golfer)
235 Lexington Rd
Glastonbury, CT 06033, USA

Elliott, John (Jumbo) (Athlete, Football Player)
17 Fieldstone Ln
Oyster Bay, TX 11771, USA

Elliott, Matt (Athlete, Football Player)
540 Lost Hunters Cyn
China Spring, TX 76633, USA

Elliott, Michael (Misc)
45 Larkfield
Ewhurst Cranleigh
Surrey GU6 7QU, UNITED KINGDOM (UK)

Elliott, Missy (Actor, Musician, Producer)
c/o Mona Scott-Young *Monami Entertainment*
100 Church St
8th Floor
New York, NY 10007, USA

Elliott, Paul H (Cinematographer)
Sandra Marsh Mgmt
9150 Wilshire Blvd #220
Beverly Hills, CA 90212, USA

Elliott, Peggy Gordon (Educator)
929 Harvey Dunn St
Brookings, SD 57006, USA

Elliott, Pete3
003 Dunbarton Ave. NW
Canton, OH 44708-1818

Elliott, Peter R (Pete) (Athlete, Coach, Football Coach, Football Player)
3003 Dunbarton Ave NW
Canton, OH 44708, USA

Elliott, Randy (Athlete, Baseball Player)
PO Box 834
Somis, CA 93066-0834, USA

Elliott, R Keith (Business Person)
Hercules Inc
Hercules Plaza 1313 N Market St
Wilmington, DE 19894, USA

Elliott, Robert (Athlete, Basketball Player)
6760 East Fieldstone Lane
Tucson, AZ 8S750-2075, USA

Elliott, Sam (Actor)
c/o Iris Grossman *ICM Partners (ICM-LA)*
10250 Constellation Blvd Fl 7
Los Angeles, CA 90067, USA

Elliott, Sean (Athlete, Basketball Player)
1726 Greystone Ridge
San Antonio, TX 78258-4506, USA

Elliott, Stephen (Writer)
The Rumpus
490 2nd St #200
San Francisco, CA 94107, USA

Elliott, Steve (Horse Racer)
1070 Club House Blvd
New Smyrna, FL 32168-7964, USA

Elliott, Ted (Writer)
c/o Brian Siberell *Creative Artists Agency (CAA-LA)*
2000 Ave Of The Stars
Los Angeles, CA 90067, USA

Ellis, A J (Athlete, Baseball Player)
3252 Mannington Ct
Lexington, KY 40503-1330, USA

Ellis, Albert (Doctor)
Institute of Rational-Emotional Therapy
75 W End Ave #C14J
New York, NY 10023-7862, USA

Ellis, Alex (Athlete, Basketball Player)
914 South Front Street
Hamilton, OH 45011, USA

Ellis, Allan (Athlete, Football Player)
7352 S Dante Ave
Chicago, IL 60619, USA

Ellis, Anita
130 East End Ave.
New York, NY 10021

Ellis, Aunjanue (Actor)
c/o Howard Axel *TMT Entertainment Group*
648 Broadway
Suite 1002
New York, NY 10012, USA

Ellis, Bo (Athlete, Basketball Player)
516 North 14th Street
Milwaukee, WI 53233, USA

Ellis, Bret Easton (Writer)
International Creative Mgmt
40 W 57th St #1800
New York, NY 10019, USA

Ellis, Caroline (Actor)
8060 Saint Clair Ave
North Hollywood, CA 91605, USA

Ellis, Chris (Athlete, Football Player)
c/o Adam Heller *Vantage Management Group*
518 Reamer Ave
Carnegie, PA 15106, USA

Ellis, Cliff (Basketball Player, Coach)
Auburn University
Athletic Dept
Auburn, AL 36831, USA

Ellis, Dale (Athlete, Basketball Player)
3564 West Hampton Drive NW
Marietta, GA 30064-1775, USA

Ellis, Dan (Athlete, Hockey Player)
1505 N 188th St
Elkhorn, NE 68022-4522, USA

Ellis, Danny (Athlete, Golfer)
1543 Cherry Lake Way
Lake Mary, FL 32746-1906, USA

Ellis, Don (Bowler)
34 Crestwood Circle
Suger Land, TX 77478-3914, USA

Ellis, Elmer (Historian)
3300 New Haven Ave #223
Columbia, MO 65201, USA

Ellis, Gerry (Athlete, Football Player)
250 Cavil Way
De Pere, WI 54115, USA

Ellis, Gregory (Athlete, Football Player)
P.O. Box 96075
Southlake, Texas 76092, USA

Ellis, Harold (Athlete, Basketball Player)
9420 Parkwood Avenue
Douglasville, GA 30135-7504, USA

Ellis, Hunter (Actor, Reality TV Star)
c/o Lauren Feeney *Ideal Management*
172 81st St
Brooklyn, NY 11209, United States

Ellis, Janet (Actor)
Arlington Entertainments
1/3 Charlotte St
London W1P 1HD, UNITED KINGDOM (UK)

Ellis, Jim (Athlete, Baseball Player)
13608 Avenue 224
Tulare, CA 93274-9304, USA

Ellis, Joe (Athlete, Basketball Player)
Perfect Shot Skills
PO Box 8055
Foster City, CA 94404-8055, USA

Ellis, John (Athlete, Baseball Player)
Connecticut Sports Foundation
455 Boston Post Rd Ste 203B
Old Saybrook, CT 06475-1554, USA

Ellis, Joseph J (Writer)
Mount Holyoke College
History Dept
South Hadley, MA 01075, USA

Ellis, Kathleen (Kathy) (Swimmer)
3024 Woodshor Court
Carmel, IN 46033, USA

Ellis, Kenneth (Athlete, Football Player)
13826 Brantley Dr
Baker, LA 70714, USA

Ellis, LaPhonso (Athlete, Basketball Player)
51215 Shannon Brook Ct
Granger, IN 46530-7905, USA

Ellis, Larry R (General)
Deputy Chief of Staff Operations/Plans
HqUSA Pentagon
Washington, DC 20310, USA

Ellis, Luther (Athlete, Football Player)
527 Riverside Ave
Mancos, CO 81328, USA

Ellis, Mark (Athlete, Baseball Player)
19301 N 100th Way
Scottsdale, AZ 85255-2606, USA

Ellis, Mark (Stylist)
c/o Staff Member *Ennis*
119 Braintree St
Boston, MA 02134, USA

Ellis, Maurice (Bo) (Athlete, Basketball Player)
1229 East 158th Street
South Holland, IL 60473-1804, USA

Ellis, Michelle (Athlete, Golfer)
30842 Temple Stand Ave
Wesley Chapel, FL 33543, USA

Ellis, Nelsan (Actor)
c/o Emily Gerson Saines *Brookside Artists Management (NY)*
250 W 57th St
Suite 2303
New York, NY 10107, USA

Ellis, Osian G (Misc)
90 Chandos Ave
London N20 9DZ, UNITED KINGDOM (UK)

Ellis, Patrick (H J) (Educator)
Catholic University
President's Office
Washington, DC 20064, USA

Ellis, Ray (Athlete, Football Player)
4666 E Olney Ave
Gilbert, AZ 85234, USA

Ellis, Rob (Athlete, Baseball Player)
2020 Krislin Dr NE
Grand Rapids, MI 49505-7160, USA

Ellis, Robert (Athlete, Baseball Player)
2066 75th Ave
Baton Rouge, LA 70807-5836, USA

Ellis, Romallis (Athlete, Boxer, Olympic Athlete)
2062 San Marco Dr
Ellenwood, GA 30294, USA

Ellis, Ronald J E (Ron) (Athlete, Hockey Player)
c/o Staff Member *Hockey Hall of Fame*
Brookfield Place
30 Yonge St
Toronto ON M5E 1X8, CANADA

Ellis, Sammy (Athlete, Baseball Player)
12511 Forest Highlands Dr
Dade City, FL 33525-8273, USA

Ellis, Samuel J (Sam) (Baseball Player)
12511 Forest Highlands Dr
Dade City, FL 33525, USA

Ellis, Scott (Director)
420 Central Park West #5B
New York, NY 10025, USA

Ellis, Sedrick (Athlete, Football Player)
c/o Eugene Parker *Maximum Sports Management*
6435 W Jefferson Blvd
#197
Fort Wayne, IN 46804, USA

Ellis, Shuan (Athlete, Football Player)
1000 Fulton Ave
Hempstead, NY 11550, USA

Ellis, Terry (Music Group)
East West Records
75 Rockefeller Plaza #1200
New York, NY 10019, USA

Ellis-Bextor, Sophie (Actor, Musician)
c/o Staff Member *Universal Music Ltd (UK)*
22 St Peters Square
London W6 9NW, UNITED KINGDOM

Ellis Brothers (Music Group, Musician)
P.O. Box 50221
Nashville, TN 37203, USA

Ellis Jr, Clarence J (Athlete, Football Player)
120 Hights Hollow
Fayetteville, GA 30215, USA

Ellison, Chase (Actor)
c/o Staff Member *Artistry Management*
340 N. Camden Dr
Suite 302
Beverly Hills, CA 90210, USA

Ellison, David (Actor)
c/o Eddie Michaels *Insignia Public Relations*
1507 20th St
Santa Monica, CA 90404, USA

Ellison, Faye E (Stylist)
5501 Ewing Circle
South Edina, MN 55410, USA

Ellison, Harlan
PO Box 55548
Sherman Oaks, CA 91423-0548

Ellison, Harlan j (Writer)
Kilimajaro Group
P O Box 55548
Sherman Oaks, CA 91413-0548, USA

Ellison, Jason (Athlete, Baseball Player)
3745 248th Ave SE
Issaquah, WA 98029-7717, USA

Ellison, Jennifer (Actor)
c/o Colette Fenlon *Colette Fenlon Management*
2A Eaton Rd
West Derby
Liverpool L2 7JJ, UNITED KINGDOM

Ellison, Keith (Congressman, Politician)
1027 Longworth HOB
Washington, DC 20515, USA

Ellison, Larry (Business Person)
Oracle Corporation
500 Oracle Pkwy
Redwood Shores, CA 94065, USA

Ellison, Lawrence J (Business Person)
Oracle Systems
500 Oracle Parkway
Redwood City, CA 94065, USA

Ellison, Pervis (Athlete, Basketball Player)
4602 Kettering Drive NE
Roswell, GA 30075-3190, USA

Ellison, Riki (Athlete, Football Player)
11 Wharf St
Alexandria, VA 22314, USA

Ellison, William H (Willie) (Athlete, Football Player)
3503 Mosley Ct
Houston, TX 77004, USA

Elliss, Luther (Athlete, Football Player)
3760 Evelyn Dr
Salt Lake City, UT 84124, USA

Ellroy, James (Writer)
Sobel Weber Assoc
146 E 19th St
New York, NY 10003, USA

Ellsberg, Daniel (Politician)
90 Norwood Ave
Kensington, CA 94707-1150, USA

Ellsburv, Jacoby (Athlete, Baseball Player)
2007 Boston Red Sox
3636 SE Midvale Dr, Corvallis OR, 97333-3229

Ellsbury, Jacoby (Athlete, Baseball Player)
c/o Scott Boras *Boras Corporation*
18 Corporate Plaza
Newport Beach, CA 92660, USA

Ellsworth, Dick (Athlete, Baseball Player)
1099 W Morris Ave
USA

Ellsworth, Frank L (Educator)
465 W 23rd St #15L
New York, NY 10011-2118, USA

Ellsworth, Kiko (Actor)
c/o Staff Member *Psycho Rock Productions*
PO Box 55305
Sherman Oaks, CA 91413, USA

Ellsworth, Percy (Athlete, Football Player)
11261 Fortsville Rd
Drewryville, VA 23829, USA

Ellsworth, Steve (Athlete, Baseball Player)
546 W Enterprise Ave
Clovis, CA 93619-8356, USA

Ellwood, Paul M Jr (Physicist)
Jackson Hole Group
P O Box 270
Bondurant, WY 82922, USA

Ellzey, Charley (Athlete, Football Player)
116 Roosevelt St
Quitman, MS 39355, USA

Elman, Jamie (Actor)
c/o Staff Member *Kohner Agency, The*
9300 Wilshire Blvd
Suite 555
Beverly Hills, CA 90212, USA

Elmendorf, Dave (Athlete, Football Player)
17990 FM 1452 W
Normangee, TX 77871, USA

Elmore, Henry (Athlete, Baseball Player)
4311 43rd Pl N
Birmingham, AL 35217-3925, USA

Elmore, Len (Athlete, Basketball Player)
P.O. Box 22
Highland, MD 20777-0022, USA

Elrod, Jack (Cartoonist)
7240 Hunter's Branch Dr NE
Atlanta, GA 30328, USA

Elrod, James (Athlete, Football Player)
10124 S Maplewood Ave
Tulsa, OK 74137, USA

Elrod, Scott (Actor)
c/o Steven Jensen *Direct Management Group*
6363 Wilshire Blvd
Suite 115
Los Angeles, CA 90048, USA

Els, Ernie (Athlete, Golfer)
c/o Andrew "Chubby" Chandler
International Sports Management Ltd (ISM UK)
Cherry Tree Farm
Cherry Tree Lane
Rostherne, Cheshire WA14 3RZ, UNITED KINGDOM

Elshire, Neil (Athlete, Football Player)
2441 NW Torsway St
Bend, OR 97701, USA

El Sitio (Moris y Santiago) (Musician)
c/o Gabriel Blanco *Gabriel Blanco Iglesias (Mexico)*
Rio Balsas 35-32
Colonia Cuauhtemoc
DF 06500, Mexico

Elsna, Hebe (Writer)
Curtis Brown
162/168 Regent St
London W1R 5TB, UNITED KINGDOM (UK)

Elsner, Hannelore
ZBF Leopoldstr. 19
Munich, GERMANY D-80802

Elson, Francisco (Athlete, Basketball Player)
92 Foxton Drive
San Antonio, TX 78260-7749, USA

Elson, Karen (Model)
Ford Models Agence
9 Rue Scribe
Paris 75009, FRANCE

Elster, Kevin (Athlete, Baseball Player)
5801 Marshall Dr
Huntington Beach, CA 92649-2727, USA

Elston, Darrell (Athlete, Basketball Player)
2596 West State Road 28
Tipton, IN 46072-9787, USA

Elston, Gene (Commentator)
10810 Ashcroft Dr
Houston, TX 77096-6021, USA

Elsworth, Michael (Actor)
Sharon Power
PO Box 1243
Wellington, NEW ZEALAND

Elswrit, Richard (Rik) (Music Group)
Artists Int'l Mgmt
9850 Sandalwood Blvd #458
Boca Raton, FL 33428, USA

Elton, Ben (Actor, Comedian)
Phil McIntyre Mgmt
35 Soho Square
London W1V 5DG, UNITED KINGDOM (UK)

E. Lungren, Daniel (Congressman, Politician)
2313 Rayburn HOB
Washington, DC 20515, USA

Elvin, Violetta (Ballerina)
Marina di Equa
80066 Seiano
Bay of Naples, ITALY

Elvira
Queen B Productions
16830 Ventura Blvd #501
Encino, CA 91436, USA

Elvira, Narciso (Athlete, Baseball Player)
Dom Conocida El
Concuite Mun Tlalix, Mexico, USA

Elway, John A (Athlete, Football Player)
Elway's
4763 S Elizabeth Ct
Englewood, CO 80113, USA

Elwes, Cary (Actor)
c/o Staff Member *Kritzer Levine Wilkins Entertainment (KLWG)*
11872 La Grange Ave
1st Floor
Los Angeles, CA 90025, USA

Ely, Alexandre (Soccer Player)
5526 N 2nd St
Philadelphia, PA 19120, USA

Ely, Jack (Music Group)
Jeff Hubbard Productions
P O Box 53664
Indianapolis, IN 46253, USA

Ely, Joe (Music Group, Songwriter, Writer)
Fitzgerald-Hartley
34 N Palm St #100
Ventura, CA 93001, USA

Ely, Larry (Athlete, Football Player)
12190 Waters Edge Ct
Loveland, OH 45140, USA

Ely, Melvin (Basketball Player)
Los Angeles Clippers
Staples Center 1111 S Figueroa St
Los Angeles, CA 90015, USA

Elynuik, Pat (Athlete, Hockey Player)
143 Aspen Green
Calgary, AB T3Z 3B9, Canada

Eman, J H A (Henny) (Prime Minister)
Prime Minister's Office
Oranjestad, ARUBA

Emanuel, Alphonsia (Actor)
Marina Martin
12/13 Poland St
London W1V 2DE, UNITED KINGDOM (UK)

Emanuel, Bert (Athlete, Football Player)
15 Bees Creek Ct
Missouri City, TX 77459, USA

Emanuel, Elizabeth F (Designer, Fashion Designer)
42A Warrington Crescent
Maida Vale
London W9 1EP, UNITED KINGDOM (UK)

Emanuel, Frank (Athlete, Football Player)
10211 Deercliff Dr
Tampa, FL 33647, USA

Emanuel, Rahm (Government Official, Journalist)
c/o Staff Member *White House, The*
1600 Pennsylvania Ave NW
Washington, DC 20500, USA

Embach, Carsten (Athlete)
BSR Rennsteig e V
Grafenrodaer Str 2
Oberhof 98559, GERMANY

Emberg, Kelly (Actor, Model)
P.O. Box 675401
Rancho Santa Fe, CA 92067-5401, USA

Embery, Joan
. San Diego Zoo
Park Blvd, San Diego 92104

Embrace (Music Group)
c/o Staff Member *Paradigm (Monterey)*
404 W Franklin St
Monterey, CA 93940, USA

Embree, Alan (Athlete, Baseball Player)
29400 NE 70th Cir
Camas, WA 97702-9185, USA

Embree, Jon (Athlete, Football Player)
2300 S Rock Creek Pkwy Apt 14201
Superior, CO 80027, USA

Embry, Ethan (Actor)
c/o Brad Schenck *Paradigm (LA)*
360 N Crescent Dr
North Bldg
Beverly Hills, CA 90210, USA

Embry, Wayne (Athlete, Basketball Player, Misc)
Toronto Raptors
400-40 Bay St
Attn: Senior Advisor To President
Toronto, ON M5J 2X2, Canada

Emburey, John E (Cricketer)
Northantshire Cricket Club
Wantage Road
Northampton NN1 4TJ, UNITED KINGDOM (UK)

Emerick, Kate (Actor)
c/o Matt Sherman *Matt Sherman Management*
7510 W Sunset Blvd
Suite 1413
Los Angeles, CA 90046, USA

Emerson, Alice F (Educator)
Andrew Mellon Fondation
140 E 62nd St
New York, NY 10021, USA

Emerson, Chris (Actor)
c/o Lorraine Berglund *Lorraine Berglund Management*
11537 Hesby St.
North Hollywood, CA 91601, USA

Emerson, David F (Admiral)
P.O. Box 90892
Brooklyn, NY 11209-0892, USA

Emerson, Douglas (Actor)
1450 Belfast Dr
Los Angeles, CA 90069, USA

Emerson, George H (Educator)
Utah State University
President's Office
Logan, UT 84322, USA

Emerson, J Martin (Misc)
American Federation of Musicians
1501 Broadway
New York, NY 10036, USA

Emerson, Jo Ann (Congressman, Politician)
2230 Rayburn HOB
Washington, DC 20515, USA

Emerson, Keith (Musician)
c/o Staff Member *Carlini Group*
445 Park Ave Fl 9
New York, NY 10022, USA

Emerson, Michael (Actor)
c/o Staff Member *Vanguard Management Group*
8060 Melrose Ave
4th Floor
Los Angeles, CA 90046, USA

Emerson, Nelson (Athlete, Hockey Player)
717 33rd St
Manhattan Beach, CA 90266-3425, USA

Emerson, Nelson
Los Angeles Kings 1111 S Figueroa St
Attn Player Development Dept
Ste, Los Angeles 90015-1333, Canada

Emerson, Roy (Athlete, Tennis Player)
2221 Alta Vista Dr
Newport Beach, CA 92660-4128, USA

Emerson Drive (Music Group)
c/o Staff Member *Creative Artists Agency (CAA-TN)*
3310 West End Ave
5th Floor
Nashville, TN 37203, USA

Emery, Brent (Athlete, Cycler, Olympic Athlete)
N62W15 Teepee Court
Menomonee Falls, WI 53051

Emery, John (Athlete)
2001 Union St
San Fransisco, CA 94123, USA

Emery, Julie Ann (Actor)
c/o Stacey Bock-McLaughlin *Principal Entertainment (LA)*
1964 Westwood Blvd #400
Los Angeles, CA 90025, USA

Emery, Kenneth O (Oceanographer)
35 Horseshoe Lane
North Falmouth, MA 02556, USA

Emery, Lin (Artist, Misc)
7820 Dominican St
New Orleans, LA 70118, USA

Emery, Oren D (Religious Leader)
Wesleyan International
6060 Castelway West Dr
Indianapolis, IN 46250, USA

Emery, Ralph (Entertainer)
PO Box 23470
Nashville, TN 37202, USA

Emery, Ray (Athlete, Hockey Player)
C A A Hockey
204-822 11 Ave SW
Attn J P Barry
Calgary, AB T2R OE5, Canada

Emery, Victor (Athlete)
61 Walton St
London SW 3J, UNITED KINGDOM (UK)

Emick, Jarrod (Actor)
Gersh Agency
232 N Canon Dr
Beverly Hills, CA 90210, USA

Emilio (Music Group)
Refugee Mgmt
209 10th Ave S #347 Cummins Station
Nashville, TN 37203, USA

Emin, Tracey (Director)
European Graduate School
Alter Kehr 20
Leuk-Stadt CH-3953, Switzerland

Eminem (Actor, Musician, Producer)
c/o Paul Rosenberg *Goliath Artists*
151 Lafayette St Fl 6
New York, NY 10013, USA

Eminger, Steve (Athlete, Hockey Player)
145 Triton Ave
Woodbridge, ON L4L 6R8, Canada

Emir of Bahrain
721 Fifth Ave.60th Flr.
New York, NY 10022

Emir of Kuwait
Banyan Palace
Kuwait City, KUWAIT

Emma, David (Athlete, Hockey Player, Olympic Athlete)
193 Eugenia Dr
Naples, FL 34108-2929, USA

Emmanuel (Musician)
Sendyk Leonard
532 Colorado Ave
Santa Monica, CA 90401, USA

Emmanuel, Tommy (Musician)
c/o Staff Member *Paradigm (Monterey)*
404 W Franklin St
Monterey, CA 93940, USA

Emme (Model)
c/o Daniel Strone *Trident Media Group LLC*
41 Madison Ave
36th Floor
New York, NY 10010, USA

Emmel, Paul (Athlete, Baseball Player)
2989 N Lakeview Dr
Sanford, MI 34202-2216, USA

Emmerich, Noah (Actor, Producer)
c/o Jason Gutman *Gersh (NY)*
41 Madison Ave
New York, NY 10010, USA

Emmerich, Roland (Director, Producer)
c/o Staff Member *Centropolis Entertainment*
1445 N Stanley Fl 3
Los Angeles, CA 90046, USA

Emmerson, Michael (Actor)
c/o Staff Member *Vanguard Management Group*
8060 Melrose Ave
4th Floor
Los Angeles, CA 90046, USA

Emmert, Mark (Educator)
Louisiana State University
President's Office
Baton Rouge, LA 70803, USA

Emmerton, Bill (Athlete, Track Athlete)
615 Ocean Ave
Santa Monica, CA 90402, USA

Emmett, John C (Inventor)
Oak House Hatfield Broad Oak
Bishop's Stortford
Herts CM22 7HG, UNITED KINGDOM (UK)

Emmons, Howard W (Engineer)
1010 Waltham St #443B
Lexington, MA 02421, USA

Emmons, John (Athlete, Hockey Player)
67589 Rachael Ln
Washington, MI 48095-1844, USA

Emmott, Bill (Editor)
Economist Magazine
25 Saint James's St
London SW1A 1HG, UNITED KINGDOM (UK)

Emory, Sonny (Musician)
Great Scott Productions
137 N Wetherly Dr #403
Los Angeles, CA 90048, USA

Emotions (Music Group)
c/o Staff Member *Diva Central Inc*
7510 W Sunset Blvd Ste 1445
Los Angees, CA 90046, USA

Empey, James (General)
8602 Park Olympia
Universal City, TX 78148-3256, USA

Empson, Gay MOrris (Stylist)
c/o Staff Member *Bryan Bantry*
900 Broadway Ste 400
New York, NY 10003, USA

Emrich, Tom (General)
2820 N 42nd Way
Phoenix, AZ 85008-1432, USA

Emrick, Mike "Doc" (Athlete, Hockey Player)
PO Box 246
Marysville, MI 48040-0246, USA

Emtman, Steven C (Steve) (Athlete, Football Player)
19601 S Cheney Spangle Rd
Cheney, WA 99004, USA

Ena, Justin (Athlete, Football Player)
1398 W 1525 S
Cedar City, UT 84720, USA

Enan, Susan (Musician)
c/o Staff Member *Paradigm (Monterey)*
404 W Franklin St
Monterey, CA 93940, USA

Enau, Ron (Race Car Driver)
Bunch Racing
9009-B Topsail Cove
Huntersville, NC 28078, USA

Enberg, Alexander (Actor)
c/o Staff Member *TalentWorks (LA)*
3500 W Olive Ave
Suite 1400
Burbank, CA 91505, USA

Enberg, Dick (Commentator)
1275 Virginia Way
La Jolla, CA 92037-5231, USA

En Blanco Y Negro (Music Group)
c/o Staff Member *Sony Music Miami*
605 Lincoln Rd Fl 7
Miami Beach, FL 33139, USA

Enbom, John (Writer)
c/o Staff Member *Creative Artists Agency (CAA-LA)*
2000 Ave Of The Stars
Los Angeles, CA 90067, USA

Encarnacion, Luis (Athlete, Baseball Player)
6 las Cabos De Herrer
Manz 9 Santo Domingo, Dominican Republic, USA

Endean, Craig (Athlete, Hockey Player)
650 Garnet Rd
Kamloops, BC V2B 6K1, Canada

Endelman, Stephen (Composer, Musician)
c/o Staff Member *Robert Urband & Associates*
8981 W Sunset Blvd #311
W Hollywood, CA 90069-1881, USA

Ender, Grummt Kornelia (Swimmer)
DSV
Postfach 420140
Kassel 34070, GERMANY

Enders, Erica (Race Car Driver)
c/o Staff Member *Big Machine Media*
780 3rd Ave
15th Floor
New York, NY 10017, USA

Enders, Trevor (Athlete, Baseball Player)
25906 Silver Timbers Ln
Katy, TX 77494, USA

Endicott, Bill (Athlete, Baseball Player)
14219 Oak Knoll Rd
Sonora, CA 95370-8822, USA

Endicott, Lori (Athlete, Olympic Athlete, Volleyball Player)
351 Dogwood Rdg
Rogersville, MO 65742-8183, USA

Endicott, Shane (Athlete, Hockey Player)
1025 2nd St E
Saskatoon, SK S7H 1R2, Canada

End of Fashion (Music Group)
c/o Staff Member *Paradigm (Monterey)*
404 W Franklin St
Monterey, CA 93940, USA

Endress, Albert (al) (Athlete, Football Player)
201 Oregon Ave
Louisville, OH 44641, USA

Endress, Belinda (Race Car Driver)
God Speed on Wheels
PO Box 501
Newbury Park, CA 91319, USA

Endress, Ned (Athlete, Basketball Player)
1632 Highbridge Road
Cuyahoga Falls, OH 44223-2363, USA

E. Neal, Richard (Congressman, Politician)
2208 Rayburn HOB
Washington, DC 20515, USA

Enevoldsen, Einar (Aviator)
103 City Limits Cir
Emeryville, CA 94608-1058, USA

Enfield, Berry (Misc)
3401 N Thompkins Ave
Bethany, OK 73008-3646, USA

Eng, Chris (Stylist)
4 Stuyvesant Oval
#B
New York, NY 10009, USA

Engblom, Brian (Athlete, Hockey Player)
824 Ridgemont Cir
Highlands Ranch, CO 80126-5576, USA

Engblom, Brian
Winnipeg Jets 300 Portage Ave
Attn: Broadcast Dept
Winnioeg, MB R3C 5S4, Canada

Engel, Albert E (Geophysicist, Physicist)
University of California
Scripps Institute Geology Dept
La Jolla, CA 92093, USA

Engel, Albert J (Judge)
US Court of Appeals
110 Michigan Ave NW
Grand Rapids, MI 94503, USA

Engel, Bob (Athlete, Baseball Player)
3500 Harmony Dr
Bakersfield, CA 93306-1219, USA

Engel, Georgia (Actor)
c/o Staff Member *Peter Strain & Associates Inc (LA)*
5455 Wilshire Blvd
Suite 1812
Los Angeles, CA 90036-4368, USA

Engel, Steve (Athlete, Baseball Player)
6212 Old Stone Ct
Hamilton, OH 45224-12471, USA

Engel, Susan
43A Princess Rd. Regents Park
London, ENGLAND NW1 8JS

Engelauf, Philip (Scientist)
4506 Water Elm Ct
Houston, TX 77059-3416, USA

Engelbart, Douglas C (Scientist)
89 Catalpa Dr
Menlo Park, CA 94027-2167, USA

Engelberger, John (Athlete, Football Player)
8176 Cliffview Ave
Springfield, VA 22153, USA

Engelberger, Joseph F (Engineer)
Transition Research Corp
15 Durant Ave
Bethel, CT 06801, USA

Engelhard, David H (Religious Leader)
Cristian Reformed Church
2850 Kalamazoo Ave SE
Grand Rapids, MI 49560, USA

Engelhardt, Thomas A (Tom) (Cartoonist, Editor)
Saint Louis Post-Dispatch
Editorial Dept 900 N Tucker
Saint Louis, MO 63101, USA

Engelke, Janice (Stylist)
24 W Cedar Ave
Merchantville, NJ 08109, USA

Engen, D Travis (Business Person)
ITT Industries
4 W Red Oak Lane
White Plains, NY 10604, USA

Enger, John (Athlete, Golfer)
c/o Jim Lehrman *SFX Golf*
36855 W Main St Ste 200
Purcellville, VA 20132, USA

Engerman, Stanley L (Economist, Historian)
181 Warrington Dr
Rochester, NY 14618, USA

Engholm, Bjorn (Government Official)
Jurgen-Wallenwever-Str 9
Lubeck, GERMANY

Engibous, Thomas J (Business Person)
Texas Instruments
8505 Forest Lane P O Box 660199
Dallas, TX 75266, USA

England, Anthony (Astronaut, Geophysicist, Physicist)
7949 Ridgeway Court
Dexter, MI 48130, USA

England, Anthony W Dr (Astronaut)
7949 Ridgeway Ct
Dexter, MI 48130-9700, USA

England, Audie
6100 Wilshire Blvd. #1170
Los Angeles, CA 90048

England, Dan
PO Box 82
Great Neck, NY 10021

England, Gordon R (Secretary)
Homeland Security Department
Washington, DC 20528, USA

England, Richard (Architect)
26/1 Merchants St
Valletta, MALTA

England, Tyler (Music Group)
Buddy Lee
38 Music Square E #300
Nashville, TN 37203, USA

Englander, Herold R (Doctor, Scientist)
11502 Wisper Bluff St
San Antonio, TX 78230, USA

Englander, Israel (Misc)
740 Park Ave FI14B
New York, NY 10021-4288, USA

Engle, Dave (Athlete, Baseball Player)
5343 Castle Hills Dr
San Diego, CA 92109-1926, USA

Engle, Doug (Baseball Player)
Montreal Expos
17282 Helser Rd
Berlin Center, OH 44401 9784, USA

Engle, Eleanor (Commentator)
Archives
319 W Main St
Camp Hill, PA 17011-6333, USA

Engle, Joe (Astronaut, General)
3280 Cedar Heights Dr
Colorado Springs, CO 80904, USA

Engle, Jon (Race Car Driver)
Engle Motorsports
960 St. Andrews Lane
Louisville, CO 80027, USA

Engle, Joseph H Majgen (Astronaut)
1906 Back Bay Ct
Houston, TX 77058-4202, USA

Engle, Rick (Athlete, Baseball Player)
6413 Seneca Trl
Mentor, OH 44060-3416, USA

Engle, Robert F (Nobel Prize Laureate)
New York University
Stem Business School
New York, NY 10012, USA

Engleberg, Mort (Producer)
Mort Engelberg Productions, Inc.
1504 Rising Glen Rd
West Hollywood, CA 90069, USA

Englehart, Robert W (Bob) Jr (Cartoonist, Editor)
Hartford Courant
Editorial Dept 280 Broad St
Hartford, CT 06105, USA

Englehorn, Shirley (Athlete, Golfer)
849 Shrine Vw
Colorado Springs, CO 80906, USA

Engler, Erich (Scientist)
80 Valley Way Cir SE
Huntsville, AL 35802-2572, USA

Engler, James (Politician)
PO Box 3037
Mount Pleasant, MI 48804, USA

Engler, John M (Ex-Governor)
The Hill
1625 K St NW
Suite 900
Washington, DC 20006, USA

Engler, Michael (Director, Producer)
c/o Staff Member *United Talent Agency (UTA)*
9336 Civic Center Dr
Beverly Hills, CA 90210, USA

Engles, Rick (Athlete, Football Player)
11307 S Vine St
Jenks, OK 74037, USA

English, A J (Athlete, Basketball Player)
8 Morning Dew Dr
Middletown, DE 19709-2416, USA

English, Alex (Athlete, Basketball Player)
596 Rimer Pond Rd
Blythewood, SC 29016-9448, USA

English, Claude (Athlete, Basketball Player)
14041 Switzer Road
Overland Park, KS 66221-9735, USA

English, Corri (Actor)
c/o Staff Member *Silver Massetti & Sztmary (SMS) Talent Inc*
8383 Wilshire Blvd
Suite 230
Beverly Hills, CA 90211, USA

English, Diane (Writer)
c/o Staff Member *Shukovsky/English Entertainment*
4605 Lankershim Blvd #510
North Hollywood, CA 91602

English, Edmond J (Business Person)
TJX Companies
770 Cochituate Road
Framingham, MA 01701, USA

English, Floyd L (Business Person)
Andrew Corp
10500 W 153rd St
Orland Park, IL 60462, USA

English, James F Jr (Educator)
31 Potter St
Groton, CT 06340, USA

English, JoJo (Athlete, Basketball Player)
133 Ramblewood Drive
Columbia, SC 29209-4439, USA

English, Joseph T (Doctor)
Saint Vincent's Hospital
203 W 12th St
New York, NY 10011, USA

English, Kim (Musician)
c/o Staff Member *Diva Central Inc*
7510 W Sunset Blvd Ste 1445
Los Angees, CA 90046, USA

English, L Douglas (Doug) (Athlete, Football Player)
4306 Benedict Ln
Austin, TX 78746, USA

English, Madeline (Athlete, Baseball Player)
55 Clinton St
Everett, MA 02149-4640, USA

English, Michael (Music Group)
Trifecta Entertainment
209 10th Ave S #302
Nashville, TN 37203, USA

English, Paul (Actor)
Wurzel Talent Mgmt
19528 Ventura Blvd #501
Tarzana, CA 91356, USA

English, Ralna (Musician)
Box 14522
Scottsdale, AZ 86267, USA

English, Scott (Athlete, Basketball Player)
10740 East Placita Metate
Tucson, AZ 85749-8808, USA

English, Todd (Chef)
c/o Staff Member *Grand Productions*
2811 Champion Rd
Naperville, IL 60654, USA

Engluand, Robert (Actor)
1616 Santa Cruz St
Laguna Beach, CA 92651, USA

Englund, Robert (Actor)
1278 Glenneyre #73
Laguna Beach, CA 92651, USA

Engram, Simon (Bobby) (Athlete, Football Player)
1104 Black River Rd
Camden, SC 29020, USA

Engstrom, Molly (Athlete, Hockey Player, Olympic Athlete)
7560 Southshore Dr
Siren, WI 54872

Engstrom, Ted W (Misc)
World Vision
919 W Huntington Dr
Arcadia, CA 91007, USA

Engvall, Bill (Actor, Comedian, Producer)
c/o J P Williams *Parallel Entertainment*
9420 Wilshire Blvd #250
Beverly Hills, CA 90212, USA

Enigma (Music Group)
c/o Staff Member *Virgin Records (NY)*
150 5th Ave
New York, NY 10010, USA

Enis, Curtis (Athlete, Football Player)
10972 Comanche Dr
Sidney, OH 45365, USA

Enis, Hunter (Athlete, Football Player)
2521 Marley Rd
Jacksboro, TX 76458, USA

Enke, Fred (Athlete, Football Player)
206 E McMurray Blvd
Casa Grande, AZ 85222, USA

Enke, Werner
Moltkestr. 6
Munich, GERMANY D-80803

Enke-Kania, Karin (Skier)
Tolstoistr 3
Dresden 01326, GERMANY

Enkhbayar, Nambaryn (Prime Minister)
Prime Minister's Office
Great Hural
Ulan Bator 12, MONGOLIA

Enlow, Johnny (Religious Leader, Writer)
DAYSTAR
3434 Pleasantdale Rd
Atlanta, GA 30340, USA

Enn, Hans (Skier)
Hinterglemm 400
Saalbach 5754, AUSTRIA

Ennis, John (Athlete, Baseball Player)
2231 Agate Ct
Simi Valley, CA 91402-1917, USA

Ennis, Ralph (Musician)
2 Kirklake Bank
Formby
Liverpool L37 2Y5, UNITED KINGDOM (UK)

Ennis, Ray (Musician)
2 Kirklake Bank
Formby
Liverpool L37 2Y5, UNITED KINGDOM (UK)

Ennis Sisters, The (Music Group)
c/o Staff Member *Paradigm (Monterey)*
404 W Franklin St
Monterey, CA 93940, USA

Eno, Brian (Composer, Musician)
Opal Music
3 Pembridge Mews
London W11 3Eq, UNITED KINGDOM (UK)

Eno, Brian (Actor)

Enoch, Russell
43A Princess Rd. Regents Park
London, ENGLAND NW1 8JS

Enos, John (Actor)
c/o Lara Rosenstock *Lara Rosenstock Management*
8371 Blackburn Ave #1
Los Angeles, CA 90048, USA

Enos, Lisa (Actor, Producer)
c/o Staff Member *ICM Partners (ICM-LA)*
10250 Constellation Blvd Fl 7
Los Angeles, CA 90067, USA

Enos, Mireille (Actor)
c/o Howard Green *Framework Entertainment (LA)*
9057 Nemo St
Suite C
West Hollywood, CA 90069, USA

Enos, Randal (Cartoonist)
402 N Park Ave
Easton, CT 06612-1248, USA

Enright, Barry (Athlete, Baseball Player)
11627 E Regal Ct
Chandler, AZ 85249-4545, USA

Enright, George (Athlete, Baseball Player)
3075 Strawflower Way
Lake Worth, FL 33467-1465, USA

Enrique, Luis
c/o Staff Member *Verve Music Group*
1755 Broadway Fl3
New York, NY 10019, USA

Enriquez, Jocelyn
1135 Francisco St. #7
San Francisco, CA 94109

Ensberg, Morgan (Athlete, Baseball Player)
5535 Memorial Dr
Unit F-114
Houston, TX 92075-2047, USA

Ensher, Jason R (Physicist)
University of Colorado
Physics Dept
Boulder, CO 80309, USA

Ensign, John
9808 Moon Valley Pl
Las Vegas, NV 89134-6738, USA

Ensign, Michael (Actor)
Abrams Artists
9200 Sunset Blvd
#1125
Los Angeles, CA 90069, USA

Ensler, Eve (Actor, Producer, Writer)
c/o Staff Member *Little, Brown Book Group*
100 Victoria Embankment
London EC4Y 0DY, UK

Ensley, Frank (Athlete, Baseball Player)
241 Webster Ave
Grambling, LA 71245, USA

Entner, Warren (Music Group)
Thomas Cassidy
11761 E Speedway Blvd
Tucson, AZ 85748, USA

Entremont, Philippe (Musician)
10 Rue de Castuglione
Paris 75001, FRANCE

Entremont, Philippe
Schwarzenbergplatz 10/7
Vienna, AUSTRIA A-1040

Entwhistle, John
PO Box 241
Lake Peekskill, NY 10537

Enya (Composer, Musician)
c/o Staff Member *Warner Music Germany GmbH (WMI-Germany)*
Alter Wandrahm 14
Hamburg D - 20457, Germany

Enzensberger, Hans M (Writer)
Lindenstr 29
Frankfurt am Maim 60325, GERMANY

Enzi, Michael (Politician)
431 Circle Dr
Gillette, WY 82716-4903, USA

Eotvos, Peter (Composer)
Naardeweg 56
Blaircum 1261 BV, NETHERLANDS

E. Petri, Thomas (Congressman, Politician)
2462 Rayburn HOB
Washington, DC 20515, USA

Ephraim, Alonzo (Athlete, Football Player)
1713 Five Acre Rd
Dolomite, AL 35061, USA

Ephraim, Molly (Actor)
c/o Josh Katz *United Talent Agency (UTA)*
9336 Civic Center Dr
Beverly Hills, CA 90210, USA

Ephriam, Mablean (Judge)
c/o Sean Perry *WME (LA)*
9601 Wilshire Blvd Fl 3
Beverly Hills, CA 90210, USA

Epic (Artist, Musician)
Wyze Mgmt
34 Maple St
London W1 5GD, UNITED KINGDOM (UK)

Eppard, Jim (Athlete, Baseball Player)
23115 153rd Ave
Rapid City, SD 57703-9041, USA

Epper, Tony (Actor)
927 Hwy 93S #5349
Salmon, ID 83467, USA

Epperson-Doumani, Brenda (Actor)
kazarian/Spencer
11365 Ventura Blvd
#100
Studio City, CA 91604, USA

Eppinger, Dale L (War Hero)
101 Windy Hollow St
Victoria, TX 77904, USA

Epple, Maria (Skier)
Gunzesried 3
Blaicach 87544, GERMANY

Epple-Beck, Irene (Skier)
Autmberg 235
Seeg 87637, GERMANY

Eppler, Dieter
Franziskaweg 17
Stuttgart, GERMANY D-70599

Eppridge, Bill (Photographer)
923 Saw Mill River Rd # 106
Ardsley, NY 10502-1106, USA

Epps, Bobby (Athlete, Football Player)
934 Illinois Ave
Pittsburgh, PA 15221, USA

Epps, Jeanette J (Astronaut)
4727 Five Knolls Dr
Friendswood, TX 77546-3160, USA

Epps, Mike (Actor, Comedian)
c/o Niles Kirchner *Niles Ahead Productions*
5441 Bevis Ave
Sherman Oaks, CA 91411, USA

Epps, Omar (Actor, Producer)
c/o Eli Selden *Anonymous Content (LA)*
3531 Hayden Ave
Culver City, CA 90232, USA

Epps, Phil (Athlete, Football Player)
212 Boulder Creek Dr
Desoto, TX 75115, USA

Epps, Raymond (Athlete, Basketball Player)
4030 Old Warwick Road
Richmond, VA 23234-1975, USA

E. Price, David (Congressman, Politician)
2162 Rayburn HOB
Washington, DC 20515, USA

Epstein, Daniel M (Writer)
843 W University Parkway
Baltimore, MD 21210, USA

Epstein, Gabriel (Architect)
3 Rue Mazet
Paris 75006, FRANCE

Epstein, Jason (Editor)
Random House
1745 Broadway
#B1
New York, NY 10019, USA

Epstein, Joseph (Educator, Writer)
522 Church St
#6B
Evanston, IL 60201, USA

Epstein, Mike (Athlete, Baseball Player)
6384 South Blackhawk Way
Aurora, CO 80016, USA

Epstein, Theo (Commentator)
75 Peterborough Street
Apt 703
Boston, MA 02215-4315, USA

Erardi, Greg (Athlete, Baseball Player)
42 Westgate Rd
Massapequa Park, NY 11762-1953, USA

Erasure (Music Group)
c/o Jonny (Jon) Podell *Podell Talent Agency LLC*
22 W 21st St
9th Floor
New York, NY 10010, USA

Erat, Martin (Athlete, Hockey Player)
4 Crooked Stick Ln
Brentwood, TN 37027-8938, USA

Erautt, Eddie (Athlete, Baseball Player)
7252 Walte Dr
La Mesa, CA 91941-7631, USA

Erb, Christy (Athlete, Golfer)
4043 Country Trl
Bonita, CA 91902-3025, USA

Erb, Donald J (Composer)
2073 Blusestone Road
Cleveland, OH 44121, USA

Erb, Richard D (Government Official)
International Monetary Fund
700 19th St NW
Washington, DC 20431, USA

Erbe, Kathryn (Actor)
LMR
1964 Westwood Blvd
#400
Los Angeles, CA 90025, USA

Erburu, Robert F (Business Person, Publisher)
1518 Blue Jay Way
Los Angeles, CA 90069, USA

Erdman, Dennis (Actor, Director, Producer)
c/o Staff Member *ICM Partners (ICM-LA)*
10250 Constellation Blvd Fl 7
Los Angeles, CA 90067, USA

Erdman, Paul E (Writer)
1817 Lytton Springs Road
Healdsburg, CA 95448, USA

Erdman, Richard (Actor)
5655 Greenbush Ave
Van Nuys, CA 91401, USA

Erdmann, Susi-Lisa (Athlete)
Karwendelstr 8A
Munich 81369, GERMANY

Erdo, Peter Cardinal (Religious Leader)
Mindszenty Hercegprimas Ter 2
Esztergom Magyarirszay 2501, HUNGARY

Erdogan, Recep Tayyip (Prime Minister)
Premier's Office
Eski Basbakanlik
Bakanliklar
Ankara, TURKEY

Erdos, Todd (Athlete, Baseball Player)
118 Windsor Ct
Cranberry Twp, PA 16066-3216, USA

Erenberg, Richard (Athlete, Football Player)
318 Snowberry Cir
Venetia, PA 15367, USA

Ergen, Charles W (Misc)
EchoStar Communications Corp
5330 Lakeshore Dr
Littleton, CO 80123-1541, USA

Erhardt, Warren R (Publisher)
455 Wakefield Dr
Metuchen, NJ 08840, USA

Erhuero, Oris (Actor)
c/o Staff Member *Midwest Talent Management Inc*
4821 Lankershim Blvd #F
PMB 149
N Hollywood, CA 91601, USA

Eric, B (Music Group, Musician)
Rush Artists
1600 Varick St
New York, NY 10013, USA

Eric Kaplan, Bruce (Producer)
c/o Staff Member *WmE2 (WMA-LA)*
1 William Morris Pl
Beverly Hills, CA 90212, USA

Ericks, John (Athlete, Baseball Player)
17000 Oketo Ave
Tinley Park, IL 60477-2630, USA

Erickson, Arthur C (Architect)
Arthur Erickson Architects
1672 W 1st Ave
Vancouver, BC V6J 1G1, CANADA

Erickson, Bryan (Athlete, Hockey Player)
40207 County Rd 2
Suite A
Roseau, MN 56751, USA

Erickson, Bud (Athlete, Football Player)
14523 165th Pl NE
Woodinville, WA 98072, USA

Erickson, Chad (Athlete, Hockey Player)
56213 349th St
Warroad, MN 56763-9127, USA

Erickson, Craig (Athlete, Football Player)
420 N Country Club Dr
Lake Worth, FL 33462, USA

Erickson, Dennis (Athlete, Coach, Football Coach, Football Player)
4949 Centennial Blvd
Santa Clara, CA 95054, USA

Erickson, Emily (Stylist)
P.O. Box 11121
Oakland, CA 94611-0121, USA

Erickson, Ethan (Actor)
c/o Staff Member *Diverse Talent Group*
9911 W Pico Blvd Ste 340W
Los Angeles, CA 90035, USA

Erickson, Grant (Athlete, Hockey Player)
222 Parks St
Whitewood, SK S0G 5C0, Canada

Erickson, Jennifer (Stylist)
c/o Staff Member *Directions USA*
3717-C W Market St
Greensboro, NC 27403, USA

Erickson, Keith (Athlete, Basketball Player, Volleyball Player)
333 23rd St
Santa Monica, CA 90402-2513, USA

Erickson, Matt (Athlete, Baseball Player)
1408 S Fidelis St
Appleton, WI 54915-4Q_, USA

Erickson, Millard J. (Writer)
c/o Staff Member *Crossway Books*
1300 Crescent St
Wheaton, IL 60187, USA

Erickson, Robert (Composer)
University of California
Music Dept
La Jolla, Ca 92093, USA

Erickson, Roger (Athlete, Baseball Player)
P.O. Box 235
Sautee Nacoochee, GA 30571-0235, USA

Erickson, Scott (Actor)
501 Chicago Ave S
Minneapolis, MN 55415, USA

Erickson, Scott G (Athlete, Baseball Player)
1183 Corral Ave
Sunnyvale, CA 94086-7010, USA

Erickson, Steve (Writer)
Poseidon Press
1230 Ave of Americas
New York, NY 10020, USA

Erickson-Sauer, Louise (Athlete, Baseball Player, Commentator)
917 Pleasant Ave
Arcadia, WI 54612-1859, USA

Ericson, John (Actor)
7 Avenida Vista Grande
#310
Santa Fe, NM 87508, USA

Ericsson, Jonathan (Athlete, Hockey Player)
c/o Staff Member *Newport Sports Management*
201 City Centre Dr
Suite 400
Mississauga, ON L58 2T4, Canada

E. Rigell, Scott (Congressman, Politician)
327 Cannon HOB
Washington, DC 20515, USA

Erik, Erik (Athlete, Olympic Athlete, Skier)
731 Martingale Ln
Park City, UT 84098-7559, USA

Eriksen, Stein (Skier)
7700 Stein Way
Park City, UT 84060, USA

Erikson, Duke (Misc)
Borman Entertainment
1250 6th St
#401
Santa Monica, CA 90401, USA

Erikson, Raymond L (Doctor)
Harvard University
Medical School
25 Shattuck St
Boston, MA 02115, USA

Eriksson, Loui
6323 Meadow Rd
Dallas, TX 75230-5140, USA

Eriksson, Roland (Athlete, Hockey Player)
Falkvagen 6
Vasteras S-72223, Sweden

Erin Gray, Erin Gray (Actor)

Erixon, Jan (Athlete, Hockey Player)
Stenbackav 58
Skelleftea S-93142, Sweden

Erkiletian, Lynda (Reality TV Star)
c/o Staff Member *Bravo (NY)*
30 Rockefeller Plaza
New York, NY 10112, USA

Erlandson, Eric (Songwriter, Writer)
Artist Group International
9560 Wilshire Blvd
#400
Beverly Hills, CA 90212, USA

Erlandson, Tom Sr (Athlete, Football Player)
1045 E Possee Rd
Castle Rock, CO 80108, USA

Erman, John (Director)
c/o Johnnie Planco *Parseghian Planco LLC*
322 8th Ave
Suite 601
New York, NY 10001, USA

Ermey, R Lee (Actor)
4348 W Ave N3
Palmdale, CA 93551, USA

Ermy, R Lee
4348 W Avenue N3
Palmdale, CA 9355l, USA

Erna, Sully (Actor, Music Group)
c/o Staff Member *WmE2 (WMA-LA)*
1 William Morris Pl
Beverly Hills, CA 90212, USA

Ernaga, Frank (Athlete, Baseball Player)
50 N Roop St
Susanville, CA 46011-1609, USA

Ernest, Dixon (Athlete, Football Player)
324 Viceroy Curv
Stockbridge, GA 30281, USA

Erni, Hans (Artist)
6045 Meggen
Lucerne, SWITZERLAND

Ernie, Nimmons (Athlete, Baseball Player)
500 Pine Hollow Blvd Apt 103D
Lorain, OH 44055-3003, USA

Ernman, Malena (Musician)
c/o Staff Member *Eliasson Artists*
Stockholm
Skeppargatan 86
Stockholm 114 59, Sweden

Ernst, Bret (Actor, Comedian)
c/o Joan Green *Joan Green Management*
1836 Courtney Terr
Los Angeles, CA 90046, USA

Ernst, Mark A (Business Person)
H & R Block Inc
4400 Main St
Kansas City, MO 64111, USA

Ernst, Richard R (Nobel Prize Laureate)
Laboratorium fur Physikalische Chemie
ETH-Zentrum
Zurich CH-8092, SWITZERLAND

Ernster, Paul (Athlete, Football Player)
6954 S Fultondale Cir
Aurora, CO 80016, USA

Eroy, Iran (Actor)
c/o Staff Member *Televisa*
Blvd Adolfo Lopez Mateos 232
Colonia San Angel INN
DF CP 01060, MEXICO

Errazuriz Ossa, Francisco J Cardinal (Religious Leader)
Casilla 30D
Erasmo Escala 1894
Santiago, CHILE

Errey, Bob (Athlete, Hockey Player)
156 Hickory Heights Dr
Birdgeville, PA 15017, USA

Errico, Melissa (Actor)
c/o Richard Schmenner *Paradigm (LA)*
360 N Crescent Dr
North Bldg
Beverly Hills, CA 90210, USA

Erricson, Charlene (Stylist)
c/o Staff Member *Judy Inc*
1 Yorkville Ave
Toronto ON M4W 1L1, Canada

Erskine, Carl D (Athlete, Baseball Player)
4031 Fallbrook Ln
Anderson, IN 46011, USA

Erskine, Peter (Musician)
1727 Hill St
Santa Monica, CA 90405, USA

Erskine, Ralph (Architect)
Box 156
Gustav III's Vag
Drottningholm 170 11, SWEDEN

Erstad, Darin C (Athlete, Baseball Player)
12 Secret Cv
Newport Coast, CA 68516-6105, USA

Ertel, Mark (Athlete, Basketball Player)
1721 Cloister Drive
Indianapolis, IN 46260-1066, USA

Ertl, Gerhard (Nobel Prize Laureate)
Fritz-Haber Institut
Max-Pianck-Gesellschaft Faradayweg 4- 6
Attn:Fritz-Haber-Institut
Berlin D-14195, Germany

Ertl, Martina (Skier)
Erthofe 17
Lenggries 83661, GERMANY

Ertl, Sue (Athlete, Golfer)
4707 Sabal Key Dr
Bradenton, FL 34203, USA

Eruzione, Mike (Athlete, Hockey Player, Olympic Athlete)
1 Sherborn St Fl 7
Boston, MA 02215, USA

Ervin, Janice (Stylist)
2014 Central Ave NE
Minneapolis, MN 55418, USA

Erving, Julius (Athlete, Basketball Player)
108 Windrush Road
Winston Salem, NC 27106-2594, USA

Ervins, Ricky (Athlete, Football Player)
20984 Nightshade Pl
Ashburn, VA 20147, USA

Ervolino, Frank (Politician)
Laundry & Dry Cleaning Union
107 Delaware Ave
Buffalo, NY 14202, USA

Erwin, Hank
4213rd St. NE
Leeds, AL 35094

Erwin, Mike (Actor)
c/o Loch Powell *Leverage Management*
3030 Pennsylvania Ave
Santa Monica, CA 90404, USA

Erwin, Terry (Athlete, Football Player)
5596 S Lansing Way
Englewood, CO 80111, USA

Erwitt, Elliott R (Photographer)
88 Central Park West
New York, NY 10023-5299, USA

Erxleban, Russell (Athlete, Football Player)
306 Saddlehorn Dr
Dripping Springs, TX 78620-2740, USA

Erxleben, Russell A (Athlete, Football Player)
306 Saddlehorn Dr
Drippping Springs, TX 78620, USA

Esaki, Leo (Nobel Prize Laureate)
2484 Uenomuro
Tsukuba Ibaraki 305, JAPAN

Esasky, Nick (Athlete, Baseball Player)
1779 Starlight Dr
Marietta, GA 30062, USA

Esau, Len (Athlete, Hockey Player)
809 1st St W
Meadow Lake, SK S9X 1E2, Canada

Escalera, Nino (Athlete, Baseball Player)
DK20 Calle 201
Carolina, PR 00983-3715, USA

Escape (DJ)
c/o Len Evans *Project Publicity*
312 West 53rd St
Suite 202
New York, NY 10019, USA

Escarpeta, Arlen (Actor)
c/o Jerry Shandrew *Shandrew Public Relations*
1050 S Stanley Ave
Los Angeles, CA 90019-6634, USA

Esch, Eric (Butterbean) (Boxer)
Rt 13 Box 254
Jasper, MI 35501, USA

Eschbach, Jesse E (Judge)
US Court of Appeals
US Courthouse
701 Clematis St
West Palm Beach, FL 33401, USA

Esche, Robert (Athlete, Hockey Player, Olympic Athlete)
6750 W Carter Rd
Rome, NY 13440-1326, USA

Eschelman, Vaughn (Baseball Player)
Boston Red Sox
30106 Falher Dr
Spring, TX 77386 1683, USA

Eschen, larrv (Athlete, Baseball Player)
3649 Garden Blvd
Gainesville, GA 30506-1552, USA

Eschen, Larry (Athlete, Baseball Player)
3649 Garden Blvd
Gainesville, GA 30506, USA

Eschenbach, Christoph (Musician)
Maspalomas
Monte Leon 760625
Gran Canaria, SPAIN

Eschenbach, Christoph
2 Ave. d'Alena
Paris, FRANCE 75016

Eschenmoser, Albert J (Misc)
Bergstra 9
Kusnacht, ZH 8700, SWITZERLAND

Eschert, Jurgen (Athlete)
Tornowstr 8
Potsdam 1447, GERMANY

Escobar, Kelvim (Athlete, Baseball Player)
1292 Biscaya Dr
Surfside, FL 33154-3316, USA

Escobar, Yunel (Athlete, Baseball Player)
15763 SW 43rd St
Miami, Fl 33185-3815, USA

Escovedo, Pete (Musician)
c/o Victor Pamiroyan
PO Box 1741
Alameda, CA 94501, USA

E. Serrano, Jose (Congressman, Politician)
2227 Rayburn HOB
Washington, DC 20515, USA

Eshelman, Vaughn (Athlete, Baseball Player)
30106 Falher Dr
Spring, TX 77386-1683, USA

Eshman, Rob (Writer)
c/o Emile Gladstone ICM Partners (ICM-LA)
10250 Constellation Blvd Fl 7
Los Angeles, CA 90067, USA

Esiason, Norman J (Boomer) (Athlete, Football Player)
25 Heights Rd
Manhasset, NY 11030, USA

Eskell, Diana
41 Bushgrove Stanmore
Middlesex, ENGLAND HA7 2DY

Eskridge, Jack (Athlete, Basketball Player)
15297 K4 Hwy
Valley Falls, KS 66088-1293, USA

Esler-Smith, Frank (Misc)
Agency for Peroforming Arts
9200 Sunset Blvd
#900
Los Angeles, CA 90069, USA

Espada, Joey (Athlete, Baseball Player)
1409 Islamorada Dr
Jupiter, Fl 33458-8765, USA

Esparaza, Michael (Actor)
c/o Carl Scott Simmons & Scott Entertainment
4110 W. Burbank Blvd.
Burbank, CA 91505, USA

Esparza, Marlen (Athlete, Boxer)
c/o Staff Member United Talent Agency (UTA)
9336 Civic Center Dr
Beverly Hills, CA 90210, USA

Esparza, Moctesuma (Producer)
c/o Staff Member ICM Partners (ICM-LA)
10250 Constellation Blvd Fl 7
Los Angeles, CA 90067, USA

Esparza, Raul (Actor)
c/o Elin McManus-Flack Elin Flack Management
435 West 57th Street #3M
New York, NY 10019, USA

Espenson, Jane (Producer)
c/o Melanie Marquez M4 Publicity
11684 Ventura Blvd #213
Studio City, CA 91604, USA

Esperon, Natalia (Actor)
c/o Staff Member Televisa
Blvd Adolfo Lopez Mateos 232
Colonia San Angel INN
DF CP 01060, MEXICO

Espineli, Geno (Athlete, Baseball Player)
1222 Park ln
Katy, TX 77450-4613

Espino, Gaby (Actor)
c/o Gabriel Blanco Gabriel Blanco Iglesias (Mexico)
Rio Balsas 35-32
Colonia Cuauhtemoc
DF 06500, Mexico

Espinosa, Danny (Athlete, Baseball Player)
2326 N Towner St
Santa Ana, CA 92706-1942, USA

Espinoza, Alvaro (Athlete, Baseball Player)
1601 SE Alroso Blvd
Port Saint Lucie, FL 34953-7341, USA

Espinoza, Mark (Actor)
c/o Staff Member Howard Entertainment
10850 Wilshire Blvd
Suite 1260
Los Angeles, CA 90024, USA

Esposito, Brian (Athlete, Baseball Player)
364 Twinbark Ave
Holbrook, NY 11741-5722, USA

Esposito, Frank (Bowler)
200 N State Route 17
Paramus, NJ 07652-2902, USA

Esposito, Giancarlo (Actor)
c/o Staff Member Untitled Entertainment (LA)
350 S. Beverly Dr #200
Beverly Hills, CA 90212, USA

Esposito, Jennifer (Actor)
c/o Katherine Atkinson Washington Square Arts (LA)
1041 N Formosa Ave
The Lot Writers Bldg, Room 305
West Hollywood, CA 90046, USA

Esposito, Laura (Actor)
Gersh Agency
232 N Canon Dr
Beverly Hills, CA 90210, USA

Esposito, Mike (Athlete, Football Player)
35 Hampton Town Est
Hampton, NH 03842, USA

Esposito, Philip A (Phil) (Athlete, Hockey Player)
4003 W Tacon St
Tampa, FL 33629-8544, USA

Esposito, Sammv (Athlete, Baseball Player)
P^icallyUnable To Sign Autographs

Esposito, Sammy (Athlete, Baseball Player)
8303 Amber Leaf Ct
Raleigh, NC 27612, USA

Esposito, Tony (Athlete, Hockey Player)
418 55th Ave
Saint Petersburg Beach, FL 33706, USA

Esposito, Tony
418 55th Ave.
St. Petersburg, FL 33706-2311

EsPv., Duane
9032 E Hannibal St
Mesa, AZ 85207-4234, USA

Espy, Cecil (Athlete, Baseball Player)
5480 Encino Dr
San Diego, CA 92114-6307, USA

Espy, Mike (Politician)
819 7th St NW Ste 205
Washington, DC 20001-3762, USA

Esquivel, Laura (Actor, Producer, Writer)
c/o Staff Member Doubleday/RandomHouse
1745 Broadway
New York, NY 10019, USA

Esquivel, Manuel (Prime Minister)
United Democratic Party
19 King St
PO Box 1143
Belize City, BELIZE

Essany, Michael (Actor, Talk Show Host)
Michael Essany Show
c/o Mike Randazzo
139 Concord Circle
Valparaiso, IN 46385, USA

Essegian, Chuck (Athlete, Baseball Player)
15639 Bronco Dr
Canyon Country, CA 91387-4717, USA

Essensa, Bob (Athlete, Hockey Player)
1130 Iroqouis Trl
Oxford, MI 48371, USA

Esser, Mark (Athlete, Baseball Player)
208 Ridge Rd
Jupiter, FL 33477-5915, USA

Essex, David
5 Stratford Saye 20-22 Wellington
Bournemouth Dorset, ENGLAND BG8 8JN

Essex, Myron E (Biologist)
Harvard School of Public Health
665 Huntington Ave
Boston, MA 02115, USA

Essex, Trai (Athlete, Football Player)
c/o Eugene Parker Maximum Sports Management
6435 W Jefferson Blvd
#197
Fort Wayne, IN 46804, USA

Essian, James (Jim) (Athlete, Baseball Player, Coach)
134 Eckford Dr
Troy, MI 48085-4745, USA

Essink, Ron (Athlete, Football Player)
P.O. Box 265
Hamilton, MI 49419, USA

Esslinger, Hartmut (Designer)
FrogDesign
1327 Chesapeake Terrace
Sunnyvale, CA 94089, USA

Essman, Susie (Comedian)
c/o Lee Kernis Brillstein Entertainment Partners
9150 Wilshire Blvd #350
Beverly Hills, CA 90212, USA

Esswood, Paul L V (Opera Singer)
Jasmine Cottage
42 Ferring Lane
West Sussex BN12 6QT, UNITED KINGDOM (UK)

Estabrook, Mike (Athlete, Baseball Player)
502 Titus Rd
Lambertville, NJ 08530-2235, USA

Estabrook, Wayne (Athlete, Football Player)
6219 S Los Lagos CV
Fort Mohave, AZ 86426-7046, USA

Estacea, Elizabeth (Musician)
PO Box 691481
Charlotte, NC 28227

Estalella, Bobby (Athlete, Baseball Player)
453 Cinnamon Dr
Kissimmee, Fl 34759-5405, USA

Esteban, Samantha (Actor)
c/o Staff Member James/Levy/Jacobson Management Inc
3500 W Olive Ave
Suite 1470
Burbank, CA 91505, USA

Estefan, Emilio (Business Person, Musician)
Estefan Enterprises
420 Jefferson Ave
Miami Beach, FL 33139, USA

Estefan, Gloria (Musician)
39 Star Island Dr
Miami Beach, FL 33139, USA

Estefan, Lili (Actor)
c/o Staff Member Univision
605 3rd St. Fl12
New York, NY 10158, USA

Estefan, Manuel A (Educator)
California State University
President's Office
Chico, CA 95929, USA

Estelle (DJ, Musician)
c/o Tracy Nguyen IPR + MKTG
1515 Broadway
40th Floor
New York, NY 10036, USA

Estelle, Dick (Athlete, Baseball Player)
2221 Taylor St
Point Pleasant Boro, NJ 08742-3839, USA

Esten, Charles (Actor)
c/o Staff Member Stone Manners Salners Agency (LA)
9911 W Pico Blvd Ste 1400
Los Angeles, CA 90035, USA

Estern, Neil (Artist)
432 Cream Hill Road
West Cornwall, CT 06796-1210, USA

Estes, A Shawn (Athlete, Baseball Player)
6659 E Meadowlark Ln
Paradise Valley, AZ 85253-3620, USA

Estes, Billy Sol
1004 S. College
Brady, TX 76825

Estes, Bob (Athlete, Golfer)
4408 Long Champ Dr
Apt 21
Austin, TX 78746-1186, USA

Estes, Ellen (Misc)
Stanford University
Athletic Dept
Stanford, CA 94305, USA

Estes, Howell M Jr (Business Person, General)
7603 Shadywood Road
Bethesda, MD 20817, USA

Estes, James (Cartoonist)
1103 Callahan St
Amarillo, TX 79106-4201, USA

Estes, Larry (Athlete, Football Player)
115 Alida St
Hammond, LA 70403, USA

Estes, Rob (Actor)
1020 91st Ave NE
Bellevue, WA 98004, USA

Estes, Simon L (Opera Singer)
c/o Staff Member *Opera Et Concert*
37, rue de la Chaussée d'Antin
Paris F-75009, France

Estes, Will (Actor)
c/o Jason Barrett *Alchemy Entertainment*
7024 Melrose Ave
Suite 420
Los Angeles, CA 90038, USA

Estes, William K (Physicist)
1145 Linden Drive
Bloomington, IN 47408-1277, USA

Esteve-Coll, Elizabeth (Misc)
27 Ursula St
London SW11 3DW, UNITED KINGDOM
(UK)

Estevez, Emilio (Actor, Director)
c/o Scott Melrose *Scott Melrose*
Prefers to be contacted via email or
telephone
CA, USA

Estevez, Ramon (Actor)
837 Ocean Ave
#101
Santa Monica, CA 90402, USA

Estevez, Renee (Actor)
Michael Mann Talent
617 S Olive St
#311
Los Angeles, CA 90014, USA

Esthero (Musician)
c/o Staff Member *ArtistDirect*
9046 Lindblade St
Culver City, CA 90232, USA

Estill, Michelle (Athlete, Golfer)
642 Yacavona St
Kent, OH 44240-3318, USA

Estleman, Loren Daniel (Writer)
5552 Walsh Road
Whitmore Lake, MI 48189, USA

Estrada, Charle L (Chuck) (Athlete,
Baseball Player)
1289 Manzanita Way
San Luis Obispo, CA 93401-7838, USA

Estrada, Erik (Actor, Producer)
c/o Konrad Leh *Creative Talent Group*
1900 Avenue of the Stars
Suite 2475
Los Angeles, CA 90067, USA

Estrada, Erik-Michael (Musician)
c/o PJ Shapiro *Ziffren Brittenham LLP*
1801 Century Park W
Los Angeles, CA 90067, USA

estrada, Johnny (Athlete, Baseball Player)
20 Winged Foot Rdg
Newnan, GA 30265-2083, USA

Estrella, Alberto (Actor)
c/o Staff Member *Televisa*
Blvd Adolfo Lopez Mateos 232
Colonia San Angel INN
DF CP 01060, MEXICO

Estrella, Leo (Athlete, Baseball Player)
5462 NW Boydga Ave
Port Saint Lucie, FL 34986:4038, USA

Estrich, Susan (Attorney, Attorney
General, General)
9255 Doheny Road
#802
West Hollywood, CA 90069, USA

Estrin, Zack (Writer)
c/o Staff Member *WME (LA)*
9601 Wilshire Blvd Fl 3
Beverly Hills, CA 90210, USA

Eszterhas, Joe (Writer)
c/o Craig Baumgarten *Baumgarten
Management*
11925 Wilshire Blvd
Suite 310
Los Angeles, CA 90025, USA

Eszterhas, Joseph A (Writer)
c/o Craig Baumgarten *Baumgarten
Management*
11925 Wilshire Blvd
Suite 310
Los Angeles, CA 90025, USA

Etaix, Pierre (Actor, Director)
Cirque Fratellini
2 Rue de la Cloture
Paris 75019, France

Etchebarren, Andy (Athlete, Baseball
Player)
1488 Vermeer Dr
Nokomis, FL 17401-2401, USA

Etchegaray, Roger Cardinal (Religious
Leader)
Piazza San Calisto
Vatican City 00120

Etcheverry, Marco (Soccer Player)
DC United
14120 Newbrook Dr
Chantilly, VA 20151, USA

Etcheverry, Michel (Actor)
47 Rue du Borrego
Paris 75020, FRANCE

Etebari, Eric (Actor)
c/o Staff Member *Agency for the
Performing Arts (APA-LA)*
405 S Beverly Dr
Suite 500
Beverly Hills, CA 90212-4425, USA

Etel, Alex (Actor)
c/o Staff Member *ICM Partners (ICM-LA)*
10250 Constellation Blvd Fl 7
Los Angeles, CA 90067, USA

Etharton, Seth (Baseball Player)
Anaheim Angels
16 Saint John
Dana Point, CA 92629 4127, USA

Ethelle, Chuck (Race Car Driver)
124-126 Pomfret St.
Putnam, CT 06260, USA

Etheredge, Carlos (Athlete, Football
Player)
1231 Tuscumbia Rd
Collierville, TN 38017, USA

Etheridge, Bobby (Athlete, Baseball
Player)
118 Portland Rd
Eudora, AR 71640-2174, USA

Etheridge, Joe (Athlete, Football Player)
900 E Bryan St
Kermit, TX 79745, USA

Etheridge, Melissa (Musician, Songwriter,
Writer)
c/o Bill Leopold *W.F. Leopold
Management*
4425 Riverside Dr
Suite 102
Burbank, CA 91505, USA

Etherton, Seth (Athlete, Baseball Player)
16 Saint John
Dana Point, CA 92629-4127, USA

Ethier, Andre (Athlete, Baseball Player)
c/o Nez Balelo *CAA Sports (LA)*
2000 Avenue of the Stars
Los Angeles, CA 90067, USA

Ethridge, Mark F III (Editor)
5516 Gorham Dr
Charlotte, NC 28226, USA

Etienne, Treva (Actor)
c/o Staff Member *London Flair PR*
7119 W. Sunset Blvd #170
Los Angeles, CA 90046, USA

Etienne-Martin (Artist)
7 Rue du Pot de Fer
Paris 75005, FRANCE

Etrog, Sorel (Artist)
PO Box 67034
23 Yonge St
Toronto, ON M4P 1E0, CANADA

Etsel, Edward (Ed) (Misc)
University of Virginia
Athletic Dept
Charlottesville, VA 22906, USA

Etsou-Nzabi-Bamungwabi, Frederic
(Religious Leader)
Archdiocese of Kinshasa
BP 8431
Kinshasa 1, CONGO DEMOCRATIC
REPUBLIC

Etter, Bob (Athlete, Football Player)
8609 La Riviera Dr
Apt F
Sacramento, CA 95826, USA

Ettinger, Cynthia (Actor)
c/o Dan Barnhardt *Thruline Entertainment*
9250 Wilshire Blvd
Ground Fl
Beverly Hills, CA 90212, USA

Ettles, Mark (Athlete, Baseball Player)
3-10 Rose Avenue
South Perth, AU 6151, Australia

E-Type (Music Group)
c/o Staff Member *Agency Group Ltd, The
(Denmark)*
Slotsgade 2 Fl 2
Copenhagen 2200, DENMARK

Etzel, Edward (Athlete, Olympic Athlete,
Shooter)
1934 Van Voorhis Rd
Morgantown, WV 26508-1429

Etzel, Gregory A M (War Hero)
7822 Wonder St
Citrus Heights, CA 95610, USA

Etzioni, Amitai W (Activist)
7110 Arran Place
Bethesda, MD 20817, USA

Etzwiler, Donnell D (Doctor)
7611 Bush Lake Dr
Minneapolis, MN 55438, USA

Eubank, Chris (Boxer)
9 Upper Dr
Hove, East Sussex BN3 6GR, UNITED
KINGDOM

Eubank, Karen (Stylist)
c/o Staff Member *Campbell Agency, The*
3838 Oak Lawn Ave
Suite 900
Dallas, TX 75219-4510, USA

Eubank, Shari (Actor)
2965 N 625 E rd
Farmer City, IL 61842, USA

Eubanks, Bob (Motivational Speaker,
Television Host)
P.O. Box 1634
Santa Ynez, CA 93460-1634, USA

Eubanks, Dwight (Reality TV Star, Stylist)
Purple Door Salon
321 Edgewood Ave
Atlanta, GA 30312, USA

Eubanks, Kevin (Musician)
c/o Staff Member *NBC Universal (NY)*
30 Rockefeller Plaza
New York, NY 10112, USA

Eufemia, Frank (Athlete, Baseball Player)
433 6th Ave
Seaside Heights, NJ 07645-2323, USA

Euhus, Tim (Athlete, Football Player)
3520 SE Shoreline Dr
Corvallis, OR 97333, USA

Eunice, Cecil (Race Car Driver)
Rt. 3
Box 77
Blackshear, GA 31515, USA

Eure, Wesley (Actor)
Irv Schechter
9300 Wilshire Blvd
#410
Beverly Hills, CA 90212, USA

Europe (Music Group, Musician)
Box 22036
Stockholm S-10422, Sweden

Europe, Tom (Athlete, Football Player)
Groundwork Athletics
10-736 Granville St
Vancouver, BC V6Z 1G3, Canada

Eusebio, Tony (Athlete, Baseball Player)
2078 Shannon Lakes Blvd
Kissimmee, FL 34743, USA

Evan & Jaron (Music Group)
c/o Billy Lazarus *United Talent Agency
(UTA)*
9336 Civic Center Dr
Beverly Hills, CA 90210, USA

Evancho, Jackie (Musician)
P.O. Box 11184
Pittsburgh, PA 15237, USA

Evanescence (Music Group)
c/o Kim Estlund *Baker Winokur Ryder
Public Relations (BWR-LA)*
9100 Wilshire Blvd
Suite 500, West Tower
Beverly Hills, CA 90212, USA

Evangelista, Christine (Actor)
c/o Myrna Jacoby *MJ Management*
130 W 57th St
Suite 11A
New York, NY 10019, USA

Evangelista, Daniella (Actor)
c/o Steve Chasman *Current Entertainment*
9378 Wilshire Blvd
Sutie 210
Beverly Hills, CA 90212, USA

Evangelista, Linda (Actor, Model)
c/o Didier Fernandez *DNA Model Management*
555 W 25th St
New York, NY 10001, USA

Evanovich, Janet (Writer)
c/o Robert Gottlieb *Trident Media Group LLC*
41 Madison Ave
36th Floor
New York, NY 10010, USA

Evans, Aja (Actor)
c/o Staff Member *Precision Entertainment*
6338 Wilshire Blvd
Los Angeles, CA 90048, USA

Evans, Alice (Actor)
c/o Mary Ellen Mulcahy *Framework Entertainment (LA)*
9057 Nemo St
Suite C
West Hollywood, CA 90069, USA

Evans, Andrea (Actor)
ARL
8075 W 3rd St
#303
Los Angeles, CA 90048, USA

Evans, Anthony H (Educator)
California State University
President's Office
San Bermardino, CA 92407, USA

Evans, Barry (Athlete, Baseball Player)
8303 Seven Oaks Dr
Jonesboro, GA 30236, USA

Evans, Bart (Athlete, Baseball Player)
8323 Rolling HIlls Dr
Nixa, MO 65807-8680, USA

Evans, Bill (Athlete, Basketball Player, Olympic Athlete)
24360 Sandpiper Isle Way #105
Bonita Springs, FL 34134, USA

Evans, Byron (Athlete, Football Player)
1763 E Carter Rd
Phoenix, AZ 85042, USA

Evans, Caryl (Athlete, Hockey Player)
22403 Marjorie Ave
Torrance, CA 90505, USA

Evans, Charlie (Athlete, Football Player)
406 Ozzie St NW
Orting, WA 98360-7405, USA

Evans, Chris

Evans, Chris (Athlete, Hockey Player)

Evans, Chris (Athlete, Hockey Player)
c/o Erwin Stoff *3 Arts Entertainment Inc*
9460 Wilshire Blvd
7th Floor
Beverly Hills, CA 90210, USA

Evans, Dale (Athlete, Football Player)
8878 N State Highway 5
Unit 3
Camdenton, MO 65020, USA

Evans, Dan (Commentator)
1356 Linda Vista Ave
Pasadena, CA 91103-2346, USA

Evans, Daniel J (Politician)
4000-D NE 41st St
Seattle, WA 98105, USA

Evans, Darrell (Athlete, Baseball Player)
5207 Virtuoso
Irvine, CA 92620-0355, USA

Evans, Daryl (Athlete, Hockey Player)
22403 Marjorie Ave.
Torrance, CA 90505, USA

Evans, David (Edge) (Musician)
c/o Allen Grubman *Grubman, Indursky, & Schindler*
152 W 57th St
31st Floor
New York, NY 10019, USA

Evans, David Mickey (Director)
c/o Gleb Klioner *Schachter Entertainment*
1157 S Beverly Dr Fl 2
Los Angeles, CA 90035, USA

Evans, Demetric (Athlete, Football Player)
3820 Appleton Ln
Flower Mound, TX 75022, USA

Evans, Dick (Writer)
121 Morning Dove Court
Daytona Beach, FL 32119, USA

Evans, Dixie (Dancer, Model)
4525 W Twain Ave #205
Las Vegas, NV 89103, USA

Evans, Donald (Athlete, Football Player)
12407 Beauvoir St
Raleigh, NC 27614, USA

Evans, Donald L (Secretary)
Commerce Department
14th St & Constitution Ave NW
Washington, DC 20230, USA

Evans, Donna (Actor)
c/o Staff Member *United Stuntwomen's Association*
3518 Cahuenga Blvd West #206B
Hollywood, CA 90068, USA

Evans, Doug (Athlete, Hockey Player)
869 Clonsilla Ave
Peterborough, ON K9J OB7, Canada

Evans, Dwayne (Athlete)
PO Box 91219
Phoenix, AZ 85066, USA

Evans, Dwight (Athlete, Baseball Player)
c/o Staff Member *Boston Red Sox*
4 Yawkey Way
Boston, MA 02215, USA

Evans, Evans (Actor)
3114 Abington Dr
Beverly Hills, CA 90210, USA

Evans, Faith (Musician)
7518 Agnew Ave
Los Angeles, CA 90045, USA

Evans, Frank (Athlete, Baseball Player)
c/o Jeanette Kimble 6617 S Monroe St
Tacoma, WA 98409-2437, USA

Evans, George (Cartoonist)
c/o Staff Member *King Features Syndication*
300 W 57th St
15th Floor
New York, NY 10019-5238, USA

Evans, Glen (Biologist)
Salk Institute
10100 N Torrey Pines Road
La Jolla, CA 92037, USA

Evans, Greg (Cartoonist)
216 Country Garden Lane
San Marcos, CA 92069, USA

Evans, Harold J (Physicist)
17360 Holy Names Dr
Unit 2037
Lake Oswego, OR 97034-5186, USA

Evans, Harold M (Editor)
Random House
1745 Broadway
#B1
New York, NY 10019, USA

Evans, Heath (Athlete, Football Player)
242 Surfview Dr
Pacific Palisades, CA 90272, USA

Evans, Indiana (Actor)
Kermond Management
271 Goulburn St
Darlinghurst, Sydney 2010, AUSTRALIA

Evans, James B (Jim) (Baseball Player)
1801 Rogge Lane
Austin, TX 80104-5312, USA

Evans, Janet (Athlete, Olympic Athlete, Swimmer)
c/o Staff Member *Premier Management Group (PMG Sports)*
115 Crescent Commons Dr Ste 250
Cary, NC 27518, USA

Evans, Jay (Athlete, Football Player)
8878 N Highway 5
Camdenton, MO 65020, USA

Evans, Jerry (Athlete, Football Player)
4139 Ivanhoe Dr
Lorain, OH 44053, USA

Evans, J Handel (Educator)
San Jose State University
President's Office
San Jose, CA 95192, USA

Evans, Joan (Actor)
2289 Merrimack Ave
Henderson, NV 89044, USA

Evans, John (Business Person)
Alcan Aluminium
1188 Sherbrooke St W
Montreal, PC H3A 3G2, CANADA

Evans, John A (Athlete, Football Player)
North Carolina State University
P.O. Box 8501
Attn: Alumni Association
Raleigh, NC 27695, USA

Evans, John E (Business Person)
Allied Group
701 5th Ave
Des Moines, IA 50391, USA

Evans, John R (Misc)
Rocketfeller Foundation
113 Ave of Americas
New York, NY 10036, USA

Evans, John V
D L Evans Bank 397 N Overland Ave
Burlev, ID 83318-3432, USA

Evans, Josh (Athlete, Football Player)
P.O. Box 273309
Boca Raton, FL 33427, USA

Evans, J Thomas (Wrestler)
607 S Fir Court
Broken Arrow, OK 74012, USA

Evans, Karin
Laubenheimer Str. I
Berlin, GERMANY D-14197

Evans, Kellylee (Musician)
c/o Staff Member *SL Feldman & Associates (Toronto)*
8 Elm St
Toronto, ON M5G 1G7, Canada

Evans, Larry (Athlete, Football Player)
5316 S Broadway Cir
Apt 8-208
Englewood, CO 80113, USA

Evans, Lee (Actor, Comedian, Writer)
c/o Staff Member *Off The Kerb Productions*
Hammer House, 3rd Fl
113-117 Wardour St
London W1F 0UN, UK

Evans, Linda (Actor)
P.O. Box 29
Rainer, WA 98576, USA

Evans, Luke (Actor)
c/o Lena Roklin *Luber Roklin Management*
8530 Wilshire Blvd
6th Floor
Beverly Hills, CA 90211, USA

Evans, Lynn (Musician)
Richard Paul Assoc
16207 Mott
Macomb Township, MI 48044, USA

Evans, Marc (Director)
c/o Jane Villiers *Tessa Sayle Agency*
11 Jubilee Pl
London SW3 3TE, UNITED KINGDOM (UK)

Evans, Marsha Johnson (Admiral)
American Red Cross
431 18th St NW
Washington, DC 20006, USA

Evans, Martin J (Misc, Scientist)
Castle Rise 41
Rumney
Cardiff CF3 9BB, WALES

Evans, Martin Sir (Nobel Prize Laureate)
Cardiff School of Biosciences PO Box 911
Biomedical Bid!!, Cardiff CFlO 3US, England

Evans, Mary Beth (Actor, Director)
c/o Michael Bruno *The Michael Bruno Group*
13576 Cheltenham Dr
Sherman Oaks, CA 91423, USA

Evans, Mike (Athlete, Basketball Player)
9931 Cottoncreek Drive
Highlands Ranch, CO 80130-3825, USA

Evans, Mike (Athlete, Football Player)
1 Hunters Run
Greenville, SC 29615, USA

Evans, Murray (Journalist)
46 Courtside Cir
San Antonio, TX 78216-7843, USA

Evans, Natalie (Stylist)
c/o Staff Member *Crews*
828 Clemont Dr
Atlanta, GA 30306, USA

Evans, Nicholas (Nick) (Writer)
Delacorte Press
1540 Broadway
New York, NY 10036, USA

Evans, Norm (Athlete, Football Player)
360 NW Boulder Pl
Issaquah, WA 98027, USA

Evans, Norm E (Athlete, Football Player)
4143 Via Marina
Marina Del Rey, CA 90292, USA

Evans, Paul (Athlete, Hockey Player)
1033 Silverdale Rd
Peterborough, ON K9J 0B7 Canada,
Canada

Evans, Reggie (Athlete, Football Player)
2813 Juniper St
Merrifield, VA 22116, USA

Evans, Richard (Sportscaster)
Madison Square Garden
4 Pennsylvania Plaza
New York, NY 10001, USA

Evans, Richard Paul (Writer)
Richard Paul Evans Inc.
P.O. Box 712137
Salt Lake City, UT 84171, USA

Evans, Rob (Coach)
Arizona State University
Athletic Dept
Tempe, AZ 85287, USA

Evans, Robert (Producer)
Robert Evans Productions
Paramount Pictures
5555 Melrose
Los Angeles, CA 90038, USA

Evans, Robert C (Mountaineer)
Ardincaple
Capel Curig
Betws-y-Coed, Northern Wales, WALES

Evans, Robert S (Business Person)
Crane Co
100 Stamford Plaza
Stamford, CT 06902, USA

Evans, Ronald (Scientist)
Salk Institute PO Box 85800
San Diego, CA 92186-5800, USA

Evans, Ronald E
6134 E Mescal
Scottsdale, AZ 85254, USA

Evans, Ronald M (Doctor)
Salk Institute
10100 N Torrey Pines Road
La Jolla, CA 92037, USA

Evans, Sara (Musician)
11 Elm St
Mountain Brook, AL 35213, USA

Evans, Shaun (Actor)
c/o Jon Rubinstein Authentic Talent and
Literary Management
45 Main St
Suite 1004
Brooklyn, NY 11201, USA

Evans, Thomas (Business Person)
Collins & Aikman Corporation
PO Box 7054
Troy, MI 48007-7054

Evans, Tom (Athlete, Baseball Player)
32533 SE 68th St
Issaquah, WA 98027-8729, USA

Evans, Tracy (Athlete, Olympic Athlete,
Skier)
1317 Ptarmigan Loop
Park City, UT 84098-5989, USA

Evans, Troy (Actor)
PO Box 834
Lakeside, MT 59922, USA

Evans, Vince (Athlete, Football Player)
14084 Bronte Dr
Whittier, CA 90602, USA

Evans, Walker (Race Car Driver)
Walker Evans Racing
PO Box 2469
Riverside, CA 92516, USA

Evans, William (Basketball Player,
Olympic Athlete)
3110 Springstead Cir
Louisville, KY 40241-4416, USA

Evanshen, Terry (Athlete, Football Player)
19 Dorset St RR 1
Hampton, ON L0B 1J0, Canada

Evashevski, Forest (Coach, Football
Coach)
5820 Clubhouse Dr
Vero Beach, FL 32967, USA

Evason, Dean (Athlete, Hockey Player)
c/o Staff Member Washington Capitals
627 N Glebe Rd
Arlington, VA 22203, USA

Evastina, Liisa (Actor)
c/o Celia Campbell Murphy Kidman
Edwards
45 Manchester St
London W1U 7LS, UK

Evdokimova, Eva (Ballerina)
Gregori Productions
PO Box 1586
New York, NY 10150, USA

Eve (Actor)
c/o Amanda Silverman 42West (NY)
220 W 42nd St
12th Floor
New York, NY 10036, USA

Eve, Alice (Actor)
c/o Alissa Vradenburg Untitled
Entertainment (LA)
350 S. Beverly Dr #200
Beverly Hills, CA 90212, USA

Eve, Diva (Athlete, Wrestler)
c/o Staff Member World Wrestling
Entertainment (WWE)
Titan Towers
1241 E Main St
Stamford, CT 06905-3857, USA

Eve, Trevor J (Actor)
c/o Matthew Lesher Insight
1134 S Cloverdale Ave
Los Angeles, CA 90019, USA

Eveland, Dana (Athlete, Baseball Player)
37138 Liana Ln
Palmdale, CA 93551-6237, USA

Evelyn, Lionel (Athlete, Baseball Player)
2508 Edgemere Ave
Far Rockaway, NY 11691-2716, USA

Everclear (Music Group)
c/o Staff Member Tenth Street
Entertainment
270 Lafayette St
Suite 706
New York, NY 10012, USA

Everett, Adam (Athlete, Baseball Player,
Olympic Athlete)
4374 Oglethorpe Loop NW
Acworth, GA 30101-9533, USA

Everett, Carl E (Athlete, Baseball Player)
19108 Harborbridge Ln
Lutz, FL 3558-9717, USA

Everett, Chad (Actor)
5472 Island Forest Place
Westlake Village, CA 91362, USA

Everett, Danny (Athlete)
Santa Monica Track Club
1801 Ocean Park Ave
#112
Santa Monica, CA 90405, USA

Everett, Jim (Athlete, Football Player)
555 N El Camino Real
Suite A445
San Clemente, CA 92672, USA

Everett, Major (Athlete, Football Player)
P.O. Box 1441
Pine Lake, GA 30072, USA

Everett, Mark Oliver (Musician)
4046 Cromwell Ave
Los Angeles, CA 90027, USA

Everett, Rupert (Actor)
c/o Annett Wolf WKT Public Relations
(WKT-LA)
9350 Wilshire Blvd
Suite 450
Beverly Hills, CA 90212, USA

Everett, Thomas G (Athlete, Football
Player)
P.O. Box 795337
Dallas, TX 75379-5337, USA

Everham, Ray (Race Car Driver)
18917 Peninsula Point Dr
Cornelius, NC 28031-7599, USA

Everhard, Nancy (Actor)
Kazarian /Spencer
11365 Ventura Blvd
#100
Studio City, CA 91604, USA

Everhart, Angie (Actor, Producer)
7251 Pacific View Dr
Los Angeles, CA 90068, USA

Everitt, Leon (Athlete, Baseball Player)
367 Henry Everitt Rd
Marshall, TX 76001-8525, USA

Everitt, Mike (Baseball Player)
12381 Walnut Ridge Ct
Clive, IA 50325-8127, USA

Everitt, Mike (Athlete, Baseball Player)
4215 162nd St
Urbandale, IA 50323-2509, USA

Everitt, Steve (Athlete, Football Player)
17252 Snapper Ln
Summerland Key, FL 33042, USA

Everlast (Actor, Composer, Musician)
3455 Rubio Crest Dr
Altadena, CA 91001, USA

Everly Brothers (Musician)
Beehive
PO Box 3933
Seattle, WA 98124-3933, USA

Evermore (Music Group)
c/o Staff Member Paradigm (Monterey)
404 W Franklin St
Monterey, CA 93940, USA

Evernham, Ray (Race Car Driver)
18917 Peninsula Point Dr
Cornelius, NC 28031-7599, USA

Evers, Bill (Athlete, Baseball Player)
PO Box 507
Durham, NC 34654-6330, USA

Evers, Charles (Politician)
1072 J R Lynch St
Jackson, MS 39203-3344, USA

Evers, Jackson (Actor)
232 N Crescent Dr
#101
Beverly Hills, CA 90210, USA

Evers, Jay (Stylist)
c/o Staff Member Independent Artists
448 E Riverdale Ave
Orange, CA 92865, USA

Evers, John (Comedian)
PO Box 169
Mount Airy, NC 27030, USA

Evers-Euterneck, Ernest (Scientist)
4416 Shelby Ave SE
Huntsville, AL 35801-1055, USA

Eversgerd, Bryan (Baseball Player, Coach)
Swing of the Quad Cities
P.O. Box 3496
Attn: Coaching Staff
Davenport, IA 62801-7616, USA

Eversley, Frederick J (Artist)
1110 W Albert Kinney Blvd
Venice, CA 90219, USA

Everson, Cory (Actor, Athlete)
39 Hackamore Ln
Bell Canyon, CA 91307, USA

Everson, Mark (Government Official)
Internal Revenue Service
111 Constitution Ave NW
Washington, DC 20224, USA

Evert, Chris (Athlete, Olympic Athlete,
Tennis Player)
8563 Horseshoe Ln
Boca Raton, FL 33496, USA

Evert, Ray F (Biologist)
810 Woodward Dr
Madison, WI 53704, USA

Every Move A Picture (Music Group)
c/o Staff Member Paradigm (Monterey)
404 W Franklin St
Monterey, CA 93940, USA

Everything But The Girl (Music Group,
Musician)
c/o Staff Member High Road Touring
751 Bridgeway
3rd Floor
Sausalito, CA 94965, USA

Evey, Dick (Athlete, Football Player)
335 S Springview Rd
Maryville, TN 37801, USA

Evidon, Lisa J (Stylist)
4421 Beard Ave
South Minneapolis, MN 55410, USA

Evigan, Briana (Actor)
c/o Matt Luber Luber Roklin Management
8530 Wilshire Blvd
6th Floor
Beverly Hills, CA 90211, USA

Evigan, Greg (Actor)
5070 Arundel Dr
Woodland Hills, CA 91364, USA

Evo, Bill (Athlete, Hockey Player)
2723 Roundtree Dr
Troy, MI 48083-2327, USA

Evora, Cesar (Actor)
c/o Staff Member *Televisa*
Blvd Adolfo Lopez Mateos 232
Colonia San Angel INN
DF CP 01060, MEXICO

Evora, Cesaria (Musician)
Monterey International
200 W Superior
#202
Chicago, IL 60610, USA

Evraire, Ken (Athlete, Football Player)
73 Fairlawn Ave
Toronto, ON M5M 1S6, Canada

Evre, Willie (Athlete, Baseball Player)
364 S 100 E Ste 211
Cedar CitY, UT 84720-3810, USA

Evren, Kenan (General, President)
Beyaz Ev Sokak 21
Armutalan, Marmaris, TURKEY

Evron, Ephraim (Government Official)
Ministry of Foreign Affairs
Tel-Aviv, ISRAEL

Ewald, Esther (Athlete, Baseball Player,
Commentator)
8455 N Ozanam Ave
Niles, IL 60714-1935, USA

Ewald, Reinhold (Cosmonaut)
DLR Astronauterburo WT/AN
Linder Hohe
Cologne 51140, GERMANY

Ewell, Dwight (Actor)
c/o Margrit Polak *Margrit Polak
Management*
1954 Hillhurst Ave
Suite 405
Los Angeles, CA 90027, USA

Ewell, Kayla (Actor)
1330 N Lincoln St
Burbank, CA 91506, USA

Ewen, Todd (Athlete, Hockey Player)
420 Thunderhead Canyon Dr
Ballwin, MO 63011, USA

Ewing, Barbara (Actor)
Flat 4
1 Candover St
York House, London W1W 7DG,
UNITED KINGDOM (UK)

Ewing, Blake
c/o Jeff Morrone *Jeff Morrone
Entertainment*
9350 Wilshire Blvd
Suite 224
Beverly Hills, CA 90212, USA

Ewing, Lucy (Stylist)
c/o Staff Member *Katy Barker Agency Inc*
6606 10th Ave Apt 3R
Brooklyn, NY 11219, USA

Ewing, Maria L (Opera Singer)
33 Bramerton St
London SW3, UNITED KINGDOM (UK)

Ewing, Patrick (Athlete, Basketball Player,
Coach, Olympic Athlete)
37 Summit St
Englewood Cliffs, NJ 07632, USA

Ewing, Reid (Actor)
c/o Justin Grey Stone *Untitled
Entertainment (LA)*
350 S. Beverly Dr #200
Beverly Hills, CA 90212, USA

Ewing, Sam (Athlete, Baseball Player)
1048 Cedarview Ln
Franklin, TN 66604-2605, USA

Example (Music Group)
c/o Doug Smith *Coda Music Agency - UK*
229 Shoreditch High St
London E1 6PJ, UK

Exelby, Garnet (Athlete, Hockey Player)
1182 Saint Louis Pl NE
Atlanta, GA 30306, USA

Exelby, Randy (Athlete, Hockey Player)
10040 E Happy Valley Rd
Unit 210
Scottsdale, AZ 85255, USA

Exerins, Leo (Athlete, Football Player)
595 Valour Rd
Winnipeg, MB R3G 3A7, Canada

Exile
PO Box 1547
Goodlettsville, TN 37070-1547

Exley, Susan (Stylist)
11569 Hartsook St
Valley Village, CA 91601, USA

Expose (Music Group)
c/o Staff Member *Richard Walters
Entertainment, Inc*
PO Box 2789
Toluca Lake, CA 91610-0789, USA

Extreme (Music Group, Musician)
c/o Rod MacSween *International Talent
Booking*
74A Charlotte St
London W1T 4QJ, UNITED KINGDOM
(UK)

Eyes, Raymond (Publisher)
McCall's Magazine
375 Lexington Ave
New York, NY 10017, USA

Eyharts, Leopold
49 Rue Desnouttes
Paris 75015, FRANCE

Eyharts, Leopold Colonel (Astronaut)
2371 Calypso Ln
League Citv, TX 77573-0758, USA

Eyre, Richard (Director)
c/o Staff Member *Creative Artists Agency
(CAA-LA)*
2000 Ave Of The Stars
Los Angeles, CA 90067, USA

Eyre, Scott (Athlete, Baseball Player)
7010 190th St E
Bradebtob, FL 34211, USA

Eyre, Willie (Athlete, Baseball Player)
17569 Cherry Ridge Ln
Ft Myers, FL 33967, USA

Eysenck, Hans J (Misc)
10 Dorchester Dr
London SE24, UNITED KINGDOM (UK)

Eyskens, Mark (Government Official)
Graaf de Grunnelaan
Heverlee 3001, BELGIUM

Eytchison, Ronald M (Admiral)
11 Prentice Lane
Signal Mountain, TN 37377, USA

Ezarik, Justine (Internet Star)
c/o Dan Weinstein *Collective*
8383 Wilshire Blvd
Suite 1050
Beverly Hills, CA 90211, USA

Ezell, Glenn (Athlete, Baseball Player)
4790 Brittany DrS Unit B-7
Saint Petersburg, FL 33715-2606, USA

Ezersky, John (Athlete, Basketball Player)
2564 Walnut Blvd
Apt 103
Walnut Creek, CA 94596-4251, USA

Ezinicki, Bill (Athlete, Hockey Player)
166 Ballville Rd
Bolton, MA 01740, USA

Ezor, Blake (Athlete, Football Player)
10622 Salmon Leap St
Las Vegas, NV 89183, USA

Ezra, Derek (Government Official)
2 Salisbury Road
Wimbledon
London SW19 4EZ, UNITED KINGDOM
(UK)

Ezrin, Bob (Producer)
Nimbus School of Recording Arts Ltd.
238 E 2nd Ave
Suite 300
Vancouver, BC V5T 1B7, Canada

Fa, Sione (Reality TV Star)
43258 Chisolm Dr
Maricopa, AZ 85239, USA

Faas, Horst (Photographer)
12 Norwich Street
London EC4A, England

Fabac-Bretting, Elizabeth (Baseball Player)
1455 Mesa St
Redding, CA 96001-2310, USA

Fabares, Shelley (Actor)
c/o Staff Member *Innovative Artists (LA)*
1505 10th St
Santa Monica, CA 90401, USA

Fabbricini, Tiziana (Opera Singer)
Gianni Testa
Via Wrenteggio 31/6
Milan 20146, ITALY

Fabel, Brad (Athlete, Golfer)
247 Windsor Terrace Dr
Nashville, TN 37221-2279, USA

Faber, David (Actor, Writer)
c/o Staff Member *CNBC*
900 Sylvan Ave
Englewood Cliffs, NJ 07632, USA

Faber, Sandra M (Scientist)
16321 Ridgecrest Ave
Monte Sereno, CA 95030-4139, USA

Fabi, Ted
9350 Castlegate Dr.
Indianapolis, IN 46256

Fabian, John M (Astronaut)
100 Shine Rd
Port Ludlow, WA 98365, USA

Fabian, John M Dr (Astronaut)
100 Shine Rd
Port Ludlow, WA 98365-9274, USA

Fabian, Lara (Musician, Songwriter,
Writer)
Alian Productions
1 Place du Commerce
Nun's Island, PQ H3E 1A2, CANADA

Fabian, Lara
BP 37
Boussu-1, BELGIUM 7301

Fabian, Patrick (Actor)
c/o Donald Spradlin *Essential Talent
Management*
6399 Wilshire Blvd
Suite 401
Los Angeles, CA 90048, USA

Fabini, Jason (Athlete, Football Player)
17 Tappanwood Rd
Locust Valley, NY 11560, USA

Fabio (Actor, Model)
19620 Wells Dr
Tarzana, CA 91356, USA

Fabiola Moray Aragon, Dona (Royalty)
Royal Palace of Laeken
Laeken-Brussels, BELGIUM

Fabius, Laurent (Misc)
Mairie
Le Grand-Quevilly 76120, FRANCE

Fabray, Nanette (Actor, Musician)
14350 Sunset Blvd
Pacific Palisades, CA 90272, USA

Fabregas, Francesc (Soccer Player)
Arsenal Football Club
Highbury House
75 Drayton Park
London N5 1BU, UNITED KINGDOM

Fabregas, Jorge (Athlete, Baseball Player)
4936 SW 6th St
Coral Gables, FL 33134-1346, USA

Fabro, Sam (Athlete, Football Player)
724 South Dr
Winnipeg, MB R3T 0C3, Canada

Fabulous, Moolah (Wrestler)
101 Moolah Dr
Columbia, SC 29223, USA

Face, Elroy L (Roy) (Athlete, Baseball
Player)
608 Della Dr
Apt 5F
North Versailles, PA 15137, USA

Facinelli, Peter (Actor)
c/o Jason Weinberg *Untitled
Entertainment (LA)*
350 S. Beverly Dr #200
Beverly Hills, CA 90212, USA

Fadden, Stanley (Staub) (Race Car Driver)
Fadden Racing
Box 427
Main St., New Haverhill NH, 03774

Faddeyev, Ludwig D (Mathematician,
Physicist)
Streklov Math Institute
Nab Fontanki 27
Saint Petersburg D11, RUSSIA

Faddis, Jonathan (Jon) (Misc)
Carolyn McClair
PO Box 55
Radio Station
New York, NY 10101, USA

Fadeyechev, Aleksei (Dancer)
Bolshoi Theater
Teatralnaya Pl 1
Moscow 103009, RUSSIA

Fadeyechev, Nicolai B (Dancer)
Bolshoi Theater
Teatralnaya Pl 1
Moscow 103009, RUSSIA

Fadul, Francisco Jose (Prime Minister)
Prime Minister's Office
Bissau, GUINEA-BISSAU

Faedo, Len (Lenny) (Athlete, Baseball
Player)
2920 W Collins St
Tampa, FL 33607, USA

Faedo, Lenny
2920 W Collins St
Tamoa, FL 3607-6702, USA

Faerch, Daeg (Actor)
c/o Kieran Maguire *The Arlook Group*
205 S Beverly Dr
Suite 209
Beverly Hills, CA 90212, USA

Fagan, Garth (Choreographer)
Garth Fagan Dance
50 Chestnut Plaza
Rochester, NY 14604, USA

Fagan, John J (Misc)
International teamsters Brotherhood
25 Louisiana NW
Washington, DC 20001, USA

Fagan, Julian (Athlete, Football Player)
PO Box 920
Madison, MS 39130-0920, USA

Fagan, kevin (Cartoonist)
26771 Ashford
Mission Viejo, CA 92692-4106, USA

Fagan, Kevin (Athlete, Football Player)
11441 Camp Dr
Dunnellon, FL 34432, USA

Fagen, Clifford B (Basketball Player)
1021 Royal Saint George Dr
Naperville, IL 60563, USA

Fagen, Donald (Musician, Songwriter,
Writer)
Howard Rose
9460 Wilshire Blvd
#310
Beverly Hills, CA 90212, USA

Fagerbakke, Bill (Actor)
1500 Will Geer Rd
Topanga, CA 90290, USA

Fagg, George G (Judge)
US Court of Appeals
US Courthouse
East 1st & Walnut
Des Moines, IA 50309, USA

Faggin, Federico (Inventor, Physicist)
27910 Roble Blanco Dr
Los Altos Hills, CA 94022-2464, USA

Faggins, Demarcus (Athlete, Football
Player)
3002 Southworth Ln
Manvel, TX 77578, USA

Faggs, Starr H Mae (Athlete, Track
Athlete)
10152 Shady Lane
Cincinnati, OH 45215, USA

Fahd bin Ibn, Abdul al-Aziz al Saud
(King)
Royal Palace
Royal Court
Riyadh, SAUDI ARABIA

Fahey, Bill (Athlete, Baseball Player)
5740 Mona Ln
Dallas, TX 75236-1722, USA

Fahey, Brandon (Athlete, Baseball Player)
5740 Mona Ln
Dallas, TX 75236, USA

Fahey, Damien (Television Host)
c/o Michael (Mike) Esterman
Esterman.Com, LLC
Prefers to be contacted via email
MD, USA

Fahey, Jeff (Actor)
c/o Jeff Goldberg *Jeff Goldberg
Management*
817 Monte Leon Dr
Beverly Hills, CA 90210, USA

Fahey, Jim (Athlete, Hockey Player)
117 Plymouth Ave
Milton, MA 02186, USA

Fahey, Siobhan (Musician)
5700 Holly Oak Dr
Los Angeles, CA 90068, USA

Fahey, Trevor (Athlete, Hockey Player)
7629 Bayhill Ct
New Port Richey, FL 34654, USA

Fahnhorst, James (Jim) (Athlete, Football
Player)
2365 Brockton Ln N
Minneapolis, MN 55447, USA

Fahnhorst, Keith (Athlete, Football Player)
12216 Chadwick Ln
Eden Prairie, MN 55344, USA

Fahr, Alicia (Actor)
c/o Staff Member *Televisa*
Blvd Adolfo Lopez Mateos 232
Colonia San Angel INN
DF CP 01060, MEXICO

Fahrberger, Mary Lou (Stylist)
310 Oselka Dr
#452
New Buffalo, MI 49117-2014, USA

Fahy, Bill (Horse Racer)
465 Hewitt Ave
Washington, PA 15301-1538, USA

Faia, Renee (Actor)
c/o Marni Anhalt *Imperium 7 Talent
Agency*
5455 Wilshire Blvd
Suite 1706
Los Angeles, CA 90036, USA

Fain, Farris
PO Box 1357
Georgetown, CA 95634

Fain, Richard (Athlete, Football Player)
2705 62nd St W
Lehigh Acres, FL 33971-5849, USA

Faine, Jeff K (Athlete, Football Player)
Forty VII
108 Estates Cir
Unit A
Lake Mary, FL 32746-3023, USA

Fainsilber, Adrien (Architect)
7 Rue Salvador Allende
Nanterre 92000, FRANCE

Fair, Lorrie (Athlete, Olympic Athlete,
Soccer Player)
300 3rd St Apt 1515
San Francisco, CA 94107-1259

Fair, Terry (Athlete, Football Player)
1936 Mahogany Wood Trl
Knoxville, TN 37920-6298, USA

Fairbairn, Bill (Athlete, Hockey Player)
10-20W Magnacca Cres
Brandon, MB R7B 2N9, Canada

Fairbairn, Bruce (Actor)
Century Artists
PO Box 59747
Santa Barbara, CA 93150, USA

Fairband, Bill
13607 E Garigans Gulch
Vail, AZ 85641-6030, USA

Fairbank, Richard D (Financier)
Capital One Financial
1680 Capital One Dr
McLean, VA 22102-3407, USA

Fairbanks, Chuck (Athlete, Football
Coach, Football Player)
25191 N 104th Way
Scottsdale, AZ 85255, USA

Fairchild, Chad (Athlete, Baseball Player)
2700 Coconut Bay Ln
Unit 1D
Sarasota, FL 34219-5821, USA

Fairchild, Greg (Athlete, Football Player)
6604 Heege Rd
Saint Louis, MO 63123-2608, USA

Fairchild, John (Athlete, Basketball Player)
9801 Chantilly Rd NW
Albuquerque, NM 87114-4402, USA

Fairchild, Kelly (Athlete, Hockey Player)
14900 43rd Ave N
Minneapolis, MN 55446-2789, USA

Fairchild, Morgan (Actor)
P.O. Box 57593
Sherman Oaks, CA 91403, USA

Fairchild, Paul (Athlete, Football Player)
22249 W 183rd St
Olathe, KS 66062, USA

Fairchild, Thomas E (Judge)
US Court of Appeals
111 N Cancal St
Building 6
Chicago, IL 60606, USA

Faircloth, Arthur (Athlete, Football Player)
10010 Sandwedge Ct
Fredericksburg, VA 22408, USA

Faircloth, D McLauchlin (Lauch)
(Politician)
803 Beaman St
Clinton, NC 28328-2607, USA

Fairey, Jim (Athlete, Baseball Player)
218 Strawberry Ln
Clemson, SC 29631-1363, USA

Fairey, Shepard
c/o Bradley Frank *Platform Public
Relations*
2666 N Beachwood Dr
Los Angeles, CA 90068, USA

Fairholm, Jeff (Athlete, Football Player)
110 Rue Pierre-Panet
L'Ile-Bizard, QC H9C 2X3, Canada

Fairley, Nick (Football Player)
c/o Brian E. Overstreet *E.O. Sports
Management*
1314 Texas Ave
Suite 1212
Houston, TX 77002, USA

Fairly, Ronald R (Ron) (Athlete, Baseball
Player)
75369 Spyglass Dr
Indian Wells, CA 92210, USA

Fairs, Eric (Athlete, Football Player)
32707 Wales Cir
Fulshear, TX 77441-4250, USA

Faison, Donald (Actor)
c/o Glenn Rigberg *HYPHENATE*
9701 Wilshire Blvd.
10th floor
Beverly Hills, CA 90212, USA

Faison, Matthew (Actor)
13701 E Kagel Canyon Road
Sylmar, CA 91342, USA

Faison, Tiffani (Chef)
c/o Staff Member *Magical Elves Inc*
453 S Spring Street Ste
Los Angeles, CA 90013, USA

Faison, William (Earl) (Athlete, Football
Player)
2279 N Sequoia Dr
Prescott, AZ 86301-4326, USA

Faith, Paloma (Musician)
c/o Olivia Woodward *Curtis Brown
Group*
Haymarket House
28 - 29 Haymarket
London SW1Y 4SP, UNITED KINGDOM

Faithfull, Marianne (Actor, Songwriter)
Susan Dewsap
235 Gootscray Rd
New Eltham
London SE9 2EL, UNITED KINGDOM
(UK)

Faithless (Music Group)
c/o Staff Member *Paradigm (Monterey)*
404 W Franklin St
Monterey, CA 93940, USA

Fakih, Rima (Beauty Pageant Winner)
The Miss Universe Organization
1370 Avenue of the Americas
16th Floor
New York, NY 10019, USA

Fakir, Abdul (Duke) (Music Group)
c/o Staff Member *ICM Partners (ICM-NY)*
730 Fifth Ave
New York, NY 10019, USA

Falana, Lola (Dancer, Music Group)
Capital Entertainment
217 Seaton Place NE
Washington, DC 20002, USA

Falcam, Leo A (President)
President's Office
Palikjr
Kolonia
Pohnpei, FM 96941, MICRONESIA

Falcao, Jose Freire Cardinal (Religious
Leader)
QL 12-CJ12
Lote 1
Lago Sul, Brasilia DF 71630-325, BRAZIL

Falcao, Jose Friere Cardinal (Religious
Leader)
QL 12-CJ 12 Lote 1 Lago Sul
Brasilia DF 71630-325, BRAZIL

Falco, Edie (Actor)
c/o Adam Schweitzer *ICM Partners
(ICM-NY)*
730 Fifth Ave
New York, NY 10019, USA

Falcone, Ben (Actor)
c/o Staff Member *Parallel Entertainment*
9420 Wilshire Blvd #250
Beverly Hills, CA 90212, USA

Falcone, Pete (Athlete, Baseball Player)
2232 Thornton Ct
Alexandria, LA 71301, USA

Falconi, Irina (Athlete, Tennis Player)
c/o Dan Nagler *South Beach Sports Agency*
770 Claughton Island Dr
#1510
Miami, FL 33131, USA

Faldo, Nick (Athlete, Golfer)
Faldo Enterprises
18 - 20 Sheet St
Windsor
Berkshire SL4 1BG, UK

Falik, Yuri (Composer, Conductor)
Fihlyandsky Prospekt 1 #54
Saint Petersburg 194044, RUSSIA

Falk, David (Lawyer)
Falk Assoc
5335 Wiconsin Ave NW #850
Washington, DC 20015, USA

Falk, David B (Attorney, Attorney General, General, Misc)
Falk Assoc
5335 Wisconsin Ave NW #850
Washington, DC 20015, USA

Falk, Paul (Figure Skater)
Sybelstr 21
Dusseldorf 40239, GERMANY

Falk, Randall M (Religious Leader)
Temple
5015 Harding Road
Nashville, TN 37205, USA

Falkenberg, Bob (Athlete, Hockey Player)
7251 190a St NW
Edmonton, AB T5T 5S9, Canada

Falkenborg, Brian (Athlete, Baseball Player)
30233 N 125th Dr
Peoria, AZ 85383-3429, USA

Falkenborg, Brian (Athlete, Baseball Player)
30223 N 125th Dr
Peoria, AZ 85383, USA

Falkenborg, Brian (Athlete, Baseball Player)
1980 Minnesota Twins
2920 W Collins St, Tamoa FL, 33607-6702

Falkenstein, Claire (Artist)
719 Ocean Front Walk
Venice, CA 90291, USA

Falkman, Craig (Athlete, Hockey Player)
PO Box 1957
Gillette, WY 82717-1957, USA

Falkner, Keith (Musician)
Low Cottages Ilketshall Saint Margaraet
Bungay
Suffolk, UNITED KINGDOM (UK)

Fall, Jim (Actor)
c/o Staff Member *United Talent Agency (UTA)*
9336 Civic Center Dr
Beverly Hills, CA 90210, USA

Fall, Timothy (Actor)
Gersh Agency
232 N Canon Dr
Beverly Hills, CA 90210, USA

Falldin, Thorbjom (Prime Minister)
As 870 16 Ramvik
Ramvik 870 16, SWEDEN

Fallin, Mary (Governor, Politician)
Oklahoma State Capitol
2300 N Lincoln Blvd, Room 212
Oklahoma City, OK 73105, USA

Fallon, Bob (Athlete, Baseball Player)
1830 SW 81st Ave
Apt 4416
North Lauderdale, FL 33068-4253, USA

Fallon, Jimmy (Actor, Comedian, Talk Show Host)
c/o Eric Kranzler *Management 360*
9111 Wilshire Blvd
Beverly Hills, CA 90210, USA

Fallon, Tiffany (Model, Reality TV Star)
c/o Cheryl McLean *Creative Public Relations*
3385 Oak Glen Dr
Los Angeles, CA 90068, USA

Falloon, Pat (Athlete, Hockey Player)
112-155 10th St
Birtle, MB R0M 0C0, Canada

Fall Out Boy (Music Group)
c/o Bob McLynn *Crush Management*
60-62 E 11th St
7th Floor
New York, NY 10003, USA

Falls, Mike (Athlete, Football Player)
5831 Secrest Dr
Austin, TX 78759, USA

Faloona, Christopher J (Cinematographer)
138 Via La Soledad
Redondo Beach, CA 90277, USA

Falteisek, Steve (Athlete, Baseball Player)
12 Verbena Ave
Floral Park, NY 85248-4465, USA

Faltermayer, Harold (Composer)
Wasserburgerlandstrasse 16
Baldham 85598, Germany

Faltings, Gerd (Mathematician)
Princeton University
Mathematics Dept
Princeton, NJ 08544, USA

Faltskog, Agnetha (Musician)
Agnetha Faltskog Productions
Sodra Brobanken 41A
Stockholm 111 49, Sweden

Faludi, Susan C (Journalist)
1032 Irving St #204
San Francisco, CA 94122, USA

Falvey, Justin (Producer)
c/o Staff Member *Dreamworks Television*
100 Universal Plaza Bldg 5125
Universal City, CA 91608, USA

Fambrough, Charles (Musician)
Zane Mgmt
Bellvue
Broad & Walnut Sts
Philadelphia, PA 19102, USA

Fambrough, Henry (Music Group)
Buddy Allen Management
3750 Hudson Manor Terrace #3AG
Bronx, NY 10463, USA

Famiglietti, Mark (Actor)
c/o Robert Stein *Robert Stein Management*
PO Box 3797
Beverly Hills, CA 90212, USA

Famuyiwa, Rick (Director, Writer)
c/o Philip Raskind *WME (LA)*
9601 Wilshire Blvd Fl 3
Beverly Hills, CA 90210, USA

Fancher, Hampton (Director)
262 Old Topanga Cnyon
Topanga, CA 90290, USA

Fancy, Richard (Actor)
c/o Paul Kohner *Kohner Agency, The*
9300 Wilshire Blvd
Suite 555
Beverly Hills, CA 90212, USA

Faneca, Alan (Athlete, Football Player)
214 Friedrichs Ave
Metairie, LA 70005-4517, USA

Faneyte, Rikkert (Baseball Player)
San Francisco Giants
7408 E Osborn Rd
Scottsdale, AZ 85251 6424, USA

Fangio II, Juan Manuel (Race Car Driver)
All-American Racers
2334 S Broadway
Santa Ana, CA 92707, USA

Fankhauser, Merrell (Composer, Musician)
PO Box 1504
Arroyo Grande, CA 93421, USA

Fankhouser, Scott (Athlete, Hockey Player)
826 Alpine Dr
Jasper, GA 30143, USA

Fann, Al (Actor)
6051 Hollywood Blvd #207
Hollywood, CA 90028, USA

Fanning, Brent (Race Car Driver)
Udder Nonsense Racing
Rt. 4
Box 80
Stephenville, TX 76401, USA

Fanning, Dakota (Actor)
c/o JJ Harris *One Talent Management*
9220 Sunset Blvd
Los Angeles, CA 90069, USA

Fanning, Elle (Actor)
c/o Cindy Osbrink *Osbrink Talent Agency*
4343 Lankershim Blvd
Suite 100
Universal City, CA 91602, USA

Fanning, Jim (Commentator)
8-800 Commissioners Rd W
London, ON N6K 1C2 Canada, USA

Fanning, Jim (Athlete, Baseball Player, Coach)
154 Tiner Ave
Dorchester, ON N0L 1G2, Canada

Fanning, Michael L (Mike) (Athlete, Football Player)
7107 S Yale Ave # 330
Tulsa, OK 74136-6308, USA

Fanning, Neil (Actor)
c/o Staff Member *International Casting Service & Associates*
2/218 Crown St (via Kings Lane)
Darlinghurst NSW 2010, Australia

Fanning, Shawn (Business Person)
c/o Staff Member *Roxio Inc*
455 El Camino Real
Santa Clara, CA 95050, USA

Fannypack (Music Group)
Famous Celebrity Sound
29 John St
Suite 230
New York, NY 10038, USA

Fano, Robert M (Engineer, Scientist)
51 Woodland Way
North Chatham, MA 02650, USA

Fanok, Harry (Athlete, Baseball Player)
12373 Old State Rd
Chardon, OH 44024-9560, USA

Fansler, Stan (Athlete, Baseball Player)
32 Bunting Ln
Beckley, WV 25801-3656, USA

Fanta 4 (Music Group)
c/o Staff Member *Sony Music Entertainment Germany*
Neumarkter Str. 28
Muenchen 81673, Germany

Fante, Ricky (Musician)
c/o Staff Member *Virgin Records (NY)*
150 5th Ave
New York, NY 10010, USA

Fantetti, Ken (Athlete, Football Player)
1211 SE 175th Pl
Portland, OR 97233, USA

Fanucchi, Ledio (Athlete, Football Player)
5650 W Dakota Ave
Fresno, CA 93722-9749, USA

Fanucci, Mike (Athlete, Football Player)
1357 N Tercera Ave
Chandler, AZ 85226, USA

Fanzone, Carmen (Athlete, Baseball Player)
5114 Ranchito Ave
Sherman Oaks, CA 91423-1235, USA

Faracy, Stephanie (Actor)
8765 Lookout Mountain Road
Los Angeles, CA 90046, USA

Faraldo, Joe (Horse Racer)
12510 Queens Blvd Apt 1206
Kew Gardens, NY 11415-1528, USA

Faralla, Lillian (Athlete, Baseball Player, Commentator)
102 Antigua Ct
Coronado, CA 92118-3315, USA

Farar, Hassan Abshir (Prime Minister)
Prime Minister's Office
People's Palace
Mogadishy, SOMALIA

Farasopoulos, Chris (Athlete, Football Player)
195 Migues Mountain Ln
Aptos, CA 95003, USA

Farbar, Anne (Stylist)
c/o Staff Member *RJ Bennett Represents*
274 1st Ave
#8-E
New York, NY 10009, USA

Farber, Barry (Journalist)
2211 Broadway Apt 3A
New York, NY 10024-6264, USA

Farber, Enid (Photographer)
665 9th Ave Apt 2E
New York, NY 10036-3623, USA

Farber, Hap (Athlete, Football Player)
200 Dominican Dr
Madison, MS 39110, USA

Farber, Stacey (Actor)
c/o Yanick Landry *Newton-Landry Management*
19 Isabella St
Toronto ON M4Y 1M7, Canada

Farda, Richard (Athlete, Hockey Player)
Sonnenrain 10
Hor-gen, 8810 Switzerland

Far East Movement (Music Group, Musician)
c/o Staff Member *Stampede Management*
12530 Beatrice St
Los Angeles, CA 90066, USA

Faregalli, Lindy (Bowler)
113 N 5th Ave
Manville, NJ 08835, USA

Farenthold, Blake (Congressman, Politician)
2110 Rayburn HOB
Washington, DC 20515, USA

Farenthold, Frances T (Activist, Educator)
2929 Buffalo Speedway #18B
Houston, TX 77098, USA

Fares, Muhammad Ahmed Al (Cosmonaut)
PO Box 1272
Aleppo, SYRIA

Fargas, Antonio (Actor)
H David Moss
733 Seward St #PH
Los Angeles, CA 90038, USA

Fargas, Justin (Athlete, Football Player)
9839 Kessler Ave
Chatsworth, CA 91311-5506, USA

Fargis, Joe (Athlete, Horse Racer, Olympic Athlete)
11744 Marblestone Ct
Wellington, FL 33414-6041, USA

Fargo, Donna (Musician)
PO Box 210877
Nashville, TN 37221, USA

Fargo, Thomas B (Admiral)
Commander Pacific Fleet
Camp H M Smith
Honolulu, HI 96861, USA

Farha (Actor, Bollywood)
308 Dara Villa A B Nair Road
Juhu
Mumbai, MS 400049, INDIA

Farhadi, Asghar (Director)
c/o Keya Khayatian *United Talent Agency (UTA)*
9336 Civic Center Dr
Beverly Hills, CA 90210, USA

Faries, Paul (Athlete, Baseball Player)
3299 Beechwood Dr
Lafayette, CA 91423-1235, USA

Farina, Battista (Pinin) (Designer)
Pininarina SpA
Via Lesna 78
Turin
Grugliasco 10095, ITALY

Farina, David (Religious Leader)
Chrishtian Church of North America
41 Sherbrooke Road
Trenton, NJ 08638, USA

Farina, Dennis (Actor)
c/o Amy Guenther *Gateway Management Company Inc*
860 Via De La Paz
Suite F10
Pacific Palisades, CA 90272, USA

Farina, Johnny (Music Group)
Bellrose Music
308 E 6th St #13
New York, NY 10003, USA

Faris, Anna (Actor)
c/o Doug Wald *Anonymous Content (LA)*
3531 Hayden Ave
Culver City, CA 90232, USA

Faris, Sean (Actor)
c/o Dino May *Dino May Management*
6362 Hollywood Blvd #422
Hollywood, CA 90028-6323, USA

Faris, Valerie (Director, Producer)
Bob Industries
1313 5th St
Santa Monica, CA 90401, USA

Farish, William S (Diplomat)
US Embassy
Grosvenor Square 55 Upper Brook St
London W1A 2LQ, UNITED KINGDOM (UK)

Fariss, Monty (Athlete, Baseball Player)
P.O. Box 1854
Weatherford, OK 73096, USA

Fariss Montv, Montv
PO Box 249
Leedev, OK 73654-0249, USA

Farkas, Bertalan (Astronaut, Misc)
A Magyar Koztarsasag Kutato Urhajosa
Pf 25
Budapest 1885, HUNGARY

Farkas, Ferenc (Composer)
Nagyatai Utca 12
Budapest 1026, HUNGARY

Farkas, Jeff (Athlete, Hockey Player)
284 Patrice Ter
Buffalo, NY 14221, USA

Farley, Bob (Athlete, Baseball Player)
1325 Sycamore Rd
Montoursville, PA 17754-9511, USA

Farley, Carole (Music Group, Opera Singer)
270 Riverside Dr
New York, NY 10025, USA

Farley, Dale (Athlete, Football Player)
1048 Mount Carmel Church Rd
Sparta, TN 38583-5203, USA

Farley, David (Writer)
c/o Staff Member *Morra Brezner Steinberg & Tenenbaum (MBST) Entertainment*
345 N Maple Dr
Suite 200
Beverly Hills, CA 90210, USA

Farley, Dick (Athlete, Football Player)
117 Candlewood Dr
Williamstown, MA 01267-2973, USA

Farley, Jenni (JWoww) (Reality TV Star)
c/o Michael (Mike) Esterman
Esterman.Com, LLC
Prefers to be contacted via email
MD, USA

Farley, Lillian
84 Kenneth Ave.
Huntington, NY 11743

Farm, Ali (Athlete)
PO Box 160
Berrien Springs, MI 49103-0160

Farman, Melissa (Actor)
c/o Staff Member *Prodigy Talent Group*
Prefers to be contacted by telephone or email
Beverly Hills, CA, USA

Farmar, Jordan (Athlete, Basketball Player)
172 Middlesex Ave
Englewood Cliffs, NJ 07632-1532, USA

Farmer, Art
49 E. 96th St.
New York, NY 10128

Farmer, Billy (Baseball Player)
18987 E Wilshire Blvd
Jones, OK 73049, USA

Farmer, Danny (Athlete, Football Player)
332 Lorraine Blvd
Los Angeles, CA 90020, USA

Farmer, Dave (Athlete, Football Player)
141 Via Medici
Aptos, CA 95003, USA

Farmer, Ed (Athlete, Baseball Player)
4581 Camino Del Sol
Calabasas, CA 91302-3836, USA

Farmer, Ed (Athlete)
333 West 35th St
Chicago, IL 60616

Farmer, Evan (Actor, Television Host)
c/o Robert Attermann *Abrams Artists Agency (LA)*
9200 Sunset Blvd
11th Floor
Los Angeles, CA 90069, USA

Farmer, Gary (Actor)
c/o Staff Member *Gonzo Dr. Records*
P.O. Box 31096
Santa Fe, NM 87394, USA

Farmer, George (Athlete, Football Player)
332 Lorraine Blvd
Los Angeles, CA 90020, USA

Farmer, George III (Athlete, Football Player)
12422 S Denker Ave
Los Angeles, CA 90047, USA

Farmer, Howard (Athlete, Baseball Player)
1675 W 10th Pl
Gary, IN 70065-5810, USA

Farmer, James (Athlete, Basketball Player)
214 Ashborough Circle
Donthan, AL 36301-1267, USA

Farmer, John Jr (Ex-Governor)
Rutgers School Of Law-Newark
123 Washington St
Newark, NJ 07102, USA

Farmer, Mike (Athlete, Basketball Player, Coach)
2520 Lakeview Drive
Santa Rosa, CA 95405-8657, USA

Farmer, Mimsy (Actor)
Cineart
36 Rue de Ponthieu
Paris 75008, FRANCE

Farmer, Richard G (Doctor)
9126 Town Gate Lane
Bethesda, MD 20817, USA

Farmer, Robert (Athlete, Football Player)
481 Bergen Ave
Jersey City, NJ 07304-2416, USA

Farmiga, Vera (Actor)
c/o Jon Rubinstein *Authentic Talent and Literary Management*
45 Main St
Suite 1004
Brooklyn, NY 11201, USA

Farner, Donald S (Biologist, Physicist)
University of Washington
Zoology Dept
Seattle, WA 98195, USA

Farner, Mark (Music Group, Musician)
Bobby Roberts
P O Box 1547
Goodlettsville, TN 37070, USA

Farnham, John (Musician)
Box 6500 St. Kilda Rd.
Central Melbourne, AUSTRALIA 3004

Farnham, John P (Music Group)
TalentWorks
663 Victoria St
Abbottsford, VIC 3067, AUSTRALIA

Farnon, Shannon
12743 Milbank St.
Studio City, CA 91604

Farnsworth, Jeff (Athlete, Baseball Player)
704 50th Ave W
Bradenton, FL 37064, USA

Farnsworth, Kyle (Athlete, Baseball Player)
1400 Stickley Ave
Kissimmee, FL 34747-4024, USA

Faro, Michele (Stylist)
c/o Staff Member *Art Department*
48 Greene St
4th Floor
New York, NY 10013, USA

Farquhar, John W (Doctor)
Stanford University
Med School
Disease Prevention Center
Stanford, CA 94305, USA

Farquhar, Marilyn G (Biologist, Misc)
12894 Via Latina
Del Mar 92014, USA

Farquhar, Robert W (Scientist)
Johns Hopkins University
Applied Physics Laboratory
Laurel, MD 20723, USA

Farr, Bruce (Architect)
Bruce Farr Assoc
613 3rd St
Annapolis, MD 21403, USA

Farr, Diane (Actor)
c/o Josh Katz *United Talent Agency (UTA)*
9336 Civic Center Dr
Beverly Hills, CA 90210, USA

Farr, Dmarco (Athlete, Football Player)
2175 Del Monte Dr
San Pablo, CA 94806, USA

Farr, Felicia (Actor)
1143 Tower Road
Beverly Hills, CA 90210, USA

Farr, Jaime (Actor)
2316 Delaware Ave
Suite 266
Buffalo, NY 14216-2687, USA

Farr, Jamie (Actor)
53 Ranchero Rd
Bell Canyon, CA 91307, USA

Farr, Jim (Athlete, Baseball Player)
3 Tyndal Ct
Williamsburg, VA 23188-1552, USA

Farr, Kendall (Stylist)
c/o Staff Member *Judy Casey Inc*
114 E 13th St
New York, NY 10003, USA

Farr, Kimberly (Actor)
Tisherman Agency
6767 Forest Lawn Dr #101
Los Angeles, CA 90068, USA

Farr, Mel Jr (Athlete, Football Player)
4525 Lakeview Ct
Bloomefield Hills, MI 48301, USA

Farr, Melvin (Mel) Sr (Athlete, Football
Player)
10550 W 8 Mile Rd
Ferndale, MI 48220, USA

Farr, Michael (Athlete, Football Player)
3950 Paran Ridge NW
Atlanta, GA 30327, USA

Farr, Miller (Athlete, Football Player)
11815 Rowood Dr
Houston, TX 77070-5349, USA

Farr, Norman (Rocky) (Athlete, Hockey
Player)
3850 Overton Park Dr W
Fort Worth, TX 76109, USA

Farr, Sam (Congressman, Politician)
1124' Longworth HOB
Washington, DC 20515, USA

Farragut, Ken (Athlete, Football Player)
11 Ladoga Ave
Tampa, FL 33606-3803, USA

Farrakhan, Louis (Religious Leader)
Nation of Islam
734 W 79th St
Chicago, IL 60620, USA

Farrar, Brian Major (General)
12 4th Artillery Rd
Fort Leavenworth, KS 66027, USA

Farrar, Frank L (Politician)
203 Ninth Avenue
Britton, SD 57430, USA

Farrel, Franklin (Athlete, Hockey Player)
89 Notch Hill Road
Apt 223
North Branford, CT 06471, USA

Farrell, Christopher (Musician)
c/o Mike Rosen *Working Artists Agency*
13525 Ventura Blvd
Sherman Oaks, CA

Farrell, Colin (Actor)
c/o Danica Smith *PMK/BNC Public
Relations (PMK-LA)*
8687 Melrose Ave Fl 8
West Hollywood, CA 90069, USA

Farrell, Dave (Musician)
7 Sawgrass
Trabuco Canyon, CA 92679, USA

Farrell, John (Athlete, Baseball Player)
31009 Wilderness Trl
Westlake, OH 33767-8519, USA

Farrell, Mike (Actor)
3950 Paran Rdg NW
Atlanta, GA 30327-3030, USA

Farrell, Paul (Athlete, Football Player)
P.O. Box 804
Dennis Port, MA 02639, USA

Farrell, Perry (Musician)
c/o Rod MacSween *International Talent
Booking*
74A Charlotte St
London W1T 4QJ, UNITED KINGDOM
(UK)

Farrell, Sean (Athlete, Football Player)
17754 Esprit Dr
Tampa, FL 33647, USA

Farrell, Sharon (Actor)
360 S Doheny Dr
Beverly Hills, CA 90211, USA

Farrell, Shea (Actor)
Artists Agency
1180 S Beverly Dr #301
Los Angeles, CA 90035, USA

Farrell, Suzanne (Ballerina)
Kennedy Center for Performing Arts
Education Dept
Washington, DC 20566, USA

Farrell, Terence (Terry) (Architect)
17 Hatton St
London NW8 8PL, UNITED KINGDOM
(UK)

Farrell, Terry (Actor)
Don Buchwald
6500 Wilshire Blvd #2200
Los Angeles, CA 90048, USA

Farrelly, Bobby (Director, Producer,
Writer)
c/o David O'Connor *Creative Artists
Agency (CAA-LA)*
2000 Ave Of The Stars
Los Angeles, CA 90067, USA

Farrelly, Peter (Director, Producer, Writer)
c/o BeBe Lerner *ID Public Relations
(ID-LA)*
7060 Hollywood Blvd
8th Floor
Los Angeles, CA 90028, USA

Farren, Paul (Athlete, Football Player)
21 Gammons Rd
Cohasset, MA 02025, USA

Farrer, Kathy (Athlete, Golfer)
4815 Westgrove Dr #301
Addison, TX 75001, USA

Farrimond, Richard A (Athlete, Baseball
Player)
Metra Marconi Center
Gunnels Wood Rd Stevenage
Herts, Kittv Hawk 27949-3522, UNITED
KINGDOM (UK)

Farrimond, Richard Major (Astronaut)
Paradigm Secure Communications
Gunnels Wood Road Stevenage
Hertfordshire SGl 2AS, England

Farrington, Amy
c/o Staff Member *Meghan Schumacher
Management*
13351-D Riverside Dr #387
Sherman Oaks, CA 91423, USA

Farrington, Richard (Horse Racer)
32 Spring St
Wallington, NJ 07057-2045, USA

Farrington, Robert (Horse Racer)
105 Country Pl
Sanford, FL 32771-6502, USA

Farrington, Robert G (Bob) (Race Car
Driver)
201 Lake Hinsdale Dr #211
Willowbrook, IL 60527, USA

Farrior, James (Athlete, Football Player)
1004 Summerset Dr
Pittsburgh, PA 15217, USA

Farris, Dionne (Music Group)
c/o Staff Member *Creative Artists Agency
(CAA-LA)*
2000 Ave Of The Stars
Los Angeles, CA 90067, USA

Farris, Jerome
US Court of Appeals
US Courthouse 1010 5th Ave
Seattle, WA 98104, USA

Farris, Joseph (Cartoonist)
16 Long Meadow Ln
Bethel, CT 06801-2612, USA

Farris, Kris (Athlete, Football Player)
24 Allbrook Ct
Ladera Ranch, CA 92694-0246, USA

Farris, Rachel (Musician)
c/o Staff Member *Logic House Media*
3123 Traviston Dr
Franklin, TN 37064-6218, USA

Farrish, Dave (Athlete, Hockey Player)
Anaheim Ducks 2695 E Katella Ave
Attn Coaching Staff
Anaheim, CA 92806-5904, USA

Farriss, Andrew (Music Group)
8 Hayes St #1
Neutral Bay, NSW 20891, AUSTRALIA

Farriss, Jon (Music Group, Musician)
8 Hayes St #1
Neutral Bay, NSW 20891, AUSTRALIA

Farriss, Tim (Music Group, Musician)
8 Hayes St #1
Neutral Bay, NSW 20891, AUSTRALIA

Farrow, Mallory (Actor)
Hervey/Grimes
PO Box 64249
Los Angeles, CA 90064, USA

Farrow, Mia (Actor)
c/o Judy Hofflund *Hofflund/Polone*
9465 Wilshire Blvd #420
Beverly Hills, CA 90212, USA

Farrow, Yvonne (Actor)
Geddes Agency
8430 Santa Monica Blvd Ste 200
West Hollywood, CA 90069, USA

Farrow-Rapp, Elizabeth (Baseball Player)
1200 E Partridge St Unit 25A
Metamora, IL 61548-9360, USA

Farulli, Piero (Musician)
Via G D'Annunzio 153
Florence, ITALY

Farwig, Stephanie (Athlete, Golfer)
2308 E Taro Ln
Phoenix, AZ 85024-2416, USA

Faryniarz, Brett (Athlete, Football Player)
1021 S Patrick Way
Anaheim, CA 92808, USA

Fasano, John (Actor, Director, Producer,
Writer)
c/o Craig Baumgarten *Baumgarten
Management*
11925 Wilshire Blvd
Suite 310
Los Angeles, CA 90025, USA

Fasano, Sal (Athlete, Baseball Player)
905 Catherine Gin
Minooka, IL 60447-4528, USA

Fash, Robert (General)
41 Rosewood Dr
Hawthorn Woods, IL 60047-7729, USA

Fashoway, Gord (Athlete, Hockey Player)
3131 SE 167th Ave
Portland, OR 97236, USA

Fasman, Gerald D (Biologist)
180 Wells Ave #106
Newton Center, MA 02459-3328, USA

Fass, Horst (Journalist, Photographer)
12 Norwich St
London EC4A, UNITED KINGDOM (UK)

Fassbaender, Brigitte (Opera Singer)
Am Theater
Braunschweig 38100, GERMANY

Fassbender, Michael (Actor)
c/o Conor McCaughan *Troika*
74 Clerkenwell Rd
3rd Floor
London EC1M 5QA, United Kingdom

Fassel, Jim (Athlete, Coach, Football
Coach, Football Player)
345 N Quentin Rd 100
Palatine, IL 60067, USA

Fassero, Jeff (Athlete, Baseball Player)
9841 N 56th St
Paradise Valley, AZ 85253-1108, USA

Fast, Darcy (Athlete, Baseball Player)
2981 Harrison Ave
Centralia, WA 98531-9356, USA

Fast, Darrell (Religious Leader)
Mennonite Church General Conference
P O Box 347
Newton, KS 67114, USA

Fast, Larry (Composer, Musician)
Polydor Records
70 Universal City Plaza
Universal City, CA 91608, USA

Faszholz, Jack (Athlete, Baseball Player)
18338 Maries Road 308
Belle, MO 65013-2125, USA

Faszhotz, Jack (Athlete, Baseball Player)
18338 Maries Road 308
Belle, MO 65013, USA

Fatafehi, Mario (Athlete, Football Player)
279 W 1360 N
American Fork, UT 84003-2739

Fatboy Slim (Musician)
c/o David Levy *WmE2 (WMA-UK)*
103 New Oxford St
London WC1A 1DD, UK

Fatefehi, Mario (Athlete, Football Player)
279 W 1360 N
American Fork, UT 84003, USA

Fatel, Mitch (Musician)
c/o Staff Member *Paradigm (Monterey)*
404 W Franklin St
Monterey, CA 93940, USA

Fath, Farah (Actor)
c/o Kurt Patino *Rothman / Patino / Andres
Entertainment*
4370 Tujunga Ave
Suite 120
Studio City, CA 91604, USA

Fat Joe (Actor, Musician)
1203 NW 121st Ave
Plantation, FL 33323, USA

Fatone, Joey Jr (Dancer, Musician)
c/o Joe Mulvihill *LiveWire Entertainment*
100 Universal Studios Plaza
Bldg 22 A, Suite 255
Orlando, FL 32819, USA

Fattah, Chaka (Congressman, Politician)
2301 Rayburn HOB
Washington, DC 20515, USA

Faubert, Mario (Athlete, Hockey Player)
4 Ch du Canal RR 1
St-Stanislaus De Kost, QC J0S 1W0,
Canada

Faucette, Chuck (Athlete, Football Player)
4117 Hobnail Dr
Saint Charles, MO 63304-2317, USA

Faucette, Mark (Athlete, Hockey Player)
1100 Haley Ln
Dunedin, FL 34698-6120, USA

Faucher, William (Horse Racer)
42 Old Stage Rd
Hinsdale, NH 03451-2308, USA

Fauci, Anthony S (Doctor)
3012 43rd St NW
Washington, DC 20016, USA

Faucon, Bernard (Photographer)
6 Rue Barbanegre
Paris 75019, FRANCE

Faulconer, Martha (Athlete, Golfer)
374 Stratford Dr
Lexington, KY 40503, USA

Faulk, Amy (Race Car Driver)
Hypertech Inc
1215 Appling Rd.
Bartlett, TN 38135, USA

Faulk, Kevin (Athlete, Football Player)
190 Summer St
South Walpole, MA 02071, USA

Faulk, Marshall (Athlete, Football Player)
6430 Clayton Rd
Apt 305
Saint Louis, MO 63117, USA

Faulk, Trev (Athlete, Football Player)
307 Martin Oaks Dr
Lafayette, LA 70501, USA

Faulkner, Alex (Athlete, Hockey Player)
17 Adams Ave
Bishops Falls, NL A0H 1C0, Canada

Faulkner, Chris (Athlete, Football Player)
1596 E 400 S
Tipton, IN 46072, USA

Faulkner, Eric (Musician)
27 Preston Grange
Preston Pans E
Lothian, SCOTLAND

Faulkner, Jeff (Athlete, Football Player)
14150 Carlton Dr
Davie, FL 33330-4659, USA

Faulkner, John (Scientist)
Scripps Institution of Oceanography
La Jolla, CA 92093, USA

Faumui, Taase (Athlete, Football Player)
1574 Linapuni St
Honolulu, HI 96819, USA

Faure, Maurice H (Government Official)
28 Blvd Raspail
Paris 75007, FRANCE

Fauria, Christian (Athlete, Football Player)
1908 SE Abbey St
Blue Springs, MO 64014, USA

Fauser, Mark (Actor)
c/o Staff Member United Talent Agency
(UTA)
9336 Civic Center Dr
Beverly Hills, CA 90210, USA

Fauss, Ted (Athlete, Hockey Player)
6861 Lowell Rd
Rome, NY 13440, USA

Faust, Andre (Athlete, Hockey Player)
250 Heritage Rd
Cherry Hill, NJ 08034-3150, USA

Faust, August (Athlete, Hockey Player)
250 Heritage Rd.
Cherry Hill, NJ 08034-3150, USA

Faust, Chad (Actor)
c/o Evan Hainey Untitled Entertainment
(LA)
350 S. Beverly Dr #200
Beverly Hills, CA 90212, USA

Faust, Paul (Athlete, Football Player)
5522 Highwood Dr W
Minneapolis, MN 55436, USA

Faust, Paul (Athlete, Football Player)
5522 Highwood Dr W
Minneapolis, MN 55436-1227, USA

Faustino, David (Actor)
17201 Parthenia St
Northridge, CA 91325, USA

Faut-Eastman, Jean (Athlete, Baseball
Player, Commentator)
406 Warrington Pl
Rock Hill, SC 29732-7408, USA

Fauts, Dan
4020 Murphy Canyon Rd.
San Diego, CA 92123-4407

Fauza, Dario (Doctor, Misc)
Harvard Medical School
25 Shattuck St
Boston, MA 02115, USA

Favell, Doug (Athlete, Hockey Player)
8 Captain Tenbrock Terr
St Catharines, ON L2W 1B2, CANADA

Favier, Jean-Jacques (Misc)
Technologies Avances
17 Ave des Martys
Grenoble Cedex 38054, FRANCE

Favier, Jean-Jacques Dr (Astronaut)
20 rue Jeanne Marvig
Toulouse 31400, France

Favino, Pierfrancesco (Actor)
c/o Tammy Rosen Sanders Armstrong
Caserta
425 N Robertson Blvd
Los Angeles, CA 90048, USA

Favor, Mike (Athlete, Football Player)
8409 Shadow Creek Dr
Osseo, MN 55311-1570, USA

Favor-Hamilton, Suzy (Athlete, Olympic
Athlete, Track Athlete)
1014 Beloit Ct
Madison, WI 53705-2233

Favors, Gregory (Athlete, Football Player)
230 Merritt Dr
Roswell, GA 30076-3936, USA

Favre, Brett L (Athlete, Football Player)
1 Willow Bend Dr
Hattiesburg, MS 39402-8552, USA

Favreau, Jon (Actor, Writer)
c/o Ina Treciokas Slate Public Relations
9000 Sunset Blvd #915
West Hollywood, CA 90069, USA

Fawcett, Don W (Doctor, Misc)
3710 American Way
Apt 325
Missoula, MT 59808-1927, USA

Fawcett, John (Director)
c/o Scott Yoselow Gersh (NY)
41 Madison Ave
New York, NY 10010, USA

Fawcett, Joy (Athlete, Olympic Athlete,
Soccer Player)
11 Calle Marta Rancho
Santa Margarita, CA 92688-3500, USA

Fawcett, Sherwood L (Physicist, Scientist)
1852 Riverside Dr #A
Columbus, OH 43212, USA

Faxon Jr, Brad (Athlete, Golfer)
c/o Staff Member Pro Golfers Association
(PGA) Tour
112 TPC Blvd
Ponte Vedra Beach, FL 32082, USA

Fay, David B (Golfer)
US Golf Assn
Golf House
Liberty Corner Road
Far Hills, NJ 07931, USA

Fay, Meagan (Actor)
c/o Staff Member Paradigm (LA)
360 N Crescent Dr
North Bldg
Beverly Hills, CA 90210, USA

Fay, Meagen (Actor)
c/o Staff Member Main Title Entertainment
8383 Wilshire Blvd
Suite 408
Los Angeles, CA 90211, USA

Fay, Peter T (Judge)
US Court of Appeals
99 NE 4th St
Miami, FL 33132, USA

Faydoedeelay (Music Group, Musician)
Q Prime
729 7th Ave #1600
New York, NY 10019, USA

Fayed, Mohamed al- (Business Person)
Craven Cottage Stevenage Road
Fulham
London SW6 6HH, UNITED KINGDOM
(UK)

Fazande, Jermaine (Athlete, Football
Player)
460 Wilson St
Marrero, LA 70072-1124, USA

Fazio, Ernie (Athlete, Baseball Player)
2310 Royal Oaks Dr
Alamo, CA 94507-2223, USA

Fazio, Ernie
2310 Royal Oaks Dr.
Alamo, CA 94507

Fazio, Tom (Architect, Golfer)
Fazio Golf Course Designers
401 N Main St #400
Hendersonville, NV 28792, USA

Fazzini, Enrico (Doctor)
New York University
Medical Center
550 1st Ave
New York, NY 10016, USA

F. Bass, Charles (Congressman, Politician)
2350 Rayburn HOB
Washington, DC 20515, USA

F. Costello, Jerry (Congressman,
Politician)
2408 Rayburn HOB
Washington, DC 20515, USA

F. Doyle, Michael (Congressman,
Politician)
401 Cannon HOB
Washington, DC 20515, USA

Feacher, Ricky (Athlete, Football Player)
1522 Ferman Ave
Cleveland, OH 44109-3642, USA

Feagles, Jeff (Athlete, Football Player)
219 Sunset Ave
Ridgewood, NJ 07450-2420, USA

Feamster, Dave (Athlete, Hockey Player)
1058 S May Valley Dr
Pueblo, CO 81007, USA

Feamster, Tom (Athlete, Football Player)
1805 Virginia Ct
Tavares, FL 32778-2135, USA

Fear Before (Music Group, Musician)
c/o Staff Member Equal Vision Records
P.O. Box 38202
Albany, NY 12203-8202, USA

Fearnley-Whittingstall, Hugh (Chef)
c/o Staff Member BBC Artist Mail
PO Box 1116
Belfast BT2 7AJ, United Kingdom

Fearon, Douglas T (Doctor, Misc)
Wellcome Trust Immunology Unit
Hills Road
Cambridge CB2 2SP, UNITED KINGDOM
(UK)

Fears, Willie (Athlete, Football Player)
1414 S Summit St
Little Rock, AR 72202-5821, USA

Feaster, Allison (Basketball Player)
Charlotte Sting
100 Hive Dr
Charlotte, NC 28217, USA

Featherston, Katie (Actor)
c/o Jillian Fowkes ID Public Relations
(ID-LA)
7060 Hollywood Blvd
8th Floor
Los Angeles, CA 90028, USA

Featherstone, Glen (Athlete, Hockey
Player)
8 Larrabee Ave
Danvers, MA 01960, USA

Featherstone, Tony (Athlete, Hockey
Player)
Allstate Insurance Agency
3003 Danforth Ave
Danforth Shoppers World #9
Toronto, ON M4C 1M9, CANADA

Febles, Carlos (Athlete, Baseball Player,
Coach)
Lancaster Jethawks
45116 Valley Central
Attn: Coaching Staff
Lancaster, CA 01854-3602, USA

Feck, Luke M (Editor)
6880 Worthington Road
Westerville, OH 43082, USA

Fedderly, Bernie (Race Car Driver)
John Force Racing
22722 Old Canal Rd.
Yorba Linda, CA 92887-4602, USA

Federer, Mike (Race Car Driver)
Mike Federer Racing
23210 54th St. E.
Buckley, WA 98321, USA

Federer, Roger (Athlete, Tennis Player)
Postfach
Bottmingen CH-4103, Switzerland

Federico, Anthony (Athlete, Football Player)
12306 Van Nuys Blvd
Sylmar, CA 91342, USA

Federico, Creig (Athlete, Football Player)
24224 Leski Ln
Plainfield, IL 60585-2782, USA

Federko, Bernie (Athlete, Hockey Player)
2219 Devonsbrook Dr
Chesterfield, MO 63005, USA

Federko, Bernie (Athlete, Hockey Player)
St Louis Blues 1401 Clark Ave
Attn Broadcast Dept
Saint Louis, MO 63103-2700, USA

Federline, Kevin (Actor, Choreographer, Musician)
Dmand Entertainment
1777 Westwood Blvd Ste 200
Los Angeles, CA 90024, USA

Federov, Sergei (Athlete, Hockey Player)
1865 Huntingwood Ln
Boomfield Hills, MI 48304, USA

Federspiel, Joe (Athlete, Football Player)
2016 Lakeside Dr
Lexington, KY 40502, USA

Fedewa, Tim (Race Car Driver)
4403 Stough Rd.
Concord, NC 28027, USA

Fedor, Dave (Athlete, Basketball Player)
4510 Audubon Avenue
De leon Springs, FL 32130-3033

Fedorov, Sergei (Athlete, Hockey Player)
1975 Tiverton Rd
Bloomfield Hills, MI 48304-2348, USA

Fedoruk, Paul (Athlete, Hockey Player)
4578 Liam Dr
Frisco, TX 75034, USA

Fedoruk, Sylvia (Scientist)
49 Simpson Cres
Saskatoon SK S7H 3C5, Canada

Fedoruk, Todd (Athlete, Hockey Player)
4578 Liam Dr
Frisco, TX 75034-2139, USA

Fedoseyev, Vladimir I
Moscow House of Recording
Kachalova 24
Moscow 121069, RUSSIA

Fedotenko, Ruslan (Athlete, Hockey Player)
230 W 56th St #54E
New York, NY 10019, USA

Fedotov, Maxim V (Musician)
Tolbukhin Str 8 #6
Moscow 121596, RUSSIA

F. Edwards, Donna (Congressman, Politician)
318 Cannon HOB
Washington, DC 20515, USA

Fedyk, Brent (Athlete, Hockey Player)
1741 Holland St
Birmingham, MI 48009-7804, USA

Fee, Melinda (Actor)
145 S Fairfax Ave #310
Los Angeles, CA 90036, USA

Feeder (Music Group)
Feeder Central
PO Box 2539
London W1A 3HZ, UNITED KINGDOM

Feehery, Gerry (Athlete, Football Player)
5 Sharpless Ln
Media, PA 19063, USA

Feehily, Mark (Musician)
c/o Staff Member *Solo Agency Ltd (UK)*
55 Fulham High St
2nd Floor
London SW6 3JJ, United Kingdom

Feeley, A J (Athlete, Football Player)
477 Zuni Or
Del Mar, CA 92014-2445, USA

Feely, Jay (Athlete, Football Player)
7808 River Ridge Dr
Temple Terrace, FL 33637-4933, USA

Feeney, Joe
32630 Concord Dr.
Madison Heights, MI 48071

Fegan, Roshon (Actor, Musician)
c/o Bonnie Liedtke *Principato/Young Management*
9465 Wilshire Blvd
Suite 430
Beverly Hills, CA 90212, USA

Fegley, Richard (Photographer)
Playboy Magazine
Reader Services 680 N Lake Shore Dr
Chicago, IL 60611, USA

Fegley, Jr., Don (Race Car Driver)
RD 1
Box 148-J
New Ringgold, PA 17960, USA

Feher, George (Physicist)
University of California
Physics Dept 9500 Gilman Dr
La Jolla, CA 92093, USA

Feher, Raymond (Athlete, Basketball Player)
62 Cool Springs Road
Signal Mountain, TN 37377-2075, USA

Feherty, David (Athlete, Golfer)
6422 Prestonshire Ln
Dallas, TX 75225-2309, USA

Fehr, Brendan (Actor)
c/o Staff Member *ROAR (LA)*
9701 Wilshire Blvd
8th Floor
Los Angeles, CA 90212, USA

Fehr, Donald (Commentator)
34 Rockinghorse Trl
Rve Brook, NY 10573-1038, USA

Fehr, Oded (Actor)
c/o Wendy Murphey *IFA Talent Agency*
8730 Sunset Blvd
Suite 490
Los Angeles, CA 90069, USA

Fehr, Rick (Athlete, Golfer)
2869 W Haley Dr
Anthem, AZ 85086, USA

Fehr, Steve (Bowler)
1329 Castlebridge Ct
Cincinnati, OH 45233-5214, USA

Fehrenbach, Charles M (Astronomer)
Les Magnanarelles
Lourmarin 84160, FRANCE

Feick, Jamie (Athlete, Basketball Player)
3 Township Road 200
Centerburg, OH 43011-9674, USA

Feierabend, Ryan (Athlete, Baseball Player)
366 Windsor Dr
Elyria, OH 95670-6190, USA

Feiffer, Jules (Cartoonist, Writer)
PO Box 373
Southampton, NY 11969-0373, USA

Feig, Paul (Actor, Director)
c/o Renee Kurtz *Creative Artists Agency (CAA-LA)*
2000 Ave Of The Stars
Los Angeles, CA 90067, USA

Feige, Kevin (Producer)
Marvel Studios
9242 Beverly Blvd
Suite 350
Beverly Hills, CA 90210, USA

Feigenbaum, Armand V (Business Person, Engineer)
General Systems
23 South St #250
Pittsfield, MA 01201, USA

Feigenbaum, Edward A (Scientist)
1017 Cathcart Way
Stanford, CA 94305, USA

Feightner, Edward (General)
1653 32nd St NW
Washington, DC 20007-2931, USA

Feilden, Bernard M (Architect)
Stiffkey Old Hall
Wells-next-to-the-Sea
Norfolk NR23 1QJ, UNITED KINGDOM (UK)

Feinberg, Alan (Musician)
Cramer/Marder Artists
3436 Springhill Road
Lafayette, CA 94549, USA

Feinberg, Wilfred (Judge)
US Court of Appeals
US Courthouse Foley Square
New York, NY 10007, USA

Feingold, Russell (Politician)
7114 Donna Dr
Middleton, WI 53562-1709, USA

Feinstein, A Richard (Doctor, Physicist)
1760 2nd Ave #32C
New York, NY 10128, USA

Feinstein, Dianne (Politician)
c/o Staff Member *United States Senate (Hart Office)*
316 Hart Senate Office Building
Washington, DC 20510, USA

Feinstein, Jeffrey (General)
10 Whisperwood Ct
Dalzell, SC 29040-9671, USA

Feinstein, Michael (Music Group, Musician)
4647 Kingswell Ave #110
Los Angeles, CA 90027, USA

Feitle, Dave (Athlete, Basketball Player)
442 Martel Ln
Coppell, TX 75019-7592, USA

Fekkai, Frederic (Stylist)
Frederic Fekkai Salon
444 N Rodeo Dr
Beverly Hills, CA 90210, USA

Felashia
PO Box 31734
Tucson, AZ 87571

Felber, Dean (Music Group, Musician)
FishCo Mgmt
P O Box 5456
Columbia, SC 29250, USA

Felch, William C (Doctor, Physicist)
8545 Carmel Valley Road
Carmel, CA 93923, USA

Feld, Eliot (Choreographer, Dancer)
Feld Ballet
890 Broadway #800
New York, NY 10003, USA

Feldenkrais, Moshe (Doctor, Misc)
University of Tel-Aviv
Psychology Dept
Tel-Aviv, ISRAEL

Felder, Benny (Athlete, Baseball Player)
5012 N 39th St
Tampa, FL 33610, USA

Felder, Don (Musician)
PO Box 6051
Malibu, CA 90264, USA

Felder, Kenny (Athlete, Baseball Player)
2902 W Amberwood Dr
Phoenix, AZ 85045-2289, USA

Felder, Mike (Athlete, Baseball Player)
322 S 17th St
Richmond, CA 94804-2606, USA

Felder, Raoul Lionel (Attorney)
437 Madison Ave
New York, NY 10022-7030, USA

Feldhausen, Paul (Athlete, Football Player)
W137S6949 Clarendon Pl
Muskego, WI 53150, USA

Feldman, Bella (Artist)
12 Summit Lane
Berkeley, CA 94708, USA

Feldman, Ben (Actor)
c/o Michael Baum *Impression Entertainment*
9229 W Sunset Blvd #700
West Hollywood, CA 90069, USA

Feldman, Corey (Actor)
c/o Staff Member *Scott Carlson Entertainment*
5739 Bucknell Ave
Valley Village, CA 91607, USA

Feldman, Ed
7700 Wisconsin Ave
Bethesda, MD 20814

Feldman, Jerome M (Doctor, Physicist)
2744 Sevier St
Durham, NC 27705, USA

Feldman, Marty (Athlete, Football Player)
100 Louise Ct
Los Gatos, CA 95032-1608, USA

Feldman, Michelle (Bowler)
Gary Feldman
P O Box 713
Skaneateles, NY 13152, USA

Feldman, Myer (Government Official)
Ginsberg Feldman Bress
1250 Connecticut Ave NW
Washington, DC 20036, USA

Feldman, Sandra (Misc)
American Federation of Teachers
555 New Jersey Ave NW
Washington, DC 20001, USA

Feldman, Scott (Athlete, Baseball Player)
2848 Woodside St Apt 302
Dallas, TX 75204-2587, USA

Feldman, Tamara (Actor)
c/o John Pierce *The Group*
800 South Robertson Blvd
Suite 5
Los Angeles, CA 90035, USA

Feldmann, Marc (Doctor, Misc)
Charing Cross Hospital
Saint Dunstan's Road
London W6 8RP, UNITED KINGDOM
(UK)

Feldon, Barbara (Actor, Model)
14 E 74th St
New York, NY 10021, USA

Feldott, Jennifer (Athlete, Golfer)
P.O. Box 359
Glenn, MI 49416-0359, USA

Feldshuh, Tovah S (Actor)
c/o Staff Member *Brookside Artists
Management (NY)*
250 W 57th St
Suite 2303
New York, NY 10107, USA

Feldstein, Martin (Economist, Government
Official)
147 Clifton St
Belmont, MA 02478, USA

Felici, Angelo Cardinal (Religious Leader)
Piazza della Citta Leonina 9
Rome 00193, ITALY

Feliciano, Jose (Musician)
c/o John Reilly *Rogers & Cowan PR (LA)*
Pacific Design Center
8687 Melrose Ave, 7th Floor
West Hollywood, CA 90069, USA

Felipe (Prince)
Palacio de la Zarzuela
Madrid 28080, SPAIN

Felix, Allyson (Athlete, Olympic Athlete)
c/o Staff Member *Octagon (VA)*
7100 Forest Ave #201
Richmond, VA 23226, USA

Felix, Junior (Athlete, Baseball Player)
7545 Treadway Rd
Gresham, SC 29546-4210, USA

Felix the Cat
12020 Chandler Blvd. #200
No. Hollywood, CA 91607

Felke, Petra (Athlete, Track Athlete)
SC Motor Jena
Wollnitzevstr 42
Jena 07749, GERMANY

Felker, Gene (Athlete, Football Player)
945 N Pasadena Unit 160
Mesa, AZ 85201-4319, USA

Feller, Happy (Athlete, Football Player)
4225 Camacho St
Austin, TX 78723-5389, USA

Feller, Jack (Athlete, Baseball Player)
145 Oakwood Dr
Coldwater, MI 49036-8606, USA

Fellowes, Julian (Actor)
c/o Jeremy Barber *United Talent Agency
(UTA)*
9336 Civic Center Dr
Beverly Hills, CA 90210, USA

Fellows, Mark (Athlete, Football Player)
P.O. Box 517
Choteau, MT 59422, USA

Fellows, Ron (Athlete, Football Player)
202 Creekview Dr
Wylie, TX 75098, USA

Felmy, Hansjorg
Berghofen
Eching, GERMANY D-84174

Felsenstein, Lee (Inventor)
1479 Regent Street
Redwood City, CA 94061-2821, USA

Felske, John (Athlete, Baseball Player,
Coach)
3804 Ridge Rd
Spring Grove, IL 60081-9390, USA

Felsner, Brian (Athlete, Hockey Player)
28376 Lange Rd
Chesterfield, MI 48047, USA

Felsner, Denny (Athlete, Hockey Player)
16094 Haverhill Dr
Macomb, MI 48044, USA

Felt, Dick
3993 N 750 E
Provo, UT 84604-4773, USA

Felt, Richard (Athlete, Football Player)
3993 N 750 E
Provo, UT 84604, USA

Feltham, Denise (Stylist)
c/o Staff Member *Sydney Represents*
280 Mott St
New York, NY 10012, USA

Felton, Dennis (Basketball Player)
University of Georgia
Athletic Dept
Athens, GA 30602, USA

Felton, Eric (Athlete, Football Player)
P.O. Box 1355
Coppell, TX 75019, USA

Felton, John (Musician)
GMS
PO Box 1031
Montrose, CA 91021, USA

Felton, Raymond (Athlete, Basketball
Player)
15109 Redwood Valley Ln
Charlotte, NC 28277-3282, USA

Felton, Terry (Athlete, Baseball Player)
1253 Cordoba Dr
Zachary, LA 70791-6212, USA

Felton, Tom (Actor)
c/o Staff Member *Harry Potter Production*
Leavesden Studios
PO Box 3000
Leavesden, Hertfordshire WD2 7LT,
UNITED KINGDOM

Feltrin, Tony (Athlete, Hockey Player)
P.O. Box 560
Lake Cowichan, BC V0R 2G0, Canada

Felts, Narvel (Musician, Songwriter,
Writer)
2005 Narvel Felts Way
Malden, MO 63863, USA

Feltsman, Vladimir (Musician)
Columbia Artists Mgmt Inc
165 W 57th St
New York, NY 10019, USA

Feltus, Alan E (Artist)
Porziano 68
Assisi PG 06081, ITALY

Feltz, Vanessa ((Actor)
c/o Staff Member *XS Promotions*
57 Fonthill Rd
Aberdeen AB11 6UQ, UNITED
KINGDOM (UK)

Fem 2 Fem
1122 B St. #308
Hayward, CA 94541-4272

Femia, John
1650 Broadway #714
New York, NY 10019

Fencik, J Gary (Athlete, Football Player)
1134 W Schubert Ave
Chicago, IL 60614, USA

Fendrich, Rainhard (Musician)
c/o Staff Member *Agentur Rehling*
Kirchenstrasse 17c
Germering D-82110, Germany

Fenech, Edwige (Actor)
Carol Levi Co
Via Giuseppe Pisanelli
Rome 00196, ITALY

Fenech, Jeff (Boxer)
PO Box 21
Hardys Bay, NSW 2257, AUSTRALIA

Fenech-Adami, Edward (Prime Minister)
176 Main St
Birkikara, MALTA

Fenenbock, Charles (Athlete, Football
Player)
6000 S Land Park Dr
Apt 105
Sacramento, CA 95822, USA

Fenerty, Gill (Athlete, Football Player)
2452 Brookhaven Ct NE
Atlanta, GA 30319-5243, USA

Feng, Ying (Ballerina)
Central Ballet of China
3 Taiping St
Beijing 100050, CHINA

Feng-HslungHsu (Engineer)
IBM T J Watson Research Center
PO Box 218
Yorktown Heights, NY 10598, USA

Fenley, Molissa (Choreographer, Dancer)
59 Walder St #4
New York, NY 10013, USA

Fenn, John B (Nobel Prize Laureate)
4909 Cary Street Road
Richmond, VA 23226, USA

Fenn, Sherilyn (Actor)
c/o Cynthia Campos-Greenberg *Anthem
Entertainment*
9595 Wilshire Blvd
Suite 900
Los Angeles, CA 90212-2509, USA

Fennema, Carl (Athlete, Football Player)
2470 Dexter Ave N Apt 402
Seattle, WA 98109-2248, USA

Fenner, Derrick (Athlete, Football Player)
7533 33rd Ave NW
Seattle, WA 98117, USA

Fenner, Lane (Athlete, Football Player)
412 Labarre Ct
Saint Johns, FL 32259, USA

Fenney, Rick (Athlete, Football Player)
41594 Margarita Rd
Temecula, CA 92591, USA

Fenske, Chuck
3 Tattnall Pl.
Hilton Head, SC 29928

Fenson, Pete (Athlete, Olympic Athlete)
3769 Crest Ct NE
Bemidji, MN 56601-6083, USA

Fenton, James (Writer)
P F D Drury House
34-43 Russell St
London WC2B 5HA, UNITED KINGDOM
(UK)

Fenton, Paul (Athlete, Hockey Player)
16 Bridle Path Rd
Brewster, MA 02631-1611, USA

Fenton, Paul (Athlete, Hockey Player)
Nashville Predators 501 Broadway
Attn: Asst General Manager
Nashville, TN 37203-3980, USA

Fenton, Peggy (Athlete, Baseball Player,
Commentator)
11131 Cottonwood Dr
Palos Hills, IL 60465-2528, USA

Fenwick, Bobby (Athlete, Baseball Player)
51201 Hutchinson Rd
Three Rivers, MI 49093-9029, USA

Fenyves, Dave (Athlete, Hockey Player)
940 Parish Pl
Hummelstown, PA 17036, USA

Feore, Colm (Actor)
c/o Gayle Abrams *Oscars Abrams Zimel
& Associates, Inc. (OAZ)*
438 Queen St E
Toronto ON M5A 1T4, CANADA

Ferarone, Jessica (Actor)
c/o Tiffany Kuzon *Evolution Entertainment
(LA)*
901 N Highland Ave
Los Angeles, CA 90038, USA

Feraud, Gianfranco (Designer, Fashion
Designer)
25 Rue Saint Honore
Paris 75001, FRANCE

Ferdin, Pamela (Actor)
171 Pier Avenue #453
Santa Monica, CA 90405, USA

Ferdinand, Franz (Musician)
c/o Staff Member *Paradigm (Monterey)*
404 W Franklin St
Monterey, CA 93940, USA

Ferdinand, Marie (Basketball Player)
San Antonio Silver Stars
1 SBC Center
San Antonio
TX, 78219 USA

Ferdinand, Rio (Soccer Player)
c/o Staff Member *Manchester United PLC*
Sir Matt Busby Way
Old Trafford
Manchester M160RA, UNITED
KINGDOM

Ferdinand, Ron (Cartoonist)
PO Box 1997
Monterey, CA 93942

Ference, Andrew (Athlete, Hockey Player)
220 Commercial St.
Boston, MA 02109, USA

Ference, Brad (Athlete, Hockey Player)
2424 Gold Canyon Dr
San Antonio, TX 78259, USA

Ferentz, Kirk (Coach, Football Coach)
University of Iowa
Athletic Dept
Iowa City
IA 52242, USA

Fergason, James L (Jim) (Inventor)
145 Gartland Dr
Menlo Park, CA 94025, USA

Fergie (Actor, Musician)
1310 N Kenter Ave
Los Angeles, CA 90049, USA

Fergon, Vicki (Athlete, Golfer)
44 Partridge Ln
Aliso Viejo, CA 92656, USA

Fergus, Keith (Athlete, Golfer)
11515 Noblewood Crest Ln
Houston, TX 77082-6814, USA

Fergus, Tom (Athlete, Hockey Player)
Blue Leaf Ltd
1240 Springwood Cres
Oakville, ON L6M 1V8, Canada

Ferguson, Alexander C (Alex) (Soccer Player)
Manchester United FC
Old Trafford
Manchester M16 0RA, UNITED KINGDOM (UK)

Ferguson, Charles A (Editor)
1448 Joseph St
New Orleans, LA 70115, USA

Ferguson, Charley (Athlete, Football Player)
81 Stonecroft Ln
Buffalo, NY 14226, USA

Ferguson, Christopher J (Misc)
1008 Maroney Ln
Pacific Palisades, CA 90272-2451, USA

Ferguson, Christopher J Cdr (Astronaut)
16111 Park Center Way
Houston, TX 77059-4083, USA

Ferguson, Clarence C Jr (Attorney, Attorney General, Diplomat, General)
Harvard University
Law School
Cambridge, MA 02138, USA

Ferguson, Colin (Actor)
c/o Perry Zimel *Oscars Abrams Zimel & Associates, Inc. (OAZ)*
438 Queen St E
Toronto ON M5A 1T4, CANADA

Ferguson, Craig (Actor, Comedian, Television Host)
Late Late Show with Craig Ferguson
7800 Beverly Blvd #244
Los Angeles, CA 90036, USA

Ferguson, Cullum Cathy (Athlete, Olympic Athlete, Swimmer)
3107 San Gabriel Ave
Clovis, CA 93619-9272, USA

Ferguson, Deborah (Stylist)
c/o Staff Member *Judy Inc*
1 Yorkville Ave
Toronto ON M4W 1L1, Canada

Ferguson, Frederick E (General)
106 S Stellar Pkwy
Chandler, AZ 85226-3725, USA

Ferguson, George (Athlete, Hockey Player)
5765 Montville Dr
McDonald, PA 15057, USA

Ferguson, Jason (Athlete, Football Player)
15139 SW 34th St
Davie, FL 33331-2714, USA

Ferguson, Jay (Actor)
c/o Robert Marsala *Wishlab*
2225-A Hyperion Ave
Los Angeles, CA 90027, USA

Ferguson, Jesse Tyler (Actor)
c/o Jon Rubinstein *Authentic Talent and Literary Management*
45 Main St
Suite 1004
Brooklyn, NY 11201, USA

Ferguson, Joe (Athlete, Baseball Player)
11322 River Run Ln
Berlin, MD 21811-3288, USA

Ferguson, Joe (Athlete, Football Player)
12 Mason Ln
Bella Vista, AR 72715, USA

Ferguson, Keith (Athlete, Football Player)
P.O. Box 19006
Sugar Land, TX 77496, USA

Ferguson, Kent (Athlete, Diver, Olympic Athlete)
809 Olive Way Apt 954
Seattle, WA 98101-1898, USA

Ferguson, Lorne (Athlete, Hockey Player)
35 Gretna Green
Kingston, ON K7M 3J3, Canada

Ferguson, Lynda (Actor)
606 N Larchmont Blvd
#309
Los Angeles, CA 90004, USA

Ferguson, Nick (Athlete, Football Player)
1114 Arlington Ave SW
Atlanta, GA 30310, USA

Ferguson, Norm (Athlete, Hockey Player)
71 Causeway Dr
Sydney, NS B1L 1C5, Canada

Ferguson, Robert (Athlete, Football Player)
15102 Oldtown Bridge Ct
Sugar Land, TX 77498-1298, USA

Ferguson, Roger W Jr (Economist, Government Official)
Federal Reserve Board
20th & Constitution Ave NW
Washington, DC 20551, USA

Ferguson, Sarah (Royalty)
c/o Karen Sellars *ICM Partners (ICM-LA)*
10250 Constellation Blvd Fl 7
Los Angeles, CA 90067, USA

Ferguson, Thomas A Jr (Business Person)
Newell Rubbermaid Inc
Newell Center
29 E Stephenson St
Freeport, IL 61032, USA

Ferguson, Vasquero D (Vagas) (Athlete, Football Player)
Richmond High School
Richmond High School 380 Hub Etchison Pkwy
Richmond, IN 47374-5398, USA

Ferguson, Warren J (Judge)
US Courts of Appeals
34 Civic Center Plaza
Santa Ana, CA 92701, USA

Ferguson, William (Athlete, Football Player)
9433 N Newport Hwy
Spokane, WA 99218, USA

Ferguson-Winn, Mabel (Athlete, Track Athlete)
2575 S Steele Road
#206
San Bernardino, CA 92408, USA

Fergusson, Frances D (Educator)
Vassar College
President's Office
Poughkeepsie, NY 12603, USA

Fergus-Thompson, Gordo (Musician)
150 Audley Road
Hendon
London NW4 3EG, UNITED KINGDOM (UK)

Ferigno, Lou (Actor)
Lou Ferrigno Enterprises Inc
PO Box 1671
Santa Monica, CA 90406, USA

Ferland, E James (Business Person)
Public Service Enterprise
80 Park Plaza
PO Box 1171
Newark, NJ 07101, USA

Ferland, Jodelle (Actor)
c/o Vickie Petronio *Play Management*
807 Powell St
Suite 220
Vancouver V6A 1H7, CANADA

Ferlinghetti, Lawrence (Writer)
City Lights Booksellers
261 Columbus Ave
San Francisco, CA 94133-4586, USA

Ferlito, Vanessa (Actor)
c/o Jeff Golenberg *Collective*
8383 Wilshire Blvd
Suite 1050
Beverly Hills, CA 90211, USA

Fermin, Felix (Athlete, Baseball Player)
Akron Aeros
300 S Main St
Attn: Coaching Staff
Akron, OH 44308, USA

Fernandes, Ron (Athlete, Football Player)
900 Fairwood St
Inkster, MI 48141-4003, USA

Fernandez, Adrian (Athlete, Race Car Driver)
Fernandez Racing
6950 Guion Rd
#51
Indianapolis, IN 46268, USA

Fernandez, Alejandro (Musician)
Hauser Entertainment
11003 Rocks Road
Whittier, CA 90601, USA

Fernandez, Alex (Athlete, Baseball Player)
12323 SW 55th St
Suite 107
Cooper City, FL 33330-3312, USA

Fernandez, Bernardo (Athlete, Baseball Player)
6701 Dorita Ave #202
Las Vegas, NV 89108, USA

Fernandez, Chico (Athlete, Baseball Player)
1310 SW 97th Ave
Miami, FL 33351-6181, USA

Fernandez, Chico (Athlete, Baseball Player)
8401 NW 40th Ct
Sunrise, FL 33351, USA

Fernandez, Chico
3322 24th St.
Detroit, MI 48208

Fernandez, Craig (Director, Writer)
c/o Staff Member *The Gotham Group Inc*
9255 Sunset Blvd
Suite 515
Los Angeles, CA 90069, USA

Fernandez, C Sidney (Sid) (Athlete, Baseball Player)
25 Aulike St
Apt 218
Kailua, HI 96734-2262, USA

Fernandez, Evalina
5911 Allison St.
Los Angeles, CA 90022

Fernandez, Ferdinand F (Judge)
US Courts of Appeals
125 S Grand Ave
Pasadena, CA 91105, USA

Fernandez, Frank (Athlete, Baseball Player)
37 Coughlan Ave
Staten Island, NY 10310-3149, USA

Fernandez, Gigi (Tennis Player)
Gigi Tennis Camp
4202 E Fowler Ave #214
Tampa, FL 33620, USA

Fernandez, Giselle (Television Host)
NHD International Service
PO Box 498
Quakertown, PA 18951, USA

Fernandez, Jared (Athlete, Baseball Player)
4298 S 4625 W
Salt Lake City, UT 84120-4964, USA

Fernandez, Juan (Actor)
Don Buchwald
6500 Wilshire Blvd
#2200
Los Angeles, CA 90048, USA

Fernandez, Julian (Stylist)
c/o Staff Member *Independent Artists*
448 E Riverdale Ave
Orange, CA 92865, USA

Fernandez, Lisa (Athlete, Olympic Athlete, Softball Player)
1460 Homewood Rd #95B
Seal Beach, CA 90740-4627, USA

Fernandez, Manny (Athlete, Hockey Player)
Sport Prospects Inc
77 Rue de Bleury
Attn: Gilles Lupien
Rosemere, QC J7A 4L9, Canada

Fernandez, Manny (Athlete, Football Player)
1709 Poplar Ridge Rd
Ellaville, GA 31806-5935, USA

Fernandez, Mary Jo
133 1st St. NE
St. Petersburg, FL 33701

Fernandez, Mary Joe (Athlete, Olympic Athlete, Tennis Player)
3215 Roundwood Rd
Chagrin Falls, OH 44022-6635, USA

Fernandez, Mervyn (Athlete, Football Player)
2477 Briarwood Dr
San Jose, CA 95125-4918, USA

Fernandez, O Antonio (Tony) (Athlete, Baseball Player)
19232 N Gardenia Ave
Weston, FL 33332-4409, USA

Fernandez, Pedro (Musician, Songwriter)
Exclusive Artists Productions
PO Box 65948
Los Angeles, CA 90065, USA

Fernández, Pedro (Musician)
c/o Staff Member *Machete Music*
2220 Colorado Ave
Santa Monica, CA 90404, USA

Fernandez, Shiloh (Actor)
c/o Justin Grey Stone *Untitled Entertainment (LA)*
350 S. Beverly Dr #200
Beverly Hills, CA 90212, USA

Fernandez, Vicente (Musician)
Hauser Entertainment
11003 Rocks Road
Whittier, CA 90601, USA

Ferneyhough, Brian J P (Composer)
848 Allardice Way
Stanford, CA 94305, USA

Fernsten, Eric (Athlete, Basketball Player)
5634 Linden Street
Dublin, CA 94568-7704

Ferragamo, Vince (Athlete, Football Player)
Touchdown Real Estate
6200 E Canyon Rim Rd
Suite 204
Anaheim, CA 92807-4315, USA

Ferrante, Orlando (Athlete, Football Player)
1223 Adair St
San Marina, CA 91108, USA

Ferrara, Abel (Director)
International Creative Mgmt
8942 Wilshire Blvd
#219
Beverly Hills, CA 90211, USA

Ferrara, Adam (Actor)
Conversation Co
697 Middle Neck Road
Great Neck, NY 11023, USA

Ferrara, Al (Athlete, Baseball Player)
4901 Whitsett Ave Apt 207
Valley Village, CA 91607-3550, USA

Ferrara, Al (Athlete, Baseball Player)
4901 Whitsett Ave
Apt 207
Valley Village, CA 91607, USA

Ferrara, Jerry (Actor)
c/o Stephen (Steve) Levinson *Leverage Management*
3030 Pennsylvania Ave
Santa Monica, CA 90404, USA

Ferrara, Laura (Stylist)
c/o Celebrity Stylist *Bryan Bantry*
900 Broadway Ste 400
New York, NY 10003, USA

Ferrare, Cristina (Entertainer, Model)
10727 Wilshire Blvd
#1602
Los Angeles, CA 90024, USA

Ferrarese, Don (Athlete, Baseball Player)
15290 Myalon Rd
Apple Valley, CA 92307-4938, USA

Ferrari, Al (Athlete, Basketball Player)
5911 Bristlecone Court
Saint Louis, MO 63129-2917, USA

Ferrari, Anthony (Athlete, Baseball Player)
17 Bretano Way
Greenbrae, CA 94904-1180, USA

Ferrari, Michael R Jr (Educator)
570 Greenway Dr
Lake Forest, IL 60045, USA

Ferrari, Tina (Dancer, Wrestler)
2901 S Las Vegas Blvd
Las Vegas, NV 89109, USA

Ferrario, Bill (Athlete, Football Player)
116 Hensy Ct
Scranton, PA 18504, USA

Ferraris, Jan (Athlete, Golfer)
7108 N 13th Pl
Phoenix, AZ 85020, USA

Ferraro, Chris (Athlete, Hockey Player)
PO Box 155
Sound Beach, NY 11789-0155, USA

Ferraro, Dave (Bowler)
672 E Chester St
Kingston, NY 12401, USA

Ferraro, Mike (Athlete, Baseball Player, Coach)
5201 Rim View Ln
Las Vegas, NV 89130-3658, USA

Ferraro, Peter (Athlete, Hockey Player)
PO Box 155
Sound Beach, NY 11789-0155, USA

Ferraro, Ray (Athlete, Hockey Player)
c/o Staff Member *Rogers Sportsnet*
181 Keefer Pl
Suite 221
Vancouver, BC V6B 1W6, Canada

Ferratti, Rebecca (Actor, Model)
10061 Riverside Dr
#721
Toluca Lake, CA 91602, USA

Ferrazzi, Ferruccio (Artist)
Piazza delle Muse
Via G G Porro 27
Rome 00197, ITALY

Ferrazzi, Pierpaolo (Athlete)
EuroGrafica
Via del Progresso
Marano Vicenza 36035, ITALY

Ferre, Gianfranco (Designer, Fashion Designer)
Villa Della Spiga 19/A
Milan 20121, ITALY

Ferree, Jim (Athlete, Golfer)
12 Kings Tree Rd
Hilton Head Island, SC 29928-6101, USA

Ferreira, Sky (Musician)
c/o Ron Laffitte *Red Light Management (LA)*
8439 W Sunset Blvd
Suite 2
Los Angeles, CA 90069, USA

Ferreira, Tony (Athlete, Baseball Player)
3006 Merrill Ave
Clearwater, FL 99336-3401, USA

Ferreira, Wayne (Tennis Player)
Int'l Mgmt Group
1 Erieview Plaza
1360 E 9th St #1300
Cleveland, OH 44114, USA

Ferrell, Bob (Athlete, Football Player)
88 Emory Ave
Beaumont, CA 92223, USA

Ferrell, Bobby
1090 N Shooting Star Dr
Beaumont, CA 92223-8435, USA

Ferrell, Conchata (Actor)
1335 N Seward St
Los Angeles, CA 90028, USA

Ferrell, Earl (Athlete, Football Player)
107 E Forest Trl
South Boston, VA 24592, USA

Ferrell, Rachel (Musician)
Vida Music Group
19800 Cornerstone Sq #415
Ashburn, VA 20147, USA

Ferrell, Rachelle (Musician)
Vida Music Group
19800 Cornerstone Square
#415
Ashburn, VA 20147, USA

Ferrell, Tyra (Actor)
c/o Staff Member *Gersh (LA)*
9465 Wilshire Blvd
Suite 600
Beverly Hills, CA 90212, USA

Ferrell, Will (Actor, Comedian, Producer)
c/o Jimmy Miller *Mosaic Media Group*
9200 W. Sunset Blvd
10th Floor
Los Angeles, CA 90069, USA

Ferrell Edmonson, Barbara A (Athlete, Olympic Athlete, Track Athlete)
University of Newada
239 N Hillcrest Blvd
Inglewood, CA 90301-1310, USA

Ferreol, Andrea
10 Ave. George V
Paris, FRANCE F-75008

Ferrer, Alex (Judge, Television Host)
Judge Alex
4261 Southwest Fwy
Houston, TX 77027, USA

Ferrer, Danay (Musician)
Evolution Talent
1776 Broadway
#1500
New York, NY 10019, USA

Ferrer, Lupita
861 Stone Canyon Rd.
Los Angeles, CA 90077

Ferrer, Miguel (Actor)
c/o Leslie Allan-Rice *Leslie Allan-Rice Management*
1007 Maybrook Dr
Beverly Hills, CA 90210, USA

Ferrer, Sergio (Athlete, Baseball Player)
37 Coughlan Ave
Staten Island, NY 10310-3149, USA

Ferrera, America (Actor)
c/o Jon Rubinstein *Authentic Talent and Literary Management*
45 Main St
Suite 1004
Brooklyn, NY 11201, USA

Ferreras, Francisco (Pipin) (Misc)
7548 W Treasure Dr
North Bay Village, FL 33141, USA

Ferrero, Louis P (Business Person)
PO Box 675744
Rancho Santa Fe, CA 92067, USA

Ferrigno, Lou (Actor)
Lou Ferrigno Enterprises Inc
PO Box 1671
Santa Monica, CA 90406, USA

Ferrin, Arnie (Athlete, Basketball Player)
91e Donner Way
Apt 301
Salt Lake City, UT 84158-4119, USA

Ferrin, Jennifer (Actor)
c/o Staff Member *As The World Turns*
JC Studios
1268 E 14th St
New York, NY 11230, USA

Ferring, Mark (Scientist)
4002 W Pine Brook Wav
Houston, TX 77059-3017, USA

Ferris, Bob (Athlete, Baseball Player)
18259 Glen Oak Way
Leesburg, VA 20176-3992, USA

Ferris, John (Swimmer)
1961 Klamath River Dr
Rancho Cordova, CA 95670, USA

Ferris, Michael (Mike) (Producer, Writer)
c/o Staff Member *Broder Webb Chervin Silbermann Agency, The (BWCS)*
10250 Constellation Blvd
Los Angeles, CA 90067-6200, USA

Ferris, Pamela
16601 Marques Ave. #405
Pacific Palisades, CA 90272

Ferriss, Dave (Athlete, Baseball Player)
510 Robinson Dr
Cleveland, MS 38732-2214, USA

Ferriss, David M (Boo) (Athlete, Baseball Player)
510 Robinson Dr
Cleveland, MS 38732, USA

Ferriss, Timothy (Writer)
c/o Staff Member *Random House Publicity*
1745 Broadway
New York, NY 10019, USA

Ferritor, Daniel E (Educator)
University of Arkansas
Chancellor's Office
Fayetteville, AR 72701, USA

Ferro, Cindy (Athlete, Golfer)
1901 Brookside Dr
Scotch Plains, NJ 07076, USA

Ferron (Musician, Songwriter, Writer)
JR Productions
4930 Paradise Dr
Tiburon, CA 94920, USA

Ferry, Bryan (Musician, Songwriter, Writer)
c/o Staff Member *Dene Jesmond Entertainment Ltd.*
65 New Cavendish St.
London W1M 7RD, UK

Ferry, Daniel J W (Danny) (Athlete, Basketball Player)
19300 South Park Blvd
Shaker Heights, OH 44122, USA

Ferry, Danny
604 Castano Ave
San Antonio, TX 78209-3617, USA

Ferry, David R (Writer)
Wellesley College
English Dept
Wellesley, MA 02181, USA

Ferry, John D (Misc)
6175 Mineral Point Road
Madison, WI 53705, USA

Ferry, Robert (Bob) (Athlete, Basketball Player)
2129 Beach Haven Road
Annapolis, MD 21409-5744, USA

Fersen, Paul (Athlete, Football Player)
PO Box 4
Dorset, VT 05251-0004, USA

Fersht, Alan R (Misc)
2 Barrow Close
Cambridge CB2 2AT, UNITED KINGDOM (UK)

Fert, Albert (Nobel Prize Laureate)
CNRS - Thales
Unité Mixte De Physique - UMR 137
128 Route Départementale
Palaiseau F-91767, France

Fest, Howard (Athlete, Football Player)
133 Forest Cir
Bandera, TX 78003, USA

Festinger, Leon (Misc)
37 W 12th St
New York, NY 10011, USA

Festinger, Robert (Writer)
c/o Bryan Besser *Verve Talent & Literary Agency, LLC*
9696 Culver Blvd
Suite 301
Culver City, CA 90232, USA

Fetchick, Mike (Athlete, Golfer)
4 White Birch Dr
Dix Hills, NY 11746-7720, USA

Fetisov, Viacheslav (Slava) (Athlete, Hockey Player)
65 Avon Dr
Essex Fells, NJ 07021, USA

Fetisov, Viacheslav (Athlete, Hockey Player)
65 Avon Dr
Essex Fells, NJ 07021-1717, USA

Fetter, Trevor (Business Person)
13737 Noel Rd #100
Dallas, TX 75240, USA

Fetterhoff, Robert (Religious Leader)
Fellowship of Grace Brethem
PO Box 386
Winona Lake, IN 46590, USA

Fetters, Mike (Athlete, Baseball Player)
2411 E Cedar Pl
Chandler, AZ 85249-3261, USA

Fettig, Jeff M (Business Person)
Whirlpool Corp
2000 N State St
RR 63
Benton Harbor, MI 49022, USA

Fetting, Katie (Actor)
c/o Ramses Ishak *United Talent Agency (UTA)*
9336 Civic Center Dr
Beverly Hills, CA 90210, USA

Fetting, Ralner (Artist)
Hasenhelde 61
Berlin 61, GERMANY

Fettman, Martin (Astronaut)
1572 N Saguaro Cliffs Ct
Tucson, AZ 85745-8839, USA

Fettman, Martin J (Astronaut)
1572 North Saguaro Cliffs Court
Tuczon, AZ 85745-8839, USA

Feuer, Debra
9560 Wilshire Blvd. #500
Beverly Hills, CA 90212

Feuerstein, Mark (Actor)
c/o Steven Levy *Framework Entertainment (LA)*
9057 Nemo St
Suite C
West Hollywood, CA 90069, USA

Feulner, Edwin J Jr (Misc)
Heritage Foundation
214 Massachusetts Ave NE
Washington, DC 20002, USA

Feustel, Andrew J (Astronaut)
4003 Elm Crest
Houston, TX 77059-3281, USA

Fewx, Gene (Misc)
666 15th St NE
Salem, OR 97301, USA

Fey (Musician)
RAC Paseo Palmas 1005
#1
Chapultepec Lomas
Mexico City 11000, MEXICO

Fey, Michael (Cartoonist)
United Feature Syndicate
200 Madison Ave
New York, NY 10016, USA

Fey, Tina (Actor, Comedian)
500 W. End Ave. #2C
New York, NY 10024, USA

Fezler, Forrest (Athlete, Golfer)
6270 Old Water Oak Rd
Tallahassee, FL 32312-3861, USA

F. H. Faleomavaega Jr., Eni
(Congressman, Politician)
2422 Rayburn HOB
Washington, DC 20515, USA

Fiala, John (Athlete, Football Player)
12113 268th Drive NE
Duvall, WA 98019, USA

Fiala, Neil (Athlete, Baseball Player)
4709 Woody Terrace Ct
Saint Louis, MO 63129-1683, USA

Fialkowska, Janina (Musician)
Ingpen & Williams
7 St George's Ct
131 Putney Bridge Rd
London SW15 2PA, UNITED KINGDOM (UK)

Fiasco, Lupe (Musician)
c/o Cara Lewis *Creative Artists Agency (CAA-LA)*
1325 Ave of the Americas
New York, NY 10019, USA

Fibiger, Jesse (Athlete, Hockey Player)
3336 Ocean Blvd
Victoria, BC V9C 1W6, Canada

Ficca, Dan (Athlete, Football Player)
151 Kansas Ln
Kulpmont, PA 17834-2005, USA

Fichaud, Eric (Athlete, Hockey Player)
191 Rue Charron
Lemoyne, QC J4R 2K6, Canada

Fichtel, Anja
Stauferring 104
Tauberbischofsheim, GERMANY D-97941

Fichter, Mike (Athlete, Baseball Player)
8821 Jackson Ct
Munster, IN 60438-3728, USA

Fichter, Rick T (Cinematographer)
7 Kramer Place
San Francisco, CA 94133, USA

Fichtner, Hans J (Scientist)
612 Cleemont Dr SE
Huntsville, AL 35801-1870, USA

Fichtner, Ross (Athlete, Football Player)
46833 Danbridge St
Plymouth, MI 48170, USA

Fichtner, William (Actor)
c/o Andrea Pett-Joseph *Brillstein Entertainment Partners*
9150 Wilshire Blvd #350
Beverly Hills, CA 90212, USA

Fick, Robert (Athlete, Baseball Player)
164 Brodia Wav
Walnut Creek, CA 94598-4920, USA

Fiddler, Vern (Athlete, Hockey Player)
3659 Hickory Grove Ln
Frisco, TX 75033-2875, USA

Fidler, Mike (Athlete, Hockey Player)
7723 Gleason Rd
Minneapolis, MN 55439, USA

Fiedel, Brad (Composer)
Gortaine/Schwartz
13245 Riverside Dr
#430
Sherman Oaks, CA 91423, USA

Fiedler, Arthur (General)
5119 Whitecap St
Oxnard, CA 93035-1848, USA

Fiedler, Jay (Athlete, Football Player)
25 Russell Rd
Garden City, NY 11530, USA

Fiedler, Jens
Bruno-Granz-Str. 48
Chemnitz, GERMANY D-09122

Fieger, Geoffrey (Attorney, Attorney General, General)
Fieger Fieger Schwartz
19390 W Ten Mile Road
Southfield, MI 48075, USA

Field, Arabella (Actor)
S M S Talent
8730 Sunset Blvd
#440
Los Angeles, CA 90069, USA

Field, Ayda (Actor)
c/o Staff Member *Brillstein Entertainment Partners*
9150 Wilshire Blvd #350
Beverly Hills, CA 90212, USA

Field, Byron (Actor)

Field, Chelsea (Actor)
Troxell
15263 Mulholland Dr
Los Angeles, CA 90077, USA

Field, George (Scientist)
Harvard University
60 Garden StCambridge,
MA 02138-1516, USA

Field, Helen (Opera Singer)
Athole Still
Foresters Hall
25-27 Westow St
London SE19 3RY, UNITED KINGDOM (UK)

Field, Nate (Athlete, Baseball Player)
332 W Jamison Pl Unit 58
Littleton, CO 80120-5248, USA

Field, Patricia (Stylist)
c/o Ivana Savic *Grant Savic Kopaloff & Associates*
6399 Wilshire Blvd #414
Los Angeles, CA 90048, USA

Field, Sally (Actor)
c/o Judy Hofflund *Hofflund/Polone*
9465 Wilshire Blvd #420
Beverly Hills, CA 90212, USA

Field, Shirley Arin (Actor)
c/o Paul Pearson *Daly Pearson Associates*
586 King's Rd
Chelsea
London SW6 2DX, UNITED KINGDOM (UK)

Field, Todd (Actor, Director)
c/o Ari Emanuel *WME (LA)*
9601 Wilshire Blvd Fl 3
Beverly Hills, CA 90210, USA

Fielder, Cecil (Athlete, Baseball Player)
Charlotte County Redfish
6907 Smokey Brook Ln
Katty, TX 77494-1607, USA

Fielder, Guyle (Athlete, Hockey Player)
2253 Leisure World
Mesa, AZ 85206, USA

Fielder, Prince (Athlete, Baseball Player)
11171 Sun Center Dr Ste 290
Rancho Cordova, CA 95670-6190, USA

Fieldgate, Norm (Athlete, Football Player)
2510 Colwood Dr
North Vancouver, BC V7R 2R1, Canada

Fielding, Fred F (Attorney, Attorney General, General, Government Official)
Wiley Rein Fielding
7925 Jones Branch Dr
#6200
McLean, VA 22102, USA

Fielding, Helen (Writer)
c/o Beth Swofford *Creative Artists Agency (CAA-LA)*
2000 Ave Of The Stars
Los Angeles, CA 90067, USA

Fielding, Joy (Writer)
Atria Books
1230 Ave of Americas
New York, NY 10020, USA

Fielding, Susannah (Actor)
c/o Kim Callahan *Industry Entertainment Partners*
955 S Carrillo Dr
Suite 300
Los Angeles, CA 90048, USA

Fielding, Yvette (Actor)
Antix Productions
128 Grove Ln
Cheadle Hulme
Cheshire SK8 7ND, UNITED KINGDOM

Fields, Brandon (Athlete, Football Player)
4509 Holt Rd
Sylvania, OH 43560, USA

Fields, Bruce (Athlete, Baseball Player)
Cleveland Indians 2401 Ontario St Attn: Coaching Staff
cleveland, OH 44115-4003, USA

Fields, Debbi (Business Person)
Mrs. Fields Training R&D Ctr
1290 W 2320 St
Suite A
Salt Lake City, UT 84119-1483, USA

Fields, Edgar (Athlete, Football Player)
435 Musket Entry
Roswell, GA 30076, USA

Fields, Freddie
8899 Beverly Blvd. #918
Los Angeles, CA 90048-2412

Fields, Harold T Jr (General)
126 Dear Run Strut
Enterprise, AL 36330, USA

Fields, Holly (Actor)
Don Buchwald
6500 Wilshire Blvd
#2200
Los Angeles, CA 90048, USA

Fields, Jitter (Athlete, Football Player)
5776 Kensington Ave
Detroit, MI 48224, USA

Fields, Joseph C (Joe) Jr (Athlete, Football Player)
1 University Place
Chester, PA 191013, USA

Fields, Josh (Athlete, Baseball Player)
4819 61st Avenue Dr W
Bradenton, FL 34210-4033, USA

Fields, Kenny (Athlete, Basketball Player)
Iese E Ramon Rd Unit 81
Palm Springs, CA 92264-7775, USA

Fields, Kim (Actor)
c/o Adam Robinson *Southfield Village*
8228 Sunset Blvd #190
Los Angeles, CA 90046, USA

Fields, Landry (Athlete, Basketball Player)
c/o Chris Emens *Octagon Home Office*
1751 Pinnacle Dr
15th Floor
McLean, VA 22102, USA

Fields, Mark (Athlete, Football Player)
887 W Palo Brea Dr
Litchfield Park, AZ 85340, USA

Fields, Scott (Athlete, Football Player)
7513 Santa Lucia St
Fontana, CA 92336, USA

Fields, Stephen (Baseball Player)
8306 Wickham Rd
Springfield, VA 22152-1708, USA

Fields, Stephen (Athlete, Baseball Player)
8306 Wickham Rd
Springfield, VA 22152-1708, USA

Fields, Valerie
PO Box 4025
Niagara Falls, NY 14304

Fields-Rose, Debbi (Misc)
6052 Evensong Cv
Memphis, TN 38120-2360, USA

Fieldstad, Oivin
Damfaret 59
Bryn-Oslo 6, NORWAY

Fien, Casey (Athlete, Baseball Player)
7200 Santa Clara St
Buena Park, CA 90620-3116, USA

Fiennes, Joseph (Actor)
c/o Sandra Chang *Anonymous Content (LA)*
3531 Hayden Ave
Culver City, CA 90232, USA

Fiennes, Ralph (Actor)
c/o Nicole Caruso *Wolf Kasteler Van Iden & Associates (NY)*
584 Broadway
Suite 310
New York, NY 10012, USA

Fierek, Wolfgang
Ottobrunner Str. 15
Brunnthal, GERMANY D-85649

Fieri, Guy (Chef, Television Host)
2039 Marsh Rd
Santa Rosa, CA 95403, USA

Fierstein, Harvey (Actor, Musician, Writer)
c/o Ron Fierstein *RF Entertainment Inc.*
29 Haines Rd
Bedford Hills, NY 10507, USA

Fieser, Louis (Inventor)
58 Medford St
Arlington, MA 02474, USA

Fife, Dan (Danny) (Athlete, Baseball Player)
5854 Misty Hill Dr
Clarkston, MI 48346-3033, USA

Figaro, Cedric (Athlete, Football Player)
205 Staten St
Lafayette, LA 70501, USA

Figga, Mike (Athlete, Baseball Player)
16434 Turnbury Oak Dr
Odessa, FL 33556-2896, USA

Figg-Currier, Cindy (Athlete, Golfer)
109 Blue Jay Dr
Lakeway, TX 78734-5101, USA

Figgins, Chone (Athlete, Baseball Player)
16 San Sovino
Newport Coast, CA 92657, USA

Figgins, Desmond "Chone" (Athlete, Baseball Player)
6SO Bellevue Wav NE
Bellevue, WA 98004-5045, USA

Figgis, Michael (Mike) (Director)
c/o Robert Newman *WME (LA)*
9601 Wilshire Blvd Fl 3
Beverly Hills, CA 90210, USA

Figini, Luigi (Architect)
Via Perone di S Martino 8
Milan, ITALY

Figini, Michela (Skier)
Ariolo
Prato Lavenina 6799, SWITZERLAND

Figlo-Gill, Josephine (Athlete, Baseball Player, Commentator)
437 N. Fork Dr.
Lakeland, FL 33809-1426, USA

Figner, George (Athlete, Football Player)
2329 N Recker Rd Unit 116
Mesa, AZ 85215, USA

Figo, Luis (Soccer Player)
Real Madrid FC
Avda Cincha Espina 1
Madrid 28036, SPAIN

Figueras-Dotti, Marta (Athlete, Golfer)
6174 Palomino Circle
Bradenton, FL 34201-2384, USA

Figueroa, Bien (Athlete, Baseball Player)
3272 Addison Ln
Tallahassee, FL 32317-9045, USA

Figueroa, Ed (Athlete, Baseball Player)
A-N15 Calle 41
Santa Juanita, PR 00619, USA

Figueroa, Efrain (Actor)
c/o Staff Member *Mitchell K Stubbs & Assoc (MKS)*
8675 W. Washington Blvd
Suite 203
Culver City, CA 90232, USA

Figueroa, Nelson (Athlete, Baseball Player)
1950 E Woodsman Pl
Chandler, AZ 85286-2007, USA

Figura, Maria Louisa (Actor)
The Figura Studio
5716 Chauenga Blvd
North Hollywood, CA 91606, USA

Figures, Deon (Athlete, Football Player)
1520 S Visalia Ave
Compton, CA 90220, USA

Fikac, Jeremy (Athlete, Baseball Player)
PO Box 2187
Wimberley, TX 78676, USA

Fike, Dan (Athlete, Football Player)
23479 Wingedfoot Dr
Westlake, OH 44145, USA

Fikrig, Erol (Doctor)
Yale University
Medical Center
Infectious Disease Dept
New Haven, CT 06510, USA

Fila, Ivan (Writer)
c/o David Krintzman *Morris, Yorn, Barnes, Levine, Krintzman, Rubenstein and Kohner*
2000 Ave of the Stars
3rd Floor, North Tower
Los Angeles, CA 90067, USA

Filan, Shane (Musician)
c/o Staff Member *RCA Label Group UK*
9 Derry St
London W8 5HY, UK

Filardi, Peter (Director, Producer, Writer)
c/o Robert Marsala *Wishlab*
2225-A Hyperion Ave
Los Angeles, CA 90027, USA

Filarski-Steffes, Helen (Athlete, Baseball Player, Commentator)
19623 Damman St
Harper Woods, MI 48225-1753, USA

Filatova, Ludmila P (Opera Singer)
Ryleyevastr 6
#13
Saint Petersburg, RUSSIA

File, Bob (Athlete, Baseball Player)
6412 Riverfront Dr
Palmyra, NJ 08065-2149, USA

Filer, Tom (Athlete, Baseball Player)
Indianapolis Indians 501 W Maryland St
Attn Coaching Staff
indianapolis, IN 46225-1041, USA

Files, Jim (Athlete, Football Player)
6303 Fallstone Rd
Fort Smith, AR 72916, USA

Files, Jimmy (Athlete, Football Player)
6303 Fallstone Rd
Fort Smith, AR 72916, USA

Filicia, Thom (Designer, Television Host)
c/o Staff Member *WmE2 (WMA-LA)*
1 William Morris Pl
Beverly Hills, CA 90212, USA

Filiol, Jalme (Tennis Player)
Advantage International
1025 Thomas Jefferson NW
#430
Washington, DC 20007, USA

Filion, Herve (Misc)
18 Evans Ave
Alberston, NY 11507, USA

Filion, Renald (Horse Racer)
3-95 Rue des Erables
Lachute, QC, J8H IAG Canada

Filion, Rheo (Horse Racer)
187 S Franklin St # 251
Wilkes Barre, PA 18766-0998, USA

Filipacchi, Daniel (Publisher)
Hachette Filipacchi
149-51 Rue Anatole-France
Levallois 92534, FRANCE

Filipchenko, Anatoli N (Cosmonaut, General)
Potcha Kosmonavtov Moskovskoi Oblasti
Syvisdny Goroduk 141160, RUSSIA

Filipek, Ron (Athlete, Basketball Player)
933 Hillside Drive
Cookeville, TN 38501-2890, USA

Filipelli, John (Horse Racer)
1949 NE 1st St
Deerfield Beach, FL 33441-4504, USA

Filipovic, Dusanka (Scientist)
Halozone Technologies Inc 4000 Nashua Dr
Mississauga, ON, L4V 1P8 Canada

Filippo, Lou
7826 Botany St.
Downey, CA 90240-2624

Filippo (Fillipo/Filippo), Fabrizio (Fab) (Actor)
c/o David Lillard *IFA Talent Agency*
8730 Sunset Blvd
Suite 490
Los Angeles, CA 90069, USA

Fill, Shannon (Actor)
260 S Beverly Dr #200
Beverly Hills, CA 90212, USA

Fillion, Bob (Athlete, Hockey Player)
306-275 Boul Saint-Luc
Saint-Jean-Sur-Richelieu, QC J2W OB7, Canada

Fillion, Nathan (Actor)
c/o Ennis Kamcili *United Talent Agency (UTA)*
9336 Civic Center Dr
Beverly Hills, CA 90210, USA

Fillip, Chet (Race Car Driver)
PO Box 220
Ozona, TX 76943, USA

Fillmore, Greg (Athlete, Basketball Player)
12449 Blueberry Woods Circle East
Apt E
Jacksonville, FL 32258-4174

Fillon, Bob (Athlete, Hockey Player)
201-980 Rue Cayer
Saint-Jean-Sur-Richelieu, QC J3A 1N8, Canada

Filner, Bob (Congressman, Politician)
2428 Rayburn HOB
Washington, DC 20515, USA

Filppula, Valttieri (Athlete, Hockey Player)
20883 Richmond Dr
Northville, MI 48167-9501, USA

Filson, Pete (Athlete, Baseball Player)
1725 Packer Ave
Philadelphia, PA 19145, USA

Filter (Music Group)
c/o Staff Member *Warner Bros Records (NY)*
75 Rockefeller Center
New York, NY 10019, USA

Fimmel, Travis (Actor, Model)
c/o David Seltzer *Management 360*
9111 Wilshire Blvd
Beverly Hills, CA 90210, USA

Fimple, Dennis
3518 Cahuenga Blvd. W. #306
Los Angeles, CA 90068

Fimple, Jack (Athlete, Baseball Player)
8012 Cliffrose St
Windsor, CA 95492-9537, USA

Fina, John (Athlete, Football Player)
5180 E Fort Lowell Rd
Tucson, AZ 85712, USA

Finch, Frederick (General)
14722 Highland Rdg
San Antonio, TX 78233-3845, INDIA

Finch, James (Race Car Driver)
Phoenix Racing
1718 Tennessee Ave
Lynn Haven, FL 32444, USA

Finch, Jennie (Athlete, Olympic Athlete, Softball Player)
Finch Windmill
Finch Windmill PO Box 97
LaMirada, CA 90637-0097, USA

Finch, Joel (Athlete, Baseball Player)
68571 Oak Spring Rd
Edwardsburg, MI 49112-9502, USA

Finch, Jon (Actor)
London Mgmt
2-4 Noel St
London W1V 3RB, UNITED KINGDOM (UK)

Finch, Karl (Athlete, Football Player)
4408 Copper Crest Ln
Modesto, CA 95355, USA

Finch, Linda (Aviator)
World Flight
211 Switch Oaks
San Antonio, TX 78618-0124, USA

Finch, Tyrone (Comedian)
c/o Staff Member *United Talent Agency (UTA)*
9336 Civic Center Dr
Beverly Hills, CA 90210, USA

Finchem, Timothy W (Athlete, Golfer)
c/o Staff Member *Pro Golfers Association (PGA) Tour*
112 TPC Blvd
Ponte Vedra Beach, FL 32082, USA

Fincher, Alfred (Athlete, Football Player)
1267 Avenue Du Chateau
Covington, LA 70433, USA

Fincher, David (Director)
c/o Bryan Lourd *Creative Artists Agency (CAA-LA)*
2000 Ave Of The Stars
Los Angeles, CA 90067, USA

Finck, George C (War Hero)
143 Beaver Lane
Benton, LA 71006, USA

Fincke, Edward
15819 El Dorado Oaks Dr
Houston, TX 77059-4045, USA

Fincke, Edward M (Astronaut)
15819 El Dorado Oaks Dr
Houston, TX 77059-4045, USA

Fincke, E Michael (Mike) (Astronaut)
15819 El Dorado Oaks Dr
Houston, TX 77059-4045, USA

Finckel, David (Musician)
I M G Artists
3 Burlington Lane
London W4 2TH, UNITED KINGDOM (UK)

Findlay, Conn F (Athlete, Yachtsman)
1920 Oak Knoll
Belmont, CA 94002, USA

Fine, David (Director, Writer)
c/o Melissa Myers *WME (LA)*
9601 Wilshire Blvd Fl 3
Beverly Hills, CA 90210, USA

Fine, Jeanna
19 Hanover Pl. PMB 313
Hicksville, NY 11801-5103

Fine, Tom (Misc)
2605 Cascade Cove Dr
Little Slm, TX 75068-7603

Fine, Travis (Actor)
Vaughn D Hart
200 N Robertson Blvd #219
Beverly Hills, CA 90211, USA

Fine, Wendy (Stylist)
6232-A Tapia Dr
Malibu, CA 90265, USA

Finfera, Joe (Actor)
c/o Staff Member *Select Artists Ltd (CA-Westside Office)*
1138 12th Street
Suite 1
Santa Monica, CA 90403, USA

Fingaz, Sticky (Artist, Musician)
c/o David Guc *Vanguard Management Group*
8060 Melrose Ave
4th Floor
Los Angeles, CA 90046, USA

Finger Eleven (Music Group)
c/o Staff Member *Wind-up Records*
72 Madison Ave Fl 8
New York, NY 10016, USA

Fingers, Rollie (Athlete, Baseball Player)
P.O. Box 230729
Las Vegas, NV 89105-0729, USA

Fink, Gerald R (Doctor, Scientist)
40 Alston Road
West Newton, MA 02465, USA

Fink, Jason (Athlete, Football Player)
2619 Regatta Ln
Davis, CA 95618, USA

Fink, John
1680 N. Vine St. #614
Hollywood, CA 90028

Fink, Mitchell
1835 E. Michelle St.
West Covina, CA 91791

Fink, Natascha (Athlete, Golfer)
Golfclub Murhof Adriach 54
Frohnleiten A-8130, Austria

Finkbeiner, Kirsten Rowe (Activist)
MomsRising
12011 Bel-Red Rd
Suite 206
Bellevue, WA 98005, USA

Finkel, Fyvush (Actor)
c/o Dianne Busch *Leading Artists*
145 W 45th St
Suite 1000
New York, NY 10036, USA

Finkel, Henry (Hank) (Athlete, Basketball Player)
2 Pocahontas Way
Lynnfield, MA 01940-1042, USA

Finkel, Shelly
310 Madison Ave
#804
New York, NY 10017, USA

Finkelstein, Anita (Stylist)
c/o Staff Member *Elite Model Management/Atlanta*
1708 Peachtree St NW
#210
Atlanta, GA 30309, USA

Finkes, Matt (Athlete, Football Player)
5442 Cedar Springs
Columbus, OH 43228, USA

Finlay, Frank (Actor)
Ken McReddie
91 Regent St
London W1R 7TB, UNITED KINGDOM (UK)

Finlay, Jack (Athlete, Football Player)
10 La Cerra Cir
Rancho Mirage, CA 92270, USA

Finley, Brian (Athlete, Hockey Player)
84 Greenview Ln
Sault Ste Marie, ON P6A 6K9, Canada

Finley, Charles E (Chuck) (Athlete, Baseball Player)
500 McCormick Rd
West Monroe, LA 71291-1921, USA

Finley, David (Opera Singer)
1642 Milvia St
#3S
Berkeley, CA 94709, USA

Finley, Gerald H (Opera Singer)
I M G Artists
3 Burlington Lane
Chiswick
London W4 2TH, UNITED KINGDOM (UK)

Finley, Jeff (Race Car Driver)
Team Rensi Motorsports
4011 Handsmill Hwy
York, SC 29745, USA

Finley, Jermichael (Athlete, Football Player)

Finley, John L (Astronaut)
700 Colonial Road
Suite 120
Memphis, TN 38117-5191, USA

Finley, Karen (Artist)
Creative Time
59 E 4th St #6E
New York, NY 10003-8991, USA

Finley, Margot (Actor)
c/o Staff Member *Pacific Artists Management*
1285 W Broadway
Suite 685
Vancouver, BC V6H 3X8, Canada

Finley, Michael (Athlete, Basketball Player)
11 Highgate Dr
San Antonio, TX 78257-1714, USA

Finley, Steven (Steve) (Athlete, Baseball Player)
c/o Lew Weitzman *Preferred Artists*
16633 Ventura Blvd #1421
Encino, CA 91436, USA

Finn, Jim (Athlete, Football Player)
12-14 Western Dr
Fair Lawn, NJ 07410, USA

Finn, John (Actor)
c/o Gabrielle Krengel *Domain Talent*
9229 Sunset Boulevard
Suite 710
Los Angeles, CA 90069, USA

Finn, Neil (Musician, Songwriter, Writer)
c/o Staff Member *WmE2 (WMA-LA)*
1 William Morris Pl
Beverly Hills, CA 90212, USA

Finn, Patrick (Actor)
c/o Staff Member *Brillstein Entertainment Partners*
9150 Wilshire Blvd #350
Beverly Hills, CA 90212, USA

Finn, Steve (Athlete, Hockey Player)
5 De Cheverny St
Blainville, QC J7B 1M7, Canada

Finn, Steven (Athlete, Hockey Player)
8 Rue D'Angers
Blainville, QC J7B 1Y8, Canada

Finn, Tim (Musician)
Grant Thomas Mgmt
98 Surrey St
Darlinghurst, NSW 2010, AUSTRALIA

Finn, Veronica (Musician)
Evolution Talent
1776 Broadway
#1500
New York, NY 10019, USA

Finn, William (Composer, Songwriter, Writer)
New York University
Music Dept
New York, NY 10012, USA

Finnegan, Christian (Comedian)
c/o Kara Welker *Generate Management*
1545 26th St
Suite 200
Santa Monica, CA 90404, USA

Finnegan, Cortland (Athlete, Football Player)
9254 Wardley Park Ln
Brentwood, TN 37027, USA

Finneran, Brian (Athlete, Football Player)
1905 Sugarloaf Club Dr
Duluth, GA 30097, USA

Finneran, Garry (Athlete, Football Player)
17021 Paulette Pl
Granada Hills, CA 91344, USA

Finneran, Gary (Athlete, Football Player)
17021 Paulette Pl
Granada Hills, CA 91344, USA

Finneran, John G (Admiral)
2904 N Leisure World Blvd
#404
Silver Spring, MD 20906, USA

Finneran, Katie (Actor)
c/o Adena Chawke *Greenlight
Management and Production*
13848 Valleyheart Dr
Sherman Oaks, CA 91423, USA

Finneran, Rittenhouse Sharon (Swimmer)
212 Harbor Dr
Santa Cruz, CA 95062, USA

Finnerty, Dan (Actor, Musician)
c/o Staff Member *WmE2 (WMA-LA)*
1 William Morris Pl
Beverly Hills, CA 90212, USA

Finnessey, Shandi (Beauty Pageant Winner)
c/o Staff Member *Miss Universe
Organization, The*
1370 Ave of the Americas Fl 16
New York, NY 10019, USA

Finney, Albert (Actor)
Michael Simkins
45/51 Whitfield St
London W1P 6AA, UNITED KINGDOM (UK)

Finney, Allison (Athlete, Golfer)
78160 Desert Mountain Cir
Bermuda Dunes, CA 92203, USA

Finney, Tom (Soccer Player)
Preston North End FC
Deepdale
Sir Finney Way
Preston PR1 6RU, UNITED KINGDOM (UK)

Finnie, Linda A (Musician)
16 Golf Course Girvan
Ayrshire KA26 9HW, UNITED KINGDOM (UK)

Finnie, Roger (Athlete, Football Player)
937 NW 58th St
Miami, FL 33127, USA

Finnigan, Jennifer (Actor)
c/o John Carrabino *John Carrabino
Management*
5900 Wilshire Blvd Fl 4 #406
Los Angeles, CA 90036, USA

Finnvold, Gar (Athlete, Baseball Player)
1204 NE 4th Ave
Boca Raton, FL 33432-2808, USA

Finsterwald, Dow (Athlete, Golfer)
6330 Masters Blvd
Orlando, FL 32819-4869, USA

Finzer, Dave (Athlete, Football Player)
1435 Kaywood Ln
Glenview, IL 60025, USA

Fiona, Melanie (Musician)
c/o Dennis Ashley *ICM Partners (ICM-LA)*
10250 Constellation Blvd Fl 7
Los Angeles, CA 90067, USA

Fiore, Dave (Athlete, Football Player)
868 Southampton Dr
Palo Alto, CA 94303, USA

Fiore, Kathryn (Actor)
c/o Michael P Levine *Levine Management*
9028 W Sunset Blvd #PH1
Los Angeles, CA 90069, USA

Fiore, Mike (Athlete, Baseball Player)
17 Silver St
Malverne, NY 11565-1116, USA

Fiore, Teri (Stylist)
c/o Staff Member *O'Gorman/Schramm
Represents, Inc*
642 Washington St
#1-A
New York, NY 10014, USA

Fiore, Tony (Athlete, Baseball Player)
19021 Fishermans Bend Dr
Lutz, FL 33558-9754, USA

Fiorentini, Jeff (Athlete, Baseball Player)
4200 Chardonnay Dr
Rockledge, FL 32955-5133, USA

Fiorentino, Peter (Athlete, Hockey Player)
5570 Belmont Ave
Niagara Falls, ON L2H 1J7, Canada

Fiori, Ed (Athlete, Golfer)
50 Burwick St
Sugar Land, TX 77479-2997, USA

Fiori, Fernando (Actor)
c/o Staff Member *Latin World
Entertainment Agency (WEA)*
2601 South Bayshore Drive
Suite 235
Miami, FL 33133-5432, USA

Fiorillo, Elisbatta (Opera Singer)
Columbia Artists Mgmt Inc
165 W 57th St
New York, NY 10019, USA

Fiorito, Jaelle (Actor, Television Host)
c/o Staff Member *Rebel Entertainment
Partners*
5700 Wilshire Blvd
Suite 456
Los Angeles, CA 90036, USA

Firbank, Ann
76 Oxford St.
London, ENGLAND W1N OAX

Fire, Andrew Z. (Nobel Prize Laureate)
Stanford University School Of Medicine
3000 Pasteur Dr
Stanford, CA 94305, USA

Firefall
6400 Pleasant Park Dr
Chanhassen, MN 55317

Fireman, Paul B (Business Person, Misc)
Reebok International
1895 J W Foster Blvd
Canton, MA 02021, USA

Fireovid, Steve (Athlete, Baseball Player)
1408 Woodstream Dr
Bryan, OH 43506-9049, USA

Fires, Earlie S (Horse Racer)
16337 Rivervale Lane
Rivervale, AR 60640-7034, USA

Firestone, Andrew (Actor, Reality TV Star)
c/o Staff Member *Paradigm (LA)*
360 N Crescent Dr
North Bldg
Beverly Hills, CA 90210, USA

Firestone, Dennis (Race Car Driver)
5380 Via Moreno
Yorba Linda, CA 92686, USA

Firestone, Eddie
303 S. Crescent Heights
Los Angeles, CA 90048

Firestone, Roy (Sportscaster)
Seizen/Wallach Productions
257 S Rodeo Dr
Beverly Hills, CA 90212-3803, USA

Firm, The
57A Great Titchfield St.
London, ENGLAND W1P 7FL

Firova, Dan (Athlete, Baseball Player)
208 Saint John St
Refugio, TX 78377-3436, USA

First, Neal L (Misc)
9437 W Garnette Dr
Sun City, AZ 85373, USA

Firth, Colin (Actor)
c/o Jessica Kolstad *WKT Public Relations
(WKT-LA)*
9350 Wilshire Blvd
Suite 450
Beverly Hills, CA 90212, USA

Firth, Peter (Actor)
Markham & Froggatt
Julian House
4 Windmill St
London W1P 1HF, UNITED KINGDOM (UK)

Fiscella, Nicole (Model)
c/o Staff Member *New York Model
Management*
596 Broadway #701
New York, NY 10012, USA

Fischbach, Ephraim (Physicist)
5821 Farm Ridge Road
West Lafayette, IN 47906, USA

Fischbacher, Andrea (Athlete, Skier)
Hauptstr. 255
Eben/PG A-5531, Austria

Fischer, Adam
Askonas Holt Ltd
27 Chancery Lane
London WC2A 1PF, UNITED KINGDOM (UK)

Fischer, Bernard
208 King Rd.
Kuna, ID 83634

Fischer, Bill (Athlete, Baseball Player)
139 Upland Dr
Council Bluffs, IA 51503-4823, USA

Fischer, Bill (Athlete, Football Player)
23191 Shady Oak ln
Estero, FL 33928, USA

Fischer, Brad (Athlete, Baseball Player)
6110 Forest Ridge Ct
Me Farland, WI 53558-9020, USA

Fischer, Edmond H (Nobel Prize Laureate)
5540 N Windermere Road
Seattle, WA 98105-2849, USA

Fischer, Erich (Athlete, Olympic Athlete, Water Polo Player)
1405 Bluebird Canyon Dr
Laguna Beach, CA 92651-3006, USA

Fischer, Ernst Otto (Nobel Prize Laureate)
Sohnckestr 16
Munich 81479, GERMANY

Fischer, Hank (Athlete, Baseball Player)
7024 Summit Dr
Navarre, FL 32566-8745, USA

Fischer, Heinz (President)
Prasidentschaftskanzlei
Hofburg
Alderstiege
Vienna 1010, AUSTRIA

Fischer, Helmut
Kaiserplatz 5
Munich, GERMANY D-80803

Fischer, Ivan
1 Andrassy Utca 27
Budapest 1061, HUNGARY

Fischer, Jack D
PO Box 1407
Friendswood, TX 77549-1407, USA

Fischer, Jeff (Athlete, Baseball Player)
215 Worth Ct N
West Palm Beach, FL 33405-2751, USA

Fischer, Jenna (Actor)
1663 Grandview Ave
Glendale, CA 91201, USA

Fischer, Jiri (Athlete, Hockey Player)
20101 Westview Dr
Northville, MI 48167-9206, USA

Fischer, Lisa (Musician)
Alive Enterprices
3264 S Kihei Road
Kihei, HI 96753, USA

Fischer, Michael L (Misc)
California Coastal Conservancy
1330 Broadway #1100
Oakland, CA 94612, USA

Fischer, Patrick (Pat) (Athlete, Football Player)
P.O. Box 4289
Leesburg, VA 20177, USA

Fischer, Schmidt Birgit (Athlete)
Kuckuckswald 11
Kleinmachnow 14532, GERMANY

Fischer, Stanley (Business Person, Economist)
399 Park Ave Fmt 2
New York, NY 10022-4661, USA

Fischer, Sven (Athlete)
Schillerhoehe 7
Schmalkalden 98574, GERMANY

Fischer, Tiet Jen (Stylist)
c/o Staff Member *Artist Untied (LA)*
845 S Mansfield Ave
#1
Los Angeles, CA 90036, USA

Fischer, Todd (Athlete, Baseball Player)
12734 Newtown Rd
Unionville, TN 37180-5004, USA

Fischer, Todd (Athlete, Golfer)
7347 Linwood Ct
Pleasanton, CA 94588-4877, USA

Fischer, Van (Director)
Gersh Agency
232 N Canon Dr
Beverly Hills, CA 90210, USA

Fischer, Veronika
Glockengiesserwall 3
Hamburg, GERMANY D-20095

Fischer, William A (Moose) (Athlete, Football Player)
1790 Pinnacle Ridge Ln
Colorado Springs, CO 80919, USA

Fischer-Dieskau, Dietrich (Opera Singer)
Hochschule Fuer Musik
Hans Einzler Berlin
Charlottenstrasse, 55
Berlin D-10117, Germany

Fischerspooner (Music Group)
c/o Staff Member *Paradigm (Monterey)*
404 W Franklin St
Monterey, CA 93940, USA

Fischette, Charles (General)
8107 SE 169th Palownia Loop
The Villages, FL 32162-8378, USA

Fischetti, Brad (Musician)
Evolution Talent Agency
1776 roadway
15th Floor
New York, NY 10019

Fischetti, Vincent (Biologist)
Rockefeller University
Medical Center
1230 York Ave
New York, NY 10021, USA

Fischler, Patrick (Actor)
c/o Stewart Strunk *Main Title Entertainment*
8383 Wilshire Blvd
Suite 408
Los Angeles, CA 90211, USA

Fischlin, Mike (Athlete, Baseball Player)
1010 Curtright Pl
Greensboro, GA 30642-7432, USA

Fiset, Stephane (Athlete, Hockey Player)
c/o Staff Member *Newport Sports Management*
1042 Charcot
Suite 304
Bouchervulle, QC J4B 8R4, Canada

Fish, Ginger (Musician)
c/o Staff Member *Interscope Records (LA) - Main*
2220 Colorado Ave
Santa Monica, CA 90404, USA

Fish, Howard M (General)
1223 Capilano Dr
Shreveport, LA 71106, USA

Fish, Matt (Athlete, Basketball Player)
4138 E Waterman Ct
Gilbert, AZ 85297-3574, USA

Fishbacher, Siegfried (Magician)
Mirage Hotel & Casino
3400 Las Vegas Blvd S
Las Vegas, NV 89109, USA

Fishback, Joe (Athlete, Football Player)
148 Fairoaks Cir
Stockbridge, GA 30281, USA

Fishbone
PO Box 4450
New York, NY 10101

Fishburne, Laurence (Actor)
c/o Helen Sugland *Landmark Artists*
4116 W Magnolia Blvd
Suite 101
Burbank, CA 91505, USA

Fishel, Danielle (Actor)
c/o Staff Member *Innovative Artists (LA)*
1505 10th St
Santa Monica, CA 90401, USA

Fishel, John (Athlete, Baseball Player)
329 Marjoram Dr
Columbus, OH 43230-7027, USA

Fisher, Allison (Billiards Player)
Alfie Inc
9021 Hwy 105
South Boone, NC 28607

Fisher, Anna L (Astronaut)
1912 Elmen St
Houston, TX 77019-6144, USA

Fisher, Bernard F (General, War Hero)
4200 W King Road
Kuna, ID 83634, USA

Fisher, Brian (Athlete, Baseball Player)
3660 S Uravan St
Aurora, CO 80013-3458, USA

Fisher, Bryan (Actor)
c/o Jamie Freed *Paris Hilton Entertainment*
8383 Wilshire Blvd
Suite 1050
Beverly Hills, CA 90211, USA

Fisher, Carrie (Actor, Writer)
1700 Coldwater Rd
Beverly Hills, CA 90210, USA

Fisher, Charles (Athlete, Football Player)
PO Box 133
Aliquippa, PA 15001, USA

Fisher, Climie
30 Bridstow Pl.
London, ENGLAND W2 5AE

Fisher, Derek (Athlete, Basketball Player)
23808 Long Valley Rd
Hidden Hills, CA 91302, USA

Fisher, Doug (Athlete, Football Player)
4040 Hancock St
Apt 204
San Diego, CA 92110, USA

Fisher, Dunc (Athlete, Hockey Player)
2600 Regina Ave
Regina, SK S4S 0G5, Canada

Fisher, Ed (Athlete, Football Player)
4734 E Redfield Rd
Phoenix, AZ 85032, USA

Fisher, Eddie G (Athlete, Baseball Player)
408 Cardinal Cir S
Altus, OK 73521-1714, USA

Fisher, Elder A (Bud) (Bowler)
7551 Brackenwood Circle N
Indianapolis, IN 46260, USA

Fisher, Evan (Musician)
GEMS
PO Box 1031
Montrose, CA 91021, USA

Fisher, Frances (Actor)
c/o Tammy Rosen *Sanders Armstrong Caserta*
425 N Robertson Blvd
Los Angeles, CA 90048, USA

Fisher, Fritz (Athlete, Baseball Player)
3703 Barcelona Dr
Toledo, OH 43615-1203, USA

Fisher, Gerry
River Bank Hartsfield Rd.
W. Molesey Surrey, ENGLAND

Fisher, Isla (Actor)
c/o Julie Darmody *Mosaic Media Group*
9200 W. Sunset Blvd
10th Floor
Los Angeles, CA 90069, USA

Fisher, Jack (Athlete, Baseball Player)
4407 Nicholas St
Easton, PA 18045-4930, USA

Fisher, Jeff (Coach, Football Coach)
460 Great Circle Rd
Nashville, TN 37228, USA

Fisher, Jeff (Athlete, Football Coach, Football Player)
385 Lake Valley Dr
Franklin, TN 37069, USA

Fisher, Joel (Artist)
PO Box 65
Palisades, NY 10964-0065, USA

Fisher, Joely (Actor)
c/o John Carrabino *John Carrabino Management*
5900 Wilshire Blvd Fl 4 #406
Los Angeles, CA 90036, USA

Fisher, Jules E (Designer)
Jules Fisher Enterprises
126 5th Ave
New York, NY 10011, USA

Fisher, Kimberly (Model)
PO Box 69330 #703
West Hollywood, CA 90069

Fisher, Mary (Misc)
Charles Scribner's Sons
866 3rd Ave
New York, NY 10022, USA

Fisher, Matthew (Misc)
39 Croham Road
South Croydon CR2 7HD, UNITED KINGDOM (UK)

Fisher, Maurice (Maury) (Athlete, Baseball Player)
15920 Lucerne Rd
Fredericktown, OH 43019-9531, USA

Fisher, Mimi (Stylist)
c/o Staff Member *Judy Casey Inc*
114 E 13th St
New York, NY 10003, USA

Fisher, Paul C (Misc)
Fisher Space Pen Company
711 Yucca St Boulder City,
NV 89005-1905, USA

Fisher, Ray (Athlete, Football Player)
RR 2 Box 235
Fairfield, IL 62837, USA

Fisher, Raymond C (Judge)
US Courts of Appeals
125 S Grand Ave
Pasadena, CA 91105, USA

Fisher, Red (Writer)
Montreal Gazette
250 Saint Antoine W
Montreal, QC H2Y 3R7, CANADA

Fisher, Rob
45 Montague Rd.
Richmond Surrey, ENGLAND

Fisher, Robert (Business Person)
Gap Inc
2 Folsom St
San Francisco, CA 94105, USA

Fisher, Roger (Musician)
Borman Entertainment
1250 6th St
#401
Santa Monica, CA 90401, USA

Fisher, Sarah (Race Car Driver)
c/o Staff Member *NASCAR*
1801 Speedway Blvd
Daytona Beach, FL 32015, USA

Fisher, Steve (Coach)
San Diego State University
Athletic Dept
San Diego, CA 92182, USA

Fisher, Terry Louise
5314 Pacific Ave.
Marina del Rey, CA 90292-7118

Fisher, Thomas L
Nicor Inc
1844 Ferry Road
Naperville, IL 60563, USA

Fisher, Tom (Athlete, Baseball Player)
8771 Boxlev Dr Aot IH
Camby, IN 46113-8968, USA

Fisher, Tony (Athlete, Football Player)

Fisher, Trisha Leigh
243 Delfern Dr.
Los Angeles, CA 90077

Fisher, William F (Astronaut)
1119 Woodland Dr
Seabrook, TX 77586-4014, USA

Fisher-Stevens, Lorraine (Baseball Player)
120 Birdsell St
Jackson, MI 49203-4670, USA

Fishman, Jerald G (Business Person)
Analog Devices Inc
1 Technology Way
Norwood, MA 02062, USA

Fishman, Jon (Musician)
Dionyslan Productions
431 Pine St
Burlington, VT 05401, USA

Fishman, Michael (Actor)
c/o Ryan Glasgow *Bohemia Group*
1680 Vine St Ste 216
Los Angeles, CA 90028, USA

Fisichella, Giancarlo (Race Car Driver)
Benetton Formula Ltd
Whiteways Tech Centre
Enstone
Chipping Norton, Oxfordshire OX8 6XZ, UNITED KINGDOM

Fisk, Carlton (Athlete, Baseball Player)
18705 63rd Ave E
Bradenton, FL 34211-7025, USA

Fisk, Pliny III (Architect)
Maximum Potential Building Systems Center
8604 FM 969
Austin, TX 78724, USA

Fisk, Schuyler (Actor)
c/o Staff Member *Fat Dot*
87 Bedford St
Suite 1
New York, NY 10014, USA

Fiske, Robert B Jr (Attorney, Attorney General, General)
19 Juniper Road
Darien, CT 06820, USA

Fisker, Bruce L (General)
9001 S Jimson Weed Way
Highlands Ranch, CO 80126, USA

Fister, Doug (Athlete, Baseball Player)
2179 Dunn Rd
Merced, CA 95340-8679, USA

Fitch, Bill (Basketball Coach, Coach)
3714 Walden Estates Dr
Montgomery, TX 77356-8043, USA

Fitch, Leigh (Horse Racer)
RR 114
Sebag, ME 04029, USA

Fitch, Val L (Nobel Prize Laureate)
292 Hartley Ave
Princeton, NJ 08540-5656, USA

Fitchner, Bob (Athlete, Hockey Player)
138 Ross Pl
Carman, MB R0G 0J0, Canada

Fites, Donald V (Business Person)
Caterpillar Inc
100 NE Adams St
Peoria, IL 61629, USA

Fitgerald, Ann (Stylist)
c/o Staff Member *Team*
423 W Broadway
4th Floor
Boston, MA 02127, USA

Fittipaldi, Christian (Race Car Driver)
282 Alphaville Barueri
Sao Paulo 064500, BRAZIL

Fittipaldi, Emerson (Race Car Driver)
735 Crandon Blvd #503
Miami, FL 33149, USA

Fittipaldi, Lisa (Artist)
Mind's Eye Foundation
215 Beauregard San Antonio,
TX 78204-1304, USA

Fitt of Bell's Hill, Gerald (Government
Official)
irish Club
82 Eaton Square
London SW1, UNITED KINGDOM (UK)

Fitts, Rick
1903 Dracena Dr.
Los Angeles, CA 90068

Fitz, Raymond L (Educator)
University of Dayton
President's Office
Dayton, OH 45469, USA

Fitzgerald, A Ernest (Government Official,
Lawyer)
Air Force Management Systems
Pentagon
Washington, DC 20330, USA

Fitzgerald, Brian (Athlete, Baseball Player)
7226 John Taylor Mews
Ruther Glen, VA 22546-4816, USA

Fitzgerald, Caitlin (Actor)
c/o Adam Schweitzer *ICM Partners
(ICM-NY)*
730 Fifth Ave
New York, NY 10019, USA

Fitzgerald, Ed (Athlete, Baseball Player)
431 Christopher St
Folsom, CA 95630-1706, USA

Fitzgerald, Fern (Actor)
Boutique
10 Universal City Plaza
Ste 2000
Universal City, CA 91608, USA

FitzGerald, Frances (Writer)
Simon & Schuster
1230 Ave of Americas
New York, NY 10020, USA

Fitzgerald, Glenn (Actor)
c/o Sue Leibman *Barking Dog
Entertainment*
609 Greenwich St
6th Floor
New York, NY 10014, USA

FitzGerald, Helen (Actor)
Paul Lohner
9300 Wilshire Blvd
#555
Beverly Hills, CA 90212, USA

Fitzgerald, Jack (Actor)
William Kerwin Agency
1605 N Cahuenga
#202
Los Angeles, CA 90028, USA

Fitzgerald, James F (Misc)
Golden State Warriors
1001 Broadway
Oakland, CA 94607, USA

Fitzgerald, John (Athlete, Baseball Player)
1913 Greve Ave
Apt 1
Spring Lake, NJ 07762-2354, USA

Fitzgerald, John (Athlete, Football Player)
408 Arborcrest Dr
Richardson, TX 75080, USA

Fitzgerald, Kevin (Misc)
Alameda East Veterinary Hospital
9770 E Alameda Ave
Denver, CO 80247, USA

Fitzgerald, Larry (Athlete, Football Player)
6920 E Hummingbird Ln
Paradise Valley, AZ 85253, USA

Fitzgerald, Marcus (Athlete, Football
Player)
c/o Roosevelt Barnes *Maximum Sports
Management*
6435 W Jefferson Blvd
#197
Fort Wayne, IN 46804, USA

Fitzgerald, Melissa (Actor)
c/o Staff Member *Geddes Agency, The*
8430 Santa Monica Blvd
Suite 200
Los Angeles, CA 90069, USA

Fitzgerald, Mickey (Athlete, Football
Player)
4579 Somerset Rd SW
Smyrna, GA 30082, USA

Fitzgerald, Mike (Athlete, Baseball Player)
415 Parkview Dr
Rochester, IL 62563-9543, USA

Fitzgerald, Mike (Athlete, Baseball Player)
502 Flint Ave
Long Beach, CA 90814-2039, USA

Fitzgerald, Mosley Benita (Athlete)
Women in Cable/Telecommunications
14555 Avion Parkway
Chantilly, VA 20151, USA

FitzGerald, Niali W A (Business Person)
Unilever NV
Weena 455
Rotterdam, DK 3000, NETHERLANDS

Fitzgerald, Pat (Athlete, Football Player)
2271 Bracken Ln
Northfield, IL 60093

Fitzgerald, Peter
1133 Crest Ln
Me Lean, VA 22101-1805

Fitzgerald, Rusty (Athlete, Hockey Player)
4730 Dodge St
Duluth, MN 55804, USA

Fitzgerald, Tac (Actor)
c/o Staff Member *Iris Burton Agency*
10100 Santa Monica Blvd Ste 1300
Los Angeles, CA 90067, USA

Fitzgerald, Tara (Actor)
Caroline Dawson
125 Gloucester Road
London SW7 4IE, UNITED KINGDOM
(UK)

Fitzgerald, Thom (Director)
c/o Gloria Bonelli *Gloria Bonelli &
Associates*
Prefers to be contacted via email or
telephone
Pine Bush, NY 12566, USA

Fitzgerald, Tom (Athlete, Hockey Player)
3 Samuel Phelps Way
North Reading, MA 01864, USA

Fitzgerald, Tom (Athlete, Hockey Player)
Pittsburgh Penguins 66 Mario Lemieux Pl
Ste 2
Attn: Asst To General Manager
Pittsburgh, PA 15219-3504, USA

Fitzgerald-Leclair, Meryle (Baseball
Player)
909 E Hanson St
Mitchell, SD 57301-3635, USA

Fitzhugh, Steve (Athlete, Football Player)
1030 Felt' Ct Apt 330
Hopkins, MN 55343, USA

Fitzkee, Scott (Athlete, Football Player)
1611 Grafton Shop Rd
Forest Hill, MD 21050, USA

Fitzmaurice, David J (Misc)
Electrical Radio & Machinists Union
11256 156th St NW
Washington, DC 20005, USA

Fitzmaurice, Michael J (General, War
Hero)
PO Box 178
Hartford, SD 57033, USA

Fitzmaurice, Molly (Stylist)
c/o Staff Member *O'Gorman/Schramm
Represents, Inc*
642 Washington St
#1-A
New York, NY 10014, USA

Fitzmaurice, Shaun (Athlete, Baseball
Player)
1911 Normanstone Dr
Midlothian, VA 23113-9669, USA

Fitzmorris, Al (Athlete, Baseball Player)
17512 W 159th Ter
Olathe, KS 66062, USA

Fitzmorris, Al (Athlete, Baseball Player)
17512 W 159th Ter
Olathe, KS 66062-4017, USA

Fitzpatrick, Mark (Athlete, Hockey Player)
10571 SW Kelsey Way
Port Saint Lucie, FL 34987-1989, USA

Fitzpatrick, Michael (Baseball Player)
262 Lodge Ln
Kalamazoo, MI 49009-9161, USA

Fitzpatrick, Mike (Athlete, Baseball
Player)
262 Lodge Ln
Kalamazoo, MI 49009-9161, USA

Fitzpatrick, Rory (Athlete, Hockey Player)
580 Colebrook Dr
Rochester, NY 14617, USA

Fitzpatrick, Ross (Athlete, Hockey Player)
PO Box 459
Hershey_, PA 17033-0459, USA

Fitzpatrick, Ryan (Athlete, Football Player)
c/o Jimmy Sexton *CAA (Memphis)*
1100 Ridgeway Loop Rd
5th Floor
Memphis, TN 38120, USA

Fitzpatrick, Sandy (Athlete, Hockey
Player)
11250 Lakerim Rd
San Diego, CA 92131, USA

Fitzpatrick, Sonya (Psychic, Writer)
Animals Are Forever LLC
80 Garden Ct
Suite 150
Monterey, CA 93940, USA

Fitzsimmons, Greg (Actor)
c/o Kara Welker *Generate Management*
1545 26th St
Suite 200
Santa Monica, CA 90404, USA

Fitzsimonds, Roger L (Financier)
Firstar Corp
777 E Wisconsin Ave
Milwaukee, WI 53202, USA

Fitzwater, Marlin (Government Official)
851 Cedar Drive
Deale, MD 20751-9613, USA

Five for Fighting (Music Group)
c/o Staff Member *Paradigm (NY)*
360 Park Ave S Fl 16
New York, NY 10010, USA

Fix, Oliver (Athlete)
Ringstr 6
Stadtbergen, GERMANY

Fixman, Marshall (Misc)
Colorado State University
Chemistry Dept
Fort Collins, CO 80523, USA

Fizer, Marcus (Basketball Player)
Charlotte Bobcats
129 W Trade St #700
Charlotte, NC 28202, USA

Flach, Ken (Coach, Tennis Player)
Vanderbilt University
Athletic Dept
Nashville, TN 37240, USA

Flach, Thomas (Yachtsman)
Johanna-Resch-Str 13
Berlin 12439, GERMANY

Flack, Enya (Actor)
c/o Paul Barrutia *The Paradise Group*
PO Box 69451
West Hollywood, CA 90069, USA

Flack, Roberta (Musician)
c/o Staff Member *Universal Attractions*
135 W 26th St
12 Floor
New York, NY 10001, USA

Flade, H Kiaus-Dietrich (Cosmonaut)
Airbus Industries
1 Rond Point M Bellonte
Blagnac Cedex 31707, FRANCE

Flagg, Fannie (Actor, Comedian)
c/o Sally Willcox *Creative Artists Agency
(CAA-LA)*
2000 Ave Of The Stars
Los Angeles, CA 90067, USA

Flagg, Josh (Business Person, Reality TV
Star)
Coldwell Banker Beverly Hills East
9388 Santa Monica Blvd
Beverly Hills, CA 90210, USA

Flaherty, Harry (Athlete, Football Player)
23 Elizabeth Dr
Oceanport, NJ 07757, USA

Flaherty, Joe
c/o Staff Member *Silver Massetti & Szatmary (SMS-NY)*
145 W 45th St #1204
New York, NY 10036, USA

Flaherty, John (Athlete, Baseball Player)
17 Joseph Bow Ct
Pearl River, NY 10965-2868, USA

Flaherty, Maureen
PO Box 15967
Long Beach, CA 90815-0967, USA

Flaherty, Stephen (Composer)
c/o Staff Member *Gersh (LA)*
9465 Wilshire Blvd
Suite 600
Beverly Hills, CA 90212, USA

Flaherty, Wade (Athlete, Hockey Player)
c/o Art Breeze *Pro-Rep Entertainment Consulting*
113-276 Midpark Way SE
Calgary, AB T2X 1J6, Canada

Flair, Ric (Athlete, Wrestler)
c/o Elaine Gillespie *Gillespie Agency, The*
3007 Millwood Ave
Columbia, SC 29205, USA

Flake, Jeff (Congressman, Politician)
240 Cannon HOB
Washington, DC 20515, USa

Flame, Penny (Adult Film Star)
19422 Archwood St.
Reseda, CA 91335, USA

Flaming Lips, The (Music Group, Musician)
c/o Robby Fraser *WME (LA)*
9601 Wilshire Blvd Fl 3
Beverly Hills, CA 90210, USA

Flanagan, Barry (Artist)
5E Fawe St
London E14 6PD, UNITED KINGDOM (UK)

Flanagan, Crista (Actor)
c/o Kay Liberman *Liberman/Zerman Management*
252 N Larchmont Blvd
Suite 200
Los Angeles, CA 90004, USA

Flanagan, Ed (Athlete, Football Player)
10981 Clayton St
Northglenn, CO 80233, USA

Flanagan, Edward M Jr (General)
Parade Rest
12 Oyster Catcher Road
Beaufort, SC 29907, USA

Flanagan, Fionnula (Actor)
c/o Dick Guttman *Guttman Associates*
118 S Beverly Dr
Suite 201
Beverly Hills, CA 90212, USA

Flanagan, Flonnula (Actor)
Guttman
118 S Beverly Dr
Beverly Hills, CA 90212, USA

Flanagan, Helen (Actor)
c/o Staff Member *Linton Management*
3 The Rock
Greater Manchester BL9 0JP, UNITED KINGDOM

Flanagan, James L (Engineer)
Rulgers University
Computer Aids for Industry Center
Piscataway, NJ 08855, USA

Flanagan, Mike (Athlete, Football Player)
4631 Waring St
Houston, TX 77027, USA

Flanagan, Shalane (Athlete, Track Athlete)
c/o Staff Member *US Olympic Committee*
Alumni Relations
1750 E Boulder St
Colorado Springs, CO 80909-5793, USA

Flanagan, Tommy (Actor)
c/o Beth Holden-Garland *Untitled Entertainment (LA)*
350 S. Beverly Dr #200
Beverly Hills, CA 90212, USA

Flanery, Bridget
8428-C Melrose Pl.
Los Angeles, CA 90069

Flanery, Sean Patrick (Actor)
c/o Jeff Golenberg *Collective*
8383 Wilshire Blvd
Suite 1050
Beverly Hills, CA 90211, USA

Flanigan, Jim (Athlete, Football Player)
3820 Sand Bay Point Rd
Sturgeon Bay, WI 54235, USA

Flanigan, Jim (Athlete, Football Player)
4511 Wyandot Trl
Green Bay, WI 54313, USA

Flanigan, Joe (Actor)
c/o John Carrabino *John Carrabino Management*
5900 Wilshire Blvd Fl 4 #406
Los Angeles, CA 90036, USA

Flanigan, Lauren (Opera Singer)
Robert Lombardo
Harkness Plaza
61 W 62nd St #6F
New York, NY 10023, USA

Flanigan, Tom (Athlete, Baseball Player)
114 E 40th St
Covington, KY 41015-1802, USA

Flanigen, Edith (Inventor)
502 Woodland Hills Rd
White Plains, NY 10603-3136, USA

Flannery, John (Athlete, Baseball Player)
9002 Scottish Pastures Dr
Austin, TX 78750-3582, USA

Flannery, John (Athlete, Football Player)
7514 Dawn Mist Ct
Sugar Land, TX 77479, USA

Flannery, Kate (Actor)
c/o Kristopher Koller *Seven Summits Pictures & Management*
8906 W Olympic Blvd
Ground Floor
Beverly Hills, CA 90211, USA

Flannery, Susan (Actor)
Flannery-Daedy-Leona
6977 Shepard Mesa
Carpinteria, CA 93013, USA

Flannery, Thomas (Cartoonist, Editor)
911 Dartmouth Glen Way
Baltimore, MD 21212, USA

Flannery, Tim (Athlete, Baseball Player)
715 Hymettus Ave
Encinitas, CA 92024-2148, USA

Flannigan, Maureen (Actor)
Gold Marshak Liedtke
3500 W olive Ave
#1400
Burbank, CA 91505, USA

Flaska, Carrie (Actor)
3440 29th St
Astoria, NY 11106, USA

Flatley, Michael (Actor, Dancer)
c/o Staff Member *Creative Artists Agency (CAA-LA)*
2000 Ave Of The Stars
Los Angeles, CA 90067, USA

Flatley, Patrick (Pat) (Athlete, Hockey Player)
c/o Staff Member *National Hockey League (NHL)*
50 Bay St
11th Floor
Toronto, ON M5J 2X8, Canada

Flatley, Paul R (Athlete, Football Player)
795 Woods Rd
Richmond, IN 47374, USA

Flatt, Lester
PO Box 647
Hendersonville, TN 37215

Flaum, Joel M (Judge)
US District Court
219 S Dearborn St
Chicago, IL 60604, USA

Flav, Flavor (Actor, Comedian, Reality TV Star)
c/o Heather Taylor *Alliance Worldwide Communications*
12115 Magnolia Blvd
#137
North Hollywood, CA 91607, USA

Flavell, Richard A (Misc)
Yale University
Medical Center
Immunology Dept
New Haven, CT 06520, USA

Flavin, Jennifer (Model)
30 Beverly Park
Beverly Hills, CA 90210, USA

Flavin, John (Athlete, Baseball Player)
23060 16th St
Newhall, CA 91321-1054, USA

Flavio, Alfaro (Athlete, Baseball Player, Olympic Athlete)
3240 N Bass Island Rd
West Sacramento, CA 95691-5848, USA

Flay, Bobby (Chef, Television Host)
c/o Jonathan Rosen *WME (WMA-NY)*
1325 Ave of the Americas
New York, NY 10019, USA

Flchter, Michael (Baseball Player)
8821 Jackson Ct
Munster, IN 46321-2410, USA

Flea (Actor, Musician)
c/o Peter Mensch *Q Prime South*
729 Seventh Ave
16th Floor
New York, NY 10019, USA

Flebotte, Dave (Producer)
c/o Ann Blanchard *Creative Artists Agency (CAA-LA)*
2000 Ave Of The Stars
Los Angeles, CA 90067, USA

Fleck, Bela (Composer, Musician)
c/o Ted Kurland *Ted Kurland Associates*
173 Brighton Ave
Boston, MA 02134, USA

Fleck, Jack (Athlete, Golfer)
12006 Edgewater Rd
Fort Smith, AR 72903-5889, USA

Fleckman, Marty (Athlete, Golfer)
26411 Ridgestone Park Ln
Cypress, TX 77433-1279, USA

Fleder, Gary R (Director)
ACTW Filmworks
624 Sunset Ave
Venice, CA 90291, USA

Fleeshman, Richard (Actor)
Pemberton Associates
193 Wardour Street
London W1V 3FA, UNITED KINGDOM (UK)

Fleetwood, Ken (Designer, Fashion Designer)
14 Savile Row
London SW1, UNITED KINGDOM (UK)

Fleetwood, Mick (Musician)
Fleetwood Marketing
5737 Kanan Rd #237
Agoura Hills, CA 91301, USA

Fleigel, Bernie (Athlete, Basketball Player)
21 Granville Rd # 3
Cambridge, MA 02138-6806, USA

Fleischer, Arthur Jr (Attorney, Attorney General, General)
Fried Frank Harris Shriver Jacobson
1 New York Plaza
New York, NY 10004, USA

Fleischer, Charles
749 N. Crescent Heights
Los Angeles, CA 90038

Fleischer, Daniel (Religious Leader)
201 Princess Dr
Corpus Christi, TX 78410, USA

Fleischer, Richard (General)
1050 E Brigham Rd Apt 38
Saint George, UT 84790-8439, USA

Fleischman, Paul (Writer)
PO Box 646
Aromas, CA 95004, USA

Fleischmann, Peter (Director, Producer)
Filmzentrum Babelsberg
August-Bebel-Str 26-53
Potsdam 14482, GERMANY

Fleisher, Brett (Actor)
c/o Alan Somers *Pure Arts Entertainment*
1925 Century Park East
Suite 2320
Los Angeles, CA 90067, USA

Fleisher, Bruce (Athlete, Golfer)
11722 Cardena Ct
Palm Beach Gardens, FL 33418-1564, USA

Fleisher, Leon (Musician)
20 Merrymount Road
Baltimore, MD 21210, USA

Fleiss, Heidi (Misc)
Dirty Laundry
150 S Highway 160
4A
Pahrump, NV 89048-2133, USA

Fleiss, Michael (Mike) (Director, Producer)
c/o Staff Member *Next Entertainment*
3300 W Olive Ave #500
Burbank, CA 91403-3520, USA

Fleiss, Noah (Actor)
c/o Ellen Gilbert *Abrams Artists Agency (NY)*
275 Seventh Ave
26th Floor
New York, NY 10001, USA

Fleming, Cory (Athlete, Football Player)
2500 Whitney Pl Apt 8108
Metairie, LA 70002, USA

Fleming, David (Dave) (Athlete, Baseball Player)
37 Laurelwood Ln
Southbury, CT 06488-4657, USA

Fleming, Ed
RD #3 Box 261K
Greensbury, PA 15601

Fleming, Eric (Director)
c/o David Krintzman *Morris, Yorn, Barnes, Levine, Krintzman, Rubenstein and Kohner*
2000 Ave of the Stars
3rd Floor, North Tower
Los Angeles, CA 90067, USA

Fleming, George (Athlete, Football Player)
1100 Lake Washington Blvd S
Seattle, WA 98144, USA

Fleming, Gerry (Athlete, Hockey Player)
c/o Staff Member *Florida Everblades*
11000 Everblades Pkwy
Estero, FL 33928, USA

Fleming, James P (General)
PO Box 487
Manvel, TX 77578-0487, USA

Fleming, John (Congressman, Politician)
416 Cannon HOB
Washington, DC 20515, USA

Fleming, Mac A (Misc)
Maintenance of Ways Brotherhood
26555 Evergreen Road
Southfield, MI 48076, USA

Fleming, Marv (Athlete, Football Player)
909 Howard St
Marina del Rey, CA 90292, USA

Fleming, Peggy (Athlete, Figure Skater, Olympic Athlete)
Fleming Jenkins Vineyards & Winery 300 College Ave
Apt A
Los Gatos, CA 95030-7066, USA

Fleming, Peter E Jr (Attorney, Attorney General, General)
Curtis Mallet-Prevost Colt Mosle
101 Park Ave
New York, NY 10178, USA

Fleming, Reg (Athlete, Hockey Player)

Fleming, Renee (Musician, Opera Singer)
c/o Staff Member *IMG (Cleveland)*
1360 E 9th St
Suite 100
Cleveland, OH 44114, USA

Fleming, Rhonda (Actor)
10281 Century Woods Dr
Los Angeles, CA 90067, USA

Fleming, Richard C D (Engineer)
Greater Denver Chamber of Commerce
1445 Market ST
Denver, CO 80202, USA

Fleming, Scott (Government Official)
2750 Shasta Road
Berkeley, CA 94708, USA

Fleming, Troy (Athlete, Football Player)
115 Reveille Ct
Franklin, TN 37064, USA

Fleming, Troy (Athlete, Football Player)
P.O. Box 789
Knoxville, TN 37901, USA

Fleming, Vern (Athlete, Basketball Player, Olympic Athlete)
10713 Brixton Lane
Fishers, IN 46037-8707, USA

Fleming, Wendell H (Mathematician)
9 Dolly Dr
Bristol, RI 02809, USA

Fleming, Willie (Athlete, Football Player)
10295 Maggira Pl
Las Vegas, NV 89135-3249, USA

Flemister, Zeron (Athlete, Football Player)
10119 Southlawn Cir
Commerce City, CO 80022, USA

Flemming, Catherine
Goethestr. 17
Munich, GERMANY D-80336

Flemming, John (Artist)
1409 Cambronne St
New Orleans, LA 70118, USA

Flemming, William N (Bill) (Sportscaster)
ABC-TV Sports Dept
77 W 66th St
New York, NY 10023, USA

Flemyng, Gordon (Director)
1 Albert Road
Wilmslow
Cheshire SK9 5HT, UNITED KINGDOM (UK)

Flemyng, Jason (Actor)
Conway Van Gelder Robinson
18-21 Jermyn St
London SW1Y 6NB, UNITED KINGDOM (UK)

Flemyng, Robert (Actor)
4 Netherbourne Road
London SW4, UNITED KINGDOM (UK)

Flener, Huck (Athlete, Baseball Player)
2186 North Ave
Chico, CA 95926-1430, USA

Flennes, Ranulph T-W (Misc)
Greenlands Exford
Minehead
West Sussex, UNITED KINGDOM (UK)

Flerstein, Harvey F (Actor, Musician, Writer)
1479 Carla Ridge Dr
Beverly Hills, CA 90210, USA

Flesch, John (Athlete, Hockey Player)
74101 8th Ave
South Haven, MI 49090-9750, USA

Flesch, Steve (Athlete, Golfer)
10710 Meadow Stable Ln
Union, KY 41091-7986, USA

Flessel, Craig (Cartoonist)
40 Camino Alto
#2306
Mill Valley, CA 94941, USA

Fletcher, Andrew (Baseball Player)
3282 Kinderhill Ln
Germantown, TN 38138-8210, USA

Fletcher, Andy (Musician)
Reach Media
295 Greenwich St
#109
New York, NY 10007, USA

Fletcher, Andy (Athlete, Baseball Player)
7304 Lauren Ln
Olive Branch, MS 38654-6362, USA

Fletcher, Billy (Athlete, Football Player)
3216 Winners Cir
Germantown, TN 38138, USA

Fletcher, Brendan (Actor)
Seven Summits Mgmt
8447 Wilshire Blvd
#200
Beverly Hills, CA 90211, USA

Fletcher, Charles M (Physicist, Scientist)
2 Coastguard Cottages
Newtown PO30 4PA, UNITED KINGDOM (UK)

Fletcher, Chris (Athlete, Football Player)
4818 La Cruz Dr
La Mesa, CA 91941, USA

Fletcher, Cliff (Athlete, Hockey Player)
3030 Grand Bay Blvd Unit 314
Longboat Key, FL 34228-4407, USA

Fletcher, Darrin (Athlete, Baseball Player)
9146 E 2100 North Rd
Oakwood, IL 61858-6285, USA

Fletcher, Derrick (Athlete, Football Player)
79 Terra Bella Dr
Manvel, TX 77578, USA

Fletcher, Dexter
1 Kingsway House Albion Rd.
London, ENGLAND N16

Fletcher, Diane (Actor)
Ken McReddie
91 regent St
London W1R 7TB, UNITED KINGDOM (UK)

Fletcher, Ernest L (Politician)
811 Landing Pt
Stockbridge, GA 30281-9064, USA

Fletcher, Guy (Musician)
Damage Mgmt
16 Lambton Place
London W11 2SH, UNITED KINGDOM (UK)

Fletcher, Jamar (Athlete, Football Player)
11063 Worchester Dr
Saint Louis, MO 63136, USA

Fletcher, London (Athlete, Football Player)
18898 Shropshire Ct
Leesburg, VA 20176, USA

Fletcher, Louis (Athlete, Football Player)
18278 Buccaneer Ter
Leesburg, VA 20176, USA

Fletcher, Louise (Actor)
1520 Camden Ave
#105
Los Angeles, CA 90025, USA

Fletcher, Maria (Beauty Pageant Winner)
117 Regency Dr
Conway, SC 29526, USA

Fletcher, Martin (Correspondent)
NBC-TV
News Dept
4001 Nebraska Ave NW
Washington, DC 20016, USA

Fletcher, Paul (Athlete, Baseball Player)
431 Harpold Ave
Ravenswood, WV 26164-1333, USA

Fletcher, Scott B (Athlete, Baseball Player)
300 Birkdale Dr
Fayetteville, GA 30215-2720, USA

Fletcher, Simon (Athlete, Football Player)
2225 S Ensenada St
Aurora, CO 80013, USA

Fletcher, Terrell (Athlete, Football Player)
P.O. Box 711960
San Diego, CA 92171, USA

Fletcher, Tom (Athlete, Baseball Player)
9287 E 2085 North Rd
Oakwood, IL 61858-6252, USA

Fletcher, William A (Judge)
US Court of Appeals
Courts Building
95 7th St
San Francisco, CA 94103, USA

Flett, Bill "Cowboy" (Athlete, Hockey Player)

Fleury, Marc-Andre (Athlete, Hockey Player)
Octagon Sports Management
1751 Pinnacle Dr Ste 1500
Mclean, VA 22102-3833, USA

Fleury, Theoren (Theo) (Athlete, Hockey Player)
Fleury's Concrete Coatings
542 Patterson Grove SW
Calgary, AB T3H 3N6, Canada

Flichel, Todd (Athlete, Hockey Player)
Bowling Green State University Athletic
9564 Taberna Ln
Olmsted Falls, OH 44138-4257, USA

Flick, Bob (Musician)
Bob Flick Productions
300 Vine
#14
Seattle, WA 98121, USA

Flick, Mick
Sherry Netherlands 5th & 59th
New York, NY 10003

Flick, Tom (Athlete, Football Player)
9718 208th Ave NE
Redmond, WA 98053, USA

Flicker, John (Misc)
National Audubon Society
President's Office
700 Broadway
New York, NY 10003, USA

Flinelt, Flemming O (Choreographer, Dancer)
Christiansholms Parkv 24
Klampenborg 2930, DENMARK

Flinn, John (Athlete, Baseball Player)
6221 Lake Providence Ln
Charlotte, NC 28277-0565, USA

Flinn, Ryan (Athlete, Hockey Player)
21611 N 37th St
Phoenix, AZ 85050-4945, USA

Flint, George (Athlete, Football Player)
P.O. Box 2486
Prescott, AZ 86302, USA

Flint, Judson (Athlete, Football Player)
306 Federal St
Farrell, PA 16121, USA

Flint, Keith (Dancer, Musician)
c/o Staff Member *Maverick Recording Co (LA)*
3300 Warner Blvd
Burbank, CA 91505-4632, USA

Flippin, Lucy Lee (Actor)
1753 Canfield Ave
Los Angeles, CA 90035

Flitcroft, Garry (Soccer Player)
c/o Staff Member *Blackburn Rovers Football Club*
Ewood Park
Blackburn
Lancashire BB2 4JF, UNITED KINGDOM

Flitter, Josh (Actor)
c/o Ellen Gilbert *Abrams Artists Agency (NY)*
275 Seventh Ave
26th Floor
New York, NY 10001, USA

Float, Jeffrey (Athlete, Olympic Athlete, Swimmer)
1906 University Park Dr
Sacramento, CA 95825-8210, USA

Flobots (Music Group)
c/o Corrie Christopher *Agency for the Performing Arts (APA-LA)*
405 S Beverly Dr
Suite 500
Beverly Hills, CA 90212-4425, USA

Flockhart, Calista (Actor)
c/o Melissa Kates *Viewpoint Inc*
8820 Wilshire Blvd.
Suite 220
Beverly Hills, CA 90211, USA

Flockhart, Ron (Athlete, Hockey Player)
PO Box 234
Sicamous, BC V0E 2V0, Canada

Flock of Seagulls (Music Group, Musician)
c/o Carlos Keyes *Red Entertainment Agency*
505 8th Ave
Suite 1004
New York, NY 10018, USA

Floethe, Chris (Baseball Player)
5634 Mount Hood Ct
Martinez, CA 94553-5837, USA

Floetry (Music Group)
c/o Cara Lewis *Creative Artists Agency (CAA-LA)*
1325 Ave of the Americas
New York, NY 10019, USA

Flogging Molly (Music Group, Musician)
c/o Gary Schwindt *Villam Artist Management*
820 Hyperion Ave.
Los Angeles, CA 90029, USA

Flood, Ann (Actor)
15 E 91st St
New York, NY 10128, USA

Flood, Staci (Model, Musician)
Clear Talent Group
10950 Ventura Blvd
Studio City, CA 1604, USA

Flor, Claus Peter (Conductor)
Intermusica Artists
16 Duncan Terrace
London N1 8BZ, UNITED KINGDOM (UK)

Flora, Donnie (Stylist)
5805 Hansen Rd
Minneapolis, MN 55436, USA

Flora, Kevin (Athlete, Baseball Player)
25035 Portsmouth
Mission Viejo, CA 92692-2812, USA

Flora, Lars (Athlete, Olympic Athlete, Track Athlete)
6500 Michigan Blvd
Anchorage, AK 99516-1818, USA

Florance, Sheila (Actor)
Melbourne Artists
643 Saint Kikla Road
Melbourne, VIC 3004, AUSTRALIA

Florek, Dann (Actor)
145 W 45th St
#1204
New York, NY 10036, USA

Florence, Don (Athlete, Baseball Player)
144 Bedford Rd
New Boston, NH 03070-4301, USA

Florence, Tyler (Chef, Television Host)
Tyler Florence Shop
59 Throckmorton Ave
Mill Valley, CA 94941, USA

Florence + The Machine (Music Group)
c/o Mairead Nash *LuvLuvLuv Management*
106 Leonard St Fl 1
London EC2A 4RH, UNITED KINGDOM (UK)

Flores, Bill (Congressman, Politician)
1505 Longworth HOB
Washington, DC 20515, USA

Flores, Facusse Carlos (President)
Casa Presidencial
Blvd Juan Pablo II
Tegucigalpa, HONDURAS

Flores, Francisco (President)
President's Office
Casa Presidencial
San Salvador, El SALVADOR

Flores, Jose (Athlete, Baseball Player)
PO Box 81533
Corpus Christi, TX 78468-1533, USA

Flores, Nikki (Musician)
c/o Staff Member *Sony Music International*
550 Madison Ave
New York, NY 10022-3211, USA

Flores, Patrick F (Religious Leader)
Archbishop's Residence
2600 Woodlawn Ave
San Antonio, TX 78228, USA

Flores, Randy (Athlete, Baseball Player)
8230 E Hoverland Rd
Scotsdale, AZ 85255-3908, USA

Flores, Ron (Athlete, Baseball Player)
12026 Reichling Ln
Whittier, CA 90606-2561, USA

Flores, Thomas R (Tom) (Athlete, Coach, Football Coach, Football Executive, Football Player)
77741 Cove Point Cir
Indian Wells, CA 92210, USA

Flores, Tom
11220 NE 53rd St.
Kirkland, WA 98033

Floria, James J (Jim) (Ex-Congressman, Ex-Governor)
Florio, Perrucci, Steinhardt, and Fader
80 Wall St
Suite 815
New York, NY 10005, USA

Florie, Bryce (Athlete, Baseball Player)
1118 Lands End Dr
Hanahan, SC 29410-4752, USA

Florin, Krista (Stylist)
c/o Staff Member *Bulgari (NY)*
730 5th Ave
New York, NY 10019, USA

Florin, Susan (Athlete, Golfer)
1883 Lexington Pl
Tarpon Springs, FL 34688, USA

Florio, James (Politician)
76 Linden Ave
Metuchen, NJ 08840-1449, USA

Florio, Steven T (Publisher)
Conde Nast Publications
Publisher's Office
4 Times Square
New York, NY 10036, USA

Florio, Thomas A (Actor)
New Yorker Magazine
Publisher's Office
4 Times Square
New York, NY 10036, USA

Flory, Med (Actor)
6044 Ensign Ave
North Hollywood, CA 91606, USA

Flournoy, Craig (Journalist)
Dallas News
Editorial Dept
Communications Center
Dallas, TX 75265, USA

Flower, Joseph R (Religious Leader)
Assemblies of God
1445 N Boonville Ave
Springfield, MO 65802, USA

flower, tyler (Athlete, Baseball Player)
109 Newcastle Walk
Woodstock, GA 30188-6088, USA

Flowers, Bernard (Athlete, Football Player)
3819 Old Farm Rd
Lafayette, IN 47909, USA

Flowers, Brandon (Musician)

Flowers, Bruce (Athlete, Basketball Player)
276 West Grantley Avenue
Elmhurst, IL 60126-2238, USA

Flowers, Charles (Charlie) (Athlete, Football Player)
6170 Mount Brook Way NW
Atlanta, GA 30328, USA

Flowers ', Erik (Athlete, Football Player)
712 Mandalay Pkwy
McDonough, GA 30253, USA

Flowers, Frank E (Director, Writer)
c/o Aleen Keshishian *Brillstein Entertainment Partners*
9150 Wilshire Blvd #350
Beverly Hills, CA 90212, USA

Flowers, Gennifer
4859 Cedar Springs #241
Dallas, TX 75219

Flowers, Richmond (Athlete, Football Player)
3434 Indian Lake Dr
Pelham, AL 35124, USA

Flowers of Queen's Gate, Brian H (Physicist)
53 Athenaeum Road
London N2O 9AL, UNITED KINGDOM (UK)

Floyd, Bobby (Athlete, Baseball Player)
1757 SE Dominic Ave
Port Saint Lucie, FL 34952-5815, USA

Floyd, Bobby Jack (Athlete, Football Player)
4133 Tahoe Vista Dr
Rocklin, CA 95765, USA

Floyd, Carlisie (Composer)
4491 Yoakum Blvd
Houston, TX 77006, USA

Floyd, C Clifford (Cliff) (Athlete, Baseball Player)
3283 Birch Ter
Davie, FL 33330-1337, USA

Floyd, Dixon (Athlete, Football Player)
4285 Pierre Dr
Beaumont, TX 77705, USA

Floyd, Eddie (Musician, Songwriter, Writer)
Jason West
Gables House
Saddlebow Kings Lynn PE34 3AR, UNITED KINGDOM (UK)

Floyd, Eric (Athlete, Football Player)
18047 Sailfish Dr
Lutz, FL 33558, USA

Floyd, Eric "Sleepy" (Athlete, Basketball Player)
5644 Westheimer Rd
Houston, TX 77056-4002, USA

Floyd, Eric (Sleepy) (Athlete, Basketball Player)
3101 Ivy Creek Lane
Gastonia, NC 28056, USA

Floyd, Gavin (Athlete, Baseball Player)
9809 Milano Dr
Trinity, FL 34655-4668, USA

Floyd, George (Athlete, Football Player)
7056 Burlington Pike
Attn: Faculty Staff
Florence, KY 41042, USA

Floyd, Larry (Athlete, Hockey Player)
3780 Hancock St
San Diego, CA 92110, USA

Floyd, Leslie (Baseball Player)
Detroit Tigers
PO Box 7619
Texarkana, TX 75505 7619, USA

Floyd, Marlene (Athlete, Golfer)
5370 Clubhouse Ln
Hope Mills, NC 28348-9794, USA

Floyd, Ray
PO Box 545957
Surfside, FL 33154-5957

Floyd, Raymond (Athlete, Golfer)
505 S Flagler Dr
Suite 910
West Palm Beach, FL 33401, USA

Floyd, Susan
PO Box 5617
Beverly Hills, CA 90210

Floyd, Tim (Coach)
New Orleans Hornets
New Orleans Arena
1501 Girod St
New Orleans, LA 70113, USA

Floyd, William (Athlete, Football Player)
7827 Glen Echo Rd N
Jacksonville, FL 32211, USA

Fluegel, Darlanne (Actor)
Shelter Entertainment
9255 Sunset Blvd
#1010
Los Angeles, CA 90069, USA

Flueger, Patrick (Actor)
c/o Nancy Kremer *Nancy Kremer Management*
4545 Morse Ave
Studio City, CA 91604, USA

Fluevog, John (Fashion Designer)
John Fluevog Shoes
837 Granville St
Vancouver, BC V6Z 1K7, Canada

Fluno, Jere D (Business Person)
W W Grainger Inc
5500 W Howard St
Skokie, IL 60077, USA

Flutie, Darren (Athlete, Football Player)
29 Pine St
Natick, MA 01760-1203, USA

Flutie, Doug (Athlete, Football Player, Heisman Trophy Winner)
22 Chieftain Ln
Natick, MA 01760, USA

Flyleaf (Music Group)
c/o Rod MacSween *International Talent Booking*
74A Charlotte St
London W1T 4QJ, UNITED KINGDOM (UK)

F. Lynch, Stephen (Congressman, Politician)
2348 Rayburn HOB
Washington, DC 20515, USA

Flynn, Barbara (Actor)
Markham & Froggatt
Julian House
4 Windmill St
London W1P 1HF, UNITED KINGDOM (UK)

Flynn, Colleen (Actor)
LGM
10390 Santa Monica Blvd
#300
Los Angeles, CA 90025, USA

Flynn, Danny (Stylist)
c/o Staff Member *Cloutier Agency*
2632 La Cienega Ave
Los Angeles, CA 90034, USA

Flynn, Doug (Athlete, Baseball Player)
2465 Vale Dr
Lexington, KY 40514-1421, USA

Flynn, George W (Misc)
382 Summit Ave
Leonia, NJ 07605, USA

Flynn, Gillian (Writer)
c/o Annsley Rosner *Crown Publishers*
1745 Broadway
New York, NY 10019, USA

Flynn, Jackie (Comedian)
c/o Staff Member *Buchwald/Fortitude (LA)*
6500 Wilshire Blvd
Suite 2200
Los Angeles, CA 90048, USA

Flynn, Julie (Stylist)
c/o Celebrity Stylist *Bernstein & Andriulli*
58 W 40th St
New York, NY 10018, USA

Flynn, Luke (Actor, Producer, Writer)
c/o Kay Liberman *Liberman/Zerman Management*
252 N Larchmont Blvd
Suite 200
Los Angeles, CA 90004, USA

Flynn, Melissa (Actor)
c/o Staff Member *Lucie Charland Communications Inc.*
2266 rue Parthenais, bur. 303
Montreal, Quebec H2K 3T5, Canada

Flynn, Mike (Athlete, Football Player)
301 Newbury St Ste 13
Danvers, MA 01923-1029, USA

Flynn, Mike (Athlete, Basketball Player)
3934 E Battala Ave
Gilbert, AZ 85297-3550, USA

Flynn, Neil (Actor)
c/o Staff Member *Christopher Wright Management*
3207 Winnie Dr
Los Angeles, CA 90068, USA

Flynn, Raymond L (Diplomat, Politician)
Catholic Alliance
Via CatholICity
PO Box 1872
Chesapeake, VA 23327, USA

Flynn, Sean (Actor)
c/o Christopher Rockwell *Global Creative*
1051 Cole Ave # B
Los Angeles, CA 90038, USA

Flynn, Tom (Athlete, Football Player)
4008 Holiday Park Dr
Murrysville, PA 15668, USA

Flynn, Vince (Writer)
Cloak & Dagger Press
2316 Delaware Ave #266
Buffalo, NY 14216-2687, USA

Flynt, Larry (Publisher)
LFP Inc
8484 Wilshire Blvd #900
Beverly Hills, CA 90211, USA

Flynville Train (Music Group)
c/o Staff Member *Paradigm (Monterey)*
404 W Franklin St
Monterey, CA 93940, USA

Flythe, Mark (Athlete, Football Player)
505 Pheasant Run
Monmouth Junction, NJ 08852, USA

F. Napolitano, Grace (Congressman, Politician)
1610 longworth HOB
Washington, DC 20515, USA

Fo, Dario (Nobel Prize Laureate)
Pietro Sclotta
Via Alessandria 4
Milan 1-20129, ITALY

Foa, Barrett (Actor)
c/o Ethan Salter *Greene & Associates*
1901 Avenue Of The Stars Ste 130
Los Angeles, CA 90067, USA

Foale, C Michael (Doctor)
2101 Todville Rd #11
Seabrook, TX 77586, USA

Foale, C Michael Dr
2102 Todville Rd Unit 11
Seabrook, TX 77586-3732, USA

Foale, C Michael (Mike) (Astronaut)
2101 Todville Road
#11
Seabrook, TX 77586, USA

Fobbs, Brandon
c/o Todd Justice *Justice & Ponder*
P.O. Box 480033
Los Angeles, CA 90048, USA

Foege, William H (Misc)
10610 SW Cowan Road
Vashan, WA 98070, USA

Foeger, Luggi (Skier)
Christopher Foeger
230 S Balsamina Way
Portola Valley, CA 94028, USA

Foerster, Paul (Athlete, Olympic Athlete, Sailor)
126 Dunford Dr
Rockwall, TX 75032-6625, USA

Fogarty, Thomas (Inventor)
Thomas Fogarty Winery 3270 Alpine Rd
Portola Valley, CA 94028-7523, USA

Fogdoe, Tomas (Skier)
Skogsvagen 18
Gallvare 970 02, SWEDEN

Fogel, Robert W (Nobel Prize Laureate)
5321 S University Ave
Chicago, IL 60615, USA

Fogerty, John (Musician, Songwriter)
c/o Daniel Weiner *Paradigm (Monterey)*
404 W Franklin St
Monterey, CA 93940, USA

Fogg, Josh (Athlete, Baseball Player)
4910 S Quincy St
Tampa, FL 33611-3820, USA

Fogg, Kirk (Actor)
c/o Staff Member *Brady Brannon & Rich*
5670 Wilshire Blvd
Suite 820
Los Angeles, CA 90036, USA

Foggie, Fred (Athlete, Football Player)
360 Jackson Rd
Inman, SC 29349, USA

Foggs, Edward L (Religious Leader)
Church of God
PO Box 2420
Anderson, IN 46018, USA

Fogle, Larry (Athlete, Basketball Player)
72 Beechwood Street
Rochester, NY 14609, USA

Fogleman, Ronald R (Ron) (General)
406 Snowshoe Lane
Durango, CO 81301, USA

Fogler, Dan (Actor, Producer)
c/o Suzan Bymel *Management 360*
9111 Wilshire Blvd
Beverly Hills, CA 90210, USA

Fogler, Eddie (Basketball Player)
University of South Carolina
Athletic Dept
Columbia, SC 53233, USA

Foglesong, Robert H (Doc) (General)
Vice Chief of Staff
HqUSAF Pentagon
Washington, DC 20330, USA

Fogolin Jr, Lee (Athlete, Hockey Player)
352 Lessard Dr NW
Edmonton, AB T6M 1A5, Canada

Foiles, Hank (Athlete, Baseball Player)
4333 Silverleaf Ct
Virginia Beach, VA 23462-5738, USA

Foiles, Lisa (Actor)
Boutique Talent Agency
C/O Nancy Schmidt Sanford
10 Universal City Plaza #2000
Universal City, CA 91608, USA

Fokin, Vitold P (Prime Minister)
Cabinet of Ministers
Government Building
Klev, UKRAINE

Folau, Spencer (Athlete, Football Player)
14003 Woodens Ln
Reisterstown, MD 21136, USA

Folco, Peter (Athlete, Hockey Player)
6463 Rue Bannantyne
Verdun, QC H4H 1J8, Canada

Folder-Powell, Rose (Athlete, Baseball Player, Commentator)
4651 Spilman Ave
Carnation, WA 98014-6326, USA

Folds, Ben (Musician, Songwriter)
c/o Staff Member *ICM Partners (ICM-LA)*
10250 Constellation Blvd Fl 7
Los Angeles, CA 90067, USA

Foley, Christopher (Actor)
c/o Scott Zimmerman *Evolution Entertainment (LA)*
901 N Highland Ave
Los Angeles, CA 90038, USA

Foley, Dave (Comedian)
c/o Matthew Labov *Forefront Media*
8500 Melrose Ave Ste 205
West Hollywood, CA 90069, USA

Foley, Dave (Athlete, Football Player)
4500 Redmond Rd
Springfield, OH 45505, USA

Foley, ex-Speaker Tom
601 W. 1st Ave. #2W
Spokane, WA 99204-0317

Foley, Gerry (Athlete, Hockey Player)
352 Skead Rd
Garson, ON P3L 1N4, Canada

Foley, Glenn (Athlete, Football Player)
3204 Buxmont Rd
Marlton, NJ 08053, USA

Foley, Jeremy (Actor)
Academy Kids Mgmt
4942 Vineland Ave #103
North Hollywood, CA 91601, USA

Foley, John (Athlete, Basketball Player)
P.O. Box 143
Barre, MA 01005-0143, USA

Foley, Linda (Misc)
Newspaper Guild
8611 2nd Ave
Silver Spring, MD 20910, USA

Foley, Marv (Athlete, Baseball Player)
10166 Glen more Ave
Bradenton, FL 34202-4049, USA

Foley, Maurice B (Judge)
US Tax Court
400 2nd St NW
Washington, DC 20217, USA

Foley, Mick (Actor, Wrestler)
c/o Elaine Gillespie *Gillespie Agency, The*
3007 Millwood Ave
Columbia, SC 29205, USA

Foley, Robert F (General, War Hero)
Army Emergency Relief
200 Stovall St
Alexandria, VA 22314-5710, USA

Foley, Scott (Actor)
c/o Dominique Appel *Baker Winokur Ryder Public Relations (BWR-LA)*
9100 Wilshire Blvd
Suite 500, West Tower
Beverly Hills, CA 90212, USA

Foley, Steve (Athlete, Football Player)
6321 S Newport Ct
Centennial, CO 80111, USA

Foley, Sylvester R Jr (Admiral)
50 Apple Hill Dr
Tewksbury, MA 01876, USA

Foley, Thomas S (Diplomat)
PO Box 1047
Medical Lake, WA 99022, USA

Foley, Tim (Athlete, Football Player)
9816 Fairway Cir
Leesburg, FL 34788, USA

Foley, Tim J (Athlete, Football Player)
2851 Old Clifton Rd
Springfield, OH 45502, USA

Foley, Tom (Athlete, Baseball Player)
5237 Karlsburg Pl
Palm Harbor, FL 34685-3696, USA

Folger, Franklin (Cartoonist)
c/o Staff Member *King Features Syndication*
300 W 57th St
15th Floor
New York, NY 10019-5238, USA

Foli, Tim (Athlete, Baseball Player)
74 Apian Way
Ormond Beach, FL 32174-1872, USA

Foligno, Mike (Athlete, Hockey Player)
c/o Staff Member *Sudbury Wolves*
240 Elgin St
Sudbury, ON P3E 3N6, Canada

Folk, Bill (Athlete, Hockey Player)
2720 Quinn Dr
Regina, SK S4P 2W1, Canada

Folkenberg, Robert S (Religious Leader)
Seventh-Day Adventists
12501 Old Columbia Pike
Silver Spring, MD 20904, USA

Folkers, Rich (Athlete, Baseball Player)
7100 3rd Ave N
Saint Petersburg, FL 33710-7502, USA

Folkins, Lee (Athlete, Football Player)
8749 the Esplanade Apt 13
Orlando, FL 32836, USA

Folkl, Kristin (Athlete, Olympic Athlete, Volleyball Player)
4847 Langtree Dr
Saint Louis, MO 63128-2728, USA

Folkman, Judah (Scientist)
18 Chatham Cir
Brookline, MA 02446-5454, USA

Foll, Tim (Baseball Player)
New York Mets
1003 Hilltop Ln
Kodak, TN 37764 1838, USA

Follesdal, Dagfinn K (Misc)
Staverhagen 7
Slepemdem 1312, NORWAY

Follet, George (Athlete, Football Player)
6254 Parima St
Long Beach, CA 90803-2108, USA

Follett, Ken (Writer)
Box 4
Knebworth SG3 6UT, UNITED KINGDOM (UK)

Follmer, George (Race Car Driver)
3529 E Mountain View Drive
Post Falls, ID 83854, USA

Follows, Megan (Actor)
c/o Perry Zimel *Oscars Abrams Zimel & Associates, Inc. (OAZ)*
438 Queen St E
Toronto ON M5A 1T4, CANADA

Folman, Ari (Director)
c/o Maha Dakhil *Creative Artists Agency (CAA-LA)*
2000 Ave Of The Stars
Los Angeles, CA 90067, USA

Folon, Jean-Michel (Artist)
Burcy
Beaumont-du-Gatinais 77890, FRANCE

Folse, John (Chef)
Chef John Folse and Company
2517 S Philippe Ave
Gonzales, LA 70737, USA

Folsom, Allan R (Writer)
Little Brown
3 Center Plaza
Boston, MA 02108, USA

Folsom, James (Politician)
1482 Orchard Dr NE
Cullman, AL 35055-2145, USA

Folsom, Steve (Athlete, Football Player)
6 Woodhollow Trl
Round Rock, TX 78665, USA

Folsome, Claire (Biologist)
University of Hawaii
Microbiology Dept
2600 Campus Road
Honolulu, HI 96822, USA

Folston, James (Athlete, Football Player)
1450 Victoria Blvd
Rockledge, FL 32955, USA

Fonda, Bridget (Actor)
c/o Staff Member *IFA Talent Agency*
8730 Sunset Blvd
Suite 490
Los Angeles, CA 90069, USA

Fonda, Jane (Actor)
1575 Carla Ridge
Beverly Hills, CA 90210, USA

Fonda, Peter (Actor)

Fondren, Debra Jo (Actor, Model)
PO Box 4351-856
Los Angeles, CA 90078, USA

Foner, Eric (Historian)
606 W 116th St
New York, NY 10027, USA

Fong, Darryl
247 S. Beverly Dr. #102
Beverly Hills, CA 90212

Fonoti, Toniu (Athlete, Football Player)
370 Ulupaina St Apt D
Kailua, HI 96734, USA

Fonseca (Musician)
c/o Staff Member *WmE2 (WMA-Miami)*
119 Washington Ave
Suite 400
Miami, FL 33139, USA

Fonseca, Adriana (Actor)
c/o Staff Member *Televisa*
Blvd Adolfo Lopez Mateos 232
Colonia San Angel INN
DF CP 01060, MEXICO

Fonseca, Chris (Actor)
Strauss-McGarr Entertainment
1199 Boise Way
Costa Mesa, CA 92626, USA

Fonseca, David (Musician)
c/o Staff Member *Universal Music Publishing Group (Latin)*
420 Lincoln Rd
Suite 200
Miami Beach, FL 33139, USA

Fonseca, Lyndsy (Actor)
c/o Felicia Sager *Sager Management*
260 S Beverly Dr
Suite 205
Beverly Hills, CA 90212, USA

Fonsi, Luis
c/o Staff Member *Universal Music Group (UMG - LA)*
2220 Colorado Ave
Santa Monica, CA 90404, USA

Fontaine, Joan (Actor)
c/o Staff Member *Gage Group, The (LA)*
14724 Ventura Blvd
Suite 505
Sherman Oaks, CA 91403, USA

Fontaine, Levi (Athlete, Basketball Player)
805 Rollins Rd Apt 2
Burlingame, CA 94010-1265, USA

Fontaine, Lucien (General)
1680 Riverwood Ln
Coral Springs, FL RH2 2QY, England

Fontaine, Maurice A (Misc)
25 Rue Pierre Nicole
Paris 75005, FRANCE

Fontana, Isabeli (Model)
UNO BCN
Av. Marques de l'Argentera 5
Principal 3
Barcelona 08003, Spain

Fontana, Tom (Producer, Writer)
c/o Peter Benedek *United Talent Agency (UTA)*
9336 Civic Center Dr
Beverly Hills, CA 90210, USA

Fontana, Wayne (Musician)
Brian Gannon Mgmt
PO Box 106
Rochdale OL16 4HW, UNITED KINGDOM (UK)

Fontas, Jon (Athlete, Hockey Player)
9 Boggs Cir
Nashua, NH 03060-4861, USA

Fontenot, Albert (Athlete, Football Player)
4919 Gammage St
Houston, TX 77021, USA

Fontenot, Jerry (Athlete, Football Player)
938 Bristol Dr
Deerfield, IL 60015, USA

Fontenot, Joe (Athlete, Baseball Player)
2231 Doc Hughes Rd
Buford, GA 30519-4240, USA

Fontenot, Ray (Athlete, Baseball Player)
1674 S Crestview Dr
Lake Charles, LA 70605-5280, USA

Fontes, Wayne H (Athlete, Coach, Football Coach, Football Player)
2043 Harbour Watch Cir
Tarpon Springs, FL 34689, USA

Fonteyne, Inge (Stylist)
c/o Staff Member *Agency, The (NY)*
580 Broadway
#500
New York, NY 10012, USA

Fonteyne, Val (Athlete, Hockey Player)
5403 52 Ave
Wetaskiwin, AB T9A 0X8, Canada

Fontinato, Lou (Athlete, Hockey Player)
8254 Eramosa Milton Town Line
Campbellville, ON L0P 1B0, Canada

Fonville, Chad (Athlete, Baseball Player)
2338 Piney Green Rd
Midway Park, NC 28544-1112, USA

Fonville, Charles (Athlete, Track Athlete)
1845 Wintergreen Court
Ann Arbor, MI 48103, USA

Fonzi, Dolores (Actor)
c/o Staff Member *Kuranda Management*
Santo Angel, 84
Madrid 28043, Spain

Foo, Jon (Actor)
c/o Steve Chasman *Current Entertainment*
9378 Wilshire Blvd
Sutie 210
Beverly Hills, CA 90212, USA

Foo Fighters (Music Group)
c/o Steve Martin *Nasty Little Man*
110 Greene St #605
New York, NY 10012, USA

Foor, Jim (Athlete, Baseball Player)
2018 Bolsover St
Houston, TX 77005-1616, USA

Foose, Chip (Actor)
Foose Design Inc
17811 Sampson Ln
Huntington Beach, CA 92647, USA

Foote, Adam (Athlete, Hockey Player)
4656 S Ogden St
Englewood, CO 80113-5975, USA

Foote, Barry (Athlete, Baseball Player)
1990 Marsh Oak Ln
Johns Island, SC 29455-6305, USA

Foote, Chris (Athlete, Football Player)
1140 Harbin Ridge Ln
Knoxville, TN 37909, USA

Foote, Dan (Cartoonist, Editor)
Dallas Times Herald
Editorial Dept
Herald Square
Dallas, TX 75202, USA

Foote, Larry (Athlete, Football Player)
24605 Franklin Farms Dr
Franklin, MI 48025, USA

Foote II, Edward T (Educator)
University of Miami
President's Office
Coral Gables, FL 33124, USA

Footman, Dan (Athlete, Football Player)
1311 Windsor Pl
Jacksonville, FL 32205-7962, USA

Foppert, Jesse (Athlete, Baseball Player)
P.O. Box 150682
San Rafael, CA 94915-0682, USA

Foray, June (Actor)
22745 Erwin St
Woodland Hills, CA 91367, USA

Forbert, Steve (Musician, Songwriter,
Writer)
Mongrel Music
743 Center Blvd
Fairfax, CA 94930, USA

Forbes, Brian
Seven Pines Wentworth
Surrey, ENGLAND

Forbes, Bryan (Director, Writer)
Bookshop
Virginia Water, Surrey, UNITED
KINGDOM (UK)

Forbes, Colin (Writer)
Elaine Green Ltd 37 Gold Hawk Road
London, W12 8QQ, England

Forbes, Dave (Athlete, Hockey Player)
4020 Reserve Pt
Colorado Springs, CO 80904-1043, USA

Forbes, Kristin (Economist, Government
Official)
Council of Economic Advisers
Old Executive Office Bldg
Washington, DC 20500, USA

Forbes, Malcolm S (Steve) Jr (Editor,
Misc)
Forbes Magazine
Editorial Dept
60 5th Ave
New York, NY 10011, USA

Forbes, Michelle (Actor)
c/o Laura Berwick *Hofflund/Polone*
9465 Wilshire Blvd #420
Beverly Hills, CA 90212, USA

Forbes, Mike (Athlete, Hockey Player)
547 Waverly Ave
Grand Haven, MI 49417-2127, USA

Forbes, P J (Athlete, Baseball Player)
9017 Chartwell Cir
Wichita, KS 67205-1445, USA

Forbes, West (Musician)
Paramount Entertainment
PO Box 12
Far Hills, NJ 07931, USA

Force, John (Race Car Driver)
John Force Racing
22722 Old Canal Rd.
Yorba Linda, CA 92887-4602, USA

Ford, Alan (Athlete, Football Player)
1251 McNiven Ave
Regina, SK S4S 3X7, Canada

Ford, Ben (Athlete, Baseball Player)
1717 Applewood Pl NE
Cedar Rapids, IA 52402-3321, USA

Ford, Bette
1801 Ave. of the Stars #902
Los Angeles, XA 90067

Ford, Brian (Athlete, Hockey Player)
311 Queen St
Fredericton, NB E3B 1B1, CANADA

Ford, Charlie (Athlete, Football Player)
2995 South St
Beaumont, TX 77702, USA

Ford, Charlotte
25 Sutton Pl.
New York, NY 10023

Ford, Cheryl (Basketball Player)
Detroit Shock Palace
2 Championship Dr
Aubum Hills, MI 48326, USA

Ford, Chris (Athlete, Basketball Player,
Coach)
424 North Vendrome Avenue
Margate City, NJ 08402-1265, USA

Ford, Clementine (Actor)
c/o Staff Member *Schumacher
Management*
1122 San Vicente Blvd.
Santa Monica, CA 90402, USA

Ford, Colton (Musician)
c/o Staff Member *Diva Central Inc*
7510 W Sunset Blvd Ste 1445
Los Angees, CA 90046, USA

Ford, Curt (Athlete, Baseball Player)
6306 Sprig Oak Ct
Apt B
Saint Louis, MO 63128-4336, USA

Ford, Dale (Baseball Player)
678 Brethern Church Rd
Jonesborough, TN 37659-3923, USA

Ford, Dale (Athlete, Baseball Player)
678 Brethern Church Rd
Jonesborough, TN 37659-3923, USA

Ford, Dan (Athlete, Baseball Player)
1271 Linton Rd
Benton, LA 71006-8736, USA

Ford, Darren (Baseball Player)
7640 NW 79th Ave Apt L8
Tamarac, FL 33321-2868, USA

Ford, Dave (Athlete, Baseball Player)
19523 N Sagamor
Cleveland, OH 44126-1662, USA

Ford, David (Musician)
c/o Staff Member *Paradigm (Monterey)*
404 W Franklin St
Monterey, CA 93940, USA

Ford, Debbie (Motivational Speaker,
Writer)
Debbie Ford Productions
P.O. Box 8064
La Jolla, California 92037, USA

Ford, Diane
201 San Vicente Blvd. #6
Santa Monica, XA 90402

Ford, Don (Athlete, Basketball Player)
519 West Quinto Street
Apt B
Santa Barbara, CA 93105, USA

Ford, Don (Athlete, Basketball Player)
519 W Quinto St Apt B
Santa Barbara, CA 93105-4800

Ford, Doug (Athlete, Golfer)
3737 Gulfstream Ave
Delray Beach, FL 33483, USA

Ford, Eileen (Business Person)
c/o Staff Member *Ford Models (NY)*
238 E 4th St
New York, NY 10009, USA

Ford, Eileen
344 E. 59th St.
New York, NY 10022

Ford, Ervin (Baseball Player)
Indianapolis Clowns
429 Banks St
Greensboro, NC 27401-3105, USA

Ford, Faith (Actor)
c/o Rebecca (Becca) Kovacik *Hofflund/
Polone*
9465 Wilshire Blvd #420
Beverly Hills, CA 90212, USA

Ford, Frankie (Musician, Songwriter,
Writer)
Ken Keane Artists
PO Box 1875
Gretna, LA 70054, USA

Ford, Frederick (Adult Film Star)
c/o Staff Member *Diva Central Inc*
7510 W Sunset Blvd Ste 1445
Los Angees, CA 90046, USA

Ford, Garrett (Athlete, Football Player)
682 Westview Ave
Morgantown, WV 26505, USA

Ford, Gib (Athlete, Basketball Player,
Olympic Athlete)
264 Edgemere Way East
Naples, FL 34105-7150, USA

Ford, Harrison (Actor)
655 MacCulloch Dr
Los Angeles, CA 90049, USA

Ford, Henry (Athlete, Football Player)
7222 Shannon Rd
Verona, PA 15147, USA

Ford, Henry (Athlete, Football Player)
809 Glendevon Dr
McKinney, TX 75071-6543, USA

Ford, Jack (Correspondent)
CBS-TV
News Dept
51 W 52nd St
New York, NY 10019, USA

Ford, James L (Athlete, Football Player)
2168 College Cir N
Jacksonville, FL 32209, USA

Ford, Kevin A (Astronaut)
1002 Oak Park Lane
Friendswood, TX 47348-9243, USA

Ford, Lew (Athlete, Baseball Player)
2201 ladv Cornwall Dr
lewisville, TX 75056, USA

Ford, Lita (Actor, Composer, Musician)
c/o Garry Buck *Monterey International*
P.O. Box 297
Carmel-by-the-Sea, CA 93921, USA

Ford, Matt (Athlete, Baseball Player)
10837 Cypress Glen Dr
Coral Springs, FL 33071-8164, USA

Ford, Melissa (Model)
c/o Michael (Mike) Esterman
Esterman.Com, LLC
Prefers to be contacted via email
MD, USA

Ford, Melyssa (Model)
c/o Michael (Mike) Esterman
Esterman.Com, LLC
Prefers to be contacted via email
MD, USA

Ford, Mick (Actor)
c/o Staff Member *CDA*
125 Gloucheser Rd
London SW7 4TE, UK

Ford, Mike (Athlete, Football Player)
9798 Fm 1565
Terrell, TX 75160, USA

Ford, Mike (Athlete, Hockey Player)
65 Kingscrest Dr
la Salle, MB ROG OAl, Canada

Ford, Phil (Athlete, Basketball Player,
Olympic Athlete)
Po Box 90623
Raleigh, NC 27675-0623, USA

Ford, Richard (Writer)
International Creative Mgmt
40 W 57th St
#1800
New York, NY 10022-7703, USA

Ford, Robert (Athlete, Basketball Player)
202 Pathway Lane
West Lafayette, IN 47906-2162, USA

Ford, Ruth (Actor)
Dakota Hotel
1 W 72nd St
New York, NY 10023, USA

Ford, Scott (Business Person)
Alltel Corp
PO Box 96019
Charlotte, NC 28296-0019, USA

Ford, Sherell (Athlete, Basketball Player)
1509 South 6th Avenue
Maywood, IL 60153-2014, USA

Ford, Ted (Athlete, Baseball Player)
3713 N 25th ln
McAllen, TX 78501-6285, USA

Ford, Ted (Athlete, Baseball Player)
6220 N 11th St
Apt 19
McAllen, TX 78504-3275, USA

Ford, Thomas Mikal (Actor)
c/o Staff Member *TalentWorks (LA)*
3500 W Olive Ave
Suite 1400
Burbank, CA 91505, USA

Ford, T J (Basketball Player)
Milwaukee Bucks
Bradley Center
1001 N 4th St
Milwaukee, WI 53203, USA

Ford, Tom (Designer, Fashion Designer)
Gucci
845 Madison Ave
New York, NY 10021, USA

Ford, Trent (Actor)
c/o Staff Member *Paradigm (LA)*
360 N Crescent Dr
North Bldg
Beverly Hills, CA 90210, USA

Ford, Wendell H (Ex-Governor, Ex-
Senator)
220 Daviess St
Owensboro, KY 42303, USA

Ford, Whitey (Athlete, Baseball Player)
WhiteyFord.com
3750 Galt Ocean Dr Apt 1411
Fort lauderdale, FL 33308-7623, USA

Ford, Willa (Musician)
c/o Brad Marks *Apoko Group*
1550 17th St
Santa Monica, CA 90404-3402, USA

Ford, William C Jr (Business Person)
Ford Motor Co
American Road
Dearborn, MI 48121, USA

Forde, Brian (Athlete, Football Player)
20225 Bothell Everett Hwy
Apt 1131
Bothell, WA 98012, USA

Fordham, Julia (Musician, Songwriter, Writer)
Vanguard Records
2700 Pennsylvania Ave
Santa Monica, CA 90404, USA

Fordham, Tom (Athlete, Baseball Player)
14559 Miguel Ln
El Cajon, CA 92021-2843, USA

Fordham, Willie (Baseball Player)
Negro Baseball Leagues
3608 Tudor Dr
Harrisburg, PA 17109-1235, USA

Ford Jr, Gerald R (Ex-President, Politician, President)
40365 San Dune Road
Rancho Mirage, CA 92270, USA

Fordyce, Brook (Athlete, Baseball Player)
5 River Crest Ct
Stuart, FL 34996, USA

Foreigner (Music Group, Musician)
c/o Daniel Weiner *Paradigm (Monterey)*
404 W Franklin St
Monterey, CA 93940, USA

Foreman, Amanda (Actor)
c/o Gregg A Klein *Abrams Artists Agency (LA)*
9200 Sunset Blvd
11th Floor
Los Angeles, CA 90069, USA

Foreman, Carol L T (Government Official)
5600 Wisconsin Avenue
Apt 502
Chevy Chase, MD 20815-4410, USA

Foreman, Chuck (Athlete, Football Player)
9716 Mill Creek Dr
Eden Prairie, MN 55347-4307, USA

Foreman, Deborah (Actor)
P.O.Box 2305
Big Bear City, CA 92314, USA

Foreman, George (Athlete, Boxer, Olympic Athlete)
George Foreman Enterprises
PO Box 1405
Huffman, TX 77336-1405, USA

Foreman, Walter E (Chuck) (Athlete, Football Player)
9716 Mill Creek Dr
Eden Prairie, MN 55347, USA

Foremsky, Skee (Bowler)
914 Manchester Dr
Conroe, TX 77304-2713, USA

Foresman, Susan B (Stylist)
2767 N Quincy St
Arlington, VA 22207, USA

Forest, Michael (Actor)
1327 North Vista
#203
Los Angeles, CA 90046, USA

Forester, Herschel (Athlete, Football Player)
15250 Prestonwood Blvd Apt 230
Dallas, TX 75248, USA

Forester, Nicole (Actor)
c/o Doug Kesten *Paradigm (NY)*
360 Park Ave S Fl 16
New York, NY 10010, USA

Foret, Sarah (Actor)

Forey, Conley (Athlete, Hockey Player)
412-2929 4th Ave W
Vancouver, BC V6K 4T3, Canada

Forget, Guy (Tennis Player)
Rue des Pacs 2
Neuchatel 2000, SWITZERLAND

Forlani, Arnaldo (Prime Minister)
Piazzale Schumann 15
Rome, ITALY

Forlani, Claire (Actor)
c/o Marsha McManus *Principal Entertainment (LA)*
1964 Westwood Blvd #400
Los Angeles, CA 90025, USA

Forman, Al (Baseball Player)
219 W Tateway Rd Apt B
Kitty Hawk, NC 27949-4377, USA

Forman, Al (Athlete, Baseball Player)
115 Acorn Ln
Point Harbor, NC 27964, USA

Forman, Don (Athlete, Basketball Player)
1532 Gormican Lane
Naples, FL 34110-0920, USA

Forman, Milos (Director)
c/o Ari Emanuel *WME (LA)*
9601 Wilshire Blvd Fl 3
Beverly Hills, CA 90210, USA

Forman, Stanley (Journalist, Photographer)
17 Cherry Road
Beverly, MA 01915-1511, USA

Forman, Tom (Cartoonist)
10544 James Road
Celina, TX 75009, USA

Formia, Osvaldo (Horse Racer)
6501 Winfield Blvd #A10
Margate, FL 33063, USA

Forney, Carl (Athlete, Baseball Player)
169 Riddley St
Marion, NC 28752, USA

Forney, G David Jr (Scientist)
6 Coolidge Hill Road
Cambridge, MA 02138, USA

Forney, Kynan (Athlete, Football Player)
2046 Skybrooke Ln
Hoschton, GA 30548, USA

Foronjy, Richard (Actor)
c/o Staff Member *House of Representatives, The*
1434 6th St
Suite 1
Santa Monica, CA 90401, USA

Forrest, Bayard (Athlete, Basketball Player)
300A Squaw Valley Place
Pagosa Springs, CO 81147-9773, USA

Forrest, Frederic (Actor)
11300 W Olympic Blvd
#610
Los Angeles, CA 90064, USA

Forrest, Katherine Virginia (Writer)
PO Box 31613
San Francisco, CA 94131

Forrest, Lili (Designer)
600 Moulton Ave
#205
Los Angeles, CA 90031, USA

Forrest, Mark
13266 Bracken St.
Arleta, CA 91331

Forrest, Sally (Actor)
1125 Angelo Dr
Beverly Hills, CA 90210, USA

Forrest, Steve (Actor)
1605 Michael Lane
Pacific Palisades, CA 90272, USA

Forrestal, Robert P (Financier, Government Official)
3949 Vermont Road NE
Atlanta, GA 30319, USA

Forrester, James (Scientist)
Cedars-Sinai Medical Center
8700 Beverly Blvd
West Hollywood, CA 90048, USA

Forrester, Jay W (Inventor)
Massachusetts Institute of Technology Management School
Cambridge, MA 02139-4301, USA

Forrester, Patrick G (Astronaut)
3923 park Circle Way
Houston, TX 77059-3019, USA

Forrester Sisters (Music Group)
c/o Staff Member *Warner Bros Music*
4000 Warner Blvd
Burbank, CA 91522

Forsberg, Fred (Athlete, Football Player)
1727 223rd Ave SE
Sammamish, WA 98075, USA

Forsberg, Peter (Athlete, Hockey Player)
Forspro AB
Viktoriaesplanaden 1,
Ornskoldsvik 89123, Sweden

Forsch, Ken (Athlete, Baseball Player)
881 S Country Glen Way
Anaheim, CA 92808-2635, USA

Forsey, Brock (Athlete, Football Player)
8346 W Sun Disk St
Boise, ID 83714, USA

Forslund, Constance (Actor)
165 W 46th St
#1109
New York, NY 10036, USA

Forsman, Dan (Athlete, Golfer)
88 W 4500 N
Provo, UT 84604-5517, USA

Forst, Bill (Cartoonist)
2320 Byer Road
Santa Cruz, CA 95062, USA

Forstchen, William (Writer)
c/o Staff Member *Spectrum Literary Agency*
320 Central Park West
Suite 1-D
New York, NY 10025, USA

Forster, Brian
16172 Flamstead Dr.
Hacienda Heights, CA 91745

Forster, Joseph (General)
2477 Leisure World
Mesa, AZ 85206-5414, USA

Forster, Marc (Director, Producer)
c/o Guymon Casady *Management 360*
9111 Wilshire Blvd
Beverly Hills, CA 90210, USA

Forster, Robert (Actor)
c/o Eli Selden *Anonymous Content (LA)*
3531 Hayden Ave
Culver City, CA 90232, USA

Forster, Scott (Athlete, Baseball Player)
901 Sturgis ln
Ambler, PA 19002-2022, USA

Forster, Terry (Baseball Player)
Chicago White Sox
PO Box 711658
Santee, CA 92072 1658, USA

Forster, William H (General)
10245 Fairfax Dr
Fort Belvoir, VA 22060, USA

Forsyth, Bill (Director)
P F D
Drury House
34-43 Russell St
London WC2B 5HA, UNITED KINGDOM (UK)

Forsyth, Bruce (Actor, Comedian)
Kent House
Upper Ground
London SE1, UNITED KINGDOM (UK)

Forsyth, Chris (Actor)

Forsyth, Frederick (Writer)
Trans World Publishers
61-63 Oxbridge Rd
Ealing
London W5 5SA, UNITED KINGDOM (UK)

Forsythe, Bill
20 Winton Dr.
Glasgow, SCOTLAND G12 0QA

Forsythe, Gerald (Gary) (Motorcycle Race, Motorcycle Racer)
Forsythe Racing
7231 Georgetown Road
Indianapolis, IN 46268, USA

Forsythe, Gerry
9350 Castlegate Dr
Indianapolis, IN 46256

Forsythe, Rosemary (Actor)
1591 Benedict Canyon
Beverly Hills, CA 90210, USA

Forsythe, William (Actor)
c/o Kieran Maguire *The Arlook Group*
205 S Beverly Dr
Suite 209
Beverly Hills, CA 90212, USA

Forsythe, William (Choreographer)
Frankfurt Ballet
Untermainanlage 11
Frankfurt 60311, GERMANY

Fort, Edward B (Educator)
North Carolina A&T State University
Chancellor's Office
Greensboro, NC 27411, USA

Fort-Brescia, Bernardo (Architect)
Arquitectonica International
550 Brickell Ave
#200
Miami, FL 33131, USA

Forte, Deborah (Producer)
c/o Staff Member *Scholastic Entertainment*
557 Broadway
New York, NY 10012, USA

Forte, Fabian
6671 Sunset Blvd. #1502
Los Angeles, DA 90028

Forte, Ike (Athlete, Football Player)
5811 Winchester Dr
Texarkana, TX 75503, USA

Forte, Joseph (Basketball Player)
355 Elm Croft Blvd
#621
Rockville, MD 20850, USA

Forte, Matt (Athlete, Football Player)
2067 Laurel Valley Dr
Vernon Hills, IL 60061, USA

Forte, Will (Actor, Writer)
c/o Julie Darmody *Mosaic Media Group*
9200 W. Sunset Blvd
10th Floor
Los Angeles, CA 90069, USA

Fortenberry, Jeff (Congressman,
Politician)
1514 Longworth HOB
Washington, DC 20515, USA

Fortier, Claude (Misc)
1014 De Grenoble
Sainte-Foy
Quebec, QC G1V 2Z9, CANADA

Fortier, Dave (Athlete, Hockey Player)
150 Kingsmount Blvd
Sudbury, ON P3E 1K9, Canada

Fortier, Laurie (Actor)
c/o Steven Jensen *Direct Management
Group*
6363 Wilshire Blvd
Suite 115
Los Angeles, CA 90048, USA

Fortier, Suzanne (Stylist)
2529 6th St
Santa Monica, CA 90405, USA

Fortin, Ray (Athlete, Hockey Player)
899 109e Av
Drummondville, QC J2B 4Ml, Canada

Fortin, Roman (Athlete, Football Player)
10741 Bell Rd
Duluth, GA 30097, USA

Fortner, Nell (Coach)
Aubum University
Athletic Dept
Aubum, AL 36849, USA

For Today (Music Group, Musician)
c/o Shannon Quiggle *Facedown Records*
P.O. Box 477
Sun City, CA 92586, USA

Fortson, Danny (Athlete, Basketball
Player)
360 Cleveland Ave
Glendale, OH 45246-4624, USA

Fortugno, Tim (Athlete, Baseball Player)
3604 Babson Dr
Elk Grove, CA 95758-4576, USA

Fortunato, Don (Athlete, Football Player)
222 Regent Wood Rd
Northfield, IL 60093, USA

Fortunato, Joseph F (Joe) (Athlete,
Football Player)
P.O. Box 934
Natchez, MS 39121, USA

Fortune, Jimmy (Musician)
American Major Talent
8747 Highway 304
Hernando, MS 38632, USA

Fortuno, Luis (Governor, Politician)
La Fortaleza
San Juan, PR 00901, USA

Foruria, John (Athlete, Football Player)
5603 Edson St
Boise, ID 83705, USA

Forward, Susan (Writer)
c/o Staff Member *HarperCollins Publishers*
10 East 53rd St
c/o Author mail, 7th Floor
New York, NY 10022, USA

Forzano, Rick (Athlete, Football Coach,
Football Player)
3216 Interlaken St
West Bloomfield, MI 48323, USA

Fosbury, Dick (Athlete, Olympic Athlete,
Track Athlete)
PO Box 1791
Ketchum, ID 8334

Fosnow, Jerry (Athlete, Baseball Player)
7028 W Waters Ave
lTamna, FL 33634-2292, USA

Foss, Anita (Athlete, Baseball Player,
Commentator)
2107 Ashland Ave
Santa Monica, CA 90405-6025, USA

Foss, John W II (General)
16 Hampton Key
Williamsburg, VA 23185, USA

Foss, Larry (Athlete, Baseball Player)
4303 E English St
Wichita, KS 67218-1320, USA

Fossas, Tony (Athlete, Baseball Player)
11302 NW 9th St
Plantation, FL 33325-1501, USA

Fosse, Ray (Athlete, Baseball Player)
P.O. Box 567
Diablo, CA 94528-0567, USA

Fossey, Brigitte (Actor)
18 Rue Troyon
Paris 75017, FRANCE

Fossum, Casey (Athlete, Baseball Player)
18032 Glenville Cv
Austin, TX 78738-7651, USA

Fossum, Eric (Inventor)
198 Forest Rd
Wolfeboro, NH 03894-4012, USA

Fossum, Michael E (Astronaut)
822 Rolling Run Court
Houston, TX 77062-2100, USA

Foster, Alan (Athlete, Baseball Player)
10330 Grandview Dr
La Mesa, CA 91941-6844, USA

Foster, Alex (Athlete, Hockey Player)
721 S Livernois Rd
Rochester Hills, MI 48307-2770, USA

Foster, Arian (Athlete, Football Player)
c/o Rick French *French/West/Vaughan*
185 Madison Ave
Suite 401
New York, NY 10016, USA

Foster, Barry (Athlete, Football Player)
1905 Ashton Ct
Colleyville, TX 76034-4401, USA

Foster, Ben (Actor)
c/o Ken Jacobson *Ken Jacobson
Management*
Preferred to be contacted by phone or
email
Los Angeles, CA 91367, USA

Foster, Bill (Basketball Player)
Virginia Polytechnic Institute
Athletic Dept
Blacksburg, VA 24061, USA

Foster, Brendan (Athlete, Track Athlete)
Whitegates
31 Meadowfield Road
Stocksfield, Northumberland, UNITED
KINGDOM (UK)

Foster, Cecil (General)
PO Box 515
Superior, MT 59872-0515, USA

Foster, Corey (Athlete, Hockey Player)
71 Pine Ridge Dr
Arnprior, ON K7S 3G8, Canada

Foster, Coy (Misc)
5486 Glen Lakes Dr
Dallas, TX 75231, USA

Foster, David (Musician, Songwriter)
c/o Liz Rosenberg *Liz Rosenberg Media*
142 W. 57th St
6th Floor
New York, NY 10019, USA

Foster, Deshaun (Athlete, Football Player)
2391 Apple Tree Dr
Tustin, CA 92780, USA

Foster, Dwight (Athlete, Hockey Player)
721 S Livernois Rd
Rochester Hills, MI 48307, USA

Foster, George (Athlete, Football Player)
4057 Meadowbrook Dr
Mason, GA 31204, USA

Foster, George (Athlete, Baseball Player)
15 E Putnam Ave
Apt 320
Greenwich, CT 06830-5424, USA

Foster, Jeff (Athlete, Basketball Player)
333 Pickwick Court
Noblesville, IN 46062-9071, USA

Foster, Jerome (Athlete, Football Player)
18900 Goldwin St
Southfield, MI 48075, USA

Foster, Jodie (Actor, Director)
1267 Lago Vista Dr
Beverly Hills, CA 90210, USA

Foster, John (Actor)
c/o Staff Member *Windfall*
3000 W Alameda Ave
Burbank, CA 91523-0001, USA

Foster, John (Athlete, Baseball Player)
519 Airway Ave
Lewiston, ID 83501-4503, USA

Foster, Jon (Actor)
c/o Ken Jacobson *Ken Jacobson
Management*
Preferred to be contacted by phone or
email
Los Angeles, CA 91367, USA

Foster, Kris (Athlete, Baseball Player)
116 Johns Ave
Lehigh Acres, FL 33936-2135, USA

Foster, Larry (Athlete, Baseball Player)
205 W Obell St
Whitehall, MI 49461-1742, USA

Foster, Lawrence T (Conductor)
International Creative Mgmt
40 W 57th St
#1800
New York, NY 10019, USA

Foster, Leo (Athlete, Baseball Player)
699 Glensprings Dr
Cincinnati, OH 45246-2129, USA

Foster, Marty (Baseball Player)
319 W 5th Ave
Denver, CO 80204-5118, USA

Foster, Marty (Athlete, Baseball Player)
1718 Arrowhead Dr
Beloit, WI 53511-3808, USA

Foster, Meg (Actor)
c/o Chris Roe *CR Management*
23852 Pacific Coast Hwy
Suite 627
Malibu, CA 90265, USA

Foster, Norm (Athlete, Hockey Player)
632 Rewold Dr
Rochester, MI 48307, USA

Foster, Norman R (Architect)
Foster Assoc
Riverside 3
22 Hester Road
London SW11 4AN, UNITED KINGDOM
(UK)

Foster, Radney (Musician, Songwriter,
Writer)
c/o Staff Member *WmE2 (WMA-LA)*
1 William Morris Pl
Beverly Hills, CA 90212, USA

Foster, Robert W (Bob) (Boxer)
913 Valencia Dr NE
Albuquerque, NM 87108, USA

Foster, Rod (Athlete, Basketball Player)
1246 Armacost Avenue
Apt 105
Los Angeles, CA 90025-6432, USA

Foster, Ron (Athlete, Football Player)
17819 Merridy St
Apt 117
Northridge, CA 91325, USA

Foster, Roy
650 East 27th Place North
Tulsa, OK 74106-2409, USA

Foster, Roy A (Athlete, Football Player)
5824 Shenandoah Ave
Los Angeles, GA 90056, USA

Foster, Sara (Actor)
c/o Brad Marks *Apoko Group*
1550 17th St
Santa Monica, CA 90404-3402, USA

Foster, Scott M (Actor)
c/o John Tae Lee *Shapiro/West &
Associates*
141 El Camino Dr #205
Beverly Hills, CA 90212, USA

Foster, Scott Michael (Actor)
c/o John Tae Lee *Shapiro/West &
Associates*
141 El Camino Dr #205
Beverly Hills, CA 90212, USA

Foster, Steve (Athlete, Baseball Player)
1020 Heathrow Dr
Frisco, TX 75034-7806, USA

Foster, Sutton (Actor)
c/o Joe Machota *Creative Artists Agency
(CAA-NY)*
162 Fifth Ave
6th Floor
New York, NY 10010, USA

Foster, Todd (Boxer)
249 21st Ave NW
Great Falls, MT 59404, USA

Foster, William E (Bill) (Coach)
152 Hollywood Dr
Coppell, TX 75019, USA

Foster Jr, John S (Physicist)
TRW Inc
1 Space Parkway
Redondo Beach, CA 90278, USA

Foster the People (Music Group, Musician)
c/o Staff Member *Star Time Intl*
79 5th Ave
15th Floor
New York, NY 10003, USA

Foth, Robert (Athlete, Olympic Athlete, Shooter)
2221 Tesla Dr
Colorado Springs, CO 80909-1446, USA

Foti, Tony (Race Car Driver)
LAPD Racing Team
10250 Etinwanda
Northridge, CA 91325, USA

Fotiu, Nick (Athlete, Hockey Player)
16 Backus River Rd
East Falmouth, MA 02536-5205, USA

Fou, Ts'ong (Musician)
62 Aberdeen Park
London N5 2BL, UNITED KINGDOM (UK)

Foucault, Steve (Athlete, Baseball Player)
24353 Rolling View Ct
lutz, FL 33559-8642, USA

Fouch, Allison (Athlete, Golfer)
2949 Oakwood Dr SE
Grand Rapids, MI 49506, USA

Foudy, Judy (Julie) (Model, Soccer Player)
US Soccer Federation
1801 S Prairie Ave
Chicago, IL 60616, USA

Foudy, Julie
1801 S. Prairie Ave.
Chicago, IL 60616

Fought, John (Athlete, Golfer)
5747 E Via Los Ranchos
Paradise Valley, AZ 85253, USA

Foules, Elbert (Athlete, Football Player)
633 E Ohea St
Greenville, MS 38701, USA

Foulke, Keith (Athlete, Baseball Player)
4844 W Electra Ln
Glendale, AZ 85310-3833, USA

Foulkes, Llyn (Artist)
6010 Eucalyptus Lane
Los Angeles, CA 90042, USA

Fountain, Pete
237 N. Peters St. #400
New Orleans, Los Angeles 71030

Fountain, Peter D (Pete) Jr (Musician)
Paradise Artists
108 E Matilija St
Ojai, CA 93023, USA

Fountain, Rex
10475 Bellagio Rd.
Los Angeles, CA 90077

Fountaine, Jamal (Athlete, Football Player)
245 SW Lincoln St
Apt 122
Portland, OR 97201, USA

Fountains of Wayne (Music Group)
c/o Staff Member *Big Hassle Media*
40 Exchange Pl #1900
New York, NY 10005, USA

Four Aces, The
11761 E. Speedway Blvd
Tucson, AZ 85748-2017

Fourcade, John (Athlete, Football Player)
2749 Long Branch Dr
Marrero, LA 70072, USA

Four Freshman, The
PO Box 93534
Las Vegas, NV 89193-3534

Four Freshmen, The (Music Group)
c/o Staff Member *International Ventures*
25115 Avenue Stanford Ste 102
Valencia, CA 91355, USA

Four Lads, The
11761 E. Speedway Blvd.
Tucson, AZ 85748-2017

Fournier, Brigitte (Opera Singer)
EMI America Records
1370 Ave of Americas
New York, NY 10019, USA

Fournier, Francine
PO Box 935
Bear, DE 19701, USA

Four Non Blondes
PO Box 170545
San Francisco, CA 94117

Foust, Nina (Athlete, Golfer)
901 East Dr
Morehead City, NC 28557-3009, USA

Fouts, Dan (Athlete, Football Player)
16820 Varco Road
Bend, OR 97701, USA

Fowle, Lillia (Stylist)
12918 Valleyheart Dr
#5
Studio City, CA 91604-1991, USA

Fowler, Bobby (Athlete, Football Player)
12520 Mexicana Cv
Del Valle, TX 78617, USA

Fowler, Cal (Athlete, Basketball Player)
10121 Godspeed Drive
Ocean City, MD 21842-8854, USA

Fowler, Chris (Sportscaster)
c/o Staff Member *ESPN (Main)*
ESPN Plaza
935 Middle St
Bristol, CT 06010-1001, USA

Fowler, Claudia (Stylist)
2932 Polo Club Rd
Nashville, TN 37221, USA

Fowler, Dan (Athlete, Football Player)
18574 Merlon Ct
Leesburg, VA 20176, USA

Fowler, David (Athlete, Football Player)
511 Cove Rd
Shelbyville, KY 40065-7941, USA

Fowler, E Michael C (Architect)
5300 S Dragoon Dr
Chandler, AZ 85249, us

Fowler, Jim (Actor)
Wild Kingdom
Mutual of Omaha
Mutual of Omaha Plaza
Omaha, NE 68175, USA

Fowler, Kevin (Musician)
c/o Staff Member *Paradigm (Monterey)*
404 W Franklin St
Monterey, CA 93940, USA

Fowler, Melvin (Athlete, Football Player)
2850 Amsdell Rd Apt 27
Hamburg, NY 14075, USA

Fowler, Peggy Y (Business Person)
Portland General Electric
121 SW Salmon St
Portland, OR 97204, USA

Fowler, Ryan (Athlete, Football Player)
1713 Montclair Blvd
Brentwood, TN 37027, USA

Fowler, Todd (Athlete, Football Player)
10024 Fm 3053 N
Kilgore, TX 75662, USA

Fowler, Willmer (Athlete, Football Player)
471 Linwood Ave
Buffalo, NY 14209, USA

Fowler, W Wyche Jr (Diplomat, Ex-Senator)
701 A St NE
Washington, DC 20002-6031, USA

Fowlkes, Alan (Athlete, Baseball Player)
405 Emerald Lake Dr
Lumberton, NC 28358-8022, USA

Fox, Allen (Coach, Tennis Player)
Pepperdine University
Athletic Dept
Malibu, CA 90265, USA

Fox, Andy (Athlete, Baseball Player)
9087 Tarmac Ct
Fair Oaks, CA 95628-8142, USA

Fox, Bernard (Actor)
6601 Burnet Ave
Van Nuys, CA 91405, USA

Fox, Chad (Athlete, Baseball Player)
6007 Windrose Hollow Ln
Spring, TX 77379-8904, USA

Fox, Charles I (Composer, Conductor)
American Int'l Artists
356 Pine Valley Road
Hoosick Falls, NY 12090, USA

Fox, Edward (Actor)
25 Maida Ave
London W2, UNITED KINGDOM (UK)

Fox, Emilia (Actor)
125 Glouster Rd
London SW7 4TE, UNITED KINGDOM

Fox, Eric (Athlete, Baseball Player)
9527 W Littlewood Dr
Boise, ID 83709-5397, USA

Fox, Everett (Misc)
Clark University
Jewish Studies Program
Worcester, MA 01610, USA

Fox, George
4950 Yonge St. #2400
Toronto, . CANADA Ont M2N 6K

Fox, Greg (Athlete, Hockey Player)
635 Glendalough Ct
Alpharetta, GA 30004-3056, USA

Fox, Harold (Athlete, Basketball Player)
6511 Wilburn Drive
Capitol Heights, MD 20743-3351, USA

Fox, Jackie
23368 Ostronic Dr.
Woodland Hills, CA 91367

Fox, Jake (Athlete, Baseball Player)
7028 Bellona Ave
Baltimore, MD 21212-1111, USA

Fox, James (Actor)
International Creative Mgmt
76 Oxford St
London W1N 0AX, UNITED KINGDOM (UK)

Fox, Jessica (Actor)
Associated International Management
Nederlander House 7 Great Russell Street
London
WC1B 3NH UK

Fox, Jim (Athlete, Hockey Player)
224 S Juanita Ave
#A
Redondo Beach, CA 90277, USA

Fox, Jim (Athlete, Basketball Player)
4136 North 52nd Street
Phoenix, AZ 85018-4402, USA

Fox, Jim
Los Angeles Kings 1111 S Figueroa St Ste 3100
Los Angeles, CA 90015-1333, USA

Fox, John (Athlete, Coach, Football Coach, Football Player)
11137 McClure Manor Dr
Charlotte, NC 28277, USA

Fox, Jorja (Actor)
c/o Peg Donegan *Framework Entertainment (LA)*
9057 Nemo St
Suite C
West Hollywood, CA 90069, USA

Fox, Marye Anne (Misc)
1530 Soledad Avenue
La Jolia, CA 91037-3815, USA

Fox, Matthew (Actor, Director)
18625 MacAlpine Loop
Bend, OR 97702, USA

Fox, Matthew (Religious Leader)
Grace Episcopal Cathedral
1 Nob Hill Circle
San Francisco, CA 94108, USA

Fox, Matthew (Athlete, Baseball Player)
3379 Caruso Pl
Oviedo, Fl 32765-8749, USA

Fox, Maurice S (Biologist)
983 Memorial Dr
#401
Cambridge, MA 02138, USA

Fox, Megan (Actor)
c/o Dominique Appel *Baker Winokur Ryder Public Relations (BWR-LA)*
9100 Wilshire Blvd
Suite 500, West Tower
Beverly Hills, CA 90212, USA

Fox, Michael J (Actor)
The Michael J. Fox Foundation For Parkinson's Research
Grand Central Station
P.O. Box 4777
New York, NY 10163, USA

Fox, Neil (Actor)
c/o Staff Member *MPC Entertainment*
MPC House
15-16 Maple Mews
London NW6 5UZ, UNITED KINGDOM

Fox, Rick (Actor, Athlete, Basketball Player)
10727 Wilshire Blvd
Apt 302
Los Angeles, CA 90024-4400, USA

Fox, Samantha (Model, Musician)
Fox 2000
PO Box 7834
London NW3 3ZT, UNITED KINGDOM (UK)

Fox, Shayna
6212 Banner Ave.
Los Angeles, CA 90038

Fox, Sheldon (Architect)
Kohn Pederson Fox Assoc
111 W 57th St
New York, NY 10019, USA

Fox, Spencer (Actor)
c/o Maggie Schuster *J Mitchell Management*
440 Park Ave S
New York, NY 10016, USA

Fox, Terry (Athlete, Baseball Player)
2312 Sugar Mill Rd
New Iberia, LA 70563-8648, USA

Fox, Tim (Athlete, Football Player)
11 Glover Ave
Hull, MA 02045, USA

Fox, Tim (Athlete, Football Player)
10 Longmeadow Dr
Westwood, MA 02090, USA

Fox, Vernon (Athlete, Football Player)
6704 Willow River Ct
Las Vegas, NV 89108, USA

Fox, Vicente (Politician, President)
Patacio Nacional
Patio de Honor
2 Piso
Mexico City DF 06067, MEXICO

Fox, Vivica (Actor)
c/o Lita Richardson *Richardson Entertainment*
13400 Chandler Blvd.
Sherman Oaks, CA 91401, USA

Fox, Wesley L (General, War Hero)
855 Deercraft Dr
Blacksburg, VA 24060-0272, USA

Fox Brothers
Rt. 6 Bending Chestnut
Franklin, TN 37064

Foxton, Simon (Stylist)
c/o Staff Member *Katy Barker Agency Inc*
6606 10th Ave Apt 3R
Brooklyn, NY 11219, USA

Foxworth, Domonique (Athlete, Football Player)
3533 5 Sherwood Rd SE
Smyrna, GA 30082, USA

Foxworth, Robert (Actor)
c/o Chris Schmidt *Paradigm (LA)*
360 N Crescent Dr
North Bldg
Beverly Hills, CA 90210, USA

Foxworthy, Jeff (Actor, Comedian)
365 High Bridge Chase
Alpharetta, GA 30022, USA

Foxx, Dion (Athlete, Football Player)
6457 Springcrest Ln
Henrico, VA 23231, USA

Foxx, Jamie (Actor, Comedian)
c/o Jamie King *Foxx-King Entertainment*
9229 Sunset Blvd
Suite 830
Los Angeles, CA 90069, USA

Foxx, Shyla (Adult Film Star)
c/o Staff Member *Atlas Multimedia Inc*
9005 Eton Ave Ste C
Canoga Park, CA 91304-1743, USA

Foxx, Tanya
901-G Victoria St.
Compton, CA 90220

Foxx, Virginia (Congressman, Politician)
1230 Longworth HOB
Washington, DC 20515, USA

Foy, Eddie III (Actor)
3003 W Olive Ave
Burbank, CA 91505, USA

Foyle, Adonal (Athlete, Basketball Player)
174 Crestview Drive
Orinda, CA 94563-3922, USA

Foyt, Larry (Race Car Driver)
AJ Foyt Racing
128 Commercial Dr
Mooresville, TN 28116, USA

Foytack, Paul (Athlete, Baseball Player)
1910 Portview Dr
Spring Hill, TN 37174-8249, USA

Foyt IV, A.J. (Race Car Driver)
Vision Racing
19480 Stokes Rd
Waller, TX 77484, USA

Foyt, Jr., A.J. (Race Car Driver)
19480 Stokes Road
Waller, TX 77484, USA

Frabotta, Don (Actor)
PO Box 962
Douglas, MA 01516-0962, USA

Fradkov, Mikhail (Prime Minister)
Prime Minister's Office
Kremlin
Staraya Pl 4
Moscow 103132, RUSSIA

Fradon, Dana (Cartoonist)
2 Brushy Hill Road
Newtown, CT 06470, USA

Fradon, Ramona (Cartoonist)
Tribune Media Services
435 N Michigan Ave
#1500
Chicago, IL 60611, USA

Frailing, Ken (Athlete, Baseball Player)
2150 Shadow Oaks Rd
Sarasota, FL 34240-9324, USA

Frain, James (Actor)
c/o Melanie Greene *Affirmative Entertainment*
425 N Robertson Blvd
Los Angeles, CA 90048, USA

Fraiture, Nikolai (Musician)
MVO Ltd
370 7th Ave
#807
New York, NY 10001, USA

Frakes, Jonathan (Actor, Director)
c/o Doug MacLaren *ICM Partners (ICM-LA)*
10250 Constellation Blvd Fl 7
Los Angeles, CA 90067, USA

Fralic, William (Bill) (Athlete, Football Player)
280 Galsworthy Ct
Roswell, GA 30075, USA

Frampton, Peter (Musician, Songwriter)
c/o Nicki Loranger *Vector Management (LA)*
1100 Glendon Ave.
Suite 2000
Los Angeles, CA 90024, USA

Franca, Celia (Ballerina, Choreographer)
157 King St E
Toronto, ON M5C 1G9, CANADA

France, Brian (Race Car Driver)
1151 N. Halifax Ave.
Daytona Beach, FL 32118-3654, USA

France, Doug (Athlete, Football Player)
6056 Great Falls Ave
Las Vegas, NV 89110, USA

France, James (Misc)
1147 N Halifax Ave
dayetona beach, FL 32118-3654, USA

France, Jim (Business Person)
Nascar
PO Box 2875
Daytona Beach, FL 32120, USA

Francekevich, Al (Photographer)
73 5th Ave Apt 2B
New York, NY 10003-3023, USA

Francella, Meaghan (Athlete, Golfer)
16 Maywood Ave
Port Chester, NY 10573, USA

Franceschetti, Lou (Athlete, Hockey Player)
72 Orchardcroft Cres
Toronto, ON M3J 1S8, Canada

Franchi, Rudy (Misc)
1228 S. Holt
Los Angeles, CA 90035, USA

Franchione, Dennis (Coach, Football Coach)
Texas A&M University
Athletic Dept
College Station, TX 77843, USA

Franchitti, Dario (Race Car Driver)
Team Green
7615 Zionsville Road
Indianapolis, IN 46268, USA

Franci, Jason (Athlete, Football Player)
336 Vintage Glen Ct
Santa Rosa, CA 95403, USA

Francis, Betty (Baseball Player)
11750 S Homan Ave Trlr 19A
Merrionette Park, IL 60803-4513, USA

Francis, Black (Musician)
3970 N Shasta Loop
Eugene, OR 97405, USA

Francis, Bob (Athlete, Coach, Hockey Player)
23725 N 75th Pl
Scottsdale, AZ 85258-6128, USA

Francis, Clarence (Bevo) (Basketball Player)
18340 Steubenyille Pike Road
Salineville, OH 43945, USA

Francis, Connie (Actor, Musician)
6413 NW 102nd Ter
Parkland, Fl 33076-2357, USA

Francis, Don (Scientist)
Genentech Inc
460 Point San Bruno Blvd
South San Francisco, CA 94080, USA

Francis, Donna (Stylist)
c/o Staff Member *Bryan Bantry*
900 Broadway Ste 400
New York, NY 10003, USA

Francis, Emile (Athlete, Hockey Player)
7220 Crystal Lake Dr
West Palm Beach, FL 33411, USA

Francis, Emile P (Coach)
7220 Crystal Lake Dr
West Palm Beach, FL 33411, USA

Francis, Fred (Correspondent)
NBC-TV
News Dept
4001 Nebraska Ave NW
Washington, DC 20016, USA

Francis, Genie (Actor)
10990 Wilshire Blvd
#1600
Los Angeles, CA 90024, USA

Francis, Harrison (Athlete, Football Player)
207 S Susan Ave
Wagoner, OK 74467, USA

Francis, Jeff (Athlete, Baseball Player)
3191 Quitman St
Denver, CO 80212-1457, USA

Francis, Joe (Producer)
c/o Staff Member *Mantra Films*
PO Box 150
Hollywood, CA 90078, USA

Francis, Joe (Athlete, Football Player)
45-570 Kaaluna Pl
Kaneohe, HI 96744, USA

Francis, Paul (Actor)
c/o Staff Member *Gilbertson Management*
1334 3rd St Promenade #201
Santa Monica, CA 90401, USA

Francis, Ron (Athlete, Hockey Player)
12312 Birchfalls Dr
Raleigh, NC 27614-7900, USA

Francis, Ron (Athlete, Football Player)
3315 Ashton Park Dr
Houston, TX 77082, USA

Francis, Russ (Athlete, Football Player)
800 Putney Rd
Brattleboro, VT 05301, USA

Francis, Steve (Athlete, Basketball Player)
632 Pifer Road
Houston, TX 77024-5434, USA

Francis, Wallace (Athlete, Football Player)
2452 Wilshire Way
Douglasville, GA 30135-8129, USA

Francis, Wally (Athlete, Football Player)
1307 Walton Ln SE
Smyrna, GA 30082, USA

Francis, William (Bill) (Musician)
Artists International
9850 Sandalwood Blvd
#458
Boca Raton, FL 33428, USA

Francisco, Aaron (Athlete, Football Player)
7081 S St Ruben Ave
Gilbert, AZ 85298-4147, USA

Francisco, Ben (Athlete, Baseball Player)
689 S Scout Trl
Anaheim, CA 92807-4757, us

Francisco, Don (Television Host)
c/o Staff Member *Univision*
605 3rd St. Fl12
New York, NY 10158, USA

Francisco, George J (Misc)
Fireman & Oilers Union
1100 Circle 75 Parkway
Atlanta, GA 30339, USA

Francisco, Pablo (Comedian)
c/o Matt Schuler *Levity Entertainment
Group*
6701 Center Drive West
Suite 1111
Los Angles, CA 90045, USA

Franckowiak, Mike (Athlete, Football
Player)
73 Fitch Way
Princeton, NJ 08540, USA

Francks, Rainbow Sun (Actor)
c/o Staff Member *Sci-FI Channel, The*
100 Universal Plaza
Bldg 1280/12
Universal City, CA 91608, USA

Franco, Brian (Athlete, Football Player)
155 Oceanwalk Dr S
Atlantic Beach, FL 32233-4679

Franco, Carlos (Athlete, Golfer)
10561 NW 51st St
Doral, FL 33178, USA

Franco, Dave (Actor)
c/o Miles Levy *James/Levy/Jacobson
Management Inc*
3500 W Olive Ave
Suite 1470
Burbank, CA 91505, USA

Franco, James (Actor)
2430 Hidalgo Ave
Los Angeles, CA 90039, USA

Franco, John (Athlete, Baseball Player)
111 Cliffwood Avenue
Staten Island, NY 10304, USA

Franco, Julio (Athlete, Baseball Player)
651 NE 23rd Ct
Pompano Beach, FL 33064-5504, USA

Franco, Liliana (Actor)
c/o Staff Member *Eileen O'farrell Personal
Management*
11653 Blix Street Suite 5
Studio City, CA 91602, United States

Franco, Matt (Athlete, Baseball Player)
1008 Clear Sky Pl
Simi Valley, CA 93065-8331, USA

Francoeur, Jeff (Athlete, Baseball Player)
3111 Willowstone Dr
Duluth, GA 30096-4023, USA

Francois-Poncet, Jean A (Financier,
Government Official)
6 Blvd Suchet
Paris 75116, FRANCE

Francona, Terry (Athlete, Baseball Player,
Coach)
750 Newton S
Chestnut Hill, MA 02467-2606, USA

Francona, Tito (Athlete, Baseball Player)
1109 Penn Ave
New Brighton, PA 15066-1632, USA

Frandsen, Kevin (Athlete, Baseball Player)
11000 N 77th Pl Unit 1007
Scottsdale, AZ 85260-5599, USA

Frangoulis, Mario (Musician)
c/o Staff Member *Sony Music
International*
550 Madison Ave
New York, NY 10022-3211, USA

Frank, Anthony M (Financier,
Government Official)
Independent Bancorp
3800 N Central
Phoenix, AZ 85012, USA

Frank, Barney (Politician)
Congressman Barney Frank
2252 Rayburn HOB
Washington, DC 20515-2104, USA

Frank, Charles (Actor)
S D B Partners
1801 Ave of Stars
#902
Los Angeles, CA 90067, USA

Frank, Claude (Musician)
Columbia Artists Mgmt Inc
165 W 57th St
New York, NY 10019, USA

Frank, Darryl (Producer)
c/o Staff Member *Dreamworks Television*
100 Universal Plaza Bldg 5125
Universal City, CA 91608, USA

Frank, Diana (Actor)
The Agency
1800 Ave of Stars
#400
Los Angeles, CA 90067, USA

Frank, Donald (Athlete, Football Player)
2039 Weston Green Loop
Cary, NC 27513-2268, USA

Frank, Gary (Actor)
1401 S Bentley Ave
#202
Los Angeles, CA 90025, USA

Frank, Howard (Business Person)
Carnival Corp
3655 NW 87th Ave
Miami, FL 33178, USA

Frank, Jason David (Actor, Comedian)
Richard Stone
2 Henrietta St
London WC2E 8PS, UNITED KINGDOM
(UK)

Frank, Jerome D (Educator)
818 W 40th St
#K
Baltimore, MD 21211, USA

Frank, Joanna (Actor)
1274 Capri Dr
Pacific Palisades, CA 90272, USA

Frank, Joe (Entertainer)
KCRW-FM
1900 Pico Blvd
Santa Monica, CA 90405, USA

Frank, John (Athlete, Football Player)
Medical Hair Restoration
200 W End Ave Apt 17E
New York, NY 10023-4856, USA

Frank, Larry (Race Car Driver)
Larry Frank Auto Body Works
832 Fork Shoals Rd .
Greenville, SC 29605, USA

Frank, Lawrence
51 Edward St
Demarest, NJ 07627-2205

Frank, Louis A (Astronomer)
University of Iowa
Astronomy Dept
Iowa City, IA 52242, USA

Frank, Mike (Athlete, Baseball Player)
1343 W 19th St
Upland, CA 91784-7433, USA

Frank, Neil L (Misc)
National Hurricane Center
1320 S Dixie Highway
Coral Gables, FL 33146, USA

Frank, Phil (Cartoonist)
500 Turley St
Sausalito, CA 94965, USA

Frank, Robert (Photographer)
Edwynn Houk Gallery
745 Fifth Ave
4th Floor
New York, NY 10151, USA

Frank, Scott (Actor, Director, Writer)
c/o Staff Member *Arroyo Films*
50 W Dayton St
#308
Pasadena, CA 91105, USA

Frank, Tellis (Athlete, Basketball Player)
4936 Van Noord Avenue
Sherman Oaks, CA 91423-2214, USA

Frank-Dummerth, Edna (Baseball Player)
5044 Tealby Ln
Saint Louis, MO 63128-2952, USA

Franke, Robert (Writer)
c/o Allen Fischer *Principato/Young
Management*
9465 Wilshire Blvd
Suite 430
Beverly Hills, CA 90212, USA

Frankel, Bethenny (Chef, Reality TV Star)
195 Hudson St #5B
New York, NY 10013, USA

Frankel, Felice (Artist, Photographer)
Massachusetts Institute of Technology
Edgerton Center
Cambridge, MA 02139, USA

Frankel, Max (Journalist)
New York Times 229 W 43rd St Attn
Editorial Dept
New York, NY 10036-3913, USA

Franken, Al (Actor, Comedian, Writer)
c/o Staff Member *Creative Artists Agency
(CAA-LA)*
2000 Ave Of The Stars
Los Angeles, CA 90067, USA

Frankenthaler, Helen (Artist)
19 Contentment Island Rd
Darien, CT 06820-6208, USA

Frankl, Peter (Musician)
5 Gresham Gardens
London NW11 8NX, UNITED KINGDOM
(UK)

Frankl, Viktor (Scientist)
Mariannengasse 1
Vienna A-1090, Austria

Franklin, Anthony R (Tony) (Athlete,
Football Player)
117 Shady Trail St
San Antonio, TX 78232, USA

Franklin, Aretha (Musician)
8450 Linwood St
Detroit, MI 48206, USA

Franklin, Arnold (Athlete, Football Player)
131 Ruskin Dr
Cincinnati, OH 45246-2418, USA

Franklin, Aubrayo (Athlete, Football
Player)
1 Castleton Ct
Johnson City, TN 37615-4949, USA

Franklin, Barbara Hackman (Secretary)
1875 Perkins St
Bristol, CT 06010-8910, USA

Franklin, Bobby (Athlete, Football Player)
384 Country Club Dr
Senetobia, MS 38668, USA

Franklin, Bonnie (Actor)
c/o Staff Member *Cunningham Escott
Slevin & Doherty (CESD-LA)*
10635 Santa Monica Blvd
130
Los Angeles, CA 90025, USA

Franklin, Byron (Athlete, Football Player)
2613 Singapore Dr
Birmingham, AL 35211, USA

Franklin, Carl M (Director)

Franklin, Cleveland (Athlete, Football
Player)
60 Hillary Cir
New Castle, DE 19720-8620, USA

Franklin, Dennis (Athlete, Football Player)
15474 Edmore Dr
Detroit, MI 48205-1351, USA

Franklin, Diane (Actor)
Third Hill Entertainment
195 S Beverly Dr
#400
Beverly Hills, CA 90212, USA

Franklin, Don
10101 Santa Monica Blvd. #2500
Los Angeles, CA 90067

Franklin, Don (Actor)
Paradigm Agency
10100 Santa Monica Blvd
#2500
Los Angeles, CA 90067, USA

Franklin, Dwaine (General)
12826 E 42nd St
Yuma, AZ 85367-6037, USA

Franklin, Farrah (Musician)
8391 Beverly Blvd.
Los Angeles, CA 90048, USA

Franklin, George (Athlete, Football Player)
6727 Feather Creek Dr
Houston, TX 77086-2005, USA

Franklin, Howard (Director, Writer)
c/o Staff Member *Agency for the
Performing Arts (APA-LA)*
405 S Beverly Dr
Suite 500
Beverly Hills, CA 90212-4425, USA

Franklin, Jay (Baseball Player)
San Diego Padres
2450 Massanutten Ter
Winchester, VA 22601 2774, USA

Franklin, Jerell (Athlete, Football Player)
2512 Nettleton St
Houston, TX 77004-2042, USA

Franklin, Jethro (Athlete, Football Player)
4806 Keneshaw Dr
Sugar Land, TX 77479-3984, USA

Franklin, Joe
Box 1
Lynbrook, NY 11563

Franklin, John (Actor)
Gilla Roos
9744 Wilshire Blvd
#203
Beverly Hills, CA 90212, USA

Franklin, Jon D (Journalist)
9650 Strickland Road
Raleigh, NC 27615, USA

Franklin, Kirk (Musician)
c/o Gwendolyn Quinn *GQ Media &
Public Relations*
1650 Broadway
Suite 1011
New York, NY 10019, USA

Franklin, Larry (Athlete, Football Player)
9390 Afton Grove Rd
Cordova, TN 38018, USA

Franklin, Melissa (Physicist)
Harvard University
Physics Dept
Cambridge, MA 02138, USA

Franklin, Micah (Athlete, Baseball Player)
3948 E Lafayette Ave
Gilbert, AZ 85298-9139, USA

Franklin, Missy (Athlete, Olympic Athlete,
Swimmer)
c/o Staff Member *USA Swimming
Association*
1 Olympic Plz
Colorado Springs, CO 80909-5770, USA

Franklin, P J (Athlete, Football Player)
903 S Laurel St
Amite, LA 70422-3525, USA

Franklin, Robert (Business Person)
Placer Dome Inc
1600-1055 Dunsmuir St
Vancouver, BC V7X 1P1, CANADA

Franklin, Roshawn (Actor)
c/o Staff Member *Freeze Frame
Entertainment*
5225 Wilshire Blvd #303
Los Angeles, CA 90036, USA

Franklin, Ryan (Athlete, Baseball Player,
Olympic Athlete)
1009 Muirfield Dr
Shawnee, OK 74801-0515, USA

Franklin, Shirley (Politician)
Mayor's Office
City Hall
55 Trinity Ave S
Atlanta, GA 30303, USA

Franklin, Wayne (Athlete, Baseball Player)
15 S Mauldin Ave
North East, MD 21901-4023, USA

Franklin, William (Boxer, Misc)
920 La Sombra Dr
San Marcos, CA 92069, USA

Franklin, Willie (Athlete, Football Player)
P.O. Box 62
Lake Dallas, TX 75065, USA

Franklyn, Sabina (Actor)
CCA Mgmt
4 Court Lodge
48 Sloane Square
London SW1W 8AT, UNITED KINGDOM
(UK)

Frankman, Betty Skelton (Astronaut)
651 Allenwood Loop
The Villages, FL 32162-1004, USA

Frank-Martin, Tobi (Stylist)
4102 Old Topanga Canyon Rd
Calabasas, CA 91302, USA

Franks, Daniel (Bubba) (Athlete, Football
Player)
1 Cavil Way
De Pere, WI 54115, USA

Franks, Dennis (Athlete, Football Player)
4 Westmount Ct
Greensboro, NC 27410, USA

Franks, Elvis (Athlete, Football Player)
2147 Rusk St
Beaumont, TX 77701, USA

Franks, Frederick M Jr (General)
6364 Brampton Court
Alexandria, VA 22304, USA

Franks, Gerold
1745 Camino Palmero
Los Angeles, CA 90046

Franks, Hermine (Baseball Player)
422 Pecor St
Oconto, WI 74153-1800, USA

Franks, Michael (Musician, Songwriter,
Writer)
c/o Staff Member *Agency for the
Performing Arts (APA-LA)*
405 S Beverly Dr
Suite 500
Beverly Hills, CA 90212-4425, USA

Franks, Ray (Race Car Driver)
PO Box 151
New Carlisle, OH 45344, USA

Franks, Tommy General (War Hero)
15273 N 2280 Rd
Roosevelt, OK 73564-5042, USA

Franks, Tommy Ray (General)
4 Star Ranch
15273 N 2280 Rd
Roosevelt, OK 73564, USA

Franks, Trent (Congressman, Politician)
2435 Rayburn HOB
Washington, DC 20515, USA

Frankston, Robert M (Bob) (Designer)
State Corp
15035 N 73rd St
Scottsdale, AZ 85260, USA

Fransen, Libby (Stylist)
15121 Woodruff Rd
Wayzata, MN 55391, USA

Fransioli, Thomas A (Artist)
55 Dodges Row
Wenham, MA 01984, USA

Franti, Michael (Actor, Composer,
Musician)
c/o Jamie Simon *PFA Media NYC*
285 W Broadway
Suite 630
New York, NY 10013, USA

Frantz, Adrienne (Actor)
c/o Marnie Sparer *Innovative Artists (LA)*
1505 10th St
Santa Monica, CA 90401, USA

Frantz, Chris (Musician)
Premier Talent
3 E 54th St
#1100
New York, NY 10022, USA

Franz, Arthur (Art) (Athlete, Baseball
Player)
P.O. Box 974
El Prado, NM 87529-0974, USA

Franz, Dennis (Actor)
c/o Alisa Adler *Paradigm (LA)*
360 N Crescent Dr
North Bldg
Beverly Hills, CA 90210, USA

Franz, Frederick W (Religious Leader)
Jehovah's Witnesses
25 Columbia Heights
Brooklyn, NY 11201, USA

Franz, John E (Inventor)
9831 Meadowfern Dr
Saint Louis, MO 63126-2417, USA

Franz, Judy R (Physicist)
American Physical Society
1 Physics Eclipse
College Park, MD 20740, USA

Franz, Mary (Stylist)
4349 Hillside Ave
Slinger, WI 53086, USA

Franz, Nolan (Athlete, Football Player)
327 31st St
Gulfport, MS 39507, USA

Franz, Rodney T (Rod) (Athlete, Football
Player)
1448 Engberg Ct
Carmichael, CA 95608, USA

Franz, Ron (Athlete, Basketball Player)
8590 Beaverwood Drive
Germantown, TN 38138-7715, USA

Franz, Todd (Athlete, Football Player)
5629 N Classen Blvd
Oklahoma City, OK 73118-4015, USA

Franzen, Johan (Athlete, Hockey Player)
22726 Summer Ln
Novi, MI 48374-3648, USA

Franzen, Jonathan (Writer)
c/o Richard Green *Creative Artists Agency
(CAA-LA)*
2000 Ave Of The Stars
Los Angeles, CA 90067, USA

Franzen, Ulrich J (Architect)
975 Park Ave
New York, NY 10028, USA

Frappi, Luigi (Artist)
Via Del Cirone, 6
Bevagna I-06031, Italy

Frasca, Robert J (Architect)
Zimmer Gunsul Frasca
320 SW Oak St
#500
Portland, OR 97204, USA

Frascatore, John (Athlete, Baseball Player)
3121 Saturn Rd
Brooksville, FL 34604-7032, USA

Frasconi, Antonio (Artist)
26 Dock Road
Norwalk, CT 06854, USA

Frase, Paul (Athlete, Football Player)
124 Crossroad Lakes Dr
Ponte Vedra Beach, FL 32082, USA

Fraser, Antonia (Writer)
Curtis Brown
Haymarket House
28/29 Haymarket
London SW1Y 4SP, UNITED KINGDOM
(UK)

Fraser, Brad (Writer)
Great North Artists Mgmt
350 Dupont Ave
Toronto, ON M5R 1V9, CANADA

Fraser, Brendan (Actor)
c/o JoAnne Colonna *Brillstein
Entertainment Partners*
9150 Wilshire Blvd #350
Beverly Hills, CA 90212, USA

Fraser, Brooke (Musician)
c/o Jonathan Adelman *Paradigm (NY)*
360 Park Ave S Fl 16
New York, NY 10010, USA

Fraser, Curt (Athlete, Hockey Player)
Grand Rapids Griffins 130 Fulton St W
Ste 111
Grand Rapids, MI 49503-2601, USA

Fraser, Dawn (Athlete, Swimmer)
87 Birchgrove Road
Balmain NSW, Australia

Fraser, Douglas (Misc)
United Auto Workers
8000 E Jefferson Ave
Detroit, MI 48214, USA

Fraser, George MacDonald (Writer)
Curtis Brown
28/29 Haymarket
London SW1Y 4SP, UNITED KINGDOM
(UK)

Fraser, Gretchen
5023 236th Pl. SE
Woodinville, WA 98072-8610

Fraser, Hon
MalcolmThurulgoona
Redhill, AUSTRALIA Vic. 3937,
AUSTRALIA

Fraser, Honor (Model)
c/o Staff Member *Fam*
boul. Vital Bouhot 30
Neuilly-sur-Seine,Paris 75008, FRANCE

Fraser, Hugh (Actor)
Jonathan Altaras
13 Shorts Gardens
London WC2H 9AT, UNITED KINGDOM
(UK)

Fraser, Iain
2938 Grinstead Dr
Louisville, KY 40206-2645, USA

Fraser, Laura (Actor)
c/o Tammy Rosen *Sanders Armstrong
Caserta*
425 N Robertson Blvd
Los Angeles, CA 90048, USA

Fraser, Malcolm (Prime Minister)
Thurulgoona
Redhill, VIC 3937, AUSTRALIA

Fraser, Neale (Tennis Player)
21 Bolton Ave
Hampton, VIC 3188, AUSTRALIA

Fraser, Ware Dawn (Swimmer)
403 Darling St
Balmain, NSW 2041, AUSTRALIA

Fraser, Willie (Athlete, Baseball Player)
3 Turano
Laguna Niguel, CA 92677-8927, USA

Frashilla, Fran (Coach)
New Mexico University
Athletic Dept
Albuquerque, NM 87131, USA

Frasor, Jason (Athlete, Baseball Player)
12611 SE Old Cypress Dr
Hobe Sound, FL 33455, USA

Fratello, Michael R (Mike) (Athlete,
Basketball Player, Coach, Sportscaster)
7642 Fisher Island Drive
Miami Beach, FL 33109, USA

Fratianne, Linda S (Athlete, Figure Skater,
Olympic Athlete)
3352 Whispering Glen Ct
Simi Valley, CA 93065-0596, USA

Frattare, Lanny (Commentator)
Pittsburgh Pirates
2032 Croghan Dr
Carnegie, PA 15106-1593, USA

Frauenfelder, Mark (Internet Star)
Boing Boing
13547 Ventura Blvd #91
Sherman Oaks, CA 91423, USA

Fraumeni, Joseph F Jr (Inventor)
National Cancer Institute
Cancer Etiology Division
Bethesda, MD 20892, USA

Frawley, Dan
4110 County Road 16
Brinston, ON K0E lC0, Canada

Frayn, Michael (Writer)
Greene & Heaton
37A Goldhawk Road
London W12 8QQ, UNITED KINGDOM
(UK)

Frazar, Harrison (Athlete, Golfer)
3208 Villanova St
Dallas, TX 75225-4839, USA

Frazer, Liz (Actor)
Peter Charlesworth
68 Old Brompton Road
#200
London SW7 3LQ, UNITED KINGDOM
(UK)

Frazier, Al (Athlete, Football Player)
17240 133rd Avve
Apt 12A
Jamaica, NY 11434, USA

Frazier, Albert (Baseball Player)
Jacksonville Red Caps
5749 Copper Hill Ln E
Jacksonville, FL 32218-7311, USA

Frazier, Andre (Athlete, Football Player)
9650 Fallshill Cir
Cincinnati, OH 45231-2886, USA

Frazier, Charley (Athlete, Football Player)
4018 Brookston St
Houston, TX 77045, USA

Frazier, Dallas (Musician, Songwriter,
Writer)
RR 5 Box 133
Longhollow Pike
Gallatin, TN 37066, USA

Frazier, George (Athlete, Baseball Player)
6886 S Evanston Ave
Tulsa, OK 74136-4554, USA

Frazier, Guy (Athlete, Football Player)
3944 Dickson Ave
Cincinnati, OH 45229, USA

Frazier, Herman (Athlete, Olympic
Athlete, Track Athlete)
1777 Ala Moana Blvd
Honolulu, HI 96815, USA

Frazier, Ian (Writer)
Farrar Straus Giroux
19 Union Square W
New York, NY 10003, USA

Frazier, Kevin (Actor, Television Host)
c/o Staff Member *Entertainment Tonight*
(ET)
4024 Radford Ave.
Studio City, CA 91604, USA

Frazier, Leslie (Athlete, Football Player)
17559 Bearpath Trl
Eden Prairie, MN 55347-3488, USA

Frazier, Lisa (Musician)
c/o Staff Member *Diva Central Inc*
7510 W Sunset Blvd Ste 1445
Los Angees, CA 90046, USA

Frazier, Lou (Athlete, Baseball Player)
1371 N Concord Ave
Chandler, AZ 85225-8624, USA

Frazier, Mavis (Boxer)
2917 N Broad St
Philadelphia, PA 19132, USA

Frazier, Owsley B (Business Person)
Brown-Forman Corp
850 Dixie Highway
Louisville, KY 40210, USA

Frazier, Sheila (Actor)
c/o Daniel Hoff *Daniel Hoff Agency*
5455 Wilshire Blvd
Suite 1100
Los Angeles, CA 90036, USA

Frazier, Walt (Athlete, Basketball Player)
381 Malcolm X Blvd Ph A
New York, NY 10027-2173, USA

Frazier, Will (Athlete, Basketball Player)
P.O. Box 380772
Duncanville, TX 75138-0772, USA

Frazier, Willie (Athlete, Football Player)
6203 Bankside Dr
Houston, TX 77096, USA

Frears, Stephen A (Director)
93 Talbot Road
London W2, UNITED KINGDOM (UK)

Freberg, Stanley V (Stan) (Actor,
Comedian)
Radio Spirits
PO Box 3107
Wallingford, CT 06492, USA

Frechette, Peter (Actor)
c/o Staff Member *Buchwald/Fortitude (LA)*
6500 Wilshire Blvd
Suite 2200
Los Angeles, CA 90048, USA

Freddie, Douglas (Athlete, Football Player)
24 Pheasant Run Dr
Cabot, AR 72023-3608, USA

Frederic, Dreux (Lil Fizz) (Musician)
c/o Douglas Mark *Mark Music and Media*
Law
Prefers to be contacted via telephone
Los Angeles, CA 90069, USA

Frederick, Andrew B (Athlete, Football
Player)
7247 Alexander Dr
Dallas, TX 75214, USA

Frederick, Andy
7247 Alexander Dr
Dallas, TX 75214-3216, USA

Frederick, Justin (Stylist)
PO Box 412
Rancocas, NJ 08073, USA

Frederick, Kevin (Athlete, Baseball Player)
20512 N Clarice Ave
Lincolnshire, IL 60069-9618, USA

Frederick, Mike (Athlete, Football Player)
425 Fairmont Dr
Chester Springs, PA 19425-3657, USA

Fredericks, Frank (Frankie) (Athlete, Track
Athlete)
4497 Wimbledon Dr
Provo, UT 84604, USA

Fredericks, Fred (Cartoonist)
PO Box 475
Eastham, MA 02642-0475, USA

Frederickson, Ivan C (Tucker) (Athlete,
Football Player)
12414 Indian Rd
North Palm Beach, FL 33408, USA

Frederickson, Rob (Athlete, Football
Player)
5942 E Caballo Ln
Paradise Valley, AZ 85253, USA

Frederickson, Scott (Athlete, Baseball
Player)
20703 Turning Leaf Lake Ct
Cypress, TX 77433, USA

Fredrickson, George M (Historian)
741 Esplanada Way
Palo Alto, CA 94305, USA

Fredrickson, Rob (Athlete, Football Player)
8312 N 50th St
Paradise Valley, AZ 85253-2005, USA

Fredrickson, Scott (Athlete, Baseball
Player)
20703 Turning Leaf Lake Ct
Cypress, TX 77433-4612, USA

Fredriksson, Gert (Athlete)
Bruunsgat 13
Nykoping 61122, SWEDEN

Fredriksson, Marie (Musician, Songwriter,
Writer)
D &D Mgmt
Lilla Nygatan 19
Stockholm 11128, SWEDEN

Free (Actor, Musician)
c/o Damu Bobb *Identity Talent Agency*
(ID)
9107 Wilshire Blvd
Suite 500
Beverly Hills, CA 90210, USA

Free, Helen M (Inventor)
3752 E Jackson Blvd
Elkhart, IN 46516, USA

Free, Scott (Stylist)
c/o Staff Member *Rex Agency, The*
6311 Romaine St
Los Angeles, CA 90038, USA

Free, World B (Athlete, Basketball Player,
Coach)
1 Twin Hollow Ct
Sicklerville, NJ 08081-4057, USA

Freebo
740 N. Hayworth Ave.
Los Angeles, CA 90046

Freed, Andy (Commentator)
4611 Noble Pl
Parrish, FL 34219-7599, USA

Freed, Curt R (Biologist)
University of Colorado
Health Science Center
4200 E 9th Ave
Denver, CO 80220, USA

Freed, Jack H (Misc)
108 Homestead Circle
Ithaca, NY 14850, USA

Freed, Jill (Stylist)
2112 Iris Ct
Santa Rosa, CA 95404, USA

Freedman, Alix M (Journalist)
Wall Street Journal
Editorial Dept
200 Liberty St
New York, NY 10281, USA

Freedman, David A (Mathematician)
901 Alvarado Road
Berkeley, CA 94705, USA

Freedman, Gerald A (Director, Opera
Singer)
Theatre Julliard School
Lincoln Center Plaza
New York, NY 10023, USA

Freedman, James O (Educator)
Dartmouth College
President's Office
Hanover, NH 03755, USA

Freedman, Ronald (Activist)
1200 Earhart Road
#228
Ann Arbor, MI 48105, USA

Freedman, Russell (Writer)
280 Riverside Dr Apt lOK
New York, NY 10025-9028, USA

Freedman, Wendy L (Astronomer)
Camegie Observatories
813 Santa Barbara St
Pasadena, CA 91101, USA

Freeh, LouisFBI
9th & Pennsylvania Ave. NW
Washington, DC 20035

Freehan, Bill (Athlete, Baseball Player)
6999 Indian Garden Rd
Petoskey, MI 49770-8708, USA

Freelon, Nnenna (Musician)
Ted Kurland
173 Brighton Ave
Boston, MA 02134, USA

Freelon, Solomon (Athlete, Football
Player)
2021 Burg Jones Ln
Monroe, LA 71202-4406, USA

Freeman, Antonio (Athlete, Football
Player)
11201 NW 18th St
Plantation, FL 33323-2226, USA

Freeman, Arturo (Athlete, Football Player)
14420 Stirling Rd
Southwest Ranches, FL 33330, USA

Freeman, Bernard (Bun B) (Musician)
c/o Marty Diamond *Paradigm (NY)*
360 Park Ave S Fl 16
New York, NY 10010, USA

Freeman, Bobby (Musician)
Lustig Talent
PO Box 770850
Orlando, FL 32877, USA

Freeman, Cassidy (Actor)
c/o Janice Lee *Entertainment Fusion Group*
7080 Hollywood Blvd
Suite 903
Los Angeles, CA 90028, USA

Freeman, Cathy (Athlete, Track Athlete)
PO Box 700
South Melbourne, VIC 3205, AUSTRALIA

Freeman, Charles W Jr (Diplomat)
Project International
1800 K St NW
#1010
Washington, DC 20006, USA

Freeman, Crispin (Actor, Writer)
c/o Staff Member *Arlene Thornton & Associates*
12711 Ventura Blvd
Suite 490
Studio City, CA 91604, USA

Freeman, Gary (Athlete, Basketball Player)
P.O. Box 1399
Albany, OR 97321-0548, USA

Freeman, Gregory A (Writer)
4880 Lower Roswell Rd Ste 165210
Marietta, GA 30068-4375, USA

Freeman, Isaac (Musician)
Keith Case Assoc
1025 17th Ave S
#200
Nashville, TN 37212, USA

Freeman, Issac (Fatman Scoop)
(Musician)
c/o Staff Member *PhreQuency Entertainment*
1830 South Rd.
Unit 24 #178
Wappingers Falls, NY 12590, USA

Freeman, J E (Actor)
Gersh Agency
232 N Canon Dr
Beverly Hills, CA 90210, USA

Freeman, Jennifer Nicole (Actor)
c/o Nils Larsen *Principato/Young Management*
312 W 5th St Apt 815
Los Angeles, CA 90013, USA

Freeman, Jimmy (Athlete, Baseball Player)
4716 E 106th St
Tulsa, OK 74137-6805, USA

Freeman, K Todd (Actor)
c/o Staff Member *Steppenwolf Theatre Co*
758 W North Ave Fl 4
Chicago, IL 60610, USA

Freeman, La Vel (Athlete, Baseball Player)
8941 Laguna Place Way
Elk Grove, CA 95758-5351, USA

Freeman, Martin (Actor)
c/o Jo Yao *United Talent Agency (UTA)*
9336 Civic Center Dr
Beverly Hills, CA 90210, USA

Freeman, Marvin (Athlete, Baseball Player)
20135 Mohawk Trl
Olympia Fields, IL 60461-1135, USA

Freeman, Meg (Stylist)
c/o Staff Member *Jam Arts, Inc*
154 W 57th St
New York, NY 10019, USA

Freeman, Michael WIlliam (Actor)
c/o Scott Zimmerman *Evolution Entertainment (LA)*
901 N Highland Ave
Los Angeles, CA 90038, USA

Freeman, Mike (Athlete, Football Player)
6020 Danny Kaye Dr
Apt 1502
San Antonio, TX 78240, USA

Freeman, Mona (Actor)
608 N Alpine Dr
Beverly Hills, CA 90210, USA

Freeman, Morgan (Actor)
c/o Stan Rosenfield *Stan Rosenfield & Associates*
2029 Century Park E
Suite 1190
Los Angeles, CA 90067, USA

Freeman, Phil (Athlete, Football Player)
1222 S Stanley Ave
Los Angeles, CA 90019, USA

Freeman, Reggie (Athlete, Football Player)
P.O. Box 1694
Clewiston, FL 33440, USA

Freeman, Robin (Athlete, Golfer)
115 Chelsea Cir
Palm Desert, CA 92260-4688, USA

Freeman, Rod (Athlete, Basketball Player)
6308 Murray Lane
Brentwood, TN 37027-6210, USA

Freeman, Russ (Athlete, Football Player)
4090 Summit Crossing Dr
Decatur, GA 30034, USA

Freeman, Russell (Football Coach, Football Player)
4090 Summit Crossing Dr
Decatur, GA 30034-3542, USA

Freeman, Sandi (Correspondent)
Cable News Network
News Dept
820 1st ST NE
Washington, DC 20002, USA

Freeman, Steve (Athlete, Football Player)
Mississippi State University
P.O. Box 5308
Attn: Alumni Association
Mississippi State, MS 39762, USA

Freeman, Yvette (Actor, Musician)
Stone Manners
6500 Wilshire Blvd
#550
Los Angeles, CA 90048, USA

Freeney, Dwight (Athlete, Football Player)
8484 Wilshire Blvd Ste 220
Beverly Hills, CA 90211-3223, USA

Freer, Mark (Athlete, Hockey Player)
823 Linden Rd
Hershey, PA 17033-1735, USA

Freese, David (Athlete, Baseball Player)
16559 Thunderhead Canyon Court
Ballwin, MO 63011-1853, USA

Freese, Gene (Athlete, Baseball Player)
6504 Glendale St
Metairie, LA 70003-3011, USA

Freese, George (Athlete, Baseball Player)
3341 SW Marigold St
Portland, OR 97219-5309, USA

Freese, Louis (Musician)
c/o Jack Iannaci *Brass Artists & Associates*
9025 Wilshire Blvd
Suite 400
Beverly Hills, CA 90211, USA

Fregosi, Jim (Athlete, Baseball Player, Coach)
1092 Copeland Ct
Tarpon Springs, FL 34688-7622, USA

Fregoso, Ramon (Actor)
c/o Staff Member *TV Azteca*
Periferico Sur 4121
Colonia Fuentes del Pedregal
DF CP 14141, Mexico

Frehley, Ace (Musician)
c/o Staff Member *Creative Artists Agency (CAA-LA)*
2000 Ave Of The Stars
Los Angeles, CA 90067, USA

Frei, Emil III (Misc)
Dana-Farber Cancer Institute
44 Binney St
Boston, MA 02115, USA

Freidheim, Cyrus (Business Person)
Chiquita Brands International
250 E 5th St
Cincinnati, OH 45202, USA

Freigang, Stephan
Strasse der Jugend 58
Cottbus, GERMANY D-03050

Freilicher, Jane (Artist)
Fishbach Gallery
210 11th Ave
#801
New York, NY 10001, USA

Freire, Nelson (Musician)
Columbia Artists Mgmt Inc
165 W 57th St
New York, NY 10019, USA

Freireich, Emil J (Doctor)
M D Anderson Medical Center
1515 Holcombe Blvd
Houston, TX 77030, USA

Frei Ruiz-Tagle, Eduardo (President)
President's Office
Palacio de la Monedo
Santiago, CHILE

Freis, Edward DJ (Doctor)
4515 Willard Ave
Chevy Chase, MD 20815, USA

Freisleben, Dave (Athlete, Baseball Player)
1326 Diamante Dr
Pasadena, TX 77504-1479, USA

Freitas, Jesse (Athlete, Football Player)
8405 Florissant Ct
San Diego, CA 92129-4408, USA

Freitas, Rocky (Athlete, Football Player)
2667 E Manoa Rd
Honolulu, HI 96822, USA

Freitas - CA, Camille (Stylist)
7929 Selma
#7
West Hollywood, CA 90046, USA

Freitas - TX, Camille (Stylist)
12124 Dixfield Dr
Dallas, TX 75218, USA

French, Dawn (Actor, Comedian)
P F D Drury House
34-43 Russell St
London WC2B 5HA, UNITED KINGDOM (UK)

French, Ernest (Athlete, Football Player)
1004 Moran St
Bay Minette, AL 36507, USA

French, Florence (Stylist)
6414 Pontiac Dr
La Grange, IL 60525, USA

French, Heather (Beauty Pageant Winner)
1361 Tyler Park Dr
Louisville, KY 40204-1539, USA

French, Jane (Musician)
c/o Staff Member *Pixie Publishing*
9611 Ross Ave
Cincinnati, OH 45242

French, Jim (Athlete, Baseball Player)
PO Box 39 49594 Ke Rd
Mesa, CO 81643-0039, USA

French, John (Athlete, Hockey Player)
142 Woodbury Cres
Newmarket, ON L3X 2SS, Canada

French, Julie (Stylist)
c/o Staff Member *Industry Representation*
448 E Riverdale Ave
Orange, CA 92865, USA

French, Kate (Actor)
c/o Brooklyn Weaver *Energy Entertainment*
999 N Doheny Dr
#711
Los Angeles, CA 90069, USA

French, Leigh (Actor)
1850 N Vista St
Los Angeles, CA 90046, USA

French, Luke (Athlete, Baseball Player)
10090 Severn Ln
Parker, CO 80134-3617, USA

French, Marilyn (Writer)
Charlotte Sheedy Agency
65 Bleecker St
#1200
New York, NY 10012, USA

French, Niki (Musician)
Mega Artists Mgmt
PO Box 89
Edam, ZJ 1135, NETHERLANDS

French, Paige (Actor)
Gersh Agency
232 N Canon Dr
Beverly Hills, CA 90210, USA

French, Rufus (Athlete, Football Player)
P.O. Box 10628
Green Bay, WI 54307, USA

French, Sarah (Model, Television Host)
221 Trumbull St
Hartford, CT 06103, USA

French, Susan
110 E. 9th St. #C-1005
Los Angeles, CA 90079

Freni, Mirelia (Opera Singer)
John Coast Mgmt
31 Sinclair Road
London W14 0NS, UNITED KINGDOM (UK)

Freni, Mirella (Opera Singer)
Decca/Universal Classics Records
825 8th Ave
New York, NY 10019, USA

Frenkiel, Richard H (Engineer, Inventor)
Rutgers University
WINLAB
PO Box 909
Piscataway, NJ 08855, USA

Frentzen, Heinz-Harald (Race Car Driver)
Formula One Ltd
Silverstone Circuit
Northamptonshire NN12 8TN, UNITED KINGDOM (UK)

Freon, Franck (Race Car Driver)
434 E .Ma i n St.
Brownsburg, IN 46112, USA

Freotte, Gus (Athlete, Football Player)
10040 Litzsinger Rd
Saint Louis, MO 63124, USA

Freotte, Mitch (Athlete, Football Player)
445 Reynolds Ave
Kittanning, PA 16201, USA

Frerotte, Gus (Athlete, Football Player)
10040 Litzsinger Rd
Saint Louis, MO 63124, USA

Fresco, Paolo (Business Person)
Fiat SpA
Corso Marconi 10/20
Turin 10125, ITALY

Fresh, Doug E (Musician)
c/o Reg Reg Askew *Fly Guy Management*
1 W 34th St #201
New York, NY 10016, USA

Fresh, Mannie (Musician, Producer)
c/o Staff Member *Universal Music Group (UMG - LA)*
2220 Colorado Ave
Santa Monica, CA 90404, USA

Freston, Kathy (Writer)
c/o Staff Member *St Martins Press*
Publicity Dept
175 5th Ave
New York, NY 10010, USA

Freud, Bella (Designer, Fashion Designer)
48 Rawstorne St
London EC1V 7ND, UNITED KINGDOM (UK)

Freudenthal, David (Politician)
10020 Yellowstone Rd
Cheyenne, VVY 82009-8943, USA

Freudenthal, Thor (Director)
c/o Peter McHugh *The Gotham Group Inc*
9255 Sunset Blvd
Suite 515
Los Angeles, CA 90069, USA

Freund, Lambert B (Engineer)
9720 Glen Eden Ct
Brentwood, TN 37027-8356

Freundlich, Bart (Director, Producer, Writer)
c/o Bart Walker *ICM Partners (ICM-LA)*
555 W 25th St
4th Floor
New York, NY 10001, USA

Frewer, Matt (Actor)
c/o Carol Gettko *Warren Cowan & Associates PR*
8899 Beverly Blvd #919
Los Angeles, CA 90048, USA

Frey, Bob (Race Car Driver)
605 Harvest Lane
Waterford, NJ 08089, USA

Frey, Christopher
The Toft E. Dean nr. Chichester
Sussex, ENGLAND

Frey, Dick
23618 Powder Mill Dr
Tomball, TX 77377-3920, USA

Frey, Glenn (Actor, Musician, Songwriter, Writer)
5020 Brent Knoll Ln
Suwanee, GA 30024, USA

Frey, James (Writer)
c/o Richard Green *Creative Artists Agency (CAA-LA)*
2000 Ave Of The Stars
Los Angeles, CA 90067, USA

Frey, Jim (Commentator)
12101 Tullamore Ct Unit 406
Lutherville Timonium, MD 21093-8148, USA

Frey, Richard (Athlete, Football Player)
P.O. Box 1967
Tomball, TX 77377-1967, USA

Frey, Sami
21 Place des Vosges
Paris, FRANCE F-75003

Frey, Steve (Athlete, Baseball Player)
1414 2nd Street Pike
Southampton, PA 18966-3931, USA

Freyer, Marina (Stylist)
30 Northway
Old Greenwich, CT 06870, USA

Freyndlikh, Alisa B (Actor)
Rubinstein Str 11
#7
Saint Petersburg 191002, RUSSIA

Freytag, Arny (Photographer)
22735 MacFarlane Dr
Woodland Hills, CA 91364, USA

Friberg, Arnold (Artist)
Friberg Fine Arts
5206 Pinemont Dr
Salt Lake City, UT 84123, USA

Frick, Gottlob (Opera Singer)
Eichelberg-Haus Waldfrieden
Olbronn-Durrn 75248, GERMANY

Frick, Stephen N (Astronaut)
4322 Towering Oak Court
Houston, TX 93923-8429, USA

Fricke, Janie (Musician)
Janie Fricke Concerts
PO Box 798
Lancaster, TX 75146, USA

Fricker, Brenda (Actor)
c/o Staff Member *IFA Talent Agency*
8730 Sunset Blvd
Suite 490
Los Angeles, CA 90069, USA

Frickman, Andy (Director)
c/o Staff Member *WME (LA)*
9601 Wilshire Blvd Fl 3
Beverly Hills, CA 90210, USA

Frid, David (Stylist)
c/o Staff Member *Ford Models (Chicago)*
311 W Superior St
Chicago, IL 60654, USA

Friday, Bill (Athlete, Hockey Player)
34 South brook Dr Unit 43
Binbrook, ON LOR ICO, Canada

Friday, Tim (Athlete, Hockey Player)
81 Fisher Rd
Southborough, MA 01772-1004, USA

Friday Jr, Elbert W (Government Official)
US National Weather Service
1125 East-West Highway
Silver Spring, MD 20910, USA

Fridell, Squire
13563 Ventura Blvd. #200
Sherman Oaks, CA 91403

Fridgen, Dan (Athlete, Hockey Player)
1524 Boulton Rd
Troy, NY 12180-3630, USA

Fridman, Mikhail (Business Person)
Alfa Group
1 Arbat St
Moscow 119019, Russia

Fridovich, Irwin (Misc)
3517 Courtland Dr
Durham, NC 27707, USA

Fridriksson, Fridrik T (Director)
Bjarkgata 8
Reykjavik 101, ICELAND

Friebe, Anika
111 E. 22nd St. #200
New York, NY 10010

Fried, Charles (Educator, Government Official)
Harvard University
Law School
Cambridge, MA 02138, USA

Friede, Mike (Athlete, Football Player)
6943 County Road 56
Johnstown, CO 80534-8237, USA

Friedel, Jacques (Physicist)
2 Rue Jean-Francois Gerbillon
Paris 75006, FRANCE

Friedericy, Bonita (Actor)
8480 Hillside Ave
Los Angeles, CA 90069, USA

Friedgen, Ralph (Coach, Football Coach)
University of Maryland
Athletic Dept
College Park, MD 20742, USA

Friedkin, William (Director)
c/o Renee Tab *Sentient*
1617 Broadway Mezzanine Suite
Santa Monica, CA 90404, USA

Friedlander, Judah (Comedian, Writer)
c/o Jennifer Konawal *Gersh (NY)*
41 Madison Ave
New York, NY 10010, USA

Friedlander, Lee (Artist, Photographer)
44 S Mountain Road
New City, NY 10956-2315, USA

Friedle, Gerry (DJ Otzi) (Musician)
C/O Karin Neuwirth
Pollau 31
Jagerberg A-8091, Austria

Friedle, Will (Actor)
c/o Steven Muller *Innovative Artists (LA)*
1505 10th St
Santa Monica, CA 90401, USA

Friedman, Andrew (Commentator)
1265 Snell Isle Blvd NE
Saint Petersburg, FL 33704-3035, USA

Friedman, Doug (Athlete, Hockey Player)
226 Falmouth Rd
Falmouth, ME 04105-2053, USA

Friedman, Emanuel A (Educator)
Beth-Israel Hospital
330 Brookline Ave
Boston, MA 02215, USA

Friedman, Jeffrey (Misc)
Rockefeller University
Hughes Medical Institute
New York, NY 10021, USA

Friedman, Jerome I (Nobel Prize Laureate)
75 Greenough St
Brookline, MA 02445-6152, USA

Friedman, Kinky (Writer)
906 1/2 Congress
Austin, TX 78701, USA

Friedman, Lawrence M (Educator, Lawyer)
724 Frenchmans Road
Palo Alto, CA 94305, USA

Friedman, Lennie (Athlete, Football Player)
1300 Adams Mountain Rd
Raleigh, NC 27614, USA

Friedman, Peter (Actor, Musician)
J Michael Bloom
233 Park Ave S
#1000
New York, NY 10003, USA

Friedman, Philip (Writer)
Ivy Books/Random House Inc
1745 Broadway
#B1
New York, NY 10019, USA

Friedman, Sonya
208 Harristown Rd
Glen Rock, NJ 07452

Friedman, Stephen (Financier, Government Official)
White House
1600 Pennsylvania Ave NW
Washington, DC 20500, USA

Friedman, Thomas (Journalist)
7117 Bradley Blvd
Bethesda, MD 20817-2125, USA

Friedman, Yona (Architect)
33 Blvd Garibaldi
Paris 75015, FRANCE

Friedmann, Phil (Musician)
Overland Productions
156 W 56th St
#500
New York, NY 10019, USA

Friel, Anna (Actor)
c/o Abi Harris *Ken McReddie Ltd*
11 Connaught Pl
London W2 2ET, UNITED KINGDOM

Friel, Brian (Writer)
Drumaweir House
Greencastle, County Donegal, IRELAND

Friels, Colin (Actor)
129 Brooke St
Woollomooloo
Sydney, NSW 2011, AUSTRALIA

Friend, Bob (Athlete, Baseball Player)
4 Salem Cir
Pittsburgh, PA 15238-2525, USA

Friend, Lionel (Conductor)
136 Rosendale Road
London SE21 8LG, UNITED KINGDOM (UK)

Friend, Patricia A (Misc)
1275 K St NW
#5
Washington, DC 20005, USA

Friend, Richard H (Misc)
Cavendish Laboratory
Chemistry Dept
Cambridge, UNITED KINGDOM (UK)

Friend, Rupert (Actor)
c/o Boomer Malkin *WME (LA)*
9601 Wilshire Blvd Fl 3
Beverly Hills, CA 90210, USA

Frier, Mike (Athlete, Football Player)
180 Jackson St NE Apt 1615
Atlanta, GA 30312-1358, USA

Fries, Chuck
6922 Hollywood Blvd.
Los Angeles, CA 90028

Fries, Donald B (Publisher)
Life Magazine
Time-Life Building
New York, NY 10020, USA

Friesen, David (Musician)
Thomas Cassidy
11761 E Speedway Blvd
Tucson, AZ 85748, USA

Friesen, Don (Musician)
c/o Staff Member *Paradigm (Monterey)*
404 W Franklin St
Monterey, CA 93940, USA

Friesen, Jeff (Athlete, Hockey Player)
47 Christopher St
Ladera Ranch, CA 92694-1527, USA

Friesinger, Anni (Speed Skater)
WIGE Media AG
Geilbelweg 24
Fellbach 70736, GERMANY

Friest, Ron (Athlete, Hockey Player)
456 St John St
Windsor, ON N8S 3T7, Canada

Friesz, John (Athlete, Football Player)
1454 E West Pebblestone Ct
Hayden, ID 83835, USA

Frig, Len (Athlete, Hockey Player)
7556 Wynford St
Salt Lake City, UT 84121-5449, USA

Frigid Pink
32885 Northampton
Warren, MI 48093

Friis, Janus (Business Person)
50 New Bond St
London W1S 1BJ, UK

Frimout, Dirk D (Astronaut)
c/o Staff Member *NASA*
Johnson Space Center
2101 NASA Rd
Houston, TX 77058, USA

Frimout, Dirk D Dr (Astronaut)
Laurierlaan 1
Sint-Pieters-Woluwe B-1150, Belgium

Frisbee, Rob (Athlete)
c/o Jerry Shandrew *Shandrew Public Relations*
1050 S Stanley Ave
Los Angeles, CA 90019-6634, USA

Frisch, Byron (Athlete, Football Coach, Football Player)
3304 Corte Cadiz
Carlsbad, CA 92009-8956, USA

Frisch, David (Athlete, Football Player)
3 Pebble Acres Ct
High Ridge, MO 63049-1665, USA

Frischman, Daniel
145 S. Fairfax Ave. #310
Los Angeles, CA 90036

Frischmann, Justine (Musician)
CMO Mgmt
Ransomes Dock
357-37 Parkgate Road
London SW11 4NP, UNITED KINGDOM (UK)

Frisell, William R (Bill) (Musician)
Nonesuch Records
75 Rockefeller Plaza
New York, NY 10019, USA

Frishberg, David L (Composer, Musician)
c/o Staff Member *Irvin Arthur Assoc*
1441 3rd Ave #12C
New York, NY 10028-1976, USA

Frist, William (Politician)
703 Bowling Ave
Nashville, TN 37215-1048, USA

Fritsch, Jamie
2745 Conway Rd
Odenton, MD 21113-2324, USA

Fritsch, Ted Jr (Athlete, Football Player)
5014 Odins Way
Marietta, GA 30068, USA

Fritsche, Dan (Athlete, Hockey Player)
116 Olentangy Pt
Columbus, OH 43202-1905, USA

Fritsche, Jim (Athlete, Basketball Player)
470 Emerson Avenue West
Saint Paul, MN 55118-2034, USA

Fritz, Harold A (General)
1017 W Scottwood Dr
Peoria, IL 61615-1056, USA

Fritz, Nikki (Actor)
PO Box 57764
Sherman Oaks, CA 91413, USA

Frizzell, David (Musician)
4694 E Robertson Road
Cross Plains, TN 37049, USA

Frizzell, John (Composer)
B M I
8730 Sunset Blvd
#300
Los Angeles, CA 90069, USA

Frizzelle, William J (Athlete, Football Player)
8001 Tylerton Dr
Raleigh, NC 27613, USA

Frobel, Doug (Athlete, Baseball Player)
169 Springwater Dr
Kanata, ON K2M 1Z8, Canada

Froboess, Cornelia (Musician)
Rinklhof
Kleinholzhausen
Raubling, GERMANY D-83064

Froemming, Bruce (Athlete, Baseball Player)
702 W Haddonstone Pl
Thiensville, WI 53092-5966, USA

Froese, Bob (Athlete, Hockey Player)
11701 Clarence Center Rd
Akron, NY 14001, USA

Frogren, Jonas (Athlete, Hockey Player)
Newport Sports Management
400-201 City Centre Dr
Attn Don Meehan
Mississauga, ON L5B 2T4, Canada

Frohnmayer, David B (Dave) (Educator)
University of Oregon
President's Office
Eugene, OR 97403, USA

Frohnmayer, John E (Government Official)
1335 SW Timian Street
Corvallis, OR 97333-3932, USA

Frohwirth, Todd (Athlete, Baseball Player)
S66W24360 Skvline Ave
Waukesha, WI 53189-9254, USA

Froines, John (Activist, Educator)
University of California
Public Health School
Los Angeles, CA 90024, USA

Frolov, Alexander (Athlete, Hockey Player)
1467 3rd St
Manhattan Beach, CA 90266, USA

Frolov, Diane (Actor)
c/o Richard Weitz *WME (LA)*
9601 Wilshire Blvd Fl 3
Beverly Hills, CA 90210, USA

Fromherz, Peter (Physicist)
Max Pianck Biochemistry Institute
Biophysics Dept
Martinsried, GERMANY

Fromm, Fritz (Misc)
An der Bismarckschule 64
Hannover 30173, GERMANY

Frommelt, Paul (Skier)
Liechtenstein Ski Federation
Vaduz, LIECHTENSTEIN

Fron, Kenneth (Designer)
Kenneth Fron Designs
333 W North Ave #133
Chicago, IL 60610, USA

Frongillo, John (Athlete, Football Player)
10230 Elmhurst Dr NW
Albuquerque, NM 87114, USA

Froning-O'Meara, Mary (Athlete, Baseball Player, Commentator)
417 Bay Hill Dr
Madison, WI 53717-2650, USA

Fronius, Hans (Artist)
Guggenbergasse 18
Perchtoldadorf bel Vienna 2380, AUSTRIA

Frontiere, Dominic
280 S. Beverly Dr. #411
Beverly Hills, CA 90212

Froom, Mitchell (Misc)
Gary Stamler Mgmt
3055 Overland Ave
#200
Los Angeles, CA 90034, USA

Frosch, Robert (Scientist)
56 McCallum D
Falmouth, MA 02540-2232, USA

Frost, Craig (Misc)
Lustig Talent
PO Box 770850
Orlando, FL 32877, USA

Frost, Dave (Athlete, Baseball Player)
2206 Ocana Ave
Long Beach, CA 90815-2125, USA

Frost, David (Athlete, Golfer)
4245 N Central Expy
Suite 350
Dallas, TX 75205-4570, USA

Frost, David P (Actor, Entertainer, Producer, Writer)
4245 North Central Expy
Suite 350
Dallas, TX 75205-4570, USA

Frost, Jo (Actor, Reality TV Star)
c/o J P Williams *Parallel Entertainment*
9420 Wilshire Blvd #250
Beverly Hills, CA 90212, USA

Frost, Ken (Athlete, Football Player)
22842 Stinnett Hollow Rd
Athens, AL 35614, USA

Frost, Lindsay (Actor)
c/o Staff Member *Allman/Rea Management*
9255 W Sunset Blvd Ste 600
Los Angeles, CA 90069, USA

Frost, Mark (Writer)
Mark Frost Productions
PO Box 1723
North Hollywood, CA 91614, USA

Frost, Nick (Actor)
c/o Tom Drumm *The Safran Company*
8748 Holloway Dr
Los Angeles, CA 90069, USA

Frost, Sadie (Actor)
Julian Belfarge
46 Albemarle St
London W1X 4PP, UNITED KINGDOM (UK)

Frost, Scott (Athlete, Football Player)
99 Thomas Lk
Ashland, NE 68003, USA

Frost, Sir David
BBC Centre Wood Lane
London, ENGLAND W12 7RJ

Froud, Brian (Artist)
c/o Robert Gould *IMAGINOSIS*
4195 Crisp Canyon
Sherman Oaks, CA 91403, USA

Froud, Wendy (Artist)
c/o Robert Gould *IMAGINOSIS*
4195 Crisp Canyon
Sherman Oaks, CA 91403, USA

Fruedek, Jacques (Physicist)
2 Rue Jean-Francois Gerbillon
Paris 70006, FRANCE

Fruh, Eugen (Artist)
Romergasse 9
Zurich 8001, SWITZERLAND

Fruhbeck de Burgos, Rafael (Conductor)
Avenida dek Mediterraneo 21
Madrid 28007, SPAIN

Fruhwirth, Amy (Athlete, Golfer)
26431 N 44th Way
Phoenix, AZ 85050-8579, USA

Frusciante, John (Musician)
Boeing
8942 Wilshire Blvd
Everett, WA 98208, USA

Fruton, Joseph S (Misc)
123 York St
New Haven, CT 06511, USA

Fry, Arthur L (Inventor)
2270 Valley View Ave E
Saint Paul, MN 55119-5856, USA

Fry, Bob (Athlete, Football Player)
1604 Bexley Dr
Wilmington, NC 28412-2049, USA

Fry, Hayden (Athlete, Football Player)
1069 Calais Cir
Mesquite, NV 89027-8803, USA

Fry, Jay (Athlete, Football Player)
P.O. Box 53
College Corner, OH 45003, USA

Fry, Jerry (Athlete, Baseball Player)
3300 Stanton St
Springfield, IL 62703^4830, USA

Fry, Jordan (Actor)
c/o Carlyne Grager *Dramatic Artists Agency*
103 W. Alameda Ave
Suite 139
Burbank, CA 91502, USA

Fry, Michael (Cartoonist)
United Feature Syndicate
200 Madison Ave
New York, NY 10016, USA

Fry, Robert (Athlete, Football Player)
1604 Bexley Dr
Wilmington, NC 28412, USA

Fry, Scott A (Admiral)
Director Joint Staff Operations
Pentagon
Washington, DC 20318, USA

Fry, Stephen J (Actor, Comedian, Writer)
c/o Christian Hodell *Hamilton Hodell Ltd*
66-68 Margaret St Fl 5
London W1W 8SR, UK

Fry, Thornton C (Mathematician)
500 Mohawk Dr
Boulder, CO 80303, USA

Fryar, Irving D (Athlete, Football Player, Sportscaster)
51 Applegate Rd
Jobstown, NJ 08041, USA

Fryberger, Dates (Athlete, Hockey Player, Olympic Athlete)
PO Box 564 114 Gin Ridge Rd
Sun Valley, ID 83353-0564, USA

Fryce, Trevor (Athlete, Football Player)
20293 E Lake Cir
Centennial, CO 80016, USA

Frydman, Romy (Stylist)
c/o Staff Member *Sarah Laird Inc*
12 Charles Ln
New York, NY 10014, USA

Frye, Jeff (Athlete, Baseball Player)
6833 Lahontan Dr
Fort Worth, TX 76132-5457, USA

Frye, Meno
2713 N. Keystone
Burbank, CA 91504

Frye, Shawn
2713 N. Keystone
Burban, CA 91504

Frye, Soleil Moon (Actor)
The Little Seed
219 N. Larchmont Blvd
Los Angeles, CA 90004, USA

Fryer, Bernie (Athlete, Basketball Player)
471 E Glacier View Dr
Sequim, WA 98382-3127, USA

Fry-Irvin, Shirley (Tennis Player)
1970 Asylum Ave
West Hartford, CT 06117, USA

Fryling, Victor J (Business Person)
CMS Energy Fairlane Plaza South
330 Town Center Dr
Dearborn, MI 48126, USA

Fryman, Travis (Athlete, Baseball Player)
2600 Highway 196
Molino, FL 32577-9502, USA

F. Sensenbrenner Jr., James
(Congressman, Politician)
2449 Rayburn HOB
Washington, DC 20515, USA

Ftorek, Robert B (Robbie) (Athlete, Hockey Player, Olympic Athlete)
79 Sunset Point Rd.
Wolfeborn, NH 03894-4907, USA

Fu, Mingxia (Swimmer)
General Physical Culture Bureau
9 Tiyuguan Road
Bejing, CHINA

Fucarino, Frank (Athlete, Basketball Player)
21 Heathcote Court
Shirley, NY 11967-4423, USA

Fuchs, Joseph L (Publisher)
Mademoiselle Magazine
350 Madison Ave
New York, NY 10017, USA

Fuchs, Leo
609 N. Kilkea Dr.
Los Angeles, CA 90048

Fuchs, Michael J (Television Host)
Home Box Office
1100 Ave of Americans
New York, NY 10036, USA

Fuchs, Victor R (Economist)
796 Cedro Way
Stanford, CA 94305, USA

Fuchsberger, Joachim (Actor)
Hubertusstr 62
Grunwald 82031, GERMANY

Fuell, Don (Athlete, Football Player)
Commodore Blvd Apt 2504
1750
Cocoa Beach, FL 32931-3270, USA

Fuente, David I (Business Person)
Office Depot Inc
2200 Old Germantown Road
Delray Beach, FL 33445, USA

Fuente, Luis (Dancer)
98 Rue Lepic
Paris 75018, FRANCE

Fuentealba, Victor W (Misc)
4501 Arabia Ave
Baltimore, MD 21214, USA

Fuentes, Alison (Stylist)
c/o Staff Member *Directions USA*
3717-C W Market St
Greensboro, NC 27403, USA

Fuentes, Brian (Athlete, Baseball Player)
1342 El Portal Dr
Merced, CA 95340-0774, USA

Fuentes, Daisy (Entertainer, Model)
c/o Ray McKigney *Shelter Entertainment*
9454 Wilshire Blvd.
Suite 715
Beverly Hills, CA 90212, USA

Fuentes, Julio M (Judge)
US Court of Appeals
US Courthouse
50 Walnut St
Newark, NJ 07102, USA

Fuentes, Mike (Athlete, Baseball Player)
9626 Sycamore Ct
Davie, FL 33328-6768, USA

Fuentes, Rigoberto (Tito) (Athlete, Baseball Player)
61 S Maddux Dr
Reno, NV 89512, USA

Fuentes, Tito (Athlete, Baseball Player)
61 S. Maddux Dr.
Reno, NV 89512-1832, USA

Fugard, Athol H (Writer)
PO Box 5090
Walmer
Port Elizabeth 6065, SOUTH AFRICA

Fugate, Katherine (Writer)
c/o Bayard Maybank *Hohman Maybank Lieb*
9229 Sunset Blvd
Suite 700
Los Angeles, CA 90069, USA

Fugees, The
83 Riverside Dr.
New York, NY 10024

Fugelsang, John (Actor, Comedian)
c/o Staff Member *WmE2 (WMA-LA)*
1 William Morris Pl
Beverly Hills, CA 90212, USA

Fugere, Joe (Baseball Player)
1150 Hillsboro Mile Apt 404
Hillsboro Beach, FL 33062-1737, USA

Fugere, Joe (Athlete, Baseball Player)
1150 Hillsboro Mile
Apt 404
Hillsboro Beach, FL 28139-6876, USA

Fugett, Jean (Athlete, Football Player)
4801 West Pkwy
Baltimore, MD 21229, USA

Fugger, Edward (Biologist)
305 Island View Dr
Penhook, VA 24137, USA

Fugit, Patrick (Actor)
c/o Brett Norensberg *Gersh (LA)*
9465 Wilshire Blvd
Suite 600
Beverly Hills, CA 90212, USA

Fuglesang, Christer (Astronaut)
108 Englewood St
Bellaire, TX 77401, USA

Fuglesang, Christer Dr (Astronaut)
PO Box 555
Bellaire, TX 77402-0555, USA

Fuhr, Grant (Athlete, Hockey Player)
c/o Staff Member *Phoenix Coyotes*
6751 N White Out Way
Suite 200
Glendale, AZ 85305, USA

Fuhrman, Isabelle (Actor)
c/o Susie Mains *Trilogy Talent*
13425 Ventura Blvd
2nd Floor
Sherman Oaks, CA 91423, USA

Fuhrman, Mark (Attorney)
P.O. Box 333
Sagle, ID 83860-0333, USA

Fujisaki, Judge Hiroshi
1705 Main St. #Q
Santa Monica, CA 90401

Fujita, Hiroyuki (Engineer)
1-9-14 Senkawa
Toshimaku, Tokyo 171, JAPAN

Fujita, Scott (Athlete, Football Player)
27350 Upper Forty Dr
Carmel Valley, CA 93924-9250, USA

Fujita, Yoshio (Astronomer)
6-21-7 Renkoji
Tamashi 206, JAPAN

Fujiwara, Midori (Stylist)
c/o Staff Member *Judy Inc*
1 Yorkville Ave
Toronto ON M4W 1L1, Canada

Fukuto, Maru (Director)
Jim Preminger Agency
450 N Roxbury Dr
#1050
Beverly Hills, CA 90210, USA

Fukuyarna, Francis (Activist)
George Mason University
Public Policy Dept
Fairfax, VA 22030, USA

Fulcher, Bill (Athlete, Football Player)
18 Eagle Pointe Dr
Augusta, GA 30909-6056, USA

Fulcher, David (Athlete, Football Player)
4140 Fieldsedge Dr
Mason, OH 45040-8538, USA

Fulcher, Modriel (Athlete, Football Player)
6010 S Westmoreland Rd
Apt 1012
Dallas, TX 75237, USA

Fulchino, Jeff (Athlete, Baseball Player)
11 Laurel Dr
Monroe, CT 06468-1649, USA

Fuld, Richard S Jr (Financier)
Lehman Bros
745 7th Ave
New York, NY 10019, USA

Fuld, Sam (Athlete, Baseball Player)
284 Marlberry Cir
Jupiter, FL 33458-2848, USA

Fulford, Carlton W Jr (General)
Deputy CinC
US European Command Stuttgart-Vaihingen Germany
APO, AE 09128, USA

Fulgham, John (Athlete, Baseball Player)
769 Cricklewood Ter
Lake Mary, FL 32746-5310, USA

Fulghum, Robert (Writer)
Random House
1015 Violeta Dr
Alhambra, CA 91801-5332, USA

Fulghum, Robert (Writer)
c/o Staff Member *HarperCollins Publishers*
10 East 53rd St
c/o Author mail, 7th Floor
New York, NY 10022, USA

Fulhage, Scott (Athlete, Football Player)
2340 N Rd
Beloit, KS 67420, USA

Fulks, Robbie (Musician, Songwriter, Writer)
Mongrel Music
743 Center Blvd
Fairfax, CA 94930, USA

Fuller, Amanda (Actor)
c/o Amy Abell *Glick Agency*
1505 10th St
Santa Monica, CA 90401, USA

Fuller, Bob B (Writer)
37 Langton Way
London 5E3, UNITED KINGDOM (UK)

Fuller, Bryan (Writer)
c/o Ari Greenburg *WME (LA)*
9601 Wilshire Blvd Fl 3
Beverly Hills, CA 90210, USA

Fuller, Carl (Athlete, Basketball Player)
8302 Kirkville Drive
Houston, TX 77089-2194, USA

Fuller, Corey (Athlete, Football Player)
4161 Ballard Rd
Tallahassee, FL 32305-6308, USA

Fuller, Curtis D (Athlete, Football Player)
Denon Records
1711 Players Mill Rd
Franklin, TN 37067-8582, USA

Fuller, Deiores (Actor, Songwriter, Writer)
3628 Ottawa Circle
Las Vegas, NV 89109, USA

Fuller, Drew (Actor)
c/o Stephanie Simon *Untitled Entertainment (LA)*
350 S. Beverly Dr #200
Beverly Hills, CA 90212, USA

Fuller, Eddie (Athlete, Football Player)
36422 the Bluffs Ave
Prairieville, LA 70769-3197, USA

Fuller, Jack W (Editor, Publisher)
Chicago Tribune
Editorial Dept
435 N Michigan
Chicago, IL 60611, USA

Fuller, Jeff (Race Car Driver)
Jeff Fuller Motorsports
P.O. Box 3336
Mooresville, NC 28117, USA

Fuller, Jim (Athlete, Baseball Player)
5107 Bur Oak Dr
Pasadena, TX 77505-3028, USA

Fuller, Joe (Athlete, Football Player)
8906 Farnsworth Ave N
Minneapolis, MN 55443, USA

Fuller, John (Athlete, Baseball Player)
31912 Paseo Terraza
San Juan Capistrano, CA 92675-3060, USA

Fuller, Johnny (Athlete, Football Player)
1925 Highland Dr
Salado, TX 76591-5792, USA

Fuller, Kathryn S (Misc)
World Wildlift Fund
1250 24th St NW
Washington, DC 20037, USA

Fuller, Kurt (Actor)
c/o Rick Ax *Gold Coast Management*
438 S Venice Blvd Apt 5
Venice, CA 90291, USA

Fuller, Lance
1900 Longwood Ave.
Los Angeles, CA 90016

Fuller, Linda (Activist)
Habitat for Humanity
121 Habitat St
Americus, GA 31709, USA

Fuller, Mark (Artist)
Wet Design
90 Universal City Plaza
Universal City, CA 91608, USA

Fuller, Marvin D (General)
6799 Patton Dr
Fort Hood, TX 76544, USA

Fuller, Mike (Athlete, Football Player)
4241 Abingdon Trl
Birmingham, AL 35243, USA

Fuller, Penny (Actor)
12428 Hesby St
North Hollywood, CA 91601, USA

Fuller, Randy (Athlete, Football Player)
2257 Patsy Ln
Columbus, GA 31903, USA

Fuller, Robert (Actor)
PO Box 272
Era, TX 76238-0272, USA

Fuller, Rod (Race Car Driver)
David Powers Motorsports
10205 Westheimer Rd.
#100
Houston, TX 77042-3164, USA

Fuller, Simon (Producer)
c/o Jeff Frasco *Creative Artists Agency (CAA-LA)*
2000 Ave Of The Stars
Los Angeles, CA 90067, USA

Fuller, Steve (Athlete, Football Player)
81 Oak Tree Ln
Bluffton, SC 29910, USA

Fuller, Tony (Athlete, Basketball Player)
4222 Lost Springs Dr
Agoura Hills, CA 91301-5326, USA

Fuller, Vem (Athlete, Baseball Player)
155 Ironwood Cir
Aurora, OH 44202, USA

Fuller, Vern (Athlete, Baseball Player)
155 Ironwood Cir
Aurora, OH 44202-9156, USA

Fuller, Vincent (Athlete, Football Player)
3186 Parthenon Ave
Apt J
Nashville, TN 37203, USA

Fuller, William H Jr (Athlete, Football Player)
1014 Fairway Dr
Chesapeake, VA 23320-8200, USA

Fullerton, C Gordon (Astronaut)
44046 28th St W
Bldg 4800D
Lancaster, CA 93536, USA

Fullerton, C Gordon Colonel (Astronaut)
44046 28th St W Bldg 4800D
Lancaster, CA 93536-6026, USA

Fullerton, Ed (Athlete, Football Player)
135 Point Vue Dr
Pittsburgh, PA 15237, USA

Fullerton, Fiona (Actor)
London Mgmt
2-4 Noel St
London W1V 3RB, UNITED KINGDOM (UK)

Fullerton, Larry (Inventor)
Time Domain
6700 Odyssey Dr NW
Huntsville, AL 35806, USA

Fullington, Darrell (Athlete, Football Player)
1023 W Patrick Cir
Daytona Beach, FL 32117, USA

Fullmer, Brad (Athlete, Baseball Player)
400 S Barrington Ave Aot 202
Los Angeles, CA 90049-6413, USA

Fullmer, Gene (Boxer)
9250 S 2200 West
West Jordan, UT 84088, USA

Fullone, Sam (Race Car Driver)
Fullone Motorsports
10743 Mileback Rd
North Collins, NY 14111, USA

Fullwood, Brent (Athlete, Football Player)
4002 Maybreeze Rd
Marietta, GA 30306, USA

Fullwood, Troy (Athlete, Baseball Player)
317 Manning Ln
Hampton, VA 33767-1805, USA

Fulmer, Phillip (Coach, Football Coach)
University of Tennessee
Athletic Dept
Knoxville, TN 37996, USA

Fulsher, Sharon (Stylist)
c/o Staff Member *Arlene Wilson Management*
807 N Jefferson St
#200
Milwaukee, WI 53202, USA

Fulton, Bill (Athlete, Baseball Player)
3001 Lexington Ct
Export, PA 15632-9061, USA

Fulton, Eileen (Actor, Musician)
"As the World Turns Show" CBS-TV
524 W 57nd St
New York, NY 10019, USA

Fulton, Fitz
1023 E Ave J-5
Lancaster, CA 93535, USA

Fulton, Fitzhugh (Aviator)
43129 41st St W
Lancaster, CA 93536-5003, USA

Fulton, Robert (Politician)
PO Box 2634
Waterloo, IA 50704-2634, USA

Fulton, Soren (Actor)
c/o Staff Member *Savage Agency*
6212 Banner Ave
Los Angeles, CA 90038, USA

Fultz, Aaron (Athlete, Baseball Player)
PO Box41
Munford, TN 38058-0041, USA

Fultz, Frank (Athlete, Baseball Player)
310 Willow Glade Pt
Aloharetta, GA 30022-1025, USA

Fultz, Jeff (Race Car Driver)
JCR3 Racing
PO Box 561001
Charlotte, NC 28256, USA

Fultz, Mike (Athlete, Football Player)
1900 W Foothills Rd
Lincoln, NE 68523, USA

Fu Manchu (Music Group, Musician)
c/o Staff Member *Agency for the Performing Arts (APA-LA)*
405 S Beverly Dr
Suite 500
Beverly Hills, CA 90212-4425, USA

Fumero, David (Actor)
c/o Jerome Martin *Jerome Martin Management*
1655 N Cherokee Ave
2nd Floor
Hollywood, CA 90028, USA

Fumusa, Dominic (Actor)
c/o Robert Stein *Robert Stein Management*
PO Box 3797
Beverly Hills, CA 90212, USA

Fun. (Music Group, Musician)
c/o Dalton Sim *Nettwerk - Boston*
33 Richdale Ave
Suite 121
Cambridge, MA 02140, USA

Fun Affairs
Flossergasse 7
Munich, GERMANY D-81369

Funaki, Kazuyoshi (Skier)
Japanese Olympic Committee
1-1-1 Jinan Shilbuya-Ku
Tokyo 150, JAPAN

Func, Eric (Composer)
PO Box 1073
Helena, MT 59624, USA

Funchess, Tom (Athlete, Football Player)
1015 Funchess St
Crystal Springs, MS 39059, USA

Fund, John (Writer)
c/o Staff Member *The American Spectator*
1611 N Kent St
Suite 9
Arlington, VA 22209, USA

Funderburk, Leonard J (War Hero)
2311 Lathan Road
Monroe, NC 28112, USA

Funderburk, Mark (Athlete, Baseball Player)
6924 Old Providence Rd
Charlotte, NC 28226-7740, USA

Funderburke, Lawrence (Athlete, Basketball Player)
1688 Meadoway Court
Blacklick, OH 43004-9759, USA

Funicello, Annette (Actor, Musician)
16102 Sandy Ln
Encino, CA 91316, USA

Funk, Caribbean (Music Group)
c/o Staff Member *Sony Music Miami*
605 Lincoln Rd Fl 7
Miami Beach, FL 33139, USA

Funk, Elaine (Stylist)
307 W Haven
Arlington Heights, IL 60005, USA

Funk, Frank (Athlete, Baseball Player)
4022 S Alamandas Way
Gold Canyon, AZ 85118-1899, USA

Funk, Fred (Athlete, Golfer)
24729 Harbour View Dr
Ponte Vedra Beach, FL 32082-1509, USA

Funk, Nolan Gerard (Actor)
c/o Kim Callahan *Industry Entertainment Partners*
955 S Carrillo Dr
Suite 300
Los Angeles, CA 90048, USA

Funk, Tom (Athlete, Baseball Player)
6952 N Olive St
Kansas City, MO 64118-2876, USA

Funk, Wally Col (Aviator)
PO Box 1219
Roanoke, TX 76262-1219, USA

Funke, Alex (Cinematographer)
1176 Fiske St
Pacific Palisades, CA 90272, USA

Funkmaster Flex (DJ, Musician)
c/o Ron Rivlin *Coast II Coast Entertainment*
8671 Wilshire Blvd Ste 500
Beverly Hills, CA 90211, USA

Funt, Peter
PO Box 827
Monterey, CA 93942

Fuqua, Antoine (Director)
3332 Clerendon Rd
Beverly Hills, CA 90210, USA

Fuqua, John (Athlete, Football Player)
13983 Glastonbury Ave
Detroit, MI 48223, USA

Fuqua, John Frenchy
13983 Glastonbury Ave
Detroit, MI 48223-2921, USA

Furay, Richie (Musician)
c/o Staff Member *Agency Group Ltd, The (NY)*
142 West 57th St
6th Floor
New York, NY 10019, USA

Furcal, Rafael (Athlete, Baseball Player)
397 Sweet Bav Ave
Plantation, FL 33324-8227, USA

Furey, John (Actor)
c/o Staff Member *Hartig Hilepo Agency Ltd*
54 W 21st St #610
New York, NY 10010, USA

Furgler, Kurt (President)
Dufourstr 34
Saint-Gail 9000, SWITZERLAND

Furian, Mira (Actor)
6410 Blarney Stone Court
Springfield, VA 22152, USA

Furianetto, Ferruccio (Opera Singer)
Metropolitan Opera Assn
Lincoln Center Plaza
New York, NY 10023, USA

Furie, Sidney (Director, Producer, Writer)
c/o Jack Gilardi *ICM Partners (ICM-LA)*
10250 Constellation Blvd Fl 7
Los Angeles, CA 90067, USA

Furjanic, Anthony (Athlete, Football Player)
15220 Cottonwood Ct
Orland Park, IL 60467, USA

Furjanic, Tony
15220 Cottonwood Ct
Orland Park, IL 60467-7346, USA

Furlan, Mira (Actor)
c/o Chris Roe *CR Management*
23852 Pacific Coast Hwy
Suite 627
Malibu, CA 90265, USA

Furlong, Edward (Actor)
c/o Mark Rousso *New Wave Entertainment (LA)*
2660 W Olive Blvd
Burbank, CA 91505, USA

Furlong, Shirley (Athlete, Golfer)
16412 S 18th Dr
Phoenix, AZ 85045-1628, USA

Furman, Andrew (Race Car Driver)
Latonio Racing
PO Box 75007
Cincinnati, OH 45275, USA

Furmaniak, J J (Athlete, Baseball Player)
12502 Larksour Ln
Plainfield, IL 60585-5545, USA

Furmann, Benno (Actor)
c/o Staff Member *Artists Independent Management (UK)*
32 Tavistock St
London WC2E 7PB, UNITED KINGDOM (UK)

Furness, Deborra-Lee (Actor, Director, Producer)
c/o Staff Member *Seed Productions*
10201 W Pico Blvd
Bldg 52, Rm 105
Los Angeles, CA 90035, USA

Furniss, Bruce (Athlete, Olympic Athlete, Swimmer)
18452 Old Lamplighter Cir
Villa Park, CA 92861-4528, USA

Furniss, Steve (Athlete, Olympic Athlete, Swimmer)
6478 Frampton Cir
Huntington Beach, CA 92648-6620, USA

Furno, Carlo Cardinal (Religious Leader)
Piazza Della Citta Leonina
Rome 92807, ITALY

Furr, Brad (Race Car Driver)
8242 Creekside Dr.
Dublin, CA 94568, USA

Furrer, Will (Athlete, Football Player)
420 Logan Ranch Rd
Georgetown, TX 78628, USA

Furrey, Mike (Athlete, Football Player)
8579 Newbury Ct N
Canton, MI 48187, USA

Furst, Anthony (Athlete, Football Player)
3001 Big Hill Rd
Dayton, OH 45419, USA

Furst, Janos K (Conductor)
I M G Artists
3 Burlington Lane
Chiswick
London W4 2TH, UNITED KINGDOM (UK)

Furst, Nathan (Musician)
c/o Mike Rosen *Working Artists Agency*
13525 Ventura Blvd
Sherman Oaks, CA

Furst, Stephen (Actor, Comedian)
Gold Marshak Liedtke
3500 W Olive Ave
#1400
Burbank, CA 91505, USA

Furstenfeld, Jeremy (Musician)
Ashley Talent
2002 Hogback Road
#20
Ann Arbor, MI 48105, USA

Furstenfeld, Justin (Musician)
827 W Hopkins St
San Marcos, TX 78666, USA

Furtado, Nelly (Musician, Songwriter, Writer)
c/o Chris Smith *Chris Smith Management Inc*
21 Camden St
5th Floor
Toronto, ON M5V 1V2, Canada

Furuhashi, Hironshin (Swimmer)
3-9-11 Nozawa
Setagayaku
Tokyo, JAPAN

Furukawa, Masaru (Swimmer)
5-5-12 Shinohara Honmachi
Nadaku
Kobe, JAPAN

Furukawa, Satoshi (Astronaut)
NASDA
Tsukuba Space Center
2-1-1 Sengen
Tukuhashi, Ibaraka 305, JAPAN

Furukawa, Satoshi Dr (Astronaut)
NASDA, Tsukuba Space Center 2-1-1 Sengen
Tukuba-shi Ibaraka 305, Japan

Furuseth, Ole Christian (Skier)
John Colletts Alle 74
Oslo 0854, NORWAY

Fury, Ed (Actor)
6729 Babcock Ave
N Hollywood, CA 91606-1310

Furyk, Jim (Athlete, Golfer)
240 Deer Haven Dr
Ponte Vedra Beach, FL 32082-2107, USA

Fusco, Cosimo (Actor)
Studio Segre
Piazzale Di Ponte Milvio 28
Rome 00191, Italy

Fusco, John (Writer)
c/o Michael Sugar *Anonymous Content (LA)*
3531 Hayden Ave
Culver City, CA 90232, USA

Fusco, Mark (Athlete, Hockey Player, Olympic Athlete)
155 Grove St
Westwood, MA 02090, USA

Fusco, Scott (Athlete, Hockey Player, Olympic Athlete)
41 Wedgemere Ave
Winchester, MA 01890-2439, USA

Fusina, Chuck A (Athlete, Football Player)
1548 King James St
Pittsburgh, PA 15237, USA

Fussell, Chris (Athlete, Baseball Player)
3238 N Eastmoreland Dr
Oregon, OH 43616-2933, USA

Futey, Bohdan A (Judge)
US Claims Court
717 Madison Place NW
Washington, DC 20439, USA

Futral, Elizabeth (Opera Singer)
Neil Funkhouser Mgmt
105 Arden St
#5G
New York, NY 10040, USA

Futrell, Mary H (Misc)
George Washington University Education School
Washington, DC 20052, USA

Futter, Ellen V (Educator)
American Natural History Museum
Park Ave West & 79th St
New York, NY 10034, USA

Futterman, Dan (Actor)
Gersh Agency
232 N Canon Dr
Beverly Hills, CA 90210, USA

Future (Musician)
c/o Michael Forman *Michael Forman Management*
409 N. Camden Drive
Suite 205
Beverly Hills, CA 90210, USA

Futureheads, The (Music Group)
c/o Staff Member *Paradigm (Monterey)*
404 W Franklin St
Monterey, CA 93940, USA

Fyfe, William S Dr (Scientist)
59 Harcove St
St Catharines, ON L2N 6L9, CANADA

Fyhrie, Mike (Athlete, Baseball Player)
4 Wellesley Ct
Trabuco Canyon, CA 92679-4725, USA

Fylstra, Daniel (Engineer)
Visicorp
2895 Zanken Road
San Jose, CA 95134, USA

G, Franky (Actor)
c/o Jimmy Darmody *Creative Artists Agency (CAA-LA)*
2000 Ave Of The Stars
Los Angeles, CA 90067, USA

G, Kenny (Musician)
c/o Irving Azoff *Azoff Music Management/Front Line*
1100 Glendon Ave
Los Angeles, CA 90024, USA

Gaarder, Jostein (Misc)
Gullkroken 22A
Oslo 0377, NORWAY

Gabaldon, Diana (Writer)
10810 N. Tatum Blvd.
#102-321
Phoenix, AZ 85028, USA

Gabalier, Andreas (Musician)
c/o Staff Member *Armin Rahn Agency and Management*
Dreimuehlenstr. 7
Muenchen 80469, Germany

Gabarra, Carin (Athlete, Olympic Athlete, Soccer Player)
305 Rosslare Dr
Arnold, MD 21012-3007, USA

Gabbana, Stefano (Designer, Fashion Designer)
Doice & Gabbana
Via Santa Cecilia 7
Milan, 20122 ITALY

Gabbard, Kason (Athlete, Baseball Player)
855 D011town Dr
Savannah, TN 38372-3713, USA

Gabbard, Steve (Athlete, Football Player)
7038 Bradfordville Rd
Tallahassee, FL 32309-1806, USA

Gabbert, Blaine (Football Player)
c/o Tom Condon *CAA - St. Louis*
222 S Central Ave
Suite 1008
St Louis, MO 63105, USA

Gabel, Seth (Actor)
c/o Peter Kiernan *Management 360*
9111 Wilshire Blvd
Beverly Hills, CA 90210, USA

Gaberino, Geoffrey (Athlete, Olympic
Athlete, Swimmer)
747 Bear Creek Cv
Gulf Shores, AL 36542-3040, USA

Gable, Brian (Cartoonist)
The Globe and Mail 444 Front St W
Toronto, ON M5V 2S9, CANADA

Gable, Brian (Cartoonist)
67 Riverside Dr
#1D
New York, NY 10024, USA

Gable, Daniel M (Danny) (Athlete,
Olympic Athlete, Wrestler)
4343 Treefarm Ln NE
Iowa City, IA 52240-7829, USA

Gable, John Clark
Jack Scagnetti Talent Agency
5118 Vineland Avenue Ste #102
North Hollywood, CA 91601

Gabler, Bill (Baseball Player)
Chicago Cubs
4443 Mattis Rd
Saint Louis, MO 63128 3136, USA

Gabler, Wally (Athlete, Football Player)
RR 1
Heathcote, ON N0H 1N0, Canada

Gabler, William (Gabe) (Athlete, Baseball
Player)
3227 Bayshore Pkwy
Arnold, MO 63010-4009, USA

Gabor, William (Athlete, Basketball
Player)
101 Ocean Bluffs Blvd
Apt 503
Jupiter, FL 33477-7362, USA

Gabor, Zsa Zsa (Actor)
1001 Bel Air Rd
Los Angeles, CA 90077, USA

Gaborik, Marian (Athlete, Hockey Player)
Icy Luck Inc
720 Manhattan Ave
Manhattan Beach, CA 90266-5653, USA

Gabriel, Ana (Musician)
AG Ediciones Musicales
Peten 117 Col Narvarte
Mexico City 03020, MEXICO

Gabriel, Charles A (General)
Flight International
International Airport
Newport News, VA 23602, USA

Gabriel, Eric (Stylist)
c/o Staff Member *Rex Agency, The*
6311 Romaine St
Los Angeles, CA 90038, USA

Gabriel, Feliciano (Stylist)
c/o Celebrity Stylist *Camilla Lowther
Managment (CLM Represents)*
30-32 Ericsson Pl
New York, NY 10013, USA

Gabriel, Gunter
Vorhelmer Str. 63
Ennigerloh-Enniger, GERMANY D-59320

Gabriel, Juan (Musician)
c/o Staff Member *Universal Music
Publishing Group (Latin)*
420 Lincoln Rd
Suite 200
Miami Beach, FL 33139, USA

Gabriel, Michael (Artist)
Dlouha 32
Prague 1 110 00, CZECH REPUBLIC

Gabriel, Peter (Musician, Songwriter)
c/o Staff Member *Real World Records*
Box Mill
Box Corsham
Wiltshire SN1 38PN, United Kingdom

Gabriel, Roman
16817 McKee Rd.
Charlotte, NC 28278

Gabriel, Seychelle (Actor)
c/o TJ Stein *Stein Entertainment Group*
1351 N Crescent Heights Blvd #312
West Hollywood, CA 90046, USA

Gabriel Jr, Roman I (Athlete, Football
Player)
P.O. Box 4173
Calabash, NC 28467, USA

Gabrielle, Josefina (Actor)
c/o Staff Member *Stone Manners Salners
Agency (LA)*
9911 W Pico Blvd Ste 1400
Los Angeles, CA 90035, USA

Gabrielle, Monique (Actor, Model)
2436 N. Federal Hwy. #332
Pompano, FL 33064-6854, USA

Gabriels, Ed (Stylist)
c/o Staff Member *Halley Resources*
37 W 20th St
#603
New York, NY 10011, USA

Gabrielson, Len (Athlete, Baseball Player)
24230 Hillview Rd
Los Altos, CA 94024-5221, USA

Gacki, Sebastian (Actor)
c/o Staff Member *Lizbell Agency*
216-309 W Cordova St
Vancouver, BC V6B 1E5, USA

Gad, Josh (Actor)
c/o Aleen Keshishian *Brillstein
Entertainment Partners*
9150 Wilshire Blvd #350
Beverly Hills, CA 90212, USA

Gaddis, John L (Historian)
Ohio University
Contemporary History Institute
Brown House
Athens, OH 45701, USA

Gaddis, Robert (Athlete, Football Player)
1022 Gaddis Rd
Edwards, MS 39066, USA

Gade, Ariel (Actor)
c/o Jennifer Millar *Paradigm (LA)*
9200 Sunset Blvd
11th Floor
Los Angeles, CA 90069, USA

Gadinsky, Brian (Producer)
c/o Staff Member *WmE2 (WMA-LA)*
1 William Morris Pl
Beverly Hills, CA 90212, USA

Gadot, Gal (Actor)
c/o Darren Goldberg *Global Creative*
1051 Cole Ave # B
Los Angeles, CA 90038, USA

Gadsby, William A (Bill) (Athlete, Hockey
Player)
28765 E Kalong Cir
Southfield, MI 48034-5650, USA

Gadsden, Oronde (Athlete, Football
Player)
11241 NW 15th St
Plantation, FL 33323, USA

Gadzhiev, Raul S O (Composer)
Azerbaijan State Popular Orchestra
Baku, AZERBAIJAN

Gadzuric, Dan (Athlete, Basketball Player)
1312 Villa Barolo Ave
Henderson, NV 89052-4175, USA

Gaechter, Mike (Athlete, Football Player)
13 Horizon Pt
Frisco, TX 75034, USA

Gaerte, Joe (Race Car Driver)
Gaerte Engines
615 Monroe
Rochester, IN 46975, USA

Gaeta, John (Designer, Special Effects
Designer)
c/o Staff Member *ICM Partners (ICM-LA)*
10250 Constellation Blvd Fl 7
Los Angeles, CA 90067, USA

Gaetti, Gary (Athlete, Baseball Player)
2704 Barbara Ln
Houston, TX 77005-3420, USA

Gaff, Brent (Athlete, Baseball Player)
5925 S State Road 9
Albion, IN 46701-9623, USA

Gaffigan, Jim (Actor, Comedian)
c/o Estelle Lasher *Principal Entertainment
(NY)*
1964 Westwood Blvd
Suite 400
Los Angeles, CA 90025, USA

Gaffney, Derrick T (Athlete, Football
Player)
11750 Cherry Bark Dr E
Jacksonville, FL 32218, USA

Gaffney, Drew Dr (Astronaut)
6613 Chatsworth Pl
Nashville, TN 37205-3955, USA

Gaffney, Jabar (Athlete, Football Player)
10142 Hatton Cir
Orlando, FL 32832-6174, USA

Gaffney, Janice (Athlete, Skier)
8118 Vantage Ave
North Hollywood, CA 91605-1437, USA

Gaffney, Mo (Actor)
c/o Staff Member *Stone Manners Salners
Agency (LA)*
9911 W Pico Blvd Ste 1400
Los Angeles, CA 90035, USA

Gaffney, Paul F (Admiral)
President National Defense University
Fort Lesley McNair
Washington, DC 20319, USA

Gaga, Lady (Dancer, Musician)
c/o Amanda Silverman *42West (NY)*
220 W 42nd St
12th Floor
New York, NY 10036, USA

Gage, Fred H (Misc)
Salk Biological Study Institute
10110 N Torrey Pines Road
La Jolla, CA 92037, USA

Gage, Jody (Athlete, Hockey Player)
91 W Forest Dr
Rochester, NY 14624-3755, USA

Gage, Nathaniel L (Educator)
85 Peter Courts Circle
Palo Alto, CA 94305, USA

Gage, Nicholas (Journalist)
37 Nelson St
North Grafton, MA 01536, USA

Gage, Paul (Inventor)
Craig Research
Highway 178 N
Chippewa Falls, WI 55402, USA

Gagliano, Phil (Athlete, Baseball Player)
1095 Crescent Dr
Hollister, MO 65672-4884, USA

Gagliano, Ralph (Athlete, Baseball Player)
1756 Overton Park Ave
Memphis, TN 38112-5344, USA

Gagliano, Robert F (Bob) (Athlete,
Football Player)
822 Fitzgerald Ave
Ventura, CA 93003-0228, USA

Gagliardi, John (Coach, Football Coach)
Saint John's University
16446 Jasmine Ct
Cold Spring, MN 56320-9655, USA

Gagne, Eric S (Athlete, Baseball Player)
c/o Scott Boras *Boras Corporation*
18 Corporate Plaza
Newport Beach, CA 92660, USA

Gagne, Greg (Athlete, Baseball Player)
746 Whetstone Hill Rd
Somerset, MA 02726-3702, USA

Gagne, Lynn (Stylist)
1252 Ash St
Winnetka, IL 60093, USA

Gagne, Paul (Athlete, Hockey Player)
Lot 13 Aurora
Iroquois Falls, ON P0K 6K1, Canada

Gagne, Simone (Athlete, Hockey Player)
116710th St
Manhattan Beach, CA 90266-6019, USA

Gagner, Dave (Athlete, Coach, Hockey
Player)
c/o Staff Member *London Knights*
99 Dundas St
London, ON N6A 6K1, Canada

Gagner, Larry (Athlete, Football Player)
205 W Curtis St
Tampa, FL 33603, USA

Gagner, Sam (Athlete, Hockey Player)
Pulver Sports
479 Bedford Park Ave
Attn Ian Pulver
Toronto, ON M5M 1K2, Canada

Gagnier, Holly (Actor)
Stone Manners
6500 Wilshire Blvd
#550
Los Angeles, CA 90048, USA

Gagnon, Andre Philippe
89 Rue Alexandra
Granby, CANADA PQ J2C 2P4

Gagnon, Dave
56670 Inland Ct
Macomb, MI 48042-1189, USA

Gago, Jenny (Actor)
c/o Bill Rogin *Bill Rogin Management*
427 N Canon Dr #215
Beverly Hills, CA 90210, USA

Gagosian, Larry (Business Person)
Gagosian Gallery
980 Madison Ave
#PH
New York, NY 10021, USA

Gaikowski, Steve (Athlete, Baseball Player)
416 Turner St NE
Olympia, WA 98506-4663, USA

Gail, David
c/o Staff Member *Henze Management*
1925 Century Park E #2320
Los Angeles, CA 90067, USA

Gail, Joseph G (Biologist)
107 Bellemore Road
Baltimore, MD 21210, USA

Gail, Max (Actor)
c/o Laura Pallas *Pallas Management*
5301 Bellaire Ave
Valley Vilage, CA 91607, US

Gaile, Jeri
880 Hilldale Ave. #3
Los Angeles, CA 90069

Gailer, Frank (General)
2 Waterford Gln
San Antonio, TX 78257-1249, USA

Gailes, Jason (Athlete, Olympic Athlete, Rower)
17 Mark Vincent Dr
Westford, MA 01886-4505, USA

Gailey, T Chandler (Chan) (Athlete, Coach, Football Coach, Football Player)
191 Sterling Hills Dr
Clarkesville, GA 30523-6817, USA

Gaillard, Bob (Coach)
50 Bonnie Brae Dr
Novato, CA 94949, USA

Gaillard, Eddie (Athlete, Baseball Player)
134 Sweet Bav Cir
Juoiter, FL 33458-2816, USA

Gaillard, Mary Katharine (Physicist)
University of California
Physics Dept
Berkeley, CA 94720, USA

Gaim, Andre (Nobel Prize Laureate)
University of Manchester Oxford Road
Attn: School of Physics
Manchester M13 9PL, United Kingdom

Gaiman, Neil (Writer)
Cat Mihos
4470 W Sunset Blvd #339
Los Angeles, CA 90027, USA

Gain, Robert (Bob) (Athlete, Football Player)
11 Nokomis Dr
Eastlake, OH 44095, USA

Gainer, Derrick (Athlete, Football Player)
733 E McDonald Rd
Plant City, FL 33567, USA

Gainer, Jay (Athlete, Baseball Player)
1035 East 8th St
Panama City, FL 32401-3594, USA

Gaines, Bill (Athlete, Basketball Player)
921 Berverly Cir
Cedar Hill, TX 75104-1236, USA

Gaines, Boyd (Actor, Musician)
c/o Elin McManus-Flack *Elin Flack Management*
435 West 57th Street #3M
New York, NY 10019, USA

Gaines, Clark (Athlete, Football Player)
21364 Scara Pl
Broadlands, VA 20148, USA

Gaines, Corey (Athlete, Basketball Player)
3968 Windansea Street
Las Vegas, NV 89147-6544, USA

Gaines, Davis
315 W. 57th St. #4H
New York, NY 10019

Gaines, Ernest J (Writer)
PO Box 81
Oscar, LA 70762-0081, USA

Gaines, Joe (Athlete, Baseball Player)
77 Anair Way
Oakland, CA 94605-4874, USA

Gaines, Lawrence (Athlete, Football Player)
4963 Cherry Blossom Cir
West Bloomfield, MI 48324, USA

Gaines, Reese (Baseball Player)
Houston Rockets
Toyota Center
2 E Greenway Plaza
Houston, TX 77046, USA

Gaines, Rowdy (Athlete, Olympic Athlete, Swimmer)
6800 Hawaii Kai Dr
Honolulu, HI 96825, USA

Gaines, Wentford (Athlete, Football Player)
20 Sheffield St
Jersey City, NJ 07305, USA

Gaines, William C (Journalist)
Chicago Tribune
1326 Marks Ave
Jackson, MS 39213-7113, USA

Gainey, Robert M (Bob) (Athlete, Coach, Hockey Player)
c/o Staff Member *Montreal Canadiens*
1275 Rue Saint-Antoine O
Montreal, QB H3C 5L2, Canada

Gainey, Steve (Athlete, Hockey Player)
900 McGill Road Box 3010
Attn: Hockey Coaching Staff
Kamloops, BC V2C SN3, USA

Gainey, Telmanch "Ty" (Athlete, Baseball Player)
123 Presidential Dr Aot D
19807-3213, DE Wilmine:ton, USA

Gainey, Ty (Athlete, Baseball Player)
3040 West Market Street Ext
Cheraw, SC 29520, USA

Gainsbourg, Charlotte (Actor)
c/o Frederique Moidon *ArtMedia*
20 avenue Rapp
Paris 75008, France

Gair, Joanne (Stylist)
c/o Staff Member *Mercury Artists*
8460 Higuera St Fl 2
Culver City, CA 90232, USA

Gaiser, George (Athlete, Football Player)
28752 Kalkallo Dr
Boerne, TX 78015, USA

Gaison, Blane (Athlete, Football Player)
45-444 Koa Kahiko St
Kaneohe, HI 96744, USA

Gaitan, Paulina (Actor)
c/o Dar Rollins *ICM Partners (ICM-LA)*
10250 Constellation Blvd Fl 7
Los Angeles, CA 90067, USA

Gaiter, Tony (Athlete, Football Player)
9235 NW 35th Ct
Miami, FL 33147, USA

Gaiters, Bob (Athlete, Football Player)
6909 Knowlton Pl
Apt 206
Los Angeles, CA 90045, USA

Gaither, Bill (Musician, Songwriter)
Gaither Music Co
PO Box 737
Alexandria, VA 22314, USA

Gajan, Hokie (Athlete, Football Player)
213 Cottonwood Ln
Mandeville, LA 70471, USA

Gajarsa, Arthur J (Judge)
Us Court of Appeals
717 Madison Place NW
Washington, DC 20439, USA

Gajdusek, D Carieton (Nobel Prize Laureate)
Human Virology Institute
725 W Lombard St
#N460
Baltimore, MD 21201, USA

Gajdusek, Karl (Writer)
c/o Jill McElroy *Management 360*
110 S Fairfax Ave
Suite 350
Los Angeles, CA 90036, USA

Gajkowski, Steve (Athlete, Baseball Player)
416 Turner St NE
Olympia, WA 98506, USA

Gakeler, Dan (Athlete, Baseball Player)
3714 Sawe:rass Rd
Greensboro, NC 27410-9068, USA

Gal, Sandra (Athlete, Golfer)
Callaway Golf Company
2180 Rutherford Rd
Carlsbad, CA 92008-7328, USA

Galabru, Michael
11 rue Boissiere
Paris, FRANCE F-75116

Galambos, Robert (Misc)
8826 La Jolla Scenic Dr
La Jolla, CA 92037, USA

Galanos, James (Designer, Fashion Designer)
1316 Sunset Plaza Dr
Los Angeles, CA 90069, USA

Galanos, Mike (Television Host)
Prime News Tonight
CNN
1 Time Warner Center
New York, NY 10019, USA

Galante, Matt (Baseball Player, Coach)
Houston Astros
85 Hei11hts Ter
Middletown, NJ 07748-3405, USA

Galarraga, Andres (Athlete, Baseball Player)
1639 Enclave Cir
West Palm Beach, FL 33411-1862, USA

Galarrage, Andres J P (Baseball Player)
Barrio Nuevo Chapellin
Clejon Soledad #5
Caracas, VENEZUELA

Galasso, Bob (Athlete, Baseball Player)
267 Adelaide Rd
Connellsville, PA 15425-6215, USA

Galati, Frank J (Director)
2990 Emathia Street
Miami, FL 33133-3223, USA

Galbraith, Clint (Horse Racer)
PO Box 902
Scottsville, NY 14546-0902, USA

Galbraith, Scott (Athlete, Football Player)
3700 Plymouth Dr
North Highlands, CA 95660, USA

Galbreath, Scott (Athlete, Football Player)
3649 Plymouth Dr
North Highlands, CA 95660, USA

Galbreath, Tony (Athlete, Football Player)
411 W 9th St
Fulton, MO 65251, USA

Galdikas, Birute M F (Misc)
Orangutan Foundation International
822 Wellesley Ave
Los Angeles, CA 90049, USA

Gale, Ed (Actor)
c/o Cindy Osbrink *Osbrink Talent Agency*
4343 Lankershim Blvd
Suite 100
Universal City, CA 91602, USA

Gale, Greg (Stylist)
c/o Staff Member *Bryan Bantry*
900 Broadway Ste 400
New York, NY 10003, USA

Gale, Joseph H (Judge)
US Tax Court
400 2nd St NW
Washington, DC 20217, USA

Gale, Megan (Actor)
c/o Ann Churchill-Brown *Shanahan Management*
Level 3 Berman House
Surry Hills 2010, AUSTRALIA

Gale, Mike (Athlete, Basketball Player)
18003 4th Avenue South
Burien, WA 98148-1803, USA

Gale, Rich (Athlete, Baseball Player)
869 Center Park St
Daniel Island, SC 29492-7569, USA

Gale, Robert P (Inventor)
980 Bluegrass Lane
Los Angeles, CA 90049, USA

Gale, Tommy (Race Car Driver)
P.O. Box 375
Elizabeth, PA 15037, USA

Galecki, Johnny (Actor)
c/o Ryan Revel *Benderspink*
5870 W Jefferson Blvd
Studio E
Los Angeles, CA 90016, USA

Galella, Ron (Photographer)
12 Nelson Ln
Montville, NJ 07045-9306, USA

Galeotti, Bethany Joy (Actor)
c/o Jill Fritzo *PMK/BNC Public Relations (PMK-NY)*
622 3rd Ave
8th Floor
New York, NY 10017, USA

Galer, Robert E (General)
3525 Turtle Creek Blvd
Apt 6D
Dallas, TX 75219-5515, USA

Galiena, Anna (Actor)
c/o Dominique Besnehard *ArtMedia*
20 avenue Rapp
Paris 75008, France

Galifianakis, Zach (Actor, Producer, Writer)
c/o Marc Gurvitz *Brillstein Entertainment Partners*
9150 Wilshire Blvd #350
Beverly Hills, CA 90212, USA

Galigher, Ed (Athlete, Football Player)
1025 Prospect St Ste 150
La Jolla, CA 92037-4163, USA

Galik, Denise (Actor)
Badgley Connor Talent
9229 Sunset Blvd
#311
Los Angeles, CA 90069, USA

Galina, Stacy (Actor)
c/o Mark Scroggs *David Shapira & Associates*
193 N Robertson Blvd
Beverly Hills, CA 90211, USA

Galindo, Rudy (Figure Skater)
c/o Staff Member *Champions on Ice*
Tom Collins Enterprises Inc
3500 W 80th St
Minneapolis, MN 55431, USA

Gall, Hugues (Opera Singer)
Grand Theatre de Geneva
11 Blvd du Theatre
Geneva 1211, SWITZERLAND

Gall, John (Athlete, Baseball Player)
20 Corte Del Sol
Millbrae, CA 94030-2111, USA

Gallacher, Kevin (Soccer Player)
Blackbum Rovers
Ewood Park
Blackbum
Lancashire BB2 4JF, UNITED KINGDOM (UK)

Gallagher (Misc)
14984 Roan Court
Wellington, FL 33414, USA

Gallagher, Al (Athlete, Baseball Player)
1810 N Parkwood Dr
Harlingen, KS 78550-8027, USA

Gallagher, Bob (Athlete, Baseball Player)
315 Fair Ave
Santa Cruz, CA 95060, USA

Gallagher, Brian (Misc)
United Way of America
701 N Fairfax Ave
Alexandria, VA 22314, USA

Gallagher, Bronagh (Actor)
Marmont Mgmt
Langham House
302/8 Regent St
London W1R 5AL, UNITED KINGDOM (UK)

Gallagher, Chad (Athlete, Basketball Player)
482 Wynstone Way
Rockton, IL 61072-3434, USA

Gallagher, Dave (Athlete, Baseball Player)
315 Fair Ave
Santa Cruz, CA 95060-6343, USA

Gallagher, Dave (Athlete, Football Player)
2740 California Ct
Columbus, IN 47201, USA

Gallagher, David (Actor)
c/o Abby Bluestone *Innovative Artists (LA)*
1505 10th St
Santa Monica, CA 90401, USA

Gallagher, Delia (Anchor)
c/o Staff Member *CNN (LA)*
6430 Sunset Blvd #300
Hollywood, CA 90028, USA

Gallagher, Doug (Athlete, Baseball Player)
11 Cherokee Dr
Hamilton, OH 45013-4909, USA

Gallagher, Frank (Athlete, Football Player)
6572 Enclave Dr
Clarkston, MI 48348, USA

Gallagher, Helen (Actor, Musician)
260 W End Ave
New York, NY 10023, USA

Gallagher, John (Religious Leader)
Advent Christian Church
PO Box 551
Presque Isle, ME 04769, USA

Gallagher, Liam (Musician)
Ignition Mgmt
54 Linhope St
London NW1 6HL, UNITED KINGDOM (UK)

Gallagher, Mary (Actor)
c/o Michael Greenwald *Buchwald/Fortitude (LA)*
6500 Wilshire Blvd
Suite 2200
Los Angeles, CA 90048, USA

Gallagher, Megan (Actor)
Don Buchwald
6500 Wilshire Blvd
#2200
Los Angeles, CA 90048, USA

Gallagher, Mike (Radio Personality)
Gallagher Networks
350 5th Ave #1818
New York, NY 10118, USA

Gallagher, Noel (Musician, Songwriter, Writer)
c/o Staff Member *Ignition Management*
54 Linhope St
London NW1 6HL, UNITED KINGDOM

Gallagher, Patrick (Actor)
c/o Harold Augenstein *Abrams Artists Agency (LA)*
9200 Sunset Blvd
11th Floor
Los Angeles, CA 90069, USA

Gallagher, Peter (Actor)
c/o John Carrabino *John Carrabino Management*
5900 Wilshire Blvd Fl 4 #406
Los Angeles, CA 90036, USA

Gallagher, Sean (Athlete, Baseball Player)
4434 NW 99th Ter
Sunrise, FL 33351-4747, USA

Gallagher Jr, Jim (Athlete, Golfer)
P.O. Box 507
Greenwood, MS 38935-0507, USA

Gallagher-Smith, Jackie (Athlete, Golfer)
193 Paradise Cir
Jupiter, FL 33458-2853, USA

Gallant, Gerard (Athlete, Coach, Hockey Player)
c/o Staff Member *New York Islanders*
1535 Old Country Rd
Plainview, NY 11803, USA

Gallant, Matt (Actor, Television Host)
608 Idaho Ave 8
Santa Monica, CA 90403, USA

Gallant, Mavis (Writer)
14 Rue Jean Ferrandi
Paris 75006, FRANCE

Gallardo, Camillio (Actor)
Innovative Artists
1505 10th St
Santa Monica, CA 90401, USA

Gallardo, Carlos (Actor)
c/o Michael Henderson *Heresun Management*
4119 West Burbank Blvd.
Burbank, CA 91505, USA

Gallardo, Silvana (Actor)
10637 Burbank Blvd
No. Hollywood, CA 91601

Gallardo, Yovani (Athlete, Baseball Player)
8556 Waterfront Ct
Fort Worth, TX 76179-2504, USA

Gallatin, Harry (Athlete, Basketball Player, Coach)
2010 Madison Ave
Edwardsville, IL 62025-2623, USA

Gallegly, Elton (Congressman, Politician)
2309 Rayburn HOB
Washington, DC 20515, USA

Gallego, Gina (Actor)
The Agency
1800 Ave of Stars
#400
Los Angeles, CA 90067, USA

Gallego, Mike (Athlete, Baseball Player)
11 Sunnin11dale
Trabuco Canyon, CA 92679-5103, USA

Gallegos, Gilbert G (Misc)
Fraternal Order of Police
1410 Donaldson Pike
Nashville, TN 37217, USA

Gallery, Robert (Athlete, Football Player)
3163 20th St
Masonville, IA 50654, USA

Galles, Jamie (Race Car Driver)
109-C Gasoline Alley
Indianapolis, IN 46222, USA

Galles, John (Misc)
National Small Business United
1156 15th St NW
#1100
Washington, DC 20005, USA

Galletti, Carl (Business Person)
P.O. Box 3934
Sedona, AZ 86340, USA

Galley, Garry (Athlete, Hockey Player)
c/o Staff Member *CBC TV*
P.O. Box 500
STN A, 5H100
Toronto, ON M5W 1E6, Canada

Galliano, John C (Designer, Fashion Designer)
House of Dior
60 Rue D'Avron
Paris 75020, FRANCE

Gallico, Gregory III (Doctor, Inventor)
Massachusetts General Hospital
275 Cambridge St
Boston, MA 02114, USA

Galligan, Zach (Actor, Comedian)
c/o Aine Leicht *Horror & Hilarity*
Prefers to be contacted via telephone
Los Angeles, CA 90067, USA

Gallimore, Jamie (Athlete, Hockey Player)
10931 62 Ave NW
Edmonton, AB T6H 1N3, Canada

Gallison, Joe (Actor)
PO Box 10187
Wilmington, NC 28404, USA

Gallner, Kyle (Actor)
c/o Sarah Shyn *3 Arts Entertainment Inc*
9460 Wilshire Blvd
7th Floor
Beverly Hills, CA 90210, USA

Gallo, Carla (Actor)
c/o Stacy Abrams *Abrams Entertainment*
5225 Wilshire Blvd #515
Suite 515
Los Angeles, CA 90036, USA

Gallo, Frank (Artist)
University of Illinios
Art Dept
Urbana, IL 61801, USA

Gallo, George (Director)
c/o Todd Hoffman *ICM Partners (ICM-LA)*
10250 Constellation Blvd Fl 7
Los Angeles, CA 90067, USA

Gallo, Mike (Athlete, Baseball Player)
1415 Christine St
Houston, TX 77017-4003, USA

Gallo, Robert C (Scientist)
University of Maryland
Study of Viruses Institute
Baltimore, MD 21228, USA

Gallo, Vincent (Actor, Director)
c/o Danny Goldberg *Gold Village Entertainment*
37 W 17th St
Suite 7W
New York, NY 10011, USA

Gallop, Tom (Actor)
c/o Dan Baron *Agency for the Performing Arts (APA-LA)*
405 S Beverly Dr
Suite 500
Beverly Hills, CA 90212-4425, USA

Galloway, David (Athlete, Football Player)
5441 NW 184th St
Miami Gardens, FL 33055-5344, USA

Galloway, Jean (Religious Leader)
Volunteers of America
1660 Duke St
Alexandria, VA 22314, USA

Galloway, Joey (Athlete, Football Player)
4340 Hanna Hills Dr
Dublin, OH 43016-9518, USA

Galotti, Ronald A (Publisher)
Conde Nast Publications
Publisher's Office
4 Times Square
New York, NY 10036, USA

Galston, Arthur W (Biologist)
200 Leeder Hill Drive
Apt 410
Hamden, CT 06517-2728, USA

Galvez, Balvino (Athlete, Baseball Player)
3986 SW 190th Ave
Miramar, FL 33029-2726, USA

Galvin, James (Writer)
University of Iowa
Writer's Workshop
Iowa City, IA 52242, USA

Galvin, John General (General)
2714 Jodeco Cir
Jonesboro, GA 30236-5329, USA

Galvin, John R (Athlete, Football Player)
136 Parkview Ave
Lowell, MA 01852-3811, USA

Galway, James (Musician)
Benzeholzstr 11
Meggen 6045, SWITZERLAND

Galyon, Gregory (Athlete, Football Player)
2352 Monticello Dr
Maryville, TN 37803, USA

Galyon, Scott (Athlete, Football Player)
4631 Horseshoe Trl
Morristown, TN 37814-8035, USA

Gam, Rita (Actor)
180 W 58th St
#8B
New York, NY 10019, USA

Gamar, Charles D
7660 N 159th St E
Benton, KS 67017, USA

Gambaccini, Sciascia (Stylist)
c/o Staff Member *Art + Commerce*
531 W 25th St # 4
New York, NY 10001, USA

Gambee, Dave (Athlete, Basketball Player)
6175 SW Arrow Wood Lane
Portland, OR 97223-7261, USA

Gamble, Chris (Athlete, Football Player)
13335 Pierre Reverdy Dr
Davidson, NC 28036, USA

Gamble, David (Athlete, Football Player)
16804 Royal Poinciana Dr
Weston, FL 33326-1582, USA

Gamble, Dick (Athlete, Hockey Player)
1 Vantage Dr
Pittsford, NY 14534-3205, USA

Gamble, Ed (Cartoonist)
Florida Times-Union
Editorial Dept
1 Riverside Ave
Jacksonville, FL 32202, USA

Gamble, Fred (Race Car Driver)
P.O. Box 5274
Snowmass Village, CO 81615, USA

Gamble, John (Athlete, Baseball Player)
369 Caliente St
Reno, NV 89509-2729, USA

Gamble, Kenny (Ken) (Athlete, Football
Player)
4 Algonquin Dr
Wilbraham, MA 01095, USA

Gamble, Kevin (Athlete, Basketball Player)
41 W Huckleberry Rd
Lynnfield, MA 01940-7261, USA

Gamble, Mason (Actor)
United Talent Agency
9560 Wilshire Blvd
#500
Beverly Hills, CA 90212, USA

Gamble, Oscar (Athlete, Baseball Player)
9705 Bent Brook Dr
Montgomery, AL 36117-7445, USA

Gamble, Trent
4481 NW 42nd Ter
Coconut Creek, FL 33073-4721, USA

Gamble, Troy (Athlete, Hockey Player)
12038 Terraza Cove Ln
Houston, TX 77041-6230, USA

Gamboa, Juan Pablo (Actor)
c/o Staff Member *Televisa*
Blvd Adolfo Lopez Mateos 232
Colonia San Angel INN
DF CP 01060, MEXICO

Gamboa, Tom (Athlete, Baseball Player)
318 Loch Lomond Rd
Rancho Mira11e, CA 92270-5606, USA

Gambol, Chris (Athlete, Football Player)
PO Box 2154
Glen Ellyn, IL 60138-2154, USA

Gambon, Michael (Actor)
c/o Paul Lyon-Maris *Independent Talent
Group (ITG-UK)*
Oxford House
76 Oxford St
London W1D 1BS, UK

Gambon, Michael J (Actor)
International Creative Mgmt
40 W 57th St
#1800
New York, NY 10019, USA

Gambon, Sir Michael (Actor)
c/o Staff Member *ICM Partners (ICM-LA)*
10250 Constellation Blvd Fl 7
Los Angeles, CA 90067, USA

Gambrell, Bill (Athlete, Football Player)
341 Osceola Ave
Bogart, GA 30622, USA

Gambrell, David (Politician)
3205 Arden Road NW
Atlanta, GA 30305-1918, USA

Gambril, Don (Coach)
4409 Soring Row
Northport, AL 35473-5231, USA

Gambucci, Andre (Athlete, Hockey
Player, Olympic Athlete)
4365 Carriage View Rd.
Colorado Springs, CO 80906, USA

Gambucci, Gary (Athlete, Hockey Player)
9241 Yukon Ave S
Minneapolis, MN 55438-1446, USA

Gambucci, Sergio (Athlete, Hockey
Player)
4365 Carriage House Vw
Colorado Springs, CO 80906-8702, USA

Gamester, Russ (Race Car Driver)
150 W. Warren St.
Peru, IN 46970, USA

Gamez, Robert (Athlete, Golfer)
1128 Wllde Dr
Kissimmee, FL 34747, USA

Gammino, Thomas (Race Car Driver)
875 Phenix Ave
Cranston, RI 02920, USA

Gammon, John (Actor)
c/o Jason Solomon *Full Circle
Management*
4932 Lankershim Blvd
Suite 202
North Hollywood, CA 91601, USA

Gammon, Kendall (Athlete, Football
Player)
14429 Maple St
Overland Park, KS 66223, USA

Gammons, Peter (Commentator)
Boston Globe
36 Glen Rd
Brookline, MA 02445-7721, USA

Gampel, Michele (Stylist)
24617 Stagg St
West Hills, CA 91304, USA

Ganassi, Floyd (Chip) (Race Car Driver)
7777 Woodland Dr.
Indianapolis, IN 46278, USA

Ganassi, Sonia (Opera Singer)
Columbia Artists Mgmt Inc
165 W 57th St
New York, NY 10019, USA

Ganatra, Nisha (Director)
c/o Sheryl Peterson *Agency for the
Performing Arts (APA-LA)*
405 S Beverly Dr
Suite 500
Beverly Hills, CA 90212-4425, USA

Ganchar, Perry (Athlete, Hockey Player)
8043 Summerhouse Dr W
ADublin, OH 43016-7062, USA

Gand, Gale (Chef, Television Host)
c/o Staff Member *Food Network, The*
1180 Ave of the Americas Fl 11
New York, NY 10036, USA

Gandarillas, Gus (Athlete, Baseball Player)
6320 NW 114th St
Hialeah, FL 33012-2334, USA

Gandee, Sherman (Sonny) (Athlete,
Football Player)
148 Viking Way
Naples, FL 34110, USA

Gandhi, Sonia (Government Official,
Politician)
All India Congress Party
24 Akbar Road
New Delhi, New Delhi 110011, INDIA

Gandhimathi (Actor, Bollywood)
59 Saidapet Road
Chennai, TN 600026, INDIA

Gandler, Markus (Skier)
Sinwell 22
Kitzbuhel 6370, AUSTRIA

Gandolfi, Michael (Model)
c/o Staff Member *Ford Models (NY)*
238 E 4th St
New York, NY 10009, USA

Gandolfini, James (Actor)
c/o Mark Armstrong *Sanders Armstrong
Caserta*
2120 Colorado Blvd
Suite 120
Santa Monica, CA 90404, USA

Gandolfo, Joseph (Horse Racer)
4 Cameron Rd
Saddle River, NJ 07458-2934, USA

Gandy, David (Model)
c/o Staff Member *Heffner Management*
80 Vine St.
Suite 203
Seattle, WA 98121, USA

Gandy, Dylan (Athlete, Football Player)
41302 Scarborough Ln
Novi, MI 48375-2893, USA

Gandy, Mike (Athlete, Football Player)
8508 E Sweetwater Ave
Scottsdale, AZ 85260-4110, USA

Gandy, Wayne L (Athlete, Football Player)
406 Pinecrest Rd NE
Atlanta, GA 30342-3827, USA

Ganellin, Charon Robin (Inventor)
University College 20 Gordon Street
Chemistry Dept
London WC1H OAJ, ENGLAND

Ganellin, C Robin (Inventor)
University College
Chemistry Dept
20 Gordon
London WC1H OAJ, UNITED KINGDOM
(UK)

Ganesan, Bhanurekha Gemini (Rekha)
(Actor, Bollywood)
c/o Simone Sheffield *Canyon
Entertainment*
P.O. Box 256
Palm Springs, CA 92263, USA

Ganesh, Gemini (Actor)
6 Nungambakkam High Road
Chennai, TN 600 034, INDIA

Ganev, Tzetzi
1751 N. Berendo St. #21
Los Angeles, CA 90027

Ganga (Actor)
6 South Mada Street
Mylapore
Chennai, TN 600 004, INDIA

Gangel, Jamie (Correspondent)
NBC-TV News Dept
30 Rockefeller Plaza
New York, NY 10112, USA

Gangloff, Mark (Athlete, Olympic Athlete,
Swimmer)
5318 Camden Dr
Stow, OH 44224-5526, USA

Gang of Four (Music Group)
c/o Staff Member *Paradigm (Monterey)*
404 W Franklin St
Monterey, CA 93940, USA

Gann, Mike (Athlete, Football Player)
1479 Ashford Pl NE
Atlanta, GA 30319, USA

Gannascoli, Joseph (Joe) (Actor)
c/o Greg Meyer *Meyer Management
Group (MMG)*
1400 Atlantic Ave
Suite 274
Long Beach, CA 90814, USA

Gannon, Coleen (Stylist)
c/o Staff Member *Team*
423 W Broadway
4th Floor
Boston, MA 02127, USA

Gannon, Richard J (Rich) (Athlete,
Football Player, Sportscaster)
6472 Smithtown Rd
Excelsior, MN 55331-8211, USA

Gansler, Bob (Coach, Soccer Player)
Kansas City Wizards
2 Arrowhead Dr
Kansas City, MO 64129, USA

Ganson, Arthur (Artist)
Massachusetts Institute of Technology
Compton Gallery
Cambridge, MA 02139, USA

Gant, Harry (Race Car Driver)
7531 Millersville Rd
Taylorsville, NC 28681, USA

Gant, Kenneth (Athlete, Football Player)
1820 West 10th St
Lakeland, FL 33805, USA

Gant, Kenneth (Kenny) (Athlete, Football Player)
3906 Carrollwood Place Cir
Apt 243
Tampa, FL 33624, USA

Gant, Mtume (Actor)
c/o Maggie Woods *Online Talent Group*
Prefers to be contacted via email or telephone
Los Angeles, CA 90069, USA

Gant, Reuben (Athlete, Football Player)
P.O. Box 3051
Tulsa, OK 74101, USA

Gant, Robert (Actor)
c/o British Reece *PMK/BNC Public Relations (PMK-LA)*
8687 Melrose Ave Fl 8
West Hollywood, CA 90069, USA

Gant, Ron (Athlete, Baseball Player)
40 Hartz Way Ste 10
secaucus, NJ 30189-6910, USA

Gantin, Bernardin Cardinal (Religious Leader)
Congregation for Bishops
Plazza Pio XII 10
Rome 00193, ITALY

Gantner, Jim (Athlete, Baseball Player)
P.O. Box 156
Eden, WI 53019-0156, USA

Gantos, Jack (Writer)
Farrar Straus Giroux
19 Union Square W
New York, NY 10003, USA

Gantt, Harvey
Rt. #1 Box 587
Taylorsville, NC 28681

Gantt, Jerome (Athlete, Football Player)
2035 Long Point Trl
Sanford, NC 27332-7449, USA

Gantt, Jerry (Athlete, Football Player)
1511 Atwick Dr
Fayetteville, NC 28304, USA

Ganz, Bruno (Actor)
Mgmt Ema Baumbauer
Keplerstrasse 2
München 81679, GERMANY

Ganzel, Teresa (Actor)
Irv Schechter
9300 Wilshire Blvd
#410
Beverly Hills, CA 90212, USA

Gao, Xiang (Musician)
Columbia Artists Mgmt Inc
165 W 57th St
New York, NY 10019, USA

Gao, Xingjian (Nobel Prize Laureate)
Chinese University of Hong Kong Press
Shatin
Hong Kong, CHINA

Gaona, Jessica (Actor)
c/o Staff Member *Abrams Artists Agency (LA)*
9200 Sunset Blvd
11th Floor
Los Angeles, CA 90069, USA

Gap Band, The
89 Fifth Ave. #700
New York, NY 10003

Garabaldi, Bob
2143 Oregon Ave.
Stockton, CA 95204

Garagiola, Joe (Commentator)
4555 E Mavo Blvd
Unit 3331
Phoenix, AZ 85050-6990, USA

Garagiola, Joe (Commentator)
7235 E Paradise Dr
Scottsdale, AZ 85260-5433, USA

Garagozzo, Keith (Athlete, Baseball Player)
16 Foxcroft Way
Mount Laurel, NJ 08054-5732, USA

Garai, Romola (Actor)
c/o Billy Lazarus *United Talent Agency (UTA)*
9336 Civic Center Dr
Beverly Hills, CA 90210, USA

Garalczyk, Mark (Athlete, Football Player)
8096 N 85th Way
Suite 101
Scottsdale, AZ 85258, USA

Garamendi, John (Congressman, Politician)
228 Cannon HOB
Washington, DC 20515, USA

Garan, Ronald J Jr (Astronaut)
2002 Sea Cove Court
Houston, TX 77058, USA

Garan, Ronald J Lt Colonel (Astronaut)
2002 Sea Cove Ct
Houston, TX 77058-4228, USA

Garant, Robert Ben (Actor, Director, Producer, Writer)
c/o Joseph Cohen *Creative Artists Agency (CAA-LA)*
2000 Ave Of The Stars
Los Angeles, CA 90067, USA

Garas, Kaz (Actor)
10145 N Buchanan Ave
Portland, OR 97203, USA

Garavani, Valentino (Designer, Fashion Designer)
Palazzo Mignanelli
Piazza Mignanelli 22
Rome 00187, Italy

Garavito, R Michael (Misc)
Michigan State University
Biochemistry Dept
East Lansing, MI 48824, USA

Garbacz, Lori (Athlete, Golfer)
777 Albany Post Rd
Briarcliff Manor, NY 10510, USA

Garbage (Music Group)
c/o Jenna Adler *Creative Artists Agency (CAA-LA)*
2000 Ave Of The Stars
Los Angeles, CA 90067, USA

Garbarek, Jan (Musician)
Niels Juels Gate 42
Oslo 0257, NORWAY

Garber, Gene (Athlete, Baseball Player)
771 Stonemill Dr
Elizabethtown, PA 17022-9717, USA

Garber, Terri (Actor)
c/o Maggie Smith *Maggie Smith Management*
3365 Paseo Del Sol
Calabasas, CA 91302, USA

Garber, Victor (Actor)
c/o Bill Butler *Industry Entertainment Partners*
955 S Carrillo Dr
Suite 300
Los Angeles, CA 90048, USA

Garbey, Barbaro (Athlete, Baseball Player)
14094 Woodside St
Livonia, MI 48154-5206, USA

Garces, Paula (Actor)
c/o Staff Member *Untitled Entertainment (NY)*
322 8th Ave #601
New York, NY 10001-6715, USA

Garces, Rich (Athlete, Baseball Player)
605 Swigert St
Kerrville, TX 78028-3140, USA

Garcetti, Gil
139 N Cliffwood
Los Angeles, CA 90049, USA

Garci, Jose Luis (Director)
Direccion General del Libro
Paseo de la Castellana 109
Madrid 16, SPAIN

Garcia, Adam (Actor)
c/o Peter Safran *The Safran Company*
8748 Holloway Dr
Los Angeles, CA 90069, USA

Garcia, Aimee (Actor)
c/o William Mercer *Thruline Entertainment*
9250 Wilshire Blvd
Ground Fl
Beverly Hills, CA 90212, USA

Garcia, Andrew (Musician)
c/o Simon Fuller *XIX Entertainment*
35-37 Parkgate Rd
32/33 Ransomes Dock
London SW11 4NP, UNITED KINGDOM (UK)

Garcia, Andy (Actor, Musician)
c/o JoAnne Colonna *Brillstein Entertainment Partners*
9150 Wilshire Blvd #350
Beverly Hills, CA 90212, USA

Garcia, Carlos (Athlete, Baseball Player)
5208 William St
Lancaster, NY 14086-9448, USA

Garcia, Danay (Actor)
CW Talent Management
c/o L Travis Clark
PO Box 532
Hollywood, CA 90078, USA

Garcia, Danna (Actor)
c/o Staff Member *Telemundo*
2470 West 8th Avenue
Hialeah, FL 33010, USA

Garcia, Danny (Athlete, Baseball Player)
22 Silo Ln
Levittown, NY 11756-3807, USA

Garcia, Dave (Athlete, Baseball Player, Coach)
17842 Avenida Cordillera
Unit 28
San Diego, CA 92128-1514, USA

Garcia, Eddie (Athlete, Football Player)
4912 Oreilly Rd
Omro, WI 54963-9643, USA

Garcia, Freddy A (Baseball Player)
Quisquella Qta
Etapa M22 #52
La Romana, DOMINICAN REPUBLIC

Garcia, Gonzalo (Stylist)
c/o Staff Member *Mark Edward Inc*
325 W 8th St
#1011
New York, NY 10018, USA

Garcia, Gretchen (Stylist)
c/o Staff Member *Ford Models (Chicago)*
311 W Superior St
Chicago, IL 60654, USA

Garcia, Guillermo (Athlete, Baseball Player)
3806 Shoma Dr
West Palm Beach, FL 33414-4374, USA

Garcia, James (Athlete, Football Player)
999 E Basse Rd
Suite 180
San Antonio, TX 78209, USA

Garcia, Jeff (Athlete, Football Player)
PO Box 8977
Rancho Santa Fe, CA 92067-8977, USA

Garcia, Jesus (Actor)
c/o Staff Member *Columbia Artists Mgmt Inc*
1790 Broadway Fl 6
New York, NY 10019-1412, USA

Garcia, Jim (Athlete, Football Player)
999 E Basse Rd Ste 180
San Antonio, TX 78209-1807, USA

Garcia, Joanna (Actor)
c/o Pamela Kohl *3 Arts Entertainment Inc*
9460 Wilshire Blvd
7th Floor
Beverly Hills, CA 90210, USA

Garcia, Jorge (Actor)
c/o Erik Kritzer *Kritzer Levine Wilkins Entertainment (KLWG)*
11872 La Grange Ave
1st Floor
Los Angeles, CA 90025, USA

Garcia, Jsu (Actor)
c/o Phyllis Carlyle *Carlyle Productions & Management*
2050 Laurel Canyon Blvd
Los Angeles, CA 90046, USA

Garcia, Juan Carlos (Actor)
c/o Gabriel Blanco *Gabriel Blanco Iglesias (Mexico)*
Rio Balsas 35-32
Colonia Cuauhtemoc
DF 06500, Mexico

Garcia, Karim (Athlete, Baseball Player)
38 Agnew Farm Rd
Armonk, NY 10504, USA

Garcia, Kiko (Athlete, Baseball Player)
526 Trailview Cir
Martinez, CA 94553-3563, USA

Garcia, Leo (Athlete, Baseball Player)
11264 W Buchanan St
Avondale, AZ 85323-6824, USA

Garcia, Leonardo (Actor)
c/o Staff Member *TV Azteca*
Periferico Sur 4121
Colonia Fuentes del Pedregal
DF CP 14141, Mexico

Garcia, Lilian
1100 Valley Brook Ave
Lyndhurst, NJ 07071, USA

Garcia, Mike (Athlete, Baseball Player)
25931 Calle Agua
Moreno Valley, CA 92551-1620, USA

Garcia, Nina (Designer, Editor, Reality TV Star)
Elle Magazine
1633 Broadway 44th Fl
New York, NY 10019, USA

Garcia, Odalys (Actor)
c/o Staff Member *Univision*
605 3rd St. Fl12
New York, NY 10158, USA

Garcia, Pedro (Athlete, Baseball Player)
L4 Parq Del Condado
Caguas, PR 00727-1224, USA

Garcia, Ralph (Athlete, Baseball Player)
7441 Brian Ln
La Palma, CA 90623-1312, USA

Garcia, Rich (Baseball Player)
PO Box 3276
Clearwater Beach, FL 33767-8276, USA

Garcia, Rich (Athlete, Baseball Player)
P.O. Box 3276
Clearwater Beach, FL 33767, USA

Garcia, Rodrigo (Director)
c/o Adriana Alberghetti *WME (LA)*
9601 Wilshire Blvd Fl 3
Beverly Hills, CA 90210, USA

Garcia, Russell (Composer)
18558 Citronia
#15
Northridge, CA 91324, USA

Garcia, Teddy (Athlete, Football Player)
2203 Cook Rd
Oak Grove, LA 71263-3705, USA

Garcia Marquez, Gabriel (Nobel Prize Laureate, Writer)
Fuego 144
Pedregal de San Angel
Mexico City, DF, MEXICO

Garciaparra, Nomar (Athlete, Baseball Player, Olympic Athlete)
613 15th St
Manhattan Beach, CA 90266-4804, USA

Gardeazabal, Marcela (Actor)

Gardell, Billy (Actor)
c/o Nick Nuciforo *Creative Artists Agency (CAA-LA)*
2000 Ave Of The Stars
Los Angeles, CA 90067, USA

Gardener, Daryl (Athlete, Football Player)
8925 Legacy Ct Apt 106
Kissimmee, FL 34747-3018, USA

Gardenhire, Ron (Athlete, Baseball Player, Coach)
585 Country Road B2 E
Saint Paul, MN 55117-1610, USA

Gardin, Ron (Athlete, Football Player)
P.O. Box 66051
Tucson, AZ 85728, USA

gardiner, Bruce (Athlete, Hockey Player)
Barrie Police Headquarters 29 Sperling Dr
Barrie, ON L4M 6K9, Canada

Gardiner, John Eliot (Conductor)
Gore Farm
Ashmore
Salisbury, Wilts SP5 5AR, UNITED KINGDOM (UK)

Gardiner, Mike (Athlete, Baseball Player)
26 Read Dr
Hanover, MA 02339-2632, USA

Gardiner, Robert K A (Misc)
PO Box 9274
The Airport
Accra, GHANA

Gardner, Art (Athlete, Baseball Player)
1953 Hi^hway 35 S
Walnut Grove, MS 39189-5025, USA

Gardner, Ashley (Actor)
c/o Staff Member *Forster Entertainment*
12533 Woodgreen St
Los Angeles, CA 90066, USA

Gardner, Barry (Athlete, Football Player)
15415 Ashland Ave
Harvey, IL 60426, USA

Gardner, Bill (Athlete, Hockey Player)
c/o Staff Member *Chicago Wolves*
2301 Ravine Way
Chicago, IL 60025, USA

Gardner, Billy (Athlete, Baseball Player, Coach)
35 Dayton Rd
Waterford, CT 06385-4205, USA

Gardner, Booth (Politician)
8012nd Ave
Seattle, WA 98104-1576, USA

Gardner, Brett (Athlete, Baseball Player)
331 Foxglove Ave
Summerville, SC 29483-5567, USA

Gardner, Carwell (Athlete, Football Player)
9603 Galene Dr
Louisville, KY 40299, USA

Gardner, Chris (Athlete, Baseball Player)
2304 SW Abalon Cir
Port Saint Lucie, FL 34953-5718, USA

Gardner, Christopher (Business Person, Writer)
Rubenstein Communications
c/o Rachel Nagler
1345 Avenue of the Americas 30th Fl
New York, NY 10105, USA

Gardner, Cory (Congressman, Politician)
213 Cannon HOB
Washington, DC 20515, USA

Gardner, Dale (Astronaut)
c/o Staff Member *NASA*
Johnson Space Center
2101 NASA Rd
Houston, TX 77058, USA

Gardner, Dale A Captain (Astronaut)
433 Choke Cherry Ct
Golden, CO 80403-1941, USA

Gardner, Dave (Athlete, Hockey Player)
Brick Brewing
181 King St S
Waterloo, ON N2J 1P7, Canada

Gardner, David P (Educator)
Hewlett Foundation
2121 Sand Hill Road
Menlo Park, CA 94025, USA

Gardner, George (Athlete, Hockey Player)

Gardner, Guy S (Astronaut)
P.O. Box 2730
Gainesville, GA 30503-2730, USA

Gardner, Guy S Colonel (Astronaut)
PO Box 4109
Media, PA 19063-7109, USA

Gardner, Howard E (Physicist)
Harvard University
Graduate Education School
Cambridge, MA 02138, USA

Gardner, James H (Basketball Player, Coach)
5465 Bromely Dr
Oak Park, CA 91377, USA

Gardner, Jeff (Athlete, Baseball Player)
1850 Boa Vista Cir
Costa Mesa, CA 92626-4701, USA

Gardner, John (Dancer)
American Ballet Theatre
890 Broadway
New York, NY 10003, USA

Gardner, Ken (Athlete, Basketball Player)
3795 Hawkeye Street
Salt Lake City, UT 84120-3390, USA

Gardner, Lee (Athlete, Baseball Player)
1354 Blue Heron Dr
Highland, MI 48357-3910, USA

Gardner, Lori (Stylist)
c/o Staff Member *Judy Inc*
1 Yorkville Ave
Toronto ON M4W 1L1, Canada

Gardner, Mark (Athlete, Baseball Player)
15216 Mesa View Ave
Friant, CA 93626-9780, USA

Gardner, Martin (Writer)
c/o *St. Martin's Press*
ATTN: PUBLICITY DEPT
175 Fifth Ave
New York, NY 10010, USA

Gardner, Moe (Athlete, Football Player)
11017 Lorin Way
Duluth, GA 30097-8482, USA

Gardner, Nancy P (Stylist)
2215 W Melrose St
#2
Chicago, IL 60618, USA

Gardner, Paul (Athlete, Hockey Player)
3687 May Pointe Cv
Southaven, MS 38672-6513, USA

Gardner, Philip (General)
Wakehurst 19 Princes Crescent Hove
Sussex BN3 4GS, ENGLAND

Gardner, Racine (Race Car Driver)
P.O. Box 934
Buellton, CA 93427, USA

Gardner, Randy (Athlete, Figure Skater, Olympic Athlete)
4640 Glencove Ave #6
Marina del Rey, CA 90292, USA

Gardner, Rob (Athlete, Baseball Player)
2001 Gas^rilla Rd Lot D21
Placida, FL 33946-2635, USA

Gardner, Rod (Athlete, Football Player)
1883 Executive Dr
Duluth, GA 30096-8922, USA

Gardner, Rulon (Athlete, Olympic Athlete, Wrestler)
121 Eugene St North
Salt Lake, UT 84054-1764

Gardner, Rulon (Actor)
6791 Brook Forest Drive
Evergreen, CO 80439-6827, USA

Gardner, Slick (Race Car Driver)
P.O. Box 277
Buellton, CA 93427, USA

Gardner, Wee Willie (Athlete, Basketball Player)
Harlem Globetrotters
400 E. Van Buren
Suite 300
Phoenix, AZ 85004, USA

Gardner, Wes (Athlete, Baseball Player)
305 Ruth
Benton, AR 72019-2226, USA

Gardner, Wilford R (Physicist)
University of California
Natural Resources College
Berkeley, CA 94720, USA

Gardocki, Christopher A (Chris) (Athlete, Football Player)
63 Yokshire Dr
Hilton Head Island, SC 29928, USA

Gardos, Eva (Director)
c/o Staff Member *ICM Partners (ICM-LA)*
10250 Constellation Blvd Fl 7
Los Angeles, CA 90067, USA

Gare, Danny (Athlete, Hockey Player)
Buffalo Sabres 1 Seymour H Knox III Plz
Ste 1
Attn: Broadcast Dept
Buffalo, NY 14203-3096, USA

Gare, Danny (Athlete, Hockey Player)
6 Regent St
Nelson, BC V1L 2Pl, Canada

Garelick, Jeremy (Producer)
c/o Staff Member *Principato/Young Management*
9465 Wilshire Blvd
Suite 430
Beverly Hills, CA 90212, USA

Garewal, Simi (Actor, Bollywood)
Paviova 6th Floor Little Gibb's Road
Malabar Hill
Bombay, MS 400 006, INDIA

Garfat, Jance (Musician)
Artists Int'l Mgmt
9850 Sandalwood Blvd
#458
Boca Raton, FL 33428, USA

Garfield, Allen (Actor)
c/o Brian McCabe *Venture IAB*
3211 Cahuenga Blvd W Ste 104
Los Angeles, CA 90068, USA

Garfield, Andrew (Actor)
1853 Noel Pl
Beverly Hills, CA 90210, USA

Garfinkel, Jack (Athlete, Basketball Player)
300 Ocean Pkwy
Apt 2E
Brooklyn, NY 11218-4078, USA

Garfinkle, David (Producer)
c/o Staff Member *Renegade 83 Entertainment*
5700 Wilshire Blvd
6th Floor
Los Angeles, CA 90036, USA

Garfunkel, Art (Actor, Musician)
120 E 87th St #P14E
New York, NY 10128, USA

Garibaldi, Bob (Athlete, Baseball Player)
2143 Oregon Ave
Stockton, CA 95204-4617, USA

Garity, Troy (Actor)
c/o Jason Weinberg *Untitled Entertainment (LA)*
350 S. Beverly Dr #200
Beverly Hills, CA 90212, USA

Garko, Ryan (Athlete, Baseball Player)
9267 E Trailside Vw
Scottsdale, AZ 85255-6214, USA

Garland, Beverly (Actor)
8014 Briar Summit Dr
Los Angeles, CA 90046, USA

Garland, Carrington
8014 Briar Summit Dr
Los Angeles, CA 90046

Garland, George D (Physicist)
5 Mawhiney Court
Huntsville, ON P0A 1K0, CANADA

Garland, Jon (Athlete, Baseball Player)
16833 Armstead St
Granada Hills, CA 91344-2704, USA

Garland, Merrick B (Judge)
US Court of Appeals
333 Constitution Ave NW
Washington, DC 20001, USA

Garland, Travis (Musician)
c/o Simon Fuller *XIX Entertainment*
35-37 Parkgate Rd
32/33 Ransomes Dock
London SW11 4NP, UNITED KINGDOM (UK)

Garland, Wayne (Athlete, Baseball Player)
7556 Mossback St
Las Vegas, NV 89123-1581, USA

Garland, Winston (Athlete, Basketball Player)
2304 Cleveland Street
Gary, IN 46404-3423, USA

Garlick, Scott (Soccer Player)
Colorado Rapids
555 17th St
#3350
Denver, CO 80202, USA

Garlin, Jeff (Actor, Producer)
c/o Staff Member *3 Arts Entertainment Inc*
9460 Wilshire Blvd
7th Floor
Beverly Hills, CA 90210, USA

Garlits, Donald G (Big Daddy) (Race Car Driver)
Garlits Racing Museum
13700 SW 16th Ave
Ocala, FL 34473, USA

Garlitz, Don (Big Daddy) (Race Car Driver)
13700 SW 16th Ave.
Ocala, FL 34473, USA

Garlock, Bradley (Stylist)
c/o Staff Member *Judy Casey Inc*
114 E 13th St
New York, NY 10003, USA

Garmaker, Dick (Athlete, Basketball Player)
5824 East 111th Street
Tulsa, OK 74137-7703, USA

Garman, Mike (Athlete, Baseball Player)
15144 Kings Row Rd
Caldwell, ID 83607-8371, USA

Garman-Hosted, Ann (Athlete, Baseball Player, Commentator)
6582 N 100 E
Wawaka, IN 46794-9724, USA

Garmon, Kelvin (Athlete, Football Player)
1424 Creekview Dr
Lewisville, TX 75067, USA

Garn, Jake Brig Gen (Astronaut)
1267 Chandler Cir
Salt Lake City, UT 84103-4237, USA

Garn, Stanley M (Misc)
1200 Earhart Road
#223
Ann Arbor, MI 48105, USA

Garneau, Jean-Claude (Athlete, Hockey Player)
497 Av Glazier
Quebec, QC G1M 3R6, Canada

Garneau, Marc (Astronaut)
Space Agency
6767 Route de Aeroport
Sainte-Hubert, QC J3Y 8Y9, CANADA

Garneau, Marc Capt (Astronaut)
5282 Rue Drolet
Montreal, QC H2T 2H4, CANADA

Garner, Charlie (Athlete, Football Player)
12944 Royal George Ave
Odessa, FL 33556, USA

Garner, Hal (Athlete, Football Player)
698 S 180 E
Smithfield, UT 84335-1669, USA

Garner, James (Actor)
2515 Fountain Hill Loop
Lincoln, CA 95648, USA

Garner, Jennifer (Actor)
1700 San Remo Dr
Pacific Palisades, CA 90272, USA

Garner, Kelli (Actor)
c/o John Carrabino *John Carrabino Management*
5900 Wilshire Blvd Fl 4 #406
Los Angeles, CA 90036, USA

Garner, Phil (Athlete, Baseball Player, Coach)
2 Sapling Pl
Spring, TX 77382-2636, USA

Garner, Tyrone (Athlete, Hockey Player)
Halton Regional Police Department 3800 Southampton Blvd
Burlington, ON L7M 3Y2, Canada

Garner, Wendell R (Physicist)
PO Box 650
Branford, CT 06405, USA

Garner, William S (Cartoonist)
Memphis Commercial Appeal
Editorial Dept
495 Union Ave
Memphis, TN 38103, USA

Garnes, Sam (Athlete, Football Player)
101 Hearthstone Dr
West Milford, NJ 07480, USA

Garnett, Dave (Athlete, Football Player)
4527 Tyrone Ave
Sherman Oaks, CA 91423, USA

Garnett, Kevin (Athlete, Basketball Player)
450 Orono Orchards Rd S
Wayzata, MN 55391

Garnett, Scott (Athlete, Football Player)
1637 28th St SE
Puyallup, WA 98372, USA

Garnett, Winfield (Athlete, Football Player)
2029 S 16th Ave
Broadview, IL 60155, USA

Garnica, Ron (Stylist)
c/o Staff Member *Zenobia Agency Inc*
PO Box 909
Groveland, CA 95321, USA

Garofalo, Janeane (Actor)
c/o Kara Welker *Generate Management*
1545 26th St
Suite 200
Santa Monica, CA 90404, USA

Garouste, Gerard (Artist)
La Mesangere
Marcilly-sur-Eure 27810, FRANCE

Garpeniov, Johan (Athlete, Hockey Player)
Vikvagen 1
Tyreso S-13562, Sweden

Garpenlov, Johan (Athlete, Hockey Player)
Breviksvagen 133
Tyresso A-13569, Sweden

Garr, Ralph (Athlete, Baseball Player)
22314 Auburn Canyon Ln
Richmond, TX 77469-5639, USA

Garr, Teri (Terri/Terry) (Actor)
9150 Wilshire Blvd
#350
Beverly Hills, CA 90212, USA

Garrahy, Joseph (Politician)
63 Starr Dr.
Narragansett, RI 02882-3129, USA

Garrard, David (Athlete, Football Player)
12450 Royal Troon Ln
Jacksonville, FL 32224-5675, USA

Garrard, Rose (Artist)
105 Carpenters Road
#21
London E18, UNITED KINGDOM (UK)

Garreis, Robert M (Geophysicist, Physicist)
South Florida University
Marine Science Dept
Saint Petersburg, FL 33701, USA

Garrelts, Scott (Athlete, Baseball Player)
11070 Ashland Way
Shreveport, LA 71106-9348, USA

Garret, Dean
6226 Stevens Ave
Minneapolis, MN 55423-1606, USA

Garret, Peter (Musician)
PO Box 249
Maroubra, NSW 2035, Australia

Garrett, Adrian (Athlete, Baseball Player)
Louisville Bats 401 E Main St
Louisville, KY 40202-1110, USA

Garrett, Alvin (Athlete, Football Player)
2600 Napoleon Ct
Birmingham, AL 35243, USA

Garrett, Beau (Actor)
c/o Sean Fay *Kritzer Levine Wilkins Entertainment (KLWG)*
11872 La Grange Ave
1st Floor
Los Angeles, CA 90025, USA

Garrett, Brad (Actor, Comedian)
c/o Glenn Robbins *Raw Talent Management*
545 Veterans Ave
Los Angeles, CA 90024, USA

Garrett, Carl (Athlete, Football Player)
203 S Crawford St
Denton, TX 76205-6215, USA

Garrett, Clifton (Athlete, Baseball Player)
7504 Kenicott Lane
Plainfield, IL 60586-4173, USA

Garrett, Dick (Athlete, Basketball Player)
7100 North Park Manor Dr
Milwaukee, WI 53224-4642, USA

Garrett, Drake (Athlete, Football Player)
32600 Concord Dr
Apt 724
Madison Heights, MI 48071, USA

Garrett, Jason (Athlete, Football Player)
3512 Lindenwood Ave
Dallas, TX 75205, USA

Garrett, Jeremy (Actor)
c/o Staff Member *Paradigm (LA)*
360 N Crescent Dr
North Bldg
Beverly Hills, CA 90210, USA

Garrett, John (Athlete, Hockey Player)
c/o Staff Member *Rogers Sportsnet*
181 Keefer Pl
Suite 221
Vancouver, BC V6B 1W6, Canada

Garrett, John (Athlete, Football Player)
1402 Meadow Ln
Southlake, TX 76092, USA

Garrett, Judd (Athlete, Football Player)
900 Meadow Ln
Southlake, TX 76092, USA

Garrett, Kathleen (Actor)
The Agency
1800 Ave of Stars
#400
Los Angeles, CA 90067, USA

Garrett, Kenneth (Photographer)
National Geographic Magazine
1145 17th St NW
Washington, DC 20036, USA

Garrett, Kenny (Musician)
Von Productions
1915 Cullen Ave
Austin, TX 78757, USA

Garrett, Leif (Actor, Musician)
c/o Barbara Papageorge *Barbara Papageorge Publicity*
790 Amsterdam Ave
New York, NY 10025, USA

Garrett, Len (Athlete, Football Player)
9413 W Tampa Dr
Baton Rouge, LA 70815, USA

Garrett, Lesley (Opera Singer)
PV Productions
Park Offices
121 Dora Road
London SW19 7JT, UNITED KINGDOM (UK)

Garrett, Lila (Director)
1245 Laurel Way
Beverly Hills, CA 90210, USA

Garrett, Mike (Athlete, Football Player, Heisman Trophy Winner)
1507 E Mountain St
Pasadena, CA 91104-3910, USA

Garrett, MJ (Reality TV Star)
c/o Michael (Mike) Esterman
Esterman.Com, LLC
Prefers to be contacted via email
MD, USA

Garrett, Pat (Musician, Songwriter, Writer)
Patrick Sickafus
PO Box 84
Strausstown, PA 19559, USA

Garrett, Peter (Musician, Politician)
P.O. Box 186
Glebe NSW 2037, Australia

Garrett, Reggie (Athlete, Football Player)
3 Martino Way
Somerset, NJ 08873, USA

Garrett, Rowland (Athlete, Basketball Player)
219 Western Hills Dr
Jackson, MS 39212-3216, USA

Garrett, Scott (Congressman, Politician)
2244 Raybury HOB
Washington, DC 20515, USA

Garrett, Spencer (Actor)
c/o Erik Kritzer *Kritzer Levine Wilkins Entertainment (KLWG)*
11872 La Grange Ave
1st Floor
Los Angeles, CA 90025, USA

Garrett, Wayne (Athlete, Baseball Player)
4331 Linwood St
Sarasota, FL 34232-3905, USA

Garrett, Wilbur E (Editor)
National Geographic Magazine
17th & M Sts
Washington, DC 20036, USA

Garrett, William E (Photographer)
209 Seneca Road
Great Falls, VA 22066, USA

Garrett III, H Lawrence (Government Official)
RR1 Box 136-18
Boyce, VA 22620, USA

Garrick, Tom (Athlete, Basketball Player)
235 Providence Street
West Warwick, RI 02893-2552, USA

Garrido, Gil (Athlete, Baseball Player)
11311 SW 200th St
Apt 110D
Miami, FL 33157-8281, USA

Garrido, Norberto (Athlete, Football Player)
15633 Briarbank St
La Puente, CA 91744, USA

Garrigus, Thomas (Athlete, Olympic Athlete, Shooter)
PO Box 681
Plains, MT 59859-0681, USA

Garriott, Owen E (Doctor)
111 Lost Tree Dr SW
Huntsville, AL 35824-1313, USA

Garriott, Owen K (Astronaut)
111 Lost Tree Dr SW
Huntsville, AL 35824-1313, USA

Garris, John (Athlete, Basketball Player)
308 Carroll Street
New Bedford, MA 02740-1415, USA

Garris, Kiwane (Athlete, Basketball Player)
23 East Rocket Circle
Park Forest, IL 60466-1613, USA

Garrison, David (Actor)
630 Estrada Redona
Santa Fe, NM 87501, USA

Garrison, Gary (Athlete, Football Player)
993 N Vulcan Ave
Apt 7
Encinitas, CA 92024, USA

Garrison, John (Athlete, Hockey Player)
Old Concord Rd
Lincoln, MA 01773, USA

Garrison, Lane (Actor)
c/o Dannielle Thomas *Untitled Entertainment (LA)*
350 S. Beverly Dr #200
Beverly Hills, CA 90212, USA

Garrison, Walt (Athlete, Football Player)
3475 E Hickory Hill Rd
Argyle, TX 76226, USA

Garrison, Webster (Athlete, Baseball Player)
2038 Rue Racine
Marrero, LA 70072-4729, USA

Garrison-Jackson, Zina (Athlete, Olympic Athlete, Tennis Player)
PO Box 2077
Bowie, MD 20718-2077, USA

Garrity, Gregg (Athlete, Football Player)
86 Seldom Seen Rd
Bradfordwoods, PA 15015, USA

Garrity, Jack (Athlete, Hockey Player, Olympic Athlete)
100 Gas Light Dr Apt 9
South Weymouth, MA 02190-2149, USA

Garrity, Pat (Athlete, Basketball Player)
85 Harrison Ave
New Cannan, CT 06840-5802, USA

Garron, Larry (Athlete, Football Player)
987 Pleasant St
Framingham, MA 01701, USA

Garror, Leon (Athlete, Football Player)
259 Stocking St
Mobile, AL 36604, USA

Garrum, Larry (Athlete, Hockey Player)
987 Pleasant St
Framingham, MA 01701, USA

Garson, Willie (Actor)
c/o Gladys Gonzalez *John Carrabino Management*
5900 Wilshire Blvd Fl 4 #406
Los Angeles, CA 90036, USA

Garten, Ina (Writer)
Clarkson Potter
Author Mail
1745 Broadway
New York, NY 10019, USA

Garth, Jennie (Actor)
c/o Randy James *James/Levy/Jacobson Management Inc*
3500 W Olive Ave
Suite 1470
Burbank, CA 91505, USA

Garth, Leonard I (Judge)
US Court of Appeals
US Courthouse
50 Walnut St
Newark, NJ 07102, USA

Gartner, Claus-Theo
Postfach 230313
Essen, GERMANY 45071

Gartner, Mike (Athlete, Hockey Player)
c/o Staff Member *Hockey Hall of Fame*
Brookfield Place
30 Yonge St
Toronto ON M5E 1X8, CANADA

Garver, Cathy (Actor)
550 Mountain Home Road
Woodside, CA 94062, USA

Garver, Kathy (Actor)
170 Woodridge Rd
Hillsborough, CA 94010, USA

Garver, Lori B (Scientist)
Nasa Headquarters 300 ESt NW MS 9042
Washington, DC 20001-2712, USA

Garver, Ned (Athlete, Baseball Player)
1121 Town Line Rd
Unit 164
Bryan, OH 43506-8732, USA

Garvey, Mike (Race Car Driver)
Competitive Edge
1033 Louisiana Ave.
#1101
Winter Park, FL 32789, USA

Garvey, Steve (Athlete, Baseball Player)
74923 US Highway 111
Indian Wells, CA 92210-7134, USA

Garvey-Truhan, Cyndy
13924 Panay Way #309
Marina del Rey, CA 90292-6102

Garvin, Jerry (Athlete, Baseball Player)
1797 E 700 S
Sorineville, UT 84663-3241, USA

Garwasiuk, Ron (Athlete, Hockey Player)
34 Fieldstone Dr
Spruce Grove, AB T7X 3C2, Canada

Garwin, Richard L (Scientist)
1 Christie Pl Unit 402W
Scarsdale, NY 10583-8305, USA

Gary, Cleveland (Athlete, Football Player)
720 SE Martin Luther King Jr Blvd
Stuart, FL 34994, USA

Gary, Cleveland E (Athlete, Football Player)
1446 SW 169th Ave
Indiantown, FL 37956, USA

Gary, Dunn (Athlete, Football Player)
243 Navajo St
Tavernier, FL 33070-2119, USA

Gary, Keith (Athlete, Football Player)
450 Massachusetts Ave NW
Apt 903
Washington, DC 20001, USA

Gary, Leonard (Athlete, Basketball Player)
3318 North Decatur Blvd
Unit 2086
Las Vegas, NV 89130, USA

Gary, Lorraine (Actor)
1158 Tower Dr
Beverly Hills, CA 90210, USA

Garza, David (Musician)
Partisan Arts
PO Box 5085
Larkspur, CA 94977, USA

Garza, Emilio M (Judge)
US Court of Appeals
US Courthouse
8200 1-10 W
San Antonio, TX 78230, USA

Garza, Joselle (Race Car Driver)
865 Comstock Ave.
#11-A
Los Angeles, CA 90024, USA

Garza, Nicole (Actor)
c/o David Rudy *Armada Partners*
815 Moraga Drive
Los Angeles, CA 90049, USA

Garza, Rene (Stylist)
c/o Celebrity Stylist *Oliver Piro Inc*
725 Riverside Dr Apt 3A
New York, NY 10031, USA

Gascoigne, Paul J (Soccer Player)
Arran Gardner
Holborn Hall
10 Grays Inn Road
London WC1X 8BY, UNITED KINGDOM
(UK)

Gascoine, Jill (Actor)
Marina Martin
12/13 Poland St
London W1V 3DE, UNITED KINGDOM
(UK)

Gascolgne, Sheryl
Stanstead Abbots
Hertfordshire, ENGLAND

Gascon, Eileen (Athlete, Baseball Player, Commentator)
249 Trowbridge Rd
Elk Grove Village, IL 60007-3820, USA

Gascon, Elleen (Baseball Player)
249 Trowbridge Rd
Elk Grove Village, IL 60007-3820, USA

Gash, Samuel L (Sam) (Athlete, Football Player)
46544 Galway Dr
Novi, MI 48374, USA

Gash, Thane (Athlete, Football Player)
201 Whispering Hills Dr
Hendersonville, NC 28792, USA

Gaskill, Brian (Actor)
c/o Marie Mathews *Marie Mathews Management*
8730 Sunset Blvd #200
Los Angeles, CA 90069, USA

Gaskill, Michael (Stylist)
c/o Celebrity Stylist *Photogenics Media*
8549 Higuera St
Building B
Culver City, CA 90232, USA

Gasol, Pau (Athlete, Basketball Player)
c/o Arn Tellem *Wasserman Media Group*
10960 Wilshire Blvd
Suite 2200
Los Angeles, CA 90024, USA

Gaspar, Rod (Athlete, Baseball Player)
28771 Peach Blossom
Mission Viejo, CA 92692-1072, USA

Gaspari, Rich (Misc)
PO Box 29
Milltown, NJ 08850, USA

Gass, William H (Writer)
6304 Westminster Place
Saint Louis, MO 63130, USA

Gassert, Ron (Athlete, Football Player)
11 Sheffield Pl
Southampton, NJ 08088, USA

Gasslyev, Nikolal T (Opera Singer)
Mariinsky Theater
Teartainaya Pl 1
Saint Petersburg, RUSSIA

Gassman, Alessandro (Actor)
Christian Cucchini Mgmt
Lungotevere del Mellini 10
Rome 00193, ITALY

Gassner, Dave (Athlete, Baseball Player)
N1376 Woodland Dr
Greenville, WI 54942-8035, USA

Gassoff, Brad (Athlete, Hockey Player)
P.O. Box 85
Wells, BC V0K 2R0, Canada

Gast, Leon (Director, Editor, Producer)
c/o Staff Member *WmE2 (WMA-LA)*
1 William Morris Pl
Beverly Hills, CA 90212, USA

Gast, Paul (Race Car Driver)
120 Industrial Dr.
Grand Island, NY 14072, USA

Gasteyer, Ana (Actor, Comedian)
c/o Staff Member *Dontanville/Frattaroli (D/F)*
270 Lafayette St
Suite 402
New York, NY 10012, USA

Gastineau, Brittny (Actor, Reality TV Star)
c/o Dana-Lee Schuman *ICM Partners (ICM-LA)*
10250 Constellation Blvd Fl 7
Los Angeles, CA 90067, USA

Gastineau, Lisa (Actor, Reality TV Star)
c/o Staff Member *True Entertainment*
601 W 26th St
Suite 1336
New York, NY 10001, USA

Gastineau, Marcus D (Mark) (Athlete, Football Player)
22202 N 48th St
Phoenix, AZ 85054, USA

Gastineau, Mark (Athlete, Football Player)
PO Box 816
Eagar, AZ 85925-0816, USA

Gaston, Cito (Athlete, Baseball Player, Coach)
1454 Woodstream Dr
Oldsmar, FL 34677-4832, USA

Gaston, Hiram (Baseball Player)
Birmingham Black Barons
18 Burntwood Cres
Winnipeg, AB R2J 3A1, CANADA

Gaston, Michael (Actor)
c/o Lisa Lieberman *Innovative Artists (NY)*
235 Park Ave S
7th Floor
New York, NY 10003, USA

Gates, Antonio (Athlete, Football Player)
c/o Staff Member *EAG Sports Management*
12910 Agustin Pl
Playa Vista, CA 90094, USA

Gates, Bill (Misc)
c/o Staff Member *Microsoft Corporation*
1 Microsoft Way
Redmond, WA 98052-8300, USA

Gates, Brent (Athlete, Baseball Player)
2125 Shawnee Dr SE
Grand Raoids, MI 49506-5332, USA

Gates, Daryl (Actor)
24876 Sunstar Ln
Dana Point, CA 92629, USA

Gates, David (Musician, Songwriter, Writer)
Paradise Artists
108 E Matilija St
Ojai, CA 93023, USA

Gates, Gareth (Musician)
c/o Staff Member *19 Entertainment*
33/32 Ransomes Dock
35-37 Parkgate Rd
London SW11 4NP, UK

Gates, Henry Lewis Jr (Educator)
Harvard University
Afro-American Studies Dept
Cambridge, MA 02138, USA

Gates, Josh (Actor)
c/o Noreen Savides *323 Talent Management*
P.O. Box 3234
Quartz Hill, CA 93586, USA

Gates, Mike (Athlete, Baseball Player)
131 Edgewater Rd
Kooskia, ID 83539-5024, USA

Gates, Robert M (Educator, Government Official)
19031 W Big Lake Blvd
Mount Vernon, WA 98274, USA

Gatewood, Aubrey (Athlete, Baseball Player)
5 Pine Tree Loop
North Little Rock, AR 72116-8313, USA

Gatewood, Les (Athlete, Football Player)
P.O. Box 414
Kirbyville, TX 75956, USA

Gatewood, Tom (Athlete, Football Player)
101 Cambridge Dr
Nutley, NJ 07110, USA

Gathegi, Edi (Actor)
c/o Mary Ellen Mulcahy *Framework Entertainment (LA)*
9057 Nemo St
Suite C
West Hollywood, CA 90069, USA

Gatherum, Dave (Athlete, Hockey Player)
1457 Mountain Rd
Thunder Bay, ON P7C 1R5, Canada

Gathright, Joey (Athlete, Baseball Player)
20100 Park Row Dr Aot 1307
Katv, TX 77449-4985, USA

Gatlin, Justin (Athlete, Track Athlete)
c/o Staff Member *USA Track & Field*
132 E Washington St
Suite 800
Indianapolis, IN 46204, USA

Gatlin, Larry (Musician)
5100 Harris Ave.
Kansas City, MO 64133-2331, USA

Gatling, Chris (Athlete, Basketball Player)
175 Canon Drive
Orinda, CA 94563, USA

Gatti, Bill (Athlete, Football Player)
1400 Regal Springs Ct
Louisville, KY 40205-3334

Gatti, Jennifer (Actor)
S D B Partners
1801 Ave of Stars
#902
Los Angeles, CA 90067, USA

Gatting, Michael W (Cricketer)
Middlesex Cricket Club
Saint John's Wood Road
London NW8 8QN, UNITED KINGDOM (UK)

Gattison, Kenny (Athlete, Basketball Player)
1115 I St NE
Washington, DC 20002-7117, USA

Gattorno, Francisco (Actor)
c/o Gabriel Blanco *Gabriel Blanco Iglesias (Mexico)*
Rio Balsas 35-32
Colonia Cuauhtemoc
DF 06500, Mexico

Gatzos, Steve (Athlete, Hockey Player)
McThirsty's Pint
Porch and Pint 172 Lansdowne St E
Peterborough, ON K9J 7N9, Canada

Gaubatz, Dennis (Athlete, Football Player)
1250 County Road 943
West Columbia, TX 77486, USA

Gaucho, Ronaldinho (Soccer Player)
Futbol Club Barcelona
Avenida Aristides Mailol
Barcelona 08028, SPAIN

Gauci, Miriam (Opera Singer)
Kunstleragentur Raab & Bohm
Plankengasse 7
Vienna 1010, AUSTRIA

Gaudet, Jim (Athlete, Baseball Player)
3336 Vineville Ave
Macon, GA 31204-2328, USA

Gaudiani, Claire L (Educator)
53 Neptune Dr
Groton, CT 06340, USA

Gaudin, Chad (Athlete, Baseball Player)
108 Citrus Rd
New Orleans, LA 70123-2504, USA

Gaudreau, Rob (Athlete, Hockey Player)
22 Briarbrooke Ln
Cranston, RI 02921, USA

Gaudreault, Armand (Athlete, Hockey Player)
301-425 Boui de L'Atrium
Quebec, QC G1H OA8, Canada

Gaughan, Brendan (Race Car Driver)
Rusty Wallace Racing
1459 Knob Hill Rd.
Mooresville, NC 28117, USA

Gaul, Frank (Athlete, Football Player)
3420 Balsam Dr
Westlake, OH 44145, USA

Gaul, Gilbert M (Journalist)
Philadelphia Inquirer
Editorial Dept
400 N Broad St
Philadelphia, PA 19130, USA

Gaul, Michael (Athlete, Hockey Player)
Webster Hockey Academy
22 Hampton Gardens
Attn: Coaching Staff
Pointe-Claire, QC H9S 5B8, Canada

Gaulin, Jean-Marc (Athlete, Hockey Player)
273 Rue Principale
St-Basile-Le-Grand, QC J3N 1J7, Canada

Gault, Bill (Athlete, Football Player)
P.O. Box 105
Bangs, TX 76823, USA

Gault, William Campbell (Writer)
481 Mountain Dr
Santa Barbara, CA 93103, USA

Gaultier, Jean Paul (Designer, Fashion Designer)
30, rue du Faubourg St Antoine
Paris 75012, FRANCE

Gaume, Dallas (Athlete, Hockey Player)
4350 Gallaghers Fairway S
Kelowna, BC V1W 4X4, Canada

Gaurav, Kumar (Actor)
Dimple 7 Pali Hill
Bandra
Bombay, MS 400 050, INDIA

Gaustad, Paul (Athlete, Hockey Player)
55 Saybrook Pl
Buffalo, NY 14209, USA

Gauthier, Dan (Actor)

Gauthier, Daniel (Athlete, Hockey Player)
17 Rue Nicoud
Charlemagne, QC J5Z 1Z2, Canada

Gauthier, Jean (Athlete, Hockey Player)
415 Av Vinet
Dorval, QC H9S 2M7, Canada

Gauthier, Luc (Athlete, Hockey Player)
c/o Staff Member *Colorado Avalanche*
Pepsi Center
1000 Chopper Cir
Denver, CO 80204, USA

Gauthier, Jr., Denis (Athlete, Hockey Player)
1658 9th St
Manhattan Beach, CA 90266-6129, USA

Gauthreaux, Joe (DJ)
c/o Staff Member *Diva Central Inc*
7510 W Sunset Blvd Ste 1445
Los Angees, CA 90046, USA

Gautier, Dick (Actor)
c/o Staff Member *Beacon Talent Agency*
170 Apple Ridge Rd
Woodcliff, NJ 07677, USA

Gautlier, Jean-Paul (Designer, Fashion Designer)
Jean-Paul Gaultier SA
325 Rue Du Faubaurg St Martin
Paris 75003, FRANCE

Gauvreau, Jocelyn (Athlete, Hockey Player)
19 Rue le Vasseur
Gatineau, QC J8V 2M8, Canada

Gava, Cassandra (Actor)
1745 Camino Palmero #210
Los Angeles, CA 90046, USA

Gavankar, Janina (Actor)
c/o Arlene Forster *Forster Entertainment*
12533 Woodgreen St
Los Angeles, CA 90066, USA

Gavaskar, Sunil M (Cricketer)
40 Bhalchandra Road #A Dadar
Bombay, MS 400014, INDIA

Gavilan, Kid
1 Hall of Fame Dr.
Canastota, NY 13032

Gavin, Charles E (Chuck) (Athlete, Football Player)
2800 Grape St
Denver, CO 80207, USA

Gavin, Diarmuid (Actor)
c/o Staff Member *John Noel Management*
10A Belmont St
Floor 2
London NW1 8HH, UNITED KINGDOM
(UK)

Gavin, Erica
c/o Siouxzan Perry *Girlwerks Management*
3395 E Camino Rojos
Palm Springs, CA 92262, USA

Gavin, John (Actor, Diplomat)
2100 Century Park W #10263
Los Angeles, CA 90067, USA

Gaviria, Trujillo Cesar (President)
Organization of American States
17th & Constitution NW
Washington, DC 20006, USA

Gavitt, Dave (Basketball Player, Misc)
Boston Celtics
151 Merrimac St #1
Boston, MA 02114, USA

Gavrilov, Andrei V (Musician)
c/o Mark Stephan *Mark Stephan Buhl Artists Management*
Geylinggasse 1
Wien 1130, AUSTRIA

Gavron, Rafi (Actor)
c/o Peter McGrath *Affirmative Entertainment*
425 N Robertson Blvd
Los Angeles, CA 90048, USA

Gay, Billy (Athlete, Football Player)
824 Lisdowney Dr
Lockport, IL 60441, USA

Gay, Brian (Athlete, Golfer)
6809 Valhalla Way
Windermere, FL 34786, USA

Gay, Don
1818 Rodeo Dr.
Mesquite, TX 75149

Gay, Everett (Athlete, Football Player)
700 E Johnson St
Waco, TX 76705, USA

Gay, George
588 Charlton Ct. NW
Marietta, GA 30064

Gay, Jerry (Photographer)
2121 Madison St Ste C
Everett, WA 98203-5375, USA

Gay, Peter J (Historian)
270 Riverside Dr #8C
New York, NY 10025-5211, USA

Gay, Randall (Athlete, Football Player)
116 Cocasset St
Apt 14
Foxboro, MA 02035, USA

Gay, Rudy (Athlete, Basketball Player)
91 W Galloway Dr
Memphis, TN 38111-6839, USA

Gay, William (Athlete, Football Player)
8200 E Jefferson Ave
Apt 804
Detroit, MI 48214, USA

Gaydos, Joey (Actor)
c/o Staff Member *Cunningham Escott Slevin & Doherty (CESD-LA)*
10635 Santa Monica Blvd
130
Los Angeles, CA 90025, USA

Gaydos, Kent (Athlete, Football Player)
1107 Mallard Ct
Granbury, TX 76048-2676, USA

Gaydos Jr, Joey (Actor)
20436 Martinsville Rd
Belleville, MI 48111, USA

Gaydukov, Sergei N (Astronaut, Misc)
Potchta Kosmonavtov
Moskovskoi Oblasti
Syvisdny Goroduk 141160, RUSSIA

Gaye, Nona (Actor)
c/o Steven Muller *Innovative Artists (LA)*
1505 10th St
Santa Monica, CA 90401, USA

Gayheart, Rebecca (Actor, Model)
2101 N Beverly Dr
Beverly Hills, CA 90210, USA

Gayle, Crystal (Actor, Musician)
c/o Staff Member *Webster & Associates PR*
3573 Couchville Pike
Hermitage, TN 37076, USA

Gayle, Sami (Actor)
c/o David Guillod *Intellectual Artists Management*
10585 Santa Monica Blvd
Suite 135
Los Angeles, CA 90025, USA

Gayle, Shaun (Athlete, Football Player)
1530 N Elk Grove Ave
Apt I
Chicago, IL 60622, USA

Gaylor, Noel (Admiral)
2111 Mason Hill Dr
Alexandria, VA 22306, USA

Gaylor, Robert (General)
4114 Antlers Lodge Rd
San Antonio, TX 78251-4300, USA

Gaylor, Trevor (Athlete, Football Player)
5855 Hammond Dr
Norcross, GA 30071, USA

Gaylord, Frank (Artist)
25 Delmont Ave
Barre, VT 05641, USA

Gaylord, Mitch (Athlete, Gymnast, Olympic Athlete)
4824 Cargill Cir
Ft Worth, TX 76244-6073, USA

Gaylord, Scott (Race Car Driver)
Scott Gaylord Racing
1451 Depen
Lakewood, CO 80214, USA

Gaylords, The
32630 Concord Dr.
Madison Heights, MI 48071

Gaynes, George (Actor)
3344 Campanil Dr
Santa Barbara, CA 93109, USA

Gaynor, Gloria (Music Group, Musician)
c/o Staff Member *Richard De La Font Agency*
3808 W South Park Blvd
Broken Arrow, OK 74011, USA

Gaynor, Mitzi (Actor, Dancer, Musician)
610 Arden Dr
Beverly Hills, CA 90210, USA

Gayoom, Maumoon Abdul (President)
Presidential Palace
Orchid Magu
Male 20-05, MALDIVES

Gayson, Eunice (Actor)
Spotlight
7 Leicester Place
London WC2H 7BP, UNITED KINGDOM
(UK)

Gayton, Joe (Writer)
c/o David Saunders *Agency for the Performing Arts (APA-LA)*
405 S Beverly Dr
Suite 500
Beverly Hills, CA 90212-4425, USA

Gayton, Tony (Writer)
c/o Matt Ochacher *Agency for the Performing Arts (APA-LA)*
405 S Beverly Dr
Suite 500
Beverly Hills, CA 90212-4425, USA

Gaze, Andrew (Athlete, Basketball Player)
Australian Basketball Resources
P.O. Box 2222
Ivanhoe, East 3029, Australia

Gbagbo, Laurent (President)
President's Office
Boulevard Clozel
Abidijan, IVORY COAST

Gbaja-Biamila, Akbar (Athlete, Football Player)
1050 Armitage St
Alameda, CA 94502, USA

Gbaja-Biamila, Kabeer (Athlete, Football Player)
1071 Hill Dr
Oneida, WI 54155, USA

G. Bartlett, Roscoe (Congressman, Politician)
2412 Rayburn HOB
Washington, Washington DC, USA

Geale, Rob (Athlete, Hockey Player)
4167 NW 178th Pl
Portland, OR 97229, USA

Gearan, Mark (Educator, Government Official)
Hobart & William Smith College
President's Office
Geneva, NY 14456, USA

Gearhart, John (Biologist, Doctor)
Johns Hopkins Univesity
Medical Center
Baltimore, MD 21218, USA

Geary, Anthony (Actor)
7010 Pacific View Dr
Los Angeles, CA 90068, USA

Geary, Cynthia (Actor)
Baumgarten/Prophet
1041 N Formosa Ave #200
West Hollywood, CA 90046, USA

Geary, Geoff (Athlete, Baseball Player)
2735 Callaway Ln
Kissimmee, FL 34744-8533, USA

Geary, Tony
7010 Pacific View Dr.
Los Angeles, CA 90068

Geater, Ron (Athlete, Football Player)
3012 Oceanside Ct
Plainfield, IL 60586, USA

Geathers, James (Athlete, Football Player)
200 Tony Dr
Georgetown, SC 29440, USA

Geathers, Robert (Athlete, Football Player)
1 Dab Dr
Georgetown, SC 29440, USA

Gebert, Gordon (Actor)
8 Dwight St
Poughkeepsie, NY 12601, USA

Gebhard, Bob (Commentator)
5242 E Otero Pl
Centennial, CO 80122-3889, USA

Gebo, Daniel (Scientist)
Northern Illinois University
Paleontology Dept
De Kalb, IL 60115, USA

Gebrselassie, Haile (Athlete, Track Athlete)
Ethiopian Athletic Federation
P O Box 3241
Addis Ababa, ETHIOPIA

Geck, Thea (Stylist)
180 Brannan St
Apt 227
San Francisco, CA 94107-2052, USA

Gedda, Nicolai (Opera Singer)
Valhallavagen 128
Stockholm 11441, SWEDEN

Geddes, Anne (Photographer)
Kel Geddes Management
2 York Street
Parnell
Auckland 1001, NEW ZEALAND

Geddes, Bob (Athlete, Football Player)
79251 Tom Fazio Ln S
La Quinta, CA 92253, USA

Geddes, Jane (Athlete, Golfer)
60 Buckingham Dr
Stamford, CT 06902-8310, USA

Geddes, Jim (Athlete, Baseball Player)
6738 Harrisburg London Rd
Orient, OH 43146-9454, USA

Geddes, Ken (Athlete, Football Player)
7702 147th Ave NE
Redmond, WA 98052, USA

Gedman, Rich (Athlete, Baseball Player)
10 Parmenter Rd
Framingham, MA 01701-3019, USA

Gedmintas, Ruta (Actor)
c/o Olivia Homan *United Agents*
12-26 Lexington St
London W1F OLE, UK

Gedney, Chris (Athlete, Football Player)
4981 Boneta Rd
Medina, OH 13215-9303, USA

Gedrick, Jason (Actor)
c/o Staff Member *IFA Talent Agency*
8730 Sunset Blvd
Suite 490
Los Angeles, CA 90069, USA

Gee, Dillon (Athlete, Baseball Player)
413 SHill Dr
Cleburne, TX 76033-4539, USA

Gee, E Gordon (Educator)
Vanderbilt University
Chancellor's Office
Nashville, TN 37240, USA

Gee, James D (Religious Leader)
Penecostal Church of God
4901 Pennsylvania
Joplin, MO 64804, USA

Gee, Prunella (Actor)
Michael Ladkin Mgmt
1Duchess St #1
London W1N 3DE, UNITED KINGDOM
(UK)

Geer, Charlotte (Athlete, Olympic
Athlete, Rower)
PO Box 324
Hinesburg, VT 05461-0324, USA

Geer, Dennis (Financier)
Federal Deposit Insurance
550 17th St NW
Washington, DC 20429, USA

Geer, Ellen (Actor)
21418 W Entrada Road
Topanga, CA 90290, USA

Geer, Josh (Athlete, Baseball Player)
10836 Peach Cir
Fornev, TX 75126-6666, USA

Geer, Julia (Athlete, Olympic Athlete,
Rower)
243 Lyle McKee Rd
Morrisville, VT 05661-8902, USA

Geertz, Clifford J (Misc)
Institute for Advanced Study
Social Science Dept
Princeton, NJ 08540, USA

Geeson, Judy (Actor)
Media Artists Group
6300 Wilshire Blvd
#1470
Los Angeles, CA 90048, USA

Geeson, Sally (Actor)
c/o Staff Member *Michael Summerton
Management*
Martin Taylor-Brown
Mimosa House, Mimosa St
London SW6 4DS, UK

Gee-Soo, Kim (Actor)
Sidus HQ
88 Sam-sung dong
Sambo Building 1st Fl.
Kang-nam gu, Seoul 135 090, Korea

Geffen, Aviv
Bugroashov 26
Tel Aviv, ISRAEL 63342

Geffen, David (Business Person, Producer)
1801 Angelo Dr
Beverly Hills, CA 90210, USA

Geffner, Glenn (Commentator)
4058 Palm Pl
Weston, FL 33331-5035, USA

Gegenhuber, John
9171 Wilshire Blvd. #441
Beverly Hills, CA 90210

Gehlhausen, Spike (Race Car Driver)
5456 Meadowwood Dr.
Speedway, IN 46222, USA

Gehman, Martha
2488 Cheremoya Ave
Los Angeles, CA 90068

Gehring, Frederick W (Mathematician)
2139 Melrose Ave
Ann Arbor, MI 48104, USA

Gehring, Walter J (Doctor, Misc,
Scientist)
Hochfeldstr 32
Therwill 4106, SWITZERLAND

Gehringer, Rick (Musician)
c/o Staff Member *Brothers Management
Associates Inc*
141 Dunbar Ave
Fords, NJ 08863

Gehrke, Jack (Athlete, Football Player)
9200 Cherry Creek South Dr
Apt 40
Denver, CO 80231, USA

Gehry, Frank (Architect)
Gehry And Associates 12541 Beatrice St
Los Angeles, CA 90066-7001, USA

Gehry, Franko O (Architect)
Gehry Partners
12541 Beatrice St
Los Angeles, CA 90066, USA

Geiberger, Al (Athlete, Golfer)
73091 Country Club Dr
Suite A4
Palm Desert, CA 92260, USA

Geiberger, Brent (Athlete, Golfer)
113 Chelsea Cir
Palm Desert, CA 92260, USA

Geiduschek, E Peter (Biologist)
University of California
Biology Dept 9500 Gilman Dr
La Jolla, CA 92093, USA

Geier, Philip H Jr (Business Person)
Interpublic Group
1271 Ave of Americas
New York, NY 10020, USA

Geiger, Ken (Journalist, Photographer)
Dallas Mornig News
Communications Center
Dallas, TX 75265, USA

Geiger, Matt (Athlete, Basketball Player)
12506 Twin Branch
Acres Rd
Tampa, FL 33626-4423, USA

Geiger, Teddy (Musician)
c/o John Geiger
11 Tamarron Way
Pittsford, NY 14534, USA

Geii-Mann, Murray (Nobel Prize
Laureate)
Santa Fe Institute 1399 Hyde Park Rd
Santa Fe, NM 87501-8943, USA

Geimer, Samantha
4245 Waipua
Kilauea, HI 96754

Geingob, Hage G (Prime Minister)
Prime Minister's Office
Private Bag 13338
Windhoek 9000, NAMIBIA

Geisel, Dave (Athlete, Baseball Player)
4 Blacksmith Ln
Media, PA 19063-4411, USA

Geishert, Vern (Athlete, Baseball Player)
984 N Park St
Richland Center, WI 53581-1428, USA

Geisinger, Justin (Athlete, Football Player)
441 Summit Oaks Dr
Nashville, TN 37221, USA

Geismar, Thomas H (Architect)
Cambridge Seven Assoc
1050 Massachusetts Ave
Cambridge, MA 02138, USA

Geiss, Johannes (Physicist)
University of Beme
Physics Instit Sidlerstr 5
Beme 3012, SWITZERLAND

Geissendorfer, Hans
An den Herrenbergen 21a
Neustadt/Aisch, GERMANY D-91413

Geissinger-Harding, Jean (Athlete,
Baseball Player, Commentator)
539 Hodunk Rd
Coldwater, MI 49036-9273, USA

Geist, Bill (Correspondent)
c/o Staff Member *N.S. Bienstock*
1740 Broadway
24th Floor
New York, NY 10019, USA

Geithner, Timothy (Financier, Politician)
Dept of Treasury
1500 Pennsylvania Ave NW
Washington, DC 20220, USA

Gelb, Leslie H (Educator)
Council of Foreign Relations
58 E 68th St
New York, NY 10021, USA

Gelbaugh, Stan (Athlete, Football Player)
10819 Hob Nail Ct
Potomac, MD 20854, USA

Geldart, Gary (Athlete, Hockey Player)
1136 Morning Creek Ln
League City, TX 77573-1893, USA

Geldof, Bob (Actor, Musician)
c/o Rick Shoor *Red Entertainment Agency*
505 8th Ave
Suite 1004
New York, NY 10018, USA

Gelfand, Izrael M (Mathematician)
118 N 5th Ave
Highland Park, NJ 18904, USA

Gelfant, Alan (Actor)
Peter Strain
5724 W 3rd #302
Los Angeles, CA 90036, USA

Gelinas, Gratien (Actor, Writer)
316 Girouard St #207
Oka, QC J0N 1E0, CANADA

Gelinas, Martin (Athlete, Hockey Player)
c/o Staff Member *National Sports
Development Ltd*
7475 Flint Rd SE
Calgary, AL T2H 1G3, Canada

Gellar, Sarah Michelle (Actor)
c/o JoAnne Colonna *Brillstein
Entertainment Partners*
9150 Wilshire Blvd #350
Beverly Hills, CA 90212, USA

Gellard, Sam (Athlete, Hockey Player)
35 Dancers Dr
Markham, ON L6C 2C4, Canada

Geller, Glenn (Business Person)
c/o Staff Member *CBS Paramount
Network Television*
CBS Studios
4024 Radford Ave
Studio City, CA 91604, USA

Geller, Margaret (Scientist)
Harvard Center For Astrophysics 60
Garden St
Cambridge, MA 02138-1516, USA

Geller, Uri (Actor)
c/o Staff Member *Celeb Agents*
77 Oxford St
London ON W1D 2ES, UNITED
KINGDOM (UK)

Gell-Mann, Murray (Nobel Prize
Laureate)
Santa Fe Institute
1399 Hyde Park Road
Santa Fe, NM 87501, USA

Gelman, Larry (Actor)
5121 Greenbush Ave
Sherman Oaks, CA 91423, USA

Gelman, Michael
7 Lincoln Sq.
New York, NY 10023

Gelnar, John (Athlete, Baseball Player)
1811 Suzanne Dr Aot 2
Weatherford, OK 73096-2383, USA

Gemar, Charles D (Astronaut)
7660 N 159th St Court E
Benton, KS 67017, USA

Gemar, Charles D Lt Colonel (Astronaut)
7660 N 159th Street Ct E
Benton, KS 67017-8926, USA

Gemma, Giuliano
Via dei Riari 66
Rome, ITALY 00165

Genaux, Vivicia (Opera Singer)
Robert Lombardo
Harkness Plaza 61 W 62nd St #6F
New York, NY 10023, USA

Gendron, George (Editor)
Inc Magazine
Editorial Dept 77 N Washington St
Boston, MA 02114, USA

Gendron, Jean-Guy (Athlete, Hockey
Player)
122 Rue de la Chaudiere
Saint-Nicholas, QC G7A 2R8, Canada

Gene, Marc (Race Car Driver)
Minardi Team
Via Spallanzani 21
Faenza 48018, ITALY

Generation, The X
184 Glochester Pl.
London, ENGLAND NW1

Genesis (Music Group)
c/o Staff Member *Hit and Run Music Ltd*
25 Ives Street
South Kensington
London SW3 2ND, United Kingdom

Genet, Sabryn
7800 Beverly Blvd. #3305
Los Angeles, CA 90036

Genilas, Eric (Athlete, Hockey Player)
165 Mulberry St.
Newark, NJ 07102, USA

Genitallica (Music Group)
c/o Staff Member *Sony Music Miami*
605 Lincoln Rd Fl 7
Miami Beach, FL 33139, USA

Genovese, George (Athlete, Baseball
Player)
11474 Erwin St
North Hollywood, CA 91606-4126, USA

Genscher, Hans-Dietrich
Am Kottenforst 16
Wachtberg 3 5307, GERMANY

Gensler, M Arthur Jr (Architect)
Gensler & Assoc Architects
550 Keamy St
San Francisco, CA 94108, USA

Gentile, Jim (Athlete, Baseball Player)
1016 S Neptune Rd
Edmond, OK 73003-6071, USA

Gentile, Troy (Actor)
c/o Leonard Torgan *Collective*
8383 Wilshire Blvd
Suite 1050
Beverly Hills, CA 90211, USA

Gentilozzi, Paul (Race Car Driver)
201 N. Washington Square
#900
Lansing, MI 48933, USA

Gentry, Alvin (Basketball Player, Coach, Misc)
New Orleans Homets
New Orleans Arena 1501 Girod St
New Orleans, LA 70113, USA

Gentry, Bobbie (Music Group)
269 S Beverly Dr #368
Beverly Hills, CA 90212, USA

Gentry, Craig (Athlete, Baseball Player)
1209 Cartwright st
72956-2809, AR 72956-2809, USA

Gentry, Curtis (Athlete, Football Player)
387 Meadow Green Ln
Round Lake Beach, IL 60073, USA

Gentry, Dennis (Athlete, Football Player)
916 Queen Elizabeth Dr
McGregor, TX 76657, USA

Gentry, Harvey (Athlete, Baseball Player)
109 Eaton Ln
Bristol, TN 37620-2820, USA

Gentry, Jerald Col (Aviator)
1439 Rue Desiree
Baton Rouge, LA 70810-3150, USA

Gentry, Montgomery (Music Group)
c/o John Dorris Sr *Hallmark Direction Company*
713 18th Avenue South
Nashville, TN 37203-3214, USA

Gentry, Race
2379 Mountain View Dr
Escondido, CA 92116

Gentry, Teddy W (Music Group, Musician)
P O Box 529
Fort Payne, AL 35968, USA

Gentry, Troy (Musician)
c/o Staff Member *Hallmark Direction Company*
713 18th Avenue South
Nashville, TN 37203-3214, USA

Genzel, Carrie (Actor)
Pakula/King
9229 Sunset Blvd #315
Los Angeles, CA 90069, USA

Genzman, Andy (Race Car Driver)
Genzman Racing
2145 Napoleon St.
Fremont, OH 43420, USA

Genzmer, Harald (Composer)
Eisensteinstr 10
Munich 81679, GERMANY

Geoffrion, Dan (Athlete, Hockey Player)
413 Overall Dr
Brentwood, TN 37027, USA

Geoffrion, Daniel (Athlete, Hockey Player)
413 Overall Dr
Brentwood, TN 37027-7649, USA

Geoffrion, Scott (Race Car Driver)
Team Mopar
27608 La Paz
#506
Laguna Rills, CA 92656, USA

George, Alex (Athlete, Baseball Player)
8432 Linden Ln
Prairie Village, KS 66207-1834, USA

George, Alicia (Stylist)
714 N Idlewild
Memphis, TN 38107, USA

George, Boy (Musician)
c/o Ian Fintak *Agency Group Ltd, The (LA)*
1880 Century Park E
Suite 711
Los Angeles, CA 90067, USA

George, Cardinal Francis Eugene (Religious Leader)
Palazzo Del S Uffizio LI
Rome 00193, ITALY

George, Chris (Athlete, Baseball Player, Olympic Athlete)
428 Kathv Lvnn Dr
Pittsbureh, PA 15239-1708, USA

George, Christopher S (Chris) (Baseball Player)
121 E Maranta Road
Mooresville, NC 28117, USA

George, Devean (Athlete, Basketball Player)
1285 French Creek Dr
Wayzata, MN 55391-9105, USA

George, Ed (Athlete, Football Player)
1220 S Orange Ave
Sarasota, FL 34239-2028, USA

George, Ed (Athlete, Football Player)
1220 S Orange Ave
Sarasota, FL 34239, USA

George, Eddie (Athlete, Football Player, Heisman Trophy Winner)
9538 Sanctuary Pl
Brentwood, TN 37027, USA

George, Eddie (Actor)
c/o Peter Schaffer *All Pro Sports and Entertainment*
36 Steele St
Suite 100
Denver, CO 80206, USA

George, Edward A J (Financier)
Bank of England
Threadneedle St
London EC2R 8AH, UNITED KINGDOM (UK)

George, Elizabeth (Writer)
c/o Robert Gottlieb *Trident Media Group LLC*
41 Madison Ave
36th Floor
New York, NY 10010, USA

George, Eric (Actor)
Lasher McManus Robinson
1964 Westwood Blvd #400
Los Angeles, CA 90025, USA

George, Francis E Cardinal (Religious Leader)
Chicago Archidiocese
1555 N State Parkway
Chaicago, IL 60610, USA

George, Gotz
Terrassenstr. 32
Berlin, GERMANY D-14129

George, Jason Winston (Actor)
c/o Peter Kiernan *Management 360*
9111 Wilshire Blvd
Beverly Hills, CA 90210, USA

George, Jeffrey S (Jeff) (Athlete, Football Player)
1908 Schwier Ct
Indianapolis, IN 46229, USA

George, Lynda Day
10310 Riverside Dr. #104
Toluca Lake, CA 91602-2457

George, Matt (Athlete, Football Player)
24403 Newhall Ave Apt 3
Newhall, CA 91321-2771, USA

George, Melissa (Actor)
c/o Pamela Kohl *3 Arts Entertainment Inc*
9460 Wilshire Blvd
7th Floor
Beverly Hills, CA 90210, USA

George, Peter (Athlete, Olympic Athlete, Weightlifter)
1649 Kalakaua Ave Ste 204
Honolulu, HI 96826-2494, USA

George, Phyllis (Beauty Pageant Winner, Television Host)
c/o Staff Member *WmE2 (WMA-LA)*
1 William Morris Pl
Beverly Hills, CA 90212, USA

George, Ron (Athlete, Football Player)
13720 Piedmont Vista Dr
Haymarket, VA 20169, USA

George, Steve (Athlete, Football Player)
5922 W Airport Blvd
Houston, TX 77035, USA

George, Susan (Actor)
McKorkindale & Holton
1-2 Langham Place
London W1A 3DD, UNITED KINGDOM (UK)

George, Tate (Athlete, Basketball Player)
55 Georgetown Road
Bristol, CT 06010-5510, USA

George, Terry (Writer)
c/o Ari Emanuel *WME (LA)*
9601 Wilshire Blvd Fl 3
Beverly Hills, CA 90210, USA

George, Tim (Athlete, Football Player)
77 Saddle Ln
Easton, PA 18045, USA

George, Tony (Race Car Driver)
Vison Racing
6803 Coffman Rd
Indianapolis, IN 46268, USA

George, Wes (Athlete, Hockey Player)
442 O'Regan Crt
Saskatoon, SK S7L 6N8, Canada

George, William W (Business Person)
Medtronic Inc
7000 Central Ave NE
Minneapolis, MN 55432, USA

Georgel, Pierre (Misc)
24 Rue Richer
Paris 76009, FRANCE

George-McFaul, Jean (Baseball Player)
2432 Kilkeer Ste 9
N Battleford, SK S9I 3Y5, CANADA

Georges, Anne (Baseball Player)
407 Oak St
Des Plaines, IL 60016-4429, USA

Georgi, Howard (Physicist)
Harvard University
Physics Dept Lyman Laboratory
Cambridge, MA 02138, USA

Georgian, Theodore J (Religious Leader)
Orthodox Presbyterian Church
P O Box P
Willow Grove, PA 19090, USA

Georgievski, Ljubisa (Ljupco) (Prime Minister)
Prime Minister's Office
Dame Grueva 6
Skopje 91000, MACEDONIA

Georgije, Bishop (Religious Leader)
Serbian Orthodox Church
Sava Monastery P O Box 519
Libertyville, IL 60048, USA

Georgoulis, Alexis (Actor)
c/o Ali Sages *Sages Entertainment Group*
9107 Wilshire Blvd.
Suite 450
Beverly Hills, CA 90210, USA

Gephardt, Richard (Politician)
DLA Piper
PO Box 9945
Me Lean, VA 22102-0945, USA

Geraci, Sonny (Music Group)
Mars Talent
27 L'Ambiance Court
Bardonia, NY 10954, USA

Geraghty, Brian (Actor)
c/o Lena Roklin *Luber Roklin Management*
8530 Wilshire Blvd
6th Floor
Beverly Hills, CA 90211, USA

Gerard, Bobby (Stylist)
c/o Staff Member *Artists by Timothy Priano (CA)*
8447 Wilshire Blvd
#301
Beverly Hills, CA 90211, USA

Gerard, Gil (Actor)
23679 Calabasas Road #325
Calabasas, CA 91302, USA

Gerard, Gus (Athlete, Basketball Player)
614 Cypresswood Drive
Spring, TX 77388-5913, USA

Gerard, Jean Shevlin (Diplomat)
American Embassy
22 Blvd Emannanuel Servais
2535, LUXEMBOURG

Gerard, Tara (Reality TV Star)
c/o Michael (Mike) Esterman
Esterman.Com, LLC
Prefers to be contacted via email
MD, USA

Gerber, Craig (Athlete, Baseball Player)
4297 N Pershine Ave
San Bernardino, CA 92407-3737, USA

Gerber, H Joseph (Business Person)
Gerber Scientific Inc
83 Gerber Road W
South Windsor, CT 06074, USA

Gerber, Joel (Judge)
US Tax Court
400 2nd St NW
Washington, DC 20217, USA

Gerber, Michael (Business Person, Writer)
E-Myth Worldwide
2235 Mercury Way Ste 200
Santa Rosa, CA 95407, USA

Gerber, Rande (Business Person)
33246 Pacific Coast Hwy
Malibu, CA 90265, USA

Gerberding, Julie (Doctor, Government Official, Physicist)
Centers for Disease Control
1600 Clifton Road NE
Atlanta, GA 30329, USA

Gerberman, George (Athlete, Baseball Player)
1501 Michael St
El Campo, TX 77437-9345, USA

Gercke, Lena (Model)
c/o Staff Member *REDSEVEN Artists & Events GmbH*
Medienallee 7
Unterfoehring D-85774, Germany

Gere, Richard (Actor)
c/o Alan Nierob *Rogers & Cowan PR (LA)*
Pacific Design Center
8687 Melrose Ave, 7th Floor
West Hollywood, CA 90069, USA

Geredine, Tom (Athlete, Football Player)
1155 Woodlands Dr
Kyle, TX 78640-5530, USA

Gerela, Roy (Athlete, Football Player)
3933 Ramrod Frg
Las Cruces, NM 88012, USA

Geren, Bob (Athlete, Baseball Player, Coach)
32 Bottlebrush Ct
Danville, CA 94506-4743, USA

Gerena, Samuel (Gringo) (Musician)
c/o Staff Member *Universal Music Publishing Group (Latin)*
420 Lincoln Rd
Suite 200
Miami Beach, FL 33139, USA

Gerety, Tom Jr (Educator)
Amherst College
President's Office
Amherst, MA 01002, USA

Gerg, Hilde (Skier)
Brauneck Tolzer Hutte
Lenggries 83661, GERMANY

Gergen, David R (Politician)
31 Ash St
Cambridge, MA 02138-4840, USA

Gergiev, Valery A
Kunstleragentur Raab & Bohm
Plankengasse 7
Vienna 1010, AUSTRIA

Gerg-Leitner, Michaela (Skier)
Jachenauer Str 26
Lenggries 83661, GERMANY

Gerhardt, Alben (Musician)
Columbia Artists Mgmt Inc
165 W 57th St
New York, NY 10019, USA

Gerhardt, Don (Athlete, Football Player)
1465 Waterford Dr
Golden Valley, MN 55422-4274, USA

Gerhardt, Jason (Actor)
Hollywood Entertainment
C/O Ron Scott
9255 Sunset BlvdSte 803
Los Angeles, CA 90069, USA

Gerhardt, Rusty (Athlete, Baseball Player)
P.O. Box 426
New London, TX 75682-0426, USA

Gerhart, Bobby (Race Car Driver)
305 Lights St.
Lebanon, PA 17042, USA

Gerhart, Ken (Athlete, Baseball Player)
1603 Ashford Ct
Murfreesboro, TN 37129-5888, USA

Gering, Galen (Actor)
c/o Staff Member *Schumacher Management*
1122 San Vicente Blvd.
Santa Monica, CA 90402, USA

Gering, Jenna (Actor)
c/o Jonathan Bluman *WME (LA)*
9601 Wilshire Blvd Fl 3
Beverly Hills, CA 90210, USA

Gerlach, Gary (Publisher)
Des Moines Register & Tribune
715 Locust St
Des Moines, IA 50309, USA

Gerlach, Jim (Congressman, Politician)
2442 Raybury HOB
Washington, DC 20515, USA

Germain, Dorothy (Athlete, Golfer)
202 Nc Highway 62 W
Randleman, NC 27317, USA

Germain, Eric (Athlete, Hockey Player)
46 Dawes Ave
Hamden, CT 06517, USA

Germain, Paul M (Engineer)
3 Ave de Xhampaubert
Paris 75015, FRANCE

Germain, Stephanie (Producer)
c/o Staff Member *Creative Artists Agency (CAA-LA)*
2000 Ave Of The Stars
Los Angeles, CA 90067, USA

German, Aleksei G (Director)
Marsovo Pole 7 #37
Saint Petersburg 191041, RUSSIA

German, Jammi (Athlete, Football Player)
3702 Highland Ave
Fort Myers, FL 33916, USA

German, Lauren (Actor)
c/o Doug Wald *Anonymous Content (LA)*
3531 Hayden Ave
Culver City, CA 90232, USA

German, William (Editor)
San Francisco Chronicle
Editorial Dept 901 Mission
San Francisco, CA 94103, USA

Germane, Geoffrey J (Engineer)
Brigham Young University
Mechanical Engineering Dept
Provo, UT 84602, USA

Germani, Fernando (Music Group, Musician)
Via Delle Terme Decians 11
Rome, ITALY

Germann, Greg (Actor, Director)
c/o Jeff Golenberg *Collective*
8383 Wilshire Blvd
Suite 1050
Beverly Hills, CA 90211, USA

Germano, Justin (Athlete, Baseball Player)
1006 N E 15th St
Caoe Coral, FL 33909-1455, USA

Germano, Lisa (Music Group, Musician)
Artists & Audience Entertainment
P O Box 35
Pawling, NY 12564, USA

Germany, Reggie (Athlete, Football Player)
246 Haystack Ave
Pataskala, OH 43062-7359, USA

Germany, Willie (Athlete, Football Player)
4401 Pratt St
Omaha, NE 68111, USA

Germar, Manfred (Athlete, Track Athlete)
DLV
Alsfelder Str 27
Darmstadt 642889, GERMANY

Germeshausen, Bernhard (Athlete)
Hinter Dem Salon 39
Schwansee 99195, GERMANY

Germond, Jack
1627 K St NW #1100
Washington, DC 20006

Gernander, Ken (Athlete, Hockey Player)
355 Eddy Glover Blvd
New Britain, CT 06053-2411, USA

Gerner, Robert (Doctor, Misc)
University of California
Neuropsychiatric Institute
Los Angeles, CA 90024, USA

Gernert, David (Publisher)
The Gernet Co
136 E 57th St
New York, NY 10022, USA

Gernert, Dick (Athlete, Baseball Player)
1801 Cambridge Ave APt C12
Reading, PA 19610-2669, USA

Gernhardt, Michael L (Astronaut)
2022 Lakeside Lndg
Seabrook, TX 77586-8301, USA

Gernon, Bruce (Writer)
c/o Staff Member *Llewellyn Worldwide, LTD*
2143 Wooddale Drive
Saint Paul, MN 55125-2989, USA

Gero, Gary D (Cinematographer)
2 McLaren #A
Irvine, CA 92618, USA

Geronimo, Cesar F (Baseball Player)
Tefeda Flo #46
Santo Domingo, DOMINICAN REPUBLIC

Gerrard, Steven (Athlete, Soccer Player)
Liverpool FC
Anfield Road
Liverpool
Merseyside L4 OTH, UNITED KINGDOM

Gerring, Cathy (Athlete, Golfer)
3328 Tarrant Springs Trl
Fort Wayne, IN 46804, USA

Gerry, Alan (Misc)
105 Loomis Rd
Liberty, NY 12754-2710, USA

Gersbach, Carl (Athlete, Football Player)
P.O. Box 433
Devon, PA 19333, USA

Gershon, Gina (Actor)
6 Varick St. #7C
New York, NY 10013, USA

Gerson, Mark (Photographer)
3 Regal Lane Regent's Park
London NW1 7TH, UNITED KINGDOM (UK)

Gerstell, A Frederick (Business Person)
CalMat Co
3200 San Fernando Road
Los Angeles, CA 90065, USA

Gerstner, Lou (Business Person)
IBM Corp
1 North Castle Drive
Armonk, NY 10504, USA

Gertz, Jami (Actor)
c/o Jason Barrett *Alchemy Entertainment*
7024 Melrose Ave
Suite 420
Los Angeles, CA 90038, USA

Gerut, Jody (Athlete, Baseball Player)
623 Rochdale Cir
Lombard, IL 60148, USA

Gerut, Joseph "Jody" (Athlete, Baseball Player)
746 N Cuvler Ave
Oak Park, IL 60302-1775, USA

Gervais, Ricky (Actor, Director, Producer)
c/o Duncan Hayes *United Agents*
12-26 Lexington St
London W1F OLE, UK

Gervin, Derrick (Athlete, Basketball Player)
8147 Babe Ruth St
San Antonio, TX 78240-2902, USA

Gervin, George (Athlete, Basketball Player, Coach)
44 Gervin Pass
Spring Branch, TX 78070-6370, USA

Gerwick, Ben C Jr (Architect, Engineer)
5727 Country Club Dr
Oakland, CA 94618, USA

Geschke, Charles (Business Person)
Adobe Systems
345 Park Ave
San Jose, CA 95110, USA

Gesek, John (Athlete, Football Player)
105 Sand Point Ct
Coppell, TX 75019, USA

G. Eshoo, Anna (Congressman, Politician)
205 Cannon HOB
Washington, DC 20515, USA

Gesinger, Michael (Photographer)
1136 Umatilla Ave
Port Townsend, WA 98368, USA

Gessendorf, Mechthild (Opera Singer)
Columbia Artists Mgmt Inc
165 W 57th St
New York, NY 10019, USA

Gessford, Jim (Athlete, Football Player)
6515 Teton Dr
Lincoln, NE 68510-4123

Gessle, Per (Music Group, Musician)
D&D Mgmt
Lilla Nygatan 19
Stockholm 111 28, SWEDEN

Gest, David (Actor, Producer)
c/o Staff Member *Ultra DJ Management*
42 City Business Centre
Lower Road
London SE16 2XB, UK

Getherall, Joey (Athlete, Football Player)
3105 Las Marias Ave
Hacienda Heights, CA 91745, USA

Gethers, Peter (Writer)
c/o Catherine Brackey *ICM Partners*
(ICM-LA)
10250 Constellation Blvd Fl 7
Los Angeles, CA 90067, USA

Gets, Malcolm (Actor)
c/o Lisa Loosemore *Viking Entertainment*
445 W 23rd St
Suite 1A
New York, NY 10011, USA

Gettelfinger, Ron (Misc)
United Auto Workers
800 E Jefferson Ave
Detroit, MI 48214, USA

Gettinger, Ruby (Reality TV Star)
c/o Glenn Rigberg *Inphenate*
9701 Wilshire Blvd.
10th Floor
Beverly Hills, CA 90212, USA

Gettis, Byron (Athlete, Baseball Player)
6313 Whalen Ave
East Saint Louis, IL 62207-1051, USA

Getty, Andrew
2936 Montcalm Ave.
W. Hollywood, CA 90046

Getty, Balthazar (Actor)
c/o Jeff Golenberg *Collective*
8383 Wilshire Blvd
Suite 1050
Beverly Hills, CA 90211, USA

Getty, Charlie (Athlete, Football Player)
3736 W Morningside St
Springfield, MO 65807, USA

Getty, Gordon
2880 Broadway
San Francisco, CA 94115

Get Up Kids (Music Group)
c/o Staff Member *Creative Artists Agency*
(CAA-LA)
2000 Ave Of The Stars
Los Angeles, CA 90067, USA

Getz, John (Actor)
4124 Wade St
Los Angeles, CA 90066, USA

Getzlaf, Ryan (Athlete, Hockey Player)
The Sports Corporation
2735-10088 102 Ave NW
Attn Rich Winter
Edmonton, AB T5J 2Z1, Canada

Getzlaff, James (Actor)
c/o Staff Member *Douglas Gorman*
Rothacker & Wilhelm Inc
1501 Broadway
Suite 703
New York, NY 10036, USA

Geyer, Georgie Anne (Journalist)
The Plaza Suite 800 25th St NW
Washington, DC 20037-2208, USA

Geyer, Hugh (Music Group)
2218 Ridge Road
McKeesport, PA 15135, USA

Geyer, Renee (Actor, Composer)
c/o Staff Member *The Harbour Agency*
135 Forbes St
Woolloomooloo NSW 2011, Australia

G. Fitzpatrick, Michael (Congressman, Politician)
1224 Longworth HOB
Washington, DC 20515, USA

G. Grimm, Michael (Congressman, Politician)
512 Cannon HOB
Washington, DC 20515, USA

Ghadie, Samia (Actor)
c/o *Granada TV*
Quay Street
Manchester M60 9EA

Ghaffari, Matt (Athlete, Olympic Athlete, Wrestler)
32834 Fox Chappel Ln
Avon Lake, OH 44012-2331, USA

Ghai, Subhash (Bollywood, Director, Filmmaker, Producer)
12 Cliff Tower
Mount Mary Church Road Bandra (W)
Mumbai, MS 400050, INDIA

Ghannouchi, Mohamed (Prime Minister)
Prime Minister's Office
Place du Gouvernement
Tunis, TUNISIA

Ghattas, Stephenos II Cardinal (Religious Leader)
Patriarcat Copte Catholique
BP 69 Rue Ibn Sandar
Cairo 11712, EGYPT

Ghauri, Yasmeen (Model)
c/o Staff Member *Next Model Management (NY)*
15 Watts St
6th Floor
New York, NY 10013, USA

Ghelfi, Tony (Athlete, Baseball Player)
3414 Geneva Ln
La Crosse, WI 54601-8302, USA

Gheorghiu, Angela (Opera Singer)
Levon Sayan
2 Rue du Prieure
Nyon 1260, SWITZERLAND

Gheorghiu, Ion A (Artist)
27-29 Emil Pangratti St
Bucharest, ROMANIA

Ghesquiere, Nicolas (Fashion Designer)
11 Avenue dlena
Balenciaga, Paris 75016, UNITED KINGDOM

Ghiardi, John F L (Economist, Government Official)
12 Park Overlook Court
Bathesda, MD 20817, USA

Ghiglia, Oscar A (Music Group, Musician)
Helfembergstr 14
Basel 4059, SWITZERLAND

Ghiglotti, Marilyn (Actor)
Redrock Entertainment Development
118 South Cordova St
3rd Fl
Burbank, CA 91505, USA

Ghiuselev, Nicola (Opera Singer)
Villa della Pisana 370/B-2
Rome 00163, ITALY

Ghizikis, Phaidon (General, President)
25 Kountouriotou
Pefki 151 21, GREECE

Ghosh, Gautam (Director)
28/1-A Gariahat Road Block 5 #50
Calcutta, WB 700029, INDIA

Ghosh, Partho (Bollywood, Director, Filmmaker, Producer)
D1 Hawa Apartments Opp Holy Spirit
Hospital
Mahakali Caves Road Andheri (E)
Bombay, MS 400 093, INDIA

Ghost, Amanda (Musician)
c/o Staff Member *Basina Recording Company*
PO Box 8121
Pittsburgh, PA 15217-0121, USA

Ghostface, Killa (Music Group, Musician)
Famous Artists Agency
250 W 57th St
New York, NY 10107, USA

Ghostland Observatory (Music Group)
c/o Staff Member *Paradigm (Monterey)*
404 W Franklin St
Monterey, CA 93940, USA

Ghuman Jr, JB (Actor)
c/o Harry Gold *TalentWorks (LA)*
3500 W Olive Ave
Suite 1400
Burbank, CA 91505, USA

Giacconi, Riccardo (Nobel Prize Laureate)
1440 16th St NW #730
Washington, DC 20036-2252, USA

Giacomarro, Ralph (Athlete, Football Player)
3945 Mantle Ridge Dr
Cumming, GA 30041, USA

Giacomin, Edward (Eddie) (Athlete, Hockey Player)
6575 Red Maple Ln
Bloomfield Hills, MI 48301-3225, USA

Giaever, Ivar (Nobel Prize Laureate)
2080 Van Antwerp Road
Schenectady, NY 12309, USA

Giaever, Ivar (Nobel Prize Laureate)
2080 Van Antwerp Rd
Schenectady, NY 12309-1124, USA

Giaffone, Felipe (Race Car Driver)
Conquest Racing
5062 W. 79th St.
Indianapolis, IN 46268, USA

Giallombardo, Bob (Athlete, Baseball Player)
7903 Antique Cir
Waxhaw, NC 28173-7858, USA

Giallonardo, Mario (Athlete, Hockey Player)
94 Queen Mary Ave
Burlington, ON L7T 2G7, Canada

Giamatti, Marcus
c/o Mitchell Stubbs *Mitchell K Stubbs & Assoc (MKS)*
8675 W. Washington Blvd
Suite 203
Culver City, CA 90232, USA

Giamatti, Paul (Actor)
187 Hicks St. #4D
Brooklyn, NY 11201, USA

Giambalvo, Louis (Actor)
c/o Staff Member *Judy Schoen & Associates*
606 N Larchmont Blvd #309
Los Angeles, CA 90004, USA

Giambastiani, Edmund P Jr (Admiral)
Deputy CNO for Resources/Warfare
Requirements
HqUSN
Washington, DC 20350, USA

Giambi, Jason (Athlete, Baseball Player)
34 Isleworth Dr
Henderson, NV 89052-6465, USA

Giambi, Jeremy (Athlete, Baseball Player)
23360 S Power Rd
Gilbert, AZ 85298-8904, USA

Giambra, Joey (Boxer)
7950 W Flamingo Road #1188
Las Vegas, NV 89147, USA

Giambrone, Art (Horse Racer)
398 Brickyard Rd
Freehold, NJ 07728-8414, USA

Giammona, Louie (Athlete, Football Player)
525 Parrish St
Philadelphia, PA 19123, USA

Gian, Joey (Musician)
Joey Gian Entertainment
13351 D Riverside Dr #294
Sherman Oaks, CA 91423, USA

Gian, Joseph
8271 Melrose Ave. #110
Los Angeles, CA 90046

Gianas, Maria (Stylist)
c/o Staff Member *Ford Models (Chicago)*
311 W Superior St
Chicago, IL 60654, USA

Giancanelli, Hal (Athlete, Football Player)
2227 Portola Ln
Westlake Village, CA 91361, USA

Giancola, Sammi (Reality TV Star)
c/o Sal Bonaventura *CEG Talent*
251 W. 39th St
7th Floor
New York, NY 10011, USA

Gianelli, John (Athlete, Basketball Player)
PO Box 1097
Pinecrest, CA 95364-0097, USA

Giannelli, Ray (Athlete, Baseball Player)
56 E Saltaire Rd
Lindenhurst, NY 11757-6829, USA

Giannini, Andriano (Actor)
c/o Lindy King *United Agents*
12-26 Lexington St
London W1F OLE, UK

Giannini, Giancario (Actor)
Via Salaria 292
Rome 00199, ITALY

Giannoulas, Ted (Commentator)
6549 Mission Gorge Rd
Ste 247
San Diego, CA 92120-2306, USA

Gianopoulos, David (Actor)
c/o Staff Member *GVA Talent Agency Inc*
8981 Sunset Blvd.
Suite 101
Los Angeles, CA 90069, USA

Gianulias, Nicole (Nikki) (Bowler)
Ladies Professional Bowling Tour
7200 Harrison Ave #7171
Rockford, IL 61112, USA

Giaquinto, Nick (Athlete, Football Player)
316 3rd Ave
Stratford, CT 06615, USA

Giarraputo, Jack (Producer, Writer)
c/o Staff Member *Happy Madison Productions*
10202 W Washington Blvd
Judy Garland Bldg
Culver City, CA 90232, USA

Giarratano, Tony (Athlete, Baseball Player)
14 Skytop Gdns Apt 6
Parlin, NJ 08859-2118, USA

Gibara, Samir (Business Person)
Goodyear Tire & Rubber
1144 W Market St
Akron, OH 44316, USA

Gibb, Barry (Musician, Songwriter)
c/o Paul Bloch *Rogers & Cowan PR (LA)*
Pacific Design Center
8687 Melrose Ave, 7th Floor
West Hollywood, CA 90069, USA

Gibb, Cynthia (Actor)
c/o Scott Hart *Scott Hart Entertainment*
14622 Ventura Blvd
#746
Sherman Oaks, CA 91403, USA

Gibb, Donald (Actor)
Ashby/Rojo Entertainment
1485 South Beverly Dr
Los Angeles, CA 90035, USA

Gibberd, Frederick (Architect)
House Marsh Lane Old Harlow
Essex CM17 0NA, UNITED KINGDOM
(UK)

Gibbon, Joe (Athlete, Baseball Player)
26 County Road 24142
Newton, MS 39345-8946, USA

Gibbons, Beth (Music Group, Songwriter, Writer)
Fruit
Saga Center 326 Kensal Road
London W10 5BZ, UNITED KINGDOM
(UK)

Gibbons, Billy (Music Group, Musician)
c/o Rick Canny *Sanctuary Artist Management*
8750 Wilshire Blvd Ste 200
Beverly Hills, CA 90211, USA

Gibbons, Brian (Athlete, Baseball Player)
51788 Whitestale Lane
South Bend, IN 46628-1242, USA

Gibbons, Brian (Athlete, Hockey Player)
4 Twillingate Pl
St. John's, NL AlE 3R4, Canada

Gibbons, James F (Engineer)
15 Red Berry Ridge
Portola Valley, CA 94028-8077, USA

Gibbons, Jay (Athlete, Baseball Player)
29408 Malibu View Ct
Agoura Hills, CA 91301-6237, USA

Gibbons, Jim (Athlete, Football Player)
891 Valley Rd
Carbondale, CO 81623-9712, USA

Gibbons, John (Athlete, Baseball Player, Coach)
3602 Hunters Quail
San Antonio, TX 78230-2052, USA

Gibbons, John D (Prime Minister)
Leeward 5 Leeside Dr
Pembroke HM 05, BERMUDA

Gibbons, Kaye (Writer)
c/o Lynn Pleshette *Lynn Pleshette Literary Agency*
2700 N. Beachwood Dr.
Los Angeles, CA 90068, USA

Gibbons, Leeza (Entertainer, Producer)
c/o Staff Member *Leeza Gibbons Enterprises*
11925 Wilshire Blvd #300
Los Angeles, CA 90025, USA

Gibbons, Tim (Producer)
c/o Staff Member *ICM Partners (ICM-LA)*
10250 Constellation Blvd Fl 7
Los Angeles, CA 90067, USA

Gibbons, Walter (Athlete, Baseball Player)
103 E North St
Tampa, FL 33604-6156, USA

Gibbs, Barry (Athlete, Hockey Player)
6176 Stinson Way NW
Edmonton, AB T6R OK31967, Canada

Gibbs, Bob (Congressman, Politician)
329 Cannon HOB
Washington, DC 20515, USA

Gibbs, Connor (Actor)
c/o Geoff Cheddy *Brillstein Entertainment Partners*
9150 Wilshire Blvd #350
Beverly Hills, CA 90212, USA

Gibbs, Coy (Race Car Driver)
c/o Staff Member *NASCAR*
1801 Speedway Blvd
Daytona Beach, FL 32015, USA

Gibbs, H Jarrell (Business Person)
Texas Utilities Co
Energy Plaza 1601 Bryan St
Dallas, TX 75201, USA

Gibbs, Jake (Athlete, Baseball Player)
223 Saint Andrews Cir
Oxford, MS 38655-2518, USA

Gibbs, Joe (Athlete, Football Coach, Football Player, Race Car Driver)
Joe Gibbs Racing
19122 Peninsula Point Dr.
Cornelius, NC 2803-7603, USA

Gibbs, Joe (Athlete, Football Player)
19133 Peninsula Point Dr
Cornelius, NC 28031-7603, USA

Gibbs, Lawrence B (Government Official)
Miller & Chevaliar
655 15th St NW #900
Washington, DC 20005, USA

Gibbs, L Richard (Cricketer)
276 Republic Park
Peter's Hall EBD, GUYANA

Gibbs, Marla (Actor, Music Group)
c/o Robert Depp *Beverly Hecht Agency*
3500 W Olive Ave
Suite 1180
Burbank, CA 91505, USA

Gibbs, Martin (Biologist, Scientist)
5 Arbor Ct
Burlington, MA 01803-3800, USA

Gibbs, Mickey (Race Car Driver)
3 Grandview Circle
Gadsden, AL 35905, USA

Gibbs, Pat (Athlete, Football Player)
4835 Corley St
Beaumont, TX 77707, USA

Gibbs, Patt (Misc)
Flght Attendants Assn
1275 K St NW #500
Washington, DC 20005, USA

Gibbs, Sonny (Athlete, Football Player)
2708 Halbert St
Fort Worth, TX 76112-5531, USA

Gibbs, Terri (Musician, Songwriter)
1439 Clary Cut Rd
Appling, GA 30802, USA

Gibbs, Terry (Music Group, Musician)
Thomas Cassidy
11761 E Speedway Blvd
Tucson, AZ 85748, USA

Gibbs, Timothy (Actor)
c/o Julia Buchwald *Buchwald/Fortitude (LA)*
6500 Wilshire Blvd
Suite 2200
Los Angeles, CA 90048, USA

Gibgot, Adam (Writer)
c/o Adriana Alberghetti *WME (LA)*
9601 Wilshire Blvd Fl 3
Beverly Hills, CA 90210, USA

Giblett, Eloise R (Doctor, Misc)
6533 53rd St NE
Seattle, WA 98115, USA

Giblin, Robert (Athlete, Football Player)
2818 Reynolds Ln
Port Neches, TX 77651, USA

Gibney, Rebecca (Actor)
128 Rupert St.
Collingwood, Vic. 3066, AUSTRALIA

Gibney, Susan (Actor)
c/o Matthew Lesher *Insight*
1134 S Cloverdale Ave
Los Angeles, CA 90019, USA

Gibralter, Steve (Athlete, Baseball Player)
2512 Crooked Crk
Megjuite, TX 75181-4214, USA

Gibraltor, Steve (Athlete, Baseball Player)
3651 Asbury St
Dallas, TX 75205, USA

Gibran, Kahill (Artist, Misc)
160 W Canton St
Boston, MA 02118, USA

Gibson, Aaron (Athlete, Football Player)
1777 Timber Creek Rd Apt 2122
Flower Mound, TX 75028-7342, USA

Gibson, Andy (Musician)
c/o Staff Member *Curb Records (Nashville)*
48 Music Sq E
Nashville, TN 37203, USA

Gibson, Antonio (Athlete, Football Player)
2320 Jaguar Dr
Apt 502
Bryan, TX 77807, USA

Gibson, Bob (Athlete, Basketball Player)
1717 S 56th St
Omaha, NE 68106-2215, USA

Gibson, Bob (Athlete, Baseball Player)
1717 S 56th St
Omaha, NE 68106-2215, USA

Gibson, Bob (Athlete, Baseball Player)
215 Bellevue Blvd S
Bellevue, NE 68005, USA

Gibson, Charles (Television Host)
c/o Staff Member *ABC News*
77 W 66th St
3rd Floor
New York, NY 10023, USA

Gibson, Claude (Athlete, Football Player)
47 Gladstone Rd
Asheville, NC 28805, USA

Gibson, Damon (Athlete, Football Player)
4332 Dell Rd
Apt J
Lansing, MI 48911-8126, USA

Gibson, Deborah (Debbie) (Actor, Musician)
8491 W Sunset Blvd #1650
W Hollywood, CA 90069

Gibson, Dennis (Athlete, Football Player)
6900 NE 11th Ct
Ankeny, IA 50023, USA

Gibson, Derrick (Athlete, Football Player)
303 Avenue O NW
Winter Haven, FL 33881-4906, USA

Gibson, Derrick (Athlete, Baseball Player)
138 Buckeye Loop Rd
Winter Haven, FL 33881, USA

Gibson, Doug (Athlete, Hockey Player)
1220 Cartier Blvd
Peterborough, ON K9H 6S1, Canada

Gibson, Edward G (Astronaut)
Aviation Management Services
1658 S Litchfield Road
Goodyear, AZ 85338, USA

Gibson, Edward G Dr (Astronaut)
34022 N 85th St
Scottsdale, AZ 85266-1345, USA

Gibson, Ellie (Athlete, Golfer)
35705 N 29th Ln
Phoenix, AZ 85086, USA

Gibson, Ernest (Athlete, Football Player)
1749 Kinsman Cv
Marietta, GA 30062-8173, USA

Gibson, Everett K Jr (Geophysicist, Misc, Physicist)
1015 Trowbridge Dr
Houston, TX 77062, USA

Gibson, Fred (Athlete, Golfer)
2006 Avenel St
Orlando, FL 32828, USA

Gibson, Greg (Baseball Player)
3628 Briarwood Dr
Catlettsburg, KY 41129-9298, USA

Gibson, Greg (Athlete, Baseball Player)
20305 Country Club Dr
Cattlesburg, KY 41129-8602, USA

Gibson, Janice (Athlete, Golfer)
9747 S Granite Ave
Tulsa, OK 74137, USA

Gibson, John (Correspondent)
c/o Staff Member *Fox News Channel (NY)*
1211 Ave of the Americas
Level C1
New York, NY 10036-8701, USA

Gibson, Kelly (Athlete, Golfer)
700 S Peters St
Apt 419
New Orleans, LA 70130, USA

Gibson, Kirk (Athlete, Baseball Player)
33 Sunset Ln
Grosse Pointe Farms, MI 48236-3730,
USA

Gibson, Laurie-Anne (Laurieann)
(Choreographer)
c/o Stephanie Molina *Rogers & Cowan PR (LA)*
Pacific Design Center
8687 Melrose Ave, 7th Floor
West Hollywood, CA 90069, USA

Gibson, Leah (Actor)
c/o Kim Matuka *Online Talent Group*
Prefers to be contacted via email or
telephone
Los Angeles, CA 90069, USA

Gibson, Mark (Race Car Driver)
Mark Gibson Racing
308 Wages Rd.
Auburn, GA 30011-2856, USA

Gibson, Mel (Actor, Director, Producer)
c/o Alan Nierob *Rogers & Cowan PR (LA)*
Pacific Design Center
8687 Melrose Ave, 7th Floor
West Hollywood, CA 90069, USA

Gibson, Oliver (Athlete, Football Player)
1448 E 52nd St
#406
Chicago, IL 60615, USA

Gibson, Paul (Athlete, Baseball Player)
23421 Water Cir
Boca Raton, FL 33486-8547, USA

Gibson, Quentin H (Biologist, Misc)
3 Woods End Road
Etna, NH 03750, USA

Gibson, Ralph (Photographer)
331 W Broadway
New York, NY 10013-2265, USA

Gibson, Reginald W (Judge)
US Claims Court
717 Madison Place NW
Washington, DC 20439, USA

Gibson, Robert L
1709 Shagbark Trail
Murfreesboro, TN 37130, USA

Gibson, Robert L Captain (Astronaut)
1709 Shagbark Trl
Murfreesboro, TN 37130-1136, USA

Gibson, Robert L (Hoot) (Astronaut)
1709 Shagbark Trail
Murfreesboro, TN 37130, USA

Gibson, Roy (Scientist)
Residence Les Hesperides 51 Allee Jean
de Be ins
Montpellier F-34000, France

Gibson, Russ (Athlete)
495 Gardners Neck Rd
Swansea, MA 02777, USA

Gibson, Suzanne (Stylist)
1608 Amberwood Dr
#6
South Pasadena, CA 91030, USA

Gibson, Thomas (Actor, Director)
215 W Kings Hwy
San Antonio, TX 78212, USA

Gibson, Tyrese (Actor, Musician,
Producer)
c/o Jerome Martin *Jerome Martin
Management*
1655 N Cherokee Ave
2nd Floor
Hollywood, CA 90028, USA

Gibson, William (Writer)
General Delivery
Stockbridge, MA 01262-9999, USA

Gick, George (Athlete, Baseball Player)
875 Elston Rd
Lafayette, IN 47909, USA

Gidada, Negasso (President)
President's Office
P O Box 5707
Addis Ababa, ETHIOPIA

Giddish, Kelli (Actor)
c/o Jean-Louis Diamonika *One
Entertainment (NY)*
12 W 57th St
Penthouse
New York, NY 10019, USA

Gideon, Brett (Athlete, Baseball Player)
P.O. Box 822
Georgetown, TX 78627-0822, USA

Gideon, Jim (Athlete, Baseball Player)
2509 McCallum Dr
Austin, TX 78703-2520, USA

Gideon, Raynold (Actor, Writer)
3524 Multiview Dr
Los Angeles, CA 90068, USA

Gidley, Pamela (Actor)
c/o Tom Harrison *Diverse Talent Group*
9911 W Pico Blvd Ste 340W
Los Angeles, CA 90035, USA

Gidzenko, Yuri P (Astronaut, Misc)
Potchta Kosmonavtov
Moskovskoi Oblasti
Syvisdny Goroduk 141160, RUSSIA

Gielen, Michael A (Composer, Conductor)
Hans Ulrich Schmid
Postfach 1617
Hanover 30016, GERMANY

Giella, Joseph (Cartoonist)
191 Morris Dr
East Meadow, NY 11554, USA

Gien, Pamela (Actor, Writer)
c/o Heather Schroder *ICM Partners
(ICM-NY)*
730 Fifth Ave
New York, NY 10019, USA

Gienger, Eberhard
Friedrich-Schaal-Str. 53
Tubingen, GERMANY D-72074

Gierasch, Stefan (Actor)
c/o Staff Member *Brandon's Commercials
Unlimited*
8383 Wilshire Blvd
Suite 850
Beverly Hills, CA 90211, USA

Gierer, Vincent A Jr (Business Person)
UST Inc
100 W Putnam Ave
Greenwich, CT 06830, USA

Gierowski, Stefan (Artist)
Ul Gagarina 15 m 97
Warsaw 00-753, POLAND

Giesler, Jon (Athlete, Football Player)
129 Umbrella Pl
Jupiter, FL 33458, USA

Giessinger, Andrew (Athlete, Football
Player)
1667 Union Ave
Barberton, OH 44203, USA

Gietzen, Pam (Athlete, Golfer)
603 Woodland West Dr
Woodway, TX 76712, USA

Giffin, Lee (Athlete, Hockey Player)
RR 4
Blenheim, ON N0P 1A0, Canada

Gifford, Frank N (Athlete, Football Player,
Sportscaster)
Lambchop Productions PO Box 275
Cos Cob, CT 06807-0275, USA

Gifford, Gloria (Actor)
Schiowitz/Clay/Rose
1680 N Vine St #1016
Los Angeles, CA 90028, USA

Gifford, Kathie Lee (Correspondent,
Entertainer)
c/o Staff Member *Today Show, The*
30 Rockefeller Plz
New York, NY 10112, USA

Giffords, Gabrielle (Congressman,
Politician)
1030 Longworth HOB
Washington, DC 20515, USA

Gift, Roland (Actor, Music Group)
Primary Talent Int'l
1-12 Petonville Road
London N1 9PL, UNITED KINGDOM
(UK)

Gigandet, Cam (Actor)
c/o Matt Luber *Luber Roklin Management*
8530 Wilshire Blvd
6th Floor
Beverly Hills, CA 90211, USA

Giggie, Bob (Athlete, Baseball Player)
8 Royal Lake Dr Apt 3
Braintree, MA 02184-5457, USA

Gigli, Romeo (Designer, Fashion
Designer)
37 W 57th St #900
New York, NY 10019, USA

Gigliotti, Lou (Race Car Driver)
LG Motorsports
4314 Action St.
Garland, TX 75042, USA

Gigon, Norm (Athlete, Baseball Player)
2503 Rio Vista Dr
Mahwah, NJ 07430-4506, USA

Gigot, Paul (Journalist)
Wall Street Journal
Editorial Dept 200 Liberty St
New York, NY 10281, USA

Giguere, Jean-Sebastien (Athlete, Hockey
Player)
2066 Port Bristol Cir
Newport Beach, CA 92660, USA

Giguere, Russ (Music Group, Musician)
Variety Artists
1924 Spring St
Paso Robles, CA 93446, USA

Giheno, John (President)
Prime Minister's Office
Marera Hau
Port Moresby, PAPUA NEW GUINEA

Gil, Ariadna (Actor)
Cineart
36 Rue de Ponthieu
Paris 75008, FRANCE

Gil, Benii (Athlete, Baseball Player)
11712 Wild Pear Ln
Fort Worth, TX 76244-8815, USA

Gil, Geronimo (Athlete, Baseball Player)
c/o Staff Member *Baltimore Orioles*
333 W Camden St
Baltimore, MD 21201, USA

Gil, Gilberto (Music Group, Songwriter,
Writer)
BPR
36 Como St Ramford
Essex RM 7 7DR, UNITED KINGDOM
(UK)

Gil, Gus (Athlete, Baseball Player)
2240 SW 42nd Ter
Fort Lauderdale, FL 33317-6618, USA

Gil, R Benjamin (Benji) (Athlete, Baseball
Player)
504 Unbridled Ln
Keller, TX 76248-8724, USA

Gilbert, Brad
888 17th St. NW #1200
Washington, DC 20006

Gilbert, Bradley (Brad) (Tennis Player)
ProServe
1101 Woodrow Wilson Blvd #1800
Arlington, VA 22209, USA

Gilbert, Brantley (Musician)
c/o Staff Member *Paradigm (Monterey)*
404 W Franklin St
Monterey, CA 93940, USA

Gilbert, Buddy (Athlete, Baseball Player)
1913 Belcaro Dr
Knoxville, TN 37918-3709, USA

Gilbert, Chris (Athlete, Football Player)
6619 Blue Hills Rd
Houston, TX 77069-2412, USA

Gilbert, Daren (Athlete, Football Player)
13926 Villanova Ave
Chino, CA 91710, USA

Gilbert, David (Cartoonist)
c/o Staff Member *King Features
Syndication*
300 W 57th St
15th Floor
New York, NY 10019-5238, USA

Gilbert, Ed (Athlete, Hockey Player)
657 Jacksonville Rd
Warminster, PA 18974-1508, USA

Gilbert, Elizabeth (Writer)
c/o Sarah Chalfant *The Andrew Wylie
Agency*
250 W 57th St
Suite 2114
New York, NY 10107, USA

Gilbert, Elsie
1016 N. Orange Grove #4
Los Angeles, CA 90046

Gilbert, Felix (Historian)
918 Bluffwood Dr
Iowa City, IA 52245, USA

Gilbert, Freddie (Athlete, Football Player)
110 Camden Rd
Griffin, GA 30223-1677, USA

Gilbert, Gary (Producer)
c/o Staff Member *Gilbert Films*
9255 Sunset Blvd
Suite 711
West Hollywood, CA 90069, USA

Gilbert, Gibby (Athlete, Golfer)
7070 Sunset Mountain Dr
Chattanooga, TN 37421, USA

Gilbert, Gilles (Athlete, Hockey Player)
9964 Rue de la Farriniere
Quebec, QC G2K 1L7, Canada

Gilbert, Greg (Athlete, Coach, Hockey Player)
c/o Staff Member *Toronto Marlies*
100 Princes Blvd
Toronto, ON M6K 3C3, Canada

Gilbert, J Freeman (Geophysicist, Physicist)
780 Kalamath Dr
Del Mar, CA 92014, USA

Gilbert, Joe (Athlete, Baseball Player)
512 W Martin Luther King Blvd
Jasper, TX 75951-2527, USA

Gilbert, Kenneth A (Music Group, Musician)
23 Cloitre Notre-Dame
Chartres 28000, FRANCE

Gilbert, Lawrence I (Biologist)
1105 Phils Creek Road
Chapel Hill, NC 27516, USA

Gilbert, Lewis (Director, Producer)
19 Blvd de Suisse
Monte Carlo, MONACO

Gilbert, Lewis (Athlete, Football Player)
6331 SW 1st St
Plantation, FL 33317, USA

Gilbert, Mark (Athlete, Baseball Player)
2340 NW 45th St
Boca Raton, FL 33431-8437, USA

Gilbert, Martin J (Historian)
Merton College
Oxford OX1 4JD, UNITED KINGDOM (UK)

Gilbert, Melissa (Actor)
18600 Ringling St
Tarzana, CA 91356, USA

Gilbert, O'Neill (Athlete, Coach, Football Coach, Football Player)
460 Great Circle Rd
Nashville, TN 37228, USA

Gilbert, Peter (Director)
Innovative Artists
1505 10th St
Santa Monica, CA 90401, USA

Gilbert, Richard W (Publisher)
Des Moines Register & Tribune
715 Locust St
Des Moines, IA 50309, USA

Gilbert, Rod
New York Rangers 2 Penn Plz Fl 22
Attn: Director, Special Projects
New York, NY 10121-2299, USA

Gilbert, Rodrique G (Rod) (Athlete, Hockey Player)
52 E End Ave
Apt 33-A
New York, NY 10028, USA

Gilbert, Ronnie (Music Group)
Donna Korones Mgmt
P O Box 8388
Berkeley, CA 94707, USA

Gilbert, Sara (Actor)
1355 Devlin Dr
West Hollywood, CA 90069, USA

Gilbert, Sean (Athlete, Football Player)
7912 Baltusrol Ln
Charlotte, NC 28210, USA

Gilbert, Shawn (Athlete, Baseball Player)
9656 Kathleen Dr
Cypress, CA 90630-4023, USA

Gilbert, Simon (Music Group, Musician)
Interceptor Enterprises
98 White Lion St
London N1 9PF, UNITED KINGDOM (UK)

Gilbert, S J Sr (Religious Leader)
Baptist Convention of America
6717 Centennial Blvd
Nashville, TN 37209, USA

Gilbert, Walter (Nobel Prize Laureate)
15 Gray Gardens W
Cambridge, MA 02138-2311, USA

Gilberto, Astrud (Music Group)
Absolute Artists
530 Howard Ave #200
San Francisco, CA 94105, USA

Gilberto, Bebel (Music Group)
Miracle Prestige
1 Water Lane Camden Town
London NW1 8NZ, UNITED KINGDOM (UK)

Gilbertson, Bob (Race Car Driver)
2250 Toomey Ave.
Charlotte, NC 28203, USA

Gilbertson, Harrison (Actor)
c/o Laina Cohn *Laina Cohn Management*
15066 Sutton St
Sherman Oaks, CA 91403, USA

Gilbertson, Keith (Coach, Football Coach)
University of Washington
Athletic Dept
Seattle, WA 98195, USA

Gilbertson, Stan (Athlete, Hockey Player)
2924 Mosswood Dr
Lodi, CA 95242-2051, USA

Gilbreath, Rod (Athlete, Baseball Player)
1438 Ridgeland Way SW
Lilburn, GA 30047-4352, USA

Gilbreth, Bill (Athlete, Baseball Player)
709 Gary Ln
Abilene, TX 79601-5537, USA

Gilbride, Kevin (Athlete, Coach, Football Player)
3400 S Water St
Pittsburgh, PA 15203, USA

Gilburg, Tom (Athlete, Football Player)
35 Hess Blvd
Lancaster, PA 17601-4043, USA

Gilchrist, Adam (Athlete, Cricketer)
c/o Staff Member *Western Australia Cricket Association*
WACA Ground
P.O. Box 6045
East Perth, WA 6892, Australia

Gilchrist, Brent (Athlete, Hockey Player)
Bank of Montreal
200-3200 30 Ave
Vernon, BC V1T 2C5, Canada

Gilchrist, Guy (Cartoonist)
20 Bristol Dr
Canton, CT 06019-2214, USA

Gilchrist, Jeanne (Baseball Player)
218-67 Miner Street
New Westminster, BC V3L 5N5, CANADA

Gilchrist, Keir (Actor)
c/o Willie Mercer *Thruline Entertainment*
9250 Wilshire Blvd
Ground Fl
Beverly Hills, CA 90212, USA

Gilchrist, Pual R (Religious Leader)
Presbyterian Church in America
1862 Century Place
Atlanta, GA 30345, USA

Gilder, Bob (Athlete, Golfer)
1977 NW Bonney Dr
Corvallis, OR 97330, USA

Gilder, George F (Economist, Writer)
Main Road
Tyringham, MA 01264, USA

Gildon, Jason (Athlete, Football Player)
1562 Barrington Dr
Wexford, PA 15090, USA

Gile, Don (Athlete, Baseball Player)
570 Seahorse Ln
Redwood City, CA 94065-1223, USA

Giles, Bill (Commentator)
Philadelphia Phillies
1755 Cedar Ln
Vilanova, PA 19085-2018, USA

Giles, Brian (Athlete, Baseball Player)
136 Coronation Ave
Las Vegas, NV 89123-1153, USA

Giles, Curt (Athlete, Hockey Player)
5225 Grandview Sq
Apt 402
Minneapolis, MN 55436, USA

Giles, Jimmie (Athlete, Football Player)
3959 Van Dyke Rd #298
Lutz, FL 33558, USA

Giles, Marcus (Athlete, Baseball Player)
2285 Marquand Ct
Alpine, CA 91901-6201, USA

Giles, Nancy (Actor)
12047 178th St
Jamaica, NY 11434, USA

Giles, Sandra
350 N. Crescent Dr.
Beverly Hills, CA 90210-4847

Giles, Selina (Actor)
Edward Hill Management
Dolphin House
2-5 Manchester St
BN2 1TF, United Kingdom

Giletti, Alain (Figure Skater)
103 Place de L'Eglise
Chamonix 74400, FRANCE

Gilfillan, Jason (Athlete, Baseball Player)
153 Gilfillan Rd
Blacksburg, SC 29702-8521, USA

Gilford, David (Athlete, Golfer)
Andrew Murray
19 Higher Lane
Lymm Cheshire WA13 0AR, United Kingdom

Gilford, Zach (Actor)
c/o Charles Mastropietro *Circle of Confusion (NY)*
270 Lafayette St
Suite 402
New York, NY 10012, USA

Gilfry, Rodney (Opera Singer)
Columbia Artists Mgmt Inc
165 W 57th St
New York, NY 10019, USA

Gilgorov, Kiro (President)
President's Office
Skopje, MACEDONIA

Gilhen, Randy (Athlete, Hockey Player)
c/o Staff Member *Manitoba Moose*
260 Hargrave St
Winnipeg, MB R3C 5S5, Canada

Gilk, Shelley (Athlete, Golfer)
10537 Toledo Dr N
Minneapolis, MN 55443, USA

Gilkey, Bernard (Athlete, Baseball Player)
2200 Dunhill Way Ct
Chesterfield, MO 63005-4511, USA

Gill, George N (Publisher)
Louisville Courier-Journal & Times
525 W Broadway
Louisville, KY 40202, USA

Gill, Hal (Athlete, Hockey Player)
11 Reiling Pond Rd
Lincoln, MA 01773-2311, USA

Gill, Janis (Music Group)
Monty Hitchcock Mgmt
5101 Overton Road
Nashville, TN 37220, USA

Gill, Johnny (Music Group, Musician, Songwriter, Writer)
4924 Balboa Blvd #366
Encino, CA 91316, USA

Gill, Johnny Ray (Actor)
c/o Jordyn Palos *Persona PR*
8840 Wilshire Blvd
Suite 212
Beverly Hills, CA 90211, USA

Gill, Kendall (Athlete, Basketball Player)
c/o Staff Member *Milwaukee Bucks*
1001 North 4th Street
Milwaukee, WI 53203

Gill, Priya (Actor, Bollywood)
606 Nestle - B 4th Cross Road
Lokhandwala Complex Andheri (W)
Mumbai, MS 400058, INDIA

Gill, Tanya (Stylist)
c/o Staff Member *Solo Artists*
2148 Federal Ave
Los Angeles, CA 90025, USA

Gill, Thea (Actor)
c/o Cynthia Campos-Greenberg *Anthem Entertainment*
9595 Wilshire Blvd
Suite 900
Los Angeles, CA 90212-2509, USA

Gill, Tim (Business Person, Designer, Engineer)
Gill Foundation
2215 Market St
Denver, CO 80205, USA

Gill, Todd (Athlete, Hockey Player)
c/o Staff Member *Brockville Braves*
1030 Montrose St
Brockville, ON K6V 7G1, Canada

Gill, Tonya (Athlete, Golfer)
3655 Habersham Rd NE
Apt B2229
Atlanta, GA 30305, USA

Gill, Vince (Musician, Songwriter)
c/o Larry Fitzgerald *Fitzgerald Hartley Co*
(Nashville)
1908 Wedgewood Ave
Nashville, TN 37212, USA

Gill, William A Jr (Government Official,
Misc)
15975 Cove Lane
Dumfries, VA 22026, USA

Gillan, Ian (Musician)
Miracle Prestige
1 Water Lane
Camden Town
London NW1 8N2, UNITED KINGDOM
(UK)

Gillanders, David (Athlete, Olympic
Athlete, Swimmer)
1617 Briarwood Dr
Jonesboro, AR 72401-4632, USA

Gillaspie, Conor (Athlete, Baseball Player)
5601 Pacific St
Omaha, NE 68106-1640, USA

Gillbreath, Rod (Baseball Player)
Atlanta Braves
1438 Ridgeland Way SW
Lilbum, GA 30047 4352, USA

Gillen, Aidan (Actor)
c/o Leanne Coronel *Coronel Group*
1100 Glendon Ave
17th Floor
Los Angeles, CA 90046, USA

Gillen, Don (Athlete, Hockey Player)
21 Capilano Dr
Saskatoon, SK S7K 4A4, Canada

Giller, Walter
Via Tamporiva 26
Castagnola, SWITZERLAND CH-6976

Gilles, Daniel (Writer)
161 Ave Churchill
Brussels 1180, BELGIUM

Gilles, Tom (Athlete, Baseball Player)
14615 W Southern St
Princeville, IL 61559-9375, USA

Gillespie, Ann (Actor)
Greene Assoc
7080 Hollywood Blvd #1017
Los Angeles, CA 90028, USA

Gillespie, Charles A Jr (Diplomat)
Scowcroft Group
900 17th St #500
Washington, DC 20006, USA

Gillespie, Cole (Athlete, Baseball Player)
5455 Summit St
West Linn, OR 97068-2822, USA

Gillespie, Craig (Director)
c/o Simon Millar *Rumble Media*
1620 Broadway
Santa Monica, CA 90403, USA

Gillespie, Darlene (Actor)
2117 Bermuda Dunes Pl
Oxnard, CA 93036, USA

Gillespie, Jack (Athlete, Basketball Player)
600 6th Avenue North
Great Falls, MT 59401-2342, USA

Gillespie, Rhondda (Music Group,
Musician)
2 Princess Road
Saint Leonards-on-Sea
East Sussex TN37 6EL, UNITED
KINGDOM (UK)

Gillespie, Robert (Financier)
KeyCorp
127 Public Square
Cleveland, OH 44114, USA

Gillespie, Ronald J (Doctor, Misc)
McMaster University
Chemistry Dept
Hamilton, ON L8S 4M1, CANADA

Gillespie, Ronald J Dr (Scientist)
McMaster University 20-1280 Main St W
Attn: Chemistry Dept
Hamilton, ON L8S 4L8, CANADA

Gillespie, Willie (Athlete, Football Player)
102 Aztec Dr
Starkville, MS 39759-2006, USA

Gillette (Musician)
c/o Staff Member *Diva Central Inc*
7510 W Sunset Blvd Ste 1445
Los Angees, CA 90046, USA

Gillette, Anita (Actor)
501 S Beverly Dr #3
Beverly Hills, CA 90212, USA

Gillette, Walker (Athlete, Football Player)
401 N College Dr
Franklin, VA 23851, USA

Gilley, J Wade (Educator)
University of Tennessee
President's Office
Knoxville, TN 37996, USA

Gilley, Mickey (Music Group, Songwriter,
Writer)
Gilley's Interests
PO Box 1242
Pasadena, TX 77501, USA

Gilliam, Burton
1427 Tascosa Ct.
Allen, TX 75013

Gilliam, Dondre (Athlete, Football Player)
6858 Sturbridge Dr Apt D
Baltimore, MD 21234-7426, USA

Gilliam, Elijah (Baseball Player)
Birmingham Black Barons
1617 5th Ave N
Birmingham, AL 35203-1953, USA

Gilliam, John (Athlete, Football Player)
4045 Moheb St SW
Atlanta, GA 30331-6418, USA

Gilliam, Jon (Athlete, Football Player)
440 S Walnut Grove Rd
Midlothian, TX 76065-6206, USA

Gilliam, Seth (Actor)
c/o Jason Gutman *Gersh (NY)*
41 Madison Ave
New York, NY 10010, USA

Gilliam, Terry (Actor, Animator, Writer)
Old Hall South Grove
Highgate
London N6 6BP, UNITED KINGDOM
(UK)

Gilliand, David (Race Car Driver)
7777 Woodland Dr.
Indianapolis, IN 46278, USA

Gilliand, Herman (Baseball Player)
Chicago Cubs
1833 Kern Mountain Way
Antioch, CA 94531 7497, USA

Gilliard, Cory (Athlete, Football Player)
3951 Zinsle Ave
Cincinnati, OH 45213-2348, USA

Gilliatt, Penelope
31 Chester Sq.
London, ENGLAND SW1W 9HT

Gillick, Pat (Commentator)
3011 W Garfield St
Seattle, WA 98199-4243, USA

Gillie, Nick (Producer)
c/o Staff Member *Metropolitan (MTA)*
4526 Wilshire Blvd
Los Angeles, CA 90010, USA

Gillies, Ben (Music Group, Musician)
John Watson Mgmt
P O Box 281
Sunny Hills, NSW 2010, AUSTRALIA

Gillies, Clark (Athlete, Hockey Player)
17 Pinta Ct
Greenlawn, NY 11740-2314, USA

Gillies, Daniel (Actor, Director, Writer)
c/o Ben Levine *Kritzer Levine Wilkins
Entertainment (KLWG)*
11872 La Grange Ave
1st Floor
Los Angeles, CA 90025, USA

Gillies, Elizabeth (Actor)
c/o Amy Zvi *Thruline Entertainment*
9250 Wilshire Blvd
Ground Fl
Beverly Hills, CA 90212, USA

Gilliford, Paul (Athlete, Baseball Player)
7 Woodland Dr
Malvern, PA 19355-3308, USA

Gillig, Tony (Race Car Driver)
Gillig Motorsports
Box 823
Lake Zurich, IL 60047, USA

Gilligan, Carol (Educator)
Harvard University
Gender Studies Dept
Cambridge, MA 02138, USA

Gilligan, John (Politician)
3618 Hedgerow Ln
Cincinnati, Oh 45220-1508, USA

Gillilan, William J III (Business Person)
Centex Corp
P O Box 199000
Dallas, TX 75219, USA

Gilliland, Butch (Race Car Driver)
Gilliland Racing
912 N. Anaheim
Anaheim, CA 92805, USA

Gilliland, David (Race Car Driver)
The Racers Group
292 Rolling Hills Rd.
Mooresville, NC 28117, USA

Gilliland, Richard (Actor)
c/o Anthony DeMichele *Beacon Talent
Agency*
170 Apple Ridge Rd
Woodcliff, NJ 07677, USA

Gilliland, Robert J (Aviator)
PO Box 84
Palm Desert, CA 92261-0084, USA

Gillingwater, Leah (Reality TV Star)
c/o Staff Member *Real World, The*
6007 Sepulveda Blvd
Van Nuys, CA 91411, USA

Gillis, Don (Athlete, Football Player)
4658 Oso Pkwy
Corpus Christi, TX 78413, USA

Gillis, Louis (Baseball Player)
Birmingham Black Barons
2920 33rd Way N
Birmingham, AL 35207-3720, USA

Gillis, Malcolm (Educator)
Rice University
President's Office
Houston, TX 77251, USA

Gillis, Mike (Athlete, Hockey Player)
Gillis and Association
Vancouver Canucks 800 Griffiths Way
Attn: General Manager
Vancouver, BC V6B 6G1, Canada

Gillis, Paul
2210 Medford Ct
Odessa, TX 79762-4504, USA

Gillis, Tom (Athlete, Golfer)
527 Tanview Dr
Oxford, MI 48371, USA

Gillom, Jennifer (Basketball Player)
c/o Staff Member *LA Sparks*
555 N Nash Street
El Segundo, CA 90245, USA

Gillooly (Stone), Jeff
10408 SE 82nd Ave.
Portland, OR 97266

Gillow, Russ (Athlete, Hockey Player)
1517 W Songbird Dr
StGeorge, UT 84790-7261, USA

Gilman, Alfred G (Nobel Prize Laureate)
10996 Crooked Creek Dr
Dallas, TX 75229-4304, USA

Gilman, Billy (Music Group)
c/o Rodney Essig *Creative Artists Agency
(CAA-TN)*
3310 West End Ave
5th Floor
Nashville, TN 37203, USA

Gilman, Dorothy (Writer)
1200 King St Apt 338
Port Chester, NY 10573-7005, USA

Gilman, Kenneth B (Business Person)
Limited Inc
3 Limited Parkway
P O Box 1600
Columbus, OH 43216, USA

Gilman, Richard H (Publisher)
Boston Globe
Publisher's Office
135 W T Morrissey Blvd
Dorchester, MA 02125, USA

Gilman, Sid (Doctor, Misc)
3441 Geddes Road
Ann Arbor, MI 48105, USA

Gilmartin, Paul (Comedian)
c/o Staff Member *Agency for the
Performing Arts (APA-LA)*
405 S Beverly Dr
Suite 500
Beverly Hills, CA 90212-4425, USA

Gilmartin, Raymond V (Business Person)
Merck Co
1 Merck Dr P O Box 100
Whitehouse Station, NJ 08889, USA

Gilmer, Harry V (Athlete, Football Player)
7467 Highway N
O Fallon, MO 63366, USA

Gilmore, Artis (Athlete, Basketball Player)
11043 Turnbridge Dr
Jacksonville, FL 32256-2329, USA

Gilmore, Bryan (Athlete, Football Player)
123 Houston St
Lufkin, TX 75904, USA

Gilmore, Clarence P (Editor)
1629 Boston Post Road
Westbrook, CT 06498-2047, USA

Gilmore, Jared (Actor)
c/o David Dean Portelli *David Dean Management*
Prefers to be contacted via telephone or email
Los Angeles, CA, USA

Gilmore, Jimmie Dale (Music Group, Songwriter, Writer)
c/o Staff Member *Concerted Efforts*
P.O. Box 440326
Somerville, MA 02144, USA

Gilmore, Kenneth O (Editor)
Charles Road
Mount Kisco, NY 10549, USA

Gilmore, Tom (Athlete, Hockey Player)
Partition Systems
1647 70 Ave NW
Edmonton, AB T6P INS, Canada

Gilmore, Walt (Athlete, Basketball Player)
257 Benjamin Blvd
Bear, DE 19701-1693, USA

Gilmour, Buddy (Horse Racer)
50 Merrick Ave Unit 410
East Meadow, NY 11554-1593, USA

Gilmour, David (Music Group, Musician)
c/o Steve Martin *Agency Group Ltd, The (NY)*
142 West 57th St
6th Floor
New York, NY 10019, USA

Gilmour, Doug (Athlete, Hockey Player)
c/o Staff Member *Toronto Maple Leafs*
Air Canada Centre
400-40 Bay St
Toronto, ON M5J 2X2, Canada

Gilmour, Doug (Athlete, Hockey Player)
Kingston Frontenacs PO Box 665
Attn: General Manager
Kingston, ON K7L 4X1, Canada

Gilmour, George (Horse Racer)
1445 NW 69th Ave
Margate, FL 33063-2552, USA

Gilmour of Craigmillar, Ian (Government Official)
Ferry House Old Isleworth
Middx, UNITED KINGDOM (UK)

Gilmur, Chuck (Athlete, Basketball Player)
PO Box 64290
Tacoma, WA 98464-0290, USA

Gilpin, Peri (Actor)
c/o Scott Henderson *WME (LA)*
9601 Wilshire Blvd Fl 3
Beverly Hills, CA 90210, USA

Gilpin Faust, Drew (Educator)
76 Brattle St
Cambridge, MA 02138, USA

Gilroy, Frank (Writer)
8 Mangin Rd
Monroe, NY 10950-2203, USA

Gilroy, Frank D (Writer)
6 Magnin Rd
Monroe, NY 10950, USA

Gilroy, Tom (Actor, Director, Producer, Writer)
c/o Staff Member *WmE2 (WMA-LA)*
1 William Morris Pl
Beverly Hills, CA 90212, USA

Gilroy, Tony (Director, Writer)
c/o Risa Gertner *Creative Artists Agency (CAA-LA)*
2000 Ave Of The Stars
Los Angeles, CA 90067, USA

Gilsig, Jessalyn (Actor)
c/o Steven Levy *Framework Entertainment (LA)*
9057 Nemo St
Suite C
West Hollywood, CA 90069, USA

Gilson, Hal (Athlete, Baseball Player)
15247 E Sage Dr
Fountain Hills, AZ 85268-4373, USA

Gilyard Jr, Clarence (Actor)
24040 Camino Del Avion #A239
Monarch Bay, CA 92629, USA

Gimbel, Norman (Songwriter, Writer)
P O Box 50013
Santa Barbara, CA 93150, USA

Gimbrone, Michael A Jr (Doctor, Misc)
Brigham & Women's Hospital
Vascular Pathlogy Dept
Boston, MA 02115, USA

Gimenez, Chris (Athlete, Baseball Player)
781 Eschenburg Dr
Gilroy, CA 95020-5610, USA

Gimeno, Andres (Tennis Player)
Paseo de la Bnanova 38
Barcelona 6, SPAIN

Gimpel, Erica
c/o Staff Member *Innovative Artists (LA)*
1505 10th St
Santa Monica, CA 90401, USA

Gina G (Music Group)
What Mgmt
P O Box 1463
Culver City, CA 90232, USA

Gin Blossoms (Music Group)
PO Box 429094
San Francisco, CA 94142, USA

Ging, Jack (Actor)
48701 San Pedro St
La Quinta, CA 92253, USA

Gingerich, Philip D (Misc, Scientist)
University of Michigan
Paleontology Dept
Ann Arbor, MI 48109, USA

Gingras, Gaston (Athlete, Hockey Player)
50 Rue du Docteur
Pierrefonds, QC H8Z 1L2, Canada

Gingrey, Phil (Congressman, Politician)
442 Cannon HOB
Washington, DC 20515, USA

Gingrich, Newton L (Newt) (Politician)
7410 Windy Hill Ct
Me Lean, VA 22102-2800, USA

Ginibre, Jean-Louis (Editor)
Hachett Filipacchi
1633 Broadway
New York, NY 10019, USA

Ginn, Chad (Athlete, Golfer)
c/o Staff Member *Signature Sports Group*
4150 Olson Memorial Hey
Suite 110
Minneapolis, MN 55422, USA

Ginn, Hubert (Athlete, Football Player)
16 Egrets Nest Dr
Savannah, GA 31406, USA

Ginn, William H Jr (General)
1002 Priscilla Lane
Alexandria, VA 22308, USA

Ginn Jr, Ted (Athlete, Football Player)
18289 SW 54th St
Miramar, FL 33029-5091, USA

Ginobili, Emanuel (Manu) (Athlete, Basketball Player)
10 Queens HI
San Antonio, TX 78257-1724, USA

Ginsberg, Joe (Athlete, Baseball Player)
12635 SW Kingsway Cir
#D1
Lake Suzy, FL 34269-4585, USA

Ginsberg, Justice Ruth Bader
700 New Hampshire Ave. NW
Washington, DC 20037

Ginsburg, Douglas H (Judge)
US Court of Appeals
333 Constitution Ave NW
Washington, DC 20001, USA

Ginsburg, Ruth Bader (Judge, Lawyer, Misc)
US Supreme Court
1 1st St NE
Washington, DC 20543, USA

Ginsburg, William
10100 Santa Monica Blvd #800
Los Angeles, CA 90067, USA

Ginter, Keith (Athlete, Baseball Player)
2907 Maple Ave
Fullerton, CA 92835-2126, USA

Ginter, Matt (Athlete, Baseball Player)
3320 Boonesboro Rd
Winchester, KY 40391-9292, USA

Ginter-Brooker, Susan (Athlete, Golfer)
314 Yorkshire Dr
Greenville, SC 29615, USA

Gintner, Heidi (Stylist)
c/o Staff Member *Zenobia Agency Inc*
PO Box 909
Groveland, CA 95321, USA

Ginzburg, Vitaly L (Nobel Prize Laureate)
PN Lebedev Physical Institute Leninskii Pr 53
Moscow 117924, RUSSIA

Ginzton, Edward L (Business Person, Engineer)
Varian Assoc
3100 Hansen Way
Palo Alto, CA 94304, USA

Giofriddo, Al
64 Bristol Pl.
Goleta, CA 93117

Gioia (Musician)
c/o Staff Member *Diva Central Inc*
7510 W Sunset Blvd Ste 1445
Los Angees, CA 90046, USA

Giola, Dana (Government Official, Writer)
National Endowment for Arts
1100 Pennsylvania Ave NW
Washington, DC 20506, USA

Gionta, Brian (Athlete, Hockey Player, Olympic Athlete)
Sports Consulting Group
65 Monroe Ave Ste D
Pittsford, NY 14534-1318, USA

Giordano, Tommy (Athlete, Baseball Player)
176 Riverside Ave
Amityville, NY 11701-3738, USA

Giosia, Nadia (Nadia G) (Chef)
c/o Jason Pinyan *Artist and Brand Management - LA*
8687 Melrose Ave
8th Floor
Los Angeles, CA 90069, USA

Giovanelli, Gordon (Athlete, Olympic Athlete, Rower)
332 Pico De La Loma
Escondido, CA 92029-7912, USA

Giovanni, Joseph (Architect)
Giovanni Assoc
140 E 40th St
New York, NY 10016, USA

Giovanni, Nikki E (Writer)
Virginia Polytechnic Institute
English Dept
Blacksburg, VA 24061, USA

Giovanola, Ed (Athlete, Baseball Player)
1741 Nomark Ct
San Jose, CA 95125-3948, USA

Giovinazzo, Carmine (Actor)
6626 Cahuenga Terr
Los Angeles, CA 90068, USA

Gipson, Charles (Athlete, Baseball Player)
632 S Earlham St
Orange, CA 92869-5406, USA

Gipsy Kings (Music Group)
c/o Staff Member *Podell Talent Agency LLC*
22 W 21st St
9th Floor
New York, NY 10010, USA

Giradeau, Bernard
37 rue Froidevaux
Paris, FRANCE 75014

GiradelII, Marc (Skier)
9413 Oberegg-Sulzbach
SWITZERLAND

Giraldo, Neil (Musician, Producer)
0 Hana Hwy
Hana, HI 96713, USA

Girard, Ken (Athlete, Hockey Player)
6-519 Riverside Dr
London, ON N6H 5J3, Canada

Girardi, Dan (Athlete, Hockey Player)
Newport Sports Management
400-201 City Centre Dr
Attn Don Meehan
Mississauga, ON L5B 2T4, Canada

Girardi, Joseph E (Joe) (Athlete, Baseball Player)
6 Fairwav Dr
Purchase, NY 10577-1139, USA

Girardi, Serge (Stylist)
c/o Staff Member *Management + Artists + Organization*
330 W 38th St
#1401
New York, NY 10018, USA

Giraudeau, Bernard (Actor)
Cineart
36 Rue de Ponthieu
Paris 75008, FRANCE

Giri, Tulsi (Prime Minister)
Jawakpurdham
District Dhanuka, NEPAL

Girls Aloud (Music Group)
Polydor
72 Black Lion Ln
London W6 9BE, UNITED KINGDOM

Girls Aloud
c/o Staff Member *Concorde Intl Artists Ltd*
101 Shepherds Bush Rd
London W6 7LP, UNITED KINGDOM
(UK)

Girone, Remo (Actor)
Cineart
36 Rue de Ponthieu
Paris 75008, FRANCE

Giroux, Bonny (Actor)
c/o Staff Member *Deborah Harry Talent*
408-1917 W 4th Ave
Vancouver, BC V6J 1M7, CANADA

Giroux, Larry (Athlete, Hockey Player)
10 Colleen Dr
Edwardsville, IL 62025, USA

Giroux, Rejean (Athlete, Hockey Player)
1060 Av de Salaberry
Quebec, QC GIR 2VS, Canada

Giscard, d'Estaing Valery (Politician, President)
11 Rue Benouville
Paris F-75116, FRANCE

Gish, Annabeth (Actor)
c/o Joan Hyler *Hyler Management*
20 Ocean Park Blvd
Suite 25
Santa Monica, CA 90405, USA

Gisler, Mike (Athlete, Football Player)
407 Tampa Dr
Victoria, TX 77904-1649, USA

Gismonti, Egberto (Music Group, Musician)
International Music Network
278 S Main St #400
Gloucester, MA 01930, USA

Gissell, Chris (Athlete, Baseball Player)
4310 NW 121st Cir
Vancouver, WA 98685-2052, USA

Gissinger, Andy (Athlete, Football Player)
1667 Union Ave
Barberton, OH 44203, USA

Gitai, Yael (Stylist)
c/o Celebrity Stylist *Workgroup (San Francisco)*
35 Beideman Pl
San Francisco, CA 94115, USA

Gitlin, Todd (Historian)
New York University
Culture & Communications Dept
New York, NY 10012, USA

Gitomer, Jeffrey (Business Person)
BuyGitomer Inc
310 Arlington Ave
Lot 329
Charlotte, NC 28203, USA

Giudice, Teresa (Reality TV Star)
c/o Michael (Mike) Esterman
Esterman.Com, LLC
Prefers to be contacted via email
MD, USA

Giuffre, Carlo
Via Massimi 45
Rome, ITALY I-00136

Giuffre, James P (Jimmy) (Music Group, Musician)
Legacy Records
550 Madison Ave #1700
New York, NY 10022, USA

Giuliani, Rudolph (Politician)
Giuliani Partners LLC 5 Times Sq Fl 6
New York, NY 10036-6528, USA

Giuliani, Rudy (Politician)
Giuliani Partners
1251 Ave of the Americas
New York, NY 10020-1100, USA

Giuliano, Jeff (Athlete, Hockey Player)
46 Lutheran Dr
Nashua, NH 03063-2914, USA

Giuliano, Louis J (Business Person)
ITT Industries
4 W Red Oak Lane
White Plains, NY 10604, USA

Giuliano, Tom (Music Group)
6929 N Hayden Road
Scottsdale, AZ 85250, USA

Giullani, Rudolph W (Misc, Politician)
Guiliani Partners
5 Times Square
New York, NY 10036, USA

Giuntoli, David (Actor)
c/o Judy Hofflund *Hofflund/Polone*
9465 Wilshire Blvd #420
Beverly Hills, CA 90212, USA

Giuranna, Bruno (Music Group, Musician)
Via Bembo 96
Asolo TV 31011, ITALY

Giusti, David J (Dave) (Athlete, Baseball Player)
524 Clair Dr
Pittsburgh, PA 15241-2013, USA

Given, Dave (Athlete, Hockey Player)
1250 Parkside Dr f._
Seattle, WfL 98112-3718, USA

Givens, Adele (Actor, Comedian)
c/o Staff Member *Gersh (LA)*
9465 Wilshire Blvd
Suite 600
Beverly Hills, CA 90212, USA

Givens, Brian (Athlete, Baseball Player)
811 Deer Clover Cir
Castle Pines, CO 80108-8202, USA

Givens, Jack (Athlete, Basketball Player, Misc)
9610 Leeside Court
Windermere, FL 34786-6200, USA

Givens, Robin (Actor)
c/o Darryl Marshak *Marshak/Zachary Company, The*
8840 Wilshire Blvd
1st Floor
Beverly Hills, CA 90210, USA

Givins, Brian (Athlete, Baseball Player)
719 Stonemont Ct
Castle Rock, CO 80108, USA

Givins, Ernest (Athlete, Football Player)
Boca Ciega High School 924 58th St S
Gulfport, FL 31707-2547, USA

Gizzi, Claudio (Composer)
SIAE
Viaile dell Letteratura 30
Rome 00100, ITALY

Gjertsen, Douglas (Athlete, Olympic Athlete, Swimmer)
7130 Haven ridge Way
McDonough, GA 30253-8511, USA

G K (Actor)
11 Shyamala Vadana Street
Koyathoppu
Chennai, TN 600 024, INDIA

Gladden, Danny (Dan) (Athlete, Baseball Player)
6543 Pinnacle Dr
Eden Prairie, MN 55346-1906, USA

Gladding, Fred (Athlete, Baseball Player)
436 Marsh Pointe Dr
Columbia, SC 29229-7025, USA

Gladieux, Robert (Athlete, Football Player)
802 Arch Ave
South Bend, IN 46601, USA

Gladwell, Malcolm (Business Person, Writer)
c/o Bill Leigh *The Leigh Bureau*
92 E Main St
Suite 200
Somerville, NJ 08876, USA

Glance, Harvey (Athlete, Track Athlete)
2408 Old Creek Road
Montgomery, AL 36117, USA

Glanville, Brandi (Reality TV Star)
c/o Staff Member *Persona PR*
8840 Wilshire Blvd
Suite 212
Beverly Hills, CA 90211, USA

Glanville, Doug (Athlete, Baseball Player)
209 Hillcrest Rd
Raleigh, NC 27605-1719, USA

Glanville, Jerry (Athlete, Coach, Football Coach, Football Player, Sportscaster)
130 Holly Dr
Dawsonville, GA 30534, USA

Glasbergen, Randy (Cartoonist)
c/o Staff Member *King Features Syndication*
300 W 57th St
15th Floor
New York, NY 10019-5238, USA

Glaser, Donald A (Nobel Prize Laureate)
University of California
Molecular Biology Laboratory
Berkeley, CA 94720-0001, USA

Glaser, Jim (Music Group)
Joe Taylor Artist Agency
2802 Columbine Place
Nashville, TN 37204, USA

Glaser, Jon (Actor, Writer)
c/o Staff Member *3 Arts Entertainment Inc*
9460 Wilshire Blvd
7th Floor
Beverly Hills, CA 90210, USA

Glaser, Milton (Artist, Misc)
Milton Glaser Assoc
207 E 32nd St
New York, NY 10016, USA

Glaser, Paul Michael (Actor, Director)
c/o Mark Teitelbaum *Teitelbaum Artists Group*
8840 Wilshire Blvd
3rd Floor
Beverly Hills, CA 90212, USA

Glaser, Rose Mary (Athlete, Baseball Player, Commentator)
8929 Long Ln
Cincinnati, OH 45231-5024, USA

Glaser Brothers
91619th Ave
Nashville, TN 37212, US

Glasgow, Brian (Athlete, Football Player)
5 Sage Ct
Bolingbrook, IL 60490, USA

Glasgow, Nesby (Athlete, Football Player)
13429 122nd Ave NE
Kirkland, WA 98034, USA

Glasgow, Walter (Athlete, Olympic Athlete, Sailor)
781 Silver Spur Dr
Weatherford, TX 76087-6417, USA

Glashow, Sheldon Lee (Nobel Prize Laureate)
30 Prescott St
Brookline, MA 02446-4038, USA

Glaspie, April (Diplomat)
State Department
2201 C St NW
Washington, DC 20520, USA

Glass, Chip (Athlete, Football Player)
7704 NE 140th St
Bothell, WA 98011, USA

Glass, David (Commentator)
Kansas City Royals
17 Glenbrook
Bentonville, AK 72712-3840, USA

Glass, Gerald (Athlete, Basketball Player)
1123 Tillman Road
Port Gibson, MS 39150-2890, USA

Glass, Glenn (Athlete, Football Player)
301 Portsmouth Rd
Knoxville, TN 37909, USA

Glass, H Bentley (Biologist)
P O Box 65
East Setauket, NY 11733, USA

Glass, Ira (Writer)
c/o Steven Barclay *Steven Barclay Agency*
12 Western Ave
Petaluma, CA 94952, USA

Glass, Leland (Athlete, Football Player)
9 Bayou Ct
Sacramento, CA 95831, USA

Glass, Nancy (Journalist)
Glass DiFede Productions
345 Montgomery Ave
Bala Cynwyd, PN 19004

Glass, Philip (Composer)
48 E 3rd St #2
New York, NY 10003, USA

Glass, Ron (Actor)
c/o Mitchell Stubbs *Mitchell K Stubbs & Assoc (MKS)*
8675 W. Washington Blvd
Suite 203
Culver City, CA 90232, USA

Glass, Todd (Actor)
c/o Alex Murray *McDonald-Murray Management*
11846 Ventura Blvd Ste 202
Studio City, CA 91604, USA

Glass, William S (Bill) (Athlete, Football Player)
Bill Glass Ministries
P.O. Box 761101
Dallas, TX 75376, USA

Glasser, Erika (Actor)
c/o Gabriel Blanco *Gabriel Blanco Iglesias (Mexico)*
Rio Balsas 35-32
Colonia Cuauhtemoc
DF 06500, Mexico

Glasser, Ira S (Activist, Attorney, Attorney General, General, Lawyer, Misc)
American Civil Liberties Union
132 W 43rd St
New York, NY 10036, USA

Glasser, Isabel (Actor)
c/o Kyle Luker *The Group Entertainment*
141 West 28th St Ste 300
New York, NY 10001, USA

Glasser, William (Doctor, Misc)
11633 San Vincente Blvd
Los Angeles, CA 90049, USA

Glassford, Bill (Athlete, Football Player)
3212 N Miller Rd Apt 216
Scottsdale, AZ 85251-6985, USA

Glassic, Tom (Athlete, Football Player)
1030 S Pine Dr
Bailey, CO 80421, USA

Glassman, Adam (Stylist)
c/o Staff Member *Bryan Bantry*
900 Broadway Ste 400
New York, NY 10003, USA

Glasson, Bill (Athlete, Golfer)
2917 S Deer Crk
Stillwater, OK 74074, USA

Glass Tiger
238 Davenport #126
Toronto, CANADA Ont.M5R 1J

Glasvegas (Music Group, Musician)
c/o Ben Winchester *Primary Talent International (UK)*
The Primary Building
10-11 Jockeys Fields
London WC1R 4BN, UK

Glatter, Lesli L (Director)
United Talent Agency
9560 Wilshire Blvd #500
Beverly Hills, CA 90212, USA

Glatz, Fred (Athlete, Football Player)
224 Perkins Row
Topsfield, MA 01983, USA

Glatzeder, Winfried
Gosslerstrasse 24
Berlin, GERMANY D-12161

Glau, Summer (Actor)
c/o Mimi DiTrani *Schiff Company, The*
9465 Wilshire Blvd
Suite 480
Beverly Hills, CA 90212, USA

Glauber, Keith (Athlete, Baseball Player)
20 Highland Ct
Freehold, NJ 07728-9041, USA

Glauber, Roy J. (Nobel Prize Laureate)
221 Pleasant St
Arlington, MA 02476-8131, USA

Glaudini, Lola (Actor, Producer)
c/o Staff Member *Mosaic Media Group*
9200 W. Sunset Blvd
10th Floor
Los Angeles, CA 90069, USA

Glaus, Troy (Athlete, Baseball Player)
4300 Bibleway Ct
Holly Springs, NC 27540, USA

Glave, Matthew (Actor)
17628 McCormick St
Encino, CA 91316, USA

Glavin, Denis Joseph (Misc)
Electrical Radio & Machine Worders Union
11 E 1st St
New York, NY 10003, USA

Glavine, Mike (Athlete, Baseball Player)
89 Treble Cove Rd
North Billeria, MA 01862-2215, USA

Glavine, Tom (Athlete, Baseball Player)
920 Hurleston Ln
Alpharetta, GA 30022-6251, USA

Glazer, Jay (Sportscaster)
CBS-TV
Sports Dept 51 W 52nd St
New York, NY 10019, USA

Glazer, Jonathan (Director, Writer)
c/o David Naylor *David Naylor & Associates*
6535 Santa Monica Blvd
Hollywood, CA 90038, USA

Glazer, Malcolm (Business Person, Football Executive)
1482 S Ocean Blvd
Palm Beach, FL 33480-5019, USA

Glazer, Mitch (Producer)
c/o Staff Member *Creative Artists Agency (CAA-LA)*
2000 Ave Of The Stars
Los Angeles, CA 90067, USA

Glazer, Nathan (Activist)
12 Scott St
Cambridge, MA 02138, USA

Glazier, Nancy (Artist)
Somerset House Publishing
10688 Haddington
Houston, TX 77043, USA

Glazkov, Yuri N (Astronaut, General, Misc)
Potchta Kosmonavtov
Moskovskoi Oblasti
Syvisdny Goroduk 141160, RUSSIA

Glazunov, Ilya S (Artist)
Razhviz Academy
Kamergersky Per 2
Moscow 103009, RUSSIA

Gleason, Andrew M (Mathematician)
110 Larchwood Dr
Cambridge, MA 02138, USA

Gleason, Joanna (Actor)
c/o Vera Mihailovich *Forward Entertainment*
9255 Sunset Blvd
Suite 805
Los Angeles, CA 90069, USA

Gleason, Mary Pat (Actor, Writer)
c/o Tim Stone *Stone Manners Salners Agency (LA)*
9911 W Pico Blvd Ste 1400
Los Angeles, CA 90035, USA

Gleason, Matthew (Stylist)
c/o Staff Member *Pat Bates & Associates*
300 W 12th St
New York, NY 10014, USA

Gleason, Roy (Athlete, Baseball Player)
41654 Margarita Rd
APT 180
Temecula, CA 92591-2921, USA

Gleason, Tim (Athlete, Hockey Player)
1196 Stone Kirk Dr
Raleigh, NC 27614-7289, USA

Gleaton, Jerry Don (Athlete, Baseball Player)
3008 Avenue K
Brownwood, TX 76801-6016, USA

Gleeson, Brendan (Actor)
c/o Larry Taube *Principal Entertainment (LA)*
1964 Westwood Blvd #400
Los Angeles, CA 90025, USA

Glemp, Jozef Cardinal (Religious Leader)
Sekretariat Prymasa Kolski
Ul Miodowa 17
Warsaw 00 246, POLAND

Glen, John (Director)
Spyros Skouras
1015 Gayley Ave #300
Los Angeles, CA 90024, USA

Glenesk, Dean (Athlete, Olympic Athlete, Pentathlete)
1705 Ben Crenshaw Way
Austin, TX 78746-6120, USA

Glenn, Aaron (Athlete, Football Player)
30 Commanders Cove
Missouri City, TX 77459, USA

Glenn, Dorsey (Athlete, Football Player)
4242 NE Edmonson Ct
Lees Summit, MO 64064-1681, USA

Glenn, Jason (Athlete, Football Player)
15530 Ella Blvd
Apt 501
Houston, TX 77090, USA

Glenn, John (Athlete, Baseball Player)
514 E 12th Ave
Cordele, GA 31015-1334, USA

Glenn, Mike (Athlete, Basketball Player)
3571 Kilpatrick Lane
Snellville, GA 30039-8643, USA

Glenn, Scott (Actor)
c/o Johnnie Planco *Parseghian Planco LLC*
322 8th Ave
Suite 601
New York, NY 10001, USA

Glenn, Stanley (Athlete, Baseball Player)
9 Baily Rd
Lansdowne, PA 19050, USA

Glenn, Tarik (Athlete, Football Player)
10481 Titan Run
Carmel, IN 46032, USA

Glenn, Terry
1619 Fair Oaks Ct
Westlake, TX 76262-8224, USA

Glenn, Vencie (Athlete, Football Player)
718 Casita Ln
San Marcos, CA 92069-7397, USA

Glenn, Wayne E (Misc)
United Paperworkers Int'l Union
3340 Perimeter Hill Dr
Nashville, TN 37211, USA

Glennan, Robert E Jr (Educator)
Emporia State University
President's Office
Emporia, KS 66801, USA

Glennie, Brian (Athlete, Hockey Player)
4 Curling Rd
Bracebridge, ON P1L 1M6, Canada

Glennie, Evelyn E A (Music Group, Musician)
P O Box 6 Sawtry Huntingdon
Cambs PE17 5WE, UNITED KINGDOM (UK)

Glennie-Smith, Nick (Composer)
Vangelos Mgmt
15233 Ventura Blvd #200
Sherman Oaks, CA 91403, USA

Glenn Jr, John H (Astronaut, Ex-Senator)
Ohio State University
Stillman Hall 1947 College Road
Columbus, OH 43210, USA

Glennon, Matt (Athlete, Hockey Player)
6 Gardner Street
Hingham, MA 02043, USA

Glenwright, Brian (Athlete, Hockey Player)

Gless, Sharon (Actor)
Rosenzweig Productions
P O Box 48005
Los Angeles, CA 90048, USA

Glick, Alexis (Correspondent)
c/o Staff Member *Fox News Channel (NY)*
1211 Ave of the Americas
Level C1
New York, NY 10036-8701, USA

Glick, Frederick (Freddie) (Athlete, Football Player)
4226 Antlers Ct
Fort Collins, CO 80526, USA

Glick, Gary (Athlete, Football Player)
2801 Middlesborough Ct
Fort Collins, CO 80525, USA

Glickman, Daniel R (Misc, Secretary)
Harvard University
Kennedy Government School
Cambridge, MA 02138, USA

Glidden, Bob (Race Car Driver)
Rt. 1
Box 236
Whiteland, IN 46184, USA

Glidden, Robert (Educator)
Ohio University
President's Office
Athens, OH 45701, USA

Glidewell, Iain (Judge)
Rough Heys Farm Macclesfield
Cheshire SK11 9PF, UNITED KINGDOM (UK)

Glimcher, Arnold O (Arne) (Artist, Misc)
Pace Gallery
32 E 57th St
New York, NY 10022, USA

Glimm, James (Scientist)
120 E 81st St
Apt 12E
New York, NY 10028-1429, USA

Glinatsis, George (Athlete, Baseball Player)
13742 W 59th Ave
Arvada, CO 80004-3740, USA

Glisson, Lane (Stylist)
303 11th St
Brooklyn, NY 11215, USA

Glitman, Maynard W (Diplomat)
P O Box 438
Jeffersonville, VT 05464, USA

Glitter, Gary (Music Group, Songwriter, Writer)
Jef Hanlon Mgmt
1 York St
London W1H 1PZ, UNITED KINGDOM (UK)

Glmble, Johnny (Misc)
Nancy Fly Agency
6618 Wolfcreek Pall
Austin, TX 78749, USA

Gload, Ross (Athlete, Baseball Player)
23 Harrison Ave
East Hampton, NY 11937-2051, USA

Globensky, Alan (Athlete, Hockey Player)
20 Myrtle St apt 2
Augusta, ME 04330-4736

Globke, Rob (Athlete, Hockey Player)
8 Barron Dr
Hampton, VA 23669-3202, USA

Glockner, Michael
Kaiserslautener Str. 54
Saarbrucken, GERMANY D-66123

Gloden, Fred (Athlete, Football Player)
3821 Andrea Rd
Philadelphia, PA 19154, USA

Gloeckner, Lorry (Athlete, Hockey Player)
11671 King Rd.
Richmond, BC V7A 3B5, Canada

Gloor, Danny (Athlete, Hockey Player)
172 Henry
Mitchell, ON N0K 1N0, Canada

Gloriana (Music Group, Musician)
c/o Staff Member *Emblem*
22301 Mulholland Hwy
Calabasas, CA 91302, USA

Glory, New Found (Music Group)
c/o Staff Member *Ellis Industries Inc*
234 Shoreward Drive
Great Neck, NY 11021, USA

Glosson, Clyde (Athlete, Football Player)
5803 Lake Falls Dr
San Antonio, TX 78222, USA

Glotzbach, Charlie (Race Car Driver)
2513 Coopers lane
Sellersburg, IN 47172, USA

Glotzbatch, Charles (Race Car Driver)
2513 Cooper's Lane
Sellersburg, IN 47172, USA

Glouberman, Michael (Producer)
c/o Staff Member *United Talent Agency (UTA)*
9336 Civic Center Dr
Beverly Hills, CA 90210, USA

G Love & Special Sauce (Music Group)
c/o Staff Member *Paradigm (Monterey)*
404 W Franklin St
Monterey, CA 93940, USA

Glover, Andrew (Athlete, Football Player)
33226 Magnolia Cir
Magnolia, TX 77354-1523, USA

Glover, Bloc (Motorcycle Race, Motorcycle Racer)
American Motorcycle Assn
13515 Yormouth Dr
Pickerington, OH 43147, USA

Glover, Brian (Actor)
DeWolfe
Manfield House
376/378 Strand
London WC2R 0LR, UNITED KINGDOM

Glover, Bruce (Actor)
11449 Woodbine St
Los Angeles, CA 90066, USA

Glover, Chris (Musician)
c/o Staff Member *Paradigm (Monterey)*
404 W Franklin St
Monterey, CA 93940, USA

Glover, Clarence (Athlete, Basketball Player)
811 Lake Forest Pkwy
Louisville, KY 40245-5138, USA

Glover, Crispin (Actor, Director, Producer)
3573 Carnation Ave
Los Angeles, CA 90026, USA

Glover, Danny (Actor)
P O Box 170069
San Francisco, CA 94117, USA

Glover, Dion (Athlete, Basketball Player)
3691 Seton Hall Way
Decatur, GA 30034-5509, USA

Glover, Donald (Actor, Writer)
c/o Greg Walter *3 Arts Entertainment Inc*
9460 Wilshire Blvd
7th Floor
Beverly Hills, CA 90210, USA

Glover, Gary (Athlete, Baseball Player)
19704 Kell Estates Ln
Lutz, FL 33549-4092, USA

Glover, Howie (Athlete, Hockey Player)
15 Wendy Cres
Kitchener, ON N2A 1N0, Canada

Glover, Jane A
Kaylor Mgmt
130 W 57thSt #8G
New York, NY 10019, USA

Glover, John (Actor)
c/o Nevin Dolcefino *Innovative Artists (LA)*
1505 10th St
Santa Monica, CA 90401, USA

Glover, Julian (Actor)
200 Fulham Road
London SW10 9PN, United Kingdom

Glover, Kevin B (Athlete, Football Player)
11553 Manor Stone Ln
Columbia, MD 21044, USA

Glover, La'Roi (Athlete, Football Player)
PO Box 410589
Saint Louis, MO 63141-0589, USA

Glover, Lucas (Athlete, Golfer)
105 Annas Pl
Simpsonville, SC 29681, USA

Glover, Richard E (Rich) (Athlete, Football Player)
215 Claremont Ave
Jersey City, NJ 07305-3623, USA

Glover, Stephen (Steve-O) (Actor, Writer)
c/o Mike Liotta *True Public Relations*
6725 W Sunset Blvd #470
Los Angeles, CA 90028-7180, USA

Glowacki, Janusz (Writer)
845 W End Ave #4B
New York, NY 10025, USA

Gloy, Tom (Race Car Driver)
Rahal/Gloy Racing
804A Performance Dr.
Mooresville, NC 28115, USA

Gluck, Carol (Historian)
440 Riverside Dr
New York, NY 10027, USA

Gluck, Griffin (Actor)
c/o Leslie Allan-Rice *Leslie Allan-Rice Management*
1007 Maybrook Dr
Beverly Hills, CA 90210, USA

Gluck, Louise E (Writer)
14 Ellsworth Park
Cambridge, MA 02139-1011, USA

Glueck, Larry (Athlete, Football Player)
10 Cooper Rd
East Falmouth, MA 02536, USA

Glushchenko, Fedor I
1st Prydilnaya Str 11 #5
Moscow 105037, RUSSIA

Glymph, Junior (Athlete, Football Player)
7300 Fontana Dr
Columbia, SC 29209, USA

Glynn, Bill (Athlete, Baseball Player)
6916 51st St
San Diego, CA 92120-1212, USA

Glynn, Brian (Athlete, Hockey Player)
City of Prince Albert
City of Prince Albert 1084 Central Ave
Attn: Police Dept
Prince Albert, SK S6V 7P3, Canada

Glynn, Carlin (Actor)
1165 5th Ave
New York, NY 10029, USA

Glynn, Ed (Athlete, Baseball Player)
5212 Stratford Chase Dr
Virginia Beach, VA 23464-5621, USA

Glynn, Gene (Athlete, Baseball Player)
15329 Snake Trl
Waseca, MN 56093-4733, USA

Glynn, Ian M (Misc, Physicist)
Daylesford Conduit Head Road
Cambridge CB3 0EY, UNITED KINGDOM (UK)

Glynn, Robert D Jr (Business Person)
PG&E Corp
Spear Tower 1 Market St
San Francisco, CA 94105, USA

Glynn, Ryan (Athlete, Baseball Player)
14010 W Hyde Park Dr #201
Ft Myers, FL 33912, USA

G. McCotter, Thaddeus (Congressman, Politician)
1632 Longworth HOB
Washington, DC 20515, USA

G. Miller, Gary (Congressman, Politician)
2349 Rayburn HOB
Washington, DC 20515, USA

Gminski, Mike (Athlete, Basketball Player, Sportscaster)
1309 Canterbury Hill Circle
Charlotte, NC 28211-1454, USA

Gnarls Barkley (Music Group)
Downtown Records
73 Spring St #504
New York, NY 10012, USA

Gnedovsky, Yuri P (Architect)
Union of Architects
Granatny Per 22
Moscow 103001, RUSSIA

Goad, Tim (Athlete, Football Player)
138 Birchwood Dr
Pittsboro, NC 27312, USA

Goalby, Bob (Athlete, Golfer)
904 Briar Hill Rd
Belleville, IL 62223, USA

Gob, Art (Athlete, Football Player)
123 Hiscott Dr
Pittsburgh, PA 15241, USA

Gobble, Jimmy (Athlete, Baseball Player)
150 Lake View Estates Dr
Bristol, VA 37620-1307, USA

Goble, Les (Athlete, Football Player)
21 Dodge Ave
Waverly, NY 14892, USA

Goc, Marcel (Athlete, Hockey Player)
12348 NW 69th Ct
Parkland, FL 33076-3334, USA

Gocke, Justin
6763 Pistachio Pl.
Palmdale, CA 93551-1622

Gocong, Chris (Athlete, Football Player)
PO Box 93
Berea, OH 44017-0093, USA

Godard, Eric (Athlete, Hockey Player)
2330 Larkins Way
Pittsburgh, PA 15203-2218, USA

Godard, Jean-Luc (Director)
15 Rue du Nord
Roulle 1180, SWITZERLAND

Goday, Dale (Stylist)
55 E 11th St
New York, NY 10003, USA

Godbold, John C (Judge)
P.O. Box 3038
Montgomery, AL 36109-0038, USA

Godboldo, Dale (Actor)
c/o Joanna (Joanie) Burstein *Burstein Company, The*
15304 Sunset Blvd
suite 208
Pacific Palisades, CA 90272, USA

Godby, Danny (Athlete, Baseball Player)
RR 2 Box 17A
Chapmanville, WV 25508-9773, USA

Godchaux, Stephen (Producer)
c/o Staff Member *WmE2 (WMA-LA)*
1 William Morris Pl
Beverly Hills, CA 90212, USA

Goddard, Daniel (Actor)
c/o Staff Member *Luber Roklin Management*
8530 Wilshire Blvd
6th Floor
Beverly Hills, CA 90211, USA

Goddard, Joe (Athlete, Baseball Player)
304 Ridgepark Dr
Beckley, WV 25801-9593, USA

Goddard, John (Misc, Scientist)
4224 Beulah Dr
La Canada, CA 91011, USA

Goddard, Mark (Actor)
P O Box 778
Middleboro, MA 02346, USA

Godden, Ernie (Athlete, Hockey Player)
31 Rinaldo Rd
Keswick, ON L4P 3X9, Canada

Godecki, Marzena (Actor)
Jonethan M. Shiff Productions
373 Bay Street
Port Melbourne
Victoria, Australia 3207

Godfread, Dan (Athlete, Basketball Player)
622 Michigan St
Eagle River, WI 54521-8929, USA

Godfrey, Chris (Athlete, Football Player)
52383 Swanson Dr
South Bend, IN 46635, USA

Godfrey, Paul V (Publisher)
Toronto Sun
333 King St E
Toronto, ON M5A 3X5, CANADA

Godfrey, Randall (Athlete, Football Player)
4102 Mount Zion Church Rd
Valdosta, GA 31605, USA

Godin, Seth (Business Person, Writer)
Do You Zoom Inc
PO Box 305
Irvington, NY 10533, USA

Godina, John
PO Box 120
Indianapolis, IN 46204-0120

Godley, Georgina (Designer, Fashion Designer)
42 Bassett Road
London W10 6UL, UNITED KINGDOM (UK)

Godley, Kevin (Music Group, Musician)
Heronden Hall Tenterden
Kent, UNITED KINGDOM (UK)

Godmanis, Ivars (Politician)
Palasta St 1
Riga 1954, LATVIA

Godreche, Judith (Actor, Writer)
c/o Staff Member *Zelig Films*
57 rue Reaumur
Paris 75002, France

Godsmack (Music Group)
c/o John Branigan *WME (LA)*
9601 Wilshire Blvd Fl 3
Beverly Hills, CA 90210, USA

Godson, Lindley (General)
PO Box 237
Greenville, ME 04441-0237, USA

Godsted, Patricia Martin (Stylist)
8931 S Oakley St
Chicago, IL 60620, USA

Godwin, Fay S (Photographer)
Fay Godwin Network
3-4 Kerby St
London E4N 8TS, UNITED KINGDOM (UK)

Godwin, Gail K (Writer)
P O Box 946
Woodstock, NY 12498, USA

Godwin, Linda M (Astronaut, Physicist)
16923 Cottonwood Way
Houston, TX 77059, USA

Godynyuk, Alexander (Athlete, Hockey Player)
217 Fallen Rd
Lexington, MA 02421-5802, USA

Goeas, Leo (Athlete, Football Player)
113 Shady Ln
Longwood, FL 32750-2867, USA

Goebel, Brad (Athlete, Football Player)
P.O. Box 4006
Horseshoe Bay, TX 78657, USA

Goebel, Timothy (Athlete, Figure Skater, Olympic Athlete)
c/o Staff Member *Champions on Ice*
Tom Collins Enterprises Inc
3500 W 80th St
Minneapolis, MN 55431, USA

Goebeler, Hans (General)
PO Box 135
Holder, FL 34445-0135, USA

Goeddeke, George (Athlete, Football Player)
45575 N Stonewood Rd
Canton, MI 48187-6645, USA

Goehr, Alexander
11 West Rd.
Cambridge, ENGLAND

Goehr, P Alexander (Composer)
University of Cambridge
Music Faculty 11 West Road
Cambridge, UNITED KINGDOM (UK)

Goel, Jyotin (Actor, Bollywood)
258 Famous Cine Building
Mahalaxmi
Bombay, MS 400 011, INDIA

Goellner, Marc-Kevin (Athlete, Tennis Player)
Blau-Weiss Neuss
Tennishall Jahnstrasse
Neuss 41464, GERMANY

Goen, Bob (Entertainer)
21767 Plainwood Dr
Woodland Hills, CA 91364, USA

Goerke, Glenn A (Educator)
University of Houston
President's Office
Houston, TX 77204, USA

Goestenkors, Gail (Basketball Player, Coach)
Duke University
Athletic Dept
Durham, NC 27708, USA

Goestschi, Renate (Skier)
Schwarzenbach 3
Obdach 8742, AUSTRIA

Goettmann, Georgia
344 E. 59th St.
New York, NY 10022

Goetz, Bernhard
55 W. 14th St.
New York, NY 10011

Goetz, Dick (Athlete, Golfer)
4301 Fillbrook Ln
Tyler, TX 75707, USA

Goetz, Eric (Misc, Yachtsman)
Eric Goetz Marine & Technology
15 Broad Common Road
Bristol, RI 02809, USA

Goetz, Peter Michael (Actor)
c/o Staff Member *Silver Massetti & Szatmary (SMS) Talent Inc*
8383 Wilshire Blvd
Suite 230
Beverly Hills, CA 90211, USA

Goetz, Russ (Baseball Player)
937 Fawcett Ave
Mc Keesport, PA 15132-1409, USA

Goetz, Russ (Athlete, Baseball Player)
937 Fawcett Ave
McKeesport, PA 15132, USA

Goetze-Ackerman, Vicki (Athlete, Golfer)
3621 Sally Parrish Trl
Valrico, FL 33596, USA

Goetzman, Gary (Producer)
c/o Staff Member *Creative Artists Agency (CAA-LA)*
2000 Ave Of The Stars
Los Angeles, CA 90067, USA

Goff, Jerry (Athlete, Baseball Player)
3 Oak Valley Dr
Novato, CA 94947-1964, USA

Goff, Mike (Athlete, Baseball Player)
7320 W Surrey Ave
Peoria, AZ 85381-6017, USA

Goff, Mike (Athlete, Football Player)
2225 5th St
Peru, IL 61354, USA

Goff, Willard (Athlete, Football Player)
441 E 10th Ave
Springfield, CO 81073, USA

Goffin, David (Producer)
c/o Staff Member *ICM Partners (ICM-LA)*
10250 Constellation Blvd Fl 7
Los Angeles, CA 90067, USA

Goffin, Gerry (Musician, Songwriter)
9171 Hazen Dr
Beverly Hills, CA 90210, USA

Goffin, Louise (Musician)
c/o Staff Member *Evolution Music Partners*
1680 N. Vine St.
Hollywood, CA 90028, USA

Goforth, Bart (Athlete, Football Player)
7000 Greenbriar St Apt 20
Houseton, TX 77030-3244, USA

Gofourth, Derrel (Athlete, Football Player)
1119 S Woodcrest Dr
Stillwater, OK 74074, USA

Gogan, Kevin (Athlete, Football Player)
4643 286th Ave SE
Fall City, WA 98024, USA

Goganious, Keith (Athlete, Football Player)
4173 Cheswick Ln
Virginia Beach, VA 23455, USA

Gogel, Matt (Athlete, Golfer)
3509 W 68th St
Mission Hills, KS 66208, USA

Goggin, Chuck (Athlete, Baseball Player)
1224 Roundhouse Ln
Alexandria, VA 22314-5908, USA

Goggins, Walton (Actor, Producer)
c/o Darris Hatch *Daris Hatch Management*
10027 Rossbury Pl
Los Angeles, CA 90064-4825, USA

Gogolak, Charlie (Athlete, Football Player)
PO Box 361
Northeast Harbor, ME 04662-0361, USA

Gogolak, Peter (Pete) (Athlete, Football Player)
24 Arrowhead Way
Darien, CT 06820, USA

Gogolewski, Bill (Athlete, Baseball Player)
1522 Graham Ave
Oshkosh, WI 54902-2623, USA

Go-Go's, The (Musician)
c/o Bradford Cobb *Direct Management Group*
947 N La Cienega Blvd
Suite G
Los Angeles, CA 90069, USA

Goh, Kun (Prime Minister)
Prime Minister's Office
77 Sejonh-no
Chongnoku
Seoul, SOUTH KOREA

Goh, Michelle (Actor)
c/o Leonard Bonnell *Characters Talent Agency (Toronto)*
8 Elm St
2nd Floor
Toronto, ON M5G 1G7, CANADA

Goh, Rex (Music Group, Musician)
Agency for Performing Arts
9200 Sunset Blvd #900
Los Angeles, CA 90069, USA

Goh Chok Tong (Prime Minister)
Prime Minister's Office
Istana Annexe
Singapore 0923, SINGAPORE

Goheen, Robert F (Diplomat, Educator)
1 Orchard Circle
Princeton, NJ 08540, USA

Gohmert, Louie (Congressman, Politician)
2440 Rayburn HOB
Washington, DC 20515, USA

Gohr, Greg (Athlete, Baseball Player)
77 Scotland Rd
Reading, MA 01867-3323, USA

Goich, Dan (Athlete, Football Player)
PO Box 19068
Las Vegas, NV 89132, USA

Going, Joanna (Actor)
c/o Nevin Dolcefino *Innovative Artists (LA)*
1505 10th St
Santa Monica, CA 90401, USA

Goings, E V (Business Person)
Tupperware Corp
P O Box 2353
Orlando, FL 32802, USA

Goings, Nick (Athlete)
c/o Staff Member *Carolina Panthers*
800 S Mint St
Charlotte, NC 28202, USA

Goings, Nick (Athlete, Football Player)
9603 Sunset Grove Dr
Huntersville, NC 28078, USA

Goitschel-Beranger, Marielle (Skier)
Val Thorens
Saint-Martin de Belleville 73440, FRANCE

Gokey, Danny (Musician)
c/o Staff Member *19 Entertainment - LA*
9000 W Sunset Blvd #1574
West Hollywood, CA 90069, USA

Gola, Thomas J (Tom) (Athlete, Basketball Player)
15 Kings Oak Ln
Philadelphia, PA 19115-4008, USA

Golay, Jeanne (Athlete, Cycler, Olympic Athlete)
PO Box 1697
Glenwood Springs, CO 81602-1697, USA

Gold, Ari (Musician)
c/o Staff Member *Grapevine Public Relations*
5237 N Cahuenga Blvd #2
N Hollywood, CA 91601, USA

Gold, Brandy (Actor)
Gold Marshak Liedtke
3500 W Oliva Ave #1400
Burbank, CA 91505, USA

Gold, Elon (Actor, Comedian)
c/o Ruthanne Secunda *United Talent Agency (UTA)*
9336 Civic Center Dr
Beverly Hills, CA 90210, USA

Gold, Herbert (Writer)
1051 Broadway #A
San Francisco, CA 94133, USA

Gold, Ian (Athlete, Football Player)
10275 Tradition Pl
Lone Tree, CO 80124, USA

Gold, Jack (Director)
24 Wood Vale
London N1O 3DP, UNITED KINGDOM (UK)

Gold, Jaime (Misc)
Buzznation LLC
11601 Wilshire Blvd Ste 22
Los Angeles, CA 90025, USA

Gold, Jimmy
11990 San Vicente Blvd. #340
Los Angeles, CA 90049

Gold, Judy (Comedian)
c/o Rick Dorfman *Rick Dorfman Management*
450 W 15th St #500
New York, NY 10011, USA

Gold, Missy
3500 W. Olive Ave. #1400
Burbank, CA 91505

Gold, Murray (Musician)
Manners McDade Artist Management
c/o Catherine Manners
18 Broadwick St 4th Fl
London W1F 8HS, UNITED KINGDOM

Gold, Seth (DJ)
c/o Len Evans *Project Publicity*
312 West 53rd St
Suite 202
New York, NY 10019, USA

Gold, Thomas (Scientist)
63 Waterwagon Rd
Ithaca, NY 14850-9703, USA

Gold, Todd
c/o Daniel Strone *Trident Media Group LLC*
41 Madison Ave
36th Floor
New York, NY 10010, USA

Gold, Tracey (Actor)
c/o Harry Gold *TalentWorks (LA)*
3500 W Olive Ave
Suite 1400
Burbank, CA 91505, USA

Goldberg, Adam (Actor)
c/o Nancy Iannios *Nancy Iannios PR*
PO Box 430
Signal Mountain, TN 37377, USA

Goldberg, Bernard (Writer)
c/o Staff Member *HarperCollins Publishers*
10 East 53rd St
c/o Author mail, 7th Floor
New York, NY 10022, USA

Goldberg, Bill (Athlete, Football Player, Wrestler)
7082 Eagle Mountain Rd
Bonsall, CA 92003, USA

Goldberg, Edward D (Geophysicist, Misc, Physicist)
750 Val Sereno Dr
Encinitas, CA 92024, USA

Goldberg, Eric (Animator)
c/o Ellen Goldsmith-Vein *The Gotham Group Inc*
9255 Sunset Blvd
Suite 515
Los Angeles, CA 90069, USA

Goldberg, Gary David (Actor, Director, Producer, Writer)
c/o Staff Member *UBU Productions*
4024 Radford Ave
Bungalow 14
Studio City, CA 91604, USA

Goldberg, Hank (Sportscaster)
11111 Biscayne Blvd # 353
Miami, FL 33181-3404, USA

Goldberg, Leonard (Producer)
Spectradyne Inc
1198 Commerce Dr
Richardson, TX 75081, USA

Goldberg, Lucianne
255 W. 84th St. #6A
New York, NY 10024-4321

Goldberg, Luella G (Educator)
7019 Tupa Dr
Minneapolis, MN 55439, USA

Goldberg, Marshall (Biggie) (Artist)
222 Bowery Place
New York, NY 10012, USA

Goldberg, Richard W (Judge)
US International Trade Court
1 Federal Plaza
New York, NY 10278, USA

Goldberg, Stan (Cartoonist)
16241 Powells Cove Blvd
Apt 4G
Whitestone, NY 11357-1435, USA

Goldberg, Whoopi (Actor, Comedian, Talk Show Host)
c/o Brad Cafarelli *PMK/BNC - LA*
8687 Melrose Ave
8th Floor
West Hollywood, CA 90069, USA

Goldberger, Andi
Bleckenwegen 4
Waldzell, AUSTRIA 4924

Goldberger, Andreas (Skier)
Bleckenwegen 4
Waldzell 4924, AUSTRIA

Goldberger, Marvin L (Educator, Physicist)
621 Mira Monte
La Jolla, CA 92037, USA

Goldblum, Jeff (Actor)
c/o Keith Addis *Industry Entertainment Partners*
955 S Carrillo Dr
Suite 300
Los Angeles, CA 90048, USA

Golden, Arthur (Writer)
c/o Lynn Pleshette *Lynn Pleshette Literary Agency*
2700 N. Beachwood Dr.
Los Angeles, CA 90068, USA

Golden, Clyde (Athlete, Baseball Player)
26 E 59th St
Apt 503
Jacksonville, FL 32208, USA

Golden, Harry (Bowler, Misc)
Professional Bowlers Assn
719 2nd Ave #701
Seattle, WA 98104, USA

Golden, Jim (Athlete, Baseball Player)
8630 SW 10th Ave
Topeka, KS 66615-9688, USA

Golden, Kate (Athlete, Golfer)
969 HUnterwood Dr
Jasper, TX 75951, USA

Golden, Kit (Producer)
c/o Staff Member *Manhattan Project*
1775 Broadway
Suite 410
New York, NY 10019, USA

Golden, Tim (Athlete, Football Player)
P.O. Box 278052
Miramar, FL 33027, USA

Golden, William Lee (Musician, Songwriter)
1764 Saundersville Rd
Hendersonville, TN 37075, USA

Goldens, The
Box 1795
Hendersonville, TN 37077

Goldenthal, Elliot (Composer, Musician)
c/o Staff Member *Chasen & Company*
8899 Beverly Blvd
Suite 405
Los Angeles, CA 90048, USA

Goldfaden, Ben (Athlete, Basketball Player)
5819 Bounty Circle
Tavares, FL 32778-9293, USA

Goldfinger, Sarah (Actor)
c/o Staff Member *Creative Artists Agency (CAA-LA)*
2000 Ave Of The Stars
Los Angeles, CA 90067, USA

Goldfrapp, Alison (Musician)
c/o Staff Member *Mute Records*
1 Albion Pl
London W6 0QT, UK

Goldin, Claudia D (Economist)
Harvard University
Economics Dept
Cambridge, MA 02138, USA

Goldin, Daniel S (Scientist)
The Intellisis Corporation 10350 Science Center Dr Ste 10 Attn: Presidents Office
San Diego, CA 92121-1135, USA

Goldin, Judah (Educator)
3300 Darby Road
Haverford, PA 19041, USA

Goldin, Nan (Photographer)
334 Bowry
New York, NY 10012, USA

Goldin, Ricky Paull (Actor)
c/o Staff Member *Stone Manners Salners Agency (LA)*
9911 W Pico Blvd Ste 1400
Los Angeles, CA 90035, USA

Golding, Meta (Actor)
c/o Charlton Blackburne *A Management*
9107 Wilshire Blvd.
Suite 650
Beverly Hills, CA 90210, USA

Goldman, Bo (Producer, Writer)
c/o David O'Connor *Creative Artists Agency (CAA-LA)*
2000 Ave Of The Stars
Los Angeles, CA 90067, USA

Goldman, Duff (Chef)
Charm City Cakes
2936 Remington Ave
Baltimore, MD 21211, USA

Goldman, Hersh
62 Essex St
Swampscott, MA 01907-1713, USA

Goldman, Julie (Actor, Comedian)
427 Union Street
#3
Brooklyn, New York 11215, USA

Goldman, Les (Athlete, Football Player)
800 E Cypress Creek Rd
Suite 203
Fort Lauderdale, FL 33334, USA

Goldman, Matt (Musician)
Blue Man Group
Luxor Hotel
3900 Las Vegas Blvd. S.
Las Vegas, NV 89119, USA

Goldman, William (Writer)
Janklow & Nesbit
50 E 77th St Apt 30
New York, NY 10075-1842, USA

Goldoni, Lelia
15459 Wyandotte St.
Van Nuys, CA 91405

Goldreich, Peter M (Astronomer)
471 S Catalina Ave
Pasadena, CA 91106, USA

Goldrup, Ray
2383 Broderick
West Jordan, UT 84084

Goldsboro, Bobby (Musician, Songwriter)
La Rana Productions
PO Box 5250
Ocala, FL 34478, USA

Goldsbury, Christopher (Misc)
112 Torcido Dr
San Antonio, TX 78209-5643, USA

Goldschmidt, Neil (Politician)
1150 SW King Ave
Portland, OR 97205-1116, USA

Goldsman, Akiva (Director)
c/o Simon Halls *Slate Public Relations*
9000 Sunset Blvd #915
West Hollywood, CA 90069, USA

Goldsmith, Bethany (Baseball Player)
1000 E Michigan St Apt A
Orlando, FL 32806-4736, USA

Goldsmith, Jonathan (Actor)
c/o Stephanie Gabriel James/Levy/
Jacobson Management Inc
3500 W Olive Ave
Suite 1470
Burbank, CA 91505, USA

Goldsmith, Judy (Activist)
National Organization for Women
425 13th St NW
Washington, DC 20002, USA

Goldsmith, Kelly (Actor)
c/o Dede Binder-Goldsmith Defining
Artists Agency
10 Universal City Plaza
Suite 2000
Universal City, CA 91608, USA

Goldsmith, Paul (Race Car Driver)
1705 E. Main St.
Griffith, IN 46319, USA

Goldsmith, Stephen (Politician)
Governor's Office
State House
Indianapolis, IN 46204, USA

Goldspink, Calvin (Actor)
c/o Staff Member Reel Talent
Management
P.O. Box 491035
Los Angeles, CA 90049, USA

Goldstein, Allan L (Biologist, Misc,
Scientist)
800 25th St NW #1005
Washington, DC 20037, USA

Goldstein, Avram (Misc)
620 Sand Hill Rd
Apt 120D
Palo Alto, CA 94304-2095, USA

Goldstein, Jenette
3932 Marathon St.
Los Angeles, CA 90029

Goldstein, Joseph L (Nobel Prize
Laureate)
3831 Turtle Creek Blvd #22B
Dallas, TX 75219, USA

Goldstein, Lonnie (Athlete, Baseball
Player)
3401 Premier Dr
APt 213
Plano, TX 75023-7093, USA

Goldstein, Lori (Stylist)
c/o Staff Member Art + Commerce
531 W 25th St # 4
New York, NY 10001, USA

Goldstein, Murray (Misc, Physicist)
United Cerebral Palsey Foundation
1660 L St NW #700
Washington, DC 20036, USA

Goldstine, Herman H (Mathematician,
Scientist)
56 Pasture Lane
Bryn Mawr, PA 19010, USA

Goldstone, Jeffrey (Physicist)
77 Massachusetts Ave #6-313
Cambridge, MA 02139, USA

Goldstone, Richard J (Judge)
Constitutional Court Private Bag X32
Braamfontein 2017, SOUTH AFRICA

Goldsworthy, Andrew C (Andy) (Artist,
Photographer)
Hue-Williams Fine Art
21 Cork St
London W1X 1HB, UNITED KINGDOM
(UK)

Goldsworthy, Bill (Athlete, Hockey
Player)

Goldthwait, Bob (Bobcat) (Actor,
Comedian)
c/o Rick Greenstein Gersh (LA)
9465 Wilshire Blvd
Suite 600
Beverly Hills, CA 90212, USA

Goldup, Glenn (Athlete, Hockey Player)
31 Elizabeth St
Etobicoke, ON M8V 2R9, Canada

Goldwasser, Eugene (Biologist, Misc)
5656 S Dorchester Ave
Chicago, IL 60637, USA

Goldwater Jr, Barry
4401 Connecticut Ave NW PMB 850
Washington, DC 20077-3548, USA

Goldwire, Anthony
2007 Birnam Glen Dr
Sugar Land, TX 77479-6421

Goldwyn, Tony (Actor, Director)
c/o Peter Levine Creative Artists Agency
(CAA-LA)
2000 Ave Of The Stars
Los Angeles, CA 90067, USA

Goldwyn Jr, Samuel (Producer)
c/o Staff Member Samuel Goldwyn
Company
9570 W Pico Blvd #400
Los Angeles, CA 90035, USA

Golembiewski, Billy (Bowler)
4966 N Wise Road
Coleman, MI 48618, USA

Golembrosky, Frank (Athlete, Hockey
Player)
4 Francis Cir
Newark, DE 19711-2625

Golenbock, Peter (Sportscaster)
849 Jennings Ave N
Saint Petersburg, FL 33704-1142, USA

Golic, Bob (Athlete, Football Player,
Sportscaster)
6130 Loch Lomond Ct
Solon, OH 44139, USA

Golic, Mike (Athlete, Football Player)
108 Westland Rd
Avon, CT 06001, USA

Goligoski, Alex
916 Golf Course Rd
Grand Rapids, MN 55744-3440, USA

Golimowski, David A (Scientist)
515 Holden Road
Towson, MD 21286-5637, USA

Golina, Stacy
325 S. Swall Dr. #502
Los Angeles, CA 90048-3078

Golino, Valeria (Actor, Producer)
c/o Michael (Mike) Jelline United Talent
Agency (UTA)
9336 Civic Center Dr
Beverly Hills, CA 90210, USA

Golisano, B Thomas (Business Person)
Paychex Inc
911 Panorama Trail S
Rochester, NY 14625, USA

Golisano, Tom (Business Person)
911 Panorama Trail S
Rochester, NY 14625-0397, USA

Gollat, Mike (Baseball Player)
Philadelphia Phillies
2650 Greenlawn Dr
Seven Hills, OH 44131 3623, USA

Golodryga, Bianna (Actor, Anchor)
c/o Staff Member Good Morning America
(NY)
ABC
147 Columbus Ave Fl 6
New York, NY 10023, USA

Golonka, Arlene (Actor)
Silver/Kass/Massetti
8730 Sunset Blvd #480
Los Angeles, CA 90069, USA

Golovin, Tatiana (Athlete, Tennis Player)
c/o Staff Member Women's Tennis
Association (WTA (UK))
Palliser House
Palliser Rd
London W149EB, UK

Golson, Benny (Composer, Music Group,
Musician)
Abby Hoffer
223 1/2 E 48th St
New York, NY 10017, USA

Golson, Greg (Athlete, Baseball Player)
2670 Ravenwood Dr
Round Rock, TX 78665-7926, USA

Golsteyn, Jerry (Athlete, Football Player)
243 Tadcaster Ct
Raeford, NC 28376, USA

Goltz, Dave (Athlete, Baseball Player)
1009 Stony Brook Mnr
Fergus Falls, MN 56537-4413, USA

Gomes, Jonny (Athlete, Baseball Player)
9438 E Sera Brisa
Scottsdale, AZ 85255, USA

Gomes, Wayne (Athlete, Baseball Player)
5104 W Creek Ct
Suffolk, VA 23435-3523, USA

Gomez (Music Group)
c/o Jason Colton Red Light Management
(VA)
PO Box 1467
Charlottesville, VA 22902, USA

Gomez, Andres (Tennis Player)
ProServe
1101 Woodrow Wilson Blvd #1800
Arlington, VA 22209, USA

Gomez, Carlos
15520 Flyboat Ln
Saint Paul, MN 55124-6021, USA

Gomez, Carlos (Actor)
c/o Billy Miller Billy Miller Management
8322 Ridpath Dr
Los Angeles, CA 90046, USA

Gomez, Chris (Athlete, Baseball Player)
8 Vernal Spg
Irvine, CA 92603-0405, USA

Gomez, Edgar (Eddie) (Music Group,
Musician)
Integrity Talent
P O Box 961
Burlington, MA 01803, USA

Gomez, Hector (Actor)
c/o Staff Member Televisa
Blvd Adolfo Lopez Mateos 232
Colonia San Angel INN
DF CP 01060, MEXICO

Gomez, Ian (Actor)
c/o Staff Member Handprint Entertainment
1100 Glendon Ave #100
Los Angeles, CA 90024-3593, USA

Gomez, Javier (Actor)
c/o Gabriel Blanco Gabriel Blanco
Iglesias (Mexico)
Rio Balsas 35-32
Colonia Cuauhtemoc
DF 06500, Mexico

Gomez, Jeff (Cartoonist)
Starlight Runner Entertainment 5 Union
Sq W Fl 4 Attn: Office of the President
New York, NY 10003-3312, USA

Gomez, Jill (Opera Singer)
16 Milton Park
London N6 5QA, UNITED KINGDOM
(UK)

Gomez, Juan "A Orlando" (Athlete,
Baseball Player)
Frederick Keys
21 Stadium Dr
Attn: Manager's Office
Fredrick, MD 21703-6553, USA

Gomez, Leo (Athlete, Baseball Player)
273 Portofino Dr
North Venice, FL 34275-6654, USA

Gomez, Luis (Athlete, Baseball Player)
676 Chesterfield Dr
Lawrenceville, GA 30044-5624, USA

Gomez, Marga (Comedian)
PO Box 460368
San Francisco, California 94146, USA

Gomez, Natalie (Actor)
c/o Staff Member Advance LA
7904 Santa Monica Blvd
West Hollywood, CA 90046

Gomez, Nick (Director)
c/o Staff Member Evolution Entertainment
(LA)
901 N Highland Ave
Los Angeles, CA 90038, USA

Gomez, Panchito (Actor)
240 N Hollywood Way
Burbank, CA 91505, USA

Gomez, Pat (Athlete, Baseball Player)
2257 Quarry Way
Rocklin, CA 95765-4292, USA

Gomez, Ralph E (Mathematician, Misc)
Alfred P Sloan Foundation
President's Office 630 5th Ave
New York, NY 10111, USA

Gomez, Randy (Athlete, Baseball Player)
50 Oak St
San Martin, CA 95046-9592, USA

Gomez, Rick (Actor)
c/o Sam Maydew Collective
8383 Wilshire Blvd
Suite 1050
Beverly Hills, CA 90211, USA

Gomez, Scott (Athlete, Hockey Player,
Olympic Athlete)
Pulver Sports
479 Bedford Park Ave
Attn Ian Pulver
Toronto, ON M5M 1K2, Canada

Gomez, Selena (Actor)
19241 Wells Dr
Tarzana, CA 91356, USA

Gomez, Wilfredo (Athlete, Boxer)
Boxing Hall of Fame
1 Hall of Fame Dr
Casastota, NY 13032, USA

Gomez-Preston, Reagan (Actor)
c/o Mara Santino *Luber Roklin Management*
8530 Wilshire Blvd
6th Floor
Beverly Hills, CA 90211, USA

Gomez-Preston, Reagen (Actor)
c/o Staff Member *Jeff Morrone Entertainment*
9350 Wilshire Blvd
Suite 224
Beverly Hills, CA 90212, USA

Gomory, Ralph E (Scientist)
260 Douglas Rd
Chappaqua, NY 10514-3100, USA

Gompers, Bill (Athlete, Football Player)
1060 Montego Bay Dr N
Merritt Island, FL 32953, USA

Gompf, Thomas (Tom) (Athlete, Diver, Olympic Athlete)
2716 Barrel Ave
Plant City, FL 33566, USA

Goncalves, Vascos dos Santos (General, Prime Minister)
Ave Estados Unidos da America 86
5 Esq
Lisbon 1700, PORTUGAL

Gonchar, Sergei (Athlete, Hockey Player)
2331 Fisher Island Dr Apt 4301
Miami Beach, FL 33109-0094, USA

Gondrezick, Grant (Athlete, Basketball Player)
5906 Etiwanda Avenue
Unit 19
Tarzana, CA 91356-1649, USA

Gondry, Michel (Director, Writer)
c/o Dan Aloni *WmE2 (WMA-LA)*
1 William Morris Pl
Beverly Hills, CA 90212, USA

Gong, Julie (Stylist)
Julie Gong
Prefers to be contacted
via telephone or email
New York, NY 10012, USA

Gonick, Larry (Cartoonist)
247 Missouri St
San Francisco, CA 94107-2404, USA

Gonnenwein, Wolfgang
Opera et Concert
Maximilianstr 22
Munich 80539, GERMANY

Gonshaw, Francesca (Actor)
Greg Mellard
12 D'Arblay St #200
London W1V 3FP, UNITED KINGDOM (UK)

Gonsoulin, Austin (Goose) (Athlete, Football Player)
5966 Reeves Dr
Silsbee, TX 77656, USA

Gonzales, Alberto (Government Official, Judge)
White House
1600 Pennsylvania Ave NW
Washington, DC 20500, USA

Gonzales, Carlos (Cinematographer)
1549 1/2 N Commonwealth Ave
Los Angeles, CA 90027, USA

Gonzales, Dan (Athlete, Baseball Player)
429 W Silvertip Rd
Tucson, AZ 85737-3704, USA

Gonzales, Jaslene (Model)
c/o Lizzie Grubman *Lizzie Grubman Public Relations*
270 Lafayette St
Suite 504
New York, NY 10012, USA

Gonzales, Larry (Athlete, Baseball Player)
3800 Bradford St
Spc 248
La Verne, CA 91750-3151, USA

Gonzales, Raul (Soccer Player)
Sergio Cerro Luengas
Alcala 694 1
Madrid 28019, SPAIN

Gonzales, Rene (Athlete, Baseball Player)
755 E Orangewood Dr
Covina, CA 91723-3620, USA

Gonzalez, Alex (Athlete, Baseball Player)
7743 SW 119th Ct
Miam, FL 33183-3854, USA

Gonzalez, Ana (Stylist)
2122-A Clinton Ave
Alameda, CA 94501, USA

Gonzalez, Anthony (Athlete, Football Player)
13271 Dumbarton St
Carmel, IN 46032-7321, USA

Gonzalez, Araceli (Actor)
c/o Staff Member *Telefe - Argentina*
Pavon 2444 (C1248AAT)
Buenos Aires, ARGENTINA

Gonzalez, Arthur (Judge)
US Bankruptcy Court
1 Bowling Green
New York, NY 10004, USA

Gonzalez, Charles (Congressman, Politician)
1434 Longworth HOB
Washington, DC 20515, USA

Gonzalez, edgar (Athlete, Baseball Player)
144 Avenida Loretta
Chula Vista, CA 91914-4631, USA

Gonzalez, Edith (Actor)
c/o Staff Member *Televisa*
Blvd Adolfo Lopez Mateos 232
Colonia San Angel INN
DF CP 01060, MEXICO

Gonzalez, Fredi (Athlete, Baseball Player, Coach)
2768 Pete Shaw Rd
Marietta, GA 30066-2206, USA

Gonzalez, Gabe (Athlete, Baseball Player)
920 Cerritos Ave
Long Beach, CA 90813-4812, USA

Gonzalez, gio
920 Cerritos Ave
Long Beach, CA 33012-3349, United States

Gonzalez, Hector (Religious Leader)
Baptist Churches USA
P O Box 851
Valley Forge, PA 19482, USA

Gonzalez, Jeremi (Athlete, Baseball Player)
1120 N La Salle Dr
Apt 14N
Chicago, IL 60610, USA

Gonzalez, Juan (Athlete, Baseball Player)
c/o Staff Member *Texas Rangers*
1000 Ballpark Way
Arlington, TX 76011, USA

Gonzalez, Juan A (Baseball Player)
Ext Catoni A9
Vega Baja, PR 00693, USA

Gonzalez, Lazaro Naranjo (Cholly) (Athlete, Baseball Player)
8306 NW 7th St #32
Miami, FL 33126-3924, USA

Gonzalez, Leon (Athlete, Football Player)
4025 Leonnie Rd
Jacksonville, FL 32208, USA

Gonzalez, Luis (Athlete, Baseball Player)
8902 Ilona Ln Apt 8
Houston, TX 77025-3636, USA

Gonzalez, Macchi Luis (President)
Palacio de Gobiemo
Ave Marisol Lopez
Asuncion, PARAGUAY

Gonzalez, Mike (Athlete, Baseball Player)
2414 Pine Brook Ct
Deer Park, TX 77536-1518, USA

Gonzalez, Miriam (Actor, Model)
c/o Staff Member *Playboy Productions*
2706 Media Center Drive
Los Angles, CA 90065, USA

Gonzalez, Nicholas (Actor)
c/o Chuck James *ICM Partners (ICM-LA)*
10250 Constellation Blvd Fl 7
Los Angeles, CA 90067, USA

Gonzalez, Orlando (Athlete, Baseball Player)
12460 NW 11th Ln
Miami, FL 33182-2463, USA

Gonzalez, Pedro (Athlete, Baseball Player)
104 Gen Cabral
San Pedro de Macoris, Dominican Republic

Gonzalez, Phoenix (Actor)
c/o Staff Member *Select Artists Ltd (CA-Westside Office)*
1138 12th Street
Suite 1
Santa Monica, CA 90403, USA

Gonzalez, Raul (Soccer Player)
Real Madrid FC
Avda Concha Espina 1
Madrid 28036, SPAIN

Gonzalez, Rick (Actor)
c/o Stephanie Nese *Framework Entertainment (LA)*
9057 Nemo St
Suite C
West Hollywood, CA 90069, USA

Gonzalez, Susana (Actor)
c/o Staff Member *Televisa*
Blvd Adolfo Lopez Mateos 232
Colonia San Angel INN
DF CP 01060, MEXICO

Gonzalez, Tony (Athlete, Baseball Player)
8011 SW 196th Ter
Cutler Bay, FL 33764-2863, USA

Gonzalez, Tony (Athlete, Football Player)
c/o Denise White *EAG Sports Management*
12910 Agustin Pl
Playa Vista, CA 90094, USA

Gonzalez, Victor (Actor)
c/o Gabriel Blanco *Gabriel Blanco Iglesias (Mexico)*
Rio Balsas 35-32
Colonia Cuauhtemoc
DF 06500, Mexico

Gonzalez Zumarraga, Antonio J Cardinal (Religious Leader)
Arzobispado
Apartado 17-01-00106
Called Chile
Quito 1140, ECUADOR

Gonzalo, Julie (Actor)
c/o Sharon Lane *Lane Management Group*
13017 Woodbridge St
Studio City, CA 91604, USA

Gooch, Jeff (Athlete, Football Player)
12709 Seronera Valley Ct
Spring Hill, FL 34610-7658, USA

Good, Andrew (Athlete, Baseball Player)
1433 S Belcher Rd
Apt G4
Clearwater, FL 33764-2863, USA

Good, David (Reality TV Star, Writer)
c/o Inna Shamis *AvantGarde Communications Group*
Prefers to be contacted via telephone or email
USA

Good, Hugh W (Religious Leader)
Primitive Advent Christian Church
273 Frame Road
Elkview, WV 25071, USA

Good, Meagan (Actor)
c/o Evan Hainey *Untitled Entertainment (LA)*
350 S. Beverly Dr #200
Beverly Hills, CA 90212, USA

Good, Melanie (Actor)
c/o Staff Member *Bobby Ball Talent Agency*
4116 W Magnolia Blvd Ste 205
Burbank, CA 91505-2700, USA

Good, Michael T (Astronaut)
2617 Broussard Court
Seabrook, TX 77586, USA

Good, Michael T Lt Colonel (Astronaut)
3874 Cherry Plum Dr
Colorado Springs, CO 80920-2802

Goodacre, Connick Jill (Model)
Harry Connick
Wilkins Mgmt 323 Broadway
Cambridge, MA 02139, USA

Goodacre, Glenna (Artist, Misc)
National Academy Museum
1083 5th Ave
New York, NY 10126, USA

Goodall, Caroline (Actor)
P F D Drury House
34-43 Russell St
London WC2B 5HA, UNITED KINGDOM (UK)

Goodall, Jane (Writer)
4245 Fairfax Dr Ste 600
Arlington, VA 22203-1698, USA

Goodburn, Kelly (Athlete, Football Player)
3710 W 52nd Pl
Mission, KS 66205, USA

Good Charlotte (Music Group)
81 Pondfield Rd #358
Bronxville, NY 10708, USA

Goode, Chris (Athlete, Football Player)
1428 Egret Ln
Birmingham, AL 35214, USA

Goode, David R (Business Person)
Norfolk Southern Corp
3 Commercial Place
Norfolk, VA 23510, USA

Goode, Irvin (Irv) (Athlete, Football Player)
1030 Schnucks Woodsmill Plz
Chesterfield, MO 63017, USA

Goode, Kerry (Athlete, Football Player)
639 Herron Ct
Fairburn, GA 30213, USA

Goode, Matthew (Actor)
c/o Craig Bankey *WKT Public Relations (WKT-LA)*
9350 Wilshire Blvd
Suite 450
Beverly Hills, CA 90212, USA

Goode, Rob (Athlete, Football Player)
1902 Oakridge Trl
Bridgeport, TX 76426, USA

Goode, Tom (Athlete, Football Player)
9190 Tom Goode Rd
West Point, MS 39773, USA

Goodell, Brian S (Athlete, Olympic Athlete, Swimmer)
27040 S Ridge Dr
Mission Viejo, CA 92692, USA

Goodell, Roger (Business Person, Football Executive)
National Football League
Commissioner's Office
280 Park Ave Fl 12W
New York, NY 10017-1206, USA

Gooden, Drew (Basketball Player)
Orlando Magic
Waterhouse Center
8701 Maitland Summit Blvd
Orlando, FL 32810, USA

Gooden, Dwight (Athlete, Baseball Player)
20114 Nob Oak Ave
Tampa, FL 33647-3359, USA

Gooden, Harry (Athlete, Football Player)
5001 Rime Vlg
Brimingham, Al 35216-6456, USA

Goodenough, Larry (Athlete, Hockey Player)
3677 Spruce Hill Rd
Ottsville, PA 18942-9508, USA

Goodenough, Ward H (Misc)
3300 Darby Road #5306
Haverford, PA 19041, USA

Goodeve, Charles P (Athlete, Football Player)
30177 Tattersail Way
Menifee, CA 92584-7366, USA

Goodeve, Grant (Actor)
21416 NE 68th Court
Redmond, WA 98053, USA

Goodfellow, Peter N (Misc, Scientist)
Cancer Research Fund
Lincoln Inn Fields
London WC2A 3PX, UNITED KINGDOM (UK)

Goodfriend, Lynda (Actor)
c/o Lynda Goodfriend *Lynda Goodfriend Management*
338 S Beachwood Dr
Burbank, CA 91506, USA

Goodfriend, Lynda (Actor)
338 S Beachwood Dr
Burbank, CA 91506, USA

Gooding, Cuba Jr (Actor)
c/o Nancy Kane *Kane & Associates*
319 N Venice Blvd
Venice, CA 90291, USA

Gooding, Omar (Actor)
c/o Ericalane Brown *The Kartel Company*
1304 W 2nd St
Suite 310
Los Angeles, CA 90026, USA

Goodlatte, Bob (Congressman, Politician)
2240 Rayburn HOB
Washington, DC 20515, USA

Goodlin, Chalmers (Misc)
7620 Red River Road
West Palm Beach, FL 33411, USA

Goodman, Alfred (Composer)
Bodenstedtstr 31
Munich 81241, GERMANY

Goodman, Allegra (Writer)
Dial Press
375 Hudson St
New York, NY 10014, USA

Goodman, Andre (Athlete, Football Player)
125 Island View Cir
Elgin, SC 29045-9182, USA

Goodman, Brian (Actor)
c/o Paul Santana *Agency for the Performing Arts (APA-LA)*
405 S Beverly Dr
Suite 500
Beverly Hills, CA 90212-4425, USA

Goodman, Brian (Athlete, Football Player)
15009 S 14th Pl
Phoenix, AZ 85048, USA

Goodman, Corey S (Biologist, Misc)
Howard Hughes Medical Institute
Molecular/Cell Biology Dept
Berkeley, CA 94720, USA

Goodman, David A. (Writer)
c/o Jon Huddle *United Talent Agency (UTA)*
9336 Civic Center Dr
Beverly Hills, CA 90210, USA

Goodman, Drew (Commentator)
5721 Green Oaks Dr
Greenwood Village, CO 80121-1336, USA

Goodman, Ellen H (Editor, Misc)
Boston Globe
Editorial Dept 135 W T Morrissey Blvd
Dorchester, MA 02125, USA

Goodman, Harvey (Athlete, Football Player)
2689 County Road 318
Westcliffe, CO 81252, USA

Goodman, Henry
2015 Broad Street
Apt 108
Cranston, RI 02905-3346, USA

Goodman, Jo (Stylist)
1103 E California Ave
Glendale, CA 91206, USA

Goodman, John (Actor, Musician, Producer)
c/o Bob Gersh *Gersh (LA)*
9465 Wilshire Blvd
Suite 600
Beverly Hills, CA 90212, USA

Goodman, John (Athlete, Football Player)
800 E 9th St
Edmond, OK 73034, USA

Goodman, Joseph W (Engineer)
570 University Terrace
Los Altos, CA 94022, USA

Goodman, Oscar (Attorney, Attorney General, General)
520 S 4th St
Las Vegas, NV 89101, USA

Goodman, Richard (Producer)
c/o Staff Member *WME (LA)*
9601 Wilshire Blvd Fl 3
Beverly Hills, CA 90210, USA

Goodmann, Terrence (Stylist)
723 E Fairmont Rd
Burbank, CA 91501, USA

Goodnight, James (Jim) (Business Person)
SAS Institute Inc
100 SAS Campus Dr
Cary, NC 27513-2414, USA

Goodnoff, Irvin (Cinematographer)
29997 Mulholland Highway
Agoura Hills, CA 91301, USA

Goodrem, Delta (Actor, Musician)
c/o Staff Member *The Harbour Agency*
135 Forbes St
Woolloomooloo NSW 2011, Australia

Goodrich, Dwayne (Athlete, Football Player)
533 Oakcrest Dr
Coppell, TX 75019, USA

Goodrich, Gail (Actor, Athlete, Basketball Player, Sportscaster)
P.O. Box 4969
Greenwich, CT 06830-3911, USA

Goodrich, Jon (Baseball Player)
123 W Agua Caliente Rd
Sonoma, CA 95476-3340, USA

Goodrich Jr, Gail C (Athlete, Basketball Player)
270 Oceano Dr
Los Angeles, CA 90049, USA

Goodrum, Charles (Athlete, Football Player)
117 Pico Rd
East Palatka, FL 32131, USA

Goodson, Ed (Athlete, Baseball Player)
2330 Cold Springs Ln
Galax, VA 24333-3763, USA

Goodson, James A (War Hero)
37 Carolina Trail
Marshfield, MA 02050, USA

Goodwill, Oliver (Actor)
Asylum Entertainment
C/O Marcello Robinson
7920 Sunset Blvd 2nd Fl
Los Angeles, CA 90046, USA

Goodwin, Curtis (Athlete, Baseball Player)
14939 Western Ave
San Leandro, CA 94578-3627, USA

Goodwin, Danny (Athlete, Baseball Player)
1555 Linksview Close
Stone Mountain, GA 30088-3768, USA

Goodwin, Doris Kearns (Historian)
General Delivery
1649 Monument Lane
Concord, MA 01742, USA

Goodwin, Doug (Athlete, Football Player)
400 Waverly Place Cir Apt B1
North Charleston, SC 29418-2010, USA

Goodwin, Ginnifer (Actor)
c/o John Carrabino *John Carrabino Management*
5900 Wilshire Blvd Fl 4 #406
Los Angeles, CA 90036, USA

Goodwin, Hunter (Athlete, Football Player)
1011 Lyceum Ct
College Station, TX 77840-2342, USA

Goodwin, Louise (Stylist)
c/o Staff Member *Mel Bryant Management*
611 Broadway #623
New York, NY 10012

Goodwin, Michael (Actor)
8271 Melrose Ave #110
Los Angeles, CA 90046, USA

Goodwin, Randy (Race Car Driver)
Randy Goodwin Racing
2009 Somerset Lane
Fullerton, CA 92633, USA

Goodwin, Ron (Athlete, Football Player)
3702 Sul Ross St
San Angelo, TX 76904, USA

Goodwin, Tom
8 Maple st
Massapequa, NY 11758-5717, USA

Goodwin, Tom (Athlete, Baseball Player, Olympic Athlete)
8 Maple St
Massapequa, NY 11758-5717, USA

Goodwin, Trudie (Actor)
Bosun House
1 Deer Park Rd
Merton
London SW19 3TL, ENGLAND

Goody, Joan E (Architect)
Goody Clancy Assoc
334 Boylston St
Boston, MA 02116, USA

Goodyear, Scott (Race Car Driver)
Scott Goodyear Racing
PO Box 589
Carmel, IN 46082, USA

Goo Goo Dolls (Music Group)
c/o David Levine *WME (LA)*
9601 Wilshire Blvd Fl 3
Beverly Hills, CA 90210, USA

Goolagong-Cawley, Evonne (Athlete, Tennis Player)
c/o Staff Member *Ovations*
P.O. Box 1337
Rozelle, NSW 2039, Australia

Goolagong Cawley, Evonne F (Tennis Player)
Private Bag 6060
Richmond, SV 3121, AUSTRALIA

Goorjian, Michael (Actor)
Evolution Entertainment
901 N Highland Ave
Los Angeles, CA 90038, USA

Goosen, Don (Boxer, Misc)
6320 Van Nuys Blvd
Van Nuys, CA 91401, USA

Goosen, Retief (Athlete, Golfer)
14 N Park
Sunninghill
Ascot SL59B, United Kingdom

Gopi (Actor)
M3/F Anugraha Colony 3rd Avenue
Ashok Nagar
c, TN 600 083, INDIA

Gopi Krishna, B M (Actor)
14 Soundara Rajan Street
T Nagar
Chennai, TN 600 017, INDIA

Goranson, Alicia (Actor)
c/o Staff Member *Paradigm (LA)*
360 N Crescent Dr
North Bldg
Beverly Hills, CA 90210, USA

Gorbachev, Mikhail S (General, Nobel Prize Laureate, Politician, Secretary)
Leningradsky Prospekt 49
Moscow 125468, RUSSIA

Gorbachev, Yuri (Artist)
Adrienne Editions
377 Geary St
San Francisco, CA 94102, USA

Gorbatko, Viktor V (Astronaut, General, Misc)
Potchta Kosmonavtov
Moskovskoi Oblasti
Svyisdny Goroduk 141160, RUSSIA

Gorchakova, Galina (Opera Singer)
Askonas Holt Ltd
27 Chancery Lane
London WC2A 1PF, UNITED KINGDOM (UK)

Gordeeva, Ekaterina (Athlete, Figure Skater)
c/o Staff Member *IMG (LA)*
717 N Alta Vista Blvd
Los Angeles, CA 90046, USA

Gorder, Genevieve (Designer, Television Host)
c/o Ken Slotnick *WME (WMA-NY)*
1325 Ave of the Americas
New York, NY 10019, USA

Gordeyev, Vyacheslav M (Ballerina, Choreographer, Dancer)
Tverskaya Str 9 #78
Moscow 103009, RUSSIA

Gordimer, Nadine (Nobel Prize Laureate)
7 Frere Road Parktown
Johannesburg 2193, SOUTH AFRICA

Gordin, Charles (Actor)
187 Chestnut Hill Road
Wilton, CT 06897, USA

Gordon, Barry (Actor, Music Group)
1912 Kaweah Dr
Pasadena, CA 91105, USA

Gordon, Ben (Athlete, Basketball Player)
c/o Raymond Brothers *International Athlete Management, Inc*
433 N. Camden Dr
Suite 600
Beverly Hills, CA 90210, USA

Gordon, Bert I (Director)
9640 Arby Dr
Beverly Hills, CA 90210, USA

Gordon, Bing
Kleiner, Perkins, Caufield, Byers
2750 Sand Hill Rd
Menlo Park, CA 94025, USA

Gordon, Bobby (Race Car Driver)
6300 Valley View Ave
Buena Park, CA 90620, USA

Gordon, Bridgette (Athlete, Basketball Player, Olympic Athlete)
3400 Sweetwater Rd #1309
Lawrenceville, GA 30044-2495, USA

Gordon, Carl
8661 Pine Tree Pl.
Los Angeles, CA 90069

Gordon, Carolyn (Stylist)
c/o Staff Member *L'Agence*
5901-C Peachtree Dunwoody Rd
#60
Atlanta, GA 30328, USA

Gordon, Cornell (Athlete, Football Player)
4029 Spring Meadow Crest
Chesapeake, VA 23321, USA

Gordon, Danso (Actor)
c/o Paul Nicholls *Artistry Management*
340 N. Camden Dr
Suite 302
Beverly Hills, CA 90210, USA

Gordon, Darrien (Athlete, Football Player)
1500 Pecos Dr
Southlake, TX 76092, USA

Gordon, David (Choreographer)
47 Great Jones St #2
New York, NY 10012, USA

Gordon, Dick (Athlete, Football Player)
5017 Anderson Pl
Cincinnati, OH 45227, USA

Gordon, Don
6853 Pacific View Dr
Los Angeles, CA 90068

Gordon, Don (Athlete, Baseball Player)
711 Sunset Mountain Dr
Chattanooga, TN 37421-2076, USA

Gordon, Don (Actor)
Acme Talent
4727 Wilshire Blvd #333
Los Angeles, CA 90010, USA

Gordon, Don (Athlete, Baseball Player)
711 Sunset Mountain Dr
Chattanooga, TN 37421-2076, USA

Gordon, Ed (Correspondent)
NBC-TV
News Dept 30 Rockefeller Plaza
New York, NY 10112, USA

Gordon, Eve
10100 Santa Monica Blvd. #2500
Los Angeles, CA 90067

Gordon, Hannah Taylor (Actor)
Hutton Mgmt
4 Old Manor Close Askett
Buckinghamshire HP27 9NA, UNITED KINGDOM (UK)

Gordon, Harold P (Business Person)
Hasbro Inc
1027 Newport Ave
Pawtucket, RI 02861, USA

Gordon, Herold (Athlete, Baseball Player)
8798 Traverse St
Detroit, MI 48213, USA

Gordon, Howard (Producer, Writer)
c/o Rick Rosen *WME (LA)*
9601 Wilshire Blvd Fl 3
Beverly Hills, CA 90210, USA

Gordon, Ira (Athlete, Football Player)
PO Box 24526
Federal Way, WA 98093-1526, USA

Gordon, Jack (Athlete, Hockey Player)
17-1725 Southmere Cres
Surrey, BC V4A 7A7, Canada

Gordon, Jeff (Race Car Driver)
c/o Jon Edwards *Performance PR Plus*
520 N College St
Charlotte, NC 28202, USA

Gordon, John (Commentator)
13011 Milford Pl
Fort Myers, FL 33913-8454, USA

Gordon, Keith (Actor, Director, Writer)
c/o Dan Aloni *WmE2 (WMA-LA)*
1 William Morris Pl
Beverly Hills, CA 90212, USA

Gordon, Keith (Athlete, Baseball Player)
4601 Thornhurst Dr
Olney, MD 20832-1826, USA

Gordon, Kiowa (Actor)
c/o Ryan Martin *Agency for the Performing Arts (APA-LA)*
405 S Beverly Dr
Suite 500
Beverly Hills, CA 90212-4425, USA

Gordon, Lamar (Athlete, Football Player)
4331 N 16th St
Milwaukee, WI 53209-6924, USA

Gordon, Lancaster (Athlete, Basketball Player)
550 Robinhood Rd
Jackson, MS 39206-5403, USA

Gordon, Lawrence (Business Person)
Largo Entertainment
20th Century Fox 10201 W Pico Blvd
Los Angeles, CA 90064, USA

Gordon, Leo
9977 Wornon Ave.
Sunland, CA 91040

Gordon, Lincoln (Diplomat, Economist)
10450 Lottsford Road
Apt 253
Bowie, MD 20721-3303, USA

Gordon, Mikalah (Musician)
c/o Staff Member *11-16 Entertainment*
11048 La Maida
Suite 9
North Hollywood, CA 91601, USA

Gordon, Mike (Musician)
c/o Jason Colton *Red Light Management (VA)*
PO Box 1467
Charlottesville, VA 22902, USA

Gordon, Mike (Athlete, Baseball Player)
35 Longview Rd
Brockton, MA 02301-5637, USA

Gordon, Milton A (Educator)
California State University
President's Office
Fullerton, CA 99264, USA

Gordon, Nina (Musician)
c/o Staff Member *Paradigm (Monterey)*
404 W Franklin St
Monterey, CA 93940, USA

Gordon, Pamela (Prime Minister)
United Bermuda Party
Burrows Bldg
Hamilton HM, CX, BERMUDA

Gordon, Phil (Misc)
Much and House Public Relations
8075 West Third Street 500
Los Angeles, CA 90048, USA

Gordon, Richard (Astronaut)
65 Woodside Dr
Prescott, AZ 86305-5092, USA

Gordon, Richard F Jr (Astronaut)
65 Woodside Dr
Prescott, AZ 86305, USA

Gordon, Robby (Race Car Driver)
Robby Gordon Motorsports
10615 Twin Lakes Parkway
Charlotte, NC 28269, USA

Gordon, Scott (Athlete, Coach, Hockey Player)
c/o Staff Member *Providence Bruins*
1 La Salle Sq
Providence, RI 02903, USA

Gordon, Sean (Model)
c/o Staff Member *IMG*
304 Park Ave S Fl 12
New York, NY 10010, USA

Gordon, Stuart (Director, Producer)
c/o Staff Member *Red Hen Productions*
3607 West Magnlia
Suite L
Burbank, CA 91505, USA

Gordon, Tom (Athlete, Baseball Player)
2006 Lake Lotela Dr
Avon Park, FL 33825-8030, USA

Gordon, Tracy (Race Car Driver)
Beal's General Store
Main St.
Strong, ME 02983, USA

Gordon, William E (Physicist)
Rice University
Space Physics Dept
PO Box 1892
Houston, TX 77251, USA

Gordon, Zachary (Actor)
c/o Daniel Spilo *Industry Entertainment Partners*
955 S Carrillo Dr
Suite 300
Los Angeles, CA 90048, USA

Gordon-Levitt, Joey
4024 Radford Ave Bldg. 3
Studio City, CA 91604

Gordon-Levitt, Joseph (Actor)
c/o Stephen Huvane *Slate Public Relations*
9000 Sunset Blvd #915
West Hollywood, CA 90069, USA

Gordy, Berry
878 Stradella Rd.
Los Angeles, CA 90077

Gordy, Walter (Physicist)
2521 Perkins Road
Durham, NC 27705, USA

Gore, Al (Ex-Senator, Ex-Vice President, Politician)
The Office of Al & Tipper Gore
3810 Bedford Ave #250
Nashville, TN 37215-2563, USA

Gore, Frank (Athlete, Football Player)
6641 SW 159th Pl
Miami, FL 33193, USA

Gore, Lesley (Musician, Songwriter, Writer)
World Entertainment Assoc
297101 Kinderkamack Road
#128
Oradell, NJ 07649, USA

Gore, Martin (Musician)
c/o Staff Member *Mute Records*
1 Albion Pl
London W6 0QT, UK

Gore, Michael
15622 Royal Oak Rd
Encino, CA 91436

Gore, Robert W (Inventor)
465 Polly Drummond Hill Rd
Newark, DE 19711-4340, USA

Gore, Tipper (Politician)
The Office of Al & Tipper Gore
3810 Bedford Ave #250
Nashville, TN 37215-2563, USA

Gorecki, Reid (Athlete, Baseball Player)
1017 Crestdale
Crossing Dr
Avon Park, FL 33825-8030, USA

Gorecki, Rick (Athlete, Baseball Player)
8703 Powers Ct
Orland Park, IL 60462-5695, USA

Gore Jr, Albert A (President, Vice President)
312 Lunnwood Blvd
Nashville, TN 37205, USA

Goren, Shlomo (General, Religious Leader)
Chief Rabbinate
Hechal Shlomo
Jerusalem, ISRAEL

Gorence, Tom (Athlete, Hockey Player)
120 Hanapepe Loop
Honolulu, HI 96825, USA

Gorenstein, Mark B (Conductor)
Rublevskoye Shosses 28
#25
Moscow 121609, RUSSIA

Gores, Alec (Misc)
49 Beverly Park Cir
Beverly Hills, CA 90210-1566, USA

Goreski, Brad (Stylist)
c/o Eric Kranzler *Management 360*
9111 Wilshire Blvd
Beverly Hills, CA 90210, USA

Goretta, Claude (Director)
10 Tour de Boel
Geneva 1204, SWITZERLAND

Gorgal, Ken (Athlete, Football Player)
4 The Court Of Harborside
Northbrook, IL 60062, USA

Gorgl, Elisabeth (Athlete, Skier)
Kapfenberger Sportvereinigung
Franz Fekete Stadion
J.-Brandl-Gasse 25
Kapfenberg A-8605, Austria

Gorham, Christopher (Actor)
c/o Glenn Rigberg *HYPHENATE*
9701 Wilshire Blvd.
10th floor
Beverly Hills, CA 90212, USA

Gorham, Eville (Misc)
1933 E River Terrace
Minneapolis, MN 55414, USA

Gorie, Docominic L
13656 Hidden Valley Ln
Salida, CO 81201-9760, USA

Gorie, Dominic L (Astronaut)
16522 Craighurst Dr
Houston, TX 77059, USA

Gorillaz (Music Group)
c/o Staff Member *Virgin Records (LA)*
1750 Vine St
Los Angeles, CA 90028-5209, USA

Gorin, Brandon (Athlete, Football Player)
11031 Mirador Ln
Fishers, IN 46037-7555, USA

Gorin, Charles
2617 First Dr.
Austin, TX 78731

Gorin, Charlie (Athlete, Baseball Player)
2617 Fiset Dr
Austin, TX 78731-5613, USA

Goring, Robert T (Butch) (Athlete, Hockey Player)
New York Islanders 1255 Hempstead Tpke
Attn: Broadcast Dept
Uniondale, NY 11553-1200, USA

Gorinski, Bob (Athlete, Baseball Player)
758 Claypike Rd
Acme, PA 15610-2177, USA

Goris, Eva (Actor)
International Creative Mgmt
8942 Wilshire Blvd
#219
Beverly Hills, CA 90211, USA

Gorlin, Alexander (Architect)
Alexander Gorlin Architect
137 Varick St
New York, NY 10013, USA

Gorman, Brian (Baseball Player)
PO Box 1208
Somis, CA 93066-1208, USA

Gorman, Brian (Athlete, Baseball Player)
1381 Via Latina Dr
Camarillo, CA 93012-9294, USA

Gorman, Bryan (Athlete, Golfer)
The Auld Course
525 Hunte Pkwy
Chula Vista, CA 91914, USA

Gorman, Burn (Actor)
c/o Staff Member *Luber Roklin Management*
8530 Wilshire Blvd
6th Floor
Beverly Hills, CA 90211, USA

Gorman, Cliff
333 W. 57th St.
New York, NY 10019

Gorman, Dave (Athlete, Hockey Player)
6821 Domenic Cres
Niagara Falls, ON L2J 4L5, Canada

Gorman, E J (Writer)
PO Box 669
Cedar Rapids, IA 52406-0669, USA

Gorman, Joseph T (Business Person)
TRW Inc
1900 Richmond Road
Cleveland, OH 44124, USA

Gorman, Paul F Jr (General)
9175 Batesville Road
Alton, VA 22920, USA

Gorman, R C (Artist)
PO Box 1258
El Prado, NM 87529, USA

Gorman, Steve (Musician)
c/o Staff Member *Mitch Schneider Organization (MSO)*
14724 Ventura Blvd #410
Sherman Oaks, CA 91403, USA

Gorman, Tom (Athlete, Baseball Player)
1615 SW 5th Ave
Portland, OR 97201-5403, USA

Gorman, Tom (Tennis Player)
ProServe
1101 Woodrow Wilson Blvd
#1800
Arlington, VA 22209, USA

Gorman-Cahill, Margaret
4216 38th St. NW
Washington, DC 20016-2258

Gorme, Eydie (Musician)
944 Pinehurst Dr
Las Vegas, NV 89109, USA

Gormley, Antony (Artist)
13 South Villas
London NW1 9BS, UNITED KINGDOM (UK)

Gorneault, Nick (Athlete, Baseball Player)
94 Seymour Ave
Springfield, MA 01109-1330, USA

Gorney, Karen Lynn (Actor)
Karen Company
Po Box 23-1060
New York, NY 10023, USA

Gorouuch, Edward Lee (Educator)
University of Alaska
President's Office
Anchorage, AK 99508, USA

Gorrell, Bob (Cartoonist)
Creators Syndicate
5777 W Century Blvd
#700
Los Angeles, CA 90045, USA

Gorrell, Fred (Misc)
501 E Port au Prince Lane
Phoenix, AZ 85022, USA

Gorris, Marleen (Director, Writer)

Gorski, Mark (Athlete, Cycler, Olympic Athlete)
17 Colonial Hills Pkwy
Saint Louis, MO 63141-7765, USA

Gorski, Tamara (Actor)
Steve Young & Associates
18 Gloucester Lane #200
Toronto M4Y 1L5, CANADA

Gorter, Cornelis J (Physicist)
Klobeniersburgwal 29
Amsterdam, NETHERLANDS

Gortman, Shaunzinski (Basketball Player)
Charlotte Sting
100 Hive Dr
Charlotte, NC 28217, USA

Gortner, Marjoe (Actor)
P.O. Box 0356
Sun Valley, ID 83353-0356, USA

Gorvl, John (Athlete, Baseball Player)
1888 Cranberrv Isles
Way
Apopka, FL 32712-2138, USA

Goryl, John (Athlete, Baseball Player, Coach)
528 Dry Run Rd
Monongahela, PA 15063, USA

Gorzelanny, Tom (Athlete, Baseball Player)
10522 Louetta Ln
Orland Park, IL 60467-1350, USA

Gosar, Paul (Congressman, Politician)
504 Cannon HOB
Washington, DC 20515, USA

Gosger, Jim (Athlete, Baseball Player)
1823 7th St
Port Huron, MI 48060-6301, USA

Goslin, Thomas B Jr (General)
Deputy CinC
US Strategic Command
Offutt Air Force Base, NE 68113, USA

Gosling, James (Scientist)
Sun Microsystems
75 Fox Hollow Ln
Redwood City, CA 94062-4158, USA

Gosling, Mike (Athlete, Baseball Player)
2016 Crest Dr
Encinitas, CA 92024-5218, USA

Gosling, Ryan (Actor)
c/o Carolyn Govers *Artist Management*
1119 Colorado Ave
Suite 12
Santa Monica, CA 90401, USA

Gosnell, Raja (Director)
c/o Staff Member *Creative Artists Agency (CAA-LA)*
2000 Ave Of The Stars
Los Angeles, CA 90067, USA

Goss, Luke (Actor)
Insomnia Media Group
100 Universal Dr Bungalow 7151
Universal City, CA 91608, USA

Goss, Matt (Actor)
c/o Staff Member *Andrew Freedman Public Relations*
9127 Thrasher Ave
Los Angeles, CA 90069, USA

Goss, Porter (Misc)
Central Intelligence Agency
Office of Public Affairs
Washington, DC 20505

Goss, Robert F (Misc)
Oil Chemical & Atomic International
1636 Champa St
Denver, CO 80202, USA

Gossage, Goose (Athlete, Baseball Player)
Wish You Were Here Productions
303 East 83rd St #6A
New York, NY 10028, USA

Gossage, Rich (Athlete, Baseball Player)
35 Marland Rd
Colorado Springs, CO 80906-4328, USA

Gosselaar, Mark-Paul (Actor)
c/o Staff Member *James/Levy/Jacobson Management Inc*
3500 W Olive Ave
Suite 1470
Burbank, CA 91505, USA

Gosselin, Guy (Athlete, Hockey Player, Olympic Athlete)
Mlkern sports
131 Bissen st
Caledonia, MN 55921-1811, USA

Gosselin, Jonathan (Reality TV Star)
c/o Mike Heller *Talent Resources*
124 E 36 St
Suite A
New York, NY 10116, USA

Gosselin, Kate (Reality TV Star)
c/o Julie May *Media Motion International (MMI)*
15332 Antioch St
#726
Pacific Palisades, CA 90272, 310-459-7310

Gosselin, Mario (Athlete, Hockey Player)
c/o Staff Member *Ecole de Hockey Energie*
70 Rue des Fauvettes
Saint-Basile-Le-Grand, QC J3N 1P4, Canada

Gosselin, Mario (Race Car Driver)
Wing's Racing
270 Parkside Lane
Rocky Mount, VA 24151, USA

Gossett, David (Athlete, Golfer)
4501 Spanish Oaks Club Blvd
Apt 9
Austin, TX 78738, USA

Gossett, D Bruce (Athlete, Football Player)
6109 Puerto Dr
Rancho Murieta, CA 95683, USA

Gossett, Jeff (Athlete, Football Player)
6 Lake Forest Ct
Roanoke, VA 76262, USA

Gossett, Robert (Actor)
c/o Staff Member *Leavitt Talent Group*
8255 W Sunset Blvd
West Hollywood, CA 90046, USA

Gossett Jr, Louis (Actor)
c/o Hillard Elkins *Elkins Entertainment*
8306 Wilshire Blvd
Suite 438
Beverly Hills, CA 90211, USA

Gossick, Sue (Athlete, Diver, Olympic Athlete)
11738 Villageview Ct
Moorpark, CA 93021-3759, USA

Gossick Crockatt, Sue (Swimmer)
13768 Christian Barrett Dr
Moorpark, CA 93021, USA

Gossip (Music Group)
c/o Sara Newkirk *WME (LA)*
9601 Wilshire Blvd Fl 3
Beverly Hills, CA 90210, USA

Gossom, Thom (Athlete, Football Player)
25 Bay Dr SE
Fort Walton Beach, FL 32548-5701, USA

Gostkowski, Stephen (Athlete, Football Player)
2104 Old Bridge Ln
Bellingham, MA 02019, USA

Goswami, Kunal (Director)
47 Jaihind Society 11th N S Road
JVPD Scheme
Bombay, MS 400 049, INDIA

Gotch, Karl
18530 Wayne Rd.
Odessa, FL 33556-4739

Gothard, Michael
18 Shirlock Rd.
London, ENGLAND NW3 2HS

Gothard, Preston (Athlete, Football Player)
448 Merry Way
Pike Road, AL 36064, USA

Goto, Joji (Stylist)
c/o Staff Member *Ennis*
119 Braintree St
Boston, MA 02134, USA

Gotshalk, Len (Athlete, Football Player)
1200 Butler Creek Rd
Ashland, OR 97520-9370, USA

Gotshalk, Leonard (Athlete, Football Player)
1200 Butler Creek Rd
Ashland, OR 97520, USA

Gott, Jim (Athlete, Baseball Player)
2275 Huntil'lgton
Dr Unit 177
San Marino, CA 91108-2640, USA

Gott, Karel (Musician)
Nad Bertramkou 18
Prague 160 00, CZECH REPUBLIC

Gottfried, Brian (Tennis Player)
129 Teal Pointe Lane
Ponte Vedra Beach, FL 32082, USA

Gottfried, Gilbert (Actor, Comedian)
c/o Steve Honig *Honig Company, The*
4804 Laurel Canyon Blvd.
#828
Studio City, CA 91607, USA

Gotti, Carmine (Reality TV Star)
c/o Staff Member *Growing Up Gotti*
13400 Riverside Dr #300
Sherman Oaks, CA 91423, USA

Gotti, John, Jr (Reality TV Star)
c/o Staff Member *Growing Up Gotti*
13400 Riverside Dr #300
Sherman Oaks, CA 91423, USA

Gotti, Victoria (Actor, Producer, Reality TV Star)
c/o Tammy Brook *FYI Public Relations*
174 5th Ave
Suite 404
New York, NY 10010, USA

Gottlieb, Michael (Director)
2436 Washington Ave
Santa Monica, CA 90403, USA

Gottlieb, Robert A (Editor, Publisher)
237 E 48th St
New York, NY 10017, USA

Gottman, John (Writer)
The Gottman Institute, Inc
P.O. Box 15644
Seattle, WA 98115-0644, USA

Gottwald, Lukasz (Dr. Luke) (Producer)
Kemosabe Entertainment, LLC
9111 Sunset Blvd
Los Angeles, CA 90069, USA

Goude, Ingrid (Model)
511 Las Fuentes Dr
Santa Barbara, CA 93108, USA

Gougeon, Donni (Misc)
Variety Artists
1924 Spring St
Paso Robles, CA 93446, USA

Gough, Alfred (Writer)
c/o Renee Kurtz *Creative Artists Agency (CAA-LA)*
1 William Morris Pl
Beverly Hills, CA 90212, USA

Gough, Tommy (Musician)
Brothers Mgmt
141 Dunbar Ave
Fords, NJ 08863, USA

Goulart, Izabel (Actor, Model)
c/o Staff Member *Women Model Management*
199 Lafayette Street
7th Floor
New York, NY 10012, USA

Gould, Alexander (Actor)
c/o TJ Stein *Stein Entertainment Group*
1351 N Crescent Heights Blvd #312
West Hollywood, CA 90046, USA

Gould, Bob (Athlete, Hockey Player)
3651 Oil Springs Line
Oil Springs, ON N0N 1P0, Canada

Gould, Dana (Actor, Producer, Writer)

Gould, Eileen (Stylist)
31275 Labaya St
Westlake Village, CA 91361, USA

Gould, Elizabeth (Doctor)
Princeton University
Medical Center
Neurosciences Dept
Princeton, NJ 08544, USA

Gould, Elliott (Actor)
c/o Jeff Witjas *Agency for the Performing Arts (APA-LA)*
405 S Beverly Dr
Suite 500
Beverly Hills, CA 90212-4425, USA

Gould, Hal (Athlete, Baseball Player)
126 Rogers Ave
Millville, NJ 08332-9723, USA

Gould, John (Athlete, Hockey Player)
99 Main St
Beeton, ON L0G 1A0, Canada

Gould, Kelly (Actor)
c/o TJ Stein *Stein Entertainment Group*
1351 N Crescent Heights Blvd #312
West Hollywood, CA 90046, USA

Gould, Larry (Actor)
2918 Wright St
Port Huron, MI 48060-8529

Gould, Lawrence M (Misc)
201 E Rudasill Road
Tucson, AZ 85704, USA

Gould, Matt Kennedy (Reality TV Star)
c/o Staff Member *WmE2 (WMA-LA)*
1 William Morris Pl
Beverly Hills, CA 90212, USA

Gould, Nolan (Actor)
c/o Jamie Malone *MC Talent Management*
4821 Lankershim Blvd #F329
N Hollywood, CA 91601, USA

Gould, Robbie
22394 N Prairie Ln
Kildeer, IL 60047-9771, USA

Gould, Ronald M (Judge)
US Court of Appeals
US Courthouse
1010 5th Ave
Seattle, WA 98104, USA

Gould, Shane
207 Kent St.Level 18
Sydney, AUSTRALIA NSW 2000

Gould, Terry (Producer)
c/o Staff Member *Lenhoff & Lenhoff*
830 Palm Ave
West Hollywood, CA 90069

Gould, Thomas W (General)
Orton Gold Hay 6 Howlands
Peterborough
Cambridgeshire, USA

Goulding, Ellie (Musician)
c/o Staff Member *Next Model Management (LA)*
8447 Wilshire Blvd #PH
Beverly Hills, CA 90211, USA

Gould Innes, Shane (Swimmer)
207 Kent St
Level 18
Sydney, NSW 2000, AUSTRALIA

Goulet, Michael (Athlete, Hockey Player)
1283 Buffalo Ridge Rd
Castle Rock, CO 80108, USA

Goulet, Michel (Athlete, Hockey Player)
1283 Buffalo Ridge Rd
Castle Rock, CO 80108-8192, USA

Goulet, Patrice (Stylist)
c/o Staff Member *Ford Models (Chicago)*
311 W Superior St
Chicago, IL 60654, USA

Goundamani (Actor)
7 Cenatop Ist Cross Street
Teynampet
Chennai, TN 600 018, INDIA

Gourdine, Jerome (Musician)
9413 Canyon Mesa Dr
Las Vegas, NV 89144, USA

Gouveia, Kurt (Athlete, Football Player)
138 Seagrove Ln
Mooresville, NC 28117, USA

Govan, Gerald (Athlete, Basketball Player)
30 Newport Pkwy
Apt 2112
Jersey City, NJ 07310-1512, USA

Gove, David
59 Blackthorn Rd
Marstons Mills, MA 02648-1026

Gove, Jeff (Athlete, Golfer)
21323 31st Ave SE
Bothell, WA 98021-7871, USA

Govedaris, Chris (Athlete, Hockey Player)
325 Brewster Rd
Bristol, CT 06010, USA

Govedaris, David (Athlete, Hockey Player)
3838B Lower Union Rd
Orlando, FL 32814, USA

Goverde, David (Athlete, Hockey Player)
3838B Lower Union Rd
Orlando, FL 32814-6508

Govich, Milena (Actor)
c/o Rhonda Price *Gersh (NY)*
41 Madison Ave
New York, NY 10010, USA

Gov't Mule (Music Group)
c/o Staff Member *Paradigm (Monterey)*
404 W Franklin St
Monterey, CA 93940, USA

Gowan, Caroline (Athlete, Golfer)
209 Crescent Ave
Greenville, SC 29605-2814, USA

Gowan, James (Architect)
2 Linden Gardens
London W2 4ES, UNITED KINGDOM
(UK)

Gowan, Lawrence (Musician)
c/o Sterling Bacon *TBA Artist Management (Atlanta)*
1111 Alderman Dr #285
Alpharetta, GA 30005-5433, USA

Gowdy, Cornell (Athlete, Football Player)
4611 John St
Suitland, MD 20746, USA

Gowdy, Trey (Congressman, Politician)
1237 Longworth HOB
Washington, DC 20515, USA

Gowell, Larry (Athlete, Baseball Player)
45 Seventh St Apt 2
Auburn, ME 04210-5692, USA

Gower, David I (Cricketer)
David Gower Promotions
6 George St
Nottingham NG1 3BE, UNITED
KINGDOM (UK)

Gower, Jessica (Actor)
c/o Jason Newman *Untitled Entertainment (LA)*
350 S. Beverly Dr #200
Beverly Hills, CA 90212, USA

Gowers, W Timothy (Mathematician)
Cambridge University
16 Mill Lane
Cambridge CB2 1SB, UNITED KINGDOM
(UK)

Gowin, Toby (Athlete, Football Player)
1605 Oak Creek Cir
Tyler, TX 75703-0433, USA

Gowon, Yakub (General, President)
National Oil/Chemical Marketing Co
38-39 Marina
Lagos 2052, NIGERIA

Gowrie, Earl of (Government Official)
Government Securities
Stag Place
London SW1E 5DS, UNITED KINGDOM
(UK)

Gowtham (Actor)
9 Pooram prakash Rao Road
Balaji Nagar
Chennai, TN 600 014, INDIA

Gowthami (Actor, Bollywood)
2-B, Syamvilla 2nd Main Road
C.I.T.Colony Mylapore
Chennai, TN 600004, INDIA

Goycoechea, Sergio (Soccer Player)
Argentine Football Assn
Via Monte 1366-76
Buenos Aires 1053, ARGENTINA

Goydos, Paul (Athlete, Golfer)
1864 Stearnlee Ave
Long Beach, CA 90815, USA

Goyer, David (Director, Producer, Writer)
c/o Dan Aloni *WmE2 (WMA-LA)*
1 William Morris Pl
Beverly Hills, CA 90212, USA

Goyer, Gerry (Athlete, Hockey Player)
205-1963 Durnin Rd
Kelowna, BC V1X 7Y4, Canada

Goyette, Danielle (Athlete, Hockey
Player, Olympic Athlete)
131 Silver Springs Dr NW
Calgary, AB T3B 3G6, Canada

Goyette, J G Philippe (Phil) (Athlete,
Hockey Player)
815 38-E Ave
Lachine, QC H8T 2C4, Canada

Goyo, Dakota (Actor)
c/o Steven Kavovit *Thruline Entertainment*
9250 Wilshire Blvd
Ground Fl
Beverly Hills, CA 90212, USA

Goyri, Sergio (Actor)
c/o Staff Member *Televisa*
Blvd Adolfo Lopez Mateos 232
Colonia San Angel INN
DF CP 01060, MEXICO

Gozzo, Mauro (Athlete, Baseball Player)
156 Newton St
Berlin, CT 06037-1254, USA

G Ponnambalam (Actor)
10 Dr Subbarray Nagar
II Street Kodambakkam
Chennai, TN 600 024, INDIA

Grabarkewitz, Billy (Athlete, Baseball
Player)
2162 Estes Park Rd
Southlake, TX 76092-3835, USA

Grabe, Ronald J (Astronaut)
13302 E Country Shadows Road
Chandler, AZ 85249, USA

Grabe, Ronald J Colonel (Astronaut)
2653 E Scorpio Pl
Chandler, AZ 85249-5257, USA

Grabeel, Lucas (Actor)
c/o Robert C. Thompson *Group III Management*
13914 Addison St
Sherman Oaks, CA 91423, USA

Graber, Bill (Athlete, Track Athlete)
PO Box 5019
Upland, CA 91785, USA

Graber, Rod (Athlete, Baseball Player)
4674 Mount Armet Dr
San Diego, CA 92117-4719, USA

Graber, Susan P (Judge)
US Courts of Appeals
Pioneer Courthouse
555 SW Yamhill St
Portland, OR 97204, USA

Grabois, Neil R (Educator)
Colgate University
President's Office
Hamilton, NY 13346, USA

Grabow, John (Athlete, Baseball Player)
6810 S Amethyst Dr
Chndler, AZ 85249-7195, USA

Grabowski, James S (Jim) (Athlete,
Football Player)
1523 Withorn Ln
Inverness, IL 60067, USA

Grabowski, Jason (Athlete, Baseball
Player)
131 Beach Park Rd
Clinton, CT 06413-2335, USA

Grace, Alexis (Musician)

Grace, April (Actor)
c/o Lenore Zerman *Liberman/Zerman Management*
252 N Larchmont Blvd
Suite 200
Los Angeles, CA 90004, USA

Grace, Bud (Cartoonist)
PO Box 66
Oakton, VA 22124, USA

Grace, Maggie (Actor)
c/o Darren Goldberg *Global Creative*
1051 Cole Ave # B
Los Angeles, CA 90038, USA

Grace, Mark (Athlete, Baseball Player)
5624 E Via Buena Vis
Paradise Valley, AZ 85253-8129, USA

Grace, Mike (Athlete, Baseball Player)
12791 Big Lake Rd
Davisburg, MI 48350-3419, USA

Grace, Mike (Athlete, Baseball Player)
12791 Big Lake Rd
Davisburg, MI 48350, USA

Grace, Nancy (Lawyer, Television Host)
c/o Staff Member *CNN (Atlanta)*
One CNN Center
PO Box 105366
Atlanta, GA 30303, USA

Grace, Robert Bud (Cartoonist)
3037 Fox Den Ln
Oakton, VA 22124-1307, USA

Grace, Topher (Actor)
8707 Sunset Plaza Pl
West Hollywood, CA 90069, USA

Graceland
3765 Elvis Presley Blvd
Memphis, TN 38116

Gracey, James S (Admiral, Business
Person)
1 Westin Center
2445 M St NW #260
Washington, DC 20037, USA

Grach, Eduard D (Musician)
1st Smolensky Per 9
#98
Moscow 113324, RUSSIA

Grachev, Pavel S (General)
Ovchinnikovskaya Nab 18/1
Moscow 113324, RUSSIA

Gracheva, Nadezhda A (Ballerina)
1st Truzhennikov Per 17
#49
Moscow 119121, RUSSIA

Grachvogel, Maria (Designer, Fashion
Designer)
c/o Staff Member *Maria Grachvogel*
5 South Molton Street
London, England W11 1LT, United
Kingdom

Gracie, Charlie (Musician)
Jeff Hubbard Productions
PO Box 53664
Indianapolis, IN 46253, USA

Gracie, Royce (Athlete, Wrestler)
KhonKhor Enterprises Inc
9806 Zackery Ave
Charlotte, NC 28277, USA

Gracin, Joshua (Musician)
c/o Rob Beckham *WmE2 (WMA-TN)*
1600 Division St
Suite 300
Nashville, TN 37203, USA

Grad, Harold (Mathematician)
248 Overlook Road
New Rochelle, NY 10804, USA

Graddy, Sam (Athlete, Football Player)
4792 Brasac Dr
Stone Mountain, GA 30083, USA

Gradin, Thomas (Athlete, Hockey Player)
c/o Staff Member *Vancouver Canucks*
800 Griffiths Way
Vancouver V6B 6G1, Canada

Gradishar, Randy C (Athlete, Football
Player)
7628 Pineridge Ter
Castle Rock, CO 80108, USA

Gradison, Ronnie (Athlete, Basketball
Player)
6151 Chappellfield Drive
West Chester, OH 45069, USA

Gradkowski, Bruce (Athlete, Football
Player)
1120 Peermont Ave
Pittsburgh, PA 15216-2214, USA

Grady, Ellen
150 E. Olive #111
Burbank, CA 91502

Grady, James T (Politician)
International Teamsters Brotherhood
25 Louisiana Ave NW
Washington, DC 20001, USA

Grady, Wayne (Athlete, Golfer)
PO Box 78
Coolum Beach QLD 4573, Australia

Graeber, Clark (Tennis Player)
411 Harbor Road
Fairfield, CT 06431, USA

Graef, Jed (Athlete, Olympic Athlete,
Swimmer)
PO Box 880
Shelburne, VT 05482-0880, USA

Graelis, Francisco (Pancho) (Cartoonist,
Editor)
Le Monde
Editorial Dept
21 Bis Rue Claude Bernard
Paris 75005, FRANCE

Graf, Bianca
Oppenheimstr. 6b
Wolfen, GERMANY D-06766

Graf, Dave (Athlete, Football Player)
1825 SE 21st Ave
Pompano Beach, FL 33062, USA

Graf, Hans
Houston Symphony
Jesse Jones Hall
615 Louisiana St
Houston, TX 77002, USA

Graf, Richard (Athlete, Football Player)
11108 Bluestem Ln
Eden Priarie, MN 55347, USA

Graf, Rick (Athlete, Football Player)
6609 Biscayne Blvd
Minneapolis, MN 55436-1703, USA

Graf, Stefanie M (Steffi) (Tennis Player)
8921 Andre Dr
Las Vegas, NV 89148, USA

Graf, Stephanie (Athlete, Model, Track Athlete)
9804 Camden Hills Ave
Las Vegas, NV 89145, USA

Graff, Ilena (Actor)
11455 Sunshine Terrace
Studio City, CA 91604, USA

Graff, Neil (Athlete, Football Player)
Graff Capital Management
P.O. Box 2696
Sioux Falls, SD 57101, USA

Graff, Randy (Actor)
Peter Strawn Assoc
1501 Broadway
#2900
New York, NY 10036, USA

Graff, Todd
547 Hudson St.
New York, NY 10014

Graffanino, Tony (Athlete, Baseball Player)
6875 W Cottontail Ln
Peoria, AZ 85260-7044, USA

Graffin, Guillaume (Ballerina)
American Ballet Theatre
890 Broadway
New York, NY 10003, USA

Graffman, Gary (Musician)
Curtis Institute of Music
1726 Locust St
Philadelphia, PA 19103, USA

Grafstein, Bernice (Physicist, Scientist)
Weill Medical College
Physiology Dept
1300 York Ave
New York, NY 10021, USA

Grafstein, Bernice Dr (Scientist)
Weill Medical College 1300 York Ave
Attn Physiology Dept
New York, NY 10065-4805, USA

Grafton, Sue (Writer)
PO Box 41446
Santa Barbara, CA 93140-1446, USA

Gragg, Scott (Athlete, Football Player)
583 Cash Nichols Rd
Stevensville, MY 59870, USA

Graham, Art (Athlete, Football Player)
P.O. Box 785
South Orleans, MA 02662, USA

Graham, Bill (Athlete, Football Player)
11013 Sierra Verde Trl
Austin, TX 78759, USA

Graham, Bob (Politician)
14814 Breckness Pl
Miami Lakes, FL 33016-1458, USA

Graham, Brendan (Musician, Writer)
c/o Staff Member PeerMusic USA
3260 Blume Dr
Suite 405
Richmond, CA 94806, USA

Graham, Brian (Athlete, Baseball Player)
11995 El Camino Real
San Diego, CA 92130-2544, USA

Graham, Charles P (General)
134 Wabler Way
Georgetown, TX 78628, USA

Graham, Chris (Director)
c/o Simon Millar Rumble Media
1620 Broadway
Santa Monica, CA 90403, USA

Graham, Currie
c/o Vera Mihailovich Forward Entertainment
9255 Sunset Blvd
Suite 805
Los Angeles, CA 90069, USA

Graham, Dan (Athlete, Baseball Player)
6444 Little Pine Way
Las Vegas, AZ 89108-3420, USA

Graham, Daniel O (General)
High Frontier Inc 1010 Vermont Ave NW
Washington, DC 20005-4902, USA

Graham, David (Athlete, Golfer)
99 Mountainside Dr
Whitefish, MT 59937-4997, USA

Graham, Demingo (Athlete, Football Player)
179 Hillside Ter
Irvington, NJ 07111-1506

Graham, Derrick (Athlete, Football Player)
203 Pine Hill Rd
West End, NC 27376, USA

Graham, Dick (Athlete, Hockey Player)
13580 Technology Dr.
#3314
Eden Prairie, MN 55344, USA

Graham, Dirk (Athlete, Coach, Hockey Player)
17001 S Blackfoot Dr
Lockport, IL 60441-4367

Graham, Donald E (Publisher)
Washington Post Co
1150 15th St NW
Washington, DC 20071, USA

Graham, Ed (Musician)
c/o Sue Whitehouse Whitehouse Management
PO Box 43829
London NW6 3PJ, UNITED KINGDOM

Graham, Franklin (Religious Leader)
Samantan's Purse
PO Box 3000
Boone, NC 28607, USA

Graham, Gail (Golfer)
Landmark Sport Group 277 Richmond St NW
Toronto, ON M5V 1X1, CANADA

Graham, Gerrit (Actor)
S M S Talent
8730 Sunset Blvd
#440
Los Angeles, CA 90069, USA

Graham, Glen (Musician)
Shapiro Co
9229 Sunset Blvd
#607
Los Angeles, CA 90069, USA

Graham, Greg (Athlete, Basketball Player)
12636 Wolf Run Rd
Noblesville, IN 46060-8001, USA

Graham, Hason (Athlete, Football Player)
140 Shoreline Dr
Fayetteville, GA 30215, USA

Graham, Heather (Actor, Producer)
c/o Risa Shapiro Schiff Company, The
9465 Wilshire Blvd
Suite 480
Beverly Hills, CA 90212, USA

Graham, Jeff (Athlete, Football Player)
1840 Infirmary Rd
Dayton, OH 45418, USA

Graham, John R (Writer)
University of California
Astronomy Dept
Berkeley, CA 94720, USA

Graham, Jorie (Writer)
General Delivery
12 Quincy St
West Tisbury, MA 02138-3804, USA

Graham, Kat (Actor, Musician)
c/o Jon Simmons Simmons & Scott Entertainment
4110 W. Burbank Blvd.
Burbank, CA 91505, USA

Graham, Kenny (Athlete, Football Player)
P.O. Box 7402
Santa Monica, CA 90406, USA

Graham, Kent (Athlete, Football Player)
1001 N Washington St
Wheaton, IL 60187, USA

Graham, Larry (Musician)
c/o Staff Member Variety Artists International Inc
793 Higuera Street
Suite 6
San Luis, CA 93401-0500, USA

Graham, Lauren (Actor)
c/o John Carrabino John Carrabino Management
5900 Wilshire Blvd Fl 4 #406
Los Angeles, CA 90036, USA

Graham, Lee (Athlete, Baseball Player)
481 Richmond Rd
Cleveland, OH 44143-2745, USA

Graham, Linda (Bowler)
4147 E Seneca Ave
Des Moines, IA 50317--8123, USA

Graham, Lindsey (Politician)
PO Box 486
Seneca, SC 29679-0486, USA

Graham, Loren R (Historian)
7 Francis Ave
Cambridge, MA 02138, USA

Graham, Lou (Athlete, Golfer)
85 Concord Park W
Nashville, TN 37205-4707, USA

Graham, Mal (Athlete, Basketball Player)
122 Christina Street
Newton Heights, MA 02461-1916, USA

Graham, Mikey (Musician)
JC Music
84A Strand on the Green
London W43 PU, UNITED KINGDOM (UK)

Graham, Milt (Athlete, Football Player)
21 Wildflower Ln
Yarmouth Port, MA 02675-1474, USA

Graham, Parker (Musician)
Performers of the World
8901 Melrose Ave
#200
West Hollywood, CA 90069, USA

Graham, Pat (Athlete, Hockey Player)
Dundas University Health Clinic
200-438 University Ave
Toronto, ON M5G 2K8, Canada

Graham, Paul (Athlete, Basketball Player)
5255 North Marshall Street
Philadelphia, PA 19120-3134, USA

Graham, Roger (Athlete, Football Player)
1996 Jacksonville Jaguars
Monroe, NY 10950-4946, USA

Graham, Samaria
c/o Steven Jensen Direct Management Group
6363 Wilshire Blvd
Suite 115
Los Angeles, CA 90048, USA

Graham, Stedman (Business Person)
S. Graham & Associates
455 N Cityfront Plaza 15th Fl
Chicago, IL 60611, USA

Graham, Stephen (Actor)
c/o Ben Levine Kritzer Levine Wilkins Entertainment (KLWG)
11872 La Grange Ave
1st Floor
Los Angeles, CA 90025, USA

Graham, Susan (Opera Singer)
Columbia Artists Mgmt Inc
165 W 57th St
New York, NY 10019, USA

Graham, Tommy (Athlete, Football Player)
4084 S Wisteria Way
Denver, CO 80237, USA

Graham, Wayne (Athlete, Baseball Player)
2017 Dryden Rd
Houston, TX 77030-1205, USA

Graham, William B (Business Person)
40 Devonshire Lane
Kenilworth, IL 60043, USA

Graham, William F (Billy) (Religious Leader, Writer)
Billy Graham Evangelistic Assoc
1 Billy Graham Pkwy
Charlotte, NC 28201, USA

Graham, William R (Government Official)
Xsirius Inc
1110 N Glebe Road
#620
Arlington, VA 22201, USA

Graham-Douglas, Mary Lou (Baseball Player)
9990 N Hillview Dr
Tucson, AZ 85737-7940, USA

Grahame, John (Athlete, Hockey Player, Olympic Athlete)
9000 E Jewell Cir
Denver, CO 80231-3450

Grahame, Ron (Athlete, Hockey Player)
9000 E Jewell Cir
Denver, CO 80231-3450

Grahame-Smith, Seth (Writer)
c/o Melissa Kates Viewpoint Inc
8820 Wilshire Blvd.
Suite 220
Beverly Hills, CA 90211, USA

Grahame-Smith, Francis (Astronomer)
Old School House
Henbury
Macclesfield, Cheshire SK11 9PH, UNITED KINGDOM (UK)

Grahe, Joe (Athlete, Baseball Player)
2317 N Wallen Dr
West Palm Beach, FL 33410-2558, USA

Grahn, Nancy
4910 Agnes Ave.
No. Hollywood, CA 91607

Grahn, Nancy Lee (Actor)
c/o Staff Member *Innovative Artists (LA)*
1505 10th St
Santa Monica, CA 90401, USA

Grainger, David W (Business Person)
WW Grainger Inc
100 Grainger Parkway
Lake Forest, IL 60045, USA

Grainger, Holliday (Actor)
c/o Conor McCaughan *Troika*
74 Clerkenwell Rd
3rd Floor
London EC1M 5QA, United Kingdom

Gralish, Tom (Journalist, Photographer)
203 E Cottage Ave
Haddonfield, NJ 08033-1824, USA

Gralla, Milton (Publisher)
Gralla Publications
1515 Broadway
New York, NY 10036, USA

Graman, Alex (Athlete, Baseball Player)
450 E Sunset Dr
Huntingburg, IN 47542-9316, USA

Gramanis, Paul (Athlete, Football Player)
989 Parkview Dr
Tallahassee, FL 32311, USA

Gramatica, Guillermo (Bill) (Athlete, Football Player)
3912 Northampton Way
Tampa, FL 33618, USA

Gramatica, Martin (Athlete, Football Player)
8905 Promise D
Tampa, FL 33626, USA

Gramlich, Edward M (Economist, Government Official)
Federal Reserve Board
20th & Constitution Aves NW
Washington, DC 20551, USA

Gramly, Tommy (Athlete, Baseball Player)
16485 Red Wood Cir W
McKinney, TX 75071-6198, USA

Gramm, Lou (Musician)
c/o Staff Member *Creative Artists Agency (CAA-LA)*
2000 Ave Of The Stars
Los Angeles, CA 90067, USA

Gramm, Wendy L (Government Official)
Commodity Futures Trading Commission
2033 K St NW
Washington, DC 20006, USA

Gramm, W Philip (Phil) (Politician)
UBS Warburg
PO Box 1559
Helotes, FL 78023-1559, USA

Grammas, Alex (Athlete, Baseball Player, Coach)
4030 Vestview Dr
Vestavia, AL 35242-2554, USA

Grammer, Camille (Actor, Reality TV Star)
c/o Jill Fritzo *PMK/BNC Public Relations (PMK-NY)*
622 3rd Ave
8th Floor
New York, NY 10017, USA

Grammer, Kathy (Actor)
Artists Agency
1180 S Beverly Dr
#301
Los Angeles, CA 90035, USA

Grammer, Kelsey (Actor)
c/o Stan Rosenfield *Stan Rosenfield & Associates*
2029 Century Park E
Suite 1190
Los Angeles, CA 90067, USA

Grammer, Spencer (Actor)
c/o Evan Hainey *Untitled Entertainment (LA)*
350 S. Beverly Dr #200
Beverly Hills, CA 90212, USA

Grams, Rod (Politician)
1215 Brainerd Ave
Duluth, MN 55811-2427, USA

Gran, Phyllis
Penguin/Pitnam Publishing
200 Madison Ave
New York, NY 10016

Granaderos, Alyson (Stylist)
c/o Staff Member *Montana Artists Agency*
9150 Wilshire Blvd Ste 100
Beverly Hills, CA 90212, USA

Granatelli, Andy (Race Car Driver)
1468 Edgec1iff Lane
Montecito, CA 93108-2810, USA

Granato, Catherine (Cammi) (Athlete, Hockey Player, Olympic Athlete)
Hockey Hall of Fame Brookfield Place 30 Yonge St
Toronto, ON MSE 1X8, Canada

Granato, Tony (Athlete, Hockey Player)
Pittsburgh Penguins
66 Mario Lemieux Pl Ste 2
Pittsburgh, PA 15219-3504

Granato, Tony (Athlete, Hockey Player, Olympic Athlete)
1481 Hollow Tree Dr
Pittsburgh, PA 15241-2962

Granby, John (Athlete, Football Player)
2870 Addison Cir S
Rochester, MI 48306-4923, USA

Grand, Katie (Stylist)
c/o Staff Member *Camilla Lowther Managment (CLM Represents)*
30-32 Ericsson Pl
New York, NY 10013, USA

Grandberry, Ken (Athlete, Football Player)
108 E Mark Rd
Harker Heights, TX 76548, USA

Grandberry, Omari (Omarion) (Actor)
c/o Guido Giordano *ICM Partners (ICM-LA)*
10250 Constellation Blvd Fl 7
Los Angeles, CA 90067, USA

Grande, Ariana (Actor)
c/o Jennifer Merlino *Untitled Entertainment (LA)*
350 S. Beverly Dr #200
Beverly Hills, CA 90212, USA

Grande, George (Commentator)
70 Four Rod Rd
Hamden, CT 06514-1615, USA

Grandelius, Everett (Sonny) (Athlete, Football Player)
31531 Robinhood Dr
Beverly Hills, MI 48025, USA

Granderson, Curtis (Athlete, Baseball Player)
1450 S Emerald St
Chicago, IL 60607-4440, USA

Granderson, Rufus (Athlete, Football Player)
1717 Paris Ave SE
Grand Rapids, MI 49507, USA

Grand Funk Railroad (Musician)
c/o Staff Member *Paradigm (Monterey)*
404 W Franklin St
Monterey, CA 93940, USA

Grandholm, Jim (Athlete, Basketball Player)
211 Spring Park Ave
Sawyer, MI 49125-8353, USA

Grandin, Temple (Scientist)
2918 Silver Plume Dr
#C3
Fort Collins, CO 80526, USA

Grandison, Ronnie (Athlete, Basketball Player)
6151 Chappellfield Dr
West Chester, OH 45069-6648, USA

Grandmaster, Mele-Mel (Musician)
Groove Entertainment
1005 N Alfred St
#2
West Hollywood, CA 90069, USA

Grandmont, Jean-Michel (Economist)
55 Blvd de Charonne
Les Doukas 23
Paris 75011, FRANCE

Grand Ole Opry
2804 Opryland Dr
Nashville, TN 37214

Grand-Pierre, Jean-Luc (Athlete, Hockey Player)
8432 Galdino Dr
New Albany, OH 43054-7149

Grandpre, Mary (Designer)
Scholastic Press
555 Broadway
New York, NY 10012, USA

Grandy, Fred (Politician)
9417 Spruce Tree Cir
Bethesda, MD 20814-1654, USA

Granger, Charley (Athlete, Football Player)
621 Burbridge St
Port Allen, LA 70767, USA

Granger, Clive W J (Nobel Prize Laureate)
University of California
Economics Dept
9500 Gilman Dr
La Jolla, CA 92093, USA

Granger, Danny (Athlete, Basketball Player)
3801 Pete Dye Blvd
Carmel, IN 46033-8170, USA

Granger, David (Athlete)
Ingalls & Snyder
61 Broadway
#3100
New York, NY 10006, USA

Granger, Hoyle (Athlete, Football Player)
10611 Cranbrook Rd
Houston, TX 77042, USA

Granger, Jeff (Athlete, Baseball Player)
2905 Glasgow Dr
Arlington, TX 76015-2226, USA

Granger, Kay (Congressman, Politician)
320 CaJ1Illon HOB
Washington, DC 20515, USA

Granger, Stewart (Athlete, Basketball Player)
552 E 53rd
Brooklyn, NY 11203-5323, USA

Granger, Wayne (Athlete, Baseball Player)
133 Redtail Pl
Winter Springs, FL 32708-5626, USA

Granholm, Jennifer (Politician)
2066 Asilomar Dr
Oakland, CA 94611-2646, USA

Grannis, Paul D (Physicist)
Fermi Nat Accelerator Lab
CDF Collaboration
PO Box 500
Batavia, IL 60510, USA

Grant, Alan (Athlete, Football Player)
2474 40th Ave
San Francisco, CA 94116, USA

Grant, Alexander (Alex da Kid) (Musician)
9126 Cordell Dr
West Hollywood, CA 90069, USA

Grant, Amy (Musician, Songwriter)
c/o Staff Member *The M Collective*
P.O. Box 273
Franklin, TN 37065, USA

Grant, Beth
2852 Hollyridge Dr.
Los Angeles, CA 90068

Grant, Bob (Athlete, Football Player)
10153 Riverside Dr
Toluca Lake, CA 91602-2562, USA

Grant, Bob (Journalist)
WABC Radio 2 Pennsylvania Plaza
New York, NY 10121, USA

Grant, Boyd (Coach)
Colorado State University
Athletic Dept
Fort Collins, CO 80523, USA

Grant, Brea (Actor)
c/o Nicole Perna *Baker Winokur Ryder Public Relations (BWR-LA)*
9100 Wilshire Blvd
Suite 500, West Tower
Beverly Hills, CA 90212, USA

Grant, Brian (Athlete, Basketball Player)
24152 SW Petes
Mountain Rd
west Linn, OR 97068-4500, USA

Grant, Bud (Athlete, Football Coach, Football Player)
8134 Oakmere Rd
Minneapolis, MN 55438-1333, USA

Grant, Charles (Actor)
Media Artists Group
6300 Wilshire Blvd
#1470
Los Angeles, CA 90048, USA

Grant, Danny (Athlete, Hockey Player)
1163 Route 101
Nasonworth, NB E3C 2C3, Canada

Grant, Darryl (Athlete, Football Player)
6931 Compton Ln
Centreville, VA 20121, USA

Grant, David (Athlete, Football Player)
c/o Michael Katcher *Creative Artists Agency (CAA-LA)*
2000 Ave Of The Stars
Los Angeles, CA 90067, USA

Grant, Deborah (Actor)
Larry Datzall
17 Broad Ct #12
London WC2B 5QN, UNITED KINGDOM

Grant, Deon (Athlete, Football Player)
2001 Carolina Panthers
Evans, GA 30809-4526, USA

Grant, Edmond (Eddy) (Musician, Songwriter, Writer)
Consolidated Ale
PO Box 87
Tarporley CW6 9FN, UNITED KINGDOM (UK)

Grant, Faye (Actor)
13000 Brentwood Ter
Los Angeles, CA 90049-4807, USA

Grant, Frank (Athlete, Football Player)
2126 Glencourse Ln
Reston, VA 20191, USA

Grant, Gil (Producer)
c/o Staff Member *Principal Entertainment (LA)*
1964 Westwood Blvd #400
Los Angeles, CA 90025, USA

Grant, Gogi (Musician)
10323 Alamo Ave
#202
Los Angeles, CA 90064, USA

Grant, Harry (Race Car Driver)
7531 Millersville Rd.
Taylorsville, NC 28681, USA

Grant, Harvey (Athlete, Basketball Player)
11802 Woodbrook Ct
Bowie, MD 20721-4102, USA

Grant, Horace (Athlete, Basketball Player)
195 Michael Ln
Arroyo Grande, CA 93420-5323, USA

Grant, Hugh (Actor)
c/o Leslee Dart *42West (NY)*
220 W 42nd St
12th Floor
New York, NY 10036, USA

Grant, HUgh (Horse Racer)
35 E 84th St Apt 8B
New York, NY 10028-0871, USA

Grant, James T (Mudcat) (Athlete, Baseball Player)
1020 S Dunsmuir Ave
Los Angeles, CA 90019, USA

Grant, Jennifer (Actor)
c/o Mark Teitelbaum *Teitelbaum Artists Group*
8840 Wilshire Blvd
3rd Floor
Beverly Hills, CA 90212, USA

Grant, Jim "Mudcat" (Athlete, Baseball Player)
1020 S Dunsmuir Ave
Los Angeles, CA 90019-6754, USA

Grant, John (Athlete, Football Player)
623 Clayton St
Denver, CO 80206-3812, USA

Grant, Josh (Athlete, Basketball Player)
3191 S Davis Blvd
Bountiful, UT 84010-5764, USA

Grant, Kate Jennings (Actor)
c/o Tammy Rosen *Sanders Armstrong Caserta*
2120 Colorado Blvd
Suite 120
Santa Monica, CA 90404, USA

Grant, Lee (Actor, Director)
c/o Joel Dean *TalentWorks (LA)*
3500 W Olive Ave
Suite 1400
Burbank, CA 91505, USA

Grant, Leonard (Uncle Murda) (Musician)
c/o Staff Member *Violator Management*
36 W 25th St
2nd Floor
New York, NY 10010, USA

Grant, Mark (Commentator)
2837 Via Dieguenos
Alpine, CA 91901-3638, USA

Grant, Martin (Athlete, Hockey Player)
17 Mount View Crt
Collingwood, ON L9Y 5A9, Canada

Grant, Mickie (Actor)
250 W 94th St
#6G
New York, NY 10025, USA

Grant, Orantes (Athlete, Football Player)
5103 Ashford Gables Dr
Atlanta, GA 30338-6780, USA

Grant, Orantes (Athlete, Football Player)
385 Creekview Blvd
Covington, GA 30016, USA

Grant, Paul (Basketball Player)
Milwaukee Bucks
Bradley Center
1001 N 4th St
Milwaukee, WI 53203, USA

Grant, Rachel (Actor)
Bloomfields Management
34 South Molton Street
London W1K 5BP, UNITED KINGDOM

Grant, Reggie
PO Box 15602
Los Angeles, CA 90015-0602, USA

Grant, Reginald (Athlete, Football Player)
P.O. Box 15602
Los Angeles, CA 90015, USA

Grant, Richard E (Actor)
International Creative Mgmt
76 Oxford St
London W1N 0AX, UNITED KINGDOM (UK)

Grant, Robert M (Educator)
RR 1 Box 1423
Berlin, NH 03570, USA

Grant, Rodney A. (Actor)
c/o Anne Geddes *Geddes Agency, The*
8430 Santa Monica Blvd
Suite 200
Los Angeles, CA 90069, USA

Grant, Steve (Athlete, Football Player)
20134 SW 123rd Dr
Miami, FL 33177, USA

Grant, Susannah (Director, Writer)
c/o Risa Gertner *Creative Artists Agency (CAA-LA)*
2000 Ave Of The Stars
Los Angeles, CA 90067, USA

Grant, Tom (Athlete, Baseball Player)
36 Millville Rd
Mendon, MA 01756-1231, USA

Grant, Toni (Misc)
610 S Ardmore Ave
Los Angeles, CA 90005, USA

Grant, Travis (Athlete, Basketball Player)
3314 Pointe Bleue Court
Decatur, GA 30034-5118, USA

Grant, Wally (Athlete, Hockey Player)
4853 Lone Oak Ct
Ann Arbor, MI 48108-8575

Grant, Wes (Athlete, Football Player)
3014 North St # B
Atlanta, GA 30344-4355, USA

Grant, Wesley (Athlete, Football Player)
3870 Crenshaw Blvd
Apt 926
Los Angeles, CA 90008, USA

Grantham, Larry (Athlete, Football Player)
1971 Tissington Dr
Horn Lake, MS 38637, USA

Granville, Billy (Athlete, Football Player)
PO Box 3426
Sugar Land, TX 77487-3307, USA

Grapenthin, Dick (Athlete, Baseball Player)
5040 170th Ave
Linn Grove, IA 51033, USA

Grapenthin, Rick (Athlete, Baseball Player)
500 Argylls Crst
Alpharetta, GA 30022-6118, USA

Grasmanis, Paul (Athlete, Football Player)
1073 Watkins Creek Dr
Franklin, TN 37067-7830, USA

Grasmick, Lou (Athlete, Baseball Player)
6715 Quad Ave
Rosedale, MD 21237-2406, USA

Grass, Darren (Athlete, Baseball Player, Olympic Athlete)
1086 174th Street
Hammond, WI 54015-4831, USA

Grass, Gunter (Nobel Prize Laureate)
Glockengiesstrasse 21
Lubeck D-23552, Germany

Grass, Gunter (Nobel Prize Laureate)
Sekfretariat Glockengiesserstr 21
Lubeck 23552, GERMANY

Grass, Gunther
Glockengiesserstr. 21
Lubeck D-23552, GERMANY

Grassie, Karen (Actor)
PO Box 913
Pacific Palisades, CA 900272, USA

Grassle, Karen (Actor)
2646 Francisco Way
El Cerrito, CA 94530-1531, USA

Grassley, charles (Politician)
2342 S Rolfe St
Arlington, VA 22202-1545, USA

Grassroots, The
108 E. Matilija St.
Ojai, CA 93023

Grata, Enrique (Actor)
c/o Staff Member *Univision*
605 3rd St. Fl12
New York, NY 10158, USA

Grate, Carl (Athlete, Football Player)
205 Wind Ship Ln
Woodstock, GA 30189, USA

Grate, Don (Athlete, Basketball Player)
1245 NW 203rd Street
Miami, FL 33169-2312, USA

Grate, Don (Athlete, Baseball Player)
1245 NW 203rd St
Miami, FL 33169, USA

Grater, Mark (Athlete, Baseball Player)
1136 Indiana Ave
Monaca, PA 15061, USA

Graterol, Belker (Athlete, Baseball Player)
2301 Lakeland Hills Blvd
Lakeland, FL 33805, USA

Gratham, Larry (Athlete, Football Player)
1971 Tissington Dr
Horn Lake, MS 38637, USA

Gratton, Chris (Athlete, Hockey Player)
8801 Fazio Ct
Tampa, FL 33647-2292

Gratton, Gilles (Athlete, Hockey Player)
4980 des Chenes St
Sainte-Catherine, QC J5C 1L1, CANADA

Gratton, Jean-Guy (Athlete, Hockey Player)
1320 Rue des Patriotes
Laval, QC H7L 2N6, Canada

Gratton, Norm (Athlete, Hockey Player)
2144 De Maricourt St
Montreal, QC H4E 1W1, Canada

Grau, Dieter (Scientist)
2004 Max Luther Dr NW Apt 220
Huntsville, AL 35810-3853, USA

Grau, Shirley Ann (Writer)
12 Nassau Dr
Metairie, LA 70005-4434, USA

Grausman, Philip (Artist)
21 Barnes Road
Washington, CT 06793, USA

Gravel, Gerry (Ge Ge) (Race Car Driver)
52 Mt. Auburn St.
Somersworth, NH 03878, USA

Gravel, Maurice R (Mike) (Politician)
3133 Frontera Way Apt 341
Burlingame, CA 94010-5767, USA

Graveline, Duane (Astronaut)
4414 Cormorant Ln
Merritt Island, FL 32953-8504, USA

Graveline, Duane E (Astronaut)
494 Pleasant St
Island Pond, VT 05846, USA

Gravelle, Gordon (Athlete, Football Player)
2208 Cordoba Ct
Antioch, CA 94509, USA

Gravelle, Leo (Athlete, Hockey Player)
725-70 Rue de la Futaie
Gatineau, QC J8T 8S2, Canada

Gravelle, Louisa (Stylist)
c/o Staff Member *Solo Artists*
2148 Federal Ave
Los Angeles, CA 90025, USA

Graves, Adam (Athlete, Hockey Player)
c/o Staff Member *New York Rangers*
2 Pennsylvania Plaza
Rm 2200
New York, NY 10121, USA

Graves, Alex (Producer)
c/o Staff Member *ICM Partners (ICM-LA)*
10250 Constellation Blvd Fl 7
Los Angeles, CA 90067, USA

Graves, Danny (Athlete, Baseball Player)
5041 Rishley
Run Way
Mount Dora, FL 32757-8010, USA

Graves, Denyce (Opera Singer)
Columbia Artists Mgmt Inc
165 W 57th St
New York, NY 10019, USA

Graves, Denyce (Opera Singer)

Graves, Earl (Athlete, Basketball Player)
123 Random Farms Drive
Chappaqua, NY 10514-1018, USA

Graves, Earl G (Writer)
Earl G Graves Publishing130 5th Ave
New York, NY 10011-4355, USA

Graves, Ernest Jr (General)
2328 S Nash St
Arlington, VA 22202, USA

Graves, Harold N Jr (Government
Official, Journalist)
4816 Grantham Ave
Chevy Chase, MD 20815, USA

Graves, Hilliard (Athlete, Hockey Player)
AMCA Sales Ltd
100 Simmonds Dr
Dartmouth, NS B3B 1N9, Canada

Graves, Marsharne (Athlete, Football
Player)
7544 E Hannibal Cir
Mesa, AZ 85207, USA

Graves, Michael (Architect)
341 Nassau St
Princeton, NJ 08540-4602, USA

Graves, Ray (Athlete, Coach, Football
Coach, Football Player)
4230 Hartwood Ln
Tampa, FL 33624, USA

Graves, Richard G (General)
12069 Sage Hollow Cir
Kamas, UT 84036-9348, USA

Graves, Rory (Athlete, Football Player)
7585 Shadow Wood Dr
Jonesboro, GA 30236, USA

Graves, Rupert (Actor)
c/o Barry McPherson *Agency for the
Performing Arts (APA-LA)*
405 S Beverly Dr
Suite 500
Beverly Hills, CA 90212-4425, USA

Graves, Sam (Congressman, Politician)
1415 Longworth HOB
Washington, DC 20515, USA

Graves, Tom (Athlete, Football Player)
1902 Montclair Ave
Norfolk, VA 23523, USA

Graves, Tom (Congressman, Politician)
1113 Longworth HOB
Washington, DC 20515, USA

Graves, White (Athlete, Football Player)
2610 Birchwood Dr
Monroe, LA 71201, USA

Gravitte, Beau (Actor)
Paradigm Agency
10100 Santa Monica Blvd
#2500
Los Angeles, CA 90067, USA

Gray, Alasdair J (Writer)
McAlpine
2 Marchmont Terrace
Glasgow G12 9LT, SCOTLAND

Gray, Alec (Actor)
c/o Delaney Andrews *Strategic Talent
Group*
4804 Laurel Canyon Blvd
#149
Valley Village, CA 91607, USA

Gray, Alfred M (General)
6317 Chaucer View Cir
Alexandria, VA 22304-3548, USA

Gray, Alfred M Jr (General)
6317 Chaucer View Circle
Alexandria, VA 22304, USA

Gray, Billy (Actor)
19612 Grandview Dr
Topanga Canyon, CA 90290, USA

Gray, Carlton (Athlete, Football Player)
11981 Kenn Rd
Cincinnati, OH 45240-1313, USA

Gray, C Boyden (Government Official)
Wilmer Cutler Pickering
2445 M St NW
Washington, DC 20037, USA

Gray, Coleen (Actor)
2337 Roscomare Road
#2-112
Los Angeles, CA 90077, USA

Gray, Colleen
2337 Roscomare Rd. #2-112
Los Angeles, CA 90077-1851

Gray, Dave (Athlete, Baseball Player)
416 E 1050 N
Ogden, UT 84404, USA

Gray, David (Musician, Songwriter)
c/o Rob Holden *Mondo Management*
26-32 Voltaire Rd #2D
London SW6 6DH, UNITED KINGDOM
(UK)

Gray, Dick (Athlete, Baseball Player)
503 S Hampton St
Anaheim, CA 92804, USA

Gray, Dobie (Musician)
2211 Elliott Ave
Nashville, T N 37204, USA

Gray, Doug (Musician)
Ron Rainey Mgmt
315 S Beverly Dr
#407
Beverly Hills, CA 90212, USA

Gray, Duicie (Actor)
Barry Burnett
31 Coventry St
London W1V 8AS, UNITED KINGDOM
(UK)

Gray, Dulcie
44 Brunswick Gardens #2
London W8 4AN, ENGLAND

Gray, D'Wayne (General)
3423 Barger Dr
Falls Church, VA 22044, USA

Gray, Earnest (Athlete, Football Player)
6746 Kirby Oaks Ln
Memphis, TN 38119, USA

Gray, Ed (Basketball Player)
Houston Rockets
Toyota Center
2 E Greenway Plaza
Houston, TX 77046, USA

Gray, Erin (Actor, Model)
10921 Alta View Dr
Studio City, CA 91604, USA

Gray, Erin (Actor)
c/o Geneva Bray *GVA Talent Agency Inc*
8981 Sunset Blvd.
Suite 101
Los Angeles, CA 90069, USA

Gray, F Gary (Director)
c/o Staff Member *Management 360*
9111 Wilshire Blvd
Beverly Hills, CA 90210, USA

Gray, Fred Sr (Attorney, Attorney
General, General)
1005 Lakeshore Dr
Tuskegee, AL 36083, USA

Gray, Gary (Athlete, Basketball Player)
541 Janice Ln
La Place, LA 70068-5680, USA

Gray, Gary G. (Athlete, Baseball Player)
P.O. Box 98
La Place, LA 70069, USA

Gray, George W (Misc)
Juniper House
Furzehill
Wimborne, Dorset BH21 4HD, UNITED
KINGDOM (UK)

Gray, Harrison
1141 Hillcrest Manor Estate
Strathmore, AB TIP OB9, Canada

Gray, Harry B (Misc)
1415 E California Blvd
Pasadena, CA 91106, USA

Gray, Hector (Athlete, Football Player)
Miami Springs High School
751 Dove Ave
Miami Springs, FL 33166, USA

Gray, James (Director, Writer)
c/o Todd Feldman *Creative Artists Agency
(CAA-LA)*
2000 Ave Of The Stars
Los Angeles, CA 90067, USA

Gray, Jeff (Athlete, Baseball Player)
3229 Stonebridge Trl
Valrico, FL 33596-9252, USA

Gray, Jerry (Athlete, Football Player)
PO Box 280869
Nashville, TN 37228-0869, USA

Gray, Jim (Actor)
3325 Blair Drive
Los Angeles, CA 90068, USA

Gray, John (Writer)
John Gray's Mars Venus
20 Sunnyside Ave
#A130
Mill Valley, CA 94941, USA

Gray, John (Director, Writer)
c/o Steve Rabineau *United Talent Agency
(UTA)*
9336 Civic Center Dr
Beverly Hills, CA 90210, USA

Gray, John (Athlete, Hockey Player)
23 Bear Path
Hampton, NH 03842-1300

Gray, John (Johnny) (Athlete, Baseball
Player)
10645 Greenbriar Ct
Boca Raton, FL 33498-1644, USA

Gray, Johnnie (Athlete, Football Player)
220 Short St
Wrightstown, WI 54180-1154, USA

Gray, Ken (Athlete, Football Player)
1114 Willow
Kingsland, TX 78639-3864, USA

Gray, Lester (General)
19307 W Clarendon Ave
Litchfield Park, AZ 85340-9504, USA

Gray, Linda (Actor)
PO Box 5064
Sherman Oaks, CA 91403, USA

Gray, Lorenzo (Athlete, Baseball Player)
2680 E 19th St
Apt 1
Signal Hill, CA 90755-1106, USA

Gray, Macy (Musician, Songwriter)
c/o Staff Member *Gold Levin Talent*
8424-A Santa Monica Blvd
Suite 706
Los Angeles, CA 90069, USA

Gray, Mel (Athlete, Football Player)
4507 Skyline Dr
Rockford, IL 61107-3718, USA

Gray, Mel (Athlete, Football Player)
137 Winterset Pass
Williamsburg, VA 23188, USA

Gray, Michael
9294 Civic Center Dr.
Beverly Hills, CA 90210

Gray, Michael (Stylist)
c/o Staff Member *Artists Management, Inc*
11906 Lawler St
Los Angeles, CA 90066, USA

Gray, Moses (Athlete, Football Player)
1331 Aggie Ln
Indianapolis, IN 46260, USA

Gray, Nel (Athlete, Football Player)
6549 Samantha Ln
Rockford, IL 61107, USA

Gray, Scott (Cartoonist)
c/o Staff Member *Marvel Entertainment,
Inc.*
417 5th. Ave
New York, NY 10016, USA

Gray, Spaiding (Artist, Writer)
22 Wooster St
New York, NY 10013, USA

Gray, Stuart (Athlete, Basketball Player)
909 Andover Grn
Lexington, KY 40509-2930, USA

Gray, Sylvester (Athlete, Basketball
Player)
4929 Bilrae Circle South
Millington, TN 38053-1612, USA

Gray, Tamrya (Actor)
c/o Staff Member *19 Entertainment*
33/32 Ransomes Dock
35-37 Parkgate Rd
London SW11 4NP, UK

Gray, Tamyra (Musician)
c/o Jeff Frasco *Creative Artists Agency
(CAA-LA)*
2000 Ave Of The Stars
Los Angeles, CA 90067, USA

Gray, Terry (Athlete, Hockey Player)
PO Box 371
Richmond, ON KOA 2ZO, Canada

Gray, Tim (Athlete, Football Player)
6109 Crane St
Houston, TX 77026, USA

Gray, Torrian (Athlete, Football Player)
370 Oaktree Blvd
Christiansburg, VA 24073-4740, USA

Gray, Vincent (Governor, Politician)
One Judiciary Square
441 Forth St NW
Washington, DC 20001, USA

Gray, William H III (Misc)
United Negro College Fund
500 E 62nd St
New York, NY 10021, USA

Graybiel, Ann M (Scientist)
Massachusetts Institute of Technology
Cognitive Sci Dept
Cambridge, MA 02139, USA

Gray Cabey, Noah (Actor)
c/o Blake Bandy *Kritzer Levine Wilkins Entertainment (KLWG)*
11872 La Grange Ave
1st Floor
Los Angeles, CA 90025, USA

Grayden, Sprague (Actor)
c/o Katie Rhodes *Untitled Entertainment (LA)*
350 S. Beverly Dr #200
Beverly Hills, CA 90212, USA

Graydon, Joe
1870 Caminito Del Cielo
Glendale, CA 91208

Graydon, Michael (General)
Lloyds Bank 7 Pall Mall Cox and king's
Branch London
SWlY SNA, England

Graye, Devon (Actor)
c/o Adam Griffin *Kritzer Levine Wilkins Entertainment (KLWG)*
11872 La Grange Ave
1st Floor
Los Angeles, CA 90025, USA

Grayer, Jeff (Athlete, Basketball Player)
1617 Barbara Dr
Flint, MI 48504-1637, USA

Grayhm, Steven (Actor, Director, Writer)
c/o Adam Griffin *Kritzer Levine Wilkins Entertainment (KLWG)*
11872 La Grange Ave
1st Floor
Los Angeles, CA 90025, USA

Graynor, Ari (Actor)
c/o Jill Kaplan *Principal Entertainment (NY)*
130 W 42nd St
Suite 614
New York, NY 10036, USA

Graysmith, Robert (Cartoonist, Editor)
San Francisco Chronicle
901 Mission St
San Francisco, CA 94103, USA

Grayson, C Jackson Jr (Educator, Government Official)
123 N Post Oak Lane
Houston, TX 77024, USA

Grayson, David Lee (Athlete, Football Player)
5962 Rancho Mission Rd Unit 218
San Diego, CA 92108-2552, USA

Grayson, Mel (Stylist)
c/o Staff Member *St Rage & Company*
270 N Canon Dr
#1611
Beverly Hills, CA 90210, USA

Grayson Sr, Dave (Athlete, Football Player)
7116 Los Soneto Ct
San Diego, CA 92114, USA

Gray-Stanford, Jason (Actor)
c/o Scott Zimmerman *Evolution Entertainment (LA)*
901 N Highland Ave
Los Angeles, CA 90038, USA

Grazer, Brian (Producer)
c/o Staff Member *Imagine Films Entertainment*
1925 Century Park E
Los Angeles, CA 90067, USA

Grazia, Eugene (Athlete, Hockey Player)
2421 NE 49th St
Fort Lauderdale, FL 33308, USA

Graziadei, Michael (Actor)
c/o Amy Abell *Glick Agency*
1505 10th St
Santa Monica, CA 90401, USA

Graziani, Ariel (Soccer Player)
San Jose Earthquakes
3550 Stevens Creek Blvd
#200
San Jose, CA 95117, USA

Graziano, Renee
c/o Staff Member *Maniac Management*
NA
NA NA

Grazioso, Claudia (Producer, Writer)
c/o Nicole Clemens *ICM Partners (ICM-LA)*
10250 Constellation Blvd Fl 7
Los Angeles, CA 90067, USA

Grazzola, Kenneth E (Publisher)
Aviation Week Magazine
1221 Ave of Americas
New York, NY 10020, USA

Grba, Eli (Athlete, Baseball Player)
106 Fox Run
Florence, AL 35633-1465, USA

Grbac, Elvis (Athlete, Football Player)
17361 Coldwater Trl
Chargin Falls, OH 44023, USA

Greacen, Bob (Athlete, Basketball Player)
333 Reeder Street
Easton, PA 18042-7663, USA

Greason, Bill (Athlete, Baseball Player)
4536 Hillman Dr SW
Birmingham, AL 35221-1816, USA

Greason, Staci
8831 Sunset Blvd. #304
Los Angeles, CA 90069

Greason, William (Baseball Player)
Birmingham Black Barons
4536 Hillman Dr SW
Birmingham, AL 35221-1816, USA

Great Big Sea (Musician)
Fleming & Associates
733-735 North Main
Ann Arbor, MI 48104-1030

Greaves, Gary (Athlete, Football Player)
8221 SW 176th St
Palmetto Bay, FL 33157, USA

Grebeck, Craig (Athlete, Baseball Player)
24202 Juanita Dr
Laguna Niguel, CA 92677-4064, USA

Grebenshchikov, Boris (Musician)
2 Marata St
#3
Saint Petersburg, RUSSIA

Grechko, Georgi M (Cosmonaut)
Potcha Kosmonavtov
Moskovskoi Oblasti
Syvisdny Goroduk 141160, RUSSIA

Greco, Buddy (Musician)
Zane Mgmt
5 Monte Verde Way
Palm Desert, CA 92260, USA

Greco, Emilio (Artist)
Viale Cortina d'Ampezzo 132
Rome 00135, ITALY

Greco, Juliette (Actor, Musician)
Maurice Maraouani
37 Rue Marbeuf
Paris 75008, FRANCE

Greco, Marco (Race Car Driver)
11717 W. Rockville Rd.
Indianapolis, IN 46232, USA

Greco, Michael (Actor)
c/o Pedro Pinto *Gregg Millard Management*
38 Barton House
Sable St
London N1 2AF, UK

Greczyn, Alice (Actor)
c/o Adam Griffin *Kritzer Levine Wilkins Entertainment (KLWG)*
11872 La Grange Ave
1st Floor
Los Angeles, CA 90025, USA

Greeley, Andrew
6030 S. Ellis
Chicago, IL 60637

Greeley, Andrew M (Andy) (Writer)
6030 S Ellis Ave
Chicago, IL 60637, USA

Green, A C
904 Silver Spur Rd
Rolling Hills Estates, CA 90274-3800, USA

Green, A C (Athlete, Basketball Player)
904 Silver Spur Road
Rolling Hills Estates, CA 90274, USA

Green, Adolph
211 Central Park W. #19E
New York, NY 10024

Green, Ahman (Athlete, Football Player)
1750 Limestone Trl
De Pere, WI 54115-7973, USA

Green, A.J. (Football Player)
c/o Tom Condon *CAA - St. Louis*
222 S Central Ave
Suite 1008
St Louis, MO 63105, USA

Green, Al (Musician, Religious Leader, Songwriter)
PO Box 456
Millington, TN 38083, USA

Green, Al (Congressman, Politician)
220.1 Rayburn HOB
Washington, DC 20515, USA

Green, Al (Musician)
c/o Staff Member *Shore Fire Media*
32 Court St
16th Floor
Brooklyn, NY 11201, USA

Green, Andy (Athlete, Baseball Player)
1025 Lakefront Dr
Lexington, KY 40517-2658, USA

Green, Anthony (Athlete, Football Player)
9611 Wesland Cir
Randallstown, MD 21133, USA

Green, Barrett (Athlete, Football Player)
1004 Green Pine Blvd
Apt D1
West Palm Beach, FL 33409, USA

Green, Barry (Misc)
Team Green
7615 Zionsville Road
Indianapolis, IN 46268, USA

Green, Benny (Musician)
Jazz Tree
211 Thompson St
#1D
New York, NY 10012, USA

Green, B Eric (Athlete, Football Player)
13131 Luntz Point Ln
Windermere, FL 34786, USA

Green, Boyce (Athlete, Football Player)
4156 1st Street Pl NW
Hickory, NC 28601, USA

Green, Brian Austin (Actor, Director, Producer)
1605 San Vicente Blvd
Santa Monica, CA 90402, USA

Green, Cee-Lo (Musician)
165 Pointer Ridge Trail
Fayetteville, GA 30214, USA

Green, Charlie (Athlete, Football Player)
255 S Kyrene Rd
Unit 214
Chandler, AZ 85226, USA

Green, Charlie (Athlete, Football Player)
c/o Staff Member *Bryan Bantry*
900 Broadway Ste 400
New York, NY 10003, USA

Green, Chris (Athlete, Football Player)
331 Patio Village Ter
Weston, FL 33326, USA

Green, Chris (Athlete, Baseball Player)
4054 Uppergate Ln
Charlotte, NC 28215-3831, USA

Green, Cleveland (Athlete, Football Player)
5537 Robinson Road Ext
Jackson, MS 39204, USA

Green, Cornell (Athlete, Football Player)
2106 Trinidad Dr
Dallas, TX 75232, USA

Green, Dallas (Athlete, Baseball Player, Coach)
846 Conowingo Rd
Conowingo, MD 21918-1307, USA

Green, Dallas
846 Conowingo Rd
Conowingo, MD 21918-1307

Green, Darrell (Athlete, Football Player)
20998 Rostormel Dr
Ashburn, VA 20147, USA

Green, Dave (Athlete, Football Player)
8311 Pat Blvd
Tampa, FL 33615-1810, USA

Green, David (Race Car Driver)
118 Reel Brook Lane
Mooreslli1e, NC 28117-8801, USA

Green, David (Director)
International Creative Mgmt
76 Oxford St
London W1N 0AX, UNITED KINGDOM
(UK)

Green, David (Athlete, Baseball Player)
Colinia Managua Grupo H47
Managua, Nicaragua

Green, David E (Misc)
5339 Brody Dr
Madison, WI 53705, USA

Green, David E (Athlete, Football Player)
8311 Pat Blvd
Tampa, FL 33615, USA

Green, David Gordon (Director,
Producer, Writer)
c/o Staff Member *The Gotham Group Inc*
9255 Sunset Blvd
Suite 515
Los Angeles, CA 90069, USA

Green, David T (Inventor)
US Surgical Corp
401 Black Rock Tpke
Easton, CT 06612 -1545, USA

Green, Debbie (Athlete, Olympic Athlete,
Volleyball Player)
239 5th St
Seal Beach, CA 90740, USA

Green, Dennis (Athlete, Coach, Football
Coach, Football Player)
3930 Torrey Hill Ln
San Diego, CA 92130, USA

Green, Dick (Athlete, Baseball Player)
3924 Ridgemoor Dr
Rapid City, SD 57702-5328, USA

Green, Donnie (Athlete, Football Player)
11 S Walnut St Apt 316
Hagerstown, MD 21740-5499, USA

Green, E G (Athlete, Football Player)
3505 45th Ter W Unit 105
Bradenton, FL 34210-3177, USA

Green, E.G. (Athlete, Football Player)
26620 Castleview Way
Wesley Chapel, FL 33544, USA

Green, Eric (Athlete, Football Player)
PO Box 204
Clewiston, FL 33440-0204, USA

Green, Ernie (Athlete, Football Player)
424 Rue Marseille
Dayton, OH 45429, USA

Green, Eva (Actor)
c/o Angharad Wood *Tavistock Wood
Management*
32 Tavistock St
London WC2B 5HA, UK

Green, Gary (Athlete, Baseball Player)
939 Kennebec St
Pittsburgh, PA 15217-2604, USA

Green, Gary F (Athlete, Football Player)
16330 Walnut Creek Dr
San Antonio, TX 78247, USA

Green, Gaston (Athlete, Football Player)
13524 Stanford Ave
Los Angeles, CA 90059-3538, USA

Green, Gene (Congressman, Politician)
2470 Rayburn HOB
Washington, DC 20515, USA

Green, George (Athlete, Baseball Player)
1718 S Oxford Ave Apt 1
Los Angeles, CA 90006-5130, USA

Green, George
1718 S Oxford Ave Apt 1
Los Angeles, CA 90006-5130, USA

Green, George (Athlete, Baseball Player)
1718 S Oxford Ave Apt 1
Los Angeles, CA 90006-5130, USA

Green, George
1718 S Oxford Ave Apt 1
Los Angeles, CA 90006-5130, USA

Green, Gerald (Writer)
88 Arrowhead Trail
New Canaan, CT 06840, USA

Green, Hamilton (Prime Minister)
Plot D Lodge
Georgetown, GUYANA

Green, Harold (Athlete, Football Player)
145 Folk Rd
Blythewood, SC 29016, USA

Green, Howard (Physicist)
Harvard Medical School
Physiology & Biophysics Dept
Boston, MA 02115, USA

Green, Hubert (Athlete, Golfer)
5141 Gulf Dr
Panama City, FL 32408, USA

Green, Hugh (Athlete, Football Player)
4758 Highway 61
Fayette, MS 39069, USA

Green, Jacob (Athlete, Football Player)
4921 Whistling Straits Loop
College Station, TX 77845-3866, USA

Green, Jacquez (Athlete, Football Player)
5102 Madison Lakes Cir W
Davie, FL 33328, USA

Green, Janine (Actor)
c/o David Sweeney *Sweeney
Management*
6253 Hollywood Blvd
Suite 201
Los Angeles, CA 90028, USA

Green, Jarvis (Athlete, Football Player)
10438 Dunsford Dr
Lone Tree, CO 80124-9796, USA

Green, Jeff (Athlete, Basketball Player)
c/o Staff Member *Oklahoma City Thunder*
Two Leadership Square
211 N Robinson Ave, Suite 300
Oklahoma City, OK 73102, USA

Green, Jeff (Race Car Driver)
Haas CNC Racing
6001 Haas Way
Kannapolis Gateway Business Park
Kannapolis, NC 28081, USA

Green, Jenna Leigh (Actor)
c/o Aaron Kogan *Sovereign Talent Group*
8421 Wilshire Blvd
Suite 200
Beverly Hills, CA 90211, USA

Green, Jessie (Athlete, Football Player)
638 County Road 2470
Mount Pleasant, TX 75455-9255, USA

Green, Jimmy (Athlete, Golfer)
2130 Keystone Dr
Auburn, AL 36830, USA

Green, John (Athlete, Football Player)
7417 Jester Ct
Ooltewah, TN 37363, USA

Green, John M (Johnny) (Athlete,
Basketball Player)
9 Susan Lane
Dix Hills, NY 11746-5140, USA

Green, John N (Jack) Jr
(Cinematographer)
516 Esplanade
#E
Redondo Beach, CA 90277, USA

Green, Jordan-Claire (Actor)
c/o Staff Member *Cunningham Escott
Slevin & Doherty (CESD-LA)*
10635 Santa Monica Blvd
130
Los Angeles, CA 90025, USA

Green, Kate (Writer)
Bantam/Delacorte/Dell/Doubleday Press
1540 Broadway
New York, NY 10036, USA

Green, Ken (Athlete, Golfer)
4520 Feivel Road
Apt 56
West Palm Beach, FL 33417-8078, USA

Green, Lamar (Athlete, Basketball Player)
P.O. Box 490208
Chicago, IL 60649-0208, USA

Green, Lenny (Athlete, Baseball Player)
18693 Sunset St
Detroit, MI 48234-2043, USA

Green, Leonard I (Business Person)
Rite Aid Corp
30 Hunter Lane
Camp Hill, PA 17011, USA

Green, Litterial (Athlete, Basketball
Player)
160 McIntosh Place Dr
Fayetteville, IL 30214-7318, USA

Green, Lucinda (Misc)
Appleshaw House
Andover
Hants, UNITED KINGDOM (UK)

Green, Marilyn (Race Car Driver)
601 Norwalk St.
Greensboro, NC 27407, USA

Green, Mark (Race Car Driver)
Hensley Racing
1542 J.S. Holland Rd.
Ridgeway, VA 23148, USA

Green, Mark (Race Car Driver)
Trackside Marketing Group
345 Marblerock Way
Lexington, KY 40503, USA

Green, Mark A (Athlete, Football Player)
1087 Creek Bend Dr
Vernon Hills, IL 60061, USA

Green, Mark J (Activist, Attorney General)
Democracy Project
43 E 19th St Fl 3
New York, NY 10003-1304, USA

Green, Maurice Spurgeon (Editor)
Hermitage
Twyford House
Hants, UNITED KINGDOM (UK)

Green, Michael (Cinematographer)
11 Stevenson Lane
Upper Saddle River, NJ 07458, USA

Green, Mike
1615 N Queen St Unit M603
Arlington, VA 22209-2801

Green, Mike (Athlete, Football Player)
15271 Peach St
Chino Hills, CA 91709, USA

Green, Nick (Athlete, Baseball Player)
1380 Lake Washington
Cir
Lawrenceville, GA 30022-6118, USA

Green, Pat (Musician)
c/o Staff Member *WmE2 (WMA-TN)*
1600 Division St
Suite 300
Nashville, TN 37203, USA

Green, Patricia (Producer, Writer)
c/o David Greenblatt *Greenlit*
1800 N Highland Ave
Suite 500
Los Angeles, CA 90028, USA

Green, Paul (Athlete, Football Player)
1635 N Formosa Ave Apt 208
Los Angeles, CA 90046, USA

Green, Pumpsie (Athlete, Baseball Player)
2105 Harper St
El Cerrito, CA 94530-172, USA

Green, Ray (Athlete, Football Player)
2738 S University Dr Apt 15A
Davie, FL 33328-1428, USA

Green, Rick (Athlete, Hockey Player)
1260 W. de la Gauchetiere st.
Montreal, QC H3B 5E8, Canada

Green, Rick (Producer)
c/o Glenn Cockburn *Meridian Artists*
2 College St
Suite 207
Toronto, ON M5G 1K3, Canada

Green, Rickey (Athlete, Basketball Player)
20584 Tyler Drive
Lynwood, IL 60411-8571, USA

Green, Robin (Writer)
c/o Staff Member *Broder Webb Chervin
Silbermann Agency, The (BWCS)*
10250 Constellation Blvd
Los Angeles, CA 90067-6200, USA

Green, Robson (Actor)
c/o Staff Member *Coastal Productions*
25B Broadchare
The Quayside
Newcastle-Upon-Tyne NE1 3DQ,
UNITED KINGDOM (UK)

Green, Sarah (Producer)
c/o Staff Member *ICM Partners (ICM-LA)*
10250 Constellation Blvd Fl 7
Los Angeles, CA 90067, USA

Green, Scarborough (Athlete, Baseball
Player)
2020 Crimson
Meadows Dr
O'Fallon, MO 63366-4186, USA

Green, sean
3823 Fieldside Cir
Louisville, KY 40299-6545, USA

Green, Seth (Actor, Comedian, Producer)
c/o Staff Member *Koopman Management*
851 Oreo Pl
Pacific Palisades, CA 90272, USA

Green, Shawn (Athlete, Baseball Player)
3801 Sandune Ln
Corona Del Mar, CA 92625-1623, USA

Green, Sidney (Basketball Player, Coach)
Florida Atlantic University
Athletic Dept
Boca Raton, FL 33431, USA

Green, Skylar (Athlete, Football Player)
3121 Thomas Ave
Dallas, TX 75204, USA

Green, Steve (Athlete, Basketball Player)
942 Round Table Court
Indianapolis, IN 46260-4923, USA

Green, Suzy (Athlete, Golfer)
26006 Carol Ave
Franklin, MI 48025, USA

Green, Tammie (Athlete, Golfer)
4990 Township Road 147 NE
Somerset, OH 43783-9753, USA

Green, Taylor (Athlete, Baseball Player)
Double Diamond Sports Management
7640 NW 79th Ave
Apt L8
Tamarac, FL 33321-2&6&, USA

Green, Timothy J (Tim) (Athlete, Football
Player, Sportscaster)
1194 Breenfield Ln
Skaneateles, NY 13152, USA

Green, Tom (Actor, Comedian)
c/o Howard Lapides *Core/Lapides Lear
Entertainment*
14724 Ventura Blvd.
Penthouse
Sherman Oaks, CA 91403, USA

Green, Travis (Athlete, Hockey Player)
2 Riverside
Irvine, CA 92602-0903, USA

Green, Trent (Athlete, Football Player)
570 Chestnut Forest Cv
Fort Wayne, IN 46814, USA

Green, Tyler (Athlete, Baseball Player)
15065 S 39th St
Phoenix, AZ 85044-6676, USA

Green, Van (Athlete, Football Player)
311 Leta St
Auburndale, FL 33823, USA

Green, Victor (Athlete, Football Player)
245 Woodscape Ct
Alpharetta, GA 30022, USA

Green, Vivian (Actor)
c/o Staff Member *WME (LA)*
9601 Wilshire Blvd Fl 3
Beverly Hills, CA 90210, USA

Green, Willie (Athlete, Football Player)
152 Farmington Rd
Shelby, NC 28150, USA

Green, Woody (Athlete, Football Player)
702 SE Palmblad Pl
Portland, OR 97080-1496, USA

Green, Yatil (Athlete, Football Player)
2000 Island Blvd
Apt 3002
Aventura, FL 33160, USA

Greenaway, Peter (Director)
Allarts Ltd
387B King St
London W6 9NH, UNITED KINGDOM
(UK)

Greenberg, Adam (Athlete, Baseball
Player)
79 Fernwood Dr
Guilford, CT 06437-2367, USA

Greenberg, Adam (Cinematographer)
Gersh Agency
232 N Canon Dr
Beverly Hills, CA 90210, USA

Greenberg, Alan C (Financier)
Bear Steams Co
383 Madison Ave
New York, NY 10017, USA

Greenberg, Bernard (Biologist, Scientist)
1463 E 55th Place
Chicago, IL 60637, USA

Greenberg, Bryan (Actor)
c/o Ellen Meyer *Ellen Meyer Management*
8899 Beverly Blvd
Suite 612
West Hollywood, CA 90048, USA

Greenberg, Carl (Journalist)
6001 Canterbury Dr
Culver City, CA 90230, USA

Greenberg, Evan (Business Person)
American International Group
70 Pine St
New York, NY 10270, USA

Greenberg, Jack (Attorney, Attorney
General, Educator, General)
118 Riverside Dr
New York, NY 10024, USA

Greenberg, Maurice R (Business Person)
American International Group
70 Pine St
New York, NY 10270, USA

Greenberg, Mike (Sportscaster, Television
Host)
c/o Lou Oppenheim *Headline Media
Management*
888 7th Ave #503
New York, NY 10106, USA

Greenberg, Morton I (Judge)
US Court of Appeals
Judicial Complex
402 E State St
Trenton, NJ 08608, USA

Greenberg, Peter (Television Host)
c/o Staff Member *Today Show, The*
30 Rockefeller Plz
New York, NY 10112, USA

Greenberg, Robbie S (Cinematographer)
11 Reef St
Marina del Rey, CA 90292, USA

Greenberg, Ross (Producer, Writer)
c/o Staff Member *Shed Media US*
3800 Barham Blvd
Suite 410
Los Angeles, CA 90068, USA

Greenberg, Sarah T (Stylist)
180 West End Ave
#17-B
New Buffalo, NY 10023, USA

Greenberg, Susin Ross (Stylist)
1262 Deerfield Pl
Highland Park, IL 60035, USA

Greenblatt, Stephen J (Writer)
Harvard University
English Dept
Cambridge, MA 02138, USA

Greenblatt, William
30710 Monte Lado Dr.
Malibu, CA 90265

Greenburg, Dan (Writer)
323 E 50th St
New York, NY 10022, USA

Greenburg, Paul (Journalist)
5900 Scenic Dr
Little Rock, AR 72207, USA

Greenbush, Rachel Lindsay (Actor)
Gold Marshak Liedtke
3500 W Olive Ave
#1400
Burbank, CA 91505, USA

Greenbush, Sidney Robin (Actor)
Gold Marshak Liedtke
3500 W Olive Ave
#1400
Burbank, CA 91505, USA

Green Day (Music Group)
c/o John Dehais *Pat's Management
Company*
5900 Wilshire Blvd #1720
Los Angeles, CA 90036, USA

Greene, A J (Athlete, Football Player)
3900 Braxton Dr
Charlotte, NC 28226-7003, USA

Greene, Al (Athlete, Baseball Player)
18294 Marlowe St
Detroit, MI 48235-2762, USA

Greene, Andrew
330 Richmond Ave
South Orange, NJ 07079-2134

Greene, Ashley (Actor)
c/o Staff Member *McKeon-Myones
Management*
3500 Olive Ave
Suite 770
Burbank, CA 91505, USA

Greene, Biloah (Actor)
c/o Vincent Cirrincione *Vincent
Cirrincione Associates*
1516 N Fairfax Ave
Los Angeles, CA 90046, USA

Greene, Bob (Fitness Expert)
c/o Tyler Delaney *Westport Entertainment
Associates*
1700 Post Rd
Suite C-15
Fairfield, CT 06824, USA

Greene, Brian (Mathematician, Physicist)
Columbia University
Physics Dept
New York, NY 10027, USA

Greene, Charles E (Charlie) (Athlete,
Olympic Athlete, Track Athlete)
P.O. Box 6938
Lincoln, NE 68506-0938, USA

Greene, Charlie (Athlete, Baseball Player)
1449 Oldfield Dr
Tallahassee, FL 32308-0534, USA

Greene, David (Football Coach, Football
Player)
c/o Lenore Zerman *Liberman/Zerman
Management*
252 N Larchmont Blvd
Suite 200
Los Angeles, CA 90004, USA

Greene, Dawn (Philanthropist)
Jerome L Greene Foundation
950 3rd Avenue
New York, New York 10022, USA

Greene, Ellen (Musician)
Innovative Artists
1505 10th St.
Santa Monica, CA 90401, USA

Greene, Graham (Actor)
c/o Susan Smith *Susan Smith Company,
The*
1344 N Wetherly Dr
Los Angeles, CA 90069-1817, USA

Greene, Jack (Musician)
Ace Productions
PO Box 428
Portland, TN 37148, USA

Greene, Jack P (Historian)
1974 Division Road
East Greenwich, RI 02818, USA

Greene, James
60 Pope's Grove Twickenham
Middlesex, ENGLAND

Greene, Jay (Scientist)
16502 Craighurst Dr
Houston, TX 77059-6518, USA

Greene, Jay
16502 Craighurst Dr
Houston, TX 77059-6518, USA

Greene, Jennifer (Stylist)
c/o Celebrity Stylist *Oliver Piro Inc*
725 Riverside Dr Apt 3A
New York, NY 10031, USA

Greene, Joe (Athlete, Football Player)
P.O. Box 270953
Flower Mound, TX 75027, USA

Greene, Julie (Stylist)
c/o Staff Member *Fifty8 Artists*
58 W Huron St
Chicago, IL 60610, USA

Greene, Ken (Athlete, Football Player)
5569 Nevil Pt
Brentwood, TN 37027-8281, USA

Greene, Kenneth E (Ken) (Athlete,
Football Player)
7607 Hazard Center Dr
San Diego, CA 92108, USA

Greene, Kevin (Athlete, Football Player)
c/o David Dunn *Athletes First, LLC*
9140 Irvine Center Dr
Irvine, CA 92618, USA

Greene, Khalil (Athlete, Baseball Player)
10 Green Hill Dr
Simpsonville, SC 29681-4148, USA

Greene, Leonard M (Inventor)
1010 Greacen Point Rd
Mamaroneck, NY 10543, USA

Greene, Maurice (Athlete, Track Athlete)
c/o Staff Member *Exposure Marketing
Group*
348 S Hauser Blvd #PH414
Los Angeles, CA 90046, USA

Greene, Michele (Actor, Musician)
PO Box 29117
Los Angeles, CA 90029, USA

Greene, Michelle
PO Box 29117
Los Angeles, CA 90029-0117, USA

Greene, Pat (Writer)
c/o Staff Member *Playscripts, Inc.*
325 W 38th St
Suite 305
New York, NY 10018, USA

Greene, Paul (Actor)
c/o Jessica Cohen *JCPR*
9903 Santa Monica Blvd
Suite 983
Beverly Hills, CA 90212, USA

Greene, Shecky (Actor, Comedian)
1642 S La Verne Way
Palm Springs, CA 92264, USA

Greene, Todd (Athlete, Baseball Player)
725 Pine Leaf Ct
Alpharetta, GA 30022-1026, USA

Greene, Tommy (Athlete, Baseball Player)
6001 Dalecross Way
Glen Allen, VA 23059-6962, USA

Greene, Tony (Athlete, Football Player)
1890 Briarcliff Cir NE
Apt D
Atlanta, GA 30329, USA

Greene, Tony (Athlete, Football Player)
9001 Brookville Rd
Silver Spring, MD 20910, USA

Greene, Willie (Athlete, Baseball Player)
1044 GA Highway 22 E
Haddock, GA 31033-2360, USA

Greenfield, James L (Journalist)
470 Park Ave
#9A
New York, NY 10022, USA

Greenfield, Jeff (Correspondent)
Cable News Network
News Dept
820 1st St NE
Washington, DC 20002, USA

Greenfield, Jerry (Inventor)
2779 South Rd
Williston, VT 05495-8883, USA

Greenfield, Lauren (Director,
Photographer, Producer)
Lauren Greenfield Photography
2417 McKinley Ave
Venice, CA 90291, USA

Greenfield, Max (Actor, Producer)
c/o Loch Powell *Leverage Management*
3030 Pennsylvania Ave
Santa Monica, CA 90404, USA

Greenfield-Sanders, Timothy (Artist,
Photographer)
821 Broadway Fl 4
New York, NY 10003, USA

Greengard, Paul (Nobel Prize Laureate)
500 E 63rd St Apt 24A
New York, NY 10065-7956, USA

Greengrass, Jim (Athlete, Baseball Player)
232 Talking Rock Creek Pro Rd
Chatsworth, GA 30705-6895, USA

Greengrass, Paul (Director)
c/o Beth Swofford *Creative Artists Agency
(CAA-LA)*
2000 Ave Of The Stars
Los Angeles, CA 90067, USA

Greenlaw, Jeff (Athlete, Hockey Player)
9213 Colberg Dr
Austin, TX 78749, USA

Greenlaw, Linda (Writer)
c/o Eliot Gunner *Keppler Associates*
3030 Clarendon Blvd
7th Floor
Arlington, VA 22201, USA

Greenlay, Mike (Athlete, Hockey Player)
c/o Staff Member *Minnesota Wild*
317 Washington St
Saint Paul, MN 55102, USA

Greenlay, Mike (Athlete, Hockey Player)
3338 Richmond Bay
Saint Paul, MN 55129-4925

Greenlee, David (Actor)
1811 N Whitley
#800
Los Angeles, CA 90028, USA

Greenspan, Alan (Politician)
Greenspan Associates LLC
2710 Chain Bridge Rd NW
Washington, DC 20016-3404, USA

Greenspan, Jerry (Athlete, Basketball
Player)
60 Herbert Ter
West Orange, NJ 07052-1021, USA

Greenspan, Melissa (Actor)
c/o Jeff Danis *Danis, Panaro, Nist (DPN)*
9201 W Olympic Blvd
Beverly Hills, CA 90212, USA

Greenstein, Jeff (Producer)
c/o Staff Member *ICM Partners (ICM-LA)*
10250 Constellation Blvd Fl 7
Los Angeles, CA 90067, USA

Greenville, Georgina (Model)
Next Model Mgmt
188 Rue de Rivoli
Paris 75001, FRANCE

Greenwald, Milton (Misc)
University of California
Museum of Paleontology
Berkeley, CA 94720, USA

Greenwalt, T Jack (Misc)
2444 Madison Road
#1501
Cincinnati, OH 45208, USA

Greenway, Chad (Athlete, Football Player)
39448 250th St
Mount Vernon, SD 57363, USA

Greenwell, Mike (Athlete, Baseball Player)
18500 State Road 31
Alva, FL 33920-3016, USA

Greenwood, Bruce (Actor)
c/o Chuck Binder *Binder & Associates*
1465 Lindacrest Dr
Beverly Hills, CA 90210, USA

Greenwood, Colin (Musician)
Nasty Little Man
72 Spring St
#1100
New York, NY 10012, USA

Greenwood, David (Athlete, Basketball
Player)
18857 Whitney Pl
Rowland Heights, CA 91748-4873, USA

Greenwood, Jonny (Musician)
Nasty Little Man
72 Spring St
#1100
New York, NY 10012, USA

Greenwood, L C (Athlete, Football Player)
Badgeley Promotions PO Box 3528
Parkersburg, WV 26103-3528, USA

Greenwood, Lee (Musician, Songwriter)
Lee Greenwood Inc
PO Box 22025
Huntsville, AL 35814, USA

Greenwood, Michael
Princes Gate1 4 Kingston House E
London, ENGLAND SW7

Greenwood, Morlon (Athlete, Football
Player)
2 Waters Lake Blvd
Missouri City, TX 77459, USA

Greenwood, Norman (Misc)
University of Leeds
Chemistry Dept
Leeds, LS2 9JT, UNITED KINGDOM (UK)

Greer, Brian (Athlete, Baseball Player)
307 Bagnall Ave
Placentia, CA 92870-1904, USA

Greer, Brodie
300 S. Raymond Ave. #II
Pasadena, CA 91105

Greer, David S (Misc)
Brown University
PO Box G
Providence, RI 02912, USA

Greer, Donovan (Athlete, Football Player)
3423 Shadowside Ct
Houston, TX 77082-8303, USA

Greer, Germaine (Writer)
Atkin & Stone
Atkin and Stone29 Fernshaw Road
London SW10 0TG, UNITED KINGDOM

Greer, Gordon G (Editor)
Better Homes & Gardens Magazine
1716 Locust St
Des Moines, IA 50309, USA

Greer, Hal (Athlete, Basketball Player)
c/o Staff Member *Naismith Memorial
Basketball Hall of Fame*
1000 West Columbus Avenue
Springfield, MA 01105, USA

Greer, Howard (Admiral)
8539 Prestwick Dr
La Jolia, CA 92037, USA

Greer, Judy (Actor)
c/o Staff Member *Principato/Young
Management*
9465 Wilshire Blvd
Suite 430
Beverly Hills, CA 90212, USA

Greer, Kenny (Athlete, Baseball Player)
17 Hill St
Cohasset, MA 02025-2218, USA

Greer, Rusty (Athlete, Baseball Player)
4703 Patterson Ln
Colleyville, TX 76034-4507, USA

Greezyn, Alice (Actor)
c/o Staff Member *Windfall*
3000 W Alameda Ave
Burbank, CA 91523-0001, USA

Gregerson, Luke (Athlete, Baseball Player)
109 N Aldine Ave
Park Ridge, IL 60068-3007, USA

Gregg, Clark (Actor)
c/o Paulette Bartlett *Paulette Bartlett
Management*
3000 West Olympic Blvd
Suite 1364
Santa Monica, CA 90404, USA

Gregg, Forrest (Athlete, Coach, Football
Coach, Football Executive, Football
Player)
2985 Plaza Azul
Santa Fe, NM 87507, USA

Gregg, John
1/1 Punch St.
Mosman, AUSTRALIA NSW 2088

Gregg, Judd A (Politician)
1234 Ocean Blvd
Rye, NH 03870-2209, USA

Gregg, Kelly (Athlete, Football Player)
13800 Hollow Glen Rd
Edmond, OK 73013, USA

Gregg, Kevin (Athlete, Baseball Player)
1907 SW Brooklane Dr
Corvallis, OR 97333-1627, USA

Gregg, Randy (Athlete, Hockey Player)
13021 104th Ave. NW
Edmonton, AB T5N 0V9, Canada

Gregg, Stephen (Writer)
c/o Staff Member *Creative Artists Agency
(CAA-LA)*
2000 Ave Of The Stars
Los Angeles, CA 90067, USA

Gregg, Stephen R (War Hero)
280 Main Street
Spt 310
Little Falls, NJ 07424-1375, USA

Gregg, Tommy (Athlete, Baseball Player)
Omaha Storm Chasers 12356 Ballpark
Way
Attn: Coaching Staff
Paoillion, NE 68046-4817, USA

Gregg, Tommy (Athlete, Baseball Player)
10 Cambridge Ln
Sharpsburg, GA 30277-2462, USA

Gregoire, Chris (Governor, Politician)
Legislative Bldg
P.O. Box 40002
Olympia, WA 98504-0002, USA

Gregoire, Gabriel (Athlete, Football
Player)
575 Rang Saint-Joseph
RR 2
Sainte-Martine, QC J0S 1V0, Canada

Gregoire, Stephan (Race Car Driver)
Dick Simon Racing
25801 Victoria Blvd.
Dana Point, CA 92624, USA

Gregor, Bob (Athlete, Football Player)
14128 180th Ave NE
Redmond, WA 98052, USA

Gregor, Gary (Athlete, Basketball Player)
444 Dove Ridge Rd
Columbia, SC 29223-5589, USA

Gregorian, Vartan (Educator)
Camegie Corp
President's Office
437 Madison Ave
New York, NY 10022, USA

Gregorio, Rose (Actor)
29 W 10th St #3
New York, NY 10011, USA

Gregorio, Tom (Athlete, Baseball Player)
2929 W Windsong Dr
Phoenix, AZ 85045, USA

Gregorios, Metropolitan Paulos M
(Religious Leader)
Orthodox Seminary
PO Box 98
Kottayam, Kerala 686001, INDIA

Gregory, Adam (Actor)
c/o Beverly Strong *Strong Management*
3532 Hayden Ave
Culver City, CA 90232, USA

Gregory, Andre (Actor)
c/o Jeff Hunter *WME (WMA-NY)*
1325 Ave of the Americas
New York, NY 10019, USA

Gregory, Bettina L (Correspondent)
ABC-TV
News Dept
5010 Creston St
Hyattsville, MD 20781, USA

Gregory, Bill (Athlete, Football Player)
4317 Cityview Dr
Plano, TX 75093-, USA

Gregory, Claude (Athlete, Basketball Player)
14621 Blackburn Rd
Burtonsville, MD 20866-1303, USA

Gregory, Cynthia (Ballerina)
American Ballet Theatre
890 Broadway
New York, NY 10003, USA

Gregory, Damian (Athlete, Football Player)
2100 Walmar Dr
Lansing, MI 48917, USA

Gregory, Dick (Activist, Actor, Comedian)
Dick Gregory Health Enterprise
PO Box 3270
Plymouth, MA 02361, USA

Gregory, Dorian (Actor, Television Host)
c/o Staff Member *Creative Management Entertainment Group (CMEG)*
2050 S Bundy Dr
Suite 280
Los Angeles, CA 90025, USA

Gregory, Frederick D (Astronaut)
506 Tulip Road
Annapolis, MD 21403, USA

Gregory, Frederick D Colonel (Astronaut)
506 Tulip Rd
Annapolis, MD 21403-1326, USA

Gregory, Glynn (Athlete, Football Player)
7007 Joyce Way
Dallas, TX 75225, USA

Gregory, Jim (Athlete, Hockey Player)
c/o Staff Member *National Hockey League (NHL)*
50 Bay St
11th Floor
Toronto, ON M5J 2X8, Canada

Gregory, Kathy (Cartoonist)
Playboy Magazine
Reader Services
680 N Lake Shore Dr
Chicago, IL 60611, USA

Gregory, Lee (Athlete, Baseball Player)
6456 N Tellman Ave
Fresno, CA 93711-1315, USA

Gregory, Nick (Actor)
c/o Staff Member *Kerin-Goldberg Associates*
155 E 55th St #5D
New York, NY 10022, USA

Gregory, Paul (Actor)
PO Box 415
Desert Hot Springs, CA 92240-0415, USA

Gregory, Philippa (Writer)
c/o Staff Member *Independent Talent Group (ITG-UK)*
Oxford House
76 Oxford St
London W1D 1BS, UK

Gregory, Roberta (Artist)
c/o Staff Member *Fantagraphics Books*
7563 Lake City Way
Seattle, WA 98115, USA

Gregory, Stephen (Actor)
Carey
64 Thornton Ave
London W4 1QQ, UNITED KINGDOM (UK)

Gregory, William G (Astronaut)
2027 E Freeport Lane
Gilbert, AZ 85234, USA

Gregory, William G Lt Colonel (Astronaut)
2027 E Freeport Ln
Gilbert, AZ 85234-2829, USA

Gregory, William H (Editor)
Aviation Week Magazine
1221 Ave of Americas
New York, NY 10020, USA

Gregory, William Jr (Athlete, Football Player)
4317 Cityview Dr
Plano, TX 75093, USA

Gregory, Wilton D (Religious Leader)
Illinois Diocese
Chancery Office
222 S 3rd St
Belleville, IL 62220, USA

Gregson, Glenn (Athlete, Baseball Player)
719 Touchstone Dr
Helena, MT 59601-5488, USA

Gregson, Wallace C (General)
Commanding General
Marine Forces Pacific
Camp HM Smith, HI 96861, USA

Gregson-Williams, Harry (Composer, Musician)
c/o Staff Member *Chasen & Company*
8899 Beverly Blvd
Suite 405
Los Angeles, CA 90048, USA

Grehl, Michael (Editor)
Memphis Commercial Appeal
Editorial Dept
495 Union Ave
Memphis, TN 38103, USA

Greider, Carol (Nobel Prize Laureate)
John Hopkins University
4327 Wickford Rd
Baltimore, MD 21205-2825, USA

Greif, Bill (Athlete, Baseball Player)
807 E 31st St
Austin, TX 78705-3205, USA

Greig, John (Athlete, Basketball Player)
2031 218th Pl NE
Sammamish, WA 98074-4049, USA

Greig, Mark (Athlete, Hockey Player)
c/o Art Breeze *Pro-Rep Entertainment Consulting*
113-276 Midpark Way SE
Calgary, AB T2X 1J6, Canada

Greiner, William R (Educator)
State University of New York
President's Office
Buffalo, NY 14221, USA

Greiner-Petter-Memm, Simone (Athlete)
Am Sportplatz 14
Waldau 98667, GERMANY

Greinke, Zack (Athlete, Baseball Player)
8629 Vista Pine Ct
Orlando, FL 32826-6307, USA

Greise, Bob (Athlete)
3195 Ponce de Leon Blvd #412
Coral Gables, FL 33134

Greisen, Chris (Athlete, Football Player)
1710 Arabian Dr
Green Bay, WI 54313, USA

Greisen, Nick (Athlete, Football Player)
c/o Brad Leshnock *BTI Sports Advisors*
615 South Blvd
Suite C
Oak Park, IL 60302, USA

Greisinger, Seth (Athlete, Baseball Player, Olympic Athlete)
6460 Overbrook St
Falls Church, VA 22043-1914, USA

Greiss, Gabrielle (Stylist)
c/o Staff Member *Management + Artists + Organization*
330 W 38th St
#1401
New York, NY 10018, USA

Greist, Kim (Actor)
Innovative Artists
1505 10th St
Santa Monica, CA 90401, USA

Grelf, Michael (Director)
La Jolla Playhouse
PO Box 12039
La Jolla, CA 92039, USA

Grenier, Adrian (Actor)
430 Grand Ave
Brooklyn, NY 11238, USA

Grenier, Gillies (Stylist)
c/o Staff Member *Fifty8 Artists*
58 W Huron St
Chicago, IL 60610, USA

Grenier, Richard (Athlete, Hockey Player)
234 Rue Lanoue
Repentigny, QC J6A 1W'1, Canada

Grenier, Zach (Actor)
c/o Staff Member *Hartig Hilepo Agency Ltd*
54 W 21st St #610
New York, NY 10010, USA

Grennes, Janet (Stylist)
2706 Rosedale Ave
Raleigh, NC 27607, USA

Grentz, Theresa Shank (Coach)
University of Illinois
Athletic Dept
Champaign, IL 61820, USA

Greschner, Ron (Athlete, Hockey Player)
PO Box 4513
Greenwich, CT 06831-8513

Gresham, Bob (Athlete, Football Player)
314 Meadowview Dr Apt 709
Boone, NC 28607, USA

Gretch, Joel (Actor)
c/o Molly Madden *3 Arts Entertainment Inc*
9460 Wilshire Blvd
7th Floor
Beverly Hills, CA 90210, USA

G. Retcnert, David (Congressman, Politician)
1730 Longworth HOB
Washington, DC 20515, USA

Gretsch, Joel (Actor)
c/o David (Dave) Fleming *Mosaic Media Group*
9200 W. Sunset Blvd
10th Floor
Los Angeles, CA 90069, USA

Gretzky, Wayne (Athlete, Hockey Player)
6436 E Gainsborough Rd
Scottsdale, AZ 852Sl-1950

Grevey, Kevin (Athlete, Basketball Player)
528 River Bend Road
Great Falls, VA 22066-4049, USA

Grevioux, Kevin (Actor)
c/o Scott Agostini *WME (LA)*
9601 Wilshire Blvd Fl 3
Beverly Hills, CA 90210, USA

Grewal, Alexi (Athlete, Cycler, Olympic Athlete)
1 Echo Canyon Rd
Pagosa Springs, CO 81147-9747, USA

Grey, Alex (Artist)
Cosm
46 Deer Hill Rd
Wappingers Falls, NY 12590, USA

Grey, Beryl E (Ballerina)
Fernhill Priory Road
Forest Row
East Sussex RH18 5JE, UNITED KINGDOM (UK)

Grey, Dick (Athlete, Baseball Player)
503 S Hampton St
Anaheim, CA 92804-2233, USA

Grey, Jennifer (Actor)
c/o Greg Clark *Untitled Entertainment (LA)*
350 S. Beverly Dr #200
Beverly Hills, CA 90212, USA

Grey, Joel (Actor)
c/o Nevin Dolcefino *Innovative Artists (LA)*
1505 10th St
Santa Monica, CA 90401, USA

Grey, Sasha (Actor, Adult Film Star)
P.O. Box 1480
Studio City, CA 91614, USA

Grey, Skylar (Musician)
c/o Sara Newkirk *WME (LA)*
9601 Wilshire Blvd Fl 3
Beverly Hills, CA 90210, USA

Grey, Zena (Actor)
c/o Abby Bluestone *Innovative Artists (LA)*
1505 10th St
Santa Monica, CA 90401, USA

Greyeyes, Michael
3500 W. Olive Ave. #1400
Burbank, CA 91505

Gribbon, Melissa (Actor)
c/o Dianne Hooper *Starcraft Talent Agency*
265 E Orange Grove #D
Burbank, CA 91502, USA

Gribow, Patti
3303 Clarendon Rd.
Beverly Hills, CA 90210

Grich, Bobby (Athlete, Baseball Player)
Major League Protection Systems 7668 El Camino Real
Ste 104-435
Carlsbad, CA 92009-7932, USA

Grieco, Richard (Actor)
c/o Tracy Quinn *Quinn Management*
17328 Ventura Blvd
Suite 416
Encino, CA 91316, USA

Grieder, William (Journalist)
Simon & Schuster
1230 Ave of Americas
New York, NY 10020, USA

Griem, Helmut (Actor)
Mgmt Erna Baumbauer
Keplerstr 2
Munich 81679, GERMANY

Grier, David Alan (Actor, Comedian)
c/o Staff Member *ROAR (LA)*
9701 Wilshire Blvd
8th Floor
Los Angeles, CA 90212, USA

Grier, Herbert E (Engineer)
9648 Blackgold Road
La Jolla, CA 92037, USA

Grier, Marrio (Athlete, Football Player)
826 Almora Dr
Charlotte, NC 28216, USA

Grier, Mike (Athlete, Hockey Player)
72 Stonecrest Dr
Needham, MA 02492-2783

Grier, Pam (Actor)
c/o Harry Gold *TalentWorks (LA)*
3500 W Olive Ave
Suite 1400
Burbank, CA 91505, USA

Grier, Roosevelt (Rosey) (Athlete, Football Player)
1250 4th St
6th Floor
Santa Monica, CA 90401, USA

Grierson, Don (Athlete, Hockey Player)
2066 Mountain Grove Ave
Burlington, ON L7P 2H9, Canada

Gries, Jonathan (Jon) (Actor, Director, Producer)
c/o Steve Lovett *Lovett Management*
1327 Brinkley Ave
Los Angeles, CA 90049, USA

Griese, Brian (Athlete, Football Player)
17 Polo Club Dr
Denver, CO 80209-, USA

Griese, Robert A (Bob) (Athlete, Football Player, Sportscaster)
12044 SE Birkdale Run
Jupiter, FL 33469, USA

Griesemer, John N (Government Official)
RR 2 Box 204B
Springfield, MO 65802, USA

Grieser, Sylvia (Stylist)
c/o Staff Member *Frame Representatives*
275 West St
New York, NY 10013, USA

Grieve, Ben (Athlete, Baseball Player)
6906 Fairway Rd
La Jolla, CA 92037-5619, USA

Grieve, Brent (Athlete, Hockey Player)
Cardinal Group of Companies Ltd
1595 16th Ave
Suite 602
Richmond Hill, ON L4B 3N9, Canada

Grieve, Pierson M (Business Person)
Ecolab Inc
Ecolab Center
370 Wabasha St N
Saint Paul, MN 55102, USA

Grieve, Tom (Commentator)
4107 Carnation Dr
Arlington, TX 76016-3922, USA

Grieve, Tom (Athlete, Baseball Player)
Texas Rangers PO Box 90111
Attn Broadcast Dept
Arlington, TX 76004-3111, USA

Griffey, Ken (Athlete, Baseball Player)
Bakersfield Blaze PO Box 10031
Attn: Managers Office
Bakersfield, CA 93389-0031, USA

Griffey, Ken (Athlete, Baseball Player)
1102 Portmoor Way
Winter Garden, FL 34787-4619, USA

Griffey Jr, Ken (Athlete, Baseball Player)
8921 Charleston Park
Orlando, FL 32819-4444, USA

Griffin, Alfredo (Athlete, Baseball Player)
9731 NW 41st St
Doral, FL 33178-2944, USA

Griffin, Alfredo (Athlete, Baseball Player)
Los Angeles Angels Of Anaheim 2000 E Gene Autry Way
Attn: Coaching Staff
Anaheim, CA 92806-6143, USA

Griffin, Archie (Athlete, Football Player, Heisman Trophy Winner)
6845 Temperance Point Pl
Westerville, OH 43082, USA

Griffin, Blake (Athlete, Basketball Player)
c/o Jeff Schwartz *Excel Sports Management*
9665 Wilshire Blvd #500
Los Angeles, CA 90212, USA

Griffin, Bo (Correspondent, Television Host)
c/o Staff Member *Good Day Live*
20th Century Fox Television
10201 W Pico Blvd Blg 88 Rm 29
Los Angeles, CA 90035, USA

Griffin, Cecelia (Stylist)
c/o Staff Member *Punch Artists*
305 Madison Ave
#449
New York, NY 10165, USA

Griffin, Cedric (Athlete, Football Player)
10567 Parker Dr
Eden Prairie, MN 55347-, USA

Griffin, Cornelius (Athlete, Football Player)
224 Countryside Dr
Troy, AL 36079, USA

Griffin, Courtney (Athlete, Football Player)
6302 N Selland Ave
Fresno, CA 93711, USA

Griffin, Damon (Athlete, Football Player)
1608 Radford Pl
Monrovia, CA 91016, USA

Griffin, David (Athlete, Football Player)
PO Box 1443
Roswell, GA 30077, USA

Griffin, Doug (Athlete, Baseball Player)
15811 El Soneto Dr
Whittier, CA 90603-1446, USA

Griffin, Eddie (Actor, Comedian, Producer)

Griffin, Eric (Boxer)
PO Box 964
Jasper, TN 37347, USA

Griffin, Forrest (Athlete, Wrestler)
c/o Jervis L Cole
5 River Park Pl W Ste #203
Fresno, CA 93720, USA

Griffin, Gerald (Scientist)
PO Box 526
Hunt, TX 78024-0526, USA

Griffin, Greg (Athlete, Basketball Player)
12051 Bayport St Apt
1-208
Garden Grove, CA 92840-4404, USA

Griffin, Jim (Athlete, Football Player)
217 Packing House Rd
Lake Charles, LA 70615, USA

Griffin, John-Ford (Athlete, Baseball Player)
PO Box 1359
Sarasota, FL 34230-1359, USA

Griffin, John W (Athlete, Football Player)
10315 Herons Ridge Dr
Lakeland, TN 38002, USA

Griffin, Kathy (Actor, Comedian, Reality TV Star)
c/o Steve Levine *ICM Partners (ICM-LA)*
10250 Constellation Blvd Fl 7
Los Angeles, CA 90067, USA

Griffin, Keith (Athlete, Football Player)
4330 Canada Hills Ct
Waldorf, MD 20602, USA

Griffin, Larry (Athlete, Football Player)
5617 Silchester Ln
Charlotte, NC 28215, USA

Griffin, Leonard (Athlete, Football Player)
P.O. Box 480
Calhoun, LA 71225, USA

Griffin, Mike (Athlete, Baseball Player)
1620 Grove Ave
Woodland, CA 95695-5149, USA

Griffin, Mike (Athlete, Baseball Player)
Norfolk Tides 150 Park Ave
Attn Coaching Staff
Norfolk, VA 23510-2712, USA

Griffin, Nikki (Actor)
c/o Staff Member *Agency for the Performing Arts (APA-LA)*
405 S Beverly Dr
Suite 500
Beverly Hills, CA 90212-4425, USA

Griffin, Patty (Musician, Songwriter, Writer)
Monterey Peninsula Artists
509 Hartnell St
Monterey, CA 93940, USA

Griffin, Paul (Athlete, Basketball Player)
903 Great Tree Dr
San Antonio, TX 78260-7744, USA

Griffin, Ray (Athlete, Football Player)
5395 Anacala Ct
Westerville, OH 43082, USA

Griffin, Robert P (Politician)
Michigan Supreme Court
3950 Sumac Dr Apt 126
Traverse City, MI 49684-7012, USA

Griffin, Rod L (Writer)
c/o Staff Member *$olvency International Inc*
PO Box 4433
Clearwater, FL 33758, USA

Griffin, Taylor (Athlete, Basketball Player)
c/o Jeff Schwartz *Excel Sports Management*
9665 Wilshire Blvd #500
Los Angeles, CA 90212, USA

Griffin, Thomas N Jr (General)
3935 School Section Rd Aot 1
Cincinnati, OH 45211-3369, USA

Griffin, Timothy (Congressman, Politician)
1232 Longworth HOB
Washington, DC 20515, USA

Griffin, Tom (Athlete, Baseball Player)
13147 Avenida La Valencia
Poway, CA 92064-1905, USA

Griffin, Tony (Actor, Director, Writer)
c/o Staff Member *Merv Griffin Entertainment*
130 South El Camino Drive
Beverly Hills, CA 90212

Griffin, Ty (Athlete, Baseball Player, Olympic Athlete)
7803 N River Shore Dr
Tampa, FL 33604-3903, USA

Griffin, Wade (Athlete, Football Player)
2937 Highway 72
Holly Springs, MS 38635, USA

Griffin, Warren (Warren G) (Actor, Musician)
c/o Johnny Gallo *Artist Representation Group*
9701 Wilshire Blvd.
10th Floor
Beverly Hills, CA 90212, USA

Griffin D, Gerry (Scientist)
PO Box 526
Hunt, TX 78024-0526, USA

Griffing, Glynn (Athlete, Football Player)
2318 Irving Pl
Jackson, MS 39211, USA

Griffith, Alan R (Financier)
Bank of New York
1 Wall St
New York, NY 10286, USA

Griffith, Bill (Cartoonist)
Pinhead Productions
PO Box 88
Hadlyme, CT 06439, USA

Griffith, Calvin (Baseball Player)
Minnesota Twins
501 Chicago Ave
Minneapolis, MN 55415-1517, USA

Griffith, Clint (Athlete, Football Player)
878 13th Ave S
Jacksonville Beach, FL 32250-4122, USA

Griffith, Darrell (Athlete, Basketball Player)
PO Box 24841
Louisville, KY 40224-0841, USA

Griffith, Derrell (Athlete, Baseball Player)
201 E Central Blvd
Anadarko, OK 73005-3431, USA

Griffith, Emile A (Boxer)
150 Washington St
#6J
Hempstead, NY 11550, USA

Griffith, H. Morgan (Congressman, Politician)
1108 Longworth HOB
Washington, DC 20515, USA

Griffith, Howard (Athlete, Football Player)
9152 S Clyde Ave
Chicago, IL 60617, USA

Griffith, James (Business Person)
Timken Co
1835 Dueber Ave SW
Canton, OH 44706, USA

Griffith, Mary A (Activist)
1304 Rudgear Rd
Walnut Creek, CA 94596, USA

Griffith, Melanie (Actor, Producer)
611 S Muirfield Rd
Los Angeles, CA 90005-3832, USA

Griffith, Rhiana (Actor)
c/o Staff Member *Darlene Kaplan Entertainment*
4450 Balboa Ave
Encino, CA 91316, USA

Griffith, Robert (Athlete, Football Player)
3525 Del Mar Heights Rd Unit 331
San Diego, CA 92130, USA

Griffith, Thomas Ian (Actor)
c/o Lou Pitt *Pitt Group, The*
9465 Wilshire Blvd
Suite 420
Beverly Hills, CA 90212, USA

Griffith, Thomas Ian (Actor)
Endeavor Talent Agency
9701 Wilshire Blvd
#1000
Beverly Hills, CA 90212, USA

Griffith, Tom W (Misc)
Rural Letter Carriers Assn
1448 Duke St
#100
Alexandria, VA 22314, USA

Griffith, Wendy (Religious Leader, Television Host)
c/o Staff Member *CBN News*
Christian Broadcasting Network
977 Centerville Turnpike
Virginia Beach, VA 23464, USA

Griffith, Yolanda (Basketball Player)
Sacramento Monarchs
Arco Arena
1 Sports Parkway
Sacramento, CA 95834, USA

Griffiths, Brian (Baseball Player)
16022 SE Goosehollow Dr
Clackamas, OR 97015-7859, USA

Griffiths, Isobel
Tower Bridge House
St Katharine's Way
London, not applicable E1W 1AA, United Kingdom

Griffiths, Jeremy (Athlete, Baseball Player)
120 Beachdale Dr
Avon Lake, OH 44012-1611, USA

Griffiths, Lucy (Actor)
c/o Larry Taube *Principal Entertainment (LA)*
1964 Westwood Blvd #400
Los Angeles, CA 90025, USA

Griffiths, Nick (Stylist)
c/o Staff Member *Management + Artists + Organization*
330 W 38th St
#1401
New York, NY 10018, USA

Griffiths, Phillip A (Mathematician)
Advanced Study Institute
Director's Office
Olden Lane
Princeton, NJ 08540, USA

Griffiths, Rachel (Actor)
c/o Michael D Aglion *Signpost*
250 S Beverly Dr
Suite 201
Beverly Hills, CA 90212, USA

Griffiths, Richard (Actor)
c/o Staff Member *Paradigm (LA)*
360 N Crescent Dr
North Bldg
Beverly Hills, CA 90210, USA

Griffiths, Susan
9300 Wilshire Blvd. #410
Beverly Hills, CA 90212

Griggs, Acle (Baseball Player)
Birmingham Black Barons
820 Newwau Ave SW
Birmingham, AL 35221-3854, USA

Griggs, Perry (Athlete, Football Player)
1275 Carlysle Park Dr
Lawrenceville, GA 30044, USA

Griggs, William E (Athlete, Football Player)
18 Summerhill Ln
Medford, NJ 08055, USA

Grigorian, Irina (Figure Skater)
c/o Staff Member *Champions on Ice*
Tom Collins Enterprises Inc
3500 W 80th St
Minneapolis, MN 55431, USA

Grigsby, Benji (Baseball Player)
118 Teakwood Dr SW
Huntsville, AL 35801-3453, USA

Grijalva, Lucy (Writer)
PO Box 1634
Benicia, CA 94510

Grijalva, Victor E (Business Person)
Schlumberger Ltd
277 Park Ave
New York, NY 10172, USA

Grilli, Guido (Athlete, Baseball Player)
250 Sloan Ln
Locust Grove, AR 72550-9000, USA

Grilli, Jason (Athlete, Baseball Player)
9037 Point Cypress Dr
Orlando, FL 32836-5475, USA

Grilli, Steve (Athlete, Baseball Player)
8637 Briar Patch
Baldwinsville, NY 13027, USA

Grillo, Frank
c/o Chris Huvane *Management 360*
9111 Wilshire Blvd
Beverly Hills, CA 90210, USA

Grim, Robert (Bob) (Athlete, Football Player)
18 NW Saginaw Ave
Bend, OR 97701, USA

Grimaldi, Dan (Actor)

Grimaud, Helene (Musician)
I C M Artists
40 W 57th St
New York, NY 10019, USA

Grimes, Gary
4578 W. 165th St.
Lawndale, CA 90260

Grimes, Kareem
c/o Adam Robinson *Southfield Village*
6255 W. Sunset Blvd
Suite 923
Los Angeles, CA 90028, USA

Grimes, Karolyn (Actor)
PO Box 145
Carnation, WA 98014, USA

Grimes, Martha (Writer)
115 D St SE
#G-6
Washington, DC 20003, USA

Grimes, Paul (Stylist)
c/o Staff Member *Mark Edward Inc*
325 W 8th St
#1011
New York, NY 10018, USA

Grimes, Randy (Athlete, Football Player)
13214 Halifax St
Houston, TX 77015, USA

Grimes, Sally (Stylist)
Selene Studios
820 Wenonah Ave
Oak Park, IL 60304-1036, USA

Grimes, Scott (Actor)
c/o Adam Levine *Levine Okwu Erickson Management*
9601 Wilshire Blvd
3rd Floor
Beverly Hills, CA 90210, USA

Grimes, Shenae (Actor)
c/o Amanda Rosenthal *Amanda Rosenthal Talent Agency*
543 Richmond St W
Suite 123
Toronto, ON M5V 1Y6, Canada

Grimes, Tammy (Actor, Musician)
Don Buchwald
10 E 44th St
New York, NY 10017, USA

Grimes, Tinsley (Actor)
c/o Staff Member *Innovative Artists (LA)*
1505 10th St
Santa Monica, CA 90401, USA

Griminelli, Andrea (Musician)
Columbia Artists Mgmt Inc
165 W 57th St
New York, NY 10019, USA

Grimm, Dan (Athlete, Football Player)
2514 Smith Harbour Dr
Denver, NC 28037, USA

Grimm, Russ (Athlete, Coach, Football Coach, Football Player)
2654 E Mead Pl
Chandler, AZ 85249, USA

Grimm, Tim (Actor)
Abrams Artists
9200 Sunset Blvd
#1125
Los Angeles, CA 90069, USA

Grimmette, Mark (Athlete, Luge Player, Olympic Athlete)
21 Snowberry Ln
Lake Placid, NY 12946-3102, USA

Grimshaw, Nicholas T (Architect)
1 Conway St
Fitzroy Square
London W1P 5HA, UNITED KINGDOM (UK)

Grimsley, Jason (Athlete, Baseball Player)
13315 Timberwild Ct
Tomball, TX 77375-2939, USA

Grimsley, Ross (Athlete, Baseball Player)
Richmond Flying Squirrels
3001 N Boulevard
Richmond, VA 23230-4331, USA

Grimsley, Ross (Athlete, Baseball Player)
92 Conewago Ct
Owings Mills, MD 21117-5049, USA

Grimson, Stu (Athlete, Hockey Player)
c/o Staff Member *NHL Players Association*
1700-20 Bay St
Toronto, ON M5J 2R8, Canada

Grimsson, Olafur Ragnar (President)
President's Office
Sto'marradshusini v/Lackjartog
Reykjavik, ICELAND

Grinberg, Anouk (Actor)
Artmedia
20 Ave Rapp
Paris 75007, FRANCE

Grindenko, Tatyana T (Musician)
Moscow State Philharmonic
Tverskaya Str 31
Moscow 103050, RUSSIA

Grinder, Scott (Baseball Player)
1323 14th Ave N
Birmingham, AL 35204-2712, USA

Grinder, Scott (Athlete, Baseball Player)
1323 14th Ave N
Birmingham, AL 35173-5218, USA

Griner, Paul (Writer)
Random House
1745 Broadway
#B1
New York, NY 10019, USA

Grinham, Rawley Judy (Swimmer)
103 Green Lane Northwood
Middx HA6 1AP, UNITED KINGDOM (UK)

Grinnell, Alan D (Physicist)
University of California
Medical School
Lewis Center
Los Angeles, CA 90024, USA

grinnell, todd (Actor)
c/o DEBRA MANNERS *Daniel Hoff Agency*
5455 Wilshire Blvd
Suite 1100
Los Angeles, CA 90036, USA

Grinstead, Irish (Musician)
c/o Staff Member *Creative Artists Agency (CAA-LA)*
2000 Ave Of The Stars
Los Angeles, CA 90067, USA

Grinstead, LeMisha (Musician)
c/o Staff Member *Creative Artists Agency (CAA-LA)*
2000 Ave Of The Stars
Los Angeles, CA 90067, USA

Grinstein, Gerald (Business Person)
Delta Airlines
Hartsfield International Airport
Atlanta, GA 30320, USA

Grint, Rupert (Actor)
c/o Clair Dobbs *Public Eye Communications*
535 Kings Rd
Suite 313 Plaza
London SW10 0SZ, United Kingdom

Grinville, Patrick (Writer)
Academie Goncourt
38 Rue du Faubourg Saint Jacques
Paris 75014, FRANCE

Grisanti, Eugene P (Business Person)
International Flavors
521 W 57th St
New York, NY 10019, USA

Grisdale, John (Athlete, Hockey Player)
A-455 Bromley St
Coquitlam, BC V3K 6N7, Canada

Grise, Pascale (Stylist)
c/o Staff Member *Loox Agency*
12 Desbrosses St
New York, NY 10013, USA

Grisez, Germain (Misc)
Mount Saint Mary's College
Christain Ethics Dept
Emmitsburg, MD 21727, USA

Grisham, John (Writer)
Oakwood Books
PO Box 1780
Oxford, MS 38655, USA

Grishin, Evgenil (Speed Skater)
Committee of Physical Culture
Skatertny Pl 4
Moscow, RUSSIA

Grishuk, Pasha
Luzhnetskaia nab. 8
Moscow, RUSSIA 119871

Grisman, David (Composer, Musician)
CM Mgmt
5749 Larryan Dr
Woodland Hills, CA 91367, USA

Grissom, Marquis (Athlete, Baseball Player)
110 Fiddlers Rdg
Fayetteville, GA 30214-2684, USA

Grissom, Scott (Race Car Driver)
Grissom Motorsports
395 Sawdust Rd. #2019
The Woodlands, TX 77380, USA

Grissom, Steve (Race Car Driver)
Source International
5901 Orr Road
Charlotte, NC 28211, USA

Grist, Reri (Opera Singer)
Columbia Artists Mgmt Inc
165 W 57th St
New York, NY 10019, USA

Griswold, Sandra (Stylist)
963 Noth Point St
San Francisco, CA 94109, USA

Grizzard, George (Baseball Player, Basketball Player)
Champion Lakes
PO Box 288
Bolivar, PA 15923, USA

Grizzard, George (Actor)
400 E 54th St
New York, NY 10022, USA

Groat, Dick (Athlete, Baseball Player)
320 Beech St
Pittsburgh, PA 15218-1406, USA

Groat, Dick (Athlete, Basketball Player)
320 Beech St
Pittsburgh, PA 15218-1406, USA

Grob, Mike (Athlete, Golfer)
3611 Quimet Cir
Billings, MT 59106-1009, USA

Groban, Josh (Musician, Songwriter)
c/o Cliff Burnstein *Q Prime Inc*
729 Seventh Ave
16th Floor
New York, NY 10019, USA

Grobell, Werner (Mr Frick) (Misc)
PO Box 7886
Incline Village, NV 89452, USA

Groce, Clifton (Clif) (Athlete, Football Player)
1632 Park Pl
College Station, TX 77840, USA

Groce, Dejuan (Athlete, Football Player)
1443 Oxbow Dr
Cedar Hill, TX 75104, USA

Groce, Ron (Athlete, Football Player)
3624 5th Ave S
Minneapolis, MN 55409, USA

Grocholewski, Zenon Cardinal (Religious Leader)
Palazzo della Congregazioni
Piazzo Pio XII #3
Rome 00193, ITALY

Grode, Jarrett (Actor)
c/o Ruthanne Secunda *United Talent Agency (UTA)*
9336 Civic Center Dr
Beverly Hills, CA 90210, USA

Grodin, Charles
187 Chestnut Hill Rd.
Wilton, CT 06897-4106, USA

Groener, Harry (Actor)
c/o Susan Smith *Susan Smith Company, The*
1344 N Wetherly Dr
Los Angeles, CA 90069-1817, USA

Groening, Matthew (Matt) (Cartoonist)
c/o Michael A Neidorf *Caplan-Groening Family Foundation*
11400 W Olympic Blvd #590
Los Angeles, CA 90064-1574, USA

Groetzinger Jr, Jon (Business Person)
American Greetings Corp
1 American Road
Cleveland, OH 44144, USA

Grofe Jr, Ferde
18139 W Coastline
Malibu, CA 90265, USA

Groff, Angela (Stylist)
c/o Staff Member *Ennis*
119 Braintree St
Boston, MA 02134, USA

Groff, Jonathan (Actor)
c/o Tony Lipp *Anonymous Content (LA)*
3531 Hayden Ave
Culver City, CA 90232, USA

Groff, Mike (Race Car Driver)
270 Wigmore Drive
Pasadena, CA 91105, USA

Grogan, John (Writer)
HarperCollins Publishers L.L.C.
1000 Keystone Industrial Park
Scranton, PA 18512, USA

Grogan, Steven J (Steve) (Athlete, Football Player)
6 Country Club Ln
Foxboro, MA 02035, USA

Groh, Al (Coach, Football Coach)
University of Virginia
Athletic Dept
Charlottesburg, VA 22903, USA

Groh, Gary (Athlete, Golfer)
331 Signe Ct
Lake Bluff, IL 60044-1219, USA

Grohl, Dave (Musician)
c/o Staff Member *RCA Records (LA)*
8750 Wilshire Blvd Fl 2
Beverly Hills, CA 90211, USA

Grollman, Rabbi Earl (Religious Leader, Writer)
c/o Staff Member *Beacon Press*
25 Beacon St
Boston, MA 02108, USA

Groman, Bill (Athlete, Football Player)
7906 Scherzo ln
Houston, TX 77040-, USA

Groman, William (Athlete, Football Player)
7906 Scherzo Ln
Houston, TX 77040-2529, USA

Gromov, Mikhael L (Mathematician)
91 Rue de la Sante
Paris 75013, FRANCE

Gronberg, Mathias (Athlete, Golfer)
247 Plymouth Rd
West Palm Beach, FL 33405, USA

Gronemeyer, Herbert (Musician)
c/o Antje Winter *Agentur Winter*
Meienbergstr. 24
Erfurt 99084, Germany

Gronk (Artist)
Saxon-Lee Gallery
7525 Beverly Blvd
Los Angeles, CA 90036, USA

Gronkiewicz, Lee (Athlete, Baseball Player)
227 S Marion St Apt D
Columbia, SC 29205-3271, USA

Gronkowski, Rob (Athlete, Football Player)
c/o Drew Rosenhaus *Rosenhaus Sports Representation*
6400 Allison Road
Miami Beach, FL 33141, USA

Gronman, Tuomas (Athlete, Hockey Player)
66 Mario Lemieux Pl
Pittsburgh, PA 15219, USA

Gronstrand, Jari (Athlete, Hockey Player)
c/o Staff Member *Toronto Maple Leafs*
Air Canada Centre
400-40 Bay St
Toronto, ON M5J 2X2, Canada

Groom, Buddy (Athlete, Baseball Player)
1991 Saint Andrews Dr
Red Oak, TX 75154-5837, USA

Groom, Sam (Actor)
8730 Sunset Blvd
#440
Los Angeles, CA 90069, USA

Groom, Winston (Writer)
18096 Woodland Drive
Point Clear, AL 36564, USA

Grootegoed, Matt (Athlete, Football Player)
17302 Destry Cir
Huntington Beach, CA 92647, USA

Gropp, Louis Oliver (Editor)
140 Riverside Dr
#6G
New York, NY 10024, USA

Gros, Earl (Athlete, Football Player)
17424 Airline Hwy
Suite 12
Prairieville, LA 70769, USA

Gros, Francois (Misc)
102 Rue de la Tour
Paris 75116, FRANCE

Grosek, Michal (Athlete, Hockey Player)
5 Samba Cir
Sandwich, MA 02563-2597

Gros Louis, Kenneth R R (Educator)
Indiana University
President's Office
Bloomington, IN 47405, USA

Gross, Al (Athlete, Football Player)
3203 Greenwood St
Stockton, CA 95205-5708, USA

Gross, Alfred E (Athlete, Football Player)
8227 Grandstaff Dr
Sacramento, CA 95823, USA

Gross, Arye
c/o Paul Greenstone *Paul Greenstone Entertainment*
3008 Sorrelwood Dr
San Ramon, CA 94582-5008, USA

Gross, Charles G (Psychic)
45 Woodside Lane
Princeton, NJ 08540, USA

Gross, Clayton (General)
2306 SE Spyglass Dr
Vancouver, WA 98683-5102, USA

Gross, David (Nobel Prize Laureate)
Kavli Inst. For Theoretical Physics
30 Pueblo Vista Rd
Santa Barbara, CA 93103-2159, USA

Gross, David (Comedian)
c/o Staff Member *United Talent Agency (UTA)*
9336 Civic Center Dr
Beverly Hills, CA 90210, USA

Gross, Don (Athlete, Baseball Player)
1299 E Farrand Rd
Clio, MI 48420-9137, USA

Gross, Gabe (Athlete, Baseball Player)
1756 Ravmer Pl
Auburn, AL 36830-2185, USA

Gross, Greg (Athlete, Baseball Player)
802 Hallowell Dr
West Chester, PA 19382-5243, USA

Gross, Henry (Musician)
c/o Pat Horgan *Pat Horgan Talent*
2789 West Main St #5
Wappingers Falls, NY 12590, USA

Gross, Jordan (Athlete, Football Player)
12725 Ninebark Trl
Charlotte, NC 28278, USA

Gross, Kevin (Athlete, Baseball Player)
2058 N Mills Ave
PO Box 144
Claremont, CA 91711-2812, USA

Gross, Kip (Athlete, Baseball Player)
2015 Ridgeview Ct
Redlands, CA 92373-6979, USA

Gross, Lance (Actor)
c/o Kenneth (Kenny) Goodman *Schiff Company, The*
9465 Wilshire Blvd
Suite 480
Beverly Hills, CA 90212, USA

Gross, Lee (Athlete, Football Player)
871 Holland Rd
Newton, AL 36352, USA

Gross, Mary (Actor, Comedian)
c/o Staff Member *Pakula/King & Associates*
9229 Sunset Blvd
Suite 315
Los Angeles, CA 90069, USA

Gross, Michael (Actor)
4431 Woodleigh Ln
Canada, CA 91011, USA

Gross, Michael (Swimmer)
Paul-Ehrlich-Str 6
Frankfurt/Main 60596, GERMANY

Gross, Paul (Actor)
c/o John S Kelly *Bresler Kelly & Associates*
11500 W Olympic Blvd
Suite 510
Los Angeles, CA 90064, USA

Gross, Ricco (Athlete)
Waldbahnstr 34A
Ruhpolding 83324, GERMANY

Gross, Robert A (Physicist)
14 Sunnyside Way
New Rochelle, NY 10804, USA

Gross, Robert (Bob) (Athlete, Basketball Player)
13466 SE Red Rose Ln
Happy Valley, OR 97086-9752, USA

Gross, Terry R (Correspondent)
WHYY-Radio
News Dept
Independence Mall W
Philadelphia, PA 19104, USA

Gross, Wayne (Athlete, Baseball Player)
45 Leonard Ct
Danville, CA 94526-1911, USA

Grosscup, Lee (Athlete, Football Player)
703 Atlantic Ave
Apt 110
Alameda, CA 94501, USA

Grosser, Heinz (Scientist)
Rontgenstrasse 4
Hainburg D-63512, Germany

Grossfeld, Stanley (Photographer)
Boston Globe
Boston Globe PO Box 55819
Boston, MA 02205-5819, USA

Grosshuesch, Lee (General)
1239 Kupau St
Kailua, HI 96734-3645, USA

Grossman, Allen R (Writer)
4 Jeffrey Terrace
Lexington, MA 02420-1324, USA

Grossman, Burt (Athlete, Football Player)
1482 Antioch Ave
Chula Vista, CA 91913-1477, USA

Grossman, Judith (Writer)
Warren Wilson College
English Dept
Swannanoa, NC 28778, USA

Grossman, Judith (Athlete, Football Player)
1000 Football Dr
Lake Forest, IL 60045, USA

Grossman, Leslie (Actor)
c/o Staff Member *Metropolitan (MTA)*
4526 Wilshire Blvd
Los Angeles, CA 90010, USA

Grossman, Randy (Athlete, Football Player)
204 Ridge Rd
Pittsburgh, PA 15238, USA

Grossman, Rex (Athlete, Football Player)
2552 S Smith Rd
Bloomington, IN 47401-8923, USA

Grossman, Rex (Athlete, Football Player)
17230 Crawley Rd
Odessa, FL 33556, USA

Grosvenor, Gerald Cavendish (Business Person, Royalty)
The Grosvenor Estate
Eaton Estate Office
Eccleston, Chester CH49ET, United Kingdom

Grosvenor, Gilbert M (Publisher)
National Geographic Society
17th & M NW
Washington, DC 20036, USA

Grote, Jerry (Athlete, Baseball Player)
2608 N Main St Ste B
#21
Belton, TX 76513-1547, USA

Grote, Jerry C. (Athlete, Basketball Player)
3 Balboa Way
Hot Springs Valley, AR 71909-6913, USA

Grotenfelt, Georg E J (Architect)
Kapteeninkatu 20D
Helsinki 00140, FINLAND

Grotewold, Jeff (Athlete, Baseball Player)
PO Box 3439
Crestline, CA 92325-3439, USA

Groth, Jeff (Athlete, Football Player)
13824 Driftwood Dr
Carmel, IN 46033, USA

Groth, Johnny (Athlete, Baseball Player)
170 N Ocean Blvd Apt 307
Palm Beach, FL 33480-3931, USA

Grott, Matt (Athlete, Baseball Player)
19431 N Concho Cir
Sun City, AZ 85373-1201, USA

Grottkau, Bob (Athlete, Football Player)
255 Atlantic Dr
Rio Vista, CA 94571, USA

Grottkau, Robert (Athlete, Football Player)
5105 Muirfield Ln
Spokane, WA 99223, USA

Grouch, Roger K (Astronaut)
Life/Microgravity Sciences Office
NASA Headquarters
Washington, DC 20546, USA

Groulx, Pierre (Coach, Hockey Player)
156 NW 118th Drive
Coral Springs, FL 33071-8072, USA

Groulx, Wayne (Athlete, Hockey Player)
552 Montee de L'Eglise
St-Colomban, QC J5K 2J2, Canada

Grove, Andrew (Business Person)
Intel Corp
2200 Mission College Blvd
Santa Clara, CA 95054, USA

Grover, Gulshan (Actor, Bollywood)
c/o Michael Livingston *Leavitt Talent Group*
8255 W Sunset Blvd
West Hollywood, CA 90046, USA

Groves, Napiera Danielle (Actor)
c/o Christine Thomas *Sweet Mud Group*
648 Broadway #1002
New York, NY 10012, USA

Groves, Philip (Stylist)
c/o Staff Member *Ford Models (Chicago)*
311 W Superior St
Chicago, IL 60654, USA

Groves, Richard H (General)
400 Madison St
#1302
Alexandria, VA 22314, USA

Grow, Carol (Actor, Model)
c/o Jon Orlando *WNWN Media*
348 S. Hauser Blvd #PH414
Los Angeles, CA 90036, USA

Grroms, Charles R (Red) (Artist)
85 Walker St
New York, NY 10013, USA

Grubar, Richard (Athlete, Basketball Player)
1804 Milan Rd
Greensboro, NC 27410-3028, USA

Grubb, John (Athlete, Baseball Player)
6618 Bel Lac Dr
Chester, VA 23831, USA

Grubb, Kevin (Race Car Driver)
c/o *Grubb Motorsports*
5120 Jefferson Davis Hwy
Richmond, VA 23234, USA

Grubb, Robert (Actor)
c/o Staff Member *Shanahan Management*
Level 3 Berman House
Surry Hills 2010, AUSTRALIA

Grubb, Wayne (Race Car Driver)
Grubb Motorsports
5120 Jefferson Davis Hwy
Richmond, VA 23234, USA

Grubbs, Gary (Actor)
Parasigm Agency
10100 Santa Monica Blvd
#2500
Los Angeles, CA 90067, USA

Grubbs, Robert H (Nobel Prize Laureate)
California Institute of Technology
1700 SpruceSt
South Pasadena, CA 91030-4721, USA

Gruber, Bob (Athlete, Football Player)
1704 W Call St Apt 107
Tallahassee, FL 32304-4959, USA

Gruber, Jonathan (Director, Writer)
c/o Josh Adler *New Wave Entertainment (LA)*
2660 W Olive Blvd
Burbank, CA 91505, USA

Gruber, Kelly (Athlete, Baseball Player)
3306 Blue Jay Ln
Austin, TX 78732-1601, USA

Gruber, Paul (Athlete, Football Player)
P.O. Box 4239
Edwards, CO 81632, USA

Gruberova, Edita (Opera Singer)
Opera et Concert
Maximillianstr 22
Munich 80539, GERMANY

Grubman, Allen J (Lawyer)
Grubman Indursky Schindler Goldstein
152 W 57th St
New York, NY 10019, USA

Grubnic, Dave (Race Car Driver)
John Mitchell Racing
392 Highway 287
Ennis, MT 29729, USA

Gruden, John (Athlete, Hockey Player)
1287 Essex Dr
Rochester Hills, MI 48307-3139

Gruden, Jon (Athlete, Coach, Football Coach, Football Player)
c/o Bob LaMonte *Professional Sports Representation*
1220 Plumas St
Reno, NV 89509, 775-828-1864

Grudens, Richard
Box 344 Main St.
Stony Brook, NY 11790

Grudzielanek, Mark (Athlete, Baseball Player)
PO Box 1581
Rancho Santa Fe, CA 92067-1581, USA

Gruen, Danny (Athlete, Hockey Player)
RR 1 RPO
South Glllies, ON P0T 2V0, Canada

Gruen, Sara (Writer)
c/o Staff Member *HarperCollins Publishers*
10 East 53rd St
c/o Author mail, 7th Floor
New York, NY 10022, USA

Gruenberg, Erich (Musician)
80 Northway
Hampstead Garden Suburb
London NW11 6PA, UNITED KINGDOM (UK)

Gruenwald, Jim (Athlete, Olympic Athlete, Wrestler)
Northern Michigan University 1401
Presque Isle Ave Attn Usoec
Marquette, MI 49855-5301, USA

Gruffudd, Ioan (Actor)
c/o Sam Maydew *Collective*
8383 Wilshire Blvd
Suite 1050
Beverly Hills, CA 90211, USA

Gruhl, Scott (Athlete, Hockey Player)
8732 Laumic Dr
North Chesterfield, VA 23235-4655

Grum, Anselm (Religious Leader)
Sekretariat P Anselm Grun
Schweinfurter Strabe 40
Munsterschwarzach, Abtei 97359, GERMANY

Grum, Clifford J (Business Person)
Temple-Inland Inc
303 S Temple Dr
Diboll, TX 75941, USA

Grumman, Cornelia (Journalist)
Chicago Tribune
Editorial Dept
435 N Michigan Ave
Chicago, IL 60611, USA

Grummer, Elisabeth (Opera Singer)
Am Schlachtensee 104
Berlin 14163, GERMANY

Grunberg, Greg (Actor)
c/o Susan Calogerakis *Thruline Entertainment*
9250 Wilshire Blvd
Ground Fl
Beverly Hills, CA 90212, USA

Grunberg, Peter (Nobel Prize Laureate)
Juelich
Forschungszentrum
Unternehmenskommunikation
Juelich D-52425, Germany

Grunberg-Manago, Marianne (Misc)
80 Boulevard Pasteur
Paris 75015, FRANCE

Grundfest, Joseph A (Government Official)
Stanford University
Law School
Stanford, CA 94305, USA

Grundhofer, Jerry A (Financier)
Firstar Corp
777 E Wisconsin Ave
Milwaukee, WI 53202, USA

Grundhofer, John F (Business Person, Financier)
Donaldson Company, Inc
1400 W 94th St
Bloomington, MN 55431, USA

Grundman, Bernie (Musician)
Bernie Grundman Mastering
1640 N Gower St
Hollywood, CA 90028, USA

Grundt, Ken (Athlete, Baseball Player)
4814 W Parker Ave
Chicago, IL 60639-1712, USA

Grundy, Hugh (Musician)
Lustig Talent
PO Box 770850
Orlando, FL 32877, USA

Grune, George V (Publisher)
PO Box 2348
Ponte Vedra Beach, FL 32004, USA

Gruneisen, Sam (Athlete, Football Player)
569 Finsbay Ct
Ocoee, FL 34761, USA

Grunewald, Barbara (Stylist)
2120 W Waveland Ave
Chicago, IL 60618, USA

Grunfeld, Ernie (Athlete, Basketball Player, Olympic Athlete)
10121 Counselman Rd
Potomac, MD 20854-5021, USA

Grunhard, Tim (Athlete, Football Player)
2005 Arno Rd
Mission Hills, KS 66208, USA

Grunseth, Jon (Politician)
Lennonville Orchards 259 Lennon Road
North Bruny TAS 7150, Australia

Grunsfeld, John M (Astronaut)
PO Box 279
Highland, MD 20777-0279, USA

Grunwald, Ernie (Actor)
c/o Suzanne (Sue) Wohl *TalentWorks (LA)*
3500 W Olive Ave
Suite 1400
Burbank, CA 91505, USA

Grunwald, Henry A (Diplomat, Editor)
62A Barkers Point Rd
Port Washington, NY 11050-1323, USA

Grunwald, Norten
Nyborggade Strandboulevarden 160-162
DK-2100
Copenhagen, DENMARK

Grupo Mania (Music Group)
c/o Staff Member *Sony Music Miami*
605 Lincoln Rd Fl 7
Miami Beach, FL 33139, USA

Grupp, Robert (Athlete, Football Player)
305 Hill Ave
Langhorne, PA 19047, USA

Grushin, Dave
200 W. Superior #202
Chicago, IL 60710

Grushin, Pyotr D (Engineer)
Academy of Sciences
14 Lenisky Prospekt
Moscow, RUSSIA

Grusin, Dave (Composer, Musician)
Monterey International
200 W Superior
#202
Chicago, IL 60610, USA

Grutman, N Roy (Lawyer)
Grutman Miller Greenspoon Hendler
505 Park Ave
New York, NY 10022, USA

Gruttadauria, Mike (Athlete, Football Player)
4250 Swift Rd
Sarasota, FL 34231-6547, USA

Gryboski, Kevin (Athlete, Baseball Player)
127 Castlebrooke Dr
Venetia, PA 15367-1391, USA

Grygiel, George (Athlete, Baseball Player)
451 West Bazille Way
Green Valley, AZ 85614-5270, USA

Grygiel, George (Athlete, Baseball Player)
451 W Bazille Way
Green Valley, AZ 85614, USA

Grylls, Bear (Television Host)
Bear Grylls Ventures
401 Wilshire Blvd
Suite 1055
Santa Monica, CA 90401, USA

Grymes, Darrell (Athlete, Football Player)
1737 Minnesota Ave SE Apt 1
Washington, DC 20020-4755, USA

Gryp, Bob (Athlete, Hockey Player)
11 Duren Ave
Woburn, MA 01801-5304

Grzanich, Mike (Athlete, Baseball Player)
176 Holliday Trce
Raymond, MS 39154-9569, USA

Grzebien, Anna (Athlete, Golfer)
c/o Staff Member *Ladies Pro Golf Association (LPGA)*
100 International Golf Dr
Daytona Beach, FL 32124-1092, USA

Grzenda, Joe (Athlete, Baseball Player)
40 Hillcrest Dr
Covington Township, PA 18424-7852, USA

G. Thompson, Bennie (Congressman, Politician)
2466 Rayburn HOB
Washington, DC 20515, USA

Guadagnino, Kathy Baker (Athlete, Golfer)
1535 SW 4th Cir
Boca Raton, FL 33486-4414, USA

Guadagnino, Vinny (Reality TV Star)
c/o Sal Bonaventura *CEG Talent*
251 W. 39th St
7th Floor
New York, NY 10011, USA

Guangbiao, Chen (Business Person)
Jiangsu Huangpu Investment
Nanjing, Jiangsu Province, China

Guard, Christopher
76 Oxford St.
London, ENGLAND W1N OAX

Guardado, Eddie (Athlete, Baseball Player)
11268 Overlook Pt
Tustin, CA 92782-4314, USA

Guardino, Harry (Actor)
2949 E Via Vaquero Road
Palm Springs, CA 92262, USA

Guare, John (Writer)
R Andrew Boose 1 Dag Hammarskjold Plz
New York, NY 10017-2201, USA

Guarilia, Gene (Athlete, Basketball Player)
86 Main St
Duryea, PA 18642-1023, USA

Guarini, Justin (Musician)
c/o Jeff Ballard *Jeff Ballard PR*
4814 N Lemona Ave
Sherman Oaks, CA 91403, USA

Guarnere, William (General)
2800 Dogwood Ln
Broomall, PA 19008-1015, USA

Guarriello, Taimak (Actor)
c/o Staff Member *Chasin Agency, The*
8899 Beverly Blvd
Suite 716
Los Angeles, CA 90048-2449, USA

Guaty, Camille (Actor)
c/o Michael Baum *Impression Entertainment*
9229 W Sunset Blvd #700
West Hollywood, CA 90069, USA

Guay, Paul (Athlete, Hockey Player, Olympic Athlete)
34 Kirkbrae Dr
Lincoln, RI 02865-1019

Gubaidulina, Sofia A (Composer)
2D Pugachevskaya 8
Korp 5 #130
Moscow 107061, RUSSIA

Gubanich, Creighton (Athlete, Baseball Player)
10 Galicia Dr
Phoenixville, PA 19460-2010, USA

Gubarev, Aleksei A (Cosmonaut, General)
Potchta Kosmonavtov
Moskovskoi Oblasti
Syvisdny Goroduk 141160, RUSSIA

Gubelmann, Fiona (Actor)
c/o Brady McKay *Flutie Entertainment (LA)*
9320 Wilshire Blvd
Suite 202
Beverly Hills, CA 90212, USA

Guber, Peter (Producer)
Mandaly Entertainment
10202 W Washington Blvd
#1070
Culver City, CA 90232, USA

Gubert, Walter A (Financier)
J P Morgan Chase
270 Park Ave
New York, NY 10017, USA

Gubicza, Mark (Athlete, Baseball Player)
11808 Macoda Ln
Chatsworth, CA 91311-1271, USA

Gubler, Matthew Gray (Actor, Director, Writer)
c/o Colton Gramm *Brillstein Entertainment Partners*
9150 Wilshire Blvd #350
Beverly Hills, CA 90212, USA

Gubner, Gary (Athlete, Olympic Athlete, Weightlifter)
1 Renaissance Sq Unit 24F
White Plains, NY 10601-3006, USA

Gucci (Designer, Fashion Designer)
Gucci
Rembrandt Tower, 1
Amstelplein 1096 HA
Amsterdam, The Netherlands

Gucciardo, Pat (Athlete, Football Player)
2406 Kenmoore Rd
Maumee, OH 43537, USA

Guccione, Chris (Athlete, Baseball Player)
88 Paloma Ave
Brighton, CO 80601, USA

Guccione, Christopher (Baseball Player)
88 Paloma Ave
Brighton, CO 80601-8791, USA

Guckel, Henry (Engineer)
University of Wisconsin
Engineering Dept
Madison, WI 53706, USA

Guckert, Elmer (Baseball Player)
1212 Balmoral Dr
Pittsburgh, PA 15237-5092, USA

Guckert, Elmer (Athlete, Baseball Player)
1212 Balmoral Dr
Pittsburgh, PA 15237, USA

Gudmundson, Scott (Athlete, Football Player)
11 Guindola Way
Apt 268
Hot Springs Village, AR 71909, USA

Gudmundsson, Petur (Athlete, Basketball Player)
2423 Vibrant Oak
San Antonio, TX 78232-2616, USA

Guelleh, Ismail Omar (President)
President's Office
8-10 Ahmed Nessim St
Djibouti, DJIBOUTI

Guennel, Joe (Soccer Player)
835 Front Range Road
Littleton, CO 80120, USA

Gueno, James (Athlete, Football Player)
8173 Drexel Ct
Eden Prairie, MN 55347-2189, USA

Guenther, Johnny (Bowler)
23826 115th Place W
Woodway, WA 98020-5212, USA

Guerard, Michael E (Chef)
Les Pres d'Eugenie
Eugenie les Bains 40320, FRANCE

Guerard, Stephane (Athlete, Hockey
Player)
123 Rue Principale
Saint-Fiavien, QC G0S 2MO, Canada

Guerin, Bill (Athlete, Hockey Player)
Pittsburgh Penguins
66 Mario Lemieux Pl Ste 2
Pittsburgh, PA 15219-3504

Guerin, Bill (Athlete, Hockey Player,
Olympic Athlete)
12 North Rd
Oyster Bay, NY 11771-1904

Guerin, Richie (Athlete, Basketball Player)
1355 Bear Island Dr
West Palm Beach, FL 33409-2042, USA

Guerra, Blanca (Actor)
c/o Staff Member *Televisa*
Blvd Adolfo Lopez Mateos 232
Colonia San Angel INN
DF CP 01060, MEXICO

Guerra, Eddie (Actor)
c/o Peter Micelli *Creative Artists Agency
(CAA-LA)*
2000 Ave Of The Stars
Los Angeles, CA 90067, USA

Guerra, Jackie (Comedian)
c/o Staff Member *Brillstein Entertainment
Partners*
9150 Wilshire Blvd #350
Beverly Hills, CA 90212, USA

Guerra, Juan Luis (Musician)
c/o Staff Member *EMI Music Group (NY)*
150 Fifth Avenue
New York, NY 10011, USA

Guerra, Saverio (Actor)
c/o Susan Ferris *Bohemia Group*
1680 Vine St Ste 216
Los Angeles, CA 90028, USA

Guerra, Vida (Actor, Model)
c/o Staff Member *Britto Agency PR*
234 W 56th St
Penthouse
New York, NY 10019, USA

Guerrero, Julen (Soccer Player)
AC Bilbao
Alameda Mazarredo 23
Bilbao 48009, SPAIN

Guerrero, Mario (Athlete, Baseball Player)
Calle Duarte#450
Santa Domingo, Dominican Republic,
USA

Guerrero, Pedro (Athlete, Baseball Player)
10720 NW 66th St
Apt 408
Doral, FL 33178-3657, USA

Guerrero, Roberto (Race Car Driver)
PO Box 381
Cl ay, KY 42404, USA

Guerrero, Vladimir (Athlete, Baseball
Player)
5160 E Copa De Oro Dr
Anaheim, CA 92807-3639, USA

Guerrero Coles, Lisa (Actor, Sportscaster)
c/o Lorraine Berglund *Lorraine Berglund
Management*
11537 Hesby St.
North Hollywood, CA 91601, USA

Guerrier, Matt (Athlete, Baseball Player)
200 Highland View Dr
Birmingham, AL 35242-6874, USA

Guers, Paul
40 rue de Buci
Paris, FRANCE 75006

Guess Who
31 Hemlock Pl. Winnepeg
Man., CANADA R2H 1L8

Guest, Christopher (Actor, Director)
463 Mesa Rd
Santa Monica, CA 90402, USA

Guest, Cornelia (Model)
1419 Donhill Dr
Beverly Hills, CA 90210, USA

Guest, Douglas (Misc)
Gables
Minchinhampton
Gloscester GL6 9JE, UNITED KINGDOM
(UK)

Guest, Lance
2269 La Granada Dr.
Los Angeles, CA 90068

Guetary, Francois (Actor)
Cineart
36 Rue de Ponthieu
Paris 75008, FRANCE

Guetta, David (DJ, Musician)
c/o Maria May *CAA (London)*
1 Beadon Rd
4th Floor, Space One
London W6 0EA, UNITED KINGDOM
(UK)

Guetterman, Lee (Athlete, Baseball
Player)
108 1/2 E Broadway St
Lenoir City, TN 37771-2908, USA

Guevara, Carlos (Athlete, Baseball Player)
501 S Crisp St
Uvalde, TX 78801-5905, USA

Guevremont, Jocelyn (Athlete, Hockey
Player)
4303 NW 70th Ln
Coral Springs, FL 33065, USA

Guffey, Cary (Actor)
236 Eagle Park Ln
Birmingham, AL 35242, USA

Guffey Jr, John W (Business Person)
Coltec Industries
2550 W Tyvola Road
Charlotte, NC 28217, USA

Gugelmin, Mauricio (Race Car Driver)
PacWest Reacing Group
4476 60 602
Cuiriba, PR 80250-210, BRAZIL

Guggemos, Neal (Athlete, Football Player)
8173 Drexel Ct
Eden Prairie, MN 55347, USA

Guggenheim, Alan (Inventor)
Northwest Power Systems
PO Box 5339
Bend, OR 97708, USA

Guggenheim, Marc (Actor)
c/o Eddie Michaels *Insignia Public
Relations*
1507 20th St
Santa Monica, CA 90404, USA

Gugino, Carla (Actor)
c/o Jason Weinberg *Untitled
Entertainment (LA)*
350 S. Beverly Dr #200
Beverly Hills, CA 90212, USA

Guglielmi, Ralph (Athlete, Football Player)
159 Red Berry Dr
Wallace, NC 28466, USA

Gugliotta, Tom (Athlete, Basketball
Player)
992 Wadsworth Dr NW
Atlanta, GA 30318-1654, USA

Guice, Jackson (Cartoonist)
DC Comics
1700 Broadway
New York, NY 10019, USA

Guida, Gloria
Via Francesco Denza 48
Rome, ITALY I-00197

Guida, Lou (Misc)
4800 N Highway A1A
#505
Vero Beach, FL 32963, USA

Guidinger, Jay (Athlete, Basketball Player)
N39W22702 Grandview Dr
Pewaukee, WI 53072-2735, USA

Guido, Med Mutke Dr (Scientist)
Drvgalski-Allee 118
Munich D-81477, Germany

Guidolin, Aldo (Athlete, Hockey Player)
34 Blair Dr
Guelph, ON N1l 1N7, Canada

Guidoni, Umberto (Astronaut)
Via Leonardo Libera 34
Rome 00173, Italy

Guidry, Kevin (Athlete, Football Player)
4045 W Briarfield St
Lake Charles, LA 70607, USA

Guidry, Mark
1264 Camelot Lane
Lemont, IL 60439

Guidry, N T (Engineer)
23971 Coral Springs Lane
Tehachapi, CA 93561, USA

Guidry, Paul (Athlete, Football Player)
880 Noel Dr
Mount Juliet, TN 37122, USA

Guidry, Ron (Athlete, Baseball Player)
P.O. Box 666
Scott, LA 70583-0666, USA

Guiel, Aaron (Athlete, Baseball Player)
18944 69 Ave
Surrey, BC V4N 5K1, Canada

Guilbaut, Jeremy (Actor)
c/o Russ Mortensen *Pacific Artists
Management*
1285 W Broadway
Suite 685
Vancouver, BC V6H 3X8, Canada

Guilbe, Felix (Baseball Player)
Baltimore Elite Giants
Los Cabos Calle Carambala
Ponce, PR 00716, USA

Guilbert, Ann (Actor)
550 Erskine Dr
Pacific Palisades, CA 90272, USA

Guilford, Eric (Athlete, Football Player)
8111 W Wacker Rd
Unit 51
Peoria, AZ 85381, USA

Guilfoyle, Kimberly (Television Host)
c/o Staff Member *Fox News Channel (NY)*
1211 Ave of the Americas
Level C1
New York, NY 10036-8701, USA

Guilfoyle, Paul (Actor)
c/o Donna Massetti *Silver Massetti &
Szatmary (SMS) Talent Inc*
8383 Wilshire Blvd
Suite 230
Beverly Hills, CA 90211, USA

Guill, Juliana (Actor)
c/o Tim Taylor *Luber Roklin Management*
8530 Wilshire Blvd
6th Floor
Beverly Hills, CA 90211, USA

Guillaume, Robert (Actor)
c/o Alan David *Alan David Management*
8840 Wilshire Blvd
Suite 200
Beverly Hills, CA 90211, USA

Guillem, Sylvie (Ballerina)
c/o Staff Member *Royal Ballet*
Covent Garden
Bow St
London WC2E 9DD, UK

Guillemin, Roger C L (Nobel Prize
Laureate)
7316 Encelia Ave
La Jolla, CA 92037-5728, USA

Guillemots (Music Group, Musician)
c/o Staff Member *MCT Management*
520 8th Ave Rm 2205
New York, NY 10018, USA

Guillen, Carlos
17121 Collins Ave Apt 4301
Sunny Isles Beach, FL 33160-4373, USA

Guillen, Francesca (Actor)
c/o Staff Member *Televisa*
Blvd Adolfo Lopez Mateos 232
Colonia San Angel INN
DF CP 01060, MEXICO

Guillen, Ozzie (Athlete, Baseball Player)
19462 38th Ct
Golden Beach, FL 33160-2298, USA

Guillen, Ozzie (Athlete, Baseball Player)
Florida Marlins
2267 NW 199th St
Miami gardens, FL 33056-2664, USA

Guillerman, John (Director)
309 S Rockingham Ave
Los Angeles, CA 90049, USA

Guillermin, John
309 S. Rockingham Ave.
Los Angeles, CA 90049

Guillo, Dominque (Actor)
Cineart
36 Rue de Ponthieu
Paris 75008, FRANCE

Guillory, Bennet
1519 Galaxy Ct.
Rohnert Park, CA 94928-5611

Guillory, Sienna (Actor)
c/o Holly Shakoor *42West (LA)*
11400 W Olympic Blvd
Suite 1100
Los Angeles, CA 90064, USA

Guillory, Tony (Athlete, Football Player)
2605 Blanchette St
Beaumont, TX 77701-6615, USA

Guinan, Francis
606 N. Larchmont Blvd. #309LA
, CA 90004

Guindon, Bob (Athlete, Hockey Player)
2109 Tsse Jourdain
Sainte-Sophie, QC JSJ 1K1, Canada

Guindon, Bob (Athlete, Baseball Player)
2109 Tsse Jourdain
Sainte-Sophie, QC J5J IKl, Canada

Guindon, Richard G (Cartoonist)
321 W Lafayette Blvd Lbby
Detroit, MI 48226-2703, USA

Guinee, Tim (Actor)
c/o Jonathan Howard *Innovative Artists (LA)*
1505 10th St
Santa Monica, CA 90401, USA

Guiney, Bob (Game Show Host, Reality TV Star)
c/o Anthony Embry *AE Entertainment Public Relations*
124 Evening Shade Dr
Charleston, SC 29414, USA

Guinier, Lani (Educator, Lawyer)
University of Pennsylvania
Law School
3400 Chestnut
Philadelphia, PA 19104, USA

Guinn, Skip (Athlete, Baseball Player)
PO Box 911
Stilwell, OK 74960-0911, USA

Guinney, Bob (Reality TV Star)
c/o Kim Jakwerth *Marleah Leslie & Associates PR*
1645 N Vine St
Suite 712
Los Angeles, CA 90028, USA

Guinta, Frank (Congressman, Politician)
1223 Longworth HOB
Washington, DC 20515, USA

Guirgis, Stephen Adly (Comedian)
c/o Staff Member *Gersh (LA)*
9465 Wilshire Blvd
Suite 600
Beverly Hills, CA 90212, USA

Guiry, Thomas (Actor)
c/o Rhonda Price *Gersh (NY)*
41 Madison Ave
New York, NY 10010, USA

Guisewite, Cathy L (Cartoonist)
4039 Camellia Ave
Studio City, CA 91604-3007, USA

Guite, Ben (Athlete, Hockey Player)
3735 E Ellsworth Ave Apt A
Denver, CO 80209-5629

Guite, Pierre (Athlete, Hockey Player)
96085 Marsh Lakes Dr
Fernandina Beach, FL 32034-0825

Gujral, Inder Kumar (Prime Minister)
5 Janpath
New Delhi, Delhi 110011, INDIA

Gujral, Namrata
c/o Mike Eistenstadt *Amsel, Eisenstadt & Frazier Talent Agency (AEF)*
5055 Wilshire Blvd
Suite 860
Los Angeles, CA 90036-6108, USA

Gulager, Clu (Actor)
Clu Gulager Acting
320 Wilshire Blvd
Santa Monica, CA 90401, USA

Gulan, Mike (Athlete, Baseball Player)
4409 Fairway Dr
Steubenville, OH 43953-3305, USA

Gulbinowicx, Henryk Roman Cardinal (Religious Leader)
Metropolita Wroclawski
UL Katedraina 11
Wroclaw 50-328, POLAND

Gulbis, Natalie (Athlete, Golfer)
30 Strada Principale
Henderson, NV 89011-3603, USA

Guldelli, Giovanni (Actor)
Carol Levi Co
Via Giuseppe Pisanelli
Rome 00196, ITALY

Gulden, Brad (Athlete, Baseball Player)
15820 Lundstead Rd
Carver, MN 55315-9702, USA

Guleghina, Maria (Opera Singer)
Askonas Holt Ltd
27 Chancery Lane
London WC2A 1PF, UNITED KINGDOM (UK)

Guliford, Eric (Athlete, Football Player)
8111 W Wacker Rd Unit 51
Peoria, AZ 85381-4943, USA

Gulka, Budd (Athlete, Hockey Player)
20945 42 Ave
Langley, BC V3A 4Z9, Canada

Gulledge, David (Athlete, Football Player)
1064 Inverness Cove Way
Birmingham, AL 35242-4217, USA

Gullett, Donald E (Don) (Athlete, Baseball Player)
194 Kingswav Dr
South Shore, KY 41175-7934, USA

Gulli, Franco (Musician)
Columbia Artists Mgmt Inc
165 W 57th St
New York, NY 10019, USA

Gullickson, William L (Bill) (Athlete, Baseball Player)
3 Banchory Ct
Palm Beach Gardens, FL 33418-6811, USA

Gullikson, Tom (Athlete)
Tim & Tom Gullikson Foundation
8000 Sears Tower
Chicago, IL 60606

Gullit, Ruud (Soccer Player)
FC Chelsea
Stamford Bridge
Fulham Road
London SW6 1HS, UNITED KINGDOM (UK)

Gulliver, Dorothy
28792 Lajos Lane
Valley Center, A 92082

Gulliver, Glenn (Athlete, Baseball Player)
8123 Cortland Ave
Allen Park, MI 48101-2215, USA

Gulliver, Harold (Editor)
Atlanta Constitution
Editorial Dept
72 Marieta St NW
Atlanta, GA 30303, USA

Gulman, Gary (Musician)
c/o Staff Member *Paradigm (Monterey)*
404 W Franklin St
Monterey, CA 93940, USA

Gulseth, Don (Athlete, Football Player)
100 2nd St SE
Apt 202
Minneapolis, MN 55414, USA

Gulutzan, Glen (Athlete, Hockey Player)
Dallas Stars
2601 Avenue of the Stars Ste 100
Frisco, TX 75034-9016

Gulyas, Denes (Opera Singer)
Hungarian State Opera
Andrassy Utca 22
Budapest 1062, HUNGARY

Gulzar (Bollywood, Songwriter, Writer)
Boskiyana Pali Hill
Bandra (W)
Mumbai, MS 400050, INDIA

Guman, Michael D (Mike) (Athlete, Football Player)
3913 Pleasant Ave
Allentown, PA 18103, USA

Gumbel, Bryant C (Sportscaster)
NFL Network
30 Rockefeller Plz Ste 1508
New York, NY 10112-0015, USA

Gumbel, Greg (Sportscaster, Television Host)
c/o Staff Member *CBS Television*
51 W 52nd St
New York, NY 10019, USA

Gummer, Grace (Actor)
c/o Michelle Benson *42West (NY)*
220 W 42nd St
12th Floor
New York, NY 10036, USA

Gummer, Henry (Musician)
c/o Matthew Berkson *Undermountain Records*
1918 Weepah Way
Los Angeles, CA 90046, USA

Gummer, Mamie (Actor)
c/o Michelle Benson *42West (NY)*
220 W 42nd St
12th Floor
New York, NY 10036, USA

Gummersall, Devon (Actor)
c/o Peg Donegan *Framework Entertainment (LA)*
9057 Nemo St
Suite C
West Hollywood, CA 90069, USA

Gummoe, John (Musician)
6812 Apperson St
Tujunga, CA 91042, USA

Gump, Scott (Athlete, Golfer)
11225 Willow Gardens Dr
Windermere, FL 34786-6020, USA

Gumpert, Dave (Athlete, Baseball Player)
68371 Fleetwood Dr
South Haven, MI 49090-8357, USA

Gun, Jang Dong (Actor)
152-4-4 bukit gembira condo
off jalan kuchai lama
kuala lumpur, wilayah
persekutuan 58200, Mylasia

Gund, Agnes (Misc)
Museum of Modern Art
11 W 53rd St
New York, NY 10019, USA

Gund, Graham (Architect)
47 Thorndike St Ste 1
Cambridge, MA 02141-1799, USA

Gunderman, Robert (Athlete, Football Player)
11 Post Brook Rd S
West Milford, NJ 07480, USA

Gunderson, Eric (Athlete, Baseball Player)
19809 SE 10th St
Camas, WA 98607-7273, USA

Gundi (Actor)
RR1
Roseneath, ON KOK 2XO, CANADA

Gundu, Kalyanam (Actor)
D-1 Block Lloyds Colony
Royapettah
Chennai, TN 600 014, INDIA

G Unit (Music Group)
c/o Staff Member *Interscope Records (NY)*
1755 Broadway
New York, NY 10019, USA

Gunmuddsson, Petur (Athlete, Basketball Player)
2423 Vibrant Oak
San Antonio, TX 78232, USA

Gunn, Anna (Actor)
c/o Christian Donatelli *Schiff Company, The*
9465 Wilshire Blvd
Suite 480
Beverly Hills, CA 90212, USA

Gunn, Chanda (Athlete, Hockey Player, Olympic Athlete)
74 Rockcroft Rd
Weymouth, MA 02188, USA

Gunn, James (Actor, Director, Writer)
c/o Peter Safran *The Safran Company*
8748 Holloway Dr
Los Angeles, CA 90069, USA

Gunn, James P (Astronomer)
Princeton University
Princeton Universitv Astrophysics
Princeton, NJ 08544-0001, USA

Gunn, Lance (Athlete, Football Player)
10600 Arrowhead Dr Ste 225
Fairfax, VA 22030-7306, USA

Gunn, Nathan (Opera Singer)
c/o Staff Member *Opus 3 Artists*
5670 Wilshire Blvd
Suite 1790
Los Angeles, CA 90036, USA

Gunn, Richard (Actor)
c/o Chris Henze *Thruline Entertainment*
9250 Wilshire Blvd
Ground Fl
Beverly Hills, CA 90212, USA

Gunn, Sean (Actor)
c/o Mitch Clem *Shadow Entertainment*
10 Universal City Plz
20th Floor
Universal City, CA 91608, USA

Gunn, Tim (Educator, Reality TV Star, Television Host)
c/o Staff Member *Project Runway*
915 Broadway 20th Fl
New York, NY 10010, USA

Gunnarsson, Martin (Athlete, Olympic Athlete, Shooter)
3536 Saint Marys Rd Lot D24
Columbus, GA 31906-4594, USA

Gunnell, Sally (Athlete, Track Athlete)
18 Shepherd's Croft
Brighton
East Sussex, UNITED KINGDOM (UK)

Gunnels, Riley (Athlete, Football Player)
606 Wesley Ave
Ocean City, NJ 08226, USA

Gunner, Harry (Athlete, Football Player)
248 Emory Ln
Port Arthur, TX 77642-4769, USA

Guns N' Roses (Music Group)
c/o Staff Member *Geffen Records*
9126 Sunset Blvd
West Hollywood, CA 90069, USA

Gunter, Dan (Actor)
Century Artists
PO Box 59747
Santa Barbara, CA 93150, USA

Gunther, David (Athlete, Basketball Player)
4510 Cherry St
Grand Forks, ND 58201-7742, USA

Gunvalson, Vicki (Reality TV Star)
c/o Richard Heard *Vicki Gunvalson Entertainment*
Prefers to be contacted via telephone and email
New York, NY, USA

Guokas Jr, Matt (Athlete, Basketball Player, Coach)
2410 South 19th St
Philadelphia, PA 19145-4226, USA

Guolla, Steve (Athlete, Hockey Player)
729 Rutgers Rd
Rochester Hills, MI 48309-2546

Gupta, Neena (Actor)
129 Aram Nagar II Versova Road
Andheri
Bombay, MS 400 061, INDIA

Gupta, Raj (Business Person)
Rohm & Haas Co
100 S Independence Mall W
#1A
Philadelphia, PA 19106, USA

Gupta, Sanjay (Correspondent, Doctor)
c/o Staff Member *CNN (Atlanta)*
One CNN Center
PO Box 105366
Atlanta, GA 30303, USA

Gupta, Sudhir (Misc)
University of California
Medicine Dept
Irvine, CA 92717, USA

Gur, Mordechai (General)
25 Mishmeret St
Afeka
Tel-Aviv 69694, ISRAEL

Gura, Larry C (Athlete, Baseball Player)
P.O. Box 94
Litchfield Park, AZ 85340-0094, USA

Gurdon, John B (Misc)
Magdalene College
Master's Cottage
Cambridge CB3 0AG, UNITED KINGDOM (UK)

Guren, Peter (Cartoonist)
Creators Syndicate
5777 W Century Blvd
#700
Los Angeles, CA 90045, USA

Gurewitz, Brett (Musician)
c/o Staff Member *WmE2 (WMA-LA)*
1 William Morris Pl
Beverly Hills, CA 90212, USA

Gurganus, Alan (Writer)
Vintage/Anchor Publicity
1745 Broadway Fl 20
New York, NY 10019, USA

Gurian, Michael (Writer)
417 W 32nd Ave
Spokane, WA 99203, USA

Gurley, Buck (Athlete, Football Player)
103 Neetle Close Dr
Woodstock, GA 30188-7077, USA

Gurney, Alex (Race Car Driver)
Dan Gurney Racing
2334 S. Broadway
Santa Ana, CA 92707, USA

Gurney, Daniel S (Dan) (Race Car Driver)
All-American Racers Inc
2334 So. Broadway
Santa Ana, CA 92707, USA

Gurney, Hilda (Horse Racer)
8430 Waters Road
Moorpark, CA 93021, USA

Gurney, James (Writer)
PO Box 693
Rhinebeck, NY 12572-0693, USA

Gurney, Scott (Actor)
c/o Staff Member *Guttman Associates*
118 S Beverly Dr
Suite 201
Beverly Hills, CA 90212, USA

Gurney Jr, Albert R (A R) (Writer)
40 Wellers Bridge Road
Roxbury, CT 06783, USA

Gurode, Andre (Athlete, Football Player)
15827 Maple Shores Dr
Houston, TX 77044-4485, USA

Gurry, Kick (Actor)
c/o Robert Stein *Robert Stein Management*
PO Box 3797
Beverly Hills, CA 90212, USA

Gursky, Al (Athlete, Football Player)
54 Securda Rd
Reading, PA 19607, USA

Gurwitch, Annabelle (Actor)
Don Buchwald
6500 Wilshire Blvd
#2200
Los Angeles, CA 90048, USA

Gusarov, Alexei (Athlete, Hockey Player)
9695 E Kansas Cir #41
Denver, CO 80247

Gusella, James (Inventor)
Harvard Medical School
25 Shattuck St
Boston, MA 02115, USA

Gusev, Sergei (Athlete, Hockey Player)
16001 Ridley Pl
Apt 2-A
Tampa, FL 33647, USA

Gus Gus (Music Group)
c/o Andrew Curley *International Talent Booking*
74A Charlotte St
London W1T 4QJ, UNITED KINGDOM (UK)

Gushiken, Koji (Gymnast)
Nippon Physical Education College
Judo School
Tokyo, JAPAN

Gusmao, Jose Alexandre (Xanana) (President)
President's Office
Dili, EAST TIMOR

Gustafson, Derek (Athlete, Hockey Player)
3309 NE 165th Ave
Vancouver, WA 98682-8653

Gustafson, Ed (Athlete, Football Player)
6209 Mineral Point Rd
Apt 1007
Madison, WI 53705, USA

Gustafson, Kathryn (Architect)
Gustafson Guthrie Nichol
Pier 55
#31101 Alaskan Way
Seattle, WA 98101, USA

Gustafson, Sophie (Athlete, Golfer)
6043 Jamestown Park
Orlando, FL 32819, USA

Gustafson, Steven (Musician)
Agency for Performing Arts
9200 Sunset Blvd
#900
Los Angeles, CA 90069, USA

Gustafsson, Per (Athlete, Hockey Player)
5605 NE 3rd Ave
Fort Lauderdale, FL 33334, USA

Gustav, H.M. King Carl XVI (Royalty)
Kungl. Slottet
Stockholm SE-111 30, Sweden

Guster (Music Group)
c/o Staff Member *Nettwerk Management (NY)*
345 Seventh Ave Fl 24
New York, NY 10001, USA

Gustin, Grant
c/o Robert Stein *Robert Stein Management*
PO Box 3797
Beverly Hills, CA 90212, USA

Gutensohn-Knopf, Katrin (Skier)
Oberfeldweg 12
Oberaudorf 83080, GERMANY

Guterman, Lawrence M (Director)
c/o Staff Member *WME (LA)*
9601 Wilshire Blvd Fl 3
Beverly Hills, CA 90210, USA

Gutfeld, Greg (Television Host)
c/o Staff Member *Fox News Channel (NY)*
1211 Ave of the Americas
Level C1
New York, NY 10036-8701, USA

Guth, Alan H (Physicist)
Massachusetts Institute of Technology
Physics Dept
Cambridge, MA 02139, USA

Guth, Bucky (Athlete, Baseball Player)
202 Morris Dr
Salisbury, MD 21804-7229, USA

Guth, Forrest (General)
349 Dewey Dr
Annapolis, MD 21401-2246, USA

Guthe, Manfred (Cinematographer)
122 Collier St
Toronto, ON M4W 1M3, CANADA

Gutherie, Arlo (Actor, Composer, Musician)
c/o Dora Whitaker *Whitaker Agency, The*
4924 Vineland Avenue
N Hollywood, CA 91601, USA

Gutherie, Jeremy (Athlete, Baseball Player)
1004 Clay St
Ashland, OR 97520, USA

Guthrie, Arlo (Musician, Songwriter)
c/o Annie Guthrie *Rising Son Records*
Clamzo's Court
218 Beach Rd
Washington, WA 01223, USA

Guthrie, Brett (Congressman, Politician)
308 Cannon HOB
Washington, DC 20515, USA

Guthrie, Janet (Race Car Driver)
Janet Guthrie Racing
PO Box 505
Aspen, CO 81612, USA

Guthrie, Jennifer (Actor)
Don Buchwald
6500 Wilshire Blvd #2200
Los Angeles, CA 90048, USA

Guthrie, Jeremy (Athlete, Baseball Player)
3106 Millcreek Rd
Pleasant Grove, UT 84062-8790, USA

Guthrie, Mark (Athlete, Baseball Player)
3129 Donald Ross Rd E
Sarasota, FL 34240-7628, USA

Guthrie, Savannah (Correspondent)
c/o Michael Glantz *Headline Media Management*
888 7th Ave #503
New York, NY 10106, USA

Gutierrez, Alexander (Stylist)
c/o Staff Member *Workgroup (Hollywood)*
8491 Sunset Blvd
#368
West Hollywood, CA 90069, USA

Gutierrez, Brock (Athlete, Football Player)
1040 Pueblo Pass
Weidman, MI 48893, USA

Gutierrez, Carlos M (Business Person)
Kellogg Co
1 Kellogg Square
PO Box 3599
Battle Creek, MI 49016, USA

Gutierrez, Diego (Actor)
c/o Staff Member *Creative Artists Agency (CAA-LA)*
2000 Ave Of The Stars
Los Angeles, CA 90067, USA

Gutierrez, Franklin (Athlete, Baseball Player)
5130 Preferred Pl
Hilliard, OJ 43026, USA

Gutierrez, Gustavo (Misc)
Instituto Bartolome Las Casas-Rimac
Apartado 3090
Lima 100, PERU

Gutierrez, Horacio (Music Group, Musician)
I C M Artists
40 W 57th St
New York, NY 10019, USA

Gutierrez, Jackie (Athlete, Baseball Player)
10631 SW 126th Ave
Miami, FL 33186-3744, USA

Gutierrez, Jennifer (Athlete, Olympic Athlete, Triathlete)
5232 Fullerton Ln Highlands
Ranch, CO 80130-6614, USA

Gutierrez, Luclo (President)
Palacio de Gobiemo
Garcia Moreno
Quito 1043, ECUADOR

Gutierrez, Ricky (Athlete, Baseball Player)
13803 NW lOth Ct
Pembroke Pines, FL 33028-2350, USA

Gutierrez, Sidney M (Astronaut)
324 Sarah Lane NW
Albuquerque, NM 87114, USA

Gutierrez, Sidney M Colonel (Astronaut)
324 Sarah Ln NW
Albuquerque, NM 87114-1026, USA

Gutman, Natalia G (Music Group, Musician)
Askonas Holt Ltd
27 Chancery Lane
London WC2A 1PF, UNITED KINGDOM (UK)

Gutman, Roy W (Journalist)
1349 Windy Hill Road
McLean, VA 22102-2803, USA

Gutmann, Amy (Educator)
Princeton University
President's Office
Princeton, NJ 08544, USA

Gutsche, TorstenHans- (Athlete)
Hans-Marchwitza-Ring 51
Potsdam 14473, GERMANY

Gutschewski, Scott (Basketball Player, Golfer)
20110 Douglas St
Elkhorn, NE 68022, USA

Guttenberg, Steve (Actor)
c/o Staff Member *Binder & Associates*
1465 Lindacrest Dr
Beverly Hills, CA 90210, USA

Gutz, Julie (Athlete, Baseball Player, Commentator)
9940 Gappa Rd
Kabetogama, MN 56669-8048, USA

Guy, Buddy (Music Group, Musician)
Buddy Guy Legends
734 S Wabash Ave
Chicago, IL 60603, USA

Guy, Cristy (Stylist)
c/o Staff Member *It's All in the Clothes*
5720 Martway St
Suite 102
Mission, KA 66202, USA

Guy, Francois-Frederic (Music Group, Musician)
Van Walsum Mgmt
4 Addison Bridge Place
London W14 8XP, UNITED KINGDOM (UK)

Guy, Jasmine (Actor)
c/o Staff Member *Stone Manners Salners Agency (LA)*
9911 W Pico Blvd Ste 1400
Los Angeles, CA 90035, USA

Guy, Kevan (Athlete, Hockey Player)
10127 Dunsinane Dr
South Jordan, UT 84095-9066

Guy, Lou (Athlete, Football Player)
2127 Sheffield Dr
Jackson, MS 39211-5851, USA

Guy, Melwood (Athlete, Football Player)
345 Castle St
Lowell, IN 46356, USA

Guy, Ray (Athlete, Football Player)
936 Central Rd SW
Thomson, GA 30824-8278, USA

Guy, Sebastien (Actor)
c/o Staff Member *Acme Talent & Literary (LA)*
1400 Atlantic Ave
Suite 274
Long Beach, CA 90814, USA

Guy, William L (Ex-Governor, Politician)
225 13th Ave W Apt 204
West Fargo, ND 58078-2690, USA

Guyer, Cindy (Actor)
c/o Marta Michaud *Cinematic Management*
249 1/2 E 13th St
New York, NY 10003, USA

Guyer, David B (Misc)
Save the Children Foundation
514 2nd St
Owyhee, NV 89832, USA

Guynn, Jack (Financier, Government Official)
Federal Reserve Bank
1000 Peachtree St NE
Atlanta, GA 30309, USA

Guyon, John C (Educator)
Southern Illinois Univesity
President's Office
Carbondale, IL 62901, USA

Guyot, Paul (Actor, Producer, Writer)
c/o Kathy White *Creative Artists Agency (CAA-LA)*
2000 Ave Of The Stars
Los Angeles, CA 90067, USA

Guyton, Myron (Athlete, Football Player)
302 Shadow Glen
McDonough, GA 30253, USA

Guzman, Alejandra (Musician)
c/o Staff Member *BMG*
1540 Broadway
New York, NY 10036, USA

Guzman, Andrea (Actor)
c/o Staff Member *TV Caracol*
Calle 76 #11 - 35
Piso 10AA
Bogota DC 26484, COLOMBIA

Guzman, Cristian (Athlete, Baseball Player)
10727 Cory Lake Dr
Tampa, FL 33647-2725, USA

Guzman, Jose (Athlete, Baseball Player)
4401 Shadycreek Ln
Colleyville, TX 76034-4729, USA

Guzman, Juan (Athlete, Baseball Player)
176 Dockside Cir
Weston, FL 33327-1100, USA

Guzman, Luis (Actor)
Gersh Agency
232 N Canon Dr
Beverly Hills, CA 90210, USA

Guzman, Ryan
c/o Tim Taylor *Luber Roklin Management*
8530 Wilshire Blvd
6th Floor
Beverly Hills, CA 90211, USA

Guzman, Santiago (Baseball Player)
St Louis Cardinals
1712 N Douty St
Hanford, CA 93230 2155, USA

Guzy, Carol (Journalist, Photographer)
2412 Fort Scott Dr
Arlington, VA 22202-2266, USA

Gwathmey, Charles (Architect)
Gwathmey Siegel Architects
475 10th Ave
New York, NY 10018, USA

Gwathmey, Charles (Architect)
Gwathmey Siegel & Assoc
475 Tenth Ave
New York, NY 10018, USA

Gwinn, Mary Ann (Journalist)
Seattle Times
Seattle Times Fairview Avenue NAnd John Street Attn: Editorial Dept
Seattle, WA 98111, USA

Gwinn, Ross (Athlete, Football Player)
1736 Washington St
Natchitoches, LA 71457, USA

Gwosdz, Doug (Athlete, Baseball Player)
2108 Rose Rd
Pearland, TX 77581-3844, USA

Gwyn, Marcus (Athlete, Baseball Player)
150 E Elm Cres
Spring, TX 77382-1047, USA

Gwynn, Chris (Athlete, Baseball Player, Olympic Athlete)
10975 Hillside Rd
Rancho Cucamonga, CA 91737, USA

Gwynn, Darrell (Race Car Driver)
4850 SW 52nd St
Davie, FL 33314, USA

Gwynn, Tony (Athlete, Baseball Player)
c/o John Boggs *John Boggs & Associates*
5675 Ruffin Rd
Suite 350
San Diego, CA 92123, USA

Gwynn, Tony (Athlete, Baseball Player)
San Diego State University
5500 Campanile Dr
Attn: Head Baseball Coach
San Diego, CA 92182, USA

Gwynne, A Patrick (Architect)
Homewood Esher
Surrey KT10 9JL, UNITED KINGDOM (UK)

Gwynn Jr, Tony (Athlete, Baseball Player)
15643 Boulder Ridge Ln
Poway, CA 92064, USA

Gyanendra (King)
Royal Palace
Narayanhiti Durbag Marg
Kathmandu, NEPAL

Gyll, J Soren (Business Person)
Volvo AB
Goteborg 405 08, SWEDEN

Gyllenhaal, Jake (Actor)
c/o Evelyn O'Neill *Management 360*
9111 Wilshire Blvd
Beverly Hills, CA 90210, USA

Gyllenhaal, Maggie (Actor)
c/o Courtney Kivowitz *Schiff Company, The*
9465 Wilshire Blvd
Suite 480
Beverly Hills, CA 90212, USA

Gyllenhaal, Stephen G (Director, Producer, Writer)
c/o Staff Member *WmE2 (WMA-LA)*
1 William Morris Pl
Beverly Hills, CA 90212, USA

Gyllenhammer, Pehr G (Business Person)
CHU PLC Saint Helen's 1 Undershaft
London EC3P 3DQ, UNITED KINGDOM (UK)

Gym Class Heroes (Music Group)
c/o Bob McLynn *Crush Management*
60-62 E 11th St
7th Floor
New York, NY 10003, USA

Gyokuban, Sal (Chef)
Kanmeiho Restaurant
7-6-47 Akasaka Akasaka New Plaza 105
USA

GZA (Musician)
c/o Staff Member *Agency Group Ltd, The (NY)*
142 West 57th St
6th Floor
New York, NY 10019, USA

Haag, Ulrika (Stylist)
c/o Staff Member *Wilhelmina Miami Beauty*
927 Lincoln Rd
#200
Miami Beach, FL 33139, USA

Haakon (Prince)
Det Kongeligel Slottet
Drammensveien 1
Oslo 0010, NORWAY

Haas, Andrew T (Misc)
Auto Aero & Agricultural Union
1300 Connecticut NW
Washington, DC 20036, USA

Haas, Dave (Athlete, Baseball Player)
160 E 6th Pl
Mesa, AZ 85201-5068, USA

Haas, Ed (Photographer)
180 W End Ave Apt 11C
New York, NY 10023-4940, USA

Haas, Eddie (Athlete, Baseball Player, Coach)
8314 Alpena Way
Louisville, KY 40242-2502, USA

Haas, Ernest (Photographer)
853 7th Ave
New York, NY 10019, USA

Haas, Ernst (Photographer)
853 7th Ave Apt lOB
New York, NY 10019-5222, USA

Haas, Hunter (Athlete, Golfer)
4078 Lively Ln
Dallas, TX 75220-1825, USA

Haas, Jay (Athlete, Golfer)
4 Tuscany Ct
Greer, SC 29650-4021, USA

Haas, Jerry (Race Car Driver)
Jerry Haas Motorsports
350 Haas Lane
Fenton, MO 63025, USA

Haas, Lucas (Actor)
Lighthouse
409 N Camden Dr #202
Beverly Hills, CA 90210, USA

Haas, Lukas (Actor)
c/o Jason Weinberg *Untitled Entertainment (LA)*
350 S. Beverly Dr #200
Beverly Hills, CA 90212, USA

Haas, Moose (Athlete, Baseball Player)
4351 E Lariat Ln
Phoenix, AZ 85050-8905, USA

Haas, Rachel (Stylist)
c/o Staff Member *Apostrophe (NY)*
527 W 29th St
New York, NY 10001, USA

Haas, Richard J (Artist)
29 Overcliff St
Yonders, NY 10705-1418, USA

Haas, Robert D (Business Person)
Levi Strauss Assoc
1155 Battery St
San Francisco, CA 94111, USA

Haas, Thomas (Tommy) (Tennis Player)
TC Weiden am Postkeller
Schmiritzer Weg
Weiden 92637, GERMANY

Haas, Waltraud
Kuniglberggasse 45
Vienna, AUSTRIA A-1130

Haase, Andy (Athlete, Football Player)
1508 Bon Homme Richard Dr
Fort Collins, CO 80526, USA

Haavelmo, Trygve (Nobel Prize Laureate)
University of Oslo Box 1095
Blindern N-0317, Norway

Haayer, Adam (Athlete, Football Player)
2362 Stonecrest Path NW
Prior Lake, MN 55372, USA

Habel, Karl (Misc, Scientist)
Reading Institute of Rehabilitation
RR 1 Box 252
Reading, PA 19607, USA

Habel, Sarah (Actor)
c/o Everly Lee *Agency for the Performing Arts (APA-LA)*
405 S Beverly Dr
Suite 500
Beverly Hills, CA 90212-4425, USA

Haber, Norman (Inventor)
Haber Inc
470 Main Road
Towaco, NJ 07082, USA

Habermann, Eva
Kuckuchsberg 9
Lutiansee, GERMANY D-22952

Habermas, Jurgen (Misc)
Ringstr 8B
Stamberg 82319, GERMANY

Habib, Brian (Athlete, Football Player)
17235 Sangallo Ln
San Diego, CA 92127, USA

Habib, Munir (Astronaut, Misc)
Potchta Kosmonavtov
Moskovskoi Oblasti
Syvisdny Goroduk 141160, RUSSIA

Habibie, Baharuddin Jusuf (President)
President's Office
15 Jalan Merdeka Utara
Jakarta, INDONESIA

Habiger, Eugene E (Gene) (General)
Energy Department
Security Ops 1000 Independence NW
Washington, DC 20585, USA

Habraken, Nicolaas J (Architect)
63 Wildemislaan
Apeldoom 7313 BD, NETHERLAND

Habscheid, Marc (Athlete, Hockey Player)
4 Sussex Rd
Winchester, MA 01890, USA

Habyan, John (Athlete, Baseball Player)
4 Dorfer Ln
Nesconset, NY 11767-1067, USA

Hachette, Jean-Louis (Publisher)
Hachette Livre
83 Ave Marceau
Paris 75116, FRANCE

Hachten, Bill (Athlete, Football Player)
6205 Mineral Point Rd Apt 210
Madison, WI 53705-4577, USA

Hachten, William (Athlete, Football Player)
6205 Mineral Point Rd
Apt 210
Madison, WI 53705, USA

Hack, Olivia (Actor)
c/o Bonnie Ventis *Clear Talent Group (LA)*
10950 Ventura Blvd
Studio City, CA 91604, USA

Hack, Shelley (Actor, Model)
1208 Georgina
Santa Monica, CA 90402, USA

Hackbart, Dale (Athlete, Football Player)
2541 Cowley Dr
Lafayette, CO 80026, USA

Hacker, Carol (Stylist)
2534 Plk St
San Francisco, CA 94109, USA

Hacker, Eric (Athlete, Baseball Player)
526 Shellv Ct
Duncanville, TX 75137-4128, USA

Hacker, Rich (Athlete, Baseball Player)
2900 18th Fairway Dr
Belleville, IL 62220-4840, USA

Hackerman, Norman (Scientist)
5842 Westslope Dr
Austin, TX 78731-3633, USA

Hackett, Dino (Athlete, Football Player)
1152 Kearns Hackett Rd
Pleasant Garden, NC 27313, USA

Hackett, D.J. (Athlete, Football Player)
6510 S Delmar Pl
Gilbert, AZ 85298-4061, USA

Hackett, Grant (Swimmer)
PO Box 940
Dickson, ACT 2602, AUSTRALIA

Hackett, Jeff (Athlete, Hockey Player)
c/o Staff Member *Colorado Avalanche*
Pepsi Center
1000 Chopper Cir
Denver, CO 80204, USA

Hackett, Joey (Athlete, Football Player)
1147 Kearns Hackett Rd
Pleasant Garden, NC 27313, USA

Hackett, Martha (Actor)
Vaughn D Hart
8899 Beverly Blvd #815
Los Angeles, CA 90048, USA

Hackett, Paul (Politician)
Hackett for US Senate
PO Box 43281
Cincinnati, OH 45243, USA

Hackett, Rudy (Athlete, Baseball Player)
10330 Downey Ave
Unit 30
Downey, CA 9e241-5914, USA

Hackett, Ryan (Race Car Driver)
J&R Supply Corp.
4380 Hackett Pl.
White Plains, MD 20695-3859, USA

Hackford, Taylor (Director, Producer, Writer)
c/o Stan Rosenfield *Stan Rosenfield & Associates*
2029 Century Park E
Suite 1190
Los Angeles, CA 90067, USA

Hackl, Georg (Athlete)
Caftehaus Soamatl Ramsauerstr 100
Berchtesgaden-Engedey 83471, GERMANY

Hackman, Gene (Actor)
c/o Susan Madore *Guttman Associates*
118 S Beverly Dr
Suite 201
Beverly Hills, CA 90212, USA

Hackman, Luther (Athlete, Baseball Player)
1406 12th Ave N
Apt 16G
Columbus, MS 39701-3602, USA

Hackney, David (Artist)
19-B Buckingham Avenue
Slough Berks, England SLI 4QB, USA

Hackney, Lisa (Basketball Player, Golfer)
c/o Staff Member *Signature Sports Group*
4150 Olson Memorial Hey
Suite 110
Minneapolis, MN 55422, USA

Hackney, Roderick P (Architect)
Saint Peter's House
Windmill St Macclesfield
Cheshire SK11 7HS, UNITED KINGDOM (UK)

Hackwith, Scott (Music Group, Musician, Songwriter, Writer)
Overland Productions
156 W 56th St #500
New York, NY 10019, USA

Hadas, Rachel C (Educator, Writer)
Faculty of Art & Sciences - Newark, Department of English
360 Dr. Martin Luther King Jr. Blvd.
520 Hill Hail
Newark, NJ 07102-1801, USA

Haddad, Drew (Athlete, Football Player)
2597 Wakefield Ln
Westlake, OH 44145-3838, USA

Haddix, Margaret (Writer)
c/o Joshua Adams *Adams Literary*
7845 Colony Rd
C4 #215
Charlotte, NC 28226, USA

Haddix, Michael (Athlete, Football Player)
614 Fox Run Rd
Sewell, NJ 08080-4254, USA

Haddix, Wayne (Athlete, Football Player)
8117 S Pole CvDr
Memphis, TN 38125-4610, USA

Haddock, Karen (Race Car Driver)
Haddock Racing
PO Box 2455
2811 Ocean Hwy.
Shallote, NC 28459, USA

Haddock, Sherry (Stylist)
115 E 9th St
#5-G
New York, NY 10003, USA

Haddon, Dayle (Actor, Model)
Hyperion Books
114 5th Ave
New York, NY 10011, USA

Haddon, Lawrence (Actor)
14950 Sutton St
Sherman Oaks, CA 91403, USA

Haddon, Lloyd (Athlete, Hockey Player)
16806 94 Ave NW
Edmonton, AB T5R 5L5, Canada

Haden, Charles E (Charlie) (Composer, Music Group, Musician)
Merlin Co
17609 Ventura Blvd #212
Encino, CA 91316, USA

Haden, Nate (Actor)
c/o Staff Member *Diverse Talent Group*
9911 W Pico Blvd Ste 340W
Los Angeles, CA 90035, USA

Haden, Nick (Athlete, Football Player)
114 Julianna Dr
Coraopolis, PA 15108, USA

Haden, Patrick C (Pat) (Athlete, Football Player, Sportscaster)
1525 Wilson Ave
San Marino, CA 91108, USA

Haden Church, Thomas (Actor)
2366 Station C Rd
Vanderpool, TX 78885, USA

Hader, Bill (Actor)
c/o Naomi Odenkirk *Odenkirk Provissiero Entertainment*
Raleigh Studios
650 N. Bronson Ave, Bldg. B145
Los Angeles, CA 90004, USA

Hadfield, Chris A (Astronaut)
638 Shorewood Dr
Kemah, TX 77565, USA

Hadfield, Chris Colonel
638 Shorewood Dr
Seabrook, TX 77586-4610, USA

Hadfield, Chris Colonel (Astronaut)
638 Shorewood Dr
Seabrook, TX 77586-4610, USA

Hadfield, Vic (Athlete, Hockey Player)
438-1011 Upper Middle Rd E
Oakville, ON L6H 5Z9, Canada

Hadid, Zaha (Architect)
Studio 9
10 Bowling Green Lane
London WC1R 0BD, UNITED KINGDOM (UK)

Hadl, John W (Athlete, Football Player)
University Of Kansas 1651 Drive
Naismith 105 Parrott Athletic Center
Lawrence, KS 66045-0001, USA

Hadlee, Richard J (Cricketer)
PO Box 29186
Christchurch, NEW ZEALAND

Hadley, Brett (Actor)
5070 Woodley Ave
Encino, CA 91436, USA

Hadley, Ron (Athlete, Football Player)
4533 131st Pl SW
Mukilteo, WA 98275, USA

Hadley, Tony (Music Group, Musician)
c/o Staff Member *Shout! Promotions*
P.O. Box 42
Manchester M46 0WX, UK

Hadnot, James (Athlete, Football Player)
5521 48th St
Apt 84
Lubbock TX, 79414

Hadnot, Rex (Athlete, Football Player)
2677 Center Court
Dr
Weston, FL 33332, USA

Haebler, Ingrid (Music Group, Musician)
Ibbs & Tillett
420-452 Edgware Road
London W2 1EG, UNITED KINGDOM (UK)

Haechen, Hartmut (Conductor)
Organisation Int'l Artistique
16 Ave F D Roosevelt
Paris 75008, FRANCE

Haefner, Ruby (Athlete, Baseball Player)
1436 Union Road
Apt 329
Gastonia, NC 28054-2310, USA

Haegele, Patricia (Publisher)
Good Housekeeping Magazine
959 8th Ave
New York, NY 10019, USA

Haegg, Gunder (Athlete, Track Athlete)
Swedish Olympic Committee
Idrottens Hus
Farsta 12387, SWEDEN

Haendel, Ida (Music Group, Musician)
Harlod Holt
31 Sinclair Road
London W14 0NS, UNITED KINGDOM (UK)

Haenel, Hal (Athlete, Olympic Athlete, Sailor)
3049 Landa St
Los Angeles, CA 90039-3011, USA

Haenicke, Diether H (Educator)
Western Michigan University
President's Office
Kalamazoo, MI 49008, USA

Hafen, Barney (Athlete, Football Player)
1125 Goldenrod Cir
Saint George, UT 84790, USA

Hafer, Fred D (Business Person)
GPU Inc
300 Madison Ave
Morristown, NJ 07960, USA

Haffner, Scott (Athlete, Basketball Player)
5e62 Sweetwater Dr
Noblesville, IN 46e62-7164, USA

Hafner, Dudley H (Misc)
140 Estrada Maya
Santa Fe, NM 87506, USA

Hafner, Travis (Athlete, Baseball Player)
32696 Lake Rd
Avon Laker, OH 44012-1646, USA

Hafstein, Johann (Prime Minister)
Sjalfstaedisflokkurinn Laufasvegi 46
Reykjavik, ICELAND

Hag, Sid (Actor)
Kathleen Schultz Associates Talent Agency
6442 Coldwater Canyon #206
Valley Glen, CA 91606, USA

Hagan, Cliff (Athlete, Basketball Player)
8839 Lakeside Cir
Vero Beach, FL 32963-4082, USA

Hagan, Derek (Football Player)
830 Madison St Apt 523
Hoboken, NJ 07030-6857, USA

Hagan, Glenn (Athlete, Basketball Player)
34 Roth St
Rochester, NY 14621-5320, USA

Hagan, Marianne (Actor)
c/o Scott Zimmerman *Evolution Entertainment (LA)*
901 N Highland Ave
Los Angeles, CA 90038, USA

Hagan, Molly (Actor)
c/o Staff Member *Kohner Agency, The*
9300 Wilshire Blvd
Suite 555
Beverly Hills, CA 90212, USA

Hagan, Sarah (Actor)
c/o Staff Member *Mark Robert Management*
2208 Patricia Ave
Los Angeles, CA 90064, USA

Hagar, Sammy (Musician, Songwriter)
c/o Irving Azoff *Azoff Music Management/ Front Line*
1100 Glendon Ave
Los Angeles, CA 90024, USA

Hagee, Michael W (General)
Commandant HqUSMC
2 Navy Annex
Washington, DC 20380, USA

Hagee, Michael W General (General)
1011 Homestead Dr
Fredericksburg, TX 78624-7347, USA

Hagee, Pastor John (Religious Leader)
John Hagee Ministries
P.O. Box 1400
San Antonio, TX 78295-1400, USA

Hagegard, Hakan (Opera Singer)
Gunnarsbyn
Edane 670 30, SWEDEN

Hagel, Chuck (Politician, Senator)
920 Towlston Rd
Me Lean, VA 22102-1036, USA

Hageman, Fred (Athlete, Football Player)
4608 Merion Ct
Lawrence, KS 66047, USA

Hagemeister, Charles C (General)
1908 Canterbury Court
Leavenworth, KS 66048-6525, USA

Hagen, Alexander
Mittelweg 58
Hamburg, GERMANY D-20149

Hagen, Cosma Shiva (Actor)
c/o Nicole Walter *Metro Public Relations*
6525 W Sunset Blvd
6th Floor
Hollywood, CA 90028, USA

Hagen, Halvor (Athlete, Football Player)
32 Algonquin Rd
Canton, MA 02021, USA

Hagen, Kevin (Athlete, Baseball Player)
24826 164th Ave SE
Covington, WA 98042-5232, USA

Hager, Bob
4001 Nebraska Ave. NW
Washington, DC 20016

Hager, Britt (Athlete, Football Player)
6200 Indian Canyon Dr
Austin, TX 78746-6352, USA

Hager, Kristen (Actor)
c/o Shelley Browning *Magnolia Entertainment (LA)*
9595 Wilshire Blvd
Suite 601
Beverly Hills, CA 90212, USA

Hager, Robert (Correspondent)
NBC-TV
News Dept 4001 Nebraska Ave NW
Washington, DC 20016, USA

Hagerstrom, Anastasia (Stylist)
420 Argonaut Ave
San Francisco, CA 94134, USA

Hager Twins
PO Box 1516
Champaign, IL 61824

Hagerty, Julie (Actor)
c/o Steven Levy *Framework Entertainment (LA)*
9057 Nemo St
Suite C
West Hollywood, CA 90069, USA

Hagerty, Michael (Actor)

Haggans, Clark (Athlete, Football Player)
3165 S Alma School Rd Ste 29-225
Chandler, AZ 85248-3760, USA

Haggard, Merle (Musician, Songwriter)
7691/7733/7735/7737 Silver Bridge Rd
Palo Cedro, CA 96073, USA

Hagge, Marlene (Athlete, Golfer)
PO Box 2212
Palm Desert, CA 92261-2212, USA

Haggerty, Dan (Actor)
C/O Doc Cleland
2134 62nd Pl SE
Auburn, WA 98092, USA

Haggerty, Jonathan (Athlete, Football Player)
c/o Staff Member *Synergy Sports, Inc.*
14001 Dallas Pkwy
Suite 1200
Dallas, TX 75240, USA

Haggerty, Sean (Athlete, Hockey Player)
200 Highland Rd
Rye, NY 10580-1883

Haggerty, Steve (Athlete, Football Player)
3313 E Costilla Ave
Centennial, CO 80122, USA

Haggerty, Tim (Cartoonist)
United Feature Syndicate
200 Madison Ave
New York, NY 10016, USA

Haggins, Odell (Athlete, Football Player)
8125 Blenheim Ln
Tallahassee, FL 32312-6803, USA

Haggins, Raymond (Athlete, Baseball Player)
2825 E Lynchburg Ct
Montgomery, AL 36116-3335, USA

Haggis, Paul (Director, Producer, Writer)
c/o Staff Member *Paul Haggis Productions*
9200 Sunset Blvd #820
Los Angeles, CA 90069, USA

Hagin, Wayne (Commentator)
2236 Thistle Ridge Cir
Highlands Ranch, CO 80126-2638, USA

Hagins, Isaac (Ike) (Athlete, Football Player)
9008 Tudor Dr Apt 105
Tampa, FL 33615-3749, USA

Hagler, Marvin (Boxer)
c/o Valerie Swett *Deutsch Williams*
One Design Center Pl Ste 600
Boston, MA 02210

Hagman, Matti (Athlete, Hockey Player)
Finnish Hockey Hall of Fame
PO Box 487
Tampere F-33101, Finland

Hagman, Niklas (Athlete, Hockey Player)
Thompson, Dorfman, Sweatman
PO Box 639 Stn Main
Attn: Donald Baizley
Winnipeg, MB R3C 2K6, Canada

Hagn, Johanna (Athlete)
ASG Elsdorf
Behrgasse 6
Elsdorf 50198, GERMANY

Hagner, Meredith (Actor)
c/o James Suskin *James Suskin Management*
2 Charlton St Ste 5K
New York, NY 10014, USA

Hagon, Garrick (Actor)
c/o Staff Member *Coolwaters Productions*
10061 Riverside Dr.
Box 531
Toluca Lake, CA 91602, USA

Hagood, Oksana (Stylist)
c/o Staff Member *Help Me Rhonda*
541 10th St NW #294
Atlanta, GA 30318, USA

Hague, William MP (Government Official)
House of Commons
Westminster
London SW1A 0AA, UNITED KINGDOM (UK)

Hahn, Beatrice H (Biologist)
University of Alabama
Medical School Microbiology Dept
Bermingham, AL 35294, USA

Hahn, Don (Athlete, Baseball Player)
1046 Boise Dr
Campbell, CA 95008-0306, USA

Hahn, Erwin L (Physicist)
69 Stevenson Ave
Berkeley, CA 94708, USA

Hahn, Frank H (Economist)
61 Adams Road
Cambridge CB3 9AD, UNITED KINGDOM (UK)

Hahn, Hilary (Music Group, Musician)
Hans Ulrich Schmid
Postfach 1617
Hanover 30016, GERMANY

Hahn, James (Politician)
Mayor's Office
City Hall 200 N Spring St
Los Angeles, CA 90012, USA

Hahn, Joseph (Music Group)
Artist Group International
9560 Wilshire Blvd #400
Beverly Hills, CA 90212, USA

Hahn, Kathryn (Actor)
c/o Lindsey Porter *Gersh (NY)*
41 Madison Ave
New York, NY 10010, USA

Hahn, Mary Downing (Writer)
c/o Staff Member *Clarion Books*
215 Park Ave South
New York, NY 10013, USA

Hai, Do Thi (Actor)
c/o Barry McPherson *Agency for the Performing Arts (APA-LA)*
405 S Beverly Dr
Suite 500
Beverly Hills, CA 90212-4425, USA

Haid, Charles (Athlete, Baseball Player)
4376 Forman Ave
Toluca Lake, CA 91602, USA

Haidee, Findlay-Levin (Stylist)
c/o Staff Member *Creative Exchange Agency*
53 Gansevoort St
3rd Floor
New York, NY 10014, USA

Haig, Sid (Actor)
c/o Staff Member *Kathleen Schultz Associates Talent Agency*
6442 Coldwater Canyon
Suite 117
North Hollywood, CA 91606-1137, USA

Haigh, Denise (Athlete, Golfer)
198 Barbados Dr
Jupiter, FL 33458, USA

Haight, Mike (Athlete, Football Player)
105 Windsor Rd
IA, North Liberty 52317-8009, USA

Haignere, Jean-Pierre (Misc)
CNES
2Place Maurice Quentin
Paris Cedeux 75039, FRANCE

Haik, Mac (Athlete, Football Player)
11738 Wood Ln
Houston, TX 77024, USA

Hailer, Bill (Athlete, Baseball Player)
RR 2 Box 82C
Brownstow, IL 62418-9630, USA

Hailey, Ken (Athlete, Football Player)
241 Festival Dr
Oceanside, CA 92057-5135, USA

Hailey, Leisha (Actor, Musician, Songwriter)
c/o Geordie Frey *GEF Entertainment*
122 N Clark Dr
Suite 401
Los Angeles, CA 90048, USA

Hailey, Oliver
11747 Canton Pl.
Studio City, CA 91604

Haill, Gary H (Athlete, Football Player)
6207 Surflanding Ln
Huntington Beach, CA 92648, USA

Hailston, Earl B (General)
Commanding General
Marine Corps Forces Pacific
Camp H M Smith, HI 96861, USA

Haimovitz, Matt (Music Group, Musician)
Columbia Artists Mgmt Inc
165 W 57th St
New York, NY 10019, USA

Haine-Daniels, Audrey (Athlete, Baseball Player, Commentator)
618 Revere Dr
Bay Village, OH 44140-1971, USA

Haines, Byron (Athlete, Football Player)
16625 1st Ave S
Apt 202
Burien, WA 98148, USA

Haines, Emily (Musician)
c/o Staff Member *Paradigm (Monterey)*
404 W Franklin St
Monterey, CA 93940, USA

Haines, John (Athlete, Football Player)
4000 Chamisa Dr
Austin, TX 78730, USA

Haines, Kris (Athlete, Football Player)
2828 N Talman Ave Unit K
Chicago, IL 60618-7829, USA

Haines, Lee M (Religious Leader)
Wesleyan Church
PO Box 50434
Indianapolis, IN 46250, USA

Haines, Martha (Athlete, Baseball Player, Commentator)
144 Langshire Ct
Florence, KY 41042-3542, USA

Haines, Randa (Director)
1429 Avon Park Terrace
Los Angeles, CA 90026, USA

Hainsev, Ron (Athlete, Hockey Player)
2154 Wynnton Pt
Duluth, GA 30097-5007

Hainsey, Ron (Athlete, Hockey Player)
Olympic Sports Management
9 Alden Rd
Wellesley, MA 02481-6702, USA

Hair, Harlod (Athlete, Baseball Player)
1645 W 20th Street
Jacksonville, FL 32209-4817, USA

Hair, Harold (Athlete, Baseball Player)
1645 W 20th St
Jacksonville, FL 32209-4817, USA

Haire, John E (Business Person)
Highland Capital Partners
92 Hayden Ave
Lexington, MA 02421, USA

Hairi, Gisue (Architect)
Hairi & Hairi
18 E 12th St
New York, NY 10003, USA

Hairi, Moigan (Architect)
Hairi & Hairi
18 E 12th St
New York, NY 10003, USA

Hairston, Alan (Athlete, Basketball Player)
6120 South 125th St
Seattle, WA 98178-3546, USA

Hairston, Carl (Athlete, Football Player)
3514 Spyglass Hill Dr
Green Bay, WI 54311-6122, USA

Hairston, Harold (Baseball Player)
Homestead Grays
542 E 107th St
Cleveland, OH 44108-1432, USA

Hairston, John (Johnny) (Athlete, Baseball Player)
4226 NE 22nd Ave
Portland, OR 97211-5757, USA

Hairston, Scott (Athlete, Baseball Player)
4658 S Banning Dr
Gilbert, AZ 85297-5257, USA

Hairston, Stacey (Athlete, Football Player)
1928 Creeksedge Dr
Columbus, OH 43209-3348, USA

Hairston Jr, Jerry (Athlete, Baseball Player)
2205 Warwick Wav Ste 200
Marriottsville, MD 21104-1632, USA

Hairston Sr, Jerry (Athlete, Baseball Player)
7831 W Peace Pipe Rd
Tucson, AZ 85743-5207, USA

Haise, Fred W
14316 FM 2354 Rd
Baytown, TX 77520, USA

Haise, Fred W Jr (Astronaut, Aviator)
PO Box 5765
Pasadena, TX 77508-5765, USA

Haise, Jim (Baseball Player)
Washington Senators
2425 Albion Ave
Orlando, FL 32833 3981, USA

Haislett, Nicole (Athlete, Olympic Athlete, Swimmer)
275 N Poplar St
Massapequa, NY 11758-25S1, USA

Haislip, Marcus (Basketball Player)
Milwaukee Bucks
Bradley Center 1001 N 4th St
Milwaukee, WI 53203, USA

Haitink, Bernard J H (Conductor)
Harold Holt
31 Sinclair Road
London W14 0NS, UNITED KINGDOM (UK)

Hajak, Ron
17420 Ventura Blvd. #4
Encino, CA 91316

Hajdu, Richard (Athlete, Hockey Player)
1236 Janet Pl
Duncan, BC V9L5R6, Canada

Hajek, Andreas (Athlete)
Weissbundenweg 18
Halle/Saale 06128, GERMANY

Hajek, Dave (Athlete, Baseball Player)
5190 Bitterweed Ln
Colorado Springs, CO 80917-1302, USA

Ha Jin (Writer)
Emory University
English Dept
Atlanta, GA 30332, USA

Haji-Sheikh, Ali (Athlete, Football Player)
550 S Spinningwheel Ln
Bloomfield Township, MI 48304, USA

Hajt, Bill (Athlete, Hockey Player)
215 Old Lyme Dr
Buffalo, NY 14221-2208

Hajt, Chris (Athlete, Hockey Player)
12 Eugene Dr
Guelph, ON NlL 1P6, Canada

Hakim, Az-Zahir (Athlete, Football Player)
210 Canaan Glen Way SW
Atlanta, GA 30331, USA

Hakkinen, Jay (Athlete, Biathlete, Olympic Athlete)
PO Box 701
Kasilof, AK 99610-0701, USA

Hakkinen, Mikka (Race Car Driver)
McLaren International
Albert Dr
Woking
Surrey GU21 5JY, UNITED KINGDOM (UK)

Halama, John (Athlete, Baseball Player)
7615 Fort Hamilton Pkwy
Brooklyn, NY 11228-2325, USA

Haland, Bjoro
Sor-Audnedal, NORWAY N-4520

Halas, John (Animator)
Educational Film Center
5-7 Kean St
London WC2B 4AT, UNITED KINGDOM (UK)

Halbert, Charles (Athlete, Basketball Player)
100 E Whidbey Ave Apt 35
Oak Harbor, WA 98277-2579, USA

Halbert, David (Business Person)
Advance PCS
750 W John Carpenter Fwy #1200
Irving, TX 75039-2507

Halbreich, Kathy (Director, Misc)
Walker Art Center
725 Vineland Place
Minneapolis, MN 55403, USA

Haldeman, Charles (Ed) (Financier)
Putnam Investments
1 Post Office Square
Boston, MA 02109, USA

Haldeman, Tim (Actor)
4257 Lincoln Ave
Culver City, CA 90232, USA

Haldorson, Burdette (Athlete, Basketball Player, Olympic Athlete)
2868 Stonewall Hts
Colorado Springs, CO 80909-1735, USA

Hale, Alan (Astronomer)
Southwest Space Research Institute
15 E Spur Road
Cloudcraft, NM 88317, USA

Hale, Alan (Scientist)
89116 Springs Canyon Rd
Cloudcroft, NM 88317-9404, USA

Hale, Alan Spencer
5476 St. Paul Rd
Morristown, NJ 07813

Hale, Barbara (Actor)
PO Box 6061-261
Sherman Oaks, CA 91413, USA

Hale, Bob (Athlete, Baseball Player)
616 Overhill Ave
Park Ridge, IL 600683455, USA

Hale, Chip (Athlete, Baseball Player)
190 Driftwood Ct
Aptos, CA 95003, USA

Hale, Chris (Athlete, Football Player)
327 E El Sur St
Monrovia, CA 91016, USA

Hale, Dave (Athlete, Football Player)
1204 S Maple St Apt B
Ottawa, KS 67460, 66067-3460

Hale, David (Athlete, Hockey Player)
3470 Cortina Dr
Colorado Springs, CO 80918-1814

Hale, Demarlo (Athlete, Baseball Player)
4560 Woodlands Village Dr
Orlando, FL 32835-2717, USA

Hale, Georgina (Actor)
74A St John's Wood High St
London NW8, UNITED KINGDOM (UK)

Hale, Jean (Actor)
715 Napoli Dr
Pacific Palisades, CA 90272, USA

Hale, John (Athlete, Baseball Player)
2200 Pine St
Bakersfield, CA 93301-3429, USA

Hale, Larry (Athlete, Hockey Player)
795 Chase Ave
Penticton, BC V2A 2H8, Canada

Hale, Lucy (Actor)
c/o Elissa Leeds-Fickman *Reel Talent Management*
P.O. Box 491035
Los Angeles, CA 90049, USA

Hale, walter"chip" (Athlete, Baseball Player)
7555 E Sabino Vista Dr
Tucson, AZ 85750-2710, USA

Haley, Charles J (Athlete, Football Player)
3787 Royal Cove Dr
Dallas, TX 75229, USA

Haley, Dick (Athlete, Football Player)
5248 Shoreline Cir
Sanford, FL 32771, USA

Haley, Jack (Athlete, Basketball Player)
5e9 Ocean Ave
Seal Beach, CA 9e74e-6le6, USA

Haley, Jackie Earle (Actor)
c/o Leslie Allan-Rice *Leslie Allan-Rice Management*
1007 Maybrook Dr
Beverly Hills, CA 90210, USA

Haley, Jermaine (Athlete, Football Player)
16806 Heather Knolls Pl
Hamilton, VA 20158, USA

Haley, Katie (Athlete, Golfer)
24312 138th Ave SE
Kent, WA 98042, USA

Haley, Len (Athlete, Hockey Player)
724 Balmer Cres
Creston, BC V0B 1G0, Canada

Haley, Maria (Financier)
Arkansas Commision of Economic Development
One Capitol Mall
Little Rock, AR 72201, USA

Haley, Nikki (Governor, Politician)
Office of the Governor
PO box 11369
Columbia, SC 29211, USA

Halffter, Cristobal J (Composer, Conductor)
Jurgen Erlebach
Grillparsestr 24
Hamburg 22085, GERMANY

Halford, Rob (Music Group)
International Creative Mgmt
40 W 57th St #1800
New York, NY 10019, USA

Halfpenny, Jill (Actor)
c/o Staff Member *Talking Heads*
2-4 Noel St
London W1F 8GB, UNITED KINGDOM

Halfvarson, Eric (Opera Singer)
Munro Artist Mgmt
786 Darthmouth St
South Darthmouth, MA 02748, USA

Hali, Tamba (Athlete, Football Player)
13227 Outlook Dr
Leawood, KS 66209, USA

Haliburton, Ronnie (Athlete, Football Player)
3460 Lake Arthur Dr
Port Arthur, TX 77642-7604, USA

Halicki, Ed (Athlete, Baseball Player)
19605 Paddlewheel Ln
Reno, NV 89521-7850, USA

Halimon, Shaler (Athlete, Basketball Player)
9535 SW Millen Dr
Portland, OR 97224-6510, USA

Halkidis, Bob (Athlete, Hockey Player)
Hal kid is Hockey Training
3419 Lake Park Rd
Indian Trail, NC 28079-6561

Halko, Steve (Athlete, Hockey Player)
124 Crystlewood Ct
Morrisville, NC 27560-7569

Hall, Adam (Athlete, Hockey Player)
1230 Fletcher Ave
Kalamazoo, MI 49006-2432

Hall, Ahmard (Athlete, Football Player)
4541 Winfield Dr
Nashville, TN 37211, USA

Hall, Alaina Reed (Actor)
10636 Rathburn
Northridge, CA 91326, USA

Hall, Albert (Athlete, Baseball Player)
1628 Spaulding Ishkooda Rd
Birmingham, AL 35211-5520, USA

Hall, Amy (Stylist)
c/o Staff Member *Margaret Maldonado Agency*
1100 Glendon #1000
Los Angeles, CA 90024, USA

Hall, Andy (Athlete, Football Player)
Cardinal Gibbons High School 4601
Bayview Dr
Fort Lauderdale, FL 33308, USA

Hall, Anthony Michael (Actor)
c/o Staff Member *Morra Brezner Steinberg & Tenenbaum (MBST) Entertainment*
345 N Maple Dr
Suite 200
Beverly Hills, CA 90210, USA

Hall, Arsenio (Actor, Musician, Television Host)
c/o Staff Member *Career Management*
9229 W Sunset Blvd #720
Los Angeles, CA 90069, USA

Hall, Art (Athlete, Football Player)
Cardinal Gibbons High School
4601 Bayview Dr
Fort Lauderdale, FL 33308, USA

Hall, Barbara (Producer, Writer)
c/o Chris Harbert *Creative Artists Agency (CAA-LA)*
2000 Ave Of The Stars
Los Angeles, CA 90067, USA

Hall, Bill (Athlete, Baseball Player)
4935 E Berneil Dr
Paradise Valley, AZ 85253-1521, USA

Hall, Bobby
20122 Hall Dr.
Brooksville, FL 34601

Hall, Brett A. (Athlete, Hockey Player)
3520 Eden Way
Stillwater, MN 55082, USA

Hall, Bridget (Model)
I M G Models
304 Park Ave S #1200
New York, NY 10010, USA

Hall, Bruce Michael (Actor)
c/o Jerry Shandrew *Shandrew Public Relations*
1050 S Stanley Ave
Los Angeles, CA 90019-6634, USA

Hall, Bug (Actor)
c/o Laina Cohn *Laina Cohn Management*
15066 Sutton St
Sherman Oaks, CA 91403, USA

Hall, Chad (Athlete, Football Player)
c/o Chad Speck *Allegiant Athletic Agency*
35 Market Sq
Suite 201
Knoxville, TN 37902, USA

Hall, Charles (Inventor)
Basic Designs
5815 Bennett Valley Road
Santa Rosa, CA 95404-8565, USA

Hall, Charlie (Football Player)
602 Lavaca St
Yoakum, TX 77995-4136, USA

Hall, Cory (Athlete, Football Player)
1202 E Swift Ave
Fresno, GA 93704-3836, USA

Hall, Courtney (Athlete, Football Player)
19912 Enslow Dr
Carson, CA 90746, USA

Hall, Dana (Athlete, Football Player)
9730 Diamond St
Yucaipa, CA 92399, USA

Hall, Dante (Athlete, Football Player)
13314 Barbstone Dr
Houston, TX 77044, USA

Hall, Dante (Athlete)
c/o Staff Member *Kansas City Chiefs*
1 Arrowhead Dr
Kansas City, MO 64129, USA

Hall, Darren (Athlete, Baseball Player)
3508 Castlewood Ct
Flower Mound, TX 75022-7814, USA

Hall, Darryl (Athlete, Football Player)
21013 E Crestline Cir
Centennial, CO 80015, USA

Hall, Daryl (Music Group, Songwriter)
c/o Staff Member *Creative Artists Agency (CAA-LA)*
2000 Ave Of The Stars
Los Angeles, CA 90067, USA

Hall, Deangelo (Athlete, Football Player)
5553 Legends Dr
Braselton, GA 30517, USA

Hall, Dean Scott (Race Car Driver)
PO Box 2589
Olympic Valley, CA 96146, USA

Hall, Debi (Actor)
c/o Linda McAlister *Linda McAlister Talent*
100 Oak Ln
Waxahachie, TX 75167-8412, USA

Hall, Deidre (Actor)
1223 Wilshire Blvd #825
Santa Monica, CA 90403, USA

Hall, Del (Athlete, Hockey Player)
1057 E 6160 S
Salt Lake City, UT 84121-6712

Hall, Delores (Actor, Music Group)
Agency for Performing Arts
485 Madison Ave
New York, NY 10022, USA

Hall, Delton (Athlete, Football Player)
9 Mystic Ct
Greensboro, NC 27406, USA

Hall, Dick (Athlete, Baseball Player)
403 Plumbridge Ct
Unit 403
Lutherville Timonium, MD 21093-8275, USA

Hall, Dino (Football Player)
355 Chestnut Neck Rd
Port Republic, NJ 08241-9703, USA

Hall, Donald (Writer)
Eagle Point Farm
Eagle Pond Farm Eagle Pond Road
Wilmot, NH 03287, USA

Hall, Donald J (Business Person)
Hallmark Cards
2501 McGee St
Kansas City, MO 64108, USA

Hall, Donald R (Athlete, Football Player)
355 Chestnut Neck Rd
Port Republic, NJ 08241, USA

Hall, Drew (Athlete, Baseball Player)
4107 Spreading Oaks Ct
Waxhaw, NC 28173-7814, USA

Hall, Edward T (Doctor, Writer)
8 Calle Jacinta
Santa Fe, NM 87508, USA

Hall, Ervin (Erv) (Athlete, Track Athlete)
Citicorp Mortgage
670 Mason Ridge Center Dr
Saint Louis, MO 63141, USA

Hall, Fawn (Misc)
9008 Norma Pl
West Hollywood, CA 90069-4832, USA

Hall, Galen (Coach, Football Coach, Football Player)
Pennsylvania State University
200 Presidents Dr
State College, PA 16803-1802, USA

Hall, Gary C (Engineer)
PO Box 715
Rosamond, CA 93560, USA

Hall, Glenn H (Athlete, Hockey Player)
PO Box 2483 Stn Main
Stony Plain, AB T7Z 1X9, Canada

Hall, Greff Kaye (Swimmer)
906 3rd St
Mukilteo, WA 98275, USA

Hall, Irma P. (Actor)
3202 O'Bannon Dr
Dallas, TX 75224, USA

Hall, James E (Jim) (Race Car Driver)
RR 7 Box 640
Midland, TX 79706, USA

Hall, James S (Jim) (Music Group, Musician)
Jazz Tree
211 Thompson St #LD
New York, NY 10012, USA

Hall, Jeff (Athlete, Football Player)
2201 Lake Ave
Apt 205
Knoxville, TN 37916, USA

Hall, Jerry (Doctor, Misc)
George Washington University
Med Center 2300 St NW
Washington, DC 20037, USA

Hall, Jerry (Actor, Model)
c/o Staff Member *TESS Management*
9-10 Market Pl
4th Floor
London W1W 8AQ, UK

Hall, Jimmie (Athlete, Baseball Player)
8622 Carter Grove Dr
Elm City, NC 27822-7926, USA

Hall, Joe (Athlete, Baseball Player)
961 Peachers Mill Rd
Clarksville, TN 37042-7629, USA

Hall, Joe B (Basketball Player, Coach)
Central Bank & Trust Co
300 W Vine St
Lexington, KY 40507, USA

Hall, John L. (Nobel Prize Laureate)
University Of Colorado JILA
3748 Davidson Pl
Boulder, CO 80305-5533, USA

Hall, Josh (Athlete, Baseball Player)
3512 Hawkins Mill Rd
Lynchburg, VA 24503-4923, USA

Hall, Ken (Football Player)
PO Box 567
Fredericksburg, TX 78624-0567, USA

Hall, Kristen (Musician)
c/o Staff Member *Gail Gellman Management*
23852 Pacific Coast Highway
Malibu, CA 90265, USA

Hall, Lani (Music Group)
31930 Pacific Coast Highway
Malibu, CA 90265, USA

Hall, Lanny (Educator)
Hardin-Simmons University
President's Office
Abilene, TX 79698, USA

Hall, Lemanski (Athlete, Football Player)
2336 Wimbledon Cir
Franklin, TN 37069, USA

Hall, Leon (Athlete, Football Player)
2343 Clydes Xing
Cincinnati, OH 45244-2800, USA

Hall, Lloyd M Jr (Religious Leader)
Congregation Christian Church Assn
PO Box 1620
Oak Creek, MI 53154, USA

Hall, L Parker (Athlete, Football Player)
4712 Cole Rd
Memphis, TN 38117, USA

Hall, Michael C (Actor, Producer)
c/o Jon Rubinstein *Authentic Talent and Literary Management*
45 Main St
Suite 1004
Brooklyn, NY 11201, USA

Hall, Monty
519 N. Arden Dr.
Beverly Hills, CA 90210

Hall, Murray (Athlete, Hockey Player)
21-1357 ontario st
Burlington, ON L7S 1E9, Canada

Hall, Nigel J (Artist)
11 Kensington Park Gardens
London W11 3HD, UNITED KINGDOM
(UK)

Hall, Peter R F (Director)
Peter Hall Co
18 Exeter St
London WC2E 7DU, UNITED KINGDOM
(UK)

Hall, Philip Baker (Actor)

Hall, Pooch (Actor)
c/o Mark Turner *Abrams Artists Agency (NY)*
9200 Sunset Blvd
11th Floor
Los Angeles, CA 90069, USA

Hall, Randy (Athlete, Football Player)
P.O. Box 447
Genesee, ID 83832, USA

Hall, Reamy (Actor)
c/o Gloria Hinojosa *Amsel, Eisenstadt & Frazier Talent Agency (AEF)*
5055 Wilshire Blvd
Suite 860
Los Angeles, CA 90036-6108, USA

Hall, Rebecca (Actor)
c/o Staff Member *Julian Belfrage & Associates*
9 Argyll St
3rd Floor
London W1F 7TG, UK

Hall, Regina (Actor)
c/o Paul Young *Principato/Young Management*
9465 Wilshire Blvd
Suite 430
Beverly Hills, CA 90212, USA

Hall, Rhett (Athlete, Football Player)
15605 Oak Glen Ave
Morgan Hill, CA 95037-8804, USA

Hall, Robert David (Actor)
c/o Cynthia Snyder *Cynthia Snyder Public Relations*
5739 Colfax Ave
N Hollywood, CA 91601-1636, USA

Hall, Robert N (Inventor)
2315 Gurenson Lane
Niskayuna, NY 12309-5908, USA

Hall, Samuel (Sam) (Athlete, Swimmer)
5759 Wilcke Way
Dayton, OH 45459, USA

Hall, Shane (Race Car Driver)
Stegall Motorsports
515 Putnam Rd
Fountain Inn, SC 29644, USA

Hall, SheldonO (General)
7871 State Route 366
Russells Point, OH 43348-9531, USA

Hall, Sonny (Misc)
Transport Workers Union
80 W End Ave
New York, NY 10023, USA

Hall, Taylor (Athlete, Historian)
4833 Saratago Blvd
#276
Corpus Christi, TX 78413, USA

Hall, Toby (Athlete, Baseball Player)
5206 Avenue La Crosse
Lutz, FL 33558-2827, USA

Hall, Tom (Athlete, Football Player)
75 the Laurels
Enfield, CT 06082-2356, USA

Hall, Tom (Athlete, Baseball Player)
3592 Lillian St
Riverside, CA 92504-3609, USA

Hall, Tom T (Musician, Songwriter)
Tom T Hall Enterprises
PO Box 1246
Franklin, TN 37065, USA

Hall, Walter (Athlete, Golfer)
271 Orchard Park Dr
Advance, NC 27006-7481, USA

Hall, Willie (Athlete, Football Player)
717 S Hacienda St
Anaheim, CA 92804, USA

Hall, Windlan (Athlete, Football Player)
13609 Pleasant Ln
Burnsville, MN 55337, USA

Halla, Brian L (Business Person)
National Semiconductor
2900 Semiconductor Dr
Santa Clara, CA 95051, USA

Halladay, H Leroy (Roy) (Athlete, Baseball Player)
18509 Council Crest Dr
Odessa, FL 33556-5039, USA

Hallam, John
51 Lansdowne Gardens
London, ENGLAND SW8 2EL

Hall & Oates (Music Group)
c/o Jonathan Wolfson *Wolfson Public Relations*
22201 Ventura Blvd
Suite 207
Woodland Hills, CA 91364, USA

Hallberg, Gary (Athlete, Golfer)
12516 Ventana Mesa Cir
Castle Rock, CO 80108-9147, USA

Halldorson, Dan (Athlete, Golfer)
209 South Rd
Cambridge, IL 61238-1429, USA

Hallen, Bob (Athlete, Football Player)
7052 Rushmore Way
Painesville, OH 44077, USA

Haller, Alan (Athlete, Football Player)
1265 Lobelia Ln
Dewitt, MI 48820, USA

Haller, Bill (Baseball Player)
RR 2 Box 82C
Brownstown, IL 62418-9630, USA

Haller, Gordon (Athlete)
20514 E Caley Dr
Centennial, CO 80016, USA

Haller, Kevin (Athlete, Hockey Player)
c/o Staff Member *Hockey Ministries International*
1100 De La Gauchetiere St W
Unit 265 7
Montreal, QC H3B 2S2, Canada

Hallervorden, Dieter
Nurnberger Str. 33
Berlin, GERMANY D-10777

Hallet, Jim (Athlete, Golfer)
18 Oliver St
South Yarmouth, MA 02664, USA

Hall-Garmes, Ruth (Actor)
432 Alandele Ave
Los Angeles, CA 90036, USA

Halliburton, Jeff (Athlete, Basketball Player)
113 Wake Forest Dr
O'Fallon, MO 63368-3786, USA

Hallick, Tom
13900 Tahiti Way #108
Marina del Rey, CA 90292

Halliday, Nathan (Actor)
c/o Sharon Lane *Lane Management Group*
13017 Woodbridge St
Studio City, CA 91604, USA

Hallier, Lori (Actor)
c/o Richard Lucas *Lucas Talent Inc*
100 W. Pender St
Sun Tower, 7th Floor
Vancouver, BC V6B 1R8, Canada

Hallin, Mats (Athlete, Hockey Player)
c/o Staff Member *Chicago Blackhawks*
1901 W Madison St
Chicago, IL 60612, USA

Hallinan, Joseph T (Journalist)
Random House
1745 Broadway #B1
New York, NY 10019, USA

Hallion, Tom (Baseball Player)
4040 Ormond Rd
Louisville, KY 40207-2036, USA

Hallion, Tom (Athlete, Baseball Player)
4040 Ormond Rd
Louisville, KY 40207, USA

Hallisay, Brian (Actor)
c/o Justin Grey Stone *Untitled Entertainment (LA)*
350 S. Beverly Dr #200
Beverly Hills, CA 90212, USA

Hallisey, Caroline (Athlete, Olympic Athlete, Speed Skater)
44 New Zealand Rd Apt 26
Seabrook, NH 03874-4181, USA

Halliwell, Geri (Music Group)
c/o Gina Hoffman *Baker Winokur Ryder Public Relations (BWR-LA)*
9100 Wilshire Blvd
Suite 500, West Tower
Beverly Hills, CA 90212, USA

Hall Jr, Gary (Athlete, Olympic Athlete, Swimmer)
4335 N Meridian Ave
Miami Beach, FL 33140, USA

Hallman, Tom Jr (Journalist)
Portland Oregonian
Editorial Dept
1320 SW Broadway
Portland, OR 97201, USA

Hallman, Victoria (Actor)
2006 Lombardy Ave
Nashville, TN 37215, USA

Hallock, Ty (Athlete, Football Player)
3676 Hunters Way Dr SE
Ada, MI 49301, USA

Hall Sr, Gary (Athlete, Olympic Athlete, Swimmer)
The Race Club
151 Kahiki Dr
Tavernier, FL 33140, USA

Hallstrom, Lasse (Director)
c/o Tracey Jacobs *United Talent Agency (UTA)*
9336 Civic Center Dr
Beverly Hills, CA 90210, USA

Hallstrom, Ron (Athlete, Football Player)
P.O. Box 379
Woodruff, WI 54568, USA

Hallwachs, Hans-Peter
Lindenstr. 9a
Grunwald, GERMANY 83021

Hallworth, Nina & Clare (Stylist)
c/o Staff Member *Artists by Timothy Priano (CA)*
8447 Wilshire Blvd
#301
Beverly Hills, CA 90211, USA

Hallyday, Johnny (Actor, Music Group)
CC Productions
6 Rue Daubigny
Paris 75017, FRANCE

Halonen Tarja, Kaarina (President)
Presidential Palace
Pohjoisesplandi 1
Helsinki 17 00170, FINLAND

Halperin, Bertrand I (Physicist)
Harvard University
Physics Dept
Cambridge, MA 02138, USA

Halpern, Daniel (Writer)
9 Mercer St
Princeton, NJ 08540, USA

Halpern, Jack (Misc)
5801 S Dorchester Ave #4A
Chicago, IL 60637, USA

Halpern, James S (Judge)
US Tax Court
400 2nd St NW
Washington, DC 20217, USA

Halpern, Jeff (Athlete, Hockey Player)
9212 Sprinklewood Ln
Potomac, MD 20854, USA

Halpin, Brandan Dean (Actor)
c/o Dino May *Dino May Management*
6362 Hollywood Blvd #422
Hollywood, CA 90028-6323, USA

Halpin, Luke (Actor)
227 Caddy Rd
Rotonda West, FL 33947, USA

Halprin, Lawrence (Architect)
125 E Sir Francis Drake Blvd
Larkspur, CA 94939-1860, USA

Halsell, James D Colonel (Astronaut)
Nasa Johnson Space Center 2101 Nasa
Pkwy Attn Assist Dir for Airc
Houston, TX 77058-3696, USA

Halsell Jr, James D (Astronaut)
257 River Cove Rd
Huntsville, AL 35811-8010, USA

Halstead, Greg (Model, Reality TV Star)
c/o Anthony Embry *AE Entertainment Public Relations*
124 Evening Shade Dr
Charleston, SC 29414, USA

Halstead, Thomas (Stylist)
c/o Staff Member *Zenobia Agency Inc*
PO Box 909
Groveland, CA 95321, USA

Halsteadt, Dirck (Photographer)
204 Lisa Dr
Austin, TX 78733-2411, USA

Halter, Shane (Athlete, Baseball Player)
2701 W 140th St
Overland Park, KS 66224, USA

Halter, Shane (Athlete, Baseball Player)
2701 West 140th Street
Overland Park, KS 66224-3940, USA

Halterman, Aaron (Athlete, Football Player)
524 W Northlane Dr
Bloomington, IN 47404-2205, USA

Haluska, Jim (Athlete, Football Player)
4325 W Cleveland Ave
Milwaukee, WI 53219, USA

Halverson, Dean (Athlete, Football Player)
45971 State Highway 74
Palm Desert, CA 92260, USA

Halvorsen, Gail Col (General)
1525 W Dove Way
Amado, AZ 85645-9731, USA

Halward, Doug (Athlete, Hockey Player)
16 Creekstone Pl
Port Moody, BC V3H 4L6, Canada

Ham, Darvin (Athlete, Basketball Player)
13e8 Yucatan Dr SE
Rio Rancho, NM 87124-8922, USA

Ham, Jack (Athlete, Football Player)
Jack Ham Enterprises Inc
540 Lindbergh Dr
Coraopolis, PA 15108, USA

Ham, Kenneth T (Astronaut)
1315 Falling Leaf Dr
Friendswood, TX 77546-4615, USA

Ham, Kenneth T Cdr (Astronaut)
1315 Falling Leaf Dr
Friendswood, TX 77546-4615, USA

Ham, Tracy (Athlete, Football Player)
164 Cotton Creek Dr
McDonough, GA 30252-9012, USA

Hamari, Julia (Opera Singer)
Max Brod-Weg 14
Stuttgart 70437, GERMANY

Hamasaki, Ayumi (Actor, Musician)
c/o Staff Member *Avex Entertainment*
3-1-30-7F Minami Aoyama
Minato
Tokyo 107-0062, Japan

Hambling, Maggi (Artist)
Morley College
Westminster Bridge Road
London SE1 7HT, UNITED KINGDOM (UK)

Hambrick, Darren (Athlete, Football Player)
38632 Patti Lane
Lacoochee, FL 33537, USA

Hambrick, Troy (Athlete, Football Player)
1103 Pineland Rd
Columbia, SC 29223, USA

Hambright, Roger (Athlete, Baseball Player)
8709 NE 37th Ave
Vancouver, WA 98665-1065, USA

Hamburger, Michael P L (Writer)
John Johnson
45/47 Clerkenwell Green
London EC1R 0HT, UNITED KINGDOM (UK)

Hamed, Nihad (Religious Leader)
Islamic Assn in US/Canada
25351 Five Mile Road
Redford Township, MI 48239, USA

Hamed, Prince Naseem (Athlete, Boxer)
Mowbray House
Mowbray Street
Stockport, Cheshire SK1 3EJ, UNITED KINGDOM

Hamel, Alan
PO Box 827
Monterey, CA 93942

Hamel, Dean (Athlete, Football Player)
1009 Hawthorne Dr NE
Lenoir, NC 28645-, USA

Hamel, Gilles (Athlete, Hockey Player)
1484 Rue du McOn
Sherbrooke, QC J1N 1V4, Canada

Hamel, Jean (Athlete, Hockey Player)
5 Rue Lebeau
Asbestos, QC J1T 4L4, Canada

Hamel, Michael A (Astronaut)
1032 Werbel Pl
San Pedro, CA 90731-1166, USA

Hamel, Pierre (Athlete, Hockey Player)
1613 Beechwood Rd
Yadkinville, NC 27055, USA

Hamel, Veronica (Actor, Model)
c/o Staff Member *Cunningham Escott Slevin & Doherty (CESD-LA)*
10635 Santa Monica Blvd
130
Los Angeles, CA 90025, USA

Hamel, William (Religious Leader)
Evangelical Free Church
901 E 78th St
Minneapolis, MN 55420, USA

Hamelin, Bob (Athlete, Baseball Player)
51 Patton Ct SE
Concord, NC 28025-3742, USA

Hamels, Cole (Athlete, Baseball Player)
c/o Jon Orlando *WNWN Media*
348 S. Hauser Blvd #PH414
Los Angeles, CA 90036, USA

Hamhuis, Dan (Athlete, Hockey Player)
9553 Hampton Reserve Dr
Brentwood, TN 37027, USA

Hamill, Dorothy (Athlete, Figure Skater, Olympic Athlete)
PO Box 39549
Baltimore, MD 21212, USA

Hamill, Mark (Actor)
20358 Big Rock Dr
Malibu, CA 90265, USA

Hamill, W Pete (Editor, Writer)
8 Whiskey Hill Road
Wallkitt, NY 12589, USA

Hamilton, Al (Athlete, Hockey Player)
2452 115 St NW
Edmonton, AB T6J 3S1, Canada

Hamilton, Allan G (Al) (Athlete, Hockey Player)
2452 115th St NW
Edmonton, AB T6J 3S1, Canada

Hamilton, Anthony (Musician)
c/o Mark Cheatham *Creative Artists Agency (CAA-NY)*
162 Fifth Ave
6th Floor
New York, NY 10010, USA

Hamilton, Arthur Lee (Athlete, Baseball Player)
2243 College Cir N
Jacksonville, FL 32209-5916, USA

Hamilton, Ashley (Actor)
c/o Staff Member *TalentWorks (LA)*
3500 W Olive Ave
Suite 1400
Burbank, CA 91505, USA

Hamilton, Ben (Athlete, Football Player)
5240 Golden Ridge Ct
Parker, CO 80134, USA

Hamilton, Bethany (Athlete, Writer)
P.O. Box 863
Hanalei, HI 96714, USA

Hamilton, Bobby Jr (Race Car Driver)
Motorsports Decisions
PO Box 190
Greenbrier, TN 37073, USA

Hamilton, Charles (Musician)
c/o Staff Member *Violator Management*
36 W 25th St
2nd Floor
New York, NY 10010, USA

Hamilton, Conrad (Athlete, Football Player)
19619 N 35th Pl
Phoenix, AZ 85050, USA

Hamilton, Darrell (Athlete, Football Player)
22 Sunrise Ct
Randallstown, MD 21133, USA

Hamilton, Darryl (Athlete, Baseball Player)
4721 Southwind Dr
Baton Rouge, LA 70816-4738, USA

Hamilton, Dave (Athlete, Baseball Player)
9464 Cherry Hills Ln
San Ramon, CA 94583-3935, USA

Hamilton, Davey (Race Car Driver)
6415 Toledo St.
Houston, TX 77008, USA

Hamilton, David (Photographer)
41 Blvd du Montpamasse
Paris 75006, FRANCE

Hamilton, Dennis (Athlete, Basketball Player)
24215 South Agate Dr
Sun Lakes, AZ 85248, USA

Hamilton, Dennis (Athlete, Basketball Player)
1493 E Zion Way
Chandler, AZ 85249-5196, USA

Hamilton, Derek (Actor)
c/o PJ Shapiro *Ziffren Brittenham LLP*
1801 Century Park W
Los Angeles, CA 90067, USA

Hamilton, Derrick (Athlete, Football Player)

Hamilton, Forestom (Chico) (Composer, Music Group, Musician)
c/o Staff Member *Concerted Efforts*
P.O. Box 440326
Somerville, MA 02144, USA

Hamilton, George (Actor)
c/o Jeffrey Lane *Jeffrey Lane & Associates*
9255 Doheny Rd
Suite 2003
Los Angeles, CA 90069, USA

Hamilton, Guy (Director)
Puerto de Andraitz
Apartado III
Palma de Mallorca, SPAIN

Hamilton, Harry (Athlete, Football Player)
P.O. Box 986
Lemont, PA 16851, USA

Hamilton, Jack (Athlete, Baseball Player)
Jack's Plaza View Restaurant 245 N
Wildwood Dr
Branson, MO 65616-2193, USA

Hamilton, James (Athlete, Football Player)
242 McGirt Rd
Hamlet, NC 28345, USA

Hamilton, James (Athlete, Football Player)
242 McGirt Rd
Hamlet, NC 28345-9124, USA

Hamilton, Jeff (Athlete, Baseball Player)
2485 Golfview Cir
Fenton, MI 48430-9633, USA

Hamilton, Joe (Athlete, Basketball Player)
9e2 Loveall Ln
Louisville, KY 40223-3470, USA

Hamilton, Joey (Athlete, Baseball Player)
4035 Wellington Mist Pl
Duluth, GA 30097-2352, USA

Hamilton, Josh (Athlete, Baseball Player)
1215 Perdenalas Trail
Westlake, TX 76262, USA

Hamilton, Keith (Athlete, Football Player)
6 Bonnieview Ln
Towaco, NJ 07082, USA

Hamilton, Laird (Athlete, Producer)
c/o Jane Kachmer *Jane Kachmer Management*
P.O. Box 2246
Malibu, CA 90265, USA

Hamilton, Laurell K (Writer)
Ma Petite Enterprises, L.L.C.
P.O. Box 270375
St. Louis, Missouri 63127, USA

Hamilton, Lee H (Politician)
Wilson Int'l Schorlars Center
1300 Pennsylvania Ave NW
Washington, DC 20004, USA

Hamilton, Leonard (Basketball Player, Coach)
Florida State University
Athletic Dept
Tallahassee, FL 32306, USA

Hamilton, Lewis (Race Car Driver)
Hamilton Motorsport Ltd.
Corporatec Ltd.
32 St. James'S St
London SW1A 1HD, UK

Hamilton, Linda (Actor)
c/o Bobbie Edrick *Bobbie Edrick*
8955 Norma Pl
Los Angeles, CA 90069, USA

Hamilton, Lisa Gay (Actor)
c/o Stacy Boniello *Firm, The*
2049 Century Park E #2550
Los Angeles, CA 90067, USA

Hamilton, Lynn
1042 S. Burnside Ave.
Los Angeles, CA 90019

Hamilton, Marcus (Actor)
Hank Ketchum Enterprises
PO Box 1997
Monterey, CA 93942, USA

Hamilton, Marcus (Cartoonist)
12225 Ranburne Rd
Mint Hill, NC 28227-5623, USA

Hamilton, Michael (Athlete, Football Player)
6755 Mira Mesa Blvd
123-227
San Diego, CA 92121, USA

Hamilton, Michael (Artist)
2012 N 19th St
Boise, ID 83702, USA

Hamilton, Mike (Athlete, Baseball Player)
1070 Thorndale Cir
Prospe, TX 75078-9391, USA

Hamilton, Milo (Commentator)
Houston Astros
2001 Holcombe Blvd Unit 901
Houston, TX 77030-4214, USA

Hamilton, Natasha (Musician)
c/o Staff Member *Concorde Intl Artists Ltd*
101 Shepherds Bush Rd
London W6 7LP, UNITED KINGDOM (UK)

Hamilton, Paula (Actor)
PFD Drury House
34-43 Russell St
London WC2B 5HA, UNITED KINGDOM (UK)

Hamilton, Ray (Athlete, Football Player)
920 Rock Elm Dr
Auburn, GA 30011-4609, USA

Hamilton, Richard (Athlete, Basketball Player)
c/o Staff Member *Detroit Pistons*
2 Championship Dr
Auburn Hills, MI 48326, USA

Hamilton, Roy Lee (Athlete, Basketball Player)
1644 Del Mar Rd
Oceanside, CA 92057-4910, USA

Hamilton, Ruffin (Athlete, Football Player)
236 Sumac Trl
Woodstock, GA 30188-5154, USA

Hamilton, Scott (Athlete, Figure Skater, Olympic Athlete)
2451 Hidden River Ln
Franklin, TN 37069-6933, USA

Hamilton, Suzanna (Actor)
Julian Belfarge
46 Albermarie St
London W1X 4PP, UNITED KINGDOM (UK)

Hamilton, Tanya (Director)
c/o Adam Robinson *Southfield Village*
8228 Sunset Blvd #190
Los Angeles, CA 90046, USA

Hamilton, Todd (Athlete, Golfer)
2004 Rock Dove Ct
Westlake, TX 76262-9076, USA

Hamilton, Tom (Musician)
P.O. Box 67039
Newton, MA 02167, USA

Hamilton, Tom (Commentator)
31704 Sailors Cv
Avon Lake, OH 44012-2931, USA

Hamilton, Tom (Stylist)
1433 W Edgewater Ave
Chicago, IL 60660, USA

Hamilton, Tyler (Artist, Cycler, Olympic Athlete)
40 Cloutmans Ln
Marblehead, MA 01945-1S45, USA

Hamilton, Victoria (Actor)
c/o Michael Lazo *Untitled Entertainment (LA)*
350 S. Beverly Dr #200
Beverly Hills, CA 90212, USA

Hamilton, Wes
18905 4th Ave N
Minneapolis, MN 55447-3307

Hamilton-Klemperer, Kim
44 W. 62nd St.10th Flr.
New York, NY 10023

Hamiter, Uhuru (Athlete, Football Player)
5737 Hazel Ave
Philadelphia, PA 19143, USA

Hamlin, Brooke (Actor)
c/o Staff Member *Coast to Coast Talent Group*
3350 Barham Blvd
Los Angeles, CA 90068, USA

Hamlin, Denny (Race Car Driver)
Denny Hamlin Racing, Inc
13415 Reese Blvd. W.
Huntersville, NC 28075, USA

Hamlin, Eugene (Athlete, Football Player)
3571 Silver Farms Ln
Traverse City, MI 49684-8827, USA

Hamlin, Harry (Actor)
3007 LK Glen Dr
Beverly Hills, CA 90210, USA

Hamlin, Ken (Athlete, Baseball Player)
5242 County Road 413
McMillan, MI 49853-9266, USa

Hamlin, Shelley (Athlete, Golfer)
4311 W Ardmore Rd
Laveen, AZ 85339-2112, USA

Hamm, Jon (Actor)
c/o Vera Mihailovich *Forward Entertainment*
9255 Sunset Blvd
Suite 805
Los Angeles, CA 90069, USA

Hamm, Mia (Athlete, Olympic Athlete, Soccer Player)
Mia Hamm Foundation
61315th St
Manhattan Beach, CA 90266-4804, USA

Hamm, Morgan (Athlete, Gymnast, Olympic Athlete)
W229S3827 Milky Way Rd
Waukesha, WI 53189-7909, USA

Hamm, Nick (Director)
International Creative Mgmt
8942 Wilshire Blvd #219
Beverly Hills, CA 90211, USA

Hamm, Paul (Athlete, Gymnast, Olympic Athlete)
c/o Sheryl Shade *Shade Global*
10 E 40th St Fl 48
New York, NY 10016, USA

Hamm, Pete (Athlete, Baseball Player)
525 Lockhart Gulch Rd
Scotts Valley, CA 95066-3034, USA

Hamm, Richard L (Religious Leader)
Christian Church Disciples of Christ
PO Box 1986
Indianapolis, IN 46206, USA

Hammad al-Bassam, Abd al-Mohsin (Cosmonaut)
Royal Embassy of Saudi Arabia
22 Holland Park
London W11, UNITED KINGDOM (UK)

Hammaker, Atlee (Athlete, Baseball Player)
12740 Manning Ln
Knoxville, TN 37932-1001, USA

Hammarstrom, Inge (Athlete, Hockey Player)
c/o Staff Member *Philadelphia Flyers*
First Union Spectrum
3601 S Broad St, Suite 2
Philadelphia, PA 19148, USA

Hammel, Eugene A (Misc)
2332 Piedmont Ave
Berkeley, CA 94720, USA

Hammel, Jason
6 Holly Ln
Rehoboth, MA 02769-1437, USA

Hammel, Penny (Athlete, Golfer)
4786 Orchard Ln
Delray Beach, FL 33445-5306, USA

Hammer (Music Group, Musician)
Terrie Williams Agency
1500 Broadway Front
#7
New York, NY 10036, USA

Hammer, AJ (Television Host)
Showbiz Tonight
CNN
1 Time Warner Center
New York, NY 10019, USA

Hammer, Armie (Actor)
c/o Megan Moss Pachon *ID Public Relations (ID-LA)*
7060 Hollywood Blvd
8th Floor
Los Angeles, CA 90028, USA

Hammer, Jaime (Adult Film Star)
8033 Sunset Blvd #535
W Hollywood, CA 90046, USA

Hammer, MC (Actor, Musician, Songwriter)
7683 West Erb Way
Tracy, CA 95304, USA

Hammer, Victor S (Cinematographer)
PO Box 10788
Marina del Rey, CA 90295, USA

Hammergren, John H (Business Person)
McKesson HBOC Inc
1 Post St
San Francisco, CA 94104, USA

Hammer Jr, Jan (Composer, Musician)
Elliott Sears Management
7 Dunham Dr
New Fairfield, CT 06812, USA

Hammes, Gordon G (Misc)
11 Staley Place
Durham, NC 27705, USA

Hammett, Kirk (Music Group, Musician)
2505 Divisadero St
San Francisco, CA 94115, USA

Hammink, Geert (Athlete, Basketball Player)
2619 Clementon Park Ct
Orlando, FL 32835-6160, USA

Hammock, Robby (Athlete, Baseball Player)
12026 W Leather Ln
Peoria, AZ 85383-5849, USA

Hammon, Becky (Athlete, Basketball Player)
c/o Mike Cound *Sportalents*
Ctra de l'Escladella, 11
El Meu Poblet - Bloc 3E
La Massana, Andorra

Hammon, Ira (Athlete, Football Player)
17715 NE 38th Way
Vancouver, WA 98682-3683, USA

Hammon, Jennifer
270 N. Canon Dr. #1064
Beverly Hills, CA 90210

Hammond, Albert Jr (Music Group, Musician)
MVO Ltd
370 7th Ave #807
New York, NY 10001, USA

Hammond, Beresford (Musician)

Hammond, Beresford (Musician)
c/o Jeff Epstein Universal Attractions
135 W 26th St
12 Floor
New York, NY 10001, USA

Hammond, Bobby (Athlete, Football Player)
2535 Butler St
East Elmhurst, NY 11369, USA

Hammond, Chris (Athlete, Baseball Player)
908 Old Highway 431
Wedowee, AL 36278-4612, USA

Hammond, Darrell (Actor, Comedian)
c/o Geoff Cheddy Brillstein Entertainment Partners
9150 Wilshire Blvd #350
Beverly Hills, CA 90212, USA

Hammond, Donnie (Athlete, Golfer)
1642 Bridgewater Dr
Lake Mary, FL 32746-4103, USA

Hammond, Fred (Music Group)
Face to Face
21421 Hilltop St Blvd 20
Southfield, MI 48034, USA

Hammond, Gary (Athlete, Football Player)
5321 Seascape Ln
Plano, TX 75093, USA

Hammond, James T (Religious Leader)
Pentecostal Free Will Baptist Church
PO Box 1568
Dunn, NC 28335, USA

Hammond, Joan H (Opera Singer)
Private Bag 101
Geelong Mail Center, VIC 3221, AUSTRALIA

Hammond, John (Music Group, Musician)
c/o Staff Member Shore Fire Media
32 Court St
16th Floor
Brooklyn, NY 11201, USA

Hammond, Josh (Actor)
c/o Staff Member Hines and Hunt Entertainment
1213 W Magnolia Blvd
Burbank, CA 91506, USA

Hammond, Julie (Athlete, Basketball Player)
2943 S Ulster St
Denver, CO 80231-4170, USA

Hammond, Katherine (Stylist)
c/o Celebrity Stylist Oliver Piro Inc
725 Riverside Dr Apt 3A
New York, NY 10031, USA

Hammond, Ken (Athlete, Hockey Player)
38325 McDowell Dr
Solon, OH 44139, USA

Hammond, Kim (Athlete, Football Player)
9 Creek Bluff Run
Flagler Beach, FL 32136, USA

Hammond, L Blaine Colonel (Astronaut)
17595 Harvard Ave
Irvine, CA 92614-8516, USA

Hammond, Lisa B (Stylist)
c/o Staff Member Celestine - CA
1666 20th St
#200-B
Santa Monica, CA 90404, USA

Hammond, Richard (Actor, Correspondent)
c/o Staff Member BBC Television Centre
Incoming Mail
Wood Lane
London W12 7RJ, United Kingdom

Hammond, Robert D (General)
219 Del Mesa Carmel
Carmel, CA 93923-7951, USA

Hammond, Steve (Athlete, Baseball Player)
11104 Lake Butler Blvd
Windermere, FL 34786-7808, USA

Hammond, Tom (Sportscaster)
NBC-TV
Sprots Dept 30 Rockefeller Plaza
New York, NY 10112, USA

Hammond Jr, Caleb D (Misc, Publisher)
P.O. Box 194
Mendham, NJ 07945-0194, USA

Hammonds, Jeffrey (Jeff) (Athlete, Baseball Player, Olympic Athlete)
113 Grand Cove Pl
Madison, AL 35758-3034, USA

Hammonds, Tom (Athlete, Basketball Player)
122 Windsor Dr
Crestview, FL 32539-8601, USA

Hammons, David (Artist)
Studio Museum in Harlem
144 W 125th St
New York, NY 10027, USA

Hammons, Roger (Religious Leader)
Primitive Advent Christian Church
273 Frame Road
Elkview, WV 25071, USA

Hamner, Earl (Writer)
11575 Amanda Dr.
Studio City, CA 91604-4144, USA

Hamnett, Katharine (Designer, Fashion Designer)
Katharine Hamnett Ltd
202 New North Road
London N1, UNITED KINGDOM (UK)

Hampel, Olaf (Athlete)
Pommenweg 2
Bielefeld 33689, GERMANY

Hampshire, Susan (Actor)
123A Kings Rd
London SW3 4PL, UNITED KINGDOM (UK)

Hampson, Blake (Actor)
c/o Staff Member Nickelodeon UK
PO Box 6425
LONDON W1A 6UR, UNITED KINGDOM

Hampson, Justin (Athlete, Baseball Player)
7018 Richmond Dr
Glen Carbon, IL 62034-3058, USA

Hampson, Ted (Athlete, Hockey Player)
4436 Claremore Dr
Minneapolis, MN 55435-4136, USA

Hampson, Thomas (Opera Singer)
Starktriedgasse 53
Vienna 1180, AUSTRIA

Hampton, Brenda (Producer)
c/o Clifford Gilbert-Lurie Ziffren Brittenham LLP
1801 Century Park W
Los Angeles, CA 90067, USA

Hampton, Casey (Athlete, Football Player)
105 Conover Rd
Pittsburgh, PA 15208, USA

Hampton, Christopher J (Writer)
2 Kensington Park Gardens
London W11, UNITED KINGDOM (UK)

Hampton, Daniel O (Dan) (Athlete, Football Player)
9191 Falling Waters Dr
Burr Ridge, IL 60527, USA

Hampton, Ike (Baseball Player)
New York Mets
4415 E Ridge Gate Rd
Anaheim, CA 92807-3507, USA

Hampton, James (Actor)
102 Forest Hill Dr
Roanoke, TX 76262, USA

Hampton, Locksley (Slide) (Music Group, Musician)
Charismic Productions
2604 Mozart Place NW
Washington, DC 20009, USA

Hampton, Lorenzo (Athlete, Football Player)
1251 Nottoway Trl
Marietta, GA 30066, USA

Hampton, Michael W (Mike) (Athlete, Baseball Player)
8601 N 59th Pl
Paradise Valley, AZ 85253-2212, USA

Hampton, Millard (Athlete, Track Athlete)
201 W Mission St
San Jose, CA 95110, USA

Hampton, Ralph C Jr (Religious Leader)
Free Will Baptist Bible College
3606 W End Ave
Nashville, TN 37205, USA

Hampton, Rick (Athlete, Hockey Player)
King City Community Center
King City Community_ Center 25 Doctors Lane
King City, ON L7B 1G2, Canada

Hampton, Rodney (Athlete, Football Player)
5603 Grand Floral Blvd
Houston, TX 77041, USA

Hampton, Shanola (Actor)
c/o Elissa Leeds-Fickman Reel Talent Management
P.O. Box 491035
Los Angeles, CA 90049, USA

Hamri, Sanaa
c/o Larry Kennar Code Entertainment
9229 Sunset Blvd #615
Los Angeles, CA 90069, USA

Hamrlik, Roman (Athlete, Hockey Player)
56 Alhambra Dr
Oceanside, NY 11572-5425, USA

Hamulack, Tim (Athlete, Baseball Player)
530 Campbell Rd
York, PA 17402-3335, USA

Hamway, Mark (Athlete, Hockey Player)
2865 Rubbins Rd
Howell, MI 48843-7924, USA

Hamway, Marl (Athlete, Hockey Player)
3758 Lcoh Bend Dr
Commerce Township, MI 48382, USA

Hamzah (Prince)
Crown Prince's Office
Royal Palace
Amman, JORDAN

Han, Heejun (Musician)
c/o Staff Member 19 Entertainment - LA
9000 W Sunset Blvd #1574
West Hollywood, CA 90069, USA

Hanafusa, Hidesaburo (Biologist)
Rockefeller University
1230 York Ave
New York, NY 10021, USA

Hanauer, Chip (Yachtsman)
Hanauer Enterprises
2702 NE 88th St
Seattle, WA 98115, USA

Hanauer, Terri
8271 Melrose Ave. #110
Los Angeles, CA 90046

Hanburger, Christian (Chris) Jr (Athlete, Football Player)
708 Winter Hill Dr
Apex, NC 27502-1376, USA

Hanbury-Tension, Robin (Scientist)
Maidenwell
Cardinham Bodmin
Comwall PL3O 4DW, UNITED KINGDOM (UK)

Hance Jr, James H (Financier)
Bank of America Corp
100 N Tyron St
Charlotte, NC 28255, USA

Hancock, Anthony (Athlete, Football Player)
8233 Corteland Dr
Knoxville, TN 37909, USA

Hancock, Eddie(murphy) (Athlete, Baseball Player)
2104 W 15th St
Pueblo, CO 81003-1126, USA

Hancock, Garry (Athlete, Baseball Player)
2217 Greenhills Dr
Valrico, FL 33596-5215, USA

Hancock, Herbert J (Herbie) (Composer, Musician)
c/o Seth Malasky Paradigm (NY)
360 Park Ave S Fl 16
New York, NY 10010, USA

Hancock, John D (Director)
7355 N Fail Road
La Porte, IN 46350, USA

Hancock, John Lee (Director, Producer, Writer)
c/o David O'Connor Creative Artists Agency (CAA-LA)
2000 Ave Of The Stars
Los Angeles, CA 90067, USA

Hancock, Lee (Athlete, Baseball Player)
8338 Brentwood Blvd
Brentwood, CA 94513-1113, USA

Hancock, Leroy (Athlete, Baseball Player)
2010 Haywood Ave
Forest City, AR 72335-4518, USA

Hancock, Mike (Athlete, Football Player)
5513 Coloma Cir
Simi Valley, CA 93063-5029, USA

Hancock, Phillip (Athlete, Golfer)
3215 W Swann Ave
Apt 30
Tampa, FL 33609-4663, USA

Hancock, Ryan (Athlete, Baseball Player)
542 Aiden Ridge Dr
Draper, UT 84020-7305, USA

Hancock, Terri (Athlete, Golfer)
115 Devereux Dr
Athens, GA 30606, USA

Hand, Jon T (Athlete, Football Player)
13013 Broad St
Carmel, IN 46032, USA

Hand, Larry (Athlete, Football Player)
4414 Robinhood Rd
Winston Salem, NC 27106, USA

Hand, Rich (Athlete, Baseball Player)
3824 Bay Ct
Fort Worth, TX 76179-3831, USA

Handelsman, J B (Cartoonist)
New Yorker Magazine
Editorial Dept 4 Times Square
New York, NY 10036, USA

Handelsman, Walt (Cartoonist, Editor)
Newsday
Editorial Dept 235 Pinelawn Road
Melville, NY 11747, USA

Handford, Martin (Cartoonist)
Walker Books
87 Vauxhall Walk
London SE11 5HU, UNITED KINGDOM
(UK)

Handler, Chelsea (Comedian, Television Host)
c/o Stephen Huvane *Slate Public Relations*
9000 Sunset Blvd #915
West Hollywood, CA 90069, USA

Handler, Daniel (Actor, Writer)
c/o Esther Newberg *ICM Partners (ICM-NY)*
730 Fifth Ave
New York, NY 10019, USA

Handler, Evan (Actor)
c/o Lenore Zerman *Liberman/Zerman Management*
252 N Larchmont Blvd
Suite 200
Los Angeles, CA 90004, USA

Handley, Ray (Athlete, Football Coach, Football Player)
P.O. Box 355
Glenbrook, NV 89413, USA

Handley, Taylor (Actor)
c/o Booh Schut *Booh Schut Company*
11365 Sunshine Terrace
Studio City, CA 91604, USA

Handloser, Sandy (Stylist)
752 West End Ave
New York, NY 10025, USA

Handrahan, Vern (Athlete, Baseball Player)
36 Newland Cres
Charlottetown, PE C1A 4H5, Canada

Hands, Terence (Director)
Clwyd Theater Cymru
Mold
Flintshire, NORTH WALES

Hands, William A (Bill) (Athlete, Baseball Player)
P.O. Box 334
Orient, NY 11957-0334, USA

Handsome
9255 Sunset Blvd. #200
Los Angeles, CA 90069-3309

Handy, John (Music Group, Musician)
Integrity Talent
PO Box 961
Burlington, MA 01803, USA

Handy, John W (General)
Commander-in-Chief
Transportation Command
Scott Air Force Base, IL 62225, USA

Handzus, Michal (Athlete, Hockey Player)
123 29th St
Hermosa Beach, CA 90254-2358, USA

Hanes, Ken
8281 Melrose Ave #200
Los Angeles, CA 90046

Hanescu, Victor (Athlete, Tennis Player)
c/o Staff Member *SFX Sports Management*
5335 Wisconsin Ave NW #850
Washington, DC 20015, USA

Haney, Chris (Athlete, Baseball Player)
P.O. Box 135
Barboursville, VA 22923-0135, USA

Haney, Hank (Golfer)
Hank Haney Golf Ranch
2791 S Stemmons Fwy
Lewisville, TX 75067, USA

Haney, Larry (Athlete, Baseball Player)
P.O. Box 157
Barboursville, VA 22923-0157, USA

Haney, Lee (Writer)
Lee Haney Enterprises
105 Trail Point Circle
Fairburn, GA 30213, USA

Haney, Merv (Athlete, Hockey Player)
249 Lindsay St
Kimberley, BC V1A 1L4, Canada

Haney, Todd (Athlete, Baseball Player)
5404 Pointwood Cir
Waco, TX 76710-1265, USA

Hanfmann, George M A (Archaeologist)
Harvard University
Fogg Art Museum
32 Quincy St
Cambridge, MA 02138, USA

Hanford, Dixon (Athlete, Football Player)
1512 Hunters Chase Dr
Apt 2C
Westlake, OH 44145-6126, USA

Hanft, Ruth S (Scientist)
3340 Brookside Dr
Charlottesville, VA 22901, USA

Hangartner, Geoff (Athlete, Football Player)
805 Park Slope Dr
Charlotte, NC 28209, USA

Hangsleben, Alan (Athlete, Hockey Player)
5760 Little Rd
Lothian, MD 20711-9543

Hanie, Caleb (Athlete, Football Player)
2435 Wincrest Dr
Rockwall, TX 75032-7008, USA

Hanifan, Jim (Athlete, Football Coach, Football Player)
1217 Grey Fox Run
Weldon Spring, MO 63304, USA

Hanigan, Ryan
55 Bailev Rd
Andover, MA 01810-4200, USA

Hanin, Roger (Actor)
9 rue du Boccador
Paris 75008, FRANCE

Hanke, Christopher (Actor)
c/o Shea Martin *SLATE Public Relations - NY*
307 7th Ave
Suite 2401
New York, NY 10001, USA

Hankins, Jay (Athlete, Baseball Player)
26509 E Outer Belt Rd
Greenwood, MO 64034-9387, USA

Hankinson, Ben (Athlete, Hockey Player)
6515 Biscayne Blvd.
Minneapolis, MN 55436, USA

Hankinson, Casey (Athlete, Hockey Player)
6615 Parkwood Ln
Minneapolis, MN 55436-1733, USA

Hankinson, Tim (Coach, Soccer Player)
Columbus Crew
2121 Velman Ave
Columbus, OH 43211, USA

Hanks, Colin (Actor)
c/o Courtney Kivowitz *Schiff Company, The*
9465 Wilshire Blvd
Suite 480
Beverly Hills, CA 90212, USA

Hanks, Eugene (General)
5813 Nugget Ave NE
Albuquerque, NM 87111-5926, USA

Hanks, Merton (Athlete, Football Player)
855 E Davisburgild
Holly, MI 48442-8597, USA

Hanks, Sam (Race Car Driver)
17766 Tramonto Dr.
Pacific Palisades, CA 90272, USA

Hanks, Tom (Actor, Producer)
c/o Leslee Dart *42West (NY)*
220 W 42nd St
12th Floor
New York, NY 10036, USA

Hanks, Zach (Actor)
c/o Michael Henderson *Heresun Management*
4119 West Burbank Blvd.
Burbank, CA 91505, USA

Hankton, Cortez (Athlete, Football Player)
11180 Castlemain Cir W
Jacksonville, FL 32256, USA

Hankton, Karl (Athlete, Football Player)
12532 Hennigan Place Ln
Charlotte, NC 28214-1464, USA

Hanley, Bridget
12021 Hesby St.
Valley Village, CA 91607-3115

Hanley, Dick (Athlete, Olympic Athlete, Swimmer)
266 Lake Dr
Hurley, WI 54534, USA

Hanley, Frank (Misc)
Int'l Union of Operating Engineers
1125 17th St NW
Washington, DC 20036, USA

Hanley, Jeffrey (Scientist)
16411 Havenhurst Dr
Houston, TX 77059-5306, USA

Hanley, Jenny (Actor)
MGA
Southbank House
Black Prince Road
London SE1 7SJ, UNITED KINGDOM
(UK)

Hanley, Kay (Music Group)
c/o Staff Member *Paradigm (Monterey)*
404 W Franklin St
Monterey, CA 93940, USA

Hanley, Richard (Swimmer)
E266 Lake Road
Ironwood, MI 49938, USA

Hanlon, Edward Jr (General)
Commanding General
Marine Combat Development Command
Quantico, VA 22134, USA

Hanlon, Glen (Athlete, Hockey Player)
Vancouver Giants 100 Renfrew St N
Attn Coaching Staff
Vancouver, BC Vancouver, Canada

Hanlon, Glen (Athlete, Hockey Player)
c/o Staff Member *Washington Capitals*
627 N Glebe Rd
Arlington, VA 22203, USA

Hanmer, Craig (Athlete, Hockey Player)

Hann, Judith
56 Wood Lane
London, ENGLAND W12 7RJ

Hanna, Jack
PO Box 400
Powell, OH 43065

Hanna, Jen (Athlete, Golfer)
9 Zelma Dr
Greenville, SC 29617, USA

Hanna, Jerome (Music Group)
Paramount Entertainment
PO Box 12
Far Hills, NJ 07931, USA

Hanna, John (Athlete, Hockey Player)

Hanna, Preston (Athlete, Baseball Player)
5555 Mayfair Dr
Pensacola, FL 32506-5390, USA

Hannah, Bob (Motorcycle Race, Motorcycle Racer)
American Motorcycle Assn
13515 Yarmouth Dr
Pickerington, OH 43147, USA

Hannah, Bob (Baseball Player, Coach)
University of Delaware
Athletic Dept
Newark, DE 19716, USA

Hannah, Charles A (Charley) (Athlete, Football Player)
P.O. Box 2671
Lutz, FL 33548, USA

Hannah, Daryl (Actor)
c/o Chuck Binder *Binder & Associates*
1465 Lindacrest Dr
Beverly Hills, CA 90210, USA

Hannah, John (Actor)
c/o Sue Latimer *Artists Rights Group (ARG)*
4 Great Portland St
London W1W 8PA, UNITED KINGDOM (UK)

Hannah, John (Athlete, Football Player)
2407 Hideaway Place SE
Decatur, AL 35603, USA

Hannah, Travis (Athlete, Football Player)
10807 Lemoli Ave
Inglewood, CA 90303, USA

Hannah, Wayne (Religious Leader)
Fellowship of Grace Brethren Churches
PO Box 386
Winona Lake, IN 46590, USA

Hannahan, Jack
1995 Bayard Ave
Saint Paul, MN 55116-1214, USA

Hannahs, Gerald (Gerry) (Athlete, Baseball Player)
1411 Andover Rdg
Little Rock, AR 72227-3971, USA

Hannam, Ryan (Athlete, Football Player)
213 S School St
Saint Ansgar, IA 50472-1495, USA

Hannan, Dave (Athlete, Hockey Player)
408 Timberlake Dr
Venetia, PA 15367, USA

Hannan, Jacquie (Stylist)
Prefers to be contacted
via email

Hannan, Jim (Athlete, Baseball Player)
3907 Cherry Hill Way
Annandale, VA 22003-2220, USA

Hannan, Scott (Athlete, Hockey Player)
35 S Bellaire St
Denver, CO 80246-1010, USA

Hannawald, Sven (Skier)
WH Sport Int'l GmbH
Im Sabel 4
Trier 54294, GERMANY

Hannelius, Geneveive (Actor)
c/o Karl Hofheinz *Synergy Talent*
13251 Ventura Blvd
Studio City, CA 91604, USA

Hanneman, Craig (Athlete, Football Player)
4350 Gibson Rd NW
Salem, OR 97304, USA

Hanneman, Steve (Actor)
c/o Staff Member *Abrams Artists Agency (LA)*
9200 Sunset Blvd
11th Floor
Los Angeles, CA 90069, USA

Hannigan, Alyson (Actor)
c/o Staff Member *Lovett Management*
1327 Brinkley Ave
Los Angeles, CA 90049, USA

Hannigan, Mackenzie (Actor)
c/o Staff Member *Martin Weiss Management*
PO Box 5656
Santa Monica, CA 90409-5656, USA

Hannigan, Ray (Athlete, Hockey Player)
1717 S Woodland Dr Spc 36
Kalispell, MT 59901-9103, USA

Hannity, Sean (Correspondent)
c/o Staff Member *Fox News Channel (NY)*
1211 Ave of the Americas
Level C1
New York, NY 10036-8701, USA

Hannon, Tom (Athlete, Football Player)
17398 Roxbury Ave
Southfield, MI 48075, USA

Hannuia, Dick (Coach, Swimmer)
1021 Westley Dr
Tacoma, WA 98465, USA

Hanrahan, Don (Athlete, Basketball Player)
416 Valley Rd
Cos Cob, CT 06807-1622, USA

Hanrahan, Joel (Athlete, Baseball Player)
4152 River Marsh Dr
Fernandina Beach, Fl 32034-1644, USA

Hanratty, Sammi (Actor)
c/o Linda Henrie *Go Talent Management*
12930 Ventura Blvd
Suite 904
Studio City, CA 91604, USA

Hanratty, Terrance R (Terry) (Athlete, Football Player)
31 Gower Rd
New Canaan, CT 06840-6630, USA

Hans, Rollen (Athlete, Basketball Player)
12607 100th Ln NE
Apt L156
Kirkland, WA 98034-8830, USA

Hans-Adam II (Prince)
Schloss Vaduz
9490 Vaduz
LIECHTENSTEIN

Hansbrough, Tyler (Athlete, Basketball Player)
c/o Jeff Schwartz *Excel Sports Management*
9665 Wilshire Blvd #500
Los Angeles, CA 90212, USA

Hansch, Theodor W. (Nobel Prize Laureate)
LMU
Hans-Kopfermannstrasse 1
Garching D-80799, Germany

Hansell, Greg (Athlete, Baseball Player)
1791 W Prescott Dr
Chandler, AZ 85248-4845, USA

Hansen, Beck (Beck) (Musician, Songwriter, Writer)
c/o Staff Member *Nasty Little Man*
110 Greene St #605
New York, NY 10012, USA

Hansen, Bob (Athlete, Basketball Player)
710 36th St
West Des Moines, IA 50265-3166, USA

Hansen, Bob (Athlete, Baseball Player)
19 N Kelsey Ave
Evansville, IN 47711-6051, USA

Hansen, Brendan (Athlete, Olympic Athlete, Swimmer)
8704 Farmdale Cv
Austin, TX 78749-3439, USA

Hansen, Brian (Athlete, Football Player)
101 W Hazeltine Ln
Sioux Falls, SD 57108, USA

Hansen, Bruce (Athlete, Football Player)
480 N 1100 E
American Fork, UT 84003, USA

Hansen, Chris (Correspondent, Television Host)
c/o Staff Member *Dateline NBC*
NBC News
30 Rockefeller Plz
New York, NY 10112, USA

Hansen, Courtney (Actor)
c/o Liza Anderson *Anderson Group Public Relations*
8060 Melrose Ave Fl 4
Los Angeles, CA 90046, USA

Hansen, Craig (Athlete, Baseball Player)
1180 Washington St
Apt 508
Boston, MA 11542-2904, USA

Hansen, David (Dave) (Athlete, Baseball Player)
9852 Orchard Ln
Villa Park, CA 92861-3105, USA

Hansen, Deborah (Stylist)
PO Box 204
Brookline, MA 02146, USA

Hansen, Don (Athlete, Football Player)
3290 Spain Rd
Snellville, GA 30039-8503, USA

Hansen, Frederick M (Fred) (Athlete, Track Athlete)
201 Vanderpool Lane #12
Houston, TX 77024, USA

Hansen, Gale (Actor)
721 SE 29th Ave
Portland, OR 97214, USA

Hansen, Gunnar (Actor)
PO Box 368
North East Harbor, ME 04662, USA

Hansen, Gus (Actor)
c/o Staff Member *Poker Royalty, LLC*
10789 W. Twain Ave.
Suite 200
Las Vegas, NV 89135, USA

Hansen, Guy (Athlete, Baseball Player)
3876 Red Rock St
Las Vegas, NV 89103-2333, USA

Hansen, Jacqueline (Athlete, Track Athlete)
1133 9th St
Santa Monica, CA 90403, USA

Hansen, James E (Physicist, Scientist)
Goddard Institute for Space Studies
2880 Broadway
New York, NY 10025-7886, USA

Hansen, Jed (Athlete, Baseball Player)
1534 12th Lane Fi
Fox Island, WA 98584-7977, USA

Hansen, Lars (Athlete, Basketball Player)
1230 Horn Ave
Apt 504
West Hollywood, CA 90069-2175, USA

Hansen, Marcia (Stylist)
2411 Colony Ct
Ann Arbor, MI 48104, USA

Hansen, Mark Victor (Business Person, Motivational Speaker, Writer)
Mark Victor Hansen and Associates
711 W 17th St #D-2
Costa Mesa, California 92627, USA

Hansen, Neil (Race Car Driver)
4018 E. 5th Ave.
Spokane, WA 9920r, USA

Hansen, Patti (Model)
Redlands W Wittering
Chichester
Sussex, UNITED KINGDOM (UK)

Hansen, Peter (Actor)
Stone Manners
6500 Wilshire Blvd
#550
Los Angeles, CA 90048, USA

Hansen, Phil (Athlete, Football Player)
24921 N Melissa Dr
Detroit Lakes, MN 56501, USA

Hansen, Rich (Athlete, Hockey Player)
78 Eatons Neck Rd
Northport, NY 11768, USA

Hansen, Rick (Athlete)
Rick Hansen Man In Motion Foundation
520 West 6th Ave 5th Fl
Vancouver, BC V5Z 1A1, CANADA

Hansen, Roger (Athlete, Baseball Player)
14618 Kayak Point Rd
Stanwood, WA 98292-5301, USA

Hansen, Ron (Athlete, Baseball Player)
13602 Alliston Dr
Baldwin, MD 21013-9748, USA

Hansen, Roscoe (Athlete, Football Player)
638 Sooy Ln
Absecon, NJ 08201, USA

Hansen, Ryan (Actor)
c/o Nate Steadman *Gersh (LA)*
9465 Wilshire Blvd
Suite 600
Beverly Hills, CA 90212, USA

Hansen, Tavis (Athlete, Hockey Player)
3821 51st Ave SW
Seattle, WA 98116-3614, USA

Hansis, Ron (Athlete, Hockey Player)
112 Stegal Cir
Longs, SC 29568-8841

Hansis, Van (Actor)
c/o Kathy Kanner *Kanner Entertainment*
30 W 74th St #PH1
New York, NY 10023, USA

Hanson (Music Group)
1045 W 78th St
Tulsa, OK 74132, USA

Hanson, Carl T (Admiral)
900 Birdseye Road
Orient, NY 11967, USA

Hanson, Curtis (Director, Producer)
c/o David Kramer *United Talent Agency (UTA)*
9336 Civic Center Dr
Beverly Hills, CA 90210, USA

Hanson, Dave (Athlete, Hockey Player)
304 Timberlake Dr
Venetia, PA 15367-1376

Hanson, Erik (Athlete, Baseball Player)
20333 N 83rd Pl
Scottsdale, AZ 85255-3931, USA

Hanson, Isaac (Musician)
c/o Jeffrey Hasson *Paradigm (Nashville)*
124 12th Ave S
Suite 410
Nashville, TN 37203, USA

Hanson, Janet (Stylist)
74 Kensington Ave
Norwood, NJ 07648, USA

Hanson, Jason D (Athlete, Football Player)
27272 Ovid Ct
Franklin, MI 48025-1036, USA

Hanson, Jennifer (Musician)
c/o Staff Member Creative Artists Agency
(CAA-TN)
3310 West End Ave
5th Floor
Nashville, TN 37203, USA

Hanson, Joselio (Athlete, Football Player)
2531 Hudspeth St
Inglewood, CA 90303, USA

Hanson, Stan
PO Box 970
Hotchkiss, CO 81419-0970

Hanson, Taylor (Musician, Songwriter)
c/o Neil Warnock Agency Group Ltd, The
(UK)
361-373 City Rd
London EC1V 1PQ, UK

Hanson, Tommy (Athlete, Baseball Player)
102 Ferndale Ct
Redlands, CA 92374-4285, USA

Hanson, Tracy (Athlete, Golfer)
89 S Atlantic Ave
Apt 1403
Ormond Beach, FL 32176, USA

Hanson, William R (Artist)
78 W Notre Dame St
Glens Falls, NY 12801, USA

Hanson, Zac (Musician)
c/o Jeffrey Hasson Paradigm (Nashville)
124 12th Ave S
Suite 410
Nashville, TN 37203, USA

Hanson-Sfingi, Beverly (Athlete, Golfer)
79915 Horseshoe Rd
La Quinta, CA 92253, USA

Hanspard, Byron (Athlete, Football Player)
P.O. Box 792
Desoto, TX 75123, USA

Hansraj, Jugal (Actor, Bollywood)
14-A Queens Apt
Pali Hill Bandra (W)
Mumbai, MS 400050, INDIA

Hanss, Ted (Scientist)
Information Technology Intergration
Center
3025 Boardwalk
Ann Arbor, MI 48108, USA

Hantak, Bob (Athlete, Baseball Player)
526 Summerplace Ct
Saint Louis, MO 63125-5545, USA

Hantla, Bob (Athlete, Football Player)
7815 E Monte Vista Rd
Scottsdale, AZ 85257-2209, USA

Hantla, Robert (Athlete, Football Player)
7815 E Monte Vista Rd
Scottsdale, AZ 85257, USA

Hantuchova, Daniela (Tennis Player)
c/o Staff Member Women's Tennis
Association (WTA (US))
One Progress Plaza
Ste 1500
St Petersburg, FL 33701, USA

Hanuja (Actor, Bollywood)
No 20 Periyar Street
Gandhi Nagar
Chennai, TN, INDIA

Hanulak, Chet (Athlete, Football Player)
225 Canal Park Dr
Apt 6
Salisbury, MD 21804, USA

Hanzal, Martin (Athlete, Hockey Player)
19550 N Grayhawk Dr Unit 1091
Scottsdale, AZ 85255-3993, USA

Hanzlik, Bill (Athlete, Basketball Player,
Olympic Athlete)
5701 Green Oaks Dr
Greenwood Village, CO 80121-1336,
USA

Hape, Patrick (Athlete, Football Player)
105 Sutton Cir
Birmingham, AL 35242, USA

Hapke, Bruce (Misc)
1702 Georgetown Place
Pittsburgh, PA 15235, USA

Happ, J A (Athlete, Baseball Player)
3832 N Ashland Ave Apt 3S
Chicago, IL 60613-5235, USA

Harada, Masahiko (Fighting) (Boxer)
2-21-5 Azabu-Juban
Minatoku
Tokyo 106, JAPAN

Harald V (King)
Det Kongelige Slott
Drammensvelen 1
Oslo 0010, NORWAY

Harang, Aaron (Athlete, Baseball Player)
6411 Glenroy St
San Diego, CA 92120, USA

Harang, Aaron (Athlete, Baseball Player)
6392 Camino Corto
San Diego, CA 92120-3108, USA

Harb, Fred (Race Car Driver)
815 E. Fairfield Rd.
High Point, NC 27263, USA

Harbach, Otto
3455 Congress St
Fairfield, CT 06430-2036

Harbaruk, Nick

Harbaugh, David (Cartoonist)
1649 Stone Mansion Dr
Sewickley, PA 15143-8600, USA

Harbaugh, Gregory J (Astronaut)
1936 Thornwood Avenue
Wilmette, IL 60091-1403, USA

Harbaugh, James (Jim) (Athlete, Football
Player)
c/o David Dunn Athletes First, LLC
9140 Irvine Center Dr
Irvine, CA 92618, USA

Harbaugh, Robert E (Doctor)
Dartmouth-Hitchcock Medical Center
Surgery Dept
Hanover, NH 03756, USA

Harbert, Marguerite (Misc)
2700 Woodridge Rd
Mountain Brk, AL 35223-2912, USA

Harbison, John H (Composer)
479 Franklin St
Cambridge, MA 02139, USA

Harbour, David (Actor)
c/o Meg Mortimer Principal Entertainment
(NY)
130 W 42nd St
Suite 614
New York, NY 10036, USA

Harbo-Weidmann, Claire (Stylist)
476 E Cypress Ave
#M
Burbank, CA 91501, USA

Harbutt, Charles (Photographer)
1 5th Ave Apt 16G
New York, NY 10003-4317, USA

Harcourt, Ed (Musician)
c/o Staff Member Paradigm (Monterey)
404 W Franklin St
Monterey, CA 93940, USA

Hard, Darlene R (Tennis Player)
22924 Erwin St
Woodland Hills, CA 91367, USA

Hardaway, Anfemee (Penny) (Athlete,
Basketball Player, Olympic Athlete)
3217 Point Hill CV
Memphis, TN 38125, USA

Hardaway, Anfernee (Athlete, Basketball
Player, Olympic Athlete)
3217 Point Hill Cv
Memphis, TN 38125-889e, USA

Hardaway, Tim (Athlete, Basketball
Player, Olympic Athlete)
10050 SW 62nd Ave
Miami, FL 33156-3378, USA

Hardeman, Buddy (Athlete, Football
Player)
5711 Heming Ave
Springfield, VA 22151, USA

Hardeman, Don (Athlete, Football Player)
901 S Valley Mills Dr
Apt 207-B
Waco, TX 76711, USA

Hardeman, Tami (Stylist)
1921 Brian Way
Decatur, GA 30033, USA

Harden, Bobby (Athlete, Football Player)
1750 NW 36th Ter
Fort Lauderdale, FL 33311, USA

Harden, Marcia Gay (Actor)
God of Carnage
Bernard B Jacobs Theater
242 W 45th St
New York, NY 10036, USA

Harden, Michael (Athlete, Football Player)
7150 Leetsdale Dr
Apt 315
Denver, CO 80224, USA

Harden, Mike (Athlete, Football Player)
21512 E Portland Pl
Aurora, CO 80016-2343, USA

Hardenberger, Hahan (Music Group,
Musician)
Columbia Artists Mgmt Inc
165 W 57th St
New York, NY 10019, USA

Hardesty, Brandon (Actor)
c/o Brandt Joel WME (LA)
9601 Wilshire Blvd Fl 3
Beverly Hills, CA 90210, USA

Hardesty Jr, David C (Educator)
West Virginia University
President's Office
Morgantown, WV 26506, USA

Hardie, Kate (Actor)
Jonathan Altaras
13 Shorts Gardens
London WC2H 9AT, UNITED KINGDOM
(UK)

Hardiek, Kevin (Stylist)
c/o Staff Member Maximum Talent
1873 S Bellaire St
Suite 915
Denver, CO 80222-4356, USA

Hardin, Jerry
3033 Vista Crest Dr.
Los Angeles, CA 90068

Hardin, Melora (Actor)
c/o Staff Member Kohner Agency, The
9300 Wilshire Blvd
Suite 555
Beverly Hills, CA 90212, USA

Hardin, Paul III (Educator)
University of North Carolina
Chancellor's Office
Chapel Hill, NC 27599, USA

Hardin, Ty (Actor)
2210 87Street Court NW
Gig Harbor, WA 98332-7550, USA

Harding, Daniel (Musician)
c/o Staff Member ICM Partners (ICM-LA)
10250 Constellation Blvd Fl 7
Los Angeles, CA 90067, USA

Harding, Ian (Actor)
c/o Gina Hoffman Baker Winokur Ryder
Public Relations (BWR-LA)
9100 Wilshire Blvd
Suite 500, West Tower
Beverly Hills, CA 90212, USA

Harding, John Wesley (Actor, Composer,
Music Group, Songwriter, Writer)
c/o Staff Member Concerted Efforts
P.O. Box 440326
Somerville, MA 02144, USA

Harding, Josh (Athlete, Hockey Player)
1415 Brown St
Regina, SK S4N 5C9, Canada

Harding, Peter (General)
Ministry of Defense Whitehall
London SW1, England

Harding, Sarah (Musician)
c/o Sarah Camlett Independent Talent
Group (ITG-UK)
Oxford House
76 Oxford St
London W1D 1BS, UK

Harding of Petherton, John (General)
Lower Farm Nether Compton
Sherborne, Dorset, England

Hardis, Stephen R (Business Person)
Eaton Corp
Eaton Center 1111 Superior Ave
Cleveland, OH 44114, USA

Hardison, Dee (Athlete, Football Player)
756 Belvin Maynard Rd
Harrells, NC 28444-9308, USA

Hardison, Kadeem (Actor)
19743 Valleyview Dr
Topanga, CA 90290, USA

Hardisty, Huntington (Admiral)
Lexington Institute
1600 Wilson Blvd #900
Arlington, VA 22209, USA

Hardman, Cedrick (Athlete, Football Player)
250 Moss St
Laguna Beach, CA 92651, USA

Hardman, Earl
1400 E. Carson
Pittsburgh, PA 15302

Hardnett, Charles (Charlie) (Athlete, Basketball Player, Coach)
1906 Swainsboro Dr
Louisville, KY 40218-2417, USA

Hardrict, Cory (Actor)
c/o Staff Member *Burstein Company, The*
15304 Sunset Blvd
suite 208
Pacific Palisades, CA 90272, USA

Hardt, Michael (Educator)
Duke Univesity
English Dept
Durham, NC 27708, USA

Hardtke, Jason (Athlete, Baseball Player)
1538 Bouchard Dr
San Jose, CA 95118-3917, USA

Hardwick, Billy
1576 S. White Station
Memphis, TN 38117

Hardwick, Chris (Actor)
c/o Alex Murray *McDonald-Murray Management*
11846 Ventura Blvd Ste 202
Studio City, CA 91604, USA

Hardwick, Gary C (Director, Producer, Writer)
c/o Bruce Kaufman *ICM Partners (ICM-LA)*
10250 Constellation Blvd Fl 7
Los Angeles, CA 90067, USA

Hardwick, Johnny (Artist, Voice Over Artist, Writer)
c/o Staff Member *Creative Artists Agency (CAA-LA)*
2000 Ave Of The Stars
Los Angeles, CA 90067, USA

Hardwick, William B (Billy) (Bowler)
1576 S White Station Road
Memphis, TN 38117-7220, USA

Hardwicke, Catherine (Director)
c/o BeBe Lerner *ID Public Relations (ID-LA)*
7060 Hollywood Blvd
8th Floor
Los Angeles, CA 90028, USA

Hardy, Adrian (Athlete, Football Player)
7530 Kingsport Blvd
New Orleans, LA 70128, USA

Hardy, Alan (Athlete, Basketball Player)
13841 Gratiot Avenue
Detroit, MI 48205-2805, USA

Hardy, Bruce A (Athlete, Football Player)
252 W 325 N
Ivins, UT 84738-6132, USA

Hardy, Carroll (Athlete, Baseball Player, Football Player)
1514 Whitehall Dr
Longmont, CO 80504-7971, USA

Hardy, Darrell (Athlete, Basketball Player)
3126 Knoll St
Houston, TX 77080-3011, USA

Hardy, David (Athlete, Football Player)
P.O. Box 1270
New Waverly, TX 77358-1270, USA

Hardy, Hagood (Composer, Musician)
SOCAN
41 Valleybrook Dr
Don Mills, ON M3B 2S6, CANADA

Hardy, Hugh (Architect)
Hardy Holzman Pfeiffer
902 Broadway
New York, NY 10010, USA

Hardy, James (Athlete, Basketball Player)
1682 Lakewood Dr
Salt Lake City, UT 84117-7518, USA

Hardy, James (Athlete, Football Player)
c/o Eugene Parker *Maximum Sports Management*
6435 W Jefferson Blvd
#197
Fort Wayne, IN 46804, USA

Hardy, Jeff (Wrestler)
c/o Kerry Rodgerson *World Wrestling Entertainment (WWE)*
Titan Towers
1241 E Main St
Stamford, CT 06905-3857, USA

Hardy, Jim (Athlete, Football Player)
48490 San Vicente St
La Quinta, CA 92253, USA

Hardy, J J (Athlete, Baseball Player)
5070 S Roosevelt St
Tempe, AZ 85282-6599, USA

Hardy, Joe (Athlete, Hockey Player)
1256 Rte De Fossambault
RR 2
Saint-Augustin-De-Desmaures, QC G3A 1W8, Canada

Hardy, John C (Scientist)
48 Rathnelly Ave
Toronto, ON M4V 2M3, Canada

Hardy, John (Jack) (Athlete, Baseball Player)
1260 NW 192nd Ln
Pembroke Pines, FL 33029, USA

Hardy, Kevin (Athlete, Football Player)
1228 Windsor Harbor Dr
Jacksonville, FL 32225, USA

Hardy, Kevin (Athlete, Football Player)
298 Paraiso Dr
Danville, CA 94526, USA

HardY, Larry (Athlete, Baseball Player)
17 Jennifer Ct
Roanoke, TX 76262-5402, USA

Hardy, Larry (Athlete, Baseball Player)
7 Jennifer Ct
Roanoke, TX 76262, USA

Hardy, Larry (Athlete, Football Player)
1711 Fairwood Dr
Jackson, MS 39213, USA

Hardy, Mark (Athlete, Hockey Player)
220 21st St
Manhattan Beach, CA 90266-4547, USA

Hardy, Matt (Wrestler)
c/o Kerry Rodgerson *World Wrestling Entertainment (WWE)*
Titan Towers
1241 E Main St
Stamford, CT 06905-3857, USA

Hardy, Rob (Actor)
c/o Adam Robinson *Southfield Village*
8228 Sunset Blvd #190
Los Angeles, CA 90046, USA

Hardy, Sophie (Doctor)
332 Ave du Marechal Juin
Boulogne, FRANCE 92100, FRANCE

Hardy, Terry (Athlete, Football Player)
3109 S Rick Dr
Montgomery, AL 36108, USA

Hardy, Tom (Actor)
c/o Mick Sullivan *Creative Artists Agency (CAA-LA)*
2000 Ave Of The Stars
Los Angeles, CA 90067, USA

Hardy, Willis (General)
26523 Calle Lorenzo San Juan
Capistrano, CA 92675-1672, USA

Hare, David (Writer)
95 Linden Gardens
London WC2, UNITED KINGDOM (UK)

Hare, Eddie (Athlete, Football Player)
802 Walker School Rd
Sugar Land, TX 77479, USA

Hare, Frederick K (Scientist)
301 Lakeshore Rd W
Oakville, ON L6K 1G2, Canada

Hare, Shawn (Athlete, Baseball Player)
1975 Deer Path Trl
Oxford, MI 48371-6062, USA

Harelik, Mark (Actor)
c/o Staff Member *Gersh (LA)*
9465 Wilshire Blvd
Suite 600
Beverly Hills, CA 90212, USA

Haren, Dan (Athlete, Baseball Player)
c/o Joe Urbon *Creative Artists Agency (CAA-NY)*
162 Fifth Ave
6th Floor
New York, NY 10010, USA

Harer, Richard (Aviator)
3032 Barrington Dr
Toledo, OH 43606-3007, USA

Harewood, Dorian (Actor)
c/o Tracy Quinn *Quinn Management*
17328 Ventura Blvd
Suite 416
Encino, CA 91316, USA

Hargain, Tony (Athlete, Football Player)
PO Box 116
Fair Oaks, CA 95628, USA

Hargan, Steve (Athlete, Baseball Player)
2502 E Morongo Trl
Palm Springs, CA 92264, USA

Harge, Ira (Athlete, Basketball Player)
328 Yucca Dr NW
Albuquerque, NM 87105-1935, USA

Hargesheimer, Al (Athlete, Baseball Player)
107 N Evanston Ave
Arlington Heights, IL 60004-6617, USA

Hargesheimer, Alan (Athlete, Baseball Player)
107 N Evanston Ave
Arlington Heights, IL 60004, USA

Hargett, Edd (Athlete, Football Player)
379 County Road 222
Nacogdoches, TX 75965-4806, USA

Hargis, Gary (Athlete, Baseball Player)
157 Gemini St
Lompoc, CA 92679-3702, USA

Hargitay, Mariska (Actor)
c/o Leslie Sloane *Baker Winokur Ryder Public Relations BWR (BWR-NY)*
292 Madison Ave
12th Floor
New York, NY 10017, USA

Hargrove, D Michael (Mike) (Athlete, Baseball Player, Coach)
3925 Ramblewood Dr
Richfield, OH 44286-9642, USA

Hargrove, Jim (Athlete, Football Player)
805 S Key Ave
Lampasas, TX 76550-3153, USA

Hargrove, Linda (Coach)
Washington Mystics
MCI Center
601 E St NW
Washington, DC 20004, USA

Hargrove, Marion (Writer)
401 Montana Ave. #6
Santa Monica, A 90403-1303, USA

Hari, Rene (Stylist)
3153 Bloomington Ave
South Minneapolis, MN 55407, USA

Harikkala, Tim (Athlete, Baseball Player)
W6132 Everglade Rd
Greenville, WI 54942-8590, USA

Harington, Kit (Actor)
c/o Gene Parseghian *Parseghian Planco LLC*
322 8th Ave
Suite 601
New York, NY 10001, USA

Haris, Niki (Musician)
c/o Staff Member *Diva Central Inc*
7510 W Sunset Blvd Ste 1445
Los Angees, CA 90046, USA

Harker, Al (Athlete, Soccer Player)
409 2nd Street
Lafayette Hill, PA 19444-1403, USA

Harker, Susannah
55 Ashburnham Grove Greenwich
London, ENGLAND SW10 8UJ

Harket, Morten (Music Group)
Bandana Mgmt
11 Elvaston Place #300
London SW7 5QC, UNITED KINGDOM (UK)

Harkey, Mike (Athlete, Baseball Player)
23930 Strange Creek Dr
Diamond Bar, CA 91709-1761, USA

Harkey, Steve (Athlete, Football Player)
6582 Cherry Tree Ln NE
Atlanta, GA 30328, USA

Harkin, Kenan (Sportscaster)
c/o Staff Member *WmE2 (WMA-LA)*
1 William Morris Pl
Beverly Hills, CA 90212, USA

Harkin, Tom (Politician, Senator)
731 Hart Senate Office Bldg
Washington, DC 20510-0001, USA

Harkins, Brett (Athlete, Hockey Player)
4701 Duhme Rd
Apt 1D
Saint Petersburg, FL 33708, USA

Harkleroad, Ashley (Tennis Player)
c/o Jill Smoller *WME (LA)*
9601 Wilshire Blvd Fl 3
Beverly Hills, CA 90210, USA

Harkless, Burkley (Athlete, Football Player)
2308 E Windsor Dr
Denton, TX 76209, USA

Harkness, Jerry (Athlete, Basketball Player)
8340 Misty Dr
Indianapolis, IN 46236-9190, USA

Harkness, Tim (Athlete, Baseball Player)
70 Homefield Sq
Courtice, ON L1E 1L3, Canada

Harkrider, Kip (Athlete, Baseball Player, Olympic Athlete)
120 Deercrest Dr
Carthage, TX 75633-5688, USA

Harlan, Bob (Business Person, Football Executive)
2621 Forestville Dr
Green Bay, WI 54304-1359, USA

Harlan, Jack R (Scientist)
University of Illinois
Agronomy Dept
Urbana, IL 61801, USA

Harlan, Kevin (Sportscaster)
CBS-TV
Sprots Dept
51 W 52nd St
New York, NY 10019, USA

Harlem Globetrotters
400 E. Van Buren #300
Phoenix, AZ 85004

Harley, Steve (Music Group)
Work Hard
19D Pinfold Road
London SW16 2SL, UNITED KINGDOM (UK)

Harlicka, Skip (Athlete, Basketball Player)
2643 Saint Marys St
Raleigh, NC 27609-7644, USA

Harlin, Renny (Director, Producer)
Midnight Sun Pictures
8800 Sunset Blvd #400
Los Angeles, CA 90069, USA

Harlock, David (Athlete, Hockey Player)
4714 Oak Hollow Ct
Dexter, MI 48130, USA

Harlow, Larry (Athlete, Baseball Player)
26348 W Burnett Rd
Buckeye, AZ 85396-9239, USA

Harlow, Larry (Athlete, Baseball Player)
26348 W Burnett Rd
Buckeye, AZ 85396, USA

Harlow, Pat (Athlete, Football Player)
230 W Avenida San Antonio
San Clemente, CA 92672, USA

Harlow, Scott (Athlete, Hockey Player)
285 Harvest Ln
Bridgewater, MA 02324-2457, USA

Harlow, Shalom (Model)
c/o Heather Reynolds One Entertainment (NY)
12 W 57th St
Penthouse
New York, NY 10019, USA

Harman, Denham (Biologist)
9817 Hamey Parkway S
Omaha, NE 68114, USA

Harman, Jane (Congressman, Politician)
2400 Rq,yburn HOB
Washington, DC 20515, USA

Harman, Jennifer (Misc)
c/o Staff Member Poker Royalty, LLC
10789 W. Twain Ave.
Suite 200
Las Vegas, NV 89135, USA

Harman, Katie (Beauty Pageant Winner)
c/o Staff Member The Miss America Organization
Two Miss America Way #1000
Atlantic City, NJ 08401, USA

Harman, Walter (General)
1003 Vista Ave
Escondido, CA 92026-1543, USA

Harman, Andrew P (Athlete, Football Player)
1258 Waters Edge Dr
Dayton, OH 45458, USA

Harmon, Andy (Football Player)
1258 Waters Edge Dr
Dayton, OH 45458-3937, USA

Harmon, Chuck (Athlete, Baseball Player)
6035 Ridgeacres Dr
Unit A
Cincinnati, OH 45237-4733, USA

Harmon, Clarence (Athlete, Football Player)
P.O. Box 571
Verona, MS 38879, USA

Harmon, Dan (Writer)
c/o Blair Kohan United Talent Agency (UTA)
9336 Civic Center Dr
Beverly Hills, CA 90210, USA

Harmon, Ed (Football Player)
136 Juniper Hill Rd NE
Albuquerque, NM 87122-1913, USA

Harmon, Joy (Actor)
9901 Poole Ave
Sunland, CA 91040, USA

Harmon, Kelly (Actor, Model)
13224 Old Oak Lane
Los Angeles, CA 90049, USA

Harmon, Manny -
8350 Santa Monica Blvd
Los Angeles, CA 90069

Harmon, Mark (Actor)
564 N Cliffwood Ave
Los Angeles, CA 90049, USA

Harmon, Merle (Sportscaster)
424 E Lamar Blvd #210
Arlington, TX 76011, USA

Harmon, Michael (Athlete, Football Player)
336 Hayat Loop
Oxford, MS 38655-9017, USA

Harmon, Mike (Race Car Driver)
Donlavey Racing
5011 Old Midlothian Pike
Richmond, VA 27263, USA

Harmon, Nigel (Astronaut)
Church Crookham
Aldershot, UNITED KINGDOM (UK)

Harmon, Robert (Director)
c/o Andrew Ruf Paradigm (LA)
360 N Crescent Dr
North Bldg
Beverly Hills, CA 90210, USA

Harmon, Ronnie K (Athlete, Football Player)
13022 218th St
Springfield Gardens, NY 11413, USA

Harmon, Terry (Athlete, Baseball Player)
62 Oakwood Dr
Medford, NJ 08055, USA

Harmon, Tom (Athlete, Baseball Player)
6101 Bon Terra Dr
Austin, TX 78731-3849, USA

Harmon, Winsor
c/o Jerry Shandrew Shandrew Public Relations
1050 S Stanley Ave
Los Angeles, CA 90019-6634, USA

Harmonica Rascals, The
4585 N. River Rd.
E. Zanesville, OH 43701-8174

Harmon-Sehorn, Angie (Actor)
5314 Round Meadow Rd
Hidden Hills, CA 91302, USA

Harms, Alfred G Jr (Admiral)
Chief Education/Training
Naval Air Station
Pensacola, FL 32508, USA

Harms, Kristin (Producer)
c/o Staff Member Creative Artists Agency (CAA-LA)
2000 Ave Of The Stars
Los Angeles, CA 90067, USA

Harnden, Arthur (Art) (Athlete, Olympic Athlete, Track Athlete)
7218 Pepper Ridge
Corpus Christi, TX 78413, USA

Harnes, Robert (Baseball Player)
Chicago Giants
833 E Drexel Sq
Chicago, IL 60615-3705, USA

Harness, William E (Opera Singer)
PO Box 328
Washougal, WA 98671, USA

Harnick, Sheldon
General Delivery
Kirtland Afb, NM 87117-9999, USA

Harnick, Sheldon (Writer)
Bell And Company_ 122 E 42nd St Fl 31
New York, NY 10168-3100, USA

Harnisch, Peter T (Pete) (Athlete, Baseball Player)
35 Bretwood Dr S
Colts Neck, NJ 07722-2402, USA

Harnois, Elisabeth (Actor)
c/o Ted Schachter Schachter Entertainment
1157 S Beverly Dr Fl 2
Los Angeles, CA 90035, USA

Harnoncourt, Nikolaus
38 Piaristangasse
Vienna 1080, AUSTRIA

Harnos, Christine (Actor)
Gersh Agency
232 N Canon Dr
Beverly Hills, CA 90210, USA

Harnoy, Ofra (Musician)
437 Spadina Road
PO Box 23046
Toronto, ON M5P 2W0, CANADA

Harold, Gale (Actor)
c/o Larry Taube Principal Entertainment (LA)
1964 Westwood Blvd #400
Los Angeles, CA 90025, USA

Harout, Magda (Actor)
13452 Vose St
Van Nuys, CA 91405, USA

Harp, George
5456 Youngs Rd
Vernon, NY 13476-4712, USA

Harper, Alvin C (Athlete, Football Player)
501 Harry S Truman Dr Apt 109
Upper Marlboro, MD 20774, USA

Harper, Ben (Musician, Songwriter)
2314 La Mesa Dr
Santa Monica, CA 90402, USA

Harper, Bob (Fitness Expert)
c/o Joyce Sevilla Entertainment Fusion Group
8899 Beverly Blvd
Suite 412
West Hollywood, CA 90046, USA

Harper, Brandon (Athlete, Baseball Player)
1612 Iris St
Broomfield, CO 80020-3433, USA

Harper, Brian (Athlete, Baseball Player)
8319 E Shetland Trl
Scottsdale, AZ 85258-1343, USA

Harper, Bruce (Athlete, Football Player)
311 Lindbergh Ave
Closter, NJ 07624, USA

Harper, Bryce (Athlete, Basketball Player)
c/o Scott Boras Boras Corporation
18 Corporate Plaza
Newport Beach, CA 92660, USA

Harper, Charles M (Business Person)
6625 State St
Omaha, NE 68152, USA

Harper, Charlie (Athlete, Football Player)
2115 Augusta
McKinney, TX 75070, USA

Harper, Dave (Athlete, Football Player)
4494 Cedar St
Eureka, CA 95503, USA

Harper, David (Athlete, Football Player)
4494 Cedar St
Eureka, CA 95503-8901, USA

Harper, Dawn (Athlete, Track Athlete)
c/o Staff Member HS International Sports Management, Inc.
9871 Irvine Center Dr
Irvine, CA 92618, USA

Harper, Derek (Athlete, Basketball Player)
3el W 53rd St Apt 14F
New York, NY leel9-5772, USA

Harper, Deveron (Athlete, Football Player)
2749 Huntsville St
Kenner, LA 70062, USA

Harper, Donald D W (Don) (Athlete, Diver, Olympic Athlete)
1765 Lynnhaven Dr
Columbus, OH 43221, USA

Harper, Dwayne (Athlete, Football Player)
104 Cue St
Orangeburg, SC 29115, USA

Harper, Ed (General)
2733 Fairway Oaks Dr
Lake Saint Louis, MO 63367-2940, USA

Harper, Edward J (Composer)
7 Morningside Park
Edinburgh EH10 5HD, SCOTLAND

Harper, Gregg (Congressman, Politician)
307 Cq,nnQn HOB
Washington, DC 20515, USA

Harper, Heather M (Opera Singer)
20 Milverton Road
London NW6 7AS, UNITED KINGDOM
(UK)

Harper, Heck
13647 Gaffney #17
Oregon City, OR 97045

Harper, Herschel (Baseball Player)
Negro Baseball Leagues
3302 Hazelwood Dr SW
Atlanta, GA 30311-3038, USA

Harper, Hill (Actor)
c/o Marvet Britto *Britto Agency PR*
234 W 56th St
Penthouse
New York, NY 10019, USA

Harper, Jessica (Actor, Music Group)
15430 Brownwood Place
Los Angeles, CA 90077, USA

Harper, John
9700 Kessler Ave.
Chatsworth, CA 91311

Harper, Judson M (Engineer)
1818 Westview Road
Fort Collins, CO 80524, USA

Harper, Mark (Athlete, Football Player)
2162 Albany Ave
Memphis, TN 38108, USA

Harper, Michael (Athlete, Basketball
Player)
2387 College Hill Pl
West Linn, OR 97068-1222, USA

Harper, Nick (Athlete, Football Player)
9549 Sanctuary Pl
Brentwood, TN 37027-8499, USA

Harper, Robert (Actor)
Karg/Weissenbach
329 N Wetherly Dr
#101
Beverly Hills, CA 90211, USA

Harper, Roger (Athlete, Football Player)
1921 Holburn Ave
Columbus, OH 43207, USA

Harper, Roland (Athlete, Football Player)
1391 Westbourne Pkwy
Algonquin, IL 60102, USA

Harper, Roman (Athlete, Football Player)
c/o Bill Johnson *SportsTrust Advisors - GA*
3340 Peachtree Rd NE
16th Floor
Atlanta, GA 30326, USA

Harper, Ron (Athlete, Basketball Player)
8934 Brecksville Rd
#417
Brecksville, OH 44141-2318, USA

Harper, Ron (Actor)
c/o Staff Member *Tisherman Gilbert
Motley Drozdoski Talent Agency (TGMD)*
6767 Forest Lawn Dr
Suite 101
Los Angeles, CA 90068, USA

Harper, Shane (Actor)
c/o Nicole David *WME (LA)*
9601 Wilshire Blvd Fl 3
Beverly Hills, CA 90210, USA

Harper, Stephen (Prime Minister)
Prime Minister's Office
Langevin Block
Ottawa, ON K1A 0A1, CANADA

Harper, Terry (Athlete, Baseball Player)
4225 Jailette Rd
Atlanta, GA 30349-1848, USA

Harper, Terry (Athlete, Hockey Player)
PO Box 5227
El Dorado Hills, CA 95762, USA

Harper, Terry (Athlete, Baseball Player)
4225 Jailette Rd
Atlanta, GA 30349, USA

Harper, Tess (Actor)
c/o David Guc *Vanguard Management
Group*
8060 Melrose Ave
4th Floor
Los Angeles, CA 90046, USA

Harper, Tommy (Athlete, Baseball Player)
5 Cow Hill Rd
Sharon, MA 02067-2987, USA

Harper, Travis (Athlete, Baseball Player)
10 Brook Ridge Ln
Morgantown, WV 26508-2542, USA

Harper, Valerie (Actor)
PO Box 7187
Beverly Hills, CA 90212-7187, USA

Harper, Willie M (Athlete, Football
Player)
2525 Berryessa Ct
Tracy, CA 95304, USA

Harpring, Matt (Athlete, Basketball
Player)
c/o Staff Member *Utah Jazz*
301 West South Temple
Salt Lake City, UT 84101, USA

Harptones, The
55 W. 119th St.
New York, NY 10026

Harrah, Colbert D (Toby) (Athlete,
Baseball Player, Coach)
316 Leewood Cir
Azle, TX 76020-4913, USA

Harrah, Dennis W (Athlete, Football
Player)
925 Rockin One Way
Paso Robles, CA 93446-8433, USA

Harrar, J George (Misc)
125 Puritan Dr
Scarsdale, NY 10583, USA

Harraway, Charley (Athlete, Football
Player)
7961 Megan Hammock Way
Sarasota, FL 34240-8244, USA

Harraway, Charlie (Athlete, Football
Player)
7961 Megan Hammock Way
Sarasota, FL 34240, USA

Harrell, Anthony (Actor)

Harrell, Billy (Athlete, Baseball Player)
253 Mount Hope Dr
Albany, NY 12202-1017, USA

Harrell, Graham (Athlete, Football Player)
c/o Chad Speck *Allegiant Athletic Agency*
35 Market Sq
Suite 201
Knoxville, TN 37902, USA

Harrell, James (Athlete, Football Player)
17826 Crystal Preserve Dr
Lutz, FL 33548-6408, USA

Harrell, James A (Geophysicist, Physicist)
University of Toledo
Geology Dept
Toledo, OH 43606, USA

Harrell, John (Athlete, Baseball Player)
756 Erie Cir
Milpitas, CA 95035-3551, USA

Harrell, Justin (Athlete, Football Player)
c/o Eugene Parker *Maximum Sports
Management*
6435 W Jefferson Blvd
#197
Fort Wayne, IN 46804, USA

Harrell, Lucas (Athlete, Baseball Player)
2453 E Raynell St
Springfield, MO 65804-4510, USA

Harrell, Lynn M (Musician)
I M G Artists
420 W 45th St
New York, NY 10036, USA

Harrell, Sam (Athlete, Football Player)
5758 Hirondel St
Houston, TX 77033-2302, USA

Harrell, Tom (Music Group, Musician)
Joel Chriss
300 Mercer St #3J
New York, NY 10003, USA

Harrell, Willard (Athlete, Football Player)
8 Scarlet Oak Ct
Lake Saint Louis, MO 63367, USA

Harrelson, Bill (Athlete, Baseball Player)
6900 Kimberly Ave
Bakersfield, CA 93308-3923, USA

Harrelson, Brett (Actor)
Agency for Performing Arts
9200 Sunset Blvd #900
Los Angeles, CA 90069, USA

Harrelson, Derrell M (Bud) (Athlete,
Baseball Player, Coach)
357 Ridgefield Rd
Hauppauge, NY 11788-2314, USA

Harrelson, Ken (Commentator)
9006 Shawn Park Pl
Orlando, FL 11722-4605, USA

Harrelson, Woody (Actor)
c/o Ina Treciokas *Slate Public Relations*
9000 Sunset Blvd #915
West Hollywood, CA 90069, USA

Harrer, Tim (Athlete, Hockey Player)
7030 W 113th St
Minneapolis, MN 55438-2446, USA

Harrick, Jim (Basketball Player, Coach)
Denver Nuggets
Pepsi Center
1000 Chopper Circle
Denver, CO 80204, USA

Harriet, Judy (Actor)
12400 Ventura Blvd
Studio City, CA 91604, USA

Harrigan, Lori (Athlete, Olympic Athlete,
Softball Player)
828 Rainbow Rock St
Las Vegas, NV 89123-3121, USA

Harriger, Denny (Athlete, Baseball Player)
902 N Water St
Kittanning, PA 16201-1121, USA

Harring, Laura Elena (Actor, Beauty
Pageant Winner)
12335 Santa Monica Blvd #302
Los Angeles, CA 90025, USA

Harrington, Al (Athlete, Basketball Player)
16124 Chancellors Ridge Way
Noblesville, IN 46062-7137, USA

Harrington, Bill (Athlete, Baseball Player)
7219 Cleveland School Rd
Garner, NC 27529-8928, USA

Harrington, Dan (Misc)
PO Box 1659
Santa Monica, CA 90406-1659, USA

Harrington, David (Music Group,
Musician)
Kronos Quartet
1235 9th Ave
San Francisco, CA 94122, USA

Harrington, Dennis (Athlete, Golfer)
Stanford Roberts
5668 S Rex Rd #101
Memphis, TN 38119, USA

Harrington, Desmond (Actor)
c/o Stephanie Simon *Untitled
Entertainment (LA)*
350 S. Beverly Dr #200
Beverly Hills, CA 90212, USA

Harrington, Donald J (Educator)
Saint John's Univesity
President's Office
Jamaica, NY 11439, USA

Harrington, Jay (Actor)
c/o Abe Hoch *A Management*
9107 Wilshire Blvd.
Suite 650
Beverly Hills, CA 90210, USA

Harrington, Joey (Athlete, Football Player)
708 NE Royal Ct
Portland, OR 97232-2671, USA

Harrington, John (Athlete, Hockey Player,
Olympic Athlete)
StJohn's University
PO Box 7277 Attn Hockey Program
Collegeville, MN 56321-7277, USA

Harrington, Mickev (Athlete, Baseball
Player)
135 Scenic Dr
Hattiesburg_, MS 39401-8403, USA

Harrington, Mike (Mickey) (Athlete,
Baseball Player)
135 Scenic Dr
Hattiesburg, MS 39401, USA

Harrington, Othella (Athlete, Basketball
Player)
1602 Rika Pt
Houston, TX 77077-3432, USA

Harrington, Padraig (Golfer)
c/o Staff Member *Pro Golfers Association
(PGA) Tour*
112 TPC Blvd
Ponte Vedra Beach, FL 32082, USA

Harrington, Pat
730 Marzella Ave.
Los Angeles, A 90049

Harrington, Pat Jr (Actor)
730 Marzella Ave
Los Angeles, CA 90049, USA

Harrington, Perry (Athlete, Football Player)
1302 Roxbury Ct
Jackson, MS 39211, USA

Harrington, Robert (Race Car Driver)
2609 Woodshade Ave
Kannapolis, NC 28127, USA

Harrington, Scott (Race Car Driver)
920 Ardmore Dr.
Louisville, KY 40217, USA

Harriott, Ainsley
12 Ogle St.
London, ENGLAND W1P 7LG

Harris, Al (Athlete, Football Player)
4200 Coral Hills Dr
Coral Springs, FL 33065, USA

Harris, Al (Athlete, Football Player)
12 Stone Ridge Dr
South Barrington, IL 60010, USA

Harris, Alonzo (Candy) (Athlete, Baseball Player)
7378 Tyler Ln
Fontana, CA 92336-5772, USA

Harris, Andy (Congressman, Politician)
506 Callinon HOB
Washington, DC 20515, USA

Harris, Antwan (Athlete, Football Player)
7413 Ray Rd
Raleigh, NC 27613, USA

Harris, Archie (Athlete, Football Player)
17 Hawthorne Ct NE
Washington, DC 20017, USA

Harris, Arlen (Athlete, Football Player)
223 Wellsmont Ct
Saint Charles, MO 63304-2326, USA

Harris, Barbara
159 W. 53rd St. #12-D
New York, NY 10019-6005

Harris, Barbara C (Activist, Religious Leader)
Episcopal Diocese of Massachusetts
138 Tremont St
Boston, MA 02111, USA

Harris, Barry (DJ, Music Group, Musician)
Brad Simon Organization
122 E 57th St #300
New York, NY 10022, USA

Harris, Bernard A Dr
3411 Erin Knoll Ct
Houston, TX 77059-3716, USA

Harris, Bernard A Jr (Astronaut)
3411 Erin Knoll Court
Houston, TX 77059, USA

Harris, Billy (Athlete, Baseball Player)
205 FellowshiP Dr
Hamlet, NC 28345-3507, USA

Harris, Billy (Athlete, Hockey Player)
Muskoka Candle Company PO Box 233
Rosseau, ON POC 1JO, Canada

Harris, Bishop Barbara
138 Tremont St.
Boston, MA 02111

Harris, Bo (Athlete, Football Player)
P.O. Box 52539
Shreveport, LA 71135, USA

Harris, Boyd (Gail) (Athlete, Baseball Player)
9008 Weir St
Manassas, VA 20155-1252, USA

Harris, Brendan (Athlete, Baseball Player)
30 Fox Hollow Ln
Queensbury, NY 12804-1139, USA

Harris, Buddy (Athlete, Baseball Player)
2305 Carol Ln
Norristown, PA 19128-4926, USA

Harris, Calvin (DJ, Musician)
c/o Alexandra Greenberg *Mitch Schneider Organization (MSO)*
14724 Ventura Blvd #410
Sherman Oaks, CA 91403, USA

Harris, Charlaine (Writer)
PO Box 354
Magnolia, AR 71754, USA

Harris, Charles (Bubba) (Athlete, Baseball Player)
P.O. Box 159
Nobleton, FL 34661, USA

Harris, Chris (Athlete, Basketball Player)
1ee Oakmont Ln Apt 8e8
Belleair, FL 33756-1975, USA

Harris, Cliff (Athlete, Football Player)
722 Kentwood Dr
Rockwall, TX 75032, USA

Harris, Clifford (T.I.) (Musician)
c/o Brian Sher *Category 5 Entertainment*
9229 Sunset Blvd.
Suite 601
Los Angeles, CA 90069, USA

Harris, Corey (Athlete, Football Player)
933 N Tremont St
Indianapolis, IN 46222, USA

Harris, Cristi Ellen
c/o Staff Member *House of Representatives, The*
1434 6th St
Suite 1
Santa Monica, CA 90401, USA

Harris, Damian (Director)
International Creative Mgmt
8942 Wilshire Blvd #219
Beverly Hills, CA 90211, USA

Harris, Danielle (Actor, Director)
c/o Felicia Sager *Sager Management*
260 S Beverly Dr
Suite 205
Beverly Hills, CA 90212, USA

Harris, Danneel (Actor)
c/o Jason Newman *Untitled Entertainment (LA)*
350 S. Beverly Dr #200
Beverly Hills, CA 90212, USA

Harris, Del (Basketball Coach, Coach)
1134 Osage Cir
St George, UT 84790-6810, USA

Harris, Devin (Athlete, Basketball Player)
8 Green Park Dr
Dallas, TX 75248-2798, USA

Harris, Dickie (Athlete, Football Player)
801 Fuller Ave
Kelowna, BC V1Y 6X2, Canada

Harris, Donald (Athlete, Baseball Player)
916 Hubert St
Waco, TX 76704, USA

Harris, Duriel (Athlete, Football Player)
3875 San Pablo Rd S Apt 1212
Jacksonville, FL 32224-6819, USA

Harris, Ed (Actor)
c/o Catherine Olim *PMK/BNC Public Relations (PMK-LA)*
8687 Melrose Ave Fl 8
West Hollywood, CA 90069, USA

Harris, Emmylou (Musician, Songwriter)
P.O. Box 158568
Nashville, TN 37215-8568, USA

Harris, Ernest (Athlete, Baseball Player)
1007 46th St Ensley
Birmingham, AL 35208-1434, USA

Harris, Estelle (Actor)
c/o Joel Dean *TalentWorks (LA)*
3500 W Olive Ave
Suite 1400
Burbank, CA 91505, USA

Harris, Franco (Athlete, Football Player)
200 Chauser Ct S
Sewickley, PA 15143, USA

Harris, Gail (Baseball Player)
New York Giants
9008 Weir St
Manassas, VA 20110 4913, USA

Harris, Gail Robyn (Actor)
Don Gerler
3349 Cahuenga Blvd W #1
Los Angeles, CA 90068, USA

Harris, George (Athlete, Hockey Player)
1467 Miller Dr
Sarnia, ON N7S 3M5, Canada

Harris, Greg (Athlete, Baseball Player)
12613 Richmond Run Ct
Raleigh, NC 02653-6665, USA

Harris, Greg (Athlete, Baseball Player)
P.O. Box 2665
Orleans, MA 02653, USA

Harris, Henry (Biologist)
William Dunn Pathology School
South Parks Road
Oxford OX1 3RE, UNITED KINGDOM (UK)

Harris, Hernando (Pep) (Athlete, Baseball Player)
995 Ten Oaks Dr
Lancaster, SC 29720, USA

Harris, Hugh (Athlete, Hockey Player)
9784 Herons Cv
Indianapolis, IN 46280-2787, USA

Harris, Ike (Athlete, Football Player)
Bellsouth Corporation
26 N Waterview Dr
Palm Coast, FL 32137-1619, USA

Harris, Jackie (Athlete, Football Player)
716 W Barraque St
Pine Bluff, AR 71601-4064, USA

Harris, James L (Athlete, Football Player)
9838 Old Baymeadows Rd
Jacksonville, FL 32256, USA

Harris, Jared (Actor)
c/o Amy Guenther *Gateway Management Company Inc*
860 Via De La Paz
Suite F10
Pacific Palisades, CA 90272, USA

Harris, Jay (Cartoonist)
c/o Staff Member *King Features Syndication*
300 W 57th St
15th Floor
New York, NY 10019-5238, USA

Harris, Jeff (Athlete, Baseball Player)
Lake County Captains 35300 Vine St Attn: Coaching Staff, OH 44095-3142, USA

Harris, Joe (Athlete, Football Player)
4747 River Rd
Ellenwood, GA 30294, USA

Harris, Joe Frank (Ex-Governor)
712 West Ave
Cartersville, GA 30120, USA

Harris, John (Athlete, Golfer)
4316 Fremont Ave S
Minneapolis, MN 55409-1721, USA

Harris, John (Athlete, Hockey Player)
Somerset Downs
11-4311 20 St
Vernon, BC V1T 4E4, Canada

Harris, John (Athlete, Baseball Player)
7064 Chelsea Dr
Amarillo, TX 79119-6588, USA

Harris, John (Athlete, Football Player)
270 NW 120th St
Miami, FL 33168, USA

Harris, John R (Architect)
24 Devonshire Place
London W1N 2BX, UNITED KINGDOM (UK)

Harris, Jon (Athlete, Football Player)
110 Cedar Ct
Swedesboro, NJ 08085, USA

Harris, Joshua (Actor)
1800 Vine St #305
Los Angeles, CA 90028, USA

Harris, Julie (Actor)
c/o Staff Member *WmE2 (WMA-LA)*
1 William Morris Pl
Beverly Hills, CA 90212, USA

Harris, Juliette (Actor)
c/o Staff Member *It Girl Public Relations*
5301 Beethoven St
Suite 220
Los Angeles, CA 90066, USA

Harris, Katherine
c/o Daniel Strone *Trident Media Group LLC*
41 Madison Ave
36th Floor
New York, NY 10010, USA

Harris, Kwame (Athlete, Football Player)
4949 Centennial Blvd
Santa Clara, CA 95054, USA

Harris, Lara (Actor)
c/o Peter Kaiser *Talent House (NY)*
325 W 38th St #605
New York, NY 10018, USA

Harris, Larry (Athlete, Football Player)
41 Alta Ave
Yonkers, NY 10705, USA

Harris, Laura (Actor)
c/o Kami Putnam-Heist *Creative Artists Agency (CAA-LA)*
9601 Wilshire Blvd
3rd Floor
Beverly Hills, CA 90210, USA

Harris, Lenny (Athlete, Baseball Player)
JD Legends Promotions
Attn: Jack DeLance
10808 Foothill Blvd #160-454
Rancho Cucamonga, CA 33015-2050,
USA

Harris, Leon (Correspondent)
Cable News Network
News Dept
1050 Techwood Dr NW
Atlanta, GA 30318, USA

Harris, Leonard (Athlete, Football Player)
1817 Trilogy Park Dr
Hoschton, GA 30548, USA

Harris, Leotis (Athlete, Football Player)
2815 Stephanie Dr
Little Rock, AR 72206-5421, USA

Harris, Leroy (Athlete, Football Player)
1919 Live Oak St
Savannah, GA 31404, USA

Harris, Lou (Athlete, Football Player)
5606 Windsor Ct
Suitland, MD 20746-4410, USA

Harris, Louis (Mathematician)
200 E 66th St
#2004
New York, NY 10021, USA

Harris, Lucious (Athlete, Basketball Player)
1149 W 62nd Street
Los Angeles, CA 90044-3733, USA

Harris, Major (Athlete, Football Player)
c/o Staff Member *College Football Hall Of Fame*
111 South St. Joseph St
South Bend, IN 46601, USA

Harris, Marilyn
217 N. San Marino Ave.
San Gabriel, CA 91775

Harris, Mel (Actor)
c/o Joanna (Joanie) Burstein *Burstein Company, The*
15304 Sunset Blvd
suite 208
Pacific Palisades, CA 90272, USA

Harris, Meredith Gray (Stylist)
c/o Staff Member *Anyway Productions*
870 Avenue of the Americas
New York, NY 10001, USA

Harris, M L (Athlete, Football Player)
M L Harris Outreach
15589 Apple Valley Rd
Apple Valley, CA 92307, USA

Harris, Moira (Actor)
c/o Staff Member *Creative Artists Agency (CAA-LA)*
2000 Ave Of The Stars
Los Angeles, CA 90067, USA

Harris, Naomie (Actor)
c/o Christina Papadopoulos *Baker Winokur Ryder Public Relations BWR (BWR-NY)*
292 Madison Ave
12th Floor
New York, NY 10017, USA

Harris, Napoleon (Athlete, Football Player)
c/o Staff Member *EAG Sports Management*
12910 Agustin Pl
Playa Vista, CA 90094, USA

Harris, Neil (Historian)
5555 S Everett Ave
Chicago, IL 60637, USA

Harris, Neil Patrick (Actor)
3946 Stone Canyon Ave
Sherman Oaks, CA 91404, USA

Harris, Nick (Athlete, Football Player)
2035 Kingsway Dr
Troy, MI 48098-4173, USA

Harris, Odie L Jr (Athlete, Football Player)
821 S Polk St Apt 127
Desoto, TX 75115, USA

Harris, Quentin (Athlete, Football Player)
3013 W Glass Ln
Phoenix, AZ 85041, USA

Harris, Rachael (Actor, Comedian)
c/o Peter Principato *Principato/Young Management*
9465 Wilshire Blvd
Suite 430
Beverly Hills, CA 90212, USA

Harris, Raymont (Athlete, Football Player)
1144 Aroya Ct
New Albany, OH 43054, USA

Harris, Reggie (Athlete, Baseball Player)
35 Ashleigh Dr
Waynesboro, VA 22980-7479, USA

Harris, Rickie (Athlete, Football Player)
4225 Mozart Brigade Ln Apt 1
Fairfax, VA 22033-3960, USA

Harris, Robert (Athlete, Football Player)
4533 River Gem Ave
Windermere, FL 34786-3128, USA

Harris, Rolf (Entertainer)
c/o Suzanne Westrip *Billy Marsh Associates*
76A Grove End Rd
St John's Wood
London NW8 9ND, UK

Harris, Ron (Athlete, Hockey Player)
7 Bachman Terr
Kanata, ON K2L 1W2, Canada

Harris, Ronald W (Ronnie) (Boxer)
1365 Glenview St NE
Canton, OH 44721, USA

Harris, Ronnie (Athlete, Football Player)
16911 123rd Pl NE
Bothell, WA 98011-7135, USA

Harris, Rosemary (Actor)
International Creative Mgmt
76 Oxford St
London W1N 0AX, UNITED KINGDOM (UK)

Harris, Ross
6542 Fulcher Ave.
No. Hollywood, CA 91606

Harris, Ryan (Athlete, Football Player)
c/o Eugene Parker *Maximum Sports Management*
6435 W Jefferson Blvd
#197
Fort Wayne, IN 46804, USA

Harris, Sam (Actor, Music Group, Writer)
c/o Barry Krost *Barry Krost Management*
9220 W Sunset Blvd Ste 106
Los Angeles, CA 90069, USA

Harris, Samantha (Actor)
c/o David Brady *Bx2 Management*
1333 2nd St
Suite 620
Santa Monica, CA 90401, USA

Harris, Sean (Athlete, Football Player)
2255 W Germann Rd Apt 1162
Chandler, AZ 85286-7270, USA

Harris, Sidney (Cartoonist)
302 W 86th St #9A
New York, NY 10024, USA

Harris, Stefon (Misc)
Joel Chriss
300 Mercer St
#3J
New York, NY 10003, USA

Harris, Steve (Athlete, Basketball Player)
3005 W Fort Worth St
Broken Arrow, OK 74012-3276, USA

Harris, Steve (Actor)
c/o Colton Gramm *Brillstein Entertainment Partners*
9150 Wilshire Blvd #350
Beverly Hills, CA 90212, USA

Harris, Steve (Musician)
Sanctuary Music Mgmt
82 Bishop's Bridge Road
London W2 6BB, UNITED KINGDOM (UK)

Harris, Susan (Producer)
LaGrange Management
11828 La Grange Ave #200
Los Angeles, CA 90025, USA

Harris, Ted (Athlete, Hockey Player)
1 Stonegate Ct
Blackwood, NJ 08012, USA

Harris, Thomas (Director, Writer)
c/o Robert (Bob) Bookman *Creative Artists Agency (CAA-LA)*
2000 Ave Of The Stars
Los Angeles, CA 90067, USA

Harris, Tim (Athlete, Football Player)
843 North N St
Livermore, CA 94551, USA

Harris, Tomas (Writer)
c/o Robert (Bob) Bookman *Creative Artists Agency (CAA-LA)*
2000 Ave Of The Stars
Los Angeles, CA 90067, USA

Harris, Tommie (Athlete, Football Player)
1000 Football Dr
Lake Forest, IL 60045, USA

Harris, Tony (Athlete, Football Player)
530 Venice Way
Apt 6
Inglewood, CA 90302, USA

Harris, Tyrone (Gene) (Athlete, Baseball Player)
1267 NE 16th Ave
Okeechobee, FL 34972-3066, USA

Harris, Vic (Athlete, Baseball Player)
5420 S Garth Ave
Los Angeles, CA 90056-1116, USA

Harris, Walt (Athlete, Football Player)
4103 Shinault Ln
Olive Branch, MS 38654, USA

Harris, Wendell (Athlete, Football Player)
10338 Westwood Ave
Baton Rouge, LA 70809-3268, USA

Harris, William M (Athlete, Football Player)
2118 Laurel Forest Way
Houston, TX 77014, USA

Harris, Willie (Athlete, Baseball Player)
1176 Willie C Harris Dr
Cairo, GA 39828, USA

Harris, Wilmer (Baseball Player)
Philadelphia Stars
441 Tomlinson Rd Apt F3
Philadelphia, PA 19116-3227, USA

Harris, Wood (Actor)
Gersh Agency
232 North Canon Drive
Beverly Hills, CA 90210, USA

Harris III, James S. (Jimmy Jam) (Composer, Producer)
c/o Staff Member *Flyte Tyme Productions*
P.O. Box 398045
Edina, MN 55435, USA

Harris Jr, Clifford (TI) (Musician)
c/o Brian Sher *Category 5 Entertainment*
9229 Sunset Blvd.
Suite 601
Los Angeles, CA 90069, USA

Harrison, Alvin (Athlete, Track Athlete)
Octagon
1751 Pinnacle Dr #1500
McLean, VA 22102, USA

Harrison, Bertram C (General)
P.O. Box 209
Leesburg, VA 20178-0209, USA

Harrison, Bob (Athlete, Baseball Player)
16777 Loch Cir
Noblesville, IN 46060-4482, USA

Harrison, Bob (Athlete, Football Player)
3 Westwind Cir
Stamford, TX 79553, USA

Harrison, Brett (Actor)
1539 N. Laurel Ave. #305
Los Angeles, CA 90046, USA

Harrison, Chris (Actor, Reality TV Star)
c/o Staff Member *Creative Public Relations*
3385 Oak Glen Dr
Los Angeles, CA 90068, USA

Harrison, Chuck (Athlete, Baseball Player)
222 Buckskin Rd
Abilene, TX 79602-4508, USA

Harrison, C Richard (Business Person)
Parametric Technology
140 Kendrick St
Needham Heights, MA 02494, USA

Harrison, David (Athlete, Basketball Player)
11593 Larkspur Ln
Carmel, IN 46e32-8614, USA

Harrison, Dennis (Athlete, Football Player)
1048 Hickory Hollow Rd
Nashville, TN 37221, USA

Harrison, Dwight (Athlete, Football Player)
2265 Buchanan St
Beaumont, TX 77703, USA

Harrison, Glynn (Athlete, Football Player)
485 Huntington Rd
Suite 203
Athens, GA 30606, USA

Harrison, Greg (Actor)
c/o Staff Member *Stone Manners Salners Agency (LA)*
9911 W Pico Blvd Ste 1400
Los Angeles, CA 90035, USA

Harrison, James (Athlete, Football Player)
2525 Matterhorn Dr
Wexford, PA 15090, USA

Harrison, Jane (Stylist)
455 W 23rd St
New York, NY 10011, USA

Harrison, Jenilee (Actor)
JLeeCorp
19528 Ventura Blvd #365
Tarzana, CA 91356, USA

Harrison, Jerome (Athlete, Football Player)
7500 Paradise Rd Lot 75
San Antonio, TX 78244-2293, USA

Harrison, Jerry (Musician)
Sire/Warner Bros Records
3300 Warner Blvd
Burbank, CA 91505, USA

Harrison, Jim (Athlete, Football Player)
6038 Royal Crk
San Antonio, TX 78239-1614, USA

Harrison, Jim (Athlete, Hockey Player)
102-645 Barrera Rd
Kelowna, BC V1W 3C9, Canada

Harrison, Kathryn (Writer)
Random House
1745 Broadway #B1
New York, NY 10019, USA

Harrison, Landon (General)
7517 Tamarron PINE
Albuquerque, NM 87109-3836, USA

Harrison, Linda (Actor)
9846 Portola Drive
Beverly Hills, CA 90210-1421, USA

Harrison, Lisi (Writer)
c/o Richard Abate *3 Arts Entertainment - NY*
49 West 27th St.
5th Floor
New York, NY 10001, USA

Harrison, Mark (Editor)
The Gazette
250 Saint Antoine St W
Montreal, QC H2Y 2R7, CANADA

Harrison, Martin (Athlete, Football Player)
6160 S Featherstone Cir
Reno, NV 89511-4349, USA

Harrison, Marvin (Athlete, Football Player)
10 Breyer Ct
Elkins Park, PA 19027-1350, USA

Harrison, Matt (Athlete, Baseball Player)
160Irvil'lg Pl
Creedmoo, NC 27522-7028, USA

Harrison, Matthew (Director)
Rigberg Roberts Rugolo
1180 S Beverly Dr #601
Los Angeles, CA 90035, USA

Harrison, Michael Allen (Composer, Musician)
MAH Records
1610 NE Tillamook St
#1
Portland, OR 97212, USA

Harrison, (Mya) Marie (Actor)
c/o Melissa Berger *Melissa Berger Public Relations*
613 W. Knoll
#C
West Hollywood, CA 90069, USA

Harrison, Nolan (Athlete, Football Player)
2121 N Westmoreland St Apt 543
Arlington, VA 22213-1069, USA

Harrison, Patti Boyd (Photographer)
Friar Park Road
Henley on Thames, England

Harrison, Paul (Athlete, Hockey Player)
486 Elm St S
Timmins, ON P4N 1X9, Canada

Harrison, Randy (Actor, Producer)
c/o Staff Member *Paradigm (LA)*
360 N Crescent Dr
North Bldg
Beverly Hills, CA 90210, USA

Harrison, Reggie (Athlete, Football Player)
1912 Halifax Rd
Woodbridge, VA 22191, USA

Harrison, Robert (Athlete, Basketball Player)
13405 NW Wax Myrtle Trl
Palm City, FL 34990-4826, USA

Harrison, Rodney (Athlete, Football Player)
2825 Darlington Pointe
Duluth, GA 30097-4318, USA

Harrison, Roric (Athlete, Baseball Player)
18662 Macarthur Blvd
Suite 200
Irvine, CA 92612, USA

Harrison, Rorie (Athlete, Baseball Player)
680 Glenneyre St
Laguna Beach, CA 92651-2420, USA

Harrison, Schae
7800 Beverly Blvd. #3371
Los Angeles, CA 90036

Harrison, Tom (Athlete, Baseball Player)
2932 Channing Way
Los Alamitos, CA 90720-4049, USA

Harrison, Tony (Writer)
Gordon Dickinson
2 Crescent Grove
London SW4 7AH, UNITED KINGDOM (UK)

Harrison, Tyreo (Athlete, Football Player)
8619 Braun Hill Dr
San Antonio, TX 78254, USA

Harrison, William B Jr (Financier)
JP Morgan Chase Corp
270 Park Ave
New York, NY 10017, USA

Harrison, William H (General)
7302 Amber Lane SW
Tacoma, WA 98498, USA

Harrison Breetzke, Joan (Swimmer)
16 Clevedon Road
East London 5201, SOUTH AFRICA

Harris-Stewart, Luisa (Basketball Player, Olympic Athlete)
1002 Cherry St
Greenwood, MS 38930-6506, USA

Harris-Stewart, Lusia M (Lucy) (Athlete, Basketball Player, Olympic Athlete)
1002 Cherry Street
Greenwood, MS 38930, USA

Harrold, Peter (Athlete, Hockey Player)
9385 Baldwin Rd
Mentor, OH 44060-8055, USA

Harron, Mary (Director, Producer, Writer)
c/o Staff Member *Dontanville/Frattaroli (D/F)*
270 Lafayette St
Suite 402
New York, NY 10012, USA

Harrow, Lisa
46 Albemarle St
London, ENGLAND W1X 4PP

Harry (Prince)
Clarence House
Stable Yard Gate
London SW1, UNITED KINGDOM (UK)

Harry, Debbie (Actor, Musician, Songwriter)
c/o Linda Carbone *Press Here Publicity*
138 W. 25th St
9th Floor
New York, NY 10001, USA

Harry, Deborah (Actor, Musician)
c/o Jason Weinberg *Untitled Entertainment (LA)*
350 S. Beverly Dr #200
Beverly Hills, CA 90212, USA

Harry, Emile (Athlete, Football Player)
34 Villa Vista Dr
Brownsville, TX 78520, USA

Harry, Jackee (Actor, Director)
c/o Christopher Barrett *Metropolitan (MTA)*
4526 Wilshire Blvd
Los Angeles, CA 90010, USA

Harryhausen, Ray F (Director)
2 Ilchester Place
W Kensington
London W14 8AA, UNITED KINGDOM (UK)

Harsch, Eddie (Musician)
c/o Staff Member *Mitch Schneider Organization (MSO)*
14724 Ventura Blvd #410
Sherman Oaks, CA 91403, USA

Harshman, Jack (Athlete, Baseball Player)
320 Yukon Ter
Georgetown, NY 78633-5098, USA

Harshman, Margo (Actor)

Harshman, Marv (Athlete, Basketball Player, Coach)
1653 S Geiger St
Tacoma, WA 98465-1509, USA

Hart, Bethany (Athlete, Bobsledder, Olympic Athlete)
13 Elm St
North Grafton, MA 01536-1403, USA

Hart, Bo (Athlete, Baseball Player)
P.O. Box 1761
Freedom, CA 95062-4918, USA

Hart, Bob (Bowler)
5740 Laurel Oak Dr
Suwanee, GA 30024-3370, USA

Hart, Bret
435 Patina Place SE
Calgary, CANADA Alb T3H 2P

Hart, Christopher
1423 N. Martel Ave. #4
Los Angeles, CA 90046-4204

Hart, Clinton (Athlete, Football Player)
2894 County Road 730
Webster, FL 33597, USA

Hart, Corey (Athlete, Baseball Player)
1445 Lambert Close #300
Montreal, CANADA 42101-5220, USA

Hart, Dick (Athlete, Football Player)
273 Oarlock Cir
East Syracuse, NY 13057, USA

Hart, Dolores Hart (Actor)
Regina Laudis Abbey
275 Flanders Road
Bethlehem, CT 06751, USA

Hart, Doris (Tennis Player)
600 Biltmore Way #306
Coral Gables, FL 33134, USA

Hart, Dorothy
43 Martindale Rd.
Asheville, NC 28804

Hart, Doug (Athlete, Football Player)
2192 Medina Rd
Long Lake, MN 55356-9501, USA

Hart, Dudley (Athlete, Golfer)
5130 Rockledge Dr
Clarence, NY 14031-2442, USA

Hart, Freddie (Music Group, Musician, Songwriter, Writer)
317 N Kenwood
Burbank, CA 91505, USA

Hart, Gary (Politician)
27925 Troublesome Gulch Rd
Evergreen, CO 80439-9260, USA

Hart, Gary W (Ex-Senator, Politician, Writer)
c/o Staff Member *Henry Holt & Company*
175 Fifth Avenue
New York, NY 10010, USA

Hart, Gerry (Athlete, Hockey Player)
10 Parkridge Ct
Huntington, NY 11743, USA

Hart, Harold J (Athlete, Football Player)
1016 Brook View Ave
Atlanta, GA 30340-3842, USA

Hart, Herbert L A (Lawyer)
11 Manor Place
Oxford, UNITED KINGDOM (UK)

Hart, Ian (Actor)
P F D
Drury House 34-43 Russell St
London WC2B 5HA, UNITED KINGDOM (UK)

Hart, James V (Director, Producer, Writer)
c/o Jon Levin *Creative Artists Agency (CAA-LA)*
2000 Ave Of The Stars
Los Angeles, CA 90067, USA

Hart, James W (Jim) (Athlete, Football Player, Misc)
3141 Dominica Way
Naples, FL 34119, USA

Hart, Jane (Aviator)
18584 Lancashire Way
San Diego, CA 92128-1032, USA

Hart, Jason (Athlete, Baseball Player)
19317 Nestor Ave
Carson, CA 9e746-26e7, USA

Hart, Jeff (Athlete, Football Player)
1307 SE 14th Ave
Canby, OR 97013, USA

Hart, Jeff (Athlete, Golfer)
105 Guanajuato Ct
Solana Beach, CA 92075-2510, USA

Hart, Jim (Athlete, Football Player)
3141 Dominica Way
Naples, FL 34119, USA

Hart, Jimmy (Actor, Composer, Wrestler)
c/o Nick Cordasco *Prince Marketing Group*
18 Carillon Cir
Livingston, NJ 07039, USA

Hart, Jim Ray (Athlete, Baseball Player)
17074 Templeton Ln
Lathrop, CA 95330, USA

Hart, John (Commentator)
5205 Latrobe Dr
Windermere, FL 34786-8959, USA

Hart, John (Athlete, Baseball Player)
5205 Latrobe Dr
Windermere, FL 34786-8959, USA

Hart, John R (Correspondent)
International Creative Mgmt
40 W 57th St #1800
New York, NY 10019, USA

Hart, Kevin (Athlete, Baseball Player)
5605 Plantation Cir
Plano, TX 75093-4205, USA

Hart, Kevin (Actor, Comedian)
c/o David (Dave) Becky *3 Arts Entertainment Inc*
9460 Wilshire Blvd
7th Floor
Beverly Hills, CA 90210, USA

Hart, Larry (Athlete, Football Player)
c/o Jordan Woy *Willis and Woy Management*
3030 Olive St #520
Dallas, TX 75219, USA

Hart, Leo (Athlete, Football Player)
1014 Arbor Trce NE
Atlanta, GA 30319-5378

Hart, Linda (Actor)
c/o Staff Member *Gage Group, The (LA)*
14724 Ventura Blvd
Suite 505
Sherman Oaks, CA 91403, USA

Hart, Marcy (Athlete, Golfer)
886 Meadowlands Dr
Winston Salem, NC 27107, USA

Hart, Margie
228 S. Hudson Ave.
Los Angeles, CA 90004

Hart, Melissa Joan (Actor)
c/o Kieran Maguire *The Arlook Group*
205 S Beverly Dr
Suite 209
Beverly Hills, CA 90212, USA

Hart, Mickey (Music Group, Musician)
c/o Staff Member *Agency Group Ltd, The (NY)*
142 West 57th St
6th Floor
New York, NY 10019, USA

Hart, Mike (Athlete, Baseball Player)
409 Larkspur Ave
Portage, MI 49002, USA

Hart, Mike (Athlete, Baseball Player)
16552 W Crescent Dr
New Berlin, WI 53151, USA

Hart, Parker T (Diplomat)
4705 Berkeley Terrace NW
Washington, DC 20007, USA

Hart, Richard (Athlete, Football Player)
273 Oarlock Clr
East Syracuse, NY 13057, USA

Hart, Roxanne
c/o Staff Member *Seven Summits Pictures & Management*
8906 W Olympic Blvd
Ground Floor
Beverly Hills, CA 90211, USA

Hart, Stanley R (Geophysicist, Physicist)
53 Quonset Road
Falmouth, MA 02540, USA

Hart, Terry J (Astronaut)
PO Box V
Hellertown, PA 18055, USA

Hart, Terry J Dr (Astronaut)
PO Box V
Hellertown, PA 18055-0218, USA

Hart, Tommy (Athlete, Football Player)
3503 Highland Ave
Redwood City, CA 94062, USA

Hartack, Bill (Horse Racer)
4215 W 6th Ave
Hialeah, FL 33012-3815, USA

Harte, Houston H (Publisher)
Harte-Hanks Communications
200 Concord Plaza Dr
San Antonio, TX 78216, USA

Hartenstein, Chuck (Athlete, Baseball Player)
10735 Cassia Dr
Austin, TX 78759-6452, USA

Hartenstine, Michael A (Mike) (Athlete, Football Player)
322 Winchester Ct
Lake Bluff, IL 60044, USA

Hartgraves, Dean (Athlete, Baseball Player)
1741 S Sierra Vista Dr
Tempe, AZ 85281, USA

Hartigan, Grace (Artist)
1701 1/2 Eastern Ave
Baltimore, MD 21231, USA

Hartigan, Mark (Athlete, Hockey Player)
17925 48th Ct N
Minneapolis, MN 55446-1948, USA

Hartings, Jeff (Athlete, Football Player)
171 Manchester Cir
Pittsburgh, PA 15237-8701, USA

Hartler, Vicky (Congressman, Politician)
1023 Longworth HOB
Washington, DC 20515, USA

Hartley, Bob (Athlete, Coach, Hockey Player)
13 South Ave SE
Atlanta, GA 30315, USA

Hartley, Frank (Athlete, Football Player)
4022 Fishermans Cove Ct
Lutz, FL 33558-9749, USA

Hartley, Hal (Director)
True Fiction Pictures
39 W 14th St #406
New York, NY 10011, USA

Hartley, Harry J (Educator)
University of Connecticut
President's Office
Storrs, CT 06269, USA

Hartley, Justin (Actor)
c/o Theodore B Gekis *Gekis Management*
4217 Verdugo View Dr
Los Angeles, CA 90065-4317, USA

Hartley, Ken (Athlete, Football Player)
4615 S Bridge Ave
Weslaco, TX 78596-1393, USA

Hartley, Mariette (Actor)
Dayton Milrad Cho Management
c/o Judy Milrad
8306 Wilshire Blvd #56
Beverly Hills, CA 90211, USA

Hartley, Mike (Athlete, Baseball Player)
9485 Quail Canyon Rd
El Cajon, CA 92021-6709, USA

Hartley, Nina (Actor, Director, Producer)
7095 Hollywood Blvd
#648
Los Angeles, CA 90028, USA

Hartley, Shaunya (Stylist)
557 Empire Blvd
Brooklyn, NY 11225, USA

Hartley, Ted
524 N. Rockingham Ave.
Los Angeles, CA 90049

HartleyJ, Bob (Athlete, Hockey Player)
2713 Bonar Hall Path
Duluth, GA 30097-7463, USA

HartleyJ, Bob (Athlete, Hockey Player)
Ottawa Senators 110-1000 Palladium Dr
Attn: Broadcast Dept
Ottawa, ON K2V IAS, Canada

Hartline, Mary (Actor)
c/o Staff Member *Pierce & Shelly*
13775-A Mono Way #220
Sonora, CA 95370, USA

Hartman, Arthur A (Diplomat)
APCO Consulting Group
1615 L St NW
Washington, DC 20036, USA

Hartman, David
16-00 Rt. 208 Box 770
Fair Lawn, NJ 07410

Hartman, George E (Architect)
107 Hesketh Street
Chevy Chase, MD 20815-4222, USA

Hartman, J C (Athlete, Baseball Player)
3425 Rosedale St
Houston, TX 77004-6312, USA

Hartman, Kevin (Soccer Player)
Los Angeles Galaxy
1010 Rose Bowl Dr
Pasadena, CA 91103, USA

Hartman, Mike (Athlete, Hockey Player)
P.O. Box 472405
Charlotte, NC 28247, USA

Hartman, Rhonda (Race Car Driver)
5611 Hwy.
81 North
Williamston, SC 29697, USA

Hartman, Richard (Race Car Driver)
1340 Keone Circle
Williamston, SC 29697, USA

Hartmann, Frederick W (Editor)
Florida Times-Union
Editorial Dept
1 Riverside Ave
Jacksonville, FL 32202, USA

Hartmann, Robert T (Government Official)
4129 Estate La Grande Princess #C
Christiansted, VI 00820, USA

Hartnell, Scott (Athlete, Hockey Player)
111 Church St
Philadelphia, PA 19106-2209, USA

Hartnett, Josh (Actor)
c/o Suzan Bymel *Management 360*
9111 Wilshire Blvd
Beverly Hills, CA 90210, USA

Hartog, Jan de (Writer)
Andrew Nurnberg Assoc
45/47 Clerkenwell Green
London EC1R 0HT, UNITED KINGDOM (UK)

Harts, Greg (Athlete, Baseball Player)
829 Humphries St SW
Atlanta, GA 30310-2165, USA

Harts, Shaunard (Athlete, Football Player)
5304 Tamarindo Ln
Elk Grove, CA 95758-6821, USA

Hartsburg, Craig (Athlete, Hockey Player)
c/o Staff Member *Soo Greyhounds Hockey Club*
201-212 Queen Street E
Sault Ste Marie, ON P6A 5X8, Canada

Hartsfield, Henry W
422 Willow Vista Dr
Seabrook, TX 77586-7338, USA

Hartsfield, Henry W Colonel (Astronaut)
422 Willow Vista Dr
El Lago, TX 77586-6020, USA

Hartsfield, Henry W (Hank) Jr (Astronaut)
422 Willow Vista Dr
Seabrook, TX 77586, USA

Hartsfield, Roy (Athlete, Baseball Player)
159 Preserve Pkwv
Ball Ground, GA 30107-3233, USA

Hartshorn, Lawrence (Athlete, Football Player)
P.O. Box 1542
Cedar Ridge, CA 95924, USA

Hartsock, Ben (Athlete, Football Player)
1274 Wheatley Forest Dr
Brentwood, TN 37027, USA

Hartsock, Jeffrey (Jeff) (Athlete, Baseball Player)
1720 Swannanoa Dr
Greensboro, NC 27410-3932, USA

Hartung, James (Athlete, Gymnast, Olympic Athlete)
6425 Tanglewood Ln
Lincoln, NE 68516-2355, USA

Hartwell, Edgerton (Athlete, Football Player)
3830 Galendo Dr
North Las Vegas, NV 89032-0623, USA

Hartwell, Erin (Athlete, Cycler, Olympic Athlete)
PO Box 917
Trexlertown, PA 18087-0917, USA

Hartwell, Leland (Nobel Prize Laureate)
University Of Seattle
1100 Fairview Ave N Attn Hutchinson Cancer Researc Seattle, WA 98109-4433, USA

Hartwell, Leland H (Lee) (Nobel Prize Laureate)
Hutchinson Cancer Research Center
PO Box 19024
Seattle, WA 98109, USA

Hartwell, Lisa Wu (Reality TV Star)
c/o Staff Member *Bravo (NY)*
30 Rockefeller Plaza
New York, NY 10112, USA

Hartwig, Carter (Athlete, Football Player)
5539 FM 762 Rd
Richmond, TX 77469-8320, USA

Hartwig, Justin (Athlete, Football Player)
4009 Overland Dr
Lawrence, KS 66049-4122, USA

Hartzell, Paul (Athlete, Baseball Player)
PO Box 2860
Hailey, ID 83333-2860, USA

Hartzog, George B Jr (Government Official)
1643 Chain Bridge Road
McLean, VA 22101, USA

Haruf, Kent (Writer)
Southern Illinois University
English Dept
Carbondale, IL 62901, USA

Harvey, Anthony (Director)
Arthur Greene
101 Park Ave #4300
New York, NY 10178, USA

Harvey, Antonio (Athlete, Basketball Player)
59e6 Yaupon Ave
Moss Point, MS 39563-6046, USA

Harvey, Bryan (Athlete, Baseball Player)
1224 Astoria Pkwy
Catawba, NC 28609-8885, USA

Harvey, Claude (Athlete, Football Player)
2918 Dragonwick Dr
Houston, TX 77045, USA

Harvey, Cynthia T (Ballerina)
American Ballet Theater
890 Broadway
New York, NY 10003, USA

Harvey, David R (Business Person)
Sigme-Aldrich Corp
3050 Spruce St
Saint Louis, MO 63103, USA

Harvey, Don
6310 San Vicente Blvd. #520
Los Angeles, CA 90048

Harvey, Donnell (Basketball Player)
Orlando Magic
Waterhouse Center
8701 Maitland Summit Blvd
Orlando, FL 32810, USA

Harvey, Doug (Athlete, Baseball Player)
32398 River Island Dr
Springville, CA 93265-9632, USA

Harvey, Fred (Athlete, Hockey Player)
397 Parkhurst Dr.
Fredericton, Fredericton Junction NB E3B 2K2, Canada

Harvey, Guy (Artist)
Guy Harvey Enterprises
4350 Oakes Rd
#518
Davie, FL 33314, USA

Harvey, Harry (Educator, Horse Racer)
34 Deep Hollow Lane N
Columbus, NJ 08022-1018, USA

Harvey, H Douglas (Doug) (Athlete, Baseball Player)
32398 River Island Dr
Springville, CA 93265-9632, USA

Harvey, James B (Athlete, Football Player)
3685 Clairice Cv
Memphis, TN 38133, USA

Harvey, Jan
169 Queensgate #8A
London, ENGLAND SW7 5EH

Harvey, Jim (Athlete, Football Player)
3685 Clairice Cv
Memphis, TN 38133-0979, USA

Harvey, Ken (Athlete, Football Player)
11600 Great Falls Way
Great Falls, VA 22066, USA

Harvey, Ken (Athlete, Baseball Player)
5012 Grand Ave APt C
Kansas Citv, MO 64112-2761, USA

Harvey, Marvin (Athlete, Football Player)
901 Riggins Rd Apt 522
Tallahassee, FL 32308-2202, USA

Harvey, Maurice (Athlete, Football Player)
27 Clark St
Apt 4
Pontiac, MI 48342, USA

Harvey, Nancy (Athlete, Golfer)
7006 E Jenson St
Unit 62
Mesa, AZ 85207-2833, USA

Harvey, PJ (Musician)
c/o Staff Member *Island Records*
825 Eighth Ave
New York, NY 10019, USA

Harvey, Polly Jean (P J) (Music Group, Musician, Songwriter, Writer)
Helter Skelter
Plaza 535 Kings Road
London SW10 0S, UNITED KINGDOM (UK)

Harvey, Richard (Athlete, Football Player)
3414 Baltimore Ave
Pascagoula, MS 39581, USA

Harvey, Steve (Actor, Comedian)
c/o Staff Member *HarperCollins Publishers*
10 East 53rd St
c/o Author mail, 7th Floor
New York, NY 10022, USA

Harvey, Terry (Baseball Player)
US Olympic Team
215 Annandale Dr
Cary, NC 27511-6503, USA

Harvey, Todd (Athlete, Hockey Player)
Hockey Training Above 353 McCarthy Rd
PO Box 818
Stratford, ON NSA 7S7, Canada

Harvick, Kevin (Race Car Driver)
Childress Racing
425 Industrial Dr
Welcome, NC 27374, USA

Harville, Chad (Athlete, Baseball Player)
261 Farmington Rd
Savannah, TN 38372-5635, USA

Harvin, Percy (Athlete, Football Player)
c/o Joel Segal *Lagardere Unlimited - NY*
845 UN Plaza
New York, NY 10017, USA

Harwell, Steve (Actor, Music Group)
c/o Staff Member *Creative Artists Agency (CAA-LA)*
2000 Ave Of The Stars
Los Angeles, CA 90067, USA

Hary, Armin (Athlete, Track Athlete)
Schloss
Diessen/Ammersee 86911, GERMANY

Hasbrook, Annette (Scientist)
107 Drift Wood Dr
Seabrook, TX 77586-4701, USA

Hase, Dagmar (Swimmer)
Niederndodeleber Str 14
Magdeburg 29110, GERMANY

Hasegawa, Shigetoshi (Athlete, Baseball Player)
29 Summer House
Irvine, CA 92603-0211, USA

Hasek, Dominik (Athlete, Hockey Player)
c/o Dominator Areal Dutreva, Delnicka 54/1020 Praha 7
Holesovice 170 00, Czech Republic

Haselkorn, Robert (Scientist)
5834 S Stony Island Ave
Chicago, IL 60637, USA

Haselman, Bill (Athlete, Baseball Player)
14501 SE 85th St
Newcastle, WA 98059-9218, USA

Haselrig, Carlton (Athlete, Football Player)
386 William Penn Ave
Johnstown, PA 15901, USA

Haseltine, Dan (Music Group)
Flood Bumstead McCarthy
1700 Hayes St #304
Nashville, TN 37203, USA

Haseltine, William A (Biologist)
Human Genome Sciences
9410 Key West Ave
Rockville, MD 20850, USA

Hasen, Irvin H (Cartoonist)
68 E 79th St
New York, NY 10021, USA

Hasen, Irwin (Cartoonist)
68 E !9th St Apt E
New York, NY 10075-0224, USA

Hasenmayer, Don (Athlete, Baseball Player)
721 Golf Dr
Warrington, PA 18976-2053, USA

Hasham, Josephine (Athlete, Baseball Player, Commentator)
575 11th St
Miami, FL 33161-7157, USA

Hashimoto, Ryutaro (Politician)
Prime Ministers Office 6-1 Nagata-cho 1 chome Chiyoda-Ku
Tokyo, Japan 35214-4826, USA

Hashu, Nick (Athlete, Basketball Player)
2514 W Orangethrope Ave
Spc 27
Fullerton, CA 92833-4238, USA

Haskell, Colleen Marie (Actor)
c/o Andy Cohen *Gersh (LA)*
10250 Constellation Blvd Fl 7
Los Angeles, CA 90067, USA

Haskin, Scott (Athlete, Basketball Player)
3078 South Roxbury Dr
West Linn, OR 97068-8295, USA

Haskins, Clem (Athlete, Basketball Player, Coach)
2632 Roberts Rd
Campbellsville, KY 42718, USA

Haskins, Dennis (Actor)
c/o Arlene Thornton *Arlene Thornton & Associates*
12711 Ventura Blvd
Suite 490
Studio City, CA 91604, USA

Haskins, Jon (Athlete, Football Player)
4055 Higel Ave
Sarasota, FL 34242, USA

Haskins, Michael D (Admiral)
Inspector General HqUSN
Pentagon
Washington, DC 20350, USA

Haslam, Bill (Governor, Politician)
State Capitol
Nashville, TN 37243, USA

Haslem, Udonis (Athlete, Basketball Player)
1331 Brickell Bay Dr
Apt 3311
Miami, FL 33332-3325, USA

Hasler, Otmar (Prime Minister)
Primier's Office
Regierungsgebaude
Vaduz 9490, USA

Haslett, James D (Jim) (Athlete, Coach, Football Coach, Football Player)
118 Crandon Dr
Saint Louis, MO 63105, USA

Hasluck, Paul M C (Government Official)
2 Adams Road
Dalkeith, WA 6009, AUSTRALIA

Hass, Robert (Writer)
University of California
English Dept
Berkeley, CA 94720, USA

Hassan, Ahmed (Television Host)
5417 Prewitt Ranch Dr.
Antioch, CA 94531, USA

Hassan, Fred (Business Person)
Schering-Plough Corp
1 Giralda Farms
Madison, NJ 07940, USA

Hassan Ibn Talal (Prince)
Deputy King's Office
Royal Palace
Amman, JORDAN

Hassel, Gerald L (Financier)
Bank of New York
1 Wall St
New York, NY 10286, USA

Hassel, Trenton (Athlete, Baseball Player)
4776 Mickle Ln
Clarksville, TN 37043-8263, U S A

Hasselbach, Harald (Athlete, Football Player)
17919 E Dorado Dr
Centennial, CO 80015-5916, USA

Hasselbeck, Donald W (Don) (Athlete, Football Player)
38 Noon Hill Ave
Norfolk, VA 02056, USA

Hasselbeck, Elisabeth (Reality TV Star, Television Host)
c/o Staff Member *View, The*
320 W 66th St
New York, NY 10023-6338, USA

Hasselbeck, Matt (Athlete, Football Player)
9027 NE 1st St
Bellevue, WA 98004, USA

Hasselbeck, Tim (Athlete, Football Player)
38 Noon Hill Ave
Norfolk, MA 02056, USA

Hasselhoff, David (Actor, Music Group)
c/o Jan McCormack *JSO Management*
1746 S. Britain Rd
Southbury, CT 06488, USA

Hasselmo, Nils (Educator)
Assn of American Universities
1200 New York Ave #1200
Washington, DC 20005, USA

Hassenfeld, Alan G (Business Person)
Hasbro Inc
1027 Newport Ave
Pawtucket, RI 02861, USA

Hassett, Joe (Athlete, Basketball Player)
28 Marigold Cir
North Providence, RI 02904, USA

Hassett, Marilyn (Actor)
8905 Rosewood Ave
West Hollywood, CA 90048, USA

Hassey, Ron (Athlete, Baseball Player)
Jupiter Hammerheads 4751 Main St Attn:
Managers Office
jupiter, FL 33458-5203, USA

Hassler, Andy (Athlete, Baseball Player)
P.O. Box 15932
Phoenix, AZ 85060-5932, USA

Hassmann, Derek (Scientist)
2112 Shadow Bay Cir
League City, TX 77573-6620, USA

Hasson, Maurice (Musician)
18 West Heath Court
North End Road
London NW11, UNITED KINGDOM (UK)

Hast, Adele (Editor)
Newberry Library
60 W Walton St
Chicago, IL 60610, USA

Hastert, Dennis (Ex-Congressman)
27 N River St
Batavia, IL 60510-2666, USA

Hastert, J Dennis (Politician)
PO Box 153
Plano, IL 60545-0153, USA

Hastings, Andre (Athlete, Football Player)
700 N Dobson Rd
Unit 37
Chandler, AZ 85224, USA

Hastings, Barry G (Financier)
Northern Trust Corp
50 S La Salle St
Chicago, IL 60603, USA

Hastings, Bob (Actor)
620 S. Sparks St.
Burbank, CA 91505, USA

Hastings, Doc (Congressman, Politician)
1203 Longworth HOB
Washington, DC 20515, USA

Hastings, Don (Actor)
524 W 57th St #5330
New York, NY 10019, USA

Hastings, Scott (Athlete, Basketball Player)
5414 E Nichols Pl
Centennial, CO 80122, USA

Haston, Kirk (Athlete, Basketball Player)
2600 S Main St
Lobelville, TN 37097, USA

Hasty, James (Athlete, Football Player)
8212 127th Ave SE
Newcastle, WA 98056, USA

Hatalsky, Morris (Athlete, Golfer)
201 S Ocean Grande Dr
Ph 5
Ponte Vedra Beach, FL 32082-6514, USA

Hatch, Annia (Athlete, Gymnast, Olympic Athlete)
1800 Sans Souci Blvd #239
N Miami, FL 33181-3069, USA

Hatch, Harold A (General)
8655 White Beach Way
Vienna, VA 22182, USA

Hatch, Henry J (General)
2715 Silkwood Court
Oakton, VA 22124, USA

Hatch, Monroe W Jr (General)
8210 Thomas Ashleigh Lane
Clifton, VA 20124, USA

Hatch, Orrin (Senator)
104 Hart Office Building
Washington, DC 20510, USA

Hatch, Orrin (Politician)
2127 Galloping Way
Vienna, VA 22181-2934, USA

Hatch, Richard (Actor, Reality TV Star)
c/o Michael Kaliski *Omniquest Entertainment (LA)*
1416 N La Brea Ave
Hollywood, CA 90028, USA

Hatchell, Sylvia (Basketball Player)
University of North Carolina Athletic Dept
Chapell Hill, NC 27515, USA

Hatcher, Billy (Athlete, Baseball Player)
Cincinnati Reds 100 Joe Nuxhall Way
Attn Coaching Staff
Cincinnati, OH 45202-4109, USA

Hatcher, Chris (Athlete, Baseball Player)
1406 250th St
Audubon, IA 50025-7356, USA

Hatcher, Derian (Athlete, Hockey Player, Olympic Athlete)
567 Chews Landing Rd
Haddonfield, NJ 08033, USA

Hatcher, Derian (Athlete, Hockey Player)
Philadelphia Flyers 3601 S Broad St Ste 2
Attn Coaching Staff
Philadelphia, PA 19148-5297, USA

Hatcher, Kevin (Athlete, Hockey Player, Olympic Athlete)
1225 S Water St
Marine City, MI 48039, USA

Hatcher, Mickey (Athlete, Baseball Player)
Los Angeles Angels Of Anaheim 2000 E
Gene Autry Way I
attn coaching staff
anaheim, CA 92806-6143, USA

Hatcher, R Dale (Athlete, Football Player)
906 White Plains Rd
Gaffiney, SC 29340, USA

Hatcher, Teri (Actor)
c/o Jeremy Barber *United Talent Agency (UTA)*
9336 Civic Center Dr
Beverly Hills, CA 90210, USA

Hatchett, Derrick (Athlete, Football Player)
7811 Westshire Dr
San Antonio, TX 78227, USA

Hatchett, Joseph W (Judge)
US Court of Appeals
810 Lewis State Bank Building
Tallahassee, FL 32302, USA

Hatchett, Judge Glenda (Judge, Reality TV Star)
c/o Elizabeth Much *Much and House Public Relations*
8075 W 3rd St
Suite 500
Los Angeles, CA 90048, USA

Hatchette, Matthew (Athlete, Football Player)
3222 Winding Pine Trl
Longwood, FL 32779, USA

Hatfield, Juliana (Musician, Songwriter)
c/o Staff Member *Concerted Efforts*
P.O. Box 440326
Somerville, MA 02144, USA

Hathaway, Amy
c/o Beverly Strong *Strong Management*
3532 Hayden Ave
Culver City, CA 90232, USA

Hathaway, Anne (Actor)
c/o Suzan Bymel *Management 360*
9111 Wilshire Blvd
Beverly Hills, CA 90210, USA

Hathaway, Hilly (Athlete, Baseball Player)
2672 Forest Blvd
Jacksonville, FL 32246-3414, USA

Hathaway, Noah (Actor)
5150 Choppers & Hot Rods
228 Grand Ave
Perryville, MO 63775, USA

Hathaway, Ray (Athlete, Baseball Player)
25 Leisure Mountain Rd
Asheville, NC 28804-1147, USA

Hathaway, William (Politician)
6707 Wemberly Way
Mclean, VA 22101-1529, USA

Hathaway, William D (Ex-Senator)
6707 Wemberly Way
McLean, VA 22101-1529, USA

Hathcock, Dave (Athlete, Football Player)
417 Rolling Mill Rd
Old Hickory, TN 37138, USA

Hatori, Miho (Music Group)
Billions Corp
833 W Chicago Ave #101
Chicago, IL 60622, USA

Hatosy, Shawn (Actor)
c/o Staff Member *Mary Erickson Entertainment*
2122 Hillhurst Ave #A
Los Angeles, CA 90027, USA

Hatoum, Ed (Athlete, Hockey Player)
Hatoum Auto Sales 5711 No 3 Rd
Richmond, BC VGX 2C9, Canada

Hatsopoulos, George N (Business Person, Engineer)
Thermo Electron Corp
81 Wyman St
PO Box 9046
Waltham, MA 02454, USA

Hatteberg, Scott (Athlete, Baseball Player)
802 Berg Ct NW
Gig Harbor, WA 98335-7709, USA

Hatten, Tom (Actor)
1759 Sunset Plaza Dr
Los Angeles, CA 90069, USA

Hattersley, Roy S G (Government Official)
House of Lords
Westminster
London SW1A 0PW, UNITED KINGDOM (UK)

Hattestad, Stine Lise (Skier)
Sundlia 1B
Nesoya 1315, NORWAY

Hatton, Grady (Athlete, Baseball Player, Coach)
P.O. Box 97
Warren, TX 77664-0097, USA

Hatton, Noah (Stylist)
c/o Staff Member *Karlee Artist Management*
2658 Griffith Park Blvd
#171
Los Angeles, CA 90039, USA

Hatton, Ricky (Athlete, Boxer)
Banner Promotions
1231 Bainbridge Street
Philadelphia, PA 19147, USA

Hatton, Vernon (Vern) (Athlete, Basketball Player)
1492 Copper Run Blvd
Lexington, KY 40533-8405, USA

Hattori, Shige (Race Car Driver)
4377 Triple Crown Dr.
Concord, NC 28027, USA

Hattori, Shigeaki (Race Car Driver)
Bettenhausen Motorsports
57A Gasolina Alley
Indianapolis, IN 46143, USA

Hau, Lene Vestergaard (Physicist)
Harvard University
Applied Physics Dept
Cambridge, MA 01238, USA

Hauck, Frederick H (Rick) (Astronaut)
2 Redwood Lane
Falmouth, ME 04105-1368, USA

Hauck, Frederick H "Rick" Captain (Astronaut)
2 Redwood Ln
Falmouth, ME 04105-1368, USA

Hauck, Silke 16
Mt. Bundt Verlag K2
Mannheim, GERMANY 69159

Hauck, Tim (Athlete, Football Player)
460 Great Circle Rd
Nashville, TN 37228-1404, USA

Haudenschild, Jack (Race Car Driver)
Wildchild Designs
628 Maple St.
Vermillion, OH 44089, USA

Hauer, Brett (Athlete, Hockey Player)
2921 Branch St
Duluth, MN 55812-2340, USA

Hauer, Rutger (Actor)
1601 Cloverfield Blvd #5000N
Santa Monica, CA 90404, USA

Hauerwas, Stanley (Religious Leader)
Duke University
Divinity School
Durham, NC 27706, USA

Haughey, Chris (Athlete, Baseball Player)
4117 Stevenson Blvd Ant 283
Fremont, CA 94538-5001, USA

Haught, Gary (Athlete, Baseball Player)
16445 Lynn St
Choctaw, OK 73020-7926, USA

Haughton, Tom
6011 NW 69th Mnr
Parkland, FL 33067-4507, USA

Hauk, A Andrew (Judge, Skier)
US Court House
312 N Spring St
Los Angeles, CA 90012, USA

Haun, Darla
300 S. Raymond Ave. #11
Pasadena, CA 91105

Haun, Lindsey (Actor)
c/o Staff Member *Margie Weiner Management*
8205 Santa Monica Blvd
Suite 1-450
Los Angeles, CA 90046, USA

Haus, Herman A (Engineer, Scientist)
38 Jeffrey Terrace
Lexington, MA 02420, USA

Hausen, Harald Zur (Nobel Prize Laureate)
German Cancer Research Centre lm
Neuenheimer Feld 280
Heidelberg, German 35214-4826, USA

Hauser, Art (Athlete, Football Player)
2816 Walsh Rd
Cincinnati, OH 45208, USA

Hauser, Cole (Actor)
c/o Michael Gruber *After Dark Management Group*
Prefers to be contacted via telephone
Los Angeles, CA 90069, USA

Hauser, Erich (Artist)
Saline 36
Rottweil 78628, GERMANY

Hauser, Tim (Music Group)
c/o Staff Member *The Merlin Company*
16574 Bosque Dr
Encino, CA 91436, USA

Hauser, Wings (Actor)
9450 Chivers Ave
Sun Valley, CA 91352, USA

Hausman, Jerry A (Economist)
Massachussetts Institute of Technology
Economics Dept
Cambridge, MA 02139, USA

Hausman, Tom (Athlete, Baseball Player)
3165 Westfield Cir
Las Vegas, NV 89121-3332, USA

Hauss, Lenard M (Len) (Athlete, Football Player)
110 Portmere Dr
Jesup, GA 31546, USA

Hauver, Charles (General)
6300 E Speedway Blvd Apt 1157
Tucson, AZ 85710-1154, USA

Havelange, Jean M F G (Joao) (Soccer Player)
Ave Rio Branco 89B
Conj 602 Centro
Rio de Janiero 20040-004, BRAZIL

Havelange, JoaoRua
Prudente de Marosa 1700 Apto. 1001
Rio de Janeiro, BRAZIL BR 20420-0

Havelid, Niclas (Athlete, Hockey Player)
Prestige Hocey Group
PO Box 129
Point Roberts, WA 98281-0129, USA

Haven, Annette
PO Box 1244
Sausalito, CA 94966

Haven, James (Actor)
c/o Staff Member *Saffron Management*
9171 Wilshire Blvd #441
Beverly Hills, CA 90210, USA

Havens, Brad (Athlete, Baseball Player)
3227 Eden Trl
Brighton, MI 48114-9185, USA

Havens, Frank B (Athlete)
PO Box 55
Harborton, VA 23389, USA

Havens, Richie (Musician, Songwriter)
177 Woodland Ave
Westwood, NJ 07675, USA

Haverdink, Kevin (Athlete, Football Player)
15844 Prairie Ronde Rd
Schoolcraft, MI 49087, USA

Haverland, Charles (General)
1708 University Ln Apt 505
Cocoa, FL 32922-5635, USA

Havers, Nigel (Actor)
c/o John Crosby *Crosby/Spilo Management*
1310 N Spaulding Ave
Los Angeles, CA 90046, USA

Havig, Dennis (Athlete, Football Player)
5964 Old Stilesboro Rd NW
Acworth, GA 30101, USA

Havin, Alexa (Actor)
c/o Staff Member *Mattie Management*
1438 N Gower St #57
Los Angeles, CA 90028-8358, USA

Havins, Alexa (Actor)
c/o Noreen Konkle *AKA Talent Agency*
6310 San Vicente Blvd
Suite 200
Los Angeles, CA 90048, USA

Havlicek, John (Athlete, Basketball Player)
24 Beech Rd
Weston, MA 02493-1915, USA

Havlish, Jean (Bowler)
PO Box 122
Rockville, MN 56369-0122, USA

Havlish, Jean (Athlete, Baseball Player, Commentator)
PO Box 122
Rockville, MN 56369-0122, USA

Havrilak, Sam (Athlete, Football Player)
1 Trojan Horse Dr
Phoenix, MD 21131, USA

Havrilla, Jo Ann
9751 Old Route 99
McKean, PA 16426-1725

Hawass, Zahi (Writer)
Supreme Council of Antiquities
3 Al-Adel Bakr St
Zamalek, Cairo, EGYPT

Hawblitzel, Ryan (Athlete, Baseball Player)
7972 S Four Oaks Pt
Floral City, FL 34436-2623, USA

Hawerchuck, Dale (Athlete, Hockey Player)
Grande Farms
RR 5
LCD Main
Orangeville, ON L9W 2Z2, Canada

Hawerchuk, Dale (Athlete, Hockey Player)
Grande Farms RR 5 LCD Main
Orangeville, ON L9W 2Z2, CANADA

Hawes, Roy (Athlete, Baseball Player)
P.O. Box 854
Ringgold, GA 30736-0854, USA

Hawes, Steve (Athlete, Basketball Player)
400 W Highland Dr
Seattle, WA 98119-3532, USA

Hawgood, Greg (Athlete, Hockey Player)
1230 Saint Andrews Way
Kamloops, BC V1S 1S6, Canada

Hawk, AJ (Athlete, Football Player)
4349 Windemer Ln
Oneida, WI 54155-8648, USA

Hawk, John D (General)
3243 Solie Ave
Bremerton, WA 98310-2821, USA

Hawk, Tony (Actor, Athlete, Skateboarder)
Tony Hawk Inc
1611-A S Melrose Dr #362
Vista, CA 92081, USA

Hawke, Ethan (Actor)
c/o Mara Buxbaum *ID PR (LA)*
7060 Hollywood Blvd
8th Floor
Los Angeles, CA 90028, USA

Hawke, Jason (Adult Film Star)
c/o Staff Member *Diva Central Inc*
7510 W Sunset Blvd Ste 1445
Los Angees, CA 90046, USA

Hawke, Robert J L (Prime Minister)
GPO Box 36
Sydney, NSW 2001, AUSTRALIA

Hawkes, Christopher (Archaeologist)
19 Walton St
Oxford OX1 2HQ, UNITED KINGDOM (UK)

Hawkes, John (Actor)
c/o JB Roberts *Thruline Entertainment*
9250 Wilshire Blvd
Ground Fl
Beverly Hills, CA 90212, USA

Hawking, Lucy (Writer)
c/o Staff Member *Simon & Schuster*
1230 Avenue of the Americas
New York, NY 10020, USA

Hawking, Stephen (Physicist, Scientist)
DAMTP University Of Cambridge
c/o Judith Croasdell
Centre For Mathematical Sciences,
Wilberforce Road
Cambridge CB3 0WA, UK

Hawking, Stephen (Scientist)
Cambridge University Applied
Mathematics Dept
Cambridge, CB3 9EW
Englanc 10168-3100, USA

Hawkins, Alex (Athlete, Football Player)
215 Bonanza Rd
Denmark, SC 29042, USA

Hawkins, Andy (Athlete, Baseball Player)
Texas Rangers PO Box 90111 Attn
Coaching Staff
Arlington, TX 76004-3111, USA

Hawkins, Artrell (Athlete, Football Player)
12166 Peak Dr
Cincinnati, OH 45246, USA

Hawkins, Barbara (Music Group)
Superstars Unlimited
PO Box 371371
Las Vegas, NV 89137, USA

Hawkins, Benjamin C (Ben) (Athlete, Football Player)
606 11th Ave
Belmar, NJ 07719-2412, USA

Hawkins, Bill (Athlete, Football Player)
19183 SE Jupiter River Dr
Jupiter, FL 33458, USA

Hawkins, Brad
47 Music Sq. E.
Nashville, TN 37203

Hawkins, Chauncey (Loon) (Musician)
c/o Michael (Mike) Esterman
Esterman.Com, LLC
Prefers to be contacted via email
MD, USA

Hawkins, Connie (Athlete, Basketball Player)
2994 E Pony Ct
Gilbert, AZ 85295-3775, USA

Hawkins, Courtney (Athlete, Football Player)
8305 Gale Rd
Goodrich, MI 48438, USA

Hawkins, Dan (Musician)
c/o Sue Whitehouse *Whitehouse Management*
PO Box 43829
London NW6 3PJ, UNITED KINGDOM

Hawkins, Edwin (Music Group)
PAZ Entertainment
2041 Locust St
Philadelphia, PA 19103, USA

Hawkins, Frank (Athlete, Football Player)
2300 Alta Dr
Las Vegas, NV 89107, USA

Hawkins, Heather (Stylist)
8949 Gamesford Dr
Charlotte, NC 28277, USA

Hawkins, Hersey (Athlete, Basketball Player, Olympic Athlete)
18168 W Narramore Rd
Goodyear, AZ 85338, USA

Hawkins, Jennifer (Actor, Beauty Pageant Winner)
c/o Staff Member *Ovations*
P.O. Box 1337
Rozelle, NSW 2039, Australia

Hawkins, Justin (Musician)
Must Destroy Music
PO Box 40008
London N6 5XT, UNITED KINGDOM

Hawkins, Latroy (Athlete, Baseball Player)
3521 Amberwood Ln
Prosoer, TX 75078-9126, USA

Hawkins, Michael Daly (Judge)
US Court of Appeals
230 N 1St
Phoenix, AZ 85025, USA

Hawkins, Mike (Athlete, Football Player)
2320 Bordeaux Dr
Bay City, TX 77414, USA

Hawkins, Rip (Athlete, Football Player)
100 Tower Carlile Rd
Devils Tower, WY 82714, USA

Hawkins, Ronnie (Music Group)
Agency Group Ltd
59 Berkeley St
Toronto, ON M5A 2W5, CANADA

Hawkins, Rosa (Music Group)
Superstars Unlimited
PO Box 371371
Las Vegas, NV 89137, USA

Hawkins, Rowena
PO Box 15277
Chattanooga, TN 37415-0277

Hawkins, Sally (Actor)
c/o Larry Taube *Principal Entertainment
(LA)*
1964 Westwood Blvd #400
Los Angeles, CA 90025, USA

Hawkins, Sophie B (Music Group,
Musician, Songwriter, Writer)
Trumpet Swan Productions
520 Washington Blvd #337
Marina del Rey, CA 90292, USA

Hawkins, Thomas (Tommy) (Athlete,
Basketball Player)
1745 Manzanita Park Ave
Malibu, CA 90265-3013, USA

Hawkins, Todd (Athlete, Hockey Player)
300 Lamoreaux Dr
Elk Rapids, MI 49629, USA

Hawkins, Wayne (Athlete, Football Player)
1 Dogwood Ct
San Ramon, CA 94583-3908, USA

Hawkins, Wynn (Athlete, Baseball Player)
5326 Cottage Dr
Cortland, OH 44410-9521, USA

Hawkinson, Tim (Artist)
Ace Gallery
5514 Wilshire Blvd
Los Angeles, CA 90036, USA

Hawksworth, Blake (Athlete, Baseball
Player)
20811 NE 25th St
Sammamish, WA 98074-6350, USA

Hawksworth, John
24 Cottesmore Gardens #2
London, ENGLAND W8 5PR

Hawlata, Franz (Opera Singer)
I M G Artists
3 Burlington Lane
Chiswick
London W4 2TH, UNITED KINGDOM
(UK)

Hawley, Frank (Race Car Driver)
Frank Hawley Drag Racing School
County Road 225
Gainesville, FL 32609, USA

Hawley, Richard (Musician)
c/o Staff Member *Alias Production*
22, Rue Douai
Paris F-75009, France

Hawley, Sandy (Jockey)
9625 Merrill Road
Silverwood, MI 48760, USA

Hawley, Steven (Astronaut)
University of Kansas
3303 Calvin Dr
Lawrence, KS 66045-7582, USA

Hawn, Goldie (Actor, Director, Producer)
c/o Alan Nevins *Renaissance Literary &
Talent*
P.O. Box 17379
Beverly Hills, CA 90209, USA

Haworth, Alan (Athlete, Hockey Player)
2614 Rue de la Commune
Drummondville, QC J2B OB5, Canada

Haworth, David Capt (General)
General Delivery
Kirtland Afb, NM 87117-9999, USA

Haworth, Gord (Athlete, Hockey Player)
2780 Rue Lalancette
Drummondville, QC J2B 3X9, CANADA

Hawpe, Brad (Athlete, Baseball Player)
Colorado Rockies Foundation 2001 Blake
St Unit A
denver, CO 80205-2060, USA

Hawpe, David V (Editor)
Louisville Courier-Journal
Editorial Dept
525 Broadway
Louisville, KY 40202, USA

Hawryliw, Neil (Athlete, Hockey Player)
1366 Seminole Rd
Norton Shores, MI 49441-4349, Canada

Hawthorne, Duane (Athlete, Football
Player)
11481 Pineview Crossing Dr
Maryland Heights, MO 63043-5103, USA

Hawthorne, Greg (Athlete, Football
Player)
1428 E Jefferson Ave
Fort Worth, TX 76104, USA

Hawthorne, Sir Nigel
Febdens Park Cold Christmas Lane
Thundridge Herts, ENGLAND SG12 QUE

Hax, Carolyn (Writer)
Washington Post
Editorial Dept
1150 15th St NW
Washington, DC 20071, USA

Hay, Bill (Athlete, Hockey Player)
4020 Crestview Rd SW
Calgary, AB T2T 2L4, Canada

Hay, Colin (Music Group)
TPA
PO Box 125
Round Corner, NSW 2158, AUSTRALIA

Hay, Don (Athlete, Hockey Player)
Vancouver Giants 100 Renfrew St N
Attn Coaching Staff
Vancouver, BC V5K 3N7, Canada

Hay, Jim (Athlete, Hockey Player)
2024 NE 76th Ave
Portland, OR 97213, USA

Hay, Louise L (Writer)
Hay House
P.O. Box 5100
Carlsbad, CA 92018-5100, USA

Hayaishi, Osamu (Biologist)
1-29 Izumigawacho
Shimogamo Sakyoku
Kyoto 606-0807, JAPAN

Hayareet, Haya
Herons Flight Marlow
Buckinghamshire, ENGLAND

Hayashi, Henry
5127 Klump Ave
No. Hollywood, CA 91601-3725

Hayashi, Izuo (Engineer)
OptoElectrics Research Lab
5-5 Tohkodai
Tsukuba
Ibaraki 300-26, JAPAN

Hayashi, Shizuya (War Hero)
1331 Hoowai St
Pearl City, HI 96782, USA

Hayashida, Erica (Athlete, Golfer)
1470 NW 107th Ave
Suite R
Doral, FL 33172, USA

Haycox, Marie (Stylist)
337 The Boulevard
Glen Rock, NJ 07452, USA

Haydee, Marcia (Ballerina)
Stuttgart Ballet
Oberer Schlossgarten 6
Stuttgart 70173, USA

Haydel, Hal (Athlete, Baseball Player)
304 Lynwood Dr
Houma, LA 70360-6228, USA

Hayden
431-67 Mowat Ave
Toronto, CANADA Ont. M6K 3

Hayden, Aaron (Athlete, Football Player)
504 Stone Oaks Cv
Collierville, TN 38017, USA

Hayden, Frederick (Biologist)
University of Virginia
Med Ctr
Microbiology Dept
Charlottesville, VA 22903, USA

Hayden, Gene (Athlete, Baseball Player)
424 W Locust St
Lodi, CA 95240-2018, USA

Hayden, Jim (Publisher)
Philadelphia Inquirer
400 N Broad St
Philadelphia, PA 19130, USA

Hayden, J Michael (Mike) (Ex-Governor,
Government Official)
Office Of The Secretary
Kansas Dept. Of Wildlife & Parks
1020 S. Kansas, Rm 200
Topeka, KS 66612, USA

Hayden, John (Race Car Driver)
Hayden Enterprises
107 Flat Ridge Rd
Goodlettsville, TN 37072, USA

Hayden, Leo (Athlete, Football Player)
33 Preston Rd
Columbus, OH 43209-1652, USA

Hayden, Linda (Actor)
Michael Ladkin Mgmt
1 Duchess St #1
London W1N 3DE, UNITED KINGDOM
(UK)

Hayden, Michael (Actor)
H W A Talent
3500 W Olive Ave #1400
Burbank, CA 91505, USA

Hayden, Michael (Politician)
5809 Sagamore Ct
Lawrence, KS 66047-2071, USA

Hayden, Michael V (General)
Director National Security Agency
Fort George C Meade, MD 20755, USA

Hayden, Neil Steven (Publisher)
1755 York Ave #19A
New York, NY 10128, USA

Hayden, Nicky (Athlete, Motorcycle
Racer)
Nicky Hayden Inc
419 Medina Road
Medina, OH 44256, USA

Hayden, Tom (Politician)
152 Wadsworth Ave
Santa Monica, CA 90405-3510, USA

Haydon, Jones Ann (Tennis Player)
85 Westerfield Road
Edgloaston
Birmingham 15, UNITED KINGDOM
(UK)

Haydon, Nicky (Motorcycle Racer)
c/o Steve Dicterow *International Racers,
Inc*
8001 Irvine Center Dr Ste 820
Irvine, CA 92618, USA

Haydu, Beatrice (Aviator)
4200 N Ocean Dr
Riviera Beach, FL 33404-2856, USA

Haye, David (Athlete, Boxer)
Hayemaker Boxing
57 Jackson Rd
Bromley
Kent BR2 8NT, UK

Hayek, Julie
5645 Burning Tree Dr.
La Canada, CA 91011

Hayek, Peter (Athlete, Hockey Player)
5644 Upton Ave S
Minneapolis, MN 55410, USA

Hayek, Salma (Actor, Model, Producer)
c/o Evelyn O'Neill *Management 360*
9111 Wilshire Blvd
Beverly Hills, CA 90210, USA

Hayers, Sidney A (Director)
John Redway
5 Denmark St
London WC2H 8LP, UNITED KINGDOM
(UK)

Hayes, Amy (Model, Sportscaster)
641 N Hardin Heights
Harrodsburg, KY 40330, USA

Hayes, Ben (Athlete, Baseball Player)
3501 10th St NE
Saint Petersburg, FL 33704-1605, USA

Hayes, Bill (Actor)
4528 Beck Ave
North Hollywood, CA 91602, USA

Hayes, Bill (Athlete, Baseball Player)
San Francisco Giants 24 Willie Mays Plz
Attn Coaching Staff
san fransisco, CA 94107-2199, USA

Hayes, Billie (Athlete, Football Player)
2876 Avalon St
Riverside, CA 92509, USA

Hayes, Bob
2717 King Cole Dr.
Dallas, TX 75216-3430

Hayes, Brian
60 Charlotte St.
London, ENGLAND W1P 1LS

Hayes, Charlie (Athlete, Baseball Player)
22503 Holly Creek Trl
Tomball, TX 77377-3656, USA

Hayes, Chris (Race Car Driver)
R&H Motorsports
10134 6th St.
#G
Rancho Cucamonga, CA 91730, USA

Hayes, Dade
c/o Daniel Strone Trident Media Group
LLC
41 Madison Ave
36th Floor
New York, NY 10010, USA

Hayes, Darren (Music Group, Musician)
PO Box 193
Jimboomba, QLD 4280, AUSTRALIA

Hayes, Dawn (Stylist)
c/o Staff Member Dawn to Dusk Image
Agency
8306 Wilshire Blvd
#412
Beverly Hills, CA 30211, USA

Hayes, Denis A (Geophysicist, Misc,
Physicist)
Green Seal
PO Box 18237
Washington, DC 20036, USA

Hayes, Dennis (Engineer, Inventor)
Hayes Microcomputer Products
865 United Nations Plz Unit 16A
New York, NY 10017-1803, USA

Hayes, Elvin (Athlete, Basketball Player)
PO Box 3688
Santa Clara, CA 95055-3688, USA

Hayes, Erinn (Actor)
c/o David Sweeney Sweeney
Management
6253 Hollywood Blvd
Suite 201
Los Angeles, CA 90028, USA

Hayes, Gemma (Musician)
c/o Staff Member Paradigm (Monterey)
404 W Franklin St
Monterey, CA 93940, USA

Hayes, Gerald (Athlete, Football Player)
3841 E Windsong Dr
Phoenix, AZ 85048, USA

Hayes, Hunter (Musician)
c/o Christian Carino Creative Artists
Agency (CAA-LA)
2000 Ave Of The Stars
Los Angeles, CA 90067, USA

Hayes, Jarvis (Basketball Player)
Washington Wizards
MCI Center 601 F St NW
Washington, DC 30326-1240, USA

Hayes, Jim (Athlete, Basketball Player)
31 Curley St
Long Beach, NY 11561, USA

Hayes, Jocelyn (Producer)

Hayes, John
1117 Robin Lane
Allentown, NJ 08501, USA

Hayes, Jonathan (Athlete, Football Player)
1231 Obannon Creek Ln
Loveland, OH 45140, USA

Hayes, J P (Athlete, Golfer)
740 Camino Real Ave
El Paso, TX 79922-2010, USA

Hayes, Larry (Athlete, Football Player)
6128 Stonehaven Dr
Nashville, TN 37215-5624, USA

Hayes, Louis S (Music Group, Musician)
P.O. Box 482
Desoto, TX 75123-0482, USA

Hayes, Mark (Athlete, Golfer)
1014 Saint Andrews Dr
Edmond, OK 73025, USA

Hayes, Mercury (Athlete, Football Player)
138 W Whitney St
Houston, TX 77018, USA

Hayes, Patty (Athlete, Golfer)
3436 Sipsey St
The Villages, FL 32162, USA

Hayes, Ray (Athlete, Football Player)
5000 Laur Rd
North Branch, MI 48461, USA

Hayes, Reggie (Actor)
c/o Staff Member TalentWorks (LA)
3500 W Olive Ave
Suite 1400
Burbank, CA 91505, USA

Hayes, Robert M (Activist)
National Coalition for the Homeless
105 E 22nd St
New York, NY 10010, USA

Hayes, Rudy (Athlete, Football Player)
354 Red Hill Rd
Pickens, SC 29671-9188, USA

Hayes, Sean (Actor)
c/o Staff Member Principato/Young
Management
9465 Wilshire Blvd
Suite 430
Beverly Hills, CA 90212, USA

Hayes, Steve (Athlete, Basketball Player)
1630 Mercoal Dr
Spring, TX 77386-2959, USA

Hayes, Von (Athlete, Baseball Player)
435 E Illinois Rd
Lake Forest, IL 60045, USA

Hayes, Wade (Music Group)
Trey Turner Assoc
40 Music Square W
Nashville, TN 37203, USA

Hayes, Wendell (Athlete, Football Player)
1935 E 30th St
Apt 23
Oakland, CA 94606, USA

Haygood, Clyde (Stylist)
c/o Staff Member Independent NY
15 E 30th St #401
New York, NY 10016, USA

Haygood, Herb (Athlete, Football Player)
1735 Central Ave
Sarasota, FL 34234, USA

Hayhoe, Bill (Athlete, Football Player)
5146 Santa Anita Dr
Sparks, NV 89436, USA

Hayhurst, Dirk (Athlete, Baseball Player)
64 Division St
Hudson, OH 44236, USA

Haylett, Alice (Athlete, Baseball Player)
243 Pearl Avenue
Lakeland, FL 33815-3737, USA

Hayman, Conway (Athlete, Football
Player)
6811 Stiller Dr
Missouri City, TX 77489-3419, USA

Hayman, David T (Actor, Director)
c/o Staff Member Independent Talent
Group (ITG-UK)
Oxford House
76 Oxford St
London W1D 1BS, UK

Hayman, Fred (Designer, Fashion
Designer)
6946 Wildlife Road
Malibu, CA 90265, USA

Hayman, Gorgon I (Cinematographer)
54 Lakes Lane
Beaconsfield
London HP9 2LB, UNITED KINGDOM
(UK)

Hayman, James (Director)
c/o Staff Member Creative Artists Agency
(CAA-LA)
2000 Ave Of The Stars
Los Angeles, CA 90067, USA

Haymond, Alvin (Athlete, Football Player)
2857 Mantis Dr
San Jose, CA 95148, USA

Haynes, Abner (Athlete, Football Player)
1950 Fm 489
Oakwood, TX 75855, USA

Haynes, Al (Misc)
4410 S 182nd St
Seatac, WA 98188, USA

Haynes, Betsy (Writer)
5973 Sandhill Cir
The Colony, TX 75056-3678, USA

Haynes, Colton (Actor)
c/o Eric Podwall Podwall Entertainment
710 N Orlando Ave
Loft 203
Los Angeles, CA 90069, USA

Haynes, Haynes
7200 Sandering Ct.
Carlsbad, CA 92009-5173

Haynes, Heath (Athlete, Baseball Player)
1525 S Carmelina Ave
Los Angeles, CA 90025-3621, USA

Haynes, Jimmy (Athlete, Baseball Player)
516 Riverside Dr
Lagrange, GA 30240-9633, USA

Haynes, Mark (Athlete, Football Player)
220 S Oneida St
Denver, CO 80230-6951, USA

Haynes, Marques (Athlete, Baseball
Player)
1300 County Road 4627
Winnsboro, TX 75494-7340, U S A

Haynes, Michael (Athlete, Football Player)
2375 Saddlesprings Dr
Alpharetta, GA 30004-3254, USA

Haynes, Michael (Athlete, Football Player)
1580 Arbour Glenn Dr
Lawrenceville, GA 30043, USA

Haynes, Mike (Athlete, Football Player)
8141 Santaluz Village Gm n S
San Diego, CA 92127-2518, USA

Haynes, Mike (Athlete, Football Player)
8 Morningside Ln
Westport, CT 06880, USA

Haynes, Nathan (Athlete, Baseball Player)
609 N Ventura St
Apt 4
Anaheim, CA 92801-3740, USA

Haynes, Reggie (Athlete, Football Player)
2324 Antiqua Ct
Reston, VA 20191, USA

Haynes, Richard (Attorney, Attorney
General, General)
2701 Fannin St
Houston, TX 77002, USA

Haynes, Roy O (Musician)
Ted Kurland
173 Brighton Ave
Boston, MA 02134, USA

Haynes, Todd (Director)
c/o Staff Member Creative Artists Agency
(CAA-LA)
2000 Ave Of The Stars
Los Angeles, CA 90067, USA

Haynes, Verron (Athlete, Football Player)
2500 Northwinds Pkwy
Suite 275
Alpharetta, GA 30004, USA

Haynes, Warren (Musician)
c/o Staff Member Paradigm (Monterey)
404 W Franklin St
Monterey, CA 93940, USA

Haynes Jr, Cornell (Nelly) (Musician)
c/o Dana Sims ICM Partners (ICM-LA)
10250 Constellation Blvd Fl 7
Los Angeles, CA 90067, USA

Haynesworth, Albert (Athlete, Football
Player)
c/o Chad Speck Allegiant Athletic Agency
35 Market Sq
Suite 201
Knoxville, TN 37902, USA

Haynie, Jim
10100 Santa Monica Blvd. #2500
Los Angeles, CA 90067

Haynie, Sandra (Athlete, Golfer)
6 Brookfield Ct
Roanoke, TX 76262, USA

Hays, Harold (Athlete, Football Player)
10410 Ravenswood Rd
Granbury, TX 76049, USA

Hays, Kathryn (Actor)
c/o Staff Member As The World Turns
JC Studios
1268 E 14th St
New York, NY 11230, USA

Hays, Robert (Actor)
919 Victoria Ave
Venice, CA 90291, USA

Hays, Ronald J (Admiral)
869 Kamoi Place
Honolulu, HI 96825, USA

Hays, Thomas C (Business Person)
Fortune Brands Inc
300 Tower Parkway
Lincolnshire, IL 60069, USA

Haysbert, Dennis (Actor)
c/o Geevani Singh GS Management
861 S. Windsor Blvd #105
Los Angeles, CA 90005, USA

Hayter, David (Writer)
c/o Staff Member *Kaplan/Perrone Entertainment*
9744 Wilshire Blvd
Suite 300
Beverly Hills, CA 90212, USA

Hayward, Brian (Athlete, Hockey Player)
7648 E Hollow Oak Rd
Anaheim, CA 92808-1425, USA

Hayward, Brian (Athlete, Hockey Player)
Anaheim Ducks 2695 E Katella Ave
Attn Broadcast Dept
Anaheim, CA 92806-5904, USA

Hayward, Brooke
305 Madison Ave. #956
New York, NY 10165-1001

Hayward, Charles E (Publisher)
Little Brown Co
Time-Life Building
Rockefeller Center
New York, NY 10020, USA

Hayward, Gordon (Athlete, Baseball Player)
Gordon and Jody Hayward 76 Brandywine Ct
Brownsburg, IN 46112-1076, U S A

Hayward, Hurley (Race Car Driver)
1445 Ponte Vedra Blvd.
Ponte Vedra Beach, FL 32082, USA

Hayward, Justin (Musician)
The Threshold Record Co Ltd
53 High St
Cobham, Surrey KT11 3DP, UNITED KINGDOM (UK)

Hayward, Lazar (Athlete, Basketball Player)
c/o Sam Goldfelder *Excel Sports Management*
9665 Wilshire Blvd #500
Los Angeles, CA 90212, USA

Hayward, Ray (Athlete, Baseball Player)
5113 Deerhurst Dr
Norman, OK 73072-3882, USA

Hayward, Reggie (Athlete, Football Player)
4651 Swilcan Bridge Ln S
Jacksonville, FL 32224, USA

Hayward, Thomas B (Admiral)
2200 Ross Ave #3800
Dallas, TX 75201, USA

Haywood, Alfred (Athlete, Football Player)
69 Waters Edge Way
Fayetteville, GA 30215, USA

Haywood, Bill (Athlete, Baseball Player)
867 VIlla Dr
North Myrtle Beach, SC 29582-2575, USA

Haywood, Spencer (Athlete, Basketball Player, Olympic Athlete)
49447 Plymouth Way
Plymouth, MI 48170-6439, USA

Hayworth, Nan (Congressman, Politician)
1440 Longworth HOB
Washington, DC 20515, USA

Hayworth, Tracy (Athlete, Football Player)
155 Knights Church Rd
Decherd, TN 37324, USA

Hazanavicius, Michael (Director)
c/o Maha Dakhil *Creative Artists Agency (CAA-LA)*
2000 Ave Of The Stars
Los Angeles, CA 90067, USA

Hazard, Geoffrey C Jr (Attorney, Attorney General, Educator, General)
200 W Willow Grove Ave
Philadelphia, PA 19118, USA

Haze, Jonathan
3636 Woodhill Canyon
Studio City, CA 91604

Hazell, Keeley (Actor)
98 De Beauvoir Rd
London N1 4EN, United Kingdom

Hazelton, Major (Athlete, Football Player)
6803 S Crandon Ave
Chicago, IL 60649, USA

Hazen, Maya (Actor)
c/o Adam Griffin *Kritzer Levine Wilkins Entertainment (KLWG)*
11872 La Grange Ave
1st Floor
Los Angeles, CA 90025, USA

Hazewood, Drungo (Athlete, Baseball Player)
7991 Westboro Way
Sacramento, CA 95823-4934, USA

Haziza, Shlomi (Artist)
H Studio
8640 Tamarack Ave
Sun Valley, CA 91352, USA

Hazzard, Johnny (Adult Film Star)
c/o Staff Member *Diva Central Inc*
7510 W Sunset Blvd Ste 1445
Los Angees, CA 90046, USA

Hazzard, Shirley (Writer)
200 E 66th St
New York, NY 10021, USA

H. Bishop, Timothy (Congressman, Politician)
306 Cannon HOB
Washington, DC 20515, USA

Heacock, Raymond L (Engineer)
Jet Production Laboratory
4800 Oak Grove Dr
Pasadena, CA 91109, USA

Head, Anthony (Actor)
Gordon & French
12-13 Poland St
London W1F 8QB, ENGLAND

Head, Anthony Stewart (Actor)
c/o Staff Member *Innovative Artists (LA)*
1505 10th St
Santa Monica, CA 90401, USA

Head, Don (Athlete, Hockey Player)
15240 NE Knott St
Portland, OR 97230, USA

Head, Emily (Actor)
c/o Kate Bryden *Gordon and French*
12-13 Poland St
London W1F 8QB, UNITED KINGDOM (UK)

Head, James W (Scientist)
Brown University
Geological Sciences Dept
Providence, RI 02912, USA

Head, John (Baseball Player)
Kansas City Monarchs
12677 Tremblewood Dr
Florissant, MO 63033-4729, USA

Head, Roy (Musician)
Texas Sounds Entertainment
2317 Pecan
Dickinson, TX 77539, USA

Headden, Susan M (Journalist)
Indianapolis Star
Editorial Dept
307 N Pennsylvania
Indianapolis, IN 46204, USA

Headen, Andy (Athlete, Football Player)
P.O. Box 821
Liberty, NC 27298, USA

Headey, Lena (Actor)
c/o Tina Thor *TMT Entertainment Group*
648 Broadway
Suite 1002
New York, NY 10012, USA

Headington, Timothy (Misc)
7823 Marquette St
Dallas, TX 75225-4400, USA

Headley, Chase (Athlete, Baseball Player)
1128 Re2alitv Wav
Knoxville, TN 37923-6799, USA

Headley, Glenne
8942 Wilshire Blvd.
Beverly Hills, CA 90211

Headley, Heather (Actor, Musician)
40 W 56th St #5F
New York, NY 10019, USA

Headley, Shari
112-26 178th St.
Jamaica, NY 11433

Headly, Glenne (Actor)
c/o Brian Mann *ICM Partners (ICM-LA)*
10250 Constellation Blvd Fl 7
Los Angeles, CA 90067, USA

Headon, Topper (Musician)
c/o Staff Member *Premier Talent*
3 E 54th St
#1100
New York, NY 10022, USA

Headrick, CC (Stylist)
c/o Staff Member *Page.214*
3303 Lee Pkwy
#205
Dallas, TX 75219, USA

Heafner, Vance (Athlete, Golfer)
6212 Godfrey Dr
Raleigh, NC 27612-6717, USA

Heald, Anthony (Actor)
Endeavor Talent Agency
9701 Wilshire Blvd #1000
Beverly Hills, CA 90212, USA

Healey, Danis W (Government Official)
Pingles Place
Alfriston
East Sussex BN26 5TT, UNITED KINGDOM (UK)

Healey, Derek E (Composer)
29 Stafford Road
Ruislip Gardens
Middx H4A 6PB, UNITED KINGDOM (UK)

Healey, James
415 S. Spalding Dr. #306
Beverly Hills, CA 90212

Healey, John G (Misc)
Amnesty International USA
322 8th Ave
New York, NY 10001, USA

Healey, Mary (Actor)
c/o Staff Member *Rabbit Vocal Management*
27 Poland St
3rd Floor
London W1F 8QW, UK

Healey, Rich (Athlete, Hockey Player)
1085 Carter Crest Rd NW
Edmonton, AB T6R 2N2, Canada

Healy, Chip (Football Player)
1903 Lathan Ct
Nashville, TN 37207-4812, USA

Healy, Cornelius T (Misc)
Plate Die Engravers Union
228 S Swarthmore Ave
Ridley Park, PA 19078, USA

Healy, Don (Athlete, Football Player)
3427 Boca Ciega Dr
Naples, FL 34112, USA

Healy, Fran (Athlete, Baseball Player)
1 Primrose Ln
Holyoke, MA 01040-1523, USA

Healy, Fran (Music Group)
Wildlife Entertainment
21 Heathmans Road
London SW6 4TJ, UNITED KINGDOM (UK)

Healy, Glenn (Athlete, Hockey Player)
c/o Staff Member *The Sports Network*
9 Channel Nine Ct
Toronto, ON M1S 4B5, Canada

Healy, Jane E (Journalist)
Orlando Sentinel
Editrial Dept
633 N Orange Ave
Orlando, FL 32801, USA

Healy, Jeramiah (Writer)
186 Commonwealth Ave Apt 31
Boston, MA 02116-2719, USA

Healy, Jeremiah (Writer)
PO Box 442
Kents Mill, ME 04349-0442, USA

Healy, Matthew L. (Matt) (Writer)
c/o Simon Millar *Rumble Media*
1620 Broadway
Santa Monica, CA 90403, USA

Healy, Patricia (Actor)
Shelter Entertainment
9255 Sunset Blvd #1010
Los Angeles, CA 90069, USA

Heames, Darin (Actor)
c/o Andrew Stawiarski *ADS Management*
269 S. Beverly Dr #441
Beverly Hills, CA 90212, USA

Heaney, Brian (Athlete, Basketball Player)
153 Spinnaker Dr
Halifax, Nova Scotia B3N 3C3, Canada

Heaney, Gerald W (Judge)
US Court of Appeals
Federal Building
Duluth, MN 55802, USA

Heaney, Seamus (Nobel Prize Laureate)
Faber and Faber 3 Queens Square
London, ENGLAND WC1N 3AU, USA

Heap, Imogen (Musician)
c/o Staff Member *Solar Management*
13 Rosemont Rd
London NW3 6NG, UK

Heap, Joseph (Athlete, Football Player)
410 Laurelleaf Ln
Covington, LA 70433, USA

Heap, Todd (Athlete, Football Player)
4320 N Essex Cir
Mesa, AZ 85207-7167, USA

Heaphy, Shawn (Athlete, Hockey Player)
73 Lakeview Dr
Charlton, Charlton 01507-5429, USA

Heard, Amber (Actor)
c/o Geyer Kosinski *Media Talent Group*
9200 Sunset Blvd
Suite 550
Los Angeles, CA 90069, USA

Heard, G Alexander (Educator, Politician, Scientist)
2100 Golf Club Lane
Nashville, TN 37215, USA

Heard, Garfield (Athlete, Basketball Player)
1735 Peachtree St NE #133
Atlanta, GA 30309, USA

Heard, Herman Jr (Athlete, Football Player)
P.O. Box 938
Broomfield, CO 80038, USA

Heard, Jerry (Athlete, Golfer)
293 Talawah Rd
Purvis, MS 39475-5047, USA

Heard, John (Actor)
Odyssey Theatre Emsemble
2055 S Sepulveda Blvd
Los Angeles, CA 90025, USA

Hearn, Chick (Misc)
4362 Avocado Ave
Yorba Linda, CA 92886-2506, USA

Hearn, Ed (Athlete, Baseball Player)
5737 Theden St
Shawnee, KS 66218-9199, USA

Hearn, George (Actor, Music Group)
211 S Beverly Dr #211
Beverly Hills, CA 90212, USA

Hearn, J Woodrow (Religious Leader)
United Methodist Church
PO Box 320
Nashville, TN 37202, USA

Hearn, Kevin (Musician)
c/o Staff Member *Six Shooter Management*
98038, 970 Queen St East
Toronto, ON M4M 1Jo, Canada

Hearn, Thomas K Jr (Educator)
Wake Forest University
President's Office
Winston Salem, NC 27109, USA

Hearn, Tom (Golfer)
Links Mmg
5068 W Plano Pkwy Ste 256
Plano, TX 75093-4441, USA

Hearne, Bill (Music Group, Musician)
Class Act Entertainment
PO Box 160236
Nashville, TN 37216, USA

Hearns, Shane (Athlete, Baseball Player, Olympic Athlete)
8165 Brians Ct
Lambertville, MI 48144-9583, USA

Hearns, Tommy (Boxer)
c/o Staff Member *National Organization of Professional Athletes*
1806 Watermere Ln
Windermere, FL 34786, USA

Hearrell, Frank (General)
762 Saint Pius Dr
Corpus Christi, TX 78412-3065, USA

Hearron, Jeff (Athlete, Baseball Player)
5820 Hill Rd
Powder Sorines, GA 30127-4041, USA

Hearst, Amanda Randolph (Model)
c/o Keya Morgan *Keya Morgan Productions*
P.O. Box 18447
Beverly Hills, CA 90209, USA

Hearst, Donald P (Engineer)
Langley Research Center
NASA
Hampton, VA 23665, USA

Hearst, Garrison (Athlete, Football Player)
3753 Augusta Hwy
Lincolnton, GA 30817, USA

Hearst, Lydia (Model)
c/o Ryan Brown *Factory PR*
580 Broadway #600
New York, NY 10012, USA

Hearst, Patricia (Writer)
110 5th St
San Francisco, CA 94103-2918

Hearst, Rick (Actor)
Stone Manners
6500 Wilshire Blvd #550
Los Angeles, CA 90048, USA

Hearst, Victoria
865 Comstock Ave.
Los Angeles, CA 90024

Hearst Shaw, Patty (Actor)
66 E Meadow Rd
Wilton, CT 06897, USA

Heart (Musician)
c/o Jeff Frasco *Creative Artists Agency (CAA-LA)*
2000 Ave Of The Stars
Los Angeles, CA 90067, USA

Heaslip, Mark (Athlete, Hockey Player)
11 Leland Ct
Chevy Chase, MD 20815, USA

Heater, Don (Athlete, Football Player)
8704 Manchester Ave
Kansas City, MO 64138, USA

Heater, Larry (Athlete, Football Player)
3711 Royal Fern Cir
Las Vegas, NV 89115, USA

Heath, Albert (Tootie) (Music Group, Musician)
Ted Kurland
173 Brighton Ave
Boston, MA 02134, USA

Heath, Bill (Athlete, Baseball Player)
1626 Lake Charlotte Ln
Richmond, TX 77406-7016, USA

Heath, Brandon
c/o Staff Member *Creative Trust, Inc.*
5141 Virginia Way
Suite 320
Brentwood, TN 37027, USA

Heath, Carey (Race Car Driver)
Carey Heath Motorsports
12 Worster Rd.
Eliot, ME 03903, USA

Heath, James E (Jimmy) (Composer, Music Group, Musician)
Ted Kurland
173 Brighton Ave
Boston, MA 02134, USA

Heath, Kelly (Athlete, Baseball Player)
2249 Portofino Pl
Apt 2222
Palm Harbor, FL 34683-7740, USA

Heath, Mike (Athlete, Baseball Player)
2107 Timothy Ter
Valrico, FL 33594-3145, USA

Heath, Rodney (Athlete, Football Player)
6673 Red Pine Dr
Liberty Township, OH 45044-8765, USA

Heath, Shona (Stylist)
c/o Staff Member *Camilla Lowther Managment (CLM Represents)*
30-32 Ericsson Pl
New York, NY 10013, USA

Heath, Tommy (Musician)
c/o JD Sobol *RPM Talent Agency*
741 N Cahuenga Blvd
Suite 101
Los Angeles, CA 90038, USA

Heathcock, Clayton H (Misc)
5235 Alhambra Valley Road
Martinez, CA 94553, USA

Heathcock, Jeff (Athlete, Baseball Player)
24962 Calle Vecindad
Lake Forest, CA 92630, USA

Heathcote, Bella (Actor)
c/o Brian Medavoy *Medavoy Management*
10203 Santa Monica Blvd
Suite 400
Los Angeles, CA 90067, USA

Heathcote, Jud (Athlete, Basketball Player, Coach)
5418 S Quail Ridge Cir
Spokane, WA 99223, USA

Heathcott, Mike (Athlete, Baseball Player)
12445 E Saddlehorn Trl
Scottsdale, AZ 85259, USA

Heatherly, Eric (Actor)
c/o Staff Member *The Bazel Group Inc*
4636 Lebanon Pike #308
Hermitage, TN 37076, USA

Heath-Stubbs, John F A (Writer)
22 Artesian Road
London W2 5AR, UNITED KINGDOM (UK)

Heaton, Neal (Athlete, Baseball Player)
3 Nursery Ct
East Patchogue, NY 11772-6152, USA

Heaton, Patricia (Actor)
c/o CeCe Yorke *True Public Relations*
6725 W Sunset Blvd #470
Los Angeles, CA 90028-7180, USA

Heatwave
6464 Sunset Blvd. #1010
Hollywood, CA 90028

Heaver, Paul (Athlete, Hockey Player)
20 Raiford St
Aurora, ON L4G 6J2, Canada

Heaverlo, Dave (Athlete, Baseball Player)
3720 W Lakeshore Dr
Moses Lake, WA 98837-3003, USA

Hebenton, Andy (Athlete, Hockey Player)
3295 SW Sandalwood Ln
Gresham, OR 97080, USA

Hebenton, Clay (Athlete, Hockey Player)
13457 Whitewater Dr
Poway, CA 92064, USA

Hebert, Ashley (Reality TV Star)
University Of Pennsylvania
School Of Dental Medicine
240 S 40th St
Philadelphia, PA 19104, USA

Hebert, Bobby (Athlete, Football Player)
530 Avala Ct
Alpharetta, GA 30022, USA

Hebert, Bud (Athlete, Football Player)
P.O. Box 250342
Plano, TX 75025, USA

Hebert, Guy (Athlete, Hockey Player, Olympic Athlete)
8 Gleneagles Dr
Newport Beach, CA 92660-4296, USA

Hebert, Johnny (Race Car Driver)
Team Lotus
Kettering Hamm Hall
Wymondham
Norfolk NR18 7HW, UNITED KINGDOM (UK)

Hebert, Ken (Athlete, Football Player)
7001 Mount Sharp Rd
Wimberly, TX 78676, USA

Hebner, Rich (Richie) (Athlete, Baseball Player)
6 Tetreault Dr
Walpole, MA 02081-2224, USA

Hebron, Vaughn (Athlete, Football Player)
154 Madison Ct
Southampton, PA 18966, USA

Hebson, Bryan (Athlete, Baseball Player)
1151 Fairmont Ln
Auburn, AL 36830-2105, USA

Heche, Anne (Actor)
c/o Jason Weinberg *Untitled Entertainment (LA)*
350 S. Beverly Dr #200
Beverly Hills, CA 90212, USA

Hecht, Albie (Producer, Writer)
c/o Staff Member *Spike TV*
1515 Broadway
New York, NY 10036, USA

Hecht, Duvall (Misc)
2910 W Garry Ave
Santa Ana, CA 92704, USA

Hecht, Jessica (Actor)
c/o Staff Member *Innovative Artists (LA)*
1505 10th St
Santa Monica, CA 90401, USA

Hecht, Jochen (Athlete, Hockey Player)
95 Levin Ln
East Amherst, NY 14051, USA

Hechter, Daniel (Designer, Fashion Designer)
4 Ave Ter Hoche
Paris 75008, FRANCE

Hecht-Herskowitz, Gina (Actor)
5930 Foothill Dr
Los Angeles, CA 90068, USA

Heck, Andy (Athlete, Football Player)
221 Deer Haven Dr
Ponte Vedra Beach, FL 32082, USA

Heck, Bob (Athlete, Football Player)
1939 Tarpon Rd
Naples, FL 34102-1565, USA

Heck, Ralph (Athlete, Football Player)
1906 Wicks Ridge Ln
Marietta, GA 30062-6777, USA

Heck, Richard (Nobel Prize Laureate)
University Of Delaware Attn: Chemistry
Dept
Newark, DE 19716, USA

Heck, Robert (Athlete, Football Player)
1939 Tarpon Rd
Naples, FL 34102, USA

Heckard, Steve (Athlete, Football Player)
671 Glendale Dr
Rock Hill, SC 29732-2309, USA

Heckard, Tae (Actor)
c/o Staff Member *Pakula/King &
Associates*
9229 Sunset Blvd
Suite 315
Los Angeles, CA 90069, USA

Hecker, Zvi (Architect)
19 Elzar St
Tel Aviv 65157, ISRAEL

Heckerling, Amy (Director, Producer)
1330 Schuyler Road
Beverly Hills, CA 90210, USA

Heckler, Margaret (Politician)
1401 N Oak St Apt 904
Arlington, VA 22209-3650, USA

Heckler, Margaret M (Secretary)
1401 N Oak St
Arlington, VA 22209, USA

Heckman, James (Athlete)
4807 S Greenwood Ave
Chicago, IL 60615-1913, USA

Heckman, James J (Nobel Prize Laureate)
4807 S Greenwood Ave
Chicago, IL 60615, USA

Heckscher, August (Writer)
333 E 68th St
New York, NY 10021, USA

Hector, Johnny (Athlete, Football Player)
101 Grandville Dr
101 Grandville Dr, LA 70508-6448, USA

Hector, Willie (Athlete, Football Player)
138 Lower Ter
San Francisco, CA 94114-1443, USA

Hedaya, Dan (Actor)
Gersh Agency
232 North Canon Dr
Beverly Hills, CA 90210, USA

Hedbera, Anders
Krabbvagen 18
Lidingo 18130, Sweden

Hedberg, Anders (Athlete, Hockey Player)
7305 Campeau Dr
Kanata, ON K2K 3M2, Canada

Hedberg, Johan (Athlete, Hockey Player)
c/o Jay Grossman *PuckAgency LLC*
555 Pleasantville Rd
North Building, Suite 210
Briarcliff Manor, NY 10510, USA

Hedberg, Randy (Athlete, Football Player)
137 Twelve Oaks Dr
Murphysboro, IL 62966-6572, USA

Hedderick, Herman (Athlete, Basketball
Player)
2913 Homestead Dr
Erie, PA 16506, USA

Hedeman, Richard (Tuff) (Misc)
PO Box 224
Morgan Mill, TX 76465, USA

Heder, Jon (Actor, Producer)
c/o Julie Darmody *Mosaic Media Group*
9200 W. Sunset Blvd
10th Floor
Los Angeles, CA 90069, USA

Hedford, Eric (Music Group, Musician)
Monqui Mgmt
PO Box 5908
Portland, OR 97228, USA

Hedgepeth, Whitney (Athlete, Olympic
Athlete, Swimmer)
9801 Westward Dr
Austin, TX 78733-3145, USA

Hedges, Clifton
10475 Crosspoint Blvd.
Indianapolis, IN 46256-3323

Hedges, Peter (Director, Writer)
c/o Richard Lovett *Creative Artists Agency
(CAA-LA)*
2000 Ave Of The Stars
Los Angeles, CA 90067, USA

Hedican, Bret (Athlete, Hockey Player,
Olympic Athlete)
290 Las Quebradas Ln
Alamo, CA 94507, USA

Hedin, Pierre (Athlete, Hockey Player)
Lakasund 158
Bonassund 891 78, Sweden

Hedington, Tim (Producer)
c/o Staff Member *GK Films*
1411 5th St
Suite 200
Santa Monica, CA 90401, USA

Hedison, Alexandra (Actor)
Hedison Photography
PO Box 691636
Los Angeles, CA 90069, USA

Hedison, Bret (Athlete, Hockey Player)
1848 Torrington
Raleigh, NC 27619, USA

Hedison, David (Actor)
779 Carissa Dr
West Palm Beach, FL 33411-3412, USA

Hedlund, Garrett (Actor)
c/o Cynthia Pett-Dante *Brillstein
Entertainment Partners*
9150 Wilshire Blvd #350
Beverly Hills, CA 90212, USA

Hedlund, Mike (Athlete, Baseball Player)
2412 Klinger Rd
Arlington, TX 76016-1143, USA

Hedquist, Julien
c/o Staff Member *IMG*
304 Park Ave S Fl 12
New York, NY 10010, USA

Hedren, Tippi (Actor)
The Roar Foundation
6867 Soledad Canyon Rd
Acton, CA 93510, USA

Hedrick, Chad (Athlete, Olympic Athlete,
Speed Skater)
18203 Stockton Springs Dr
Spring, TX 77379-6926, USA

Hedrick, Joan (Writer)
300 Summit St
Hartford, CT 06106-3105, USA

Hedrick, Joan D (Writer)
Trinity College
Women's Studies Program
300 Summit St
Hartford, CT 06106, USA

Hedrick, Larry (Race Car Driver)
Larry Hedrick Motorsports
Box 511
114 Victory Lane
Stateville, NC 28677, USA

Heeger, Alan (Nobel Prize Laureate)
1042 Las Alturas Rd
Santa Barbara, CA 93103-1608, USA

Heeger, Alan J (Nobel Prize Laureate)
1042 Las Alturas Road
Santa Barbara, CA 93103, USA

Heenan, Pat (Athlete, Football Player)
10007 Raynor Rd
Silver Spring, MD 20901, USA

Heep, Danny (Athlete, Baseball Player)
18610 Crosstimber
San Antonio, TX 782S8-4587, USA

Heera (Actor, Bollywood)
Nungambakkam
Chennai, TN 600034, INDIA

Heeschen, David S (Astronomer)
702 Copa D'Oro
Marathon, FL 33050, USA

Heesters, Johannes
Heimgartenstr. 21
Starnberg, GERMANY D-82319

Heeter, Carrie (Inventor)
Michigan State Univesity
Communication Technology Lab
East Lansing, MI 48824, USA

Heeter, Gene (Athlete, Football Player)
11 Symphony Dr
Lake Grove, NY 11755-1313, USA

Heffern, Meghan (Actor)
c/o Barb Godfrey *Parent Management*
530 Queen St East
Toronto
ON M5A 1V2, CANADA

Heffernan, Bert (Athlete, Baseball Player)
130 Eagle Ct
Locust Grove, VA 22508-5432, USA

Heffernan, Dave (Athlete, Football Player)
8101 SW 79th Ter
Miami, FL 33143, USA

Heffernan, Kevin (Actor, Comedian,
Producer, Writer)
Broken Lizard Industries
4000 Warner Blvd
Building 139 #102
Burbank, CA 91522, USA

Heffner, Bob (Athlete, Baseball Player)
910 N 12th St
Allentown, PA 18102-1102, USA

Heffner, Kyle (Actor)
c/o Melanie Sharp *Sharp Talent*
117 N Orlando Ave
Los Angeles, CA 90048, USA

Heffron, Edward (Misc)
420 Mifflin St
Philadelphia, PA 19148-1823, USA

Heffron, John (Actor, Comedian)
c/o Peter Rosegarten *Conversation
Company*
1044 Northern Blvd
Suite 304
Roslyn, NY 11576, USA

Heffron, Richard T (Director)
c/o Staff Member *Shapiro-Lichtman Talent
Agency*
1333 Beverly Green Drive
Los Angeles, CA 90035-1018, USA

Heflin, Bronson (Athlete, Baseball Player)
1004 Pintail Pl
Hendersonville, TN 37075-8897, USA

Heflin, Milt (Scientist)
15506 Seahorse Dr
Houston, Tx 77062-3617, USA

Heflin, Vince (Athlete, Football Player)
4811 Lake Ontario Way
Bowie, MD 20720-, USA

Hefner, Christie (Business Person,
Publisher)
Playboy Enterprises
680 N Lake Shore Dr
Chicago, IL 60611, USA

Hefner, Hugh (Producer, Publisher)
Playboy Mansion
10236 Charring Cross Rd
Los Angeles, CA 90077, USA

Hefner, Larry (Athlete, Football Player)
1208 Arboretum Dr
Lewisville, NC 27023, USA

Hefner, Lene
15127 Califa St.
Van Nuys, CA 91411

Heft, Bob
4098 Green St.
Saginaw, MI 48603-6618

Heft, Robert (Bob) (Designer)
PO Box 20404
Saginaw, MI 48602, USA

Hegamin, George (Athlete, Football
Player)
1409 S Lamar St
Apt 616
Dallas, TX 75215, USA

Hegan, Mike (Athlete, Baseball Player)
7 Wild Turkey Run
Hilton Head Island, SC 29926-1901, USA

Heger, Rene (Actor)
c/o Jerry Shandrew *Shandrew Public
Relations*
1050 S Stanley Ave
Los Angeles, CA 90019-6634, USA

Hegerland, Anita
1315 Nesoya
, NORWAY

Hegg, Steve (Athlete, Cycler, Olympic
Athlete)
3898 Westhaven Dr
Carlsbad, CA 92008-2754, USA

Heggtveit, Ann Hamilton (Skier)
General Delivery
Grand Isle, VT 05458, USA

Hegland, Jean (Writer)
5450 Mill Creek rd
Healdsburg, CA 95448, USA

Hegman, Bob (Athlete, Baseball Player)
3529 NW Winding Woods Dr
Lees Summit, MO 64064-1879, USA

Hegman, Mike (Athlete, Football Player)
2958 Suesand Dr
Memphis, TN 38128, USA

Hehn, Sascha
Postfach 100823
Munich, GERMANY D-80082

Heidei, James (Athlete, Football Player)
1425 Wisteria Dr
Vicksburg, MS 39180, USA

Heidelberger, Charles (Misc)
1495 Poppy Peak Dr
Pasadena, CA 91105, USA

Heidemann, Jack (Athlete, Baseball Player)
1816 S Salida Del Sol Cir
Mesa, AZ 85202-5529, USA

Heiden, Elizabeth L (Beth) (Athlete, Olympic Athlete, Speed Skater)
915 Swarthmore Ct
Madison, WI 53705-2118, USA

Heiden, Eric (Athlete, Olympic Athlete, Speed Skater)
1219 Cottonwood Ln
Park City, UT 84098-7602, USA

Heiden, Steve (Athlete, Football Player)
18186 Lake Forest Cir
Lakeville, MN 55044-5284, USA

Heiden, Steve (Athlete, Football Player)
2600 Rushford Village
Rushford, MN 55971, USA

Heidmann, Manfred
Borbecker Str. 237
Essen, GERMANY D-45355

Heidt, Mike (Athlete, Hockey Player)
8 Creekside Way
Sprice Grove, AB T7X 3Y7, Canada

Heidt Jr, Horace (Musician)
4155 Witzel Dr
Sherman Oaks, CA 91423, USA

Heier, William (Misc)
620 E Fairmont Dr
Tempe, AZ 85282-3725, USA

Heigl, Jennifer (Actor)
Writers & Artists
8383 Wilshire Blvd #550
Beverly Hills, CA 90211, USA

Heigl, Katherine (Actor, Model)
c/o Jill Fritzo *PMK/BNC Public Relations (PMK-NY)*
622 3rd Ave
8th Floor
New York, NY 10017, USA

Heilbron, Lorna (Actor)
Brunskill
169 Queen's Gate
London SW7 5HE, UNITED KINGDOM (UK)

Heilbroner, Robert L (Economist)
412 W End Ave #3E
New York, NY 10024-5775, USA

Heilman, Aaron (Athlete, Baseball Player)
39W272 Sheldon Ln
Geneva, IL 60134-5309, USA

Heilmeier, Ann (Stylist)
120 Leonard Pl
Dover, NJ 07801, USA

Heilmeier, George (Inventor)
17612 Woods Edge Dr
Dallas, TX 75287-7546, USA

Heim, Val (Athlete, Baseball Player)
1050 Louden St
Superior, NE 68978, USA

Heimbold, Charles A Jr (Business Person)
Bristol-Myers Squibb
345 Park Ave
New York, NY 10154, USA

Heimburger, Craig (Athlete, Football Player)
311 Flagstone Dr
Belleville, IL 62221, USA

Heimel, Cynthia (Writer)
Simon & Schuster
1230 Ave of Americas
New York, NY 10020, USA

Heimkreiter, Steve (Athlete, Football Player)
45 Devils Den Apt 208
Fort Thomas, KY 41075-4045, USA

Heimlich, Henry (Scientist)
3939 Erie Ave Apt 4060
Cincinnati, OH 45208-1976, USA

Heimlich, Henry J (Doctor, Physicist)
2347 Bedford Ave #1D
Cincinnati, OH 45208, USA

Heim-McDaniel, Kay (Athlete, Baseball Player, Commentator)
3390 143rd St W
Rosemount, MN 55068-4057, USA

Heimrath, Jr., Ludwig (Race Car Driver)
26117 -34th Ave. East
Spanaway, WA 98387, USA

Heimueller, Gorman (Athlete, Baseball Player)
2148 Glen Ave
Riverton, UT 84065-7079, USA

Heimuli, Lakei (Athlete, Football Player)
1963 W 1870 S
Woods Cross, UT 84087-2181, USA

Heine, Jutta (Athlete, Track Athlete)
Blaue Muhle
Burglahr 57614, GERMANY

Heineman, Dave (Governor)
Office of the Governor
P.O. Box 94848
Lincoln, NE 68509-4848, USA

Heineman, Ken (Athlete, Football Player)
15982 Serenity Point Ln
Rogers, AR 72756-8615, USA

Heinen, Mike (Athlete, Golfer)
4518 E Meadow Ln
Lake Charles, LA 70605-5318, USA

Heinkel, Don (Athlete, Baseball Player)
508 Covineton Ave
Birmineham, AL 35206-3057, USA

Heinle, Amelia (Actor)
c/o John Carrabino *John Carrabino Management*
5900 Wilshire Blvd Fl 4 #406
Los Angeles, CA 90036, USA

Heinrich, Keith (Athlete, Football Player)
21011 Pricewood Manor Ct
Cypress, TX 77433-2075, USA

Heinrich, Lionel (Athlete, Hockey Player)
19-617 27th Av S
Cranbrook, BC V1C 6L1, Canada

Heinrich, Martin (Congressman, Politician)
336 Cannon HOB
Washington, DC 20515, USA

Heins, Shawn (Athlete, Hockey Player)
c/o Staff Member *Sports Personnel Services*
125 Lake St W
Suite 200
Wayzata, MN 55391, USA

Heinsohn, Tom (Athlete, Basketball Player, Coach)
PO Box 422
Newton Upper Falls, MA 02464-0002, USA

Heintz, Bob (Athlete, Golfer)
2213 Highland Woods Dr
Dunedin, FL 34698, USA

Heintz, Chris (Athlete, Baseball Player)
7128 Wareham Dr
Tampa, FL 33647-1132, USA

Heintzelman, Laura (Stylist)
c/o Staff Member *Ford Models (Chicago)*
311 W Superior St
Chicago, IL 60654, USA

Heintzelman, Tom (Athlete, Baseball Player)
1500 W 8th St
Unit 82
Mesa, AZ 85201-3825, USA

Heinz, Bob (Athlete, Football Player)
516 Mansion Ct Unit 502
Santa Clara, CA 95054-4336, USA

Heinz, Rick (Athlete, Hockey Player)
264 Van Allen Gate
Milton, ON L9T 5Y8, Canada

Heinz, W C (Sportscaster, Writer)
1150 Nichols Hill Road
Dorset, VT 05251, USA

Heinze, Steve (Athlete, Hockey Player, Olympic Athlete)
4659 La Espada Dr
Santa Barbara, CA 93111, USA

Heinzer, Franz (Skier)
Lauenen
Rickenbach/Schwyz 6432, SWITZERLAND

Heise, Bob (Athlete, Baseball Player)
537 Live Oak Dr
Angels Camp, CA 95222-9898, USA

Heiser, Rolland (Misc)
4721 Ocean Blvd # W7
Sarasota, FL 34242, USA

Heiser, Roy (Athlete, Baseball Player)
1038 Grovehill Rd
Halethorpe, MD 21227^38()2, USA

Heiserman, Rick (Athlete, Baseball Player)
17252 Adams St
Omaha, NE 68135-3078, USA

Heiskala, Earl (Athlete, Hockey Player)
982 Ocean Ln
Imperial Beach, CA 91932, USA

Heiss Jenkins, Carol (Athlete, Figure Skater, Olympic Athlete)
3183 Regency Place
Westlake, OH 44145, USA

Heisten, Barrett (Athlete, Hockey Player)
4621 Pavalof St
Anchorage, AK 99503-1016, USA

Heitmann, Eric (Athlete, Football Player)
21511 Grand Hollow Ln
Katy, TX 77450-8809, USA

Heitmeyer, Jayne
4450 Lakeside Dr. #350
Burbank, CA 91505

Heizer, Miles (Actor)
c/o Staff Member *Stein Entertainment Group*
1351 N Crescent Heights Blvd #312
West Hollywood, CA 90046, USA

Hejda, Jan (Athlete, Hockey Player)
7778 Cromwell End
New Albany, OH 43051-8849, USA

Hejduk, Milan (Athlete, Hockey Player)
8651 Sawgrass Dr
Lone Tree, CO 80121-8504, USA

Helander, Peter (Athlete, Hockey Player)
Vastergatan 3A
Goteborg 411 23, Sweden

Helberg, Simon (Actor)
c/o Tim Sarkes *Brillstein Entertainment Partners*
9150 Wilshire Blvd #350
Beverly Hills, CA 90212, USA

Held, Archie (Artist, Misc)
A New Leaf Garden
1286 Gilman St
Berkeley, CA 94706, USA

Held, Carl
1817 Hillcrest Rd. #51
Los Angeles, CA 90068

Held, Franklin (Bud) (Athlete, Olympic Athlete, Track Athlete)
13367 Caminito Mar Villa
Del Mar, CA 92014, USA

Held, Mel (Athlete, Baseball Player)
103 Hogan Ln
Bryan, OH 43506-9161, USA

Held, Paul (Athlete, Football Player)
29055 Blue Moon Dr
Menifee, CA 92584, USA

Held, Richard M (Doctor)
Massachusetts Institute of Technology
Psychology Dept
Cambridge, MA 02139, USA

Helde, Annette
8430 Santa Monica Blvd. #200
Los Angeles, CA 90036

Heldt, Mike (Athlete, Football Player)
12711 Corral Rd
Tampa, FL 33626-4405, USA

Helf, Mark (Stylist)
c/o Celebrity Stylist *Photogenics Media*
8549 Higuera St
Building B
Culver Clty, CA 90232, USA

Helfand, David (Astronomer)
Columbia Univesity
Astronomer Dept
New York, NY 10027, USA

Helfand, Eric (Athlete, Baseball Player)
7314 Jackson Dr
San Diego, CA 92119-2317, USA

Helfer, Ricki Tigert (Financier)
Federal Deposit Insurance
550 17th St NW
Washington, DC 20429, USA

Helfer, Tricia (Actor)
c/o Gordon Gilbertson *Gilbertson Management*
1334 3rd St Promenade #201
Santa Monica, CA 90401, USA

Helford, Bruce (Producer, Writer)
c/o Staff Member *United Talent Agency (UTA)*
9336 Civic Center Dr
Beverly Hills, CA 90210, USA

Helgeland, Brian (Director)
c/o Robert Newman *WME (LA)*
9601 Wilshire Blvd Fl 3
Beverly Hills, CA 90210, USA

Helgenberger, Marg (Actor)
c/o Nancy Sanders *Sanders Armstrong Caserta*
2120 Colorado Blvd
Suite 120
Santa Monica, CA 90404, USA

Helinski, Donald R (Biologist)
University of California
Molecular Genetics Center
La Jolla, CA 92093, USA

Helix
1505 W. 2nd Ave. #200
Vancouver, CANADA BC V6H 3Y4

Hellawell, Keith (Government Official, Lawyer)
Government Offices
Great George St
London SW1A 2AL, UNITED KINGDOM (UK)

Hellemond, Andy Van (Athlete, Hockey Player)
4 St Catharine St
Guelph, ON N1E 4L5, Canada

Heller, Andre
Singerstr. 8
Vienna, AUSTRIA A-1010

Heller, Daniel M (Attorney, Attorney General, General)
Israel Discount Bank Building
14 NE 1st Ave
Miami, FL 33132, USA

Heller, Jane (Writer)
1014 Ladera Ln
Santa Barbara, CA 93108-1630, USA

Heller, Jeffrey M (Business Person)
Electronic Data Systems
5400 Legacy Dr
Plano, TX 75024, USA

Heller, John H (Scientist)
74 Horsehoe Road
Wilton, CT 06897, USA

Heller, Ron (Athlete, Football Player)
538 Stillwater River Rd
Absarokee, MT 59001-6218, USA

Hellerman, Fred (Music Group, Songwriter, Writer)
83 Goodhill Road
Weston, CT 06883, USA

Hellestrae, Dale (Athlete, Football Player)
11705 E Charter Oak Dr
Scottsdale, AZ 85259, USA

Hellickson, Russell (Russ) (Athlete, Olympic Athlete, Wrestler)
6893 Lauren Place
Columbus, OH 43235, USA

Helling, Rick A (Ricky) (Athlete, Baseball Player, Olympic Athlete)
3672 Landings Dr
Excelsior, MN 55331-9709, USA

Hellion
18653 Ventura Blvd. #307
Tarzana, CA 91356

Hellman, Bonnie
1680 N. Vine St. #614
Hollywood, CA 90028

Hellman, Martin (Inventor)
730 Alvarado Ct
Stanford, CA 94305-1074, USA

Hellman, Monte (Director)
8588 Appian Way
Los Angeles, CA 90046, USA

Hellmann, Martina (Athlete, Track Athlete)
Neue Leipziger Str 14
Leipzig 04205, GERMANY

Hellmuth, George F (Architect)
10111 Ingleside Dr
Saint Louis, MO 63124, USA

Hellmuth, Phillip (Misc)
1101 University Ave
Palo Alto, CA 94301-2239, USA

Hellstrand, Kristoffer (Biologist)
Goteborg University
Virology Dept
Goteborg 405 30, SWEDEN

Helluin, Francis (Athlete, Football Player)
3930 Southdown Mandalay Rd
Houma, LA 70360, USA

Helluin, Jerry (Athlete, Football Player)
3930 Southdown Mandalay Rd
Houma, LA 70360-3001, USA

Hellwig, James (Ultimate Warrior) (Athlete, Wrestler)
Ultimate Creations, Inc.
43A County Road 119 North
Sante Fe, NM 87506, USA

Hellwig, Jim (Athlete, Wrestler)
Ultimate Creations, Inc.
43A County Road 119 North
Santa Fe, NM 87506, USA

Hellyer, Paul T (Government Official)
65 Harbour Square #506
Toronto, ON M5J 2L4, CANADA

Helm, Darren (Athlete, Hockey Player)
c/o Staff Member *Detroit Red Wings*
Joe Luis Arena
600 Civic Center Dr
Detroit, MI 48226, USA

Helm, Peter
1480 S. Wild Oaks Dr.
Nixa, MO 65714

Helm, Val (Athlete, Baseball Player)
Chicago White Sox
PO Box 423
Superior, NE 68978-0423, USA

Helmberger, Don V (Misc)
California Institute of Technology
Seismology Dept
Pasadena, CA 91125, USA

Helmer, Frank (Stylist)
c/o Staff Member *Exclusive Artists Mgmt*
7700 Sunset Blvd
#205
Los Angeles, CA 90046, USA

Helmerich, Hans C (Business Person)
Helmerich & Payne Inc
Utica & 21st St
Tulsa, OK 74114, USA

Helmerich, Walter H III (Business Person)
Helmerich & Payne Inc
Utica & 21st St
Tulsa, OK 74114, USA

Helmerson, Frans (Music Group, Musician)
Columbia Artists Mgmt Inc
165 W 57th St
New York, NY 10019, USA

Helmly, James R (General)
Commander
US Army Reserves
HqUSA Pentagon
Washington, DC 20310, USA

Helmond, Katherine (Actor)
2035 Davies Way
Los Angeles, CA 90046, USA

Helmreich, Ernst J M (Misc)
University of Wurzburg Biozentrum
Am Hubland
Wurzburg 97074, GERMANY

Helms, Ed (Actor, Comedian)
c/o Peter Principato *Principato/Young Management*
9465 Wilshire Blvd
Suite 430
Beverly Hills, CA 90212, USA

Helms, Jimmy (Race Car Driver)
6230 Rock Island Rd.
Charlotte, NC 28278, USA

Helms, L S (Financier)
KeyCorp
127 Public Square
Cleveland, OH 44114, USA

Helms, Susan J (Astronaut)
NASA
Johnson Space Center
2101 NASA Road
Houston, TX 77058, USA

Helms, Susan J Biggen
10824 W Coco Pl
Littleton, CO 80127-4112, USA

Helms, Tommy (Athlete, Baseball Player, Coach)
5427 Bluesky Dr
Cincinnati, OH 45247-7865, USA

Helms, Wes (Athlete, Baseball Player)
9314 Bear Creek Rd
Sterrett, Al 35147-9166, USA

Helmstetter, Shad (Motivational Speaker, Writer)
Goals-On-Line.com Corporate Offices
362 Gulf Breeze Parkway
Suite 104
Gulf Breeze, FL 32561, USA

Helmut
1775 Broadway #433
New York, NY 10019

Helmuth, Phil (Misc)
1101 University Ave
Palo Alto, CA 94301, USA

Helnwein, Gottfried (Artist)
Aul der Burg 2
Burgbrol 56659, GERMANY

Heloise
PO Box 795000
San Antonio, TX 78279

Heloise, (Cruse Evans) (Journalist)
PO Box 795000
San Antonio, TX 78279, USA

Helpern, Joan G (Designer, Fashion Designer)
Joan & David Helpern Inc
46 W 56th St #200
New York, NY 10019, USA

Heltau, Michael (Actor, Music Group)
Sulzweg 11
Vienna 1190, AUSTRIA

Helton, Barry (Athlete, Football Player)
3325 Clubview Ter
Colorado Springs, CO 80906-4479, USA

Helton, Bill D (Business Person)
New Century Energies
1225 17th St
Denver, CO 80202, USA

Helton, Mike (Race Car Driver)
PO Box 2875
Daytona Beach, FL 32120, USA

Helton, RJ (Musician)
PO Box 246
1400 Market Place Blvd
Cumming, GA 30041, USA

Helton, Todd (Athlete, Baseball Player)
Colorado Rockies Foundation 2001 Blake St Unit A
Denver, CO 80602=8111, USA

Helvin, Marie (Model)
IMG Models
23 Eyot Gardens
London W6 9TN, UNITED KINGDOM (UK)

Hely, Steve (Actor)
c/o Cori Wellins *WME (LA)*
9601 Wilshire Blvd Fl 3
Beverly Hills, CA 90210, USA

Heman, Russ (Athlete, Baseball Player)
5555 Canyon Crest Dr
Apt 3D
Riverside, CA 92507-6453, USA

Hemandez, Angel (Baseball Player)
500 Cypress Xing
Wellington, FL 33414-6368, USA

Hemecker, Ralph (Director)
c/o Staff Member *Mythic Films*
225 East Broadway
Suite 115B
Glendale, CA 91205, USA

Hemenway, Robert E (Educator)
University of Kansas
President's Office
Lawrence, KS 66045, USA

Hemingway, Gerardine (Designer, Fashion Designer)
Red or Dead Ltd
Courtney Road Bldg 201
Wembley
Middx HA9 7PP, UNITED KINGDOM (UK)

Hemingway, Mariel (Actor, Model)
c/o Gregg Edwards *Gregg Edwards Management*
6072 Franklin Ave
#304
Los Angeles, CA 90028, USA

Hemingway, Rose (Actor)
c/o Charles Mastropietro *Circle of Confusion (NY)*
270 Lafayette St
Suite 402
New York, NY 10012, USA

Hemingway, Toby (Actor)
c/o Sarah Shyn *3 Arts Entertainment Inc*
9460 Wilshire Blvd
7th Floor
Beverly Hills, CA 90210, USA

Hemingway, Wayne (Designer, Fashion Designer)
Red or Dead Ltd
Courtney Road Bldg 201
Wembley
Middx HA9 7PP, UNITED KINGDOM (UK)

Hemme, Christy (Actor)
c/o Liza Anderson *Anderson Group Public Relations*
8060 Melrose Ave Fl 4
Los Angeles, CA 90046, USA

Hemmens, Heather (Actor)
c/o Stephanie Simon *Untitled Entertainment (LA)*
350 S. Beverly Dr #200
Beverly Hills, CA 90212, USA

Hemmer, Bill (Correspondent)
c/o Staff Member *Fox News Channel (NY)*
1211 Ave of the Americas
Level C1
New York, NY 10036-8701, USA

Hemmi, Heini (Skier)
Chalet Bel-Lia
Valbella 7077, SWITZERLAND

Hemming, Lindy (Designer, Stylist)
c/o Robert Arakelian *United Talent Agency (UTA)*
9336 Civic Center Dr
Beverly Hills, CA 90210, USA

Hemmis, Paige (Actor, Reality TV Star)
c/o Staff Member *Extreme Makeover: Home Edition*
Endemol Entertainment USA
9225 Sunset Blvd #1100
Los Angeles, CA 90069, USA

Hemond, Roland (Commentator)
1332 W Edgemont Ave
Phoenix, AZ 85007-1117, USA

Hemond, Scott (Athlete, Baseball Player)
263 Florida Ave
Dunedin, FL 34698-7530, USA

Hemphill., Bret (Athlete, Baseball Player)
1273 Trehowell Dr
Roseville, CA 95678-6110, United States

Hemphill, Darryl (Athlete, Football Player)
10218 Aurora Fld
San Antonio, TX 78245-2622, USA

Hemphill, Joel (Music Group)
Harper Agency
PO Box 144
Goodlettsville, TN 37070, USA

Hemphill, Labreeska (Music Group)
Harper Agency
PO Box 144
Goodlettsville, TN 37070, USA

Hemphill, Richard (Baseball Player)
Kansas City Monarchs
422 Barnes St
Rockhill, SC 29730-5044, USA

Hempstead, Hessley (Athlete, Football Player)
14823 Dunbeth Dr
Huntersville, NC 28078-3308, USA

Hempstone, Smith Jr (Diplomat, Writer)
7611 Fairfax Road
Bethesda, MD 20814, USA

Hemric, Dick (Athlete, Basketball Player)
1220 7th St NE
North Canton, OH 44720-2116, USA

Hemsky, Ales (Athlete, Hockey Player)
Jiri Crha Sports Representation
16390 Braeburn Ridge Trl
Delray Beach, FL 33446-9508, USA

Hemsley, Nate (Athlete, Football Player)
26 Roberts Pl
Willingboro, NJ 08046, USA

Hemsley, Stephen J (Business Person)
United HealthCare Corp
Opus Center
9900 Bren Road E
Minnetonka, MN 55343, USA

Hemsworth, Chris (Actor)
c/o Will Ward *ROAR (LA)*
9701 Wilshire Blvd
8th Floor
Los Angeles, CA 90212, USA

Hemsworth, Liam (Actor)
c/o Will Ward *ROAR (LA)*
9701 Wilshire Blvd
8th Floor
Los Angeles, CA 90212, USA

Hemus, Solly (Athlete, Baseball Player, Coach)
5100 San Felipe St
Unit 194E
Houston, TX 77056-3688, USA

Henao, Zulay (Actor)
c/o Jean-Louis Diamonika *One Entertainment (NY)*
12 W 57th St
Penthouse
New York, NY 10019, USA

Hencken, John F (Athlete, Olympic Athlete, Swimmer)
PO Box 2540
Weaverville, NC 28787-2540, USA

Hendershot, Larry (Athlete, Football Player)
6201 W Riviera Dr
Glendale, IN 85304-2523, USA

Hendershot, Ray (Artist)
1007 Lakeview Terrace
Pennsburg, PA 18073, USA

Henderson, Alan (Basketball Player)
Atlanta Hawks
190 Marieta St SW
Atlanta, GA 30303, USA

Henderson, Anthony (Krayzie Bone) (Actor, Composer, Musician)
c/o Staff Member *RBC Records*
150 E. Olive
Suite 114
Burbank, CA 91502, USA

Henderson, Cedric (Athlete, Basketball Player)
P.O. Box 148
Smyrna, GA 30081-0148, USA

Henderson, Chris (Soccer Player)
Columbus Crew
2121 Velman Ave
Columbus, OH 43211, USA

Henderson, David (Athlete, Basketball Player)
805 Sweet Hollow Ct
Middletown, DE 19709-8645, USA

Henderson, David L (Dave) (Athlete, Baseball Player)
6004 142nd Ct SE
Bellevue, WA 98006-4901, USA

Henderson, Devery (Athlete, Football Player)
835 E Bellevue St
Opelousas, LA 70570, USA

Henderson, Donald A (Educator, Misc)
3802 Greenway
Baltimore, MD 21218, USA

Henderson, Felicia (Writer)
c/o Scott Schwartz *Vision Art Management*
9465 Wilshire Blvd Ste 870
Beverly Hills, CA 90212, USA

Henderson, Florence (Actor, Music Group)
FHB Productions
PO Box 11295
Marina del Rey, CA 90295, USA

Henderson, Gerald (Athlete, Basketball Player)
185 Birkdale Dr
Blue Bell, PA 19422-3276, USA

Henderson, James A (Business Person)
Cummins Engine Co
PO Box 3005
500 Jackson St
Columbus, IN 47201, USA

Henderson, Jerome (Athlete, Football Player)
11051 Berkely Club Dr Apt 201
Raleigh, NC 27617-8543, USA

Henderson, Jerome (Athlete, Basketball Player)
3208 Potterstone Way
Avon, OH 44011-4202, USA

Henderson, Joe (Athlete, Baseball Player)
525 Agua Clara St
El Paso, TX 79928-9011, USA

Henderson, John (Athlete, Football Player)
11667 Blackstone River Dr
Jacksonville, FL 32256-2919, USA

Henderson, John (Athlete, Football Player)
18130 19th Ave N
Plymouth, MN 55447, USA

Henderson, Josh (Actor)
c/o Michael Baum *Impression Entertainment*
9229 W Sunset Blvd #700
West Hollywood, CA 90069, USA

Henderson, Julie (Model)
596 Broadway #701
New York, NY 10012, USA

Henderson, Karen LeCraft (Judge)
US Court of Appeals
333 Constitution Ave NW
Washington, DC 20001, USA

Henderson, Keith (Athlete, Football Player)
PO Box 2754
Cartersville, GA 30120, USA

Henderson, Ken (Athlete, Baseball Player)
200 Winchester Cir Apt D104
Los Gatos, CA 95032-1872, USA

Henderson, Kevin (Athlete, Basketball Player)
2960 Champion Way
Apt 2203
Tustin, CA 92782, USA

Henderson, Logan (Musician)
c/o Remington Franklin *ICM Partners (ICM-LA)*
10250 Constellation Blvd Fl 7
Los Angeles, CA 90067, USA

Henderson, Martin (Actor)
c/o Peter Kiernan *Management 360*
9111 Wilshire Blvd
Beverly Hills, CA 90210, USA

Henderson, Murray (Athlete, Hockey Player)
18 Gatehead Rd.
North York, ON M2J 2P5, Canada

Henderson, Neale (Athlete, Baseball Player)
341 Los Soneto Dr
San Diego, CA 92114-5922, USA

Henderson, Othello (Athlete, Football Player)
323 Silent Spring Dr
Cedar Park, TX 78613-4217, USA

Henderson, Paul (Athlete, Hockey Player)
The Leadership Group
Leader Impact Group 2-2855 Argentia Rd
Mississauga, ON L5N 8G6, Canada

Henderson, Paul III (Journalist)
Seattle Times
Editorial Dept
1120 John St
Seattle, WA 98109, USA

Henderson, Reuben (Athlete, Football Player)
3918 Hunters Ridge Dr Apt 4
Lansing, MI 48911, USA

Henderson, Richard (Actor, Musician)

Henderson, Richard (Biologist)
MRC Molecular Biology Laboratory
Hills Road
Cambridge CB2 2QH, UNITED KINGDOM (UK)

Henderson, Rickey (Athlete, Baseball Player)
10561 Englewood Dr
Oakland, CA 94605-5013, USA

Henderson, Rod (Athlete, Baseball Player)
552 Winter Hill Ln
Lexington, KY 40509-2932, USA

Henderson, Shirley (Actor)
c/o Lorraine Hamilton *Hamilton Hodell Ltd*
66-68 Margaret St Fl 5
London W1W 8SR, UK

Henderson, Steve (Athlete, Baseball Player)
10509 Gretna Green Dr
Tampa, FL 33626-1830, USA

Henderson, Thomas (Athlete, Basketball Player, Olympic Athlete)
6822 Baron Gate Ct
Spring, TX 77379-5094, USA

Henderson, Thomas (Athlete, Football Player)
3106 E 13th St
Austin, TX 78702-2506, USA

Henderson, Thomas
7 Seafield Lane
Westhampton Beach, NY 11978

Henderson, Wymon (Athlete, Football Player)
634 Braidwood Dr NW
Acworth, GA 30101-3529, USA

Henderson, Zachary (Athlete, Football Player)
16005 Sheffield Blvd
Edmond, OK 73013-2043, USA

Henderson III, Joe (Race Car Driver)
1435 W. Morehead St.
#170
Charlotte, NC 28208, USA

Hendler, Lauri
4034 Stone Canyon
Sherman Oaks, CA 91403

Hendley, Bob (Athlete, Baseball Player)
645 Wimbish Rd
Macon, GA 31210-4328, USA

Hendley, Dick (Athlete, Football Player)
6 Sun Flare Ct
Greer, SC 29650, USA

Hendren, Jerry (Athlete, Football Player)
14826 N Chesapeake Ln
Mead, WA 99021-9270, USA

Hendrick, George (Athlete, Baseball Player)
Tampa Bay Rays 1 Tropicana Dr Attn Coaching Staff
saint petersburg, FL 33705-1703, USA

Hendricks, Barbara (Opera Singer)
I M G Artists
420 W 45th St
New York, NY 10036, USA

Hendricks, Christina (Actor)
c/o Ben Levine Kritzer Levine Wilkins Entertainment (KLWG)
11872 La Grange Ave
1st Floor
Los Angeles, CA 90025, USA

Hendricks, Jon (Music Group)
Virginia Wicks
2737 Edwin Place
Los Angeles, CA 90046, USA

Hendricks, L H (Baseball Player)
Negro Baseball Leagues
12 Sunset Blvd
Beaufort, SC 29907-1421, USA

Hendricks, Matt (Athlete, Hockey Player)
12410 25th Ave N
Minneapolis, MN 55441-4008, USA

Hendricks, Susan (Anchor)
c/o Staff Member CNN (Atlanta)
One CNN Center
PO Box 105366
Atlanta, GA 30303, USA

Hendricks, Theodore P (Ted) (Athlete, Football Player)
165 Sunset Way
Miami Springs, FL 33166, USA

Hendrickson, Darby (Athlete, Hockey Player, Olympic Athlete)
Minnesota Wild 317 Washington St
Saint Paul, MN 55102-1667, USA

Hendrickson, Elizabeth (Actor)
c/o Staff Member Creative Partners Group
1522 2nd St
Santa Monica, CA 90401, USA

Hendrickson, Jack (Athlete, Hockey Player)
4161 Jeddo Rd
Burtchville, MI 48059-1121, USA

Hendrickson, Mark (Athlete, Baseball Player)
1585 Wyndham Dr
York, PA 17403-5925, USA

Hendrickson, Steve (Athlete, Football Player)
210 W 15th Ave
Escondido, CA 92025-5714, USA

Hendrix, Elaine (Actor)
Rigberg Roberts Rugolo
1180 S Beverly Dr #601
Los Angeles, CA 90035, USA

Hendrix, Harville (Writer)
c/o Staff Member Henry Holt & Company
175 Fifth Avenue
New York, NY 10010, USA

Hendrix, John W (General)
Commanding General
Army Forces Command
Fort McPherson, GA 30330, USA

Hendrix, Terri (Musician)
Wilory Records
PO Box 2340
San Marcos, TX 78667, USA

Hendrix, Tim (Athlete, Football Player)
7251 Hamilton Dr
Midlothian, TX 76065-6974, USA

Hendry, Gloria (Actor)
256 S Robertson Blvd
Beverly Hills, CA 90211, USA

Hendry, Jim (Commentator)
1400 S Western Ave
Park Ridge, IL 60068-5062, USA

Hendry, Joel (Athlete, Golfer)
c/o Jim Lehrman SFX Golf
36855 W Main St Ste 200
Purcellville, VA 20132, USA

Hendry, Ted (Baseball Player)
14740 N 90th Pl
Scottsdale, AZ 85260-2700, USA

Hendry, Ted (Athlete, Baseball Player)
14740 N 90th Pl
Scottsdale, AZ 85260, USA

Hendryx, Nona (Musician)
Black Rock
6201 Sunset Blvd #329
Hollywood, CA 90028, USA

Hendy, John (Athlete, Football Player)
590 N Bayview Ave
Sunnyvale, CA 94085-3633, USA

Henenlotter, Frank (Director)
81 Bedford St #6E
New York, NY 10014, USA

Hengel, Dave (Athlete, Baseball Player)
2642 Kingfisher Ln
Lincoln, CA 95648-8753, USA

Hengge, Helga (Mountaineer)
Gabriel-von-Seidl-Str. 31e
Gruenwald D-82031, Germany

Henin-Hardenne, Justine (Tennis Player)
Octagon
1751 Pinnacle Dr #1500
McLean, VA 22102, USA

Henke, Brad (Athlete, Football Player)
3412 Troy Dr
Los Angeles, CA 90068-1436, USA

Henke, Brad (Actor)
c/o Matt Schwartz Christopher Wright Management
930 South Orange Grove Avenue
Los Angeles, CA 90036, USA

Henke, Ed (Athlete, Football Player)
11381 Madrone Ct
Auburn, CA 95602-8380, USA

Henke, Karl (Athlete, Football Player)
1180 Bogota Ct
Oxnard, CA 93035, USA

Henke, Nolan (Athlete, Golfer)
1323 Florida Ave
Fort Myers, FL 33901, USA

Henke, Tom (Athlete, Baseball Player)
6200 Saint Francis Dr
Jefferson City, MO 65101-9292, USA

Henkel, Andrea (Athlete)
TKW Sport-Promotion
Lerchenstr 39
Memmingen 87700, GERMANY

Henkel, Heike (Athlete, Track Athlete)
Tannenbergstr 57
Leverkusen 51373, GERMANY

Henkel, Herbert L (Business Person)
Ingersoll-Rand Co
200 Chestnut Ridge Road
Woodcliff Lake, NJ 07677, USA

Henkin, Louis (Attorney, Attorney General, Educator, General)
460 Riverside Dr
New York, NY 10027, USA

Henle, Gertrude (Scientist)
533 Ott Road
Bala Cynwyd, PA 19004, USA

Henley, Belth
William Morris Agency 1350 Avenue of the Americas
New York, NY 10019-4702, USA

Henley, Bob (Athlete, Baseball Player)
11050 Moreland Dr E
Grand Bay, AL 36541-6626, USA

Henley, Carey (Athlete, Football Player)
1611 S Clayton Ave
Chattanooga, TN 37412, USA

Henley, Darryl (Athlete, Football Player)
10178 Woodridge Dr
Rancho Cucamonga, CA 91737, USA

Henley, Don (Music Group, Songwriter)
c/o Irving Azoff Azoff Music Management/ Front Line
1100 Glendon Ave
Los Angeles, CA 90024, USA

Henley, Drewe (Actor)
Granary Cottage Bed & Breakfast
1 Granary Cottages
Combpyne, Axminster
Devon EX13 8SX, UK

Henley, Edward T (Misc)
Hotel & Restaurant Employees Union
1219 28th St NW
Washington, DC 20007, USA

Henley, Gail (Athlete, Baseball Player)
7338 Alta Vis
La Verne, CA 91750-1115, USA

Henley, Garney (Athlete, Football Player)
857 Nebraska Ave
SW
Huron, SD 57350-2347, USA

Henley, Georgie (Actor)
c/o Christian Hodell Hamilton Hodell Ltd
66-68 Margaret St Fl 5
London W1W 8SR, UK

Henley, J Smith (Judge)
US Court of Appeals
200 Federal Building
Harrison, AR 72601, USA

Henley, Larry (Composer)
Creative Directions
PO Box 335
Brentwood, TN 37024, USA

Henley, Patricia
PO Box 259
Battle Ground, IN 47920

Henley, Robert (Ballerina)
Montreal Expos
11050 Moreland Dr E
Grand Bay, AL 36541 6626, USA

Henman, Graham (Director)
Agency for Performing Arts
9200 Sunset Blvd #900
Los Angeles, CA 90069, USA

Henman, Tim (Tennis Player)
14497 N Dale Mabry Hwy
#205 N
Tampa, FL 33618, USA

Henn, Mark (Animator)
Walt Disney Animation
PO Box 10200
Lake Buena Vista, FL 32830, USA

Henn, Sean (Athlete, Baseball Player)
3658 Snow Creek Dr
Aledo, TX 76008-3677, USA

Henn, Walter (Architect)
Ramsachleite 13
Mumau 82418, GERMANY

Hennagan, Monique (Athlete, Olympic Athlete, Track Athlete)
505 Winter View Way
Stockbridge, GA 30281-7799, USA

Henneman, Brian (Music Group)
Hard Head Productions
180 Varick St #800
New York, NY 10014, USA

Henneman, Mike (Athlete, Baseball Player)
806 Lake Creek Dr
McKinney, TX 75070-5590, USA

Hennen, Thomas J (Astronaut)
522 Villa Dr
Seabrook, TX 77586, USA

Hennen, Thomas J Chief (Astronaut)
16315 Cascade Caverns Ln
Houston, TX 77044-1240, USA

Henner, Marilu (Actor)
c/o Rory Rosegarten Conversation Company
1044 Northern Blvd
Suite 304
Roslyn, NY 11576, USA

Hennessey, Brad (Athlete, Baseball Player)
6657 Brentridge Ln
Lambertville, MI 48144-9374, USA

Hennessey, Wally (Horse Racer)
4141 NW 9th Ct
Coconut Creek, FL 33066-1644, USA

Hennessy, Jill (Actor)
c/o Matthew Saver *Matthew Saver Law Offices*
269 S Beverly Dr
Beverly Hills, CA 90210, USA

Hennessy, John (Educator)
Stanford University
President's Office
Stanford, CA 94305, USA

Hennessy, John B (Archaeologist)
497 Old Windsor Road
Kellyville, NSW 2153, AUSTRALIA

Henney, Daniel (Actor)
c/o Staff Member *WmE2 (WMA-LA)*
1 William Morris Pl
Beverly Hills, CA 90212, USA

Henney, Jane (Government Official)
Food & Drug Administration
5600 Fishers Lane
Rockville, MD 20852, USA

Hennig, Shelley (Actor)
c/o Allan Grifka *Alchemy Entertainment*
7024 Melrose Ave
Suite 420
Los Angeles, CA 90038, USA

Hennigan, Charley (Athlete, Football Player)
3875 Line Ave Apt 108
Shreveport, LA 71106-1160, USA

Hennigan, John (Athlete, Wrestler)
c/o Staff Member *World Wrestling Entertainment (WWE)*
Titan Towers
1241 E Main St
Stamford, CT 06905-3857, USA

Hennigan, Mike (Athlete, Football Player)
542 N Washington Ave
Cookeville, TN 38501, USA

Hennigan, Phil (Athlete, Baseball Player)
P.O. Box 1212
Center, TX 75935-1212, USA

Henning, Dan (Athlete, Football Coach, Football Player)
116 Meeting Way
Ponte Vedra Beach, FL 32082-3947, USA

Henning, John F Jr (Publisher)
Sunset Magazine
80 Willow Road
Menlo Park, CA 94025, USA

Henning, Larry
7426 43rd Ave. SE.
St. Cloud, MN 53704-9579

Henning, Linda (Actor)
10765 Wrightwood Dr
Studio City, CA 91604, USA

Henning, Lorne (Athlete, Coach, Hockey Player)
Vancouver Canucks 800 Griffiths Way
Vancouver, BC V6B 6G1, Canada

Henning, Paul (Athlete, Hockey Player)
4250 Navajo Ave.
Toluca Lake, CA 91602, USA

Henninger, Brian (Athlete, Golfer)
25481 SW Newland Rd
Wilsonville, OR 97070, USA

Henninger, Rick (Athlete, Baseball Player)
98 Park Ln
Pottsboro, TX 75076-3990, USA

Hennings, Chad W (Athlete, Football Player)
6101 Bay Valley Ct
Flower Mound, TX 75022, USA

Henning-Walker, Anne (Athlete, Olympic Athlete, Speed Skater)
12359 E Lasalle Pl
Aurora, CO 80014-1921, USA

Hennis, Randy (Athlete, Baseball Player)
1747 Sienna Dr
Melbourne, FL 32934-9030, USA

Henrich, Bobby (Athlete, Baseball Player)
1531 Via Los Coyotes
La Habra, CA 90631-7655, USA

Henrich, Dieter (Misc)
Gerlichstr 7A
Munich 81245, GERMANY

Henrich, Tom
1547 Albino Trail
Dewey, AZ 86327

Henrichs, Jeff (Athlete, Baseball Player)
6192 Riverside Blvd Apt C46
Sacramento, CA 95831-1222, USA

Henrichsen, Brett (DJ)
c/o Len Evans *Project Publicity*
312 West 53rd St
Suite 202
New York, NY 10019, USA

Henricks, Jon N (Swimmer)
254 Laurel Ave
Des Plaines, IL 60016, USA

Henricks, Terence Colonel (Astronaut)
3811 Cole Ave
Dallas, TX 75204-1514, USA

Henricks, Terence T (Tom) (Astronaut)
Timken Aerospace
PO Box 547
Keene, NH 03431, USA

Henrie, David (Actor)
c/o Jason Weinberg *Untitled Entertainment (LA)*
350 S. Beverly Dr #200
Beverly Hills, CA 90212, USA

Henrik (Prince)
Amalienborg Palace
Copenhagen K 1257, DENMARK

Henrikse, Lance (Actor)
c/o Jean-Pierre (JP) Henraux *Henraux Management*
Prefers to be contacted by telephone
CA, USA

Henriksen, Donald (Athlete, Basketball Player)
18160 Cottonwood Rd
Bend, OR 97707-9317, USA

Henriksen, Jan (Horse Racer)
PO Box 176
Crosswicks, NJ 08515-0176, USA

Henrikson, Lance (Actor)
c/o Jeff Witjas *Agency for the Performing Arts (APA-LA)*
405 S Beverly Dr
Suite 500
Beverly Hills, CA 90212-4425, USA

Henriques, Sean Paul (Actor, Musician)
c/o Staff Member *WmE2 (WMA-LA)*
1 William Morris Pl
Beverly Hills, CA 90212, USA

Henriquez, Ron (Actor)
PO Box 38027
Los Angeles, CA 90038, USA

Henry, Albert (Athlete, Basketball Player)
2410 N 52nd St
Philadelphia, PA 19131-1409, USA

Henry, Anthony (Athlete, Football Player)
1999 McKinney Ave #1605
Dallas, TX 75201-1712, USA

Henry, Bill (Athlete, Baseball Player)
47 Oyster Landing Ln
Hilton Head Island, SC 29928-3045, USA

Henry, Bill (Athlete, Baseball Player)
2313 Kilkenny Ln
Deer Park, TX 77536-3955, USA

Henry, Brad (Politician)
Governor's Office
State Capitol Bldg #212
Oklahoma City, OK 73105, USA

Henry, Brad (Politician)
PO Box 156
Shawnee, OK 74802-0156, USA

Henry, Buck (Actor, Writer)
117 E 57th St
New York, NY 10022, USA

Henry, Buck (Writer)
117 W 57th St
New York, NY 10019-2209, USA

Henry, Butch (Athlete, Baseball Player)
12072 Paseo De Amor Ln
El Paso, TX 79936-4499, USA

Henry, Chris (Athlete, Football Player)
545 Summit Oaks Ct
Nashville, TN 37221-1429, USA

Henry, Clarence (Forgman) (Music Group, Songwriter, Writer)
3309 Lawrence St
New Orleans, LA 70114, USA

Henry, Conner (Athlete, Basketball Player)
1122 N College Ave
Claremont, CA 91711-3927, USA

Henry, Dale (Attorney, Hockey Player)
8611 Datapoint Dr
Apt 43
San Antonio, TX 78229, USA

Henry, David (Actor)
c/o Dallas Smith *United Agents*
12-26 Lexington St
London W1F OLE, UK

Henry, Doug (Athlete, Baseball Player)
2804 Burries Rd
Hartland, WI 53029-8823, USA

Henry, Dwayne (Athlete, Baseball Player)
407 E Hampstead Ct
Middletown, DE 19709-1631, USA

Henry, Geoffrey A (Prime Minister)
PO Box 281
Rarotonga, COOK ISLANDS

Henry, Gloria (Actor)
849 N Harper Ave
Los Angeles, CA 90046, USA

Henry, Gregg (Actor)
8956 Appian Way
Los Angeles, CA 90046, USA

Henry, J J (Athlete, Golfer)
6901 Sanctuary Ln
Fort Worth, TX 76132-7101, USA

Henry, Joe (Athlete, Baseball Player)
220 N 7th St
Lovejoy, IL 62059, USA

Henry, Joe (Music Group, Songwriter, Writer)
Monterey Peninsula Artists
509 Hartnell St
Monterey, CA 93940, USA

Henry, John (Baseball Player)
Florida Marlins
4698 Sanctuary Ln
Boca Raton, FL 33431-5206, USA

Henry, John (Commentator)
40 Cottage St
Brookline, MA 02445-5938, USA

Henry, Joseph L (Doctor)
60 Marinita Ave
San Rafael, CA 94901, USA

Henry, Justin (Actor)
c/o Staff Member *Phoenix Organization, The*
1990 South Bundy Dr #630
Los Angeles, CA 90025, USA

Henry, Kevin (Athlete, Football Player)
3378 Aberrone Pl
Buford, GA 30519-7981, USA

Henry, Lenny (Actor)
c/o Staff Member *WmE2 (WMA-LA)*
1 William Morris Pl
Beverly Hills, CA 90212, USA

Henry, Mark (Athlete, Wrestler)
c/o Staff Member *World Wrestling Entertainment (WWE)*
Titan Towers
1241 E Main St
Stamford, CT 06905-3857, USA

Henry, Mike (Actor)
Pittsburgh Steelers
10803 Blix St Unit 3
North Hollywood, CA 91602-3822, USA

Henry, Pat (Stylist)
c/o Staff Member *Punch Productions*
11661 San Vicente Blvd #222
Los Angeles, CA 90049, USA

Henry, Pierre (Composer)
32 Rue Toul
Paris 75012, FRANCE

Henry, Piper
1680 N. Vine St. #614
Hollywood, CA 90028

Henry, Robert H (Judge)
US Court of Appeals
PO Box 1767
Oklahoma City, OK 73101, USA

Henry, Ron (Athlete, Baseball Player)
2160 Downing St
Denver, CO 80205-5261, USA

Henry, Steve (Athlete, Football Player)
1907 Darlene Way
Emporia, KS 66801-6024, USA

Henry, Thierry (Athlete, Soccer Player)
c/o Nicola Richardson *QVoice*
161 Drury Ln, Covent Garden
3rd Floor
London WC2B 5PN, UK

Henry, Travis (Athlete, Football Player)
6698 S Shawnee Ct
Aurora, CO 80016-2473, USA

Henry, Wally (Athlete, Football Player)
3444 Bernadette Ct Apt A
West Covina, CA 91792-4702, USA

Henry, William H Jr (Producer)
Time-Life Books
Rockefeller Center
New York, NY 10020, USA

Hensarling, Jeb (Congressman, Politician)
129 Cannon HOB
Washington, DC 20515, USA

Hensby, Mark (Athlete, Golfer)
8121 E Echo Canyon St
Mesa, AZ 85207-7185, USA

Hensel, Bruce (Doctor)
17526 Tramanto Dr
Pacific Palisades, CA 90272, USA

Hensel, Robert M (World Record Holder)
wheelierecord@yahoo.com
138 E 3rd St #A
Oswego, NY 13126, USA

Hensel, Witold (Archaeologist)
Ul Marszalkowska 84/92M
Warsaw 109 00-514, POLAND

Hensick, T J
2950 Charann Dr
Howell, MI 48843-8611, USA

Hensilwood, Christopher (Misc, Scientist)
Iziko Museum
25 Queen Victoria St
Cape Town, SOUTH AFRICA

Henslee, Jimmie (Stylist)
c/o Staff Member *Independent Artists*
448 E Riverdale Ave
Orange, CA 92865, USA

Hensley, Chuck (Athlete, Baseball Player)
259 Bonanza Dr
Erie, CO 80516-8451, USA

Hensley, Clay (Athlete, Baseball Player)
3601 Dogwood Blossom Ct
Pearland, TX 77581-5038, USA

Hensley, Dick (Athlete, Football Player)
6319 Roberto Dr
Huntington, WV 25705-2529, USA

Hensley, Elaine (Stylist)
511 Gun Club Rd
Nashville, TN 37205, USA

Hensley, Jimmy (Race Car Driver)
2570 Horse Pasture Price Rd
Ridgeway, VA 24148, USA

Hensley, John (Actor)
c/o Vincent Cirrincione *Vincent
Cirrincione Associates*
1516 N Fairfax Ave
Los Angeles, CA 90046, USA

Hensley, Jon (Actor)
c/o Staff Member *Innovative Artists (LA)*
1505 10th St
Santa Monica, CA 90401, USA

Hensley, Kirby J (Religious Leader)
Universal Life Church
601 3rd St
Modesto, CA 95351, USA

Henson, Brian (Actor, Director, Producer)

Henson, Champ (Athlete, Football Player)
P.O. Box 3
Ashville, OH 43103, USA

Henson, Darrin Dewitt (Actor)
c/o Adam Griffin *Kritzer Levine Wilkins
Entertainment (KLWG)*
11872 La Grange Ave
1st Floor
Los Angeles, CA 90025, USA

Henson, Drew (Athlete, Baseball Player)
4629 Lorraine Ave
Dallas, TX 75209-6013, USA

Henson, Drew (Athlete, Football Player)
4629 Lorraine Ave
Dallas, TX 75209-6013, USA

Henson, Elden (Actor)
c/o Chuck Binder *Binder & Associates*
1465 Lindacrest Dr
Beverly Hills, CA 90210, USA

Henson, Gary (Athlete, Football Player)
5032 Vermillion Dr
Castle Rock, CO 80108-9032, USA

Henson, Harold (Athlete, Football Player)
15367 Lockbourne Eastern Rd
Ashville, OH 43103-9476, USA

Henson, John (Actor, Comedian)
Conversation Co
1044 Northern Blvd #304
Roslyn, NY 11576, USA

Henson, Lisa (Producer)
Columbia Pictures
2400 Riverside Dr
Burbank, CA 91505, USA

Henson, Lou (Basketball Player, Coach)
New Mexico State University
Athletic Dept
Las Cruces, NM 88033, USA

Henson, Luther (Athlete, Football Player)
5395 Maple Grove Ave
Blanchester, OH 45107, USA

Henson, Sammie (Athlete, Olympic
Athlete, Wrestler)
Henson Wrestling 3017 24th Ave SE
Norman, OK 73071-1731, USA

Henson, Taraji P (Actor)
c/o Vincent Cirrincione *Vincent
Cirrincione Associates*
1516 N Fairfax Ave
Los Angeles, CA 90046, USA

Henstridge, Natasha (Actor, Model)
c/o David (Dave) Fleming *Mosaic Media
Group*
9200 W. Sunset Blvd
10th Floor
Los Angeles, CA 90069, USA

Hentgen, Pat (Athlete, Baseball Player)
Toronto Blue Jays 1 Blue Jays Way Suite
3200 Attn: Special Assistant
toronto, ON, USA

Hentoff, Nat (Writer)
Village Voice 36 Cooper Sq Frnt 1
New York, NY 10003-7149, USA

Hentoff, Nathan I (Nat) (Critic, Musician)
Village Voice
Editorial Dept
36 Cooper Square
New York, NY 10003, USA

Henton, Anthony (Athlete, Football
Player)
1026 Avenue G
Bessemer, AL 35020-7200, USA

Henton, John (Actor)
c/o Staff Member *Gersh (LA)*
9465 Wilshire Blvd
Suite 600
Beverly Hills, CA 90212, USA

Hentrich, Craig (Athlete, Football Player)
604 Canters Ct
Franklin, TN 37067, USA

Hentrich, Helmut (Architect)
Dusseldorfer Str 67
Dusseldorf-Oberkassel 40545, GERMANY

Hepburn, Cassandra (Actor)
c/o Glenn Hughes III *Gem Entertainment
Group*
10701 Wilshire Blvd.
Ste. 1202
Los Angeles, CA 90024, USA

Hepburn, Lonnie (Athlete, Football Player)
1875 NW 59th St
Miami, FL 33142-2429, USA

Hepler, Bill (Athlete, Baseball Player)
12518 Fort King Rd
Dade City, FL 33525-5609, USA

Heppel, Leon A (Biologist)
Cornell University
Biochemistry Dept
Ithaca, NY 14850, USA

Hepple, Alan (Athlete, Hockey Player)
Colorado Avalanche 1000 Chopper Cir
Denver, CO 80204-5805, USA

Heppner, Ben (Opera Singer)
Columbia Artists Mgmt Inc
165 W 57th St
New York, NY 10019, USA

Heppner, Peter (Musician)
c/o Staff Member *Warner Music Germany
GmbH (WMI-Germany)*
Alter Wandrahm 14
Hamburg D - 20457, Germany

Herb, Marvin (Business Person)
Coca-Cola Bottling Company of Chicago
7400 North Oak Park Avenue
Niles, IL 60714

Herbers, Ian (Athlete, Hockey Player)
1135 Ridgeway Rd
Brookfield, WI 53045-2423, USA

Herbert, Doug (Race Car Driver)
1443 E. Gaston St.
Lincolnton, NC 28092, USA

Herbert, Gary (Governor, Politician)
20 State Capitol
Salt Lake City, UT 84114, USA

Herbert, Holly (Journalist)
Celebrity Justice c/o Warner Bros
4000 Warner Blvd
Burbank, CA 91522, USA

Herbert, James (Writer)
David Higham Associates
5-8 Lower John St
London W1R 4HA, UNITED KINGDOM
(UK)

Herbert, Johnny (Race Car Driver)
PP Sayber AG
Wildbachstr 9
Hinwil 8340, SWITZERLAND

Herbert, Michael K (Editor)
990 Grove St
Evanston, IL 60201, USA

Herbert, Raymond E (Ray) (Athlete,
Baseball Player)
9360 Taylors Turn
Stanwood, MI 49346-9686, USA

Herbert, Vincent (Musician)
c/o Kenny (Kenneth) Meiselas *Grubman,
Indursky, & Schindler*
152 W 57th St
31st Floor
New York, NY 10019, USA

Herbert, Walter W (Wally) (Scientist)
Rowan Cottage
Catlodge
Laggan
Inverness-shire PH20 1AH, UNITED
KINGDOM (UK)

Herbert of Hemingford, D Nicholas
(Publisher)
Old Rectory
Hemingford Abbots
Huntington Cambs PE18 9AN, UNITED
KINGDOM (UK)

Herbig, George (Scientist)
2176 Halekoa Dr
Honolulu, HI 96821-1055, USA

Herbig, George H (Astronomer)
University of Hawaii
Astronomy Institute
2680 Woodlawn Dr
Honolulu, HI 96822, USA

Herbig, Gunther
Toronto Symphony
60 Simcoe St #C116
Toronto, ON MJ5 2H5, CANADA

Herbst, William (Astronomer)
Wesleyan Univesity
Astronomy Dept
Middletown, CT 06459, USA

Herczegh, Gezar G (Judge)
Int'l Court of Justice
Camegieplein 2
KJ Hague 2517, NETHERLANDS

Herd, Carla
8281 Melrose Ave. #200
Los Angeles, CA 90046

Herd, Richard (Actor)
PO Box 56297
Sherman Oaks, CA 91413, USA

Herda, Frank A (War Hero)
PO Box 34239
Cleveland, OH 44134, USA

Herda, Frank A (Misc)
PO Box 30967
Cleveland, OH 44130-0914, USA

Heredia, Felix (Athlete, Baseball Player)
P.O. Box 4842
Hialeah, FL 33014-0842, USA

Heredia, Gil (Athlete, Baseball Player)
Missoula Osprey 412 WAlder St Attn
Coaching Staff
missoula, MT 59802-4122, USA

Heredia, Wilson (Actor)
c/o Sarah Fargo *Paradigm (NY)*
360 Park Ave S Fl 16
New York, NY 10010, USA

Heredia, Wilson Jermaine (Actor)
c/o Leanne Coronel *Coronel Group*
9601 Wilshire Blvd
3rd Floor
Beverly Hills, CA 90210, USA

Herek, Stephen R (Director)
Endeavor Talent Agency
9701 Wilshire Blvd #1000
Beverly Hills, CA 90212, USA

Herera, Sue (Correspondent, Television Host)
c/o Staff Member *CNBC*
900 Sylvan Ave
Englewood Cliffs, NJ 07632, USA

Herger, Wally (Congressman, Politician)
242 Cannon HOB
Washington, DC 20515, USA

Hergert, Joe (Athlete, Football Player)
875 Tater Rd
New Smyrna Beach, FL 32168, USA

Herges, Matt (Athlete, Baseball Player)
21019 N 79th Pl
Scottsdale, AZ 85255-6421, USA

Hergesheimer, Wally (Athlete, Hockey Player)
301b-15 Valhalla Dr
Winnipeg, MB R2G 4G8, Canada

Herincx, Raimund (Opera Singer)
Monk's Vineyard
Larkbarrow
Shepton Mallet
Somerset BA4 4NR, UNITED KINGDOM (UK)

Herjavec, Robert (Business Person)
c/o Monique Moss *Integrated PR*
9025 Wilshire Blvd
Suite 400
Beverly Hills, CA 90211, USA

Herkenhoff, Matt (Athlete, Football Player)
16000 Baywood Ln
Eden Prairie, MN 55346, USA

Herles, Kathleen (Actor)
c/o Shirley Grant *Shirley Grant Management*
PO Box 866
Teaneck, NJ 07666, USA

Herlihy, Tim (Actor, Comedian)
c/o Staff Member *WME (LA)*
9601 Wilshire Blvd Fl 3
Beverly Hills, CA 90210, USA

Herline, Alan (Athlete, Football Player)
610 Post Oak Cir
Brentwood, TN 37027, USA

Herman, Alexis (Politician)
892 Linganore Dr
Me Lean, MA 22102-2141, USA

Herman, Axel (Model)
c/o Celebrity Stylist *Ford Models (NY)*
238 E 4th St
New York, NY 10009, USA

Herman, Bill (Horse Racer)
478 Sycamore Springs St
Debary, FL 32713-4828, USA

Herman, Bill (Athlete, Basketball Player)
200 Laurel Lake Dr
Apt 305
Hudson, OH 44236-2156, USA

Herman, Dave (Athlete, Football Player)
19 Stephens Ln
Valhalla, NY 10595, USA

Herman, David J (Business Person)
Adam Opel AG
Bahnhofplatz 1
Russelsheim 65429, GERMANY

Herman, Jerry (Composer, Musician)
455 N Palm Dr #3
Beverly Hills, CA 90210, USA

Herman, Micah (Director)
c/o Joanna (Joanie) Burstein *Burstein Company, The*
15304 Sunset Blvd
suite 208
Pacific Palisades, CA 90272, USA

Herman, Pee-Wee (Actor, Comedian)
PO Box 29373
Los Angeles, CA 90029

Hermann, Allen M (Physicist)
2704 Lookout View Dr
Golden, CO 80401, USA

Hermann, Mark (Athlete, Football Player)
8525 Tidewater Dr
Indianapolis, IN 46236, USA

Hermannson, Dustin M (Baseball Player)
9002 E Rimrock Dr
Scottsdale, AZ 85255, USA

Hermansen, Chad (Athlete, Baseball Player)
2104 Rhonda Ter
Henderson, NV 89074-0651, USA

Hermanson, Dustin (Athlete, Baseball Player)
9002 E Rimrock Dr
Scottsdale, AZ 85255-9133, USA

Hermaszewski, Miroslav (Astronaut, General)
Ul Czeczota 25
Warsaw 02-650, POLAND

Hermeling, Terry (Athlete, Football Player)
717 NW 16th Ave
Portland, OR 97208, USA

Hermida, Jeremy (Athlete, Baseball Player)
3728 Paces Park Cir SE
Smyrna, GA 30080-6874, USA

Hermiston, Michael (Stylist)
c/o Staff Member *Mark Edward Inc*
325 W 8th St
#1011
New York, NY 10018, USA

Hermits s/ Peter Noone, Herman's (Music Group, Musician)
Herman's Hermits Inc
1482 E Valley Rd
Suite 515
Monteicto, CA 93108, USA

Hermlin, Stephan (Writer)
Hermann-Hesse-Str 39
Berlin 13156, GERMANY

Hermon, John C (Government Official, Lawyer)
Warren Road
Donaghadee
County Down, NORTHERN IRELAND

Herms, George (Artist)
Jack Rutberg Fine Arts
357 N La Brea Ave
Los Angeles, CA 90036, USA

Hern, Tom (Actor)
c/o Simon Millar *Rumble Media*
1620 Broadway
Santa Monica, CA 90403, USA

Hernandez, Adrian (Athlete, Baseball Player)
1723 Alden Rd Aot 1
Janesville, WI 53545-0886, USA

Hernandez, Angel (Athlete, Baseball Player)
501 Cypress Xing
Wellington, FL 33414-6369, USA

Hernandez, Carlos (Athlete, Baseball Player)
San Diego Padres
P.O. Box 122000
Attn: Player Development Dept
San Diego, CA 92112, USA

Hernandez, Chuck (Athlete, Baseball Player)
3113 River Cove Dr
Tampa, FL 33614-2828, USA

Hernandez, David (Athlete, Baseball Player)
9618 McKenn(l D(
Elk Grove, CA 95757-4024, USA

Hernandez, David (Musician)

Hernandez, Evelio (Athlete, Baseball Player)
3004 SW 113th Ave
Miami, FL 33165-2228, USA

Hernandez, Jackie (Athlete, Baseball Player)
13390 NE 7th Ave
Apt 103
North Miami, FL 33161-7509, USA

Hernandez, Jay (Actor)
United Talent Agency
9560 Wilshire Blvd #500
Beverly Hills, CA 90212, USA

Hernandez, Jeremy (Athlete, Baseball Player)
861 Hemlock Ridge Ct
Simi Valley, CA 93065-5540, USA

Hernandez, Jose (Astronaut)
4015 N Water Iris Ct
Houston, TX 77059-3013, USA

Hernandez, Jose (Athlete, Baseball Player)
Delmarva Shorebirds PO Box 1557
Attn: Coaching Staff
Salisbury, MD 21802-1557, USA

Hernandez, Jose (Athlete, Baseball Player)
2700 Coconut Bay Ln Unit 3G
Sarasota, FL 34237-3063, USA

Hernandez, Julio (Stylist)
c/o Staff Member *Mercury Artists*
8460 Higuera St Fl 2
Culver City, CA 90232, USA

hernandez, keith (Athlete, Baseball Player)
New York Mets 12301 Roosevelt Ave
Attn Broadcast Dept
Flushing, NY 11368-1629, USA

Hernandez, Keith (Athlete, Baseball Player)
c/o Staff Member *SportsNet New York*
75 Rockefeller Plz
New York, NY 10019, USA

Hernandez, Leo (Athlete, Baseball Player)
1352 SW 75th Ave
Miami, FL 33144, USA

Hernandez, Livan (Athlete, Baseball Player)
560 Gate Ln
Miami, FL 33137-3361, USA

Hernandez, Los Bros (Artist)
c/o Staff Member *Fantagraphics Books*
7563 Lake City Way
Seattle, WA 98115, USA

Hernandez, Matt (Athlete, Football Player)
P.O. Box 682
Eastpointe, MI 48021, USA

Hernandez, Michel (Athlete, Baseball Player)
18857 Maisons Dr
Lutz, FL 33558-2879, USA

Hernandez, Orlando (Athlete, Baseball Player)
1001 Brickell Bay Dr
Suite 1710
Miami, FL 33131, USA

Hernandez, Ramon (Athlete, Baseball Player)
19498 S Coquina Way
Weston, FL 33332-2423, USA

Hernandez, Robert J (Business Person)
USX Corp
600 Grant St
Pittsburgh, PA 15219, USA

Hernandez, Roberto (Athlete, Baseball Player)
5965 Bavview Cir S
Gulfoort, FL 33707-3929, USA

Hernandez, Rodolfo p (General)
5328 Bluewater Pl
Fayetteville, NC 28311-1224, USA

Hernandez, Rodolfo P (War Hero)
5328 Bluewater Place
College Lakes
Fayetteville, NC 28311, USA

Hernandez, Rudy (Athlete, Baseball Player)
8 Calle Rodriguez Serra
San Juan, PR 00907, USA

Hernandez, Rudy (Athlete, Baseball Player)
Beloit Snappers
P.O. Box 855
Attn: Coaching Staff
Beloit, WI 53512, USA

Hernandez, Runelvys (Athlete, Baseball Player)
18717 E 24th Street Ct S
Independence, MO 64057-2474, USA

Hernandez, Willie (Athlete, Baseball Player)
PO Box 125 Bo Espina
Calle C Buzon
Aguada, PR 00602-0125, USA

Hernandez, Xavier (Athlete, Baseball Player)
3002 E Autumn Run Cir
Sugar Land, TX 77479-2636, USA

Hernandez Colon, Rafael (Ex-Governor)
P.O. Box 4071
San Juan, PR 00902, USA

Herndon, David (Athlete, Baseball Player)
337 Dusty Ln
Panama, FL 32409-2203, USA

Herndon, Junior (Athlete, Baseball Player)
1477 Sequoia Ave
Craig, CO 81625-3732, USA

Herndon, Kelly (Athlete, Football Player)
1968 Cambridge St
Twinsburg, OH 44087, USA

Herndon, Larry (Athlete, Baseball Player)
Lakeland Flying Tigers 2125 N Lake Ave
Attn: Coaching Staff
Lakeland, FL

Herndon, Larry (Athlete, Baseball Player)
6149 Brunswick Rd
Arlington, TN 38002-6936, USA

Herndon, Mark J (Music Group, Musician)
RR 1 Box 239A
Mentone, AL 35984, USA

Herndon, Ty (Music Group)
PO Box 121858
Nashville, TN 37212, USA

Heroux, Yves (Athlete, Hockey Player)
8 Village Ln
Middletown, NJ 07748-1854, CANADA

Herr, John C (Scientist)
University of Virginia
Med Center
Immunology Dept
Charlottesville, VA 22903, USA

Herr, Matt (Athlete, Hockey Player)
1951 Holly Creek Pl
Concord, CA 94521-1550, USA

Herr, Tom (Athlete, Baseball Player)
1077 Olde Forge Xing
Lancaster, PA 17601-1738, USA

Herranz Casado, Julian Cardinal (Religious Leader)
Legislative Texts Curia
Piazza Pio XII #10
Rome 00193, ITALY

Herren, James (Athlete, Football Player)
224 Monongahela Ave
Glassport, PA 15045, USA

Herrera, Anthony (Athlete, Football Player)
c/o Chad Speck *Allegiant Athletic Agency*
35 Market Sq
Suite 201
Knoxville, TN 37902, USA

Herrera, Augustine (Race Car Driver)
Marty Kane Motorsports
Box 908
Brea, CA 92822, USA

Herrera, Carolina (Designer, Fashion Designer)
Carolina Herrera Ltd
501 Fashion Ave
#1700
New York, NY 10018, USA

Herrera, Caroline (Designer, Fashion Designer)
501 Seventh Ave Fl 17
New York, NY 10018, USA

Herrera, Efren (Athlete, Football Player)
861 Atlanta Ct
Claremont, CA 91711, USA

Herrera, Jaime (Congressman, Politician)
1130 Longworth HOB
Washington, DC 20515, USA

Herrera, Johnny (Race Car Driver)
Johnny Herrera Racing Inc
2333 E. Southern Ave.
#1013
Tempe, AZ 85282, USA

Herrera, Kristin (Actor)
c/o David Eisenberg *Protege Entertainment*
710 E. Angeleno Ave
Burbank, CA 91501, USA

Herrera, Pamela (Ballerina)
American Ballet Theatre
890 Broadway
New York, NY 10003, USA

Herrera, Silvestre S (War Hero)
7222 W Windsor Blvd
Glendale, AZ 85303, USA

Herriman, Don (Athlete, Hockey Player)
640 Homewood Ave
Peterborough, ON K9J 4V6, Canada

Herring, Harold (Athlete, Football Player)
8673 Laurel Dr
Pinellas Park, FL 33782, USA

Herring, Laura
4702 N. 36th St.
Phoenix, AZ 85018-3423

Herring, Lynn (Actor)
37900 Road 800
Raymond, CA 93653, USA

Herring, Vincent (Composer, Musician)
Fat City Artists
1906 Chet Atkins Place #502
Nashville, TN 37212, USA

Herring-James, Katie (Athlete, Baseball Player, Commentator)
143 Grouse Ridge Rd
Tamuqua, PA 18252-5442, USA

Herrington, John B (Astronaut)
4367 Bays Water Dr
Colorado Springs, CO 80920-7636, USA

Herrington, John B Cdr (Astronaut)
4367 Bays Water Dr
Colorado Springs, VO 80920-7636, USA

Herrington, John S (Business Person, Secretary)
Harcourt Brace
525 B St
San Diego, CA 92101, USA

Herrman, Ed (Athlete, Baseball Player)
13153 Toblasson Rd
Poway, CA 92064, USA

Herrmann, Don (Athlete, Football Player)
P.O. Box 318
Brookside, NJ 07926, USA

Herrmann, Ed (Athlete, Baseball Player)
13153 Tobiasson Rd
Poway, CA 92064-4308, USA

Herrmann, Mark (Athlete, Football Player)
8525 Tidewater Dr W
Indianapolis, IN 46236, USA

Herrnstein, John (Athlete, Baseball Player)
603 Seminole Rd
Chillicothe, OH 45601-1547, USA

Herrod, Jeff (Athlete, Football Player)
20129 Tamiami Trl
Tampa, FL 33647-3370, USA

Herron, Bruce (Athlete, Football Player)
8504 S Calumet Ave
Chicago, IL 60619, USA

Herron, Cindy (Music Group)
East West Records
75 Rockefeller Plaza #1200
New York, NY 10019, USA

Herron, Denis (Athlete, Hockey Player)
12841 Marsh Point Way
West Palm Beach, FL 33418-6973, USA

Herron, Keith (Athlete, Basketball Player)
5374 Chew Ave
Apt G2
Philadelphia, PA 19138-2804, USA

Herron, Robert J (Architect)
Herron Assoc
28-30 Rivington St
London EC2A 3DU, UNITED KINGDOM (UK)

Herron, Tim (Athlete, Golfer)
20440 Linden Rd
Excelsior, MN 55331, USA

Herrscher, Rick (Athlete, Baseball Player)
7714 Marquette St
Dallas, TX 75225-4413, USA

Hersch, Fred (Music Group, Musician)
SRO Artists
PO Box 9532
Madison, WI 53715, USA

Hersch, Michael (Composer)
21C Music Publishing
30 W 63rd St #15S
New York, NY 10023, USA

Herschbach, Dudley (Nobel Prize Laureate)
116 Conant Rd
Lincoln, MA 01773-3908, USA

Herschler, E David (Artist)
PO Box 5859
Santa Barbara, CA 92150, USA

Hersh, Earl (Athlete, Baseball Player)
682 Morning Glory Dr
Hanover, PA 17331-7828, USA

Hersh, Kristin (Composer, Music Group, Songwriter, Writer)
c/o Staff Member *Concerted Efforts*
P.O. Box 440326
Somerville, MA 02144, USA

Hersh, Seymour (Journalist, Writer)
1211 Connecticut Ave NW
Washington, DC 20036-2709, USA

Hershey, Barbara (Actor)
c/o Jill Littman *Impression Entertainment*
9229 W Sunset Blvd #700
West Hollywood, CA 90069, USA

Hershey, Erin (Actor)
PO Box 16212
Irvine, CA 92623, USA

Hershey, Maralyn
37337 Green Level Rd.
Wakefield, VA 23888

Hershey-Reeser, Esther Anne (Athlete, Baseball Player, Commentator)
3450 Compass Rd
Gap, PA 17527-9006, USA

Hershiser, Orel (Athlete, Baseball Player)
2167 Orchard Mist St
Las Vegas, NVTX 89135-1563, USA

Hershko, Avram (Nobel Prize Laureate)
Technion Israel Inst. Of Technology
Taub Building
Haifa 32000, Israel

Herta, Bryan (Race Car Driver)
Bryan Herta Racing, Inc
24803 Los Altos Dr.
Santa Clarita, CA 91355-4955, USA

Hertel, Rob (Athlete, Football Player)
1707 Camden Pkwy
South Pasadena, CA 91030, USA

Herter, Jason (Athlete, Hockey Player)
5325 Roosevelt Dr
Hermantown, MN 55811-3679, USA

Hertford, Chelsea (Actor)
345 E. Tujunga Ave
Burbank, CA 91502, USA

Hertweck, Neal (Athlete, Baseball Player)
111 Leesburg Ln
Troutman, NC 28166-7600, USA

Hertz, C Hellmuth (Physicist)
Lund INstitute of Technology
Physics School
Lund, SWEDEN

Hertz, Steve (Athlete, Baseball Player)
10211 SW 96th Ter
Miami, FL 33176, USA

Hertzberg, Daniel (Journalist)
Wall Street Journal
Editorial Dept
200 Liberty St
New York, NY 10281, USA

Hertzberger, Herman (Architect)
Architectourstudio
Box 74665
Amsterdam, BR 1070, NETHERLANDS

Hervey, Jason (Actor)
2049 Century Park E #2500
Los Angeles, CA 90067, USA

Hervey, Matt (Athlete, Hockey Player)
38635 Maracaibo Cir W
Palm Springs, CA 92264-0208, USA

Herzenberg, Caroline Littlejohn (Physicist)
1700 E 56th St #2707
Chicago, IL 60637, USA

Herzfeld, John (Director)
c/o Staff Member *WME (LA)*
9601 Wilshire Blvd Fl 3
Beverly Hills, CA 90210, USA

Herzfeld, John M (Director)
Industry Entertainment
955 Carillo Dr #300
Los Angeles, CA 90048, USA

Herzigova, Eva (Model)
c/o Scott Lipps *One Model Management*
42 Bond St
2nd Floor
New york, NY 10012, USA

Herzlinger, Brian (Director)
c/o Naren Desai *Brillstein Entertainment Partners*
9150 Wilshire Blvd #350
Beverly Hills, CA 90212, USA

Herzner, Uli (Stylist)
c/o Staff Member *Ford Models (Miami)*
311 Lincoln Rd
#205
Miami Beach, FL 33139, USA

Herzog, Arthur III (Writer)
4 E 81st St
New York, NY 10028, USA

Herzog, Jacques (Architect)
Herzog & De Meuron Architekten
Rheinschanze 6
Basel 4056, SWITZERLAND

Herzog, Roman (Ex-President, Politician, President)
Schloss Bellevue
Spreeweg 1
Berlin 10557, GERMANY

Herzog, Roman (Politician)
Schlostrasse Bellevue Spreeweg 1
Berlin, Germany D-10557, USA

Herzog, Werner (Director)
Werner Herzog Filmproduktion
Spiegelgasse 9
Vienna 1010, Austria

Herzog, Whitey (Athlete, Baseball Player, Coach)
9426 Sappington Estates Dr
Saint Louis, MO 63127-1664, USA

Hesburgh, Father Theodore
1320 Hesburgh Library
South Bend, IN 46566

Hesburgh, Theodore M (Educator)
University of Natre Dame
1301 Hesburgh Library
Notre Dame, IN 46556, USA

Heseltine, Michael R D (Government Official)
Thenford House near Banbury
Oxon OX17 2BX, UNITED KINGDOM (UK)

Hesketh, Joe (Athlete, Baseball Player)
202 Glenridge Rd
East Aurora, NY 14052-2625, USA

Heskin, Kam (Actor)
c/o Susan Calogerakis *Thruline Entertainment*
9250 Wilshire Blvd
Ground Fl
Beverly Hills, CA 90212, USA

Heslov, Grant (Actor, Director)
c/o Rick Ax *Gold Coast Management*
438 S Venice Blvd Apt 5
Venice, CA 90291, USA

Hess, Bob (Athlete, Hockey Player)
PO Box 598
Chesterfield, MO 63006-0598, USA

Hess, Erika (Skier)
Aeschi
Gratenort 6388, SWITZERLAND

Hess, Ilse
Gailenberg 22
Hindelang/Allgau, GERMANY D-87541

Hess, Jared (Director, Writer)
Moxie Pictures
2644 30th St.
Santa Monica, CA 90405, USA

Hess, John B (Business Person)
Amerada Hess Corp
1185 Ave of Americas
New York, NY 10036, USA

Hess, Sandra (Actor)
c/o Chris Henze *Thruline Entertainment*
9250 Wilshire Blvd
Ground Fl
Beverly Hills, CA 90212, USA

Hesseman, Howard (Actor)
Innovative Artists
1505 10th St
Santa Monica, CA 90401, USA

Hessenland, Dagmar
Amsterdamer Str. 3
Munich, GERMANY D-80805

Hession, Therese (Athlete, Golfer)
3871 Stonesthrow Ln
Hilliard, OH 43026, USA

Hessler, Curtis A (Publisher)
Times-Mirror Co
Times-Mirror Square
Los Angeles, CA 90053, USA

Hessler, Gordon (Director)
8910 Holly Place
Los Angeles, CA 90046, USA

Hessler, Robert R (Oceanographer)
Scripps Institute of Oceanography
Biodiversity Dept
La Jolla, CA 92037, USA

Hessman, Mike (Athlete, Baseball Player)
524 Saint James Dr
Loris, SC 29569-2550, USA

Hest, Ari (Musician)
c/o Staff Member *Paradigm (Monterey)*
404 W Franklin St
Monterey, CA 93940, USA

Hester, Dan (Athlete, Basketball Player)
13846 N Sunset Dr
Fountain Hills, AZ 85268-3173, USA

Hester, Devin (Athlete, Football Player)
514 Yates Ave
Calumet City, IL 60409-3165, USA

Hester, Jessie L (Athlete, Football Player)
12813 Pine Acre Ct
Wellington, FL 33414, USA

Hester, John (Athlete, Baseball Player)
125 Okoni Ln
Eatonton, GA 31024-1098, USA

Hester, Paul V (General)
Commander
Special Operations Command
Hurlburt Field, FL 32544, USA

Heston, Fraser (Actor)
7990 Briar Summit Dr
Los Angeles, CA 90046, USA

Hetfield, James (Musician)
2020 Union St
San Francisco, CA 94123, USA

Hetherington, Eileen M (Doctor)
University of Virginia
Psychology Dept
Gilmer Hall
Charlottesville, VA, USA

Hetki, Johnny (Athlete, Baseball Player)
4004 Stary Dr
Cleveland, OH 44134-5823, USA

Hetrick, Jennifer (Actor)
c/o Staff Member *AKA Talent Agency*
6310 San Vicente Blvd
Suite 200
Los Angeles, CA 90048, USA

Hettema, Dave (Athlete, Football Player)
31 Desert Sky Rd SE
Albuquerque, NM 87123-3983, USA

Hettich, Arthur M (Editor)
606 Shore Acres Dr
Mamaroneck, NY 10543, USA

Hettiger, Julie (Stylist)
c/o Staff Member *JH Creative*
3830 Westerman St
Houston, TX 77005, USA

Hetzel, Eric (Athlete, Baseball Player)
2271 Hetzel Rd
Crowley, LA 70526-8318, USA

Hetzel, Fred (Athlete, Basketball Player)
218 Cornwall St NW
Leesburg, VA 20176-7170, USA

Heuring, Lori (Actor)
c/o Holly Shakoor *42West (LA)*
11400 W Olympic Blvd
Suite 1100
Los Angeles, CA 90064, USA

Heverly-Williams, Ruth (Baseball Player)
520 Tennis Ave
Ambler, PA 19002-6015, USA

Heveron, Doug (Race Car Driver)
PO Box 250
Denver, NC 28037, USA

Heward, Jamie (Athlete, Hockey Player)
159 Bentley Dr
Regina, SK S4N 4S7, Canada

Hewett, Christopher
1422 N. Sweetzer #110
Los Angeles, CA 90069

Hewett, Howard (Music Group)
GHR Entertainment
6014 N Pointe Place
Woodland Hills, CA 91367, USA

Hewgley, Claude (Athlete, Football Player)
55 Silvermont Dr
Spring, TX 77382, USA

Hewish, Anthony (Nobel Prize Laureate)
Pryor's Cottage
Kingston
Cambridge CB3 7NQ, UNITED KINGDOM (UK)

Hewish, Antony (Nobel Prize Laureate)
Pryor's Cottage Kingston
CaiTibridge, England CB3 7NQ, USA

Hewitt, Angela (Musician)
Cramer/Marder Artists
3436 Springhill Road
Lafayette, CA 94549, USA

Hewitt, Bill (Athlete, Baseball Player)
923 Vance Jackson Rd Apt 1107
San Antonio, TX 78201-2739, USA

Hewitt, Bob (Tennis Player)
822 Boylston St #203
Chestnut Hill, MA 02467, USA

Hewitt, Christopher (Actor)
154 E 66th St
New York, NY 10021, USA

Hewitt, Heather
6324 Tahoe Dr.
Los Angeles, CA 90068

Hewitt, Jennifer Love (Actor)
c/o Danielle Thomas *Untitled Entertainment (LA)*
350 S. Beverly Dr #200
Beverly Hills, CA 90212, USA

Hewitt, John (Race Car Driver)
Hewitt Racing
37 Hewitt Lane
Troy, NY 12180, USA

Hewitt, Martin (Actor)
1346 Madonna Rd
San Luis Obispo, CA 93405, USA

Hewitt, Paul (Basketball Player, Coach)
Georgia Institute of Technology
Athletic Dept
Atlanta, GA 30332, USA

Hewitt, Peter (Director, Producer, Writer)
c/o Jenne Casarotto *Casarotto Ramsay & Associates Ltd (UK)*
Waverley House
7-12 Noel St
London W1F 8GQ, UK

Hewko, Robert (Athlete, Football Player)
100 Lincoln Rd
Apt 634
Miami, FL 33139, USA

Hewlett, David (Actor)
c/o Shelley Browning *Magnolia Entertainment (LA)*
9595 Wilshire Blvd
Suite 601
Beverly Hills, CA 90212, USA

Hewlett, Howard (Music Group)
Green Light Talent Agency
PO Box 3172
Beverly Hills, CA 90212, USA

Hewlett, Mark (Reality TV Star)
c/o Jerry Shandrew *Shandrew Public Relations*
1050 S Stanley Ave
Los Angeles, CA 90019-6634, USA

Hewson, Jack (Athlete, Basketball Player)
114 Tahlequah Ln
Loudon, TN 37774-3143, USA

Hewson, John (Government Official)
ABN Amro Australia
10 Spring St #14
Sydney, NSW 2000, AUSTRALIA

Hextall, Bryan
908-6880 Wallace Dr
Brentwood Bay, BC V8M 1N8, Canada

Hextall, Dennis H (Athlete, Hockey Player)
2631 Harvest Hills Dr
Brighton, MI 48114-8299, USA

Hextall, Ronald (Ron) (Athlete, Hockey Player)
Los Angeles Kings 1111 S Figueroa St Ste 3100
Los Angeles, CA 90015-1333, USA

Hextall Jr, Brian (Athlete, Hockey Player)
908-6880 Wallace Dr
Brentwood Bay, BC V8M 1N8, Canada

Hey, John D (Economist, Mathematician)
University of York
Economics Dept
Heslington
York YO1 5DD, UNITED KINGDOM (UK)

Hey, Virginia (Actor)
c/o Michael Henderson *Heresun Management*
4119 West Burbank Blvd.
Burbank, CA 91505, USA

Heydeman, Greg (Athlete, Baseball Player)
702 Ramona Ave
Monterey, CA 93940-5430, USA

Heyer, Kirk (Athlete, Football Player)
4264 Center Street
Omaha, NE 68105, USA

Heyer, Ingeburg
PO Box 143
Burtonsville, MD 20866-0143, USA

Heyer, Shane
345 Toyon Ter
San Marcos, CA 92069-8120, USA

Heyland, Rob
The Manor Middle Lyttleton
Worcestershire, ENGLAND

Heyman, Abigail (Photographer)
40 W 12th St Apt 1
New York, NY 10011-8693, usA

Heyman, Richard (Biologist)
Ligand Pharmaceuticals
9393 Town Center Dr #100
San Diego, CA 92121, USA

Heyward, Cameron (Football Player)
c/o Pat Dye Jr *SportsTrust Advisors - GA*
3340 Peachtree Rd NE
16th Floor
Atlanta, GA 30326, USA

Heyward, Jason (Athlete, Baseball Player)
2443 Crescent Park Ct Aot 1180
Apt 1180
Atlanta, GA 30339-6024, USA

Heyward-Bey, Darrius (Athlete, Football Player)
c/o Ben Dogra *CAA - St. Louis*
222 S Central Ave
Suite 1008
St Louis, MO 63105, USA

Heywood, Anne (Actor)
9966 Liebe Dr
Beverly Hills, CA 90210, USA

H. Hoyer, Steney (Congressman, Politician)
1705 Longworth HOB
Washington, DC 20515, USA

Hiatt, Andrew (Biologist)
Scripps Research Foundation
10666 N Torrey Pines Road
La Jolla, CA 92037, USA

Hiatt, Jack (Athlete, Baseball Player)
715 E 1st St
Coquille, OR 97423-1904, USA

Hiatt, John (Music Group, Musician, Songwriter, Writer)
c/o Staff Member *United Talent Agency (UTA)*
9336 Civic Center Dr
Beverly Hills, CA 90210, USA

Hiatt, Phil (Athlete, Baseball Player)
30 Littleton St
Cantonment, FL 32533-6558, USA

Hiatt, Shana (Actor, Model)
c/o Jerry Shandrew *Shandrew Public Relations*
1050 S Stanley Ave
Los Angeles, CA 90019-6634, USA

Hibbard, Greg (Athlete, Baseball Player)
Mahoning Valley Scrappers 111 Eastwood Mall Blvd
Attn Coaching Staff
Niles, OH 44446-4841, USA

Hibbard, Greg (Athlete, Baseball Player)
5287 Conifer View Ln
Lakeland, TN 38002-4874, USA

Hibbert, Edward (Actor)
Gage Group
14724 Ventura Blvd #505
Sherman Oaks, CA 91403, USA

Hibbs, Jim (Athlete, Baseball Player)
4659 Foothill Rd
Ventura, CA 93003-1903, USA

Hick, Graeme A (Cricketer)
Worcestershire County Cricket Club
New Road
Worcester, UNITED KINGDOM (UK)

Hick, John H (Religious Leader)
144 Oak Tree Lane
Selly Oak
Birmingham B29 6HU, UNITED KINGDOM (UK)

Hick', Ray (Athlete, Football Player)
801 Evergreen Dr
Friendswood, TX 77546-4757, USA

Hickam, Homer (Writer)
9532 Hemlock Dr SE
Huntsville, AL 35803-1165, USA

Hickam, Homer H Jr (Writer)
9532 Hemlok Dr SE
Huntsville, AL 35803, USA

Hicke, Bill (Athlete, Hockey Player)

Hicke, Ernie (Athlete, Hockey Player)
5287 S Sugarberry Ct
Gilbert, AZ 85298-4657, USA

Hickenbottom, Michael (Wrestler)
c/o Kerry Rodgerson *World Wrestling Entertainment (WWE)*
Titan Towers
1241 E Main St
Stamford, CT 06905-3857, USA

Hickenlooper, John (Governor, Politician)
136 State Capitol
Denver, CO 80203-1792, USA

Hickerson, Bryan (Athlete, Baseball Player)
275 S Hunters Rdg
Warsaw, IN 46582-5645, USA

Hickerson, Gene (Athlete)
4471 Nagel Road
Avon, OH 44011, USA

Hickey, Bo (Athlete, Football Player)
94 Field Crest Rd
New Canaan, CT 06840-6330, USA

Hickey, Jim (Athlete, Baseball Player)
3911 Story Rd
Saint Cloud, FL 34772-7589, USA

Hickey, John Benjamin (Actor)
c/o Sarah Fargo *Paradigm (NY)*
360 Park Ave S Fl 16
New York, NY 10010, USA

Hickey, Maurice (Publisher)
Denver Post
65015th St
Denver, CO 80202, USA

Hickey, Pat (Athlete, Hockey Player)
2 Alexis St
Red Deer, AB T4R 3E6, Canada

Hickey, Thomas J (General)
2127 Bobbyber Dr
Vienna, VA 22182, USA

Hickey, William V (Business Person)
Sealed Air Corp
Park 80 E
Saddle Brook, NJ 07663, USA

Hickland, Catherine (Actor)
255 W 84th St #2A
New York, NY 10024, USA

Hickman, Dallas (Athlete, Football Player)
6521 E Dreyfus Ave
Scottsdale, AZ 85254, USA

Hickman, Darryl (Actor)
171 Hermosillo Road
Santa Barbara, CA 93108, USA

Hickman, Dwayne (Actor)
PO Box 17226
Encino, CA 91416, USA

Hickman, Fred (Sportscaster)
Cable News Network
Sports Dept
1050 Techwood Dr NW
Atlanta, GA 30318, USA

Hickman, Jesse (Athlete, Baseball Player)
2004 Simmons St #A
Alexandria, LA 71301-3739, USA

Hickman, Jim (Race Car Driver)
PO Box455
Henning, TN 38041-0455, USA

Hickman, Larry (Athlete, Football Player)
5519 Westchester Dr
Tyler, TX 75703, USA

Hickman, Tracy (Writer)
c/o Staff Member *HarperCollins Publishers*
10 East 53rd St
c/o Author mail, 7th Floor
New York, NY 10022, USA

Hickox, Edwin (Attorney, Baseball Player)
1721 Baron Court
Port Orange, FL 32128-6789, USA

Hickox, Edwin (Athlete, Baseball Player)
1721 Baron Ct
Port Orange, FL 32128, USA

Hickox, Marc
10 St. Mary St. #308
Toronto, CANADA Ont. M4Y 1

Hickox, Richard S (Conductor)
35 Ellington St
London N7 8PN, UNITED KINGDOM (UK)

Hicks, Adam (Actor)
c/o Mona Loring *MLC PR*
7080 Hollywood Blvd
Suite 903
Los Angeles, CA 90028, USA

Hicks, Alex (Athlete, Hockey Player)
7511 E Tailspin Ln
Scottsdale, AZ 85255-4632, USA

Hicks, Artis (Athlete, Football Player)
1804 Woods Edge Dr NE
Leesburg, VA 20176-6618, USA

Hicks, Betty (Athlete, Golfer)
10357 Mary Ave
Cupertino, CA 95014, USA

Hicks, Brandon
4907 Pocahontas Dr
Pasadena, TX 77505-2915, USA

Hicks, Buddy (Athlete, Baseball Player)
1526 N Dixie Downs Rd
Unit 26
Saint George, UT 84770-4105, USA

Hicks, Catherine (Actor)
c/o Margrit Polak *Margrit Polak Management*
1954 Hillhurst Ave
Suite 405
Los Angeles, CA 90027, USA

Hicks, Dan (Sportscaster)
NBC-TV
Sports Dept
30 Rockefeller Plaza
New York, NY 10112, USA

Hicks, Dan (Music Group)
Leslie Wiener
PO Box 245
Sausalito, CA 94966, USA

Hicks, Doug (Athlete, Hockey Player)
117 Selkirk Blvd
Red Deer, AB T4N OG8, Canada

Hicks, Dwight (Athlete, Football Player)
PO Box 342
Sierra Madre, CA 91025-0342, USA

Hicks, Eric (Athlete, Football Player)
6714 W 148th Ter
Overland Park, KS 66223-2929, USA

Hicks, Esther (Motivational Speaker, Writer)
P.O. Box 690070
San Antonio, Texas 78269, USA

Hicks, Glenn (Athlete, Hockey Player)
2 Alexis St
Red Deer, AB T4R 3E6, Canada

Hicks, Glenn
2 Alexis St
Red Deer, AB T4R 3E6, Canada

Hicks, Jerry (Motivational Speaker, Writer)
P.O. Box 690070
San Antonio, Texas 78269, USA

Hicks, Jim (Athlete, Baseball Player)
9331 Portal Dr
Houston, TX 77031-2210, USA

Hicks, Jimmy (Musician)
4110 N Shore Dr
West Palm Beach, FL 33047, USA

Hicks, Joe (Athlete, Baseball Player)
2707 Brookmere Rd
Charlottesville, VA 22901-1106, USA

Hicks, Michele (Actor)
c/o Eric Black *Crestview Entertainment*
521 Montana Ave
Santa Monica, CA 90403, USA

Hicks, Michelle (Actor)
c/o Staff Member *Innovative Artists (LA)*
1505 10th St
Santa Monica, CA 90401, USA

Hicks, Robert (Athlete, Football Player)
2544 Hightower Ct NW
Atlanta, GA 30318, USA

Hicks, Scott (Director)
PO Box 824
Kent Town 5071, SOUTH AFRICA

Hicks, "Sonny" Osceola (Athlete, Football Player)
1626 Wood Grove Rd
Memphis, TN 38117-2350, USA

Hicks, Sylvester (Athlete, Football Player)
144 Sweetbay Dr
Jackson, TN 38301, USA

Hicks, Taylor (Musician, Reality TV Star)
c/o K. Blaine Johnston *Rogues Gallery*
20 Clinton St
Suite C-7
New York, NY 10002, USA

Hicks, Thomas O (Commentator)
Texas Rangers
10000 Hollow Wav Rd
Dallas, TX 75229-6631, USA

Hicks, Tom (Athlete, Football Player)
207 Rivershire Ln
Apt 106
Lincolnshire, IL 60069, USA

Hicks, Vicki Cheung (Stylist)
2 S Hill Ct
Morristown, NJ 07960-3368, USA

Hicks, Wayne (Athlete, Hockey Player)
7726 E Buteo Dr
Scottsdale, AZ 85255-4656, USA

Hicks, W K (Athlete, Football Player)
10149 Kemp Forest Dr
Houston, TX 77080, USA

Hicks Jr, John C (Athlete, Football Player)
3287 Green Cook Rd
Johnstown, OH 43031, USA

Hidalgo, John (Government Official)
May's Valentine Davenport Moore
1899 L St NW
Washington, DC 20036, USA

Hiddleston, Tom (Actor)
c/o Jon Rubenstein *Authentic Talent and Literary Management*
45 Main St
Suite 1004
Brooklyn, NY 11201, USA

Hide, Herbie (Boxer)
Matchroom
10 Western Road
Romford
Essex RM1 3JT, UNITED KINGDOM (UK)

Hide, Raymond (Geophysicist, Physicist)
University of Oxford
Jesus College
Oxford OX1 3DW, UNITED KINGDOM (UK)

Hidi, Andre (Athlete, Hockey Player)
38 Avoca Ave
Toronto, ON M4T 2B9, Canada

Hieb, Richard J (Astronaut)
Allied Signal Tech Services
2712 Lighthouse Dr
Houston, TX 77058-4318, USA

Hiebert, Erwin N (Historian)
40 Payson Road
Belmont, MA 02478, USA

Hiemstra, Ed (Athlete, Football Player)
100 Hamilton Ct Unit D
Manhattan, MT 59741-8162, USA

Hier, Marvin (Activist, Religious Leader)
Simon Wiesenthal Holocaust Center
9766 W Pico Blvd
Los Angeles, CA 90035, USA

Hieronymus, Clara W (Journalist)
50 Spring St
Sevannah, TN 38372, USA

Hietala, Brad (Race Car Driver)
85 North St.
Enfield, CT 06082, USA

Hietpas, Joe (Athlete, Baseball Player)
611 E Timberline Dr
Appleton, WI 54913-7104, USA

Hi-Five
PO Box 3030
Jamaica, NY 11431

Higashi, Satoshi (Athlete, Golfer)
Bridgestone Sports
45 Higashi-Matsushita-Cho Kanda
Chiyoda-ku
Tokyo 101, Japan

Higdon, Bruce (Cartoonist)
210 Canvasback Court
Murfreesboro, TN 37130-8855, USA

Higginbotham, Joan E (Astronaut)
1409 Mija Lane
Seabrook, TX 77586-2406, USA

Higginbotham, Patrick E (Judge)
US Court of Appeals
US Courthouse
1100 Commerce St
Dallas, TX 75242, USA

Higgins, Al (Producer)
c/o Staff Member *Creative Artists Agency (CAA-LA)*
2000 Ave Of The Stars
·Los Angeles, CA 90067, USA

Higgins, Brian (Congressman, Politician)
2459 Rayburn HOB
Washington, DC 20515, USA

Higgins, Christopher
34 Colgate Dr
Smithtown, NY 11787-2017, USA

Higgins, David (Actor)
c/o Ben Feigin *Anonymous Content (LA)*
3531 Hayden Ave
Culver City, CA 90232, USA

Higgins, Dennis (Athlete, Baseball Player)
1123 Boonville Rd
Jefferson City, MO 65109-0621, USA

Higgins, Earle (Athlete, Basketball Player)
29128 Chateau Ct
Farmington Hills, MI 48334-4112, USA

Higgins, Jack (Cartoonist, Editor)
59 Waverly Ave
Clarendon Hills, IL 60514-1236, USA

Higgins, Jack (Writer)
September Tide
Mont de la Rocque Jersey
Channel Island, UNITED KINGDOM (UK)

Higgins, J Kenneth (Misc)
Boeing Commercial Airplane Group
PO Box 3707
Seattle, WA 98124, USA

Higgins, J Kenneth Capt
Boeing Commercial Airplane Group PO Box 3707
Seattle, WA 98124-2207, USA

Higgins, John (Coach, Swimmer)
40 Williams Dr
Annapolis, MD 21401, USA

Higgins, Kevin (Athlete, Baseball Player)
10551 Haywood Dr
Las Vegas, NV 89135-2851, USA

Higgins, Mark (Athlete, Baseball Player)
2999 Abbotts Oak Way
Duluth, GA 30097-2193, USA

Higgins, Mike (Athlete, Basketball Player)
137 48th Ave
Greeley, CO 80634-4307, USA

Higgins, Missy (Musician)
c/o Staff Member *EMI Music (Australia)*
98-100 Glover St
P.O. Box 311
Cremorne, NSW 2090, Australia

Higgins, Pam (Athlete, Golfer)
5 Pea Pine Ln
Newport Beach, CA 92660, USA

Higgins, Paul (Athlete, Hockey Player)
c/o Staff Member *Toronto Young Nationals Hockey Club*
233-1080 Tapscott Rd
Scarborough, ON M1X 1E7, Canada

Higgins, Robert (Business Person)
Fleet Boston Corp
1 Federal St
Boston, MA 02110, USA

Higgins, Rod (Athlete, Basketball Player)
743 Mendenhall Ct
Fort Mill, SC 29715-7852, USA

Higgins, Rosalyn (Judge)
International Court of Justice
Peace Palace
Hague, KJ 2517, NETHERLANDS

Higgins, Scott (Athlete, Baseball Player)
3591 Indian Clover Street
Plumas Lake, CA 95961-8740, USA

Higgins, Scott (Athlete, Baseball Player)
3591 Indian Clower St
Plumas Lake, CA 95961, USA

Higgins, Tim (Athlete, Hockey Player)
c/o Staff Member *Chicago Blackhawks*
1901 W Madison St
Chicago, IL 60612, USA

Higgins, Tom (Athlete, Football Player)
506-251 Queens Quay W
Toronto, ON M5J 2N6, Canada

Higginson, Bobby (Athlete, Baseball Player)
2039 Indian Sky Cir
Lakeland, FL 33813-4859, USA

Higginson, John (Doctor)
16 Sundew Road
Savannah, GA 31411, USA

Higginson, Torri (Actor)
c/o Staff Member *Sci-FI Channel, The*
100 Universal Plaza
Bldg 1280/12
Universal City, CA 91608, USA

Higgs, Kenny (Athlete, Basketball Player)
746 Sargent Dr
Owensboro, KY 42301-833, USA

Higgs, Mark (Athlete, Football Player)
45 NW 156th Ln
Pembroke Pines, FL 33028, USA

Higham, Scott (Journalist)
Washington Post
Editorial Dept
1150 15th St NW
Washington, DC 20071, USA

Highley, Ray (Race Car Driver)
Red Line Racing
1650 Linda Vista Dr.
San Marcos, CA 92069, USA

Highman, Charles
4027 Farmouth Dr.
Los Angeles, CA 90027

Highmore, Freddie (Actor)
c/o Sue Latimer *Artists Rights Group (ARG)*
4 Great Portland St
London W1W 8PA, UNITED KINGDOM (UK)

Highsmith, Alonzo (Athlete, Football Player)
3703 E Valley Dr
Missouri City, TX 77459-4305, USA

Highsmith, Don (Athlete, Football Player)
221 S 9th Ave
Highland Park, NJ 08904, USA

High Speed Scene, The (Music Group)
c/o Staff Member *Paradigm (Monterey)*
404 W Franklin St
Monterey, CA 93940, USA

Hightower, John B (Director)
394 Emily Dickinson North
Newport News, VA 23606-1486, USA

Hightower, Rosella (Ballerina, Choreographer, Dancer)
Villa Piege Luiere
Parc Florentina Ave Vallauris
Cannes 06400, FRANCE

Highway 101
PO Box 1547
Goodlettsville, TN 37050-1547

Higuera, Teddy (Athlete, Baseball Player)
1567 S Sycamore Pl
Chandler, AZ 85286-6818, USA

Hiii-Westerman, Joyce (Athlete, Baseball Player, Commentator)
1565 47th Ave
Kenosha, WI 53144-1289, USA

Hijeulos, Oscar (Writer)
Harriet Wasserman Literary Agency 132 E 43rd St
NewYork, NY 10017-4019, USA

Hijuelos, Oscar (Writer)
Hofstra University
English Dept
10000 Fulton Ave
Hempstead, NY 11550, USA

Hikaru, Utada (Musician)
c/o Staff Member *Island Records*
825 Eighth Ave
New York, NY 10019, USA

Hiken, Gerald
910 Moreno Ave.
Palo Alto, CA 94303

Hilario, Maybyner (Nene) (Basketball Player)
Denver Nuggets
Pepsi Center
1000 Chopper Circle
Denver, CO 80204, USA

Hilario, Nene (Athlete, Basketball Player)
c/o Dan Fegan *Lagardere Unlimited - (LA)*
10866 Wilshire Blvd
Los Angeles, CA 90024, USA

Hilbert, Andy (Athlete, Hockey Player)
419 N Michigan Ave
Howell, MI 48843, USA

Hilbert, Jon (Athlete, Football Player)
8701 Key Ct
Louisville, KY 40299-1317, USA

Hildebrand, Jeffrey (Misc)
3780 Willowick Rd
Houston, TX 77019-1116, USA

Hildebrand, John G (Biologist)
629 N Olsen Ave
Tucson, AZ 85719, USA

Hildebrand, Madison (Business Person, Reality TV Star)
Coldwell Banker
29178 Heathercliff Rd
Malibu, CA 90265, USA

Hildebrandt, Dieter
Rollenhagenstr. 3a
Munich, GERMANY D-81739

Hildebrandt, Greg (Cartoonist)
Dark Horse
10956 SE Main St
Milwaukie, OR 97222, USA

Hildreth, Eugene A (Doctor)
2000 Cambridge Avenue
Apt 129
Reading, PA 19610-2741, USA

Hilfiger, Tommy (Designer, Fashion
Designer)
Tommy Hilfiger USA
601 W 26th St #500
New York, NY 10001, USA

Hilgenberg, Jay W (Athlete, Football
Player)
1296 Kimmer Ct
Lake Forest, IL 60045, USA

Hilgenberg, Joel (Athlete, Football Player)
2027 Ridgeway Dr
Iowa City, IA 52245, USA

Hilgenbrinck, Tad (Actor)
c/o Jonathan Howard *Innovative Artists
(LA)*
1505 10th St
Santa Monica, CA 90401, USA

Hilgendorf, Tom (Athlete, Baseball Player)
P.O. Box 124
Camanche, IA 52730-0124, USA

Hilger, Rusty (Athlete, Football Player)
2625 SW 67th St
Oklahoma City, OK 73159-2735, USA

Hiljus, Erik (Athlete, Baseball Player)
2253 Demaray Dr
Grants Pass, OR 97527-9147, USA

Hill, Aaron (Actor)
c/o Siri Garber *Platform Public Relations*
2666 N Beachwood Dr
Los Angeles, CA 90068, USA

Hill, Aaron (Athlete, Baseball Player)
1147 Skye Ln
Palm Harbor, FL 34683-1460, USA

Hill, A Derek (Artist)
National Art Collections Fund
20 John Islip St
London SW1, UNITED KINGDOM (UK)

Hill, Al (Athlete, Hockey Player)
4807 Margaret Ln
Harrisburg, PA 17110-3365, United States

Hill, Al (Athlete, Hockey Player)
4807 Margaret Ln
Harrisbury, PA 17110, USA

Hill, Anita (Educator)
600 Third Ave #200
New York, NY 10016, USA

Hill, Armand (Athlete, Basketball Player)
1626 Laurens Way SW
Atlanta, GA 30311-3718, USA

Hill, Bernard (Actor)
c/o Staff Member *Seven Summits Pictures
& Management*
8906 W Olympic Blvd
Ground Floor
Beverly Hills, CA 90211, USA

Hill, Bob (Basketball Coach, Coach)
205 Rio Cordillera
Boerne, TX 78006, USA

Hill, Bobby (Athlete, Baseball Player)
1874 Drv Creek Rd
San Jose, CA 95124-1005, USA

Hill, Brendan (Musician)
c/o Staff Member *ArtistDirect*
9046 Lindblade St
Culver City, CA 90232, USA

Hill, Bruce (Athlete, Football Player)
1919 E Citation Ln
Tempe, AZ 85284, USA

Hill, Calvin (Athlete, Football Player)
10300 Walker Lake Dr
Great Falls, VA 22066, USA

Hill, Carolyn (Athlete, Golfer)
5906 Skimmer Point Blvd S
Gulfport, FL 33707-3938, USA

Hill, Cindy (Athlete, Golfer)
2852 NW 8th St
Fort Lauderdale, FL 33311, USA

Hill, Damon G D (Race Car Driver)
PO Box 100
Nelson
Lanscashire BB9 8AQ, UNITED
KINGDOM (UK)

Hill, Dan (Music Group, Songwriter,
Writer)
Paquin Entertainment
1067 Sherwin Road
Winnipeg, MB R3H 0TB, CANADA

Hill, Dan
1407 Mt. Pleasant Rd.
Toronto, CANADA Ont. M4N 2

Hill, Daniel W (Dan) (Athlete, Football
Player)
171 Montrose Dr
Durham, NC 27707, USA

Hill, Dave (Athlete, Baseball Player)
125 Jenny Lind Dr
Hendersonville, NC 28791-1321, USA

Hill, David H (Athlete, Football Player)
921 Clements Cir
Moody, AL 35004, USA

Hill, David L (Tex) (War Hero)
317 Elizabeth Road
San Antonio, TX 78209, USA

Hill, Derek (Athlete, Football Player)
8939 Gallatin Rd
Pico Rivera, CA 90660, USA

Hill, Donnie (Athlete, Baseball Player)
6 Knob Hl
Laguna Niguel, CA 92677-5903, USA

Hill, Draper (Cartoonist, Editor)
368 Washington Road
Grosse Pointe Woods, MI 48230, USA

Hill, Dule (Actor)
12603 Moorpark St #305
Studio City, CA 91604, USA

Hill, Dusty (Music Group, Musician)
Lone Wolf Mgmt
PO Box 163690
Austin, TX 78716, USA

Hill, Eddie (Race Car Driver)
National Hot Rod Association
2035 Financial Hwy.
Glendora, CA 91741, USA

Hill, Eric (Athlete, Football Player)
5500 Palm Cir
Galveston, TX 77551, USA

Hill, Erica (Television Host)
Prime News Tonight
CNN
1 Time Warner Center
New York, NY 10019, USA

Hill, Faith (Musician)
c/o Coran Capshaw *Red Light
Management (VA)*
PO Box 1467
Charlottesville, VA 22902, USA

Hill, Fred (Athlete, Football Player)
31441 Paseo Riobo
San Juan Capistrano, CA 92675, USA

Hill, Garry (Athlete, Baseball Player)
9602 Willowglen Trl
Charlotte, NC 28215-9767, USA

Hill, Gary (Athlete, Basketball Player,
Football Player)
9957 Hickory Hollow Rd
Shawnee, OK 74804-9059, USA

Hill, Geoffrey W (Writer)
Boston University
University Professors
745 Commonwealth St
Boston, MA 02215, USA

Hill, Glenallen (Athlete, Baseball Player)
108 Calvin Pl
Santa Cruz, CA 95060-3124, USA

Hill, Grant (Athlete, Basketball Player,
Olympic Athlete)
9600 McCormick Pl
Lawrence, KS 66049-2400, USA

Hill, Greg (Athlete, Football Player)
Audio Video Unplugged
14580 Beltwood Pkwy E
Farmers Branch, TX 75244, USA

Hill, Greg (Athlete, Football Player)
P.O. Box 43210
Port Hueneme, CA 93044, USA

Hill, Greg L (Athlete, Football Player)
P.O. Box 43210
Port Hueneme, CA 93044, USA

Hill, Gregory (Director)
c/o Staff Member *Paul Lane Entertainment*
468 N Camden Dr.
Beverly Hills, CA 90210, USA

Hill, Harlon (Athlete, Football Player)
RR 2 Box 276
Killen, AL 35645, USA

Hill, Ike (Athlete, Football Player)
412 Randolph St
Oak Park, IL 60302, USA

Hill, Jack (Director, Producer, Writer)
1445 North Fairfax Avenue
Apt 205
West Hollywood, CA 90046-3927, USA

Hill, James (General)
7424 Kilbourn Ave
Skokie, IL 60076-3842, USA

Hill, James C (Judge)
US Court of Appeals
56 Forsyth St NW
Atlanta, GA 30303, USA

Hill, James T (General)
Commanding General
Army Forces Command
Fort McPherson, GA 30330, USA

Hill, J D (Athlete, Football Player)
2543 N 53rd Dr
Phoenix, AZ 85035, USA

Hill, J.D. (Athlete, Football Player)
1550 South Yucca St
Chandler, AZ 85286, USA

Hill, Jeremy (Athlete, Baseball Player)
10050 Gooding Dr
Dallas, TX 75229-6209, USA

Hill, Jessie (Music Group, Musician)
1210 Caffin Ave
New Orleans, LA 70117, USA

Hill, Jim (Sportscaster)
ABC-TV
Sprots Dept
77 W 66th St
New York, NY 10023, USA

Hill, Jim (Athlete, Football Player)
4120 Parva Ave
Los Angeles, CA 90027, USA

Hill, John S (Athlete, Football Player)
2005 Boyce Bridge Rd
Creedmoor, NC 27522, USA

Hill, Jonah (Actor)
c/o Sharon Jackson *WME (LA)*
9601 Wilshire Blvd Fl 3
Beverly Hills, CA 90210, USA

Hill, Julia Butterfly (Misc)
Circle of Life Foundation
PO Box 3764
Oakland, CA 94609, USA

Hill, Ken (Athlete, Baseball Player)
1360 Shady Oaks Dr
Southlake, TX 76092-4208, USA

Hill, Kenneth (Athlete, Football Player)
121 Hawkins Pl
Boonton, NJ 07005, USA

Hill, Kent (Athlete, Football Player)
630 Hawthorne Pl
Fayetteville, GA 30214, USA

Hill, Kent A (Athlete, Football Player)
630 Hawthorne Pl
Fayetteville, GA 30214, USA

Hill, Kim (Music Group)
Ambassador Artist Agency
PO Box 50358
Nashville, TN 37205, USA

Hill, King (Athlete, Football Player)
7611 Sands Terrace Ln
Spring, TX 77389, USA

Hill, Koyie (Athlete, Baseball Player)
2405 NW 151st St
Edmond, OK 73013-9227, USA

Hill, Koyle (Athlete, Baseball Player)
5216 N Valentine Rd
Park City, KS 67219, USA

Hill, Lauryn (Actor, Musician)
c/o Nicole David *WME (LA)*
9601 Wilshire Blvd Fl 3
Beverly Hills, CA 90210, USA

Hill, Madre (Athlete, Football Player)
18 Charleston Ct
Elgin, SC 29045, USA

Hill, Marc (Athlete, Baseball Player)
203 Maple St
Elsberry, MO 63343-1604, USA

Hill, Michael (Commentator)
11231 NW 18th St
Plantation, FL 33323-2226, USA

Hill, Mike (Athlete, Golfer)
6750 Jefferson Rd
Brooklyn, MI 49230-9717, USA

Hill, Milt (Athlete, Baseball Player)
8401 Avalon Ct
Cumming, GA 30041-5724, USA

Hill, Norm (Athlete, Football Player)
340 Dromore Ave
Winnipeg, MB R3M OJ5, Canada

Hill, Pat (Football Player)
California State University
Athletic Dept
Fresno, CA 93740, USA

Hill, Perry (Athlete, Baseball Player)
8916 Wyatt Cir
Argyle, TX 76226-6513, USA

Hill, Randal (Athlete, Football Player)
5360 SW 130th Ter
Weston, FL 33027, USA

Hill, Rich
17 Soafford Rd
Milton, MA 02186-4408, USA

Hill, Rich (Athlete, Baseball Player)
17 Spafford Rd
Milton, MA 02186, USA

Hill, Ron (Athlete, Track Athlete)
PO Box 11
Hyde
Cheshire SK14 1RD, UNITED KINGDOM
(UK)

Hill, Roy (Race Car Driver)
Roy Hill Drag Racing School
4926 Walker Mill Rd.
Sophia, NC 27350, USA

Hill, Sean (Athlete, Hockey Player,
Olympic Athlete)
2735 E Carob Dr
Chandler, AZ 85286-3118, USA

Hill, Simmie (Athlete, Basketball Player)
1470 Elizabeth Blvd
1470 Elizabeth Blvd, PA 15221-1223,
USA

Hill, Steven (Actor)
18 Jill Lane
Monsey, NY 10952, USA

Hill, Susan E (Writer)
Longmoor Farmhouse Ebrington
Chipping Campden
Glos GL55 6NW, UNITED KINGDOM
(UK)

Hill, Tamia (Musician)
c/o Staff Member *HUFF Events and PR*
325 W 38th St
Suite 805
New York, NY 10018, USA

Hill, Terence (Actor)
3 Los Pinos Road
Santa Fe, NM 87505, USA

Hill, Terrell L (Biologist, Physicist)
3400 Paul Sweet Road #C220
Santa Cruz, CA 95065, USA

Hill, Thomas (Tom) (Athlete, Track
Athlete)
428 Elmcrest Dr
Norman, OK 73071, USA

Hill, Tony (Athlete, Football Player)
729 Forest Bend Dr
Plano, TX 75025, USA

Hill, Tyrone (Baseball Player)
Pinnacle
5594 Electric Ave
San Bernardino, CA 92407-2713, USA

Hill, Virgil (Boxer)
1618 Santa Gertrudis Loop
Bismarck, ND 58503, USA

Hill, Virgil L Jr (Admiral)
1000 Glendon Court
Ambler, PA 19002, USA

Hill, Walter (Director)
836 Greenway Dr
Beverly Hills, CA 90210, USA

Hill, Winston (Athlete, Football Player)
101 Lane Dr
Gladewater, TX 75647, USA

Hillaby, John (Writer)
Constable Co
Lanchesters
102 Fulham Palace Road
London W6 9ER, UNITED KINGDOM
(UK)

Hillaker, Harry (Engineer)
1802 Palace Dr
Grand Prairie, TX 75050, USA

Hillan, Patrick (Actor)
11005 Morrison St #206
N Hollywood, CA 91601

Hillary, Edmund P (Mountaineer,
Scientist)
278A Remuera Road
Auckland SE2, NEW ZEALAND

Hille, Bertil (Doctor)
10630 Lakeside Ave NE
Seattle, WA 98125, USA

Hille, Einar (Mathematician)
8862 La Jolla Scenic Dr N
La Jolla, CA 92037, USA

Hillebrand, Gerald (Athlete, Football
Player)
23 Madison Cir
Davenport, IA 52806, USA

Hillebrecht, Rudolf F H (Architect)
Gneiststr 7
Hanover 30169, GERMANY

Hillegas, Shawn (Athlete, Baseball Player)
1409 116th Dr SE
Lake Stephens, WA 98258-7935, USA

Hillel, Shlomo (Government Official)
14 Gelber St
Jerusalem 96755, ISRAEL

Hillen, Bobby (Race Car Driver)
Donlavey Racing
5011 Midlothian Turnpike
Richmond, VA 23225, USA

Hillenbrand, Daniel A (Business Person)
Hillenbrand Industries
700 State RR 46 E
Batesville, IN 47006, USA

Hillenbrand, Laura (Writer)
c/o Tina Bennett *WME (WMA-NY)*
1325 Ave of the Americas
New York, NY 10019, USA

Hillenbrand, Martin J (Diplomat)
University of Georgia
International Trade/Security Center
Athens, GA 30602, USA

Hillenbrand, Shea (Athlete, Baseball
Player)
2614 E Via De Palmas
Gilbert, AZ 85298-2068, USA

Hillenburg, Stephen (Animator, Producer,
Writer)
c/o Staff Member *Perry & Neidorf CPA*
9720 Wilshire Bvld
Suite 300
Beverly Hills, CA 90212-2015, USA

Hiller, Arthur (Director)
1218 Benedict Canyon
Beverly Hills, CA 90210, USA

Hiller, Jim (Athlete, Coach, Hockey
Player)
c/o Staff Member *Chilliwack Bruins*
45323 Hodgins Ave
Chilliwack, BC V2P 8G1, Canada

Hiller, John (Athlete, Baseball Player)
W8085 Becker Dr
Iron Mountain, MI 49801-9385, USA

Hiller, Lee (Journalist)
c/o Staff Member *Artistic Agency*
P.O. Box 68538
Portland, OR 97268, USA

Hiller, Susan (Artist)
83 Loudoun Road
London NW8 0DL, UNITED KINGDOM
(UK)

Hillerman, John (Actor)
1110 Bade St
Houston, TX 77055, USA

Hillery, Patrick J (President)
Grasmere Greenfield Road
Sutton
Dublin 13, IRELAND

Hill Hearth, Amy
c/o Daniel Strone *Trident Media Group
LLC*
41 Madison Ave
36th Floor
New York, NY 10010, USA

Hilliard, Dalton (Athlete, Football Player)
23 Hermitage Dr
Destrehan, LA 70047, USA

Hilliard, Ike (Athlete, Football Player)
c/o Neil Schwartz *Schwartz & Feinsod*
contact via telephone or email
New York, NY 10603

Hilliard, Issac (Athlete, Football Player)
8240 SW 164th Ter
Palmetto Bay, FL 33157, USA

Hillier, James (Inventor)
22 Arreton Road #CR31
Princeton, NJ 08540, USA

Hillier, Randy (Athlete, Hockey Player)
308 Brookhaven Ln
Pittsburgh, PA 15241-2582, USA

Hillier, Steve (Music Group, Musician)
Primary Talent Int'l
2-12 Petonville Road
London N1 9PL, UNITED KINGDOM
(UK)

Hillin Jr, Bobby (Race Car Driver)
c/o Staff Member *NASCAR*
1801 Speedway Blvd
Daytona Beach, FL 32015, USA

Hillis, Ali (Actor, Producer)
c/o Staff Member *Pinnacle Public
Relations*
8265 Sunset Blvd
Suite 201
Los Angeles, CA 90064, USA

Hillis, Robert (Rib) (Actor)
c/o John Guglielmetti *Continuum
Entertainment*
303 Park Ave S
Suite 1220
New York, NY 10010, USA

Hillis, W Daniel (Danny) (Scientist)
Applied Minds
1209 Grand Central Ave
Glendale, CA 91201, USA

Hillman, Avriel (Actor)
203 Comstock St
#11
Seattle, WA 98119, USA

Hillman, Chris (Music Group, Musician,
Songwriter, Writer)
McMullen Co
433 N Camden Dr #400
Beverly Hills, CA 90210, USA

Hillman, Darnell (Athlete, Basketball
Player)
6011 Medora Dr
Indianapolis, IN 46228-1397, USA

Hillman, Dave (Athlete, Baseball Player)
849 Mimosa Dr
Kingsport, TN 37660-2563, USA

Hillman, Eric (Athlete, Baseball Player)
157 Bellaire St
Denver, CO 80220-5632, USA

Hillman, Floyd "Bud"
28 Cheyenne Crt
Leamington, ON N8H 5E3, Canada

Hillman, Floyd (Bud) (Athlete, Hockey
Player)
28 Cheyenne Crt
Leamington, ON N8H 5E3, Canada

Hillman, Larry (Athlete, Hockey Player)
57 Westland St
St Catharines, ON L2S 3W8, Canada

Hillman, Trey (Athlete, Baseball Player,
Coach)
301 Appaloosa Run
Liberty Hill, TX 78642-3862, USA

Hillman, Wayne (Athlete, Hockey Player)

Hills, Carla (Secretary)
3125 Chain Bridge Road NW
Washington, DC 20016, USA

Hills, Carla (Politician)
3125 Chain Bridge Rd NW
Washington, DC 20016-3411, USA

Hills, Nate (Danja) (Musician, Producer)
8045 Mulholland Dr
Los Angeles, CA 90046, USA

Hills, Roderick M (Business Person,
Government Official)
Mudge Rose Guthrie Alexander Ferdon
1200 19th St NW
Washington, DC 20036, USA

Hill Smith, Marilyn (Opera Singer)
Music International
13 Ardilaun Road
Highbury
London N5 2QR, UNITED KINGDOM
(UK)

Hillsong (Musician)
c/o Staff Member *Integrity Music*
1000 Cody Rd.
Mobile, AL 36695, USA

Hillton, Dave (Athlete, Baseball Player)
4910 E Sunnyside Dr
Scottsdale, AZ 85254, USA

Hill-Westerman, Joyce (Baseball Player)
1565 47th Ave
Kenosha, WI 53144-1289, USA

Hilmers, David C (Astronaut)
2846 Bellefontaine St
Houston, TX 77025-1610, USA

Hilmers, David C Colonel (Astronaut)
2846 Bellefontaine St
Houston, TX 77025-1610, USA

Hilmes, Jerome B (General)
4900 Windsor Park
Sarasota, FL 34235, USA

Hilson, Keri (Musician)
c/o Dana Sims *ICM Partners (ICM-LA)*
10250 Constellation Blvd Fl 7
Los Angeles, CA 90067, USA

Hil St Soul (Music Group)
c/o Staff Member *Paradigm (Monterey)*
404 W Franklin St
Monterey, CA 93940, USA

Hilten, Heinz (Scientist)
2815 Carl T Jones Dr SE Apt 308
Huntsville, AL 35802-1262, USA

Hilton, Barron (Business Person,
Philanthropist)
Hilton Hotels Corp
9336 Civic Center Dr
Beverly Hills, CA 90210, USA

Hilton, Dave (Athlete, Baseball Player)
4910 E Sunnyside Dr
Scottsdale, AZ 85254-4671, USA

Hilton, Fred (Athlete, Basketball Player)
6169 Mourning Dove Dr
Baton Rouge, LA 70817-1107, USA

Hilton, Janet (Music Group, Musician)
Holly House E Downs Road
Bowdon Altrincham
Cheshire WA14 2LH, UNITED
KINGDOM (UK)

Hilton, John J (Athlete, Football Player)
3911 S Fairway Dr
Powhatan, VA 23139, USA

Hilton, Kathy
c/o Catherine Saxton *The Saxton Group*
535 Fifth Ave
19th Floor
New York, NY 10017, USA

Hilton, Nicky (Designer, Heir/Heiress)
Nicky Hilton Worldwide
7521 Melrose Ave
Los Angeles, CA 90046, USA

Hilton, Paris (Heir/Heiress, Reality TV
Star)
c/o Jamie Freed *Paris Hilton Entertainment*
2934 1/2 Beverly Glen Cir
Suite 383
Bel Air, CA 90077, USA

Hilton, Perez (Entertainer, Writer)
c/o Ben Russo *EMC / Bowery*
8145 Santa Monica Blvd
Suite 200
West Hollywood, CA 90046, USA

Hilton, Rick (Business Person)
Hilton & Hyland
250 N Canon Dr
Beverly Hills, CA 90210, USA

Hilton, Roy (Athlete, Football Player)
8332 Merrymount Dr
Baltimore, MD 21244, USA

Hilton, Tyler (Actor)
c/o Victoria Blake *Victoria Blake
Management*
23622 Calabasas Road
Suite 230
Calabasas, CA 91302, USA

Hilty, Megan (Actor)
c/o Erica Tuchman *One Entertainment
(NY)*
12 W 57th St
Penthouse
New York, NY 10019, USA

Hiltz, Nichole (Actor)
c/o Steve Caserta *Sanders Armstrong
Caserta*
2120 Colorado Blvd
Suite 120
Santa Monica, CA 90404, USA

Hiltzik, Michael A (Journalist)
Los Angeles Times
Editorial Dept
202 W 1st
Los Angeles, CA 90012, USA

Hilworth, John (Athlete, Hockey Player)
11084 State Road 37 E
New Haven, IN 46774-9770, USA

HIM (Music Group, Musician)
c/o Tim Edwards *Flowerbooking*
1532 N Milwaukee Ave
Suite 201
Chicago, IL 60622, USA

Himelstein, Aaron (Actor)
c/o Paul Brown *New Wave Entertainment
(LA)*
2660 W Olive Blvd
Burbank, CA 91505, USA

Himes, Dick (Athlete, Football Player)
431 Prairie Ln
Luxemburg, WI 54217, USA

Himes, James (Congressman, Politician)
119 Cannon HOB
Washington, DC 20515, USA

Himes, Larry (Commentator)
6516 W Montego Ln
Glendale, AZ 85306-3144, USA

Himmelfarb, Gertrude (Historian)
2510 Virginia Ave NW
Washington, DC 20037, USA

Himmelman, Peter (Composer, Musician)
230 22nd. Street
Brentwood, California 94513, USA

Hinault, Bernard (Athlete)
Les Poteries
Quessoy
Yffiniac F-22120, France

Hincapie, George (Athlete, Cycler,
Olympic Athlete)
11 Bella Citta Ct
Greenville, SC 29609-2724, USA

Hinch, A J (Athlete, Baseball Player,
Olympic Athlete)
841S Avenida De Las Ondas
La Jolla, CA 92037-3026, USA

Hinch, AJ (Athlete, Baseball Player)
8415 Avenida De Las Ondas
La Jolla, CA 92037-3026, USA

Hinchliffe, Brett (Athlete, Baseball Player)
5117 Melbourne St Unit 4204
Punta Gorda, FL 33980-3034, USA

Hinckley, Mike (Athlete, Baseball Player)
525 Allison Ln
Moore, OK 73160-0006, USA

Hinckley Jr, John (Misc)
St. Elizabeths Hospital
1100 Alabama Ave SE
Washington, DC 20005, USA

Hinder (Music Group)
Universal Motown Records
1755 Broadway
New York, NY 10019, USA

Hindi, Dion (Race Car Driver)
Hindi Motorsports
1421 Wagon Train
Albueuerque, NM 87123, USA

Hindle, Art (Actor)
Buzz Halliday & Assoc
8899 Beverly Blvd #715
Los Angeles, CA 90048, USA

Hindman, Stan (Athlete, Football Player)
824 Creed Rd
Okaland, CA 94610, USA

Hindmarch, Dave (Athlete, Hockey
Player)
3341 Beach Ave
Roberts Creek, BCq V0N 2W2, Canada

Hinds, Aisha (Actor)
c/o Michael Greene *Greene & Associates*
1901 Avenue Of The Stars Ste 130
Los Angeles, CA 90067, USA

Hinds, Ciaran (Actor)
c/o Larry Dalzell *Dalzell & Beresford Ltd*
26 Astwood Mews
London SW7 4DE, UNITED KINGDOM
(UK)

Hinds, Cirian (Actor)
c/o Staff Member *WME (LA)*
9601 Wilshire Blvd Fl 3
Beverly Hills, CA 90210, USA

Hinds, Sam (Athlete, Baseball Player)
2151 Sunnyside Ave
Apt 132
Clovis, CA 93611, USA

Hinds, Samuel A A (Prime Minister)
Prime Minister's Office
Public Buildings
Georgetown, GUYANA

Hinds, William (Cartoonist)
1301 Spring Oaks Circle
Houston, TX 77055-4703, USA

Hine, Maynard K (Doctor)
1121 W Michigan St
Indianapolis, IN 46202, USA

Hine, Patrick (General)
Lloyds Bank 7 Pall Mall Cox and kings
Branch
London, England SWl 5NA, USA

Hine, Patrick (Misc)
Lloyd's Bank
Cox's & Kings
7 Pall Mall
London SW1 5NA, UNITED KINGDOM
(UK)

Hiner, Glen H (Business Person)
Owens-Coming
1 Owens Coming Parkway
Toledo, OH 43659, USA

Hines, Andre (Athlete, Football Player)
1906 North 44th St
Kansas City, KS 66102, USA

Hines, Ben (Athlete, Baseball Player)
2709 2nd St
La Verne, CA 91750-5006, USA

Hines, Bruce (Athlete, Baseball Player)
4155 E Fairfield St
Mesa, AZ 85205-5008, USA

Hines, Byron (Race Car Driver)
14010 Marquard
Santa Fe Springs, CA 90670, USA

Hines, Cheryl (Actor)
c/o Paul Young *Principato/Young
Management*
9465 Wilshire Blvd
Suite 430
Beverly Hills, CA 90212, USA

Hines, Clint (Race Car Driver)
Hines Racing
8324 -140th St. W
Taylor Ridge, IL 61284, USA

Hines, Deni (Music Group)
Peter Rix Mgmt
49 Hume St #200
Crows Nest, NSW 2065, AUSTRALIA

Hines, Glen Ray (Athlete, Football Player)
861 N Queen Annes Lace Dr
Fayetteville, AR 72704-5106, USA

Hines, Grainger (Actor, Producer)
c/o Staff Member *Austingrai Productions*
11747 Sunset Blvd
Suite 128
Los Angeles, CA 90049, USA

Hines, Mimi (Actor)
2540 S Maryland Pkwy
Las Vegas, NV 89109-1627

Hingis, Martina (Athlete, Tennis Player)
Inselweg 28
Hurden CH-8640, Switzerland

Hingorani, Narain G (Engineer)
1286 Lexington Lane
Lake Zurich, IL 60047, USA

Hings, Donald L (Inventor)
281 Howard Ave
North Burnaby, BC V5B 4Y7, CANADA

Hingsen, Jurgen (Athlete, Track Athlete)
655 Circle Dr
Santa Barbara, CA 93108, USA

Hinkle, Lon (Athlete, Golfer)
P.O. Box 1347
Bigfork, MT 59911-1347, USA

Hinkle, Marin (Actor)
c/o Staff Member *Innovative Artists (LA)*
1505 10th St
Santa Monica, CA 90401, USA

Hinkle, Robert (Actor)
389 Old Wagon Rd
Royse City, TX 75189, USA

Hinkley, Brent (Actor)
c/o Staff Member *Gage Group, The (LA)*
14724 Ventura Blvd
Suite 505
Sherman Oaks, CA 91403, USA

Hinman, Dayle (Misc)
c/o Staff Member *Story House
Productions, Inc*
2233 Wisconsin Ave NW #420
Washington, DC 20007, USA

Hinn, Benny (Religious Leader)
PO Box 162000
Irving, TX 75016-2000, USA

Hinnant, Michael (Athlete, Football Player)
43 Ashford Way
Schwenksville, PA 19473, USA

Hinners, Noel (Government Official)
7 Greyswood Court
Rockville, MD 20854, USA

Hinners, Noel (Scientist)
42 Mule Deer Trl
Littleton, CO 80127-5789, USA

Hinojosa, Ricardo H (Judge)
US District Court
PO Box 5007
McAllen, TX 78502, USA

Hinojosa, Ruben (Congressman, Politician)
2262 Rayburn HOB
Washington, DC 20515, USA

Hinojosa, Tish (Music Group, Songwriter, Writer)
PO Box 3304
Austin, TX 78764, USA

Hinote, Dan (Athlete, Hockey Player)
Columbus Blue Jackets 200 W
Nationwide Blvd Unit 1
Columbus, OH 43215-2564, USA

Hinrich, Kirk (Basketball Player)
c/o Staff Member *Chicago Bulls*
1901 W Madision St
Chicago, IL 60612, USA

Hinrichs, Paul (Athlete, Baseball Player)
1982 Brett Dr
Madisonville, KY 42431-9115, USA

Hinse, Andre (Athlete, Hockey Player)
PO Box 237
Fort Cobb, OK 73038-0237, USA

Hinshaw, Alex (Athlete, Baseball Player)
3367 Yankton Ave
Claremont, CA 91711-2004, USA

Hinshaw, George (Athlete, Baseball Player)
15125 S Raymond Ave
Apt 14
Gardena, CA 90247-3433, USA

Hinske, Eric (Athlete, Baseball Player)
9460 E Sierra Pinta Dr
Scottsdale, AZ 85255-9196, USA

Hinsley, Jerry (Athlete, Baseball Player)
4255 Holliday Ln
Las Cruces, NM 88007-5760, USA

Hinson, Jordan (Actor)
c/o Bonnie Liedtke *Principato/Young Management*
9465 Wilshire Blvd
Suite 430
Beverly Hills, CA 90212, USA

Hinson, Larry (Athlete, Golfer)
Route 4 Box 397
Douglas, GA 31533, USA

Hinson, Roy (Athlete, Basketball Player)
4272 State Highway 27
Monmouth Junction, NJ 08852, USA

Hinson, Roy (Athlete, Basketball Player)
8167 Quail Meadow Way
West Palm Beach, FL 33412-1506, USA

Hinterseer, Ernst (Skier)
Hahnenkammstr
Kitzbuhel 6370, AUSTRIA

Hinterseer, Hans (Hansi) (Athlete, Musician, Skier)
Charlet-Sonnenhofweg 16
Kitzbuhel A-6370, Austria

Hintikka, Jaakko J (Misc)
University of Helsinki
PO Box 24
Helsinki 00014, FINLAND

Hinton, Charles R (Athlete, Football Player)
124 Tanglewood Rd
Natchez, MS 39120, USA

Hinton, Chris (Athlete, Football Player)
650 Galway Dr
Roswell, GA 30076, USA

Hinton, Christopher J (Chris) (Athlete, Football Player)
5136 Falcon Chase Ln
Atlanta, GA 30342, USA

Hinton, Chuck (Athlete, Baseball Player)
6330 16th St NW
Washington, DC 20011-8010, USA

Hinton, Chuck (Athlete, Football Player)
124 Tanglewood Rd
Natchez, MS 39120-4526, USA

Hinton, Darby (Actor)
1267 Bel Air Road
Los Angeles, CA 90077, USA

Hinton, Eddie (Athlete, Football Player)
34 Auburn Rdg
Spring Branch, TX 78070, USA

Hinton, James David (Actor)
c/o Staff Member *Cunningham Escott Slevin & Doherty (CESD-LA)*
10635 Santa Monica Blvd
130
Los Angeles, CA 90025, USA

Hinton, Jill (Athlete, Golfer)
8976 SW 44th Ln
Gainesville, FL 32608, USA

Hinton, Marcus (Athlete, Football Player)
63 Farrell Breland Rd
Wiggins, MS 39577-9119, USA

Hinton, Rich (Athlete, Baseball Player)
7447 Hawkins Rd
Sarasota, FL 34241-9376, USA

Hinton, Sam (Musician, Songwriter)
1719 Addison St
Berkeley, CA 94703-1501, USA

Hinton, S E
8955 Beverly Blvd
Los Angeles, CA 90048, USA

Hinton of Bankside, Christopher (Engineer, Government Official)
Tiverton Lodge
Dulwich Common
London SG2 7EW, UNITED KINGDOM (UK)

Hintz, Donald C (Business Person)
Entergy Corp
10055 Grogans Mill Road #5A
The Woodlands, TX 77380, USA

Hinzo, Tommy (Athlete, Baseball Player)
635 Imperial Beach Blvd
Imperial Beach, CA 91932-2720, USA

Hiort, Esbjonm (Architect)
Bel Colles Farm
Parkvej 6
Rungsted Kyst 2960, DENMARK

Hipp, I M (Athlete, Football Player)
1216 Hickman Arch
Virginia Beach, VA 23454-5878, USA

Hipp, Paul (Actor)
c/o Staff Member *Stone Manners Salners Agency (LA)*
9911 W Pico Blvd Ste 1400
Los Angeles, CA 90035, USA

Hipple, Eric (Athlete, Football Player)
7155 Driftwood Dr
Fenton, MI 48430, USA

Hipps, Claude (Athlete, Football Player)
1535 Dartmouth Rd
Columbus, GA 31904, USA

Hipwell, Elizabeth
18 Gramercy Park So
New York, NY 10003-1724

Hirase, Mayumi (Athlete, Golfer)
I M G
1360 E 9th St
Ste 100
Cleveland, OH 44114-1730, USA

Hirata-Chalfin, Gail (Athlete, Golfer)
15539 Quiet Oak Dr
Chino Hills, CA 91709, USA

Hire, Kathryn P Cdr (Astronaut)
PO Box 580146
Houston, TX 77258-0146, USA

Hire, Kathryn P (Kay) (Astronaut)
PO Box 580146
Houston, TX 77258, USA

Hiroshima
1460 4th St. #205
Santa Monica, CA 90401

Hirosue, Ryoyo (Actor)
c/o Omiotek Maciej *OmniotComp*
Sowinskiego 27A
Grodzisk
Mazowiecki, POLAND

Hirsch, Corey (Athlete, Hockey Player)
c/o Staff Member *Hockey Canada*
2424 University Dr NW
Calgary, AB T2N 3Y9, Canada

Hirsch, David
6255 Sunset Blvd. #627
Los Angeles, CA 90028

Hirsch, E D Jr (Educator)
University of Virginia
Education Dept
Charlottesville, VA 22906, USA

Hirsch, Emile (Actor)
c/o Sam Maydew *Collective*
8383 Wilshire Blvd
Suite 1050
Beverly Hills, CA 90211, USA

Hirsch, Hallee (Actor, Musician)
c/o Amy Abell *Glick Agency*
1505 10th St
Santa Monica, CA 90401, USA

Hirsch, Judd (Actor)
c/o Joel Rudnick *Paradigm (LA)*
360 N Crescent Dr
North Bldg
Beverly Hills, CA 90210, USA

Hirsch, Laurence E (Business Person)
Centex Corp
2728 N Harwood
Dallas, TX 75201, USA

Hirsch, Lee (Director)
c/o Mark Ross *Paradigm (LA)*
360 N Crescent Dr
North Bldg
Beverly Hills, CA 90210, USA

Hirsch, Leon C (Inventor)
150 Glover Ave
Norwalk, CT 06850, USA

Hirsch, Robert P (Actor)
1 Pl du Palais Bourbon
Paris 75007, FRANCE

Hirsch, Stan
16027 Ventura Blvd. #206
Encino, CA 91436-2733

Hirsch, Tom (Athlete, Hockey Player)
8469 Zanzibar Ln N
Osseo, MN 55311-1814, USA

Hirschbeck, John (Baseball Player)
8730 Raintree Run
Youngstown, OH 44514-2987, USA

Hirschbeck, John (Athlete, Baseball Player)
8730 Raintree Run
Youngstown, OH 44514, USA

Hirschbeck, Mark (Baseball Player)
15 Blackberry Ln
Shelton, CT 06484-3774, USA

Hirschbeck, Mark (Athlete, Baseball Player)
15 Blackberry Ln
Shelton, CT 06484, USA

Hirschbein, Jonathan (Writer)
c/o Melissa Breaux *Washington Square Arts (LA)*
1041 N Formosa Ave
The Lot Writers Bldg, Room 305
West Hollywood, CA 90046, USA

Hirschbiegel, Oliver (Director)
c/o Tobin Babst *Kaplan/Perrone Entertainment*
9560 Wilshire Blvd Fl 5
Beverly Hills, CA 90212, USA

Hirscher, Marcel (Athlete, Skier)
Atomic GMBH
Lackengasse 301
Altenmarkt A-5541, Austria

Hirschfeld, Marie (Stylist)
330 Sir Walter Dr
Cheshire, CT 06410, USA

Hirschfelder, David (Composer)
APRA
PO Box 567
Crows Nest, NSW 2065, Australia

Hirschfielder, Gerald J (Cinematographer)
425 Ashland St
Ashland, OR 97520, USA

Hirschmann, Ralph F (Misc)
711 Radcliffe Court
Lansdale, PA 19446-5895, USA

Hirson, Alice (Actor)
Halpem Assoc
PO Box 5597
Santa Monica, CA 90409, USA

Hirst, Damien (Artist)
White Cube Gallery
Saint James's
44 Duke St
London SW1Y 6DD, UNITED KINGDOM (UK)

Hirtz, Dagmar
Jollystr. 14
Munich, GERMANY D-81545

Hirzebruch, Friedrich E P
(Mathematician)
Thuringer Allee 127
Saint Augustin 53757, GERMANY

Hisaishi, Joe (Composer, Musician)
c/o Staff Member *Greenspan Artist Management*
8760 W Sunset Blvd
West Hollywood, CA 90069, USA

Hiser, Gene (Athlete, Baseball Player)
1450 Caldwell Ln
Hoffman Estates, IL 60169-1202, USA

Hiskey, Babe (Athlete, Golfer)
1706 12th St
Galena Park, TX 77547-2302, USA

Hisle, Larry E (Athlete, Baseball Player)
2404A N 23rd St
Sheboygan, WI 53083-4447, USA

Hislop, Ian (Actor)
c/o Jenne Casarotto *Casarotto Ramsay & Associates Ltd (UK)*
Waverley House
7-12 Noel St
London W1F 8GQ, UK

Hislop, Jamie (Athlete, Hockey Player)
10852 Mapleshire Cres SE
Calgary, AB T2J 1Y9, Canada

Hisner, Harley (Athlete, Baseball Player)
14322 Monroeville Rd
Monroeville, IN 46773-9555, USA

Hitchcock, Jimmy (Athlete, Football Player)
616 Briar Patch Ter
Waxhaw, NC 28173-6822, USA

Hitchcock, Ken (Athlete, Hockey Player)
St Louis Blues 1401 Clark Ave Attn Coaching Staff
Saint Louis, MO 63103-2700, USA

Hitchcock, Michael (Actor)
c/o Staff Member *Gersh (LA)*
9465 Wilshire Blvd
Suite 600
Beverly Hills, CA 90212, USA

Hitchcock, Ray (Athlete, Football Player)
2190 Arcade St
Saint Paul, MN 55109, USA

Hitchcock, Robyn (Musician, Songwriter)
c/o Amanda Howard *Amanda Howard Associates*
21 Berwick St
London W1F 0PZ, UNITED KINGDOM (UK)

Hitchcock, Russell (Musician)
Agency for Performing Arts
9200 Sunset Blvd #900
Los Angeles, CA 90069, USA

Hitchcock, Sterling (Athlete, Baseball Player)
255 Yucca Rd
Naples, FL 34102-5318, USA

Hitchins, Christopher
2022 Columbia Rd. NW
Washington, DC 20009

Hite, Robert (General)
18 Annandale
Nashville, TN 37215-5818, USA

Hite, Shere (Writer)
75 Haywood St Apt 312
Asheville, NY 28801-2841, USA

Hite-James, Kathy (Athlete, Golfer)
38651 Nyasa Dr
Palm Desert, CA 92211, USA

Hitt, Joel (Athlete, Football Player)
800 Founders Pointe Blvd
Franklin, TN 37064, USA

Hitt, John C (Educator)
1000 Central Florida Blvd
Orlando, FL 32826, USA

Hitt, Lee (Athlete, Football Player)
4318 N Hall St
Dallas, TX 75219-2731, USA

Hitzges, Jennifer (Stylist)
c/o Staff Member *Jed Root Inc*
61-A Walker St
New York, NY 10013, USA

Hix, William (Athlete, Football Player)
5070 White Dr
Batesville, AR 72501, USA

Hjejle, Iben (Actor, Writer)
c/o Staff Member *Kasper Notlev*
Gl. Kongevej 86A 3.Th
Frederiksberg C1850, Denmark

Hjertstedt, Gabriel (Athlete, Golfer)
100 Sawgrass Corners Dr
Ponte Verde Beach, FL 32082, USA

Hjorth, Maria (Athlete, Golfer)
608 Henley Cir
Davenport, FL 33896, USA

Hlass, I Jerry (Engineer)
National Space Technology Laboratories
NSTL Station, MS 39529, USA

Hlavac, Jan (Athlete, Hockey Player)
1033 Royal Pass Road
Tampa, FL 33602-5724, USA

Hlushko, Todd (Athlete, Hockey Player)
16 Elderberry Crt
Guelph, ON N1L 1K3, Canada

H. Michaud, Michael (Congressman, Politician)
1724 Longworth HOB
Washington, DC 20515, USA

Hnatiuk, Glen (Athlete, Golfer)
8746 Mississippi Run
Weeki Wachee, FL 34613, USA

Hnidy, Shane (Athlete, Hockey Player)
3 Iris
Irvine, CA 92620, USA

Hnidy, Shane
Winnipeg Jets 300 Portage Ave
Attn: Broadcast Dept
Winnipeg, MB R3C 5S4, Canada

Hnilicka, Milan (Athlete, Hockey Player)
1111 S Figueroa St
Los Angeles, CA 90015, USA

Ho, David (Scientist)
A Diamond Aids Research Center 445 1st Ave
New York, NY 10016, USA

Ho, David (Scientist)
Aaron Diamond AIDS Research Center
455 1st Ave
New York, NY 10016, USA

Ho, Don
PO Box 90039
Honolulu, HI 96825-0039

Ho, Donald T (Don) (Music Group)
277 Lewers St
Honolulu, HI 96815, USA

Ho, Tao (Architect)
Upper Deck North Point West
Passenger Ferry Pier
North Point, HONG KONG

Hoag, Jan
855 N. Martel Ave.
Los Angeles, CA 90046

Hoag, Judith W (Actor)
HWA Talent
3500 W Olive Ave
#1400
Burbank, CA 91505, USA

Hoag, Peter C (Misc)
3566 Little Rock Dr
Provo, UT 84604, USA

Hoag, Tami (Writer)
Delacorte Press
1540 Broadway
New York, NY 10036, USA

Hoage, Terrell L (Terry) (Athlete, Football Player)
870 Arbor Rd
Paso Robles, CA 93446, USA

Hoagland, Ashley (Athlete, Golfer)
803 26th Ave W
Palmetto, FL 34221, USA

Hoagland, Edward (Writer)
P.O. Box 51
Barton, VT 05822-0051, USA

Hoagland, Jimmie L (Jim) (Journalist)
Washington Post
Editorial Dept
1150 15th St NW
Washington, DC 20071, USA

Hoaglin, Fred (Athlete, Coach, Football Coach, Football Player)
7 Governors Rd
Hilton Head, SC 29928, USA

Hoak, Dick (Athlete, Football Player)
162 Crest View Dr
Greensburg, PA 15601, USA

Hoar, Joseph P (General)
386 13th St
Del Mar, CA 92014, USA

Hoard, Leroy (Athlete, Football Player)
13141 NW 8th Ct
Sunrise, FL 33325-1326, USA

Hoare, C Antony R (Engineer)
Oxford University
Computing Lab
Parks Road
Oxford OX1 3QD, UNITED KINGDOM (UK)

Hoare, Sarajane (Stylist)
c/o Staff Member *Vernon Jolly Inc*
180 Varick St
#912
New York, NY 10014, USA

Hoare, Tony
430 Edgware Rd
London, ENGLAND W2 1EG

Hoban, Mike (Athlete, Football Player)
1917 Holly Ave
Darien, IL 60561, USA

Hoban, Russell C (Writer)
6 Musgrave Crescent
London SW6 4PT, UNITED KINGDOM (UK)

Hobart, Ken (Athlete, Football Player)
531 18th Ave
Lewiston, ID 83501-3823

Hobart, Nick (Cartoonist)
5632 Indiana Ave
New Port Richey, FL 34652, USA

Hobaugh, Charles 0 Lt Colonel (Astronaut)
2009 Charter Pointe Ct
League City, TX 77573-9021, USA

Hobaugh, Charles O (Astronaut)
NASA
Johnson Space Center
2101 NASA Road
Houston, TX 77058, USA

Hobaugh, Ed (Athlete, Baseball Player)
1420 3rd Ave
Ford City, PA 16226-1303, USA

Hobault, John (Scientist)
15 Piper Rd Apt K301
Scarborough, ME 04074-7560, USA

Hobbie, Glen (Athlete, Baseball Player)
RR2 Box 234A
Ramsey, IL 62080-9398, USA

Hobbs, Becky (Musician)
Entertainment Artists
2409 21st Ave S
#100
Nashville, TN 37212, USA

Hobbs, Chelsea (Actor)
c/o Sam Maydew *Collective*
8383 Wilshire Blvd
Suite 1050
Beverly Hills, CA 90211, USA

Hobbs, Ellis (Athlete, Football Player)
8885 Old Southwick Pass
Alpharetta, GA 30022-7137, USA

Hobbs, Franklin (Fritz) (Misc)
151 E 79th St
New York, NY 10021, USA

Hobbs, Jack (Athlete, Baseball Player)
3 Wade Dr
Cherry Hill, NJ 08034-1741, USA

Hobbs, Rebecca (Actor)
c/o Kathryn Rawlings *Kathryn Rawlings Actors Agency*
4/28 Williamson Ave.
Grey Lynn
Auckland, New Zealand

Hobby, Marion (Athlete, Football Player)
708 Nytol Cir
Birmingham, AL 35210, USA

Hobel, Mara (Actor)
17 Cunningham Dr
Lagrangeville, NY 12540, USA

Hobgood, CJ (Athlete)
c/o Steven Astephen *Wasserman Media Group - Carlsbad*
2052 Corte Del Nogal
150
Carlsbad, CA 92001, USA

Hobin, Mike
176 Childs Rd
Basking Ridge, NJ 07920-3326

Hoblit, Gregory (Director, Producer)
c/o JC Spink *Benderspink*
5870 W Jefferson Blvd
Studio E
Los Angeles, CA 90016, USA

Hobson, Clell L (Butch) (Athlete, Baseball Player)
6302 Catarata St
Bakersfield, CA 93311-9638, USA

Hobson, J Allan (Scientist)
Harvard University
Sleep Laboratory
Cambridge, MA 02138, USA

Hobson, Jeff (Misc)
Jack Grenier Productions
32630 Concord Dr
Madison Heights, MI 48071, USA

Hobson, Mellody (Producer)
c/o Staff Member *DreamWorks SKG*
1000 Flower St
Glendale, CA 91201, USA

Hoch, Carin (Athlete, Golfer)
I M G
1360 E 9th Ste 100
Cleveland, OH 44114-1730, USA

Hoch, Danny (Artist)
c/o Staff Member *Gersh (LA)*
9465 Wilshire Blvd
Suite 600
Beverly Hills, CA 90212, USA

Hoch, Greg (Horse Racer)
18 Summer Wind Loop
Murrells Inlet, SC 29576-5690, USA

Hoch, Scott (Athlete, Golfer)
8800 Lake Sheen Ct
Orlando, FL 32836-5482, USA

Hochevar, Luke (Athlete, Baseball Player)
2452 Glen Meadow Rd
Knoxville, TN 37909-1092, USA

Hochhuth, Rolf (Writer)
PO Box 661
Basel 4002, SWITZERLAND

Hochstein, Russ (Athlete, Football Player)
6618 Green River Dr Unit E
Highlands Ranch, CO 80130-6742, USA

Hochstrasser, Robin M (Misc)
University of Pennsylvania
Chemistry Dept
Philadelphia, PA 19104, USA

Hochwald, Bari (Actor)
Tuscan Film Commission
Via San Gallo, 25
Florence 50129, Italy

Hock, Dee Ward (Business Person)
Visa International
900 Metro Center Blvd
Foster City, CA 94404, USA

Hocke, Stefan (Skier)
Sportgymnasium
Am Harzwald 3
Oberhof 98558, GERMANY

Hockenberry, Chuck (Athlete, Baseball Player)
1546 Birka Ln
Onalaska, WI 54650, USA

Hockenberry, John (Actor, Correspondent, Writer)
c/o Sally Willcox *Creative Artists Agency (CAA-LA)*
2000 Ave Of The Stars
Los Angeles, CA 90067, USA

Hockenbery, Chuck (Athlete, Baseball Player)
1546 Birka Ln
Onalaska, WI 54650-2087, USA

Hocking, Dennis (Athlete, Baseball Player)
2592 N Falconer Way
Orange, CA 92867, USA

Hocking, Denny (Athlete, Baseball Player)
7384 E Villanueva Dr
Orange, CA 92867-6440, USA

Hocking, Justin (Athlete, Hockey Player)
3726 E 52nd Ct
Spokane, WA 99223, USA

Hockney, David (Artist)
7508 Santa Monica Blvd
Los Angeles, CA 90046, USA

Hocott, Brenda (Athlete, Golfer)
261 Cave Ln
San Antonio, TX 78209, USA

Hodder, Kane (Actor)
3701 Senda Calma
Calabasas, CA 91302, USA

Hodder, Kenneth (Religious Leader)
Salvation Army
615 Slaters Lane
Alexandria, VA 22314, USA

Hoddick, Steve (Race Car Driver)
782 Aero Dr.
Cheektowaga, NY 14225, USA

Hoddinott, Alun (Composer)
64 Gowerton Road
Three Crosses
Swansea SA4 3PX, WALES

Hoddle, Glenn (Soccer Player)
Football Assn
16 Lancaster Gate
London W2 3LW, UNITED KINGDOM (UK)

Hodel, Donald (Politician)
2200 Simms Pl
Lakewood, CO 80215-1183, USA

Hodel, Donald P (Secretary)
1801 Sara Dr
#L
Chesapeake, VA 23320, USA

Hodel, Nathan (Athlete, Football Player)
19197 W Fairview Dr
Mundelein, IL 60060-3497, USA

Hodge, Aldis (Actor)
c/o Matt Luber *Luber Roklin Management*
8530 Wilshire Blvd
6th Floor
Beverly Hills, CA 90211, USA

Hodge, Charles E (Charlie) (Athlete, Hockey Player)
27111 25a Ave
Aldergrove, BC V4W 3N4, Canada

Hodge, Daniel A (Dan) (Wrestler)
General Delivery
Perry, OK 73077, USA

hodge, donald
901 Lawrence St NE
Washington, DC 20017-3520, USA

Hodge, Douglas (Actor)
c/o Lindy King *United Agents*
12-26 Lexington St
London W1F OLE, UK

Hodge, Ed (Athlete, Baseball Player)
127 Jewell St
Johnson City, TN 37601-5209, USA

Hodge, Edwin (Actor)
c/o Matt Luber *Luber Roklin Management*
8530 Wilshire Blvd
6th Floor
Beverly Hills, CA 90211, USA

Hodge, John (Scientist)
1951 Sagewood Ln Af>!_l23
Reston, VA 20191-5411, USA

Hodge, Patricia (Actor)
International Creative Mgmt
76 Oxford St
London W1N 0AX, UNITED KINGDOM (UK)

Hodge, Sedrick (Athlete, Football Player)
120 Victoria Pl
Fayetteville, GA 30214, USA

Hodge, Stephanie (Actor)
Gersh Agency
232 N Canon Dr
Beverly Hills, CA 90210, USA

Hodge, Sue
82 Constance Rd. Twickenham
Middlesex A, ENGLAND TW2 7J

Hodge Jr, Kenneth R (Ken) (Athlete, Hockey Player)
1115 Main St
Lynnfield, MA 01940, USA

Hodges, Bill (Basketball Player, Coach)
Georgia College
Athletic Dept
Milledgeville, GA 31061, USA

Hodges, Bob (Athlete, Hockey Player)
43 Karch St
Cambridge, ON N3C 1Y4, Canada

Hodges, Craig (Athlete, Basketball Player)
67 Elm St
Park Forest, IL 60466-1702, USA

Hodges, Eric (Actor)
3800 West Alameda Ave
Burbank, CA 91505

Hodges, Jean (Stylist)
Showgrits
Prefers to be contacted
via telephone or email
Burbank, CA 91501, USA

Hodges, Kevin (Athlete, Baseball Player)
19506 Kuykendahl Rd
Spring, TX 77379-3408, USA

Hodges, Louise
31A St. George's Rd Leyton
London, ENGLAND E1O 5RH

Hodges, Mike (Director)
Wesley Farm Durweston
Blanford Forum
Dorset DT11 0QG, UNITED KINGDOM (UK)

Hodges, Morris (Athlete, Baseball Player)
1520 River Haven Ln
Birmingham, AL 35080-3287, USA

Hodges, Morris (Athlete, Baseball Player)
404 Park Lake Ter
Helena, AL 35080, USA

Hodges, Pat (Actor, Musician)
c/o Staff Member *Diva Central Inc*
7510 W Sunset Blvd Ste 1445
Los Angees, CA 90046, USA

Hodges, Ron (Athlete, Baseball Player)
55 Hajo Ln
Rocky Mount, VA 24151-6819, USA

Hodges, Trey (Athlete, Baseball Player)
19506 Kuykendahl Rd
Spring, TX 77379-3408, USA

Hodge Sr, Ken (Athlete, Hockey Player)
13 Longfellow Dr
Newburyport, MA 01950-3325, USA

Hodgkin, Howard (Artist)
Anthony D'Offay Gallery
9/24 Dering St
London W1R 9AA, UNITED KINGDOM (UK)

Hodgman, John (Actor)
c/o Jay Gassner *United Talent Agency (UTA)*
9336 Civic Center Dr
Beverly Hills, CA 90210, USA

Hodgson, James D (Politician)
28802 Grayfox St
Malibu, CA 90265-4253, USA

Hodgson, James D (Secretary)
10132 Hillgrove Dr
Beverly Hills, CA 90210, USA

Hodgson, Pat (Athlete, Football Player)
816 Commons Park
Statham, GA 30666-2539, USA

Hodgson, Roger (Musician)
c/o Colin Lewis *Agency Group Ltd, The (Canada)*
2 Berkeley Street
Suite 202
Toronto M5A 4J5, Canada

Hodgson, Ted (Athlete, Hockey Player)
PO Box 162
Hobbema, AB TOC 1NO, Canada

Hodnett, Greg (Race Car Driver)
PO Box 34725
Bartlett, TN 38134, USA

Hodo, David (Music Group)
8255 Sunset Blvd
West Hollywood, CA 90046, USA

Hodson, Kevin (Athlete, Hockey Player)
390 McNabb St
Unit 2
Sault Sainte Marie, ON P6B 1, Canada

Hodson, Tom (Athlete, Football Player)
17938 Crossing Blvd
Baton Rouge, LA 70810, USA

Hoebel, Bret (Reality TV Star)
c/o Staff Member *Abrams Artists Agency (LA)*
9200 Sunset Blvd
11th Floor
Los Angeles, CA 90069, USA

Hoechlin, Tyler (Actor)
c/o Matt Luber *Luber Roklin Management*
8530 Wilshire Blvd
6th Floor
Beverly Hills, CA 90211, USA

Hoeft, Roberta (Stylist)
c/o Staff Member *Ford Models (Chicago)*
311 W Superior St
Chicago, IL 60654, USA

Hoegh, Leo (Politician)
1472 W Desert Hills Dr
Green Valley, AZ 85622-8287, USA

Hoekstra, Cecil (Athlete, Hockey Player)
303 St. Paul St W
St Catharines, ON L2S 2E8, Canada

Hoelscher, David (Athlete, Football Player)
8931 N Star Fort Loramie Rd
Yorkshire, OH 45388-9750, USA

Hoelscher, Joel (Athlete, Football Player)
8931 N Star Fort Loramine Rd
Yorkshire, OH 45388, USA

Hoelzer, Margaret (Athlete, Olympic Athlete, Swimmer)
4400 Wallingford Ave N
Apt 13
Seattle, WA 98103-7544, USA

Hoene, Ohil (Athlete, Hockey Player)
1110 Mississippi Ave
Duluth, MN 55811, USA

Hoene, Phil (Athlete, Hockey Player)
1110 Mississippi Ave
Duluth, MN 55811-4920, USA

Hoenig, Michael (Composer, Musician)
c/o Staff Member *Gorfaine/Schwartz Agency Inc*
4111 W Alameda Ave
Suite 509
Burbank, CA 91505, USA

Hoenig, Thomas M (Financier, Government Official)
615 W Meyer Blvd
Kansas City, MO 64113, USA

Hoernig, Otto W Lt Colonel
Spacelink International L L C 12930
Worldgate Dr Ste 700
Herndon, VA 20170-6036, USA

Hoernig, Otto W Lt Colonel (Astronaut)
Spacelink International L L C 12930
Worldgate Dr Ste 700
Herndon, VA 20170-6036, USA

Hoerr, Irv (Race Car Driver)
541 Division St.
Campbell, CA 95008, USA

Hoest, Bunny (Cartoonist)
William Hoest Enterprises
27 Watch Way
Lloyd Neck
Huntington, NY 11743-9707, USA

Hoeven, john (Politician)
PO Box 2572
Bismarck, ND 58502-2572, USA

Hoey, George (Athlete, Football Player)
13635 Clermont Ct
Thornton, CO 80602-6965, USA

Hoey, Jim (Athlete, Baseball Player)
2360 Highwav 33
Ste 207
Trenton, NJ 08691-1417, USA

Hofer, Paul (Athlete, Football Player)
7093 Cedardale Rd
Olive Branch, MS 38654-1307, USA

Hoff, Katie (Athlete, Olympic Athlete, Swimmer)
c/o Staff Member *USA Swimming Association*
1 Olympic Plz
Colorado Springs, CO 80909-5770, USA

Hoff, Marcian (Inventor)
26541 Taaffe Rd
Los Altos Hills, CA 94022-4313, USA

Hoff, Philip (Politician)
214 Prospect Pkwy
Burlington, VT 05401-4148, USA

Hoffa, James
2593 Hounds Chase Dr
Troy, MI 48098-2338, USA

Hoffa, James P (Misc)
2593 Hounds Chase Dr
Troy, MI 48098, USA

Hoffman, Al (Race Car Driver)
Al Hoffman Racing
17818 Willis McCall Rd.
Umatilla, FL 32784, USA

Hoffman, Alan J (Mathematician)
IBM Research Center
PO Box 218
Yorktown Heights, NY 10598, USA

Hoffman, Alice (Writer)
3 Hurlbut St
Cambridge, MA 02138-1603, USA

Hoffman, Alice (Writer)
3 Hurlbut St
Cambridge, MA 02138, USA

Hoffman, Barbara (Athlete, Baseball Player, Commentator)
318 E Mill St
Millstadt, IL 62260-1218, USA

Hoffman, Basil (Actor)
26 Aller Court
Glendale, CA 91206, USA

Hoffman, Darleane C (Physicist)
Lawrence Berkeley Laboratory
1 Cyctotron Road
Berkeley, CA 94720, USA

Hoffman, Dustin (Actor, Director, Producer)
c/o Kelly Bush *ID PR (LA)*
7060 Hollywood Blvd
8th Floor
Los Angeles, CA 90028, USA

Hoffman, Elizabeth (Actor)
Bauman Assoc
5750 Wilshire Blvd
#473
Los Angeles, CA 90036, USA

Hoffman, Elizabeth (Educator)
University of Colorado
President's Office
Boulder, CO 80309, USA

Hoffman, Glenn E (Athlete, Baseball Player)
201 S Old Bridge Rd
Anaheim, CA 92808-1326, USA

Hoffman, Guy (Athlete, Baseball Player)
313 Fairwav Dr Apt S
Bloomington, IL 61701-8219, USA

Hoffman, Ingrid (Chef, Television Host)
c/o Staff Member *Food Network, The*
1180 Ave of the Americas Fl 11
New York, NY 10036, USA

Hoffman, Jackie (Actor)
c/o Hannah Roth *Buchwald/Fortitude (LA)*
6500 Wilshire Blvd
Suite 2200
Los Angeles, CA 90048, USA

Hoffman, Jamie (Athlete, Baseball Player)
909 N Jefferson St
New Ulm, MN 56073-1433, USA

Hoffman, Jeffrey A (Astronaut)
US Embassy
2 Ave Gabriel
PSC 116/NASA
Paris Cedex 75382, FRANCE

Hoffman, Jeffrey A Dr (Astronaut)
10 Saint Charles St
Boston, MA 02116-6233, USA

Hoffman, John (Athlete, Football Player)
3303 E Kentucky Ave
Denver, CO 80209-4929, USA

Hoffman, John Robert (Writer)
c/o Rosalie Swedlin *Anonymous Content (LA)*
3531 Hayden Ave
Culver City, CA 90232, USA

Hoffman, Jorg (Swimmer)
Saarmunder Str 74
Potsdam 14478, GERMANY

Hoffman, Kara (Actor)
c/o Rod Baron *Baron Entertainment*
13848 Ventura Blvd
Suite A
Sherman Oaks, CA 91423-3654

Hoffman, Marguerite (Business Person, Philanthropist)
Dallas Museum of Art
1717 North Harwood
Dallas, Texas 75201, USA

Hoffman, Matt (Actor)
c/o Staff Member *Liberation Management*
1412 12th Ave
Los Angeles, CA 90019, USA

Hoffman, Michael (Director)
c/o Doug MacLaren *ICM Partners (ICM-LA)*
10250 Constellation Blvd Fl 7
Los Angeles, CA 90067, USA

Hoffman, Mim (Stylist)
c/o Staff Member *Arlene Wilson Management*
807 N Jefferson St
#200
Milwaukee, WI 53202, USA

Hoffman, Paul Felix (Geophysicist, Physicist)
162 Cypress St
Brookline, MA 02445, USA

Hoffman, Philip Seymour (Actor, Producer)
c/o Staff Member *Cooper's Town Productions*
302A West 12th St #214
New York, NY 10014, USA

Hoffman, Rick (Actor)
c/o Staff Member *Jeff Morrone Entertainment*
9350 Wilshire Blvd
Suite 224
Beverly Hills, CA 90212, USA

Hoffman, Robert (Actor, Dancer)
c/o Michael Baum *Impression Entertainment*
9229 W Sunset Blvd #700
West Hollywood, CA 90069, USA

Hoffman, Ted Jr (Bowler)
1568 Partarian Way
San Jose, CA 95129, USA

Hoffman, Toby (Music Group, Musician)
Columbia Artists Mgmt Inc
165 W 57th St
New York, NY 10019, USA

Hoffman, Trevor (Athlete, Baseball Player)
2220 Ocean Front
Del Mar, CA 92014-2134, USA

Hoffman, William M (Songwriter, Writer)
190 Prince St
New York, NY 10012, USA

Hoffmann, Christian (Skier)
Frunwald 7
Aigen 4160, AUSTRIA

Hoffmann, Frank N (Nordy) (Athlete, Football Player)
400 N Capitol St NW
Apt 327
Washington, DC 20001, USA

Hoffmann, Gaby
8942 Wilshire Blvd
Beverly Hills, CA 90211

Hoffmann, Isabella
6500 Wilshire Blvd. #2200
Los Angeles, CA 90048

Hoffmann, Jules (Nobel Prize Laureate)
Institut de Biologie Moleculaire et Cellulaire 15 rue Rene Descartes Attn: Molecular and Cellular Biology Institut
Strasbourg Cedex, France 67084, USA

Hoffmann, Roald (Nobel Prize Laureate)
4 Sugarbush Ln
Ithaca, NY 14850-6326, USA

Hoffmann, Roald (Nobel Prize Laureate)
4 Sugarbush Lane
Ithaca, NY 14850, USA

Hoffmeyer, Bob (Athlete, Hockey Player)
c/o Staff Member *New Jersey Devils*
Continental Arena
165 Mulberry St
Newark, NJ 07102-3611, USA

Hofford, Jim (Athlete, Hockey Player)
5 Vanderberg Dr
Fairport, NY 14450-8427, USA

Hoffort, Bruce (Athlete, Hockey Player)
N1778 Hyacinth Ln
Greenville, WI 54942-9005, USA

Hoffpauir, Jarrett (Athlete, Baseball Player)
2043 Viking St
Vidalia, LA 71373-3011, USA

Hoffpauir, Micah (Athlete, Baseball Player)
2105 Stanford St
Jacksonville, TX 75766-5246, USA

Hoffs, Susanna (Musician)
Bangles Mall
1341W Fullerton Ave
Box 180
Chicago, IL 60614, USA

Hofheimer, Charlie (Actor)
c/o Abby Bluestone *Innovative Artists (LA)*
1505 10th St
Santa Monica, CA 90401, USA

Hofmann, Al (Race Car Driver)
PO Box 346
Umatilla, FL 32784, USA

Hofmann, Detief (Athlete)
Saarlandstr 164
Karlsruhe 76187, GERMANY

Hofmann, Douglas (Artist)
8602 Saxon Circle
Baltimore, MD 21236, USA

Hofmann, Isabella (Actor)
Don Buchwald
6500 Wilshire Blvd #2200
Los Angeles, CA 90048, USA

Hofmann, Kenneth (Commentator)
Oakland A's
1380 Galaxy Way
Concord, CA 94520-4912, USA

Hofschneider, Marco (Actor)
Progressive Artists Agency
400 S Beverly Dr #216
Beverly Hills, CA 90212, USA

Hofstatter, Peter R (Doctor, Psychic)
Lehmkuhleweg 16
Buxtehude 21614, GERMANY

Hofstetter, Steve (Writer)
c/o David Krintzman *Morris, Yorn, Barnes, Levine, Krintzman, Rubenstein and Kohner*
2000 Ave of the Stars
3rd Floor, North Tower
Los Angeles, CA 90067, USA

Hogaboam, Bill (Athlete, Hockey Player)
1317 Mountainview St
Kelowna, BC V1Y 4M9, Canada

Hogan, Brooke (Musician, Reality TV Star)
Brookestar
130 Willadel Drive
Belleair, FL 33756, USA

Hogan, Chris (Actor)
c/o Staff Member *Rugolo Entertainment*
195 S Beverly Dr
Suite 400
Beverly Hills, CA 90212, USA

Hogan, Chuck (Writer)
c/o Richard Abate *3 Arts Entertainment - NY*
49 West 27th St.
5th Floor
New York, NY 10001, USA

Hogan, Craig (Astronomer)
University of Washington
Astronomy Dept
Seattle, WA 98195, USA

Hogan, Darrell (Athlete, Football Player)
14988 Scenic Loop Rd
Helotes, TX 78023, USA

Hogan, Hulk (Actor, Wrestler)
c/o Darren Prince *Prince Marketing Group*
18 Carillon Cir
Livingston, NJ 07039, USA

Hogan, John (Horse Racer)
4947 State Route 40
Argyle, NY 12809-3468, USA

Hogan, Linda (Writer)
University of Colorado
English Dept
Boulder, CO 80309, USA

Hogan, Linda (Actor)
c/o Peter Young *Sovereign Talent Group*
8421 Wilshire Blvd
Suite 200
Beverly Hills, CA 90211, USA

Hogan, Marc (Athlete, Football Player)
3761 Colby St
Pittsburgh, PA 15214, USA

Hogan, Michael (Actor)
c/o Jamie Levitt *Lauren Levitt & Associates Inc*
1525 W 8th St 3rd Fl
Vancouver V6J 1T5, British Columbia

Hogan, Mike (Athlete, Football Player)
11 Walton Creek Dr SW
Rome, GA 30165, USA

Hogan, Nick (Actor, Reality TV Star)
c/o Darren Prince *Prince Marketing Group*
18 Carillon Cir
Livingston, NJ 07039, USA

Hogan, Paul (Actor)
7022 Grasswood Ave
Malibu, CA 90265, USA

Hogan, Paul (Reality TV Star)
c/o Staff Member *Acme Talent & Literary (LA)*
1400 Atlantic Ave
Suite 274
Long Beach, CA 90814, USA

Hogan, Paul (PJ) (Director, Producer, Writer)
c/o Richard Lovett *Creative Artists Agency (CAA-LA)*
2000 Ave Of The Stars
Los Angeles, CA 90067, USA

Hogan, Robert (Actor)
344 W 89th St #1B
New York, NY 10024, USA

Hogan, Terry
130 Willadel Dr.
Belleair, FL 34616

Hoganson, Paul (Athlete, Hockey Player)
1070 W Eagle Landing Pt
Tucson, AZ 85737-9230, USA

Hogarth, Freddie
69 St. Quentin Ave. #1
London, ENGLAND W10 6PA

Hogdon, Marilinda (Stylist)
225 E 9th St
#19-K
New York, NY 10128, USA

Hoge, Merril (Athlete, Football Player)
105 Stanbery Rdg
Fort Thomas, KY 41075, USA

Hogeboom, Gary (Athlete, Football Player)
13635 Hofma Ct
Grand Haven, MI 49417-9669, USA

Hogestyn, Drake (Actor)
c/o Staff Member *Hines and Hunt Entertainment*
1213 W Magnolia Blvd
Burbank, CA 91506, USA

Hogg, Christopher A (Business Person)
Courtaulds
18 Hanover Square
London W1A 2BB, UNITED KINGDOM (UK)

Hogg, James R (Admiral)
Prescott Farm
2556 W Main Road
Portsmouth, RI 02871, USA

Hoggard, Jay (Music Group, Musician)
Creative Music Consultants
181 Christie St #300
New York, NY 10002, USA

Hoggarth, Ron (Athlete, Hockey Player)
1109 Woodland Dr
Orillia, ON L3V 6H1, CANADA

Hogland, Doug (Athlete, Football Player)
1514 4th St
Tillamook, OR 97141, USA

Hoglund, Jonas (Athlete, Hockey Player)
Ringvagen 28
Skoghall 66333, Sweden

Hogosta, Goran (Athlete, Hockey Player)
Hosjostrand 109
Falun S-79147, Sweden

Hogue, Beniot (Athlete, Hockey Player)
488 Village Oaks Ln
Babylon, NY 11702, USA

Hogue, Benoit (Athlete, Hockey Player)
488 Village Oaks Ln
Babylon, NY 11702-3124, USA

Hogue, Linda (Stylist)
5374 Whitehall Pl
Atlanta, GA 30126, USA

Hogue, Stacey
10474 Santa Monica Blvd. #380
Los Angeles, CA 90025

Hogwood, Christopher J H (Conductor, Musician)
10 Brookside
Cambridge CB2 1JE, UNITED KINGDOM (UK)

Hohensee, Mike (Athlete, Football Player)
6N568 Burr Rd
Saint Charles, IL 60175-6109, USA

Hohlmayer, Alice (Athlete, Baseball Player, Commentator)
5155 Cedarwood Rd Apt 47
Bonita, CA 91902-1946, USA

Hohmann, John (Misc)
Louis Berger Assoc
1110 E Missouri Ave
#200
Phoenix, AZ 85014, USA

Hohn, Bill (Athlete, Baseball Player)
1406 Royal Oak Dr
Blue Bell, PA 19525-9270, USA

Hohn, Robert (Athlete, Football Player)
2624 N 78th St
Lincoln, NE 68507, USA

Hohne, Claus
An der Kiesgrube 3
Holzkirchen, GERMANY D-83607

hoiberg, fred
2129 Quail Ridge Rd
Ames, IA 50010-9476, USA

Hoiles, Chris (Athlete, Baseball Player)
8688 Jerry City Rd
Wayne, OH 43466-9837, USA

Hoisington, Allan (Athlete, Football Player)
71371 Biskra Rd
Rancho Mirage, CA 92270, USA

Hoke, Chris (Athlete, Football Player)
121 Cardinal Cir
Pittsburgh, PA 15237-1067, USA

Hoke, Jon (Athlete, Football Player)
4906 Cambridge St
Sugar Land, TX 77479, USA

Hoku (Musician)
c/o Staff Member *United Talent Agency (UTA)*
9336 Civic Center Dr
Beverly Hills, CA 90210, USA

Holahan, Dennis
9250 Wilshire Blvd. #208
Beverly Hills, CA 90212

Holberg, Fred (Athlete, Basketball Player)
2851 Timberview Trl
Chaska, MN 55318, USA

Holbert, Aaron (Athlete, Baseball Player)
32015 Teague Way
Wesley Chapel, FL 33545-1612, USA

Holbert, Jerry (Cartoonist, Editor)
Boston Herald
Editorial Dept
1 Herald St
Roxbury, MA 02118, USA

Holbert, Ray (Athlete, Baseball Player)
18436 W Palo Verde Ave
Waddell, AZ 85355-4330, USA

Holbrook, Bill (Cartoonist)
c/o Staff Member *King Features Syndication*
300 W 57th St
15th Floor
New York, NY 10019-5238, USA

Holbrook, Bill (Cartoonist)
940 Providence Club Dr
Monroe, GA 30656-6214, USA

Holbrook, Hal (Actor)
9100 Hazen Dr
Beverly Hills, CA 90210, USA

Holbrook, Karen (Educator)
Presidint's Office
Ohio State University
Columbus, OH 43210, USA

Holbrook, Sam (Athlete, Baseball Player)
2620 Sungale Ct
Lexington, KY 40513-1463, USA

Holbrook, Terry (Athlete, Hockey Player)
251 Meriden Rd
Painesville, OH 44077-3733, USA

Holcomb, Corey (Comedian)
c/o Staff Member *WmE2 (WMA-LA)*
1 William Morris Pl
Beverly Hills, CA 90212, USA

Holden, Alexandra (Actor)

Holden, Amanda (Actor)
c/o Melanie Greene *Affirmative Entertainment*
425 N Robertson Blvd
Los Angeles, CA 90048, USA

Holden, Andrew (Stylist)
c/o Staff Member *AFG Management*
Pier 62
Chelsea Piers #203
New York, NY 10011, USA

Holden, Carl (Athlete, Baseball Player)
12755 Henderson Ln
Madison, AL 35756-3327, USA

Holden, Gina (Actor)
c/o Staff Member *Collective*
8383 Wilshire Blvd
Suite 1050
Beverly Hills, CA 90211, USA

Holden, Henry (Misc)
1140 Bloomfield Ave Ste 220
West Caldwell, NJ 07006-7126, USA

Holden, Jennifer
115 S. Topanga Canyon #153
Topanga, CA 90290

Holden, Joyce (Actor)
444 N El Camino Real #89
Encinitas, CA 92024-1313

Holden, Laurie (Actor)
c/o Jason Newman *Untitled Entertainment (LA)*
350 S. Beverly Dr #200
Beverly Hills, CA 90212, USA

Holden, Mari (Athlete, Cycler, Olympic Athlete)
2109 Caminito Del Barco
Del Mar, CA 92014-3603, USA

Holden, Mariean (Actor)
L A Talent
8335 Sunset Blvd #200
Los Angeles, CA 90069, USA

Holden, Mark (Athlete, Hockey Player)
4837 Spruce Pine Way
North Spruceville, OH 44039-2341, USA

Holden, Robert (Politician)
1937 Wind river Dr
Jefferson City, MA 65101-4375, USA

Holden, Steve (Athlete, Football Player)
1202 N Nevada Way
Mesa, AZ 85203, USA

Holden, Tim (Congressman, Politician)
2417 Rayburn HOB
Washington, DC 20515, USA

Holden, William Wildlife Foundation
PO Box 67981
Los Angeles, CA 90067

Holden-Reid, Kristen (Actor)
c/o Staff Member *Paradigm (LA)*
360 N Crescent Dr
North Bldg
Beverly Hills, CA 90210, USA

Holder, Christopher (Actor)
H David Moss
733 Seward St #PH
Los Angeles, CA 90038, USA

Holder, Geoffrey (Actor, Dancer)
565 Broadway
New York, NY 10012, USA

Holder, Livingston L (Astronaut)
18422 SE 58th St
Issaquah, WA 98027-8618, USA

Holderer, Oskar
2304 Oakwood Ave NW
Huntsville, AL 35810-4408, USA

Holderness, Joan (Athlete, Baseball Player, Commentator)
1037 Summerwind Drive
Crossville, TN 38571-3691, USA

Holderness, Sue
10 Rectory Close Windsor
Berks., ENGLAND SL4 5ER

Holdman, Warrick (Athlete, Football Player)
c/o Fletcher Smith *Blueprint Sports Group*
221 W. Jefferson Ave
Naperville, IL 60540, USA

Holdorf, Willi (Athlete, Track Athlete)
Adidas KG
Herzogenaurach 91074, GERMANY

Holdridge, David (Athlete, Baseball Player)
39364 N Parisi Cir
San Tan Valley, AZ 85140-5721, USA

Holdsclaw, Chamique (Basketball Player)
Washington Mystics
MCI Center
601 F St NW
Washington, DC 20004, USA

Holdsworth, Fred (Athlete, Baseball Player)
578 Upland Hills Dr
Chelsea, MI 48118-9650, USA

Hole
150 E. 58th St. #1900
New York, NY 10155-0002

Holecek, John (Athlete, Football Player)
1876 N Wilmot Ave
Chicago, IL 60647, USA

Holgren, Paul H
724 Southwick Cir
Somerdale, NJ 08083, USA

Holiday, Corey (Athlete, Football Player)
315 Columbia Pl E
Chapel Hill, NC 27516, USA

Holiday, Debby (Musician)
c/o Staff Member *Diva Central Inc*
7510 W Sunset Blvd Ste 1445
Los Angees, CA 90046, USA

Holiday, Ron (Athlete, Football Player)
229 Balance Meeting Rd
Peach Bottom, PA 17563, USA

Holik, Bobby (Athlete, Hockey Player)
P.O. Box 9236
Jackson, WY 83002-9236, USA

Holl, Steven M (Architect)
Steven Holl Architects
435 Hudson St #400
New York, NY 10014, USA

Holladay, Robert (Athlete, Football Player)
2369 Timberland Dr NE
Conyers, GA 30207, USA

Holladay, Wilhelmina Cole (Misc)
National Museum of Women in Arts
1250 New York NW
Washington, DC 20005, USA

Holland, Agnieszka (Director, Writer)
Agence Nicole Cann
1 Rue Alfred de Vigny
Paris 75008, FRANCE

Holland, Al (Athlete, Baseball Player)
4443 Lewiston St NW
Roanoke, VA 24017-1009, USA

Holland, Al (Athlete, Baseball Player)
4443 Lewiston St NW
Roanoke, VA 24017, USA

Holland, Bill (Race Car Driver)
4790 W. 16th St.
Indianapolis, IN 46222-2573, USA

Holland, Brad (Athlete, Basketball Player)
1374 Sparrow Rd
Carlsbad, CA 92011-3961, USA

Holland, Darius (Athlete, Football Player)
13972 Meadowbrook Dr
Broomfield, CO 80020, USA

Holland, Derek (Athlete, Baseball Player)
13316 W Ocotillo Ln
Surprise, AZ 85374-5255, USA

Holland, Dexter (Musician)
Rebel Waltz
31652 2nd Ave
Laguna Beach, CA 92651, USA

Holland, Heinrich D (Geophysicist, Physicist)
14 Rangely Road
Winchester, MA 01890, USA

Holland, Jamie L (Athlete, Football Player)
Ohio State University
410 Woody Hayes Dr
Attn: Alumni Association
Columbus, OH 43210, USA

Holland, Jennifer (Actor)
c/o Jon Simmons *Simmons & Scott Entertainment*
4110 W. Burbank Blvd.
Burbank, CA 91505, USA

Holland, Jerry (Athlete, Hockey Player)
115 Douglasbank Pl SE
Calgary, AB T2Z 2J4, Canada

Holland, John (Athlete, Football Player)
3117 Flagstone Dr
Garland, TX 75044, USA

Holland, Johnny (Athlete, Football Player)
3303 Prestwick Sq
Missouri City, TX 77459, USA

Holland, John R (Religious Leader)
Foursquare Gospel Int'l Church
1910 W Sunset Blvd
Los Angeles, CA 90026, USA

Holland, Jools (Music Group)
c/o Staff Member *Miracle Artists*
1 York Street
London
England W1U 6PA, United Kingdom

Holland, Josh
4533 Willis Ave.
Sherman Oaks, CA 91403-2710

Holland, Juliam M (Jools) (Musician)
One Fifteen
Gallery 28 Wood Wharf
Horseferry
London SE10 9BT, UNITED KINGDOM (UK)

Holland, Ken (Athlete, Hockey Player)
Detroit Red Wings 600 Civic Center Dr
Attn: General Manager
Detroit, MI 48226-4419, USA

Holland, Ken (Athlete, Hockey Player)
967 McDonald Dr
Northville, MI 48167-1072, USA

Holland, Paul (Musician)
Variety Artists
1924 Spring St
Paso Robles, CA 93446, USA

Holland, Richard (Actor)
453 Frederick St
San Francisco, CA 94117-2719, USA

Holland, Todd (Director)
c/o David Lonner *Oasis Media Group*
8730 W. Sunset Blvd
Suite 700
Los Angeles, CA 90036, USA

Holland, Wilbur (Athlete, Basketball Player)
538 Georgia Dr
Columbus, GA 31907-5091, USA

Holland, Willa (Actor)
c/o Ellen Meyer *Ellen Meyer Management*
8899 Beverly Blvd
Suite 612
West Hollywood, CA 90048, USA

Holland, Willard R Jr (Business Person)
FirstEnergy Corp
76 S Main St
Akron, OH 44308, USA

Hollander, Dan (Figure Skater)
c/o Staff Member *Champions on Ice*
Tom Collins Enterprises Inc
3500 W 80th St
Minneapolis, MN 55431, USA

Hollander, John (Writer)
Yale University
English Dept
New Haven, CT 06520, USA

Hollander, Lorin (Musician)
I C M Artists
40 W 57th St
New York, NY 10019, USA

Hollander, Nicole (Cartoonist)
Sylvia Syndicate
1440 N Dayton St
Chicago, IL 60622, USA

Hollander, Xaviera
Stadionweg 17
Amsterdam, HOLLAND 1077 RU

Hollander, Zander (Writer)
3805 Yuma Street NW
Washington, DC 20016-2213, USA

Hollandsworth, Todd M (Athlete, Baseball Player)
1310 Macalpin Drive
Inverness, IL 60010-6424, USA

Hollas, Donald (Athlete, Football Player)
22015 Gold Leaf Trl
Cypress, TX 77433, USA

Holldobler, Berthold K (Biologist, Writer)
University of Wurzburg
Zoologie II
Am Nubland
Wurzburg 97074, GERMANY

Holle, Eric (Athlete, Football Player)
6646 Whitemarsh Valley Walk
Austin, TX 78746, USA

Holle, Gary (Athlete, Baseball Player)
820 5th Ave
Watervliet, NY 12189-3612, USA

Hollein, Hans (Architect)
Eiskellerstr 1
Dusseldorf 40213, GERMANY

Holler, Ed (Athlete, Football Player)
4500 Ivy Hall Dr
Columbia, SC 29206, USA

Holleran, Leslie (Producer)
c/o Staff Member *Laha Films*
115 East 92nd Street
7C
New York, NY 10128, USA

Hollerer, Walter F (Writer)
Heerstr 99
Berlin 14055, GERMANY

Holler Thompson, Alana (Honey Boo Boo Child) (Beauty Pageant Winner)
PO Box 72
McIntrye, GA 31054, USA

Holliday, Charles O (Business Person)
E I DuPont de Nemours
1007 Market St
Wilmington, DE 19801, USA

Holliday, Cheryl (Writer)
c/o Staff Member *United Talent Agency (UTA)*
9336 Civic Center Dr
Beverly Hills, CA 90210, USA

Holliday, Fred (Actor)
4610 Forman Ave
Toluca Lake, CA 91602, USA

Holliday, Jennifer (Actor, Music Group)
Universal Attractions
W 57th St #1500
New York, NY 10019, USA

Holliday, Johnny (Commentator)
Washington Nationals 1500 S Capitol St
SE
Attn: Broadcast Dept
Washington, DC 20003-3599, USA

Holliday, Kathy
345 N. Maple Dr. #397
Beverly Hills, CA 90210

Holliday, Kene
9300 Wilshire Blvd. #400
Beverly Hills, CA 90212

Holliday, Matt (Athlete, Baseball Player)
4 Ravenswood Rd
Englewood, CO 80113-4138, USA

Holliday, Polly D (Actor, Music Group)
c/o Staff Member *The Blake Agency*
23441 Malibu Colony Rd
Malibu, CA 90265, USA

Hollie, Doug (Athlete, Football Player)
3917 Midvale Ave
Oakland, CA 94602, USA

Hollier, Dwight (Athlete, Football Player)
5012 Woodview Ln
Matthews, NC 28104, USA

Hollies, The
Hill Farm Hackleton
Northants., ENGLAND NN7 2DH

Holliger, Heinz (Composer, Musician)
Konzertgellschaft
Hochstr 51
Basel 4002, SWITZERLAND

Holliman, Earl (Actor)
PO Box 1969
Studio City, CA 91614, USA

Hollimon, Mike (Athlete, Baseball Player)
9922 Glen Canyon Dr
Dallas, TX 75243-4608, USA

Hollimon, Ulysses (Athlete, Baseball
Player)
3726 Benton Blvd
Kansas City, MO 64128-2515, USA

Hollings, Ernest (Politician)
1415 N Utah St
Arlington, VA 22201-4823, USA

Hollings, Ernest (Ex-Senator)
261 Calhoun St Rm 304
Charleston, SC 29401, USA

Hollings, Michael R (Religious Leader)
Saint Mary of Angels
Moorhouse Road Bayswater
London W2 5DJ, UNITED KINGDOM
(UK)

Hollingsworth, Ben (Actor)
c/o Shelley Browning *Magnolia
Entertainment (LA)*
9595 Wilshire Blvd
Suite 601
Beverly Hills, CA 90212, USA

Hollingsworth, Shawn (Athlete, Football
Player)
6 Broyhill Ct
Stafford, VA 22554, USA

Hollinquest, Lamont (Athlete, Football
Player)
13709 S San Pedro St
Los Angeles, CA 90061, USA

Hollins, Damon (Athlete, Baseball Player)
1135 Camellia Ln
Suisun City, CA 94585-3804, USA

Hollins, Dave (Athlete, Baseball Player)
3221 Southwestern Blvd
Orchard Park, NY 14127-1230, USA

hollins, Essie (Athlete, Basketball Player)
9102 NW 48th St
Sunrise, FL 33351-5214, USA

Hollins, Lionel (Athlete, Basketball Player,
Coach)
7594 Tagg Dr
Germantown, TN 38138-5827, USA

Hollis, Essie (Athlete, Basketball Player)
9102 NW 48th St
Sunrise, FL 33351, USA

Hollis, James (Writer)
5200 Montrose Blvd
Houston, TX 77006, USA

Hollis, Michael (Athlete, Football Player)
24 Falling Waters
Oakland, NJ 07436, USA

Hollister, Dave (Actor, Music Group)
c/o Staff Member *Richard De La Font
Agency*
3808 W South Park Blvd
Broken Arrow, OK 74011, USA

Hollister, Ken (Athlete, Football Player)
8772 Linksway Dr
Powell, OH 43065, USA

Hollit, Raye (Zapp)
2554 Lincoln Blvd. #638
Marina del Rey, CA 90292

Holloman, Laurel (Actor)
c/o Tammy Rosen *Sanders Armstrong
Caserta*
425 N Robertson Blvd
Los Angeles, CA 90048, USA

Hollomon, Gus (Athlete, Football Player)
2489 County Road 139
Cameron, TX 76520, USA

Holloway, Brenda (Musician)
Universal Attractions
145 W 57th St
#1500
New York, NY 10019, USA

Holloway, Brian (Athlete, Football Player)
742 New York Route 43
Stephentown, NY 12168, USA

Holloway, James (General)
4800 Fillmore Ave Apt 1058
Alexandria, VA 22311-5076, USA

Holloway, James L III (Admiral)
4800 Fillmore Ave #1058
Alexandria, VA 22311, USA

Holloway, Johnny (Athlete, Football
Player)
1500 W 9th St
Apt 5
Lawrence, KS 66044, USA

Holloway, Joseph
25 Broad St Ste 5 # 283
Freehold, NJ 07728-1962, USA

Holloway, Josh (Actor)
c/o Jai Khanna *Brillstein Entertainment
Partners*
9150 Wilshire Blvd #350
Beverly Hills, CA 90212, USA

Holloway, Ken (Music Group)
World Class/Berry Mgmt
1848 Tyne Blvd
Nashville, TN 37215, USA

Holloway, Matt (Writer)
c/o Staff Member *Nine Yards
Entertainment*
8530 Wilshire Blvd Fl 5
Beverly Hills, CA 90211, USA

Holloway, Robin G (Composer)
Gonville & Caius College
Music Dept
Cambridge CB2 1TA, UNITED
KINGDOM (UK)

Holloway, Tommy (Scientist)
28612 Post Oak Run
Magnolia, TX 77355-4664, USA

Holloway, William J Jr (Judge)
US Court of Appeals
PO Box 1767
Oklahoma City, OK 73101, USA

Hollowell, Matt (Baseball Player)
8 Oldwick Rd
Whitehouse Station, NJ 08889-3719, USA

Hollowell, Matt (Athlete, Baseball Player)
8 Oldwick Rd
Whitehouse Station, NJ 33458-5250, USA

Hollweg, Ryan (Athlete, Hockey Player)
340 Treeline Park
Apt 1226
San Antonio, TX 78209-1843, USA

Holly, Buddy Memorial Society
PO Box 6123
Lubbock, TX 79413

Holly, Jeff (Athlete, Baseball Player)
1201 Walnut Ave
Apt 57
Tustin, CA 92780-5739, USA

Holly, Lauren (Actor)
c/o Ben Press *Buchwald/Fortitude (LA)*
6500 Wilshire Blvd
Suite 2200
Los Angeles, CA 90048, USA

Holly, Molly (Wrestler)
c/o Staff Member *World Wrestling
Entertainment (WWE)*
Titan Towers
1241 E Main St
Stamford, CT 06905-3857, USA

Hollyday, Christopher (Musician)
Ted Kurland
173 Brighton Ave
Boston, MA 02134, USA

Holm, Ian (Actor)
Markham & Froggatt
Julian House
4 Windmill St
London W1P 1HF, UNITED KINGDOM
(UK)

Holm, Joan (Bowler)
5829 N Magnolia Ave
Chicago, IL 60660, USA

Holm, Peter
1 rue de Fer Achevel Port Grimaud
Cogolin, FRANCE F- 83310

Holm, Richard H (Misc)
483 Pleasant St #10
Belmont, MA 02478, USA

Holm, Sir Ian
46 Albermarle St.
London, ENGLAND W1X 4PP

Holm, Steve (Athlete, Baseball Player)
10205 Garden Hwy
Sacramento, CA 95837-9100, USA

Holman, Brad (Athlete, Baseball Player)
4720 N Ridge Rd
Wichita, KS 67205-8837, USA

Holman, Brian (Athlete, Baseball Player)
15821 Parkhill St
Overland Park, KS 66221-2549, USA

Holman, C Ray (Business Person)
Mallinckrodt Inc
675 McDonell Blvd
Saint Louis, MO 63134, USA

Holman, Gary (Athlete, Baseball Player)
8073 Camino Montego
Carlsbad, CA 92009-9545, USA

Holman, Marshall (Athlete, Bowler)
288 Island Pointe Drive
Medford, OR 97504-9453, USA

Holman, Ralph T (Biologist)
1403 2nd Ave SW
Austin, MN 55912, USA

Holman, Rodney (Athlete, Football Player)
41460 Herwig Bluff Rd
Slidell, LA 70461, USA

Holman, Scott (Athlete, Football Player)
4 Comiso
Irvine, CA 92614, USA

Holman, Scott (Athlete, Baseball Player)
25 Delbert Ln
Santa Rosa Beach, FL 32459-3678, USA

Holman, Shawn (Athlete, Baseball Player)
105 Edgewood Rd
Sewickley, PA 15143-9681, USA

Holmberg, Dennis (Athlete, Baseball
Player)
2079 Monica Ct
Palm Harbor, FL 34683-5030, USA

Holmberg, Mark (Musician)
MOB Agency
6404 Wilshire Blvd #505
Los Angeles, CA 90048, USA

Holmberg, Rob (Athlete, Football Player)
316 Coppersmith Ln
Strasburg, PA 17579, USA

Holmes, A M (Writer)
Columbia Univesity
English Dept
New York, NY 10027, USA

Holmes, Ashton (Actor)
c/o Jeff Morrone *Jeff Morrone
Entertainment*
9350 Wilshire Blvd
Suite 224
Beverly Hills, CA 90212, USA

Holmes, Charlie (Athlete, Hockey Player)
7567 NE Meadowmeer Ln
Bainbridge Island, WA 98110-1223, USA

Holmes, Clayton (Athlete, Football Player)
1142 Hollings Ave
Florence, SC 29506, USA

Holmes, Clint (Music Group)
Conversation Co
697 Middle Neck Road
Great Neck, NY 11023, USA

Holmes, Dame Kelly (Athlete)
*International Association of Athletics
Federations*
17 rue Princesse Florestine
BP 359
MC98007, MONACO

Holmes, Darren (Athlete, Baseball Player)
1 Emerald Ct
Arden, NC 28704-9594, USA

Holmes, D Brainerd (Business Person, Engineer)
Bay Colony Corp Center
950 Winter St #4350
Waltham, MA 02451, USA

Holmes, Earl (Athlete, Football Player)
2978 Stonybrook Ct
Tallahassee, FL 32309, USA

Holmes, Eric (Race Car Driver)
Beebe Racing
801-10th St. Fl 5-1
Modesto, CA 95354, USA

Holmes, Howdy (Race Car Driver)
301 Barton Shore Drive
Ann Arbor, MI 48105, USA

Holmes, JB (Athlete, Golfer)
7410 Cypress Grove Rd
Orlando, FL 32819, USA

Holmes, Jennifer (Actor)
PO Box 6303
Carmel, CA 93921, USA

Holmes, Jerry (Athlete, Football Player)
107 Chatham Ter
Hampton, VA 23666, USA

Holmes, Katie (Actor)
c/o Nanci Ryder *Baker Winokur Ryder Public Relations (BWR-LA)*
9100 Wilshire Blvd
Suite 500, West Tower
Beverly Hills, CA 90212, USA

Holmes, Kenneth (Athlete, Football Player)
P.O. Box 273309
Boca Raton, FL 33427, USA

Holmes, Larry (Boxer)
91 Larry Holmes Dr #200
Easton, PA 18042, USA

Holmes, Lester (Athlete, Football Player)
3760 Motor Ave
Los Angeles, CA 90034, USA

Holmes, Pat (Athlete, Football Player)
221 Mack Hollimon Dr
Kerrville, TX 78028, USA

Holmes, Priest (Athlete, Football Player)
9727 Autumn Arbor
San Antonio, TX 78240, USA

Holmes, Ray (Athlete, Baseball Player)
1 S Washington St Apt 101
Denver, CO 80209-2038, us

Holmes, Rudell (Athlete, Football Player)
1713 Lisa Ave
Vista, CA 92084, USA

Holmes, Rudy (Athlete, Football Player)
2151 Ronda Granada Unit A
Laguna Woods, CA 92637-0718, USA

Holmes, Santonio (Athlete, Football Player)
c/o Peter Miller *Jabez Marketing Group*
516 East 2nd St #3
Boston, MA 02127, USA

Holmes, Sherlock Society
221B Baker St.
London, ENGLAND W1

Holmes, Susan (Actor, Model)
c/o Jerry Shandrew *Shandrew Public Relations*
1050 S Stanley Ave
Los Angeles, CA 90019-6634, USA

Holmes, Tina (Actor)
c/o Mike Smith *Principal Entertainment (LA)*
1964 Westwood Blvd #400
Los Angeles, CA 90025, USA

Holmes, TJ (Anchor)
CNN
1 Cnn Center
Atlanta, GA 30303

Holmes Norton, Eleanor (Congressman, Politician)
2136 Rayburn HOB
Washington, DC 20515, USA

Holmgren, Janet L (Educator)
Mills College
President's Office
Oakland, CA 94613, USA

Holmgren, Michael G (Mike) (Athlete, Coach, Football Coach, Football Player)
17 Shoreby Dr
Cleveland, OH 44108-1161, USA

Holmgren, paul (Athlete, Hockey Player)
Philadelphia Flyers
724 Southwick Cir
Somerdale, NJ 08083-2312

Holmgren, Paul (Athlete, Coach, Hockey Player)
724 Southwick Cir
Somerdale, NJ 08083-2312

Holmoe, Tom (Athlete, Football Player)
1674 N 1670 W
Provo, UT 84604, USA

Holmquest, Donald L (Astronaut)
205 Princeton Rd
Menlo Park, CA 94025-5217, USA

Holmquest, Donald L Dr (Astronaut)
205 Princeton Rd
Menlo Park, CA 94025-5217, USA

Holmquist, Leif (Athlete, Hockey Player)
Glasving_evagen 3
Huskvarna 56148, 56148

Holmstrom, Carl (Skier)
1703 E 3rd St #101
Duluth, MN 55812, USA

Holmstrom, Peter (Musician)
Monqui Mgmt
PO Box 5908
Portland, OR 97228, USA

Holmstrom, Tomas (Athlete, Hockey Player)
43479 McLean Ct
Novi, MI 48375-4017, USA

Holohan, Pete (Athlete, Football Player)
2945 Curie St
San Diego, CA 92122-4105, USA

Holonyak, Nick (Inventor)
101 W Windsor Rd
Urbana, IL 61802-6663, USA

Holroyd, Michael (Writer)
85 Saint Marks Road
London W10 6JS, UNITED KINGDOM (UK)

Holroyd, Scott (Actor)
c/o Christopher Wright *Christopher Wright Management*
3207 Winnie Dr
Los Angeles, CA 90068, USA

Holst, Per (Producer)
Per Holst Film A/S
Rentemestervej 69A
Copenhagen, NV 2400, DENMARK

Holt, Chris (Athlete, Baseball Player)
152 Hollywood Dr
Coppell, TX 75019-7302, USA

Holt, Claire (Actor)
c/o Melanie Greene *Affirmative Entertainment*
425 N Robertson Blvd
Los Angeles, CA 90048, USA

Holt, David Lee (Musician)
AristoMedia
1620 16th Ave S
Nashville, TN 34212, USA

Holt, Gary (Athlete, Hockey Player)
5820 S Sorrel Ct
Spokane, WA 99224-8298, USA

Holt, Glenn L (Athlete, Football Player)
North Miami High School
800 NE 137th St
North Miami, FL 33161, USA

Holt, Glynn Dr (Astronaut)
Boston University 110 Cummington St Dept of
Boston, MA 02215-2407, USA

Holt, Harry (Athlete, Football Player)
5608 S Vine Ave
Tucson, AZ 85706-2116, USA

Holt, Issac (Athlete, Football Player)
4028 Fairmont Pl
Birmingham, AL 35207, USA

Holt, Issiac (Athlete, Football Player)
4028 Fairmont Pl
Birmingham, AL 35207-2732, USA

Holt, Jim (Athlete, Baseball Player)
150 Judge Sharpe Rd
Graham, NC 27253-8202, USA

Holt, Lester (Correspondent)
NBC-TV
News Dept
30 Rockefeller Plaza
New York, NY 10112, USA

Holt, Milton (Athlete, Football Player)
1461 N School St
Honolulu, HI 96817-1915, USA

Holt, Pierce (Athlete, Football Player)
5101 County Road 430
San Angelo, TX 76901-9506, USA

Holt, Robert J (Athlete, Football Player)
1332 Williams Ave
Desoto, TX 75115, USA

Holt, Roger (Athlete, Baseball Player)
804 Hilltop St
Fruitland Park, FL 34731-2061, USA

Holt, Sandrine (Actor)
c/o Jennifer Goldhar *Characters Talent Agency (Toronto)*
8 Elm St
2nd Floor
Toronto, ON M5G 1G7, CANADA

Holt, Torry (Athlete, Football Player)
c/o Mark Lepselter *Maxx Sports & Entertainment*
546 Fifth Ave Fl 6
New York, NY 10036, USA

Holtgrave, Vern (Athlete, Baseball Player)
389 N 8th St
Breese, IL 62230-1107, USA

Holt Jr, Jack
504 Temple Dr
Harrah, OK 73045, USA

Holt Jr., Rush (Congressman, Politician)
1214 Longworth HOB
Washington, DC 20515, USA

Holt-Kramer, Toni
1229 Santa Monica Blvd
Santa Monica, CA 90404

Holton, A Linwood Jr (Physicist)
64 Francis Ave
Cambridge, MA 02138, USA

Holton, Brian (Athlete, Baseball Player)
3214 Estate Dr
Oakdale, PA 15071-1445, USA

Holton, Linwood (Politician)
3883 Black Stump Rd
Weems, VA 22576-2017, USA

Holton, Mark (Actor)
c/o Staff Member *Gage Group, The (LA)*
14724 Ventura Blvd
Suite 505
Sherman Oaks, CA 91403, USA

Holton, Michael (Athlete, Basketball Player, Coach)
5822 NW Redfox Dr
Portland, OR 97229-2657, USA

Holtz, Louis L (Lou) (Athlete, Coach, Football Coach, Football Player)
9209 Cromwell Park Pl
Orlando, FL 32827, USA

Holtz, Mike (Athlete, Baseball Player)
515 Double Dam Rd
Northern Cambria, PA 15714-7404, USA

Holtzman, Elizabeth (Liz) (Misc, Politician)
2 Park Ave Fl 21
New York, NY 10016-9301, USA

Holtzman, Jerome (Baseball Player, Writer)
1225 Forest Ave
Evanston, IL 60202-1409, USA

Holtzman, Kenneth D (Ken) (Athlete, Baseball Player)
256 Waterside Dr
Grover, MO 63040-1632, USA

Holtzman, Wayne H (Doctor)
2500 Barton Creek Blvd
Apt 1504
Austin, TX 78735-1622, USA

Holub, Dick (Athlete, Basketball Player)
16159 W Wildflower Dr
Surprise, AZ 85374-5048, USA

Holub, E J (Athlete, Football Player)
2311 S County Road 1120
Midland, TX 79706, USA

Holum, Dianne (Athlete, Olympic Athlete, Speed Skater)
961 E 1st Ave Apt 605
Broomfield, CO 80020, USA

Holum, Kirstin (Athlete, Olympic Athlete, Speed Skater)
961 E 1st Ave
Apt 605
Broomfield, CO 80020-3724, USA

Holway, Jerome F (Cinematographer)
448 Spruce Dr
Exton, PA 19341, USA

Holy, Steve (Musician)
c/o Staff Member *Paradigm (Nashville)*
124 12th Ave S
Suite 410
Nashville, TN 37203, USA

Holyfield, Evander (Boxer)
794 Evander Holyfield Highway
Fairburn, GA 30213, USA

Holz, Gordon (Athlete, Football Player)
730 South Plaza Dr
Apt 222
Saint Paul, MN 55120, USA

Holzemer, Mark (Athlete, Baseball Player)
10044 Macalister Trl
Highlands Ranch, CO 80129-6248, USA

Holzer, Helmut (Scientist)
2103 Greenwood Place SW
Huntsville, AL 35802, USA

Holzer, Jenny (Artist)
80 Hewitts Road
Hoosick Falls, NY 12090, USA

Holzer, Kristine (Athlete, Olympic Athlete, Speed Skater)
10410 W Whispering Cliffs Dr
Boise, ID 83704-1911, USA

Holzier, James (Actor)
c/o Bob Willems *Champion Entertainment*
2620 Fountainview
Suite 220
Houston, TX 77057, USA

Holzinger, Brian (Athlete, Hockey Player)
1005 Ledgemont Dr
Broadview Heights, OH 44147-4021, USA

Holzman, Malcolm (Architect)
Hardy Holzman Pfeiffer
902 Broadway
New York, NY 10010, USA

Hom, Aaron (Stylist)
c/o Staff Member *Zenobia Agency Inc*
PO Box 909
Groveland, CA 95321, USA

Homa, Lisa (Stylist)
875 W 81 St
New York, NY 10033, USA

Homan, Dennis (Athlete, Football Player)
1950 Charlotte Ct
Florence, AL 35630, USA

Homeier, Skip (Actor, Director)
75381 Desert Valley Lane
Indian Wells, CA 92210-8316, USA

Homfeld, Conrad (Athlete, Horse Racer, Olympic Athlete)
Sandron
11744 Marblestone Court
Wellington, FL 33414, USA

Honda, Yuka (Music Group)
Billions Corp
833 W Chicago Ave #101
Chicago, IL 60622, USA

Honderich, Beland H (Publisher)
Toronto Star
1 Yonge St
Toronto, ON M5E 1E6, CANADA

Honderich, John H (Editor)
Toronto Star
Editorial Dept
1 Yonge St
Toronto, ON M5E 1E6, CANADA

Honegger, Fritz (President)
Schloss-Str 29
Ruschlidon 8803, SWITZERLAND

Honeycutt, Rick (Athlete, Baseball Player)
207 Forrest Rd.
Fort Oglethorpe, GA 30742-3706, USA

Honeycutt, Rick (Athlete, Baseball Player)
207 Forrest Rd
Fort Oglethrope, GA 30742, USA

Honeycutt, Van B (Business Person)
Computer Sciences Corp
2100 E Grand Ave
El Segundo, CA 90245, USA

Honeycyt (Music Group)
c/o Staff Member *Paradigm (Monterey)*
404 W Franklin St
Monterey, CA 93940, USA

Honeyghan, Lloyd (Boxer)
50 Barnfield Wood Road
Park Langley
Beckenham
Kent, UNITED KINGDOM (UK)

Honeymoon Suite
1505 W. 2nd Ave. #200
Vancouver, CANADA BC V6H 3Y4

Hong, James (Actor)
c/o Carol Weiss *Stage 9 Talent*
1249 Lodi Pl
Hollywood, CA 90038, USA

Hong Song Nam (Prime Minister)
Premier's Office
Pyongyong, NORTH KOREA

Honig, Donald (Commentator)
2322 Cromwell Hills Dr
Cromwell, CT 06416-1803, USA

Honore, Jean Cardinal (Religious Leader)
Archeveche
BP 1117
27 Rue Jules-Simon
Tours Cedex 37011, FRANCE

Hoobastank (Music Group)

Hood, Bruce
B-5497 Sixth Line RR 2B
Hillsburgh, ON NOB 1ZO, Canada

Hood, Don (Athlete, Baseball Player)
20753 Charing Cross Cir
Estero, FL 33928-2542, USA

Hood, Estus (Athlete, Football Player)
2105 W Grace St
Kankakee, IL 60901, USA

Hood, Gavin (Director)
c/o Julia Tyrrell *Julia Tyrrell Management*
57 Greenham Rd
London N10 1LN, UK

Hood, Kenneth (Religious Leader)
5799 Bloomfield Ave
Verona, NJ 07044, USA

Hood, Leroy E (Inventor, Scientist)
2033 2nd Ave Apt 2300
Seattle, WA 98121-2258, USA

Hood, Robert
Boys Life Magazine
Editorial Dept
1325 Walnut Hill Lane
Irving, TX 75038, USA

Hoogstratten, Louise
12451 Mulholland Dr.
Beverly Hills, CA 90210

Hook, Chris (Athlete, Baseball Player)
30 Northfield Dr
Florence, KY 41042-8924, USA

Hook, Jay (Athlete, Baseball Player)
P.O. Box 90
Maple City, MI 49664-0090, USA

Hooker, Charles R (Artist)
28 Whippingham Road
Brighton
Sussex BN2 3PG, UNITED KINGDOM (UK)

Hooker, Fair (Athlete, Football Player)
3728 Rutherford Ct
Inglewood, CA 90305, USA

Hooks, Jan (Actor)
c/o Staff Member *Innovative Artists (LA)*
1505 10th St
Santa Monica, CA 90401, USA

Hooks, Kevin (Director)
International Creative Mgmt
8942 Wilshire Blvd #219
Beverly Hills, CA 90211, USA

Hooks, Robert (Actor)
145 N Valley St
Burbank, CA 91505, USA

Hooks, Roland (Athlete, Football Player)
3724 Calgary Dr
Reno, NV 89511, USA

Hookstratten, Edward G (Attorney, Attorney General, General)
Ed Hookstratten Mgmt
9536 Wilshire Blvd #500
Beverly Hills, CA 90212, USA

Hoop, Jesca (Musician)
c/o Staff Member *Paradigm (Monterey)*
404 W Franklin St
Monterey, CA 93940, USA

Hooper, Bobby Joe (Athlete, Basketball Player)
825 Ivywood St
Apt 4
Dayton, OH 45420-1751, USA

Hooper, Bobby Joe (Athlete, Basketball Player)
_?25 ^wood St Apt 4
Dayton, OH 45420-1751, USA

Hooper, Brandon
3003 3rd St. #4
Santa Monica, CA 90405-5488

Hooper, C Darrow (Athlete, Olympic Athlete, Track Athlete)
6 Braemore Place
Dallas, TX 75230-1958, USA

Hooper, Kevin (Athlete, Baseball Player)
2701 Century Dr
Lawrence, KS 66049-2523, USA

Hooper, Lance (Race Car Driver)
195 Poplar Grove Rd.
Mooresville, NC 28115, USA

Hooper, Tobe
PO Box 5617
Beverly Hills, CA 90210

Hooper, Tom (Director)
c/o Doug MacLaren *ICM Partners (ICM-LA)*
10250 Constellation Blvd Fl 7
Los Angeles, CA 90067, USA

Hoopes, Mitch (Athlete, Football Player)
5000 Murray Blvd
Apt F1
Salt Lake City, UT 84123-2674, USA

Hooser, Carroll (Athlete, Basketball Player)
6317 Kings Rd
Double Oak, TX 75077-7314, USA

Hooten, Burt
3619 Grandby Ct.
San Antonio, TX 78217

Hooten, Leon (Athlete, Baseball Player)
524 S 7th St
Coos Bay, OR 97420, USA

Hootie & The Blowfish (Music Group)
c/o Staff Member *Paradigm (Monterey)*
404 W Franklin St
Monterey, CA 93940, USA

Hooton, Burt C (Athlete, Baseball Player)
3619 Granby Ct
San Antonio, TX 78217-4653, USA

Hootselle, Brenda (Stylist)
c/o Staff Member *Talent Plus*
1222 Lucas Ave
Suite 300
St. Louis, MO 63103, USA

Hootselle, Meko (Stylist)
c/o Staff Member *Talent Plus*
1222 Lucas Ave
Suite 300
St. Louis, MO 63103, USA

Hoover, Alice (Athlete, Baseball Player, Commentator)
340 Roosevelt Ave
Reading, PA 19605-2337, USA

Hoover, Brad (Athlete, Football Player)
2130 Climbing Rose Ln
Matthews, NC 28104, USA

Hoover, Erna (Inventor)
87 Tanglewood Dr
Summit, NJ 07901-3120, USA

Hoover, Herbert III
200 S. Los Robles Ave. #520
Pasadena, CA 91101-2431

Hoover, Houston (Athlete, Football Player)
1216 Mareed Ave
Yazoo City, MS 39194, USA

Hoover, John (Athlete, Baseball Player)
1615 W Fountain Way
Fresno, CA 93705-3331, USA

Hoover, Lloyd N Maj (Aviator)
1520 Meadowbrook Rd
Altadena, CA 91001-3227, USA

Hoover, Paul (Athlete, Baseball Player)
2320 Anderson Rd
Cuyahoga Falls, OH 44221-3620, USA

Hoover, Robert A (Bob) (Aviator)
Bob Hoover Airshows
1100 E Imperial Ave
El Segundo, CA 90245, USA

Hoover, Tom (Race Car Driver)
207 Lowry Ave.
North Minneapolis, MN 55411, USA

Hoover, Tom (Athlete, Basketball Player)
9 Apple Manor Ln
East Brunswick, NJ 08816-2872, USA

Hoover, Vicky (Stylist)
PO Box 854
Littleton, CO 80160, USA

Hoovler, Skip (Athlete, Football Player)
8249 Broad St SW
Pataskala, OH 43062, USA

Hope, Alec D (Writer)
PO Box 7949
Alice Springs, NT 0871, AUSTRALIA

Hope, Jim (Producer)
c/o Staff Member *WME (LA)*
9601 Wilshire Blvd Fl 3
Beverly Hills, CA 90210, USA

Hope, John (Athlete, Baseball Player)
5406 Bayberry Ln
Tamarac, FL 33319-3127, USA

Hope, Leslie (Actor)
c/o Lee Wallman *Wallman Public Relations*
10323 Santa Monica Blvd
Suite 109
Los Angeles, CA 90025, USA

Hope, Maurice (Boxer)
582 Kingsland Road
London E8, UNITED KINGDOM (UK)

Hope, Tamara (Actor)
c/o Matt Schwartz *Christopher Wright Management*
6100 Wilshire Blvd #1170
Los Angeles, CA 90048, USA

Hopkins, Andy (Athlete, Football Player)
2335 Walnut Ridge Dr
Missouri City, TX 77489-5005, USA

Hopkins, Anthony (Actor)
c/o Paul Bloch *Rogers & Cowan PR (LA)*
Pacific Design Center
8687 Melrose Ave, 7th Floor
West Hollywood, CA 90069, USA

Hopkins, Antony (Composer, Writer)
Woodyard Cottage Ashridge
Berkhamsted
Herts HP4 1PS, UNITED KINGDOM (UK)

Hopkins, Bernard (Athlete, Boxer)
c/o Staff Member *Golden Boy Promotions*
626 Wilshire Blvd #350
Los Angeles, CA 90017, USA

Hopkins, Bo (Actor)
6628 Ethel Ave
North Hollywood, CA 91606, USA

Hopkins, Bob (Athlete, Basketball Player)
8421 SE 71st St
Mercer Island, WA 98040-5409, USA

Hopkins, Demetrius (Boxer)
c/o Staff Member *Top Rank Inc.*
3908 Howard Hughes Pkwy
#580
Las Vegas, NV 89109, USA

Hopkins, Don (Athlete, Baseball Player)
P.O. Box 8817
Benton Harbor, MI 49023-8817, USA

Hopkins, Gail (Athlete, Baseball Player)
120 Canterbury Dr
Parkersburg, WV 26104-8048, USA

Hopkins, Gareth (Business Person)
c/o Staff Member *EMI Recorded Music (UK)*
27 Wrights Lane
London W8 5SW, UK

Hopkins, Godfrey T (Photographer)
Wilmington Cottage Wilmington Road
Seaford
E Sussex BN25 2EH, UNITED KINGDOM (UK)

Hopkins, Jan (Correspondent)
Cable News Network
News Dept
1050 Techwood Dr NW
Atlanta, GA 30318, USA

Hopkins, Jerry (Athlete, Football Player)
6688 E Highway 6
Waco, TX 76705, USA

Hopkins, Josh (Actor)
Gersh Agency
232 N Canon Dr
Beverly Hills, CA 90210, USA

Hopkins, Kaitlin (Actor)
19528 Ventura Blvd #559
Tarzana, CA 91356, USA

Hopkins, Katherine
215 S. La Cienega Blvd. PH
Beverly Hills, CA 90211

Hopkins, Larry (Athlete, Hockey Player)
3012 S Fir Ave
Broken Arrow, OK 74012-7496, USA

Hopkins, Linda (Actor, Musician)
2055 N Ivar St #PH
Los Angeles, CA 90068, USA

Hopkins, Michael J (Architect)
27 Broadley Terrace
London NW1 6LG, UNITED KINGDOM (UK)

Hopkins, Michael S Ltcolonel (Astronaut)
910 White Pine Dr
Friendswood, TX 77546-3570, USA

Hopkins, Stephen
8942 Wilshire Blvd.
Beverly Hills, CA 90211

Hopkins, Stephen J (Director)
International Creative Mgmt
8942 Wilshire Blvd #219
Beverly Hills, CA 90211, USA

Hopkins, Sy (Music Group)
Paramount Entertainment
PO Box 12
Far Hills, NJ 07931, USA

Hopkins, Tamburo (Athlete, Football Player)
2740 Maitland Crossing Way
Apt 2208
Orlando, FL 32810, USA

Hopkins, Telma (Actor, Musician)
4122 Don Luis Dr
Los Angeles, CA 90008, USA

Hopkins, Tom (Business Person, Writer)
Tom Hopkins International
7531 E 2nd St
Scottsdale, AZ 85251, USA

Hopkins, Wesley (Athlete, Football Player)
7412 White Oak Rd
Fairfield, AL 35064, USA

Hoppe, Fred (Artist)
7401NW 105th St
Malcolm, NE 68402, USA

Hoppe, Wolfgang (Athlete)
Dieterstedter Str 11
Apolda 99510, GERMANY

Hoppen, Dave (Athlete, Basketball Player)
16341 Webster St
Omaha, NE 68118-2513, USA

Hopper, C Darrow (Athlete, Football Player)
6 Braemore Pl
Dallas, TX 75230-1958, USA

Hopper, John D Jr (General)
Commander
Air Education/Training Command
Randolph Air Force Base, TX 78155, USA

Hopper, Norris (Athlete, Baseball Player)
902 Hampton St
Shelby, NC 28152-6412, USA

Hopperdeitz, Anna (Actor)
c/o Staff Member *Agentur Fuhrmann*
Lindenstr 8A
Isen-Pemmering 84424, Germany

Hoppock, Doug (Athlete, Football Player)
13212 W 115th St
Shawnee Mission, KS 66210, USA

Hoppus, Cliff (Stylist)
c/o Staff Member *Exclusive Artists Mgmt*
7700 Sunset Blvd
#205
Los Angeles, CA 90046, USA

Hoppus, Mark (Actor, Musician, Producer)
c/o Geyer Kosinski *Media Talent Group*
9200 Sunset Blvd
Suite 550
Los Angeles, CA 90069, USA

Hopson, Dennis (Athlete, Basketball Player)
7229 Donnybrook Dr
Dublin, OH 43017-2403, USA

Horacek, Tony (Athlete, Hockey Player)
71 Clover Pl
Lebanon, PA 17042-9400, USA

Horan, Dennis
32458 Galatina St
Temecula, CA 92592-3881, USA

Horan, James (Actor)
c/o Staff Member *Angel City Talent*
4741 Laurel Canyon Blvd #101
Valley Village, CA 91607, USA

Horan, Machael W (Mike) (Athlete, Football Player)
1232 Edgeview Dr
Santa Ana, CA 92705, USA

Horbiger, Christiane
Frankengasse 28
Zurich, SWITZERLAND CH-8001

Horbul, Doug (Athlete, Hockey Player)
2562 Statts
Fruitvale, BC VOG 1LO, Canada

Hordges, Cedrick (Athlete, Basketball Player)
237 W 127th St
Apt 28
New York, NY 10027-2901, USA

Hordichuk, Darcy (Athlete, Hockey Player)
8237 NW 107th Ter
Parkland, FL 33076-4766, USA

Horecker, Bernard L (Biologist)
16517 Cypress Villa Lane
Fort Myers, FL 33908, USA

Horgan, Joe (Athlete, Baseball Player)
512 Hvland Dr
Lockoort, LA 70374-3333, USA

Horgan, Patrick (Actor)
201 E 89th St
New York, NY 10128, USA

Horinek, Ramon A (War Hero)
181 National Blvd
Universal City, TX 78148, USA

Horlacher, Gary (Scientist)
3423 E Pine Brook Way
Houston, TX 77059-3203, USA

Horlen, Joel (Athlete, Baseball Player)
3718 Chartwell Dr
San Antonio, TX 78230-3202, USA

Horlock, John H (Educator, Engineer)
2 The Avenue
Ampthill
Bedford MK45 2NR, UNITED KINGDOM (UK)

Horn, Don (Athlete, Football Player)
1336 Hazeline Lake Dr
Colorado Springs, CO 80921-4105, USA

Horn, Gyula (Prime Minister)
Parliament
Kossuth Lajor Ter 1/3
Budapest 1055, HUNGARY

Horn, Joe (Athlete, Football Player)
2408 Shenley Park Ct
Duluth, GA 30097, USA

Horn, Marian Blank (Judge)
US Claims Court
717 Madison Place NW
Washington, DC 20439, USA

Horn, Paul J (Musician)
4601 Leyns Road
Victoria, BC V8N 3A1, CANADA

Horn, Roy (Magician)
Mirage Hotel & Casino
3400 Las Vegas Blvd S
Las Vegas, NV 89109

Horn, Sam (Athlete, Baseball Player)
1305 Narragansett Blvd
Cranston, RI 02905-3825, USA

Horn, Shriley (Music Group)
1007 Towne Lane
Charlottesville, VA 22901, USA

Horn, Thomas (Actor)
c/o Jennifer Allen *Viewpoint Inc*
8820 Wilshire Blvd.
Suite 220
Beverly Hills, CA 90211, USA

Hornacek, Jeff (Athlete, Basketball Player)
5821 N 37th St
Paradise Valley, AZ 85253-5004, USA

Hornaday, Ron (Race Car Driver)
Kevin Harvick Inc
703 Park Lawn Ct.
Kernersville, NC 27284, USA

Hornbeck, Larry (Inventor)
3130 Bethel Cannon Rd
Van Alstyne, TX 75495-3571, USA

Hornburg, Hal M (General)
Commander
Air Combat Command
Langley Air Force Base, VA 23665, USA

Hornby, Nick (Writer)
Cassarotto
60/66 Wardour St
London W1V 4ND, UNITED KINGDOM
(UK)

Horne, Donald R (Writer)
53 Grosvenor St
Woollahra
Sydney, NSW 2025, AUSTRALIA

Horne, John R (Business Person)
Navistar International
PO Box 1488
Warrenville, IL 60555, USA

Horne, Marilyn (Opera Singer)
The Marilyn Horne Foundation
250 West 57th St #603
New York, NY 10019, USA

Horneber, Petra (Misc)
Ringstr 77
Kranzberg 85402, GERMANY

Horneff, Wil (Actor)
c/o Staff Member *Creative Artists Agency*
(CAA-LA)
2000 Ave Of The Stars
Los Angeles, CA 90067, USA

Horner, Bob (Athlete, Baseball Player)
209 Steeplechase Dr
Irving, TX 75062-3823, USA

Horner, Charles A (General)
2824 Jack Nicklaus Way
Shalimar, FL 32579, USA

Horner, Craig (Actor)
c/o Matt Andrews *Marquee Management*
The Gatehouse
188 Oxford St Studio B
Paddington NSW 2021, Australia

Horner, Freeman V (War Hero)
1501 Doubletree Dr
Columbus, GA 31904, USA

Horner, James (Composer, Musician)
c/o Carri McClure *McClure and*
Associates Public Relations
5225 Wilshire Blvd #909
Los Angeles, CA 90036, USA

Horner, John R (Jack) (Scientist)
70 Cougar Dr
Bozeman, MT 59718, USA

Horner, Martina S (Business Person,
Educator)
TIAA-CREF
730 3rd Ave
New York, NY 10017, USA

Horner, Richard E (Scientist)
1064 Paradise Lake Dr SE
Grand Rapids, MI 49546-3831, USA

Horner, Sam (Athlete, Football Player)
681 Duck Thurmond Rd
Dawsonville, GA 30534-2811, USA

Hornig, Donald F (Misc)
1 Little Pond Cove Road
Little Compton, RI 02837, USA

Hornish Jr, Sam (Race Car Driver)
Penske Racing
200 Renske Way
Mooresville, Nc 28115, USA

Hornsby, Bruce (Musician)
PO Box 3545
Williamsburg, VA 23187, USA

Hornsby, Ron (Athlete, Football Player)
2028 Washington St
Franklinton, LA 70438, USA

Hornsby, Russell (Actor)
c/o Leonard Torgan *Collective*
8383 Wilshire Blvd
Suite 1050
Beverly Hills, CA 90211, USA

Hornung, Larry (Athlete, Hockey Player)

Hornung, Paul (Athlete, Football Player,
Heisman Trophy Winner)
Waterfront Plaza
325 West Main St #1116
Louisville, KY 40202, USA

Horovitz, Adam (King Ad-Rock) (Artist,
Music Group, Musician)
c/o Staff Member *WME (LA)*
9601 Wilshire Blvd Fl 3
Beverly Hills, CA 90210, USA

Horovitz, Israel A (Writer)
146 W 11th St
New York, NY 10011, USA

Horovitz, Joseph (Composer)
Royal College of Music
Prince Consort Road
London SW7 2BS, UNITED KINGDOM
(UK)

Horowitz, Adam
c/o Philip Raskind *WME (LA)*
9601 Wilshire Blvd Fl 3
Beverly Hills, CA 90210, USA

Horowitz, David (Correspondent)
Fight Back !
P.O. Box 49915
Los Angeles, CA 90049-0915, USA

Horowitz, David (Misc)
1319 Bonita Ave
Berkeley, CA 94709-1924, USA

Horowitz, Jerome P (Scientist)
Michigan Cancer Foundation
110 E Warren Ave
Detroit, MI 48201, USA

Horowitz, Norman H (Biologist)
2495 Brighton Road
Pasadena, CA 91104, USA

Horowitz, Paul (Doctor, Physicist)
111 Chilton St
Cambridge, MA 02138, USA

Horowitz, Sari (Journalist)
Washington Post
Editorial Dept
1150 15th St NW
Washington, DC 20071, USA

Horowitz, Scott J (Astronaut)
5491 Freestyle Way
Park City, UT 84098-7621, USA

Horowitz, Scott J Colonel (Astronaut)
5491 Freestyle Way
Park City, UT 84098-7621, USA

Horry, Robert (Athlete, Basketball Player)
2618 Sara Ridge Ln
Katy, TX 77450-5374, USA

Horsey, David (Cartoonist, Editor)
c/o Staff Member *King Features*
Syndication
300 W 57th St
15th Floor
New York, NY 10019-5238, USA

Horsford, Anna Maria (Actor)
PO Box 48082
Los Angeles, CA 90048, USA

Horsley, Jack (Athlete, Olympic Athlete,
Swimmer)
608 N Sampson St
Ellensburg, WA 98926-3162, USA

Horsley, Lee A (Actor)
c/o Laura Walsh *Central Artists*
3310 W Burbank Blvd #A
Burbank, CA 91505-2230, USA

Horsley, Richard D (Financier)
Regions Financial Corp
417 20th St N
Birmingham, AL 35203, USA

Horsman, Vince (Athlete, Baseball Player)
1941 Pinehurst Dr
Clearwater, FL 33763-2228, USA

Horst, Lisa Ann
PO Box 8633
Lancaster CO, PA 17604

Horstman, Catherine (Athlete, Baseball
Player, Commentator)
39018 Desert Greens Dr E
Palm Desert, CA 92260-1403, USA

Horth, Annie (Stylist)
c/o Staff Member *Judy Inc*
1 Yorkville Ave
Toronto ON M4W 1L1, Canada

Horton, Ethan S (Football Player,
Sportscaster)
4602 Fairvista Dr
Charlotte, NC 28269-1098, USA

Horton, Frank E (Educator)
288 River Ranch Circle
Bayfield, CO 81122, USA

Horton, Greg (Athlete, Football Player)
1053 Lytle St
Redlands, CA 92374, USA

Horton, Jonathan (Athlete, Gymnast,
Olympic Athlete)
c/o Staff Member *USA Gymnastics*
Pan American Plz #300
201 S Capitol Ave
Indianapolis, IN 46225, USA

Horton, Larry (Athlete, Football Player)
215 Emerald St
Harrisburg, PA 17110-1013, USA

Horton, Lawrence (Athlete, Football
Player)
1442 S 13th St
Harrisburg, PA 17104, USA

Horton, Mark (Race Car Driver)
Summit Racing
PO Box 535
Richfield, OH 44286-0535, USA

Horton, Michael (Editor)
c/o Staff Member *Mirisch Agency*
8840 Wilshire Blvd
Suite 100
Beverly Hills, CA 90211, USA

Horton, Nathan (Athlete, Hockey Player)
The Orr Hockey Group
PO Box 290836
Charlestown, MA 02129-0215, USA

Horton, Peter (Actor)
409 Santa Monica Blvd #PH
Santa Monica, CA 90401, USA

Horton, Ray (Athlete, Football Player)
3400 S Water St
Pittsburgh, PA 15203-2349, USA

Horton, Ricky (Athlete, Baseball Player)
16026 Aston Ct
Chesterfield, MO 63005-4575, USA

Horton, Robert (Actor)
5317 Andasol Ave
Encino, CA 91316, USA

Horton, Steve Major (General)
571 Sandy_ Mountain Dr
Sunrise Beach, TX 78643-9264, USA

Horton, Tony (Athlete, Fitness Expert,
Television Host)
BeachBody
3301 Exposition Blvd Fl 3
Santa Monica, CA 90404, USA

Horton, Tony (Athlete, Baseball Player)
17001 Livorno Dr
Pacific Palisades, CA 90272-3232, USA

Horton, Willie (Athlete, Baseball Player)
The Athlete Connection
PO Box 380135
Llinton Township, MI 48038-0060, USA

Horton, Willie(baseball)
15124 Warwick St.
Detroit, MI 48223

Horvath, Bronco J (Athlete, Hockey
Player)
27 Oliver St
South Yarmouth, MA 02664-2901, USA

Horvitz, H Robert (Nobel Prize Laureate)
Massachusetts Institute of Technology
34 Pilgrim Rd
Wellesley Hills, MA 02481-2447, USA

Horvitz, Louis J (Director)
c/o Staff Member *Gersh (LA)*
9465 Wilshire Blvd
Suite 600
Beverly Hills, CA 90212, USA

Horwitz, Brian (Athlete, Baseball Player)
5118 E Edgemont Ave
Phoenix, AZ 85008-1642, USA

Horwitz, Tony (Journalist)
Wall Street Journal
Editorial Dept
200 Liberty St
New York, NY 10281, USA

Hosbein, Marion (Athlete, Baseball
Player, Commentator)
1347 Cliff Barnes Drive
Kalamazoo, MI 49009-8329, USA

Hosea, Bobby (Actor)
c/o Sara Schedeen *Metropolitan (MTA)*
4526 Wilshire Blvd
Los Angeles, CA 90010, USA

Hosey, Dwayne (Athlete, Baseball Player)
164 N Plum Ave
Ontario, CA 91764-4137, USA

Hosey, Steve (Athlete, Baseball Player)
2351 W Lorna Linda Ave
Fresno, CA 93711-0417, USA

Hoshide, Akihiko (Astronaut)
NASDA, Tsukuba Space Center 2-1-1,
Sengen
Tukuba-shi, Ibaraka 305, japan

Hosket, Bill (Athlete, Basketball Player,
Olympic Athlete)
7461 Worthington Galena Rd
Worthington, OH 43085-6715, USA

Hoskins, Bob (Actor)
Cassarotto
60/66 Wardour St
London W1V 4ND, UNITED KINGDOM
(UK)

Hoskins, Derrick (Athlete, Football Player)
10491 Road 842
Philadelphia, MS 39350, USA

Hosley, Tim (Athlete, Baseball Player)
112 Elena Dr
Moore, SC 29369-9657, USA

Hosmer, Bradley C (Brad) (General)
PO Box 1128
Cedar Crest, NM 87008, USA

Hospodar, Ed (Athlete, Hockey Player)
217 Orchard Way
Wayne, PA 19087-4805, USA

Hoss, Clark (Athlete, Football Player)
2709 Ridge Ln
West Linn, OR 97068-2986, USA

Hossa, Marian (Athlete, Hockey Player)
The Sports Corporation
2735-10088 102 Ave NW
Attn Rich Winter
Edmonton, AB T5J 2Z1, Canada

Hossein, Robert (Actor, Director)
Ghislaine de Wing
10 Rue du Docteur Roux
Paris 75015, FRANCE

Hosseini, Khaled
c/o Judy Lubershane *Judy Lubershane Agency*
not available
Boston, MA 02101, USA

Hostak, Al (Boxer)
11501 161st Ave SE
Renton, WA 98059, USA

Hostak, Martin (Athlete, Hockey Player)
Ceska Televize odd. kontaktu s divakem
Kavci hory
Praha 4 140 70, Czech Republic

Hostetler, Dave (Athlete, Baseball Player)
3404 Steeplechase Trl
Arlington, TX 76016-2325, USA

Hostetler, David L (Artist)
PO Box 989
Athens, OH 45701, USA

Hostetler, Jeff (Athlete, Football Player)
The Hass Foundation 50 Clay St Ste 410
Morgantown, WV 26501-5932, USA

Hostetter, G Richard (Religious Leader)
Presbyterian Church in America
1852 Century Plaza
Atlanta, GA 30345, USA

Hoston, Ricky (Baseball Player)
St Louis Cardinals
16026 Aston Ct
Chesterfield, MO 63005 4575, USA

Hoston, Tony (Baseball Player)
Boston Red Sox
17001 Livorno Dr
Pacific Palisades, CA 90272 3232, USA

Hotani, Hirokazu (Engineer)
Teikyo University
Biosciences Dept
Toyosatodai
Utsunomiya 320, JAPAN

Hot Chelle Rae (Music Group)
c/o Staff Member *Jive Records*
550 Madison Ave
New York, NY 10022-3211, USA

Hotchkiss, Rob (Musician)
Jon Landau
80 Mason St
Greenwich, CT 06830, USA

Hotchkiss, Rollin D (Doctor, Scientist)
2-4 Rolling Hills
Lenox, MA 01240, USA

Hotchner, Aaron
14 Hillandale Rd.
Westport, CT 06880

Hotchner, Aaron Edward (Producer, Writer)
c/o Staff Member *HarperCollins Publishers*
10 East 53rd St
c/o Author mail, 7th Floor
New York, NY 10022, USA

Hotham, Greg (Athlete, Hockey Player)
40 Ridgeway Ave
Barrie, ON L4N 5L2, Canada

Hottelet, Richard C (Correspondent)
120 Chestnut Hill Road
Wilton, CT 06897, USA

Hottman, Ken (Athlete, Baseball Player)
9537 2nd Ave
Elk Grove, CA 95624-1936, USA

Hoty, Dee
333 W. 56th St.
New York, NY 10019

Hou, Ya-Ming (Biologist)
Massachusetts Institute of Technology
Biology Dept
Cambridge, MA 02139, USA

Houbregs, Bob (Athlete, Basketball Player)
1949 Arena Ct SE
Olympia, WA 98501-6874, USA

Houcke, Sara (Misc)
Feld Enterprises
1313 17th St E
Palmetto, FL 34221, USA

Houda, Doug
Boston Bruins
100 Legends Way Ste 250
Attn: Coaching Staff
Boston, MA 02114-1389, USA

Houda, Doug (Athlete, Hockey Player)
10 Lovell Rd
Lynnfield, MA 01940-1818, USA

Houde, Claude
1350 Rue de la Seve
Drummondville, QC J2C 7L1, Canada

Hough, Charlie (Athlete, Baseball Player)
2266 Shade Tree Cir
Brea, CA 92821-4423, USA

Hough, Charlie (Athlete, Baseball Player)
2266 Shadetree Cir
Brea, CA 92821, USA

Hough, Derek (Dancer, Reality TV Star)
1322 N Detroit St #12
Los Angeles, CA 90046, USA

Hough, Jim (Athlete, Football Player)
2440 Christian Dr
Chaska, MN 55318, USA

Hough, John (Director)
Associated International Mgmt
5 Denmark St
London WC2H 8LP, UNITED KINGDOM
(UK)

Hough, Joseph C Jr (Educator)
Union Theological Seminary
President's Office
New York, NY 10027, USA

Hough, Julianne (Dancer, Musician)
c/o Brad Cafarelli *PMK/BNC - LA*
8687 Melrose Ave
8th Floor
West Hollywood, CA 90069, USA

Hough, Michael A (General)
Deputy Cofs Aviation
HqUSMC 2 Navy St
Washington, DC 20380, USA

Hough, Mike (Athlete, Hockey Player)
25 Marsh Harbour
Aurora, ON L4G 5Y7, Canada

Hough, Stephen A G (Musician)
Harrison/Parrott
12 Penzance Place
London W11 4PA, UNITED KINGDOM
(UK)

Houghton, James (Business Person)
Field 36 Spencer Hill Road
Corning, NY 14830, USA

Houghton, John (Physicist)
Rutherford Appleton Laboratory
Chilton
Didcot Oxon OX11 0QX, UNITED
KINGDOM (UK)

Houghton, Katherine (Actor)
Ambrosio/Mortimer
165 W 46th St
New York, NY 10036, USA

Houghton of Sowerby, Douglas
(Government Official)
110 Marsham Court
London SW1, UNITED KINGDOM (UK)

Hougland, Bill (Athlete, Basketball Player,
Olympic Athlete)
504 Canyon Dr
Lawrence, KS 66049-2400, USA

Houider, Bill (Athlete, Hockey Player)
220 Maple Cove
RR 2 North Bay, ON P1B 8G3, Canada

Houle, Rejean (Athlete, Hockey Player)
7941 Boul Lasalle
Lasalle, QC H8P 3R1, Canada

Houle, Rejean
Montreal Canadiens
1275 Rue Saint-Antoine 0
Attn Community Ambassador
Montreal, QC H3C 5L2, Canada

Houlemard, Michael (Athlete, Baseball
Player)
111 S Orange Grove Blvd
Apt 104
Pasadena, CA 91105-1756, USA

Houlton, D J (Athlete, Baseball Player)
2357 N Campus Ave
Upland, CA 91784-1303, USA

Hounsfield, Godfrey N (Nobel Prize
Laureate)
15 Crane Park Road
Whitton Twickenham
Middx TW2 6DF, UNITED KINGDOM
(UK)

Hounsou, Djimon (Actor, Model,
Producer)
c/o Peter Safran *The Safran Company*
8748 Holloway Dr
Los Angeles, CA 90069, USA

Hourde, Daniel (Artist)
37, rue Galande
Paris 75005, France

House, Craig (Athlete, Baseball Player)
8614 Brock Cir
Austin, TX 78745-6368, USA

House, David (Dave) (Business Person)
Nortel Networks Corp
8200 Dixie Road
Brampton, ON L6T 5P6, CANADA

House, James
1313 16th Ave. So.
Nashville, TN 37212

House, J R (Athlete, Baseball Player)
34 River Ridge Trl
Ormond Beach, FL 32174, USA

House, J R (Athlete, Baseball Player)
34 River Ridge Trl
Ormond Beach, FL 32174-4340, USA

House, Karen Eliot (Journalist)
Dow Jones International 1 World
Financial Ctr Fl 9 Attn Office of the
President
New York, NY 10281-1003, USA

House, Karen Ellot (Journalist)
58 Cleveland Lane
Princeton, NJ 08540, USA

House, Kathryn (Stylist)
c/o Staff Member *Crews*
828 Clemont Dr
Atlanta, GA 30306, USA

House, Kevin (Athlete, Football Player)
4004 Alexander Palm Ct
Tampa, FL 33624-2379, USA

House, Pat (Athlete, Baseball Player)
2053 White Pine Ln
Boise, ID 83706-4048, USA

House, Pat (Athlete, Baseball Player)
2554 W Penick Pointe Ct
Meridian, ID 83646, USA

House, Rick (Athlete, Football Player)
1538 McCreary Rd
Winnipeg, MB R3P0M7, Canada

House, Stormy
12334 Gorham Ave.
Los Angeles, CA 90049

House, Tom (Athlete, Baseball Player)
12794 Via Felino
Del Mar, CA 92014-3806, USA

House, Yoanna (Model, Television Host)
c/o Staff Member *Style Network*
5750 Wilshire Blvd
Los Angeles, CA 90036, USA

Householder, Paul (Athlete, Baseball
Player)
521 N Swinton Ave
Delray Beach, FL 33444-3969, USA

HouseJ, Eddie (Athlete, Basketball Player)
35 Kings Way
Waltham, MA 02451-9041, USA

House of Pain (Music Group)
c/o Staff Member *WmE2 (WMA-LA)*
1 William Morris Pl
Beverly Hills, CA 90212, USA

Houser, Huell
450 N. Rossmore Ave. #602
Los Angeles, CA 90004

Houser, Jerry (Actor)
8325 Skyline Dr
Los Angeles, CA 90046, USA

Houser, John (Athlete, Football Player)
2197 Creekside Dr
Solvang, CA 93463-2238, USA

Houser, Kevin (Athlete, Football Player)
941 Montclair Cir
Westlake, OH 44145, USA

Houser, Randolph (Randy) (Musician)
c/o Staff Member *Fitzgerald Hartley Co
(Nashville)*
1908 Wedgewood Ave
Nashville, TN 37212, USA

Houser, Susan (Stylist)
c/o Staff Member *Independent NY*
15 E 30th St #401
New York, NY 10016, USA

Houshmandzadeh, T J (Athlete, Football
Player)
16703 Greenbrook Cir
Cerritos, CA 90703, USA

Housie, Wayne (Athlete, Baseball Player)
16530 Colt Way
Moreno Valley, CA 92555-3303, USA

Housley, Phil (Athlete, Hockey Player,
Olympic Athlete)
2877 Itasca Ave S
Lakeland, MN 55043-9742, USA

Housner, George W (Engineer, Misc)
California Institute of Technology
Engineering Dept
Pasadena, CA 91125, USA

Houston (Adult Film Star)
c/o Staff Member *Atlas Multimedia Inc*
9005 Eton Ave Ste C
Canoga Park, CA 91304-1743, USA

Houston, Allan (Athlete, Basketball
Player, Olympic Athlete)
Allan Houston Foundation
350 5th Ave Fl 59
New York, NY 10118-5999, USA

Houston, Andy (Race Car Driver)
c/o *Global Performance Co*
835 F Williamson Road #36
Mooresville, NC 28117, USA

Houston, Bobby (Athlete, Football Player)
4640 Vendue Range Dr
Raleigh, NC 27604-5078, USA

Houston, Byron (Athlete, Basketball
Player)
3108 Birch Ln
Edmond, OK 73034-8249, USA

Houston, Cissy (Musician)
*The New Hope Baptist Church Youth
Choir*
106 Sussex Ave
Newark, NJ 07103, USA

Houston, Edwin A (Business Person)
Ryder System Inc
3600 NW 82nd Ave
Miami, FL 33166, USA

Houston, Jarell (J-Boog) (Actor, Musician)
c/o Michael (Mike) Esterman
Esterman.Com, LLC
Prefers to be contacted via email
MD, USA

Houston, Jim (Athlete, Football Player)
925 Trimble Pl
Northfield, OH 44067-2239, USA

Houston, Ken (Athlete, Hockey Player)
25 University Dr
Chatham, ON N7L 4V4, Canada

Houston, Kenneth R (Ken) (Athlete,
Football Player)
3603 Forest Village Drive
Kingwood, TX 77339, USA

Houston, Marques (Batman) (Actor,
Musician)
c/o Tyler Grasham *Agency for the
Performing Arts (APA-LA)*
405 S Beverly Dr
Suite 500
Beverly Hills, CA 90212-4425, USA

Houston, Marquis (Actor, Musician)

Houston, Penelope (Music Group)
Absolute Artists
8490 W Sunset Blvd #403
West Hollywood, CA 90069, USA

Houston, Russell (Artist)
General Delivery
Eagar, AZ 85925, USA

Houston, Thelma (Musician)
J Cast Productions
2550 Greenvalley Rd
Los Angeles, CA 90046, USA

Houston, Tyler (Athlete, Baseball Player)
325 Pleasant Summit Dr
Henderson, NV 89012-3486, USA

Houston, Wade (Basketball Player,
Coach)
University of Tennessee
Athletic Dept
Knoxville, TN 37901, USA

Houston Calls (Music Group)
c/o Staff Member *Drive Thru Records*
3019 Olympic Blvd
Santa Monica, CA 90404-5001, USA

Houthakker, Hendrik S (Economist)
1 Ivy Pointe Way
Hanover, NH 03755, USA

Hovan, Chris (Athlete, Football Player)
17301 Ladera Estates Blvd
Lutz, FL 33548-4817, USA

Hove, Andrew C Jr (Financier)
Federal Deposit Insurance
550 17th St NW
Washington, DC 20429, USA

Hover, Don (Athlete, Football Player)
19 Wolf Creek Rd
Winthrop, WA 98862-9767, USA

Hovind, David J (Business Person)
PACCAR Inc
777 106th Ave NE
Bellevue, WA 98004, USA

Hovis, Guy (Musician)
207 Morningside N
Ridgeland, MS 39157, USA

Hovland, Tim (Athlete, Volleyball Player)
431 Main St.
El Segundo, CA 90245, USA

Hovley, Steve (Athlete, Baseball Player)
P.O. Box 655
Oak View, CA 93022-0655, USA

Hovsepian, Vatche (Religious Leader)
Armenian Church of America West
1201 N Vine St
Los Angeles, CA 90038, USA

Howard, Adina (Musician)
International Creative Mgmt
40 W 57th St #1800
New York, NY 10019, USA

Howard, Adina (Musician)
c/o Staff Member *Diva Central Inc*
7510 W Sunset Blvd Ste 1445
Los Angees, CA 90046, USA

Howard, Alan (Actor)
Julian Belfrage
46 Albermarle St
London W1X 4PP, UNITED KINGDOM
(UK)

Howard, Andrew (Actor)
c/o Michelle Czernin von Chudenitz
Popular Press Media Group (PPMG)
468 N Camden Dr
Suite 105A
Beverly Hills, CA 90210, USA

Howard, Ann (Opera Singer)
Stafford Law Assoc
6 Barham Close
Weybridge
Surrey KT13 9PR, UNITED KINGDOM
(UK)

Howard, Arliss (Actor, Director, Writer)
c/o Gene Parseghian *Parseghian Planco
LLC*
322 8th Ave
Suite 601
New York, NY 10001, USA

Howard, Ben (Athlete, Baseball Player)
45 Cross Brook Cv
Jackson, TN 38305-3548, USA

Howard, Bob (Athlete, Football Player)
2444 56th St
San Diego, CA 92105, USA

Howard, Bobby (Athlete, Football Player)
745 Hansell St SE Apt 513
Atlanta, GA 30312-3475, USA

Howard, Brian (Athlete, Basketball Player)
619 Vermont Ave
Fort Walton Beach, FL 32547-3033, USA

Howard, Bruce (Athlete, Baseball Player)
8705 Misty Creek Dr
Sarasota, FL 34241-9562, USA

Howard, Bryce Dallas (Actor)
c/o Peter Kiernan *Management 360*
9111 Wilshire Blvd
Beverly Hills, CA 90210, USA

Howard, Chris (Athlete, Baseball Player)
8655 Jones rd
Apt 301
Jersey Village, TX 77065-5104, USA

Howard, Chris (Athlete, Baseball Player)
17 Sea View Ave
Nahant, MA 01908-1548, USA

Howard, Clark (Radio Personality, Writer)
Newstalk 750 WSB
1601 W. Peachtree St
Atlanta, GA 30309, USA

Howard, Clint (Actor)
c/o Tiffany Kuzon *Evolution Entertainment
(LA)*
901 N Highland Ave
Los Angeles, CA 90038, USA

Howard, Dana (Athlete, Football Player)
228 Oakridge Ct
Fairview Heights, IL 62208-3452, USA

Howard, David (Athlete, Football Player)
5516 E Rosedale St
Fort Worth, TX 76112-6859, USA

Howard, David (Athlete, Baseball Player)
22846 Chesterview
LoopApt 111
Land 0 Lakes, FL 34639-5343, USA

Howard, Desmond (Athlete, Football
Player, Heisman Trophy Winner)
7507 Ponce De Leon Rd
Miami, FL 33143-6107, USA

Howard, Doug (Athlete, Baseball Player)
8038 Deer Creek Rd
Salt Lake City, UT 84121-5762, USA

Howard, Dwight (Athlete, Basketball
Player)
3565 Rice Lake Loop
Longwood, FL 32779-3081, USA

Howard, Eddie (Athlete, Football Player)
1130 E Workman Ave
West Covina, CA 91790, USA

Howard, Erik (Athlete, Football Player)
23255 FM 150 W
Driftwood, TX 78619-9155, USA

Howard, Frank (Athlete, Baseball Player,
Coach)
24178 Lenah Woods Pl
Aldie, VA 20105-2369, USA

Howard, Frank O (Athlete, Baseball
Player)
24178 Lenah Woods Place
Aldie, VA 20105-2369, USA

Howard, Fred (Athlete, Baseball Player)
250 Lake Lulu Dr
Winter Haven, FL 33880-4461, USA

Howard, Gene (Athlete, Football Player)
11051 Lavender Ave
Fountain Valley, CA 92708, USA

Howard, George (Bowler)
8415 Brookwood Dr
Portage, MI 49024, USA

Howard, George (Musician)
David Rubinson
PO Box 411197
San Francisco, CA 94141, USA

Howard, Greg (Athlete, Basketball Player)
4517 W 16th Pl
Apt 2
Los Angeles, CA 90019, USA

Howard, Greg (Cartoonist)
3403 W 28th St
Minneapolis, MN 55416-4302, USA

Howard, Harry N (Historian)
6508 Greentree Road
Bradley Hills Grove
Bethesda, MD 20817, USA

Howard, James Newton (Composer,
Musician)
c/o Staff Member *Chasen & Company*
8899 Beverly Blvd
Suite 405
Los Angeles, CA 90048, USA

Howard, Jan (Music Group)
c/o Staff Member *Tessier-Marsh Talent*
505 Canton Pass
Madison, TN 37115, USA

Howard, Jeffrey R (Judge)
US Court of Appeals
US Courthouse
55 Pleasant St
Concord, NH 03301, USA

Howard, Jim (Athlete, Hockey Player)
518 Hamilton St
Ogdensburg, NY 13669-2714, USA

Howard, Joe (Athlete, Football Player)
2501 Joseph Dr
Clinton, MD 20735, USA

Howard, John W (Politician, Prime Minister)
Prime Minister's Office
Parliament House
Canberra, ACT 2600, AUSTRALIA

Howard, Josh (Athlete, Basketball Player)
PO Box 802851
Dallas, TX 75380-2851, USA

Howard, Joyce
147 Ocean Ave.
Santa Monica, CA 90403

Howard, Juwan (Athlete, Basketball Player)
11714 Bistro Ln
Houston, TX 77082-2726, USA

Howard, Ken (Director)
c/o Diane Perez *Zero Gravity Management*
1531 14th. St
Santa Monica, CA 90404, USA

Howard, Kyle (Actor)
c/o Steve Himber *Steve Himber Entertainment*
211 S Beverly Dr #601
Beverly Hills, CA 90212, USA

Howard, Larry (Athlete, Baseball Player)
207 Innwood Dr
Georgetown, TX 78628-8311, USA

Howard, Lee (Athlete, Baseball Player)
4650 Dulin Rd
Spc 203
Fallbrook, CA 92028-8766, USA

Howard, Leo (Actor)
c/o Emily Urbani *Osbrink Talent Agency*
4343 Lankershim Blvd
Suite 100
Universal City, CA 91602, USA

Howard, Lisa
247 S. Beverly Dr. #102
Beverly Hills, CA 90212

Howard, Matt (Athlete, Baseball Player)
31896 Jaybee Ln
Temecula, CA 92592-4174, USA

Howard, Michael (Government Official)
House of Commons
Westminster
London SW1A 0AA, UNITED KINGDOM (UK)

Howard, Mike (Athlete, Baseball Player)
101 Kenbridge Ln
Madison, MS 39110-9773, USA

Howard, Miki (Musician)
c/o Mike Gardner *Gardener Entertainment*
5683 Hazelcrest Dr
Thousand Oaks, CA 91362, USA

Howard, ohn
GPO Box 59
Sydney, AUSTRALIA NSW 2001, AUSTRALIA

Howard, Otis (Athlete, Basketball Player)
231 Manhattan Ave
Oak Ridge, TN 37830-7544, USA

Howard, Paige (Actor)
c/o Meredith Wechter *ICM Partners (ICM-LA)*
10250 Constellation Blvd Fl 7
Los Angeles, CA 90067, USA

Howard, Paul (Athlete, Football Player)
8502 S Jebel Way
Aurora, CO 80013, USA

Howard, Percy (Athlete, Football Player)
3525 Neely Rd
Memphis, TN 38109-3811, USA

Howard, Rance (Actor)
4286 Clybourne Ave
Burbank, CA 91505, USA

Howard, Rebecca Lynn (Musician)
c/o Staff Member *Paradigm (Monterey)*
404 W Franklin St
Monterey, CA 93940, USA

Howard, Reggie (Athlete, Football Player)
775 Tucker St
Dyersburg, TN 38024-3791, USA

Howard, Reggie (Athlete, Baseball Player)
4332 Crimson Leaf Cv
Memphis, TN 38125-2905, USA

Howard, Richard (Writer)
23 Waverly Place #5X
New York, NY 10003-6717, USA

Howard, Robert (Hardcore Holly) (Wrestler)
c/o Kerry Rodgerson *World Wrestling Entertainment (WWE)*
Titan Towers
1241 E Main St
Stamford, CT 06905-3857, USA

Howard, Ron (Actor, Director, Producer, Writer)
c/o Richard Lovett *Creative Artists Agency (CAA-LA)*
2000 Ave Of The Stars
Los Angeles, CA 90067, USA

Howard, Ron (Athlete, Football Player)
14701 NE 61st Ct
Redmond, WA 98052, USA

Howard, Ryan (Athlete, Baseball Player)
1630 Bentshire Ct
Ballwin, MO 63011-4754, USA

Howard, Sherman (Athlete, Football Player)
5125 Thomas Dr
Richton Park, IL 60471, USA

Howard, Sherri (Actor)
c/o Michael Henderson *Heresun Management*
4119 West Burbank Blvd.
Burbank, CA 91505, USA

Howard, Sherri (Athlete, Track Athlete)
14059 Bridle Ridge Road
Sylmar, CA 91342, USA

Howard, Sherry
14059 Bridle Ridge Rd.
Sylmar, CA 91342

Howard, Stephen (Athlete, Basketball Player)
3941 Legacy Dr Ste 204 # A193
Plano, Texas 75023-8331, USA

Howard, Steven (Athlete, Baseball Player)
4712 Shetland Ave
Oakland, CA 94605-5629, USA

Howard, Susan (Actor)
PO Box 1456
Boerne, TX 78006, USA

Howard, Terrence (Actor)
c/o Renee Tab *Sentient*
1617 Broadway Mezzanine Suite
Santa Monica, CA 90404, USA

Howard, Thomas (Athlete, Baseball Player)
340 Clark St
Middletown, OH 45042-2041, USA

Howard, Tim (Soccer Player)
Manchester United FC
Sir Matt Busby Way
Old Trafford
Manchester M16 0RA, ENGLAND

Howard, Todd (Athlete, Football Player)
1300 Bienville Ave
Ruston, LA 71270, USA

Howard, Traylor (Actor)
c/o John Carrabino *John Carrabino Management*
5900 Wilshire Blvd Fl 4 #406
Los Angeles, CA 90036, USA

Howard, Wilbur (Athlete, Baseball Player)
643 Walston Ln
Houston, TX 77060-5846, USA

Howard, William W Jr (Misc)
National Wildlife Federation
11100 Wildlife Center Dr
Reston, VA 20190, USA

Howarth, Elgar (Composer)
27 Cromwell Ave
London N6 5HN, UNITED KINGDOM (UK)

Howarth, Jim (Athlete, Baseball Player)
275 Santini St
Biloxi, MS 39530-2958, USA

Howarth, Judith (Opera Singer)
Lies Askonas
6 Henrietta St
London WC2E 8LA, UNITED KINGDOM (UK)

Howarth, Roger (Actor)
K&H
1212 Ave of the Americas #3
New York, NY 10036, USA

Howarth, Thomas (Architect)
University of Toronto
230 College St
Toronto, ON M5S 1R1, CANADA

Howatch, Susan (Writer)
Atiken & Stone
29 Femshaw Road
London SW10 0TG, UNITED KINGDOM (UK)

Howatt, Garry (Athlete, Hockey Player)
20314 E Bronco Dr
Queen Creek, AZ 85142-6007, USA

Howe, Adam (Stylist)
c/o Staff Member *Management & Production/MAP Inc*
48 St Marks Pl
4th Floor
New York, NY 10003, USA

Howe, Arthur (Journalist)
Philadelphia Inquirer
Editorial Dept
400 N Broad St
Philadelphia, PA 19130, USA

Howe, Brian (Musician)
c/o Samantha Crisp *Kohner Agency, The*
9300 Wilshire Blvd
Suite 555
Beverly Hills, CA 90212, USA

Howe, Delles (Athlete, Football Player)
1907 Crescent Dr
Monroe, LA 71202, USA

Howe, Garry (Athlete, Football Player)
3807 NE Gardenia Ln
Ankeny, IA 50021-9289, USA

Howe, Gordie (Athlete, Hockey Player)
Power Play International
1119 Rochester Rd
Troy, MI 48083-6013, USA

Howe, G Woodson (Editor)
Omaha World-Herald
Editorial Dept
World-Herald Square
Omaha, NE 68102, USA

Howe, Jonathan T (Admiral)
Arthur Vining Davis Foundation
225 Water St #1510
Jacksonville, FL 32202, USA

Howe, Marie (Writer)
822 Palmer Road
Apt 2A
Bronxville, NY 10708, USA

Howe, Mark (Athlete, Hockey Player, Olympic Athlete)
9 Inverness Ln
Jackson, NJ 08527-4046, USA

Howe, Marty (Athlete, Hockey Player)
40 Plank Ln
Glastonbury, CT 06033-2523, USA

Howe, Oscar (Artist)
5900 S Prairie View Court
Sioux Falls, SD 57108, USA

Howe, Sean (Writer)
c/o Staff Member *HarperCollins Publishers*
10 East 53rd St
c/o Author mail, 7th Floor
New York, NY 10022, USA

Howe, Tina (Writer)
333 W End Ave
New York, NY 10023, USA

Howe, Vic (Athlete, Hockey Player)
279 Charles Lutes Rd
Moncton, NB E1G 2R8, Canada

Howe Jr, Arthur H (Art) (Athlete, Baseball Player, Coach)
17214 Calico Peak Way
Cypress, TX 77433-2113, USA

Howell, Alex (Cartoonist)
c/o Staff Member *King Features Syndication*
300 W 57th St
15th Floor
New York, NY 10019-5238, USA

Howell, Bailey (Athlete, Basketball Player)
1567 Montgomery Rd
Starkville, MS 39759-5431, USA

Howell, Brad
Gunterring 21
Hattersheim, GERMANY D-65795

Howell, C Thomas (Actor, Director, Producer, Writer)
c/o Jean-Pierre (JP) Henraux *Henraux Management*
Prefers to be contacted by telephone
CA, USA

Howell, David (Golfer)
c/o Staff Member *International Sports Management Ltd (ISM UK)*
Cherry Tree Farm
Cherry Tree Lane
Rostherne, Cheshire WA14 3RZ, UNITED KINGDOM

Howell, Delles (Athlete, Football Player)
1907 Crescent Dr
Monroe, LA 71202-3023, USA

Howell, Francis C (Misc)
1994 San Antonio Ave
Berkeley, CA 94707, USA

Howell, Henry V (Harry) (Athlete, Hockey Player)
401-49 Robinson St
Hamilton, ON L8P 1Y7, Canada

Howell, Jack (Athlete, Baseball Player)
822 S Lehigh Dr
Tucson, AZ 85710-4741, USA

Howell, Jay (Athlete, Baseball Player)
4560 Colony Pt
Suwanee, GA 30024-3010, USA

Howell, John
8276 Sand Dollar Dr
Windsor, CO 80528-7530, USA

Howell, J P (Athlete, Baseball Player)
1706 11th St Apt 11
Sacramento, CA 95811-6547, USA

Howell, Kanin (Actor)
c/o Brandon Ross *Temptation Management*
1010 S Robertson Blvd
Suite 2
Los Angeles, CA 90035, USA

Howell, Kathleen (Engineer)
Purdue University
Aeronautical Engineering Dept
West Lafayette, IN 47907, USA

Howell, Ken (Athlete, Baseball Player)
22090 Buckingham Dr
Farmington Hills, MI 48335, USA

Howell, Margaret (Designer, Fashion Designer)
5 Garden House
8 Battersea Park Road
London SW8, UNITED KINGDOM (UK)

Howell, Mike (Athlete, Football Player)
200 Charlotte St
Monroe, LA 71202, USA

Howell, Pat (Athlete, Football Player)
7692 N Kincaid Ave
Fresno, CA 93711, USA

Howell, Patrick (Pat) (Athlete, Baseball Player)
3081 Lacoste Rd
Mobile, AL 36618-4617, USA

Howell, Roy (Athlete, Baseball Player)
276 El Portal Dr
Pismo Beach, CA 93449-1504, USA

Howell III, Charles (Athlete, Golfer)
c/o Thomas Parker *GPR Sports Management*
11715 Spinnaker Way
Hollywood, FL 33026, USA

Howells, Anne (Opera Singer)
Milestone Broom Close
Esher Surrey, UNITED KINGDOM (UK)

Howells, Michael (Stylist)
c/o Staff Member *Camilla Lowther Managment (CLM Represents)*
30-32 Ericsson Pl
New York, NY 10013, USA

Howe of Aberavon, R E Geoffrey (Government Official)
Barclays Bank
Cavendish Square Branch
4 Vere St
London W1, UNITED KINGDOM (UK)

Hower, Elizabeth (Actor)
c/o Ken Treusch *Bleecker Street Entertainment*
568 Broadway #801
New York, NY 10012, USA

Howerton, Glenn (Actor)
c/o Nick Frenkel *3 Arts Entertainment Inc*
9460 Wilshire Blvd
7th Floor
Beverly Hills, CA 90210, USA

Howes, Sally Ann (Actor, Music Group, Musician)
Saraband
265 Liverpool Road
London N1 1LX, UNITED KINGDOM (UK)

Howey, Steve (Actor)
c/o Brian Swardstrom *WME (LA)*
9601 Wilshire Blvd Fl 3
Beverly Hills, CA 90210, USA

Howfield, Bobby (Athlete, Football Player)
5529 S Lowell Blvd
Littleton, CO 80123, USA

Howfield, Ian (Athlete, Football Player)
2851 Elk Canyon Ct
Las Vegas, NV 89117, USA

Howison, Ryan (Athlete, Golfer)
245 Barbardos Dr
Jupiter, FL 33458, USA

Howitt, Dann (Athlete, Baseball Player)
PO Box 565
Douglas, MI 49406-0565, USA

Howitt, Peter (Director)
c/o Stephen Marks *Evolution Entertainment (LA)*
901 N Highland Ave
Los Angeles, CA 90038, USA

Howland, Ben (Basketball Player, Coach)
University of California
Athletic Dept
Los Angeles, CA 90024, USA

Howland, Beth (Actor)
255 Amalfi Dr
Santa Monica, CA 90402, USA

Howland, Chris
Vordersten Buchel 11
Rosrath, GERMANY D-51503

Howle, Paul (Cartoonist)
United Feature Syndicate
200 Madison Ave
New York, NY 10016, USA

Howlett, Liam (Composer, Musician)
Midi Mgmt
Jenkins Lane
Great Hallinsbury
Essex CM22 7QL, UNITED KINGDOM (UK)

Howley, Chuck (Athlete, Football Player)
5234 Ravine Dr
Dallas, TX 75220, USA

Howry, Bobby (Athlete, Baseball Player)
24108 N 73rd Ln
Peoria, AZ 85383-3290, USA

Howry, Keenan (Athlete, Football Player)
19426 Coslin Ave
Carson, CA 90746, USA

Howse, Steven (Layzie Bone) (Actor, Composer, Musician)
c/o Staff Member *Mo Thug West Records*
Prefers to be contacted via email
Los Angeles, CA, USA

Howson, Scott (Athlete, Hockey Player)
c/o Staff Member *Edmonton Oilers*
11230 110 St NW
GM, AB T5G 3H7, Canada

Howze, Leonard Earl (Actor)
c/o Jessica Berlinski *Melissa Prophet Management*
Prefers to be contacted by telephone
CA, USA

Hoy, Peter (Athlete, Baseball Player)
26 Woods Dr
Canton, NY 13617-1061, USA

Hoyda, Dave (Athlete, Hockey Player)
3305 Bahama Dr
Sand Springs, OK 74063-2912, USA

Hoye, James (Athlete, Baseball Player)
12838 Patricia Dr
North Royalton, OH 44133-1024, USA

Hoyem, Steve (Athlete, Football Player)
28 Twilight Blf
Newport Coast, CA 92657, USA

Hoyer, Jed (Commentator)
118 Huntington Ave
Boston, MA 02116-5743, USA

Hoying, Bobby (Athlete, Football Player)
9071 Tartan Fields Dr
Dublin, OH 43017, USA

Hoyos, Luis Fernando (Actor)
c/o Gabriel Blanco *Gabriel Blanco Iglesias (Mexico)*
Rio Balsas 35-32
Colonia Cuauhtemoc
DF 06500, Mexico

Hoyt, D LaMarr (Athlete, Baseball Player)
1594 Lost Creek Dr
Columbia, SC 29212-2859, USA

Hrabosky, Alan T (Al) (Athlete, Baseball Player, Sportscaster)
9 Frontenac Estates Dr
Saint Louis, MO 63131-2613, USA

Hrbek, Kent A (Athlete, Baseball Player)
2611 W 112th St
Bloomington, MN 55431-3965, USA

Hrdina, Jiri (Athlete, Hockey Player)
c/o Staff Member *Dallas Stars*
2601 Avenue of the Stars
Suite 100
Frisco, TX 75034-9016, USA

Hrdy, Sarah Blaffer (Misc)
University of California
Anthropology Dept
Davis, CA 95616, USA

Hriniak, Walt (Athlete, Baseball Player)
18 Stacy Dr
North Andover, MA 01845-1832, USA

Hrivnak, Gary (Athlete, Football Player)
1508 W Plymouth Dr
Arlington Heights, IL 60004, USA

Hrivnak, Jim (Athlete, Hockey Player)
835 Rue Pierre-Marc-Masson
L'Ile-Bizard, QC H9E 0A3, Canada

Hrkac, Tony (Athlete, Hockey Player)
6904 W Lantern Ln
Mequon, WI 53092-1575, USA

Hrudey, Kelly (Athlete, Hockey Player)
c/o Staff Member *CBC TV*
P.O. Box 500
STN A, 5H100
Toronto, ON M5W 1E6, Canada

Hrycuik, Jim (Athlete, Hockey Player)
1011 Konihowski Rd
Saskatoon, SK S7S 1K5, Canada

Hrymnak, Steve (Athlete, Hockey Player)
Site 15 Comp 125
RR 13 STN P
Thunder Bay, ON P7B 5E4, Canada

Hrynewich, Tim (Athlete, Hockey Player)
1132 North Ln
Norton Shores, MI 49441-4684, USA

H. Smith, Christopher (Congressman, Politician)
2373 Rayburn HOB
Washington, DC 20515, USA

Hu, Jintao (President)
Communist Party Central Committee
1 Zhong Nan Hai
Beijing, CHINA

Hu, Kelly (Actor)
c/o Cheryl McLean *Creative Public Relations*
3385 Oak Glen Dr
Los Angeles, CA 90068, USA

Hu, Qili (Government Official)
Consultative Conference
23 Taipingqiao St
Beijing 100283, CHINA

Huang, Helen (Musician)
I C M Artists
40 W 57th St
New York, NY 10019, USA

Huang, Henry (Biologist, Inventor)
Washington Universtiy
Biology Dept
Saint Louis, MO 63130, USA

Huang, James (Actor)
c/o Staff Member *Cunningham Escott Slevin & Doherty (CESD-LA)*
10635 Santa Monica Blvd
130
Los Angeles, CA 90025, USA

Huang, Motoko (Stylist)
242-06-B Oak Park Dr
Douglaston, NY 11362, USA

Huang, Nina
8007 Highland Terr.
Los Angeles, CA 90046

Huang, Ying (Musician)
c/o Staff Member *Sony BMG/Jive Records*
2100 Colorado Ave
Santa Monica, CA 90404, USA

Huard, Bill (Athlete, Hockey Player)
41 Massier Ln
Foothill Ranch, CA 92610-2305, USA

Huard, Brock (Athlete, Football Player)
11688 179th Pl NE
Redmond, WA 98052, USA

Huard, Damon (Athlete, Football Player)
9508 NE 18th St
Clyde Hill, WA 98004, USA

Huard, John (Athlete, Football Player)
40 Vista Dr
S Portland, ME 04106, USA

Huarte, John (Athlete, Football Player,
Heisman Trophy Winner)
Arizona Tile
8829 S Priest Dr
Tempe, AZ 85284-1905, USA

Hub (Musician)
William Morris Agency
1325 Ave of Americas
New York, NY 10019, USA

Hubbard, Elizabeth
1505 10th Street
Santa Monica, CA 90401

Hubbard, Erica (Actor)
c/o Staff Member *Jenny Delaney
Management*
3238 Fond Dr
Encino, CA 91436, USA

Hubbard, Glenn (Athlete, Baseball Player)
1515 Kings Xing
Stone Mountain, GA 30087-1914, USA

Hubbard, Gregg (Hobbie) (Music Group,
Musician)
Sawyer Brown Inc
5200 Old Harding Road
Franklin, TN 37064, USA

Hubbard, Jack
10239 Sorenstam Dr
Trinity, FL 3465S-4661, USA

Hubbard, John (Artist)
Chilcombe House
Chilcombe near Bridport
Dorset, UNITED KINGDOM (UK)

Hubbard, Marvin R (Marv) (Athlete,
Football Player)
5804 Dawn View Ct
Castro Valley, CA 94552, USA

Hubbard, Mike (Athlete, Baseball Player)
2552 Brookstone Ln
Richmond, VA 23233-6914, USA

Hubbard, Phil (Athlete, Basketball Player,
Olympic Athlete)
5130 Pleasant Forest Dr
Centreville, VA 20120-1248, USA

Hubbard, Ray Wylie (Musician)
c/o Staff Member *Davis McLarty Agency*
708 South Lamar
Suite D
Austin, TX 78704, USA

Hubbard, Robert (Athlete, Basketball
Player)
353 Piper Dr
West Springfield, MA 01089, USA

Hubbard, Stanley (Misc)
2289 River Rd S
Lakeland, MN 55043-9775, USA

Hubbard, Trenidad (Athlete, Baseball
Player)
4206 Clearwater Ct
Missouri City, TX 77459-1668, USA

Hubbard, Trent (Baseball Player)
Colorado Rockies
2654 E 77th St
Chicago, IL 60649-4725, USA

Hubbauer, Matt (Athlete, Hockey Player)
c/o Staff Member *Toronto Maple Leafs*
Air Canada Centre
400-40 Bay St
Toronto, ON M5J 2X2, Canada

Hubbert, Brad (Athlete, Football Player)
3100 Landington Dr
Austell, GA 30106-3538, USA

Hubel, David H (Nobel Prize Laureate)
54 Jonathan Ct
Lincoln, MA 01773-3408, USA

Hubenthal, Karl (Cartoonist, Editor)
3901 E Coast Hwy #15
Corona Del Mar, CA 92625, USA

Huber, Anke (Tennis Player)
Dieselstr 10
Karlsdorf-Neuthard 76689, GERMANY

Huber, Jon (Athlete, Baseball Player)
4409 S Angeline St
Seattle, WA 98118-1857, USA

Huber, Lauren (Stylist)
PO Box 112
Fort Lee, NJ 07024, USA

Huber, Max (Athlete, Football Player)
1047 Riverside ln
Orem, UT 84097-6601, USA

Huber, Mike (Athlete, Baseball Player)
509 N Hena St
Greenville, IL 62246-1313, USA

Huber, Robert (Nobel Prize Laureate)
Planck Biochemie Instiut
Am Kiopferspitz
Manrinsried D-82152, GERMANY

Hubert-Whitten, Janet
10061 Riverside Dr. #204
Toluca Lake, CA 91602-2515

Hubick, Greg (Athlete, Hockey Player)
225 Angus St
Regina, SK S4R 3K5, Canada

Hubka, Gene (Athlete, Football Player)
1065 Marshall St
Milton, PA 17847, USA

Hubley, Season (Actor)
31 Mansfield Ave
Essex Junction, VT 05452, USA

Huck, Fran (Athlete, Hockey Player)
Fran Huck and Associates
550 El Camino Rd
Kelowna, BC VlX 2R9, Canada

Huckabee, Cooper (Actor)
1800 El Cerrito Place #34
Los Angeles, CA 90068, USA

Huckabee, Michael (Politician)
1134 Silverwood Trl
North Little Rock, AR 72116-5136, USA

Huckabee, Mike (Ex-Governor, Politician)
c/o Staff Member *Fox News Channel (NY)*
1211 Ave of the Americas
Level C1
New York, NY 10036-8701, USA

Huckaby, Ken (Athlete, Baseball Player)
4490 S Rio Dr
Chandler, AZ 85249-3382, USA

Huckleby, Harlan (Athlete, Football
Player)
7473 Franklin Ridge Way
West Bloomfield, MI 48322, USA

Hucknall, Mick (Musician)
c/o Staff Member *Silentway Managment
Ltd*
34 Percy St
London W1T 2DG, UK

Huckstep, Ronald L (Doctor)
108 Sugarloaf Crescent
Castlecrag
Syndey, NSW 2068, AUSTRALIA

Huclack, Dan (Athlete, Football Player)
B-11 Apple Lane
Winnipeg, MB R2y 2G9, Canada

Hucles, Angela (Athlete, Olympic Athlete,
Soccer Player)
1641 Tether Keep
Virginia Beach, VA 23454-1332, USA

Hucul, Fred (Athlete, Hockey Player)
4550 N Flowing Wells Rd
Unit 226
Tucson, AZ 8570S-2387, USA

Hudd, Roy
652 Finchley Rd.
London, ENGLAND NW11 7NT

Huddleston, David (Actor)
9200 Sunset Blvd #612
Los Angeles, CA 90069, USA

Huddy, Charlie
Winnipeg Jets
300 Portage Ave
Attn: Coaching Staff
Winnipeg, MB R3C 5S4, Canada

Huddy, Charlie (Athlete, Hockey Player)
c/o Staff Member *Edmonton Oilers*
11230 110 St NW
GM, AB T5G 3H7, Canada

Hudecek, Vaclav (Musician)
Londynska 25
Prague 2 120 00, CZECH REPUBLIC

Hudek, John (Athlete, Baseball Player)
John Hudek's All Star Baseball Academy
7603 Shady Way Dr
Sugar Land, TX 7J479.-628A, USA

Hudepohl, Joe (Athlete, Olympic Athlete,
Swimmer)
10437 Greendale Dr
Tampa, FL 33626-5305, USA

Hudgens, Dave (Athlete, Baseball Player)
5802 E Windsor Ave
Scottsdale, AZ 85257-1039, USA

Hudgens, Vanessa (Actor)
c/o Evan Hainey *Untitled Entertainment
(LA)*
350 S. Beverly Dr #200
Beverly Hills, CA 90212, USA

Hudis, Mark (Writer)
c/o Staff Member *United Talent Agency
(UTA)*
9336 Civic Center Dr
Beverly Hills, CA 90210, USA

Hudler, Jiri (Athlete, Hockey Player)
111 Willits St
Apt 502
Birmingham, MI 48009-3332, USA

Hudler, Rex (Athlete, Baseball Player)
11745 Riehl Ave
Tustin, CA 92782-3372, USA

Hudner, Thomas J Jr (General)
31 Allen Farm Lane
Concord, MA 01742-2202, USA

Hudson, Bill
7023 Birdview
Malibu, CA 90265-4106

Hudson, Bob (Athlete, Football Player)
3408 Dalrock Rd
Rowlett, TX 75088, USA

Hudson, Brett (Actor, Producer, Writer)
c/o Staff Member *WmE2 (WMA-LA)*
1 William Morris Pl
Beverly Hills, CA 90212, USA

Hudson, C B Jr (Business Person)
Torchmark Corp
2001 3rd Ave S
Birmingham, AL 35233, USA

Hudson, Charles (Athlete, Baseball Player)
PO Box 368
Oakwood, TX 75855-0368, USA

Hudson, Charles (Charlie) (Athlete,
Baseball Player)
32 W Hooker Ave
Coalgate, OK 74538, USA

Hudson, Chris (Athlete, Football Player)
6361 Moondance Cv
Olive Branch, MS 38654, USA

Hudson, Clifford G (Business Person,
Financier)
Sonic Corporation
101 Park Ave
Oklahoma City, OK 73102-7200, USA

Hudson, Dave (Athlete, Hockey Player)
5204 Briar Tree Dr
Dallas, TX 75248-6032, USA

Hudson, Emie (Actor)
5711 Hoback Glen Road
Hidden Hills, CA 91302, USA

Hudson, Ernie (Actor, Producer)
c/o Darryl Marshak *Marshak/Zachary
Company, The*
8840 Wilshire Blvd
1st Floor
Beverly Hills, CA 90210, USA

Hudson, Garth (Music Group, Musician)
Skyline Music
32 Clayton St
Portland, ME 04103, USA

Hudson, Gary (Actor)
c/o Staff Member *Origin Talent Agency*
4705 Laurel Canyon #306
Studio City, CA 91607, USA

Hudson, Gordon (Athlete, Football Player)
12498 Falls Creek Rd
Riverton, UT 84065-1915, USA

Hudson, Hal (Athlete, Baseball Player)
422 Sandpiper Dr
Apt C
Fort Pierce, FL 34982-5112, USA

Hudson, Haley (Actor)
c/o Staff Member *Weeds*
Showtime Newtworks (LA)
10880 Wilshire Blvd #1600
Los Angeles, CA 90024, USA

Hudson, Hugh (Director)
c/o Staff Member *ICM Partners (ICM-LA)*
10250 Constellation Blvd Fl 7
Los Angeles, CA 90067, USA

Hudson, James (Doctor)
Harvard Medical School
Psychiatry Dept
25 Shattuck St
Boston, MA 02115, USA

Hudson, Jennifer (Actor, Musician)
c/o Lisa Kasteler *WKT Public Relations (WKT-LA)*
9350 Wilshire Blvd
Suite 450
Beverly Hills, CA 90212, USA

Hudson, Jesse (Athlete, Baseball Player)
341 Albert Lewis Way
Mansfield, LA 71052-5723, USA

Hudson, Jim (Athlete, Football Player)
215 Mallet Ct
Austin, TX 78737-2608, USA

Hudson, Joe (Athlete, Baseball Player)
109 Pine Valley Dr
Medford, NJ 08055-9210, USA

Hudson, John (Athlete, Football Player)
3320 Highway 77
Paris, TN 38242, USA

Hudson, Kate (Actor)
c/o Brad Cafarelli *PMK/BNC - LA*
8687 Melrose Ave
8th Floor
West Hollywood, CA 90069, USA

Hudson, Lex (Athlete, Hockey Player)
General Delivery
Flat Rock, NL ADA 3LO, Canada

Hudson, Lou (Athlete, Basketball Player)
2002 Lakeview Dr
Park City, UT 84060-7049, USA

Hudson, Lucy-Jo (Actor)
Granada Television
Quay St
Manchester M60 9EA, ENGLAND

Hudson, Luke (Athlete, Baseball Player)
9912 Aster Cir
Fountain Valley, CA 92708-2309, USA

Hudson, Marvin (Athlete, Baseball Player)
542 Metasville Rd
Washington, GA 30673-2605, USA

Hudson, Marvin (Athlete, Baseball Player)
542 Metasville Rd
Washington, GA 30673, USA

Hudson, Mike (Athlete, Hockey Player)
1856 Knox Rd
Vancouver, BC V6T 1S3, Canada

Hudson, Oliver (Actor, Producer)

Hudson, Orlando (Athlete, Baseball Player)
1416 Pocket Rd
Darlington, SC 29532-8416, USA

Hudson, Ray (Coach, Soccer Player)
DC United
14120 Newbrook Dr
Chantilly, VA 20151, USA

Hudson, Rex (Athlete, Baseball Player)
4704 Spring Meadow Ln
Midland, TX 79705-2966, USA

Hudson, Richard S (Athlete, Football Player)
Henry County High School
315 S Wilson St
Attn: Assistant Principal
Paris, TN 38242, USA

Hudson, Robert W (Athlete, Football Player)
3408 Dalrock Rd
Rowlett, TX 75088, USA

Hudson, Sally (Skier)
PO Box 2343
Olympic Valley, CA 96146, USA

Hudson, Tim (Athlete, Baseball Player)
901 Rocky Hills Dr
Auburn, AL 36830-7222, USA

Hudson, Troy (Athlete, Baseball Player)
6040 Earle Brown Dr Ste 4S0
Minneapolis, MN SS430-2589, USA

Hudspeth, Tommy (Athlete, Football Coach, Football Player)
3522 W 71st Pl
Tulsa, OK 74136, USA

Huelskamp, Tim (Congressman, Politician)
126 Cannon HOB
Washington, DC 20515, USA

Huerta, Carlos (Athlete, Football Player)
2980 Howard Hughes Pkwy
Suite 550
Las Vegas, NV 89169, USA

Huertas, Jon (Actor, Producer)
c/o Sherry Marsh *Marsh Entertainment*
12444 Ventura Blvd #203
Studio City, CA 91604, USA

Hues, Frankie
2640 NE 135th St. #302
Miami Beach, FL 33181

Hues, Matthias (Actor)
Lou Records
32 rue des Jeûneurs
Paris 75002, FRANCE

Huet, Cristobal (Athlete, Hockey Player)
Sports Consulting Group
65 Monroe Ave Ste D
Pittsford, NY 14534-1318, USA

Huff, Aubrey (Athlete, Baseball Player)
745 Bromfield Rd
Hillsborough, CA 94010-6619, USA

Huff, Brent (Actor)
c/o Erik Seastrand *WME (LA)*
9601 Wilshire Blvd Fl 3
Beverly Hills, CA 90210, USA

Huff, Gary E (Athlete, Football Player)
3175 Hawks Landing Dr
Tallahassee, FL 32309, USA

Huff, Kenneth W (Ken) (Athlete, Football Player)
105 Blackford Ct
Durham, NC 27712, USA

Huff, Marty (Athlete, Football Player)
6700 Keithcrest Dr
Temperance, MI 48182-1231, USA

Huff, Mike (Athlete, Baseball Player)
5500 S Madison St APt 18
Hinsdale, IL 60521-8115, USA

Huff, Orlando (Athlete, Football Player)
14623 196th Ave SE
Renton, WA 98059-8120, USA

Huff, Sam (Athlete, Football Player, Sportscaster)
Billie Van Pay
PO Box 963
Middleburg, VA 20118-0963, USA

Huff, Shawn
1505 10th St.
Santa Monica, CA 90401

Huff, Tanya (Writer)
c/o Staff Member *JABberwocky Literary Agency*
P.O. Box 4558
Sunnyside, NY 11104-0558, USA

Huffington, Arianna (Journalist, Writer)
c/o Staff Member *Andrew Freedman Public Relations*
9127 Thrasher Ave
Los Angeles, CA 90069, USA

Huffington, Michael (Ex-Congressman, Politician)
3005 45th Street NW
Washington, DC 20016, USA

Huffins, Chris (Athlete, Decathlon Athlete, Olympic Athlete)
1319 Wildcliff Pkwy NE
Atlanta, GA 30329-3465, USA

Huffman, Cady
c/o Alan David *Alan David Management*
8840 Wilshire Blvd
Suite 200
Beverly Hills, CA 90211, USA

Huffman, Felicity (Actor)
c/o Staff Member *Desperate Housewives*
ABC Television
2300 Riverside Dr
Burbank, CA 91506, USA

Huffman, Kerry (Athlete, Hockey Player)
5557 Sea Forest Dr.
Unit 215
New Port Richey, FL 34652-3213, USA

Huffman, Logan (Actor)
c/o Tina Thor *TMT Entertainment Group*
648 Broadway
Suite 1002
New York, NY 10012, USA

Huffman, Phil (Athlete, Baseball Player)
194 Paxton Rd
Rochester, NY 14617-4657, USA

Huffman, Tim (Athlete, Football Player)
3365 Jubilee Trl
Dallas, TX 75229, USA

Hufnagel, John (Athlete, Football Player)
12859 Biggin Church Rd S
Jacksonville, FL 32224, USA

Hufsey, Billy (Actor)
15415 Muskingam
Brook Park, OH 44142, USA

Hufstedler, Shirley M (Educator, Politician, Secretary)
720 Iverness Dr
La Canada-Flintridge, CA 91011-4149, USA

Hug, Procter R Jr (Judge)
US Court of Appeals
400 S Virginia St
Reno, NV 89501, USA

Hug, Steve (Athlete, Gymnast, Olympic Athlete)
3813 Hughes Ave
Culver City, CA 90232-2715, USA

Hugasian, Harry (Athlete, Football Player)
Arcadia Gardens
720 W Camino Real Ave
Arcadia, CA 91007-7877, USA

Huggins, Bob (Athlete, Basketball Player, Coach)
207 Beecher Hall
Cincinnati, OH 45221, USA

Hugh, Dianne (Stylist)
55 N Sunset Ave
Freeport, IL 61032, USA

Hughes, Albert (Director, Producer, Writer)
c/o David Wirtschafter *WME (LA)*
9601 Wilshire Blvd Fl 3
Beverly Hills, CA 90210, USA

Hughes, Alfredrick (Athlete, Basketball Player)
5024 S Kildare Ave
Chicago, IL 60632-4543, USA

Hughes, Allen (Director, Producer, Writer)
c/o David Wirtschafter *WME (LA)*
9601 Wilshire Blvd Fl 3
Beverly Hills, CA 90210, USA

Hughes, Bobby (Athlete, Baseball Player)
114 Montreal St
Playa Del Rey, CA 90293-7608, USA

Hughes, Bradley (Athlete, Golfer)
204 Easton Ct
Simpsonville, SC 29680, USA

Hughes, Bradley (Misc)
3657 Cross Creek Rd
Malibu, CA 90265-4929, USA

Hughes, Brent (Athlete, Hockey Player)
1641 Nile Dr
Apt 824
Corpus Christi, TX 78412-4981, USA

Hughes, Brent (Athlete, Hockey Player)
2016 Sweetgum Dr
Birmingham, AL 35244-1628, USA

Hughes, Carolyn (Actor, Sportscaster, Television Host)
c/o Staff Member *Fox Sports Television Group*
10201 W Pico Blvd Bldg 101
Los Angeles, CA 90035, USA

Hughes, Danan (Athlete, Football Player)
278 SE Sumpter Ct
Lees Summit, MO 64063-3669, USA

Hughes, Dave (Hughesy) (Comedian)
c/o Staff Member *Westside Talent*
44 Watton St
1st Floor
Werribee, Victoria 3030, Australia

Hughes, David (Athlete, Football Player)
5307 240th Ave NE
Redmond, WA 98053, USA

Hughes, Dennis (Athlete, Football Player)
360 Beechwood Dr
Athens, GA 30606, USA

Hughes, Dustin (Athlete, Baseball Player)
5226 Savannah Pkwy
Southaven, MS 38672-7513, USA

Hughes, Eddie (Athlete, Basketball Player)
4253 Deerfield Hills Rd
Colorado Springs, CO 80916-3506, USA

Hughes, Edward Z (Publisher)
American Heritage Magazine
Forbes Building
60 5th Ave
New York, NY 10011, USA

Hughes, Ernie (Athlete, Football Player)
2116 Camino Brazos
Pleasanton, CA 94566, USA

Hughes, Finola (Actor)
c/o Steven Jensen *Independent Group, The*
6363 Wilshire Blvd
Suite 115
Los Angeles, CA 90048, USA

Hughes, Frank (Athlete, Hockey Player)
PO Box 1856
Sparwood, BC V0B 2G0, Canada

Hughes, Frank John (Actor)
c/o Dan Baron *Agency for the Performing Arts (APA-LA)*
405 S Beverly Dr
Suite 500
Beverly Hills, CA 90212-4425, USA

Hughes, Glenn (Musician)
6671 W Sunset Blvd
Suite #1585-114
Los Angeles, CA 90028, USA

Hughes, Harry (Politician)
24788 Woods Dr
Denton, MD 21629-2323, USA

Hughes, Howie (Athlete, Hockey Player)
3711 27th Pl W
Apt 205
Seattle, WA 98199-2062, USA

Hughes, H Richard (Architect)
47 Chiswick Quay
London W4 3UR, UNITED KINGDOM
(UK)

Hughes, Irene
500 N. Michigan Ave. #1039
Chicago, IL 60611

Hughes, Jack (Athlete, Hockey Player)
Beanpot Financial
54 Canal St
Floor 5
Boston, MA 02114-2015, USA

Hughes, Jim (Athlete, Baseball Player)
530 S Londerry Ln
Anaheim, CA 92807-4654, USA

Hughes, John (Athlete, Hockey Player)
68 Sarah Janes Ln
Cornwall, PE C0A 1H0, CANADA

Hughes, Karen (Government Official)
US Department of State
2201 C Street NW
Washington, DC 20520, USA

Hughes, Kate (Athlete, Golfer)
275 Merlot Ln
Saint Albans, MO 63073, USA

Hughes, Kathleen (Actor)
8818 Rising Glen Place
Los Angeles, CA 90069, USA

Hughes, Keith (Athlete, Baseball Player)
176 Sycamore Rd
Havertown, PA 19083-3508, USA

Hughes, Keith W (Financier)
Pilgrim's Pride
P.O. Box 93
Pittsburg, TX 75686, USA

Hughes, Kim (Athlete, Basketball Player)
2221 Via Cerritos
Palos Verdes Estates, CA 90274-2303, USA

Hughes, Larry (Athlete, Basketball Player)
3 Hanna Ct
Cleveland, OH 44108-1162, USA

Hughes, Macon (Athlete, Football Player)
13202 Lost Creek Rd
Tomball, TX 77375-2927, USA

Hughes, Mark (Coach)
c/o Staff Member *Blackburn Rovers Football Club*
Ewood Park
Blackburn
Lancashire BB2 4JF, UNITED KINGDOM

Hughes, Mervyn G (Cricketer)
Australian Cricket Board
90 Jollimant St
Melbourne, VIC 3002, AUSTRALIA

Hughes, Miko (Actor)
Jamieson Assoc
53 Sunrise Road
Superior, MT 59872, USA

Hughes, Pat (Commentator)
13 FoxTrl
Lincolnshire, IL 60069-4010, USA

Hughes, Pat (Athlete, Hockey Player)
8388 Webster Hills Rd
Dexter, MI 48130-9365, USA

Hughes, Pat (Athlete, Football Player)
4 Woodside Dr
Stratham, NH 03885, USA

Hughes, Phil (Athlete, Baseball Player)
c/o Team Member *New York Yankees*
Yankee Stadium
161st St & River Ave
Bronx, NY 10451, USA

Hughes, Randy (Athlete, Football Player)
17608 Cedar Creek Canyon Dr
Dallas, TX 75252, USA

Hughes, Richard H (Dick) (Athlete, Baseball Player)
P.O. Box 598
Stephens, AR 71764-0598, USA

Hughes, Ryan (Athlete, Hockey Player)
21 Palmerston Pl
Basking Ridge, NJ 07920-2513, USA

Hughes, Sarah (Athlete, Figure Skater, Olympic Athlete)
John Hughes
12 Channel Dr
Great Neck, NY 11024, USA

Hughes, Suzan (Actor)
c/o Staff Member *ICM Partners (ICM-LA)*
10250 Constellation Blvd Fl 7
Los Angeles, CA 90067, USA

Hughes, Terry (Athlete, Baseball Player)
107 Woodcreek Dr
Spartanburg, SC 29303-1949, USA

Hughes, Thomas J Jr (Admiral)
400 Mar Vista Dr #4
Monterey, CA 93940, USA

Hughes, Tom (Athlete, Baseball Player)
610 Kimswick Ct
Deer Park, TX 77536-6139, USA

Hughes, Tom
c/o Kate Bryden *Gordon and French*
12-13 Poland St
London W1F 8QB, UNITED KINGDOM
(UK)

Hughes, Tyrone C (Athlete, Football Player)
4758 Eunice St
New Orleans, LA 70127, USA

Hughes, Wendy (Actor)
129 Bourke St Woolloomooloo
Sydney, NSW 2011, AUSTRALIA

Hughes-Fulford, Millie (Astronaut)
Veterans Affairs Dept
Medical Center
4150 Clement St
San Francisco, CA 94121, USA

Hughes-Fulford, Millie Dr (Astronaut)
218 Reed Cir
Mill Valley, CA 94941-2514, USA

Hughley, DL (Actor, Comedian)
c/o David (Dave) Becky *3 Arts Entertainment Inc*
9460 Wilshire Blvd
7th Floor
Beverly Hills, CA 90210, USA

Hugo, Chad (Musician)
c/o Scott Vener *Schiff Company, The*
9465 Wilshire Blvd
Suite 480
Beverly Hills, CA 90212, USA

Hugo Boss (Designer, Fashion Designer)
Hugo Boss AG
Dieselstrabe 12
Metzingen 72555, Germany

Hugstedt, Petter (Skier)
Kongsberg 3600, NORWAY

Huguenin, G Richard (Inventor)
Millitech Corp
South Deerfield, MA 01373, USA

Hui, Tammy (Actor)
c/o Lisa King *King Talent*
303-228 E 4th Ave
Vancouver V5T-1G5, CANADA

Huisgen, Rolf (Misc)
Kaulbachstr 10
Munich 80539, GERMANY

Huish, Justin (Archer, Athlete, Olympic Athlete)
3475 Indian Mesa Dr
Thousand Oaks, CA 91360-1133, USA

Huisman, Justin (Athlete, Baseball Player)
8713 Forest Glen Ct
Saint John, IN 46373-8795, USA

Huisman, Rick (Athlete, Baseball Player)
17W025 Oak Ln
Bensenville, IL 60106-2860, USA

Huismann, Mark (Athlete, Baseball Player)
5751 NW Plantation Ln
Lees Summit, MO 64064-1686, USA

Huizenga, Bill (Congressman, Politician)
1217 Longworth HOB
Washington, DC 20515, USA

Huizenga, John R (Scientist)
43 McMichael Dr
Pinehurst, NC 28374, USA

Huizenga, Wayne (Commentator)
1575 Ponce De Leon Dr
Ft Lauderdale, FL 33316-1323, USA

Hulbert, Mike (Athlete, Golfer)
7770 Apple Tree Cir
Orlando, FL 32819, USA

Hulbig, Joe (Athlete, Hockey Player)
17 Apple Blossom Ln
Stow, MA 01775-1380, USA

Hulce, Tom (Actor)
2305 Stanley Hills Dr
Los Angeles, CA 90046, USA

Hulcher, Janet
Arnold Palmer Enterprises
9000 Bay Hill Blvd
Orlando, FL 32819-4999, USA

Hulett, Tim (Athlete, Baseball Player)
799 Dumaine Dr
Bossier City, LA 71111-6273, USA

Hulett, Timothy "Tug" (Athlete, Baseball Player)
6154 Buncombe Rd
Shreveport, LA 71129-4125, USA

Hull, Bobby (Athlete, Hockey Player)
6916 Lennox Pl
University Park, FL 34201-2256, USA

Hull, Brett (Athlete, Hockey Player)
Dallas Stars
2601 Avenue of the Stars Ste 100
Attn: Executive VP
Frisco, TX 75034-9016, USA

Hull, Brett A (Athlete, Hockey Player, Olympic Athlete)
3826 Maplewood Ave
Dallas, TX 75205-2829, USA

Hull, Dennis
115 E. Maple St.
Hinsdale, IL 60521

Hull, Dennis W (Athlete, Hockey Player)
11642 County Rd 29
Roseneath, ON K0K 2X0, Canada

Hull, Don (Misc)
US Olympic Committe
1 Olympia Plaza
Colorado Springs, CO 80909, USA

Hull, Eric (Athlete, Baseball Player)
803 N 4th St
Selah, WA 98942-9411, USA

Hull, Gina (Athlete, Golfer)
479 Arricola Ave
Saint Augustine, FL 32080, USA

Hull, James D (Admiral)
Commander US Coast Guard Atlantic
4131 Crawford St
Portsmouth, VA 23704, USA

Hull, Jody (Athlete, Coach, Hockey Player)
c/o Staff Member *Peterborough Petes*
151 Lansdowne St W
Peterborough, ON K9J 1Y4, Canada

Hull, Mike (Athlete, Football Player)
3809 Vista Azul
San Clemente, CA 92672, USA

Hull, Roger H (Educator)
Union College
Chancellor's Office
Schenectady, NY 12308, USA

Hullar, Theodore L (Educator)
3 Lowell Place
Ithaca, NY 14850, USA

Hullet, Jamie (Athlete, Golfer)
1153 Lakeview Dr
Mesquite, TX 75149, USA

Hulme, Denis (Race Car Driver)
CI-6
RDTE Puke
Bay of Plenny, NEW ZEALAND

Hulme, Etta (Cartoonist, Editor)
Fort Worth Star-Telegram
Editorial Dept
400 W 7th St
Fort Worth, TX 76102, USA

Hulme, Keri (Writer)
Hodder & Stoughton
338 Euston Road
London NW1 3BH, UNITED KINGDOM
(UK)

Hulse, Cale (Athlete, Hockey Player)
c/o Art Breeze *Pro-Rep Entertainment Consulting*
113-276 Midpark Way SE
Calgary, AB T2X 1J6, Canada

Hulse, Chuck (Race Car Driver)
7341 Spruce Circle
la Palma, CA 90623, USA

Hulse, David (Athlete, Baseball Player)
1301 Kenwood Dr
San Angelo, TX 76903-7261, USA

Hulse, Russell A (Nobel Prize Laureate)
PO Box 451
Princeton, NJ 08542-0451, USA

Hultgren, Randy (Congressman, Politician)
427 Cannon HOB
Washington, DC 20515, USA

Hultz, Don (Athlete, Football Player)
5078 Pleasant Ridge Rd
Millington, TN 38053, USA

Huly, Jan C (General)
Deputy CofS Plans Policies & Ops
HqUSMC 2 Navy St
Washington, DC 20380, USA

Human League (Music Group)
c/o Staff Member *Performers of the World*
5657 Wilshire Blvd #280
Los Angeles, CA 90036, USA

Humann, L Philip (Financier)
Sun Trust Banks
303 Peachtree St NE
Atlanta, GA 30308, USA

Humayan, Mark S (Doctor)
Johns Hopkins University
Wilmer Ophthalmology Institute
Baltimore, MD 21218, USA

Humber, Philip (Athlete, Baseball Player)
PO Box 130788
Tyler, TX 75713-0788, USA

Humbert, John O (Religious Leader)
Christian Church Disciples of Christ
130 E Washington
Indianapolis, IN 46204, USA

Humbert, Richard (Athlete, Football Player)
12112 Ashton Park Dr
Glen Allen, VA 23059, USA

Hume, A Britton (Brit) (Correspondent)
3100 N St NW #9
Washington, DC 20007, USA

Hume, Alan
Deanrise Deanwood Rd.
Jordans Bucks., ENGLAND

Hume, Brit (Television Host)
c/o Staff Member *Fox News Channel (DC)*
400 N Capital ST NW #550
Washington, CA 20001, USA

Hume, John (Nobel Prize Laureate)
5 Bayview Terrace
Derry BT48 7EE, NORTHERN IRELAND

Hume, Kirsty (Model)
Viva Models Paris
15, rue Duphot
PAris 75001, FRANCE

Hume, Roger
9 Blenheim St.
London, ENGLAND W1Y 9LE

Hume, Stephen (Editor)
Vancouver Sun
2250 Granville St
Vancouver, BC V6H 3G2, CANADA

Hume, Tom (Athlete, Baseball Player)
9923 59th St E
Parrish, FL 34219-4467, USA

Humenik, Ed (Athlete, Golfer)
4746 SW Hammock Creek Dr
Palm City, FL 34990, USA

Humes, Edward (Journalist)
Simon & Schuster
1230 Ave of Americas
New York, NY 10020, USA

Humes, John P (Diplomat)
Forest Mill Road
Mill Neck, NY 11765, USA

Humes, Mary Margaret
PO Box 1168-714
Studio City, CA 91604

Humes, Mary-Margaret (Actor, Model)
Stone Manners
6500 Wilshire Blvd #550
Los Angeles, CA 90048, USA

Humiston, Mike (Athlete, Football Player)
311 N Richhill St
Waynesburg, PA 15370, USA

Humm, David (Athlete, Football Player)
4301 Via Olivero Ave
Las Vegas, NV 89102-3799, USA

Hummel, Rick (Commentator)
PO Box 270056
Saint Louis, MO 63127-0056, USA

Hummel, Tim (Athlete, Baseball Player)
1550 Kerr Rd
Whiteford, MD 21160-1318, USA

Hummer, John (Athlete, Basketball Player)
2640 Baker St
San Francisco, CA 94123-3802, USA

Hummes, Claudio Hummes Cardinal
(Religious Leader)
Avenida Higienopolis 890
CP 1670
Sao Paulo 01238-908, BRAZIL

Humperdinck, Engelbert (Actor, Musician, Producer)
c/o Arthur Andelson *Kismet Talent Agency*
3435 Ocean Park Blvd.
Suite 107
Santa Monica, CA 90405, USA

Humphery, Bobby (Athlete, Football Player)
914 E Highland Blvd
San Antonio, TX 78210-3529, USA

Humphrey, Claude (Athlete, Football Player)
3399 Lord Dunmore Cv
Bartlett, TN 38134, USA

Humphrey, Gordon J (Ex-Senator, Politician)
78 Garvin Hill Road
Chichester, NH 03258, USA

Humphrey, Jay (Athlete, Football Player)
14109 Brookridge Cir
Dallas, TX 75254, USA

Humphrey, Paul (Athlete, Football Player)
1120 East Davis Dr
Apt 515
Terre Haute, IN 47802, USA

Humphrey, Renee
9300 Wilshire Blvd. #555
Beverly Hills, CA 90212

Humphrey, Richard (Baseball Player)
21 Midland Dr
Morristown, NJ 07960-5064, USA

Humphrey, Richard (Athlete, Baseball Player)
26 Player Green Pl
Spring, TX 77340-2431, USA

Humphrey, Ryan (Basketball Player)
Memphis Grizzlies
175 Toyota Plaza #150
Memphis, TN 38103, USA

Humphrey, Terry (Athlete, Baseball Player)
7 Oakmont
Trabuco Canyon, CA 92679-4728, USA

Humphreys, Bob (Athlete, Baseball Player)
1803 Oakwood St
Bedford, VA 24523-1217, USA

Humphreys, Mike (Athlete, Baseball Player)
1402 Lost Creek Dr
Desoto, TX 75115-3662, USA

Humphreys, Todd (Race Car Driver)
Humphrey's Race Team
Route #5
Elbridge, NY 13060, USA

Humphries, Barry (Actor)
5 Soho Square
London W1V 5DE, UNITED KINGDOM
(UK)

Humphries, Jay (Athlete, Basketball Player)
22107 N 37th Ter
Phoenix, AZ 80138-8736, USA

Humphries, Kris (Athlete, Basketball Player)
c/o Liza Anderson *Anderson Group Public Relations*
8060 Melrose Ave Fl 4
Los Angeles, CA 90046, USA

Humphries, Rusty (Radio Personality)
Rusty Humphries Show
225 NE Hillcrest Dr.
Grants Pass, OR 97526, USA

Humphries, Stan (Athlete, Football Player)
4100 Chauvin Ln
Monroe, LA 71201-2057, USA

Humphries, Stefan (Athlete, Football Player)
8708 East Redwood Ln
Spokane, WA 99217, USA

Humphry, Derek (Activist)
ERGO
24828 Norris Lane
Junction City, OR 97448, USA

Hun, Sen (Prime Minister)
Prime Minister's Office
Supreme National Council
Phnom Penh, COMBODIA

Hundertwasser, FriedensreichMu
hle Odissenbach
Rapottenstein, AUSTRIA 3911

Hundley, Mandisa (Musician)
c/o Staff Member *The M Collective*
P.O. Box 273
Franklin, TN 37065, USA

Hundley, Randy (Athlete, Baseball Player)
Randy Hundley Baseball Camp
1935 5 Plum Grove
Rd # 285
Palatine, IL 60067-7258, USA

Hundley, Rod (Hot Rod) (Athlete, Basketball Player, Sportscaster)
1860 Siggard Dr
Salt Lake City, UT 85023-6222, USA

Hundley, Todd (Athlete, Baseball Player)
830 Raleigh Rd
Glenview, IL 60025-4328, USA

Hundon, James (Athlete, Football Player)
92 Kenneth Ct
Bay Point, CA 94565-1545, USA

Hundt, Reed E (Government Official)
6416 Brookside Dr
Bethesda, MD 20815, USA

Hung, Sammo (Actor)
c/o Maani Golesorkhi *Bluestone Entertainment*
9000 Sunset Blvd
Suite 700
Los Angeles, CA 90069, USA

Hung, William (Musician, Reality TV Star)
c/o Michael (Mike) Esterman
Esterman.Com, LLC
Prefers to be contacted via email
MD, USA

Hunger, Daniela (Swimmer)
SV Preussen
Hansastr 190
Berlin 13088, GERMANY

Huniford, James (Architect, Designer)
Sills Hunifor Assoc
30 E 67th St
New York, NY 10021, USA

Hunkapiller, Michael (Biologist, Inventor)
Applied Biosystems
850 Lincoln Center Dr
Foster City, CA 94404, USA

Hunley, Con (Musician)
6406 Spring View Ln
Knoxville, TN 37918, USA

Hunley, Ricky C (Athlete, Football Player)
9617 Stonemasters Dr
Loveland, OH 45140, USA

Hunnam, Charlie (Actor)
c/o Cynthia Pett-Dante *Brillstein Entertainment Partners*
9150 Wilshire Blvd #350
Beverly Hills, CA 90212, USA

Hunnicutt, Gayle (Actor)
174 Regents Park Road
London NW1, UNITED KINGDOM (UK)

Hunphrey, Bobby (Athlete, Football Player)
4209 Woodbine Ln
Hoover, AL 35226, USA

Hunsicker, Gerald (Commentator)
11914 Cobblestone Dr
Houston, TX 77024-5003, USA

Hunt, Bobby (Athlete, Football Player)
5928 Bentway Dr
Charlotte, NC 28226, USA

Hunt, Bonnie (Actor, Director, Talk Show Host)
415 25th St
Santa Monica, CA 90402, USA

Hunt, Bryan (Artist)
31 Great Jones St
New York, NY 10012, USA

Hunt, Byron (Athlete, Football Player)
P.O. Box 281
Rutherford, NJ 07070, USA

Hunt, Charlie (Athlete, Football Player)
8700 Nathans Cove Ct
Jacksonville, FL 32256, USA

Hunt, Cletidus (Athlete, Football Player)
7246 Creek Bend Dr
Memphis, TN 38125, USA

Hunt, Courtney (Director, Writer)
c/o Staff Member *WmE2 (WMA-LA)*
1 William Morris Pl
Beverly Hills, CA 90212, USA

Hunt, Crystal (Actor)
c/o Scott Zimmerman *Evolution Entertainment (LA)*
901 N Highland Ave
Los Angeles, CA 90038, USA

Hunt, Francesca (Actor)
c/o Dallas Smith *United Agents*
12-26 Lexington St
London W1F OLE, UK

Hunt, George (Athlete, Football Player)
40 N Pine Cir
Belleair, FL 33756, USA

Hunt, Helen (Actor)
c/o Stephen Huvane *Slate Public Relations*
9000 Sunset Blvd #915
West Hollywood, CA 90069, USA

Hunt, James (Politician)
6653D Governor Hunt Rd
Lucama, NC 27851-9415, USA

Hunt, Jimmy (Actor)
2279 Lansdale Court
Simi Valley, CA 93065, USA

Hunt, John (Athlete, Football Player)
8 Ulverston Way
Blythewood, SC 29016, USA

Hunt, John R (Religious Leader)
Evangelical Covenant Church
5101 N Francisco Ave
Chicago, IL 60625, USA

Hunt, Kevin (Athlete, Football Player)
11 Royal Ln
Londonderry, NH 03053, USA

Hunt, Lamar (Football Executive, Soccer Player, Tennis Player)
Thanksgiving Tower
1601 Elm St #2800
Dallas, TX 75201, USA

Hunt, Linda (Athlete, Golfer)
3016 Cypress Cir
Ball Ground, GA 30107, USA

Hunt, Linda (Actor)
c/o Tim Curtis *WME (LA)*
9601 Wilshire Blvd Fl 3
Beverly Hills, CA 90210, USA

Hunt, Marsha (Actor, Writer)
c/o Staff Member *D&M Publishers*
2323 Quebec St
Suite 201
Vancouver, BC V5T 4S7, Canada

Hunt, Marsha (Actor)
13131 Magnolia Blvd
Van Nuys, CA 91423, USA

Hunt, Nelson Bunker (Business Person)
Hunt Resources Investment Group
Fountain Place
1445 Ross at Field
Dallas, TX 75202-2785, USA

Hunt, Nicholas (General)
Eurotunnel 111 Buckingham Palace Road
London, SW 1W OST, England

Hunt, Peter (Director, Producer)
c/o Dennis Aspland *Aspland Management*
245 W 55th St
Suite 1102
New York, NY 10019, USA

Hunt, Randy (Athlete, Baseball Player)
324 Holly Ridge Dr
Montgomery, AL 36109-3904, USA

Hunt, Ray (Business Person)
Hunt Oil Company
1900 North Akard St
Dallas, TX 75201

Hunt, Ray (Misc)
5915 Steuben Ct
Dallas, TX 75248-2115, USA

Hunt, Richard
1017 W Lill Ave
Chicago, IL 60614, USA

Hunt, Ronald K (Ron) (Athlete, Baseball Player)
2806 Jackson Rd
Wentzville, MO 63385-4205, USA

Hunt, R Timothy (Nobel Prize Laureate)
Imperial Cancer Research Fund
Clare Hall Laboratories PO Box 123 Cell Cycle Control Lab Herts
London ENG 3LD, England

Hunt, Sam (Athlete, Football Player)
1708 Eliza St
Nacogdoches, TX 75961, USA

Hunt, Van (Musician)
c/o Staff Member *Creative Artists Agency (CAA-LA)*
2000 Ave Of The Stars
Los Angeles, CA 90067, USA

Hunt, Wendy (DJ)
c/o Staff Member *Diva Central Inc*
7510 W Sunset Blvd Ste 1445
Los Angees, CA 90046, USA

Hunten, Donald M (Astronomer)
10 E Calle Corts
Tucson, AZ 85716, USA

Hunter, Anthony (Athlete, Football Player)
3553 Edgeview Dr
Cincinnati, OH 45213, USA

Hunter, Anthony R (Tony) (Biologist)
Salk Institute
10100 N Torrey Pines Road
La Jolla, CA 92037, USA

Hunter, Bill (Athlete, Hockey Player)

Hunter, Billy (Athlete, Baseball Player, Coach)
104 E Seminary Ave
Lutherville Timonium, MD 21093-6127, USA

Hunter, Brian (Athlete, Baseball Player)
12141 Centralia St
Unit 219
Lakewood, CA 90715-1565, USA

Hunter, Brian (Athlete, Baseball Player)
1440 Kasten Dr
Dolton, IL 60419-2469, USA

Hunter, Buddy
Boston Red Sox
14616 Fir Cir
Plattsmouth, NE 68048-5112, USA

Hunter, Buddy (Athlete, Baseball Player)
14616 Fir Cir
Plattsmouth, NE 68048-5112, USA

Hunter, Charlie (Music Group, Musician)
Figurehead Mgmt
3470 19th St
San Francisco, CA 94110, USA

Hunter, Dale (Athlete, Hockey Player)
c/o Staff Member *London Knights*
99 Dundas St
London, ON N6A 6K1, Canada

Hunter, Daniel (Athlete, Football Player)
210 N Lakeview Dr
Farmerville, LA 71241-2504, USA

Hunter, Dave (Athlete, Hockey Player)
53350 Ran ge Rd 220
Androssan, AB T8E 2B5, Canada

Hunter, Dorothy (Baseball Player)
2607 Miller Ave NW
Grand Rapids, MI 49544-1948, USA

Hunter, Duncan (Congressman, Politician)
223 Cannon HOB
Washington, DC 20515, USA

Hunter, Herman (Athlete, Football Player)
541 Rural Hill Rd
Nashville, TN 37217-4107, USA

Hunter, Holly (Actor)
c/o David Seltzer *Management 360*
9111 Wilshire Blvd
Beverly Hills, CA 90210, USA

Hunter, Ian (Music Group, Musician, Songwriter, Writer)
Helter Skelter
Plaza
535 Kings Road
London SW10 0S, UNITED KINGDOM (UK)

Hunter, Jack D
22 Hypolita St
St. Augustine, FL 32084, USA

Hunter, Jeff (Athlete, Football Player)
3492 Monte Carlo Dr
Augusta, GA 30906, USA

Hunter, Jesse (Music Group, Musician)
Friedman & LaRosa
1334 Lexington Ave
New York, NY 10128, USA

hunter, Jim (Athlete, Baseball Player)
12939 Penshurst Ln
Windermere, FL 34786-6672, USA

Hunter, Jim (Commentator)
3010 Franklins Chance Dr
Fallston, MD 21047-1353, USA

Hunter, Jim (Skier)
Jungle Jim Hunter Mgmt
864 Woodpark Way SW
Calgary, AB T2W 2V8, CANADA

Hunter, John (Engineer)
Lawrence Livermore Laboratory
7000 East St
Livermore, CA 94550, USA

Hunter, Lauren (Stylist)
c/o Staff Member *Koko Represents*
166 Geary St
#1007
San Francisco, CA 94108, USA

Hunter, Les (Athlete, Basketball Player)
8712 W 92nd St
Overland Park, KS 66212-3817, USA

Hunter, Lindsey
4355 Hickory Ridge Ct
Plymouth, MI 48170-5123

Hunter, Mark (Athlete, Hockey Player)
c/o Staff Member *London Knights*
99 Dundas St
London, ON N6A 6K1, Canada

Hunter, Mellisa (Reality TV Star)
c/o Michael (Mike) Esterman
Esterman.Com, LLC
Prefers to be contacted via email
MD, USA

Hunter, Montgomery (Athlete, Football Player)
411 Washington St
Dover, OH 44622, USA

Hunter, Patrick (Athlete, Football Player)
880 N David Ct
Chandler, AZ 85226, USA

Hunter, Paul (Director, Editor, Writer)
c/o Rob Carlson *WME (LA)*
9601 Wilshire Blvd Fl 3
Beverly Hills, CA 90210, USA

Hunter, Rachel (Actor, Model)
c/o Chuck Binder *Binder & Associates*
1465 Lindacrest Dr
Beverly Hills, CA 90210, USA

Hunter, Rich (Athlete, Baseball Player)
3820 Agave Ct
Perris, CA 92570-7192, USA

Hunter, Robert (Politician)
US Department Of State 2201 C St NW
Washington, DC 20520-0099, USA

Hunter, Ronald (Actor)
c/o Barbara Price *Kings Highway Entertainment*
14538 Benefit St.
Suite 103
Sherman Oaks, CA 91423, USA

Hunter, Scott (Athlete, Football Player)
6386 Dolive Ct
Daphne, AL 36526, USA

Hunter, Stephen (Writer)
Washington Post
Editorial Dept
1150 15th St NW
Washington, DC 20071, USA

Hunter, Steven (Basketball Player)
Orlando Magic
Waterhouse Center
8701 Maitland Summit Blvd
Orlando, FL 32810, USA

Hunter, Tab (Actor, Writer)
PO Box 50308
Santa Barbara, CA 93150, USA

Hunter, Tim (Director)
c/o Staff Member *Gersh (LA)*
9465 Wilshire Blvd
Suite 600
Beverly Hills, CA 90212, USA

Hunter, Tim (Athlete, Coach, Hockey Player)
c/o Staff Member *San Jose Sharks*
525 W Santa Clara St
San Jose, CA 95113, USA

Hunter, Tommy (Musician)
c/o Staff Member *Rocklands Entertainment*
1135 Pasadena Ave S
St Petersburg, FL 33707, USA

Hunter, Torii (Athlete, Baseball Player)
P.O. Box 1357
Prosper, TX 75078-1357, USA

Hunter, Trent (Athlete, Hockey Player)
26 MacKay Way
Roslyn, NY 11576-2169, USA

Hunter, Willard (Athlete, Baseball Player)
2562 Poppleton Ave
Omaha, NE 68105-2303, USA

Hunter-Gault, Charlayne (Correspondent)
News Hour Show
2700 S Quincy St #250
Arlington, VA 22206, USA

Hunter-Reay, Ryan (Race Car Driver)
3200 NE 40th Court
Fort lauderdale, FL 33308, USA

Hunthausen, Raymond G (Religious Leader)
Catholic Archdiocese of Seattle
910 Marion
Seattle, WA 98104, USA

Huntington, Neal (Commentator)
332 Rve Gate St
Bay Village, OH 44140-1274, USA

Huntington, Sam (Actor)
c/o Walter Hamada *H2F Entertainment*
644 N Cherokee Ave
Los Angeles, CA 90004, USA

Huntington, Samuel P (Politician)
Harvard University
Olin Institute
Political Science Dept
Cambridge, MA 02138, USA

Huntington-Whiteley, Rosie (Actor, Model)
c/o Jeff Speich *Anonymous Content (LA)*
2000 Ave Of The Stars
Los Angeles, CA 90067, USA

Huntley, Joni (Athlete, Olympic Athlete, Track Athlete)
7148 SW 4th Ave
Portland, OR 97219-2220, USA

Huntley, Noah (Actor)
c/o Lindy King *United Agents*
12-26 Lexington St
London W1F OLE, UK

Huntley, Richard (Athlete, Football Player)
6005 Williams Rd
Apt A
Charlotte, NC 28215, USA

Huntsman, Stanley H (Coach)
5532 Timbercrest Trail
Knoxville, TN 37909, USA

Huntz, Steve (Athlete, Baseball Player)
3303 Linden Rd
Apt 405
Rocky River, OH 44116-4105, USA

Hunwlck, Matt (Athlete, Hockey Player)
37242 Mariano Dr
Sterling Heights, MI 48312-2054, USA

Hunyadfi, Steven (Coach, Swimmer)
838 Ridgewood Dr #12
Fort Wayne, IN 46805, USA

Hunyady, Emese (Speed Skater)
Beim Spitzriegel 1/2/9
Baden 2500, AUSTRIA

Hunziker, Terry (Designer)
208 3rd Ave S
Seattle, WA 98104, USA

Huo, Yaobang (General, Secretary)
Communist Party Central Committee
Zhongguo Gongchan Dang
Beijing, CHINA

Huot, Raymond P (General)
Inspector General HqUSAF
Pentagon
Washington, DC 20330, USA

Hupp, Jana Marie (Actor)
c/o Karen Forman *Domain Talent*
9229 Sunset Boulevard
Suite 710
Los Angeles, CA 90069, USA

Huppert, Dave (Athlete, Baseball Player)
6732 Stephens Path
Zephyrhills, FL 33542-0652, USA

Huppert, Isabelle (Actor)
VMA
20 Ave Rapp
Paris 75007, USA

Huras, Larry (Athlete, Hockey Player)
RR 1 PO
Allenford, ON N0H 1A0, Canada

Hurd, Douglas R (Government Official)
Hawkpoint
Crosby Court
4 Great Saint Helens
London EC3A 6HA, UNITED KINGDOM (UK)

Hurd, Gale Anne (Producer)
c/o Staff Member *Valhalla Motion Pictures*
3201 Cahuenga Blvd W
Los Angeles, CA 90068, USA

Hurd, Michelle (Actor)
1077 E Santa Anita Ave
Burbank, CA 91501, USA

Hurd, Molly (Stylist)
c/o Staff Member *Workgroup (Hollywood)*
8491 Sunset Blvd
#368
West Hollywood, CA 90069, USA

Hurdle, Clinton M (Clint) (Athlete, Baseball Player, Coach)
9068 Sturbridge Pl
Littleton, CO 80129, USA

Hurford, Peter J (Musician)
Broom House Saint Bernard's Road
Saint Albans
Herts AL3 5RA, UNITED KINGDOM (UK)

Hurlburt, Bob (Athlete, Hockey Player)
205-3169 Tillicum Rd
Victoria, BC V9A 2B4, Canada

Hurlbut, Frank (General)
95 N Paseo Laredo
Cathedral City, CA 92234-1518, USA

Hurlbut, Linda (Athlete, Golfer)
24741 Calle Coneio
Calabasas, CA 91302, USA

Hurlbut, Mike (Athlete, Hockey Player)
86 Cougar Pt
Massena, NY 13662-3176, USA

Hurley, Alfred F (Historian)
University of North Texas
President's Office
Denton, TX 76203, USA

Hurley, Bob (Athlete, Basketball Player)
1410 Shoreline Way
Hollywood, FL 07070-1975, USA

Hurley, Chad (Business Person)
YouTube, Inc
901 Cherry Ave.
San Bruno, CA 94066, USA

Hurley, Craig (Actor)
c/o Sandie Schnarr *AVOTalent Agency*
5670 Wilshire Blvd.
Suite 1930
Los Angeles, CA 90036, USA

Hurley, Douglas G (Astronaut)
700 Thomwood Dr
Friendswood, TX 77546, USA

Hurley, Douglas G Ltcol (Astronaut)
1848 Lake Landing Dr
League City, TX 77573-7781, USA

Hurley, Elizabeth (Actor, Model)
c/o Duncan Heath *Independent Talent Group (ITG-UK)*
Oxford House
76 Oxford St
London W1D 1BS, UK

Hurley, Eric (Athlete, Baseball Player)
2024 Sterling Trace Dr
Keller, TX 76248-9739, USA

Hurley, Marybeth (Stylist)
c/o Staff Member *Team*
423 W Broadway
4th Floor
Boston, MA 02127, USA

Hurlic, Philip (Actor)
1105 Caswell Ave
Compton, CA 90220, USA

Hurn, David (Photographer)
Prospect Cottage
Tintem
Gwent, WALES

Hurnick, Ilja (Composer, Musician)
Narodni Trida 35
Prague 1 11000, CZECH REPUBLIC

Hurst, Bill (Athlete, Baseball Player)
15820 SW 88th Ct
Palmetto Bay, FL 33157-2031, USA

Hurst, Bruce (Athlete, Baseball Player)
1080 N Riata St
Gilbert, AZ 85234-3466, USA

Hurst, Geoff (Athlete, Football Player)
c/o Staff Member *The FA*
25 Soho Square
London W1D 4FA, United Kingdom

Hurst, Grady (Athlete, Football Player)
5810 S 40th St Apt 118
Phoenix, AZ 85040-9018, USA

Hurst, Jackson (Actor)
c/o Staff Member *Lee Peterson and Associates*
78 San Marcos St
Austin, TX 78702, USA

Hurst, James (Athlete, Baseball Player)
221 Westricidge Blvd
Greenwood, IN 46142-2136, USA

Hurst, Jimmy (Athlete, Baseball Player)
901 University Ln
Tuscaloosa, AL 35401-7134, USA

Hurst, Jonathan (Athlete, Baseball Player)
308 Woodburn Creek Rd
Spartanburg, SC 29302-4279, USA

Hurst, Maurice (Athlete, Football Player)
P.O. Box 431068
Dallas, TX 75343, USA

Hurst, Michael (Actor)
Bruce Ugly Agency
218 Richmond Road
Grey Lynn
Auckland 2, NEW ZEALAND

Hurst, Pat (Athlete, Golfer)
7655 E Wing Shadow Rd
Scottsdale, AZ 85255, USA

Hurst, Rick (Actor)
1230 N. Horn
#401
West Hollywood, CA 90069, USA

Hurst, Ron (Athlete, Hockey Player)
8 Snowberry_Cres
Georgetown, ON L7G 6M4, Canada

Hurst, Ryan (Actor)
c/o Brian Swardstrom *WME (LA)*
9601 Wilshire Blvd Fl 3
Beverly Hills, CA 90210, USA

Hurston, Chuck (Athlete, Football Player)
9360 Prestwick Club Dr
Duluth, GA 30097, USA

Hurt, Frank (Misc)
Bakery Confectionery Tobacco Union
10401 Connecticut
Kensington, MD 20895, USA

Hurt, John (Actor)
c/o John Crosby *Crosby/Spilo Management*
1310 N Spaulding Ave
Los Angeles, CA 90046, USA

Hurt, Mary Beth (Actor)
1619 Broadway #900
New York, NY 10019, USA

Hurt, Robert (Congressman, Politician)
1516 Longworth HOB
Washington, DC 20515, USA

Hurt, William (Actor)
c/o Jessica Kolstad *WKT Public Relations (WKT-LA)*
9350 Wilshire Blvd
Suite 450
Beverly Hills, CA 90212, USA

Hurtado, Edwin (Athlete, Baseball Player)
Toronto Blue Jays
7219 134th Ct SE
Newcastle, WA 98059-3004, USA

Hurtado Larrea, Oswaldo (President)
Suecia 277 y Av Los Shyris
Quito, ECUADOR

Hurwich, Leo M (Doctor)
University of Pennsylvania
Psychology Dept
Philadelphia, PA 19104, USA

Hurwicz, Leonid (Economist, Nobel Prize Laureate)
5015 35th Avenue South
Apt 605
Minneapolis, MN 55417-1556, USA

Hurwit, Bruce (Director)
c/o Staff Member *Morra Brezner Steinberg & Tenenbaum (MBST) Entertainment*
345 N Maple Dr
Suite 200
Beverly Hills, CA 90210, USA

Hurwitz, Emanuel H (Musician)
25 Dollis Ave
London N3 1DA, UNITED KINGDOM
(UK)

Hurwitz, Jerard (Biologist)
Memorial Sioan Kettering Cancer Center
1275 York Ave
New York, NY 10021, USA

Hurwitz, Mitchell
c/o Adam Berkowitz *Creative Artists Agency (CAA-LA)*
2000 Ave Of The Stars
Los Angeles, CA 90067, USA

Husa, Karel J (Composer)
1 Bellwood Lane
Ithaca, NY 14850, USA

Husain, Mishal (Journalist)
c/o Staff Member *BBC Artist Mail*
PO Box 1116
Belfast BT2 7AJ, United Kingdom

Husaini (Actor)
T 16/2 Kalasethra Colony
Besant Nagar
Chennai, TN 600 090, INDIA

Husak, Todd (Athlete, Football Player)
100 N Sepulveda Blvd
El Segundo, CA 90245, USA

Husar, Lubomyr Cardinal (Religious Leader)
Ploscha Sviatoho Jura 5
Lviv 290000, UKRAINE

Husbands, Clifford (Governor)
c/o Private Secretary To The Governor-General
Government House
Saint Michael, Barbados

Huscroft, Jamie (Athlete, Hockey Player)
3024 38th St SE
Puyallup, WA 98374, USA

Huselius, Kristian (Athlete, Hockey Player)
Newport Sports Management
400-201 City Centre Dr
Attn Don Meehan
Mississauga, ON L5B 2T4, Canada

Husen, Torsten (Educator)
Int'l Educational Institute
Armfeltsgatan 10
Stockholm 115 34, SWEDEN

Husenov, Surat (Prime Minister)
Prime Minister's Office
Baku, AZERBAIJAN

Hush, Lizabeth
4512 Gentry Ave.
No. Hollywood, CA 91607

Huska, Ryan (Athlete, Hockey Player)
421 Quilchena Dr
Kelowna, BC V1W 4T7, Canada

Huskey, Robert L (Butch) (Athlete, Baseball Player)
P.O. Box 996
Apache, OK 73006-0996, USA

Huskins, Kent (Athlete, Hockey Player)
Octagon Sports Management
66 Slater St 23rd F
Attn Larry Kelly
Ottawa, ON K1P 5H1, Canada

Husky, Rick
13565 Lucca Dr.
Pacific Palisades, CA 90272

Husmann, Ed (Athlete, Football Player)
27266 Orth Ln
Conroe, TX 77385, USA

Huson, Jeff (Athlete, Baseball Player)
10349 Rowlock Way
Parker, CO 80134-9580, USA

Huson, Kimberly (Stylist)
2514 3rd St
Santa Monica, CA 90405, USA

Hussain, Nasir (Director, Filmmaker, Producer)
24 Pali Hill
Bandra
Bombay, MS 400 050, INDIA

Hussey, Olivia (Actor)
c/o Staff Member *Richard Schwartz Management*
2934-1/2 Beverly Glen Cir #107
Los Angeles, CA 90077, USA

Husted, Dave (Athlete, Bowler)
16231 SE Norma Road
Portland, OR 97267-5193, USA

Husted, Wayne D (Artist)
Keep Homestead Museum
Ely Road
Monson, MA 01057, USA

Huston, Anjelica (Actor, Director)
c/o Ina Treciokas *Slate Public Relations*
9000 Sunset Blvd #915
West Hollywood, CA 90069, USA

Huston, Carol
10100 Santa Monica Blvd. #2500
Los Angeles, CA 90067

Huston, Daniel (Danny) (Actor, Director)
c/o Laina Cohn *Laina Cohn Management*
15066 Sutton St
Sherman Oaks, CA 91403, USA

Huston, Geoff (Athlete, Basketball Player)
1960 Ellis Ave
Bronx, NY 10472-5006, USA

Huston, Jack (Actor)
c/o Todd Diener *Collective*
8383 Wilshire Blvd
Suite 1050
Beverly Hills, CA 90211, USA

Huston, John (Athlete, Golfer)
1134 Skye Ln
Palm Harbor, FL 34683, USA

Huston, Ron (Athlete, Hockey Player)
31-2025 Kokanee Dr N
Cranbrook, BC V1C 6J2, Canada

Hutch, Jesse (Actor)
c/o Staff Member *Pacific Artists Management*
1285 W Broadway
Suite 685
Vancouver, BC V6H 3X8, Canada

Hutch, Willie (Athlete, Hockey Player)
225 W. 57th St.
5th Flr.
New York, NY 10019, USA

Hutcherson, Josh (Actor)
c/o Ric Beddingfield *Beddingfield Company, The*
13600 Ventura Blvd
Suite B
Sherman Oaks, CA 91423, USA

Hutcherson, Robert (Bobby) (Musician)
Abby Hoffer
223 1/2 E 48th St
New York, NY 10017, USA

Hutchins, Jason (Athlete, Baseball Player)
2401 Stone Castle Cir
College Station, TX 77845-5494, USA

Hutchins, Mel (Athlete, Basketball Player)
160 Sherri Ln
Oceanside, CA 92054-5327, USA

Hutchins, Paul (Athlete, Football Player)
8818 S Jeffery Blvd
Chicago, IL 60617, USA

Hutchins, Sonny (Race Car Driver)
8114 Michaels Rd.
Richmond, VA 23229, USA

Hutchins, Will (Actor)
PO Box 371
Glen Head, NY 11545, USA

Hutchinson, Andrew (Athlete, Hockey Player)
5860 Printemp Dr
East Lansing, MI 48823, USA

Hutchinson, Anthony (Athlete, Football Player)
124 Bellaire Ct
Bellaire, TX 77401, USA

Hutchinson, Asa (Politician)
1501 North Pierce Street
Suite 102
Little Rock, AR 72207-5222, USA

Hutchinson, Barbara (Misc)
American Federation of Labor
815 15th St NW
Washington, DC 20005, USA

Hutchinson, Chad (Athlete, Baseball Player)
915 Millie Ave
Menlo Park, CA 94025-4419, USA

Hutchinson, Clyde A Jr (Misc)
University of Chicago
Searle Laboratory
Chimestry Dept
Chicago, IL 60637, USA

Hutchinson, Doug (Actor)
United Talent Agency
9560 Wilshire Blvd
#500
Beverly Hills, CA 90212, USA

Hutchinson, Doug (Actor)
c/o Ryan Martin *Agency for the Performing Arts (APA-LA)*
405 S Beverly Dr
Suite 500
Beverly Hills, CA 90212-4425, USA

Hutchinson, Frederick E (Educator)
University of Maine
President's Office
Orono, ME 04469, USA

Hutchinson, J Maxwell (Architect)
Cavendish Mansions
#61 Clerkenwell Road
London EC1R 5DH, UNITED KINGDOM
(UK)

Hutchinson, Kieran (Actor)
c/o Adam Levine *Levine Okwu Erickson Management*
9601 Wilshire Blvd
3rd Floor
Beverly Hills, CA 90210, USA

Hutchinson, Neil (Scientist)
420 NW 11th Ave Unit 901
Portland, OR 97209-2969, USA

Hutchinson, Ron (Athlete, Hockey Player)
213 Merlin Ct
Kelowna, BC V1V 1N2, Canada

Hutchinson, Scott (Athlete, Football Player)
726 Forest Glen Ct
Maitland, FL 32751, USA

Hutchinson, Steven (Athlete, Football Player)
350 Calamus Cir
Hamel, MN 55340, USA

Hutchinson, Tim (Politician)
Dickstein Shapiro LLP 1825 I St NW
Fl1200 Attn Pub Plcy and Law Dept
Washington, DC 20006-5417, USA

Hutchison, Dave (Athlete, Hockey Player)
Re/Max Centre City Realty Inc
3922 Hamilton Rd
Dorchester, ON N0L 1G2, Canada

Hutchison, Doug (Actor)
c/o Ryan Martin *Agency for the Performing Arts (APA-LA)*
405 S Beverly Dr
Suite 500
Beverly Hills, CA 90212-4425, USA

Hutchison, Kay Bailey (Politician)
4646 Shadywood Ln
Dallas, TX 75209-2018, USA

Hutchison, Melinda (Stylist)
2913 Toledo Ave S
St. Louis Park, MN 55416, USA

Huth, Edward J (Doctor, Editor)
1124 Morris Ave
Bryn Mawr, PA 19010, USA

Huth, Gerald (Athlete, Football Player)
5009 Elm Grove Dr
Las Vegas, NV 89117, USA

Huther, Bruce (Athlete, Football Player)
1156 N Bonnie Brae St
Denton, TX 76201, USA

Hutson, Brian (Athlete, Football Player)
6077 Arboretum Dr
Frisco, TX 75034, USA

Hutson, Candace
3500 W. Olive Ave. #920
Burbank, CA 91505

Hutson, Herb (Athlete, Baseball Player)
7203 W Suger Tree Ct
Savannah, GA 31410-2414, USA

Hutson, Tracy (Actor, Reality TV Star)
c/o Staff Member *Extreme Makeover: Home Edition*
Endemol Entertainment USA
9225 Sunset Blvd #1100
Los Angeles, CA 90069, USA

Hutt, Donald (Athlete, Football Player)
3167 S Hudspeth Ave
Meridian, ID 83642-4816, USA

Hutt, Peter B (Attorney, Attorney General, General)
Covington & Berlin
1201 Pennsylvania Ave NW
Washington, DC 20004, USA

Hutter, Mark (Race Car Driver)
Team Rensi Motorsports
6804 Hobson Valley Rd.
#118
Woodridge, IL 60517, USA

Hutto, Jim (Athlete, Baseball Player)
1317 John Carroll Dr
Pensacola, FL 32504-7114, USA

Hutton, Anthony (Reality TV Star)
c/o Staff Member *Big Brother (UK)*
Channel 4 Television
124 Horseferry Rd
London SW1P 2TX, UNITED KINGDOM

Hutton, Danny (Music Group, Musician)
2437 Horseshoe Canyon Road
Los Angeles, CA 90046, USA

Hutton, Gunilla (Actor)
803 Alston Ln
Santa Barbara, CA 93108, USA

Hutton, Lauren (Actor, Model)
c/o Katie Rhodes *Untitled Entertainment (LA)*
350 S. Beverly Dr #200
Beverly Hills, CA 90212, USA

Hutton, Mark (Athlete, Baseball Player)
6 Corfu Court
Westlakes Adelaide, AU 5021, Australia

Hutton, Pascale (Actor)
c/o Ben Levine *Kritzer Levine Wilkins Entertainment (KLWG)*
11872 La Grange Ave
1st Floor
Los Angeles, CA 90025, USA

Hutton, Ralph (Swimmer)
Vancouver Police Department
312 Main St
Vancouver, BC, CANADA

Hutton, Rif (Actor)
c/o Staff Member *Momentum Talent and Literary Agency*
9401 Wilshire Blvd
Suite 501
Beverly Hills, CA 90212, USA

Hutton, Timothy (Actor)
c/o Judy Hofflund *Hofflund/Polone*
9465 Wilshire Blvd #420
Beverly Hills, CA 90212, USA

Hutton, Tommy (Athlete, Baseball Player)
18 Huntly Dr
Palm Beach Gardens, FL 33418, USA

Hutton, Tommy (Athlete, Baseball Player)
Los Angeles Dodgers
18 Huntly Dr
Palm Beach Gardens, FL 33418-6812, USA

Hutzler, Brody (Actor)
c/o Staff Member *Pakula/King & Associates*
9229 Sunset Blvd
Suite 315
Los Angeles, CA 90069, USA

Huxhold, Ken (Athlete, Football Player)
8524 Stone Harbor Ave
Las Vegas, NV 89145, USA

Huxley, Hugh E (Biologist)
349 Nashawtuc Road
Concord, MA 01742, USA

Huxley, Laura (Doctor, Writer)
1795 Washington Way
Venice, CA 90291-4701, USA

Huxtable, Ada Louise (Critic)
969 Park Ave
New York, NY 10028, USA

Huyck, Willard (Director)
39 Oakmont Dr
Los Angeles, CA 90049, USA

Hvorostovsky, Dmitri (Opera Singer)
Lies Askonas
6 Henrietta St
London WC2E 8LA, UNITED KINGDOM (UK)

Hwang, David Henry (Writer)
c/o Scott Henderson *WME (LA)*
9601 Wilshire Blvd Fl 3
Beverly Hills, CA 90210, USA

Hyams, Joe
10375 Wilshire Blvd. #4D
Los Angeles, CA 90024-4722

Hyams, Joseph I (Joe) Jr (Writer)
10375 Wilshire Blvd #4D
Los Angeles, CA 90024, USA

Hyams, Peter (Director)
PO Box 10
Basking Ridge, NJ 07920, USA

Hyatt, Fred (Athlete, Football Player)
19350 SE 52nd Pl
Morriston, FL 32668, USA

Hybl, William J (Misc)
US Olympic Committe
1 Olympia Plaza
Colorado Springs, CO 80909, USA

Hyche, Heath (Comedian)
c/o Staff Member *Brillstein Entertainment Partners*
9150 Wilshire Blvd #350
Beverly Hills, CA 90212, USA

Hyche, Steve (Athlete, Football Player)
2801 Five Oaks Ln
Birmingham, AL 35243, USA

Hyde, Allan (Actor)
c/o Iris Grossman *ICM Partners (ICM-LA)*
10250 Constellation Blvd Fl 7
Los Angeles, CA 90067, USA

Hyde, Brandon (Athlete, Baseball Player)
203 Foresteria Dr
West Palm Beach, FL 33403-3413, USA

Hyde, Dick (Athlete, Baseball Player)
1506 Cambridge Dr
Champaign, IL 61821-4957, USA

Hyde, Harry
PO Box 291
Harrisburg, NC 28075

Hyde, Jonathan (Actor)
William Morris Agency
52/53 Poland Place
London W1F 7LX, UNITED KINGDOM (UK)

Hyder, Greg (Athlete, Basketball Player)
16228 Wato Rd
Apt A
Apple Valley, CA 92307-7813, USA

Hyde-White, Alex (Actor)
Borinstein Oreck Bogart
3172 Dona Susana Dr
Studio City, CA 91604, USA

Hyers, Tim (Athlete, Baseball Player)
241 Ridge Rd
Covington, GA 30016-5138, USA

Hyland, Brian (Musician)
Stone Buffalo
PO Box 101
Helendale, CA 92342, USA

Hyland, Robert (Athlete, Football Player)
30 Colonial Rd
White Plains, NY 10605, USA

Hyland, Sarah (Actor)
c/o Richard Konigsberg *RKM*
400 N Mansfield Ave
Los Angeles, CA 90036, USA

Hylton, James (Race Car Driver)
15 Avalon Rd
Martin, GA 30577, USA

Hylton, Thomas J (Journalist)
Pottstown Mercury
Editorial Dept
Hanover & Kings Sts
Pottstown, PA 19464, USA

Hyman, B D
PO Box 7107
Charlottesville, VA 22906, USA

Hyman, Dick
223 1/2 E. 48th St.
New York, NY 10017

Hyman, Dorothy
7 Norman Close Barnsley
So. Yorks, ENGLAND S71 244

Hyman, Earle (Actor)
Manhattan Towers
484 W 43rd St #33E
New York, NY 10036, USA

Hyman, Fracaswell (Producer)
c/o Staff Member *WmE2 (WMA-LA)*
1 William Morris Pl
Beverly Hills, CA 90212, USA

Hyman, Kenneth
Sherwood House Tilehouse Lane Denham
Bucks, ENGLAND.

Hyman, Misty (Swimmer)
3826 E Lupine Ave
Phoenix, AZ 85028, USA

Hyman, Misty (Athlete, Swimmer)
3826 E Lupine Ave
Phoenix, AZ 85028-2125, USA

Hyman, Richard R (Dick) (Composer, Musician)
Abby Hoffer
223 1/2 E 48th St
New York, NY 10017, USA

Hymes, Randy (Athlete, Football Player)
P.O. Box 2132
League City, TX 77574-2132, USA

Hymowitz, Kay S. (Writer)
Manhattan Institute For Policy Research
52 Vanderbilt Ave Fl 2
New York, NY 10017, USA

Hynd, Noel
c/o Susan Simons *Broder Webb Chervin Silbermann Agency, The (BWCS)*
10250 Constellation Blvd
Los Angeles, CA 90067-6200, USA

Hynd, Ronald (Ballerina, Choreographer)
Fern Cottage Up Somerton
Bury Saint Edmonds
Suffolk IP29 4ND, UNITED KINGDOM (UK)

Hynde, Chrissie (Actor, Musician)
c/o Gail Colson *Gailforce Management Ltd*
55 Fulham High St
London SW6 3JJ, UK

Hyndman, Mike (Athlete, Hockey Player)
7143 Bluebell Ct
Lakewood Ranch, FL 34202-4197

Hyneman, Jamie (Actor, Special Effects Designer)
Mythbusters Beyond Productions
1268 Missouri Street
San Francisco, CA 94107, USA

Hynes, Dave (Athlete, Hockey Player)
10 Trinity Ct
Wellesley Hills, MA 02481, USA

Hynes, David
10 TrinityCt
Wellesley Hills, MA 02481-2505

Hynes, Garry (Director)
Druid Theater Co
Chapel Lane
Galway, IRELAND

Hynes, Samuel (Writer)
130 Moore St
Princeton, NJ 08540, USA

Hynes, Tyler (Actor)
201 Laurier Ave E #202
Ottawa, ON K1N 6P1, CANADA

Hynoski, Henry (Athlete, Football Player)
P.O. Box 257
Elysburg, PA 17824, USA

Hyre, John (Business Person)
870 High St Ste #104
Worthington, OH 43085, USA

Hysong, Nick (Athlete, Track Athlete)
2822 E Cholla St
Phoenix, AZ 85028, USA

Hytner, Nicholas R (Director)
National Theatre
South Bank
London SE1 9PX, UNITED KINGDOM (UK)

Hyzdu, Adam (Athlete, Baseball Player)
7823 E Red Hawk Cir
Mesa, AZ 85207-1167, USA

Iacavazzi, Cosmo (Athlete, Football Player)
90 Vine St
Taylor, PA 18517, USA

Iacocca, Lee (Business Person)
The Iacocca Foundation
867 Boylston St
6th Floor
Boston, MA 02116, USA

Iaconelli, Mike (Athlete, Fisherman)
c/o Staff Member *Octagon Outdoors*
916 Loblolly Dr
Lewisville, NC 27023, USA

Iaconio, Frank (Race Car Driver)
250 US Highway 206
Flanders, NJ 07836, USA

Iacono, Paul (Actor)
c/o Wendi Green *Paradigm (LA)*
9200 Sunset Blvd
11th Floor
Los Angeles, CA 90069, USA

Iafrate, Al A (Athlete, Hockey Player)
17320 Fairfield St
Livonia, MI 48152, USA

Iakovas, Primate Archbishop (Religious Leader)
31 Park Dr
South Rye, NY 10021, USA

Ian, Janis (Composer, Musician)
c/o Staff Member *Cooking Vinyl USA*
P.O. Box 246
Huntington, NY 11743, USA

Iaquaniello, Mike (Athlete, Football Player)
49105 Plum Tree Dr
Plymouth, MI 48170, USA

Iassonga, Dan (Athlete, Baseball Player)
1501 Bailey Farm Ct SW
Marietta, GA 30064, USA

Iassonga, Daniel (Baseball Player)
5950 N 78th St Unit 159
Scottsdale, AZ 85250-6183, USA

Iavaroni, Marcus (Athlete, Basketball Player)
8120 N Via De Lago
Scottsdale, AZ 85258-4211, USA

Ibanez, Raul (Athlete, Baseball Player)
12961 SW 143rd Ter
Miami, FL 33186-8943, USA

Ibbetson, Arthur (Cinematographer)
Tanglewood Chalfont Lane
Chorley Wood
Herts, UNITED KINGDOM (UK)

Ibers, James A (Misc)
990 N Lake Shore Drive
Apt 17C
Chicago, IL 60611-1376, USA

Ibiam, Francis A (Religious Leader)
Ganymede Unwana
PO Box 240 Afikpo
Imo State, NIGERIA

Ibn Salman Ibn ' Abd Al-' Aziz Al-Saud (Astronaut, Misc)
PO Box 18368
Riyadh 11415, SAUDI ARABIA

Ibrahim, Barre Mainassara (Misc)
Head of State's Office
Presidential Palace
Niamey, NIGER

Ibrahimovic, Zlatan (Athlete, Soccer Player)
Paris Saint-Germain Football Club
24 Rue Du Commandant Guilbaud
Cedex 16
Paris 75781, France

Ibuka, Yaeko (Activist)
Fukusei Byoin
Leprosarium
Mount Fuji, JAPAN

Icahn, Carl (Business Person)
Icahn Co
445 Hamilton Ave #1210
White Plains, NY 10601, USA

Ice
11500 W. Olympic Blvd. #655
Los Angeles, CA 90064

Ice, Vanilla (Musician)
c/o Tommy Quon *TQ Management Agency*
2412 Piedra Dr
Plano, TX 75023, USA

Icehouse
Box KX-300 Kings Cross
Sydney, AUSTRALIA 2011

Ice T (Actor, Artist)
Coast II Coast
3350 Wilshire Blvd #1200
Los Angeles, CA 90010, USA

Ice-T (Actor, Musician, Producer, Reality TV Star)
31B Casta Ln
Edgewater, NJ 07020, USA

Ichaso, Leon (Director)
c/o Michael Pio *Innovative Artists (LA)*
1505 10th St
Santa Monica, CA 90401, USA

Ickes, Harold (Politician)
6215 TallyHo Ln
Alexandria, VA 22307-1014, USA

Ickx, Jacky (Race Car Driver)
171 Chaussee de la Hulpe
Brussels 1170, BELGIUM

Iconic Boyz (Dancer)
14 Wilson Ave
Suite 5
Englishtown, NJ 07726, USA

Idelson, Bill (Actor, Comedian)
710 Brooktree Rd
Pacific Palisade, CA, 90272

Idle, Eric (Actor, Comedian)
c/o Chris Kanarick *ID Public Relations (ID-NY)*
150 W 30th St
19th Floor
New York, NY 10001, USA

Idol, Billy (Musician, Songwriter, Writer)
c/o John Marx *WME (LA)*
9601 Wilshire Blvd Fl 3
Beverly Hills, CA 90210, USA

Iduarte Foucher, Andres (Writer)
Calle Edimburgo 3
Colonia del Valle
Mexico City, DF 12, MEXICO

Idzlak, Slawomir (Cinematographer)
Ul Wazow 1-Z
Warsaw 01-986, POLAND

Ifans, Rhys (Actor)
Endeavor Talent Agency
9701 Wilshire Blve #1000
Beverly Hills, CA 90212, USA

Ifeanyi, Israel (Athlete, Football Player)
44733 Ruthron Ave
Lancaster, CA 93536, USA

Ifill, Gwen (Writer)
c/o Staff Member *Doubleday*
1540 Broadway
New York, NY 10036

Iger, Robert A (Business Person)
Walt Disney Co
500 S Buena Vista St
Burbank, CA 91521, USA

Iginia, J. (Athlete, Hockey Player)
PO Box 1540
Sta. M
Calgary, AL T2P 3B9, CANADA

Iginla, Jarome (Athlete, Hockey Player)
c/o Donald Meehan *Newport Sports Management*
201 City Centre Dr
Suite 400
Mississauga, ON L58 2T4, Canada

Iglesias, Enrique (Musician)
c/o Fernando Giaccardi *Collective*
8383 Wilshire Blvd
Suite 1050
Beverly Hills, CA 90211, USA

Iglesias, Gabriel (Actor)
c/o Yvette Shearer *Schure Media*
1356 Grandview Ave
Glendale, CA 91201, USA

Iglesias, Julio (Musician)
7 Indian Creek Drive
Indian Creek Village, FL 33154, USA

Iglesias, Tuaquin (Athlete, Football Player)
c/o Chad Speck *Allegiant Athletic Agency*
35 Market Sq
Suite 201
Knoxville, TN 37902, USA

Ignarro, Louis J (Nobel Prize Laureate)
University of California
Medical School
10833 LeConte
Los Angeles, CA 90095, USA

Ignasiak, Gary (Athlete, Baseball Player)
1679 S Riverside Ave
St Clair, MI 48079, USA

Ignasiak, Mike (Athlete, Baseball Player)
5821 Saline Ann Arbor Rd
Saline, MI 48176-9566, USA

Ignatius, Paul R (Government Official)
3650 Fordham Road
Washington, DC 20016, USA

Ignatius Zakka I Iwas, Patriarch (Religious Leader)
Syrian Orthodox Patriarchate
Bab Toma
PB 22260
Damascus, SYRIA

Ignizo, Mildred (Bowler)
241 Shore Acres Dr
Rochester, NY 14612, USA

Iguchi, Tadahito (Athlete, Baseball Player)
Chiba Lotte Marines 1 Mihama
Mihama-ku, Chiba-shi
chiba, IL 2618581, JAPAN

Iguodala, Andre (Athlete, Basketball Player)
c/o Rob Pelinka *Landmark Sports Agency*
10990 Wilshire Blvd
Suite 1000
Los Angeles, CA 90024, USA

Igwebuike, Donald (Athlete, Football Player)
14231 Angelton Ter
Burtonsville, MD 20866, USA

Iha, James (Music Group, Musician)
1245 W Glenlake
Chicago, IL 60660, USA

Ihara, Michio (Artist)
63 Wood St
Concord, MA 01742, USA

Ihedigbo, James (Athlete, Football Player)
c/o Dave Butz *Sportstars Inc*
1350 Avenue of the Americas
28th Floor
New York, NY 10019, USA

Ihnacak, Peter (Athlete, Hockey Player)
c/o Staff Member *Toronto Maple Leafs*
Air Canada Centre
400-40 Bay St
Toronto, ON M5J 2X2, Canada

Ihnatowicz, Zbigniew (Architect)
Ul Mokotowska 31 M 15
Warsaw 00-560, POLAND

Ilkin, Tunch (Athlete, Football Player)
2610 Cedarvue Dr
Pittsburgh, PA 15241, USA

Ike, Reverend (Religious Leader)
4140 Broadway
New York, NY 10033, USA

Ikeda, Daisaku (Religious Leader)
Soka Gakkai
32 Shinanomachi
Shinjuku
Tokyo 160-8583, JAPAN

Iken, Monica
c/o Staff Member *WmE2 (WMA-LA)*
1 William Morris Pl
Beverly Hills, CA 90212, USA

Ikenberry, Stanley O (Educator)
American Council on Education
1 Dupont Circle NW
Washington, DC 20036, USA

Ikeuchi, Hiroyuki (Actor)
c/o Staff Member *LesPros Entertainment*
1-8-1-10F Shimo Meguro
Meguro
Tokyo 153-0064, Japan

Ikle, Fred C (Scientist)
7010 Glenbrook Road
Washington, DC 20014, USA

Ikola, Willard (Athlete, Hockey Player, Olympic Athlete)
5697 Green Circle Dr
Apt 316
Hopkins, MN 55343, USA

Ilavarasi (Actor, Bollywood)
69 Vedawali Street
Kannbiran Colony
Chennai, TN 600093, INDIA

Il Divo (Music Group, Musician)
c/o Meredith Plant *Octagon*
Octagon House
81-83 Fulham High St
London SW6 3JW, UK

Iler, Laura (Stylist)
c/o Staff Member *Marnie Rose Agency*
37 Lower Shad
Pound Ridge, NY 10576, USA

Iler, Robert (Actor)
J Mitchell Management
c/o Maggie Schuster
70 W 36th St Ste 1006
New York, NY 10018

Iley, Barbara (Actor)
Paradigm Agency
10100 Santa Monica Blvd #2500
Los Angeles, CA 90067, USA

Ilg, Ray (Athlete, Football Player)
252 Shindagan Rd
Wilmot, NH 03287, USA

Ilg, Raymond P (Admiral)
1830 Fountain Drive
Unit 1505
Reston, VA 20190-4475, USA

Ilgauskas, Zydrunas (Athlete, Basketball Player)
32654 Lake Road
Avon Lake, OH 44012, USA

Ilgenfritz, Mark (Athlete, Football Player)
742 Sharp Mountain Crk SE
Marietta, GA 30067, USA

Iliescu, Ion (President)
President's Office
Calea Victoriei 59-53
Bucharest, ROMANIA

Ilitch, Michael (Athlete, Hockey Player)
237670 Woodlynne Dr
Bingham Farms, MI 48025, USA

Ilkin, Tunch (Athlete, Football Player)
2610 Cedarvue Dr
Pittsburgh, PA 15241-2912, USA

Illmann, Margaret (Ballerina)
National Ballet of Canada
157 E King St
Toronto, ON M5C 1G9, CANADA

Illsley, John (Musician)
Damage Mgmt
16 Lambton Place
London W11 2SH, UNITED KINGDOM
(UK)

Iloilo, Ratu Josefa (President)
President's Office
PO Box 2513
Suva
Viti Levu, FIJI

Ilsley, Blaise (Athlete, Baseball Player)
Memphis Redbirds 175 Toyota Plz Ste
300 Attn: Coaching Staff
Memphis, TN 38103-2697, USA

Ilyenko, Yuriy G (Cinematographer)
9 Michail Koyzybinksy Str #22
Kiev 252030, UKRAINE

Imada, Ryuji (Athlete, Golfer)
16204 Sierra De Avila
Tampa, FL 33613-5221, USA

Imahara, Grant
Mythbusters Beyond Productions
1268 Missouri St.
San Francisco, CA 94107, USA

Imai, Kenji (Architect)
4-12-28 Kitazawa
Setagayaku
Tokyo, JAPAN

Imai, Nobuko (Musician)
Irene Witmer Mgmt
Kerkstrat 97
Amsterdam, GD 1017, NETHERLANDS

Iman (Actor, Model)
285 Lafayette St #7DE
New York, NY 10012, USA

Imbert, Bertrand S M (Engineer, Scientist)
50 Rue de Turenne
Paris 75003, FRANCE

Imbert, Peter M (Lawyer)
Lieutenancy Office
City Hall
Victoria St
London S1E 6QP, UNITED KINGDOM
(UK)

Imbrie, Andrew W (Composer)
2625 Rose St
Berkeley, CA 94708, USA

Imbruglia, Natalie (Actor, Musician)
c/o Joanna Milosz *Jm Agency*
143A Chapel St
Prahran VIC 3181, Australia

Imes, Mo'Nique (Actor, Comedian,
Television Host)
c/o Ricky Anderson *Anderson & Smith
P.C.*
One Arena Place
7322 Southwest Frwy, Suite 2010
Houston, TX 77074, USA

Imhoff, Darrall (Athlete, Basketball
Player, Olympic Athlete)
3637 Sterling Wood Dr
Eugene, OR 97408-7201, USA

Imhoff, Darrell (Athlete)
3637 Sterling Wood Dr
Eugene, OR 97408

Imhoff, Gary (Actor)
Samantha Group
300 S Raymond Ave
Pasadena, CA 91105, USA

Imhoff, Martin (Athlete, Football Player)
11224 Corte Playa Azteca
San Diego, CA 92124, USA

Imle, John F Jr (Business Person)
Unocal Corp
2141 Rosecrans Ave
El Segundo, CA 90245, USA

Immelman, Trevor (Athlete, Golfer)
9536 Tavistock Rd
Orlando, FL 32827, USA

Immelt, Jeffrey (Jeff) (Business Person)
General Electric Co
3135 Easton Turnpike
Fairfield, CT 06828, USA

Immerfall, Daniel (Dan) (Speed Skater)
5421 Trempeleau Trail
Madison, WI 53705, USA

Impemba, Mario (Athlete, Baseball Player)
19945 Gallahad Dr
Macomb, MI 48044-1756, USA

Imperato, Carlo
21940 Scallion Dr
Santa Clarita, CA 91350-1636, USA

Imperioli, Michael (Actor)
c/o Tina Thor *TMT Entertainment Group*
648 Broadway
Suite 1002
New York, NY 10012, USA

Imus, Don (Radio Personality)
16 West Ave
Darien, CT 06820, USA

IMX (Music Group)
c/o Staff Member *Pyramid Entertainment
Group*
377 Rector Pl #21A
New York, NY 10280-1439, USA

Inaba, Carrie Ann (Actor, Choreographer,
Dancer)
c/o Nicole Perez-Krueger *PMK/BNC
Public Relations (PMK-LA)*
8687 Melrose Ave Fl 8
West Hollywood, CA 90069, USA

Inamori, Kazuo (Business Person)
KDDI Corp
3-22 Nishi-Shinjuku
Shinjuku
Tokyo 163-8003, JAPAN

Inarritu, Alejandro (Actor)
c/o Staff Member *Anonymous Content
(LA)*
3531 Hayden Ave
Culver City, CA 90232, USA

Inbal, Eliahu (Conductor)
Heissischer Rundfunk
Bertramstr 8
Frankfurt/Main 60320, GERMANY

Incandella, Sal (Race Car Driver)
Indy Racing Regency
5811 W 73rd St
Indianapolis, IN 46278, USA

Incaviglia, Peter J (Pete) (Athlete,
Baseball Player)
PO Box 1047
Arigyle, TX 76226-1047, USA

Inclan, Rafael (Actor)
c/o Staff Member *Televisa*
Blvd Adolfo Lopez Mateos 232
Colonia San Angel INN
DF CP 01060, MEXICO

Incubus (Music Group)
c/o Marlene Tsuchii *Creative Artists
Agency (CAA-LA)*
2000 Ave Of The Stars
Los Angeles, CA 90067, USA

Indelicato, Mark (Actor)
c/o Anne Woodward *ROAR (LA)*
9701 Wilshire Blvd
8th Floor
Los Angeles, CA 90212, USA

Indhu (Actor, Bollywood)
D/o G.K.Ram Kumar
2 Circular Road United India Colony
Chennai, TN 600024, INDIA

Indiana, Robert (Artist)
PO Box 808
Vinalhaven, ME 04863-0808, USA

Indigo Girls (Music Group)
c/o Staff Member *High Road Touring*
751 Bridgeway
3rd Floor
Sausalito, CA 94965, USA

Indraja (Actor, Bollywood)
89 Krishna Nagar
Virugambakkam
Chennai, TN 600092, INDIA

Indurain, Miguel
Avendia Villava
Pamplona (Navarra), SPAIN E-31013

Infamous Stringdusters, The (Music
Group, Musician)
c/o Michael Allenby *The Artist Farm*
100 W. South St
1A
Charlottesville, VA 22902, USA

Infante, Lindy (Athlete, Coach, Football
Coach, Football Player)
6780 AlA S
Saint Augustine, FL 32080, USA

Infante, Toño (Actor)
c/o Staff Member *Televisa*
Blvd Adolfo Lopez Mateos 232
Colonia San Angel INN
DF CP 01060, MEXICO

Ing, Hout (Government Official)
Foreign Affairs Ministry
Phnom Penh, COMBODIA

ing, Peter (Athlete, Hockey Player)
Fan-Tastic Sports
21021 Heron Way_Ste 104
Lakeville, MN 55044-8085, USA

Ing, Peter (Athlete, Hockey Player)
Casino Niagara
P.O. Box 300
Stn Main
Niagara Falls, ON L2E 6T3, Canada

Ingarfield Jr, Earl (Athlete, Hockey Player)
619 Mourning Dove Dr
Sarasota, FL 34236, USA

Ingarfield Sr, Earl (Athlete, Hockey
Player)
1715 Lakehill Cres S
Lethbridge, AB T1K 3R2, Canada

Inge, Brandon (Athlete, Baseball Player)
5035 Fox Ridge Ct
Ann Arbor, MI 48103-9601, USA

Inge, Peter A (Misc)
House of Lords
Westminster
London SW1A 0PW, UNITED KINGDOM
(UK)

Ingels, Marty (Actor, Comedian)
c/o Deborah Zucker *Ingels Entertainment*
Suite One Productions
16400 Ventura Blvd #335
Encino, CA 91436, USA

Ingelsby, Tom (Athlete, Basketball Player)
1507 Canterbury Ln
Berwyn, PA 19312-1915, USA

Ingersoll, Ralph II (Publisher)
Ingersoll Publications
PO Box 1869
Lakeville, CT 06039, USA

Inghram, Mark G (Physicist)
3077 Lakeshore Drive North
Holland, MI 49424-6022, USA

Ingle, Doug (Music Group, Musician)
Entertainment Services Int'l
6400 Pleasant Park Dr
Chanhassen, MN 55317, USA

Ingle, Robert D (Editor)
San Jose Mercury News
Editorial Dept
750 Ridder Park Dr
San Jose, CA 95131, USA

Inglebright, Jim (Race Car Driver)
Roadrunner Motorsports
4984 Peabody Rd
Fairfield, CA 93432, USA

inglett, joe (Athlete, Baseball Player)
3874 Gardiner Run
Copley, OH 44321-3160, USA

Inglis, Bill (Athlete, Hockey Player)
5709 Ozark Dr
Forth Worth, TX 76131, USA

Inglis, Tim (Athlete, Football Player)
105 Crafton Park Ln
Cary, NC 27519-5575, USA

Ingman, Einar H (General)
W4053 W Silver Lake Rd
Irma, WI 54442-9726, USA

Ingman, Elnar H Jr (War Hero)
W4053 N Silver Lake Road
Irma, WI 54442, USA

Ingraham, Hubert A (Prime Minister)
Prime Minister's Office
Whitfield Center
Box CB10980
Nassau, BAHAMAS

Ingraham, Laura (Radio Personality)
c/o Staff Member *XM Satellite Radio
Studios*
1500 Eckington Pl NE
Washington, DC 20002, USA

Ingram, A John (Doctor)
4940 Sullivan Woods Cove
Memphis, TN 38117, USA

Ingram, Brian (Athlete, Football Player)
4805 White Oak Path
Stone Mountain, GA 30088-3016, USA

Ingram, Clint (Athlete, Football Player)
7812 Chase Meadows Dr E
Jacksonville, FL 32256-4641, USA

Ingram, Garey (Athlete, Baseball Player)
Mississippi Braves PO Box 97389 Attn:
Coaching Staff
pearl, ML 39288-7389, USA

Ingram, Jack (Musician)
c/o Staff Member *Capital Sports &
Entertainment*
98 San Jacinto Blvd
Suite 430
Austin, TX 78701, USA

Ingram, Jack (Race Car Driver)
699 Brevard Rd
Asheville, NC 28806, USA

Ingram, James (Musician)
c/o Staff Member *Agency for the
Performing Arts (APA-LA)*
405 S Beverly Dr
Suite 500
Beverly Hills, CA 90212-4425, USA

Ingram, James (Music Group, Musician,
Songwriter, Writer)
867 Muirfield Road
Los Angeles, CA 90005, USA

Ingram, Lonnie (Biologist)
University of Florida
Microbiology/Cell Science Dept
Gainesville, FL 32611, USA

Ingram, Mark (Football Player)
c/o Chafie Fields *Lagardere Unlimited -
NY*
845 UN Plaza
New York, NY 10017, USA

Ingram, Mark (Misc)
Mark Ingram
110 E 55th St
8th Floor
New York, NY 10012, USA

Ingram, McKoy (Athlete, Basketball
Player)
2301 33rd St
Gulfport, MS 39501-6541, USA

Ingram, Preston (Baseball Player)
Negro Baseball Leagues
174 Douglas St SE
Atlanta, GA 30317-2626, USA

Ingram, Riccardo (Athlete, Baseball
Player)
5720 Martin Grove Dr NW
Lilburn, GA 30047-6078, USA

Ingram, Robert (General)
1020 Acapulco Rd
Jacksonville, FL 32216, USA

Ingram, Vernon M (Biologist)
Massachusetts Institute of Technology
Biochemistry Dept
Cambridge, MA 02139, USA

Ingrao, Pietro (Government Official)
Centro Studie Iniziative Per La Reforma
Via Della Vite 13
Rome, ITALY

Ingrassia, Frank (Horse Racer)
39 Imlaystown Hightstown Rd
Allentown, NJ 08501-2104, USA

Ingrassia, Jacqueline (Horse Racer)
39 Imlaystown Hightstown Rd
Allentown, NJ 08501-2104, USA

Ingrassia, Paul J (Journalist)
111 Division Ave
New Providence, NJ 07974, USA

Inkeles, Alex (Activist)
1001 Hamilton Ave
Palo Alto, CA 94301, USA

Ink Spots, The
5100 DuPont Blvd. #10A
Ft. Lauderdale, FL 33308

Inkster, Juli Simpson (Athlete, Golfer)
23140 Mora Glen Dr
Los Altos, CA 94024, USA

Inman, Bobby Ray (Admiral, Government
Official)
701 Brazos St #500
Austin, TX 78701, USA

Inman, Dale (Race Car Driver)
142 Holder Inman Rd.
Ranaleman, NC 27317-8044, USA

Inman, Jerry (Athlete, Football Player)
P.O. Box 1113
Battle Ground, WA 98604, USA

Inman, Joe (Athlete, Golfer)
3599 Tuckers Farm SE
Marietta, GA 30067, USA

Inman, John (Athlete, Golfer)
2210 Chase St
Durham, NC 27707, USA

Inman, John (Actor)
AMG Ltd
8 King St
London WC2E 8HN, UNITED KINGDOM
(UK)

Inmon, Earl (Athlete, Football Player)
38429 Jamestown St
Umatilla, FL 32784, USA

Innauer, Anton (Toni) (Coach, Skier)
Steinbruckstr 8/11
Innsbruck 6024, AUSTRIA

Innes, Laura (Actor)
c/o Troy Nankin *Wishlab*
2225-A Hyperion Ave
Los Angeles, CA 90027, USA

Inness, Gary (Athlete, Hockey Player)
7 Gowan Rd
Shanty Bay, ON L0L 2L0, Canada

Inniger Jr, Ervin (Athlete, Basketball
Player)
311 11th Ave S
Apt 101
Fargo, ND 58103-2856, USA

Innis (Musician)
c/o Staff Member *Paradigm (LA)*
360 N Crescent Dr
North Bldg
Beverly Hills, CA 90210, USA

Innis, Jeff (Athlete, Baseball Player)
4920 Woodlong Ln
Cumming, GA 30040-5275, USA

Innis, Roy (Politician)
800 Riverside Dr. #6E
New York, NY 10032-7407, USA

Innis, Roy E A (Activist)
817 Broadway
New York, NY 10003, USA

Innis, Walter (General)
Watergate West 2700 Virginia Ave NW
Washington, DC 20037-1909, USA

Inogradov, Pavel (Astronaut, Misc)
Potchta Kosmonavtov
Moskovskol Oblasti
Syvisdny Goroduk 141160, RUSSIA

Inoue, Shinya (Biologist, Photographer)
Marine Biological Laboratory
167 Water St
Woods Hole, MA 02543, USA

Inoue, Yuichi (Artist)
Ohkamiyashiki 2475-2 Kurami
Samakawamachi 253-01 Kozagun
Kam, JAPAN

Inouye, Lisa (Actor)
c/o Nick Terzian *Nick Terzian Agency
(NTA)*
1445 North Stanley Avenue
2nd Floor
Los Angeles, CA 90046, USA

Insane Clown Posse (Music Group,
Musician)
c/o Staff Member *WME (LA)*
9601 Wilshire Blvd Fl 3
Beverly Hills, CA 90210, USA

Insko, Delmer M (Del) (Horse Racer)
2360 Fischer Road
South Beloit, IL 61080-9728, USA

Inslee, Jay (Congressman, Politician)
2329 Rayburn HOB
Washington, DC 20515, USA

Insley, Will (Artist)
231 Bowery
New York, NY 10002, USA

Insolla, Anthony (Editor)
Newsday
Editorial Dept
235 Pinelawn
Melville, NY 11747, USA

Insolo, Jimmy (Race Car Driver)
19636 Ermitie St.
Canyon Country, CA 91351, USA

INXS
c/o Michael Moses *Baker Winokur Ryder
Public Relations (BWR-LA)*
9100 Wilshire Blvd
Suite 500, West Tower
Beverly Hills, CA 90212, USA

Inzaghi, Filippo (Soccer Player)
c/o Team Member *AC Milan*
Via Turati 3
Milan 20221, Italy

Iommi, Tony (Musician)
c/o *Equator Music Ltd*
17 Hereford Mansions
Hereford Rd
London W2 5BA, UNITED KINGDOM

Ionatana, Ionatana (Prime Minister)
Prime Minister's Office
Vaiaku
Funafuti, TUVALU

Iorg, Dane (Athlete, Baseball Player)
5358 W Evergreen Cir
American Fork, UT 84003-9476, USA

Iorg, Garth (Athlete, Baseball Player)
Milwaukee Brewers 1 Brewers Way Stop
4 Attn Coaching Staff
Milwaukee, WI 53214-3691, USA

Ioss, Walter (Photographer)
152 De Forrest Road
Montauk, NY 11954, USA

Iovine, Jimmy (Producer)
c/o Staff Member *Interscope Records (LA)
- Main*
2220 Colorado Ave
Santa Monica, CA 90404, USA

Iqbal Rashid, Ian (Director)
c/o Staff Member *United Talent Agency
(UTA)*
9336 Civic Center Dr
Beverly Hills, CA 90210, USA

Iraheta, Allison (Musician)

Irani, Aruna (Actor, Bollywood)
603 B Gazdar Apartments
Near Juhu Hotel Juhu
Mumbai, MS 400049, INDIA

Irani, Ray R (Business Person)
Occidental Petroleum
10889 Wilshire Blvd
Los Angeles, CA 90024, USA

Irbe, Arturs (Athlete, Hockey Player)
6337 Georgetown Pike
Mclean, VA 22101-2209, USA

Iredale, Randle W (Architect)
1151 W 8th Ave
Vancouver, BC V6H 1C5, CANADA

Ireland, Dan (Director, Producer, Writer)
c/o Staff Member *Gersh (LA)*
9465 Wilshire Blvd
Suite 600
Beverly Hills, CA 90212, USA

Ireland, Kathy (Actor, Business Person,
Model)
c/o Danielle Marie Owens *Guttman
Associates*
118 S Beverly Dr
Suite 201
Beverly Hills, CA 90212, USA

Ireland, Marin (Actor)
c/o Emily Gerson Saines *Brookside Artists
Management (NY)*
250 W 57th St
Suite 2303
New York, NY 10107, USA

Ireland, Patricia (Misc, Politician)
Katz Kutler Haigler Assoc
901 New Jersey Ave NW Apt 372
Washington, DC 20001-1428, USA

Ireland, Rich (Baseball Player)
181 Glen Dr
Grants Pass, OR 97526-9018, USA

Ireland, Tim (Athlete, Baseball Player)
21001 San Ramon Valley Blvd Ste A4 Ste
A-4
san ramon, CA 94583-3454, USA

Iris, Donnie (Music Group, Musician,
Songwriter, Writer)
807 Darlington Road
Beaver Falls, PA 15010, USA

Irish Rovers, The
1505 W. 2nd Ave. #200
Vancouver, CANADA BC V6H 3Y4

Irizarry, Vincent (Actor)
c/o Douglas Warner *Warner Artist
Management*
2001 Wilshire Blvd #210
Santa Monica, CA 90403, USA

Irobe, Yoshiaki (Financier)
26-6-6 Saginomiya
Nakanoku
Tokyo, JAPAN

Iron & Wine (Music Group, Musician)
c/o Rob Challice *Coda Music Agency -
UK*
229 Shoreditch High St
London E1 6PJ, UK

Iron Butterfly
PO Box 770850
Orlando, FL 32877

Iron Maiden (Music Group)
c/o Staff Member *EMI Music Group (NY)*
150 Fifth Avenue
New York, NY 10011, USA

Irons, Gerald (Athlete, Football Player)
30010 E Legends Trail Ct
Spring, TX 77386-2998, USA

Irons, Grant (Athlete, Football Player)
30010 E Legends Trail Ct
Spring, TX 77386-2998, USA

Irons, Jeremy (Actor)
c/o Fred Specktor *Creative Artists Agency
(CAA-LA)*
2000 Ave Of The Stars
Los Angeles, CA 90067, USA

Irons, Max (Actor)
c/o Billy Lazarus *United Talent Agency
(UTA)*
9336 Civic Center Dr
Beverly Hills, CA 90210, USA

Irons, Nicholas (Actor)
Emptage Hallett
c/o Michael Emptage
24 Poland St
London W1F 8QL, UNITED KINGDOM

Irons, Robbie (Athlete, Hockey Player)
4227 Cordell Cv
Fort Wayne, IN 46845, USA

Ironside, Michael (Actor, Producer,
Writer)
c/o David Ginsberg *Insight*
1134 S Cloverdale Ave
Los Angeles, CA 90019, USA

Irrera, Dom (Actor, Comedian)
c/o Staff Member *Buchwald/Fortitude (LA)*
6500 Wilshire Blvd
Suite 2200
Los Angeles, CA 90048, USA

Irsay, Jim (Business Person, Football
Executive)
1711 W 116th St
Carmel, IN 46032-6984, USA

Irvan, Ernie (Race Car Driver)
5111 Selkirk Plantation Rd
Wadmalow Island, SC 29847, USA

Irvin, Anthony
One Olympic Plaza
Colorado Springs, CO 80909-5770

Irvin, Byron (Athlete, Basketball Player)
10940 S Parnell Ave
Chicago, IL 60628-3232, USA

Irvin, Cal (Athlete, Baseball Player)
1311 Julian St
Greensboro, NC 27406-2158, USA

Irvin, Daryl (Athlete, Baseball Player)
815 Confederacy Dr
Penn Laird, VA 22846, USA

Irvin, John (Director)
c/o Jack Gilardi *ICM Partners (ICM-LA)*
10250 Constellation Blvd Fl 7
Los Angeles, CA 90067, USA

Irvin, Ken (Athlete, Football Player)
8151 Nesbit Ferry Rd
Atlanta, GA 30350, USA

Irvin, Michael J (Athlete, Football Player)
2339 Aberdeen Bend
Carrollton, TX 75007, USA

Irvin, Monte (Athlete, Baseball Player)
1815 Enclave Pkwy #6111
Houston, TX 77077-3669, USA

Irvine, Daryl (Athlete, Baseball Player)
815 Confederacy Dr
Penn Laird, VA 22846-9633, USA

Irvine, Eddie (Race Car Driver)
Ferrari SpA
Casella Postale 589
Modena 41100, ITALY

Irvine, George (Athlete, Basketball Player)
P.O. Box 179
Indianola, WA 98342-0179, USA

Irvine, Jeremy (Actor)
c/o Jessica Kolstad *WKT Public Relations
(WKT-LA)*
9350 Wilshire Blvd
Suite 450
Beverly Hills, CA 90212, USA

Irvine, Paula
23852 Pacific Coast Hwy. PMB 195
Malibu, CA 90265

Irvine, Ted (Athlete, Hockey Player)
5-2727 Portage Ave
Winnipeg, MB R3J 0R2, Canada

Irving, Amy (Actor)
Rigberg Roberts Rugolo
1180 S Beverly Dr #601
Los Angeles, CA 90035, USA

Irving, John (Writer)
c/o Robert (Bob) Bookman *Creative Artists
Agency (CAA-LA)*
2000 Ave Of The Stars
Los Angeles, CA 90067, USA

Irving, Paul H (Attorney, Attorney
General, General)
Manatt Phelps Phillips
11355 W Olympic Blvd
Los Angeles, CA 90064, USA

Irving, Stu (Athlete, Hockey Player,
Olympic Athlete)
93 Hart St
Beverly Farms, MA 01915, USA

Irving, Terry (Athlete, Football Player)
3205 Avenue R 1/2
Apt 2
Galveston, TX 77550-9951, USA

Irvin Jr, LeRoy (Athlete, Football Player)
2905 Ruby Dr
Apt C
Fullerton, CA 92831, USA

Irwin, Bill (Actor, Writer)
20 1st Ave
Nyack, NY 10960, USA

Irwin, Bindi (Misc)
Australia Zoo
Glass House Mountains Tourist Route
Beerwah, Queensland 4519, AUSTRALIA

Irwin, Glen (Athlete, Hockey Player)
4024 Chesapeake Ave
Hampton, VA 23669-4632

Irwin, Hale (Athlete, Golfer)
5720 N Saguaro Rd
Paradise Valley, AZ 85253, USA

Irwin, Haley (Athlete, Hockey Player,
Olympic Athlete)
440 Marquette St
Thunder Bay, ON P7E ST8 Canada, USA

Irwin, Heath (Athlete, Football Player)
5530 N 115th St
Longmont, CO 80504, USA

Irwin, Ivan (Athlete, Hockey Player)
485 Maple Rd
Ajax, ON L1S 1E4, Canada

Irwin, Jennifer (Actor)
c/o Gayle Abrams *Oscars Abrams Zimel
& Associates, Inc. (OAZ)*
438 Queen St E
Toronto ON M5A 1T4, CANADA

Irwin, Lou (Athlete, Hockey Player)
485 Maple Ave.
Ajax, ON L1S 1E4, Canada

Irwin, Malcolm R (Biologist)
4720 Regent St
Madison, WI 53705, USA

Irwin, Mark (Cinematographer)
1522 Olive St
Santa Barbara, CA 93101, USA

Irwin, Mary (Writer)
3260 Gilcrest Ter
Colorado Springs, CO 80906-4510, USA

Irwin, Paul G (Misc)
Humane Society of the United States
2100 L St NW
Washington, DC 20037, USA

Irwin, Robert W (Artist)
Pace Gallery
32 E 57th St
New York, NY 10022, USA

Irwin, Steven (Athlete, Soccer Player)
Liverpool Football Club
Anfield Road
Liverpool
Merseyside L4 0TH, UK

Irwin, Tim (Athlete, Football Player)
Law Office Of Tim Irwin
P.O. Box 2186
Knoxville, TN 37901, USA

Irwin, Tom
PO Box 5617
Beverly Hills, CA 90210

Irwin, Tommy (Race Car Driver)
1724 Handley Ave.
Winchester, VA 22601, USA

Irwin-Mellencamp, Elaine (Model)
John Caugar Mellencamp
5072 W Stevens Road
Nashville, IN 47448, USA

Isaac, Oscar (Actor)
c/o Jason Spire *Inspire Entertainment*
315 7th Ave
Suite 17E
New York, NY 10001, USA

Isaacks, Levie C (Cinematographer)
6634 Sunnyslope Ave
Van Nuys, CA 91401, USA

Isaacksen, Peter
4635 Placidia Ave
No. Hollywood, CA 91602

Isaacs, Jason (Actor)
c/o Jeff Golenberg *Collective*
8383 Wilshire Blvd
Suite 1050
Beverly Hills, CA 90211, USA

Isaacs, Jeremy I (Director)
Royal Opera House
Covent Garden Bow St
London WC1 7Q4, UNITED KINGDOM
(UK)

Isaacs, Susan (Writer)
Harper Collins Publishers
10 E 53rd St
New York, NY 10022, USA

Isaacson, Julius (Misc)
Novelty & Production Workers Union
1815 Franklin Ave
Valley Stream, NY 11581, USA

Isaacson, Walter S (Journalist)
c/o Staff Member *Little, Brown Book
Group*
100 Victoria Embankment
London EC4Y 0DY, UK

Isaak, Chris (Actor, Musician, Songwriter)
c/o Howard Kaufman *HK Management
(LA)*
10866 Wilshire Blvd Ste 200
Los Angeles, CA 90024, USA

Isaak, Russell (Business Person)
CPI Corp
1706 Washington Ave
Saint Louis, MO 63103, USA

Isabel, Margarita (Actor)
c/o Staff Member *TV Azteca*
Periferico Sur 4121
Colonia Fuentes del Pedregal
DF CP 14141, Mexico

Isabelle, Katharine (Actor)
c/o Wendy Murphey *IFA Talent Agency*
8730 Sunset Blvd
Suite 490
Los Angeles, CA 90069, USA

Isabelle, Katherine (Actor)
c/o Staff Member *IFA Talent Agency*
8730 Sunset Blvd
Suite 490
Los Angeles, CA 90069, USA

Isacksen, Peter (Actor)
c/o Staff Member *JWTwo Entertainment*
2425 Olympic Blvd #200
East Tower
Santa Monica, CA 90404, USA

Isaksson, Irma Sara (Musician,
Songwriter, Writer)
United Stage Artists
PO Box 11026
Stockholm 100 61, SWEDEN

Isales, Orlando (Athlete, Baseball Player)
14710 SW 106th Ave
Miami, FL 33176-7791, USA

Isard, Walter (Economist)
3218 Garrett Road
Drexel Hill, PA 19026, USA

Isbell, Joe Bob (Athlete, Football Player)
1606 Nest Pl
Plano, TX 75093, USA

Isbin, Sharon (Musician)
Columbia Artists Mgmt Inc
165 W 57th St
New York, NY 10019, USA

Iscove, Robert (Rob) (Director)
16045 Royal Oak Road
Encino, CA 91436, USA

Isdell, E Neville (Business Person)
Coca-Cola Co
1 Coca-Cola Plaza
310 North Ave NW
Atlanta, GA 30313, USA

Isenbarger, John (Athlete, Football Player)
7808 Somerset Bay
Apt C
Indianapolis, IN 46240, USA

Isenhour, Tripp (Athlete, Golfer)
10012 N Fulton Ct
Orlando, FL 32836, USA

Isham, Mark (Composer)
Ron Moss Mgmt
2635 Griffith Park Blvd
Los Angeles, CA 90039, USA

Ishara, B R (Actor, Bollywood)
C36 North Bombay Housing Society
Juhu Tara Road
Mumbai, MS 400049, INDIA

Ishibashi, Kanichiro (Business Person)
1 Nagasakacho Azabu
Minatoku
Tokyo, JAPAN

Ishida, Jim (Actor)
871 N Vail Ave
Montebello, CA 90640, USA

Ishiguro, Kazuo (Writer)
Rogers Coleridge White
20 Powis Mews
London W11 1JN, UNITED KINGDOM
(UK)

Ishihara, Shintaro (Government Official)
Sanno Grand Building
#606 2-14-2 Nagatocho Chiyodaku
Tokyo, JAPAN

Ishii, Kazuhiro (Architect)
4-14-27 Akasaka
Minatoku
Tokyo 107, JAPAN

Ishii, Linda (Athlete, Golfer)
2607 E 3rd St
Los Angeles, CA 90033, USA

Ishikawa, Sigeru (Economist)
19-8-4 Chome Kugayama
Suginamiku
Tokyo 168-0082, JAPAN

Ishikawa, Travis (Athlete, Baseball Player)
12 Narcissus Ct
Danville, CA 94506-4795, USA

Ishimaru, Akira (Engineer)
2913 165th Place NE
Bellevue, WA 98008, USA

Ishizaka, Kimishiga (Doctor)
Allergy/Immunology Institute
11149 N Torrey Pines Road
La Jolla, CA 92037, USA

Ishizaka, Teruko (Doctor)
Good Samaritan Hospital
5601 Loch Raven Blvd
Baltimore, MD 21239, USA

Ishmael, Stephen D (Scientist)
35808 42nd St E
Palmdale, CA 93552-6212, USA

Isitt, Debbie (Director)
c/o Nick Marston *Curtis Brown Group*
Haymarket House
28 - 29 Haymarket
London SW1Y 4SP, UNITED KINGDOM

Iskander, Fazil A (Writer)
Krasnoarmeiskaya Str 23 #104
Moscow 125319, RUSSIA

Islas, Claudia (Actor)
c/o Staff Member *TV Azteca*
Periferico Sur 4121
Colonia Fuentes del Pedregal
DF CP 14141, Mexico

Islas, Mauricio (Actor)
c/o Staff Member *Televisa*
Blvd Adolfo Lopez Mateos 232
Colonia San Angel INN
DF CP 01060, MEXICO

Isler, Jennifer (Athlete, Olympic Athlete, Sailor)
6828 Country Club Dr
La Jolla, CA 92037-5605, USA

Isley, Ronald (Ron) (Musician)
Ron Weisner Mgmt
PO Box 261640
Encino, CA 91426, USA

Isley Brothers (Music Group)
c/o Carleen Donovan *Press Here Publicity*
138 W. 25th St Fl 9
New York, NY 10001, USA

Ismail, Ahmed Sultan (Engineer)
43 Ahmed Abdel Aziz St
Dokki
Cairo, EGYPT

Ismail, Qadry (Athlete, Football Player)
1506 Sunningdale Way
Bel Air, MD 21015, USA

Ismail, Raghib R (Rocket) (Athlete, Football Player)
7423 Marigold Dr
Irving, TX 75063-5505, USA

Ison, Christopher J (Journalist)
Minneapolis-Saint Paul Star Tribune
425 Portland Ave
Minneapolis, MN 55488, USA

Isozaki, Arata (Architect)
Arata Assoc
6-17-9 Adasaka
Minatoku
Tokyo 107, JAPAN

Israel, Janine (Stylist)
c/o Staff Member *Celestine - CA*
1666 20th St
#200-B
Santa Monica, CA 90404, USA

Israel, Steve (Congressman, Politician)
2457 Rayburn HOB
Washington, DC 20515, USA

Israel, Werner (Scientist)
5189 Polson Terrace
Victoria, BC V8Y 2C5, CANADA

Israelson, Larry (Athlete, Hockey Player)
PO Box 17 Site 17 RR 1
Didsbury, AB T0M 0W0, Canada

Isringhausen, Jason (Athlete, Baseball Player)
7060 N State Route 159
Moro, IL 62067-1622, USA

Issel, Dan (Athlete, Basketball Player, Coach)
325 E Palace Ave
Santa Fe, NM 87501-2275, USA

Isselbacher, Kurt J (Doctor)
20 Nobscot Road
Newton Center, MA 02459, USA

Isserlis, Steven (Musician)
Harrison/Parrott
12 Penzance Place
London W11 4PA, UNITED KINGDOM
(UK)

Ito, Lance (Attorney, Judge)
Los Angeles Superior Court
825 S Madison Ave
Pasadena, CA 91106-4404, USA

Ito, Masayoshi (Government Official)
1-28-3 Chitose-Dai
Setagayaku
Tokyo 157, JAPAN

Ito, Midori (Figure Skater)
Skating Federation
Kryshi Taaikukan 1-1-1
Shibuyaku
Tokyo 10, JAPAN

Ito, Robert (Actor)
843 N Sycamore Ave
Los Angeles, CA 90038, USA

Itskovich, Anka (Stylist)
c/o Staff Member *Jam Arts, Inc*
154 W 57th St
New York, NY 10019, USA

Itzin, Gregory (Actor)
Borinstein Oreck Bogart
3172 Dona Susana Dr
Studio City, CA 91604, USA

Iuzzolino, Mike (Athlete, Basketball Player)
1048 New London Dr
Greensburg, PA 15601-1144, USA

Ivanchenkov, Aleksandr S (Astronaut, Misc)
Potchta Kosmonavtov
Moskovskoi Oblasti
Syvisdny Goroduk 141160, RUSSIA

Ivanchenkov, Alexander
141 160 Zvezdny Gorodok
Moscow Obl., RUSSIA

Ivanek, Zeljko
101 W 12th St
Apt 18D
New York, NY 10011, USA

Ivanisevic, Goran (Tennis Player)
Alijnoviceva 28
Split 58000, SERBIA & MONTENEGRO

Ivanov, Igor S (Government Official)
Foreign Affairs Ministry
Smolenskaya-Sennaya 32/34
Moscow, RUSSIA

Ivanov, Kalina (Actor, Designer)
c/o Sandra Marsh *Sandra Marsh Management*
9150 Wilshire Blvd #220
Beverly Hills, CA 90212, USA

Ivanovic, Ana (Athlete, Tennis Player)
DH-Management AG
Holeestrasse 86
Basel 4054, Switzerland

Ivens, Teri (Actor)
c/o Stephen Rice *Pantheon Talent*
1900 Ave Of The Stars
Suite 2840
Los Angeles, CA 90067, USA

Ivens, Terri (Actor)
c/o Staff Member *Kohner Agency, The*
9300 Wilshire Blvd
Suite 555
Beverly Hills, CA 90212, USA

Iver, Bon (Music Group)
c/o Carrie Tolles *Shore Fire Media*
32 Court St
16th Floor
Brooklyn, NY 11201, USA

Ivers, Eileen (Athlete, Misc)
Sony Records
2100 Colorado Ave
Santa Monica, CA 90404, USA

Iverson, Duke (Athlete, Football Player)
616 Elm Dr
Petaluma, CA 94952, USA

Iverson, Portia (Religious Leader)
11312 Highway 75
Plattsmouth, NE 68048-8268, USA

Iverson, Willie (Athlete, Basketball Player)
14789 Rosemary St
Detroit, MI 48213, USA

Ivery, Eddie Lee (Athlete, Football Player)
1080 Wrightsboro Rd
Thomson, GA 30824, USA

Ives, J Atwood (Business Person)
Eastern Enterprises
201 Rivermoor St
West Roxbury, MA 02132, USA

Ivey, Dana (Actor)
Paradigm Agency
10100 Santa Monica Blvd #2500
Los Angeles, CA 90067, USA

Ivey, James
5845 Dahlia Dr. #7
Orlando, FL 32807-3267

Ivey, James B (Jim) (Cartoonist, Editor)
5840 Dahlia Dr #7
Orlando, FL 32807, USA

Ivey, Judith (Actor)
53 W 87th St #2
New York, NY 10024, USA

Ivey, Phil (Misc)
c/o Staff Member *Kolyma Corporation*
Full Tilt Poker
62 Lloyd G Smith Blvd
Oranjestad, AW, USA

Ivey, Royal (Athlete, Basketball Player)
6080 Indian Wood Cir SE
Mableton, GA 30126-2969, USA

Ivie, Mike (Athlete, Baseball Player)
PO Box 1565
Loganville, GA 30052-1565, USA

Ivins, Marsha S (Astronaut)
2811 Timber Briar Circle
Houston, TX 77059-2904, USA

Ivlow, John (Athlete, Football Player)
124 N Poppy Ln
Plainfield, IL 60544, USA

Ivo, Tommy (Race Car Driver)
247 S. Orchard Dr
Burbank, CA 91506

Ivor, Clark (Stylist)
c/o Staff Member *Karlee Artist Management*
2658 Griffith Park Blvd
#171
Los Angeles, CA 90039, USA

Ivory, Elvin (Athlete, Basketball Player)
1071 E Woodbury Rd
Pasadena, CA 91016-4676, USA

Ivory, Horace O (Athlete, Football Player)
5321 Diaz Ave
Fort Worth, TX 76107, USA

Ivory, James (Athlete, Baseball Player)
3026 Wenonah Park Rd SW
Birmingham, AL 35211, USA

Ivory, James F (Director, Filmmaker, Producer)
18 Patroon St
Claverach, NY 12513, USA

Ivosev, Aleksandra (Misc)
Sluzbeni put Zavoda 5
Careva Cuprija
Belgrad 11030, SERBIA & MONTENEGRO

Iwago, Mitsuaki (Photographer)
Edelhof Daichi Building #2F
8 Honsio-cho Shinjukaku
Tokyo 160, JAPAN

Iwanowski, Mark (Athlete, Football Player)
523 N 12th St
Reading, PA 19604, USA

Iwatani, Yasuko (Stylist)
c/o Staff Member *L'Agence*
5901-C Peachtree Dunwoody Rd
#60
Atlanta, GA 30328, USA

Iwerks, Donald W (Business Person)
Iwerks Entertainment
4520 W Valerio St
Burbank, CA 91505, USA

Iwerks, Leslie (Director, Producer)
c/o Scott Agostini *WME (LA)*
9601 Wilshire Blvd Fl 3
Beverly Hills, CA 90210, USA

Iyanaga, Shokichi (Mathematician)
12-4 Otsuka 6-Chome
Bunkyoku
Tokyo 112-0012, JAPAN

Iyer, Kalpana (Actor, Dancer)
E 43 Geeta Kiran Society J P Road Four Bangalows
Andheri
Bombay, MS 400 058, INDIA

Izibor, Laura (Musician)
c/o Staff Member *Paradigm (Monterey)*
404 W Franklin St
Monterey, CA 93940, USA

Izo, George (Athlete, Football Player)
PO Box 325
Alexandria, VA 22313-0325, USA

Izquierdo, Hank (Athlete, Baseball Player)
12458 71st Pl N
West Palm Beach, FL 33412-1438, USA

Izquierdo, Hansel (Athlete, Baseball Player)
8420 SW 154th Circle Ct
Apt 515
Miami, FL 33193, USA

Izturis, Cesar (Athlete, Baseball Player)
375 S 3rd St
Burbank, CA 91502, USA

Izzard, Eddie (Actor, Comedian)
c/o Caroline Chignell *PBJ Management*
22 Rathbone St
London W1T 1LA, UK

Izzo, Larry (Athlete, Football Player)
1 Snowbird Pl
The Woodlands, TX 77381, USA

Izzo, Tom (Basketball Player, Coach)
Michigan State University
Athletic Dept
East Lansing, MI 48824, USA

J, Jessie (Musician)
c/o Staff Member *Next Model Management (LA)*
8447 Wilshire Blvd #PH
Beverly Hills, CA 90211, USA

Jaa, Tony (Actor)
Sahamongkol Film International Co., Ltd
388, 9th Floor, 3B, S.P. Building (IBM)
Phaholyothin Rd
Payathai, Bangkok 10400, Thailand

Jabali, Warren (Athlete, Basketball Player)
5018 SW 168th Ave
Miramar, FL 33027-4914, USA

Jabe (Stylist)
c/o Staff Member *L'Agence*
5901-C Peachtree Dunwoody Rd
#60
Atlanta, GA 30328, USA

Jablonski, Henryk (President)
Ul Filtrowa 61 m 4
Warsaw 02-056, POLAND

Jablonski, Pat (Athlete, Hockey Player)
18814 Wimbledon Cir
Lutz, FL 33558, USA

Jabs, Matthias (Musician)
c/o Staff Member *Agency Group Ltd, The (NY)*
142 West 57th St
6th Floor
New York, NY 10019, USA

Jace, Michael (Actor)
c/o Craig Dorfman *Frontline Management*
5670 Wilshire Blvd.
Suite 1370
Los Angeles, CA 90036, USA

Jack, Beau
1 Hall of Fame Dr.
Canastota, NY 13032

Jack, Eric (Athlete, Football Player)
4206 West Ross Ave
Gelndale, AZ 85308, USA

Jack, Jarrett (Athlete, Basketball Player)
c/o Jeff Schwartz *Excel Sports Management*
9665 Wilshire Blvd #500
Los Angeles, CA 90212, USA

Jack Davis, Jack Davis (Cartoonist)
c/o Staff Member *Simon & Schuster*
1230 Avenue of the Americas
New York, NY 10020, USA

Jacke, Chris (Athlete, Football Player)
1631 Shallow Creek Ct
Green Bay, WI 54311-3963, USA

Jacke, Christoper L (Chris) (Athlete, Football Player)
P.O. Box 888
Phoenix, AZ 85001, USA

Jackee (Actor)
7250 Franklin Ave
#814
Los Angeles, CA 90046, USA

Jacklin, Tony (Athlete, Golfer)
1175 51st St
Bradenton, FL 34209-4259, USA

Jackman, Barret (Athlete, Hockey Player)
4924 Pershing Pl
Saint Louis, MO 63108-1202, USA

Jackman, Hugh (Actor)
c/o Alan Nierob *Rogers & Cowan PR (LA)*
Pacific Design Center
8687 Melrose Ave, 7th Floor
West Hollywood, CA 90069, USA

Jacks, Wayne (Race Car Driver)
Wayne Jacks Motorsports
2755 No. Lamont St.
Las Vegas, NC 89115, USA

Jacks Mannequin (Musician)
c/o Staff Member *Maverick Recording Co (LA)*
3300 Warner Blvd
Burbank, CA 91505-4632, USA

Jackson, Al (Baseball Player)
Pittsburgh Pirates
3321 SE Morningside Blvd
Port Saint Lucie, FL 34952-5906, USA

Jackson, Alan (Musician, Songwriter)
P.O. Box 121945
Nashville, TN 37212-1945, USA

Jackson, Alfonza (Athlete, Football Player)
2701 Godwin Ln
Pensacola, FL 32526, USA

Jackson, Alfred (Athlete, Football Player)
1811 Kirby Dr
Houston, TX 77019, USA

Jackson, Alphonso (Secretary)
Housing & Urban Development Department
451 7th SW
Washington, DC 20410, USA

Jackson, Alvin N (Al) (Athlete, Baseball Player)
3221 SE Morningside Blvd
Port Saint Lucie, FL 34952-5919, USA

Jackson, Anne (Actor)
140 Riverside Dr #19E
New York, NY 10024, USA

Jackson, Arthur J (General, War Hero)
1290 E Spring Court
Boise, ID 83712-8313, USA

Jackson, Barry
29 Rathcoole Ave.
London, ENGLAND N8 9LY

Jackson, Betty (Designer, Fashion Designer)
Betty Jackson Ltd
1 Netherwood Place
London W14 0BW, UNITED KINGDOM (UK)

Jackson, Bo (Athlete, Football Player, Heisman Trophy Winner)
100 Oak Ridge Dr W
Burr Ridge, IL 60527-6870, USA

Jackson, Bo (Athlete, Baseball Player)
100 Oak Ridge Dr W
Burr Ridge, IL 60527-6870, USA

Jackson, Bob (Athlete, Football Player)
30608 Salem Dr
Bay Village, OH 44140-1127, USA

Jackson, Bobby (Athlete, Football Player)
47 Tippin Dr
Huntington Station, NY 11746, USA

Jackson, Bobby (Basketball Player)
Sacramento Kings
Arco Arena
1 Sports Parkway
Sacramento, CA 95834, USA

Jackson, Brandon T (Actor, Producer)
c/o Staff Member *ML Management*
125 W 55th St Fl 8
New York, NY 10019, USA

Jackson, Brian (Athlete, Football Player)
c/o Jordan Woy *Willis and Woy Management*
3030 Olive St #520
Dallas, TX 75219, USA

Jackson, Calvin (Athlete, Football Player)
250 SW 28th Ter
Fort Lauderdale, FL 33312, USA

Jackson, Charles (Athlete, Football Player)
P.O. Box 888285
Atlanta, GA 30356, USA

Jackson, Cheyenne (Actor)
c/o Pete Sanders *Fifteen Minutes (NY)*
115 W 29th St Fl 8
New York, NY 10001, USA

Jackson, Christine W (Stylist)
368 Penning Rd
Chehalis, WA 98532, USA

Jackson, Chuck (Athlete, Baseball Player)
15821 SE 175th Pl
Renton, WA 98058-9122, USA

Jackson, Chuck (Musician)
Universal Attractions
225 W 57th St #500
New York, NY 10019, USA

Jackson, Clarence (Athlete, Football Player)
5251 Appleleaf Ct
Richmond, VA 23234, USA

Jackson, Conor (Athlete, Baseball Player)
7301 E 3rd Ave
Unit 313
Scottsdale, AZ 85251-4461, USA

Jackson, Dallas (Producer, Writer)
c/o Staff Member *Davis Entertainment*
150 S Barrington Pl
Los Angeles, CA 90049, USA

Jackson, Damian (Athlete, Baseball Player)
1955 Sunset Dr Unit 81
Escondido, CA 92025-6635, USA

Jackson, Dane (Athlete, Hockey Player)
5887 Pinehurst Ct
Grand Forks, ND 58201-2813, USA

Jackson, Danny (Athlete, Baseball Player)
16332 Larsen St
Overland Park, KS 66062-8520, USA

Jackson, Darrell (Athlete, Baseball Player)
P.O. Box 4424
Downey, CA 90241-1424, USA

Jackson, Darrell (Athlete, Football Player)
12727 SE 38th Street
Bellevue, WA 98006-1235, USA

Jackson, Darrin (Athlete, Baseball Player)
Chicago White Sox 333 W 35th St Attn
Broadcast Dept
chicago, IL 60616-3696, USA

Jackson, Daryl S (Architect)
161 Hotham St
East Melbourne, VIC 3002, AUSTRALIA

Jackson, Deanna (Basketball Player)
Indiana Fever
Conseco Fieldhouse
125 S Pennsylvania
Indianapolis, IN 46204, USA

Jackson, Don (Athlete, Hockey Player)
12308 W Texas St
Wichita, KS 67235-1431, USA

Jackson, Donald
1080 Brocks
South Pickering ON, CANADA

Jackson, Doris (Musician)
Nationwide Entertainment
2756 N Green Valley Parkway
Henderson, NV 89014, USA

Jackson, Earnest (Athlete, Football Player)
915 Cole Ave Apt 2003
Rosenberg, TX 77471-3962, USA

Jackson, Eddie (Bowler)
3961 Glenmore Ave
Cincinnati, OH 45211-3509, USA

Jackson, Edwin (Athlete, Baseball Player)
6955 Setter Dr
Columbus, GA 31909-4803, USA

Jackson, Ernie (Athlete, Football Player)
938 Pisgah N
Eads, TN 38028-9799, USA

Jackson, Francis A (Composer, Musician)
Nether Garth
East Acklam
Malton North Yorkshire YO17 9RG,
UNITED KINGDOM (UK)

Jackson, Frank (Athlete, Football Player)
5904 Gregory Ln
Allen, TX 75002, USA

Jackson, Gildart (Actor)
c/o Chuck Binder *Binder & Associates*
1465 Lindacrest Dr
Beverly Hills, CA 90210, USA

Jackson, Glenda (Actor)
Crouch Assoc
9-15 Neal St
London WC2H 9PF, UNITED KINGDOM
(UK)

Jackson, Grady (Athlete, Football Player)
PO Box 841
Braselton, GA 30517-0015, USA

Jackson, Grant (Athlete, Baseball Player)
212 Mesa Cir
Pittsburgh, PA 15241-1721, USA

Jackson, Harold (Athlete, Coach, Football
Player)
6144 Flight Ave
Los Angeles, CA 90056, USA

Jackson, Harold (Journalist)
Birmingham News
Editorial Dept
2200 N 4th Ave N
Birmingham, AL 35203, USA

Jackson, Heathermary (Stylist)
c/o Staff Member *Management + Artists +
Organization*
330 W 38th St
#1401
New York, NY 10018, USA

Jackson, Honor (Athlete, Football Player)
384 Wren Dr
Santa Rosa, CA 95401-5852, USA

Jackson, Huson (Architect)
Sert Jackson Assoc
442 Marrett Road #101
Lexington, MA 02421, USA

Jackson, Jack (Athlete, Hockey Player)
12108 Slater St
Overland Park, KS 66213-1557, USA

Jackson, James A (Jim) (Athlete,
Basketball Player)
17827 Windflower Way
Dallas, TX 75252, USA

Jackson, Janet (Actor, Dancer, Musician)
c/o Danielle Marie Owens *Guttman
Associates*
118 S Beverly Dr
Suite 201
Beverly Hills, CA 90212, USA

Jackson, Jaren (Athlete, Basketball Player)
16813 Hoffman Manor Dr
Silver Spring, MD 20905-5033, USA

Jackson, Jarious (Athlete, Football Player)
7423 Marigold Dr
Irving, TX 75063-5505, USA

Jackson, Jeff (Athlete, Baseball Player)
853 S Kingsley Dr #D
Los Angeles, CA 90005-4367, USA

Jackson, Jeff (Athlete, Football Player)
1119 Parkview Dr
Griffin, GA 30224-4738, USA

Jackson, Jeff (Athlete, Hockey Player)
c/o Staff Member *Toronto Maple Leafs*
Air Canada Centre
400-40 Bay St
Toronto, ON M5J 2X2, Canada

Jackson, Jeremy (Actor, Producer)
c/o Rachel Rothman *Rothman / Patino /
Andres Entertainment*
4370 Tujunga Ave
Suite 120
Studio City, CA 91604, USA

Jackson, Jermaine (Basketball Player)
Atlanta Hawks
190 Marietta St SW
Atlanta, GA 30303, USA

Jackson, Jermaine (Music Group,
Musician, Songwriter)
4641 Hayvenhurst Dr
Encino, CA 91436, USA

Jackson, Jesse (Activist, Politician,
Religious Leader)
400 T Street NW
Washington, DC 20001, USA

Jackson, Joe (Business Person)
c/o Staff Member *Paradigm (Monterey)*
404 W Franklin St
Monterey, CA 93940, USA

Jackson, Joe M (General, War Hero)
25320 38th Ave S
Kent, WA 98032-5679, USA

Jackson, john (Athlete, Baseball Player)
PO Box 898
Hodge, LA 71247-0898, USA

Jackson, John (Athlete, Football Player)
8183 Alpine Aster Ct
Liberty Township, OH 15044, USA

Jackson, John David (Boxer)
1022 S State St
Tacoma, WA 98405, USA

Jackson, John (Fabolous) (Musician)
c/o Tammy Brook *FYI Public Relations*
174 5th Ave
Suite 404
New York, NY 10010, USA

Jackson, John M (Actor)
JAG
5555 Melrose Ave
Clara Bow #204
Los Angeles, CA 90038, USA

Jackson, Jonathan (Actor)
c/o David Guillod *Intellectual Artists
Management*
9560 Wilshire Blvd Fl 5
Beverly Hills, CA 90212-2401, USA

Jackson, Joshua (Actor)
c/o Michael Bircumshaw *Water Street
Management*
5225 Wilshire Blvd
Suite 615
Los Angeles, CA 90036, USA

Jackson, Kate (Actor)
c/o Staff Member *WmE2 (WMA-LA)*
1 William Morris Pl
Beverly Hills, CA 90212, USA

Jackson, Keith (Race Car Driver)
8941 West Jewell Pl.
Lakewood, CO 80227, USA

Jackson, Keith (Athlete, Football Player)
1801 Champlin Dr
Apt 1707
Little Rock, AR 72223, USA

Jackson, Keith J (Athlete, Football Player)
P.O. Box 241695
Little Rock, AR 72223, USA

Jackson, Keith M (Sportscaster)
ABC-TV
Abc Sports 77 W 66th St Rm 100
New York, NY 10023-6298, USA

Jackson, Ken (Athlete, Baseball Player)
P.O. Box 613
Waskom, TX 75692-0613, USA

Jackson, Kenny (Athlete, Football Player)
1319 Linn St
State College, PA 16803-3026, USA

Jackson, Kirby (Athlete, Football Player)
373 Vista Lake Ter
Suwanee, GA 30024, USA

Jackson, Kwame (Business Person, Reality
TV Star)
c/o Staff Member *Mark Burnett
Productions*
640 N Sepulveda Blvd
Los Angeles, CA 90049, USA

Jackson, Larron (Athlete, Football Player)
20000 Mitchell Pl Unit 56
Denver, CO 80249-7231, USA

Jackson, Larry R (Misc)
Grain Millers Federation
4949 Oslon Memorial Parkway
Minneapolis, MN 55422, USA

Jackson, La Toya (Model, Musician)
c/o Jeffre Phillips *Ja-Tail Enterprises*
8306 Wilshire Blvd.
Suite 528
Beverly Hills, CA 90211, USA

Jackson, Lauren (Basketball Player)
Seattle Storm
Key Arena
351 Elliott Ave W #500
Seattle, WA 98119, USA

Jackson, Lenzie (Athlete, Football Player)
4524 E La Puente Ave
Phoenix, AZ 85044-1421, USA

Jackson, Leo (Race Car Driver)
Box 726
191 Airport Road
Arden, NC 28704, USA

Jackson, Leshon (Athlete, Football Player)
P.O. Box 957
Haskell, OK 74436, USA

Jackson, Lillian (Baseball Player)
1050 W Camino Velasquez
Green Valley, AZ 85614-4527, USA

Jackson, Luke (Athlete, Basketball Player,
Olympic Athlete)
7711 County Road 511
Rosharon, TX 77583-7286, USA

Jackson, Mannie (Athlete, Basketball
Player)
Harlem Globetrotters
400 E Van Buren St
Suite 300
Phoenix, AZ 85004-0672, USA

Jackson, Mark A (Athlete, Basketball
Player, Sportscaster)
17 Winmere Pl
Dix Hills, NY 91302-3152, USA

Jackson, Mark A (Athlete, Football Player)
1480 lloyd Ct
Wheaton, IL 60189-7368, USA

Jackson, Marlon
4641 Hayvenhurst Ave.
Encino, CA 91316

Jackson, Mel (Actor)
c/o Staff Member *Stone Manners Salners
Agency (LA)*
9911 W Pico Blvd Ste 1400
Los Angeles, CA 90035, USA

Jackson, Melvin (Athlete, Football Player)
4345 Enoro Dr
Los Angeles, CA 90008, USA

Jackson, Mervin (Athlete, Basketball
Player)
16638 Kildare Ct
Tinley Park, IL 60477-1579, USA

Jackson, Michael (Athlete, Football Player)
14207 128th Pl NE
Kirkland, WA 98034, USA

Jackson, Michelle (Stylist)
c/o Staff Member *Zenobia Agency Inc*
PO Box 909
Groveland, CA 95321, USA

Jackson, Mick (Director)
1349 Berea Place
Pacific Palisades, CA 90272, USA

Jackson, Mike (Athlete, Baseball Player)
805 11th Ave
Apt 2H
Paterson, NJ 07514-1012, USA

Jackson, Mike (Athlete, Baseball Player)
17214 Oak Dale Dr
Spring, TX 77379-8846, USA

Jackson, Milt (Athlete, Football Player)
100 McMindes Ct
Roseville, CA 95747, USA

Jackson, Monte C (Athlete, Football Player)
11010 W Ocean Air Dr Apt 363
San Diego, CA 92130-4629, USA

Jackson, Nate (Athlete, Football Player)
11968 E Lake Cir
Greenwood Village, CO 80111-5245, USA

Jackson, Neil (Actor)
c/o Staff Member *IFA Talent Agency*
8730 Sunset Blvd
Suite 490
Los Angeles, CA 90069, USA

Jackson, Nickey (Stylist)
c/o Staff Member *Help Me Rhonda*
541 10th St NW #294
Atlanta, GA 30318, USA

Jackson, Noah (Athlete, Football Player)
1640 Millburne Rd
Lake Forest, IL 60045, USA

Jackson, Paris (Actor)
c/o Ann Gurrola *Marleah Leslie & Associates PR*
1645 N Vine St
Suite 712
Los Angeles, CA 90028, USA

Jackson, Peter (Director)
c/o Ken Kamins *Key Creatives*
1800 N Highland Ave
Suite 500
Los Angeles, CA 90028, USA

Jackson, Phil (Athlete, Basketball Coach, Basketball Player, Coach)
18942 Medicine Rock Ln
Lakeside, MT 59922-9514, USA

Jackson, Phillip (Actor)
c/o Pippa Markham *Markham & Froggatt*
4 Windmill St
London W1T 1HZ, UK

Jackson, Quinton (Rampage) (Athlete, Wrestler)
c/o Staff Member *ROAR (LA)*
9701 Wilshire Blvd
8th Floor
Los Angeles, CA 90212, USA

Jackson, Ralph (Athlete, Basketball Player)
3235 W 111th Pl
Inglewood, CA 90303-2316, USA

Jackson, Randy (Musician, Reality TV Star)
c/o Harriet Sternberg *Harriet Sternberg Management*
4530 Gloria Ave
Encino, CA 91436, USA

Jackson, Randy (Athlete, Baseball Player)
250 Hunnicutt Dr
Athens, GA 30606-1708, USA

Jackson, Randy B (Athlete, Football Player)
747 Musago Run
Lake Mary, FL 32746, USA

Jackson, Ransom (Baseball Player)
Chicago Cubs
250 Hunnicutt Dr
Athens, GA 30606-1708, USA

Jackson, Rebbie (Music Group, Musician, Songwriter, Writer)
4641 Hayvenhurst Dr
Encino, CA 91436, USA

Jackson, Reggie (Athlete, Baseball Player)
c/o Staff Member *Doubleday/RandomHouse*
1745 Broadway
New York, NY 10019, USA

Jackson, R Graham (Architect)
Calhoun Tungate Jackson Dill Architects
6200 Savoy Dr
Houston, TX 77036, USA

Jackson, Richard A (Religious Leader)
North Phoenix Baptist Church
5757 N Central Ave
Phoenix, AZ 85012, USA

Jackson, Richard Lee
1815 Butler Avenue
#120
Los Angeles, CA 90025-5644

Jackson, Richard S (Richie) (Athlete, Football Player)
6000 Kingston Ct
New Orleans, LA 70131, USA

Jackson, Rickey (Athlete, Football Player)
448 Avenue I
Marrero, LA 70072-1717, USA

Jackson, Rickey A (Athlete, Football Player)
325 S Barfield Hwy
Pahokee, FL 33476, USA

Jackson, Ron (Athlete, Baseball Player)
515 White Rd
Fayetteville, GA 30214-1211, USA

Jackson, Ronald Shannon (Musician)
Worldwide Jazz
1128 Broadway #425
New York, NY 10010, USA

Jackson, Roy Lee (Athlete, Baseball Player)
8269 Lee Road 54
Auburn, AL 36830-8222, USA

Jackson, Russ (Athlete, Football Player)
4153 Vermont Cres
Burlington, ON l7M 4A9, Canada

Jackson, Ryan (Athlete, Baseball Player)
2335 Alpine Ave
Sarasota, FL 34239-4117, USA

Jackson, Samuel L (Actor)
c/o Eli Selden *Anonymous Content (LA)*
3531 Hayden Ave
Culver City, CA 90232, USA

Jackson, Sasha (Actor)
c/o Ric Beddingfield *Beddingfield Company, The*
13600 Ventura Blvd
Suite B
Sherman Oaks, CA 91423, USA

Jackson, Shar (Actor)
c/o Trisanne Marin *LA Management*
225 E. Broadway
Suite B104
Glendale, CA 91205, USA

Jackson, Sheldon (Athlete, Football Player)
4466 Teresita Ct
Chino, CA 91710, USA

Jackson, Sherry (Actor)
800 N Lucia Ave #A
Redondo Beach, CA 90277-2233, USA

Jackson, Shirley Ann (Educator, Physicist)
Rensselaer Polytechnic Institute
President's Office
Troy, NY 12180, USA

Jackson, Sonny (Athlete, Baseball Player)
117 Palm Bay Dr
Apt B
Palm Beach Gardens, FL 33418-5790, USA

Jackson, Stephen (Athlete, Basketball Player)
6945 Brazos Ave
Port Arthur, TX 77642-6581, USA

Jackson, Steve (Athlete, Football Player)
43752 Lees Mill Sq
Leesburg, VA 20176, USA

Jackson, Steve (Athlete, Football Player)
1153 Bergen Pkwy
Suite M
Evergreen, CO 80439, USA

Jackson, Steven (Athlete, Football Player)
c/o Eugene Parker *Maximum Sports Management*
6435 W Jefferson Blvd
#197
Fort Wayne, IN 46804, USA

Jackson, Steven R (Randy) (Musician)
c/o Taunya Zilkie *Zilk Inc*
686 South Arroyo Pkwy
Suite 300
Pasadena, CA 91105, USA

Jackson, Stonewall (Musician, Songwriter)
6007 Cloverland Dr
Brentwood, TN 37027, USA

Jackson, Stoney (Actor)
3151 Cahuenga Blvd W #310
Los Angeles, CA 90068, USA

Jackson, Tarvaris (Athlete, Football Player)
11171 Sun Center Dr Ste 290
Rancho Cordova, CA 95670-6190, USA

Jackson, Thomas Penfield (Judge)
US District Court
333 Constitution Ave NW
Washington, DC 20001, USA

Jackson, Thomas (Tom) (Athlete, Football Player, Sportscaster)
ESPN-TV
Sports Dept ESPN Plaza
935 Middle St
Bristol, CT 06010, USA

Jackson, Tim (Athlete, Football Player)
6501 White Oak Dr
Rowlett, TX 75089, USA

Jackson, Tito (Musician)
2467 Taylor Ave
Corona, CA 92882-6980, USA

Jackson, Tracy (Athlete, Basketball Player)
10588 Spotted Horse Ln
Columbia, MD 21044-2214, USA

Jackson, Tre (Athlete, Football Player)
680 Harrison Ave
Peekskill, NY 10566, USA

Jackson, Trina (Athlete, Olympic Athlete, Swimmer)
9271 Saltwater Way
Jacksonville, FL 32256-9606, USA

Jackson, Tyoka (Athlete, Football Player)
16312 Birkdale Dr
Odessa, FL 33556-2802, USA

Jackson, Tyson (Athlete, Football Player)
c/o Eugene Parker *Maximum Sports Management*
6435 W Jefferson Blvd
#197
Fort Wayne, IN 46804, USA

Jackson, Verdell (Baseball Player)
Memphis Red Sox
413 Lincoln St
Venice, IL 62090-1117, USA

Jackson, Vernell (Athlete, Baseball Player)
413 Lincoln St
Venice, IL 62090-1117, USA

Jackson, Vestee (Athlete, Football Player)
6554 Eagle Creek Ln
Las Vegas, NV 89156-5945, USA

Jackson, Victoria (Actor, Comedian)
c/o Kim Dorr *Defining Artists Agency*
10 Universal City Plaza
Suite 2000
Universal City, CA 91608, USA

Jackson, Victoria (Business Person)
Lola Boutique
110 S Robertson Blvd
Los Angeles, CA 90069, USA

Jackson, Vincent E (Bo) (Athlete, Baseball Player, Football Player)
P.O. Box 158
Mobile, AL 36601, USA

Jackson, Wanda (Music Group, Musician)
Wanda Jackson Enterprises
8200 S Pennsylvania Ave
Oklahoma City, OK 73159, USA

Jackson, Wardell (Athlete, Basketball Player)
185 Hamilton Ave
Columbus, OH 43216-4142, USA

Jackson, Waverly (Athlete, Football Player)
1231 Halifax St
South Hill, VA 23970, USA

Jackson, Wilbur (Athlete, Football Player)
P.O. Box 1571
Ozark, AL 36361, USA

Jackson, Willie (Athlete, Football Player)
P.O. Box 12643
Gainesville, FL 32604, USA

Jackson, Zach (Athlete, Baseball Player)
7620 Menler Dr
Austin, TX 78735-1809, USA

Jackson Hoye, Rose (Actor)
c/o Staff Member *Haldeman Business Management*
1137 2nd Street
Santa Monica, CA 90403, USA

Jackson Lee, Sheila (Congressman, Politician)
2160 Rayburn HOB
Washington, DC 20515, USA

Jacob, Francois (Nobel Prize Laureate)
15 Rue de Conde
Paris 75006, FRANCE

Jacob, Irene (Actor)
Nicole Cann
1 Rue Alfred du Vigny
Paris 75008, FRANCE

Jacob, John E (Activist)
National Urban League
120 Wall St #700
New York, NY 10005, USA

Jacob, Katerina (Actor)
Agentur Doris Mattes
Merzstr 14
Munich 81679, USA

Jacob, Ralph (Actor)
c/o Staff Member *Britto Agency PR*
234 W 56th St
Penthouse
New York, NY 10019, USA

Jacob, Stanley (Inventor)
1055 SW Westwood Court
Portland, OR 97239-2708, USA

Jacobellis, Lindsey (Athlete, Olympic
Athlete, Speed Skater)
30684 E Ski Bowl Way
Government Camp, OR 97028, USA

Jacobi, Derek G (Actor)
c/o Staff Member *ICM Partners (ICM-LA)*
10250 Constellation Blvd Fl 7
Los Angeles, CA 90067, USA

Jacobi, Walter (Scientist)
2004 Max Luther Dr NW Apt 419
Huntsville, AL 35810-3864, USA

Jacobs, Allen (Athlete, Football Player)
3050 Tolcate Ln
Salt Lake City, UT 84121, USA

Jacobs, Brandon (Athlete, Football Player)
2 Seven Trails Ln
Wayne, NJ 07470-2008, USA

Jacobs, Cam (Athlete, Football Player)
5420 Atlantic Vw
Saint Augustine, FL 32080-7148, USA

Jacobs, Darlene (Stylist)
c/o Staff Member *Mercury Artists*
8460 Higuera St Fl 2
Culver City, CA 90232, USA

Jacobs, Dave (Athlete, Football Player)
8388 Glen Eagle Dr
Manlius, NY 13104, USA

Jacobs, Gillian (Actor)
c/o Jill Kaplan *Principal Entertainment
(NY)*
130 W 42nd St
Suite 614
New York, NY 10036, USA

Jacobs, Harry (Athlete, Football Player)
108 Lenora Dr
Hamburg, NY 14075, USA

Jacobs, Irwin M (Business Person)
Qualcomm Inc
5775 Morehouse Dr
San Deigo, CA 92121, USA

Jacobs, Jack H (General, War Hero)
Bankers Trust Co
161 Liberty Corner Rd
Far Hills, NJ 07931-2588, USA

Jacobs, Jeremy (Misc)
1300 N Davis Rd
East Aurora, NY 14052-9473, USA

Jacobs, Julien I (Judge)
US Tax Court
400 2nd St NW
Washington, DC 20217, USA

Jacobs, Katie (Producer, Writer)
c/o Tony Etz *Creative Artists Agency
(CAA-LA)*
2000 Ave Of The Stars
Los Angeles, CA 90067, USA

Jacobs, Lawrence-Hilton (Actor)
PO Box 67905
Los Angeles, CA 90067, USA

Jacobs, Lou (Photographer)
296 Avenida Andorra
Cathedral City, CA 92234-1605, USA

Jacobs, Marc (Designer, Fashion
Designer)
Marc Jacobs
403 Bleeker St
New York, NY 10014, USA

Jacobs, Mike (Athlete, Baseball Player)
1583 Hikers Trail Dr
Chula Vista, CA 91915-1826, USA

Jacobs, Norman J (Publisher)
Century Publishing Co
990 Grove St
Evanston, IL 60201, USA

Jacobs, Proverb (Athlete, Football Player)
4369 Detroit Ave
Oakland, CA 94619, USA

Jacobs, Ray (Athlete, Football Player)
2402 W 5th Ave
Corsicana, TX 75110-4047, USA

Jacobs, Regina (Athlete, Olympic Athlete,
Track Athlete)
3209 Wisconsin St
Oakland, CA 94602-4029, USA

Jacobs, Tim (Athlete, Football Player)
7306 Finns Ln
Lanham, MD 20706, USA

Jacobs, Tim (Athlete, Hockey Player)
6516 County Road 301
Parachute, CO 81635, USA

Jacobs-Badini, Jane (Athlete, Baseball
Player, Commentator)
1854 4th St
Cuyahoga Falls, OH 44221-3802, USA

Jacobsen, Bucky (Athlete, Baseball Player)
1546 Boalch Ave NW
North Bend, WA 98045-8127, USA

Jacobsen, Casey (Athlete, Basketball
Player)
Phoenix Suns
201 E Jefferson St
Phoenix, AZ 85004, USA

Jacobsen, Peter (Athlete, Golfer)
27771 Marina Pointe Dr
Bonita Springs, FL 34134, USA

Jacobsen, Peter (Athlete, Golfer)
9400 SW Barnes Rd
Suite 550
Portland, OR 97225-6690, USA

Jacobsen, Stephanie (Actor)
c/o Christopher Rockwell *Global Creative*
1051 Cole Ave # B
Los Angeles, CA 90038, USA

Jacobsen, Steven C (Engineer)
University of Utah
Engineering Design Center
Salt Lake City, UT 84112, USA

Jacobs-Murk, Janet (Athlete, Baseball
Player, Commentator)
899 Olentangy Rd
Franklin Lakes, NJ 07417-2811, USA

Jacobson, A Thurl (Geophysicist,
Physicist)
7955 West Innsbrook Court
Boise, ID 83704-4487, USA

Jacobson, D D (Bowler)
8261 Rees St
Playa del Rey, CA 90293-7823, USA

Jacobson, Herbert L (Diplomat, Journalist)
Apartado 160
Escazu, COSTA RICA

Jacobson, Peter (Actor)
c/o Elizabeth Much *Much and House
Public Relations*
8075 W 3rd St
Suite 500
Los Angeles, CA 90048, USA

Jacobson, Peter Marc (Actor, Producer,
Writer)
c/o Staff Member *New York Nick*
5750 Wilshire Blvd
Los Angeles, CA 90036, USA

Jacobson, Sada (Athlete, Fencer, Olympic
Athlete)
7950 Nesbit Ferry Rd
Atlanta, GA 30350-1006, USA

Jacobson, Scott (Actor)
c/o Staff Member *Creative Artists Agency
(CAA-LA)*
2000 Ave Of The Stars
Los Angeles, CA 90067, USA

Jacoby, Billy
PO Box 46324
Los Angeles, CA 90046

Jacoby, Brook (Athlete, Baseball Player)
Cincinnati Reds 100 Joe Nuxhall Way
Attn Coaching Staff
cincinnati, OH 45202-4109, USA

Jacoby, Joe (Athlete, Football Player)
2730 Willow Dr
Vienna, VA 22181-5347, USA

Jacoby, Laura
PO Box 46324
Los Angeles, CA 90046

Jacoby, Lowell E (Admiral)
Director Defense Intelligence Agency
Washington, DC 20340, USA

Jacoby, Scott (Actor)
PO Box 461100
Los Angeles, CA 90046, USA

Jacome, Jason (Athlete, Baseball Player)
5115 N Camino Esplendora
Tucson, AZ 85718-6226, USA

Jacot, Christopher (Actor)
c/o Ted Schachter *Schachter
Entertainment*
1157 S Beverly Dr Fl 2
Los Angeles, CA 90035, USA

Jacot, Michele (Skier)
Residence du Brevent
74 Chamonix, FRANCE

Jacott, Carlos (Actor)
c/o JB Roberts *Thruline Entertainment*
9250 Wilshire Blvd
Ground Fl
Beverly Hills, CA 90212, USA

Jacox, Kendyl (Athlete, Football Player)
50 Schubach Dr
Sugar Land, TX 77479-5727, USA

Jacques, Jeff (Athlete, Hockey Player)
230 Davy Street PO Box 107
Niagara, ON LOS 1JO, Canada

Jacques, Reeves (Athlete, Football Player)
9135 Buffalo Speedway
Houston, TX 77025-4426, USA

Jacques, Russell (Artist)
48701 Shady View Dr
Palm Desert, CA 92260-6730, USA

Jacquez, Pat (Athlete, Baseball Player)
4430 Annandale Dr
Stockton, CA 95219-1782, USA

Jacquez, Thomas (Tom) (Athlete, Baseball
Player)
4430 Annandale Dr
Stockton, AZ 95219-1782, USA

Jacuzzi, Roy (Business Person)
Jacuzzi Whirlpool Bath
2121 N California Blvd
Walnut Creek, CA 94596, USA

Jadakiss (Artist, Music Group, Musician)
c/o Drew Elliot *Universal Media Artists*
140 E 46th St #PHC
New York, NY 10017, USA

Jade
c/o Staff Member *Diva Central Inc*
7510 W Sunset Blvd Ste 1445
Los Angees, CA 90046, USA

Jade, Samantha (Musician)
c/o Staff Member *Jive Records*
550 Madison Ave
New York, NY 10022-3211, USA

Jadot, Jean L O (Religious Leader)
Ave de l'Atlantique 71-B-12
Brussels 1150, BELGIUM

Jae, Jana
PO Box 35736
Tulsa, OK 74153

Jaeckel, Barry (Athlete, Golfer)
210 Falcon Cv
Brandon, MS 39047, USA

Jaeckel, Paul (Athlete, Baseball Player)
328 W 7th St
Claremont, CA 91711-4313, USA

Jaeckin, Just (Director)
8 Villa Mequillet
Neuilly/Seine 92200, FRANCE

Jaeger, Andrea (Athlete, Tennis Player)
Silver Lining Ranch
256 Rancho Milagro Way
Hesperus, CO 81326-8750, USA

Jaeger, Jeff T (Athlete, Football Player)
3026 Sahalee Dr W
Sammamish, WA 98074, USA

Jaeger, Sam (Actor)
c/o Steve Dontanville *Circle of Confusion
(NY)*
8609 E Washington Blvd #8607
Culver City, CA 90232, USA

Jaenicke, Hannes
Goetherstr. 17
Munich, GERMANY D-80336

Jae-sang, Park (PSY) (Musician)
c/o Staff Member *Universal Music Group
(TN)*
401 Commerce St #1100
Nashville, TN 37219-2489, USA

Jaffe, Arthur M (Mathematician)
27 Lancaster St
Cambridge, MA 02140, USA

Jaffe, Herold W (Doctor)
Centers for Disease Control
1600 Clifton Road
Atlanta, GA 30333, USA

Jaffe, Robert L (Physicist)
Massachusetts Institute of Technology
Physics Dept
Cambridge, MA 02139, USA

Jaffe, Stanley R (Director, Producer)
Lean Building
10202 Washington Blvd
Culver City, CA 90232, USA

Jaffe, Susan (Ballerina)
American Ballet Theatre
890 Broadway
New York, NY 10003, USA

Jaffrey, Saeed (Actor, Bollywood, Comedian)
503 Sejal New Link Road
Andheri
Bombay, MS 400 058, INDIA

Jagdeo, Bharrat (Prime Minister)
President's Office
Brickham
New Garden & South Sts
Georgetown, GUYANA

Jagendort, Andre T (Doctor)
455 Savage Farm Dr
Ithaca, NY 14850, USA

Jager, Thomas (Tom) (Athlete, Olympic Athlete, Swimmer)
1416 Chinook St
Moscow, ID 83843-2506, USA

Jager, Tom
64 Ramble Wood Blvd.
Tijeras, NM 87059

Jagge, Finn Christian (Skier)
Michelets Vei 108
Stabekk 1320, NORWAY

Jagged Edge (Music Group)
c/o Nancy Josephson *WME (LA)*
9601 Wilshire Blvd Fl 3
Beverly Hills, CA 90210, USA

Jagger, Bianca (Actor, Model)
c/o Amanda Bross *Finch & Partners - Paris*
Top Floor
29-37 Heddon St
London W1B 4BR, UNITED KINGDOM

Jagger, Jade (Business Person)
16th West 19th LLC
752 Pacific St
Brooklyn, NY 11238, USA

Jagger, Mick (Musician)
116 Richmond Hill
Richmond
Greater London TW10 6, UNITED KINGDOM

Jagland, Thorbjoern (Politician, Prime Minister)
Stortinget
Postboks 8001 Dep
Oslo N-0030, NORWAY

Jaglom, Henry (Director)
9165 W Sunset Blvd #300
Los Angeles, CA 90069, USA

Jagr, Jaromir (Athlete, Hockey Player)
c/o J P Barry *C A A Hockey*
822 11th Ave SW
Suite 204
Calgary, AB T2R 0E5, Canada

Jaguares (Music Group)
c/o Staff Member *BMG*
1540 Broadway
New York, NY 10036, USA

Jaha, John (Athlete, Baseball Player)
12776 SE Geneva Wa'i
Happy Valley, OR 97086-6182, USA

Jahan, Marine (Actor, Dancer)
Media Artists Group
6300 Wilshire Blvd #1470
Los Angeles, CA 90048, USA

Jaheim (Musician)
Diane Mill
100 Evergreen Point #402
East Orange, NJ 07018, USA

Jahn, Helmut (Architect)
2450 N Lakeview Ave
Chicago, IL 60614-2878, USA

Jahn, Robert G (Engineer)
Princeton University
Aerospace Sciences Dept
Princeton, NJ 08544, USA

Jahn, Sigmund (Astronaut, General, Misc)
Fontanestr 35
Strausberg 15344, GERMANY

Jahncke, Barton (Athlete, Olympic Athlete, Sailor)
714 Girod St Apt 2B
New Orleans, LA 70130-3523, USA

Jaidah, Ali Mohammed (Government Official)
Qatar Petroleum Corp
PO Box 3212
Doha, QATAR

Jaitley, Celina (Actor, Beauty Pageant Winner)
c/o Staff Member *Brillstein Entertainment Partners*
9150 Wilshire Blvd #350
Beverly Hills, CA 90212, USA

Jakel, Bernd (Yachtsman)
Salvador-Allende-Str 48
Berlin 12559, GERMANY

Jake Locker, Jake
c/o David Dunn *Athletes First, LLC*
9140 Irvine Center Dr
Irvine, CA 92618, USA

Jakeman, Seth (Musician)
c/o Staff Member *Paradigm (Monterey)*
404 W Franklin St
Monterey, CA 93940, USA

Jakes, Bishop T D (Musician, Writer)
c/o Staff Member *Creative Artists Agency (CAA-LA)*
2000 Ave Of The Stars
Los Angeles, CA 90067, USA

Jakes, John (Writer)
445 Meadow Lark Dr
Sarasota, Fl 34236-1901, USA

Jakes, T D (Religious Leader)
Potter's House
6777 W Kiest Blvd
Dallas, TX 75211, USA

Jakes, T D (Religious Leader)
Integrity Music
1000 Cody Rd
Mobile, AL 36695, USA

Jakes, Van (Athlete, Football Player)
305 Worthing Ln
McDonough, GA 30253, USA

Jaki, Stanley L (Misc, Physicist)
PO Box 167
Princeton, NJ 08542, USA

Jakobs, Marco (Athlete)
Oststr 1B
Unna 59427, GERMANY

Jakobson, Maggie (Actor)
c/o Kesha Williams *Affirmative Entertainment*
425 N Robertson Blvd
Los Angeles, CA 90048, USA

Jakobson, Max (Government Official, Journalist)
Rahapajankatu 3B 17
Helsinki 16 00160, FINLAND

Jakopin, John (Athlete, Hockey Player)
57 Samana Dr
Miami, FL 33133-2609, USA

Jakosits, Michael (Misc)
Karlsbergstr 140
Homburg/Saar 66424, GERMANY

Jakovac, JJ (Athlete, Golfer)
c/o Jim Lehrman *SFX Golf*
36855 W Main St Ste 200
Purcellville, VA 20132, USA

Jakowenko, George (Athlete, Football Player)
5 Aberdeen Dr
West Nyack, NY 10994, USA

Jakub, Lisa (Actor)
c/o Nancy LeFeaver *LeFeaver Talent Management Ltd*
2 College St #202
Toronto ON M5G 1K3, CANADA

Jakubo, Mike (Athlete, Hockey Player)
1164 Maureen Cres
Sudbury, ON P3A 3K5, Canada

Jal, Emmanuel (Musician, Writer)
c/o Staff Member *Sonic360, Inc.*
Top Floor East
33 Riding House St.
London W1W 7DZ, UK

Jalal, Farida (Actor, Bollywood)
3B Nandini Unik Housing Society
Opp Bon Bon J P Road Andheri
Mumbai, MS 400058, INDIA

Jalbert, Pierre
2642 N. Beverly Glen Blvd
Los Angeles, CA 90077

Jamail, Joseph D Jr (Attorney, Attorney General, General)
Jamail & Kolius
500 Dallas St #3434
Houston, TX 77002, USA

Jamal, Ahmad (Music Group, Musician)
Brad Simon Organization
122 E 57th St #300
New York, NY 10022, USA

Jambor, Agi (Music Group, Musician)
1616 Bolton St
Baltimore, MD 21217, USA

Jamerson, Dave (Athlete, Basketball Player)
13960 Salsbury Creek Dr
Carmel, IN 46077-9342, USA

James, Aaron (Athlete, Basketball Player)
3057 Orrin Ave
Youngstown, OH 44505-4436, USA

James, Alex (Composer, Musician, Producer)
c/o Staff Member *Parlophone Records*
EMI House
43 Brook Green
London W6 7EF, United Kingdom

James, Angela (Athlete, Hockey Player)
Seneca College York Campus 70 The Pond Rd
Attn: Sports Coordinator
North York, ON M3J 3M6, Canada

James, Anthony (Actor)
CNA Assoc
1875 Century Park East
#2250
Los Angeles, CA 90067, USA

James, Art (Athlete, Baseball Player)
6935 Brown Dr S
Fairburn, GA 30213-3197, USA

James, Bill (Sportscaster)
445 Tennessee St
Lawrence, KS 66044-1376, USA

James, Bill (Athlete, Baseball Player, Writer)
625 Ohio St
Lawrence, KS 66044-2357, USA

James, Billy (Athlete, Basketball Player)
12 S Sunset Dr
Lexington, IN 47138-8935, USA

James, Bob (Athlete, Baseball Player)
15844 Cindy Ct
Canyon Country, CA 91387-1881, USA

James, Boney (Musician)
c/o Staff Member *Paradigm (Monterey)*
404 W Franklin St
Monterey, CA 93940, USA

James, Bradie (Athlete, Football Player)
2509 Silver Table Dr
Lewisville, TX 75056-5680, USA

James, Bradley (Actor)
c/o Ruth Young *United Agents*
12-26 Lexington St
London W1F OLE, UK

James, Casey (Musician)
c/o Simon Fuller *XIX Entertainment*
35-37 Parkgate Rd
32/33 Ransomes Dock
London SW11 4NP, UNITED KINGDOM (UK)

James, Charlie (Athlete, Baseball Player)
3303 Tanglewood Way
Fulton, MO 65251-3981, USA

James, Charmayne (Misc)
Gold Buckle Ranch
2100 N Highway 360 #1207
Grand Prairie, TX 75050, USA

James, Cheryl (Salt) (Musician)
c/o Chris Johnston-Davies *Intrigue Management*
25 Spinney Way
Needingworth
Cambridgeshire PE27 4SR, United Kingdom

James, Chris (Athlete, Baseball Player)
1040 County Road 2707
Alto, TX 75925-5915, USA

James, Chuck (Athlete, Baseball Player)
4840 Golden Drive SW
Mableton, GA 30126, USA

James, Claudis (Athlete, Football Player)
6767 Presidential Dr
Jackson, MS 39213, USA

James, Cleo (Athlete, Baseball Player)
Major League Baseball Alumni 1631 Mesa Ave Ste B
colorado springs, CO 80906-2656, USA

James, Clifton (Actor)
500 W 43rd St #25D
New York, NY 10036, USA

James, Clive V L (Journalist, Misc)
P F D
Drury House
34-43 Russell St
London WC2B 5HA, UNITED KINGDOM
(UK)

James, Craig (Athlete, Football Player)
12714 W FM 455
Celina, TX 75009, USA

James, Dalton
303 N. Buena Vista #209
Burbank, CA 91505-3686

James, Danielle (Actor)
c/o Roger Carey *Roger Carey Associates*
Suite 909, The Old House
Shepperton Film Studios, Studios Road
Shepperton, Mddx TW17 0QD, UK

James, D Clayton (Historian)
106 Wagon Wheel Trail
Moneta, VA 24121, USA

James, Delvin (Athlete, Baseball Player)
13355 Fm 1878
Nacogdoches, TX 75961-1039, USA

James, Dion (Athlete, Baseball Player)
5 Shelter Point Ct
Sacramento, CA 95831-1415, USA

James, Don (Coach, Football Coach)
7047 Chanticleer Ave SE
Snoqualmie, WA 98065, USA

James, Donald M (Business Person)
Vulcan Materials Co
1200 Urban Center Dr
Birmingham, AL 35242, USA

James, Duncan (Musician)
c/o Staff Member *Concorde Intl Artists Ltd*
101 Shepherds Bush Rd
London W6 7LP, UNITED KINGDOM
(UK)

James, Duncan (Musician)
c/o Staff Member *BMG (UK)*
Bedford House
6979 Fulham High Street
London SW6 3JW, United Kingdom

James, Edgerrin (Athlete, Football Player)
c/o Drew Rosenhaus *Rosenhaus Sports
Representation*
6400 Allison Road
Miami Beach, FL 33141, USA

James, EL (Writer)
c/o Russell Perreault *Vintage Books*
1745 Broadway #12-1
New York, NY 10019, USA

James, Forrest (Politician)
21911vy Creek Church Rd
Rutledge, AL 36071-3913, USA

James, Geraldine (Actor)
Julian Belfarge
46 Albermarle St
London W1X 4PP, UNITED KINGDOM
(UK)

James, Gerry (Athlete, Hockey Player)
3674 Dolphin Dr
Nanoose Bay, BC V9P 9H1, Canada

James, G Larry (Athlete, Track Athlete)
Stockton State College
Atheletic Dept
Pomona, NJ 08240, USA

James, Godfrey
The Shack Western Rd. Pevensey Bay
E. Sussex, ENGLAND

James, Henry (Athlete, Basketball Player)
527 E Leith St
Fort Wayne, IN 46806-1118, USA

James, Jesse (Actor)
Austin Speed Shop
1414 S Lamar Blvd
Austin, TX 78704, USA

James, Jessie (Musician)
c/o Staff Member *Island Records*
825 Eighth Ave
New York, NY 10019, USA

James, John (Actor)
PO Box 9
Cambridge, NY 12816, USA

James, Johnny (Athlete, Baseball Player)
6037 E Larkspur Dr
Scottsdale, AZ 85254-4444, USA

James, John W (Athlete, Football Player)
23108 NE 69th Ave
Melrose, FL 32666, USA

James, Joni (Music Group, Musician)
PO Box 7027
Westchester, IL 60154, USA

James, Joshua (Musician)
c/o Brittany Pearce *Fresh and Clean
Media*
12701 Venice Blvd.
Los Angeles, CA 90066, USA

James, Kate (Model)
Men/Women Model Inc
199 Lafayette St
New York, NY 10012, USA

James, Kevin (Actor, Comedian)
c/o Jeff Sussman *Jeff Sussman
Management*
15374 Dickens St
2nd Floor
Sherman Oaks, CA 91403

James, Larry D (Astronaut)
AFELM
USS Space Command
Peterson Air Force Base, CP 80914, USA

James, LeBron (Athlete, Basketball Player)
3590 Crystal View Ct
Miami, FL 33133, USA

James, Leela (Musician)
c/o Stephanie Mahler *Creative Artists
Agency (CAA-NY)*
162 Fifth Ave
6th Floor
New York, NY 10010, USA

James, Lennie (Actor)
Castaway Voice Overs
15 Broad Ct Ste 3
London WC2B 5QN, UNITED KINGDOM

James, Lionel (Athlete, Football Player)
199 Woodbury Dr
Sterrett, AL 35147, USA

James, Michael Raymond (Actor)
c/o Mark Armstrong *Sanders Armstrong
Caserta*
2120 Colorado Blvd
Suite 120
Santa Monica, CA 90404, USA

James, Mickie (Athlete, Wrestler)
121 Dogwood Ct
Aylett, VA 23009, USA

James, Mike (Athlete, Baseball Player)
115 Austin Ct
Mary Esther, FL 32569-1396, USA

James, Oliver (Actor, Musician)
c/o Staff Member *MPG Management*
1136 Roxbury Drive
Los Angeles, CA 90035, USA

James, Oscar (Stylist)
c/o Staff Member *Ken Barboza Associates*
115 W 30th St Rm 203
New York, NY 10001, USA

James, Paul (Actor, Producer)
c/o Staff Member *HGTV/Home & Garden
Television*
9721 Sherrill Blvd
Knoxville, TN 37932, USA

James, P D (Writer)
37-A Gold hawk Road
London W12 8QQ, England

James, Po (Athlete, Football Player)
1421 E Sherman St
Hammond, IN 46320, USA

James, Ralph
205 S. Arnaz Dr. #4
Beverly Hills, CA 90211

James, Rick (Athlete, Baseball Player)
102 Stoney Creek Dr
Florence, AL 35633-1581, USA

James, Robert (Athlete, Football Player)
1511 N Highland Ave
Murfreesboro, TN 37130, USA

James, Robert (Bob) (Music Group,
Musician, Songwriter, Writer)
Monterey International
200 W Superior #202
Chicago, IL 60610, USA

James, Roland (Athlete, Football Player)
19 Spring Ln
Sharon, MA 02067, USA

James, Sheila (Actor)
3201 Pearl St
Santa Monica, CA 90405, USA

James, Sheryl (Journalist)
Saint Petersburg Times
Editorial Dept
490 1st Ave
Saint Petersburg, FL 33701, USA

James, Skip (Athlete, Baseball Player)
14429 Windsor St
Overland Park, KS 66224-3669, USA

James, Sonny (Musician, Songwriter)
c/o Staff Member *WmE2 (WMA-TN)*
1600 Division St
Suite 300
Nashville, TN 37203, USA

James, Steve (Director, Producer, Writer)
c/o Paul Canterna *Seven Summits Pictures
& Management*
8906 W Olympic Blvd
Ground Floor
Beverly Hills, CA 90211, USA

James, Tommy (Music Group, Musician)
Aura Entertainment
PO Box 4354
Clifton, NJ 07012, USA

James, Toran (Athlete, Football Player)
RR 3 Box 14-13
Ahoskie, NC 27910, USA

James, Val (Athlete, Hockey Player)
105 S 32nd St
Wyandanch, NY 11798, USA

James of Holland Park, Phyllis D (Writer)
Elaine Green Ltd
37A Goldhawk Road
London W12 SQQ, UNITED KINGDOM
(UK)

Jameson, Jenna (Actor, Adult Film Star)
16722 Baruna Ln
Huntington Beach, CA 92649, USA

Jameson, Louise
18-21 Jermyn St.
London, ENGLAND SW1Y 6HP

Jameson, Paulene
7 Warrington Gardens
London, ENGLAND W9 2QB

James-Roadman, Charmayne (Misc)
General Delivery
Clayton, NM 88415, USA

jamieson, David (General)
Drove House Thornham Hunstandton
Norfolk, England, USA

Jamieson, Janet (Athlete, Baseball Player,
Commentator)
6324 212th St SW Trlr 3
Lynnwood, WA 98036-7425, USA

Jamiroquai (Music Group)
c/o Staff Member *Nettwerk Management
(LA)*
1545 Wilcox Ace
Suite 200
Los Angeles, CA 90028, USA

Jamison, Antawn (Athlete, Basketball
Player)
Dallas Mavericks
6041 Providence Country Club Dr
Charlotte, NC 28277-2631, USA

Jamison, Jayne (Publisher)
Redbook Magazine
224 W 57th St
New York, NY 10019, USA

Jamison, Jimi (Musician)
4002 Glendale Dr
Memphis, TN 38128-2408, USA

Jamison, Mae
PO Box 580317
Houston, TX 77258-0317

Jamison, Mikki (Actor)
1501 S Latawah St
Spokane, WA 99203, USA

Jamison, Milo
1231 Tennyson St
Manhattan Beach, CA 90266

Jammeh, Yahya A J J (Misc)
President's Office
State House
Banjul, GAMBIA

Jammer, Quentin (Athlete, Football
Player)
4020 Murphy Canyon Rd
San Diego, CA 92123, USA

Jampolsky, Gerald (Writer)
Celestial Arts
PO Box 7123
Berkeley, CA 94707

Janakaraj (Actor)
8 H D Raja Street
Teynampet
Chennai, TN 600 018, INDIA

Janaki, Sowcar (Actor, Bollywood)
13 Cenetop Road
2nd Street
Chennai, TN 600018, INDIA

Jan & Dean
221 Main St. #P
Huntington Beach, CA 92648

Janaszak, Steve (Athlete, Hockey Player,
Olympic Athlete)
42 Montrose Ave
Babylon, NY 11702, USA

Jance, J A (Writer)
Avon/William Morrow
1350 Ave of Americas
New York, NY 10019, USA

Jancso, Miklos (Director)
Solyom Laszio Utca 17
Budapest II 1022, HUNGARY

Janda, Krystyna (Actor)
Teatr Powszechny
Ul Zamoyskiego 20
Warsaw, POLAND

Jande, Marine (Actor)
Gilla Roos
16 West 22nd Street
3rd Floor
New York, NY 10010

Jane, Jesse (Actor, Adult Film Star)
c/o Staff Member *Media Artists Group*
(LA)
8255 W Sunset Blvd
Los Angeles, CA 90046, USA

Jane, Thomas (Actor)
c/o Michael Katcher *Creative Artists*
Agency (CAA-LA)
2000 Ave Of The Stars
Los Angeles, CA 90067, USA

Janecyk, Bob (Athlete, Hockey Player)
5973 Pheasant View Dr NE
Ada, MI 49301-8648, USA

Janecyl, Bob (Athlete, Hockey Player)
5973 Pheasant View Dr NE
Ada, MI 49301, USA

Janeski, Jerry (Athlete, Baseball Player)
28901 Via Buena Vis
San Juan Capistrano, CA 92675-5554,
USA

Janet, Ernest (Athlete, Football Player)
21838 SE 275th St
Maple Valley, WA 98038, USA

Janeway, Michael C (Editor)
Northwestern University
Fisk Hall
Evanston, IL 60201, USA

Janeway, Richard (Doctor)
PO Box 188
Blowing Rock, NC 28605, USA

Jang, Jeong (Athlete, Golfer)
7769 Apple Tree Cir
Orlando, FL 32819, USA

Janik, Doug (Athlete, Hockey Player)
51 Senator Ave
Agawam, MA 01001, USA

Janikowski, Bruce (Athlete, Football
Player)
2716 W 112th St
Shawnee Mission, KS 66211, USA

Janis, Byron (Music Group, Musician)
Columbia Artists Mgmt Inc
165 W 57th St
New York, NY 10019, USA

Janis, Conrad (Actor, Music Group,
Musician)
1434 N Genesee Ave
Los Angeles, CA 90046, USA

Janis, Elizabeth (Actor)
c/o Michael Greenwald *Buchwald/*
Fortitude (LA)
6500 Wilshire Blvd
Suite 2200
Los Angeles, CA 90048, USA

Janish, Paul (Athlete, Baseball Player)
11926 Deep Woods Dr
Cypress, TX 77429-2741, USA

Janitz, John A (Business Person)
Textron Inc
40 Westminster St
Providence, RI 02903, USA

Jankins, Corey (Baseball Player)
Bowman
456 S Church St Apt J1
Lexington, SC 29072-3342, USA

Jankowska-Cieslak, Jadwiga (Actor)
Film Polski
Ul Mazewiecka 6/8
Warsaw 00-950, POLAND

Jankowski, Gene F (Television Host)
American Film Institute
901 15th St NW #700
Washington, DC 20005, USA

Jankowski, Peter (Producer)
c/o Staff Member *Wolf Films Inc (LA)*
100 Universal City Plz
Bldg 2252
Universal City, CA 91608-1085, USA

Jannazzo, Izzy (Boxer)
6924 62nd Ave
Flushing, NY 11379, USA

Janney, Allison (Actor)
c/o Chris Henze *Thruline Entertainment*
9250 Wilshire Blvd
Ground Fl
Beverly Hills, CA 90212, USA

Janney, Craig H (Athlete, Hockey Player)
4424 N 59th Pl
Phoenix, AZ 85018, USA

Janotta, Howard (Athlete, Basketball
Player)
18118 Brookwood Frst
San Antonio, TX 78258, USA

Janov, Arthur (Writer)
1205 Abbot Kinney Blvd
Venice, CA 90291-3315, USA

Janov, Arthur (Philanthropist, Psychic)
1205 Abbot Kinney Blvd
Venice, CA 90291, USA

Janowicz, Josh (Actor)
c/o Darren Goldberg *Global Creative*
1051 Cole Ave # B
Los Angeles, CA 90038, USA

Janowitz, Gundula (Opera Singer)
3072 Kasten
75, AUSTRIA

Janowitz, Will (Actor)
c/o David Ginsberg *Insight*
1134 S Cloverdale Ave
Los Angeles, CA 90019, USA

Janowski, Marek (Conductor)
I M G Artists
3 Burlington Lane
Chiswick
London W4 2TH, UNITED KINGDOM
(UK)

Janseen, Daniel (Business Person)
Solvay & Cie
33 Rue du Prince Albert
Brussels 1050, BELGIUM

Janseen, Famke (Actor, Model)
c/o Emily Gerson Saines *Brookside Artists*
Management (NY)
250 W 57th St
Suite 2303
New York, NY 10107, USA

Jansen, Dan (Athlete, Olympic Athlete,
Speed Skater)
PO Box 3354
Mooresville, NC 28117, USA

Jansen, Jim (Actor)
c/o Martin Gage *Gage Group, The (LA)*
14724 Ventura Blvd
Suite 505
Sherman Oaks, CA 91403, USA

Jansen, Raymond A (Publisher)
Newsday Inc
235 Pinelawn Road
Melville, NY 11747, USA

Jansons, Mariss (Conductor)
I M G Artists
3 Burlington Lane
Chiswick
London W4 2TH, UNITED KINGDOM
(UK)

Janssen, Bill (Athlete, Football Player)
4530 Pioneer Greens Dr
lincoln, NE 68526-9204, USA

Janssen, Cam (Athlete, Hockey Player)
313 Forest Run Drive
Eureka, MO 63025-2119, USA

Janssen, Casey (Athlete, Baseball Player)
232 24th St
Manhattan Beach, CA 90266-4300, USA

Janssen, Dani
2220 Avenue of the Stars #2803
Los Angeles, CA 90067

Janssen, Famke (Actor, Model)
c/o Emily Gerson Saines *Brookside Artists*
Management (NY)
250 W 57th St
Suite 2303
New York, NY 10107, USA

Janssen, Frances (Athlete, Baseball Player)
4311 Mayflower Drive
Lafayette, IN 47909-3473, USA

Janssen, Tom (Cartoonist)
Prinsengract 304, 1016 HW
Amsterdam, Netherlands

Janssens, Mark (Athlete, Hockey Player)
115 Central Park W
Apt 17-A
New York, NY 10023, USA

Jantz, Richard (Misc)
University of Tennessee
Anthropology Dept
Knoxville, TN 37996, USA

Jantzen, Linda (Stylist)
c/o Staff Member *Anyway Productions*
870 Avenue of the Americas
New York, NY 10001, USA

January, Don (Athlete, Golfer)
5006 Village Pl
Dallas, TX 75248, USA

January, Don (Golfer)
4139 Sicily Dr
Frisco, TX 75034-6659, USA

January, Lois (Actor)
PO Box 1233
Beverly Hills, CA 90213, USA

Jany, Alexandre (Alex) (Swimmer)
104 Blvd Livon
Marseille 13007, FRANCE

Janzen, Daniel H (Biologist)
University of Pennsylvania
Biology Dept
Philadelphia, PA 19104, USA

Janzen, Edmund (Religious Leader)
General Conference of Mennonite
Brethren
8000 W 21st St
Wichita, KS 67205, USA

Janzen, Henry (Athlete, Football Player)
Sport Manitoba
200 Main St Suite 100
Winnipeg, MB R3C lA8, Canada

Janzen, Lee (Athlete, Golfer)
9088 Point Cypress Dr
Orlando, FL 32836, USA

Janzen, Marty (Athlete, Baseball Player)
Lancaster Barnstormers 650 N Prince St
Attn: Coaching Staff
Lancaster, PA 17603-3025, USA

Jaqua, Jon (Athlete, Football Player)
34320 McKenzie View Dr
Eugene, OR 97408, USA

Jaquess, Pete (Athlete, Football Player)
631 Cunningham Ln
El Cajon, CA 92019, USA

Jaramillo, Jason (Athlete, Baseball Player)
6111 Madeline Ln
Caledonia, WI 53108-9557, USA

Jaramillo, Rudy (Athlete, Baseball Player)
3855 Echo Brook Ln
Dallas, TX 75229-5222, USA

Jardine, Al
Box 36
Big Sur, CA 93920

Jardine, Alan C (Al) (Musician)
PO Box 36
Big Sur, CA 93920, USA

Jarecki, Andrew (Director, Musician,
Producer)
c/o Staff Member *Hit the Ground Running*
Films
200 W 57th St #1304
New York, NY 10019, USA

Jarman Jr, Claude (Actor)
16 Tamal Vista Ln
Axminster
Kentifield, CA 94904, USA

Jarmusch, Jim (Director)
c/o Bart Walker *ICM Partners (ICM-LA)*
555 W 25th St
4th Floor
New York, NY 10001, USA

Jaroncyk, Ryan (Baseball Player)
Bowman
2923 Roseann Ave
Escondido, CA 92027-5306, USA

Jarostchuk, Ilia (Athlete, Football Player)
4 Macarthur Rd
Wellesley, MA 02482, USA

Jarreau, Al (Musician)
c/o Staff Member *Agency for the Performing Arts (APA-LA)*
405 S Beverly Dr
Suite 500
Beverly Hills, CA 90212-4425, USA

Jarrell, Tom
77 W. 66th St.
New York, NY 10023

Jarrett, Dale (Race Car Driver)
1510 46th Ave NE
Hickory, NC 28601, USA

Jarrett, Doug (Athlete, Hockey Player)
3903 Lower Coach Rd
Stevensville, ON LOS 1SO, Canada

Jarrett, Gary (Athlete, Hockey Player)
9662 E Peak View Rd
Scottsdale, AZ 85262-2352, USA

Jarrett, Jason (Race Car Driver)
Jarrett-Favre Motorsports
2025 Evans St. NE
Box 465
Conover, NC 28613, USA

Jarrett, Keith (Composer, Musician)
Stephen Cloud
PO Box 4774
Santa Barbara, CA 93140, USA

Jarrett, Ned (Race Car Driver)
3182 9th Tee Dr
Newton, NC 28658, USA

Jarriel, Thomas E (Tom) (Correspondent)
ABC-TV
News Dept
77 W 66th St
New York, NY 10023, USA

Jarrier, Jean-Pierre
17 bd. Larvotto
Monte Carlo, MONACO

Jarrin, Jaime (Athlete, Baseball Player)
725 La Mirada Ave
San Marino, CA 91108-1729, USA

Jarry, Pierre (Athlete, Hockey Player)
4141 Av Pierre-De-Coubertin
Montreal, QC H1V 3N7, Canada

Jarryd, Anders (Tennis Player)
Maaneskoldsgatan 37
Lidkoping 531 00, SWEDEN

Jars of Clay (Music Group)
c/o Janet Weir *Red Light Management (LA)*
8439 W Sunset Blvd
Suite 2
Los Angeles, CA 90069, USA

Ja Rule (Actor, Musician)
10 Lookout Dr
Saddle River, NJ 07458, USA

Jaru the Damaja (Musician)
William Morris Agency
1325 Ave of Americas
New York, NY 10019, USA

Jaruzelski, Wojciech (General, President)
Biuro Bylego
Ul Klonowa 1
Warsaw 02-001, POLAND

Jarvi, Neeme (Conductor)
PO Box 305
Sea Bright, NJ 07760, USA

Jarvi, Paavo (Conductor)
Cincinnati Symphony
Music Hall
1241 Elm St
Cincinnati, OH 45202, USA

Jarvik, Robert (Scientist)
1 Columbus Pl
New York, NY 10019-8201, USA

Jarvis, Bruce (Athlete, Football Player)
4153 Issaquah Pine Lake Rd SE
Sammamish, WA 98075, USA

Jarvis, Curtis (Athlete, Football Player)
401 Albert Dr
Gardendale, AL 35071, USA

Jarvis, Doug (Athlete, Coach, Hockey Player)
c/o Staff Member *Montreal Canadiens*
1275 Rue Saint-Antoine O
Montreal, QB H3C 5L2, Canada

Jarvis, Graham
15351 Via De Las Olas
Pacific Palisades, CA 90272

Jarvis, James (Athlete, Basketball Player)
PO Box 154
Asotin, WA 99402-0154, USA

Jarvis, Katie (Actor)
c/o Billy Lazarus *United Talent Agency (UTA)*
9336 Civic Center Dr
Beverly Hills, CA 90210, USA

Jarvis, Kevin (Athlete, Baseball Player)
1613 Whispering Hills Dr
Franklin, TN 37069-7242, USA

Jarvis, Lucy
171 W. 57th St.
New York, NY 10019

Jarvis, Martin
2-4 Noel St.
London, ENGLAND W1V 3RB

Jarvis, Pat (Athlete, Baseball Player)
4201 Providence Ln
Tucker, GA 30084-2630, USA

Jarvis, Ray (Athlete, Baseball Player)
15 Higgins St
Apt 106
Smithfield, RI 02917-4033, USA

Jarvis, Ray (Athlete, Football Player)
18320 Taywood Cir
Apt 102
Brookfield, WI 53045, USA

Jarvis, Wes (Athlete, Hockey Player)
National Training Risks
1155 Stellar Drr
Newmarket, ON L3Y 7B8, Canada

Jaso, John (Athlete, Baseball Player)
494 Weldon St
Redding, CA 96001-3642, USA

Jason, David (Actor)
c/o Staff Member *Lynda Ronan Personal Management*
Hunters House
1 Redcliffe Road
London SW20 9NR, UK

Jason, Dunn (Athlete, Football Player)
2201 Sweetleaf Ct
Lexington, KY 40513-1376, USA

Jason, Harvey
1280 Sunset Plaza Dr
Los Angeles, CA 90069

Jason, Peter (Actor)
c/o Staff Member *Diverse Talent Group*
9911 W Pico Blvd Ste 340W
Los Angeles, CA 90035, USA

Jason, Sybil (Actor)
19200 Salt lake Pl
Northridge, CA 91326, USA

Jason & deMarco (Music Group)
c/o Staff Member *RJN Music!*
8033 Sunset Blvd #574
Hollywood, CA 90046, USA

Jasontek, Rebecca (Athlete, Olympic Athlete, Swimmer)
1201 Retswood Dr
Loveland, OH 45140-8701, USA

Jasper, Edward (Athlete, Football Player)
110 N Price St
Troup, TX 75789, USA

Jasper, Herbert H (Scientist)
4501 Rue Sherbrooke 0
Westmount, QC H3Z 1E7, CANADA

Jasrai, Puntsagiin (Prime Minister)
Prime Minister's Office
Ulan Bator, MONGOLIA

Jaster, Larry (Athlete, Baseball Player)
1105 Mill Creek Dr
Saint Johns, FL 32259-8973, USA

Jastremski, Chet (Athlete, Olympic Athlete, Swimmer)
927 S Baldwin Dr
Bloomington, IN 47401-4813, USA

Jastrow, Terry L (Director)
13201 Old Oak Lane
Los Angeles, CA 90049, USA

Jastrow II, Kenneth M (Business Person)
Temple-Inland Inc
303 S Temple Dr
Diboll, TX 75941, USA

Jata, Paul (Athlete, Baseball Player)
5972 Quartz Valley Dr
Newport, KY 41076-7129, USA

Jathar, Anjali (Actor, Bollywood)
Anand Ashram 1st Floor Building 22
Pandita Rambai Road Gamdevi
Mumbai, MS 400007, INDIA

Jatoi, Ghulan Mustafa (Prime Minister)
Jatoi House
18 Khayaban-E-Shamsheer Housing #V
Karachi, PAKISTAN

Jauch, Ray (Athlete, Football Player)
5306 Harkey Rd
Waxhaw, NC 28173-8461, USA

Jaugstetter, Robert (Athlete, Olympic Athlete, Rower)
619 Mandeville St Ste 3
New Orleans, LA 70117-8501, USA

Jaumotte, Andre (Engineer)
33 Ave jeanne Bte 17
Brussels 1050, BELGIUM

Jauregui, Jessica (Stylist)
c/o Staff Member *Help Me Rhonda*
541 10th St NW #294
Atlanta, GA 30318, USA

Jauron, Dick M (Athlete, Coach, Football Coach, Football Player)
602 Wharton Dr
Lake Forest, IL 60045, USA

Jauss, Dave (Athlete, Baseball Player)
3820 13th Ave SW
Naples, FL 34117-5330, USA

Javan, Ali (Inventor)
45 Payson Rd
Belmont, MA 02478-2720, USA

Javed, Miandad Khan (Cricketer)
Pakistani Crciket Control Board
Gaddafi Stadium
Lahore, PAKISTAN

Javerbaum, David (Writer)
c/o Staff Member *3 Arts Entertainment Inc*
9460 Wilshire Blvd
7th Floor
Beverly Hills, CA 90210, USA

Javier, Julian (Athlete, Baseball Player)
P.O. Box 71
San Francisco de Macoris, USA

Javier, Stan (Athlete, Baseball Player)
11544 NW 43rd Ter
Doral, FL 33178, USA

Javier Galvan Y Fama (Music Group)
c/o Staff Member *Sony Music Miami*
605 Lincoln Rd Fl 7
Miami Beach, FL 33139, USA

Javierre Ortas, Antonio M Cardinal (Religious Leader)
Via Rusticucci 13
Rome 00193, ITALY

Jaworski, Marian Cardinal (Religious Leader)
Mytropolycha Kuria Latynskoho
Ploscha Katedraina 1
29008, UKRAINE

Jaworski, Ronald V (Ron) (Athlete, Football Player, Sportscaster)
18 Brookwood Dr
Medford, NJ 08055-8178, USA

Jax, Garth (Athlete, Football Player)
5335 S Valentia Way
Apt 137
Greenwood Village, CO 80111-3106, USA

Jay, Bob (Athlete, Hockey Player)
9 Sunnyside Ave
Burlington, MA 01803, USA

Jay, Joey (Athlete, Baseball Player)
7209 Battenwood Ct
Tampa, FL 33785-1288, USA

Jay, Ken (Musician)
Andy Gould Mgmt
9100 Wilshire Blvd
#400W
Beverly Hills, CA 90212, USA

Jay, Natalie
6230 Wilshire Blvd. #153
Los Angeles, CA 90048

Jay, Peter (Government Official)
Hensington Farmhouse
Woodstock
Oxon OX20 1LH, UNITED KINGDOM (UK)

Jay, Ricky (Actor)
Simone
1790 Broadway
#1000
New York, NY 10019, USA

Jay, Riemersma (Athlete, Football Player)
3067 Regency Pkwy
Zeeland, MI 49464-6852, USA

Jay, Tony (Actor)
c/o Staff Member *Pakula/King & Associates*
9229 Sunset Blvd
Suite 315
Los Angeles, CA 90069, USA

Jayabharathi (Actor, Bollywood)
75 4th Cross Street
Loghia Colony Saligramam
Chennai, TN 600093, INDIA

Jayachitra (Actor, Bollywood)
Lynwood Avenue 9 Lady Madhavan Nair Road
Mahalingapuram Gandhi Nagar
Chennai, TN 600093, INDIA

Jayamalini (Actor, Bollywood)
1 1st Mail Road
Thirunagar
Chennai, TN 600026, INDIA

Jay & The Americans
1045 Pomme De Pin Dr
New Port Ritchey, FL 34655

Jay & The Techniques
4250 AIA South #D-11
St. Augustine, FL 32080-7431

Jayapradha (Actor, Bollywood)
1 Hindi Prachara Sabha Road
T Nagar
Chennai, TN 600017, INDIA

Jayasudha (Actor, Bollywood)
Veenas Colony
9-13 II Street
Chennai, TN 600018, INDIA

Jayne, Billy
8521 Nash Dr.
Los Angeles, CA 90046

Jayne, Erika (Musician)
c/o Staff Member *Levine Communications Office*
9100 Wilshire Blvd
Suite 540, East Tower
Beverly Hills, CA 90212, USA

Jayston, Michael (Actor)
Michael Whitehall
125 Gloucester Road
London SW7 4TE, UNITED KINGDOM (UK)

Jay-Z (Musician, Producer)
195 Hudson St #7ABPH
New York, NY 10013, USA

Jazz Crusaders, The (Music Group)
Universal
225 W 57th St
Floor 5
New York, NY 10019

Jazzyfatnastees (Music Group)
c/o Staff Member *Paradigm (Monterey)*
404 W Franklin St
Monterey, CA 93940, USA

Jbara, Gregory (Actor)
c/o Marilyn Szatmary *Silver Massetti & Szatmary (SMS) Talent Inc*
8383 Wilshire Blvd
Suite 230
Beverly Hills, CA 90211, USA

JBJ (Musician)
Q Prime
729 7th Ave
#1600
New York, NY 10019, USA

J-Bolt (Producer)
Lightning Bolt Entertainment
3342 S Sandhill Rd
Suite 9-424
Las Vegas, NV 89121, USA

J. Dold, Robrt

J. Duncan Jr., John (Congressman, Politician)
2207 Rayburn HOB
Washington, DC 20515, USA

Jean (Royalty)
Grand Ducal Palace
PB 331
2013, LUXEMBOURG

Jean, Gloria (Actor, Musician)
3844 W Channel Islands Blvd
#166
Oxnard, CA 93035, USA

Jean, Norma (Musician)
22 Skyline Dr
Kimberling City, MO 65686, USA

Jean, Wyclef (Musician)
c/o Yvette Shearer *Schure Media*
16 Skyline Dr
#594
Montville, NJ 07045, USA

Jean-Baptiste, Marianne (Actor)
c/o Elise Konialian *Untitled Entertainment (NY)*
322 8th Ave #601
New York, NY 10001-6715, USA

Jeangerard, Bob (Athlete, Basketball Player, Olympic Athlete)
1930 Belmont Ave
San Carlos, CA 94070-4731, USA

Jean-Louis, Jimmy (Actor)
c/o Alex Cole *Elevate Entertainment*
10100 Santa Monica Blvd.
Suite 300
Los Angeles, CA 90067, USA

Jeanmaire, ZiZi (Actor, Ballerina)
Ballets Roland Petit
20 Blvd Gabes
Marseilles 13008, FRANCE

Jeanrenaud, Joan (Musician)
Kronos Quartet
1235 9th Ave
San Francisco, CA 94122, USA

Jeantot, Philippe (Yachtsman)
Jeantot Organization
Siege: BP 01
Les Sables D'Olonne 85100, FRANCE

Jecha, Ralph (Athlete, Football Player)
717 Vinewood Ave
Willow Springs, IL 60480, USA

Jee, Elizabeth (Actor)
Commercials Unlimited
8383 Wilshire Blvd
#850
Beverly Hills, CA 90211, USA

Jee, Rupert (Business Person)
Hello Deli
213 West 53rd Street
New York, NY 10019

Jeelani, Abdul (Athlete, Basketball Player)
W525 State Road 59
Palmyra, WI 53156, USA

Jeetendra (Actor, Bollywood)
Plot No 26 Greater Bombay Co-Op Society
Gulmohar Cross Road No 5 JVPD Scheme
Mumbai, MS 400049, INDIA

Jeff, Reinke (Athlete, Football Player)
13821 320th St
New Prague, MN 56071-4126, USA

Jeffcoat, Don (Actor)
c/o Staff Member *House of Representatives, The*
1434 6th St
Suite 1
Santa Monica, CA 90401, USA

Jeffcoat, James W (Jim) (Athlete, Football Player)
5135 Summit Hill Dr
Dallas, TX 75287, USA

Jeffcoat, Mike (Athlete, Baseball Player)
4224 Oak Springs Dr
Arlington, TX 76016-4508, USA

Jefferies, Gregg (Athlete, Baseball Player)
7806 Bernal Ave
Pleasanton, CA 76016, USA

Jeffers, Eve Jihan (Actor, Producer)
c/o Amanda Silverman *42West (NY)*
220 W 42nd St
12th Floor
New York, NY 10036, USA

Jeffers, Patrick (Athlete, Football Player)
5810 Buckpasser Cove
Austin, TX 78746, USA

Jeffers, Rusty (Athlete)
PO Box 30081
Phoenix, AZ 85024

Jefferson, Al (Athlete, Basketball Player)
c/o Jeff Schwartz *Excel Sports Management*
9665 Wilshire Blvd #500
Los Angeles, CA 90212, USA

Jefferson, James (Athlete, Football Player)
11220 NE 53rd St
Kirkland, WA 98033, USA

Jefferson, Jeff (Race Car Driver)
752 State Route 410
Naches, WA 98937-7400, USA

Jefferson, John L (Athlete, Football Player)
43590 Merchant Mill Ter
Leesburg, VA 20176, USA

Jefferson, Reggie (Athlete, Baseball Player)
1881 Raymond Tucker Rd
Tallahassee, FL 32311-8793, USA

Jefferson, Richard (Basketball Player)
New Jersey Nets
390 Murray Hill Parkway
East Rutherford, NJ 07073, USA

Jefferson, Roy (Athlete, Football Player)
8813 Queen Elizabeth Blvd
Annandale, VA 22003, USA

Jefferson, Stan (Athlete, Baseball Player)
2420 Hunter Ave
Apt 3E
Bronx, NY 10475-5644, USA

Jefferson, Thad (Athlete, Football Player)
P.O. Box 1552
Rialto, CA 92377, USA

Jefferson Starship (Music Group)
c/o Staff Member *Mission Control*
15030 Ventura Blvd #541
Sherman Oaks, CA 91403, USA

Jeffery, Aaron (Actor)
c/o Robert Marsala *Wishlab*
2225-A Hyperion Ave
Los Angeles, CA 90027, USA

Jeffires, Haywood (Athlete, Football Player)
3818 Hanberry Ln
Pearland, TX 77584, USA

Jeffords, James (Politician)
1314 C St SE
Washington, DC 20003-2343, USA

Jeffory, Dawn (Actor)
c/o *Network Solutions*
PO Box 447
Herndon, VA 20172-0447, USA

Jeffre, Justin (Musician)
DAS Communications
83 Riverside Dr
New York, NY 10024, USA

Jeffress, Jeremy
6901 Marlowe Rd
Richmond, VA 23225-4295, USA

Jeffrey, Arthur (General)
7305 Englewood Hill Pl
Yakima, WA 98908-1267, USA

Jeffrey, Arthur F (War Hero)
752 Juniper Glen Court
Ballwin, MO 08540, USA

Jeffrey, Larry (Athlete, Hockey Player)
35392 Blyth Rd
RR 5
Goderich, ON N7A 3Y2, Canada

Jeffrey, Richard C (Misc)
55 Patton Ave
Princeton, NJ 08540, USA

Jeffreys, Anne (Actor)
18915 Nordhoff St
#5
Northridge, CA 91324, USA

Jeffreys, Harold (Astronomer)
160 Huntingdon Road
Cambridge CB3 0LB, UNITED KINGDOM (UK)

Jeffries, Chris (Basketball Player)
Toronto Raptors
Air Canada Center
40 Bay St
Toronto, ON M5J 2NB, CANADA

Jeffries, Doug (Adult Film Star)
c/o Staff Member *Diva Central Inc*
7510 W Sunset Blvd Ste 1445
Los Angees, CA 90046, USA

Jeffries, Fran (Actor)
c/o Stanley H.Handman
10160 Cielo Dr
Beverly Hills, CA 90210, USA

Jeffries, Herb (Musician)
Flaming-O Productions
44489 Town Center Way
Palm Desert, CA 92260, USA

Jeffries, Jared (Basketball Player)
Washington Wizards
MCI Centre
601 F St NW
Washington, DC 20004, USA

Jeffries, John T (Astronomer)
1652 E Camino Cieto
Tucson, AZ 85718, USA

Jeffries, Willie (Athlete, Football Coach)
c/o Staff Member *College Football Hall Of Fame*
111 South St. Joseph St
South Bend, IN 46601, USA

Jelen, Ben (Musician)
c/o Staff Member *Maverick Recording Co (LA)*
3300 Warner Blvd
Burbank, CA 91505-4632, USA

Jelesky, Tom (Athlete, Football Player)
9556 W 1160 N
Demotte, IN 46310, USA

Jelic, Chris (Athlete, Baseball Player)
33 Allegheny Ave
Apt 5
Cuddy, PA 15031-9763, USA

Jelinek, Elfriede (Nobel Prize Laureate)
c/o Staff Member *Rowohlt Verlag*
Hamburger Strasse 17
Reinbek 21465, Germany

Jelinek, Tomas (Athlete, Hockey Player)
c/o Staff Member *Calgary Flames*
P.O. Box 1540
Stn M
Calgary, AB T2P 3B9, Canada

Jelks, Greg
Philadelphia Phillies
615 Bay Springs Rd
Centre, AL 35960-1212, USA

Jelks, Greg (Athlete, Baseball Player)
Slippery Rock Sliders
P.O. Box 501
Attn: Managers Office
Slippery Rock, PA 16057, USA

Jelley, Thomas (Athlete, Football Player)
200 Tabernacle Rd
Black Mountain, NC 28711, USA

Jellicoe, George P J R (Government Official)
Tidcombe Manor
Tidcombe near Marlborough
Wilts SN8 2SL, UNITED KINGDOM (UK)

Jeltz, Steve (Athlete, Baseball Player)
606 W 28th Pl
Lawrence, KS 66046-4621, USA

Jem (Musician)
c/o Seth Friedman *Red Light Management (LA)*
8439 W Sunset Blvd
Suite 2
Los Angeles, CA 90069, USA

Jemison, Antawn (Basketball Player)
Washington Wizards
MCI Centre
601 F St NW
Washington, DC 20004, USA

Jemison, Eddie (Actor)
c/o Gabrielle Krengel *Domain Talent*
9229 Sunset Boulevard
Suite 710
Los Angeles, CA 90069, USA

Jemison, Theodore J (Religious Leader)
National Bapist Convention USA
1620 White's Creek Pike
Nashville, TN 37207, USA

Jencks, William P (Misc)
11 Revere St
Lexington, MA 02420, USA

Jendresen, Erik (Producer, Writer)
c/o Staff Member *WME (LA)*
9601 Wilshire Blvd Fl 3
Beverly Hills, CA 90210, USA

Jendrick, Megan (Athlete, Olympic Athlete, Swimmer)
USA Swimming
Quanntum Aquatics PO Box 8844
Tacoma, WA 98419-0844, USA

Jenes Jr, Theodore G (General)
809 169th Place SW
Lynnwood, WA 98037, USA

Jeni, Richard (Comedian)
c/o Staff Member *Agency for the Performing Arts (APA-LA)*
405 S Beverly Dr
Suite 500
Beverly Hills, CA 90212-4425, USA

Jenifer, Franklyn G (Educator)
University of Texas at Dallas
President's Office
Richardson, TX 75083, USA

Jenke, Noel (Athlete, Football Player)
17665 Bonnie Ln
Brookfield, WI 53045, USA

Jenkin of Roding, Patrick F (Government Official)
703 Howard House
Dolphin Square
London SW1V 3PQ, UNITED KINGDOM (UK)

Jenkins, Alfred le Sesne (Diplomat)
Stalsama High Knob
PO Box 586
Front Royal, VA 22630, USA

Jenkins, Andrew (Actor)
c/o Jon Simmons *Simmons & Scott Entertainment*
4110 W. Burbank Blvd.
Burbank, CA 91505, USA

Jenkins, Carter (Actor)
c/o Mary Sanders *inMomentum Management*
14622 Ventura Blvd #778
Sherman Oaks, CA 91403, USA

Jenkins, Charlie (Athlete, Olympic Athlete, Track Athlete)
12826 Forest Creek Ct
Sykesville, MD 21784-5526

Jenkins, Cullen (Athlete, Football Player)
4018 S Parker Way
De Pere, WI 54115, USA

Jenkins, Daniel (Actor)
S M S Talent
8730 Sunset Blvd
#440
Los Angeles, CA 90069, USA

Jenkins, David W (Athlete, Figure Skater, Olympic Athlete)
5947 S Atlanta Ave
Tulsa, OK 74105, USA

Jenkins, Dean (Athlete, Hockey Player)
244 Fairmount St
Lowell, MA 01852-3708, USA

Jenkins, Don (General)
3770 Bowling Green Rd
Morgantown, KY 42261-8219, USA

Jenkins, Don (Athlete, Football Player)
49 W Main St
Frostburg, MD 21532, USA

Jenkins, Don J (War Hero)
3783 Bowling Green Road
Morgantown, KY 42261, USA

Jenkins, Ed (Athlete, Football Player)
1750 Washington St
Suite B1
Boston, MA 02118, USA

Jenkins, Ferguson (Athlete, Baseball Player)
Ferguson Jenkins Foundation
PO Box 664
Lewiston, NY 14092, USA

Jenkins, Fletcher (Athlete, Football Player)
2347 S J St
Tacoma, WA 98405, USA

Jenkins, Geoff (Athlete, Baseball Player)
6683 E Judson Rd
Paradise Valley, AZ 85253-4369, USA

Jenkins, George (Designer, Director)
2402 4th St #10
Santa Monica, CA 90405-3668, USA

Jenkins, Hayes Alan (Athlete, Figure Skater, Olympic Athlete)
3183 Regency Place
Westlake, OH 44145, USA

Jenkins, Izel (Athlete, Football Player)
5106 Masters Ln N
Wilson, NC 27896, USA

Jenkins, James (Baseball Player)
Cincinnati Indianapolis Clowns
630 Malcolm X Blvd
New York, NY 10037-1247, USA

Jenkins, Jay (Young Jezzy) (Musician)
c/o Laura Wright *Avid Exposure*
8721 W Sunset Blvd
Suite P3
West Hollywood, CA 90069, USA

Jenkins, Jerry B (Writer)
Tyndale House Publishers
351 Executive Dr
PO Box 80
Wheaton, IL 60189, USA

Jenkins, Kackie (Butch) (Actor)
PO Box 541G
Fairview, NC 28730, USA

Jenkins, Katherine (Musician)
c/o Staff Member *Nettwerk Management (LA)*
1545 Wilcox Ace
Suite 200
Los Angeles, CA 90028, USA

Jenkins, Ken (Actor)
c/o Chris Schmidt *Paradigm (LA)*
360 N Crescent Dr
North Bldg
Beverly Hills, CA 90210, USA

Jenkins, Kerry (Athlete, Football Player)
5492 Scout Trace Ln
Birmingham, AL 35244, USA

Jenkins, Kris (Athlete, Football Player)
309 E Morehead St
Apt 622
Charlotte, NC 28202, USA

Jenkins, Loren (Journalist)
Washington Post
Editorial Dept
1150 15th St NW
Washington, DC 20071, USA

Jenkins, Lynn (Congressman, Politician)
1122 Longworth HOB
Washington, DC 20515, USA

Jenkins, Marilyn (Athlete, Baseball Player, Commentator)
1511 Van Auken St SE
Grand Rapids, MI 49508-2511, USA

Jenkins, Mark (Writer)
c/o Staff Member *HarperCollins Publishers*
10 East 53rd St
c/o Author mail, 7th Floor
New York, NY 10022, USA

Jenkins, Patty (Director, Writer)
c/o Michael Sugar *Anonymous Content (LA)*
3531 Hayden Ave
Culver City, CA 90232, USA

Jenkins, Paul (Artist)
Image Terrae
PO Box 6833
Yorkville Station
New York, NY 10128, USA

Jenkins, Richard (Actor)
c/o Rhonda Price *Gersh (NY)*
41 Madison Ave
New York, NY 10010, USA

Jenkins, Robert (Athlete, Football Player)
2878 Fieldview Ter
San Ramon, CA 94583, USA

Jenkins, Stephan (Music Group, Musician)
c/o Eric Godtland *Eric Godtland Management*
1040 Mariposa St
Suite 200
San Francisco, CA 94107, USA

Jenkins, Tom (Athlete, Golfer)
107 Ranch Road 620 S
Lakeway, TX 78734, USA

Jenkins, Walt (Athlete, Football Player)
22570 Thorncliffe St
Southfield, MI 48033-3426, USA

Jenks, Bobby (Athlete, Baseball Player)
3958 E Northridge Cir
Mesa, AZ 85215, USA

Jenner, Brody (Reality TV Star)
c/o Eric Podwall *Podwall Entertainment*
710 N Orlando Ave
Loft 203
Los Angeles, CA 90069, USA

Jenner, Bruce (Athlete, Decathlon Athlete, Olympic Athlete, Reality TV Star)
25254 Eldorado Meadow Rd
Hidden Hills, CA 91302-1242, USA

Jenner, Kendall (Model, Reality TV Star)
25115 Eldorado Meadow Rd
Hidden Hills, CA 91302, USA

Jenner, Kris (Business Person, Reality TV Star)
25115 Eldorado Meadow Rd
Hidden Hills, CA 91302, USA

Jenney, Lucinda
1505 10th Street
Santa Monica, CA 90401

Jennings, Adam (Athlete, Football Player)
330 Suwanee Ave
Suwanee, GA 30024-6768, USA

Jennings, Brandon (Athlete, Basketball Player)
c/o Bill Duffy *BDA Sports Management (BDA-CA)*
700 Ygnacio Valley Rd
Suite 330
Walnut Creek, CA 94596, USA

Jennings, Dave (Athlete, Football Player)
1 Briarcliff Rd
Upper Saddle River, NJ 07458, USA

Jennings, David T (Dave) (Athlete, Football Player)
1 Briarcliff Rd
Upper Saddle River, NJ 07458, USA

Jennings, Delbert O (War Hero)
3701 25th Way SE
Olympia, WA 98501, USA

Jennings, Doug (Athlete, Baseball Player)
P.O. Box 812692
Boca Raton, FL 33486-6428, USA

Jennings, Doug
Oakland A's
3030 Canterbury Dr
Boca Raton, FL 33434-3348, USA

Jennings, Garth (Director)
c/o Frank Wuliger *Gersh (LA)*
9465 Wilshire Blvd
Suite 600
Beverly Hills, CA 90212, USA

Jennings, Grant (Athlete, Hockey Player)
P.O. Box 190434
Anchorage, AK 99519, USA

Jennings, Greg (Athlete, Football Player)
c/o Eugene Parker *Maximum Sports Management*
6435 W Jefferson Blvd
#197
Fort Wayne, IN 46804, USA

Jennings, Jason (Athlete, Baseball Player)
5274 Monterey Dr
Frisco, TX 75034-4087, USA

Jennings, Jonas (Athlete, Football Player)
123 Davis Rd
Fayetteville, GA 30215-4912, USA

Jennings, Keith (Athlete, Basketball Player)
695 Holly Crest Dr
Culpeper, VA 22701-3071, USA

Jennings, Keith (Athlete, Football Player)
119 Axtell Dr
Summerville, SC 29485-3403, USA

Jennings, Ken (Actor)
c/o Staff Member *JEOPARDY!*
10202 W. Washington Blvd
Culver City, CA 90232

Jennings, Lyfe (Musician)
c/o Staff Member *Sony/RCA Records*
550 Madison Ave
New York, NY 10022, USA

Jennings, Lynn (Athlete, Olympic Athlete, Track Athlete)
2124 NW Wilson St
Portland, OR 97210-2316, USA

Jennings, Paul C (Engineer)
640 S Grand Ave
Pasadena, CA 91105, USA

Jennings, Richard (Athlete, Football Player)
6499 Park Riviera Way
Sacramento, CA 95831, USA

Jennings, Rick (Athlete, Football Player)
442 Sterling Pl Apt 12
Brooklyn, NY 11238-4536, USA

Jennings, Robert B (Doctor)
Duke University
Medical Center
Pathology Dept
Durham, NC 27710, USA

Jennings, Robert Y (Judge)
61 Bridle Way
Grantchester
Cambridge CB3 9NY, UNITED KINGDOM (UK)

Jennings, Robin (Athlete, Baseball Player)
6052 Kingsford Ave
Park City, UT 84098-1191, USA

Jennings, Shooter (Musician)
c/o Michael Moses *Baker Winokur Ryder Public Relations (BWR-LA)*
9100 Wilshire Blvd
Suite 500, West Tower
Beverly Hills, CA 90212, USA

Jennings, Stanford (Athlete, Football Player)
403 G St
Beckley, WV 25801-6613, USA

Jennings, Will (Musician, Songwriter)
c/o Staff Member *Gorfaine/Schwartz Agency Inc*
4111 W Alameda Ave
Suite 509
Burbank, CA 91505, USA

Jennings Desmond, Desmond (Athlete, Baseball Player)
2482 Vera Cruz Dr
Birmimzham, AL 35235-2233, USA

Jenrette, Richard H (Business Person)
67 E 93rd St
New York, NY 10128, USA

Jenrette, Rita (Writer)
9270 Alden Dr
Beverly Hills, CA 90210, USA

Jens, Salome (Actor)
Badgley Connor Talent
9229 Sunset Blvd #311
Los Angeles, CA 90069, USA

Jens, Walter (Writer)
Sonnenstr 5
Tubingen, GERMANY

Jensen, Al (Athlete, Hockey Player)
NHL Scouting Service
50 Bay_ Street 11th Floor
Toronto, ON M5J 2X8, Canada

Jensen, Bob (Athlete, Football Player)
72420 Morningstar Rd
Rancho Mirage, CA 92270, USA

Jensen, Chris (Athlete, Hockey Player)
20310 Enright Way
Farmington, MN 55024-2022, USA

Jensen, David (Athlete, Hockey Player)
65 Cheryl Ln
Holliston, MA 01746, USA

Jensen, Derrick (Athlete, Football Player)
147 Downing St
Panama City, FL 32413, USA

Jensen, Elwood V (Misc)
Karolinska Institute
Medical Nutrition Dept
Huddinge 141 86, SWEDEN

Jensen, Flemming (Athlete, Football Player)
9775 Deer Brook Cir
Sandy, UT 84092-6035, USA

Jensen, James (Misc)
Brigham Young University
Geology Dept
Provo, UT 84602, USA

Jensen, Jerry (Athlete, Football Player)
2714 86th St SE
Everett, WA 98208, USA

Jensen, Jim (Athlete, Football Player)
9811 N Oak Knoll Cir
Davie, FL 33324, USA

Jensen, Jim D (Athlete, Football Player)
239 Habitat Cir
Windsor, CO 80550, USA

Jensen, Karen (Actor)
9363 Wilshire Blvd
#212
Beverly Hills, CA 90210, USA

Jensen, Luke (Tennis Player)
370 Ferry Landing NW
Atlanta, GA 30328

Jensen, Marcus (Athlete, Baseball Player, Olympic Athlete)
19550 N Grayhawk Dr
Unit 1134
Scottsdale, AZ 85255-3987, USA

Jensen, Maren (Actor)
Kessler Schneider Co
15260 Ventura Blvd
Suite 1040
Sheman Oaks, CA 91403

Jensen, Roger W (Ex-Senator)
3542 Pennyroyal Road
Port Charlotte, FL 33953, USA

Jensen, Ryan (Athlete, Baseball Player)
3059 S Larkspur St
Gilbert, AZ 85295-2034, USA

Jensen, Steve (Athlete, Hockey Player)
24921 Arena Dr
Deerwood, MN 56444, USA

Jensen Jr, James W (Cinematographer)
28853 Garnet Hill Court
Agoura Hills, CA 91301, USA

Jent, Chris (Athlete, Basketball Player)
445 Retreat Ln w
Powell, OH 43065-9768, USA

Jeong, Ken (Actor)
c/o Brett Carducci *Sovereign Talent Group*
8421 Wilshire Blvd
Suite 200
Beverly Hills, CA 90211, USA

Jeosen, Kevin (Athlete, Baseball Player)
4533 E County Down Dr
Chandler, AZ 85249-7339, USA

Jepsen, Carly Rae (Musician)
c/o Scooter Braun *Island Def Jam Group*
Worldwide Plaza
825 8th Ave Fl 28
New York, NY 10019, USA

Jepsen, Les (Athlete, Basketball Player)
8075 9th Street Way N
Saint Paul, MN 55128-5360, USA

Jepsen, Roger (Politician)
3542 Pennyroyal Rd
Port Charlotte, FL 33953-4606, USA

Jeray, Nicole (Athlete, Golfer)
3728 Ridgeland Ave
Berwyn, IL 60402, USA

Jeremiah (Musician)
c/o Staff Member *Siri Music Entertainment*
1324 Lexington Ave
New York, NY 10128, USA

Jeremiah, David (General)
S Pentagon
Washington, DC 20301-0001, USA

Jeremiah, David E (Admiral)
2898 Melanie Lane
Oakton, VA 22124, USA

Jeremy, Ron (Adult Film Star)
c/o Michael (Mike) Esterman
Esterman.Com, LLC
Prefers to be contacted via email
MD, USA

Jericho, Chris (Athlete, Wrestler)
c/o Michael Braverman *Braverman/Bloom Company*
14320 Ventura Blvd
Suite 632
Sherman Oaks, CA 91423, USA

Jerkens, H Allen (Horse Racer)
9509 242nd St
Floral Park, NY 11001, USA

Jermann, David (Artist)
2 Union St
Sparkill, NY 10976

Jernberg, Sixten (Skier)
Fritidsby 780
Lima 7806, SWEDEN

Jernigan, Tamara E (Tammy) (Astronaut)
4268 Brindisi Place
Pleasanton, CA 94566, USA

Jernstedt, Ken (General, War Hero)
911 Pine St
Hood River, OR 97031-1968, USA

Jerry, Reichow (Athlete, Football Player)
9 Meredith Drive
Santa Fe, NM 87506, USA

Jerusalem, Siegfried (Opera Singer)
Sudring 9
Eckental 90542, GERMANY

Jeruzelski, Wojciech (President)
Bluro Bylego
Al Jerozolimskie 91
Warsaw 02-001, POLAND

Jervey, Travis (Athlete, Football Player)
22 Sand Dollar Dr
Isle Of Palms, SC 29451-2647, USA

Jerzembeck, Mike (Athlete, Baseball Player)
10625 S Hall Dr
Charlotte, NC 28270-0285, USA

Jessamy, Charles (Athlete, Football Player)
1836 S Shenandoah St
Los Angeles, CA 90035, USA

Jessee, Michael A (Financier)
Federal Home Loan Bank of Boston
P.O. Box 990411
Boston, MA 02199-0411, USA

Jessen, Ruth (Athlete, Golfer)
2823 NE Meadow Pl
Lake Forest Park, WA 98155, USA

Jessica (lil mama)Kirkland, Niatia (Musician)
c/o Staff Member *Jive Records*
550 Madison Ave
New York, NY 10022-3211, USA

Jessie, Tim (Athlete, Football Player)
155 Cedar Ave
Shepherdsville, KY 40165, USA

Jessiman, Hugh (Athlete, Hockey Player)
480 Hollow Tree Ridge
Darien, CT 06920, USA

Jessup, Bill (Athlete, Football Player)
13341 Saint Andrews
Dr Unit 137D
Seal Beach, CA 90740-4139, USA

Jestadt, Garry (Athlete, Baseball Player)
9875 E Larkspur Dr
Scottsdale, AZ 85260-5145, USA

Jestadt, Garry (Athlete, Baseball Player)
9875 E Larkspur Dr
Scottsdale, AZ 85260, USA

Jester, Virgil (Athlete, Baseball Player)
8130 Raleigh Pl
Westminster, CO 80031, USA

Jet (Actor)
c/o Staff Member *Creative Artists Agency (CAA-LA)*
2000 Ave Of The Stars
Los Angeles, CA 90067, USA

Jeter, Brad (Race Car Driver)
PO Box 6541
Greenville, SC 29606, USA

Jeter, Derek (Athlete, Baseball Player)
Turn 2 Foundation
Attention: Memorabilia Request
215 Park Avenue S, Suite 1905
New York, NY 10003, USA

Jeter, Gary (Athlete, Football Player)
3612 Quail Ridge Dr
Plainsboro, NJ 08536-4133, USA

Jeter, Gene (Athlete, Football Player)
2369 Lower Wetumpka Rd
Montgomery, AL 36110-2610, USA

Jeter, John (Athlete, Baseball Player)
1012 N 5th St
Monroe, LA 71291-8693, USA

Jeter, Perry (Athlete, Football Player)
772 Lincoln Blvd
Steubenville, OH 43952, USA

Jeter, Shawn (Athlete, Baseball Player)
4287 Walford St
Columbus, OH 43224-2342, USA

Jeter, Tommy (Athlete, Football Player)
14 Slate Path Dr
Spring, TX 77382, USA

Jeter, Tony (Athlete, Football Player)
71 S Orange Ave
South Orange, NJ 07079, USA

Jethro Tull (Music Group)
c/o Staff Member *WmE2 (WMA-LA)*
1 William Morris Pl
Beverly Hills, CA 90212, USA

Jetsons (Music Group)
Signature Entertainment
Suite 3
5727 Topanga Canyon
Woodland Hills, CA 91367

Jett, Brent W (Astronaut)
5509 Crawford St
Houston, TX 77004-7119, USA

Jett, Jack E (Television Host)
c/o Collin Reno *WmE2 (WMA-LA)*
1 William Morris Pl
Beverly Hills, CA 90212, USA

Jett, James (Athlete, Football Player)
P.O. Box 430
Kearneysville, WV 25430, USA

Jett, Joan (Musician)
c/o Ken Laguna *Blackheart Records Group*
636 Broadway
New York, NY 10012, USA

Jett, John (Athlete, Football Player)
177 Crowder Point Dr
Reedville, VA 22539, USA

Jetton, Paul (Athlete, Football Player)
1062 Harmon Hills Rd
Dripping Springs, TX 78620-4286, USA

Jeunet, Jean-Pierre (Director)
International Creative Mgmt
8942 Wilshire Blvd
#219
Beverly Hills, CA 90211, USA

Jeung, Peggi (Stylist)
c/o Staff Member *Artist Untied (LA)*
845 S Mansfield Ave
#1
Los Angeles, CA 90036, USA

Jevanord, Oystein (Musician)
Bandana Mgmt
11 Elvaston Place
#300
London SW7 5QC, UNITED KINGDOM (UK)

Jewel (Musician, Songwriter)
c/o Irving Azoff *Azoff Music Management/ Front Line*
1100 Glendon Ave
Los Angeles, CA 90024, USA

Jewell, Buddy (Musician)
c/o Staff Member *WmE2 (WMA-TN)*
1600 Division St
Suite 300
Nashville, TN 37203, USA

Jewell, Geri (Actor)
c/o Staff Member *Kazarian Spencer Ruskin & Assoc.*
11969 Ventura Blvd
3rd Floor
Studio City, CA 91604, USA

Jewett, Bob (Athlete, Football Player)
991 N Shore Dr
Springport, MI 49284, USA

Jewett, Robert (Athlete, Football Player)
991 N Shore Dr
Springport, MI 49284, USA

Jewett, Trent (Athlete, Baseball Player)
330 Sullivan Rd
Glen Morgan, WV 25813-7604, USA

Jewett-Beckett, Christine (Athlete, Baseball Player, Commentator)
PO Box 126
Stewart Valley, SK SON 2PO, Canada

Jewison, Norman F (Actor, Director, Producer, Writer)
c/o Staff Member *Yorktown Productions Ltd*
18 Gloucester Ln
Floor 5
Toronto ON M4Y 1L5, CANADA

Jewitt-Beckett, Christine (Baseball Player)
PO Box 126
Stewart Valley, SK S0N 2P0, CANADA

J. Fleischmann, Charles (Congressman, Politician)
511 Cannon HOB
Washington, DC 20515, USA

J. Forbes, Randy (Congressman, Politician)
2438 Rayburn HOB
Washington, DC 20515, USA

Jhabvala, Ruth Prawer (Writer)
400 E 52nd St
New York, NY 10022, USA

J. Heck, Joseph (Congressman, Politician)
132 Cannon HOB
Washington, DC 20515, USA

Jhene (Musician)

Jhulka, Ayesha (Actor, Bollywood)
102 Tirupati Apartments
7 Bungalows Versova Andheri (W)
Mumbai, MS 400061, INDIA

Jia, Li (Misc)
Duke University
Medical Center
Hematology Dept
Durham, NC 27708, USA

Jiahua, Zou (Government Official)
Communist Party Central Committee
Jhong Nan Hai
Beijing, CHINA

Jiang, Tian (Musician)
Columbia Artists Mgmt Inc
165 W 57th St
New York, NY 10019, USA

Jiang, Tiefeng (Artist)
Fingerhut Gallery
690 Bridgeway
Sausalito, CA 94965, USA

Jiang, Zemin (President)
Central Military Commitee
Zhonganahai
Beijing, CHINA

Jiles, Dwayne (Athlete, Football Player)
3712 Churchill Ct
Plano, TX 75075, USA

Jiles, Pam (Athlete, Track Athlete)
2623 Wisteria St
New Orleans, LA 70122

Jiles, Pamela (Pam) (Athlete, Track Athlete)
2623 Wisteria St
New Orleans, LA 70122, USA

Jillette, Penn (Comedian)
4132 S Rainbow Blvd
Box 377
Las Vegas, NV 89103, USA

Jillian, Ann (Actor)
PO Box 57739
Sherman Oaks, CA 91413, USA

Jillson, Jeff (Athlete, Hockey Player)
14 Lincoln Dr
North Smithfield, RI 02896, USA

Jim, Ridlon (Athlete, Football Player)
4468 E Lake Rd
Cazenovia, NY 13035-9214, USA

Jimenez, Carlos (Architect)
Jimenez Architectural Design Studio
1116 Willard St
Houston, TX 77006, USA

Jimenez, Flaco (Misc)
DeLeon Artists
4031 Panama Court
Piedmont, CA 94611, USA

Jimenez, Joe (Athlete, Golfer)
P.O. Box 1737
Boerne, TX 78006, USA

Jimenez, Manny (Baseball Player)
Kansas City A's
24003 Colmar Ln
Murrieta, CA 92562-1978, USA

Jimenez, Miguel Angel (Athlete, Golfer)
Advantage International
1751 Pinnacle Dr
Suite 1500
Mc Lean, VA 22102, USA

Jimenez, Nicario (Artist)
5531 Teak Wood Dr NW
Naples, FL 34119, USA

Jimenez, Ubaldo (Athlete, Baseball Player)
c/o Pat Rooney *SFX Baseball*
400 Skokie Blvd
Suite 280
Northbrook, IL 60062, USA

Jimenez Pons, Eduardo (Writer)
c/o Gabriel Blanco *Gabriel Blanco Iglesias (Mexico)*
Rio Balsas 35-32
Colonia Cuauhtemoc
DF 06500, Mexico

Jimerson, Charlton (Athlete, Baseball Player)
22048 Betlen Way
Castro Valley, CA 77459-1553, USA

Jiminez, Houston (Athlete, Baseball Player)
Asheville Tourists
30 Buchanan Pl
Attn: Coaching Staff
Asheville, NC 28801, USA

Jiminez, Miguel (Athlete, Baseball Player)
128 Post Ave
New York, NY 10941-1814, USA

Jimmy, Deratt
4418 Saddle Run Rd N
Wilson, NC 27896, USA

Jimmy, Keyes (Athlete, Football Player)
5338 Southlake Dr
Milton, FL 32571-7000, USA

Jimmy, Richards (Athlete, Football Player)
733 Vanderbilt Ave
Virginia Beach, VA 23451-3632, USA

Jimmy Eat World (Music Group)
21 W. Berridge Ln
Phoenix, AZ 85013, USA

Jimoh, Ade (Athlete, Football Player)
41782 Bristow Manor Dr
Ashburn, VA 20148, USA

Jin, Svoboda (Director)
Na Balkane 120
Prague 3, CZECH REPUBLIC

Jindal, Bobby (Governor)
Office of the Governor
P.O. Box 94004
Baton Rouge, LA 70804, USA

Jindrak, Mark (Wrestler)
2355 Reyer Rd
Auburn, NY 13021

Jinks, Dan (Actor, Producer)
c/o Staff Member *Jinks/Cohen Company*
4000 Warner Blvd
Bldg 138
Burbank, CA 91522, USA

Jirsa, Ron (Coach)
University of Georgia
Athletic Dept
Athens, GA 30613, USA

Jirschele, Mike (Athlete, Baseball Player)
186 Robert St
Clintonville, WI 54929-1153, USA

Jiscke, Martin C (Educator)
Iowa State University
President's Office
Ames, IA 50011, USA

JJ Grey and Mofro (Music Group, Musician)
c/o Jesse Aratow *Madison House Inc.*
4760 Walnut St
#106
Boulder, CO 80301, USA

J. Kucinich, Dennis (Congressman, Politician)
2445 Rayburn HOB
Washington, DC 20515, USA

J-Kwon (Musician)
c/o Staff Member *So So Def Recordings Inc*
1350 Spring St NW #750
Atlanta, GA 30309-2870, USA

JLS (Music Group, Musician)
c/o Staff Member *Modest! Management*
91A Peterborough Rd
London SW6 3BU, UK

J. Markey, Edward (Congressman, Politician)
2108 Rayburn HOB
Washington, DC 20515, USA

Joannou, Dakis (Business Person)
Deste Foundation Centre For Contemporary Art
Filellinon 11 & Em. Pappa street
Athens 142 34, Greece

Joanou, Phil (Actor, Director)
c/o Todd Smith *Todd Smith and Associates*
11835 W Olympic Blvd
Suite 640E
Los Angeles, CA 90064-5000, USA

Job, Brian (Swimmer)
PO Box 70427
Sunnyvale, CA 94086, USA

Jobe, Brandt (Athlete, Golfer)
2224 King Fisher Dr
Westlake, TX 76262, USA

Jobe, Frank W (Doctor)
Kerlan-Jobe Orthopedic Clinic
501 E Hardy St
#200
Inglewood, CA 90301, USA

Jobert, Marlene (Actor)
c/o Staff Member *ArtMedia*
20 avenue Rapp
Paris 75008, France

Jobko, William (Athlete, Football Player)
770 Fawn Ct
Loganville, GA 30052, USA

Jobrani, Maz (Actor)
c/o Ray Moheet *Mitchell K Stubbs & Assoc (MKS)*
8675 W. Washington Blvd
Suite 203
Culver City, CA 90232, USA

Joc, Yung (Musician)
c/o Jack Iannaci *Brass Artists & Associates*
9025 Wilshire Blvd
Suite 400
Beverly Hills, CA 90211, USA

Jochum, Betsy (Athlete, Baseball Player, Commentator)
22997 Brick Rd
South Bend, IN 46628-9719, USA

Jocketty, Walt (Commentator)
520 N and South Rd A_Qt 304
Saint Louis, MO 63130-3826, USA

Jodat, Jim (Athlete, Football Player)
25032 Mammoth Cir
El Toro, CA 92630, USA

Jodie, Brett (Athlete, Baseball Player)
1359 Corley Mill Rd
Lexington, SC 29072-7635, USA

Jodzio, Rick (Athlete, Hockey Player)
31202 Boca Raton Pl
Laguna Niguel, CA 92677-2484

Joe (Musician)
c/o Staff Member *Jive Records*
550 Madison Ave
New York, NY 10022-3211, USA

Joe, Billy (Athlete, Football Player)
3964 Butler Springs Way
Birmingham, AL 35226-6234, USA

Joe, Cheryl (Stylist)
2312 Colt Rd
Rancho Palos Verdes, CA 90275-6502, USA

Joe, Devlin ʻ (Athlete, Football Player)
3715 Schintzius Rd
Eden, NY 14057, USA

Joe, Leon (Athlete, Football Player)
5250 Grand Ave Ste 14
Gurnee, IL 60031-1877, USA

Joe, Reliford (Athlete, Baseball Player)
Kiwanis Club PO Box 1007 Attn
Presidents Office
Douglas, GA 31534-1007, USA

Joe, William (Billy) (Football Player)
Florida A&M University
Athletic Dept
Tallahassee, FL 32307, USA

Joel, Billy (Musician, Songwriter)
121 Brick Kiln Rd
Sag Harbor, NY 11963, USA

Joel, Katie Lee (Actor)
c/o Jonathan Rosen *WME (WMA-NY)*
1325 Ave of the Americas
New York, NY 10019, USA

Joel, Piñeiro (Athlete, Baseball Player)
3410 Poinciana Ave
Miami, FL 33133-6525, USA

Joel, Richard M (Educator)
Yeshiva University
President's Office
500 W 185th St
New York, NY 10033, USA

Joelson, Tsianina (Actor)
c/o Sherry Marsh *Marsh Entertainment*
12444 Ventura Blvd #203
Studio City, CA 91604, USA

Joens, Michael (Writer)
c/o Natasha Kern *Natasha Kern Literary Agency*
P.O. Box 1069
White Salmon, WA 98672-1069, USA

Joey & T (Stylist)
c/o Staff Member *Fred Segal Beauty*
PO Box 5304
Beverly Hills, CA 90209, USA

Joffee, Roland V (Director, Producer)
c/o Craig Baumgarten *Baumgarten Management*
11925 Wilshire Blvd
Suite 310
Los Angeles, CA 90025, USA

Jofre, Eder (Boxer)
Alamo de Ministero Rocha
Azevedo 373 C Cesar 21-15
Sao Paulo, BRAZIL

Jogia, Avan (Actor)
c/o Alejandra Cristina *Ace PR*
4122 Sunnyslope Ave
Sherman Oaks, CA 91423, USA

Jogis, Chris (Athlete)
7 Birch Rd
Larchmont, NY 10538

Johannesen, Glenn (Athlete, Hockey Player)
10 Granby Ct
Derwood, MD 20855-1406, USA

Johannesen, Lena (Athlete)
PO Box 325
Studio City, CA 90232

Johanns, Michael (Politician)
6320 Washington Blvd
Arlington, VA 22205-1906, USA

Johannsen, Jake (Actor, Comedian)
c/o Pam Ellis *Ellis Talent Group*
4705 Laurel Canyon Blvd
Suite 300
Valley Village, CA 91607, USA

Johannson, John (Athlete, Hockey Player)
3408 Zenith Ave S
Minneapolis, MN 55416-4622, USA

Johannsson, Kristian (Opera Singer)
Herbert Breslin
119 W 57th St
#1505
New York, NY 10019, USA

Johansen, David (Musician)
c/o Nina Nisenholtz *N2N Entertainment*
1230 Montana Ave
Suite 203
Santa Monica, CA 90403, USA

Johansen, Iris (Writer)
c/o Author Mail *Bantam-Dell Publishing (NY)*
1745 Broadway
New York, NY 10019, USA

Johansen, Trevor (Athlete, Hockey Player)
6741 N Placita Acebo
Tucson, AZ 85750, USA

Johanson, Donald (Scientist)
1288 9th St
Berkeley, CA 94710-1501, USA

Johanson, Donald C (Misc)
Arizona State University
Human Origins Institute
Tempe, AZ 85287, USA

Johanson, Erika (Writer)
c/o Gabriel Blanco *Gabriel Blanco Iglesias (Mexico)*
Rio Balsas 35-32
Colonia Cuauhtemoc
DF 06500, Mexico

Johanson, Sue (Talk Show Host)
42 Pardee Ave
Toronto, ON M6K 3H5, CANADA

Johansonsci, Donald C Dr (Scientist)
Arizona State University PO Box 874101
Attn Inst of Hmn Origins
Tempe, AZ 85287-4101, USA

Johanssen, David
9200 Sunset Blvd. #900
Los Angeles, CA 90069

Johansson, Bjorn (Athlete, Hockey Player)
Stenkulla
Odensbacken S-71593, Sweden

Johansson, Calle (Athlete, Hockey Player)
1708 Mayfair Pl
Crofton, MD 21114, USA

Johansson, Kathy (Model)
PO Box 13923
Tucson, AZ 85732-3923

Johansson, Mathias (Athlete, Hockey Player)
Ringgatan 17 A
Karlstad S-65349, SWEDEN

Johansson, Ove (Athlete, Football Player)
3511 Goodfellow Ln
Amarillo, TX 79121, USA

Johansson, Paul (Actor)
c/o Gordon Gilbertson *Gilbertson Management*
1334 3rd St Promenade #201
Santa Monica, CA 90401, USA

Johansson, Per-Ulrik (Athlete, Golfer)
19489 Harbor Rd S
Jupiter, FL 33469, USA

Johansson, Roger (Athlete, Hockey Player)
Fridemsgatan 9
Karlstad S-65461, Sweden

Johansson, Scarlett (Actor)
c/o CeCe Yorke *True Public Relations*
6725 W Sunset Blvd #470
Los Angeles, CA 90028-7180, USA

Johjima, Kenji (Athlete, Baseball Player)
2412 109th Ave SE
Bellevue, WA 98004, USA

John, Caspar (Admiral)
Trethewey
Mousehole Penzance
Cornwall, UNITED KINGDOM (UK)

John, Charles (Politician)
Community State Bank 131 S Walnut St
Starke, FL 32091-3954, USA

John, David D (Misc)
7 Cyncoed Ave
Cardiff CF2 6ST, WALES

John, Daymond (Business Person)
c/o Monique Moss *Integrated PR*
9025 Wilshire Blvd
Suite 400
Beverly Hills, CA 90211, USA

John, Elton (Musician, Producer, Songwriter)
c/o Frank Presland *Twenty-First Artists Ltd (UK)*
1 Blythe Rd
London W14 OHG, UK

John, Gottfried (Actor)
Elisabethweg 4
Utting, GERMANY D-86919

John, John (Politician)
95 Hill Top Dr
East Greenwich, RI 02818-4024, USA

John, Rienstra (Athlete, Football Player)
5056 Briscoglen Dr
Colorado Springs, CO 80906-8612, USA

John, Riggins (Athlete, Football Player)
8000 Riverside Dr
Cabin John, MD 20818-1627, USA

John, Tommy (Athlete, Baseball Player)
6202 Seton House Ln
Charlotte, NC 28277-4524, USA

John, Tylyn (Model)
813 Harbor Blvd #133
W Sacramento, CA 95691

Johncock, Gordon (Race Car Driver)
8740 Wickert Road
South Branch, MI 48161-9626, USA

Johnny & The Hurricanes
195 Hannum Ave.
Rossford, OH 43460

Johns, Bibi
D-82049
Pullach, GERMANY

Johns, Cindy (Actor)
PO Box 369
Arlington, TX 76004

Johns, Daniel (Musician)
John Watson Mgmt
PO Box 281
Sunny Hills, NSW 2010, AUSTRALIA

Johns, Don (Athlete, Hockey Player)
226 Evergreen Dr
Beaconsfield, QC H9W 2A9, Canada

Johns, Doug (Athlete, Baseball Player)
1131 SW 72nd Ave
Plantation, FL 33317-4125, USA

Johns, Freeman (Athlete, Football Player)
906 Sally Cir
Wichita Falls, TX 76301, USA

Johns, Glynis (Actor)
c/o Staff Member *Marshak/Zachary
Company, The*
8840 Wilshire Blvd
1st Floor
Beverly Hills, CA 90210, USA

Johns, Jasper (Artist)
PO Box 642
Sharon, CT 06069-0642, USA

Johns, Keith (Athlete, Baseball Player)
Arkansas Travelers
P.O. Box 55066
Attn: Coaching Staff
Little Rock, AR 72215, USA

Johns, Lori (Race Car Driver)
PO Box 3667
Corpus Christi, TX 48161-9626, USA

Johns, Marcus (Actor)
c/o Sharon Lane *Lane Management Group*
13017 Woodbridge St
Studio City, CA 91604, USA

Johns, Milton (Actor)
78 Temple Sheen Rd
London SW14 7RJ, ENGLAND

Johns, Stratford
29 Mostyn Rd. Merton Park
London, ENGLAND SW19 3LL

Johnson, Aaron (Athlete, Hockey Player)
3810 Gabrielle Dr
Dublin, OH 43016, USA

Johnson, Aaron Perry (Actor)
c/o Cynthia Pett-Dante *Brillstein
Entertainment Partners*
9150 Wilshire Blvd #350
Beverly Hills, CA 90212, USA

Johnson, Abigail (Business Person)
Fidelity Investments
82 Devonshire St #V8C
Boston, MA 02109-3614, USA

Johnson, Adam (Athlete, Baseball Player)
7335 Hertiage Palms Estate Dr
Fort Myers, Fl 33966-5724, USA

Johnson, Addison (Cartoonist)
c/o Staff Member *King Features
Syndication*
300 W 57th St
15th Floor
New York, NY 10019-5238, USA

Johnson, Adrian (Athlete, Baseball Player)
8102 Meadeville St
Houston, TX 77459-3559, USA

Johnson, Albert (Athlete, Football Player)
3506 Mahejan Dr
Pearland, TX 77584-5501, USA

Johnson, Alex (Athlete, Baseball Player)
18425 Bretton Dr
Detroit, MI 48223-1311, USA

Johnson, Alexz (Actor)
c/o Staff Member *WmE2 (WMA-LA)*
1 William Morris Pl
Beverly Hills, CA 90212, USA

Johnson, Allen (Race Car Driver)
PO Box 926
Greeneville, TN 37744, USA

Johnson, Allen (Athlete, Track Athlete)
Octagon
1751 Pinnacle Dr
#1500
McLean, VA 22102, USA

Johnson, Alonzo (Athlete, Football Player)
P.O. Box 134
Stanley, NC 28164, USA

Johnson, Amy Jo (Actor)
c/o Joanna (Joanie) Burstein *Burstein
Company, The*
15304 Sunset Blvd
suite 208
Pacific Palisades, CA 90272, USA

Johnson, Andre (Athlete, Football Player)
c/o Kennard McGuire *MS World LLC*
1270 Crabb River Rd
Suite #600-104
Richmond, TX 77469, USA

Johnson, Andreas (Musician)
c/o Staff Member *United Stage Artist*
Box 11029
Stockholm S-10061, Sweden

Johnson, Andrew (Athlete, Basketball
Player)
1101 Oak Cir
Lansdale, PA 19446, USA

Johnson, Andy (Athlete, Football Player)
P.O. Box 6828
Athens, GA 30604, USA

Johnson, Anjelah (Actor)
c/o Dave Rath *Generate Management*
1545 26th St
Suite 200
Santa Monica, CA 90404, USA

Johnson, Anne-Marie (Actor)
2522 Silver Lake Terrace
Los Angeles, CA 90039, USA

Johnson, Anthony (Athlete, Football
Player)
2545 5th Ave S
St Petersburg, FL 33712-1634, USA

Johnson, Anthony (Athlete, Basketball
Player)
5162 Inwood Pl
Mableton, GA 30126-7612, USA

Johnson, April (Stylist)
c/o Staff Member *Independent Artists*
448 E Riverdale Ave
Orange, CA 92865, USA

Johnson, Arte (Actor, Comedian)
2725 Bottlebrush Dr
Los Angeles, CA 90077, USA

Johnson, Ashley (Actor)
c/o Doreen Wilcox Little *Anonymous
Content (LA)*
3531 Hayden Ave
Culver City, CA 90232, USA

Johnson, Avery (Athlete, Basketball
Coach, Basketball Player, Coach)
23 Grand Colonial Dr
Spring, TX 77382-2071

Johnson, Barry (Athlete, Football Player)
1103 Northwind Dr
Reston, VA 20194-1009, USA

Johnson, Bart (Actor)
c/o Matt Luber *Luber Roklin Management*
8530 Wilshire Blvd
6th Floor
Beverly Hills, CA 90211, USA

Johnson, Bart (Athlete, Baseball Player)
1929 N Newland Ave
Chicago, IL 60707-3308, USA

Johnson, Batsey L (Designer, Fashion
Designer)
Betsey Johnson Co
127 E 9th St
#703
Los Angeles, CA 90015, USA

Johnson, Ben (Athlete, Baseball Player)
112 Locksley Dr
Greenwood, SC 29649, USA

Johnson, Bethel (Athlete, Football Player)
817 Paisley Ln
Red Oak, TX 75154-8868, USA

Johnson, Betsey (Designer, Fashion
Designer)
c/o Staff Member *Betsey Johnson*
498 Seventh Ave Fl 21
New York, NY 10018, USA

Johnson, Beverly (Actor, Model)
c/o Nancy Chaidez *Nancy Chaidez &
Associates*
6818 Longridge Ave
North Hollywood, CA 91605, USA

Johnson, Bill (Actor)
c/o Mike Pruitt *Actors Clearinghouse*
501 N 1H35
Austin, TX 78702, USA

Johnson, Bill (Athlete, Baseball Player)
14 Rankin Rd
Newark, DE 29501-5823, USA

Johnson, Bill (Congressman, Politician)
317 Cannon HOB
Washington, DC 20515, USA

Johnson, Bob (Athlete, Football Player)
165 Magnolia Ave
Cincinnati, OH 45246, USA

Johnson, Bob (Athlete, Hockey Player)
32361 Hearthstone Rd
Farmington Hills, MI 48334-3438

Johnson, Bob D (Athlete, Baseball Player)
650 Caves Hwy
Cave Junction, OR 97538-9809, USA

Johnson, Bob W (Athlete, Baseball Player)
1474 Barclay St
Saint Paul, MN 55106, USA

Johnson, Boris
Greater London Authority
City Hal, The Queen's Walk
London SE1 2AA, UK

Johnson, Brad (Athlete, Football Player)
1911 Nellie Gray Ct
Athens, GA 30606, USA

Johnson, Brandon (Athlete, Football
Player)
1541 W Coquina Dr
Gilbert, AZ 85233-7007, USA

Johnson, Brent (Athlete, Hockey Player)
808 N Florida St
Arlington, VA 22205, USA

Johnson, Brian (Athlete, Baseball Player)
7595 E Placita Vista Del Bosque
Tucson, AZ 85715, USA

Johnson, Brian (Musician)
c/o Christopher Dalston *Creative Artists
Agency (CAA-LA)*
2000 Ave Of The Stars
Los Angeles, CA 90067, USA

Johnson, Brooks (Coach)
Stanford University
Athletic Dept
Stanford, CA 94305, USA

Johnson, Bryant (Athlete, Football Player)
5749 Legends Club Cir
Braselton, GA 30517-6028, USA

Johnson, Bryce (Actor)
c/o Staff Member *Artists Production
Group (APG)*
9348 Civic Center Dr Fl 2
Beverly Hills, CA 90210, USA

Johnson, Buck (Athlete, Basketball Player)
701 Pine Grove Rd
Harvest, AL 35749-9050, USA

Johnson, Butch (Athlete, Football Player)
9719 S Red Oakes Dr
Highlands Ranch, CO 80126, USA

Johnson, Calvin (Athlete, Football Player)
c/o Bus Cook *Bus Cook Sports, Inc*
1 Willow Bend Dr
Hattiesburg, MS 39402, USA

Johnson, Carl (Athlete, Football Player)
8818 S Shannon Dr
Tempe, AZ 85284, USA

Johnson, Carolyn Dawn (Musician,
Songwriter)
c/o Staff Member *Creative Artists Agency
(CAA-TN)*
3310 West End Ave
5th Floor
Nashville, TN 37203, USA

Johnson, Cassie (Athlete, Olympic
Athlete)
412 Birchwood Ct
Saint Paul, MN 55110-1805, USA

Johnson, Cecil (Athlete, Football Player)
1481 NW 103rd St
Apt 260
Miami, FL 33147, USA

Johnson, Chad (Athlete, Football Player)
2899 Juniper Ln
Davie, FL 33330-1349, USA

Johnson, Charles (Business Person)
17 Indian Creek Dr
Indian Creek Village, FL 33154, USA

Johnson, Charles (Athlete, Baseball
Player, Olympic Athlete)
12301 NW 7th St
Plantation, FL 33325, USA

Johnson, Charles L (Charley) (Athlete,
Football Player)
P.O. Box 1312
Mesilla, NM 88046, USA

Johnson, Charles R (Writer)
University of Washington
English Dept
Seattle, WA 98105, USA

Johnson, Charlie W (Athlete, Football
Player)
1400 Willow Ave
Louisville, KY 40204, USA

Johnson, Chris (Athlete, Golfer)
6210 W Sunset Rd
Tucson, AZ 85743, USA

Johnson, Chris (Athlete, Football Player)
c/o Denise White EAG Sports
Management
12910 Agustin Pl
Playa Vista, CA 90094, USA

Johnson, Chris (Actor)
c/o Staff Member Luber Roklin
Management
8530 Wilshire Blvd
6th Floor
Beverly Hills, CA 90211, USA

Johnson, Chuck (Athlete, Football Player)
1203 N Avenue M
Freeport, TX 77541, USA

Johnson, Clark
9560 Wilshire Blvd. #516
Beverly Hills, CA 90212

Johnson, Claude (Juan) (Musician)
Mars Talent
27 L'Ambiance Court
Bardonia, NY 10954, USA

Johnson, Clay (Athlete, Basketball Player)
6306 N Strathbury Ave
Kansas City, MO 64151-4331, USA

Johnson, Clemon (Athlete, Basketball
Player)
3574 Four Oaks Blvd
Tallahassee, FL 32311-3308, USA

Johnson, Cliff (Athlete, Baseball Player)
9618 Mediator Pass
Converse, TX 78109-1925, USA

Johnson, Cornelius (Athlete, Football
Player)
603 Dale St
Highland Springs, VA 23075, USA

Johnson, Courtney (Misc)
8472 W Granite Dr
Granite Bay, CA 95746, USA

Johnson, Craig (Athlete, Hockey Player)
26 Golden Eagle
Irvine, CA 92603-0309, USA

Johnson, Curley (Athlete, Football Player)
5512 Wedgefield Rd
Granbury, TX 76049-4411, USA

Johnson, Curt (Producer, Writer)
c/o Evan Corday Evolution Entertainment
(LA)
901 N Highland Ave
Los Angeles, CA 90038, USA

Johnson, Curtis (Baseball Player)
Kansas City Monarchs
PO Box B-188
St Rose, LA 70087, USA

Johnson, Curtis (Athlete, Football Player)
2015 Calumet Ave
Toledo, OH 43607, USA

Johnson, Dale (Actor)
c/o Staff Member LA Models/LA Talent
Agency
7700 Sunset Blvd
Los Angeles, CA 90046, USA

Johnson, Dane (Athlete, Baseball Player)
2652 Big Pine Dr
Holiday, FL 55304-7152, USA

Johnson, Danny (Athlete, Hockey Player)

Johnson, Darrius (Athlete, Football Player)
402 Thomas St
Terrell, TX 75160-3832, USA

Johnson, Dave (Misc)
United Garment Workers
4207 Lebanon Road
Hermitage, TN 37076, USA

Johnson, Dave (Athlete, Baseball Player)
3202 Woodhollow Cir
Abilene, TX 79606-4211, USA

Johnson, Dave (Athlete, Baseball Player)
7101 Mount Vista Rd
Kingsville, MD 21087, USA

Johnson, Davey (Athlete, Baseball Player,
Coach)
1064 Howell Branch Rd
Winter Park, FL 32789-1004, USA

Johnson, David (Dave) (Athlete, Track
Athlete)
Azusa Pacific University
PO Box 2713
Azusa, CA 91702, USA

Johnson, David G (Economist)
1700 E 56th St
#1306
Chicago, IL 60637, USA

Johnson, David W (Business Person)
Campbell Soup Co
1 Campbell Place
Camden, NJ 08103, USA

Johnson, Demetrios (Athlete, Football
Player)
840 Garonne Dr
Ballwin, MO 63021, USA

Johnson, Dennis (Athlete, Football Player)
PO Box 467
Hawthorne, NJ 07507-0467, USA

Johnson, DerMarr (Basketball Player)
Phoenix Suns
14610 Man 0 War Dr
Bowie, MD 20721-1295, USA

Johnson, Dick (Athlete, Baseball Player)
5001 E Main St
Lot 762
Mesa, AZ 85205-8172, USA

Johnson, D J (Athlete, Football Player)
3814 Kingsbury Dr
Louisville, KY 40207, USA

Johnson, Don (Athlete, Baseball Player)
3935 King Pl
Cincinnati, OH 45223-2407, USA

Johnson, Don (Actor)
c/o Justin Grey Stone Untitled
Entertainment (LA)
350 S. Beverly Dr #200
Beverly Hills, CA 90212, USA

Johnson, Don (Athlete, Baseball Player)
1529 NE 21st Ave
Apt 205
Portland, OR 97232-1579, USA

Johnson, Donnell (Athlete, Football
Player)
1792 Temple Ave Apt 1
Atlanta, GA 30337-2723, USA

Johnson, Dwayne (The Rock) (Actor,
Athlete, Football Player)
16875 Stratford Ct
Southwest Ranches, FL 33331-1362, USA

Johnson, Dwight (Athlete, Football Player)
1812 King Cole Dr
Waco, TX 76705, USA

Johnson, Earl (Athlete, Football Player)
340 S Keach St
Daytona Beach, FL 32114, USA

Johnson, Ed (Athlete, Basketball Player)
196 Adobe Ln
Mount Airy, NC 27030-5658, USA

Johnson, Eddie (Athlete, Basketball Player)
Santa Rosa Correctional Institution
5850 E Milton Rd
Milton, FL 32583, USA

Johnson, Elliot (Athlete, Baseball Player)
11 Pee:ram Ct
Durham, NC 27703-7970, USA

Johnson, Eric (Musician)
Joe Priesnitz Artist Mgmt
PO Box 5249
Austin, TX 78763, USA

Johnson, Eric (Athlete, Golfer)
893 Chateau Meadows Dr
Eugene, OR 97401, USA

Johnson, Eric (Actor)
c/o Jai Khanna Brillstein Entertainment
Partners
9150 Wilshire Blvd #350
Beverly Hills, CA 90212, USA

Johnson, Erik (Athlete, Baseball Player)
155 Carondelet Plaza
#505
St.Louis, MO 94583-7989, USA

Johnson, Ernest
3106 Bowdoin St
Des Moines, IA 50313-4613, USA

Johnson, Ervin (Basketball Player)
Minnesota Timberwolves
5340 Newport St
Englewood, co 80111-1659, USA

Johnson, Essex (Athlete, Football Player)
1633 E Dimondale Dr
Carson, CA 90746, USA

Johnson, Ezra (Athlete, Football Player)
330 Millhaven Lndg
Fayetteville, GA 30215-8179, USA

Johnson, Footer (Athlete, Baseball Player)
5001 E Main St
Mesa, AZ 85205, USA

Johnson, Frank (Athlete, Baseball Player)
1151 Cypress Hill Ln
Stockton, CA 95206-6245, USA

Johnson, Frank (Athlete, Basketball Player,
Coach)
4320 N 40th St
Phoenix, AZ 85018-4105, USA

Johnson, Gary (Athlete, Baseball Player)
50 Tallwood Ct
Atherton, CA 94027-6432, USA

Johnson, Gary E. (Ex-Governor, Politician)
Students For Sensible Drug Policy
1623 Connecticut Ave NW
3rd Floor
Washington, DC 20009, USA

Johnson, Gary L (Athlete, Football Player)
450 Oliver Rd
Haughton, LA 71037, USA

Johnson, Georgann (Actor)
218 N Glenroy Place
Los Angeles, CA 90049, USA

Johnson, George (Athlete, Golfer)
285 Monarch Village Way
Stockbridge, GA 30281, USA

Johnson, George T (Athlete, Basketball
Player)
630 Highland Overlook
Atlanta, GA 30349-3919, USA

Johnson, Graham R (Musician)
83 Fordwych Road
London NW2 3TL, UNITED KINGDOM
(UK)

Johnson, Greg (Athlete, Hockey Player)
1058 Runyon Rd
Rochester Hills, MI 48306, USA

Johnson, Gregory (Astronaut)
134 NASA Research Center
2100 Brookpark Rd
Attn: Chief - External Programs Division
Cleveland, OH 44135-3191, USA

Johnson, Hailey Noelle (Actor)
c/o Staff Member TalentWorks (LA)
3500 W Olive Ave
Suite 1400
Burbank, CA 91505, USA

Johnson, Hansford T (General)
USAA Capital Corp
9800 Fredericksburg Road
San Antonio, TX 78284, USA

Johnson, Harold (Boxer)
6101 Morris St
Philadelphia, PA 19144, USA

Johnson, Harry (General)
PO Box 100452
Birmingham, AL 35210-0452, USA

Johnson, Haylie (Actor)
c/o Lin Bickelmann Encore Artists
Management
3815 W Olive Ave
Suite 101
Burbank, CA 91505, USA

Johnson, Haynes (Journalist)
University Of Maryland 2100 Journalism
Bldg
College Park, MD 20742-7100, USA

Johnson, Holly (Musician)
Lustig Talent
PO Box 770850
Orlando, FL 32877, USA

Johnson, Howard (Athlete, Baseball
Player)
8597 SE Coconut St
Hobe Sound, FL 33455-2914, USA

Johnson, Ian (Journalist)
Wall Street Journal
Editorial Dept
200 Liberty St
New York, NY 10281, USA

Johnson, Jack (Musician)
59-524 Opae Rd
Haleiwa, HI 96712, USA

Johnson, Jack (Athlete, Hockey Player)
48 Malaga Way
Manhattan Beach, CA 90266-7201, USA

Johnson, James A (Financier)
Federal National Mortgage Assn
3900 Wisconsin Ave NW
Washington, DC 20016, USA

Johnson, James E (Johnnie) (War Hero)
Stables
Hargate Hall Buxton
Derbyshire SK17 8TA, UNITED
KINGDOM (UK)

Johnson, Jamey (Musician)
c/o Staff Member *Webster & Associates
PR*
3573 Couchville Pike
Hermitage, TN 37076, USA

Johnson, Jannette (Skier)
PO Box 901
Sun Valley, ID 83353, USA

Johnson, Jarit (Race Car Driver)
PO Box 3876
Mooresville, NC 28117, USA

Johnson, Jarret (Athlete, Football Player)
78 Bensmill Ct
Reisterstown, MD 21136-6461, USA

Johnson, Jason (Athlete, Football Player)
4713 Arabian Run
Indianapolis, IN 46228, USA

Johnson, Jason (Athlete, Baseball Player)
18122 Emerald Bay St
Tampa, FL 33647-3315, USA

Johnson, Jay (General)
The Pentagon 2000 Chief
Washington, DC 20350-0001, USA

Johnson, Jay (Actor, Comedian)
c/o Staff Member *WmE2 (WMA-LA)*
1 William Morris Pl
Beverly Hills, CA 90212, USA

Johnson, Jay Kenneth (Actor)
c/o Jeff Morrone *Jeff Morrone
Entertainment*
9350 Wilshire Blvd
Suite 224
Beverly Hills, CA 90212, USA

Johnson, Jeff (Athlete, Baseball Player)
424 N Hardee St
Durham, NC 28227-9307, USA

Johnson, Jenna (Coach, Swimmer)
University of Tennessee
Athletic Dept
PO Box 15016
Knoxville, TN 37901, USA

Johnson, Jerome L (Admiral)
Navy-Marine Corps Releif Society
801 N Randolph St
Arlington, VA 22203, USA

Johnson, Jerry (Athlete, Baseball Player)
16670 Espola Rd
Poway, CA 92064-1630, USA

Johnson, Jerry (Athlete, Football Player)
474 SW Meadow Ter
Port Saint Lucie, FL 34984-3545, USA

Johnson, Jesse (Athlete, Football Player)
102 Rosegill Rd
North Chesterfield, VA 23236-2748, USA

Johnson, Jim (Athlete, Hockey Player)
Interactive Coaching LLC
354 Edward Ave W
Winnipeg, MB R2C 2H8, Canada

Johnson, Jimmie (Race Car Driver)
Jimmie Johnson Fan Club
152 Woodfield Drive
Statesville, NC 28677, USA

Johnson, Jimmy (Race Car Driver)
PO Box 4283
Mooresville, NC 28117, USA

Johnson, Jimmy (Cartoonist)
United Feature Syndicate
200 Madison Ave
New York, NY 10016, USA

Johnson, Jimmy (Athlete, Football Coach,
Football Player)
656 Amaranth Blvd
Mill Valley, CA 94941, USA

Johnson, J J
648 Broadway #703
New York, NY 10012, USA

Johnson, Joanna (Actor)
c/o Staff Member *WmE2 (WMA-LA)*
1 William Morris Pl
Beverly Hills, CA 90212, USA

Johnson, Joe (Athlete, Baseball Player)
14 Evergreen Rd
Plainville, MA 02762-1902, USA

Johnson, Joe (Basketball Player)
c/o Staff Member *Atlanta Hawks*
1 CNN Center NW
Suite 405
Atlanta, GA 30303, USA

Johnson, Johari (Actor)
H W A Talent
3500 W Olive Ave
#1400
Burbank, CA 91505, USA

Johnson, John (Athlete, Football Player)
133 Plymouth Dr
Lagrange, GA 30240, USA

Johnson, John (Athlete, Basketball Player)
4751 N 18th St
Milwaukee, WI 53209-6430, USA

Johnson, John (Athlete, Golfer)
236 E Hemlock St
Oxnard, CA 93033, USA

Johnson, John (Athlete, Basketball Player)
4751 N 18th St
Milwaukee, WI 53209, USA

Johnson, John Henry (Athlete, Baseball
Player)
3345 Delna Dr
Sparks, NV 89431-1408, USA

Johnson, John Henry (Athlete, Baseball
Player)
3345 Delna Dr
Sparks, NV 89431, USA

Johnson, Johnny (Athlete, Football Player)
929 Delaware Ave
Santa Cruz, CA 95060, USA

Johnson, Jonathan (Athlete, Baseball
Player)
7 Alverston Ct
Irmo, SC 29063-2934, USA

Johnson, Joseph (Athlete, Football Player)
166 Homestead Hills Cir
Winston Salem, NC 27103, USA

Johnson, J Seward (Artist)
Sculpture Foundation
2525 Michigan Ave
#A6
Santa Monica, CA 90404, USA

Johnson, Junior (Race Car Driver)
1100 Glen Oaks Dr
Hamptonville, NC 27020, USA

Johnson, Keith (Athlete, Baseball Player)
P.O. Box 4122
Park City, UT 63038-1469, USA

Johnson, Kenneth (Athlete, Football
Player)
536 E 169th St
Carson, CA 90746, USA

Johnson, Kenneth (Athlete, Football
Player)
1334 NW 42nd St
Miami, FL 33142, USA

Johnson, Kenneth (Athlete, Basketball
Player)
1401 N Wheeler Ave
Portland, OR 97227-1831, USA

Johnson, Kenny (Actor)
c/o Josh Katz *United Talent Agency (UTA)*
9336 Civic Center Dr
Beverly Hills, CA 90210, USA

Johnson, Kermit (Athlete, Football Player)
3259 Lincoln Ave
Altadena, CA 91001, USA

Johnson, Kevin (Baseball Player,
Sportscaster)
NBC-TV
Sports Dept
30 Rockefeller Plaza
New York, NY 10112, USA

Johnson, Keyshawn (Football Player)
19232 Northfleet Way
Tarzana, CA 91356, USA

Johnson, Kym (Actor)
c/o Siri Garber *Platform Public Relations*
2666 N Beachwood Dr
Los Angeles, CA 90068, USA

Johnson, Lamar (Athlete, Baseball Player)
4105 Sangre Trl
Arlington, TX 76016-2972, USA

Johnson, Lance (Athlete, Baseball Player)
5712 Foxfire Rd
Mobile, AL 36618-2653, USA

Johnson, Landon (Athlete, Football Player)
1915 Mountain Trail Dr
Charlotte, NC 28214-5429, USA

Johnson, Larry (Athlete, Football Player)
340 Glengarry Ln
State College, PA 16801-7092, USA

Johnson, Larry (Athlete, Baseball Player)
1905 E Jean St
Tampa, FL 33610, USA

Johnson, Larry D (Basketball Player)
c/o Staff Member *Kansas City Chiefs*
1 Arrowhead Dr
Kansas City, MO 64129, USA

Johnson, Laura
1917 Weepah Way
Los Angeles, CA 90046

Johnson, Laurie (Composer)
Priority House
Camp Hill Stanmore
Middx HA7 3JQ, UNITED KINGDOM
(UK)

Johnson, Lee (Athlete, Football Player)
1173 McDaniel Ct
Alpine, UT 84004, USA

Johnson, Leon (Athlete, Football Player)
813 Vine Arden Rd
Morganton, NC 28655, USA

Johnson, Leshon (Athlete, Football Player)
15102 Beverly St
Overland Park, OK 66223-3200, USA

Johnson, Levi (Athlete, Football Player)
1202 Craig Dr
Westland, MI 48186-5504, USA

Johnson, Lonnie (Athlete, Football Player)
8500 Amber Ridge Ct
Sanford, FL 32771-8325, USA

Johnson, Lou (Athlete, Baseball Player)
4532 Valley Ridge Ave
Los Angeles, CA 90008-4827, USA

Johnson, Luci Baines (Politician)
170 Crescent Rd
Toronto, ON M4W 1V2, Canada

Johnson, Luther (Guitar Jr) (Musician)
c/o Staff Member *Concerted Efforts*
P.O. Box 440326
Somerville, MA 02144, USA

Johnson, Lynn-Holly (Actor)
Cavaleri
178 S Victory Blvd
#205
Burbank, CA 91502, USA

Johnson, Magic (Athlete, Basketball
Player, Olympic Athlete)
c/o Darren Prince *Prince Marketing
Group*
18 Carillon Cir
Livingston, NJ 07039, USA

Johnson, Mamie "Peanut" (Athlete,
Baseball Player)
623 14th St NE
Washington, DC 20002-5413, USA

Johnson, Manny (Athlete, Football Player)
c/o Chad Speck *Allegiant Athletic Agency*
35 Market Sq
Suite 201
Knoxville, TN 37902, USA

Johnson, Marc (Musician)
A Train Mgmt
PO Box 29242
Oakland, CA 94604, USA

Johnson, Margaret (Athlete, Baseball
Player)
825 Country Club Dr SE Apt 1D
Rio Rancho, NM 87124-2265, USA

Johnson, Mark (Athlete, Hockey Player, Olympic Athlete)
1609 Hidden Hill Dr
Verona, WI 53593, USA

Johnson, Mark (Athlete, Golfer)
P.O. Box 2945
Soldotna, AK 99669, USA

Johnson, Mark (Athlete, Baseball Player)
40 Helen Ave
Rye, NY 40047-7201, USA

Johnson, Mark (Athlete, Baseball Player)
109 Mossy Lake Rd
Perry, GA 10580-2447, USA

Johnson, Mark (Boxer)
1204 Howison Place SW
Washington, DC 20024, USA

Johnson, Mark (Athlete, Hockey Player)
1609 Hidden Hill Dr
Verona, WI 53593-7971, USA

Johnson, Mark Steven (Director, Writer)
c/o Eddie Michaels *Insignia Public Relations*
1507 20th St
Santa Monica, CA 90404, USA

Johnson, Marques (Athlete, Basketball Player)
5133 Dawn View Pl
Los Angeles, CA 90043-2006, USA

Johnson, Marvin (Boxer)
5452 Turfway Circle
Indianapolis, IN 46228, USA

Johnson, Marvin M (Engineer)
4413 Woodland Road
Bartlesville, OK 74006, USA

Johnson, Maurice (Athlete, Football Player)
112 Mountainview Rd
Mount Laurel, NJ 08054, USA

Johnson, Michael (Musician)
Buddy Lee
38 Music Square East
#300
Nashville, TN 37203, USA

Johnson, Michael D (Athlete, Track Athlete)
c/o Staff Member *Octagon*
2 Union St
Suite 300
Portland, ME 04101, USA

Johnson, Mickey (Athlete, Basketball Player)
3642 w Grenshaw St
Chicago, IL 60624-4207, USA

Johnson, Mike (Athlete, Baseball Player)
20251 State Highway 34
Pelican Rapids, MN 56572-7005, USA

Johnson, Mike (Athlete, Baseball Player)
124 Isle Verde Way
Palm Beach Gardens, FL 33418, USA

Johnson, Mike (Athlete, Hockey Player)
Winnipeg Jets 300 Portage Ave
Attn: Broadcast Dept
Winnipeg, MB R3C 5S4, Canada

Johnson, Mitchell (Athlete, Football Player)
2764 Unicorn Ln NW
Washington, DC 20015, USA

Johnson, Monica (Writer)
Innovative Artists
1505 10th St
Santa Monica, CA 90401, USA

Johnson, Monte (Athlete, Football Player)
2349 Hurst Dr NE
Atlanta, GA 30305-4232, USA

Johnson, Neil (Athlete, Basketball Player)
821 Plymouth Ln
Virginia Beach, VA 23451-5926, USA

Johnson, Nic (Race Car Driver)
PTG Racing
441 Victory Rd
Winchester, VA 22602, USA

Johnson, Nicholas (Lawyer, Writer)
PO Box 1876
Iowa City, IA 52244, USA

Johnson, Nick (Athlete, Baseball Player)
8008 Sacramento St
Fair Oaks, CA 95628, USA

Johnson, Norm (Athlete, Hockey Player)
16427 NE Tillamook St
Portland, OR 97230, USA

Johnson, Norm (Athlete, Football Player)
400 Peachtree Industrial Blvd
Apt 1615
Suwanee, GA 30024, USA

Johnson, Norm (Athlete, Football Player)
8523 NW Anderson Hill Rd
Silverdale, WA 98383, USA

Johnson, Norman (Musician)
Paramount Entertainment
PO Box 12
Far Hills, NJ 07931, USA

Johnson, Ollie (Athlete, Basketball Player)
1700 Spring Garden St
Philadelphia, PA 19130, USA

Johnson, Ora J (Religious Leader)
General Assn of General Baptists
100 Stinson Dr
Poplar Bluff, MO 63901, USA

Johnson, Paul (Athlete, Hockey Player, Olympic Athlete)
3305 Lanewood Ln N
Minneapolis, MN 55447-5020, USA

Johnson, Paul (Football Coach)
Georgia Tech Athletic Association
150 Bobby Dodd Way NW
Atlanta, GA 30332-0455, USA

Johnson, Paul B (Historian)
Coach House
Over Stowey near Bridgewater
Somerset TA5 1HA, UNITED KINGDOM (UK)

Johnson, Penny
121 N. San Vicente Blvd.
Beverly Hills, CA 90211

Johnson, Pepper (Athlete, Football Player)
The Sports Corner PO Box 1133
Russells Point, OH 43348-1133, USA

Johnson, Pete (Athlete, Football Player)
6304 Misty Cove ln
Columbus, OH 43231-1689, USA

Johnson, Rafer L (Actor, Athlete, Decathlon Athlete)
4217 Woodcliff Road
Sherman Oaks, CA 91403, USA

Johnson, Ralph (Athlete, Baseball Player)
5703 E 30th Ave
Tampa, FL 33619-1525, USA

Johnson, Ralph E (Architect)
Perkins & Will
330 N Wabash Ave
#3600
Chicago, IL 60611, USA

Johnson, Randy (Athlete, Baseball Player)
10645 N Tatum Blvd #C200
Phoenix, AZ 33157-7160, USA

Johnson, Raylee (Athlete, Football Player)
2010 Black Fox Or NE
Atlanta, GA 30345-4123, USA

Johnson, Raymond Edward
167 Grieb Rd.
Wallingford, CT 06492

Johnson, Ray William (Actor)
c/o David (Dave) Becky *3 Arts Entertainment Inc*
9460 Wilshire Blvd
7th Floor
Beverly Hills, CA 90210, USA

Johnson, R E (Misc)
Train Dispatchers Assn
1370 Ontario St
#1040
Cleveland, OH 44113, USA

Johnson, Reed (Athlete, Baseball Player)
30137 Mira Loma Dr
Temecula, CA 92592, USA

Johnson, Reggie (Athlete, Football Player)
17907 Souter Ln
Land Lakes, FL 34638-7887, USA

Johnson, Rian (Director, Writer)
c/o Brian Dreyfuss *Featured Artists Agency*
1880 Century Park E #1402
Los Angeles, CA 90067, USA

Johnson, Richard (Butch) (Archer, Athlete, Olympic Athlete)
234 Route 197
Woodstock, CT 06281-1637, USA

Johnson, Richard K (Actor)
c/o Staff Member *Conway van Gelder*
8-12 Broadwick St
London W1F 8HW, UK

Johnson, Rob (Athlete, Football Player)
26635 Aracena Dr
Mission Viejo, CA 92691, USA

Johnson, Robert (Business Person)
c/o Staff Member *BET - Black EntertainmentTelevision (DC)*
1235 W Place NE
Washington, DC 20018-1211, USA

Johnson, Robert L (Business Person)
Black Entertainment TV
1900 W Place NE
Washington, DC 20018, USA

Johnson, Ron (Athlete, Baseball Player)
428 S Maie Ave
Compton, CA 37357-5692, USA

Johnson, Ronald A (Ron) (Athlete, Football Player)
226 Summit Ave
Summit, NJ 07901, USA

Johnson, Rondin (Athlete, Baseball Player)
1025 S 324th Pl
Federal Way, WA 98003-5930, USA

Johnson, Rontrez (Athlete, Baseball Player)
1426 SE 18th St
Cape Coral, FL 33909-2870, USA

Johnson, Roy (Misc)
Roofers & Waterproofers Union
1125 17th St NW
Washington, DC 20036, USA

Johnson, Russ (Athlete, Baseball Player, Olympic Athlete)
3542 Russell Rd
Green Cove Springs, FL 70726-1777, USA

Johnson, Russell (Actor)
Professor's Place
PO Box 1198
Bainbridge Island, WA 98110, USA

Johnson, Sam (Congressman, Politician)
1211 Longworth HOB
Washington, DC 20515, USA

Johnson, Sammy (Athlete, Football Player)
142 Old Mill Rd Apt B
High Point, NC 27265-1283, USA

Johnson, Scarlett (Actor)
c/o Duncan Millership *WME (LA)*
9601 Wilshire Blvd Fl 3
Beverly Hills, CA 90210, USA

Johnson, Shannon (Basketball Player)
Connecticut Sun
Mohegan Sun Arena
Uncasville, CT 06382, USA

Johnson, Shawn (Athlete, Gymnast, Olympic Athlete)
Chow's Gymnastics
2210 Park Dr
W Des Moines, IA 50265, USA

Johnson, Sheila (Business Person)
Washington Mystics
401 9th Street NW
Washington, DC 20004, USA

Johnson, Shelly W (Cinematographer)
970 Jimeno Road
Santa Barbara, CA 93103, USA

Johnson, Sonia (Activist)
3318 2nd St S
Arlington, VA 22204, USA

Johnson, Spencer (Writer)
Spencer Johnson Partners
825 N 1420 E
Orem, UT 84097, USA

Johnson, Steffond (Athlete, Basketball Player)
10525 Marsh Ln
Dallas, TX 75229-5142, USA

Johnson, Steve (Race Car Driver)
3760 Mountain View Lane
Birmingham, AL 35223, USA

Johnson, Steve (Athlete, Basketball Player)
9715 SW Quail Post Rd
Portland, OR 97219-6363, USA

Johnson, Syl (Musician, Songwriter, Writer)
Blue Sky Artists
761 Washington Ave N
Minneapolis, MN 55401, USA

Johnson, Ted (Athlete, Football Player)
10 Appletree Ln
Wayland, MA 01778-1314, USA

Johnson, Terry (Athlete, Hockey Player)
Endev Energy Inc
400-777 8th Ave SW
Attn: Vice-President, Land
Calgary, AB T2P 3R5, Canada

Johnson, Teyo (Athlete, Football Player)
2222 Oak Rd
Lynnwood, WA 98087-6321, USA

Johnson, Thomas (Athlete, Baseball Player)
15107 Interlachen Dr
Apt 324
Silver Spring, MD 20906, USA

Johnson, Tim (Athlete, Football Player)
21300 Redskin Park Dr
Ashburn, VA 20147, USA

Johnson, Tim (Athlete, Football Player)
2839 Dorell Ave
Orlando, FL 32814-6757, USA

Johnson, Tim (Athlete, Baseball Player, Coach)
2700 Van Dorn St
Lincoln, NE 68502, USA

Johnson, Timothy (Correspondent, Doctor)
c/o Staff Member *Good Morning America (NY)*
ABC
147 Columbus Ave Fl 6
New York, NY 10023, USA

Johnson, Tom (Athlete, Baseball Player)
2700 Knox Ave N
Minneapolis, MN 55411-1246, USA

Johnson, Torrence V (Astronomer)
Jet Propulsion Laboratory
4800 Oak Grove Dr
Pasadena, CA 91109, USA

Johnson, Tre (Athlete, Football Player)
680 Harrison Ave
Peekskill, NY 10566, USA

Johnson, Undra (Athlete, Football Player)
1550 Cost Ave Apt 29
Clarksburg, WV 26301-4889, USA

Johnson, Vance (Athlete, Football Player)
2503 Hayes Dr
Grand Junction, CO 81505-1274, USA

Johnson, Vaughan (Athlete, Football Player)
4915 Arendell St
Apt 253
Morehead City, NC 28557, USA

Johnson, Vaughan M (Athlete, Football Player)
5800 Airline Hwy
Metairie, LA 70003, USA

Johnson, Vicki (Stylist)
8226 Cherokee Circle
Leawood, KS 66206, USA

Johnson, Vickie (Basketball Player)
c/o Staff Member *New York Liberty*
2 Penn Plz Fl 14
New York, NY 10121, USA

Johnson, Vinnie (Athlete, Basketball Player)
5236 Elmsgate Dr
Orchard Lake, MI 48324, USA

Johnson, Vinnie (Athlete, Basketball Player)
5236 Elmgate Dr
Orchard Lake, MI 48324-3017, USA

Johnson, Virginia (Ballerina)
133 W 71st St
New York, NY 10023, USA

Johnson, Virginia (Scientist)
Masters And Johnson Institute 800
Holland Rd
Ballwin, MO 63021-7230, USA

Johnson, Virginia E (Doctor)
Johnson Assoc
800 Holland Road
Ballwin, MO 63021, USA

Johnson, Wallace (Athlete, Baseball Player)
PO Box 64618
Gary, IN 46401-0618, USA

Johnson, Warren (Race Car Driver)
WJ Enterprises
700 N. Price Rd
Sugar Hill, GA 30518, USA

Johnson, Wendy (Race Car Driver)
126 Red Brook Lane
Mooresville, NC 28117, USA

Johnson, William A (Billy White Shoes) (Athlete, Football Player)
3701 Whitney Pl
Duluth, GA 30096, USA

Johnson, William B (Business Person)
Ritz-Carlton Hotels
4445 Willard Ave
#800
Chevy Chase, MD 20815, USA

Johnson, William H (Athlete, Football Player)
522 E Pleasant Grove Rd
Montgomery, AL 36105, USA

Johnson, William R (Business Person)
H J Heinz Co
PO Box 57
Pittsburgh, PA 15230, USA

Johnson, William W (Athlete, Football Player)
20 Mohawk Rd
Canton, MA 02021, USA

Johnson, Woody (Business Person, Football Executive)
1195 Lamington Rd
Bedminster, NJ 07921-2764, USA

Johnson, Zach (Athlete, Golfer)
c/o John Mascatello *SFX World Sports Management*
11921 Freedom Dr
Suite 1180
Reston, VA 20190, USA

Johnson-Goodman, Mamie (Peanut) (Athlete, Baseball Player)
618 Southern Ave SE
Washington, DC 20032, USA

Johnson III, Edward (Business Person)
Fidelity Investments
82 Devonshire St #V8C
Boston, MA 02109-3614, USA

Johnson III, Joseph E (Doctor, Physicist)
Philadelphian
2401 Pennsylvania Ave
#15C44
Philadelphia, PA 19130, USA

Johnson Jr, Benjamin S (ben) (Athlete, Track Athlete)
Ed Futerman
2 Saint Clair Ave E
#1500
Toronto, ON M4T 2R1, CANADA

Johnson Jr, Ernie (Sportscaster)
TNT-TV
Sports Department
1050 Techwood Dr
Atlanta, GA 30318, USA

Johnson Jr, G Griffith (Government Official)
300 Locust Ave
Annapolis, MD 21401, USA

Johnson Jr, Johnnie (Athlete, Football Player)
P.O. Box 114
La Grange, TX 78945, USA

Johnson Jr, Manuel H (Economist, Government Official)
Johnson Smick Int'l
2099 Pennsylvania Ave NW
#950
Washington, DC 20006, USA

Johnson, Jr., Tommy (Race Car Driver)
493 Southpoint Circle
Brownsburg, IN 46112, USA

Johnson-Noga, Arlene
1923 7th Ave E
Regina, SK S4N 4M7, CANADA

Johnson Pucci, Gail (Swimmer)
2132 Ward Dr
Walnut Creek, CA 94596, USA

Johnsson, Kim (Athlete, Hockey Player)
5308 Oaklawn Ave
Minneapolis, MN 55424-1309, USA

Johnston, Alastair (Misc)
International Mgmt Group
75490 Fairway Dr
Indian Wells, CA 92210, USA

Johnston, Allen H (Religious Leader)
Bishop's House
3 Wymer Terrace
PO Box 21
Hamilton, NEW ZELAND

Johnston, Bernie (Athlete, Hockey Player)
715 Central Park Blvd
Port Orange, FL 32127, USA

Johnston, Brian (Athlete, Football Player)
236 Hideaway Ln
Mooresville, NC 28117, USA

Johnston, Bruce (Musician)
International Creative Mgmt
8942 Wilshire Blvd
#219
Beverly Hills, CA 90211, USA

Johnston, Daryl (Moose) (Athlete, Football Player)
4414 Woodfin Dr
Dallas, TX 75230, USA

Johnston, Ed (Athlete, Hockey Player)
c/o Staff Member *Pittsburgh Penguins*
1001 Fifth Ave
Pittsburgh, PA 15219, USA

Johnston, Freedy (Musician, Songwriter, Writer)
Morebarn Music
30 Hilcrest Ave
Morristown, NJ 07960, USA

Johnston, George (Athlete, Hockey Player)
15604 B. Myrtle St.
Mead, WA 99021-5944, USA

Johnston, Gerald A (Business Person)
McDonnell Douglas Corp
PO Box 516
Saint Louis, MO 63166, USA

Johnston, Gerald E (Business Person)
Clorox Co
1221 Broadway
Oakland, CA 94612, USA

Johnston, Greg (Athlete, Hockey Player)
c/o Staff Member *Toronto Maple Leafs*
Air Canada Centre
400-40 Bay St
Toronto, ON M5J 2X2, Canada

Johnston, Harold S (Misc)
285 Franklin St
Harrisonburg, VA 22801, USA

Johnston, Jamie (Actor)
c/o Norbert Abrams *Noble Caplan Abrams*
1260 Yonge St
2nd Floor
Toronto ON M4T 1W6, Canada

Johnston, J Bennett (Politician)
Steptoe and Johnston 1330 Connecticut
Ave NW Ste 1C
Washington, DC 20036-1724, USA

Johnston, J Bennett Jr (Ex-Senator)
Johnston Assoc
2099 Pennsylvania Ave NW
#1000
Washington, DC 20006, USA

Johnston, Jimmy (Athlete, Golfer)
Pro's Inc
9 S 12th St
Fl 3
Richmond, VA 23219, USA

Johnston, Joe (Director)
c/o Adam Kanter *Creative Artists Agency (CAA-LA)*
2000 Ave Of The Stars
Los Angeles, CA 90067, USA

Johnston, Joel (Athlete, Baseball Player)
1479 Sweetwater Way
Pottstown, PA 19464-1940, USA

Johnston, Joey (Athlete, Hockey Player)
RR 4
Station Delivery Ctr
Peterborough, ON K9J 6X5, Canada

Johnston, John Dennis (Actor)
S D B Partners
1801 Ave of Stars
#902
Los Angeles, CA 90067, USA

Johnston, Ken
6300 Wilshire Blvd. #2110
Los Angeles, CA 90048

Johnston, Kristen (Actor)
c/o Judy Hofflund *Hofflund/Polone*
9465 Wilshire Blvd #420
Beverly Hills, CA 90212, USA

Johnston, Larry (Athlete, Hockey Player)
904 E Liberty St
Milford, MI 48381-2081, USA

Johnston, Levi (Misc)
c/o Rex Lamont Butler *Rex Lamont Butler & Associates*
745 West 4th Ave
Anchorage, AK 99501, USA

Johnston, Lynn (Cartoonist)
Universal Press Syndicate
4520 Main St
Kansas City, MO 64111, USA

Johnston, Mark (Athlete, Football Player)
5604 Southwest Pkwy
Apt 3535
Austin, TX 78735-6278, USA

Johnston, Marshall (Athlete, Hockey Player)
3933 Waville Rd NE
Bemidji, MN 56601, USA

Johnston, Nate (Athlete, Basketball Player)
8870 Fontainebleau Blvd
Apt 301
Miami, FL 33172-4427, USA

Johnston, Rex D (Athlete, Baseball Player, Football Player)
15117 Illinois Ave
Paramont, CA 90723-4106, USA

Johnston, Sabrina
c/o Staff Member *Diva Central Inc*
7510 W Sunset Blvd Ste 1445
Los Angees, CA 90046, USA

Johnston, Tom (Musician)
PO Box 359
Sonoma, CA 95476

Johnstone, Jay (Athlete, Baseball Player)
853 Chapea Rd
Pasadena, CA 91107-5656, USA

Johnstone, John (Athlete, Baseball Player)
9330 Clubside Cir
Unit 3305
Sarasota, FL 34238-3367, USA

Johnstone, Parker (Race Car Driver)
541 Division St.
Campbell, CA 95008, USA

Johnstone, Tony (Athlete, Golfer)
Proserv
5335 Wisconsin Ave NW
Suite 850
Washington, DC 20015, USA

Johnstone Jr, John W (Business Person)
467 Carter St
New Canaan, CT 06840, USA

Johnston-Forbes, Cathy (Athlete, Golfer)
5104 Lunar Dr
Kitty Hawk, NC 27949, USA

Johnston Jr, S K (Business Person)
Coca-Cola Enterprises
2500 Windy Ridge Parkway
Atlanta, GA 30339, USA

Johnston McKay, Marry H (Astronaut)
University of Tennessee
Space Institute
Tullahoma, TN 37388, USA

Joiner, Rusty (Actor, Athlete, Model)
c/o Marc Chancer *Origin Talent Agency*
4705 Laurel Canyon #306
Studio City, CA 91607, USA

Joiner Jr, Charles (Charlie) (Athlete, Coach, Football Coach, Football Player)
16935 W Bernardo Drive
Suite 107
San Diego, CA 92127, USA

Jokinen, Olli (Athlete, Hockey Player)
4401 N Federal HwySte 201
Boca Raton, FL 33431-5164, USA

Jolas, Betsy M (Composer)
Nat Superieur Musique Conservatoire
209 Ave Jaures
Paris 75019, FRANCE

Joli, France (Musician)
c/o Staff Member *Diva Central Inc*
7510 W Sunset Blvd Ste 1445
Los Angees, CA 90046, USA

Joliceur, David (Musician)
Famous Artists Agency
250 W 57th St
New York, NY 10107, USA

Jolie, Angelina (Actor, Philanthropist)
c/o Geyer Kosinski *Media Talent Group*
9200 Sunset Blvd
Suite 550
Los Angeles, CA 90069, USA

Joliot, Pierre A (Biologist)
16 Rue de la Glaciere
Paris 75013, FRANCE

Jolitz, Evan (Athlete, Football Player)
15 Old Kimball Rd
Brooklyn, CT 06234, USA

Jolley, Gordon (Athlete, Football Player)
1459 Navajo Dr
St George, UT 84790, USA

Jolley, Leroy (Horse Racer)
304 Paschal Ave
Franklin Sauare, NY 11010-2808, USA

Jolley, Lewis (Athlete, Football Player)
2715 Rosegate Ln
Charlotte, NC 28270, USA

Jolley, Willie (Motivational Speaker)
PO Box 55459
Washington, DC 20040, USA

Jolliff, Howie (Athlete, Basketball Player)
2346 Fallen Oak Cir NE
Massillon, OH 44646-4887, USA

Jolly, Allison (Athlete, Olympic Athlete, Sailor)
27122 Benidorm
Mission Viejo, CA 92692-3405, USA

Jolly, Allison (Yachtsman)
1275 Seville Lane NE
Saint Petersburg, FL 33704, USA

Jolly, E Grady (Judge)
US Court of Appeals
Eastland Courthouse
245 E Capitol St
Jackson, MS 39201, USA

Jolly, Ken (Athlete, Football Player)
159 Bon Aire Dr
Dallas, TX 75218, USA

Jolovitz, Jenna (Actor, Writer)
c/o Staff Member *Creative Artists Agency (CAA-LA)*
2000 Ave Of The Stars
Los Angeles, CA 90067, USA

Joltz, Joachim (Engineer)
AM Forsthof 16
Wuppertal 42119, GERMANY

Joly, Frederique (Stylist)
9401/2 Milwood Ave
Venice, CA 90291, USA

Joly, Greg (Athlete, Hockey Player)
21 McDonald Dr
Queensbury, NY 12804, USA

Joly, Yvan (Athlete, Hockey Player)
16 Hwy 3
Wainfleet, ON L0S 1V0, Canada

Jomdt, L daniel (Business Person)
Walgreen Co
200 Wilmot Road
Deerfield, IL 60015, USA

Jomphe, Jean-Francois (Athlete, Hockey Player)
6440 Sky Pointe Dr
Suite 140 MBB 39
Las Vegas, NV 89131, USA

Jonas, Don (Athlete, Football Player)
1831 Seneca Blvd
Winter Springs, FL 32708-5534, USA

Jonas, Joe (Musician)
c/o Keleigh Thomas *Sunshine, Sachs & Associates - LA*
8409 Santa Monica Blvd
West Hollywood, CA 90069, USA

Jonas, Kevin (Musician)
c/o Michael Samonte *Sunshine, Sachs & Associates - LA*
8409 Santa Monica Blvd
West Hollywood, CA 90069, USA

Jonas, Nick (Musician)
c/o Michael Samonte *Sunshine, Sachs & Associates - LA*
8409 Santa Monica Blvd
West Hollywood, CA 90069, USA

Jonathan, Stan (Athlete, Hockey Player)
RR 1
Ohsweken, ON N0A 1M0, Canada

Jonathan, Wesley (Actor)
c/o Adrienne McWhorter *Abrams Artists Agency (LA)*
9200 Sunset Blvd
11th Floor
Los Angeles, CA 90069, USA

Jones, Aaron (Athlete, Football Player)
7677 Torino Ct
Orlando, FL 32835, USA

Jones, Adam (Athlete, Baseball Player)
c/o Staff Member *Baltimore Orioles*
333 W Camden St
Baltimore, MD 21201, USA

Jones, Al (Athlete, Baseball Player)
1339 Brussels St
San Francisco, CA 94134, USA

Jones, Alex E (Journalist, Radio Personality)
3001 South Lamar
Suite 100
Austin, TX 78704, USA

Jones, Alfred (Boxer)
19303 Patton St
Detroit, MI 48219, USA

Jones, Allen (Artist)
41 Charterhouse Square
London EC1M 6EA, UNITED KINGDOM (UK)

Jones, Andruw (Athlete, Baseball Player)
2931 Grey Moss Pass
Duluth, GA 30097-6274, USA

Jones, Angus T (Actor)
c/o Wendi Green *Paradigm (LA)*
9200 Sunset Blvd
11th Floor
Los Angeles, CA 90069, USA

Jones, Anthony (Athlete, Basketball Player)
44 Hempstead Dr
Newark, DE 19702-7711, USA

Jones, Antonia (Actor)
Buzz Halliday
8899 Beverly Blvd
#620
Los Angeles, CA 90048, USA

Jones, Ashthon (Musician)
c/o Simon Fuller *XIX Entertainment*
35-37 Parkgate Rd
32/33 Ransomes Dock
London SW11 4NP, UNITED KINGDOM (UK)

Jones, Asjha (Basketball Player)
Connecticut Sun
Mohegan Sun Arena
Uncasville, CT 06382, USA

Jones, Askia (Athlete, Basketball Player)
3160 SW 132nd Ave
Miramar, FL 33027-3868, USA

Jones, Barry (Athlete, Baseball Player)
411 S Morton Ave
Centerville, IN 47330-1429, USA

Jones, Ben (Athlete, Baseball Player)
1323 Tewkesbury Pl NW
Washington, DC 20012-2921, USA

Jones, Ben J (Prime Minister)
Victoria St
Greenville
Saint Andrew's, GRENADA

Jones, Bert (Athlete, Football Player)
1492 Madera St
Ruston, LA 71270, USA

Jones, Bertram H (Bert) (Athlete, Football Player)
P.O. Box 248
Simsboro, LA 71275, USA

Jones, Bob (Bobby) (Athlete, Baseball Player)
32 Elm St
Rutherford, NJ 07070, USA

Jones, Bobby (Athlete, Basketball Player, Olympic Athlete)
Charlotte Christian School
7301 Sardis Rd
Charlotte, NC 28270-6063, USA

Jones, Bobby (Athlete, Baseball Player)
7809 S Oxford Ave
Tulsa, OK 74136-8524, USA

Jones, Bobby (Athlete, Baseball Player)
10222 N Whitney Ave
Fresno, CA 93730, USA

Jones, Bobby (Athlete, Football Player)
6824 Stewart Sharon Rd
Brookfield, OH 44403-9789, USA

Jones, Booker T (Actor, Musician)
c/o Staff Member *Concerted Efforts*
P.O. Box 440326
Somerville, MA 02144, USA

Jones, Brad (Athlete, Hockey Player)
c/o Staff Member *International Hockey League*
117 W 4th St
Rochester, MI 48307, USA

Jones, Brandon (Athlete, Football Player)
1070 Randall Rd
Texarkana, TX 75501-2102, USA

Jones, Brent M (Athlete, Football Player, Sportscaster)
756 El Pintado Rd
Danville, CA 94526, USA

Jones, Brian (Athlete, Football Player)
2501 Wickersham Ln Apt 2022
Austin, TX 78741-4674, USA

Jones, Bryn Terfel (Opera Singer)
Harlequin Agency
203 Fidlas Road
Cardiff CF4 5NA, WALES

Jones, Buckshot (Race Car Driver)
Buckshot Racing
182 Belue Rd
Spartanburg, SC 29303, USA

Jones, Caldwell (Athlete, Basketball
Player)
625 Edgecombe
Stockbridge, GA 30281-4282, USA

Jones, Calvin (Athlete, Baseball Player)
2815 Butterfield Stage Rd
Lewisville, TX 75077-3181, USA

Jones, Calvin (Athlete, Football Player)
25 Sierra St Apt E306
San Francisco, CA 94107-2855, USA

Jones, Carlton (Stylist)
c/o Staff Member *Illusions Management*
129 W 27th St
Penthouse
New York, NY 10001, USA

Jones, Carnetta (Actor)
CunninghamEscottDipene
10635 Santa Monica Blvd
#130
Los Angeles, CA 90025, USA

Jones, Cedric (Athlete, Football Player)
48B Rodwell Ave
Greenwich, CT 06830-6121, USA

Jones, Charles (Athlete, Basketball Player)
2315 Windsor Ave
Baltimore, MD 21216-3227, USA

Jones, Charles A (Athlete, Basketball
Player)
304 Chestnut St
Elizabethtown, KY 42701-9431, USA

Jones, Charles W (Misc)
Brotherhood of Boilermakers
753 S 8th Ave
Kansas City, KS 66105, USA

Jones, Charlie (Sportscaster)
33 Campbell Ln
Menlo Park, CA 94025-6353, USA

Jones, Cherry (Actor)
c/o Scott Henderson *WME (LA)*
9601 Wilshire Blvd Fl 3
Beverly Hills, CA 90210, USA

Jones, Chipper (Athlete, Baseball Player,
Olympic Athlete)
c/o Staff Member *Atlanta Braves*
755 Hank Aaron Dr SW
Atlanta, GA 30315, USA

Jones, Chris (Athlete, Baseball Player)
1821 Westward Ho Cir
El Cajon, CA 92021-3721, USA

Jones, Chris (Athlete, Baseball Player)
1312 E Thunderhill Pl
Phoenix, AZ 85048, USA

Jones, Chris T (Athlete, Football Player)
2372 Treasure Isle Dr
West Palm Beach, FL 33410-1312, USA

Jones, Christopher (Chris) (Actor, Artist)
c/o Sherry Dodd
PO Box 15714
Beverly Hills, CA 90209, USA

Jones, Christopher Michael (Actor,
Dancer)
c/o Justine Hunt *Hines and Hunt
Entertainment*
1213 W Magnolia Blvd
Burbank, CA 91506, USA

Jones, Clarence (Athlete, Baseball Player)
2641 Club Dr
Greensboro, GA 30642-3476, USA

Jones, Claude Earl (Actor)
Henderson/Hogan
8285 W Sunset Blvd
#1
West Hollywood, CA 90046, USA

Jones, Cleon (Athlete, Baseball Player)
751 Edwards St
Mobile, AL 36610-3334, USA

Jones, Clinton (Athlete, Football Player)
7559 McLaren Ave
West Hills, CA 91307-1525, USA

Jones, C L "Jack" (General)
15730 Rosanky Rd
Holland, TX 76534-5057, USA

Jones, Cobi (Soccer Player)
501 N Edinburgh Ave
Los Angeles, CA 90048, USA

Jones, Collis (Athlete, Basketball Player)
1217 Argyle Ave
Baltimore, MD 21217-2928, USA

Jones, Courtney J L (Figure Skater)
National Skating Assn
15-27 Gee St
London EC1V 3RE, UNITED KINGDOM
(UK)

Jones, Cullen (Athlete, Olympic Athlete,
Swimmer)
c/o Staff Member *Premier Management
Group (PMG Sports)*
115 Crescent Commons Dr Ste 250
Cary, NC 27518, USA

Jones, Dahntay (Athlete, Basketball
Player)
3247 Wedge Hill Cv
Memphis, TN 38125-8891, USA

Jones, Dale (Athlete, Football Player)
PO Box 2716
Boone, NC 28607-2716, USA

Jones, Dalton (Athlete, Baseball Player)
4688 S Dixon Ln
Liberty, MS 39645, USA

Jones, Damon (Athlete, Basketball Player)
c/o Staff Member *Mark Termini Associates*
Prefers to be contacted via telephone
Cleveland, OH, USA

Jones, Damon (Athlete, Football Player)
12690 Cooper Springs Rd
Jacksonville, Fl 32246, USA

Jones, Dan (Athlete, Football Player)
5150 SW 20th St
Plantation, FL 33317, USA

Jones, Daniel (Writer)
c/o Staff Member *The New York Times
Company*
229 W 43rd St
New York, NY 10036, USA

Jones, Dante (Athlete, Football Player)
326 Partridge Run Dr
Ducanville, TX 75137, USA

Jones, Darryl (Musician)
Rascoff/Zysblat
110 W 57th St
#300
New York, NY 10019, USA

Jones, Darryl (Athlete, Baseball Player)
15628 King Dr
Meadville, PA 16335-6546, USA

Jones, Daryl (Politician)
15820 SW 98th Ct
Miami, FL 33157-1758, USA

Jones, Daryll (Athlete, Football Player)
581 N Oakley Dr
Columbus, GA 31906-4369, USA

Jones, David A (Business Person)
Humana Corp
500 W Main St
Louisville, KY 40202, USA

Jones, David D (Athlete, Football Player)
3131 Mockingbird Ln
Dallas, TX 75205-2324, USA

Jones, David (Deacon) (Athlete, Football
Player)
715 S Canyon Mist Lane
Anaheim, CA 92808, USA

Jones, Davy (Race Car Driver)
TRW Racing
1397 330th Street
Adair, IA 50002, USA

Jones, Dax (Athlete, Baseball Player)
10021 W Suddard Pl
Beach Park, IL 60087-1717, USA

Jones, Dean (Actor, Musician)
PO Box 570276
Tarzana, CA 91357, USA

Jones, Dhani (Athlete, Football Player)
10300 Gary Rd
Potomac, MD 20854-4155, USA

Jones, Dick (Actor)
PO Box 7716
Northridge, CA 91322

Jones, Dickie (Actor)
PO Box 7716
Northridge, CA 91327, USA

Jones, Don (Athlete, Football Player)
8446 Wren Creek Dr
Charlotte, NC 28269-6176, USA

Jones, Donell (Musician)
c/o Ra-Fael Blanco *2R's Entertainment &
Media*
601 W. 135th St
#6E
New York, NY 10031, USA

Jones, Donta (Athlete, Football Player)
4495 Jimmy Greens Pl
La Plata, MD 20646-5852, USA

Jones, Doug (Athlete, Baseball Player)
129 E Navilla Pl
Covina, CA 91723-3023, USA

Jones, Doug (Actor)
c/o John Zander *Zander Magic*
9068 Priscilla St
Downey, CA 90242, USA

Jones, Dub (Athlete, Football Player)
904 Glendale Dr
Ruston, LA 71270-2346, USA

Jones, Dwight (Athlete, Basketball Player,
Olympic Athlete)
20119 Mayfair Park Ln
Spring, TX 77379-2436, USA

Jones, Earl (Athlete, Track Athlete)
15114 Petroskey Ave
Detroit, MI 48238, USA

Jones, Earl (Athlete, Football Player)
3127 Seiler Ct
Naperville, IL 60565, USA

Jones, Earl (Athlete, Basketball Player)
8402 Belding Ct
Brandywine, MD 20613-7107, USA

Jones, Ed (Athlete, Football Player)
Team Jones, Inc
PMB. 282
14232 Marsh Ln
Addison, TX 75001, USA

Jones, Eddie (Actor)
Gage Group
14724 Ventura Blvd
#505
Sherman Oaks, CA 91403, USA

Jones, Eddie (Athlete, Basketball Player)
3400 Paddock Rd
Weston, FL 33331-3520, USA

Jones, Edith H (Judge)
US Court of Appeals
515 Rusk Ave
Houston, TX 77002, USA

Jones, E Edward (Religious Leader)
Baptist Convention of America
777 S R L Thornton Freeway
Dallas, TX 75203, USA

Jones, E Fay (Architect)
Fay Jones/Maurice Jennings Architects
619 W Dickson
Fayetteville, AR 72701, USA

Jones, Elvin R (Musician)
DL Media
PO Box 2728
Bala Cynwyd, PA 19004, USA

Jones, Ernest (Athlete, Football Player)
17410 SW 109th Ave
Miami, FL 33157, USA

Jones, Etta
160 Goldsmith Ave.
Newark, NJ 07112

Jones, Evan (Actor)
c/o Susan Curtis *Curtis Talent
Management*
9607 Arby Dr
Beverly Hills, CA 90210, USA

Jones, Felicity (Actor)
c/o Erica Gray *Viewpoint Inc*
8820 Wilshire Blvd.
Suite 220
Beverly Hills, CA 90211, USA

Jones, Felix (Athlete, Football Player)
c/o Eugene Parker *Maximum Sports
Management*
6435 W Jefferson Blvd
#197
Fort Wayne, IN 46804, USA

Jones, Freddie (Athlete, Football Player)
120 Word Ln
Harvest, AL 35749-8800, USA

Jones, Freddie (Actor)
c/o Staff Member *Diamond Management*
31 Percy St
London W1T 2DD, UK

Jones, Garrett (Athlete, Baseball Player)
670 W Wavman St APt 1306
Chicago, IL 60661-1702, USA

Jones, Gary (Athlete, Football Player)
1410 Ten Mile Dr
Cedar Hill, TX 75104-6239, USA

Jones, Gary (Athlete, Baseball Player)
475 S Westridge Cir
Anaheim, CA 92807-3733, USA

Jones, Gemma (Actor)
Conway Van Gelder Robinson
18-21 Jermyn St
London SW1Y 6NB, UNITED KINGDOM
(UK)

Jones, George (Musician)
500 Wilson Pike Cir #200
Brentwood, TN 37027, USA

Jones, George (Athlete, Football Player)
ao Tracy Jones 2066 NW Glisan St
Apt 2
Portland, OR 97209-1151, USA

Jones, Glenn (Musician)
Universal Attractions
145 W 57th St
#1500
New York, NY 10019, USA

Jones, Gordon (Athlete, Football Player)
18919 Fishermans Bend Drive
Lutz, FL 33558, USA

Jones, Grace (Actor, Model, Musician)
Wall of Sound
24 Farm Lane Trading
London SW6 1QJ, UNITED KINGDOM

Jones, Greg (Athlete, Baseball Player)
14260 Passage Way
Seminole, FL 33776-1001, USA

Jones, Greg (Athlete, Football Player)
2331 S Frenton Dr
Lakewood, CO 80227, USA

Jones, Greg (Skier)
PO Box 500
Tahoe City, CA 96145, USA

Jones, Gregory M (Athlete, Football
Player)
3203 Kirby Ln
Walnut Creek, CA 94598, USA

Jones, Griff Rhys (Actor, Producer, Writer)
c/o Staff Member TalkBack Management
20-21 Newman St
London W1T 1PG, UNITED KINGDOM
(UK)

Jones, Grover (Deacon) (Athlete, Baseball
Player)
1015 Goldfinch Ave
Sugar Land, TX 77478-3452, USA

Jones, Gwyneth (Opera Singer)
PO Box 556
Zurich 8037, SWITZERLAND

Jones, Hal (Athlete, Baseball Player)
17700 Avalon Blvd #67
Carson, CA 90746, USA

Jones, Hassan (Athlete, Football Player)
1010 Eldridge St
Clearwater, FL 33755-4205, USA

Jones, Hayes W (Athlete, Olympic
Athlete, Track Athlete)
1040 James K Blvd
Pontiac, MI 48341, USA

Jones, Henry (Hank) (Musician)
Joel Chriss
300 Mercer St
#3J
New York, NY 10003, USA

Jones, Herita (Stylist)
908 Tipperary Dr
Greensboro, NC 27406, USA

Jones, Homer C (Athlete, Football Player)
416 S Texas St
Pittsburg, TX 75686, USA

Jones, Horace (Athlete, Football Player)
7925 Hobart Ave
Pensacola, FL 32534, USA

Jones, Howard (Musician)
Howard Jones Music
Alexander Road
Aylesbury HP20 2NR, United Kingdom

Jones, Jack (Musician)
c/o Staff Member International Ventures
25115 Avenue Stanford Ste 102
Valencia, CA 91355, USA

Jones, Jacque (Athlete, Baseball Player,
Olympic Athlete)
347 Saint Rita Ct
San Diego, CA 92113, USA

Jones, James (Athlete, Football Player)
1009 Hunters Creek Dr
Carrollton, TX 75007, USA

Jones, James (Athlete, Football Player)
P.O. Box 22694
Kansas City, MO 64113, USA

Jones, James (Athlete, Football Player)
9481 Highland Oak Dr
Unit 1815
Tampa, FL 33647, USA

Jones, James C (Athlete, Football Player)
2 Odyssey Dr
Tinley Park, IL 60477, USA

Jones, James Earl (Actor)
Horatio Productions
P.O. Box 610
Pawling, NY 12564, USA

Jones, James (Jimmy) (Athlete, Basketball
Player)
14700 Marvin Ln
Southwest Ranches, FL 33330-3404, USA

Jones, Jamie (Musician)
MPI Talent
9255 Sunset Blvd
#407
Los Angeles, CA 90069, USA

Jones, Janet (Actor)
9100 Wilshire Blvd
#1000W
Beverly Hills, CA 90212, USA

Jones, January (Actor)
c/o Paul Nelson Mosaic Media Group
9200 W. Sunset Blvd
10th Floor
Los Angeles, CA 90069, USA

Jones, Jason (Actor)
c/o Jay Gassner United Talent Agency
(UTA)
9336 Civic Center Dr
Beverly Hills, CA 90210, USA

Jones, Jason (Athlete, Baseball Player)
1125 Oakview Dr SE
Smyrna, GA 30080-7917, USA

Jones, Jeff (Coach)
University of Virginia
Athletic Dept
Charlottesville, VA 22903, USA

Jones, Jeff (Athlete, Baseball Player)
51 Emmons Ct
Wyandotte, MI 48192, USA

Jones, Jeff (Athlete, Baseball Player)
311 White Horse Pike
Haddon Heights, NJ 08035, USA

Jones, Jeffrey (Actor)
7336 Santa Monica Blvd
#691
West Hollywood, CA 90046, USA

Jones, Jenny (Comedian)
c/o Gail Stocker Gail Stocker Presents
1025 N Kings Rd #113
Los Angeles, CA 90069, USA

Jones, Jermaine (Athlete, Football Player)
1522 Victor II Blvd
Morgan City, LA 70380-2120, USA

Jones, Jermaine (Musician)
c/o Staff Member 19 Entertainment - LA
9000 W Sunset Blvd #1574
West Hollywood, CA 90069, USA

Jones, Jerry (Misc)
4400 Preston Rd
Dallas, TX 75205-3722, USA

Jones, Jerry (Business Person, Football
Executive)
4400 Preston Rd
Dallas, TX 75205-3722, USA

Jones, Jill Marie (Actor)
c/o Peggy Rudman Identity Talent Agency
(ID)
9107 Wilshire Blvd
Suite 500
Beverly Hills, CA 90210, USA

Jones, Jim (Musician)
c/o Gordon MacDonald Buchwald/
Fortitude (LA)
6500 Wilshire Blvd
Suite 2200
Los Angeles, CA 90048, USA

Jones, Jimmie (Athlete, Football Player)
2658 Unicorn Ct
Herndon, VA 20171, USA

Jones, Jimmie (Athlete, Football Player)
204 Moss Dr
Cedar Hill, TX 75104, USA

Jones, Jimmy (Athlete, Hockey Player)
12 Aspen Leaf Crt
Aurora, ON L4G 7T3, Canada

Jones, Jimmy (Athlete, Baseball Player)
3054 Newcastle Dr
Dallas, TX 75220-1636, USA

Jones, joe (Athlete, Baseball Player)
2411 Carlisle Pl
Sarasota, FL 34231-7013, USA

Jones, Joe (Athlete, Football Player)
1413 Scott Ct
Irving, TX 75060, USA

Jones, Joey (Athlete, Football Player)
4032 Royal Oak Cir
Mountain Brk, AL 35243-5831, USA

Jones, John E (Athlete, Football Player)
19610 100th Ave NE
Bothell, WA 98011, USA

Jones, John Marshall
1801 Ave. of the Stars #307
Los Angeles, CA 90067

Jones, John Paul (Musician)
Opium Arts
49 Portland Road
London W11 4LJ, UNITED KINGDOM
(UK)

Jones, Julia (Actor)
c/o Evan Hainey Untitled Entertainment
(LA)
350 S. Beverly Dr #200
Beverly Hills, CA 90212, USA

Jones, Julio (Football Player)
c/o Pat Dye Jr SportsTrust Advisors - GA
3340 Peachtree Rd NE
16th Floor
Atlanta, GA 30326, USA

Jones, June S (Athlete, Coach, Football
Coach, Football Player)
6024 Airline Road
Dallas, TX 75205, USA

Jones, K C (Athlete, Basketball Player,
Olympic Athlete)
Basketball Hall of Fame 1000 Hall of
Fame Ave
1000 Hall of Fame Ave
Ste 100
Springfield, MA 01105-2545, USA

Jones, K C (Athlete, Football Player)
102 N Atlantic Dr
Lantana, FL 33462-1914, USA

Jones, KC (Athlete, Basketball Player)
Basketball Hall of Fame
1000 Hall of Fame Ave Ste 100
Springfield, MA 01105-2545, USA

Jones, Keith (Athlete, Hockey Player)
c/o Staff Member Versus Network
281 Tresser Blvd
Floor 9
Stamford, CT 06901, USA

Jones, Keith (Athlete, Hockey Player)
Philadelphia Flyers
3601 S Broad St Ste 2
Attn Broadcast Dept
Philadelphia, PA 19148-S297, USA

Jones, Kelly (Musician)
Marsupial Mgmt
Home Farm
Welfor Newbury
Berkshire RG20 8HR, UNITED
KINGDOM (UK)

Jones, Ken (Athlete, Football Player)
4455 Porter Rd
Niagara Falls, NY 14305, USA

Jones, Kenneth V (Actor)
PRS
29/33 Berners St
London W1P 4AA, ENGLAND

Jones, Kent (Athlete, Golfer)
5108 Coyote Hill Way NW
Albuquerque, NM 87120, USA

Jones, Kim (Athlete, Football Player)
1396 Madison Ave
Apt 150
Loveland, CO 80537, USA

Jones, Kimberly (Commentator)
20 Sherry Ln
Saddle Brook, NJ 07663-5935, USA

Jones, Larry (Athlete, Basketball Player)
1442 Cottingham Ct W
Columbus, OH 43209-3144, USA

Jones, LeRoi (Imamu Amiri Baraka)
(Writer)
State University of New York
Afro American Studies Dept
Stony Brook, NY 11794, USA

Jones, Leroy (Athlete, Football Player)
347 Kantor Blvd
Casselberry, FL 32707-5760, USA

Jones, Levi (Athlete, Football Player)
1449 W Bahia Ct
Gilbert, AZ 85233-5601, USA

Jones, Lolo (Athlete, Olympic Athlete, Track Athlete)
Lolo Jones Management
c/o Angelia Jefferson
PO Box 82226
Baton Rouge, LA 70884, USA

Jones, L Q (Actor)
2144 1/2 N Cahuenga Blvd
Los Angeles, CA 90068, USA

Jones, Lyle V (Misc)
RR 7
Pittsboro, NC 27312, USA

Jones, Lynn (Athlete, Baseball Player)
9959 Dicksonburg Rd
Conneautville, PA 16406-1817, USA

Jones, Lynn (General)
1907 Miller Ave
Mission, TX 78572-2957, USA

Jones, Major (Athlete, Basketball Player)
2475 Brandy Mill Rd
Houston, TX 77067-1275, USA

Jones, Malia (Actor, Athlete)
c/o Michelle Henderson *Henderson & Romo*
100 Universal City Plz
7152
Universal City, CA 91608, USA

Jones, Mandana (Actor)
CAM
19 Denmark Street
London WC2H 8NA, England

Jones, Marcus (Athlete, Football Player)
18701 Pepper Pike
Lutz, FL 33558, USA

Jones, Marcus (Athlete, Baseball Player)
20375 Longbay Dr
Yorba Linda, CA 92887-3250, USA

Jones, Marilyn (Actor)
Kaplan-Stahler Agency
8383 Wilshire Blvd
#923
Beverly Hills, CA 90211, USA

Jones, Marvin (Athlete, Baseball Player)
4134 12th St
Ecorse, MI 48229, USA

Jones, Marvin (Athlete, Football Player)
536 N Biscayne River Dr
Miami, FL 33169, USA

Jones, Marvin M (Athlete, Football Player)
8891 NW 193rd St
Miami, FL 33157, USA

Jones, Matt (Athlete, Football Player)
13838 Bella Riva Ln
Rogers, FL 32225-5434, USA

Jones, Maurice (Athlete, Football Player)
13649 Marsh Harbor Dr N
Jacksonville, FL 32225-2642, USA

Jones, Maxine (Musician)
East West Records
75 Rockefeller Plaza
#1200
New York, NY 10019, USA

Jones, Merlakia (Basketball Player)
Cleveland Rockers
Gund Arena
1 Center Court
Cleveland, OH 44115, USA

Jones, Mick (Musician)
c/o Staff Member *Sanctuary Artist Management (UK)*
Sanctuary House
45-53 Sinclair Road
London W14 0NS, UNITED KINGDOM

Jones, Mick (Musician)
Hard to Handle Mgmt
16501 Ventura Blvd
#602
Encino, CA 91436, USA

Jones, Mickey (Actor, Musician)
c/o Staff Member *Hervey/Grimes Talent Agency*
10561 Missouri Ave
Suite 2
Los Angeles, CA 90025, USA

Jones, Mike (Athlete, Baseball Player)
6761 Atlantic Blvd
Jacksonville, FL 32211-8729, USA

Jones, Mike (Musician)
c/o Staff Member *Warner Bros*
4000 Warner Blvd
#16
Burbank, CA 91522, USA

Jones, Mike A (Athlete, Football Player)
422 Davis Rd
Lebanon, TN 37087-0901, USA

Jones, Nasir (Nas) (Actor, Musician)
c/o Staff Member *SMC Europe*
14 Bowling Green Ln
Clerkenwell
London EC1R OBD, UK

Jones, Nathan (Actor)
c/o Rick Bassman *Cunningham Escott Slevin & Doherty (CESD-LA)*
10635 Santa Monica Blvd
130
Los Angeles, CA 90025, USA

Jones, Nathaniel R (Judge)
US Court of Appeals
US Courthouse
425 Walnut St
Cincinnati, OH 45202, USA

Jones, Norah (Musician)
c/o John Silva *SAM*
722 Seward St
Los Angeles, CA 90038, USA

Jones, Odell (Athlete, Baseball Player)
5831 Opal Ave
Palmdale, CA 93552-3967, USA

Jones, Orlando (Actor)
c/o Chuck Jones *Linasea Corp*
8306 Wilshire Blvd
Suite #432
Beverly Hills, CA 90211, USA

Jones, Ozell (Athlete, Basketball Player)
2220 Chestnut Ave Apt 1
Long Beach, CA 90806-4258, USA

Jones, Parnelli (Race Car Driver)
PO Box 1 W
Torrance, CA 90507, USA

Jones, Patrick (Actor)
c/o Staff Member *Martin Weiss Management*
PO Box 5656
Santa Monica, CA 90409-5656, USA

Jones, Patti (Stylist)
10387 Howling Coyote Ave
Las Vegas, NV 89135, USA

Jones, Peter (Business Person)
Peter Jones TV
Palliser House, Palliser Rd
West Kensington
London W14 9EB, UK

Jones, P. J. (Race Car Driver)
2334 S. Broadway
Box 2186
Santa Ana, CA 02708, USA

Jones, PJ (Race Car Driver)
Patrick Racing
8431 Georgetown Road
Indianapolis, IN 46268, USA

Jones, Preston (Athlete, Football Player)
116 Hamilton Dr
Anderson, SC 29621, USA

Jones, Preston (Actor)
c/o Alan Iezman *Shelter Entertainment*
9454 Wilshire Blvd.
Suite 715
Beverly Hills, CA 90212, USA

Jones, Quincy (Actor, Musician, Producer)
Quincy Jones Music Publishing
6671 Sunset Blvd
#1574A
Los Angeles, CA 90028, USA

Jones, Randy (Athlete, Baseball Player)
Major League Protection Systems 7668 El Camino Real, Ste 104-435
Carlbad, CA 92009-7932, USA

Jones, Randy (Athlete, Hockey Player)
7 Red Fox Trail
Sicklersville, NJ 08081-3709, USA

Jones, Rashida (Actor, Musician)
c/o Andrea Pett-Joseph *Brillstein Entertainment Partners*
9150 Wilshire Blvd #350
Beverly Hills, CA 90212, USA

Jones, Rebecca (Actor)
c/o Gabriel Blanco *Gabriel Blanco Iglesias (Mexico)*
Rio Balsas 35-32
Colonia Cuauhtemoc
DF 06500, Mexico

Jones, Rees (Athlete, Golfer)
10 Belleclaire Pl
Montclair, NJ 07044, USA

Jones, Reginald V (Physicist)
8 Queen's Terrace
Aberdeen AB1 1XL, SCOTLAND

Jones, Renee (Actor)
256 S Robertson Blvd
#700
Beverly Hills, CA 90211, USA

Jones, Rich (Athlete, Basketball Player)
101 Luna Way Apt 232
Las Vegas, NV 89145-0187, USA

Jones, Richard T (Actor)
c/o Doug Wald *Anonymous Content (LA)*
3531 Hayden Ave
Culver City, CA 90232, USA

Jones, Richard Timothy
584 Broadway #1009
New York, NY 10012

Jones, Rick (Athlete, Baseball Player)
PO Box 440981
Jacksonville, FL 32222, USA

Jones, Rickie Lee (Musician, Songwriter)
c/o Ron Stone *Gold Mountain Entertainment*
2 Music Cir S #212
Nashville, TN 37203, USA

Jones, Ricky (Athlete, Baseball Player)
1832 Brickyard Rd
Comer, GA 30629-3222, USA

Jones, Robert (Athlete, Football Player)
728 Barton Creek Blvd
Austin, TX 78746-4142, USA

Jones, Robert (K C) (Athlete, Basketball Player, Coach)
c/o Staff Member *Naismith Memorial Basketball Hall of Fame*
1000 West Columbus Avenue
Springfield, MA 01105, USA

Jones, Robin (Athlete, Basketball Player)
16640 Cynthia Ct
Tinley Park, IL 60477-8209, USA

Jones, Rod (Athlete, Football Player)
1121 Angie Ln
Desoto, TX 75115-3873, USA

Jones, Roger (Athlete, Football Player)
712 Trebor Dr
Goodlettsville, TN 37072, USA

Jones, Ron (Athlete, Hockey Player)
301 Brock St
Coppell, TX 75019, USA

Jones, Ronald (Popeye) (Athlete, Basketball Player)
29 Bass Pond Dr
Frisco, TX 75034-1937, USA

Jones, Rondell (Athlete, Football Player)
421 Competition Rd
Raleigh, NC 27603-1962, USA

Jones, Rosie (Athlete, Golfer)
4895 High Point Rd NE
Atlanta, GA 30342, USA

Jones, Ross (Athlete, Baseball Player)
4135 Eastridge Cir
Pompano Beach, FL 33064-1847, USA

Jones, Rulon K (Athlete, Football Player)
4003 N 3775 E
Eden, UT 84310, USA

Jones, Ruppert (Athlete, Baseball Player)
Major League Protection Systems 7668 El Camino Real Ste 104-435
carlshbad, CA 92009-7932, USA

Jones, Rushen (Athlete, Football Player)
2316 E Fraktur Rd
Phoenix, AZ 85040-3490, USA

Jones, Sam (Athlete, Basketball Player)
338 S Hampton Club Way
Saint Augustine, FL 32092-1031, USA

Jones, Sean (Athlete, Football Player)
4602 McKeever Ln
Missouri City, TX 77459, USA

Jones, Selwyn (Athlete, Football Player)
11216 Grimes Ave
Pearland, TX 77584-5524, USA

Jones, Shelton (Athlete, Basketball Player)
8112 Lockman Ln
Charlotte, NC 28269-5192, USA

Jones, Shirley (Actor, Musician)
4531 Noeline Way
Encino, CA 91436, USA

Jones, Simon (Actor)
Innovative Artists
1505 10th St
Santa Monica, CA 90401, USA

Jones, Sir Charles
Hep'me Records
3947 Cox's Ferry Rd
Bolton, MS 39041, USA

Jones, Spike (Athlete, Football Player)
3612 Club Dr NW
Kennesaw, GA 30144, USA

Jones, Stacey (Stylist)
c/o Staff Member *Fifty8 Artists*
58 W Huron St
Chicago, IL 60610, USA

Jones, Stacy (Athlete, Baseball Player)
1777 Ponderosa Rd
Attalla, AL 35954-5653, USA

Jones, Star (Actor, Producer, Talk Show Host)
c/o Tamara Houston *Round Table Entertainment*
509 N Fairfax Ave
Suite 200
Los Angeles, CA 90036, USA

Jones, Stephen (Lawyer)
Jones & Wyatt
PO Box 472
Enid, OK 73702, USA

Jones, Stephen J M (Designer, Fashion Designer)
36 Great Queen St
London WC1E 6BT, UNITED KINGDOM (UK)

Jones, Steve (Athlete, Baseball Player)
8116 Kingsdale Dr
Knoxville, TN 37919-7005, USA

Jones, Steve (Football Player)
12774 Fee Fee Rd
Saint Louis, MO 63146-4402, USA

Jones, Steve (Musician)
Solo Agency
55 Fulham High St
London SW6 3JJ, UNITED KINGDOM (UK)

Jones, Steve (Athlete, Basketball Player)
8303 Quebec Dr
Houston, TX 77096-1034, USA

Jones, Steven (Physicist)
Brigham Young University
Physics Dept
Provo, UT 84602, USA

Jones, Tamala (Actor)
c/o Danielle Allman-Del *D2 Management*
9255 Sunset Blvd
Suite 600
Los Angeles, CA 90069, USA

Jones, Taylor (Cartoonist)
Times-Mirror Syndicate
Times-Mirror Square
Los Angeles, CA 90053, USA

Jones, Tebucky (Athlete, Football Player)
77 Ely Rd
Farmington, CT 06032-1706, USA

Jones, Terry (Actor, Director, Writer)
Python Pictures
34 Thistlewaite Rd
London E5 QQQ, UNITED KINGDOM

Jones, Thomas (Athlete, Football Player)
2742 Clinch Haven Rd
Big Stone Gap, VA 24219-4158, USA

Jones, Thomas D (Astronaut)
2026 Beacon Heights Drive
Reston, VA 77586-6475, USA

Jones, thomas F (Athlete, Baseball Player)
13846 Atlantic Blvd A_pj: 509
Jacksonville, FL 32225-3286, USA

Jones, Thomas V (Business Person)
1050 Moraga Dr
Los Angeles, CA 90049, USA

Jones, Tim (Athlete, Baseball Player)
30 Chicot Dr
Maumelle, AR 72113, USA

Jones, Tim (Athlete, Baseball Player)
6049 Roloff Way
Orangevale, CA 95662-4544, USA

Jones, Toby (Actor)
c/o Billy Lazarus *United Talent Agency (UTA)*
9336 Civic Center Dr
Beverly Hills, CA 90210, USA

Jones, Todd B G (Athlete, Baseball Player)
421 Eagle Pointe Dr
Pell City, AL 35128-7266, USA

Jones, Tom (Musician)
c/o Donna Woodward *Valley Music, Ltd*
Prefers to be contacted via telephone
Oxforshire, England

Jones, Tommy Lee (Actor)
P.O. Box 966
San Saba, TX 76877, USA

Jones, Tony (Athlete, Football Player)
Exquisite Cuts 1820 N Brown Rd Ste 40
Lawrenceville, GA 30043-1800, USA

Jones, Tracy (Athlete, Baseball Player)
101 Harbor Green Dr
Apt 602
Bellevue, KY 41073-1155, USA

Jones, Trevor (Composer)
46 Ave Road Highgate
London N6 5DR, UNITED KINGDOM (UK)

Jones, Ty (Athlete, Hockey Player)
11803 E 20th Ave
Spokane Valley, WA 99206-7002, USA

Jones, Tyler Patrick (Actor)
House of Representatives
400 S Beverly Dr #214
Beverly Hills, CA 90212, USA

Jones, Vaughan F R (Mathematician)
University of California
Mathematics Dept
Berkeley, CA 94720, USA

Jones, Victor (Athlete, Football Player)
17727 Sedona Way
Cornelius, NC 28031-8766, USA

Jones, Victor T (Athlete, Football Player)
PO Box 132241
Dallas, TX 75313-2241, USA

Jones, Vinnie (Actor, Producer)
c/o Alex Cole *Elevate Entertainment*
10100 Santa Monica Blvd.
Suite 300
Los Angeles, CA 90067, USA

Jones, Volus
625 S. Griffith Park Dr
Burbank, CA 91506

Jones, Wali (Athlete, Basketball Player)
3160 SW 132nd Ave
Miramar, FL 33027-3868, USA

Jones, Wallace (Athlete, Basketball Player, Olympic Athlete)
512 Chinoe Road
Lexington, KY 40502-2402, USA

Jones, Walter (Athlete, Football Player)
520 Raymond Pl NW
Renton, WA 98057-3432, USA

Jones, Walter Emanuel (Actor)
K & K Entertainment
1498 W Sunset Blvd
Los Angeles, CA 90026, USA

Jones, Wayne (Actor, Comedian)
Smooth Man Productions
206 Belmont Dr
Palatka, FL 32177, USA

Jones, Wesley (Architect)
Holt Hinshaw Jones
320 Florida St
San Francisco, CA 94110, USA

Jones, Wilbert (Athlete, Basketball Player)
3360 Idlecreek Way
Decatur, GA 30034-4916, USA

Jones, William A (Dub) (Athlete, Football Player)
904 Glendale Dr
Ruston, LA 71270, USA

Jones, Willie D (Athlete, Football Player)
4440 Hidden Orchard Ln
Indianapolis, IN 46228, USA

Jones Cox, Vena (Business Person)
Real Life Real Estate
PO Box 58279
Cincinnati, OH 45258, USA

Jones-Doxey, Marilyn (Athlete, Baseball Player, Commentator)
5058 Red Oak Pl
Bradenton, FL 34207-2245, USA

Jones Girls, The
PO Box 6010 #761
Sherman Oaks, CA 91413-6010

Jones III, Samuel L (Actor)
c/o Staff Member *Abrams Artists Agency (LA)*
9200 Sunset Blvd
11th Floor
Los Angeles, CA 90069, USA

Jones Jr, James L (General)
Supreme Allied Commander
Supreme Headquarters
APO, AE 09705, USA

Jones Jr, Robert Trent (Athlete, Golfer)
1900 S Ocean Dr
Apt 1612
Fort Lauderdale, FL 33316, USA

Jones Jr, Roy (Actor, Boxer, Producer, Sportscaster)
c/o Darren Prince *Prince Marketing Group*
18 Carillon Cir
Livingston, NJ 07039, USA

Jones-Thompson, Marion (Athlete, Olympic Athlete, Track Athlete)
13532 Utah Flats Dr
Austin, TX 78727-6362, USA

Jong, Erica (Writer)
121 Davis Hill Rd.
Weston, CT 06883-2015, USA

Jon-Jules, Danny (Actor)
BBC Information - Artist Mail
PO Box 1116
Belfast B3Z 7AJ, UK

Jonrowe, Dee Dee (Athlete)
PO Box 272
Willow, AK 99688, USA

Jonsen, Albert R (Doctor)
University of Washington
Med School
Medical Ethics Dept
Seattle, WA 98195, USA

Jonson, Johnny (Athlete, Football Player)
P.O. Box 4283
Mooresville, NC 28117, USA

Jonsson, Hans (Athlete, Hockey Player)
Lakasund 1S9
Bonassund, Sweden 891 78, USA

Jonsson, Jorgen (Athlete, Hockey Player)
2000 E Gene Autry Way
Anaheim, CA 92806, USA

Jonsson, Tomas
Denmark Ice Hockey Union Fodboldens
Hvs DBU Aile 1
Brondbv, Denmark 260S, USA

Jonze, Spike (Actor, Director)
c/o Staff Member *Dickhouse Productions*
5555 Melrose Ave
Los Angeles, CA 90038, USA

Joop, Wolfgang (Designer, Fashion Designer)
Joop
Harvestehuder Weg 22
Hamburg 20149, GERMANY

Joost, Henry (Director)
c/o Rowena Arguelles *Creative Artists Agency (CAA-LA)*
2000 Ave Of The Stars
Los Angeles, CA 90067, USA

Jophery, Brown (Athlete, Baseball Player)
3008 W 81st St
Inglewood, CA 90305-1425, USA

Joplin, Josh (Musician)
c/o Staff Member *MCT Management*
520 8th Ave Rm 2205
New York, NY 10018, USA

Jopling, Jay (Business Person)
White Cube
144 - 152 Bermondsey St
London SE1 3TQ, UK

Jopling, T Michael (Government Official)
Ainderby Hall
Thirsk
North Yorks YO7 4HZ, UNITED KINGDOM (UK)

Jorane (Composer, Musician)
c/o Staff Member *Greenspan Artist Management*
8760 W Sunset Blvd
West Hollywood, CA 90069, USA

Jordan, Anthony (Athlete, Football Player)
38 Albemarle St
Rochester, NY 14613, USA

Jordan, Brian (Athlete, Baseball Player)
Brian Jordan Foundation
3746 Scalding Park Dr
Norcross, GA 30092-2632, USA

Jordan, Brian (Athlete, Football Player)
3746 Spalding Park Dr
Norcross, GA 30092-2632, USA

Jordan, Buford (Athlete, Football Player)
11 Acadia St
Kenner, LA 70065, USA

Jordan, Cameron (Cam) (Football Player)
c/o Doug Hendrickson *Octagon Football*
832 Sansome St.
1st Floor
San Francisco, CA 94111, USA

Jordan, Claudia (Actor, Television Host)
c/o Laura Wright *Avid Exposure*
8721 W Sunset Blvd
Suite P3
West Hollywood, CA 90069, USA

Jordan, Curtis (Athlete, Football Player)
629 Surfside Ave
Virginia Beach, VA 23451-3658, USA

Jordan, Darin (Athlete, Football Player)
44 Connell Dr
Stoughton, MA 02072, USA

Jordan, Don (Boxer)
5100 2nd Ave
Los Angeles, CA 90043, USA

Jordan, Don D (Business Person)
Reliant Energy
1111 Louisiana Ave
Houston, TX 77002, USA

Jordan, Eddie (Athlete, Basketball Player)
158 Monroe Ave
Belle Mead, NJ 08502-4632, USA

Jordan, Glenn (Director)
9401 Wilshire Blvd
#700
Beverly Hills, CA 90212, USA

Jordan, Hamilton (Actor)
The Harry Walker Agency Inc
355 Lexington Avenue 21st Fl
New York, NY 10017, USA

Jordan, I King (Educator)
Gallaudet University
President's Office
800 Florida NW
Washington, DC 20001, USA

Jordan, Jeremy (Actor, Musician)
c/o Ted Schachter *Schachter Entertainment*
1157 S Beverly Dr Fl 2
Los Angeles, CA 90035, USA

Jordan, Jim (Congressman, Politician)
1524 Longworth HOB
Washington, DC 20515, USA

Jordan, Kathy (Tennis Player)
114 Walter Hays Dr
Palo Alto, CA 94303, USA

Jordan, Kevin (Athlete, Baseball Player)
127 Ney St
San Francisco, CA 94112-1642, USA

Jordan, Lamont (Athlete, Football Player)
1407 Alberta Dr
Forestville, MD 20747, USA

Jordan, Larry (Athlete, Football Player)
4780 Kirk Rd
Youngstown, OH 44515-5403, USA

Jordan, Larry R (General)
Deputy Commander in Chief
US Army Europe/7th Army
APO, AE 09014, USA

Jordan, Laura (Actor)
c/o Matthew Lesher *Insight*
1134 S Cloverdale Ave
Los Angeles, CA 90019, USA

Jordan, Leander (Athlete, Football Player)
1661 Peachtree Cir N
Jacksonville, FL 32207-6423, USA

Jordan, Lee Roy (Athlete, Football Player)
7710 Caruth Blvd
Dallas, TX 75225, USA

Jordan, Le Roy
2425 Burbank St.
Dallas, TX 75235-3196

Jordan, Leslie (Actor)
c/o Billy Miller *Billy Miller Management*
8322 Ridpath Dr
Los Angeles, CA 90046, USA

Jordan, Mary (Journalist)
Washington Post
Editorial Dept
1150 15th St NW
Washington, DC 20071, USA

Jordan, Michael (Athlete, Basketball Player, Olympic Athlete)
2022 Windy Hill Ln
Highland Park, IL 60035-4234, USA

Jordan, Montell (Musician)
c/o Staff Member *Richard De La Font Agency*
3808 W South Park Blvd
Broken Arrow, OK 74011, USA

Jordan, Neil (Director, Writer)
c/o Staff Member *WmE2 (WMA-LA)*
1 William Morris Pl
Beverly Hills, CA 90212, USA

Jordan, Neil P (Director)
6 Sorrento Terrace
Dalkey
County Dublin, IRELAND

Jordan, Patty (Athlete, Golfer)
4372 Twilight Ln
Hamburg, NY 14075, USA

Jordan, Randy (Athlete, Football Player)
2220 Rockingham Loop
College Station, TX 77845-4854, USA

Jordan, Ricardo (Athlete, Baseball Player)
Arcadia Road Prison 13617 SE Highway 70 # B04316
arcadia, FL 34266-7800, USA

Jordan, Ricky (Athlete, Baseball Player)
965 Moonlit Way
Folsom, CA 95630-7506, USA

Jordan, Scott (Athlete, Baseball Player)
265 Great Oak Dr
Athens, GA 30605-4504, USA

Jordan, Scott (Athlete)
1530 Carroll Drive NW
Suite 103
Atlanta, GA 30318-3600, USA

Jordan, Shelby (Athlete, Football Player)
29208 Posey Way
Rancho Palos Verdes, CA 90275, USA

Jordan, Stanley (Musician)
SJ Productions
16845 N 29th Ave
#2000
Phoenix, AZ 85053, USA

Jordan, Steve (Athlete, Football Player)
1762 Magnolia Cir
Pleasanton, CA 94566-4764, USA

Jordan, Tom (Athlete, Baseball Player)
15 Dulce Rd
Santa Fe, NM 87508-8284, USA

Jordan, Tony (Athlete, Football Player)
38 Albemarle St
Rochester, NY 14613-1402, USA

Jordanaires, The
46-19 220th Pl.
Bayside, NY 11361-3654

Jordan Jr, Vernon E (Civil Rights Activist, Politician)
Lazard Freres
30 Rockefeller Plz
#400
New York, NY 20008-2718, USA

Jordanova, Vera (Actor, Model)
c/o Alix Gucovsky *Special Artists Agency*
9465 Wilshire Blvd #820
Beverly Hills, CA 90212, USA

Jorden, Tim (Athlete, Football Player)
11402 N 26th Pl
Scottsdale, AZ 85260, USA

Jordensen, Anker (Prime Minister)
Borgbjergvej 1
Copenhagen, SV 2450, DENMARK

Jordenson, Dale W (Economist)
1010 Memorial Dr
#14C
Cambridge, MA 02138, USA

Jordison, Joey (Musician)
c/o Staff Member *Gersh (NY)*
41 Madison Ave
New York, NY 10010, USA

Jorgensen, Bodil (Actor)
c/o Lene Seested *Panorama Agency*
Ryesgade 103B
CopenHagen DK-2100, Denmark

Jorgensen, Mike (Athlete, Baseball Player, Coach)
1820 Harbor Mill Dr
Fenton, MO 63026-2653, USA

Jorgensen, Roger (Athlete, Basketball Player)
642 Woodcrest Dr
Pittsburgh, PA 15205-1520, USA

Jorgensen, Ryan (Athlete, Baseball Player)
5 Links Ct
Kingwood, TX 77339-5326, USA

Jorgensen, Terry (Athlete, Baseball Player)
1493 S Sugar Bush Rd
Luxemburg, WI 54217-9311, USA

Jorginho (Soccer Player)
Rua Levi Carreiro 420
Barra de Tijuca, BRAZIL

Jose, Felix (Athlete, Baseball Player)
6814 W Calumet Cir
Lake Worth, FL 33467-7007, USA

Jose, Jose (Musician)
Fanny Schatz Mgmt
Melchor Ocampo 309
Mexico City, DF CP 11590, MEXICO

Jose, Lind (Baseball Player)
Pittsburgh Pirates
18 Villa Santa
Dorado, PR 00646-5770, USA

Josefowicz, Leila (Musician)
I M G Artists
420 W 45th St
New York, NY 10036, USA

Joseph, Chris (Athlete, Hockey Player)
17 L'Hirondelle Crt St
Albert
Edmonton, AB T8N SX9, Canada

Joseph, Curtis (Athlete, Hockey Player)
c/o Donald Meehan *Newport Sports Management*
201 City Centre Dr
Suite 400
Mississauga, ON L58 2T4, Canada

Joseph, Daryl J (Astronaut)
615 Peachtree Ct
Campbell, CA 95008-6353, USA

Joseph, Davin (Athlete, Football Player)
17912 Bimini Isle Ct
Tampa, FL 33647-2782, USA

Joseph, James (Athlete, Football Player)
8942 Stoneridge Pl
Montgomery, AL 36117-8876, USA

Joseph, Jeffrey
400 S. Beverly Dr. #102
Beverly Hills, CA 90212

Joseph, Kevin (Athlete, Baseball Player)
8826 Lacrosse Dr
Dallas, TX 75231-4826, USA

Joseph, Stephen (Doctor)
New York City Health Department
125 Worth St
New York, NY 10013, USA

Joseph, Vance (Athlete, Football Player)
1995 E Coalton Rd Apt 35-101
Superior, CO 80027-4426, USA

Joseph, William (Athlete, Football Player)
1071 NE 107th St
Miami, FL 33161-7353, USA

Joseph, William (Musician)
c/o Staff Member *MCT Management*
520 8th Ave Rm 2205
New York, NY 10018, USA

Joseph III, Joseph E (Doctor)
University of Michigan
Taubman Center
Ann Arbor, MI 48109, USA

Josephine, Charlotte (Royalty)
Grand Ducal Palace
Luxembourg, LUXEMBOURG

Josephs, Wilfred (Composer)
4 Grand Union Walk
Kentish Town Rd Camden Town
London NW1 9LP, UNITED KINGDOM (UK)

Josephson, Brian D (Nobel Prize Laureate)
Cavendish Laboratory
Madingley Road
Cambridge CB3 0HE, UNITED KINGDOM (UK)

Josephson, Karen (Swimmer)
1923 Junction Dr
Concord, CA 94518, USA

Josephson, Lester (Josey) (Athlete, Football Player)
5388 N Genernatas Dr
Tucson, AZ 85704, USA

Josephson, Sarah (Swimmer)
1923 Junction Dr
Concord, CA 94518, USA

Joshi, Indira (Actor)
c/o Staff Member *BBC Artist Mail*
PO Box 1116
Belfast BT2 7AJ, United Kingdom

Joshi, Pallavi (Actor, Bollywood, Talk Show Host)
23 Shefalee Makrand Soc
Veer Savarkar Rd Mahim
Bombay, MS 400016, INDIA

Joshua, Larry (Actor)
c/o Judy Orbach *Judy O Productions*
6136 Glen Holly
Hollywood, CA 90068, USA

Joshua, Von (Athlete, Baseball Player)
20922 E Glen Haven Cir
Northville, MI 48167-2465, USA

Jospin, Lionel R (Prime Minister)
Haute-Garonne Conseil
Place Saint Etienne
Toulouse Cedex 31090, FRANCE

Jost, Mike (Athlete, Baseball Player)
339 W Woodward St
Vail, AZ 85641-2036, USA

Jostyn, Jennifer (Actor)
c/o Staff Member *Abrams Artists Agency (LA)*
9200 Sunset Blvd
11th Floor
Los Angeles, CA 90069, USA

Josue, Steve (Athlete, Football Player)
18711 NE 3rd Ct Apt 215
Miami, FL 33179-3808, USA

Joswick, Bob (Athlete, Football Player)
5829 W Orlando Cir
Broken Arrow, OK 74011-1153, USA

Joswick, Robert (Athlete, Football Player)
10902 Wilson Ave
Alta Loma, CA 91737, USA

Jothilakshmi (Actor, Bollywood)
32 Sarangapani Street
T Nagar
Chennai, TN 600017, INDIA

Jothimeena (Actor, Bollywood)
32 Sarangapani Street
T Nagar
Chennai, TN 600017, INDIA

Joubert, Beverly (Photographer)
National Geographic Magazine
17th & M Sts NW
Washington, DC 20036, USA

Joubert, Brian (Figure Skater)
Federation Francaise des Sports De Glace
35 rue Felicien David
Paris 75016, FRANCE

Joubert, Dereck (Photographer)
National Geographic Magazine
17th & M Sts NW
Washington, DC 20036, USA

Joulwan, George A (General)
1348 S 19th St
Arlington, VA 22202, USA

Jourdain Jr, Michel (Race Car Driver)
Team Rahal
4601 Lyman Dr
Hillard, OH 43026, USA

Jourdan, Louis (Actor)
1139 Maybrook
Beverly Hills, CA 90210, USA

Journell, Jimmy (Athlete, Baseball Player)
1511 Eastgate Rd
Springfield, OH 45503-2427, USA

Journey (Music Group)
c/o Peter Grosslight *WME (LA)*
9601 Wilshire Blvd Fl 3
Beverly Hills, CA 90210, USA

Jovanovic, Pavle (Athlete, Bobsledder, Olympic Athlete)
701 W 189th St Apt 1H
New York, NY 10040-4041, USA

Jovanovich, Peter W (Publisher)
MacMillan
1177 Ave of Americas
#1965
New York, NY 10036, USA

Jovanovski, Ed (Athlete, Hockey Player)
528 E Alexander Palm Rd
Boca Raton, FL 33432-7985, USA

Jovovich, Milla (Actor, Model, Musician)
c/o Jason Weinberg *Untitled Entertainment (LA)*
350 S. Beverly Dr #200
Beverly Hills, CA 90212, USA

Jow, Malese (Actor)
c/o Christopher Ledford *Acumen Entertainment Partners*
201 N Hollywood Way
Suite 108
Burbank, CA 91505, USA

Jow, Melise (Actor)
c/o Glenn Hughes III *Gem Entertainment Group*
10701 Wilshire Blvd.
Ste. 1202
Los Angeles, CA 90024, USA

Joy, Kathryn (Stylist)
1679 Penny Lane
Bartlett, IL 60103, USA

Joy, Megan (Musician)

Joy, Mike (Race Car Driver)
111 Mystic Lake Loop
Mooresville, NC 28117-6000, USA

Joy, Robert (Actor)
c/o Donna Massetti *Silver Massetti & Szatmary (SMS) Talent Inc*
8383 Wilshire Blvd
Suite 230
Beverly Hills, CA 90211, USA

Joyal, Eddie (Athlete, Hockey Player)
6469 Wandermere Dr
San Diego, CA 92120-3214, USA

Joyce, Andrea (Correspondent, Sportscaster)
Arts & Entertainment
235 E 45th St
New York, NY 10017, USA

Joyce, Bob
700 Windgrove Trl
Maitland, FL 327Sl-S412, USA

Joyce, Delvin (Athlete, Football Player)
355 Trott Cir
Martinsville, VA 24112, USA

Joyce, Duane (Athlete, Hockey Player)
143 W Elm St
Pemboke, MA 023S9-2136, USA

Joyce, Elaine (Actor)
724 N Roxbury Dr
Beverly Hills, CA 90210, USA

Joyce, James (Baseball Player)
9785 SW 167th Pl
Beaverton, OR 97007-8705, USA

Joyce, James (Athlete, Baseball Player)
9785 SW 167th Pl
Beaverton, OR 97007, USA

Joyce, Jim (Athlete, Baseball Player)
9785 SW 167th Pl
Beaverton, OR 97007-8705, USA

Joyce, Joan (Athlete, Golfer)
20024 Back Nine Dr
Boca Raton, FL 33498, USA

Joyce, John T (Misc)
Bricklayers & Allied Craftsmen
815 15th St NW
Washington, DC 20005, USA

Joyce, Kara Lynn (Athlete, Olympic Athlete, Swimmer)
5973 Cedar Ridge Dr
Ann Arbor, MI 48103-8791, USA

Joyce, Kevin (Athlete, Basketball Player, Olympic Athlete)
420 W Olive St Apt 9
Long Beach, NY 11561-3128, USA

Joyce, Lisa (Actor)
c/o Staff Member *Stone Manners Salners Agency (LA)*
9911 W Pico Blvd Ste 1400
Los Angeles, CA 90035, USA

Joyce, Matt (Athlete, Football Player)
6330 E Wilshire Dr
Scottsdale, AZ 85257-1122, USA

Joyce, Matt (Athlete, Football Player)
3804 Villas Del Sol Ct
Tampa, FL 33609-4440, USA

Joyce, Mike (Athlete, Baseball Player)
1609 Whitman Ln
Wheaton, IL 60187-7445, USA

Joyce, Tom (Artist)
21 Likely Road
Santa Fe, NM 87508, USA

Joyce, William (Artist, Writer)
3302 Centenary Blvd
Shreveport, LA 71104, USA

Joyce, William H (Business Person)
Union Carbide
39 Old Ridgebury Road
Danbury, CT 06810, USA

Joyeux, Odette
1 rue Seguier
Paris, FRANCE 75006

Joyner, Alrederick (Al) (Athlete, Track Athlete)
CMG World Wide
8560 Sunset Blvd
10th Fl Penthouse
West Hollywood, CA 90069, USA

Joyner, Harry (Athlete, Basketball Player)
1100 N Alyssa Cir
Payson, AZ 85541-3371, USA

Joyner, Lisa (Television Host)
4202 Klump Ave
N Hollywood, CA 91602, USA

Joyner, Mark (Business Person, Writer)
Mark Joyner Inc
7426 Cherry Ave #210-150
Fontana, CA 92336, USA

Joyner, Michelle (Actor)
Paradigm Agency
10100 Santa Monica Blvd
#2500
Los Angeles, CA 90067, USA

Joyner, Seth (Athlete, Football Player)
5138 N 79th Pl
Scottsdale, AZ 85250-7209, USA

Joyner, Tom (Radio Personality)
PO Box 630495
Irving, TX 75063

Joyner, Wally (Athlete, Baseball Player)
516 E 2800 S
Mapleton, UT 84664-4850, USA

Joyner-Kersee, Jacqueline (Jackie) (Athlete, Olympic Athlete, Track Athlete)
Women's Sports Foundation
1049 Bristol Manor Dr
Ballwin, MO 63011-5106, USA

Jozwiak, Brian J (Athlete, Coach, Football Coach, Football Player)
203 Ruby Lake Ln
Winter Haven, FL 33884, USA

J. Rahall II, Nick (Congressman, Politician)
2307 Rayburn HOB
Washington, DC 20515, USA

J. Ribble, Reid (Congressman, Politician)
1513 Longworth HOB
Washington, DC 20515, USA

J. Rogers, Mike (Congressman, Politician)
133 Cannon HOB
Washington, DC 20515, USa

J. Rooney, Thomas (Congressman, Politician)
1529!-Qn.9WQrth HQB
Washington, DC 20515, USA

J. Roskam, Peter (Congressman, Politician)
227 Ca,rtn<m HOB
Washington, DC 20515, USA

J. Tiberi, Patrick (Congressman, Politician)
106 Cannon HOB
Washington, DC 20515, USA

Ju, Ming (Artist)
28 Lane 460
Chih Shan Road Section 2
Taipei, TAIWAN

Juanes (Musician)
c/o Staff Member *Fernan Martinez Communications*
180 NE 39 St
Miami Design District, FL 33178, USA

Juantorena Danger, Alberto (Athlete, Track Athlete)
National Institute for Sports
Sports City
Havana, CUBA

Juarez, Ricardo (Rocky) (Athlete, Boxer, Olympic Athlete)
3916 Weems St
Houston, TX 77009-4747, USA

Juchheim, Alwin (Politician)
939 Ave of Pines St
Grenada, MS 38901-4609, USA

Juckes, Gordon W (Misc)
1475 Avenue B
Big Pine Key, FL 33043, USA

Judd, Ashley (Actor)
c/o Annett Wolf *WKT Public Relations (WKT-LA)*
9350 Wilshire Blvd
Suite 450
Beverly Hills, CA 90212, USA

Judd, Cledus T
KOCH Records
22 Harbor Park Drive
Port Washington, NY 11050, USA

Judd, Cris (Actor, Choreographer)
c/o Monica Barkett *Global Artists Agency*
6253 Hollywood Blvd
Suite 508
Los Angeles, CA 90028, USA

Judd, Howard L (Misc)
University of California
Medical Center
Ob-Gyn Dept
Los Angeles, CA 90024, USA

Judd, Jackie (Correspondent)
ABC-TV
News Dept
77 W 66th St
New York, NY 10023, USA

Judd, Mike (Athlete, Baseball Player)
9805 Shadow Rd
La Mesa, CA 91941-4154, USA

Judd, Naomi (Musician)
c/o Julie Colbert *WME (LA)*
9601 Wilshire Blvd Fl 3
Beverly Hills, CA 90210, USA

Judd, Wynonna (Musician)
c/o Julie Colbert *WME (LA)*
9601 Wilshire Blvd Fl 3
Beverly Hills, CA 90210, USA

Juden, Jeff (Athlete, Baseball Player)
85 Proctor St
Salem, MA 01970-2110, USA

Judge, Christopher (Actor, Writer)
c/o Christina King *Pantheon Talent*
1900 Ave Of The Stars
Suite 2840
Los Angeles, CA 90067, USA

Judge, George (Economist)
University of California
Economics Dept
Berkeley, CA 94720, USA

Judge, Mike (Actor, Animator, Producer, Writer)
c/o Michael Rotenberg *3 Arts Entertainment Inc*
9460 Wilshire Blvd
7th Floor
Beverly Hills, CA 90210, USA

Judges, Gordon (Athlete, Football Player)
1782 Meadowview Ave
Pickering, ON L1V 3G8, Canada

Judkins, Jeff (Athlete, Basketball Player)
3471 S 3570 E
Salt Lake City, UT 84109-3243, USA

Judson, Howie (Athlete, Baseball Player)
239 Fairway Cir
Winter Haven, FL 33881-8742, USA

Judson, William (Athlete, Football Player)
652 Sinclair Way
Jonesboro, GA 30238, USA

Jue, Bhawoh (Athlete, Football Player)
4514 Billingham St
Fairfax, VA 22030-6195, USA

Juenger, David (Athlete, Football Player)
790 Cliffside Dr
Chillicothe, OH 45601, USA

Juergensen, Heather (Actor)
c/o Staff Member *Generate Management*
1545 26th St
Suite 200
Santa Monica, CA 90404, USA

Jugnauth, Anerood (Prime Minister)
La Caverne 1
Vacoas, MAURITIUS

Juhl, Finn (Designer)
Kratvaenget 15
Chartottenlund 2920, DENMARK

Jules, Gary (Musician)
c/o Staff Member *Paradigm (Monterey)*
404 W Franklin St
Monterey, CA 93940, USA

Julian, Fred (Athlete, Football Player)
730 Strawberry Valley Ave NW
Comstock Park, MI 49321, USA

Julian, Janet (Actor)
Borinstein Oreck Bogart
3172 Dona Susana Dr
Studio City, CA 91604, USA

Julian, Jonathan (Actor)
c/o Susan Nathe *Nathe & Associates*
8281 Melrose Ave #200
Los Angeles, CA 90046, USA

Julian II, Alexander (Designer, Fashion Designer)
Alexander Julian Inc
PO Box 60
Georgetown, CT 06829, USA

Julich, Bobby (Athlete, Cycler, Olympic Athlete)
998 Brush Creek Ln
Glenwood Springs, CO 81601-4502, USA

Julien, Claude (Athlete, Coach, Hockey Player)
c/o Staff Member *Boston Bruins*
TD Banknorth Garden
100 Legends Way, Suite 250
Boston, MA 02114, USA

Julien, Claude (Athlete, Hockey Player)
Boston Bruins
100 Legends Way Ste 2SO
Attn: Coaching Staff
Boston, MA 02114-1389, USA

Julien, Max (Actor)
3580 Avenida del Sol
Studio City, CA 91604, USA

Julio, Jorge (Athlete, Baseball Player)
4032 E Gardenia Ave
Weston, FL 33332-2453, USA

Julius, DeAnne (Economist)
Bank of England
Threadneedle St
London EC2R 8AH, UNITED KINGDOM (UK)

Jullen, Claude (Coach)
Montreal Canadiens
1260 de la Gauchetiere W
Montreal, QC H3B 5E8, CANADA

Juma, Kevin (Athlete, Football Player)
1120 Cliff Ave Apt 501
Tacoma, WA 98402-5132, USA

Jump 5 (Music Group)
c/o Staff Member *Bobby Roberts Agency*
P.O. Box 1547
Goodlettsville, TN 37072, USA

Jumper, John P (General)
Chief of Staff
HqUSAF Pentagon
Washington, DC 20330, USA

Junck, Mary (Publisher)
Baltimore Sun
501 N Calvert St
Baltimore, MD 21202, USA

Juncker, Jean-Claude (Prime Minister)
Hotel de Bourgogne
4 Rue de la Congregation
2910, LUXEMBOURG

June, Cato (Athlete, Football Player)
13500 Van Brady Rd
Upper Marlboro, MD 20772-7905, USA

Juneau, Joe (Athlete, Hockey Player)
Harfan Technologies Inc
100-2 rue de Jardin
Attn: VIce President's Office
Port-Rouge, QC G3H 3R7, Canada

Jung, Ernst (Writer)
8815 Lagenensligen/Wiltingen
GERMANY

Jung, Ji-Hoon (Rain) (Actor)
c/o Cho Dong Won *J.tune Entertainment*
2F, M Building 221-5
NonHyunDong GangNamGu
Seoul 135010, Korea

Jung, Richard (Misc)
Waldhofstr 42
Freiburg 71691, GERMANY

Jung, Werner (Aviator)
Eichendorffstrasse 1
Wiesbaden D-65187, Germany

Junge, Eric (Athlete, Baseball Player)
89 Clinton St Apt 2R
New York, NY 10002-3889, USA

Junger, Gil (Director, Producer)
c/o Staff Member *Creative Artists Agency (CAA-LA)*
2000 Ave Of The Stars
Los Angeles, CA 90067, USA

Junger, Sebastian (Writer)
United Talent Agency
9560 Wilshire Blvd
#500
Beverly Hills, CA 90212, USA

Jungman, Eric (Actor)
c/o Staff Member *Leslie Allan-Rice Management*
1007 Maybrook Dr
Beverly Hills, CA 90210, USA

Jungueira, Bruno (Race Car Driver)
2127 Brickell Ave
#3105
Miami, FL 33129, USA

Junior, Ester J (E J) (Athlete, Football Player)
911 W Summit St
Bolivar, MO 65613, USA

Junior Balaiya (Actor)
3 Melgai Vaniyagar Street
Vadapalani
Chennai, TN 600 026, INDIA

Junior Varsity (Music Group)
Victory Records
346 N Justine St Ste 504
Chicago, IL 60607, USA

Junker, Steve (Athlete, Football Player)
17S6 Thrums Rd
Castlegar, BC VlN 4N4, Canada

Junkin, Abner (Athlete, Football Player)
5 Lakeside Ln
Newport, AR 72112, USA

Junkin, Joe (Athlete, Hockey Player)
2319 Canby St
Harrisburg, PA 17103-1720, USA

Junkin, Trey (Athlete, Football Player)
300 Wren St
Winnfield, LA 71483, USA

Junqueira, Bruno (Race Car Driver)
721 Crandon Boulevard
Apt 308
Key Biscayne, FL 33149, USA

Juppe, Alain (Politician)
57 rue de Varenne
Paris, FRANCE F-75007

Juppe, Alain M (Prime Minister)
Mairie
Place Pey-Berland
Bordeaux Cedex 33077, FRANCE

Jur, Jeffrey (Cinematographer)
10615 Northvale Road
Los Angeles, CA 90064, USA

Jurak, Ed (Athlete, Baseball Player)
3650 S Walker Ave
San Pedro, CA 90731-6046, USA

Juran, Joseph M (Engineer)
Juran Institute
11 River Road
Wilton, CT 06897, USA

Juran, Nathan (Director, Writer)
197 Desert Lakes Dr
Rancho Mirage, CA 92270-4053, USA

Jurasik, Peter (Actor)
969 1/2 Manzanita Street
Los Angeles, CA 90029, USA

Jurasin, Bobby (Athlete, Football Player)
160 Huron Woods Dr
Marquette, MI 49855-9699, USA

Jurevicius, Joe (Athlete, Football Player)
1779 Berkshire Rd
Gates Mills, OH 44040-9747, USA

Jurewicz, Mike (Athlete, Baseball Player)
13804 Evergreen Ct
Saint Paul, MN 55124-9257, USA

Jurgens, Dan (Cartoonist)
5033 Green Farms Rd.
Edina, MN 55436-1091, USA

Jurgens, Udo (Actor)
Ltg. Dominik Beckmann
Posttfach 10 08 54
Munchen, Germany 80082

Jurgensen, Sonny (Athlete, Football Player)
6963 Greentree Dr.
Naples, FL 34108, USA

Jurgensmeier-Carroll, Margaret (Athlete, Baseball Player, Commentator)
5245 Rowena Dr
Roscoe, IL 61073-7221, USA

Jurich, Tom (Athlete, Football Player)
14910 Landmark Dr
Louisville, KY 40245-6525, USA

Juriga, James (Athlete, Football Player)
3001 Easton Pl
Saint Charles, IL 60175, USA

Juriga, Jim (Athlete, Football Player)
3001 Easton Pl
Saint Charles, IL 60175, USA

Jurinac, Sena (Opera Singer)
State Opera House
Opernring 2
Vienna 1010, AUSTRIA

Jurkovic, John (Athlete, Football Player)
2212 June Dr
Schererville, IN 46375, USA

Jurkovic, Mirko (Athlete, Football Player)
68520 Garver Lake Rd
Edwardsburg, MI 49112, USA

Jurow, Martin
5833 Berkshire Lane
Dallas, TX 75209

Jury, Bob (Athlete, Football Player)
2 Sassafras Ln
Greensburg, PA 15601-9023, USA

Just, Walter (Publisher)
Milwaukee Journal
333 W State St
Milwaukee, WI 53203, USA

Just, Ward S (Writer)
36 Ave Junot
Paris, FRANCE

Juster, Norton (Writer)
259 Lincoln Ave
Amherst, MA 01002, USA

Justice, David (Athlete, Baseball Player)
18570 Old Coach Way
Poway, CA 92064-6651, USA

Justice, Donald R (Writer)
338 Rocky Shore Dr
Iowa City, IA 52246, USA

Justice, Victoria (Actor)
c/o Jonathan Shank *Red Light*
Management (LA)
8439 W Sunset Blvd
Suite 2
Los Angeles, CA 90069, USA

Justice, William
3832 Chanson Dr.
Los Angeles, CA 90043

Justin, Dan (Athlete, Hockey Player)
53 Beaufort Rd
Toronto, ON M4E 1M8, Canada

Justin, Kerry (Athlete, Football Player)
13331 W Marlette Ct
Litchfield Park, AZ 85340, USA

Justin, Paul (Athlete, Football Player)
15727 Teal Rd
Verona, KY 41092-8228, USA

Just Jinger (Music Group)
c/o Staff Member *Paradigm (Monterey)*
404 W Franklin St
Monterey, CA 93940, USA

Justman, Seth (Musician)
Nick Ben-Meir
652 N Doheny Dr
Los Angeles, CA 90069, USA

Jutze, Skip (Athlete, Baseball Player)
3395 Zephyr Ct
Wheat Ridge, CO 80033-5967, USA

Juvenile (Musician)
c/o Staff Member *ICM Partners (ICM-LA)*
10250 Constellation Blvd Fl 7
Los Angeles, CA 90067, USA

J. Visclosky, Peter (Congressman,
Politician)
2256 Rayburn HOB
Washington, DC 20515, USA

J W, Pirtle (Athlete, Baseball Player)
1205 Carver Dr
Champaign, IL 61820-2412, USA

J. Walz, Timothy (Congressman,
Politician)
1722 Longworth HOB
Washington, DC 20515, USA

Kaake, Jeff (Actor)
2533 N Carson St
#3105
Carson City, NV 89706, USA

Kaas, Carmen (Model)
Men/Women Model Inc
199 Lafayette St
#700
New York, NY 10012, USA

Kaas, Jon H (Psychic)
Vanderbilt University
Psychology Dept
Nashville, TN 37240, USA

Kaas, Patrica (Musician)
Talent Sorcier
3 Rue des Petites-Ecuries
Paris 75010, FRANCE

Kaat, Jim (Athlete, Baseball Player)
The Thrill of Victory 129 NW 13th St Ste
17
Boca Raton, FL 33432-1635, USA

Kab, Vyto (Athlete, Football Player)
18 Grissing Ct
Cedar Grove, NJ 07009-1916, USA

Kaba, Agim (Actor, Producer)
c/o Adam Griffin *Kritzer Levine Wilkins*
Entertainment (KLWG)
11872 La Grange Ave
1st Floor
Los Angeles, CA 90025, USA

Kabakov, Ilya (Artist)
Gladstone Gallery
525 W 52nd St
New York, NY 10019, USA

Kabat-Zinn, Jon (Writer)
Sounds True, Inc
413 S Arthur Avenue
Louisville, CO 80027, USA

Kabbah, Ahmad Tejan (President)
President's Office
State House
Independence Ave
Freetown, SIERRA LEONE

Kabel, Bob (Athlete, Hockey Player)
120S-6940 Henderson Hwy
Lockport, MB R1B IAS, Canada

Kabila, Joseph (General, President)
President's Office
Mont Ngaliema
Kinshaha, CONGO DEMOCRATIC
REPUBLIC

Kabua, Imata (President)
President's Office
Cabinet Building
PO Box 2
Majuro, MARSHALL ISLANDS

Kacherski, John (Athlete, Football Player)
5477 Gordon Way
Dublin, OH 43017-8870, USA

Kachowski, Mark (Athlete, Hockey Player)
113 Pine Creek Dr
Venetia, PA 1S367-1330, USA

Kachur, Ed (Athlete, Hockey Player)
GD
Upsala, ON P0T 2Y0, Canada

Kaci (Musician)
c/o Staff Member *Curb Records (LA)*
3907 W Alameda Ave #104
Burbank, CA 91505

Kacyvenski, Isaiah (Athlete, Football
Player)
1081 Beacon St # 8
Brookline, MA 02446-5610, USA

Kaczmarek, Jane (Actor)
c/o Adena Chawke *Greenlight*
Management and Production
13848 Valleyheart Dr
Sherman Oaks, CA 91423, USA

Kaczur, Nick (Athlete, Football Player)
17 K Marie Dr
Attleboro, MA 02703-6730, USA

Kadafi, Moammar
Bab el Aziziya
Tripoli, LIBYA

Kadanoff, Leo P (Physicist, Scientist)
5421 S Cornell Ave
Chicago, IL 60615-5678, USA

Kadare, Ismael (Writer)
63 Blvd Saint-Michel
Paris 75005, FRANCE

Kadela, Dave (Athlete, Football Player)
9413 Culross Ct
Dublin, OH 43017, USA

Kadenyuk, Leonld K (Cosmonaut)
Potchta Kosmonavtov
Moskovskoi Oblasti
Syvisdny Goroduk 141160, RUSSIA

Kadher, Pakkoda (Actor)
9 Ponmana Semmal Street
M G R Nagar
Chennai, TN 600 078, INDIA

Kadish, Lawrence (Horse Racer)
135 Jericho Tpke
Old Westburv, NY 11568-1508, USA

Kadish, Michael S (Mike) (Athlete,
Football Player)
7941 Sudbury Ln SE
Ada, MI 49301, USA

Kadish, Ronald T (Ron) (General)
Director
Missile Defense Agency
Washington, DC 20301, USA

Kadison, Joshua (Musician, Songwriter,
Writer)
Nick Bode
1265 Electric Ave
Venice, CA 90291, USA

Kadziel, Ron (Athlete, Football Player)
2492 Creek Dr
Park City, UT 84060, USA

Kaeding, Nate (Athlete, Football Player)
1528 1st Ave Unit A
Coralville, IA 52241-1100, USA

Kae-Kazim, Hakeem (Actor)
c/o Staff Member *Rough Diamond*
Management
1424 N Kings Rd
West Hollywood, CA 90069, USA

Kaelin, Kato
6404 Wilshire Blvd. #950
Los Angeles, CA 90048-5529

Kaelin, Todd (Stylist)
c/o Staff Member *Directions USA*
3717-C W Market St
Greensboro, NC 27403, USA

Kaese, Trent (Athlete, Hockey Player)
Cottonwood Golf Course
197S Haslam Rd
Nanaimo, BC V9X ITI, Canada

Kaestle, Carl F (Historian)
35 Charlesfield St
Providence, RI 02906, USA

Kaesviharn, Kevin (Athlete, Football
Player)
6334 Merrimac Ln N
Osseo, MN 55311-3835, USA

Kafelnikov, Yevgeny A (Tennis Player)
Int'l Mgmt Group
26 Riverside Dr
Rumson, NJ 07760, USA

Kafentzis, Kurt (Athlete, Football Player)
1305 Perkins Ave
Richland, WA 99354-3106, USA

Kafentzis, Mark (Athlete, Football Player)
15912 134th Avenue Ct E
Puyallup, WA 98374-9647, USA

Kaftan, George (Athlete, Basketball
Player)
2591 Lantern Light Way
Manasquan, NJ 08736-2247, USA

Kagan, Daryn (Correspondent)
Cable News Network
News Dept
1050 Techwood Dr NW
Atlanta, GA 30318, USA

Kagan, Daryn (Correspondent)
1579 Monroe Dr
Suite F-134
Atlanta, GA 30324, USA

Kagan, Daryn
Washington Speakers Bureau
1663 Prince St
Alexandria, VA 22314, USA

Kagan, Henri Boris (Misc)
University Paris-Sud
Institut de Chimie Moleculaire
Orsay 91405, FRANCE

Kagan, Jeremy Paul (Director)
2024 N Curson Ave
Los Angeles, CA 90046, USA

Kagasoff, Daren (Actor)
c/o John Carrabino *John Carrabino*
Management
5900 Wilshire Blvd Fl 4 #406
Los Angeles, CA 90036, USA

Kagen, David (Actor)
6457 Firmament Ave
Van Nuys, CA 91406, USA

Kagge, Erling (Skier)
Munkedamsveien 86
Oslo 0270, NORWAY

Kahan, Richard (Actor)
c/o Elena Kirschner *Lucas Talent Inc*
100 W. Pender St
Sun Tower, 7th Floor
Vancouver, BC V6B 1R8, Canada

Kahane, Jeffrey (Musician)
I M G Artists
420 W 45th St
New York, NY 10036, USA

Kahin, Brian (Educator)
Harvard University
Information Infrastructure Project
Cambridge, MA 02138, USA

Kahler, Bob (Athlete, Football Player)
5500 Salem Square Dr N
Palm Harbor, FL 34685-1146, USA

Kahler, Robert (Athlete, Football Player)
5500 Salem Square Dr N
Palm Harbor, FL 34685, USA

Kahn, Joseph (Director, Writer)
c/o Staff Member *HSI Entertainment*
3630 E Ham Dr
Culver City, CA 90232, USA

Kahn, Michael (Editor)
c/o David Gersh *Gersh (LA)*
9465 Wilshire Blvd
Suite 600
Beverly Hills, CA 90212, USA

Kahn, Robert E (Scientist)
909 Lynton Place
Mclean, VA 22102-2113, USA

Kahn, Roger (Writer)
280 Marcotte Road
Kingston, NY 12401, USA

Kahn, Roger (Commentator)
PO Box 556
Stone Ridge, NY 12484-0556, USA

Kahn, Shahid (Business Person)
Flex-N-Gate
1306 East University Ave
Urbana, IL 61802, USA

Kahne, Kasey (Race Car Driver)
c/o Jon Edwards *Performance PR Plus*
520 N College St
Charlotte, NC 28202, USA

Kahneman, Daniel (Nobel Prize Laureate)
41 Adams Dr
Princeton, NJ 10003-5121, USA

Kai, Teanna (Adult Film Star)
c/o Staff Member *Atlas Multimedia Inc*
9005 Eton Ave Ste C
Canoga Park, CA 91304-1743, USA

Kaif, Katrina (Actor)
Pepsi Foods Private Limited
3B, DLF Corporate Park, 'S' Block
Qutab Enclave, Phase-III
Gurgaon, Haryana 122002, India

Kaifu, Toshiki (Prime Minister)
House of Representatives
Diet
Tokyo 100, JAPAN

Kaimer, Karl (Athlete, Football Player)
3 Kerr Ave
Lavallette, NJ 08735, USA

Kain, Karin A (Dancer)
National Ballet of Canada
470 Queens Quay
Toronto, ON M5V 3K4, CANADA

Kain, Khalil (Actor)
c/o Staff Member *Envision Entertainment*
8840 Wilshire Blvd
3rd Floor
Beverly Hills, CA 90211, USA

Kainer, Don (Athlete, Baseball Player)
1923 Sieber Dr
Houston, TX 77017-6201, USA

Kaiser, A Dale (Misc)
832 Santa Fe Ave
Stanford, CA 94305, USA

Kaiser, Bob (Athlete, Baseball Player)
8 Independence Way
Southampton, NJ 08088-9047, USA

Kaiser, Don (Athlete, Baseball Player)
2901 E 12th St
Ada, OK 74820-7259, USA

Kaiser, George B (Financier)
Bank of Oklahoma
Bank of Oklahoma Tower
PO Box 2300
Tulsa, OK 74102, USA

Kaiser, Jason (Athlete, Football Player)
3885 Cheyenne Pl
Sedalia, CO 80135, USA

Kaiser, Jeff (Athlete, Baseball Player)
26227 James Dr
Grosse Lie, MI 48138-2172, USA

Kaiser, Ken (Baseball Player)
56 Holley Sue Ln
Rochester, NY 14626-1170, USA

Kaiser, Ken (Athlete, Baseball Player)
56 Holley Sue Ln
Rochester, NY 14626-1170, USA

Kaiser, Michael (Misc)
Kennedy Center for Performing Arts
Washington, DC 20011, USA

Kaiser, Natasha (Athlete, Track Athlete)
2601 Hickman Road
Des Moines, IA 50310, USA

Kaiser, Suki (Actor)
c/o Pam Winter *Gary Goddard Agency*
10 St Mary St
Suite 305
Toronto, ON M4Y 1P9, Canada

Kaiser, Tim (Producer)
c/o Scott Schwartz *Vision Art Management*
9465 Wilshire Blvd Ste 870
Beverly Hills, CA 90212, USA

Kaiser, Vern (Athlete, Hockey Player)
1275 Kilwinning St
Penticton, BC V2A 4P2, Canada

Kaiser Chiefs (Music Group)
c/o Staff Member *Helter Skelter (UK)*
535 Kings Rd
The Plaza
London SW10 0SZ, UNITED KINGDOM (UK)

Kaiserman, William (Designer, Fashion Designer)
29 W 56th St
New York, NY 10019, USA

Kaji, Gautam S (Financier)
Cabot Corporation
2 Seaport Lane
Suite 1300
Boston, MA 02210-2019, USA

Kajlich, Bianca (Actor)
c/o Chris Henze *Thruline Entertainment*
9250 Wilshire Blvd
Ground Fl
Beverly Hills, CA 90212, USA

Kajol (Actor, Bollywood)
c/o Bunty Bahl *Carving Dreams Entertainment*
304-305, Oberoi Chambers II
B Wing, Off New Link Road, Andheri West
Mumbai 400053, INDIA

Kaka (Athlete, Soccer Player)
c/o Staff Member *Real Madrid*
Avenida De Concha Espina, 1
Estadio Santiago Bernabéu
Madrid 28036, Spain

Kakhidze, Djansug I (Conductor)
Leselidze St 18
Tbilisi 380005, GEORGIA

Kalafat, Ed (Athlete, Basketball Player)
2323 Kingfish Rd
Naples, FL 34102-1539, USA

Kalafut, Kathy (Stylist)
329 W 55th St
#3-B
New York, NY 10019, USA

Kalam, A P J Abdul (President)
President's Office
Bharat ka Rashtrapati Bhavan
New Delhi, New Delhi 110004, INDIA

Kalangis, Ike (Financier)
Boatmen's Sunwest
303 Roma Ave NW
Albuquerque, NM 87102, USA

Kalas, Harry (Sportscaster)
Philadelphia Philies
3308 Chatham Pl
Media, PA 19063-4313, USA

Kalas, Todd (Commentator)
9417 Cavendish Drive
Apt 108
Tampa, FL 33626-5173, USA

Kalashnikov, Mikhail T (Designer, General)
A O Izhmash
426006 Izhevsk
Udmurtia Republic, RUSSIA

Kalb, Marvin (Correspondent, Educator, Journalist)
Harvard University
Shorenstein Center
79 JF Kennedy St
Cambridge, MA 20036-2007, USA

Kalem, Toni (Actor)
c/o Joy Gorman *Anonymous Content (LA)*
3531 Hayden Ave
Culver City, CA 90232, USA

Kalember, Patricia (Actor)
Innovative Artists
1505 10th St
Santa Monica, CA 90401, USA

Kalen, Herbert D (War Hero)
General Delivery
Angel Fire, NM 87710, USA

Kaler, Jamie (Actor)
c/o Sheila Wenzel *Innovative Artists (LA)*
1505 10th St
Santa Monica, CA 90401, USA

Kaleta, Patrick (Athlete, Hockey Player)
3011 Cloverbank Rd
Hamburg, NY 1407S-3400, USA

Kalichstein, Joseph (Musician)
I C M Artists
40 W 57th St
New York, NY 10019, USA

Kalikow, Peter S (Publisher)
H J Kalikow Co
101 Park Ave
New York, NY 10178, USA

Kalil, Ryan (Athlete, Football Player)
2910 Selwyn Ave
Charlotte, NC 28209-1762, USA

kalina, Richard (Artist)
44 King St
New York, NY 10014, USA

Kaline, Al (Athlete, Baseball Player)
3613 York Ct
Bloomfield Hills, MI 48301-2058, USA

Kaline, Albert W (Al) (Athlete, Baseball Player)
3613 York Ct
Bloomfield Hills, MI 48301, USA

Kaling, Mindy (Actor)
c/o Howard Klein *3 Arts Entertainment Inc*
9460 Wilshire Blvd
7th Floor
Beverly Hills, CA 90210, USA

Kalinin, Dmitri (Athlete, Hockey Player)
Puckagency LLC
555 Pleasantville Rd Ste 210N
Attn Jay Grossman
Briarcliff Manor, NY 10510-1900, USA

Kalis, Todd A (Athlete, Football Player)
900 Bayview Ct
Cranberry Township, PA 16066, USA

Kalish, Martin (Misc)
School Administrators Federation
853 Broadway
New York, NY 10003, USA

kalish, ryan
37 Obre Pl
Shrewsbury, NJ 07702-4123, USA

Kalitta, Connie (Race Car Driver)
American International Airways
1010 James L. Hart Parkway
Ypsilanti, MI 48197, USA

Kalitta, Doug (Race Car Driver)
Kalitta Motorsports
1010 James L. Hart Parkway
Ypsilandi, MI 49197, USA

Kallaugher, Kevin (Kall) (Cartoonist)
Baltimore Sun
Editorial Dept
501 N Calvert St
Baltimore, MD 21202, USA

Kallen, Jackie
c/o Daniel Strone *Trident Media Group LLC*
41 Madison Ave
36th Floor
New York, NY 10010, USA

Kallen, Kitty (Musician)
35 Winthrop Place
Englewood, NJ 07631, USA

Kallin, Catherine (Scientist)
224 Hillcrest Ave
Hamilton, ON L8P 2XS, Canada

Kallir, Lilian (Musician)
Columbia Artists Mgmt Inc
165 W 57th St
New York, NY 10019, USA

Kallman, Gerhard M (Architect)
Kallman McKinnell Wood
939 Boylston St
Boston, MA 02115, USA

Kalloniatis, Anthony (Actor, Comedian, Composer, Director)
c/o Barry Katz *New Wave Entertainment (LA)*
2660 W Olive Blvd
Burbank, CA 91505, USA

Kallur, Anders (Athlete, Hockey Player)
Utsiktsvagen 14
Falun S-79131, Sweden

Kalman, Rudolf E (Mathematician)
ETH Zentrum
Zurich 8092, SWITZERLAND

Kalmanir, Thomas (Athlete, Football Player)
425 E Shelldrake Cir
Fresno, CA 93720, USA

Kalmbach, Herbert (Politician)
1056 Santiago Dr
Newport Beach, CA 92660-5728, USA

Kalplan, Deborah (Director, Writer)
c/o Staff Member *WmE2 (WMA-LA)*
1 William Morris Pl
Beverly Hills, CA 90212, USA

Kalpokas, Donald (Prime Minister)
Prime Minister's Office
PO Box 110
Port Vila, VANUTA

Kalu, N D (Athlete, Football Player)
3719 Poplar Springs Dr
Missouri City, TX 77459-6722, USA

Kalu, Ndukwe (Athlete, Football Player)
1910 Quail Hollow Dr
Fresno, TX 77545, USA

Kalule, Ayub (Boxer)
Palle Skjulet
Bagsvaert 12
Copenhagen 2880, DENMARK

Kalyagin, Aleksander A (Actor)
1905 Goda Str 3
#91
Moscow 123100, RUSSIA

Kamal, Gray (Musician)
William Morris Agency
1325 Ave of Americas
New York, NY 10019, USA

Kamali, Norma (Designer, Fashion Designer)
OMO Norma Kamali
11 W 56th St
New York, NY 10019, USA

Kaman, Chris (Athlete, Basketball Player)
300 N Dianthus St
Manhattan Beach, CA 90266-6717, USA

Kamana III, John (Athlete, Football Player)
2319 Kapahu St
Honolulu, HI 96813-1433, USA

Kamano, Stacy (Actor)
c/o Staff Member *AKA Talent Agency*
6310 San Vicente Blvd
Suite 200
Los Angeles, CA 90048, USA

Kamanu, Lew (Athlete, Football Player)
160 Keonekai Rd
Kihei, HI 96753-7123, USA

Kamarck, Martin A (Financier)
MAKO Consulting LLC
850 Third Avenue
9th Floor
New York, NY 10022, USA

Kamb, Alexander (Misc)
300 Alberta Way
Hillsborough, CA 94010-7148, USA

Kamen, Dean (Inventor)
15 W Wind Dr
Bedford, NH 03110, USA

Kamensky, Valeri (Athlete, Hockey Player)
5 Stonehedge Dr S
Greenwich, CT 06831-3219, USA

Kamesh, Kamala (Actor, Bollywood)
4F 3rd Block
Shanthi Towers 88 ArcotRoad Vadapalani
Chennai, TN 600026, INDIA

Kamieniecki, Scott (Athlete, Baseball Player)
7800 Somerhill Ln
Clarkston, MI 48348-4383, USA

Kamin, Blair (Critic)
Chicago Tribune
Editorial Dept
435 N Michigan Ave
Chicago, IL 60611, USA

Kaminir, Lisa (Actor)
Ellis Talent Group
14241 N Maple Dr
#207
Sherman Oaks, CA 01423, USA

Kaminski, Janusz (Cinematographer)
23801 Catabasas Road
#2004
Catabasas, CA 91302, USA

Kaminski, Kevin (Athlete, Hockey Player)
4560 Venture Dr
Southaven, MS 38671-9719, USA

Kaminski, Larry (Athlete, Football Player)
31423 State Highway 3 NE
Poulsbo, WA 98370, USA

Kaminski, Marek (Misc)
Ul Dickmana 14/15
Gdansk 80-339, POLAND

Kaminsky, Walter (Misc)
Hamburg University
Martin-Luther-King Platz 6
Hamburg 20146, GERMANY

Kaminsky, Yan (Athlete, Hockey Player)
4842 Wildrose Ct NW
Kennesaw, GA 30152-77S2, USA

Kamisar, Yale (Educator, Lawyer)
2910 Daleview Dr
Ann Arbor, MI 48105, USA

Kamm, Brian (Athlete, Golfer)
479 Barnette Rd
Bluff City, TN 37618, USA

Kammen, Michael G (Historian)
Comell University
History Dept
McGraw Hall
Ithaca, NY 14853, USA

Kammerer, Carl (Athlete, Football Player)
6941 Brooke Rd
Highland, MD 20777, USA

Kamoze, Ini (Musician)
Famous Artists Agency
250 W 57th St
New York, NY 10107, USA

Kampa, Bob (Athlete, Football Player)
2001 Jennifer Dr
Aptos, CA 95003-2840, USA

Kampa, Robert (Athlete, Football Player)
2001 Jennifer Dr
Aptos, CA 95003, USA

Kampelman, Max M (Diplomat, Government Official)
3154 Highland Place NW
Washington, DC 20008, USA

Kampman, Aaron (Athlete, Football Player)
2887 Moose Creek Trl
Green Bay, WI 54313, USA

Kamprad, Ingvar (Business Person)
IKEA Svenska Försäljnings AB
Box 200
Odakra 26035, Sweden

Kamu, Okko T
Calle Mozart 7
Rancho Domingo
Benalmedina Pueblo 29369, SPAIN

Kan, Yuet Wai (Misc)
20 Yerba Buena Ave
San Francisco, CA 94127, USA

Kanaan, Tony (Race Car Driver)
Andretti Green Racing
7615 Zionsville Rd.
Indianapol is, IN 46268, USA

Kanaga (Actor)
33 1st Mall Road
R A Puram
Chennai, TN 600028, INDIA

Kanakaredes, Melina (Actor)
c/o Bill Butler *Industry Entertainment Partners*
955 S Carrillo Dr
Suite 300
Los Angeles, CA 90048, USA

Kanal, Brooke (Stylist)
1 Blackberry Ln
Framingham, MA 01701, USA

Kanal, Tony (Musician, Songwriter, Writer)
Rebel Waltz Inc
31652 2nd Ave
Laguna Beach, CA 92651, USA

Kanaly, Steve (Actor)
4663 Grand Ave
Ojai, CA 93023, USA

Kanamori, Hiroo (Physicist)
California Institute of Technology
Geophysics Dept
Pasadena, CA 91125, USA

Kanan, Sean
c/o Kim Matuka *Online Talent Group*
Prefers to be contacted via email or telephone
Los Angeles, CA 90069, USA

Kananln, Roman G (Architect)
Join-Stock Mosprojekt
13/14 1 Brestkaya Str
Moscow 125190, RUSSIA

Kancheli, Giya A (Georgy) (Composer)
Tovstonogov Str 6
Tbilisi 380064, GEORGIA

Kandel, Eric R (Nobel Prize Laureate)
9 Sigma Place
Bronx, NY 10471, USA

Kander, John H (Composer)
B M I
8730 Sunset Blvd
#300
Los Angeles, CA 90069, USA

Kane (Wrestler)
c/o Kerry Rodgerson *World Wrestling Entertainment (WWE)*
Titan Towers
1241 E Main St
Stamford, CT 06905-3857, USA

Kane, Abigail (Stylist)
c/o Staff Member *Crews*
828 Clemont Dr
Atlanta, GA 30306, USA

Kane, Andy (Handy Andy) (Actor)
c/o Staff Member *David Anthony Promotions*
PO Box 286
Warrington
Cheshire WA2 8GA, UNITED KINGDOM

Kane, Big Daddy (Musician)
c/o Ron Rivlin *Coast II Coast Entertainment*
8671 Wilshire Blvd Ste 500
Beverly Hills, CA 90211, USA

Kane, Carol (Actor)
c/o Wes Stevens *Vox*
6420 Wilshire Blvd Ste 1080
Los Angeles, CA 90048, USA

Kane, Chelsea (Actor, Musician)
8418 Lookout Mountain Ave
Los Angeles, CA 90046, USA

Kane, Christian (Actor, Musician)
9116 Wonderland Ave
Los Angeles, CA 90046, USA

Kane, Frank "Red"
1614 Northridge Dr
Arlington, TX 76012-2247, USA

Kane, John C (Business Person)
Cardinal Health
7000 Cardinal Place
Dublin, OH 43017, USA

Kane, Jonny (Race Car Driver)
7615 Zionsville Rd
Indianapolis, IN 46268, USA

Kane, Khalil (Actor)
c/o Staff Member *Envision Entertainment*
8840 Wilshire Blvd
3rd Floor
Beverly Hills, CA 90211, USA

Kane, Lorie (Athlete, Golfer)
101-5397 Eglinton Ave W
Etobicoke, Ontario M9C 5K6, Canada

Kane, Nick (Musician)
AstroMedia
1620 16th Ave S
Nashville, TN 37212, USA

Kane, Patrick (Athlete, Hockey Player)
401 N Wabash Ave Unit 33J
Chicago, IL 60611-3637, USA

Kane, Patrick (Athlete, Hockey Player)
c/o Pat Brisson *Creative Artists Agency (CAA-LA)*
2000 Ave Of The Stars
Los Angeles, CA 90067, USA

Kane, Richard (Athlete, Football Player)
2525 Greensboro Pt
Reno, NV 89509, USA

Kane Elson, Marion (Swimmer)
4669 Badger Road
Santa Rosa, CA 95409, USA

Kanell, Danny (Athlete, Football Player)
4632 Sea Grape Dr
Laud By Sea, FL 33308, USA

Kanellis, Maria (Actor, Wrestler)
c/o Jessica Cohen *JCPR*
9903 Santa Monica Blvd
Suite 983
Beverly Hills, CA 90212, USA

Kaneshiro, Takeshi (Actor)
c/o Staff Member *WME (LA)*
9601 Wilshire Blvd Fl 3
Beverly Hills, CA 90210, USA

Kanew, Jeffery R (Director)
c/o Staff Member *Directors Guild of America*
7920 Sunset Blvd
Los Angeles, CA 90046-0907, USA

Kang, Dong-Suk (Musician)
Clarion/Seven Muses
47 Whitehall Park
London N19 3TW, UNITED KINGDOM (UK)

Kang, Jimin (Athlete, Golfer)
8539 E Cactus Wren Cir
Scottsdale, AZ 85266, USA

Kang, Sung (Actor)
c/o Scott Schachter *United Talent Agency (UTA)*
9336 Civic Center Dr
Beverly Hills, CA 90210, USA

Kang, Tim (Actor)
c/o Anna Liza Recto *Vincent Cirrincione Associates*
1516 N Fairfax Ave
Los Angeles, CA 90046, USA

Kangas-Brody, Jennifer (Athlete, Golfer)
6275 Knob Bend Dr
Grand Blanc, MI 48439, USA

Kango, Mayuri (Actor, Bollywood)
21 Kala Pathar Gokul Paradise
Thakur Complex Kandivili (E)
Mumbai, MS 400101, INDIA

Kanicki, James (Athlete, Football Player)
4590 Schramling Rd
Pierpont, OH 44082, USA

Kanievska, Marek (Director)
International Creative Mgmt
8942 Wilshire Blvd
#219
Beverly Hills, CA 90211, USA

Kanin, Fay (Writer)
653 Palisades Beach Road
Santa Monica, CA 90402, USA

Kann, Donald (Stylist)
1435 12th St
Key West, FL 33040, USA

Kann, Peter R (Business Person, Journalist, Publisher)
Dow Jones Co
200 Liberty St
New York, NY 10281, USA

Kann, Stan
570 N. Rossmore Ave.
Los Angeles, CA 90004

Kannadasan, Vishali (Actor, Bollywood)
29/1 lst Cross Street
Chinmaya Nagar
Chennai, TN 600011, INDIA

Kannaiah, Ennathe (Actor)
RP Block No8 Llyods Colony
Royapet
Chennai, TN 600 014, INDIA

Kanne, Michael S (Judge)
US Court of Appeals
PO Box 1340
Lafayette, IN 47902, USA

Kannegiesser, Gordon (Gord) (Athlete, Hockey Player)
Knox Insurance
705 Cassells St
North Bay, ON PlB 4A3, Canada

Kannegiesser, Sheldon (Athlete, Hockey Player)
Knox Insurance
70S Cassells St
North Bay, ON PlB 4A3, Canada

Kannenberg, Bernd (Athlete, Track Athlete)
Sportschule
Sonthofen/Aligau 87527, GERMANY

Kannokada, Melanie (Actor, Bollywood)
c/o Asal Masomi *Asal Masomi Public Relations*
6320 Canoga Ave
Suite 1513
WoodlandHills, CA 91367, USA

Kanouse, Lyle (Actor)
c/o Staff Member *Gage Group, The (LA)*
14724 Ventura Blvd
Suite 505
Sherman Oaks, CA 91403, USA

Kansas (Music Group)
c/o Staff Member *Creative Artists Agency (CAA-LA)*
2000 Ave Of The Stars
Los Angeles, CA 90067, USA

Kansch, Heather (Artist)
Knowle
Rundlerohy Newton Abbot
Devon TQ12 2PJ, UNITED KINGDOM (UK)

Kanter, Paul (Musician)
Ron Rainey Mgmt
315 S Beverly Dr
#407
Beverly Hills, CA 90212, USA

Kantor, Michael (Mickey) (Secretary)
2709 Olive Avenue NW
Washington, DC 20007-3326, USA

Kantor, Secy
Mickey 5019 Klingle St NW
Washington, DC 20016, USA

Kantrowitz, Adrian (Doctor)
70 Gallogly Road
Lake Angelus, MI 48326, USA

Kantrowitz, Arthur R (Physicist)
4 Downing Road
Hanover, NH 03755, USA

Kanwaljit (Actor, Bollywood)
B-1001 Abhishek Apts
Juhu Versova Link Road 4 Bungalows
Andheri (W)
Mumbai, MS 400053, INDIA

Kanwar, Anita (Actor, Bollywood)
501A Anisha Apartments Yari Road
Versova Andheri
Mumbai, MS 400061, INDIA

Kanwar, Raj (Bollywood, Director, Filmmaker, Producer)
6 Mewawala Building Haidery House
Next To Arrow Studio Vakola Masjid
Santacruz (E)
Bombay, MS 400 055, INDIA

Kao, Archie (Actor)
c/o Tim Kwok *Convergence Entertainment*
9150 Wilshire Blvd
Suite 247
Beverly Hills, CA 90212, USA

Kao, Charles K (Engineer, Nobel Prize Laureate)
Yes Foundation
1 Harbour Road
#1708, Wen Chai
Hong Kong, China

Kao, Min (Misc)
Garmin International
1200 E lSlst St, Olathe KS 66062-3426, USA

Kapadia, Asif (Actor, Director, Writer)
c/o Robert (Bob) Bookman *Creative Artists Agency (CAA-LA)*
2000 Ave Of The Stars
Los Angeles, CA 90067, USA

Kapadia, Dimple (Actor, Bollywood)
201-A Vastu Bldg
Military Rd Juhu
Mumbai, MS 400049, INDIA

Kapanen, Sami (Athlete, Hockey Player)
Kalpa Hockey
Sairaalakatu l5
Attn: Owners Office
Kuopio 70110, Finland

Kapele, John (Athlete, Football Player)
45-543 Paleka Rd
Kaneohe, HI 96744, USA

Kapellusch, Kim (Stylist)
30528 Yosemite Dr
Castaic, CA 91384-3735, USA

Kapelos, John (Actor)
c/o Staff Member *McCabe Group, The*
3211 Cahuenga Blvd W Ste 104
Los Angeles, CA 90068, USA

Kapioitas, John (Business Person)
ITT Sheraton Corp
1111 Westchester Ave
West Harrison, NY 10604, USA

Kaplan, Bonnie (Stylist)
7033 N Kedzie
#1411
Chicago, IL 60645, USA

Kaplan, Gabe
2732 McConnell Dr
Los Angeles, CA 90064, USA

Kaplan, Jonathan S (Director)
4323 Ben Ave
Studio City, CA 91604, USA

Kaplan, Justin (Writer)
PO Box 219
Truro, MA 02666-0219, USA

Kaplan, Ken (Athlete, Football Player)
8313 N Fremont Ave
Tampa, FL 33604, USA

Kaplan, Marvin (Actor)
PO Box 1522
Burbank, CA 91507, USA

Kaplan, Nathan O (Misc)
8587 La Jolla Scenic Dr
La Jolla, CA 92037, USA

Kaplan, Steven (Actor)
c/o Ellen Gilbert *Abrams Artists Agency (LA)*
9200 Sunset Blvd
11th Floor
Los Angeles, CA 90069, USA

Kapler, Gabe (Athlete, Baseball Player)
30375 Morning View Dr
Malibu, CA 90265-3618, USA

Kaplon, Al (Actor)
2899 Agoura Road
Suite 172
Westlake Village, CA 91361, USA

Kaplow, Herbert E (Correspondent)
211 N Van Buren St
Falls Church, VA 22046, USA

Kapnek, Emily (Actor)
c/o Staff Member *Creative Artists Agency (CAA-LA)*
2000 Ave Of The Stars
Los Angeles, CA 90067, USA

Kapono, Jason (Athlete, Basketball Player)
c/o Staff Member *Miami Heat*
1 SE 3rd Avenue
Suite 2300
Miami, FL 33131, USA

Kapoor, Anil (Actor, Bollywood)
c/o Staff Member *ICM Partners (ICM-LA)*
10250 Constellation Blvd Fl 7
Los Angeles, CA 90067, USA

Kapoor, Anish (Artist)
33 Coleherne Road
London SW10, UNITED KINGDOM (UK)

Kapoor, Karishma (Actor, Bollywood)
2B Excellency 1101/1201
4th Cross Road, Lokhandwala Complex
Andheri (W)
Mumbai, MS 400048, INDIA

Kapoor, Karisma (Actor, Bollywood)
2B Excellency 1101 1201 4th Cross Road
Lokhandwala Complex
Bombay, MS 400 058, INDIA

Kapoor, Kunal (Actor)
c/o Staff Member *Globosport Mumbai Pvt Ltd*
Prime Plaza, 5th Flr, 501, 38 S.V. Rd
Santacruz (W).
Mumbai 400 054, India

Kapoor, Rajiv (Actor, Bollywood, Director, Filmmaker, Producer)
R K Studios
Chembur
Bombay, MS 400 071, INDIA

Kapoor, Ranbir (Actor, Bollywood)
c/o Staff Member *Globosport Mumbai Pvt Ltd*
Prime Plaza, 5th Flr, 501, 38 S.V. Rd
Santacruz (W).
Mumbai 400 054, India

Kapoor, Randhir (Actor, Bollywood, Director, Producer)
R K Studios
Chembur
Bombay, MS 400 071, INDIA

Kapoor, Ravi (Actor)
c/o Matthew Lesher *Insight*
1134 S Cloverdale Ave
Los Angeles, CA 90019, USA

Kapoor, Rishi (Actor, Bollywood)
27 Krishna Raj
Pali Hill Bandra
Mumbai, MS 400058, INDIA

Kapoor, Sanjay (Actor, Bollywood)
18 Arjun Magnum Bungalows
Lokhandwala Complex Andheri (W)
Mumbai, MS 400053, INDIA

Kapoor, Shakti (Actor, Bollywood, Comedian)
Palm Beach 7th Floor Gandhigram Road
Juhu
Bombay, MS 400 049, INDIA

Kapoor, Shashi (Actor, Bollywood)
112 Atlas Apartments
Harkness Road
Bombay, MS 400 006, INDIA

Kapor, Mitchell D (Engineer)
Open Source Application Foundation
177 Post St
#900
San Francisco, CA 94115-1126, USA

Kapp, Joseph (Joe) (Athlete, Football Player)
P.O. Box 1973
Los Gatos, CA 95031-1973, USA

Kapp Horner, Alex (Actor, Producer)
c/o Staff Member *T&A Pictures*
15233 Ventura Blvd Fl 9
Sherman Oaks, CA 91403, USA

Kappu, Satyen (Actor, Bollywood)
201 Canvera J P Road
Versova Andheri
Bombay, MS 400 061, INDIA

Kapriski, Valerie
10 Ave. George V
Paris, FRANCE F-75008

Kaprisky, Valerie (Actor)
Artmedia
20 Ave Rapp
Paris 75007, FRANCE

Kaptur, Marcy (Congressman, Politician)
2186 Rayburn HOB
Washington, DC 20515, USA

Kapture, Mitzi (Actor)
c/o Rod Baron *Baron Entertainment*
13848 Ventura Blvd
Suite A
Sherman Oaks, CA 91423-3654

Kapur, Shekhar (Actor, Bollywood, Director, Filmmaker, Producer)
42 Sheetal A B Nair Road
Juhu
Bombay, MS 400 049, INDIA

Kapur, Steve (Apache Indian) (Musician)
c/o Staff Member *Mission Control Artists Agency*
Unit 3 City Business Centre
St Olav's Court, Lower Road
London SE16 2XB, UNITED KINGDOM (UK)

Karabin, Ladislav (Athlete, Hockey Player)
8907 Russo Rd.
Ft. Pierce, FL 349S1-3826, USA

Karageorghis, Vassos (Misc)
Foundation Anastasios Leventis
28 Sofoulis St
Nicosia, CYPRUS

Karamanov, Alemdar S (Composer)
Voykova Str 2
#4
Simferopol, Crimea, UKRAINE

Karamatic, George (Athlete, Football Player)
982 Donald Way
Santa Maria, CA 93455, USA

Karan, Amara (Actor)
c/o Ciara Parkes *Public Eye Communications*
535 Kings Rd
Suite 313 Plaza
London SW10 0SZ, United Kingdom

Karan, Donna (Designer, Fashion Designer)
Donna Karan Co
550 Seventh Ave
NY 10018, USA

Karapati, Gyorgy (Misc)
Il Liva Utca 1
Budapest 1025, HUNGARY

Karath, Kym (Actor)
40 Halsey Dr
Old Greenwich, CT 06870-1226, USA

Karathanasis, Sotirios K (Scientist)
Harvard Medical School
25 Shattuck St
Boston, MA 02115, USA

Karatz, Bruce E (Business Person)
Kaufman & Broad Home
10990 Wilshire Blvd
Los Angeles, CA 90024, USA

Karbacher, Bernd
Hufnagelstrasse 13
Munich, GERMANY D-80686

Karcher, Ken (Athlete, Football Player)
373 Freemantle Ct
Saline, MI 48176-9155, USA

Karchner, Matt (Athlete, Baseball Player)
401 E 2nd St
Berwick, PA 18603-4801, USA

Kardashian, Khloe (Actor)
19011 Ashurst Ln
Tarzana, CA 91356, USA

Kardashian, Kim (Actor, Reality TV Star)
c/o Jill Fritzo *PMK/BNC Public Relations (PMK-NY)*
622 3rd Ave
8th Floor
New York, NY 10017, USA

Kardashian, Kourtney (Reality TV Star)
c/o Jill Fritzo *PMK/BNC Public Relations (PMK-NY)*
622 3rd Ave
8th Floor
New York, NY 10017, USA

Kardashian, Rob (Actor, Reality TV Star)
c/o Lance Klein *WME (LA)*
9601 Wilshire Blvd Fl 3
Beverly Hills, CA 90210, USA

Karelskaya, Rimma K (Ballerina)
Bolshol Theater
Teatralnaya Pi 1
Moscow 103009, RUSSIA

Karen, Ehrisman (Stylist)
1243 Redfield Rd
Naperville, IL 60563-0440, USA

Karen, James
4455 Los Feliz Blvd. #807
Los Angeles, CA 90027

Karialainen, Kyosti
Trodjevagen 49
Gavle 80S 96, Sweden

Karieva, Bernara (Ballerina)
Navoi Opera Theater
28 M K Otaturk St
Tashkent 700029, UZBEKISTAN

Karim, Reef (Actor)
c/o Staff Member *Daris Hatch Management*
10027 Rossbury Pl
Los Angeles, CA 90064-4825, USA

Karim-Lamrani, Mohammed (Prime Minister)
Rue du Mont Saint Michel
Anfa Superieur
Casablanca 21300, MOROCCO

Karimov, Islam M (President)
President's Office
Uzbekistansky Prosp 45
Tashkent, UZBEKISTAN

Karin, Anna (Actor)
Greene Assoc
7080 Hollywood Blvd
#1017
Los Angeles, CA 90028, USA

Karina, Anna (Actor)
Artmedia
20 Ave Rapp
Paris 75007, FRANCE

Kariya, Paul (Athlete, Hockey Player)
2493 Aquasanta
Tustin, CA 92782-1104, CANADA

Karkovice, Ron (Athlete, Baseball Player)
272 Celebration Blvd
Kissimmee, FL 34747-5082, USA

Karl, George (Coach)
10936 N Port Washington Road
Mequon, WI 53092, USA

Karl, George (Athlete, Basketball Player)
245 S Krameria St
Denver, CO 80224-1044, USA

Karl, Jan
5555 Melrose Ave. L
Los Angeles, CA 90038

Karl, Scott (Athlete, Baseball Player)
6446 Lilium Ln
Carlsbad, CA 92011-2793, USA

Karlander, Al (Athlete, Hockey Player)
4940 Deer Ridge Dr N
Carmel, IN 46033-8904, USA

Karlander, Al (Athlete, Hockey Player)
249 W. Admiral Way So.
Carmel, IN 46032, USA

Karle, Isabelia (Misc)
6304 Lakeview Dr
Falls Church, VA 22041, USA

Karle, Jerome (Nobel Prize Laureate)
6304 Lakeview Dr
Falls Church, VA 22041-1309, USA

Karlen, John (Actor)
PO Box 1195
Santa Monica, CA 90406, USA

Karlin, Ben (Producer, Writer)
c/o Staff Member *3 Arts Entertainment Inc*
9460 Wilshire Blvd
7th Floor
Beverly Hills, CA 90210, USA

Karlin, Fred
1187 Coast Village Rd. #1-339
Montecito, CA 93108

Karlin, Samuel (Mathematician)
Stanford University
Mathematics Dept
Stanford, CA 94305, USA

Karling, John S (Misc)
1219 Tuckahoe Lane
West Lafayette, IN 47906, USA

Karlis, Rich (Athlete, Football Player)
9947 Arthur Ln
Highlands Ranch, CO 80130-8009, USA

Karloff, Sara
PO Box 2424
Rancho Mirage, CA 92270

Karlson, Kristine (Athlete, Olympic Athlete, Rower)
4 Pinneo Hill Rd
Hanover, NH 03755-4600, USA

Karlson, Phil
3094 Patricia Ave.
Los Angeles, CA 90064

Karlsson, Lena (Musician)
MOB Agency
6404 Wilshire Blvd
#807
Los Angeles, CA 90048, USA

Karlstad, Geir (Speed Skater)
Hamarveien 5A
Fjellhamar 1472, NORWAY

Karlzen, Mary (Musician, Songwriter, Writer)
Little Big Man
155 Ave of Americas
#700
New York, NY 10013, USA

Karmanos Jr, Peter (Business Person)
Compuware Corp
1 Campus Martius
Detroit, MI 48226, USA

Karmi, Ram (Architect)
Karmi Architects
17 Kaplan St
Tel Aviv 64734, ISRAEL

Karmi-Melamede, Ada (Architect)
Karmi Architects
17 Kaplan St
Tel Aviv 64734, ISRAEL

Karn, Richard (Actor)
c/o Staff Member *Stone Manners Salners Agency (LA)*
9911 W Pico Blvd Ste 1400
Los Angeles, CA 90035, USA

Karnad, Girish (Actor)
Silver Cascade Mount Mary Road
Bandra
Bombay, MS 400 050, INDIA

Karnes, David K (Ex-Senator)
Kutak Rock
Omaha Building
1650 Farnam St
Omaha, NE 68102-2186, USA

Karnes, Jay (Actor)
c/o Jonathan Howard *Innovative Artists (LA)*
1505 10th St
Santa Monica, CA 90401, USA

Karnofsky, Sonny (Athlete, Football Player)
14801 Nevar Ct
Rancho Murieta, CA 95683, USA

Karnow, Stanley (Historian)
10850 Spring Knolls Dr
Potomac, MD 20854, USA

Karns, Christine (Race Car Driver)
Karns Racing
24 Grieson Rd
Honey Brook, PA 19344, USA

Karnuth, Jason (Athlete, Baseball Player)
2822 Helding Park Ct
Katv, TX 77494-8522, USA

Karol, Scott (Producer)
c/o Staff Member *Crystal Sky Pictures*
10203 Santa Monica Blvd
5th Floor
Los Angeles, CA 90067, USA

Karolyi, Bela (Athlete, Coach, Olympic Athlete)
454 Forest Service 200 Rd
Huntsville, TX 77340-2686, USA

Karon, Jan (Writer)
7060 Esmont Farm
Esmont, VA 22937, USA

Karp, Richard M (Scientist)
University of Washington
Computer Science Dept
Seattle, WA 98195, USA

Karp, Ryan (Athlete, Baseball Player)
8 Fox Run Rd
Medway, MA 02053-2242, USA

Karpa, Dave (Athlete, Hockey Player)
18 Jupiter Hills Dr
Newport Beach, CA 92660-9206

Karpatkin, Rhonda H (Publisher)
Consumer Reports Magazine
101 Truman Ave
Yonkers, NY 10703, USA

Karpinski, Keith (Athlete, Football Player)
1803 Sycamore Ave
Royal Oak, MI 48073-5020, USA

Karpluk, Erin (Actor)
c/o Staff Member *ROAR (LA)*
9701 Wilshire Blvd
8th Floor
Los Angeles, CA 90212, USA

Karplus, Martin (Misc)
Harvard University
Chemistry Dept
Cambridge, MA 02138, USA

Karpov, Anatoly (Misc)
International Peace Fund
Prechistenka 10
Moscow, RUSSIA

Karpowich, Ed (Athlete, Football Player)
P.O. Box 177
Fallon, NV 89407, USA

Karr, Mary (Writer)
Syracuse University
English Dept
Syracuse, NY 13244, USA

Karras, Louis (Athlete, Football Player)
904 Tulip Cir
Weston, FL 33327-2450, USA

Karras, Ted (Athlete, Football Player)
1122 N Shelby St
Gary, IN 46403, USA

Karros, Eric P (Athlete, Baseball Player)
PO Box 2380
Manhattan Beach, CA 90267-2380, USA

Karsay, Steve (Athlete, Baseball Player)
1861 Post Oak Pl
Westlake, TX 76262-4808, USA

Karslake, Betty L (Stylist)
1253 Andrews Ave
Lakewood, OH 44107, USA

Karstens, Jeff (Athlete, Baseball Player)
7280 Jamacha Rd
San Diego, CA 92114-3013, USA

Kartheiser, Vincent (Actor)
c/o Evan Hainey *Untitled Entertainment (LA)*
350 S. Beverly Dr #200
Beverly Hills, CA 90212, USA

Kartz, Keith (Athlete, Football Player)
19232 E Hinsdale Ln
Centennial, CO 80016, USA

Karusseit, Ursula (Actor)
Volksbunne
Rasa Luxemburg Platz
Berlin 10178, GERMANY

Karvan, Claudia (Actor, Musician)
c/o Robyn Gardiner *RGM Artist Group*
64-76 Kippax St
Level 2, Suite 202 & 206
Surry Hills, NSW 2010, Australia

Kar-Wai, Wong (Director)
Jet Tone Production
21/F Park Commercial Centre
No. 180 Tung Lo Wan Rd.
Hong Kong, China

Karyo, Tcheky (Actor)
c/o Staff Member *Current Entertainment*
9378 Wilshire Blvd
Sutie 210
Beverly Hills, CA 90212, USA

Karzai, Hamid (Prime Minister)
Prime Minister's Office
Shar Rahi Sedarat
Kabul, AFGHANISTAN

Kasabian, Kamera (Musician)
c/o Staff Member *Paradigm (Monterey)*
404 W Franklin St
Monterey, CA 93940, USA

Kasabov, Anton (Actor)
c/o Scott Karp *Crystal Sky Pictures*
10203 Santa Monica Blvd
5th Floor
Los Angeles, CA 90067, USA

Kasarova, Vesselina (Opera Singer)
Columbia Artists Mgmt Inc
165 W 57th St
New York, NY 10019, USA

Kasatkina, Natalya R (Ballerina, Choreographer)
Saint Karietny Riad
H 5/10 B 37
Moscow 103006, RUSSIA

Kasatonov, Alexei (Athlete, Hockey Player)
153 Eagle Rock Way
Montclair, NJ 07042-1621, USA

Kasay, John (Athlete, Football Player)
8812 Covey Rise Ct
Charlotte, NC 28226, USA

Kasch, Cody (Actor)
c/o Staff Member *ICM Partners (ICM-LA)*
10250 Constellation Blvd Fl 7
Los Angeles, CA 90067, USA

Kasch, Max (Actor)
c/o Staff Member *Abrams Artists Agency (LA)*
9200 Sunset Blvd
11th Floor
Los Angeles, CA 90069, USA

Kasdan, Lawrence (Actor, Director, Producer, Writer)
c/o Staff Member *Kasdan Pictures*
9220 W Sunset Blvd
Suite 108
West Hollywood, CA 90069-3500, USA

Kaselowski, Brian (Race Car Driver)
K Auto Motorsports
2790 Auburn Rd
Auburn Mills, MI 48326, USA

Kasem, Casey (Actor, Entertainer)
138 N Mapleton Dr
Los Angeles, CA 90077, USA

Kasem, Jean (Actor)
138 N Mapleton Dr
Los Angeles, CA 90077, USA

Kasem, Kerri (Actor)
c/o Steve Rohr *Lexicon Public Relations*
1901 Ave of the Stars
2nd Floor
Los Angeles, CA 90067, USA

Kaser, Helmut A (Misc)
Hitzigweg 11
Zurich 8032, SWITZERLAND

Kash, Daniel (Actor, Director)
c/o Staff Member *Coolwaters Productions*
10061 Riverside Dr.
Box 531
Toluca Lake, CA 91602, USA

Kasha, Al (Composer, Musician)
458 N Oakhurst Dr
#102
Beverly Hills, CA 90210, USA

Kashanchi, Ashkan (Actor, Bollywood)
c/o Asal Masomi *Asal Masomi Public Relations*
6320 Canoga Ave
Suite 1513
WoodlandHills, CA 91367, USA

Ka Shing, Li (Business Person)
Li Ka Shing Foundation
7/F Cheung Kong Center
2 Queens Road Central
HONG KONG

Kashkashian, Kim (Musician)
c/o Staff Member *Musicians Corporate Management*
PO Box 825
Highland, NY 12528, USA

Kashner, Sam (Writer)
c/o Staff Member *Simon & Schuster*
1230 Avenue of the Americas
New York, NY 10020, USA

Kashthuri (Actor, Bollywood)
4 Kashthuri Ranga Road
Chennai, TN 600018, INDIA

Kasich, John (Governor, Politician)
Vern Riffe Ctr
77 S High St Fl 30
Columbus, OH 43215-6108, USA

Kaskade (DJ, Musician)
c/o Barry Taylor *MCT Management*
520 8th Ave Rm 2205
New York, NY 10018, USA

Kaskey, Raymond J (Artist)
Kaskey Studio Inc
3804 38th St
Brentwood, MD 20722, USA

Kasko, Eddie (Athlete, Baseball Player, Coach)
32 Major Ginter Ct
Richmond, VA 23227-3349, USA

Kasl, Dr. Charlotte (Writer)
Many Roads, One Journey
P.O. Box 1302
Lolo, MT 59847, USA

Kasler, James (General)
8993 E !SOON Rd
Momence, IL 60954-3340, USA

Kasner, Sherrie (Stylist)
c/o Staff Member *Solo Artists*
2148 Federal Ave
Los Angeles, CA 90025, USA

Kason, Corinne (Actor)
Lovell Assoc
7095 Hollywood Blvd
#1006
Los Angeles, CA 90028, USA

Kasovitz, Mathieu (Actor)
Cineart
36 Rue de Ponthieu
Paris, FRANCE 75008

Kasparaitis, Darius (Athlete, Hockey Player)
Skeppargatan 4
Stockholm 11452, Sweden

Kasparaltis, Darius
170 Fairway Landings Dr.
Canonsburg, PA 15317-9567

Kasparov, Garri (Misc)
Russian Chess Federation
Luzhnetskaya 8
Moscow 119270, RUSSIA

Kasper, Kevin (Athlete, Football Player)
2211 Spartina Ln
Naperville, IL 60564-5033, USA

Kasper, Len (Commentator)
445 Drexel Ave
Glencoe, IL 60022-2102, USA

Kasper, Steve (Athlete, Coach, Hockey Player)
6 Swan Ln
Andover, MA 01810-2844, USA

Kasper, Walter Cardinal (Religious Leader)
Via dell Erba 1
Rome 00193, ITALY

Kasperek, Dick (Athlete, Football Player)
824 S County Line Rd
Hinsdale, IL 60521, USA

Kaspszyk, Jacek (Conductor)
Teatr Wielu
Pl Teatrainy 1
Warsaw 00-077, POLAND

Kasrashvili, Makvala (Opera Singer)
Bolshoi Theater
Teatralnaya Pl 1
Moscow 103009, RUSSIA

Kass, Carmen (Model)
City Models
Rue Jean Mermoz
Paris 75008, FRANCE

Kass, Danny (Skier)
PO Box 8549
Mammoth Lakes, CA 93546, USA

Kass, Leon R (Misc)
1150 17th St NW
#AE1
Washington, DC 20036, USA

Kass, Patricia
B.P. 203
Illkirch, FRANCE F-06700

Kassebaum, Nancy Landon (Ex-Senator)
US Embassy
Tokyo
Unit 45004 Box 200
APO, AP 37756-0008, USA

Kassebaum-Baker, Nancy (Ex-Senator)
PO Box 8
Huntsville, TN 37756-0008, USA

Kassell, Brad (Athlete, Football Player)
20117 Rancho Cielo Ct
Lago Vista, TX 78645-6046, USA

Kassell, Carl (Correspondent)
National Public Radio
635 Massachusetts Ave
Washington, DC 20001, USA

Kassian, Dennis
93 Crystal Way
Sherwood Park, AB T8H 1T8, Canada

Kassir, John (Actor)
c/o Vincent Cirrincione Vincent
Cirrincione Associates
1516 N Fairfax Ave
Los Angeles, CA 90046, USA

Kassorla, Irene C (Doctor)
908 N Roxbury Dr
Beverly Hills, CA 90210, USA

Kassovitz, Mathieu (Actor, Director, Producer)
MNP Entreprise
18 Rue Du Fbg Du Temple
Paris 75011, France

Kastelic, Ed (Athlete, Hockey Player)
1839 W Muirwood Dr
Phoenix, AZ 85045-1773

Kasten, Robert
1683 31st St NW
Washington, DC 20007-2968, USA

Kaster, Deena (Athlete, Olympic Athlete, Track Athlete)
1208 Majestic Pines Drive
Mammoth Lakes, CA 93546, USA

Kastor, Deena (Olympic Athlete, Track Athlete)
PO Box 5068
Mammoth Lakes, CA 93546, USA

Kasyanov, Mikhail M (Prime Minister)
Prime Minister's Office
Kremlin
Staraya Pl 4
Moscow 103132, RUSSIA

Kaszycki, Mike (Athlete, Hockey Player)
9 SHore Blvd
St Catharines, ON L2N 5T9, Canada

Kata, Matt (Athlete, Baseball Player)
1711 Westend Pl
Round Rock, TX 78681-2252, USA

Katchik, Joe (Athlete, Football Player)
25 Forty Oaks Rd
Whitehouse Station, NJ 08889, USA

Katchor, Ben (Cartoonist)
Little Brown
3 Center Plaza
Boston, MA 02108, USA

Kate, Lauren (Writer)
P.O. Box 461514
Los Angeles, CA 90046, USA

Kates, Kimberley (Actor)
David Talent
116 S Gardner St
Los Angeles, CA 90036, USA

Kates, Kimberly
3500 W. Olive Ave. #1400
Burbank, CA 91505

Kates, Robert W (Misc)
1081 Bar Harbor Road
Trenton, ME 04605, USA

Kathadi, Ramamurthi (Actor)
4 Krishna Avenue
C V Raman Road
Chennai, TN 600 006, INDIA

Katic, Stana (Actor)
c/o Nancy Seltzer Nancy Seltzer &
Associates
6220 Del Valle Drive
Los Angeles, CA 90048, USA

Katims, Jason (Producer)
c/o Staff Member Creative Artists Agency
(CAA-LA)
2000 Ave Of The Stars
Los Angeles, CA 90067, USA

Katims, Milton (Conductor, Musician)
Fairway Estales
8001 Sand Point Way NE
Seattle, WA 98115, USA

Katin, Peter R (Musician)
Maureen Lunn
Top Farm Parish Lane
Hedgerley
Bucks SL2 3JH, UNITED KINGDOM (UK)

Katkaveck, Leo (Athlete, Basketball Player)
1408 Jeremy Ln
Rocky Mount, NC 27803-1516, USA

Katolin, Mike (Athlete, Football Player)
308 Loyola Dr
Aptos, CA 95003-5228, USA

Katona, Kerry (Actor)
c/o Staff Member Random House Group
Limited
The Book Service Limited
20 Vauxhall Bridge Road
London SW1V 2SA, United Kingdom

Katritzky, Alan R (Misc)
1221 SW 21st Ave
Gainesville, FL 32601, USA

Katsav, Moshe (Politician, President)
President's Office
3 Hanassi
Jerusalem 92188, ISRAEL

Katsoudas, Stella (Musician, Songwriter, Writer)
Ashley Talent
2002 Hogback Road
#20
Ann Arbor, MI 48105, USA

Katt, Nicky (Actor)
c/o John Carrabino John Carrabino
Management
5900 Wilshire Blvd Fl 4 #406
Los Angeles, CA 90036, USA

Katt, William (Actor)
5860 Le Sage Ave
Woodland Hills, CA 91367, USA

Kattan, Chris (Comedian)
c/o Staff Member 3 Arts Entertainment Inc
9460 Wilshire Blvd
7th Floor
Beverly Hills, CA 90210, USA

Kattan, Mohammed Imad (Architect)
PO Box 950846
Amman 11195, JORDAN

Kattus, Eric (Athlete, Football Player)
854 Adams Rd
Loveland, OH 45140-7242, USA

Katula, Matt (Athlete, Football Player)
813 Crystal Palace Ct
Owings Mills, MD 21117-2257, USA

Katy B (Musician)
c/o Tom Schroeder Coda Music Agency -
UK
229 Shoreditch High St
London E1 6PJ, UK

Katz, Alex (Artist)
435 W Broadway
New York, NY 10012, USA

Katz, Bernard (Nobel Prize Laureate)
University College Department of
Medicine Gower Street London
WClE 6BT WClE 6BT, England

Katz, Cindy
Badgley Connor Talent Agency
1680 Vine Street #1016
Los Angeles, CA 90028, USA

Katz, Donald L (Engineer)
2011 Washtenaw Ave
Ann Arbor, MI 48104, USA

Katz, Douglas J (Doug) (Admiral)
1530 Gordon Cove Dr
Annapolis, MD 21403, USA

Katz, Harold (Misc)
Philadelphia 76ers
1st Union Center
3601 S Broad St
Philadelphia, PA 19148, USA

Katz, Hilda (Artist)
915 W End Ave
#5D
New York, NY 10025, USA

Katz, Jonathan (Actor, Animator, Comedian, Producer, Writer)
c/o Staff Member President Street
Productions
137 Fifth Avenue
Suite 9F
New York, NY 10010, USA

Katz, Michael (Misc)
1 Griggs Lane
Chappaqua, NY 10514, USA

Katz, Omri (Actor)
JH Productions
23674 Calabasas Road
#333
Calabasas, CA 91302, USA

Katz, Richard (Actor)
c/o Kirsten Wright Amanda Howard
Associates
21 Berwick St
London W1F 0PZ, UNITED KINGDOM
(UK)

Katz, Ross (Producer)
c/o Staff Member United Talent Agency
(UTA)
9336 Civic Center Dr
Beverly Hills, CA 90210, USA

Katz, Samuel L (Misc)
1917 Wildcat Creek Road
Chapel Hill, NC 27516, USA

Katz, Simon (Musician)
Searles
Chapel
26A Munster St
London SW6 4EN, UNITED KINGDOM
(UK)

Katz, Tonnie L (Editor)
Orange Country Register
Editorial Dept
625 N Grand Ave
Santa Ana, CA 92701, USA

katz, Vera (Politician)
Mayor's Office
City Hall
1221 SW 4th Ave #340
Portland, OR 97204, USA

Katzenberg, Jeffrey (Business Person)
c/o Staff Member DreamWorks SKG
1000 Flower St
Glendale, CA 91201, USA

Katzenmayer, Travis (Baseball Player)
562 N Overland
Mesa, AZ 85207-6670, USA

Katzenmeier, Travis (Athlete, Baseball Player)
1128 N Mountain Rd
Mesa, AZ 85207-2408, USA

Katzenmoyer, Andy (Athlete, Football Player)
5764 Salem Dr
Westerville, OH 43082-8186, USA

Katzur, Klaus (Swimmer)
Robert-Siewart-Str 76
Chemnitz 0912, GERMANY

Kauahi, Kani (Athlete, Game Show Host)
635 S Ellis St Apt 3054
Chandler, AZ 85224-4975, USA

kauffman, bob (Athlete, Basketball Player)
1677 Rivermist Dr SW
Lilburn, GA 30047-2451, USA

Kauffman, Joel (Race Car Driver)
Kitzbradshaw Racing
114 Meadow Hill Circle
Mooresville, NC 28115, USA

Kauffman, Marta (Producer, Writer)
c/o Staff Member Bright Kauffman Crane
Productions
4000 Warner Blvd
Bldg 160 #750
Burbank, CA 91522

Kaufman, Adam (Actor)
c/o Steven Levy Framework Entertainment
(LA)
9057 Nemo St
Suite C
West Hollywood, CA 90069, USA

Kaufman, Avy (Actor)
c/o Rick Kurtzman Creative Artists Agency
(CAA-LA)
2000 Ave Of The Stars
Los Angeles, CA 90067, USA

Kaufman, Bob (Ajax) (Athlete, Basketball Player)
1677 Rivermist Dr SW
Lilbum, GA 30047, USA

Kaufman, Charlie (Writer)
c/o Sharon Jackson WME (LA)
9601 Wilshire Blvd Fl 3
Beverly Hills, CA 90210, USA

Kaufman, Curt (Athlete, Baseball Player)
308 Hillway Dr
Glenwood, IA 51534-1210, USA

Kaufman, Dan S (Misc)
University of Wisconsin
Medical School
Hematology Dept
Madison, WI 53706, USA

Kaufman, Donald (Writer)
c/o Staff Member United Talent Agency (UTA)
9336 Civic Center Dr
Beverly Hills, CA 90210, USA

Kaufman, Henry (Financier)
Lehman Brothers
25 Bank St
30th Floor
London E14 5LE, United Kingdom

Kaufman, Joan (Athlete, Baseball Player, Commentator)
1111 Crystal Spg
San Antonio, TX 78258-6909, USA

Kaufman, Moises (Director)
c/o Patty Detroit Todd Smith and Associates
10250 Constellation Blvd
7th Floor
Los Angeles, CA 90067, USA

Kaufman, Napolean (Athlete, Football Player)
72 Incline Green Ln
Alamo, CA 94507, USA

Kaufman, Napoleon (Athlete, Football Player)
1913 Via Di Salemo
Pleasanton, CA 94566, USA

Kaufman, Tim (Race Car Driver)
Kaufman Racing
8201 S. Meade Ave.
Burbank, IL 60459, USA

Kaufusi, Steve (Athlete, Football Player)
3018 Comanche Ln
Provo, UT 84604-4344, USA

Kaulitz, Bill (Musician)
c/o Staff Member Universal Music Deutschland
Stralauer Allee 1
Berlin 10245, Germany

Kausalya (Actor)
15 A-2 Akshar
Palace Road
Bangalore, KA 52, INDIA

Kaushal, Kamini (Actor, Bollywood, Dancer)
B2 Anita Mt Pleasant Road
Malabar Hill
Bombay, MS 400 006, INDIA

Kaushik, Satish (Actor, Bollywood, Comedian, Director, Filmmaker)
1/124 Park View Zakaria Agadi Nagar
Yari Road Versova Andheri
Bombay, MS 400 061, INDIA

Kauth, Kathleen (Athlete, Hockey Player, Olympic Athlete)
13 Hillcrest Ln
Saratoga Springs, NY 12866-8528, USA

Kavana (Musician)
Tony Denton Promotions
19 S Molton Ln
Mayfair
London, England W1K 5LE

Kavanagh, Brad (Actor)
c/o Jeff Golenberg Collective
8383 Wilshire Blvd
Suite 1050
Beverly Hills, CA 90211, USA

Kavandi, Janet L (Astronaut)
3907 Park Circle Way
Houston, TX 77059, USA

Kavelaars, Ingrid (Actor)
c/o Staff Member Silver Massetti & Szatmary (SMS-NY)
145 W 45th St #1204
New York, NY 10036, USA

Kaveri (Actor, Bollywood)
114 4th Street
New Britania Nagar
Chennai, TN 600087, INDIA

Kaviya (Actor, Bollywood)
Santhi Apts
Kumaran Colony 9th Street
Chennai, TN 600026, INDIA

Kavner, Julie (Actor)
c/o Paul Martino ICM Partners (ICM-NY)
730 Fifth Ave
New York, NY 10019, USA

Kavovit, Andrew (Actor)
c/o Staff Member TalentWorks (LA)
3500 W Olive Ave
Suite 1400
Burbank, CA 91505, USA

Kawakubo, Rei (Designer, Fashion Designer)
Comme des Garcons
5-11-5 Minamiaoyana
Minatoku
Tokyo, JAPAN

Kawalerowicz, Jersy (Director, Writer)
Ul Marconich 5m 21
Warsaw 02-954, POLAND

Kay, Alan C (Engineer)
Viewpoints Research Institute
1209 Grand Capital Ave
Glendale, CA 91201, USA

Kay, Bill (Athlete, Football Player)
4266 Waterston Courtyard
Evans, GA 30809-5036, USA

Kay, Charles
18 Epple Rd.
London, ENGLAND SW6

Kay, Dianne (Actor)
1565 Calle Del Estribo
Pacific Palisades, CA 90272, USA

Kay, Jason (Jay) (Musician)
c/o Staff Member WmE2 (WMA-LA)
1 William Morris Pl
Beverly Hills, CA 90212, USA

Kay, John (Musician)
Elite Management Corp
2211 Norfolk St
#760
Houston, TX 77098, USA

Kay, Lisa (Actor)
c/o Jeremy Conway Conway van Gelder
8-12 Broadwick St
London W1F 8HW, UK

Kay, Michael (Athlete, Baseball Player)
418 Pine Grove Ln
Hartsdale, NY 10530-1157, USA

Kay, Michael (Commentator)
418 Pine Grove Ln
Hartsdale, NY 10530-1157, USA

Kay, Michael (Athlete, Baseball Player)
418 Pine Grove Ln
Hartsdale, NY 10530-1157, USA

Kay, Michael
418 Pine Grove Ln
Hartsdale, NY 10530-1157, USA

Kay, Peter (Actor)
c/o Staff Member McIntyre Management Ltd
35 Soho Sq
2nd Floor
London W1D 3QX, UK

Kay, Vanessa (Actor)
c/o Staff Member Comedy Central (LA)
2049 Century Park E #4170
Los Angeles, CA 90067, USA

Kay, William H (Athlete, Football Player)
4266 Waterston Courtyard
Evans, GA 30809, USA

Kaye, Davie A
1044 Ironwork Pass
Vancouver BC V6H 3P1, CANADA

Kaye, Jonathan (Stylist)
c/o Staff Member Katy Barker Agency Inc
6606 10th Ave Apt 3R
Brooklyn, NY 11219, USA

Kaye, Jonathan (Athlete, Golfer)
328 W El Camino Dr
Phoenix, AZ 85021-5525, USA

Kaye, Judy (Actor, Musician)
Bret Adams
448 W 44th St
New York, NY 10036, USA

Kaye, Justin (Athlete, Baseball Player)
3591 Arville St Unit 302B
Las Vegas, NV 89103-1679, USA

Kaye, Lila
47 Courtfield Rd. #9
London, ENGLAND SW7 4DB

Kaye, Melvina
PO Box 6085
Burbank, CA 91510

Kaye, Thorsten (Actor)
c/o Staff Member ICM Partners (ICM-LA)
10250 Constellation Blvd Fl 7
Los Angeles, CA 90067, USA

Kaye, Tony (Misc)
Sun Artists
9 Hillgate St
London W8 7SP, UNITED KINGDOM (UK)

Kayleigh, Layla (Actor, Television Host)
c/o Staff Member United Talent Agency (UTA)
9336 Civic Center Dr
Beverly Hills, CA 90210, USA

Kayser, Elmer L (Historian)
2921 34th St NW
Washington, DC 20008, USA

Kaz (Artist)
c/o Staff Member Fantagraphics Books
7563 Lake City Way
Seattle, WA 98115, USA

Kazan, Lainie (Actor, Musician)
9903 Santa Monica Blvd #283
Beverly Hills, CA 90212, USA

Kazan, Zoe (Actor)
c/o Michelle Benson 42West (NY)
220 W 42nd St
12th Floor
New York, NY 10036, USA

Kazankina, Tatyana (Athlete, Track Athlete)
Hoshimina St
111211
Saint Petersburg, RUSSIA

Kazanski, Ted (Athlete, Baseball Player)
1544 Dormie Dr
Gladwin, MI 48624-8104, USA

Kazarnovskaya, Lubov Y (Opera Singer)
Hohenbergstr 50
Vienna 1120, AUSTRIA

Kazer, Beau
139-A N. San Fernando Rd
Burbank, CA 91502

Kazmaier, Dick (Athlete, Football Player, Heisman Trophy Winner)
Kazmaier Associates
676 Elm St #1
Concord, MA 01742-2169, USA

Kazmar, sean
4 Los Llanos
Edgewood, NM 87015, USA

Kazmir, Scott (Athlete, Baseball Player)
16619 Rose Bay Trl
Cypress, TX 77429-4935, USA

K Bagyaraj (Actor)
Off 1 Kuppusamy Street
T Nagar
Chennai, TN 600 017, INDIA

K Balaji (Actor)
58 Pantheon Road
Egmore
Chennai, TN 600 008, INDIA

K Balasing (Actor)
86/2 Maddox Street Choolai
Chennai, TN 600 112, INDIA

K Bapaiah (Bollywood, Director)
15 Seethamma Colony 3rd Cross Road
Alwarpet
Madras, TN 600 017, INDIA

KC & The Sunshine Band (Music Group)
c/o Kirt Webster Webster & Associates PR
3573 Couchville Pike
Hermitage, TN 37076, USA

K-Ci & JoJo (Music Group)
c/o Staff Member Devour
3575 Cahuenga Blvd W
#254
Los Angeles, CA 90068, USA

K D, Dunn (Athlete, Football Player)
2264 Colleen Ct
Decatur, GA 30032-7153, USA

K. Davis, Danny (Congressman, Politician)
2159 Rayburn HOB
Washington, DC 20515, USa

Kea, Clarence (Athlete, Basketball Player)
9175 Jennifer St
Beaumont, TX 77707-2727, USA

Keach, James (Actor)
c/o Staff Member *Catfish Productions*
23852 Pacific Coast Hwy
Suite #313
Malibu, CA 90265, USA

Keach, Stacy (Actor)
101 N Robertson Blvd Ste 200
Beverly Hills, CA 90211-2191, USA

Keady, Gene (Coach)
Purdue University
Mackey Arena
West Lafayette, IN 47907, USA

Keagan, Carrie (Television Host)
c/o Staff Member *No Good TV (NGTV)*
9944 Santa Monica Blvd
Beverly Hills, CA 90212, USA

Keaggy, Phil (Musician)
c/o Staff Member *Street Level Artists Agency*
107 East Center St
Warsaw, IN 46580, USA

Keagle, Greg (Athlete, Baseball Player)
11 Wolcott Dr
Horseheads, NY 14845-1012, USA

Kealey, Steve (Athlete, Baseball Player)
1080 1700 Ave
Abilene, KS 67410-6321, USA

Kean, Jane
c/o Staff Member *Pierce & Shelly*
13775-A Mono Way #220
Sonora, CA 95370, USA

Kean, Laurel (Athlete, Golfer)
25280 Ojibway Ct
Punta Gorda, FL 33983, USA

Kean, Thomas H (Ex-Governor)
Quad Partners
21 Penn Plaza
Suite 1501
New York, NY 10001, USA

Keanan, Staci (Actor)
c/o Jennifer Goodwin *PMK/BNC - LA*
8687 Melrose Ave
8th Floor
West Hollywood, CA 90069, USA

Keane (Musician)
c/o Staff Member *Island Records*
825 Eighth Ave
New York, NY 10019, USA

Keane, Dolores (Musician)
D K Entertainments
Caherlistrane, Galway, IRELAND

Keane, Glen (Animator)
Walt Disney Studios
Animation Dept
500 S Buena Vista St
Burbank, CA 91521, USA

Keane, John M (Jack) (General)
Vice Chief of Staff HqUSA
Pentagon
Washington, DC 20310, USA

Keane, Katie Amanda (Actor)
c/o Paul Bennett *PB Management*
6523 West Sixth Street
Los Angeles, CA 90048, USA

Keane, Kerrie (Actor)
S D B Partners
1801 Ave of Stars
#902
Los Angeles, CA 90067, USA

Keane, Mike (Athlete, Hockey Player)
The Rink 91 Lawson Cres
Winnipeg, MB R3P OT3, Canada

Keane, Roy M (Soccer Player)
Sunderland FC
Sunderland
Stadium Park
Manchester, Tyne & Wear SR5 1SU,
UNITED KINGDOM (UK)

Keane, Sean (Misc)
Macklam Feldman Mgmt
1505 W 2nd Ave
#200
Vancouver, BC V6H 3Y4, CANADA

Keans, Doug (Athlete, Hockey Player)
240 Dartmouth Ave
spring Hill, FL 34606-5435

Kear, David (Misc)
34 W End
Ohope, NEW ZELAND

Kearney, Bob (Athlete, Baseball Player)
4155 Elizabeth Dr
Stevensville, MI 49127-9530, USA

Kearney, Jim (Athlete, Football Player)
Washington High School
1817 E 59th St
Kansas City, KS 64130-3329, USA

Kearney, Mat (Musician)
c/o Staff Member *First Company Management*
504 Autumn Springs Ct
Suite A8
Franklin, TN 37067, USA

Kearney, Tim (Athlete, Football Player)
2144 Dartmouth Gate Ct
Ballwin, MO 63011, USA

Kearns, Austin (Athlete, Baseball Player)
719 Haverhill Dr
Lexington, KY 40503-3426, USA

Kearns, Dennis (Athlete, Hockey Player)
1292 Esquimalt Ave
West Vancouver, BC V7T 1K3, CANADA

Kearns, Michael (Athlete, Basketball Player)
PO Box 263
Monroe, NC 28111-0263, USA

Kearns, Thomas (Athlete, Football Player)
121 Bay Colony Dr
Fort Lauderdale, FL 33308, USA

Kearns, Thomas (Athlete, Basketball Player)
27 Deepwood Rd
Darien, CT 06820-3202, USA

Kearse, Amalya L (Judge)
US Court of Appeals
US Courthouse
Foley Square
New York, NY 10007, USA

Kearse, Jevon (Athlete, Football Player)
61 Whitworth Blvd
Nashville, TN 37205-5019, USA

Keaser, Lloyd (Athlete, Olympic Athlete, Wrestler)
43960 Tavern Dr
Ashburn, VA 20147-3905, USA

Keathley, George (Director)
Missouri Repertory Theater
4949 Cherry St
Kensas City, MO 64110, USA

Keating, Bill (Athlete, Football Player)
4810 S Lafayette Ln
Englewood, CO 80113, USA

Keating, Charles (Actor)
Don Buchwald
10 E 44th St
New York, NY 10017, USA

Keating, Chris (Athlete, Football Player)
741 Canton Ave
Milton, MA 02186, USA

Keating, Dominic (Actor)
c/o Staff Member *Shelter Entertainment*
9454 Wilshire Blvd.
Suite 715
Beverly Hills, CA 90212, USA

Keating, Paul (Royalty)
31 Bligh St Level 2
Sydney 2000, AUSTRALIA

Keating, Paul J (Prime Minister)
Keating Assoc-War Mgmt
Bushy Park Road
57 Meadowbank
Dublin, IRELAND

Keating, Ronan (Musician)
Carol Assoc-War Mgmt
Bushy Park Rd
57 Meadowbank
Dublin, IRELAND

Keating, Ronan (Musician)
c/o Amanda Bross *Finch & Partners - Paris*
Top Floor
29-37 Heddon St
London W1B 4BR, UNITED KINGDOM

Keating, Thomas A (Athlete, Football Player)
3725 W St NW
Washington, DC 20007, USA

Keatley, Greg (Athlete, Baseball Player)
140 Rockridge Ct
Lexington, SC 29072-7970, USA

Keaton, Curtis (Athlete, Football Player)
246 Briarcliff Dr
Kannapolis, NC 28081, USA

Keaton, Diane (Actor, Director, Producer)
c/o Adam Venit *WME (LA)*
9601 Wilshire Blvd Fl 3
Beverly Hills, CA 90210, USA

Keaton, Joshua (Josh) (Actor)
c/o Brian Wilkins *Kritzer Levine Wilkins Entertainment (KLWG)*
11872 La Grange Ave
1st Floor
Los Angeles, CA 90025, USA

Keaton, Michael (Actor, Director, Producer)
c/o Paul Bloch *Rogers & Cowan PR (LA)*
Pacific Design Center
8687 Melrose Ave, 7th Floor
West Hollywood, CA 90069, USA

Keats, Donald H (Composer)
University of Denver
Music School
Denver, CO 80208, USA

Keats, Ele (Actor)
c/o Rob D'Avola *Rob DAvola & Associates*
9107 Wilshire Blvd #450
Beverly Hills, CA 90210, USA

Kebbel, Arielle (Actor)
c/o Martin Berneman *Precision Entertainment*
6338 Wilshire Blvd
Los Angeles, CA 90048, USA

Kebbell, Toby (Actor)
c/o Samantha Mast *Rogers & Cowan PR (LA)*
Pacific Design Center
8687 Melrose Ave, 7th Floor
West Hollywood, CA 90069, USA

Kebede, Liya (Model)
c/o Staff Member *IMG Models (NY)*
304 Park Ave S
12th Floor
New York, NY 10010, USA

Kebich, Vyacheslau F (Prime Minister)
National Assembly
K Marksa Str 38
Dom Urada
Minsk 220016, BELARUS

Keb Mo (Musician, Songwriter, Writer)
Monterey International
200 W Superior
#202
Chicago, IL 60610, USA

Keck, Donald B (Inventor)
2877 Chequers Circle
Big Flats, NY 14814-9610, USA

Keckin, Val (Athlete, Football Player)
8918 Montrose Way
San Diego, CA 92122, USA

Kecman, Dan (Athlete, Football Player)
16413 Fox Valley Ter
Rockville, MD 20853-3220, USA

Keczmer, Dan
PO Box 2883
Brentwood, TN 37024-2883

Keczmer, Don (Athlete, Hockey Player)
8303 Bridle Pl
Brentwood, TN 37027, USA

Kedah (King)
Istana Anak Bukit
Alor Setar, Kedah Darul Aman,
MALAYSIA

Keddie, Asher (Actor)
c/o Staff Member *Shanahan Management*
Level 3, Berman House
91 Campbell St
Surry Hills NSW 2010, Australia

Kedes, Maureen (Actor)
Tisherman Agency
6767 Forest Lawn Dr
#101
Los Angeles, CA 90403, USA

Kee, Lee Shau (Business Person)
Henderson Land Development Company Limited
72-76/F, Two International Finance Centre
8 Finance Street, Central
Hong Kong

Keeble, Jerry (Athlete, Football Player)
P.O. Box 367
Dunnigan, CA 95937, USA

Keeble, John (Musician)
International Talent Group
729 7th Ave
#1600
New York, NY 10019, USA

Keedy, Pat (Athlete, Baseball Player)
6308 Mountainview Cir
Gardendale, AL 35071-2088, USA

Keefe, Adam (Athlete, Basketball Player)
15933 Alcima Ave
Pacific Palisades, CA 90272-2405, USA

Keefe, Mike (Cartoonist)
Denver Post
Editorial Dept
PO Box 1709
Denver, CO 80201, USA

Keefe, Sheldon (Athlete, Hockey Player)
c/o Staff Member *Pembroke Lumber Kings*
P.O. Box 92
Stn Main
Pembroke, ON K8A 6X1, Canada

Keefer, Don (Actor)
4146 Allot Ave
Sherman Oaks, CA 91423, USA

Keeffe, Bernard (Conductor)
153 Honor Oak Road
London SE23 3RN, UNITED KINGDOM
(UK)

Keegan, Andrew (Actor)
c/o Barry McPherson *Agency for the Performing Arts (APA-LA)*
405 S Beverly Dr
Suite 500
Beverly Hills, CA 90212-4425, USA

Keegan, Ed
PO Box 764
Malaga, NJ 08328-0764, USA

Keegan, Kari (Actor)
2042 S Oxford Ave
Los Angeles, CA 90018, USA

Keehne, Virginya (Actor)
Craig Mgmt
125 S Sycamore Ave
Los Angeles, CA 90036, USA

Keeler, Don
24000 Jensen Dr.
West Hills, CA 91304

Keeler, William H Cardinal (Religious Leader)
National Conference of Catholic Bishops
3211 4th St
Washington, DC 20017, USA

Keeley, Robert V (Diplomat)
3814 Livingston St NW
Washington, DC 20015, USA

Keeling, Alexandra (Stylist)
c/o Staff Member *Artists by Timothy Priano (CA)*
8447 Wilshire Blvd
#301
Beverly Hills, CA 90211, USA

Keeling, Charles D (Musician)
Scripps Oceanography Institute
Ritler Hall
9500 Gilman Dr
La Jolla, CA 92093, USA

Keeling, Harold (Athlete, Basketball Player)
6707 Broad Oaks Dr
Richmond, TX 77406-7629, USA

Keel Jr, Alton G (Business Person, Diplomat)
Atlantic Partners
2891 S River Road
Stanardsville, VA 22973, USA

Keelor, Greg (Musician)
c/o Staff Member *ArtistDirect*
9046 Lindblade St
Culver City, CA 90232, USA

Keen, Robert Earl (Musician, Songwriter)
Rosetta
PO Box 2186
Bandera, TX 78003, USA

Keen, Sam (Writer)
16331 Norrbom Road
Sonoma, CA 95476, USA

Keena, Monica (Actor)
c/o Sarah Fargo *Paradigm (NY)*
360 Park Ave S Fl 16
New York, NY 10010, USA

Keenan, Joseph D (Misc)
2727 29th St NW
Washington, DC 20008, USA

Keenan, Larry (Athlete, Hockey Player)
132 Gordon Dr
North Bay, ON P1B 8B2, Canada

Keenan, Maynard James (Musician)
c/o Staff Member *Virgin Records (NY)*
150 5th Ave
New York, NY 10010, USA

Keenan, Mike (Misc)
550 NE 21st Ave
#13
Deerfield Beach, FL 33441, USA

Keene, Donald L (Educator)
Columbia University
Language Dept
Kent Hall
New York, NY 10027, USA

Keene, Larry (Athlete, Hockey Player)
1232 Gordon Dr.
North Bay, ON P1B 8B2, CANADA

Keene, Tommy (Musician, Songwriter, Writer)
Black Park Mgmt
PO Box 107
Sunbury, NC 27979, USA

Keene Cherot, Kyera (Actor)
c/o Staff Member *Creative Artists Agency (CAA-LA)*
2000 Ave Of The Stars
Los Angeles, CA 90067, USA

Keenen, Mary Jo
9200 Sunset Blvd. #1130
Los Angeles, CA 90069

Keener, Catherine (Actor)
c/o Staff Member *ID Public Relations (ID-LA)*
7060 Hollywood Blvd
8th Floor
Los Angeles, CA 90028, USA

Keener, Jeff (Athlete, Baseball Player)
2107 Dewey St
Murphysboro, IL 62966-2451, USA

Keener, Joe (Athlete, Baseball Player)
16915 Glendower Ave
Edwards, CA 93523-3515, USA

Keenlyside, Simon (Opera Singer)
Columbia Artists Mgmt Inc
165 W 57th St
New York, NY 10019, USA

Keeny Jr, Spurgeon M (Misc)
3600 Albernarle St NW
Washington, DC 20008, USA

Keerthana, K (Actor, Bollywood)
71 A Kamarajar Salai
R A Puram
Chennai, TN 600028, INDIA

Keeslar, Matt (Actor)
c/o Staff Member *Stone Manners Salners Agency (LA)*
9911 W Pico Blvd Ste 1400
Los Angeles, CA 90035, USA

Keesling, Barbara (Writer)
c/o Staff Member *Random House Publicity*
1745 Broadway
New York, NY 10019, USA

Keeton, Durwood (Athlete, Football Player)
1372 Diamond Gate Pl
El Paso, TX 79936, USA

Keeton, Rickey (Athlete, Baseball Player)
3433 Stathem Ave
Cincinnati, OH 45211-5723, USA

Keezer, Geoff (Misc)
DL Media
PO Box 2728
Bala Cynwyd, PA 19004, USA

Keflezighi, Meb (Athlete, Olympic Athlete, Track Athlete)
141 Mammoth Knolls Drive
Mammoth Lakes, CA 93546, USA

Kegel, Oliver (Athlete)
Am Bogen 23
Berlin 13589, GERMANY

Keggi, Caroline (Athlete, Golfer)
9228 E Happy Hollow Dr
Scottsdale, AZ 85262, USA

Ke$ha (Musician)
933 Forest Acres Ct
Nashville, TN 37220, USA

Kehoe, Rick (Athlete, Hockey Player)
1027 Highland Dr
Canonsburg, PA 15317-5227

Keibler, Stacy (Actor, Wrestler)
c/o Leslie Grossnickle *Untitled Entertainment (LA)*
350 S. Beverly Dr #200
Beverly Hills, CA 90212, USA

Keightley, David N (Historian)
University of California
History Dept
Berkeley, CA 94720, USA

Keillor, Garrison E (Correspondent, Writer)
A Prairie Home Companion
480 Cedar St
Saint Paul, MN 55101, USA

Keim, Jenny (Swimmer)
R O'Brien
Swimming Hall of Fame
1 Hall of Fame Dr
Fort Lauderdale, FL 33316, USA

Keisler, Randy (Athlete, Baseball Player)
6842 Durango Creek Dr
Magnolia, TX 77354-2749, USA

Keita, Ibrahaim Boubakar (Prime Minister)
Prime Minister's Office
BP97
Bamako, MALI

Keita, Salif (Composer, Musician)
International Music Network
278 S Main St
#400
Gloucester, MA 01930, USA

Keitel, Harvey (Actor)
c/o Toni Howard *ICM Partners (ICM-LA)*
10250 Constellation Blvd Fl 7
Los Angeles, CA 90067, USA

Keith, Duncan
1442 W Fullerton Ave Apt 4D
Chicago, IL 60614-7877

Keith, Embray (Athlete, Football Player)
1232 Sun nymede Ave
South Bend, IN 46615, USA

Keith, Louis (Doctor)
333 E Superior St
#476
Chicago, IL 60611, USA

Keith, Penelope (Actor)
66 Berkeley House
Hay Hill
London SW3, UNITED KINGDOM (UK)

Keith, Toby (Musician)
P.O. Box 8739
Rockford, IL 61126, USA

Keithley, Gary (Athlete, Football Player)
1801 W Westhill Dr
Cleburne, TX 76033, USA

Keith Rennie, Callum (Actor)
c/o Elizabeth Hodgson *Elizabeth Hodgson Management Group*
1688 Cypress St
Suite 405
Vancouver, BC V6J 5J1, Canada

Kekalainen, Jarmo (Athlete, Hockey Player)
Jokerit Helsinki Areenakuja 1
Helsinki, SF 00240, Finland

Kekich, Mike (Athlete, Baseball Player)
5314 Canada Vista Pl NW
Albuaueraue, NM 87120-2412, USA

Kelcher, Louie J (Athlete, Football Player)
10204 Carlotta Cove
Austin, TX 78733, USA

Keleti, Agnes (Misc)
Wingate Institute for Physical Education & Sport
Matanya 42902, ISRAEL

Kelis (Musician)
30 Vintage Ct
McDonough, GA 30253, USA

Kelis, Kid 'N Play (Music Group)
1650 Broadway #508
New York, NY 10019, USA

Kelker-Kelly, Robert (Actor)
4704 Whitsett Ave
Studio City, CA 91604, USA

Kell, Ayla (Actor)
c/o Scott Zimmerman *Evolution Entertainment (LA)*
901 N Highland Ave
Los Angeles, CA 90038, USA

kell, Everett "Skeeter" (Athlete, Baseball Player)
PO Box 10113
Conway, AR 72034-0001, USA

Kell, Everett (Skeeter) (Athlete, Baseball Player)
P.O. Box 10113
Conway, AR 72034, USA

Kellan (Stylist)
c/o Staff Member *Igroup + Ridecreative*
315 W 39th St
#908
New York, NY 10018, USA

Kellar, Mark (Athlete, Football Player)
3537 Fuller St W
Edina, MN 55410, USA

Kellaway, Roger (Composer)
Pat Phillips Mgmt
520 E 81st St
#PH C
New York, NY 10028, USA

Kelleher, Chris
541 Kitchen Lane
Pittston, PA 18643

Kelleher, Erhard (Misc)
Sudliche Munchneustr 6A
Grunwald 82031, GERMANY

Kelleher, Herbert D (Business Person)
144 Thelma Dr
San Antonio, TX 78212, USA

Kelleher, Mick (Athlete, Baseball Player)
1451 Alamo Pintado Rd
Solvang, CA 93463-9757, USA

Keller, Bill (Athlete, Basketball Player)
14602 Scatborough Ln
Noblesville, IN 46062-9729, USA

Keller, Cord (Producer)
c/o Staff Member *Innovative Artists (LA)*
1505 10th St
Santa Monica, CA 90401, USA

Keller, Dave (Athlete, Baseball Player)
4403 Marchmont Blvd
Land 0 Lakes, FL 34638-7760, USA

Keller, Dustin (Athlete, Football Player)
c/o Roosevelt Barnes *Maximum Sports Management*
6435 W Jefferson Blvd
#197
Fort Wayne, IN 46804, USA

Keller, Gary (Athlete, Basketball Player)
220 Estado Way NE
Saint Petersburg, FL 33704-3752, USA

Keller, Jason (Race Car Driver)
Progressive Motorsports
201 Rolling Hills Rd.
Mooresville, NC 28115, USA

Keller, Joseph B (Mathematician)
820 Sonoma Terrace
Stanford, CA 94305, USA

Keller, Joyce (Psychic, Radio Personality, Television Host, Writer)
600 Harbor Blvd
#905
Weehawken, NJ 07086, USA

Keller, Kalyn (Athlete, Olympic Athlete, Swimmer)
2809 Ellenville Place Apt R-1
Los Angeles, CA 90007, USA

Keller, Klete (Athlete, Olympic Athlete, Swimmer)
3015 N Hozoni Rd
Prescott, AZ 86305-3992, USA

Keller, Kris (Athlete, Baseball Player)
2496 Oakview Dr
Jacksonville, FL 32246-2462, USA

Keller, Larry (Athlete, Football Player)
2933 Five Oaks Ln
Brenham, TX 77833, USA

Keller, Leonard B (War Hero)
6350 Majzun Rd
Milton, FL 32570, USA

Keller, Martha (Actor)
Lemonstr 9
Munich 81679, GERMANY

Keller, Marthe (Actor)
c/o Laurent Gregoire *Agence Artistique Adequat*
108 rue Reaumur
Paris 75002, France

Keller, Mary Page (Actor)
c/o Staff Member *Silver Massetti & Szatmary (SMS) Talent Inc*
8383 Wilshire Blvd
Suite 230
Beverly Hills, CA 90211, USA

Keller, Melissa (Actor)
c/o Margie Weiner *Margie Weiner Management*
8205 Santa Monica Blvd
Suite 1-450
Los Angeles, CA 90046, USA

Keller, Ralph (Athlete, Hockey Player)
1027 Highland Dr
Canonsburg, PA 15317-5227

Keller, Rita (Baseball Player)
6410 Westchester St
Portage, MI 49024-3276, USA

Keller, Ron (Athlete, Baseball Player)
P.O. Box 3267
Cashiers, NC 28717-3267, USA

Keller, Thomas (Chef)
French Laundry
6540 Washington St
Yountville, CA 94599, USA

Kellerman, Ernie (Athlete, Football Player)
408 Fairway Vw
Chagrin Falls, OH 44023, USA

Kellerman, Faye (Writer)
Karpfinger Agency
357 W 20th St
New York, NY 10011, USA

Kellerman, Jonathan (Writer)
c/o Brian Pike *Creative Artists Agency (CAA-LA)*
2000 Ave Of The Stars
Los Angeles, CA 90067, USA

Kellerman, Max (Actor, Sportscaster)
c/o Staff Member *I, Max*
Fox Sports Television Group
10201 W Pico Blvd Bldg 101
Los Angeles, CA 90035, USA

Kellerman, Sally (Actor)
c/o Chuck Binder *Binder & Associates*
1465 Lindacrest Dr
Beverly Hills, CA 90210, USA

Kellermann, Ernie (Athlete, Football Player)
90 Glenview Dr
Aurora, OH 44202-8219, USA

Kellermeyer, Doug (Athlete, Football Player)
1028 Daisy Ave
Carlsbad, CA 92011-4820, USA

Kelley, Alexis (Stylist)
c/o Staff Member *Montana Artists Agency*
9150 Wilshire Blvd Ste 100
Beverly Hills, CA 90212, USA

Kelley, Allen (Athlete, Basketball Player, Olympic Athlete)
5900 Longleaf Dr
Lawrence, KS 66049-5801, USA

Kelley, Bill (Athlete, Football Player)
6446 US Highway 69 S
Lone Oak, TX 75453, USA

Kelley, Brian (Athlete, Football Player)
98 Constitution Way
Basking Ridge, NJ 07920, USA

Kelley, David E (Producer, Writer)
c/o Staff Member *David E Kelley Productions*
1600 Rosecrans Ave #4B
Manhattan Beach, CA 90266, USA

Kelley, Dean (Athlete, Basketball Player)
5900 Longleaf Dr
Lawrence, KS 66049, USA

Kelley, Donald R (Historian)
45 Jefferson Ave
New Brunswick, NJ 08901, USA

Kelley, Dwight (Athlete, Football Player)
1006 Clubview Blvd N
Columbus, OH 43235, USA

Kelley, Earl A (Athlete, Basketball Player)
5900 Longleaf Dr
Lawrence, KS 66049-5801, USA

Kelley, Gaynor N (Business Person)
Perkin-Elmer Corp
710 Bridgeport Ave
Shelton, CT 06484, USA

Kelley, Gordon (Athlete, Football Player)
3101 S Ocean Blvd
Apt 126
Highland Beach, FL 33487, USA

Kelley, Harold H (Psychic)
21634 Rambla Vista St
Maliby, CA 90265, USA

Kelley, Ike (Athlete, Football Player)
1006 Clubview Blvd N
Columbus, OH 432354222, USA

Kelley, Jack (Athlete, Hockey Player)
PO Box 538
Oakland, ME 04963-0538

Kelley, Jon (Television Host)
c/o Staff Member *Extra (LA)*
Telepictures Productions
1840 Victory Blvd
Glendale, CA 91201, USA

Kelley, Josh (Musician)
c/o Debbie Wilson *Wilspro Management*
P.O. Box 9
Point Pleasant, NY 10001, USA

Kelley, Kevin (Athlete, Baseball Player)
1311 Quarterpath Ct
Richmond, TX 77469, USA

Kelley, Kitty (Writer)
1228 Eton Court NW
Washington, DC 20007, USA

Kelley, Malcolm David (Actor)
c/o Nelson Parks *ESI Network*
6310 San Vicente Blvd #340
Los Angeles, CA 90048, United States

Kelley, Manon (Adult Film Star)
P.O. Box 315
Bellmore, NY 11710, USA

Kelley, Nathalie (Actor)
c/o Megan Silverman *WME (LA)*
9601 Wilshire Blvd Fl 3
Beverly Hills, CA 90210, USA

Kelley, Paul X (General)
1600 N Oak St Apt 1619
Arlington, VA 22209-2769, USA

Kelley, Paul X (General)
1600 N Oak St
#1619
Arlington, VA 22209-2769, USA

Kelley, Rich (Athlete, Basketball Player)
314 Raymundo Dr
Woodside, CA 94062-4129, USA

Kelley, Ryan (Actor)
c/o Beverly Strong *Strong Management*
9350 Wilshire Blvd
#224
Beverly Hills, CA 90212, USA

kelley, shawn
813 Worlick Way
Chattanooga, TN 37421-8234, USA

kelley, shawn (Athlete, Baseball Player)
813 Worlick Way
Chattanooga, TN 37421-8234, USA

Kelley, Sheila (Actor, Producer)
524 Lorraine Blvd
Los Angeles, CA 90020-4732, USA

Kelley, Shelia (Actor)
524 Lorraine Blvd
Los Angeles, CA 90020-4732, USA

Kelley, Steve (Cartoonist)
San Diego Union
Editorial Dept
350 Camino de la Reina
San Diego, CA 92108, USA

Kelley, Thomas G (War Hero)
600 Washington St #1100
Boston, MA 02111-1704, USA

Kelley, Tom (Athlete, Baseball Player)
710 11th Ave S
North Myrtle Beach, SC 29582-3754, USA

Kelley, William G (Business Person)
Consolidated Stores
1105 N Market St
Wilmington, DE 19801, USA

Kellgren, Christer (Athlete, Hockey Player)
Rothlinsvag 41
Saro 42942, Sweden

Kellin, Kevin (Athlete, Football Player)
12500 Capri Cir N Apt 302
Treasure Island, FL 33706-4972, USA

Kellman, Barnet (Director)
c/o Staff Member *Jackoway Tyerman Wertheimer Austen Mandelbaum Morris & Klein*
1925 Century Park E
22nd Floor
Los Angeles, CA 90067, USA

Kellner, Catherine (Actor)
c/o Michael Lazo *Untitled Entertainment (LA)*
350 S. Beverly Dr #200
Beverly Hills, CA 90212, USA

Kellner, Deborah (Actor)
c/o Jessica (Pilch) Samuel *Sanders Armstrong Caserta*
2120 Colorado Blvd
Suite 120
Santa Monica, CA 90404, USA

Kellogg, Clark (Athlete, Basketball Player)
5423 Medallion Dr E
Westerville, OH 43082-8691, USA

Kellogg, Jeffrey (Baseball Player)
22900 Cherry Hill Ct
Mattawan, MI 49071-9562, USA

Kellogg, Jeffrey (Athlete, Baseball Player)
22900 Cherry Hill Ct
Mattawan, MI 49071-9562, USA

Kellogg, Mike (Athlete, Football Player)
7497 Tabor St
Arvada, CO 80005, USA

Kellogg, Vivian (Athlete, Baseball Player, Commentator)
9145 Olcott Lk
Jackson, MI 49201-7832, USA

Kellogg, William S (Business Person)
Kohl's Corp
N56W17000 Ridgewood Dr
Menomonee Falls, WI 53051, USA

Kellogg Jr, Allan J (General, War Hero)
250 Lihau St
Kailua, HI 96734-1654, USA

Kellum, Marv (Athlete, Football Player)
235 Jamaica Ave
Pittsburgh, PA 15229, USA

Kelly, Aaron (Musician)
c/o Simon Fuller *XIX Entertainment*
35-37 Parkgate Rd
32/33 Ransomes Dock
London SW11 4NP, UNITED KINGDOM (UK)

Kelly, Annesse (Bowler)
2912 Cape Verde Lane
Las Vegas, NV 89128, USA

Kelly, Arvesta (Athlete, Basketball Player)
1040 Oxford St N
Saint Paul, MN 55103-1246, USA

Kelly, Bob (Athlete, Hockey Player)
10 Peyton Ct
Marlton, NJ 08053-4700, USA

Kelly, Bob (Athlete, Baseball Player)
6 Mohawk Dr
Niantic, CT 06357-2812, USA

Kelly, Brendan (Actor)
c/o Staff Member *Allman/Rea Management*
9255 W Sunset Blvd Ste 600
Los Angeles, CA 90069, USA

Kelly, Brendon John (Actor)
c/o Toni Scheinbaum *C3 Management Group*
4555 Matilija Avenue
Sherman Oaks, CA 91423, USA

Kelly, Brian (Athlete, Football Player)
2517 Cozumel Dr
Tampa, FL 33618-1901, USA

Kelly, Bryan (Athlete, Baseball Player)
5400 Cub Lake Dr
Apopka, FL 32703-1946, USA

Kelly, Chris
21/22 Poland St.
London, ENGLAND W1V 3DD

Kelly, Clinton
c/o Staff Member *The Learning Channel (TLC)*
10100 Santa Monica Blvd
Suite 1500
Los Angeles, CA 90067, USA

Kelly, Colleen (Stylist)
c/o Staff Member *Directions USA*
3717-C W Market St
Greensboro, NC 27403, USA

Kelly, Dale (Baseball Player)
Toronto Blue Jays
3417 Quall Meadows Dr
Santa Maria, CA 93455-2477, USA

Kelly, Dan (Athlete, Hockey Player)
165 Mulberry St.
Newark, NY 17102, USA

Kelly, Daniel (Actor)
c/o Staff Member *Epitome Pictures*
220 Bartley Dr
Toronto, ON M4A 1G1, Canada

Kelly, Daniel-Hugh (Actor)
Innovative Artists
1505 10th St
Santa Monica, CA 90401, USA

Kelly, David Patrick (Actor)
c/o Staff Member *Paradigm (LA)*
360 N Crescent Dr
North Bldg
Beverly Hills, CA 90210, USA

Kelly, Dean Lennox (Actor)
c/o Staff Member *Scott Marshall Partners Ltd*
15 Little Portland St
2nd Floor
London W1W 8BW, UK

Kelly, Diva Kelly (Athlete, Wrestler)
c/o Staff Member *World Wrestling Entertainment (WWE)*
Titan Towers
1241 E Main St
Stamford, CT 06905-3857, USA

Kelly, Don (Athlete, Baseball Player)
216 Cliffside Dr
Mars, PA 16046-4802, USA

Kelly, Eamon M (Educator)
3122 Octavia St
New Orleans, LA 70125, USA

Kelly, Elisworth (Artist)
PO Box 1708
Chatham, NY 12037, USA

Kelly, Ellison (Athlete, Football Player)
146 Manning Ave
Hamilton, ON L9A, Canada

kelly, Ellsworth (Artist)
PO Box 151
Spencertown, NY 12165-0151, USA

Kelly, Greg (Correspondent)
Fox News Channel
1211 Avenue Of The Americas
New York, NY 10036, USA

Kelly, Harold (Horse Racer)
440 Tennent Rd
Manalapan, NJ 07726-3410, USA

Kelly, James E (Jim) (Athlete, Football Player)
Jim Kelly Enterprises, Inc.
1 Regency Ct
Marlton, NJ 08053-4243, USA

Kelly, James M (Jim) (Astronaut)
403 S Northfield St
Mediapolis, IA 52637-9702, USA

Kelly, Jean Louisa (Actor)
c/o Staff Member *Levine Okwu Erickson Management*
6363 Wilshire Blvd
Suite 300
Los Angeles, CA 90048, USA

Kelly, Jeff (Athlete, Football Player)
6437 Munke Rd
La Grange, TX 78945, USA

Kelly, Jerry (Athlete, Golfer)
723 Wilder Dr
Madison, WI 53704-6011, USA

Kelly, Joanne (Actor)
c/o Joanna (Joanie) Burstein *Burstein Company, The*
15304 Sunset Blvd
suite 208
Pacific Palisades, CA 90272, USA

Kelly, John (Musician)
EMI America Records
6920 Sunset Blvd
Los Angeles, CA 90028, USA

Kelly, John D (Athlete, Football Player)
816 NE 18th Ave
Apt 4
Fort Lauderdale, FL 33304, USA

Kelly, John H (Diplomat)
International Equity Partners
1808 Overlake Dr SE
#D
Conyers, GA 30013, USA

Kelly, John Paul (Athlete, Hockey Player)
PO Box 10416 RPO 10
Lloydminster, AB T9V 3A5, Canada

Kelly, Justin (Actor)
c/o Brad Stokes *Kass & Stokes Management*
9229 Sunset Blvd
Suite 504
Los Angeles, CA 90069, USA

Kelly, Kenny (Athlete, Baseball Player)
1318 Louisiana st
Plant City, FL 33563-5828, USA

Kelly, Kevin (Baseball Player)
1311 Quarterpath Ct
Richmond, TX 77469-6502, USA

Kelly, Leonard P (Red) (Athlete, Hockey Player)
30 Dunvegan Rd
Toronto, ON M4V 2P6, Canada

Kelly, Leroy (Athlete, Football Player)
115 Eastbrook Lane
Willingboro, NJ 08046, USA

Kelly, Lisa Robin (Actor)
c/o Dan Baron *Agency for the Performing Arts (APA-LA)*
405 S Beverly Dr
Suite 500
Beverly Hills, CA 90212-4425, USA

Kelly, Malcolm (Athlete, Football Player)
c/o Chad Speck *Allegiant Athletic Agency*
35 Market Sq
Suite 201
Knoxville, TN 37902, USA

Kelly, Mark E (Astronaut)
2121 Barrington Dr
League City, TX 77573-6690, USA

Kelly, Megyn (Correspondent)
c/o Staff Member *Fox News Channel (NY)*
1211 Ave of the Americas
Level C1
New York, NY 10036-8701, USA

Kelly, Michael (Actor)
c/o Brian Liebman *Liebman Entertainment*
25 E 21st St #PH
New York, NY 10011-8503, USA

Kelly, Mike (Congressman, Politician)
515 Cannon HOB
Washington, DC 20515, USA

Kelly, Mike (Athlete, Football Player)
7941 David Kenney Farm Rd
Huntersville, NC 28078, USA

Kelly, Mike (Athlete, Baseball Player)
8490 S Maole Ave
Temoe, AZ 85284-2244, USA

Kelly, Minka (Actor)
c/o Nicole King *Management 360*
9111 Wilshire Blvd
Beverly Hills, CA 90210, USA

Kelly, Moira (Actor)
c/o Troy Nankin *Wishlab*
2225-A Hyperion Ave
Los Angeles, CA 90027, USA

Kelly, Morgan (Actor)
c/o Tina Petro *Epic Talent*
3451 St. Laurent #400
Montreal QC H2X 2T6, Canada

Kelly, Pat (Athlete, Baseball Player)
6748 Friendship Dr
Sarasota, FL 34241-5757, USA

Kelly, Pat (Athlete, Baseball Player)
10 Murray St
Bangor, PA 18013, USA

Kelly, Paul (Musician, Songwriter)
c/o Staff Member *Paradigm (Monterey)*
404 W Franklin St
Monterey, CA 93940, USA

Kelly, Raymond (Misc)
Police Commissioner's Office
1 Police Plaza
New York, NY 10038, USA

Kelly, Richard (Rich) (Director, Writer)
c/o John Campisi *Creative Artists Agency (CAA-LA)*
2000 Ave Of The Stars
Los Angeles, CA 90067, USA

Kelly, Robert (Athlete, Football Player)
5380 N 750 E
Hamlet, IN 46532, USA

Kelly, Roberto (Athlete, Baseball Player)
Augusta Greenjackets
510 Franklin Dr
Arlington, TX 76011-2244, USA

Kelly, Robert (R Kelly) (Artist, Musician, Songwriter, Writer)
c/o Derrel McDavid *Winkler & McDavid, Ltd*
308 W Madison
Oak Park, IL 60302, USA

Kelly, Roz
5161 Riverton Ave. #105
No. Hollywood, CA 91601-3943

Kelly, Ryan (Actor)
c/o Staff Member *Ambition Talent*
439 Wellington St. W.
Suite 204
Toronto, ON M5V 1E7, Canada

Kelly, Scott J (Astronaut)
2121 Barrington Dr
League City, TX 77058-3607, USA

Kelly, Thomas (Athlete, Football Player)
14524 La Mesa Dr
La Mirada, CA 90638, USA

Kelly, Thomas (Athlete, Basketball Player)
2117 Forge Rd
Santa Barbara, CA 93108, USA

Kelly, Todd (Athlete, Football Player)
237 Gwinhurst Rd
Knoxville, TN 37934-4535, USA

Kelly, Tom (Athlete, Baseball Player, Coach)
1643 Currie St N
Saint Paul, MN 55119-7160, USA

Kelly, Tom (Photographer)
PO Box 472
Pottstown, PA 19464-0472, USA

Kelly, Van (Athlete, Baseball Player)
11 Beauregard Dr
Spencer, NC 28159-1957, USA

Kelly III, Thomas J (Journalist)
PO Box 2208
Sanatoga Branch
Pottstown, PA 19464, USA

Kelly Jr, Thomas J (Biologist)
Memorial Stolan Kettering Cancer Center
1275 York Ave
New York, NY 10021, USA

Kelm, Larry (Athlete, Football Player)
67 Driftoak Cir
The Woodlands, TX 77381, USA

Kelman, Arthur (Misc)
2150 Center Avenue
Apt 20E
Fort Lee, NJ 07024-5805, USA

Kelman, James (Writer)
Weidenfeld-Nicolson
Upper Saint Martin's Lane
London WC2H 9EA, UNITED KINGDOM (UK)

Kelsay, Chris (Athlete, Football Player)
29 Peppermill Ln
Orchard Park, NY 14127-4532, USA

Kelser, Gregory (Athlete, Basketball Player)
30400 Forest Dr
Franklin, MI 48025-1598, USA

Kelsey, David (Actor)
c/o Staff Member Select Artists Ltd (CA-Westside Office)
1138 12th Street
Suite 1
Santa Monica, CA 90403, USA

Kelsey, Frances O (Misc)
Federal Drug Administration
5600 Fishers Lane
Rockville, MD 20852, USA

Kelso, Ben (Athlete, Basketball Player)
1877 Midchester Dr
West Bloomfield, MI 48025-1598, USA

Kelso, Bill (Athlete, Baseball Player)
136 NE Briarcliff Rd
Kansas City, MO 64116, USA

Kelso, Mark (Athlete, Football Player)
897 Luther Rd
East Aurora, NY 14052, USA

Kelso II, Frank B (Admiral, General)
7794 Turlock Road
Springfield, VA 37334-2270, USA

Kelton, David (Athlete, Baseball Player)
515 Riverside Dr
Lagrange, GA 30240-9635, USA

Kelvin (Stylist)
c/o Staff Member Photogenics Media
8549 Higuera St
Building B
Culver City, CA 90232, USA

Kem (Music Group)
c/o Staff Member Paradigm (Monterey)
404 W Franklin St
Monterey, CA 93940, USA

Kemal, Yashar (Writer)
PK14 Basinkoy
Istanbul, TURKEY

Kemmerer, Beatrice (Athlete, Baseball Player, Commentator)
8437 Carter St
Bremen, IN 46506-9201, USA

Kemmerer, Russ (Athlete, Baseball Player)
6335 Colebrook Dr
Indianapolis, IN 46220-4205, USA

Kemp, Gary (Musician)
International Talent Group
729 7th Ave
#1600
New York, NY 10019, USA

Kemp, Jeff (Athlete, Football Player)
22101 NE 66th Pl
Redmond, WA 98053, USA

Kemp, Jeremy (Actor)
Marina Martin
12/13 Poland St
London W1V 3DE, UNITED KINGDOM (UK)

Kemp, Martin (Musician)
Mission Control
Business Center
Lower Road
London SE16 2XB, UNITED KINGDOM (UK)

Kemp, Matt (Athlete, Baseball Player)
c/o Staff Member Los Angeles Dodgers (LA Dodgers)
1000 Elysian Park Ave
Los Angeles, CA 90012, USA

Kemp, Perry (Athlete, Football Player)
PO Box 78
Westland, PA 15378-0078, USA

Kemp, Ross (Actor)
EastEnders
BBC Elstree Centre
Clarendon Road
Borehamwood, Herts UK WD6 1JF

Kemp, Shawn (Athlete, Basketball Player)
18237 Belding Ct
Brandywine, MD 20613-7107, USA

Kemp, Steve (Athlete, Baseball Player)
1428 Colony Plz
Newport Beach, CA 92660-6362, USA

Kempainen, Robert (Athlete, Olympic Athlete, Track Athlete)
1753 Princeton Ave
Saint Paul, MN 55105-1915, USA

Kemper, Ellie (Actor)
c/o Liz Mahoney ID Public Relations (ID-LA)
7060 Hollywood Blvd
8th Floor
Los Angeles, CA 90028, USA

Kemper, Victor J (Cinematographer)
Gersh Agency
232 N Canon Dr
Beverly Hills, CA 90210, USA

Kemper II, David W (Financier)
Commerce Bancshares
1000 Walnut St
Kansas City, MO 64106, USA

Kempf, Cecil J (Admiral)
831 Olive Ave
Coronado, CA 92118, USA

Kempf, Florian (Athlete, Football Player)
8039 Pine Rd
Apt 1
Philadelphia, PA 19111, USA

Kempinska, Charles (Athlete, Football Player)
925 State St
Natchez, MS 39120, USA

Kempner, Patty (Athlete, Olympic Athlete, Swimmer)
1605 Harris Dr
Fort Collins, CO 80524-1041, USA

Kempner, Walter (Misc)
1505 Virginia Ave
Durham, NC 27705, USA

Kemppel, Nina (Athlete, Olympic Athlete, Track Athlete)
2819 McCallie Ave
Anchorage, AK 99517-1221, USA

Kempthorne, Dirk (Politician)
1949 STeal Ln
Boise, ID 83706-4049, USA

Kempton, Tim (Athlete, Basketball Player)
4131 N 43rd St
Phoenix, AZ 85018, USA

Kempton, tin (Athlete, Basketball Player)
16223 W Cambridge Ave
Goodyear, AZ 85395-2084, USA

Ken, Baird (Athlete, Hockey Player)
Lot 4 Berry Bay
White Lake, MB R0B 1M0, Canada

Ken, Reese
1010 Forest Knoll Ct
Lithia Springs, GA 30122-3639, USA

Kenady, Chris (Athlete, Hockey Player)
5042 Tuxedo Blvd
Mound, MN 55364-9254

Kenan, Sean
77 W. 66th St.
New York., NY 10033

Kendal, Felicity (Actor)
Chatto & Linnit
Prince of Wales Coventry St
London W1V 7FE, UNITED KINGDOM (UK)

Kendall, A Bruce (Yachtsman)
6 Pedersen Place
Bucklands Beach
Auckland, NEW ZELAND

Kendall, Barbara (Yachtsman)
Kendall Distributing
82B Great South Road
Auckland, NEW ZELAND

Kendall, Donald M (Business Person)
PepsiCo Inc
Anderson Hill Road
Purchase, NY 10577, USA

Kendall, Fred (Athlete, Baseball Player)
57575 Johnston Rd
Anza, CA 92539-9646, USA

Kendall, Jason (Athlete, Baseball Player)
11730 Stonehenge Ln
Los Angeles, CA 90077-1302, USA

Kendall, Jeannie (Musician)
Joe Taylor Artist Agency
2802 Columbine Place
Nashville, TN 37204, USA

Kendall, Pete (Athlete, Football Player)
P.O. Box 888
Phoenix, AZ 85001, USA

Kendall, Skip (Athlete, Golfer)
8406 Kemper Ln
Windermere, FL 34786, USA

Kendall, Tom (Race Car Driver)
International Motor Sports Assn
1394 Broadway Ave
Braselton, GA 30517, USA

Kendall, Tony
Via G. Talombini 12
Rome, ITALY 00156

Kenders, Al (Athlete, Baseball Player)
8744 Matilija Ave
Panorama City, CA 91402-3320, USA

Kendler, Bob (Misc)
US Handball Assn
4101 Dempster St
Skokie, IL 60076, USA

Kendrena, Ken (Baseball Player)
4235 Stone Mountain Dr
Chino Hills, CA 91709-6155, USA

Kendrick, Alex (Producer)
c/o Staff Member Sherwood Pictures
2201 Whispering Pines Rd
Albany, GA 31707, USA

Kendrick, Anna (Actor)
c/o Lisa Perkins Fifteen Minutes (LA)
8436 W 3rd St
Suite 650
Los Angeles, CA 90048, USA

Kendrick, Darren (Actor)
c/o Albert Giannelli Omnium Entertainment Group
444 N. Larchmont Blvd
Suite 108
Los Angeles, CA 90004, USA

Kendrick, Frank (Athlete, Basketball Player)
8355 Providence Dr
Fishers, IN 46038-5233, USA

Kendrick, Howard (Athlete, Baseball Player)
8650 E Joshua Tree Ln
Scottsdale, AZ 85250-4923, USA

Kendrick, Kyle (Athlete, Baseball Player)
7475 Wisconsin Ave Ste 600
Bethesda, MD 20814-3492, USA

Kendrick, Rodney (Composer, Musician)
Carolyn McClair
410 W 53rd St
#128C
New York, NY 10019, USA

Kendrick E G, "Ken" (Athlete, Baseball Player)
3964 E Paradise View Dr
Paradise Valley, AZ 85253-3800, USA

Keneally, Thomas M (Writer)
24 Serpentine
Bilgola Beach, NSW 2107, AUSTRALIA

Keneley, Matt (Athlete, Football Player)
25142 Sandia Ct
Laguna Hills, CA 92563, USA

Kener, Kira (Adult Film Star)
Vivid Entertainment
3599 Cahuenga Blvd. W
Los Angeles, CA 90068, USA

Kenichi, Chen (Chef)
Akasaka Shisen Hanten 2-5-5 Hiragacho
Zenkoku Ryokan Kaikan
Chiyoda-ku, Tokyo, japan

Kenilorea, Peter (Prime Minister)
Kalala House
PO Box 535 Honiara
Guadacanal, SOLOMON ISLANDS

Kenmore, Joan (Actor)
33106 Ocean Ridge
Dana Point, CA 92629, USA

Kenn, Michael L (Mike) (Athlete, Football Player)
360 Bardolier
Alpharetta, GA 30022-5129, USA

Kenna, E Douglas (Doug) (Athlete, Business Person, Football Player)
111 S Saint Joseph St
South Bend, IN 46601, USA

Kenna, Edward (General, War Hero)
121 Coleraine Road
Hamilton, VIC 3300, AUSTRALIA

Kennan, Brian (Musician)
Lustig Talent
PO Box 770850
Orlando, FL 32877, USA

Kennard, Derek (Athlete, Football Player)
15849 S 35th Way
Phoenix, AZ 85048-7278, USA

Kennard, Trevor (Athlete, Football Player)
TKM Inc
207 Oxford St
Winnipeg, MB R3M 3H8, USA

Kennard, William (Bill) (Government Official)
Carlyie Group
1001 Pennsylvania Ave NW
Washington, DC 20004, USA

Kenne, Leslie F (General)
Deputy CofS for Warfighting Integration
HqUSA Pentagon
Washington, DC 20310, USA

Kennedy, Adam (Athlete, Baseball Player)
5025 Windhill Dr
Riverside, CA 92507-0615, USA

Kennedy, Alan D (Business Person)
Tupperware Corp
PO Box 2353
Orlando, FL 32802, USA

Kennedy, Allan (Stylist)
c/o Staff Member *Katy Barker Agency Inc*
6606 10th Ave Apt 3R
Brooklyn, NY 11219, USA

Kennedy, Anthony M (Judge)
US Supreme Court
1 1st St NE
Washington, DC 20543-0002, USA

Kennedy, Claudia J (General)
c/o Staff Member *WME (WMA-NY)*
1325 Ave of the Americas
New York, NY 10019, USA

Kennedy, Coenelia G (Judge)
US Court of Appeals
US Courthouse
231 W Lafayette Blvd
Detroit, MI 48226, USA

Kennedy, Cortez (Athlete, Football Player)
121 Gary Lynn Dr
Osceola, AR 72370, USA

Kennedy, Courtney (Athlete, Hockey Player, Olympic Athlete)
13 Whispering Hill Rd
Woburn, MA 01801-4781, USA

Kennedy, Dan (Business Person, Writer)
Kennedy Inner Circle Inc
5818 N 7th St #103
Phoenix, AZ 85014, USA

Kennedy, David M (Secretary)
3838 Ruth Dr
Salt Lake City, UT 84124, USA

Kennedy, David M (Historian)
Stanford University
History Dept
Stanford, CA 94305, USA

Kennedy, Dean (Athlete, Hockey Player)
General Delivery
Pincher Creek, AB T0K 1W0, Canada

Kennedy, D James (Religious Leader)
Coral Ridge Presbyterian Church
5554 N Federal Hwy
Fort Lauderdale, FL 33308, USA

Kennedy, Donald (Educator)
Stanford University
International Studies Institute
Stanford, CA 94305, USA

Kennedy, Dwayne (Comedian)
c/o Rick Messina *Messina Baker Entertainment*
955 Carrillo Dr
Suite 100
Los Angeles, CA 90048, USA

Kennedy, Ethel (Misc)
Robert F. Kennedy Memorial
1367 Connecticut Ave
#200
Washington, DC 20036, USA

Kennedy, Eugene (Athlete, Basketball Player)
8218 Westrock Dr
Dallas, TX 75243-6524, USA

Kennedy, Forbes (Athlete, Hockey Player)
20 Oakland Dr
Charlottetown, PA C1C 1P4, Canada

Kennedy, George (Actor)
110 E Rocky Dr
Eagle, ID 83616, USA

Kennedy, Ian (Athlete, Baseball Player)
c/o Team Member *New York Yankees*
Yankee Stadium
161st St & River Ave
Bronx, NY 10451, USA

Kennedy, James C (Business Person)
Cox Enterprises
1400 Lake Hearn Dr NE
Atlanta, GA 30319, USA

Kennedy, Jamie (Actor, Producer, Writer)
c/o Stephen (Steve) Small *Paradigm (LA)*
360 N Crescent Dr
North Bldg
Beverly Hills, CA 90210, USA

Kennedy, Jim (Athlete, Baseball Player)
13940 SW Lisa Ln
Beaverton, OR 97005-4315, USA

Kennedy, Jimmy (Athlete, Football Player)
901 N Broadway
Saint Louis, MO 63101, USA

Kennedy, Joe (Athlete, Baseball Player)
P.O. Box 169
Seven Mile, OH 45062, USA

Kennedy, Joe (Athlete, Basketball Player)
201 43rd St
Virginia Beach, VA 23451-2503, USA

Kennedy, Joey D (Joe) Jr (Journalist)
1635 11th Place S
Birmingham, AL 35205, USA

Kennedy, John (Athlete, Baseball Player)
2 Rodney Rd
Peabody, MA 01960-3S17, USA

Kennedy, John Milton (Actor)
5711 Reseda Blvd
#204
Tarzana, CA 91356, USA

Kennedy, Junior (Athlete, Baseball Player)
6601 Eucalyptus Dr
Spc 215
Bakersfield, CA 93306-6844, USA

Kennedy, Kathleen (Producer)
c/o Staff Member *United Talent Agency (UTA)*
9336 Civic Center Dr
Beverly Hills, CA 90210, USA

Kennedy, Ken (Wrestler)
c/o Kerry Rodgerson *World Wrestling Entertainment (WWE)*
Titan Towers
1241 E Main St
Stamford, CT 06905-3857, USA

Kennedy, Kenoy (Athlete, Football Player)
16275 O'Conner Ave
Forney, TX 75126-7572, USA

Kennedy, Kevin (Athlete, Baseball Player, Coach, Television Host)
c/o Staff Member *Fox Sports*
1211 Avenue of the Americas
Suite 302
New York, NY 10036, USA

Kennedy, Lan (Athlete, Baseball Player)
2405 Brockton Way
Henderson, NV 89074-5471, USA

Kennedy, Lee (Business Person)
Equifax Inc
1550 Peachtree St NE
Atlanta, GA 30309, USA

Kennedy, Leon Isaac (Actor)
859 N Hollywood Way
#384
Burbank, CA 91505, USA

Kennedy, Lincoln (Athlete, Football Player)
2027 E Minton St
Mesa, AZ 85213-1438, USA

Kennedy, Mike (Athlete, Hockey Player)
DTZ Barnicke
900-50 Burnhamthorpe Rd W
Mississauga, ON L5B 3C2, Canada

Kennedy, Mimi (Actor)
c/o Todd Justice *Justice & Ponder*
P.O. Box 480033
Los Angeles, CA 90048, USA

Kennedy, M Peter (Figure Skater)
7650 SE 41st
Mercer Island, WA 98040, USA

Kennedy, Nigel (Musician)
Russels
Regency House
1-4 Warwick St
London W1R 5WB, UNITED KINGDOM (UK)

Kennedy, Page (Actor)
c/o Judy Page *Mitchell K Stubbs & Assoc (MKS)*
8675 W. Washington Blvd
Suite 203
Culver City, CA 90232, USA

Kennedy, Paul M (Historian)
409Humphrey St
New Haven, CT 06511, USA

Kennedy, Randall L (Educator, Lawyer)
Harvard University
Law School
Cambridge, MA 02138, USA

Kennedy, Ray F (Business Person)
Masco Corp
21001Van Born Road
Taylor, MI 48180, USA

Kennedy, Robert F Jr (Lawyer)
Pace Environmental Litigation Clinic
Pace University School of Law
78 N Broadway
White Plains, NY 10603, USA

Kennedy, Robert H (Athlete, Football Player)
4906 N 76th Pl
Scottsdale, AZ 85251, USA

Kennedy, Ryan (Actor)
c/o Lesa Kirk *Kirk Talent Agencies Inc*
70 East 2nd. Ave
Suite 301
Vancouver, BC V5T 1B1, Canada

Kennedy, Ted (Athlete, Hockey Player)
Physically unable to sign autographs

Kennedy, Terrence E (Terry) (Athlete, Baseball Player)
333 N Pennington Dr
Unit 23
Chandler, AZ 85224-8266, USA

Kennedy, T Lincoin (Athlete, Football Player)
3917 Spring Garden Pl
Apt 1
Spring Valley, CA 91977, USA

Kennedy, William (Athlete, Basketball Player)
9927 Galleon Dr
West Palm Beach, FL 33411-18e7, USA

Kennedy, William J (Writer)
New York State Writers Institute
Washington Ave
Albany, NY 12222-0100, USA

Kennedy, William J (Athlete, Football Player)
16383 Ronnie Ln
Livonia, MI 48154, USA

Kennedy, X Joseph (X J) (Writer)
22 Revere St
Lexington, MA 02420, USA

Kennedy-Powell, Kathleen (Judge)
Los Angeles Municipal Court
110 N Grand Ave
Los Angeles, CA 90012, USA

Kennedy Schlossberg, Caroline (Writer)
ESI Design
111 Fifth Ave 12th Fl
New York, NY 10003, USA

Kennel, Hans
605 Douglas Ln NE
Huntsville, AL 35801-1740, USA

Kenner, Ellen (Radio Personality, Talk Show Host)
P.O. Box 440
NORTH SCITUATE, Rhode Island 02857, USA

kenner, Kevin (Musician)
Columbia Artists Mgmt Inc
165 W 57th St
New York, NY 10019, USA

Kennerd, Trevor (Athlete, Football Player)
TKM Inc 207 Oxford St
Winnipeg, MB R3M 3h8, Canada

Kennerly, David Hume (Photographer)
1015 18th St
Santa Monica, CA 90403-4469, USA

Kenney, Art (Athlete, Baseball Player)
3 Timber Ln
North Reading, MA 01864-3016, USA

Kenney, Bill (Athlete, Football Player)
13450 E State Route 150
Kansas City, MO 64149-1243, USA

Kenney, Jerry (Athlete, Baseball Player)
926 E Windfield Ct
Beloit, WI 53511-6547, USA

Kenney, Stephen F (Steve) (Athlete, Football Player)
1105 Silver Oaks Ct
Raleigh, NC 27614, USA

Kenney, William P (Athlete, Football Player)
2808 SW Arthur Dr
Lees Summit, MO 64082, USA

Kennibrew, Dee Dee (Musician)
Superstars Unlimited
PO Box 371371
Las Vegas, NV 89137, USA

Kenniff, Sean (Doctor)
6 Madison Lane #2
Carle Place, NY 11514, USA

Kennington, DJ (Race Car Driver)
10206 Ford Road
St Thomas, ON N5P 3T1, CANADA

Kennison, Eddie (Athlete, Football Player)
14813 Sherwood Rd
Overland Park, KS 66224-3842, USA

Kenny, Shannon (Actor)
c/o Joanna (Joanie) Burstein *Burstein Company, The*
15304 Sunset Blvd
suite 208
Pacific Palisades, CA 90272, USA

Kenny, Shirley Strum (Educator)
State University of New York
President's Office
Stony Brook, NY 11794, USA

Kenny, Tom (Actor, Musician, Writer)
c/o Kara Welker *Generate Management*
1545 26th St
Suite 200
Santa Monica, CA 90404, USA

Kenny, Yvonne (Opera Singer)
I M G Artists
3 Burlington Lane
Chiswick
London W4 2TH, UNITED KINGDOM (UK)

Kenny G (Musician)
c/o Staff Member *Richard De La Font Agency*
3808 W South Park Blvd
Broken Arrow, OK 74011, USA

Kenon, Larry (Athlete, Basketball Player)
25057 Toutant Beauregard Rd
San Antonio, TX 78255-34e2, USA

Kenseth, Matt (Race Car Driver)
Roush/Fenway Racing
4600 Roush Pl.
Concord, NC 28027, USA

Kensing, Logan (Athlete, Baseball Player)
208 E Bandera Rd
Boerne, TX 78006-2902, USA

Kensit, Patsy (Actor, Musician)
14 Lambton Place Nottinghill
London W11 2SH, UNITED KINGDOM (UK)

Kent, Allegra (Ballerina)
c/o Staff Member *Sanford J Greenburger Associates Inc*
55 Fifth Avenue
New York, NY 10003, USA

Kent, Arthur (Correspondent)
2184 Torringford St
Torrington, CT 06790, USA

Kent, (Edward G N P Patrick) (Misc)
York House
Saint James's Place
London SW1, UNITED KINGDOM (UK)

Kent, Heather Paige
c/o Justin Grey Stone *Untitled Entertainment (LA)*
350 S. Beverly Dr #200
Beverly Hills, CA 90212, USA

Kent, Jean (Actor)
London Mgmt
2-4 Noel St
London W1V 3RB, UNITED KINGDOM (UK)

Kent, Jeff (Athlete, Baseball Player)
12006 Pleasant Panorama Vw
Austin, TX 78738-5309, USA

Kent, Joey (Athlete, Football Player)
6409 Eric St NW
Huntersville, AL 35810, USA

Kent, Jonathan (Director)
International Creative Mgmt
76 Oxford St
London W1N 0AX, UNITED KINGDOM (UK)

Kent, Julie (Ballerina)
American Ballet Theatre
890 Broadway
New York, NY 10003, USA

Kent, Marjorie
1169 Mary Circle
LaVerne, CA 91750

Kent, Peter (Misc)
43 Trinity Court Gray's Inn Road
London WC1, UNITED KINGDOM (UK)

Kent, Steve (Athlete, Baseball Player)
3118 Minthorn Dr
Killeen, TX 76542-1932, USA

Kentner, Louis (Musician)
1 Mallord St
London SW3, UNITED KINGDOM (UK)

Kentucky Headhunters
PO Box 1895
Glasgow, KY 42142, USA

Kenty, Hilmer (Boxer)
Escot Boxing
19260 Bretton Dr
Detroit, MI 48223, USA

Kenville, Bill (Athlete, Basketball Player)
59 Crary Ave
Binghamton, NY 13905-3828, USA

Kenworthy, Dick (Athlete, Baseball Player)
5551 Rue Royale
Apt D
Indianapolis, IN 46227, USA

Kenya, Wendi (Actor)
Michael Forman Management
409 N Camden Dr Ste 205
Beverly Hills, CA 90210, USA

Kenyon, Mel (Race Car Driver)
4645 S. 25 West
Lebanon, IN 46052, USA

Kenzle, Leila (Actor)
c/o Staff Member *Agency for the Performing Arts (APA-LA)*
405 S Beverly Dr
Suite 500
Beverly Hills, CA 90212-4425, USA

Kenzo (Designer, Fashion Designer)
3 Place des Victories
Paris 75001, FRANCE

Keobouphan, Sisavat (Prime Minister)
Premier's Office
Vientiane, LAOS

Keogan, Murray (Athlete, Hockey Player)
5631 E Superior St
Duluth, MN 55804-2530

Keoghan, Phil (Television Host)
c/o Staff Member *ICM Partners (ICM-LA)*
10250 Constellation Blvd Fl 7
Los Angeles, CA 90067, USA

Keohane, Nannerl O (Educator)
Duke University
President's Office
Durham, NC 27706, USA

Keoke, Kimo (Actor)
612 1/2 N Spaulding Avenue
Los Angeles, CA 90036, USA

Keon, David M (Dave) (Athlete, Hockey Player)
115 Brackenwood Rd
Palm Beach Gardens, FL 33418-9065, USA

Keough, Donald R (Financier)
200 Galleria Parkway
#970
Atlanta, GA 30339, USA

Keough, Joe (Athlete, Baseball Player)
110 Binham Hts
Shavano Park, TX 78249-2056, USA

Keough, Lainey (Designer, Fashion Designer)
42 Dawson St
Dublin 2, IRELAND

Keough, Marty (Athlete, Baseball Player)
6874 E Nightingale Star Cir
Scottsdale, AZ 85266-7044, USA

Keough, Matt (Athlete, Baseball Player)
12 Shire
Trabuco Canyon, CA 92679-4907, USA

Kepcher, Carolyn (Reality TV Star)
c/o Staff Member *The Apprentice*
The Trump Co
725 Fifth Ave
New York, NY 10022, USA

keppel, Bobby (Athlete, Baseball Player)
1297 Stephen ridge Ct
Saint Charles, MO 63304-3405, USA

Keppinger, Jeff (Athlete, Baseball Player)
1578 Cardillo Ct
Dacula, GA 30019-7750, USA

Kepshire, Kurt (Athlete, Baseball Player)
4 Stonebridge Rd
Oxford, CT 06478-1164, USA

Ke Quan, Jonathan (Actor)

Ker, Crawford (Athlete, Football Player)
214 Harbor View Ln
Largo, FL 33770, USA

Ker, Joshua (Athlete, Football Player)
2927 Lakeshore Dr
Muskegon, MI 49441, USA

Kerbow, Randall (Athlete, Football Player)
10122 Lost Hollow Ln
Missouri City, TX 77459-2494, USA

Kerbow, Randy (Athlete, Football Player)
3803 Crystal Falls Dr
Missouri City, TX 77459-4249, USA

Kercher, Dick (Athlete, Football Player)
3205 May Cir SE
Rio Rancho, NM 87124, USA

Kercheval, Ken (Actor)
Stephany Hurkos
11935 Kling St #10
Valley Village, CA 91607, USA

Kercheval, Ralph (Athlete, Football Player)
1220 Richmond Rd
Lexington, KY 40502, USA

Kerdyk, Tracy (Athlete, Golfer)
441 Valencia Ave
Apt 401
Coral Gables, FL 33134-5782, USA

Kerekorian, Kirk (Business Person)
MGM/UA Communications
2500 Broadway St
Santa Monica, CA 90404, USA

Kerekou, Mathieu A (General, President)
President's Office
Boite Postale
Cotonou 2020, BENIN

Keresztes, K Sandor (Architect)
Fo Utca 44/50
Budapest 1011, HUNGARY

Keresztury, Bill (Athlete, Football Player)
16845 FM 32
Blanco, TX 78606-5443, USA

Kerfeld, Charlie (Athlete, Baseball Player)
15402 66th Avenue Ct NW
Gig Harbor, WA 98332-8736, USA

Kerkorian, Kirk (Business Person)
Tracinda Corporation
150 Rodeo Dr #250
Beverly Hills, CA 90212, USA

Kerkovich, Rob (Actor)
c/o Lorraine Berglund *Lorraine Berglund Management*
11537 Hesby St.
North Hollywood, CA 91601, USA

Kerley, James (Television Host)
c/o Mark Morrissey And Associates
45 Oxford St
Bondi Junction NSW 2022

Kern, Bill (Athlete, Baseball Player)
625 W Green St
Allentown, PA 18102-1601, USA

Kern, Ericca
3972 Barranca Parkway #J-321
Irvine, CA 92714

Kern, Geof (Photographer)
1355 Conant St
Dallas, TX 75207, USA

Kern, Jim (Athlete, Baseball Player)
6009 Amberwood Ct
Arlington, TX 76016-1001, USA

Kern, Joey (Actor)
c/o Staff Member *Paradigm (LA)*
360 N Crescent Dr
North Bldg
Beverly Hills, CA 90210, USA

Kern, Rex W (Athlete, Football Player)
2816 Avenida de Autlan
Camarillo, CA 93010, USA

Kernaghan, Lee (Musician)
c/o Stephen White *Stephen White Management*
7 Kingslangley Rd
Greenwich, NSW 2065, Australia

Kernan, Joseph (Politician)
200 W Washington St Ste 226
Indianapolis, IN 46204-2731, USA

Kernek, George (Athlete, Baseball Player)
16423 Cotton Gin Ave
Wayne, OK 73095-3172, USA

Kerner, Gabriele (Nena) (Musician)
C/O EAS
Beethofenstrasse, 53
Hamburg D-22083, Germany

Kerner, Ian (Writer)
c/o Staff Member *HarperCollins Publishers*
10 East 53rd St
c/o Author mail, 7th Floor
New York, NY 10022, USA

Kerns, Joanna (Actor)
c/o Sean Freidin *ICM Partners (ICM-LA)*
10250 Constellation Blvd Fl 7
Los Angeles, CA 90067, USA

Kerns, Sandra
620 Resolano Dr.
Pacific Palisades, CA 90272

Kerns Jr, David V (Engineer)
Vanderbilt University
Electrical Engineering Dept
Nashville, TN 37235, USA

Kerr, Alan (Athlete, Hockey Player)
Okanagan Hockey School
201-853 Eckhardt Ave W
Penticton, BC V2A 9C4, Canada

Kerr, Allen (Musician)
419 Carrington St
Adelaide, SA 5000, AUSTRALIA

Kerr, Brook (Actor)
c/o Martin Berneman *Precision Entertainment*
6338 Wilshire Blvd
Los Angeles, CA 90048, USA

Kerr, Cristie (Athlete, Golfer)
8367 SW 137th Ave
Miami, FL 33183-4045, USA

Kerr, Edward
9701 Wilshire Blvd.10th Flr.
Beverly Hills, CA 90212

Kerr, Graham (Chef, Writer)
Kerr Corp
1020 N Sunset Dr
Camano Island, WA 98282, USA

Kerr, John G (Actor)
2975 Monterey Road
San Marino, CA 91108, USA

Kerr, Judy (Actor)
4139 Tujunga Ave
Studio City, CA 91604, USA

Kerr, Kristen (Actor)
c/o Steven Jensen *Independent Group, The*
6363 Wilshire Blvd
Suite 115
Los Angeles, CA 90048, USA

Kerr, Miranda (Model)
c/o Aleen Keshishian *Brillstein Entertainment Partners*
9150 Wilshire Blvd #350
Beverly Hills, CA 90212, USA

Kerr, Pat (Designer, Fashion Designer)
Pat Kerr Inc
200 Wagner Place
Memphis, TN 38103, USA

Kerr, Philip (Writer)
AP Watts Agents
20 John St
London WC1N 2DR, UNITED KINGDOM (UK)

Kerr, Reg (Athlete, Hockey Player)
2291 Birchwood Ln
Northfield, IL 60093-3103, USA

Kerr, Steve (Athlete, Basketball Player)
PO Box 1964
Rancho Santa Fe, CA 92e67-1964, USA

Kerr, Tim (Athlete, Coach, Hockey Player)
157 Fellswood Dr
Moorestown, NJ 08057-4015, USA

Kerr, William T (Business Person)
Meredith Corp
1716 Locust St
Das Moines, IA 50309, USA

Kerrey, J Robert (Bob) (Ex-Governor, War Hero)
21 W 11th St
New York, NY 10011, USA

Kerrick, Donald L (General)
Deputy Assistant National Security Agency
Fort George C Meade, MD 20755, USA

Kerrigan, Joseph T (Joe) (Athlete, Baseball Player, Coach)
450 Forest Ln
North Wales, PA 19454-2478, USA

Kerrigan, Marguerite (Athlete, Baseball Player, Commentator)
12179 94th St
Largo, FL 33773-4306, USA

Kerrigan, Nancy (Athlete, Figure Skater, Olympic Athlete)
7 Cedar Ave
Stoneham, MA 02180-2420, USA

Kerrigan, Pamela (Athlete, Golfer)
3205 Tuckers Ln
Hingham, MA 02043, USA

Kerrigan, Ryan (Football Player)
c/o David Dunn *Athletes First, LLC*
9140 Irvine Center Dr
Irvine, CA 92618, USA

Kerr Jr, Donald M (Physicist)
Science Applications International
1241 Cave St
La Jolla, CA 92037, USA

Kerry, Alexandra (Actor)
c/o Staff Member *TalentWorks (LA)*
3500 W Olive Ave
Suite 1400
Burbank, CA 91505, USA

Kerry, Bob (Ex-Senator)
7602 Pacific St
Omaha, NE 78114, USA

Kerry, John (Politician)
19 Louisburg Sq
Boston, MA 02108, USA

Kerry, Teresa Heinz (Misc)
Heinz Family Philanthropies
1101 Pennsylvania Ave. NW
Suite 350
Washington, DC 20004, USA

Kersee, Bob
1034 S. Brentwood Blvd. #1530
St. Louis, MO 63117-1215

Kersey, Jerome (Athlete, Basketball Player)
24140 SW Petes Mountain Rd
West Linn, OR 97068, USA

Kersey, Merritt (Athlete, Football Player)
17 Balance Mill Rd
Nottingham, PA 19362, USA

Kersey, Paul (Actor)
c/o Staff Member *TalentWorks (LA)*
3500 W Olive Ave
Suite 1400
Burbank, CA 91505, USA

Kersh, David (Musician)
Mark Hybner Entertainment
PO Box 223
Shiner, TX 77984, USA

Kershaw, Clayton (Athlete, Baseball Player)
c/o Staff Member *Los Angeles Dodgers (LA Dodgers)*
1000 Elysian Park Ave
Los Angeles, CA 90012, USA

Kershaw, Doug (Musician)
RR 1 Box 34285
Weld County Road 47
Eaton, CO 80615, USA

Kershaw, Sammy (Musician)
c/o Richard De La Font *Richard De La Font Agency*
3808 W South Park Blvd
Broken Arrow, OK 74011, USA

Kershaw, Sammy (Race Car Driver)
111 Kay Dr.
Easley, 29640 SC, USA

Kershenbaum, David (Musician, Producer)
19021 Devonport Ln
Tarzana, CA 91356, USA

kerslake, Doug (Athlete, Hockey Player)
5427 Pine Grove Ave
Norfolk, VA 23502-4924

Kersten, Wally (Athlete, Football Player)
4604 Longfellow Ave
Minneapolis, MN 55407, USA

Kertesz, Imre (Nobel Prize Laureate)
Acte Sud Paris
18 Rue Séguier
Paris 75 006, France

Kerwin, Brian (Actor)
c/o Staff Member *Paradigm (LA)*
360 N Crescent Dr
North Bldg
Beverly Hills, CA 90210, USA

Kerwin, Irene (Athlete, Baseball Player, Commentator)
610 W Albany Ave
Peoria, IL 61604-1506, USA

Kerwin, Joseph P (Astronaut)
10411 River Rd
College Station, TX 77845-6719, USA

Kerwin, Lance (Actor)
PO Box 1708
Kapaa, HI 96746-5708, USA

Kerwin, Larkin (Physicist)
2166 Bourboniere Park
Sillery, QC G1T 1B4, CANADA

Kerwin, Tom (Athlete, Basketball Player)
283 Salter Path Rd
Unit 114
Atlantic Beach, NC 28512-6178, USA

Keseday, Robert (Athlete, Football Player)
57 Linden Ave
Park Ridge, NJ 07656, USA

Keselowski, Brad (Race Car Driver)
c/o Staff Member *Penske Racing South*
200 Penske Way
Mooresville, NC 28115, USA

Keser, Dean (Athlete, Football Player)
202 Rod Cir
Middletown, MD 21769, USA

Keshishian, Alek (Director, Writer)
c/o Aleen Keshishian *Brillstein Entertainment Partners*
9150 Wilshire Blvd #350
Beverly Hills, CA 90212, USA

Kesler, Ryan (Athlete, Hockey Player)
5982 Pontiac Trl
West Bloomfield, MI 48323-2225

Kesner, Jillian (Actor)
William Carroll Agency
11360 Brill Dr
Studio City, CA 91604, USA

Kessel Jr, Phil (Athlete, Hockey Player)
Newport Sports Management
400-201 City Centre Dr
Attn Wade Arnott
Mississauga, ON L5B 2T4, Canada

Kessell, Rick (Athlete, Hockey Player)
60 Underhill Dr
North York, ON M3A 2J7, Canada

Kessell, Simone (Actor)
c/o Will Ward *ROAR (LA)*
9701 Wilshire Blvd
8th Floor
Los Angeles, CA 90212, USA

Kessinger, Donald E (Don) (Athlete,
Baseball Player, Coach)
1306 Pelican Loop
Oxford, MS 38655-7344, USA

Kessinger, Keith (Athlete, Baseball Player)
12004 Water Ridge Dr
Oxford, MS 38655-6019, USA

Kessinger, Ted (Athlete, Football Player)
612 N Washington St
Lindsborg, KS 67456-1516, USA

Kessler, Alice & Ellen
Nymphenburger Str. 86
Munich, GERMANY D-80636

Kessler, David A (Doctor, Writer)
c/o Phyllis Parsons *The Parsons Company*
1738 Almond Ave
Walnut Creek, CA 94596, USA

Kessler, Glenn (Producer, Writer)
c/o Staff Member *Creative Artists Agency
(CAA-LA)*
2000 Ave Of The Stars
Los Angeles, CA 90067, USA

Kessler, Ron (Writer)
c/o Staff Member *Trident Media Group
LLC*
41 Madison Ave
36th Floor
New York, NY 10010, USA

Kessler, Stephen
1120 S. Ridgley Dr.
Los Angeles, CA 90019-2528

Kessler, Todd (Producer, Writer)
c/o Staff Member *Creative Artists Agency
(CAA-LA)*
2000 Ave Of The Stars
Los Angeles, CA 90067, USA

Kester, Rick (Athlete, Baseball Player)
P.O. Box 623
Gardnerville, NV 89410-0623, USA

Kestner, Boyd (Actor)
Mirisch Agency
1801 Century Park E
#1801
Los Angeles, CA 90067, USA

Ketchum, Dave
2318 Waterby St.
Westlake Village, CA 91361-1834

Ketchum, Hal (Musician)
602 Wayside Dr.
Wimberley, TX 78676

Ketchum, Howard (Engineer)
3800 Washington Road
West Palm Beach, FL 33405, USA

Ketchum, Rai (Musician, Songwriter,
Writer)
602 Wayside Dr
Wimberley, TX 78676, USA

Ketola, Veli-Pekka (Athlete, Hockey
Player)
Talikkalankuja 6
Pori 28300, Finland

Ketola-Lacamera, Helen (Athlete, Baseball
Player, Commentator)
907 New York St
Edgewater, FL 32132-2373, USA

Ketter, Kerry (Athlete, Hockey Player)
3259 Majestic Dr
Courtenay, BC V9N 9X4, Canada

Ketterle, Wolfgang (Nobel Prize Laureate)
25 Bellingham Dr
Brookline, MA 02446, USA

Kettle, Roger (Cartoonist)
c/o Staff Member *King Features
Syndication*
300 W 57th St
15th Floor
New York, NY 10019-5238, USA

Keves, Gyorgy (Architect)
Keves es Epitesztarsai Rt
Melinda Utca 21
Budapest 1121, HUNGARY

Key, Jimmy (Athlete, Baseball Player)
128 Talavera Pl
Palm Beach Gardens, FL 33418-6221,
USA

Key, Keegan Michael (Actor)
c/o Joel Zadak *Principato/Young
Management*
9465 Wilshire Blvd
Suite 430
Beverly Hills, CA 90212, USA

Key, Larry (Athlete, Football Player)
9661 60th St
Attn: Church Administrations
Pinelias Park, FL 33782, USA

Key, Sean (Athlete, Football Player)
4637 Chapel Creek Dr
Plano, TX 75024, USA

Key, Ted (Cartoonist)
1694 Glenhardie Road
Wayne, PA 19087, USA

Key, Wade (Athlete, Football Player)
P.O. Box 857
Hondo, TX 78861-0857, USA

Keyes, Alan (Politician)
Loyalty to Liberty
P.O. Box 83759
Gaithersburg, MD 20883, USA

Keyes, Daniel (Writer)
222 NW 69th St
Boca Raton, FL 33487, USA

Keyes, Leroy (Athlete, Football Player)
6156 Pleasant Ave
Pennsauken, NJ 08110, USA

Keyes, Robert W (Engineer)
IBM Research Division
PO Box 218
Yorktown Heights, NY 10598, USA

Keyfitz, Nathan (Mathematician)
61 Mill Road
North Hampton, NH 03862, USA

Keymah, T'Keyah Crystal (Actor)
121 N San Vicente Blvd
Beverly Hills, CA 90211, USA

Keynes, Skander (Actor)
c/o Brian Swardstrom *WME (LA)*
9601 Wilshire Blvd Fl 3
Beverly Hills, CA 90210, USA

Keys, Alicia (Musician, Songwriter)
191 Brayton St
Englewood Cliffs, NJ 07632, USA

Keys, Brady (Athlete, Football Player)
2931 Banchory Rd
Winter Park, FL 32792-4501, USA

Keys, Ronald E (General)
Commander in Chief Allied Forces South
Europe
Box 1 PSC 813
FPO, AE 09620, USA

Keys, Rudy (Athlete, Basketball Player)
4308 Ludi Mae Ct
Charlotte, NC 28227-6638, USA

Keys, Tyrone (Athlete, Football Player)
5708 Clouds Peak Dr
Lutz, FL 33558-4974, USA

Keyser, Brian (Athlete, Baseball Player)
11983 Cypress Links Dr
Fort Myers, FL 33913-8404, USA

Keyser, Joan (Stylist)
8008 Taylor Rd
Victor, NY 14564, USA

Keyser, Richard L (Business Person)
WW Grainger Inc
100Grainger Parkway
Lake Forest, IL 60045, USA

Keyser Jr, F Ray (Ex-Governor, General)
144 E Hartford St
Hernando, FL 34442, USA

Keysey, Ken
Rt. 8 Box 477
Pleasant Hill, OR 97401

Keyworth, Jon (Athlete, Football Player)
1722 E Ridgefield Rd
Spanish Fork, UT 84660-8477, USA

Khabibulin, Nikolai (Athlete, Hockey
Player)
Puckagency LLC
555 Pleasantville Rd Ste 210N
Attn Jay Grossman
Briarcliff Manor, NY 10510-1900, USA

Khajag, Barsamian (Religious Leader)
Armenian Church of America
Eastern Diocese
630 2nd Ave
New York, NY 10016, USA

Khaled, DJ (Musician)
c/o Staff Member *5W Public Relations
(NY)*
888 7th Ave # 12
New York, NY 10106, USA

Khali, Simbi (Actor)
Innovative Artists
1505 10th St
Santa Monica, CA 90401, USA

Khalifa, Sam (Athlete, Baseball Player)
1050 N Camino Seco
Apt 1044
Tucson, AZ 85710-1770, USA

Khalifa, Sheikh Khalifa bin Sulman al
(Prime Minister)
Prime Minister's Office
Government House
Manama, BAHARIN

Khalifa, Wiz (Musician)
30 Virginia Ln
Canonsburg, PA 15317, USA

Khalifa-al-Thani, Hamad Bin (Prime
Minister, Prince)
Royal Palace
PO Box 923
Doha, QATAR

Khalil, Christel (Actor)
c/o Meredith Fine *Coast to Coast Talent
Group*
3350 Barham Blvd
Los Angeles, CA 90068, USA

Khalil, Cristel (Actor)

Khamenei, Hojatolislam Sayyed Ali
(President)
Religious Leader's Office
Teheran, IRAN

Khamtai, Siphandon (Prime Minister)
Prime Minister's Office
Council of Ministers
Vientiane, LAOS

Khan, Aamir (Actor, Bollywood)
c/o Staff Member *WME (LA)*
9601 Wilshire Blvd Fl 3
Beverly Hills, CA 90210, USA

Khan, Abdulla (Actor)
20/1 Arch Bishop Avenue
Boat Club Road
Chennai, TN 600 018, INDIA

Khan, Alia (Designer)
Asian Andaz Inc
183 Madison Ave #1719
New York, NY 10016, USA

Khan, Ali Akbar (Composer)
Gregory DiGiovine Mgmt
121 Jordan St
San Rafael, CA 94901, USA

Khan, Amjad Ali (Composer)
3 Sadhna Enclave
Panchsheel Park
New Delhi, New Delhi 110 017, INDIA

Khan, Ayub (Actor, Bollywood)
Xavier House 2nd Floor
St Peter Colony Bandra (W)
Mumbai, MS 400050, INDIA

Khan, Chaka (Actor, Musician)
Chaka Khan Enterprises
9100 Wilshire Blvd
Suite 450 East
Beverly Hills, CA 90212, USA

Khan, Farah (Director)
c/o Staff Member *Indya.com Portal Pvt
Ltd.*
Embassy Point, 3rd Floor
150, Infantry Road
Bangalore, Karnataka 560001, India

Khan, Fardeen (Actor, Bollywood)
Sunshine Jassawala Wadi
Juhu Road Juhu
Mumbai, MS 400049, INDIA

Khan, Feroz (Actor, Bollywood, Director,
Filmmaker, Producer)
Sunshine Jussawala Wadi
Juhu Church Road
Mumbai, MS 400049, INDIA

Khan, Gulam Ishaq (Ex-President,
President)
3B University Town
Jamrud Road
Peshawar, PAKISTAN

Khan, Inamullah (Religious Leader)
Muslim Congress
D26 Block 8
Gulshan-E_Iqbal
Karachi 75300, PAKISTAN

Khan, Jemima (Heir/Heiress, Journalist)
c/o Staff Member *AP Watt Ltd*
20 John St
London WC1N 2DR, UK

Khan, Kader (Actor, Bollywood)
102 Raj Kamal
2nd Hasnabad Lane Santacruz
Mumbai, MS 400054, INDIA

Khan, Niazi Imran (Cricketer)
c/o Staff Member *Emptage Hallett*
14 Rathbone Pl
London W1T 1HT, UNITED KINGDOM
(UK)

Khan, Prince Sadruddin Aga
Collonge-Bellerive,
SWITZERLAND CH-1245

Khan, Princess Yasmin
146 Central Park W
New York, NY 10023

Khan, Salman (Actor, Bollywood)
3 Galaxy Apartments
Bt Road, Bandstand
Bandra, Bombay 400 050, India

Khan, Sanjay (Actor, Bollywood, Director,
Producer)
Sanjay House 11 Silver Beach A B Nair
Road
Juhu
Bombay, MS 400 049, INDIA

Khan, Shahbaaz (Actor, Bollywood)
GB6 Agha Khan Baug
Versova Andheri
Bombay, MS 400 061, INDIA

Khan, Shahrukh (Actor, Bollywood)
c/o Staff Member *Red Chillies
Entertainment*
Lokhandwala, Andheri (West)
Mumbai, Maharashtra, India

Khan, Sohail (Actor, Bollywood, Director,
Producer)
4 Coral Reef 55 Chimbai Road
Bandra (W)
Mumbai, MS 400050, INDIA

Khan, The Aga IV
Aiglemont
Gouvieux, FRANCE F-60270

Khanh, Emanuelle (Designer, Fashion
Designer)
Emanuelle Khanh International
45 Ave Victor Hugo
Paris 75116, FRANCE

Khanna, Akshaye (Actor, Bollywood)
13/C Elplaza
Little Gibs Road Malabar Hill
Mumbai, MS 400026, INDIA

Khanna, Amit (Actor, Bollywood)
301 Sea Star Near Holiday Inn
Balraj Sahni Marg
Mumbai, MS 400049, INDIA

Khanna, Mukesh (Actor, Bollywood,
Director)
3 Parijat 95
Marine Drive
Bombay, MS 400 002, INDIA

Khanna, Rahul (Actor, Bollywood)
12/18 V.P. Road
C.P. Tank Mumbai 4
Mumbai, MS 400004, INDIA

Khanna, Rinke (Actor, Bollywood)
201-A Vastu Bldg
Military Rd Juhu
Mumbai, MS 400049, INDIA

khanna, Twinkle (Actor, Bollywood)
Samudra Mahal Birla Lane
Juhu
Mumbai, MS 400049, INDIA

Khanna, Vinod (Actor, Bollywood)
11 Palazo 13th Flr Behind WIAA
Malabar Hill
Mumbai, MS 400006, INDIA

Khanzadian, Vahan (Opera Singer)
3604 Broadway
#2N
New York, NY 10031, USA

Kharbanda, Kulbhushan (Actor)
501 Silver Cascade Mount Mary Road
Bandra
Bombay, MS 400 050, INDIA

Kharin, Sergei (Athlete, Hockey Player)
3306 N RIverwood Dr
Twin Lake, MI 49457-9789, USA

Khariton, Yuli B (Physicist)
Nuclear Energy Center
Arsamas 16
Nizhy Novgorog Region, RUSSIA

Khashoggi, Adnan
Box 6
Riyadh, SAUDI ARABIA

Khashoggi, Adnan M (Business Person)
La Baraka
Marbella, SPAIN

Khatami, Mohammad (Politician,
President)
President's Office
Dr Ali Shariati Ave
Teheran, IRAN

Khavin, Vladimir Y (Architect)
Glavmosarchitectura
Mayakovsky Square 1
Moscow 103001, RUSSIA

Khayat, Edward (Eddie) (Athlete, Coach,
Football Coach, Football Player)
7813 Haydenberry Cove
Nashville, TN 37221, USA

Khayat, Nadir (RedOne) (Producer)
c/o Alan Melina *New Heights
Entertainment*
PO Box 8489
Calabasas, CA 91372, USA

Khayat, Robert (Athlete, Football Player)
P.O. Box 667
Oxford, MS 38655, USA

Khayat, Robert (Educator)
University of Mississippi
Chancellor's Office
University, MS 38677, USA

Kher, Anupam (Actor, Bollywood)
402 Marina
Juhu Tara Road Juhu Beach
Mumbai, MS 400049, INDIA

K. Hirono, Mazie (Congressman,
Politician)
1410 Longworth HOB
Washington, DC 20515, USA

Khitty (Actor)
E3 Sea Brook Apartments 4th C'Ward
Road
Valmigi Nagar Thiruvanmiyur
Chennai, TN 600 041, INDIA

Khmylev, Yuri (Athlete, Hockey Player)
8236 Oakway Ln
Buffalo, NY 14221-2871

Khokhlov, Boris (Dancer)
Myaskovsky St 11-13
#102
Moscow 121019, USA

Khondji, Darius (Cinematographer)
International Creative Mgmt
8942 Wilshire Blvd
#219
Beverly Hills, CA 90211, USA

Khorkina, Svetlana (Gymnast, Olympic
Athlete)
Russian Gymnastics Federation
Lujnetskaya Nabereynaya 8
Moscow 119270, RUSSIA

Khotan (Musician)
c/o Gabriel Blanco *Gabriel Blanco
Iglesias (Mexico)*
Rio Balsas 35-32
Colonia Cuauhtemoc
DF 06500, Mexico

Khouna, Sheikh El Afia Quid Mohamed
(Prime Minister)
Prime Minister's Office
Nouakchott, MAURITANIA

Khouri, Callie (Director)
c/o Richard Green *Creative Artists Agency
(CAA-LA)*
2000 Ave Of The Stars
Los Angeles, CA 90067, USA

Khrennikov, Tikhon N (Composer)
Plotnikov Per 10/28
#19
Moscow 121200, RUSSIA

Khristenko, Viktor (Prime Minister)
Prime Minister's Office
Kremlin
Staraya Pl 4
Moscow 103132, RUSSIA

Khristich, Dmitri (Athlete, Hockey Player)
5002 N Convent Ln Apt E
Apt E
Philadelphia, PA 19114-3125

Khruschev, Sergei
PO Box 1948
Providence, RI 02912

Khush, Gurdev S (Scientist)
Int'l Rice Research Institute
PO Box 933
Manila 1099, PHILLIPINES

Khvorostovsky, Dimitri A (Opera Singer)
Elen Victorova
Mosfilmovskaya 26
#5
Moscow, RUSSIA

Kiana (Talk Show Host)
ESPN 2
935 Middle St
Bristol, CT 06010

Kiarostaml, Abbas (Director)
Zeitgeist Films
247 Center St
#200
New York, NY 10013, USA

Kibaki, Mwai (President)
President's Office
Harambee House
Harambee Ave
Nairobi, KENYA

Kibler, John (Athlete, Baseball Player)
2701 El Camino Real
#205
Palo Alto, CA 94306-1713, USA

Kibrick, Anne (Educator)
130 Seminary Ave
#312
Auburndale, MA 02466, USA

Kibrick, Sidney (Actor)
10490 Wilshire Blvd. #1901
Los Angeles, CA 90024-4649, USA

Kichel III, Walter (Editor)
Fortune Magazine
Editorial Dept
1291 Ave of Americas
New York, NY 10020, USA

Kickinger, Roland (Actor)
c/o Staff Member *Coralie Jr Theatrical
Agency*
907 S Victory Blvd
Burbank, CA 91502-2430, USA

Kidd, Carl (Athlete, Football Player)
2317 Peach Tree Dr
Little Rock, AR 72211-4331, USA

Kidd, Dylan (Director)
c/o Staff Member *Creative Artists Agency
(CAA-LA)*
2000 Ave Of The Stars
Los Angeles, CA 90067, USA

Kidd, Glenna Sue (Athlete, Baseball
Player, Commentator)
51 17th St
Logansport, IN 46947-2842, USA

Kidd, Ian (Athlete, Hockey Player)
2512 E 7th St
Duluth, MN 55812-1406, USA

Kidd, Jason (Athlete, Basketball Player,
Olympic Athlete)
c/o Jeff Schwartz *Excel Sports
Management*
9665 Wilshire Blvd #500
Los Angeles, CA 90212, USA

Kidd, Jodie (Model)
c/o Staff Member *IMG*
304 Park Ave S Fl 12
New York, NY 10010, USA

Kidd, John (Athlete, Football Player)
4204 Moorland Dr
Midland, MI 48640, USA

Kidd, Sue (Baseball Player)
51 17th St
Logansport, IN 46947-2842, USA

Kidd, Trevor
Mountain Bean Coffee Company
121-1325 Bear Mountain Pky
Victoria, BC V9B 6T8, Canada

Kidd, Warren (Athlete, Basketball Player)
313 River Rd
Harpersville, AL 35078-7e14, USA

Kidd, William W (Billy) (Athlete, Olympic
Athlete, Skier)
Billy Kidd Racing
2305 Mount Werner Circle
Steamboat Springs, CO 80487, USA

Kidder, Margot (Actor)
c/o Derek Maki *Coolwaters Productions*
10061 Riverside Dr.
Box 531
Toluca Lake, CA 91602, USA

Kidder Lee, Barbara (Skier)
1308 W Highland
Phoenix, AZ 85013, USA

Kidjo, Angelique (Musician)
c/o Staff Member *Red Light Management (LA)*
8439 W Sunset Blvd
Suite 2
Los Angeles, CA 90069, USA

Kidman, Nicole (Actor, Producer)
9579 Lime Orchard Dr
Beverly Hills, CA 90210, USA

Kid Rock (Musician)
c/o Ken Levitan *Vector Management*
P.O. Box 120479
Nashville, TN 37212, USA

Kiecker, Dana (Athlete, Baseball Player)
4104 Prairie Ridge Rd
Saint Paul, MN 55123-1625, USA

Kiedis, Anthony (Musician)
c/o Jason Weinberg *Untitled Entertainment (LA)*
350 S. Beverly Dr #200
Beverly Hills, CA 90212, USA

Kiefel, Ron (Athlete, Cycler, Olympic Athlete)
3893 Field Dr
Wheat Ridge, CO 80033-4372, USA

Kiefer, Adolph G (Athlete, Coach, Olympic Athlete, Swimmer)
42125 N Hunt Club Road
Wadsworth, IL 60083, USA

Kiefer, Mark (Athlete, Baseball Player)
11822 Old Fashion Way
Garden Grove, CA 92840-2117, USA

Kiefer, Nicolas (Athlete, Tennis Player)
c/o Staff Member *ATP Tour*
201 ATP Tour Blvd
Ponte Vedra Beach, FL 32082-3211, USA

Kiefer, Steve (Athlete, Baseball Player)
12389 Cloudburst Trl
Moreno Valley, CA 92555-5426, USA

Kiehl, Marina (Skier)
Hermie-Bland Str 11
Munich 81545, GERMANY

Kiehl, Stuart (Cinematographer)
4193 Concord Ave
Santa Rosa, CA 95407, USA

Kiel, John (Athlete, Football Player)
12100 Pebblepointe Pass
Carmel, IN 46033, USA

Kiel, Richard (Actor)
c/o Steve (Sr) Stevens *The Stevens Group*
14011 Ventura Blvd #201
Sherman Oaks, CA 91423, USA

Kielty, Bob (Bobby) (Athlete, Baseball Player)
21504 Appaloosa Ct
Canyon Lake, CA 92587-7628, USA

Kiely, John (Athlete, Baseball Player)
84 Brown St
Brockton, MA 02301-1006, USA

Kiely, Mark
9255 Sunset Blvd. #620
Los Angeles, CA 90069

Kieper, John (Race Car Driver)
15643 NE Siskiyou Ct.
Portland, OR 97230, USA

Kier, Miss Lady (Musician)
P.O. Box 32805
London, England N1 5WP, United Kingdom

Kier, Udo (Actor)
c/o Richard Schwartz *Richard Schwartz Management*
2934-1/2 Beverly Glen Cir #107
Los Angeles, CA 90077, USA

Kiermayer, Susanne (Misc)
Amthofplatz 5
Kirchberg 94259, GERMANY

Kieschnick, Brook (Baseball Player)
Chicago Cubs
201 Evans Ave
San Antonio, TX 78209-3721, USA

Kieschnick, Brooks (Athlete, Baseball Player)
107 Dover Rd
San Antonio, TX 78209-6169, USA

Kiesel, Theresia (Athlete, Track Athlete)
Stifterstr 24
Truan 4050, AUSTRIA

Kiewel, Jeff (Athlete, Football Player)
9923 E Karst Pl
Tucson, AZ 85748-4566, USA

Kiffin, Irv (Athlete, Basketball Player)
1441 Trellis Ln
Pembroke Pines, FL 33e26-3250, USA

Kiffin, Lane (Athlete, Football Player)
906 9th St
Manhattan Beach, CA 90266-5953, USA

Kiffin, Monte (Athlete, Football Player)
6005 Williamsburg Cv
Jonesboro, AR 72404-9636, USA

Kiggens, Lisa (Athlete, Golfer)
1504 Club View Dr
Bakersfield, CA 93309-3541, USA

Kight, Kelvin (Athlete, Football Player)
3748 Bramblevine Cir
Lithonia, GA 30038-2920, USA

Kightlinger, Laura (Actor, Comedian, Producer, Writer)
c/o David Martin *Avalon Management*
8332 Melrose Ave
2nd Floor
Los Angeles, CA 90069, USA

Kihn, Greg (Musician)
Riot Mgmt
55 Santa Clara Ave
#120
oakland, CA 94610, USA

Kiick, James F (Jim) (Athlete, Football Player)
2900 S University Dr
Apt 9112
Davie, FL 33328, USA

Kikuchi, Rinko (Actor)
c/o Staff Member *Creative Artists Agency (CAA-LA)*
2000 Ave Of The Stars
Los Angeles, CA 90067, USA

Kikutake, Kiyonori (Architect)
1-11-15 Otsuka
Bunkyoku, Tokyo, JAPAN

Kilar, Wojciech (Composer)
Ul Ksciuszki 165
Katowice 40-524, POLAND

Kilbey, Steven (Musician)
Globeshine
101 Chamberlayne Road
London NW10 3ND, UNITED KINGDOM (UK)

Kilborn, Craig (Talk Show Host)
c/o Shani Rosenzweig *United Talent Agency (UTA)*
9336 Civic Center Dr
Beverly Hills, CA 90210, USA

Kilbourne, Wendy (Actor)
9300 Wilshire Blvd
#410
Beverly Hills, CA 90212, USA

Kilburn, Terry (Actor)
Meadowbrook Theatre
Oakland University
Walton & Squirrel
Rochester, MI 48063, USA

Kilcher, Q'Orianka (Actor)
c/o Carlyne Grager *Dramatic Artists Agency*
103 W. Alameda Ave
Suite 139
Burbank, CA 91502, USA

Kilcullen, Bob (Athlete, Football Player)
400 E Division St
Pilot Point, TX 76258-4510, USA

Kiley, Ariel (Actor)
c/o Gene Parseghian *Parseghian Planco LLC*
322 8th Ave
Suite 601
New York, NY 10001, USA

Kilgallon, Robert D (Scientist)
662 Park Ave
Meadville, PA 16335, USA

Kilger, Chad (Athlete, Hockey Player)
1351 Second St E
Cornwall, ON K6H 2B6, Canada

Kilgore, Al (Cartoonist)
21655 113th Dr
Queens Village, NY 11429, USA

Kilgore, Jon (Athlete, Football Player)
2422 Glen Oaks Ct NE
Atlanta, GA 30345, USA

Kilgus, Paul (Athlete, Baseball Player)
968 Threewood Cir
Bowling Green, KY 42103-2479, USA

Kilguss-Crall, Annette (Stylist)
4438 Ethel Ave
Studio City, CA 91604, USA

Kilian, Thomas J (Business Person)
Conseco Inc
PO Box 1957
Carmel, IN 46082, USA

Kilius, Marika (Figure Skater)
Postfach 201151
Dreieich 63271, GERMANY

Kilkenny, Mike (Athlete, Baseball Player)
274 Holland St W
Bradford, ON L3Z 1J1, Canada

Killam, Taran (Actor)
c/o Joel Zadak *Principato/Young Management*
9465 Wilshire Blvd
Suite 430
Beverly Hills, CA 90212, USA

Killeen, Denise (Athlete, Golfer)
803 Golden Wood Trce
Canton, GA 30114-6572, USA

Killeen, Evans (Athlete, Baseball Player)
137 Main St
Westhampton Beach, NY 11978-2607, USA

Killens, Terry (Athlete, Football Player)
5665 Water Spring Way
Mason, OH 45040, USA

Killett, Charlie (Athlete, Football Player)
114 Forrest Heights Rd
Paris, TN 38242, USA

Kill Hannah (Music Group, Musician)
c/o Staff Member *In De Goot Entertainment*
119 W 23rd St #609
New York, NY 10011, USA

Killinger, Kerry K (Financier)
Washington Mutual Inc
1201 3rd Ave
Seattle, WA 98101, USA

Killip, Christopher D (Photographer)
Harvard University
Visual Studies Dept
24 Quincy St
Cambridge, MA 02138, USA

Killorin, Pat (Athlete, Football Player)
8304 Partridgeberry Dr
Baldwinsville, NY 13027, USA

Killum, Ernie (Athlete, Basketball Player)
710 Pennybrook Ln
Stone Mountain, GA 30087-5917, USA

Killy, Jean-Claude (Skier)
Villa Les 13 Chemin Bellefontaine
Cologny-GE 1223, SWITZERLAND

Kilmer, Val (Actor)
c/o Stephanie Simon *Untitled Entertainment (LA)*
350 S. Beverly Dr #200
Beverly Hills, CA 90212, USA

Kilmer, William O (Billy) (Athlete, Football Player)
1853 Monte Carto Way
Apt 36
Coral Springs, FL 33071, USA

Kilmore, Chris (Musician)
c/o Staff Member *ArtistDirect*
9046 Lindblade St
Culver City, CA 90232, USA

Kilner, Kevin (Actor)
Innovative Artists
1505 10th St
Santa Monica, CA 90401, USA

Kilpatrick, Carl (Athlete, Basketball Player)
10517 23rd Street Ct E
Edgewood, WA 98372-1595, USA

Kilpatrick, Eric
6330 Simpson Ave. #3
No. Hollywood, CA 91606

Kilpatrick, Kwame (Politician)
Mayor's Office
City-County Building
2 Woodward Ave
Detroit, MI 48226, USA

Kilrain, Susan L (Astronaut)
625 Cedar Ln
Virginia Beacch, VA 23452, USA

Kilrea, Brian (Athlete, Coach, Hockey Player)
2192 Saunderson Dr
Ottawa, ON K1G 2G4, Canada

Kilts, James M (Business Person)
Gillette Co
Prudential Tower Building
Boston, MA 02199, USA

Kilzer, Louis C (Lon) (Journalist)
Minneapolis-Saint Paul Star-Tribune
425 Portland Ave
Minneapolis, MN 55488, USA

Kim, Anthony (Athlete, Golfer)
c/o Clarke Jones *IMG (Cleveland)*
1360 E 9th St
Suite 100
Cleveland, OH 44114, USA

Kim, Daniel Dae (Actor)
P.O. Box 10151
Honolulu, HI 96816, USA

Kim, Jacqueline (Actor)
Innovative Artists
1505 10th St
Santa Monica, CA 90401, USA

Kim, Jaegwon (Misc)
Brown University
Philosophy Dept
Providence, RI 02912, USA

Kim, Lil' (Musician)
c/o Staff Member *Energon Entertainment*
276 5th Ave
Suite 712
New York, NY 10001, USA

Kim, Nelli V (Gymnast)
2480 Cobblehill
#A Alocove
Woodbury, MN 55125, USA

Kim, Peter S (Misc)
Whitehead Institute
9 Cambridge Center
Cambridge, MA 02142, USA

Kim, Stephan Sou-hwan Cardinal
(Religious Leader)
Archbishop's House
2 Ka 1 Myong Dong Chungku
Seoul 100, SOUTH KOREA

kim, Wendell (Athlete, Baseball Player)
3286 E ivanhoe St
Gilbert, AZ 85295-340_4_, USA

kim, Wendell
3286 E ivanhoe St
Gilbert, AZ 85295-3404, USA

kim, Wendell (Athlete, Baseball Player)
3286 E ivanhoe St
Gilbert, AZ 85295-3404, USA

Kim, Yoon-jin (Actor)
c/o Staff Member *WmE2 (WMA-LA)*
1 William Morris Pl
Beverly Hills, CA 90212, USA

Kim, Young Sam (President)
Sangdo-dong 7-6
Tongjakku
Seoul, SOUTH KOREA

Kim, Young Uck (Musician)
Columbia Artists Mgmt Inc
165 W 57th St
New York, NY 10019, USA

Kim, Yunjin (Actor)
c/o Alex Chaice *Global Creative*
1051 Cole Ave # B
Los Angeles, CA 90038, USA

Kimball, Bobby (Musician)
World Entertainment Assoc
297101 Kinderkamack Road
#128
Oradell, NJ 07649, USA

Kimball, Bruce (Athlete, Football Player)
41 Spring Rd
Rye, NH 03870, USA

Kimball, Cheyenne (Musician)

Kimball, Dick (Coach)
1540 Waltham Dr
Ann Arbor, MI 48103, USA

Kimball, Shawn (Athlete, Baseball Player)
75 Black Stream Dr
Levant, ME 04456-4427, USA

Kimball, Toby (Athlete, Basketball Player)
6859 Avenida Ave
La Jolla, CA 92037-6407, USA

Kimball, Ward
8910 Ardendale Ave.
San Gabriel, CA 91775

Kimball, Warren F (Historian)
2540 Otter Lane
Johns Island, SC 29455, USA

Kimball-Purdham, Mary Ellen (Athlete,
Baseball Player, Commentator)
15299 S 18th St
Vicksburg, MI 49097-9738, USA

Kimber, Bill (Athlete, Football Player)
7801 Point Meadows Dr Unit 3102
Jacksonville, FL 32256-9145, USA

Kimber, William (Athlete, Football Player)
7801 Point Meadows Dr
Unit 3102
Jacksonville, FL 32256, USA

Kimble, Bo (Athlete, Basketball Player)
100 Poe Ct
North Wales, PA 19454, USA

Kimble, Darin (Athlete, Hockey Player)
1202 27th St
Granite City, IL 62040-3431, USA

Kimble, Gregory "Bo" (Athlete, Basketball
Player)
100Poe Ct Unit 83
North Wales, PA 19454-4430, USA

Kimble, Warren (Artist)
RR 3Box 1038
Brandon, VT 05733, USA

Kimbrough, Charles (Actor, Musician)
255 Amalfi Dr
Santa Monica, CA 90402, USA

Kimbrough, Elbert (Athlete, Football
Player)
886 W 2nd St
Galesburg, IL 61401-5711, USA

Kimbrough, John (Athlete, Football Player)
2016 Fleming Dr
McKinney, TX 75070-3986, USA

Kimbrough, Stan (Athlete, Basketball
Player)
3922 Elm Ave
Cincinnati, OH 45236-39e8, USA

Kimbrough, Tony (Athlete, Football
Player)
3395 Sharp Rd
Sturgis, MS 39769-8764, USA

Kimbrough, Will (Musician)
Cedar Creek Music
164 Dove Creek Rd
Frankfort, KY 40601, USA

Kimery, James L (Misc)
Veterans of Foreign Wars
405 W 34th St
Kansas City, MO 64111, USA

Kimm, Bruce (Athlete, Baseball Player,
Coach)
3168 121st St
Amana, IA 52203-8046, USA

Kimmel, Frank (Race Car Driver)
KFPI/Amber Estes
102 Brookshire Dr.
Danville, KY 40422, USA

Kimmel, Jerry (Athlete, Football Player)
1411 Colesville Rd
Harpursville, NY 13787-1430, USA

Kimmel, Jimmy (Comedian, Television
Host)
Jimmy Kimmel Live
6834 Hollywood Blvd #600
Hollywood, CA 90028, USA

Kimmell, Dana (Actor)
26684 Stanford St
Hemet, CA 92544, USA

Kimmelman, Jamie (Stylist)
c/o Staff Member *Mel Bryant Management*
611 Broadway #623
New York, NY 10012

Kimmins, Kenneth (Actor)
c/o Joanna (Joanie) Burstein *Burstein
Company, The*
15304 Sunset Blvd
suite 208
Pacific Palisades, CA 90272, USA

Kims of Comedy (Comedian)
c/o Staff Member *Paradigm (Monterey)*
404 W Franklin St
Monterey, CA 93940, USA

Kimura, Doreen (Psychic, Scientist)
211 Madison Ave
Toronto, ON M5R 2S6, CANADA

Kimura, Kazuo (Designer)
Japan Design Foundation
2-2 Cenba Chuo
Higashiku
Osaka 541, JAPAN

Kimura, Motoo (Biologist)
Institute of Genetics
Yata 1
111 Mishima
Shizuokaken 411, JAPAN

Kinard, Billy (Athlete, Football Player)
41 Vail Ln
Watchung, NJ 07069, USA

Kinard, Terry (Athlete, Football Player)
PO Box 1780
Conyers, GA 30012-7954, USA

Kincade, Keylon (Athlete, Football Player)
1344 Gayle St
Burleson, TX 76028-8628, USA

Kincaid, Jamaica (Writer)
College Road
North Bennington, VT 05257, USA

Kincaid, Jim (Athlete, Football Player)
401 Tryon Dr
Goldsboro, NC 27530-9149, USA

Kinchen, Brian (Athlete, Football Player)
19052 E Pinnacle Cir
Baton Rouge, LA 70810, USA

Kinchen, Todd W (Athlete, Football
Player)
247 Guava Dr
Baton Rouge, LA 70808, USA

Kinchla, Chan (Musician)
c/o Staff Member *ArtistDirect*
9046 Lindblade St
Culver City, CA 90232, USA

Kincses, Veronika (Opera Singer)
Hungarian State Opera
Andrassy Ulca 22
Budapest 1061, HUNGARY

Kind, Danielle (Actor)
C/O Micheline Watson
Take One Talent Management Inc
PO Box 20019
Ottawa K1N 9N5, CANADA

Kind, Richard (Actor)
c/o Arlene Forster *Forster Entertainment*
12533 Woodgreen St
Los Angeles, CA 90066, USA

Kind, Ron (Congressman, Politician)
1406 Longworth HOB
Washington, DC 20515, USA

Kind, Roslyn (Actor, Musician)
Scott Stander
13707 Riverside Dr
#201
Sherman Oaks, CA 91423, USA

Kindall, Jerry (Athlete, Baseball Player)
7220 E Grey Fox Ln
Tucson, AZ 85750-1377, USA

Kinder, Melvyn (Writer)
c/o Staff Member *Random House*
1540 Broadway
New York, NY 10036, USA

Kinder, Melvyn (Psychic)
1951 San Ysidro Dr
Beverly Hills, CA 90210, USA

Kinder, Richard D (Business Person)
Kinder and Morgan
500 Dallas St
Suite 1000
Houston, TX 77002, USA

Kinderman, Keith (Athlete, Football
Player)
5837 Bradfordville Rd
Tallahassee, FL 32309, USA

Kindig, Howard (Athlete, Football Player)
8740 Bayside Ave
Baton Rouge, LA 70806, USA

Kindle, Greg (Athlete, Football Player)
7606 Heron Park Ct
Humble, TX 77396, USA

Kindler, Klaus
Am Berg 6
Schwietenkirchen, GERMANY D-85301

Kindrachuk, Orest (Athlete, Hockey
Player)
14044th Ave
Asbury Park, NJ 07712-4944, USA

Kindred, David A (Writer)
Atlanta Constitution
Editorial Dept
72 Marietta St
Atlanta, GA 30303, USA

Kindricks, Bill (Athlete, Football Player)
1466 Alma Loop
San Jose, CA 95125-1731, USA

Kiner, Ralph (Athlete, Baseball Player)
New York Mets 12301 Roosevelt Ave
Attn Broadcast Dept
Flushing, NY 11368-1629, USA

Kiner, Ralph (Athlete, Baseball Player)
200 Bradley Pl Apt 203
Palm Beach, FL 33480-3765, USA

Kiner, Steve (Athlete, Football Player)
112 N Ole Hickory Trl
Carrollton, GA 30117, USA

King, Adrienne (Actor)
c/o Aine Leicht *Horror & Hilarity*
Prefers to be contacted via telephone
Los Angeles, CA 90067, USA

King, Alan (Actor, Producer, Writer)
c/o Lisa Gallant *Gallant Management*
10250 Constellation Blvd Fl 7
Los Angeles, CA 90067, USA

King, Albert (Athlete, Basketball Player)
88 Sturbridge Circle
Wayne, NJ 07470-8402, USA

King, Alton (Athlete, Baseball Player)
8226 Esper St
Detroit, MI 48204-3120, USA

King, Angelo (Athlete, Football Player)
2922 W Royal Ln Apt 2090
Irving, TX 75063-6235, USA

King, BB (Musician)
BB King Road Show Inc
3170 W Sahara Ave #D-17
Las Vegas, NV 89102, USA

King, Ben E (Musician)
Smiling Clown Music
PO Box 1097
Teaneck, NJ 07666, USA

King, Benjamin (Actor)
c/o Peter Principato *Principato/Young Management*
9465 Wilshire Blvd
Suite 430
Beverly Hills, CA 90212, USA

King, Bernard (Athlete, Football Player)
Hollywood Christian School
1708 N State Road 7
Attn: Athletic Dept
Hollywood, FL 33021, USA

King, Bernard (Athlete, Basketball Player)
307 Jupiter Hills Dr
Dututh, GA 30097-5900 King, USA

King, Billie Jean (Athlete, Tennis Player)
101 W. 79th St.
New York, NY 10024, USA

King, Bruce (Politician)
9140 E Canyon Terrace Dr
Tucson, AZ 85715-5597, USA

King, Cammie Conlon
c/o Staff Member *Pierce & Shelly*
13775-A Mono Way #220
Sonora, CA 95370, USA

King, Candie (Athlete, Golfer)
2673 Saleroso Dr
Rowland Heights, CA 91748, USA

King, Carlos (Athlete, Football Player)
107 S Corncrib Ct
Cary, NC 27513, USA

King, Carole (Musician)
19042 Pacific Coast Highway
Malibu, CA 90265, USA

King, Carolyn Dineen (Judge)
US Court of Appeals
US Courthouse
515 Rusk Ave
Houston, TX 77002, USA

King, Cheryl (Actor)
CLInc Talent
843 N Sycamore Ave
Los Angeles, CA 90038, USA

King, Claude (Musician)
320 Green Terrace Rd
Shreveport, LA 71118, USA

King, Clyde E (Athlete, Baseball Player, Coach)
103 Stratford Rd
Goldsboro, NC 27534, USA

King, Colbert (Journalist)
Washington Post
Editorial Dept
1150 15th St NW
Washington, DC 20071, USA

King, Curtis (Athlete, Baseball Player)
2538 Beechwood Dr
Wineland, NJ 08361-2932, USA

King, Dan (Athlete, Basketball Player)
4803 Grand Dell Dr
Crestwood, KY 40299-5824, USA

King, Dana (Correspondent)
CBS-TV
News Dept
524 W 57th St
New York, NY 10019, USA

King, Dave (Athlete, Hockey Player)
7748 E Clinton St
Scottsdale, AZ 85260-5582, USA

King, Dave
Phoenix Coyotes
6751 N Sunset Blvd Ste 20
Attn: Coaching Staff
Glendale, AZ 85305-3124, USA

King, David A (Misc)
Masters Lodge
Downing College
Cambridge CB2 1DQ, UNITED KINGDOM (UK)

King, David J (Athlete, Football Player)
4365 Riverstone Shls
Ellenwood, GA 30294-6550, USA

King, Dennis (Artist)
3857 26th St
San Francisco, CA 94131, USA

King, Derek (Athlete, Hockey Player)
8184 E Wigspan Way
Scottsdale, AZ 85255-6504

King, Dexter Scott (Misc)
M L King Nonviolent Social Change Center
449 Auburn Ave NE
Atlanta, GA 30312, USA

King, Don (Business Person)
Don King Productions
501 Fairway Dr
Deerfield Beach, FL 33441, USA

King, Don (Misc)
Don King Productions
968 Pinehurst Dr
Las Vegas, NV 89109, USA

King, Donald W (Athlete, Football Player)
1621 Fox Hall Rd
Savannah, GA 31406, USA

King, Ed (Athlete, Football Player)
9903 North Blvd
Cleveland, OH 44108, USA

King, Emanuel
PO Box 41
Leroy, AL 36548-0041, USA

King, Eric (Athlete, Baseball Player)
1063 Stanford Dr
Simi Valley, CA 93065-4952, USA

King, Erik (Actor)
c/o Joanna (Joanie) Burstein *Burstein Company, The*
15304 Sunset Blvd
suite 208
Pacific Palisades, CA 90272, USA

King, Evelyn (Musician)
c/o JD Sobol *RPM Talent Agency*
741 N Cahuenga Blvd
Suite 101
Los Angeles, CA 90038, USA

King, Ezell (Athlete, Baseball Player)
P.O. Box 321154
Houston, TX 77221-1154, USA

King, Frank (Baseball Player)
Negro Baseball Leagues
415 E Rhinehill Rd SE
Atlanta, GA 30315-7403, USA

King, Gayle (Correspondent, Editor)
c/o Andrew Freedman *Andrew Freedman Public Relations*
9127 Thrasher Ave
Los Angeles, CA 90069, USA

King, Gordon (Athlete, Football Player)
2641 Highwood Dr
Roseville, CA 95661, USA

King, Gordon D (Athlete, Football Player)
2641 Highwood Dr
Roseville, CA 95661, USA

King, Graham (Producer)
c/o Joy Fehily *Prime*
9696 Culver Blvd
Suite 102
Culver City, CA 90232, USA

King, G Stephen (Athlete, Football Player)
45 Chipping Stone Rd
North Attleboro, MA 02760, USA

King, Hal (Athlete, Baseball Player)
828 Geneva Dr
Oviedo, FL 32765, USA

King, Hal (Athlete, Baseball Player)
828 Geneva Dr
Oviedo, FL 32765-9503, USA

King, Hogue Maxine (Mick) (Swimmer)
US Air Force Academy
PO Box 155
USAF Academy, CO 80840, USA

King, Horace (Athlete, Football Player)
884 Fairburn Rd NW
Atlanta, GA 30331-3341, USA

King, Jaime (Actor)
c/o Brad Cafarelli *PMK/BNC - LA*
8687 Melrose Ave
8th Floor
West Hollywood, CA 90069, USA

King, James A (Opera Singer)
Columbia Artists Mgmt Inc
165 W 57th St
New York, NY 10019, USA

King, James B (Editor)
Seattle Times
Editorial Dept
1120 John St
Seattle, WA 98109, USA

King, James C (General)
Director
National Imagery/Mapping Agency
Chantilly, VA 22021, USA

King, Jean
5510 Cahuenga Blvd
No. Hollywood, CA 91601

King, Jeff (Athlete, Baseball Player)
PO Box 60
Molt, MT 59057-0060, USA

King, Jeff (Misc)
PO Box 48
Denali National Park, AK 99755, USA

King, Jim (Athlete, Baseball Player)
720 Stokenbury Rd
Elkins, AR 72727-3214, USA

King, Joe (Athlete, Football Player)
373 Boyd Rd
Hallsville, TX 75650-7003, USA

King, John (Correspondent, Television Host)
5003 Belt Rd NW
Washington, DC 10960, USA

King, Jonathan
1 Wyndham Yard
London, ENGLAND W1H 1AR

King, Kaki (Musician)
c/o Staff Member *Paradigm (Monterey)*
404 W Franklin St
Monterey, CA 93940, USA

King, Kathryn (Katie) (Athlete, Hockey Player, Olympic Athlete)
Boston College 140 Commonwealth Ave
Attn Womens Ice Hockey Coach
Chestnut Hill, MA 02467-3858, USA

King, Kenny (Athlete, Football Player)
1184 Verde Oaks Ln
Fort Worth, TX 76135-9034, USA

King, Kent Masters (Actor)
c/o Richard Schwartz *Richard Schwartz Management*
2934-1/2 Beverly Glen Cir #107
Los Angeles, CA 90077, USA

King, Kevin (Athlete, Baseball Player)
RR 1 Box 107
Braggs, OK 74423-9739, USA

King, Kris (Athlete, Hockey Player)
c/o Staff Member *National Hockey League (NHL)*
50 Bay St
11th Floor
Toronto, ON M5J 2X8, Canada

King, Lamar (Athlete, Football Player)
5082 Springhouse Cir
Rosedale, MD 21237-3356, USA

King, Lamnar (Athlete, Football Player)
1453 Browning Dr
Essex, MD 21221, USA

King, Larry (Journalist, Talk Show Host)
c/o Geyer Kosinski *Media Talent Group*
9200 Sunset Blvd
Suite 550
Los Angeles, CA 90069, USA

King, Linden (Athlete, Football Player)
1130 S Flower St Apt 416
Los Angeles, CA 90015-2144, USA

King, Loyd (Athlete, Basketball Player)
118 Wilde Brook Dr
Asheville, NC 28806-l052, USA

King, Mark (Musician)
P.O. Box 23
Sandown PO36 9QL, UK

King, Mary-Claire (Misc)
University of Washington
Medical School
Genetics Dept
Seattle, WA 98195, USA

King, Mervyn A (Economist)
Bank of England
Threadneedle St
London EC2R 8AH, UNITED KINGDOM
(UK)

King, Michael (Business Person)
King World Productions
12400 Wilshire Blvd
Los Angeles, CA 90025, USA

King, Michael (Business Person)
c/o Staff Member *King World Productions Inc (LA)*
2401 Colorado Ave #110
Santa Monica, CA 90404

King, Michael Patrick (Producer, Writer)
c/o Simon Halls *Slate Public Relations*
9000 Sunset Blvd #915
West Hollywood, CA 90069, USA

King, Michel Patrick (Director)
c/o Simon Halls *Slate Public Relations*
9000 Sunset Blvd #915
West Hollywood, CA 90069, USA

King, Micki (Athlete, Diver, Olympic Athlete)
3S09 Colt Neck Ln
Lexington, KY 40502-3042, USA

King, Morgana (Actor, Musician)
Subrena Artists
330 W 56th St #18M
New York, NY 10019, USA

King, Nellie (Athlete, Baseball Player)
3890 Bigelow Blvd
Apt 405
Pittsburgh, PA 15213, USA

King, Patsy
6/70 Hawksburn Rd South Yarra
Victoria, AUSTRALIA 3141

King, Perry (Actor)
3647 Wrightwood Dr
Studio City, CA 91604, USA

King, Phillip (Artist)
Bernard Jackson Gallery
14A Clifford St
London W1X 1RF, UNITED KINGDOM
(UK)

King, Ray (Athlete, Baseball Player)
4220 N 161st Ave
Goodyear, AZ 85395, USA

King, Ray (Athlete, Baseball Player)
14870 W Encanto Blvd
Unit 1046
Goodyear, AZ 85395-6605, USA

King, Reggie (Athlete, Basketball Player)
4716 Chouteau St
Shawnee, KS 66226-2300, USA

King, Regina (Actor)
c/o John Carrabino *John Carrabino Management*
5900 Wilshire Blvd Fl 4 #406
Los Angeles, CA 90036, USA

King, Richard L (Business Person)
Albertson's Inc
250 Parkcenter Blvd
Boise, ID 83726, USA

King, Roger (Business Person)
King World Productions
12400 Wilshire Blvd
Los Angeles, CA 90025, USA

King, R Stacey (Athlete, Basketball Player)
5340 Rfd
Long Grove, IL 60047-9744, USA

King, Scott (Athlete, Hockey Player)
203 Maple Ave
Hershey, PA 17033-1549, USA

King, Shaun (Athlete, Football Player)
1646 41st St S
Saint Petersburg, FL 33711, USA

King, Shawn Southwick (Actor)
c/o Staff Member *WmE2 (WMA-LA)*
1 William Morris Pl
Beverly Hills, CA 90212, USA

King, Stephen (Writer)
c/o Juliann Eugley
49 Florida Ave
Bangor, ME 04401, USA

King, Steve (Athlete, Hockey Player)
2200 Buttonbush Cres
Mississauga, ON LSL 1CS, Canada

King, Steve (Congressman, Politician)
1131 Longworth HOB
Washington, DC 20515, USA

King, Steven (Athlete, Hockey Player)
55 Chestnut Dr
East Greenwich, RI 02818-2102, USA

King, Ted (Actor, Musician)
c/o Staff Member *Paradigm (LA)*
360 N Crescent Dr
North Bldg
Beverly Hills, CA 90210, USA

King, Thea (Musician)
16 Milverton Road
London NW6 7AS, UNITED KINGDOM
(UK)

King, Thomas J (Tom) (Government Official)
House of Commons
Westminster
London SW1A 0AA, UNITED KINGDOM
(UK)

King, Tom (Athlete, Basketball Player)
4930 Sea Watch Dr
Fernandina Beach, FL 32034, USA

King, Vania (Athlete, Tennis Player)
c/o John Tobias *Lagardere Unlimited - (D.C.)*
5335 Wisconsin Ave NW
Suite 850
Washington, DC 20015, USA

King, Vick (Athlete, Football Player)
255 E 23rd St
Larose, LA 70373-2136, USA

King, Wayne (Athlete, Hockey Player)
129 Seventh St
Midland, ON L4R 3Y9, Canada

King, W David (Coach)
Calgary Flames
PO Box 1540
Station M
Calgary, AB T2P 3B9, CANADA

Kingdom, Roger (Athlete, Track Athlete)
146 S Fairmont St
#1
Pittsburgh, PA 15206, USA

Kingery, Ellsworth (Athlete, Football Player)
501 Auburn Ave
Monroe, LA 71201, USA

kingery, jeff
6208 S Jamaica Ct
Englewood, CO 80111-5717, USA

Kingery, Mike (Athlete, Baseball Player)
51923 298th St
Grove City, MN 56243-4305, USA

Kingery, Wayne (Athlete, Football Player)
1045 Walters St
Apt 411
Lake Charles, LA 70607, USA

King III, Martin Luther (Activist)
Realizing the Dream, Inc.
191 Peachtree St NW
Suite 3300
Atlanta, GA 30303, USA

King Jr, Woodie (Producer)
417 Convent Ave
New York, NY 10031, USA

King Kong (Actor)
77 Sastri Street
Kaveri Nagar Saidapet
Chennai, TN 600 015, INDIA

Kinglsey, Ben (Actor)
International Creative Mgmt
76 Oxford St
London W1N 0AX, UNITED KINGDOM
(UK)

Kingman, Brian (Athlete, Baseball Player)
2939 E Avalon Dr
Phoenix, AZ 85016-7503, USA

Kingman, Dave (Athlete, Baseball Player)
P.O. Box 209
Glenbrook, NV 89413-0209, USA

Kingrea, Richard O (Athlete, Football Player)
102 N Bay View Ave
Fairhope, AL 36532, USA

Kingrea, Rick (Athlete, Football Player)
102 N Bayview St
Fairhope, AL 36532-2505, USA

Kingsale, Gene (Athlete, Baseball Player)
105 Angelfish Ln
Jupiter, FL 33477-7227, USA

King Sisters
10275 S. 2505 E.
Sandy, UT 84092-4464

Kingsley, Ben (Actor)
c/o Christina Papadopoulos *Baker Winokur Ryder Public Relations BWR (BWR-NY)*
292 Madison Ave
12th Floor
New York, NY 10017, USA

Kingsley, Patricia
371 Alma Real Dr.
Pacific Palisades, CA 90272

Kingsmen, The
1720 N. Ross Ave.
Santa Ana, CA 92706

Kings Norton, (Harold R Cox) (Engineer, Scientist)
Westcote House
Chipping Campden
Glos, UNITED KINGDOM (UK)

Kings of Convenience (Music Group)
c/o Staff Member *Paradigm (Monterey)*
404 W Franklin St
Monterey, CA 93940, USA

Kings of Leon (Music Group, Musician)
c/o Andy Mendelson *Vector Management - New York*
113 E. 55th St
New York, NY 10022, USA

Kingsriter, Doug (Athlete, Football Player)
3118 Saint Johns Dr
Dallas, TX 75205-2938, USA

Kingston, Alex (Actor)
c/o Lorrie Bartlett *ICM Partners (ICM-LA)*
10250 Constellation Blvd Fl 7
Los Angeles, CA 90067, USA

Kingston, George (Athlete, Hockey Player)
235 W Camino Descanso
Palm Springs, CA 92264-8323, USA

Kingston, Jack (Congressman, Politician)
2372 Rayburn HOB
Washington, DC 20515, USA

Kingston, Kenny
11561 Dona Dorotea Dr.
Studio City, CA 91604

Kingston, Mark
47 Courtfield Rd. #9
London, ENGLAND SW7 4DB

Kingston, Maxine Hong (Writer)
University of California
English Dept
Berkeley, CA 94720, USA

Kingston, Sean (Musician)
c/o Staff Member *Czar Entertainment*
11 W 25th St
Suite 300
New York, NY 10010, USA

Kingston Trio, The
9410 S. 46th St.
Phoenix, AZ 85044

Kinkade, Mike (Athlete, Baseball Player, Olympic Athlete)
3005 SE Spyglass Dr
Vancouver, WA 98683-3704, USA

Kinkade, Mike (Athlete, Baseball Player)
Everett Aquasox 3802 Broadway
Attn: Coaching Staff
Everett, WA 98201-5032, USA

Kinkel, Klaus (Government Official)
Auswartigen Amt
Adenauerallee 101
Bonn 53113, GERMANY

Kinks, The
29 Ruston Mews
London, ENGLAND W11 1RB

Kinley, Heather (Musician)
Epic Records
1211 S Highland Ave
Los Angeles, CA 90019, USA

Kinley, Jennifer (Musician)
Epic Records
1211 S Highland Ave
Los Angeles, CA 90019, USA

Kinleys (Music Group)
P.O. Box 128501
Nashville, TN 37212, USA

Kinley's, The
PO Box 128501
Nashville, TN 37212

Kinmont, Jill
310 Sunland Ave.
Bishop, CA 93514

Kinmont, Kathleen (Actor)
9929 Sunset Blvd
#310
Los Angeles, CA 90069, USA

Kinnaman, Melanie (Actor)
1354 N Curson Ave
Los Angeles, CA 90046, USA

Kinnan, Timothy A (General)
US Military Representative
NATO Blvd Leopold III
Brussels 1110, BELGIUM

Kinnear, Dominic (Coach)
San Jose Earthquakes
3550 Stevens Creek Blvd
#200
San Jose, CA 95117, USA

Kinnear, Geordie (Athlete, Hockey Player)
1012 Harrogate Ln
Matthews, NC 28104-6874, USA

Kinnear, Geordie (Athlete, Hockey Player)
Charlotte Checkers
210 E Trade St
Attn: Coaching Staff
Charlotte, NC 28202-2404, USA

Kinnear, Greg (Actor, Comedian)
c/o Leslie Sloane *Baker Winokur Ryder Public Relations BWR (BWR-NY)*
292 Madison Ave
12th Floor
New York, NY 10017, USA

Kinnear III, James W (Business Person)
Ten Standard Forum
PO Box 120
Stamford, CT 06904, USA

Kinnebrew, Larry (Athlete, Football Player)
216 Kingston Ave NE
Rome, GA 30161, USA

Kinney, Dallas (Journalist, Photographer)
13010 Silver Sands Drive
Fort Myers, FL 33913-6934, USA

Kinney, Dennis (Athlete, Baseball Player)
P.O. Box 304
Schnecksville, PA 18078-0304, USA

Kinney, Erron (Athlete, Football Player)
2411 Rushland Landing Rd
Johns Island, SC 29455-8712, USA

Kinney, Jeff (Writer)
c/o Sylvie Rabineau *Rabineau Wachter and Sanford Literary Agency*
522 Wilshire Boulevard Suite L
Santa Monica, CA 90401, USA

Kinney, Jeff (Athlete, Football Player)
2002 Champions Cir
Castle Rock, CO 80104-2734, USA

Kinney, Josh (Athlete, Baseball Player)
588 Uoper Portage Rd
Port Allegany, PA 16743-3230, USA

Kinney, Kathy (Actor)
c/o Billy Miller *Billy Miller Management*
8322 Ridpath Dr
Los Angeles, CA 90046, USA

Kinney, Matt (Athlete, Baseball Player)
12 Owens Way
Hermon, ME 04401-0878, USA

Kinney, Steve (Athlete, Football Player)
1714 Merrill Loop
San Jose, CA 95124, USA

Kinney, Taylor (Actor)
c/o Larry Taube *Principal Entertainment (LA)*
1964 Westwood Blvd #400
Los Angeles, CA 90025, USA

Kinney, Terry (Actor)
Gersh Agency
232 N Canon Dr
Beverly Hills, CA 90210, USA

Kinnock, Neil G (Government Official)
European Communities Commission
200 Rue de Loi
Brussels 1049, BELGIUM

Kinnunen, Mike (Athlete, Baseball Player)
5818 McKinley Pl N
Seattle, WA 98103-5711, USA

Kinsella, Brian (Athlete, Hockey Player)
1408 Longfellow Dr
Temperance, MI 48182-9296, USA

Kinsella, John P (Swimmer)
PO Box 3067
Sumas, WA 98295, USA

Kinsella, Thomas (Writer)
Killalane
Laragh
County Wicklow, IRELAND

Kinsella, William Patrick (W P) (Writer)
1952-152A St
#216
Surrey, BC V4A 9T2, CANADA

Kinsella, W P
PO Box 3067
Sumas, WA 98295, USA

Kinser, Mark (Race Car Driver)
Mark Kinser Racing
11 Vista General Delivery
Oolitic, IN 47651, USA

Kinser, Steve (Race Car Driver)
Steve Kinser Racing
280 E. Smithville Rd
Bloomington, IN 47401, USA

Kinsey, Angela (Actor)
c/o Staff Member *Jenny Delaney Management*
3238 Fond Dr
Encino, CA 91436, USA

Kinsey, James L (Misc)
Rice University
Natural Sciences School
Houston, TX 77005, USA

Kinsey, Tarence (Athlete, Basketball Player)
11328 Grand Winthrop Ave
Riverview, FL 33578-4279, USA

Kinshofer-Guthlein, Christa (Skier)
Munchnerstr 44
Rosenheim 83026, GERMANY

Kinski, Nastassja (Actor, Model)
c/o Staff Member *Artists Independent Management (LA)*
825 Nowita Pl
Venice, CA 90291, USA

Kinsler, Ian (Athlete, Baseball Player)
3516 Greenbrier D
Dallas, TX 75225-5003, USA

Kinsman, Brent (Actor)
c/o Staff Member *AKA Talent Agency*
6310 San Vicente Blvd
Suite 200
Los Angeles, CA 90048, USA

Kinsman, Shane (Actor)
c/o Staff Member *AKA Talent Agency*
6310 San Vicente Blvd
Suite 200
Los Angeles, CA 90048, USA

Kintner, William R (Scientist)
Foreign Policy Research Institute
3508 Market St
Philadelphia, PA 19104, USA

Kinzer, Matt (Athlete, Football Player)
6717 Sweetbrier Dr
Fort Wayne, IN 46814-4564, USA

Kinzer, Matt (Athlete, Baseball Player)
6717 Sweetbrier Dr
Fort Wayne, IN 46814, USA

Kinzinger, Adam (Congressman, Politician)
1218 Longworth HOB
Washington, DC 20515, USA

KioKio (DJ)
c/o Staff Member *Diva Central Inc*
7510 W Sunset Blvd Ste 1445
Los Angees, CA 90046, USA

Kiper Jr, Mel (Sportscaster)
ESPN-TV
Sports Dept ESPN Plaza
935 Middle St
Bristol, CT 06010, USA

Kipketer, Wilson (Athlete, Track Athlete)
Atletik Forbund Idraettens Hus
Brondby Stadion 20
Brondby 2605, DENMARK

Kiplinger, Austin H (Publisher)
Montevideo
1680 River Road
Poolesville, MD 20837, USA

Kipp, Fred (Athlete, Baseball Player)
6613 W 126th Ter
Leawood, KS 66209-2599, USA

Kipper, Bob (Athlete, Baseball Player)
Portland Sea Dogs PO Box 636
Attn Coaching Staff
Portland, ME 04104-0636, USA

Kipper, Bob (Athlete, Baseball Player)
117 Tuscany Way
Greer, SC 29650-4070, USA

Kipper, Thornton (Athlete, Baseball Player)
4680 W Geronimo St
Chandler, AZ 85226-5306, USA

Kiprusoff, Miikka (Athlete, Hockey Player)
c/o Staff Member *Octagon Sports Representation*
7400 Metro Blvd
Suite 280
Minneapolis, MN 55439, USA

Kiraly, Charles F (Karch) (Athlete, Coach, Olympic Athlete, Volleyball Player)
c/o Staff Member *Simon & Schuster*
1230 Avenue of the Americas
New York, NY 10020, USA

Kirby, Bruce (Actor)
629 N Orlando Ave
#3
West Hollywood, CA 90048, USA

Kirby, Durwood (Writer)
PO Box 3454
Fort Myers, FL 33918, USA

Kirby, Jim (Athlete, Baseball Player)
520 Lohman Road
Mount Juliet, TN 37122, USA

Kirby, John (Athlete, Football Player)
586 A St
David City, NE 68632-1939, USA

Kirby, Luke (Actor)
c/o Kish Igbal *Gary Goddard Agency*
10 St Mary St
Suite 305
Toronto, ON M4Y 1P9, Canada

Kirby, Pete
PO Box 1734
Madison, TN 37116

Kirby, Ronald H (Architect)
PO Box 337
Melville
Johannesburg 2109, SOUTH AFRICA

Kirby, Stuart (Race Car Driver)
832 Broadway
Bowl i ng Green, KY 42101, USA

Kirby, Terry (Athlete, Football Player)
744 Michelle Dr
Newport News, VA 23601-4626, USA

Kirby, Wayne (Athlete, Baseball Player)
Baltimore Orioles 333 W Camden St
Attn: Coaching Staff
Baltimore, MD 21201-2496, USA

Kirby, Wayne (Athlete, Baseball Player)
320 Kenya Rd
Las Vegas, NV 89123-1169, USA

Kirby, Will (Reality TV Star)
c/o Staff Member *Metropolitan (MTA)*
4526 Wilshire Blvd
Los Angeles, CA 90010, USA

Kirchbach, Gunar (Athlete)
Georgi-Dobrowoiski-Ste 10
Furstenwalde 15517, GERMANY

Kirchenbauer, Bill
3800 Barham Blvd.
Los Angeles, CA 90068-1042

Kirchhoff, Ulrich (Misc)
Hoven 258
Rosendahl 48720, GERMANY

Kirchiro, Bill (Athlete, Football Player)
9889 Fleming Ave
Bethesda, MD 20814, USA

Kirchner, Jamie Lee (Actor)
c/o Maani Golesorkhi *Bluestone Entertainment*
9000 Sunset Blvd
Suite 700
Los Angeles, CA 90069, USA

Kirchner, Mark (Athlete)
Haruptstr 74A
Scheibe-Alsbach 98749, GERMANY

Kirchner, Mark (Athlete, Football Player)
1522 Palmer St
Houston, TX 77003-4622, USA

Kirchschlager, Angelika (Opera Singer)
Mastrioanni Assoc
161 W 61st St
#17E
New York, NY 10023, USA

Kircus, David (Athlete, Football Player)
1210 Clark Rd
Lapeer, MI 48446-9401, USA

Kirgo, George (Actor, Writer)
178 N Carmelina Ave
Los Angeles, CA 90049, USA

Kiriazis, Nick (Actor)
c/o Staff Member *Pakula/King & Associates*
9229 Sunset Blvd
Suite 315
Los Angeles, CA 90069, USA

Kirilenko, Andrei
1406 Perrys Hollow Rd
Salt Lake City, UT 84103-4249, USA

Kirilenko, Maria (Tennis Player)
c/o Staff Member *Women's Tennis Association (WTA (US))*
One Progress Plaza
Ste 1500
St Petersburg, FL 33701, USA

Kirk, Bill (Athlete, Baseball Player)
16 Timber Villa
Elizabethtown, PA 17022, USA

Kirk, Gavin (Athlete, Hockey Player)
Molson Canada 33 Carlingview Dr
Toronto, ON M9W SE4, Canada

Kirk, James (Actor)
c/o Tyman Stewart *Characters Talent Agency, The (Vancouver)*
8 Elm St
2nd Floor
Toronto, ON M5G 1G7, Canada

Kirk, Justin (Actor)
c/o Lainie Sorkin Becky *Management 360*
9111 Wilshire Blvd
Beverly Hills, CA 90210, USA

Kirk, Rahsaan Roland (Musician)
Atlantic Records
9229 Sunset Blvd
#900
Los Angeles, CA 90069, USA

Kirk, Tammy Jo (Race Car Driver)
732 Peek Road
Dalton, GA 30721

Kirk, Tara (Athlete, Olympic Athlete, Swimmer)
15 W Montgomery St
Baltimore, MD 21230-3844, USA

Kirk, Thomas B (Physicist)
Brookhaven National Laboratory
Physics Dept
2 Center St
Upton, NY 11973, USA

Kirk, Walt (Athlete, Basketball Player)
3730 Pennsylvania Ave #302
Dubuque, IA 52001-3066, USA

Kirkby, Emma (Musician)
Consort of Music
54A Leamington Road Villas
London W11 1HT, UNITED KINGDOM
(UK)

Kirkconnell, Clare
Box 63
Rutherford, CA 94573-0063

Kirkeby, Per (Artist)
Margarete Roeder Gallery
545 Broadway
New York, NY 10012, USA

Kirkland, Douglas (Photographer)
9060 Wonderland Park Ave
Los Angeles, CA 90046-1432, USA

Kirkland, Gelsey (Ballerina)
500 Mount Tailac Court
Roseville, CA 95747, USA

Kirkland, Levon (Athlete, Football Player)
308 Saint Helena Ct
Greenville, SC 29607-5988, USA

Kirkland, Lori (Producer)
c/o Staff Member *Luber Roklin Management*
8530 Wilshire Blvd
6th Floor
Beverly Hills, CA 90211, USA

Kirkland, Mike (Musician)
Bob Flick Productions
300 Vine
#14
Seattle, WA 98121, USA

Kirkland, Mike (Athlete, Football Player)
3350 N Sassafras Hill Rd
Fayetteville, AR 72703-9640, USA

Kirkland, Sally (Actor)

Kirkland, Wilber (Athlete, Basketball Player)
127 Kimberwick Cir
Glenmoore, PA 19343-1124, USA

Kirkland, Willie (Athlete, Baseball Player)
19374 Northrop St
Detroit, MI 48219-5500, USA

Kirkman, Michael (Athlete, Baseball Player)
171 SW Tina Gin
Lake City, FL 32024-4898, USA

Kirkman, Rick (Cartoonist)
c/o Staff Member *King Features Syndication*
300 W 57th St
15th Floor
New York, NY 10019-5238, USA

Kirkman, Robert (Writer)
c/o David Alpert *Circle of Confusion (LA)*
8607 Washington Blvd
Culver City, CA 90232, USA

Kirkpatrick, Chris (Actor, Musician)
c/o Staff Member *Good Guy Entertainment*
3733 Oakfield Dr
Sherman Oaks, CA 91423, USA

Kirkpatrick, David (Director, Producer)
c/o Staff Member *Plymouth Rock Studios*
36 Cordage Park Cir
Suite 305
Plymouth, MA 02360, USA

Kirkpatrick, Ed (Athlete, Baseball Player)
24791 Via Larga
Laguna Niguel, CA 92677, USA

Kirkpatrick, Maggie (Actor)
Shanahan Mgmt
PO Box 1509
Darlinghurst, NSW 1300, AUSTRALIA

Kirkpatrick, Ralph (Musician)
Old Quarry
Guilford, CT 06437, USA

Kirkreit, Daron (Athlete, Baseball Player, Olympic Athlete)
161 Steeplechase Cir
Sanford, FL 32771-9540, USA

Kirksey, Roy (Athlete, Football Player)
204 Williams St
Taylors, SC 29687-2056, USA

Kirkup, James (Writer)
British Monomarks
BM-Box 2780
London WC1V 6XX, UNITED KINGDOM
(UK)

Kirkwood, Craig (Actor)
c/o Staff Member *Levine Management*
9028 W Sunset Blvd #PH1
Los Angeles, CA 90069, USA

Kirkwood, Don (Athlete, Baseball Player)
455 W Elmwood Ave
Clawson, MI 48017-1231, USA

Kirllenko, Andrei (Basketball Player)
Utah Jazz
Delta Center
301 W South Temple
Salt Lake City, UT 84101, USA

Kirner, Gary (Athlete, Football Player)
3507 Senasac Ave
Long Beach, CA 90808-2847, USA

Kirouac, Lou (Athlete, Football Player)
3630 Chattahoochee Ct
Duluth, GA 30096, USA

Kirrane, John (Jack) (Athlete, Hockey Player, Olympic Athlete)
3 Country Rd
Chestnut Hill, MA 02467-2912, USA

Kirrene, Joe (Athlete, Baseball Player)
2557 Kilpatrick Ct
San Ramon, CA 94583-1726, USA

Kirschke, Travis (Athlete, Football Player)
10196 Crooked Stick Trl
Lone Tree, CO 80124, USA

Kirschner, Carl (Educator)
Rutgers State University College
President's Office
New Brunswick, NJ 08093, USA

kirschner, David (Actor)
c/o Staff Member *WmE2 (WMA-LA)*
1 William Morris Pl
Beverly Hills, CA 90212, USA

Kirschstein, Ruth L (Doctor)
National Institute of Health
9000 Rockville Pike
Bethesda, MD 20892, USA

Kirsebom, Vendela (Model)
c/o Staff Member *Ford Models (NY)*
238 E 4th St
New York, NY 10009, USA

Kirshbaum, Laurence J (Publisher)
Warner Books
Time-Life Building
Rockefeller Center
New York, NY 10020, USA

Kirshbaum, Ralph (Musician)
Columbia Artists Mgmt Inc
165 W 57th St
New York, NY 10019, USA

Kirshner, Mia (Actor)
c/o Daniel (Danny) Sussman *Brillstein Entertainment Partners*
9150 Wilshire Blvd #350
Beverly Hills, CA 90212, USA

Kirstein, Adam (Stylist)
c/o Staff Member *Judy Inc*
1 Yorkville Ave
Toronto ON M4W 1L1, Canada

Kirszenstein, Szewinska Irena (Athlete, Track Athlete)
Ul Bagno 5m 80
Warsaw 00-112, POLAND

Kirtman, David (Athlete, Football Player)
PO Box 50743
Bellevue, WA 98015-0743, USA

Kirton, Mark (Athlete, Hockey Player)
251 North Service Rd W
Oakville, ON L6M 3E7, Canada

Kisabaka, Lisa (Athlete, Track Athlete)
Franz-Hitze-Str 22
Leverkusen 51372, GERMANY

Kiselak, Mike (Athlete, Football Player)
316 Cimarron Trl
Irving, TX 75063, USA

Kiser, Garland (Athlete, Baseball Player)
267 Carr Dr
Blountville, TN 37617-4608, USA

Kiser, Terry (Actor)
Innovative Artists
1505 10th St
Santa Monica, CA 90401, USA

Kishida, Kyoko
7-5-34-801 Akasada Miatuku
Tokyo, JAPAN

Kishlansky, Mark A (Historian)
Harvard University
History Dept
Cambridge, MA 02138, USA

Kisio, Kelly (Athlete, Hockey Player)
c/o Staff Member *Calgary Hitmen*
P.O. Box 1420
Stn Main
Calgary, AB T2P 3B9, Canada

Kison, Bruce (Athlete, Baseball Player)
1403 Riverside Cir
Bradenton, FL 34209-1244, USA

Kisor, Henry (Writer)
2800 Harrison St
Evanston, IL 60201, USA

KISS (Music Group)
c/o Doc McGhee *McGhee Entertainment*
8730 Sunset Blvd
Suite 175
Los Angeles, CA 90069, USA

Kissane, James (Athlete, Basketball Player)
6 Mellen Ln
Wayland, MA 01778, USA

Kissane, Jim (Athlete, Basketball Player)
6 Mellen Ln
Wayland, MA 01778-2015, USA

Kissell, Ed (Athlete, Football Player)
40 Sebbins Pond Dr
Bedford, NH 03110, USA

Kissell, Larry (Congressman, Politician)
1632 Longworth HOB
Washington, DC 20515, USA

Kissel-Lafser, Audrey (Athlete, Baseball Player, Commentator)
9506 Port Dr
Affton, MO 63123-6530, USA

Kissin, Evgeni I (Musician)
Harold Holt
31 Sinclair Rd
London W14 0NS, UNITED KINGDOM (UK)

Kissinger, Henry A (Politician)
350 Park Ave Fl 26
New York, NY 10022-6045, USA

Kissling, Conny (Skier)
Hubel
Messen 3254, SWITZERLAND

Kistler, Darci (Ballerina)
New York City Ballet
Lincoln Center Plaza
New York, NY 10023, USA

Kitaen, Tawny (Actor)
Talent Group
5670 Wilshire Blvd #820
Los Angeles, CA 90036, USA

Kitaj, R B (Artist)
Mariborough Fine Art
6 Albermarle St
London W1, UNITED KINGDOM (UK)

Kitano, Takeshi (Actor, Director)
Office Kitano
5-4-14 Akasaka Minataku
Tokyo 107-0052, JAPAN

Kitaro (Composer, Musician)
GLP Huetteldorferstra 259
Vienna
 1140, AUSTRIA

Kitayenko, Dmitri G (Conductor)
Chalet Kalimor
Botterens 1652, SWITZERLAND

Kitbunchu, M Michael Cardinal (Religious Leader)
122 Soi Naaksuwan
Thanon Nonsi Yannawa
Bangkok 10120, THAILAND

Kitchen, Curtis (Athlete, Basketball Player)
343 19th Ave
Seattle, WA 98122-5735, USA

Kitchen, Michael (Actor)
International Creative Mgmt
76 Oxford St
London W1N 0AX, UNITED KINGDOM (UK)

Kitchen, Mike (Athlete, Coach, Hockey Player)
c/o Staff Member *Florida Panthers*
1 Panther Pkwy
Sunrise, FL 33323, USA

Kitchens, Bobbie (Stylist)
PO Box 3352
Pasadena, CA 91109, USA

Kitchens, Jimmy (Race Car Driver)
Moy Racing
486 Withrow Rd.
Forest City, NC 28043, USA

Kite, Greg (Athlete, Basketball Player)
3060 Seigneury Dr
Windermere, FL 34786-8353, USA

Kite, Jimmy (Race Car Driver)
Blueprint Racing
6800 W. 73rd St.
Bedford Park, IL 60638-6024, USA

Kite, Tom (Athlete, Golfer)
6000 Long Champ Ct
Austin, TX 78746-1106, USA

Kithune, Robert K U (Admiral)
1597 Haloloke St
Hilo, HI 96720, USA

Kitna, Jon (Athlete, Football Player)
18898 Bella Vista Ct
Northville, MI 48168, USA

Kitsch, Taylor (Actor)
c/o Katie Rhodes *Untitled Entertainment (LA)*
350 S. Beverly Dr #200
Beverly Hills, CA 90212, USA

Kitsis, Edward (Eddy) (Producer)
c/o Philip Raskind *WME (LA)*
9601 Wilshire Blvd Fl 3
Beverly Hills, CA 90210, USA

Kitson, Syd (Athlete, Football Player)
3 Frost Ln
New Providence, NJ 07974, USA

Kitt, A J (Skier)
2437 Franklin Ave
Louisville, CO 80027, USA

Kittel, Charles (Physicist)
University of California
Physics Dept
Berkeley, CA 94720, USA

Kittinger Jr, Joseph W (Joe) (Aviator)
608 Mariner Way
Altamonte Springs, FL 32701-5434, USA

Kittle, Ron (Athlete, Baseball Player)
PO Box 1998
Valparaiso, IN 46384-1998, USA

Kittles, Kerry (Athlete, Basketball Player)
P.O. Box 233
New Vernon, NJ 07417-0641, USA

Kittles, Tory (Actor)
c/o Matt Luber *Luber Roklin Management*
8530 Wilshire Blvd
6th Floor
Beverly Hills, CA 90211, USA

Kitty, Carruthers (Athlete, Figure Skater, Olympic Athlete)
2106 White Eagle Ln
Katy, TX 77450-8689, USA

Kitzhaber, John (Governor, Politician)
160 State Capitol
900 Court St
Salem, OR 97301-4047, USA

Kiyoko, Hayley (Actor)
c/o Staff Member *AKA Talent Agency*
6310 San Vicente Blvd
Suite 200
Los Angeles, CA 90048, USA

Kiyosaki, Kim (Business Person, Writer)
CASHFLOW Technologies Inc
4330 N Civic Center Plz #100
Scottsdale, AZ 95251, USA

Kiyosaki, Robert T (Business Person, Writer)
CASHFLOW Technologies Inc
4330 N Civic Center Plz
Suite 100
Scottsdale, AZ 85251, USA

Kizer, Carolyn A (Writer)
University of Arizona
English Dept
Tucson, AZ 85721-0001, USA

Kizim, Leonid D (Cosmonaut)
Mojaysky Military School
Russian Space Forces
Saint Petersburg, RUSSIA

Kjell, Adrien (Athlete, Hockey Player)
Norumsgarde ISI
Goteborg 41743, SWEDEN

Kjer, Bodil (Actor)
Vestre Pavilion Frydenlund
Frydenlund Alle 19
Vedbaek 2950, DENMARK

Kjus, Lasse (Athlete, Skier)
LK International AG
Gewerbestr. 11
Cham 6330, Switzerland

Klabunde, Charles S (Artist)
68 W 3rd St
New York, NY 10012, USA

Klages, Fred (Athlete, Baseball Player)
2813 Crossvine Cir
Spring, TX 77380-1396, USA

Klammer, Franz (Skier)
Mooswald 22
Fresach/Ktn 9712, AUSTRIA

Klaplisch, Cedric (Director)
Cineart
36 Rue de Ponthieu
Paris 75008, FRANCE

Klares, John (Athlete, Bowler)
4600 Vegas Dr
Aot 116
Las Vegas, NV 89108-2158, USA

Klas, Eri (Conductor)
Nurme 54
Tallinn 0016, ESTONIA

Klasnic, John (Athlete, Football Player)
924 Highland Ave
Mc Keesport, PA 15133, USA

Klass, Beverly (Athlete, Golfer)
P.O. Box 244364
Boynton Beach, FL 33424, USA

Klassen, Danny (Athlete, Baseball Player)
5680 SW Pomegranate Way
Palm City, FL 34990-8627, USA

Klassen, Ralph (Athlete, Hockey Player)
826 Avenue C N
Saskatoon, SK S7L 1J8, Canada

Klatt, Trent (Athlete, Hockey Player)
267 W 12th Ave
Grand Rapids, MN 55744-3487, USA

Klatt, Trent (Athlete, Hockey Player)
New York Islanders
1255 Hempstead Tpke
Attn Player Development Dept
Uniondale, NY 11553-1200, USA

Klattenhoff, Diego (Actor)
c/o Francis Okwu *Zero Gravity Management*
6363 Wilshire Blvd
Suite 300
Los Angeles, CA 90048, USA

Klaus, Bobby (Athlete, Baseball Player)
10661 Gabacho Dr
San Diego, CA 92124-1404, USA

Klaus, Deita (Actor)
c/o Staff Member *Digigraphics/Dream Girl World*
4650 Libbit Ave
Encino, CA 91436, USA

Klaus, Vaclav (Politician, President)
c/o Staff Member *Kancelar Prezidenta Republiky (Czech Republic)*
Hradecek
Prague 1 119 08, Czech Republic

Klausing, Chuck (Coach, Football Coach)
2115 Lazor St
Indiana, PA 15701, USA

Klausner, Richard D (Biologist)
National Cancer Institute
31 Center Dr
Bethesda, MD 20892, USA

Klaveno, Mariana
c/o Alan Iezman *Shelter Entertainment*
9454 Wilshire Blvd.
Suite 715
Beverly Hills, CA 90212, USA

Klawitter, Tom (Athlete, Baseball Player)
3220 Dover Ct
Janesville, WI 53546-1956, USA

Klaxons (Music Group)
c/o Staff Member *Paradigm (Monterey)*
404 W Franklin St
Monterey, CA 93940, USA

Klebba, Martin (Actor)
c/o Staff Member *The Stevens Group*
14011 Ventura Blvd #201
Sherman Oaks, CA 91423, USA

Klebe, Giselher (Composer)
Bruchstr 16
Detmold 32756, GERMANY

Kleber, Karen (Stylist)
150 E 18th St
#4-H
New York, NY 10003, USA

Klecko, Joseph E (Joe) (Athlete, Football Player)
105 Stella Ln
Aston, PA 19014, USA

Klee, Ken (Athlete, Hockey Player)
78 W Ranch Trl
Morrison, CO 80465-9503, USA

Klees, Christian (Misc)
Eutiner Sportschutzen
Schutzenweg 26
Eutin 23701, GERMANY

Kleihues, Josef P (Architect)
Schlickweg 4
Berlin 14129, GERMANY

Klein, Alex (Misc)
Columbia Artists Mgmt Inc
165 W 57th St
New York, NY 10019, USA

Klein, Calvin (Designer, Fashion Designer)
650 Meadow Ln
Southampton, NY 11968, USA

Klein, Chris (Actor)
c/o Cynthia Pett-Dante *Brillstein Entertainment Partners*
9150 Wilshire Blvd #350
Beverly Hills, CA 90212, USA

Klein, Danny (Musician)
Nick Ben-Meir
652 N Doheny Dr
Los Angeles, CA 90069, USA

Klein, David (Misc)
National Child Health Institute
9000 Rockville Pike
Bethesda, MD 20892, USA

Klein, Edward
c/o Staff Member *St Martins Press*
Publicity Dept
175 5th Ave
New York, NY 10010, USA

Klein, Emilee (Athlete, Golfer)
7660 Beverly Blvd #315
Los Angeles, CA 90036-2743, USA

Klein, George (Biologist)
Kottlavagen 10
Lidingo 181 61, SWEDEN

Klein, Herbert G (Government Official,
Publisher)
Copley Press
350 Camino de Reina
San Diego, CA 92108, USA

Klein, Jennifer (Producer)
c/o Carlos Goodman *Bloom Hergott
Diemer Rosenthal Laviolette & Feldman*
150 S Rodeo Dr Fl 3
Beverly Hills, CA 90212, USA

Klein, Jenny
201 S. Capitol Ave. #430
Indianapolis, IN 46225

Klein, Jess (Musician, Songwriter, Writer)
Drake Assoc
177 Woodland Ave
Westwood, NJ 07675, USA

Klein, Joe (Journalist, Writer)
Newsweek Magazine
Editorial Dept
251 W 57th St
New York, NY 10019, USA

Klein, Joel (Educator, Government
Official, Lawyer)
NY City Schools
Chancellor's Office
110 Livingston St
Brooklyn, NY 11201, USA

Klein, Jonathan (Business Person)
c/o Staff Member *CNN (NY)*
1 Time Warner Center
New York, NY 10019, USA

Klein, Lawrence R (Nobel Prize Laureate)
1400 Waverly Road
Apt B035
Gladwyne, PA 19035-1260, USA

Klein, Lester A (Doctor)
Scripps Clinic
Urology Dept
10666 N Torrey Pines Road
La Jolla, CA 92037, USA

Klein, Marci (Director, Producer, Writer)
c/o Jeffrey Jacobs *Creative Artists Agency
(CAA-LA)*
2000 Ave Of The Stars
Los Angeles, CA 90067, USA

Klein, Naomi (Producer, Writer)
Klein Lewis Productions
PO Box 67746 280 Spadina Ave
Toronto, ON M5T3BO, CANADA

Klein, Perry (Athlete, Football Player)
30760 Broad Beach Rd
Malibu, CA 90265, USA

Klein, Richard J (Athlete, Football Player)
609 E 2nd St
Pana, IL 62557, USA

Klein, Robert (Actor, Musician)
c/o Rory Rosegarten *Conversation
Company*
1044 Northern Blvd
Suite 304
Roslyn, NY 11576, USA

Klein, Robert O (Bob) (Athlete, Football
Player)
15933 Alcima Ave
Pacific Palisades, CA 90272, USA

Klein Borkow, Dana (Producer)
c/o Staff Member *WmE2 (WMA-LA)*
1 William Morris Pl
Beverly Hills, CA 90212, USA

Kleindienst, Richard
3103 Crestview Dr.
Prescott, AZ 86301-5001

Kleine, Joe (Athlete, Basketball Player,
Olympic Athlete)
53 Hickory Hills Cir
Little Rock, AR 72212-2766, USA

Kleine, Joseph (Joe) (Baseball Player)
Cornwall Community Police
PO Box 87Stn Main
Cornwall, ON K6H ST7, Canada

Kleinendorst, Kurt (Athlete, Hockey
Player)
7049 Village Commons Way
Midvale, UT 84047, USA

Kleinendorst, Scot (Athlete, Hockey
Player)
35387 Lake St
Cohasset, MN 55721-2160, USA

Kleinert, Harold E (Doctor)
225 Abraham Flexner Way
Louisville, KY 40202, USA

Kleinfeld, Andrew J (Judge)
US Court of Appeals
Courthouse Square
250 Cushman St
Fairbanks, AK 99701, USA

Kleinman, Arthur M (Psychic)
Harvard University
Anthropology Dept
Cambridge, MA 02138, USA

Kleinrock, Leonard (Scientist)
318 N Rockingham Ave
Los Angeles, CA 90049, USA

Kleinsasser, Jim (Athlete, Football Player)
6835 Cardinal Cove Dr
Mound, MN 55364-9535, USA

Kleinsmith, Bruce (Cartoonist)
PO Box 1083
San Juan Bautista, CA 95045-1083, USA

Kleiser, Randal (Director)
3050 Runyan Canyon Road
Los Angeles, CA 90046, USA

Kleisinger, Terry (Athlete, Hockey Player)
37 Elisia Dr
Moose Jaw, SK S6j 1G9, Canada

Klemm, Adrian (Athlete, Football Player)
2650 Cedar Springs Rd Apt 3333
Dallas, TX 75201-1446, USA

Klemm, Jay (Athlete, Baseball Player)
47 Choctaw Ridge Rd
Branchburg, NJ 08876, USA

Klemm, Jay (Athlete, Baseball Player)
1605 Airy Hill Ct #D
Crofton, MD 08876-5441, USA

Klemm, Jon (Athlete, Hockey Player)
400 61st St
Willowbrook, IL 60527-1806, USA

Klemm, Jon (Athlete, Hockey Player)
Spokane Chiefs
700 W Mallon Ave
Attn: Coaching Staff
Sookane, WA 99201-2134, USA

Klemmer, John (Musician)
Boardman
10548 Clearwood Court
Los Angeles, CA 90077, USA

Klemp, Cardinal Jozef
Kolski U1Miodowa 17
Warsaw, POLAND PL-00-583

Klemperer, William (Misc)
53 Shattuck Road
Watertown, MA 02472, USA

Klemt, Becky (Lawyer)
Pence & MacMilan
PO Box 1285
Laramie, WY 82073, USA

Klensch, Elsa
1050 Techwood Dr. NW
Atlanta, GA 30318

Kleppe, Thomas S (Secretary)
7100 Darby Road
Bethesda, MD 20817, USA

Klesko, Ryan (Athlete, Baseball Player)
c/o Staff Member *San Diego Padres*
100 Park Blvd
San Diego, CA 92101, USA

Klesla, Rostislav (Athlete, Hockey Player)
9425 E Desert Village Dr
Scottsdale, AZ 85255-6095, USA

Klesla, Rotislav (Athlete, Hockey Player)
200 W. Nationwide
Columbus, OH 43215, USA

Klett, Peter (Musician)
11410 NE 124th St
#627
Kirkland, WA 98034, USA

Klever, Rocky (Athlete, Football Player)
3829 W 42nd Ave
Anchorage, AK 99517, USA

Kley Minnis, Chaney (Actor)
c/o Staff Member *Foundation
Management*
100 N Crescent Dr
Suite 323
Beverly Hills, CA 90212, USA

Klick, Jim (Athlete, Football Player)
4001 E Lake Estates Dr
Davie, FL 33328, USA

Klicullen, Bob (Athlete, Football Player)
400 E Division St
Pilot Point, TX 76258, USA

Klieman, Rikki (Attorney, Commentator)
5683 Holly Oak Dr
Los Angeles, CA 90068, USA

Kliks, Rudolf R (Architect)
Russian Chamber of Commerce
Ul Kuibysheva 6
Moscow, RUSSIA

Klim, Michael (Swimmer)
177 Bridge Road
Richmond, VIC 3121, AUSTRALIA

Klima, Petr (Athlete, Hockey Player)
1000 Forest Ln
Bloomfield Hills, MI 48301-4112, USA

Klimchock, Lou (Athlete, Baseball Player)
8876 S Myrtle Ave
Tempe, AZ 85284-3178, USA

Klimke, Reiner (Misc)
Krumme Str 3
Munster 48143, GERMANY

Klimuk, Pyotr I (Cosmonaut)
Potchta Kosmonavtov
Moskovskoi Oblasti
Syvisdny Goroduk 141160, RUSSIA

Kline, Bobby (Athlete, Baseball Player)
6656 31st Way S
Saint Petersburg, FL 33172-5404, USA

Kline, Jeff (Producer, Writer)
c/o Staff Member *WME (LA)*
9601 Wilshire Blvd Fl 3
Beverly Hills, CA 90210, USA

Kline, John (Congressman, Politician)
2439 Rayburn HOB
Washington, DC 20515, USA

Kline, John
2439 Rayburn HOB
Washington, DC 20515, USA

Kline, Kevin D (Actor)
c/o Judy Hofflund *Hofflund/Polone*
9465 Wilshire Blvd #420
Beverly Hills, CA 90212, USA

Kline, Owen (Actor)
c/o Staff Member *WmE2 (WMA-LA)*
1 William Morris Pl
Beverly Hills, CA 90212, USA

Kline, Richard (Actor)
c/o Harry Gold *TalentWorks (LA)*
3500 W Olive Ave
Suite 1400
Burbank, CA 91505, USA

Kline, Steve (Athlete, Baseball Player)
Augusta Greenjackets 78 Milledge Rd
Attn: Coaching Staff
Augusta, GA 30904-3022, USA

Kline, Steve (Athlete, Baseball Player)
PO Box 1525
Chelan, WA 98816-1525, USA

Kline, Steve (Athlete, Baseball Player)
258 Trutt Rd
Winfield, PA 17889-9304, USA

Kline-Randall, Maxine (Athlete, Baseball
Player, Commentator)
3751 Milnes Rd
Hillsdale, MI 49242-9313, USA

Klingbeil, Chuck (Athlete, Football Player)
47921 US Highway 41
Houghton, MI 49931-9007, USA

Klingenbeck, Scott (Athlete, Baseball
Player)
6230 Kincora Ct
Cincinnati, OH 45233-4458, USA

Klingler, David (Athlete, Football Player)
3113 N Saddlebrook Ln
Katy, TX 77494-5616, USA

Klingman, Lynzee (Actor)
c/o Staff Member *United Talent Agency
(UTA)*
9336 Civic Center Dr
Beverly Hills, CA 90210, USA

Klink, Joe (Athlete, Baseball Player)
119 Green Heron Ct
Daytona Beach, FL 32119-1393, USA

The Celebrity Black Book 2013

Klinsmann, Jurgen (Soccer Player)
3419 Via Lido
#600
Newport Beach, CA 92663, USA

Klitbo, Cynthia (Actor)
c/o Staff Member *Televisa*
Blvd Adolfo Lopez Mateos 232
Colonia San Angel INN
DF CP 01060, MEXICO

Klitschko, Wladimir (Actor, Athlete, Boxer)
Klitschko Management Group
Borselstr.28
Haus I
Hamburg 22765, Germany

Kllesmet, Robert B (Misc)
Union of Police Assns
815 16th St NW
#307
Washington, DC 20006, USA

Klosowski, Dolores (Baseball Player)
14254 Farnsworth Dr
Sterling Heights, MI 48312-4352, USA

Kloss, Ilana (Athlete, Tennis Player)
World TeamTennis
1776 Broadway
Suite 600
New York, NY 10019, USA

Klosterman, Bruce (Athlete, Football Player)
14194 Deerfield Ct
Dubuque, IA 52003, USA

Klotz, H Louis (Red) (Athlete, Basketball Player, Coach)
114 S Osbourne Ave
Margate City, NJ 08402, USA

Klotz, Irving M (Misc)
1500 Sheridan Road
#7D
Wilmette, IL 60091, USA

Klotz, Jack (Athlete, Football Player)
729 E 25th St
Chester, PA 19013-5229, USA

Klotz, John S (Athlete, Football Player)
729 E 25th St
Chester, PA 19013, USA

Klous, Patricia (Actor)
2539 Benedict Canyon Dr
Beverly Hills, CA 90210, USA

Kloves, Steve (Director, Writer)
c/o David O'Connor *Creative Artists Agency (CAA-LA)*
2000 Ave Of The Stars
Los Angeles, CA 90067, USA

Klueh, Duane (Athlete, Basketball Player)
252 Francis Avenue Ct
Terre Haute, IN 47804-510l, USA

Kluer, Duane (Athlete, Basketball Player, Coach)
252 Francis Avenue Ct
Terre Haute, IN 47804, USA

Klug, Aaron (Nobel Prize Laureate)
70 Cavendish Ave
Hills Road
Cambridge CB1 40T, England

Kluger, Richard (Writer)
c/o Staff Member *Random House Publicity*
1745 Broadway
New York, NY 10019, USA

Klugh, Earl (Musician)
c/o Staff Member *Richard De La Font Agency*
3808 W South Park Blvd
Broken Arrow, OK 74011, USA

Klum, Heidi (Model, Producer)
c/o Sara Jane Lieb *Full Picture (NY)*
915 Broadway
20th Floor
New York, NY 10010, USA

Klurfeld, Herman
445 Grand Bay Dr Apt 602
Key Biscayne, FL 33149-1909, USA

Klutts, Mickey (Athlete, Baseball Player)
6136 Maple Ave
Lake Isabella, CA 93240-9706, USA

Kluttz, Lonnie (Athlete, Basketball Player)
183 Greenwing Ln
Saint Matthews, SC 29135-8168, USA

Kluwe, Chris (Athlete, Football Player)
6686 Montford Dr
Huntington Beach, CA 92648-6625, USA

Kluzak, Gord (Athlete, Hockey Player)
770 Boylston St
Apt 27C
Boston, MA 02199-7926, USA

Kluzak, Gord (Athlete, Hockey Player)
Boston Bruins
100 Legends Way Ste 250
Attn: Broadcast Dept
Boston, MA 02114-1389, USA

Klymaxx (Music Group)
c/o Staff Member *Diva Central Inc*
7510 W Sunset Blvd Ste 1445
Los Angees, CA 90046, USA

Klymkiw, Julius (Athlete, Hockey Player)
66 Buttercup Ave
Winnipeg, MB R2V 2S5, Canada

Klyn, Vincent
4200 Ocean View Dr
Malibu, CA 90265

Klyszewski, Waclaw (Architect)
Ul Gomoslaska 16m 15A
Warsaw 00-432, POLAND

Kmak, Joe (Athlete, Baseball Player)
1021 Hatteras Ct
Foster City, CA 94404-3546, USA

Kmetko, Steve
5670 Wilshire Blvd. #200
Los Angeles, CA 90036

K'naan (Music Group, Musician)
c/o Aaron Schubert *Paquin Entertainment (Winnipeg)*
395 Notre Dame Ave
Winnipeg MT R3B 1R2, CANADA

Knackert, Brent (Athlete, Baseball Player)
16802 Leafwood Cir
Huntington Beach, CA 92647-4851, USA

Knafelc, Gary (Athlete, Football Player)
2147 Burley Ave
Clemont, FL 34711, USA

Knafelc, Greg (Athlete, Football Player)
1243 Prairie Falcon Trl
Green Bay, WI 54313-7177, USA

Knape, Lindberg Ulrike (Swimmer)
Drostvagen 7
Karlskoga 691 33, SWEDEN

Knapp, Charles B (Educator)
Aspen Institute
1333 New Hampshire Ave NW
Washington, DC 20036, USA

Knapp, Chris (Athlete, Baseball Player)
788 Rich Dr
Oviedo, FL 32765-6447, USA

Knapp, Cleon T (Publisher)
Talewood Corp
10100 Santa Monica Blvd
#2000
Los Angeles, CA 90067, USA

Knapp, Jennifer (Musician)
c/o Staff Member *Creative Artists Agency (CAA-TN)*
3310 West End Ave
5th Floor
Nashville, TN 37203, USA

Knapp, John W (Educator, General)
Virginia Military Institute
Superintendent's Office
Lexington, VA 24450, USA

Knapp, Lindsay (Athlete, Football Player)
5018 Bruce Ave
Minneapolis, MN 55424, USA

Knapp, Rick (Athlete, Baseball Player)
23427 Garrett Ave
Port Charlotte, FL 33954-2534, USA

Knapp, Sebastian (Actor)
c/o Lorraine Berglund *Lorraine Berglund Management*
11537 Hesby St.
North Hollywood, CA 91601, USA

Knapp, Stefan (Artist)
Sandhills
Godalming
Surrey, UNITED KINGDOM (UK)

Knapple, Jeff (Athlete, Football Player)
10025 Toluca Lake Ave
Toluca Lake, CA 91602-2923, USA

Knarr, Charles (Scientist)
637 Cliff Park Rd
Monterey, TN 38574-7340, USA

Knaus, William (Doctor)
George Washington University Medical Center
Washington, DC 20052, USA

Knauss, Hans (Skier)
Fastenberg 60
Schladming 8970, AUSTRIA

Kneale, R Bryan C (Artist)
10A Muswell Road
London N10 2BG, UNITED KINGDOM (UK)

Knebel, John A (Politician)
1418 Labumum St
McLean, VA 22101-2523, USA

Knechtel, Dave (Athlete, Football Player)
14 Ambroise lane
Winnipeg, MB R2M 5P2, Canada

Kneifel, Chris (Race Car Driver)
6 Timberline Lane
Riverwoods, IL 60016, USA

Knepper, Bob (Athlete, Baseball Player)
20410 Silverhorn Ln
Monument, CO 80132-8092, USA

Knepper, Robert (Actor)
c/o Ben Levine *Kritzer Levine Wilkins Entertainment (KLWG)*
11872 La Grange Ave
1st Floor
Los Angeles, CA 90025, USA

Kness, Richard M (Opera Singer)
240 Central Park South
#16M
New York, NY 10019, USA

Kneuer, Cameo (Misc)
Starshape by Cameo
2554 Lincoln Blvd
#640
Venice, CA 90291, USA

Knibbs, Darrel (Athlete, Hockey Player)
2236 Surfwood Dr
Muskegon, MI 49441-1162

Knicely, Alan (Athlete, Baseball Player)
700 Three Leagues Rd
McGaheysville, VA 22840-2680, USA

Knickle, Rick (Athlete, Hockey Player)
192 Martinwood Way NE
Calgary, AB T3J 3H8, Canada

Knickman, Clarence Roy (Athlete, Cycler, Olympic Athlete)
436 Fallbrook Ave
Newbury Park, CA 91320-4929, USA

Knief, Gayle (Athlete, Football Player)
1825 Birchwood Cir
Waukee, IA 50263, USA

Kniffin, Chuck (Athlete, Baseball Player)
420 S Deer Mountain Road
Florissant, CO 80816, USA

Knight, Andrew S B (Editor, Publisher)
News International
PO Box 495
Virginia St
London W1 9XY, UNITED KINGDOM (UK)

Knight, Beverley (Musician)
c/o Staff Member *International Talent Booking (ITB - UK)*
27A Floral St Fl 3
Covent Garden
London WC2E 9, UNITED KINGDOM

Knight, Billy (Athlete, Basketball Player)
1051 Bluffhaven Way NE
Atlanta, GA 30319-4818, USA

Knight, Brandon (Athlete, Baseball Player)
New York Yankees
PO Box 1685
Ventura, CA 93002-1685, USA

Knight, Brevin (Athlete, Basketball Player)
3226 Bedford Ln
Germantown, TN 28207-2154, USA

Knight, Brian (Athlete, Baseball Player)
1123 Stuart St
Helena, MT 59601-2138, USA

Knight, Brian (Baseball Player)
1123 Stuart St
Helena, MT 59601-2138, USA

Knight, Carlos (Actor)
c/o Ford Englerth *Redrock Entertainment Development*
118 South Cordova Street
3rd Floor
Burbank, CA 91505, USA

Knight, Charles F (Business Person)
Emerson Electric Co
8000 W Florissant Ave
Box 41000
Saint Louis, MO 63136, USA

Knight, Chris (Musician, Songwriter, Writer)
Rick Alter Mgmt
1018 17th Ave S
#12
Nashville, TN 37212, USA

Knight, Christopher (Actor)
1600 Monterey Blvd
Hermosa Beach, CA 90254, USA

Knight, Curt (Athlete, Football Player)
7230 Rio Flora Pl
Downey, CA 90241-2030, USA

Knight, Curt (Athlete, Football Player)
7230 Rio Flora Pl
Downey, CA 90241, USA

Knight, David (Athlete, Football Player)
2600 Farm Rd
Alexandria, VA 22302, USA

Knight, Douglas M (Educator)
773 Greenwood Ave
Glencoe, IL 60022-1514, USA

Knight, Gladys (Musician)
3221 La Mirada Ave
Las Vegas, NV 89120-3011, USA

Knight, Jean (Musician)
Ken Keene Artists
PO Box 1875
Gretna, LA 70054, USA

Knight, Jonathan (Musician)
c/o Staff Member *Interscope Records (LA) - Main*
2220 Colorado Ave
Santa Monica, CA 90404, USA

Knight, Jordan (Musician)
c/o Tracy Nguyen *IPR + MKTG*
1515 Broadway
40th Floor
New York, NY 10036, USA

Knight, Marcus (Athlete, Football Player)
326 Threatt ln
Sylacauga, AL 35150-8635, USA

Knight, Marion (Suge) (Actor, Musician, Producer)
c/o Staff Member *Acme Talent & Literary (LA)*
1400 Atlantic Ave
Suite 274
Long Beach, CA 90814, USA

Knight, Michael E
1344 Lexington Ave
New York, NY 10120-1307, USA

Knight, Negele (Athlete, Basketball Player)
18624 N 4th Ave
Phoenix, AZ 85027-5665, USA

Knight, Norman (Scientist)
1706 Country Club Dr
Friendswood, TX 77546-6024, USA

Knight, Paul (Producer)
c/o Anthony Jones *United Agents*
12-26 Lexington St
London W1F OLE, UK

Knight, Phil (Business Person)
Nike Inc
1 SW Bowerman Dr
Beaverton, OR 97005, USA

Knight, Ray (Athlete, Baseball Player)
Washington Nationals 1500 S Capitol St SE
Attn: Broadcast Dept
Washington, DC 20003-3599, USA

Knight, Ray (Athlete, Baseball Player)
PO Box 129
Auburn, AL 36831-0129, USA

Knight, Robert M (Bobby) (Athlete, Basketball Player, Coach)
8003 County Road 6910
Lubbock, TX 79407-5760, USA

Knight, Roger (Athlete, Football Player)
929 Flywheel Cir
De Forest, WI 53532-0910, USA

Knight, Ron (Athlete, Basketball Player)
1426 Ellsmere Ave
Los Angeles, CA 90019-3800, USA

Knight, Sandra (Actor)
626 Kaimalino St
Kailua, HI 96734, USA

Knight, Scott (Stylist)
c/o Staff Member *Artists by Timothy Priano (CA)*
8447 Wilshire Blvd
#301
Beverly Hills, CA 90211, USA

Knight, Shawn (Athlete, Football Player)
13090 Welcome Way
Reno, NV 89511-8688, USA

Knight, Shirley (Actor)
c/o Martin Gage *Gage Group, The (LA)*
14724 Ventura Blvd
Suite 505
Sherman Oaks, CA 91403, USA

Knight, Sterling (Actor)
c/o Christopher Rockwell *Global Creative*
1051 Cole Ave # B
Los Angeles, CA 90038, USA

Knight, Steve (Writer)
c/o Staff Member *Creative Artists Agency (CAA-LA)*
2000 Ave Of The Stars
Los Angeles, CA 90067, USA

Knight, Steve (Athlete, Football Player)
4503 Bevington Ln
Apt A
Indianapolis, IN 46240, USA

Knight, Summer
PO Box 9786
Marina del Rey, CA 90295

Knight, Toby (Athlete, Basketball Player)
106 Claywood Dr
Brentwood, NY 11717-5724, USA

Knight, Tom (Athlete, Football Player)
P.O. Box 888
Phoenix, AZ 85001, USA

Knight, TR (Actor)
c/o Staff Member *Gersh (LA)*
9465 Wilshire Blvd
Suite 600
Beverly Hills, CA 90212, USA

Knight, Travis (Athlete, Basketball Player)
3159 Millcreek Rd
Pleasant Give, UT 84062-8790, USA

Knight, Trevor (Adult Film Star)
c/o Staff Member *Diva Central Inc*
7510 W Sunset Blvd Ste 1445
Los Angees, CA 90046, USA

Knight, Wayne (Actor)
c/o Staff Member *Agency for the Performing Arts (APA-LA)*
405 S Beverly Dr
Suite 500
Beverly Hills, CA 90212-4425, USA

Knight, Wendi (Adult Film Star)
c/o Staff Member *Atlas Multimedia Inc*
9005 Eton Ave Ste C
Canoga Park, CA 91304-1743, USA

Knightley, Keira (Actor)
c/o Will Ward *WME (LA)*
9601 Wilshire Blvd Fl 3
Beverly Hills, CA 90210, USA

Knightlinger, Lauren (Actor)
c/o Peter Principato *Principato/Young Management*
9465 Wilshire Blvd
Suite 430
Beverly Hills, CA 90212, USA

Knighton, Zachary (Actor)
c/o Nick Frenkel *3 Arts Entertainment Inc*
9460 Wilshire Blvd
7th Floor
Beverly Hills, CA 90210, USA

Knights, Dave (Musician)
195 Sandycombe Road
Kew TW9 2EW, UNITED KINGDOM (UK)

Knipple, Bobby (Bowler)
2626 Vuelta Grande Ave
Long Beach, CA 90815-2253, USA

Knipscheer, Fred (Athlete, Hockey Player)
13404 Macaw Pl
Carmel, IN 46033-8964, USA

Knisley, Sam (Athlete, Basketball Player)
14808 Hanover Pike
Upperco, MD 21155-9735, USA

Knobbs, Brian
14804 58th St.
North Clearwater, FL 34620

Knoblauch, Chuck (Athlete, Baseball Player)
11702 Forest Glen St
Houston, TX 77024-6414, USA

Knoedler, Justin (Athlete, Baseball Player)
315 Eagle Ridge D
Chatham, IL 62629-2037, USA

Knoff, Kurt (Athlete, Football Player)
11121 Bluestem Ln
Eden Prairie, MN 55347, USA

Knoll, Andrew H (Misc)
Harvard University
Botanical Museum
26 Oxford St
Cambridge, MA 02138, USA

Knoll, Jozsef (Misc)
Semmelweis Medical University
Pharmacology Dept
Budapest 1089, HUNGARY

Knolle, Byron Maj (Aviator)
1201 Patton Way
San Marino, CA 91108-1931, USA

Knoop, Bobby (Athlete, Baseball Player)
2543 E Mountain Sky Ave
Phoenix, AZ 85048-9516, USA

Knopf, Sascha (Actor, Model)
c/o Bradley Frank *Platform Public Relations*
2666 N Beachwood Dr
Los Angeles, CA 90068, USA

Knopfler, David (Musician)
Damage Mgmt
16 Lambton Place
London W11 2SH, UNITED KINGDOM (UK)

Knopfler, Mark (Musician)
Paul Crockford Mgmt
37 Ruston Mews
London W11 1RB, UNITED KINGDOM (UK)

Knopper, Steve (Writer)
3445 W Moncrieff Pl
Denver, CO 80211, USA

Knorr, Micah (Athlete, Football Player)
10391 Whitecrown Cir
Corona, CA 92883-9267, USA

Knorr, Randy (Athlete, Baseball Player)
12134 Bishopsford Dr
Tampa, FL 33626-1319, USA

Knorr, Randy (Athlete, Baseball Player)
Syracuse Chiefs 1 Tex Simone Dr
Attn: Managers Office
Syracuse, NY 13208-1274, USA

Knostman, Richard (Dick) (Athlete, Basketball Player)
346 Crestone Ave
Salida, CO 8120l-1521, USA

Knott, Eric (Athlete, Baseball Player)
1906 Dog Leg Dr
Sebring, FL 33872-3838, USA

Knott, Jon (Athlete, Baseball Player)
4250 Vicenza Dr Unit A
Venice, FL 34293-0714, USA

Knotts, Gary (Athlete, Baseball Player)
18 Covey Rd
Decatur, AL 35603-6021, USA

Knowles, Beyonce (Actor, Musician)
195 Hudson St #7ABPH
New York, NY 10013, USA

Knowles, Darold (Athlete, Baseball Player)
1515 Whisoer Wind Ln
Oldsmar, FL 34677-5133, USA

Knowles, Darold (Athlete, Baseball Player)
Dunedin Blue Jays 373 Douglas Ave
Attn: Coaching Staff
Dunedin, FL 34698-7913, USA

Knowles, Harry (Internet Star)
PO Box 180011
Austin, TX 78718-0011, USA

Knowles, Jeremy R (Misc)
67 Francis Ave
Cambridge, MA 02138, USA

Knowles, Miki & Gregg (Stylist)
1740 Anzle Ave
Winter Park, FL 32789, USA

Knowles, Nick (Television Host)
c/o Staff Member *Hilary Knight Management*
Grange Farm
Church Lane
Old Northampton NN6 9QZ, UK

Knowles, Rodney (Athlete, Basketball Player)
3592 Island Dr
N Topsail Beach, NC 28460-8202, USA

Knowles, Solange (Actor, Musician)
c/o Staff Member *Roc Nation*
1411 Broadway
38th Floor
New York, NY 10018, USA

Knowles, Tony (Politician)
1146 SSt
Anchorage, AK 99501-4230, USA

Knowlton, Steve R (Skier)
Palmer Yeager Assoc
6600 E Hampden Ave
#210
Denver, CO 80224, USA

Knox, Bill (Athlete, Football Player)
7836 Forest Ave
Gary, IN 46403, USA

Knox, Chuck (Athlete, Football Player)
48711 San Vicente St
La Quinta, CA 92253-2220, USA

Knox, John (Athlete, Baseball Player)
3701 W Oak Shores Dr
Crossroad, TX 76227-2606, USA

Knox, Kenny (Athlete, Golfer)
3813 Dills Rd
Monticello, FL 32344-4699, USA

Knox, Terence (Actor)
c/o Lin Bickelmann *Encore Artists Management*
3815 W Olive Ave
Suite 101
Burbank, CA 91505, USA

Knox-Johnson, Robin (Yachtsman)
26 Sefton St
Putney
London SW15, UNITED KINGDOM (UK)

Knoxville, Johnny (Actor)
c/o Sean Robinson *LW1*
7257 Beverly Blvd #200
Los Angeles, CA 90036, USA

Knuble, Mike (Athlete, Hockey Player, Olympic Athlete)
K 0 Sports
501 S Cherry St Ste 580
Attn Kurt Overhardt
Attn Kurt Overhardt, CO 80246-1327, USA

Knudsen, Arthur G (Skier)
5111 Wright Ave
#104
Racine, WI 53406, USA

Knudsen, Erik (Actor)
c/o Staff Member *Burstein Company, The*
15304 Sunset Blvd
suite 208
Pacific Palisades, CA 90272, USA

Knudsen, Kurt (Athlete, Baseball Player)
5155 Patti Jo Dr
Carmichael, CA 95608-0968, USA

Knudson, Mark (Athlete, Baseball Player)
881 W 100th Ave
Northglenn, CO 80260-6255, USA

Knudson, Thomas J (Journalist)
Sacramento Bee
Editorial Dept
21st & Q Sts
Sacramento, CA 95852, USA

Knudson Jr, Alfred G (Misc)
Institute for Cancer Research
7701 Burholme Ave
Philadelphia, PA 19111, USA

Knussen, S Oliver (Composer)
Harrison/Parrott
12 Penzance Place
London W11 4PA, UNITED KINGDOM (UK)

Knuth, Donald E (Scientist)
1063 Vernier Pl
Stanford, CA 94305-1006, USA

Koalska, Matt (Athlete, Hockey Player)
95 RoseAveW
Saint Paul, MN 55117-4927, USA

Koart, Matt (Athlete, Football Player)
122 Sonora Ave
Danville, CA 94526, USA

Koba, Jeff
8899 Beverly Blvd. #705
Los Angeles, CA 90048

Koback, Nick (Athlete, Baseball Player)
71 Hopmeadow St
Apt 9A-1
Weatogue, CT 06089-9635, USA

Kobasew, Chuck (Athlete, Hockey Player)
12 Chardonnay
Osoyoos, BC V0H 1V0, CANADA

Kobashigawa, Yeiki (War Hero)
85-120 Mill St
Waianae, HI 96793, USA

Kobayashi, Makoto (Nobel Prize Laureate)
High Energy Accelerator Research Organization
1-1 Oho Tsukuba
Ibaraki 305-0801, Japan

Kobe, Katsuhiko (Chef)
Ristorante Massa
1-23-11 Ebisu
Shibuya-ku, Tokyo, Japan

Kobel, Kevin (Athlete, Baseball Player)
7650 E Williams Dr
Unit 1072
Scottsdale, AZ 85255-4810, USA

Kober, Jeff (Actor)
4544 Ethel Ave
Studio City, CA 91604, USA

Koblik, Steven (Educator)
Huntington Library & Art Gallery
1151 Oxford Road
San Marino, CA 91108, USA

Koblitz, Karen (Artist)
2919 Tilden Ave
Los Angeles, CA 90064, USA

Kobza, Jerry (Race Car Driver)
Shenandoah Valley Motorsports
11 So. Oak Lane
Waynesboro, VA 22980, USA

Koch, Aaron (Athlete, Football Player)
9 Garnet Dr
Franklin, MA 02038-4625, USA

Koch, Alan (Athlete, Baseball Player)
1714 Pebble Creek Dr
Prattville, AL 36066-7206, USA

Koch, Bill
PO Box 1011
Kula, HI 96790-1011

Koch, Billy (Athlete, Baseball Player, Olympic Athlete)
3160 Tusket Ave
North Port, FL 34286-4904, USA

Koch, Carin (Athlete, Golfer)
5231 E Herrera Dr
Phoenix, AZ 85054, USA

Koch, Charles S (Business Person)
Charles G Koch Charitable Foundation
655 15th St NW #825
Washington, DC 20005, USA

Koch, David (Business Person)
Koch Family Management
459 Columbus Ave #216
New York, NY 10024, USA

Koch, Desmond (Des) (Athlete, Football Player, Track Athlete)
23296 Gilmore St
Canoga Park, CA 91307, USA

Koch, Ed (Artist)
1211 NW Ogden Ave
Bend, OR 97701, USA

Koch, Edward I (Politician)
2 5th Ave Apt 160
New York, NY 10011-8841, USA

Koch, Gary (Athlete, Golfer)
2934 W Lawn Ave
Tampa, FL 33611-1647, USA

Koch, Gregory M (Greg) (Athlete, Football Player)
34 Valley Oaks Cir
Spring, TX 77382-1722, USA

Koch, James V (Educator)
Old Dominion University
President's Office
Norfolk, VA 23529, USA

Koch, Marianne
Am Hohenberg 27
Tutzing, GERMANY D-82327

Koch, Pete (Athlete, Football Player)
866 W 16th St
Newport Beach, CA 92663, USA

Koch, Peter (Actor)
c/o Staff Member *Fly Trap, The*
900 E 1st St
Los Angeles, CA 90012, USA

Koch, Stacey (Stylist)
52 Box St
Concord, MA 01742, USA

Koch, William (Bill) (Athlete, Olympic Athlete, Skier)
PO Box 115
Ashland, OR 97520, USA

Koch, William I (Bill) (Business Person, Yachtsman)
Oxbow Corp
1601 Forum Place
West Palm Beach, FL 33401, USA

Kochan, Dieter (Athlete, Hockey Player)
2005 Spruce Ln
Houghton, MI 49931-2721, USA

Kocharian, Robert (President, Prime Minister)
President's Office
Marshal Bagramian Prosp 19
Yerevan 375010, ARMENIA

Kocherga, Anatoli I (Opera Singer)
Gogolevskaya 37/2/47
Kiev 254053, RUSSIA

Kochi, Jay K (Misc)
4372 Faculty Lane
Houston, TX 77004, USA

Koch Jr, Howard (Producer)
Producers Guild of America
8530 Wilshire Boulevard #450
Beverly Hills, CA 90211, USA

Kochman, Roger (Athlete, Football Player)
521 Beverly Blvd
Upper Derby, PA 19082, USA

Kocourek, Dave (Athlete, Football Player)
1170 Cara Ct
Marco Island, FL 34145, USA

Kocsis, Zoltan (Composer, Musician)
Narcisa Ulca 29
Budapest 1126, HUNGARY

Kocur, Joe (Athlete, Hockey Player)
c/o Staff Member *Detroit Red Wings*
Joe Luis Arena
600 Civic Center Dr
Detroit, MI 48226, USA

Kodes, Jan (Tennis Player)
Na Berance 18
Prague 6/Dejvioe 160 00, CZECH REPUBLIC

Kodjoe, Boris (Actor, Model)
c/o Evan Hainey *Untitled Entertainment (LA)*
350 S. Beverly Dr #200
Beverly Hills, CA 90212, USA

Koecher, Dick (Athlete, Baseball Player)
3310 Grand Cypress Dr
Apt 102
Naples, FL 34119-7979, USA

Koechner, David (Actor, Writer)
c/o John Elliott *Mosaic Media Group*
9200 W. Sunset Blvd
10th Floor
Los Angeles, CA 90069, USA

Koegel, Pete (Athlete, Baseball Player)
301 The Birches
Saugerties, NY 12477-5249, USA

Koegel, Warren (Athlete, Football Player)
Coastal Carolina University
1273 N Fraser St
Georgetown, SC 29440, USA

Koehler, Horst (Financier, President)
Bundespräsidialamt
Spreeweg 1
Berlin 10557, Germany

Koelle, George B (Misc)
3300 Darby Road
#3310
Haverford, PA 19041, USA

Koelle, Heinz-Hermann (Scientist)
400 Pelham Ave SW
Apt 201
Huntsville, AL 35801, USA

Koelling, Brian (Athlete, Baseball Player)
20230 Augusta Dr
Lawrenceburg, IN 47025, USA

Koen, Karleen (Writer)
Random House
1745 Broadway
#B1
New York, NY 10019, USA

Koenekamp, Fred (Cinematographer)
9756 Shoshine Ave
Northridge, CA 91325, USA

Koenig, Brad (Model)
c/o Staff Member *Ford Models (NY)*
238 E 4th St
New York, NY 10009, USA

Koenig, Walter (Actor)
PO Box 4395
North Hollywood, CA 91617, USA

Koepfer, Karl (Athlete, Football Player)
2017 Waters Edge Dr
Westlake, OH 44145, USA

Koepke, Andreas
441 av. du Prado B.P. 124
Marseilles Cedex 08, FRANCE F-13267

Koepp, David (Director, Writer)
c/o Richard Lovett *Creative Artists Agency (CAA-LA)*
2000 Ave Of The Stars
Los Angeles, CA 90067, USA

Koerner, Catherine (Scientist)
804 W Lake Cir
Friendswood, TX 77546-5573, USA

Koester, Helmut H K E (Misc)
12 Flintlock Road
Lexington, MA 02420, USA

Koetter, Dirk (Coach, Football Coach)
Arizona State University
Athletic Dept
Tempe, AZ 85287, USA

Koffler, Pamela (Producer)
c/o Staff Member *Killer Films (US)*
526 W 26th St
Rm 715
New York, NY 10001-5524, USA

Kofoed, Bart (Athlete, Basketball Player)
10161 Foxhall Dr
Charlotte, NC 28210-7846, USA

Kogan, Pavel L (Conductor, Musician)
Bryusov Per 8/10
Moscow 103009, RUSSIA

Kogan, Theo (Actor, Musician)
Wilhelmina Creative Mgmt
300 Park Ave S
#200
New York, NY 10010, USA

Kogen, Jay (Producer)
c/o Staff Member *WME (LA)*
9601 Wilshire Blvd Fl 3
Beverly Hills, CA 90210, USA

Koger, Gene (Athlete, Baseball Player)
285 Koger Road
Reidsville, NC 27320-9555, USA

Kogut, Charles (Athlete, Football Player)
210 W 22nd St Ste 110
Oak Brook, Il 60523-4035, USA

Kohan, David (Producer)
c/o Staff Member *KoMut Entertainment*
300 Television Plaza
Burbank, CA 91505, USA

Koharski, Don (Athlete, Hockey Player)
12807 Lake Jovita Blvd
Dade City, FL 33525-8264, USA

Kohde-Kilsch, Claudia (Tennis Player)
Elsa-Brandstrom-Str 22
Saarbrucken 66119, GERMANY

Kohl, Ernest (Musician)
c/o Staff Member *Diva Central Inc*
7510 W Sunset Blvd Ste 1445
Los Angees, CA 90046, USA

Kohl, Helmut (Politician)
CDU/CSU
Marbacher Strasse 11
Ludwigshafen D-67071, GERMANY

Kohl, Herbert (Politician)
929 N Astor St
Unit 2708
Milwaukee, WI 53202-3491, USA

Kohlberg, Jerome (Misc)
155 Crow Hill Rd
Mount Kisco, NY 10549-3803, USA

Kohlbrand, Joe (Athlete, Football Player)
3709 Indian River Dr
Cocoa, FL 32926, USA

Kohler, Herbert (Misc)
441 Green Tree Rd
Kohler, WI 53044-1406, USA

Kohler, Jurgen (Soccer Player)
Borussia Dortmund
Postfach 100509
Dortmund 44005, GERMANY

Kohlhaas, Jeannette (Athlete, Golfer)
6287 Battlegate Rd
Jacksonville, FL 32258, USA

Kohli, Armaan (Actor, Bollywood)
44 Union Park Chembur
Mumbai, MS 400071, INDIA

Kohli, Raj Kumar (Bollywood, Director, Filmmaker, Producer)
Behind Lido Cinema
Juhu Road
Bombay, MS 400 049, INDIA

Kohlmeier, Ryan (Athlete, Baseball Player)
301 Vine St
Cottonwood Falls, KS 66845-9812, USA

Kohlsaat, Peter (Cartoonist)
5536 Richmond Curv
Minneapolis, MN 55410-2534, USA

Kohn, A Eugene (Architect)
Kohn Pedersen Fox Assoc
111 W 57th St
New York, NY 10019, USA

Kohn, Alfie (Writer)
c/o Staff Member *Houghton Mifflin Company (Trade Division)*
222 Berkeley St
Adult Editorial, 8th Floor
Boston, MA 02116-3764, USA

Kohn, Joseph J (Mathematician)
32 Sturges Way
Princeton, NJ 08540, USA

Kohn, Walter (Nobel Prize Laureate)
236 La Vista Grande
Santa Barbara, CA 93103-2819, USA

Kohn-Stevenson, Perri (Stylist)
5651 Willis Ave
Van Nuys, CA 91411, USA

Kohoutek, Lubos (Astronomer)
Corthumstr 5
Hamburg 21029, GERMANY

Kohrs, Bob (Athlete, Football Player)
1304 5 105th Pl Apt 3125
Mesa, AZ 85209-3877, USA

Koib, Thomas Claudia A (Coach, Swimmer)
Stanford University
Athletic Dept
Stanford, CA 94305, USA

Koirala, manicha (Actor, Bollywood)
302 Beachwood Towers, Yari Road
Versova
Andheri (W), Mumbai 400061, India

Koiv, Kerli (Musician)
c/o Staff Member *Island Def Jam Group*
Worldwide Plaza
825 8th Ave Fl 28
New York, NY 10019, USA

Koivu, Mikko (Athlete, Hockey Player)
5500 Halifax Ln
Minneapolis, MN 55424-1439, USA

Koivu, Saku (Athlete, Hockey Player)
Thompson, Dorfman, Sweatman
PO Box 639 Stn Main
Attn: Donald Baizley
Winnipeg, MB R3C 2K6, Canada

Koizumi, Junichiro (Prime Minister)
Prime Minister's Office
1-6-1 Negatoicho
Chiyodaku, Tokyo 100, JAPAN

Kojac, George (Swimmer)
33 Arboles del Norte
Fort Pierce, FL 34951, USA

Kojis, Don (Athlete, Basketball Player)
8186 Commercial St
Le Mesa, CA 91942-2926, USA

Kok, Willem (Politician)
Binnenhof 20
The Hague, EA 2500, Netherlands

Kokkonen, Elissa Lee (Musician)
Columbia Artists Mgmt Inc
165 W 57th St
New York, NY 10019, USA

Kokonin, Vladimir (Opera Singer)
Bolshoi Theater
Teatralnaya Pl 1
Moscow 103009, RUSSIA

Kokosalaki, Sophia (Designer, Fashion Designer)
c/o Staff Member *Sophia Kokosalaki*
3/138 Long Acre
Convent Garden
London, England, United Kingdom

Kokotakis, Nick
9229 Sunset Blvd. #315
Los Angeles, CA 90069

Kok Oudegeest, Mary (Swimmer)
Escuela Nacional de Natacion
Izarra
Alava, SPAIN

Kola, Joey (Comedian)
c/o Staff Member *WmE2 (WMA-LA)*
1 William Morris Pl
Beverly Hills, CA 90212, USA

Kolakowski, Leszek (Misc)
77 Hamilton Road
Oxford OX2 7QA, UNITED KINGDOM (UK)

Kolanko, Mary Lou (Baseball Player)
3109 W Henry Ave
Tampa, FL 33614-5924, USA

Kolanos, Krys (Athlete, Hockey Player)
3407 Underhill Dr NW
Calgary, AB T2N 4E9, Canada

Kolat, Cary (Athlete, Olympic Athlete, Wrestler)
2414 Scenic View Ln
Chapel Hill, NC 27516-9143, USA

Kolb, Brandon (Athlete, Baseball Player)
2043 Pin Oak Pl
Danville, CA 94506-2119, USA

Kolb, Dan (Athlete, Baseball Player)
PO Box 700
Walnut, IL 61376-0700, USA

Kolb, Danny (Athlete, Baseball Player)
1601 51st Dr
Union Grove, WI 53182, USA

Kolb, Gary (Athlete, Baseball Player)
5143 Hopewell Dr
Charleston, WV 25313-1784, USA

Kolb, Jon (Athlete, Football Player)
32 Lee Ave
Grove City, PA 16127, USA

Kolb, Kevin (Athlete, Football Player)
4711 Steepleridge Trl
Granbury, TX 76048-5001, USA

Kolber, Suzy (Sportscaster)
ESPN-TV
Sports Dept
ESPN Plaza 935 Middle St
Bristol, CT 06010, USA

Kolbert, Kathryn (Lawyer)
Center for Reproductive Law & Policy
120 Wall St
New York, NY 10005, USA

Kolden, Scott
8743 Quakertown Ave
Northridge, CA 91324

Kole, Karen (Stylist)
c/o Staff Member *The Docherty Agency - OH*
2044 Euclid Ave
Cleveland, OH 44115, USA

Kole, Warren (Actor)
c/o Staff Member *D/F Management*
8609 E Washington Blvd #8607
Culver City, CA 90232, USA

Kolehmainen, Mikko (Athlete)
Poppelitie 18
Mikkeli 50130, FINLAND

Kolen, Mike (Athlete, Football Player)
1613 Manchester Ln
Birmingham, AL 35243, USA

Kolesar, Robert (Athlete, Football Player)
5003 Lincoln Ave
Cleveland, OH 44134, USA

Kolinsky, Sue (Producer)
c/o Staff Member *Innovative Artists (LA)*
1505 10th St
Santa Monica, CA 90401, USA

Kolius, John (Athlete, Olympic Athlete, Sailor)
103 S Y St
La Porte, TX 77571-6656, USA

Kollar, Bill (Athlete, Football Player)
4899 Montrose Blvd Apt 605
Houston, TX 77006-6165, USA

Kollas, Konstantinos V (Prime Minister)
124 Vassil Sophias St
Ampelokipi
Athens, GREECE

Kollek, Mayor Teddy
22 Jaffa Rd.
Jerusalem, ISRAEL

Koller, Dagmar
Naglergasse 2
Vienna, AUSTRIA A-1010

Koller, William C (Misc)
University of Kansas
Medical School
Neurology Dept
Kansas City, KS 66160, USA

Kollner, Eberhard (Cosmonaut)
An der Trainierbahn 7
Neuenhagen 115366, GERMANY

Kollo, Rene (Opera Singer)
Opera et Concert
Maximillianstr 22
Munich 80539, GERMANY

Kolm, Henry V (Engineer)
Weir Meadow Road
Wayland, MA 01778, USA

Kolnik, Juraj (Athlete, Hockey Player)
HC Geneve-Servette Chemin de la
Graviere 4
Les Acasias CH-1227, Switzerland

Kolodner, Richard D (Scientist)
Dana-Forber Cancer Institute
44 Binnery St
Boston, MA 02115, USA

Kolodziej, Ross (Athlete, Football Player)
1753 Camelot Dr
Madison, WI 53705-1005, USA

Kolodziewjski, Chris (Athlete, Football Player)
1123 Sandalwood Dr
Lawrenceville, GA 30043, USA

Kolpakova, Irina A (Ballerina)
American Ballet Theatre
890 Broadway
New York, NY 10003, USA

Kolstad, Dean (Athlete, Hockey Player)
15492 Brooklodge Rd
Hickory Corners, MI 49060-9740, USA

Kolstad, Hal (Athlete, Baseball Player)
15149 Bel Escou Dr
San Jose, CA 95124-5032, USA

Kolsti, Paul (Cartoonist)
Dallas News
Editorial Dept
Communications Center
Dallas, TX 75265, USA

Kolta, Lajos (Cinematographer, Director)
c/o Staff Member *Gersh (LA)*
9465 Wilshire Blvd
Suite 600
Beverly Hills, CA 90212, USA

Koltsov, Konstantin (Athlete, Hockey Player)
1135 Park Overlook Dr NE
Atlanta, GA 30324-5683, USA

Kolvenbach, Peter-Hans (Religious Leader)
Borgo Santo Spirito 5
CP 6139
Rome 00195, ITALY

Kolzig, Olaf (Athlete, Hockey Player)
Pro-Rep Group
201-280 Midpark Way SE
Attn Art Breeze
Calgary, AB T2X 1J6, Canada

Komadoski, Neil (Athlete, Hockey Player)
876 Judson Manor Dr
Saint Louis, MO 63141-6057, USA

Komal (Royalty)
Royal Palace
Narayanhiti
Durbag Marg
Kathmandu, NEPAL

Koman, Bill (Athlete, Football Player)
5 Upper Ladue Rd
Saint Louis, MO 63124, USA

Koman, Michael (Writer)
c/o Staff Member *ICM Partners (ICM-LA)*
10250 Constellation Blvd Fl 7
Los Angeles, CA 90067, USA

Komarkova, Vera (Misc)
University of Colorado
INSTAAR
Boulder, CO 80302, USA

Komarniski, Zenith (Athlete, Hockey Player)
1590 37B Ave NW
Edmonton, AB T6T 0E2, CANADA

Komenich, Kim (Photographer)
111 Cornelia Ave
Mill Valley, CA 94941-4812, USA

Komenich, Nadia (Gymnast)
The Bart Conner Gymnastics Academy
PO Box 720217
Norman, OK 73070, USA

Kometani, Pam (Athlete, Golfer)
4342 Killauea Ave
Honolulu, HI 96816-5113, USA

Komine, Shane (Athlete, Baseball Player)
641 8th Ave
Hinilulu, HI 96816-2109, USA

Kominsky, Cheryl (Bowler)
Ladies Professional Bowling Tour
7200 Harrison Ave
#7171
Rockford, IL 61112, USA

Komisarek, Mike (Athlete, Hockey Player)
Olympic Sports Management
9 Alden Rd
Wellesley, MA 02481-6702, USA

Komisarz, Rachel (Athlete, Olympic Athlete, Swimmer)
9402 Magnolia Ridge Dr
Unit 201
Louisville, KY 40291-6756, USA

Komleva, Gabriela T (Ballerina)
Fontanka River 116
#34
Saint Petersburg 198005, RUSSIA

Komlos, Peter (Musician)
Torokvesz Ulca 94
Budapest 1025, HUNGARY

Komminsk, Brad (Athlete, Baseball Player)
Norfolk Tides 150 Park Ave
Attn Coaching Staff
Norfolk, VA 23510-2712, USA

Komminsk, Brad (Athlete, Baseball Player)
688 Fallside Ln
Westerville, OH 43081-5003, USA

Kompara, John (Athlete, Football Player)
13030 Coldwater Loop
Clermont, FL 34711-8014, USA

Komunyaaka, Yusef (Writer)
900 W State St
Trenton, NJ 08618-5328, USA

Konare, Alpha Oumar (President)
President's Office
BP
Bamako, MALI

Koncak, Jon (Athlete, Basketball Player, Olympic Athlete)
P.O. Box 10040
Jackson, WY 83002-0040, USA

Koncar, Mark (Athlete, Football Player)
447 N Alpine Blvd
Alpine, UT 84004, USA

Konchalovsky, Andrei (Director, Producer, Writer)

Kondakova, Elena V (Astronaut)
Russian Space Agency
42 Shchapkinst
Moscow 129857, Russia

Kondia, Tom (Athlete, Basketball Player)
3517 Cleveland Ave
Brookfield, IL 60513, USA

Kondla, Tom
3517 Cleveland Ave
Brookfield, IL 60513-Il03, USA

Kondratiyeva, Maria V (Ballerina)
Bolshoi Theater
Teatralnaya Pt1
Moscow 103009, RUSSIA

Konerko, Paul (Athlete, Baseball Player)
8053 E Leaning Rock Rd
Scottsdale, AZ 85266-1645, USA

Koneski, Jr., Walter (Race Car Driver)
Koneski Racing
368 Broezel Ave
Lancaster, NY 14086, USA

Konian, Desiree (Stylist)
c/o Staff Member *Artists by Timothy Priano (CA)*
8447 Wilshire Blvd
#301
Beverly Hills, CA 90211, USA

Konieczny, Doug (Athlete, Baseball Player)
9503 Dundalk St
Spring, TX 77379-4314, USA

Konik, George (Athlete, Hockey Player)
1027 Savannah Rd
Saint Paul, MN 55123-1543, USA

Konitz, Lee (Musician)
Bennett Morgan
1282 RR 376
Wappingers Falls, NY 12590, USA

Konner, Lawrence (Larry) (Writer)
c/o Tom Strickler *WME (LA)*
9601 Wilshire Blvd Fl 3
Beverly Hills, CA 90210, USA

Kono, Tommy (Athlete, Olympic Athlete, Weightlifter)
98-2025 Hapaki St
Aiea, HI 96701-1642, USA

Kononenko, Oleg D (Cosmonaut)
Potchta Kosmoriavtov
Moskovskoi Oblasti
Syvisdny Goroduk 141160, RUSSIA

Konopasek, Ed (Athlete, Football Player)
2336 Meadowledge Ct
De Pere, WI 54115, USA

Konowalchuk, Steve (Athlete, Hockey Player)
2628 S Adams St
Denver, CO 80210-6232, USA

Konowalchuk, Steve (Athlete, Hockey Player)
Seattle Thunderbirds
625 W James St
Attn: Coaching Staff
Kent WA, WA 98032-4406, USA

Konrad, Dorothy
10650 Missouri Ave. #2
Los Angeles, CA 90025

Konrad, John H (Astronaut)
Hughes Space-Communications Group
PO Box 92919
Los Angeles, CA 90009, USA

Konrad, Rob (Athlete, Football Player)
11884 Windmill Lake Dr
Boynton Beach, FL 33473-7846, USA

Konroyd, Steve (Athlete, Hockey Player)
317 S Park Ave
Hinsdale, IL 60521-4638, USA

Konroyd, Steve (Athlete, Hockey Player)
Chicago Blackhawks
1901 W Madison St
Attn: Broadcast Dept
Chicago, IL 60612-2459, USA

Konsalik, Heinz
Aegidienberg
Bad Honnet, GERMANY D-53604

Konstantinidis, Aris (Architect)
4 Vasilissis Sofias Blvd
Athens 106 74, GREECE

Konstantinov, Vladimir (Athlete, Hockey Player)
6782 Enclave
West Bloomfield, MI 48322-1399, USA

Kontos, Chris (Athlete, Hockey Player)
40 Beck Blvd
Penetanguishene, ON L9M 1E1, Canada

Konuszewski, Dennis (Athlete, Baseball Player)
3054 Yorkshire Dr
Bay City, MI 48706-9244, USA

Konyukhov, Fedor F (Misc)
Tourism/Sports Union
Studeniy Proyezd 7
Moscow 129282, RUSSIA

Kooistra, Scott (Athlete, Football Player)
106 Overlook Dr
Loveland, OH 45140-6689, USA

Kooks, The (Music Group)
c/o Staff Member *Paradigm (Monterey)*
404 W Franklin St
Monterey, CA 93940, USA

Kool & The Gang (Music Group)
c/o Staff Member *J Bird Entertainment Agency*
4905 S Atlantic Ave
Daytona Beach, FL 32127, USA

Koolhaas, Rem (Architect)
Metropolitan Architecture
Heer Bokelweg 149
Rotterdam 3032, NETHERLANDS

Koolhoven, Martin (Director)
c/o Daniel Koefoed *Montecatini Management*
Teerketelsteeg 1
Amsterdam 1012 TB, The Netherlands

Koonce, George (Athlete, Football Player)
925 E Wells St Apt 217
Milwaukee, WI 53202-3953, USA

Koonce, Graham (Athlete, Baseball Player)
2474 Pimlico Pl
Alpine, CA 91901-3952, USA

Koons, Jeff (Artist)
600 Broadway
New York, NY 10012, USA

Koontz, Dean (Astronaut)
PO Box 9529
Newport Beach, CA 92658-9529, USA

Koontz, Ed (Athlete, Football Player)
2860 Blackshear Ave
Pensacola, FL 32503-4874, USA

Koop, C Everett (Scientist)
3 Ivy Pointe Way
Hanover, NH 03755-1407, USA

Kooper, Al (Musician)
Legacy Records
550 Madison Ave
#1700
New York, NY 10022, USA

Koopman, A Ton G M (Conductor)
Meerweg 23
BC Bussu 1405, NETHERLANDS

Koopmans-Kint, Cor (Swimmer)
Pacific Sands C'Van Park
Nambucca Heads, NSW 2448,
AUSTRALIA

Koos, Torin (Athlete, Olympic Athlete,
Skier)
1510 Madison St
Wenatchee, WA 98801-1731, USA

Kooser, Ted (Writer)
1820 Branched Oak Rd
Garland, NE 68360, USA

Koosman, Jerry (Athlete, Baseball Player)
2483 State Road 35
Osceola, WI 54020-4216, USA

Kopacz, George (Athlete, Baseball Player)
14150 Somerset Ct
Orland Park, IL 60467-1142, USA

Kopas, Jack (Horse Racer)
PO Box 249
Ilderton, ON NOM 2AO, Canada

Kopay, Dave (Athlete, Football Player)
100 W Highland Dr Apt 102
Seattle, WA 98109-2048, USA

Kopecky, Tomas (Athlete, Hockey Player)
4401 N Federal Hwy Ste 201
Boca Raton, FL 33431-5164, USA

Kopell, Bernie (Actor)
19413 Olivos Dr
Tarzana, CA 91356, USA

Kopeloff, Eric (Director)
c/o Staff Member *WmE2 (WMA-LA)*
1 William Morris Pl
Beverly Hills, CA 90212, USA

Kopelson, Arnold (Producer)
901 N Roxbury Dr
Beverly Hills, CA 90210, USA

Koper, Herbert (Athlete, Basketball
Player)
11707 Rushmore
Oklahoma City, OK 73099-8235, USA

Kopervas, Gary (Cartoonist)
c/o Staff Member *King Features
Syndication*
300 W 57th St
15th Floor
New York, NY 10019-5238, USA

Kopicki, Joe (Athlete, Basketball Player)
47608 Cheryl Ct
Shelby Township, MI 48315-4708, USA

Kopins, Karen (Actor)
Sutton Barth Vennari
122 Old Mountain Tom Rd
Bantam, CT 06750, USA

Kopit, Arthur (Writer)
240 W 98th St
#11B
New York, NY 10025, USA

Kopitar, Anze (Athlete, Hockey Player)
c/o Staff Member *Los Angeles Kings*
1111 S. Figueroa St
Suite 3100
Los Angeles, CA 90015, USA

Koplitz, Lynne (Actor)
c/o Staff Member *Paradigm (Monterey)*
404 W Franklin St
Monterey, CA 93940, USA

Koplove, Mike (Athlete, Baseball Player)
3235 Chaucer St
Philadelphia, PA 19145-5841, USA

Kopp, David (Actor)
c/o Deb Dillistone *Red Management*
Box 3
415 West Esplanade
North Vancouver, BC V7M 1A6, Canada

Kopp, Jeff (Athlete, Football Player)
9409 Hannahs Mill Dr
Apt 403
Owings Mills, MD 21117, USA

Kopp, Larry (Race Car Driver)
Lary Kopp Racing
5511 McCormick Ave.
Baltimore, MS 31206, USA

Kopp, Wendy (Misc)
Teach for America Foundation
315 W 36th St
#6
New York, NY 10018, USA

Koppel, Edward J "Ted" (Journalist)
10701 Ardnave Pl
Potomac, MD 20854-1261, USA

Koppel, Ted (Correspondent)
10701 Ardnave Pl
Potomic, VA 20854-1261, USA

Koppelman, Chaim (Artist)
498 Broome St
New York, NY 10013, USA

Koppelman, Charles (Business Person)

Koppen, Dan (Athlete, Football Player)
1801 Old Bridge Ln
Bellingham, MA 02019-3134, USA

Kopper, Hilmar (Financier)
Deutsche Bank AG
Taunusanlage 12
Frankfurt/Main 60325, GERMANY

Koppes, Peter (Musician)
Globeshine
101 Chamberlayne Road
London NW10 3ND, UNITED KINGDOM
(UK)

Koppikar, Isha (Actor)
c/o Staff Member *Canyon Entertainment*
P.O. Box 256
Palm Springs, CA 92263, USA

Kopple, Barbara J (Director)
Cabin Creek Films
155 Ave of Americas
New York, NY 10013, USA

Kopra, Timothy L (Astronaut)
2518 Lakeside Dr
Seabrook, TX 77586, USA

Kopra, Timothy L Lt Colonel (Astronaut)
4912 Cross Creek Ln
League City, TX 77573-6267, USA

Koprowski, Hilary (Biologist)
334 Fairhill Road
Wynnewood, PA 19096, USA

Koptchak, Sergei (Opera Singer)
Robert Lombardo
Harkness Plaza
61 W 62nd St #6F
New York, NY 10023, USA

Korab, Jerry (Athlete, Hockey Player)
Korab Inc
213 Maison Ct
Palm Beach Gardens, FL 33410-2215,
USA

Korach, Ken (Commentator)
1963 Troon Dr
Henderson, NV 89074-1040, USA

Koralek, Paul G (Architect)
7 Chalcot Road
#1
London NW1 8LH, UNITED KINGDOM
(UK)

Korbut, Olga (Athlete, Gymnast, Olympic
Athlete)
16356 N Thompson Peak Pkwy #2024
Scottsdale, AZ 85260-2108, USA

Korcheck, Steve (Athlete, Baseball Player)
6424 98th St E
Bradenton, FL 34202-9769, USA

Kord, Kazimierz (Conductor)
Filharmonia Narodowa
Ul Jasna 5
Warsaw 00-950, POLAND

Korda, Maria
304 N. Screenland Dr.
Burbank, CA 91505

Korda, Michael V (Writer)
Simon & Schuster/Pocket/Summit
1230 Ave of the Americas
New York, NY 10020, USA

Korda, Petr (Tennis Player)
4909 61st Ave Dr W
Bradenton, FL 34210, USA

Korec Jan, Chryzostom Cardinal
(Religious Leader)
Biskupstvo Nitra
PP 46A
Nitra 95050, SLOVAKIA

Korecky, Bobby
A13 Lincoln Ln
Dayton, NJ 08810-1345, USA

Koreeda, Hirokazu (Director)
Directors' Guild of Japan
3-2 5F
Maruyamacho
Shibuya, Tokyo 150-0044, JAPAN

Koren, Edward B (Cartoonist)
New Yorker Magazine
Editorial Dept
4 Times Square
New York, NY 10036, USA

Koren, Steve (Producer, Writer)
c/o Staff Member *Creative Artists Agency
(CAA-LA)*
2000 Ave Of The Stars
Los Angeles, CA 90067, USA

Korf, Mia (Actor)
Paradigm Agency
10100 Santa Monica Blvd
#2500
Los Angeles, CA 90067, USA

Korince, George (Athlete, Baseball Player)
3033 Townline Rd
Stevensville, ON LOS ISI, Canada

Korjus, Tapio (Athlete, Track Athlete)
General Delivery
Lapua, FINLAND

Korloff, Sara (Actor)
Boris Karloff Enterprises
PO Box 2424
Rancho Mirage, CA 92270, USA

Korman, Maxime Carlot (Prime Minister)
Prime Minister's Office
PO Box 110
Port Vila, VANUATU

Kormann, Peter (Gymnast)
US Olympic Committee
1 Olympia Plaza
Colorado Springs, CO 80909, USA

Korn (Music Group)
c/o Mark Philips *Prospect Park*
2049 Century Park East
Suite 2550
Century City, CA 90067, USA

Korn, Jim (Athlete, Hockey Player)
19670 Sweetwater Curv
Excelsior, MN 55331-8113, USA

Kornberg, Arthur (Nobel Prize Laureate)
365 Golden Oak Dr
Portola Valley, CA 94028, USA

Kornberg, Hannah (Actor)
c/o Holly Williams *Williams Unlimited*
5010 Buffalo Ave
Sherman Oaks, CA 91423

Kornberg, Roger D. (Nobel Prize
Laureate)
345 Walsh Rd
Atherton, CA 94027-6436, USA

Kornet, Frank (Athlete, Basketball Player)
9580 Stanton Rd
Lantana, TX 76226-7304, USA

Korney, Mike (Athlete, Hockey Player)
2565 Departure Bay Rd
Nanaimo, BC V9S 3W2, Canada

Kornheiser, Tony (Sportscaster, Writer)
Washington Post
Editorial Dept
1150 15th St NW
Washington, DC 20071, USA

Koroll, Cliff (Athlete, Hockey Player)
23W569 Glendale Ter
Roselle, IL 60172-3541, USA

Koromzay, Alix (Actor)
334 Vernon Ave
Venice, CA 90291, USA

Koronka, John (Athlete, Baseball Player)
1403 lOth St
Clermont, FL 34711-2808, USA

Korpan, Richard (Business Person)
Florida Progress Corp
100 Central Ave
Saint Petersburg, FL 33701, USA

Kors, Michael (Designer, Fashion
Designer)
Michael Kors Inc
11 W 42nd St
New York, NY 10036, USA

Kors, R J (Athlete, Football Player)
956 Gardenia Way
Corona Del Mar, CA 92625, USA

Korsantiya, Alexander (Musician)
Columbia Artists Mgmt Inc
165 W 57th St
New York, NY 10019, USA

Kortas, Ken (Athlete, Football Player)
466 Brooks Ln
Simpsonville, KY 40067, USA

Korte, Steve (Athlete, Football Player)
5640 Oslo Ln
Park City, UT 84098-7708, USA

Korth, David (Scientist)
3923 Valley Green Ct
Houston, TX 77059-5556, USA

Korvald, Lars (Prime Minister)
Vinkelgaten 6
Mjondalen 3050, NORWAY

Korver, Kelvin (Athlete, Football Player)
16934 Pella Rd
Adams, NE 68301, USA

Korver, Kyle (Athlete, Basketball Player)
c/o Jeff Schwartz *Excel Sports Management*
9665 Wilshire Blvd #500
Los Angeles, CA 90212, USA

Kosar Jr, Bernie (Athlete, Football Player)
PO Box 8
Nashport, OH 43830-0008, USA

Kosberg, Robert (Producer, Writer)
Robert Kosberg Productions
1438 N Gower St Box 10
Hollywood, CA 90028, USA

Kosc, Greg (Athlete, Baseball Player)
3465 Hunting Run Rd
Medina, OH 44256, USA

Kosc, Greg (Baseball Player)
3465 Hunting Run rd
Medina, OH 44256-8200, USA

Kosco, Andy (Athlete, Baseball Player)
10324 Springfield Rd
Youngstown, OH 44514-3158, USA

Koshalek, Richard (Director)
Museum of Contemporary Art
250 S Grand Ave
Los Angeles, CA 90012, USA

Koshansky, Joe (Athlete, Baseball Player)
13314 Point Pleasant Dr
Fairfax, VA 22033-3507, USA

Koshiba, Masatoshi (Nobel Prize Laureate)
University of Tokyo
7-3-1 Hongo
Bunkyo-ku, Tokyo 113-0033, JAPAN

Koshiro IV, Matsumoto (Actor, Dancer)
Kabukiza Theatre
12-15-4 Ginza
Chuoku, Tokyo 104, JAPAN

Koshland Jr, Daniel E (Misc)
3991 Happy Valley Road
Lafayette, CA 94549, USA

Kosier, Kyle (Athlete, Football Player)
PO Box 93946
Southlake, TX 76092-0119, USA

Kosins, Gary (Athlete, Football Player)
13895 Ruffner Ln
Sebastian, FL 32958-3418, USA

Koski, Bill (Athlete, Baseball Player)
1120 Valencia Ct
Modesto, CA 95350-4665, USA

Koski, Tony (Athlete, Basketball Player)
143 King James Dr
South Dennis, MA 02660, USA

Koskie, Corey (Athlete, Baseball Player)
161 Primrose Ln
Hamel, MN 55340-3603, USA

Koskoff, Sarah (Actor)
c/o Cliff Roberts *WME (LA)*
9601 Wilshire Blvd Fl 3
Beverly Hills, CA 90210, USA

Koslo, Paul (Actor)
c/o Noreen Savides *323 Talent Management*
P.O. Box 3234
Quartz Hill, CA 93586, USA

Koslofski, Kevin (Athlete, Baseball Player)
1910 Shore Oak Dr
Decatur, IL 62521-5563, USA

Koslow, Lauren (Actor)
c/o John Crosby *Crosby/Spilo Management*
1310 N Spaulding Ave
Los Angeles, CA 90046, USA

Kosmalski, Len (Athlete, Basketball Player)
404 Washington Ave
PH 8
Miami Beach, FL 33139-6606, USA

Kosner, Edward A (Editor)
Esquire Magazine
Editorial Dept
1790 Broadway #1300
New York, NY 10019, USA

Koss, Johann Olav (Speed Skater)
Dagaliveien 21
Oslo 0387, NORWAY

Koss, John C (Inventor)
Koss Corp
4129 N Port Washington Ave
Milwaukee, WI 53212, USA

Koss, Stein (Athlete, Football Player)
5219 N Casa Blanca Dr
Apt 31
Paradise Valley, AZ 85253, USA

Kosser, Ted (Writer)
1820 Branched Oak Rd
Garland, NE 68360-9303, USA

Kostadinova, Stefka (Athlete, Track Athlete)
Rue Anghel Kantchev 4
Sofia 1000, BULGARIA

Kostecki, John (Athlete, Olympic Athlete, Sailor)
2221 Raintree Ct
Rocklin, CA 95765-4653, USA

Kostelic, Janica (Skier)
Ski Association
Trg Sportova 11
Zagreb 1000, CROATIA

Koster, Steven J (Cinematographer)
26881 Goya Circle
Mission Viejo, CA 92691, USA

Kostiuk, Mike (Athlete, Football Player)
24663 Beierman Ave
Warren, MI 48091, USA

Kostner, Isolde (Skier)
General Delivery
Hortisei BZ, ITALY

Kostopoulos, Tom (Athlete, Hockey Player)
8336 Wheatstone Ln
Raleigh, NC 27613-1479, USA

Kostro, Frank (Athlete, Baseball Player)
3161 S Jasmine Way
Denver, CO 80222-7627, USA

Kosugi, Kane (Actor)
c/o Lou Pitt *Pitt Group, The*
9465 Wilshire Blvd
Suite 420
Beverly Hills, CA 90212, USA

Kosuth, Joseph (Artist)
591 Broadway
New York, NY 10012, USA

Koszelak, Stanley N (Astronaut)
1125 Mendocino Way
Redlands, CA 92374-4975, USA

Kotalik, Ales (Athlete, Hockey Player)
Octagon Sports Management
66 Slater St 23rd Fl
Attn Larry Kelly
Ottawa, ON K1P 5H1, Canada

Kotarski, Mike (Athlete, Baseball Player)
31 Grove Street
Lexington, MA 02420-1623, USA

Kotb, Hoda (Anchor, Television Host)
c/o Staff Member *Today Show, The*
30 Rockefeller Plz
New York, NY 10112, USA

Kotcheff, W Theodore (Ted) (Director)
Ted Kotcheff Productions
13451 Firth Dr
Beverly Hills, CA 90210, USA

Kotchman, Casey (Athlete, Baseball Player)
8442 125th Ct
Seminole, Fl 33776-3200, USA

Koteas, Elias (Actor)
c/o Staff Member *WME (LA)*
9601 Wilshire Blvd Fl 3
Beverly Hills, CA 90210, USA

Koterba, Jeff (Cartoonist)
Omaha World Herald
Editorial Dept
14th & Dodge St Wichita
Omaha, NE 68102, USA

Kotero, Apollonia (Actor, Model)
c/o Staff Member *Mary Grady Agency (MGA)*
The Landmark Bldg
4400 Coldwater Canyon Ave #135
Studio City, CA 91605, USA

Kotil, Ariene (Baseball Player)
13045 S 70th Ct
Palos Heights, IL 60463-2107, USA

Kotil, Arlene (Athlete, Baseball Player, Commentator)
13045 S 70th Ct
Palos Heights, IL 60463-2107, USA

Kotite, Richard E (Rich) (Athlete, Coach, Football Coach, Football Player)
241 Fanning St
Staten Island, NY 10314, USA

Kotlarek, Gene (Skier)
4910 Walking Horse Point
Colorado Springs, CO 80917, USA

Kotlarek, George (Skier)
330 N Arlington Ave
#512
Duluth, MN 55811, USA

Kotlayakov, Vladimir M (Geophysicist, Physicist)
Geography Institute
Staromonetny per 29
Moscow 109017, RUSSIA

Kotsay, Mark (Athlete, Baseball Player)
6659 Calle Ponte Bella
Rancho Santa Fe, CA 92091-0208, USA

Kotsonis, Ieronymous (Religious Leader)
Archdiocese of Athens
Hatzichristou 8
Athens 402, Greece 53212, USA

Kotsopoulos, Chris (Athlete, Hockey Player)
1713 Midnight Ln
Stroudsburg, PA 18360-7771, USA

Kottaras, George (Athlete, Baseball Player)
11677 E Del Timbre Dr
Scottsdale, AZ 85259-5908, USA

Kottke, Leo (Musician, Songwriter)
c/o Staff Member *Paradigm (Monterey)*
404 W Franklin St
Monterey, CA 93940, USA

Kotto, Yaphet (Actor, Director, Producer, Writer)
c/o Staff Member *Diverse Talent Group*
9911 W Pico Blvd Ste 340W
Los Angeles, CA 90035, USA

Kotto, Yaphet F (Actor)
c/o Nicole Green *Rival Agency, The*
9157 Sunset Blvd #212
W Hollywood, CA 90069, USA

Kotulak, Ronald (Editor)
Chicago Tribune
Editorial Dept
435 N Michigan Ave
Chicago, IL 60611, USA

Kotzky, Alex S (Cartoonist)
20317 56th Sve
Oakland Gardens, NY 11364, USA

Kouchner, Bernard (Doctor)
L'Action d'Humanitaire
8 Ave de Segur
Paris 75350, USA

Koudelka, Josef (Photographer)
Magnum Photos
Moreland Bldgs
23 Old St
London EC1V 9HL, UNITED KINGDOM (UK)

Koufax, Sandy (Athlete, Baseball Player)
c/o Harlan Werner *Sports Placement Service*
330 W 11th St
Suite 105
Los Angeles, CA 90015, USA

Kounen, Jan (Actor, Director, Producer, Writer)
c/o Robert Newman *WME (LA)*
9601 Wilshire Blvd Fl 3
Beverly Hills, CA 90210, USA

Kournikova, Anna (Athlete, Tennis Player)
c/o Staff Member *Octagon (VA)*
7100 Forest Ave #201
Richmond, VA 23226, USA

Kournikova, Anna (Misc)
2345 Lake Ave
Sunset Isle 3
Miami Beach, FL 33140, USA

Koutouvides, Niko (Athlete, Football Player)
129 9th Ln
Kirkland, WA 98033-3992, USA

Kouzmanoff, Kevin (Athlete, Baseball Player)
28606 Evergreen Manor Dr
Evergreen, CO 80439-8387, USA

Kovac, Ed (Athlete, Football Player)
2654 Gracewood Ave
Cincinnati, OH 45239-7240, USA

Kovacevich, Richard M (Financier)
Wells Fargo Co
420 Montgomery St
San Francisco, CA 94163, USA

Kovacevich, Stephen (Conductor, Musician)
Van Walsum Mgmt
4 Addison Bridge Place
London W14 8XP, UNITED KINGDOM (UK)

Kovach, Bill (Editor)
Harvard University
Nieman Fellows Program
Cambridge, MA 02138, USA

Kovacic, Ernst (Musician)
Ingpen & Williams
14 Kensington Court
London W8 5DN, UNITED KINGDOM (UK)

Kovacic-Ciro, Zdravko (Misc)
JP Kamova 57
Rijeka 51000, SERBIA & MONTENEGRO

Kovack, Nancy (Actor)
270 Oakmont Dr
Los Angeles, CA 90049, USA

Kovacs, Andras (Director)
Magyar Jakobinusok Ter 2/3
Budapest 1122, HUNGARY

Kovacs, Denes (Musician)
Iranyi Utca 12
Budapest V, HUNGARY

Kovacs, Mijou (Actor)
c/o Staff Member *JFPM*
11 rue Chanez
Paris Cedex 16
Paris 75781, FRANCE

Kovai, Anuradha (Actor)
2 23rd Street Amirtha Apartments
Nanganallur
Chennai, TN 600 061, INDIA

Kovai, Sarala (Actor, Bollywood)
80 Nevkatesh Nagar I Street
Dhasaratha Puram
Chennai, TN 600093, INDIA

Kovalchick-Roark, Dorothy (Athlete, Commentator, Golfer)
112 Maridale Dr
West Monroe, LA 71291 2350, USA

Kovalchuk, Ilja (Athlete, Hockey Player)
2900 Pharr Court South NW
Apt 2419
Atlanta, GA 30305, USA

Kovalchuk, Ilja
5509 Long Island Dr NW
Atlanta, GA 30327-4839, USA

Kovalchuk, Ilya (Athlete, Hockey Player)
5509 Long Island Dr NW
Atlanta, GA 30327-4839, USA

Kovalenko, Alexei (Athlete, Hockey Player)
1 Trimont Ln
Unit 2000A
Pittsburg, PA 15211, USA

Kovalenok, Vladimir S (Cosmonaut, General)
3 Ap 22
Hovanskaya St
Moscow 129515, RUSSIA

Kovalev, Alexei (Athlete, Hockey Player)
Eclipse Sports Management
331 Madison Ave Fl 3
New York, NY 10017-5116, USA

Kovalevsky, Jean (Astronomer)
Villa La Padovane
8 Rue Saint Michael
Saint-Antoine, Grasse 06130, FRANCE

Kovatch, John P (Athlete, Football Player)
619 Willowglen Rd
Santa Barbara, CA 93105, USA

Kove, Martin (Actor)
c/o Michael Kaliski *Omniquest Entertainment (LA)*
1416 N La Brea Ave
Hollywood, CA 90028, USA

Kovic, Ron (Writer)
507 N Lucia Ave
Redondo Beach, CA 90277-3009, USA

Kowal, Charles T (Astronomer)
Space Telescope Science Institute
Homewood Campus
Baltimore, MD 21218, USA

Kowalczyk, Ed (Musician)
Freedman & Smith
350 W End Ave
#1
New York, NY 10024, USA

Kowalczyk, Jozef (Religious Leader)
Nuncjatura Apostolska
Al Ch Szucha 12
#163
Warsaw 00-582, POLAND

Kowalczyk, Paula (Stylist)
37 W 85th St
#1-C
New York, NY 10024, USA

Kowalczyk, Walt (Athlete, Football Player)
144 Maryknoll Rd W
Rochester Hills, MI 48309, USA

Kowalkowski, Robert (Athlete, Football Player)
2410 Correll Dr
Lake Orion, MI 48360, USA

Kowalkowski, Scott (Athlete, Football Player)
3995 Kelsey Rd
Lake Orion, MI 48360, USA

Kowalski, Ted (Musician)
GEMS
PO Box 1031
Montrose, CA 91021, USA

Kowitz, Brian (Athlete, Baseball Player)
1657 Bullock Cir
Owings Mill, MD 21117-1609, USA

Koy, Ernie (Athlete, Football Player)
P.O. Box 6
Kenney, TX 77452-0006, USA

Koy, Ted (Athlete, Football Player)
1225 County Road 155
Georgetown, TX 78626-1937, USA

Koyama, Debbie (Athlete, Golfer)
118 Tranquila Dr
Camarillo, CA 93012, USA

Koz, Dave (Musician)
c/o Staff Member *Agency for the Performing Arts (APA-LA)*
405 S Beverly Dr
Suite 500
Beverly Hills, CA 90212-4425, USA

Kozak, Don (Athlete, Hockey Player)
1510 E Beacon Dr
Gilbert, AZ 85234-2674, USA

Kozak, Harley Jane (Actor)
21336 Colina Dr
Topanga, CA 90290, USA

Kozak, Julie (Journalist)
Extra c/o Warner Bros
4000 Warner Blvd
Burbank, CA 91522, USA

Kozak, Les (Athlete, Hockey Player)
1072 Kimbro Sr
Baton Rouge, LA 70808-6042, USA

Kozak, Scott (Athlete, Football Player)
18617 S Grasle Rd
Oregon City, OR 97045, USA

Kozeev, Konstantin (Cosmonaut)
Potchta Kosmonavtov
Moskovskoi Oblasti
Syvisdny Goroduk 141160, RUSSIA

Kozelko, Tom (Athlete, Basketball Player)
6200 Peninsula Dr
Traverse City, MI 49686-1916, USA

Kozena, Magdalena (Opera Singer)
Narodni Divadlo
Dvorakova 11
Brno 60000, CZECH REPUBLIC

Kozer, Sarah (Actor)
c/o Ric Tanner
8383 Wilshire Blvd #510
Beverly Hills, CA 90211, USA

Kozerski, Bruce (Athlete, Football Player)
3088 Waterbury Ct
Edgewood, KY 41017-8124, USA

Kozinski, Alex (Judge)
US Court of Appeals
125 S Grand Ave
Pasadena, CA 91105, USA

Kozlicki, Ron (Athlete, Basketball Player)
5002 Hidden Branches Dr
Atlanta, GA 30338-3910, USA

Kozlov, Slava
4240 Irma Ct
Atlanta, GA 30327-3713, USA

Kozlov, Viktor (Athlete, Hockey Player)
106 W 74th St
Attn Paul Theofanous
New York, NY 10023-2334, USA

Kozlov, Vyacheslav (Athlete, Hockey Player)
4240 Irma Ct
Atlanta, GA 30327, USA

Kozlova, Anna (Swimmer)
c/o Staff Member *Premier Management Group (PMG Sports)*
115 Crescent Commons Dr Ste 250
Cary, NC 27518, USA

Kozlova, Valentina (Ballerina)
New York City Ballet
Lincoln Center Plaza
New York, NY 10023, USA

Kozlowski, Ben (Athlete, Baseball Player)
9083 Briarwood Dr
Seminole, FL 33772-2810, USA

Kozlowski, Brian (Athlete, Football Player)
61 E Shore Dr
Niantic, CT 06357-3833, USA

Kozlowski, Christine (Beauty Pageant Winner)
PO Box 742
Vicksburg, MS 39181, USA

Kozlowski, Glen (Athlete, Football Player)
455 Belmont Pl Unit 262
Provo, UT 84606-7612, USA

Kozlowski, Linda (Actor)
7022 Grasswood Ave
Malibu, CA 90265, USA

Kozlowski, Mike (Athlete, Football Player)
563 N 2430 W
Provo, UT 84601-7278, USA

Koznick, Kristina (Athlete, Olympic Athlete, Skier)
PO Box 85
Wolcott, CO 81655-0085, USA

Kozol, Jonathan (Writer)
PO Box 145
Byfield, MA 01922, USA

K Prabakaran (Actor)
23-C North Boag Road
T Nagar
Chennai, TN 600 017, INDIA

Kraatz, Victor (Figure Skater)
Connecticut Skating Center
300 Alumni Road
Newington, CT 06111, USA

Kraayeveld, Dave (Athlete, Football Player)
10515 124th Ave NE
Kirkland, WA 98033, USA

Krabbe, Jeroen (Actor)
Van Eeghaustraat 107
Amsterdam, EZ 1071, NETHERLANDS

Krabbe, Katrin (Athlete, Olympic Athlete)
JahnstraBe 6
Neubrandenburg D-17033, Germany

Krabbe-Zimmermann, Katrin (Athlete, Track Athlete)
Dorfstr 9
Pinnow 17091, GERMANY

Krackow, Jurgen (Business Person)
Schumannstr 100
Dusseldorf 40237, GERMANY

Kraemer, Joe (Athlete, Baseball Player)
3212 NE 401st Cir
La Center, WA 98629-5241, USA

Kraft, Chris (Scientist)
14919 Village Elm St
Houston, TX 77062-2914

Kraft, Christopher C (Chris) Jr (Misc)
14919 Village Elm St
Houston, TX 77062, USA

Kraft, Craig A (Artist)
931 R St NW
Washington, DC 20001, USA

Kraft, Greg (Athlete, Golfer)
14820 Rue De Bayonne
Apt 302
Clearwater, FL 33762-3029, USA

Kraft, Jonathan (Business Person, Football Executive)
27 Woodland Rd
Chestnut Hill, MA 02467-2318, USA

Kraft, Leo A (Composer)
45 Hill Park Ave #219
Great Neck, NY 11021, USA

Kraft, Lindsey (Actor)
c/o Matt Sherman *Matt Sherman Management*
7510 W Sunset Blvd
Suite 1413
Los Angeles, CA 90046, USA

Kraft, Robert (Business Person, Football Executive)
260 Heath St
Chestnut Hill, MA 02467-2823, USA

Kraft, Robert (Composer)
4722 Noeline Ave
Encino, CA 91436, USA

Kraft, Robert P (Physicist)
University of California
Lick Observatory
Santa Cruz, CA 95064, USA

Kraft, Ryan (Athlete, Hockey Player)
16219 Hawthorn Path
Lakeville, MN 55044-7573, USA

Kragen, Greg (Athlete, Football Player)
601 47th St
Sacramento, CA 95819-3141, USA

Kragen, Ken
240 Baroda
Los Angeles, CA 90077

Krahl, Jim (Athlete, Football Player)
514 Rolling Mill Dr
Sugar Land, TX 77498-3072, USA

Krainin, Julian (President)
Krainin Productions
25211 Summerhill Lane
Stevenson Ranch, CA 91381, USA

Krajicek, Lukas (Athlete, Hockey Player)
5319 Fishersound Ln
Apollo Beach, FL 33572-3344, USA

Krajicek, Richard (Tennis Player)
Octagon
1751 Pinnacle Dr
#1500
McLean, VA 22102, USA

Krakau, Merv (Athlete, Football Player)
706 Prairie St
Guthrie Center, IA 50115, USA

Krakauer, Jon (Writer)
c/o John Ware *John Ware Literary Agency*
392 Central Park W
New York, NY 10025, USA

Krake, Skip (Athlete, Hockey Player)
5401 37 St
Lloydminster, AB T9V 1T8, Canada

Krakoski, Joe (Athlete, Football Player)
1359 Garden Wall Cir
Reston, VA 20194, USA

Krakowski, Jane (Actor, Musician)
c/o Bill Butler *Industry Entertainment Partners*
955 S Carrillo Dr
Suite 300
Los Angeles, CA 90048, USA

Krall, Diana (Musician)
c/o Sam Feldman *Macklam Feldman Mgmt*
1505 W 2nd Ave
Suite 200
Vancouver BC V6H 3Y4, Canada

Krall, Gerald (Athlete, Football Player)
9236 Mandell Rd
Perrysburg, OH 43551, USA

Kraly, Steve (Athlete, Baseball Player)
12 Davis Ave
Johnson City, NY 13790-3007, USA

Kramarsky, David (Director, Producer)
1630 Berkeley St
Apt 1
Santa Monica, CA 90404-4134, USA

Kramer, Barry (Athlete, Basketball Player)
101 Deanna Ct
Schenectady, NY 12309-1333, USA

Kramer, Billy J (Musician)
Mars Talent
27 L'Ambiance Court
Bardonia, NY 10954, USA

Kramer, Brad (Horse Racer)
11295 E Lytle Rd
Lennon, MI 48449-9512, USA

Kramer, Chris (Actor)
c/o Deb Dillistone *Red Management*
100 W. Pender St
Sun Tower, 7th Floor
Vancouver, BC V6B 1R8, Canada

Kramer, Clare (Actor)
c/o Darren Goldberg *Global Creative*
1051 Cole Ave # B
Los Angeles, CA 90038, USA

Kramer, Eric Allen (Actor)

Kramer, Erik (Athlete, Football Player)
5950 Kingham Ct
Agoura Hills, CA 91301-4436, USA

Kramer, Gerald L (Jerry) (Athlete, Football Player)
11768 Chinden Blvd
Boise, ID 83714, USA

Kramer, Jack
231 N. Glenroy Pl
Los Angeles, CA 90049

Kramer, Jana (Actor)
c/o David Guillod *Intellectual Artists Management*
10585 Santa Monica Blvd
Suite 135
Los Angeles, CA 90025, USA

Kramer, Jim (Writer)
c/o Staff Member *3 Arts Entertainment Inc*
9460 Wilshire Blvd
7th Floor
Beverly Hills, CA 90210, USA

Kramer, Joel (Athlete, Basketball Player)
3817 E Highland Ave
Phoenix, AZ 85018-3619, USA

Kramer, Joel R (Editor)
Minneapolis Star Tribune
425 Portland Ave
Minneapolis, MN 55488, USA

Kramer, Joey (Musician)
Aero Force One
4 Brussels St
Worcester, MA 01610, USA

Kramer, John A (Jack) (Tennis Player)
231 Glenroy Pl
Los Angeles, CA 90049, USA

Kramer, Kent (Athlete, Football Player)
200 Troon Rd
McKinney, TX 75070-6783, USA

Kramer, Kyle (Athlete, Football Player)
2170 Little Miami Dr
Spring Valley, OH 45370-9789, USA

Kramer, Larry (Activist, Writer)
Gay Men's Health Crisis
119 W 24th St
New York, NY 10011, USA

Kramer, Paul
20023 Bernist Ave.
Torrance, CA 90503-2103

Kramer, Randy (Athlete, Baseball Player)
143 Camino Pacifico
Aptos, CA 95003-5886, USA

Kramer, Stepfanie (Actor, Director, Writer)
c/o Mark Teitelbaum *Teitelbaum Artists Group*
8840 Wilshire Blvd
3rd Floor
Beverly Hills, CA 90212, USA

Kramer, Steve
1126 Hollywood Way #203-A
Burbank, CA 91505

Kramer, Thomas (Tommy) (Athlete, Football Player)
123 Mirror Lk
San Antonio, TX 78260-4351, USA

Kramer, Tom (Athlete, Baseball Player)
10665 Hamilton Ave
Cincinnati, OH 45231-1703, USA

Kramer, Wayne (Musician)
Performers of the World
8901 Melrose Ave
#200
West Hollywood, CA 90069, USA

Kramer-Hartman, Ruth (Athlete, Baseball Player, Commentator)
PO Box 38
Limekiln, PA 19535-0038, USA

Kramnik, Vladmir (Misc)
Russian Chess Federation
Luchnetskaya 8
Moscow 119270, RUSSIA

Kranchick, Matt (Athlete, Football Player)
579 Crossroad School Rd
Carlisle, PA 17015-9433, USA

Kranek, Ernst
623 Chino Canyon Rd.
Palm Springs, CA 92262

Kranepool, Ed (Athlete, Baseball Player)
177 High Pond Dr
Jericho, NY 11753-2806, USA

Kranitz, Rick (Athlete, Baseball Player)
6344 W Buckskin Trl
Phoenix, AZ 85083-3452, USA

Krantz, Judith (Writer)
166 Groverton Place
Los Angeles, CA 90077-3732, USA

Kranz, Eugene (Gene) (Scientist)
1108 Shady Oak Lane
Dickinson, TX 77539-3327, USA

Kranz, Fran (Actor)
c/o Rebecca (Becca) Kovacik *Hofflund/Polone*
9465 Wilshire Blvd #420
Beverly Hills, CA 90212, USA

Kranz, Ken (Athlete, Football Player)
N57W24143 N Sycamore Cir
Sussex, WI 53089, USA

Krapek, Karl (Business Person)
United Technologies Corp
United Technologies Building
Hartford, CT 06101, USA

Krasinski, John (Actor)
1250 Foothill Rd
Ojai, CA 93023, USA

Krasniqi, Luan (Boxer)
Oschlewg 10
Rottweil 78628, GERMANY

Krasnoff, Eric (Business Person)
Pall Corp
2200 Northern Blvd
Greenvale, NY 11548, USA

Krasny, Yuri (Artist)
Sloane Gallery
Oxford Office Building
1612 17th St
Denver, CO 80202, USA

Kratch, Bob (Athlete, Football Player)
10685 County Road 24
Watertown, MN 55388, USA

Kratka, Paul (Actor)
5670 El Camino Real #F
Carlsbad, CA 92008, USA

Kratochvilova, Jarmila (Athlete, Track Athlete)
Goleuv Jenikov
582 82, CZECH REPUBLIC

Kratt, Chris (Cinematographer, Director, Producer, Television Host, Writer)

Kratt, Martin (Cinematographer, Director, Producer, Television Host, Writer)

Kratz, Erik (Athlete, Baseball Player)
1840 Manor Dr
Harrisonburg, VA 22801-7625, USA

Kratzert, Bill (Athlete, Golfer)
7470 Founders Way
Ponte Vedra Beach, FL 32082-1914, USA

Kraulis, Andrew (Actor)
c/o Staff Member *Amanda Rosenthal Talent Agency*
543 Richmond St W
Suite 123
Toronto, ON M5V 1Y6, Canada

Kraus, Daniel (Athlete, Basketball Player)
10101 Governor Warfield Pkwy Unit 222
Columbia, MD 21044-3322, USA

Kraus, Peter
Kaiserplatz 7
Munich, GERMANY D-80803

Krause, Brian (Actor)
c/o Leland LaBarre *Bleu, An Entertainment Company*
5225 Wilshire Blvd
Suite 701
Los Angeles, CA 90036, USA

Krause, Chester L (Publisher)
Krause Publications
700 E State St
Iola, WI 54990, USA

Krause, Dieter (Athlete)
Karl-Marx-Allee 21
Berlin 1017, GERMANY

Krause, Helmut (Scientist)
15311 Brandonwood Pl
Houston, TX 77069-1538, USA

Krause, Hemut
15311 Brandonwood Pl
Houston, TX 77069-1538, USA

Krause, Larry (Athlete, Football Player)
N9169 Mill Rd
Summit Lake, WI 54485-9717, USA

Krause, Nick (Actor)
c/o Rebecca Many Rosenberg *Principato/Young Management*
9465 Wilshire Blvd
Suite 430
Beverly Hills, CA 90212, USA

Krause, Paul J (Athlete, Football Player)
18099 Judicial Way N
Lakeville, MN 55044, USA

Krause, Peter (Actor)
c/o Peter Levine *Creative Artists Agency (CAA-LA)*
2000 Ave Of The Stars
Los Angeles, CA 90067, USA

Krause, Richard M (Misc)
4000 Cathedral Ave NW
#413B
Washington, DC 20016, USA

Krause, Ryan (Football Player)
14508 Jefferson St
Omaha, NE 68137-3968, USA

Kraushaar, Sitke (Athlete)
Friedr-Ludwig-Jahn-Str 34
Sonneberg 02692, GERMANY

Kraushaar, William L (Physicist)
27 Stoney Creek Road
Scarborough, ME 04074, USA

Krauss, Alison (Musician)
c/o Staff Member *Shore Fire Media*
32 Court St
16th Floor
Brooklyn, NY 11201, USA

Krauss, Barry (Athlete, Football Player)
753 Whitehall Pl
Carmel, IN 46033-3064, USA

Krauss, Lawrence M (Physicist)
Case Western Reserve University
Physics Dept
Cleveland, OH 44106, USA

Krausse, Lew (Athlete, Baseball Player)
12811 NE 186th St
Holt, MO 64048-8956, USA

Krausse, Stefan (Athlete)
Kart-Zink-Str 2
Ilmenau 96883, GERMANY

Krauthammer, Charles (Writer)
Washington Post Writers Group
1150 15th St NW
Washington, DC 20071, USA

Kravchuk, Igor (Athlete, Hockey Player)
300 chemin de la Riviere Rouge
Harrington, QC J8G 2S7, Canada

Kravec, Ken (Athlete, Baseball Player)
6752 Taeda Dr
Sarasota, FL 34241-9152, USA

Kravitch, Phyllis A (Judge)
US Court of Appeals
56 Forsyth St NW
Atlanta, GA 30303, USA

Kravits, Jason
6310 San Vicente Blvd. #520
Los Angeles, CA 90048

Kravitz, Danny (Athlete, Baseball Player)
8810 Route 487
Dushore, PA 18614-8040, USA

Kravitz, Lenny (Musician, Songwriter)
612 Dauphine St
New Orleans, LA 70112, USA

Kravitz, Zoe (Actor)
c/o Jillian Neal *Untitled Entertainment (LA)*
350 S. Beverly Dr #200
Beverly Hills, CA 90212, USA

Krawczyk, Ray (Athlete, Baseball Player)
67 Cloudcrest
Aliso Viejo, CA 92656-1323, USA

Krawitz, Jan (Filmmaker)
Bldg I20 Stanford University
Stanford, CA 94305-2050, USA

Krayzelburg, Lenny (Athlete, Olympic Athlete, Swimmer)
Octagon
1629 N Crescent Heights Blvd
Los Angeles, CA 90069-1602, USA

Kreamcheck, John (Athlete, Football Player)
2508 N Villa Ln
McHenry, IL 60051, USA

Krebbs, John (Race Car Driver)
Diamond Ridge
3232 Amoruso Way
Roseville, CA 95747, USA

Krebs, Art (Race Car Driver)
327 31st St.
Gulfport, MS 39502, USA

Krebs, Charles j (Scientist)
4640 15th Ave W
Vancouver, BC V6R 3B6, Canada

Krebs, Edwin G (Nobel Prize Laureate)
3835 E McGrawStreet
Seattle, WA 98112-2428, USA

Krebs, Robert D (Business Person)
Burlington North/Santa Fe
2650 Lou Menk Dr
Fort Worth, TX 76131, USA

Krebs, Susan (Actor)
4704 Tobias Ave
Sherman Oaks, CA 91403, USA

Kredel, Elmar Maria (Religious Leader)
Obere Karolinenstra 5
Bamber 96033, GERMANY

Kregel, Kevin R (Astronaut)
2601 Bay Shore Dr
Seabrook, TX 77586-1690, USA

Krehbiel, Frederick A (Business Person)
Molex Inc
2222 Wellington Court
Lisle, IL 60532-1682

Krehbiel, John Hammond (Business Person)
Molex Inc.
2222 Wellington Court
Lisle, IL 60532-1682

Kreider, Dan (Athlete, Football Player)
102 Fawn Hl
Millersville, PA 17551-9758, USA

Kreider, Steve (Athlete, Football Player)
350 Harrow Ln
Blue Bell, PA 19422, USA

Kreischer, Bert (Musician)
c/o Staff Member *Paradigm (Monterey)*
404 W Franklin St
Monterey, CA 93940, USA

Kreitling, Richard (Athlete, Football Player)
24017 Trout Lake Rd
Bovey, MN 55709-8548, USA

Kreitzburg, Brock (Athlete, Bobsledder, Olympic Athlete)
4504 Providence Rd Apt 1D
Charlotte, NC 28226-4109, USA

Krejc, Otomar
Kubisova 26
Praha 8 CZ-18200, Czech Republic

Krejci, David (Athlete, Hockey Player)
c/o Staff Member *Boston Bruins*
TD Banknorth Garden
100 Legends Way, Suite 250
Boston, MA 02114, USA

Kreklow, Wayne (Athlete, Basketball Player)
4001 S Old Mill Creek Rd
Columbia, MO 65203-9635, USA

krels, Jason (Soccer Player)
Dallas Burn
14800 Quorum Dr
#300
Dallas, TX 75254, USA

Krementz, Jill (Photographer)
228 E 48th St
New York, NY 10017-1567, USA

Kremer, Andrea (Sportscaster)
ESPN-TV
Sports Dept
ESPN Plaza 935 Middle St
Bristol, CT 06010, USA

Kremer, Gidon (Musician)
I C M Artists
40 W 57th St
New York, NY 10019, USA

Kremer, Howard (Comedian)
c/o Staff Member *ICM Partners (ICM-LA)*
10250 Constellation Blvd Fl 7
Los Angeles, CA 90067, USA

Kremer, Ken (Athlete, Football Player)
6116 Double Eagle Ct
Kansas City, MO 64152-4970, USA

Kremers, Jimmy (Athlete, Baseball Player)
6209 W Orlando St
Broken Arrow, OK 74011-1264, USA

Kremmel, Jim (Athlete, Baseball Player)
524 W 18th Ave
Spokane, WA 99203-2011, USA

Kremser, Karl (Athlete, Football Player)
301 W Glenview Dr
Salisbury, NC 28147-7227, USA

Krenchicki, Wayne (Athlete, Baseball Player)
2524 Hawthorne Dr
Beloit, WI 53511-2338, USA

Krenk, Mitch (Athlete, Football Player)
1822 4th Ave
Nebraska City, NE 68410, USA

Krens, Thomas (Misc)
Solomon R Guggenheim Museum
1071 5th Ave
New York, NY 10128, USA

Krentz, Dale (Athlete, Hockey Player)
71 Lodge Pl
Sylvan Lake, AB T4S 2N2, Canada

Krenwinkel, Patricia
#W8314 Bed #MA11U CA Inst. for Women16756 Chino Corona
Frontera, CA 91720

Krenz, Jan (Composer, Conductor)
Filharmonia Narodowa
Ul Jasna 5
Warsaw, POLAND

Krenzel, Craig (Athlete, Football Player)
10174 Jerome Rd
Dublin, OH 43017-7606, USA

Krepfle, Keith (Athlete, Football Player)
200 S Park Dr
Collingswood, NJ 08108-1030, USA

Kreps, David M (Economist)
Stanford University
Graduate Business School
Stanford, CA 94305, USA

Krerowicz, Mark (Athlete, Football Player)
1425 Luscombe Dr
Toledo, OH 43614, USA

Kresa, Kent (Business Person)
Northrop Grumman Corp
1840 Century Park East
Los Angeles, CA 90067, USA

Kresge, Chris (Athlete, Golfer)
834 Trailwood Dr
Apopka, FL 32712-3231, USA

Kresge, Cliff (Athlete, Golfer)
c/o Jim Lehrman *SFX Golf*
36855 W Main St Ste 200
Purcellville, VA 20132, USA

Kreskin (Misc)
444 2nd St
Pitcaim, PA 15140, USA

Kress, Chuck (Athlete, Baseball Player)
1705 Pine St Apt 104
Sandpoint, ID 83864-2044, USA

Kress, Nathan (Actor)
c/o Donna Jeanne Goheen *Young Performers Management*
14431 Ventura Blvd
#506
Sherman Oaks, CA 91423, USA

Kressley, Carson (Stylist, Television Host)
c/o Jason Weinberg *Untitled Entertainment (LA)*
350 S. Beverly Dr #200
Beverly Hills, CA 90212, USA

Kretchmer, Arthur (Editor)
Playboy Magazine
Editorial Dept
680 N Lake Shore Dr
Chicago, IL 60611, USA

Kretschmann, Thomas (Director)
c/o Staff Member *United Talent Agency (UTA)*
9336 Civic Center Dr
Beverly Hills, CA 90210, USA

Kretschmer, Christina (Stylist)
c/o Staff Member *Ennis*
119 Braintree St
Boston, MA 02134, USA

Kreuger, Rick (Athlete, Baseball Player)
4664 Sheldon Ct
Hudsonville, MI 49426-7810, USA

Kreuk, Kristin (Actor)
c/o Russ Mortensen *Pacific Artists Management*
1285 W Broadway
Suite 685
Vancouver, BC V6H 3X8, Canada

Kreuter, Chad (Athlete, Baseball Player)
5800 SW 85th St
Miami, FL 33143-8224, USA

Kreutz, Olin (Athlete, Football Player)
750 S Southmeadow Ln
Lake Forest, IL 60045-4836, USA

Kreutzer, Frank (Athlete, Baseball Player)
921 Windwhisper Ln
Annapolis, MD 21403-3486, USA

Kreutzmann, Bill (Musician)
PO Box 1073
San Rafael, CA 94915, USA

Kreuzer, Lisa
Bavariaring 32
Munich, GERMANY D-80336

Kreviazuk, Chantal (Musician, Songwriter)
c/o Staff Member *Paradigm (Monterey)*
404 W Franklin St
Monterey, CA 93940, USA

Krevis, Al (Athlete, Football Player)
78 Copperfield Rd
Worcester, MA 01602-1328, USA

Krevlazuk, Chantel
1505 W. 2nd Ave. #200
Vancouver, CANADA BC V6H 3Y4

Kribel, Joel (Athlete, Golfer)
26254 N 46th St
Phoenix, AZ 85050-8510, USA

Kricfalusi (Kricfaluci), John K (Actor, Animator, Director, Writer)
c/o Staff Member *Rough Draft Korea*
Kyejin B/D, 425-7
Togok-dong, Kannam-Gu
Seoul 135-270, Korea

Krick, Jaynie (Athlete, Baseball Player, Commentator)
911 Glen Eagle Ln
Fort Wayne, IN 46845-9501, USA

Krickstein, Aaron (Tennis Player)
7559 Fairmont Court
Boca Raton, FL 33496, USA

Krieg, Arthur M (Misc)
University of Iowa
Medical College
Immunology Dept
Iowa City, IA 52242, USA

Krieg, Dave (Athlete, Football Player)
2439 E Desert Willow Dr
Phoenix, AZ 85048-9007, USA

Krieg, Jim (Athlete, Football Player)
76690 Lark Ln
Indian Wells, CA 92210-8984, USA

Krieger, Robbie (Musician, Songwriter, Writer)
3011 Ledgewood Dr
Los Angeles, CA 90068, USA

Krieger, Robby (Musician)
c/o Mike Monterulo *The Kirby Organization - U.K.*
6 Walter Ln
Camden
London NW1 8NZ, UK

Krier, Gary (Aviator)
Dryden Flight Research Centre
PO Box 273 M/S 2003
Bldg 4800
Edwards, CA 93523-0273, USA

Krier, Leon (Architect)
16 Belsize Park
London NW3, UNITED KINGDOM (UK)

Kriewald, Doug (Athlete, Football Player)
5031 Snow Mesa Dr
Fort Collins, CO 80528, USA

Kriewaldt, Clint (Athlete, Football Player)
W3189 Center Valley Rd
Freedom, WI 54165-8214, USA

Krige, Alice (Actor)
2875 Barrymore Dr
Malibu, CA 90265, USA

Krikalev, Sergei K (Cosmonaut)
Potchta Kosmonavtov
Moskovskoi Oblasti
Syvisdny Goroduk 141160, RUSSIA

Krimm, John (Athlete, Football Player)
2565 Abington Rd
Upper Arlington, OH 43221, USA

Kring, Tim (Writer)
c/o Richard Abate *3 Arts Entertainment - NY*
49 West 27th St.
5th Floor
New York, NY 10001, USA

Kripke, Eric (Director, Producer, Writer)
c/o Staff Member *Principato/Young Management*
9465 Wilshire Blvd
Suite 430
Beverly Hills, CA 90212, USA

Kripke, Saul A (Misc)
Princeton University
Philosophy Dept
Princeton, NJ 08544, USA

Krisher, Bill (Athlete, Football Player)
5915 Over Downs Dr
Dallas, TX 75230, USA

Krishnamurthy, Suchithra (Actor, Bollywood)
402A Leela Apartments
Cuerpark Co-op Society Yari Road
Andheri (W)
Mumbai, MS 400061, INDIA

Krishnan, Ramya (Actor, Bollywood)
7 Lakshmi Sri Street
Janaki Nagar
Chennai, TN 600087, INDIA

Kriss, Gerard A (Astronomer)
Johns Hopkins University
Astronomy Dept
Baltimore, MD 21218, USA

Kristen, Marta (Actor)
375 Mesa Rd
Santa Monica, CA 90402, USA

Kristiansen, Ingrid (Athlete, Track Athlete)
Nils Collett Vogts Vei 51B
Oslo, 0765, NORWAY

Kristiansen, Kjeld Kirk (Business Person, Educator)
Lego Group
Billund 7190, DENMARK

Kristien, Dale
691 Country Club Dr.
Burbank, CA 91501

Kristina Sisco, Kristina (Actor)
c/o Staff Member *Cohen/Thomas Agency*
1888 N Crescent Heights Blvd
Los Angeles, CA 90069, USA

Kristof, Kathy M (Writer)
Los Angeles Times
Editorial Dept
202 W 1st St
Los Angeles, CA 90012, USA

Kristoff, Joe (Bowler)
4290 Meadowview Court
Columbus, OH 43224-1927, USA

Kristofferson, Kris (Actor, Musician, Songwriter)
3179 Sumac Ridge Rd
Malibu, CA 90265, USA

Kristol, Irving (Editor, Scientist)
Public Interest Magazine
1112 16th St NW
Washington, DC 20036, USA

Kristol, William
6625 Jill Ct.
McLean, VA 22101

Krivda, Rick (Athlete, Baseball Player)
112 Dolores Dr
Irwin, PA 15642-5519, USA

Krivokrasov, Sergei (Athlete, Hockey Player)
8505 E Alameda Ave #3329
Denver, CO 80230-6070, USA

Krivsky, Wayne (Commentator)
3841 Gregory Ln
Erlanger, KY 41018-3819, USA

Kriwet, Heinz (Business Person)
Thyssen AG
August-Thyssen-Str 1
Dusseldorf 40211, GERMANY

Krizmanich, Jack (Actor)
c/o Mara Santino *Luber Roklin Management*
8530 Wilshire Blvd
6th Floor
Beverly Hills, CA 90211, USA

Krmpotich, David (Athlete, Olympic Athlete, Rower)
128 Archbishop Dr
Conshohocken, PA 19428-1328, USA

Kroeger, Chad (Musician, Songwriter)
408 Monarch Pl
Lahaina, HI 96761, USA

Kroeger, Gary (Actor, Comedian)
10474 Santa Monica Blvd
#380
Los Angeles, CA 90025, USA

Kroeger, Josh (Athlete, Baseball Player)
13477 N 87th Ln
Peoria, AZ 85381-6114

Kroeger, Mike (Musician)
408 Monarch Pl
Lahaina, HI 96761, USA

Kroell, Ronnie (Actor, Model)
c/o Dino May *Dino May Management*
6362 Hollywood Blvd #422
Hollywood, CA 90028-6323, USA

Kroemer, Herbert (Nobel Prize Laureate)
University Of California At Santa Barbara
Rm 4107
Santa Barbara, CA 93106-0001, USA

Kroenke, Zach (Athlete, Baseball Player)
Double Diamond Sports Management
7640 NW 79th Ave Apt L8
Tamarac, FL 33321-2868, USA

Kroes, Doutzen (Model)
c/o Staff Member *Paparazzi Model Management*
Singel 512-2
AZ 1017, THE NETHERLANDS

Krofft, Marty (Actor, Producer)
Sid & Marty Krofft Pictures
c/o CBS Studio Center
4024 Radford Ave
Studio City, CA 91604, USA

Krofft, Sid (Misc)
7710 Woodrow Wilson Dr
Los Angeles, CA 90046, USA

Kroft, Steve (Correspondent)

Krogh, Sandy (Stylist)
14 Haggerston Aisle
Irvine, CA 92612, USA

Krohn, Jonathan (Writer)
15335 Little Stone Way
Alpharetta, GA 30004, USA

Krol, John Cardinal
222 N. 17th St.
Philadelphia, PA 19103

Kroll, Alexander S (Alex) (Athlete, Football Player)
581 Whalley Rd
Charlotte, VT 05445, USA

Kroll, Bob (Athlete, Football Player)
344 Golfside Cv
Longwood, FL 32779-4669, USA

Kroll, Gary (Athlete, Baseball Player)
9038 E 40th St
Tulsa, OK 74145-3713, USA

Kroll, Gustav (Scientist)
1206 McClung Ave SE
Huntsville, AL 35801-2507, USA

Kroll, Lucien (Architect)
Ave Louis Berlaimont 20
Boite 9
Brussels 1160, BELGIUM

Kroll, Robert L (Athlete, Football Player)
P.O. Box 8563
Maitland, FL 32751, USA

Kroll, Sylvio
Tranitzer Str. 8
Cottbus, GERMANY D-03048

Krom, Tommy (Athlete, Basketball Player)
519 Briar Hill Rd
Louisville, KY 40206-3009, USA

Kromm, Richard (Rich) (Athlete, Coach, Hockey Player)
1935 Cheyenne Dr
Evansville, IN 47715-7044, USA

Kronberger, Petra (Skier)
Ellmautal 37
Pfarrwerfen 5452, AUSTRIA

Krone, Julie (Horse Racer)
7305 Marine Pl
Carlsbad, CA 92011-4684, USA

Kroner, Gary (Athlete, Football Player)
7330 Buckingham Ct
Boulder, CO 80301, USA

Kronwall, Niklas (Athlete, Hockey Player)
22235 Picadilly Cir
Novi, MI 48375-4796, USA

Krook, Kevin (Athlete, Hockey Player)
216 20 St
Cold Lake, AB T9M 1E2, Canada

Kroon, Marc (Athlete, Baseball Player)
12617 N 56th Pl
Scottsdale, AZ 85254-4259, USA

Kropfelder, Nicholas (Soccer Player)
13803 Lighthouse Ave
Ocean City, IN 21842, USA

Kropp, Tom (Athlete, Basketball Player)
1811 W 41st St
Kearney, NE 68845-8286, USA

Krosney, Alexandra (Actor)
c/o Beverly Strong *Strong Management*
9350 Wilshire Blvd
#224
Beverly Hills, CA 90212, USA

Kross, David (Actor)
c/o Staff Member *Julian Belfrage & Associates*
9 Argyll St
3rd Floor
London W1F 7TG, UK

Kroto, Harold W (Nobel Prize Laureate)
University of Sussex
Chemistry Dept
Brighton, Sussex 9Nl 9QJ, England

Krough, Jeff (Race Car Driver)
PO Box 602
Kamiah, ID 83536, USA

Krsnich, Rocky (Athlete, Baseball Player)
5701 W 92nd St
Overland Park, KS 66207-2442, USA

KRS-One (Musician)
c/o Sasha Brookner *Heliocentric Public Relations*
5770 W. Centinela Ave
Los Angeles, CA 90045, USA

Krstic, Nenad (Basketball Player)
New Jersy Nets
390 Murray Hill Parkway
East Rutherford, NJ 07073, USA

Kruckei, Marie (Baseball Player)
52128 Woodbridge Dr
South Bend, IN 46635-1053, USA

Kruckel, Marie (Athlete, Baseball Player, Commentator)
52128 Woodridge Dr
South Bend, IN 46635-1053, USA

Kruczek, Mike (Athlete, Football Player)
4028 Gilder Rose Pl
Winter Park, FL 32792-9416, USA

Krueger, Anne O (Economist)
Stanford University
Economics Dept
Stanford, CA 94305, USA

Krueger, Bill (Athlete, Baseball Player)
30132 SE Redmond Fall City Rd
Fall City, WA 98024-7104, USA

Krueger, Charles A (Charlie) (Athlete, Football Player)
44 Regency Dr
Clayton, CA 94517, USA

Krueger, James G (Misc)
Rockefeller University
Medical Center
1230 York Ave
New York, NY 10021, USA

Krueger, Kurt
1221 La Collina Dr.
Beverly Hills, CA 90210

Krueger, Phil (Race Car Driver)
8662 Houston Rd.
Freetown, IN 47235-9624, USA

Krueger, Robert C (Bob) (Diplomat, Ex-Senator)
US Embassy-Burundl
State Department
2201 C St NW
Washington, DC 20522, USA

Krueger, Rolf (Athlete, Football Player)
P.O. Box 638
Wallis, TX 77485, USA

Krug, Chris (Athlete, Baseball Player)
40695 Posada Ct
Palm Desert, CA 92260-2317, USA

Krug, Gene (Athlete, Baseball Player)
1327 Baylor Dr
Colorado Springs, CO 80909-3301, USA

Krug, Manfred
Rankestr. 9
Berlin, GERMANY D-10789

Kruger, Christiane
Waldschmidtstr. 16
Starnberg, GERMANY 82319

Kruger, Diane (Actor, Model)
c/o Abi Harris *Ken McReddie Ltd*
11 Connaught Pl
London W2 2ET, UNITED KINGDOM

Kruger, Hardy (Actor)
PO Box 2450
Palm Springs, CA 92263-2450, USA

Kruger, Lon (Athlete, Basketball Coach, Basketball Player, Coach)
11 Quintessa Cir
Las Vegas, NV 89141-6054, USA

Kruger, Mike
Gorch-Fock-Kehre 9
Quickborn, GERMANY D-25451

Kruger, Pit (Actor)
Geleitstr 10
Frankfurt/Main 60599, GERMANY

Krugman, Paul R (Nobel Prize Laureate)
Princeton University
414 Robertson Hall
Princeton, NJ 08544-0001, USA

Kruk, John (Commentator)
ESPN-TV 935 Middle St Attn Baseball Broadcast Dept
Bristol, CT 06010-1000, USA

Kruk, John (Athlete, Baseball Player)
PO Box 7847
Naples, FL 34101-7847, USA

Krukow, Mike (Athlete, Baseball Player)
6094 Madbury Ct
San Luis Obispo, CA 93401-8244, USA

Krulak, Charles (General)
PO Box 707
Bear, DE 19701-0707, USA

Krulicki, Jim (Athlete, Hockey Player)
35 Primrose Path
58 Boiler Beach Rd RR 1 Stn Main
Kitchener, ON N2E 2X3, Canada

Krulwich, Robert (Correspondent)
CBS-TV
News Dept
524 W 57th St
New York, NY 10019, USA

Krumholtz, David (Actor)
c/o Jeff Golenberg *Collective*
8383 Wilshire Blvd
Suite 1050
Beverly Hills, CA 90211, USA

Krumrie, Tim (Athlete, Football Player)
c/o Staff Member *Kansas City Chiefs*
1 Arrowhead Dr
Kansas City, MO 64129, USA

Krupa, Joanna (Model, Reality TV Star)
c/o Steven Grossman *Collective*
8383 Wilshire Blvd
Suite 1050
Beverly Hills, CA 90211, USA

Krupicka, Jarda (Athlete, Hockey Player)
Budweiser Import GmbH
Lindenstrasse 20
Kloten 8302, Switzerland

Krupp, Uwe (Athlete, Hockey Player)
79 Park Cir NE
Atlanta, GA 30305-2771, USA

Kruschen, Jack
PO Box 10143
Canoga Park, CA 91309-1143

Kruscschev, Sergei Dr (Writer)
Brown University
PO Box 1970
Providence, RL 02912-1970, USA

Kruse, Earl J (Misc)
Roofers/Waterproofers/Allied Workers
1125 17th St NW
Washington, DC 20036, USA

Kruse, Martin (Religious Leader)
Prinz-Friedrrich-Leopold-Str 14
Berlin 14219, GERMANY

Krushelnyski, Mike (Athlete, Hockey Player)
PO Box 834
Cohoes, NY 12047-0834, USA

Krusiec, Michelle (Actor)
c/o Jennifer Wiley *Framework Entertainment (NY)*
129 W 27th St Fl 12
New York, NY 10001, USA

Kruskal, Martin D (Mathematician)
60 Littlebrook Road N
Princeton, NJ 08540, USA

Krutko, Larry (Athlete, Football Player)
1565 6th St
Waynesburg, PA 15370-1653, USA

Krygier, Todd (Athlete, Hockey Player)
23946 Wintergreen Cir
Apt 13
Novi, MI 48374-3681, USA

Krynzel, Dave (Athlete, Baseball Player)
951 Derringer Ln
Henderson, NV 89014-2595, USA

Krypreos, Nick (Athlete, Hockey Player)
9209 Copenhaven Dr
Potomac, MD 20854, USA

Kryskow, Dave (Athlete, Hockey Player)
58 Sandstone Ridge Cres
Okotoks, AB T1S 1P9, Canada

Krystkowiak, Larry (Athlete, Basketball Player)
2343 Dallin St
Salt Lake City, UT 84109-1524, USA

Krzysztof, Oliwa (Athlete, Hockey Player)
707 Derzee Ct
Delmar, NY 12054, USA

Krzyzewski, Mike (Athlete, Basketball Player, Coach)
4406 West Cornwallis Rd
Durham, NC 27705-8126, USA

K. Simpson, Michael (Congressman, Politician)
2312 Rayburn HOB
Washington, DC 20515, USA

KT Tunstall (Musician)
c/o Simon Banks *SB Management*
The Homestead Cottage
111 Church Rd
London SW13 9HL, UK

Kuba, Filip (Athlete, Hockey Player)
17216 Emerald Chase Dr
Tampa, FL 33647-2780, USA

Kubala, Ray (Athlete, Football Player)
3433 Alexandrite Way
Round Rock, TX 78681-2436, USA

Kuban, Bob (Musician)
17626 Lasiandra Dr
Chesterfield, MO 63005, USA

Kubasov, Valeri N (Cosmonaut)
Potchta Kosmonavtov
Moskovskoi Oblasti
Syvisdny Goroduk 141160, RUSSIA

Kubasov, Valery
141-160 Svyossdy Gorodok
Potchta Kosmonavtov, RUSSIA

Kubek, Anthony C (Tony) (Athlete, Baseball Player, Sportscaster)
685 Smoky Lake Dr
Phelps, WI 54554-9314, USA

Kubel, Jason (Athlete, Baseball Player)
21031 Ventura Blvd Ste 1000
Woodland Hills, CA 91364-2227, USA

Kubenka, Jeff (Athlete, Baseball Player)
9706 Endcliff
San Antonio, TX 78250-3426, USA

Kuberski, Bob (Athlete, Football Player)
13 Forwood Dr
Garnet Valley, PA 19060-1215, USA

Kuberski, Robert (Athlete, Football Player)
13 Forwood Dr
Marcus Hook, PA 19061, USA

Kuberski, Steve (Athlete, Basketball Player)
91 Lawson Rd
Winchester, MA 01890-3153, USA

Kubiak, Gary (Athlete, Coach, Football Coach, Football Player)
14 Woods Edge Ln
Houston, TX 77024-7525, USA

Kubiak, Leo (Athlete, Basketball Player)
2638 N Prestwick Way
Lecanto, FL 34461-6902, USA

Kubiak, Ted (Athlete, Baseball Player)
11956 Fernardo Plaza Drive
San Diego, CA 92128-2538, USA

Kubik, Brad (Athlete, Football Player)
3025 W Oakhaven Ln
Springfield, MO 65810-1948, USA

Kubin, Larry (Athlete, Football Player)
315 Cannery Ln
Forest Hill, MD 21050, USA

Kubina, Pavel (Athlete, Hockey Player)
1145 81st St S
Saint Petersburg, FL 33707-2726, USA

Kubinski, Tim (Athlete, Baseball Player)
384 Santa Maria Ave
San Luis Obispo, CA 93405-2140, USA

Kubiszvn, Jack (Athlete, Baseball Player)
2306 Universitv Blvd Ste A
Tuscaloosa, AL 35401-1581, USA

Kubiszyn, Jack (Athlete, Baseball Player)
2306 University Blvd
Tuscaloosa, AL 35401-1581, USA

Kubski, Gil (Athlete, Baseball Player)
4542 Scenario Dr
Huntington Beach, CA 92649-2221, USA

Kubski, Gill (Athlete, Baseball Player)
4542 Scenario Dr
Huntington Beach, CA 92649-2221, USA

Kucan, Milan (President)
President's Office
Erjavcera 17
Ljubljana 61000, SOLVENIA

Kucek, Jack (Athlete, Baseball Player)
8220 Blue Heron Ln
Canfield, OH 44406-9134, USA

Kucera, Frantisek (Athlete, Hockey Player)
Sportovni Centrum Letnany Tupolevova
ul. 699
Praha Letnany 9, Czech Republic

Kuchar, Matt (Athlete, Golfer)
121 Plantation Cir
Ponte Vedra Beach, FL 32082-3921, USA

Kuchma, Leonid D (President)
President's Office
Bankova Str 11
Kiev 252011, UKRAINE

Kuchta, Frank (Athlete, Football Player)
5021 Fairlawn Rd
Lyndhurst, OH 44124, USA

Kucinich, Dennis
12217 Milan
Cleveland, OH 44111

Kucinich, Dennis J (Misc)
14518 Drake Road
Cleveland, OH 44136, USA

Kucks, Johnny (Athlete, Baseball Player)
15 Oakland St
Hillsdale, NJ 07642-184, USA

Kuczenski, Bruce (Athlete, Basketball
Player)
135 Southshire Dr
Southington, CT 06489-4224, USA

Kuczynski, Betty (Bowler)
4515 Prescott Ave
Apt 1B
Lyons, IL 60534-1960, USA

Kudelka, James A (Choreographer,
Dancer)
National Ballet of Canada
470 Queens Quay W
Toronto, ON M5V 3K4, CANADA

Kudelski, Bob (Athlete, Hockey Player)
PO Box 351
Midway, UT 84049-0351, USA

Kuder, Mary (Artist)
Kuder Art Studio
539 Navahopi Road
Sedona, AZ 86336, USA

Kudlow, Lawrence (Television Host)
Kudlow & Company
CNBC
900 Sylvan Ave
Englewood Cliffs, NJ 07632, USA

Kudoh, Youki (Actor)
c/o Vincent Cirrincione *Vincent
Cirrincione Associates*
1516 N Fairfax Ave
Los Angeles, CA 90046, USA

Kudrave, David (Race Car Driver)
7918 Zionville Rd.
Indianapolis, IN 46268, USA

Kudrna, Julius (Athlete)
Sekaninova 36
Prague 2 120 00, CZECH REPUBLIC

Kudrow, Lisa (Actor)
c/o Jennifer Allen *Viewpoint Inc*
8820 Wilshire Blvd.
Suite 220
Beverly Hills, CA 90211, USA

Kuebler, David (Opera Singer)
Haydn Rawstron
36 Station Road
London SE20 7BQ, UNITED KINGDOM
(UK)

Kuechenberg, Robert J (Bob) (Athlete,
Football Player)
2519 SW 30th Ter
Fort Lauderdale, FL 33312, USA

Kuechenberg, Rudy (Athlete, Football
Player)
2841 NW 73rd Ave
Hollywood, FL 33024, USA

Kuehl, Ryan (Athlete, Football Player)
10409 Masters Ter
Potomac, MD 20854, USA

Kuehn, Art (Athlete, Football Player)
19520 NE 185th St
Woodinville, WA 98077, USA

Kuehn, Enrico (Athlete)
BSD
An der Schiessstatte 4
Berchtesgaden 83471, GERMANY

Kuehne, Hank (Athlete, Golfer)
11117 Grren Bayberry Dr
Palm Beach Gardens, FL 33418, USA

Kuehne, Kelli (Athlete, Golfer)
7211 Oakbluff Dr
Dallas, TX 75254-2736, USA

Kuerten, Gustavo (Tennis Player)
Octagon
1751 Pinnacle Drive
#1500
McLean, VA 22102, USA

Kuester, John (Athlete, Basketball Player)
105 Carnoustie Way
Media, PA 19063-1858, USA

Kufeldt, James (Business Person)
Winn-Dixie Stores
5050 Edgewood Court
Jacksonville, FL 32254, USA

Kufuor, John Agyekum (President)
Chairman's Office
Castle
PO Box 1627
Accra, GHANA

Kugler, Pete (Athlete, Football Player)
9984 Whitetail Ln
Littleton, CO 80127, USA

Kuharek, John (General)
4708 W Bay Ave
Tampa, FL 33616-1003, USA

Kuhaulua, Fred (Athlete, Baseball Player)
89-203 Ualakahiki Pl
Waianae, HI 96792-3937, USA

Kuhaulua, Jesse (Wrestler)
Azumazeki Stable
4-6-4 Higashi Komagata
Ryogoku
Tokyo, JAPAN

Kuhlemann, Bill (Race Car Driver)
Summit Racing
Box 535
Richfield, OH 44285, USA

Kuhlman, Ron (Actor)
5738 Willis Ave
Van Nuys, CA 91411, USA

Kuhlmann, Kathleen M (Opera Singer)
Int'l Management Group
G Paris
54 Ave Marceau
Paris 75008, FRANCE

Kuhlmann-Wilsdorf, Doris (Physicist)
University of Virginia
Materials Science Dept
Charlottesville, VA 22901, USA

Kuhn, Gustav (Conductor)
6343 Ere
AUSTRIA

Kuhn, Stephen L (Steve) (Composer,
Musician)
Berkeley Agency
2608 9th St
Berkeley, CA 94710, USA

Kuhweide, Wilhelm
10031 E. Buckskin Trail
Scottsdale, AZ 85255

Kuiper, Duane (Athlete, Baseball Player)
3665 Deer Trail Dr
Danville, CA 94506-6021, USA

Kuiper, Glen (Commentator)
321 SeQuoia Ter
Danville, CA 94506-4545, USA

Kuipers, Andre Dr (Astronaut)
European Space Centre
8-10 rue Mario Nikis
Paris Cedex F-75738, France

Kukkonen, Lasse (Athlete, Hockey Player)
Puckagency LLC
555 Pleasantville Rd Ste
210N Attn Jay Grossman
Briarcliff Manor, NY 10510-1900, USA

Kukoc, Toni (Athlete, Basketball Player)
1830 Hybernia Dr
Highland Park, IL 60035-5500, USA

Kukulowicz, Adolph (Athlete, Hockey
Player)
1342 Sea Lovers Ln
RR 5
Gabriola, BC V0R 1X5, Canada

Kukunoor, Nagesh

Kulak, Stu (Athlete, Hockey Player)
113 Sunglo Dr
Penticton, BC V2A 8X6, Canada

Kulbacki, Joe (Football Player)
PO Box 97
Colden, NY 14033-0097, USA

Kulbacki, Joseph (Athlete, Football Player)
9419 S Hill Rd
Boston, NY 14025, USA

Kuleshov, Valery (Musician)
c/o Staff Member *Musicians Corporate
Management*
PO Box 825
Highland, NY 12528, USA

Kulich, Vladimir (Actor)
c/o Jeff Goldberg *Jeff Goldberg
Management*
817 Monte Leon Dr
Beverly Hills, CA 90210, USA

Kulikov, Viktor G (Misc)
Ministry of Defense
Myasnitskaya Str 37
Moscow 10100, RUSSIA

Kulka, Konstanty A (Musician)
Filharmonia Narodowa
Ul Jasna 5
Warsaw 00-007, POLAND

Kulkarni, Mamta (Actor, Bollywood)
D Wing 7th Floor 701 RC Complex
Versova Yari Road
Mumbai, MS 400061, INDIA

Kulkarni, Shrinivas R (Astronomer)
California Institute of Technology
Astronomy Dept
Pasadena, CA 91125, USA

Kulongoski, Theodore (Politician)
4232 NE Couch St
Portland, OR 97213-1630, USA

Kulpa, Ronald (Athlete, Baseball Player)
1958 Parkland Woods Dr
Maryland Heights, MO 63304-0508, USA

Kumanyika, Shiriki K (Misc)
University of Illinois
Nutrition/Dietetics Dept
Chicago, IL 60607, USA

Kumar, Akshay (Actor, Bollywood)
203 A Wing Benzer Apartments
Lokhandwala Complex Andheri (W)
Mumbai, MS 400053, India

Kumar, Ashok (Actor, Bollywood)
47 Union Park Chembur
Mumbai, MS 400071, INDIA

Kumar, Dilip (Actor, Bollywood)
34/B Palli Hill
Nargis Dutt Road Bandra (W)
Mumbai, MS 400050, INDIA

Kumar, Kiran (Actor)
Jeevan Kiran S V Road
Bandra
Bombay, MS 400 050, INDIA

Kumar, Manoj (Actor, Director,
Filmmaker, Producer)
Lakshmi Villa Grount Floor-45
Tagore Road Santacruz (W)
Bombay, MS 400 054, INDIA

Kumar, Mehul (Bollywood, Director,
Filmmaker, Producer)
302 Atlantic J P Road
Seven Bangalows Andheri
Bombay, MS 400 061, INDIA

Kumar, Mohan (Bollywood, Director,
Filmmaker)
Prem Sagar 'B' Linking Road
Khar
Bombay, MS 400 052, INDIA

Kumar, Rajendra (Actor, Bollywood,
Director, Filmmaker, Producer)
Dimple 7 Pali Hill
Bandra
Bombay, MS 400 050, INDIA

Kumar, Sanjay (Business Person)
Computer Associates Int'l
1 Computer Associates Plaza
Islandia, NY 11749, USA

Kumar, Sarath (Actor)
16 Rajamannaar Saalai
Thyagaraya Nagar
Chennai, TN 600 017, INDIA

Kumaratunga, Chandrika B (President)
President's Office
Republic Square
Sri Jayewardenepura Kotte
SRI LANKA

Kumbernuss, Astrid (Athlete, Track Athlete)
Neubrandenburg Jahnstadion
Schwedenstr 25
Neubrandenburg 17033, GERMANY

Kumble, Roger (Actor, Director, Writer)
c/o David Kramer *United Talent Agency (UTA)*
9336 Civic Center Dr
Beverly Hills, CA 90210, USA

Kume, Mike (Athlete, Baseball Player)
6810 Woodard Rd
Andover, OH 44003-9638, USA

Kumerow, Eric (Athlete, Football Player)
736 Fairview Ln
Bartlett, IL 60103, USA

Kumin, Maxine W (Writer)
Joppa Road
Warner, NH 03278, USA

Kumin, Maxine Winokur (Writer)
Joppa Dist #30
Warner, NH 03278, USA

Kummer, Glenn F (Business Person)
Fleetwood Enterprises
3125 Myers St
Riverside, CA 92503, USA

Kump, Ernest J (Architect)
Villa Boecklin
Jupiterstr 15
Zurich 8032, SWITZERLAND

Kumpel, Mark (Athlete, Hockey Player, Olympic Athlete)
22 Oceanwood Dr
Scarborough, ME 04074, USA

Kundera, Milan (Writer)
Gallimard
5 Rue Sebastien-Bottin
Paris 75007, FRANCE

Kundla, John (Athlete, Basketball Coach, Coach)
Main Street Lodge
909 Main St NE
Apt 208
Minneapolis, MN 55413-1854, USA

Kunerth, Mark J (Producer, Writer)
c/o Ted Chervin *ICM Partners (ICM-LA)*
10250 Constellation Blvd Fl 7
Los Angeles, CA 90067, USA

Kunes, Ellen (Editor)
Oprah Magazine
224 W 57th St
#900
New York, NY 10019, USA

Kuney, Eva Lee (Actor)
8962 Shale Valley St
Las Vegas, NV 89123, USA

Kung, Hans (Misc)
Waldhauserstr 23
Tubingen 72076, GERMANY

Kung, Patrick C (Misc)
T Cell Sciences
119 4th Ave
Needham, MA 02494, USA

Kunin, Madeleine (Politician)
9 Harbor Watch Rd
Burlington, VT 05401-5269, USA

Kunis, Mila (Actor)
c/o Susan Curtis *Curtis Talent Management*
9607 Arby Dr
Beverly Hills, CA 90210, USA

Kunitz, Chris (Athlete)
3331 Annandale Dr
Presto, PA 15142-1057, USA

Kunitz, Matt (Producer)
c/o Staff Member *WmE2 (WMA-LA)*
1 William Morris Pl
Beverly Hills, CA 90212, USA

Kunkel, Jeff (Athlete, Baseball Player)
4921 County Road 605
Burleson, TX 76028-1155, USA

Kunkel, Louis M (Misc)
Children's Hospital
300 Longwood Ave
Boston, MA 02115, USA

Kunkel-Huff, Anna (Baseball Player)
9220 E Fairway Blvd
Apt C136
Sun Lakes, AZ 85248-6579, USA

Kunnert, Kevin (Athlete, Basketball Player)
8286 SW Wilderland Ct
Portland, OR 97224-7646, USA

Kunstler, Mort (Artist)
137 Cove Neck Rd
Oyster Bay, NY 11771-1824, USA

Kunstmann, Doris
Alexander Lamonstrasse 9
Munich, GERMANY D-81679

Kuntar, Les (Athlete, Hockey Player)
9721 SW 89th Loop
Ocala, FL 34481-5577, USA

Kuntz, Murray (Athlete, Hockey Player)
4571 Sugar Maple Dr
Gloucester, ON K1V 1R7, Canada

Kuntz, Rusty (Athlete, Baseball Player)
10102 W 152nd Ter
Overland Park, KS 66221-2709, USA

Kunz, Eddie (Athlete, Baseball Player)
242 NE 136th Ave
Portland, OR 97230-3345, USA

Kunz, George J (Athlete, Football Player)
8215 S Bermuda Rd
Las Vegas, NV 89123, USA

Kunz, Lee (Athlete, Football Player)
4096 Youngfield St
Wheat Ridge, CO 80033, USA

Kunze, Terry (Athlete, Basketball Player)
6931 Halifax Ave N
Minneapolis, MN 55429-1373, USA

Kunzel, Erich Jr (Conductor)
TRM Mgmt
825 S Lazelle St
Columbus, OH 43206, USA

Kunzu, Hari (Writer)
EP Dutton
375 Hudson St
New York, NY 10014, USA

Kuok Hock Nien, Robert (Business Person)
Kuok Limited
No.1 Kim Seng Promenade
#07-01 Great World City
237994, Singapore

Kupchak, Mitch (Athlete, Basketball Player, Olympic Athlete)
361 Fordyce Rd
Los Angeles, CA 90049-2009, USA

Kupcinet, Kari (Actor)
1660 Mill Trail
Highland Park, IL 60035-1502, USA

Kupec, C J (Athlete, Basketball Player)
6448 River Run
Columbia, MD 21044-6022, USA

Kupets, Courtney (Athlete, Gymnast, Olympic Athlete)
133 Falling Shoals Dr
Athens, GA 30605-5740, USA

Kupfer, Carl (Misc)
National Eye Institute
9000 Rockville Pike
Bethesda, MD 20892, USA

Kupfer, Harry (Director)
Komische Oper
Behrenstr 55-57
Berlin 10117, GERMANY

Kupferberg, Sabine (Ballerina)
Dans Theater 3
Scheldoldoekshaven 60
Gravenhage, EN 2511, NETHERLANDS

Kuplowsky, Winn (Stylist)
c/o Staff Member *Judy Inc*
1 Yorkville Ave
Toronto ON M4W 1L1, Canada

Kupp, Craig (Athlete, Football Player)
609 S 31st Ave
Yakima, WA 98902, USA

Kupp, Jacob (Jake) (Athlete, Football Player)
4801 Snowmountain Rd
Yakima, WA 98908, USA

Kupper, William P Jr (Publisher)
Business Week
1221 Ave of Americas
New York, NY 10020, USA

Kupperman, Joel (Actor)
P.O. Box 672
Mansfield Center, CT 06250-0672, USA

Kuranari, Tadashi (Government Official)
2-18-12 Daita
Setangayaku
Tokyo 155, JAPAN

Kurant, Willy (Cinematographer)
Lyons Sheldon Agency
800 S Robertson Blvd
#6
Los Angeles, CA 90035, USA

Kuras, Ellen M (Cinematographer)
54 Summit St
Nyack, NY 10960, USA

Kurasov, Georgy (Artist)
4/2 Inzenernaja St
Saint Petersburg 191011, RUSSIA

Kureishi, Hanif (Writer)
81 Comeragh Road
London W14 9HS, UNITED KINGDOM (UK)

Kurek, Ralph (Athlete, Football Player)
2373 Lime Pond Rd
South Royalton, VT 05068-4411, USA

Kurgan, Barbara (Stylist)
c/o Staff Member *Tricia Joyce Inc*
79 Chambers St
2nd Floor
New York, NY 10007, USA

Kurisko, Jamie (Athlete, Football Player)
3270 Aldrich Dr
Cumming, GA 30040-5378, USA

Kuriyama, Chiaki (Actor)
c/o Staff Member *Crystal Sky Pictures*
10203 Santa Monica Blvd
5th Floor
Los Angeles, CA 90067, USA

Kurkova, Karolina (Model)
c/o Nicole Esposito *Full Picture (NY)*
915 Broadway
20th Floor
New York, NY 10010, USA

Kurland, Bob (Athlete, Basketball Player, Olympic Athlete)
1024 Kings Crown Dr
Sanibel, FL 33957-4910, USA

Kurlander, Tom
1801 Avenue of the Stars #902
Los Angeles, CA 90067

Kurnick, Howie (Athlete, Football Player)
2339 Bretton Dr
Cincinnati, OH 45244, USA

Kurokawa, Kisho (Architect)
Aoyama Building
#11F 1-2-3 Kita Aoyama
Minatoku, Tokyo, JAPAN

Kurosaki, Ryan (Athlete, Baseball Player)
2024 Fairmont Dr
Benton, AR 72015-3163, USA

Kurosawa, Takuya (Race Car Driver)
Dale Coyne Racing
13400 Budler Rd.
Plainfield, IL 60544, USA

Kurpeikis, Justin (Athlete, Football Player)
246 Varsity Ln
State College, PA 16803-1845, USA

Kurrasch, David B (Business Person)
The Monkey Hook, LLC
25672 Raintree Rd
Laguna Hills, CA 92653, USA

Kurrasch, Roy (Athlete, Football Player)
2211 Canyon Dr
Los Angeles, CA 90068-2401, USA

Kurrat, Kiaus-Dieter (Athlete, Track Athlete)
Am Hochwald 30
28460
Klemmachow 1453, GERMANY

Kurri, Jari (Athlete, Hockey Player)
Hockey Hall of Fame Brookfield Place
30 Yonge St.
Toronto, ON M5E 1X8, Canada

Kurri, Jarri (Athlete, Hockey Player)
c/o Staff Member *Hockey Hall of Fame*
Brookfield Place
30 Yonge St
Toronto ON M5E 1X8, CANADA

Kursinski, Anne (Athlete, Horse Racer, Olympic Athlete)
107 Spring Hill Rd
Frenchtown, NJ 08825-3019, USA

Kurt, Gary (Athlete, Hockey Player)
Waterloo Regional Police
11 Wasaga Woods Cir
Wasaga Beach, ON L9Z 2N1, Canada

Kurtag, Gyorgy (Composer)
Lihego V3
Veroce 2621, HUNGARY

Kurtenbach, Orland J (Athlete, Hockey Player)
14066 29a Ave
Surrey, BC V4P 2J8, Canada

Kurth, Wallace (Wally) (Actor, Musician)
2143 N Valley Dr
Manhattan Beach, CA 90266, USA

Kurtis, Bill (Television Host)
c/o Staff Member *Kurtis Productions*
400 W Erie St #500
Chicago, IL 60610, USA

Kurtis, Dalene (Actor)
c/o Juliette Harris *It Girl Public Relations*
5301 Beethoven St
Suite 220
Los Angeles, CA 90066, USA

Kurtz, Hal (Athlete, Baseball Player)
511 Flat Iron Square Rd
Church Hill, MD 21623-1269, USA

Kurtz, Swoosie (Actor)
c/o Konrad Leh *Creative Talent Group*
1900 Avenue of the Stars
Suite 2475
Los Angeles, CA 90067, USA

Kurtzberg, Joanne (Physicist)
Duke University
Medical Center
Durham, NC 27708, USA

Kurtzman, Alex (Producer)
c/o BeBe Lerner *ID Public Relations (ID-LA)*
7060 Hollywood Blvd
8th Floor
Los Angeles, CA 90028, USA

Kurtzman, Katy (Actor, Director)
c/o Staff Member *Lynn Production & Mgmt*
20411 Chapter Dr
Woodland Hills, CA 91364, USA

Kurvers, Tom (Athlete, Hockey Player)
10146 Birch Grove Rd
Brainerd, MN 56401-3173, USA

Kurvers, Tom
Tampa Bay Lightning
401 Channelside Dr
Attn: Asst General Manager
Tamoa, FL 33602-5400, USA

Kurylenko, Olga (Actor)
c/o Joel Lubin *Creative Artists Agency (CAA-LA)*
2000 Ave Of The Stars
Los Angeles, CA 90067, USA

Kuryluk, Merve (Athlete, Hockey Player)
63 Alexandra Ave
Yorkton, SK S3N 2J6, Canada

Kurys, Sophie (Athlete, Baseball Player, Commentator)
8301 E Fairmount Ave
Scottsdale, AZ 85251-4835, USA

Kurz, Sabina (Stylist)
c/o Staff Member *Bryan Bantry*
900 Broadway Ste 400
New York, NY 10003, USA

Kurzweil, Raymond (Inventor)
Kurzwell Applied Intelligence
411 Waverly Oaks Road
Waltham, MA 02452, USA

Kusama, Karyn (Director)
Endeavor Talent Agency
9701 Wilshire Blvd
#1000
Beverly Hills, CA 90212, USA

Kusatsu, Clyde (Actor)
Paradign Agency
10100 Santa Monica Blvd
#2500
Los Angeles, CA 90067, USA

Kush, Frank (Athlete, Football Player)
113 E Loma Vista Dr
Tempe, AZ 85282-3574, USA

Kush, Rod (Athlete, Football Player)
45 Willow Point Dr
Ashland, NE 68003-9408, USA

Kushboo (Actor, Bollywood)
20/1 Arch Bshap
Mithyas Ave Boat Club Road
Chennai, TN 600018, INDIA

Kushell, Lisa (Actor)
c/o Staff Member *Abrams Artists Agency (LA)*
9200 Sunset Blvd
11th Floor
Los Angeles, CA 90069, USA

Kushner, Dale (Athlete, Hockey Player)
202-1260 Wally Rd
Comox, BC V9M 3N9, CANADA

Kushner, Dave (Musician)
4234 Babcock Ave
Studio City, CA 91604, USA

Kushner, Harold S (Writer)
145 Hartford St
Natick, MA 01760

Kushner, Robert E (Artist)
DC Moore Gallery
724 5th Ave
New York, NY 10019, USA

Kushner, Tony (Writer)
c/o Staff Member *Creative Artists Agency (CAA-LA)*
2000 Ave Of The Stars
Los Angeles, CA 90067, USA

Kuske, Kevin (Athlete)
BSD
An der Schlessstatte 4
Berchtesgaden 83471, GERMANY

Kusnitz, Jared (Actor)
c/o TJ McMurdo *McMurdo Management & Associates*
1616 N Fuller Ave
313
Los Angeles, CA 90046, USA

Kusnyer, Art (Athlete, Baseball Player)
6598 Taeda Dr
Sarasota, FL 34241-9145, USA

Kusturica, Emir (Actor, Director, Musician, Writer)
Fondazione Culturale Edison
Largo VIII Marzo, 9
Parma 43100, ITALY

Kutcher, Ashton (Actor, Producer)
c/o Stephanie Simon *Untitled Entertainment (LA)*
350 S. Beverly Dr #200
Beverly Hills, CA 90212, USA

Kutcher, Randy (Athlete, Baseball Player)
3016 Purple Sage Ln
Palmdale, CA 93550-7972, USA

Kuti, Fela (Musician)
Rosebud Agency
PO Box 170429
San Francisco, CA 94117, USA

Kutless (Musician)
c/o Staff Member *WmE2 (WMA-TN)*
1600 Division St
Suite 300
Nashville, TN 37203, USA

Kutner, Rob (Writer)
c/o Staff Member *Kaplan Stahler Agency*
8383 Wilshire Blvd
Suite 923
Beverly Hills, CA 90211, USA

Kutsugeras, Kelle (Stylist)
c/o Staff Member *Celestine - CA*
1666 20th St
#200-B
Santa Monica, CA 90404, USA

Kuttner, Robert (Writer)
c/o Staff Member *Chelsea Green Publishing*
85 N Main St
Suite 120
White River Jct, VT 05001, USA

Kuttner, Stephan G (Historian)
2270 Le Conte Ave
#601
Berkeley, CA 94709, USA

Kutty, Padmini (Actor, Bollywood)
33 1st Street Kamdar Nagar
Nungambakkam
Chennai, TN 600034, INDIA

Kutyna, Donald J (General)
4818 Kenyon Court
Colorado Springs, CO 80917, USA

Kutyna, Marty (Athlete, Baseball Player)
2255 NW 14th St
Delray Beach, FL 33445-2610, USA

Kutz, Mae
140 Buckingham Ct
Goodlettsville, TN 37072

Kutzler, Jerry (Athlete, Baseball Player)
8415 27th Ave
Kenosha, WI 53143-6232, USA

Kuykendall, Fulton (Athlete, Football Player)
1497 Rucker Cir
Woodstock, GA 30188, USA

Kuykendall, John W (Educator)
Davidson College
President's Office
Davidson, NC 28036, USA

Kuzava, Bob (Athlete, Baseball Player)
1118 Vinewood St
Wyandotte, MI 48192-4945, USA

Kuziel, Bob (Athlete, Football Player)
3375 Walnut Dr
Ellicott City, MD 21043, USA

Kuzmicz, George (Athlete, Hockey Player)
12 Devonridge Cres
Scarborough, ON M1C SAS, Canada

Kuznetsoff, Alexel (Musician)
Columbia Artists Mgmt Inc
165 W 57th St
New York, NY 10019, USA

Kuzyk, Ken
5 McEnroe Dr
Londonderry, NH 03053-3042, USA

Kuzyk, Mimi (Actor)
Artists Agency
1180 S Beverly Dr
#301
Los Angeles, CA 90035, USA

Kvapil, Travis (Race Car Driver)
Doug Yates Racing
112 Byers Creek Rd.
Mooresville, NC 28117, USA

Kvasha, Oleg (Athlete, Hockey Player)
22 Bluff Rd
Glen Cove, NY 11542, USA

Kvitova, Petra (Athlete, Tennis Player)
c/o Staff Member *Women's Tennis Association (WTA (UK))*
Palliser House
Palliser Rd
London W149EB, UK

Kwalick, Thaddeus J (Ted) (Athlete, Football Player)
755 Purdue Ct
Santa Clara, CA 95051, USA

Kwan, Jennie (Actor)
Innovative Artists
1505 10th St
Santa Monica, CA 90401, USA

Kwan, Michelle (Athlete, Figure Skater, Olympic Athlete)
c/o Staff Member *Champions on Ice*
Tom Collins Enterprises Inc
3500 W 80th St
Minneapolis, MN 55431, USA

Kwan, Nancy (Actor)
Marlin
252 7th Ave #9P
New York, NY 10001, USA

Kwanten, Ryan (Actor)
c/o Orly Adelson *Orly Adelson Management*
12304 Santa Monica Blvd
Suite 115
Los Angeles, CA 90025, USA

Kwapis, Ken (Comedian, Director, Producer)
c/o Staff Member *In Cahoots*
4024 Radford Ave
Editorial Bldg 2 #7
Studio City, CA 91604, USA

Kwasniewski, Aleksander (President)
Kancelaria Prezydenta RP
Ul Wiejska 4/8
Warsaw 00-902, POLAND

Kweli, Talib (Musician)
c/o Steve Levine *ICM Partners (ICM-LA)*
10250 Constellation Blvd Fl 7
Los Angeles, CA 90067, USA

Kweli, Talieb (Musician)
c/o Steve Levine *ICM Partners (ICM-LA)*
10250 Constellation Blvd Fl 7
Los Angeles, CA 90067, USA

Kweller, Ben (Musician)
c/o Staff Member *Paradigm (Monterey)*
404 W Franklin St
Monterey, CA 93940, USA

Kwiatkowski, Joel (Athlete, Hockey Player)
2020 Tall Pines Dr SE
Grand Rapids, MI 49546-7923, USA

Kwoh, Yik San (Engineer)
Memorial Medical Center
PO Box 1428
Long Beach, CA 90801, USA

Kwolek, Stephanie L (Inventor)
312 Spalding Road
Wilmington, DE 19803-2422, USA

Kwon, Boa (Musician)
c/o Staff Member *Creative Artists Agency (CAA-LA)*
2000 Ave Of The Stars
Los Angeles, CA 90067, USA

Kwong, Larry
178 Oakbriar Close SW
Calgary, AB T2V 5G6, Canada

Kwong, Norman Honorable (Athlete, Football Player)
178 Oakbriar Close SW
Calgary, AB T2V 5G6, Canada

Kwouk, Burt (Actor)
Diamond Mgmt
31 Percey St
London W1T 2DD, UNITED KINGDOM (UK)

Kydland, Finn (Nobel Prize Laureate)
169 Noble Ln
Worthington, PA 16262-9405, USA

Kyl, Jon (Politician)
4442 E Camelback Rd
Unit 160, Phoenix AZ, 85018-2838

Kyle, Aaron (Athlete, Football Player)
8544 Townley Rd Apt 2M
Huntersville, NC 28078-1868, USA

Kyle, David L (Business Person)
ONEOK Inc
100 W 5th St
PO Box 871
Tulsa, OK 74102, USA

Kyle, Jason (Athlete, Football Player)
16801 Jetton Rd
Cornelius, NC 28031-7445, USA

Kyle, Richardson (Athlete, Football Player)
3516 Balmar Mews Rd
Baltimore, MD 21211-1471, USA

Kyles, Stan (Athlete, Baseball Player)
827 Old Wvnd Ct
Spartanburg, SC 29301-4231, USA

Kyles, Whitney (Stylist)
c/o Staff Member *Dawn to Dusk Image Agency*
8306 Wilshire Blvd
#412
Beverly Hills, CA 30211, USA

Kylian, Jiri (Dancer)
Dance Theatre
Scheldeldoekshaven 60
Gravenhage, EN 2511, NETHERLANDS

Kyo, Machiko (Actor)
Olimpia Copu
6-35 JinguMae
Shibuyaku
Tokyo, JAPAN

Kypreos, Nick (Athlete, Hockey Player)
c/o Staff Member *Rogers Sportsnet (Toronto)*
9 Channel Nine Crt
Toronto, ON M1S 4B5, Canada

Kysar, Jeff (Athlete, Football Player)
570 June St
Rialto, CA 92376, USA

Kyte, Jim (Athlete, Hockey Player)
226 Sherwood Dr
Ottawa, ON K1Y 3V8, Canada

Laaksonen, Antti (Athlete, Hockey Player)
9225 Red Oak Dr
Victoria, MN 55386-4515, USA

Laatasi, Kamuta (Prime Minister)
Prime Minister's Office
Vaiaku
Funafuti, TUVALU

Laaveg, Paul (Athlete, Football Player)
PO Box 406
Berryville, VA 22611-0406, USA

Labaff, Ernie (Misc)
Aluminum Brick Glass Workers Union
3362 Hollenberg
Bridgeton, MO 63044, USA

Labandeira, Josh (Athlete, Baseball Player)
2166 W Cricklewood Ct
Porterville, CA 93257-6270, USA

Labarbera, Jason
8184 E Wingspan Way
Scottsdale, AZ 85255-6451, usa

L'Abbe, Moe (Athlete, Hockey Player)
4520 Golden Triangle Blvd
Fort Worth, TX 76244-6316, USA

Labeaux, Sandy (Athlete, Football Player)
PO Box 3132
San Ramon, CA 94583-8132, USA

LaBeef, Sleepy (Musician)
14469 E Highway 264
Lowell, AR 72745, USA

Labelle, Marc
5705 Eagle Creek Ct
Maineville, OH 45039-7204, USA

LaBelle, Patti (Musician)
c/o Patti Webster *W&W PR*
476 Union Ave
2nd Floor
Middlesex, NJ 08846, USA

Labelle, Rob (Actor)
c/o Staff Member *Elizabeth Hodgson Management Group*
1688 Cypress St
Suite 405
Vancouver, BC V6J 5J1, Canada

LaBeouf, Shia (Actor)
c/o John Crosby *Crosby/Spilo Management*
1310 N Spaulding Ave
Los Angeles, CA 90046, USA

Labeque, Katia (Musician)
Columbia Artists Mgmt Inc
165 W 57th St
New York, NY 10019, USA

Labeque, Marielle (Musician)
Columbia Artists Mgmt Inc
165 W 57th St
New York, NY 10019, USA

Laber, Honey Jeanne (Stylist)
235 W 102nd St
#10-D
New York, NY 10025, USA

Labeyrie, Antoine (Astronomer)
Haute-Provence Observatoire
Saint-Michael Observatolre
FRANCE

Labine, Tyler (Actor)
c/o Jason Heyman *Creative Artists Agency (CAA-LA)*
2000 Ave Of The Stars
Los Angeles, CA 90067, USA

Labiosa, David (Actor)
c/o Daryl Kane *Guinan Management*
4942 Vineland Ave
#111
North Hollywood, CA 91601, USA

Labonte, Bobby (Race Car Driver)
Petty Enterprises
112 Byers Creek Rd
Mooresville, NC 28117, USA

Labonte, Justin (Race Car Driver)
PO Box 843
Trinity, NC 27370, USA

Labonte, Terry (Race Car Driver)
1100 Clodfelter Rd
Winston Salem, NC 27107-8806, USA

Laborde, Alden J (Business Person)
63 Oriole St
New Orleans, LA 70124, USA

Labossiere, Gord (Athlete, Hockey Player)
114 Rue De Faubourg
RR 5 RPO
Saint-Ferreol-Les-Neiges, QC G0A 3R0, Canada

Labounty, Matt (Athlete, Football Player)
360 W 17th Ave
Eugene, OR 98125, USA

Labounty_, Matt (Athlete, Football Player)
360 W 17th Ave
Eugene, OR 97401-3859, USA

Labovitch, Max (Athlete, Hockey Player)
22 Ashbury Bay
Winnipeg, MB R2V 2T4, Canada

Laboy, Travis (Athlete, Football Player)
1567 E Prescott Ct
Chandler, AZ 85249-4798, USA

Labraaten, Dan (Athlete, Hockey Player)
Byrviken 303
Leksand S-79392, Sweden

Labrador, Honey (Actor, Television Host)
c/o Staff Member *Last Bastion Entertainment*
459 S Sycamore Ave
Los Angeles, CA 90036, USA

Labre, Yvon (Athlete, Hockey Player)
7812 Til mont Ave
Parkville, MD 21234-5539, USA

Labrinth (Music Group)
c/o Staff Member *WmE2 (WMA-UK)*
103 New Oxford St
London WC1A 1DD, UK

La Brode, Richard (Scientist)
2710 Village Dale Ave
Houston, TX 77059-3573, 77059-3573

LaBute, Neil (Director, Writer)
c/o Brad Gross *Brad Gross Agency, The*
161 S Arden Blvd
Los Angeles, CA 90004, USA

Labyorteaux, Matthew (Actor)
10808 Hartsook Street
N Hollywood, CA 91601, USA

Labyorteaux, Patrick (Actor)
c/o Kim Dorr *Defining Artists Agency*
10 Universal City Plaza
Suite 2000
Universal City, CA 91608, USA

Lacasse, Ryan (Athlete, Football Player)
3 Gaslight Ln
North Easton, MA 02356-2721, USA

Lacefield, Reggie (Athlete, Basketball Player)
674 Old School House Rd
Middletown, DE 19709-9690, USA

Lacefield, T Cleon (Scientist)
14202 Golf View Trl
Houston, TX 77059-4403, USA

Lacey, Bob (Athlete, Baseball Player)
7623 E Decatur St
Mesa, AZ 85207-5728, USA

Lacey, Chonn (Athlete, Football Player)
1314 W Ontario St
Philadelphia, PA 19140, USA

Lacey, Deborah (Actor)
1801 Ave of Stars #1250
Los Angeles, CA 90067, USA

Lacey, Jeff (Boxer)
Gary Shaw Productions LLC
33 Divan Way
Wayne, NJ 07470-5201, USA

Lach, Elmer J (Athlete, Hockey Player)
89 Bayview Ave.
Pointe Claire, QC H9S 5C4, Canada

Lachance, Michael (Mike) (Race Car Driver)
183 Sweetmans Lane
Englishtown, NJ 07726, USA

Lachance, Michel (Horse Racer)
183 Sweetmans Ln
Millstone Township, NJ 08535-8107, USA

Lachance, Scott (Athlete, Hockey Player, Olympic Athlete)
15 Meadow View Ln
Andover, MA 01810-4759, USA

LaChapelle, David (Artist, Photographer)
HSI Productions
601 W 26th St #1420
New York, NY 10001, USA

Lachapelle, Sean (Athlete, Football Player)
9860 Izilda Ct
Sacramento, CA 95829-8167, USA

LaChappelle, Sean P (Athlete, Football Player)
8724 Lodestone Cir
Elk Grove, CA 95624, USA

Lachemann, Bill (Athlete, Baseball Player)
208 Riverview Ln
Great falls, MT 59404-1523, USA

Lachemann, Marcel E (Athlete, Baseball Player, Coach)
PO Box 587
Penrvn, CA 95663-0587, USA

Lachemann, Rene G (Athlete, Baseball Player, Coach)
7500 E Boulders Pkwy
Unit 66
Scottsdale, AZ 85266-1212, USA

Lacher, Blaine (Athlete, Hockey Player)
29 Shannon Cres SE
Medicine Hat, AB T1B 4C2, Canada

Lachey, Drew (Musician, Television Host)
c/o Jeremy Katz *Katz Company, The*
1674 Broadway
7th Floor
New York, NY 10019, USA

Lachey, James M (Jim) (Athlete, Football Player)
1445 Roxbury Road
Apt G
Columbus, OH 43212, USA

Lachey, Nick (Musician)
c/o Colton Gramm *Brillstein Entertainment Partners*
9150 Wilshire Blvd #350
Beverly Hills, CA 90212, USA

Lachhiman, Gurung (War Hero)
Village Dahakhani
Village Development Conmelle
Ward 4, Chitwan, NEPAL

Lachowicz, Al (Athlete, Baseball Player)
1000 Sunset Bav Ct
Granburv, TX 76048-1239, USA

Lachowicz, Al (Athlete, Baseball Player)
1000 Sunset Bav Ct
Granburv, TX 76048-1239, USA

Lachter, Sylvia (Stylist)
136 W 24th St
New York, NY 10011, USA

Lacina, Corbin (Athlete, Football Player)
1550 Skyline Ct
Saint Paul, MN 55121-1148, USA

Lackey, Brad (Race Car Driver)
Badco
35 Monument Plaza
Pleasant Hill, CA 94523, USA

Lackey, John (Athlete, Baseball Player)
10 Shore Walk
Newport Coast, CA 92657-2158, USA

Lackey, Mercedes (Writer)
c/o Staff Member *JABberwocky Literary Agency*
P.O. Box 4558
Sunnyside, NY 11104-0558, USA

Laclavere, Georges (Physicist)
53 Ave de Breteuil
Paris 75007, FRANCE

Laclotte, Michel R (Director)
10 Bis Rue du Pre-aux-Clerc
Paris 75007, FRANCE

Iacocca, Lee (Misc)
430 Dalehurst Ave
Los Angeles, CA 90024-2514, USA

Lacock, Pete (Athlete, Baseball Player)
10019 Mackey Cir
Overland Park, KS 66212-3461, USA

Lacombe, Henri (Oceanographer)
20 Bis Ave de Lattre de Tassigny
Bourg-la-Reine 92340, FRANCE

Lacombe, Norman
Lacombe and Dempsey Hockey Impact Centre
103-4330 Black Gold Dr
Leduc, AB T9E 3C3, Canada

Lacorte, Frank (Athlete, Baseball Player)
1667 El Dorado Dr
Gilroy, CA 95020-3754, USA

Lacoss, Mike (Athlete, Baseball Player)
145 Countv Road 816
Higdon, AL 35979-9126, USA

Lacoste, Catherine (Golfer)
Calle B6
#4 El Soto de la Moraleja Alcobendas
Madrid, SPAIN

La Costeña, Banda (Music Group)
c/o Staff Member *BMG*
1540 Broadway
New York, NY 10036, USA

Lacouture, Dan
125 Lakeview Dr
Centerville, MA 02632-1416, USA

Lacroix, Andre J (Athlete, Hockey Player)
115 S Franklin St
Chagrin Falls, OH 44022-3214, USA

LaCroix, Christian
73 rue du Faubourg-St.-Honore
Paris, FRANCE F-75008

Lacroix, Christian M M (Designer, Fashion Designer)
73 Rue du Faubourg Saint Honore
Paris 75008, FRANCE

Lacroix, Dan
Tampa Bay Lightning
401 Channelside Dr
Attn Coaching Staff
Tampa, FL 33602-5400, USA

Iacroix, Eric (Athlete, Hockey Player)
Colorado Avalanche
1000 Chopper Cir
Denver, CO 80204-5805

Lacrosse, Dave (Athlete, Football Player)
1712 Harmon Rd
Conshohocken, PA 19428, USA

Lacy, Alan (Business Person)
Sears Roebuck Co
3333 Beverly Blvd
Hoffman Estates, IL 60179, USA

Lacy, Kerry (Athlete, Baseball Player)
145 Countv Road 816
Higdon, AL 35979-9126, USA

Lacy, Lee (Athlete, Baseball Player)
Lee Lacy Baseball Academy
6310 Neveda Ave
Apt E420
Woodland Hills, CA 91367-3437, USA

Lacy, Raymon (Athlete, Baseball Player)
2860 State Highway 63 W
Wiergate, TX 75977-9783, USA

Lacy Clay Jr., William (Congressman, Politician)
2418 Rayburn HOB
Washington, DC 20515, USA

Ladd, Andrew (Athlete, Hockey Player)
16821 Crystal Ct
Tinley Park, IL 60477-2779

Ladd, Carol (Stylist)
2867 SW Montgomery Dr
Portland, OR 97201, USA

Ladd, Cheryl (Actor)
P.O. Box 1329
Santa Ynez, CA 93460, USA

Ladd, David (Actor)
9212 Hazen Dr
Beverly Hills, CA 90210, USA

Ladd, Diane (Actor)
c/o Scott Hart *Scott Hart Entertainment*
14622 Ventura Blvd
#746
Sherman Oaks, CA 91403, USA

Ladd, Jim (Radio Personality, Writer)
3321 South La Cienega
Los Angeles, CA 90016, USA

Ladd, Jordan (Actor)
c/o Staff Member *Kritzer Levine Wilkins Entertainment (KLWG)*
11872 La Grange Ave
1st Floor
Los Angeles, CA 90025, USA

Ladd, Margaret (Actor)
c/o Staff Member *Abrams Artists Agency (LA)*
9200 Sunset Blvd
11th Floor
Los Angeles, CA 90069, USA

Ladd, Pete (Athlete, Baseball Player)
239 Town Farm Rd
New Gloucester, ME 04260-4438, USA

Ladd Jr, Alan
c/o Staff Member *Ladd Company, The*
9465 Wilshire Blvd #910
Beverly Hills, CA 90210, USA

Laden, Nina B
6750 26th Ave NW
Seattle, WA 98117-5828, USA

Laderman, Exra (Composer)
Yale University
Music School
New Haven, CT 06520, USA

Ladin, Eric (Actor)
c/o Staff Member *Main Title Entertainment*
8383 Wilshire Blvd
Suite 408
Los Angeles, CA 90211, USA

Ladouceur, L P (Athlete, Football Player)
3807 Prescott Ave Unit B
Dallas, TX 75219-2238, USA

Ladouceur, Randy (Athlete, Hockey Player)
1221 Cross Creek Cir #F7
Greenville, NC 27834-5094, CANADA

Lady Antebellum (Music Group)
c/o Daniel Miller *Borman Entertainment (TN)*
4322 Harding Pike #429
Nashville, TN 37205, USA

Ladygo, Pete (Athlete, Football Player)
124 Orchard St
Keyser, WV 26726-3153, USA

Ladysmith Black Mambazo (Musician)
326-D Ridge Road
Cedar Grove, NJ 07009, USA

Laemmle, Carla (Actor)
645 N Serrano Ave
Hollywood, CA 90004, USA

Laeru, Brad
133 Lanigan Cres
Stittsville, ON K2S 1G9, Canada

Laettner, Christian (Athlete, Basketball Player, Olympic Athlete)
1225 Church Rd
Angola, NY 14006-8831, USA

LaFave, Debra
2220 Nichols Road
Lithia, Florida 33547-2230, USA

Laferriere, Rick (Athlete, Hockey Player)
RE/MAX Chay Realty
152 Bayfield St
Barrie, ON L4M 3B5, Canada

Laffer, Arthur (Doctor)
5375 Exec Sq #330
La Jolla, CA 92037, USA

Laffer, Arthur B (Economist)
24255 Pacific Coast Highway
Malibu, CA 90263, USA

Lafferty, James (Actor)
c/o Eric Nelson *Zero Gravity Management (II)*
9255 Sunset Blvd
Suite 1010
Los Angeles, CA 90069, USA

Laffey, Aaron (Architect, Baseball Player)
32301 Monaco Pl
Avon Lake, OH 44012-2567, USA

Laffite, Jacques
Technopole de la Nievre
Magny Cours, FRANCE F-58470

Laffitte, Havana (Stylist)
c/o Staff Member *Art Department*
48 Greene St
4th Floor
New York, NY 10013, USA

Lafforgue, Laurent (Mathematician)
IHES
Mathematics Dept
Bures-sur-Yvette 91440, FRANCE

LaFleur, Art (Actor)
c/o Joel King *Pakula/King & Associates*
9229 Sunset Blvd
Suite 315
Los Angeles, CA 90069, USA

Lafleur, David (Athlete, Football Player)
3900 Thompson Rd
Sulphur, LA 70665, USA

Lafleur, Greg (Athlete, Football Player)
2911 Rene Beauregard Ave
Baton Rouge, LA 70820-5712, USA

La Fleur, Guy (Athlete, Hockey Player)
14 Pl. du Moulin
Lolle-Bizard, QC H9E 1N2, CANADA

Lafleur, Guy (Athlete, Hockey Player)
Montreal Canadiens
1275 Rue Saint-Antoine 0
Montreal, QC H3C 5L2, Canada

Lafleur, Guy D (Athlete, Hockey Player)
14 Place du Molin
L'Ile-Bizard, QC H9E 1N2, Canada

Lafley, Alan G (Business Person)
Procter & Gamble Co
1 Procter & Gamble Plaza
Cincinnati, OH 45202, USA

La Fong, Michelle
3855 Shore Parkway #1D
Brooklyn, NY 11235

Lafontaine, Oskar (Government Official)
Landtag Saarland
Postfach 101833
Saarbrucken 66018, GERMANY

LaFontaine, Patrick (Pat) (Athlete, Hockey Player, Olympic Athlete)
Companions in Courage
PO Box 768
Huntington, NY 11743-0768

Laforest, Pete (Athlete, Baseball Player)
2212 Lansing Ave
Portage, MI 49002-3630, USA

LaForge, Claude (Athlete, Hockey Player)
122-1975 Ch du Fer A Cheval
Ste-Julie, QC J3E OB7, Canada

LaFosse, Robert (Choreographer)
New York City Ballet
Lincoln Center Plaza
New York, NY 10023, USA

Laframboise, Pete (Athlete, Hockey Player)

Lafrancois, Roger (Athlete, Baseball Player)
64 Aspinook St
Jewett City, CT 06351-1802, USA

Lafrate, Al (Athlete, Hockey Player)
7975 Five Mile Rd.
Livonia, MI 48154, USA

La Frenais, Ian (Director, Producer, Writer)
c/o Bruce Kaufman *ICM Partners (ICM-LA)*
10250 Constellation Blvd Fl 7
Los Angeles, CA 90067, USA

Lafreniere, Jason (Athlete, Hockey Player)
261 Front Rd W RR 1
1 L'Orignal, ON K0B IK0, Canada

Lafreniere, Roger (Athlete, Hockey Player)
110 Eugene Rd
North Bay, ON P1B 8B7, Canada

LaFrentz, Raef (Athlete, Basketball Player)
PO Box 220
Adel, IA 50003-0220, USA

Lafton, James D (Athlete, Football Player)
15487 Mesquite Tree Trl
Poway, CA 92064, USA

Laga, Mike (Athlete, Baseball Player)
148 Maple Ridge Rd
Florence, MA 01062-9749, USA

Laga'aia, Jay (Actor)
Karen Kay Management
PO Box 446
Auckland, NEW ZEALAND

Lagace, Jean-Guy (Athlete, Hockey Player)
6420 Ziklag Cir
Birmingham, AL 35235-2160

Lagace, Pierre (Athlete, Hockey Player)
2403 Brooksboro Dr
Erie, PA 16510-4053

Lagana, Jr., Bobby (Race Car Driver)
72 Woodruff Ave.
Scarsdale, NY 10583, USA

Lagana, Sr., Bobby (Race Car Driver)
72 Woodruff Ave.
Scarsdale, NY 10583, USA

Lagarde, Thomas (Basketball Player, Olympic Athlete)
3809 E Greensboro Chapel Hill Rd
Snow Camp, NC 27349-9841, USA

Lagarde, Tom (Athlete, Basketball Player, Olympic Athlete)
3809 E Greensboro Chapel Hill Rd
Snow Camp, NC 27349-9841, USA

Lagasse, Emeril (Chef)
829 Saint Charles St
New Orleans, LA 70130, USA

Lagasse, Jr., Scott (Race Car Driver)
JTG Racing
7201 Caldwell Rd.
Harrisburg, NC 28075, USA

Lagatd, Bernar (Athlete, Olympic Athlete, Track Athlete)
9121 E Cottonwood Ct
Tucson, AZ 85749-9783, USA

Lagattuta, Bill (Correspondent)
CBS-TV
News Dept
7800 Beverly Blvd
Los Angeles, CA 90036, USA

Lagedrost, Kelly (Athlete, Golfer)
10011 Kimbrough Dr
Brooksville, FL 34601, USA

Lageman, Jeff (Athlete, Football Player)
2907 Forest Cir
Jacksonville, FL 32257, USA

Lagerberg, Bengt (Musician)
Motor SE
Gotabergs Gatan 2
Gothenburg 400 14, SWEDEN

Lagerfeld, Karl (Designer, Fashion Designer)
Chanel
29-31 Rue Cambon
Paris 75001, France

Lagerfelt, Caroline (Actor)
8730 Sunset Blvd
#480
Los Angeles, CA 90069, USA

Laghi, Pio Cardinal (Religious Leader)
Catholic Education Congregation
Piazza Pio XII 3
Rome 00193, ITALY

Lago, David (Actor)
c/o Mark Robert *Mark Robert Management*
2208 Patricia Ave
Los Angeles, CA 90064, USA

Lagod, Chet (Athlete, Football Player)
7016 Rocky Trl
Chattanooga, TN 37421, USA

Lagoo, Shreeram (Actor, Bollywood)
3 Gold Mist 36 Carter Road
Bandra
Bombay, MS 400 050, INDIA

Lagos, Richard (President)
President's Office
Palacio de la Monedo
Santiago, CHILE

Lagrand, Morris (Athlete, Football Player)
4419 Ellenwood Ave
Saint Louis, MO 63161, USA

LaGravenese, Richard (Director, Producer, Writer)
c/o Staff Member *Writers Co-Op*
4000 Warner Blvd
Bldg 1
Burbank, CA 91522, USA

Lagrone, John (Athlete, Football Player)
1416 Marigold St
Borger, TX 79007-6440, USA

Lagrossa, Stephanie (Reality TV Star)
c/o Jamie Lopez
The Actors Group
3400 Beacon Avenue South
Seattle, WA 98144, USA

Lagrow, Lerrin (Athlete, Baseball Player)
12271 E Turquoise Ave
Scottsdale, AZ 85259-5105, USA

Laguardia, Ernesto (Actor)
c/o Gabriel Blanco *Gabriel Blanco Iglesias (Mexico)*
Rio Balsas 35-32
Colonia Cuauhtemoc
DF 06500, Mexico

Laguna, Frederica de (Misc)
Quadrangle
10 South Bryn Mawr Avenue
Bryn Mawr, PA 19010-3213, USA

Laguna, Ismael (Boxer)
Panama Zona 6
Entrega General
PANAMA

Lahache, Floyd (Athlete, Hockey Player)
Kahnawake
Kahnawake, QC J0L 1B0, Canada

Lahaie, Dick (Race Car Driver)
Drag Racing HOF
13700 SW 16th Ave
Ocala, FL 34473, USA

Lahair, Bryan (Athlete, Baseball Player)
13712 W Country
Gables Dr
Surprise, AZ 85379-8335, USA

LaHaye, Tim (Writer)
Tyndale House Publishers
351 Executive Dr
PO Box 80
Wheaton, IL 60189, USA

Lahbib, Simone (Actor)
c/o Staff Member *Ken McReddie Ltd*
11 Connaught Pl
London W2 2ET, UNITED KINGDOM

Lahgenbrunner, Jamie (Athlete, Hockey Player)
94233 Warloe Shore Ln
Moose Lake, MN 55767-6713, USA

Lahiri, Jhumpa (Writer)
Houghton Mifflin
222 Berkeley St
#700
Boston, MA 02116, USA

Lahood, Mike (Athlete, Football Player)
23816 S Bronze Dr
Sun Lakes, AZ 85248-0851, USA

Lahoud, Joe (Athlete, Baseball Player)
90 Tinker Hill Rd
New Preston Marble Dale,
CT 06777-1415, USA

Lahould, Emile (President)
Presidential Palace
Baabda
Beirut, LEBANON

Lahti, Christine (Actor, Director)
c/o David Seltzer *Management 360*
9111 Wilshire Blvd
Beverly Hills, CA 90210, USA

Lahti, Jeff (Athlete, Baseball Player)
4632 Tyler Dr
Hood River, OR 97031-9742, USA

Lai, Francis (Composer)
23 Rue Franklin
Paris 75016, FRANCE

Laich, Brooks (Athlete, Hockey Player)
PO Box 471
Wawota, SK S0G SA0, Canada

Laidlaw, Scott (Athlete, Football Player)
209 Peyton Leann Pt
La Vergne, TN 37086-3293, USA

Laidlaw, Tom (Athlete, Hockey Player)
Laidlaw Sports Management
32 Ridge Blvd
Port Chester, NY 10573-2120

Laidler, Keith J (Scientist)
5 Arundel Ave
Ottawa, ON K1K 0B1, Canada

Lail, Leah (Actor)
c/o Staff Member *Diverse Talent Group*
9911 W Pico Blvd Ste 340W
Los Angeles, CA 90035, USA

Laimbeer, Bill (Athlete, Basketball Player)
470 Gray Ct
Marco Island, FL 34145-1939, USA

Laine, Cleo (Musician)
Acker's Int'l Jazz
53 Cambridge Mansions
London SW11 4RX, UNITED KINGDOM
(UK)

Laine, Dame Cleo
The Old Rectory Wavendon
Milton Keynes, ENGLAND MK17 8LT

Laine, Skylar (Musician)
c/o Staff Member *19 Entertainment - LA*
9000 W Sunset Blvd #1574
West Hollywood, CA 90069, USA

Laing, Bill (Athlete, Hockey Player)
PO Box 88
Harris, SK S0L 1K0, Canada

Laing, Quintin (Athlete, Hockey Player)
PO Box 88
Harris, SK S0L IK0, Canada

Laingen, L Bruce (Diplomat)
5627 Old Chester Road
Bethesda, MD 20814, USA

Laird, Bruce (Athlete, Football Player)
20 Stone Ridge Ct
Baltimore, MD 21239, USA

Laird, Dean (General)
160 Acacia Way
Coronado, CA 92118-2421, USA

Laird, Gerald (Athlete, Baseball Player)
13735 E Yucca St
Scottsdale, AZ 85259-4641, USA

Laird, Melvin R (Politician)
16676 Bobcat Dr
Fort Myers, FL 33908-4325, USA

Laird, Peter (Cartoonist)
PO Box 417
Haydenville, MA 01039-0417, USA

Laird, Ron (Athlete, Olympic Athlete, Track Athlete)
4706 Diane Dr.
Ashtabula, OH 44004, USA

Laird, Ronald (Ron) (Athlete, Track Athlete)
4706 Diane Dr
Ashtabuta, OH 44004, USA

Laithwaite, Eric R (Engineer)
Imperial College
Electrical Engineering Dept
London SW7 2BT, UNITED KINGDOM
(UK)

Laitman, Jeffrey (Misc)
Mount Sinai Medical Center
Anatomy Dept
1 Lavy Place
New York, NY 10029, USA

Lajeunesse, Serge (Athlete, Hockey Player)
33 Rue Larocque E
Sainte-Agathe-Des-Monts, QC J8C 1H8,
Canada

LaJoie, Jon (Comedian)
c/o Trevor Engelson *Underground Management*
447 S. Highland Ave.
Los Angeles, CA 90036, USA

LaJoie, Randy (Race Car Driver)
Phoenix Racing
S Industrial Park #7
Mooresville, NC 28115, USA

Lajole, Bill (Baseball Player)
Detroit Tigers
456 Yacht Harbor Dr
Osprey, FL 34229-9744, USA

Lakatos, Josh (Athlete, Olympic Athlete, Shooter)
3180 Milton St
Pasadena, CA 91107-4526, USA

Lake, Antwan (Athlete, Football Player)
1032 Bluebell Dr
Dacula, GA 30019-7855, USA

Lake, Carnell A (Athlete, Football Player)
P.O. Box 55048
Irvine, CA 92619, USA

Lake, Don (Actor, Writer)
c/o Gayle Divine *Divine Management*
3822 Latrobe St
Los Angeles, CA 90031

Lake, Greg (Musician)
Asia
9 Hillgate St
London W8 7SP, UNITED KINGDOM (UK)

Lake, James A (Biologist)
University of California
Molecular Biology Institute
Los Angeles, CA 90024, USA

Lake, Kenneth (General)
115 W 7th St
Red Lodge, MT 59068-9067, USA

Lake, Oliver E (Musician)
DL Media
PO Box 2728
Bala Cynwyd, PA 19004, USA

Lake, Ricki (Actor, Talk Show Host)
c/o Josh Sabarra *Breaking News PR*
9601 Wilshire Blvd
Suite 1106
Beverly Hills, CA 90210, USA

Lake, Sanoe (Actor)
c/o Staff Member *Luber Roklin Management*
8530 Wilshire Blvd
6th Floor
Beverly Hills, CA 90211, USA

Lake, Steve (Athlete, Baseball Player)
7402 N 177th Ave
Waddell, AZ 85355-9320, USA

Laker, Fredrick A (Business Person)
Princess Tower West Sunrise
Box F207 Freeport
Grand Bahamas, BAHAMAS

Laker, Jim (Cricketer)
Oak End
9 Portlinscale Road Putney
London SW15, UNITED KINGDOM (UK)

Laker, Tim (Athlete, Baseball Player)
325 SPring Breeze Ct
Simi Valley, CA 93065-6719, USA

Lakes, Gary (Opera Singer)
I C M Artists
40 W 57th St
New York, NY 10019, USA

Lakin, Christine (Actor)
c/o Gordon Gilbertson *Gilbertson Management*
1334 3rd St Promenade #201
Santa Monica, CA 90401, USA

Lakner, Yehoshua (Composer)
Postfach 7851
Luceme 7 6000, SWITZERLAND

Lakoue, Enoch Devant (Prime Minister)
Prime Minister's Office
Bangui, CENTRAL AFRICAN REPUBLIC

Lakshmi, Padma (Actor)
c/o Christina Papadopoulos *Baker Winokur Ryder Public Relations BWR (BWR-NY)*
292 Madison Ave
12th Floor
New York, NY 10017, USA

Lalaine (Actor)
c/o Beverly Strong *Strong Management*
3532 Hayden Ave
Culver City, CA 90232, USA

La Lanne, Jack (Athlete)
430 Quintana Rd
Morro Bay, CA 93442, USA

La Lanne, Jack
430 Quintana Rd. #151
Morro Bay, CA 93442-1948

La Ley (Music Group)
c/o Staff Member *United Talent Agency (UTA)*
9336 Civic Center Dr
Beverly Hills, CA 90210, USA

Laliberte, Guy (Astronaut)
Cirque de Soleil
8400 2nd Ave
Attn: Chief Executive Officer
Montreal, QC H1Z 4M6, CANADA

LaLiberte, Nicole (Actor)
c/o Allan Mindel *Framework Entertainment (LA)*
9057 Nemo St
Suite C
West Hollywood, CA 90069, USA

Laliberte-Bourque, Andree (Director)
Musee du Quebec
1 Ave Wolfe-Montcalm
Quebec, QC G1R 5H3, CANADA

Lalime, Patrick (Athlete, Hockey Player)
Pulver Sports
479 Bedford Park Ave
Attn Ian Pulver
Toronto, ON M5M 1K2, Canada

Lalitha, Devi (Actor, Bollywood)
23 Karaneeswar Koil Street
Saidapet
Chennai, TN 600015, INDIA

Lalive, Caroline (Athlete, Olympic Athlete, Skier)
30 Blue Sage Cir Steamboat
Springs, CO 80487-3024, USA

Lally, Bob (Athlete, Football Player)
18 Cartwright Dr
Princeton Junction, NJ 08550, USA

Lalonde, Bobby (Athlete, Hockey Player)
523 Broadgreen St
Pickering, ON LI W 3E8, Canada

Lalonde, Donny
2554 Lincoln Blvd. #729
Venice, CA 90291

Lalonde, Larry (Musician)
Figurehead Mgmt
3470 19th St
San Francisco, CA 94110, USA

Lalonde, Ron (Athlete, Hockey Player)
5 Forest Trail RR 1
Gormley, ON LOH lGO, Canada

Lalor, Mike (Athlete, Hockey Player)
51 Meadowbrook Rd
Needham, MA 02492-1913

Lama, Dalai (Nobel Prize Laureate, Religious Leader)
Office of His Holiness the Dalai Lama
Thekchen Choeling
PO McLeod Ganj
Himachai, Pradesh, INDIA

Lama, Ganju (General)
Shangderpa House 34 Singtam Ravangla Road
PO Ravangla
West Sikkim, INDIA

Lamar, Chuck (Commentator)
2250 Kent Pl
Clearwater, FL 33764-6623, USA

Lamar, Dwight (Bo) (Athlete, Basketball Player)
103 Claire St
Lafayette, LA 70507-4803, USA

Lamar, Kendrick (Musician)
c/o Staff Member *Interscope Records (NY)*
1755 Broadway
New York, NY 10019, USA

LaMarr, Phil (Actor, Comedian)
c/o Staff Member *Sanders Armstrong Caserta*
2120 Colorado Blvd
Suite 120
Santa Monica, CA 90404, USA

Lamas, A J (Actor)
c/o Ryan Daly *Zero Gravity Management*
1531 14th. St
Santa Monica, CA 90404, USA

Lamb, Allan J (Cricketer)
Lamb Assoc
4 Saint Giles St
#400
Northampton NN1 1JB, UNITED KINGDOM (UK)

Lamb, Brad (Athlete, Football Player)
6460 Chase Dr
Mentor, OH 44060, USA

Lamb, David (Athlete, Baseball Player)
603 Hampshire Rd #465
Westlake Village, CA 91361-2307, USA

Lamb, John (Athlete, Baseball Player)
P.O. Box 2
Sharon, CT 06069-0002, USA

Lamb, Mike (Athlete, Baseball Player)
17 Meadow Wood Dr
Trabuco Canyon, CA 92679-4737, USA

Lamb, Ray (Athlete, Baseball Player)
3 Corte Tallista
San Clemente, CA 92673-6863, USA

Lamb, Wally (Writer)
c/o Staff Member *HarperCollins Publishers*
10 East 53rd St
c/o Author mail, 7th Floor
New York, NY 10022, USA

Lamberg, Adam (Actor)
c/o Stephanie Davis *Wet Dog Entertainment*
9460 Wilshire Blvd
7th Floor
Beverly Hills, CA 90210, USA

Lambert, Adam (Musician)
c/o Staff Member *Direct Management Group*
947 N La Cienega Blvd
Suite G
Los Angeles, CA 90069, USA

Lambert, Chris (Athlete, Baseball Player)
1072 Cilley Rd Manchester
Manchester, NH 03103-2908, USA

Lambert, Christophe (Actor)
9 Ave Trempley
C/Lui
Geneva 1209, SWITZERLAND

Lambert, Christopher (Actor, Producer, Writer)
c/o Gerry Harrington *Brillstein Entertainment Partners*
9150 Wilshire Blvd #350
Beverly Hills, CA 90212, USA

Lambert, Dan (Athlete, Hockey Player)
7375 E Wingspan Way
Scottsdale, AZ 85255-4758

Lambert, Dion (Athlete, Football Player)
11157 Sunburst St
Lake View Terrace, CA 91342, USA

Lambert, Frank (Athlete, Football Player)
2550 Yeager Rd Apt 16-12
West Lafayette, IN 40242, USA

Lambert, Gordon (Athlete, Football Player)
PO Box 11
Pageton, WV 24871-0011, USA

Lambert, Jack (Athlete, Football Player)
PO Box 512
Worthington, PA 16262-4810, USA

Lambert, Jerry
PO Box 25371
Charlotte, NC 28212

Lambert, John (Athlete, Basketball Player)
884 Dolphin Dr
Danville, CA 94526-1826, USA

Lambert, Lane (Athlete, Hockey Player)
Nashville Predators
501 Broadway
Nashville, TN 37203-3980

Lambert, L W
Rt. #1
Olin, NC 28860, USA

Lambert, Mary M (Director)
International Creative Mgmt
8942 Wilshire Blvd
#219
Beverly Hills, CA 90211, USA

Lambert, Miranda (Musician)
c/o Simon Renshaw *Strategics Artist Management*
1100 Glendon Ave #1000
Los Angeles, CA 90024, USA

Lambert, Phyllis (Architect)
Centre d'Architecture
1920 Rue Baile
Montreal, QC H3H 2S6, CANADA

Lambert, Sheila (Basketball Player)
Charlotte Sting
100 Hive Dr
Charlotte, NC 28217, USA

Lamberti, Pasquale (Athlete, Football Player)
8 Wellington Ave
Everett, MA 02149, USA

Lambiel, Stephane (Figure Skater)
c/o Staff Member *Art on Ice Production*
Siewerdtstrasse 95
Zurich CH-8050, SWITZERLAND

Lamb Jr, Willis E (Nobel Prize Laureate)
315 Red Rock Dr
Sedona, AZ 86351, USA

Lamb Of God (Music Group, Musician)
c/o Larry Mazer *Entertainment Services Unlimited*
Main Street Plaza 1000
#303
Vorhees, NJ 08043, USA

Lamborn, Doug (Congressman, Politician)
437 Cannon HOB
Washington, DC 20515, USA

Lambrecht, Dietrich R (Engineer)
Rathenaustr 11
Mulheim an der Ruhr 45470, GERMANY

Lambro, Phillip (Composer)
Trigram Music
1888 Century Park East
#10
Los Angeles, CA 90067, USA

Lambros, Andy
9310 Topanga Canyon Blvd. #125
Chatsworth, CA 91311

Lamby, Dick (Athlete, Hockey Player, Olympic Athlete)
3 Ocean Ave
Salem, MA 01970-5456

Lamelin, Stephanie (Actor)
c/o Katie Mason *Luber Roklin Management*
8530 Wilshire Blvd
6th Floor
Beverly Hills, CA 90211, USA

Lamkin, Kathy (Actor)
c/o Linda McAlister *Linda McAlister Talent*
100 Oak Ln
Waxahachie, TX 75167-8412, USA

Lamm, Julie
Box B
Aspen, CO 81612-7402

Lamm, Richard D (Politician)
University of Denver
W Center Ave For Public Policy
Denver, CO 80219, USA

Lamm, Robert (Musician)
Air Tight Mgmt
115 West Road
Winchester Center, CT 06098, USA

Lammens, Hank (Athlete, Hockey Player)
11 Hilltop Rd
Norwalk, CT 06854-5001

Lammers, Esmee (Director, Writer)
Features Creative Mgmt
Entrepotdok 76A
Amsterdam, AD 101, NETHERLANDS

Lammers, Michael (Scientist)
5529 Lincrest Ln
Houston, TX 77056-6807, USA

Lammons, Pete (Athlete, Football Player)
5006 E Fallen Bough Dr
Houston, TX 70417, USA

Lamonica, Darryl (Athlete, Football Player)
8796 N 6th St
Fresno, CA 93720, USA

Lamonica, Daryle (Athlete, Football Player)
8796 N 6th St
Fresno, CA 93720-1711, USA

Lamonica, Roberto de (Artist)
Rua Anibal de Mendanca 180
AP 202
Rio de Janeiro, RJ ZC-37, BRAZIL

Lamont, Gene W (Athlete, Baseball Player, Coach)
5194 Siesta Woods Dr
Sarasota, FL 34242-1457, USA

Lamont, Norman S H (Government Official)
Balli Group PLC
5 Stanhope Gate
London W1Y 5LA, UNITED KINGDOM (UK)

Lamontagne, Donald A (General)
Commander
Air University
Maxwell Air Force Base, AL 36112, USA

LaMontagne, Ray (Musician)
c/o Staff Member *Paradigm (Monterey)*
404 W Franklin St
Monterey, CA 93940, USA

Lamoreaux, L Scott (General)
30 Topaz Way
Sequim, WA 98382-4739, USA

Lamoriello, Lou (Athlete, Hockey Player)
6D Cove Ln N
North Bergen, NJ 07047-6237

Lamorte, Gina (Stylist)
c/o Staff Member *Axis Models & Talent*
P.O. Box 367
Ringwood, NJ 07456-0367, USA

LaMorte, Robia (Actor)
c/o Rob D'Avola *Rob DAvola & Associates*
9107 Wilshire Blvd #450
Beverly Hills, CA 90210, USA

Lamothe, Marc (Athlete, Hockey Player)
248 Bruyere St
Ottawa, ON KIN 5E6, Canada

Lamott, Anne (Writer)
c/o Steven Barclay *Steven Barclay Agency*
12 Western Ave
Petaluma, CA 94952, USA

LaMotta, Jake (Boxer)
400 E 57th St
New York, NY 10022, USA

Lamp, Dennis (Athlete, Baseball Player)
30824 La Miranda
Unit 228
Rancho Santa Margarita, CA 92688-5812, USA

Lamp, Jeff (Athlete, Basketball Player)
4971 Credit River Dr
Savage, MN 55378-4610, USA

Lampa, Rachael
25 Music Sq. W.
Nashville, TN 37203

Lampanelli, Lisa (Comedian)
c/o Maggie Houlehan *Parallel Entertainment*
9420 Wilshire Blvd #250
Beverly Hills, CA 90212, USA

Lampard, Frank (Soccer Player)
Chelsea Football Club
Stamford Bridge
Fulham Road
London SW6 1HS, UNITED KINGDOM

Lampard, Keith (Athlete, Baseball Player)
6124 Highway 6 N
Houston, TX 77084-1304, USA

Lamparski, Richard (Writer)
4202 Calle Real
Apt 245
Santa Barbara, CA 93110-4081, USA

Lampert, Edward S (Business Person)
ESL Investments Inc
200 Greenwich Ave
Greenwich, CT 06830, USA

Lampert, Zohra (Actor)
Don Buchwald
6500 Wilshire Blvd
#2200
Los Angeles, CA 90048, USA

Lamphear, Dan (Athlete, Football Player)
669 Bent Ridge Ln
Barrington, IL 60010, USA

Lampkin, Tom (Athlete, Baseball Player)
3810 SE 153rd Ct
Vancouver, WA 98683-5313, USA

Lampley, Jim (Sportscaster)
c/o Staff Member *Crystal Spring Productions*
9713 Santa Monica Blvd #214
Beverly Hills, CA 90210, USA

Lampley, Jimmy (Athlete, Basketball Player)
3197 Balsam Cv
Memphis, TN 38127-7483, USA

Lamplugh, Ian (Athlete, Baseball Player)
1830 Fairburn Dr
Victoria, BC V8N 1P9, Canada

Lamplugh, Ian (Baseball Player)
1830 Fairburn Dr
Victoria, BC V8N 1P9, CANADA

Lamplugh, Ian (Athlete, Baseball Player)
1830 Fairburn Dr
Victoria BC, V8N 1P9 Canada, USA

Lampman, Bryce (Athlete, Hockey Player)
1568 Redwood Ln SW
Rochester, MN 55902-1688

Lampman, Mike (Athlete, Hockey Player)
7007 Hawaii Kai Dr Apt D22
Honolulu, HI 96825-3141

Lampson, Butler W (Engineer)
Microsoft Research Corp
16011 NE 36th Way
Redmond, WA 98073, USA

Lampton, Michael (Astronaut)
University of California
Space Science Laboratory
Berkeley, CA 94720, USA

La Mura, Mark
6399 Wilshire Blvd. #414
Los Angeles, CA 90048

Lanbros, Andy
9040 Topanga Canyon Blvd. #200
West Hills, CA 91304-1435

Lancaster, Amber
c/o Cindy Guagenti *Baker Winokur Ryder Public Relations (BWR-LA)*
9100 Wilshire Blvd
Suite 500, West Tower
Beverly Hills, CA 90212, USA

Lancaster, Les (Athlete, Baseball Player)
PO Box 1105
Dothan, AL 36302-1105, USA

Lancaster, Mark (Horse Racer)
195 Mill Ln W
Columbus, NJ 08022-1941, USA

Lancaster, Neal (Athlete, Golfer)
6 Quail Run
Smithfield, NC 27577, USA

Lancaster, Penny (Actor)
c/o Staff Member *Special Artists Agency*
9465 Wilshire Blvd #820
Beverly Hills, CA 90212, USA

Lancaster, Sarah (Actor)
c/o Amanda Glazer *Kohner Agency, The*
9300 Wilshire Blvd
Suite 555
Beverly Hills, CA 90212, USA

Lance, Bert (Politician)
409 ELine St
Calhoun, GA 30701-2265

Lance, Dirk (Musician)
c/o Staff Member *ArtistDirect*
9046 Lindblade St
Culver City, CA 90232, USA

Lance, Gary (Athlete, Baseball Player)
212 Sunset Cir
Prosperity, SC 29127-8426, USA

Lance, Leonard (Congressman, Politician)
426 Cannon HOB
Washington, DC 20515, USA

Lancellotti, Rick (Athlete, Baseball Player)
5190 Thompson Rd
Clarence, NY 14031-1127, USA

Lancelotti, Rick (Athlete, Baseball Player)
5190 Thompson Rd
Clarence, NY 14031, USA

Land, Tammi
c/o Staff Member *Osbrink Talent Agency*
4343 Lankershim Blvd
Suite 100
Universal City, CA 91602, USA

Landa, Sonny (Stylist)
c/o Staff Member *Manifest Artist Management*
1975 E Sunrise Blvd
#412
Fort Lauderdale, FL 33304, USA

Landaker, Dave (Baseball Player)
Topps
3593 Buffum St
Simi Valley, CA 93063-3215, USA

Landau, Irvin (Editor)
Consumer Reports Magazine
Editorial Dept
101 Truman Ave
Yonkers, NY 10703, USA

Landau, Jacob (Artist)
2 Pine Dr
Roosevelt, NJ 08555, USA

Landau, Jon (Director, Producer, Writer)
c/o Staff Member *LightStorm Entertainment*
919 Santa Monica Blvd
Santa Monica, CA 90401

Landau, Juliet (Actor)
Miss Juliet Productions
P.O. Box 2792
Hollywood, CA 90078

Landau, Martin (Actor)
c/o Rona Menashe *Guttman Associates*
118 S Beverly Dr
Suite 201
Beverly Hills, CA 90212, USA

Landeau, Aleksia (Actor)
c/o Staff Member *Metropolitan (MTA)*
4526 Wilshire Blvd
Los Angeles, CA 90010, USA

Landecker, John Records
MAGIC 104.3 WJMK
180 N. Stetson Suite 900
Prudential 2 Building
Chicago, IL 60601

Lander, Benjamin (Educator)
American University
President's Office
Washington, DC 20016, USA

Lander, David L (Actor)
c/o Staff Member *Arlene Thornton & Associates*
12711 Ventura Blvd
Suite 490
Studio City, CA 91604, USA

Lander, Natalie (Actor)
c/o Scott Zimmerman *Evolution Entertainment (LA)*
901 N Highland Ave
Los Angeles, CA 90038, USA

Landers, Amy (Actor)
c/o Staff Member *Badgley-Connor-King*
9229 Sunset Blvd.
Suite 311
Los Angeles, CA 90069, USA

Landers, Andy (Coach)
University of Georgia
Athletic Dept
Athens, GA 30602, USA

Landers, Audrey (Actor, Musician)
688 Eagle Watch Ln
Osprey, FL 34229, USA

Landers, Judy (Actor)
3933 Losillias Dr
Sarasota, FL 34238, USA

Landers, Kristy (Actor)
c/o Gregory (Greg) Redlitz *Robert Thorne Company*
9654 Heather Rd
Beverly Hills, CA 90210, USA

Landers, Robert (Athlete, Golfer)
P.O. Box 497
Azle, TX 76098-0497, USA

Landes, David S (Historian)
24 Highland St
Cambridge, MA 02138, USA

Landes, Michael (Actor)
c/o Chris Andrews *Creative Artists Agency (CAA-LA)*
2000 Ave Of The Stars
Los Angeles, CA 90067, USA

Landesberg, Sylven (Athlete, Basketball Player)
c/o Jeff Schwartz *Excel Sports Management*
9665 Wilshire Blvd #500
Los Angeles, CA 90212, USA

Landestoy, Rafael (Athlete, Baseball Player)
13564 SW 177th Ter
Miami, FL 33177-7777, USA

Landeta, Sean (Athlete, Football Player)
P.O. Box 422
Manhasset, NY 11030, USA

Landey, Nina (Actor)
c/o Staff Member *Bauman Redanty & Shaul Agency*
5757 Wilshire Blvd
Suite 473
Beverly Hills, CA 90212, USA

Landgrebe, Ludrun
Goethstr. 17
Munich, GERMANY D-80336

Landham, Sonny (Actor)

Landi, Sal (Actor)
c/o Craig Mobbs *AKA Talent Agency*
6310 San Vicente Blvd
Suite 200
Los Angeles, CA 90048, USA

Landig, Rhea (Stylist)
c/o Staff Member *Perrella Management*
330 W 38th St Rm 1407
New York, NY 10018, USA

Landis, Bill (Athlete, Baseball Player)
525 E Sycamore Dr
Hanford, CA 93230-1443, USA

Landis, Floyd (Athlete)
Ouch Pro Cycling Team
3530 Grand Ave
Suite 4
Oakland, CA 94610-2036, USA

Landis, Jim (Athlete, Baseball Player)
203 Alchemy Way
Napa, CA 94558-7214, USA

Landis, John D (Director)
c/o Abram Nalibotsky *Gersh (LA)*
9465 Wilshire Blvd
Suite 600
Beverly Hills, CA 90212, USA

Lando, Joe (Actor)
c/o Staff Member *Metropolitan (MTA)*
4526 Wilshire Blvd
Los Angeles, CA 90010, USA

Landon, Bruce (Athlete, Hockey Player)
250 Dewey St
West Springfield, MA 01089-1606

Landon, Howard C R (Writer)
Chateau de Foncoussieres
Rabastens
Tarn 81800, FRANCE

Landon, Jennifer (Actor)
c/o Jamie Freed *Paris Hilton Entertainment*
8383 Wilshire Blvd
Suite 1050
Beverly Hills, CA 90211, USA

Landon, Larry (Athlete, Hockey Player)
Pro Hockey Players Association
3964 Portage Rd
Niagara Falls, ON L2J 2K9, Canada

Landon, Tina (Actor, Choreographer)
c/o Staff Member *McDonald/Selznick Assoc (MSA)*
1611A N El Centro Ave
Hollywood, CA 90028, USA

Landon Jr, Michael (Actor, Director, Producer, Writer)
6401 Chesebro Rd.
Agoura Hills, CA 91301, USA

Landreaux, Ken (Athlete, Baseball Player)
JD Legends Promotions
10808 Foothill Blvd #160-454
Rancho Cucamonga, CA 91730-3889, USA

Landres, Paul
5343 Amestoy Ave
Encino, CA 91316

Landreth, Larry (Athlete, Baseball Player)
116 St Vincent St S
Stratford, ON N5A 2W8, Canada

Landri, Derek (Athlete, Football Player)
2022 Scottswood Cir
South Bend, IN 46617-1849, USA

Landrieu, Mary (Politician)
405 E Capitol St SE
Washington, DC 20003-3810, USA

Landrieu, Moon (Politician)
4301 S Prieur St
New Orleans, LA 70125-5125, USA

Landrith, Hobie (Athlete, Baseball Player)
1462 Nome Ct
Sunnyvale, CA 94087-4264, USA

Landrum, Bill (Athlete, Baseball Player)
840 Silver Point Rd
Chapin, SC 29036-7963, USA

Landrum, Bill (Athlete, Baseball Player)
840 Silver Point Rd
Chapin, SC 29036, USA

Landrum, Ced (Athlete, Baseball Player)
2425 Hillview Dr
Fort Worth, TX 76119-2722, USA

Landrum, Joe (Athlete, Baseball Player)
715 Sharpe Rd
Columbia, SC 29203-9347, USA

Landrum, Mike (Athlete, Football Player)
88 Raybourn Rd
Sumrall, MS 39482, USA

Landrum, Tito (Athlete, Baseball Player)
428 E 58th St Apt Grd
New York, NY 10022-2362, USA

Landry, Ali (Actor, Model)
c/o Staff Member *Reel Talent Management*
P.O. Box 491035
Los Angeles, CA 90049, USA

Landry, Dawan (Athlete, Football Player)
309 Kennedy St
Ama, LA 70031, USA

Landry, Gregory P (Greg) (Athlete, Coach, Football Coach, Football Player)
133 Melanie Ln
Troy, MI 48098, USA

Landsberger, Mark (Athlete, Basketball Player)
1702 8th Ave SE
Saint Cloud, MN 56304-2104, USA

Landsburg, Valerie (Actor)
22745 Chamera Lane
Topanga Canyon, CA 90290, USA

Landsee, Bob (Athlete, Football Player)
PO Box 628128
Middleton, WI 53562-8128, USA

Landsee, Robert (Athlete, Football Player)
P.O. Box 628128
Middleton, WI 53562, USA

Landy, Bernard (Government Official)
Government du Quebec
885 Grand Allee Est
Quebec, QC GLA 1A2, CANADA

Landy, Leonard (Actor)
78229 Kistler Way
Palm Desert, CA 92211, USA

Landzaat, Andre
7500 Devista Dr
Los Angeles, CA 90046

Lane, Abbe (Actor, Musician)
500 Bel Air Rd
Los Angeles, CA 90077, USA

Lane, Barry (Athlete, Golfer)
I M G
1360 E 9th St
Suite 100
Cleveland, OH 44114-1730, USA

Lane, Cristy (Musician)
PO Box 654
Madison, TN 37116, USA

Lane, Diane (Actor)
c/o Joan Hyler *Hyler Management*
20 Ocean Park Blvd
Suite 25
Santa Monica, CA 90405, USA

Lane, Dick (Athlete, Baseball Player)
2717 Legend Dr
Las Vegas, NV 89134-8829, USA

Lane, Garcia (Athlete, Football Player)
5128 Stone Ridge Rd S Apt I
Columbus, OH 43213-4141, USA

Lane, Gord (Athlete, Hockey Player)
5656 Vantage Point Rd
Columbia, MD 21044-2613

Lane, Jason (Athlete, Baseball Player)
8930 Oak Grove Ave
Sebastopol, CA 95472-2460, USA

Lane, Jerome (Athlete, Basketball Player)
1500 Marion Ave
Apt 509
Akron, OH 44313, USA

Lane, Johnny
5048 Casa Dr.
Tarzana, CA 91356-4422

Lane, John R (Jack) (Misc)
San Francisco Museum of Modem Art
151 3rd St
San Francisco, CA 94103, USA

Lane, Kenneth Jay (Designer, Fashion Designer)
Kenneth Jay Lane Inc
20 W 37th St
New York, NY 10018, USA

Lane, Lilas (Actor)
c/o Peter Himberger *Impact Artists Group LLC*
42 Hamilton Ter
New York, NY 10031, USA

Lane, MacArthur (Athlete, Football Player)
3238 Knowland Ave
Oakland, CA 94619, USA

Lane, Malcolm D (Misc)
5607 Roxbuy Place
Baltimore, MD 21209, USA

Lane, Marvin (Marv) (Athlete, Baseball Player)
40164 Gulliver Dr
Sterling Heights, MI 48310-1729, USA

Lane, Mary (Stylist)
1069 Sea Palms West Dr
St. Simons Island, GA 31522, USA

Lane, Max (Athlete, Football Player)
16 Strong St
Newburyport, MA 01950-2411, USA

Lane, Melvin B (Publisher)
99 Tallwood Court
Menlo Park, CA 94027, USA

Lane, Mike (Cartoonist)
Baltimore Sun
Editorial Dept
501 N Calvert St
Baltimore, MD 21202, USA

Lane, Nathan (Actor, Musician)
c/o Simon Halls *Slate Public Relations*
9000 Sunset Blvd #915
West Hollywood, CA 90069, USA

Lane, Perry (General)
30 Monica Dr
Nashua, NH 03062-2363, USA

Lane, Skip (Athlete, Business Person, Football Player)
14 Roosevelt Rd
Westport, CT 06880, USA

Lanegan, Mark (Musician)
Helter Skelter Plaza
535 Kings Road
London SW1O 0S, UNITED KINGDOM (UK)

Lane of St Ippollitts, Geoffrey D (Judge)
Royal Courts of Justice
Strand
London WC2A 2LL, UNITED KINGDOM (UK)

Laneuville, Eric (Actor)
5138 W Slauson Ave
Los Angeles, CA 90056, USA

Laney, James T (Diplomat, Educator)
2015 Grand Prix Dr NE
Atlanta, GA 30345, USA

Lang, Andrew (Athlete, Basketball Player)
1048 Woodruff Plantation Pkwy SE
Marietta, GA 30067-9106, USA

Lang, Antonio (Athlete, Basketball Player)
2255 Barretts Ln
Mobile, AL 36617-2734, USA

Lang, Belinda (Actor)
Ken McReddie
91 Regent St
London W1R 7TB, UNITED KINGDOM (UK)

Lang, Chip (Athlete, Baseball Player)
132 Westminister Dr
Pittsburgh, PA 15229-3165, USA

Lang, Ed (Photographer)
Elysium Growth Press
16255 Ventura Blvd
#515
Encino, CA 91436, USA

Lang, Gene (Athlete, Football Player)
11526 Azalea Trace
Gulfport, MS 39503, USA

Lang, George C (War Hero)
3786 Clark St
Seaford, NY 11783, USA

Lang, Helmut (Designer, Fashion Designer)
Helmut Lang New York
819 Washington St
New York, NY 10012, USA

Lang, Jack (Government Official)
Mairie
Blois 41000, FRANCE

Lang, Jack (Writer)
4 Barry Dr
E Northport, NY 11731, USA

Lang, Jonny (Musician)
Blue Sky Artists
761 Washington Ave N
Minneapolis, MN 55401, USA

Lang, June (Actor)
12756 Kahlenberg Lane
North Hollywood, CA 91607, USA

Lang, Katherine Kelly (Actor, Model)
"The Bold and The Beautiful"
Bell-Phillip Television Productions Inc
7800 Beverly Blvd Ste 3371
Los Angeles, CA 90036, USA

Lang, KD (Actor, Musician)
1314 NW Irving St #713/#714
Portland, OR 97209, USA

Lang, Kenard (Athlete, Football Player)
1781 Oakbrook Dr
Longwood, FL 32779, USA

Lang, Lang (Musician)
c/o Staff Member *Columbia Artists Mgmt Inc*
1790 Broadway Fl 6
New York, NY 10019-1412, USA

Lang, Le-Lo (Athlete, Football Player)
19436 E Maplewood Pl
Aurora, CO 80016-3868, USA

Lang, Pearl (Choreographer, Dancer)
382 Central Park West
New York, NY 10025, USA

Lang, Stephen (Actor)
c/o Susan Calogerakis *Thruline Entertainment*
9250 Wilshire Blvd
Ground Fl
Beverly Hills, CA 90212, USA

Langbo, Arnold G (Business Person)
Kellogg Co
1 Kellogg Square
PO Box 3599
Battle Creek, MI 49016, USA

Langdon, Brooke
1180 S. Beverly Dr. #608
Los Angeles, CA 90035

Langdon, Darren (Athlete, Hockey Player)
1 Oake's Rd
Deer Lake, NL A8A IXS, Canada

Langdon, Harry (Photographer)
PO Box 16816
Beverly Hills, CA 90209, USA

Langdon, Michael
34 Arnham Ct. Grand Ave.
Hove E. Sussex, ENGLAND

Langdon, Sue Ane (Actor)
4618 Park Mirasol
Calabasas, CA 91302-1731, USA

Langdon, Sue Ann (Actor)
4618 Park Marasol
Calabasas, CA 91302, USA

Lange, Allison
3500 W. Olive Ave. #1400
Burbank, CA 91505

Lange, Andre (Athlete)
BSD
An der Schiessstatte 4
Berchtesgaden 83471, GERMANY

Lange, Artie (Actor)
c/o Richard Abate *3 Arts Entertainment - NY*
49 West 27th St.
5th Floor
New York, NY 10001, USA

Lange, Bonnie
PO Box 3827
Beverly Hills, CA 90212

Lange, Detective Tom
12021 Wilshire Blvd. #846
Los Angeles, CA 90025

Lange, Dick (Athlete, Baseball Player)
39744 Salvatore Dr
Sterling Heights, MI 48313-5165, USA

Lange, Ernst (Scientist)
904 Speake Rd NW
Huntsville, AL 35816-3532, USA

Lange, Jessica (Actor)
c/o Jason Weinberg *Untitled Entertainment (LA)*
350 S. Beverly Dr #200
Beverly Hills, CA 90212, USA

Lange, Niklaus (Actor)
c/o Staff Member *Schumacher Management*
1122 San Vicente Blvd.
Santa Monica, CA 90402, USA

Lange, Ted (Actor)
c/o Staff Member *Schiowitz Connor Ankrum Wolf*
1680 N Vine St
Suite 1016
Los Angeles, CA 90028, USA

Lange, Thomas (Athlete)
ratzeburger Ruderclub
Domhof 57
Ratzburg 23909, GERMANY

Langehorne, Reggie (Athlete, Football Player)
12260 Smiths Neck Rd
Carrollton, VA 23314, USA

Langella, Frank (Actor)
c/o Toni Howard *ICM Partners (ICM-LA)*
10250 Constellation Blvd Fl 7
Los Angeles, CA 90067, USA

Langen, Christoph (Athlete)
BC Onterhaching
Ottobrunner Str 16
Unterhaching 82008, GERMANY

Langenbrunner, Jamie (Athlete, Hockey Player, Olympic Athlete)
2 Maywood Ct
Caldwell, NJ 07006-4316

Langencamp, Reather (Actor)
156 F St SE
Washington, DC 20003, USA

Langenkamp, Heather (Actor)
c/o Harrison Cheung *Harrison Cheung & Associates*
11617 Natrona Dr
Austin, TX 78759-4123, USA

Langer, AJ (Actor)
c/o Staff Member *Valeo Entertainment*
8265 Sunset Blvd
Suite 103
Los Angeles, CA 90046, USA

Langer, Alois A (Inventor)
111 Saddlebrook Dr
Harrison City, PA 15636, USA

Langer, Bernhard (Athlete, Golfer)
3667 Princeton Pl
Boca Raton, FL 33496, USA

Langer, James J (Jim) (Athlete, Football Player)
14280 Wolfram Street NW
Ramsey, MN 55303, USA

Langer, James S (Physicist)
1130 Las Canoas Lane
Santa Barbara, CA 93105, USA

Langer, Robert (Doctor)
Massachusetts Institute of Technology
Chem Engineer Dept
Cambridge, MA 02139, USA

Langerhans, Ryan (Athlete, Baseball Player)
18911 Angel Mountain Dr
Leander, TX 78641-3805, USA

Langevin, Dave (Athlete, Hockey Player)
1090 W Circle Ct
Saint Paul, MN 55118-4148

Langevin, Jim (Politician)
Jim Langevin for Congress
181-A Knight Street
Warwick, RI 02886, USA

Langfeld, Josh (Athlete, Hockey Player)
13050 Linnet St NW
Minneapolis, MN 55448-7078

Langford, Jevon (Athlete, Football Player)
1 Paul Brown Stadium
Cincinnati, OH 45202, USA

Langford, John (Engineer)
Aurora Flight Sciences
9950 Wakerman Dr
Manassas, VA 20110, USA

Langford, Rick (Athlete, Baseball Player)
8330 9th Avenue Ter NW
Bradenton, FL 34209-9678, USA

Langham, C Antonio (Athlete, Football Player)
P.O. Box 232
Town Creek, AL 35672, USA

Langham, Franklin (Athlete, Golfer)
P.O. Box 3428
Peachtree City, GA 30269-7428, USA

Langham, Wallace (Actor)
10264 Rochester Ave
Los Angeles, CA 90024, USA

Langham, Wally (Actor)
c/o Josh Katz *United Talent Agency (UTA)*
9336 Civic Center Dr
Beverly Hills, CA 90210, USA

Langhorne, Reggie (Athlete, Football Player)
12260 Smiths Neck Rd
Carrollton, VA 23314-3802, USA

Langkow, Daymond (Athlete, Hockey Player)
7940 E Quill Ln
Scottsdale, AZ 85255-6428

Langley, Neva (Beauty Pageant Winner)
6300 Rivioli Dr
Macon, GA 31210, USA

Langley, Roger (Skier)
Broad St
Barre, MA 01005, USA

Langlois, Lisa (Actor)
c/o Staff Member *Leavitt Talent Group*
8255 W Sunset Blvd
West Hollywood, CA 90046, USA

Langlois, Paul (Musician)
Management Trust
219 Dufferin St
#309B
Toronto, ON M5K 3J1, CANADA

Langlois Jr, Albert (Athlete, Hockey Player)
2473 Crest View Dr
Los Angeles, CA 90046-1406

Langmann, Thomas (Producer)
La Petite Reine
20, rue de Saint-Petersbourg
Paris F-75008, France

Langone, Kenneth (Business Person)
Invemed Associates
375 Park Ave
Suite 2205
New York, NY 10152, USA

Langone, Stefano (Musician)
c/o Simon Fuller *XIX Entertainment*
35-37 Parkgate Rd
32/33 Ransomes Dock
London SW11 4NP, UNITED KINGDOM (UK)

Langston, J William (Doctor)
Parkinson's Foundation
2444 Moorpark Ave
San Jose, CA 95128, USA

Langston, Mark E (Athlete, Baseball Player)
56 Golden Eagle
Irvine, CA 92603-0309, USA

Langston, Murray (Actor, Comedian)
Entertainment Alliance
PO Box 4734
Santa Rosa, CA 95402, USA

Langton, Brooke (Actor)
Rigberg Roberts Rugolo
1180 S Beverly Dr
#601
Los Angeles, CA 90035, USA

Langton, Brooke (Actor)
c/o Mark Measures *Abrams Artists Agency (LA)*
9200 Sunset Blvd
11th Floor
Los Angeles, CA 90069, USA

Langway, Rod (Athlete, Hockey Player)
Brookfield Place
30 Yonge St
Toronto, ON M5E 1X8, CANADA

Lanier, Bob (Athlete, Basketball Player, Coach)
Bob Lanier Enterprises Inc.
N93W14575 Whittaker Way
Menomonee Falls, WI 53051-1652, USA

Lanier, Chris (Artist)
c/o Staff Member *Fantagraphics Books*
7563 Lake City Way
Seattle, WA 98115, USA

Lanier, Harold C (Hal) (Athlete, Baseball Player, Coach)
3270 Countryside View Dr
Saint Cloud, FL 34772-7050, USA

Lanier, Jaron (Engineer)
Advanced Network Services
200 Business Park Dr
Armonk, NY 10504, USA

Lanier, Ken (Athlete, Football Player)
21923 E Ridge Trail Cir
Aurora, CO 80016-2665, USA

Lanier, Lorenzo "Rimp" (Athlete, Baseball Player)
4515 E Frontenac Dr
Cleveland, OH 44128-5004, USA

Lanier, Lorenzo (Rimp) (Athlete, Baseball Player)
4515 E Frontenac Dr
Cleveland, OH 44128, USA

Lanier, Willie E (Athlete, Football Player)
2911 E Brigstock Road
Midlothian, VA 23113, USA

Lankford, Frank (Athlete, Baseball Player)
104 Lakeview Ave NE
Atlanta, GA 30305-3725, USA

Lankford, James (Congressman)
509 Cannon HOB
Washington, DC 20515, USA

Lankford, Kim (Actor)
6071 US Highway 64
Bloomfield, New Mexico 87413, USA

Lankford, Paul (Athlete, Football Player)
3838 Biggin Church Rd W
Jacksonville, FL 32224, USA

Lankford, Ray (Athlete, Baseball Player)
1520 Lake Whitney Dr
Windermere, FL 34786-6041, USA

Lannetta, Chris
7422 E 7th Ave Unit 14
Denver, CO 80230-6230, USA

Lanois, Daniel (Actor, Musician)
c/o Staff Member *Paradigm (Monterey)*
404 W Franklin St
Monterey, CA 93940, USA

Ianotta, Howard (Athlete, Basketball Player)
18118 Brookwood Frst
San Antonio, TX 78258-4474, USA

Lanphear, Dan (Athlete, Football Player)
669 Bent Ridge Ln
Barrington, IL 60010, USA

LanSala, James (Misc)
Amalgamated Transit Union
5025 Wisconsin Ave NW
Washington, DC 20016, USA

Lansberry, Ross (Athlete, Hockey Player)
32610 Big Springs Rd
Acton, CA 93510-1501

Lansbury, Angela (Actor, Musician)
c/o Tim Curtis *WME (LA)*
9601 Wilshire Blvd Fl 3
Beverly Hills, CA 90210, USA

Lansbury, David (Actor)
Don Buchwald
6500 Wilshire Blvd
#2200
Los Angeles, CA 90048, USA

Lansdale, Joe R
113 Timberridge St
Nacogdoches, TX 75961, USA

Lansford, Alex (Athlete, Football Player)
P.O. Box 905
Lampasas, TX 76550, USA

Lansford, Carney (Athlete, Baseball Player)
Colorado Rockies 2001 Blake St Attn Coaching Staff
Denver, CO 80205-2000, USA

Lansford, Jody (Athlete, Baseball Player)
5730 San Lorenzo Dr
San Jose, CA 95123-2967, USA

Lansford, Mike (Athlete, Football Player)
6200 E Canyon Rim Rd
Apt 205
Anaheim, CA 92807, USA

Lansing, Mike (Athlete, Baseball Player)
9691 Sun Meadow St
Highlands Ranch, CO 80129-6925, USA

Lansing, Sherry L (Producer)
10741 Levico Way
Los Angeles, CA 90077-1918, USA

Lanter, Matt (Actor)
c/o Faras Rabadi *Emerald Talent Group*
10 Universal City Plaza
20th Floor
Universal City, CA 91608, USA

Lantz, Stu (Athlete, Basketball Player)
5270 Mount Burnham Dr
San Diego, CA 92111-3948, USA

Lanus, Valentino (Actor)
c/o Angel Hidalgo *Angel Hidalgo Management*
Gral Mendez #3 Int. C001
Col Ampliacion Daniel Garza
Mexico City 11830, MEXICO

Lanvin, Bernard (Designer, Fashion Designer)
22 Rue du Faubourg Saint Honore
Paris 70008, FRANCE

Lanz, David (Musician)
c/o *Narada*
4650 N Port Washington Rd
Milwaukee, WI 53212, USA

Lanz, Rick (Athlete, Hockey Player)
18962 20 Ave
Surrey, BC V3S 9V2, Canada

Lanza, Charles (Athlete, Football Player)
19 Snowberry Ct
Cockeysville, MD 21030, USA

Lanza, Suzanne
345 N. Maple Dr. #397
Beverly Hills, CA 90210

La Oreja de Van Gogh (Music Group)
c/o Staff Member *Sony Music Miami*
605 Lincoln Rd Fl 7
Miami Beach, FL 33139, USA

Laoretti, Larry (Athlete, Golfer)
712 Baytree Dr
Titusville, FL 32780-2310, USA

LaPage, Paul (Governor)
Office of the Governor
#1 State House Station
Augusta, ME 04333-0001, USA

LaPaglia, Anthony (Actor)
c/o Jennifer Allen *Viewpoint Inc*
8820 Wilshire Blvd.
Suite 220
Beverly Hills, CA 90211, USA

LaPaglia, Jonathan
1505 10th St.
Santa Monica, CA 90401

Lapaine, Daniel (Actor)
Envision Entertainment
409 Santa Monica Blvd
Santa Monica, CA 90401, USA

Laperriere, Ian (Athlete, Hockey Player)
C A A Sports
2000 Avenue of the Stars
Fl3
Los Angeles, CA 90067-4704, USA

Laperriere, J Jacques H (Athlete, Coach, Hockey Player)
6 Governors Ct
Palm Beach Gardens, FL 33418-7159

Laperrlere, Jacques
New Jersey Devils
165 Mulberry St
Newark, NJ 07102-3607

Lapham, Bill (Athlete, Football Player)
136 S 52nd St
West Des Moines, IA 50265, USA

Lapham, Dave (Athlete, Football Player)
8254 Sunfish Ln
Maineville, OH 45039, USA

Lapham, Lewis H (Editor)
Harper's Magazine
Editorial Dept
666 Broadway
New York, NY 10012, USA

Lapidus, Alan (Architect)
Lapidus Assoc
43 W 61st St
New York, NY 10023, USA

Lapidus, Edmond (Ted) (Designer, Fashion Designer)
66 Blvd Maurice-Barres
Neuilly-sur-Seine 92200, FRANCE

Lapierre, Dominique (Historian)
Les Bignoles
Ramatuelle 83350, FRANCE

Lapin, Kathy (Stylist)
1440 Wilmot Rd
Deerfield, IL 60015, USA

Lapine, James E (Director, Writer)
c/o Staff Member *Judi Farkas Management*
116 N. Mansfield Ave.
Los Angeles, CA 90036, USA

Lapira, Liza (Actor)
c/o Eric Nelson *Zero Gravity Management (II)*
9255 Sunset Blvd
Suite 1010
Los Angeles, CA 90069, USA

Lapka, Myron (Athlete, Football Player)
3982 Hemway Ct
Simi Valley, CA 93063, USA

La Placa, Alison (Actor)
c/o Staff Member *Marshak/Zachary Company, The*
8840 Wilshire Blvd
1st Floor
Beverly Hills, CA 90210, USA

LaPlaca, Alison (Actor)
1614 N Argyle Ave
Hollywood, CA 90028, USA

LaPlanche, Rosemary (Actor)
13914 Hartsook St
Sherman Oaks, CA 91423, USA

LaPlante, Lynda (Writer)
Random House
1745 Broadway
#B1
New York, NY 10019, USA

Lapli, John (General)
Governor General's House
Box 252
Honiara, GUADACANAL SOLOMON
ISLANDS

Lapoint, Dave (Athlete, Baseball Player)
11704 Stonewood Gate Dr
Riverview, FL 33579-4025, USA

Lapointe, Claude (Athlete, Hockey Player)
105 Runnymede Dr
Lansdale, PA 19446-6366

Lapointe, Guy
4568 E. des Bousquets
Augustin, CANADA PQ 6A3 1C4

Lapointe, Martin (Athlete, Hockey Player)
Minnesota Wild 317 Washington St
Saint Paul, MN 55102-1667

Lapointe, Ron (Athlete, Football Player)
940 E Haverford Rd
Bryn Mawr, PA 19010-3845, USA

Laport, Osvaldo (Actor)
c/o Staff Member *Telefe - Argentina*
Pavon 2444 (C1248AAT)
Buenos Aires, ARGENTINA

LaPorte, Danny (Race Car Driver)
949 Via Del Monte
Palos Verdes Estates, CA 90274, USA

Laposata, Joseph S (General)
Battle Monuments Commission
20 Massachusetts
Washington, DC 20314, USA

Lapotaire, Jane (Actor)
92 Oxford Gardens
#C
London W10, UNITED KINGDOM (UK)

Lappalainen, Markku (Musician)
Island Def Jam Records
8920 Sunset Blvd
#200
Los Angeles, CA 90069, USA

Lappas, Steve (Coach)
Villanova University
Athletic Dept
Villanova, PA 19085, USA

Lappe, Frances Moore (Writer)
989 Market Street
San Francisco, CA 94103, USA

Lappin, Peter (Athlete, Hockey Player)
1258 Meadows Rd
Geneva, IL 60134-3214

La Prada, Edgar (Athlete, Hockey Player)
12 Shuniah St.
Thunder Bay, ON P7A 2Y8, CANADA

Laprade, Edgar (Athlete, Hockey Player)
12 Shuniah St.
Thunder Bay, ON P7A 2Y8, Canada

LaPraed, Ronald (Ron) (Musician)
Management Assoc
1920 Benson Ave
Saint Paul, MN 55116, USA

Laquer, Walter (Historian)
Georgetown University
Strategic Studies
1800 K St NW
Washington, DC 20006, USA

Lara, Brian C (Cricketer)
West Indies Cricket Club
PO Box 616
Saint John's, ANTIGUA

Lara, Claude Autant
66 rue Lepic
Paris, FRANCE 75018

Lara, Joe (Actor)
c/o Peter Giagni *Peter Giagni Management*
8981 Sunset Blvd #103
West Hollywood, CA 90069, USA

Laragh, John H (Doctor, Educator)
435 E 70th St
New York, NY 10021, USA

Laraki, Azeddine (Prime Minister)
Islamic Conference
Kilo 6
Mecca Road
Jeddah 21411, SAUDI ARABIA

Laraway, Jack (Athlete, Football Player)
5250 Fox Hollow Dr Apt 530
Naples, FL 34104-5191, USA

Lardner Jr, George (Journalist)
Washington Post
Editorial Dept
1150 15th St NW
Washington, DC 20071, USA

Lardon, Brad (Athlete, Golfer)
17334 Sioux Springs Dr
College Station, TX 77845-4589, USA

Lardy, Henry A (Misc)
1829 Thorstrand Road
Madison, WI 53705, USA

Laredo, Jaime (Musician)
Harold Holt
31 Sinclair Road
London W14 0NS, UNITED KINGDOM
(UK)

Laredo, Ruth (Musician)
I C M Artists
40 W 57th St
New York, NY 10019, USA

Larena, John (Designer)
c/o Staff Member *Mirisch Agency*
8840 Wilshire Blvd
Suite 100
Beverly Hills, CA 90211, USA

Laresca, Vincent (Actor)
c/o Brandy Gold *TalentWorks (LA)*
3500 W Olive Ave
Suite 1400
Burbank, CA 91505, USA

Larese, York (Athlete, Basketball Player)
22 Grove Pl
Unit 15
Winchester, MA 01890-3863, USA

Large, Kiersten (Stylist)
c/o Staff Member *Solo Artists*
2148 Federal Ave
Los Angeles, CA 90025, USA

Large, Storm (Musician)
The Dowd Agency
444 Park Ave S
Penthouse
New York, NY 10016, USA

Largent, Steve (Politician)
3835 N Randolph Ct
Arlington, USA

Largent, Steve (Athlete, Football Player)
3835 N Randolph Ct
Arlington, VA 22207-4577, USA

Larionov, Igor (Athlete, Hockey Player)
2363 Tilbury Pl
Bloomfield Hills, MI 48301-2732

Larish, Jeff (Baseball Player)
5229 E Baker Dr
Cave Creek, AZ 85331-2458

Lariviere, Garry (Athlete, Hockey Player)
44 Royal Oak Dr St
Catharines, ON L2N 6K7, Canada

Lark, Maria (Actor)
c/o Staff Member *Frontier Booking International*
1560 Broadway
Suite 1110
New York, NY 10036, USA

Larkin, Andy (Athlete, Baseball Player)
2844 E Flower St
Gilbert, AZ 85298-5754, USA

Larkin, Barry (Athlete, Baseball Player)
5410 Osprey Isle Ln
Orlando, FL 32819-4015, USA

Larkin, Barry L (Athlete, Baseball Player, Olympic Athlete)
5410 Osprey Isle Ln
Orlando, FL 32819-4015, USA

Larkin, Gene (Athlete, Baseball Player)
9496 Abbott Ct
Eden Prairie, MN 5S347-2817, USA

Larkin, Pat (Athlete, Baseball Player)
23400 Canzonet St
Woodland Hills, CA 91367-6013, USA

Larkin, Patty (Musician, Songwriter, Writer)
SRO Artists
6629 University Ave
#206
Middleton, WI 53562, USA

Larkin, Sheila
9229 Sunset Blvd. #311
Los Angeles, CA 90069

Larkin, Stephen (Athlete, Baseball Player)
9178 Solon Dr
Cincinnati, OH 45242-4616, USA

Larmer, Jeff (Athlete, Hockey Player)
27 Donald Ave RR 1
Nottawa, ON LOM 1PO, Canada

Larmer, Steve (Athlete, Hockey Player)
1664 Poplar Point Rd RR 4
Peterborough, ON K9J GXS, Canada

Larmore, Jennifer (Opera Singer)
I C M Artists
40 W 57th St
New York, NY 10019, USA

Larner, Stevan (Cinematographer)
1209 Ballard Canyon Road
Solvang, CA 93463, USA

Laro, David (Judge)
US Tax Court
400 2nd St NW
Washington, DC 20217, USA

Larocca, Greg (Athlete, Baseball Player)
14 Tinker Rd
Bedford, NH 03110-4429, USA

Laroche, Adam (Athlete, Baseball Player)
1735 E Oak St
Fort Scott, KS 66701-1841, USA

Laroche, Andy
815 W 18th St
Fort Scott, KS 66701-3400

Laroche, Dave (Athlete, Baseball Player)
815 W 18th St
Fort Scott, KS 66701-3400, USA

LaRoche, Philippe (Skier)
Club de Ski Acrobatique
Lac Beauport, QC G0A 20Q, CANADA

LaRocque, Gene R (General)
5015 Macomb St NW
Washington, DC 20016, USA

Laroque, Michele (Actor)
Artmedia
20 Ave Rapp
Paris 75007, FRANCE

LaRosa, Julius (Musician)
67 Sycamore Lane
Irvington, NY 10533, USA

La Rosa, Linda (Stylist)
c/o Staff Member *Ford Models (Chicago)*
311 W Superior St
Chicago, IL 60654, USA

Larose, Chad (Athlete, Hockey Player)
Newport Sports Management
400-201 City Centre Dr
Attn Patrick Morris
Mississauga, ON L5B 2T4, Canada

Larose, Claude (Athlete, Hockey Player)
Sher-Wood 2745 Rue de la Sherwood
Sherbrooke, QC JIK 1E1, Canada

Larose, Claude (Athlete, Hockey Player)
5060 NW 54th St
Coconut Creek, FL 33073-3713, USA

Larose, Dan (Athlete, Football Player)
4873 N Raymond Rd
Luther, MI 49656, USA

Larose, Guy (Athlete, Hockey Player)
5 Tip Cart Rd.
Sutton, MA 01590-4801

Larose, John (Athlete, Baseball Player)
99 Roland St
Cumberland, RI 02864-5515, USA

Larose, Paul (Athlete, Hockey Player)
170 Rue Taschereau
Trois-Rivieres, QC G8W 1G9, Canada

Larose, Vic (Athlete, Baseball Player)
2908 E Svlvia St
Phoenix, AZ 85032-71351968, USA

LaRouche, Lyndon
15820 Round Top Lane
Round Hill, VA 20141-2052

Larouche, Pierre (Athlete, Hockey Player)
112 Vanderbilt Dr
Pittsburgh, PA 15243-1323

LaRouche Jr, Lyndon H (Politician)
18520 Round Top Lane
Round Hill, VA 20141-2052, USA

La Roux (Musician)
c/o Marty Diamond *Paradigm (NY)*
360 Park Ave S Fl 16
New York, NY 10010, USA

Larrieux, Amel (Musician)
Bliss Life
2114 Pico Blvd #B
Santa Monica, CA 90405, USA

Larroquette, John (Actor)
c/o Staff Member *Brillstein Entertainment Partners*
9150 Wilshire Blvd #350
Beverly Hills, CA 90212, USA

Larry, Rentz (Athlete, Football Player)
2 Grove Isle Dr Apt 1504
Miami, FL 33133-4112, USA

Larry, Wendy (Coach)
Old Dominion University
Athletic Dept
Norfolk, VA 23529, USA

Larry Sanitsky, Larry Sanitsky (Producer)
c/o Nancy Josephson *WME (LA)*
9601 Wilshire Blvd Fl 3
Beverly Hills, CA 90210, USA

Larsen, Art (Tennis Player)
203 Lorraine Blvd
San Leandro, CA 94577, USA

Larsen, Blaine (Musician)
c/o Staff Member *Paradigm (Monterey)*
404 W Franklin St
Monterey, CA 93940, USA

Larsen, Bruce (Editor)
Vancouver Sun
2250 Granville St
Vancouver, BC V6H 3G2, CANADA

Larsen, Don (Athlete, Baseball Player)
P.O. Box 2863
Hayden Lake, ID 83835-2863, USA

Larsen, Gary L (Athlete, Football Player)
4317 San Juan St NE
Lacey, WA 98516, USA

Larsen, Larry (Actor)
24680 Road N
Cortez, CO 81321, USA

Larsen, Libby (Composer)
2205 Kenwood Parkway
Minneapolis, MN 55405, USA

Larsen, Paul E (Religious Leader)
Evangelical Convenant Church
5101 N Francisco Ave
Chicago, IL 60625, USA

Larsen, Ralph S (Business Person)
Johnson & Johnson
1 Johnson & Johnson Plaza
New Brunswick, NJ 08933, USA

Larson, Bill (Athlete, Football Player)
1365 Redwood Dr
Windsor, CO 80550-4603, USA

Larson, Brandon (Athlete, Baseball Player)
8922 Rich Way
San Antonio, TX 78251-2971, USA

Larson, Brie (Actor)
c/o Anne Woodward *ROAR (LA)*
9701 Wilshire Blvd
8th Floor
Los Angeles, CA 90212, USA

Larson, Bruce (Race Car Driver)
PO Box 71
Dauphin, PA 17018, USA

Larson, Charles R (Chuck) (Admiral)
Northrop Gruman Corp
1840 Century Park E
Los Angeles, CA 90067, USA

Larson, Dan (Athlete, Baseball Player)
797 Oxen Street
Paso Robles, CA 93446-4656, USA

Larson, Darrell
8380 Melrose Ave. #207
Los Angeles, CA 90069

Larson, Gary (Cartoonist)
Universal Press Syndicate
4520 Main St
Kansas City, MO 64111, USA

Larson, Gerald (Jerry Lacy) (Actor)
c/o Staff Member *Sutton Barth & Vennari Inc*
145 S Fairfax
Suite 310
Los Angeles, CA 90036, USA

Larson, Greg (Athlete, Football Player)
P.O. Box 393
Nisswa, MN 56468, USA

Larson, Jack (Actor)
449 N Skyewiay Road
Los Angeles, CA 90049, USA

Larson, Jay (Musician)
c/o Staff Member *Paradigm (Monterey)*
404 W Franklin St
Monterey, CA 93940, USA

Larson, Jill (Actor)
Innovative Artists
1505 10th St
Santa Monica, CA 90401, USA

Larson, Kent (Adult Film Star)
c/o Staff Member *Diva Central Inc*
7510 W Sunset Blvd Ste 1445
Los Angees, CA 90046, USA

Larson, Kurt (Athlete, Football Player)
N66W35796 W Spring Hollow Cir
Oconomowoc, WI 53066, USA

Larson, Kyle (Athlete, Football Player)
5203 I Ave
Kearney, NE 68847-8461, USA

Larson, Lance (Athlete, Olympic Athlete, Swimmer)
1131 La Limonar Rd
Santa Ana, CA 92705-2302, USA

Larson, Lyndon (Athlete, Football Player)
4117 E Encanto St
Mesa, AZ 85205, USA

Larson, Lynn (Athlete, Football Player)
12209 N 66th St
Scottsdale, AZ 85254-4521, USA

Larson, Paul (Athlete, Football Player)
3718 W Harding Rd
Turlock, CA 95380, USA

Larson, Pete (Athlete, Football Player)
3901 N Ridgeview Rd
Arlington, VA 22207-4664, USA

Larson, Peter N (Business Person)
Brunswick Corp
1 N Field Court
Lake Forest, IL 60045, USA

Larson, Reed (Athlete, Hockey Player)
14334 Fairway Dr.
Eden Prairie, MN 55344-1955

Larson, Rick (Congressman, Politician)
108 Cannon HOB
Washington, DC 20515, USA

Larson, Sarah (Model)
c/o Kenya Knight *Nous Model Management*
117 N Robertson Blvd
Los Angeles, CA 90048, USA

Larson, Shana (Producer, Writer)
c/o Lucy Stille *Paradigm (LA)*
360 N Crescent Dr
North Bldg
Beverly Hills, CA 90210, USA

Larson, William H (Athlete, Football Player)
1365 Redwood Dr
Windsor, CO 80550, USA

Larson, Wolf (Actor)
10600 Holman Ave
1
Los Angeles, CA 90024, USA

Larson-Pessolano, Becky (Athlete, Golfer)
121 Manor Ct
Springfield, MA 01118, USA

Larsson, Curt (Athlete, Hockey Player)
Nygatan 9
Sodertalje 15173, Sweden

Larsson, Dean (Athlete, Golfer)
Advantage International
1751 Pinnacle Dr
Suite 1500
Mc Lean, VA 22102-3833, USA

Larsson, Lars-Eric
Master Ernsts gata 6A
Helsingborg, SWEDEN S-25435

Larsson, Magnus
Pier House Strand on the Green Chiswick
London, ENGLAND W4

Larter, Al
6100 Wilshire Blvd. #1170
Los Angeles, CA 90048

Larter, Ali (Actor)
2501 Astral Dr
Los Angeles, CA 90046, USA

LaRue, Chi Chi (Director, DJ)
c/o Staff Member *Diva Central Inc*
7510 W Sunset Blvd Ste 1445
Los Angees, CA 90046, USA

La Rue, Danny
57 Gr. Cumberland Pl
London, ENGLAND W1M 7LJ

La Rue, Eva (Actor, Television Host)
c/o Marv Dauer *Marv Dauer Management*
11661 San Vicente Blvd
Suite 104
Los Angeles, CA 90049, USA

La Rue, Florence
4300 Louise Ave.
Encino, CA 91316

LaRue, Florence (Actor, Musician)
Sterling Winters
10877 Wilshire Blvd
#15
Los Angeles, CA 90024, USA

Larue, Jason (Athlete, Baseball Player)
30020 Twin Ridge Dr
Bulverde, TX 78163-2400, USA

Larue, Renee (Adult Film Star)
c/o Staff Member *Atlas Multimedia Inc*
9005 Eton Ave Ste C
Canoga Park, CA 91304-1743, USA

Larussa, Tonv (Baseball Player)
338 Golden Meadow Pl
Alamo, CA 94507-2711

LaRussa, Tony (Athlete, Baseball Player, Coach)
c/o Staff Member *Saint Louis Cardinals (St Louis Cardinals)*
700 Clark Ave
St Louis, MO 63102, USA

LaRusso, Vincent
419 Park Ave. So. #1009
New York, NY 10016

Larv, Frank (Baseball Player)
11813 Baseball Dr
Northport, AL 35475-4908

Lary, Frank (Athlete, Baseball Player)
11813 Baseball Dr
Northport, AL 35475-4908, USA

Lary, R Yale (Athlete, Football Player)
6366 Lansdale Road
Fort Worth, TX 76116, USA

LaSalle, Denise (Musician)
CAI Entertainment Agency
PO Box 9267
Jackson, MS 39286, USA

LaSalle, Eriq (Actor, Director)
PO Box 2369
Beverly Hills, CA 90213, USA

Lasardo, Robert (Actor)
c/o Staff Member *Silver Massetti & Szatmary (SMS) Talent Inc*
8383 Wilshire Blvd
Suite 230
Beverly Hills, CA 90211, USA

La Scala, Nancy (Actor)
c/o Victor (Viktor) Kruglov *Victor Kruglov Talent Management*
7461 Beverly Blvd Ste 403
Los Angeles, CA 90036, USA

Lascher, David (Actor)
c/o Staff Member *Vanguard Management Group*
8060 Melrose Ave
4th Floor
Los Angeles, CA 90046, USA

LaScola, Judith (Artist)
Compositions Gallery
317 Sutter St
San Francisco, CA 94108, USA

Lash, Bill (Skier)
17438 Bothell Way NE
#C305
Bothell, WA 98011, USA

Lash, Jim (Athlete, Football Player)
597 Van Everett Ave
Akron, OH 44306, USA

Lashar, Tim (Athlete, Football Player)
4056 Nicole Pl
Norman, OK 73072, USA

Lashay, Gia (Adult Film Star)
GL Productions
P.O.Box 70741
Sunnyvale, CA Sunnyvale, USA

Lasher, Fred (Athlete, Baseball Player)
N9596 County Road K
Merrillan, WI 54754-8038, USA

Lashley, Nick (Musician)
1034 Garfield Ave
Venice, CA 90291, USA

Lasker, Deedee (Athlete, Golfer)
1665 Chamisal Ct
Carlsbad, CA 92011, USA

Lasker, Greg (Athlete, Football Player)
2521 Yeoman Ln
West Lafayette, IN 47906, USA

Las Ketchup (Music Group)
c/o Staff Member *Sony Music Miami*
605 Lincoln Rd Fl 7
Miami Beach, FL 33139, USA

Laskey, Bill (Athlete, Football Player)
P.O. Box 734
3257 N Manitou Trl
Leland, MI 49654, USA

Laskey, Bill (Athlete, Baseball Player)
PO Box 1556
Burlingame, CA 94011-1556, USA

Laskey, Frank (Athlete, Football Player)
584 Battle Branch Vista Dr
Franklin, NC 28734, USA

Laskin, Melissa (Stylist)
c/o Staff Member *Celestine - CA*
1666 20th St
#200-B
Santa Monica, CA 90404, USA

Laskoski, Gary (Athlete, Hockey Player)
10SummitVw
Goshen, NY 10924-5713

Laskowski, John (Athlete, Basketball Player)
216 E Lakewood Dr
Bloomington, IN 47408-1040 ----, USA

Lasky, Scott (Sportscaster)
c/o Staff Member *Maxx Sports & Entertainment*
546 Fifth Ave Fl 6
New York, NY 10036, USA

Laslavic, Jim (Athlete, Football Player)
648 A Ave
Coronado, CA 92118, USA

Lasorda, Tommy (Athlete, Baseball Player, Coach)
c/o Staff Member *WmE2 (WMA-LA)*
1 William Morris Pl
Beverly Hills, CA 90212, USA

Lassally, Walter (Cinematographer)
6 Ladbroke Gardens
London W11 2PT, UNITED KINGDOM (UK)

Lasse, Dick (Athlete, Football Player)
111 Windcrest Ct
Beaver Falls, PA 15010-1178, USA

Lasse, Richard S (Athlete, Football Player)
111 Windcrest Ct
Beaver Falls, PA 15010, USA

Lasser, Louise (Actor, Comedian)
200 E 71st St
#20C
New York, NY 10021, USA

Lasseter, John (Animator, Director)
c/o Staff Member *Pixar Animation Studios*
1200 Park Avenue
Emeryville, CA 94608, USA

Lassetter, Don (Athlete, Baseball Player)
P.O. Box 326
Lyon, MS 38645-0326, USA

Lassez, Sarah (Actor)
Innovative Artists
1505 10th St
Santa Monica, CA 90401, USA

Lassic, Derrick (Athlete, Football Player)
353 Shawnee Indian Ct
Suwanee, GA 30024, USA

Lassick, Sydney
2734 Bellevue
Los Angeles, CA 90026

Lassiter, Amanda (Basketball Player)
Minnesota Lunx
Target Center
600 1st Ave N
Minneapolis, MN 55403, USA

Lassiter, Ike (Athlete, Football Player)
2812 Rawson St
Oakland, CA 94619-3348, USA

Lassiter, Isaac (Athlete, Football Player)
2812 Rawson St
Oakland, CA 94619, USA

Lassiter, Kwamie (Athlete, Football Player)
1222 W Sunrise Pl
Chandler, AZ 85248, USA

Last, James (Musician)
Schone Aussicht 16
Hamburg 22085, GERMANY

Laster, Danny B (Scientist)
Hruska Meal Animal Research Center
PO Box 166
Clay Center, NE 68933, USA

Laswell, Greg (Musician)
c/o Jena Vuylsteke *Vanguard Records*
2700 Pennsylvania Ave
Santa Monica, CA 90404, USA

Latarte, Steve (Race Car Driver)
18420 Nantz Rd.
Cornelius, NC 28031, USA

Lateef (Music Group, Musician)
c/o Staff Member *Madison House Inc.*
4760 Walnut St
#106
Boulder, CO 80301, USA

Lateef, Yusef (Composer, Musician)
Rhino Records
10635 Santa Monica Blvd
Los Angeles, CA 90025, USA

Latham, Bill (Athlete, Baseball Player)
211 Magnolia St
Trussville, AL 35173-1307, USA

Latham, Chris (Athlete, Baseball Player)
6331 Buzz Aldrin Dr
Las Vegas, NV 89149-1389, USA

Latham, David (Astronomer)
Harvard University
Astronomy Dept
Cambridge, MA 02138, USA

Latham, Jim (Composer)
c/o John Tempereau *Soundtrack Music Assoc*
1460 4th St
Suite 308
Santa Monica, CA 90401, USA

Latham, Jody (Actor)
c/o Lindy King *United Agents*
12-26 Lexington St
London W1F OLE, UK

Latham, Louise (Actor)
300 Hot Springs Rd
Santa Barbara, CA 93108-2038, USA

Latham, Tom (Congressman, Politician)
2217 Rayburn HOB
Washington, DC 20515, USA

Lathan, Sanaa (Actor)
c/o Philip Grenz *ICM Partners (ICM-LA)*
9601 Wilshire Blvd Fl 3
Beverly Hills, CA 90210, USA

Lathan, Stan (Director, Producer, Writer)
c/o Staff Member *Simmons Lathan Media Group*
6100 Wilshire Blvd
Suite 1111
Los Angeles, CA 90048, USA

Lathon, Lamar L (Athlete, Football Player)
23 Westpoint Dr
Missouri City, TX 77459, USA

Latifah, Queen (Actor, Musician)
c/o Amanda Silverman *42West (NY)*
220 W 42nd St
12th Floor
New York, NY 10036, USA

Latimer, Don (Athlete, Football Player)
562 S Kalispell Way
Aurora, CO 80017, USA

Latimore (Musician)
Rodgers Redding
1048 Tatnall St
Macon, GA 31201, USA

Latimore, Joseph
1505 10th St.
Santa Monica, CA 90401, USA

Latin, Jerry (Athlete, Football Player)
2312 Clover Ave
Rockford, IL 61102-3412, USA

Latman, Barry (Athlete, Baseball Player)
2726 Shelter Island Dr
P.O. Box 519
San Diego, CA 92106-2731, USA

Laton, Gary (Race Car Driver)
Gary Laton Motorsports
4011 Hands Mill Hwy
York, SC 29745, USA

Latortue, Gerard (Prime Minister)
Prime Minister's Office
Palais Ministeres
Port-au-Prince, HAITI

Latos, Jim (Athlete, Hockey Player)
1026 Whitewood Cres
Saskatoon, SK S7J 4L1, Canada

Latourelle, Ron (Athlete, Football Player)
2366 Portage Ave Suite 4A
Winnipeg, MB R3J 0N4, Canada

LaTourette, John E (Educator)
218 S Deerview Circle
Prescott, AZ 86303, USA

Latreille, Phil (Athlete, Hockey Player)
360 Park St.
Menasha, WI 54952-3428

Latta, David (Athlete, Hockey Player)
1419 MoodieSt E
Thunder Bay, ON P7E 4Y8, Canada

Lattanzi, Chloe (Musician)
c/o Staff Member *Innovative Artists (NY)*
235 Park Ave S
7th Floor
New York, NY 10003, USA

Lattimore, Brian (Athlete, Football Player)
1790 Santa Blas Walk
Apt 503
Saint Louis, MO 63138, USA

Lattimore, Kenny (Actor)
c/o Sara Ramaker *Paradigm (LA)*
360 N Crescent Dr
North Bldg
Beverly Hills, CA 90210, USA

Lattin, David (Athlete, Basketball Player)
8230 Twin Tree Ln
Houston, TX 77071-2918, USA

Lattisaw, Stacy (Musician)
9537 Fort Foote Rd
Ft Washington, MD 20744, USA

Lattlmore, Kenny (Musician)
Rhythm Jazz Entertainment Group
4465 Don Milagro Dr
Los Angeles, CA 90008, USA

Lattner, Johnny (Athlete, Football Player, Heisman Trophy Winner)
1700 Riverwoods Dr
Apt 503
Melrose Park, IL 60160, USA

Latzke, Paul (Athlete, Football Player)
1123 Escalona Dr
Santa Cruz, CA 95060, USA

Lau, Andy (Actor, Producer)
c/o Staff Member *Focus Films*
18/F, Futura Plaza
111-113 How Ming St
Kwun Tong, Kowloon, Hong Kong

Lauda, Andreas-Nikolaus (Niki) (Race Car Driver)
San Costa de Baix
Santa Eulalia
Ibiza, SPAIN

Lauda, Niki
San Costa de Baix
Santa Eularia des Riu (Ibiza),
SPAIN E-07840

Laude, Bill (Athlete, Baseball Player)
662 Franklin Ave
Frankfort, IL 60423-1206, USA

Lauder, Leonard A (Business Person)
Estee Lauder Companies
767 5th Ave
New York, NY 10153, USA

Lauder, Ronald (Business Person)
Estee Lauder Companies
767 5th Ave
New York, NY 10153, USA

Laudner, Tim (Athlete, Baseball Player)
P.O. Box 10
Hamel, MN 55340-0010, USA

Lauen, Michel (Athlete, Hockey Player)
4535 W 56th St
Minneapolis, MN 55435, USA

Lauer, Andrew (Actor)
3018 3rd St
Santa Monica, CA 90405, USA

Lauer, Andy (Actor)
c/o Andrea Pett-Joseph *Brillstein Entertainment Partners*
9150 Wilshire Blvd #350
Beverly Hills, CA 90212, USA

Lauer, Bonnie (Athlete, Golfer)
525 Via Laguna Vis
San Luis Obispo, CA 93405, USA

Lauer, Brad (Athlete, Hockey Player)
10 Deer Moss Trail
Stittsville, ON K2S 1C9, CANADA

Lauer, Martin (Athlete, Track Athlete)
Hardstr 41
Lauf 77886, GERMANY

Lauer, Matt (Journalist)
2301 Deerfield Rd
Sag Harbor, NY 11963-2016, USA

Lauer, Matt (Correspondent)
c/o Staff Member *Today Show, The*
30 Rockefeller Plz
New York, NY 10112, USA

Lauer, Tod R (Astronomer)
6471 N Tierra de Las Catalina
Tucson, AZ 85718, USA

Laufenberg, Brandon (Athlete, Football
Player)
5917 Azalea Ln
Dallas, TX 75230-3403, USA

Laughlin, Craig (Athlete, Hockey Player)
2217 Mount Tabor Rd
Gambrills, MD 21054-1801

Laughlin, Craig (Athlete, Hockey Player)
Washington Capitals
627 N Glebe Rd Ste 850
Arlington, VA 22203-2144

Laughlin, John (Actor)
Laughlin Enterprises
13116 Albers St
Sherman Oaks, CA 91401, USA

Laughlin, Robert B (Nobel Prize Laureate)
Stanford University
960 Mears Ct
Stanford, CA 94305-1029, USA

Laughlin, Teresa (TC) (Actor, Designer)
TC Laughlin Design Group Inc
8 Larchmont Ave
Larchmont, NY 10538-4220, USA

Laughlin, Tom (Actor)
PO Box 840
Moorpark, CA 93020-0840, USA

Laughlin, Jr., Mike (Race Car Driver)
Laughlin Racing
114 Pride Dr.
Simpsonville, SC 29681, USA

Laukkanen, Janne (Athlete, Hockey
Player)
401 Channelside Dr
Tampa, FL 33602, USA

Lauper, Cyndi (Musician, Songwriter)
c/o Lisa Barbaris *So What Management*
890 W End Ave
#1A
New York, NY 10025, USA

Laurance, Ashley (Actor)
c/o Leland LaBarre *Bleu, An
Entertainment Company*
5225 Wilshire Blvd
Suite 701
Los Angeles, CA 90036, USA

Laurance, Dale (Business Person)
Occidental Petroleum
10889 Wilshire Blvd
Los Angeles, CA 90024, USA

Laurance, Matthew (Actor)
1951 Hillcrest Rd
Los Angeles, CA 90068, USA

Laure, Carole (Actor, Musician)
Cineart
36 Rue de Ponthieu
Paris 75008, FRANCE

Laurel, Rich (Athlete, Basketball Player)
706 Antelope Way
Kissimmee, FL 34759-4212, USA

Lauren, Dylan (Misc)
c/o Jeffrey Jacobs *Creative Artists Agency
(CAA-LA)*
2000 Ave Of The Stars
Los Angeles, CA 90067, USA

Lauren, Joy (Actor)
c/o Mary Sanders *inMomentum
Management*
14622 Ventura Blvd #778
Sherman Oaks, CA 91403, USA

Lauren, Ralph (Designer, Fashion
Designer)
Polo Ralph Lauren Corp
867 Madison Ave
New York, NY 10021, USA

Lauren, Ralph (Misc)
867 Madison Ave
New York, NY 10021-4103, USA

Lauren, Tammy (Actor)
Gage Group
14724 Ventura Blvd
#505
Sherman Oaks, CA 91403, USA

Laurent, Melanie (Actor, Writer)
c/o Cecile Felsenberg *UBBA*
6 rue de Braque
Paris 75003, France

Laurente, Dennis (Boxer)
c/o Staff Member *Top Rank Inc.*
3908 Howard Hughes Pkwy
#580
Las Vegas, NV 89109, USA

Laurents, Arthur (Writer)
608 Northville Tpke
Riverhead, NY 11901-4717, USA

Laurer, Joanie (Chyna) (Actor, Wrestler)
c/o Michael (Mike) Esterman
Esterman.Com, LLC
Prefers to be contacted via email
MD, USA

Lauria, Dan (Actor)
c/o Harry Gold *TalentWorks (LA)*
3500 W Olive Ave
Suite 1400
Burbank, CA 91505, USA

Lauria, Matt (Actor)
c/o Jillian Fowkes *ID Public Relations
(ID-LA)*
7060 Hollywood Blvd
8th Floor
Los Angeles, CA 90028, USA

Lauricella, Francis E (Hank) (Athlete,
Football Player)
1200 5 Clearview Pkwy
Suite 1166
Harahan, LA 70123, USA

Lauridsen, Morten (Composer, Musician)
University of Southern California
Music Dept
Los Angeles, CA 90089, USA

Laurie, Greg (Religious Leader)
Harvest Christian Fellowship Church
6115 Arlington Ave
Riverside, CA 92504, USA

Laurie, Harry (Athlete, Basketball Player)
540 Bramhall Ave
Apt 3
Jersey City, NJ 07304-2323, USA

Laurie, Hugh (Actor, Comedian)
c/o Christian Hodell *Hamilton Hodell Ltd*
66-68 Margaret St Fl 5
London W1W 8SR, UK

Laurie, Piper (Actor)
2118 Wilshire Blvd
#931
Santa Monica, CA 90403, USA

Laurinaitis, James (Athlete, Football
Player)
867 McCauley Ct
Saint Charles, MO 63303-1732, USA

Laurita, Jacqueline (Reality TV Star)
c/o Staff Member *Bravo (NY)*
30 Rockefeller Plaza
New York, NY 10112, USA

Lauro, Lindore (Athlete, Football Player)
111 Scott Dr
New Castle, PA 16105, USA

Laus, Paul (Athlete, Hockey Player)
44 Chardonnay Pl
Grimsby, ON L3M 5SG, Canada

Laut, David (Athlete, Olympic Athlete)
421 Eastwood Dr
Oxnard, CA 93030-4014, USA

Lautenberg, Frank (Senator)
506 Hart Senate Office Bldg.
Washington, DC 20510, USA

Lautenberg, Frank (Politician)
100 Winston Dr Apt 9G
Cliffside Park, NJ 07010-3240, USA

Lautenschlaeger, Fred (Athlete, Football
Player)
612 Breton Pl
Arnold, MD 21012, USA

Lauter, Ed (Actor)
9165 Sunset Blvd
#202
Los Angeles, CA 90069, USA

Lauterbur, Paul C (Nobel Prize Laureate)
2702 Holcomb Dr
Urbana, IL 61802, USA

Lauterstein, Alex (DJ)
c/o Staff Member *Diva Central Inc*
7510 W Sunset Blvd Ste 1445
Los Angees, CA 90046, USA

Lautner, Georges C (Director)
9 Chemin des Basses Ribes
Grasse 06130, FRANCE

Lautner, Taylor (Actor)
c/o Peter Kiernan *Management 360*
9111 Wilshire Blvd
Beverly Hills, CA 90210, USA

Lauzerique, George (Athlete, Baseball
Player)
601 Oleaster Ave
Wellington, FL 33414-8197, USA

Lavalais, Chad (Athlete, Football Player)
3460 Tupelo In
Auburn, GA 30011-4601, USA

Lavallee, Kevin (Athlete, Hockey Player)
1210 Butterfly Ct
Marco Island, FL 34145-2308

Lavalliere, Mike (Athlete, Baseball Player)
216 81st St W
Bradenton, FL 34209-2154, USA

Lavarre, Mark
2028 Walters Ave
Northbrook, IL 60062-4526

Lave, Lester B (Economist)
1008 Devonshire Road
Pittsburgh, PA 15213, USA

Laveikin, Aleksandr I (Cosmonaut)
Potchta Kosmonavtov
Moskovskoi Oblasti
Syvisdny Goroduk 141160, RUSSIA

Lavelle, Gary (Athlete, Baseball Player)
1100 Worthington Ct
Virginia Beach, VA 23464-5855, USA

Lavelle, James (DJ, Musician)
c/o Joel Zimmerman *WME (WMA-NY)*
1325 Ave of the Americas
New York, NY 10019, USA

Lavender, Brian (Athlete, Hockey Player)
11585 Decatur St Apt C
Denver, CO 80234-3567

Lavender, Jay (Producer)
c/o Staff Member *Principato/Young
Management*
9465 Wilshire Blvd
Suite 430
Beverly Hills, CA 90212, USA

Lavender, Jody (Race Car Driver)
Jody Lavender Racing
PO Box 1527
Hartsville, SC 29551-1527, USA

Lavender, Joseph (Athlete, Football
Player)
1215 Alma St
Glendale, CA 91202, USA

Laventhol, Henry L (Hank) (Artist)
445 Heritage Hills
#F
Somers, NY 10589, USA

Laver, Rodney G (Rod) (Tennis Player)
PO Box 4798
Hilton Head Island, SC 29938, USA

Lavery, Sean (Dancer)
New York City Ballet
Lincoln Center Plaza
New York, NY 10023, USA

Lavi, Daliah (Actor)
134 W Wainman Ave
Asheboro, NC 27203, GERMANY

Lavigne, Avril (Musician, Songwriter)
c/o Nicole Perna *Baker Winokur Ryder
Public Relations (BWR-LA)*
9100 Wilshire Blvd
Suite 500, West Tower
Beverly Hills, CA 90212, USA

Lavin, Bernice E (Business Person)
Alberto-Culver
2525 Armitage Ave
Melrose Park, IL 60160, USA

Lavin, Leonard H (Business Person)
Alberto-Culver
2525 Armitage Ave
Melrose Park, IL 60160, USA

Lavin, Linda (Actor, Musician)
c/o Staff Member *Lavin Entertainment
Group*
411 S Front St
Wilmington, NC 28401, USA

Lavin, TJ (Athlete, Television Host)
c/o Staff Member *Dragon Talent*
8444 Wilshire Blvd #PH
Beverly Hills, CA 90211, USA

Laviolette, Peter (Athlete, Hockey Player)
Philadelphia Flyers
3601 S Broad St Ste 2
PhiladelPhia, PA 19148-5297

Laviolette, Peter (Athlete, Coach, Hockey
Player, Olympic Athlete)
7000 Firehouse Rd
Longboat Key, FL 34228-1138

Lavoie, Dominic (Athlete, Hockey Player)
5081 Garlenda Dr
El Dorado Hills, CA 95762-5456

Lavoine, Marc (Actor)
c/o Staff Member *ArtMedia*
20 avenue Rapp
Paris 75008, France

Lavon, Peaches (Musician)
c/o Janice Gaffney *Butterscotch Castle*
535 Geary St #612
San Francisco, CA 94102, USA

LaVoo, George (Director, Producer, Writer)
c/o Jon Rubinstein *Authentic Talent and Literary Management*
45 Main St
Suite 1004
Brooklyn, NY 11201, USA

LaVorgna, Adam (Actor)
c/o Beverly Strong *Strong Management*
9350 Wilshire Blvd
#224
Beverly Hills, CA 90212, USA

Lavoy, Robert (Athlete, Basketball Player)
613 Wood Rd
Seffner, FL 33584, USA

Lavrosky, Mikhail L (Ballerina)
Voznesesenky Per 16/4
#7
Moscow 103009, RUSSIA

Lavrov, Kyrill Y (Actor)
Michurinskaya 1
#36
Saint Petersburg 197046, RUSSIA

Law, Bernard F Cardinal (Religious Leader)
Saint Mary Major Basilica
00120, VATICAN CITY

Law, Jude (Actor)
c/o Rick Yorn *LBI Entertainment*
2000 Avenue of the Stars
3rd Floor, North Tower
Los Angeles, CA 90067, USA

Law, Ron (Baseball Player)
Cleveland Indians
3 Mountainview Rd
Greenwood Village, CO 80111-1736, USA

Law, Rudy (Athlete, Baseball Player)
JD Legends Promotions
PO Box 107
Hawthorne, CA 90251-0107, USA

Law, Ty (Athlete, Football Player)
10862 Hawks Vista St
Plantation, FL 33324, USA

Law, Vance (Athlete, Baseball Player)
1682 N 1950 W
Provo, UT 84604-1177, USA

Law, Vern (Athlete, Baseball Player)
1718 N 1050 W
Provo, UT 1980 Pittsburgh, USA

Lawanson, Ruth (Athlete, Olympic Athlete, Volleyball Player)
2050 Dickerson Rd
Reno, NV 89503-4904, USA

Lawford, Christopher (Actor)
c/o Christine Holder *Zero Gravity Management (II)*
9255 Sunset Blvd
Suite 1010
Los Angeles, CA 90069, USA

Lawler, Jerry (Wrestler)
415 Saint Nick Dr
Memphis, TN 38117, USA

Lawler, John (General)
824 Lisburn Rd Apt 609
Camp Hill, PA 17011-7101, USA

Lawler, Kate (Reality TV Star)
c/o Staff Member *Channel 4 Television Corporation*
124 Horseferry Road
London SW1P 2

Lawler, Steve (DJ, Musician)
c/o Joel Zimmerman *WME (WMA-NY)*
1325 Ave of the Americas
New York, NY 10019, USA

Lawless, Burton (Athlete, Football Player)
2035 Oak Glen Dr
Mc Gregor, TX 76657, USA

Lawless, Lucy (Actor)
c/o Alex Martinetti *Fifteen Minutes (LA)*
8436 W 3rd St
Suite 650
Los Angeles, CA 90048, USA

Lawless, Paul
4231 N Winfield Scott Plz Ste 1
Scottsdale, AZ 85251-3912

Lawless, Tom (Athlete, Baseball Player)
Corpus Christi Hooks 734 E Port Ave
Attn: Managers Office
corous christi, TX 63011-1879, USA

Lawn, John C (Lawyer)
New York Yankees
Yankee Stadium
161st St & River Ave
Bronx, NY 10451, USA

Lawrence, Andrew (Actor)
c/o Staff Member *Kass & Stokes Management*
9229 Sunset Blvd
Suite 504
Los Angeles, CA 90069, USA

Lawrence, Bill (Writer)
c/o Staff Member *Broder Webb Chervin Silbermann Agency, The (BWCS)*
10250 Constellation Blvd
Los Angeles, CA 90067-6200, USA

Lawrence, Braxton Janice (Basketball Player)
Cleveland Rockers
Gund Arena
1 Center Court
Cleveland, OH 44115, USA

Lawrence, Brian (Athlete, Baseball Player)
3379 County Road 1132
Linden, TX 75563-7375, USA

Lawrence, Carol (Actor)
12337 Ridge Circle
Los Angeles, CA 90049, USA

Lawrence, Cynthia (Opera Singer)
Herbert Breslin
119 W 57th St
#1505
New York, NY 10019, USA

Lawrence, David Jr (Publisher)
Miami Herald
1 Herald Plaza
Miami, FL 33132, USA

Lawrence, Don (Athlete, Football Player)
12620 Cedar St
Shawnee Mission, KS 66209, USA

Lawrence, Donald (Stylist)
c/o Lara Funod *Bernstein & Andriulli*
58 W 40th St
New York, NY 10018, USA

Lawrence, Francis (Director)
c/o Erwin Stoff *3 Arts Entertainment Inc*
9460 Wilshire Blvd
7th Floor
Beverly Hills, CA 90210, USA

Lawrence, Francis (Actor)
c/o Gretchen Rush *Hansen, Jacobson, Teller, Hoberman, Newman, Warren & Richman*
450 N Roxbury Dr
8th Floor
Beverly Hills, CA 90210, USA

Lawrence, Francis L (Educator)
Rutgers University
President's Office
New Brunswick, NJ 08903, USA

Lawrence, Henry (Athlete, Football Player)
2110 2nd Ave E
Palmetto, FL 34221, USA

Lawrence, James (Loz) (Musician)
PO Box 33
Pontypool, Gwent NP4 6YU, UNITED KINGDOM (UK)

Lawrence, Jennifer (Actor)
c/o Liz Mahoney *ID Public Relations (ID-LA)*
7060 Hollywood Blvd
8th Floor
Los Angeles, CA 90028, USA

Lawrence, Jim (Athlete, Baseball Player)
225 Haddington St
Caledonia, ON N3W 1G1, Canada

Lawrence, Joe (Athlete, Baseball Player)
4358 Poydras St
Lake Charles, LA 70605-4400, USA

Lawrence, Joseph (Joey) (Actor)
c/o Mark Rousso *New Wave Entertainment (LA)*
2660 W Olive Blvd
Burbank, CA 91505, USA

Lawrence, Kent (Athlete, Football Player)
150 Charter Ct
Athens, GA 30605, USA

Lawrence, Linda
4926 Commonwealth
La Canada, CA 91011

Lawrence, Marjie
13 Glenhurst Ave.
London, ENGLAND NW5

Lawrence, Mark (Athlete, Hockey Player)
49754 Churchill St
Mattawan, MI 49071-7805

Lawrence, Martin (Actor, Comedian)
c/o Sam Maydew *Collective*
8383 Wilshire Blvd
Suite 1050
Beverly Hills, CA 90211, USA

Lawrence, Matthew (Actor)
c/o Robbie Kass *Kass & Stokes Management*
9229 Sunset Blvd
Suite 504
Los Angeles, CA 90069, USA

Lawrence, Nigel (Musician)
c/o Staff Member *Paradigm (Monterey)*
404 W Franklin St
Monterey, CA 93940, USA

Lawrence, Patricia
33 St. Luke's St.
London, ENGLAND SW3

Lawrence, Richard D (General)
7301 Valbum Dr
Austin, TX 78731, USA

Lawrence, Robert S (Physicist)
Highfield House
4000 Charles St #1112
Baltimore, MD 21218, USA

Lawrence, Rolland (Athlete, Football Player)
317 Sugarcreek Dr
Franklin, PA 16323, USA

Lawrence, Russell
7800 Beverly Blvd. #3305
Los Angeles, CA 90036

Lawrence, Sean (Athlete, Baseball Player)
336 S Poplar Ave
Elmhurst, IL 60126-3565, USA

Lawrence, Sharon (Actor, Producer)
c/o David Lust *Rogers & Cowan PR (LA)*
9171 Wilshire Blvd
Suite 441
Beverly Hills, CA 90210, USA

Lawrence, Steve (Musician)
944 Pinehurst Dr
Las Vegas, NV 89109, USA

Lawrence, Tracy (Musician, Songwriter)
c/o Staff Member *WmE2 (WMA-TN)*
1600 Division St
Suite 300
Nashville, TN 37203, USA

Lawrence, Vicki (Actor, Musician)
6000 Lido Ln
Long Beach, CA 90803, USA

Lawrence, Wendy B (Astronaut)
National Reconnaissance Office
14675 Lee Road
Chantilly, VA 20151, USA

Lawrence, Wendy B Captain (Astronaut)
6225 Argyle St
Ferndale, WA 98248-8995, USA

Laws, Hubert
1078 S. Ogden Dr.
Los Angeles, CA 90019

Laws, Mary Jane (Stylist)
921 Lawn Circle
Western SPrings, IL 60558, USA

Laws, Ronnie (Musician)
c/o Staff Member *Pyramid Entertainment Group*
377 Rector Pl #21A
New York, NY 10280-1439, USA

Lawson, Ana Maria (Beauty Pageant Winner)
PO Box 59064
Potomac, MD 20859, USA

Lawson, Bianca (Actor)
c/o Staff Member *Luber Roklin Management*
8530 Wilshire Blvd
6th Floor
Beverly Hills, CA 90211, USA

Lawson, Danny (Athlete, Hockey Player)

Lawson, Denis (Actor, Director, Writer)
c/o Staff Member *Yakety Yak*
8-A Bloomsbury Sq
London WC1A 2NE, UNITED KINGDOM
(UK)

Lawson, Doyle (Musician)
c/o Staff Member *Paradigm (Monterey)*
404 W Franklin St
Monterey, CA 93940, USA

Lawson, Josh (Actor, Writer)
c/o Gabriel Cohen *Management 360*
9111 Wilshire Blvd
Beverly Hills, CA 90210, USA

Lawson, Kara (Basketball Player)
c/o Staff Member *Sacramento Monarchs*
ARCO Arena
One Sports Parkway
Sacramento, CA 95834, USA

Lawson, Ken (Ken L) (Actor)
c/o Staff Member *Agency West
Entertainment*
6255 West Sunset Blvd
Suite 908
Hollywood, CA 90028, USA

Lawson, Leigh (Actor)
P F D Drury House
34-43 Russell St
London WC2B 5HA, UNITED KINGDOM
(UK)

Lawson, Maggie (Actor)
c/o Ellen Meyer *Ellen Meyer Management*
8899 Beverly Blvd
Suite 612
West Hollywood, CA 90048, USA

Lawson, Nigella (Chef, Writer)
c/o Staff Member *Uitgeverij Contact*
Portbus 218
Amsterdam 1000 AE, The Netherlands

Lawson, Richard (Actor)
8840 Wilshire Blvd
#200
Beverly Hills, CA 90211, USA

Lawson, Richard L (General)
6910 Clifton Road
Clifton, VA 20124, USA

Lawson, Steve (Athlete, Baseball Player)
P.O. Box 5630
Brookings, OR 97415-0120, USA

Lawson, Twiggy (Actor, Model)
c/o Maureen Vincent *United Agents*
12-26 Lexington St
London W1F OLE, UK

Lawson, William (Athlete, Baseball Player)
8800 E McClellan St
Tucson, AZ 85710, USA

Lawson, William (Baseball Player)
8800 E McClellan St
Tucson, AZ 85710-4419, USA

Lawson of Blaby, Nigel (Government
Official)
32 Sutherland Walk
London SE17, UNITED KINGDOM (UK)

Lawston, Marlene (Actor)
c/o Victoria Kress *Don Buchwald &
Associates Inc (NY)*
10 E 44th St
New York, NY 10017

Lawton, Brian (Athlete, Hockey Player)
5012 Oak Bend Ln
Minneapolis, MN 55436-1167

Lawton, Jared (Stylist)
c/o Staff Member *Loox Agency*
12 Desbrosses St
New York, NY 10013, USA

Lawton, Jonathan (J.F.) (Writer)
c/o Sara Bottfeld *Industry Entertainment
Partners*
955 S Carrillo Dr
Suite 300
Los Angeles, CA 90048, USA

Lawton, Liam (Musician)
GM Publicity
86 Haddington Rd
Ballsbridge, Dublin 4
IRELAND

Lawton, Marcus (Athlete, Baseball Player)
110 Connie Dr
Gulfport, MS 39503-3254, USA

Lawton, Mary (Cartoonist)
Chronicle Features
901 Mission St
San Francisco, CA 94103, USA

Lawton, Matthew (Matt) (Athlete,
Baseball Player)
27264 Highway 67
Saucier, MS 39574-9020, USA

Lawton, Robert B (Educator)
Loyola Marymount University
President's Office
Los Angeles, CA 90045, USA

Lawwill, Theodore (Misc)
7609 Tallwood Road
Prospect, KY 40059, USA

Lax, John (Athlete, Hockey Player)
3 Greendale Ln
Harwich, MA 02645, USA

Lax, Melvin (Physicist)
12 High St
Summit, NJ 07901, USA

Lax, Peter D (Mathematician)
251 Mercer St
New York, NY 10012, USA

Laxalt, Paul (Ex-Governor, Ex-Senator,
Politician)
750 9th St NW Ste 750
#750
Washington, DC 20001-4589, USA

Laxamana, ROn (Stylist)
c/o Staff Member *Blink Management*
421 Washington Ave
#202
Miami Beach, FL 33139, USA

Laxdal, Derek
4147 E Aphrodite Dr
Boise, ID 83716-7059

Laxmikant, Berde (Actor, Bollywood)
105 Nirakar B-Wing
1st Floor Kalyan Complex Yari Road
Versova Andheri
Bombay, MS 400061, INDIA

Laxton, Bill (Athlete, Baseball Player)
261 Mansion Ave
Audubon, NJ 08106-1529, USA

Laxton, Brett (Athlete, Baseball Player)
13216 Montrose South Dr
Denham Sorings, LA 70726-7447, USA

Laxton, Gordie (Athlete, Hockey Player)
2843 Big Timber Dr NE
Grand Rapids, MI 49525-3018

Lay, Donald P (Judge)
US Court of Appeals
316 Robert St N
Saint Paul, MN 55101, USA

Layda, Gary (Photographer)
3606 Meadowbrook Ave
Nashville, TN 37205-2350, USA

Layden, Frank (Basketball Coach, Coach)
241 North Vine Street
Apt 1204W
Salt Lake City, UT 84103, USA

Layevska, Anna (Actor)
c/o Staff Member *Cesar Carrera*
C/ Isabel Serrano, 12
Madrid 28029, Spain

Layman, Jason (Athlete, Football Player)
163 New Center Rd
Sevierville, TN 37876, USA

Layne, Jerry (Athlete, Baseball Player)
2323 Cypress Gardens Blvd
Winter Haven, FL 32503-5785, USA

Layne, Jerry (Baseball Player)
2323 Cypress Gardens Blvd
Winter Haven, FL 33884-2120, USA

Layne, Shontelle (Musician)
c/o Carl Sturken *SRC - Street Records
Corporation*
Universal - Motown
1755 Broadway New Media
New York, NY 10019, USA

Layton, Dennis (Athlete, Basketball
Player)
872 S 14th St
Newark, NJ 07108-1320, USA

Layton, Les (Athlete, Baseball Player)
6424 Washington St SQc 76
Yountville, CA 94599-9461, USA

Lazar, Danny (Athlete, Baseball Player)
8444 Oakwood Ave
Munster, IN 46321-1915, USA

Lazar, Laurence (Religious Leader)
Romanian Orthodox Episcopate
2522 Grey Tower Road
Jackson, MI 49201, USA

Lazard, Justin
9350 Wilshire Blvd. #324
Beverly Hills, CA 90212

Lazarev, Alexander N
Christopher Tennant Artists
39 Taderna ROad
#2
London SW10 0PY, UNITED KINGDOM
(UK)

Lazaro, Jeff (Athlete, Hockey Player)
6422 Memphis St
New Orleans, LA 70124-3151

Lazaroff, Barbara
805 N. Sierra Dr.
Beverly Hills, CA 90210

Lazarus, Lisa (Actor, Beauty Pageant
Winner)
c/o Michael (Mike) Esterman
Esterman.Com, LLC
Prefers to be contacted via email
MD, USA

Lazarus, Mell (Cartoonist)
Creators Syndicate
5777 W Century Blvd
#700
Los Angeles, CA 90045, USA

Lazarus, Shelly (Business Person)
Ogilvy & Mather Worldwide
309 W 49th St
New York, NY 10019, USA

Lazear, Edward P (Economist)
277 Old Spanish Trail
Portola Valley, CA 94028, USA

Lazenby, George (Actor)
c/o Staff Member *Hervey/Grimes Talent
Agency*
10561 Missouri Ave
Suite 2
Los Angeles, CA 90025, USA

Lazetich, Bill (Athlete, Football Player)
3840 Rimrock Rd
Apt 2100
Billings, MT 59102, USA

Lazetich, Pete (Athlete, Football Player)
185 Martin St
Reno, NV 89509, USA

Lazier, Buddy (Race Car Driver)
Dreyer & Reinbold Racing
9375 Whitley Dr
Indianapolis, IN 46240, USA

Lazier, Jacques (Race Car Driver)
5485 Carriage Place
Rancho Cucamonga, CA 91737, USA

Lazier, Robert (Buddy) (Race Car Driver)
130 Gasoline Alley
Indianapolis, IN 46222, USA

Lazlo, Viktor
56 rue de Lisbonne
Paris, FRANCE F-75008

Lazorko, Jack (Athlete, Baseball Player)
1360 Meandering Way
Rockwall, TX 75087-2309, USA

Lazuktin, Alexander I (Cosmonaut)
Potcha Kosmonavtov
Moskovskoi Oblasti
Syvisdny Goroduk 141160, RUSSIA

Lazure, Gabrielle (Actor)
Cineart
36 Rue de Ponthieu
Paris 75008, FRANCE

Ibbetson, Bruce (Athlete, Olympic
Athlete, Rower)
424 San Bernardino Ave
Newport Beach, CA 92663-4811, USA

L. Berman, Howard (Congressman,
Politician)
2221 Rayburn HOB
Washington, DC 20515, USA

L. Boswell, Leonard (Congressman,
Politician)
1026 Longworth HOB
Washington, DC 20515, USA

L. Braley, Bruce (Congressman, Politician)
1727 Longworth HOB
Washington, DC 20515, USA

Icahn, Carl (Misc)
*Icahn Associates Corporation 767 5th Ave
Ste 4700*
New York, NY 10153-4798, USA

L. Delauro, Rosa (Congressman,
Politician)
2413 Rayburn HO
Washington, DC 20515, USA

Le, Cung (Actor)
c/o Scott Karp *Crystal Sky Pictures*
10203 Santa Monica Blvd
5th Floor
Los Angeles, CA 90067, USA

Lea, Nicholas (Actor)
c/o Adam Levine *Levine Okwu Erickson Management*
9601 Wilshire Blvd
3rd Floor
Beverly Hills, CA 90210, USA

Leabu, Tristan Lake (Actor)
LA Talent
c/o Tracy Dwyer
7700 Sunset Blvd
Los Angeles, CA 90046, USA

Leach, Brent
150 Pleasant Grove Dr
Brandon, MS 39042-2617

Leach, Jalal (Athlete, Baseball Player)
3718 Phillip Island Rd
West Sacramento, CA 95691-5939, USA

Leach, Jamie (Athlete, Hockey Player)
St Boniface Golf Club 100 Youville St
Winnipeg, MB R2H 2S1, Canada

Leach, Larry (Athlete, Hockey Player)
PO Box 995
Lloydminster, SK S9V 0Y9, Canada

Leach, Penelope (Misc)
3 Tanza Lane
London NW3 2UA, UNITED KINGDOM (UK)

Leach, Reggie (Athlete, Hockey Player)
906 Clydesdale Dr
Bear, DE 19701-2205

Leach, Rick (Athlete, Baseball Player)
593 Layman Creek Cir
Grand Blanc, MI 48439-1384, USA

Leach, Robin (Entertainer, Producer, Television Host)
c/o Staff Member *Diverse Talent Group*
9911 W Pico Blvd Ste 340W
Los Angeles, CA 90035, USA

Leach, Rosemary (Actor)
Felix de Wolfe
51 Maida Vale
London W9 1SD, UNITED KINGDOM (UK)

Leach, Sheryl (Animator)
Lyons Group
300 E Bethany Road
Allen, TX 75002, USA

Leach, Steve (Athlete, Hockey Player, Olympic Athlete)
197 South St
Reading, MA 01867-3934

Leach, Terry (Athlete, Baseball Player)
2135 SW Locks Rd
Stuart, FL 34997-7011, USA

Leachman, Cloris (Actor)
21344 Colina Dr
Topanga, CA 90290, USA

Leadbetter, Kelly (Athlete, Golfer)
9606 Tavistock Ct
Orlando, FL 32827-7018, USA

Leader, George M (Ex-Governor, Politician)
Providence Place
830 Cherry Dr
Hershey, PA 17033-2007, USA

Leader, Tom (Architect)
537 Golden Gate Avenue
Richmond, CA 94801-3709, USA

Leadon, Bernie (Musician)
Joe's Garage
4405 Belmont Park Terrace
Nashville, TN 37215, USA

Leaf, Alexander (Physicist)
5 Sussex Road
Winchester, MA 01890, USA

Leaf, Ryan (Athlete, Football Player)
John And Marcia Leaf 1508 1/2 1st Ave S
Great Falls, MT 59401-3805, USA

League, Brandon (Athlete, Baseball Player)
72385 Lake Heather Heights Ct
Dunedin, FL 34698-5649, USA

Leah, Rachelle (Actor, Athlete)
c/o Ivo Fischer *WME (LA)*
9601 Wilshire Blvd Fl 3
Beverly Hills, CA 90210, USA

Leahy, Bob (Athlete, Football Player)
2701 Rosedale Dr
Monroe, LA 71201, USA

Leahy, Gerry (Athlete, Football Player)
5129 Oakridge Dr
Beaverton, MI 48612-8591, USA

Leahy, Pat (Athlete, Hockey Player)
1 Bristol Dr
Duxbury, MA 02332-4117

Leahy, Patrick (Politician, Senator)
31 Green Acres Dr
Burlington, VT 05408-2415, USA

Leak, Jennifer (Actor)
James D'Auria Associates
PO Box 2219
Amagansett, NY 11930, USA

Leak, Justice (Actor)
c/o Staff Member *People Store*
645 Lambert Drive NE
Atlanta, GA 30324-4125, USA

Leake, Brett (Comedian)
3561 Leatherwood Lane
Maidens, VA 23102, USA

Leakes, NeNe (Reality TV Star)
c/o Steven Grossman *Collective*
8383 Wilshire Blvd
Suite 1050
Beverly Hills, CA 90211, USA

Leakey, Meave G (Biologist)
PO Box 24926
Nairobi, KENYA

Leakey, Richard (Scientist)
PO Box 24926
Nairobi, Kenya, Kenya

Leakey, Richard E F (Biologist)
PO Box 24926
Nairobi, KENYA

Leaks, Manny (Athlete, Basketball Player)
9912 North Blvd
Cleveland, OH 44108-3430, USA

Leaks Jr, Roosevelt (Athlete, Football Player)
11525 Glen Falloch Ct
Austin, TX 78754-5807, USA

Leal, Luis
Calle 28 #30-60
Barauisimeto
Lara, Venezuela

Leal, Sharon (Actor, Musician)
c/o Scott Wexler *Brillstein Entertainment Partners*
9150 Wilshire Blvd #350
Beverly Hills, CA 90212, USA

Leanderson, Matthew (Athlete, Olympic Athlete, Rower)
1301 N Highlands Pkwy Apt 110
Tacoma, WA 98406-2182, USA

Leandros, Vicky
Postfach 31 28
Kiel, GERMANY D-24030

LeAnn, Summer (Actor)
c/o Rebecca Wood *Triple Threat*
7070 Sunset Blvd Ste 126
Los Angeles, CA 90028, USA

Leannette (Stylist)
c/o Staff Member *Ken Barboza Associates*
115 W 30th St Rm 203
New York, NY 10001, USA

Lear, Evelyn (Opera Singer)
414 Sailboat Circle
Weston, FL 33326, USA

Lear, Harold (Athlete, Basketball Player)
8960 E Gail Rd
Scottsdale, AZ 85259-3119, USA

Lear, Norman M (Director, Producer, Writer)
c/o Staff Member *Act III Productions*
100 N Crescent Dr #250
Beverly Hills, CA 90210, USA

Learn, Ed (Athlete, Football Player)
1154 lakeshore Rd W RR 3
St Catharines, ON l2R 6P9, Canada

Learned, Michael (Actor)
1600 N Beverly Dr
Beverly Hills, CA 90210, USA

Leary, Denis (Actor, Comedian, Producer, Writer)
c/o Heidi Slan *42West (LA)*
11400 W Olympic Blvd
Suite 1100
Los Angeles, CA 90064, USA

Leary, Tim (Athlete, Baseball Player)
2461 Santa Monica Blvd
Santa Monica, CA 90404-2138, USA

Leatherdale, Douglas W (Business Person)
Saint Paul Companies
385 Washington St
Saint Paul, MN 55102, USA

Leaud, Jean-Pierre (Actor)
Artmedia
20 Ave Rapp
Paris 75007, FRANCE

Leavell, Allen (Athlete, Basketball Player)
7007 Windy Pines Dr
Spring, TX 77379-4733, USA

Leavell, Chuck (Musician)
Charlane Plantation
665 Charlane Dr
Dry Branch, GA 31020, USA

Leavelle, James
5701 Drexel Dr
Garland, TX 75043, USA

Leavenworth, Scotty (Actor)
c/o Susan Curtis *Curtis Talent Management*
9607 Arby Dr
Beverly Hills, CA 90210, USA

Leaves (Music Group)
c/o Staff Member *Paradigm (Monterey)*
404 W Franklin St
Monterey, CA 93940, USA

Leavitt, Allan (Athlete, Football Player)
2261 Royal Fern Ln S
Jacksonville, FL 32223-1875, USA

Leavitt, Michael O (Ex-Governor, Politician)
Leavitt Partners
Leavitt Partners 229 S Main St
Ste 2300
Salt Lake City, UT 84111-2203, USA

Leavitt, Phil (Musician)
GEMS
PO Box 1031
Montrose, CA 91021, USA

Leavy, Edward (Judge)
US Court of Appeals
555 SW Yamhill St
Portland, OR 97204, USA

Leavy, Jon (Race Car Driver)
Leavy Racing Enterprises
7700 NW 37th Ave.
Miami, FL 33147, USA

Lebadang (Artist)
Circle Gallery
303 E Wacker Dr
Chicago, IL 60601, USA

LeBaron, Edward W (Eddie) Jr (Athlete, Football Player)
7524 Pineridge Ln
Fair Oaks, CA 95628, USA

Lebda, Brett (Athlete, Hockey Player)
557 Chatham Cir
Buffalo Grove, IL 60089-3343

LeBeau, Becky
9461 Charleville Blvd. #602
Beverly Hills, CA 90212

LeBeau, C Richard (Dick) (Athlete, Coach, Football Player)
10405 Stone Ct
Cincinnati, OH 45242, USA

LeBeauf, Sabrina (Actor)
735 Kappock St
#6F
Bronx, NY 10463, USA

Lebedev, Valentin V (Cosmonaut)
Potcha Kosmonavtov
Moskovskoi Oblasti
Syvisdny Goroduk 141160, RUSSIA

LeBel, B Harper (Athlete, Football Player)
3379 Scadlock Ln
Sherman Oaks, CA 91403, USA

LeBel, Robert (Bob) (Misc)
25 Rue Saint Pierre
Cite de Chambly, QC J3L 1L7, CANADA

Leber, Ben (Athlete, Football Player)
5 Bridge Ln
Minneapolis, MN 55424-1224, USA

Lebis, Attilo (Choreographer, Dancer)
Opera de Paris
120 Rue Lyon
Paris 75012, FRANCE

LeBlanc, Christian LeBlanc (Actor)
c/o Staff Member *The Young and The Restless*
7800 Beverly Blvd
Suite 3305
Los Angeles, CA 90036, USA

LeBlanc, Jean-Paul (Athlete, Hockey Player)
120 Gadwell Lane
Manius, NY 13104-9679

LeBlanc, Matt (Actor)
c/o Michael Rotenberg *3 Arts Entertainment Inc*
9460 Wilshire Blvd
7th Floor
Beverly Hills, CA 90210, USA

Leblanc, Ray (Athlete, Hockey Player)
3070 19th Pl SW
Largo, FL 33774-1437

LeBlanc, Wade (Baseball Player)
1477 Mary Carla Ln
Lake Charles, LA 70605-7196

Lebo, Jeff (Athlete, Basketball Player)
500 Hidden Lake Way
Santa Rosa Beach, FL 27858-3715, USA

Leboeuf, Laurence (Actor)
KL Benzakein Talent
c/o Karen Benzakein
1445 Lambert Closse
Montreal H3H 1Z5, CANADA

LeBoeuf, Raymond W (Business Person)
PPG Industries
1 PPG Place
Pittsburg, PA 15272, USA

LeBon, Simon (Musician, Songwriter, Writer)
c/o Staff Member *DD Productions*
93A Westbourne Park Villas
London W2 5ED, UNITED KINGDOM (UK)

Le Bon, Yasmin (Model)
c/o Staff Member *Ford Models (NY)*
238 E 4th St
New York, NY 10009, USA

Leboutillier, Peter (Athlete, Hockey Player)
35 Wandsworth Bridge Way
Lutherville Timonium, MD 21093-3963

Lebowitz, Fran (Writer)
Random House
1745 Broadway #B1
New York, NY 10019, USA

Lebowitz, Joel L (Mathematician)
Rutgers University
Mathematics Dept
New Brunswick, NJ 08903, USA

Leboyer, Frederick (Physicist)
Georges Borchardt
136 E 57th St
New York, NY 10022, USA

LeBrock, Kelly (Actor, Model)
Bartels Co
PO Box 57593
Sherman Oaks, CA 91413, USA

Lebron, Juan (Baseball Player)
Bowman
PO Box 242
Arroya, PR 00714-0242, USA

LeBrun, Christopher M (Artist)
Marlborough Fine Art
6 Albermarle St
London W1X 4BY, UNITED KINGDOM (UK)

Lecaine, Bill (Athlete, Hockey Player)
10484 Tracewood Cir
Littleton, CO 80130-8893

LeCarre, John (Writer)
9 Gainsborough Gardens
London NW3 1BJ, UK

Lecause, Carl (Horse Racer)
124 Asbury Ave
Freehold, NJ 07728-8187, USA

LeCavalier, Vincent (Athlete, Hockey Player)
c/o Staff Member *Tampa Bay Lightning*
Ice Palace
401 Channelside Dr
Tampa, FL 33602, USA

Lechler, Shane (Athlete, Football Player)
2115 Countryshire Ln
Richmond, TX 77406-3192, USA

Lechner, Ed (Athlete, Football Player)
6305 Burnham Cir Apt 122
Inver Grove Heights, MN 55076-1665, USA

Lechter, Sharon L (Writer)
Cashflow Technologies
4330 N Civic Center Plaza
Scottsdale, AZ 85251, USA

Leckey, Nick (Athlete, Football Player)
1056 E Windsor Dr
Gilbert, AZ 85296-4254, USA

Leckner, Eric (Athlete, Basketball Player)
608 27th St
Manhattan Beach, CA 90266-2231, USA

Leckonby, William (Athlete, Football Player)
1311 Santee Mill Rd
Bethlehem, PA 18017, USA

LeClair, James M (Jim) (Athlete, Football Player)
32 4th Ave NE
Mayville, ND 58257, USA

Leclair, Jim (Athlete, Football Player)
600 Plymouth Way
Burlingame, CA 94010, USA

Le Clair, John (Athlete, Hockey Player)
208 Turnbridge Circle
Haverford, PA 19041, USA

Leclair, John (Athlete, Hockey Player, Olympic Athlete)
108 Tunbridge Cir
Haverford, PA 19041-1058

Leclaire, Pascal (Athlete, Hockey Player)
250 Daniel Burnham Square #250
Columbus, OH 43215-2693, USA

LeClerc, Jean (Actor)
19 W 44th St
#1500
New York, NY 10036, USA

Leclerc, Katie (Actor)
c/o Stephanie Moy *Luber Roklin Management*
8530 Wilshire Blvd
6th Floor
Beverly Hills, CA 90211, USA

Leclerc, Mike (Athlete, Hockey Player)
473 Abbie Way
Costa Mesa, CA 92627-3162

Leclerc, Rene (Athlete, Hockey Player)
4265 Av Laurin
Quebec, QC G1P 1T6, Canada

Leclerc, Roger (Athlete, Football Player)
257 Elm St
Agawam, MA 01001, USA

LeClere, Jennifer
5601 Navigation Blvd
Houston, TX 77011

LeClezio, Jean-Marie (Writer)
Editions Gallimard
5 Rue Sebastien-Bottin
Paris 75007, USA

Lecomte, Benoit (Swimmer)
Cross Atlantic Swimming Challenge
3005 S Lamar
#D109-353
Austin, TX 78704, USA

Leconte, Henri (Tennis Player)
IMG
Pier House
Strand-on-Green
Chiswick, London W4 3NN, UNITED KINGDOM (UK)

Leconte, Patrice (Director, Writer)
c/o Staff Member *ArtMedia*
20 avenue Rapp
Paris 75008, France

Le Corre, Erwan (Misc)
21 rue du pere chevrier
Lyon 75020, France

Lecoultre, Francine (Stylist)
2175 Lemoyne St
Los Angeles, CA 90026, USA

Lecount, Terry (Athlete, Football Player)
1288 Branchfield Ct
Riverdale, GA 30296, USA

Lecroy, Matt (Athlete, Baseball Player, Olympic Athlete)
Potomac Nationals PO Box 2148 Attn: Managers Office
Woodbridge, VA 22195-2148, USA

Lecuyer, Doug (Athlete, Hockey Player)
9203 210 St NW
Edmonton, AB T5T 6X2, Canada

Ledbetter, Monte (Athlete, Football Player)
340 Sawgrass Dr
Valdosta, GA 31602, USA

Ledee, Ricky (Athlete, Baseball Player)
PO Box 22024
Hilton Head, SC 29925-2024, USA

Leder, Mimi (Director)
c/o Sara Bottfeld *Industry Entertainment Partners*
955 S Carrillo Dr
Suite 300
Los Angeles, CA 90048, USA

Leder, Philip (Scientist)
Howard Hughes Med Institute
4000 Jones Bridge Road
Chevy Chase MD, 20815

Lederberg, Joshua (Nobel Prize Laureate)
Rockefeller University
President's Office
1230 York Ave
New York, NY 10021, USA

Lederhandler, Marty (Photographer)
307 Prospect Ave Apt 10C
Hackensack, NJ 07601-2555, USA

Lederman, Leon M (Nobel Prize Laureate)
I M SA 1500 Sullivan Rd
Aurora, IL 60506-1067, USA

Ledesma, Aaron (Athlete, Baseball Player)
13820 Cherry Creek Dr
Charleston, SC ?941 '1-0R4Q, USA

Ledet, Joshua (Musician)
c/o Staff Member *19 Entertainment - LA*
9000 W Sunset Blvd #1574
West Hollywood, CA 90069, USA

Ledford, Brandy (Actor)
c/o Leonard Bonnell *Characters Talent Agency (Toronto)*
8 Elm St
2nd Floor
Toronto, ON M5G 1G7, CANADA

Ledford, Frank F Jr (General)
Southwest Biomed Research Foundation
PO Box 760549
San Antonio
TX, 78245 USA

Ledford, Judith
11365 Ventura Blvd. #100
Studio City, CA 91604

Ledingham, Walt (Athlete, Hockey Player)
5421 Glenwood St.
Duluth, MN 55804-1333, USA

Ledoyen, Virginie (Actor, Model)
c/o Beatrice Hall *ArtMedia*
20 avenue Rapp
Paris 75008, France

Le Duc, Anh (General, President)
President's Office
Hoang Hoa Tham
Hanoi, VIETNAM

Leduc, Bob (Athlete, Hockey Player)
385 Buxton St
Harrisville, RI 02830-1704

Leduc-Alverson, Noella (Athlete, Baseball Player, Commentator)
5 Leonard Ave
Leonardo, NJ 07737-1536, USA

Ledyard, Courtney (Athlete, Football Player)
419 Miller Ave
Freeport, NY 11520, USA

Ledyard, Grant (Athlete, Hockey Player)
5072 Old Goodrich Rd
Clarence, NY 14031-1515

Lee, Alexandra (Actor)
c/o Staff Member *Loeb & Loeb (Office 1)*
10100 Santa Monica Blvd
Suite 2200
Century City, CA 90067, USA

Lee, Andy (Radio Personality, Television Host)
2DayFM Studios
Level 15
50 Goulburn St
Sidney, NSW 2000, Australia

Lee, Andy Scott (Musician)
c/o Staff Member *DCM International & Dance Crazy Management*
Suite 3, 294-296 Nether St
Finchley
London N3 1RJ, UK

Lee, Ang (Director, Producer, Writer)
206 Hommocks Rd
Larchmont, NY 10538, USA

Lee, Anthonia W (Amp) (Athlete, Football Player)
990 Brickyard Rd
Chipley, FL 32428, USA

Lee, Barbara (Congressman, Politician)
2267 Rayburn HOB
Washington, DC 20515, USA

Lee, Bertram M (Misc)
Denver Nugglets
Pepsi Center
1000 Chopper Circle
Denver, CO 80204, USA

Lee, Beverly (Musician)
Bevi Corp
PO Box 100
Clifton, NJ 07015, USA

Lee, Bill (Athlete, Baseball Player)
305 Common View Dr
Craftsbury, VT 05826-9779, USA

Lee, Bobby (Actor)
c/o Staff Member *Gersh (LA)*
9465 Wilshire Blvd
Suite 600
Beverly Hills, CA 90212, USA

Lee, Bracken (Politician)
PO Box 58371
Salt Lake City, UT 84158-0371, USA

Lee, Brandon (Adult Film Star)
c/o Staff Member *Diva Central Inc*
7510 W Sunset Blvd Ste 1445
Los Angees, CA 90046, USA

Lee, Brenda (Musician)
306 Elberta St
Nashville, TN 37210, USA

Lee, Briana (Adult Film Star)
8033 Sunset Blvd #851
W Hollywood, CA 90046, USA

Lee, Butch (Athlete, Basketball Player)
6616 Bluestone Ct
Charlotte, NC 28212-6431, USA

Lee, Carl (Athlete, Football Player)
1 Stonegate Dr
Hurricane, WV 25526, USA

Lee, Carlos (Athlete, Baseball Player)
1400 N 11th Ave
Melrose Park, IL 60160, USA

Lee, Catherine J (Artist)
PO Box 132
Condon, OR 97823, USA

Lee, Chang-Rae (Writer)
International Creative Mgmt
40 W 57th St
#1800
New York, NY 10019, USA

Lee, Charles R (Business Person)
GTE Corp
1255 Corporate Dr
Irving, TX 75038, USA

Lee, Christopher (Congressman,
Politician)
1711 Longworth HOB
Washington, DC 20515, USA

Lee, Christopher F C (Actor)
c/o Jean Diamond *Diamond Management*
31 Percy St
London W1T 2DD, UK

Lee, Cliff (Athlete, Baseball Player)
c/o Darek Braunecker *Braunecker Sports
Counseling*
226 Trelon Cir
Little Rock, AR 72223, USA

Lee, Clyde (Athlete, Basketball Player)
1118 Crater Hill Dr
Nashville, TN 37215-4510, USA

Lee, Corey (Athlete, Baseball Player)
278 Lancashire Run
Smithfield, NC 27577-8025, USA

Lee, C.S. (Actor, Director)
c/o Andrew Tetenbaum *ATA Management*
12 Desbrosses St
New York, NY 10013, USA

Lee, David (Director, Writer)
Jim Preminger Agency
450 N Roxbury Dr
#1050
Beverly Hills, CA 90210, USA

Lee, David (Actor)
c/o Paula Rosenberg *ICA Talent*
818 12th Street Ste 9
Santa Monica, CA 90403, USA

Lee, David (Athlete, Basketball Player)
c/o Mark Bartelstein *Priority Sports &
Entertainment - Chicago*
312 N La Salle
Suite 650
Chicago, IL 60610, USA

Lee, David (Athlete, Baseball Player)
56 Terrace Drive
Pittsburgh, PA 15205-4312, USA

Lee, David A (Athlete, Football Player)
2518 N Waverly Dr
Bossier City, LA 71111, USA

Lee, David H (Astronomer, Writer)
Plenum Publishing Group
233 Spring St
New York, NY 10013, USA

Lee, David L (Business Person)
Global Crossing Ltd
Wessex House
45 Reid St
Hamilton, HM 12, Bermuda

Lee, David M (Nobel Prize Laureate)
Comell University
Cornell University
159 Sapsucker Woods Rd
Ithaca, NY 14850-1923, USA

Lee, Denise (Actor)
c/o Terry Loftis *Verve Communications
Group*
325 N St. Paul St Ste2360
Dallas, TX 75201, USA

Lee, Derek (Athlete, Baseball Player)
8834 Liatris Dr
Frankfort, IL 60423-1742, USA

Lee, Derek (Athlete, Baseball Player)
3576 Brittany Way
El Dorado Hills, CA 95762, USA

Lee, Derek
5230 Hyland Hills Ave
Unit 1311
Sarasota, FL 34241-7154, USA

Lee, Derrek
First Touch Foundation
5098 Foothills Blvd #3-492
Roseville, CA 95747

Lee, Dickey (Musician)
Mars Talent
27 L'Ambiance Court
Bardonia, NY 10954, USA

Lee, Don
9101 E Palm Tree Dr
Tucson, AZ 85710-8626

Lee, Don (Athlete, Baseball Player)
9101 E Palm Tree Dr
Tucson, AZ 85710, USA

Lee, Doug (Athlete, Basketball Player)
10770 Procyon St
Las Vegas, NV 89141-8844, USA

Lee, Dwight (Athlete, Football Player)
P.O. Box 480397
New Haven, MI 48048, USA

Lee, Ed (Athlete, Hockey Player)
6 Normand St Apt D
Bristol, RI 02809-4719

Lee, Edward (Writer)
Necro Publications/Bedlam Press
PO Box 540298
Orlando, FL 32854-0298, USA

Lee, Edward (Athlete, Football Player)
1781 Verbena St NW
Washington, DC 20012, USA

Lee, Eugene (Actor)
c/o Vincent Cirrincione *Vincent
Cirrincione Associates*
1516 N Fairfax Ave
Los Angeles, CA 90046, USA

Lee, Eunice (Musician)
Columbia Artists Mgmt Inc
165 W 57th St
New York, NY 10019, USA

Lee, Geddy (Musician)
Macklam Feldman Mgmt
1505 W 2nd Ave
#200
Vancouver, BC V6H 3Y4, CANADA

Lee, Grandma (Actor, Comedian)
Lee Strong
626 Staffordshire Dr
Jacksonville, FL 32225, USA

Lee, Gregory (Athlete, Basketball Player)
8077 Wild Flower Way
San Diego, CA 92120-1622, USA

Lee, Harper (Writer)
McIntosh & Otis
353 Lexington Ave
#1500
New York, NY 10016, USA

Lee, Harper (Writer)
PO Box 278
Monroeville, AL 36461-0278, USA

Lee, H Douglas (Educator)
Stetson University
President's Office
Deland, FL 32720, USA

Lee, Homer & The Braschler's
PO Box 1408
Branson, MO 65616

Lee, Howard V (General)
529 King Arthur Dr
Virginia Beach, VA 23464-2235, USA

Lee, Jack R (Athlete, Football Player)
6306 Mid Pines Dr
Houston, TX 11069, USA

Lee, Jacky (Athlete, Football Player)
Jack Lee Interests Inc 6306 Mid Pines Dr
Houston, TX 77069-1346, USA

Lee, James Kyson (Actor)
c/o Staff Member *Kass & Stokes
Management*
9229 Sunset Blvd
Suite 504
Los Angeles, CA 90069, USA

Lee, Jared B (Cartoonist)
Jared B Lee Studio
2942 Hamilton Rd
Lebanon, OH 45036-8857, USA

Lee, Jason (Actor, Producer, Writer)
c/o Gay Ribisi *Ribisi Entertainment*
3278 Wilshire Blvd
Suite 702
Los Angeles, CA 90010, USA

Lee, Jason Scott (Actor)
c/o Cynthia Shelton-Droke *Sweet Mud
Group*
648 Broadway #1002
New York, NY 10012, USA

Lee, Jeahette (Billiards Player)
Octagon
1751 Pinnacle Dr
#1500
McLean, VA 22102, USA

Lee, Jeanette (Billiards Player)
c/o Arlene dela Cruz dela Cruz *Octagon
(VA)*
1751 Pinnacle Dr #1500
McLean, VA 22102, USA

Lee, Jenny (Athlete, Golfer)
c/o Staff Member *Ladies Pro Golf
Association (LPGA)*
100 International Golf Dr
Daytona Beach, FL 32124-1092, USA

Lee, Joe (Business Person)
Darden Restaurants
5900 Lake Ellenor Dr
Orlando, FL 32809, USA

Lee, Jon (Actor, Musician)
c/o Staff Member *McLean-Williams
Management*
Gainsborough House
81 Oxford St
London W1D 2EU, UK

Lee, Jonna (Actor)
8721 Sunset Blvd
#103
Los Angeles, CA 90069, USA

Lee, Julia (Actor)
c/o Staff Member *Privilege Talent Agency*
PO Box 260860
Encino, CA 91426-0860, USA

Lee, Kathy
204 River Edge Lane
Seiverville, TN 37862

Lee, Keith (Athlete, Basketball Player)
11653 Metz Pl
Eads, TN 38028-6912, USA

Lee, Kuan Yew (Prime Minister)
Senoir Minister's Office
Istana Annexe
Istana
Singapore 0923, SINGAPORE

Lee, Kurk (Athlete, Basketball Player)
2745 Scarborough Cir
Windsor Mill, MD 21244-8024, USA

Lee, Larry (Athlete, Football Player)
PO Box 3889
Highland Park, MI 48203-0889, USA

Lee, Laura
155 N. Beverwyck PMB 245
Lake Hiawatha, NJ 07034

Lee, Laurie Ann (Athlete, Baseball Player,
Commentator)
19528 Cohasset St
Reseda, CA 91335-2436, USA

Lee, Lela (Actor)
c/o Marilyn Szatmary *Silver Massetti & Szatmary (SMS) Talent Inc*
8383 Wilshire Blvd
Suite 230
Beverly Hills, CA 90211, USA

Lee, Leron (Athlete, Baseball Player)
8150 Warren Ct
Granite Bay, CA 95746-9576, USA

Lee, Lloyd (Athlete, Football Player)
635 Homewood Ave
Highland Park, IL 60035-2420, USA

Lee, London
1650 Broadway #1410
New York, NY 10019

Lee, Malcolm D (Actor, Director, Writer)
c/o Adam Kanter *Creative Artists Agency (CAA-LA)*
2000 Ave Of The Stars
Los Angeles, CA 90067, USA

Lee, Mark (Athlete, Football Player)
14120 NE 183rd St Unit 233
Woodinville, WA 98072-7073, USA

Lee, Mark (Athlete, Baseball Player)
130 N Rosemont St
Amarillo, TX 79106-5214, USA

Lee, Mark (Athlete, Baseball Player)
3580 Brunswick Dr
Colorado Springs, CO 80920-7338, USA

Lee, Mark C (Astronaut)
4574 Bishops Court
Middleton, WI 53562-2326, USA

Lee, Mark C Colonel (Astronaut)
79 S Player Crest Cir
Spring, TX 77382-1809, USA

Lee, Michele (Actor)
830 Birchwood
Los Angeles, CA 90024, USA

Lee, Michelle (Actor)
c/o Michael Henderson *Heresun Management*
4119 West Burbank Blvd.
Burbank, CA 91505, USA

Lee, Mike (Athlete, Baseball Player)
1790 Calmin Dr
Fallbrook, CA 92028-4303, USA

Lee, Min-ho (Actor)
c/o Staff Member *Starhaus Entertainment*
L#601 Hill B/D
563-4 Shinsa-dong, Kangnam-gu
Seoul, Korea

Lee, Natasha (Actor, Dancer, Model)
c/o Staff Member *Don Capo Entertainment*
Ste 5 South Bank Terrace
Surbiton
Surrey KT6 6DG, UNITED KINGDOM (UK)

Lee, Raphael C (Doctor)
Massachusetts Institute Technology
Engineering Dept
Cambridge, MA 02139, USA

Lee, Reggie (Actor)
c/o Adam Griffin *Kritzer Levine Wilkins Entertainment (KLWG)*
11872 La Grange Ave
1st Floor
Los Angeles, CA 90025, USA

Lee, Rex (Actor)
c/o Marc Hamou *Thruline Entertainment*
9250 Wilshire Blvd
Ground Fl
Beverly Hills, CA 90212, USA

Lee, Robert M (Athlete, Football Player)
363 Parker Ave
San Francisco, CA 94118, USA

Lee, Robinne (Actor)
c/o Darren Goldberg *Global Creative*
1051 Cole Ave # B
Los Angeles, CA 90038, USA

Lee, Rock (Athlete, Basketball Player)
4616 Blackfoot Ave
San Diego, CA 92117-6230, USA

Lee, Ron (Athlete, Basketball Player)
35788 Woodridge Ct
Farmington, MI 48335, USA

Lee, Ronnie (Athlete, Football Player)
139 Shady Trl
Mc Gregor, TX 76657-3768, USA

Lee, RonReaco
c/o Brett Carella *Lab, The*
5540 Hollywood Blvd #200
Hollywood, CA 90028, USA

Lee, Russell (Athlete, Basketball Player)
1457 Smokehouse Ln
Stone Mountain, GA 30088-3312, USA

Lee, Ruta (Actor)
2623 Laurel Canyon Road
Los Angeles, CA 90046, USA

Lee, Sammy (Athlete, Diver, Olympic Athlete)
16537 Harbour Ln
Huntington Beach, CA 92649-2105, USA

Lee, Sammy (Doctor)
16537 Harbour Ln
Huntington Beach, CA 92649, USA

Lee, Samuel (Sammy) (Coach)
16537 Harbour Lane
Huntington Beach, CA 92649, USA

Lee, Sandra (Chef, Television Host)
c/o Staff Member *Food Network, The*
1180 Ave of the Americas Fl 11
New York, NY 10036, USA

Lee, Shannon (Actor)
c/o Steven Younger *Myman Abell Fineman Fox Greenspan Light*
11601 Wilshire Blvd
Suite 2200
Los Angeles, CA 90025, USA

Lee, Sheryl (Actor)
c/o Daniel (Danny) Sussman *Brillstein Entertainment Partners*
9150 Wilshire Blvd #350
Beverly Hills, CA 90212, USA

Lee, Spike (Director, Producer)
c/o Staff Member *40 Acres & A Mule Filmworks Inc (NY)*
75 S Elliott Pl
Brooklyn, NY 11217, USA

Lee, Stan (Cartoonist, Publisher)
Marvel Entertainment
1440 S Sepulveda Blvd
#114
Los Angeles, CA 90025-3458, USA

Lee, Steven (Television Host)
c/o Staff Member *Travel Channel*
1 Discovery Pl
Silver Spring, MD 20910, USA

Lee, Sung Hi (Actor)
c/o Staff Member *TalentWorks (LA)*
3500 W Olive Ave
Suite 1400
Burbank, CA 91505, USA

Lee, Terry (Athlete, Baseball Player)
4650 Wendover St
Eugene, OR 97404-1348, USA

Lee, Tommy (Musician)
c/o David Weise *David Weise and Associates*
16000 Ventura Blvd
Suite 600
Encino, CA 91436-2753, USA

Lee, Tony (Actor)
c/o Dave Phillips *Edmonds Management*
1635 N Cahuenga Blvd Fl 5
Los Angeles, CA 90028, USA

Lee, Travis (Athlete, Baseball Player, Olympic Athlete)
PO Box 231081
Encinitas, CA 92023-1081, USA

Lee, Tsung-Dao (Nobel Prize Laureate)
25 Claremont Ave
New York, NY 10027-6813, USA

Lee, Vernon R (Religious Leader)
Wyatt Baptist Church
4621 W Hillsboro St
El Dorado, AR 71730, USA

Lee, Vincent (Baseball Player)
Baltimore Black Sox
3228 Avondale Ave
Baltimore, MD 21215-4702, USA

Lee, Wayne (Engineer)
Jet Propulsion Laboratory
4800 Oak Grove Dr
Pasadena, CA 91109, USA

Lee, William Gregory (Actor)
c/o Jeff Witjas *Agency for the Performing Arts (APA-LA)*
405 S Beverly Dr
Suite 500
Beverly Hills, CA 90212-4425, USA

Lee, Willie James (Athlete, Baseball Player)
400 5th Way
Birmingham, AL 35214-5706, USA

Lee, Yuan T (Nobel Prize Laureate)
19 Las Piedras
Orinda, CA 94563-2045, TAIWAN

Lee, Zeph (Athlete, Football Player)
7417 1/2 S Normandie Ave
Los Angeles, CA 90044, USA

Leech, Beverly
9150 Wilshire Blvd. #175
Beverly Hills, CA 90212

Leech, Richard (Opera Singer)
Thea Dispeker Artists
59 E 54th St
New York, NY 10022, USA

Leede, Ed (Athlete, Basketball Player)
307 Roca Pl
Castle Rock, CO 80108-9020, USA

Lee-Dries, Dolores (Athlete, Baseball Player, Commentator)
1950 Barcelona Rd SW
Deming, NM 88030-8552, USA

Lee Fincher, Stephen (Congressman, Politician)
1118 Longworth HOB
Washington, DC 20515, USA

Lee-Harmon, Annabelle (Baseball Player)
960 Senate St
Costa Mesa, CA 92627-3332, USA

Leek, Gene (Athlete, Baseball Player)
4055 Hamilton St Apt 5
San Diego, CA 92104-6108, USA

Leek, Sybil (Misc)
Prentice-Hall
RR 9W
Englewood Cliffs, NJ 07632, USA

Leeman, Gary (Athlete, Hockey Player)
12-1027 Old Bridge Rd RR 2
Port Carling, ON P0B IJO, Canada

Leen, Bill (Musician)
William Morris Agency
2100 W End Ave
#1000
Nashville, TN 37203, USA

Leeper, Dave (Athlete, Baseball Player)
23997 Kaleb Dr
Corona, CA 92883-9385, USA

Leerhsen, Erica (Actor)
c/o Staff Member *Kritzer Levine Wilkins Entertainment (KLWG)*
11872 La Grange Ave
1st Floor
Los Angeles, CA 90025, USA

Leese, Howard (Musician)
219 2st Ave N
#333
Seattle, WA 98109, USA

Leestma, David C (Astronaut)
4314 Lake Grove Dr
Seabrook, TX 77586, USA

Leestma, David C Captain (Astronaut)
4314 Lake Grove Dr
Seabrook, TX 77586-4114, USA

Leetch, Brian (Athlete, Hockey Player)
40 Battery_ St PH 12
Boston, MA 02109-1907

Leetch, Brian J (Athlete, Hockey Player, Olympic Athlete)
c/o Staff Member *PuckAgency LLC*
555 Pleasantville Rd
North Building, Suite 210
Briarcliff Manor, NY 10510, USA

Leetsma, David C
2101 NASA Rd
Houston, TX 77058, USA

Leetzow, Max (Athlete, Football Player)
4744 E Caley Pl
Centennial, CO 80121-3202, USA

Leeuwenburg, Jay (Athlete, Football Player)
6268 S Conventry Ln W
Littleton, CO 80123, USA

Leeves, Jane (Actor)
c/o Molly Madden *3 Arts Entertainment Inc*
9460 Wilshire Blvd
7th Floor
Beverly Hills, CA 90210, USA

Lefcourt, Peter (Actor)
c/o Staff Member *Creative Artists Agency (CAA-LA)*
2000 Ave Of The Stars
Los Angeles, CA 90067, USA

Lefebvre, Jim (Athlete, Baseball Player, Coach)
10160 E Whispering Wind Dr
Scottsdale, AZ 85255-3007, USA

Lefebvre, Joe (Athlete, Baseball Player)
12 Blake St
Concord, NH 03301-4010, USA

Lefebvre, Ryan (Commentator)
622 N Winnebago Dr
Greenwood, MO 64034-9419, USA

Lefebvre, Sylvain (Athlete, Hockey Player)
7833 Valla_gio Ln
Englewood, CO 80112-5872

Lefebvre, Sylvain
Colorado Avalanche
1000 Chopper Cir
Denver, CO 80204-5805

Lefevre, Rachelle (Actor)
c/o Lee Wallman *Wallman Public Relations*
10323 Santa Monica Blvd
Suite 109
Los Angeles, CA 90025, USA

Lefferts, Craig (Athlete, Baseball Player)
Stockton Ports 404 W Fremont St Attn: Coaching Staff
Stockton, CA 95203-2806, USA

Lefkowitz, Louis (Politician)
575 Park Ave
New York, NY 10065-7332, USA

Lefley, Chuck (Athlete, Hockey Player)
PO Box 65
Grosse Isle, MB ROC IGO, Canada

Leflore, Ron (Athlete, Baseball Player)
6263 93rd Ter
Apt 4206
Pinellas Park, FL 33782-4640, USA

Lefton, Jacqui (Stylist)
c/o Staff Member *Susan Price Inc*
333 Hudson St
#1002
New York, NY 10013, USA

Leftwich, Byron (Athlete, Football Player)
12025 New Dominion Pkwy #401
Reston, VA 20190-6268, USA

Leftwich, Phil (Athlete, Baseball Player)
15819 S 31st St
Phoenix, AZ 85048-7775, USA

Legace, Jean-Guy (Athlete, Hockey Player)
126 Cassa Grande Ln
Santa Rosa Beach, FL 32459, USA

Legace, Manny (Athlete, Hockey Player)
40708 Village Oaks
Novi, MI 48375-4464

LeGault, Lance (Actor)
c/o Staff Member *Tisherman Gilbert Motley Drozdoski Talent Agency (TGMD)*
6767 Forest Lawn Dr
Suite 101
Los Angeles, CA 90068, USA

Legend, John (Actor, Musician)
72 E. 3rd St. #1A
New York, NY 10003, USA

Legette, Burnie (Athlete, Football Player)
1118 Doyle Pl
Colorado Springs, CO 80915, USA

Legette, Tyrone (Athlete, Football Player)
1304 Hancock St
Columbia, SC 29205, USA

Legg, Greg (Athlete, Baseball Player)
Lakewood Blueclaws 2 Stadium Way
Attn: Coaching Staff
lakewood, NJ 08701-4536, USA

Leggat, Ashley (Actor)
c/o Staff Member *Walt Disney Co, The (Buena Vista Motion Picture Group)*
500 S Buena Vista St
Ink And Paint Building Rm230
Burbank, CA 91521-

Leggatt, Ian (Athlete, Golfer)
9726 E Mountain Spring Rd
Scottsdale, AZ 85255, USA

Legge, Barry (Athlete, Hockey Player)
Division 12 Police Station 210 Lyje St
Winnipeg, MB R3J 2Cl, Canada

Legge, Katherine (Race Car Driver)
307 Park Ave.
Chardon, OH 44024, USA

Legge, Michael (Actor)
c/o Staff Member *Hatton McEwan*
3 Chocolate Studios
7 Shepherdess Place
London N1 7LJ, UK

Legge, Randy (Athlete, Hockey Player)
322 Primrose Lane
Newmarket, ON L3Y 5Z2, CANADA

Leggero, Natasha (Actor)
c/o Geoff Cheddy *Brillstein Entertainment Partners*
9150 Wilshire Blvd #350
Beverly Hills, CA 90212, USA

Leggett, Anthony J (Nobel Prize Laureate)
607 W Pennsylvania Ave
Urbana, IL 61801-4818, USA

Leggett, Dave (Athlete, Football Player)
3251 Templeton Gap Rd
Colorado Springs, CO 80907-5735, USA

Leggett, Jay (Actor, Producer, Writer)
c/o Lenore Zerman *Liberman/Zerman Management*
252 N Larchmont Blvd
Suite 200
Los Angeles, CA 90004, USA

Legien, Waldemar (Athlete)
Ul Grottgera 10
Bytom 41-902, POLAND

Legler, Tim (Athlete, Basketball Player)
275 82nd St
Stone Harbor, NJ 08210-3817, USA

Legorreta, Vilchis Ricardo (Architect)
Palacio de Versalles
#285A
C Lomas Reforma
Mexico City 11020, MEXICO

Legrand, Michel (Composer, Musician)
c/o Staff Member *Kraft-Engel Management*
15233 Ventura Blvd
Suite 200
Sherman Oaks, CA 91403, USA

Legrande, Larry (Athlete, Baseball Player)
1331 Leon St NW
Roanoke, VA 24017-6011, USA

Legree, Lance (Athlete, Football Player)
25 Ardmore Ave
Clifton, NJ 07012-1807, USA

Legris, Manuel C (Ballerina)
National Theater of Paris Opera
8 Rue Scribe
Paris 75009, FRANCE

LeGros, James (Actor)
I F A Talent Agency
8730 Sunset Blvd
#490
Los Angeles, CA 90069, USA

Leguin, Ursula (Writer)
Virginia Kidd PO Box 278
Milford, PA 18337-0278, USA

LeGuin, Ursula K (Writer)
PO Box 10541
Portland, OR 97296, USA

Leguizamo, John (Actor, Comedian, Producer)
c/o Jeff Golenberg *Collective*
8383 Wilshire Blvd
Suite 1050
Beverly Hills, CA 90211, USA

Legwand, David (Athlete, Hockey Player)
333 Lake Valley Dr
Franklin, TN 37069-4652

Lehan, Michael (Athlete, Football Player)
418 Madison Ave S
Hopkins, MN 55343-8469, USA

Lehane, Dennis (Writer)
341 Kerrville South Dr
Kerrville, TX 78028, USA

Lehew, Jim (Athlete, Baseball Player)
3086 Fairview Rd
Grantsville, MD 21536-2239, USA

Lehman, I Robert (Scientist)
895 Cedro Way
Palo Alto, CA 94305, USA

Lehman, Jeffrey (Educator)
Cornell University
President's Office
Ithaca, NY 14853, USA

Lehman, Kristen (Actor)
c/o Perry Zimel *Oscars Abrams Zimel & Associates, Inc. (OAZ)*
438 Queen St E
Toronto ON M5A 1T4, CANADA

Lehman, Manny (DJ)
c/o Len Evans *Project Publicity*
312 West 53rd St
Suite 202
New York, NY 10019, USA

Lehman, Tom (Athlete, Golfer)
9820 E Thompson Peak Pkwy
Unit 704
Scottsdale, AZ 85255-6656, USA

Lehmann, Edie (Actor)
24844 Malibu Road
Malibu, CA 90265, USA

Lehmann, Erich L (Misc)
Research Statistics Group
Education Testing Service
Princeton, NJ 08541, USA

Lehmann, Karl Cardinal (Religious Leader)
Bischofliches Ordinariat
PF 1560
Bischofsplatz 2
Mainz 55116, GERMANY

Lehmann, Michael (Director, Producer)
c/o Staff Member *Industry Entertainment Partners*
955 S Carrillo Dr
Suite 300
Los Angeles, CA 90048, USA

Lehmberg, Stanford E (Historian)
1005 Calle Largo
Santa Fe, NM 87501, USA

Lehmkuhl, Reichen (Model, Reality TV Star, Writer)
c/o Mara Santino *Luber Roklin Management*
8530 Wilshire Blvd
6th Floor
Beverly Hills, CA 90211, USA

Lehn, Jean Marie
21 rue d'Oslo
Strasbourg, FRANCE F-67000

Lehn, Jean-Marie P (Nobel Prize Laureate)
Louis Pasteur Universite
4 Rue Blaise Pascal
Strasbourg F-67000, FRANCE

Lehne, Fredric (Actor)
c/o Staff Member *Bauman Redanty & Shaul Agency*
5757 Wilshire Blvd
Suite 473
Beverly Hills, CA 90212, USA

Lehninger, Albert L (Misc)
15020 Tanyard Road
Sparks, MD 21152, USA

Lehr, John (Actor, Producer, Writer)
c/o Staff Member *WmE2 (WMA-LA)*
1 William Morris Pl
Beverly Hills, CA 90212, USA

Lehr, Justin (Athlete, Baseball Player)
1281 W Derringer Way
Chandler, AZ 85286-6424, USA

Lehr, Zella (Musician)
1961 NE 31st St
Lighthouse Point, FL 33064, USA

Lehrer, Jim (Journalist)
The NewsHour with Jim Lehrer
3556 Macomb St NW
Washington, DC 20016-3162, USA

Lehrer, Robert I (Biologist)
University of California
Med Center
Hematology Dept
Los Angeles, CA 90024, USA

Lehrman, Logan (Actor)
c/o Joseph (Joe) Rice *Abrams Artists Agency (LA)*
9200 Sunset Blvd
11th Floor
Los Angeles, CA 90069, USA

Lehtinen, Dexter (Attorney, Attorney General, General, Government Official)
US Attorney's Office
Justice Dept
155 Miami Ave
Miami, FL 33130, USA

Lehtinen, Jere (Athlete, Hockey Player)
622 Stratford Ln
Coppell, TX 75019-6129, USA

Lehto, JJ (Race Car Driver)
Hogan Racing LLC
3473 Rider Trail So.
Earth City, MO 63045, USA

Lehtonen, Kari (Athlete, Hockey Player)
3230 Bryn Mawr Dr
Dallas, TX 75225-7645

Lehuep, John (Athlete, Football Player)
205 Bud Nalley Dr
Easley, SC 29642-3578, USA

Lehvonen, Hank (Athlete, Hockey Player)
4000 N Federal Hwy #207
Boca Raton, FL 33431-4527, USA

Leiba, Freddie (Stylist)
c/o Staff Member *Bryan Bantry*
900 Broadway Ste 400
New York, NY 10003, USA

Leibel, Rudolph (Misc)
464 Riverside Dr
#95
New York, NY 10027, USA

Leibman, Ron (Actor)
c/o Staff Member *Agency for the Performing Arts (APA-LA)*
405 S Beverly Dr
Suite 500
Beverly Hills, CA 90212-4425, USA

Leibovitz, Annie (Artist, Photographer)
Annie Leibovitz Photography
443 W 18th St Ste 4
New York, NY 10011-3817, USA

Leibovitz, Mitchell G (Business Person)
Pep Boys-Manny Moe & Jack
3111 W Allegheny Ave
Philadelphia, PA 19132, USA

Leibowitz, Barry (Athlete, Basketball Player)
10670 NW 17th Pl
Plantation, FL 33318-5353, USA

Leibrandt, Charlie (Athlete, Baseball Player)
1235 Stuart Ridge
Alpharetta, GA 30022-6364, USA

Leicester, Jon (Athlete, Baseball Player)
17151 Corbina Ln
Apt 112
Huntington Beach, CA 90403-3029, USA

Leick, Hudson (Actor)
c/o Staff Member *Geddes Agency, The*
8430 Santa Monica Blvd
Suite 200
Los Angeles, CA 90069, USA

Leier, Ed (Athlete, Hockey Player)
2250 Christopherson Rd Suite 10
Surrey, BC V4A 3L3, Canada

Leifer, Carol (Actor, Comedian)
c/o Howard Klein *3 Arts Entertainment Inc*
9460 Wilshire Blvd
7th Floor
Beverly Hills, CA 90210, USA

Leifer, Neil (Photographer)
235 W 56th St Apt 21B
New York, NY 10019-4330, USA

Leiferkus, Sergei P (Opera Singer)
5 The Paddocks
Abberbury Road
Iffley, Oxford OX4 4ET, UNITED KINGDOM (UK)

Leifheit, Sylvia (Model)
Agentur Reed
Treppendorfer Weg 13
Berlin 12527, GERMANY

Leigeb, Brian (Football Player)
c/o Team Member *Oakland Raiders*
1220 Harbor Bay Pkwy
Alameda, CA 94502, USA

Leigh, Barbara (Actor)
GRA
9320 Wilshire Blvd Ste 302
Beverly Hills, CA 90212, USA

Leigh, Chyler (Actor)
c/o Joanna (Joanie) Burstein *Burstein Company, The*
15304 Sunset Blvd
suite 208
Pacific Palisades, CA 90272, USA

Leigh, Danni (Musician)
c/o Bridget Bauer *Bismeaux Productions*
PO Box 463
Austin, TX 78767, USA

Leigh, Jennifer Jason (Actor)
c/o Greg Clark *Untitled Entertainment (LA)*
350 S. Beverly Dr #200
Beverly Hills, CA 90212, USA

Leigh, Mike (Director)
Thin Man Films
9 Greek St
Soho
London W1D 4DQ, UNITED KINGDOM (UK)

Leigh, Mitch (Composer)
29 W 57th St
#1000
New York, NY 10019, USA

Leigh, Regina (Musician)
Bobby Roberts
909 Meadowlark Lane
Goodlettsville, TN 37072, USA

Leighton, Brad (Race Car Driver)
c/o Staff Member *NASCAR*
1801 Speedway Blvd
Daytona Beach, FL 32015, USA

Leighton, GB (Musician)
c/o Staff Member *Paradigm (Monterey)*
404 W Franklin St
Monterey, CA 93940, USA

Leighton, Laura (Actor)
c/o Paul Santana *Agency for the Performing Arts (APA-LA)*
405 S Beverly Dr
Suite 500
Beverly Hills, CA 90212-4425, USA

Leija, James (Jesse) (Athlete, Boxer)
154 Octavia Place
San Antonio, TX 78214-1236, USA

Leiker, Tony (Athlete, Football Player)
411 E 21st St
Hays, KS 67601, USA

Leimkuehler, Paul (Business Person, Skier)
351 Darbys Run
Bay Village, OH 44140, USA

Leinart, Matt (Athlete, Football Player, Heisman Trophy Winner)
6966 Turf Dr
Huntington Beach, CA 92648-1546, USA

Leinbach, Michael (Scientist)
3595 Coral Ave
Mims, FL 32754, USA

Leinonen, Mikko (Athlete, Hockey Player)
Tappara Tampere Liiga-Tapparan Toimisto
Kissanmaankatu 9
Tampere, SF 33520, Finland

Leiper, Dave (Athlete, Baseball Player)
13082 N 103rd St
Scottsdale, AZ 85260-7272, USA

Leipheimer, Levi (Athlete, Cycler, Olympic Athlete)
1755 Crystal Springs Ct
Santa Rosa, CA 95404-1095, USA

Leipzig, Arthur (Photographer)
378 Glen Ave
Sea Clif, NY 11579-1525, USA

Leister, John (Athlete, Baseball Player)
304 Devon Dr
Saint Louis, MI 48880-9427, USA

Leisure, David (Actor)
26807 Fairlain Dr
Valencia, CA 91355, USA

Leitch, Donovan
8794 Lookout Mountain Ave.
Los Angeles, CA 90046-1859

Leitch, Matthew (Actor)
c/o Colleen Schlegel *Frontline Management*
5670 Wilshire Blvd.
Suite 1370
Los Angeles, CA 90036, USA

Leiter, Al (Athlete, Baseball Player)
181 E 90th St Apt 9B
New York, NY 10128-2389, USA

Leiter, Al
181 E 90th St Apt 9B
New York, NY 10128-2389

Leiter, Alois T (Al) (Athlete, Baseball Player)
New York Yankees
161st Street and River Avenue
Attn: Broadcast Dept
Bronx, NY 10451, USA

Leiter, Bob (Athlete, Hockey Player)
1921 Shore point Village
Gimli, MB ROC 1BO, Canada

Leiter, Ken (Athlete, Hockey Player)
30098 Warley Ct
Novi, MI 48377, USA

Leiter, Mark (Athlete, Baseball Player)
1959 Vermont Ave
Toms River, NJ 08731-5843, USA

Leith, Emmett N (Engineer)
4028 Oella Court
San Jose, CA 95124-4832, USA

Leith, Virginia (Actor)
2120 N Cardillo Ave
Palm Springs, CA 92262, USA

Leitner, Patric-Fritz (Athlete)
BSD
An der Schiessstatte 4
Berchtesgaden 83471, GERMANY

Leitner, Ted (Commentator)
PO Box 8926
Rancho Santa Fe, CA 92067-8926, USA

Leitso, Tyron (Actor)
c/o Deb Dillistone *Red Management*
100 W. Pender St
Sun Tower, 7th Floor
Vancouver, BC V6B 1R8, Canada

Leitzel, Joan (Educator)
University of Nebraska
President's Office
Lincoln, NE 68588, USA

Leius, Scott (Athlete, Baseball Player)
12620 42nd Pl N
Minneapolis, MN 55442-2344, USA

Lekakis, Paul (Musician)
c/o Staff Member *Diva Central Inc*
7510 W Sunset Blvd Ste 1445
Los Angees, CA 90046, USA

Lekang, Anton (Skier)
47 Pratt St
Winsted, CT 06098, USA

Lelbrandt, Charlie (Athlete, Baseball Player)
Cincinnati Reds
1235 Stuart Rdg
Alpharetta, GA 30022-6364, USA

Lelliott, Jeremy (Actor)
c/o Joan Green *Joan Green Management*
1836 Courtney Terr
Los Angeles, CA 90046, USA

L. Ellmers, Renee (Congressman, Politician)
1533 Longworth HOB
Washington, DC 20515

Lelong, Pierre J (Mathematician)
9 Place de Rungis
Paris 75013, FRANCE

LeLouch, Claude (Director)
15 Ave Hoche
Paris 75008, FRANCE

Lemaire, Jacques (Athlete, Hockey Player)
PO Box 1207
Palmetto, FL 34220-1207

Lemaire, Jacques G (Athlete, Coach, Hockey Player)
803 Riveria Dunes Way
Palmetto, FL 34221, USA

Lemaire, Pascale (Stylist)
c/o Elizabeth Centenari *T.H.E. Artist Agency*
1207 Potomac St., NW
Georgetown, DC 20007, USA

Lemanczyk, Dave (Athlete, Baseball Player)
24 Lehigh Ct
Rockville Centre, NY 11570-2016, USA

Lemaster, Denny (Athlete, Baseball Player)
4833 Carlene Way SW
Lilburn, GA 30047-4705, USA

Lemaster, Denny (Athlete, Baseball Player)
4833 Carlene Way SW
Lilburn, GA 30047, USA

Lemaster, Frank (Athlete, Football Player)
P.O. Box 159
Birchrunville, PA 19421, USA

Lemaster, Johnnie (Athlete, Baseball Player)
317 4th St
Paintsville, KY 41240-5225, USA

Lemaster, Jr., Ron (Race Car Driver)
3705 Brandon Rd
Huntingtonn, WV 25704, USA

Le Mat, Paul (Actor)
6300 Wilshire Blvd #1460
Los Angeles, CA 90048-5200, USA

Lemay, Dick (Athlete, Baseball Player)
1741 Holland Ln
Wichita, KS 67212-6242, USA

Lemay, Dick
1741 N Holland Ln
Wichita, Ks 67212-6242

Lemay, Moe (Athlete, Hockey Player)
6296 Lanark St
Chilliwack, BC V2R 3G9, Canada

Le May Doan, Catriona (Speed Skater)
Landmark Sport Group
1 City Centre Dr Ste 301
Mississauga, ON L5B 1M2, CANADA

LeMay-Doan, Michelle (Speed Skater)
Landmark Sport Group
277 Richmond St W
Toronto, ON M5V 1X1, CANADA

Lembeck, Michael (Actor, Director)
23852 Pacific Coast Highway
#355
Malibu, CA 90265, USA

Lemche, Kris (Actor)
c/o Brian Wilkins *Kritzer Levine Wilkins Entertainment (KLWG)*
11872 La Grange Ave
1st Floor
Los Angeles, CA 90025, USA

Lemelin, Jacques (Athlete, Hockey Player)
1301 Av Mathieu-Choret
Quebec, QC G2L1V1, Canada

Lemelin, Reggie (Athlete, Hockey Player)
10 Benevento Cir
Peabody, MA 01960-1268

Lemelson, Jerome H (Inventor)
48 Parkside Dr
Princeton, NJ 08540, USA

LeMesurier, John (Actor)
56 Barron's Keep
London W14, UNITED KINGDOM (UK)

Lemieux, Alain (Athlete, Hockey Player)
113 Wyngate Rd
Coraopolis, PA 15108-1028

Lemieux, Claude (Athlete, Hockey Player)
6008 No. Saquaro Rd
Paradise Valley, AZ 85253-4223

Lemieux, Jean (Athlete, Hockey Player)
113 Wyngate Rd
Coraopolis, PA 15108-1028

Lemieux, Jocelyn (Athlete, Hockey Player)
15 Rue de Montauban
Blainville, QC J7B 1T4, Canada

Lemieux, Joseph H (Business Person)
Owens-Illinois Inc
1 Sea Gate
Toledo, OH 43666, USA

LeMieux, Kathryn (Cartoonist)
c/o Staff Member *King Features Syndication*
300 W 57th St
15th Floor
New York, NY 10019-5238, USA

Lemieux, Mario (Athlete, Hockey Player)
Pittsburgh Penguins
66 Mario Lemieux Pl Ste 2
Pittsburgh, PA 15219-3504

Lemieux, Mario (Athlete, Hockey Player)
630 Academy Ave.
Sewickley, PA 15143-1172

Lemieux, Raymond U (Misc)
7602 119th St
Edmonton, AB T6G 1W3, CANADA

Lemieux, Raymond U Dr (Scientist)
University of Alberta
lA University Campus NW
Canada, AB T6G 2E1, USA

Lemieux, Richard
po Box1077
Temiscaming, QC JOZ3RO, Canada

Lemke, Anthony (Actor)
c/o Jennifer Goldhar *Characters Talent Agency (Toronto)*
8 Elm St
2nd Floor
Toronto, ON M5G 1G7, CANADA

Lemke, Cheryl (Television Host)
The Weather Channel
300 Interstate North Pkwy
Atlanta, Georgia 30339

Lemke, Mark (Athlete, Baseball Player)
3 Olena Dr
Whitesboro, NY 13492-2103, USA

Lemme, Steve (Comedian)
c/o Staff Member *United Talent Agency (UTA)*
9336 Civic Center Dr
Beverly Hills, CA 90210, USA

Lemmerman, Bruce (Athlete, Football Player)
621 Silverado Way
Eagle Point, OR 97524, USA

Lemmon, Chris (Actor)
80 Murray Dr
South Glastonbury, CT 06073, USA

Lemmon, Christopher (Actor)
80 Murray Dr
S Glastonbury, CT 06073, USA

Lemmons, Kasi (Actor, Director)
c/o Frank Wuliger *Gersh (LA)*
9465 Wilshire Blvd
Suite 600
Beverly Hills, CA 90212, USA

Lemoine, Tobe (Stylist)
533 N Malden Ave
La Grange Park, IL 60526, USA

Lemon, Chet (Athlete, Baseball Player)
38150 Timberlane Dr
Umatilla, Fl 32784-9302, USA

Lemon, Cleo (Athlete, Football Player)
1525 Harrington Park Dr
Jacksonville, FL 32225-4919, USA

Lemon, Don (Correspondent, Journalist)
c/o Staff Member *CNN (Atlanta)*
One CNN Center
PO Box 105366
Atlanta, GA 30303, USA

Lemon, Meadowlark (Actor, Athlete, Basketball Player)
6501 E Greenway Pkwy
Ste 102
Scottsdale, AZ 85254-2066, USA

Lemon, Mike (Athlete, Football Player)
455 Whitree Ln
Chesterfield, MO 63017-2450, USA

Lemon, Peter C (General)
6245 Viewfield Heights
Colorado Springs, CO 80919-3747, USA

Lemond, Greg (Athlete, Cycler, Olympic Athlete)
3000 Willow Dr
Hamel, MN 55340-9799, USA

Lemonds, Dave (Athlete, Baseball Player)
1501 Aringill Ln
Matthews, NC 28104-8049, USA

Lemongelio, Mark (Baseball Player)
Houston Astros
13437 S 47th St
Phoenix, AZ 85044-4833, USA

Lemongello, Mark (Athlete, Baseball Player)
13437 S 47th St
Phoenix, AZ 85044-4833, USA

Lemonheads
1775 Broadway #433
New York, NY 10019

Lemon Jelly (Music Group)
c/o Staff Member *Paradigm (Monterey)*
404 W Franklin St
Monterey, CA 93940, USA

Lemons, Abe
4314 St. Thomas
Oklahoma City, OK 73120

Lemos, Richie (Boxer)
18658 Klum Place
Rowland Heights, CA 91748, USA

Lemper, Ute (Actor, Dancer, Musician)
Les Visiteurs du Soir
40 Rue de la Folie Regnault
Paris 75011, FRANCE

Lenarcic, Spela (Stylist)
c/o Staff Member *Michele Filomeno New York LLC*
515 Greenwich St Ste 503
New York, NY 10013, USA

Lenard, Michael B (Misc)
US Olympic Committee
1 Olympia Plaza
Colorado Springs, CO 80909, USA

Lenard, Voshon (Athlete, Basketball Player)
22694 Nottingham Ln
Southfield, MI 48033-3393, USA

Lenardon, Tim (Athlete, Hockey Player)
1435 Appleridge Rd
Kelowna, BC VIW 3A6, Canada

Lenarduzzl, Mlke (Athlete, Hockey Player)
18165 pine ridge dr
Prairieville, LA 70769-3455

Lendl, Ivan (Athlete, Tennis Player)
400 5 1/2 Mile Road
Goshen, CT 06756, USA

Lenehan, Nancy (Actor)
c/o Meghan Schumacher *Meghan Schumacher Management*
13351-D Riverside Dr #387
Sherman Oaks, CA 91423, USA

Lenfant, Claude J M (Physicist)
PO Box 83027
Gaithersburg, MD 20883, USA

L. Engel, Eliot (Congressman, Politician)
2161 Rayburn HOB
Washington, DC 20515, USA

Lengies, Vanessa (Actor)
c/o Joanna (Joanie) Burstein *Burstein Company, The*
15304 Sunset Blvd
suite 208
Pacific Palisades, CA 90272, USA

L'Engle, Madeleine (Writer)
924 W End Ave Apt 95
New York, NY 10025-3542, USA

Lenhardt, Don (Athlete, Baseball Player)
13317 Woodlake Village Ct W
Saint Louis, MO 63017-5582, USA

Leningrad CowboysBMG Ariola
Steinhauser Str. 3
Munich, GERMANY D-81677

Lenk, Maria (Swimmer)
Rua Cupertino Durao 16
Leblon
Rio de Janeiro 22441, BRAZIL

Lenk, Thomas (Artist)
Gemeinde Braunsbach
Schloss Tierberg 7176, GERMANY

Lenk, Tom (Actor)
c/o Bernard Kira *Vanguard Management Group*
8060 Melrose Ave
4th Floor
Los Angeles, CA 90046, USA

Lenkaitis, Bill (Athlete, Football Player)
26 Rose Court Way
East Walpole, MA 02032-1185, USA

Lenkaitis, William E (Athlete, Football Player)
26 Rose Court Way
East Walpole, MA 02032, USA

Lenkin, Elysha (Stylist)
c/o Staff Member *Mark Edward Inc*
325 W 8th St
#1011
New York, NY 10018, USA

Lennie, Angus (Actor)
Jean Drysdale
15 Pembroke Gardens
London W8, UNITED KINGDOM (UK)

Lennix, Harry (Actor)
c/o Staff Member *Creative Artists Agency (CAA-LA)*
2000 Ave Of The Stars
Los Angeles, CA 90067, USA

Lennon, Cynthia (Artist, Writer)
c/o Staff Member *Crown Publishers*
1745 Broadway
New York, NY 10019, USA

Lennon, Diane (Musician)
1984 State Highway 165
Branson, MO 65616, USA

Lennon, Janet (Musician)
223 Devonshire Dr
Branson, MO 65616, USA

Lennon, Julian (Musician, Songwriter)
30 Ives St
London SW3 2ND, UNITED KINGDOM (UK)

Lennon, Kathy (Musician)
Overlook Dr
#10
Branson, MO 65616, USA

Lennon, Patrick (Athlete, Baseball Player)
60 Meister Blvd
Freeport, NY 11520-5938, USA

Lennon, Peggy (Musician)
1984 State Highway 165
Branson, MO 65616, USA

Lennon, Richard G (Religious Leader)
Archdiocese of Boston
2121 Commonwealth Ave
Boston, MA 02135, USA

Lennon, Sean (Musician)
Dakota Hotel
1 W 72nd St
New York, NY 10023, USA

Lennon, Thomas (Actor, Producer, Writer)
c/o Peter Principato *Principato/Young Management*
9465 Wilshire Blvd
Suite 430
Beverly Hills, CA 90212, USA

Lennon Sisters
1984 State Highway 165
Branson, MO 65616-8936

Lennox, Annie (Musician)
c/o Simon Fuller *XIX Entertainment*
35-37 Parkgate Rd
32/33 Ransomes Dock
London SW11 4NP, UNITED KINGDOM (UK)

Lennox, Kai (Actor)
c/o Gabrielle Allabashi *Ellis Talent Group*
4705 Laurel Canyon Blvd
Suite 300
Valley Village, CA 91607, USA

Lennox, William Jr (Educator, General)
Superintendent
US Military Academy
West Point, NY 10996, USA

Lenny, Rick H. (Business Person)
Hershey Foods
100 Crystal A Dr.
Hershey, PA 17033, USA

Leno, Jay (Actor, Comedian, Talk Show Host)
1151 Tower Rd
Beverly Hills, CA 90210, USA

Lenon, Paris (Athlete, Football Player)
1505 Taylor St
Lynchburg, VA 24504-3437, USA

Lenox, Adriane (Actor)
c/o Staff Member *Leading Artists*
145 W 45th St
Suite 1000
New York, NY 10036, USA

Lenox, Jack (General)
2362 Haddington Ct
The Villages, FL 32162-3574, USA

Lenska, Rula (Actor, Model)
David Daley Assoc
586A Kings Road
London SW6 2DX, UNITED KINGDOM (UK)

Lentine, Jim (Athlete, Baseball Player)
1066 Calle Del Cerro
Unit 1411
San Clemente, CA 92672-6075, USA

Lentinen, Jere (Athlete, Hockey Player)
2601 Ave. of the Stars
Frisco, TX 75043, USA

Lenton, Lisbeth (Athlete, Olympic Athlete)
Australian Swimming Inc
Unit 12/7 Beissel Street
Canberra, Belconnen 2617, AUSTRALIA

Lentz, Jack (Athlete, Football Player)
1035 Park Ave # 5B
New York, NY 10028-0912, USA

Lentz, Leary (Athlete, Basketball Player)
1309 Whispering Pines Dr
Houston, TX 77055-6854, USA

Lenz, Kay (Actor)
5916 Filaree Heights
Malibu, CA 90265, USA

Lenz, Kim (Musician, Songwriter, Writer)
Mark Pucia Media
5000 Oak Bluff Court
Atlanta, GA 30350, USA

Lenz, Nicole (Actor)
c/o Staff Member *Kazarian Spencer Ruskin & Assoc.*
11969 Ventura Blvd
3rd Floor
Studio City, CA 91604, USA

Lenz, Rick (Actor)
12955 Calvert St
Van Nuys, CA 91401, USA

Leo, Jim (Athlete, Hockey Player)
201 Old Oak Pl
Thurmont, MD 21788-1854, USA

Leo, Melissa (Actor)
c/o Jason Weinberg *Untitled Entertainment (LA)*
350 S. Beverly Dr #200
Beverly Hills, CA 90212, USA

Leon
1180 S. Beverly Dr. #608
Los Angeles, CA 90035

Leon, Carlos
4519 Cockerham Dr.
Los Angeles, CA 90027-1223

Leon, Eddie (Athlete, Baseball Player)
5285 N Strada De Rubino
Tucson, AZ 85750-1038, USA

Leon, Kenny (Actor, Director, Producer)
True Colors Theatre Company
659 Auburn Ave #257
Atlanta, GA 30312, USA

Leon, Lourdes (Lola) (Actor)
c/o Liz Rosenberg *Liz Rosenberg Media*
142 W. 57th St
6th Floor
New York, NY 10019, USA

Leon, Melina (Musician)
c/o Staff Member *Sony Music Miami*
605 Lincoln Rd Fl 7
Miami Beach, FL 33139, USA

Leon, Sarah (Stylist)
5990 NW 31st Ave
Fort Lauderdale, FL 33309-2208, USA

Leon, Valerie (Actor)
Essanay Ltd
2 Conduit St
London, W1R 9TG, UNITED KINGDOM (UK)

Leonard, Bob (Slick) (Athlete, Basketball Player, Coach)
1241 Hillcrest Dr
Carmel, IN 46033-2343, USA

Leonard, Brian (Athlete, Football Player)
20 Countryside Court Dr
Gouverneur, NY 13642-4306, USA

Leonard, Dennis (Athlete, Baseball Player)
4102 SW Evergreen St
Blue Springs, MO 64015-9713, USA

Leonard, Elmore (Writer)
2192 Yarmouth Road
Bloomfield Village, MI 48301, USA

Leonard, Gary (Athlete, Basketball Player)
2406 Ridgefield Rd
Columbia, MO 65203-1532, USA

Leonard, James (Athlete, Football Player)
RR 332 Box 349
Mullica Hill, NY 10862, USA

Leonard, Jeffrey (Athlete, Baseball Player)
Reno Silver Sox
205 Redfield Pkwy, Suite 201
Attn: Manager's Office
Reno, NV 95765-5108, USA

Leonard, Jim (Athlete, Football Player)
119 Cress Rd
Santa Cruz, CA 95060-1001, USA

Leonard, Joanne (Photographer)
University of Michigan
Art Dept
Ann Arbor, MI 48109, USA

Leonard, Joe (Motorcycle Race, Motorcycle Racer, Race Car Driver)
Motorsports Hall of Fame
PO Box 194
130 Gasoline Alley
Indianapolis, IN 46222, USA

Leonard, Joshua (Actor)
c/o Laina Cohn *Laina Cohn Management*
15066 Sutton St
Sherman Oaks, CA 91403, USA

Leonard, Justin (Athlete, Golfer)
3700 Euclid Ave
Dallas, TX 75205-3162, USA

Leonard, Mark (Athlete, Baseball Player)
22042 Hibiscus Dr
Cupertino, CA 95014-0109, USA

Leonard, Pauline (Stylist)
c/o Staff Member *Cloutier Agency*
2632 La Cienega Ave
Los Angeles, CA 90034, USA

Leonard, Robert Sean (Actor)
c/o Scott Henderson *WME (LA)*
9601 Wilshire Blvd Fl 3
Beverly Hills, CA 90210, USA

Leonard, Robert (Slick) (Athlete, Basketball Coach, Basketball Player, Coach)
5398 Baltimore Ct
Carmel, IN 46033-8882, USA

Leonard, Sugar Ray (Athlete, Boxer, Olympic Athlete)
PO Box 1433
Pacific Palisades, CA 0272-1433, USA

Leonard, Wayne (Business Person)
Entergy Corp
10055 Grogans Mill Road
#5A
The Woodlands, TX 77380, USA

Leonard-Linehan, Rhoda (Athlete, Baseball Player, Commentator)
84 Bruce Rd
Norwood, MA 02062-3103, USA

Leone, Justin (Athlete, Baseball Player)
5605 Dawnbreak Dr
Las Vegas, NV 89149-5137, USA

Leone, Sunny (Adult Film Star)
c/o Staff Member *Vivid Entertainment*
3599 Cahuenga Blvd #400
Los Angeles, CA 90068, USA

Leonetti, Jean-Baptiste (Director)
c/o Jerome Duboz *WME (LA)*
9601 Wilshire Blvd Fl 3
Beverly Hills, CA 90210, USA

Leonetti, John R (Cinematographer)
5251 Genesta Ave
Encino, CA 91316, USA

Leonetti, Matthew (Cinematographer)
1362 Bella Oceana Vista
Pacific Palisades, CA 90272, USA

Leong, Page (Actor)
C N A Assoc
1925 Century Park East
#750
Los Angeles, CA 90067, USA

Leonhard, Dave (Athlete, Baseball Player)
87 Corning St
Beverly, MA 01915-3732, USA

Leonhart, William (Diplomat)
119 Oak Terrace
Lake Bluff, IL 60044-2717, USA

Leoni, Tea (Actor, Producer)
170 E 78th St #124C
New York, NY 10075, USA

Leonidas, Stephanie (Actor)
c/o Andrew Rogers *ICM Partners (ICM-LA)*
10250 Constellation Blvd Fl 7
Los Angeles, CA 90067, USA

Leonov, Aleksei A (Cosmonaut, General)
Alfa Capital
Acad Sakharov Prospect 12
Moscow 107078, RUSSIA

Leonskaja, Elisabeth (Musician)
Columbia Artists Mgmt Inc
165 W 57th St
New York, NY 10019, USA

Leopold, Bobby (Athlete, Football Player)
801 Beckleymeade Ave
Apt 1116
Dallas, TX 75232, USA

Leopold, Jordan (Athlete, Hockey Player, Olympic Athlete)
Octagon Athlete Representation
8000 Norman Center
Dr Ste 400
Minneapolis, MN 55437-1180, USA

Leopold, Tom (Comedian)
c/o Staff Member *Gersh (LA)*
9465 Wilshire Blvd
Suite 600
Beverly Hills, CA 90212, USA

Lepage, Kevin (Race Car Driver)
618 Rice Hill Rd.
Franklin, VT 05457, USA

LeParmentier, Richard (Actor)
12A Russel St
Bath BA1 2QF, UK

Lepchenko, Varvara (Athlete, Tennis Player)
1362 Doe Trail Rd
Allentown, PA 18104, USA

Lepcio, Ted (Athlete, Baseball Player)
263 Greenlodge St
Dedham, MA 02026-6400, USA

Lepcio, Ted
263 Greenlodge St
Dedham, MA 02026-6400, USA

LePelley, Guernsey (Cartoonist, Editor)
35 Saint Germain St
Boston, MA 02115, USA

LePichon, Xavier (Geophysicist, Physicist)
Ecole Normale Superieure
24 Rue Lhomond
Paris 75005, FRANCE

Lepore, Amanda (Actor, Model)
c/o Staff Member *Grapevine Public Relations*
5237 N Cahuenga Blvd #2
N Hollywood, CA 91601, USA

Leppard, Raymond J
Indianapolis Symphony
32 E Washington St
#600
Indianapolis, IN 46204, USA

Lepperd, Thomas (Baseball Player)
5962 Wistful Vista Dr
West Des Moines, IA 50266-2864, USA

Lepperd, Thomas (Athlete, Baseball Player)
5962 Wistful Vista Dr
West Des Moines, IA 50266-2864, USA

Leppert, Don (Athlete, Baseball Player)
9226 Rami Ave
Columbus, OH 43240, USA

Leppert, Don (Athlete, Baseball Player)
1630 Epping Forest Dr
Southaven, MS 38671-8849, USA

Le Prevost, Nicholas
43A Princess Rd. Regents Park
London, ENGLAND NW1 8JS

Le Prevost, Nigel
43A Princess Rd.
London, ENGLAND W1

Lepsis, Matt (Athlete, Football Player)
6787 Trailing Oaks Dr
Frisco, TX 75034-5883, USA

Lequia-Barker, Joan (Athlete, Baseball Player, Commentator)
3236 34th St SW
Grandville, MI 49418-1905, USA

Lerach, William (Bill) (Attorney, Attorney General, General)
Milberg Weiss Hynes Lerach
1600 W Broadway
#1800
San Diego, CA 92101, USA

L'Erario, Joe
7700 Wisconsin Ave
Bethesda, MD 20814

Lerch, Randy (Athlete, Baseball Player)
19490 Monterey St
Morgan Hill, CA 95037-2606, USA

Lerche, Sondre (Musician)
c/o Staff Member *Paradigm (Monterey)*
404 W Franklin St
Monterey, CA 93940, USA

Lerchen, George (Athlete, Baseball Player)
354 E Rose Ave
Garden City, MI 48135-2645, USA

Lerew, Anthony (Athlete, Baseball Player)
6 Summer Dr
Dillsburg, PA 17019-9544, USA

Lerman, Logan (Actor)
c/o Kami Putnam-Heist *Creative Artists Agency (CAA-LA)*
9601 Wilshire Blvd
3rd Floor
Beverly Hills, CA 90210, USA

Lerner, Harriet (Writer)
c/o Staff Member *HarperCollins Publishers*
10 East 53rd St
c/o Author mail, 7th Floor
New York, NY 10022, USA

Lerner, Michael (Actor)
Innovative Artists
1505 10th St
Santa Monica, CA 90401, USA

Le Rosa, Stefan (Actor)
c/o Staff Member *Nickelodeon UK*
PO Box 6425
LONDON W1A 6UR, UNITED KINGDOM

LeRoux, Francois (Opera Singer)
I M G Artists
507 Hickory Grade Rd
Bridgeville, PA 15017-3609

Leroux, Nicolette (Athlete, Golfer)
4786 Orchard Ln
Delray Beach, FL 33445, USA

Leroy, Emarlos (Athlete, Football Player)
10135 Gate Pkwy N
Jacksonville, FL 32246, USA

LeRoy, Gloria (Actor)
Shelly & Pierce
13775A Mono Way
#220
Sonora, CA 95370, USA

Leroy, Philippe
77 rue Pigalle
Paris, FRANCE F-75009

Les, Jim (Athlete, Basketball Player)
4030 Shadvbrooke Ct
Granite Bay, CA 95746-8839, USA

Les, Jim (Athlete, Basketball Player)
3221 W Summerbend Ct
Peoria, IL 61615, USA

Lesane, Jimmy (Athlete, Football Player)
3629 Coronado Rd
Baltimore, MD 21244, USA

Lesar, David (Business Person)
Halliburton Co
Lincoln Plaza
500 N Akard St
Dallas, TX 75201, USA

Leschin, Luisa (Producer, Writer)
c/o Staff Member *WmE2 (WMA-LA)*
1 William Morris Pl
Beverly Hills, CA 90212, USA

Lesh, Phil (Musician)
c/o Jonathan Levine *Paradigm (Monterey)*
404 W Franklin St
Monterey, CA 93940, USA

Leshana, David C (Educator)
8246 E Hoverland Rd
Scottsdale, AZ 85255-3908, USA

Lesher, Brian (Athlete, Baseball Player)
217 Vassar Dr
Newark, DE 19711-3158, USA

Leskanic, Curt (Athlete, Baseball Player)
2032 Alaqua Dr
Longwood, FL 32779-3116, USA

Leskanich, Katrina (& the Waves) (Music Group, Musician)
c/o Staff Member *International Artists Holland*
P.O. Box 32
Grave 5360 AA, The Netherlands

Lesko, Matthew (Writer)
HiRise Promotions Inc
C/O Kim McCoy
1555 N Dearborn Pkwy Fl25
Chicago, IL 60610, USA

Lesley, Brad (Athlete, Baseball Player)
5235 Kester Ave
Apt 207
Sherman Oaks, CA 91411-4076, USA

Leslie, Aleen
1700 Lexington Rd.
Beverly Hills, CA 90210

Leslie, Ed (Actor, Wrestler)
c/o Nick Cordasco *Prince Marketing Group*
18 Carillon Cir
Livingston, NJ 07039, USA

Leslie, Fred W (Astronaut)
2038 Springhouse Rd S
Huntsville, AL 35802-1890, USA

Leslie, Joan (Actor)
2228 N Catalina
Los Angeles, CA 90027, USA

Leslie, Lisa (Athlete, Basketball Player, Model, Olympic Athlete)
5639 S La Cienga Blvd
Los Angeles, CA 90056, USA

Leslie, Robbie (DJ)
c/o Staff Member *Diva Central Inc*
7510 W Sunset Blvd Ste 1445
Los Angees, CA 90046, USA

Leslie, Ryan (Musician)
c/o Chris Chambers *The Chamber Group*
416 West 13th St
Suite 105
New York, NY 10014, USA

Lesnar, Brock (Athlete, Wrestler)
c/o Staff Member *UFC*
P.O. Box 26959
Las Vegas, NV 89126-0959, USA

Lesniak, John (Race Car Driver)
47 Industrial Park Access Rd.
Box 198
Middlefield, CT 06455, USA

Lesnie, Andrew (Cinematographer)
c/o Wayne Fitterman *United Talent Agency (UTA)*
9336 Civic Center Dr
Beverly Hills, CA 90210, USA

L'esperance, Carrie (Stylist)
c/o Staff Member *Zenobia Agency Inc*
PO Box 909
Groveland, CA 95321, USA

Lessard, Rick (Athlete, Hockey Player)
125 Chocolay River Trl
Marquette, M I 49855-9589

Lesseos, Mimi (Actor, Athlete)
2484 Vista Del Monte Dr
Acton, CA 93510, USA

Lessin, Leslie (Stylist)
c/o Staff Member *Katy Barker Agency Inc*
6606 10th Ave Apt 3R
Brooklyn, NY 11219, USA

Lessing, Doris (Nobel Prize Laureate)
11 Kingscroft Road #3
London, England NW 2 3QE, UK

Lessing, Doris M (Writer)
c/o Staff Member *Hoffmann und Campe Verlag GmbH*
Harvestehuder Weg 42
Hamburg 20149, Germany

Lester, Adrian (Actor)
c/o William Baylock *Seven Summits Pictures & Management*
8906 W Olympic Blvd
Ground Floor
Beverly Hills, CA 90211, USA

Lester, Bill (Race Car Driver)
6224 Viewcrest Dr.
Oakland, CA 94605, USA

Lester, Jon (Architect, Baseball Player)
7 Bernard St
Newton Highlands, MA 02461-1903, USA

Lester, Ketty (Actor, Musician)
5931 Comey Ave
Los Angeles, CA 90034, USA

Lester, Mark (Actor)
Carlton Clinic
1 Carlton St
Cheltenham
Glou GLS2 6AG, UNITED KINGDOM (UK)

Lester, Mark L (Director)
17268 Camino Yatasto
Pacific Palisades, CA 90272, USA

Lester, Richard (Dick) (Director)
c/o Staff Member *Creative Artists Agency (CAA-LA)*
2000 Ave Of The Stars
Los Angeles, CA 90067, USA

Lester, Ronnie (Athlete, Basketball Player)
1204 20th St
Manhattan Beach, CA 32505-3478, USA

Lester, Tim (Athlete, Football Player)
1160 Bream Dr
Alpharetta, GA 30004, USA

Lester, Tom
c/o Gary Moore *Gary Moore Management*
55 Karen Dr
Greenville, SC 29607, USA

Lester of Herne Hill, Anthony P (Attorney, Attorney General, General)
Blackstone Chambers
Blackstone House
Temple
London EC4Y 9BW, UNITED KINGDOM (UK)

Lesueur, Emily (Athlete, Olympic Athlete, Swimmer)
2208 E Nora St
Mesa, AZ 85213-1562, USA

Lesuk, Bill (Athlete, Hockey Player)
40 Bracken Ave
East St Paul, MB R2E OK2, Canada

Lesure, James (Actor)
c/o Vincent Cirrincione *Vincent Cirrincione Associates*
1516 N Fairfax Ave
Los Angeles, CA 90046, USA

Letarte, Pierre (Cinematographer)
551 W Pinacle
Albercom, QC J0E 1B0, CANADA

Letbetter, R Steve (Business Person)
Reliant Energy
1111 Louisiana
Houston, TX 77002, USA

Leterrier, Louis (Director)
c/o Guymon Casady *Management 360*
9111 Wilshire Blvd
Beverly Hills, CA 90210, USA

Letho, JJ (Race Car Driver)
Champion Racing
2901 Center Port Cir
Pompano Beach, FL 33064, USA

Le Tigre (Music Group)
Esther Creative Group
c/o Tom Sarig
27 W 24th St Ste 404
New York, NY 10010, USA

Letlow, W R (Russ) (Athlete, Football Player)
1876 Thelma Dr
San Luis Obispo, CA 93405, USA

Letner, Robert (Athlete, Football Player)
6515 Patty Ln
Harrison, TN 37341, USA

Leto, Jared (Actor)
c/o Jason Weinberg *Untitled Entertainment (LA)*
350 S. Beverly Dr #200
Beverly Hills, CA 90212, USA

Letowski, Trevor (Athlete, Hockey Player)
3612 Lion Ridge Ct
Raleigh, NC 27612, USA

Letowskl, Trevor (Athlete, Hockey Player)
1455 London Road
lSarnia Sting, ON N7S 6K4, Canada

Letscher, Matt (Actor)
c/o Nancy Sanders *Sanders Armstrong Caserta*
2120 Colorado Blvd
Suite 120
Santa Monica, CA 90404, USA

Letsie III (King)
Royal Palace
PO Box 524
Maseru, LESOTHO

Lett, Clifford (Athlete, Basketball Player)
7067 Rampart Way
Pensacola, FL 32505-3478, USA

Lett, Jim (Athlete, Baseball Player)
5751 State Route 34
Winfield, WV 25213-9323, USA

Lett, Leon (Athlete, Football Coach, Football Player)
ULM Athletics
308 Warhawk Way
Monroe, LA 71209, USA

Letterle, Daniel (Actor)
c/o Geordie Frey *GEF Entertainment*
122 N Clark Dr
Suite 401
Los Angeles, CA 90048, USA

Letterman, David (Comedian, Talk Show Host)
Late Show with David Letterman
CBS
1697 Broadway Fl 11
New York, NY 10019, USA

Lettermen, The
9255 Sunset Blvd. #407
Los Angeles, CA 90069

Letts, Tracy (Actor, Writer)
c/o Staff Member *Dewalt & Musik Management*
623 N. Parish Place
Burbank, CA 91506, USA

Leung, Ken (Actor)
c/o Paul Hilepo *Hartig Hilepo Agency Ltd*
54 W 21st St #610
New York, NY 10010, USA

Leuwerik, Ruth
Zuccalistr. 31
Munich, GERMANY D-80639

Levandowski, Leo (Athlete, Football Player)
1823 Twin House Rd
Oxford, PA 19363-3918, USA

Levang, Neil (Actor)
15630 Condor Ridge Rd
Canyon Country, CA 91387, USA

Levangie, Gigi (Writer)
c/o David Lubliner *WmE2 (WMA-LA)*
1 William Morris Pl
Beverly Hills, CA 90212, USA

Levasseur, Louis (Athlete, Hockey Player)
499 Av Murdoch
Rouyn-Noranda, QC J9X 1H3, Canada

LeVay, Simon (Scientist)
970 Palm Ave
West Hollywood, CA 90069, USA

Levchenko, Alexander
141 Sryosdny Gorodok
Potchta Kosmonavtov, RUSSIA

Level 42 (Music Group, Musician)
c/o Guy Richard *Agency Group Ltd, The (LA)*
1880 Century Park E
Suite 711
Los Angeles, CA 90067, USA

Levellers (Music Group)
c/o Staff Member *Paradigm (Monterey)*
404 W Franklin St
Monterey, CA 93940, USA

Levels, Dwayne (Athlete, Football Player)
3614 Colonial Ave
Dallas, TX 75215-3640, USA

Levene, Ben (Artist)
Royal Academy of Arts
Piccadilly
London W1V 2LP, UNITED KINGDOM (UK)

Levene, Keith (Musician)
c/o Staff Member *Taang! Records*
3830 5th Ave
San Diego, CA 92103, USA

Levenick, Dave (Athlete, Football Player)
1749 SE Hondo Ave
Port Saint Lucie, FL 34952-5743, USA

Levens, Dorsey (Athlete, Football Player)
4249 Olde Mill Ln NE
Atlanta, GA 30349, USA

Levenseller, Mike (Athlete, Football Player)
1570 SW Wadleigh Dr
Pullman, WA 99163-2049, USA

Levenseller, Mike (Athlete, Football Player)
1570 SW Wadleigh Dr
Pullman, WA 99163, USA

Levenstein, John (Comedian)
c/o Staff Member *ICM Partners (ICM-LA)*
10250 Constellation Blvd Fl 7
Los Angeles, CA 90067, USA

Leveque, Michel (Politician)
Minister of State's Office
BP 522
Monaco Cedex 98015, MONACO

Lever, Don (Athlete, Hockey Player)
247 Quail Hollow Ln
East Amherst, NY 14051-1633

Lever, Johny (Actor, Bollywood, Comedian)
151/152 Oxford Tower Yamuna Nagar Lokhandwala Complex Andheri
Bombay, MS 400 058, INDIA

Lever, Lafayette (Athlete, Basketball Player)
1702 W Lynx Way
Chandler, AZ 85248-5425, USA

Leverette, Otis (Athlete, Football Player)
716 N Lee St
Americus, GA 31719-3093, USA

Levering, Kate (Actor)
c/o Staff Member *Forward Entertainment*
9255 Sunset Blvd
Suite 805
Los Angeles, CA 90069, USA

Leverington, Shelby
1801 Ave. of the Stars #1250
Los Angeles, CA 90067

Leveritt, Mara (Writer)
c/o Staff Member *St Martins Press*
Publicity Dept
175 5th Ave
New York, NY 10010, USA

Le Vert
110-112 Lantoga Rd. #D
Wayne, PA 19087

Levert, Eddie (Musician)
c/o Staff Member *Associated Booking Corp*
PO Box 2055
New York, NY 10021-0051, USA

Leverton, Irene (Aviator)
1100 Willow Lake Rd
Prescott, AZ 86301, USA

Levesque, Joanna (Jojo) (Musician)
c/o Diana Levesque *Momma D's Management*
151 Lafayette St
6th Floor
New York, NY 10013, USA

Levesque, Paul (Triple H) (Athlete, Wrestler)
c/o Kerry Rodgerson *World Wrestling Entertainment (WWE)*
Titan Towers
1241 E Main St
Stamford, CT 06905-3857, USA

Levet, Thomas (Athlete, Golfer)
108 Via Quantera
Palm Beach Gardens, FL 33418, USA

Levi, Alan J. (Actor)
c/o Debbee Klein *Paradigm (LA)*
360 N Crescent Dr
North Bldg
Beverly Hills, CA 90210, USA

Levi, Wayne (Athlete, Golfer)
17 Ironwood Rd
New Hartford, NY 13413-3902, USA

Levi, Yoel
Askonas Holt Ltd
27 Chancery Lane
London WC2A 1PF, UNITED KINGDOM (UK)

Levi, Zachary (Actor)
c/o Tej Bhatia Herring *Rogers & Cowan PR (LA)*
Pacific Design Center
8687 Melrose Ave, 7th Floor
West Hollywood, CA 90069, USA

LeVias, Jerry (Athlete, Football Player)
3322 Chris Dr
Houston, TX 77063, USA

Levie, Craig (Athlete, Hockey Player)
44 Rockvalley Villas NW
Calgary, AB T3G SX3, Canada

Levieva, Margarieta (Actor)
c/o Shani Rosenzweig *United Talent Agency (UTA)*
9336 Civic Center Dr
Beverly Hills, CA 90210, USA

Levi-Montalcini, Rita (Nobel Prize Laureate)
Cell Biology Institute
Institute for Neurobiology Viale Marx 15
Rome 1-00137, ITALY

Levin, Amy Colvin (Stylist)
c/o Staff Member *Maximum Talent*
1873 S Bellaire St
Suite 915
Denver, CO 80222-4356, USA

Levin, Carl (Politician)
1017 E Capitol St SE
Washington, DC 20003-3905, USA

Levin, Drake (Musician)
Paradise Artists
108 E Matilija St
Ojai, CA 93023, USA

Levin, Harvey (Journalist)
TMZ
4000 Warner Blvd
Burbank, CA 91522-0002, USA

Levin, Mark (Radio Personality, Talk Show Host)
Citadel Communications
7201 West Lake Mead
Las Vegas, Nevada 89128, USA

Levin, Richard C (Educator)
Yale University
President's Office
New Heaven, CT 06520, USA

Levin Downey, Susan (Producer)
c/o Peter Micelli *Creative Artists Agency (CAA-LA)*
2000 Ave Of The Stars
Los Angeles, CA 90067, USA

Levine, Adam (Musician)
2880 Benedict Canyon Dr
Beverly Hills, CA 90210, USA

Levine, Alan (Athlete, Baseball Player)
10916 E Paradise Dr
Scottsdale, AZ 85259-7007, USA

Levine, Arnold (Biologist, Educator)
Rockefeller University
President's Office
1230 York Ave
New York, NY 10021, USA

Levine, Ellen R (Editor)
Good Housekeeping Magazine
959 8th Ave
New York, NY 10019, USA

Levine, Irene (Writer)
Chicago Tribune
C/O Travel
435 N Michigan Ave
Chicago, IL 60611, USA

Levine, Jack (Artist)
68 Morton St
New York, NY 10014, USA

Levine, James
Boston Symphony Orchestra
301 Massachusetts Ave
Boston, MA 02115, USA

Levine, Jerry
1505 10th St.
Santa Monica, CA 90401

Levine, Jonathan (Director)
c/o Ragna Nervik *The Ragna Nervik Company*
Prefers to be contacted via telephone
Los Angeles, CA, USA

Levine, Ken (Writer)
c/o Staff Member *Broder Webb Chervin Silbermann Agency, The (BWCS)*
10250 Constellation Blvd
Los Angeles, CA 90067-6200, USA

Levine, Michael (Business Person)
Levine Communications
1180 S Beverly Dr #301
Los Angeles, CA 90035, USA

Levine, Philip (Writer)
4549 N Van Ness Blvd
Fresno, CA 93704, USA

Levine, Philip
4549 N Van Ness Blvd
Fresno, CA 93704-3727, USA

Levine, Rachmiel (Misc)
614 Walnut St
Newton 02460, USA

Levine, Samm (Actor, Producer)
c/o Melanie Marquez *M4 Publicity*
11684 Ventura Blvd #213
Studio City, CA 91604, USA

Levine, Samuel A (Actor)
c/o Staff Member *Badgley-Connor-King*
9229 Sunset Blvd.
Suite 311
Los Angeles, CA 90069, USA

Levine, Seymour (Biologist)
1512 Notre Dame Dr
Davis, CA 95616, USA

Levine, Sol (Activist)
30 Powell St
Brookline, MA 02446, USA

Levine, S Robert (Business Person)
Cabletron Systems
PO Box 5005
Rochester, NH 03866, USA

Levine, Ted (Actor, Voice Over Artist)
c/o Robbie Kass *Kass & Stokes Management*
9229 Sunset Blvd
Suite 504
Los Angeles, CA 90069, USA

Levingston, Cliff (Basketball Player)
Denver Nuggets
Pepsi Center
1000 Chopper Circle
Denver, CO 80204, USA

Levingstone, Ken (Government Official)
House of Commons
Westminster
London SW1A 0AA, UNITED KINGDOM (UK)

LevinIra, Ira (Writer)
40 E 49th St
New York, NY 10017, USA

Levins, Scott (Athlete, Hockey Player)
815 Covered Bridge Dr
Delaware, OH 43015-3193, USA

Levinsohn, Gary (Producer)
c/o Staff Member *Mutual Film Company*
650 Bronson Ave
Clinton Bldg
Los Angeles, CA 90004, USA

Levinson, Barry (Actor, Director, Producer, Writer)
c/o Carol Goll *ICM Partners (ICM-LA)*
10250 Constellation Blvd Fl 7
Los Angeles, CA 90067, USA

Levinson, Chris (Writer)
c/o Staff Member *WME (LA)*
9601 Wilshire Blvd Fl 3
Beverly Hills, CA 90210, USA

Levinson, Jay Conrad (Business Person, Writer)
Guerilla Marketing Intl
3700 S Westport Ave #2994
Sioux Falls, SD 57106, USA

Levinson, Sanford V (Attorney, Attorney General, Educator, General)
3410 Windsor Road
Austin, TX 78703, USA

Levinthal, Cyrus (Biologist)
Columbia University
Biological Sciences Dept
New York, NY 10027, USA

Levis, Jesse (Athlete, Baseball Player)
1219 Highland Ave
Fort Washington, PA 19034-1605, USA

Levis, Patrick (Actor)
c/o Staff Member *Defining Artists Agency*
10 Universal City Plaza
Suite 2000
Universal City, CA 91608, USA

Levi-Strauss, Claude (Misc)
2 Rue des Marronniers
Paris 75016, FRANCE

Levitas, Andrew (Actor)
c/o Justin Grey Stone *Untitled Entertainment (LA)*
350 S. Beverly Dr #200
Beverly Hills, CA 90212, USA

Levitt, Arthus Jr (Financier, Government Official)
Carlyle Group
1001 Pennsylvania Ave NW
Washington, DC 20004, USA

Levitt, Chad (Athlete, Football Player)
104 Towanda Ave
Melrose Park, PA 19027, USA

Levitt, Gene
9200 Sunset Blvd. PH 25
Los Angeles, CA 90069

Levitt, George (Misc)
82 Via Del Corso
Palm Beach Gardens, FL 33418, USA

Levrault, Allen (Athlete, Baseball Player)
P.O. Box 1316
Westport, MA 02790-4911, USA

Levy, David (Government Official)
New Way Party
Knesset
Kiryat Ben Gurion
Jerusalem 91950, ISRAEL

Levy, David H (Astronomer)
Mount Palomar Observatory
Palomar Mountain
Mount Palomar, PA 92060, USA

Levy, Eugene (Actor, Director)
c/o Ben Feigin *Anonymous Content (LA)*
3531 Hayden Ave
Culver City, CA 90232, USA

Levy, Julia (Scientist)
1701-1888 Alberni St
Vancouver, BC V6G 1B3, Canada

Levy, Kenneth (Business Person)
KLA-Tencor Corp
160 Rio Robles
San Jose, CA 95134, USA

Levy, Leonard W (Historian)
1025 Timberline Terrace
Ashland, OR 97520, USA

Levy, Mariana (Actor)
c/o Staff Member *Televisa*
Blvd Adolfo Lopez Mateos 232
Colonia San Angel INN
DF CP 01060, MEXICO

Levy, Marv (Coach, Football Coach, Football Player)
2800 N Lake Shore Dr
Apt 1516
Chicago, IL 60657, USA

Levy, Marvin David (Composer)
Sheldon Sofer Mgmt
130 W 56th St
New York, NY 10019, USA

Levy, Mary (Athlete, Football Player)
2800 N Lake Shore Dr Apt 1516
Chicago, IL 60657-6269, USA

Levy, Michael R (Publisher)
Texas Monthly Magazine
PO Box 1569
Austin, TX 78767, USA

Levy, Peter (Cinematographer)
International Creative Mgmt
8942 Wilshire Blvd
#219
Beverly Hills, CA 90211, USA

Levy, Richard C (Business Person, Inventor)
c/o Staff Member *Penguin Group*
90 Eglinton Ave E #700
Toronto, Ontario M4P 2Y3, CANADA

Levy, Sara (Stylist)
c/o Staff Member *Crews*
828 Clemont Dr
Atlanta, GA 30306, USA

Levy, Shawn (Actor, Director)
c/o Amanda Lundberg *42West (NY)*
220 W 42nd St
12th Floor
New York, NY 10036, USA

Levy, William (Actor)
c/o John Carrabino *John Carrabino Management*
5900 Wilshire Blvd Fl 4 #406
Los Angeles, CA 90036, USA

Levya, Danell (Athlete, Gymnast, Olympic Athlete)
Universal Gymnastics
13439 Southwest 131st St
Miami, FL 33186, USA

Lewallyn, Dennis (Athlete, Baseball Player)
2900 Breckenridge Dr
Pensacola, FL 32526-2903, USA

Lewicki, Danny (Athlete, Hockey Player)
7169 Shallford Rd
Mississauga, ON L4T 2P6, Canada

Lewin, Josh (Commentator)
1081 W Winding Creek Dr
Grapevine, TX 76051-7837, USA

Lewinsky, Monica
7250 Franklin Ave Unit 908
Los Angeles, CA 90046-3044, USA

Lewis, Aaron (Musician)
Staind/Elektra Records
75 Rockefeller Plz
New York, NY 10019

Lewis, Albert R (Athlete, Football Player)
3532 Macedonia Rd
Centreville, MS 39631, USA

Lewis, Al (Grandpa) (Actor)
PO Box 277
New York, NY 10044, USA

Lewis, Allan (Athlete, Baseball Player)
Urb La Florida R-15
David Chiriqui, Panama, USA

Lewis, Allen (Government Official)
Beaver Lodge
Mom PO Box 1076
Castries, Sanit Lucia, WEST INDIES

Lewis, Ananda (Actor)
c/o Staff Member *Britto Agency PR*
234 W 56th St
Penthouse
New York, NY 10019, USA

Lewis, Anthony (Athlete, Football Player)
New York Times
22663 Wildwood St
Hayward, CA 94541-3227, USA

Lewis, Ashton (Race Car Driver)
Lewis Motorsports
4317 Triple Crown Dr.
Concord, NC 28027, USA

Lewis, Barbara (Musician)
Hello Stranger Productions
PO Box 300488
Fern Park, FL 32730, USA

Lewis, Bernard (Historian)
Princeton University
Near Eastern Studies Dept
Princeton, NJ 08544, USA

Lewis, Bill (Coach, Football Coach)
Georgia Institute of Technology
Arizona Cardinals 8701 S Hardy Dr
Tempe, AZ 85284-2800, USA

Lewis, Blake (Musician)

Lewis, Bob (Athlete, Basketball Player)
63910 E Squash Blossom Ln
Tucson, AZ 85739-1264, USA

Lewis, Bobby (Musician)
Lustig Talent
PO Box 770850
Orlando, FL 32877, USA

Lewis, Brooke (Actor)
c/o Staff Member *Coolwaters Productions*
10061 Riverside Dr.
Box 531
Toluca Lake, CA 91602, USA

Lewis, Bubba (Actor)
c/o Ryan Daly *Zero Gravity Management*
1531 14th. St
Santa Monica, CA 90404, USA

Lewis, Carl (Actor, Athlete, Olympic Athlete, Track Athlete)
c/o Cat Stone *Stone Management*
121 Ave Of The Stars #3000
Los Angeles, CA 90067, USA

Lewis, Chad (Athlete, Football Player)
4529 N 100 W
Provo, UT 84604-5511, USA

Lewis, Charlotte (Athlete, Basketball
Player, Olympic Athlete)
2814 N Sheridan Road
Peoria, IL 61604-2716, USA

Lewis, Clea (Actor)
1659 S Highland Ave
Los Angeles, CA 90019, USA

Lewis, Colby (Athlete, Baseball Player)
6880 Shoreway Drive
Mansfield, TX 76063, USA

Lewis, Crystal (Musician)
Proper Mgmt
PO Box 150867
Nashville, TN 37215, USA

Lewis, Damian (Actor)
Markham & Froggalt
Julian House
4 Windmill St
London W1P 1HF, UNITED KINGDOM
(UK)

Lewis, Damione (Athlete, Football Player)
9601 Gato Del Sol Ct
Waxhaw, NC 28173-0113, USA

Lewis, Dan (Athlete, Football Player)
460 S Park St
Detroit, MI 48215, USA

Lewis, Darren (Athlete, Football Player)
641 Seabeach Rd
Dallas, TX 75232, USA

Lewis, Darryl (Athlete, Football Player)
2441 S Nadine Atreet Apt 1
West Covina, CA 91792, USA

Lewis, Dave (Athlete, Football Player)
14015 Tahiti Way
Apt 111
Marina Del Rey, CA 90292, USA

Lewis, Dave (Athlete, Coach, Hockey
Player)
2040 Ranch Rd
Holly, MI 48442-8027

Lewis, Dave (Athlete, Hockey Player)
Carolina Hurricanes
1400 Edwards Mill Rd
Raleigh, NC 27607-3624

Lewis, David Levering (Writer)
Rutgers University
History Dept
East Rutherford, NJ 08903, USA

Lewis, David R (Athlete, Football Player)
406 142nd St
Ocean City, MD 21842, USA

Lewis, Dawnn (Actor)
c/o Staff Member *Gage Group, The (LA)*
14724 Ventura Blvd
Suite 505
Sherman Oaks, CA 91403, USA

Lewis, D D (Athlete, Football Player)
1624 Northcrest Dr
Plano, TX 75075-8749, USA

Lewis, D D (Athlete, Football Player)
2530 Dolly Wright St
Houston, TX 77088-7528, USA

Lewis, D D (Athlete, Football Player)
1624 Northcrest Dr
Plano, TX 75075, USA

Lewis, Dion (Athlete, Football Player)
10 Twiller St
Albany, NY 12209-2128, USA

Lewis, Drew (Business Person, Politician,
Secretary)
PO Box 70
Lederach, PA 19450-0070, USA

Lewis, Emmanuel (Actor)
859 Hwy 92 N
Fayetteville, GA 30214, USA

Lewis, Frank (Athlete, Football Player)
118 Presque Isle Dr
Houma, LA 70363, USA

Lewis, Freddie (Athlete, Basketball Player)
4122 Illinois Ave NW
Washington, DC 20011, USA

Lewis, Garry (Athlete, Football Player)
1000 Alcorn Dr
Apt 737
Alcorn State, MS 39096, USA

Lewis, Gary (Athlete, Football Player)
10610 59th Ave S
Seattle, WA 98178-2406, USA

Lewis, Gary (Athlete, Football Player)
10 N Farm Road 144
Mount Pleasant, TX 75455-8809, USA

Lewis, Geoffrey (Actor, Writer)
c/o Joel Stevens *Joel Stevens
Entertainment*
5627 Allott Ave
Van Nuys, CA 91401, USA

Lewis, Glenn (Musician)
c/o Staff Member *Creative Artists Agency
(CAA-LA)*
2000 Ave Of The Stars
Los Angeles, CA 90067, USA

Lewis, Grady (Athlete, Basketball Player)
8926 W Topeka Dr
Peoria, AZ 85382-8590

Lewis, Huey (Actor, Musician)
c/o Bob Brown *Bob Brown Management*
PO Box 779
Mill Valley, CA 94942, USA

Lewis, Jamal (Athlete, Football Player)
210 Stratton Place Way SW
Atlanta, GA 30331-6835, USA

Lewis, Jason (Actor)
c/o Alissa Vradenburg *Untitled
Entertainment (LA)*
350 S. Beverly Dr #200
Beverly Hills, CA 90212, USA

Lewis, Jazsmin
c/o Daniel Spilo *Industry Entertainment
Partners*
955 S Carrillo Dr
Suite 300
Los Angeles, CA 90048, USA

Lewis, Jeff (Athlete, Football Player)
230 N 2nd St Trlr 6
Berthoud, CO 80513-1327, USA

Lewis, Jeff (Designer, Reality TV Star)
c/o Nicole Perez-Krueger *PMK/BNC
Public Relations (PMK-LA)*
8687 Melrose Ave Fl 8
West Hollywood, CA 90069, USA

Lewis, Jenifer (Actor)
c/o Arnold M Preston *Preston
Entertainment Inc*
8033 Sunset Blvd #7250
Los Angeles, CA 90046

Lewis, Jenna (Reality TV Star)
c/o Juliette Harris *It Girl Public Relations*
5301 Beethoven St
Suite 220
Los Angeles, CA 90066, USA

Lewis, Jensen (Athlete, Baseball Player)
5311 Salem Rd
Cincinnati, OH 45230-1327, USA

Lewis, Jermaine (Athlete, Football Player)
4919 Pleasant Grove Rd
Reisterstown, MD 21136-3913, USA

Lewis, Jerry (Congressman, Politician)
2112 Rayburn HOB
Washington, DC 20515, USA

Lewis, Jerry (Actor, Comedian, Director)
1701 Waldman Ave
Las Vegas, NV 89102, USA

Lewis, Jerry Lee (Musician)
1595 Malone Rd
Nesbit, MS 38651, USA

Lewis, Jim (Athlete, Baseball Player)
5311 Hansel Ave
Apt D12
Orlando, FL 32809-3415, USA

Lewis, Jim (Athlete, Baseball Player)
676 Sparks St
Jackson, MI 49202, USA

Lewis, J L (Athlete, Golfer)
2504 Orleans Dr
Cedar Park, TX 78613-4727, USA

Lewis, John (Race Car Driver)
524 El Cerrito
Hillsborough, CA 94010, USA

Lewis, John (Congressman, Politician)
343 Cannon HOB
Washington, DC 20515, USA

Lewis, Johnny (Athlete, Baseball Player)
810 Tara Cir
Cantonment, FL 32533-9700, USA

Lewis, Jon Peter (Musician, Reality TV
Star)
PO Box 533
Newbury Park, CA 91319, USA

Lewis, Judy
71359 Cypress Dr.
Rancho Mirage, CA 92270-3553

Lewis, Juliette (Actor)
c/o Brandy Lewis *BL Management*
3940 Laurel Canyon Blvd
Suite 612
Studio City, CA 91604, USA

Lewis, Karen (Writer)
c/o James Sarnoff *The Sarnoff Company
Inc*
10 Universal City Plz #2000
Universal City, CA 91608, USA

Lewis, Kenneth D (Financier)
Bank of America Corp
100 N Tryon St
Charlotte, NC 28255, USA

Lewis, Kevin (Athlete, Football Player)
4417 Roy St
Orlando, FL 32812, USA

Lewis, Lennox (Boxer)
XS Promotions
57 Fonthill Road
Aberdeen AB11 6UQ, UNITED STATES

Lewis, Leona (Actor, Musician)
2668 Astral Dr
Los Angeles, CA 90046, USA

Lewis, Marcedes (Athlete, Football Player)
3725 Bouton Dr
Lakewood, CA 90712, USA

Lewis, Mark (Athlete, Football Player)
P.O. Box 11021
Spring, TX 77391, USA

Lewis, Mark (Athlete, Baseball Player)
1753 Cleveland Ave
Hamilton, OH 45013-5114, USA

Lewis, Marvin (Coach, Football Coach)
Cincinnati Bengals
6655 Alberly Ln
Cincinnati, OH 45243-2847, USA

Lewis, Mary (Christianni Brand) (Writer)
88 Maida Vale
London W9, UNITED KINGDOM (UK)

Lewis, Matthew (Actor)
c/o Sarah Spear *Curtis Brown Ltd*
Hay Market House
28-29 Hay Market
London SW1Y 4SP, UK

Lewis, Memory (Scientist)
7915 Park Dr
Saint Louis, MO 63117-1431, USA

Lewis, Michael (Writer)
c/o Matthew Snyder *Creative Artists
Agency (CAA-LA)*
2000 Ave Of The Stars
Los Angeles, CA 90067, USA

Lewis, Mike (Athlete, Football Player)
3350 Blodgett St
Houston, TX 27284-7013, USA

Lewis, Mike (Athlete, Basketball Player)
490 Windsor Park Rd
Kernersville, NC 27284, USA

Lewis, Mo (Athlete, Baseball Player)
2212 Rosemount Ln
San Ramon, CA 94582-5719, USA

Lewis, Mo (Athlete, Football Player)
3280 Northwide Pkwy NW
Apt 314
Atlanta, GA 30327, USA

Lewis, Monica (Musician)
Lang
1100 Alta Loma Road
#16A
Los Angeles, CA 90069, USA

Lewis, Nate (Athlete, Football Player)
3374 Brooksong Way
Dacula, GA 30019-1199, USA

Lewis, Peter B (Business Person)
Progressive Corp
6300 Wilson Mills Road
Cleveland, OH 44143, USA

Lewis, Phill (Actor)
c/o Gregg A Klein *Abrams Artists Agency
(LA)*
9200 Sunset Blvd
11th Floor
Los Angeles, CA 90069, USA

Lewis, Ralph (Athlete, Basketball Player)
3004 Maryannes Ct
North Wales, PA 19454-2024, USA

Lewis, Ramsey (Composer, Musician)
c/o Ted Kurland *Ted Kurland Associates*
173 Brighton Ave
Boston, MA 02134, USA

Lewis, Rashard (Basketball Player)
Seattle SuperSonics
351 Elliott Ave W
#500
Seattle, WA 7042-2513, USA

Lewis, Ray (Athlete, Football Player)
c/o David Dunn *Athletes First, LLC*
9140 Irvine Center Dr
Irvine, CA 92618, USA

Lewis, Richard (Actor, Comedian)
c/o Mike Eistenstadt *Amsel, Eisenstadt & Frazier Talent Agency (AEF)*
5055 Wilshire Blvd
Suite 860
Los Angeles, CA 90036-6108, USA

Lewis, Richard J (Producer)
c/o Carel Cutler *ICM Partners (ICM-LA)*
10250 Constellation Blvd Fl 7
Los Angeles, CA 90067, USA

Lewis, Richie (Athlete, Baseball Player)
13209 E County Road 700 S
Losantville, IN 47354-9514, USA

Lewis, Robert (Athlete, Basketball Player)
3656 Bay Dr
Edgewater, MD 21037-4143, USA

Lewis, Rommie (Athlete, Basketball Player)
5511 Mountville Rd
Adamstown, MD 21710-9612, USA

Lewis, Ron (Athlete, Football Player)
12821 Haverford Rd W
Apt 1
Jacksonville, FL 32218, USA

Lewis, Scott (Athlete, Baseball Player)
2584 Fairway Dr
Costa Mesa, CA 92627-1312, USA

Lewis, Shane (Race Car Driver)
209 Ridge Rd
Jupiter, FL 33477, USA

Lewis, Shaznay (Musician)
c/o Staff Member *Concorde Intl Artists Ltd*
101 Shepherds Bush Rd
London W6 7LP, UNITED KINGDOM (UK)

Lewis, Sherman (Athlete, Football Player)
45822 Bristol Cir
Novi, MI 48377, USA

Lewis, Terry (Stylist)
c/o Celebrity Stylist *Oliver Piro Inc*
725 Riverside Dr Apt 3A
New York, NY 10031, USA

Lewis, Thomas (Athlete, Football Player)
1545 E Villa Theresa Dr
Phoenix, AZ 85022-1282, USA

Lewis, Tim (Athlete, Football Player)
2938 Major Ridge Trl
Duluth, GA 30097-4985, USA

Lewis, Vaughan A (Prime Minister)
United Workers Party
1 Riverside Road
Castries, SAINT LUCIA

Lewis, Vicki (Actor, Comedian)
c/o Staff Member *Stone Manners Salners Agency (LA)*
9911 W Pico Blvd Ste 1400
Los Angeles, CA 90035, USA

Lewis, Walter (Scientist)
7915 Park Dr
Saint Louis, MO 63117-1431, USA

Lewis, Will (Athlete, Football Player)
1980 Seattle Seahawks
Samrnamish, WA 98074-3473, USA

Lewis, W Paul (Race Car Driver)
3408 Bristol Hwy
Johnson City, TN 37601, USA

Lewis III, Leo (Athlete, Football Player)
1400 N Countryshire Dr
Columbia, MO 65202-9769, USA

Lewis III, Randy (Race Car Driver)
4101 Big Ranch Road
Napa, CA 94558, USA

Lewit-Nirenberg, Julie (Publisher)
Mademoiselle Magazine
350 Madison Ave
New York, NY 10017, USA

Ley, Rick (Athlete, Hockey Player)
18 Stonehaven Rd
Dunnville, ON N1A 2W6, Canada

Ley, Terry (Athlete, Baseball Player)
2955 SE Custer Rd
Prineville, OR 97754-9424, USA

Leyden, Paul (Actor)
c/o Rhonda Price *Gersh (NY)*
41 Madison Ave
New York, NY 10010, USA

Leygue, Louis Georges (Artist)
6 Rue de Docteur Blanche
Paris 75016, FRANCE

Leyland, Jim (Athlete, Baseball Player, Coach)
261 Tech Rd
Pittsburgh, PA 15205-1734, USA

Leyritz, Jim (Athlete, Baseball Player)
11060 Cameron Ct #304
Davie, FL 33324-4188, USA

Leyton, John (Actor, Musician)
53 Keyes House
Dolphin Square
London SW1V 3NA, UNITED KINGDOM (UK)

Leyva, Nick (Athlete, Baseball Player, Coach)
1098 Tilghman Rd
Chesterbrook, PA 19087-5878, USA

Leyva, Victor (Athlete, Football Player)
17690 Road 320
Springville, CA 93265-9635, USA

Lezak, Jason (Athlete, Olympic Athlete, Swimmer)
c/o Evan Morgenstein *Premier Management Group (PMG Sports)*
115 Crescent Commons Dr Ste 250
Cary, NC 27518, USA

Lezcano, Carlos (Athlete, Baseball Player)
3870 S Dewdrop Ln
Gilbert, AZ 85297, USA

Lezcano, Sixto (Athlete, Baseball Player)
7828 Bardmoor Hill Cir
Orlando, FL 32835-8158, USA

LFO (Musician)
Evolution Talent Agency
1776 Broadway
15th Floor
New York, NY 10019

L. Fudge, Marcia (Congressman, Politician)
1019 Longworth HOB
Washington, DC 20515, USA

Ignarro, Louis J (Nobel Prize Laureate)
U C LA School Of Medicine 23 Chase# 315
Los Angeles, CA 90095-0001, USA

Ignasiak, Gary (Athlete, Baseball Player)
3084 Angelus Dr
Waterford, MI 48329-2506, USA

Ignizio, Mildred (Bowler)
241 Shore Acres Dr
Rochester, NY 14612-5807, USA

L. Hanna, Richard (Congressman, Politician)
319 CaJimon HOB
Washington, DC 20515, USA

L. Hastings, Alcee (Congressman, Politician)
2353 Rayburn HOB
Washington, DC 20515, USA

L'Hermitte, Thierry (Actor)
ICE 3
13 Rue Yves-Toudic
Paris 75010, France

Li, Frederick (Biologist)
Dana-Farber Cancer Institute
44 Binney St
Boston, MA 02115, USA

Li, Gong (Actor, Model)
c/o Julie Moore *The J-Line Group Inc*
8671 Wilshire Blvd
4th Floor
Beverly Hills, CA 90211, USA

Li, Jet (Actor)
c/o Steve Chasman *Current Entertainment*
9378 Wilshire Blvd
Sutie 210
Beverly Hills, CA 90212, USA

Li, Ka-shing (Business Person)
Computershare Hong Kong Investor Services Limited
Rooms 1712 - 1716, 17th Floor, Hopewell Centre
183 Queen's Road East
Hong Kong, Hong Kong

Li, Keyu (Designer, Fashion Designer)
21 Gong-Jian Hutong
Di An-Men
Beijing 100009, CHINA

Li, Lanqing (Government Official)
Communist Party Central Committee
Zhong Nan Hai
Beijing, CHINA

Li, Peng (President)
Communist Party Central Committee
Zhong Nan Hai
Beijing, CHINA

Li, Richard (Business Person)
38th Floor, Citibank Tower. Citibank Plaza
3 Garden Road
Central, Hong Kong, Hong Kong

Li, Yiyun (Writer)
c/o Richard Abate *3 Arts Entertainment - NY*
49 West 27th St.
5th Floor
New York, NY 10001, USA

Liacouras, Peter J (Educator)
Temple University
President's Office
Philadelphia, PA 19122, USA

Liaklev, Reidar (Speed Skater)
2770 Jaren
NORWAY

Liars (Music Group)
c/o David T Viecelli *Billions Corporation, The*
833 W Chicago Ave
Suite 101
Chicago, IL 60622-5497, USA

Liars Inc (Music Group)
c/o Staff Member *Foodchain Records*
6464 W Sunset Blvd #200
W Hollywood, CA 90028-8011, USA

Libano Christo, Carlos A (Activist, Writer)
Rua Atibaia 420
Sao Paulo 01235-010, BRAZIL

Libby, Jeff (Athlete, Hockey Player)
24 Foxwell Dr
Scarborough, ME 04074-7608

Liber, Jon (Baseball Player)
Pittsburgh Pirates
2805 Churchbell Ct
Moblle, AL 36695-2528, USA

Liberace, Dora
1775 E. Tropicana
Las Vegas, NV 89119

Libertini, Richard (Actor)
2313 McKinley Ave
Venice, CA 90291, USA

Liberty, Marcus (Athlete, Basketball Player)
3923 N Drake Ave
Chicago, IL 60618-3205, USA

Liberty, Richard
225 SW 6th St.
Dania, FL 33004

Libeskind, Daniel (Architect)
Studio Daniel Libeskund
Windscheidtr 18
Berlin 10627, GERMANY

Libett, Nick (Athlete, Hockey Player)
4272 N McNay Ct
West Bloomfield, MI 48323-2839

Liboiron, Landon (Actor)
c/o Kimberlin Dalehite *Magnolia Entertainment (LA)*
9595 Wilshire Blvd
Suite 601
Beverly Hills, CA 90212, USA

Libran, Frankie (Athlete, Baseball Player)
PO Box 312
Mayaguez, PR 00681-0312, USA

Libutti, Frank (General, Misc)
New York City Deputy Commissioner's Office
Police Plaza
New York, NY 10038, USA

Licad, Cecile (Musician)
Columbia Artists Mgmt Inc
165 W 57th St
New York, NY 10019, USA

Licari, Tony (Athlete, Hockey Player)
811-1485 Baseline Rd
Ottawa, ON K2C 3L8, Canada

Lichfield, Earl of (Photographer)
Lichfield Studios
133 Oxford Gardens
London, W10 6NE, UNITED KINGDOM (UK)

Licht, Jeremy (Actor)
4355 Clybourn Ave
Toluca Lake, CA 91602, USA

Licht, Louis (Scientist)
Ecoltree
3017 Valley View Lane NE
North Liberty, IA 52317, USA

Lichtenberg, Byron K (Astronaut)
5701 Impala South Road
Athens, TX 75752, USA

Lichtenberg, Byron K Dr (Astronaut)
570Ilmpala South Rd
Athens, TX 75752-6053, USA

Lichtenberger, H W (Business Person)
Praxair Inc
39 Old Ridgebury Road
Danbury, CT 06810, USA

Lichtenstein, Harvey (Music Group)
Brooklyn Academy of Music
30 Lafayette Ave
Brooklyn, NY 11217, USA

Lichti, Todd (Athlete, Basketball Player)
2331 Holly View Dr
Martinez, CA 94553, USA

Lichtwardt, Nancy (Stylist)
3114 NE 36th Ave
Portland, OR 97212, USA

Lick, Dennis A (Athlete, Football Player)
6140 S Knox Ave
Chicago, IL 60629, USA

Lickert, John (Athlete, Baseball Player)
P.O. Box 279
North Scituate, RI 02857-0279, USA

Lickliter, Frank (Athlete, Golfer)
846 S Main St
Franklin, OH 45005, USA

Licon, Jeffrey (Actor)
c/o Katie Mason *Luber Roklin Management*
8530 Wilshire Blvd
6th Floor
Beverly Hills, CA 90211, USA

Lidback, Jenny (Athlete, Golfer)
1130 Graystone Xing
Alpharetta, GA 30005-7436, USA

Liddell, Chuck (Iceman) (Athlete, Wrestler)
c/o Staff Member *UFC*
P.O. Box 26959
Las Vegas, NV 89126-0959, USA

Liddell, Dave (Athlete, Baseball Player)
2631 Preakness Way
Norco, CA 92860-4201, USA

Liddington, Bob (Athlete, Hockey Player)
2538 E Sahuaro Dr
Phoenix, AZ 85028-2538

Liddle, Steve (Athlete, Basketball Player)
437 Heath Pl
Smyrna, TN 37167-2636, USA

Liddy, Edward M (Business Person)
Allstate Corp
Allstate Plaza
2775 Sanders Road
Northbrook, IL 60062, USA

Liddy, G Gordon (Politician)
9112 Riverside Dr
Fort Washington, MD 20744-6863, USA

Liddy, G Gordon (Actor)
9112 Riverside Dr
Fort Washington, MD 20744, USA

Lidge, Brad (Athlete, Baseball Player)
4833 Front St
Castle Rock, CO 80104-7902, USA

Lidov, Arthur (Artist)
Pleasant Ridge Rd
Poughquag, NY 12570, USA

Lidster, Doug (Athlete, Hockey Player)
770 Taylor St
Chelsea, MI 48118-1443

Lidstrom, Nicklas (Athlete, Hockey Player)
Newport Sports Management
400-201 City Centre Dr
Attn Don Meehan
Mississauga, ON L5B 2T4, Canada

Lidstrom, Niklas (Attorney, Hockey Player)
47725 Bellagio Dr
Northville, MI 48167-9803

Liebenstein, Todd (Athlete, Football Player)
4486 Chain 0 Lakes Rd
Eagle River, WI 54521-8856, USA

Liebensteuin, Todd (Athlete, Football Player)
4486 Chain O Lakes Rd
Eagle River, WI 54521, USA

Lieber, Jon (Athlete, Baseball Player)
3060 Isle of Palms Dr W
Mobile, AL 36695-2576, USA

Lieber, Larry (Cartoonist)
c/o Staff Member *King Features Syndication*
300 W 57th St
15th Floor
New York, NY 10019-5238, USA

Lieber, Paul (Actor)
c/o Margrit Polak *Margrit Polak Management*
1954 Hillhurst Ave
Suite 405
Los Angeles, CA 90027, USA

Lieber, Rob (Writer)
c/o Staff Member *ICM Partners (ICM-LA)*
10250 Constellation Blvd Fl 7
Los Angeles, CA 90067, USA

Liebergot, Sy (Scientist)
2714 E Bainbridge Cir
Pearland, TX 77584-5906, USA

Lieberman, Andrea (Stylist)
c/o Staff Member *Margaret Maldonado Agency*
1100 Glendon #1000
Los Angeles, CA 90024, USA

Lieberman, Joseph I (Politician, Senator)
392Ilvy Terrace Ct NW
Washington, DC 20007-2139, USA

Lieberman, Nancy (Athlete, Basketball Player)
5756 Quebec Ln
Plano, TX 75024-2904, USA

Lieberman, Wendy
PO Box 5617
Beverly Hills, CA 90210

Lieberman, William S (Misc)
Metropolitan Museum of Art
5th Ave & 82nd St
New York, NY 10028, USA

Lieberman-cline, Nancy (Athlete, Basketball Player, Olympic Athlete)
2636 Creekway Drive
Carrollton, TX 75010-4227, USA

Liebert, Ottmar (Musician)
Jones & O'Malley
10123 Camarillo St
Toluca Lake, CA 91602, USA

Lieberthal, Michael S (Mike) (Athlete, Baseball Player)
1740 Larkfield Ave
Westlake Village, CA 91362-4245, USA

Liebeskind, John (Doctor)
University of California Medical Center
Surgery Dept
Los Angeles, CA 90024, USA

Liebesman, Jonathan (Director)
c/o David Gardner *Principato/Young Management*
9465 Wilshire Blvd
Suite 430
Beverly Hills, CA 90212, USA

Liebman, David (Musician)
2206 Brislin Road
Stroudsberg, PA 18360, USA

Liebowitz, Fran
205 W. 57th St.
New York, NY 10019

Liebrich, Barbara (Athlete, Baseball Player)
16608 North 51st Street
Scottsdale, AZ 85254-1063, USA

Liefeld, Bob (Cartoonist)
3845 Welsh Pony Ln
Yorba Linda, CA 92886-7929, USA

Liefeld, Rob (Artist, Cartoonist)
1942 University Ave #305
Berkeley, CA 94704, USA

Liefer, Jeff (Athlete, Baseball Player)
1116 W Bay Ave
Newport Beach, CA 92661-1017, USA

Lien, Chan (Prime Minister)
Prime Minister's Office
1 Chunghsiano East Road
Sec 1
Taipei, TAIWAN

Lien, Jennifer (Actor)
9932 Lemon Ave
Alta Loma, CA 91737, USA

Lienas, Winston (Baseball Player)
California Angels
Apartado #92
Santiago Dominican Republic

Lienhard, Bill (Athlete, Basketball Player, Olympic Athlete)
1320 Lawrence Ave
Lawrence, KS 66049-2938, USA

Liepa, Andris (Ballerina)
Bryusov Per 17
#12
Moscow 103009, RUSSIA

Liepa, Iisa (Ballerina)
Bryusov Per 17
#12
Moscow 103009, RUSSIA

Liepmann, Hans W (Engineer, Physicist)
55 Haverstock Road
La Canada-Flintridge, CA 91011, USA

Lietzke, Bruce (Athlete, Golfer)
P.O. Box 177
Larue, TX 75770-0177, USA

Lifehouse (Music Group)
c/o Staff Member *Creative Artists Agency (CAA-TN)*
3310 West End Ave
5th Floor
Nashville, TN 37203, USA

Life On Repeat (Music Group, Musician)
c/o Steve Taylor *Anthem Artist Management*
9048 Woodland Trail
Alpharetta, GA 30096, USA

Lifeson, Alex (Musician)
Macklam Feldman Mgmt
1505 W 2nd Ave
#200
Vancouver, BC V6H 3Y4, CANADA

Lifford, Tina (Actor)
c/o Nancy Sanders *Sanders Armstrong Caserta*
2120 Colorado Blvd
Suite 120
Santa Monica, CA 90404, USA

Lifvendahl, Harold R (Publisher)
Orlando Sentinel
633 N Orange Ave
Orlando, FL 32801, USA

Ligarde, Sebastian (Actor)
c/o Staff Member *Televisa*
Blvd Adolfo Lopez Mateos 232
Colonia San Angel INN
DF CP 01060, MEXICO

Light, John (Actor)
c/o Arlene Forster *Forster Entertainment*
12533 Woodgreen St
Los Angeles, CA 90066, USA

Light, Judith (Actor)
c/o Bob Gersh *Gersh (LA)*
9465 Wilshire Blvd
Suite 600
Beverly Hills, CA 90212, USA

Light, Matt (Athlete, Football Player)
261 East St
Foxboro, MA 02035-3023, USA

Lightfoot, Gordon (Musician, Songwriter, Writer)
c/o Staff Member *Early Morning Productions, Inc.*
1365 Yonge St
Suite 207
Toronto, ON M4T 2P7, Canada

Lightfoot, Leonard
446 S. Orchard Dr.
Burbank, CA 91506-2738

Lightner, Candy (Activist)
22653 Pacific Coast Highway
#289
Malibu, CA 90265, USA

Ligon, Bill (Athlete, Basketball Player)
P.O. Box 1432
Gallatin, TN 37066-1432, USA

Ligon, Tom
227 Waverly Pl.
New York, NY 10014

Ligouri, James A (Educator)
Iona College
President's Office
New Rochelle, NY 10801, USA

Ligtenberg, Kerry (Athlete, Baseball Player)
9274 Albright Ct
Inver Grove Heights, MN 55077-4546, USA

Likens, Gerie E (Biologist)
Ecosystem Studies Institute
PO Box AB
Millbrook, NY 12545, USA

Likens, Peter W (Educator)
Lehigh University
President's Office
Bethlehem, PA 18015, USA

Lil' Cease (Musician)
Famous Artists Agency
250 W 57th St
New York, NY 10107, USA

Liles, John-Michael (Athlete, Hockey Player)
Top Shelf Sports Management
21 Hopperton Dr
Attn Joseph Resnick
North York, ON M2L 2S5, Canada

Liles, Kevin (Business Person)
75 Rockefeller Plaza 32nd Fl
New York, NY 10019, USA

Liles, Robert (General)
19520 Tiber Ct
Montgomery Village, MD 20886-3913, USA

Lilienfeld, Abraham M (Biologist)
3203 Old Post Dr
Pikesville, MD 21208, USA

Lil' J (Actor, Musician, Television Host)
c/o Staff Member *Thruline Entertainment*
9250 Wilshire Blvd
Ground Fl
Beverly Hills, CA 90212, USA

Lilja, Andreas (Athlete, Hockey Player)
6501 N Federal Hwy Ste 2
Boca Raton, FL 33487-3137

Lilja, George (Athlete, Football Player)
335 Breeze Point Cir
Warren, PA 16365-2548, USA

Liljeberg, Rebecka (Actor)
Kolbäcksgränd 33
Bagarmossen 12846, Sweden

Lil Jon (Musician)
c/o David Wirtschafter *WME (LA)*
9601 Wilshire Blvd Fl 3
Beverly Hills, CA 90210, USA

Lill, John R (Musician)
Harold Holt
31 Sinclair Road
London W14 0NS, UNITED KINGDOM (UK)

Lillard, Bill (Bowler)
5418 Imogene St
Houston, TX 77096-2206, USA

Lillard, Mathew (Actor, Director, Producer)

Lillard, Matthew (Actor, Producer)
c/o Melissa Kates *Viewpoint Inc*
8820 Wilshire Blvd.
Suite 220
Beverly Hills, CA 90211, USA

Lillee, Dennis K (Cricketer)
Swan Sport
PO Box 158
Byron Bay, NSW 2481, AUSTRALIA

Lilley, Chris (Actor)
RGM Associates
c/o Sharne MacDonald
PO Box 128
Surry Hills NSW 2010, AUSTRALIA

Lilley, James R (Diplomat)
2801 New Mexico Ave NW
#407
Washington, DC 20007, USA

Lilley, John (Athlete, Hockey Player)
25 Curtis St
Wakefield, MA 01880-5109, USA

Lillibridge, Brent (Athlete, Baseball Player)
22714 43rd Dr SE
Bothell, WA 98021-9070, USA

Lillien, Lisa (Writer)
c/o Bill Stankey *Westport Entertainment Associates*
1700 Post Rd
Suite C-15
Fairfield, CT 06824, USA

Lilliquist, Derek (Athlete, Baseball Player)
226 10th Ave
Vero Beach, FL 32962-2819, USA

Lillis, Bob (Athlete, Baseball Player, Coach)
5107 Cherry Tree Ln
Orlando, FL 32819-3848, USA

Lillis, Charles M (Business Person)
MediaOne Group
188 Iverness Dr W
Englewood, CO 80112, USA

Lillix (Music Group)
c/o Staff Member *Bruce Allen Talent*
425 Carrall St
Suite 500
Vancouver, BC V6B 6E3, Canada

Lilly, Bob (Athlete, Football Player)
104 Aster Cir
Georgetown, TX 78633-4537, USA

Lilly, Evangeline (Actor)
c/o David Miner *3 Arts Entertainment Inc*
9460 Wilshire Blvd
7th Floor
Beverly Hills, CA 90210, USA

Lilly, John (Scientist)
Dolphins Foundation
11930 Oceanaire Ln
Malibu, CA 90265-2253, USA

Lilly, Kristine (Athlete, Soccer Player)

Lilly, Ted (Athlete, Baseball Player)
1305 W Waveland Ave
Chicago, IL 60613-3720, USA

Lilly, Theodore (Baseball Player)
Montreal Expos
PO Box 257
Bass Lake, CA 93604-0257, USA

Lilly, Tony (Athlete, Football Player)
13815 Holly Forest Dr
Manassas, VA 20112-3864, USA

Lilly-Heavey, Kristine (Athlete, Olympic Athlete, Soccer Player)
359 Grove St
Needham, MA 02492-1009, USA

Lillywhite, Verl (Athlete, Football Player)
1828 North Barkley
Mesa, AZ 85203, USA

Lil Wayne (Musician)
c/o Cortez Bryant *Bryant Management*
555 Washington Ave
Suite 240
Miami Beach, FL 33139, USA

Lily, Morgan (Actor)
c/o Casey Crawford *Origin Talent Agency*
4705 Laurel Canyon #306
Studio City, CA 91607, USA

Lilyholm, Len (Athlete, Hockey Player, Olympic Athlete)
4376 Thielen Ave
Minneapolis, MN 55436-1523, USA

Lim, Kwan Hi
1660 Piikoi St.
Honolulu, HI 96822

Lim, Siew-Ai (Athlete, Golfer)
304 Morning Sun Dr
Birmingham, AL 35242, USA

Lima, Adriana (Actor, Model)
c/o Chris Kiely *Marilyn Model Management*
32 Union Square East #PH
New York, NY 10003, USA

Lima, Devin
LFO/BMG Records
8750 Wilshire Blvd
Beverly Hills, CA 90211

Lima, Floriana (Actor)
c/o Adam Levine *Industry Entertainment Partners*
955 S Carrillo Dr
Suite 300
Los Angeles, CA 90048, USA

Lima, Luis (Opera Singer)
1950 Redondela Dr
Rancho Palos Verdes, CA 90275, USA

Liman, Doug (Director, Producer, Writer)
c/o Adam Kanter *Creative Artists Agency (CAA-LA)*
2000 Ave Of The Stars
Los Angeles, CA 90067, USA

Limato, Ed
456 S. Plymouth Blvd
Los Angeles, CA 90020

Limbaugh, Rush (Politician)
PO Box 2795
Palm Beach, FL 33480-2795, USA

Limbrick, Garrett (Athlete, Football Player)
PO Box 472
Hempstead, TX 77445-0472, USA

Lime, Yvonne (Actor)
Fedderson
6135 E McDonald Dr
Paradise Valley, AZ 85253, USA

Limelighters, The
11761 E. Speedway Blvd
Tucson, AZ 85748-2017

Limelights
11761 E. Speedway Blvd.
Tucson, AZ 85748-2917

Limos, Tiffany (Actor)
c/o Staff Member *Paradigm (LA)*
360 N Crescent Dr
North Bldg
Beverly Hills, CA 90210, USA

Lin, Bridget (Actor)
8 Fei Ngo Shan Road
Kowloon
Hong Kong, CHINA

Lin, Ching-Hsia (Actor)
Taiwan Cinema-Drama Assn
196 Chunghua Road
10/F Sec 1
Taipei, TAIWAN

Lin, Cho-Laing
473 West End Ave. #15A
New York, NY 10024

Lin, Cho-Liang (Musician)
Hilliard School
60 Lincoln Center Plaza
New York, NY 10023, USA

Lin, Jeremy (Linsanity) (Athlete, Basketball Player)
c/o Roger Montgomery *Montgomery Sports Group*
19141 Stone Oak
San Antonio, TX 78258, USA

Lin, Justin (Director)
c/o Rowena Arguelles *Creative Artists Agency (CAA-LA)*
2000 Ave Of The Stars
Los Angeles, CA 90067, USA

Lin, Maya Ying (Architect, Artist)
Sidney Janis Gallery
120 E 75th St
Apt 6-A
New York, NY 10021-3240, USA

Lin, Ting Ting (Stylist)
c/o Staff Member *Jed Root Inc*
61-A Walker St
New York, NY 10013, USA

Lin, Yu Ping (Athlete, Golfer)
1000 S Romney Dr
Walnut, CA 91789, USA

Linares, Julio (Athlete, Baseball Player)
PO Box 62
San Pedro De Macoris, Dominican Republic

Lincecum, Tim (Athlete, Baseball Player)
c/o Rick Thurman *Beverly Hills Sports Council*
131 S Rodeo Dr
Beverly Hills, CA 90212, USA

Lincicome, Brittany (Athlete, Golfer)
7971 Idlewild Ln
Seminole, FL 33777, USA

Linck, Anthony (Photographer)
221 Champlain Dr
Plattsburgh, NY 12901-4206, USA

Lincoln, Andrew (Actor)
c/o Staff Member *Independent Talent Group (ITG-UK)*
Oxford House
76 Oxford St
London W1D 1BS, UK

Lincoln, Blanche (Politician)
3942 27th Rd N
Arlington, VA 22207-5242, USA

Lincoln, Brad (Athlete, Baseball Player)
331 S Shanks St
Clute, TX 77531, USA

Lincoln, Craig (Athlete, Diver, Olympic Athlete)
20930 Almazan Rd
Woodland Hills, CA 91364-5501, USA

Lincoln, Howard (Commentator)
Seattle Mariners
6 Holly Hill Dr
Mercer Island, WA 98040-5326, USA

Lincoln, Jeremy (Athlete, Football Player)
71 Broadway
Apt 20A
New York, NY 10006, USA

Lincoln, Keith P (Athlete, Football Player)
550 SE Crestview St
Pullman, WA 99163, USA

Lincoln, Lar Park
8899 Beverly Blvd. #510
Los Angeles, CA 90048

Lincoln, Michael (Mike) (Athlete, Baseball Player)
8269 Moss Oak Ave
Citrus Heights, CA 95610-0763, USA

Lind, Adam (Athlete, Baseball Player)
6520 Turf Way
Anderson, IN 46013-9588, USA

Lind, DeDe
PO Box 1712
Boca Raton, FL 33429

Lind, Don L (Astronaut)
51 N 376 E
Smithfield, UT 84335, USA

Lind, Don L Dr (Astronaut)
51 N 376 E
Smithfield, UT 84335-1111, USA

Lind, Jack (Athlete, Baseball Player)
6132 E Redmont Dr
Mesa, AZ 85215, USA

lind, Jack (Baseball Player)
Milwaukee Brewers
6132 E Redmont Dr
Mesa, AZ 85215-0878, USA

Lind, Joan (Athlete)
240 Euclid Ave
Long Beach, CA 90803, USA

Lind, Jose (Athlete, Baseball Player)
18 Brisas Del Plata
Dorado, PR 00646-5123, USA

Lind, Juha (Athlete, Hockey Player)
1260 de la Gauchetiere W
Montreal, QC H3B 5E8, Canada

Lind, Marshall L (Educator)
University of Alaska Southeast
Chancellor's Office
Janeau, AK 99801, USA

Lind, Sarah (Actor)
c/o Staff Member Lucas Talent Inc
100 W. Pender St
Sun Tower, 7th Floor
Vancouver, BC V6B 1R8, Canada

Lindahl, David (Business Person)
PHP Inc
75 Old High St
Whitman, MA USA

Lindahl, George III (Business Person)
Union Pacific Resources
PO Box 1330
Houston, TX 77251, USA

Lindbeck, Assar (Economist)
50 Ostermalmsgatan
Stockholm 114 26, SWEDEN

Lindberg, Chad (Actor)
c/o Staff Member Michael Black
Management
9701 Wilshire Blvd
10th Floor
Beverly Hills, CA 90212, USA

Lindbergh, Reeve (Writer)
Simon and Schuster, Inc
1230 Avenue of the Americas 11th Fl
New York, NY 10020, USA

Lindbom, Johan (Athlete, Hockey Player)
Torplyckevagen 7
Bankeryd 564 34, Sweden

Lindelind, Liv (Model)
PO Box 1029
Frazier Park, CA 93225, USA

Lindell, Heather (Actor)
c/o Alan Ellsweig Shadow Entertainment
10 Universal City Plz
20th Floor
Universal City, CA 91608, USA

Lindell, Rian (Athlete, Football Player)
45 Stoughton Ln
Orchard Park, NY 14127-2083, USA

Lindelof, Damon (Producer, Writer)
c/o Ted Miller Creative Artists Agency
(CAA-LA)
2000 Ave Of The Stars
Los Angeles, CA 90067, USA

Lindeman, Jim (Athlete, Baseball Player)
2278 S Scott St
Des Plaines, IL 60018-3147, USA

Lindemann, Tony (Bowler)
6250 Roosevelt Blvd Lot 80
Clearwater, FL 33760-2583, USA

Linden, Eric (Athlete, Hockey Player)
1 Pattison Pl.
Philadelphia, PA 19148, USA

Linden, Hal (Actor)
c/o Staff Member Stone Manners Talent &
Literary (NY)
900 Broadway
Suite 803
New York, NY 10003, USA

Linden, Todd (Athlete, Baseball Player)
7825 NW Anderson Hill Rd
Silverdale, WA 98383-9313, USA

Linden, Walt (Athlete, Baseball Player)
4432 Harvey Ave
Western Springs, IL 60558-1645, USA

Lindenlaub, Karl W (Cinematographer)
3021 Nicholas Canyon Road
Los Angeles, CA 90046, USA

Lindenmann, Tony (Bowler)
35096 Jefferson Ave
#216
Harrison Township, MI 48045, USA

Lindenmeyer, Hans (Scientist)
Kaiser-Ludwig-Str 29A
Grunwald, Germany D-82031, UK

Linder, Kate (Actor)
c/o Sandra Siegal Siegal Company, The
9025 Wilshire Blvd #400
Beverly Hills, CA 90211, USA

Lindes, Hal (Musician)
Damage Mgmt
16 Lambton Place
London W11 2SH, UNITED KINGDOM
(UK)

Lindgren, Kjell N Dr (Astronaut)
2612 White Ibis Ct
League City, TX 77573-7750, USA

Lindh, Hilary (Skier)
PO Box 33036
Juneau, AK 99803, USA

Lindh, Mats
Ladspikaregatan 16
Goteborg 416 80, Sweden

Lindholm, Ingvar
Hringe Hages Vag 33
Ronninge, SWEDEN 14400

Lindholm, Mikael (Athlete, Hockey
Player)
Norra Abyggebyvagen 44
Gavle, 805 98 Sweden

Lindhome, Riki (Actor, Director, Writer)
c/o Mary Ellen Mulcahy Framework
Entertainment (LA)
9057 Nemo St
Suite C
West Hollywood, CA 90069, USA

Lindig, Bill M (Business Person)
Sysco Corp
1390 Enclave Parkway
Houston, TX 77077, USA

Lindland, Matt (Athlete, Olympic Athlete,
Wrestler)
26501 SE Mattson Ln
Eagle Creek, OR 97022-9606, USA

Lindlar, Renate (Stylist)
c/o Staff Member Bransch
131 Varick St
#1006
New York, NY 10013, USA

Lindley, Christina (Model)
Lindley Enterprises
114 Rhine Dr
Madison, TN 37115-3561, USA

Lindley, Leta (Athlete, Golfer)
104 Alegria Way
Palm Beach Gardens, FL 33418-1635,
USA

Lindner, William G (Misc)
Transport Workers Union
80 W End Ave
New York, NY 10023, USA

Lindo, Delroy (Actor)
c/o Brian Swardstrom WME (LA)
9601 Wilshire Blvd Fl 3
Beverly Hills, CA 90210, USA

Lindon, Vincent (Actor)
Artmedia
20 Ave Rapp
Paris 75007, FRANCE

Lindquist, Susan L (Biologist)
Whitehead Institute
9 Cambridge Circle
Cambridge, MA 02142, USA

Lindros, Brett (Athlete, Hockey Player)
85 Crescent Rd
Toronto, ON M4W 1 T7, Canada

Lindros, Eric (Athlete, Hockey Player)
Lindros Legacy Foundation
PO Box 5010
London, ON N6A SW9, Canada

Lindroth, Eric (Misc)
13151 Dufresne Place
San Diego, CA 92129, USA

Lindsay, Bill (Athlete, Hockey Player)
700 NW 7th Ave
Boca Raton, FL 33486-3518

Lindsay, Bill (Athlete, Hockey Player)
Florida Panthers
1 Panther Pkwy
Sunrise, FL 33323-5315

Lindsay, Everett (Athlete, Football Player)
101 Wildwood Beach Rd Apt 13.101
Wildwood Beach Rd Apt 13.
Saint Paul, MN 55115-1684, USA

Lindsay, Jack (Writer)
56 Maids Causeway
Cambridge, UNITED KINGDOM (UK)

Lindsay, Mark (Musician, Songwriter,
Writer)
Mars Talent
27 L'Ambiance Court
Bardonia, NY 10954, USA

Lindsay, Mort
6970 Fernhill Dr.
Malibu, CA 90265

Lindsay, R B Theodore (Ted) (Athlete,
Hockey Player)
2598 Invitational Dr.
Oakland, MI 48363-2453, USA

Lindsay, Robert (Actor, Musician)
c/o Christian Hodell Hamilton Hodell Ltd
66-68 Margaret St Fl 5
London W1W 8SR, UK

Lindsay, Ted (Athlete, Hockey Player)
25981nvitational Dr
Oakland, MI 48363-2453

Lindsey, Bill (Athlete, Baseball Player)
1317 Winterberry Dr
Reidsville, NC 27320-7154, USA

Lindsey, Dale (Athlete, Football Player)
4020 Murphy Canyon Rd
San Diego, CA 92123, USA

Lindsey, Doug (Athlete, Baseball Player)
2410 Silver Spur Ln
Leander, TX 78641-7883, USA

Lindsey, Hub (Athlete, Football Player)
1320 Frebis Ave
Columbus, OH 43206-3717, USA

Lindsey, James E (Athlete, Football Player)
1165 E Joyce Blvd
Fayetteville, AR 72703, USA

Lindsey, Jim
1165 E Joyce Blvd
Fayetteville, AR 72703-5183, USA

Lindsey, Rodney (Rod) (Athlete, Baseball
Player)
610 Comanchee Dr
Lot 43
Opelika, AL 36804-6500, USA

Lindsey, Steven W (Athlete, Football
Player)
1327 County Road 123
Water Valley, MS 38965-6114, USA

Lindsey, Steven W Colonel (Astronaut)
635 Eldorado Blvd Apt 1111
Broomfield, CO 80021-8831, USA

Lindsey, Terry (Athlete, Football Player)
324 W Brookdale Pl
Fullerton, CA 92832-1426, USA

Lindsey, Tracy
651 N. Kilkea Dr.
Los Angeles, CA 90048

Lindsley, Blake (Actor)
Gold Marshak Liedtke
3500 W Olive Ave
#1400
Burbank, CA 91505, USA

Lindsley, Donald B (Physicist)
517 11th St
Santa Monica, CA 90402, USA

Lindstrand, Per (Misc)
Thunder & Colt
Maesbury Road
Oswestry, Shropshire SY10 8HA, UNITED
KINGDOM (UK)

Lindstrom, Charlie (Chuck) (Athlete,
Baseball Player)
P.O. Box 486
Atlanta, IL 61723-0486, USA

Lindstrom, Chris (Athlete, Football Player)
70 Dudley Hill Rd
Dudley, MA 01571, USA

Lindstrom, David (Dave) (Athlete,
Football Player)
13209 Woodson St
Overland Park, KS 66209, USA

Lindstrom, Jack (Cartoonist)
United Feature Syndicate
200 Madison Ave
New York, NY 10016, USA

Lindstrom, Jon (Actor)
c/o Staff Member *Gilbertson Management*
1334 3rd St Promenade #201
Santa Monica, CA 90401, USA

Lindstrom, Matt (Athlete, Baseball Player)
316 Mohawk Ave
Rexburg, ID 83440-2227, USA

Lindstrom, Pia (Journalist)
30 Rockefeller Plz Ste 700
New York, NY 10112-0015, USA

Lindstrom, Willy (Athlete, Hockey Player)
Verkebrovagan 40
Galve 80591, SWEDEN

Lindvall, Angela (Actor, Model)
c/o Brett Norensberg *Gersh (LA)*
9465 Wilshire Blvd
Suite 600
Beverly Hills, CA 90212, USA

Lindvall, Olle (Doctor)
University of Lund
Medical Cell Research Dept
Lund 23362, SWEDEN

Lindwall, Raymond R (Cricketer)
3 Wentworth Court
Endeavour St Mt Ommaney
Brisbane, QLD 4074, AUSTRALIA

Line, Bill (Athlete, Football Player)
6048 Plumas St Apt E
Reno, NV 89519-6024, USA

Line, Lorie (Musician)
Lorie Line
222 Minnetonka Ave S
Wayzata, MN 55391, USA

Linebrink, Scott (Athlete, Baseball Player)
2100 County Road 156
Granger, TX 76530-5328, USA

Lineger, Jerry (Astronaut)
c/o Staff Member *Washington Speakers
Bureau*
1663 Prince St
Alexandria, VA 22314, USA

Linehan, Scott (Athlete, Football Player)
30246 Inkster Rd
Franklin, MI 48025-1409, USA

Lineker, Gary W (Soccer Player)
Markee UK
6 Saint George St
Nottingham NG1 3BE, UNITED
KINGDOM (UK)

Linenger, Jerry M (Astronaut)
550 S Stoney Point Road
Suttons Bay, MI 49682, USA

Linenger, Jerry M Dr (Astronaut)
550 S Stony Point Rd
Suttons Bay, MI 49682-9575, USA

Lines, Dick (Athlete, Baseball Player)
1716 Pebble Beach Ln
Lady Lake, FL 32159-2238, USA

Liney, John (Cartoonist)
c/o Staff Member *King Features
Syndication*
300 W 57th St
15th Floor
New York, NY 10019-5238, USA

Ling (Model)
I M G Models
304 Park Ave S
#1200
New York, NY 10010, USA

Ling, Bai (Actor)
c/o Matt Luber *Luber Roklin Management*
8530 Wilshire Blvd
6th Floor
Beverly Hills, CA 90211, USA

Ling, David (Athlete, Hockey Player)
I 53 Green Rd
Sydney, NS B1P 3E4, Canada

Ling, Lisa (Correspondent, Journalist)
c/o Henry Reisch *WME (WMA-NY)*
1325 Ave of the Americas
New York, NY 10019, USA

Ling, Sergei S (Prime Minister)
Prime Minister's Office
Pl Nezavisimosti
Minsk 220010, BELARUS

Ling, Victor (Scientist)
5671 Trafalgar St
Vancouver, BC V6N 1C2, Canada

Lingenfelter, Bob (Football Player)
Cleveland Browns
53144 865 Rd
Plainview, NE 68769-2505, USA

Lingenfelter, John (Race Car Driver)
Summit Racing
Box 535
Richfield, OH 44286, USA

Lingenfelter, Steve (Athlete, Basketball
Player)
17378 Ithaca Ct
Lakeville, MN 55044-8742 ----, USA

Lingle, Linda (Politician)
520 Lunalilo Home Rd Unit 8425
Honolulu, HI 96825-1760, USA

Lingmerth, Goran (Athlete, Football
Player)
624 Enfield Ct
Delray Beach, FL 33444-1749, USA

Lingner, Adam (Athlete, Football Player)
70 Stoughton Ln
Orchard Park, NY 14127, USA

Linhart, Anton (Athlete, Football Player)
13 Summer Run Ct
Timonium, MD 21093, USA

Linhart, Carl (Athlete, Baseball Player)
2647 Delmar Ave
Granite City, IL 62040-3439, USA

Linhart, Toni (Athlete, Football Player)
13 Summer Run Ct
Lutherville Timonium, MD 21093, USA

Liniak, Cole (Athlete, Baseball Player)
P.O. Box 235625
Encinitas, CA 92023-5625, USA

Linke, Paul (Actor)
Zealous Artists
139 S Beverly Dr
#225
Beverly Hills, CA 90212, USA

Linkert, Lo (Artist, Cartoonist)
9541 Lenore Dr
Garden Grove, CA 92841, USA

Linklater, Hamish (Actor)
c/o Leanne Coronel *Coronel Group*
1100 Glendon Ave
17th Floor
Los Angeles, CA 90046, USA

Linklater, Hamish (Actor)
c/o Hildy Gottlieb *ICM Partners (ICM-LA)*
10250 Constellation Blvd Fl 7
Los Angeles, CA 90067, USA

Linklater, Richard (Director, Producer,
Writer)
Detour Filmproduction
P.O. Box 13351
Austin, TX 78711, USA

Linkletter, John A (Editor)
Popular Mechanics Magazine
Editorial Dept
224 W 57th St
New York, NY 10019, USA

Linkletter, Nicole (Model)
c/o Staff Member *Ford Models (NY)*
238 E 4th St
New York, NY 10009, USA

Linley, Cody (Actor)
c/o Staff Member *Reel Talent
Management*
P.O. Box 491035
Los Angeles, CA 90049, USA

Linn, Jack (Athlete, Football Player)
8418 Trillium Rd
Fort Myers, FL 33967-3486, USA

Linn, Richard (Judge)
US Court of Appeals
717 Madison Place NW
Washington, DC 20439, USA

Linn, Teri Ann (Actor)
Sutton Barth Vennari
145 S Fairfax Ave
#310
Los Angeles, CA 90036, USA

Linn-Baker, Mark (Actor)
27702 Fairweather St
Canyon Country, CA 91351, USA

Linne, Aubrey (Athlete, Football Player)
4606 Lanham St
Midland, TX 79705, USA

Linne, Larry (Athlete, Football Player)
6861 Pumpkin Ridge Dr
Windsor, CO 80550-7015, USA

Linneha, Richard M Dr (Astronaut)
16802 Hartwood Way
Houston, 77058-2305 TX, USA

Linnehan, Richard M (Astronaut)
16802 Hartwood Way
Houston, TX 77058, USA

Linney, Laura (Actor)
c/o Aleen Keshishian *Brillstein
Entertainment Partners*
9150 Wilshire Blvd #350
Beverly Hills, CA 90212, USA

Linnin, Chris (Athlete, Football Player)
1037 Purple Sage Loop
Castle Rock, CO 80104, USA

Linowitz, Sol M (Diplomat)
2230 California St NW
#4B
Washington, DC 20008, USA

Linsalata, Joe (Athlete, Baseball Player)
4017 Washington St
Hollywood, FL 33021, USA

Linsalata, Joe (Baseball Player)
4017 Washington St
Hollywood, FL 33021-7349, USA

Linseman, Ken (Athlete, Hockey Player)
1070 Ocean Blvd.
Hampton, NH 03842-1500

Linskey, Mike (Baseball Player)
Bowman
18826 Polo Meadow Dr
Humble, TX 77346-8121, USA

Linson, Art (Director, Producer)
Art Linson Productions
Warner Bros
4000 Warner Blvd
Burbank, CA 91522, USA

Lintel, Michelle (Actor)
c/o John Paradise *The Paradise Group*
PO Box 69451
West Hollywood, CA 90069, USA

Linteris, Gregory T (Astronaut)
US Commerce Dept
Fire Science Division
Gaithersburg, MD 20899, USA

Linteris, Gregory T Dr (Astronaut)
15325 Turkey Foot Rd
Gaithersburg, MD 20878-3640, USA

Linton, Doug (Athlete, Baseball Player)
201 Ellison St
Rochester, NY 14609-4047, USA

Lintz, Larry (Athlete, Baseball Player)
8529 Sun Sprite Way
Elk Grove, CA 95624-3816, USA

Linville, Joanne (Actor)
345 N Maple Dr
#302
Beverly Hills, CA 90210, USA

Linz, Alex D (Actor)
Innovative Artists
1505 10th St
Santa Monica, CA 90401, USA

Linz, Phil (Athlete, Baseball Player)
20 Rocky Raplds Rd
Stamford, CT 06903-3131, USA

Linzy, Frank (Athlete, Baseball Player)
38947 E 151st St S
Coweta, OK 74429-8550, USA

Lioeanjie, Rene (Misc)
National Maritime Union
1150 17th St NW
Washington, DC 20036, USA

Lionetti, Donald M (General)
4517 West Rosemere Road
Tampa, FL 33609-4209, USA

Lions, Jacques-Louis (Mathematician)
7 Rue Paul Barruel
Paris 75015, USA

Lions, Pierre-Louis (Mathematician)
Paris University
Place Marechal Lattre-de-Tessigny
Paris 75775, FRANCE

Liotta, Ray (Actor)
c/o Beth Holden-Garland *Untitled Entertainment (LA)*
350 S. Beverly Dr #200
Beverly Hills, CA 90212, USA

Lioutas, Tommy (Actor)
c/o Norbert Abrams *Noble Caplan Abrams*
1260 Yonge St
2nd Floor
Toronto ON M4T 1W6, Canada

Lipa, Elisabeta (Athlete)
Str Reconstructiei 1
#78
Bucharest, ROMANIA

Lipetri, Angelo (Athlete, Baseball Player)
150 Yoakum Ave
Farmingdale, NY 11735-5034, USA

Lipinski, Ann Marie (Journalist)
Chicago Tribune
Editorial Dept
435 N Michigan Ave
Chicago, IL 60611, USA

Lipinski, Daniel (Congressman, Politician)
1717 Longworth HOB
Washington, DC 20515, USA

Lipinski, Tara (Actor, Athlete, Figure Skater, Olympic Athlete)
c/o Tracy Quinn *Quinn Management*
17328 Ventura Blvd
Suite 416
Encino, CA 91316, USA

Lipman, Maureen (Actor, Writer)
c/o Staff Member *Talking Concepts*
19 Bird Street
Lichfield
Staffordshire WS13 6PW, UNITED KINGDOM

Lipnicki, Jonathan (Actor)
c/o Jason Egenberg *United Talent Agency (UTA)*
9336 Civic Center Dr
Beverly Hills, CA 90210, USA

Lipovsek, Marjana (Opera Singer)
Artists Mgmt Zurich
Rutistr 52
Zurich-Gockhausen 8044, SWITZERLAND

Lippard, Stephen (Scientist)
975 Memorial Dr Apt 602
Cambridge, MA 02138-5803, USA

Lippard, Stephen J (Misc)
975 Memorial Dr
#602
Cambridge, MA 02138, USA

Lippett, Ronnie (Athlete, Football Player)
610 Foundry St
South Easton, MA 02375-1318, USA

Lippincott, Philip E (Business Person)
Campbell Soup Co
Campbell Place
Cemden, NJ 08103, USA

Lipporien, Paavo Tapio (Prime Minister)
Premier's Office
Snellmaninkatu 1
Helsinki 00170, FINLAND

Lipps, Lisa (Adult Film Star)
Moonlite Bunny Ranch
69 Moonlight Rd
Carson City, NV 89706, USA

Lipps, Louis (Athlete, Football Player)
132 Ruth St
Pittsburgh, PA 15211-2308, USA

Lipset, Seymour M (Misc)
900 N Strafford St
#2131
Arlington, VA 22203, USA

Lipsett, Mortimer B (Physicist)
National Institute of Health
9000 Rockville Pike
Bethesda, MD 20892, USA

Lipshutz, Bruce H (Misc)
University of California
Chemistry Dept
Santa Barbara, CA 93106, USA

Lipski, Bob (Athlete, Baseball Player)
1 Snook St
Scranton, PA 18505-2865, USA

Lipson, D Herbert (Publisher)
Philadelphia Magazine
1500 Walnut St
Philadelphia, PA 19102, USA

Lipton, Bruce (Motivational Speaker)
2574 Pine Flat Rd
Santa Cruz, CA 95060, USA

Lipton, Holly (Musician)
c/o Staff Member *Charles Rapp Enterprises Inc*
88 Pine St
New York, NY 10005, USA

Lipton, James (Actor, Producer, Television Host)
c/o Staff Member *James Lipton Productions*
120A E 23rd St Fl 3
New York, NY 10010, USA

Lipton, Martin (Attorney, Attorney General, General)
Wachtell Lipton Rosen Katz
51 W 52nd St
New York, NY 10019, USA

Lipton, Peggy (Actor, Writer)
c/o Staff Member *St Martins Press*
Publicity Dept
175 5th Ave
New York, NY 10010, USA

Lipton, Robert (Actor)
c/o Staff Member *Judy Fox Personal Talent Management*
Prefers to be contacted via telephone
Los Angeles, CA 90069, USA

Lipuma, Chris (Athlete, Hockey Player)
16032 Crystal Creek Dr Apt 1B
Orland Park, IL 60462-53SS

Liquor, Shirley Q (Comedian)
c/o Staff Member *Diva Central Inc*
7510 W Sunset Blvd Ste 1445
Los Angees, CA 90046, USA

Liquori, Martin (Marty) (Athlete, Olympic Athlete, Sportscaster, Track Athlete)
2915 NW 58th Blvd
Gainesville, FL 32606, USA

Liriano, Francisco (Athlete, Baseball Player)
2900 Thomas Ave S
Minneapolis, MN 55416-4477, USA

Liriano, Nelson (Athlete, Baseball Player)
Burlington Royals
PO Box 1143
Burlington, NC 27216-1143, USA

Lisbe, Mike (Writer)
c/o Brian Sher *Category 5 Entertainment*
10250 Constellation Blvd
7th Floor
Los Angeles, CA 90067, USA

Lisbon, Don (Athlete, Football Player)
201 Woodbine Ave
Struthers, OH 44471-2350, USA

Lisch, Russell (Athlete, Football Player)
206 Country Club Ln
Belleville, IL 62223, USA

Lisch, Rusty (Athlete, Football Player)
206 Country Club Ln
Belleville, IL 62223-1910, USA

Liscio, Patti (Golfer)
7803 Glenneagle Dr
Dallas, TX 75248-2335, USA

Liscio, Tony (Athlete, Football Player)
10348 Trailcliff Dr
Dallas, TX 75238, USA

Lisi, Rick (Athlete, Baseball Player)
143 Pinto Rd
Rogers, AR 72756-7148, USA

Lisi, Virna (Actor)
Via di Filomarino 4
Rome, ITALY

Lisin, Vladimir (Business Person)
Novolipstek Steel
2, pl. Metallurgov
Lipetsk 398040, Russia

Lisitsa, Valentina (Musician)
Columbia Artists Mgmt Inc
165 W 57th St
New York, NY 10019, USA

Liska, Stephen (Actor)
c/o Larry Metzger *Grant Savic Kopaloff & Associates*
6399 Wilshire Blvd #414
Los Angeles, CA 90048, USA

Liske, Pete (Athlete, Football Player)
116 E Mountain Brook Ln
Wenatchee, WA 98801-9159, USA

Liskov, Barbara H (Engineer)
Massachusetts Institute of Technology
Computer Sci Lab
Cambridge, MA 02139, USA

Liss, Joe (Actor)
c/o Scott Howard *Howard Entertainment*
10850 Wilshire Blvd
Suite 1260
Los Angeles, CA 90024, USA

Lissie (Musician)
c/o Staff Member *Paradigm (Monterey)*
404 W Franklin St
Monterey, CA 93940, USA

Lissner, Stephane (Opera Singer)
Theatre du Chatelet
2 Rue Eduouard Colonne
Paris 75001, FRANCE

List, Peyton (Actor)
c/o Abby Bluestone *Innovative Artists (LA)*
1505 10th St
Santa Monica, CA 90401, USA

List, Robert (Politician)
50 W Liberty St # 210
Reno, NV 89501-1940, USA

Listach, Pat (Athlete, Baseball Player)
6030 Durande Dr
Baton Rouge, LA 70820-5421, USA

Listach, Pat (Athlete, Baseball Player)
Chicago Cubs
1060 W Addison St Ste 1 Attn: Coaching Staff
chicago, IL 60613-4398

Lister, Alton (Athlete, Basketball Player)
5413 Kirkridge Pl
Garland, TX 75044, USA

Lister Jr, Tommy (Tiny Zeus) (Actor)
c/o Staff Member *Cindy Cowan Entertainment*
8265 Sunset Blvd
Suite 205
Los Angeles, CA 90046, USA

Listopad, Ed (Athlete, Football Player)
6719 Roberts Ave
Dundalk, MD 21222, USA

Listowel, Earl of (William F Hare) (Government Official)
10 Downshire Hill
London NW3, UNITED KINGDOM (UK)

Lit (Music Group)
c/o Ruta Seopetys *Sepetys Entertainment Group*
5543 Edmonton Pike
Suite 8A
Nashville, TN 37211, USA

Liteky, Angelo J "Charles" (General)
167 Staples Ave
San Francisco, CA 94112-1834, USA

Lithgow, John (Actor)
c/o Mandi Warren *Viewpoint Inc. - NY*
Prefers to be contacted via telephone
New York, NY 10012, USA

Litsch, Jesse (Athlete, Baseball Player)
6948 80th TerN
Pinellas Park, FL 33781-2011, USA

Littell, Mark (Athlete, Baseball Player)
27358 N 88th Ln
Peoria, AZ 85383-4853, USA

Littenberg, Barbara (Architect)
Peterson/Littenberg Achitecture
13 E 66th St
New York, NY 10021, USA

Litterell, Brian (Musician)
The Firm
9100 Wilshire Blvd
#100W
Beverly Hills, CA 90210, USA

Little, Bernie (Race Car Driver)
PO Box 194
Novi, MI 48376-0194, USA

Little, Big Tiny
W. 3985 Taft Dr.
Spokane, WA 99208

Little, Bryan (Athlete, Baseball Player)
4766 Tiffany Park Cir
Bryan, TX 77802-5822, USA

Little, Chad (Race Car Driver)
8718 Statesville Rd
Charlotte, NC 28269, USA

Little, Charles L (Misc)
United Transportation Union
14600 Detroit Ave
Cleveland, OH 44107, USA

Little, Dwight H (Director)
c/o Robert Lazar *ICM Partners (ICM-LA)*
10250 Constellation Blvd Fl 7
Los Angeles, CA 90067, USA

Little, Eric (Choreographer)
USA Pro Dance
11135 Knott Ave
Suite C
Cypress, CA 90630, USA

Little, Everett (Athlete, Football Player)
5219 Kingsbury St
Houston, TX 70213, USA

Little, Floyd D (Athlete, Football Player)
33207 Pacific Highway S
Federal Way, WA 98003, USA

Little, George (Athlete, Football Player)
1805 Powers St
Mc Keesport, PA 15132, USA

Little, Grady (Athlete, Baseball Player)
13115 Odell Hejg_hts Dr
Mint Hill, NC 28227-4390, USA

Little, Jack (Athlete, Football Player)
PO Box 23528
Waco, TX 76702-3528, USA

Little, Jeff (Athlete, Baseball Player)
5711 W Camper Rd
Genoa, OH 43430-9300, USA

Little, Larry C (Athlete, Coach, Football
Player)
14761 SW 169th Lane
Miami, FL 33187, USA

Little, Leonard (Athlete, Football Player)
c/o Chad Speck *Allegiant Athletic Agency*
35 Market Sq
Suite 201
Knoxville, TN 37902, USA

Little, Mark (Athlete, Baseball Player)
28014 Moss Fern Dr
Katv, TX 77494-3240, USA

Little, Milton (Musician)
Camil Productions
6606 Solitary Ave
Las Vegas, NV 89110, USA

Little, Rich (Actor, Comedian)
c/o David Martin *David Martin
Management*
13849 Riverside Dr
Sherman Oaks, CA 91423, USA

Little, Robert A (Chef)
49 Firth St
London W1V 5TE, UNITED KINGDOM
(UK)

Little, Sally (Athlete, Golfer)
3210 S Ocean Blvd
Apt 702
Highland Beach, FL 33487, USA

Little, Scott (Athlete, Baseball Player)
1321 Rosebud Dr
Jackson, MO 63755-1086, USA

Little, Steven (Musician)
Premier Talent
3 E 54th St
#1100
New York, NY 10022, USA

Little, Tasmin E (Musician)
harold Holt
31 Sinclair Road
London W14 0NS, UNITED KINGDOM
(UK)

Little, Tawny
5515 Melrose Ave.
Los Angeles, CA 90038

Little, Tawny Godin (Beauty Pageant
Winner, Entertainer)
17941 Sky Park Circle
#F
Irvine, CA 92614, USA

Little, Tony
12750 59th Way North
Clearwater, FL 33760, USA

Little, W Grady (Athlete, Baseball Player,
Coach)
130 National Dr
Pinehurst, NC 28374, USA

Little, William (Athlete, Baseball Player)
4889 Horn Lake Rd
Memphis, TN 38109-6625, USA

Little Big Town (Music Group)
c/o Jason Owen *Sandbox Entertainment*
54 Music Sq E
Suite 200
Nashville, TN 37203, USA

Little Eva
1161 NW 76th Ave.
Ft. Lauderdale, FL 33322

Littlefield, David (Commentator)
105 Spenser Ln
Sewickley, PA 15143-8725, USA

Littlefield, John (Athlete, Baseball Player)
1935 Ramar Rd
Bullhead City, AZ 86442-6949, USA

Littlefield, John (Actor)
c/o Judy Orbach *Judy O Productions*
6136 Glen Holly
Hollywood, CA 90068, USA

Littlefield, Warren (Producer)
815 Brooktree Rd.
Pacific Palisades, CA 90272, USA

Littleford, Beth (Actor)
c/o Karen Forman *Domain Talent*
9229 Sunset Boulevard
Suite 710
Los Angeles, CA 90069, USA

Little JJ (Actor)
c/o Charles King *WME (LA)*
9601 Wilshire Blvd Fl 3
Beverly Hills, CA 90210, USA

Littlejohn, Dennis (Athlete, Baseball
Player)
6813 Klamath Way
Apt D
Bakersfield, CA 93309-7899, USA

Little Man Tate (Music Group)
c/o Staff Member *Paradigm (Monterey)*
404 W Franklin St
Monterey, CA 93940, USA

Little Ones, The (Music Group)
c/o Jason Colton *Red Light Management
(VA)*
PO Box 1467
Charlottesville, VA 22902, USA

Littler, Gene (Athlete, Golfer)
PO Box 1949
Rancho Santa Fe, CA 92067-1949, USA

Little Richard (Musician)
c/o Dick Alen *WME (LA)*
9601 Wilshire Blvd Fl 3
Beverly Hills, CA 90210, USA

Little River Band
9850 Sandalfoot Blvd. #458
Boca Raton, FL 33428

Littles, Gene (Athlete, Basketball Player)
6421 E Beck Ln
Scottsdale, AZ 85254-2005, USA

Littleton, Harvey K (Artist)
RR 1 Box 843
Spruce Pine, NC 28777, USA

Littleton, Larry (Athlete, Baseball Player)
1076 Dunbarton Trce NE
Atlanta, GA 30319-2674, USA

Littleton, Wes (Athlete, Baseball Player)
14770 W Laurel Ln
Surprise, AZ 85379-6309, USA

Littman, David (Athlete, Hockey Player)
3761 Spring House Ct SE
Marietta, GA 30067-4929

Littman, Jonathan (Producer)
c/o Staff Member *Creative Artists Agency
(CAA-LA)*
2000 Ave Of The Stars
Los Angeles, CA 90067, USA

Litton, Andrew
IMG Artists
Media House
3 Burlington Lane
London W4 2TH, UNITED KINGDOM
(UK)

Litton, Bruce (Race Car Driver)
Bruce Litton Racing
PO Box 34174
Indianapolis, IN 46234, USA

Litton, Drew (Cartoonist, Editor)
Rocky Mountain News
Editorial Dept
400 W Colfax Ave
Denver, CO 80204, USA

Litton, Greg (Athlete, Baseball Player)
22 Hill brook Way
Pensacola, FL 32503-2850, USA

Littrell, Brian (Musician)
c/o Johnny Wright *Wright Entertainment
& Sports Productions*
9452 Thurloe Pl
Orlando, FL 32827, USA

Littrell, Gary L (General)
4302 Belle Vista Dr
St Pete Beach, FL 33706-3825, USA

Litzinger, Elin (Stylist)
2333 Hidalgo Ave
Los Angeles, CA 90039, USA

Liu, Lucy (Actor)
c/o Mary Ellen Mulcahy *Framework
Entertainment (LA)*
9057 Nemo St
Suite C
West Hollywood, CA 90069, USA

Liu, Matthew Stephen
10635 Santa Monica Blvd. #130
Los Angeles, CA 90025

Liu, Nancy
9057-C Nemo St.
W. Hollywood, CA 90069

Liuget, Corey (Football Player)
c/o Tony Fleming *Impact Sports - LA*
11331 Ventura Blvd Ste 1A
Studio City, CA 91604, USA

Liukin, Nastia (Athlete, Gymnast,
Olympic Athlete)
c/o Staff Member *Premier Management
Group (PMG Sports)*
115 Crescent Commons Dr Ste 250
Cary, NC 27518, USA

Liut, Mike (Athlete, Hockey Player)
26011 German Mill Rd
Franklin, MI 48025-1139

Livage, Jacques (Misc)
College de France
11 Place M Berthelot
Paris Cedex 05 75231, FRANCE

Live (Music Group)
c/o Staff Member *Paradigm (Monterey)*
404 W Franklin St
Monterey, CA 93940, USA

Lively, Blake (Actor)
c/o Jason Weinberg *Untitled
Entertainment (LA)*
350 S. Beverly Dr #200
Beverly Hills, CA 90212, USA

Lively, Bud (Athlete, Baseball Player)
8605 Esslinger Ct SE
Huntsville, AL 35802-3640, USA

Lively, Eric (Actor)
c/o Justin Grey Stone *Untitled
Entertainment (LA)*
350 S. Beverly Dr #200
Beverly Hills, CA 90212, USA

Lively, Penelope M (Writer)
c/o David Higham Associates
5-8 Lower John Street
London W1R 4HA, UNINTED KINGDOM

Lively, Robyn (Actor)
c/o Staff Member *Innovative Artists (LA)*
1505 10th St
Santa Monica, CA 90401, USA

Livermore, Ann (Business Person)
Hewlett-Packard Co
300 Hanover St
Palo Alto, CA 94304, USA

Livers, Virgil (Athlete, Football Player)
234 Johnson Ct
Tulare, CA 93274-3199, USA

Living Colour
6201 Sunset Blvd. #329
Hollywood, CA 90028

Livingston, Andrew (Athlete, Football
Player)
650 E Century Ave
Gilbert, AZ 85296, USA

Livingston, Andy (Athlete, Football Player)
650 E Century Ave
Gilbert, AZ 85296-1118, USA

Livingston, Barry (Actor)
11310 Blix St
North Hollywood, CA 91602, USA

Livingston, Bruce (Athlete, Football
Player)
511 25th Ave W
Bradenton, FL 34205, USA

Livingston, James E (General, War Hero)
3146 Pignatelli Cres
Mt Pleasant, SC 29466-8059, USA

Livingston, Julia Bassett (Stylist)
7206 Strawberry Rd
Summerfield, NC 27358, USA

Livingston, Mike (Athlete, Football Player)
8181 Monrovia St
Shawnee Mission, KS 66215, USA

Livingston, Robert L Jr (Politician)
Livingston Group
499 S Capitol St SW
#600
Washington, DC 20003, USA

Livingston, Ron (Actor)
Rigberg Roberts Rugolo
1180 S Beverly Dr
#601
Los Angeles, CA 90035, USA

Livingston, Shaun (Basketball Player)
Los Angeles Clippers
Staples Center
1111 S Figueroa St
Los Angeles, CA 90015, USA

Livingston, Stanley (Actor)
PO Box 1782
Studio City, CA 91614, USA

Livingston, Warren (Athlete, Football
Player)
308 E Malibu Dr
Tempe, AZ 85282, USA

Livingstone, Bob (Athlete, Football Player)
1625 Bluebird Ln
Munster, IN 46321, USA

Livingstone, Scott (Athlete, Baseball
Player)
1303 Pecos Dr
Southlake, TX 76092-5915, USA

Livinston (Actor)
45 Thackers Street
Pursawakkam
Chennai, TN 600 084, INDIA

Lizalde, Enrique (Actor)
c/o Staff Member Televisa
Blvd Adolfo Lopez Mateos 232
Colonia San Angel INN
DF CP 01060, MEXICO

Lizarazo, Carolina (Actor)
*c/o Gabriel Blanco Gabriel Blanco
Iglesias (Mexico)*
Rio Balsas 35-32
Colonia Cuauhtemoc
DF 06500, Mexico

Lizaso, Saul (Actor)
c/o Staff Member Televisa
Blvd Adolfo Lopez Mateos 232
Colonia San Angel INN
DF CP 01060, MEXICO

L. Jackson Jr., Jesse (Congressman,
Politician)
2419 Rayburn HOB
Washington, DC 20515, USA

Ljungberg, Fredrik (Model, Soccer Player)
*c/o Noelle Keshishian PMK/BNC Public
Relations (PMK-LA)*
8687 Melrose Ave Fl 8
West Hollywood, CA 90069, USA

Llaca, Patricia (Actor)
c/o Staff Member TV Azteca
Periferico Sur 4121
Colonia Fuentes del Pedregal
DF CP 14141, Mexico

Llamosa, Carlos (Soccer Player)
New England Revolution
CMGI Field
1 Patriot Place
Foxboro, MA 02035, USA

LL Cool J (Actor, Musician)
LL COOL J Inc.
6311 Romaine St
Hollywood, CA 90210, USA

Llenas, Winston (Athlete, Baseball Player)
Apartado #92
Santiago, Dominican Republic

Llewellyn, John A (Astronaut)
University of South Florida
4202 E Fowler Ave
Tampa, FL 33620, USA

Llewellyn, John Dr (Astronaut)
141140th Ave E
Madeira Beach, FL 33708-2204, USA

Llewellyn, Robert (Actor, Writer)
c/o Maureen Vincent United Agents
Drury House
34-43 Russell St
London WC2B 5HA, UK

Llewelyn, Doug
8075 W. 3rd St. #303
Los Angeles, CA 90048

Llewelyn-Bowen, Laurence (Actor,
Designer)
c/o Staff Member Fresh Partners LTD
Centre Square
Hardwicks Way
Wandsworth SW18 4AW, UK

Llitch, Michael (Misc)
c/o Staff Member Detriot Tigers
Comerica Park
2100 Woodward Ave
Detroit, MI 48201 - 3474, USA

Llosa, Mario Vargas (Writer)
Las Magnolias 295
6 Piso
Barranco, Lima 4, PERU

Lloyd, Arroyn (Actor)
*c/o Michael Bircumshaw Water Street
Management*
5225 Wilshire Blvd
Suite 615
Los Angeles, CA 90036, USA

Lloyd, Brandon (Athlete, Football Player)
21109 E 50th Street Ct S
Blue Springs, MO 64015-2254, USA

Lloyd, Charles (Composer, Musician)
Joel Chriss
300 Mercer St
#3J
New York, NY 10003, USA

LLoyd, Cher (Musician)
c/o Staff Member Hackford Jones PR
19 Nassau St
London W1W 7AF, UK

Lloyd, Christopher (Actor)
Managemint
PO Box 491246
Los Angeles, CA 90049, USA

Lloyd, Clive H (Cricketer)
Harefield
Harefield Dr
Wilmslow, Cheshire SK9 1NJ, UNITED
KINGDOM (UK)

Lloyd, Danny (Athlete, Football Player)
6025 Miwok Dr
San Jose, CA 95123-4113, USA

Lloyd, Dave (Athlete, Football Player)
24432 County Road 3107
Gladewater, TX 75647, USA

Lloyd, Earl (Athlete, Basketball Coach,
Basketball Player, Coach)
15 Pineridge Ct
Crossville, TN 38558-6532, USA

Lloyd, Emily Ann (Actor)
*c/o Staff Member United Talent Agency
(UTA)*
9336 Civic Center Dr
Beverly Hills, CA 90210, USA

Lloyd, Eric (Actor)
*c/o Mark Schumacher Schumacher
Management*
1122 San Vicente Blvd.
Santa Monica, CA 90402, USA

Lloyd, Gary (Race Car Driver)
Thee Dixon Racing
410 Marly Dr.
Durham, NC 21703, USA

Lloyd, Geoffrey E R (Misc)
2 Prospect Row
Cambridge CB1 1DU, UNITED
KINGDOM (UK)

Lloyd, Georgina (Writer)
Bantam Books
1540 Broadway
New York, NY 10036, USA

Lloyd, Graeme (Athlete, Baseball Player)
455 Oceanview Ave
Palm Harbor, Fl 34683-1816, USA

Lloyd, Greg (Athlete, Football Player)
144 Memory Ln
Stockbridge, GA 30281-6263, USA

Lloyd, Jake (Actor)
Osbrink Talent
4343 Lankershim Blvd
#100
North Hollywood, CA 91602, USA

Lloyd, Madison (Actor)
Osbrink Talent
4343 Lankershim Blvd
#100
North Hollywood, CA 91602, USA

Lloyd, Norman (Actor)
*c/o Staff Member Marion Rosenberg
Office, The*
PO Box 69826
Los Angeles, CA 90069-0826, USA

Lloyd, Robert A (Opera Singer)
67B Fortis Green
London SE1 9HL, UNITED KINGDOM
(UK)

Lloyd, Sabrina (Actor)
*c/o Rachel Sheedy Don Buchwald &
Associates Inc (NY)*
10 E 44th St
New York, NY 10017

Lloyd, Sam (Actor)
*c/o Staff Member Heidi Rotbart
Management*
1810 Malcolm Ave.
Suite 207
Los Angeles, CA 90025, USA

Lloyd, Scott (Athlete, Basketball Player)
6838 Alexander Dr
Dallas, TX 75214-3208, USA

Lloyd, Tony (Athlete, Baseball Player)
6536 Cherokee Dr
Fairfield, AL 35064-1703, USA

Lloyd, Walt (Cinematographer)
22287 Mulhotlland Highway
#393
Calabasas, CA 91302, USA

Llyod, Tony (Baseball Player)
Birmingham Black Barons
6536 Cherokee Dr
Fairfield, AL 35064-1703, USA

LMFAO (Music Group)
c/o Johnny Maroney Moodswing 360
135 W 26th St Fl 12
New York, NY 10019, USA

L. Mica, John (Congressman, Politician)
2187 Rayburn HOB
Washington, DC 20515, USA

Immerfall, Dan (Athlete, Olympic Athlete,
Speed Skater)
5421 Trempealeau Trl
Madison, WI 53705-4662, USA

Impe, Ed Van (Athlete, Hockey Player)
Philadelphia Flyers
3601 S Broad St Ste 2
Philadelohia, PA 19148-5297

Impemba, Mario (Commentator)
19945 Gallahad Dr
Macomb, MI 48044-1756, USA

Imus, Don (Journalist)
16 West Ave
Darien, CT 06820-4401, USA

Inhofe, James (Politician)
117 4th St SE
Washington, DC 20003-1002, USA

L. Noem, Kristi (Congressman, Politician)
226 Cannon HOB
Washington, DC 20515, USA

Intranuovo, Ralph
418 Huntsmill Blvd
Scarborough, ON MlW 3X6, Canada

Lo, Ismael (Musician)
Mad Minute Music
5-7 Rue Paul Bert
Saint Ouen 93400, FRANCE

Loach, Ken C (Director)
c/o Staff Member Sixteen Films
187 Wardour St
Floor 2
London W1F 8ZB, ENGLAND

Loach, Kenneth (Ken) (Director)
Parallax Pictures
7 Denmark St
London WC2H 8LS, UNITED KINGDOM
(UK)

Loach, Lonnie (Athlete, Hockey Player)
125 Dixon Ave
New Liskeard, ON P0J 1P0, CANADA

Loaf, Meat (Actor, Musician, Producer)
*c/o Irving Azoff Azoff Music Management/
Front Line*
1100 Glendon Ave
Los Angeles, CA 90024, USA

Loaiza, Esteban (Athlete, Baseball Player)
1404 Lands End Ct
Southlake, TX 76092-4224, USA

Loar, John (Producer)
c/o Staff Member Red Bird Cinema
P.O. Box 826
166 Montair Dr
Danville, CA 94526-0826, USA

Lobdell, Erinn (Reality TV Star)
2472 Bremen St
Milwaukee, WI 53212, USA

Lobdell, Frank (Artist)
Pier 70
San Francisco, CA 94102, USA

Lobel, Bruno
Ramering 4
Heldenstein, GERMANY 84431

Lobenstein, Bill (Athlete, Football Player)
3272 Deerfield Rd
Deerfield, WI 53531-9733, USA

Lobenstein, William (Athlete, Football Player)
3272 Deerfield Rd
Deerfield, WI 53531, USA

Lo Bianco, Tony
c/o Staff Member *Artists Only Management*
10203 Santa Monica Blvd
Los Angeles, CA 90067, USA

LoBiondo, Frank (Congressman, Politician)
2427 Rayburn HOB
Washington, DC 20515, USA

Lobkowicz, Nicholas (Misc)
Katholische Universitat
Eichstatt 85071, GERMANY

Lobo, Rebecca (Athlete, Basketball Player, Olympic Athlete)
P.O. Box 734
Granby, CT 06035-0734, USA

Loc, Tone
7932 Hillside Ave.
Los Angeles, CA 90046

Loc, Tone (Music Group)
c/o Staff Member *Universal Attractions*
135 W 26th St
12 Floor
New York, NY 10001, USA

Local, Ivars Godmanis (Prime Minister)
Brivibus Bluv 36
Riga, PDP 226170, LATVIA

Locane, Amy (Actor)
c/o Staff Member *Buchwald/Fortitude (LA)*
6500 Wilshire Blvd
Suite 2200
Los Angeles, CA 90048, USA

Locas, Jacques (Athlete, Hockey Player)

Loceff, Michael (Producer)
c/o Staff Member *Luber Roklin Management*
8530 Wilshire Blvd
6th Floor
Beverly Hills, CA 90211, USA

Lochead, Bill (Athlete, Hockey Player)
Fauerbacher Str 16
Ober-Morlen D-61239, Germany

Locher, Dick
435 N. Michigan Ave.
Chicago, IL 60611

Locher, Richard (Dick) (Cartoonist, Editor)
Chicago Tribune
Editorial Dept
435 N Michigan Ave
Chicago, IL 60611, USA

Lochhead, Kenneth C (Artist)
35 Wilton Crescent
Ottawa, ON K1S 2T4, CANADA

Lochmueller, Robert (Athlete, Basketball Player)
18 William Tell Blvd
Tell City, IN 47586-2030, USA

Lochner, Philip R Jr (Business Person, Government Official)
Time Warner Inc
75 Rockfeller Plaza
New York, NY 10019, USA

Lochner, Rudi
Hofreitstr. 15
Schonau, GERMANY D-83471

Lochte, Ryan (Athlete, Olympic Athlete, Swimmer)
1524 NW 22nd St
Gainesville, FL 32605-5231, USA

Lock, Don (Athlete, Baseball Player)
11725 West Alderny Ct
Unit 42
Wichita, KS 67212-6510, USA

Lockbaum, Gordie (Athlete, Football Player)
35 Brookshire Rd
Worcester, MA 01609, USA

Locke, Bobby (Athlete, Baseball Player)
194 Eighty Acres Rd
Dunbar, PA 15431-2274, USA

Locke, Bruce (Actor)
5670 Wilshire Blvd #820
Los Angeles, CA 90048

Locke, Chuck (Athlete, Baseball Player)
1560 Haven Hills Rd
Poplar Bluff, MO 63901-2749, USA

Locke, Gary (Politician)
Unit 7300 Box 10
DPO, AP 96521-0010, USA

Locke, Kimberley (Actor, Musician)
c/o Mark Measures *Abrams Artists Agency (LA)*
9200 Sunset Blvd
11th Floor
Los Angeles, CA 90069, USA

Locke, Larry (Baseball Player)
Cleveland Indians
155 Eighty Acres Rd Apt 2
Dunbar, PA 15431-2275, USA

Locke, Ron (Athlete, Baseball Player)
11140 Caravel Cir Apt 102
Fort Myers, FL 33908-3996, USA

Locke, Sonda (Actor)
c/o Staff Member *David Shapira & Associates*
193 N Robertson Blvd
Beverly Hills, CA 90211, USA

Locke, Sondra (Actor)
7465 Hillside Ave
Los Angeles, CA 90046, USA

Locke, Spencer (Actor)
c/o Sharon Lane *Lane Management Group*
13017 Woodbridge St
Studio City, CA 91604, USA

Locke, Tembi (Actor)
c/o Bob McGowan *McGowan Management*
8733 W Sunset Blvd
Suite 103
West Hollywood, CA 90069, USA

Locker, Bob (Athlete, Baseball Player)
PO Box 157
Harrison, MT 59735-0157, USA

Lockerman, Brad
300 S. Raymond Ave. #11
Pasadena, CA 91105

Lockett, Frank (Athlete, Football Player)
2705 Cerritas Via
Harvey, LA 70058-2936, USA

Lockett, Ken (Athlete, Hockey Player)
89 Germorda Dr
Oakville, ON L6H 2P9, Canada

Lockett, Kevin (Athlete, Football Player)
1319 W Xyler St
Tulsa, OK 74127, USA

Lockhart, Anne (Actor)
c/o Linda McAlister *Linda McAlister Talent*
100 Oak Ln
Waxahachie, TX 75167-8412, USA

Lockhart, Eugene (Athlete, Football Player)
2215 High Country Dr
Carrollton, TX 75007, USA

Lockhart, Ian (Athlete, Basketball Player)
Q25 Calle Excelsa Villas Del Cafetal II
Yauco, PR 00698-3172, USA

Lockhart, James
105 Woodcock Hill
Harrow, Middx HA3 0JJ, UNITED KINGDOM (UK)

Lockhart, June (Actor)
c/o Staff Member *Agency for the Performing Arts (APA-LA)*
405 S Beverly Dr
Suite 500
Beverly Hills, CA 90212-4425, USA

Lockhart, Keith
Boston Pops Orchestra
Symphony Hall
301 Massachusetts Ave
Boston, MA 02115, USA

Lockhart, Keith (Athlete, Baseball Player)
3330 McKinley Point Dr
Dacula, GA 30019-1599, USA

Lockhart, Paul S (Astronaut)
3142 Pleasant Cove Court
Houston, TX 77059, USA

Lockhart, Paul S Lt Colonel (Astronaut)
PSC 802 Box 74
APO, AE 09607, USA

Lockington, David
Cramer/Marder Artists
3436 Springhill Road
Lafayette, CA 94549, USA

Locklear, Gene (Athlete, Baseball Player)
1811 Penasco Rd
El Cajon, CA 92019-3708, USA

Locklear, Heather (Actor)
c/o Daniel (Danny) Sussman *Brillstein Entertainment Partners*
9150 Wilshire Blvd #350
Beverly Hills, CA 90212, USA

Locklear, Sean (Athlete, Football Player)
11250 SE 60th St
Bellevue, WA 98006-6360, USA

Locklin, Kerry (Athlete, Football Player)
2087 E Emilie Ave
Fresno, CA 93730-4731, USA

Locklin, Stu (Athlete, Baseball Player)
532 Carfax Pl SW
Albuquerque, NM 87121-2273, USA

Lockwood, Gary (Actor)
1065 E Loma Alta Dr
Altadena, CA 91001, USA

Lockwood, Scott (Athlete, Football Player)
870 West Ln
Estes Park, CO 80517-9624, USA

Lockwood, Skip (Athlete, Baseball Player)
47 John Druce Ln
Wrentham, MA 02093-1390, USA

Locorriere, Dennis (Musician)
P.O. Box 4444
Worthing BN11 3WJ, SUSSEX

Lodboa, Dan (Athlete, Hockey Player)
1 Garden St
Thorold, ON L2V 3H9, Canada

Loder, Anne Marie (Actor)
c/o Jamie Levitt *Lauren Levitt & Associates Inc*
1525 W 8th St 3rd Fl
Vancouver V6J 1T5, British Columbia

Loder, Kevin (Athlete, Basketball Player)
505 W 4th St
Mishawaka, IN 46544-1818, USA

Loder, Kurt (Journalist, Television Host)
c/o Staff Member *MTV News*
1515 Broadway Fl 29
New York, NY 10036, USA

Lodge, David
8 Sydney Rd.
Richmond Surrey, ENGLAND

Lodge, David John (Writer)
University of Birmingham
English Dept
Birmingham B15 2TT, UNITED KINGDOM (UK)

Lodge, Roger (Actor, Television Host)
c/o Michelle Bega *Rogers & Cowan PR (LA)*
Pacific Design Center
8687 Melrose Ave, 7th Floor
West Hollywood, CA 90069, USA

Lodish, Harvey F (Biologist)
195 Fisher Ave
Brookline, MA 02445, USA

Lodish, Mike (Athlete, Football Player)
1150 Trailwood Path
Bloomfield Hills, MI 48301, USA

Loduca, Paul (Athlete, Baseball Player)
3227 Medaris Ln
San Antonio
Rancho Cucamonga, TX 78258-1624, USA

Lodwick, Todd (Athlete, Olympic Athlete, Skier)
907 Merritt Steamboat
Springs, CO 80487, USA

Loe, Harald A (Doctor)
National Dental Research Institute
9000 Rockville Pike
Bathesda, MD 20892, USA

Loe, Kameron (Athlete, Baseball Player)
2323 N Houston St Apt 312
Dallas, TX 75219-7623, USA

Loeb, Jerome T (Business Person)
May Department Stores
611 Olive St
Saint Louis, MO 63101, USA

Loeb, Lisa (Musician, Songwriter)
c/o Alix Gucovsky *Special Artists Agency*
9465 Wilshire Blvd #820
Beverly Hills, CA 90212, USA

Loeb, Marshall R (Editor)
31 Montrose Road
Scarsdale, NY 10583, USA

Loeber, Jerry (Athlete, Baseball Player)
578 Bayville Rd
Locust Valley, NY 11560-1211, USA

Loebsak, David (Congressman, Politician)
1527 Longworth HOB
Washington, DC 20515, USA

Loehr, Bet (Actor)
c/o Staff Member *Coast to Coast Talent Group*
3350 Barham Blvd
Los Angeles, CA 90068, USA

Loehr, Bret (Actor)
c/o Staff Member *Coast to Coast Talent Group*
3350 Barham Blvd
Los Angeles, CA 90068, USA

Loengard, John (Photographer)
20 W 86th St
New York, NY 10024-3604, USA

Loewen, Adam (Athlete, Baseball Player)
12302 N 136th Pl
Scottsdale, AZ 85259-2311, USA

Loewen, Darcy (Athlete, Hockey Player)
10611 Kearney Mountain Ave
Las Vegas, NV 89166-5042

Loewen, James W (Historian)
Catholic University
History Dept
Washington, DC 20064, USA

Loewer, Carlton (Athlete, Baseball Player)
PO Box 3590
Alpine, WY 83128-0590, USA

Lofgren, Nils (Musician, Songwriter, Writer)
Vision Music
8012 Old Georgetown Road
Bathesda, MD 20814, USA

Lofgren, Zoe (Congressman, Politician)
1401 Longworth HOB
Washington, DC 20515, USA

Lofthouse, Mark (Athlete, Hockey Player)
Mark Lofthouse
Surrey, BC V3S 8K4, Canada

Loftin, Lennie (Actor)
c/o Scott Zimmerman *Evolution Entertainment (LA)*
901 N Highland Ave
Los Angeles, CA 90038, USA

Lofton, Cirroc (Actor)
c/o Staff Member *Innovative Artists (LA)*
1505 10th St
Santa Monica, CA 90401, USA

Lofton, Fred C (Religious Leader)
Progressive National Baptist Convention
601 50th St NE
Washington, DC 20019, USA

Lofton, James (Athlete, Baseball Player)
14103 Cerise Ave Apt 18
Hawthorne, CA 90250-8843, USA

Lofton, James D (Athlete, Football Player)
13177 Via Mesa Dr
San Diego, CA 92129, USA

Lofton, Kenny (Athlete, Baseball Player)
PO Box 68473
Tucson, AZ 85737-8473, USA

Lofton, Oscar (Athlete, Football Player)
823 Oak Hollow Dr
Hammond, LA 70401-8260, USA

logan, bob (Athlete, Hockey Player)
11 White Pine Rd
Amherst, MA 01002-3467

Logan, Chuck (Athlete, Football Player)
2526 Lawndale Ave
Evanston, IL 60201, USA

Logan, Daniel (Actor)
c/o Staff Member *Entertainment Legends Management*
1100 Irvine Blvd #66
Tustin, CA 92780, USA

Logan, Dave (Athlete, Hockey Player)
142 Acorn Ln
Shelburne, VT 05482-7330

Logan, Dick (Athlete, Football Player)
475 Chapple Hill Dr NE
North Canton, OH 44720, USA

Logan, Don (Publisher)
Time Inc
Time-Life Building
Rockefeller Center
New York, NY 10020, USA

Logan, Ernie (Athlete, Football Player)
609 Francis Ct
Spring Lake, NC 28390, USA

Logan, Exavier (Nook) (Athlete, Baseball Player)
19410 Creek Bend Dr
Spring, TX 77388-3095, USA

Logan, Jack (Musician)
William Morris Agency
1325 Ave of Americas
New York, NY 10019, USA

Logan, James K (Athlete, Football Player)
US Court of Appeals
301 Danley Ave
Opp, AL 36467-3204, USA

Logan, Jerry (Athlete, Football Player)
1624 Hillcrest Dr
Graham, TX 76450-4702, USA

Logan, John (Producer, Writer)
c/o David O'Connor *Creative Artists Agency (CAA-LA)*
2000 Ave Of The Stars
Los Angeles, CA 90067, USA

Logan, Johnny (Athlete, Baseball Player)
6115 W Cleveland Ave
Milwaukee, WI 53219-2653, USA

Logan, Marc (Athlete, Football Player)
PO Box 11886
Lexington, KY 40578-1886, USA

Logan, Melissa (Musician)
K Records
924 Jefferson St SE
#101
Olympia, WA 98501, USA

Logan, Phyllis
47 Courtfield Rd. #9
London, ENGLAND SW7 4DB

Logan, Randy (Athlete, Football Player)
330 W Fornance St
Norristown, PA 19401, USA

Logan, Rayford W (Historian)
3001 Veazey Terrace NW
Washington, DC 20008, USA

Logano, Joey (Race Car Driver)
c/o Staff Member *Joe Gibbs Racing*
13415 Reese Blvd West
Huntersville, NC 28078, USA

Loges, Stephan (Opera Singer)
Van Walsum Mgmt
4 Addison Bridge Place
London W14 8XP, UNITED KINGDOM (UK)

Logg, Charles (Athlete, Olympic Athlete, Rower)
3634 Shady Oak Trl
Gainesville, GA 30506-4542, USA

Loggia, Robert (Actor)
c/o Steve Lovett *Lovett Management*
1327 Brinkley Ave
Los Angeles, CA 90049, USA

Loggins, Kenny (Musician, Songwriter)
1100 Calle Malaga
Santa Barbara, CA 93109, USA

Logue, Donal (Actor)
c/o Perri Kipperman *Kipperman Management*
420 West End Avenue
Suite 1G
New York, NY 10024, USA

Logue, Karina (Actor)
c/o Justin Evans *The Independent Group*
6363 Wilshire Blvd
Suite 115
Los Angeles, CA 90048, USA

Loh, John M (Mike) (General)
125 Captain Graves
Williamsburg, VA 23185, USA

Lohan, Ali (Actor)
c/o Glenn Gulino *G2 Entertainment LLC*
1 Columbus Pl #S-25E
New York, NY 10019, USA

Lohan, Lindsay (Actor)
1500 San Ysidro Dr
Beverly Hills, CA 90210, USA

Lohan, Sinead (Musician, Songwriter, Writer)
Pat Egan Sound
Merchant's Court
24 Merchant's Quay
Dublin, IRELAND

Lohaus, Brad (Athlete, Basketball Player)
55 Tartan Dr
North Liberty, IA 52317-8002, USA

Lohman, Alison (Actor)
c/o Nicole King *Management 360*
9111 Wilshire Blvd
Beverly Hills, CA 90210, USA

Lohmann, Katie (Actor)
c/o Giovanni Elmore *WNWN Media*
348 S. Hauser Blvd #PH414
Los Angeles, CA 90036, USA

Lohmeyer, Eddie (Horse Racer)
63 Red Valley Rd
Cream Ridge, NJ 08514-2007, USA

Lohmiller, Chip (Athlete, Football Player)
PO Box 810
Crosslake, MN 56442-0810, USA

Lohr, Aaron (Actor)
c/o Beth Rosner *Beth Rosner Management*
15 Stuyvesant Oval
New York, NY 10009, USA

Lohr, Bob (Athlete, Golfer)
8225 Breeze Cove Ln
Orlando, FL 32819-5078, USA

Lohrke, Jack (Athlete, Baseball Player)
2817 Lucena Dr
San Jose, CA 95132, USA

Lohse, Kyle (Athlete, Baseball Player)
8613 E Artisan Pass
Scottsdale, AZ 85266-1643, USA

Loiola, Jose (Athlete, Volleyball Player)
3521 Maple Dr
Manhattan Beach, CA 90266, USA

Loiselle, Claude (Athlete, Hockey Player)
7 Orchard Dr
Queensbury, NY 12804-6206

Loiselle, Claude (Athlete, Hockey Player)
Toronto Maple Leafs
400-40 Bay St
Toronto, ON M5J 2X2, Canada

Loiselle, Rich (Athlete, Baseball Player)
560 Timber Dr
Harvard, IL 60033-7823, USA

Loken, Kristanna (Actor)
c/o Staff Member *ICM Partners (ICM-LA)*
10250 Constellation Blvd Fl 7
Los Angeles, CA 90067, USA

Lokey, Lorey (Business Person)
Business Wire
44 Montgomery St 39th Fl
San Francisco, CA 94104, USA

Lokoloko, Tore (Ex-Governor)
P.O. Box 5622
Boroko, NCD, Papua New Guinea

Lolich, Mickey (Athlete, Baseball Player)
6252 Robin Hl
Washington, MI 48094-2186, USA

Lolich, Ron (Athlete, Baseball Player)
7055 SW Dogwood Pl
Portland, OR 97225-1571, USA

Lolita
Grossmain
, AUSTRIA - A-5084

Lollar, Tim (Athlete, Baseball Player)
16626 W Bayaud Dr
Golden, CO 80401-6577, USA

Lollobrigida, Gina (Actor)
Via Appia Antica 223
Rome 00178, ITALY

Loman, Doug (Athlete, Baseball Player)
25 Lincoln St
Bakersfield, CA 93305-3412, USA

Lomas, Mark (Athlete, Football Player)
P.O. Box 17781
Irvine, CA 92623, USA

Lomasney, Steve (Athlete, Baseball Player)
7 Arnold Rd
Peabody, MA 01960-5203, USA

Lomax, Melanie
5900 Wilshire Blvd
Los Angeles, CA 90036

Lomax, Michael (Educator)
United Negro Fund
500 E 62nd St
New York, NY 10021, USA

Lomax, Neil V (Athlete, Football Player)
13090 Knaus Rd
Lake Oswego, OR 97034-1551, USA

Lombard, George (Athlete, Baseball Player)
2275 Rhinehill Rd SE
Atlanta, GA 30315-7413, USA

Lombard, Karina (Actor, Model)
EOS Entertainment Corporation
1209 Orange St
Wilmington, DE 19081, USA

Lombard, Louise (Actor)
c/o Lena Roklin *Luber Roklin Management*
8530 Wilshire Blvd
6th Floor
Beverly Hills, CA 90211, USA

Lombardi, John V (Educator)
University of Florida
President's Office
Gainesville, FL 32611, USA

Lombardi, Leigh (Actor)
c/o Staff Member *Abrams Artists Agency (NY)*
275 Seventh Ave
26th Floor
New York, NY 10001, USA

Lombardi, Louis (Actor)
c/o Erik Kritzer *Kritzer Levine Wilkins Entertainment (KLWG)*
11872 La Grange Ave
1st Floor
Los Angeles, CA 90025, USA

Lombardi, Phil (Athlete, Baseball Player)
26440 Brooks Cir
Stevenson Ranch, CA 91381-1417, USA

Lombardo, John (Musician)
Agency for Performing Arts
9200 Sunset Blvd
#900
Los Angeles, CA 90069, USA

Lombardozzi, Domenick (Actor)
c/o Michael Garnett *Leverage Management*
3030 Pennsylvania Ave
Santa Monica, CA 90404, USA

Lombardozzi, Steve (Athlete, Baseball Player)
12404 Hall Shop Rd
Fulton, MD 20759-9746, USA

Lomenda, Mark (Athlete, Hockey Player)
52 Everwoods Close SW
Calgary, AB T2Y 5AG, Canada

Lomma, Jonathan
1120 S. Washington Ave
Scranton, PA 18505

Lommi, Tony (Musician)
Red Light Communications
3305 Lobban Pl
Charlottesville, VA 22903, USA

Lomon, Kevin (Athlete, Baseball Player)
13397 Morris Loop
Cameron, OK 74932-2173, USA

Lonborg, Jim (Athlete, Baseball Player)
498 First Parish Rd
Scituate, MA 02066-3201, USA

Lonchakov, Yuri V (Cosmonaut)
Potcha Kosmonavtov
Moskovskoi Oblasti
Syvisdny Goroduk 141160, RUSSIA

London, Antonio (Athlete, Football Player)
108 Oak Forest Way
Pelham, AL 35124-2516, USA

London, Carolyn (Producer)
c/o Staff Member *Bankable Productions*
226 W 26th St
4th Floor
New York, NY 10001-6700, USA

London, Irving M (Physicist)
Harvard-MIT Health Sciences
77 Massachusetts Ave
Cambridge, MA 02139, USA

London, Jason (Actor)
c/o Staff Member *Levine Okwu Erickson Management*
6363 Wilshire Blvd
Suite 300
Los Angeles, CA 90048, USA

London, Jeremy (Actor, Director, Producer)
c/o Jean-Pierre (JP) Henraux *Henraux Management*
Prefers to be contacted by telephone
CA, USA

London, Lauren (Actor)
c/o John Carrabino *John Carrabino Management*
5900 Wilshire Blvd Fl 4 #406
Los Angeles, CA 90036, USA

London, Lisa (Actor, Model)
8949 Sunset Blvd
#201
Los Angeles, CA 90069, USA

London, Michael (Producer)
c/o Staff Member *Groundswell Productions / Michael Landon Productions*
9350 Wilshire Blvd
Suite 324
Beverly Hills, CA 90212, USA

London, Rick (Cartoonist)
c/o Staff Member *Artistic Licensing Agency*
240 Central Ave
Suite 224
Hot Springs, AR 71901, USA

London, Stacy (Reality TV Star, Television Host)
c/o Staff Member *The Learning Channel (TLC)*
10100 Santa Monica Blvd
Suite 1500
Los Angeles, CA 90067, USA

Loneker, Keith (Athlete, Football Player)
56 W Lincoln Ave
Roselle Park, NJ 07204, USA

Lonergan, Kenneth (Writer)
c/o Staff Member *WmE2 (WMA-LA)*
1 William Morris Pl
Beverly Hills, CA 90212, USA

Lonestar (Music Group)
c/o Gary Borman *Moir / Borman Entertainment*
1250 6th St
Suite 401
Santa Monica, CA 90401, USA

Lonetto, Sarah (Baseball Player)
26560 Burg Rd
Apt 132
Warren, MI 48089-3594, USA

Loney, James (Athlete, Baseball Player)
c/o Joe Urbon *Creative Artists Agency (CAA-NY)*
162 Fifth Ave
6th Floor
New York, NY 10010, USA

Loney, Troy (Athlete, Hockey Player)
4245 Glasgow Rd.
Valencia, PA 16059-1729

Long, Anthony A (Educator)
1088 Telvin St
Albany, CA 94706, USA

Long, Bill (Athlete, Baseball Player)
7699 Dimmick Rd
Cincinnati, OH 45241-1166, USA

Long, Billy (Congressman, Politician)
1541 Longworth HOB
Washington, DC 20515, USA

Long, Bishop Eddie (Religious Leader)
New Birth
6400 Woodrow Rd
Lithonia, GA 30038, USA

Long, Bob (Athlete, Baseball Player)
3646 Willow Lake Cir
Chattanooga, TN 37419-1459, USA

Long, Bob (Athlete, Football Player)
630 N 4th St Unit 614
Milwaukee, WI 53203-2809, USA

Long, Bob (Athlete, Football Player)
1413 W Via De La Gloria
Green Valley, AZ 85614, USA

Long, Bob (Athlete, Football Player)
P.O. Box 245
Ashland, PA 17921, USA

Long, Carl (Athlete, Baseball Player)
401 Duggins Dr
Kinston, NC 28501-8211, USA

Long, Carson (Athlete, Football Player)
1618 Walnut St
Ashland, PA 17921-1724, USA

Long, Charles F (Chuck) II (Athlete, Football Player)
2425 N MacArthur Blvd
Oklahoma City, OK 73127, USA

Long, Chris (Athlete, Football Player)
c/o Steve Rosner *16W Marketing LLC*
75 Union Ave
Rutherford, NJ 07070, USA

Long, Chuck (Athlete, Football Coach, Football Player)
Kansas University 1651 Naismith Dr Attn Football Coaching Staff
Lawrence, KS 66045-4069, USA

Long, Dallas (Athlete, Olympic Athlete, Track Athlete)
PO Box 355
Whitefish, MT 59937, USA

Long, Dave (Athlete, Football Player)
309 16th St
Marion, IA 52302-4356, USA

Long, David L (Publisher)
Sports Illustrated Magazine
Rockefeller Center
New York, NY 10020, USA

Long, Dennis (Denny) (Soccer Player)
RR 5
Poplar Bluff, MO 63901, USA

Long, Don (Athlete, Baseball Player)
747 Puget Ln
Edmonds, WA 98020-2643, USA

Long, Elizabeth Valk (Business Person)
J.M. Smucker Co
One Strawberry Ln
Orville, OH 44667-0280, USA

Long, Grant (Athlete, Basketball Player)
8501 Morton Taylor Rd
Belleville, MI 48111-5313, USA

Long, Howie (Actor, Football Player, Sportscaster)
c/o Jack Gilardi *ICM Partners (ICM-LA)*
10250 Constellation Blvd Fl 7
Los Angeles, CA 90067, USA

Long, Jackie
c/o Tammy Brook *FYI Public Relations*
174 5th Ave
Suite 404
New York, NY 10010, USA

Long, Jeoff (Athlete, Baseball Player)
11 Flower Ct
Lakeside Park, KY 41017-2102, USA

Long, Jessica (Athlete, Swimmer)
c/o Peter Carlisle *Octagon Olympics & Action Sports*
1751 Pinnacle Dr
15th Floor
McLean, VA 22102, USA

Long, Joan D (Producer)
La Burrage Place
Lindfield, NSW 2070, AUSTRALIA

Long, Joey (Athlete, Baseball Player)
5541 Kiser Lake Rd
Conover, OH 45317-9643, USA

Long, John (Athlete, Basketball Player)
11976 Hunt St
Romulus, MI 48174-3830, USA

Long, Justin (Actor)
c/o Paul Young *Principato/Young Management*
9465 Wilshire Blvd
Suite 430
Beverly Hills, CA 90212, USA

Long, Kevin (Athlete, Baseball Player)
6 Southpine Ct
Columbia, SC 29212-2918, USA

Long, Kevin
5753 E Night Glow Cir
Scottsdale, AZ 85266-5250, USA

Long, Khari (Athlete, Football Player)
4405 Call Field Rd
Wichita Falls, TX 76308-2445, USA

Long, Mark (Reality TV Star)
c/o Staff Member *MTV Networks (LA)*
2600 Colorado Blvd
Santa Monica, CA 90405

Long, Matthew (Matt) (Actor)
c/o Robert Glennon *Authentic Talent and Literary Management*
45 Main St
Suite 1004
Brooklyn, NY 11201, USA

Long, Mel (Athlete, Football Player)
837 Imani Cir
Toledo, OH 43602, USA

Long, Nia (Actor)
c/o Priscilla Moralez *One Talent Management*
9220 Sunset Blvd
Los Angeles, CA 90069, USA

Long, Richard (Artist)
Old School
Lower Failand
Bristol BS8 3SL, UNITED KINGDOM (UK)

Long, Rien (Athlete, Football Player)
460 Great Circle Rd
Nashville, TN 37228, USA

Long, Robert (Misc)
University of California
Paleontology Museum
Berkeley, CA 94720, USA

Long, Robert M (Business Person)
Longs Drug Stores
141 N Civic Dr
Walnut Creek, CA 94596, USA

Long, Rocky (Athlete, Football Player)
San Dego State University
5500 Campanile Dr
San Diego, CA 92182-0003, USA

Long, Ryan (Athlete, Baseball Player)
3102 Winchester Ranch Trl
Katy, TX 77493-4400, USA

Long, Scott (Actor, Reality TV Star)
c/o Staff Member *Big Brother*
Arnold Shapiro Productions
12925 Riverside Dr Fl 4
Sherman Oaks, CA 91423, USA

Long, Shelley (Actor)
P.O. Box 45530
Los Angeles, CA 90045, USA

Long, Ted (Athlete, Hockey Player)
188 Abbott Pl
Woodstock, ON N4S 8J7, Canada

Long, Terrance (Athlete, Baseball Player)
3433 Cross Creek Dr
Montgomery, AL 36116-3648, USA

Long, Tim (Athlete, Football Player)
112 Towns Walk Dr
Athens, GA 38017, USA

Long, William Ivey (Designer)
International Creative Mgmt
40 W 57th St
#1800
New York, NY 10019, USA

Longdon, Johnny
5401 Palmer Dr.
Banning, CA 92220

Longet, Claudine (Actor)
Ronald D Austin
6000 E Hopkins
Aspen, CO 81611, USA

Longfield, William (Business Person)
CR Bard Inc
730 Central Ave
New Providence, NJ 07974, USA

Longhi, Rick (Stylist)
2041 W Carroll
Chicago, IL 60612, USA

Longley, Clint (Athlete, Football Player)
13602 Camino De Oro Ct
Corpus Christi, TX 78418, USA

Longley, Luc (Athlete, Basketball Player)
Basketball Australia Hall of Fame
PO Box 7141 Alexandria, NSW 2015
Australi< 87102, USA

Longmire, Sam (Athlete, Football Player)
3220 W Ina Rd Apt 15103
Tucson, AZ 85741-2170, USA

Longmire, Tony (Athlete, Baseball Player)
419 Fleming Ave E
Valleio, CA 94591-4030, USA

Longmuir, Alan (Musician)
27 Preston Grange
Preston Pans E
Lothian, SCOTLAND

Longmuir, Derek (Musician)
27 Preston Grange
Preston Pans E
Lothian, SCOTLAND

Longo, Cody (Actor)
c/o Mara Santino *Luber Roklin Management*
8530 Wilshire Blvd
6th Floor
Beverly Hills, CA 90211, USA

Longo, Lenny (Musician)
Texas Sounds
PO Box 1644
Dickinson, TX 77539, USA

Longo, Robert (Artist)
Longo Studio
224 Center St
New York, NY 10013, USA

Longo, Tom (Athlete, Football Player)
2 Donna Ln
Wayne, NJ 07470, USA

Longo, Tony
24 Westwind St.
Marina del Rey, CA 90292

Longoria, Eva (Actor)
c/o Liza Anderson *Anderson Group Public Relations*
8060 Melrose Ave Fl 4
Los Angeles, CA 90046, USA

Longoria, Evan (Athlete, Baseball Player)
c/o Staff Member *Tampa Bay Devil Rays*
Tropicana Field
1 Tropicana Drive
Saint Petersburg, FL 33705, USA

Longuet-Higgins, H Christopher (Misc)
Sussex University
Exper Psych Lab
Falmer, Brighton BN1 9QG, UNITED KINGDOM (UK)

Long-View (Music Group)
c/o Staff Member *Paradigm (Monterey)*
404 W Franklin St
Monterey, CA 93940, USA

Longwell, Ryan (Athlete, Football Player)
5169 Fairway Oaks Dr
Windermere, FL 34786-8934, USA

Lonneke (Model)
Pauline's Talent Corp
379 W Broadway
#502
New York, NY 10012, USA

Lonow, Claudia (Comedian)
c/o Staff Member *ICM Partners (ICM-LA)*
10250 Constellation Blvd Fl 7
Los Angeles, CA 90067, USA

Lonsbrough, Porter Anita (Swimmer)
6 Rivendell Gardens
Tettendall
Wolverhampton WV6 8SY, UNITED KINGDOM (UK)

Lonsdale, Gordon (Cinematographer, Director)
4513 West 10600 North
Highland, UT 84003-9552, USA

Lonsdale, Laurie (Writer)
49 Lighthouse St
Whitby, Ontario L1N 9R9, CANADA

Lonsdale, Michael
25 rue de General-Foy
Paris, FRANCE F-75008

Loob, Hakan (Athlete, Hockey Player)
Farjestads BK Box 318
Karlstad S-65108, Sweden

Loob, Peter (Athlete, Hockey Player)
Nadendalsvagen 5
Vadstena S-59232, SWEDEN

Look, Bruce (Athlete, Baseball Player)
4298 Maitland Rd
Williamsburg, MI 49690-9575, USA

Look, Bruce
Minnesota Twins
4298 Maitland Rd
Williamsburg, MI 49690-9575, USA

Look, Dean (Athlete, Baseball Player)
80 Victorian Hills Dr
Okemos, MI 48864-3160, USA

Look, Dean Z (Athlete, Football Player)
80 Victorian Hills Dr
Okemos, MI 48864, USA

Looker, Dane (Athlete, Football Player)
7213 41st Avenue Ct E
Tacoma, WA 98443-1811, USA

Lookinland, Mike (Actor)
PO Box 9968
Salt Lake City, UT 84109, USA

Loomis, Robbie (Race Car Driver)
Hendrick Racing
4414 Pappa Joe Hendrtck Blvd.
Charlotte, NC 28262, USA

Loomis, Rod
5114 Vineland Ave.
Universal City, CA 91601

Loon (Musician)
c/o Michael (Mike) Esterman
Esterman.Com, LLC
Prefers to be contacted via email
MD, USA

Looney, Brian (Athlete, Baseball Player)
188 Romulus Rd
Cheshire, CT 06410-3535, USA

Looney, Don (Athlete, Football Player)
8955 Reata Place Trl
Benbrook, TX 76126-1650

Looney, Shelley (Athlete, Hockey Player, Olympic Athlete)
PO Box 170
New Vernon, NJ 07976-0170, USA

Looney, William R III (General)
Commander
Electronic Systems Center
Hanscom Air Force Base, MA 01731, USA

Looper, Aaron (Athlete, Baseball Player)
1405 Manchester Dr
Shawnee, OK 74804-2327, USA

Looper, Braden (Athlete, Baseball Player, Olympic Athlete)
442 Shadow Creek Dr
Palos Heights, IL 60463-2912, USA

Loose, A Mohan (Actor)
15A/4 Kesavaperumal East Street
Chennai, TN 600 004, INDIA

Loose, John W (Business Person)
Coming Corp
Houghton Park
Corning, NY 14831, USA

Looseleaf, Victoria
144 S. Doheny Dr. #304
Los Angeles, CA 90048

Iooss, Walter (Photographer)
152 Deforest Rd
Montauk, NY 11954-9619, USA

Lopardo, Frank (Opera Singer)
7 Suzanne B Court
Massapeque, NY 11758, USA

Lopasky, Bill (Athlete, Football Player)
476 Jackson Rd
Dallas, PA 18612-3073, USA

Lopasky, William (Athlete, Football Player)
Huntsville Ceasetown Rd
Dallas, PA 18612, USA

Lopata, Stan (Athlete, Baseball Player)
2239 Leisure World
Mesa, AZ 85206-5384, USA

Loper, Daniel (Athlete, Football Player)
115 Stillwater Trl
Hendersonville, TN 37075-4305, USA

Lopert, Tanya (Actor)
Cineart
36 Rue de Pnthieu
Paris 75008, FRANCE

Lopes, Davey (Athlete, Baseball Player)
309 San Elijo St
San Diego, CA 92106-3455, USA

Lopes, Davey (Athlete, Baseball Player)
Los Angeles Dodgers
1000 Elysian Park Ave Attn Coaching Staff
Los angeles, CA 90090-1112, USA

Lopes, Lisa
1505 10th St.
Santa Monica, CA 90401

Lopez, Adamari (Actor)
c/o Staff Member *Telemundo*
2470 West 8th Avenue
Hialeah, FL 33010, USA

Lopez, Albie (Athlete, Baseball Player)
1019 S Roles Dr
Gilbert, AZ 85296-8606, USA

Lopez, Areliano Oswaldo (General, President)
Servico Aereo de Honduras
Apdo 129
Tegucigalpa, DC, HONDURAS

Lopez, Arturo (Athlete, Baseball Player)
1425 Tobias Dr SE
Washington, DC 20020-2953, USA

Lopez, Danny (Little Red) (Boxer)
16531 Aguamarine Court
Chino Hills, CA 91709, USA

Lopez, Feliciano (Athlete, Tennis Player)
IMG Center
1360 E 9th St #100
Cleveland, OH 44114, USA

Lopez, Felipe (Athlete, Baseball Player)
11171 Sun Center Dr Ste 290
Rancho Cordova, CA 95670-6190, USA

Lopez, George (Actor, Comedian, Producer, Talk Show Host)
c/o Ina Treciokas *Slate Public Relations*
9000 Sunset Blvd #915
West Hollywood, CA 90069, USA

Lopez, Hector (Athlete, Baseball Player)
11415 Faldo Ct
Hudson, FL 34667-8540, USA

Lopez, Israel (Cachao) (Musician)
c/o Staff Member *Paradigm (Monterey)*
404 W Franklin St
Monterey, CA 93940, USA

Lopez, Javier (Athlete, Baseball Player)
73 Cutter Cir
Bluffton, SC 29909-4322, USA

Lopez, Javy (Athlete, Baseball Player)
4644 Whitestone Way
suwanee, GA 30024-7380, USA

Lopez, Jennifer (Actor, Musician)
25067 Jim Bridger Rd
Hidden Hills, CA 91302, USA

Lopez, Juan (Athlete, Baseball Player)
1451 Lavilla Ct
Deltona, FL 32725-4759, USA

Lopez, Luis (Athlete, Baseball Player)
1701 Pleasant Run Rd
Carrollton, TX 75006-7537, USA

Lopez, Luis (Athlete, Baseball Player)
Greenville Drive
945 S Main St Attn Coaching Staff
Greenville, SC 29601-3334, USA

Lopez, Luis (Athlete, Baseball Player)
636 40th St
Brooklyn, NY 11232-3108, USA

Lopez, Lynda (Television Host)
c/o Staff Member *Style Network*
5750 Wilshire Blvd
Los Angeles, CA 90036, USA

Lopez, Marga (Actor)
c/o Staff Member *Televisa*
Blvd Adolfo Lopez Mateos 232
Colonia San Angel INN
DF CP 01060, MEXICO

Lopez, Maria (Judge)
c/o Staff Member *Rebel Entertainment Partners*
5700 Wilshire Blvd
Suite 456
Los Angeles, CA 90036, USA

Lopez, Mario (Actor, Television Host)
c/o Mark Schulman *3 Arts Entertainment Inc*
9460 Wilshire Blvd
7th Floor
Beverly Hills, CA 90210, USA

Lopez, Mickey (Athlete, Baseball Player)
17430 SW 117th Ave
Miami, FL 33177-2203, USA

Lopez, Raul (Basketball Player)
Utah Jazz
Delta Center
301 W South Temple
Salt Lake City, UT 84101, USA

Lopez, Robert S (Historian)
41 Richmond Ave
New Haven, CT 06515, USA

Lopez, Rodrigo (Baseball Player)
Baltimore Orioles
Oriole Park
333 W Camden St
Baltimore, MD 21201, USA

Lopez, Sal (Actor, Musician)
c/o Ivan De Paz *DePaz Management*
2011 N Vermont Ave.
Los Angeles, CA 90027, USA

Lopez, Sergi (Actor)
c/o Staff Member *ICM Partners (ICM-LA)*
10250 Constellation Blvd Fl 7
Los Angeles, CA 90067, USA

Lopez, Steven (Athlete)
P.O. Bix 678
Sugarland, TX 77487, USA

Lopez, Trini (Actor, Musician)
1139 Abrigo Road
Palm Springs, CA 92262, USA

Lopez-Cobos, Jesus
Terry Harrison Mgmt
1 Clarendon Court
Charlbury, Oxon OX7 3PS, UNITED KINGDOM (UK)

Lopez-Garcia, Antonio (Artist)
Marlborough Fine Art
6 Albermarle St
London W1, UNITED KINGDOM (UK)

Lopez Rodriguez, Nicolas de J Cardinal (Religious Leader)
Archdiocese of Santo Domingo
Santo Domingo, AP 186, DOMINICAN REPUBLIC

Lopez Tarso, Ignacio (Actor)
c/o Staff Member *Televisa*
Blvd Adolfo Lopez Mateos 232
Colonia San Angel INN
DF CP 01060, MEXICO

Lopez Trujillo, Alfonso Cardinal (Religious Leader)
Arzobispado
Calle 57 N 48-28
Medellin, COLUMBIA

Lopienski, Tom (Athlete, Football Player)
128 Blackberry Dr
Hudson, OH 44236-4701, USA

Lopitalier, Phil (Athlete, Baseball Player)
231 N Kings Ave
Massapequa, NY 11758-3325, USA

Lopresti, Pete (Athlete, Hockey Player)
5100 Tifton Dr
Minneapolis, MN 55439-1457

Loquasto, Santo (Designer)
Paradigm Agency
10100 Santa Monica Blvd
#2500
Los Angeles, CA 90067, USA

Lorant, Stefan
215 W. Mountain Rd.
Lenox, MA 01240

Lorca, Valeria (Actor)
c/o Staff Member *Telefe - Argentina*
Pavon 2444 (C1248AAT)
Buenos Aires, ARGENTINA

Lorch, Karl (Athlete, Football Player)
92-861 Palailai St
Kapolei, HI 96707, USA

Lord, Albert L (Business Person)
SLM Holding Corp
11600 Sallie Mae Dr
Reston, VA 20193, USA

Lord, Jammal (Athlete, Football Player)
3110 Travis Creek Way
Fresno, TX 77545-7079, USA

Lord, Lance W (General)
Commander
US Space Command
Peterson Air Force Base, CO 80914, USA

Lord, Marjorie (Actor)
1110 Maytor Place
Beverly Hills, CA 90210, USA

Lord, M G (Cartoonist, Editor)
Newsday
Editorial Dept
235 Pinetawn Road
Melville, NY 11747, USA

Lord, Peter (Animator, Director)
Aardman Animations
Gas Ferry Road
Bristol BS1 6UN, UNITED KINGDOM (UK)

Lord, Walter
116 E. 68th St.
New York, NY 10021

Lord, Winston (Diplomat)
740 Park Ave
New York, NY 10021, USA

Lords, Traci
c/o Staff Member *Juliet Green Management*
9025 Wilshire Blvd #400
Beverly Hills, CA 90212, USA

Loree, Brad (Actor)
c/o Brenda Wong *TalentCo*
111 Water St #308
Vancouver BC V6B 1A7, CANADA

Loren, Josie (Actor)
c/o Scott Wine *Osbrink Talent Agency*
4343 Lankershim Blvd
Suite 100
Universal City, CA 91602, USA

Loren, Sophia (Actor)
c/o Leonard Hirshan *Leonard Hirshan Management*
9171 Wilshire Boulevard
Suite 400
Beverly Hills, CA 90210, USA

Loren, Veronica (Actor)
c/o Staff Member *International Artists PR & Talent Management*
3010 Wilshire Blvd #594
Los Angeles, CA 90010, USA

Lorentz, Jim (Athlete, Hockey Player)
2555 Staley Rd.
Grand Island, NY 14072-2040

Lorenz, Danny (Athlete, Hockey Player)
Kent Valley Ice Centre 6015 S 240th St
Kent, WA 98032-3406

Lorenz, Edward N (Scientist)
Massachusetts Institute of Technology
Earth Sciences Dept
Cambridge, MA 02139, USA

Lorenz, Ericka (Athlete, Olympic Athlete, Water Polo Player)
2604 Fulton St
Berkeley, CA 94704-3229, USA

Lorenz, Lee (Cartoonist)
PO Box 131
Easton, CT 06612-0131, USA

Lorenzen, Fred (Race Car Driver)
906 Burr Oak Ct.
Hinsdale, IL 60523-1514, USA

Lorenzo, Blas (Actor)
PO Box 2127
Los Angeles, CA 90078

Lorenzo, Francisco (Boxer)
c/o Staff Member *Top Rank Inc.*
3908 Howard Hughes Pkwy #580
Las Vegas, NV 89109, USA

Lorenzoni, Andrea (Astronaut)
Via B Vergine del Carmelo 168
Rome 00144, ITALY

Loretta, Mark (Athlete, Baseball Player)
PO Box 9505
Rancho Santa Fe, CA 92067-4505, USA

Lorey, Dean (Writer)
25540 Colette Way
Calabasas, CA

Loria, Christopher (Gus) (Astronaut)
102 Sea Mist Dr
League City, TX 77573, USA

Loria, Christopher J Lt Colonel (Astronaut)
102 Sea Mist Dr
League City, TX 77573-6928, USA

loria, jeffrey (Commentator)
19 E 72nd St APt 14C
New York, NY 10021-4193, USA

Loria, Jeffrey (Baseball Player)
Florida Marlins
44 Cocoanut Row Unit 407-B
Palm Beach, FL 33480-4069, USA

Lorick, Tony (Athlete, Football Player)
349 Burney Ln
Kerrville, TX 78028, USA

Lorimer, Bob (Athlete, Hockey Player)
24 Cranberry Lane
Aurora, ON L4G 5Y3, Canada

Loring, Gloria (Actor, Musician)
PO Box 1243
Cedar Glen, CA 92321, USA

Loring, John R (Artist)
621 Avon Rd
W Palm Beach, FL 33401-7803, USA

Loring, Lynn (Actor)
4910 Petit Ave
Encino, CA 91436-1131, USA

Lorius, Claude (Scientist)
Glaciologies Laboratoire
Rue Moliere
Saint-Martin d'Heres 38402, FRANCE

Lorraine, Andrew (Athlete, Baseball Player)
10436 E Acoma Dr
Scottsdale, AZ 85255-1711, USA

Lorraine, Andrew (Athlete, Baseball Player)
Everett Aquasox
3802 Broadway Attn: Coaching Staff
Everett, WA 98201-5032, USA

Lorre, Chuck (Producer, Writer)
c/o Pam Wilson *Ink Media Corp*
27734 Avenue Scott
Suite 110
Valencia, CA 91355, USA

Lorring, Joan
345 E. 68th St.
New York, NY 10021

Lorscheider, Aloisio Cardinal (Religious Leader)
Guna Metropolitana
CP 05 Tone Basilica
Aparecida, SP 12570-000, BRAZIL

Lorthridge, Ryan (Athlete, Basketball Player)
PO Box 68693
Jackson, MS 39286-8693, USA

Lortie, Louis (Musician)
Cramer/Marder Artists
3436 Springhill Road
Lafayette, CA 94549, USA

Los, Marinus (Misc)
American Cyanamid Corp
4201 Quakebridge Road
Princeton Junction, NJ 08550, USA

Loscutoff, James (Jim) (Athlete, Basketball Player, Coach)
166 Jenkins Rd
Andover, MA 01810-2304, USA

Losier, Michael (Writer)
605 827 Fairfield Road
Victoria, British Columbia V8V 5B2, Canada

Los Lagos, Banda (Music Group)
c/o Staff Member *Sony Music Miami*
605 Lincoln Rd Fl 7
Miami Beach, FL 33139, USA

Los Lobos (Music Group)
c/o Staff Member *Paradigm (Monterey)*
404 W Franklin St
Monterey, CA 93940, USA

Los Lonely Boys (Music Group)
Loophole Entertainment
PO Box 162045
Austin, TX 78716, USA

Losman, J P (Athlete, Football Player)
70 Oakland Pl
Buffalo, NY 14222-2040, USA

Los Mauricios (Writer)
c/o Staff Member *Gabriel Blanco Iglesias (Colombia)*
Dg 127A #20-36
Conjunto Plenitud, Apto 132
Bogota, Colombia

Los Rabanes (Music Group)
c/o Staff Member *Sony Music Miami*
605 Lincoln Rd Fl 7
Miami Beach, FL 33139, USA

Los Sementales de Nuevo Leon (Music Group)
c/o Staff Member *Sony Music Miami*
605 Lincoln Rd Fl 7
Miami Beach, FL 33139, USA

Los Super Reyes (Music Group, Musician)
c/o Staff Member *Warner Music International (WMI-USA)*
75 Rockefeller Plaza
New York, NY 10019, USA

Lost Boys
1775 Broadway #433
New York, NY 10019

Lostprophets (Music Group)
c/o Staff Member *Sony Music International*
550 Madison Ave
New York, NY 10022-3211, USA

Lothamer, Ed (Athlete, Football Player)
14545 W 183rd St
Olathe, KS 66062, USA

Lott, Felicity A (Opera Singer)
Kunstleragentur Raab & Bohm
Plankengasse 7
Vienna 1010, AUSTRIA

Lott, John (Athlete, Football Player)
14 E Oakwood Hills Dr
Chandler, AZ 85248-6200, USA

Lott, Phil (Producer)
c/o Staff Member *ICM Partners (ICM-LA)*
10250 Constellation Blvd Fl 7
Los Angeles, CA 90067, USA

Lott, Pixie (Musician)
c/o Staff Member *Mercury Records UK*
1 Sussex Pl
London W6 9XS, UK

Lott, Ronald M (Ronnie) (Sportscaster)
Fox-TV
Sports Dept
PO Box 900
Beverly Hills, CA 90213, USA

Lott, Ronnie (Athlete, Football Player)
11342 Canyon View Cir
Cupertino, CA 95014, USA

Lott, Thomas (Athlete, Football Player)
3617 Sailmaker Ln
Plano, TX 75023-3712, USA

Lott, Trent (Politician, Senator)
2401 Pennsylvania Ave NW Apt 806
Washington, DC 20037-1735, USA

Lotti, Helmut
Bevrijdingstraat 39
Turnhout, BELGIUM 2300

Lotz, Anne Graham (Religious Leader)
AnGel Ministries
3246 Lewis Farm Road
Raleigh, NC 27607, USA

Louboutin, Christian (Designer)
Christian Louboutin
306 West 38th St
3rd Floor
New York, NY 10018, USA

Louchiey, Corey (Athlete, Football Player)
8 Misty Creek Ln
Greenville, SC 29611, USA

Loucks, Scott (Athlete, Baseball Player)
1801 Viola Dr
Sierra Vista, AZ 85635-2149, USA

Loucks, Vernon R Jr (Business Person)
Baxter International
1 Baxter Parkway
Deerfield, IL 60015, USA

Louden, Stephanie (Athlete, Golfer)
621 Verbena Ln
Frisco, TX 75034, USA

Louderback, Tom (Athlete, Football Player)
P.O. Box 6879
Oakland, CA 94603, USA

Loudon, Rodney (Physicist)
3 Gaston St
East Bergholt
Colchester, Essex CO7 6SD, UNITED KINGDOM (UK)

Louganis, Greg (Athlete, Swimmer)
PO Box 4130
Malibu, CA 90265, USA

Loughery, Kevin (Athlete, Basketball Player, Coach)
4474 Club Dr NE
Atlanta, GA 30319-1122, USA

Loughlin, Kimerley (Stylist)
1445 N Harlem
#A
Oak Park, IL 60302, USA

Loughlin, Lori (Actor)
c/o Joanna (Joanie) Burstein *Burstein Company, The*
15304 Sunset Blvd
suite 208
Pacific Palisades, CA 90272, USA

Loughlin, Mary Anne (Correspondent)
WTBS-TV News Dept
1050 Techwood Dr NW
Atlanta, GA 30318, USA

Loughran, James
34 Cleveden Dr
Glasgow G12 0RX, SCOTLAND

Louis, Clercine (Stylist)
1080 E 57th St
Brooklyn, NY 11234, USA

Louis, Jin Luxian (Religious Leader)
Shesshan Catholic Seminary
Beijing, CHINA

Louis, Murray (Choreographer, Dancer)
Nikolais/Louis Foundation
375 W Broadway
New York, NY 10012, USA

Louisa, Maria (Model)
Next Model Mgmt
23 Watts St
New York, NY 10013, USA

Louis-Dreyfus, Julia (Actor, Comedian)
c/o Judy Hofflund *Hofflund/Polone*
9465 Wilshire Blvd #420
Beverly Hills, CA 90212, USA

Louis-Dreyfus, Robert L M (Business Person)
Adidas AG
Adi Dassier Str 2
Herzogenaurach 91702, GERMANY

Louise, Tina (Actor, Musician)
310 E 46th St #24G
New York, NY 10011, USA

Louiso, Todd (Actor)
S M S Talent
8730 Sunset Blvd
#440
Los Angeles, CA 90069, USA

Louisy, C Pearlette (Governor)
Government House
Morne Fortune
Castries, Saint Lucia, West Indies

Loukas, Angelo (Athlete, Football Player)
1535 Robin Rd
Bannockburn, IL 60015, USA

Loun, Don (Athlete, Baseball Player)
9095 Wexford Dr
Vienna, VA 22182-2152, USA

Lourdusamy, D Simon Cardinal (Religious Leader)
Palazzo dei Convertendi
64 Via della Conciliazione
Rome 00193, ITALY

Lourie, Alan D (Judge)
US Court of Appeals
717 Madison Place NW
Washington, DC 20439, USA

Louris, Gary (Musician, Songwriter, Writer)
Sussman Assoc
1222 16th Ave S
#300
Nashville, TN 37212, USA

Lousma, Jack R (Astronaut)
2722 Roseland St
Ann Arbor, MI 48103, USA

Lousma, Jack R Colonel (Astronaut)
2722 Roseland Dr
Ann Arbo, MI 48103-2137, USA

Loustel, Ron (Athlete, Hockey Player)
7-116 Wellington Cres
Winnipeg, MB R3M 0A9, Canada

Loutty, All (Prime Minister)
29 Ahmed Hesmat St
Zamalek
Cairo, EGYPT

Louvier, Alain (Composer)
53 Ave Victor Hugo
Boulogne-Billancourt 92100, FRANCE

Loux, Shane (Athlete, Baseball Player)
3105 E Sparrow Pl
Chandler, AZ 85286-5612, USA

Lovano, Joe (Composer)
International Music Network
278 S Main St
#400
Gloucester, MA 01930, USA

Lovato, Demi (Actor)
c/o Patrick Confrey *Sunshine, Sachs & Associates*
149 Fifth Ave
7th Floor
New York, NY 10010, USA

Love, Alexis
PO Box 491205
Los Angeles, CA 90049

Love, Ben H (Misc)
Boy Scouts of America
1327 Anne Court
Cedar Park, TX 78613-4022, USA

Love, Courtney (Musician, Songwriter)
c/o Jonathan Daniel *Crush Management*
60-62 E 11th St
7th Floor
New York, NY 10003, USA

Love, Darlene (Actor, Musician)
Greater Talent
437 5th Ave
New York, NY 10016, USA

Love, Duval (Athlete, Football Player)
8985 Yuba River Ave
Fountain Valley, CA 92708, USA

Love, Faizon (Actor)
c/o Paula Rosenberg *ICA Talent*
818 12th Street Ste 9
Santa Monica, CA 90403, USA

Love, Gael (Editor)
Connoisseur Magazine
Editorial Dept
1790 Broadway
New York, NY 10019, USA

Love, Ian (Musician)
c/o Staff Member *Paradigm (Monterey)*
404 W Franklin St
Monterey, CA 93940, USA

Love, Kevin (Athlete, Basketball Player)
c/o Jeff Schwartz *Excel Sports Management*
9665 Wilshire Blvd #500
Los Angeles, CA 90212, USA

Love, Loni (Actor, Comedian)
c/o Staff Member *Power Entertainment*
9100 Wilshire Blvd #700
Beverly Hills, CA 90212, USA

Love, Michael E (Mike) (Musician)
24563 Ebelden Ave.
Santa Clarita, CA 91321, USA

Love, Patricia (Writer)
c/o Author Mail *Bantam-Dell Publishing (NY)*
1745 Broadway
New York, NY 10019, USA

Love, Randy (Athlete, Football Player)
2202 Fairlands Dr
Garland, TX 75040, USA

Love, Sean (Athlete, Football Player)
121 Hunter St
Tamaqua, PA 18252, USA

Love, Stan (Athlete, Basketball Player)
1950 Egan Way
Lake Oswego, OR 97034-2728, USA

Love, Stanley G (Astronaut)
4315 Indian Sunrise Court
Houston, TX 77059, USA

Love, Stanley G Dr (Astronaut)
4315 Indian Sunrise Ct
Houston, TX 77059-5582, USA

Love & Rockets (Music Group)
4 The Lakes Bushey
Hertfordshire WD2 1HS, UK

Love III, Davis (Athlete, Golfer)
Love Golf Design
100 Brunswick Ave
Saint Simons Island, GA 31522, USA

Lovelace, Alan (Astronaut)
10960 S Tropical Trl
Merritt Island, FL 32952-7014, USA

Lovelace, Vance (Athlete, Baseball Player)
5608 12th Ave S
Tampa, FL 33619-3756, USA

Lovelady, Edwin (Athlete, Football Player)
2707 Glenwood Pkwy
Chattanooga, TN 37404, USA

Loveless, Patty (Musician, Songwriter)
c/o Staff Member *WME (LA)*
9601 Wilshire Blvd Fl 3
Beverly Hills, CA 90210, USA

Lovell, James A Captain (Astronaut)
964 Lake Rd
Lake Forest, IL 60045-2223, USA

Lovell, James A, Jr (Astronaut)
Lovell Communications
PO Box 49
Lake Forest, IL 60045, USA

Lovell, Jim (Astronaut, Writer)
c/o Staff Member *Cunningham Escott Slevin & Doherty (CESD-LA)*
10635 Santa Monica Blvd
130
Los Angeles, CA 90025, USA

Lovell, Marilyn
7840 Torreyson Dr
Los Angeles, CA 90046

Lovellette, Clyde (Athlete, Basketball Player, Olympic Athlete)
8 Woodspoint Cir
North Manchester, IN 46962-9123, USA

Lovelock, James E (Inventor, Scientist)
Coombe Mill
Saint Giles-on-Heath
Launceston, Cornwall PL 15 9RY,
UNITED KINGDOM (UK)

Lovemark, Jaime (Athlete, Golfer)
16449 La Via Feliz
Rancho Santa Fe, CA 92067, USA

Lover, Seth (Engineer, Inventor)
4 Village Dr
Saint Louis, MO 63146, USA

Loverboy
1505 W. 2nd St. #200
Vancouver, CANADA BC V6H 3Y4

Loverne, David (Athlete, Football Player)
2307 Amber Falls Dr
Rocklin, CA 95765, USA

Lovetere, John (Athlete, Football Player)
445 Old Statesville Rd
Watertown, TN 37184-4827, USA

Lovett, Lyie (Musician, Songwriter, Writer)
Haber Corp
1016 17th Ave S
#1
Nashville, TN 37212, USA

Lovett, Lyle (Musician)
c/o Ken Levitan *Vector Management*
P.O. Box 120479
Nashville, TN 37212, USA

Lovett, Ruby (Musician)
Myers Media
PO Box 378
Canton, NY 13617, USA

Lovett, Steve (Actor)
c/o Steve Lovett *Lovett Management*
1327 Brinkley Ave
Los Angeles, CA 90049, USA

Lovibond, Ophelia (Actor)
c/o Brantley Brown *Schachter Entertainment*
1157 S Beverly Dr Fl 2
Los Angeles, CA 90035, USA

Loviglio, Jay (Athlete, Baseball Player)
23 3rd Ave
East Islip, NY 11730-2015, USA

Loville, Derek (Athlete, Football Player)
B D L Financial 3020 E Camelback Rd Ste 213
Phoenix, AZ 85016-4423, USA

Lovine, Vicki
c/o Daniel Strone *Trident Media Group LLC*
41 Madison Ave
36th Floor
New York, NY 10010, USA

Loving, Candy (Actor, Model)
c/o Staff Member *Playboy Enterprises Inc*
680 North Lake Shore Drive
Chicago, IL 60611, USA

Loving, George (General)
5211 Patriots Colony Dr
Williamsburg, VA 23188-1392, USA

Lovins, Amory B (Physicist)
Hypercar Inc
220 Cody Lane
Basalt, CO 81621, USA

Lovin' Spoonful
Duryea Entertainment
35 White Birch Rd
Ridgefield, CT 06877, USA

Lovitz, Jon (Actor, Comedian, Producer, Writer)
c/o Jason Shapiro *United Talent Agency (UTA)*
9336 Civic Center Dr
Beverly Hills, CA 90210, USA

Løvland, Rolf (Composer, Musician)
c/o Staff Member *Continental Artist Management AS*
Sandakerveien 24 D, F2
Oslo N-0473, Norway

Lovrich, Pete (Athlete, Baseball Player)
19626 Beechnut Dr
Mokena, IL 60448-9333, USA

Lovsin, Ken (Athlete, Hockey Player)
Freson Bros 114-440148 St
Stony Plain, AB T7Z 1N3, Canada

Lovullo, Torey (Athlete, Baseball Player)
32108 Sailview Ln
Westlake Village, CA 91361-3619, USA

Lovuolo, Frank (Athlete, Football Player)
6 Pleasant Ct
Binghamton, NY 13905, USA

Low, Francis E (Physicist)
7102 Plantation Lane
Rockville, MD 20852-4421, USA

Low, G David (Astronaut)
Orbital Science Group
21839 Atlantic Blvd
Sterling, VA 20166, USA

Low, James (General)
122 Windward Way
Davenport, FL 33837-5110, USA

Low, Reed (Athlete, Hockey Player)
1869 Pomme Rd
Arnold, MO 63010-2453

Low, Stephen (Diplomat)
2855 Tilden St NW
Washington, DC 20008, USA

Lowder, Kyle (Actor)
c/o Michael P Levine *Levine Management*
9028 W Sunset Blvd #PH1
Los Angeles, CA 90069, USA

Lowdermilk, Dwayne (Athlete, Hockey Player)
National Training Rink
110-20740 Mufford Cres
Langley, BC V2Y 1N9, Canada

Lowdermilk, R Kirk (Athlete, Football Player)
8080 Apollo Rd NE
Kensington, OH 44427-9626, USA

Lowe, Barry
31S. Audley St.
London, ENGLAND W1

Lowe, Chad (Actor)
c/o David Rose *Innovative Artists (LA)*
1505 10th St
Santa Monica, CA 90401, USA

Lowe, Chan (Cartoonist, Editor)
Fort Lauderdale Sun-Sentinel
200 E Olas Blvd
Fort Lauderdale, FL 33301, USA

Lowe, Cortland (Athlete, Golfer)
713 Taylor Ridge Rd
Winston Salem, NC 27106, USA

Lowe, Crystal (Actor, Model)
Characters Talent Agency
8 Elm Street
Toronto, ON M5G 1G&, CANADA

Lowe, Darren (Athlete, Hockey Player)
University of Toronto 55 Harbord St
Toronto, ON M5S 2W6, Canada

Lowe, Derek (Athlete, Baseball Player)
12711 Terabella Way
Fort Myers, FL 33912-0910, USA

Lowe, Gary (Athlete, Football Player)
16940 Lauderdale Ave
Beverly Hills, MI 48025, USA

Lowe, Kevin (Athlete, Coach, Hockey Player)
Edmonton Oilers
11230 110th St
Edmonton, AB T5G 3H7, Canada

Lowe, Lloyd (Athlete, Football Player)
8805 Deerwood Dr
Rowlett, TX 75088, USA

lowe, Mark
13688 W Jesse Red Dr
Peoria, AZ 85383-7944, USA

Lowe, Nick (Musician, Songwriter, Writer)
MVO Ltd
307 7th Ave
#807
New York, NY 10001, USA

Lowe, Norman Odie (Athlete, Hockey Player)
137-5484 25 Ave
Vernon, BC VlT 7 A8, Canada

Lowe, Paul (Athlete, Football Player)
3906 Marine View Ave
San Diego, CA 92113, USA

Lowe, QV
125 Palomino Ln
Wetumpka, AL 36093-2103, USA

Lowe, Rob (Actor)
c/o David McIlvain *Brillstein Entertainment Partners*
9150 Wilshire Blvd #350
Beverly Hills, CA 90212, USA

Lowe, Sean (Athlete, Baseball Player)
802 Oak Dr
Mesquite, TX 75149-4028, USA

Lowe, Sidney (Athlete, Basketball Player, Coach)
2631 Wallingford Rd
Winston Salem, NC 27101-1923, USA

Lowe, Stephanie (Athlete, Golfer)
2004 Delancey Dr
Norman, OK 73071-3872, USA

Lowe, Woodrow (Athlete, Coach, Football Player)
Jackson-Olin High School
282 Grande View Pkwy
Maylene, AL 35114-6073, USA

Loweecey, Alice (Writer)
c/o Staff Member *Midnight Ink*
2143 Wooddale Dr
Woodbury, MN 55125-2989, USA

Lowell, Carey (Actor)
c/o Sue Leibman *Barking Dog Entertainment*
609 Greenwich St
6th Floor
New York, NY 10014, USA

Lowell, Charlie (Musician)
Flood Burnstead McCready McCarthy
1700 Hayes St
#304
Nashville, TN 37203, USA

Lowell, Christopher (Designer, Television Host)
The Christopher Lowell Show
2800 Olympic Blvd Fl 2
Santa Monica, CA 90404, USA

Lowell, Mike (Athlete, Baseball Player)
620 Santurce Ave
Coral Gables, FL 33143-6360, USA

Lowell, Scott
6500 Wilshire Blvd. #2200
Los Angeles, CA 90048

L. Owens, William (Congressman, Politician)
431 Cannon HOB
Washington, DC 20515, USA

Lowenstein, Evan (Actor, Musician)
c/o Ruthanne Secunda *United Talent Agency (UTA)*
9336 Civic Center Dr
Beverly Hills, CA 90210, USA

Lowenstein, Jaron (Actor, Musician)
c/o Ruthanne Secunda *United Talent Agency (UTA)*
9336 Civic Center Dr
Beverly Hills, CA 90210, USA

Lowenstein, John (Athlete, Baseball Player)
7017 Via Locanda Ave
Las Vegas, NV 89131-0114, USA

Lowenstein, Louis (Attorney, Attorney General, Educator, General)
5 Oak Lane
Larchmont, NY 10538, USA

Lowery, Devon (Baseball Player)
112 Catawba St
Belmont, NC 28012-3306, USA

Lowery, Nick (Athlete, Football Player)
8416 E Via De Jardin
Scottsdale, AZ 85258-3207, USA

Lowery, Steve (Athlete, Golfer)
1073 Royal Mile
Birmingham, AL 35242, USA

Lowery, Terrell (Athlete, Baseball Player)
3565 Antigua Pl
West Sacramento, CA 95691-5822, USA

Lowes, Katie (Actor)
c/o David Sweeney *Sweeney Management*
6253 Hollywood Blvd
Suite 201
Los Angeles, CA 90028, USA

Lown, Bernard (Doctor)
Lown Cardiovascular Group
21 Longwood Ave
Brookline, MA 02446, USA

Lown, Turk (Athlete, Baseball Player)
1106 Van Buren St
Pueblo, CO 81004-2832, USA

Lowndes, Jessica (Actor)
c/o Jeff Witjas *Agency for the Performing Arts (APA-LA)*
405 S Beverly Dr
Suite 500
Beverly Hills, CA 90212-4425, USA

Lowrey, Dawn (Stylist)
412 N Coast Hwy
PMB #221
Laguna Beach, CA 92651, USA

Lowrie, Jed
2958 N Evergreen St
Buckeye, AZ 85396-7783, USA

Lowry, Calvin (Athlete, Football Player)
3500 N Capital of Texas Hwy Apt 1211
Austin, TX 78746-3385, USA

Lowry, Dave (Athlete, Hockey Player)
Calgary Flames PO Box 1540 Stn M
Calgary, AB T2P 3B9, Canada

Lowry, Lois (Writer)
205 Brattle St
Cambridge, MA 02138-3345, USA

Lowry, Mark
MLP Inc
PO Box 1405
Hendersonville, TN 37077, USA

Lowry, Noah (Athlete, Baseball Player)
2621 Matera Ln
San Diego, CA 92108-6737, USA

Lowry, Shanti (Actor)

Low Stars (Music Group)
c/o Staff Member *Paradigm (Monterey)*
404 W Franklin St
Monterey, CA 93940, USA

Loy, Frank E (Misc)
Marshall German Fund
11 Dupont Circle NW
Washington, DC 20036, USA

Loy, James M (Admiral, Government Official)
Transportation Security Administration
400 7th St SW
Washington, DC 20590, USA

Loynd, Mike (Athlete, Baseball Player)
16652 Benton Taylor Dr
Chesterfield, LO 63005-4861, USA

Lozada, Johnny (Actor)
c/o Staff Member *Televisa*
Blvd Adolfo Lopez Mateos 232
Colonia San Angel INN
DF CP 01060, MEXICO

Lozado, Willie (Athlete, Baseball Player)
3032 Shagbark Trl
Sellersburg, IN 47172-9117, USA

Lozano, Conrad (Musician)
Gold Mountain
3575 Cahuenga Blvd W
#450
Los Angeles, CA 90068, USA

Lozano, Ignacio E Jr (Editor)
La Opinion
700 S Flower St #3000
Los Angeles, CA 90017, USA

Lozano, Karyme (Actor)
c/o Ivan De Paz *DePaz Management*
2011 N Vermont Ave.
Los Angeles, CA 90027, USA

Lozano, Silvia (Choreographer)
Ballet Folklorico
31 Esq Con Riva Palacio
Mexico City, DF, MEXICO

Lozano Barragan, Javier Cardinal (Religious Leader)
Health Care Workers Assistance
Via Conciliazione 3
Rome 00193, ITALY

L. Richmond, Cedric (Congressman, Politician)
415 Cannon HOB
Washington, DC 20515, USA

L. Rush, Bobby (Congressman, Politician)
2268 Rayburn HOB
Washington, DC 20515, USA

Ishinabe, Yutaka (Chef)
Queen Alice GuestHouse 3-2-33 Nishi Azabu
Minato-ku, Tokyo, Japan

Isikoff, Michael (Writer)
123 Main St #A
Irvington, NY 10533-1718, USA

Lu, Amy (Stylist)
c/o Staff Member *Judy Inc*
1 Yorkville Ave
Toronto ON M4W 1L1, Canada

Lu, Cindy (Actor)
c/o Kim Matuka *Online Talent Group*
Prefers to be contacted via email or telephone
Los Angeles, CA 90069, USA

Lu, Edward T (Ed) (Astronaut)
12332 Kosich Pl
Saratoga, CA 95070-3575, USA

Lu, Lisa
1737 N. Orange Grove Ave
Los Angeles, CA 90046

Lu, Qihui (Artist)
100-301
398 Xin-Pei Road
Xin-Zuan, Shanghai, CHINA

Lualdi, Antonella
via Cassia Antica 35
Rome, ITALY

Lubanski, Ed (Bowler)
5326 Christi Dr
Warren, MI 48091, USA

Lubbers, Ruud (Politician)
2462 N Prospect Ave Apt 623
Milwaukee, WI 53211-4456, NETHERLANDS

Lubchenco, Jane (Biologist)
Oregon State University
Marine Biology Dept
Corvallis, OR 97331, USA

Lubezki, Emmanuel (Cinematographer)
c/o Julia Kole *Jacob & Kole Agency, The*
6715 Hollywood Blvd #216
Los Angeles, CA 90028, USA

Lubich, Bronko (Wrestler)
3146 Whitemarsh Circle
Dallas, TX 75234, USA

Lubich, Silvia Chiara (Misc)
Focolare Movement
306 Via di Frascati
Rocca di Papa, RM 00040, ITALY

Lubin, Arthur
5737 Newcastle Ave.
Encino, CA 91316

Lubin, Steven (Musician)
State University of New York
School of Arts
Purchase, NY 10577, USA

Lubischer, Steve (Athlete, Football Player)
6 Fiore Ct
Oceanport, NJ 07757, USA

Lublin, Nancy (Business Person)
Do Something
24-32 Union Square E
4th Floor
New York, NY 10003, USA

Lubotsky, Mark (Musician)
Overtoom 329 III
Amsterdam, JM 1054, NETHERLANDS

Lubovitch, Lar (Choreographer, Dancer)
Lar Lubovitch Dance Co
229 W 42nd St
#8
New York, NY 10036, USA

Lubratich, Steve (Athlete, Baseball Player)
24 Sackett Rd
Lee, NH 03861-6616, USA

Lubs, Herbert A (Scientist)
5133 SW 71st Place
Miami, FL 33155, USA

Lubsen, Chip (Athlete, Olympic Athlete, Rower)
13215 Stable
Brook Way Herndon, VA 20171-2926, USA

Luc, Tone (Actor, Musician)
Headline Talent
1650 Broadway
#508
New York, NY 10019, USA

Lucado, Max (Religious Leader, Writer)
Oak Hills Church of Christ
6929 Camp Bullis Rd
San Antonio, TX 78256, USA

Lucaro, Carlos (Judge)
US Court of Appeals
1929 Stout St
Denver, CO 80294, USA

Lucas, Aubrey K (Educator)
University of Southern Mississippi
President's Office
Hattiesburg, MS 39406, USA

Lucas, Craig (Director, Producer, Writer)
c/o Staff Member *Gersh (LA)*
9465 Wilshire Blvd
Suite 600
Beverly Hills, CA 90212, USA

Lucas, Dan (Athlete, Hockey Player)
609 Forest Ave
Portland, ME 04101-1515

Lucas, Dave (Athlete, Hockey Player)
15 Peels Lane
Lindsay, ON K9V 2X8, CANADA

Lucas, Dick (Athlete, Football Player)
1269 Estate Dr
West Chester, PA 19380-4258, USA

Lucas, Erin (Actor, Reality TV Star)
c/o Staff Member *Creative Management Entertainment Group (CMEG)*
2050 S Bundy Dr
Suite 280
Los Angeles, CA 90025, USA

Lucas, Gary (Athlete, Baseball Player)
1511 High St
Rice Lake, WI 54868-1874, USA

Lucas, George (Business Person, Director, Producer)
c/o Staff Member *LucasFilm Ltd*
5858 Lucas Valley Rd
Nicasio, CA 94946, USA

Lucas, Geralyn (Writer)
1349 Lexington Ave
New York, NY 10012, USA

Lucas, Isabel (Actor)
c/o Staff Member *Schiff Company, The*
9465 Wilshire Blvd
Suite 480
Beverly Hills, CA 90212, USA

Lucas, Jerry (Athlete, Basketball Player, Olympic Athlete)
Dr Memorabilia
231 E 2nd St
Chillicothe, OH 45601, USA

Lucas, Jessica (Actor)
c/o Staff Member *Thruline Entertainment*
9250 Wilshire Blvd
Ground Fl
Beverly Hills, CA 90212, USA

Lucas, John (Athlete, Basketball Player)
21 Pin Oal Estates Ct
Bellaire, TX 77401, USA

Lucas, Josh (Actor)
8459 Ridpath Dr
Los Angeles, CA 90046, USA

Lucas, Ken (Athlete, Football Player)
1108 Stamps Cv
Cleveland, MS 38732, USA

Lucas, Matt (Actor, Producer, Writer)
c/o Kevin McLaughlin *Baker Winokur Ryder Public Relations (BWR-LA)*
9100 Wilshire Blvd
Suite 500, West Tower
Beverly Hills, CA 90212, USA

Lucas, Michael (Adult Film Star, Director)
Lucas Entertainment
589 Eighth Ave Fl 2
New York, NY 10018, USA

Lucas, Ray (Athlete, Football Player)
44 Harrison Ave # 2
Harrison, NJ 07029-1331, USA

Lucas, Richard J (Richie) (Athlete, Football Player)
1238 Old Boalsburg Rd
State College, PA 16801-6152, USA

Lucas, Robert E Jr (Nobel Prize Laureate)
5448 S East View Park
#3
Chicago, IL 60615, USA

Lucas, Tim (Athlete, Football Player)
5081 S Florence Dr
Greenwood Village, CO 80111-3613, USA

Lucas, William (Government Official)
Justice Department
Constitution & 10th NW
Washington, DC 20530, USA

Lucca, Lou (Baseball Player)
Topps
10211 Willow Bend Cir Apt 1B
Charlotte, NC 28210-8424, USA

Lucchesi, Frank (Athlete, Baseball Player, Coach)
4703 Mill Creek Dr
Colleyville, TX 76034-3646, USA

Lucchesini, Andrea (Musician)
Arts Management Group
1133 Broadway
#1025
New York, NY 10010, USA

Lucci, Mike (Athlete, Football Player)
3184 Middlebelt Rd
West Bloomfield, MI 48323, USA

Lucci, Susan (Actor)
c/o Fran Curtis *Rogers & Cowan PR (NY)*
919 Third Ave
18th Floor
New York, NY 10022, USA

Lucci, Vince Sr (Bowler)
1182 Queens Way
West Chester, PA 19382, USA

Luce, Derrel (Athlete, Football Player)
4112 Green Oak Dr
Waco, TX 76710, USA

Luce, Don
67 Tartan Ln
Buffalo, NY 14221-2616

Luce, Don
Philadelphia Flyers
3601 S Broad St Ste 2
Philadelohia, PA 19148-5297

Luce, Henry III (Publisher)
Mill Hill Road
Mill Neck, NY 11765, USA

Luce, Lew (Athlete, Football Player)
850 Symphony Isles Blvd
Ruskin, FL 33572, USA

Luce, R Duncan (Misc)
20 Whitman Court
Irvine, CA 92612, USA

Luce, Richard N (Government Official)
The House Of Lords
London SW1A 0PW, UK

Luce, William (Bill) (Writer)
PO Box 370
Depoe Bay, OR 97341, USA

Lucebert (Artist, Writer)
Boendermakerhof 10
Bergen N-H, TB 1861, NETHERLANDS

Lucero (Musician)
c/o Staff Member *Sony Music Miami*
605 Lincoln Rd Fl 7
Miami Beach, FL 33139, USA

Lucey, Dorothy (Actor, Correspondent, Television Host)
c/o Staff Member *Good Day Live*
20th Century Fox Television
10201 W Pico Blvd Blg 88 Rm 29
Los Angeles, CA 90035, USA

Luchento, Tom (Horse Racer)
3 Hedge Row Ct
Columbus, NJ 08022-1129, USA

Luchko, Klara S (Actor)
Kotelmicheskaya Nab 1/15 Korp B
#308
Moscow 109240, RUSSIA

Luchsinger, Susie (Musician)
Psalms Ministries
PO Box 990
Atoka, OK 74525, USA

Lucic, Milan (Athlete, Hockey Player)
50 Fleet St #301
Boston, MA 02109-1129, USA

Lucid, Shannon W (Astronaut, Physicist)
1622 Gunwale Road
Houston, TX 77062, USA

Lucid, Shannon W Dr (Astronaut)
1622 Gunwale Rd
Houston, TX 77062-4538, USA

Lucie, Milan (Athlete, Hockey Player)
6256 Brooks St
Vancouver, BC V5S 3J1, Canada

Lucier, Lou (Athlete, Baseball Player)
7 Jaclyn Rae Dr
Millbury, MA 01527-3372, USA

Lucier, Wayne (Athlete, Football Player)
13 Jana Rd
Salem, NH 03079-2261, USA

Lucin, Arthur
5737 Newcastle Ave
Encino, CA 91316

Lucio, Shannon (Actor)
c/o Justin Grey Stone *Untitled Entertainment (LA)*
350 S. Beverly Dr #200
Beverly Hills, CA 90212, USA

Luck, Andrew (Athlete, Football Player)
c/o Noeleen Meehan *Wasserman Media Group*
10960 Wilshire Blvd
Suite 2200
Los Angeles, CA 90024, USA

Luck, Frank (Athlete)
Lerchenweg 9
Springstille 98587, GERMANY

Luck, George E (Aviator)
5709 147th St SE
Everett, WA 98208-9376, USA

Luck, Oliver (Athlete, Football Player)
925 Riverview Dr
Morgantown, WV 26505-4633, USA

Luck, Terry (Athlete, Football Player)
334 N Brooke Dr
Canton, GA 30114-9402, USA

Luckenbill, Laurence
PO Box 636
Cross River, NY 10518

Luckenbill, Theodore (Athlete, Basketball Player)
1100 E Goliad Ave
Crockett, TX 75835-2231, USA

Luckett, Letoya (Actor)
c/o Everly Lee *Agency for the Performing Arts (APA-LA)*
405 S Beverly Dr
Suite 500
Beverly Hills, CA 90212-4425, USA

Luckhurst, Mick (Athlete, Football Player)
103 Pierre Point Isle
Duluth, GA 30097, USA

Luckinbill, Laurence (Actor)
RR 3 Flintlock Ridge Rd
Katonah, NY 10536, USA

Luckinbill, Lawrence (Actor)
PO Box 330
Georgetown, CT 06829, USA

Luckinbill, Thad (Actor)
c/o Marnie Sparer *Innovative Artists (LA)*
1505 10th St
Santa Monica, CA 90401, USA

Lucking, William (Actor)
c/o Staff Member *Twentieth Century Artists*
15760 Ventura Blvd
Ste 700
Encino, CA 91436, USA

Luckovich, Mike (Cartoonist, Editor)
Atlanta Constitution
Editorial Dept
72 Marietta St
Atlanta, GA 30303, USA

Lucky, Lillian (Baseball Player)
243 Owens St
Niles, MI 49120-4150, USA

Lucky, Mike (Athlete, Football Player)
4156 N Morning Dove Cir
Mesa, AZ 85207, USA

Lucky, Robert W (Engineer)
48 Gillespie Ave
Fair Haven, NJ 07704, USA

Lucroy, Jonathan (Athlete, Baseball Player)
9 Huntington Rd Apt 10-E
Scarsdale, NY 10583-2039

Lucy, Donny (Athlete, Baseball Player)
3674 Oak Cliff Dr
Fallbrook, CA 92028-9413, USA

Luczo, Stephen J (Business Person)
Seagate Technology
920 Disc Dr
Scotts Valley, CA 95066, USA

Ludacris (Actor, Musician, Producer)
c/o Chaka Zulu *Disturbing Tha Peace*
1451 Woodmont Lane NW
Atlanta, GA 30318, USA

Ludaker, Dave (Baseball Player)
3593 Buffum St
Simi Valley, CA 93063-3215, USA

Luddy, Barbara
119 Sultan Ave.
Capitol Heights, MD 20743-1954

Luder, Owen H (Architect)
Communication in Construction
2 Smith Square
London SW1P 3H5, UNITED KINGDOM (UK)

Ludes, John T (Business Person)
Fortune Brands Inc
300 Tower Parkway
Lincolnshire, IL 60069, USA

Luding-Rothenburger, Christa (Speed Skater)
Dresdener Eisspot-Club
Pieschener Allee 1
Dresden 01067, GERMANY

Ludington, Ronald (Athlete, Figure Skater, Olympic Athlete)
611 Thompson Station Rd
Newark, DE 19711-7505, USA

Ludlum, Robert (Actor)
c/o Ben Smith *ICM Partners (ICM-LA)*
10250 Constellation Blvd Fl 7
Los Angeles, CA 90067, USA

Ludwick, Eric (Athlete, Baseball Player)
7146 Madarang Ave
Las Vegas, NV 89178-8002, USA

Ludwick, Ryan (Athlete, Baseball Player)
115 Roberts Cir
Georgetown, TX 78633-1960, USA

Ludwig, Alexander (Actor)
c/o Guido Giordano *ICM Partners (ICM-LA)*
10250 Constellation Blvd Fl 7
Los Angeles, CA 90067, USA

Ludwig, Christa (Opera Singer)
Calliopie
162 Chemin du Santon
Mougins 06250, FRANCE

Ludwig, Craig (Athlete, Hockey Player)
8401 Albritton Dr
Frisco, TX 75034-7702, USA

Ludwig, George Dr (Scientist)
215 Aspen Trl
Winchester, VA 22602-1404, USA

Ludwig, George H (Physicist)
215 Aspen Trail
Winchester, VA 22602, USA

Ludwig, Ken (Writer)
c/o Peter Franklin *WME (WMA-NY)*
1325 Ave of the Americas
New York, NY 10019, USA

Ludzik, Steve (Athlete, Hockey Player)
2508 Silvan St
Niagara Falls, ON L2J 4K5, Canada

Luebber, Steve (Athlete, Baseball Player)
3302 Moorhead Dr
Joplin, MO 64804-5323, USA

Luebbers, Larry (Athlete, Baseball Player)
844 Issac Shelby Cir E
Frankfort, KY 40601-8806, USA

Luebbert, Eric (Stylist)
c/o Staff Member *Talent Plus*
1222 Lucas Ave
Suite 300
St. Louis, MO 63103, USA

Luebke, Cory (Athlete, Baseball Player)
2190 Oak St
Maria Stein, OH 45860-9509, USA

Lueck, Bill (Athlete, Football Player)
409 E Bird Ln
Litchfield Park, AZ 85340-4214, USA

Luecken, Rick (Athlete, Baseball Player)
2902 Fontana Dr
Houston, TX 77043-1305, USA

Luetkemeyer, Blaine (Congressman, Politician)
1740 Longworth HOB
Washington, DC 20515, USA

Luft, Joey (Actor)
108 E. Matilija St
Ojai, CA 93023

Luft, Lorna (Actor, Musician)
280 Coldwater Canyon Dr
Beverly Hills, CA 90210, USA

Lugar, Richard (Politician, Senator)
7841 Old Dominion Dr
McLean, VA 22102-2425, USA

Lugavere, Max (Television Host)
c/o Rob Levy *Untitled Entertainment (LA)*
350 S. Beverly Dr #200
Beverly Hills, CA 90212, USA

Lugbill, Jon (Athlete, Olympic Athlete)
American Cance Assn
8810 Wishart Rd
#B232
Richmond, VA 23229-7147, USA

Luger, Lex
52B49 uford Hwy.
Atlanta, GA 30340

Lugner, Richard (Actor)
Lugner Einkaufszentrum
Lugner City Gablenzgasse 5-13
Vienna 1150, Austria

Lugo, Julio (Athlete, Baseball Player)
1555 Gants Cir
Kissimmee, FL 34744-6459, USA

Lugo, Ruddy (Athlete, Baseball Player)
1555 Gants Cir
Kissimmee, FL 34744-6459, USA

Lugosi Jr, Bela
520 N Central Ave #800
Glendale, CA 91203, USA

Luhrmann, Baz (Director, Producer)
c/o Staff Member *Bazmark Inq (AUS)*
PO Box 430
Kings Cross
NSW 2011, AUSTRALIA

Lui, Stephen
10635 Santa Monica Blvd. #130
Los Angeles, CA 90025

luis, isaac (Athlete, Baseball Player)
PO Box 1167
Carolina, PR 00986-1167, USA

Luisi, Caesar (Actor)
c/o Christopher Smith *Paradigm (LA)*
360 N Crescent Dr
North Bldg
Beverly Hills, CA 90210, USA

Luisi, James
22562 Seaver Ct.
Santa Clarita, CA 91350-1389

Lujack, Johnny (Athlete, Football Player, Heisman Trophy Winner)
6321 Crow Valley Dr
Bettendorf, IA 52722-6219, USA

Lujan, Ben Ray (Congressman, Politician)
330 Cannon HOB
Washington, DC 20515, USA

Lujan, Fernando (Actor)
c/o Staff Member *TV Azteca*
Periferico Sur 4121
Colonia Fuentes del Pedregal
DF CP 14141, Mexico

Lujan, Manuel Jr (Politician, Secretary)
Manuel Lujan Agencies
PO Box 3727
Albuquerque, NM 87190-3727, USA

Lukachyk, Rob (Athlete, Baseball Player)
100 High St
Woodbridge, NJ 07095-3018, USA

Lukas, D Wayne (Coach)
5242 katella Ave
#103
Los Alamitos, CA 90720, USA

Lukas, D Wayne (Race Car Driver)
5699 Happy Canyon Rd.
Santa Ynez, CA 93460^9373, USA

Lukas, DWayne (Horse Racer)
1034 Oak Canyon Ln
Glendora, CA 91741-2256, USA

Lukashenko, Aleksandr (President)
President's Office
JK Marks St 38
Minsk 220016, BELARUS

Lukasiewicz, Mark (Athlete, Baseball Player)
8035 Fir Dr
Clay, NY 13041-8646, USA

Lukather, Steve (Musician)
Fitzgerald-Hartley
34 N Palm St
Ventura, CA 93001, USA

Luke (Musician)
Richard Walters
1800 Argyle Ave
#408
Los Angeles, CA 90028, USA

Luke, Derek (Actor)
c/o Lisa Kasteler *WKT Public Relations (WKT-LA)*
9350 Wilshire Blvd
Suite 450
Beverly Hills, CA 90212, USA

Luke, John A Jr (Business Person)
Westvaco Corp
299 Park Ave
New York, NY 10171, USA

Luke, Matt (Athlete, Baseball Player)
5262 Eucalyptus Hill Rd
Yorba Linda, CA 92886-4209, USA

Luke, Steve (Athlete, Football Player)
812 Bluffview Dr
Columbus, OH 43235, USA

Luke, Tommy (Athlete, Football Player)
116 W Shore Dr
Saltillo, MS 38866-5745

Luke, Triandos (Athlete, Football Player)
PO Box 324
Phoenixville, PA 19460-0324, USA

Luken, Tom (Athlete, Football Player)
4708 Virginia Ln
Minneapolis, MN 55424-1763, USA

Lukens, Max L (Business Person)
Baker Hughes Inc
3900 Essex Lane
Houston, TX 77027, USA

Lukens, Susan (Stylist)
5200 Knox Ave
South Minneapolis, MN 55419, USA

Luker, Rebecca (Actor)
c/o Staff Member *WmE2 (WMA-LA)*
1 William Morris Pl
Beverly Hills, CA 90212, USA

Luketic, Robert (Actor)
c/o Paul Nelson *Mosaic Media Group*
9200 W. Sunset Blvd
10th Floor
Los Angeles, CA 90069, USA

Lukin, Matt (Musician)
Legends of 21st Century
7 Trinity Row
Florence, MA 01062, USA

Lukkarinen, Marjut (Skier)
Lohja Ski Team
Lohja, FINLAND

Lukowich, Bernie
833 Gannet Crt
Victoria, BC V9B 6V6, Canada

Lukowich, Bernie (Athlete, Hockey Player)
833 Gannet Crt
Victoria, BC V9B 6V6, Canada

Lukowich, Brad (Athlete, Hockey Player)
2402 Arroyo Grande
Leander, TX 78641-8885

Lukowich, Morris (Athlete, Hockey Player)
212 Scimitar Bay NW
Calgary, AL T3L 1L7, CANADA

Luksa, Chuck (Athlete, Hockey Player)
362 Kirby Cres
Newmarket, ON L3X 1G8, Canada

Lulabel & Scottie
PO Box 171132
Nashville, TN 37217

Lula da Silva, Luis Ignacio (President)
Palacio do Planotto
Praca dos 3 Poderas
Brasilia, DF 70 150, BRAZIL

lulo, Ken (Horse Racer)
165 Prospect St Fl 2
Passaic, NJ 07055-5160, USA

Lulu (Actor, Musician)
CIA
101 Shepherds Bush
Concorde House
London W6 7LP, UNITED KINGDOM (UK)

Lum, Hadrien (Stylist)
c/o Staff Member *Judy Inc*
1 Yorkville Ave
Toronto ON M4W 1L1, Canada

Lum, Mike (Athlete, Baseball Player)
3476 Cochise Dr SE
Atlanta, GA 30339-4324, USA

Luma, James (General)
28303 Sound View Dr S Aot 108
Des Moines, WA 98198-8266, USA

Lumbly, Carl (Actor)
c/o Karen Forman *Domain Talent*
9229 Sunset Boulevard
Suite 710
Los Angeles, CA 90069, USA

Lumenti, Ralph (Athlete, Baseball Player)
9 Tomaso Rd
Milford, MA 01757-2224, USA

Lumley, Dave (Athlete, Hockey Player)
PO Box 610
Murfreesboro, AR 71958-0610

Lumley, Joanna (Actor)
c/o Staff Member *Conway van Gelder*
8-12 Broadwick St
London W1F 8HW, UK

Lumley, John L (Physicist)
743 Snyder Hill Road
Ithaca, NY 14850, USA

Lumme, Jyrki (Athlete, Hockey Player)
40 Bay St
Toronto, ON M5J 2K2, Canada

Lumpe, Jerry (Athlete, Baseball Player)
732 S Pearson Dr
Springfield, MO 65809-1613, USA

Lumpkin, Elgin (Ginuwine) (Musician)
c/o Michael Irving *Emancipated Talent*
215 Clinton St
Brooklyn, NY 11201, USA

Lumpkin, Sean (Athlete, Football Player)
4708 Virginia Ln
Minneapolis, MN 55424-1763, USA

Lumpp, Ray (Athlete, Basketball Player, Olympic Athlete)
21 Hewlett Dr
East Williston, NY 11596-2003, USA

Lumsden, David J
Melton House
Soham, Cambridgeshire, UNITED KINGDOM (UK)

Luna, Barbara (Actor)
18026 Rodarte Way
Encino, CA 91316, USA

Luna, Diego (Actor)
c/o Brandon Liebman *WME (LA)*
9601 Wilshire Blvd Fl 3
Beverly Hills, CA 90210, USA

Luna-Hill, Betty (Baseball Player)
19887 Red Feather Rd
Apple Valley, CA 92307-5514, USA

Lunar, Fernando (Athlete, Baseball Player)
3125 Zuni Pl
Alamogordo, NM 88310-4029, USA

Lunatics, St (Musician)
c/o Staff Member *Team Lunatics (MO)*
4246 Forest Park Avenue
Suite 2C
St Louis, MO 63108, USA

Lund, Don (Athlete, Baseball Player)
1200 Earhart Rd
Ann Arbor, MI 48105-2768, USA

Lund, Gordy (Athlete, Baseball Player)
1602 S Harvard Ave
Arlington Heights, IL 60005-3517, USA

Lund, Katia (Director)
c/o Sandra Lucchesi *Gersh (LA)*
9465 Wilshire Blvd
Suite 600
Beverly Hills, CA 90212, USA

Lund, Larry (Athlete, Hockey Player)
101-4593 Lakeside Rd
Penticton, BC V2A 8W4, Canada

Lund, Pennti
408-165 Court St N
Thunder Bay, ON P7A 7V1, Canada

Lunday, James (Actor)
c/o Staff Member *The Learning Channel (TLC)*
10100 Santa Monica Blvd
Suite 1500
Los Angeles, CA 90067, USA

Lunday, Kenneth (Athlete, Football Player)
1419 W Locust St
Durant, OK 74701-3458, USA

Lundberg, Anders (Misc)
Goteberg University
Physiology Dept
Box 33033
Goteborg 40 033, SWEDEN

Lundberg, Brian (Athlete, Hockey Player)
7284 Walton
Lake Cowichan, BC VOR 2GO, Canada

Lunde, Len (Athlete, Hockey Player)
15416 74 Ave NW
Edmonton, AB TSR 2Y4, Canada

Lundeen, George (Artist)
328 E 4th St
Loveland, CO 80537, USA

Lunden, Joan (Correspondent, Producer)
c/o Bill Stankey *Westport Entertainment Associates*
1700 Post Rd
Suite C-15
Fairfield, CT 06824, USA

Lundgren, Dolph (Actor)
c/o Craig Baumgarten *Baumgarten Management*
11925 Wilshire Blvd
Suite 310
Los Angeles, CA 90025, USA

Lundgren, Terry (Business Person)
Federated Department Stores
151 W 34th St
New York, NY 10001, USA

Lundholm, Bengt (Athlete, Hockey Player)
Ovre Gruvriset
Falun 79161, Sweden

Lundholm, Mark (Actor, Comedian)
c/o Staff Member *WmE2 (WMA-LA)*
1 William Morris Pl
Beverly Hills, CA 90212, USA

Lundi, Monika
Viktoriastr. 24
Munich, GERMANY D-80803

Lundquist, Dave (Athlete, Baseball Player)
714 12th Ave NE
Hickory, NC 28601-2707, USA

Lundquist, David (Athlete, Baseball Player)
Hickory Crawdads
P.O. Box 1268
Attn: Coaching Staff
Hickory, NC 28603, USA

Lundquist, Gus Briggen (Aviator)
5100 john D Ryan Blvd Apt 616
San Antonio, TX 78245-3535, USA

Lundquist, Steve (Athlete, Olympic Athlete, Swimmer)
246 Northwind Dr
Stockbridge, GA 30281-6216, USA

Lundquist, Verne (Sportscaster)
NBC-TV
1710 Natches Way
Steamboat Springs, CO 80487-9045, USA

Lundqvist, Alex (Model)
c/o Staff Member *Boss Models*
80 8th Ave
New York, NY 10011-5126, USA

Lundqvist, Henrik (Athlete, Hockey Player)
225 W 83rd St #20G
New York, NY 10024-4952, USA

Lundrigan, Joe
9427 67 ave Nw
Edmonton, AB T6E 0N6, Canada

Lundstedt, Tom (Athlete, Baseball Player)
PO Box 409
^raim, WI 54211-0409, USA

Lundstrom, Tord (Athlete, Hockey Player)
Bryn as Bygg_nads AB
Gavle 80133, Sweden

Lundy, Carmen (Musician)
Abby Hoffer
223 1/2 E 48th St
New York, NY 10017, USA

Lundy, Jessica (Actor)
c/o Staff Member *Metropolitan (MTA)*
4526 Wilshire Blvd
Los Angeles, CA 90010, USA

Lundy, Victor A (Architect)
Victor A Lundy Assoc
701 Mulberry Lane
Bellaire, TX 77401, USA

Luner, Jaime (Actor)
Martin Hurwitz
427 N Canon Dr
#215
Beverly Hills, CA 90210, USA

Luner, Jamie (Actor)
c/o Martin Berneman *Precision Entertainment*
6338 Wilshire Blvd
Los Angeles, CA 90048, USA

Lunghi, Cherie (Actor)
Yakety Yak
8A Bloomsbury Square
London WC1A 2NE, UNITED KINGDOM

Lunka, Zoltan (Boxer)
Weinheimer Str 2
Schriesheim 69198, GERMANY

Lunke, Hilary (Athlete, Golfer)
11701 Broad Oaks Dr
Austin, TX 78759, USA

Lunn, Bob (Athlete, Golfer)
P.O. Box 1495
Woodbridge, CA 95258-1495, USA

Lunney, Bryan (Scientist)
3250 Mossy Elm Ct
Houston, TX 77059-3228, USA

Lunney, Glenn (Scientist)
United Space Alliance
1150 Gemini Dr
Houston, TX 77058, USA

Lunney, Glynn (Scientist)
1902 Orchard Country Ln
Houston, TX 77062-2300, USA

Lunsford, Scott (Actor)
c/o Robert Yaffee *Infinity Management*
7923 Hollywood Blvd
Los Angeles, CA 90046, USA

Lunsford, Stephen (Actor)
c/o Bonnie Liedtke *Principato/Young Management*
9465 Wilshire Blvd
Suite 430
Beverly Hills, CA 90212, USA

Lunsford, Trey (Athlete, Baseball Player)
3955 Nail Rd
Southaven, MS 38672-6739, USA

Luongo, Chris (Athlete, Hockey Player)
103 Arabian Dr
Madison, AL 35758-6634, USA

Luongo, Roberto (Athlete, Hockey Player)
7280 Lemon Grass Dr
Parkland, FL 33076-3950, USA

Lupaschek, Ross (Athlete, Hockey Player)
11347164 Ave NW
Edmonton, AB TSX 3W1, Canada

Lupberger, Edwin A (Business Person)
Entergy Corp
10055 Grogans Mill Road
#5A
The Woodlands, TX 77380, USA

Lupica, Mike (Writer)
87 Bald Hill Rd
New Canaan, CT 06840-2404, USA

Lupien, Gilles (Athlete, Hockey Player)
Sport Prospects Inc 77 Rue de Bleury
Rosemere, QC J7A 4L9, Canada

Luplow, Al (Baseball Player)
4250 Lakecress Dr E
Saginaw, MI 48603-1687, USA

Luplow, Al (Athlete, Baseball Player)
4250 Lakecress Dr E
Saginaw, MI 48603, USA

Lupo, Benedetto (Musician)
Gerhild Baron Mgmt
Dombacher Str 41/III/3
Vienna 1170, AUSTRIA

Lupo, Frank (Producer, Writer)
c/o Stephen Marks *Evolution Entertainment (LA)*
901 N Highland Ave
Los Angeles, CA 90038, USA

LuPone, Patti (Actor, Musician)
c/o Gary Gersh *Innovative Artists (NY)*
235 Park Ave S
7th Floor
New York, NY 10003, USA

Luppi, Daniele (Composer, Musician)
c/o Staff Member *Greenspan Artist Management*
8760 W Sunset Blvd
West Hollywood, CA 90069, USA

Lupu, Radu (Musician)
Terry Harrison Mgmt
3 Clarendon Court
Charlbury, Oxon OX7 3PS, UNITED KINGDOM (UK)

Lupul, Jaffrey (Athlete, Hockey Player)
600 1/2 36th St
New_Qort Beach, CA 92663-6203, USA

Lupus, Peter (Actor)
2401 S 24th St
#110
Phoenix, AZ 85034, USA

Lurie, Alison (Writer)
Cornell University 159 Sapsucker Woods Rd
Ithaca, NY 14850-1923, USA

Lurie, Alison (Writer)
Cornell University
English Dept
Ithaca, NY 14850, USA

Lurie, Jeffrey (Business Person, Football Executive)
312 Llanfair Rd
Wynnewood, PA 19096-1216, USA

Lurie, Ranan R (Cartoonist, Editor)
Cartoonnews International
PO Box 698
Greenwich, CT 06836, USA

Lurie, Rod (Director)
c/o Staff Member *WME (LA)*
9601 Wilshire Blvd Fl 3
Beverly Hills, CA 90210, USA

Lurtsema, Bob (Athlete, Football Player)
16920 Judicial Rd
Lakeville, MN 55044, USA

Lusader, Scott (Athlete, Baseball Player)
4169 Bold Mdws
Oakland Township, MI 48306-4701, USA

Lusby, Vaughn (Athlete, Football Player)
4011 N Belt Line Rd Apt 928
Irving, TX 75038-8419, USA

Luscinski, Jim (Athlete, Football Player)
49 Pleasant St
Pembroke, MA 02359-2302, USA

Luse, Bernadette (Athlete, Golfer)
2528 Reading Dr
Orlando, FL 32804, USA

Lush, Mike (Athlete, Football Player)
910 Rebecca Ln
Crefield, PA 18069, USA

Lusha, Masiela (Actor, Producer)
Illuminary Films
7046 Hollywood Blvd.
Los Angeles, CA 90028, USA

Lusis, Janis (Athlete, Track Athlete)
Vesetas 8-3
Riga, 1013, LATVIA

Lusk, Herbert (Athlete, Football Player)
71 Palomar Real
Campbell, CA 95008, USA

Lusk, Jacob (Musician)
c/o Simon Fuller *XIX Entertainment*
35-37 Parkgate Rd
32/33 Ransomes Dock
London SW11 4NP, UNITED KINGDOM (UK)

Lustig, Aaron (Actor)
c/o Staff Member *House of Representatives, The*
1434 6th St
Suite 1
Santa Monica, CA 90401, USA

Lustig, William (Producer)
15016 Marble Dr
Sherman Oaks, CA 91403-4521, USA

Lustiger, Jean-Marie Cardinal (Religious Leader)
Maison Dioceine
8 Rue de la Ville-l'Eveque
Paris 75008, FRANCE

Lusztig, George (Mathematician)
106 Grant Ave
Newton, MA 02459, USA

Lutes, Eric (Actor)
c/o Kate Edwards *Grand View Management*
578 Washington Blvd #688
Marina del Rey, CA 90292, USA

Luther, Bobbi Sue (Actor, Model)
c/o Staff Member *Urge Artists*
9107 Wilshire Blvd. #500
Beverly Hills, CA 90210, USA

Luther, Ed (Athlete, Football Player)
30486 Le Port
Laguna Niguel, CA 92677, USA

Luther, Tina (Stylist)
580 Andrieux St
Sonoma, CA 95476-7327, USA

Lutt, Jorg-UweProf
Mensing-Str 17
Flensburg D-24937, GERMANY

Luttig, J Michael (Judge)
US Appeals Court
200 S Washington St
Alexandria, VA 22314, USA

Luttrell, Rachel (Actor)
c/o Staff Member *Silver Massetti & Szatmary (SMS) Talent Inc*
8383 Wilshire Blvd
Suite 230
Beverly Hills, CA 90211, USA

Lutui, Taitusi "Deuce" (Athlete, Football Player)
4514 E Mountain Sage Dr
Phoenix, AZ 85044-6086, USA

Lutz, Bob (Tennis Player)
101 Via Ensueno
San Clemente, CA 92672, USA

Lutz, Joleen (Actor)
H David Moss
733 Seward St
#PH
Los Angeles, CA 90038, USA

Lutz, Kellan (Actor)
c/o Nicole Perna *Baker Winokur Ryder Public Relations (BWR-LA)*
9100 Wilshire Blvd
Suite 500, West Tower
Beverly Hills, CA 90212, USA

Lutz, Mark (Actor)
c/o Nancy LeFeaver *LeFeaver Talent Management Ltd*
2 College St #202
Toronto ON M5G 1K3, CANADA

Lutz, Robert A (Business Person)
3600 Green Court
#720
Ann Arbor, MI 48105, USA

Lutz, Robin (Stylist)
11409 Frances Green Dr
North Potomac, MD 20878, USA

Luu, Chan (Designer)
818 South Broadway
6th Floor
Los Angeles, CA 90014, USA

Luuloa, Keith (Athlete, Baseball Player)
30905 Young Dove St
Menifee, CA 92584-8358, USA

LuValle, James (Athlete, Track Athlete)
1174 Los Altos Ave
#160
Los Altos, CA 94022, USA

Luvana, Carmen (Adult Film Star)
c/o Adam & Eve Productions
9445 DeSoto Ave
Chatsworth, CA 91311, USA

Luxon, Benjamin M (Opera Singer)
Mazet
Relubbus Lane
Saint Hillary
Penzance, Cornwall TR20 9DS, UNITED KINGDOM (UK)

Luyties, Ricci (Athlete, Olympic Athlete, Volleyball Player)
University of California - San Diego
2215 Hartford St San
Diego, CA 92110-2336, USA

Lu Yu, Chen (Talk Show Host, Television Host)
c/o Staff Member *Phoenix TV / HongKong Shenzhen*
No. 2-6 Dai King St
Tai Po Industrial Estate
Tai Po, N. T. Hong Kong

Luz, Franc
606 N. Larchmont Blvd. #309
Los Angeles, CA 90004

Luzhkov, Yuri M (Politician)
Government of Moscow
Tverskaya Str 13
Moscow 103032, RUSSIA

Luzi, Mario (Writer)
Via Belle Riva 20
Florence 50136, ITALY

Luzinski, Greg (Athlete, Baseball Player)
25680 Streamlet Ct
Bonita Springs, FL 34135-7829, USA

Luzinski, Ryan (Athlete, Baseball Player)
25680 Streamlet Ct
Bonita Springs, FL 34135, USA

Ivey, James (Cartoonist)
5840 Dahlia Dr
Apt 7
Orlando, FL 32807-3251, USA

Iwamura, Akinori (Athlete, Baseball Player)
623 Saxony Blvd
saint petersburg, FL 33716-1297, USA

L. Watt, Melvin (Congressman, Politician)
2304 Rayburn HOB
Washington, DC 20515, USA

Lyakhov, Vladimir A (Cosmonaut)
Potcha Kosmonavtov
Moskovskoi Oblasti
Syvisdny, Goroduk 141160, RUSSIA

Lyden, Mitch (Athlete, Baseball Player)
6055 NW 72nd Ct
Parkland, FL 33067-2441, USA

Lydman, Toni (Athlete, Hockey Player)
6035 Corinne Ln
Clarence Center, NY 14032-9510, USA

Lydon, James (Jimmy) (Actor)
3538 Lomacitas Lane
Bonita, CA 91902, USA

Lydon, John (Johnny Rotten) (Musician)
31962 Pacific Coast Highway
Malibu, CA 90265, USA

Lydon, Malcolm (Astronaut)
684 E Pelham Rd NE
Atlanta, GA 30324-5202, USA

Lydy, Scott (Athlete, Baseball Player)
4278 S Leoma Ln
Chandler, AZ 85249-4782, USA

Lye, Mark (Athlete, Golfer)
4484 Wayside Dr
Naples, FL 34119, USA

Lyfe (Musician)
c/o Staff Member *Sony/RCA Records*
550 Madison Ave
New York, NY 10022, USA

Lyght, Todd (Athlete, Football Player)
1598 Martingale St
Eugene, OR 97401-6964, USA

Lyle, Garry (Athlete, Football Player)
222 Beach Dr NE
Saint Petersburg, FL 33701, USA

Lyle, George (Athlete, Hockey Player)
33754 N 69th St
Scottsdale, AZ 85266-7014, USA

Lyle, Jarrod (Athlete, Golfer)
c/o Jim Lehrman *SFX Golf*
36855 W Main St Ste 200
Purcellville, VA 20132, USA

Lyle, Kami (Musician, Songwriter, Writer)
DS Mgmt
2814 12th Ave S
#202
Nashville, TN 37204, USA

Lyle, Keith (Athlete, Football Player)
9615 Maypan Pl
Seminole, FL 33777-4906, USA

Lyle, Sandy (Athlete, Golfer)
4905 Duck Creek Ln
Ponte Vedra Beach, FL 32082-3023, USA

Lyle, Sparky (Athlete, Baseball Player)
17 Signal Hill Dr
Voorhees, NJ 08043-2948, USA

Lyles, A C
2115 Linda Flora
Los Angeles, CA 90024, USA

Lyles, Leonard (Athlete, Football Player)
2315 Cross Hill Rd
Louisville, KY 40206, USA

Lyles, Lester (Athlete, Football Player)
6315 14th St NW
Washington, DC 20011, USA

Lyles, Lester L (Les) (General)
Commander Air Material Command
Wright-Patterson Air Force Base,
OH 45433, USA

Lyles, Robert (Athlete, Football Player)
1012 Merritt Rd Apt C
West Point, NY 10996-1347, USA

Lyman, Arthur
508 Kaanini Circle
Hilo, HI 96720

Lyman, Dorothy
c/o Staff Member *Stone Manners Salners Agency (LA)*
9911 W Pico Blvd Ste 1400
Los Angeles, CA 90035, USA

Lyman, Dustin (Athlete, Football Player)
10529 Dacre Pl
Lone Tree, CO 80124-9788

Lymon, Frankie
1650 Broadway #508
New York, NY 10019

Lympany, Moura (Musician)
Transart
8 Bristol Gardens
London W9 2JG, UNITED KINGDOM (UK)

Lyn, Mai
190 W. Kern St.
McFarland, CA 93250

Lynch, Allen J (General)
438 Belie Plaine Ave
Gurnee, IL 60031-2902, USA

Lynch, Claire
1 Camp St
Cambridge, MA 02140

Lynch, Cynthia (Athlete, Wrestler)
4205 Bridgepath Pl
Louisville, KY 40245-1971, USA

Lynch, Dan (Cartoonist, Editor)
Fort Wayne-Journal-Gazette
Editorial Dept
600 W Main St
Fort Wayne, IN 46802, USA

Lynch, David (Director)
David Lynch Foundation
654 Madison Ave
Suite 806
New York, NY 10065, USA

Lynch, Dustin (Musician)
c/o Staff Member *WmE2 (WMA-TN)*
1600 Division St
Suite 300
Nashville, TN 37203, USA

Lynch, Ed (Athlete, Baseball Player)
7832 E Parkview Ln
Scottsdale, AZ 85255-2704, USA

Lynch, Edele (Musician)
Clintons
55 Drury Lane
Covent Garden
London WC2B 5SQ, UNITED KINGDOM (UK)

Lynch, Evanna (Actor)
c/o Ricky Rollins *Schumacher Management*
1122 San Vicente Blvd.
Santa Monica, CA 90402, USA

Lynch, Fran (Athlete, Football Player)
2553 Lake Vista Dr
Broomfield, CO 80023-4528, USA

Lynch, George (Basketball Player)
5930 Royal Ln
Dallas, TX 75230-3849, USA

Lynch, Holly (Actor)
c/o Scott Karp *Crystal Sky Pictures*
10203 Santa Monica Blvd
5th Floor
Los Angeles, CA 90067, USA

Lynch, Jack (Athlete, Hockey Player)
23 Cynthia Crt
Barrie, ON L4M 2X3, Canada

Lynch, Jair (Athlete, Gymnast, Olympic Athlete)
9207 Three Oaks Dr
Silver Spring, MD 20901-3363, USA

Lynch, James E (Jim) (Athlete, Football Player)
1009 W 67th St
Kansas City, MO 64113, USA

Lynch, Jane (Actor)
8610 Lookout Mountain Ave
Los Angeles, CA 90046, USA

Lynch, Jennifer (Director, Producer)
1894 El Cerrito Place
Los Angeles, CA 90068, USA

Lynch, Jessica (Beauty Pageant Winner)
c/o Staff Member *Miss New York City Scholarship Organization*
35 East 19th Street
2nd Floor
New York, NY 10003, USA

Lynch, Jessica (War Hero)
c/o Gregory Lynch
RR #1
Palestine, WV 26160-9801, USA

Lynch, John (Football Player)
c/o Staff Member *Denver Broncos*
13655 E Broncos Pkwy
Englewood, CO 80112, USA

Lynch, John (Governor)
Office of the Governor, State House
107 N Main St
Concord, NH 03301, USA

Lynch, John Carroll (Actor)
c/o James Suskin *James Suskin Management*
2 Charlton St Ste 5K
New York, NY 10014, USA

Lynch, Keavy (Musician)
Clintons
55 Drury Lane
Covent Garden
London WC2B 5SQ, UNITED KINGDOM (UK)

Lynch, Kelly (Actor, Model)
c/o Staff Member *Crestview Entertainment*
521 Montana Ave
Santa Monica, CA 90403, USA

Lynch, Lorenzo (Athlete, Football Player)
864 Bentwater Pkwy
Cedar Hill, TX, USA

Lynch, Marshawn (Athlete, Football Player)
10650 NE 9th Pl Unit 2022
Bellevue, WA 98004-5077, USA

Lynch, Peg
304 11th St Box 339
Becket, MA 01223

Lynch, Peter S (Financier)
27 State St
Boston, MA 02109, USA

Lynch, Richard (Actor)
Richard Sindell
1910 Holmby Ave
#1
Los Angeles, CA 90025, USA

Lynch, Ross (Actor)
c/o Nils Larsen *Principato/Young Management*
9465 Wilshire Blvd
Suite 430
Beverly Hills, CA 90212, USA

Lynch, Sandra L (Judge)
US Appeals Court
McCormack Federal Building
Boston, MA 02109, USA

Lynch, Shane (Musician)
Carol Assoc-War Mgmt
Bushy Park Road
57 Meadowbank
Dublin, IRELAND

Lynch, Stephen (Comedian)
c/o Staff Member *WmE2 (WMA-LA)*
1 William Morris Pl
Beverly Hills, CA 90212, USA

Lynch, Thomas C (Admiral)
751 Eagle Farm Road
Villanova, PA 19085-2035, USA

Lynche, Michael (Musician)
c/o Simon Fuller *XIX Entertainment*
35-37 Parkgate Rd
32/33 Ransomes Dock
London SW11 4NP, UNITED KINGDOM (UK)

Lynde, Janice (Actor)
c/o David Moore *Moore Artist's Management*
310 Washington Blvd
Ste. 117
Marina Del Rey, CA 90292, USA

Lynden-Bell, Donald (Astronomer)
Institute of Astronomy
MAdingley Road
Cambridge CB3 0HA, UNITED KINGDOM (UK)

Lynden-Bell, Donald (Scientist)
University of Cambridge Madingley Road
Astronomy Dept
Cambridge, Englanc CB3 OHA, UK

Lyndon, Frank (Musician)
Paramount Entertainment
PO Box 12
Far Hills, NJ 07931, USA

Lynds, Roger (Astronomer)
Kitt Peak National Observatory
Tucson, AZ 85726, USA

Lyne, Adrian
9876 Beverly Grove Dr.
Beverly Hills, CA 90210

Lynette, Lady (Actor)
11979 Rochester Ave #6
Los Angeles, CA 90025, USA

Lyngstad, Anni-Frida (Musician, Songwriter, Writer)
Mono Music
Sodra Brobaeken 41A
Skeppsholmen
Stockholm 111 49, Sweden

Lynley, Carol (Actor)
Don gerler
3349 Cahuenga Blvd
#1
Los Angeles, CA 90068, USA

Lynn, Anthony (Athlete, Football Player)
1508 Brook Ln
Celina, TX 75009, USA

Lynn, Bari (Stylist)
c/o Staff Member *Mel Bryant Management*
611 Broadway #623
New York, NY 10012

Lynn, Betty (Actor)
The Surry Arts Council
P.O. Box 141
218 Rockford St
Mount Airy, NC 27030, USA

Lynn, Cheryl (Actor, Musician)
c/o Jeff Epstein *Universal Attractions*
135 W 26th St
12 Floor
New York, NY 10001, USA

Lynn, Eleanor (Actor)
136 Lonford Dr S
San Francisco, CA 94080, USA

Lynn, Fred (Athlete, Baseball Player)
7336 El Fuerte St
Carlsbad, CA 92009-6409, USA

Lynn, Greg (Architect)
University of California
Architecture School
Los Angeles, CA 90024, USA

Lynn, Janet (Athlete, Olympic Athlete, Speed Skater)
4215 Marsh Ave
Rockford, IL 61114-6143, USA

Lynn, Johnnie (Athlete, Football Player)
5 Wood Valley Ct
Reisterstown, MD 21136, USA

Lynn, Johnny (Athlete, Football Player)
238 Hidden Or
Blackwood, NJ 08012-4432, USA

Lynn, Jonathan (Director)
c/o Mike Marcus *Echo Lake Productions*
421 S Beverly Dr Fl 8
Beverly Hills, CA 90212, USA

Lynn, Keith (Race Car Driver)
Schnitz Racing
222 N. 3rd St.
Decatur, IN 46733, USA

Lynn, Loretta (Musician, Songwriter)
44 Hurricane Mills Rd
Hurricane Mills, TN 37078, USA

Lynn, Meredith Scott (Actor)
Rigberg Roberts Rugolo
1180 S Beverly Dr
#601
Los Angeles, CA 90035, USA

Lynn, Salomon Janet (Figure Skater)
PO Box 1026
Haymarket, VA 20168, USA

Lynn, Therese
PO Box 6057
Hoboken, NJ 07030

Lynn, Vera (Actor, Musician)
Ditchling, Sussex, UNITED KINGDOM (UK)

Lynn Allen, Ginger (Adult Film Star)
5965 Nora Lynn Dr
Woodland Hills, CA 91367, USA

Lynn Chadwick, Aimee (Actor)
c/o Melanie Sharp *Sharp Talent*
117 N Orlando Ave
Los Angeles, CA 90048, USA

Lynne, Bobbe
22732 Foothill Rd. #6
Hayward, CA 94541

Lynne, Gillian (Choreographer, Dancer)
Lean-2 Productions
18 Rutland St
Knightsbridge
London SW7 1EF, UNITED KINGDOM (UK)

Lynne, Gloria (Musician)
Subrena Artists
330 W 56th St
#18M
New York, NY 10019, USA

Lynne, Shelby (Musician, Songwriter, Writer)
c/o Staff Member *WmE2 (WMA-LA)*
1 William Morris Pl
Beverly Hills, CA 90212, USA

Lynskey, Melanie (Actor)
c/o Susan Smith *Susan Smith Company, The*
1344 N Wetherly Dr
Los Angeles, CA 90069-1817, USA

Lynyrd Skynyrd (Music Group)
c/o Staff Member *Vector Management*
P.O. Box 120479
Nashville, TN 37212, USA

Lyon, Brandon (Athlete, Baseball Player)
526 W 8thS
Preston, ID 83263-1459, USA

Lyon, Sue (Actor)
1244 N Havenhurst Dr
West Hollywood, CA 90046, USA

Lyon, William (Business Person, General)
William Lyon Co
4490 Von Karman Ave
Newport Beach, CA 92660, USA

Lyonne, Natasha (Actor, Producer)
c/o Tammy Rosen *Sanders Armstrong Caserta*
425 N Robertson Blvd
Los Angeles, CA 90048, USA

Lyons, Barry (Athlete, Baseball Player)
1079 Frank P Corso St
Biloxi, MS 39530-1922, USA

Lyons, Bill (Athlete, Baseball Player)
811 Tomahawk
Heyworth, IL 61745-9309, USA

Lyons, Brooke (Actor)
c/o Staff Member *Burstein Company, The*
15304 Sunset Blvd
suite 208
Pacific Palisades, CA 90272, USA

Lyons, Curt (Athlete, Baseball Player)
124 Virginia Dr
Richmond, KY 40475-8631, USA

Lyons, David (Actor)
c/o Annabelle Sheehan *RGM Artist Group*
64-76 Kippax St
Level 2, Suite 202 & 206
Surry Hills, NSW 2010, Australia

Lyons, Elena (Actor)
c/o Brian McCabe *Venture IAB*
3211 Cahuenga Blvd W Ste 104
Los Angeles, CA 90068, USA

Lyons, James A Jr (Admiral)
9481 Piney Mountain Road
Warrenton, VA 20186, USA

Lyons, Jeffrey (Journalist)
205 W 57th St Apt 5DD
New York, NY 10019-2112, USA

Lyons, Jeffrey
205 W. 57th St.
New York, NY 10019

Lyons, Lamar (Athlete, Football Player)
3726 Bluff Pl
San Pedro, CA 90731, USA

Lyons, Marty (Athlete, Football Player)
8 White Pine Ct
Smithtown, NY 11787, USA

Lyons, Mitchell W (Mitch) (Athlete,
Football Player)
8344 Woodcrest Dr NE
Rockford, MI 49341, USA

Lyons, Phyllis
9171 Wilshire Blvd. #441
Beverly Hills, CA 90210

Lyons, Robert F (Actor)
1801 Ave of Stars
#1250
Los Angeles, CA 90067, USA

Lyons, Steve (Athlete, Baseball Player)
JD Legends Promotions
3012nd St
Hermosa Beach, CA 90254-4662, USA

Lyons, Thomas L (Athlete, Football Player)
2814 Drummond Pt SE
Atlanta, GA 30339, USA

Lysacek, Evan (Figure Skater)
Toyota Sports Center
555 North Nash Street
El Segundo, CA 90245, USA

Lysander, Rick (Athlete, Baseball Player)
12667 Gaillon Ct
San Diego, CA 92128-6179, USA

Lysiak, Tom (Athlete, Hockey Player)
1050 Cedar Grove Rd
Buckhead, GA 30625, USA

Lyst, John H (Editor)
Indianopolis Star
Editorial Dept
307 N Pennsylvania
Indianapolis, IN 46204, USA

Lythgoe, Nigel (Producer)
c/o Staff Member 19 Entertainment
33/32 Ransomes Dock
35-37 Parkgate Rd
London SW11 4NP, UK

Lytle, Jason
c/o Staff Member Paradigm (Monterey)
404 W Franklin St
Monterey, CA 93940, USA

Lytle, Matt (Athlete, Football Player)
4602 Irish Creek Rd
Bernville, PA 19506, USA

Lytle, Roland (Athlete, Football Player)
902 Press St
Houston, TX 77020-8646, USA

Lyttle, Jim (Athlete, Baseball Player)
751 Camino Lakes Cir
Boca Raton, FL 33486-6961, USA

Lyttle, Kevin (Musician)
c/o Michael (Mike) Esterman
Esterman.Com, LLC
Prefers to be contacted via email
MD, USA

Lytton, Louisa (Actor)
Milton Keynes Theatre
Marlborough Gate
Central Milton Keynes MK9 3NZ, United
Kingdom

Lyubimov, Alexey B (Musician)
Klimentovskiy Per 9
#12
Moscow, RUSSIA

Lyubimov, Yuri P (Actor, Director)
Tanganka Theater
Chkalova Str 76
Moscow, RUSSIA

Lyubshin, Stanislav A (Actor)
Vernadskogo Prosp 123
#171
Moscow 117571, RUSSIA

Izauierdo, Hansel (Athlete, Baseball
Player)
10003 NW 9th Street Cir Apt 9-17
Miami, FL 33172-5181, USA

Izturis, Cesar (Athlete, Baseball Player)
7901 Hispanola Ave Aot 607
North Bay Village, FL 33141-4153, USA

M, Banumathi (Actor, Bollywood)
15 Poes Road
4th Street
Chennai, TN 600018, INDIA

M2M (Music Group)
c/o Staff Member Creative Artists Agency
(CAA-LA)
2000 Ave Of The Stars
Los Angeles, CA 90067, USA

Ma, Tzi (Actor)
Greene & Associates
526 North Larchmont Blvd
#201
Los Angeles, CA 90004

Ma, Yo-Yo (Musician)
54 Highland St
Cambridge, MA 02138, USA

Maarleveld, John (Athlete, Football
Player)
42 Carlton Pl
Rutherford, NJ 07070, USA

Maas, Alex
6962 Wildlife
Malibu, CA 90265-4309

Maas, Bill (Athlete, Football Player)
653 NE Shoreline Dr
Lees Summit, MO 64064, USA

Maas, Kevin (Athlete, Baseball Player)
17672 Hillside Ct
Castro Valley, CA 94546-1403, USA

Maas, William T (Bill) (Athlete, Football
Player)
P.O. Box 2175
Lees Summit, MO 64063, USA

Maathai, Wangari (Activist)
Green Belt Movement
PO Box 67545
Nairobi, KENYA

Mabe, Manabu (Artist)
Rua das Canjeranas 321
Jabaquara
Sao Paulo, SP, BRAZIL

Mabeus, Chris (Athlete, Baseball Player)
151 Shady Ln
Soldotna, AK 99669-7519, USA

Mabius, Eric (Actor)
c/o Geordie Frey GEF Entertainment
122 N Clark Dr
Suite 401
Los Angeles, CA 90048, USA

Mably, Luke (Actor)
c/o Stephanie Ritz WME (LA)
9601 Wilshire Blvd Fl 3
Beverly Hills, CA 90210, USA

Mabon, Lee (Athlete, Baseball Player)
2084 Vollintine Ave
Memphis, TN 38107, USA

Mabra, Ron (Athlete, Football Player)
155 Thornton Ct
Fayetteville, GA 30214, USA

Mabrey, Sunny (Actor)
c/o Chris Schmidt Paradigm (LA)
360 N Crescent Dr
North Bldg
Beverly Hills, CA 90210, USA

Mabrey, Vicki (Correspondent, Journalist)
c/o Staff Member Nightline
1717 DeSales St NW
Washington, DC 20036-4401, USA

Mabry, John (Athlete, Baseball Player)
715 Bellerive Manor Dr
Saint Louis, MO 63141, USA

Mabus, Raymond (Politician)
325 N Pitt St
Alexandria, VA 22314, USA

Mac, Fleetwood (Music Group)
c/o Staff Member Agency for the
Performing Arts (APA-LA)
405 S Beverly Dr
Suite 500
Beverly Hills, CA 90212-4425, USA

Macadam, AL (Athlete, Hockey Player)
PO Box 232
Morell, PE COA ISO, Canada

MacAfee Sr, Ken (Athlete, Football Player)
26 W Elm Ter
Brockton, MA 02301, USA

Macaluso, mike (Basketball Player)
1054 Cypress Way
Castle Rock, CO 80108-3465, USA

Macapagal-Arroyo, Gloria (President)
Malacanang Palace
JP Laurel St
Metro Manila 100, PHILIPPINES

MacArthur, Ellen (World Record Holder)
Offshore Challenges Events
Whitegates
Arctic Rd
Cowes, Isle of Wight PO31 7PG, UNITED
KINGDOM

MacArthur, Robb (Reality TV Star)
c/o Staff Member Boy Meets Boy
299 Queen Street West
Toronto ON M5V 2Z5, Canada

Macat, Julio G (Cinematographer)
Gersh Agency
232 N Canon Dr
Beverly Hills, CA 90210, USA

MacAvoy, Paul W (Economist)
6 Mechanic St
Woodstock, VT 05091, USA

MacBeth, Lois
4095 Athenia Way
Los Angeles, CA 90043

Macc, Willie (Actor)
Charles Belk Management
c/o Charles Belk
8939 S Sepulveda Blvd 110-240
Los Angeles, CA 90045, USA

Maccarone, Sam (Director)
c/o David Krintzman Morris, Yorn,
Barnes, Levine, Krintzman, Rubenstein
and Kohner
2000 Ave of the Stars
3rd Floor, North Tower
Los Angeles, CA 90067, USA

Macchio, Ralph (Actor)
c/o Rob Levy Untitled Entertainment (LA)
350 S. Beverly Dr #200
Beverly Hills, CA 90212, USA

MacCormac, Richard C (Architect)
9 Heneage St
London E1 5LJ, UNITED KINGDOM (UK)

Maccormack, Frank (Athlete, Baseball
Player)
2 Schmidts Pl
Secaucus, NJ 07094-4110, USA

MacCormack, Jean F (Educator)
University of Massachusetts
President's Office
Boston, MA 02125, USA

MacCready, Paul B (Engineer)
AeroVironment Inc
222 E Huntlington Dr
Monrovia, CA 91016, USA

Macdermid, Paul (Athlete, Hockey Player)
Owen Sound Attack 1900 3rd Ave E
Attn: Owners Office
Owen Sound, ON N4K 2M6, Canada

MacDermid, Paul (Athlete, Hockey
Player)
81 Lakeland Dr
Sauble Beach, ON N0H 2G0, Canada

MacDermot, Galt (Composer)
MacDermot Assoc
12 Silver Lake Road
Staten Island, NY 10301, USA

MacDiarmid, Alan G (Nobel Prize
Laureate)
635 Drexel Ave
Drexel Hill, PA 19026, USA

Macdissi, Peter (Actor)
c/o Melissa Stone 42West (LA)
11400 W Olympic Blvd
Suite 1100
Los Angeles, CA 90064, USA

MacDonald, Adam (Actor)
c/o Staff Member Characters Talent
Agency, The (Vancouver)
1505 W 2nd Ave
#200
Vancouver, BC V6H 3Y4, Canada

MacDonald, Ann-Marie (Writer)
c/o Staff Member Simon & Schuster
1230 Avenue of the Americas
New York, NY 10020, USA

Macdonald, Bob (Athlete, Baseball Player)
522 Harbor Grove Cir
Safety Harbor, FL 34695-4977, USA

MacDonald, C Parker (Athlete, Hockey
Player)
3 Miller Rd.
Northford, CT 07472, USA

MacDonald, Jeffrey (Athlete, Football
Player)
9334 Cody Dr
Broomfield, CO 80021-5325, USA

MacDonald, Julien (Designer, Fashion Designer)
c/o Staff Member *Julien MacDonald*
Haydens Place
247A Portobello Road
London, England W11 1LT, United Kingdom

MacDonald, Kelly (Actor)
c/o Emily Yomtobian *PMK/BNC Public Relations (PMK-LA)*
8687 Melrose Ave Fl 8
West Hollywood, CA 90069, USA

MacDonald, Lowell (Athlete, Hockey Player)
178 Amblewood Lane
Naples, FL 34105-7147, USA

MacDonald, Mark (Athlete, Football Player)
19178 Echo Ln
Farmington, MN 55024, USA

Macdonald, Norm (Actor, Comedian)
c/o Marc Gurvitz *Brillstein Entertainment Partners*
9150 Wilshire Blvd #350
Beverly Hills, CA 90212, USA

MacDonald, Paul (Athlete, Hockey Player)
81 Lakeland Dr.
Sauble Beach, ON N0H 2G0, CANADA

MacDonald, Ryan
5000 Delita Pl.
Woodland Hills, CA 91364

Macdougal, Mike (Athlete, Baseball Player)
2429 N Travis
Mesa, AZ 85207-2539, USA

MacDowell, Andie (Actor)
8 Fairway Pl
Asheville, NC 28803, USA

Mace, Major Timothy (Aviator)
327-B Polaris Avenue
Waterkloof Ridge, Pretoria, South Africa

Macek, Don (Athlete, Football Player)
3615 Monte Real
Escondido, CA 92029, USA

Macfadyen, Matthew (Actor)
c/o Hylda Queally *Creative Artists Agency (CAA-LA)*
2000 Ave Of The Stars
Los Angeles, CA 90067, USA

MacFarlane, Luke (Actor)
c/o Bonnie Bernstein *ICM Partners (ICM-NY)*
730 Fifth Ave
New York, NY 10019, USA

Macfarlane, Mike (Athlete, Baseball Player)
14909 Alhambra St
Overland Park, KS 66224-3905, USA

MacFarlane, Seth (Actor, Director)
c/o John Jacobs *Smart Entertainment*
9595 Wilshire Blvd #900
Beverly Hills, CA 90212, USA

MacGowan, Shane (Musician)
Free Trade Agency
Chapel Place
Rivington St
London EC2A 3DQ, UNITED KINGDOM (UK)

MacGraw, Ali (Actor)
c/o Laina Cohn *Laina Cohn Management*
15066 Sutton St
Sherman Oaks, CA 91403, USA

MacGregor, Bruce (Athlete, Hockey Player)
8112 NW l33rd St.
Edmonton, AB T5R OBl, CANADA

MacGregor, Ian K (Government Official)
Castleton House
Lochgilphead
Argyll, SCOTTLAND

MacGregor, Jeff (Actor, Writer)
c/o Katherine Herring *HarperCollins Publishers*
10 East 53rd St
c/o Author mail, 7th Floor
New York, NY 10022, USA

MacGregor, Joanna C (Musician)
Columbia Artists Mgmt Inc
165 W 57th St
New York, NY 10019, USA

MacGregor, Katherine (Actor)
1900 N Vine St #306
Los Angeles, CA 90068, USA

Macgregor, Randy (Athlete, Hockey Player)
3857 Pembrooke Ln
Vestal, NY T5R OB1, Canada

MacGuigan, Garth (Athlete, Hockey Player)
3555 Glen Field Ct Apt 279
Arlington, TX 76015-3431, USA

Mach, Brian (Athlete, Hockey Player)
8715 Osprey Ln
Chanhassen, MN 55317-8565, USA

Macha, Ken (Athlete, Baseball Player, Coach)
1118 Winnie Way
Latrobe, PA 15650-9080, USA

Macha, Mike (Athlete, Baseball Player)
PO Box 3844
Victoria, TX 77903-3844, USA

Machado, J P (Athlete, Football Player)
810 Aston Way Dr
0 Fallon, MO 63368-8652, USA

Machado, Justina (Actor)
c/o Danielle Allman-Del *D2 Management*
141 S. Barrington Ave
Los Angeles, CA 90049, USA

Machado, Mario
5750 Briarcliff Rd.
Los Angeles, CA 90068

Machado, Robert (Athlete, Baseball Player)
Chicago White Sox
1308 Canarv Island Dr
Weston, FL 33327-2347, USA

Machado-Van Sant, Helene (Athlete, Baseball Player, Commentator)
1221 Marion Ave
San Bernardino, CA 92407-1217, USA

Macharski, Franciszak Cardinal (Religious Leader)
Metropolita Krakowski
Ul Franciszkanska 3
Krakow 31-004, POLAND

Machel, Graca (Activist)
United Nations Foundation
1800 Massachusetts Ave NW
Suite 400
Washington, D.C. 20036, USA

Machemehl, Chuck (Baseball Player)
809 Charlotte Dr
McKinney, TX 75071-6081, USA

Machemer, Dave (Athlete, Baseball Player)
2159 Alpine Ct
Stevensville, MI 49127-9554, USA

Machida, Lyoto (Athlete, Boxer)
c/o Staff Member *UFC*
P.O. Box 26959
Las Vegas, NV 89126-0959, USA

Machover, Tod (Composer)
Massachusetts Institute of Technology
Media Laboratory
Cambridge, MA 02139, USA

Macht, Gabriel (Actor)
c/o Staff Member *Management 360*
9111 Wilshire Blvd
Beverly Hills, CA 90210, USA

Macht, Stephen (Actor)
248 S Rodeo Dr
Beverly Hills, CA 90212, USA

Machurek, Mike (Athlete, Football Player)
686 N Senita Way
Eagle, ID 83616-6890, ID

Macias, Eduardo R (Director)
c/o Gabriel Blanco *Gabriel Blanco Iglesias (Mexico)*
Rio Balsas 35-32
Colonia Cuauhtemoc
DF 06500, Mexico

Macias, Jose (Athlete, Baseball Player)
c/o Staff Member *Montreal Expos*
4549 Avenue Pierre de Coubertin
Montreal
Quebec H1V 3N7, CANADA

macieod, Bill (Athlete, Baseball Player)
14 Heritage Way
Marblehead, MA 01945-2332, USA

Macinnis, AL
StLouis Blues 1401 Clark Ave
Attn: VP, Hockey Operations
Saint Louis, MO 63103-2700, USA

Macinnis, Allan (Athlete, Hockey Player)
1132 Highland Pointe Dr
St. Louis, MO 63013-1408, USA

MacIntosh, Craig (Cartoonist)
3403 W 28th St
Minneapolis, MN 55416-4302, USA

MacIntosh, Sir Cameron
1 Bedford Sq.
London, ENGLAND WC1B 3RA

MacIntyre, Colin (Musician)
c/o Staff Member *Paradigm (Monterey)*
404 W Franklin St
Monterey, CA 93940, USA

Macintyre, Marguerite (Actor)
c/o Donna Massetti *Silver Massetti & Szatmary (SMS) Talent Inc*
8383 Wilshire Blvd
Suite 230
Beverly Hills, CA 90211, USA

MacIntyre, Scott (Musician)

Macio (Musician)
c/o Staff Member *Paradigm (Monterey)*
404 W Franklin St
Monterey, CA 93940, USA

Macionis, John (Athlete, Olympic Athlete, Swimmer)
2600 Barracks Rd Apt 246
Charlottesville, VA 22901-4216, USA

Maciver, Norm (Athlete, Hockey Player)
2119 Ponderosa Cir
Duluth, MN 55811-1960, USA

Mack, Allison (Actor)
c/o Sheila Wenzel *Innovative Artists (LA)*
1505 10th St
Santa Monica, CA 90401, USA

Mack, Bill (Athlete, Football Player)
51910 N Shoreham Ct
South Bend, IN 46637-1357, USA

Mack, Cedric (Athlete, Football Player)
116 Chestnut St
Lake Jackson, TX 77566, USA

Mack, Connie (Congressman, Politician)
627 26th St S
Arlington, VA 22202-2503, USA

Mack, J Kevin (Athlete, Football Player)
29359 Hummingbird Cir Dr
Westlake, OH 44145-5287, USA

Mack, Lonnie (Musician)
Concerted Efforts
59 Parsons St
West Newton, MA 02465, USA

Mack, Quinn (Athlete, Baseball Player)
35324 Marsh Ln
Wildomar, CA 92595-9019, USA

Mack, Rico (Athlete, Football Player)
1200 R D Mack Rd
Statham, GA 30666, USA

Mack, Sam (Athlete, Basketball Player)
8142S S Prairie Park Pl
Chicago, IL 60619-4800, USA

Mack, Shane (Athlete, Baseball Player, Olympic Athlete)
35324 Marsh Ln
Wildomar, CA 92595-9019, USA

Mack, Stacey (Athlete, Football Player)
1431 19th St
Orlando, FL 32805-4415, USA

Mack, Thomas (Tom) (Athlete, Football Player)
52 Grand Miramar Dr
Henderson, NV 89011-2202, USA

Mack, Tony (Baseball Player)
California Angels
431 Rogers Rd Apt 18
Lexington, KY 40505-1961, USA

Mack, Tremain (Athlete, Football Player)
3604 Rock Creek Dr
Tyler, TX 75707, USA

Mack, Warner (Musician)
National Talent Agency
2260 E Apple Ave
Muskegon, MI 49442, USA

Mack, William (Athlete, Football Player)
51910 N Shoreham Ct
South Bend, IN 46637, USA

Mackall, Michelle (Athlete, Golfer)
2057 Oxford Ave
Cardiff by the Sea, CA 92007-1719, USA

Mackanin, Pete (Athlete, Baseball Player, Coach)
11563 E Bronco Trl
Scottsdale, AZ 85255-8243, USA

Mackasey, Blair
Minnesota Wild 317 Washington St
Attn Dir Player Personnel
Saint Paul, MN 55102-1667, USA

Mackasey, Blair (Athlete, Hockey Player)
188 Centennial Ave
Beaconsfield, QC H9W 2J7, Canada

Mackay, David (Director)
Gersh Agency
232 N Canon Dr
Beverly Hills, CA 90210, USA

Mackay, David William Donald
(Astronaut)
Pear Tree Cottage
Road Winterburne Dauntsey Salisbury
Wiltshire SP46EW, UK

Mackay, Harvey (Business Person, Writer)
Mackay Envelope Corp
2100 Elm St SE
Minneapolis, MN 55414, USA

Macke, Richard C (Admiral)
1887 Alaweo St
Honolulu, HI 96821, USA

Mackell, Fleming (Athlete, Hockey Player)
104 Rue Martel
Vaudreuii-Dorion, QC J7V 1H2, Canada

MacKenney, Tamara
4935 Parkers Mill Rd.
Lexington, KY 40501

Mackenroth, Jack (Designer, Reality TV Star)
c/o Steve Le Vine *Grapevine Public Relations*
5237 N Cahuenga Blvd #2
N Hollywood, CA 91601, USA

MacKenzie, Aaron (Athlete, Hockey Player)
1510 Zamia Ave Apt 202
Boulder, CO 80304-4434, USA

Mackenzie, Barry (Athlete, Hockey Player)
562 Summerhill Cres
Sudbury, ON P3A 4Y6, Canada

MacKenzie, Benjamin (Actor)
c/o Staff Member *Management 360*
9111 Wilshire Blvd
Beverly Hills, CA 90210, USA

Mackenzie, Brock (Athlete, Golfer)
c/o Jim Lehrman *SFX Golf*
36855 W Main St Ste 200
Purcellville, VA 20132, USA

MacKenzie, Eric (Athlete, Baseball Player)
2002 James East
Bright Grove, ON N0N 1C0, Canada

Mackenzie, Gordy (Athlete, Baseball Player)
36535 Micro Racetrack RdRd
Fruitland Park, FL 34731-5163, USA

MacKenzie, J C
3500 W Olive Ave #1400
Burbank, CA 91505, USA

Mackenzie, Jeremy J G (General)
Royal Hospital
Chelsea
London Sw3 4SR, UNITED KINGDOM
(UK)

Mackenzie, Ken (Athlete, Baseball Player)
15 Fair St
Guilford, CT 06437-2601, USA

MacKenzie, Patch
3500 W. Olive #1400
Burbank, CA 91505

MacKenzie, Peter (Actor)

Mackenzie, Warren (Artist)
8695 68th St N
Stillwater, MN 55082, USA

Mackenzie, Will (Athlete, Golfer)
35 Laurel Oaks Cir
Jupiter, FL 33469, USA

Mackerras, A Charles M
10 Hamilton Terrace
London NW8 9UG, UNITED KINGDOM
(UK)

Mackey, Cindy (Athlete, Golfer)
1190 Millstone Run
Bogart, GA 30622-3062, USA

Mackey, George W (Mathematician)
25 Coolidge Hill Road
Cambridge, MA 02138, USA

Mackey, Kyle (Athlete, Football Player)
136 Brookwood Dr
Silsbee, TX 77656-8912, USA

Mackey, Louis (Athlete, Football Player)
7002 Winter Blossom Dr
Humble, TX 77346-3387, USA

Mackey, Malcolm (Athlete, Basketball Player)
504 Hemphill Ave
Chattanooga, TN 37411-2910, USA

Mackey, Rick (Misc)
5938 Four Mile Rd
Nanana, AK 99760, USA

Macki, Debra (Stylist)
c/o Sandie Torres *Lily Artist Management*
PO Box 610
Southborough, MA 01772-0610, USA

Mackie, Anthony (Actor)
c/o Jason Spire *Inspire Entertainment*
315 7th Ave
Suite 17E
New York, NY 10001, USA

Mackie, Bob (Fashion Designer)
Bob Mackie Design Group, Ltd
230 Park Ave #446
New York, NY 10169, USA

MacKinney, Steven (Stylist)
c/o Staff Member *Katy Barker Agency Inc*
6606 10th Ave Apt 3R
Brooklyn, NY 11219, USA

MacKinnon, Catherine (Lawyer)
University of Michigan
Law School
Ann Arbor, MI 48109, USA

MacKinnon, Gillies (Director)
c/o Patty Detroit *Todd Smith and Associates*
10250 Constellation Blvd
7th Floor
Los Angeles, CA 90067, USA

MacKinnon, Roderick (Nobel Prize Laureate)
53 Winchester S
Brookline, MA 02446-2748, USA

Mackintosh, Cameron A (Producer)
Cameron Mackintosh Ltd
1 Bedford Sq
London WC1B 3RA, UNITED KINGDOM
(UK)

Mackintosh, Steven (Actor)
c/o Staff Member *Yakety Yak*
8-A Bloomsbury Sq
London WC1A 2NE, UNITED KINGDOM
(UK)

Macklin, David (Athlete, Football Player)
16042 S 14th Dr
Phoenix, AZ 85045-0613, USA

Macklin, Rudy (Athlete, Basketball Player)
9336 Jefferson Hwy
Baton Rouge, LA 70809-2474, USA

Macknowski, John (Athlete, Basketball Player)
1920 Garnet Ln
Dandridge, TN 37725-4428, USA

Macknowski, Stephan (Athlete, Kayaker, Olympic Athlete)
462 Kimball Ave
Yonkers, NY 10704-2329, USA

Macknowski, Stephen (Athlete, Kayaker, Olympic Athlete)
462 Kimball Ave
Yonkers, NY 10704-2329, USA

Mackovic, John (Athlete, Football Coach, Football Player)
79295 Rancho La Quinta Dr
La Quinta, CA 92253-6217, USA

Mackowiak, Rob (Athlete, Baseball Player)
2414 W Superior St
Chicago, IL 60612-1214, USA

Mackrides, Bill (Athlete, Football Player)
23 Roberts Rd
Newtown Square, PA 19073-2011, USA

Mackrides, William (Athlete, Football Player)
23 Roberts Rd
Newton Square, PA 19073, USA

MacLachian, Kyle (Actor)
Industry Entertainment
955 Carillo Dr
#300
Los Angeles, CA 90048, USA

MacLachlan, Kyle (Actor)
c/o David Seltzer *Management 360*
9111 Wilshire Blvd
Beverly Hills, CA 90210, USA

MacLachlan, Patricia (Writer)
21 Unquomonk Road
Williamsburg, MA 01096, USA

Maclachlan, Patricia (Writer)
21 Unquomonk Rd
Williamsburg, MA 01096-9718, USA

MacLaine, Shirley (Actor, Writer)
Maclaine Enterprises
Box 25962
Munds Park, AZ 86017, USA

MacLane, Saunders (Mathematician)
5401 Westbard Avenue
Unit 115
Bethesda, MD 20816-1480, USA

MacLean, Bonnie (Artist)
P.O. Box 103
Buckingham, PA 18912, USA

MacLean, Don (Athlete, Basketball Player)
216 Los Padres Dr
Thousand Oaks, CA 91361-1333, USA

Maclean, Doug (Athlete, Hockey Player)
466 Notre Dame St
Summerside, PE CIN 1T3, Canada

MacLean, Doug (Coach)
330 Tucker Dr
Worthington, OH 43085, USA

Maclean, John (Athlete, Hockey Player)
44 Old Farm Rd
Basking Ridge, NJ 07920-3309, USA

MacLean, John (Athlete, Coach, Hockey Player)
44 Old Farm Rd
Basking Ridge, NJ 07920-3309, USA

Maclean, Paul (Athlete, Hockey Player)
41544 Glade Rd
Canton, MI 48187-3770, USA

MacLean, Paul (Athlete, Hockey Player)
Ottawa Senators 110-1000 Palladium Dr
Attn: Coaching Staff
Ottawa, ON K2V lAS, Canada

MacLean, Steven G (Astronaut)
Astronaut Program
6767 Rt de Aeroport
Saint-Hubert, QC J3Y 8Y9, CANADA

Maclean, Steven G Dr (Astronaut)
President, Canadian Space Agency
Saint-Hubert, QC BY 8Y9, Canada

MacLean-Ross, Lucella (Athlete, Baseball Player, Commentator)
115-4202 54 Ave
Lloydminster, AB T9V 0G1, CANADA

Macleay, Lachlan (Astronaut)
5105 Saddleback Hts
Colorado Springs, CO 80923-1113, USA

MacLeish, Rick (Athlete, Hockey Player)
5612 Bay Ave.
Ocean City, NJ 08226, USA

Maclellan, Brian (Athlete, Hockey Player)
Washington Capitals 627 N Glebe Rd Ste 850
Attn Dir Player Personnel
Arlington, VA 22203-2144, USA

Maclennan, Robert A R (Government Official)
74 Abingdon Villas
London W8 6XB, UNITED KINGDOM
(UK)

Macleod, Bill (Athlete, Baseball Player)
14 Heritage Way
Marblehead, MA 01945, USA

MacLeod, Gavin (Actor)
1877 Michael Lane
Pacific Palisades, CA 90272, USA

MacLeod, John (Basketball Coach, Coach)
4610 East Fanfol Dr
Phoenix, AZ 85028, USA

MacLeod, Lewis (Actor)
c/o Staff Member *Hobsons International*
62 Chiswick High Road
London W4 1SY, United Kingdom

Macleod, Pat (Athlete, Hockey Player)
7467 Ivy Hills Pl
Cincinnati, OH 45244-3041, USA

Macleod, Tom (Athlete, Football Player)
15412 N Hazard Rd
Spokane, WA 99208-8289, USA

Maclin, Lonnie (Athlete, Baseball Player)
9635 Meeks Blvd
Saint Louis, MO 63132-1507, USA

MacMahon, Brian (Misc)
89 Warren St
Needham, MA 02492, USA

MacMahon, Julian (Actor)

MacManus, Tristan (Dancer)
c/o Staff Member *Dancing With The Stars*
500 S Buena Vista St
Burbank, CA 91521, USA

Macmillan, Bill (Athlete, Hockey Player)
Upper Meadowbank Rd RR 2
Cornwall, PE C0A IHO, Canada

Macmillan, Bob (Athlete, Hockey Player)
The Sport Page Club 236 Kent St
Charlottetown PE CIA 1P3, Canada

MacMillan, John (Athlete, Hockey Player)
2672 W Conifer Dr
Eagle, ID 83616-4667, USA

MacMillan, Shannon (Soccer Player)
Portland University
Athletic Dept
Portland, OR 97203, USA

Mac Mohan (Actor)
Gulam Cottage Four Bungalows
Andheri
Bombay, MS 400 058, INDIA

MacMurray, Jamie (Race Car Driver)
211 Milford Cir
Mooresville, NC 28117, USA

MacMurray, William (Engineer)
200 Deer Run Road
Schaghticoke, NY 12154, USA

MacNabb, B Gordon (Engineer)
1406 Praine Ave
Cheyenne, WY 82009, USA

Macnee, Patrick (Actor)
PO Box 1853
Rancho Mirage, CA 92270, USA

Macneil, AL (Athlete, Hockey Player)
151 Parkview Way SE
Calgary, AB T2J 4N3, Canada

MacNeil, Bernie (Athlete, Hockey Player)
1014 Cunningham Rd
Kingston, ON K7L 4V3, Canada

MacNeil, Karen (Writer)
Karen MacNeil & Company
1335 Main St
St. Helena, CA 94574, USA

MacNeil, Robert (Correspondent, Writer)
c/o Staff Member *Penguin Press HC*
375 Hudson St
New York, NY 10014, USA

Macneil, Robert (Journalist)
2700 S Quincy St
Arlington, VA 22206-2242, USA

MacNichol, Peter (Actor)
International Creative Mgmt
8942 Wilshire Blvd
#219
Beverly Hills, CA 90211, USA

MacNicol, Peter (Actor)
c/o Ron West *Thruline Entertainment*
9250 Wilshire Blvd
Ground Fl
Beverly Hills, CA 90212, USA

Macoherson, Harry (Athlete, Baseball Player)
971 BaY. Vista Blvd
Englewood, FL 34223-240S, USA

Macomber, Debbie (Writer)
c/o Irene Goodman *Irene Goodman Literary Agency*
27 W 24th St
Suite 700B
New York, NY 10010, USA

Macomber, Dick (Horse Racer)
6720 NW 28th Ter
Fort Lauderdale, FL 33309-1320, USA

Macomber, Dick (Jockey)
6720 NW 28th Terrace
Fort Lauderdale, FL 33309, USA

Macomber, George B H (Skier)
1 Design Center Place
#600
Boston, MA 02210, USA

Macon, Eddie (Athlete, Football Player)
140 Westmoor Ave
Daly City, CA 94015-3842, USA

Macosko, Anna (Athlete, Golfer)
304 Earl Drive
Kerrville, TX 78028-7019, USA

Macphail, Andy (Commentator)
12403 Hunters Gin
Owings Mills, MD 21117-1040, USA

MacPhail, Andy (Baseball Player)
Chicago Cubs
1080 Sunset Rd
Winnetka, IL 60093-3625, USA

Macpherson, Daniel (Actor)
c/o Staff Member *Morrissey Management*
77 Glebe Point Road
Sydney NSW 2037, AUSTRALIA

MacPherson, Dick (Athlete, Football Coach, Football Player)
6202 The Hamlet
Jamesville, NY 13078-9785, USA

MacPherson, Duncan I (Cartoonist, Editor)
Toronto Star
Editorial Dept
1 Yonge St
Toronto, ON M5E 1E6, CANADA

Macpherson, Elle (Model)
c/o Michael McConnell *Buchwald/ Fortitude (LA)*
6500 Wilshire Blvd
Suite 2200
Los Angeles, CA 90048, USA

Macpherson, Harry (Athlete, Baseball Player)
971 Bay Vista Blvd
Englewood, FL 34223, USA

Macpherson, Wendy (Bowler)
PO Box 93433
Henderson, NV 89009, USA

Mac Quayle (DJ)
c/o Staff Member *Diva Central Inc*
7510 W Sunset Blvd Ste 1445
Los Angees, CA 90046, USA

MacQuitty, Jonathan (Inventor)
Abingworth Mgmt Inc
2465 E Bayshore Road
#348
Palo Alto, CA 94303, USA

Macrae, Scott (Athlete, Baseball Player)
1164 Forest Brook Ct
Marietta, GA 30068-2827, USA

MacRae, Sheila (Actor, Musician)
666 West End Ave
#10H
New York, NY 10025, USA

MacSweyn, Ralph (Athlete, Hockey Player)

MacTavish, Craig (Athlete, Coach, Hockey Player)
Chicago Wolves 2301 Ravine Way
Attn: Coaching Staff
Glenview, IL 60025-7627, USA

Maculan, Tim (Actor)
c/o Christopher Black *Opus Entertainment*
5225 Wilshire Blvd #905
Los Angeles, CA 90036, USA

Macwhorter, Keith (Athlete, Baseball Player)
75 Martin St
Rehoboth, MA 02769-2114, USA

Macy, Bill (Actor)
10130 Angelo Cir
Beverly Hills, CA 90210, USA

Macy, Geoffrey W (Astronomer)
University of California
Integrative Planetary Science Ctr
Berkeley, CA 94720, USA

Macy, Kyle (Athlete, Basketball Player)
3320 Overbrook Dr
Lexington, KY 40502-3352, USA

Macy, William H (Actor)
c/o Jessica Kolstad *WKT Public Relations (WKT-LA)*
9350 Wilshire Blvd
Suite 450
Beverly Hills, CA 90212, USA

Maczuzak, John (Athlete, Football Player)
9070 Lucia Ln
Irwin, PA 15642, USA

Madadian, Andy (Actor, Bollywood)
c/o Staff Member *Cherokee Productions*
8491 Sunset Blvd #277
Los Angeles, CA 90069, USA

Madball (Musician)
c/o Paul Gourlie *Agency Group Ltd, The (LA)*
1880 Century Park E
Suite 711
Los Angeles, CA 90067, USA

Maddalena, Julie (Actor)
c/o Staff Member *Tisherman Gilbert Motley Drozdoski Talent Agency (TGMD)*
6767 Forest Lawn Dr
Suite 101
Los Angeles, CA 90068, USA

Maddaloni, Martin J (Misc)
Plumbing & Pipe Fitting Union
901 Massachusetts Ave NW
Washington, DC 20001, USA

Madden, Beezie (Athlete, Horse Racer, Olympic Athlete)
3980 Stone Bridge Rd
Cazenovia, NY 13035-9535, USA

Madden, Benji (Musician)
c/o Staff Member *Creative Artists Agency (CAA-LA)*
2000 Ave Of The Stars
Los Angeles, CA 90067, USA

Madden, Dave (Actor)
4790 Blossom Dr
Delray Beach, FL 33445, USA

Madden, David (Writer)
Louisiana State University
US Civil War Center
Baton Rouge, LA 70803, USA

Madden, Diane (Dancer)
Trisha Brown Dance Co
211 W 61st St
New York, NY 10023, USA

Madden, D S (Religious Leader)
American Baptist Assn
4605 N State Line
Texarkana, TX 75503, USA

Madden, Joe (Athlete, Baseball Player)
2515 S Ysabella Ave
Tampa, FL 33629-6238, USA

Madden, Joel (Musician)
c/o Brian Greenbaum *Creative Artists Agency (CAA-LA)*
2000 Ave Of The Stars
Los Angeles, CA 90067, USA

Madden, John (Director)
c/o Jenne Casarotto *Casarotto Ramsay & Associates Ltd (UK)*
Waverley House
7-12 Noel St
London W1F 8GQ, UK

Madden, John (Athlete, Football Coach, Football Player, Sportscaster)
5955 Coronado Blvd
Pleasanton, CA 94588, USA

Madden, John (Athlete, Hockey Player)
5713 Ayrshire Blvd
Edina, MN 55436-2003, USA

Madden, John P (Director)
William Morris Agency
52/53 Poland Place
London W1F 7LX, UNITED KINGDOM (UK)

Madden, Mike (Athlete, Baseball Player)
4733 Frankfort Way
Denver, CO 80239-5922, USA

Madden, Morris (Athlete, Baseball Player)
105 Jennings St
Laurens, SC 29360-3317, USA

Madden, Richard (Actor)
c/o Duncan Millership *WME (LA)*
9601 Wilshire Blvd Fl 3
Beverly Hills, CA 90210, USA

Madden, Steve (Designer)
Steve Madden Ltd
52-16 Barnett Ave.
Long Island City, NY 11104, USA

Maddix, Raydell (Athlete, Baseball Player)
3724 E North Bay St
Tampa, FL 33610-7959, USA

Maddock, Robert (Athlete, Football Player)
3541 Geranium Ave
Corona Del Mar, CA 92625, USA

Maddon, Joe (Athlete, Baseball Player, Coach)
2560 N Lindsay Rd
Unit 32
Mesa, AZ 85213, USA

Maddow, Rachel (Actor, Journalist, Radio Personality)
c/o Staff Member *MSNBC*
30 Rockfeller Plz
New York, NY 10112, USA

Maddox, Bob (Athlete, Football Player)
7612 Colson Dr
Louisville, KY 40220-3358, USA

Maddox, Elliott (Athlete, Baseball Player)
980 Coral Ridge Dr
Apt 104
Coral Springs, FL 33071-4148, USA

Maddox, Garry (Athlete, Baseball Player)
312 Wynne Ln
Penn Valley, PA 19072-1338, USA

Maddox, Jerry (Athlete, Baseball Player)
20647 Thundersky Cir
Riverside, CA 92508-3177, USA

Maddox, Mark (Athlete, Football Player)
1241 S Wagon Wheel Dr
Chandler, AZ 85286, USA

Maddox, Robert (Athlete, Football Player)
7612 Coison Dr
Louisville, KY 40220, USA

Maddox, Tommy (Athlete, Football Player)
210 Ridge View Ln
Roanoke, TX 76262-5617, USA

Maddux, Greg (Athlete, Baseball Player)
36 Innisbrook Ave
Las Vegas, NV 89113-1225, USA

Maddux, Mike (Athlete, Baseball Player)
PO Box 90111
IArlinIlton, TX 76004-3111, USA

Maddy, Penelope Jo (Misc)
University of California
Philosophy Dept
Irvine, CA 92717, USA

Madekwe, Ashley (Actor)
c/o Jeff Golenberg Collective
8383 Wilshire Blvd
Suite 1050
Beverly Hills, CA 90211, USA

Madeley, Darrin (Athlete, Hockey Player)
Lake Forest Academy 1500 W Kennedy Rd
Lake Forest, IL 60045-1047, USA

Mader, Gunther (Skier)
Am Brenner 28
Gries 6156, AUSTRIA

Mader, Rebecca (Actor)
c/o Paul Nelson Mosaic Media Group
9200 W. Sunset Blvd
10th Floor
Los Angeles, CA 90069, USA

Maderos, George (Athlete, Football Player)
12 Spinnaker Way
Chico, CA 95926, USA

Madfai, Kahtan al (Architect)
22 Vassileos Constantinou
Athens 11635, GREECE

Madhavi (Actor, Bollywood)
21/C Neha Ave
Juhu Tara Road
Mumbai, MS 400049, INDIA

Madhoo (Actor, Bollywood)
Krishna Kutir
Sagarika Society Juhu Tara Road
Bombay, MS 400049, INDIA

Madhubala (Actor, Bollywood)
Krishna Kutir
1 Juhu Tara Road
Mumbai, MS 400049, INDIA

Madi, Ferenc (President)
Egyetem Ter 1-3
Budapest 1364, HUNGARY

Madigan, Amy (Actor)
c/o Staff Member Industry Entertainment Partners
955 S Carrillo Dr
Suite 300
Los Angeles, CA 90048, USA

Madigan, Connie (Athlete, Hockey Player)
7655 NE Alameda St
Portland, OR 97213-5931, USA

Madigan, John W (Business Person, Publisher)
Tribune Co
435 N Michigan Ave
#1800
Chicago, IL 60611, USA

Madigan, Kathleen (Comedian)
c/o Staff Member Gersh (LA)
9465 Wilshire Blvd
Suite 600
Beverly Hills, CA 90212, USA

Madigan, Martha (Photographer)
Tyler School of Art Beech & Penrose Aves
Philadelphia, PA 19126, USA

Madigan, Sam (Athlete, Football Player)
3685 Heron Ridge Ln
Weston, FL 33331, USA

Madill, Jeff (Athlete, Hockey Player)
6812 NW 104th St
Kansas City, MO 64154-1882, USA

Madio, James (Actor)
c/o Melisa Spamer Domain Talent
9229 Sunset Boulevard
Suite 710
Los Angeles, CA 90069, USA

Madise, Adrian (Athlete, Football Player)
1561 Drury Dr
Dallas, TX 75232-1939, USA

Madison, Bailee (Actor)
c/o Chris Rossi Core Public Relations Group
4401 Wilshire Blvd.
Los Angeles, CA 90010, USA

Madison, Holly (Model, Reality TV Star)
c/o Jason Verona Marc Entertainment
9903 Santa Monica Blvd. #523
Beverly Hills, CA 90212, USA

Madison, Martha (Actor)
c/o Jason Egenberg United Talent Agency (UTA)
9336 Civic Center Dr
Beverly Hills, CA 90210, USA

Madison, Sam (Athlete, Football Player)
13153 SW 25th Pl
Davie, FL 33325-5140, USA

Madison, Sarah Danielle (Actor)
c/o Connie Tavel Forward Entertainment
9255 Sunset Blvd
Suite 805
Los Angeles, CA 90069, USA

Madison, Scotti (Athlete, Baseball Player)
5397 Thornapple Ln NW
Acworth, GA 30101-7886, USA

Madison, Scotty (Athlete, Baseball Player)
5397 Thornapple Ln NW
Acworth, GA 30101, USA

Madkins, Gerald (Athlete, Basketball Player)
528 W 8th St
Merced, CA 95341-6023, USA

Madlock, Bill (Athlete, Baseball Player)
104 Prairie Ave
Highwood, IL 60040-1714, USA

Madoff, Bernard (Bernie) (Business Person)
Butner Low FCI
#61727-054
PO Box 999
Butner, NC 27509, USA

Madonna (Actor, Dancer, Musician, Songwriter)
9425 Sunset Blvd
Beverly Hills, CA 90210, USA

Madore, Joe (Race Car Driver)
Jam Motorsports
400 S. Vermont
#125
Oklahoma City, OK 73108, USA

Madrazo, Ignacio N (Doctor)
Av Paseo de la Reforma
#476 1er Piso
Col Juarez CP, DF 6698, MEXICO

Madrid, Alex (Athlete, Baseball Player)
P.O. Box 1974
Saint Johns, AZ 85936-1974, USA

Madrigali, Jeff (Athlete, Olympic Athlete, Sailor)
6212 Green bower Ln
Clinton, WA 98236, USA

Madritsch, Bobby (Athlete, Baseball Player)
8628 Linder Ave
Burbank, IL 60459-2928, USA

Madrugada (Music Group)
c/o Staff Member Paradigm (Monterey)
404 W Franklin St
Monterey, CA 93940, USA

Madsen, Loren (Artist)
426 Broome St
New York, NY 10013, USA

Madsen, mark (Basketball Player)
10132 Gristmill Rdg
Eden Prairie, MN 55347-4760, USA

Madsen, Michael (Actor)
c/o Chuck Binder Binder & Associates
1465 Lindacrest Dr
Beverly Hills, CA 90210, USA

Madsen, Virgina (Actor)
c/o Katie Rhodes Untitled Entertainment (LA)
350 S. Beverly Dr #200
Beverly Hills, CA 90212, USA

Madsen, Virginia (Actor)
c/o Katie Rhodes Untitled Entertainment (LA)
350 S. Beverly Dr #200
Beverly Hills, CA 90212, USA

Madson, Michael (Actor)
The Firm
9100 Wilshire Blvd
#100W
Beverly Hills, CA 90210, USA

Madson, Ryan (Athlete, Baseball Player)
16 Thomas Rd
Ladera Ranch, CA 92694, USA

Madura, Ricardo (President)
Casa Presidencial
Blvd Juan Pablo II
Tegucigalpa, HONDURAS

Maduro, Calvin (Athlete, Baseball Player)
793 Springdale Dr
Millersville, MD 21108, USA

Maduro, Calvin (Athlete, Baseball Player)
793 Springdale Dr
Millersville, MD 21108-1435, USA

Mae, Vanessa (Actor, Musician)
c/o Staff Member Agency Group Ltd, The (UK)
361-373 City Rd
London EC1V 1PQ, UK

Maegle, Dick (Athlete, Football Player)
4207 Deforest Ridge Cir
Katy, TX 77494-, USA

Maese, Joe (Athlete, Football Player)
3202 Murray Rd
Finksburg, MD 21048-2408, USA

Maestri, Hector (Athlete, Baseball Player)
581 SW 89th Ct
Miami, FL 33174-2338, USA

Maestro, Mia (Actor)
c/o Pamela Kohl 3 Arts Entertainment Inc
9460 Wilshire Blvd
7th Floor
Beverly Hills, CA 90210, USA

Maffay, Peter
Klenzestr. 1
Tutzing, GERMANY D-82327

Maffett, Debra
1525 McGavock St.
Nashville, TN 37203

Maffett, Debra Sue (Debbie) (Beauty Pageant Winner)
1525 McGavock St
Nashville, TN 37203, USA

Maffia, Roma (Actor)
c/o Staff Member Stone Manners Salners Agency (LA)
9911 W Pico Blvd Ste 1400
Los Angeles, CA 90035, USA

Maga, Mickey (Actor)
123 Jasper St #24
Encinitas, CA 92024, USA

Magadan, Dave (Athlete, Baseball Player)
3733 Johnathon Ave
Palm Harbor, FL 34685-3605, USA

Magallanes, Ever (Athlete, Baseball Player)
834 Governor St
Costa Mesa, CA 92627-3342, USA

Magaw, John W (Government Official, Lawyer)
Transportation Security Administration
400 7th St SW
Washington, DC 20590, USA

Magaziner, Henry J (Architect)
1504 South St
Philadelphia, PA 19146, USA

Magee, Alex (Athlete, Football Player)
c/o Roosevelt Barnes Maximum Sports Management
6435 W Jefferson Blvd
#197
Fort Wayne, IN 46804, USA

Magee, Andrew (Andy) (Athlete, Golfer)
6100 E Huntress Dr
Paradise Valley, AZ 85253-4217, USA

Magee, Calvin (Athlete, Football Player)
1985 2320 Comanche Trl
Grand Prairie, TX 75052-8595, USA

Magee, Dave (Horse Racer)
5S350 Deer Ridge Path
Big Rock, IL 60511-9777, USA

Magee, Dave (Race Car Driver)
5S350 Deer Ridge Path
Big Rock, IL 60511, USA

Magee, Wendell (Athlete, Baseball Player)
6500 Muskogee Cv
Leeds, AL 35094-3868, USA

Maggard, Amy (Stylist)
c/o Staff Member *Creative Talent Columbus*
5864 Nike Dr
Hilliard, OH 43026, USA

Maggard, Dave (Athlete, Track Athlete)
University of Houston
Athletic Dept
Houston, TX 77204, USA

Maggart, Brandon (Actor)
8730 Sunset Blvd #480
Los Angeles, CA 90069

Maggart, Garett (Actor)
c/o Staff Member *SDB Partners Inc*
1801 Ave of the Stars
Suite 902
Los Angeles, CA 90067, USA

Maggert, Jeff (Athlete, Golfer)
62 W Bracebridge Cir
Spring, TX 77382, USA

Maggette, Corey (Basketball Player)
Los Angeles Clippers
Staples Center
1111 S Figueroa St
Los Angeles, CA 90015, USA

Maggs, Darryl (Athlete, Hockey Player)
20918 E US Highway 24
Woodland Park, CO 80863-8002, USA

Maggs, Don (Athlete, Football Player)
38335 Tamarac Blvd Apt 212
Willoughby, OH 44094-8193, USA

Magic Numbers, The (Music Group)
c/o Staff Member *Paradigm (Monterey)*
404 W Franklin St
Monterey, CA 93940, USA

Magill, Frank J (Judge)
US Court of Appeals
Federal Building
657 2nd Ave N
Fargo, ND 58102, USA

Magilton, Gerald E (Jerry) (Astronaut)
Marlin Marietta Astro Space
100 Campus Dr
Newtown, PA 18940, USA

Magilton, Gerard (Astronaut)
1705 Powderhorn Rd
Newtown, PA 18940-9406, USA

Maginnes, John (Athlete, Golfer)
612 Topwater Ln
Greensboro, NC 27455, USA

Magistretti, Vico (Architect)
Via Conservatorio 20
Milan, ITALY

Magliozzi, Ray (Television Host)
c/o Staff Member *Car Talk Plaza*
Box 3500 Harvard Square
Cambridge, MA 02238, USA

Magliozzi, Tom (Actor, Television Host)
c/o Staff Member *Car Talk Plaza*
Box 3500 Harvard Square
Cambridge, MA 02238, USA

Magnante, Mike (Athlete, Baseball Player)
5305 Via Quinto
Newbury Park, CA 91320-6937, USA

Magnus, Dr Kurt (Scientist)
Luitpoldstrasse 4
Gauting, Germany

Magnus, Edie (Correspondent)
NBC-TV
News Dept
30 Rockefeller Plaza
New York, NY 10112, USA

Magnus, Robert (General)
Deputy CofS Programs/Resources
HqUSMC
2 Navy St
Washington, DC 20380, USA

Magnus, Sandra H (Sandy) (Astronaut)
2010 Legend Grove Ct
Houston, TX 77062-8046, USA

Magnus, Siobhan (Musician)
c/o Simon Fuller *XIX Entertainment*
35-37 Parkgate Rd
32/33 Ransomes Dock
London SW11 4NP, UNITED KINGDOM
(UK)

Magnuson, Ann
1317 Maltman Ave
Los Angeles, CA 90026

Magnussen, Jan (Race Car Driver)
5294 Winder Hwy
Brasselton, GA 30517, USA

Magnussen, Karen
2852 Thorndiff Dr.
N. Vancouver BC, CANADA V7R 2B5

Magoon, Bob (Misc)
1688 Meridian Ave
Miami Beach, FL 33139, USA

Magowan, Peter (Commentator)
San Francisco Giants
2100 Washington St
San Francisco, CA 94109-2845, USA

Magrane, Joe (Athlete, Baseball Player)
705 Guisando De Avila
Tampa, FL 33613-5204, USA

Magrane, Shannon (Musician)
c/o Staff Member *19 Entertainment - LA*
9000 W Sunset Blvd #1574
West Hollywood, CA 90069, USA

Magrann, Tom (Athlete, Baseball Player)
910 N 31st Ct
Hollywood, FL 33021-5509, USA

Magrath, Kelly (Race Car Driver)
Jim Dunn Racing
840 Kallin Ave.
Long Beach, CA 90815, USA

Magri, Charles G (Charlie) (Boxer)
345 Bethnal Green Road
Bethnal Green
London E2 6LG, UNITED KINGDOM
(UK)

Magrini, Pete (Athlete, Baseball Player)
2402 Rancho Cabeza Dr
Santa Rosa, CA 95404-2326, USA

Magro, Ronnie (Fist Pump) (Reality TV Star)
c/o Matt Cohen *IAG Entertainment & Sports*
5189 Argonne Ct
San Diego, CA 92117, USA

Magruder, Chris (Athlete, Baseball Player)
1740 Leisure Ln
Yakima, WA 98908-9224, USA

Magsamen, Sandra (Artist, Writer)
Orchard Books/Scholastic
557 Broadway
New York, NY 10012, USA

Maguire, Adrian E (Jockey)
Jockey Club
42 Portman Square
London W1H 0EM, UNITED KINGDOM
(UK)

Maguire, Gregory (Writer)
HarperCollins Children's Books
1350 Avenue of Americas
New York, NY 10019, USA

Maguire, Kevin (Athlete, Hockey Player)
Toronto Maple Leafs
400-40 Bay St
Alumni Association President
Toronto, ON M5J 2X2, CANADA

Maguire, Les (Musician)
Barry Collins
21A Cliftown Road
Southend-on-Sea
Essex SS1 1AB, UNITED KINGDOM (UK)

Maguire, Paul L (Athlete, Football Player, Sportscaster)
707 Ocean Blvd
Isle of Palms, SC 29451, USA

Maguire, Richard W (Cinematographer)
26 Condesa Road
Santa Fe, NM 87508, USA

Maguire, Sean (Actor)
c/o Staff Member *The Management Company*
2030 Pinehurst Road
Los Angeles, CA 90068, USA

Maguire, Tobey (Actor)
193 N Carmelina Ave
Los Angeles, CA 90049, USA

Maguson, Keith A (Athlete, Hockey Player)
265 King Muir Rd
Lake Forest, IL 60045, USA

Magyar, Derek (Actor)
c/o Staff Member *Wilkins Management*
12200 Olympic Blvd #400
Los Angeles, CA 90064, USA

Mahaffey, Art (Athlete, Baseball Player)
3140 W Tilgham St
PO Box 261
Allentown, PA 18104, USA

Mahaffey, John (Athlete, Golfer)
594 Sawdust Rd
Unit 229
Spring, TX 77380, USA

Mahaffey, Randy (Athlete, Basketball Player)
25 Berkeley Rd
Avondale Estates, GA 30002-1468, USA

Mahaffey, Valerie (Actor)
c/o Steven Muller *Innovative Artists (LA)*
1505 10th St
Santa Monica, CA 90401, USA

Mahaffey, Valerio
121 N. San Vicente Blvd
Beverly Hills, CA 90211

Mahaffy, John (Athlete, Hockey Player)
6 Av Argyle Apt 903
Saint-Lambert, QC J4P 2H5, Canada

Mahal, Taj (Musician, Songwriter, Writer)
c/o Staff Member *Red Light Management (LA)*
8439 W Sunset Blvd
Suite 2
Los Angeles, CA 90069, USA

Mahalic, Drew (Athlete, Football Player)
2114 SW Sunset Dr
Portland, OR 97239-2066, USA

Mahalingam, Gemini (Actor)
47 Harrington Road
Chennai, TN 600 031, INDIA

Mahan, Hunter (Athlete, Golfer)
24 Lakeview Dr
Trabuco Canyon, CA 92679-5119, USA

Mahan, Larry
Box 41
Camp Verde, TX 78010

Mahan, Lawrence (Larry) (Rodeo Rider)
4771 Fruitland Road
Sunset, TX 76270, USA

Mahar, kevin (Baseball Player)
2506 E Wheeler St
Midland, MI 48642-3178, USA

Maharidge, Date D (Writer)
Stanford University
Communications Dept
Stanford, CA 94305, USA

Maharis, George (Actor)
9401 Wilshire Blvd.
700
Beverly Hills, CA 90212, USA

Mahay, Ron (Athlete, Baseball Player)
13177 E Cochise Rd
Scottsdale, AZ 85259-5304, USA

Mahe, Reno (Athlete, Football Player)
2619 Knollbrook Ln
Spring, TX 77373-9130, USA

Maher, Bill (Talk Show Host)
c/o Marc Gurvitz *Brillstein Entertainment Partners*
9150 Wilshire Blvd #350
Beverly Hills, CA 90212, USA

Maher, Sean
c/o Staff Member *Gersh (LA)*
9465 Wilshire Blvd
Suite 600
Beverly Hills, CA 90212, USA

Maheswari (Actor, Bollywood)
9 North Ave
Sree Nagar Colony Saidapet
Chennai, TN 600015, INDIA

Maheu, Robert (Government Official, Misc)
2140 Vista Famosa Ct
Las Vegas, NV 89123-4304, USA

Mahfouz, Robbie (Athlete, Football Player)
181 Belle Terre Blvd
Covington, LA 70433-4734, USA

Mahfuz, Nagib (Nobel Prize Laureate)
American University of Cairo 113
113 Sharia Kasr el Aini Attn
Egypt

Mahindra, Anan (Business Person)
Mahindra & Mahindra
Mahindra Towers
G.M. Bhosale Marg, Worli
Mumbai 400 018, India

Mahlberg, Greg (Athlete, Baseball Player)
5100 N Placita Del Lazo
Tucson, AZ 85750-1535, USA

Mahler, Mickey (Athlete, Baseball Player)
7911 Quirt St
San Antonio, TX 78227-2636, USA

Mahlum, Eric (Athlete, Football Player)
17794 NW Solano Ct
Portland, OR 97229, USA

Mahogany, Kevin (Actor, Musician)
Ted Kurland
173 Brighton Ave
Boston, MA 02134, USA

Maholm, Paul (Athlete, Baseball Player)
135 Wild Mdws W
Hattiesburg, MS 39402-8108, USA

Mahomes, Pat (Baseball Player)
Minnesota Twins
3110 Oleander Dr
Tyler, TX 75707-2000, USA

Mahon, Keith (General)
1502 34th Ave
Vero Beach, FL 32960-2744, USA

Mahon, Sean (Actor)
c/o Staff Member *McCabe Group, The*
3211 Cahuenga Blvd W Ste 104
Los Angeles, CA 90068, USA

Mahone, Austin (Internet Star, Musician)
P.O. Box 409009
Fort Lauderdale, FL 33340, USA

Mahoney, Brian (Athlete, Basketball
Player)
96 Greystone Rd
Rockville Centre, NY 11570-4515, USA

Mahoney, Dan (Writer)
13 Swan Ln
Levittown, NY 11756-3921, USA

Mahoney, David L (Business Person)
McKesson HBOX Inc
1 Post St
San Francisco, CA 94104, USA

Mahoney, Jim (Athlete, Baseball Player)
345 Hawthorne Ave # 2
Apt R19
Hawthorne, NJ 07506-1244, USA

Mahoney, John (Actor)
c/o Staff Member *ICM Partners (ICM-NY)*
730 Fifth Ave
New York, NY 10019, USA

Mahoney, Marie (Athlete, Baseball Player,
Commentator)
207 Birdsall St
Houston, TX 77007-8107, USA

Mahoney, Marle (Baseball Player)
207 Birdsall St
Houston, TX 77007-8107, USA

Mahoney, Mike (Athlete, Baseball Player)
4412 98th St
Urbandale, IA 50322-1362, USA

Mahony, Cardinal Roger
1531 W. 9th St.
Los Angeles, CA 90012

Mahood, Beverly (Musician)
c/o Staff Member *Paquin Entertainment
(Winnipeg)*
395 Notre Dame Ave
Winnipeg MT R3B 1R2, CANADA

Mahorn, Rick (Athlete, Basketball Player)
3091 Mapleridge Ct
Rochester Hills, MI 48309, USA

Mahovlich, Francis W (Frank) (Athlete,
Hockey Player)
The Senate of Canada 908 Victoria Bldg
Room 908-VB
Ottawa, ON K1A OA4, Canada

Mahovlich, Peter (Athlete, Hockey Player)
116 Farr Ln
Queensbury, NY 12804-1989, USA

Mahre, Phil (Athlete, Olympic Athlete,
Skier)
4114 122nd St NE
Marysville, WA 98271-8572, USA

Mahre, Phil
PO Box 100
Park City, UT 84060, USA

Mahre, Steve (Athlete, Olympic Athlete,
Skier)
7610 West Chestnut Avenue
Yakima, WA 98908-1553, USA

Maida, Adam J Cardinal (Religious
Leader)
Archdiocese of Detroit
1234 Washington Blvd
Detroit, MI 48226, USA

Maida, Raine (Musician)
c/o Staff Member *Paradigm (Monterey)*
404 W Franklin St
Monterey, CA 93940, USA

Maiden-Naccarato, Jeanne (Bowler)
1 N Stadium Way
#4
Tacoma, WA 98406, USA

Maidlow, Steve (Athlete, Football Player)
1311 Garfield Ave
Springfield, OH 45504-1430, USA

Maier, Hermann (Athlete, Skier)
Im 8 ErJet
Unterbergasse
Flachau 5542, Austria

Maier, Mitch (Baseball Player)
435 Amelia Cir
South Lyon, MI 48178-8211, USA

Maier, Pat (Stylist)
c/o Staff Member *Arlene Wilson
Management*
807 N Jefferson St
#200
Milwaukee, WI 53202, USA

Maier, Pauline R (Historian)
60 Larchwood Dr
Cambridge, MA 02138, USA

Maier, Sepp (Soccer Player)
Parkstr 62
Anzing 84405, GERMANY

Maietta, Mike (Race Car Driver)
154 Pleasant Hill Rd.
Scarborough, ME 04074, USA

Mailhot, Jacques (Athlete, Hockey Player)
2303 Canyon Spgs
Belton, TX 76513-1055

Mailhouse, Robert (Actor)
1623 Dillon St
Los Angeles, CA 90026, USA

Mailinvaud, Edmond (Economist)
42 Ave de Saxe
Paris 75007, FRANCE

Maillard, Carol (Musician)
Sweet Honey Agency
PO Box 600099
Newtonville, MA 02460, USA

Maiman, Theodore H (Ted) (Inventor)
1849 Utah St
Fairfield, CA 94533-4459, USA

Maine, John (Athlete, Baseball Player)
13825 Island Dr
Huntersville, NC 28078-8903, USA

Maine, scott (Baseball Player)
470 Bella Vista Ct N
Juoiter, FL 33477-5560, USA

Maines, Natalie (Musician)
c/o Simon Renshaw *Strategics Artist
Management*
1100 Glendon Ave #1000
Los Angeles, CA 90024, USA

Mair, Adam (Athlete, Hockey Player)
25 San Fernando Ln
East Amherst, NY, 14051-2235

Maire, Annie (Stylist)
c/o Staff Member *Ford Models (Miami)*
311 Lincoln Rd
#205
Miami Beach, FL 33139, USA

Mairena, Oswaldo (Athlete, Baseball
Player)
160 E 6th Pl
Mesa, AZ 85201-5068, USA

Maisel, Jay (Photographer)
190 Bowery
New York, NY 10012-4203, USA

Maisel, Lucian (Actor)
c/o Marc Hamou *Thruline Entertainment*
9250 Wilshire Blvd
Ground Fl
Beverly Hills, CA 90212, USA

Maisel, Sherman J (Economist)
2164 Hyde St
San Francisco, CA 94109, USA

Maisenberg, Olega (Musician)
In Der Gugl 9
Klostemeuburg, AUSTRIA

Maisky, Mischa M (Musician)
Columbia Artists Mgmt Inc
165 W 57th St
New York, NY 10019, USA

Maisonneuve, Brian (Soccer Player)
Columbus Crew
2121 Volman Ave
Columbus, OH 43211, USA

Maitland, Jack (Athlete, Football Player)
3079 N Palm Aire Dr
Pompano Beach, FL 33069-3457, USA

Majdarzavyn, Ganzorig (Cosmonaut)
Academy of Sciences
Peace Ave 54B
Ulan Bator 51, MONGOLIA

Majerle, Dan (Athlete, Basketball Player,
Olympic Athlete)
4534 E Oregon Ave
Phoenix, AZ 85018-1718, USA

Majewski, Gary (Athlete, Baseball Player)
1103 Chamboard Ln
Houston, TX 77018-3212, USA

Majewski, Val (Athlete, Baseball Player)
890 Oakley Dr
Freehold, NJ 07728-8237, USA

Majkowski, Don (Athlete, Football Player)
1593 Bayhill Dr
Duluth, GA 30097-5980, USA

Majoli, Iva (Tennis Player)
27 Framingham Lane
Pittsford, NY 14534, USA

Major, Bruce
6 Ridgeview Rd
Topsfield, MA 01983-1530, USA

Major, Clarence L (Writer)
University of California
English Dept
Voorhies Hall
Davis, CA 95616, USA

Major, John (Politician)
House of Commons
London, England

Majoras, Deborah (Government Official)
Federal Trade Commission
Pennsylvania Ave & 6th St NW
Washington, DC 20580, USA

Majorino, Tina (Actor)
c/o Sarah Lum *Leverage Management*
3030 Pennsylvania Ave
Santa Monica, CA 90404, USA

Majors, Austin
Major Minors
3940 Lauren Canyon Blvd #177
Studio City, CA 91604

Majors, Bobby (Athlete, Football Player)
9631 Pecan Springs Cir
Chattanooga, TN 37421-4722, USA

Majors, John I (Johnny) (Athlete, Coach,
Football Coach, Football Player)
4207 Beechwood Rd
Knoxville, TN 37920, USA

Majors, Lee (Actor)
c/o David Shapira *David Shapira &
Associates*
193 N Robertson Blvd
Beverly Hills, CA 90211, USA

MajorSundararajan (Actor)
9 Pooram Prakash Rao Street
Balaji Nagar Royapeta
Chennai, TN 600 014, INDIA

Majtyka, Roy (Baseball Player)
2082 Orangeside Rd
Palm Harbor, FL 34683-3340, USA

Majumder, Shaun (Musician)
c/o Staff Member *Paradigm (Monterey)*
404 W Franklin St
Monterey, CA 93940, USA

Makarov, Askold A (Dancer)
Plutalova Str 18-4
Saint Petersburg 197136, RUSSIA

Makarov, Sergei (Athlete, Hockey Player)
4072 Teale Ave
San Jose, CA 95117, USA

Makarova, Inna V (Actor)
Ukrainian Blvd 11
Moscow 121059, RUSSIA

Makarova, Natalia R (Ballerina)
Herbert Breslin
119 W 57th St
#1505
New York, NY 10019, USA

Makatsch, Heike (Actor)
c/o Sybille Breitbach *Wasted Management*
Dieffenbachstrasse 33
Berlin D-10967, Germany

Make Good Your Escape (Music Group)
c/o Staff Member *Paradigm (Monterey)*
404 W Franklin St
Monterey, CA 93940, USA

Makela, Mikko (Athlete, Hockey Player)
Mikko Makela's Develpmental Hockey 27
Rivermont Cres W
Lethbridge, AB TlK 8A4, Canada

Maker, Marvin (Horse Racer)
RR 1 Box 201
Pemberton, NJ 08068, USA

Makhalina, Yufia (Ballerina)
Kirov Ballet Theater
1 Pl Iskusstr
Saint Petersburg 190000, RUSSIA

Maki, Chico (Athlete, Hockey Player)
Norfolk County Sports Hall of Fame 95
Culver St Attn Heather King
Simcoe, ON N3Y 2VS, Canada

Makings, Elizabeth (Athlete, Golfer)
10063 E San Bernardo Dr
Scottsdale, AZ 85258-5665, USA

Makinson, Jessica (Comedian)
c/o Staff Member *OmniPop Talent Group*
10700 Ventura Blvd.
2nd Floor
Studio Clty, CA 91604, USA

Makk, Karoly (Director)
Hanoczy Jeno Utca 15
Budapest 1022, HUNGARY

Makkena, Wendy (Actor)
c/o Staff Member *Schumacher Management*
1122 San Vicente Blvd.
Santa Monica, CA 90402, USA

Mako (Actor)
6477 Pepper Tree Lane
Somis, CA 93066, USA

Mako, C Gene (Tennis Player)
430 S Burnside Ave
#MC
Los Angeles, CA 90036, USA

Makowski, Tom (Athlete, Baseball Player)
6686 Omphali us Rd
Colden, NY 14033-9763, USA

Maksimoya, Yekaterina S (Ballerina)
Bolshoi Theater
Teatrainsya Pl 1
Moscow 103009, RUSSIA

Maksudian, Mike (Athlete, Baseball Player)
12148 E San Simeon Dr
Scottsdale, AZ 85259-6049, USA

Maksymiuk, Jerzy
Hoza 5A m 13
Warsaw 00-528, POLAND

Malahide, Patrick (Actor)
International Creative Mgmt
76 Oxford St
London W1N 0AX, UNITED KINGDOM
(UK)

Malakar, Sanjaya (Musician, Reality TV Star)
c/o Staff Member *SUM Company*
10736 Jefferson Blvd #140
Culver City, CA 90230, USA

Malakhov, Vladimir (Athlete, Hockey Player)
PO Box 420536
Kissimmee, FL 34742-0536, USA

Malakian, Daron (Musician)
Velvet Hammer
9911 W Pico Blvd
#350
Los Angeles, CA 90035, USA

Malamala, Siupeli (Athlete, Football Player)
122 110th Ave SE
Bellevue, WA 98004-6332, USA

Malandrino, Catherine (Designer, Fashion Designer)
468 Bromme St
New York, NY 10013, USA

Malandro, Kristina (Actor)
2518 Cardigan Court
Los Angeles, CA 90077, USA

Malanowski-Marlowe, Jean (Baseball Player)
100 Smallacombe Dr
#205-24
Scranton, PA 18508-2650, USA

Malarchuk, Clint (Athlete, Hockey Player)
1308 Myers Dr
Gardnerville, NV 89410-6166, USA

Malarchuk, Clint (Athlete, Hockey Player)
Calgary Flames PO Box 1540 Stn M
Attn: Coaching Staff
Calgary, AB T2P 3B9, Canada

Malarkey, Donald (General)
4795 Skyline Rd S Apt 106
Salem, OR 97306-2558, USA

Malaska, Mark (Athlete, Baseball Player)
3823 Cumberland Dr
Youngstown, OH 44515-4610, USA

Malatesta, Romina Herrera (Stylist)
c/o Staff Member *Michele Filomeno New York LLC*
515 Greenwich St Ste 503
New York, NY 10013, USA

Malave, Omar (Athlete, Baseball Player)
2448 Moore Haven Dr W
Clearwater, 33763-1618 33763-1618, FL

Malavoy, Christopher
9 sq. de Montsouris
Paris, FRANCE F-75014

Malaysia Vasudevan (Actor)
5 Kaman Street SFI Apts
6-B Samiyar Matt
Chennai, TN 600 024, INDIA

Malchow, Tom (Athlete, Olympic Athlete, Swimmer)
10220 NW Edgewood Dr
Portland, OR 97229-7617, USA

Malco, Romany (Actor)
c/o Staff Member *Mosaic Media Group*
9200 W. Sunset Blvd
10th Floor
Los Angeles, CA 90069, USA

Malcolm, George J (Musician)
99 Wimbledon Hill Road
London SW19 4BE, UNITED KINGDOM
(UK)

Malcomson, Paula (Actor, Producer)
c/o Sean Fay *Kritzer Levine Wilkins Entertainment (KLWG)*
11872 La Grange Ave
1st Floor
Los Angeles, CA 90025, USA

Maldacena, Juan (Physicist)
Harvard University
Physics Dept
Cambridge, MA 02138, USA

Maldini, Paolo (Coach, Soccer Player)
AC Milan
Via Turati 3
Milan 20221, ITALY

Maldonado, Candy (Athlete, Baseball Player)
HC 2 Box 16800
Arecibo, PR 00612-9396, USA

Maleeva, Katerina (Tennis Player)
Mladostr 1 #45
NH 14
Sofia 1174, BULGARIA

Maleeva-Fragniere, Manuela (Tennis Player)
Bourg-Dessous 28
La Tour de Peitz 1814, SWITZERLAND

Malek, Rami (Actor)
c/o Kyle Fritz *Kyle Fritz Management*
6325 Heather Dr
Los Angeles, CA 90068, USA

Malenchenko, Yuri I (Cosmonaut)
Potcha Kosmonavtov
Moskovskoi Oblasti
Syvisdny Goroduk 141160, RUSSIA

Maler, Jim (Athlete, Baseball Player)
5132 SW 129th Ter
Miramar, FL 33027-5839, USA

Malerba, Dr Franco (Astronaut)
Atlantis Via Cantore 14/2
Genova, Italy

Malerba, Franco E (Astronaut)
Via Cantore 10
Genova 16149, ITALY

Malerba, Luigi
Via Tro Millina 31
Rome, CA ITALY

Maley, David (Athlete, Hockey Player)
1366 Norelius Ct
San Jose, CA 95120-3849, USA

Malgunas, Stewart (Athlete, Hockey Player)
6784 Westmount Cres
Prince George, BC V2N 6R3, Canada

Malhotra, Harmesh (Bollywood, Director, Filmmaker, Producer)
32A Sunset Heights 59 Pali Hill
Nargis Dutt Road Bandra
Bombay, MS 400 050, INDIA

Malick, Terrence (Director, Producer)
c/o Roeg Sutherland *Creative Artists Agency (CAA-LA)*
2000 Ave Of The Stars
Los Angeles, CA 90067, USA

Malick, Wendie (Actor, Model)
721 N Henry Ridge Mtwy
Topanga, CA 90290, USA

malicki-Sanchez, Keram (Actor)
c/o Tiffany Kuzon *Evolution Entertainment (LA)*
901 N Highland Ave
Los Angeles, CA 90038, USA

Malicky, Neal (Educator)
Baldwin-Wallace College
President's Office
Berea, OH 44017, USA

Malielegaoi, Tuilaepa Sailele (Prime Minister)
Prime Minister's Office
PO Box L1861
Vailima, Apia, SAMOA

Malige, Didier (Stylist)
c/o Staff Member *Mercury Artists*
8460 Higuera St Fl 2
Culver City, CA 90232, USA

Malik, Art
18 Sydney Mews
London SW3 6HL, UNITED KINGDOM
(UK)

Malik, Marek (Athlete, Hockey Player)
919 Anchorage Rd
Tampa, FL 33602-5755, USA

Malil, Shelley (Actor)
c/o Mark Measures *Abrams Artists Agency (LA)*
9200 Sunset Blvd
11th Floor
Los Angeles, CA 90069, USA

Malina, Josh
2262 Cloverfield Blvd.
Santa Monica, CA 90405

Malina, Joshua (Actor, Producer)
c/o David Ginsberg *Insight*
1134 S Cloverdale Ave
Los Angeles, CA 90019, USA

Malinchak, Bill (Athlete, Football Executive)
6422 NW 65th Way
Parkland, FL 33067-1503, USA

Malinger, Ross
6212 Banner Ave.
Los Angeles, CA 90038

Malingri, Micaela (Stylist)
c/o Staff Member *Artist Untied (LA)*
845 S Mansfield Ave
#1
Los Angeles, CA 90036, USA

Malini, Hema (Actor, Bollywood)
17 Jai Hind Society
12th Road Juhu Scheme
Mumbai, MS 400049, INDIA

Malinowski, Merlin (Athlete, Hockey Player)
St Marys Lincolns PO Box 42 Stn Main
St Marys, ON N4X 1A9, Canada

Maliponte, Adrianna (Opera Singer)
Gorlinsky Promotions
35 Darer
London W1, UNITED KINGDOM (UK)

Malizia, Mike (Athlete, Golfer)
570 SE Southwood Trl
Stuart, FL 34997, USA

Malkan, Matthew A (Astronomer)
University of Arizona
Steward Observatory
Tucson, AZ 85721, USA

Malkhov, Vladimir (Ballerina)
American Baliet Theatre
890 Broadway
New York, NY 10003, USA

Malkin, Evgenl (Athlete, Hockey Player)
66 Mario Lemieux Pl
Pittsburgh, PA 15219, USA

Malkin, Evgeny (Athlete, Hockey Player)
C A A Hockey
204-822 11 Ave SW
Attn J P Barry
Calgary, AB T2R OE5, Canada

Malkin, Laurence (Writer)
c/o Josh Kesselman *Thruline Entertainment*
9250 Wilshire Blvd
Ground Fl
Beverly Hills, CA 90212, USA

Malkin, Michelle (Correspondent)
c/o Staff Member *Creators Syndicate*
5777 W Century Blvd #700
Los Angeles, CA 90045, USA

Malkmus, Bobby (Athlete, Baseball Player)
400 Wallingford Ter
Union, NJ 07083-7328, USA

Malkovich, John (Actor)
c/o Liz Mahoney *ID Public Relations (ID-LA)*
7060 Hollywood Blvd
8th Floor
Los Angeles, CA 90028, USA

Mallard, Josh (Athlete, Football Player)
175 International Dr
Athens, GA 30605-6650, USA

Mallard, Wesly (Athlete, Football Player)
8007 SW Cedarcrest St
Portland, OR 97223-8937, USA

Mallary, Robert (Artist)
PO Box 97
Conway, MA 01341-0097, USA

Mallea, Eduardo (Writer)
Posadas 1120
Buenos Aires, ARGENTINA

Mallee, John (Athlete, Baseball Player)
7426 Hamlin St
Schererville, IN 46375-3454, USA

Mallet, Jeff (Horse Racer)
1375 Chinquapin Rd
Southampton, PA 18966-4609, USA

Mallett, Jerry (Athlete, Baseball Player)
4070 Cascade Trl
Me Gregor, TX 76657-4102, USA

Mallett, Ronnie (Athlete, Football Player)
22113 Liberty Cemetery Rd
Jennings, LA 70546-8804, USA

Mallette, Alfred J (General)
7040 Quail Hill Rd
Charlotte, NC 28210, USA

Mallette, Brian (Athlete, Baseball Player)
1179 Lowery Fire House Rd
Glenwood, GA 30428-2214, USA

Mallette, Troy (Athlete, Hockey Player)
1550 Bum Rd
PO Box 764
Windy Lake Levack, ON POM 2CO, CANADA

Malley, Kenneth C (Admiral)
136 Riverside Road
Edgewater, MD 21037, USA

Mallick, Dan (Misc)
42045 N Tilton Dr
Quartz Hill, CA 93536, USA

Mallick, Don (Aviator)
42045 Tilton Dr
Lancaster, CA 93536-7321, USA

Mallick, Fran (Athlete, Football Player)
42 Republic Dr Apt 135
Bloomfield, CT 06002-5462, USA

Mallicoat, Rob (Athlete, Baseball Player)
6205 214th Ave NE
Redmond, WA 98053-2310, USA

Mallinger, John (Athlete, Golfer)
2020 Beverly Plaza
Long Beach, CA 90815, USA

Mallon, Meg (Athlete, Golfer)
5105 N Ocean Blvd
Apt C
Boynton Beach, FL 33435, USA

Mallon, Thomas (Writer)
801 25th St NW
Washington, DC 20037-2209, USA

Mallory, Carole (Actor)
2300 5th Ave
New York, NY 10037, USA

Mallory, Charles (General)
230 Baker Ln
Charleston, WV 25302-2936, USA

Mallory, Glynn C Jr (General)
19221 Heather Forest
San Antonio, TX 78258, USA

Mallory, Irvin (Athlete, Football Player)
3 Paula Ln
Waterford, CT 06385-1521, USA

Mallory, John (Athlete, Football Player)
151B Mountain Ave
Summit, NJ 07901-4172, USA

Mallory, Larry (Athlete, Football Player)
1911 Stonebrook Dr
Arlington, TX 76012, USA

Mallory, Rick (Athlete, Football Player)
920 W Emerson St
Seattle, WA 98119-1419, USA

Mallory, Sheldon (Athlete, Baseball Player)
21353 Old North Church Rd
Frankfort, IL 60423-3016, USA

Malloy, Bob (Athlete, Baseball Player)
1904 San Carlos Ave
Allen, TX 75002-2626, USA

Malloy, Dan (Governor, Politician)
State Capitol
210 Capitol Ave
Hartford, CT 06106, USA

Malloy, Edward A (Educator)
University of Notre Dame
President's Office
Notre Dame, IN 46556, USA

Malloy, Marty (Athlete, Baseball Player)
PO Box 1644 Chiefland
Chiefland, FL 32644-1644, USA

Malloy, Matt (Actor)
c/o Mark A. Schlegel *Cornerstone Talent Agency*
37 W 20th St
New York, NY 10011, USA

Malloy, Robert (Pete Hamil) (Actor, Writer)
c/o Staff Member *ICM Partners (ICM-LA)*
10250 Constellation Blvd Fl 7
Los Angeles, CA 90067, USA

Malloy, Tommy
1687 Amsterdam Ave Merrick
LI, NY 11566

Malloys, The (Music Group)
c/o Staff Member *Creative Artists Agency (CAA-LA)*
2000 Ave Of The Stars
Los Angeles, CA 90067, USA

Malo, Raul (Musician, Songwriter, Writer)

Maloff, Sam (Designer)
PO Box 51
Alta Lorna, CA 91701, USA

Malone, Arthur L (Art) (Athlete, Football Player)
1619 E Carmen St
Tempe, AZ 85283, USA

Malone, Beverly L (Misc)
American Nurses Assn
Maryland Ave SW
Washington, DC 20002, USA

Malone, Brendan (Coach)
Indiana Pacers
Conseco Fieldhouse
125 S Pennsylvania
Indianapolis, IN 46204, USA

Malone, Chuck (Athlete, Baseball Player)
310 Libertv St
Marked Tree, AR 72365-2209, USA

Malone, Dorothy (Actor)
PO Box 7287
Dallas, TX 75209, USA

Malone, Greg (Athlete, Hockey Player)
7014 Clubview Dr
Bridgeville, PA 15017-1097, USA

Malone, Jeff (Athlete, Basketball Player)
415 Lee Road 313
Smiths Station, AL 36877-3168, USA

Malone, Jena (Actor)
c/o Allison Band *Gersh (LA)*
9465 Wilshire Blvd
Suite 600
Beverly Hills, CA 90212, USA

Malone, John (Business Person)
Liberty Media
12300 Liberty Blvd
Englewood, CO 80012

Malone, Karl (Athlete, Basketball Player, Olympic Athlete)
105 W Charter St
Farmerville, LA 71241-2841, USA

Malone, Kevin (Commentator)
21345 Placerita Canyon Rd
Newhall, CA 91321-1845, USA

Malone, Maicel (Athlete, Olympic Athlete, Track Athlete)
4064 Bothwell Ter
Tallahassee, FL 32317-8545, USA

Malone, Moses (Athlete, Basketball Player)
310 S Keswick Ct
Sugar Land, TX 77478-3952, USA

Malone, Patricia (Business Person)
c/o Staff Member *Gucci America*
50 Hartz Way
Secaucus, NJ 07094, USA

Malone, Ryan (Athlete, Hockey Player)
Octagon Sports Management
1751 Pinnacle Dr
Ste 1500
Mclean, VA 22102-3833, USA

Malone, Shannon (Actor, Television Host)
c/o Jerry Shandrew *Shandrew Public Relations*
1050 S Stanley Ave
Los Angeles, CA 90019-6634, USA

Malone, Van (Athlete, Football Player)
4762 S 203rd East Ave
Broken Arrow, OK 74014-8820, USA

Maloney, Dan (Athlete, Hockey Player)
RR 2
Hawkestone, ON LOL lTO, CANADA

Maloney, Dave (Athlete, Hockey Player)
122 Dolphin Cove Quay
Stamford, CT 06902-7718, USA

Maloney, Dave (Athlete, Hockey Player)
New York Rangers 2 Penn Plz Fl 22
Attn: Broadcast Dept
New York, NY 10121-2299, USA

Maloney, Don (Athlete, Hockey Player)
21 Guilford Ln
Greenwich, CT 06831-4121, USA

Maloney, Don (Athlete, Hockey Player)
Phoenix Coyotes 6751 N Sunset Blvd Ste 200
Attn: General Manager
Glendale, AZ 85305-3124, USA

Maloney, Jim (Athlete, Baseball Player)
9722 Groffs Mill Dr Ste 107
Unit 102
Owings Mills, MD 21117-6341, USA

Maloney, Phil (Athlete, Hockey Player)
3626 Yellowpoint Rd.
RR 3
Ladysmith, BC V9G 1E8, CANADA

Maloney, Sean (Athlete, Baseball Player)
244 Pheasant Run
Saunderstown, RI 02874-2033, USA

Maloof, Adrienne (Business Person, Reality TV Star)
c/o Shaila Arora *Arora/Wasserman Entertainment Media*
23679 Calabasas Rd
Suite 633
Calabasas, CA 91302, USA

Maloof, Gavin (Business Person)
c/o Staff Member *Sacramento Kings*
1 Sports Parkway
Sacramento, CA 95834

Maloof, Mary Lou Metzger (Musician)
5100 Stern Ave
Sherman Oaks, CA 91423, USA

Maloog, Jack (Athlete, Baseball Player)
3140 S Vista Dr
Chandler, AZ 85248-3728, USA

Malouf, Kerry (Stylist)
c/o Staff Member *Mercury Artists*
8460 Higuera St Fl 2
Culver City, CA 90232, USA

Malrena, Oswaldo (Baseball Player)
Chicago Cubs
160 E 6th Pl
Mesa, AZ 85201-5068, USA

Maltais, Steve (Athlete, Hockey Player)
646 Country Club Dr
Itasca, IL 60143-1681, USA

Maltbie, Roger (Athlete, Golfer)
179 Longmeadow Dr
Los Gatos, CA 95032-5655, USA

Maltby, Kirk (Athlete, Hockey Player)
58 Putnam Pl
Grosse Pointe Shores, MI 48236-1224, USA

Maltin, Leonard (Correspondent)
c/o Staff Member *Entertainment Tonight (ET)*
4024 Radford Ave.
Studio City, CA 91604, USA

Maltin, Leonard (Journalist)
10424 Whipple St
Toluca Lake, CA 91602-2809, USA

Maltz, Rachel (Stylist)
c/o Staff Member *Ford Models (Chicago)*
311 W Superior St
Chicago, IL 60654, USA

Malubay, Ramiele (Musician)

Maly, Arturo (Actor)
c/o Staff Member *Telefe - Argentina*
Pavon 2444 (C1248AAT)
Buenos Aires, ARGENTINA

Malzone, Frank (Athlete, Baseball Player)
16 Aletha Rd
Needham, MA 02492-4302, USA

Mamas & The Papas, The
61 Purchase St. #2
Rye, NY 10580

Mambo, Kevin
3500 W. Olympic Blvd. #1400
Burbank, CA 91505

Mamet, David (Writer)
c/o Jeff Berg *ICM Partners (ICM-LA)*
10250 Constellation Blvd Fl 7
Los Angeles, CA 90067, USA

Mamoa, Jason (Actor)
c/o Jeff Witjas *Agency for the Performing Arts (APA-LA)*
405 S Beverly Dr
Suite 500
Beverly Hills, CA 90212-4425, USA

Mana (Music Group)
c/o Staff Member *Creative Artists Agency (CAA-LA)*
2000 Ave Of The Stars
Los Angeles, CA 90067, USA

Manafort, Jason (Race Car Driver)
414 New Britain Ave
Plainville, CT 06082, USA

Manahan, Austin (Athlete, Baseball Player)
21150 N Tatum Blvd
Apt 2079
Phoenix, AZ 85050-7209, USA

Manca, Massimo (Athlete, Football Player)
3867 Miriam Dr
Doylestown, PA 18902-9176, USA

Manchester, Kenneth (Inventor)
147 Worcester Rd
Princeton, MA 01541-1521, USA

Manchester, Melissa (Musician)
c/o Staff Member *Columbia Artists Mgmt Inc*
1790 Broadway Fl 6
New York, NY 10019-1412, USA

Mancina, Mark (Actor)
c/o Staff Member *Gorfaine/Schwartz Agency Inc*
4111 W Alameda Ave
Suite 509
Burbank, CA 91505, USA

Mancini, Ray
12524 Indianapolis St
Los Angeles, CA 90066-1512

Mancuso, Nick (Actor)
c/o Joel Dean *TalentWorks (LA)*
3500 W Olive Ave
Suite 1400
Burbank, CA 91505, USA

Mancuso Jr, Frank (Producer)
c/o Staff Member *FGM Entertainment*
201 N Canon Dr #328
Beverly Hills, CA 90210

Mandan, Robert
Jim Moore & Associates
16700 Celtic St
Granada Hills, CA 91344

Mandarich, Tony (Athlete, Football Player)
12767 E Altadena Dr
Scottsdale, AZ 85259-3418, USA

Mandel, Howie (Comedian, Game Show Host, Television Host)
c/o Michael Rotenberg *3 Arts Entertainment Inc*
9460 Wilshire Blvd
7th Floor
Beverly Hills, CA 90210, USA

Mandel, Johnny
28946 Cliffside Dr
Malibu, CA 90265

Mandel, Loring
555 W. 57th St. #1230
New York, NY 10019

Mandela, Nelson (Nobel Prize Laureate)
Private Bag X70000
Houghton 2041, South Africa

Mandela, N Winnie Madikizela (Activist)
Orlando West
Soweto
Johannesburg, SOUTH AFRICA

Mandelbaum, Michael (Writer)
Basic Books
387 Park Avenue South
New York, NY 10016, USA

Manderson, Stephen Paul (Professor Green) (Musician)
c/o Andy Duggan *Primary Talent International (UK)*
The Primary Building
10-11 Jockeys Fields
London WC1R 4BN, UK

Mandich, Dan (Athlete, Hockey Player)
9075 Hyland Creek Cir
MinneapolisBovey, MN 55437-1907, USA

Mandley, Pete (Athlete, Football Player)
103 E Smoke Tree Rd
Gilbert, AZ 85296-2250, USA

Mandrell, Barbara (Musician)
B.M.I.F.C.
P.O. Box 620
Hendersonville, TN 37077-0620, USA

Mandrell, Louise (Actor)
c/o Staff Member *Morris Artists Management*
818 19th Ave S
Nashville, TN 37203, USA

Mandvi, Aasif (Actor)
c/o Lillian LaSalle *LaSalle Holland*
141 West 28th St Ste 300
New York, NY 10001, USA

Mandylor, Costas (Actor)
c/o Staff Member *Evolution Entertainment (LA)*
901 N Highland Ave
Los Angeles, CA 90038, USA

Mandylor, Louis (Actor)
c/o Erik Kritzer *Kritzer Levine Wilkins Entertainment (KLWG)*
11872 La Grange Ave
1st Floor
Los Angeles, CA 90025, USA

Mane, Gucci (Musician)
c/o Nick Carcaterra *Susan Blond Inc (NY)*
50 W 57th St
14th Floor
New York, NY 10019, USA

Mane, Tyler (Actor)
c/o Lesa Kirk *Open Entertainment*
1051. N Cole Ave
Suite B
Los Angeles, CA 90038, USA

Maneche, Daria (Stylist)
c/o Staff Member *Ennis*
119 Braintree St
Boston, MA 02134, USA

Manell, George (Race Car Driver)
5455 So. Polaris Ave.
Las Vegas, NV 89118, USA

Maneluk, george (Athlete, Hockey Player)
39 Weeping Willow Dr
Winnipeg, MB R2M 4H9, Canada

Manery, Kris (Athlete, Hockey Player)
48568 Quail Run Dr S
Plymouth, MI 48170-5717, USA

Manery, Randy (Athlete, Hockey Player)
6587 Garrett Rd
Buford, GA 30518-1109

Maness, James (Athlete, Football Player)
1001 Jarvis Ln
Azle, TX 76020-3321, USA

Manetti, Larry (Actor)
4615 Winnetka
Woodland Hills, CA 91364

Manfra, Fred (Commentator)
3001 Lvndebrooke Ct
Fallston, MD 21047-1362, USA

Manganiello, Joe (Actor)
c/o Colleen Schlegel *Frontline Management*
5670 Wilshire Blvd.
Suite 1370
Los Angeles, CA 90036, USA

Mangelsdorff, AlbertEmil-
Claar-Str. 23
Frankfurt/Main, GERMANY 60322

Manges, Mark (Athlete, Football Player)
701 White Ave
Cumberland, MD 21502, USA

Mangieri, Dino (Athlete, Football Player)
108 Lamport Blvd
Staten Island, NY 10305, USA

Mangini, Eric (Athlete, Football Player)
59 Moss ln
Brewster, MA 02631-2618, USA

Mangione, Chuck (Musician)
476 Hampton Blvd.
Rochester, NY 14612

Mangold, James Allen (Director, Producer, Writer)
c/o Bo Morrison *Block-Korenbrot Public Relations*
North Market Building
110 S Fairfax, Suite 310
Los Angeles, CA 90036, USA

Mangold, Nick (Athlete, Football Player)
361 Shunpike Rd
Chatham, NJ 07928-1634, USA

Mangual, Angel (Baseball Player)
Pittsburgh Pirates
1406 R Del Valle
Ponce, PR 00728, USA

Mangual, Pepe (Athlete, Baseball Player)
2325 Calle Tabonuco
Urb Los Caobos
Ponce, PR 00716-2712, USA

Mangum, John (Athlete, Football Player)
150 Summerwood Dr
Pearl, MS 39208-9074, USA

Mangum, Jonathan (Actor)
c/o Staff Member *Shapiro/West & Associates*
141 El Camino Dr #205
Beverly Hills, CA 90212, USA

Mangum, Kris (Athlete, Football Player)
16720 Krishna Ln
Charlotte, NC 28277-1638, USA

Manheim, Camryn (Actor, Producer)
c/o Peg Donegan *Framework Entertainment (LA)*
9057 Nemo St
Suite C
West Hollywood, CA 90069, USA

Maniaci, Joe (Athlete, Football Player)
3215 Rankin Ave
Windsor, ON N9E 3C2, Canada

Maniago, Cesare (Athlete, Hockey Player)
19-788 Citadel Dr
Port Coquitlam, BC V3C 6G9, CANADA

Manic Street Preachers (Music Group)
c/o Staff Member *Paradigm (Monterey)*
404 W Franklin St
Monterey, CA 93940, USA

Manigault-Stallworth, Omarosa (Actor, Reality TV Star)

Manilow, Barry (Composer, Musician, Producer)
c/o Garry Kief *Stiletto Entertainment*
8295 S La Cienega Blvd
Inglewood, CA 90301-1521, USA

Manis, Randy (Producer)
c/o Staff Member *Killer Films (US)*
526 W 26th St
Rm 715
New York, NY 10001-5524, USA

Manisha, Koirala (Actor, Bollywood)
302 Beachwood Towers
Yari Road Versova Andher (W)
Mumbai, MS 400061, INDIA

Manjia, Nicki (Musician)
c/o Staff Member *Motown Records (NY)*
1755 Broadway
7th Floor
New York, NY 10019, USA

Manke, John (Aviator)
3803 W Avenue JIS
Lancaster, CA 93536-6339, USA

Mankell, Henning (Writer)
c/o Staff Member *Leopard förlag AB*
S:t Paulsgatan 11
Stockholm 118 46, Sweden

Mankiewicz, Frank
The Wyoming Columbia Rd. NW
Washington, DC 20009

Mankiewicz, Tom
1609 Magnetic Terrace
Los Angeles, CA 90069

Mankiller, Wilma P (Activist)
c/o Staff Member *Cherokee Nation*
PO Box 948
Tahlequah, OK 74465, USA

Mankins, Logan (Athlete, Football Player)
1 Mockingbird Ln
North Attleboro, MA 02760-2775, USA

Mankowitz, Wolf
Ahakista County Cork
Kilcrohane, IRELAND 11

Mankowski, Phil (Athlete, Baseball Player)
2280 Southwestern Blvd
Buffalo, NY 14224-4423, USA

Manley, Dexter (Athlete, Football Player)
PO Box 25049
Washington, DC 20027-8049, USA

Manley, Elizabeth (Figure Skater)
Marco Enterprises
74830 Velie Dr
#A
Palm Desert, CA 92260, USA

Manley, Joe (Athlete, Football Player)
3365 County Road 92
Rogersville, AL 35652-2736, USA

Manley, Leon (Athlete, Football Player)
1207 Knollpark Cir
Austin, TX 78758, USA

Manlikova, Hana
Vymolova 8
Prague 5 15000, Czech Republic

Mann, Aimee (Musician)
Girlie Action Media And Marketing
59 W 19th St Ste 4A
New York, NY 10011, USA

Mann, Almee (Musician, Songwriter, Writer)
Michael Hausman Mgmt
511 Ave of Americas
#197
New York, NY 10011, USA

Mann, Art (Producer, Television Host)
HDNet Films
122 Hudson St.
5th Floor
New York, New York 10013, USA

Mann, Barry (Composer)
1010 Laurel Way
Beverly Hills, CA 90210, USA

Mann, Carol (Athlete, Golfer)
6 Cape Chestnut Dr
Spring, TX 77381, USA

Mann, Catherine
9417 Spruce Tree Circle
Bethesda, MD 20814-1654

Mann, Charles (Athlete, Football Player)
1518 Night Shade Ct
Vienna, VA 22182, USA

Mann, David W (Religious Leader)
10550 S 200 W
Columbia City, IN 46725, USA

Mann, Dick (Motorcycle Racer)
Motorsports HOF
PO Box 194
Novi, MI 48376-0194, USA

Mann, Errol (Athlete, Football Player)
5521 Bonanza Pl
Missoula, MT 59808, USA

Mann, Gabriel (Actor)
c/o Van Johnson *Van Johnson Company*
10250 Constellation Blvd
Suite 2320
Los Angeles, CA 90067, USA

Mann, Garbriel (Actor)
United Talent Agency
9560 Wilshire Blvd
#500
Beverly Hills, CA 90212, USA

Mann, H Thompson (Athlete, Swimmer)
23 Pleasant St #501
Newburyport, MA 01950-2634, USA

Mann, Jim (Athlete, Baseball Player)
197 N Franklin St
Holbrook, MA 02343-1111, USA

Mann, Jimmy (Athlete, Hockey Player)
1538 Scio Ridge Rd
Ann Arbor, MI 48103-8991

Mann, Johnny (Composer, Conductor)
78516 Gorman Lane
Indio, CA 92203, USA

Mann, Kelly (Athlete, Baseball Player)
750 Napoli Dr
Pacific Palisades, CA 90272, USA

Mann, Leslie (Actor)
c/o Jodi Gottlieb *Independent Public Relations*
7060 Hollywood Blvd
8th Floor
Los Angeles, CA 90028, USA

Mann, Ltc Hiram (Aviator)
1205 Pollyanna Dr
Titusville, FL 32796-1948, USA

Mann, Manfred (Misc)
EMI Records
43 Brook Green
London W6 7EF, UNITED KINGDOM (UK)

Mann, Marvin L (Business Person)
Lexmark International
740 W New Circle Road
Lexington, KY 40550, USA

Mann, Michael K (Actor, Director, Producer, Writer)
c/o Staff Member *Forward Pass Inc*
12233 W Olympic Blvd #340
Los Angeles, CA 90064

Mann, Monroe (Actor, Producer, Writer)
c/o Staff Member *Loco Dawn Films, LLC*
499 Seventh Avenue
12th Floor North
New York, NY 10018, USA

Mann, Robert (Athlete, Football Player)
515 SW Hampton Ct
Port Saint Lucie, FL 34986, USA

Mann, Robert W (Engineer)
85 Murray Ave
Port Washington, NY 11050-3527, USA

Mann, Shelley I (Swimmer)
1301 S Scott St
#638S
Arlington, VA 22204, USA

Mann, Terrence V (Actor)
c/o Steve Stone *Cornerstone Talent Agency*
37 W 20th St
New York, NY 10011, USA

Mannelly, Patrick (Athlete, Football Player)
1128 Kildare Ave
Libertyville, IL 60048-1203, USA

Manners, Miss
1651 Harvard St. NW
Washington, DC 20009

Mannheim Steamroller (Music Group)
9120 Mormon Bridge Rd
Omaha, NE 68152, USA

Manning, Aaron (Athlete, Football Player)
6906 27th Ave
Kenosha, WI 53143-5214, USA

Manning, Archie (Athlete, Football Player)
1420 1st St
New Orleans, LA 70130-5713, USA

Manning, Charlie (Athlete, Baseball Player)
PO Box 964
Winter Haven, FL 33882-0964, USA

Manning, Danny (Athlete, Basketball Player, Olympic Athlete)
205 Running Ridge Rd
Lawrence, KS 66049-2180, USA

Manning, Eli (Athlete, Football Player)
1500 Hudson St #7I/#7J/#7K
Hoboken, NJ 07030, USA

Manning, Jane (Opera Singer)
2 Wilton Square
London N1, UNITED KINGDOM (UK)

Manning, Jim (Athlete, Baseball Player)
41 Fox Run Dr
Weaverville, NC 28787-8307, USA

Manning, Peyton (Athlete, Football Player)
c/o Tom Condon *CAA - St. Louis*
222 S Central Ave
Suite 1008
St Louis, MO 63105, USA

Manning, Rick (Athlete, Baseball Player)
22447 N 49th Pl
Phoenix, AZ 85054-7102, USA

Manning, Rob (Engineer)
Jet Propulsion Laboratory
4800 Oak Grove Dr
Pasadena, CA 91109, USA

Manning, Taryn (Actor, Musician)
c/o Heather Weiss *Much and House Public Relations*
8075 W 3rd St
Suite 500
Los Angeles, CA 90048, USA

Manning, Wade (Athlete, Football Player)
5133 Malaya St
Denver, CO 80249, USA

Mannion, Pace (Athlete, Basketball Player)
4190 Achilles Dr
Salt Lake City, UT 84124-3266, USA

Mannix, Ernie (Actor, Composer, Musician)
c/o Staff Member *Greenspan Artist Management*
8760 W Sunset Blvd
West Hollywood, CA 90069, USA

Manno, Bob (Athlete, Hockey Player)
5643 Peer St
Niagara Falls, ON L2G 1W8, Canada

Manoa, Tim (Athlete, Football Player)
1285 Boardman Canfield Rd
Youngstown, OH 44512-4058, USA

Manoff, Dinah (Actor)
Innovative Artists
1505 10th St
Santa Monica, CA 90401, USA

Manon, Julio (Athlete, Baseball Player)
4726 15th Ave S
Saint Petersburg, FL 33711, USA

Manoogian, RIchard A (Business Person)
Masco Corp
2100 Van Born Road
Taylor, MI 48180, USA

Manor, Brison (Athlete, Football Player)
285 Spruce St
Bridgeton, NJ 08302, USA

Manorama (Actor, Bollywood)
5 Neelagandan Street
T Nagar
Chennai, TN 600017, INDIA

Manos, Sam (Athlete, Football Player)
1424 E Normandy Blvd
Deltona, FL 32725, USA

Manoukian, Don (Athlete, Football Player)
5405 Mae Anne Ave
Reno, NV 89253-1813, USA

Manowar (Music Group)
Prefers to be contacted via email

Manrique, Fred (Baseball Player)
Toronto Blue Jays
1775 SW 2nd Ave
Boca Raton, FL 33432-7230, USA

Mansell, Kevin (Business Person)
Kohl's Corp
N56W17000 RIdgewood Dr
Menomonee Falls, WI 53051, USA

Mansell, Nigel (Race Car Driver)
Nigel Mansell Racing
Brands Hatch
Longfield, Kent DA3 8NG, UNITED KINGDOM (UK)

Manser, Michael J (Architect)
Morton House
Chiswick Mall
London W4 2PS, UNITED KINGDOM (UK)

Mansfield, Mike (Ex-Senator, Senator)
1101 Pennsylvania Ave NW #900
Washington, DC 20004-2514, USA

Mansfield, Peter (Nobel Prize Laureate)
Notingham University
Physics Dept
Nottingham NG7 2RD, UNITED KINGDOM (UK)

Mansfield, Von (Athlete, Football Player)
3530 194th St
Homewood, IL 60430-4325, USA

Mansfield-Kelley, Marie (Athlete, Baseball Player, Commentator)
9 Eastland Rd
Jamaica Plain, MA 02130-4616, USA

Mansholt, Sicco L (Government Official)
Oosteinde 16
Wapserveen, HB 8351, NETHERLANDS

Mansolino, Doug (Athlete, Baseball Player)
106 Santee Wav
Loudon, TN 37774-2123, USA

Manson, Charles (Misc)
B-33920, 4A 4R-23
P.O. Box 3476
Corcoran, CA 93212, USA

Manson, Dave (Athlete, Hockey Player)
211 Cowboys Pkwy
Irving, TX 75063, USA

Manson, Marilyn (Musician)
c/o Tony Cuilla *Ciulla Management*
1509 N. Crescent Heights Blvd
#4
Los Angeles, CA 90046, USA

Manson, Shirley (Musician)
c/o Staff Member *Untitled Entertainment (LA)*
350 S. Beverly Dr #200
Beverly Hills, CA 90212, USA

Mansour, Nicole (Actor)

Mansouri, Lotfi (Director, Musical Director)
San Francisco Opera House
301 Van Ness Ave
San Francisco, CA 94102, USA

Mant, Cathy (Athlete, Golfer)
326 Broadmoor Way
McDonough, GA 30253, USA

Mantador, Steve (Athlete, Hockey Player)
6301 Osprey Ter
Coconut Creek, FL 33073-2624, USA

Mantee, Paul (Actor)
PO Box 687
Malibu, CA 90265, USA

Mantegna, Joe (Actor, Producer, Writer)
c/o Jack Gilardi *ICM Partners (ICM-LA)*
10250 Constellation Blvd Fl 7
Los Angeles, CA 90067, USA

Mantei, Matt (Athlete, Baseball Player)
4709 Chicago Path
Stevensville, MI 49127-9356, USA

Mantel, Hilary (Writer)
A W Heath
79 St Martin's Ln
London WC2N 4AA, UNTED KINGDOM (UK)

Mantel, Hillary M (Writer)
AM Heath
79 Saint Martin's Lane
London WC2N 4AA, UNITED KINGDOM (UK)

Mantello, Joe (Actor, Director)
c/o Staff Member *Creative Artists Agency (CAA-LA)*
2000 Ave Of The Stars
Los Angeles, CA 90067, USA

Mantenuto, Michael (Actor)
c/o Kim Hodgert *Creative Artists Agency (CAA-LA)*
2000 Ave Of The Stars
Los Angeles, CA 90067, USA

Mantha, Mo
8423 Tally Ho Rd.
Lutherville, MD 20193

Mantha, Moe (Athlete, Hockey Player, Olympic Athlete)
1538 Scio Ridge Rd
Ann Arbor, MI 48103-8991, USA

Manthey, Jerri (Actor)
P.O. Box 801507
Valencia, California 91380

Manthra (Actor, Bollywood)
5-A Block 2 Vijay Shanti Apts
Arcot Road Vadapalani
Chennai, TN 600026, INDIA

Mantilla, Felix (Athlete, Baseball Player)
6973 N Tacoma St
Milwaukee, WI 53224-4759, USA

Mantis, Nick (Athlete, Basketball Player)
2344 Autumn Dr
Crown Point, IN 46307-9668, USA

Mantle, Anthony (Cinematographer)
c/o Staff Member *ICM Partners (ICM-LA)*
10250 Constellation Blvd Fl 7
Los Angeles, CA 90067, USA

Mantley, John
4121 Longridge Ave.
Sherman Oaks, CA 91423

Manto, Jeff (Athlete, Baseball Player)
725 Radcliffe St
Bristol, PA 19007-5223, USA

Mantooth, Randolph (Actor)
c/o Staff Member *Stone Manners Salners Agency (LA)*
9911 W Pico Blvd Ste 1400
Los Angeles, CA 90035, USA

Mantranga, Jonah (Musician)
c/o Staff Member *Paradigm (Monterey)*
404 W Franklin St
Monterey, CA 93940, USA

Mantreola, Patricia
c/o Staff Member *BMG*
1540 Broadway
New York, NY 10036, USA

Mantz, Michael R (Astronaut)
1940 Elanita Dr
San Pedro, CA 90732-4430, USA

Mantzoukas, Jason (Actor)
c/o Christie Smith *Mosaic Media Group*
9200 W. Sunset Blvd
10th Floor
Los Angeles, CA 90069, USA

Manucci, Dan (Athlete, Football Player)
1208 W Sand Dune Dr
Gilbert, AZ 85233, USA

Manuel, Barry (Athlete, Baseball Player)
805 Oak St
Mamou, LA 70554-2715, USA

Manuel, Charles F (Chuck) (Baseball Player)
2931 Plantation Road
Winter Haven, FL 33884, USA

Manuel, Charlie (Athlete, Baseball Player, Coach)
2931 Plantation Rd
Winter Haven, FL 33884-1233, USA

Manuel, Jay (Reality TV Star, Television Host)
c/o Lisa Shotland *Creative Artists Agency (CAA-LA)*
2000 Ave Of The Stars
Los Angeles, CA 90067, USA

Manuel, Jerry (Athlete, Baseball Player, Coach)
5556 Ridge Park Dr
Loomis, CA 95650-9400, USA

Manuel, Lionel (Athlete, Football Player)
827 E Cedar Dr
Chandler, AZ 85249, USA

Manuel, Marquand (Athlete, Football Player)
3672 Churchill Downs Dr
Davie, FL 33328-1307, USA

Manuel, Robert (Actor)
La Maison du Buisson
22-26 Rue Jules Regnier
Plaisir 78370, FRANCE

Manuelidis, Laura (Misc)
Yale University Medical School
Neuropathology Dept
New Haven, CT 06520, USA

Manumaleuna, Brandon (Athlete, Football Player)
1218 Koleeta Dr
Harbor City, CA 90710-1824, USA

Manusky, Greg (Athlete, Football Player)
4939 Eastbourne Ct
San Jose, CA 95138, USA

Manville, Dick (Athlete, Baseball Player)
1436 Lake Francis Dr
Apopka, FL 32712-2007, USA

Manwaring, Kirt (Athlete, Baseball Player)
San Francisco Giants
20 Prospect Rdg
Horseheads, NY 14845-7988, USA

Manwaring, Kurt D (Athlete, Baseball Player)
20 Prospect Rdg
Horseheads, NY 14845, USA

Manz, Wolfgang (Musician)
Pasteuralle 55
Hanover 30655, GERMANY

Manza, Ralph
550 Hygeia Ave.
Leucadia, CA 92024

Manzanero, Armando (Musician)
Pro Art
Paz Soidan 170
Of 903
San Isidro, Lima 27, PERU

Manzanillo, Josias (Athlete, Baseball Player)
274 Kennebec St
Mattapan, MA 02126-1106, USA

Manzarek, Ray (Musician)
c/o Dan Devita *The Kirby Organization - U.K.*
6 Walter Ln
Camden
London NW1 8NZ, UK

Manzella, Tommy (Athlete, Baseball Player)
3213 Veronica Dr
Chalmette, LA 70043-3555, USA

Manzi, Catello (Horse Racer)
1 Hickory Lane
Freehold, NJ 07728, USA

Manzi, Louis (Horse Racer)
4036 Grace Ave
Bronx, NY 10466-2210, USA

Manzi, Rocco (Horse Racer)
112 Willow Meadow Way
Oneida, NY 13421-1852, USA

Manzo, Caroline (Business Person, Reality TV Star)
c/o Sal Bonaventura *CEG Talent*
251 W. 39th St
7th Floor
New York, NY 10011, USA

Manzo, Dina (Business Person, Reality TV Star)
705 Ewing Ave
Franklin Lakes, NJ 07417, USA

Manzoni, Giacomo (Composer)
Viale Papiniano 31
Milan 20123, ITALY

Manzullo, Donald (Congressman, Politician)
2228 Rayburn HOB
Washington, DC 20515, USA

Mapes, Cliff
PO Box 872
Pryor, OK 74362

Maple, Eddie (Horse Racer)
25 Spartina Cres
Bluffton, SC 29910-4702, USA

Maple, Eddie (Race Car Driver)
420 Fair Hill Dr.
#1
Elkton, MD 21921, USA

Maples, Marla (Actor)
c/o Jonathan Todd *Sabre Entertainment*
5737 Kanan Rd #237
Agoura Hills, CA 91301, USA

Mapother, William (Actor)
c/o Brian Medavoy *Medavoy Management*
10203 Santa Monica Blvd
Suite 400
Los Angeles, CA 90067, USA

Mar, Marcela (Actor)
c/o Luis Balaguer *Latin World Entertainment Agency (WEA)*
2601 South Bayshore Drive
Suite 235
Miami, FL 33133-5432, USA

Mara, Kate (Actor)
c/o Kenneth (Kenny) Goodman *Schiff Company, The*
9465 Wilshire Blvd
Suite 480
Beverly Hills, CA 90212, USA

mara, Paul
48472 Meadow Ct
Plymouth, MI 48170-3204

Mara, Ratu Sir Kamisese K T (President)
11 Ballery Road
Suva, FIJI

Mara, Rooney (Actor)
c/o Steve Caserta *Sanders Armstrong Caserta*
2120 Colorado Blvd
Suite 120
Santa Monica, CA 90404, USA

Marachuk, Steve
568 Hana Hwy.
Pai Maui, HI 96779

Maradona, Diego (Athlete, Soccer Player)
Brandsen 805
Capital Federal 1161, ARGENTINA

Marak, Paul (Athlete, Baseball Player)
1211 Comanche Trl
Alamogordo, NM 88310-4010, USA

Maramorosch, Karl (Scientist)
1050 George St
New Brunswick, NJ 08901, USA

Maran, Josie (Actor)
c/o Darren Goldberg *Global Creative*
1051 Cole Ave # B
Los Angeles, CA 90038, USA

Marangi, Gary (Athlete, Football Player)
26 Morton St
Port Jefferson Station, NY 11776, USA

Maraniss, David (Journalist)
Washington Post
Editorial Dept
1150 15th St NW
Washington, DC 20071, USA

Marano, Laura (Actor)
c/o Jennifer Millar *Paradigm (LA)*
360 N Crescent Dr
North Bldg
Beverly Hills, CA 90210, USA

Marasca, Dana (Stylist)
c/o Staff Member *Celestine - CA*
1666 20th St
#200-B
Santa Monica, CA 90404, USA

Maratos, Terry (Actor)
c/o Staff Member *Cage Group, The*
14724 Ventura Blvd #505
Sherman Oaks, CA 91423

Maratos-Flier, Elftheria (Doctor)
Joslin Diabetes Center
1 Joslin Place
Boston, MA 02215, USA

Marber, Patrick (Writer)
Judy Daish
2 Saint Charles Place
London W10 6EG, UNITED KINGDOM
(UK)

Marble, Roy (Athlete, Basketball Player)
1355 Wagon Wheel Ln
Grand Blanc, MI 48439-4863, USA

Marbley, Harlan (Athlete, Boxer, Olympic
Athlete)
6113 Parkview Ln
Clinton, MD 20735-3850, USA

Marbury, Joseph (Athlete, Baseball Player)
1472 21st St N
Birmingham, AL 35234, USA

Marbury, Kerry (Athlete, Football Player)
1201locust Ave
Fairmont, WV 26554-2451, USA

Marbury, Rendon (Athlete, Baseball
Player)
1472 21st St N
Birmingham, AL 35234-2708, USA

Marbury, Stephan (Athlete, Basketball
Coach, Olympic Athlete)
2940 W 31st St Apt 4G
Brooklyn, NY 11224-1734, USA

Marbury, Stephon (Athlete, Basketball
Player, Olympic Athlete)
2940 W 31st St Apt 4G
Brooklyn, NY 11224-1734, USA

Marbut, Robert G (Publisher)
Argyle Communications
100 NE Loop
#1400
San Antonio, TX 78216, USA

Marc, Alessandra (Opera Singer)
Columbia Artists Mgmt Inc
165 W 57th St
New York, NY 10019, USA

Marceau, Sophie (Actor)
Artmedia
20 Ave Rapp
Paris 75007, FRANCE

Marcelino, Mario
1418 N. Highland Ave. #102
Los Angeles, CA 90028

Marcetta, Milan (Athlete, Hockey Player)
435 Gunther-Ellison Rd
Enderby, BC V0E 1 V3, Canada

March, Forbes (Actor)
c/o Staff Member *Innovative Artists (LA)*
1505 10th St
Santa Monica, CA 90401, USA

March, Jane (Actor, Model)
Storm Model Mgmt
5 Jubilee Place
#100
London SW3 3TD, UNITED KINGDOM
(UK)

March, Joan
Whale Rock Ranch Rd.
Ojai, CA 93023

March, Little Peggy (Musician)
Cape Entertainment
1161 NW 76th Ave
Plantation, FL 33822, USA

March, Peggy
1161 NW 76th Ave.
Ft. Lauderdale, FL 33322

March, Stephanie (Actor)
c/o Erica Tarin *ID Public Relations (ID-LA)*
7060 Hollywood Blvd
8th Floor
Los Angeles, CA 90028, USA

Marchand, Guy
40 rue Francois Ier
Paris, FRANCE F-75008

Marchant, Kenny (Congressman,
Politician)
1110 Longworth HOB
Washington, DC 20515, USA

Marchant, Todd (Athlete, Hockey Player,
Olympic Athlete)
10448 Caribou Way
Tustin, CA 92782-1470, USA

Marchette, Josh
6500 Wilshire Blvd. #2200
Los Angeles, CA 90048

Marchetti, Gino J (Athlete, Football
Player)
324 Devon Way
West Chester, PA 19380, USA

Marchetti, Leo V (Misc)
Fraternal Order of Police
5615 Belair Road
Baltimore, MD 21206, USA

Marchibroda, Ted (Athlete, Football
Player)
90 Orchard Point Dr
Weems, VA 22576, USA

Marchinko, Jhoni (Producer)
c/o Staff Member *United Talent Agency
(UTA)*
9336 Civic Center Dr
Beverly Hills, CA 90210, USA

Marchiol, Ken (Athlete, Football Player)
6489 5 Olathe St
Centennial, CO 80016-1052, USA

Marchionne, Sergio (Business Person)
Fiat SpA
Via Nizza 250
Turin 10126, ITALY

Marchisano, Francesco Cardinal
(Religious Leader)
Cancelleria Apostolica Palazzo
Plazza Cancelleria 1
Rome 00186, ITALY

Marchlewski, Frank (Athlete, Football
Player)
428 Toledo Dr
Lower Burrell, PA 15068, USA

Marchuk, Guri I (Mathematician)
Numerical Mathematics Institute
Gubkin Str 8
Mascow 117333, RUSSIA

Marchuk, Yevhen K (Prime Minister)
Verkovna Rada
M Hrushevskoho Str 5
Kiev 252008, UKRAINE

Marciano, David (Actor)
c/o Staff Member *Buchwald/Fortitude (LA)*
6500 Wilshire Blvd
Suite 2200
Los Angeles, CA 90048, USA

Marciano, Rob (Anchor)
c/o Staff Member *CNN (Atlanta)*
One CNN Center
PO Box 105366
Atlanta, GA 30303, USA

Marcikic, Ivan (Inventor, Physicist)
Geneva University
24 Rue du General Dufour
Geneva 1211, SWITZERLAND

Marcil, Vanessa (Actor)
c/o Adena Chawke *Greenlight
Management and Production*
13848 Valleyheart Dr
Sherman Oaks, CA 91423, USA

Marciniak, Ron (Athlete, Football Player)
2222 Hopespring Loop
The Villages, FL 32162-7044, USA

Marcinkevicius, Iustinus M (Writer)
Mildos Str 33
#6
Vilnius 232055, LITHUANIA

Marcinko, Richard (Writer)
c/o Kimberly Witherspoon *Inkwell
Management*
521 Fifth Ave
New York, NY 10175, USA

Marcinyshyn, Dave (Athlete, Hockey
Player)
36 Doucette Pl
St. Albert, AB T8N 6S6, Canada

Marcis, Dave (Race Car Driver)
Marcis Auto Racing
10 Greenleaf Road
Arden, NC 28704, USA

Marciulionis, Sarunas (Athlete, Basketball
Player)
Hotel Sarunas
Hotel Sarunas Raitininku Street 4 Attn
Vilnius 2051, Lithuania

Marco, Gian (Musician)
c/o Staff Member *Creative Artists Agency
(CAA-LA)*
2000 Ave Of The Stars
Los Angeles, CA 90067, USA

Marcol, Czeslaw C (Chester) (Athlete,
Football Player)
P.O. Box 466
Dollar Bay, MI 49922, USA

Marcon, Lou (Athlete, Hockey Player)
927 Mountdale Ave
Thunder Bay, ON P7E 2Z8, Canada

Marcontell, Ed (Athlete, Football Player)
P.O. Box 884
Rusk, TX 75785, USA

Marcos (Musician)
East West America Records
75 Rockefeller Plaza
New York, NY 10019, USA

Marcos, Imelda
Leyte Providencia Dept
Tolosa Leyte, PHILIPPINES

Marcotte, Don (Athlete, Hockey Player)
12 Cote St
Amesbury, MA 1913, 01913-3804

Marcovicci, Andrea (Actor, Musician)
Donald Smith Promotions
1640 E 48th St
#14U
New York, NY 10017, USA

Marcum, Art (Writer)
c/o Staff Member *Nine Yards
Entertainment*
8530 Wilshire Blvd Fl 5
Beverly Hills, CA 90211, USA

Marcum, Shaun (Athlete, Baseball Player)
1413 Jill Ln
Excelsior Springs, MO 64024-9790, USA

Marcus, Bernard (Business Person)
Marcus Foundation
2455 Paces Ferry Rd SE
Bldg. C, 22nd
Atlanta, GA 30339, USA

Marcus, John (Race Car Driver)
PO Box 1018
Talladega, AL 35161-1018, USA

Marcus, Jurgen
Pestalozzistr. 23a
Munich, GERMANY D-80469

Marcus, Ken (Photographer)
6916 Melrose Ave
Los Angeles, CA 90038, USA

Marcus, Rudolph (Nobel Prize Laureate)
600 S Burnside Ave Apt 11
Los Angeles, CA 90036-3906, USA

Marcus, Sparky (Actor)
910 Arlene Ct
Yreka, CA 96097, USA

Marcus, Trula M (Actor)
The Agency
1800 Ave of the Stars
#400
Los Angeles, CA 90067, USA

Marcy, Geoffrey (Astronomer)
San Francisco State University
Astronomy Dept
San Francisco, CA 94132, USA

Mardall, Cyril L (Architect)
5 Boyne Terrace Mews
London W11 3LR, UNITED KINGDOM
(UK)

Marden, Brice (Artist)
6 Saint Lukes Place
New York, NY 10014-3974, USA

Marder, Barry
c/o Daniel Strone *Trident Media Group LLC*
41 Madison Ave
36th Floor
New York, NY 10010, USA

Marderian, Greg (Athlete, Football Player)
1400 Barton Rd Apt 1701
Redlands, CA 92373-1404, USA

Mardones, Benny (Musician)
Tony Cee
PO Box 410
Utica, NY 13503, USA

Mare, Olindo (Athlete, Football Player)
5 Serenity Dr
Mandeville, LA 70471, USA

Maree, Sydney (Athlete, Track Athlete)
2 Braxton Road
Bryn Mawr, PA 19010, USA

Marek, Marcus (Athlete, Football Player)
26 Nora Ct
New Ipswich, NH 03071-3504, USA

Maren, Elizabeth (Actor)
3126 Oakcrest Dr
Los Angeles, CA 90068, USA

Maren, Jerry (Actor)
3126 Oakcrest Dr.
Los Angeles, CA 90068

Marentette, Leo (Athlete, Baseball Player)
33606 Beechwood St
Westland, MI 48185-3002, USA

Margal, Albert M (Prime Minister)
8 Hornsey Rise Gardens
London N19, UNITED KINGDOM (UK)

Margalit, Israela (Musician)
Columbia Artists Mgmt Inc
165 W 57th St
New York, NY 10019, USA

Margarita, Henry R (Athlete, Football Player)
4 Drury Ln
Stoneham, MA 02180, USA

Margavage, Dave (Athlete, Football Player)
474 Woodview Dr
lexington, KY 40515-5945, USA

Margeot, Jean Cardinal (Religious Leader)
Bonne Terre
Vacoas, MAURITIUS

Margera, Bam (Actor, Producer, Writer)
PO Box 671
Westtown, PA 19395, USA

Margera, Vincent (Actor)
c/o Michael (Mike) Esterman
Esterman.Com, LLC
Prefers to be contacted via email
MD, USA

Margerum, Ken (Athlete, Football Player)
494 Riverview Dr
Capitola, CA 95010-2778, USA

Margison, Richard (Opera Singer)
George Martynuk
352 7th Ave
New York, NY 10001, USA

Margo, Philip (Musician)
American Mgmt
19948 Mayall St
Chatsworth, CA 91311, USA

Margoliash, Emmanuel (Scientist)
554 Oakdale
Glencoe, IL 60022-2043, USA

Margolin, Phillip (Writer)
c/o Jean V Naggar *Jean Naggar Literary Agency*
216 East 75th St #1E
New York, NY 10021, USA

Margolin, Stuart (Actor)
Three Owl Productions
Box 478
Ganges, BC V0S 1E0, CANADA

Margolis, Cindy (Actor, Model)
c/o Glenn Gulino *G2 Entertainment LLC*
1 Columbus Pl #S-25E
New York, NY 10019, USA

Margolis, Lawrence S (Judge)
US Claims Court
717 Madison Place NW
Washington, DC 20439, USA

Margolyes, Miriam (Actor)
c/o Staff Member *The Rights House (UK)*
Drury House
34-43 Russell St
London WC2B 5HA, UK

Margon, Bruce H (Astronomer)
University of Washington
Astronomy Dept
PO Box 351580
Seattle, WA 98195, USA

Margoneri, Joe (Athlete, Baseball Player)
341 Turkeytown Rd
West Newton, PA 15089-1850, USA

Margot, Sandra (Athlete, Wrestler)
PO Box 1168
Studio City, CA 91603, USA

Margoyles, Miriam (Actor)
P F D Drury House
34-43 Russell St
London WC2B 5HA, UNITED KINGDOM (UK)

Margrave, John L (Misc)
4511 Vrone
Bellaire, TX 77401, USA

Margret, Ann (Actor, Dancer, Musician)
2707 Benedict Canyon Dr
Beverly Hills, CA 90210, USA

Margrethe II (Royalty)
Amalienborg Palace
Copenhgen K 1257, DENMARK

Margulies, Donald (Writer)
Yale University
English Dept
New Haven, CT 06520, USA

Margulies, James H (Jimmy) (Cartoonist, Editor)
Hackensack Record
Editorial Dept
150 River St
Hackensack, NJ 07601, USA

Margulies, Julianna (Actor)
c/o Annick Muller *ID Public Relations (ID-NY)*
150 W 30th St
19th Floor
New York, NY 10001, USA

Margulis, Lynn (Biologist)
2 Cummington St
Boston, MA 02215, USA

Mariago, Cesare
19 788 Citadel Dr.#120
Pt. Coquitlam, CANADA BC V3C 6G

Mariam, Mengistu Haile (President)
PO Box 1536
Gunhill Enclave
Harare, ZIMBABWE

Mariano, Jarah (Model)
c/o Staff Member *IMG Models (NY)*
304 Park Ave S
12th Floor
New York, NY 10010, USA

Mariategui, Sandro (Prime Minister)
Ave Ramirez Gaston 375
Miraflores, Lima, PERU

Marichal, Juan (Athlete, Baseball Player)
9458 NW 54th Doral Circle Ln
Doral, FL 33178-2048, USA

Marie, Ann (Actor)
1608 N Cahuenga
#354
Hollywood, CA 90028, USA

Marie, Aurelius J B L (President)
Zicack
Portsmouth, DOMINICA

Marie, Constance (Actor)
c/o Staff Member *Kass & Stokes Management*
9229 Sunset Blvd
Suite 504
Los Angeles, CA 90069, USA

Marie, Lisa (Actor, Model)
c/o Staff Member *WmE2 (WMA-LA)*
1 William Morris Pl
Beverly Hills, CA 90212, USA

Marie, Princess (Royalty)
Schloss Vaduz
Vaduz 9490, LIECHTENSTEIN

Marie, Rose (Actor)
c/o Leanna Levy *Cassell-Levy Inc*
843 N Sycamore Ave
Los Angeles, CA 90038, USA

Marienthal, Eli (Actor)
c/o Lisa Gallant *Gallant Management*
10250 Constellation Blvd Fl 7
Los Angeles, CA 90067, USA

Marienthal, Eric (Musician)
15030 Ventura Blvd #710
Sherman Oaks, CA 91403, USA

Marillion (Musician)
c/o Staff Member *Paradigm (Monterey)*
404 W Franklin St
Monterey, CA 93940, USA

Marilyn
33-34 Cleveland St.
London, ENGLAND W1

Marimow, William K (Journalist)
1942 Panama Street
Philadelphia, PA 19103-6610, USA

Marin, Christian
27 rue de Richelieu
Paris, FRANCE F-75001

Marin, Jack (Athlete, Basketball Player)
3909 Regent Rd
Durham, NC 27707-5311, USA

Marin, Maguy (Choreographer)
Compagnie Maguy Marin
Place Salvador Allende
Creteil 94000, FRANCE

Marin, Mindy (Director)
c/o Jeremy Plager *Creative Artists Agency (CAA-LA)*
2000 Ave Of The Stars
Los Angeles, CA 90067, USA

Marin, Nole (Stylist)
c/o Staff Member *Bernstein & Andriulli*
58 W 40th St
New York, NY 10018, USA

Marin, Richard (Stylist)
c/o Staff Member *Cloutier Agency*
2632 La Cienega Ave
Los Angeles, CA 90034, USA

Marin, Richard A (Cheech) (Actor, Comedian)
c/o Ben Feigin *Anonymous Content (LA)*
3531 Hayden Ave
Culver City, CA 90232, USA

Marin, Rosario (Government Official, Writer)
Fuerza, Inc.
1340 E. McWood St.
West Covina, CA 91790, USA

Marinaro, Ed (Athlete, Football Player)
1466 N Doheny Dr
Los Angeles, CA 90069, USA

Marinelli, Rod (Athlete, Football Player)
1981 W Southmeadow Ln
Lake Forest, IL 60045-4831, USA

Marini, Gilles (Actor, Model)
c/o Vikram Dhawer *Authentic Talent and Literary Management*
45 Main St
Suite 1004
Brooklyn, NY 11201, USA

Marini, Hector (Athlete, Hockey Player)
4534 Gatineau Ave
Mississauga, ON L4Z 2X6, Canada

Marinin, Maxim (Figure Skater)
c/o Staff Member *Champions on Ice*
Tom Collins Enterprises Inc
3500 W 80th St
Minneapolis, MN 55431, USA

Marino, Cathy (Athlete, Golfer)
6313 Willowdale Dr
Plano, TX 75093, USA

Marino, Dan (Football Player)
c/o Staff Member *Miami Dolphins*
7500 SW 30th Street
Davie, FL 33314, USA

Marino, Ken (Actor)
I F A Talent Agency
8730 Sunset Blvd
#490
Los Angeles, CA 90069, USA

Marino, Stephen (Athlete, Golfer)
203 Evergrene Pkwy
Unit 18-B
Palm Beach Gardens, FL 33410, USA

Marino, Tom (Congressman, Politician)
410 Cannon HOB
Washington, DC 20515, USA

Marinovich, Greg (Photographer)
223 Lake Al manor W
Westwood, CA 96137, USA

Marinovich, Marv (Athlete, Football Player)
1/2 Santa Margarita Pkwy
Rancho Santa Margarita, CA 92688, USA

Marinovich, Todd (Athlete, Football Player)
132 E Balboa Blvd
Newport Beach, FL 92661, USA

Marinucci, Chris (Athlete, Hockey Player)
30300 Laplant Rd
Grand Rapids, MN 55744-6062

Marinus, Martin
Postbus 724
AS Gouda, THE NETHERLANDS 2800

Mario (Musician)
c/o Staff Member J Erving Group
555 Whitehall St
Suite N
Atlanta, GA 30313, USA

Mario, Ernest (Business Person)
ALZA Corp
1950 Charleston Road
Mountain View, CA 94043, USA

Marion, Brock (Athlete, Football Player)
10 NW 42nd St
Ocala, FL 34475, USA

Marion, Frank (Athlete, Football Player)
15920 SW 99th Ct
Miami, FL 33157, USA

Marion, Fred (Athlete, Football Player)
10032 Oak Quarry Dr
Orlando, FL 32832-5645, USA

Marion, Jerry (Athlete, Football Player)
12411 Riverfront Park Dr
Bakersfield, CA 93311-5112, USA

Marion, Shawn (Athlete, Basketball Player)
5434 E Cannon Dr
Paradise Valley, AZ 85253-1155, USA

Mariotti, Ray (Editor)
Austin American-Statesman
Editorial Dept
166 E Riverside
Austin, TX 78704, USA

Maris, Ada
10100 Santa Monica Blvd#2500
Los Angeles, CA 90067

Marisol (Artist)
Marlborough Gallery
40 W 57th St
New York, NY 10019, USA

Mariucci, Steve (Athlete, Football Player)
15940 Romita Ct
Monte Sereno, CA 95030-3092, USA

Mariye, Lily (Director, Writer)
c/o Staff Member Bauman Redanty &
Shaul Agency
5757 Wilshire Blvd
Suite 473
Beverly Hills, CA 90212, USA

Mark, Albert J (Beauty Pageant Winner)
Miss American Pageant
1325 Broadway
Atlantic City, NJ 08401, USA

Mark, Bruce (Artist, Ballerina, Director)
Boston Ballet Co
19 Clarendon St
Boston, MA 02116, USA

Mark, Greg (Athlete, Football Player)
2920 Washington St
Miami, FL 33133, USA

Mark, Hans (Scientist)
1710 Rockmoor Ave Apt 3
Austin, TX 78703-2064, USA

Mark, Hans M (Educator, Government Official, Physicist)
1715 Scenic Dr
Austin, TX 78703, USA

Mark, Hans Michael (General)
1909 Hill Oaks Ct
Austin, TX 78703-2810, USA

Mark, Marky
63 Pilgrim Rd.
Braintree, MA 02184-6003

Mark, Mary Ellen (Photographer)
143 Price St
New York, NY 10012-3113, USA

Mark, Reed (Athlete, Football Player)
3724 Falcon Way
Saint Paul, MN 55123-2491, USA

Mark, Reuben (Business Person)
Colgate-Palmolive Co
300 Park Ave
New York, NY 10022, USA

Mark, Robert (Government Official, Lawyer)
Esher
Surrey KT10 8LU, UNITED KINGDOM (UK)

Markakis, Nick (Athlete, Baseball Player)
949 Piney Hill Rd
Monkton, MD 21111-1426, USA

Markaryants, Vladimir S (Government Official)
Council of Ministers
Yerevan, ARMENIA

Markbreit, Jerry (Athlete, Football Player)
9739 Keystone Ave
Skokie, IL 60076, USA

Markell, Jack (Governor, Politician)
Legislative Hall
William Penn St Fl 2
Dover, DE 19901, USA

Markell, John
7540 Spring Mill Dr
Canal Winchester, OH 43110-8831

Marken, William R (Editor)
Sunset Magazine
Editorial Dept
80 Willow Road
Mento Park, CA 94025, USA

Marker, Laurie (Biologist, Scientist)
Cheetah Conservation Fund
PO Box 2496
Alexandria, VA 22301-0496, USA

Marker, Steve (Musician)
Borman Entertainment
1250 6th St
#401
Santa Monica, CA 90401, USA

Markey, Lucille P (Misc)
18 La Gorce Circle Lane
La Gorce Island
Miami Beach, FL 33141, USA

Markgraf-Sobrero, Kathryn (Athlete, Olympic Athlete, Soccer Player)
5055 N Cumberland Blvd
Milwaukee, WI 53217-5745, USA

Mark Green, Mark
c/o Brewco Motorsports Inc
P.O. Box 3453
Dana Point, CA 92633, USA

Markham, Dale (Athlete, Football Player)
1832 Valley Dr
Bismarck, ND 58503-0195, USA

Markham, Monte (Actor)
PO Box 607
Malibu, CA 90265, USA

Markie, Biz (Actor, Musician)
c/o Ron Rivlin Coast II Coast Entertainment
8671 Wilshire Blvd Ste 500
Beverly Hills, CA 90211, USA

Markland, Jeff (Athlete, Football Player)
1135 Thornfield Ln
Las Vegas, NV 89123-0828, USA

Markle, C Wilson (Engineer)
Colorization Inc
26 Scho St
Toronto, ON M5T 1Z7, CANADA

Markle, Meghan (Actor)
c/o Pearl Servat PMK/BNC Public Relations (PMK-LA)
8687 Melrose Ave Fl 8
West Hollywood, CA 90069, USA

Markle, Paul (Athlete, Football Player)
413 Beresford Ave
Toronto, ON M6S 3B6, Canada

Markle, Peter F (Director)
7510 W Sunset Blvd
#509
Los Angeles, CA 90046, USA

Markov, Danny (Athlete, Hockey Player)
17875 Collins Ave
Apt 3402
Sunny Isles Beach, FL 33160-2718, USA

Markovich, Mark (Athlete, Football Player)
400 W Thousand Oaks Dr
Peoria, IL 61615-1394, USA

Markowitz, Barry (Cinematographer)
225 W 83rd St
#20G
New York, NY 10024, USA

Markowitz, Harry M (Nobel Prize Laureate)
1010 Turquoise St
Ste 245
San Diego, CA 92109-1266, USA

Markowitz, Michael (Artist)
23rd Street Gallery
3747 23rd St
San Francisco, CA 94114, USA

Markowitz, Robert (Director, Producer)
11521 Amanda Dr
Studio City, CA 91604, USA

Marks, Chandler
PO Box 184
Franklin, TN 37065

Marks, John (Athlete, Hockey Player)
2733 47th St S Apt 205
Fargo, ND 58104-8539

Marks, Paul A (Biologist)
25680 Military Road
Watertown, NY 13601, USA

Marks, Sean
2702 Circle Dr
Newport Beach, CA 92663-5619

Markstein, Gary (Cartoonist, Editor)
Milwaukee Journal
Editorial Dept
333 W State St
Milwaukee, WI 53203, USA

Markwart, Nevin (Athlete, Hockey Player)
24 Old Barn Rd
Hanover, MA 02339-3504

Marlatt, Harvey (Athlete, Basketball Player)
10145 Lakeview Dr
Atlanta, MI 49709-9224, USA

Marleau, Patrick (Athlete, Hockey Player)
12021 Magnolia Ct
Saratoga, CA 95070-5386

Marler, Serena (Stylist)
c/o Staff Member Team
423 W Broadway
4th Floor
Boston, MA 02127, USA

Marley, Damian (Musician)
c/o Staff Member Red Light Management (LA)
8439 W Sunset Blvd
Suite 2
Los Angeles, CA 90069, USA

Marley, Ziggy (Musician, Songwriter)
Jack's Hill
Kingston, JAMAICA

Marlin, Sterling (Race Car Driver)
Phoenix Racing
195 Jones Rd
Spartanburg, SC 29307, USA

Marling, Laura (Musician)
c/o Linda Carbone Press Here Publicity
138 W. 25th St
9th Floor
New York, NY 10001, USA

Marlohe, Berenice (Actor)
c/o Andy Coleman ICM Partners (ICM-LA)
10250 Constellation Blvd Fl 7
Los Angeles, CA 90067, USA

Marlow, Jean
32 Exeter Rd.
London, ENGLAND NW2

Marlowe, Marion (Actor)
6790 Calle La Paz
Tucson, AZ 85715, USA

Marlowe, Scott
6399 Wilshire Blvd. #414
Los Angeles, CA 90048

Marm, Walter J (General)
PO Box 2017
Fremont, NC 27830-1217, USA

Marmol, Carlos (Athlete, Baseball Player)
3786 W PiPPin St
Chicago, IL 60652-1347, USA

Marmolejo, Sylvia (Stylist)
1052 S Burnside Ave
Los Angeles, CA 90019, USA

Marnay, Audrey (Actor)
c/o Elisabeth Simpson *Agence Elisabeth Simpson*
62 Boulevard Du Montparnasse
Paris 75015, FRANCE

Marnie, Larry (Coach, Football Coach)
Arizona State University
Athletic Dept
Tempe, AZ 85287, USA

Marohn, James (Horse Racer)
700 Birchwood Dr
Westbury, NY 11590-5807, USA

Marohn, William D (Business Person)
Whirlpool Corp
2000 N State St
RR 63
Benton Harbor, MI 49022, USA

Marois, Daniel (Athlete, Hockey Player)
Hockey Specific Training
19 51 Ave.
Notre Dame-De-L1lle, QC J7V 7L8,
CANADA

Marolewski, Fred (Athlete, Baseball Player)
15705 W Waterford Ln
Manhattan, IL 60442-8160, USA

Maron, Marc (Comedian)
c/o Staff Member *United Talent Agency (UTA)*
9336 Civic Center Dr
Beverly Hills, CA 90210, USA

Marone, Lou (Athlete, Baseball Player)
10851 Carbet Pl
San Diego, CA 92124-2042, USA

Maroney, Daniel V Jr (Misc)
Amalgamated Transil Union
5025 Wilconsin Ave NW
Washington, DC 20016, USA

Maroney, Kelli (Actor, Producer)
c/o Staff Member *Bohemia Group*
1680 Vine St Ste 216
Los Angeles, CA 90028, USA

Maroney, Laurence (Athlete, Football Player)
12560 Grandview Forest Dr
Saint Louis, MO 63127-0030, USA

Maroney, McKayla (Athlete, Gymnast)
c/o Staff Member *WME (LA)*
9601 Wilshire Blvd Fl 3
Beverly Hills, CA 90210, USA

Maroon 5 (Music Group)
c/o Brian Manning *Creative Artists Agency (CAA-LA)*
2000 Ave Of The Stars
Los Angeles, CA 90067, USA

Maroth, Mike (Athlete, Baseball Player)
909 Johna Pointe Dr
Oakland, FL 34787-8953, USA

Maroto, Enrique (Athlete, Baseball Player)
701 NW 136th Ave
Miami, FL 33182-2291, USA

Marotte, Carl
438 Queen E
Toronto, CANADA Ont. M5A 1

Marotte, Gilles (Athlete, Hockey Player)

Maroulis, Constantine (Musician)
c/o Paul Reisman *Abrams Artists Agency (NY)*
275 Seventh Ave
26th Floor
New York, NY 10001, USA

Marquand, Christian
45 rue de Bellechasse
Paris, FRANCE F-75007

Marquardt, Bridget (Model, Reality TV Star)
c/o Jonathan Stone *SW PR Shop*
142 S. Crescent Dr
Beverly Hills, CA 90212, USA

Marques, Maria Elena
Nubes 723 Pedregal
Mexico DF, MEXICO

Marques, Tarso (Race Car Driver)
Payton-Coyne Racing
13400 Budler Rd
Plainfield, IL 60433, USA

Marquette, Chris (Actor)
c/o Holly Williams *Williams Unlimited*
5010 Buffalo Ave
Sherman Oaks, CA 91423

Marquez, Alfonso (Athlete, Baseball Player)
P.O. Box 413
Arbuckle, CA 85297-9668, USA

Marquez, Alfonso (Baseball Player)
4102 E Skyline Drive
Gilbert, AZ 85297, USA

Marquez, Garcia Gabriel (Nobel Prize Laureate)
Agencie Literaria
Barcelona E-08021, USA

Marquez, Gonzalez Felipe (Politician)
Secretario General
PSOE
Madrid 28023, SPAIN

Marquez, Raul -
14611 Maisemore
Houston, TX 77015

Marquis, Jason (Athlete, Baseball Player)
300 Vogel Ave
Staten Island, NY 10309-2905, USA

Marr, Aileen (Stylist)
c/o Staff Member *Kramer + Kramer*
156 5th Ave#420
New York, NY 10010, USA

Marraccini, Matt (Actor)
c/o Cynthia Campos-Greenberg *Anthem Entertainment*
9595 Wilshire Blvd
Suite 900
Los Angeles, CA 90212-2509, USA

Marrero, Connie (Athlete, Baseball Player)
129 Gordon St
Perth Amboy, NJ 08861, USA

Marrero, Eli (Athlete, Baseball Player)
10230 SW 64th St
Miami, FL 33173-2807, USA

Marrin, Pete (Athlete, Hockey Player)
1276 Mapleridge Cres
Oakville, ON LGM 2G9, Canada

Marriner, Neville
Academy Saint Martin in Fields
Raine St
London E1 9RG, UNITED KINGDOM (UK)

Marriott, Craig (Actor)
c/o Staff Member *Nickelodeon UK*
PO Box 6425
LONDON W1A 6UR, UNITED KINGDOM

Marriott, Evan (Reality TV Star)
c/o Michael (Mike) Esterman
Esterman.Com, LLC
Prefers to be contacted via email
MD, USA

Marriott, J Willard Jr (Business Person)
Marriott International
10400 Fernwood Road
Bethesda, MD 20817, USA

Marriott, Richard E (Business Person)
Host Marriott Corp
10400 Fernwood Road
Bethesda, MD 20817, USA

Marro, Anthony J (Editor)
Newsday
Editorial Dept
235 Pinelawn Road
Melville, NY 11747, USA

Marron, Donald B (Financier)
Lightyear Capital
375 Park Avenue
11th Floor
New York, NY 10152, USA

Marrone, Doug (Athlete, Football Player)
Georgia Tech
6100 Waitsfield Dr S
Jamesville, NY 13078-9306, USA

Marrow, Tracy (Ice T) (Musician)
c/o Jorge Hinojosa *Jorge Hinojosa*
6606 Maryland Dr
Los Angeles, CA 90048-4614, USA

Marryshow, Bryan (Stylist)
c/o Staff Member *Jam Arts, Inc*
154 W 57th St
New York, NY 10019, USA

Mars, Bruno (Musician)
7979 Mulholland Dr
Los Angeles, CA 90046, USA

Mars, Jacqueline (Business Person)
Mars Inc
6885 Elm St
McLean, VA 22101, USA

Mars, John (Business Person)
Mars Inc
6885 Elm St
McLean, VA 22101, USA

Mars, Mick (Musician)
c/o Staff Member *HarperCollins Publishers*
10 East 53rd St
c/o Author mail, 7th Floor
New York, NY 10022, USA

Marsalis, Branford (Composer, Musician)
Wilkins Mgmt
323 Broadway
Cambridge, MA 02139, USA

Marsalis, James (Athlete, Football Player)
101 Royal Oak Ct
Kathleen, GA 31047, USA

Marsalis, Wynton (Composer, Musician)
c/o Staff Member *Creative Artists Agency (CAA-LA)*
2000 Ave Of The Stars
Los Angeles, CA 90067, USA

Marsan, Edward (Eddie) (Actor)
c/o Marsha McManus *Principal Entertainment (LA)*
1964 Westwood Blvd #400
Los Angeles, CA 90025, USA

Marschall, Marita (Actor)
Agentur Alexander
Lamontstr 9
Munich 81679, GERMANY

Marsden, Bernie (Musician)
Int'l Talent Booking
27A Floral St
#300
London WC2E 9DQ, UNITED KINGDOM (UK)

Marsden, Freddie (Musician)
Barry Collins
21A Cliftown Road
Southend-on-Sea
Essex SS1 1AB, UNITED KINGDOM (UK)

Marsden, Gerald (Gerry) (Musician)
Barry Collins
21A Cliftown Rd
Southend-on-Sea
Essex SS1 1AB, UNITED KINGDOM (UK)

Marsden, James (Actor)
c/o Andrea Pett-Joseph *Brillstein Entertainment Partners*
9150 Wilshire Blvd #350
Beverly Hills, CA 90212, USA

Marsden, Jason (Actor)
c/o Staff Member *Cunningham Escott Slevin & Doherty (CESD-LA)*
10635 Santa Monica Blvd
130
Los Angeles, CA 90025, USA

Marsden, Matthew (Actor)
c/o Paul Nelson *Mosaic Media Group*
9200 W. Sunset Blvd
10th Floor
Los Angeles, CA 90069, USA

Marsden, Roy (Actor)
London Mgmt
2-4 Noel St
London W1V 3RB, UNITED KINGDOM (UK)

Marsh, Brad (Athlete, Hockey Player)
1000 Palladium Dr
Kanata, ON K2V 1A4, Canada

Marsh, Carol
7 Leicester Pl. #100
London, ENGLAND WC2H 7B1

Marsh, Doug (Athlete, Football Player)
629 Forest Ave
Saint Louis, MO 63135-2050, USA

Marsh, Frank (Athlete, Baseball Player)
304 Bay Shore Ave
Apt 426
Mobile, AL 36607-2059, USA

Marsh, Gary (Athlete, Hockey Player)
1871 Cardiff Crest
Courtenay, BC V9N 3Z5, Canada

Marsh, Graham (Athlete, Golfer)
Graham Marsh Golf Design
29 Commerce Drive
P.O. Box 300
Rogina, Queensland 4226, Australia

Marsh, Graham (Golfer)
112 PGA Tour Blvd
Ponte Vedra Beach, FL 32082-3046, USA

Marsh, Henry (Athlete, Track Athlete)
General Delivery
Bountiful, UT 84010, USA

Marsh, Jean (Actor)
c/o Staff Member *Diamond Management*
31 Percy St
London W1T 2DD, UK

Marsh, Jodie (Model)
c/o Staff Member *Page 3*
News International Newspapers Ltd
1 Virginia St
London E98 1XY, UNITED KINGDOM

Marsh, John (General)
Department of Army
Washington, DC 20310-0001, USA

Marsh, Julian (DJ)
c/o Staff Member *Diva Central Inc*
7510 W Sunset Blvd Ste 1445
Los Angees, CA 90046, USA

Marsh, Kym (Musician)
c/o Staff Member *Safe Management*
111 Guildford Rd
Lightwater
Surrey GU18 5RA, UNITED KINGDOM
(UK)

Marsh, Linda (Actor)
170 W End Ave
22P
New York, NY 10023, USA

Marsh, Little Peggy
8236 NW 9th St.
Plantation, FL 33324

Marsh, Marian (Actor)
PO Box 1
Palm Desert, CA 92261, USA

Marsh, Michael (Mike) (Athlete, Track
Athlete)
2425 Holly Hall St
#152
Houston, TX 77054, USA

Marsh, Mike
2847 Indian Trail Dr.
Missouri City, TX 77489

Marsh, Miles L (Business Person)
Fort James Corp
1919 S Broadway
Green Bay, WI 54304, USA

Marsh, Peter (Athlete, Hockey Player)
210 Coe Rd
Clarendon Hills, IL 60514-1002, USA

Marsh, Randy (Athlete, Baseball Player)
3023 Winterbourne Rd
Edgewood, KY 41017-9683, USA

Marsh, Randy (Baseball Player)
3023 Winterbourne Rd
Edgewood, KY 41017-9683, USA

Marsh, Robert T (Business Person,
General)
6659 Avignon Blvd
Falls Church, VA 22043, USA

Marsh, Thomas (Tom) (Athlete, Baseball
Player)
9140 Summerfield Rd
Temperance, MI 48182-9757, USA

Marshall, Albert L (Ben) (Athlete, Hockey
Player)
9603 166th Street Ct E
Puyullup, WA 98375, USA

Marshall, Amanda (Musician)
c/o Staff Member *Creative Artists Agency
(CAA-LA)*
2000 Ave Of The Stars
Los Angeles, CA 90067, USA

Marshall, Amanda (Actor)
Macklam Feldman Mgmt
1505 W 2nd Ave
#200
Vancouver, BC V6H 3Y4, CANADA

Marshall, Amanda (Musician)
c/o Rob Light *Creative Artists Agency
(CAA-LA)*
2000 Ave Of The Stars
Los Angeles, CA 90067, USA

Marshall, Arthur (Athlete, Football Player)
4821 Rocky Shoals Cir
Evans, GA 30809-7042, USA

Marshall, Barry (Nobel Prize Laureate)
Queen Elizabeth II Medical Centre
NHMRC Research Laboratory Room 1.11
L Block
Nedlands, WA 6009, AUSTRALIA

Marshall, Brandon (Athlete, Football
Player)
c/o Harlan Werner *Sports Placement
Service*
330 W 11th St
Suite 105
Los Angeles, CA 90015, USA

Marshall, Brian (Musician)
Agency Group
1776 Broadway
#430
New York, NY 10010, USA

Marshall, Burchard (Athlete, Baseball
Player)
60 Crouch Ave
Apt C12B
Norwich, CT 06360, USA

Marshall, Carolyn M (Religious Leader)
United Methodist Church
204 N Newlin St
Veedersburg, IN 47987, USA

Marshall, Chan (Cat Power) (Actor,
Composer, Musician)
c/o Staff Member *Matador Records (NY)*
304 Hudson St
7th Floor
New York, NY 10013, USA

Marshall, Charles (Athlete, Football
Player)
4605 Preston Bend Dr
Arlington, TX 76016, USA

Marshall, Chuck (Athlete, Football Player)
11215 Ponderosa Ln
Franktown, CO 80116-9306, USA

Marshall, Dale Rogers (Educator)
Whealon COllege
President's Office
Norton, MA 02766, USA

Marshall, Dave (Athlete, Baseball Player)
4802 E Centralia St
Long Beach, CA 90808-1312, USA

Marshall, David (Athlete, Football Player)
2740 Towne Village Dr
Duluth, GA 30097, USA

Marshall, Don
5887 SE Riverboat Dr
Stuart, FL 34997-1511

Marshall, Donny (Athlete, Basketball
Player)
410 N 63rd St
Seattle, WA 98103-5526, USA

Marshall, Donyell (Athlete, Basketball
Player)
55 Ridgecreek Trl
Chagrin Falls, OH 44022-2379, USA

Marshall, Ed (Athlete, Football Player)
7010 Monarch St
Corpus Christi, TX 78413, USA

Marshall, Frank (Filmmaker, Producer)
c/o Staff Member *Kennedy/Marshall
Company*
619 Arizona Ave
Santa Monica, CA 90401, USA

Marshall, F Ray (Politician)
PO Box Y
Austin, TX 78713-8925, USA

Marshall, Garry K (Actor, Director)
c/o Michelle Bega *Rogers & Cowan PR
(LA)*
Pacific Design Center
8687 Melrose Ave, 7th Floor
West Hollywood, CA 90069, USA

Marshall, Grant (Athlete, Hockey Player)
29 Garside Ave
Wayne, NJ 07470-2410

Marshall, James (Actor)
1833 Rulgers Dr
Thousands Oaks, CA 91360, USA

Marshall, James (Horse Racer)
700 Anderson Rd
Jackson, NJ 08527-5340, USA

Marshall, James L (Jim) (Athlete, Football
Player)
5258 Brookleigh Dr
Byram, MS 39272-6009, USA

Marshall, Jason
438 Begonia Ave
Corona Del Mar, CA 92625-2839

Marshall, Jim (Athlete, Football Player)
4241 Basswood Rd
Minneapolis, MN 55416-3848, USA

Marshall, Jim (Athlete, Baseball Player,
Coach)
19700 N 76th St
Apt 1119
Scottsdale, AZ 85255-4787, USA

Marshall, Johnston (Athlete, Hockey
Player)
Carolina Hurricanes
1400 Edwards Mill Rd
Attn Dir Pro Scouting
Raleigh, NC 27607-3624, USA

Marshall, Keith (Athlete, Baseball Player)
334 Beckwith Rd
Pine City, NY 14871, USA

Marshall, Ken (Actor)
Marshall Artists
345 N Maple Dr
#302
Beverly Hills, CA 90210, USA

Marshall, Kris (Actor)
c/o Claire Maroussas *Independent Talent
Group (ITG-UK)*
Oxford House
76 Oxford St
London W1D 1BS, UK

Marshall, Larry (Athlete, Football Player)
4605 SW Hickory Ln
Blue Springs, MO 64015, USA

Marshall, Leonard (Athlete, Football
Player)
PO Box 272016
Boca Raton, FL 33427-2016, USA

Marshall, Margaret A (Opera Singer)
Woodside
Main St
Gargunnock, Stirling FKS 3BP,
SCOTLAND

Marshall, Michael A (Mike) (Athlete,
Baseball Player)
Yuma Scorpions
1280 W Desert Sun Dr
Attn: Manager's Office
Yuma, AZ 85365-4556, USA

Marshall, Michael G (Mike) (Athlete,
Baseball Player)
38324 Jendral Ave
Zephyrhills, FL 33542-7830, USA

Marshall, Mike
4436 Plum St.
Zephyrhills, FL 33541

Marshall, Patricia
807 N. Alpine Dr.
Beverly Hills, CA 90210

Marshall, Paula (Actor)
c/o Nevin Dolcefino *Innovative Artists
(LA)*
1505 10th St
Santa Monica, CA 90401, USA

Marshall, Penny (Actor, Director)
c/o Staff Member *Parkway Productions*
7095 Hollywood Blvd
#1009
Hollywood, CA 90028, USA

Marshall, Peter (Television Host)
16714 Oak View Dr
Encino, CA 91436, USA

Marshall, Rob (Director)
Moxie Pictures
2644 30th St.
Santa Monica, CA 90404, USA

Marshall, Scott (Actor, Director)
c/o Staff Member *Creative Artists Agency
(CAA-LA)*
2000 Ave Of The Stars
Los Angeles, CA 90067, USA

Marshall, Sean (Athlete, Baseball Player)
6515 N Kilbourn Ave
lincolnwood, Il 60712-3436, USA

Marshall, Theda (Athlete, Baseball Player)
708 East Phillips Drive North
Littleton, CO 80122-2864, USA

Marshall, Thurgood (Politician)
6546 28th St N
Arlington, VA 22213-1207, USA

Marshall, Tom (Athlete, Basketball Player)
9548 Mariners Cove Ln
Fort Myers, FL 33919-4592, USA

Marshall, Tony (Stylist)
c/o Staff Member *Directions USA*
3717-C W Market St
Greensboro, NC 27403, USA

Marshall, Vester (Athlete, Basketball
Player)
2204 1st Ave
Apt 201
Seattle, WA 98121-1600, USA

Marshall, Warren (Athlete, Football Player)
10108 Clairbourne Pl
Raleigh, NC 27615-1323, USA

Marshall, Whit (Athlete, Football Player)
497 King Rd NW
Atlanta, GA 30342-4046, USA

Marshall, Wilber B (Athlete, Football Player)
4553 Sir Page Ln
Titusville, FL 32796-1444, USA

Marshall, Willard
204 Main St.
Forrt Lee, NJ 07024

Marshall, Willie (Athlete, Hockey Player)
2110 Acorn Ct
Lebanon, PA 17042-5769

Marshall, Winton W (General)
4389 Malia St Apt 429
Honolulu, HI 96821-1171, USA

Marshall, W W (Bones) (General, War Hero)
1517 Ehupua Place
Honolulu, HI 96821, USA

Marshall Green, Logan (Actor)
c/o Nick Frenkel *3 Arts Entertainment Inc*
9460 Wilshire Blvd
7th Floor
Beverly Hills, CA 90210, USA

Marshall of Knightsbridge, Colin M
(Business Person)
British Airways
Heathrow Airport
Hounslow
Middx TW6 2JA, UNITED KINGDOM
(UK)

Marshall Tucker Band
100 W. Putnam
Greenwich, CT 06830

Marshburn, Thomas H Dr (Astronaut)
11810 Shoal Landing St
Pearland, TX 77584-8751, USA

Marsh of Mannington, Richard W
(Government Official)
House of Lords
Westminster
London SW1A 0PW, UNITED KINGDOM
(UK)

Mars Jr, Forrest E (Misc)
Mars Inc
6885 Elm St
McLean, VA 22101, USA

Marson, Lou (Athlete, Baseball Player)
1680 Glendola Rd
Wall Township, NJ 07719-4506, USA

Marsonek, Sam (Athlete, Baseball Player)
712 Welton Rd
Lutz, FL 33548-5039, USA

Marsters, James (Actor)
c/o Staff Member *Steve Himber Entertainment*
211 S Beverly Dr #601
Beverly Hills, CA 90212, USA

Marston, Joshua (Director, Writer)
c/o Cliff Roberts *WME (LA)*
9601 Wilshire Blvd Fl 3
Beverly Hills, CA 90210, USA

Marston, Natalie Elizabeth (Actor)
c/o Shepard Smith *Archetype*
1608 Argyle Ave
Los Angeles, CA 90028, USA

Marston, Nathanial (Actor)
c/o Staff Member *Donegan Entertainment*
129 W 27th St
New York, NY 10001, USA

Marston, Nathaniel (Actor)
c/o Staff Member *One Life to Live*
56 West 66th St.
New York, NY 10023, USA

Marta, Lynn (Actor)
c/o Staff Member *Bobby Ball Talent Agency*
4116 W Magnolia Blvd Ste 205
Burbank, CA 91505-2700, USA

Marte, Judy (Actor)
c/o Michael Cooper *Creative Artists Agency (CAA-LA)*
1 William Morris Pl
Beverly Hills, CA 90212, USA

Martel, Arlene (Actor)
2109 S Wilbur Ave
Walla Walla, WA 99362, USA

Martell, Donna
PO Box 3335
Granada Hills, CA 91394

Martemucci, Anna (Director)
c/o Chad Hamilton *Anonymous Content (LA)*
3531 Hayden Ave
Culver City, CA 90232, USA

Martens, Wilfried (Prime Minister)
Europese Volkspartij
16 Rue de la Victoire
Brussels 1060, BELGIUM

Martensen, Gayle (Stylist)
c/o Staff Member *Independent Artists*
448 E Riverdale Ave
Orange, CA 92865, USA

Martha, Paul (Athlete, Football Player)
5008 Starfish Way
San Diego, CA 92154-8420, USA

Marti, Benita (Actor)
c/o Staff Member *Select Artists Ltd (CA-Valley Office)*
PO Box 4359
Burbank, CA 91503, USA

Martika (Musician)
Entertainment Artists
2409 21st Ave S
#100
Nashville, TN 37212, USA

Martin, Aaron (Athlete, Football Player)
3605 Seth Ct
Springdale, MD 20774, USA

Martin, Agnes B (Artist)
414 Placilas Road
Taos, NM 87571, USA

Martin, Al (Athlete, Baseball Player)
11000 N 77th Pl
Unit 1005
Scottsdale, AZ 85260-5599, USA

Martin, AL (Athlete, Baseball Player)
15251 S 50th St
Apt 2054
Phoenix, AZ 85044-9117, USA

Martin, Albert C (Architect)
Albert C Martin Assoc
811 W 7th St
#800
Los Angeles, CA 90017, USA

Martin, Amos (Athlete, Football Player)
11824 Duane Point Cir Apt 201
Louisville, KY 40243-2725, USA

Martin, Andrea (Actor)
c/o Staff Member *Innovative Artists (LA)*
1505 10th St
Santa Monica, CA 90401, USA

Martin, Ann (Correspondent)
KCBS-TV
News Dept
6121 Sunset Blvd
Los Angeles, CA 90028, USA

Martin, Ann M (Writer)
c/o Staff Member *Scholastic Entertainment*
557 Broadway
New York, NY 10012, USA

Martin, Babe (Athlete, Baseball Player)
114 N Holloway Rd
Ballwin, MO 63011, USA

Martin, Barri (Stylist)
c/o Staff Member *Seaminx Artist Management*
2806 Greenville Ave
#B
Dallas, TX 75206, USA

Martin, Billy (Athlete, Football Player)
PO Box 2969
Cumming, GA 30028-6513, USA

Martin, Billy (Musician)
c/o Brian Greenbaum *Creative Artists Agency (CAA-LA)*
2000 Ave Of The Stars
Los Angeles, CA 90067, USA

Martin, Blanche (Athlete, Football Player)
1621 Stoney Point Dr
Lansing, MI 48917, USA

Martin, Bob (Athlete, Basketball Player)
5812 44th Ave S
Minneapolis, MN S5417-3017, USA

Martin, Bob (Athlete, Football Player)
14200 N 27th St
Davey, NE 68336-3638, USA

Martin, Boris "Babe" (Athlete, Baseball Player)
5660 N Kolb Rd
Apt 150
Tucson, AZ 85750-3204

Martin, Boyce F Jr (Judge)
US Court of Appeals
US Courthouse
601 W Broadway
Louisville, KY 40202, USA

Martin, Brian (Athlete)
777 San Antonio
#132
Palo Alto, CA 94303, USA

Martin, Casey (Athlete, Golfer)
University of Oregon
2727 Leo Harris Pkwy
Attn: Athletic Dept
Eugene, OR 97401, USA

Martin, Casey
PO Box 109601
Palm Beach Gardens, FL 33410

Martin, Chris (Actor)
c/o Barry McPherson *Agency for the Performing Arts (APA-LA)*
405 S Beverly Dr
Suite 500
Beverly Hills, CA 90212-4425, USA

Martin, Chris (Musician)
1701 Westridge Rd
Los Angeles, CA 90049, USA

Martin, Chris (Athlete, Football Player)
c/o Jeff Lynch *Sports Management Worldwide*
1100 NW Glisan St
Suite 2B
Portland, OR 97209, USA

Martin, Christy (Boxer)
1203 Foxtree Trail
Apopka, FL 32712, USA

Martin, Cuonzo (Athlete, Basketball Player)
4315 Thistlewood Way
Knoxville, TN 37919-7884, USA

Martin, Curtis (Athlete, Football Player)
100 Hilton Ave Apt PH-1
Garden City, NY 11530-1564, USA

Martin, Dave (Chef)
c/o Staff Member *Magical Elves Inc*
453 S Spring Street Ste
Los Angeles, CA 90013, USA

Martin, Dave (Athlete, Football Player)
9306 E Berry Ave
Greenwood Village, CO 80111, USA

Martin, David (Correspondent)
CBS-TV
News Dept
2020 M St NW
Washington, DC 20036, USA

Martin, Deana (Actor)
c/o Jeffrey Lane *Jeffrey Lane & Associates*
9255 Doheny Rd
Suite 2003
Los Angeles, CA 90069, USA

Martin, Demetri (Actor, Comedian)
c/o Jason Heyman *Creative Artists Agency (CAA-LA)*
2000 Ave Of The Stars
Los Angeles, CA 90067, USA

Martin, Denise B (Editor)
MOney Magazine
Editorial Dept
Time-Life Building
New York, NY 10020, USA

Martin, Don (Athlete, Football Player)
1003 Hilltop Dr
Carrollton, MO 64633-1909, USA

Martin, Doug (Athlete, Golfer)
1406 Meadowlake Way
Union, KY 41091-7118, USA

Martin, Duane (Actor)
22401 S Summit Ridge Cir
Chatsworth, CA 91311, USA

Martin, Ed (Baseball Player)
Philadelphia Stars
6666 Brookmont Ter Apt 407
Nashville, TN 34205-4622, USA

Martin, Ed F (Actor)
c/o Steven Neibert *Imperium 7 Talent Agency*
5455 Wilshire Blvd
Suite 1706
Los Angeles, CA 90036, USA

Martin, Edward H (Admiral)
729 Guadalupe Ave
Coronado, CA 92118, USA

Martin, Eric (Athlete, Football Player)
111 Windfall Pl
Clinton, MS 39056, USA

Martin, Eric Band
PO Box 5952
San Francisco, CA 94101

Martin, Gene (Athlete, Baseball Player)
133 Winchester Dr
Leesburg, GA 31763-5064, USA

Martin, George (Athlete, Football Player)
50 Cheshire Ln
Ringwood, NJ 07456, USA

Martin, Greg (Musician)
Mitchell Fox Mgmt
212 3rd Ave N
#301
Nashville, TN 37201, USA

Martin, Gregory S (General)
Commander
US Air Forces Europe
Ramstein Air Base
APO, AE 09094, USA

Martin, Helen
1440 N. Fairfax Ave. #109
Los Angeles, CA 90046

Martin, Henry R (Cartoonist)
1382 Newtown Langhorne Road
#G206
Newtown, PA 18940-2418, USA

Martin, Ingle (Athlete, Football Player)
320 Red Feather Ln
Brentwood, TN 37027-4771, USA

Martin, Jacques (Athlete, Coach, Hockey Player)
Florida Panthers
1275 Rue Saint-Antoine 0
Montreal, QC H3C 5L2, Canada

Martin, James G (Ex-Governor, Politician)
McGuire Woods Consulting
Carolina Medical Center PO Box 32861
Charlotte, NC 28232-2861, USA

Martin, J C (Athlete, Baseball Player)
112 Oakmont Ct
Advance, NC 27006, USA

Martin, J C (Athlete, Baseball Player)
112 Oakmont Ct
Advance, NC 27006-7097, USA

Martin, Jennifer (Stylist)
c/o Staff Member *Zenobia Agency Inc*
PO Box 909
Groveland, CA 95321, USA

Martin, Jerry (Athlete, Baseball Player)
109 Chelton Ct
Columbia, SC 29212-8522, USA

Martin, Jesse L (Actor)
c/o Bob McGowan *McGowan Management*
8733 W Sunset Blvd
Suite 103
West Hollywood, CA 90069, USA

Martin, Joe (Cartoonist)
Weederman Grafix
C/O Neatly Chiseled Features
1870 Loramoor Lane
Lake Geneva, WI 53147, USA

Martin, John (Athlete, Baseball Player)
2037 SW Stratford Way
Palm City, FL 34990-2033, USA

Martin, John H (Educator)
JHM Corp
3930 RCA Blvd
#3240
Palm Beach Gardens, FL 33410, USA

Martin, Judith (Miss Manners) (Journalist)
1651 harvard St NW
Washington, DC 20009, USA

Martin, Justin (Actor)
c/o Ellen Meyer *Ellen Meyer Management*
8899 Beverly Blvd
Suite 612
West Hollywood, CA 90048, USA

Martin, Kellie (Actor)
c/o William Mercer *Thruline Entertainment*
9250 Wilshire Blvd
Ground Fl
Beverly Hills, CA 90212, USA

Martin, Kelvin (Athlete, Football Player)
608 Guadalupe Rd
Keller, TX 76248-7337, USA

Martin, Kenyon (Athlete, Basketball Player)
924 Bentwater Pkwy
Cedar Hill, TX 75104-8269, USA

Martin, Larue (Athlete, Basketball Player)
1236 Harvest Ln
University Park, IL 60484-3320, USA

Martin, LeRoy (Government Official, Lawyer)
Chicago Police Dept
Superintendent's Office
Chicago, IL 60602, USA

Martin, Lynn M (Politician, Secretary)
171 Willabay Dr
Williams Bay, WI 53191-9673, USA

Martin, Madeleine (Actor)
c/o Jill Fritzo *PMK/BNC Public Relations (PMK-NY)*
622 3rd Ave
8th Floor
New York, NY 10017, USA

Martin, Maria (Actor)
c/o Staff Member *Select Artists Ltd (CA-Valley Office)*
PO Box 4359
Burbank, CA 91503, USA

Martin, Mark (Athlete, Hockey Player)
5887 E. Riverboat Dr.
Stuart, FL 34997, USA

Martin, Mark (Race Car Driver)
c/o Staff Member *Hendrick Motorsports*
4400 Papa Joe Hendrick Blvd
Charlotte, NC 28262, USA

Martin, Marsha P (Financier)
Farm Credit Administration
1501 Farm Credit Dr
McLean, VA 22102, USA

Martin, Meaghan Jette (Actor)
c/o Myrna Lieberman *Myrna Lieberman Management*
3001 Hollyridge Drive
Hollywood, CA 90068, USA

Martin, Medeski (Musician)
c/o Staff Member *Paradigm (Monterey)*
404 W Franklin St
Monterey, CA 93940, USA

Martin, Mike (Athlete, Baseball Player)
7904 Waterfalls Ave
Las Vegas, NV 89128-6709, USA

Martin, Millicent (Actor, Musician)
London Mgmt
2-4 Noel St
London W1V 3RB, UNITED KINGDOM (UK)

Martin, Nicole (Stylist)
c/o Staff Member *Fifty8 Artists*
58 W Huron St
Chicago, IL 60610, USA

Martin, Norberto (Athlete, Baseball Player)
Helena Brewers
P.O. Box 6756
Attn: Coaching Staff
Helena, MT 59604, USA

Martin, Paul (Government Official)
Finance Department
140 O'Connor St
Ottawa, ON K1A 0G5, CANADA

Martin, Preston (Financier, Government Official)
1130 N Lake Shore Dr
#4E
Chicago, IL 60611, USA

Martin, Ray (Athlete, Baseball Player)
383 Adams St
Quincy, MA 02169-1703, USA

Martin, Ray (Billiards Player)
11-05 Cadmus Place
Fair Lawn, NJ 07410, USA

Martin, R Bruce (Misc)
University of Virginia
Chemistry Dept
Charlottesville, VA 22903, USA

Martin, Renie (Athlete, Baseball Player)
509 Little Eagle Ct
Valrico, FL 33594-3973, USA

Martin, Ricky (Musician)
641 Ocean Blvd
Golden Beach, FL 33160, USA

Martin, Rod (Athlete, Football Player)
PO Box 23
Manhattan Beach, CA 90267-0023, USA

Martin, Roland (Correspondent)
c/o Staff Member *CNN (Atlanta)*
One CNN Center
PO Box 105366
Atlanta, GA 30303, USA

Martin, Ronald D (Editor)
Atlanta Journal-Constitution
Editorial Dept
72 Marietta
Atlanta, GA 30303, USA

Martin, Rudolf (Actor)
c/o Amanda Glazer *Kohner Agency, The*
9300 Wilshire Blvd
Suite 555
Beverly Hills, CA 90212, USA

Martin, Rudolph (Actor)
c/o Staff Member *Treusch/Erickson Associates*
8955 Norma Place
Los Angeles, CA 90067, USA

Martin, Sammy (Athlete, Football Player)
114 Summit Dr
Carriere, MS 39426-7665, USA

Martin, Sammy
114 Summit Dr
Carriere, MS 39426-7665, USA

Martin, Sandy (Actor)
CNA Assoc
1875 Century Park East
#2250
Los Angeles, CA 90067, USA

Martin, Seth (Athlete, Hockey Player)
1200 Heather Pl
Trail, BC V1R 4Y2, Canada

Martin, Steve (Actor, Comedian, Producer, Writer)
c/o Alan Nierob *Rogers & Cowan PR (LA)*
Pacific Design Center
8687 Melrose Ave, 7th Floor
West Hollywood, CA 90069, USA

Martin, Susan (Stylist)
307 W Tremont Ave
#C
Charlotte, NC 28203, USA

Martin, Sylvia Wene (Bowler)
2701 Clark Towers Ct #125
Las Vegas, NV 89102, USA

Martin, Terry (Athlete, Hockey Player)
185 Hampton Hill Dr.
Williamsville, NY 14221-5841, USA

Martin, Todd (Athlete, Olympic Athlete, Tennis Player)
156 Coach Lamp Way
Ponte Vedra Beach, FL 32082-1904, USA

Martin, Tom (Athlete, Baseball Player)
8001 Surf Dr
Panama City, FL 32408-8530, USA

Martin, Tony (Athlete, Football Player)
1198 B Green Rd
Boston, GA 31626, USA

Martin, Victor Hugo (Actor)
c/o Staff Member *TV Azteca*
Periferico Sur 4121
Colonia Fuentes del Pedregal
DF CP 14141, Mexico

Martin, Wayne (Athlete, Football Player)
PO Box 4
Cherry Valley, AR 72324-0004, USA

Martin Chase, Deborah (Debra) (Producer)
c/o Staff Member *WmE2 (WMA-LA)*
1 William Morris Pl
Beverly Hills, CA 90212, USA

Martindale, Kate (Stylist)
c/o Staff Member *Cloutier Agency*
2632 La Cienega Ave
Los Angeles, CA 90034, USA

Martindale, Margo (Actor)
c/o Andrew Freedman *Andrew Freedman Public Relations*
9127 Thrasher Ave
Los Angeles, CA 90069, USA

Martindale, Wink (Entertainer, Musician)
5744 Newcastle Lane
Calabasas, CA 91302, USA

Martine, Suzanne (Stylist)
92 Grove St
New York, NY 10014, USA

Martinek, Radek (Athlete, Hockey Player)
64 Hope Dr
Plainview, NY 11803-5650, USA

Martines, Alessandra (Actor)
c/o Francois-Xavier Molin *ArtMedia*
20 avenue Rapp
Paris 75008, France

Martinez, A (Actor)
PO Box 6387
Malibu, CA 90264, USA

Martinez, Alfredo (Athlete, Baseball Player)
2346 Thomas St
Los Angeles, CA 90031-2820, USA

Martinez, Anais (Musician)
Univision Music Group
5820 Canoga Ave # 300
Woodland Hills, CA 91367, USA

Martinez, Ana Maria (Opera Singer)
JF Mastroianni
151 W 51st St
#17E
New York, NY 10023, USA

Martinez, Angela (Television Host)
c/o Staff Member *Abrams Artists Agency (LA)*
9200 Sunset Blvd
11th Floor
Los Angeles, CA 90069, USA

Martinez, Angie (Musician)
395 Hudson Street
7th Floor
New York, NY 10014, USA

Martinez, Billy Joe (Actor)
c/o Linda McAlister *Linda McAlister Talent*
100 Oak Ln
Waxahachie, TX 75167-8412, USA

Martinez, Buck (Athlete, Baseball Player, Coach)
10315 Long Beach Blvd
Long Beach Township, NJ 08008, USA

Martinez, Carmelo (Athlete, Baseball Player)
32 Brisas Del Plata
Dorado, PR 00646-5118, USA

Martinez, Chito (Athlete, Baseball Player)
100 Legacy Barn
Dr Apt 101
Collierville, TN 38017-8726, USA

Martinez, Constantino (Tino) (Athlete, Baseball Player)
324 Blanca Ave
Tampa, FL 33606, USA

Martinez, Daniel J (Artist)
University of California
Studio Art Dept
Irvine, CA 92717, USA

Martinez, Dave (Athlete, Baseball Player)
3315 Enterprise Rd E
Safety Harbor, FL 34695, USA

Martinez, Edgar (Athlete, Baseball Player)
3036 249th Ave SE
Sammamish, WA 98075-9421, USA

Martinez, Fred (Baseball Player)
California Angels
2346 Thomas St
Los Angeles, CA 90031-2820, USA

Martinez, Greg (Athlete, Baseball Player)
1596 Palora Ave
Las Vegas, NV 89169-2504, USA

Martinez, J Dennis (Athlete, Baseball Player)
9400 SW 63rd Ct
Miami, FL 33156-1817, USA

Martinez, Jorge (Actor)
c/o Staff Member *Telefe - Argentina*
Pavon 2444 (C1248AAT)
Buenos Aires, ARGENTINA

Martinez, Jose (Athlete, Baseball Player)
14601 SW 33rd Ct
Miramar, FL 33027-3729, USA

Martinez, Jose Rene (J R) (Actor, Reality TV Star)
c/o Cynthia Snyder *Cynthia Snyder Public Relations*
5739 Colfax Ave
N Hollywood, CA 91601-1636, USA

Martinez, Mel (Politician)
140 W Fawsett Rd
Winter Park, FL 32789-6016, USA

Martinez, Natalie (Actor)
c/o Sean Fay *Kritzer Levine Wilkins Entertainment (KLWG)*
11872 La Grange Ave
1st Floor
Los Angeles, CA 90025, USA

Martinez, Olivier (Actor)
c/o Staff Member *Parseghian Planco LLC*
322 8th Ave
Suite 601
New York, NY 10001, USA

Martinez, Patrice (Actor)
c/o Staff Member *Select Artists Ltd (CA-Valley Office)*
PO Box 4359
Burbank, CA 91503, USA

Martinez, Pedro (Athlete, Baseball Player)
3029 Birkdale
Weston, FL 33332, USA

Martinez, Pedro A (Baseball Player)
186 Fairmont Ave
Hyde Park, MA 02136, USA

Martinez, Ramon J (Athlete, Baseball Player)
Dominican Repubic
Bo San Miguel #9
Managuayaba Santo, Domingo, USA

Martinez, Robert (Bob) (Ex-Governor, Politician)
100 N Tampa St
Suite 4100
Tampa, FL 33602, USA

Martinez, Rosealee (Stylist)
c/o Staff Member *Team*
423 W Broadway
4th Floor
Boston, MA 02127, USA

Martinez, Silvio (Athlete, Baseball Player)
4914 103rd St Fl 2
Corona, NY 11368-3121, USA

Martinez, Susana (Governor)
State Capitol
300 Old Santa Fe Trl
Santa Fe, NM 87501, USA

Martinez, Tino (Athlete, Baseball Player, Olympic Athlete)
324 Blanca Ave
Tampa, FL 33606-3630, USA

Martinez, Tippy (Athlete, Baseball Player)
1524 Dellsway Rd
Towson, MD 21286-5901, USA

martinez, Victor (Athlete, Baseball Player)
10157 Tavistock Rd
Orlando, FL 32827-7054, USA

Martinez Somalo, Eduardo Cardinal (Religious Leader)
Palazzo delle Congregazioni
Piazza Pio XII 3
Rome 00193, ITALY

Martini, Max (Actor, Director)
c/o Vera Mihailovich *Forward Entertainment*
9255 Sunset Blvd
Suite 805
Los Angeles, CA 90069, USA

Martinkovic, John (Athlete, Football Player)
1001 Ernst Dr
Green Bay, WI 54304, USA

Martino, Frank D (Misc)
Chemical Workers Union
1655 W Market St
Akron, OH 44313, USA

Martino, Pat (Composer, Musician)
2318 S 16th St
Philadelphia, PA 19145, USA

Martino, Renato R Cardinal (Religious Leader)
Justice & Peace Curia
Piazzo S Calisto 16
Vatican City 00120, VATICAN CITY

Martins, Joao Carlos (Musician)
c/o Staff Member *Musicians Corporate Management*
PO Box 825
Highland, NY 12528, USA

Martins, Nilas (Ballerina, Dancer, Director)
c/o Staff Member *New York City Ballet*
New York State Theater
20 Lincoln Center
New York, NY 10023, USA

Martins, Steve (Athlete, Hockey Player)
22475 N Linden Dr
Lake Barrington, IL 60010-5956

Martinson, Leslie
2288 Coldwater Canyon
Beverly Hills, CA 90210

Martinson, Lestie H (Director)
2288 Coldwater Canyon Dr
Beverly Hills, CA 90210, USA

Martinson, Steve (Athlete, Hockey Player)
394 N Pier Dr
Machesney Park, IL 61115-4018

Martlin, Marlee (Actor)
10340 Santa Monica Blvd
Los Angeles, CA 90025, USA

Marton, Eva (Opera Singer)
Opera et Concert
Maximilianstr 22
Munich 80539, GERMANY

Marton, Katalin (Kati) (Writer)
c/o Amanda Urban *ICM Partners (ICM-NY)*
730 Fifth Ave
New York, NY 10019, USA

Martone, Lino (Musician)
c/o Gabriel Blanco *Gabriel Blanco Iglesias (Mexico)*
Rio Balsas 35-32
Colonia Cuauhtemoc
DF 06500, Mexico

Marts, Lonnie (Athlete, Football Player)
13650 Bromley Point Dr
Jacksonville, FL 32225, USA

Marty, Martin E (Religious Leader)
175 E Delaware Pl
Apt 8508
Chicago, IL 60611-7750, USA

Marty, Mike (Coach, Football Coach)
Saint Louis Rams
901 N Broadway
Saint Louis, MO 63101, USA

Martyn, Bob (Athlete, Baseball Player)
PO Box 778
Pacific City, OR 97135-0778, USA

Martz, Gary (Athlete, Baseball Player)
525 Sage Hills Dr
Wenatchee, WA 98801, USA

Martz, Judy (Politician)
119092 Juniper Acres Rd
Butte, MT 59750-9705, USA

Martz, Mike (Athlete, Football Coach, Football Player)
222 Republic Dr
Allen Park, MI 48101, USA

Martz, Randy (Athlete, Baseball Player)
211 Hi Pointe Pl
East Alton, IL 62024-1641, USA

Martzke, Rudy (Writer)
USA Today
Editorial Dept
1000 Wilson Blvd
Arlington, VA 22209, USA

Maruk, Dennis (Athlete, Hockey Player)
15 Berry Creek Dr
Etobicoke, ON M9W 4A1, Canada

Marusha
Kaiser-Friedrich-Str. 41
Berlin, GERMANY D-10627

Marusin, Yury M (Opera Singer)
Mariinsky Theater
Teatralnaya Pl 1
Saint Petersburg, RUSSIA

Maruskin, Chelsea (Stylist)
c/o Staff Member *Art House Management*
1548 16th St
Santa Monica, CA 90404, USA

Maruyama, Karen (Actor)
c/o Staff Member *Halpern Management*
P.O. Box 5042
Santa Monica, CA 90409-5042, USA

Maruyama, Shigeki (Athlete, Golfer)
15210 Antelo Pl
Los Angeles, CA 90077, USA

Marvaso, Tommy (Athlete, Football Player)
2 W Melrose St
Chevy Chase, MD 20815, USA

Marve, Eugene (Athlete, Football Player)
4516 W Lamb Ave
Tampa, FL 33629, USA

Marvel, Elizabeth (Actor)
c/o Robert Glennon *Authentic Talent and Literary Management*
45 Main St
Suite 1004
Brooklyn, NY 11201, USA

Marvelettes, The (Music Group)
9936 Majorca Pl
Boca Raton, FL 33434, USA

Marx, Gilda (Designer, Fashion Designer)
Gilda Marx Industries
11755 Exposition Blvd
Los Angeles, CA 90064, USA

Marx, Greg (Athlete, Football Player)
18721 Jamestown Cir
Northville, MI 48168-3532, USA

Marx, Gyorgy (Physicist)
Fehervari Utca 119
Budapest 1119, HUNGARY

Marx, Jeffrey A (Journalist)
Lexington Herald-Leader
Editorial Dept
Main & Midland
Lexington, KY 40507, USA

Marx, Melissa (Stylist)
c/o Staff Member *Axis Models & Talent*
P.O. Box 367
Ringwood, NJ 07456-0367, USA

Marx, Richard (Musician, Songwriter)
700 Arbor Dr
Lake Bluff, IL 60044, USA

Marx, Timothy (Producer)
c/o Staff Member *ICM Partners (ICM-LA)*
10250 Constellation Blvd Fl 7
Los Angeles, CA 90067, USA

Maryland, Russell (Athlete, Football Player)
1330 Eagle Bend
Southlake, TX 76092, USA

Mary Mary (Music Group)
c/o Richard De La Font *Richard De La Font Agency*
3808 W South Park Blvd
Broken Arrow, OK 74011, USA

Marzich, Andy (Bowler)
1421 Cravens Ave
#318
Torrance, CA 90501, USA

Marzoli, Andrea (Misc)
Berkeley Geochronolgoy Center
2455 Ridge Road
Berkeley, CA 94709, USA

Mas, Adrian (Actor)
c/o Gabriel Blanco *Gabriel Blanco Iglesias (Mexico)*
Rio Balsas 35-32
Colonia Cuauhtemoc
DF 06500, Mexico

Masak, Ron (Actor)
5440 Shirley Ave
Tarzana, CA 91356, USA

Masakayan, Liz (Athlete, Volleyball Player)
2864 Palomino Cir
La Jolla, CA 92037, USA

Masako, Princess (Royalty)
Imperial Palace
1-1 Chiyoda-ku
Tokyo, JAPAN

Masaoka, Onan (Athlete, Baseball Player)
1323 Auwae Rd
Hilo, HI 96720-6906, USA

Mascaras, Mil
200 W. 16th St. #10
New York, NY 10011-6150

Masco, Judit
Paseo De Gracia 67 Pral. IA
Barcelona, SPAIN 08008

Mascolo, Joseph (Actor)
c/o Staff Member *Bold and The Beautiful, The*
7800 Beverly Blvd #3371
Los Angeles, CA 90036

Mase (Musician)
c/o Staff Member *Interscope Records (NY)*
1755 Broadway
New York, NY 10019, USA

Masekela, Hugh (Musician)
c/o Staff Member *Opus 3 Artists*
5670 Wilshire Blvd
Suite 1790
Los Angeles, CA 90036, USA

Masekela, Sal (Television Host)
c/o Staff Member *ROAR (LA)*
9701 Wilshire Blvd
8th Floor
Los Angeles, CA 90212, USA

MaShay, Pepper (Actor, Musician)
c/o Staff Member *Diva Central Inc*
7510 W Sunset Blvd Ste 1445
Los Angees, CA 90046, USA

Mashburn, Jamal (Athlete, Basketball Player)
5625 Pine Tree Dr
Miami Beach, FL 33140-2149, USA

Mashburn, Jesse (Athlete, Track Athlete)
8520 S Pennsylvania Ave
Oklahoma City, OK 73159, USA

Mashkov, Vladimir L (Actor)
Oleg Tabakov Theater
Chaokygina Str 12A
Moscow, RUSSIA

Mashore, Clyde (Athlete, Baseball Player)
590 Valmore Pl
Brentwood, CA 94513-6909, USA

Mashore, Damon (Athlete, Baseball Player)
1538 W Rush Rd
Eagle, ID 83616-3630, USA

Masiello, Tony (Politician)
Mayor's Office
City Hall
65 Niagara Square
Buffalo, NY 14202, USA

Masire, Q Ketumile J (President)
PO Box 70
Gaborone, BOTSWANA

Maskawa, Toshihide (Nobel Prize Laureate)
Kyoto Sangyo University
Kyoto University Yukawa Institute for Theoretical Physics Kitashirakawa Oiwake-Cho
Kyoto-City 606-8502, Japan

Maske, Henry (Boxer)
Sauerland Promotion
Hochstadenstr 1-3
Cologne 50674, GERMANY

Maskin, Eric (Nobel Prize Laureate)
112 Mercer St
Princeton, NJ 08540-6827, USA

Maslansky, Paul (Director, Filmmaker, Producer)
Henry Barnberger
10866 Wilshire Blvd
#1000
Los Angeles, CA 90024, USA

Masloff, Sophie (Politician)
Mayor's Office
City-County Building
414 Grant St
Pittsburgh, PA 15219, USA

Maslow, Emilie (Stylist)
c/o Staff Member *Celestine - CA*
1666 20th St
#200-B
Santa Monica, CA 90404, USA

Maslow, James (Actor, Musician)
c/o Liza Anderson *Anderson Group Public Relations*
8060 Melrose Ave Fl 4
Los Angeles, CA 90046, USA

Maslowski, Matt (Athlete, Football Player)
22281 Destello
Mission Viejo, CA 92691, USA

Masnick, Paul (Athlete, Hockey Player)
303-155 Hillcrest Ave
Cooksville, ON L5B 3Z2, Canada

Mason, Anthony (Athlete, Basketball Player)
9 Brownstone Way_ A[lt 308
En_g_lewood, NJ 07631-1216, USA

Mason, Birny Jr (Engineer)
6 Island Dr
Rye, NY 10580, USA

Mason, B John (Misc)
64 Christchurch Road
East Sheen
London SW14, UNITED KINGDOM (UK)

Mason, Bob (Athlete, Hockey Player, Olympic Athlete)
9549 Yukon AveS
Minneapolis, MN 55438-1651, USA

Mason, Bob (Athlete, Hockey Player)
Minnesota Wild
317 Washington St
Saint Paul, MN 55102-1667

Mason, Bobbie Ann (Writer)
PO Box 518
Lawrenceburg, KY 40342, USA

Mason, Chris (Athlete, Hockey Player)
450 Beauchamp Cir
Franklin, TN 37067, USA

Mason, Dave (Athlete, Football Player)
37 Jackson Ave
Winchester, WI 22601-4933, USA

Mason, Dave (Musician, Songwriter)
3130 E Ojai Ave
Ojai, CA 93023, USA

Mason, Debbi (Stylist)
c/o Staff Member *Bryan Bantry*
900 Broadway Ste 400
New York, NY 10003, USA

Mason, Derrick (Athlete, Football Player)
8665 Ritchboro Rd
District Heights, MD 20747-2658, USA

Mason, Don (Athlete, Baseball Player)
8 Fawn Rd
South Yarmouth, MA 02664-1808, USA

Mason, Glen (Coach, Football Coach)
University of Minnesota
Athletic Dept
Minneapolis, MN 55455, USA

Mason, Hank (Athlete, Baseball Player)
5004 W Leyburn Ct
Apt 102
Henrico, VA 23228-4852, USA

Mason, Jackie (Actor, Comedian)
World According to Me
146 W 57th St
#68D
New York, NY 10019, USA

Mason, James Appreciation Society
PO Box 3552
London, ENGLAND SWl9 3QH

Mason, Jim (Athlete, Baseball Player)
11410 Queens Way
Theodore, AL 36582, USA

Mason, Larry B (War Hero)
826 Cinebar Road
Cinebar, WA 98533, USA

Mason, Laurence (Actor)
c/o Mara Santino *Luber Roklin Management*
8530 Wilshire Blvd
6th Floor
Beverly Hills, CA 90211, USA

Mason, Lindsey (Athlete, Football Player)
3 Elwell Ct
Randallstown, MD 21133-4307, USA

Mason, Marilyn
27 Glen Oak
Medford, OR 97504

Mason, Marlyn (Actor, Musician)
27 Glen Oak Court
Medford, OR 97504, USA

Mason, Marsha (Actor)
c/o Alexa Pagonas *Michael Black Management*
9701 Wilshire Blvd
10th Floor
Beverly Hills, CA 90212, USA

Mason, Marty (Athlete, Baseball Player)
8255 SE Angelina Ct
Hobe Sound, FL 33455-8948, USA

Mason, Mike (Athlete, Baseball Player)
2711 Piper Ridge Ln
Excelsior, MN 55331-7803, USA

Mason, Monica (Ballerina)
Royal Opera House
Convent Garden
Bow St
London WC2, UNITED KINGDOM (UK)

Mason, Nick (Musician)
Agency Group
370 City Road
London EC1V 2QA, UNITED KINGDOM (UK)

Mason, Roger (Athlete, Baseball Player)
322 Park St
Bellaire, MI 49615-9411, USA

Mason, Ron (Coach)
Michigan State University
Athletic Dept
East Lansing, MI 48224, USA

Mason, Stephen (Musician, Songwriter)
c/o Janet Weir *Red Light Management (LA)*
8439 W Sunset Blvd
Suite 2
Los Angeles, CA 90069, USA

Mason, Steve (Musician)
Agency Group Ltd
370 City Road
London EC1V 2QA, UNITED KINGDOM (UK)

Mason, Sully
4043 Irving Pl.
Culver City, CA 90230

Mason, Tom (Actor)
870 Heights Place
Oyster Bay, NY 11771, USA

Mason, Tommy (Athlete, Football Player)
240 S Orange Acres Dr
Anaheim, CA 92807, USA

Mason, Vince (Musician)
Famous Artists Agency
250 W 57th St
New York, NY 10107, USA

Mason, Willy (Musician)
c/o Staff Member *Paradigm (Monterey)*
404 W Franklin St
Monterey, CA 93940, USA

Mason Dixon
PO Box 214 Flint
TX, CA 75762

Mason of Barnsley, Roy (Government Official)
12 Victoria Ave
Barnsley
South Yorks S7O 2BH, UNITED KINGDOM (UK)

Masri, Tahir Nashat (Prime Minister)
PO Box 5550
Amman, JORDAN

Mass, Jochen (Race Car Driver)
RTL-Sportredaktion
Cologne 50570, GERMANY

Mass, Marychris (Stylist)
1903 SE Umatilla St
Portland, OR 97202, USA

Mass, Wayne (Athlete, Football Player)
71 Eagle View
Durango, CO 81303, USA

Massa, Felipe (Race Car Driver)
c/o Staff Member *Jaguar Racing Ltd*
Bradbourne Drive
Tilbrook
Milton Keynes MK7 8BJ, United Kingdom

Massa, Gordon (Athlete, Baseball Player)
8255 Bonanza Ln
Cincinnati, OH 45255-2504, USA

Massari, Lea
Viale Parioli 59
Rome, ITALY I-00197

Massaro, Ashley (Wrestler)
c/o Kerry Rodgerson *World Wrestling Entertainment (WWE)*
Titan Towers
1241 E Main St
Stamford, CT 06905-3857, USA

Masse, Bill (Baseball Player)
US Olympic Team
2501 Amherst Ct Apt 25A
Boybnton Beach, FL 33436-9017, USA

Massen, Osa
10501 Wilshire Blvd. #704
Los Angeles, CA 90024

Massenburg, Tony (Athlete, Basketball Player)
13265 Tony Ln
Stony Creek, VA 23882-3209, USA

Masset, Andrew
11635 Huston
No. Hollywood, CA 91607

Masset, Nick (Athlete, Baseball Player)
14575 W Mountain View Blvd
Unit 11107
Surprise, AZ 85374-8674, USA

Massevitch, Alla G (Astronomer)
6 Pushkurev Per
#4
Moscow 103045, RUSSIA

Massey, Debbie (Athlete, Golfer)
PO Box 116
Cheboygan, MI 49721-0116, USA

Massey, Kent (Athlete, Olympic Athlete, Sailor)
4085 Foothill Rd
Carpinteria, CA 93013-3093, USA

Massey, Kyle (Actor)
Boy-O-Boy Entertainment
Creekmoor Ln POB 6811
Riverdale, GA 30296, USA

Massey, Robert (Athlete, Football Player)
6746 Terry Ln
Charlotte, NC 28215-3672, USA

Massey, Vincent (Misc)
University of Michigan
Biochemistry Dept
Ann Arbor, MI 48109, USA

Massey, Waiter E (Educator, Physicist)
Morehouse College
President's Office
830 Westview Dr SW
Atlanta, GA 30314, USA

Massie, Giddeon (Athlete, Cycler, Olympic Athlete)
PO Box 31
Zionhill, PA 18981-0031, USA

Massie, Rick (Athlete, Football Player)
238 Doyle Ave
Paris, KY 40361-1223, USA

Massie, Robert K (Writer)
52 W Clinton Ave
Irvington, NY 10533, USA

Massie, Toby (Race Car Driver)
Massie Flying Hillbilly Racing
RR #1
Box 231-A.
LeRoy, IL 61752, USA

Massimino, Michael J (Astronaut)
15814 Elk Park Lane
Houston, TX 77062, USA

Massimino, Michael J Dr (Astronaut)
15814 Elk Park Ln
Houston, TX 77062-4775, USA

Massimino, Rollie (Coach)
18578 ES Ferland Court
Jupiter, FL 33469, USA

Massive Attack (Music Group)
c/o Staff Member *Paradigm (Monterey)*
404 W Franklin St
Monterey, CA 93940, USA

Massoglia, Chris (Actor)
c/o Sandra Chang *Anonymous Content (LA)*
955 S Carrillo Dr
Suite 300
Los Angeles, CA 90048, USA

Mast, Dick (Athlete, Golfer)
15831 Tower View Dr
Clermont, FL 34711, USA

Mast, Rick (Race Car Driver)
4909 Stough Rd.
Concord, NC 28027-8969, USA

Mastan, Abbas (Director, Producer)
Abbas Mastan Productions
B/8
Juhu Tara Road
Mumbai 400059, India

Mastanddrea, Katlin (Actor)
c/o DebraLynn Findon *Discover Inc Management*
11425 Moorpark St
Studio City, CA 91602, USA

Masteller, Dan (Athlete, Baseball Player)
1530 Bav Laurel Dr
Menlo Park, CA 94025-5808, USA

Master P (Actor, Musician)
c/o Adam Robinson *Southfield Village*
6255 W. Sunset Blvd
Suite 923
Los Angeles, CA 90028, USA

Masters, Ben (Actor)
c/o Staff Member *Silver Massetti & Szatmary (SMS) Talent Inc*
8383 Wilshire Blvd
Suite 230
Beverly Hills, CA 90211, USA

Masters, Billy (Athlete, Football Player)
501 SW Silver Spur Cir
Lees Summit, MO 64081, USA

Masters, Geoff (Tennis Player)
De Lorain St
Wavell Heights, QLD 4012, AUSTRALIA

Masters, Jamie (Athlete, Hockey Player)
178 Clitheroe Rd
Grafton, ON KOK 2GO, Canada

Masters, Margie (Athlete, Golfer)
8440 E Hazeltine Ln
Tucson, AZ 85710, USA

Masterson, Christopher (Chris) Kennedy (Actor)
c/o Staff Member *United Talent Agency (UTA)*
9336 Civic Center Dr
Beverly Hills, CA 90210, USA

Masterson, Connie (Athlete, Golfer)
4004 Island Bay Cir
Sanford, FL 32771-6344, USA

Masterson, Danny (Actor, Producer)
c/o Jenni Weinman *Patricola Lust PR*
9171 Wilshire Blvd
Suite 441
Beverly Hills, CA 90210, USA

Masterson, Fay (Actor)
c/o Francis Okwu *Zero Gravity Management*
6363 Wilshire Blvd
Suite 300
Los Angeles, CA 90048, USA

Masterson, Justin (Athlete, Baseball Player)
4095 White Oak Dr
Beavercreek, OH 45432-1927, USA

Masterson, Lisa (Talk Show Host)
Masterson MD
1333 Ocean Ave
Santa Monica, CA 90401, USA

Masterson, Mary Stuart (Actor)
c/o John Carrabino *John Carrabino Management*
5900 Wilshire Blvd Fl 4 #406
Los Angeles, CA 90036, USA

Masterson, Peter (Director, Producer, Writer)
1165 5th Ave
#15A
New York, NY 10029, USA

Masterson, Sean (Actor, Writer)
c/o Melanie Truhett *Messina Baker Entertainment*
955 Carrillo Dr
Suite 100
Los Angeles, CA 90048, USA

Masterson, Valerie (Opera Singer)
Music International
13 Ardilaun Road
London N5 2QR, UNITED KINGDOM (UK)

Mastny, Tom (Athlete, Baseball Player)
302 Lochleven Ct
Grovetown, GA 30813-5830, USA

Mastodon (Music Group, Musician)
c/o Jon Goldwater *Pinnacle Entertainment*
30 Glenn St
White Plains, NY 10603, USA

Maston, Le'shai (Athlete, Football Player)
7856 Overridge Dr
Dallas, TX 75232, USA

Mastracchio, Richard A
1910 Hillside Oak Ln
Houston, TX 77062, USA

Mastracchio, Richard A (Rick) (Astronaut)
1423 Roden Blvd Sheppard Afb
Houston, TX 76311-1378, USA

Mastrangelo, Carlo (Musician)
Paramount Entertainment
PO Box 12
Far Hills, NJ 07931, USA

Mastrantonio, Mary Elizabeth (Actor, Musician)
International Creative Mgmt
8942 Wilshire Blvd
#219
Beverly Hills, CA 90211, USA

Mastrogiacomo, Gina (Actor)
Pakula/King
9229 Sunset Blvd
#315
Los Angeles, CA 90069, USA

Mastroianni, Chiara (Actor)
P F D Drury House
34-43 Russell St
London WC2B 5HA, UNITED KINGDOM (UK)

Mastroianni, Darin (Athlete, Baseball Player)
16906 Hampton Trace Rd
Huntersville, NC 28078-6449, USA

Mastronardi, Alessandra (Actor)
c/o Staff Member *Creative Artists Agency (CAA-LA)*
2000 Ave Of The Stars
Los Angeles, CA 90067, USA

Mastrov, Mark (Sportscaster)
c/o Staff Member *WmE2 (WMA-LA)*
1 William Morris Pl
Beverly Hills, CA 90212, USA

Masui, Yoshio (Biologist, Scientist)
401-640 Sheppard Ave E
North York, ON M2K 1B8, CANADA

Masur, Andy (Commentator)
206 Park Blvd Unit 504
San Diego, CA 92101-7449, USA

Masur, Kurt
Leipzing Gweandhausorchester
Augustusplatz 8
Leipzig 04109, GERMANY

Masur, Richard (Actor)
10340 Santa Monica Blvd
Los Angeles, CA 90025, USA

Mata, Victor (Athlete, Baseball Player)
Juan Pablo Pina
#16 Alto
Santo Domingo, Dominican Republic,
USA

Mata'aho (Royalty)
Royal Palace
PO Box 6
Nuku'alofa, TONGA

Matalin, Mary (Journalist, Talk Show
Host, Writer)
Gaslight Inc
325 Fishers Rd
Maurertown, VA 22644-2760, USA

Matalon-Degni, Francine (Stylist)
260 RIverside Dr
#5-A
New York, NY 10025, USA

Matamoros, Kristi (Stylist)
c/o Staff Member Rex Agency, The
6311 Romaine St
Los Angeles, CA 90038, USA

Matan, Bill (Athlete, Football Player)
1660 Peachtree St NW Apt 6109
Atlanta, GA 30309-2485, USA

Matarazzo, Heather (Actor)
c/o Kieran Maguire The Arlook Group
205 S Beverly Dr
Suite 209
Beverly Hills, CA 90212, USA

Matarazzo, Len (Athlete, Baseball Player)
2715 Carlisle St
New Castle, PA 16105-1714, USA

Matchbox 20 (Music Group)
c/o Michael Lippman Lippman
Entertainment
23586 Calabasas Road
Suite 208
Calabasas, CA 91302, USA

Matchefts, John (Athlete, Hockey Player,
Olympic Athlete)
2415 N Chelton Rd
Colorado Springs, CO 80909-1350, USA

Matchett, Kari (Actor)
c/o Staff Member Brillstein Entertainment
Partners
9150 Wilshire Blvd #350
Beverly Hills, CA 90212, USA

Matchetts, John (Athlete, Hockey Player)
2415 Chelton Rd
Colorado Springs, CO 80909, USA

Matchick, Tom (Athlete, Baseball Player)
7700 Pilliod Rd
Holland, OH 43528-8077, USA

Matenopoulos, Debbie (Actor, Producer)
c/o Staff Member Fifteen Minutes (LA)
8436 W 3rd St
Suite 650
Los Angeles, CA 90048, USA

Mateo, Guillermo (Athlete, Baseball
Player)
c/o Staff Member Montreal Expos
4549 Avenue Pierre de Coubertin
Montreal
Quebec H1V 3N7, CANADA

Matesa, Zlatko (Prime Minister)
Prime Minister's Office
Jordanovac 71
Zagreb 41000, CROATIA

Mateschitz, Dietrich (Business Person)
Red Bull
Am Brunnen 1
Fuschl am See 5330, Austria

Matheny, Jim (Athlete, Football Player)
16 San Bernardino Ave
Ventura, CA 93004, USA

Matheny, Mike (Athlete, Baseball Player)
15 West Dr
Chesterfield, MO 63017-0721, USA

Mather, John (Scientist)
3400 Rosemary Ln Apt 419
Hyattsville, MD 20782-1033, USA

Mather, John C. (Nobel Prize Laureate)
Goddard Space Flight
3400 Rosemary Ln
Hyattsville, MD 20782-1033, USA

Mather, Paul (Stylist)
c/o Staff Member Creative Exchange
Agency
53 Gansevoort St
3rd Floor
New York, NY 10014, USA

Mathers, Jerry (Actor)
Boutique
10 Universal City Plaza
Ste 2000
Universal City, CA 91608, USA

Matherson, Tim (Actor, Director)
246 Miramar Ave
Montecito, CA 93108, USA

Matheson, Chris (Writer)
c/o Rima Greer Above the Line Agency
468 N. Camden Dr
Suite 200
Beverly Hills, CA 90210, USA

Matheson, Jim (Congressman, Politician)
2434 Rayburn HOB
Washington, DC 20515, USA

Matheson, Richard (Writer)
PO Box 81
Woodland Hills, CA 91365-0081, USA

Matheson, Richard C. (Producer)
c/o Jon Karas Infinity Management
7923 Hollywood Blvd
Los Angeles, CA 90046, USA

Matheson, Tim (Actor, Director)
c/o Michael Nilon Kritzer Levine Wilkins
Entertainment (KLWG)
2000 Ave Of The Stars
Los Angeles, CA 90067, USA

Mathews, Byron (Baseball Player)
557 Golfwood Dr
Ballwin, MO 63021-6316, USA

Mathews, Carole (Actor)
39668 Old Spring Rd
Murietta, CA 92563, USA

Mathews, F David (Politician, Secretary)
Charles F Kettering Foundation 200
Commons Rd
Dayton, OH 45459-2799, USA

Mathews, Greg (Athlete, Baseball Player)
4007 Layang Layang
Cir Apt H
Carlsbad, CA 92008-4166, USA

Mathews, Harlan (Senator)
420 Hunt Club Road
Nashville, TN 37221, USA

Mathews, Nelson (Athlete, Baseball
Player)
211 E Crestview Dr
Columbia, IL 62236-1203, USA

Mathews, Ray (Athlete, Football Player)
P.O. Box 108
Harrisville, PA 16038, USA

Mathews, Rick (Athlete, Baseball Player)
837 Drake Ave
Centerville, IA 52544-2524, USA

Mathews, T J (Athlete, Baseball Player)
211 E Crestview Dr
Columbia, IL 62236-1203, USA

Mathias, Bob (Athlete)
7469 E. Pine Ave.
Fresno, CA 93727

Mathias, Buster Jr (Boxer)
4409 Carol Ave SW
Wyoming, MI 49509, USA

Mathias, Carl (Athlete, Baseball Player)
567 Long Ln
Oley, PA 19547-9009, USA

Mathias, Ric (Athlete, Football Player)
13753 Cardinal Point Trl
Verona, WI 53593-8152

Mathias, William (Composer)
Y Graigwen Cadnant Road
Menai Bridge
Anglesey, Gwynedd LL59, WALES

Mathieson, Jim (Athlete, Hockey Player)
88 Shaws Mill Rd
Gorham, ME 04038-2231

Mathieson, John (Director)
c/o Spyros Skouras The Skouras Agency
1149 Third Street Fl 3
Santa Monica, CA 90403, USA

Mathieu, Georges V A (Artist)
125 Ava de Makakoff
Paris 75116, FRANCE

Mathieu, Marquis (Athlete)
113 W Lake Shore Dr
Hallandale, FL 33009-6026

Mathieu, Mireille (Actor, Musician)
Info Stelle Deutschland
Görrestr.13
Fulda D - 36041, Germany

Mathieu, Philip (Musician)
Lindy S MArtin Mgmt
5 Lob Lolly Court
Executive Suite
Pinehurst, NC 28374, USA

Mathilde, Princess (Royalty)
Koninklijk Palace
Rue de Brederode
Brussels 1000, BELGIUM

Mathis, Alonzo (Gorilla Zoe) (Musician)
c/o Staff Member Atlantic Records (NY)
1290 Ave of the Americas
New York, NY 10104

Mathis, Bill (Athlete, Football Player)
43 West Paces Dr NW
Atlanta, GA 30327, USA

Mathis, Clint (Soccer Player)
New York/New Jersey MetroStars
1 Harmon Plaza
#300
Secaucus, NJ 07094, USA

Mathis, Edith (Opera Singer)
Ingpen & Williams
14 Kensington Court
London W8 5DN, UNITED KINGDOM
(UK)

Mathis, Evan (Athlete, Football Player)
11938 N 113th Pl
Scottsdale, AZ 85259, USA

Mathis, Jeff (Athlete, Baseball Player)
4420 Spring Valley Dr
Marianna, FL 32448-5414, USA

Mathis, Johnny (Musician)
c/o David Snyder WME (LA)
9601 Wilshire Blvd Fl 3
Beverly Hills, CA 90210, USA

Mathis, Judge Greg (Judge)
c/o Admire Entertainment
PO Box 152
Palisades, NY 10964, USA

Mathis, Rashean (Athlete, Football Player)
26200 Marsh Landing Pkwy
Ponte Vedra Beach, FL 32082, USA

Mathis, Ron (Athlete, Baseball Player)
2922 Kismet Ln
Houston, TX 77043-1322, USA

Mathis, Samantha (Actor)
c/o Courtney Kivowitz Schiff Company,
The
9465 Wilshire Blvd
Suite 480
Beverly Hills, CA 90212, USA

Mathis, Terance (Athlete, Football Player)
3415 Camellia Ln
Suwanee, GA 30024, USA

Mathis Jr, Buster
4409 Carol SW
Wyoming, MI 49509, USA

Mathison, Bruce (Athlete, Football Player)
1228 E Squawbush Pl
Phoenix, AZ 85048, USA

Mathison, Cameron (Actor)
c/o Marcia Hurwitz Innovative Artists (LA)
1505 10th St
Santa Monica, CA 90401, USA

Mathison, Camerson (Actor)
c/o Staff Member Innovative Artists (LA)
1505 10th St
Santa Monica, CA 90401, USA

Mathison, Melissa (Writer)
655 MacCulloch Dr
Los Angeles, CA 90049, USA

Matias, John (Athlete, Baseball Player)
98-1616 Hoolauae St
Aiea, HI 96701-1801, USA

Matiko, Marie (Actor)
c/o Staff Member Sovereign Talent Group
8421 Wilshire Blvd
Suite 200
Beverly Hills, CA 90211, USA

Matine-Coburn, Persia (Stylist)
fabulousface
Prefers to be contacted
via telephone or email
CA, USA

Matisyahu (Musician)
c/o Don Van Cleave The Artists
Organization
212 Marine St
Suite 307
Santa Monica, CA 90045, USA

Matkevich, Mark (Actor)
c/o Staff Member *Glasser/Black Management*
283 Cedarhurst Ave
Cedarhurst, NY 11516, USA

Matlack, Jon (Athlete, Baseball Player)
2495 Sawdust Rd
Aot 1101
Spring, TX 77380-3365, USA

Matlack-Sagrati, Ruth (Athlete, Baseball Player, Commentator)
1086 Bristol Pike Apt 312
Bensalem, PA 19020-5664, USA

Matlin, Marlee (Actor, Producer)
c/o Lisa Perkins *Fifteen Minutes (LA)*
8436 W 3rd St
Suite 650
Los Angeles, CA 90048, USA

Matlock, Glen (Musician)
Solo Agency
55 Fulham High St
London SW6 3JJ, UNITED KINGDOM (UK)

Matlock, Jack F Jr (Diplomat)
940 Princeton Kingston Road
Princeton, NJ 08540, USA

Matola, Sharon (Misc)
Belize Zoo & Tropical Education Center
PO Box 1787
Belize City, BELIZE

Matondkar, Urmila (Actor, Bollywood)
93/14 Sanman, Lokhandwala Road
Andheri (W)
Bombay 400058, India

Matorin, Vladimir A (Opera Singer)
Ulansky Per 21 Korp 1
#53
Moscow 103045, RUSSIA

Matos, Francisco (Athlete, Baseball Player)
Arkansas Travelers
PO Box 55066 Attn
Coaching Staff
little Rock, AR 72215-5066, USA

Matos, Julius (Athlete, Baseball Player)
12823 Valimar Rd
New Port Richey, FL 34654-4815, USA

Matranga, Dave (Athlete, Baseball Player)
303 N Park Ln
Orange, CA 92867-7642, USA

Matricaria, Ronald (Business Person)
Saint Jude Medical Inc
1 Lillehei Plaza
Saint Paul, MN 55117, USA

Matsch, Richard P (Judge)
US District Court
1929 Stout St
Denver, CO 80294, USA

Matsik, George A (Business Person)
Ball Corp
10 Longs Peak Dr
Broomfield, CO 80021, USA

Matson, April (Actor)
c/o Jennifer Millar *Paradigm (LA)*
9200 Sunset Blvd
11th Floor
Los Angeles, CA 90069, USA

Matson, J Randel (Randy) (Athlete, Track Athlete)
1002 Park Place
College Station, TX 77840, USA

Matson, Pat (Athlete, Football Player)
987 Village Circle Dr
Greenwood, IN 46143-8509, USA

Matson, Randy (Athlete, Olympic Athlete, Track Athlete)
1002 Park Pl.
College Station, TX 77840-3008, USA

Matsos, Arch (Athlete, Football Player)
1410 Coventry Close St
East Lansing, MI 48823, USA

Matsos, Archie (Athlete, Football Player)
1410 Coventry Close St
East Lansing, MI 48823, USA

Matsuda, Naomi (Actor)
c/o Staff Member *AKA Talent Agency*
6310 San Vicente Blvd
Suite 200
Los Angeles, CA 90048, USA

Matsuda, Seiko (Actor, Musician)
Propaganda Films Mgmt
1741 Ivar Ave
Los Angeles, CA 90028, USA

Matsui, Hideki (Athlete, Baseball Player)
845 United Nations Plz
Apt 52C
New York, NY 10017, USA

Matsui, Kaz (Athlete, Baseball Player)
229 N Almont Dr
Beverly Hills, CA 90211-1615, USA

Matsui, Keiko (Musician)
Ted Kurland
173 Brighton Ave
Boston, MA 02134, USA

Matsui, Kosei (Artist)
Ibaraki-ken
Kasama-shi
Kasama 350, JAPAN

Matsukisa, Nobuyaki (Nobu) (Chef)
c/o Staff Member *Verve Entertainment*
5900 Wilshire Blvd #1720
Los Angeles, CA 90036-5021, USA

Matsumoto, Shigeharu (Writer)
International House of Japan
11-16 Roppongi
Minatuku
Tokyo, JAPAN

Matsushita, Hiro (Race Car Driver)
1600 Avenida Salvador
San Clemente, CA 92674, USA

Matsuzaka, Daisuke (Athlete, Baseball Player)
c/o Scott Boras *Boras Corporation*
18 Corporate Plaza
Newport Beach, CA 92660, USA

Matt, Morris (Athlete, Hockey Player)
9 Elmdale Blvd
Brandon, MB R7B 1B5, Canada

Matta, del Meskin (Religious Leader)
Deir el Makarios Monastery
Cairo, EGYPT

Matte, Thomas R (Tom) (Athlete, Football Player)
11309 Old Carriage Rd
Glen Arm, MD 21057, USA

Mattea, Kathy (Actor, Musician)
PO Box 1776
Orem, UT 84059, USA

Mattei, Frank (Musician)
Joe Taylor Mgmt
PO Box 1017
Turnersville, NJ 08012, USA

Mattek-Sands, Bethanie (Athlete, Tennis Player)
c/o Staff Member *CMPR*
2121 Rosecrans Ave.
Suite 3375
El Segundo, CA 90245, USA

Matter, Niall (Actor)
c/o Trina Allen *Play Management*
807 Powell St
Suite 220
Vancouver V6A 1H7, CANADA

Mattes, Eva (Actor)
Agentur Carola Studlar
Neurieder Str
#1C
Planegg 92152, GERMANY

Mattes, Ron (Athlete, Football Player)
1718 Moreland Wood Trl
Concord, NC 28027, USA

Mattes, Troy (Athlete, Baseball Player)
2932 Lexington St
Sarasota, FL 34231-6118, USA

Mattesich, Rudi (Skier)
General Delivery
Troy, VT 05868, USA

Matteson, Troy (Athlete, Golfer)
6518 Old Shadburn Ferry Rd
Buford, GA 30518, USA

Matteucci, Matt (Athlete, Hockey Player)
4282 W Timberwood Dr
Traverse City, MI 49686-3844

Matthes, Roland (Swimmer)
Luitpoldstr 35A
Marktheidenfeld 97828, GERMANY

Matthes, Ulrich (Actor)
Kuno-Fischer-Str 14
Berlin 14057, GERMANY

Matthew, Catriona (Athlete, Golfer)
I M G
Pler House Strand on the Green
Chiswick
London W4 3NN, United Kingdom

Matthews, Al (Athlete, Football Player)
19541 Diablo Dr
Pflugerville, TX 78660-5088, USA

Matthews, Amy (Stylist)
c/o Staff Member *Crews*
828 Clemont Dr
Atlanta, GA 30306, USA

Matthews, Aubrey (Athlete, Football Player)
15 Saint Charles Pl
Madison, MS 39110, USA

Matthews, Bill (Athlete, Football Player)
32 Olde Farm Rd
South Easton, MA 02375, USA

Matthews, Bo (Athlete, Football Player)
10053 Vine Ct
Denver, CO 80229, USA

Matthews, Bruce R (Athlete, Football Player)
6423 Oilfield Rd
Sugar Land, TX 77479, USA

Matthews, Cerys (Musician)
c/o Staff Member *Agency Group Ltd, The (UK)*
361-373 City Rd
London EC1V 1PQ, UK

Matthews, Chris (Television Host)
c/o Staff Member *MSNBC*
30 Rockfeller Plz
New York, NY 10112, USA

Matthews, Clay (Athlete, Football Player)
6068 Canterbury Dr
Agoura Hills, CA 91301, USA

Matthews, Clay (Athlete, Football Player)
c/o David Dunn *Athletes First, LLC*
9140 Irvine Center Dr
Irvine, CA 92618, USA

Matthews, Dakin (Actor)
c/o Staff Member *McCabe Group, The*
3211 Cahuenga Blvd W Ste 104
Los Angeles, CA 90068, USA

Matthews, Dave (Musician, Songwriter)
c/o Coran Capshaw *Red Light Management (VA)*
PO Box 1467
Charlottesville, VA 22902, USA

Matthews, DeLane (Actor)
Don Buchwald
5500 Wilshire Blvd
#2200
Los Angeles, CA 90048, USA

Matthews, Denny (Commentator)
11816 Norwood Dr
Leawood, KS 66211-3006, USA

Matthews, Gary N (Athlete, Baseball Player)
1542 W Jackson Blvd
Chicago, IL 60607-5304, USA

Matthews, Ian (Musician)
Geoffrey Blumenauer
11846 Balboa Blvd
#204
Granada Hills, CA 91344, USA

Matthews, Keith (Astronomer)
California Institute of Technology
Astronomy Dept
Pasadena, CA 91125, USA

Matthews, Liesel (Actor)
c/o Staff Member *Creative Artists Agency (CAA-LA)*
2000 Ave Of The Stars
Los Angeles, CA 90067, USA

Matthews, Mike (Athlete, Baseball Player)
14326 Bakerwood Pl
Haymarket, VA 20169-2638, USA

Matthews, Pat Stanley (Actor)
210 Stanton
Walla Walla, WA 99362, USA

Matthews, Rachel (Stylist)
c/o Staff Member *Judy Inc*
1 Yorkville Ave
Toronto ON M4W 1L1, Canada

Matthews, Robert C O (Economist)
Clare College
Cambridge
CB2 1TL, UNITED KINGDOM (UK)

Matthews, Ross (Correspondent)

Matthews, Shane (Athlete, Football Player)
848 NW 136th St
Newberry, FL 32669, USA

Matthews, Steve (Athlete, Football Player)
342 Short Springs Rd
Tullahoma, TN 37388, USA

Matthews, Vincent (Vince) (Athlete, Track Athlete)
6755 193rd Lane
Fresh Meadows, NY 11365, USA

Matthews Jr, Gary (Athlete, Baseball Player)
4721 Dorchester Rd
Corona Del Mar, CA 92625-2717, USA

Matthias, Shawn (Athlete, Hockey Player)
Newport Sports Management
400-201 City Centre Dr
Attn Don Meehan
Mississauga, ON L5B 2T4, Canada

Matthies, Nina (Athlete, Coach, Volleyball Player)
Pepperdine University
Athletic Dept
24255 Pacific Coast Hwy
Malibu, CA 90265, USA

Matthiesen, David H Dr (Astronaut)
3770 E Surrey Ct
Rocky River, OH 44116-4206, USA

Matthiessen, Peter (Writer)
Bridge Lane
Sagaponack, NY 11962, USA

Mattiace, Len (Athlete, Golfer)
12803 Hunt Club Rd N
Jacksonville, FL 32224-7654, USA

Mattiello, Matthew (Stylist)
c/o Staff Member *Perrella Management*
330 W 38th St Rm 1407
New York, NY 10018, USA

Mattila, Karita M (Opera Singer)
45B Croxley Road
London W9 3HJ, UNITED KINGDOM (UK)

Mattingly, Don (Athlete, Baseball Player)
7601 Newburgh Rd
Evansville, IN 47715-4527, USA

Mattingly, Mack F (Politician, Senator)
4315 10th St
East Beach
Saint Simons Island, GA 31522-3004, USA

Mattingly, Thomas K II (Admiral, Astronaut)
Rocket Development Co
1501 Quail St
#102
Newport Beach, CA 92660, USA

Mattingly, Thomas K Radm (Astronaut)
_L)niversal Space Network Inc 1500
Quail St Ste 103
Newport Beach, CA 92660-2732, USA

Mattiussi, Dick (Athlete, Hockey Player)
6 Varley Cres
Brantford, ON N3R 7Z3, Canada

Mattos, Grant (Athlete, Football Player)
1392 Miller Pl
Los Angeles, CA 90069, USA

Mattox, Gus (Adult Film Star)
c/o Staff Member *Diva Central Inc*
7510 W Sunset Blvd Ste 1445
Los Angees, CA 90046, USA

Mattson, Riley (Athlete, Football Player)
12 Coconut Grove Ln
Lahaina, HI 96761, USA

Mattson, Robin (Actor)
Stan Kamens Mgmt
7772 Torreyson Dr
Los Angeles, CA 90046, USA

Mattson-Baumgart, Jacqueline (Athlete, Baseball Player, Commentator)
4814 W Fillmore Dr
Milwaukee, WI 53219-2364, USA

Mattsson, Helena (Actor)
c/o Liza Anderson *Anderson Group Public Relations*
8060 Melrose Ave Fl 4
Los Angeles, CA 90046, USA

mattsson, Markus (Athlete, Hockey Player)
Instrumentointi-OY Sarankulmankatu 20
tampere, SF 33900, Finland

Matula, Rick (Athlete, Baseball Player)
1817 Chapel Hts
Wharton, TX 77488-4459, USA

Matusz, Brian (Athlete, Baseball Player)
6420 N 52nd Pl
Paradise Valley, AZ 85253-4157, USA

Matuszek, Len (Athlete, Baseball Player)
10326 Deerfield Rd
Cincinnati, OH 45242-5105, USA

Matvichuk, Richard (Athlete, Hockey Player)
8 Chapel Hill Ct
Cedar Grove, NJ 07009-1302, USA

Matz, Johanna
Opernring 4
Vienna, AUSTRIA 1010

Matzdorf, Pat (Athlete, Track Athlete)
1252 Bainbridge Dr
Naperville, IL 60563, USA

Mauban, Maria
4 sq. Vitruve
Paris, FRANCE 75020

Mauch, Billy & Bobby
538-C W. Northwest Hwy
Palatine, IL 60067

Mauch, Billy (Bill) (Actor)
538 W Northwest Highway
#C
Palatine, IL 60067, USA

Mauck, Carl (Athlete, Football Player)
2129 Winthrop Hill Rd
Argyle, TX 76226, USA

Mauck, Matt (Athlete, Football Player)
3 Coral Pl
Greenwood Village, CO 80111, USA

Mauer, Joe (Athlete, Baseball Player)
671 Lexington Pkwy N
Saint Paul, MN 55104-2025, USA

Maugham, R H (Religious Leader)
Christian & Missionary Alliance
PO Box 35000
Colorado Springs, CO 80935, USA

Maughan, Deryck (Financier)
GlaxoSmithKline
980 Great West Rd
Brentford, Middlesex TW8 9GS, United Kingdom

Maulden, Jerry L (Business Person)
Entergy Corp
10055 Grogans Mill Road
#5A
The Woodlands, TX 77380, USA

Mauldin, Greg (Athlete, Hockey Player)
69 Zain Cir
Milford, MA 01757-2831

Mauldin, William H (Cartoonist)
Loomis-Watkins Agency
150 E 35th St
New York, NY 10016

Maule, Brad (Actor)
c/o Hank Hedland *Opus Entertainment*
5225 Wilshire Blvd #905
Los Angeles, CA 90036, USA

Maumenee, Alfred E (Misc)
1700 Hillside Road
Stevenson, MD 21153, USA

Maura, Carmen (Actor)
GRPC SL
Calle Fuencarral 17
Madrid 28004, SPAIN

Maurer, Andy (Athlete, Football Player)
30 Perrydale Ave
Medford, OR 97501, USA

Maurer, Dave (Athlete, Baseball Player)
6845 Lake Harrison Cir
Chanhassen, MN 55317-4589, USA

Maurer, Rob (Athlete, Baseball Player)
3114 E Gum St
Evansville, IN 47714-2614, USA

Maurer, Robert D (Inventor)
2572 W 28th Ave
Eugene, OR 97405-1456, USA

Mauresmo, Amelie (Amy) (Tennis Player)
Athleteline
2 rue du chemin vert
Clichy 92110, FRANCE

Maurey, Nicole (Actor)
Residence Les Tuilerie
6 Square De Caustiglione
BP 9005
Le Chesnay F-78150, FRANCE

Mauriac, Claude (Writer)
24 Quai de Bethune
Paris 75004, FRANCE

Maurice, Ann (Actor)
c/o Lucy Inskip *House Doctor Network*
Gladstone Forge, Gladstone Ln
Cold Ash
Berkshire RG18 9PR, UK

Maurice, Paul (Athlete, Hockey Player)
3032 Cone Manor Ln
Raleigh, NC 27613-6604

Maurice, Paul (Athlete, Hockey Player)
Carolina Hurricanes
1400 Edwards Mill Rd
Raleigh, NC 27607-3624

Mauriello, Julianna Rose (Actor)
c/o Nancy Carson *Carson-Adler Agency*
250 West 57 St
Suite 2030
New York, NY 10107, USA

Mauriello, Ralph (Athlete, Baseball Player)
4241 Persimmon St
Moorpark, CA 93021-3515, USA

Maurier, Claire
Il rue de la Montague-le-Breuil
Epinay Orge, FRANCE 91360

Maurin, Laurence (Skier)
PO Box 1980
West Bend, WI 53095, USA

Mauroy, Pierre (Prime Minister)
17-19 Rue Voltaire
Lille 59800, FRANCE

Maurstad, Toralv (Actor, Director)
National Theatre
Storlingsgt 15
Osto 1, NORWAY

Maury, Duncan (Athlete, Football Player)
1554 Fallbrook Ave
Clovis, CA 93611-7348, USA

Mauser, Tim (Athlete, Baseball Player)
114 Shadow Creek Ln
Aledo, TX 76008-3111, USA

Mauti, Rich (Athlete, Football Player)
304 Plantation Dr
Mandeville, LA 70471, USA

Mauz, Henry H (Hank) Jr (Admiral)
1608 Viscaine Road
Pebble Beach, CA 93953, USA

Maven, Max
PO Box 3819
La Mesa, CA 91944-3819

Mavericks, The (Music Group)
c/o Staff Member *Asgard Promotions*
125 Parkway
London NW1 7PS, United Kingdom

Mavety, Larry (Athlete, Hockey Player)
243 Olympus Ave
Kingston, ON K7M 5S3, Canada

Mawae, Kevin J (Athlete, Football Player)
3704A Estes Rd
Nashville, TN 37215, USA

Mawby, Russell G (Misc)
WK Kellogg FOundation
1 Michigan Ave E
Battle Creek, MI 49017, USA

Max, Peter (Artist)
PeterMax.com
118 Riverside Dr
New York, NY 10024-3708, USA

Maxa, Rudy (Radio Personality, Television Host)
SavTrav Productions, Inc.
P.O. Box 65066
St. Paul, MN 55165-0066, USA

Maxcy, Brian (Athlete, Baseball Player)
982 Cobble Creek Dr
Birmingham, AL 35226-2867, USA

Maxey, Caty (Designer)
c/o Staff Member *Mirisch Agency*
8840 Wilshire Blvd
Suite 100
Beverly Hills, CA 90211, USA

Maxey, Marlon (Athlete, Basketball Player)
9013 S Blackstone Ave
Chicago, IL 60619-7909, USA

Maxey, Virginia
16414 Pick Pl.
Riverside, CA 92504

Maxi, Fumihiko (Architect)
5-16-22 Higashi Gotanda
Shinagawaku
Tokyo, JAPAN

Maxie, Brett (Athlete, Football Player)
1610 Fair Oaks Dr
Westlake, TX 76262, USA

Maxie, Larry (Athlete, Baseball Player)
296 Verdugo Way
Upland, CA 91786-7138, USA

Maximova, Ekaterina (Ballerina)
Bolshoi Theater
Teatralnaya Pi 1
Moscow 103009, RUSSIA

Maxson, Alvin (Athlete, Football Player)
17377 E Adriatic Pl Apt S302
Aurora, CO 80013, USA

Maxson, Robert (Educator)
California State University
President's Office
Long Beach, CA 90840, USA

Maxvill, Dal (Athlete, Baseball Player, Commentator)
1115 Eagle Creek Rd
Chesterfield, MO 63005-6606, USA

Maxwell, Arthur E (Oceanographer)
P.O. Box 31249
Santa Fe, NM 87594-1249, USA

Maxwell, Brad (Athlete, Hockey Player)
27285 Natchez Ave.
Elko, MN 55020, USA

Maxwell, Brad (Athlete, Hockey Player)
27285 Natchez Ave
Elko, MN 55020-9563

Maxwell, Cedric (Athlete, Basketball Player)
151 Tremont St Apt 25R
Apt 25R
Boston, MA 02111-1123, USA

Maxwell, Charlie (Athlete, Baseball Player)
730 Mapleview Dr
Paw Paw, MI 49079-1185, USA

Maxwell, Chester (General)
1516 Evergreen Park Ln SW
Olympia, WA 98502-5903, USA

Maxwell, Dobie (Comedian)
333 W North Ave #343
Chicago, IL 60610, USA

Maxwell, Frank (Politician)
Federation of TV-Radio Artists
260 Madison Ave
New York, NY 10016, USA

Maxwell, Ian (Publisher)
Eaton Terrace
London SW1, UNITED KINGDOM (UK)

Maxwell, Jacqui (Actor)
c/o Karen Goldberg *HYPHENATE*
9701 Wilshire Blvd.
10th floor
Beverly Hills, CA 90212, USA

Maxwell, Jason (Athlete, Baseball Player)
406 Hicks Rd
Nashville, TN 37221-2002, USA

Maxwell, John (Business Person, Writer)
The John Maxwell Company
2170 Satellite Blvd #195
Duluth, GA 30097, USA

Maxwell, Julie (Writer)
c/o Staff Member *Rogers, Coleridge & White Ltd.*
20 Powis Mews
London W11 1JN, UK

Maxwell, Kevin (Athlete, Hockey Player)
16 Morton Ln
West Hartford, CT 06117-1427

Maxwell, Kevin F H (Publisher)
Hill Burn
Hailey near Wallingford
Oxford OX10 6AD, UNITED KINGDOM (UK)

Maxwell, Kim (Stylist)
3450 Mission Ridge Circle
Atlanta, GA 30339, USA

Maxwell, Robert (General)
25 Lakeview Cir
Columbia, SC 29206-3222, USA

Maxwell, Robert D (General)
1001 SE 15th St Unit 44
Bend, OR 97702-2351, USA

Maxwell, Ronald F (Director, Writer)
c/o Staff Member *Phoenix Organization, The*
1990 South Bundy Dr #630
Los Angeles, CA 90025, USA

Maxwell, Tommy (Athlete, Football Player)
1634 Rockview Dr
Granbury, TX 76049-5733, USA

Maxwell, Vernon (Athlete, Football Player)
1955 E Citation Ln
Tempe, AZ 85284, USA

Maxwell, Vernon (Athlete, Basketball Player)
2601 NW 23rd Blvd Apt 170
Gainesville, FL 32605-59S4, USA

May, Alan (Athlete, Hockey Player)
c/o Staff Member *Boston Bruins*
TD Banknorth Garden
100 Legends Way, Suite 250
Boston, MA 02114, USA

May, Alan (Athlete, Hockey Player)
Washington Capitals
627 N Glebe Rd Ste 850
Arlington, VA 22203-2144

May, Arthur (Architect)
Kohn Pedersen Fox Assoc
111 W 57th St
New York, NY 10019, USA

May, Bob (Athlete, Golfer)
420 Grand Augusta Ln
Las Vegas, NV 89144-4300, USA

May, Brad (Athlete, Hockey Player)
9167 E Mountain Spring Rd
Scottsdale, AZ 85255-9151

May, Briane (Musician, Songwriter, Writer)
Old Bakehouse
16A High St Barnes
London SW13, UNITED KINGDOM (UK)

May, Carlos (Athlete, Baseball Player)
6102 Amherst Pl
Matteson, IL 60443-1988, USA

May, Chad (Athlete, Football Player)
1300 S Jesse St
Chandler, AZ 85286, USA

May, Darrell (Athlete, Baseball Player)
3315 Windsor Rd
Austin, TX 78703-2263, USA

May, David (Actor)
c/o Staff Member *Cunningham Escott Slevin & Doherty (CESD-LA)*
10635 Santa Monica Blvd
130
Los Angeles, CA 90025, USA

May, Dean (Athlete, Football Player)
7487 Alhambra Ct
Spring Hill, FL 34606, USA

May, Deborah (Actor)
Artists Agency
1180 S Beverly Dr
#301
Los Angeles, CA 90035, USA

May, Deems (Athlete, Football Player)
3922 Ayscough Rd
Charlotte, NC 28211, USA

May, Derrick (Athlete, Baseball Player)
2 Jaymar Blvd
Newark, DE 19702-2877, USA

May, Don (Athlete, Basketball Player)
1128 Colwick Dr
Dayton, OH 4S420-2206, USA

May, Don (Athlete, Basketball Player)
P.O. Box 331
Lake Ariel, PA 18436, USA

May, Donald
733 N. Seward St
PH, LA 90038

May, Elaine (Actor, Director, Writer)
c/o Staff Member *WmE2 (WMA-LA)*
1 William Morris Pl
Beverly Hills, CA 90212, USA

May, Joe (Misc)
General Delivery
Thome Bay, AK 99919, USA

May, Lee (Athlete, Baseball Player)
5533 Hill and Dale Dr
Cincinnati, OH 45213-2615, USA

May, Mark E (Football Player, Sportscaster)
c/o Staff Member *ESPN (Main)*
ESPN Plaza
935 Middle St
Bristol, CT 06010-1001, USA

May, Mathilda (Actor)
Artmedia
20 Ave Rapp
Paris 75007, FRANCE

May, Milt (Athlete, Baseball Player)
2200 Manatee Ave W
Bradenton, FL 34205-5430, USA

May, Ralphie (Actor, Comedian, Producer, Writer)

May, Ray (Athlete, Football Player)
1921 Wellington Rd
Los Angeles, CA 90016, USA

May, Rudy (Athlete, Baseball Player)
PO Box 84
Friant, CA 93626-0084, USA

May, Scott (Athlete, Basketball Player, Olympic Athlete)
2001 E Hillside Dr
Bloomington, IN 47401-6203, USA

may, Scott (Athlete, Baseball Player)
1630 Raven Cir Unit H
Estes Park, CO 80517-9477, USA

May, Suzanne (Actor)
c/o Staff Member *Frontline Management*
5670 Wilshire Blvd.
Suite 1370
Los Angeles, CA 90036, USA

May, Torsten (Boxer)
Sauerland Promotion
Hans-Bockler-Str 163
Hurth 50354, GERMANY

Mayaki, Ibrahim Hassane (Prime Minister)
Prime Minister's Office
State House
Niamey, NIGER

Mayall, John (Composer, Musician)
Monterey International
200 W Superior
#202
Chicago, IL 60610, USA

Mayall, Rik (Actor, Comedian)
Brunskill Mgmt
169 Queen's Gale
London SW7 5HE, UNITED KINGDOM (UK)

Mayasich, John (Athlete, Hockey Player)
801 McKinley Ave Apt 108
Eveleth, MN 55734-1476

Mayasich, John (Athlete, Hockey Player, Olympic Athlete)
801 McKinley Ave Apt 108
Eveleth, MN 55734-1476, USA

Maybank, Anthuan (Athlete, Olympic Athlete, Track Athlete)
171 N Porter St
Elgin, IL 60120-4476, USA

Mayberry, Doug (Athlete, Football Player)
PO Box 1390
Williams, CA 95987, USA

Mayberry, Jermane (Athlete, Football Player)
2208 Court Del Rey
Round Rock, TX 78681, USA

Mayberry, John C (Athlete, Baseball Player)
11115 W 121st Ter
Overland Park, KS 66213-1945, USA

Mayberry, Lee (Athlete, Basketball Player)
4115 E 36th St N
Tulsa, OK 74115-1709, USA

Mayberry, Tony (Athlete, Football Player)
15704 Cochester Rd
Tampa, FL 33647, USA

Mayberry, Jr., John (Athlete, Baseball Player)
11115 W 121st Ter
Overland Park, KS 66213-1945, USA

Maybin, Cameron (Athlete, Baseball Player)
85 Brompton Rd
Arden, NC 28704-8607, USA

Maybury, John (Director)
c/o Staff Member *WME (LA)*
9601 Wilshire Blvd Fl 3
Beverly Hills, CA 90210, USA

Maydan, Dan (Business Person)
Applied Materials
3050 Bowers Ave
Santa Clara, CA 95054, USA

Mayer, Christian (Skier)
Siedlerweg 18
Finkelstein 9884, AUSTRIA

Mayer, Ed (Athlete, Baseball Player)
440 Oakland Ave
Corte Madera, CA 94925-1524, USA

Mayer, Gene (Tennis Player)
115 South St
Glen Dale, MD 20769, USA

Mayer, Gil (Athlete, Hockey Player)
85 Woodland St
Lincoln, RI 02865-2804

Mayer, H Robert (Judge)
US Court of Appeals
717 Madison Place NW
Washington, DC 20439, USA

Mayer, John (Musician, Songwriter, Writer)
c/o Michael McDonald *Mick Management*
35 Washington St
Brooklyn, NY 11201, USA

Mayer, Joseph E (Physicist)
2345 Via Siena
La Jolla, CA 92037, USA

Mayer, Martin J (Admiral)
Deputy CinC
Joint Forces Command
116 Lake View Parkway
Suffolk, VA 23435, USA

Mayer, Pat
6417 Livernois Rd
Troy, MI 48098-1542

Mayer, P Augustin Cardinal (Religious Leader)
Ecclesia Dei
Vatican City 00120, VATICAN CITY

Mayer, Phil
Rt. 9 Box 715-M
Yakima, WA 98901

Mayer, Shawn (Athlete, Football Player)
378 Zion Rd
Hillsborough, NJ 08844, USA

Mayer, Travis (Skier)
37050 Williams St
Steamboat Springs, CO 80487, USA

Mayers, Jamal (Athlete, Hockey Player)
9800 Countryshire Place
S1. Louis, MO 63141-7914, USA

Mayes, Alonzo (Athlete, Football Player)
3000 SE 56th St
Oklahoma City, OK 73135, USA

Mayes, clyde
502 Dove Tree Rd
Greenville, SC 29615-4434, USA

Mayes, David (Athlete, Football Player)
3018 Kingsley Rd
Shaker Heights, OH 44122, USA

Mayes, Derrick (Athlete, Football Player)
3335 N Keystone Ave
Indianapolis, IN 46218, USA

Mayes, Rob (Actor)
c/o Christina Gualazzi *Collective*
8383 Wilshire Blvd
Suite 1050
Beverly Hills, CA 90211, USA

Mayes, Rueben (Athlete, Football Player)
2953 Lord Byron Pl
Eugene, OR 97408, USA

Mayes, Tharon
29 Winnett St
Hamden, CT 06517-2720, USA

Mayes, Wendell
1504 Bel Air Rd.
Los Angeles, CA 90077

Mayfair, Billy (Athlete, Golfer)
P.O. Box 25844
Scottsdale, AZ 85255-0114, USA

Mayfield, Corey (Athlete, Football Player)
1009 Ellis Way
Forney, TX 75126, USA

Mayfield, Jeremy (Race Car Driver)
Mayfield Motorsports
2220 Hwy 49 N
Harrisburg, NC 28117, USA

Mayhew, Lauren (Actor)
c/o David Eisenberg *Protege Entertainment*
710 E. Angeleno Ave
Burbank, CA 91501, USA

Mayhew, Martin (Athlete, Football Player)
4035 Sonnet Dr
Tallahassee, FL 32303, USA

Mayhew, Patrick B B (Government Official)
House of Lords
Westminster
London SW1A 0PW, UNITED KINGDOM (UK)

Maynard, Aaron (Race Car Driver)
33 Lake Rd.
Milton, VT 05468

Maynard, Andrew (Boxer)
Mike Trainer
3922 Fairmont Ave
Bethesda, MD 20814, USA

Maynard, Brad (Athlete, Football Player)
4915 Sage Ln
Long Grove, IL 60047, USA

Maynard, Don (Athlete, Football Player)

Maynard, Emily (Reality TV Star)
3025 Greystone
Morgantown, WV 26508, USA

Maynard, Mimi (Actor)
Badgley Connor Talent
9229 Sunset Blvd
#311
Los Angeles, CA 90069, USA

Maynard, Mujaahid (Athlete, Olympic Athlete, Wrestler)
18769 E Linvale Cir
Aurora, CO 80013-4796, USA

Mayne, Brent (Athlete, Baseball Player)
1863 Parkglen Cir
Costa Mesa, CA 92627-4506, USA

Mayne, D Roger (Photographer)
Colway Manor
Colway Lane
Lyme Regis, Dorset DT7 3HD, UNITED KINGDOM (UK)

Mayne, Kenny (Sportscaster)
ESPN-TV
Sports Dept ESPN Plaza
935 Middle St
Bristol, CT 06010, USA

Mayne, Lew (Athlete, Football Player)
PO Box 701
Daingerfield, TX 75638, USA

Mayne, Roy (Race Car Driver)
24 Reynolds Rd
Sumter, SC 29150, USA

Mayne, Thomas (Architect)
Morphosis Architects
2041 Colorado Ave
Santa Monica, CA 90404, USA

Maynor, Asa
PO Box 1641
Beverly Hills, CA 90213

Maynor, Stephanie (Athlete, Golfer)
6213 Three Apple Downs
Columbia, MD 21045-7419, USA

mayo, 0 J
3576 Golf Walk Cir
Memphis, TN 38125-8908, USA

Mayo, Jackie (Athlete, Baseball Player)
94 7 AUIWSta Dr
Youngstown, OH 44512-7923, USA

Mayo, Itzhak Ltcolonel
Nasa Johnson Space Center 2101 Nasa Pkwy Bldg 4
Houston, TX 77058-3607, USA

Mayo, Ron (Athlete, Football Player)
3995 Warner Ave
Hyattsville, MD 20784, USA

Mayock, Michael (Athlete, Football Player)
607 Georges Ln
Ardmore, PA 19003, USA

Mayock, Mike (Athlete, Football Player)
607 Georges Ln
Ardmore, PA 19003, USA

Mayor, Michel (Astronomer)
Univerisity of Geneva
Geneva Observatory
Geneva, SWITZERLAND

Mayor, Zaragoza Federico (Government Official)
UNESCO
7 Place de Fonteroy
Paris 75352, FRANCE

Mayotte, Tim (Athlete, Olympic Athlete, Tennis Player)
266 W 115th St Apt 4A
New York, NY 10026-2862, USA

Mayotte, Timothy S (Tim) (Tennis Player)
SFX Sports Group
2665 S Bayshore Dr
#602
Miami, FL 33133, USA

Mayron, Melanie (Actor, Director)
1435 N Ogden Dr
Los Angeles, CA 90046, USA

Mays, Alvoid (Athlete, Football Player)
3903 Cape Vista Dr
Bradenton, FL 34209, USA

Mays, Damon (Athlete, Football Player)
12705 N 57th Dr
Glendale, AZ 85304, USA

Mays, Jayma (Actor)
2317 Richland Ave
Los Angeles, CA 90027, USA

Mays, Jeryn (Actor)
28318 Birdie St
Moreno Valley, CA 92555-6358, USA

Mays, Joe (Athlete, Baseball Player)
10314 Riverbank Ter
Bradenton, FL 34212-5256, USA

Mays, Lyle (Musician)
Ted Kurland
173 Brighton Ave
Boston, MA 02134, USA

Mays, Melinda (Race Car Driver)
2221 Peachtree Rd NE
#D-440
Atlanta, GA 30309, USA

Mays, Rueben
7306 172nd St. SW
Edmonds, WA 98026-5121

Mays, Stafford (Athlete, Football Player)
2235 W Viewmont Way W
Seattle, WA 98199, USA

Mays, Willie (Athlete, Baseball Player)
Say Hey Foundation
PO Box 2410
Menlo Park, CA 94026, USA

Maysey, Matt (Athlete, Baseball Player)
10190 Katy Fwy Ste 350
Houston, TX 77043-5239, USA

May-Treanor, Misty (Athlete, Olympic Athlete, Volleyball Player)
1440 Coral Ridge Dr
Coral Springs, FL 33071-5433, USA

Mayweather Jr., Floyd (Athlete, Boxer)
4720 Laguna Vista
Las Vegas, NV 89109, USA

Mazach, John J (Admiral)
5423 Grist Mills Woods Road
Alexandria, VA 22309, USA

Mazar, Debi (Actor)
c/o Peg Donegan *Framework Entertainment (LA)*
9057 Nemo St
Suite C
West Hollywood, CA 90069, USA

Mazarella, Jacqueline (Actor)
c/o Tony Martinez *GVA Talent Agency Inc*
8981 Sunset Blvd.
Suite 101
Los Angeles, CA 90069, USA

Mazaroski, William S (Bill) (Baseball Player)
RR 6 Box 130
Greensburg, PA 15601, USA

Maze, Krista (Race Car Driver)
PO Box 7791
Huntington Beach, CA 92649, USA

Mazer, Bill (Sportscaster)
140 Kent Dr
Berkeley Heights, NJ 07922-2332, USA

Mazeroski, Bill (Athlete, Baseball Player)
281 Walton Tea Room Rd
Greensburg, PA 15601-6406, USA

Maznicki, Frank (Athlete, Football Player)
2 Coaches Ct
West Warwick, RI 02893, USA

Mazor, Stanley (Stan) (Inventor)
FTI/Teklicon
1169 Saint Anthony Ct
Los Altos, CA 94024-7049, USA

Mazowiecki, Tadeusz (Prime Minister)
Sejm RP Ul Qiekska 4/6/8
Warsaw 00-902, POLAND

Mazur, Jay (Athlete, Hockey Player)
148 Elderberry Dr
South Portland, ME 04106-6890

Mazur, Jay J (Misc)
Industrial Textile Employees Needletrades
1710 Broadway
New York, NY 10019, USA

Mazur, John (Athlete, Football Coach, Football Player)
672 Cornwallis Dr
Mount Laurel, NJ 08054, USA

Mazur, Monet (Actor)
c/o Marsha McManus *Principal Entertainment (LA)*
1964 Westwood Blvd #400
Los Angeles, CA 90025, USA

Mazurek, Fred (Athlete, Football Player)
79340 Citrus
La Quinta, CA 92253, USA

Mazursky, Paul (Director)
c/o Larry Shapiro *Nine Yards
Entertainment*
8530 Wilshire Blvd Fl 5
Beverly Hills, CA 90211, USA

Mazza, Valeria (Model)
Riccardo Ga
8/10 Via Revere
Milan 20123, ITALY

Mazzanti, Geno (Athlete, Football Player)
4188 E Highway 82
Lake Village, AR 71653, USA

Mazzanti, Jerry (Athlete, Football Player)
1712 S Lakeshore Dr
Lake Village, AR 71653, USA

Mazzara, Glen (Producer)
c/o Staff Member *Creative Artists Agency
(CAA-LA)*
2000 Ave Of The Stars
Los Angeles, CA 90067, USA

Mazzarello, Marcelo (Actor)
c/o Staff Member *Telefe - Argentina*
Pavon 2444 (C1248AAT)
Buenos Aires, ARGENTINA

Mazzaro, Vin (Athlete, Baseball Player)
48 Avalon Way
Waretown, NJ 08758-2698, USA

Mazzello, Joseph (Actor)
46691 Mission Blvd #536
Fremont, CA 94539

Mazzetti, Tim (Athlete, Football Player)
2 N LaSalle St #800
Chicago, IL 60602, USA

Mazzie, Marin (Actor, Musician)
J Michael Bloom
233 Park Ave S
#1000
New York, NY 10003, USA

Mazzilli, Lee L (Athlete, Baseball Player, Coach)
67 Stonehedge Dr S
Greenwich, CT 06831-3220, USA

Mazzo, Kay (Ballerina)
American Ballet School
144 W 66th St
New York, NY 10023, USA

Mazzola, Anthony T (Editor)
Town & Country Magazine
Editorial Dept
1790 Broadway
New York, NY 10019, USA

Mazzone, Leo (Athlete, Baseball Player)
4518 Mystique WayNE
Roswell, GA 30075-2087, USA

Mba, Casimir Oye (Prime Minister)
Prime Minister's Office
Boile Postale 546
Libreville, GABON

Mbasogo, Teodoro Obiang Nguema (President)
President's Office
Malabo, EQUATORIAL GUINEA

Mbatha-Raw, Gugu (Actor)
c/o Meg Mortimer *Principal Entertainment
(NY)*
130 W 42nd St
Suite 614
New York, NY 10036, USA

Mbeki, Thabo (President)
President's Office
Union Buildings
Pretoria 0001, SOUTH AFRICA

Mbenga, D J (Athlete, Basketball Player)
6112 Winton St
Dallas, TX 75214-2636, USA

M. Bilirakis, Gus (Congressman, Politician)
407 Cannon HOB
Washington, DC 20515, USA

M'Bow, Amadou-Mahtar (Government Official)
BP 5276
Dakar-Fann, SENEGAL

McAdam, Gary
34 Meadow Ln
Portland, ME 04103-3727

McAdams, Bob (Athlete, Football Player)
271 S French Broad Ave
Asheville, NC 28801, USA

McAdams, Carl (Athlete, Football Player)
206 E Main St
Antlers, OK 74523, USA

McAdams, Carl (Athlete, Football Player)
HC 82 Box 526
Atoka, OK 74525, USA

McAdams, Rachel (Actor)
c/o Shelley Browning *Magnolia
Entertainment (LA)*
9595 Wilshire Blvd
Suite 601
Beverly Hills, CA 90212, USA

McAddley, Jason (Athlete, Football Player)
3600 S Tower Ave
Chandler, AZ 85286, USA

McAdoo, Bob (Athlete, Basketball Player, Coach)
20970 Via Alamanda Apt 1
Boca Raton, FL 33428-1335, USA

McAfee, John (Business Person, Engineer)
McAfee Inc
2821 Mission College Blvd
Santa Clara, CA 95054, USA

McAfee, Ken
8 Deerfield Rd.
Medfield, MA 02052-1318

McAillister-Morton, Susie (Athlete, Golfer)
40241 Club View Dr
Rancho Mirage, CA 92270, USA

McAleese, Mary P (Politician, President)
President's Office
Office of the President Upper Marion
Street Government Complex
Dublin 2, IRELAND

McAleese, Peter (Producer)
c/o Lisa Helsing Lenhoff *Lenhoff &
Lenhoff*
830 Palm Ave
West Hollywood, CA 90069

McAleney, Ed (Athlete, Football Player)
981 Shore Rd
Cape Elizabeth, ME 04107, USA

McAlister, Chris (Athlete, Football Player)
8206 Pumpkin Hill Ct
Pikesville, MD 21208, USA

McAlister, James E (Athlete, Football Player, Track Athlete)
155 Glorietta St
Pasadena, CA 91103, USA

McAllister, Chris (Athlete, Hockey Player)
162 Eastlawn St
Fairfield, CT 06824-6480

McAllister, Deuce (Athlete, Football Player)
c/o Staff Member *Philadelphia Eagles*
1 NovaCare Way
Philadelphia, PA 19145, USA

McAlpine, Chris (Athlete, Hockey Player)
199 Oakhill Dr
Saint Paul, MN 55126-4835

McAlpine, Donald M (Cinematographer)
377 Placer Creek Lane
Henderson, NV 89014, USA

McAnally, Ernie (Athlete, Baseball Player)
PO Box 492
Mt Pleasant, TX 75456-0492, USA

McAnally, Mac (Musician, Songwriter)
c/o Staff Member *Paradigm (Monterey)*
404 W Franklin St
Monterey, CA 93940, USA

McAnally, Ron (Race Car Driver)
Motorsports HOF
191 Union Ave
Saratoga Springs, NY 12866, USA

McAnany, Jim (Athlete, Baseball Player)
1723 Cochran St Apt G
Simi Valley, CA 93065-2174, USA

McAndrew, James (Race Car Driver)
Team Matthew Inc
420-A S First St
Bangor, PA 18013, USA

McAndrew, Jamie (Athlete, Baseball Player)
9620 E Diamond Rim Dr
Scottsdale, AZ 85255-3330, USA

McAndrew, Jim (Athlete, Baseball Player)
16540 E El Lago Blvd
Unit 41
Fountain Hills, AZ 85268-4732, USA

McAndrew, Tracey (Nell) (Actor, Model)
c/o Staff Member *Adult Model SEM
Group*
98 Cockfosters Rd
Barnet
Hertfordshirt EN4 0DP, UNITED
KINGDOM

McAneeley, Bob (Athlete, Hockey Player)
40 Flagstone Cres
St. Albert, AB T8N 1R3, Canada

McAneeley, Ted (Athlete, Hockey Player)
234 Aikane St
Kailua, HI 96734-1603, USA

McAnulty, Paul (Athlete, Baseball Player)
921 Palomar Way
Oxnard, CA 93033-5111, USA

McArdle, Andrea (Actor, Musician)
Edd Kalehoff
14 Shady Glen Court
New Rochelle, NY 10805, USA

McArdle, John (Athlete, Baseball Player)
6640 Lynford St
Philadelphia, PA 19149-2124, USA

McArthur, Alex (Actor)
10435 Wheatland Ave
Sunland, CA 91040, USA

McArthur, Kevin (Athlete, Football Player)
3817 Meredith Ln
Mesquite, TX 75180, USA

McArthur, K Megan (Astronaut)
103 Harborcrest Dr
Seabrook, TX 77586-4601, USA

McArthur, William S (Bill) Jr (Astronaut)
14503 Sycamore Lake Road
Houston, TX 77062, USA

McArthur, William S Colonel (Astronaut)
NASA Johnson Space Center 2101 Nasa
Pkwy Atn: Safety and Mission Assurance
Houston, TX 77058-3696, USA

McAtee, Jud (Athlete, Hockey Player)
54 Bada10na Dr.
Hot Springs Village, AR 71909, USA

McAuley, Alphonso (Actor)
c/o David (Dave) Fleming *Mosaic Media
Group*
9200 W. Sunset Blvd
10th Floor
Los Angeles, CA 90069, USA

McAuley, Jordan (Business Person, Writer)
Contact Any Celebrity
8721 Santa Monica Blvd. #431
Los Angeles, CA 90069, USA

McAuliffe, Callan (Actor)
c/o Nicholas Bogner *Affirmative
Entertainment*
425 N Robertson Dr
Los Angeles, CA 90048, USA

McAuliffe, Dennis P (General)
9076 Belvoir Woods Parkway
Fort Belvoir, VA 22060, USA

McAuliffe, Dick (Athlete, Baseball Player)
32 Worthington Dr
Farmington, CT 06032-1493, USA

McAvoy, James (Actor)
c/o Meredith O'Sullivan *42West (LA)*
11400 W Olympic Blvd
Suite 1100
Los Angeles, CA 90064, USA

McBain, Andrew (Athlete, Hockey Player)
87 Balsam Ave
Toronto, ON M4E 3B8, Canada

McBain, Diane (Actor)
20185 Canyon View Dr
#1
Canyon Country, CA 91351, USA

McBain, Jason (Athlete, Hockey Player)
17558 SW 104th Ave
Tualatin, OR 97062-8605

McBath, Mike (Athlete, Football Player)
5044 Sailwind Cir
Orlando, FL 32810, USA

McBean, Al (Athlete, Baseball Player)
PO Box 4475
St Thomas, VI 00801, USA

McBean, Wayne (Athlete, Hockey Player)
555 Lakeside Greens Dr
Chestermere, AB TIX 1C5, Canada

McBee, Rives (Athlete, Golfer)
1504 Canyon Oaks Dr
Irving, TX 75061-2116, USA

McBeth, Marcus (Athlete, Baseball Player)
4719 E Mountain
Sage Dr
Phoenix, AZ 85044-6204, USA

McBratney, Sam (Writer)
c/o Staff Member *HarperCollins Publishers*
10 East 53rd St
c/o Author mail, 7th Floor
New York, NY 10022, USA

McBrayer, Jack
c/o Jo Yao *United Talent Agency (UTA)*
9336 Civic Center Dr
Beverly Hills, CA 90210, USA

McBriar, Mat (Athlete, Football Player)
4020 Buena Vista St
Dallas, TX 75204, USA

McBride, Bake (Athlete, Baseball Player)
4077 Reliant Cir
Owensboro, KY 42301-0024, USA

McBride, Chi (Actor)
c/o Sam Maydew *Collective*
8383 Wilshire Blvd
Suite 1050
Beverly Hills, CA 90211, USA

McBride, Danny (Actor)
c/o Lindsay Williams *The Gotham Group Inc*
9255 Sunset Blvd
Suite 515
Los Angeles, CA 90069, USA

McBride, Jeff
4185 Paradise Rd. #2081
Las Vegas, NV 89109-6508

McBride, Jon A (Astronaut)
Image Development Group
1018 Kanawha Blvd
#901
Charleston, WV 25301, USA

McBride, Jon A Captain (Astronaut)
2705 N Indian River Dr
Cocoa, FL 32922-7075, USA

McBride, Justin (Misc)
PBR
101 W. River Walk
Pueblo, CO 81003, USA

McBride, Ken (Athlete, Baseball Player)
3446 Cypress Cir
Westlake, OH 44145-4409, USA

McBride, Macay (Athlete, Baseball Player)
608 McDonald Rd
Sylvania, GA 30467-5718, USA

McBride, Martina (Musician)
c/o Jake Basden *Big Machine Records*
1219 16th Ave South
Nashville, TN 37212, USA

McBride, Oscar (Athlete, Football Player)
11 Algerwood
Ladera Ranch, CA 92694, USA

McBride, Patricia (Ballerina)
Sharon Wagner Artists
150 W End Ave
New York, NY 10023, USA

Mcbride, Susan (Writer)
8712 Garden Court
Brentwood, MO 63144-1116, USA

McBride, Turk (Athlete, Football Player)
c/o Eugene Parker *Maximum Sports Management*
6435 W Jefferson Blvd
#197
Fort Wayne, IN 46804, USA

McBride, William J (Misc)
Gorse Lodge
Ballyclare
County Antrim BT39 9DE, NORTHERN IRELAND

McBroom, Amanda (Musician, Songwriter, Writer)
167 Fairview Road
Ojai, CA 93023, USA

McBurney, Jim (Athlete, Hockey Player)
161 Louise Ave
Sault Ste. Marie, ON P6A 5X1, Canada

McCabe, Bryan (Athlete, Hockey Player)
c/o Staff Member *Toronto Maple Leafs*
Air Canada Centre
400-40 Bay St
Toronto, ON M5J 2X2, Canada

McCabe, Frank (Athlete, Basketball Player, Olympic Athlete)
6712 N White Fir Dr
Edwards, IL 61528-9424, USA

McCabe, Joe (Athlete, Baseball Player)
3003 Gardens Blvd
Naples, FL 34105-6647, USA

McCabe, John (Musician)
Novello Co
8/9 Firth St
London W1V 5TZ, UNITED KINGDOM (UK)

McCabe, Marcia
1990 Broadway Box 417 Ansonia Sta
. New York, NY 10023

McCabe, Patrick (Writer)
Picador
Macmillan Books
25 Ecckeston Place
London SW1W 9NF, UNITED KINGDOM (UK)

McCabe, Zia (Musician)
Mongui Mgmt
PO Box 5908
Portland, OR 97228, USA

McCafferty, Donald F (Don) Jr (Coach, Football Coach)
167 E Shore Road
Halesite, NY 11743, USA

McCaffery, Marcia (Stylist)
629 COle Ranch Rd
Encinitas, CA 92024, USA

McCaffrey, Barry R (General)
506 Crown View Dr
Alexandria, VA 22314, USA

McCaffrey, Mike (Athlete, Football Player)
341 W Muncie Ave
Fresno, CA 93711, USA

McCahill, John
1547 Henley Cres
Sarnia, ON N7S 5Z7, Canada

McCain, Edwin (Songwriter, Writer)
c/oMelissa Simmons
Harrington Management
PO Box 1267
Decatur, GA 30031-1267, USA

McCain, John (Politician)
U.S. Senate
2211 E Camelback Rd Unit 1105
Phoenix, AZ 85016-9059, USA

McCain, Meghan
U.S. Senate
241 Russell
Senate Office Bldg
Washington, DC 20510, USA

McCall, Brett (Stylist)
c/o Staff Member *Seaminx Artist Management*
2806 Greenville Ave
#B
Dallas, TX 75206, USA

McCall, Brian (Athlete, Baseball Player)
550 Tremont Ave
Greenburg, PA 15601-4263, USA

McCall, Davina (Actor)
c/o Staff Member *John Noel Management*
10A Belmont St
Floor 2
London NW1 8HH, UNITED KINGDOM (UK)

McCall, Don (Athlete, Football Player)
16830 Kingsbury St
Apt 131
Granada Hills, CA 91344, USA

McCall, Joe (Athlete, Football Player)
1011 SW 100th Ter
Pembroke Pines, FL 33025, USA

McCall, John (Athlete, Baseball Player)
8043 E Ragweed Dr
Tucson, AZ 85710, USA

McCall, John "windy" (Athlete, Baseball Player)
8043 E Ragweed Dr
Tucson, AZ 85710-8580, USA

McCall, Larry (Athlete, Baseball Player)
354 Justice Ridge Rd
Candler, NC 28715-9576, USA

McCall, Mitzi (Actor)
c/o Staff Member *Cunningham Escott Slevin & Doherty (CESD-LA)*
10635 Santa Monica Blvd
130
Los Angeles, CA 90025, USA

McCall, Reese (Athlete, Football Player)
1311 1st Ave N
Bessemer, AL 35020, USA

McCallany, Holt (Actor)
c/o David (Dave) Fleming *Mosaic Media Group*
9200 W. Sunset Blvd
10th Floor
Los Angeles, CA 90069, USA

McCallister, Blaine (Athlete, Golfer)
1878 Epping Forest Way S
Jacksonville, FL 32217, USA

McCall Smith, Alexander (Writer)
c/o Staff Member *Random House*
1540 Broadway
New York, NY 10036, USA

McCallum, David (Actor)
40 E 62nd St #9W
New York, NY 10065, USA

McCallum, Dunc (Athlete, Hockey Player)

McCallum, John
1740 Pittwater Rd.
Bayview, AUSTRALIA NSW 2104

McCallum, Napoleon (Athlete, Football Player)
314 Doe Run Cir
Henderson, NV 89012, USA

McCambridge, Mercedes (Astronaut)
210932 Pleasant Park Dr
Conifer, CO 80433, USA

McCament, Randy (Athlete, Baseball Player)
17338 N Del Webb Blvd
Sun City, AZ 85373-1951, USA

McCammon, Bob (Athlete, Hockey Player)
200-322 Water St
vancouver, BC V6B 1B6, Canada

McCandless, Bruce (Astronaut)
21852 Pleasant Park Dr
Conifer, CO 80433, USA

McCandless, Bruce Captain (Astronaut)
21932 Pleasant Park Rd
Conifer, CO 80433-6802, USA

McCanlies, Tim (Director, Producer, Writer)
c/o Lindsay Williams *The Gotham Group Inc*
9255 Sunset Blvd
Suite 515
Los Angeles, CA 90069, USA

McCann, Brendan (Athlete, Basketball Player)
3599 Shinnecock Ln
Green Cove Springs, FL 32043-8028, USA

McCann, Brian (Athlete, Baseball Player)
869 Big Horn Holw
Suwanee, GA 30024-1764, USA

McCann, Chuck (Actor, Comedian)
2941 Briar Knoll Dr
Los Angeles, CA 90046, USA

McCann, Kate (Stylist)
c/o Staff Member *Marnie Rose Agency*
37 Lower Shad
Pound Ridge, NY 10576, USA

McCann, Les (Composer, Musician)
DeLeon Artists
4031 Panama Court
Piedmont, CA 94611, USA

McCann, Lila (Musician)
c/o Rick Shipp *WmE2 (WMA-TN)*
1600 Division St
Suite 300
Nashville, TN 37203, USA

McCann, Michelle
1200 Singer Dr.
West Palm Beach, FL 33404

McCann, Tim (Director)
c/o Jennifer Konawal *Gersh (NY)*
41 Madison Ave
New York, NY 10010, USA

McCants, Darnerien (Athlete, Football Player)
43847 Chadwick Ter
Ashburn, VA 20148, USA

McCants, Keith (Athlete, Football Player)
6650 Cottage Hill Rd Apt 401
Mobile, AL 36695, USA

McCants, Mel (Athlete, Basketball Player)
6404 Somis Way
Sacramento, CA 95828-1523, USA

McCants, Rashad (Athlete, Basketball Player)
c/o Jeff Schwartz *Excel Sports Management*
9665 Wilshire Blvd #500
Los Angeles, CA 90212, USA

McCardell, Keenan (Athlete, Football Player)
4918 Newpoint Dr
Fresno, TX 77545-9200, USA

McCareins, Justin (Athlete, Football Player)
7707 Andes Ln
Parkland, FL 33067, USA

McCarren, Larry (Athlete, Football Player)
520 W Chickadee Ln
Green Bay, WI 54313, USA

McCarrick, Theodore E Cardinal (Religious Leader)
Archdiocesan Pastoral Center
5001 Eastern Ave
Washington, DC 20017, USA

McCarroll, Jay (Fashion Designer)
c/o Nancy Kane *Kane & Associates*
319 N Venice Blvd
Venice, CA 90291, USA

McCarron, Chris
PO Box 861
Sierra Madre, CA 91025

McCarron, Chris (Horse Racer)
1372 Sugar Maple Ln
Lexington, KY 40511-2325, USA

McCarron, Christopher (Chris) (Jockey)
Dun Roamin
318 N Terrace View Dr
Monrovia, CA 91016, USA

McCarron, Douglas J (Misc)
Carpenters/Joiners Brotherhood
101 Connecticut Ave NW
Washington, DC 20001, USA

McCarron, Scott (Athlete, Golfer)
1835 Manzanita Cir
Reno, NV 89509, USA

McCarry, Charles (Writer)
Random House
1745 Broadway
#B1
New York, NY 10019, USA

McCartan, Jack (Athlete, Hockey Player, Olympic Athlete)
15504 Almond Ln
Eden Prairie, MN 55347-2554, USA

McCarter, Andre (Athlete, Basketball Player)
3257 Kibbe Ct
Lawrenceville, GA 30044-3263, USA

McCarter, Willie (Athlete, Basketball Player)
5925 Campfield St
Jackson, MI 49201-8355, USA

McCarter Sisters
PO Box 121551
Nashville, TN 37212

McCarthy, Andrew (Actor)
c/o Emily Gerson Saines *Brookside Artists Management (NY)*
250 W 57th St
Suite 2303
New York, NY 10107, USA

McCarthy, Bill (Athlete, Football Player)
1640 Walnut Ave
Winter Park, FL 32789, USA

McCarthy, Brandon (Athlete, Baseball Player)
34457 N Legend Trail
Pkwy Unit 1018
Scottsdale, AZ 85262-4428, USA

McCarthy, Carolyn (Congressman, Politician)
2346 Rayburn HOB
Washington, DC 20515, USA

McCarthy, Cormac (Writer)
1101 N Mesa
El Paso, TX 79002, USA

McCarthy, Dan (Athlete, Hockey Player)
1346 Wolf Hill Rd
Cheshire, CT 06410-1739

McCarthy, Dennis (Composer)
Vangelos Mgmt
15233 Ventura Blvd
#200
Sherman Oaks, CA 91403, USA

McCarthy, Dennis M (General)
Commander Forces Reserve
HqUSMC
2 Navy St
Washington, DC 20380, USA

McCarthy, Donald W (Astronomer)
Stewart Observatory
University of Arizona
Tucson, AZ 85721, USA

McCarthy, Greg (Athlete, Baseball Player)
56 Wakelee Avenue Ext
Shelton, CT 06484-3954, USA

McCarthy, Jenny (Actor)
Jenny McCarthy Productions
150 S Rodeo Dr #300
Beverly Hills, CA 90212, USA

McCarthy, Joey (Race Car Driver)
McCarthy/Pritchard Motorsports
Box 1494
Dover, NJ 08802-1494, USA

McCarthy, John (Athlete, Basketball Player)
1350 Union Rd Apt 2F
Apt 2F
West Seneca, NY 14224-2940, USA

McCarthy, Julianna (Actor)
Stone Manners
6500 Wilshire Blvd
#550
Los Angeles, CA 90048, USA

McCarthy, Kevin (Athlete, Hockey Player)
Philadelphia Flyers
3601 S Broad St Ste 2
Philadelphia, PA 19148-5297

McCarthy, Kevin (Athlete, Hockey Player)
1139 Warf Rd
Lexington, NC 27292-1929, USA

McCarthy, Kevin (Congressman, Politician)
326 Cannon HOB
Washington, DC 20515, USA

McCarthy, Lin
233 N. Swall Dr.
Beverly Hills, CA 90210

McCarthy, Mary Frances (Educator, Writer)
Trinity College
English Dept
Washington, DC 20017, USA

McCarthy, Melissa (Actor)
c/o Christian Donatelli *Schiff Company, The*
9465 Wilshire Blvd
Suite 480
Beverly Hills, CA 90212, USA

McCarthy, Nobu
9229 Sunset Blvd. #311
Los Angeles, CA 90069

McCarthy, Norma
818385 Mead Lane SLU Box 9063
Victorville, CA 92392

McCarthy, Sandy (Athlete, Hockey Player)
1826 Quantz Cres
Innisfil, ON L9S 1X2, Canada

McCarthy, Shawn (Athlete, Football Player)
300 N Lakeshore Rd
Payson, AZ 85541, USA

McCarthy, Tim (Stylist)
c/o Staff Member *Judy Inc*
1 Yorkville Ave
Toronto ON M4W 1L1, Canada

McCarthy, Timothy
8686 Butterfield Lane
Orland Park, IL 60462

McCarthy, Tom (Athlete, Baseball Player)
P.O. Box 38
Limington, ME 04049-0038, USA

McCarthy, Tom (Director)
c/o Rhonda Price *Gersh (NY)*
41 Madison Ave
New York, NY 10010, USA

McCarthy, Tom (Athlete, Hockey Player)
Huntsville Muskoka Otters
20 Park Dr
Huntsville, ON P1H 1P5, Canada

McCarthy, Tom (Commentator)
2229 Union Blvd
Allentown, PA 18109, USA

McCarthy, Tony (Songwriter, Writer)
29/33 Berners Road
London W1P 4AA, UNITED KINGDOM (UK)

McCartney, Jesse (Musician)
c/o Nicole Perna *Baker Winokur Ryder Public Relations (BWR-LA)*
9100 Wilshire Blvd
Suite 500, West Tower
Beverly Hills, CA 90212, USA

McCartney, Paul (Musician, Songwriter)
c/o Scott Rodger *Quest Management*
36 Warple Way
Unit 1D
London W3 0RG, UK

McCartney, Ron (Athlete, Football Player)
10722 Bell Valley Dr
Knoxville, TN 37934, USA

McCartney, Stella (Designer, Fashion Designer)
The Larches, Farm Hill
Furze Road
Bishampton, Pershore WR10 2NA, UNITED KINGDOM (UK)

McCarty, Chris
9105 Carmelita Ave. #101
Beverly Hills, CA 90210-3543

McCarty, Darren (Athlete)
c/o Staff Member *Detroit Red Wings*
Joe Luis Arena
600 Civic Center Dr
Detroit, MI 48226, USA

McCarty, Darren
640 Oak Ave
Birmingham, MI 48009-1379

McCarty, David (Athlete, Baseball Player)
110 Waldo Ave
Piedmont, CA 94611-3943, USA

McCarty, Mary (Baseball Player)
9455 N Genesee Rd
Mount Morris, MI 48458-9734, USA

McCarty, Walter (Athlete, Basketball Player)
7525 Pine Valley Ln
Indianapolis, IN 46250-2379, USA

McCarver, J Timothy (Tim) (Athlete, Baseball Player, Sportscaster)
5825 Riegels Harbor Rd
Sarasota, FL 34242, USA

McCarver, Shonna
13280 NW Fwy. F-252
Houston, TX 77040

McCarver, Tim (Athlete, Baseball Player)
San Francisco Giants
5825 Riegels Harbor Road
Sarasota, FL 34242-1779, USA

McCary, Michael (Musician)
Southpaw Entertainment
10675 Santa Monica
Los Angeles, CA 90025, USA

McCashin, Constance (Actor)
66 Fountain Street
West Newton, MA 02465-3023, USA

McCaskill, Kirk E (Athlete, Baseball Player)
P.O. Box 451
Rancho Santa Fe, CA 92067-0451, USA

McCaskill, Ted (Athlete, Hockey Player)
4101 E Columbine Dr
Phoenix, AZ 85032-7403

McCatty, Steve (Athlete, Baseball Player)
1075 Woodbriar Dr
Oxford, MI 48371-6069, USA

McCauley, Alyn (Athlete, Hockey Player)
Newport Sports Management
400-201 City Centre Dr
Mississauga, ON L5B 2T4, Canada

McCauley, Barry (Opera Singer)
598 Ridgewood Road
Oradell, NJ 07649, USA

McCauley, Don (Athlete, Football Player)
1005 Tuscany Dr
Hillsborough, NC 27278, USA

McCauley, Frank (General)
215 Hilltop Dr
Hamilton, MT 59840-9317, USA

McCauley, Herb (Horse Racer)
69 Horseshoe Ct
Oceanpor, NJ 07757-1170, USA

McCauley, Wes (Athlete, Hockey Player)
251 Elderberry Dr
South Portland, ME 04106-7810

McCauley, William F (Admiral)
570 Margarita Ave
Coronado, CA 92118, USA

McCay, Peggy (Actor)
2714 Carmar Dr
Los Angeles, CA 90046, USA

McChesney, Robert (Bob) (Writer)
1103 S Douglas Ave
Urbana, IL 61801, USA

McChrystal, Stanley A (General)
Office Of The Chairman Of The Joint Chiefs Of Staff
9999 Joint Staff Pentagon
Washington, DC 20318-9999, USA

McCkorkle, Kevin (Actor)
c/o Peter Himberger *Impact Artists Group LLC*
42 Hamilton Ter
New York, NY 10031, USA

McClain, Cady (Actor)
c/o Marnie Sparer *Innovative Artists (LA)*
1505 10th St
Santa Monica, CA 90401, USA

McClain, Charly (Musician)
John Lentz
PO Box 198888
Nashville, TN 37219, USA

McClain, China Anne (Actor)
c/o Wendi Green *Paradigm (LA)*
9200 Sunset Blvd
11th Floor
Los Angeles, CA 90069, USA

McClain, Dewey (Athlete, Football Player)
1032 Flagg Way
Lawrenceville, GA 30044, USA

McClain, Eugene (Athlete, Baseball Player)
828 West 8th Street
Chester, PA 19013-3712, USA

McClain, Joe (Athlete, Baseball Player)
1370 Milligan Hwy
Johnson City, TN 37601-5518, USA

McClain, Katrina (Athlete, Basketball Player, Olympic Athlete)
Naismith HOF
PO Box 40893
Charleston, SC 29416, USA

McClain, Scott (Athlete, Baseball Player)
660 Golden Gate Pt
Apt 61
Sarasota, FL 34236-6645, USA

McClain, Ted (Athlete, Basketball Player)
104 Eaton Ct
Nashville, TN 37218-1003, USA

McClairen, Jack (Athlete, Football Player)
1337 Idlewild Dr
Daytona Beach, FL 32114, USA

McClairen, Jack (Cy) (Coach, Football Coach)
Pittsburgh Steelers
1337 Idlewild Dr
Daytona Beach, FL 32114-1614, USA

McClanahan, Brent (Athlete, Football Player)
1100 Sayword Ct
Bakersfield, CA 93312, USA

McClanahan, Randy (Athlete, Football Player)
8107 W Via Del Sol
Peoria, AZ 85383, USA

McClanahan, Rob (Athlete, Hockey Player, Olympic Athlete)
3310 Watertown Rd
Long Lake, MN 55356-9207, USA

McClard, Bill (Athlete, Football Player)
149 N Pleasant Ridge Dr
Rogers, AZ 72756, USA

McClarnon, Zahn (Actor)
c/o Gloria Hinojosa *Amsel, Eisenstadt & Frazier Talent Agency (AEF)*
5055 Wilshire Blvd
Suite 860
Los Angeles, CA 90036-6108, USA

McClary, Thomas (Tom) (Athlete, Football Player)
Management Assoc
PO Box 701341
Dallas, TX 75370, USA

McClatchy, Kevin (Baseball Player, Commentator)
Pittsburgh Pirates
350 S Highland Ave AQ_t 1
Pittsburgh, PA 15206-3955, USA

McCleary, Norris (Athlete, Football Player)
115 Ferguson Dr
Kings Mountain, NC 28086, USA

McCleary, Trent (Athlete, Hockey Player)
442 Curry Cres
Swift Current, SK S9H 4X4, Canada

McCleery, Finnis D (War Hero)
616 North Jackson Street
San Angelo, TX 76901-2520, USA

McClellan, Kyle (Athlete, Baseball Player)
253 Fox Haven Dr
0 Fallon, MO 63368-6584, USA

McClellan, Lloyd (Athlete, Baseball Player)
1082 Mission Hills Ct
Chesterton, IN 46304-9605, USA

McClellan, Paul (Athlete, Baseball Player)
PO Box 5184
Napa, CA 94581-0184, USA

McClellan, Scott (Government Official, Writer)
c/o Staff Member *Public Affairs*
250 West 57th Street
Suite 1321
New York, NY 10107

McClellan, Zach (Athlete, Baseball Player)
4262 W Geranium Ln
Bloomington, IN 47404-1440, USA

McClelland, Dave (Race Car Driver)
980 Eilinita Ave
Glendale, CA 91208, USA

McClelland, David C (Psychic)
81 Washington Ave
Cambridge, MA 02140, USA

McClelland, Kevin
1993 Ba_yfront Dr
Windsor, CO 80550-3589

McClelland, Kevin (Athlete, Hockey Player)
Wichita Thunder
505 W Maple St # 100
Wichita, KS 67213-4616

McClelland, Melissa (Musician)
c/o Staff Member *Paradigm (Monterey)*
404 W Franklin St
Monterey, CA 93940, USA

McClelland, Tim (Athlete, Baseball Player)
5405 Woodland Ave
West Des Moines, IA 50266-7259, USA

McClelland, Tim (Baseball Player)
5405 Woodlans Ave
West Des Moines, IA 50266-7259, USA

McClendon, Lloyd (Athlete, Baseball Player, Coach)
1082 Mission Hills Ct
Chesterton, IN 46304, USA

McClendon, Reiley (Actor)
c/o Staff Member *Kritzer Levine Wilkins Entertainment (KLWG)*
11872 La Grange Ave
1st Floor
Los Angeles, CA 90025, USA

McClendon, Sarah
3133 Connecticut Ave. NW #215
Washington, DC 20008

McClendon, Skip (Athlete, Football Player)
1456 E Pecos Rd Apt 3063
Gilbert, AZ 85295, USA

McClendon, Willie (Athlete, Football Player)
575 Cativo Dr SW
Atlanta, GA 30311, USA

McCleon, Dexter (Athlete, Football Player)
1901 Post Oak Blvd Apt 509
Houston, TX 77056, USA

McClintock, Eddie (Actor)
c/o Ric Beddingfield *Beddingfield Company, The*
13600 Ventura Blvd
Suite B
Sherman Oaks, CA 91423, USA

McClintock, Jessica (Designer, Fashion Designer)
Jessica McClintock Co
1400 16th St
San Francisco, CA 94103, USA

McClintock, Tom (Congressman, Politician)
428 Cannon HOB
Washington, DC 20515, USA

McClinton, Curtis (Athlete, Football Player)
McClinton Development Company
11714 Jefferson St
Kansas City, MC 64114, USA

McClinton, Delbert (Musician)
c/o Staff Member *Alligator Records*
P.O. Box 60234
Chicago, IL 60660, USA

McCloskey, Jack (Basketball Player)
Minnesota Timberwolves
Target Center
600 1st Ave N
Minneapolis, MN 55403, USA

McCloskey, Jim (Activist)
221 Witherspoon St
Princeton, NJ 08542, USA

McCloskey, J Michael (Misc)
Sierra Club
85 2ns St
#200
San Francisco, CA 94105, USA

McCloskey, Leigh
6032 Philip Ave.
Malibu, CA 90265

McCloskey, Leigh J (Actor)
6032 Philip Ave
Malibu, CA 90265, USA

McCloskey, Mike (Athlete, Football Player)
108 Summer Ridge Dr
Lansdale, PA 19446, USA

McCloskey, Pete (Politician)
2200 Geng Rd
Palo Alto, CA 94303-3358, USA

McCloskey, Rep (Politician)
580 Mountain Home Rd
Woodside, CA 94062

McCloskey, Robert J (Diplomat)
111 Hesketh St
Chevy Chase, MD 20815, USA

McCloskey-Rogers, Gloria (Athlete, Baseball Player, Commentator)
PO Box 512
Macon, MO 63552-0512, USA

McCloud, George (Athlete, Basketball Player)
19501 W Country Club Dr Apt 1603
Aventura, FL 33180-2478, USA

McCloud, Tyrus (Athlete, Football Player)
2850 NW 8th St
Pompano Beach, FL 33069, USA

McCloughan, Dave (Athlete, Football Player)
2225 W 46th St
Loveland, CO 80538, USA

McCloughan, Kent (Athlete, Football Player)
2241 Woody Creek Cir
Loveland, CO 80538, USA

McClover, Darrell (Athlete, Football Player)
6120 SW 19th St
Pompano Beach, FL 33068, USA

McClover, Stanley (Athlete, Football Player)
4720 Buckminister Ct
Charlotte, NC 28269, USA

McClung, Seth (Athlete, Baseball Player)
13588 Park Blvd
Seminole, FL 33776-3432, USA

McClure, Bob (Athlete, Baseball Player)
3834 SE Fairway E
Stuart, FL 34997-6120, USA

McClure, Bryton (Actor)
c/o Jeff Witjas *Agency for the Performing Arts (APA-LA)*
405 S Beverly Dr
Suite 500
Beverly Hills, CA 90212-4425, USA

McClure, Donald S (Misc)
23 Hemlock Circle
Princeton, NJ 08540, USA

McClure, Eric (Race Car Driver)
Rensi Hamilton Racing
4011 Handsmill Hwy.
York, SC 2945, USA

McClure, Kandyse (Actor)
c/o Richard Lucas *Lucas Talent Inc*
100 W. Pender St
Sun Tower, 7th Floor
Vancouver, BC V6B 1R8, Canada

McClure, Larry (Race Car Driver)
Morgan-McClure Racing
26502 Newbanks Rd
Abington, VA 24210, USA

McClure, Lisi (Stylist)
388 NE 88th St
El Portal, FL 33138, USA

McClure, Marc
1420 Beaudry Blvd.
Glendale, CA 91208

McClure, Molly
12456 Ventura Blvd. #1
Studio City, CA 91604

McClure, Tane (Actor)
Don Gerler
3349 Cahuenga Blvd W
#1
Los Angeles, CA 90068, USA

McClurg, Edie
9229 Sunset Blvd. #315
Los Angeles, CA 90069

McClurkin, Donnie (Musician)
c/o Staff Member *The Alliance Agency*
1035 Bates Ct.
Hendersonville, TN 37075, USA

McCluskey, David (Athlete, Football
Player)
22 Tannassee Ln NW Apt E8
Rome, GA 30165, USA

McCole Bartusiak, Skye (Actor)
c/o Mitchell Gossett *Cunningham Escott
Slevin & Doherty (CESD-LA)*
9560 Wilshire Blvd Fl 5
Beverly Hills, CA 90212, USA

McColister, Antoine (Ace Hood)
(Musician)

McColl, Bill (Football Player)
Chicago Bears
5166 Chelsea St
La Jolla, CA 92037-7908, USA

McColl, Peggy (Writer)
Dynamic Destinies, Inc
1 Stafford Road
Suite 312
NePean, Ontario K2H 1B9, Canada

McCollough, Cynthia (Stylist)
c/o Staff Member *Mark Edward Inc*
325 W 8th St
#1011
New York, NY 10018, USA

McCollough, David (Writer)
Jacklow And Nesbit Associates 445 Park
Ave Fl13
New York, NY 10022-8628, USA

McCollum, Andy (Athlete, Football Player)
3933 Autumn Farms Dr
Pacific, MO 63069, USA

McCollum, Betty (Congressman,
Politician)
1714 Longworth HOB
Washington, DC 20515, USA

McColm, Matt (Actor)
c/o Bob Read *ReBar Management*
10061 Riverside Drive
#722
Toluca Lake, CA 91602

McColms, Matt (Actor)
c/o Staff Member *Agency for the
Performing Arts (APA-LA)*
405 S Beverly Dr
Suite 500
Beverly Hills, CA 90212-4425, USA

McComas, Brian (Musician)
c/o Staff Member *Leon Medica
Management*
187 Hidden Lake Rd
Hendersonville, TN 37075, USA

McComb, Jeremy (Musician)
c/o Staff Member *Paradigm (Monterey)*
404 W Franklin St
Monterey, CA 93940, USA

McComb, Joanne (Athlete, Baseball
Player, Commentator)
105 Nottingham Rd
Bloomsburg, PA 17815-3021, USA

McCombs, BIUy Joe (Misc)
755 E Mulberry Ave Ste 600
San Antonio, TX 78212-6013, USA

McCombs, Red (Business Person, Football
Executive)
825 Contour Dr
San Antonio, TX 78212-1700, USA

McConathy, John (Athlete, Basketball
Player)
2320 Belmont Blvd
Bossier City, LA 71111-2427, USA

McConaughey, Matthew (Actor)
c/o Nicole Perez-Krueger *PMK/BNC
Public Relations (PMK-LA)*
8687 Melrose Ave Fl 8
West Hollywood, CA 90069, USA

McConkey, Phil (Athlete, Football Player)
1856 Viking Way
La Jolla, CA 92037-3354, USA

McConneii-Serio, Suzie (Athlete,
Basketball Player, Olympic Athlete)
2590 Rossmoor Dr
Pittsburgh, PA 15241-2584, USA

McConnell, Dave (Race Car Driver)
Dave McConnell Racing
101 Lantern Circle
McMurray, PA 15317, USA

McConnell, Harden (Scientist)
421 El Escarpado
Stanford, CA 94305-8430, USA

McConnell, Harden M (Misc)
Stanford University
Chemistry Dept
Stanford, CA 94305, USA

McConnell, John P (Business Person)
Worthington Industries
1205 Dearborn Dr
Columbus, OH 43085, USA

McConnell, Mitch (Politician)
2318 Dundee Rd
Louisville, KY 40205-2070, USA

McConnell, Page (Musician)
c/o Staff Member *Paradigm (Monterey)*
404 W Franklin St
Monterey, CA 93940, USA

McConnell, Robert M G (Rob) (Musician)
Thomas Cassidy
11761 E Speedway Blvd
Tucson, AZ 85748, USA

McConnell, Sam (Athlete, Baseball Player)
301 McKinley St
Middletown, OH 45042-3256, USA

McConnell-Serio, Suzie (Athlete,
Basketball Player)
2590 Rossmoor Dr
Pittsburgh, PA 15241-2584, USA

McConville, Frank (Misc)
Union of Plant Guard Workers of America
25510 Kelly Road
Roseville, MI 48066, USA

McCoo, Marilyn (Actor, Musician)
P.O. Box 7905
Beverly Hills, CA 90212, USA

McCook, John (Actor)
10245 Briarwood
Los Angeles, CA 90077, USA

McCool, Bill (Athlete, Baseball Player)
9250 SE 121st Loop
Summerfield, FL 34491, USA

McCool, Billy (Athlete, Baseball Player)
9250 SE 121st Loop
Summerfield, FL 34491-9477, USA

McCool, Michelle (Wrestler)
c/o Kerry Rodgerson *World Wrestling
Entertainment (WWE)*
Titan Towers
1241 E Main St
Stamford, CT 06905-3857, USA

McCord, Alex (Reality TV Star)
c/o Staff Member *Bravo (NY)*
30 Rockefeller Plaza
New York, NY 10112, USA

McCord, AnnaLynne (Actor)
c/o Gary Mantoosh *Baker Winokur Ryder
Public Relations (BWR-LA)*
9100 Wilshire Blvd
Suite 500, West Tower
Beverly Hills, CA 90212, USA

McCord, Bob (Athlete, Hockey Player)
11540 Donley Dr
Parker, CO 8013^-8027

McCord, Clinton (Athlete, Baseball
Player)
1821 Knowles St
Nashville, TN 37208, USA

McCord, Darris (Athlete, Football Player)
6160 W Surrey Rd
Bloomfield Hills, MI 48301, USA

McCord, Gary (Athlete, Golfer)
5318 E Desert Vista Rd
Paradise Valley, AZ 85253-3365, USA

McCord, Keith (Athlete, Basketball Player)
1609 Five Acre Rd
Dolomite, Al 35061-1036, USA

McCord, Kent
c/o Staff Member *Tisherman Gilbert
Motley Drozdoski Talent Agency (TGMD)*
6767 Forest Lawn Dr
Suite 101
Los Angeles, CA 90068, USA

McCord, Mack (Race Car Driver)
Gorilla AA/FA
PO Box 2608
Phoenix, AZ 85012, USA

McCord, Quentin (Athlete, Football
Player)
4194 Berwick Farm Dr
Duluth, GA 30096, USA

McCord, Susie (Race Car Driver)
Gorilla AA/FA
PO Box 2608
Phoenix, AZ 85002, USA

McCorkle, Kevin (Actor)
c/o Staff Member *Impact Artists Group
LLC*
42 Hamilton Ter
New York, NY 10031, USA

McCormack, Catherine (Actor)

McCormack, Don (Athlete, Baseball
Player)
866 Glenfield Dr
Palm Harbor, FL 34684-3218, USA

McCormack, Eric (Actor)
10155 Valley Spring Ln
Toluca Lake, CA 91602, USA

McCormack, John (Athlete, Hockey
Player)
415-45 cumberlandLane
AJax, ON L1s 7K3, canada

McCormack, Mary (Actor)
PO Box 67335
Los Angeles, CA 90067-0035, USA

McCormack, Mike (Athlete, Football
Coach, Football Player)
265 Bouquet Canyon Dr
Palm Desert, CA 92211, USA

McCormack, Patty (Actor)
c/o Staff Member *House of
Representatives, The*
1434 6th St
Suite 1
Santa Monica, CA 90401, USA

McCormack, Will (Actor)
c/o Greg Clark *Untitled Entertainment
(LA)*
350 S. Beverly Dr #200
Beverly Hills, CA 90212, USA

McCormick, Carolyn (Actor)
Bresler Kelly Assoc
11500 W Olympic Blvd
#510
Los Angeles, CA 90064, USA

McCormick, John (Athlete, Football
Player)
2615 Oak Dr
Unit 34
Lakewood, CO 80215, USA

McCormick, Kelly
Box 250
Seal Beach, CA 90740

McCormick, Len (Athlete, Football Player)
514 Bolton Pl
Houston, DC 77024, USA

McCormick, Malcolm (Mac Miller)
(Musician)
c/o Staff Member *Rostrum Records*
1712 Sarah St
Pittsburgh, PA 15203, USA

McCormick, Maureen (Actor, Musician)
c/o Debra Goldfarb *Rebel Entertainment
Partners*
5700 Wilshire Blvd
Suite 456
Los Angeles, CA 90036, USA

McCormick, Mike (Athlete, Baseball
Player)
10 Sawgrass Pl
Pinehurst, NC 28374-7114, USA

McCormick, Pat (Athlete, Diver, Olympic
Athlete)
92 Riversea Rd
Seal Beach, CA 90740-5971, USA

McCormick, Richard (Educator)
Rutgers State University
President's Office
East Rutherford, NJ 08903, USA

McCormick, Tim (Athlete, Basketball
Player)
2S00 Leroy Ln
West Bloomfield, MI 48324-2234, USA

McCormick, Tom (Athlete, Football
Player)
397 Wehmeyer Loop
Mountain Home, AR 72653, USA

McCornack, Bill (Race Car Driver)
McCornack Racing
PO Box 12265
Lexington, KY 40582, USA

McCorvey, Kez (Athlete, Football Player)
3704 Randall St
Tallahassee, FL 32309, USA

McCorvey, Norma
12730 Thomas Sumpter St.
San Antonio, TX 78223

McCorvey, Norma (Attorney)
11343 Cactus Ln
Dallas, Dallas 75238-3805, USA

McCosh, Shawn (Athlete, Hockey Player)
18992 N 74th Dr
Glendale, AZ 85308-5668

McCouch, Grayson
c/o Dan Baron *Agency for the Performing Arts (APA-LA)*
405 S Beverly Dr
Suite 500
Beverly Hills, CA 90212-4425, USA

McCourt, Dale (Athlete, Hockey Player)
1341 West Bay Rd
Garson, ON P3L 1V3, Canada

McCourt, Frank (Commentator)
22426 Pacific Coast Hwy
Malibu, CA 90265-5033, USA

McCourt, James (Actor, Television Host)
c/o Staff Member *Princess Productions*
Newcombe House
45 Notting Hill Gate
London W11 3LQ, UNITED KINGDOM

McCourt, Malachy (Actor, Writer)
c/o Marc Bass *Beacon Talent Agency*
170 Apple Ridge Rd
Woodcliff, NJ 07677, USA

McCoury, Del (Musician)
c/o Staff Member *Paradigm (Monterey)*
404 W Franklin St
Monterey, CA 93940, USA

McCovey, Willie (Athlete, Baseball Player)
P.O. Box 620342
Redwood City, CA 94062-0342, USA

McCowen, Sir Alec
3 Goodwin's Ct. St. Martin's Lane
London, ENGLAND WG2

McCown, Josh (Athlete, Football Player)
1312 Lookout Cir
Waxhaw, NC 28173, USA

McCown, Luke (Athlete, Football Player)
30963 US Highway 69 N
Rusk, TX 75785, USA

McCoy, Charlie (Musician)
PO Box 50455
Nashville, TN 37205, USA

McCoy, Colt (Athlete, Football Player)
c/o Jordan Bazant *The Legacy Agency*
230 Park Ave
Suite 851
New York, NY 10169, USA

McCoy, Dave (Misc)
Mammoth Mountain Chairlifts
PO Box 24
Mammoth Lakes, CA 93546, USA

McCoy, Gerald (Athlete, Football Player)
c/o Kelli Masters *Kelli Masters Management*
100 N Broadway
Suite 1700
Oklahoma City, OK 73102, USA

McCoy, James (General, War Hero)
13705 S 22nd Cir
Bellevue, NE 68123-4761, USA

McCoy, John B (Financier)
Corillian
3400 NW John Olsen Place
Hillsboro, OR 97124, USA

McCoy, Larry (Athlete, Baseball Player)
5758 Highway 139
Greenway AR, 72430-7045 USA, USA

McCoy, Larry (Baseball Player)
5758 Highway 139
Greenway, AR 72430-7045, USA

McCoy, LeRon (Athlete, Football Player)
761 Cattail Dr
Harrisburg, PA 17111, USA

McCoy, LisaRaye (Actor)
c/o Staff Member *The Forum Entertainment Group*
10940 Wilshire Blvd
Suite 1600
Los Angeles, CA 90024, USA

McCoy, Mark
7120 Hawthorne #18
Los Angeles, CA 90046

McCoy, Matt (Actor)
Artists Agency
1180 S Beverly Dr
#301
Los Angeles, CA 90035, USA

McCoy, Mike (Athlete, Football Player)
2224 Cotton Gin Row
Jefferson, GA 30549, USA

McCoy, Neal (Musician)
c/o Joey Lee *WmE2 (WMA-TN)*
1600 Division St
Suite 300
Nashville, TN 37203, USA

McCoy, Rosero (Choreographer)
c/o Tim O'Brien *Clear Talent Group (LA)*
10950 Ventura Blvd
Studio City, CA 91604, USA

McCoy, Sandra (Actor)
c/o Staff Member *Metropolitan (MTA)*
4526 Wilshire Blvd
Los Angeles, CA 90010, USA

McCoy, Sonya (Stylist)
c/o Staff Member *Mark Edward Inc*
325 W 8th St
#1011
New York, NY 10018, USA

McCoy, Tony (Athlete, Football Player)
9200 Oak Island Ln
Clermont, FL 34711, USA

McCracken, Jeff
15760 Ventura Blvd. #1730
Encino 91436

McCracken, Paul (Athlete, Basketball Player)
914 Westwood Blvd Aet 256
Apt 256
Los Angeles, CA 90024-2905, USA

McCracken, Quinton (Athlete, Baseball Player)
11308 E Autumn Sage Dr
Scottsdale, AZ 85255-8949, USA

McCrane, Paul (Actor)
VOX
5670 Wilshire Blvd
#820
Los Angeles, CA 90036, USA

McCrary, Bill (Athlete, Baseball Player)
2 Escocia Ln
Hot Springs Village, AR 71909-7604, USA

McCrary, Darius (Actor)
19518 Branding Iron Rd
Walnut, CA 91789, USA

McCrary, Fred (Athlete, Football Player)
134 Grandmar Chase
Canton, GA 30115, USA

McCrary, Joel (Actor)
c/o Holly Shelton *Precision Entertainment*
6338 Wilshire Blvd
Los Angeles, CA 90048, USA

McCrary, Michael (Athlete, Football Player)
9907 Chase Hill Ct
Vienna, VA 22182, USA

McCrary, Prentice (Athlete, Football Player)
5414 E Dolphin Cir
Mesa, AZ 85206, USA

McCraw, Tommy (Athlete, Baseball Player)
3142 SE Monte Vista Ct
Port Saint Lucie, FL 34952-6062, USA

McCray, Bobby (Athlete, Football Player)
c/o Staff Member *EAG Sports Management*
12910 Agustin Pl
Playa Vista, CA 90094, USA

McCray, Nikki (Athlete, Basketball Player, Olympic Athlete)
4278 Fox Hills Dr
Louisville, TN 37777-5105, USA

McCray, Prentice (Athlete, Football Player)
2109 N Argonaut St
Stockton, CA 95204, USA

McCray, Rick (Race Car Driver)
McCray Racing
28746 Glen Heather Dr
Highland, CA 92346, USA

McCray, Rodney (Athlete, Baseball Player)
45365 Horseshoe Cir
Canton, MI 48187-5042, USA

McCray, Rodney (Athlete, Basketball Player)
33 Bonita Vista Rd
Mount Vernon, NY 10552-1301, USA

McCready, Mindy (Musician)
c/o Staff Member *Iconic Records, LLC*
61 Jackson St.
Unit F
Denver, CO 80206, USA

McCreary, Bill
4318 Highcrest Dr Apt 1
Brighton, MI 48116-9798

McCreary, Bob (Athlete, Football Player)
1473 Knolls Dr
Newton, NC 28658, USA

McCreary, Scotty (Musician)
c/o Simon Fuller *XIX Entertainment*
35-37 Ransomes Rd
32/33 Ransomes Dock
London SW11 4NP, UNITED KINGDOM (UK)

McCreary, Tex
PO Box 405
Mill Neck, NY 11765-0405

McCreary, Sr., Bill (Athlete, Hockey Player)
3979 Broad moor Ct
Howell, MI 48843-7464

McCree, Marlon (Athlete, Football Player)
15590 Camden Pl
San Diego, CA 92131, USA

McCreey, Scotty (Musician)
c/o Ann Edelblute *XIX Entertainment*
35-37 Parkgate Rd
32/33 Ransomes Dock
London SW11 4NP, UNITED KINGDOM (UK)

McCrills, John W (Writer)
McCrillis & Eldredge Insurance
17 Depot St
Newport, NH 03773, USA

McCrimmon, Jim (Athlete, Hockey Player)
734 Adelaide St
Pincher Creek, AB TOK IWO, Canada

McCrindle, Andrea (Stylist)
c/o Staff Member *Judy Inc*
1 Yorkville Ave
Toronto ON M4W 1L1, Canada

McCrlmmon, jim (Athlete, Hockey Player)
734 Adelaide St
Pincher Creek, AB TOK 1 WO, Canada

McCrory, Bob (Athlete, Baseball Player)
30 Rebecca Ln
Hattiesbur11, MS 39402-8224, USA

McCrory, Glenn (Boxer)
Holborn 35 Station Road
County Durham, UNITED KINGDOM (UK)

McCrory, Helen (Actor)
c/o Clair Dobbs *Public Eye Communications*
535 Kings Rd
Suite 313 Plaza
London SW10 0SZ, United Kingdom

McCrory, Milton (Milt) (Boxer)
Escot Boxing Enterprises
19244 Bretton Dr
Detroit, MI 48223, USA

McCrudden, Ian (Actor)
c/o Josh Silver *Silver Mine Entertainment*
6705 Sunset Blvd.
Hollywood, CA 90028, USA

McCullers, Dale (Athlete, Football Player)
1613 Tupelo Dr
Waycross, GA 31501, USA

McCullers, Lance (Athlete, Baseball Player)
3309 Hoedt Ro
Tampa, FL 33618-1611, USA

McCulley, Michael J (Astronaut)
365 Private Road 652
Bay City, TX 77414-2451, USA

McCulley, Michael J Captain (Astronaut)
100 Yacht Haven Dr
Cocoa Beach, FL 32931-2627, USA

McCullin, Donald (Don) (Photographer)
Holly Hill House
Batcombe Shepton Mallet
Somerset BA4 6BL, UNITED KINGDOM (UK)

McCulloch, Ed (Race Car Driver)
Schumacher Racing
1397 Cherry Tree Road
Avon, IN 46123, USA

McCulloch, Frank W (Educator, Lawyer)
5604 Kirkside Dr
Chevy Chase, MD 20815, USA

McCulloch, Nan (Stylist)
200 Broken Lane Pl
Alpharetta, GA 30022, USA

McCulloch (McCullough), Bruce (Actor)

McCullouch, Earl (Athlete, Football Player)
2108 Santa Fe Ave Apt 15
Long Beach, CA 90810, USA

McCullough, Bob (Athlete, Football Player)
2225 Deerfield Ln
Helena, MT 59601, USA

McCullough, Colleen (Writer)
PO Box 333
Norfolk Island, NSW 2899, AUSTRALIA

McCullough, David (Writer)
Janklow & Nesbit Assoc
445 Park Ave
#1300
New York, NY 10022, USA

McCullough, David (Actor)
c/o Staff Member *Creative Artists Agency (CAA-LA)*
2000 Ave Of The Stars
Los Angeles, CA 90067, USA

McCullough, Earl (Athlete, Football Player, Track Athlete)
2108 Santa Fe Ave
Long Beach, CA 90810, USA

McCullough, John (Scientist)
412 N Shadowbend Ave
Friendswood, TX TX 77546-3839, USA

McCullough, Julian (Musician)
c/o Staff Member *Paradigm (Monterey)*
404 W Franklin St
Monterey, CA 93940, USA

McCullough, Julie (Actor)
c/o Hillard Elkins *Elkins Entertainment*
8306 Wilshire Blvd
Suite 438
Beverly Hills, CA 90211, USA

McCullough, Kimberly
9229 Sunset Blvd. #315
Los Angeles, CA 90069

McCullough, Mike (Athlete, Golfer)
6334 Evening Glow Dr
Scottsdale, AZ 85266, USA

McCullough, Rich (Athlete, Football Player)
910 Cypress Station Dr Apt 506
Houston, TX 77090, USA

McCullough, Shanna
7920 Alabama Ave.
Canoga Park, CA 91304

McCullough, Wayne (Athlete, Boxer)
9972 Shady Glade Court
Las Vegas, NV 89135-1719, USA

McCullum, Sam (Athlete, Football Player)
7701 88th Pl SE
Mercer Island, WA 98040, USA

McCully, Kilmer (Doctor)
Veteran Affairs Med Center
Pathology Dept
Davis Park
Providence, RI 02908, USA

McCumber, Josh (Athlete, Golfer)
2121 Sea Hawk Dr
Ponte Verda Beach, FL 32082, USA

McCumber, Mark (Athlete, Golfer, Sportscaster)
527 Le Master Dr
Ponte Vedra Beach, FL 32082-2312, USA

McCune, Don (Bowler)
3551 Coventry Gardens
Dr Las Vegas, NV 89135-2838, USA

McCune, Lisa (Actor)
c/o Staff Member *RGM Artist Group*
64-76 Kippax St
Level 2, Suite 202 & 206
Surry Hills, NSW 2010, Australia

McCurdy, Cindy (Golfer)
18 Cottage Dr
Newnan, GA 30265-5513, USA

McCurdy, Jennette (Actor)
c/o Chris Huvane *Management 360*
9111 Wilshire Blvd
Beverly Hills, CA 90210, USA

McCurry, Jeff (Athlete, Baseball Player)
9015 Linkmeadow Ln
Houston, TX 7702.5-4122, USA

McCurry, Margaret (Architect)
Tigerman McCurry Architects
444 N Wells St
Chicago, IL 60610, USA

McCurry, Mike (Journalist, Politician)
Cable News Network
News Dept
1050 Techwood Dr NW
Atlanta, GA 30318, USA

McCusker, Jim (Athlete, Football Player)
209 N Main St
Jamestown, NY 14701, USA

McCutchen, Andrew (Athlete, Baseball Player)
6895 Bushnell Dr
Lakeland, FL 33813-3738, USA

McCutchen, Daniel (Athlete, Baseball Player)
310 Texas Country Dr
New Braunfels, TX 78132-4429, USA

McCutcheon, Brian (Athlete, Hockey Player)
133 Iradell Rd
Ithaca, NY 14850-9265

McCutcheon, Darwin (Athlete, Hockey Player)
PO Box 5556
Vail, CO 81658-5556, USA

McCutcheon, Daylon (Athlete, Football Player)
4393 Hiwassee
Claremont, CA 91711, USA

McCutcheon, Dayton (Athlete, Football Player)
901 Golden Springs Dr # F-G
Diamond Bar, CA 91765, USA

McCutcheon, Lawrence (Athlete, Football Player)
16721 Sims Ln Apt C
Huntington Beach, CA 92649, USA

McCutcheon, Linda (Publisher)
AARP Publications
Director's Office
601 E St NW
Washington, DC 20049, USA

McCutcheon, Martine (Musician)
P F D Drury House
34-43 Russell St
London WC2B 5HA, UNITED KINGDOM (UK)

McDaniel, Ed (Athlete, Football Player)
13111 Brenwood Trl
Hopkins, MN 55343, USA

McDaniel, James (Actor)
c/o Craig Shapiro *ICM Partners (ICM-LA)*
10250 Constellation Blvd Fl 7
Los Angeles, CA 90067, USA

McDaniel, Jeremy (Athlete, Football Player)
309 Rocky Run Rd
New Bern, NC 28562, USA

McDaniel, John (Cinematographer, Musician, Producer)
c/o Glenn Daniels *Glenn Daniels Arts Management*
56 Warren St #5E
New York, NY 10007, USA

McDaniel, John (Athlete, Football Player)
586 Janney Rd
Ohatchee, AL 36271, USA

McDaniel, Lecharls (Athlete, Football Player)
12844 Starwood Ln
San Diego, CA 92131, USA

McDaniel, Lindy (Athlete, Baseball Player)
1095 Meadow Hill Dr
Lavon, TX 75166-1262, USA

McDaniel, Lindy
Rt. #2 Box 353A
Hollis, OK 73550

McDaniel, Orlando (Athlete, Football Player)
1012 N Goos Blvd
Lake Charles, LA 70601, USA

McDaniel, Randall C (Athlete, Football Player)
20405 Manor Rd
Excelsior, MN 55331, USA

McDaniel, Terry (Athlete, Baseball Player)
1441 E 75th St
Kansas City, MO 64131-1867, USA

McDaniel, Terry (Athlete, Football Player)
730 Shenandoah
Cedar Hill, TX 75104, USA

McDaniel, Xavier (Athlete, Basketball Player)
2 Oakmist Ct
Blythewood, SC 29016-8707, USA

McDaniel, Xavier (Athlete, Basketball Player)
2 Oakmist Ct
Blythewood, SC 29016, USA

McDaniels, Darryl (Darryl M) (Music Group, Musician)
Entertainment Artists
2409 21st Ave S
#100
Nashville, TN 37212, USA

McDaniels, Jim
2549 Smallhouse Rd
Bowling Green, KY 42104-4345, USA

McDaniels, Pellom (Athlete, Football Player)
333 W Meyer Blvd Apt 608
Kansas City, MO 64113, USA

McDavid, Ray (Athlete, Baseball Player)
1245 Market St #1348
San Diego, CA 92101-7358, USA

McDermott, Alice (Writer)
Farrar Straus Giroux
19 Union Square W
New York, NY 10003, USA

McDermott, Brian
27 Upper Berkeley St.
London, ENGLAND W1

McDermott, Charlie (Actor)
c/o Adam Griffin *Kritzer Levine Wilkins Entertainment (KLWG)*
11872 La Grange Ave
1st Floor
Los Angeles, CA 90025, USA

McDermott, Dean (Actor)
c/o Gleb Klioner *Schachter Entertainment*
1157 S Beverly Dr Fl 2
Los Angeles, CA 90035, USA

McDermott, Dylan (Actor, Director)
c/o Geyer Kosinski *Media Talent Group*
9200 Sunset Blvd
Suite 550
Los Angeles, CA 90069, USA

McDermott, Edward A (Government Official)
Lake House South
875 E Camino Real
Boca Raton, FL 33432, USA

McDermott, Jim (Congressman, Politician)
1035 Longworth HOB
Washington, DC 20515, USA

McDermott, R Terrance (Terry) (Speed Skater)
5078 Chainbridge
Bloomfield Hills, MI 48304, USA

McDermott, Shane
200 W. 57th St. #900
New York, NY 10106

McDermott, Terry (Athlete, Baseball Player)
7205 Sunlight Peak Dr NE
Rio Rancho, NM 87144-7508, USA

McDiarmid, Ian (Actor)
Wood Lane
London W12 7RJ, UNITED KINGDOM (UK)

McDill, Allen (Athlete, Baseball Player)
244 Richwoods Rd
Arkadelphia, AR 71923-8836, USA

McDivitt, James
9146 Cherry Ave.
Rapid City, MI 49676

McDivitt, James A Brig Gen (Astronaut)
3530 E Calle Puerta De Acero
Tucson, AZ 85718-6000, USA

McDivitt, James A (Jim) (Astronaut, General)
3530 E Calle Puerta den Acero
Tucson, AZ 85718, USA

McDole, Ron (Athlete, Football Player)
2083 Lockes Mill Rd
Berryville, VA 22611, USA

McDonagh, Bill (Athlete, Hockey Player)
11 Market St PO Box 284
Copper Cliff, ON P0M 1N0, Canada

McDonagh, John Michael (Director, Writer)
c/o Jeremy Barber *United Talent Agency (UTA)*
9336 Civic Center Dr
Beverly Hills, CA 90210, USA

McDonagh, Martin (Director, Writer)
c/o Staff Member *The Rod Hall agency*
6th Floor Fairgate House
78 New Oxford Street
London WC1A 1HB, United Kingdom

McDonald, Alvin B (Ab) (Athlete, Hockey Player)
419 Thompson Dr
Winnipeg, MB R3J 3E7, Canada

McDonald, Audra (Actor, Musician)
c/o David Kalodner *WME (WMA-NY)*
1325 Ave of the Americas
New York, NY 10019, USA

McDonald, Ben (Athlete, Baseball Player, Olympic Athlete)
8780 Henderson Rd
Denham Springs, LA 70726-6705, USA

McDonald, Bruce (Director, Producer)
c/o Bill Douglass *Paradigm (LA)*
360 N Crescent Dr
North Bldg
Beverly Hills, CA 90210, USA

McDonald, Christopher
c/o Daniel (Danny) Sussman *Brillstein Entertainment Partners*
9150 Wilshire Blvd #350
Beverly Hills, CA 90212, USA

McDonald, Country Joe (Musician)
PO Box 7054
Berkeley, CA 94707, USA

McDonald, Darnell (Athlete, Football Player)
13551 Bentley Cir
Woodbridge, VA 22192, USA

McDonald, Darnell (Athlete, Baseball Player)
542 W Windsor Ave Frnt
Phoenix, AZ 85003-1062, USA

McDonald, Dave (Athlete, Baseball Player)
2545 SE 3rd St
Pompano Beach, FL 33062-5401, USA

McDonald, David L (Admiral)
PO Box 45214
Jacksonville, FL 32232, USA

McDonald, Devon (Athlete, Football Player)
10812 Green Meadow Pl
Indianapolis, IN 46229, USA

McDonald, Donzell (Athlete, Baseball Player)
3225 Scranton St
Aurora, CO 80011-1827, USA

McDonald, Forrest (Historian)
Po Box 155
Coker, AL 35452, USA

McDonald, Gerry
41reland Rd
Wethersfield, CT 06109-2105

McDonald, Glenn (Athlete, Basketball Player)
8132JI@rina__F'acifica Dr I'J_
Long Beach, CA 90803-3806, USA

McDonald, Jiggs (Sportscaster)
8331 Arborfield Court
Fort Myers, FL 33912-4684, USA

McDonald, Joe
17337 Ventura Blvd. #208
Encino, CA 9l316-3058

McDonald, John (Athlete, Baseball Player)
411 Tilden Rd
Scituate, MA 02066-2124, USA

McDonald, Keith (Athlete, Baseball Player)
5162 E Greensboro Ln Aot A
Anaheim, CA 92807-4612, USA

McDonald, Kevin Hamilton (Actor, Writer)

McDonald, Lanny (Athlete, Hockey Player)
23 Springside St
Calgary, AB T3Z 3M1, Canada

McDonald, Michael H (Musician, Songwriter, Writer)
c/o Staff Member *WmE2 (WMA-LA)*
1 William Morris Pl
Beverly Hills, CA 90212, USA

McDonald, Michael James (Actor, Director, Writer)
c/o Staff Member *3 Arts Entertainment Inc*
9460 Wilshire Blvd
7th Floor
Beverly Hills, CA 90210, USA

McDonald, Mike (Athlete, Football Player)
1067 E Angeleno Ave
Burbank, CA 91501, USA

McDonald, Miriam (Actor)
c/o Brantley Brown *Schachter Entertainment*
1157 S Beverly Dr Fl 2
Los Angeles, CA 90035, USA

McDonald, Paul (Athlete, Football Player)
1815 Tradewinds Ln
Newport Beach, CA 92660, USA

McDonald, Ramos (Athlete, Football Player)
11620 Audelia Rd Apt 715
Dallas, TX 75243, USA

McDonald, Ricardo (Athlete, Football Player)
425 E 25th St
Paterson, NJ 07514, USA

McDonald, Richie (Musician)
PO Box 128648
Nashville, TN 37212, USA

McDonald, Roderick
982 Walglen Ct
San Jose, CA 95136-1463, USA

McDonald, Terry
2990 Surf Cres
Coquitlam, BC V3C 3S8, Canada

McDonald, Thomas F (Tommy) (Athlete, Football Player)
537 W Valley Forge Rd
King of Prussia, PA 19406, USA

McDonald, Tim (Athlete, Attorney, Football Player)
10851 N Maple Ave
Fresno, CA 93730, USA

McDonell, R Terry (Editor)
US Weekly
Editorial Dept
1290 Ave of Americas
New York, NY 10104, USA

McDonell, Thomas (Actor)
c/o Annabel Gualazzi *WME (LA)*
9601 Wilshire Blvd Fl 3
Beverly Hills, CA 90210, USA

McDonnell, Bob (Governor, Politician)
State Capitol
1111 E Broad St
Richmond, VA 23219, USA

McDonnell, Joe (Athlete, Hockey Player)
Detroit Red Wings
600 Civic Center Dr
Detroit, MI 48226-4419

McDonnell, John F (Business Person)
McDonnell Douglas Corp
PO Box 516
Saint Louis, MO 63166, USA

McDonnell, Mary (Actor)
c/o Perri Kipperman *Kipperman Management*
420 West End Avenue
Suite 1G
New York, NY 10024, USA

McDonnell, Patrick (Cartoonist)
c/o Staff Member *King Features Syndication*
300 W 57th St
15th Floor
New York, NY 10019-5238, USA

McDonough, Al (Athlete, Hockey Player)
288 Edgewater Cres
Kitchener, ON N2A 4M1, Canada

McDonough, Hubie (Athlete, Hockey Player)
65 Holmes Dr.
Manchester, NH 03104-2890, USA

McDonough, Hubie (Athlete, Hockey Player)
Manchester Monarchs
555 Elm St Ste 3
Manchester, NH 03101-2535

McDonough, Mary (Actor)
6858 Canteloupe Ave
Van Nuys, CA 91405, USA

McDonough, Neal (Actor)
c/o JJ Harris *One Talent Management*
9220 Sunset Blvd
Los Angeles, CA 90069, USA

McDonough, Neil (Actor)
Rigberg Robert Rugolo
1180 S Beverly Dr
#601
Los Angeles, CA 90035, USA

McDonough, Patrick (Athlete, Cycler, Olympic Athlete)
64 Myrtle St Apt 2
Boston, MA 02114-4577, USA

McDonough, Sean (Sportscaster)
ABC-TV
Sports Dept
77 W 66th St
New York, NY 10023, USA

McDonough, William (Architect)
410 E Water St
Charlottesville, VA 22902, USA

McDonough, William J (Financier)
Public Company Accounting Oversight Board
1666 K NW
Washington, DC 20006, USA

McDorman, Jake (Actor)
c/o Elissa Leeds-Fickman *Reel Talent Management*
P.O. Box 491035
Los Angeles, CA 90049, USA

McDormand, Frances (Actor)
23 Rafael Ave
Bolinas, CA 94924, USA

McDougal, Mike (Athlete, Hockey Player)
2892 Tanglewood Dr
Kimball, MI 48074-1535

McDougal, Susan
350 S. Grand Ave. #3900
Los Angeles, CA 90071-3460

McDougale, Stockar (Athlete, Football Player)
15 Bradford Ct
Dearborn, MI 48126, USA

McDougall, Charles (Writer)
c/o Staff Member *Industry Entertainment Partners*
955 S Carrillo Dr
Suite 300
Los Angeles, CA 90048, USA

McDougall, Ian (Producer)
c/o Staff Member *Gersh (LA)*
9465 Wilshire Blvd
Suite 600
Beverly Hills, CA 90212, USA

McDougall, Marshall (Athlete, Baseball Player)
213 Bell Branch Ln
Saint Johns, FL 32259-4438, USA

McDougall, Walter A (Historian)
University of Pennsylvania
History Dept
Philadelphia, PA 19104, USA

McDowel, Michael (Race Car Driver)
20310 Chartwell Center Dr.
Cornelius, NC 28031, USA

McDowell, Bubba (Athlete, Football Player)
6353 Richmond Ave
Houston, TX 77057, USA

McDowell, Frank (Doctor)
100 N Kalaheo Place
#F
Kailua Kona, HI 96734, USA

McDowell, Jack (Athlete, Baseball Player)
2875 Calle Rancho Vis
Encinitas, CA 92024-6672, USA

McDowell, Malcolm (Actor)
c/o Staff Member *Dontanville/Frattaroli (D/F)*
270 Lafayette St
Suite 402
New York, NY 10012, USA

McDowell, Michael (Race Car Driver)
Michael Waltrip Racing
20310 Chartwell Center Dr
Cornelius, NC 28031, USA

McDowell, Oddibe (Athlete, Baseball Player)
5240 SW 18th St
West Park, FL 33023-3157, USA

McDowell, Roger (Athlete, Baseball Player)
2690 Pete Shaw Rd
Marietta, GA 30066-2224, USA

McDowell, Ronnie (Musician)
c/o Bobby Roberts *Bobby Roberts Agency*
P.O. Box 1547
Goodlettsville, TN 37072, USA

McDowell, Sam (Athlete, Baseball Player)
City Of Le11ends 1925 Don Wickham Dr
Clermont, FL 34711-1915, USA

McDsyes, Antonio (Athlete, Basketball Player)
979 County Road 473
Meridian, MS 393el-9636, USA

McDuffe, Peter (Athlete, Hockey Player)
85 Mill St
Milton, ON L9T 1R8, Canada

McDuffie, George (Athlete, Football Player)
819 Independence Rd
Toledo, OH 43607, USA

McDuffie, Otis J (O J) (Athlete, Football Player)
1333 NW 121st Ave
Plantation, FL 33323, USA

McDuffie, Robert (Musician)
Columbia Artists Mgmt Inc
165 W 57th St
New York, NY 10019, USA

McDyess, Antonio (Athlete, Basketball Player, Olympic Athlete)
979 County Road 473
Meridian, MS 39301-9636, USA

McEachern, Shawn (Athlete, Hockey Player, Olympic Athlete)
71 Beach St
Marblehead, MA 01945-2957, USA

McEldowney, Brooke (Cartoonist)
United Feature Syndicate
200 Madison Ave
New York, NY 10016, USA

McElhenney, Rob (Actor)
c/o Nick Frenkel *3 Arts Entertainment Inc*
9460 Wilshire Blvd
7th Floor
Beverly Hills, CA 90210, USA

McElhenny, Hugh (Athlete, Football Player)
3013 Via Venezia
Henderson, NV 89052, USA

McElhone, Natascha (Actor)
c/o Christina Papadopoulos *Baker Winokur Ryder Public Relations BWR (BWR-NY)*
292 Madison Ave
12th Floor
New York, NY 10017, USA

McElhorne, Natascha (Artist)
c/o Staff Member *ICM Partners (ICM-LA)*
10250 Constellation Blvd Fl 7
Los Angeles, CA 90067, USA

McElligott, Sarah (Actor)
c/o Monica Barkett *Global Artists Agency*
6253 Hollywood Blvd
Suite 508
Los Angeles, CA 90028, USA

McElman, Andy (Athlete, Hockey Player)
260 Beach Dr
Algonquin, IL 60102-2502

McElmury, Jim (Athlete, Hockey Player, Olympic Athlete)
9122 78th St S
Cottage Grove, MN 55016, USA

McElroy, Chuck (Athlete, Baseball Player)
1049 Nederland Ave
Port Arthur, TX 77640-4338, USA

McElroy, Hugh (Athlete, Football Player)
3899 Fonville Ave
Beaumont, TX 77705, USA

McElroy, Reggie (Athlete, Football Player)
Route 1 Box 109A
Preston, MO 65732, USA

McElroy, Vann (Athlete, Football Player)
HC 34 Box 1011
Uvalde, TX 78801, USA

McElwain, Jason (Sportscaster)
c/o Staff Member *WmE2 (WMA-LA)*
1 William Morris Pl
Beverly Hills, CA 90212, USA

McEnaney, Will (Athlete, Baseball Player)
169 Roycourt Cir
Royal Palm Beach, FL 33411-8295, USA

McEnery, Peter (Actor)
International Creative Agency
76 Oxford St
London W1N 0AX, UNITED KINGDOM (UK)

McEnroe, John (Athlete, Tennis Player)
211 Central Park W
New York, NY 10024, USA

McEnroe, John P (Attorney, Lawyer)
LLP L, Weiss, Rifkind, Warton & Garrison,
Ll 1285 Avenue of the Americas
New York, NY 10019-6031, USA

McEntee, Gerald W (Politician)
State County Municipal Employees Union
1625 L St NW
Washington, DC 20036, USA

McEntire, Reba (Musician)
c/o Narvel Blackstock *Starstruck Entertainment*
40 Music Square West
Nashville, TN 37203, USA

McEvoy, Thomas (Misc)
9651 Gisborn Dr
Las Vegas, NV 89147-8215, USA

McEwan, Geraldine (Actor)
Marmont Mgmt
Langham House
302/8 Regent St
London W1R 5AL, UNITED KINGDOM (UK)

McEwan, Ian R (Writer)
15 Park Town
Oxford OX2 6SN, UNITED KINGDOM (UK)

McEwen, Bruce S (Scientist)
Rockefeller University
Immunology Dept
1230 York Ave
New York, NY 10021, USA

McEwen, Craig (Athlete, Football Player)
1610 Hilton Head Ct
Apt 1265
El Cajon, CA 92019, USA

McEwen, Mark (Correspondent)
CBS TV
News Dept
51 W 52nd St
New York, NY 10019, USA

McEwen, Mike
3712 N Peniel Ave
Bethanv, OK 73008-3441

McEwen, Tom (Race Car Driver)
Motorsports HOF
Box 194
Novi, MI 48376, USA

McEwen, Tom (Writer)
Tampa Tribune
Editorial Dept
202 S Parker St
Tampa, FL 33606, USA

McEwing, Joe (Athlete, Baseball Player)
630 Deerbrook Dr
Yardley, PA 19067-4537, USA

McFadden, Cynthia (Correspondent, Journalist, Television Host)
c/o Staff Member *Nightline*
1717 DeSales St NW
Washington, DC 20036-4401, USA

McFadden, Daniel L (Nobel Prize Laureate)
41 Southampton Ave
Berkeley, CA 94707-2034, USA

McFadden, Davenia (Actor)
c/o Felicia Sager *Sager Management*
260 S Beverly Dr
Suite 205
Beverly Hills, CA 90212, USA

McFadden, Gates (Actor)
c/o Marcia Hurwitz *Innovative Artists (LA)*
1505 10th St
Santa Monica, CA 90401, USA

McFadden, Leon (Athlete, Baseball Player)
8617 S 10th Ave
Inglewood, CA 90305-2346, USA

McFadden, Paul (Athlete, Football Player)
7395 Christopher Dr
Youngstown, OH 44514, USA

McFadden-Rusynyk, Betty Jean (Athlete, Baseball Player, Commentator)
7267 W 130th St
Cleveland, OH 44130-7814, USA

McFadin, Bud
1467 Albrecht Rd
Victoria, TX 77905-2613

McFadyen, Angus (Actor)
c/o Douglas Urbanski *Douglas Management Group*
9713 Little Santa Monica Blvd
Beverly Hills, CA 90210, USA

McFall, Dan (Athlete, Hockey Player)
475 N Williston Rd
Williston, VT 05495-9572

McFarland, Anthony (Athlete, Football Player)
7733 Stll Lakes Dr
Odessa, FL 33556, USA

McFarland, Jim (Athlete, Football Player)
5102 S 90th St
Lincoln, NE 68526, USA

McFarland, Kay (Athlete, Football Player)
7394 S Monaco St
Centennial, CO 80112, USA

McFarland, Kirsten (Writer)
c/o Staff Member *ICM Partners (ICM-LA)*
10250 Constellation Blvd Fl 7
Los Angeles, CA 90067, USA

McFarland, Mike (Race Car Driver)
PO Box 330
Mooresville, NC 28115, USA

McFarlane, Andrew (Actor)
c/o Staff Member *Jeff Morrone Entertainment*
9350 Wilshire Blvd
Suite 224
Beverly Hills, CA 90212, USA

McFarlane, Robert C (Government Official)
2010 Prospect St NW
Washington, DC 20037, USA

McFarlane, Todd (Cartoonist)
PO Box 12230
Tempe, AZ 85284-0038, USA

McFaull, David (Athlete, Olympic Athlete, Sailor)
109 Poloke Pl
Honolulu, HI 96822-5007, USA

McFayden, Brian (Actor)
c/o Babette Perry *IMG (LA)*
717 N Alta Vista Blvd
Los Angeles, CA 90046, USA

McFeeley, William S (Historian, Writer)
35 Concord Avenue
Apt 2
Cambridge, MA 02138-2339, USA

McFerrin, Bobby (Actor, Songwriter, Writer)
Original Artists
826 Broadway
#400
New York, NY 10003, USA

Mcfly (Music Group)
c/o Staff Member *Universal Music Group (UMG - LA)*
2220 Colorado Ave
Santa Monica, CA 90404, USA

McG (Director, Producer)
Wonderland Sound and Vision
8739 Sunset Blvd
West Hollywood, CA 90069, USA

McGaffigan, Andy (Athlete, Baseball Player)
6243 Forestwood Dr E
Lakeland, FL 33811-2402, USA

McGahee, Willis (Athlete, Football Player)
1 Bills Dr
Orchard Park, NY 14127, USA

McGahern, John (Writer)
Faber & Faber
3 Queen Square
London WC1N 3AU, UNITED KINGDOM (UK)

McGahey, James C (Misc)
Plant Guard Workers Union
25510 Kelly Road
Roseville, MI 48066, USA

McGahey, Kathleen (Athlete, Hockey Player, Olympic Athlete)
7427 W 81st St
Los Angeles, CA 90045-2303, USA

McGann, Michelle (Athlete, Golfer)
1200 Singer Dr
West Palm Beach, FL 33404-2765, USA

McGann, Paul (Actor)
Marina Martin
12/13 Poland St
London W1V 3DE, UNITED KINGDOM (UK)

McGarity, Vernon (General, War Hero)
6901 Andrews Road
Memphis, TN 38135-3010, USA

McGarity, Wane (Athlete, Football Player)
4622 Lavender Ln
San Antonio, TX 78220, USA

McGarrahan, Scott (Athlete, Football Player)
6636 W William Cannon Dr
Austin, TX 78735, USA

McGarrigle, Anne (Composer, Musician)
c/o Staff Member *Concerted Efforts*
P.O. Box 440326
Somerville, MA 02144, USA

McGarry, John (Athlete, Football Player)
5725 S Woodlawn Ave
Chicago, IL 60637, USA

McGarry, Kelly (Actor)
c/o Staff Member *Heresun Management*
4119 W Burbank Blvd.
Burbank, CA 91505, USA

McGarry, Steve (Cartoonist)
United feature Syndicate
200 Madison Ave
New York, NY 10016, USA

McGaugh, James L (Biologist)
2327 Aralia St
Newport Beach, CA 92660, USA

McGaughey, Shug (Horse Racer)
20941 NE 38th Ave
Miami, FL 33180-3783, USA

McGauley, Diane (Stylist)
330 Miller Ave
MidValley, CA 94941, USA

McGaw, Patrick (Actor)
Banner Entertainment
8265 W Sunset Blvd
#200
West Hollywood, CA 90046, USA

McGee, Ben (Athlete, Football Player)
35 Castle Cv
Jackson, MS 39212, USA

McGee, Charles Col (Aviator)
5002 Elsmere Pl
Bethesda, MD 20814-2826, USA

McGee, Donald (General, War Hero)
9009 Gnarled Pine Ln
Knoxville, TN 37922-7614, USA

McGee, Henry
19 Sydney Mews
London, ENGLAND SW3 6HL

McGee, Herb (Athlete, Basketball Player)
PO Box 67
Southeastern, PA 19399-0067, USA

McGee, Jake (Athlete, Baseball Player)
2739 Waterfield Dr
Sparks, NV 89434-1700, USA

McGee, Michael B (Mike) (Athlete, Football Player)
University Of South California
2 Medical Park Rd
Suite 502
Columbia, SC 29203, USA

McGee, Pamela (Pam) (Basketball Player)
Los Angeles Sparks
Staples Center
1111 S Figueroa St
Los Angeles, CA 90015, USA

McGee, Stephen (Athlete, Football Player)
c/o Staff Member *Dallas Cowboys*
1 Cowboys Pkwy
Irving, TX 75063, USA

McGee, Tim (Athlete, Football Player)
4226 Maxwell Dr
Mason, OH 45040, USA

McGee, Tony (Athlete, Football Player)
170 Tana Dr
Fayetteville, GA 30214, USA

McGee, Trina (Actor)
c/o Stephen Rice *Pantheon Talent*
1900 Ave Of The Stars
Suite 2840
Los Angeles, CA 90067, USA

McGee, Willie (Athlete, Baseball Player)
2081 Luoine Rd
Hercules, CA 94547-1104, USA

McGeever, John (Athlete, Football Player)
3479 Norwich Dr
Birmingham, AL 35243, USA

McGegan, Nicholas (Conductor)
Schwalbe Partners
170 E 61st St
#5N
New York, NY 10021, USA

McGehee, Kevin (Athlete, Baseball Player)
8639 Rid11emont Dr
Pineville, LA 71360-2629, USA

McGehee, Robby (Race Car Driver)
16 Lynnbrook Road
St Louis, MO 63131, USA

McGeorge, Missie (Athlete, Golfer)
1836 Willow Springs Ct
Haslet, TX 76052, USA

McGeorge, Rich (Athlete, Football Player)
2200 Trail Wood Dr
Durham, NC 27705, USA

McGhee, Carla (Athlete, Basketball Player, Olympic Athlete)
986 Dearborn Ln
Auburn, AL 36830-3374, USa

McGhee, George C (Government Official)
36276 Mountville Road
Middleburg, VA 20117, USA

McGhee-Anderson, Kathleen (Producer)
c/o Staff Member *Creative Artists Agency (CAA-LA)*
2000 Ave Of The Stars
Los Angeles, CA 90067, USA

McGiffin, Carol (Actor, Talk Show Host)
c/o Staff Member *ITV Network*
200 Gray's Inn Rd
London, CA WC1X 8HF, United Kingdom

McGiinchy, Kevin (Athlete, Baseball Player)
388 Medford St
Malden, MA 02148-7209, USA

McGilberry, Randy (Athlete, Baseball Player)
2110 Foxford St
Cantonment, FL 32533-6851, USA

McGill, Billy (Athlete, Basketball Player)
5129 W 58th Pl
Los Angeles, CA 9ees6-16el, USA

McGill, Bob (Athlete, Hockey Player)
116 Oriole Dr
Holland Landing, ON L9N 1H1, Canada

McGill, Bob (Athlete, Hockey Player)
Toronto Maple Leafs
400-40 Bay St
Toronto, ON M5J 2X2

McGill, Bruce (Actor)
c/o Scott Manners *Stone Manners Salners Agency (LA)*
9911 W Pico Blvd Ste 1400
Los Angeles, CA 90035, USA

McGill, Bryant (Writer)
11C Lower Dorset St
Dubline 1, IRELAND

McGill, Everett (Actor)
c/o Staff Member *WmE2 (WMA-LA)*
1 William Morris Pl
Beverly Hills, CA 90212, USA

McGill, Jill (Athlete, Golfer)
3765 Carmel View Rd
Unit 3
San Diego, CA 92130, USA

McGill, Karmeeleyah (Athlete, Football Player)
1626 N Greenwood Ave
Clearwater, FL 33755, USA

McGill, Mike (Athlete, Football Player)
8930 Louis Ct
Saint John, IN 46373, USA

McGill, Paul (Actor)
c/o Jill Fritzo *PMK/BNC Public Relations (PMK-NY)*
622 3rd Ave
8th Floor
New York, NY 10017, USA

McGill, Ryan (Athlete, Hockey Player)
958 Yoeman Hall Rd
Kalispell, MT 59901-7610

McGill, William J (Educator)
2624 Costebelle Dr
La Jolla, CA 92037, USA

McGillin, Howard (Actor)
c/o Staff Member *Cunningham Escott Slevin & Doherty (CESD-LA)*
10635 Santa Monica Blvd
130
Los Angeles, CA 90025, USA

McGillis, Kelly (Actor, Producer)
c/o Staff Member *David Williams Management*
9614 Olympic Blvd
Suite F
Beverly Hills, CA 90212, USA

McGinest, Willie (Athlete, Football Player)
2211 Easy Ave
Long Beach, CA 90810, USA

McGinley, John C (Actor)
Innovative Artists
1505 10th St
Santa Monica, CA 90401, USA

McGinley, Ted (Actor)
c/o Mark Teitelbaum *Teitelbaum Artists Group*
8840 Wilshire Blvd
3rd Floor
Beverly Hills, CA 90212, USA

McGinn, Bernard J (Misc)
5702 Kenwood Ave
Chicago, IL 60637, USA

McGinn, Dan (Athlete, Baseball Player)
1309 S 189th Ct
Omaha, NE 68130-2842, USA

McGinnis, Dave (Athlete, Coach, Football Coach, Football Player)
Arizona Cardinals
PO Box 888
Phoenix, AZ 85001, USA

McGinnis, George (Athlete, Basketball Player)
811e Bounty Ct
Indianapolis, IN 46236-8941, USA

McGinnis, Joe (Writer)
Janklow & Nesbit
445 Park Ave
#1300
New York, NY 10020, USA

McGinnis, Russ (Athlete, Baseball Player)
10368 Craftsman Wav Aot 101
San Diego, CA 92127-3523, USA

McGinnis, Susan (Television Host)
c/o Staff Member *CBS News*
Viacom Inc
524 W 57th St
New York, NY 10019, USA

McGinty, Damian (Actor)
c/o Paul Lyttle *Twenty Four Seven PR*
Prefers to be contacted via telephone or email
Los Angeles, CA, USA

McGinty, John J (General, War Hero)
7617 Joe Allen Dr
Beaufort, SC 29906-9737, USA

McGirt, James (Buddy) (Boxer)
195 Suffolk Ave
Brentwood, NY 11717, USA

McGlinchy, Kevin (Athlete, Baseball Player)
10 West St
Malden, MA 02148, USA

McGlockin, Jon (Athlete, Basketball Player)
5281 State Road
#83
Heartland, WI 53029, USA

McGlocklin, Jon
5281 State Road 83
Hartland, WI 53e29-93e6, USA

McGlothin, Pat (Athlete, Baseball Player)
1454 Kenesaw Ave
Knoxville, TN 37919-7749, USA

McGlynn, Dennis (Race Car Driver)
Dover Downs Speedway
PO Box 843
Dover, DE 19903, USA

McGlynn, Dick (Athlete, Hockey Player)
38 Rock Glen Rd
Medford, MA 02155-1946, USA

McGlynn, Dick (Athlete, Hockey Player, Olympic Athlete)
38 Rock Glen Rd
Medford, MA 02155-1946, USA

McGlynn, Pat (Musician)
27 Preston Grange
Preston Pans E
Lothian, SCOTLAND

McGlynn, Ryan (Race Car Driver)
Raynard McGlynn Motorsports
1246 Sane Souci Pkwy
Wilkes Barre, PA 18702, USA

McGoon, Dwight C (Doctor)
211 2nd St NW
#2016
Rochester, MN 55901, USA

McGovern, Elizabeth (Actor)
c/o Staff Member *Anonymous Content (LA)*
3531 Hayden Ave
Culver City, CA 90232, USA

McGovern, Jim (Athlete, Golfer)
384 Francis Ct
Oradell, NJ 07649-1308, USA

McGovern, Maureen (Actor, Musician)
MM Productions Inc
c/o Jennifer Howe
12087 Evergreen St NW
Minneapolis, MN 55448, USA

McGovern, Rob (Athlete, Football Player)
419 E 57th St
Apt 2D
New York, NY 10022, USA

McGowan, Alistair (Actor)
c/o Oriana Elia *Rights House, The*
Drury House
34-43 Russell St
London WC2B 5HA, UK

McGowan, Charles E (Religious Leader)
Presbyterian Church in America
1852 Century Place
Atlanta, GA 30345, USA

McGowan, Dustin (Athlete, Baseball Player)
P.O. Box 1281
Ludowici, GA 31316-1281, USA

McGowan, Michael (Director)
c/o Bill Douglass *Paradigm (LA)*
360 N Crescent Dr
North Bldg
Beverly Hills, CA 90210, USA

McGowan, Pat (Athlete, Golfer)
P.O. Box 88
Southern Pines, NC 28388-0088, USA

McGowan, Rose (Actor)
c/o Oren Segal *Management Production Entertainment (MPE)*
9200 Sunset Blvd
Suite 550
Los Angeles, CA 90069, USA

McGrady, Michael (Actor)
c/o Staff Member *Main Title Entertainment*
8383 Wilshire Blvd
Suite 408
Los Angeles, CA 90211, USA

McGrady, Tracy (Athlete, Basketball Player)
23 Beacon Hl
Sugar Land, TX 77479-2551, USA

McGrath, Alister (Writer)
c/o Staff Member *HarperCollins Publishers*
10 East 53rd St
c/o Author mail, 7th Floor
New York, NY 10022, USA

McGrath, Doug (Director)
c/o Staff Member *ICM Partners (ICM-LA)*
10250 Constellation Blvd Fl 7
Los Angeles, CA 90067, USA

McGrath, Douglas (Actor, Director, Writer)
c/o Staff Member *Creative Artists Agency (CAA-LA)*
2000 Ave Of The Stars
Los Angeles, CA 90067, USA

McGrath, Eugene R (Business Person)
Consolidated Edison
4 Irving Place
New York, NY 10003, USA

McGrath, James (Scientist)
Yale University
Genetics Dept
New Haven, CT 06520, USA

McGrath, Jeremy (Motorcycle Race, Motorcycle Racer)
American Motorcycle Assn
13515 Yarmouth Dr
Pickerington, OH 43147, USA

McGrath, Judy (Business Person)
c/o Staff Member *MTV Networks (LA)*
2600 Colorado Blvd
Santa Monica, CA 90405

McGrath, Mark (Musician, Television Host)
c/o John Marx *WME (LA)*
9601 Wilshire Blvd Fl 3
Beverly Hills, CA 90210, USA

McGrath, Michael (Actor)
Imperial Theatre
C/O NICE WORK IF YOU CAN GET IT
249 W 45th St
New York, NY 10036, USA

McGrath, Mike (Bowler)
738 Colusa Ave
El Cerrito, CA 94530-3313, USA

McGratton, Tom (Athlete, Hockey Player)
919-690 Regency Crt
Burlington, ON L7N 3H1, Canada

McGraw, Harold W Jr (Publisher)
McGraw-Hill Inc
1221 Ave of Americas
New York, NY 10020, USA

McGraw, Jay (Writer)
c/o Staff Member *The Dr. Phil Show*
5555 Melrose Ave
Mae West Bldg
Los Angeles, CA 90038, USA

McGraw, Joseph (General, War Hero)
2578 San Juan St
Coupeville, WA 98239-9765, USA

McGraw, Melinda (Actor)
c/o Staff Member *McKeon-Myones Management*
3500 Olive Ave
Suite 770
Burbank, CA 91505, USA

McGraw, Mike (Athlete, Football Player)
P.O. Box 529
Medicine Bow, WY 82328, USA

McGraw, Phil Dr (Doctor, Misc, Talk Show Host)
c/o Staff Member *The Dr. Phil Show*
5555 Melrose Ave
Mae West Bldg
Los Angeles, CA 90038, USA

McGraw, Robin (Writer)
c/o Staff Member *Peteski Productions Inc*
137 N Larchmont Blvd
#705
Los Angeles, CA 90004, USA

McGraw, Tim (Musician)
c/o Coran Capshaw *Red Light Management (VA)*
PO Box 1467
Charlottesville, VA 22902, USA

McGraw, Tom (Athlete, Baseball Player)
11300 NE 379th St
La Center, WA 98629-4307, USA

McGraw III, Harold W (Business Person, Publisher)
McGraw-Hill Inc
1221 Ave of Americas
New York, NY 10020, USA

McGreevey, James (Politician)
109A Green St
Woodbridge, NJ 07095-2910, USA

McGregor, Ewan (Actor)
c/o Nanci Ryder *Baker Winokur Ryder Public Relations (BWR-LA)*
9100 Wilshire Blvd
Suite 500, West Tower
Beverly Hills, CA 90212, USA

McGregor, Gilbert (Athlete, Basketball Player)
3700 Orleans Ave
Apt 4411
New Orleans, LA 7e119-4854, USA

McGregor, Maurice (Doctor)
Royal Victoria Hospital
687 Pine Ave W
Montreal, QC H3A 1A1, CANADA

McGregor, Scott (Athlete, Baseball Player)
1514 Providence Rd
Towson, MD 21286-1523, USA

McGrew, Reggie (Athlete, Football Player)
1247 Lakeside Dr
Apt 2039
Sunnyvale, CA 94085, USA

McGriff, Elton (Athlete, Basketball Player)
4011 Shoreline Dr
Dallas, TX 75233-3709, USA

McGriff, Fred (Athlete, Baseball Player)
16314 Millan De Avila
Tampa, FL 33610-1089, USA

McGriff, Hershel (Race Car Driver)
General Delivery
Green Valley, AZ 85622, USA

McGriff, Lee (Athlete, Football Player)
3501 W University Ave
Suite A
Gainesville, FL 35607, USA

McGriff, Terry (Athlete, Baseball Player)
2905 Langston Dr
Ft Pierce, FL 34946-1180, USA

McGriff, Tery (Athlete, Baseball Player)
2905 Langston Dr
Fort Pierce, FL 34946, USA

McGriff, Travis (Athlete, Football Player)
5910 NW 19th Pl
Gainesville, FL 32605, USA

McGriggs, Lamar (Athlete, Football Player)
1209-115 Main St E
Hamilton, ON L8N 1G5, Canada

McGruder, Aaron (Cartoonist)
Universal Press Syndicate
4520 Main St
Kansas City, MO 64111, USA

McGuane III, Thomas F (Writer)
410 S 3rd Ave
Bozeman, MT 59715, USA

McGuigan, Frank (Athlete, Football Player)
2715 Willits Rd
Philadelphia, PA 19114-3410, USA

McGuinn, Martin G (Financier)
Mellon Financial Corp
Mellon Bank Center
500 Grant St
Pittsburgh, PA 15258, USA

McGuinn, Roger (Musician)
c/o Staff Member *Shore Fire Media*
32 Court St
16th Floor
Brooklyn, NY 11201, USA

McGuire, Allie
4 Tanglewood Lane
Winchester, MA 01890

McGuire, Betty (Actor)
H David Moss
733 Seward St
#PH
Los Angeles, CA 90038, USA

McGuire, Bill (Athlete, Baseball Player)
17209 I St
Omaha, NE 68135-3626, USA

McGuire, Christine (Musician)
100 Rancho Circle
Las Vegas, NV 89107, USA

McGuire, Kevin E (Athlete, Basketball Player)
20 Blue Jay Ln
North Oaks, MN 55127, USA

Mcguire, Maeve
c/o Staff Member *Gage Group, The (LA)*
14724 Ventura Blvd
Suite 505
Sherman Oaks, CA 91403, USA

McGuire, Marcy (Actor)
681 Red Arrow Trail
Palm Desert, CA 92211, USA

McGuire, Mickey (Athlete, Baseball Player)
1521 Middle Park Dr
Dayton, OH 45414-1500, USA

McGuire, Patricia A (Educator)
Trinity College
President's Office
Washington, DC 20017, USA

McGuire, Phyllis (Musician)
7373 N. Scottsdale Rd
#A130
Scottsdale, AZ 85253, USA

McGuire, Ryan (Athlete, Baseball Player)
10 Atwater
Irvine, CA 92602-2028, USA

McGuire, Walter E (Gene) (Athlete, Football Player)
3229 Country Club Dr
Lynn Haven, FL 32444, USA

McGuire, Willard H (Misc)
National Education Assn
1201 16th St NW
Washington, DC 20036, USA

McGuire, William Biff (Actor)
McKenrick
1443 Pandoza Ave
Los Angeles, CA 90024, USA

McGuire, William W (Business Person)
United HealthCare Corp
Opus Center
9900 Bren Road E
Minnetonka, MN 55343, USA

McGuire-Leveque, Sarah (Athlete, Golfer)
2433 S 15th St
Springfield, IL 62703, USA

McGuire Sisters (Music Group)
c/o Stan Scottland *Stan Scottland Entertainment*
157 E 57th St #18-B
New York, NY 10022, USA

McGwire, Mark (Athlete, Baseball Player, Olympic Athlete)
StLouis Cardinals 700 Clark St Attn: Coaching Staff
Saint Louis, MO 63102-1727, USA

McHale, Christina (Athlete, Tennis Player)
c/o Staff Member *Women's Tennis Association (WTA (US))*
One Progress Plaza
Ste 1500
St Petersburg, FL 33701, USA

Mchale, Joel (Actor, Television Host)
c/o James Dolin *Sonesta Entertainment*
150 Ocean Park Blvd. #423
Santa Monica, CA 90405, USA

McHale, Kevin (Athlete, Basketball Player)
20 Blue Jay Ln
Saint Paul, MN 55127-2015, USA

McHale, Kevin (Actor)
c/o Jamie Malone *MC Talent Management*
4821 Lankershim Blvd #F329
N Hollywood, CA 91601, USA

McHattie, Stephen (Actor)
c/o Christopher Wright *Christopher Wright Management*
3207 Winnie Dr
Los Angeles, CA 90068, USA

McHattle, Stephen (Actor)
Macklam Feldman Mgmt
1505 W 2nd Ave
#200
Vancouver, BC V6H 3Y4, CANADA

McHenry, Donald F (Diplomat)
Georgetown University
Foreign Service School
Washington, DC 20057, USA

McHenry, Vance (Athlete, Baseball Player)
2396 Brown St
Durham, CA 95938-9620, USA

M. Christensen, Donna (Congressman, Politician)
1510 Longworth HOB
Washington, DC 20515, USA

McHugh, Heather (Writer)
University of Washington
English Dept
PO Box 35330
Seattle, WA 98195, USA

McHugh, Mike (Athlete, Hockey Player)
945 Parish Pl
Hummelstown, PA 17036-8986

Mcilhargey, Jack (Athlete, Hockey Player)
2120 Birch St
Point Roberts, WA 98281-9507

McIlhenny, Don (Athlete, Football Player)
8505 Edgemere Rd
Apt 101
Dallas, TX 75225-3520, USA

Mcilravy, Lincoln (Athlete, Olympic Athlete)
4220 210th St NE
Solon, IA 52333-9657, USA

McIlroy, Rory (Athlete, Golfer)
c/o Neil McLaughlin *Horizon Sports Management*
Prefers to be contacted via telephone and email

McIlvaine, Jim (Athlete, Basketball Player)
Camp Anokijig
Camp Anokijig W5639 Anokijig Ln
Plymouth, WI 53e73-2879, USA

Mcilvaine, Joe (Commentator)
106 Stonev Brook Blvd
Newtown Sauare, PA 19073-3974, USA

McInerney, Jay (Actor, Writer)
c/o Doug MacLaren *ICM Partners (ICM-LA)*
10250 Constellation Blvd Fl 7
Los Angeles, CA 90067, USA

McInnis, Hugh (Athlete, Football Player)
290 Rockwell Church Rd NE
Winder, GA 30680, USA

Mcinnis, Jeffrey (Athlete, Basketball Player)
34e4 Lazy Day Ln
Charlotte, NC 28269-e144, USA

McInnis, Marty (Athlete, Hockey Player, Olympic Athlete)
21 Peter Hobart.Dr.
Hingham, MA 02043-3751, USA

McIntosh, Bill (Athlete, Golfer)
5263 SW Bimini Cir N
Palm City, FL 34990-1246, USA

Mcintosh, Bradley (Actor, Musician)
c/o Becky Thompson *Action Talent International*
Moray House
23 - 31 Great Titchfield Street
London W1W 7PA, United Kingdom

McIntosh, Chris (Athlete, Football Player)
526 Dublin Dr
Hartford, WI 53027, USA

McIntosh, Damion (Athlete, Football Player)
1221 SW Summit Crossing Dr
Lees Summit, MO 64081, USA

McIntosh, Joe (Athlete, Baseball Player)
9120 SE 54th St
Mercer Island, WA 98040-5148, USA

Mcintosh, Robert H Col (Aviator)
22969 Ardwick St
Woodland Hills, CA 91364-4825, USA

McIntosh, Tim (Athlete, Baseball Player)
1815 S Talbott Pl
Waynesboro, VA 22980-2250, USA

McIntosh Slaughter, Louise (Congressman, Politician)
2469 Rayburn HOB
Washington, DC 20515, USA

McIntyre, Guy (Athlete, Football Player)
257 Arrowhead Way
Hayward, CA 94544, USA

McIntyre, Joe (Actor)
c/o Gina Rugolo-Judd *Rugolo Entertainment*
195 S Beverly Dr
Suite 400
Beverly Hills, CA 90212, USA

McIntyre, Joey (Musician)
c/o Jason Gutman *Gersh (NY)*
41 Madison Ave
New York, NY 10010, USA

Mcintyre, Larry (Athlete, Hockey Player)
9420 E 116th St S
Bixby, OK 74008-1733

McIntyre, Melissa (Actor)
Creative Drive Artists
c/o Dani De Lio
20 Carlton St #123
Toronto, ON M5B 2H5, CANADA

McIntyre, Mike (Congressman, Politician)
2133 Rayburn HOB
Washington, DC 20515, USA

McIntyre, Secedrick (Athlete, Football Player)
4801 Tannery Ave
Tampa, FL 33624, USA

Mcintyre, Vonda (Writer)
PO Box 31041
Seattle, WA 98103-1041, USA

McIver, Everett (Athlete, Football Player)
1205 Avignon Dr SW
Conyers, GA 30094, USA

McIvor, Richard (Athlete, Football Player)
P.O. Box 148
Fort Davis, TX 79734, USA

Mc.Julien, Paul (Athlete, Football Player)
12111 Gibbens Rd
Baton Rouge, LA 70807, USA

McJulien, Paul (Athlete, Football Player)
20300 SE Morrison Ter #H
Gresham, OR 97030-2233, USA

McKagan, Duff (Musician)
c/o Ian Sales *International Talent Booking*
74A Charlotte St
London W1T 4QJ, UNITED KINGDOM (UK)

McKagen, Duff
8647 Edwin Dr.
Los Angeles, CA 90046

McKay, Adam (Actor, Director, Writer)
c/o Jimmy Miller *Mosaic Media Group*
9200 W. Sunset Blvd
10th Floor
Los Angeles, CA 90069, USA

McKay, Bob (Athlete, Football Player)
4110 Bluffridge Dr
Austin, TX 78759, USA

McKay, Cody (Athlete, Baseball Player)
7830 S Yarrow St
Littleton, CO 80128-5492, USA

McKay, Dave (Athlete, Baseball Player)
9702 E La Posada Cir
Scottsdale, AZ 85255-3716, USA

McKay, David (Scientist)
NASA
Nasa Johnson Space Center 2101 Nasa Pkwy
Houston, TX 77058-3696, USA

McKay, Gardner (Actor, Director, Writer)
1040 Lunalilo St
Ph 2
Honolulu, HI 96822-5712, USA

McKay, Heather (Athlete)
48 Nesbitt Dr
Toronto, ON M4W 2G3, CANADA

McKay, John (Athlete, Football Player)
16601 Calle Haleigh
Pacific Palisades, CA 90272, USA

McKay, Mhairi (Athlete, Golfer)
898 W Ashbourne Dr
Eagle, ID 83616-6433, USA

McKay, Nellie (Actor)
c/o Staff Member *Kid Logic*
156 Liberty St
#12
Little Ferry, NJ 07643, USA

McKay, Peggy (Actor)
8811 Wonderland Ave
Los Angeles, CA 90046, USA

McKay, Randy (Athlete, Hockey Player)
44640 US Highway 41
Chassell, MI 49916-9102

McKay, Ray (Athlete, Hockey Player)
PO Box 182
Ilderton, ON N0M 2A0, Canada

McKay, Ross (Athlete, Hockey Player)
1401 Thornwood Dr
Downers Grove, IL 60516-1224

McKay, Tom (Actor)
c/o Jason Spire *Inspire Entertainment*
315 7th Ave
Suite 17E
New York, NY 10001, USA

McKean, Eddy (Race Car Driver)
Enerjetix Motors
20520 E. First Ave
Greenacres, WA 99016, USA

McKean, Jim (Athlete, Baseball Player)
740 Sand Pine Dr NE
Saint Petersburg, FL 33703-3181, USA

McKean, Jim (Athlete, Baseball Player)
740 Sand Pine Dr NE
Saint Petersburg, FL 33703, USA

McKean, Michael (Actor, Comedian)
3202 Club Dr
Los Angeles, CA 90064, USA

McKechnie, Walt (Athlete, Hockey Player)
McKeck's Place
P.O Box 752
Haliburton, ON K0M 1S0, CANADA

McKee, Bonnie (Musician)
15353 SE 49th Pl
Bellevue, WA 98006-3652, USA

McKee, Frank S (Misc)
United Steelworkers Union
5 gateway Center
Pittsburgh, PA 15222, USA

McKee, Gina (Actor)
Rozane Vacca
8 Silver Place
London W1R 3LJ, UNITED KINGDOM (UK)

McKee, Jay (Athlete, Hockey Player)
Rochester Americans
1 War Memorial Sq Ste 228
Rochester, NY 14614-2192

McKee, Jay (Athlete, Hockey Player)
20 Douglas Ln
Elma, NY 14059-9022

McKee, Kinnaird R (Admiral)
7100 Wheeler Park Circle
Easton, MD 21601-8448, USA

McKee, Lonette (Actor)
New Artist Group
c/o Keith Perkins
545 8th Ave Ste 401
New York, NY 10018, USA

McKee, Lucky (Director)
9300 Wilshire Blvd
Suite 555
Beverly Hills, CA 90212, USA

McKee, Maria (Musician)
Eleven Thirty
449 A Trollingwood Rd
Haw River, NC 27258, USA

McKee, Mike (Athlete, Hockey Player)
6 Linden Point Rd
Branford, CT 06405-5709

McKee, Rogers (Athlete, Baseball Player)
409 Forest Hill Dr
Shelby, NC 28150-5520, USA

McKee, Susan (Stylist)
c/o Staff Member *Clutts Agency, The*
1400 Turtle Creek Blvd
#171
Dallas, TX 75207, USA

McKee, Theodore A (Judge)
US Appeals Court
US Couthouse
601 Market St
Philadelphia, PA 19106, USA

McKee, Todd (Actor)
611 N Flores St
#2
West Hollywood, CA 90048, USA

McKeehan, Pat
PO Box 486
Louisville, TN 37777

McKeel, Walt (Athlete, Baseball Player)
7669 NC Highway 58 N
Stantonsburg, NC 27883-8635, USA

McKeever, Vito (Athlete, Football Player)
6823 Coral Reef St
Lake Worth, FL 33467, USA

McKegney, ian
467 St Albert St
Kincardine, ON N2Z 2W6, Canada

McKellar, Danica (Actor)
c/o Andrew Edwards *Wishlab*
2225-A Hyperion Ave
Los Angeles, CA 90027, USA

McKellen, Ian (Actor)
c/o Chris Andrews *Creative Artists Agency (CAA-LA)*
2000 Ave Of The Stars
Los Angeles, CA 90067, USA

McKeller, Keith (Athlete, Football Player)
1972 Waccamaw Path
Winston Salem, NC 27127, USA

McKelvey, Rob (Athlete, Golfer)
1814 Duke Rd
Atlanta, GA 30341, USA

McKendry, Alex (Athlete, Hockey Player)
151 Courthouse Rd.
Franklin Square, NY 11010, USA

McKenna, Alex (Actor)
c/o Staff Member *Grey Media Group*
16848 Charmel Lane
Pacific Palisades, CA 90272, USA

McKenna, Aline Brosh (Writer)
c/o Todd Feldman *Creative Artists Agency (CAA-LA)*
2000 Ave Of The Stars
Los Angeles, CA 90067, USA

McKenna, Andrew J (Business Person)
McDonald's Corp
1 McDonald's Plaza
1 Kroc Dr
Oak Brook, IL 60523, USA

McKenna, David (Dave) (Musician)
Thomas Cassidy
11761 E Speedway Blvd
Tucson, AZ 85748, USA

McKenna, Kevin (Athlete, Basketball Player)
3068 Cimarron Pl
Eugene, OR 97405, USA

McKenna, Paul (Motivational Speaker)
c/o Staff Member *United Agents*
12-26 Lexington St
London W1F OLE, UK

McKenna, Sean
La Corporation Inglasco Ltd
2745 Rue de la Sherwood
Sherbrooke, QC JIK IEI, Canada

McKenna, Virginia (Actor)
8 Buckfast Court
Runcorn, Cheshire WA7 1QJ, UNITED KINGDOM (UK)

McKenney, Donald H (Don) (Athlete, Hockey Player)
16 Edgewater Dr
Norton, MA 02766-2123

McKennitt, Loreena (Musician)
c/o Staff Member *Quinlan Road*
P.O. Box 933
Stratford, Ontario N5A 7M3, Canada

McKennitt, Lorena (Musician, Songwriter, Writer)
Quinlan Road
PO Box 933
Stratford, ON N5A 7M3, CANADA

McKennon, Keith R (Business Person)
6079 N Paradise View Dr
Paradise Valley, AZ 85253, USA

McKenny, Jim (Athlete, Hockey Player)
City TV
299 Queen St W
Toronto, ON M5V 2Z5, Canada

McKenry, Michael (Athlete, Baseball Player)
8364 David TipQit Way
Knoxvill, TN 37931-4478, USA

McKenzie, Andrew (Misc)
Leather Goods Plastics Novelty Union
265 W 14th St
New York, NY 10011, USA

McKenzie, Benjamin (Actor)
c/o David Seltzer *Management 360*
9111 Wilshire Blvd
Beverly Hills, CA 90210, USA

McKenzie, Bill (Athlete, Hockey Player)
9461 Timberbank Cir
Pickerington, OH 43147-8501

McKenzie, Constance
3360 Barham Blvd.
Los Angeles, CA 90068

McKenzie, Dan P (Misc)
Bullard Labs
Madingley Rise
Madingley Road
Cambridge CB3 0EZ, UNITED KINGDOM (UK)

McKenzie, Forrest (Athlete, Basketball Player)
2516 S Laurelwood
Santa Ana, CA 927e4-5439, USA

McKenzie, Jacqueline (Actor)
c/o Brett Carella *Lab, The*
5540 Hollywood Blvd #200
Hollywood, CA 90028, USA

McKenzie, Jim (Athlete, Hockey Player)
9266 Chevoit Dr
Brentwood, TN 37027-6138

McKenzie, John (Athlete, Hockey Player)
144 Marble St Apt 104
Stoneham, MA 02180-2714

McKenzie, Julia
Kingston Richmond Park
Surrey, ENGLAND

McKenzie, Kareem (Athlete, Football Player)
131 Desilvio Dr
Sicklerville, NJ 08081, USA

McKenzie, Kevin (Ballerina)
American Ballet Theatre
890 Broadway
New York, NY 10003, USA

McKenzie, Melanie (Stylist)
430 E 65th St
#2-D
New York, NY 10021, USA

McKenzie, Raleigh (Athlete, Football Player)
715 Huntsman Pl
Herndon, VA 20170, USA

McKenzie, Reggie (Athlete, Football Player)
411 Carta Rd
Knoxville, TN 37914, USA

McKenzie, Reginald (Reggie) (Athlete, Football Player)
13853 Trumbull St
Highland Park, MI 48203, USA

McKenzie, Roger (Stylist)
c/o Staff Member *Tapestry Creative Management, Inc*
274 W 132nd St #3
New York 10027, USA

McKenzie, Stan (Athlete, Basketball Player)
8316 Governor Grayson Way
Ellicott City, MD 21e43-345e, USA

McKenzie, Vashti (Religious Leader)
Payne Memorial Church
1714 Madison Ave
#16
Baltimore, MD 21217, USA

McKeon, Doug (Actor)
c/o Raymond Miller *Archetype*
1608 Argyle Ave
Los Angeles, CA 90028, USA

McKeon, Jack (Athlete, Baseball Player, Coach)
1529 Charleigh Ct
Elon, NC 27244-9770, USA

McKeon, Joel (Athlete, Baseball Player)
1901 Pierce St
Apt 7
Hollywood, FL 33020-4047, USA

McKeon, Lindsey (Actor)
c/o Robbie Kass *Kass & Stokes Management*
9229 Sunset Blvd
Suite 504
Los Angeles, CA 90069, USA

McKeon, Matt (Soccer Player)
Kansas City Wizards
2 Arrowhead Dr
Kansas City, MO 64129, USA

McKeon, Nancy (Actor)
PO Box 6778
Burbank, CA 91510, USA

McKeown, Bob (Correspondent)
CBS-TV
News Dept
51 W 52nd St
New York, NY 10019, USA

McKeown, Les
27 Preston Grange Preston Pans
E. Lothian, SCOTLAND

McKeown, Leslie (Les) (Music Group, Musician)
Brian Gannon Mgmt
PO Box 106
Rochdale, OL 16 4HW, UNITED KINGDOM (UK)

McKeown, M Margaret (Judge)
US Court of Appeals
US Courthouse
1010 5th Ave
Seattle, WA 98104, USA

McKernan, John (Ex-Governor, Politician)
Education Management Corporation
77 Sanderson Rd
Cumberland Foreside, ME 04110-1436, USA

McKey, Derrick (Athlete, Basketball Player)
8 Woodard Pl
Zionsville, IN 46e77-8189, USA

McKibben, Mike (Athlete, Football Player)
2523 Forest Brook Dr
Pittsburgh, PA 15241, USA

McKibbin, Nikki (Actor, Musician)
c/o JD Sobol *RPM Talent Agency*
741 N Cahuenga Blvd
Suite 101
Los Angeles, CA 90038, USA

McKichan, Steve (Athlete, Hockey Player)
29830 Centre Rd
Strathroy, ON N7G 3H7, Canada

McKidd, Kevin (Actor)
c/o Peter Kiernan *Management 360*
9111 Wilshire Blvd
Beverly Hills, CA 90210, USA

McKie, Aaron (Athlete, Basketball Player)
14ee Youngs Ford Rd
Gladwyne, PA 19035-1233, USA

McKie, Jason (Athlete, Football Player)
4431 W Lawn Ave
Waukegan, IL 60085, USA

McKiernan, David (General)
Commanding General
3rd Army
Fort PcPherson, GA 30330, USA

McKim, Peggy (Actor)
15801 Wyandotte St #111
Van Nuys, CA 91406, USA

McKinley, Alvin (Athlete, Football Player)
45274 W Miraflores St
Maricopa, AZ 85139, USA

McKinley, Dennis (Athlete, Football Player)
150 McKinley Rd
Mc Cool, MS 39108, USA

McKinley, John (Misc)
952 Bloomfield Village
Auburn Hills, MI 48326, USA

McKinley, Robin (Writer)
Writer's House
Writer's House Inc 21 W 26th St Fl1
New York, NY 10010-1003, USA

McKinley, Rodney (General, War Hero)
3134 Fox Hill Ter
Edmond, OK 73034-2339, USA

McKinley-Uselmann, Therese (Athlete, Baseball Player, Commentator)
1644 N Greenwood Ave
Park Ridge, IL 60068-1215, USA

McKinnely, Phil (Athlete, Football Player)
585 Edgehill Pl
Alpharetta, GA 30022, USA

McKinney, Carlton (Athlete, Basketball Player)
310 E 4th Ave
Nixon, TX 7814e-2939, USA

Mckinney, Demetria
c/o Staff Member *Serendipity Entertainment*
1041 N Formosa Ave
Suite 206A
West Hollywood, CA 90046, USA

Mckinney, Frank (Business Person)
PO BOX 388
Boynton Beach, FL 33425, USA

McKinney, Gil (Actor)
c/o Steven Levy *Framework Entertainment (LA)*
9057 Nemo St
Suite C
West Hollywood, CA 90069, USA

McKinney, Greg
1800 Ave. of the Stars #400
Los Angeles, CA 90067

McKinney, Jack (Basketball Coach, Coach)
St Joseph's University
5600 City Ave
Hawk's Hall of Fame
Philadelphia, PA 19131-1376, USA

McKinney, Kurt
9200 Sunset Blvd. #1130
Los Angeles, CA 90069

McKinney, Mark (Actor)
c/o Staff Member *WmE2 (WMA-LA)*
1 William Morris Pl
Beverly Hills, CA 90212, USA

McKinney, Odis (Athlete, Football Player)
23126 Collins St
Woodland Hills, CA 91367, USA

McKinney, Rich (Athlete, Baseball Player)
2495 E Peterson Rd
Troy, OH 45373-7790, USA

McKinney, Royce (Athlete, Football Player)
1930 N Beech Daly Rd
Dearborn Heights, MI 48127, USA

McKinney, Seth (Athlete, Football Player)
2403 Crown Ct
College Station, TX 77845, USA

McKinney, Steve (Athlete, Football Player)
2403 Crown Ct
College Station, TX 77845, USA

McKinney, Tamara (Athlete, Olympic Athlete, Skier)
4935 Parkers Mill Rd
Lexington, KY 40513-9760, USA

McKinnie, Bryant (Athlete, Football Player)
12535 Stoneway Ct
Davie, FL 33330, USA

McKinnie, Silas (Athlete, Football Player)
22875 Summer House Ct
Apt 205
Novi, MI 48375, USA

McKinnis, Hugh (Athlete, Football Player)
4759 NW El Camino Blvd
Bremerton, WA 98312, USA

McKinnney, Kurt (Actor)
5003 Tilden Ave
#206
Sherman Oaks, CA 91423, USA

McKinnney, Richard (Rick) (Athlete)
7659 Kavooras Dr
Sacramento, CA 95831, USA

McKinnney, Tamara (Skier)
4935 Parkers Mill Road
Lexington, KY 40513, USA

McKinnon, Bruce (Cartoonist, Editor)
Halifax Herald
Editorial Dept
PO Box 610
Halifax, NS B3J 2T2, CANADA

McKinnon, Dan (Athlete, Hockey Player)
610 E River Dr
Warroad, MN 56763, USA

McKinnon, Dennis (Athlete, Football Player)
PO Box 47661
Chicago, IL 60647, USA

McKinnon, Ray (Actor)
Judy Schoen
606 N Larchmont Blvd
#309
Los Angeles, CA 90004, USA

McKinnon, Ronald (Athlete, Football Player)
1063 Grand Oaks Dr
Bessemer, AL 35022, USA

McKinny, Laura Hart
3224 Nottingham Rd
Winston Salem, NC 27104-1839

Mckinzie, Gordon (Engineer)
Boeing Co
777 Program Po BOx 3707
Seattle, WA 98124, USA

McKissock, Gary S (General)
Deputy CofS for Installations/Logistics
HqUSMC
2 Navy St
Washington, DC 20380, USA

McKnight, Brian (Musician, Songwriter)
c/o Ann Gurrola *Marleah Leslie & Associates PR*
1645 N Vine St
Suite 712
Los Angeles, CA 90028, USA

McKnight, Clarence E Jr (General)
1624 Linway Park Dr
McLean, VA 22101, USA

McKnight, Ira (Athlete, Baseball Player)
8417 Laurel Valley Dr
Indianapolis, IN 46250-3906, USA

McKnight, James (Athlete, Football Player)
16705 Berkshire Ct
Southwest Ranches, FL 33331, USA

McKnight, Jeff (Athlete, Baseball Player)
3296 Highway 92 W
Bee Branch, AR 72013-8937, USA

McKnight, Joe (Athlete, Football Player)
c/o Roosevelt Barnes *Maximum Sports Management*
6435 W Jefferson Blvd
#197
Fort Wayne, IN 46804, USA

McKnight, Lauren (Actor)
c/o Mia Hansen *MLC PR*
7080 Hollywood Blvd
Suite 903
Los Angeles, CA 90028, USA

McKnight, Scotty (Athlete, Football Player)
15 Manchester Ct
Coto De Caza, CA 92679, USA

McKnight, Steven L (Biologist)
4518 Fairway St
Dallas, TX 75219-1605, USA

McKnight, Ted (Athlete, Football Player)
10236 Cedarbrooke Ln
Kansas City, MO 64131, USA

McKnight, Tom (Athlete, Golfer)
78 Lexington Dr
Bluffton, SC 29910, USA

McKnight, Tony (Athlete, Baseball Player)
406 Dundee Rd
Texarkana, AR 71854-9768, USA

McKoy, Bill (Athlete, Football Player)
585 Wexford Hollow Run
Roswell, GA 30075, USA

McKuen, Rod (Musician, Songwriter, Writer)
1155 Angelo Dr
Beverly Hills, CA 90210-2703, USA

McKyer, Tim (Athlete, Football Player)
11201 Golden Dr
Charlotte, NC 28216, USA

McLachlan, Craig
Box 176
Potts Point, AUSTRALIA NSW 2011

Mclachlan, Murray (Athlete, Hockey Player)
16 Oneida Ct
Chester Springs, PA 19425-2934

McLachlan, Sarah (Musician, Songwriter)
c/o Michael McDonald *Mick Management*
35 Washington St
Brooklyn, NY 11201, USA

McLafferty, Fred W (Scientist)
103 Needham Place
Ithaca, NY 14850, USA

McLagien, Andrew V (Director)
Stanmore Productions
PO Box 1056
Friday Harbor, WA 98250, USA

McLaglen, Andrew (Director)
Box 1056
Friday Harbor, WA 98250, USA

McLain, Denny (Athlete, Baseball Player)
4432 Golf View Dr
Brighton, MI 48116-9187, USA

McLain, Kevin (Athlete, Football Player)
2551 State St
Apt 222
Carlsbad, CA 92008, USA

McLane, Drayton (Baseball Player, Commentator)
Houston Astros
100 N Apache Dr
Temple, TX 76504-2863, USA

McLane, James P (Jimmy) Jr (Swimmer)
85 Pinckney St
Boston, MA 02114, USA

McLaren, John (Athlete, Baseball Player, Coach)
Seattle Mariners
7942 W Briden Ln
Peoria, AZ 85383-1016, USA

Mclaren, Kyle (Athlete, Hockey Player)
10744 Green Valley Dr
Gilroy, CA 95020-9333

McLaren, Richard (Photographer)
Rocket Photographic
580 Paseo Miramar
Pacific Palisades, CA 90272, USA

McLaren, Sally
28 Berkeley Sq.
London, ENGLAND W1X 6HD

Mclaughlin, Ann (Politician, Secretary)
390 Sopris Mountain Ranch Rd
Basalt, CO 81621-9178, USA

McLaughlin, Audrey (Government Official)
New Democratic Party
House of Commons
Ottawa, ON K1A 0A6, CANADA

McLaughlin, Bo (Athlete, Baseball Player)
536 N Grand
Mesa, AZ 80922.-2500, USA

McLaughlin, Byron (Baseball Player)
Seattle Mariners
7030 Alamitos Ave
San Diego, CA 92154-4764, USA

McLaughlin, Carol (Musician)
Columbia Artists Mgmt Inc
165 W 57th St
New York, NY 10019, USA

Mclaughlin, Dan (Commentator)
45 Ballas Ct
Saint Louis, MO 63131-3000, USA

McLaughlin, Joe (Athlete, Football Player)
65 Pells Fishing Rd
Brewster, MA 02631, USA

McLaughlin, Joey (Athlete, Baseball Player)
1611 S Troost Ave
Tulsa, OK 74120-6615, USA

McLaughlin, John (Athlete, Football Player)
5415 Kansas St
Houston, TX 77007, USA

McLaughlin, John (Government Official)
Central Intelligence Agency
Deputy Director's Office
Washington, DC 20505, USA

McLaughlin, John J (Television Host)
The McLaughlin Group
Oliver Productions Inc
1717 Rhode Island Ave NW #640
Washington, DC 20036, USA

McLaughlin, Mike (Race Car Driver)
PO Box 45
Waterloo, NY 13165, USA

McLean, AJ (Actor, Musician)
c/o Eric Podwall *Podwall Entertainment*
710 N Orlando Ave
Loft 203
Los Angeles, CA 90069, USA

McLean, Barney (Athlete, Skier)
9555 West 59th Avenue
Apt 303
Arvada, CO 80004-5396, USA

McLean, Constance (Stylist)
24572 Harbor View Dr
Unit A
Dana Point, CA 92629-1749, USA

McLean, Deborah (Stylist)
c/o Staff Member *Zenobia Agency Inc*
PO Box 909
Groveland, CA 95321, USA

McLean, Don (Musician, Songwriter, Writer)
c/o Jim Lenz *Paradise Artists*
P.O. Box 1821
Ojai, CA 93024-1821, USA

McLean, Greg (Director)
c/o Staff Member *WME (LA)*
9601 Wilshire Blvd Fl 3
Beverly Hills, CA 90210, USA

McLean, James (Athlete, Golfer)
c/o Jim Lehrman *SFX Golf*
36855 W Main St Ste 200
Purcellville, VA 20132, USA

Mclean, Jeff (Athlete, Hockey Player)
47 Iron Bottom Ln
Daniel Island, SC 29492-8415

McLean, Kirk (Athlete, Hockey Player)
Colorado Avalanche
1000 Chopper Cir
Denver, CO 80204-5805

McLean, Rene (Musician)
Brad Simon Organization
122 E 57th St
#300
New York, NY 10022, USA

McLean, Ron (Athlete, Football Player)
761 Fairmont Ave
Santa Maria, CA 93455, USA

McLean, Sally (Actor, Producer)
c/o Staff Member *Salmac Management*
PO Box 526
Mt Martha VIC 3934, AUSTRALIA

McLean, Scott (Athlete, Football Player)
375 Bear Ln
Lake Placid, FL 33852, USA

McLeary, Marty (Athlete, Baseball Player)
2120 Long Meadow Dr
Spring Hill, TN 37174-7129, USA

Mclellan, Todd (Athlete, Hockey Player)
San Jose Sharks
525 W Santa Clara St
SanJose, CA 95113-1500

Mclellan, Zoe (Actor)
c/o Mandi Warren *Viewpoint Inc. - NY*
700 San Vicente Ave
Suite G910
West Hollywood, CA 90069, USA

Mclelland, Dave (Athlete, Hockey Player)
714 Westminster Ave E
Penticton, BC V2A 1J3, Canada

McLemore, Dana (Athlete, Football Player)
125 Seagate Dr
San Mateo, CA 94403, USA

McLemore, LaMonte (Musician)
Sterling/Winters
10877 Wilshire Blvd
#15
Los Angeles, CA 90024, USA

McLemore, Mark (Athlete, Baseball Player)
533 S White Chapel Blvd
Southlake, TX 76092-7316, USA

McLemore, Mark (Athlete, Baseball Player)
7965 Eagle View Ln
Granite Bay, CA 95746-7333, USA

McLendon-Covey, Wendi (Actor)
c/o John Carrabino *John Carrabino Management*
5900 Wilshire Blvd Fl 4 #406
Los Angeles, CA 90036, USA

Mcleod, Al (Athlete, Hockey Player)
8021 N 14th Ave
Phoenix, AZ 85021-5631

Mcleod, Don (Athlete, Hockey Player)
305 Sylvia Cres
Trail, BC VlR 1A4, Canada

McLeod, George (Athlete, Basketball Player)
834 Greenpark Dr
Houston, TX 77e79-45e2, USA

Mcleod, Jack (Athlete, Hockey Player)
13 John Hair Cres
Saskatoon, SK S7J 2K6, Canada

Mcleod, Jimmy (Athlete, Hockey Player)
3929 NE 78th Ave Apt 10
Portland, OR 97213-6400

McLeod, Robert D (Athlete, Football Player)
600 Spring Creek Rd
Brenham, TX 77833, USA

McLerie, Allyn Ann (Actor, Dancer)
3344 Campanil Dr
Santa Barbara, CA 93109, USA

McLerran, Joshua (Actor)
c/o Staff Member *The Craze Agency*
9176 S. 300 W
Suite 3
Sandy, UT 84070, USA

McIlwain, Dave (Athlete, Hockey Player)
Yacht Club Woods
Grand Bend, ON N0M lT0, Canada

McInally, Pat (Athlete, Football Player)
19321 Ocean Heights Ln
Huntington Beach, CA 92648, USA

McIntyre, Donald C (Opera Singer)
Foxhill Farm
Jackass Lane Keston Bromley
Kent BR2 6AN, UNITED KINGDOM (UK)

McLouth, Nate (Athlete, Baseball Player)
5476 Olds Ln
Whitehall, MI 49461-9355, USA

McIvor, Rick (Athlete, Football Player)
PO Box 148
Fort Davis, TX 79734, USA

McMahan, Jack (Athlete, Baseball Player)
131 Forest View Cir
Hot Springs National Park,
AR 71913-6557, USA

McMahon, Art (Athlete, Football Player)
319 Stearns St Unit 32
Carlisle, MA 01741, USA

McMahon, James R (Jim) (Athlete, Football Player)
22431 N Violetta Dr
Scottsdale, AZ 85255, USA

McMahon, Jenna (Actor)
PO Box 5033
Carmel by the Sea, CA 93921-5033, USA

McMahon, Julian (Actor, Producer)
c/o Will Ward *ROAR (LA)*
9701 Wilshire Blvd
8th Floor
Los Angeles, CA 90212, USA

McMahon, Mike (Athlete, Football Player)
313 Oak Grove Ct
Wexford, PA 15090

McMahon, Shane (Wrestler)
c/o Kerry Rodgerson *World Wrestling Entertainment (WWE)*
Titan Towers
1241 E Main St
Stamford, CT 06905-3857, USA

McMahon, Stephanie (Wrestler)
c/o Kerry Rodgerson *World Wrestling Entertainment (WWE)*
Titan Towers
1241 E Main St
Stamford, CT 06905-3857, USA

McMahon, Jr., Mike (Athlete, Hockey Player)
1475 St. Clair Ave.
#1
St. Paul, MN 55105-2340, USA

McMahon Jr, Vincent (Vince) K (Business Person)
47 Hurtingham Dr
Greenwich, CT 06831, USA

McMakin, John (Athlete, Football Player)
PO Box 863
Anacortes, WA 98221, USA

McMann, Harry (Stylist)
408 N Lakewood Ave
Baltimore, MD 21224-1112, USA

McManus, Don (Actor)
c/o Staff Member *Principal Entertainment (LA)*
1964 Westwood Blvd #400
Los Angeles, CA 90025, USA

McManus, Jim (Athlete, Baseball Player)
2352 Hopkins Mill Rd
Duluth, GA 30096-4524, USA

McManus, Michelle (Musician)

McManus, Rove (Actor, Talk Show Host)
c/o Staff Member *Token*
1st Floor
274 Brunswick St
Fitzroy, Victoria 3065, Australia

McMartin, John (Actor, Musician)
Artists Agency
1180 S Beverly Dr
#301
Los Angeles, CA 90035, USA

McMath, Herb (Athlete, Football Player)
1515 E Glenn Ave
Springfield, IL 62703, USA

McMath, Jimmy (Athlete, Baseball Player)
3321 22nd St
Tuscaloosa, AL 35401, USA

McMenamin, Mark (Misc)
Mount Holyoke College
Geology Dept
South Hadley, MA 01075, USA

McMichael, Greg (Athlete, Baseball Player)
240 Parkside Club Ct
Duluth, GA 30097-7847, USA

McMichael, Randy (Athlete, Football Player)
5503 Highland Preserve Dr
Mableton, GA 30126, USA

McMichael, Steve D (Athlete, Football Player)
1268 Holiday Dr
Somonauk, IL 60552, USA

McMichen, Robert S (Misc)
International Typographical Union
PO Box 157
Colorado Springs, CO 80901, USA

McMillan, Audray (Athlete, Football Player)
1230 Hahlo St
Houston, TX 77020, USA

McMillan, Bob (Athlete, Hockey Player)
P.O Box 909
Sta. Central
Charlottetown, QC C1A BL9, CANADA

McMillan, Caroline (Athlete, Golfer)
5101 N Casa Blanca Dr
Unit 206
Paradise Valley, AZ 85253-6987, USA

McMillan, Caroline (Athlete, Golfer)
7525 E Phantom Way
Scottsdale, AZ 85255, USA

McMillan, Courtenay (Scientist)
1618 Missouri St
Houston, TX 77006-2528, USA

McMillan, Eddie (Athlete, Football Player)
6204 222nd St SW
Mountlake Terrace, WA 98043, USA

McMillan, Erik (Athlete, Football Player)
17209 Chesterfield Airport Rd # 308
Chesterfield, MO 63005, USA

McMillan, Ernie (Athlete, Football Player)
14816 Sycamore Manor Ct
Chesterfield, MO 63017, USA

McMillan, Nate (Athlete, Basketball Player, Coach)
c/o Lonnie Cooper *Career Sports and Entertainment*
600 Galleria Pkwy
Suite 1900
Atlanta, GA 30339, USA

McMillan, Randy (Athlete, Football Player)
6832 Hayley Ridge Way
Baltimore, MD 21209, USA

McMillan, Susan Carpenter
1744 Oak Lane
San Marino, CA 91108

McMillan, Terry (Writer)
PO Box 2408
Danville, CA 94526, USA

McMillan, Todd (Athlete, Football Player)
6113 W Spur Dr
Phoenix, AZ 85083, USA

McMillan, Tommy (Athlete, Baseball Player)
712 Spring Lake Rd
Thomasville, GA 31792-8605, USA

McMillan, William (Bill) (Misc)
1930 Sandstone Vista
Encinitas, CA 92024, USA

McMillen, Robert (Athlete, Olympic Athlete, Track Athlete)
5708 Golden West Ave
Temple City, CA 91780-2503, USA

McMillen, Tom (Athlete, Basketball Player, Olympic Athlete)
1103 S Carolina Ave SE
Washington, DC 20003-2205, USA

McMillian, Audray G (Athlete, Football Player)
1230 Hahlo St
Houston, TX 77020, USA

McMillian, Jim (Athlete, Basketball Player)
179e Polo Rd
Winston Salem, NC 27le6-4541, USA

McMillian, Mark (Athlete, Football Player)
13820 S 44th St
Phoenix, AZ 85044, USA

McMillian, Michael (Actor)
c/o Abby Bluestone *Innovative Artists (LA)*
1505 10th St
Santa Monica, CA 90401, USA

McMillin, James R (Athlete, Football Player)
7985 Westview Dr
Lakewood, CO 80214, USA

McMillon, Billy (Athlete, Baseball Player)
1516 Lost Creek Dr
Columbia, SC 29212-2859, USA

McMonagle, Donald R (Astronaut)
7737 E Shadow Vista Ct
Tucson, AZ 85750, USA

McMonagle, Donald R Colonel (Astronaut)
7737 E Shadow Vista Ct
Tucson, AZ 85750-0742, USA

McMorris, Cathy (Congressman, Politician)
2421 Rayburn HOB
Washington, DC 20515, USA

McMorris, Jerry (Baseball Player)
Colorado Rockies
PO Box 217
Timnath, CO 80547-0217, USA

McMullen, Curtis T (Mathematician)
Harvard University
Science Center
Cambridge, MA 02138, USA

McMullen, Kathy (Athlete, Golfer)
526 Harrison St
Emmaus, PA 18049, USA

McMullen, Ken (Athlete, Baseball Player)
10 Estaban Dr
Camarillo, CA 93010-1610, USA

McMullen, Kirk (Athlete, Football Player)
4108 County Line Rd
Macedon, NY 14502, USA

McMurchy, Tom (Athlete, Hockey Player)
2060 Cape Horn Ave
Coquitlam, BC V3K 1J3, Canada

McMurray, Jamie (Race Car Driver)
211 Milford Circle
Mooresville, NC 28117-7011, USA

McMurray, Sam
11500 W. Olympic Blvd. #510
Los Angeles, CA 90064-1524

McMurray, W Grant (Religious Leader)
Reorganized Church of Latter Day Saints
PO Box 1059
Independence, MO 64051, USA

McMurtry, Craig (Athlete, Baseball Player)
2835 Bottoms East Rd
Troy, TX 76579-3008, USA

McMurtry, Greg (Athlete, Football Player)
755 Oak Point Ln
Madison Heights, MI 48071, USA

McMurtry, James (Musician, Songwriter, Writer)
High Road
751 Bridgeway
#300
Sausalito, CA 94965, USA

McMurtry, Larry (Writer)
PO Box 552
Archer City, TX 76351-0552, USA

McMurtry, Tom (Aviator)
4008 Derby Cir
Lancaster, CA 93536-2400, USA

McNab, Mercedes (Actor)
c/o Jason Egenberg *United Talent Agency (UTA)*
9336 Civic Center Dr
Beverly Hills, CA 90210, USA

McNab, Peter (Athlete, Hockey Player)
10311 Rancho Montecito Dr
Parker, CO 80138-7862

McNab, Peter (Athlete, Hockey Player)
Colorado Avalanche
1000 Chopper Cir
_Denver, CO 80204-5805

McNabb, Dexter (Athlete, Football Player)
1449 Pat Tillman St
De Pere, WI 54115, USA

McNabb, Donovan (Athlete, Football Player)
c/o Fletcher Smith *Blueprint Sports Group*
221 W. Jefferson Ave
Naperville, IL 60540, USA

McNair, Kelly (Actor)
c/o Staff Member *GVA Talent Agency Inc*
8981 Sunset Blvd.
Suite 101
Los Angeles, CA 90069, USA

McNair, Sylvia (Opera Singer)
Kunstleragentur Raab & Bohm
Plankengasse 7
Vienna 1010, AUSTRIA

McNairy, Scoot (Actor)
c/o Mia Hansen *MLC PR*
7080 Hollywood Blvd
Suite 903
Los Angeles, CA 90028, USA

McNally, Kevin (Actor)
c/o Mark A. Schlegel *Cornerstone Talent Agency*
37 W 20th St
New York, NY 10011, USA

McNally, Stephen (Ste) (Musician)
Day Time
Crown House
225 Kensington High St
London W8 8SA, UNITED KINGDOM (UK)

McNally, Terrence (Writer)
c/o Jonathan Lomma *WME (LA)*
9601 Wilshire Blvd Fl 3
Beverly Hills, CA 90210, USA

McNamara, Bob (Athlete, Football Player)
4909 Prescott Cir
Minneapolis, MN 55436, USA

McNamara, Brian (Actor)
c/o Staff Member *Pathway Entertainment*
1739 Berkeley St #110C
Santa Monica, CA 90404, USA

McNamara, Eileen (Journalist)
Boston Globe
Editorial Dept
135 W T Morrissey Blvd
Dorchester, MA 02125, USA

McNamara, Jim (Baseball Player)
San Francisco Giants
15317 Surrey House Way
Centreville, VA 20120-1196, USA

McNamara, John (Athlete, Baseball Player, Coach)
1206 Beech Hill Rd
Brentwood, TN 37027-5530, USA

McNamara, John F (Athlete, Baseball Player)
15317 Surrey House Way
Centreville, VA 20120, USA

McNamara, Julianne L (Actor, Gymnast)
Barry Axelrod
2236 Encinitas Blvd
#A
Encinitas, CA 92024, USA

McNamara, Julie (Business Person)
c/o Staff Member *CBS Paramount Network Television*
CBS Studios
4024 Radford Ave
Studio City, CA 91604, USA

McNamara, Katherine (Actor)
c/o Bonnie Liedtke *Principato/Young Management*
9465 Wilshire Blvd
Suite 430
Beverly Hills, CA 90212, USA

McNamara, Mark
PO Box 134
Strawberry, CA 95375-e134, USA

McNamara, Melissa (Athlete, Golfer)
7715 S Quebec Ave
Tulsa, OK 74136, USA

McNamara, William (Actor)
c/o Frederick Levy *Management 101*
11271 Ventura Blvd
#102
Studio City, CA 91604, USA

McNamee, Peter (Athlete, Hockey Player)
47 Rolling Acres Dr
Whitby, ON LlR 2Al, Canada

McNanie, Sean (Athlete, Football Player)
14915 Rancho Real
Del Mar, CA 92014, USA

McNaught, Erin (Beauty Pageant Winner)
c/o Ursula Hufnagl *Chic Management*
36 Jersey Road
Woollahra NSW 2025, AUSTRALIA

McNaught, Judith (Writer)
Pocket Books
1230 Ave of Americas
New York, NY 10020, USA

McNaughton, John D (Director)
1370 N Milwaukee Ave
Chicago, IL 60622, USA

McNaughton, Robert F Jr (Scientist)
2511 15th St
Troy, NY 12180, USA

McNeal, Donald (Don) (Athlete, Football Player)
3311 Toledo Plz
Coral Gables, FL 33134, USA

McNeal, Krista (Beauty Pageant Winner)
NW Pageants
12708 Northrup Hwy #101
Bellevue, WA 98005, USA

McNeal, Travis (Athlete, Football Player)
4707 40th Pl N
Birmingham, AL 35217, USA

McNealey, Christopher (Athlete, Basketball Player)
30 Shady Oak Ct
Danville, CA 945e6-6145, USA

McNealy, Rusty (Athlete, Baseball Player)
3301 Bozeman St
Sacramento, CA 95838-4105, USA

McNealy, Scott (Business Person)
Sun Microsystems
4150 Network Circle
Santa Clara, CA 95054, USA

McNeeley, Big Jay (Misc)
Ray Lawrence
PO Box 1967
Studio City, CA 91614, USA

McNeely, Jeff (Athlete, Baseball Player)
405 Everette St
Monroe, NC 28112-5622, USA

McNeely, Tom (Artist)
9 Blythwood Gardens
Toronto, ON M4N 3L2, Canada

McNeice, Ian (Actor)
c/o Renee Jennett *Renee Jennett Management*
5757 Wilshire Blvd #473
Los Angeles, CA 90036, USA

McNeil, Clifton (Athlete, Football Player)
1001 Westbury Dr
Mobile, AL 36609, USA

McNeil, Emanuel (Athlete, Football Player)
2 University Ct Apt G17
Martin, TN 38237, USA

McNeil, Frederick A (Fred) (Athlete, Football Player)
9667 W Olympic Blvd
Apt 5
Beverly Hills, CA 90212, USA

McNeil, Freeman (Athlete, Football Player)
52 Dunlop Rd
Huntington, NY 11743, USA

McNeil, Gerald (Athlete, Football Player)
215 Haven Brook Ln
Richmond, TX 77406, USA

McNeil, Kate (Actor)
1743 N Dillon St
Los Angeles, CA 90026, USA

McNeil, Lori (Tennis Player)
Int'l Mgmt Group
1 Erieview Plaza
1360 E 9th St #1300
Cleveland, OH 44114, USA

McNeil, Mike (Athlete, Hockey Player)
1723 Bader Ave.
South Bend, IN 46617, USA

McNeil, Pat (Athlete, Football Player)
2117 US Highway 80 E
Mesquite, TX 75150, USA

McNeil, Ryan (Athlete, Football Player)
4702 Avenue Q
Fort Pierce, FL 34947, USA

McNeill, Bill (Athlete, Hockey Player)
8-1711 -l40th St.
Surrey, BC B4A 4H1, CANADA

McNeill, Fred (Athlete, Football Player)
801 E Walnut St Apt 1502
Pasadena, CA 91101, USA

McNeill, Mike (Athlete, Hockey Player)
52425 Spring Wood Ct
Granger, IN 46530-7438

McNeill, Robert (Athlete, Basketball Player)
1318 Wooded Way
Wayne, PA 19ele-1781, USA

McNeill, Rod (Athlete, Football Player)
1048 S Magnolia Ave
West Covina, CA 91791, USA

McNeill, Stu (Athlete, Hockey Player)
1840 StDenis Pl
West Vancouver, BC V7V 3W7, Canada

McNeill, Tom (Athlete, Football Player)
31019 Torrey Rd
Waller, TX 77484, USA

McNeill, W Donald (Don) (Tennis Player)
2165 15th Ave
Vero Beach, FL 32960, USA

McNeish, Richard (Archaeologist)
Andover Archaeology Research Foundation
1 Woodland Road
Andover, MA 01810, USA

McNell, Rufus (Baseball Player)
Indianapolis Clowns
205 Heard St
Kingston, NC 28501-5850, USA

McNerney, David H (War Hero)
20322 New Moon Trail
Crosby, TX 77532, USA

McNerney, Jerry (Congressman, Politician)
1210 Longworth HOB
Washington, DC 20515, USA

McNerney, Moisette (Stylist)
711 S Ridge Ave
Arlington Heights, IL 60005, USA

McNertney, Jerry (Athlete, Baseball Player)
112410th St
Nevada, IA 50201-1708, USA

McNett, Wendy (Stylist)
c/o Sydney Oliver *Oliver Piro Inc*
725 Riverside Dr Apt 3A
New York, NY 10031, USA

McNichol, Brian (Athlete, Baseball Player)
3511 E Merlot St
Gilber, AZ 85298-9264, USA

McNichol, Kristy (Actor)
c/o Staff Member *Good Guy Entertainment*
3733 Oakfield Dr
Sherman Oaks, CA 91423, USA

McNichols, Stephen (Politician)
6481 S Kearney Cir
Centennial, CO 80111-4315, USA

McNorton, Bruce (Athlete, Football Player)
P.O. Box 672
Bloomfield Hills, MI 48303, USA

McNown, Cade (Athlete, Football Player)
200 Lorraine Blvd
Los Angeles, CA 90004, USA

McNulty, Bill (Athlete, Baseball Player)
32716 74th Avenue Ct E
Eatonville, WA 98328-8967, USA

McNulty, Carl (Athlete, Basketball Player)
212 Westmoreland Dr E
Kokomo, IN 469el-5155, USA

McPartlin, Ant (Television Host)
c/o Kevin McLaughlin *Baker Winokur Ryder Public Relations (BWR-LA)*
9100 Wilshire Blvd
Suite 500, West Tower
Beverly Hills, CA 90212, USA

McPartlin, Ryan (Actor)
c/o Miles Levy *James/Levy/Jacobson Management Inc*
3500 W Olive Ave
Suite 1470
Burbank, CA 91505, USA

McPartlnad, Marian M (Musician)
Abby Hoffer
223 1/2 E 48th St
New York, NY 10017, USA

McPeak, Holly (Athlete, Volleyball Player)
1400 The Strand
Manhattan Beach, CA 90266, USA

McPeak, Merrill (General)
123 Furnace St
Lake Oswego, OR 97034-3954, USA

McPeak, Merrill A (Tony) (General)
123 Furnace St
Lake Oswego, OR 97034-3954, USA

McPhail, Coleman (Athlete, Football Player)
104 Flagstone Ct
Chapel Hill, NC 27517, USA

McPhail, Jerris (Athlete, Football Player)
1820 Lake Glen Dr
Fuquay Varina, NC 27526, USA

McPhee, George (Athlete, Hockey Player)
6723 Landon Ln
Bethesda, MD 20817-5639

McPhee, George (Athlete, Hockey Player)
Washington Capitals
627 N Glebe Rd Ste 850
Arlington, VA 22203-2144

McPhee, John A (Writer)
475 Drake's Corner Road
Princeton, NJ 08540, USA

McPhee, Katharine (Musician, Reality TV Star)
c/o David Schiff *The Schiff Company*
9465 Wilshire Blvd
Suite 480
Beverly Hills, CA 90212, USA

McPhee, Mike (Athlete, Hockey Player)
16 Brook Point Rd
Tantallon, NS B3Z 2R3, Canada

McPherson, Charles (Misc)
Joel Chriss
300 Mercer St
#3J
New York, NY 10003, USA

McPherson, Dallas (Athlete, Baseball Player)
133 Shellbark Dr
McDonough, GA 30252-1622, USA

McPherson, Don (Athlete, Football Player)
3 Salem Ridge Dr
Huntington, NY 11743, USA

McPherson, Donald (General, War Hero)
629 8th St
Adams, NE 68301-6012, USA

McPherson, James (Writer)
Little Brown And Company
3 centre plz ste 100
Boston, MA 02108-2084, USA

McPherson, James M (Historian)
15 Randall Road
Princeton, NJ 08540, USA

McPherson, John (Cartoonist)
Universal Press Syndicate
4520 Main St
Kansas City, MO 64111, USA

McPherson, Miles (Athlete, Football Player)
12088 Avenida Sivrita
San Diego, CA 92128, USA

McPherson, M Peter (Educator)
Michigan State University
President's Office
East Lansing, MI 48824, USA

McQuagg, Sam (Race Car Driver)
8886 Hamilton Road
Midland, GA 31820, USA

McQuarrie, Christopher (Director, Producer)
c/o Ken Kamins *Key Creatives*
1800 N Highland Ave
Suite 500
Los Angeles, CA 90028, USA

McQuarters, R W (Athlete, Football Player)
1548 E 54th St N
Tulsa, OK 74126, USA

McQueen, Chad (Actor)
c/o Staff Member *MSI Entertainment*
9229 Sunset Blvd #710
Los Angeles, CA 90069, USA

McQueen, Cozell (Athlete, Basketball Player)
100 E Charing Cross
Cary, NC 27513-3e24, USA

McQueen, Mike (Athlete, Baseball Player)
15018 Marlebone Dr
Houston, TX 77069-2022, USA

Mcqueen, Sam (Race Car Driver)
8866 Hamilton Rd
Midland, GA 31820, USA

McQueen, Steven R (Actor)
c/o Risa Shapiro *Schiff Company, The*
9465 Wilshire Blvd
Suite 480
Beverly Hills, CA 90212, USA

McQueen, Steve R (Director, Writer)
c/o Maha Dakhil *Creative Artists Agency (CAA-LA)*
2000 Ave Of The Stars
Los Angeles, CA 90067, USA

McQueeney, Barbara (Stylist)
c/o Staff Member *Campbell Agency, The*
3838 Oak Lawn Ave
Suite 900
Dallas, TX 75219-4510, USA

McQuilken, Kim (Athlete, Football Player)
801 Moore Rd
Newnan, GA 30263, USA

McRae, Basil (Athlete, Hockey Player)
Basil McRae and Associates
759 Hyde Park Rd Suite 252
London, ON N6H 3S2, Canada

McRae, Bennie (Athlete, Football Player)
532 W 143rd St Apt 63
New York, NY 10031, USA

McRae, Brian (Athlete, Baseball Player)
6721 W 121st St
Leawood, KS 66209-2003, 34212

McRae, Charles (Athlete, Football Player)
601 Self Hollow Rd
Rockford, TN 37853, USA

McRae, Donyale (Stylist)
c/o Staff Member *Montana Artists Agency*
9150 Wilshire Blvd Ste 100
Beverly Hills, CA 90212, USA

McRae, Frank (Actor)
Marshak/Zachary Company
8840 Wilshire Blvd 1st Fl
Beverly Hills, CA 90211, USA

McRae, Gord (Athlete, Hockey Player)
8168 S Wabash Ct
Centennial, CO 80112-3329

McRae, Hal (Athlete, Baseball Player, Coach)
519 Sand Crane Ct
Bradenton, FL 34212-6203, USA

McRae, Jerrold (Athlete, Football Player)
208 Grovedale Trce
Antioch, TN 37013, USA

McRae, Mo (Actor)
c/o Staff Member *Harrison Stokes*
8730 W. Sunset Blvd
Suite 270
West Hollywood, CA 90069, USA

McRae, Tom (Musician)
c/o Staff Member *Paradigm (Monterey)*
404 W Franklin St
Monterey, CA 93940, USA

McRaney, Gerald (Actor)
4270 Farmdale Ave
Studio City, CA 91604, USA

McReynolds, Jesse (Musician)
J&J Music
P.O. Box 1385
Gallatin, TN 37066, USA

McReynolds, Kevin (Athlete, Baseball Player)
2 Country Pl
Roland, AZ 72135-9763, USA

McReynolds, Larry (Race Car Driver)
123 Mystic Lake Loop
Mooresville, NC 28117-9408, USA

McReynolds, Madison (Actor)
c/o Bonnie Ventis *Clear Talent Group (LA)*
10950 Ventura Blvd
Studio City, CA 91604, USA

McRoberts, James (Aviator)
5430 Lake Washington Blvd SE
Bellevue, WA 98006-2643, USA

McRoy, Spike (Athlete, Golfer)
15019 Collier Dr SE
Huntsville, AL 35803-3631, USA

McShane, Ian (Actor)
c/o Staff Member *McShane Productions*
New Bridge Street House
30 New Bridge St
London EC4V 6BJ, UNITED KINGDOM
(UK)

McShane, Jamie (Actor)
c/o Staff Member *Select Artists Ltd (CA-Westside Office)*
1138 12th Street
Suite 1
Santa Monica, CA 90403, USA

McShane, Jennifer (Jenny) (Actor)
c/o Laura Pallas *Pallas Management*
5301 Bellaire Ave
Valley Vilage, CA 91607, US

McShane, Michael (Actor)
c/o Maureen Vincent *United Agents*
Drury House
34-43 Russell St
London WC2B 5HA, UK

McShann, James C (Jay) (Musician)
Ozark Talent
718 Schwarz Road
Lawrence, KS 66049, USA

McSheffrey, Bryan (Athlete, Hockey Player)
PO Box 866 Stn Main
Renfrew, ON K7V 4H3, Canada

McSorley, Gerard (Actor)
c/o Staff Member *Insight*
1134 S Cloverdale Ave
Los Angeles, CA 90019, USA

McSorley, Marty (Athlete, Hockey Player)
3301 the Strand
Hermosa Beach, CA 90254-2053

McSwain, Chuck (Athlete, Football Player)
PO Box 603
Caroleen, NC 28019, USA

McSwain, Rod (Athlete, Football Player)
5393 Stonewood Dr
Hickory, NC 28602, USA

McSween, Don (Athlete, Hockey Player)
4954 Glen Meadow Ct SE
Grand Rapids, MI 49546-7927

McSween, John (Athlete, Hockey Player)
4954 Glen Meadows Ct. St.
Grand Rapids, MI 49546, USA

McSweeney, Alex
c/o Staff Member *EastEnders*
1 Mortimer St
London W1T 3JA, UNITED KINGDOM

McTaggart, Jim (Athlete, Hockey Player)
Seattle Thunderbirds
625 W James St
Kent, WA 98032-4406

McTavish, Gord (Athlete, Hockey Player)
McTavish Design
13 Nanaimo Dr
Ottawa, ON K2H 6X6, Canada

McTeer, Janet (Actor)
c/o Michael Foster *The Rights House (UK)*
Drury House
34-43 Russell St
London WC2B 5HA, UK

McTeer Jr, Robert D (Financier, Government Official)
National Center for Policy Analysis
601 Pennsylvania Avenue NW
Suite 900, South Building
Washington, DC 20004, USA

McTeigue, James (Director)
c/o Lawrence Mattis *Circle of Confusion (NY)*
107-23 71st Rd #300
Forest Hills, NY 11375, USA

McTiernan, John C (Director)
The Firm
9100 Wilshire Blvd
#100W
Beverly Hills, CA 90210, USA

McVay, John (Athlete, Football Coach, Football Player)
7300 Sierra Dr
Granite Bay, CA 95746, USA

McVeigh, John (Athlete, Football Player)
1404 W Beach Dr
Panama City, FL 32401, USA

McVey, Robert (Athlete, Hockey Player, Olympic Athlete)
3333 NE 34th St Apt 1522
Fort Lauderdale, FL 33308-6914, USA

McVicar, Daniel (Actor)
1704 Oak St
Santa Monica, CA 90405, USA

McVie, Christine (Actor, Musician)
c/o Staff Member *Sugaroo! LLC*
3650 Helms Ave
Culver City, CA 90232, USA

McVie, John (Musician, Songwriter)
3124 Noela St
Honolulu, HI 96815, USA

McVie, Tom (Athlete, Hockey Player)
3013 SE Spyglass Dr
Vancouver, WA 98683-3704

McWashington, Shawn (Athlete, Football Player)
3400 S King St
Seattle, WA 98144, USA

McWatters, Bill (Athlete, Football Player)
3300 Thornway Dr
Columbus, OH 43231, USA

McWethy, John F (Correspondent)
4850 Meredith Way
Apt 304
Boulder, CO 80303-9105, USA

McWilliam, Edward (Artist)
8A Holland Villas Road
London W14 8DP, UNITED KINGDOM
(UK)

McWilliams, David (Football Executive, Football Player)
University of Texas
Athletic Dept
Austlin, TX 78712, USA

McWilliams, Eric (Athlete, Basketball Player)
798 Hearst Way
Corona, CA 92882-6396, USA

McWilliams, John (Athlete, Football Player)
4540 E Blue Spruce Ln
Gilbert, AZ 85298-4637, USA

McWilliams, Larry (Athlete, Baseball Player)
4102 Becklev Ct
Collevville, TX 76034-4670, USA

McWilliams, Robert H (Judge)
US COurt of Appeals
US Courthouse
1929 Stout St
Denver, CO 80294, USA

MDO (Music Group)
c/o Staff Member *Sony Music Miami*
605 Lincoln Rd Fl 7
Miami Beach, FL 33139, USA

Meacham, Bobby (Athlete, Baseball Player)
20610 Prince Creek Dr
Katy, TX 77450-4908, USA

Meacham, Jon (Editor, Writer)
c/o Staff Member *Royce Carlton*
866 United Nations Plaza
Suite 587
New York, NY 10017, USA

Meacham, Mildred (Athlete, Baseball Player, Commentator)
4027 Winedale Ln
Charlotte, NC 28205-4524, USA

Meacham, Rusty (Athlete, Baseball Player)
1906 Eden Glen Ln
Pearland, TX 77581-1700, USA

Mead, Amber (Actor)
c/o Courtney Kivowitz *Schiff Company, The*
9465 Wilshire Blvd
Suite 480
Beverly Hills, CA 90212, USA

Mead, Carver (Inventor)
PO Box 620204
Redwood City, CA 94062-0204, USA

Mead, Charlie (Athlete, Baseball Player)
7482 Svl Box
Victorville, CA 92395-5157, USA

Mead, John (Athlete, Football Player)
401 Westwood Dr
Apt 2
Sister Bay, WI 54234, USA

Mead, Matt (Governor, Politician)
State Capitol
200 W 24th St
Cheyenne, WY 82002-0010, USA

Mead, Richelle (Writer)
c/o Staff Member *Kensington Publishing Corp.*
119 W 40th St
New York, NY 10018, USA

Mead, Shepherd (Writer)
53 Rivermead Court
London SW6 3RY, UNITED KINGDOM
(UK)

Meade, Carl J (Astronaut)
5711 Blenveneda Terrace
Palmdale, CA 93551, USA

Meade, Carl J Colonel (Astronaut)
15013 Live Oak Springs Canyon Rd
Canyon Country, CA 91387-4804, USA

Meade, Glenn (Writer)
Saint Martin's Press
175 5th Ave
New York, NY 10010, USA

Meade, Julia
1010 Fifth Ave.
New York, NY 10021

Meade, Robin (Television Host)
CNN Headline News
100 International Blvd NW
Atlanta, GA 30303, USA

Meaden, Deborah (Business Person, Talk Show Host)
Moortown Lane
Curry Rivel
Langport, Somerset TA10 0AB, United Kingdom

Meador, Eddle D (Ed) (Athlete, Football Player)
1135 Padgett Hill Rd
Natural Bridge, VA 24578, USA

Meador, Vaughn
1096 Middle 2 Rock Rd.
Petaluma, CA 94952

Meadows, Bernard W (Artist)
34 Belsize Grove
London NW3, UNITED KINGDOM (UK)

Meadows, Brian (Athlete, Baseball Player)
218 Palos Verdes Dr
Troy, AL 36079-1701, USA

Meadows, Jayne (Actor)
16185 Woodvale Road
Encino, CA 91436, USA

Meadows, Louie (Athlete, Baseball Player)
110 Heavens Ln
Maysville, NC 28555-9479, USA

Meadows, Stephen (Actor)
1760 Courtney Ave
Los Angeles, CA 90046, USA

Meadows, Tim (Actor, Comedian)
c/o Geoff Cheddy *Brillstein Entertainment Partners*
9150 Wilshire Blvd #350
Beverly Hills, CA 90212, USA

Meads, Dave (Athlete, Baseball Player)
3220 Cypress Way
Santa Rosa, CA 95405-7512, USA

Meads, Johnny (Athlete, Football Player)
9419 Pine Lilly Ct
Navarre, FL 32566, USA

Meagher, Mary T (Athlete, Olympic Athlete, Swimmer)
404 Vanderwall
Peachtree City, GA 30269-3335, USA

Meagher, Rick (Athlete, Hockey Player)
2698 Innisfil Rd
Mississauga, ON L5M 4J2, Canada

Mealey, Rondell (Athlete, Football Player)
2952 N Nobile St
Paulina, LA 70763, USA

Meals, Gerald (Baseball Player)
2164 Shamrock Arbor Dr
Salem, OH 44460-7639, USA

Meals, Gerry (Athlete, Baseball Player)
2164 Shamrock Arbor Dr
Salem, OH 44460-1723, USA

Meamber, Tim (Athlete, Football Player)
3410 Grant St
Vancouver, WA 98660, USA

Meaney, Colm (Actor)
11921 Laurel Hills Road
Studio City, CA 91604, USA

Meaney, Kevin (Actor, Comedian)
28 Beech Lane
Tarrytown, NY 10591, USA

Means, Jimmy (Race Car Driver)
Jimmy Means Racing
102 Greenbriar Dr
Forest City, NC 28042, USA

Means, Marianne (Journalist)
2555 Pennsylvania Ave NW Apt 902
Washington, DC 20037-1637, USA

Means, Natrone J (Athlete, Football Player)
14602 Greenpoint Ln
Huntersville, NC 28078, USA

Means, Winslow (Athlete, Basketball Player)
1336 Arch St
Zanesville, OH 437el-5714, USA

Meany, Charlie (Actor)

Meara, Anne (Actor, Comedian)
c/o Staff Member *Innovative Artists (LA)*
1505 10th St
Santa Monica, CA 90401, USA

Meares, Pat (Athlete, Baseball Player)
8405 E Bridlewood St
Wichita, KS 67206-4408, USA

Mears, Casey (Race Car Driver)
c/o Staff Member *Valvoline*
P.O. Box 14000
Lexington, KY 40512, USA

Mears, Clint (Race Car Driver)
Team Mears
416 W. Fairview Rd
Bakersfield, CA 93307, USA

Mears, Derek (Actor)
c/o Staff Member *Kazarian Spencer Ruskin & Assoc.*
11969 Ventura Blvd
3rd Floor
Studio City, CA 91604, USA

Mears, Gary (Musician)
12170 Country Road 215
Tyler, TX 75707, USA

Mears, Rick (Race Car Driver)
204 Spyglass Lane
Jupiter, FL 33477, USA

Mears, Roger (Race Car Driver)
PO Box 520
Terell, NC 28682, USA

Mears, Walter R (Journalist)
Associated Press
Editorial Dept
2021 K St NW
Washington, DC 20006, USA

Mebane, Brandon (Athlete, Football Player)
2310 SE 2nd Ct
Renton, WA 98056, USA

Mecchi, Irene (Actor)
c/o Staff Member *WME (LA)*
9601 Wilshire Blvd Fl 3
Beverly Hills, CA 90210, USA

Mechalides, Louie (Race Car Driver)
8 Davis St.
Tyngsboro, MA 01879, USA

Meche, Gil (Athlete, Baseball Player)
PO Box 932
Scott, LA 70583-0932, USA

Mechlowicz, Scott (Actor)
c/o Eric Kranzler *Management 360*
9111 Wilshire Blvd
Beverly Hills, CA 90210, USA

Mechoso, Julio Oscar (Actor)
c/o Staff Member *Gage Group, The (LA)*
14724 Ventura Blvd
Suite 505
Sherman Oaks, CA 91403, USA

Meciar, Vladimir (Prime Minister)
Urad Vlady SR
Nam Slobody 1
Bratislava 81370, SLOVAKIA

Mecir, Jim (Athlete, Baseball Player)
21219 W Creekside Dr
Kildeer, IL 60047-7847, USA

Mecir, Miloslav (Tennis Player)
Julova 1
Bratislava 83101, CZECH REPUBLIC

Mecklenburg, Karl (Football Player)
6372 S Zenobia Ct
Littleton, CO 80123-6740, USA

Mecko, Joe (Athlete, Baseball Player)
2219 Temoleton Dr
Arlington, TX 76006-5769, USA

Medak, Peter (Director)
c/o Jon Brown *Ensemble Entertainment*
10474 Santa Monica Blvd #380
Los Angeles, CA 90025, USA

Medaris, J Bruce (General)
Po Box 415
Fem Park, FL 32751, USA

Medavoy, Mike (Producer)
c/o Staff Member *Phoenix Pictures*
10202 W Washington Blvd
Frankovich Bldg
Culver City, CA 90232, USA

Medcalf, Kim (Actor)
London Mgmt
2-4 Noel St
London W1V 3RB, UNITED KINGDOM (UK)

Medders, Brandon (Athlete, Baseball Player)
9732 Charolais Dr
Tuscaloosa, AL 35405-9771, USA

Meddick, Jim (Cartoonist)
United Feature Syndicate
200 Madison Ave
New York, NY 10016, USA

Meddine, Raya (Actor)
c/o Audrey Caan *Audrey Caan Management*
8665 Burton Way
Suite 520
Los Angeles, CA 90048, USA

Medearis, Angela Shelf (Chef, Writer)
c/o Staff Member *Diva Productions, Inc*
P.O. Box 91625
Austin, TX 78709-1625, USA

Medeiros, Glenn (Musician)
PO Box 8
Lawai, HI 96765, USA

Medgyessy, Peter (Prime Minister)
Prime Minister's Office
Kossuth Lajos Ter 1-3
Budapest 1055, HUNGARY

Mediate, Rocco (Athlete, Golfer)
8425 NE 12th St
Medina, WA 98039, USA

Medich, George Doc (Athlete, Baseball Player)
3007 Woodfield Dr
Aliquippa, PA 15001-1163, USA

Medieros-Baker, Deborah (Stylist)
c/o Staff Member *Ken Barboza Associates*
115 W 30th St Rm 203
New York, NY 10001, USA

Medina, Benny (Producer)
c/o Staff Member *Handprint Entertainment*
1100 Glendon Ave #100
Los Angeles, CA 90024-3593, USA

Medina, Luis (Athlete, Baseball Player)
16630 S Mountain Stone Trl
Phoenix, AZ 85048-2081, USA

Medina, Rafael (Baseball Player)
Florida Marlins
2964 Peachtree Road Apt 330
Kissimmee, FL 33015-3423, USA

Medina Estevez, Jorge Arturo Cardinal (Religious Leader)
Congregation for Divine Worship
Vatican City 00120, VATICAN CITY

Medlen, Kris (Athlete, Baseball Player)
6633 Sutherland St
Abilene, TX 79606-1635, USA

Medley, Bill (Musician)
c/o Staff Member *WmE2 (WMA-LA)*
1 William Morris Pl
Beverly Hills, CA 90212, USA

Medley, Charles R O (Artist)
Charterhouse
Charterhouse Square
London EC1M 6AN, UNITED KINGDOM (UK)

Medlin, Dan (Athlete, Football Player)
712 Guilford Rd
Jamestown, NC 27282, USA

Medlock, Mark (Musician)
Postfach 206143
Berlin 13537, GERMANY

Medrano, Frank (Actor)
c/o Kate Ward *Ward Agency*
1617 N El Centro Ave #15
Hollywood, CA 90028, USA

Medress, Henry (Musician)
Brothers Mgmt
141 Dunbar Ave
Fords, NJ 08863, USA

Medved, Aleksandr V (Wrestler)
Central Soviet Sports Federation
Skatertny p 4
Moscow, RUSSIA

Medved, David (Journalist)
8501 SE 82nd St
Mercer Island, WA 98040-5642, USA

Medved, Michael (Radio Personality, Writer)
c/o Staff Member *Greater Talent Network Inc*
437 Fifth Ave
7th Floor
New York, NY 10016, USA

Medved, Ron (Athlete, Football Player)
6615 239th Ave E
Buckley, WA 98321, USA

Medvedenko, Stanislav (Athlete, Basketball Player)
5721 S Crescent Park #404
Playa Vista, CA 90094-4002, USA

Medvedev, Zhores A (Biologist)
4 Osborn Gardens
London NW7 1DY, UNITED KINGDOM (UK)

Medvin, Scott (Athlete, Baseball Player)
673 Lynbrook Ave
Tonawanda, NY 14150-7309, USA

Medwin, Michael (Actor)
International Creative Mgmt
76 Oxford St
London W1N 0AX, UNITED KINGDOM (UK)

Mee, Darnell (Athlete, Basketball Player)
2005 Westland Dr SW
Apt 708
Cleveland, TN 37311-818e, USA

Meehan, Gerry (Athlete, Hockey Player)
2 Dafoe Crt
Aurora, ON L4G 7C8, Canada

Meehan, Greg (Athlete, Football Player)
1511 Verde Ridge Ln
Westlake Village, CA 91361, USA

Meehan, Kim (Stylist)
c/o Staff Member *Walter Schupfer Management Corp*
413 W 14th St
3rd Floor
New York, NY 10014, USA

Meehan, Patrick (Congressman, Politician)
613 Cannon HOB
Washington, DC 20515, USA

Meehan, Thomas E (Musician, Writer)
Brook House
Obtuse Road
Newtown, CT 06470, USA

Meehl, Paul E (Misc)
1544 E River Terrace
Minneapolis, MN 55414, USA

Meek, Carrie (Politician)
6830 NW 28th Ave
Miami, FL 33147-6766, USA

Meek, Heidi (Stylist)
c/o Celebrity Stylist *Cloutier Agency*
2632 La Cienega Ave
Los Angeles, CA 90034, USA

Meek, Jeffrey
c/o Anne Geddes *Geddes Agency, The*
8430 Santa Monica Blvd
Suite 200
Los Angeles, CA 90069, USA

Meeke, Brent (Athlete, Hockey Player)
11331 Whitetail Run St. NW
Bolivar, OH 44612-9230

Meeker, Howie (Athlete, Hockey Player, Sportscaster)
979 Dickinson Way
Parksville, BC V9P 1Z7, Canada

Meeks, Aaron (Actor)
c/o Staff Member *Showtime Networks (LA)*
10880 Wilshire Blvd #1600
Los Angeles, CA 90024, USA

Meeks, Bob (Athlete, Football Player)
PO Box 29734
Denver, CO 80229, USA

Meeler, Phil (Athlete, Baseball Player)
102 Pine St
Knightdale, NC 27545-9443, USA

Meely, Cliff (Athlete, Basketball Player)
3240 Iris Ave
Apt 204
Boulder, CO 8e3el-1969, USA

Meena (Actor, Bollywood)
58 Second Street
Venkatesh Nagar
Chennai, TN 600093, INDIA

Meents, Scott (Athlete, Basketball Player)
4231 155th Pl SE
Bellevue, WA 98ee6-2579, USA

Meese (Music Group)
c/o Staff Member *Red Light Management (LA)*
8439 W Sunset Blvd
Suite 2
Los Angeles, CA 90069, USA

Meese, edwin (Politician)
1075 Spring Hill Rd
Me Lean, VA 22102-2304, USA

Meese, Edwin III (Attorney, Attorney General, General)
1075 Springhill Road
McLean, VA 22102, USA

Meester, Brad (Athlete, Football Player)
7644 Chipwood Ln
Jacksonville, FL 32256, USA

Meester, Leighton (Actor)
c/o Loch Powell *Leverage Management*
3030 Pennsylvania Ave
Santa Monica, CA 90404, USA

Meeuwsen, Terry (Religious Leader, Television Host)
c/o 700 Club *Christian Broadcasting Network (CBN)*
977 Centerville Tpke
Virginia Beach, VA 23464, USA

Me First And The Gimme Gimmes (Music Group)
c/o Staff Member *Fat Wreck Chords*
PO Box 193690
San Francisco, CA 94119, USA

Meger, Paul (Athlete, Hockey Player)
215-140 Letitia St.
Barrie, ON L4N 1P5, CANADA

Meggett, Dave (Athlete, Football Player)
Lieber Correctional Institute
PO Box 205
SCDC ID: 00343610
Ridgeville, SC 29472, USA

Meggysey, Dave (Athlete, Football Player)
2528 Benvenue Ave
Berkeley, CA 94704, USA

Megrew, Mike (Athlete, Baseball Player)
25 Karen Dr
25 Karen Dr, RI 02832-1267, USA

Meher, Bill (Comedian, Correspondent)
Agency for Performing Arts
9200 Sunset Blvd
#900
Los Angeles, CA 90069, USA

Mehl, Lance A (Athlete, Football Player)
44920 Kacsmar Estates Dr
Saint Clairsville, OH 43950, USA

Mehra, Prakash (Bollywood, Director, Filmmaker, Producer)
30 Sumeet Bangalow 11th Road
JVPD Scheme
Bombay, MS 400 049, INDIA

Mehra, Smirti (Athlete, Golfer)
4038 Greystone Drive
Clermont, FL 34711-7197, USA

Mehrabian, Robert (Educator)
Carnegie Mellon University
President's Office
Pittsburgh, PA 15213, USA

Mehregany, Mehran (Engineer)
Case Western Reserve University
Electrical Engineer Dept
Cleveland, OH 44106, USA

Mehringer, David M (Astronomer)
University of Illinois
Astronomy Dept
Champaign, IL 61820, USA

Mehta, Shailesh J (Business Person)
Providian Financial Corp
201 Mission St
San Francisco, CA 94105, USA

Mehta, Sujata (Actor, Bollywood)
56 Dev Chhaya Tardeo Haji Ali Road
Tardeo
Bombay, MS 400 034, INDIA

Mehta, Ved (Writer)
139 E 79th St
New York, NY 10021, USA

Mehta, Zubin (Conductor)
Israel Philharmonic
1 Huberman St
Tel Aviv 61112, ISRAEL

Mehta (Metha) Saltzman, Deepa (Director, Editor, Producer, Writer)
Echo Lake Entertainment
421 South Beverly Dr 8th Fl
Beverly Hills, CA 90212, USA

Meier, Dave (Athlete, Baseball Player)
523 W Stuart Ave
Fresno, CA 93704-1430, USA

Meier, Richard A (Architect)
Richard Meier Partners
475 10th Ave
New York, NY 10018, USA

Meier, Shad (Athlete, Football Player)
4001 Skyline Dr
Nashville, TN 37215, USA

Meier, Waltraud (Opera Singer)
Festspielhugel 3
Bayreuth 95445, GERMANY

Meighan, Ron (Athlete, Hockey Player)
1692 Liberty Way
Orleans, ON K4A 4Y8, Canada

Meigs, Henry (General)
2811 Rainbow Dr
Louisville, KY 40206-2935, USa

Meiias, Roman (Athlete, Baseball Player)
27325 Terrytown Rd
Sun City, CA 92586-5220, United States

Meiko (Musician)
c/o Michael Moses *Baker Winokur Ryder Public Relations (BWR-LA)*
9100 Wilshire Blvd
Suite 500, West Tower
Beverly Hills, CA 90212, USA

Meilinger, Steve (Athlete, Football Player)
719 Camino Rd
Lexington, KY 40502, USA

Meineke, Don (Athlete, Basketball Player)
1266 Westcliff Ct
Dayton, OH 45459-4441, USA

Meinhold, Carl (Athlete, Basketball Player)
5 Courtleigh Pl
Reading, PA 196e6-2941, USA

Meinwald, Jerrold (Misc)
Cornell University
Chemistry Dept
Ithaca, NY 14853, USA

Meira, Vitor (Race Car Driver)
Team Rahel
4601 Lyman Dr.
Hilliard, OH 43026, USA

Meirelles, Fernando (Director, Producer)
c/o Staff Member *WME (LA)*
9601 Wilshire Blvd Fl 3
Beverly Hills, CA 90210, USA

Meirelles, Priscilla (Model)
Carousel Productions, Inc
8 San Manuel St., Capitol
Pasig City, Metro Manila 1603, PHILIPPINES

Meisel, Stephen (Photographer)
1271 Ave of Americas
New York, NY 10020, USA

Meiselas, Susan (Photographer)
256 Mott St
New York, NY 10012, USA

Meisenhelder, Glen (Race Car Driver)
Glen-Ken
77 Peros Dr.
Agawam, MA 01001, USA

Meisner, Greg (Athlete, Football Player)
419 Glenmeade Rd
Greensburg, PA 15601, USA

Meisner, Joachim Cardinal (Religious Leader)
Archbishop's Diocese
Marzellenstr 32
Cologne 50668, GERMANY

Meisner, Randy (Musician)
3706 Eureka Dr
Studio City, CA 91604, USA

Meissner, Kimmie (Figure Skater)
Office of Public Relations
The Academy Building
105 East Main St.
Newark, DE 19716-2701, USA

Meja (Musician)
Basic Music Mgmt
Norrtullsgatan 51
Stockholm 113 45, SWEDEN

Mejdani, Rexhep (President)
President's Office
Keshilli i Ministrave
Tirana, ALBANIA

Mejia, Hipolito (President)
Palacio Nacional
Calle Moises Garcia
Santo Domingo, DOMINICAN REPUBLIC

Mejia, Jorge Maria Cardinal (Religious Leader)
Biblioteca Apostolica Vaticina
Vatican City 00120, VATICAN CITY

Mejia, Paul R (Ballerina, Choreographer)
Fort Worth Ballet
6848 Green Oaks Road
Fort Worth, TX 76116, USA

Mejias, Roman (Athlete, Baseball Player)
27325 Terrytown Rd
Sun City, CA 92586-5220, USA

Mekka, Eddie (Actor)
Cosden Morgan
129 W Wilson St
#202
Costa Mesa, CA 92627, USA

Mel, Renfro (Athlete, Football Player)
8211 Hunnicut Rd
Dallas, TX 75228-5930, USA

Melametsa, Anssl (Athlete, Hockey Player)
Kivirinne 8B
Esooo, 02760 Finland

Melamld, Aleksandr (Artist)
Ronald Freeman Fine Arts
31 Mercer St
New York, NY 10013, USA

Melancon, Mei (Actor)
c/o Lena Roklin *Luber Roklin Management*
8530 Wilshire Blvd
6th Floor
Beverly Hills, CA 90211, USA

Melander, Jon (Athlete, Football Player)
8255 Kelzer Pond Dr
Victoria, MN 55386, USA

Melanie (Musician, Songwriter, Writer)
53 Baymont St
#5
Clearwater Beach, FL 33767, USA

Melanson, Rollie (Athlete, Hockey Player)
728 Rue Pierre-Baird
Boucherville, QC 3YB 7R3, CANADA

Melanson, Rollle (Athlete, Hockey Player)
728 Rue Pierre-Biard
Boucherville, QC J4B 7R3, Canada

Melanson, Rollle (Athlete, Hockey Player)
Vancouver Canucks
800 Griffiths Way
Vancouver, BC V6B 6G1, Canada

Melato, Mariangela (Actor)
Carol Levi Co
Via Giuseppe Pisanelli
Rome 00196, ITALY

Melby, Russ (Athlete, Football Player)
8208 Spanish Meadows Ave
Las Vegas, NV 89131-1447, USA

Melcher, John (Senator)
2519 Wylie Avenue
Missoula, MT 59802-3260, USA

Melcher, John (Politician)
2519 Wylie Ave
Missoula, MT 59802-3260, USA

Melchionni, Bill (Athlete, Basketball Player)
ne Bay Tree Ct
Naples, FL 341e8-3429, USA

Melchionni, Gary (Athlete, Basketball Player)
1040 Grandview Blvd
Lancaster, PA 176el-51e8, USA

Melchior, Ib (Writer)
8228 Marmont Lane
Los Angeles, CA 90069, USA

Melchoir, Tracy Lindsay
c/o Michael Bruno *The Michael Bruno Group*
13576 Cheltenham Dr
Sherman Oaks, CA 91423, USA

Meldgaard, Gitte (Stylist)
c/o Staff Member *Mercury Artists*
8460 Higuera St Fl 2
Culver City, CA 90232, USA

Mele, Sam (Athlete, Baseball Player, Coach)
340 Adams St
Quincy, MA 02169-1702, USA

Melendez, A J (Musician)

Melendez, John (Actor, Writer)
c/o Staff Member *Chapter 2 Productions*
3500 W Olive Ave
Suite 300
Burbank, CA 91505, USA

Melendez, John (Musician)
c/o Staff Member *Paradigm (Monterey)*
404 W Franklin St
Monterey, CA 93940, USA

Melendez, Kiki (Musician)
c/o Staff Member *Paradigm (Monterey)*
404 W Franklin St
Monterey, CA 93940, USA

Melendez, Lisette (Musician)
Famous Artists Agency
250 W 57th St
New York, NY 10107, USA

Melendez, Ron
12533 Woodgreen St
Los Angeles, CA 90066

Meler, Dave (Baseball Player)
Minnesota Twins
523 W Stuart Ave
Fresno, CA 93704-1430, USA

Meler, Raymond (Photographer)
Raymond Meier Photography
532 Broadway
New York, NY 10012, USA

Melges, Harry (Athlete, Olympic Athlete, Sailor)
730 Arrowhead Dr
Fontana, WI 53125-1253, USA

Melhuse, Adam (Athlete, Baseball Player)
758 Center St
San Luis Obisoo, CA 93405-2312, USA

Melillo, Kevin (Athlete, Baseball Player)
5630 Fairway View Dr
Charlotte, NC 28277-2568, USA

Melinda (Artist)
M Entertainment
120 E Flamingo Road
Las Vegas, NV 89109, USA

Mellanby, Scott (Athlete, Hockey Player)
2548 Town and Country Ln
Saint Louis, MO 63131-1121

Mellanby, Scott (Athlete, Hockey Player)
St Louis Blues
1401 Clark Ave
Saint Louis, MO 63103-2700

Mellekas, John (Athlete, Football Player)
498 Broadway
Newport, RI 02840, USA

Mellen, Polly (Stylist)
c/o Staff Member *Art + Commerce*
531 W 25th St # 4
New York, NY 10001, USA

Mellenby, Scott (Athlete, Hockey Player)
2548 Town and Country Ln
Saint Louis, MO 63131-1121, USA

Mellencamp, John (Musician, Songwriter)
P.O. Box 6777
Bloomington, IN 47408-6777, USA

Mellers, Wilfrid H (Composer, Writer)
Oliver Sheldon House
17 Aldwark
York YO1 2BX, UNITED KINGDOM (UK)

Melles, Carl
Grunbergstr 4
Vienna 1130, AUSTRIA

Melling, O R (Writer)
C/O Geraldine Whlean
26 Wolfe Tone Square E
Bray, Co Wicklow, IRELAND

Mellinkoff, Sherman M (Educator, Physicist)
University of California
Med Center
10833 LeConte Ave
Los Angeles, CA 90095, USA

Mello, Craig C (Nobel Prize Laureate)
25 Fessenden Rd
Barrington, RI 02806-4711, USA

Mello, Craig C. (Nobel Prize Laureate)
University Of Massachusetts Medical School
Biotech Two, Suite 219
373 Plantation St
Worcester, MA 01605, USA

Mello, Tamara (Actor)
c/o Brandy Gold *TalentWorks (LA)*
3500 W Olive Ave
Suite 1400
Burbank, CA 91505, USA

Mellons, Ken (Musician)
c/o Staff Member *Buddy Lee Attractions Inc*
38 Music Square E #300
Nashville, TN 37203-4396, USA

Mellor, John W (Economist)
John Mellor Assoc
801 Pennsylvania Ave NW
#PH18
Washington, DC 20004, USA

Mellor, Tom (Athlete, Hockey Player, Olympic Athlete)
63 Spoonhill Ave
Marlborough, MA 01752-2500

Melnick, Bruce E (Astronaut)
Boeing Aerospace
PO Box 21233
Kennedy Space Center, FL 32815, USA

Melnick, Bruce E Cdr (Astronaut)
30 Captains Cove Rd
Inglis, FL 34449-9129, USa

Melnick, Daniel (Producer)
1123 Sunset Hills Dr
Los Angeles, CA 90069, USA

Melniker, Benjamin (Producer)
Batfilm Productions
123 W 44th St
#10-K
New York, NY 10036, USA

Melnikov, Vitaly V (Director)
Svetianovsky Proyezd 105
#20
Saint Petersburg 195269, RUSSIA

Melnyk, Larry (Athlete, Hockey Player)
1748 Sugarpine Crt
Coquitlam, BC V3E 3E4, Canada

Melnyk, Steve (Athlete, Golfer)
5015 Pirates Cove Rd
Jacksonville, FL 32210-8309, USA

Meloan, Jon (Athlete, Baseball Player)
8017 Lichtenauer Dr
Lenexa, KS 66219-2037, USA

Meloche, Gilles (Athlete, Hockey Player)
Pittsburgh Penguins
66 Mario Lemieux Pl Ste 2
Pittsburgh, PA 15219-3504

Meloche, Gilles (Athlete, Hockey Player)
401 Church Hill Rd
Venetia, PA 15367-1142

Melody (Musician)
c/o Staff Member *Sony Music Miami*
605 Lincoln Rd Fl 7
Miami Beach, FL 33139, USA

Meloff, Chris (Athlete, Hockey Player)
8568 NW 52nd Pl
Coral Springs, FL 33067-2839, USA

Meloni, Christopher (Actor)
982 Oenoke Ridge
New Canaan, CT 06840, USA

Melrose, Barry J (Athlete, Coach, Hockey Player)
10 Windy Ridge Rd
Glens Falls, NY 12801-2473

Melroy, Pamela A (Astronaut)
3910 Valley Green Court
Houston, TX 77059, USA

Melroy, Pamela A Colonel (Astronaut)
920 N Barton St
Arlington, VA 22201-1910, USA

Melton, Bill (Athlete, Baseball Player)
9609 E Roadrunner Dr
Scottsdale, AZ 85262-1444, USA

Melton, Dave (Athlete, Baseball Player)
10253 Richwood Dr
Cupertino, CA 95014, USA

Meltzer, Allan L (Economist)
Camegie Mellon University
Economics Dept
Pittsburgh, PA 15260, USA

Melua, Katie (Musician)
c/o Rob Zifarelli *Agency Group Ltd, The (Canada)*
2 Berkeley Street
Suite 202
Toronto M5A 4J5, Canada

Meluskey, Mitch (Athlete, Baseball Player)
26 Meadowbrook Rd
Yakima, WA 98903-9505, USA

Melvill, Michael W (Astronaut)
24120 Jacaranda Dr
Tehachapi, CA 93561-8309, USA

Melvin, Bob (Athlete, Baseball Player, Coach)
8711 E Pinnacle Peak Rd
Scottsdale, AZ 85255-3517, USA

Melvin, Donnie
45 Overlook Terr.
New York, NY 10033

Melvin, Doug (Commentator)
4111 W Stonefield Rd
Meauon, WI 53092-2770, USA

Melvin, Leland D (Astronaut)
312 15th St NE
Washington, DC 20002-6502, USA

Melvin, Murray
Joy Jameson
Plaza
535 Kings Road
London SW10 OSZ, UNITED KINGDOM (UK)

Melvin, Rachel (Actor)
c/o Anne Woodward *ROAR (LA)*
9701 Wilshire Blvd
8th Floor
Los Angeles, CA 90212, USA

Melvoin, Wendy (Actor)
c/o Rick Jacobellis *First Artists Management*
4764 Park Granada
Suite 210
Calabasas, CA 91302, USA

Melzack, Ronald (Scientist)
51 Ch Banstead
Montreal-Ouest, QC H4X 1P1, USA

Melzack, Ronald (Misc)
51 Banstead Road
Montreal, QC H4X 1P1, CANADA

Melzer, Jurgen (Athlete, Tennis Player)
Champ Events
Salmgasse 5/25
Wien 1030, Austria

Member, Tim (Athlete, Football Player)
3410 Grant St
Vancouver, WA 98660, USA

Members, Swollen (Music Group, Musician)
c/o Staff Member *Agency Group Ltd, The (LA)*
1880 Century Park E
Suite 711
Los Angeles, CA 90067, USA

Memmel, Chellsie (Athlete, Gymnast, Olympic Athlete)
PO Box 510474
New Berlin, WI 53151, USA

Men, Baha (Music Group)
Evolution Talent
1776 Broadway
15th Floor
New York, NY 10019

Menafee, Cornell (Athlete, Football Player)
403 Elm Ct
Opelika, AL 36801, USA

Menaker, Mitchell G
5062 Isleworth Country Club Dr
Windermere, FL 34786-8920, USA

Menand, Louis (Historian, Writer)
New Yorker Magazine
Editorial Dept
4 Times Square
New York, NY 10036, USA

Menard, Hillary "Minnie" (Athlete, Hockey Player)
8141 Wellington Blvd
Johnston, IA 50131-8740

Menard, Howie (Athlete, Hockey Player)
8 Springfield Lane
Courtice, ON L1E 1L9, Canada

Menard, Marc (Actor)
Infinite Artists
10 - 206 E 6th Ave
Vancouver, BC V5T 1J8, CANADA

Menard, Renry W (Misc)
Scripps Institute of Oceanography
Geology Dept
La Jolla, CA 92093, USA

Mench, Kevin (Athlete, Baseball Player)
1305 Danbury Parks Dr
Keller, TX 76248-5271, USA

Menchu Tum, Rigoberta (Nobel Prize Laureate)
UN Working Group on Indigenous Populations
UN Plaza
New York, NY 10017, USA

Mencia, Carlos (Actor)
c/o Tim Sarkes *Brillstein Entertainment Partners*
9150 Wilshire Blvd #350
Beverly Hills, CA 90212, USA

Mendenhall, John (Athlete, Football Player)
PO Box 235
Cullen, LA 71071-0235, USA

Mendenhall, Ken (Athlete, Football Player)
1708 S Rankin St
Edmond, OK 73013, USA

Mendenhall, Ted
12907 Papago Dr
Poway, CA 92064-4513, USA

Mendes, Eva (Actor)
c/o David Seltzer *Management 360*
9111 Wilshire Blvd
Beverly Hills, CA 90210, USA

Mendes, Jonna (Athlete, Olympic Athlete, Track Athlete)
PO Box 92
Nixon, NV 89424-0092, USA

Mendes, Sam (Director)
c/o Simon Halls *Slate Public Relations*
9000 Sunset Blvd #915
West Hollywood, CA 90069, USA

Mendez, April Jeanette (Misc)
Florida Championship Wrestling
4535 South Dale Mabry
Tampa, FL 33611, USA

Mendez, Carlos (Athlete, Baseball Player)
Rome Braves 755 Braves Blvd NE
Rome, GA 30161-2983, USA

Mendez, Lazaro (DJ Laz) (Radio Personality)
Power 96
194 N.W. 187th St
Miami, FL 33169, USA

Mendez, Lucia (Actor)
c/o Staff Member *TV Azteca*
Periferico Sur 4121
Colonia Fuentes del Pedregal
DF CP 14141, Mexico

Mendler, Bridgit (Actor)
c/o Elaine Lively *Elaine Entertainment*
Prefers to be contacted via telephone
Northridge, CA 91324, USA

Mendonca, Albert (Stylist)
c/o Staff Member *Celestine - CA*
1666 20th St
#200-B
Santa Monica, CA 90404, USA

Mendoza, Dayana (Beauty Pageant Winner)
c/o Chris Rossi *Core Public Relations Group*
4401 Wilshire Blvd.
Los Angeles, CA 90010, USA

Mendoza, Jessica (Athlete)
Amateur Softball Association (USA Softball)
2801 N.E. 50th Street
Oklahoma City, OK 73111-7203, USA

Mendoza, June (Artist)
34 Inner Park Road
London SW19 6DD, UNITED KINGDOM (UK)

Mendoza, Linda (Director)
c/o Staff Member *Creative Artists Agency (CAA-LA)*
2000 Ave Of The Stars
Los Angeles, CA 90067, USA

Mendoza, Mike (Athlete, Baseball Player)
14207 S 20th St
Phoenix, AZ 85048-4519, USA

Mendoza, Minnie (Athlete, Baseball Player)
2866 Charlotte Dr
Murrells Inlet, SC 29576-8481, USA

Mendoza, Ramiro (Athlete, Baseball Player)
18706 Pepper Pike
Lutz, FL 33558-5303, USA

Mendoza, Reynol (Baseball Player)
2408 2nd St
Eagle Pass, TX 78852-4119, USA

Mendoza, Zuleyka Rivera (Beauty Pageant Winner)
c/o Richie Walls *International Talent Agency (ITA)*
10 NBC Universal Studios Plaza
20th Floor
Universal City, CA 91608, USA

Mendte, Larry
330 Bob Hope Dr.
Burbank, CA 91523

Menechino, Frank (Athlete, Baseball Player)
522 Arlene St
Staten Island, NY 10314-3818, USA

Menedez, Steven (Stylist)
c/o Staff Member *Artists by Timothy Priano (CA)*
8447 Wilshire Blvd
#301
Beverly Hills, CA 90211, USA

Menendez, Erik
#1878449 CSP-Sac.
Box 290066
Represa, CA 95671-0066, USA

Menendez, Lyle
California Correctional Institute
#1887106
CCI-Box 1031
Tehachapi, CA 93581, USA

Menendez, Tony (Athlete, Baseball Player)
18730 NW 48th Ct
Miami Gardens, FL 33055-2536, USA

Meneses, Alex (Actor)
c/o Cindy Schultzel-Ambers *Art/Work Entertainment*
5900 Wilshire Blvd
Suite 1720
Los Angeles, CA 90036, USA

Meneses, Antonio (Musician)
Columbia Artists Mgmt Inc
165 W 57th St
New York, NY 10019, USA

Menew (Music Group, Musician)
c/o Staff Member *REDCORE MUSIC GROUP*
520 8th Ave.
#2001
New York, NY 10018, USA

Menez, Bernard
119 Blvd. de Grenelle
Paris, FRANCE 75015

Mengatti, John
8322 Beverly Blvd. #200
Los Angeles, CA 90048

Mengelt, John (Athlete, Basketball Player)
1270 Breckenridge Ct
Lake Forest, IL 6ee45-3875, USA

Mengers, Sue
938 Bel Air Rd.
Los Angeles, CA 90077

Menhart, Paul (Athlete, Baseball Player)
725 Kelsall Drive
Richmond Hill, GA 31324-7707, USA

Menheer-Zoromapal, Marie (Baseball Player)
8871 Lake Marion Creek Rd
Haines City, FL 33844-2004, USA

Menichetti, Roberto (Designer, Fashion Designer)
3 Loc Monteleto
Gubbio, ITALY

Menke, Andrea (Stylist)
c/o Staff Member *Ford Models (Miami)*
311 Lincoln Rd
#205
Miami Beach, FL 33139, USA

Menke, Denis (Athlete, Baseball Player)
1246 Berkshire Ln
Tarpon Springs, FL 34688-7626, USA

Menken, Alan (Composer)
Shukat Co
670 W End Ave
#8A
New York, NY 10025, USA

Mennea, Pietro (Athlete, Track Athlete)
Via Cassia 1041
Rome 00189, ITALY

Mennell, Laura (Actor)
c/o Craig Schneider *Pinnacle Public Relations*
8265 Sunset Blvd
Suite 201
Los Angeles, CA 90064, USA

Menneron, Laurence (Stylist)
c/o Staff Member *Fifty8 Artists*
58 W Huron St
Chicago, IL 60610, USA

Menninga, Chris (Race Car Driver)
Conquest Racing
5062 W. 79th St.
Indianapolis, IN 46268, USA

Meno, Chorepiscopus John (Religious Leader)
263 Elm Ave
Teaneck, NJ 07666, USA

Menon, Krishnan (Actor)
c/o Jai Khanna *Brillstein Entertainment Partners*
9150 Wilshire Blvd #350
Beverly Hills, CA 90212, USA

Menon, Mambillikalathil G K (Physicist)
C-63 Tarang Apts
Mother Dairy Road
Patparganj, Delhi 110092, INDIA

Menounos, Maria (Actor, Correspondent)
c/o Staff Member *Extra (LA)*
Telepictures Productions
1840 Victory Blvd
Glendale, CA 91201, USA

Mensah, Peter (Actor)
c/o Cheri Barner *Artist Management*
1119 Colorado Ave
Suite 12
Santa Monica, CA 90401, USA

Menshov, Vladimir V (Actor, Director)
3D Tverskaya-Yamskaya 52
Moscow 125047, RUSSIA

Mentez, Chris (Musician)
Arsisanian Assoc
6671 Sunset Blvd
#1502
Los Angeles, CA 90028, USA

Menudo
2895 Biscayne Blvd. #455
Miami, FL 33137

Men Women & Children (Music Group)
c/o Staff Member *Paradigm (Monterey)*
404 W Franklin St
Monterey, CA 93940, USA

Menzel, Idina (Actor, Musician)
c/o Heather Reynolds *One Entertainment (NY)*
12 W 57th St
Penthouse
New York, NY 10019, USA

Menzel, Jiri (Director)
Studio 89
Kratky Film Jindrisska 34
Prague 1 112 07, CZECH REPUBLIC

Menzies, Peter G Jr (Cinematographer)
903 Tahoe Blvd
#802
Incline Village, NV 89451, USA

Meola, Eric (Photographer)
535 Greenwich St
New York, NY 10013, USA

Meola, Tony (Soccer Player)
488 Forest St
Keamy, NJ 07032, USA

Meoli, Christian (Actor)
c/o Brian McCabe *Venture IAB*
3211 Cahuenga Blvd W Ste 104
Los Angeles, CA 90068, USA

Meoli, Rudy (Athlete, Baseball Player)
1211 San Gabriel Ave
Henderson, NV 89002-9402, USA

Meraz, Alex (Actor)
c/o Jeb Brandon *Kritzer Levine Wilkins Entertainment (KLWG)*
11872 La Grange Ave
1st Floor
Los Angeles, CA 90025, USA

Merbold, Ulf (Astronaut)
Am Sonnenhang 4
Siegburg 53721, GERMANY

Merbold, Ulf D Dr (Astronaut)
Am Sonnenhang 4
Siegburg, Germany D-53721, USA

Mercado, Orlando (Athlete, Baseball Player)
5292 Bishop St Apt 10
Cypress, CA 90630-3082, USA

Mercado, Syesha (Musician)

Merced, Orlando (Athlete, Baseball Player)
PO Box 190494
SanJuan, PR 00919-0494, USA

Mercein, Chuck (Athlete, Football Player)
746 Mamaroneck Ave
Apt 1320
Mamaroneck, NY 10543, USA

Mercer, Mark (Athlete, Baseball Player)
10607 Penn Ave S
Minneapolis, MN 55431-3445, USA

Mercer, Mike (Athlete, Football Player)
64463 McGrath Rd
Bend, OR 97701, USA

Mercer, Ron (Athlete, Basketball Player)
San Antonio Spurs
1843 Glenhill Dr
Lexington, KY 4e5e2-2817, USA

Mercer, Toby (Artist)
Mercer Studios
316 E Reserve Dr
Kalispell, MT 59901, USA

Merchant, Andy (Athlete, Baseball Player)
PO Box 8
Malcolm, AL 36556-0008, USA

Merchant, Natalie (Musician, Songwriter, Writer)

Merchant, Stephen (Actor, Director, Producer, Writer)
c/o Staff Member *WME (LA)*
9601 Wilshire Blvd Fl 3
Beverly Hills, CA 90210, USA

Mercker, Kent (Athlete, Baseball Player)
5340 Mulrfield Ct
Dublin, OH 43017-7629, USA

Merckx, Eddy (Athlete)
s'Herenweg 11
Meise 1860, Belgium

Mercredi, Vic (Athlete, Hockey Player)
GD
Fort Chipewyan, AB TOP 1BO, Canada

Mercredi, VIctor (Athlete, Hockey Player)
GD
Fort Chioewyan, AB TOP IBO, Canada

Mercurio, Nicole (Actor)
Innovative Artists
1505 10th St
Santa Monica, CA 90401, USA

Mercurio, Paul (Actor, Musician)
Beyond Films
53-55 Brisbane St Surreyhills
Sydney, NSW 2010, AUSTRALIA

Mercurio, Steven
Columbia Artists Mgmt Inc
165 W 57th St
New York, NY 10019, USA

Mercurio, Tara (Actor)
c/o Aaron Ray *Collective*
8383 Wilshire Blvd
Suite 1050
Beverly Hills, CA 90211, USA

Mercy Me (Music Group, Musician)
c/o Scott Bickell *Brickhouse Entertainment*
106 Mission Court
Suite 1202
Franklin, TN 37067, USA

Meredith, Cla (Athlete, Baseball Player)
3807 Kensington Ave
Richmond, VA 23221-2009, USA

Meredith, Greg (Athlete, Hockey Player)
111 W 67th St Apt 36A
New York, NY 10023-5960

Meredith, james (Politician)
929 Meadowbrook Rd
Jacksonville, MS 39206-5945, USA

Meredith, James H (Misc)
929 Meadowbrook Road
Jackson, MS 39206, USA

Meredith, Richard (Athlete, Hockey Player, Olympic Athlete)
26580 Hickory Blvd
Bonita Springs, FL 34134-8203, USA

Meredith, William (Writer)
Connecticut College
PO Box 1498
New London, CT 06320, USA

Meridith, Ron (Athlete, Baseball Player)
308 Via Promesa
San Clemente, CA 92673-6820, USA

Merigan Jr, Thomas C (Scientist)
148 Goya Road
Portola Valley, CA 94028, USA

Merila, Mark (Athlete, Baseball Player)
11819 Westview Pkwy
San Diego, CA 92126-8540, USA

Merisola, Linda (Stylist)
3702 E Shangri La Rd
Phoenix, AZ 85028, USA

Meritano, Lorena (Actor)
c/o Gabriel Blanco *Gabriel Blanco Iglesias (Mexico)*
Rio Balsas 35-32
Colonia Cuauhtemoc
DF 06500, Mexico

Meriweather, Joe C (Athlete, Basketball Player)
5316 NW 84th Ter
Kansas City, MO 64154-1445, USA

Meriweather, Lee (Actor, Beauty Pageant Winner)
12139 Jeanette Pl
Granada Hills, CA 91344, USA

Meriwether, Chick (Baseball Player)
2409 Seifried St
Nashville, TN 37208-1344, USA

Meriwether, Chuck (Athlete, Baseball Player)
2409 Seifried St
Nashville, TN 37208-1344, USA

Meriwether, Lee (Actor)
c/o Scott Stander *Scott Stander & Associates*
13701 Riverside Dr
Suite 201
Sherman Oaks, CA 91423, USA

Meriwether, Porter (Athlete, Basketball Player)
8137 S Saint Lawrence Ave
Chicago, IL 6e619-see7, USA

Merkens, Guido (Athlete, Football Player)
2301 S Millbend Dr
Apt 405
Spring, TX 77380, USA

Merkerson, S Epatha (Actor)
c/o Jillian Fowkes *ID Public Relations (ID-LA)*
7060 Hollywood Blvd
8th Floor
Los Angeles, CA 90028, USA

Merkin, Daphne (Writer)
c/o Staff Member *The New York Times Company*
229 W 43rd St
New York, NY 10036, USA

Merkosky, Glenn (Athlete, Hockey Player)
113 Farr Ln
Queensbury, NY 12804-1996

Merle, Carole (Skier)
Chalet La Calette
Super-Sauze 04400, FRANCE

Merletti, Lewis C (Lawyer)
Cleveland Browns
76 Lou Groza Blvd
Berea, OH 44017, USA

Merlin, Jan (Actor)
347 N California St
Burbank, CA 91505, USA

Merlo, James L (Athlete, Football Player)
1547 E Starpass Dr
Fresno, CA 93720, USA

Merloni, Lou (Athlete, Baseball Player)
333 Ricciuti Dr Apt 1728
Quincy, MA 02169-6396, USA

Merlyn-Rees, Merlyn (Government Official)
House of Lords
Westminster
London SW1A 0PW, UNITED KINGDOM (UK)

Meron, Neil (Producer)
c/o Staff Member *WmE2 (WMA-LA)*
1 William Morris Pl
Beverly Hills, CA 90212, USA

Merovich, Pete (Soccer Player)
945 Spruce St
Pittsburgh, PA 15234, USA

Merow, James F (Judge)
US Claims Court
717 Madison Place NW
Washington, DC 20439, USA

Merrells, Jason (Actor)
c/o Nicola Richardson *QVoice*
161 Drury Ln, Covent Garden
3rd Floor
London WC2B 5PN, UK

Merrick, Dawn
8281 Melrose Ave. #200
Los Angeles, CA 90046

Merrick, Robert (Athlete, Olympic Athlete, Sailor)
470 Sea Meadow Dr
Portsmouth, RI 02871-3935, USA

Merrick, Wayne (Athlete, Hockey Player)
68 Chesham Ct.
London, ON N6G 3T4, CANADA

Merrifield, R Bruce (Nobel Prize Laureate)
43 Mezzine Dr
Cresskill, NJ 07626, USA

Merrill, Carl (Stump) (Athlete, Baseball Player, Coach)
18 Merrymeeting Dr
Topsham, ME 04086-1839, USA

Merrill, Casey (Athlete, Football Player)
78395 Avenue 41
Indio, CA 92201, USA

Merrill, Catherine (Artist)
Old Church Pottery
1456 Florida St
San Francisco, CA 94110, USA

Merrill, Dina (Actor)
Sue Siegel
405 E 54th St #12A
New York, NY 10022, USA

Merrill, Edward W (Engineer)
90 Somerset St
Belmont, MA 02478, USA

Merrill, John O (Architect)
101 Gardner Place
Colorado Springs, CO 80906, USA

Merrill, Mark (Athlete, Football Player)
782 Mimosa Ln
New Brighton, MN 55112, USA

Merriman, Brent (Athlete, Baseball Player)
907 N Cobblestone St
Gilbert, AZ 85234-8742, USA

Merriman, Brett (Athlete, Baseball Player)
1429 W Bentrup St
Chandler, AZ 85224-1386, USA

Merriman, Randy
PO Box 70025
Houston, TX 77270

Merriman, Ryan (Actor)
c/o Beth Holden-Garland *Untitled Entertainment (LA)*
350 S. Beverly Dr #200
Beverly Hills, CA 90212, USA

Merriman, Shawne (Athlete, Football Player)
c/o David Dunn *Athletes First, LLC*
9140 Irvine Center Dr
Irvine, CA 92618, USA

Merriott, Ronald (Athlete, Diver, Olympic Athlete)
1271 McDole Dr
Sugar Grove, IL 60554-5473, USA

Merritt, C C (General)
431-1645 14th Ave W
Vancouver, Canada Bc V6J 2J4, USA

Merritt, Chris (Opera Singer)
George M Martynuk
352 7th Ave
New York, NY 10001, USA

Merritt, David (Athlete, Football Player)
479 Hartford Dr
Nutley, NJ 07110, USA

Merritt, Gilbert S (Judge)
US Court of Appeals
US Courthouse
701 Broadway
Nashville, TN 37203, USA

Merritt, Jack N (General)
US Army Assn
2425 Wilson Blvd
Arlington, VA 22201, USA

Merritt, Jim (Athlete, Baseball Player)
2777 Blue Spruce Dr
Hemet, CA 92545-8701, USA

Merritt, Lloyd (Athlete, Baseball Player)
4703 Wlld Iris Dr
Apt 301
Myrtle Beach, SC 29577-8718, USA

Merritt, Tift (Musician)
c/o Staff Member *Red Light Management (LA)*
8439 W Sunset Blvd
Suite 2
Los Angeles, CA 90069, USA

Merriweather, Daniel (Musician)
c/o Staff Member *Allido*
19 Mercer St
#5
New York, NY 10013, USA

Merriweather, Mike (Athlete, Football Player)
P.O. Box 8351
Stockton, CA 95208, USA

Merrow, Susan (Misc)
Sierra Club
85 2nd St
#200
San Francisco, CA 94105, USA

Merson, Michael (Government Official)
World Health Organization
Ave Appia
Geneva 27 1211, SWITZERLAND

Merten, Lauri (Athlete, Golfer)
1010 Del Harbour Dr
Delray Beach, FL 33483, USA

Mertens, Alan (Misc)
PacWest Racing Group
150 Gasoline Alley Road
Indianapolis, IN 46222, USA

Mertens, Jerry (Athlete, Football Player)
465 Woodside Dr
Woodside, CA 94062, USA

Merton, Robert (Nobel Prize Laureate)
75 Cambridge Pkwy Unit E1108
Cambridge, MA 02142-1270, USA

Merton, Robert C (Nobel Prize Laureate)
Harvard University
Business School
Boston, MA 02163, USA

Mertz, Edwin T (Misc)
1504 Via Delta Scala
Henderson, NV 89052, USA

Mertz, Francis J (Educator)
Farleigh Dickinson University
President's Office
Teaneck, NJ 07666, USA

Mertzig, Jan (Athlete, Hockey Player)
Krokvagen 78
Huddinge 14131, Sweden

Meruelo, Alex (Business Person)
36 Indian Creek Dr
Indian Creek Village, FL 33154, USA

Merullo, Lennie (Athlete, Baseball Player)
159 Summer Ave
Reading, MA 01867-2825, USA

Merullo, Matt (Athlete, Baseball Player)
8 Fox Run Rd
Madison, CT 06443-2052, USA

Merwin, John D (Ex-Governor)
P.O. Box 1029
Hudson, OH 44236-6229, USA

Merwin, William Stanley (Writer)
Farleigh Dickinson University Press
285 Madison Ave
Madison, NJ 07940, USA

Merz, Curt (Athlete, Football Player)
1111 W Seminole St
Springfield, MO 65807, USA

Merz, Sue (Athlete, Hockey Player, Olympic Athlete)
5 Douglas Dr
Greenwich, CT 06831-3612, USA

Mesa, Carlos (President)
President's Office
Palacio de Gobierno
Plaza Murilla
La Paz, BOLIVIA

Mesa, Jose (Athlete, Baseball Player)
13173 SW 51st St
Miramar, FL 33027-5522, USA

Meschery, Tom (Athlete, Basketball Player)
1216 Versailles Ave
Alameda, CA 945el-5453, USA

Meselson, Matthew S (Misc)
Harvard University
Fairchild Biochemistry Laboratories
Cambridge, MA 02138, USA

Mesereau, Thomas (Lawyer)
1875 Century Park E
Los Angeles, CA 90067, USA

Meseroll, Mark (Athlete, Football Player)
450 Roger Dr
Salisbury, NC 28147, USA

Mesguich, Daniel (Actor, Director)
Agence Monita Derrieux
17-21 Rue Duret
Paris 75116, FRANCE

Mesic, Stipe (President)
Presidential Palace
Pantovcak 241
Zagreb 10000, CROATIA

Mesina Stanley, Dianne (Producer)
c/o Staff Member *United Talent Agency (UTA)*
9336 Civic Center Dr
Beverly Hills, CA 90210, USA

Meskill, Thomas (Politician)
218 Stony Mill Ln
East Berlin, CT 06023-1042, USA

Mesner, Bruce (Athlete, Football Player)
3178 NW 60th St
Boca Raton, FL 33496, USA

Mesnil Du Buisson, Robert (Archaeologist)
Chateau de Champobert
Par Exmes
Orne 61310, FRANCE

Mesquida, Roxane (Actor)
c/o Elisabeth Simpson *Agence Elisabeth Simpson*
62 Boulevard Du Montparnasse
Paris 75015, FRANCE

Messager, Annette (Artist)
146 Blvd Camelinat
Colombier-Fontaine 92240, FRANCE

Messenger, Melinda (Model)
Arcadia Mgmt
2-3 Golden Square
London W1R 3AD, UNITED KINGDOM (UK)

Messenger, Randy (Athlete, Baseball Player)
455 Market St Ste 2240
San Francisco, CA 94105-2446, USA

Messer, Dale (Athlete, Football Player)
5449 N Brooks Ave
Fresno, CA 93711, USA

Messer, Thomas M (Misc)
1105 Park Ave
New York, NY 10128, USA

Messerschmid, Ernst (Astronaut)
Universitat Stuttgart
Der Schone Weg 6
Reutlingen D-72766, GERMANY

Messerschmidt, J Alexander (Andy) (Baseball Player)
200 Lagunita Dr
Soquel, CA 95073, USA

Messer Simms, Leah (Reality TV Star)
c/o Lindsay Rielly *Continuum Entertainment*
303 Park Ave S
Suite 1220
New York, NY 10010, USA

Messersmith, Andy (Athlete, Baseball Player)
200 Lagunita Dr
Soquel, CA 95073-9594, USA

Messi, Lionel (Athlete, Soccer Player)
FC Barcelona
Av. Aristides Maillol S/n
Barcelona 08028, SPAIN

Messier, Joby (Athlete, Hockey Player)
PO Box 116
Wilcox, SK SOG SED, Canada

Messier, Mark (Athlete, Hockey Player)
45 Birchwood Dr
Greenwich, CT 06831-3311

Messina, Chris (Actor)
c/o Jon Rubinstein *Authentic Talent and Literary Management*
45 Main St
Suite 1004
Brooklyn, NY 11201, USA

Messina, Jim (Musician)
c/o Staff Member *Agency for the Performing Arts (APA-LA)*
405 S Beverly Dr
Suite 500
Beverly Hills, CA 90212-4425, USA

Messina, Jo Dee (Musician, Songwriter)
McGee Entertainment
21 Music Square W
Nashville, TN 37203, USA

Messing, Debra (Actor)
c/o Molly Madden *3 Arts Entertainment Inc*
9460 Wilshire Blvd
7th Floor
Beverly Hills, CA 90210, USA

Messner, Heinrich (Heini) (Skier)
Huebenweg 11
Steinach 6150, AUSTRIA

Messner, Johnny (Actor)
c/o Staff Member *McKeon-Myones Management*
3500 Olive Ave
Suite 770
Burbank, CA 91505, USA

Messner, Reinhold (Mountaineer)
Schloss Juval
Kastelbell, Tschars 39040, ITALY

Mestnik, Frank (Athlete, Football Player)
730 Eagles Mere Ct
Alpharetta, GA 30005, USA

Mestrik, Frank (Athlete, Football Player)
730 Eagles Mere Ct
Alpharetta, GA 30005, USA

Meszaros, Andrej (Athlete, Hockey Player)
581/2 Martinique Ave
Tampa, FL 33606-4039

Meszaros, Maria (Director)
Malfilm Studio
Lumumba Utca 174
Budapest 1149, HUNGARY

Metallica (Music Group)
c/o Cliff Burnstein *Q Prime Inc*
729 7th Ave
16th Floor
New York, NY 10019, USA

Metaxas, Eric (Writer)
c/o Staff Member *HarperCollins Publishers*
10 East 53rd St
c/o Author mail, 7th Floor
New York, NY 10022, USA

Metcalf, Eric Q (Athlete, Football Player)
5112 S Fountain St
Seattle, WA 98178, USA

Metcalf, John (Writer)
128 Lewis St
Ottawa, ON K2P 0S7, CANADA

Metcalf, Joseph III (Admiral)
4658 Charleston Terrace NW
Washington, DC 20007, USA

Metcalf, Laurie (Actor)
Steppenwolf Theatre Company
1650 N. Halsted St
Chicago, IL 60614, USA

Metcalf, Mark (Actor)
c/o Staff Member *Peter Strain & Associates Inc (LA)*
5455 Wilshire Blvd
Suite 1812
Los Angeles, CA 90036-4368, USA

Metcalf, Shelby (Coach)
Texas A & M University
Athletic Dept
College Station, TX 77843, USA

Metcalf, Terrance R (Terry) (Athlete, Football Player)
5112 S Fountain St
Seattle, WA 98178, USA

Metcalf, Terrence (Athlete, Football Player)
1524 Jackson Ave E Unit 9
Oxford, MS 38655, USA

Metcalf, Tom (Athlete, Baseball Player)
1390 Wisconsin River Dr
Port Edwards, WI 54469-1042, USA

Metcalf, Travis (Athlete, Baseball Player)
610 Tenna Lorna Ct
Dallas, TX 75208-3133, USA

Metcalfe, Burt
11800 Brookdale Lane
Studio City, CA 91604

Metcalfe, Jesse (Actor)
c/o Beth Holden-Garland *Untitled Entertainment (LA)*
350 S. Beverly Dr #200
Beverly Hills, CA 90212, USA

Metcalfe, Mike (Athlete, Baseball Player)
9 Cottage Pl
Ashland, NH 03217-4370, USA

Metcalfe, Robert M (Inventor)
300 Bowie St Apt 4103
Austin, TX 78703-4688, USA

Metcalfe, Robert M (Scientist)
Polaris Venture Partners
1000 Winter St
#3350
Waltham, MA 02451, USA

Metcalfe, Scott (Athlete, Hockey Player)
36 Town Pump Cir
Spencerport, NY 14559-9734

Metcalf-Lindenburger, Dorothy M
(Astronaut)
2235 Water Way
Seabrook, TX 77586-2814, USA

Metesh, Bernice (Athlete, Baseball Player,
Commentator)
1210 Kelly Ave
Joliet, IL 60435-4251, USA

Metheny, Pat (Musician)
c/o Ted Kurland *Ted Kurland Associates*
173 Brighton Ave
Boston, MA 02134, USA

Metheny, Patrick B (Pat) (Composer,
Musician)
Ted Kurland
173 Brighton Ave
Boston, MA 02134, USA

Metrano, Art (Actor)
131 N Croft Ave
#402
Los Angeles, CA 90048, USA

Metric (Music Group)
c/o Staff Member *Paradigm (Monterey)*
404 W Franklin St
Monterey, CA 93940, USA

Metrolis, Norma (Baseball Player)
175 Sea Dunes Dr
Melbourne Beach, FL 32951-3313, USA

Metropolit, Glen (Athlete, Hockey Player)
1070 Redwine Cove Rd SW
Dalton, GA 30720-4954

Metro Station (Music Group, Musician)
c/o Staff Member *Sony Music
Entertainment*
555 Madison Avenue
New York, NY 10022-3211, USA

Mette-Marit, Princess (Royalty)
Det Kongelige
Slottet Drammensvein 1
Oslo 0010, NORWAY

Metwally, Omar (Actor)
c/o James Suskin *James Suskin
Management*
2 Charlton St Ste 5K
New York, NY 10014, USA

Metz, Alfred P
10101 Westridg.e ^d
Fort Worth, TX 76126-1709, USA

Metzelaars, Pete (Athlete, Football Player)
292 Point Carpenter Rd
Fort Mill, SC 29715, USA

Metzenbaum, Howard M (Senator)
Consumer Federation of America
1424 16th St NW
Washington, DC 20036, USA

Metzger, Butch (Athlete, Baseball Player)
641 Rivergate Way
Sacramento, CA 95831-3345, USA

Metzger, Clarence (Butch) (Athlete,
Baseball Player)
641 Rivergate Way
Sacramento, CA 95831, USA

Metzger, Henry (Misc)
3410 Taylor St
Chevy Chase, MD 20815, USA

Metzger, Roger (Athlete, Baseball Player)
3560 Bluebonnet Blvd
Brenham, TX 77833-7180, USA

Metzig, Bill (Athlete, Baseball Player)
221 Chuck Wagon Rd
Lubbock, TX 79404-1903, USA

Metzler, Jim
6300 Wilshire Blvd. #2110
Los Angeles, CA 90048

Metzner, Evyan (Stylist)
c/o Staff Member *Jed Root Inc*
61-A Walker St
New York, NY 10013, USA

Meulens, Hensley (Athlete, Baseball
Player)
Inidianapolis Indians
555 Mission Rock St
San Francisco, CA 94158-2119, USA

Meunier-Lebouc, Patricia (Athlete, Golfer)
152 Porto Vecchio Way
Palm Beach Gardens, FL 33418, USA

Mewes, Jason (Actor)
c/o Andrew Weitz *WME (LA)*
9601 Wilshire Blvd Fl 3
Beverly Hills, CA 90210, USA

Mey, Reinhard
Sigismundkorso 63
Berlin, GERMANY D-13465

Mey, Uwe-Jens (Speed Skater)
Vulkanstr 22
Berlin 10367, GERMANY

Meyer, Alejandra (Actor)
c/o Staff Member *Televisa*
Blvd Adolfo Lopez Mateos 232
Colonia San Angel INN
DF CP 01060, MEXICO

Meyer, Armin H (Diplomat)
6624 Rannoch Road
Bethesda, MD 20817-5411, USA

Meyer, Bess
PO Box 5617
Beverly Hills, CA 90210

Meyer, Bob
Dryden Flight Historical Society PO Box
57
Edwards, CA 93523-0057, USA

Meyer, Bob (Athlete, Baseball Player)
24446 Caswell Ct
Laguna Niguel, CA 92677-7008, USA

Meyer, Breckin (Actor)
c/o Ashley Franklin *Thruline
Entertainment*
9250 Wilshire Blvd
Ground Fl
Beverly Hills, CA 90212, USA

Meyer, Brian (Athlete, Baseball Player)
33 Bank St
Medford, NJ 08055-2635, USA

Meyer, Dan (Athlete, Baseball Player)
11540 Marsh Creek Rd
Cla'llon, CA 94517-9759, USA

Meyer, Daniel J (Business Person)
Milacron Inc
2090 Florence Ave
Cincinnati, OH 45206, USA

Meyer, Debbie (Athlete, Olympic Athlete,
Swimmer)
PO Box 2076
Carmichael, CA 95609-2076, USA

Meyer, Dina (Actor)
c/o Stephen (Steve) LaManna *Innovative
Artists (LA)*
1505 10th St
Santa Monica, CA 90401, USA

Meyer, Edgar (Composer, Musician)
c/o Staff Member *Studio Art Concert
Agency*
Viale Della Resistenza 9
Ospedalicchio 06080, Italy

Meyer, Edward C (General)
1101 S Arlington Ridge Road
#1116
Arlington, VA 22202, USA

Meyer, Gregory (Stylist)
c/o Staff Member *Halley Resources*
37 W 20th St
#603
New York, NY 10011, USA

Meyer, Jerome J (Business Person)
Tektronix Inc
26600 Southwest Parkway
Wilsonville, OR 97070, USA

Meyer, Joey (Athlete, Baseball Player)
392 Kaimake Loop
Kailua, HI 96734-2019, USA

Meyer, John (Athlete, Football Player)
2085 Lost Dauphin Rd
De Pere, WI 54115, USA

Meyer, Joyce (Religious Leader)
Joyce Meyers Ministries
P.O. Box 655
Fenton, MO 63026, USA

Meyer, Karl H (Misc)
642 Wyndham Road
Teaneck, NJ 07666, USA

Meyer, Lawrence H (Economist,
Government Official)
Federal Reserve Board
20th & Constitution NW
Washington, DC 20551, USA

Meyer, Nicholas (Director, Producer,
Writer)
c/o Alan Gasmer *Alan Gasmer
Management Company*
10877 Wilshire Blvd.
Suite 603
Los Angeles, CA 90024, USA

Meyer, Robert K (Misc)
3 Rawlings Place
Fadden, ACT 2904, AUSTRALIA

Meyer, Ron (Athlete, Football Player)
628 18th St
Windom, MN 56101, USA

Meyer, Ron (Business Person, Producer)
c/o Staff Member *NBC Universal (LA)*
100 Universal City Plz
Universal City, CA 91608, USA

Meyer, Scott (Athlete, Baseball Player)
9311 E Calle De Valle Dr
Scottsdale, AZ 85255-4303, USA

Meyer, Stephenie (Writer)
c/o Jodi Reamer *Writers House*
21 W 26th St
New York, NY 10010, USA

Meyerowitz, Elliot M (Biologist)
California Institute of Technology
Biology Dept
Pasadena, CA 91125, USA

Meyerowitz, Joel (Photographer)
817 W End Ave
New York, NY 10025-5322, USA

Meyer-Petrovic, Anna (Athlete, Baseball
Player, Commentator)
1125 N Nema Ave
Tucson, AZ 85712-4723, USA

Meyer Reyes, Deborah E (Debbie)
(Swimmer)
Po Box 2076
Carmichael, CA 95609, USA

Meyerriecks, Jeffrey (Director, Musical
Director)
Lindy Martin Mgmt
5 Lob Lolly court
Pinehurst, NC 28374, USA

Meyers, Anne Akiko (Musician)
ICM Artists
40 W 57th St
New York, NY 10019, USA

Meyers, Ari (Actor)
c/o Holly Lebed *Holly Lebed Personal
Management*
10535 Wilshire Boulevard
Suite 808
Los Angeles, CA 90024, USA

Meyers, Augie (Musician)
Encore Talent
2137 Zercher Road
San Antonio, TX 78209, USA

Meyers, Chad (Athlete, Baseball Player)
816 Summit RidRe Dr
Papillion, NE 68046-8096, USA

Meyers, Dave (Athlete, Basketball Player)
40629 Carmelina Cir
Temecula, CA 92591-16e9, USA

Meyers, David (Dave) (Director)
c/o Ramses Ishak *United Talent Agency
(UTA)*
9336 Civic Center Dr
Beverly Hills, CA 90210, USA

Meyers, Josh (Comedian)
c/o Staff Member *WmE2 (WMA-LA)*
1 William Morris Pl
Beverly Hills, CA 90212, USA

Meyers, Krystal (Musician)
5902 Parham Rd
Franklin, TN 37064-9220, USA

Meyers, Nancy (Director)
c/o Jeff Berg *ICM Partners (ICM-LA)*
10250 Constellation Blvd Fl 7
Los Angeles, CA 90067, USA

Meyers, Patricia (Athlete, Golfer)
2784 Moran Dr
Waldorf, MD 20601, USA

Meyers, Seth (Actor, Comedian)
c/o Tim Sarkes *Brillstein Entertainment
Partners*
9150 Wilshire Blvd #350
Beverly Hills, CA 90212, USA

Meyers-Drysdale, Ann (Athlete, Basketball
Player, Olympic Athlete)
6621 Doral Dr
Huntington Beach, CA 92648-6129, USA

Meyerson, Martin (Educator)
2016 Spruce St
Philadelphia, PA 19103, USA

Meyfarth, Ulrike
Friedensweg 59
Wesseling, GERMANY D-50389

Meyfarth, Ulrike Nasse (Athlete, Track Athlete)
Buschweg 53
Odenthal 51519, GERMANY

Meyjes, Menno (Director, Producer, Writer)
c/o Gabi Morgerman *WmE2 (WMA-LA)*
1 William Morris Pl
Beverly Hills, CA 90212, USA

Meysel, Inge
Sudstrand 13
Bullenhausen, GERMANY D-21217

Mezei, Branislav (Athlete, Hockey Player)
8017 Laurel Ridge Ct
Delray Beach, FL 33446-9537

Mezentseva, Galina (Ballerina)
Kirov Ballet Theatre
1 Ploshchad Iskusstr
Saint Petersburg, RUSSIA

Mezzogiorno, Giovanna (Actor)
c/o Estelle Lasher *Principal Entertainment (NY)*
1964 Westwood Blvd
Suite 400
Los Angeles, CA 90025, USA

Mfume, Kweisi (Politician)
Naacp 4805 Mount Hope Dr
Baltimore, MD 21215-3297, USA

Mfume, Kweisi (Misc)
NAACP
President's Office
P.O. Box 1557
Baltimore, MD 21203-1557, USA

MGMT (Music Group)
c/o Staff Member *Columbia Records (NY) - Main*
550 Madison Ave
New York, NY 10022

M. Grijalva, Raul (Congressman, Politician)
1511 Longworth HOB
Washington, DC 20515, USA

M. Hall, Ralph (Congressman, Politician)
2405 Rayburn HOB
Washington, DC 20515, USA

M. Honda, Michael (Congressman, Politician)
1713 Longworth HOB
Washington, DC 20515, USA

MIA (Musician)
c/o Todd Jacobs *WME (LA)*
9601 Wilshire Blvd Fl 3
Beverly Hills, CA 90210, USA

Miadich, Bart (Athlete, Baseball Player)
17841 Hillside Dr
Lake Oswego, OR 97034-7525, USA

Mialik, Larry (Athlete, Football Player)
100 Wisconsin Ave
Apt 900
Madison, WI 53703, USA

Miami Sound Machine
6205 Bird Rd.
Miami, FL 33155

Miano, Rich (Athlete, Football Player)
Miano Sports Bar
7168 Makaa St
Honolulu, HI 96825, USA

Micalef, Corrado (Athlete, Hockey Player)
12098 Av Camille-Tessier
Montreal, QC H1E 6A4, Canada

Micalef, Corrado (Athlete, Hockey Player)
P E I Rocket
46 Kensington
Charlottetown, PE C1A SH7, Canada

Micech, Phil (Athlete, Football Player)
3029 N 91st St
Milwaukee, WI 53222, USA

Miceli, Dan (Athlete, Baseball Player)
1712 Cottonwood Dreek Pl
Lake Mary, FL 32746-4407, USA

Miceli, Joe
189 Vanderbilt Ave.
Brentwood LI, NY 11717

Micell, Justine (Actor)
Don Buchwald
6500 Wilshire Blvd
#2200
Los Angeles, CA 90048, USA

Micelotta, Mickey (Athlete, Baseball Player)
3266 Jog Park Dr
Greenacres, FL 33467, USA

Micelotta, Robert P "Mickey" (Athlete, Baseball Player)
2035 E Warm Springs Rd Unit 1007
Las Vegas, NV 89119-0454, USA

Michael (King)
Villa Serena
77 Chemin Louis-Degalliet
Versoix-Geneva 1290, SWITZERLAND

Michael, Alum E (Government Official)
National Assembly for Wales
Cardiff Bay
Cardiff CF99 1NA, WALES

Michael, Archbishop (Religious Leader)
Antiochian Orthodox Christian Church
358 Mountain Road
Englewood, NJ 07631, USA

Michael, Bob (Politician)
1029 N. Glenwood St.
Peoria, IL 61606

Michael, Eugene R (Gene) (Misc)
49 Union Ave
Upper Saddle River, NJ 07458, USA

Michael, ex-King
77 Chemin Louis Degallier
Versoix, SWITZERLAND 1290

Michael, Gene (Athlete, Baseball Player, Coach, Commentator)
49 Union Ave
Upper Saddle River, NJ 07458-2024, USA

Michael, George (Musician, Songwriter)
c/o Michael Lippman *Lippman Entertainment*
23586 Calabasas Road
Suite 208
Calabasas, CA 91302, USA

Michael, Gregory (Actor)
c/o Mitchell Gossett *Cunningham Escott Slevin & Doherty (CESD-LA)*
9560 Wilshire Blvd Fl 5
Beverly Hills, CA 90212, USA

Michael, Kevin (Musician)
c/o Staff Member *Paradigm (Monterey)*
404 W Franklin St
Monterey, CA 93940, USA

Michael, Prince & Princess of Kent
Kensington Palace
London, ENGLAND W8 5AF

Michael, Thomas (Actor, Producer, Writer)
Peeping Tom Films

Michael Carroll, Jason (Musician)
c/o Staff Member *Creative Artists Agency (CAA-TN)*
3310 West End Ave
5th Floor
Nashville, TN 37203, USA

Michael E Captain, Lopez-Aiegria (Astronaut)
_1_8715 Point Lookout Dr
Houston, TX 77058-4030, USA

Michaels, Al (Commentator)
401 S Bristol Ave
Los Angeles, CA 90049-3820, USA

Michaels, Al
47 W. 66th St
New York, NY 10023

Michaels, Alan R (Al) (Sportscaster)
ABC-TV
Sports Dept
77 W 66th St
New York, NY 10023, USA

Michaels, Beverly
11921 Weddington
No. Hollywood, CA 91601

Michaels, Bret (Musician, Reality TV Star)
c/o Joann Mignano *Krupp Kommunications*
59 West 19th St Fl 4 #4C
New York, NY 10011, USA

Michaels, Eugene H (Misc)
Alzheimer's Disease Research
15825 Shady Grove Road
Rockville, MD 20850, USA

Michaels, Fern (Writer)
1006 S Main St
Summerville, SC 29483-4231, USA

Michaels, Gianna (Adult Film Star)
Look North Promotions
7 - 9 Clifford St
Unit 101
York, Yorkshire YO1 9RA, UK

Michaels, James W (Editor)
Forbes Magazine
Editorial Dept
60 5th Ave
New York, NY 10011, USA

Michaels, Jason (Athlete, Baseball Player, Coach)
5019 Avenue Avignon
Lutz, FL 33558-2826, USA

Michaels, Jillian (Fitness Expert, Reality TV Star)
c/o Giancarlo Chersich *Empowered Media*
9100 Wilshire Blvd
Suite 520E
Los Angeles, CA 90212, USA

Michaels, Lori (Musician)
352 Seventh Ave #202
New York, NY 10001, USA

Michaels, Lorne (Producer, Writer)
c/o Staff Member *Broadway Video Entertainment*
5555 Melrose Ave
Dressing Room Bldg #105
Los Angeles, CA 90038-3197

Michaels, Louis A (Lou) (Athlete, Football Player)
69 Grace St
Swoyersville, PA 18704, USA

Michaels, Marilyn
185 West End Ave.
New York, NY 10023

Michaels, Mia (Choreographer)
c/o Tim O'Brien *Clear Talent Group (LA)*
10950 Ventura Blvd
Studio City, CA 91604, USA

Michaels, Shawn (Wrestler)
7700 Bloomington Ave
Minneapolis, MN 55423, USA

Michaels, Tammy Lynn (Actor)
c/o Marcel Pariseau *True Public Relations*
6725 W Sunset Blvd #470
Los Angeles, CA 90028-7180, USA

Michaels, Walter (Walt) (Athlete, Coach, Football Coach, Football Player)
282 Michaels Rd
Shickshinny, PA 18655, USA

Michaelsen, Kari (Actor)
Kazarian/Spencer
11365 Ventura Blvd
#100
Studio City, CA 91604, USA

Michaelson, Ingrid (Musician)
c/o Patrick Confrey *Sunshine, Sachs & Associates*
149 Fifth Ave
7th Floor
New York, NY 10010, USA

Michalak, Chris (Athlete, Baseball Player)
1108 Mockingbird Ln
Keller, TX 76248-2903, USA

Michaleczewski, Dariusz (Boxer)
Universum Box-Promotion
Am Stadtrand 27
Hamburg 22047, GERMANY

Michalek, Zbynek (Athlete, Hockey Player)
21455 N 81st St
Scottsdale, AZ 85255-6479, USA

Michalik, Art (Athlete, Football Player)
33400 Gafford St
Wildomar, CA 92595, USA

Michalka, Aly (Actor, Musician)
c/o Hilary Hansen *PMK/BNC - LA*
8687 Melrose Ave
8th Floor
West Hollywood, CA 90069, USA

Michalka, Amanda (Musician)
c/o Staff Member *Lynda Goodfriend Management*
338 S Beachwood Dr
Burbank, CA 91506, USA

Michals, Duane (Photographer)
109 E 19th St
New York, NY 10003-9603, USA

Michaud, Olivier (Athlete, Hockey Player)
289 Rue Saint-Jean-Baptiste
Beloeil, QC J3G 2V7, Canada

Michayluk, Dave (Athlete, Hockey Player)
Farm
Wakaw, SK SDK 4PO, Canada

Micheaux, Larry (Athlete, Basketball Player)
2914 Calender Lake Dr
Missouri City, TX 77459-392e, USA

Micheaux, Nicki (Actor)
c/o Charlton Blackburne *A Management*
9107 Wilshire Blvd.
Suite 650
Beverly Hills, CA 90210, USA

Micheel, Shaun (Athlete, Golfer)
3100 Kenney Dr
Germantown, TN 38139-8041, USA

Michel, Alex (Reality TV Star)
PO Box 46605
Los Angeles, CA 90046, USA

Michel, F Curtis (Astronaut)
2101 University Blvd
Houston, TX 77030, USA

Michel, F Curtis Dr (Astronaut)
2101 University Blvd
Houston, TX 77030-1218, USA

Michel, Hartmut (Nobel Prize Laureate)
Max-Planck Institut
Heinrich-Hoffmann-Str 7
Frankfort 60528, GERMANY

Michel, Hartmut (Nobel Prize Laureate)
Max-Planck Institut Heinrich-Hoffmann-Str 7
Frankfort, Germany D-60528, USA

Michel, Jean-Louis (Oceanographer, Scientist)
IFREMER
Center de Toulon
La Seyne dur Mer, Toulon 83500, FRANCE

Michel, Mike (Athlete, Football Player)
378 Drexel Ave
Ventura, CA 93003, USA

Michel, Paul R (Judge)
US Court of Appeals
717 Madison Place NW
Washington, DC 20439, USA

Michel, Robert (Politician)
322 8th St SE
Washington, DC 20003-2109, USA

Michele, Chrisette (Musician)
c/o Staff Member *Selverne & Co.*
6565 Sunset Blvd
Suite 200
Hollywood, CA 90228, USA

Michele, Draya (Reality TV Star)
c/o Marcus Blassingame *TSD Agency*
Prefers to be contacted by telephone or email
USA

Michele, Lea (Actor, Musician)
c/o Jason Weinberg *Untitled Entertainment (LA)*
350 S. Beverly Dr #200
Beverly Hills, CA 90212, USA

Michele, Lisa (Stylist)
c/o Staff Member *Ennis*
119 Braintree St
Boston, MA 02134, USA

Michele, Michael (Actor)
c/o Staff Member *A Management*
9107 Wilshire Blvd.
Suite 650
Beverly Hills, CA 90210, USA

Micheler, Elisabeth (Athlete)
Gruntenstr 45
Augsburg 86163, GERMANY

Micheletti, Joe (Athlete, Hockey Player)
12 Riverpointe Rd
Hastings On Hudson, NY 10706-3812

Micheletti, Joe (Athlete, Hockey Player)
New York Rangers
2 Penn Plz Fl 22
New York, NY 10121-2299

Micheletti, joe (Athlete, Hockey Player)
12 Riverpointe Rd
Hastings On Hudson, NY 10706-3812

Micheletti, Pat (Athlete, Hockey Player)
832 Ivy Ln
Saint Paul, MN 55123-2425

Michell, Keith (Actor)
Chatto & Linnit
Prince of Wales
Coventry St
London W1V 7FE, UNITED KINGDOM (UK)

Michell, Roger (Director)
Duncan Heath
Paramount House
162 Wardour
London, W1V 3AT, UNITED KINGDOM (UK)

Michelle, Candice (Actor, Model)
c/o Jerry Donato *Abraxas Talent Agency*
4260 Troost Ave #1
Studio City, CA 91604, USA

Michelle, Sheley (Actor)
c/o Mike Simpson *WME (LA)*
9601 Wilshire Blvd Fl 3
Beverly Hills, CA 90210, USA

Michelmore, Guy
72 Goldsmith Ave.
London, ENGLAND W3 6HN

Michelmore, Lawrence (Government Official)
4924 Sentinel Dr
Bethesda, MD 20816, USA

Michels, John (Athlete, Football Player)
4544 Alveo Rd
La Canada Flintridge, CA 91011, USA

Michels, John (Athlete, Football Player)
504 Matterhorn Dr
Gatinburg, TN 37738, USA

Michels, Rinus (Coach, Football Coach)
Hotel Breitenbacher Hof
H-Heine-Allee 36
Dusseldorf 40213, GERMANY

Michelson, Gary (Inventor)
13140 Boca De Canon Ln
Los Angeles, CA 90049-2220, USA

Michener, Charles D (Misc)
1706 W 2nd St
Lawrence, KS 66044, USA

Michiba, Rokusaburo (Chef)
Ginza Rokusan-Tei 8-8-7 Ginza Dai San
Sowaredo Building Chyuo-ku
Tokyo, Japan, USA

Michibata, Jessica (Model)
c/o Staff Member *The Tanabe Agency*
2-21-4 Aobadai
Meguro
Tokyo 153-0042, JAPAN

Michie, Donald (Scientist)
6 Inveralmond Grove
Cramond
Edinburg EH4 6RA, SCOTLAND

Michiko (Royalty)
Imperial Palace
1-1 Chiyoda-ku
Tokyo 100, JAPAN

Michner, Andy (Race Car Driver)
PO Box 24697
Indianapolis, IN 46224, USA

Michnik, Adam (Editor)
Czerha 8/10
Warsaw 00732, POLAND

Michos, Anastas N (Cinematographer)
Gersh Agency
232 N Canon Dr
Beverly Hills, CA 90210, USA

Mickal, Abe (Athlete, Football Player, Physicist)
774 Topaz St
New Orleans, LA 70124, USA

Mickell, Darren (Athlete, Football Player)
9250 Chelsea Dr
Miramar, FL 33025, USA

Mickelson, Ed (Athlete, Baseball Player)
1532 Charlemont Dr
Chesterfield, MO 63017-4604, USA

Mickelson, Phil (Athlete, Golfer)
c/o Steve Loy *Gaylord Sports Management*
13845 N Northsight Blvd
Suite 200
Scottsdale, AZ 85260, USA

Mickens, Glenn (Athlete, Baseball Player)
5920 Kini Pl
Kapaa, HI 96746-8938, USA

Mickey, Joey (Athlete, Football Player)
6213 Canyon Dr
Oklahoma City, OK 73105, USA

Mickolio, Kam (Athlete, Baseball Player)
1036 N 15th Ave
Bozeman, MT 59715-3265, USA

Middendorf, Dave (Athlete, Football Player)
P.O. Box 525
Port Orchard, WA 98366, USA

Middendorf, J William II (Diplomat, Secretary)
565 W Main Road
Little Compton, RI 02837, USA

Middendorf, Max (Athlete, Hockey Player)
7791 E San Fernando Dr
Scottsdale, AZ 85255-4020

Middendorf, Tracy (Actor)
PO Box 480410
Los Angeles, CA 90048, USA

Middendorf, William (General)
565 W Main Rd
Little Compton, RI 02837-1131, USA

Middlebrook, Jason (Athlete, Baseball Player)
3309 Glenview Ave
Austin, TX 78703-1446, USA

Middlebrook, Lindsay (Athlete, Hockey Player)
2060 Flamingo Dr
Florissant, MO 63031-3516

Middlebrooks, Charley (Athlete, Baseball Player)
Indianapolis Clowns
528 Rigby St NE
Marrietta, GA 30063-0001, USA

Middlebrooks, Willie (Athlete, Football Player)
18775 SW 78th Ct
Cutler Bay, FL 33157, USA

Middle of the Road
18 Irvine Dr. Linwood
Refrewshire, ENGLAND

Middleton, Kate (Catherine, Duchess of Cambridge) (Princess, Royalty)
St James Palace
London SW1A 1BS, UNITED KINGDOM

Middleton, Mike (Model)
Louisa Models
Ebersberger Str 9
Munich 81679, GERMANY

Middleton, Rick (Athlete, Hockey Player)
PO Box 1161
Hampton, NH 03843-1161

Middleton, Terdell (Athlete, Football Player)
1893 Prospect St
Memphis, TN 38106, USA

Middleton-Gentry, Ruth (Baseball Player)
28 Grandview Heights
Hamilton, IN 46742, USA

Midkiff, Dale (Actor)
c/o John Frazier *Amsel, Eisenstadt & Frazier Talent Agency (AEF)*
5055 Wilshire Blvd
Suite 860
Los Angeles, CA 90036-6108, USA

Midler, Bette (Actor, Musician)
c/o Ken Sunshine *Sunshine, Sachs & Associates*
149 Fifth Ave
7th Floor
New York, NY 10010, USA

Midnight Fish
Samlandstr. 32
Munich, GERMANY D-81825

Midnight Oil
Box 186 Glebe
Sydney, AUSTRALIA NSW 2037

Midon, Raul (Musician)
c/o Barry Dickins *International Talent Booking*
74A Charlotte St
London W1T 4QJ, UNITED KINGDOM (UK)

Midori (Musician)
Midori Foundation
850 7th Ave
#705
New York, NY 10019, USA

Miechur, Thomas F (Misc)
Cement & Allied Workers Union
2500 Brickdale
Elk Grove Village, IL 60007, USA

Mieczko, A J (Athlete, Hockey Player)
295 Central Park W
Apt 9G
New York, NY 10024, USA

Mieczko, AJ (Athlete, Hockey Player, Olympic Athlete)
3 Hinckley Ln
Nantucket, MA 02554-2006, USA

Miehm, Kevin (Athlete, Hockey Player)
500 Victoria St W
Whitby, ON L1N 9G4, canada

Mielke, Gary (Athlete, Baseball Player)
1718 Orchid Dr S
North Mankato, MN 56003-1435, USA

Mientkiewicz, Doug (Athlete, Baseball Player, Olympic Athlete)
125 Bawiew Isle Dr
Islamorada, FL 33036-3308, USA

Mierkowicz, Ed (Athlete, Baseball Player)
7530 Macomb St Apt 1A
Grosse Ile, MI 48138-1522, USA

Mieske, Matt (Athlete, Baseball Player)
2199 E BombaY Rd
Midland, MI 48642-8351, USA

Mieto, Juha (Skier)
General Delivery
Mieto, FINLAND

Migay, Rudy (Athlete, Hockey Player)
485 Belrose Rd
Thunder Bav, ON P7G 1K1, Canada

Miggins, Larry (Athlete, Baseball Player)
2405 Kingston St
Houston, TX l7ID9-66Q3, USA

Mighty Clouds of Joy (Music Group)
c/o Staff Member EMI Recorded Music (UK)
27 Wrights Lane
London W8 5SW, UK

Mighty Mighty Bosstones (Music Group)
c/o Staff Member Paradigm (Monterey)
404 W Franklin St
Monterey, CA 93940, USA

Migliazzo, Paul (Athlete, Football Player)
605 W 68th Ter
Kansas City, MO 64113, USA

Migliore, Richard (Horse Racer)
48 Killearn Rd
Millbrook, NY 12545-6216, USA

Migliore, Richard (Race Car Driver)
420 Fair Hill Dr #1
Elkton, MD 21921-2573, USA

Mignola, Mike (Cartoonist)
c/o Staff Member Dark Horse Entertainment
1438 N Gower St
Box 23 Bldg 28 #200
Hollywood, CA 90028, USA

Miguel (Musician)
c/o Phillanda Williams TPF Management
511 Ave of the Americas #320
New York, NY 10011, USA

Mihaly, Andras (Composer)
Verhalom Ter 9B
Budapest II 1025, HUNGARY

Mihm, Chris (Athlete, Basketball Player)
Celeland Cavaliers
47e8 Peace Pipe Path
Austin, TX 78746-24e9, USA

Mihok, Dash (Actor)
c/o Staff Member Untitled Entertainment (LA)
350 S. Beverly Dr #200
Beverly Hills, CA 90212, USA

Mikan, Larry (Athlete, Basketball Player)
891 Carmona Ct
Chula Vista, CA 91910-8012, USA

Mikawos, Stan (Athlete, Football Player)
8 John Huyda Dr
Winnipeg, MB R2G 4C9, Canada

Mike, Dennery (Athlete, Football Player)
6419 Oakley St
Philadelphia, PA 19111, USA

Mikel, Liz (Actor)
c/o Terry Loftis Verve Communications Group
325 N. St. Paul St Ste2360
Dallas, TX 75201, USA

Mikell, George
23 Shuttleworth Rd
London, ENGLAND SW11

Mike-Mayer, Istvan (Steve) (Athlete, Football Player)
681 Lincoln Ave
Glen Rock, NJ 07452, USA

Mike-Mayer, Nicholas (Nick) (Athlete, Football Player)
681 Lincoln Ave
Glen Rock, NJ 07452, USA

Mike Rizzo, Mike (DJ)
c/o Staff Member Diva Central Inc
7510 W Sunset Blvd Ste 1445
Los Angees, CA 90046, USA

Mikeska, Russ (Athlete, Football Player)
148 Phoenix Dr
Eatonton, GA 31024, USA

Mikhalchenko, Alla A (Ballerina)
Malaya Gruzinskaya St 12/18
Moscow 123342, RUSSIA

Mikhalkov, Nikita (Director)
Maly Kozikhinksy Per 4
#16-17
Moscow 103001, RUSSIA

Mikhalkov-Konchalovsky, Andrei S (Director)
Malaya Gruzinskaya 28 #130
Moscow 123557, RUSSIA

Miki, Minouri (Composer)
1-11-6 Higashi Nogawa
Komae-shi
Tokyo 201, JAPAN

Mikita, Stan (Athlete, Hockey Player)
57 Chesterfield Ct
Burr Ridge, IL 60527-7932

Mikita, Valerie (Actor)
c/o Staff Member The Stevens Group
14011 Ventura Blvd #201
Sherman Oaks, CA 91423, USA

Mikkelsen, Mads (Actor)
c/o Theresa Peters United Talent Agency (UTA)
9336 Civic Center Dr
Beverly Hills, CA 90210, USA

Mikkelsen, Vern (Athlete, Basketball Player, Golfer)
17715 Breconwood Rd
Wayzata, MN 55391-3303, USA

Mikkelson, Bill (Athlete, Hockey Player)
47 Glen Meadow Cres
St. Albert, AB T8N 3A2, Canada

Miklich, William (Athlete, Football Player)
Highway 106
Dousman, WI 53118, USA

Miklos, Arpad (Adult Film Star)
c/o Staff Member Diva Central Inc
7510 W Sunset Blvd Ste 1445
Los Angees, CA 90046, USA

Miko, Izabella (Actor)
c/o Kesha Williams Affirmative Entertainment
425 N Robertson Blvd
Los Angeles, CA 90048, USA

Mikol, Jim (Athlete, Hockey Player)
17350 SE 82nd Roslyn Ct
The Villages, FL 32162-2881

Mikolajczyk, Ron (Athlete, Football Player)
18323 Oakde Rd
Odessa, FL 33556-4918, USA

Mikolajewski, Pete (Athlete, Football Player)
2520 Singing Vista Way
El Cajon, CA 92019, USA

Miksis, Al (Athlete, Basketball Player)
522 E Algonquin Rd
Apt 203
Schaumburg, IL 60173-3801, USA

Mikulski, Barbara (Politician)
3704 N Charles St Unit 1003
Baltimore, MD 21218-2325, USA

Mikulski, Barbara (Senator)
212 W Main ST #200
Salisbury, MD 21801-5006, USA

Mikva, Abner J (Judge)
442 New Jersey Ave SE
Washington, DC 20003, USA

Mikvy, Bill (Athlete, Basketball Player)
586 Linton Hill Rd
Newtown, PA 18940, USA

Milacki, Bob (Athlete, Baseball Player)
Reading Phillies PO Box 15050 Attn: Coaching Staff
Attn: Coaching Staff Reading,
PA 19612-5050, USA

Milan, Don (Athlete, Football Player)
P.O. Box 126
Gardnerville, NV 89410, USA

Milandro, Kristina
2518 Cardigan Ct.
Los Angeles, CA 90077-1337

Milani, Denise
Periscope Media
60027 Via St
Cathedral City, CA 92234, USA

Milani, Tom (Athlete, Hockey Player)

Milano, Alyssa (Actor)
c/o Jason Barrett Alchemy Entertainment
7024 Melrose Ave
Suite 420
Los Angeles, CA 90038, USA

Milano, Fred (Musician)
Paramount Entertainment
PO Box 12
Far Hills, NJ 07931, USA

Milbourne, Larry (Athlete, Baseball Player)
747 Yale Ter
Vineland, NJ 08360-5818, USA

Milbrett, Tiffeny (Athlete, Olympic Athlete, Soccer Player)
1902 SW Broadleaf Dr
Portland, OR 97219-6375, USA

Milburn, Darryl (Athlete, Football Player)
270 E Harding St
Baton Rouge, LA 70802, USA

Milburn, Glyn (Athlete, Football Player)
8815 S 2nd Ave
Inglewood, CA 90305, USA

Milbury, Mike (Athlete, Hockey Player)
Boston Bruins
100 Legends Way Ste 250
Boston, MA 02114-1389

Milbury, Mike (Athlete, Coach, Hockey Player)
61 Edwardel Rd
Needham, MA 02492-4001

Milchan, Arnon (Producer)
c/o Staff Member New Regency Productions
10201 W Pico Blvd
Bldg 12
Los Angeles, CA 90035, USA

Milchin, Mike (Athlete, Baseball Player, Olympic Athlete)
13651 Glynshel Dr
Winter Garden, FL 34787-5001, USA

Miledi, Ricardo (Biologist)
9 Gibbs Court
Irvine, CA 92612, USA

Milem, John (Athlete, Football Player)
PO Box 5236
Salisbury, NC 28147, USA

Miles, Aaron (Athlete, Baseball Player)
1716 San Jose Dr
Antioch, CA 94509-4217, USA

Miles, Carl (Athlete, Baseball Player)
3710 S lenoir St
Columbia, MO 65201-5463, USA

Miles, Darius (Athlete, Basketball Player)
1906 Llewellyn Rd
Belleville, IL 62223-7904, USA

Miles, Don (Athlete, Baseball Player)
400 Central Ave
Palacios, TX 77465-2000, USA

Miles, Eddie (Athlete, Football Player)
960 NW 48th Ave
Coconut Creek, FL 33063, USA

Miles, Jim (Athlete, Baseball Player)
134 Moores Creek Rd
Maben, MS 39750-5532, USA

Miles, Joanna (Actor)
2062 N Vine St
Los Angeles, CA 90068, USA

Miles, John (Baseball Player)
Chicago American Giants
4130 Treehouse Dr
San Antonio, TX 78222-3510, USA

Miles, John "Mule" (Athlete, Baseball Player)
4130 Treehouse Dr
San Antonio, TX 78222-3510, USA

Miles, John R (Jack) (Writer)
3568 Mountain View Ave
Pasadena, CA 91107, USA

Miles, John W (Geophysicist, Physicist, Scientist)
16800 Academy Dr #30
Palos Verdes Peninsula, CA 90274-3975, USA

Miles, Mark (Athlete, Tennis Player)
Assn of Tennis Pros
200 Tournament Players Road
Ponte Vedra Beach, FL 32082, USA

Miles, Ostell (Athlete, Football Player)
9400 W 11th Ave
Lakewood, CO 80215, USA

Miles, Paige (Musician)
c/o Simon Fuller *XIX Entertainment*
35-37 Parkgate Rd
32/33 Ransomes Dock
London SW11 4NP, UNITED KINGDOM
(UK)

Miles, Sarah (Actor)
Chithurst Manor
Trotton near Petersfield
Hants GU31 5EU, UNITED KINGDOM
(UK)

Miles, Sylvia (Actor)
c/o Staff Member *Agency for the
Performing Arts (APA-LA)*
405 S Beverly Dr
Suite 500
Beverly Hills, CA 90212-4425, USA

Miles, Vera (Actor)
PO Box 1599
Palm Desert, CA 92261, USA

Miles-Clark, Jearl (Athlete, Track Athlete)
J J Clark
University of Florida
Athletic Dept
Gainsville, FL 32604, USA

Miley, Dave (Athlete, Baseball Player, Coach)
Scranton/Wilkes Barre Yankees 235
Montage Mountain Rd
Attn:Managers Office Moosic,
PA 18507-1765, USA

Milgliore, Richard (Race Car Driver)
420 Fair Hill Dr.
#1
Elkton, MD 21921-2573, USA

Milhoan, Michael (Actor)
c/o Staff Member *Sanders Armstrong
Caserta*
2120 Colorado Blvd
Suite 120
Santa Monica, CA 90404, USA

Mili, Itula (Athlete, Football Player)
4468 Glenmoor Hills Dr
South Jordan, UT 84095, USA

Milian, Christina (Actor)
c/o Carmen Milian *Milian Management*
16830 Ventura Blvd #501
Encino, CA 91436, USA

Milian, Marilyn (Judge, Television Host)
The Peoples Court
401 Fifth Ave.
New York, NY 10016, USA

Milicevic, Ivana (Actor, Model)
c/o Staff Member *One Talent
Management*
9220 Sunset Blvd
Los Angeles, CA 90069, USA

Milicic, Darko
5460 Whitehall Blvd
Oakland Township, MI 48306-2277

Milinchik, Joe (Athlete, Football Player)
9329 Barker Rd
New Hill, NC 27562, USA

Milinichik, Joe (Athlete, Football Player)
653 Ryan Dr
Allentown, PA 18103, USA

Militano, Mark (Athlete, Figure Skater,
Olympic Athlete)
10940 Johnson St NE
Minneapolis, MN 55434-3777, USA

Militello, Sam (Athlete, Baseball Player)
3217 W Saint John St
Tampa, FL 33607-2127, USA

Milius, John F (Director, Writer)
888 Linda Flora Dr
Los Angeles, CA 90049, USA

Milken, Michael R (Financier,
Philanthropist)
4543 Tara Dr
Encino, CA 91436, USA

Mill, Andy (Athlete, Olympic Athlete,
Skier)
69 Danielson Dr
Aspen, CO 81611-9707, USA

Milla, Roger (Soccer Player)
Federation Camerounaise de Football
BP 1116
Yaounde, CAMEROON

Millan, Cesar (Television Host)
Cesar Millan Inc
1033 N Hollywood Way
Suite C
Burbank, CA 91505, USA

Millan, Felix (Athlete, Baseball Player)
G16 Calle Camarero Parq Ecuestre
Carolina, PR 00987-8523, USA

Millar, Jeff (Cartoonist)
1301 Spring Oaks Cir
Houston, TX 77055-4703, USA

Millar, Jeffrey L (Jeff) (Cartoonist)
1301 Spring Oaks Circle
Houston, TX 77055, USA

Millar, Kevin (Athlete, Baseball Player)
Major league Baseball Network 40 Hartz
Way Ste 10
Attn: On Air Personality ""/""/""/""<,
NJ 07094-2403, USA

Millar, Miles (Writer)
c/o Staff Member *Millar/Gough Ink*
3800 Barham Blvd
Suite 503
Los Angeles, CA 90068, USA

Millard, Bryan (Athlete, Football Player)
507 Sabine St Apt 502
Austin, TX 78701, USA

Millard, Keith (Athlete, Football Player)
3739 Oakhurst Way
Dublin, CA 94568, USA

Millbern, David (Actor)
c/o Staff Member *Barry Krost Management*
9220 W Sunset Blvd Ste 106
Los Angeles, CA 90069, USA

Millcic, Darko (Basketball Player)
Detroit Pistons
Palace
2 Championship Dr
Auburn Hills, MI 48326, USA

Milledge, Lastings (Athlete, Baseball
Player)
11114 Sailbrooke Dr
Riverview, FL 33579-7074, USA

Millegan, Eric (Actor)
c/o Peter Young *Sovereign Talent Group*
8421 Wilshire Blvd
Suite 200
Beverly Hills, CA 90211, USA

Millen, Corey (Athlete, Hockey Player,
Olympic Athlete)
8400 Cormorant Cove Cir
Anchorage, AK 99507, USA

Millen, Greg (Athlete, Hockey Player)
980 Orch
Bridgenorth, ON KOL lHO, Canada

Millen, Greg (Athlete, Hockey Player)
Toronto Maple Leafs
400-40 Bay St
Toronto, ON M5J 2X2, Canada

Millen, Hugh (Athlete, Football Player)
6836 Cascade Ave SE
Snoqualmie, WA 98065, USA

Millen, Matt (Athlete, Football Player)
PO Box 196
Durham, PA 18039, USA

Miller, Aaron (Athlete, Hockey Player,
Olympic Athlete)
147 Appletree Point Rd
Burlington, VT 05408-2446

Miller, Aaron David (Writer)
c/o Staff Member *Random House*
1540 Broadway
New York, NY 10036, USA

Miller, Abby Lee (Choreographer, Reality
TV Star)
Abby Lee Miller Dance Company
7123 Saltsburg Rd
Pittsburgh, PA 15235, USA

Miller, Alan (Journalist)
Los Angeles Times
Editorial Dept
202 W 1st St
Los Angeles, CA 90012, USA

Miller, Alan (Athlete, Football Player)
3118 Erie Dr
Orchard Lake, MI 48324, USA

Miller, Alice (Athlete, Golfer)
2 Log Church Rd
Wilmington, DE 19807-1724, USA

Miller, Allan (Actor)
Douglas Gorman Rothacker Wilhelm
1501 Broadway #703
New York, NY 10036, USA

Miller, Allison (Actor)
c/o Staff Member *Beth Goldstein
Management*
4433 Colbath Ave
Suite 34
Sherman Oaks, CA 91423, USA

Miller, Andre (Basketball Player)
Denver Nuggets
Pepsi Center
1000 Chopper Circle
Denver, CO 80204, USA

Miller, Andrew (Athlete, Baseball Player)
Detroit Tigers Foundation
417 SW 129th Ter
Newberry, FL 32669-2761, USA

Miller, Anthony (Athlete, Basketball
Player)
1083 Superior St
Benton Harbor, MI 49022-5310, USA

Miller, Anthony
2302 Via Camille
San Dimas, CA 91773, USA

Miller, Ben (Actor, Producer)
c/o Staff Member *Independent Talent
Group (ITG-UK)*
Oxford House
76 Oxford St
London W1D 1BS, UK

Miller, Bennett (Director)
c/o Bryan Lourd *Creative Artists Agency
(CAA-LA)*
2000 Ave Of The Stars
Los Angeles, CA 90067, USA

Miller, Bill (Athlete, Baseball Player)
P.O. Box 2681
Aptos, CA 95001-2681, USA

Miller, Bill (Race Car Driver)
4895 Convair Dr.
Carson City, NV 89706, USA

Miller, Billy (Actor)
c/o Staff Member *James/Levy/Jacobson
Management Inc*
3500 W Olive Ave
Suite 1470
Burbank, CA 91505, USA

Miller, Billy (Athlete, Football Player)
465 Cosmos Ct
Westlake, CA 91362, USA

Miller, Billy (Athlete, Football Player)
13745 Elkton Ct
Moorpark, CA 93021, USA

Miller, Bob (Athlete, Baseball Player)
3133 Coventry Dr
Waterford, MI 48329-3213, USA

Miller, Bob (Athlete, Baseball Player)
17397 Glenmore
Redford, MI 48240, USA

Miller, Bob (Athlete, Hockey Player)
1429 Main St
Marshfield, MA 02050-2072

Miller, BobG
1702 Keirn Trl
Saint Charles, IL 60174-5827

Miller, Bode (Athlete, Olympic Athlete,
Skier)
65 Easton Valley Rd
Franconia, NH 03580-5412, USA

Miller, Brad (Athlete, Basketball Player)
Sacramento Kings
5960 Via De La Rosa
Granite Bay, CA 95746-9040, USA

Miller, Brad (Congressman, Politician)
1127 Longworth HOB
Washington, DC 20515, USA

Miller, Brandon (Race Car Driver)
Childress Racing
236 Industrial Dr.
Box 1189
Welcome, NC 27374, USA

Miller, Bruce (Athlete, Baseball Player)
2126 Parkland Dr
Fort Wayne, IN 46825-3929, USA

Miller, Buddy (Musician)
Mark Pucci Media
5000 Oak Bluff Court
Atlanta, GA 30350, USA

Miller, Calvin (Athlete, Football Player)
1602 Fairfield Dr
Stillwater, OK 74074, USA

Miller, C Arden (Doctor)
350 Caroline Meadows Villa
Capel Hill, NC 27517, USA

Miller, Carl (Athlete, Football Player)
P.O. Box 773
Crowley, TX 76036-0773, USA

Miller, Charles D (Business Person)
Avery Dennison Corp
150 N Organge Grove Blvd
Pasadena, CA 91103, USA

Miller, Cheryl (Athlete, Basketball Player,
Olympic Athlete)
3206 Ellington Dr
Los Angeles, CA 90068-1741, USA

Miller, Cheryl D (Athlete, Basketball
Player, Coach)
3206 Ellington Drive
Los Angeles, CA 90068, USA

Miller, Chris (Director)
c/o Joy Fehily *Prime*
9696 Culver Blvd
Suite 102
Culver City, CA 90232, USA

Miller, Chris (Athlete, Football Player)
2114 Elkhorn Dr
Eugene, OR 97408, USA

Miller, Christa (Actor)
c/o Jill Littman *Impression Entertainment*
9229 W Sunset Blvd #700
West Hollywood, CA 90069, USA

Miller, Christine Cook (Judge)
US Claims Court
717 Madison Place NW
Washington, DC 20439, USA

Miller, Chryste Gaines (Athlete, Olympic
Athlete, Track Athlete)
5408 E Saddleridge Ln
Lithonia, GA 30038-3976, USA

Miller, Coco (Basketball Player)
Washington Mystics
MCI Center
601 F St NW
Washington, DC 20004, USA

Miller, Corey (Athlete, Football Player)
2528 Crofton Way
Columbia, SC 29223, USA

Miller, Corky (Athlete, Baseball Player)
1115 7th St
Calimesa, CA 92320-1013, USA

Miller, C Ray (Religious Leader)
United Brethren in Christ
302 Lake St
Huntington, IN 46750, USA

Miller, Damian (Athlete, Baseball Player)
N1276 Wuensch Rd
La Crosse, WI 54601-2655, USA

Miller, Dan (Musician)
Trans Continental Records
7380 Sand Lake Road
#350
Orlando, FL 32819, USA

Miller, Danny (Actor)
c/o Staff Member *Celeb Agents*
77 Oxford St
London ON W1D 2ES, UNITED
KINGDOM (UK)

Miller, Darrell (Athlete, Baseball Player)
21159 Via Alisa
Yorba Linda, CA 92887-2510, USA

Miller, Dave (Cartoonist)
1401 Folkstone
Edmond, OK 73034-3305, USA

Miller, dave
Cleveland Indians 2401 Ontario St Attn:
Coaching
Cleveland, OH 44115-4003

Miller, David (Cartoonist)
167 Tremont St
Reheboth, MA 02769, USA

Miller, Denise (Actor, Producer)
c/o Richard Sindell *Bob Waters Agency*
9301 Wilshire Blvd
Suite 300
Beverly Hills, CA 90210, USA

Miller, Dennis (Actor, Comedian)
c/o Marc Gurvitz *Brillstein Entertainment
Partners*
9150 Wilshire Blvd #350
Beverly Hills, CA 90212, USA

Miller, Denny (Actor)
9612 Gavin Stone Ave
Las Vegas, NV 89145, USA

Miller, Dyar (Athlete, Baseball Player)
8816 Admirals Bay Dr
Indianapolis, IN 46236-9292, USA

Miller, Eddie (Athlete, Baseball Player)
1819 Alfreda Blvd
San Pablo, CA 94806-4715, USA

Miller, Eddie (Athlete, Football Player)
1503 Summerwood Dr
Clarkston, GA 30021, USA

Miller, Elizabeth C (Doctor, Educator)
1822 Masters Lane
Madison, WI 53719, USA

Miller, Eugene A (Financier)
Comerica Inc
500 Woodward Ave
Detroit, MI 48226, USA

Miller, Frank (Actor, Writer)
c/o Staff Member *Shapiro-Lichtman Talent
Agency*
1333 Beverly Green Drive
Los Angeles, CA 90035-1018, USA

Miller, Frank (Cartoonist)
Dark House Publishing
10956 SE Main St
Milwaukie, OR 97222, USA

Miller, Fred (Athlete, Football Player)
7143 Sawmill Trail
Houston, TX 77040, USA

Miller, Fred D (Athlete, Football Player)
4535 Black Rock Rd
Upperco, MD 21155, USA

Miller, Gabrielle (Actor)
c/o Staff Member *Corner Gas*
PO Box 9
Station O
Scarborough, ON M4A 2M9, CANADA

Miller, George (Congressman, Politician)
2205 Rayburn HOB
Washington, DC 20515, USA

Miller, George D (General)
20 Phillips Pond South
Natick, MA 01760, USA

Miller, George T (Kennedy) (Director)
30 Orwell St
King's Cross
Sydney, NSW 2011, AUSTRALIA

Miller, Glenn Birthplace Society
PO Box 61
Clarinda, IA 51632

Miller, Glenn (Orchestra)
605 Crescent Exec. Ct. #300
Lake Mary, FL 32746

Miller, Glenn Society
18 Crendon St.
High Wycombe, Bucks. ENGLAND

Miller, Harvey R (Attorney, Attorney
General, General)
Weil Gotshal Manges
797 5th Ave
New York, NY 10153, USA

Miller, Jack (Politician)
11507 Orilla Del Rio Pl
Temple Terrace, FL 33617-2624, USA

Miller, Jack (Race Car Driver)
Arizona Motorsports
30-F Gasoline Alley
Indianapolis, IN 46222, USA

Miller, Jamir (Athlete, Football Player)
331 Grenadine Way
Hercules, CA 94547, USA

Miller, Janet (Stylist)
7344 W 85th St
Los Angeles, CA 90045, USA

Miller, Jarod (Scientist, Talk Show Host)
c/o Staff Member *NS Bienstock Inc*
250 W 57th St
Suite 333
New York, NY 10107, USA

Miller, Jason (Writer)
10000 Santa Monica Blvd Ste 305
Los Angeles, Ca 90067, USA

Miller, Jason (Mayhem) (Athlete)
c/o Jeff Sussman *Jeff Sussman
Management*
15374 Dickens St
2nd Floor
Sherman Oaks, CA 91403

Miller, Jay (Athlete, Hockey Player)
175 Chester St
North Falmouth, MA 02556-2302

Miller, Jeff
1301 Spring Oaks Circle
Houston, TX 77055

Miller, Jeff (Congressman, Politician)
2416 Rayburn HOB
Washington, DC 20515, USA

Miller, Jeffrey W (Stylist)
c/o Staff Member *Art Department*
48 Greene St
4th Floor
New York, NY 10013, USA

Miller, Jeremy (Actor)
5255 Vesper Ave
Sherman Oaks, CA 91411, USA

Miller, Jerry (Admiral)
Smithsonian Institution Press
750 9th St NW #4300
Washington, DC 20560, USA

Miller, Jim (Athlete, Football Player)
P.O. Box 863
Ripley, MS 38663, USA

Miller, Jody (Musician)
PO Box 413
Blanchard, OK 73010, USA

Miller, Joel McKinnon (Actor)
c/o Michael Greene *Greene & Associates*
1901 Avenue Of The Stars Ste 130
Los Angeles, CA 90067, USA

Miller, Joey (Race Car Driver)
Country Joe Racing
22222 Dodd Blvd
Lakeville, MN 55044-8553, USA

Miller, John (Athlete, Baseball Player)
5105 River Ave
Apt A
Newport Beach, CA 92663-2415, USA

Miller, John (Athlete, Baseball Player)
13443 Old Annapolis Rd
Mount Airy, MD 21771-7732, USA

Miller, John (Correspondent)
ABC-TV
News Dept
77 W 66th St
New York, NY 10023, USA

Miller, Johnny (Athlete, Golfer)
P.O. Box 2260
Napa, CA 94558, USA

Miller, Johnny (Athlete, Football Player)
94 Beach St
Revere, MA 02151, USA

Miller, Jon (Baseball Player,
Commentator, Sportscaster)
San Francisco Giants
401 Nevada Ave
Moss Beach, CA 94038-9643, USA

Miller, Jonathan (Director)
63 Gloucester Crescent
London NW1, UNITED KINGDOM (UK)

Miller, Jonny Lee (Actor)
c/o Ina Treciokas *Slate Public Relations*
9000 Sunset Blvd #915
West Hollywood, CA 90069, USA

Miller, Josh (Athlete, Football Player)
16 Summer Heights Dr
Franklin, MA 02038, USA

Miller, Joyce D (Misc)
Amalgamated Clothing & Textile Workers
1710 Broadway
#3
New York, NY 10019, USA

Miller, J Ronald (Religious Leader)
Int'l Community Churches Council
21116 Washington Parkway
Frankfort, IL 60423, USA

Miller, Julie (Musician, Songwriter,
Writer)
Mark Pucci Media
5000 Oak Bluff Court
Atlanta, GA 30350, USA

Miller, Justin (Athlete, Baseball Player)
2087 Bonnie Ave
Palm Harbor, FL 34683-5059, USA

Miller, Justin (Athlete, Football Player)
c/o Eugene Parker *Maximum Sports
Management*
6435 W Jefferson Blvd
#197
Fort Wayne, IN 46804, USA

Miller, Keith (Athlete, Baseball Player)
190 Water St # 2
Highland, MI 48381-1869, USA

Miller, Keith (Athlete, Baseball Player)
1831 W Alamosa Dr
Terrell, TX 75160-0811, USA

Miller, Keith (Politician)
3705 Arctic Blvd
Anchorage, AK 99503-5774, USA

Miller, Keith H (Ex-Governor)
3705 Arctic Blvd
Anchorage, AK 99503, USA

Miller, Kelly (Athlete, Hockey Player)
3783 ChipJ>endale Cir
Okemos, MI 48864-3861

Miller, Kelly (Basketball Player)
Indiana Fever
3763 Chippendale Circle
Okemos, MI 48864, USA

Miller, Kenny
5312 Eagle Lake Dr.
Palm Beach Gardens, FL 33418

Miller, Kevin (Athlete, Hockey Player, Olympic Athlete)
4243 Redbud Trail
Williamson, MI 48895-9103

Miller, Kip (Athlete, Hockey Player)
1933 Birch Bluff Dr
Okemos, MI 48864-5915

Miller, Kristen (Actor)
Lighthouse
409 N Camden Dr
#202
Beverly Hills, CA 90210, USA

Miller, Lajos (Opera Singer)
Balogh Adam Utca 28
Budapest 1026, HUNGARY

Miller, Larry (Athlete, Baseball Player)
3205 E Desert Cove Ave
Phoenix, AZ 85028-2735, USA

Miller, Larry
311 Mulberry St
Catasauqua, PA 18032-1825, USA

Miller, Larry (Actor, Comedian)
c/o Staff Member *Brillstein Entertainment Partners*
9150 Wilshire Blvd #350
Beverly Hills, CA 90212, USA

Miller, Larry (Athlete, Football Player)
3 Cour De La Reine
Palos Hills, IL 60465, USA

Miller, Lemmie (Athlete, Baseball Player)
Rockford Riverhawks
4503 Interstate Blvd
Attn: Coaching Staff
Loves Park, IL 61111, USA

Miller, Lennox (Athlete, Track Athlete)
2120 Pinecrest Dr
Altadena, CA 91001-2121, USA

Miller, Lenore (Misc)
Retail/Wholesale/Department Store Union
30 E 29th St
New York, NY 10016, USA

Miller, Linda G
242 Conway Ave
Los Angeles, CA 90024-2602, USA

Miller, LW (Race Car Driver)
Miller Racing
206 Performance Rd
Mooresville, NC 28115, USA

Miller, Marisa (Actor, Model)
c/o Zoe Lee *Cartel Management*
665 Lillian Way
Los Angeles, CA 90004, USA

Miller, Mark (Athlete, Football Player)
6020 Poling Rd
Elida, OH 45807, USA

Miller, Mark (Musician)
Sawyer Brown Inc
5200 Old Hardling Road
Franklin, TN 37064, USA

Miller, Mark Thomas (Actor)
PCC Inc
2554 Lincoln Blvd
#124
Venice, CA 90291, USA

Miller, Matt (Athlete, Baseball Player)
3203 61st St
Lubbock, TX 79413-5519, USA

Miller, Matt (Athlete, Football Player)
15 Highgate Cir
Ithaca, NY 14850, USA

Miller, McKaley (Actor)
c/o Kelly-Marie Smith *Brilliant Public Relations*
6260 W 3rd St
Suite 425
Los Angeles, CA 90036, USA

Miller, Michael (Athlete, Football Player)
116 E McClellan St
Flint, MI 48505, USA

Miller, Mike (Athlete, Basketball Player)
2308 Bay Dr
Pompano Beach, FL 33062-2915, USA

Miller, Mildred (Opera Singer)
PO Box 110108
Pittsburgh, PA 15232, USA

Miller, M Lynn (Stylist)
434 Bronxville Rd
Bronxville, NY 10708, USA

Miller, Mulgrew (Musician)
3725 Farmersville Road
Easton, PA 18045, USA

Miller, Nancy (Writer)
c/o Michael Donkis *Prime*
9696 Culver Blvd
Suite 102
Culver City, CA 90232, USA

Miller, Nate (Boxer)
1214 Allengrove St
Philadelphia, PA 19124, USA

Miller, Nicole J (Designer, Fashion Designer)
780 Madison Ave
New York, NY 10021, USA

Miller, Norm (Athlete, Baseball Player)
43 Columbia Crest Pl
Spring, TX 77382-1331, USA

Miller, Oliver (Athlete, Basketball Player)
2912 S Meadow Dr
Fort Worth, TX 76133-7214, USA

Miller, Omar Benson (Actor)
c/o Stephen Tenenbaum *Morra Brezner Steinberg & Tenenbaum (MBST) Entertainment*
345 N Maple Dr
Suite 200
Beverly Hills, CA 90210, USA

Miller, Paul (Athlete, Hockey Player)
5 Celtic Ave
Billerica, MA 01821-1203

Miller, Paul (Athlete, Baseball Player)
252 Redbud Ln
Batavia, IL 60510-3623, USA

Miller, Penelope Ann (Actor)
c/o Greg Clark *Untitled Entertainment (LA)*
350 S. Beverly Dr #200
Beverly Hills, CA 90212, USA

Miller, Perry (Athlete, Hockey Player)
471 McNaughton Ave
Winnipeg, MB R3L 1S5, Canada

Miller, Peter North (Business Person)
Dawson House
5 Jewry St
London EC3N 2EX, UNITED KINGDOM (UK)

Miller, Randy (Athlete, Baseball Player)
22523 Oak Mist Ln
Katy, TX 77494-2256, USA

Miller, Raymond (Ray) (Athlete, Baseball Player, Coach)
P.O. Box 41
New Athens, OH 43981-0041, USA

Miller, Reggie (Athlete, Basketball Player, Olympic Athlete)
14301 E 113th St
Fishers, IN 46040-9660, USA

Miller, Reginald W (Reggie) (Athlete, Basketball Player)
3785 Puerco Canyon Rd
Malibu, CA 90265-4551, USA

Miller, Renee (Stylist)
1200 W Monroe St
#510
Chicago, IL 60607, USA

Miller, Rick (Athlete, Baseball Player)
12790 Silverthorn Ct
Bonita Springs, FL 34135-2452, USA

Miller, Robert
Capitol Complex
Carson City, NV 89710, USA

Miller, Robert M (Athlete, Football Player)
8475 Knox Rd
Clarkston, MI 48348, USA

Miller, Robert N (Red) (Athlete, Coach, Football Coach, Football Player)
3841 S Narcissis Way
Denver, CO 80237, USA

Miller, Rod (Athlete, Baseball Player)
413 Cabarton Rd
Cascade, ID 83611-5004, USA

Miller, Romeo (Musician)
c/o Shannon Barr *Shannon Barr Public Relations*
1600 Rosecrans Ave
Media Center Bldg. 7, 4th Floor
Manhattan Beach, CA 90266-3708, USA

Miller, Ron (Athlete, Football Player)
6392 Washington
Youngville, CA 94599, USA

Miller, Ryan (Athlete, Hockey Player)
700 Walbert Dr.
East Lansing, MI 48823-2176

Miller, Scott (Athlete, Football Player)
26432 Charford Way
Lake Forest, CA 92630, USA

Miller, Shannon (Athlete, Gymnast, Olympic Athlete)
505 Lancaster St Apt 10ab
Jacksonville, Fl 32204, USA

Miller, Shawn (Athlete, Football Player)
3070 W Old Highway Rd
Morgan, UT 84050, USA

Miller, Sienna (Actor)
9 The Grove Camden
London N6 6JU, UNITED KINGDOM

Miller, Stanley L (Misc)
University of California
Chemistry Dept
La Jolla, CA 92093, USA

Miller, Stephanie (Comedian, Television Host)
KTLK AM 1150
3400 W. Olive Avenue
Suite 550
Burbank, CA 91505, USA

Miller, Steve (Musician, Songwriter)
PO Box 12680
Seattle, WA 98111, USA

Miller, Stu (Athlete, Baseball Player)
3701 Ocaso Ct
Cameron Park, CA 95682, USA

Miller, Stuart L (Stu) (Baseball Player)
St Louis Cardinals
3701 Ocaso Ct
Cameron Park, CA 95682-8961, USA

Miller, Tangi (Actor)
c/o Adam Robinson *Southfield Village*
8228 Sunset Blvd #190
Los Angeles, CA 90046, USA

Miller, Terry (Athlete, Football Player)
9015 W 2nd Ave
Stillwater, OK 74074, USA

Miller, Tom (Athlete, Hockey Player)
RR 1 PO
Mitchell, ON NOK INO, Canada

Miller, Tracie (Stylist)
c/o Staff Member *Help Me Rhonda*
541 10th St NW #294
Atlanta, GA 30318, USA

Miller, Travis (Athlete, Baseball Player)
51 Whisper Way
Eaton, OH 45320-9597, USA

Miller, Trever (Athlete, Baseball Player)
24155 Hideout Tr
Land O Lakes, FL 34639-8111, USA

Miller, Ty (Actor)
c/o Staff Member *Tedesco Management*
Prefers to be contacted via telephone
Los Angeles, CA 90069, USA

Miller, Valarie Rae
3500 W. Olive Ave. #1400
Burbank, CA 91505

Miller, Von (Football Player)
c/o David Dunn *Athletes First, LLC*
9140 Irvine Center Dr
Irvine, CA 92618, USA

Miller, Wade (Athlete, Baseball Player)
12 Woods Way
Reading, PA 19610-1199, USA

Miller, Warren (Photographer)
505 Pler Ave
Hermosa Beach, CA 90254, USA

Miller, Warren (Athlete, Hockey Player)
937 21st Ave N
South Saint Paul, MN 55075-1316, USA

Miller, Wentworth (Actor)
c/o Lee Stollman *The Gotham Group Inc*
9255 Sunset Blvd
Suite 515
Los Angeles, CA 90069, USA

Miller, Wiley (Artist, Cartoonist)
8 Granite Heights Rd
Kennebunkport, ME 04046, USA

Miller, Wiley (Cartoonist)
8 Granite Heights Rd
Kennebunkport, ME 04046-5262, USA

Miller, William (Athlete, Baseball Player)
P.O. Box 2681
Aptos, CA 95001-2681, USA

Miller, Willie T (Athlete, Football Player)
308 Martin Dr
Birmingham, AL 35215, USA

Miller, Zell (Government Official, Politician)
709 Miller St
Young Harris, GA 30582-4019, USA

Millett, Kate (Writer)
20 Old Overlook Rd
Poughkeepsie, NY 12603, USA

Millette, Joe (Athlete, Baseball Player)
759 Solana Dr
Lafayette, CA 94549-5206, USA

Millhauser, John (Stylist)
c/o Staff Member *Exclusive Artists Mgmt*
7700 Sunset Blvd
#205
Los Angeles, CA 90046, USA

Millhauser, Steven (Writer)
235 Caroline St
Saratoga Springs, NY 12866, USA

Milliard, Ralph (Baseball Player)
101 Runaway Bay Dr APt 304
Virginia Beach, VA 23452-8157

Milligan, Dustin (Actor)
c/o Deb Dillistone *Red Management*
100 W. Pender St
Sun Tower, 7th Floor
Vancouver, BC V6B 1R8, Canada

Milligan, Randy (Athlete, Baseball Player)
6905 Real Princess Ln
Gwynn Oak, MD 21207-4577, USA

Millikan, Joe (Race Car Driver)
4671 Bull Creek Rd
Franklinville, NC 27248, USA

Milliken, Robert (General)
955 N 14th St
Laramie, WY 82072-2814, USA

Milliken, William (Politician)
6103 Peninsula Dr
Traverse City, MI 49686-1913, USA

Millionaire, Tony (Artist)
c/o Staff Member *Fantagraphics Books*
7563 Lake City Way
Seattle, WA 98115, USA

Millionaires (Music Group)
c/o Jonathan Daniel *Crush Management*
60-62 E 11th St
7th Floor
New York, NY 10003, USA

Millman, Dan (Writer)
PO Box 6148
San Rafael, CA 94930, USA

Millman, Irving (Inventor)
310 Windsor Cir
Cherry Hill, NJ 08002-2423, USA

Millner, eddie
491 Stambaugh Ave
Columbus, OH 43207-2565

Millns, James (Athlete, Figure Skater, Olympic Athlete)
7603 Dunbridge Dr
Odessa, FL 33556-2259, USA

Millns, Jim (Athlete, Figure Skater, Olympic Athlete)
16306 Doune Ct
Tampa, FL 33647-2761, USA

Millo, Aprile E (Opera Singer)
Columbia Artists Mgmt Inc
165 W 57th St
New York, NY 10019, USA

Milloy, Lawyer (Athlete, Football Player)
1 Bills Dr
Orchard Park, NY 14127, USA

Mills, Alan (Athlete, Baseball Player)
1811 Bellgrove St
Lakeland, FL 33805-2523, USA

Mills, Alley (Actor)
444 Carol Canal
Venice, CA 90291, USA

Mills, Bill (Athlete, Baseball Player)
4344 Commercial St
Port Charlotte, FL 33953-5945, USA

Mills, Billy (Athlete, Olympic Athlete, Track Athlete)
c/o Staff Member *Billy Mills Speakers Bureau, The*
7760 Winding Way #723
Fair Oaks, CA 95628, USA

Mills, Brad (Athlete, Baseball Player)
723 N 22nd Pl
Mesa, AZ 85213-6706, USA

Mills, Chris (Athlete, Basketball Player)
2223 Camden Ave
Los Angeles, CA 90064-1905, USA

Mills, Curtis (Athlete, Track Athlete)
328 Lake St
Lufkin, TX 75904, USA

Mills, Dick (Athlete, Baseball Player)
10345 E Desert Cove Ave
Scottsdale, AZ 85260-6304, USA

Mills, Donna (Actor)
c/o Staff Member *Darlene Kaplan Entertainment*
4450 Balboa Ave
Encino, CA 91316, USA

Mills, Eddie (Actor)
c/o Staff Member *Peter Strain & Associates Inc (LA)*
5455 Wilshire Blvd
Suite 1812
Los Angeles, CA 90036-4368, USA

Mills, Erie (Opera Singer)
John J Miller
801 W 18th St
#20
New York, NY 10033, USA

Mills, Ernie (Athlete, Football Player)
21246 SW Plantation St
Dunnellson, FL 34431-3482, USA

Mills, Frank (Composer, Musician)
Rocklands Talent
PO Box 1282
Peterborough, ON K9L 7H5, CANADA

Mills, Hayley (Actor)
c/o Alan Willig *Don Buchwald & Associates Inc (NY).*
10 E 44th St
New York, NY 10017

Mills, Heather (Activist)
MPL Communications Ltd
1 Soho Square
London, W1V 6BQ, ENGLAND

Mills, John Henry (Athlete, Football Player)
755 Bahia Cir
Ocala, FL 34472, USA

Mills, Jordan
6500 Wilshire Blvd. #2200
Los Angeles, CA 90048, USA

Mills, Judson (Actor)
c/o Dino May *Dino May Management*
6362 Hollywood Blvd #422
Hollywood, CA 90028-6323, USA

Mills, Juliet (Actor, Writer)
5252 Lennox Ave
Sherman Oaks, CA 91401, USA

Mills, Kyle (Writer)
c/o Staff Member *Vanguard Press*
387 Park Ave S
12th Floor
New York, NY 10016, USA

Mills, Leigh Ann (Athlete, Golfer)
1919 W Carmen St
Tampa, FL 33606, USA

Mills, Mary (Athlete, Golfer)
310 S Ocean Blvd
Apt 106
Boca Raton, FL 33432, USA

Mills, Mike (Musician)
c/o Staff Member *ICM Partners (ICM-LA)*
10250 Constellation Blvd Fl 7
Los Angeles, CA 90067, USA

Mills, Noah (Actor, Model)
c/o Melissa Stone *42West (LA)*
11400 W Olympic Blvd
Suite 1100
Los Angeles, CA 90064, USA

Mills, Pete (Football Player)
Buffalo Bills
27 Langfield Dr
Buffalo, NY 14215-3321, USA

Mills, Stephanie (Actor, Musician)
Associated Booking Corp
1995 Broadway
#501
New York, NY 10023, USA

Mills, Terry (Athlete, Basketball Player)
Indiana Pacers
37840 Scoutt Pine Dr
New Boston, IN 48164-9190, USA

Mills, William M (Billy) (Athlete, Track Athlete)
7760 Winding Way
Fair Oaks, CA 95628, USA

Mills, Zach (Actor)
c/o Judy Savage *Savage Agency*
6212 Banner Ave
Los Angeles, CA 90038, USA

Millsaps, Knox (Engineer)
323 NW 24th St
Gainesville, FL 32607, USA

millwood, Kevin
1204 Suncast Ln Ste 2
El Dorado Hills, CA 95762-9665

Millwood, Kevin A (Athlete, Baseball Player)
330 Las Colinas Blvd E
Apt 1722
Irving, TX 75039, USA

Milmoe, Caroline (Actor)
Nigel Martin-Smith
41 S King St
Manchester M2 6DE, UNITED KINGDOM (UK)

Milner, Anthony F D (Composer)
147 Heythorp St
Southfields
London SW18 5BT, UNITED KINGDOM (UK)

Milner, Brian (Athlete, Baseball Player)
11825 Elko Ln
Fort Worth, TX 76108-4783, USA

Milner, Eddie (Athlete, Baseball Player)
491 Stambaugh Ave
Columbus, OH 43207, USA

Milner, Martin (Actor)
3106 Azahar Street
Carlsbad, CA 92009, USA

Milnes, Sherrill E (Opera Singer)
Herbert Barrett
266 W 37th St
#2000
New York, NY 10018, USA

Milnor, John W (Mathematician)
3 Laurel Lane
Setauket, NY 11733, USA

Milo, Sandra
Viale Liegi 42
Rome, ITALY I-00198

Milonakis, Andy (Actor)
c/o Jason Cunningham *Paradigm (LA)*
360 N Crescent Dr
North Bldg
Beverly Hills, CA 90210, USA

Milongo, Andre (Prime Minister)
Union for Democracy & Republic
Brazzaville, CONGO REPUBLIC

Milos, Sofia (Actor)
Sofia Milos Fan Club
8950 West Olympic
P.O. Box 173
Beverly Hills, CA 90211, USA

Milow, Keith (Artist)
32 W 20th St
New York, NY 10011, USA

Milsap, Ronnie (Musician, Songwriter)
c/o Staff Member *Buddy Lee Attractions Inc*
38 Music Square E #300
Nashville, TN 37203-4396, USA

Milsome, Doug (Cinematographer)
Simth/Gosnell/Nicholson
PO Box 1156
Studio City, CA 91614, USA

Milstead, Charles (Football Player)
Houston Oilers
10043 Meadow Lake Ln
Houston, TX 77042-2915, USA

Milstead, Rod (Athlete, Football Player)
11815 Brookeville Landing Ct
Bowie, MD 20721, USA

Milstein, Elliott (Educator)
American University
President's Office
Washington, DC 20016, USA

Milteer, Lee (Business Person, Writer)
Lee Milteer Inc.
2100 Thoroughgood Rd
Virginia Beach, VA 23455, USA

Milton, DeLisha (Basketball Player)
Los Angeles Sparks
Staples Center
1111 S Figueroa St
Los Angeles, CA 90015, USA

Milton, Eric (Athlete, Baseball Player)
1133 Asquith Dr
Arnold, MD 21012-2153, USA

Milva
9 via Gabrio Serbelloni
Milan, ITALY I-20122

Mimbs, Michael (Athlete, Baseball Player)
2761 Mimbs Rd
Alamo, GA 30411, USA

Mimbs, Mike (Basketball Player)
950 Huntcliffe Ct
Macon, GA 31210, USA

Mimbs, Robert (Athlete, Football Player)
115 Hastings Cres
Regina, SK S4T 7N6, Canada

Mimoun, Alain (Athlete, Track Athlete)
27 Ave Edouard-Jenner
Champigny-sur-Marne 94500, FRANCE

Mims (Musician)

Mims, Madeline Manning (Athlete, Track Athlete)
7477 E 48th St
#83-4
Tulsa, OK 74145, USA

Min, Gao (Misc)
Olympic Committee
9 Tuyuguan
Beijing, CHINA

Minaj, Nicki (Musician)
c/o Gee Roberson *Hip Hop Since 1978*
1290 Ave of the Americas
26th Floor
New York, NY 10104, USA

Minarcin, Rudy (Athlete, Baseball Player)
1037 1st St
Vandergrift, PA 15690-1007, USA

Minarik, Henry (Athlete, Football Player)
1001 N Linda Ln
Lake City, MI 49561, USA

Minaya, Omar (Athlete, Baseball Player, Commentator)
c/o Staff Member *San Diego Padres*
100 Park Blvd
San Diego, CA 92101, USA

Mincer, Jacob (Economist)
448 Riverside Dr
New York, NY 10027, USA

Minchey, Nate (Athlete, Baseball Player)
1212 Ramble Creek Dr
Pflugerville, TX 78660-2155, USA

Minchin, Tim (Actor, Comedian)
c/o Max Burgos *Agency for the Performing Arts (APA-LA)*
8383 Wilshire Blvd
Suite 1050
Beverly Hills, CA 90211, USA

Mincy, Charles (Athlete, Football Player)
1142 W 79th St
Los Angeles, CA 90044, USA

Mincy, Purnell (Baseball Player)
Philadelphia Stars
127 W 96th St Apt 160
New York, NY 10025-6482, USA

Mindel, Lee F (Architect)
Shelton Mindel Assoc
56 W 22nd St Fl 12
New York, NY 10010-7279, USA

Mindell, Earl (Writer)
Hay House
PO Box 5100
Carlsbad, CA 92018-5100

Mindless Behavior (Music Group)
c/o Troy Carter *Atom Factory/Coalition Media Group*
1630 Colorado Ave
Santa Monica, CA 90404, USA

Minds, Simple (Music Group)
c/o Staff Member *Solo Agency Ltd (UK)*
55 Fulham High St
2nd Floor
London SW6 3JJ, United Kingdom

Minear, Tim (Director, Writer)
c/o Lawrence Shuman *Shuman Company*
3815 Hughes Ave
4th Floor
Culver City, CA 90232, USA

Minehan, Cathy E (Financier, Government Official)
Federal Reserve Bank
600 Atlantic Ave
Boston, MA 02210, USA

Mineo, Gordon (Race Car Driver)
Flash Gordon Racing
214 Windy Lane
Rockwall, TX 75087, USA

Miner, Harold (Athlete, Basketball Player)
5067 Mountain Foliage Dr
Las Vegas, NV 89148-1438, USA

Miner, Steve (Director)
1137 2nd St
#103
Santa Monica, CA 90403, USA

Miner, Zack (Baseball Player)
108 Glencullen Cir
Jupiter, FL 33458-6534

Minervini, Craig (Athlete, Baseball Player)
229 Cameron Drive
Weston, FL 33326-3515, USA

Mineta, Norman Y (Secretary)
Transportation Department
400 7th St SW
Washington, DC 20590, USA

Minetto, Craig (Athlete, Baseball Player)
1809 Lakeshore Dr
Lodi, CA 95242-4230, USA

Ming, Tsai (Chef)
Food Network
1180 Ave of Americas
#1200
New York, NY 10036, USA

Ming, Yao (Athlete, Basketball Player)
c/o Bill Duffy *BDA Sports Management (BDA-CA)*
700 Ygnacio Valley Rd
Suite 330
Walnut Creek, CA 94596, USA

Mingenbach, Louise (Designer)
c/o Wayne Fitterman *United Talent Agency (UTA)*
9336 Civic Center Dr
Beverly Hills, CA 90210, USA

Minghella, Max (Actor)
c/o Tony Lipp *Anonymous Content (LA)*
3531 Hayden Ave
Culver City, CA 90232, USA

Ming-Na, Wen (Actor)
c/o Troy Nankin *Wishlab*
2225-A Hyperion Ave
Los Angeles, CA 90027, USA

Mingo, Gene (Athlete, Football Player)
5701 E Colorado Ave
Denver, CO 80224, USA

Mingori, Steve (Athlete, Baseball Player)
8841 North Congress Ave
Apt 637
Kansas City, MO 64153, USA

Mingus, Charles
484 W. 43rd St. #43-S
New York, NY 10036

Ming Wang, Chien (Athlete, Baseball Player)
c/o Team Member *New York Yankees*
Yankee Stadium
161st St & River Ave
Bronx, NY 10451, USA

Minh, Tran (Choreographer, Dancer)
2014 NE 47th Ave
Portland, OR 97123, USA

Miniefield, Kevin (Athlete, Football Player)
1030 Lakehurst Rd
Waukegan, IL 60085, USA

Mink, Rep (Politician)
PO Box 50144
Honolulu, HI 96850

Minka (Adult Film Star)
USP Entertainment Inc
8635 W Sahara Ave #564
Las Vegas, NV 89117, USA

Minkoff, Rob (Director, Producer)
c/o Rand Holston *Creative Artists Agency (CAA-LA)*
2000 Ave Of The Stars
Los Angeles, CA 90067, USA

Minnelli, Liza (Actor, Musician, Producer)
150 E 69th St #21G
New York, NY 10021, USA

Minnick, Don (Athlete, Baseball Player)
215 Bernard Rd
Rocky Mount, VA 24151-2243, USA

Minniear, Randy (Athlete, Football Player)
739 Westport Rd
Easton, CT 06612, USA

Minniefield, Dick (Athlete, Basketball Player)
10902 Little Gap Dr
Sugar Land, TX 77478, USA

Minniefield, Dirk
10902 Little Gap Ct
Sugar Land, TX 77498-0946

Minnifield, Frank (Athlete, Football Player)
4809 Chaffey Ln
Lexington, KY 40515, USA

Minnillo, Vanessa (Actor, Television Host)
c/o Melissa Raubvogel *Baker Winokur Ryder Public Relations BWR (BWR-NY)*
292 Madison Ave
12th Floor
New York, NY 10017, USA

Minogue, Dannii (Actor, Musician)
c/o Melissa LeGear *Melissa LeGear Management*
329 Montague St
Albert Park, Victoria 3206, Australia

Minogue, Kylie (Actor, Musician)
c/o Allsion MacGregor *Terry Blamey Management*
PO Box 13196
London SW6 4WF, UNITED KINGDOM (UK)

Minor, Blas (Athlete, Baseball Player)
7139 Dean St
Winton, CA 95388-9766, USA

Minor, Claudie (Athlete, Football Player)
730 17th St
Suite 520
Denver, CO 80202, USA

Minor, Damon (Athlete, Baseball Player)
New Orleans Zephyrs 6000 Airline Dr
Attn: Coaching Staff
Metairie, LA 70003-4373, USA

Minor, Gerry (Athlete, Hockey Player)
6516 Jackson Dr.
San Diego, CA 92119-3309

Minor, Greg (Athlete, Basketball Player)
6543 Merrick Landing Blvd
Windermere, FL 34786-7351, USA

Minor, Kory (Athlete, Football Player)
1402 W Farlington St
West Covina, CA 91790, USA

Minor, Larry (Race Car Driver)
PO Box 398
San Jacinto, CA 92581-0398, USA

Minor, Lincoln (Athlete, Football Player)
5036 Coldwater Canyon Ave #104
Sherman Oaks, CA 91423, USA

Minor, Mark (Athlete, Basketball Player)
5693 Muldoon Ct
Dublin, OH 43016-4332, USA

Minor, Mike (Baseball Player)
4036 Cottonwood Ct
Lewisburg, TN 37091-6693

Minor, Rickey (Director, Musical Director)
c/o Staff Member *WmE2 (WMA-LA)*
1 William Morris Pl
Beverly Hills, CA 90212, USA

Minor, Ronald R (Religious Leader)
Pentecostal Church of God
4901 Pennsylvania
Joplin, MO 64804, USA

Minor, Ryan (Athlete, Baseball Player)
Delmarva Shorebirds PO Box 1557 Attn: Managers
Salisbury, MD 21802-1557, USA

Minor, Shane (Musician)
ESP Mgmt
838 N Doheny Dr
#302
West Hollywood, CA 90069, USA

Minor, Susie (Stylist)
1544 Michigan Ave
Miami, FL 33139, USA

Minor, Travis (Athlete, Football Player)
PO Box 1635
Hallandale, FL 33008, USA

Minoso, Minnie (Basketball Player, Coach)
3700 N Lake Shore Dr Apt 303
Chicago, IL 60613-4244, USA

Minoso, Minnie (Athlete, Baseball Player)
3700 N Lake Shore Dr
Apt 303
Chicago, IL 60613, USA

Minow, Newton
375 Palos Rd
Glencoe, IL 60022-1951, USA

Minow, Newton (Journalist)
375 Palos Rd
Glencoe, IL 60022-1951, USA

Minow, Newton N (Government Official)
179 E Lake Shore Dr
#15W
Chicago, IL 60611, USA

Minshall, Jim (Athlete, Baseball Player)
225 Marv Ingles Hwy
Melbourne, KY 41059-8217, USA

Minshew, Alicia (Actor)
c/o Seth Greenky *Green Key Mgmt (NY)*
251 W 89th St
Suite 4-A
New York, NY 10024, USA

Minsky, Marvin L (Scientist)
Massachusetts Institute of Technology
Computer Sci Dept
Cambridge, MA 02139, USA

Mint Condition (Musician)
c/o Staff Member *Green Light Talent Agency*
P.O. Box 3172
Beverly Hills, CA 90212, USA

Minter, Barry (Athlete, Football Player)
2626 Garcitas Crk
Richmond, TX 77406, USA

Minter, Cedric (Athlete, Football Player)
5653 E Bay Trail Ct
Boise, ID 83716, USA

Minter, Kelly (Actor)
c/o John Ly *John Ly Agency*
1601 N Gower #202
Hollywood, CA 90028, USA

Minter, Kristin (Actor)
c/o Charles Silver *Silver Massetti & Szatmary (SMS) Talent Inc*
8383 Wilshire Blvd
Suite 230
Beverly Hills, CA 90211, USA

Minter, Mike (Athlete, Football Player)
3661 Richwood Cir
Kannapolis, NC 28081, USA

Minter, Patricia (Stylist)
2056 W Belle Plaine Ave
Chicago, IL 60618, USA

Minton, Greg (Athlete, Baseball Player)
7819 E Buena Terra Way
Scottsdale, AZ 85250-650, USA

Minton, Madge Rutherford
6431 N Oxford St
Indianapolis, IN 46220-2244, USA

Minton, Yvonne F (Opera Singer)
Ingpen & Williams
26 Wadham Road
London SW15 2LR, UNITED KINGDOM (UK)

Mintz, Shiomo (Musician)
I C M Artists
40 W 57th St
New York, NY 10019, USA

Mintz, Steve (Athlete, Baseball Player)
Fort Myers Miracle 14400 Six Mile
Cypress Pkwy A
Fort Myers, FL 33912-4326, USA

Mintz-Plasse, Christopher (Actor)
c/o Josh Katz *United Talent Agency (UTA)*
9336 Civic Center Dr
Beverly Hills, CA 90210, USA

Minutelli, Gino (Athlete, Baseball Player)
3305 Foxtrot Ct
Spring Hill, TN 37174-7116, USA

Mio, Eddie (Athlete, Hockey Player)
PO Box 252745
West Bloomfield, MI 48325-2745

Miou-Miou (Actor)
VMA
20 Ave Rapp
Paris 75008, FRANCE

Mir, Isabelle (Athlete, Skier)
Saint-Lary 65170, France

Mira, George (Athlete, Football Player)
19225 SW 128th Ct
Miami, FL 33177, USA

Mirabella, Erin (Athlete, Cycler, Olympic Athlete)
914 N Idaho St
La Habra, CA 90631, USA

Mirabella, Paul (Athlete, Baseball Player)
125 Jenks Rd
Morristown, NJ 07960-8701, USA

Mirabelli, Doug (Athlete, Baseball Player)
9788 Edgewood Ave
Traverse City, MI 49685-8173, USA

Miracles, The
141 Dunbar Ave.
Fords, NJ 08863

Miraldi, Dean (Athlete, Football Player)
14015 Live Oak Ln
Grass Valley, CA 95945, USA

Miranda, Christianne (Musician, Songwriter, Writer)
c/o Staff Member *Kult Records*
38 West 36 Street Third Floor
New York, NY 10018, USA

Miranda, Lin-Manuel (Actor)
c/o Brian Liebman *Liebman Entertainment*
25 E 21st St #PH
New York, NY 10011-8503, USA

Miranda, Patricia (Wrestler)
Stanford Wrestling - Department of Athletics
Stanford University
Arrillaga Family Sports Center
Stanford, CA 94305-6150, USA

Miranda, Willie
5502 Whitwood Rd.
Baltimore, MD 21208

Mirchoff, Beau (Actor)
c/o Scott Fish *Vital Management Group (VMG)*
5225 Wilshire Blvd #303
Los Angeles, CA 90036, USA

Mirer, Rick
11220 NE 53rd St.
Kirkland, WA 98033

Mirer, Rick (Athlete, Football Player)
Mirror Wine Company 1360 Main St Ste A Attn: Owners Office
Saint Helena, CA 94574, USA

Mirich, Rex (Athlete, Football Player)
620 W Yaqui Dr
Tucson, AZ 85704, USA

Miriciolu, Nelly (Opera Singer)
53 Midhurst Ave
Muswell Hill
London N10, UNITED KINGDOM (UK)

Mirikitani, Janice (Writer)
Glide Memorial United Methodist Church
330 Ellis St
San Francisco, CA 94102, USA

Mirisch, Walter M (Producer)
647 Warner Ave
Los Angeles, CA 90024, USA

Mirkerevic, Dragen (Prime Minister)
Premier's Office
Vojvode Putnkia 3
Sarajevo 71000, BOSNIA & HERZEGOVINA

Mirkin, David (Actor, Director)
c/o David Gersh *Gersh (LA)*
9465 Wilshire Blvd
Suite 600
Beverly Hills, CA 90212, USA

Mirnyi, Max (Athlete, Tennis Player)
c/o Staff Member *ATP Tour*
201 ATP Tour Blvd
Ponte Vedra Beach, FL 32082-3211, USA

Mironov, Boris (Athlete, Hockey Player)
110 E Parsonage Way
Manalapan, NJ 07726-7949

Mironov, Dmitri (Athlete, Hockey Player)
2911 Bayview Ave.
North York, ON M2K 1E8, Canada

Mironov, Yevgeniy V (Actor)
Oleg Tabajiv Theater
Chaokygina Str 12A
Moscow, RUSSIA

Miroslav, Frycer (Athlete)
Frycer Sports Agency Pelclova 5
Ostrava 702 00, Czech Republic

Mirra, Dave (Athlete)
Wasserman Media Group, LLC
12100 Olympic Blvd
#400
Los Angeles, CA 92054, USA

Mirren, Helen (Actor, Director, Producer)
c/o Melissa Sun *Stan Rosenfield & Associates*
2029 Century Park E
Suite 1190
Los Angeles, CA 90067, USA

Mirrlees, James (Nobel Prize Laureate)
Trinity College Economics Dept
Cambridge, England CB2 ITQ, USA

Mirrlees, James A (Nobel Prize Laureate)
Trinity College
Economics Dept
Cambridge CB2 1TQ, UNITED KINGDOM (UK)

Mirza, Dia (Actor)
Globosport India Pvt Ltd
G-41, Saket
New Delhi 110017, India

Mirza, Sania (Athlete, Tennis Player)
c/o Staff Member *Globosport India Pvt Ltd*
G-41, Saket
New Dehli 110017, India

Mirzoev, Akbar (Prime Minister)
Prime Minister's Office
Dushaube, TAJIKISTAN

Misaka, Walt (Athlete, Basketball Player)
173 Aruba Dr
Saratoga Springs, UT 84045, USA

Misaka, Wataru "Wat"
288 E 2450 S
Bountiful, UT 84010-5638

Misch, Patrick (Athlete, Baseball Player)
725 N Dobson Rd
Apt 255
Chandler, AZ 85224-9110, USA

Mischak, Bob (Athlete, Football Player)
73 Brookwood Rd Unit 12
Orinda, CA 94563, USA

Mischka, Badgley (Designer, Fashion Designer)
525 Seventh Ave Fl 14
New York, NY 10018, USA

Mischke, Carl H (Religious Leader)
1034 Buena Vista Dr
Sun Prairie, WI 53590, USA

Misersky, Antje (Athlete)
Grenzgraben 3A
Stutzerbach 98714, GERMANY

Misiano, Christopher (Director)
c/o Staff Member *Creative Artists Agency (CAA-LA)*
2000 Ave Of The Stars
Los Angeles, CA 90067, USA

Misiano, Vincent (Director)
c/o Staff Member *Creative Artists Agency (CAA-LA)*
2000 Ave Of The Stars
Los Angeles, CA 90067, USA

Misko, John (Athlete, Football Player)
33252 Tule Oak Dr
Springville, CA 93265, USA

Mison, Tom (Actor)
c/o Ben Mison
32 St Johns Rd
Woking GU21 7SA, GB

Misraki, Paul
35 av. Bugeaud
Paris, FRANCE F-75116

Missick, Dorian (Actor)
c/o Myrna Jacoby *MJ Management*
130 W 57th St
Suite 11A
New York, NY 10019, USA

Missing Persons
11935 Laurel Hills Rd
Studio City, CA 91604

Miss Teen USA
6420 Wilshire Blvd.
Los Angeles, CA 90048

Misterek, Hope (Stylist)
10812 Forbes Creek Dr
#V-307
Kirkland, WA 98033, USA

Mistler, John (Athlete, Football Player)
3111 E Desert Flower Ln
Phoenix, AZ 85048, USA

Mistral, Fernanda (Actor)
c/o Staff Member *Telefe - Argentina*
Pavon 2444 (C1248AAT)
Buenos Aires, ARGENTINA

Mistry, Jimi (Actor)
c/o Staff Member *WME (LA)*
9601 Wilshire Blvd Fl 3
Beverly Hills, CA 90210, USA

Misuraca, Mike (Athlete, Baseball Player)
250 N College Park Dr Apt F26
Upland, CA 91786-9467, USA

Miszak, Anna Cepinska (Beauty Pageant Winner)
c/o Staff Member *Miss World Ltd*
21 Golden Sq
London W1R 3PA, UNITED KINGDOM (UK)

Miszuk, John (Athlete, Hockey Player)
4 Willowglen Crt
Dundas, ON L9H 6Z9, CANADA

Mitchell, Aaron (Athlete, Football Player)
3613 Frankford Rd Apt 738
Dallas, TX 75287, USA

Mitchell, Andrea (Correspondent)
2710 Chain Bridge Rd NW
Washington, DC 20016, USA

Mitchell, Basil (Athlete, Football Player)
806 Baker Ave
Mount Pleasant, TX 75455, USA

Mitchell, Betsy (Athlete, Olympic Athlete, Swimmer)
Laurel High School
Laurel High School 1 Lyman Cir Athletic Office
Beachwood, OH 44122-2199, USA

Mitchell, Beverley (Actor)
c/o Barry McPherson *Agency for the Performing Arts (APA-LA)*
405 S Beverly Dr
Suite 500
Beverly Hills, CA 90212-4425, USA

Mitchell, Beverly (Actor)
c/o Staff Member *Forster Entertainment*
12533 Woodgreen St
Los Angeles, CA 90066, USA

Mitchell, Bill (Athlete, Hockey Player)
13 Exeter Rd
Perrysburg, OH 43551-3117

Mitchell, Billy (Misc)
Rickey's Restaurant
4799 Hollywood Blvd
Hollywood, FL 33021, USA

Mitchell, Bobby (Athlete, Golfer)
435 Wimbish Dr
Danville, VA 24541-5823, USA

Mitchell, Bobby (Athlete, Baseball Player)
8697 Tiogawoods Dr
Sacramento, CA 95828-5116, USA

Mitchell, Bobby (Athlete, Baseball Player)
13887 Torrey Bella Ct
San Diego, CA 92129-4628, USA

Mitchell, Bobby (Athlete, Football Player)
450 Blue Beech Way
Chesapeake, VA 23320, USA

Mitchell, Brandon (Athlete, Football Player)
806 Schlessinger St
Abbeville, IA 70510, USA

Mitchell, Brian (Actor)
5307B Wilkinson Ave
#20
Valley Village, CA 91607, USA

Mitchell, Brian (Athlete, Football Player)
5435 Chandley Farm Cir
Centreville, VA 20120, USA

Mitchell, Brian (Athlete, Football Player)
1205 Addison Ct
Winterville, NC 28590, USA

Mitchell, Brian Stokes (Actor, Musician)
243 W 98th St
#5C
New York, NY 10025, USA

Mitchell, Charlie (Athlete, Baseball Player)
5017 Hasty Dr
Nashville, TN 37211-5345, USA

Mitchell, Charlie (Athlete, Football Player)
6300 Seward Park Ave S
Seattle, WA 98118, USA

Mitchell, Craig (Athlete, Baseball Player)
P.O. Box 174
Elk, CA 95432-0174, USA

Mitchell, Dale (Athlete, Football Player)
1837 Tanner Ave SW
Canton, OH 44706, USA

Mitchell, Darryl (Actor)
c/o Staff Member *Forster Entertainment*
12533 Woodgreen St
Los Angeles, CA 90066, USA

Mitchell, Daryl (Chill) (Actor)
c/o Jenny Delaney *Jenny Delaney Management*
3238 Fond Dr
Encino, CA 91436, USA

Mitchell, Don (Actor)
4139 Cloverdale Ave
Los Angeles, CA 90008, USA

Mitchell, Donald (Athlete, Football Player)
5620 Minner Dr
Beaumont, TX 77708, USA

Mitchell, Eddy
40 av. Sainte Foy
Neuilly, FRANCE 92200

Mitchell, Edgar D (Astronaut)
PO Box 540037
Greenacres, FL 33454, USA

Mitchell, Edgar D Captain (Astronaut)
PO Box 540037
Greenacres, FL 33454-0037, USA

Mitchell, Elizabeth (Actor)
c/o Ben Levine *Kritzer Levine Wilkins Entertainment (KLWG)*
11872 La Grange Ave
1st Floor
Los Angeles, CA 90025, USA

Mitchell, Elvis (Producer, Radio Personality, Writer)
KCRW
1900 Pico Blvd
Santa Monica, CA 90405, USA

Mitchell, Freddie (Athlete, Football Player)
606 N Brunnell Pkwy
Lakeland, FL 33815, USA

Mitchell, George (Politician)
151 Crandon Blvd Apt 110
Key Biscayne, FL 33149-1529, USA

Mitchell, George J (Politician, Senator)
DLA Piper Rudnick Gray Cary
1251 Ave of the Americas
New York, NY 10020, USA

Mitchell, Harris A (War Hero)
2701 Dees St
San Marcos, TX 78666, USA

Mitchell, Helen (Stylist)
c/o Staff Member *Judy Casey Inc*
114 E 13th St
New York, NY 10003, USA

Mitchell, Jack (Photographer)
1413 Live Oak St
New Smyrna Beach, FL 32168, USA

Mitchell, Jeff (Athlete, Hockey Player)
Suburban Hockey Schools
23995 Freeway Park Dr Ste 200
Farmington Hills, MI 48335-2829

Mitchell, Jeff (Athlete, Football Player)
12151 Roseland Dr
New Port Richey, FL 34654, USA

Mitchell, Jessie (Baseball Player)
Birmingham Black Barons
124 Dugan Ave Apt A
Birmingham, AL 35214-5182, USA

Mitchell, Jim H (Athlete, Football Player)
120 Twin Creek Ter
Forest, VA 24551, USA

mitchell, John (Athlete, Basketball Player)
1708 Castleberry Way
BIrmingham, AL 35214-4826, USA

Mitchell, John (Athlete, Baseball Player)
5017 Hasty Dr
Nashville, TN 37211, USA

Mitchell, John Cameron (Actor, Director)
c/o Richie Jackson *Jackson Group Entertainment*
345 W 13th St
New York, NY 10014, USA

Mitchell, Joni (Musician)

Mitchell, Kawika (Athlete, Football Player)
971 N Lake Sybelia Dr
Maitland, FL 32751, USA

Mitchell, Keith (Athlete, Baseball Player)
731 S 42nd St
San Diego, CA 92113-1813, USA

Mitchell, Keith C (Prime Minister)
Ministerial Complex 6th Fl
Botanical Gardens
Saint George's, GRENADA

Mitchell, Kel (Actor)
c/o Staff Member *Nine Yards Entertainment*
8530 Wilshire Blvd Fl 5
Beverly Hills, CA 90211, USA

Mitchell, Ken (Athlete, Football Player)
4313 Cityview Dr
Plano, TX 75093, USA

Mitchell, Kenneth (Actor)
c/o Stephen (Steve) Small *Paradigm (LA)*
360 N Crescent Dr
North Bldg
Beverly Hills, CA 90210, USA

Mitchell, Kevin (Athlete, Baseball Player)
3869 Ocean View Blvd
San Diego, CA 92113-1736, USA

Mitchell, Kim (Musician)
41 Britain St.
#305
Toronto, ON M5A 1R7, Canada

Mitchell, Larry (Athlete, Baseball Player)
1040 Preston Ave
Charlottesville, VA 22903-2109, USA

Mitchell, Leland (Athlete, Basketball Player)
558 Southgate Dr
Starksville, MS 39759-5035, USA

Mitchell, Leona (Opera Singer)
Columbia Artists Mgmt Inc
165 W 57th St
New York, NY 10019, USA

Mitchell, Leroy (Athlete, Football Player)
6598 N Pinewood Dr
Parker, CO 80134, USA

Mitchell, Lydell D (Athlete, Football Player)
702 Reservoir St
Baltimore, MD 21217, USA

Mitchell, Lynne (Stylist)
c/o Staff Member *Crews*
828 Clemont Dr
Atlanta, GA 30306, USA

Mitchell, Mack (Athlete, Football Player)
1200 Maynard St
Diboll, TX 75941, USA

Mitchell, Michael (Actor)
c/o Abby Bluestone *Innovative Artists (LA)*
1505 10th St
Santa Monica, CA 90401, USA

Mitchell, Mike (Director)
c/o Gregory McKnight *Creative Artists Agency (CAA-LA)*
2000 Ave Of The Stars
Los Angeles, CA 90067, USA

Mitchell, Murray (Athlete, Basketball Player)
401 Northshore Blvd
Apt 905
Portland, TX 78374-3807, USA

Mitchell, Paul (Athlete, Baseball Player)
23 Carr Rd
Berlin, MA 01503-1116, USA

Mitchell, Pete (Athlete, Football Player)
100 Paddock Pl
Ponte Vedra Beach, FL 32082, USA

Mitchell, Radha (Actor)
c/o Rick Ax *Gold Coast Management*
438 S Venice Blvd Apt 5
Venice, CA 90291, USA

Mitchell, Rick (DJ)
c/o Staff Member *Diva Central Inc*
7510 W Sunset Blvd Ste 1445
Los Angees, CA 90046, USA

Mitchell, Robert (Athlete, Baseball Player)
Cleveland Buckeyes
2009 Elmwood Ave
Tampa, FL 33605-6625, USA

Mitchell, Roger (Director, Producer)
c/o Beth Swofford *Creative Artists Agency (CAA-LA)*
2000 Ave Of The Stars
Los Angeles, CA 90067, USA

Mitchell, Roger (Athlete, Football Player)
Chaminade-Madonna College Prep
500 E Chaminade Dr
Hollywood, FL 33021, USA

Mitchell, Roland (Athlete, Football Player)
P.O. Box 5701
Lake Charles, LA 70606, USA

Mitchell, Roscoe E Jr (Composer, Musician)
SRO Artists
6629 University Ave
#206
Middleton, WI 53562, USA

Mitchell, Roy (Athlete, Hockey Player)
14449 W Stockwell Dr
Boise, ID 83713-0949

Mitchell, Russ (Correspondent, Television Host)
c/o Staff Member *CBS News Productions*
524 W 57th St
8th Floor
New York, NY 10019, USA

Mitchell, Sam (Athlete, Basketball Player, Coach)
73 Smokerise Pt
Peachtree City, GA 30269-4068, USA

Mitchell, Sasha (Actor)
Flick East-West
9057 A Nemo St
#A
West Hollywood, CA 90069, USA

Mitchell, Scott (Athlete, Football Player)
5060 Franklin Rd
Bloomfield Hills, MI 48302, USA

Mitchell, Shareen (Actor)
J Michael Bloom
9255 Sunset Blvd
#710
Los Angeles, CA 90069, USA

Mitchell, Sharon
1122 White Rock
Dixon, IL 61021

Mitchell, Shay (Actor)
c/o David Dean Portelli *David Dean Management*
Prefers to be contacted via telephone or email
Los Angeles, CA, USA

Mitchell, Shirley
10635 Santa Monica Blvd. #130
Los Angeles, CA 90025

Mitchell, Steve (Actor)
c/o Staff Member *Select Artists Ltd (CA-Westside Office)*
1138 12th Street
Suite 1
Santa Monica, CA 90403, USA

Mitchell, Susan (Writer)
Florida Atlantic University
English Dept
Boca Raton, FL 33431, USA

Mitchell, Todd (Athlete, Basketball Player)
4134 Emmajean Rd
Toledo, OH 43607-1015, USA

Mitchell, Tom (Athlete, Football Player)
1421 SW 49th Ter
Cape Coral, FL 33914, USA

Mitchell, Vernessa (Musician)
c/o Staff Member *Diva Central Inc*
7510 W Sunset Blvd Ste 1445
Los Angees, CA 90046, USA

Mitchell, Warren
28 Sheldon Ave.
London, ENGLAND N6

Mitchison, N Avrion (Biologist)
14 Belitha Villas
London N1 1PD, UNITED KINGDOM (UK)

Mitchum, Carrie (Actor)
Camden ITG Talent
1501 Main St
#204
Venice, CA 90291, USA

Mithun, Chakraborty (Actor, Bollywood)
Monarch Hotel
Ooty, TN, INDIA

Mitra, Rhona (Actor)
c/o Jason Weinberg *Untitled Entertainment (LA)*
350 S. Beverly Dr #200
Beverly Hills, CA 90212, USA

Mitre, Sergio (Athlete, Baseball Player)
1707 Summer Sky St
Chula Vista, CA 91915-1846, USA

Mitrione, Matt (Athlete, Football Player)
729 Toddsbury Ln
Richmond, IN 47374-7152, USA

Mitrov, Miliana (Stylist)
c/o Staff Member *Perrella Management*
330 W 38th St Rm 1407
New York, NY 10018, USA

Mitsotakis, Constantine (Prime Minister)
1 Aravantinou St
Athens 106 74, GREECE

Mitsoula, Jana (Actor)
Collingwood Management Inc
c/o Dylan Thomas Collingwood
#300 - 100 West Pender St
Vancouver, BC V6B 1R8, CANADA

Mitta, Aleksander N (Director)
Malaya Gruzinskaya Str 28
#105
Moscow 123557, RUSSIA

Mittal, Lakshmi (Business Person)
LNM Group
15th Floor
Hofplein 20
Rotterdam 3032, NETHERLANDS

Mitte, RJ (Actor)
c/o Addison Witt *Witt Management*
255 S. Grand Avenue #1505
Los Angeles, CA 90012, USA

Mittermaier, Rosi
Winklmoosalm
Reit im Winkl, GERMANY D-83242

Mittermaier-Neureuther, Rosi (Skier)
Winkelmoosalm
Reit Im Winkel 83242, GERMANY

Mittermayer, Tatjana (Skier)
Bucha 2A
Lenggries, GERMANY

Mitterwald, George (Athlete, Baseball Player)
5314 Kenvon Rd
Orlando, FL 32810-1714, USA

Mitts, Heather (Soccer Player)
US Soccer/ Heather Mitts
18400 Avalon Blvd #500
Carson, CA 90746, USA

Mitz, Alonzo (Athlete, Football Player)
2609 NE 4th St
Apt 216
Renton, WA 98056, USA

Mitzelfeld, Jim (Journalist)
969 N Lebanon St
Arlington, VA 22205, USA

Mivelaz, Betty (Bowler)
6671 Shadygrove St
Tujunga, CA 91042, USA

Mivelaz, Betty (Bowler)
6671 Shadygrove St
Tujunga, Ca 91042-3348, USA

Mix, Bryant (Athlete, Football Player)
37 Greenwood Plantation Rd
Natchez, MS 39120, USA

Mix, Ronald J (Ron) (Athlete, Football Player)
2317 Camino Recodo
San Diego, CA 92107, USA

Mix, Steve (Athlete, Basketball Player)
25743 Willowbend Rd
Perrrysburg, OH 43551-9787, USA

Mix Master Mike (DJ)
c/o Staff Member *Agency Group Ltd, The (UK)*
361-373 City Rd
London EC1V 1PQ, UK

Mixon, Ken (Athlete, Football Player)
12741 Kapok Ln
Davie, FL 33330, USA

Mixon, Wayne (Politician)
2219 Demeron Rd
Tallahassee, FL 32308-0943, USA

Mixson, J Wayne (Ex-Governor)
2219 Demeron Rd
Tallahassee, FL 32308, USA

Miyamura, Hiroshi H (War Hero)
1905 Mossman Ave
Gallup, NM 87301, USA

Miyamura, Hiroshi H (General)
659 Kaimalino St
Kailua, HI 96734-1616, USA

Miyazaki, Hayao (Animator)
Studio Ghibli
1-4-25 Kajinocho
Koganeishi 184, JAPAN

Miyazawa, Kiichi (Prime Minister)
6-34-1 Jingu-Mae
Shibuyaku
Tokyo 150, JAPAN

Miza, Ola L
211 Hartwood Dr
Gadsden, AL 35901-6228, USA

Mize, John D (War Hero)
112 Sunset Dr
Belmond, IA 50421, USA

Mize, Larry (Athlete, Golfer)
106 Graystone Ct
Columbus, GA 31904-4300, USA

Mize, Ola L (War Hero)
211 Hartwood Dr
Gadsden, AL 35901, USA

Mize, Ola Lee (General)
311 Hartwood Dr
Gadsden, AL 35901, USA

Mizerak, Steve (Billiards Player)
140 Alfred St
Edison, NJ 08820, USA

Mizerock, John (Athlete, Baseball Player, Coach)
1189 Leasure Run Rd
Rochester Mills, PA 15771-7507, USA

Mizrahi, Isaac (Fashion Designer, Television Host)
Isaac Mizrahi Studio
475 Tenth Ave Fl 4
New York, NY 10018, USA

Mizrahie, Barbara (Athlete, Golfer)
6440 Park Lake Cir
Boynton Beach, FL 33437, USA

Mkapa, Benjamin William (President)
President's Office
State House
PO Box 9120
Dar es Salaam, TANZANIA

M. Landry, Jeffrey (Congressman, Politician)
206 Cannon HOB
Washington, DC 20515, USA

M. Levin, Sander (Congressman, Politician)
1236 Longworth HOB
Washington, DC 20515, USA

Mlicki, Dave (Athlete, Baseball Player)
5350 Reserve Dr
Dublin, OH 43017, USA

Mlkvy, Bill (Athlete, Basketball Player)
586 Linton Hill Road
Newtown, PA 18940-1204, USA

Mlneta, Norman (Politician)
1631 Cliff Dr
Edgewater, MD 21037-4922, USA

Mlnner, Ruth (Politician)
1056 Church Hill Rd
Milford, DE 19963-5539, USA

M. Lowey, Nita (Congressman, Politician)
2365 Raybur'n HOB
Washington, DC 20515, USA

M. Lumis, Cynthia (Congressman, Politician)
113 Cannon HOB
Washington, DC 20515, USA

Mmahat, Kevin (Athlete, Baseball Player)
5500 Erlanger Rd
Kenner, LA 70065-1534, USA

Mnookin, Robert H (Attorney, Attorney General, Educator, General)
10 Follen St
Cambridge, MA 02138, USA

Mnouchkine, Ariane (Director)
Theater du Soleil
Cartoucherie
Paris 75012, FRANCE

Moakler, Shanna (Actor, Model, Reality TV Star)
c/o Lizzie Grubman *Lizzie Grubman Public Relations*
270 Lafayette St
Suite 504
New York, NY 10012, USA

Moates, Dave (Athlete, Baseball Player)
7924 24th Ave W
Bradenton, FL 34209-3254, USA

Moats, David (Journalist)
Rutland Herald
Editorial Dept
PO Box 668
Rutland, VT 05702, USA

Moats, Sanford (General)
59-635 Akanoho Pl
Haleiwa, HI 96712-9504, USA

Mobb Deep (Music Group)
c/o Staff Member *Interscope Records (NY)*
1755 Broadway
New York, NY 10019, USA

Mobley, Cuttino (Athlete, Basketball Player)
11706 Empress Oaks Ct
Houston, TX 77082-6842, USA

Mobley, Mary Ann (Actor, Beauty Pageant Winner)
2751 Hutton Dr
Beverly Hills, CA 90210, USA

Mobley, Singor (Athlete, Football Player)
2123 US Highway 80 E
Mesquite, TX 75150, USA

Mobley, William H (Educator)
4312 Ravine Ridge Trl
Austin, TX 78746-1283, USA

Moby (Actor, Composer, Musician)
c/o Staff Member *Mute Records*
1 Albion Pl
London W6 0QT, UK

Moceanu, Dominique (Gymnast)
2387 Glendon Rd
University Heights, OH 44118-3840, USA

Mochrie, Colin (Actor)
385 Adelaide St W
Toronto, ON M5V 1S4, CANADA

Mochrie, Dottie (Athlete, Golfer)
15 Blazing Star Trl
Landrum, SC 29356, USA

Mock, Garrett (Athlete, Baseball Player)
13850 Maisemore Rd
Houston, TX 77015-2303, USA

Mockett, Cathy (Athlete, Golfer)
1601 Antigua Way
Newport Beach, CA 92660-4345, USA

Mocumbi, Pascoal (Prime Minister)
Prime Minister's Office
Avenida Julius Nyerere 1780
Maputo, MOZAMBIQUE

Moczynski, Betty (Athlete, Baseball Player, Commentator)
4912 S 19th St Apt B
Milwaukee, WI 53221-2830, USA

Modano, Mike (Athlete, Hockey Player, Olympic Athlete)
6424 Mimosa Ln
Dallas, TX 75230-5137, USA

Modean, Jayne (Actor)
1030 Windsor Ave
Piedmont, CA 94610, USA

Modell, Frank (Cartoonist)
295 Central Park West
Apt 11E
New York, NY 10024-3023, USA

Modell, Frank (Cartoonist)
115 Three Mile Crse
Guilford, CT 06437-2522, USA

Modernaires, The
11761 E. Speedway Blvd
Tucson, AZ 85748-2017

Modern Talking
Modern Talking Fan Club
56200 Hoehr-Grenzhausen
, GERMANY

Modin, Fredrik (Athlete, Hockey Player)
8955 Dunn Court
Dublin, OH 43017-8880, USA

Modine, Matthew (Actor, Director, Producer)
420 W 25th St #9C
New York, NY 10001, USA

Modrow, Hans (Prime Minister)
Frankfurter Tor 6
Berlin 10243, GERMANY

Modry, Jaroslav (Athlete, Hockey Player)
7 Castle Ct
Albany, NY 12211-1910

Modrzejewski, Robert J (War Hero)
4725 Oporto Court
San Diego, CA 92124, USA

Modrzejewski, Robert J (General)
4725 Oporto Ct
San Diego, CA 92124-2446, USA

Modugno, Lori (Stylist)
c/o Staff Member *Stockland Martel*
343 E 18th St
New York, NY 10003, USA

Modzelewski, Ed (Athlete, Football Player)
P.O. Box 4207
Sedona, AZ 86340, USA

Modzelewski, Richard B (Dick) (Athlete, Football Player)
1 Pier Pointe
New Bern, NC 28562, USA

Moe (Music Group)
c/o Staff Member *Paradigm (Monterey)*
404 W Franklin St
Monterey, CA 93940, USA

moe. (Music Group)
45 Hadlock Rd
Falmouth, ME 04105, USA

Moe, Douglas E (Doug) (Athlete, Basketball Player)
13 Arnold Palmer
San Antonio, TX 78257, USA

Moe, Tommy (Athlete, Olympic Athlete, Skier)
1556 Hidden Ln
Anchorage, AK 99501-4916, USA

Moe, Tommy
2138 Churchill Dr
Anchorage, AK 99517

Moegle, Dickey (Athlete, Football Player)
4207 DeForest Ridge Cir
Katy, TX 77494, USA

Moehler, Brian (Athlete, Baseball Player)
4492 Belvedere Pl SE
Marietta, GA 30067, USA

Moe-Humphreys, Karen (Swimmer)
505 Augusta Dr
Moraga, CA 94556, USA

Moeller, Chad (Athlete, Baseball Player)
11058 E Raintree Dr
Scottsdale, AZ 85255-1809, USA

Moeller, Dennis (Inventor)
25 Cobbie Ridge Dr
Chapel Hill, NC 27516, USA

Moeller, Dennis (Athlete, Baseball Player)
2324 Ridgemont Dr
Birmingham, AL 91381-1735, USA

Moeller, Dennis L (Inventor)
147 Florence Dr
Jupiter, FL 33458-8714, USA

Moeller, Edward (Athlete, Basketball Player)
1011 Kelton Cottage Way
Morrisville, NC 27560-7031, USA

Moeller, Joe (Athlete, Baseball Player)
1505 Avenida Dr Nogales
San Clemente, CA 92672-9464, USA

Moeller, Ralf (Actor)
c/o Chuck Binder *Binder & Associates*
1465 Lindacrest Dr
Beverly Hills, CA 90210, USA

Moeller, Ron (Athlete, Baseball Player)
7355 Appleridge Ct
Cincinnati, OH 45247, USA

Moeller, Walter L (Stylist)
7420 Cove Dr
Cary, IL 60013-1717, USA

Moellering, John H (General)
50130 Manly
Chapel Hill, NC 27517, USA

Moen, Travis (Athlete, Hockey Player)
Newport Sports Management
400-201 City Centre Dr
Attn Don Meehan
Mississauga, ON L5B 2T4, Canada

Moennig, Katherine (Actor)
c/o Peg Donegan *Framework Entertainment (LA)*
9057 Nemo St
Suite C
West Hollywood, CA 90069, USA

Moesta-Anderson, Rebecca (Writer)
Anderzone
P.O. Box 767
Monument, CO 80132-0767, USA

Moffat, Donald (Actor)
c/o Staff Member *Jenny Delaney Management*
3238 Fond Dr
Encino, CA 91436, USA

Moffat, Katherine (Kitty) (Actor)
Henderson/Hogan
8285 W Sunset Blvd
#1
West Hollywood, CA 21230, USA

Moffat, Lyle (Athlete, Hockey Player)
111-1027 Pandora Ave
Victoria, BC V8V 3P6, Canada

Moffat, Mike (Athlete, Hockey Player)
17 Riverbend Rd
Markham, ON L3R 1K4

Moffat, Steven (Writer)
c/o Charlie Ferraro *United Talent Agency (UTA)*
9336 Civic Center Dr
Beverly Hills, CA 90210, USA

Moffatt, Henry K (Mathematician, Physicist)
6 Banhams Close
Cambridge CB4 1HX, UNITED KINGDOM (UK)

Moffatt, John
59A Warrington St.
London, ENGLAND W9

Moffatt, Katy (Musician, Songwriter, Writer)
PO Box 334
O Fallon, IL 62269, USA

Moffet, Jane (Athlete, Baseball Player, Commentator)
501 Tidewater Ave
Rio Grande, NJ 08242-2807, USA

Moffett, D W (Actor)
Three Arts Entertainment
9460 Wilshire Blvd
#700
Beverly Hills, CA 90212, USA

Moffett, James R (Business Person)
Freeport-McMoRan Inc
1615 Poydras St
New Orleans, LA 70112, USA

Moffett, Randy
110 Lakeover Dr.
Athens, GA 30606

Moffett, Tim (Athlete, Football Player)
115 County Road 213
Oxford, MS 38655, USA

Moffitt, Randy (Athlete, Baseball Player)
1725 Baltic Ave
Prescott, AZ 86301-6501, USA

Mofford, Ian (Athlete, Football Player)
PO Box 1158
Waitsfield, VT 05673-1158, USA

Mofford, Rose (Ex-Governor)
330 W Maryland Ave
Unit 104
Phoenix, AZ 85013, USA

Mofford, Rose (Politician)
330 W Maryland Ave Unit 104
Phoenix, AZ 85013-1340, USA

Mogae, Festus G (President)
President's Office
State House
Private Bag 001
Gaborone, BOTSWANA

Mogenburg, Dietmar (Athlete, Track Athlete)
Alter Garfen 34
Leverkusen 51371, GERMANY

Moger, Sandy (Athlete, Hockey Player)
Vernon Minor Hockey Association
PO Box 1894
Vernon, BC VlT 8Z7, Canada

Mogilevsky, Evgeny (Musician)
Columbia Artists Mgmt Inc
165 W 57th St
New York, NY 10019, USA

Mogilny, Alexander (Athlete, Hockey Player)
27543 Pacific Coast Hwy
Malibu, CA 90265-4339, USA

Mohacsi, Mary (Bowler)
15445 Sunset St
Livonia, MI 48154, USA

Mohacsi, Mary (Bowler)
15445 Sunset St
Livonia, MI 48154-3215, USA

MoHair (Music Group)
c/o Staff Member *Paradigm (Monterey)*
404 W Franklin St
Monterey, CA 93940, USA

Mohammed VI (King)
Royal Palais
Rabat, MOROCCO

Mohan (Actor, Bollywood)
8 Mylai Ranganathan Street
T Nagar
Chennai, TN 600017, INDIA

Mohler, Mike (Athlete, Baseball Player)
1627 S Shirley Ave
Gonzales, LA 70737-3917, USA

Mohler, R Albert
Southern Baptist Theological Seminary
Office Of The President
2825 Lexington Rd
Louisville, KY 40280, USA

Mohmand, Abdul Ahad (Cosmonaut)
Potchta Kosmonavtov
Moskovkoi Oblasti
Syvlsdny Goroduk 141160, RUSSIA

Mohns, Doug (Athlete, Hockey Player)
6 Mitchell Grand Way
Bedford, MA 01730-1200

Mohns, Lloyd (Athlete, Hockey Player)
Unit 2 3334 Hwy 144 Hwy
Chelmsford, ON P0M lL0, Canada

Mohoney, J Daniel (Judge)
US Court of Appeals
40 FOley Square
New York, NY 10007, USA

Mohoney, John (Actor)
International Creative Mgmt
8942 Wilshire Blvd
#219
Beverly Hills, CA 90211, USA

Mohoney, Roger (Cartoonist)
c/o Staff Member *King Features Syndication*
300 W 57th St
15th Floor
New York, NY 10019-5238, USA

Mohony, Roger Cardinal (Religious Leader)
Archdiocese of Los Angeles
3424 Wilshire Blvd
Los Angeles, CA 90010, USA

Mohorcic, Dale (Athlete, Baseball Player)
15501 Rockside Rd
Maple Heights, OH 44137-3948, USA

Mohr, Chris (Athlete, Football Player)
P.O. Box 1232
Thomson, GA 30824, USA

Mohr, Dustan (Athlete, Baseball Player)
103 Parkwood Dr
Hattiesburg, MS 39402, USA

Mohr, Jay (Actor, Comedian)
737 El Medio Ave
Pacific Palisades, CA 90272, USA

Mohr, Todd (Musician)
Morris Bliessner
1658 York St
Denver, CO 80206, USA

Mohri, Mamoru (Astronaut)
NASDA
2-1-2 Sengen
Tukubashi
Ibaraki 305, JAPAN

Mohri, Mamoru Dr (Astronaut)
NASDA, Tsukuba Space Center 2-1-1, Sengen, Tububa-shi General Manager's Office
lbaraki, Japar 305, USA

Moiler, Randy (Athlete, Hockey Player)
3950 NW 23rd Ter
Boca Raton, FL 33431-5405

Moine, Marc Forne (President)
President's Office
Casa de la Valle
Andorra la Vella, ANDORRA

Moir, Richard (Actor)
Shanahan Mgmt
PO Box 1509
Darlinghurst, NSW 1300, AUSTRALIA

Moisan, Bill (Athlete, Baseball Player)
P.O. Box 41
Newton, NH 03858, USA

Moise, Patty (Race Car Driver)
Atkins Motorsports
222 Raceway Dr.
Mooresville, NC 28117, USA

Moiseyev, Igor A (Choreographer, Director)
Moiseyev Dance Co
20 Triumfalnaya Pl
Moscow, RUSSIA

Moiseyev, Jack (Horse Racer)
499 Scotland Dr
Jackson, NJ 08527-1188, USA

Mojsiejenko, Ralf (Athlete, Football Player)
11334 Baldwin Rd
Bridgman, MI 49106, USA

Mojslejenko, Ralf (Athlete, Football Player)
11334 Baldwin Rd
Bridgeman, MI 49106, USA

Mok, Karen (Actor)
c/o Staff Member *Creative Artists Agency (CAA-LA)*
2000 Ave Of The Stars
Los Angeles, CA 90067, USA

Mok, Ken (Director, Producer)
c/o Steve Wohl *Paradigm (LA)*
360 N Crescent Dr
North Bldg
Beverly Hills, CA 90210, USA

Mokeski, Paul (Athlete, Basketball Player)
4004 Crestwood Dr
Carrollton, TX 75007-1645, USA

Mokosak, Carl (Athlete, Hockey Player)
5076 Montauk Dr NW
Comstock Park, Ml 49321-9352

Mokri, Amir (Cinematographer)
c/o Staff Member *Montana Artists Agency*
9150 Wilshire Blvd Ste 100
Beverly Hills, CA 90212, USA

Mokrzynski, Jerzy (Architect)
Ul Marszalkowska 140 m 18
Warsaw 00 061, POLAND

Mokus (Stylist)
c/o Staff Member *Mokus de Barcza*
53 E 96th St
#5-C
New York, NY 10128, USA

Mol, Gretchen (Actor)
c/o John Carrabino *John Carrabino Management*
5900 Wilshire Blvd Fl 4 #406
Los Angeles, CA 90036, USA

Molale, Brandon (Actor)
c/o Staff Member *DDC Entertainment*
8416 Campion Dr
Los Angeles, CA 90045, USA

Molden, Alex (Athlete, Football Player)
2083 Wellington Dr
West Linn, OR 97068, USA

Moldoff, Sheldon (Cartoonist)
3710 Inverrary Dr Apt lW
Lauderhill, FL 33319-5142, USA

Moldofsky, Philip J (Scientist)
Fox Chase Cancer Center
7701 Burholme Ave
Philadelphia, PA 19111, USA

Mole, Fenton (Athlete, Baseball Player)
738 Glen Eagle Ct
Danville, CA 94526-6209, USA

Moler, Jason (Athlete, Baseball Player, Olympic Athlete)
2918 Ranch Road 620 N Apt 281
Austin, TX 78734-2269, USA

Molin, Lars (Athlete, Hockey Player)
Ostra Prinsgatan 30A
Umea 90322, Sweden

Molina, Alfred (Actor)
c/o Joan Hyler *Hyler Management*
20 Ocean Park Blvd
Suite 25
Santa Monica, CA 90405, USA

Molina, Beniie (Athlete, Baseball Player)
6475 E Crabtree Pl
Yuma, AZ 85365-1115, USA

Molina, Gabe (Athlete, Baseball Player)
501 E 102nd Ave
Thornton, CO 80229, USA

Molina, Islay (Izzy) (Athlete, Baseball Player)
369 Atwater St
Port Charlotte, FL 33954, USA

Molina, Jose (Athlete, Baseball Player)
c/o Team Member *New York Yankees*
Yankee Stadium
161st St & River Ave
Bronx, NY 10451, USA

Molina, Izzy (Athlete, Baseball Player)
18132 NW 19th St
Pembroke Pines, FL 33029-3026, USA

Molina, Mario J (Nobel Prize Laureate)
PO Box 12406
La Jolia, CA 92039-2406, USA

Molina, Morio
PO Box 12406
La Jolla, CA 92039-2406, USA

Molina, Yadier (Athlete, Baseball Player)
7150 Terra Vista Dr
Peoria, IL 62232-2831, USA

Molinari, Susan (Politician)
3 Friendship Dr Unit A-3
West Bridgewater, MA 02379-1266, USA

Molinaro, Al (Actor)
1530 Arboles Dr
Glendale, CA 91207, USA

Molinaro, Bob (Athlete, Baseball Player)
1 Harbourside Dr
Apt 2312
Delray Beach, FL 33483-5170, USA

Molitor, Paul L (Athlete, Baseball Player, Coach)
c/o Staff Member *John Boggs & Associates*
5675 Ruffin Rd
Suite 350
San Diego, CA 92123, USA

Molko, Brian (Musician)
c/o Rod MacSween *International Talent Booking*
74A Charlotte St
London W1T 4QJ, UNITED KINGDOM (UK)

Moll, Georgia
229A v. Pineta Sacchetti
Rome, CA ITALY

Moll, John L (Engineer)
4111 Old Trace Road
Palo Alto, CA 94306, USA

Moll, Kurt (Opera Singer)
Voigtelstr 22
Cologne 50933, GERMANY

Moll, Richard (Actor)
1119 Amalfi Dr
Pacific Palisades, CA 90272, USA

Molla, Jordi (Actor)
Kuranda Movies SL
Calle Segre 14
Madrid 28002, SPAIN

Moller, Andreas (Soccer Player)
Borussia Dortmund
Postfach 100509
Dortmund 44005, GERMANY

Moller, Frank (Athlete)
Sportclub Berlin
Weissenseer Weg 51-55
Berlin 13051, GERMANY

Moller, Gunnar
6 Cloverdale Rd.
London, ENGLAND NW2

Moller, Hans (Artist)
2207 W Allen St
Allentown, PA 18104, USA

Moller, Mike (Athlete, Hockey Player)
70 Oaklands Cres
Red Deer, AB T4P 0C4, Canada

Moller, Paul (Engineer, Inventor)
Moller International
1222 Research Park Dr
Davis, CA 95616, USA

Moller, Randy (Athlete, Hockey Player)
Florida Panthers
1 Panther Pkwy
Sunrise, FL 33323-5315

Moller-Gladisch, Silke (Athlete, Track Athlete)
Lange Str 6
Rostock 18055, GERMANY

Mollo-Christiansen, Erik L (Oceanographer)
10 Barberry Road
Lexington, MA, USA

Molloy, Bryan B (Inventor)
7948 Beaumont Green Place
Indianapolis, IN 46250, USA

Molloy, Irene
PO Box 5617
Beverly Hills, CA 90210

Molloy, Matt (Musician)
Macklam Feldman Mgmt
1505 W 2nd Ave
#200
Vancouver, BC V6H 3Y4, CANADA

Moloney, Janel (Actor)
c/o Staff Member *Gersh (LA)*
9465 Wilshire Blvd
Suite 600
Beverly Hills, CA 90212, USA

Moloney, Michael (Actor, Reality TV Star)
c/o Staff Member *Extreme Makeover: Home Edition*
Endemol Entertainment USA
9225 Sunset Blvd #1100
Los Angeles, CA 90069, USA

Moloney, Paddy (Musician)
Macklam Feldman Mgmt
1505 W 2nd Ave
#200
Vancouver, BC V6H 3Y4, CANADA

Moloney, Rich (Athlete, Baseball Player)
125 Mallard Way
Waltham, MA 02452-8117, USA

Molssnor, Barrio
419 Bronson Cres
Saskatoon, SK S7J SE1, Canada

Molyneux, Juan Pablo (Architect)
J P Molyneux Studio
29 E 69th St
New York, NY 10021, USA

Momaday, N scott (Writer)
University Of Arizona English Dept 1600E
Univ Dept 1600E
Tucson, AZ 85721-0001, USA

Momaday, N Scott (Writer)
University of Arizona
English Dept
Tucson, AZ 85721, USA

Momesso, Sergio (Athlete, Hockey Player)
Momesso Caffe
1850 Rue Des Loisirs
Saint-Lazare, QC J7T 3B4, CANADA

Momoa, Jason (Actor)
c/o Jeff Witjas *Agency for the Performing Arts (APA-LA)*
405 S Beverly Dr
Suite 500
Beverly Hills, CA 90212-4425, USA

Momolu-Briggs, Korto (Fashion Designer)
Art Scene and Art Market
200 E. Third Street
Little Rock, AR 72201, USA

Mom Rajawong, Sirikit Kitiyarara (Royalty)
Royal Residence
Chirtalad a Villa
Bangkok, Thailand

Momsen, Robert (Athlete, Football Player)
4730 Glendale Ave
Apt 102
Toledo, OH 43614, USA

Momsen, Taylor (Musician)
c/o John Stratton *DAS Communications*
83 Riverside Dr
New York, NY 10024, USA

Momyer, William (General)
105 E Crisafulli Rd
Merritt Island, FL 32953-7304, USA

Mon, Randy (Stylist)
179 Arbor St
San Francisco, CA 94131-2920, USA

Monacelli, Amieto (Bowler)
Professional Bowlers Assn
719 2nd Ave
#701
Seattle, WA 98104, USA

Monaco, Kelly (Actor)
c/o Alejandra Cristina *Ace PR*
4122 Sunnyslope Ave
Sherman Oaks, CA 91423, USA

Monaghan, Dominic (Actor)
c/o Jeff Raymond *Rogers & Cowan PR (LA)*
Pacific Design Center
8687 Melrose Ave, 7th Floor
West Hollywood, CA 90069, USA

Monaghan, Kris (Athlete, Golfer)
54 Golf Course Dr
Ranchos De Taos, NM 87557-7914, USA

Monaghan, Marjorie
2109 S. Wilbur Ave
Walla Walla, WA 99362, USA

Monaghan, Michelle (Actor)
c/o Frank Frattaroli *Circle of Confusion (NY)*
270 Lafayette St
Suite 402
New York, NY 10012, USA

Monaghan, Thomas (Misc)
3001 Earhart Rd
Ann Arbor, MI 48105, USA

Monaghan, Thomas L
3001 Earhart
Ann Arbor, MI 48106, USA

Monaghan, Tom (Business Person)
The Ave Maria Foundation
One Ave Maria Dr
PO Box 373
Ann Arbor, MI 48106-0373, USA

Monahan, Dan (Actor)
c/o Helene Sokol *Cuzzins Management*
499 N Canon Dr
Beverly Hills, CA 90210, USA

Monahan, David (Actor, Director)
c/o Staff Member *Metropolitan (MTA)*
4526 Wilshire Blvd
Los Angeles, CA 90010, USA

monahan, Garry (Athlete, Hockey Player)
4665 Piccadilly North
West Vancouver, BC V7W 1E3, Canada

Monahan, Hartland (Athlete, Hockey Player)
624 Stickley Oak Way
Woodstock, GA 30189-3781

Monahan, Pat (Musician)
Jon Landau
80 Mason St
Greenwich, CT 06830, USA

Monahan, Shane (Athlete, Baseball Player)
624 Stickley Oak Way
Woodstock, GA 30189-3781, USA

Monan, J Donald (Educator)
Boston College
President's Office
Chestnut Hill, MA 02167, USA

Mon&raln, Bob (Athlete, Hockey Player)
55 Stonehaven Cres
Dartmouth, NS B2V 2S7, Canada

Monbouauette, Bill (Athlete, Baseball Player)
46 Doonan St
Medford, MA 02155-1333, USA

Monbouquette, William C (Bill) (Athlete, Baseball Player)
46 Doonan St
Medford, MA 02155, USA

Monchak, Alex (Al) (Athlete, Baseball Player)
7414 8th Ave W
Bradenton, FL 34209-3425, USA

Moncrief, Sidney (Athlete, Basketball Player)
2019 Wilson Rd
Little Rock, AR 72205, USA

Moncrieff, Karen (Actor)
c/o Brad Gross *Brad Gross Agency, The*
161 S Arden Blvd
Los Angeles, CA 90004, USA

Mond, Philip (Photographer)
PO Box 8906
Fort Lauderdale, FL 33310, USA

Mondale, Walter (Politician)
600 S 2nd St Apt 405
Minneapolis, MN 55401-2162, USA

Mondale, Walter F (President, Senator, Vice President)
50 S 6th
#1500
Minneapolis, MN 55402, USA

Monday, Kenny (Athlete, Olympic Athlete, Wrestler)
4119 W Deer Crossing Dr
Stillwater, OK X OK 74074-2192, USA

Monday, Rick (Athlete, Baseball Player)
811 Gavfeather Ln
Vero Beac, FL 32963-2048, USA

Monday, Rick (Athlete, Baseball Player)
811 Gayfeather Ln
Vero Beach, FL 32963, USA

Monday, Robert J (Rick) (Baseball Player, Sportscaster)
811 Gayleather Lane
Vero Beach, FL 32963, USA

Mondesi, Raul (Athlete, Baseball Player)
Los Angeles Dodgers
1169 Old Phillips Rd
Glendale, CA 91207-1153, USA

Mondou, Pierre (Athlete, Hockey Player)
239 Rue Wildor-Larouchelle
Sorel-Tracy, QC J3P 6R2, CANADA

Monds, Wonderful (Athlete, Baseball Player)
665 NW Fairhaven Dr
Port St Lucie, FL 34983, USA

Monduzzi, Dino Cardinal (Religious Leader)
Via Monfe della Farina 64
Rome 00186, ITALY

Moneo, J Fafael (Architect)
Calle Mino 5
Madrid 28002, SPAIN

Monet, Daniella (Actor)
c/o Staff Member *Elaine Entertainment*
Prefers to be contacted via telephone
Northridge, CA 91324, USA

Money, Don (Athlete, Baseball Player)
282 Old Forest Rd
Vineland, NJ 08360-1667, USA

Money, Eddie (Musician)
c/o Josh Humiston *Agency for the Performing Arts (APA-LA)*
405 S Beverly Dr
Suite 500
Beverly Hills, CA 90212-4425, USA

Money, Eric (Athlete, Basketball Player)
457 S Harvard Ave
Tucson, AZ 85710-4630, USA

Money, John W (Misc)
2104 E Madison St
Baltimore, MD 21205, USA

Money, Ken (Astronaut)
DCIEM
1133 Sheppard Ave W
#2000
Downsview, ON M3M 3B9, CANADA

Moneyham, Bill (Baseball Player)
Oakland A's
5731 White Crane Rd
Merced, CA 95340-8573, USA

Moneymaker, Chris (Misc)
1302 Braygood Dr
Collierville, TN 38017-3779, USA

Monfort, Charles (Athlete, Baseball Player)
PO Box G
Greeley, CO 80632, USA

Monge, Sid (Athlete, Baseball Player)
10 Lilah Ln
Reading, MA 01867-1075, USA

Monger, Matt (Athlete, Football Player)
1306 N Douglas Dr
Claremore, OK 74017, USA

Monheim, Annett (Stylist)
c/o Staff Member *Streeters*
560 Broadway
Suite 203
New York, NY 10012, 212-219-9566

Monheit, Jane (Musician)
c/o Cynthia B. Herbst *American International Artists*
356 Pine Valley Rd
Hoosick Falls, NY 12090, USA

Monica (Musician)
c/o Cara Lewis *Creative Artists Agency (CAA-LA)*
1325 Ave of the Americas
New York, NY 10019, USA

Monin, Clarence V (President)
Locomotive Engineers Brotherhood
1370 Ontario St
Cleveland, OH 44113, USA

Moniz, Karletta (Stylist)
903 Pine St
#30
San Francisco, CA 94108, USA

Moniz, Wendy (Actor)
c/o Nancy Sanders *Sanders Armstrong Caserta*
2120 Colorado Blvd
Suite 120
Santa Monica, CA 90404, USA

Monk, Arthur (Art) (Athlete, Football Player, Sportscaster)
10896 Lake Windermere Dr
Great Falls, VA 22066, USA

Monk, Debra (Actor)
Gage Group
315 W 57th St
#4H
New York, NY 10019, USA

Monk, Meredith J (Choreographer, Composer)
House Foundation for Arts
131 Varick St
New York, NY 10013, USA

Monk, Quincy (Athlete, Football Player)
104 White Oak Blvd
Apt 104
Jacksonville, NC 28546, USA

Monk, Sophie (Actor)
c/o Jenni Weinman *Patricola Lust PR*
9171 Wilshire Blvd
Suite 441
Beverly Hills, CA 90210, USA

Monkees, The (Music Group)
c/o Staff Member *Primary Talent International (UK)*
The Primary Building
10-11 Jockeys Fields
London WC1R 4BN, UK

Monk Jr, Thelonious
173 Brighton Ave
Boston, MA 02134, USA

Monreal Luque, Alberto (Government Official)
Eurotabac Monte Esquinza 28
Madrid 28010, SPAIN

Monroe, A L (Mike) (Misc)
International Brotherhood pf Painters
1750 New York NW
Washington, DC 20006, USA

Monroe, Betty (Actor)
c/o Staff Member *TV Azteca*
Periferico Sur 4121
Colonia Fuentes del Pedregal
DF CP 14141, Mexico

Monroe, Craig (Athlete, Baseball Player)
4123 Lynn Dr
Texarkana, TX 75503-2816, USA

Monroe, Earl (Athlete, Basketball Player)
1925 Adam Clayton Powel
Jr Blvd Apt 60
New York, NY 10026-2214, USA

Monroe, Larry (Athlete, Baseball Player)
725 N Hundley St
Hoffman Estates, IL 60169-4559, USA

Monroe, Lola (Model, Musician)
c/o Staff Member *New Era Agency, The*
Prefers to be contacted via telephone or email
Atlanta, GA, USA

Monroe, Meredith (Musician)
c/o Ame Van Iden *PMK/BNC Public Relations (PMK-LA)*
8687 Melrose Ave Fl 8
West Hollywood, CA 90069, USA

Monroe, Mircea (Actor)
c/o Tiffany Kuzon *Evolution Entertainment (LA)*
901 N Highland Ave
Los Angeles, CA 90038, USA

Monroe, Rodney (Athlete, Basketball Player)
892 Forest Glen Ln
Wellington, FL 33414-6328, USA

Monroe, Zach (Athlete, Baseball Player)
1 Sandalwood Ln
Bartonville, IL 61607-2145, USA

Monsilovich, Larry (Athlete, Football Player)
35 Alice Ln
Oxford, PA 19363-1025, USA

Monson, Dan (Basketball Player, Coach)
University of Minnesota
Bierman Athletic Building
Minneapolis, MN 55455, USA

Monsters, The (Music Group)
c/o Staff Member *Paradigm (Monterey)*
404 W Franklin St
Monterey, CA 93940, USA

Mont, Tommy (Athlete, Football Player)
15414 W Sky Hawk Dr
Sun City, AZ 85375, USA

Monta, Francoise (Nobel Prize Laureate)
Institut Pasteur 25 rue du Docteur Roux
Retroviralnfections Unit
Paris Cedex, France 75724, USA

Montador, Steve (Athlete, Hockey Player)
5857 NW 122 Terrace
Coral Springs, FL 33076-4012, USA

Montag, Holly (Reality TV Star)
c/o Anna Babbitt *New Wave Entertainment (LA)*
2660 W Olive Blvd
Burbank, CA 91505, USA

Montagnier, Luc (Nobel Prize Laureate)
World Foundation For AIDS Research 1
rue Miollis
Paris Cedex, France 75732, USA

Montagnier, Luc (Scientist)
Institut Pasteur
25 Rue du Docteur
Paris Cedux 15 75015, FRANCE

Montague, Diana (Opera Singer)
91 Saint Martin's Lane
London WC2, UNITED KINGDOM (UK)

Montague, Ed (Athlete, Baseball Player)
1521 Cherrywood Dr
San Mateo, CA 94403-3903, USA

Montague, John (Athlete, Baseball Player)
6001 Vineyard Ln
Montgomery, AL 36853-4275, USA

Montague, Lee (Actor)
Conway Van Gelder Robinson
18-21 Jermyn St
London SW1Y 6NB, UNITED KINGDOM (UK)

Montague-Smith, Patrick W (Editor)
Brereton
197 Park Road
Kingston-upon-Thames
Surrey, UNITED KINGDOM (UK)

Montalban, Paolo (Actor)
c/o Staff Member *Innovative Artists (LA)*
1505 10th St
Santa Monica, CA 90401, USA

Montalbano, Chuck (Athlete, Golfer)
4725 Farmdale Ave
North Hollywood, CA 91602-1109, USA

Montalbano, Joel (Scientist)
14210 Silver Sky Ct
Houston, TX 77062-2058, USA

Montalvo, Rafael (Athlete)
Hudson Valley Renegades
P.O. Box 661
Attn: Coaching Staff
Fishkill, NY 12524, USA

Montana, Claude (Designer, Fashion Designer)
131 Rue Saint-Denis
Paris 75001, FRANCE

Montana, French (Musician)
c/o Staff Member *Mizay Entertainment*
Prefers to be contacted via telephone
Atlanta, GA, USA

Montana, Joe (Athlete, Football Player)
9010 Franz Valley Rd
Calistoga, CA 94515-9517, USA

Montanez, Luis (Athlete, Baseball Player)
5745 SW 34th St
Miami, FL 33155-4912, USA

Montanez, Phillip (Stylist)
c/o Staff Member *Clutts Agency, The*
1400 Turtle Creek Blvd
#171
Dallas, TX 75207, USA

Montanez, Willie (Athlete, Baseball Player)
HC 5 Box 52020
Caguas, PR 00725-9201, USA

Montano, Sumalee (Actor)
c/o Kim Dorr *Defining Artists Agency*
10 Universal City Plaza
Suite 2000
Universal City, CA 91608, USA

Montazeri, Ayatollah Hussein Ali (Religious Leader)
Madresseh Faizieh
Qom, IRAN

Monte, Chante
c/o Staff Member *WME (WMA-NY)*
1325 Ave of the Americas
New York, NY 10019, USA

Montefusco, John (Athlete, Baseball Player)
1 Oakdale Dr
Apt 3D
Middletown, NJ 07748-2124, USA

Monteiro, Antonio M (President)
President's Office
Cia de la Republica
Sao Tiago Praia, CAPE VERDE

Monteith, Cory (Actor)
c/o Melissa Fonzino *Viewpoint Inc*
8820 Wilshire Blvd.
Suite 220
Beverly Hills, CA 90211, USA

Monteith, Hank (Athlete, Hockey Player)
PO Box 1598
St Marys, ON N4X 1B9, CANADA

Monteith, Kelly
PO Box 11669
Knoxville, TN 37939-1669

Monteleone, John (Inventor)
365 Smith Ave
Islip, NY 11751-4718, USA

Monteleone, Rich (Athlete, Baseball Player)
441 Lucerne Ace
Tampa, FL 33606-3838, USA

Montermini, Andrea (Race Car Driver)
434 E Main St
Brownsburg, IN 46112, USA

Montero, Agustin (Athlete, Baseball Player)
4600 Parkview Dr
McCullom Lake, IL 60050-2455, USA

Montero, Gabriela (Musician)
c/o Staff Member *Paradigm (Monterey)*
404 W Franklin St
Monterey, CA 93940, USA

Montero, Miguel (Athlete, Baseball Player)
683 W Honevsuckle Dr
Chandler, AZ 85248-3840, USA

Montero, Pablo (Actor)
c/o Staff Member *Televisa*
Blvd Adolfo Lopez Mateos 232
Colonia San Angel INN
DF CP 01060, MEXICO

Monterola, Pablo (Musician)
c/o Staff Member *BMG*
1540 Broadway
New York, NY 10036, USA

Montevecchi, Liliane (Musician)
Buzz Halliday
8899 Beverly Blvd
#620
Los Angeles, CA 90048, USA

Montez, Chris
6671 Sunset Blvd. #1502
Hollywood, CA 90028

Montgomerie, Colin (Athlete, Golfer)
c/o Staff Member *IMG (UK)*
McCormack House, Hogarth Business Park
Burlington Lane
Chiswick London W4 2TH, UNITED KINGDOM (UK)

Montgomerv, Jeff (Athlete, Baseball Player)
3701 W 140th St
Overland Park, KS 66224-8406, USA

Montgomery, Alton (Athlete, Football Player)
925 Meriwether St
Apt B
Griffin, GA 30224, USA

Montgomery, Anthony (Actor)
c/o Jerry Shandrew *Shandrew Public Relations*
1050 S Stanley Ave
Los Angeles, CA 90019-6634, USA

Montgomery, Belinda (Actor)
Epstein-Wyckoff
280 S Beverly Hills
#400
Beverly Hills, CA 90212, USA

Montgomery, Bob (Athlete, Baseball Player)
2 Parkway Dr
Saugus, MA 01906-1957, USA

Montgomery, Chase (Race Car Driver)
Tomar Motorsports
232 Main St.
Box 68
Peterson, IA 51047, USA

Montgomery, Chuck (Actor)
c/o Staff Member *Buchwald/Fortitude (LA)*
6500 Wilshire Blvd
Suite 2200
Los Angeles, CA 90048, USA

Montgomery, Cleo (Athlete, Football Player)
404 Dakota Trl
Irving, TX 75063, USA

MontgomerY, David (Athlete, Baseball Player)
8525 Ardmore Ave
Glenside, PA 19038-8454, USA

Montgomery, David (Photographer)
11 Edith Grove #B
London SW10, UNITED KINGDOM (UK)

Montgomery, Delmonico (Athlete, Football Player)
3011 Pecan Way Ct
Richmond, TX 77469, USA

Montgomery, Dorothy (Baseball Player)
2621 Berkley Dr
Chattanooga, TN 46614-5701, USA

Montgomery, Eddie (Musician)
c/o Staff Member *Hallmark Direction Company*
713 18th Avenue South
Nashville, TN 37203-3214, USA

Montgomery, Grady (Athlete, Baseball Player)
Baltimore Elite Giants
11904 Fort Washington Rd
Fort Washington, MD 20744-5908, USA

Montgomery, James P (Jim) (Athlete, Olympic Athlete, Swimmer)
1537 Bella Vista Dr
Dallas, TX 75218-3510, USA

Montgomery, Jeff (Athlete, Baseball Player)
2713 W 116th St
Leawood, KS 66211, USA

Montgomery, Jim (Athlete, Hockey Player)
Dubuque Fighting Saints PO Box 357
Dubuaue, IA 52004-0357, USA

Montgomery, John Michael (Musician)
c/o John Dorris Sr *Hallmark Direction Company*
713 18th Avenue South
Nashville, TN 37203-3214, USA

Montgomery, John W (Misc)
2 Rue de Rome
Starsbourg 67000, FRANCE

Montgomery, Lisa Kennedy (Actor)
Game Show Network
10202 W Washington Blvd
Culver City, CA 90232, USA

Montgomery, Marv (Athlete, Football Player)
1509 S Macon St
Aurora, CO 80012, USA

Montgomery, Melba (Musician)
Joe Taylor Artist Agency
2802 Columbine Place
Nashville, TN 37204, USA

Montgomery, Mike (Basketball Player, Coach)
Golden State Warriors
1001 Broadway
Oakland, CA 94607, USA

Montgomery, Mike (Athlete, Football Player)
4224 High Star Ln
Dallas, TX 75287, USA

Montgomery, Monique (Stylist)
1756 Marin Ave
Berkeley, CA 94707, USA

Montgomery, Monty (Athlete, Baseball Player)
807 Corn Tassel Trl
Martinsville, VA 24112-5601, USA

Montgomery, Poppy (Actor)
c/o Peg Donegan *Framework Entertainment (LA)*
9057 Nemo St
Suite C
West Hollywood, CA 90069, USA

Montgomery, Ray (Athlete, Baseball Player)
3107 S Webber Ct
Pearland, TX 06070-3030, USA

Montgomery, Ryan (Royce da 5'9) (Musician)
c/o Peter Schwartz *Agency Group Ltd, The (NY)*
142 West 57th St
6th Floor
New York, NY 10019, USA

Montgomery, Steve (Athlete, Baseball Player)
13731 Mercado Dr
Del Mar, CA 92014-3415, USA

Montgomery, Wilbert (Athlete, Football Player)
45990 Tournament Dr
Northville, MI 48168, USA

Montgomery Jr, Dan (Actor)
c/o Karyn Spencer *Peter Strain & Associates Inc (LA)*
5455 Wilshire Blvd
Suite 1812
Los Angeles, CA 90036-4368, USA

Montiel, Fernando (Boxer)
c/o Staff Member *Top Rank Inc.*
3908 Howard Hughes Pkwy
#580
Las Vegas, NV 89109, USA

Montiel, H Pierre
102 W 73rd St
New York, NY 10023, USA

Montler, Mike (Athlete, Football Player)
479 Tiara Vista Dr
Grand Junction, CO 81503, USA

Montminy, Marc R (Scientist)
Salk Institute
10100 N Torrey Pines Road
La Jolla, CA 92037, USA

montovo, Charlie (Athlete, Baseball Player)
202 Stoneridge Dr
Duson, LA 70529-3951, USA

Montoya, Al (Athlete, Hockey Player)
2410 Indian Ridge Dr
Glenview, IL 60026-1030, USA

Montoya, Al (Athlete, Hockey Player)
2 Penn Plaza
New York, NY 10121, USA

Montoya, Juan Pablo (Race Car Driver)
Ganassi Racing
8500 Westmoreland Dr
Concord, NC 28027, USA

Montoyo, Jose Carlos (Charlie) (Athlete, Baseball Player)
438 Summer Sails Dr
Valrico, FL 85629-8506, USA

Montreuil, Allan (Athlete, Baseball Player)
2016 Laurel St
Gretna, LA 70056, USA

Montross, Eric (Athlete, Basketball Player)
4668 S NC Highway 150
Lexington, NC 27295-8026, USA

Montsho, Este (Musician)
William Morris Agency
1325 Ave of Americas
New York, NY 10019, USA

Montvidas, Edgaras (Opera Singer)
Van Walsum Mgmt
4 Addison Bridge Place
London W14 8XP, USA

Montville, Leigh (Writer)
Boston Globe
Editorial Dept
135 WT Morrissey Blvd
Dorchester, MA 02125, USA

Monty, Harry
1600 N. Bronson Ave. #17
Hollywood, CA 90028

Monty Q (DJ)
c/o Staff Member *Diva Central Inc*
7510 W Sunset Blvd Ste 1445
Los Angees, CA 90046, USA

Monzikova, Anya (Actor)
c/o Greg Meyer *Meyer Management Group (MMG)*
1901 Avenue Of The Stars #365
Century City, CA 90067, USA

Moock, Joe (Athlete, Baseball Player)
12432 Pecos Ave
Greenwell Springs, LA 70739-3039, USA

Moodie, Janice (Athlete, Golfer)
10746 Woodchase Cir
Orlando, FL 32836, USA

Moody, Eric (Athlete, Baseball Player)
336 Gleneagle Cir
Irmo, SC 29063-8432, USA

Moody, Keith M (Athlete, Football Player)
4632 Riverview Ct
Tracy, CA 95377, USA

Moody, Lynne (Actor)
8708 Skyline Dr
Los Angeles, CA 90046, USA

Moody, Micky (Musician)
Int'l Talent Booking
27A Floral St #300
London WC2E 9DQ, UNITED KINGDOM (UK)

Moody, Orville (Athlete, Golfer)
9221 Chesapeake Ln
McKinney, TX 75071, USA

Moody, Ritchie (Baseball Player)
1696 Rockleigh Rd
Dayton, OH 45458-6048, USA

Moody, Ron (Actor)
Eric Glass
28 Berkeley Square
London W1X 6HD, UNITED KINGDOM (UK)

Moody-Luckhurst, Terri (Athlete, Golfer)
103 Pierrepont Isle
Duluth, GA 30097, USA

Moodysson, Lukas (Director)
Hantverkaregatan 12
Malmo 21155, Sweden

Moog, Andy (Athlete, Hockey Player)
530 Rolling Hills Rd
Coppell, TX 75019-4049, USA

Moomaw, Donn D (Athlete, Football Player)
3124 Corda Dr
Los Angeles, CA 90049, USA

Moon, Lynne (Stylist)
9629 Carnegie Dr
Dallas, TX 75228, USA

Moon, Philip
449 N. Highland Ave.
Los Angeles, CA 90036

Moon, Wallace W (Wally) (Athlete, Baseball Player)
702 Ellen Lee Ct
Bryan, TX 77802-1146, USA

Moon, Wally
1415 Angeline Circle
College Station, TX 77840

Moon, Warren (Athlete, Football Player)
24610 NE 126th St
Duvall, WA 98019-9006, USA

Mooney, Debra (Actor)
c/o Mike Smith *Principal Entertainment (LA)*
1964 Westwood Blvd #400
Los Angeles, CA 90025, USA

Mooney, Ed (Athlete, Football Player)
4105 63rd St
Lubbock, TX 79413, USA

Mooney, Harold A (Biologist)
2625 Ramona St
Palo Alto, CA 94306, USA

Mooney, John (Musician)
Intrepid Artists
Midtown Plaza
1300 Baxter St #405
Charlotte, NC 28204, USA

Mooney, Michael J (Educator)
Lewis & Clark College
President's Office
Portland, OR 97219, USA

Mooney, Peter (Actor)
c/o Fisher Pence *PMK/BNC Public Relations (PMK-LA)*
9460 Wilshire Blvd
7th Floor
Beverly Hills, CA 90210, USA

Mooneyham, Bill (Athlete, Baseball Player)
5731 White Crane Rd
Atwater, CA 95301-8573, USA

Mooneyhan, Bill (Athlete, Baseball Player)
5731 White Crane Rd
Atwater, CA 95301, USA

Moonsammy, Camille (Stylist)
c/o Staff Member *Pat Bates & Associates*
300 W 12th St
New York, NY 10014, USA

Moonves, Leslie (Business Person, Producer)
CBS-TV
51 W 52nd St
New York, NY 10019, USA

Moon Zombie, Sherrie (Actor)
8491 Sunset Blvd
#125
Hollywood, CA 90069, USA

Moordyukova, Nonna V (Actor)
Rublevskoye Shosse 34
Korp 2 #549
Moscow 121609, RUSSIA

Moore, Abra (Musician)
Haber Corp
16830 Ventura Blvd
#501
Encino, CA 91436, USA

Moore, Adam (Athlete, Baseball Player)
2030 County Road 2260
Mineola, TX 75773-6448, USA

Moore, Andre (Athlete, Basketball Player)
12137 S Justine St
Chicago, IL 60643-5443, USA

Moore, Ann S (Publisher)
People Magazine
Publisher's Office
Time & Life Building
New York, NY 10020, USA

Moore, Arch (Politician)
PO Box 5
Glen Dale, WV 26038-0005, USA

Moore, Archie (Athlete, Baseball Player)
201 Courtland Rd
Indiana, PA 15701-3202, USA

Moore, Arthur (Misc)
Sheet Metal Workers Int'l Assn
1750 New York Ave NW
Washington, DC 20006, USA

Moore, Balor (Athlete, Baseball Player)
901 W Viejo Rd
Friendswood, TX 77546-5836, USA

Moore, Barry (Athlete, Baseball Player)
6702 Conifer Cir
Indian Trail, NC 28079-7588, USA

Moore, Benjamin (Artist)
3123 39th Place S
Seattle, WA 98144, USA

Moore, Bill (Billy) (Athlete, Baseball Player)
10849 Mirador Dr
Rancho Cucamonga, CA 91737-6991, USA

Moore, Billie (Athlete, Basketball Player, Coach)
2247 Meadow Lane
Fullerton, CA 92831-2122, USA

Moore, Bob (Athlete, Baseball Player)
2500 Wellington Rd
Los Angeles, CA 90245-5842, USA

Moore, Bobby (Athlete, Baseball Player)
3703 Hyde Park Ave
Cincinnati, OH 45209-2321, USA

Moore, Brad (Athlete, Baseball Player)
3135 Challenger Point Dr
Loveland, CO 80538-7222, USA

Moore, Brandon (Athlete, Football Player)
15010 S 47th St
Phoenix, AZ 85044, USA

Moore, Brent (Athlete, Football Player)
137 Wild Horse Valley Rd
Novato, CA 94947, USA

Moore, Bud (Race Car Driver)
PO Box 2916
Spartanburg, SC 29303, USA

Moore, Calvin C (Mathematician)
1408 Eagle Pointe Court
Lafayette, CA 94549, USA

Moore, Chante (Musician, Songwriter)
Artistic Control
1350 Spring St NW #700
Atlanta, GA 30309, USA

Moore, Chante
c/o Staff Member *Creative Artists Agency (CAA-LA)*
2000 Ave Of The Stars
Los Angeles, CA 90067, USA

Moore, Charlie (Athlete, Baseball Player)
342 County Road 276
Cullman, AL 35057-4976, USA

Moore, Chris (Producer)
c/o Staff Member *LivePlanet*
11150 Santa Monica Blvd Ste 1200
Los Angeles, CA 90025, USA

Moore, Christina (Actor)
c/o Paul Rosicker *Gersh (LA)*
9465 Wilshire Blvd
Suite 600
Beverly Hills, CA 90212, USA

Moore, Christopher (Chris) (Director, Producer)
c/o Staff Member *WME (LA)*
9601 Wilshire Blvd Fl 3
Beverly Hills, CA 90210, USA

Moore, Christopher (Lil Twist) (Musician)
c/o Cortez Bryant *Bryant Management*
555 Washington Ave
Suite 240
Miami Beach, FL 33139, USA

Moore, Christy (Musician)
c/o Paul Charles *Asgard Promotions*
125 Parkway
London NW1 7PS, United Kingdom

Moore, Corwin (Writer)
c/o Staff Member *Creative Artists Agency (CAA-LA)*
2000 Ave Of The Stars
Los Angeles, CA 90067, USA

Moore, Darla (Business Person)
Rainwater, Inc
777 Main St
#2250
Fort Worth, TX 76102, USA

Moore, Darryl (Athlete, Football Player)
503 High St
Minden, LA 71055, USA

Moore, Dave (Football Player)
c/o Team Member *Tampa Bay Buccaneers*
1 Buccaneer Pl
Tampa, FL 33607, USA

Moore, Dayton (Athlete, Baseball Player)
2508 W 118th St
Leawood, KS 66211-3032, USA

Moore, Demi (Actor)
c/o Jason Weinberg *Untitled Entertainment (LA)*
350 S. Beverly Dr #200
Beverly Hills, CA 90212, USA

Moore, Derland P (Athlete, Football Player)
1917 Madison St
Mandeville, LA 70448, USA

Moore, Derrick (Athlete, Football Player)
3164 Jackson Creek Dr
Stockbridge, GA 30281, USA

Moore, Dick (Cartoonist)
Dick Moore Assoc
1560 Broadway
New York, NY 10036, USA

Moore, Dickie
150 West End Ave. #26C
New York, NY 10023-5743

Moore, Dominic (Athlete, Hockey Player)
Octagon Sports Management
66 Slater St 23rd Fl
Attn Larry Kelly
Ottawa, ON K1P 5H1, Canada

Moore, Dorothy (Musician)
Sirius Entertainment
13531 Claimont Way #8
Oregon City, OR 97045, USA

Moore, Earl
215 West End Blvd.
Winston-Salem, NC 27101-1203

Moore, Eric P (Athlete, Football Player)
2225 Lindsay Ln
Florissant, MO 63031, USA

Moore, Gary (Athlete, Baseball Player)
7985 Roundrock Rd
Dallas, TX 75248-5341, USA

Moore, George E (Doctor)
12048 S Blackhawk Dr
Conifer, CO 80433, USA

Moore, Gorden (Inventor)
100 Canada Rd
Redwood City, CA 94062-4104, USA

Moore, Gwen (Congressman, Politician)
2245 Rayburn HOB
Washington, DC 20515, USA

Moore, Harold G General (Writer)
585 Moores Mill Rd
Auburn, AL 36830-6027, USA

Moore, Henry (Athlete, Football Player)
2200 Pleasure Dr
Bryant, AR 72019, USA

Moore, Herman J (Athlete, Football Player)
Simple One Media 4840 N Adams Rd Ste 503
Rochester Hills, MI 48306, USA

Moore, Jackie (Musician)
T-Best Talent Agency
508 Honey Lake Court
Danville, CA 94506, USA

Moore, Jackie (Athlete, Basketball Player)
2721 Laurel Valley Ln
Arlington, TX 76006-4019, USA

Moore, Jacqueline (Wrestler)
15030 Ventura Blvd.
Suite 525
Sherman Oaks, CA 91403, USA

Moore, James E Jr (General)
18940 Joaquin Court
Salinas, CA 93908, USA

Moore, James R "Red" (Athlete, Baseball Player)
1886 Ravenwood WayNE
Atlanta, GA 30329-2734, USA

Moore, Jeffrey B (Athlete, Football Player)
2090 Dogwood Estates Cv
Germantown, TN 38139, USA

Moore, Jerald (Athlete, Football Player)
1806 Sabine Ln
Richmond, TX 77469, USA

Moore, Jerry (Athlete, Football Player)
401 Ivory Dr
Little Rock, AR 72205, USA

Moore, Jesse W (Engineer)
Ball Aerospace Corp
Boulder Industrial Park
Boulder, CO 80306, USA

Moore, J Jeremy (General)
Lloyds Bank
Cox's & King's Branch
7 Pall Mall
London SW1, UNITED KINGDOM (UK)

Moore, Joe
2410 Memorial Dr. #3C
Bryan, TX 77802

Moore, Joel David (Actor)
Coattails Entertainment
11271 Ventura Blvd Ste 434
Studio City, CA 91604, USA

Moore, John (Director, Producer, Writer)
c/o Rowena Arguelles *Creative Artists Agency (CAA-LA)*
2000 Ave Of The Stars
Los Angeles, CA 90067, USA

Moore, John A (Biologist)
11522 Tulane Ave
Riverside, CA 92507, USA

Moore, John W (Educator)
Indiana State University
President's Office
Terre Haute, IN 47809, USA

Moore, Juanita (Actor)
5001 W Florida Ave #529
Hemet, CA 92545, USA

Moore, Julianne (Actor)
c/o Evelyn O'Neill *Management 360*
9111 Wilshire Blvd
Beverly Hills, CA 90210, USA

Moore, Junior (Athlete, Baseball Player)
3728 Wall Ave
Richmond, CA 94804-3346, USA

Moore, Justin (Musician)
c/o Jake Basden *Big Machine Records*
1219 16th Ave South
Nashville, TN 37212, USA

Moore, Kelly (Race Car Driver)
PO Box 1210
Scarborough, ME 04070-1210, USA

Moore, Kelvin (Athlete, Football Player)
1564 W 110th Pl
Los Angeles, CA 90047, USA

Moore, Kelvin (Athlete, Baseball Player)
75 Stoney Point Ter
Covington, GA 30014-7070, USA

Moore, Kenya (Beauty Pageant Winner, Reality TV Star)
c/o Brian Dickens *BD Management*
16605 Pleasant Colony Dr
Upper Marlboro, MD 20774, USA

Moore, Kerwin (Athlete, Baseball Player)
18137 Goddard St
Detroit, MI 48033-2272, USA

Moore, Kip (Musician)
c/o Shawn McSpadden *Red Light Management (Nashville)*
39 Music Square East
Nashville, TN 37203, USA

Moore, Leonard E (Lenny) (Athlete, Football Player)
8815 Stonehaven Rd
Randallstown, MD 21133, USA

Moore, Leroy (Athlete, Football Player)
842 Golf Dr
Apt 201
Pontiac, MI 48341, USA

Moore, Lloyd (Race Car Driver)
152 Frew Run Rd
Frewsburg, NY 14738, USA

Moore, Lorrie (Writer)
University of Wisconsin
English Dept
Madison, WI 53706, USA

Moore, Lowes
21 Hutchinson Blvd
Mount Vernon, NY 10552-2509, USA

Moore, Lucille (Baseball Player)
6450 Miami Cir
South Bend, IN 46614-6480, USA

Moore, Malcolm A S (Scientist)
Memorial Sloan-Dettering Cancer Center
1275 York Ave
New York, NY 10021, USA

Moore, Mandy (Actor, Musician)
c/o Jon Leshay *Storefront Entertainment*
647 N Martel Ave
Suite 102
Los Angeles, CA 90036, USA

Moore, Manfred (Athlete, Football Player)
1672 Buckingham Rd
Los Angeles, CA 90019, USA

Moore, Marcus (Athlete, Baseball Player)
P.O. Box 5144
Richmond, CA 94565-7235, USA

Moore, Mary (Athlete, Baseball Player)
4225 Lake Grove Ct
White Lake, MI 48383-1528, USA

Moore, Mary Tyler (Actor)
510 E 86th St #21A
New York, NY 10028, USA

Moore, McNeil (Athlete, Football Player)
1212 Woodlawn Dr
Center, TX 75935, USA

Moore, Melanie
3500 W. Olive Ave. #920
Burbank, CA 91505-4628

Moore, Melba (Actor, Musician)
Artist Services Inc
1017 O St NW
#B
Washington, DC 20001, USA

Moore, Melissa Anne (Actor)
PO Box 55
Versailles, KY 40383, USA

Moore, Michael (Director)
c/o Ari Emanuel *WME (LA)*
9601 Wilshire Blvd Fl 3
Beverly Hills, CA 90210, USA

Moore, Michael K (Mike) (Prime Minister)
World Trade Organization
154 Rue Lausanne
Geneva 21 1211, SWITZERLAND

Moore, Michael (Mike) (Attorney, Attorney General, General)
Attorney General's Office
PO Box 220
Jackson, MS 39205, USA

Moore, Mike (Athlete, Baseball Player)
1472 E Calle De Caballos
Tempe, AZ 85284-2406, USA

Moore, Mindy (Athlete, Golfer)
36 Black Hickory Way
Ormond Beach, FL 32174, USA

Moore, Moulty (Athlete, Football Player)
5781 S Sable Cir
Margate, FL 33063, USA

Moore, Nathanlel (Nat) (Athlete, Football Player)
20041 E Oakmont Dr
Hialeah, FL 33015, USA

Moore, Otis (Baseball Player)
Pittsburgh Pirates
2923 178th Dr Apt 3
Hammond, IN 46323-3245, USA

Moore, Patrick (Athlete, Golfer)
4638 E Dartmouth St
Mesa, AZ 85205, USA

Moore, Paul (Bud) (Race Car Driver)
PO Box 2916
Spartanburg, SC 29303, USA

Moore, Rachel (Actor, Model)
c/o Staff Member *WNWN Media*
348 S. Hauser Blvd #PH414
Los Angeles, CA 90036, USA

Moore, Ralph (Musician)
Denon Records
135 W 50th St
#1915
New York, NY 10020, USA

Moore, Red (Baseball Player)
Atlanta Black Crackers
2450 Perry Blvd NW
Atlanta, GA 30318-8809, USA

Moore, Richard (Actor)
London Mgmt
2-4 Noel St
London W1V 3RB, UNITED KINGDOM (UK)

Moore, Richard W (Dickie) (Athlete, Hockey Player)
Dickie Moore Rentals 4955 Ch Saint-Francais
Saint Laurent, QC 1P3, Canada

Moore, Rob (Athlete, Football Player)
14239 S 8th St
Phoenix, AZ 85048, USA

Moore, Robert A (Athlete, Football Player)
1906 E Gate Dr
Stone Mountain, GA 30087, USA

Moore, Robert R (Athlete, Football Player)
20 Sally Ann Rd
Orinda, CA 94563, USA

Moore, Roger (Actor, Director)
c/o Tom Chasin *Chasin Agency, The*
8899 Beverly Blvd
Suite 716
Los Angeles, CA 90048-2449, USA

Moore, Ron (Athlete, Football Player)
5730 Oakwood St
Spencer, OK 73084, USA

Moore, Ronald D (Producer, Writer)
c/o Brett Loncar *Creative Artists Agency (CAA-LA)*
2000 Ave Of The Stars
Los Angeles, CA 90067, USA

Moore, Sam (Musician)
I'ma Da Wife Enterprises
7119 E Shea Blvd #109-436
#109-436
Scottsdale, AZ 85254, USA

Moore, Scott (Athlete, Baseball Player)
3503 Orange Ave
Long Beach, CA 90807-4828, USA

Moore, Scotty (Musician)
5340 Simpkins Rd
Whites Creek, TN 37189, USA

Moore, Shawn (Athlete, Football Player)
573 Brookfield Dr
Centreville, MD 21617, USA

Moore, Shemar (Actor)
c/o Charlton Blackburne *A Management*
9107 Wilshire Blvd.
Suite 650
Beverly Hills, CA 90210, USA

Moore, Stephen (Actor)
Lyttelton
Royal National Theatre
South Bank
London SE1 9PX, UK

Moore, Sterling (Athlete, Football Player)
c/o Jordan Woy *Willis and Woy Management*
3030 Olive St #520
Dallas, TX 75219, USA

Moore, Tamara
Phoenix Mercury
American West Arena
201 E Jefferson St
Phoenix, AZ 85004, USA

Moore, Terry (Actor)
c/o Budd Burton Moss *Burton Moss*
10533 Strathmore Dr
Los Angeles, CA 90024, USA

Moore, Toby (Actor)
c/o Staff Member *Sanders Armstrong Caserta*
2120 Colorado Blvd
Suite 120
Santa Monica, CA 90404, USA

Moore, Tom (Athlete, Football Player)
1038 Forest Harbor Dr
Hendersonville, TN 37075, USA

Moore, Tommy (Athlete, Baseball Player)
PO Box 336
Pioneertown, CA 92268, USA

Moore, Tracy (Athlete, Basketball Player)
12116 E 37th Pl
Tulsa, OK 74146-3104, USA

Moore, Trey (Athlete, Baseball Player)
5128 Bellerive Bend Dr
College Station, TX 77845-4477, USA

Moore, Vanessa (Stylist)
c/o Staff Member *Art Department*
48 Greene St
4th Floor
New York, NY 10013, USA

Moore, W Edward C (Biologist)
1607 Boxwood Dr
Blacksburg, VA 24060, USA

Moore, Zeke (Athlete, Football Player)
3422 Prudence Ct
Houston, TX 77045, USA

Moore Capito, Shelley (Congressman, Politician)
2443 Rayburn HOB
Washington, DC 20515, United States

Moorehead, Emery (Athlete, Football Player)
1005 Sussex Dr
Northbrook, IL 60062, USA

Moorehouse, Adrian
St. Helier Bradford Rd. Bringley
W. York., ENGLAND BD16 1PA

Moore Jr, Charles (Athlete, Track Athlete)
10 Barclay Street
New York, NY 1007-2705, USA

Moore (Paxson), Melanie Deanne (Actor)
c/o Melisa Spamer *Domain Talent*
9229 Sunset Boulevard
Suite 710
Los Angeles, CA 90069, USA

Moorer, Allison (Actor, Musician, Songwriter, Writer)
TKO Artist Mgmt
1107 17th Ave S
Nashville, TN 37212, USA

Moorer, Llana (MC Lyte) (Musician)
Sunni Gyrl Inc
PO Box 691394
Los Angeles, CA 90069, USA

Moores, John (Athlete, Baseball Player)
8022 Oxfordshire Dr
Spring, TX 77379-4665, USA

Moore-Warner, Eleanor (Athlete, Baseball Player)
2172 Kinney Ave NW
Grand Rapids, MI 49544-1160, USA

Moore-Watkins, Pauline (Actor)
4077 SW Sunset Dr
#202
Lake Oswego, OR 97035, USA

Mooring, John (Athlete, Football Player)
1901 Pat Booker Rd
Universal City, TX 78148, USA

Moorman, Dorothea Johnson
2400 E Howell St Apt I
Seattle, Wa 98122-3070, USA

Moorman, Mo (Athlete, Football Player)
9641 Shelbyville Rd
Simpsonville, KY 40067, USA

Moorse, Kiki (Musician)
K Records
924 Jefferson St SE
#101
Olympia, WA 98501, USA

MOP (Music Group)
c/o Staff Member *Interscope Records (NY)*
1755 Broadway
New York, NY 10019, USA

Mora, Danny (Actor)
c/o Staff Member *Acme Talent & Literary (LA)*
1400 Atlantic Ave
Suite 274
Long Beach, CA 90814, USA

Mora, Gene (Cartoonist)
United Feature Syndicate
200 Madison Ave
New York, NY 10016, USA

Mora, Melvin (Athlete, Baseball Player)
2316 Willow Vale Dr
Fallston, MD 21047, USA

Mora, Philippe (Director)
Altman Co
9255 Sunset Blvd
#901
Los Angeles, CA 90069, USA

Mora, Sergio (Reality TV Star)
c/o Staff Member *The Contender*
NBC Entertainment
3000 W. Alameda Ave #5366
Burbank, CA 91523, USA

Morabito, Rocky (Journalist, Photographer)
3036 Gilmore St
Jacksonville, FL 32205, USA

Morabito, Tim (Athlete, Football Player)
P.O. Box 152
Garnerville, NY 10923, USA

Moraga, David (Athlete, Baseball Player)
608 Peach Ct
Fairfield, CA 94534-1522, USA

Mora Gramunt, Gabriel (Architect)
Passtage Sant Felip
12 Bis
Barcelona 08006, SPAIN

Morahan, Christopher T (Director)
Highcombe
Devil's Punchbowl
Thursley
Godalming, Surrey GU8 6NS, UNITED
KINGDOM (UK)

Mora Jr, James E (Jim) (Coach, Football
Coach)
c/o Bob LaMonte *Professional Sports
Representation*
1220 Plumas St
Reno, NV 89509, 775-828-1864

Morales, Esai (Actor)
c/o Jai Khanna *Brillstein Entertainment
Partners*
9150 Wilshire Blvd #350
Beverly Hills, CA 90212, USA

Morales, Esal (Actor)
7527 Woodrow Wilson Dr
Los Angeles, CA 90046, USA

Morales, Jerry (Athlete, Baseball Player,
Coach)
Washington Nationals
2400 E Capitol St NE
Attn: Coaching Staff
Washington, DC 20003, USA

Morales, Jose M (Athlete, Baseball Player)
17411 Fosgate Rd
Montverde, FL 34777-0985, USA

Morales, Kendry (Athlete, Baseball Player)
c/o Staff Member *Los Angeles Dodgers
(LA Dodgers)*
1000 Elysian Park Ave
Los Angeles, CA 90012, USA

Morales, Natalie (Actor)
c/o Vincent Nastri *Bleecker Street
Entertainment*
568 Broadway #801
New York, NY 10012, USA

Morales, Natalie (Correspondent)
c/o Staff Member *NBC Universal (NY)*
30 Rockefeller Plaza
New York, NY 10112, USA

Morales, Pedro (Athlete, Wrestler)
118 Willery St
Woodbridge, NJ 96712, USA

Morales, P Pablo (Swimmer)
University of Nebraska
Athletic Dept
Lincoln, NE 68588, USA

Morales, Rich (Athlete, Baseball Player)
1650 Rosita Rd
Pacifica, CA 94044, USA

Morales, Willie (Athlete, Baseball Player)
5001 W Camino Del Desierto
Tucson, AZ 85745-9119, USA

Moran, Al (Athlete, Baseball Player)
34134 Banbury St
Farmington Hills, MI 48331-2216, USA

Moran, Al (Athlete, Baseball Player)
34134 Banbury St
Farmington Hills, MI 48331, USA

Moran, Bill (Athlete, Baseball Player)
200 Shore Dr
Portsmouth, VA 23701-1241, USA

Moran, Billy (Athlete, Baseball Player)
107 Emerling Ln
Peachtree City, GA 33947-2149, USA

Moran, Carl (Baseball Player)
Chicago White Sox
200 Shore Dr
Portsmouth, VA 23701-1241, USA

Moran, Erin (Actor)
444 Desert Springs Rd
Palmdale, CA 93551, USA

Moran, Ian (Athlete, Hockey Player)
84 S Station St
Duxbury, MA 02332, USA

Moran, John (Religious Leader)
Missionary Church
PO Box 9127
Fort Wayne, IN 46899, USA

Moran, Ian (Athlete, Hockey Player)
427 Bay Rd
Duxbury, MA 02332-5228, USA

Moran, Nick (Actor)
c/o Staff Member *Diverse Talent Group*
9911 W Pico Blvd Ste 340W
Los Angeles, CA 90035, USA

Moran, Pauline
275 Kensington Rd.
London, ENGLAND SW1 6BY

Moran, Richard J (Rich) (Athlete, Football
Player)
7252 Mimosa Dr
Carlsbad, CA 92009, USA

Moran, Sean (Athlete, Football Player)
13577 W 84th Dr
Arvada, CO 80005-5825, USA

Moran, Tommy (Actor)
c/o Staff Member *Creative Artists Agency
(CAA-LA)*
2000 Ave Of The Stars
Los Angeles, CA 90067, USA

Moran, Tony (DJ)
c/o Len Evans *Project Publicity*
312 West 53rd St
Suite 202
New York, NY 10019, USA

Morandini, Mickey (Athlete, Baseball
Player, Olympic Athlete)
1045 Walker Pass
Chesterton, IN 46304-3473, USA

Moranis, Rick (Actor)
c/o Staff Member *WmE2 (WMA-LA)*
1 William Morris Pl
Beverly Hills, CA 90212, USA

Morante, Laura (Actor)
Carol Levi Co
Via Giuseppe Pisanelli
Rome 00196, ITALY

Morasca, Jenna (Reality TV Star)
M Morasca
6027 Belle Terre Ct
Bridgeville, PA 15017, USA

Morast, Daniel J (Misc)
International Wildlife Coalition
634 N Falmouth Hwy
North Falmouth, MA 02556, USA

Morath, Max (Musician)
Producers Inc
1186 N 56th St
Tampa, FL 33617, USA

Morauta, Mekere (Prime Minister)
Premier's Office
Marea Haus
Walgani
Port Moresby, PAPUA NEW GUINEA

Moravec, Ivan (Musician)
Cramer/Marder Artists
3436 Springhill Road
Lafayette, CA 94549, USA

Morawetz, Cathleen (Scientist)
3298 Monteith Ave
Cincinnati, OH 45208-2814, USA

Morceli, Noureddine (Athlete, Track
Athlete)
Youth & Sports Minitry
3 Rue Mohamed Belouizdad
Algiers, ALGERIA

Morcott, Southwood J (Business Person)
Dana Corp
PO Box 1000
Toledo, OH 43697, USA

Mordashov, Alexei (Business Person)
2/3 Klara Tsetkin St
Moscow RU-127299, Russia

Mordecai, Mike (Athlete, Baseball Player)
10 Cross Creek Ln
Dothan, AL 36303-9320, USA

Mordillo, Guillermo (Cartoonist)
Haye Top Present
Oberweg 8
Unterhacing 82008, GERMANY

Mordkovitch, Lydia (Musician)
25B Belsize Ave
London NW3 3BL, UNITED KINGDOM
(UK)

More, Camilla (Actor)
Sharon Kemp
477 S Robertson Blvd
#204
Beverly Hills, CA 90211, USA

More, Jayson (Athlete, Hockey Player)
9532 Thoroughbred Way
Brentwood, TN 37027-8922, USA

Moreau, Doug (Athlete, Football Player)
5875 Highland Rd
Baton Rouge, LA 70808, USA

Moreau, Jeanne (Actor)
Agence Intertalent
5 Rue Clemont Marot
Paris 75008, FRANCE

Moreau, Marguerite (Actor)
c/o Heather Reynolds *One Entertainment
(NY)*
12 W 57th St
Penthouse
New York, NY 10019, USA

Moreau, Sylvie
11 av. Corentin Cariou
Paris, FRANCE 75019

Morehead, Dave (Athlete, Baseball Player)
13872 Glenmere Dr
Santa Ana, CA 92705-2812, USA

Moreino, Joe (Athlete, Football Player)
25 Gemini Dr
East Providence, RI 02914, USA

Moreira, Airto (Musician)
A Train Mgmt
PO Box 29242
Oakland, CA 94604, USA

Morejon, Dan (Athlete, Baseball Player)
22625 SW 207th Ave
Miami, FL 33170, USA

Moreland, Keith (Athlete, Baseball Player)
4209 Hidden Canyon Cv
Austin, TX 78746-1256, USA

Morelli, Oscar (Actor)
c/o Staff Member *Televisa*
Blvd Adolfo Lopez Mateos 232
Colonia San Angel INN
DF CP 01060, MEXICO

Morello, Tom (Musician)
GAS Entertainment
8935 Lindblade St
Culver City, CA 90232, USA

Morelos, Lisette (Actor)
c/o Staff Member *Televisa*
Blvd Adolfo Lopez Mateos 232
Colonia San Angel INN
DF CP 01060, MEXICO

Moreno, Arturo "Arte" (Business Person)
c/o Staff Member *Los Angeles Angels Of
Anaheim*
Angels Stadium Of Anaheim
2000 Gene Autry Way
Anaheim, CA 92806, USA

Moreno, Azucar (Music Group)
c/o Staff Member *Sony Music Miami*
605 Lincoln Rd Fl 7
Miami Beach, FL 33139, USA

Moreno, Catalina Sandino (Actor)
c/o Staff Member *Creative Artists Agency
(CAA-LA)*
2000 Ave Of The Stars
Los Angeles, CA 90067, USA

Moreno, Isabel (Actor)
c/o Gabriel Blanco *Gabriel Blanco
Iglesias (Mexico)*
Rio Balsas 35-32
Colonia Cuauhtemoc
DF 06500, Mexico

Moreno, Jaime (Musician)
New York/New Jersey Mtrostars
1 Harmon Plaza
#300
Secaucus, NJ 07094, USA

Moreno, Jaime (Race Car Driver)
252 Montclaire Circle
Weston, FL 33326, USA

Moreno, Jose Elias (Actor)
c/o Staff Member *Televisa*
Blvd Adolfo Lopez Mateos 232
Colonia San Angel INN
DF CP 01060, MEXICO

Moreno, Lea
4739 Lankershim Blvd.
No. Hollywood, CA 91602-1803

Moreno, Moses (Athlete, Football Player)
11627 Lakeside Ave
Lakeside, CA 92040, USA

Moreno, Orber (Athlete, Baseball Player)
5250 Los Palma Vista Dr
Orlando, FL 34746-5102, USA

Moreno, Rita (Actor)
7027 Devon Way
Berkeley, CA 94705-1722, USA

Moreno, Roberto (Race Car Driver)
Herdez Competition
57A Gasoline Alley
Indianapolis, IN 46222, USA

Moresco, Robert (Actor, Director, Producer, Writer)
c/o Chris Silbermann *ICM Partners (ICM-LA)*
10250 Constellation Blvd Fl 7
Los Angeles, CA 90067, USA

Moresco, Tim (Athlete, Football Player)
2413 Pond Rd
Duluth, GA 30096, USA

Moret, Rogelio (Roger) (Athlete, Baseball Player)
HC 1 P.O. Box 5225
Guaynabo, PR 00971, USA

Moretti, Fabrizio (Musician)
MVO Ltd
370 7th Ave
#807
New York, NY 10001, USA

Moretz, Chloe (Actor)
c/o Pamela Kohl *3 Arts Entertainment Inc*
9460 Wilshire Blvd
7th Floor
Beverly Hills, CA 90210, USA

Moretz, Chloe Grace (Actor)
c/o Pamela Kohl *3 Arts Entertainment Inc*
9460 Wilshire Blvd
7th Floor
Beverly Hills, CA 90210, USA

Morey, Bill (Actor)
Kazarian/Spencer
11365 Ventura Blvd
#100
Studio City, CA 91604, USA

Morfogen, George (Actor)
c/o Staff Member *Gersh (LA)*
9465 Wilshire Blvd
Suite 600
Beverly Hills, CA 90212, USA

Morgado, Arnold (Athlete, Football Player)
1750 Kaahumanu St
Apt 53-C
Pearl City, HI 96782, USA

Morgan, Angelique (Reality TV Star)
c/o Anthony Embry *AE Entertainment Public Relations*
124 Evening Shade Dr
Charleston, SC 29414, USA

Morgan, Barbara R (Astronaut)
2996 S Rookery Ln
Boise, ID 83706-5484, USA

Morgan, Bill (Writer)
c/o Staff Member *Da Capo Press*
Eleven Cambridge Center
Cambridge, MA 02142, USA

Morgan, Bobby (Athlete, Baseball Player)
3004 Stonybrook Rd
Oklahoma City, OK 73120-5716, USA

Morgan, Bobby (Athlete, Baseball Player)
3004 Stonybrook Rd
Oklahoma City, OK 73120, USA

Morgan, Brit (Actor)
c/o Jessica Cohen *JCPR*
9903 Santa Monica Blvd
Suite 983
Beverly Hills, CA 90212, USA

Morgan, Chad (Actor)
c/o Staff Member *Silver Massetti & Szatmary (SMS) Talent Inc*
8383 Wilshire Blvd
Suite 230
Beverly Hills, CA 90211, USA

Morgan, Craig (Musician)
c/o Staff Member *WmE2 (WMA-TN)*
1600 Division St
Suite 300
Nashville, TN 37203, USA

Morgan, Dan (Athlete, Football Player)
1915 Funny Side Dr
Waxhaw, NC 29173, USA

Morgan, Debbi (Actor)
c/o Elissa Leeds-Fickman *Reel Talent Management*
P.O. Box 491035
Los Angeles, CA 90049, USA

Morgan, Debelah (Musician)
DAS Communications
83 Riverside Dr
New York, NY 10024, USA

Morgan, Derrick (Athlete, Football Player)
26826 Morgan Run
Westlake, OH 44145, USA

Morgan, Donald M (Cinematographer)
15826 Mayall St
North Hills, CA 91343, USA

Morgan, Elaine
24 Aberford Rd. Mt. Ash
Glamorgan, ENGLAND

Morgan, Frank (Musician)
Integrity Talent
PO Box 961
Burlington, MA 01803, USA

Morgan, Gil (Athlete, Golfer)
P.O. Box 806
Edmond, OK 73083-0806, USA

Morgan, Glen (Director, Producer, Writer)
c/o Staff Member *WME (LA)*
9601 Wilshire Blvd Fl 3
Beverly Hills, CA 90210, USA

Morgan, James C (Business Person)
Applied Materials
3050 Bowers Ave
Santa Clara, CA 95054, USA

Morgan, James N (Economist)
1217 Bydding Road
Ann Arbor, MI 48103, USA

Morgan, Jane (Musician)
27740 Pacific Coast Highway
Malibu, CA 90265, USA

Morgan, Jaye P (Actor, Musician)
1185 La Grange Ave
Newbury Park, CA 91320, USA

Morgan, Jeffrey Dean (Actor)
4176 Farmdale Ave
Studio City, CA 91604, USA

Morgan, Joe (Athlete, Baseball Player, Coach)
15 Oak Hill Dr
Walpole, MA 02081-2713, USA

Morgan, Joe (Athlete, Baseball Player)
1988 MGR: Boston Red Sox
Walpole, MA 02081-2713, USA

Morgan, Joseph (Actor)
c/o Richard Konigsberg *RKM*
400 N Mansfield Ave
Los Angeles, CA 90036, USA

Morgan, Katie (Actor)
18663 Ventura Blvd
Suite 703
Tarzana, CA 91356, USA

Morgan, Kevin (Athlete, Baseball Player)
205 Yearling Rd
Lot 10
Duson, LA 70529-3118, USA

Morgan, Larry (Race Car Driver)
5399 Horn's Hill Rd.
Newark, OH 43055, USA

Morgan, Lewis R (Judge)
US Court of Appeals
25 Elmtree Dr
Sharpsburg, GA 30277, USA

Morgan, Lorrie (Actor, Musician)
c/o Staff Member *Webster & Associates PR*
3573 Couchville Pike
Hermitage, TN 37076, USA

Morgan, Marabel (Writer)
Total Woman Inc
1300 NW 167th St
Miami, FL 33169, USA

Morgan, Mia (Stylist)
c/o Staff Member *Ford Models (Chicago)*
311 W Superior St
Chicago, IL 60654, USA

Morgan, Michael (Scientist)
Wellcome Trust
183 Euston Road
London NW1 2BE, UNITED KINGDOM (UK)

Morgan, Michele (Actor, Musician)
5 Rue Jacques Dulud
Neuillysur-Seine 92200, FRANCE

Morgan, Michelle (Actor)
c/o Staff Member *Levine Okwu Erickson Management*
6363 Wilshire Blvd
Suite 300
Los Angeles, CA 90048, USA

Morgan, Mike (Athlete, Baseball Player)
P.O. Box 681130
Park City, UT 84068-1130, USA

Morgan, Mike (Cartoonist)
Creators Syndicate
5777 W Century Blvd
#1700
Los Angeles, CA 90045, USA

Morgan, Munden (Athlete, Basketball Player)
149 Windrush Rd
Winston Salem, NC 27106-2593, USA

Morgan, Peter (Director, Producer, Writer)
c/o Jeremy Barber *United Talent Agency (UTA)*
9336 Civic Center Dr
Beverly Hills, CA 90210, USA

Morgan, Piers (Reality TV Star, Television Host)
c/o Tracey Chapman *James Grant Media Group Ltd*
94 Strand On the Green
Chiswick
London W4 3NN, UK

Morgan, Quincy (Athlete, Football Player)
4654 N Jupiter Rd
Apt 1411
Garland, TX 75044, USA

Morgan, Rob (Race Car Driver)
Morgan DollarMotorsports
Hwy 81 South
Box 646
Hennessey, OK 77342, USA

Morgan, Robert (Politician)
1362 Keith Hills Rd
Lillington, NC 27546-8264, USA

Morgan, Robert B (Senator)
Morgan and Gilchrist
101 E Front St
Lillington, NC 27546, USA

Morgan, Shelly Taylor (Actor)
Pakula/King
9229 Sunset Blvd
#315
Los Angeles, CA 90069, USA

Morgan, Sonja (Reality TV Star)
c/o Staff Member *Bravo (NY)*
30 Rockefeller Plaza
New York, NY 10112, USA

Morgan, Stanley D (Athlete, Football Player)
P.O. Box 383048
Germantown, TN 38183, USA

Morgan, Tracy (Actor, Comedian)
c/o David (Dave) Becky *3 Arts Entertainment Inc*
9460 Wilshire Blvd
7th Floor
Beverly Hills, CA 90210, USA

Morgan, Trevor (Actor)
c/o Beverly Strong *Strong Management*
3532 Hayden Ave
Culver City, CA 90232, USA

Morgan, Walter (Athlete, Golfer)
15536 Fishermans Rest Ct
Cornelius, NC 28031, USA

Morgan, Walter T J (Misc)
57 Woodbury Dr
Sutton
Surrey, UNITED KINGDOM (UK)

Morgan, William N (Architect)
William Morgan Architects
220 E Forsyth St
Jacksonville, FL 32202, USA

Morgan, W Jason (Misc)
Princton University
Geophysic Dept
Princeton, NJ 08544, USA

Morganna (Entertainer, Model)
PO Box 20281
Columbia, OH 43220, USA

Morgenstern, Maia (Actor)
c/o Catherine Davray *Catherine Davray Agency*
16 bis rue de l'Abbe de l'Epee
Paris 75005, FRANCE

Morgenstern, Thomas (Athlete, Skier)
Eichenweg 15
Lieserbrucke 9851, Austria

Morgenthau, Robert (Politician)
1 Hogan Pl
New York, NY 10013-4311, USA

Morgenthau, Robert M (Attorney, Attorney General, General)
1085 Park Ave
New York, NY 10028, USA

Morgridge, John P (Business Person)
Cisco Systems
170 W Tasan Dr
San Jose, CA 95134, USA

Morhardt, Moe (Athlete, Baseball Player)
219 Spencer Hill Rd
Winsted, CT 06098-2214, USA

Mori, Barbara (Actor)
c/o Eric Rovner WmE2 (WMA-Miami)
119 Washington Ave
Suite 400
Miami, FL 33139, USA

Mori, Hanae (Designer, Fashion Designer)
Hanae Mori Haute Couture
17-19 Ave Montaigne
Paris, 75008, FRANCE

Mori, Yoshiro (Prime Minister)
Prime Minister's Office
1-6-1 Nagatoicho
Chiyodaku
Tokyo 100, JAPAN

Moriarty, Cathy (Actor)
c/o Brian Liebman Liebman Entertainment
25 E 21st St #PH
New York, NY 10011-8503, USA

Moriarty, Evelyn
6251 Coldwater Canyon #102
No. Hollywood, CA 91606

Moriarty, Michael (Actor)
200 W 58th St
#3B
New York, NY 10019, USA

Moriarty, Mike (Athlete, Baseball Player)
5 E Oleander Dr
Mount Laurel, NJ 08054-3601, USA

Moriarty, Tom (Athlete, Football Player)
28800 Fairmount Blvd
Cleveland, OH 44124, USA

Morimoto, Masaharu (Chef)
280 Park Ave S Apt 18M
New York, NY 10010-6132, USA

Morimoto, Masaharu
105 Hudson St.
New York, NY 10013-2331

Morin, Alan (Athlete, Golfer)
139 Jay Ct
Royal Palm Beach, FL 33411, USA

Morin, Jim (Cartoonist, Editor)
Miami Herald
Editorial Dept
Herald Plaza
Miami, FL 33101, USA

Morin, Lee M Captain (Astronaut)
10 Marys Creek Ln
Friendswood, TX 77546-3492, USA

Morin, Lee M E (Astronaut)
10 Marys Creek Lane
Friendswood, TX 77546, USA

Morison, Patricia (Actor, Musician)
Craig Mgmt
125 S Sycamore Ave
Los Angeles, CA 90036, USA

Morissette, Alanis (Musician, Songwriter, Writer)
c/o Larry Jacobson Collective
8383 Wilshire Blvd
Suite 1050
Beverly Hills, CA 90211, USA

Morissette, Dave (Athlete, Hockey Player)
6565 Rue Champetre
Saint-Hyacinthe, QC J2R 181, Canada

Moritz, Brett (Athlete, Football Player)
613 Cameron Ridge Ct
Parkton, MD 21120, USA

Moritz, Louisa
405 Cliffwood Ave.
Los Angeles, CA 90049

Moritz, Neal (Producer)
c/o Tracey Jacobs United Talent Agency (UTA)
9336 Civic Center Dr
Beverly Hills, CA 90210, USA

Moriyama, Raymond (Architect)
32 Daveport Road
Toronto, ON 1H3, CANADA

Mork, Truis (Musician)
Harrison/Parrott
12 Penzance Place
London W11 4PA, UNITED KINGDOM (UK)

Morkis, Dorothy (Athlete, Horse Racer, Olympic Athlete)
17 Farm St
Dover, MA 02030-2303, USA

Morlan, John (Athlete, Baseball Player)
3290 Belgreen Dr
Grove City, OH 43123-8297, USA

Morland, David (Athlete, Golfer)
5531 Oxford Moor Blvd
Windermere, FL 34786-7012, USA

Morley, Joanne (Athlete, Golfer)
I M G
Pier House Strand on the Ocean
Chiswick
London W4 3NN, United Kingdom

morley, Lawrence (Scientist)
90 Hemlock St
Thomas, ON NSR 1X9, Canada

Morley, Lawrence W (Geophysicist, Physicist)
90 Hemlock St
Saint Thomas, ON N5R 1X9, CANADA

Morley, Malcolm (Artist)
Pace Gallery
32 E 57th St
New York, NY 10022, USA

Morley, W I (Editor)
London Free Press
369 York St
London, ON N6A 4G1, UNITED KINGDOM (UK)

Morman, Alvin (Athlete, Baseball Player)
117 Philadelphia Dr
Rockingham, NC 28379-8607, USA

Morman, Russ (Athlete, Baseball Player)
Fresno Grizzlies 1800 Tulare St Attn: Coaching Staff
Frespo, CA 93721-2505, USA

Mormon, Russ (Athlete, Baseball Player)
1200 SW Stonecreek Dr
Blue Springs, MO 64015, USA

Morneau, Justin (Athlete, Baseball Player)
1829 Forestview Ln N
Plymouth, MN 55441-4105, USA

Mornell, Sara
9300 Wilshire Blvd. #555
Beverly Hills, CA 90212

Mornhinweg, Marty (Athlete, Football Coach, Football Player)
3507 Trevi Ct
Philadelphia, PA 19145, USA

Morning After Girls, The (Music Group)
c/o Staff Member Paradigm (Monterey)
404 W Franklin St
Monterey, CA 93940, USA

Morningstar, Darren (Athlete, Basketball Player)
1515 W Ingomar Rd
Pittsburgh, PA 15237-1644, USA

Morningwood (Music Group)
Anton Brooks
Bad Moon PR
19 B All Saints Rd
London W11 1HE, UNITED KINGDOM

Moroder, Giorgio (Composer)
1880 Century Park East
#900
Los Angeles, CA 90067, USA

Morogiello, Dan (Athlete, Baseball Player)
99 Distillery Rd
Whitehouse Station, NJ 08889-3005, USA

Moronko, Jeff (Athlete, Baseball Player)
3903 Bartons Ct
Sugar Land, TX 77479-1941, USA

Moroski, Mike (Athlete, Football Player)
1214 Pine Ln
Davis, CA 95616, USA

Morozov, Aleksey (Athlete, Hockey Player)
c/o Staff Member Pittsburgh Penguins
1001 Fifth Ave
Pittsburgh, PA 15219, USA

Morozov, Vladimir M (Opera Singer)
Kirov Opera
Mariinsky Theater
Reatralnaya 1
Saint Petersburg, RUSSIA

Morphet, David
101 Honor Oak Rd.
London, ENGLAND SE23 3LB

Morphine
48 Laight St.
New York, NY 10013

Morrall, Earl (Athlete, Football Player)
2751 68th St SW
Naples, FL 34105, USA

Morrell, David (Writer)
c/o Staff Member Vanguard Press
387 Park Ave S
12th Floor
New York, NY 10016, USA

Morretti, Tobias (Actor)
ZBF Agentur
Ordensmeisterstr 15-16
Berling 12099, GERMANY

Morrey, Charles B Jr (Mathematician)
210 Yale Ave
Kensington, CA 94708, USA

Morrice, Norman A (Ballerina, Choreographer)
Royal Ballet
Covent Garden
Bow St
London WC2E 9DD, UNITED KINGDOM (UK)

Morricone, Ennio (Composer)
Viale delle Letteratura
#30
Rome 00144, ITALY

Morrin, Wayne (Athlete, Hockey Player)
12 Carpenter Dr
Quispamsis, NB E2E 1T4, Canada

Morris, Ashley Austin (Actor)
c/o Rob Kolker Red Letter Entertainment
437 W. 48th St
Suite D
New York, NY 10036, USA

Morris, Betty (Bowler)
2169 Donovan Dr
Lincoln, Ca 95648-2967, USA

Morris, Betty (Bowler)
225 Lemming Dr
Reno, NV 89523, USA

Morris, Byron (Bam) (Athlete, Football Player)
251 NE 4th St
Cooper, TX 75432, USA

Morris, Charles R. (Writer)
The Century Foundation
1333 H St NW
10th FL
Washington, DC 20005, USA

Morris, Chris (Athlete, Basketball Player)
3097 Milford Chase SW
Marietta, GA 30008-6883, USA

Morris, Colleen
8271 Melrose Ave. #110
Los Angeles, CA 90046

Morris, Danny (Athlete, Baseball Player)
802 E Main St
Petersburg, IN 47567-1232, USA

Morris, Derek (Athlete, Hockey Player)
Thunder Creek Management
453-230 22nd St E
Attn Brad Devine
Saskatoon, SK S7K OE9, Canada

Morris, Desmond (Doctor)
78 Danbury Rd
Oxford, ENGLAND

Morris, Desmond J (Biologist, Writer)
Jonathan Cape Ltd
20 Vauxhall Bridge Road
London SW1V 2SA, UNITED KINGDOM (UK)

Morris, Dick (Misc)
64 Twin Lakes Road
South Salem, NY 10590-1009, USA

Morris, Donnie Joe (Athlete, Football Player)
1414 NW 13th Ave
Amarillo, TX 79107, USA

Morris, Doug (Business Person)
c/o Staff Member Universal Music Group (UMG - LA)
2220 Colorado Ave
Santa Monica, CA 90404, USA

Morris, Dwaine (Athlete, Football Player)
4002 Kilkenny Dr
Baton Rouge, LA 70814, USA

Morris, Edmund (Educator, Writer)
222 Central Park S
#14A
New York, NY 10019, USA

Morris, Errol (Director)
c/o Staff Member Block-Korenbrot Public Relations
North Market Building
110 S Fairfax, Suite 310
Los Angeles, CA 90036, USA

Morris, Eugene (Athlete, Football Player)
11315 SW 243rd Ter
Homestead, FL 33032, USA

Morris, Gary (Musician)
Gary Morris Productions
PO Box 176
Chromo, CO 81128, USA

Morris, Hal (Athlete, Baseball Player)
Los Angeles Angels Of Anaheim 2000 E
Gene Autry Way
anaheim, CA 92806-6143, USA

Morris, Heather (Actor)
c/o Jennifer Merlino *Untitled*
Entertainment (LA)
350 S. Beverly Dr #200
Beverly Hills, CA 90212, USA

Morris, Isaiah (Athlete, Basketball Player)
4308 W Cermak Rd
Chicago, IL 60623-2901, USA

Morris, Jack (Athlete, Baseball Player)
Minnesota Twins 1 Twins Way Attn
Broadcast Dept
Minneapolis, MN 55403-1418, USA

Morris, James P (Opera Singer)
Colbert Artists
111 W 57th St
New York, NY 10019, USA

Morris, Jan (Writer)
Trefan Morys
Llanystumdwy
Criccieth, Gwymedd, WALES

Morris, Jason (Athlete, Olympic Athlete)
575 Swaggertown Rd
Schenectady, NY 12302-9628, USA

Morris, Jenny (Musician)
Artist & Event Mgmt
PO Box 537
Randwick, NSW 2031, AUSTRALIA

Morris, Jim (Athlete, Baseball Player)
2216 Rock Creek Dr
Kerrville, TX 78028-6502, USA

Morris, John (Athlete, Baseball Player)
5538 E Paradise Ln
Scottsdale, AZ 85254-1165, USA

Morris, John (Athlete, Baseball Player)
2645 Elm Dr
North Bellmore, NY 11710-1303, USA

Morris, Johnny (Athlete, Football Player)
753 Shoreline Rd
Lake Barrington, IL 60010, USA

Morris, Jon (Athlete, Football Player)
16 Gail St.
Chelmsford, MA 01824, USA

Morris, Jon (Athlete, Hockey Player)
16 Gail St
Chelmsford, MA 01824-3510, USA

Morris, Julian (Actor)
c/o Jai Khanna *Brillstein Entertainment*
Partners
9150 Wilshire Blvd #350
Beverly Hills, CA 90212, USA

Morris, Kathryn (Actor)
c/o David (Dave) Fleming *Mosaic Media*
Group
9200 W. Sunset Blvd
10th Floor
Los Angeles, CA 90069, USA

Morris, Keith (Musician)
International Creative Mgmt
8942 Wilshire Blvd
#219
Beverly Hills, CA 90211, USA

Morris, Lamorne (Actor)
c/o Staff Member *11-16 Entertainment*
11048 La Maida
Suite 9
North Hollywood, CA 91601, USA

Morris, Larry (Artist)
105 N Union St
#4
Alexandria, VA 22314, USA

Morris, Marianne (Athlete, Golfer)
4013 Lisa Ln
Middletown, OH 45042-2832, USA

Morris, Mark W (Choreographer)
Mark Morris Dance Group
3 Lafayette Ave
#504
Brooklyn, NY 11217, USA

Morris, Matt (Musician)
c/o Staff Member *WME (LA)*
9601 Wilshire Blvd Fl 3
Beverly Hills, CA 90210, USA

Morris, Matt (Athlete, Baseball Player)
397 Old Jupiter Beach Rd
Jupiter, FL 33477-5034, USA

Morris, Mitch (Actor)
c/o Benjamin Tappan *Tappan*
Entertainment
8324 Fountain Ave
Suite C
Los Angeles, CA 90069, USA

Morris, Nathan (Musician)
c/o Staff Member *Southpaw Entertainment*
1710 N Fuller Ave
Apt 323
Los Angeles, CA 90046-3064, USA

Morris, Oswald (Ossie)
(Cinematographer)
Holbrook Church St
Fontmell Magna
Shaftesbury SP7 0NY, UNITED
KINGDOM (UK)

Morris, Phil (Actor)
704 Strand
Manhattan Beach, CA 90266, USA

Morris, Phil (Race Car Driver)
Blue RidgeMotorsports
32 Eastside Hwy
VA 22980, USA

Morris, Reginald H (Cinematographer)
255 Bambaugh Circle #308
Scarborough, ON M1W 3T6, CANADA

Morris, Robert (Artist)
Hunter College
Art Dept
New York, NY 10021, USA

Morris, Ron (Athlete, Olympic Athlete,
Track Athlete)
330 S Reese Place
Burbank, CA 91506-2724, USA

Morris, Sarah Ann (Actor)
c/o Staff Member *TalentWorks (LA)*
3500 W Olive Ave
Suite 1400
Burbank, CA 91505, USA

Morris, Sarah Jane (Actor)
c/o Melissa Stone *42West (LA)*
11400 W Olympic Blvd
Suite 1100
Los Angeles, CA 90064, USA

Morris, Seth Irvin (Architect)
2 Waverly Court
Houston, TX 77005, USA

Morris, Shellee
RR #2 Box 138
Lake City, AR 72437

Morris, Wanya (Musician)
c/o Staff Member *Creative Artists Agency*
(CAA-LA)
2000 Ave Of The Stars
Los Angeles, CA 90067, USA

Morris, Warren (Athlete, Baseball Player,
Olympic Athlete)
1215 Wilshire Dr
Alexandria, LA 71303-3141, USA

Morris, Wayna (Musician)
c/o Staff Member *Southpaw Entertainment*
1710 N Fuller Ave
Apt 323
Los Angeles, CA 90046-3064, USA

Morris, Wayne (Athlete, Football Player)
5715 Old Ox Rd
Dallas, TX 75241, USA

Morris, Wingerter Pam (Swimmer)
PO Box 14381
New Bern, NC 28561, USA

Morrison, Adam (Athlete, Basketball
Player)
c/o Team Member *Los Angeles (LA)*
Lakers
555 N Nash St
El Segundo, CA 90245, USA

Morrison, Allan E (Athlete, Football
Player)
2303 Reading Hills Ave
Henderson, NV 89052-5836, USA

Morrison, Amy (Actor)
c/o Linda Bridges *Talent Banque*
661 Dominion Rd Balmoral
Auckland 1334, New Zealand

Morrison, Christopher (Mink) (Director)
c/o Staff Member *ICM Partners (ICM-LA)*
10250 Constellation Blvd Fl 7
Los Angeles, CA 90067, USA

Morrison, Dan (Athlete, Baseball Player)
7069 Key Haven Rd
Apt 401
Seminole, FL 33776-2430, USA

Morrison, Dan (Athlete, Baseball Player)
7069 Key Haven Road
Apt 401
Seminole, FL 33777-3856, USA

Morrison, Darryl (Athlete, Football Player)
703 Brigadier Ct SE
Leesburg, VA 20175, USA

Morrison, Don (Athlete, Football Player)
P.O. Box 432
Wolfe City, TX 75496, USA

Morrison, Doug (Athlete, Hockey Player)
2112 Shannon Woods Way
Westbank, BC V4T 2R5, Canada

Morrison, Dwight (Athlete, Basketball
Player)
6112 E Singletree St
Apache Junction, AZ 85119-9548, USA

Morrison, Felton (Baseball Player)
Philadelphia Stars
3860 N Bouvier St
Philadelphia, PA 19140-3528, USA

Morrison, Fred (Athlete, Football Player)
38189 Greywalls Dr
Murrieta, CA 92562, USA

Morrison, George

Morrison, Ian (Scotty) (Misc)
Kennisis Lake
RR 1 PO Box 314
Haliburton, ON K0M 1S0, CANADA

Morrison, James (Actor)
c/o Mitch Clem *Shadow Entertainment*
10 Universal City Plz
20th Floor
Universal City, CA 91608, USA

Morrison, Jennifer (Actor)
c/o John Carrabino *John Carrabino*
Management
5900 Wilshire Blvd Fl 4 #406
Los Angeles, CA 90036, USA

Morrison, Jim (Athlete, Baseball Player)
Philadelphia Phillies
Charlotte Stone Crabs 2300 El Jobean Rd
Bldg A
Charlotte, FL 33948-1108, USA

Morrison, Jim (Athlete, Hockey Player)
1 Potts Lane
Port Hope, ON L1A OA4, Canada

Morrison, Kevin (Athlete, Hockey Player)
671 George St
Sydney, NS B1P 1L2, Canada

Morrison, Kirk (Athlete, Football Player)
c/o Staff Member *EAG Sports*
Management
12910 Agustin Pl
Playa Vista, CA 90094, USA

Morrison, Lew (Athlete, Hockey Player)
406 Souris St.
Hartney, MB R0M 0Z0, CANADA

Morrison, Mark (Musician)
Atlantic Records
1290 Ave of Americas
New York 10104, USA

Morrison, Matthew (Actor)
c/o Evelyn Karamanos *WKT Public*
Relations (WKT-LA)
9350 Wilshire Blvd
Suite 450
Beverly Hills, CA 90212, USA

Morrison, Mike (Athlete, Basketball
Player)
113 Rivana Ln
Greenville, SC 29607-5488, USA

Morrison, Patricia (Musician)
400 S Hauser Blvd #9L
Los Angeles, CA 90036, USA

Morrison, Robert S (Bob) (Business
Person)
Quaker Oats Co
Quaker Tower
PO Box 049001
Chicago, IL 60604, USA

Morrison, Scotty (Athlete, Hockey Player)
1017 Land Rd RR 1
Haliburton, ON K0M 1S0, Canada

Morrison, Shelley (Actor)
1209 South Alfred St.
Los Angeles, CA 90028, USA

Morrison, Stacy (Editor)
c/o Staff Member *Redbook Magazine*
300 W 57th St
New York, NY 10019-3796, USA

Morrison, Temuera (Actor)
c/o Staff Member *Abrams Artists Agency (LA)*
9200 Sunset Blvd
11th Floor
Los Angeles, CA 90069, USA

Morrison, Temuera (Actor)
c/o Joseph (Joe) Rice *Abrams Artists Agency (LA)*
9200 Sunset Blvd
11th Floor
Los Angeles, CA 90069, USA

Morrison, Toni (Writer)
185 Nassau St
Princeton, NJ 08544-2003, USA

Morrison, Toni (Nobel Prize Laureate, Writer)
c/o Staff Member *ICM Partners (ICM-LA)*
10250 Constellation Blvd Fl 7
Los Angeles, CA 90067, USA

Morrison, Van (Musician, Songwriter)
c/o Jim Flammia *Lost Highway Records*
54 Music Square East
Suite 300
Nashville, TN 37203, USA

Morrison-Gamberdella, Ester (Baseball Player)
3179 Pleasant Creek Rd
Rogue River, OR 97537-9803, USA

Morrison-Gamberdella, Esther (Athlete, Baseball Player)
3179 Pleasant Creek Rd
Rogue River, OR 97537-9803, USA

Morriss, Guy (Athlete, Football Player)
2013 Creekview Dr
Commerce, TX 75428-3946, USA

Morrissette, Billy (Actor, Director, Writer)
c/o Brian Inerfeld *Protocol Entertainment (LA)*
8899 Beverly Blvd #600
Los Angeles, CA 90048, USA

Morrissey, David (Actor)
c/o Laura Symons *Premier PR (UK)*
91 Berwick St
London W1F 0NE, UK

Morrissey, Jim (Athlete, Football Player)
48 Fox Trl
Lincolnshire, IL 60069, USA

Morrissey, Neil (Actor)
c/o Staff Member *ICM Partners (ICM-LA)*
10250 Constellation Blvd Fl 7
Los Angeles, CA 90067, USA

Morrissey, Steven Patrick (Actor, Composer, Music Group, Songwriter, Writer)
c/o Todd Jacobs *WME (LA)*
9601 Wilshire Blvd Fl 3
Beverly Hills, CA 90210, USA

Morrone, Joe (Coach, Football Coach)
University of Connecticut
Athletic Dept
Storrs Mansfield, CT 06269, USA

Morrow, Bobby (Athlete, Olympic Athlete, Track Athlete)
2022 Elmwood Dr
Harlingen, TX 78550-8078, USA

Morrow, Bobby Joe (Athlete, Track Athlete)
PO Box 9
Beeville, TX 78104, USA

Morrow, Brandon (Athlete, Baseball Player)
3638 N 51st Dr
Phoenix, AZ 85033-4604, USA

Morrow, Brenden (Athlete, Hockey Player)
3528 Centenary Ave
Dallas, TX 75225-5013, USA

Morrow, Bruce (Cousin Brucie) (Radio Personality)
c/o Staff Member *Sirius Satellite Radio*
1221 Avenue of the Americas
New York, NY 10020, USA

Morrow, Harold (Athlete, Football Player)
3390 US Highway 82
Maplesville, AL 36750, USA

Morrow, Jo (Actor)
17000 Ramsey Rd
White City, OR 97503, USA

Morrow, Joshua (Actor)
c/o Marv Dauer *Marv Dauer Management*
11661 San Vicente Blvd
Suite 104
Los Angeles, CA 90049, USA

Morrow, Ken (Athlete, Hockey Player)
New York Islanders 1255 Hempstead Tpke
Attn Dir Pro Scouting
Uniondale, NY 11553-1200, USA

Morrow, Ken (Athlete, Hockey Player, Olympic Athlete)
6732 r-bnticello Dr.
Kansas City, MO 64152, USA

Morrow, Mari (Actor)
c/o David Ziff *Cunningham Escott Slevin & Doherty (CESD-LA)*
10635 Santa Monica Blvd
130
Los Angeles, CA 90025, USA

Morrow, Rob (Actor)
c/o Judy Hofflund *Hofflund/Polone*
9465 Wilshire Blvd #420
Beverly Hills, CA 90212, USA

Morse, Cathy (Athlete, Golfer)
6228 Celadon Cir
West Palm Beach, FL 33418, USA

Morse, Cheryl (Stylist)
c/o Staff Member *Team*
423 W Broadway
4th Floor
Boston, MA 02127, USA

Morse, David (Actor)
Yvette Bikoff
1040 1st Ave
#1126
New York, NY 10022, USA

Morse, David (Musician)
Agency for Performing Arts
9200 Sunset Blvd
#900
Los Angeles, CA 90069, USA

Morse, David E (Publisher)
Christian Science Monitor
Publisher's Office
1 Norway St
Boston, MA 02115, USA

Morse, Helen (Actor)
147 King St #A
Sydney, NSW 2000, AUSTRALIA

Morse, John (Athlete, Golfer)
9291 17 Mile Rd
Marshall, MI 49068-9755, USA

Morse, Mike (Athlete, Baseball Player)
417 NW 97th Ave
Plantation, FL 33324-7075, USA

Morse, Natalie (Actor)
William Morris Agency
52/53 Poland Place
London W1F 7LX, UNITED KINGDOM (UK)

Morse, Philip M (Physicist)
126 Wildwood St
Winchester, MA 01890, USA

Morse, Ray
989 NW Spruce Ave. #207
Corvallis, OR 97330

Morse, Robert (Actor)
13830 Davana Terrace
Sherman Oaks, CA 91423, USA

Morse, Steve (Athlete, Football Player)
32743 Weybridge St
Fulshear, TX 77441, USA

Mortensen, Chris (Sportscaster)
ESPN-TV
Sports Dept ESPN Plaza
935 Middle St
Bristol, CT 06010, USA

Mortensen, Clayton (Athlete, Baseball Player)
1340 Fairview Ave
Rexburg, ID 83440-5078, USA

Mortensen, Dale T (Nobel Prize Laureate)
1420 Sheridan Rd Apt 7G
Wilmette, IL 60091-1870, USA

Mortensen, J D (Doctor)
Cardipulmonics Inc
5060 W Amelia Earhart Dr
Salt Lake City, UT 84116, USA

Mortensen, Viggo (Actor)
c/o Lynn Rawlins *Rawlins Company*
Prefers to be contacted via telephone or email
CA 91301, USA

Mortier, Gerard (Opera Singer)
Saizburg Festpiele
Hofstallgasse 1
Saizburg 5020, AUSTRIA

Mortimer, Barrett Angela (Tennis Player)
Oaks
Coombe Hill
Kingston-on-Thames, Surrey, UNITED KINGDOM (UK)

Mortimer, Emily (Actor)
c/o Aleen Keshishian *Brillstein Entertainment Partners*
9150 Wilshire Blvd #350
Beverly Hills, CA 90212, USA

Mortimer, John (Stylist)
c/o Staff Member *Seaminx Artist Management*
2806 Greenville Ave
#B
Dallas, TX 75206, USA

Mortimer, Kenneth P (Educator)
University of Hawaii Manoa
President's Office
Honolulu, HI 96822, USA

Mortimer, Tinsley (Reality TV Star)
c/o Jan Planit *Planit Management*
11 East 26th St
New York, NY 10010, USA

Mortita, Pat (Noriyuki) (Actor)
6399 Wilshire Blvd
#444
Los Angeles, CA 90048, USA

Mortola, Alessandra (Stylist)
c/o Staff Member *Artist Untied (LA)*
845 S Mansfield Ave
#1
Los Angeles, CA 90036, USA

Morton, Alicia (Actor)
c/o Staff Member *WmE2 (WMA-LA)*
1 William Morris Pl
Beverly Hills, CA 90212, USA

Morton, Bruce A (Correspondent)
Cable News Network
News Dept
820 1st St NE
Washington, DC 20002, USA

Morton, Charie (Athlete, Baseball Player)
5122 Sea Forest Dr
Johns Island, SC 29455-^450, USA

Morton, Craig (Athlete, Football Player)
9850 N 73rd St
Unit 2037
Scottsdale, AZ 85258, USA

Morton, Guy (Athlete, Baseball Player)
567 Femdale Ave
Vermilion, OH 44089-2437, USA

Morton, Joe (Actor)
Judy Schoen
605 N Larchont Blvd
#309
Los Angeles, CA 90004, USA

Morton, John (Athlete, Football Player)
39991 Purmice Dr
Cassel, CA 96016, USA

Morton, Johnnie (Athlete, Football Player)
2911 Oakwood Ln
Torrance, CA 90505, USA

Morton, Kevin (Athlete, Baseball Player)
12 Glen Pines Ln
Norwalk, CT 06850-1800, USA

Morton, Kristopher (Colt) (Athlete, Baseball Player)
3245 Santa Barbara Dr
Wellington, FL 33414-7267, USA

Morton, Richard (Athlete, Basketball Player)
1111 Gilman Ave
San Francisco, CA 94124-3622, USA

Morton, Samantha (Actor)
c/o Troy Nankin *Wishlab*
2225-A Hyperion Ave
Los Angeles, CA 90027, USA

Mortson, Cleland (Athlete, Hockey Player)

Mortson, Gus (Athlete, Hockey Player)
Central Gas Ontario PO Box 2005
Stn Main Timmins, ON P4N 7X4, CANADA

Morukov, Boris V (Cosmonaut)
Potcha Kosmonavtov
Moskovskoi Oblasti
Syvisdny Goroduk 141160, RUSSIA

Mosca, Angelo (Athlete, Football Player)
PO Box 144
Niagara on the Lake, ON LOS 1JO,
Canada

Moschen, Michael (Artist)
PO Box 178
Cornwall Bridge, CT 06754, USA

Moschitta Jr, John
11601 Dunston Way #206
Los Angeles, CA 90049, USA

Moschitto, Ross (Athlete, Baseball Player)
1200 Warburton Ave Apt 47
Yonkers, NY 10701-1062, USA

Moscoso, Guillermo (Athlete, Baseball Player)
3667 Victoria Manor Dr Apt 103
Lakeland, FL 33805-2989, USA

Moscow, David (Actor)
c/o Robert Stein *Robert Stein Management*
PO Box 3797
Beverly Hills, CA 90212, USA

Mosebar, Donald H (Don) (Athlete, Football Player)
1713 Walnut Ave
Manhattan Beach, CA 90266, USA

Moseby, Lloyd (Athlete, Baseball Player)
9140 Los Lagos Cir S
Granite Bay, CA 95746-5842, USA

Mosel, Tad (Writer)
149 E Side Dr Apt 26-B
Concord, NH 03301-5410, USA

Moseley, Bill (Actor)
c/o Peter Young *Sovereign Talent Group*
8421 Wilshire Blvd
Suite 200
Beverly Hills, CA 90211, USA

Moseley, Dustin (Athlete, Baseball Player)
6013 Timberwood Ln
Texarkana, AR 71854-8170, USA

Moseley, John (Athlete, Football Player)
408 Manor Dr
Columbia, MO 65203-1734, USA

Moseley, Jonny (Athlete, Olympic Athlete, Skier)
167 Trinidad Dr
Belvedere Tiburon, CA 94920-1037, USA

Moseley, Mark (Athlete, Football Player)
7250 Middle Rd
Middletown, VA 22645, USA

Moseley, Roy
152 Ivor Ct Gloucester Pl.
London, ENGLAND NW1

Moseley, T Michael (Buzz) (General)
Vice Cheif of Staff
HqUSAF Pentagon
Washington, DC 20330, USA

Moseley, William (Actor)
c/o David Guillod *Intellectual Artists Management*
10585 Santa Monica Blvd
Suite 135
Los Angeles, CA 90025, USA

Moselle, Dominic (Athlete, Football Player)
2019 Hammond Ave
Superior, WI 54880, USA

Moser, Barry (Misc)
115 Pantry Rd
North Hatfield, MA 01066, USA

Moser, Casey (Athlete, Baseball Player)
9013 Fm 368 N
Iowa Park, TX 85053-4908, USA

Moser, Donald B (Don) (Editor)
Smithsonian Magazine
Editorial Dept
900 Jefferson SW
Washington, DC 20560, USA

Moser, Rick (Athlete, Football Player)
1616 Esplanada Ave
Apt 10
Redondo Beach, CA 90277, USA

Moser, Thomas (Opera Singer)
Lies Askonas
6 Henrietta St
London WC2E 8LA, UNITED KINGDOM (UK)

Moser-Proll, Annemarie (Skier)
Moser Cafe-Bar
#92
Kleinari 115 5602, AUSTRIA

Moses, Albert
15 Overstone Rd
Harpenden Herts., ENGLAND AL5 5PN

Moses, Billy E
409 N Camden Dr #202
Beverly Hills, CA 90210, USA

Moses, Ed (Athlete)
c/o Staff Member *Premier Management Group (PMG Sports)*
115 Crescent Commons Dr Ste 250
Cary, NC 27518, USA

Moses, Edwin (Athlete, Olympic Athlete, Track Athlete)
1184 Daventry Way NE
Atlanta, GA 30319-4547, USA

Moses, Haven C (Athlete, Football Player)
1140 Cherokee St
Unit 640
Denver, CO 80204, USA

Moses, Jerry (Athlete, Baseball Player)
9 Court Ln
IPswich, MA 01938-3027, USA

Moses, John (Athlete, Baseball Player)
Corpus Christi Hooks 734 E Port Ave
Attn: Coaching Staff
corpus Christi, TX 78401-1006, USA

Moses, Kim (Producer)
c/o Staff Member *WmE2 (WMA-LA)*
1 William Morris Pl
Beverly Hills, CA 90212, USA

Moses, Lincoln E (Mathematician)
Stanford University
Medical Center
Statistics Dept
Stanford, CA 94305, USA

Moses, Mark (Actor)
c/o Suzanne (Sue) Wohl *TalentWorks (LA)*
3500 W Olive Ave
Suite 1400
Burbank, CA 91505, USA

Moses, Michael (Scientist)
817 Mystic Dr Apt 306
Cape Canaveral, FL 32920-5320, USA

Moses, Rick (Actor, Musician)
Calder Agency
19919 Redwing St
Woodland Hills, CA 91364, USA

Moses, Robert (Bob) (Activist, Educator)
99 Bishop Allen Dr
Cambridge, MA 02139, USA

Moses, William R. (Actor, Producer)
c/o Richard Caplan *Noble Caplan Abrams*
1260 Yonge St
2nd Floor
Toronto, ON M4T 1W6, Canada

Moses, Yolanda T (Educator)
City College of New York
President's Office
New York, NY 10031, USA

Mosher, Gregory D (Director, Producer)
c/o Patrick Herold *Helen Merrill Ltd*
295 Lafayette St #915
New York, NY 10012-2700, USA

Moshinsky, Elijah (Opera Singer)
28 Kidbrooke Groove
London SE3 0LG, UNITED KINGDOM (UK)

Mosimann, Anton (Chef)
Mosimann's
11B W Halkin St
London SW1X 8JL, UNITED KINGDOM (UK)

Mosisilli, Pakalitha (Prime Minister)
Chairman's Office
Military Council
PO Box 527
Maseru 100, LESOTHO

Moskau, Paul (Athlete, Baseball Player)
5041 N Apache Hills Trl
Tucson, AZ 85750-5912, USA

Mosko, Lisa (Stylist)
c/o Staff Member *De Facto*
41 Union Square West
#1001
New York, NY 10003, USA

Moskow, Michael (Financier, Government Official)
Federal Reserve Bank
230 S LaSalle St
Chicago, IL 60604, USA

Moskowitz, Robert (Artist)
81 Leonard St
New York, NY 10013, USA

Mosler, John (Athlete, Football Player)
12604 Cambridge Rd
Leawood, KS 66209, USA

Mosley, Brian (Actor)
After Dinner
Saga Court
S Heath G Missenden
Bucks HP16 9QQ, UNITED KINGDOM (UK)

Mosley, J Brooke (Religious Leader)
1604 Foulkeways
Gwynedd, PA 19436, USA

Mosley, Max R (Race Car Driver)
Int'l Automobile Fed
2 Chermin Blandonnet
Geneva 1215, SWITZERLAND

Mosley, Michael (Actor)
c/o Laurie Smith *Smith Talent Group*
14 Minetta St.
1st Floor
New York, NY 10012, USA

Mosley, Mike (Athlete, Football Player)
109 Heritage Hill Rd
Wimberley, TX 78676, USA

Mosley, Norm (Athlete, Football Player)
1056 53rd St S
Birmingham, AL 35222, USA

Mosley, Roger E (Actor)
4470 Sunset Blvd
#107-342
Los Angeles, CA 90027, USA

Mosley, Sugar Shane (Boxer)
c/o Larry O. Williams Jr. *Williams Talent Agency*
1438 N. Gower St.
Bldg. 35, Ste. 266, Box 43
Hollywood, CA 90028, USA

Mosley, Timothy (Timbaland) (Musician, Producer)
c/o David Zedeck *Creative Artists Agency (CAA-NY)*
162 Fifth Ave
6th Floor
New York, NY 10010, USA

Mosley, Walter (Writer)
c/o Bruce Miller *Washington Square Arts (NY)*
310 Bowery
2nd Floor
New York, NY 10012, USA

Mosoke, Kintu (Prime Minister)
Prime Minister's Office
PO Box 341
Kampala, UGANDA

Mosquera, Julio (Athlete, Baseball Player)
1419 Stone Creek Dr
Tarpon Springs, FL 34689-3045, USA

Moss, Carrie-Anne (Actor)
c/o Staff Member *WmE2 (WMA-LA)*
1 William Morris Pl
Beverly Hills, CA 90212, USA

Moss, Cynthia (Misc)
African Wildlife Foundation
Mara Road
PO Box 48177
Nairobi, KENYA

Moss, Damian (Athlete, Baseball Player)
1877 Ga Highway 19 S
Dublin, GA 31021-1480, USA

Moss, Eddie (Athlete, Football Player)
15404 Eagle Estates Ct
Florissant, MO 63034, USA

Moss, Elisabeth (Actor)
c/o Gay Ribisi *Ribisi Entertainment*
3278 Wilshire Blvd
Suite 702
Los Angeles, CA 90010, USA

Moss, Elza (Religious Leader)
Primitive Advent Christian Church
273 Frame Road
Elkview, WV 25071, USA

Moss, Eric Owen (Architect)
8557 Higuera St
Culver City, CA 90232, USA

Moss, Geoffrey (Cartoonist)
315 E 68th St
New York, NY 10021, USA

Moss, Jon
64 Knighton Park Rd
London, ENGLAND SE26 5RL

Moss, Kate (Model)
3 The Grove Highgate
London N6 6JU, UNITED KINGDOM

Moss, Lance (Race Car Driver)
Moss Motorsports
100 West First St.
Dallas, NC 29021, USA

Moss, Les (Athlete, Baseball Player, Coach)
420 Tullis Ave
Longwood, FL 32750, USA

Moss, Paige (Actor)
c/o Staff Member *Marshak/Zachary Company, The*
8840 Wilshire Blvd
1st Floor
Beverly Hills, CA 90210, USA

Moss, P Buckley (Artist)
1 Poplar Grove Ln
Mathews, VA 23109, USA

Moss, Perry (Athlete, Football Player, Golfer)
5660 S Lakeshore Dr
Apt 505
Shreveport, LA 71119, USA

Moss, Perry (Athlete, Basketball Player)
165 Columbia Dr
Amherst, MA 01002-3107, USA

Moss, Randy (Athlete, Football Player)
c/o Greg Barnett *Lagardere Unlimited - Miami*
927 Lincoln Rd
Suite 200
Miami, FL 33139, USA

Moss, Roland (Athlete, Football Player)
411 Camelot Dr
Salisbury, NC 28144, USA

Moss, Ronn (Actor)
2401 Nottingham Ave
Los Angeles, CA 90027, USA

Moss, Santana (Athlete, Football Player)
18619 SW 50th Ct
Miramar, FL 33029, USA

Moss, Shirley (Artist)
Moss Studios
PO Box 18104
Anaheim, CA 92817, USA

Moss, Sterling (Race Car Driver)
46 Shepherd St.
Mayfair
London W1Y 8JN, UNITED KINGDOM

Moss, Stirling (Race Car Driver)
Stirling Moss Ltd
46 Shephard St
London W1Y 8JN, UNITED KINGDOM
(UK)

Moss, Tegan (Actor)
c/o Tyman Stewart *Characters Talent Agency, The (Vancouver)*
8 Elm St
2nd Floor
Toronto, ON M5G 1G7, Canada

Moss, Zefross (Athlete, Football Player)
126 Kinsington Dr
Madison, AL 35758, USA

Mosser, Jonell (Musician)
Phil Mayo Co
PO Box 304
Bomoseen, VT 05732, USA

Mossi, Don (Athlete, Baseball Player)
23250 Canyon Ln
Caldwell, ID 83607-7709, USA

Mossman, Doug
999 Kalapaki St.
Honolulu, HI 96825

Most, Don (Actor)
6643 Buttonwood Ave
Agoura, CA 91301, USA

Mostardo, Rich (Athlete, Football Player)
3376 Summit Rd
Ravenna, OH 44266, USA

Mosteller, Frederick (Mathematician)
Harvard University
Statistics Dept
Cambridge, MA 02138, USA

Mostert, Dutch (Artist)
93696 Mallard Lane
North Bend, OR 97459, USA

Mostow, George D (Mathematician)
25 Beechwood Road
Woodbridge, CT 06525, USA

Mostow, Jonathan (Director)
Creative Artists Agency
9830 Wilshire Blvd
Beverly Hills, CA 90212, USA

Mostowicz, Jeanette (Stylist)
41 Koclas Dr
Netcong, NJ 07857, USA

Mota, Andres (Athlete, Baseball Player)
P.O. Box 2820
Toluca Lake, CA 91610-0820, USA

Mota, Andy (Athlete, Baseball Player)
9068 NW 50th Ct
Coral Springs, FL 33067-1933, USA

Mota, Guillermo (Athlete, Baseball Player)
c/o Staff Member *Los Angeles Dodgers (LA Dodgers)*
1000 Elysian Park Ave
Los Angeles, CA 90012, USA

Mota, Jose (Athlete, Baseball Player)
19058 E La Crosse St
Glendora, CA 91741-1918, USA

Mota, Manny (Athlete, Baseball Player)
Los Angeles Dodgers 1000 Elysian Park Ave Attn Coaching Staff
LOs Angeles, CA QOOQ0-111 7, USA

Mota, Ross (Athlete, Track Athlete)
R Teatro 194 4 Esq
Porto 4100, PORTUGAL

Mote, Bobby (Rodeo Rider)
6510 SW King Ln
Culver, OR 97734, USA

Mote, Kelley (Athlete, Football Player)
41121 Ocean View Dr
Avon, NC 27915, USA

Moten, Mike (Athlete, Football Player)
706 Loomis Ave
Daytona Beach, FL 32114, USA

Mother Mother (Music Group)
c/o Staff Member *Paradigm (Monterey)*
404 W Franklin St
Monterey, CA 93940, USA

Mothersbaugh, Mark (Composer, Musician)
c/o Staff Member *Greenspan Artist Management*
8760 W Sunset Blvd
West Hollywood, CA 90069, USA

Motion, Andrew (Writer)
University of East Anglia
English Dept
Norwich NR4 7TJ, UNITED KINGDOM
(UK)

Motion City Soundtrack (Music Group)
Asquared Management
2336 W Belmont
Chicago, IL 60618, USA

Motley, Darryl (Athlete, Baseball Player)
10800 W 65th St
Shawnee, Ks 66203-3810, USA

Motley Crue (Music Group)
c/o Staff Member *10th Street Entertainment (NY)*
38 W 21st St
Suite 300
New York, NY 10010, USA

Motooka, Jackie (Stylist)
1516 W Edgewater Ave
Chicago, IL 60660, USA

Motorhead (Music Group)
98 Puddleton Cres Poole
Dorset, ENGLAND, United Kingdom

Mott, Darwin (Athlete, Hockey Player)
3078 Cranbourn Cres
Regina, SK S4V 3B3, Canada

Mott, John C (Athlete, Football Player)
215 Thistledown Ln
Hamilton, MT 59840, USA

Mott, Morris (Athlete, Hockey Player)
9 Elmdale Blvd
Brandon, MB R7B 1B5, Canada

Mott, Steve (Athlete, Football Player)
7018 N Highfield Dr
Birmingham, AL 35242, USA

Mott, Stewart R (Politician)
515 Madison Ave
New York, NY 10022, USA

Motta, Dick (Basketball Coach, Coach)
423 Highway 89
Fish Haven, ID 83287-5109, USA

Mottau, CHristine (Stylist)
c/o Staff Member *Judy Casey Inc*
114 E 13th St
New York, NY 10003, USA

Mottau, Mike (Athlete, Hockey Player)
154 Cove Neck Rd
Oyster Bay, NY 11771-1826, USA

Mottelson, Ben (Nobel Prize Laureate)
Nordita
Roslagstullsbacken 23
Stockholm, Denmark 106 91, SWEDEN

Mottola, Chad (Athlete, Baseball Player)
6479 Lake Pembroke Pl
Orlando, FL 32829-7620, USA

Mottola, Greg (Director, Writer)
c/o Staff Member *United Talent Agency (UTA)*
9336 Civic Center Dr
Beverly Hills, CA 90210, USA

Mottola, Thomas (Tommy) (Business Person)
c/o Staff Member *Mottola Company, The*
745 5th Ave #800
New York, NY 10151, USA

Motton, Curt (Athlete, Baseball Player)
19903 Quiet Valley Ct
Parkton, MD 21120, USA

Motulsky, Amo G (Scientist)
4347 53rd St NE
Seattle, WA 98105, USA

Motz, Diana Gribbon (Judge)
US Appeals Court
101 W Lombard St
Baltimore, MD 21201, USA

Mouawad, Jerry (Director)
Imago Theater
17 SE 8th Ave
Portland, OR 97214, USA

Mouchawar, Alan (Athlete, Olympic Athlete, Water Polo Player)
1943 Port Trinity Pl
Newport Beach, CA 92660-7127, USA

Mould, Bob (Musician, Songwriter, Writer)
c/o Staff Member *High Road Touring*
751 Bridgeway
3rd Floor
Sausalito, CA 94965, USA

Moulder-Brown, John
193 Wardour St.
London, ENGLAND W1V 3FA

Mouli (Actor, Bollywood)
12 Srinivasa Ave
Chennai, TN 600028, INDIA

Moulton, Sara (Chef, Television Host)
c/o Staff Member *Grand Productions*
2811 Champion Rd
Naperville, IL 60654, USA

Mounce, Tony (Athlete, Baseball Player)
3901 W 46th Ave
Kennewick, WA 99337-2781, USA

Mounsey, Tara (Athlete, Hockey Player, Olympic Athlete)
22 Forge Pond Unit B
Canton, MA x MA 02021-2990, USA

Mount, Anson (Actor)
William Morris Agency
1325 Ave of Americas
New York, NY 10019, USA

Mount, Rick (Athlete, Basketball Player)
904 Hopkins Rd
Lebanon, IN 46052-1436, USA

Mount, Thomas H (Tom) (Producer)
c/o Staff Member *Mount Film Company*
9245 Cordell Dr
Los Angeles, CA 90069, USA

Mountcastle, Vernon (Scientist)
6605 Walnutwood Cir
Baltimore, MD 21212-1214, USA

Mountcastle Jr, Vernon B (Misc)
6605 Walnutwood Circle
Baltimore, MD 21212-1214, USA

Mourning, Alonzo (Athlete, Basketball Player, Olympic Athlete)
33 Arvida Pkwy
Coral Gables, FL 33156-2310, USA

Mouse, Mickey Club
PO Box 10200
Lake Buena Vista, FL 32830-0200

Mouskouri, Nana J (Musician, Songwriter)
12 Rue Gitenberg
Boulogne 92000, FRANCE

Moussier, Sabine (Actor)
c/o Staff Member *Televisa*
Blvd Adolfo Lopez Mateos 232
Colonia San Angel INN
DF CP 01060, MEXICO

Moustaki, Georges (Musician)
PolyGram Records
20 Rue des Fosses-Saint-Jacques
Paris 75005, FRANCE

Mouton, James (Athlete, Baseball Player)
4710 Lakeside Meadow Ct
Missouri City, TX 77459-1630, USA

Mouton, Leslie (Journalist)
1333 Northland Drive
Mendota Heights, MN 55120

Mouton, Lyle (Athlete, Baseball Player)
4101 Auston Way
Palm Harbor, FL 34685-4014, USA

Moverman, Oren (Director)
c/o Staff Member *WmE2 (WMA-LA)*
1 William Morris Pl
Beverly Hills, CA 90212, USA

Movessian, Victoria (Viki) (Athlete, Hockey Player)
17 Webb St
Lexington, MA 02420, USA

Movita
2766 Motor Ave.
Los Angeles, CA 90064

Movsessian, Vicki (Athlete, Hockey Player, Olympic Athlete)
17 Webb St
Lexington, MA x MA 02420-2219, USA

Mowat, Farley M (Writer)
18 King St
Port Hope, ON L1A 2R4, CANADA

Mowatt, Ezekial (Athlete, Football Player)
245 Prospect Ave
Apt 2B
Hackensack, NJ 07601, USA

Mower, Patrick (Actor)
c/o Staff Member *Burnett Granger & Assoc*
Prince of Wales Theatre
31 Coventy St
London W1D 6AS, UNITED KINGDOM (UK)

Mowers, Mark (Athlete, Hockey Player)
10 Pollock Dr
Middleton, MA 01949-1747, USA

Mowerson, Robert (Swimmer)
2601 Kenzle Terrace
#324
Minneapolis, MN 55418, USA

Mowrey, Caitlin (Actor)

Mowrey, Dude (Musician)
Joe Taylor Artist Agency
2802 Columbine Place
Nashville, TN 37204, USA

Mowry, Tahj (Actor)
c/o Jason Egenberg *United Talent Agency (UTA)*
9336 Civic Center Dr
Beverly Hills, CA 90210, USA

Mowry, Tamera (Actor, Producer)
c/o Tracy Steinsapir *Main Title Entertainment*
8383 Wilshire Blvd
Suite 408
Los Angeles, CA 90211, USA

Mowry-Hardrict, Tia (Actor)
c/o Adam Griffin *Kritzer Levine Wilkins Entertainment (KLWG)*
11872 La Grange Ave
1st Floor
Los Angeles, CA 90025, USA

Moxey, Jim (Athlete, Hockey Player)
7 Blue Heron Dr
Orangeville, ON L9W 5K6, Canada

Moxness, Barbara (Athlete, Golfer)
5512 Mirror Lakes Dr
Minneapolis, MN 55436, USA

Moyer, Jamie (Athlete, Baseball Player)
2426 32nd Ave W
Seattle, WA 98199-3202, USA

Moyer, Ken (Athlete, Football Player)
3896 Magma Ct
Mason, OH 45040, USA

Moyer, Paul (Correspondent)
12742 Highwood St
Los Angeles, CA 90049, USA

Moyer, Stephen (Actor)
c/o Lena Roklin *Luber Roklin Management*
8530 Wilshire Blvd
6th Floor
Beverly Hills, CA 90211, USA

Moyers, Bill (Journalist)
151 Central Park W Apt SN
New York, NY 10023-1577, USA

Moyers, Bill D (Correspondent)
c/o Staff Member *HarperCollins Publishers*
10 East 53rd St
c/o Author mail, 7th Floor
New York, NY 10022, USA

Moyet, Alison (Musician)
Primary Talent
2-12 Petonville Road
London N1 9PL, UNITED KINGDOM (UK)

Moylan, Peter
1889 Point River Dr
Duluth, GA 30097-7957, USA

Moyle, Allan (Director, Writer)
c/o Staff Member *Wisdom Literary*
287 S. Robertson Blvd
Suite 258
Beverly Hills, CA 90211, USA

Moynahan, Bridget (Actor, Model)
c/o Andrea Pett-Joseph *Brillstein Entertainment Partners*
9150 Wilshire Blvd #350
Beverly Hills, CA 90212, USA

Moynihan, Bobby (Actor, Comedian)
c/o Staff Member *Odenkirk Provissiero Entertainment*
Raleigh Studios
650 N. Bronson Ave, Bldg. B145
Los Angeles, CA 90004, USA

Moynihan, Christopher (Actor)
c/o Ron West *Thruline Entertainment*
9250 Wilshire Blvd
Ground Fl
Beverly Hills, CA 90212, USA

Moynihan, Colin B (Government Official)
Crown Reach
16 Grosvenor Road
London SW1V 3JV, UNITED KINGDOM (UK)

Mozeliak, John (Athlete, Baseball Player)
5 Marvhill Dr
Saint Louis, MO 63124-1368, USA

Mozo, Rebecca (Actor)
c/o Staff Member *Insight*
1134 S Cloverdale Ave
Los Angeles, CA 90019, USA

M. Palazzo, Steven (Congressman, Politician)
331 Cannon HOB
Washington, DC 20515, USA

Mphahele, Ezekiel (Writer)
5444 Zone 5
Pimville
Johannesburg, SOUTH AFRICA

Mraz, Jason (Musician, Songwriter)
c/o Bill Silva *Bill Silva Management*
8255 Santa Monica Blvd
W Hollywood, CA 90046-5912, USA

Mrazek, Jerome (Athlete, Hockey Player)
673 8th St E
Prince Albert, SK S6V OW8, Canada

Mrazovich, Chuck (Athlete, Basketball Player)
7260 W 12th Ave
Hialeah, FL 33014-4618, USA

Mrosko, Robert (Athlete, Football Player)
2874 Coleridge Rd
Cleveland, OH 44118, USA

Mroudjae, Ali (Prime Minister)
BP 58 Rond Point Gobadjou
Moroni, COMOROS

Mrozik, Rick
2234 Kelly Ave
Cloquet, MN 55720-2224, USA

Msuya, Cleopa D (Prime Minister)
Prime Minister's Office
PO Box 980
Dodoma, TANZANIA

Mswati III (King)
Royal Palace
PO Box 1
Mbabane, SWAZILAND

Mu'all, Sheikh Rashid bin Ahmed al (Politician)
Ruler's Place
Umm Al Quwain
UNITED ARAB EMIRATES

Mubarak, Muhammad Hosni (General, President)
Presidential Palace
Abdeen
Cairo, EGYPT

Muccino, Gabriele (Director)
c/o Simon Halls *Slate Public Relations*
9000 Sunset Blvd #915
West Hollywood, CA 90069, USA

Mucha, Barb (Athlete, Golfer)
5922 Crystal View Dr
Orlando, FL 32819-4207, USA

Muchlinski, Mike (Athlete, Baseball Player)
3908 243rd Pl SE
Apt Q301
Bothell, WA 98021-6918, USA

Muckalt, Bill (Athlete, Hockey Player)
3800 Portage Cv
Houghton, MI 49931-2904, USA

Muckalt, Bill
Michigan Tech University Athletics 1400 Townsend Dr
Attn: Ice Hockey Coaching Staff
Houghton, MI 49931-1295, USA

Mucke, Manuela (Athlete)
Charlottenstr 13
Berlin 10315, GERMANY

Muckensturm, Jerry (Athlete, Football Player)
4209 Hickory Ln
Jonesboro, AR 72401, USA

Muckier, John (Athlete, Hockey Player)
387 Wood Acres Dr
East Amherst, NY 14051-1660, USA

Muckler, John (Coach)
Ottawa Senators
1000 Palladium Dr
Kanata, ON K2V 1A4, CANADA

Mudcrutch (Music Group)
c/o Staff Member *Warner Bros Records (LA)*
P.O. Box 6868
Burbank, CA 91510, USA

Mudd, Howard E (Athlete, Coach, Football Player)
311 W Walnut St
Indianapolis, IN 46202, USA

Mudd, Jodie (Athlete, Golfer)
3512 Mildred Dr
Louisville, KY 40216, USA

Mudd, Roger (Journalist)
7167 Old Dominion Dr
Me Lean, VA 22101-2705, USA

Mudd, Roger
7167 Old Dominion Dr.
McLean, VA 22101

Mudd, Roger H (Correspondent)
7167 Old Dominion Dr
McLean, VA 22101, USA

Mudge, Nancy (Athlete, Baseball Player)
23019 County Road 1
Elk River, MN 55330-9437, USA

Mudra, Darrell (Coach, Football Coach)
424 Tiger Hammock Road
Crawfordville, FL 32327, USA

Mudrock, Phil (Athlete, Baseball Player)
2548 E 6600 S
Salt Lake City, UT 84121-2346, USA

Mudvayne (Music Group)
c/o Chuck Toler *Anger Management*
6907 University Ave #199
Middleton, WI 53562-2763, USA

Muelhaupt Jr, Chuck (Athlete, Football Player)
4111 Tonawanda Dr
Des Moines, IL 50312, USA

Muelier, Charles W (Business Person)
Ameren Corp
1901 Chouteau Ave
Saint Louis, MO 63103, USA

Mueller, Bill (Athlete, Baseball Player)
570 W Canyon Wav
Chandler, AZ 85248-5123, USA

Mueller, George (Scientist)
R P K 4300 Amelia Earhart Dr
Attn Chairmans Office
Oklahoma City, OK 73159-1110, USA

Mueller, George E (Engineer)
Kistler Aerospace Corp
3760 Carillon Point
Kirkland, WA 98033, USA

Mueller, Les (Athlete, Baseball Player)
P.O. Box 294
Millstadt, IL 62260-0294, USA

Mueller, Vance (Athlete, Football Player)
8141 Damico Dr
El Dorado Hills, CA 95762, USA

Mueller, Willard (Willie) (Athlete, Baseball Player)
2320 Tolbert Ln
West Bend, WI 53090-1234, USA

Mueller-Bajda, Dolores (Baseball Player)
2913 N Linder Ave
Chicago, IL 60641-4812, USA

Mueller-Stahl, Armin (Actor)
c/o ZBF
Ordensmeisterstr. 15-16
Berlin, GERMANY D-12099

Muellner, William (Athlete, Football Player)
727 Sherwood Rd
La Grange Park, IL 60526, USA

Muench, David (Photographer)
PO Box 30500
Santa Barbara, CA 93130, USA

Muetterties, Earl L (Misc)
University of California
Chemistry Dept
Berkeley, CA 94720, USA

Muetzelfeldt, Bruno (Religious Leader)
Lutheran World Federation
150 Rt de Femey
Geneva 20 1211, SWITZERLAND

Mugabe, Robert G (President)
President's Office
Munhumutapa Bldg
Samora Machel Ave
Harare, ZIMBABWE

Mugler, Thierry (Designer, Fashion Designer)
4-6 Rue Aux Ours
Paris 75003, FRANCE

Muhammad, Elijah
7351 S. Stony Island
Chicago, IL 60617

Muhammad, Muhsin (Athlete, Football Player)
c/o Staff Member Golden Peak Sports & Entertainment LLC
11352 Haswell Drive
Parker, CO 80134, USA

Muhammad, Wallace D (Religious Leader)
American Muslim Mission
7351 S Stony Island Blvd
Chicago, IL 60649, USA

Muir, Roger
10 Drewid Hill Ave.
Methuen, MA 01844

Muir DeGraad, Karen (Swimmer)
Applebosch State Hospital
Ozwatini
Natal, SOUTH AFRICA

Muirhead, Brian (Astronomer, Scientist)
Jet Propulsion Laboratory
4800 Oakgrove Dr
Pasadena, CA 91109, USA

Muirsheil of Kilmacolm, Viscount (Government Official)
Knapps
Kilmacolm
Renfrewshire, SCOTLAND

Muise, Andi (Model)

Muise, Andi (Model)
c/o Staff Member Premier Model Management
40-42 Parker St
London WC2B 5PQ, UK

Mujica, Aylin (Actor)
c/o Staff Member TV Azteca
Periferico Sur 4121
Colonia Fuentes del Pedregal
DF CP 14141, Mexico

Mukaddam, Ali (Actor)
c/o Yanick Landry Edward G Agency
19 Isabella St
Toronto ON M4Y 1M7, CANADA

Mukai, Chiaki Naito (Astronaut)
100 Cyberonics Blvd Ste 201
Houston, TX 77058-2074, USA

Mukhamedov, Irek J (Ballerina)
Royal Ballet
Covent Garden Bow St
London WC2E 9DD, UNITED KINGDOM (UK)

Mukherjee, Bharati (Writer)
130 Rivoli St
San Francisco, CA 94117, USA

Mukherjee, Hrishikesh (Bollywood, Director, Filmmaker, Producer)
123A Anupama Carter Road
Bandra
Bombay, MS 400 050, INDIA

Mukherjee, Rani (Actor, Bollywood)
B/405 Shakti Apartments
Kaylan Complex Yari Road Versova
Mumbai, MS 400061, INDIA

Mulari, Tarja (Speed Skater)
Motion Oy
Vanhan Mankkaantie 33
Espoo 02180, FINDLAND

Mularkey, Mike (Athlete, Football Coach, Football Player)
1719 Beach Ave
Atlantic Beach, FL 32233-5838, USA

Mulcahy, Anne
Xerox Corp
800 Long Ridge Road
Stamford, CT 06902, USA

Mulcahy, J Patrick (Business Person)
Raiston Purina Co
Checkerboard Square
Saint Louis, MO 63164, USA

Mulcahy, Russell (Director)
c/o Staff Member Agency for the Performing Arts (APA-LA)
405 S Beverly Dr
Suite 500
Beverly Hills, CA 90212-4425, USA

Muldaur, Maria (Musician, Songwriter, Writer)
Piedmont Talent
PO Box 680006
Charlotte, NC 28216, USA

Mulder, Karen (Model)
c/o Staff Member Elite Model Management (NY)
404 Park Ave S Fl 9
New York, NY 10016, USA

Mulder, Mark (Athlete, Baseball Player)
10295 E Cholla St
Scottsdale, AZ 85260-6038, USA

Muldoon, Leslie L (Doctor)
Oregon Health Sciences University
Neurology Dept
Portland, OR 97201, USA

Muldoon, Patrick (Actor, Model)
27652 Eastvale Rd.
Palos Verdes Peninsula, CA 90274, USA

Muldoon, Paul B (Writer)
Princeton University
Creative Writing Program
Princeton, NJ 08544, USA

Muldowney, Dominic J (Composer)
Royal National Theater
Music Dept
South Bank
London SE1 1PX, UNITED KINGDOM (UK)

Mulgrew, Kate (Actor)
c/o Lisa Loosemore Viking Entertainment
445 W 23rd St
Suite 1A
New York, NY 10011, USA

Mulhern, Matt (Actor)
Gold Marshak Liedtke
3500 W Olive Ave
#1400
Burbank, CA 91505, USA

Mulhern, Richard (Athlete, Hockey Player)
397 Walpole Ave
Beaconsfield, QC H9W 2G6, Canada

Mulhern, Ryan (Athlete, Hockey Player)
19 Beachview Ter
Middletown, RI 02842-5904, USA

Mulhern, Sinead (Opera Singer)
Van Walsum Mgmt
4 Addison Bridge Place
London W14 8XP, UNITED KINGDOM (UK)

Mulholland, Terry (Athlete, Baseball Player)
11655 N 18th Pl
Phoenix, AZ 85020-1319, USA

Mulis, Kary B (Nobel Prize Laureate)
Vyrex
2519 Avenida de la Palaya
La Jolla, CA 92037, USA

Mulitalo, Edwin (Athlete, Football Player)
110 Santa Barbara Ave
Daly City, CA 94014, USA

Mulkerin, Ted (Writer)
c/o Staff Member WME (LA)
9601 Wilshire Blvd Fl 3
Beverly Hills, CA 90210, USA

Mulkey, Chris (Actor)
Paradigm Agency
10100 Santa Monica Blvd
#2500
Los Angeles, CA 90067, USA

Mulkey-Robertson, Kim (Basketball Player, Coach)
Baylor University
Athletic Dept
Waco, TX 76798, USA

Mull, Clay (Athlete, Olympic Athlete, Speed Skater)
4344 S New Hope Rd
Gastonia, NC 28056-8454, USA

Mull, Martin (Actor)
338 S Chadbourne Ave
Los Angeles, CA 90049, USA

Mullady, Tom (Athlete, Football Player)
2855 Crooked Oak Dr
Germantown, TN 38138, USA

Mullally, Megan (Actor, Musician)
1775 Stone Canyon Rd
Los Angeles, CA 90077, USA

Mullan, Peter (Writer)
c/o Staff Member ICM Partners (ICM-LA)
10250 Constellation Blvd Fl 7
Los Angeles, CA 90067, USA

Mullane, Richard M Colonel (Astronaut)
1301 Las Lomas Rd NE
Albuquerque, NM 87106-4527, USA

Mullane, Richard M (Mike) (Astronaut)
1301 Las Lomas Road NE
Albuquerque, NM 87106, USA

Mullaney, Mark (Athlete, Football Player)
13490 Essex Ct
Eden Prairie, MN 55347, USA

Mullavey, Greg (Actor)
1818 Thayer Ave
#303
Los Angeles, CA 90025, USA

Mullavy, Greg
1818 Thayer Ave. #303
Los Angeles, CA 90025-4962

Mullen, Bill (Stylist)
c/o Staff Member Art + Commerce
531 W 25th St # 4
New York, NY 10001, USA

Mullen, Brian (Athlete, Hockey Player)
124 Berkeley Circle
Basking Ridge, NJ 07920-2023, USA

Mullen, Ford (Moon) (Athlete, Baseball Player)
20505 Marine Dr
Unit 3
Stanwood, WA 98292-7852, USA

Mullen, Joe (Athlete, Hockey Player)
Philadelphia Flyers 3601 S Broad St Ste 2
Attn Coaching Staff
Philadelphia, PA 19148-5297, USA

Mullen, Josep P (Joey) (Athlete, Hockey Player)
36 Friends Ln
South Dennis, MA 02660-2549, USA

Mullen, Larry Jr (Musician)
Principle Mgmt
30-32 Sir John Rogerson Quay
Dublin 2, IRELAND

Mullen, Michael G (Admiral)
Chairman Of The Joint Chiefs Of Staff
9999 Joint Staff Pentagon
Washington, DC 20318-9999, USA

Mullen, Nicole (Musician)
c/o Staff Member Word Records
25 Music Square West
Nashville, TN 37203, USa

Mullen, Rodney (Skateboarder)
c/o Staff Member HarperCollins Publishers
10 East 53rd St
c/o Author mail, 7th Floor
New York, NY 10022, USA

Mullen, Scott (Athlete, Baseball Player)
73 Walling Grove Rd
Beaufort, SC 29907-1067, USA

Mullen, Tom (Athlete, Football Player)
107 Greenbriar Ridge Ct
Saint Louis, MO 63122, USA

Mullen, Tony (Race Car Driver)
11825 Upper Manatee River Rd
Bradenton, FL 34202, USA

Muller, Egon (Motorcycle Race, Motorcycle Racer)
Dorfstr 17
Rodenbek, Kiel 24247, GERMANY

Muller, Elisabeth
. Feld 14
Sempach/Lu, SWITZERLAND 6204

Muller, Gerd (Soccer Player)
Neuestr 21
Munich 81479, GERMANY

Muller, Herta (Writer)
c/o Staff Member *Henry Holt & Company*
175 Fifth Avenue
New York, NY 10010, USA

Muller, Jennifer (Choreographer, Dancer)
Muller/Works Foundation
131 W 24th St
New York, NY 10011, USA

Muller, Jorg (Race Car Driver)
Insert Motorsport
Fassoldshof 1
Mainleus 95336, GERMANY

Muller, K ALex (Nobel Prize Laureate)
IBM Research Laboratory
IBM Research Lab
Saumerstrasse 4
Ruschlikon CH-8803, SWITZERLAND

Muller, Kirk (Athlete, Hockey Player)
Milwaukee Admirals 1001 N 4th St Ste 3
Attn: Coaching Staff
Milwaukee, WI 53203-1313, USA

Muller, Kirk
3852 Corkey RR 1
Inveray, ON K0H 1X0, Canada

Muller, Lisel (Writer)
LSU Press
PO Box 25053
Baton Rouge, LA 70894, USA

Muller, Marcia (Writer)
Mysterious Press
Warner Books
1271 6th Ave
New York, NY 10020, USA

Muller, Michel (Actor, Writer)
c/o Celine Kamina *UBBA*
6 rue de Braque
Paris 75003, France

Muller, Peter (Skier)
Haldenstr 18
Adliswil 8134, SWITZERLAND

Muller, Peter (Architect)
PO Box 545
Clare, SA 5453, AUSTRALIA

Muller, Richard S (Engineer)
University of California
Sensor/Acutator Center
Berkeley, CA 94720, USA

Muller, Robby (Cinematographer)
Smith/Gosnell/Nicholson
PO Box 1156
Studio City, CA 91614, USA

Muller, Robert (Misc)
Federal Bureau of Investigation
9th & Pennsylvania NW
Washington, DC 20535, USA

Muller, Steven (Educator)
21st Century Foundation
919 18th St NW #800
Washington, DC 20006, USA

Muller-Stahl, Armin (Actor)
Gartenweg 31
Sierksdorf 23730, GERMANY

Muller-Westernhagen, Marius
Mittelweg 69
Hamburg, GERMANY D-20149

Mulley of Manor Park, Frederick W
(Government Official)
House of Lords
Westminster
London SW1A 0PW, UNITED KINGDOM
(UK)

Mulligan, Carey (Actor)
c/o Jessica Kolstad *WKT Public Relations*
(WKT-LA)
9350 Wilshire Blvd
Suite 450
Beverly Hills, CA 90212, USA

Mulligan, Gerry (Writer)
c/o Staff Member *3 Arts Entertainment Inc*
9460 Wilshire Blvd
7th Floor
Beverly Hills, CA 90210, USA

Mulligan, Richard C (Biologist)
11 Sumner Road
Cambridge, MA 02138, USA

Mulligan, Sean (Athlete, Baseball Player)
24474 Eastgate Dr
Diamond Bar, CA 91765-4626, USA

Mulligan, Wayne (Athlete, Football
Player)
2410 The Haul Over
Johns Island, SC 29455, USA

Mulliken, William (Bill) (Swimmer)
4216 N Keeler Ave
Chicago, IL 60641, USA

Mullin, Chris (Athlete, Basketball Player,
Olympic Athlete)
116 Laurelwood Dr
Danville, CA 94506-1408, USA

Mullin, Chris (Baseball Player)
116 Laurelwood Dr
Danville, CA 94506, USA

Mullin, J Stanley (Skier)
Sheppard Mullin Richter Hampton
333 S Hope St
Los Angeles, CA 90071, USA

Mulliniks, Rance (Athlete, Baseball Player)
2614 S Peppertree St
Visalia, CA 93277-5507, USA

Mullins, Eric (Athlete, Football Player)
3249 Parkwood Dr
Houston, TX 77021, USA

Mullins, Fran (Athlete, Baseball Player)
9226 Ritenour Ct
Lone Tree, CO 80124-8971, USA

Mullins, Gerry (Athlete, Football Player)
1108 Mohawk Rd
Mc Donald, PA 15057, USA

Mullins, Greg (Athlete, Baseball Player)
P.O. Box 443
Florahome, FL 32140, USA

Mullins, Jeff (Athlete, Basketball Player,
Olympic Athlete)
8866 N Sea Oaks Way
Apt 202
Vero Beach, FL 32963-4195, USA

Mullins, Larry (Model)
U2
30-32 Sir John Rogerson's Quarry
Dublin, IRELAND

Mullins, Shawn (Musician, Songwriter,
Writer)
High Road
751 Bridgeway
#300
Sausalito, CA 94965, USA

Mullins, Terry (Race Car Driver)
105 Arlesia Dr.
Oak Ridge, TN 37830, USA

Mullis, Kary B
400 Goldenrod Ave
Corona Del Mar, CA 92625-2914, USA

Mullis, Kary B (Nobel Prize Laureate)
400 Goldenrod Ave
Corona Del Mar, CA 92625-2914, USA

Mullova, Viktoria Y (Musician)
Askonas Holt Ltd
27 Chancery Lane
London WC2A 1PF, UNITED KINGDOM
(UK)

Mulloy, Gardner (Tennis Player)
800 NW 9th Ave
Miami, FL 33136, USA

Muloin, Wayne (Athlete, Hockey Player)
2991 Hayes St
Avon, OH 44011-2178, USA

Mulroney, Dermot (Actor)
c/o Stephen Huvane *Slate Public
Relations*
9000 Sunset Blvd #915
West Hollywood, CA 90069, USA

Mulroney, Kieran
6100 Wilshire Blvd. #1170
Los Angeles, CA 90048

Mulroney, M Brian (Prime Minister)
47 Forden Crescent
Westmount, QC H3Y 2Y5, CANADA

Muluzi, Bakili (President)
President's Office
Private Bag 301
Capitol City
Lilongwe 3, MALAWI

Mulva, James J (Business Person)
Conoco/Philips Inc
600 N Daisy Ashford
Houston, TX 77029, USA

Mulvaney, Mick (Congressman, Politician)
1004 Longworth HOB
Washington, DC 20515, USA

Mulvenna, Glenn (Athlete, Hockey Player)
1480 Kilrush Dr
Ormond Beach, FL 32174-2882, USA

Mulvey, Grant (Athlete, Hockey Player)
491 S Hampshire Ave
Elmhurst, IL 60126-4105, USA

Mulvey, Kevin (Athlete, Baseball Player)
8149 Mulligan Cir
Port Saint Lucie, FL 34986-3310, USA

Mulvey, Paul (Athlete, Hockey Player)
8009 Oak Hollow Ln
Fairfax Station, VA 22039-2651, USA

Mulvey, Peter (Musician)
c/o Staff Member *Young / Hunter
Management*
350 Massachusetts Ave
#230
Arlington, MA 02474, USA

Mulvhill, Robert (Athlete, Basketball
Player)
57 Elmwood Ter
Wayne, NJ 07470, USA

Mulvihill, Kristen (Stylist)
c/o Staff Member *Sarah Laird Inc*
12 Charles Ln
New York, NY 10014, USA

Mulvihill, Robert
53 Pike Dr Apt 1C
Wayne, NJ 07470-1933, USA

Mulvoy, Mark (Editor, Publisher)
Sports Illustrated Magazine
Rockefeller Center
New York, NY 10020, USA

Mumba, Samantha (Actor, Musician)
Polydor Records
1 Sussex Place
London W6 9XT, UNITED KINGDOM
(UK)

Mumford, David B (Mathematician)
65 Milton St
Milton, MA 02186, USA

Mumford & Sons (Music Group)
c/o Staff Member *Dew Process*
PO Box 401
Fortitude Valley, QLD 4006, Australia

Mumley, Nick (Athlete, Football Player)
1432 Audubon Dr
Columbus, IN 47203, USA

Mumphord, Lloyd (Athlete, Football
Player)
2316 Mumphord St
Victoria, TX 77901, USA

Mumphrey, Jerry (Athlete, Baseball
Player)
7709 Fm 850
Tyler, TX 75705-2135, USA

Mumy, Bill (Actor)
11333 Moorpark St
PO Box 433
Studio City, CA 91602, USA

Mumy, Billy (Actor)
11333 Moorpark St
PO Box 433
Studio City, CA 91602, USA

Mumy, Liliana (Actor)
c/o Meredith Fine *Coast to Coast Talent
Group*
3350 Barham Blvd
Los Angeles, CA 90068, USA

Muna, Solomon Tandeng (Prime Minister)
PO Box 15 Mbengwi
Mono Division
North West Province, CAMEROON

Munchak, Michael A (Mike) (Athlete,
Football Player)
9155 Saddlebow Dr
Brentwood, TN 37027, USA

Muncrief, Kevin (Athlete, Golfer)
939 S Flood Ave
Norman, OK 73069-4504, USA

Mundae, Misty (Actor)
PO Box 447
Ringwood, NJ 07456

Mundell, Robert A (Nobel Prize Laureate)
35 Claremont Ave
New York, NY 10027-6815, USA

Mundie, Craig (Business Person)
Waggener Edstrom Worldwide - Rapid
Response Team
Three Centerpointe Drive, Suite 300
Lake Oswego, OR 97035

Mundy, Carl E General (General)
9308 Ludgate Dr
Alexandria, VA 22309-2740, USA

Mundy, Carl E Jr (General)
9308 Ludgale Dr
Alexandria, VA 22309, USA

Muni, Craig (Athlete, Hockey Player)
9291 Via Cimato Dr.
Clarence Center, NY 14032-9152, USA

Munitz, Barry A (Educator)
California State University Syetem
400 Golden Shore St
Long Beach, CA 90802, USA

Muniz, Frankie (Actor)
c/o Michael Rotenberg *3 Arts
Entertainment Inc*
9460 Wilshire Blvd
7th Floor
Beverly Hills, CA 90210, USA

Muniz, Manuel (Athlete, Baseball Player)
P.O. Box 6301
Caguas, PR 00726, USA

Munk, Chris (Athlete, Basketball Player)
14 Hillview Ct
San Francisco, CA 94124-2487, USA

Munk, Peter (Business Person)
Barrick Gold Corp
200 Bay St
Toronto, ON M5J 2J3, CANADA

Munk, Walter (Scientist)
9530 La Jolla Shores Dr
La Jolla, CA 92037-1138, USA

Munk, Walter H (Geophysicist, Physicist)
9530 La Jolta Shores
La Jolla, CA 92037, USA

Munn, Allison (Actor)
c/o Steve Caserta *Sanders Armstrong
Caserta*
2120 Colorado Blvd
Suite 120
Santa Monica, CA 90404, USA

Munn, Jeff (Athlete, Baseball Player)
7055 S Kachina Dr
Tempe, AZ 85283-4268, USA

Munn, Olivia (Actor, Talk Show Host)
c/o David (Dave) Fleming *Mosaic Media
Group*
9200 W. Sunset Blvd
10th Floor
Los Angeles, CA 90069, USA

Munninghoff, Scott (Athlete, Baseball
Player)
866 Laverty Ln
Cincinnati, OH 45230-3558, USA

Munos, Maria (Television Host)
c/o Staff Member *Entertainment Tonight
(ET)*
4024 Radford Ave.
Studio City, CA 91604, USA

Munoz, Bobby (Athlete, Baseball Player)
9040 NW 20th St
Pembroke Pines, FL 33024-3211, USA

Munoz, M Anthony (Athlete, Football
Player, Sportscaster)
6529 Irwin Simpson Rd
Mason, Ohio 45040, USA

Munoz, Mike (Athlete, Baseball Player)
1000 Carroll Meadows Ct
Southlake, TX 76092-3830, USA

Munoz, Oscar (Athlete, Baseball Player)
14161 Leaning Pine Dr
Hialeah, FL 33014-2512, USA

Munro, Alice (Writer)
PO Box 1133
Clinton, ON N0M 1L0, CANADA

Munro, Caroline (Admiral)
PO Box 2589
London W1A 3NQ, UNITED KINGDOM
(UK)

Munro, Dana G (Diplomat)
PO Box 317
Media, PA 19063, USA

Munro, Glen (Stylist)
c/o Staff Member *Judy Inc*
1 Yorkville Ave
Toronto ON M4W 1L1, Canada

Munro, Lochlyn (Actor)
International Creative Mgmt
8942 Wilshire Blvd
#219
Beverly Hills, CA 90211, USA

Munro, Peter (Athlete, Baseball Player)
4311 Westmoreland St
Little Neck, NY 11363-1943, USA

Munroe, George (Athlete, Basketball
Player)
870 United Nations Plz
Apt 13E
New York, NY 10017, USA

Munsel, Patrice (Opera Singer)
PO Box 472
Schroon Lake, NY 12870, USA

Munson, Eric (Athlete, Baseball Player)
5550 Wilshire Blvd Aot 314
LOs Angeles, CA 90036-4858, USA

Munson, Jeanne L (Stylist)
22-48 41st St
Astoria, NY 11105, USA

Munson, John (Musician)
Monterey Peninsula Artists
509 Hartnell St
Monterey, CA 93940, USA

Munter, Leilani (Race Car Driver)
Maia Motorsports
PO Box 3355
Mooresville, NC 38117, USA

Munter, Scott (Athlete, Baseball Player)
13024 Jessie Ave
Omaha, NE 68164-1375, USA

Muntyan, Mikhail (Opera Singer)
16 N Iorga Str
#13
Chisnau 277012, MOLDOVA

Muppets, The
PO Box 20750
New York, NY 10023-1488

Mura, Steve (Athlete, Baseball Player)
31892 Old Oak Rd
Trabuco Canyon, CA 92679-3245, USA

Murad, Ferid (Nobel Prize Laureate)
2121 W Holcombe Blvd
Houston, TX 77030-3303, USA

Murad, Raza (Actor, Bollywood)
B 104 Mayfair Raviraj Oberoi Complex
Near Lakxmi Industrial Estate New Link
Road Andheri
Bombay, MS 400 058, INDIA

Murakami, Masanori (Athlete, Baseball
Player)
1-4-15-1506 Nisho Ohi Shinagawa-Ku
Tokyo 140-0015, Japan

Murakami, Ryu (Writer)
Kodansha Books
2-12-21 Otowa
Bunkyoku
Tokyo 112-8001, JAPAN

Murali (Actor, Bollywood)
3-77th Street
Chennai, TN 600083, INDIA

Muraliyev, Amangeldy (Prime Minister)
Prime Minister's Office
Ul Perromayskaya 57
Bishkek, KYRGYZSTAN

Muransky, Ed (Athlete, Football Player)
16221 Villarreal De Avila
Tampa, FL 33613, USA

Muratore, John (Scientist)
1030 Montour Dr
Houston, TX 77062-2723, USA

Muratova, Kira G (Director)
Proletarsjy Blvd 14B
#15
Odessa 270015, RUSSIA

Murayama, Makio (Scientist)
5010 Benton Ave
Bathesda, MD 20814, USA

Murayama, Tomiichi (Politician, Prime
Minister)
Sorifu 1-6-1 Nagatacho Chiyada-ku
Oita, Tokyo 100, JAPAN

Murchison, Ira (Athlete, Track Athlete)
10113 S Sangamon St
Chicago, IL 60643, USA

Murchison, Lee (Athlete, Football Player)
2429 W Euclid Ave
Stockton, CA 95204, USA

Murciano, Jr, Enrique (Actor)
c/o Ilene Feldman *IFA Talent Agency*
8730 Sunset Blvd
Suite 490
Los Angeles, CA 90069, USA

Murdoch, Don (Athlete, Hockey Player)
Hockey In The Rockies School
PO Box 383 Stn Main
Attn Owners Office
Cranbrook, BC VlC 4H9, Canada

Murdoch, Robert J (Bob) (Athlete, Coach,
Hockey Player)
410 11th Ave S
Cranbrook, BC V1C 2P9, Canada

Murdoch, Rupert (Publisher)
News America Publishing
1211 Ave of Americas
New York, NY 10036, USA

Murdoch, Sarah (Actor)
c/o Staff Member *WME (LA)*
9601 Wilshire Blvd Fl 3
Beverly Hills, CA 90210, USA

Murdoch, Stuart (Musician, Songwriter,
Writer)
Legends of 21st Century
7 Trinity Row
Florence, MA 01062, USA

Murdock, David H (Business Person)
10900 Wilshire Blvd
#1600
Los Angeles, CA 90024, USA

Murdock, George (Actor)
5733 Sunfield Ave
Lakewood, CA 90712, USA

Murdock, George P (Doctor)
Wynnewood Plaza
#107
Wynnewood, PA 19096, USA

Murdock, Guy (Athlete, Football Player)
106 Medinah Ln
Tower Lakes, IL 60010, USA

Murdock, Rupert (Publisher)
1330 Angelo Dr
Beverly Hills, CA 90210-2016, USA

Murdock, Shirley (Musician)
Millennium Entertainment Group
1319 Fifth Ave N
Nashville, TN 37208, USA

Muresan, Georghe (Actor, Basketball
Player)
New Jersey Nets
390 Murray Hill Parkway
East Rutherford, NJ 07073, USA

Muresan, Gheorghe
12250 Glen Rd
Potomac, MD 20854-1017

Murgatroyd, Peta (Dancer)
c/o Staff Member *Continuum
Entertainment*
303 Park Ave S
Suite 1220
New York, NY 10010, USA

Muris, Timothy (Government Official)
Federal Trade Commission
Pennsylvania Ave & 6th St NW
Washington, DC 20580, USA

Muris, Timothy J (Educator, Government
Official)
George Mason University
Law School
Fairfax, VA 22030, USA

Murkowsk, Frank (Politician)
PO Box 70049
Fairbanks, AK 99707-0049, USA

Murkowski, Lisa (Politician)
232 S Carolina Ave
Washington, DC 20003-1940, USA

Murley, Matt (Athlete, Hockey Player)
32 Hialeah Dr
Troy, NY 12182-9770, USA

Murphey, Michael Martin (Musician,
Songwriter, Writer)
Wildfire Productions
PO Box 450
Rancho de Taos, NM 87557, USA

Murphy, Ben (Actor)
2690 Rambla Pacifico St
Malibu, CA 90265, USA

Murphy, Bill (Athlete, Football Player)
Excel Communications
6411 SW 25th St
Miramar, FL 33023, USA

Murphy, Billy (Athlete, Baseball Player)
5309 66th Avenue Ct W
University Place, WA 98467, USA

Murphy, Bob (Baseball Player, Sportscaster)
New York Mets
220 Coral Cay Ter
Palm Beach Gardens, FL 33418-4003, USA

Murphy, Bob (Athlete, Golfer)
11910 N Lake Dr
Boynton Beach, FL 33436-5556, USA

Murphy, Brian
265 Liverpool Rd
London, ENGLAND N1 1LX

Murphy, Calvin (Athlete, Basketball Player)
8218 Cliffshire Ct
Houston, TX 77083-6526, USA

Murphy, Carolyn (Model)
c/o Staff Member *IMG World (NY)*
420 W 45th St
New York, NY 10036, USA

Murphy, Caryle M (Journalist)
Washington Post
Editorial Dept
1150 15th St NW
Washington, DC 20071, USA

Murphy, Charles Q (Actor)
c/o Lorrie Bartlett *ICM Partners (ICM-LA)*
10250 Constellation Blvd Fl 7
Los Angeles, CA 90067, USA

Murphy, Charles S (Government Official)
100 Bluff View Dr #503C
Belleair Bluffs, FL 33770, USA

Murphy, Cillian (Actor)
c/o Craig Bankey *WKT Public Relations (WKT-LA)*
9350 Wilshire Blvd
Suite 450
Beverly Hills, CA 90212, USA

Murphy, Dale (Athlete, Baseball Player)
467 Aspen Ridge Ln
Alpine, UT 84004-1223, USA

Murphy, Dan (Athlete, Baseball Player)
19661 Symeron Rd
Apple Valley, CA 92307, USA

Murphy, Daniel
2878 Dickie Ct
Jacksonville, FL 32216-5397, USA

Murphy, Danny (Actor)
c/o Staff Member *Kazarian Spencer Ruskin & Assoc.*
11969 Ventura Blvd
3rd Floor
Studio City, CA 91604, USA

Murphy, Danny (Athlete, Baseball Player)
120 N Ocean Blvd Aot S-4
Delrav Beach, FL 33483-7013, USA

Murphy, David (Athlete, Baseball Player)
3508 Rolling Oaks Dr
Flower Mound, TX 75022-2907, USA

Murphy, David Lee (Musician)
c/o Staff Member *Agency for the Performing Arts (APA-LA)*
405 S Beverly Dr
Suite 500
Beverly Hills, CA 90212-4425, USA

Murphy, Dennis A (Athlete, Hockey Player)
22790 Kentfield St
Grand Terrace, CA 92313-5763, USA

Murphy, Diana E (Judge)
US Court of Appeals
300 S 4th St
Minneapolis, MN 55415, USA

Murphy, Dick (Athlete, Baseball Player)
6890 Connie Dr
Avon, IN 46123-8532, USA

Murphy, Dick (Athlete, Baseball Player)
6890 Connie Dr
Avon, IN 46123, USA

Murphy, Donna (Actor, Musician)
Gerson Saines
250 W 57th St
#2303
New York, NY 10107, USA

Murphy, Donnie (Athlete, Baseball Player)
7272 E Gainev Ranch Rd Unit 53
Scottsdale, AZ 85258-1508, USA

Murphy, Dwayne (Athlete, Baseball Player)
1811 S Karen Dr
Chandler, AZ 85286-6350, USA

Murphy, Ed (Basketball Player, Coach)
University of Mississippi
Smith Coliseum
University, MS 38677, USA

Murphy, Eddie (Actor, Comedian)
c/o Arnold Robinson *Rogers & Cowan PR (LA)*
Pacific Design Center
8687 Melrose Ave, 7th Floor
West Hollywood, CA 90069, USA

Murphy, Erin (Actor)
c/o Staff Member *James/Levy/Jacobson Management Inc*
3500 W Olive Ave
Suite 1470
Burbank, CA 91505, USA

Murphy, Gord (Athlete, Hockey Player)
10041 Cartgate Ct
Dublin, OH 43017-8865, USA

Murphy, Gord (Athlete, Hockey Player)
Florida Panthers
1 Panther Pkwy
Attn: Coaching Staff
Sunrise, FL 33323-5315, USA

Murphy, James (Athlete, Football Player)
1-1420 Clarence Ave
Winnipeg, MB R3T 1T6, Canada

Murphy, Joe (Athlete, Hockey Player)
10292 Horton Rd
Goodrich, MI 48438-9473, USA

Murphy, Larry (Athlete, Hockey Player)
1167 Connaught Dr
Ennismore, ON KOL lTO, Canada

Murphy, Lawrence T (Larry) (Athlete, Hockey Player)
Detroit Red Wings
600 Civic Center Dr
Broadcast Dept, MI 48226-4419, USA

Murphy, Mark (Athlete, Football Player)
736 Michigan Ave
Evanston, IL 60202, USA

Murphy, Mark H (Musician)
Prince/SF Productions
1450 Southgate Ave #206
Daly City, CA 94015, USA

Murphy, Mark S (Athlete, Football Player)
1020 Ruby St NW
Hartville, OH 44632, USA

Murphy, Mary (Choreographer, Reality TV Star)
Champion Ballroom Academy
3580 Fifth Ave
San Diego, CA 92103, USA

Murphy, Mary (Athlete, Golfer)
3111 N 400 W
West Lafayette, IN 47906, USA

Murphy, Michael (Actor)
c/o Gayle Abrams *Oscars Abrams Zimel & Associates, Inc. (OAZ)*
438 Queen St E
Toronto ON M5A 1T4, CANADA

Murphy, Michael Martin
4077 State Hwy. 68
Rancho de Taos, NM 87557

Murphy, Michael R (Judge)
US Court of Appeals
Federal Building
125 S State St
Salt Lake City, UT 84138, USA

Murphy, Mike (Athlete, Coach, Hockey Player)
National Hockey League
50 Bay Street 11th Floor
Attn: Hockev Operations Deot
Toronto, ON M5J 2X8, Canada

Murphy, Peter (Musician)

Murphy, Raymond D (War Hero)
4677 Sutton St NW
Albuquerque, NM 87114, USA

Murphy, Reg (Editor, Publisher)
National Geographic Society
1145 17th St NW
Washington, DC 20036, USA

Murphy, Richard W (Diplomat)
16 Sutton Place #9A
New York, NY 10022, USA

Murphy, Rob (Athlete, Baseball Player)
44 S Sewalls Point Rd
Stuart, FL 34996-6728, USA

Murphy, Rob (Athlete, Hockey Player)
Hockey Stall Inc
35 Mika St
Stittsville, ON K2S 1K8, Canada

Murphy, Roisin (Musician)
c/o Staff Member *Spectrum*
9107 Wilshire Blvd
Suite 450
Beverly Hills, CA 90210, USA

Murphy, Ron (Athlete, Hockey Player)
1 Valley Rd.
Nanticoke, ON NOH 1LO, Canada

Murphy, Ron (Athlete, Basketball Player)
14800 Hanover Pike
Upperco, MD 21155-9735, USA

Murphy, Rosemary (Actor)
220 E 73rd St
New York, NY 10021, USA

Murphy, Ryan (Director, Producer, Writer)
Ryan Murphy Productions
5555 Melrose Ave
Modular Bldg Fl 1
Los Angeles, CA 90038, USA

Murphy, Sean (Athlete, Golfer)
1004 June Pl
Lovington, NM 88260-4521, USA

Murphy, Terry (Journalist)
77 W 66th St
New Yor, NY 10023-6201, USA

Murphy, Terry (Entertainer)
Sherry Ingram
3575 Cahuenga Blvd W
#600
Los Angeles, CA 90068, USA

Murphy, Tim (Congressman, Politician)
322 Cannon HOB
Washington, DC 20515, USA

Murphy, Tod (Athlete, Basketball Player)
23 Parsons Hill Rd
Wenham, MA 01984-1823, USA

Murphy, Tom (Athlete, Baseball Player)
26561 Via Sacramento
Capistrano Beach, CA 92624-1337, USA

Murphy, Tommy (Athlete, Baseball Player)
1824 Dunsford Rd
Jacksonville, FL 32207-4206, USA

Murphy, Troy (Basketball Player)
404 W Mountain Road
Sparta, NJ 07871, USA

Murphy-O'Connor, Cormac Cardinal (Religious Leader)
Archbishop's House
Ambrosden Ave
London SW1P 1QJ, UNITED KINGDOM (UK)

Murray, Aj (Athlete, Baseball Player)
2154 E 4500 S
Vernal, UT 84078-9207, USA

Murray, Albert L (Writer)
45 W 132nd St
New York, NY 10037, USA

Murray, Andy (Athlete, Tennis Player)
c/o Staff Member *ACE Group*
21 Quayside William Morris Way
London SW6 2UZ, UK

Murray, Anne (Opera Singer)
Helge Rudolf Augstein
Sebastianplatz 3
Munich 80331, GERMANY

Murray, Anne (Musician)
Box 69030
12 St. Clair Ave East
Toronto, ON M4T 1K0, CANADA

Murray, Bill (Actor, Comedian)
Charleston Riverdogs
P.O. Box 20849
Charleston, SC 29413, USA

Murray, Bob (Athlete, Hockey Player)
445 S Bridge View Dr
Anaheim, CA 92808-1346, USA

Murray, Bob (Athlete, Hockey Player)
Anaheim Ducks
2695 E Katella Ave
Attn: General Manager
Anaheim, CA 92806-5904, USA

Murray, Bob (Athlete, Hockey Player)
3137 Beacon Dr
Coquitlam, BC V3C 3W7, Canada

Murray, Brain Doyle (Actor)
Abrams Artists
9200 Sunset Blvd
#1125
Los Angeles, CA 90069, USA

Murray, Bruce C (Scientist)
Jet Propulsion Laboratory
4800 Oak Grove Dr
Pasadena, CA 91109, USA

Murray, Bryan C (Athlete, Hockey Player)
Ottawa Senators
110-1000 Palladium Dr
Attn: General Manager
Ottawa, ON K2V IAS, Canada

Murray, Calvin (Athlete, Baseball Player, Olympic Athlete)
17434 Courtney Pine Cir
Spring, TX 77379-8505, USA

Murray, Chad Michael (Actor)
5327 Coldwater Canyon Ave #C
Sherman Oaks, CA 91401, USA

Murray, Chad Micheal (Actor)
c/o JoAnne Colonna *Brillstein Entertainment Partners*
9150 Wilshire Blvd #350
Beverly Hills, CA 90212, USA

Murray, Charles A (Scientist)
American Enterprise Institute
1150 17th St NW
Washington, DC 20036, USA

Murray, Cherry A (Business Person, Physicist)
700 Mountain Ave
New Providence, NJ 07974, USA

Murray, Chris (Misc)
IBM T J Watson Research Center
PO Box 218
Yorktown Heights, NY 10598, USA

Murray, Dale (Athlete, Baseball Player)
5695 FM 2718
Yorktown, TX 78164-1939, USA

Murray, Dan (Athlete, Baseball Player)
4312 W 78th St
Prairie Village, Ks 66208-4352, USA

Murray, Dan (Athlete, Football Player)
9 Washington Rd
Ogdensburg, NJ 07439, USA

Murray, Dave (Musician)
Sanctuary Music Mgmt
82 Bishop's Bridge Road
London W2 6BB, UNITED KINGDOM
(UK)

Murray, David K (Musician)
Joel Chriss
300 Mercer St
#3J
New York, NY 10003, USA

Murray, Devon (Actor)
PO Box 814
Maynooth
Co. Kildare, IRELAND

Murray, Don (Actor)
1201 La Patera Canyon Road
Goleta, CA 93117, USA

Murray, Doug (Cartoonist)
Marvel Comic Group
10 E 40th St
#900
New York, NY 10016, USA

Murray, Eddie C (Athlete, Baseball Player)
15609 Bronco Dr
Canyon Country, CA 91387-4717, USA

Murray, Edward P (Eddie) (Athlete, Football Player)
1070 Forest Bay Dr
Waterford, MI 48328, USA

Murray, Gerald (General)
1068 Polo Club Dr NW
Marietta, GA 30064-1284, USA

Murray, Glen (Athlete, Hockey Player)
1320 lOth St
Manhattan Beach, CA 90266-6036, USA

Murray, Glenn (Athlete, Baseball Player)
2 Spalding St
Nashua, NH 03060-4737, USA

Murray, Heath (Athlete, Baseball Player)
2605 Greenlawn Dr
Troy, OH 45373-4362, USA

Murray, Heath (Athlete, Baseball Player)
2605 Greenlawn Dr
Troy, OH 45373, USA

Murray, Iain (Yachtsman)
Int'l Management Group
75490 Fairway Dr
Indian Wells, CA 92210, USA

Murray, Jaime (Actor)
c/o Lena Roklin *Luber Roklin Management*
8530 Wilshire Blvd
6th Floor
Beverly Hills, CA 90211, USA

Murray, James D (Biologist)
University of Washington
Applied Math Dept
PO Box 352420
Seattle, WA 98195, USA

Murray, Jasmine (Musician)

Murray, Jim (Athlete, Hockey Player)
37 Viceroy Cres
Brandon, MB R7B 3R7, Canada

Murray, Joe (Athlete, Football Player)
12900 Ridgemoor Dr
Prospect, KY 40059, USA

Murray, Joel (Actor)
PO Box 5617
Beverly Hills, CA 90210

Murray, John E Jr (Educator)
Duquesne University
President's Office
Pittsburg, PA 15282, USA

Murray, Jonathan (Producer)
c/o Staff Member *Bunim/Murray Productions Inc*
6007 Sepulveda Blvd
Van Nuys, CA 91411, USA

Murray, Keith (Artist, Musician)
Famous Artists Agency
250 W 57th St
New York, NY 10107, USA

Murray, Larry (Athlete, Baseball Player)
3200 Round HIll Dr
Hayward, CA 94542-2122, USA

Murray, Margaret (Baseball Player)
1320 S Desert Meadows Cir Apt 3109
Green Valley, AZ 85614-1832, USA

Murray, Marty (Athlete, Hockey Player)
1301 34th Ave SW
Minot, ND 58701-7221, USA

Murray, Matt (Athlete, Baseball Player)
109 Greenwood Ave
Swampscott, MA 01907-2124, USA

Murray, Michael (Musician)
4436 Zeller Rd
Columbus, OH 43214-2620, USA

Murray, Mike (Athlete, Hockey Player)
4942 Fragrant Cloud Ln
Knoxville, TN 37918-8143, USA

Murray, Neil (Musician)
Int'l Talent Booking
27A Floral St
#300
London WC2E 9DQ, UNITED KINGDOM
(UK)

Murray, Patty (Politician)
2419 8th Ave N Apt 301
Seattle, WA 98109-2285, USA

Murray, Peg (Actor)
800 Light House Road
Southold, NY 11971, USA

Murray, Randy (Athlete, Hockey Player)
1016 68 Ave SW Suite 200
Calgary, AB T2V 4J2

Murray, Rem (Athlete, Hockey Player)
60593 Balmoral Way
Rochester, MI 48306-2064, USA

Murray, Rich (Athlete, Baseball Player)
435 E 108th St
Los Angeles, CA 90061-2507, USA

Murray, Rob (Athlete, Hockey Player)
Alaska Aces
724 E 15th Ave
Attn: Coaching Staff
Anchorage, AK 99501-5462, USA

Murray, Sean (Actor)
c/o Al Onorato *Unified Management*
4231 National Ave
Burbank, CA 91505, USA

Murray, Terence R (Terry) (Athlete, Hockey Player)
11 Kirkwood Rd
Scarborough, ME 04074-9456, USA

Murray, terry (Athlete, Hockey Player)
Los Angeles Kings
1111 S Figueroa St Ste 3100
Attn Coaching Staff
Los Angeles, CA 90015-1333, USA

Murray, Timothy V (Architect)
444 Springfield Road
Ottawa, ON K1M 0K4, CANADA

Murray, Tracy (Athlete, Basketball Player)
25519 Brassie Ln
La Verne, CA 91750-5918, USA

Murray, Troy (Athlete, Hockey Player)
409 6th Ave
La Grange, IL 60525-2439, USA

Murray, Troy (Athlete, Hockey Player)
Chicago Blackhawks
1901 W Madison St
Attn: Broadcast Dept
Chicago, IL 60612-2459, USA

Murray, Ty (Rodeo Rider)
1660 Private Rd #1213
Stephenville, TX 76401, USA

Murray-Leslie, Alex (Musician)
K Records
924 Jefferson St SE
#101
Olympia, WA 98501, USA

Murray of Epping Forest, Lionel (Len) (Misc)
29 Crescent
Loughton
Essex 1G10 4PY, UNITED KINGDOM
(UK)

Murrey, Dorie (Athlete, Basketball Player)
230 NE 178th St
Shoreline, WA 98155-3500, USA

Murro, Noam (Director)
c/o Staff Member *Management 360*
9111 Wilshire Blvd
Beverly Hills, CA 90210, USA

Murs, Olly (Musician)
c/o Staff Member *Modest! Management*
91A Peterborough Rd
London SW6 3BU, UK

Murtagh, Kate (Actor)
5104 Greenbush Ave
Sherman Oaks, CA 91423-1508, USA

Murton, Matt (Athlete, Baseball Player)
2304 Silver Palm Dr Apt 302
Kissimmee, FL 34747-2738, USA

Murukarni, Masanori (Baseball Player)
1-4-15-1506 Nisho Ohi Shinagawaku
Tokyo 140-0015, JAPAN

Murzyn, Dana (Athlete, Hockey Player)
41 Sunset Way SE
Calgary, AB T2X 3H6, Canada

Musa, Said (Prime Minister)
Prime Minister's Office
East Bloc
Belmopan, BELIZE

Musabayev, Talgat A (Cosmonaut)
Potcha Kosmonavtov
Moskovskoi Oblasti
Syvisdny Goroduk 141160, RUSSIA

Musante, Tony (Actor)
38 Bedford St
New York, NY 10014, USA

Musberger, Brent
47 W. 66th St.
New York, NY 10023

Musburger, Brent (Sportscaster)
286 Locha Dr
Jupiter, FL 33458-7733, USA

Muscarello, Carl
720 NW 71st Ave.
Ft. Lauderdale, FL 33317

Muse (Music Group)
c/o Cliff Burnstein *Q Prime Inc*
729 7th Ave
16th Floor
New York, NY 10019, USA

Muse, William V (Educator)
Aubum University
President's Office
Aubum University, AL 36849, USA

Muser, Tony (Athlete, Baseball Player, Coach)
11222 Martha Ann Dr
Los Alamitos, CA 90720-2956, USA

Museveni, Yoweri K (President)
President's Office
PO Box 7108
Kampala, UGANDA

Musgrave, Bill (Athlete, Football Player)
4062 Leprechan Way
Duluth, GA 30097, USA

Musgrave, F Story (Astronaut)
8572 Sweetwater Trail
Kissimmee, FL 34747, USA

Musgrave, F Story Dr (Astronaut)
8572 Sweetwater Trl
Kissimmee, FL 34747-1519, USA

Musgrave, Mandy (Actor)
c/o Adam Levine *Levine Okwu Erickson Management*
9601 Wilshire Blvd
3rd Floor
Beverly Hills, CA 90210, USA

Musgrave, R Kenton (Judge)
US Court of International Trade
1 Federal Plaza
New York, NY 10278, USA

Musgrave, Spain (Athlete, Football Player)
9727 Mount Pisgah Rd
Apt 811
Silver Spring, MD 20903, USA

Musgrave, Ted (Race Car Driver)
175 Lakeside Dr E
Port Orange, FL 32128, USA

Musgrave, Thea (Composer)
Virginia Opera Assn
PO Box 2580
Norfolk, VA 23501, USA

Musgraves, Dennis (Athlete, Baseball Player)
17100 N Highway 124
Centralia, MO 65240-3830, USA

Musgrove, Spain (Athlete, Football Player)
2350 Deckman Ln
Silver Spring, MD 20906, USA

Musharraf, Parvez (President)
President's Office
Aiwan-e-Sadr
Mall & Mayo Roads
Islamabad, PAKISTAN

Mushok, Mike (Musician)
c/o Staff Member *Agency Group Ltd, The (UK)*
361-373 City Rd
London EC1V 1PQ, UK

Musial, Stan (Athlete, Baseball Player)
Stan the Man Inc
1650 Des Peres Rd #125
St Louis, MO 63131, USA

Music, The (Music Group)
c/o Staff Member *Paradigm (Monterey)*
404 W Franklin St
Monterey, CA 93940, USA

Musil, Frank (Athlete, Hockey Player)
1606-4769 Hazel St
Burnaby, BC VSH 1S7, Canada

Musiol, Bogdan (Athlete)
Fitness-Studio
Talstr 50
Zella-Mehlis 98544, GERMANY

Musiq (Musician)
Def Soul Records
825 8th Ave
#2700
New York, NY 10019, USA

Musiq Soulchild (Music Group)
c/o Staff Member *Paradigm (Monterey)*
404 W Franklin St
Monterey, CA 93940, USA

Musk, Elon (Business Person)
SpaceX
1 Rocket Rd
Hawthorne, CA 90250, USA

Musker, John (Animator, Director)
c/o Staff Member *Creative Artists Agency (CAA-LA)*
2000 Ave Of The Stars
Los Angeles, CA 90067, USA

Musonge, Pater Mafani (Prime Minister)
Prime Minister's Office
Yaounde, BP 1057, CAMEROON

Musselman, Jeff (Athlete, Baseball Player)
1842 Port Tiffin Pl
Newport Beach, CA 92660-7121, USA

Musselman, Ron (Athlete, Baseball Player)
5313 Autumn Dr
Wilmington, NC 28409-5701, USA

Musselwhite, Charlie (Musician)
c/o Kevin Morrow *Morrow Management*
5003 Westpark Dr
Suite 102
Valley Village, CA 91601, 818-985-8592

Musser, Neal (Athlete, Baseball Player)
6140 NW Gavlord Ter
Port Saint Lucie, FL 34986-3766, USA

Mussill, Barney (Athlete, Baseball Player)
912 Moorland Dr
Grosse Pointe Woods, MI 48236-1131, USA

Mussina, Mike (Athlete, Baseball Player)
737 White Church Rd
Muncy, PA 17756-8004, USA

Musso, John (Athlete, Football Player)
242 E 3rd St
Hinsdale, IL 60521, USA

Musso, Mitchel (Actor)
c/o Elissa Leeds-Fickman *Reel Talent Management*
P.O. Box 491035
Los Angeles, CA 90049, USA

Mussolini, Alessandra (Government Official)
Italian Social Movement (MSI)
Chamber of Deputies
Rome 00100, ITALY

Musson, Ron (Race Car Driver)
Motorsports HOF
PO Box 194
Nov, MI 48050, USA

Must (Music Group)
c/o Staff Member *Wind-up Records*
72 Madison Ave Fl 8
New York, NY 10016, USA

Mustaf, Jerrod
7724 Hanover Pkwy
Apt 302
Greenbelt, MD 20770-2625, USA

Mustafa, Isaiah (Actor)
c/o Siri Garber *Platform Public Relations*
2666 N Beachwood Dr
Los Angeles, CA 90068, USA

Mustaine, Dave (Musician)
ESP Mgmt
838 N Doheny Dr #302
West Hollywood, CA 90069, USA

Mustalov, Abdulkhashim M (Prime Minister)
Government House
Tashkent 700008, UZBEKISTAN

Mustan, Abbas (Actor, Bollywood)
119 Haveliwala Building 1st Floor
E R Road
Mumbai, MS 400003, INDIA

Muster, Brad (Athlete, Football Player)
2017 Stony Oak Ct
Santa Rosa, CA 95403, USA

Muster, Thomas (Tennis Player)
370 Felter Ave
Hewlett, NY 11557, USA

Mustin, Henry C (Admiral)
2347 S Rolle St
Arlington, VA 22202, USA

Musto, Michael (Writer)
Village Voice
36 Cooper Square
New York, NY 10003

Mustonen, Olli (Composer, Musician)
Shuman Assoc
120 W 58th St
#8D
New York, NY 10019, USA

Mutchie, Marjorie Ann
1169 Mary Circle
La Verne 91750

Mutchnick, Max (Producer)
c/o Staff Member *KoMut Entertainment*
300 Television Plaza
Burbank, CA 91505, USA

Muteba II, Ronald Muwenda (King)
Royal Palace
Kampala, UGANDA

Muth, Ellen (Actor)
c/o Barbara Gale *Envoy Entertainment*
2637 Centinela Ave #8
Santa Monica, CA 90405, USA

Muth, Rene (Coach)
Pennsylvania State University
Athletic Dept
University Park, PA 16802, USA

Muthu, Kumari (Actor)
A-6 53 South West Boag Road
T Nagar
Chennai, TN 600 017, INDIA

Muti, Ornella (Actor)
c/o Staff Member *Agentur Reuter*
Feldbrunnenstr. 50
Hamburg 20148, Germany

Muti, Riccardo
Via Corti Alle Mura 25
Ravenna 48100, ITALY

Muti, Richard
via Corti alle Mura 25
Ravenna, ITALY 48100

Mutis, Jeff (Athlete, Baseball Player)
630 E Wyoming St
C/O Thomas Mutis
Allentown, PA 18103-3536, USA

Mutombo, Dikembe (Athlete, Basketball Player)
c/o Staff Member *Houston Rockets*
Toyota Center
1510 Polk St
Houston, TX 77003-5028, USA

Mutscheller, Jim (Athlete, Football Player)
12350 Rosslare Ridge Rd Unit 102
Lutherville Timonium, MD 21093, USA

Mutschler, Carlfried (Architect)
E7
7
Mannheim 68159, GERMANY

Mutter, Anne-Sophie (Musician)
Effnerstr 48
Munich 81925, GERMANY

Mutter, Carol (General)
United States Marine
Corps the Pentagon
Washington, DC 20301-0001, USA

Mutter, Carol A (General)
Women Marines Assn
PO Box 1907
Woodbridge, VA 22195, USA

Muxworthy, Jake (Actor)
c/o Staff Member *United Talent Agency (UTA)*
9336 Civic Center Dr
Beverly Hills, CA 90210, USA

Muzzatti, Jason (Athlete, Hockey Player)
4581 Dun morrow Dr
Okemos, MI 48864-1256, USA

M. Velazquez, Nydia (Congressman, Politician)
2302 Rayburn HOB
Washington, DC 20515, USA

Mwine, Ntare (Actor)
c/o August Kammer *TalentWorks (LA)*
3500 W Olive Ave
Suite 1400
Burbank, CA 91505, USA

Mwinyi, Ali Hassam (President)
President's Office
State House
PO Box 9120
Dar es Salaam, TANZANIA

Mya (Actor, Musician)
c/o Gina Hoffman *Baker Winokur Ryder Public Relations (BWR-LA)*
9100 Wilshire Blvd
Suite 500, West Tower
Beverly Hills, CA 90212, USA

My Chemical Romance (Music Group)
c/o Matt Galle *Paradigm (NY)*
360 Park Ave S Fl 16
New York, NY 10010, USA

Myer, Steve (Athlete, Football Player)
423 East Mead Dr
Chandler, AZ 85249, USA

Myers, A Maurice (Business Person)
Waste Management Inc
1001 Fannin St
Houston, TX 77002, USA

Myers, Anne M (Religious Leader)
Church of the Brethren
1451 Dundee Ave
Elgin, IL 60120, USA

Myers, Barton (Architect)
Barton Myers Assoc
9348 Civic Center Dr
Beverly Hills, CA 90210, USA

Myers, Billie
PO Box 12198
Miami, FL 33101

Myers, Brett (Athlete, Baseball Player)
312 s Pimlico St
Saint Augustine, FL 32092-3003, USA

Myers, Cynthia (Actor, Model)
PO Box 10
Liano, CA 93544, USA

Myers, Dale (Scientist)
7835 Rush Rose Dr Unit 214
Carlsbad, CA 92009-6830, USA

Myers, Dale D (Engineer)
7835 Rush Rose Dr #214
Carlsbad, CA 92009-6830, USA

Myers, Danny (Race Car Driver)
Childress Racing
PO Box 1189
Industrial Dr
Welcome, NC 27374, USA

Myers, Dave (Athlete, Baseball Player)
4221 71st Avenue Ct NW
Gig Harbor, WA 98335-6517, USA

Myers, Dee Dee (Actor, Writer)
c/o Ari Greenburg *WME (LA)*
9601 Wilshire Blvd Fl 3
Beverly Hills, CA 90210, USA

Myers, Donnie (Stylist)
c/o Staff Member *De Facto*
41 Union Square West
#1001
New York, NY 10003, USA

Myers, Frank (Athlete, Football Player)
3874 Woodhollow Dr
Apt 410
Euless, TX 76040, USA

Myers, Greg (Athlete, Baseball Player)
7917 Brasado Wav
Riverside, CA 92508-8719, USA

Myers, Hap (Athlete, Hockey Player)
604 Wolf Willow Rd NW
Edmonton, AB TST 1E6, Canada

Myers, Jack (Athlete, Football Player)
25 Biltmore Ln
Menlo Park, CA 94025, USA

Myers, Jack D (Physicist)
University of Pittsburg
1291 Scaife Hall
Pittsburg, PA 15261, USA

Myers, Jimmy (Athlete, Baseball Player)
1312 NW 14th Pl
Moore, OK 73160, USA

Myers, Lisa (Correspondent)
NBC-TV
News Dept
4001 Nebraska Ave NW
Washington, DC 20016, USA

Myers, Margaret J (Dee Dee)
(Government Official)
Equal Time Show
CBS-TV
1233 20th St NW #302
Washington, DC 20036, USA

Myers, Mike (Athlete, Baseball Player)
337 High Ridge Way
Castle Rock, CO 80108-3422, USA

Myers, Mike (Actor, Comedian)
c/o Ina Treciokas *Slate Public Relations*
9000 Sunset Blvd #915
West Hollywood, CA 90069, USA

Myers, Norman (Scientist)
Upper Meadow Old Road
Headington
Oxford OX3 8SZ, UNITED KINGDOM
(UK)

Myers, Pete (Athlete, Basketball Player)
19W011 13th St
Lombard, IL 60148-4758, USA

Myers, Randy (Athlete, Baseball Player)
15525 NE Caples Rd
Brush Prairie, WA 98606-8504, USA

Myers, Reginald R (War Hero)
PO Box 803
Annandale, VA 22003, USA

Myers, Richard (Scientist)
Stanford University
Human Genome Center
Stanford, CA 94305, USA

Myers, Richard B (Dick) (General)
Chairman Joint Chiefs of Staff
Pentagon
Washington, DC 20318, USA

Myers, Robert (Bob) (Athlete)
c/o Staff Member *SFX Sports Management*
5335 Wisconsin Ave NW #850
Washington, DC 20015, USA

Myers, Rochelle (Writer)
3827 California St
San Francisco, CA 94118, USA

Myers, Roderick (Rod) (Athlete, Baseball
Player)
1816 S 3rd St
Conroe, TX 77301-5131, USA

Myers, Rodney (Rod) (Athlete, Baseball
Player)
229 E Tanya Rd
Phoenix, AZ 85086-9253, USA

Myers, Russell (Cartoonist)
Tribune Media Services
435 N Michigan Ave
#1500
Chicago, IL 60611, USA

Myers, Tikalsky Linda (Skier)
RR 5 Box 2651
Santa Fe, NM 87506, USA

Myers, Tom (Athlete, Football Player)
6015 Rapid Creek Ct
Kingwood, TX 77345-1954, USA

Myers, Walter Dean (Photographer)
Scholastic Press
555 Broadway
New York, NY 10012, USA

Myers Jr, Harry J (Publisher)
46 W Ranch Trail
Morrison, CO 80465, USA

Myerson, Bess (Actor, Beauty Pageant
Winner, Lawyer)
3 E 71st St
#9A
New York, NY 10021, USA

Myerson, Harvey (Attorney, Attorney
General, General)
Finley Kumble Wagner Assoc
425 Park Ave
New York, NY 10022, USA

Myerson, Jacob M (Diplomat, Economist)
2 Rue Lucien-Gaulard
Paris 75018, FRANCE

Myette, Aaron (Athlete, Baseball Player)
5138 236 St
Langley, BC V2Z 2P5, Canada

Myhre, Wencke
Im Vendla 22
Nesoya, NORWAY N-1315

Myhres, Brantt (Athlete, Hockey Player)
The Sports Corporation
2735-10088 102 Ave NW
Edmonton, AB TSJ 2Zl, Canada

Myles, Alannah (Musician)
Miracle Prestige
1 Water Lane
Camden Town
London NW1 8N2, UNITED KINGDOM
(UK)

Myles, Eve (Actor)
c/o Torchwood Production Office
BBC Television Centre
Cardiff, Wales, UNITED KINGDOM

Myles, Sophia (Actor)
c/o Christian Hodell *Hamilton Hodell Ltd*
66-68 Margaret St Fl 5
London W1W 8SR, UK

Mylnlkov, Sergel (Athlete, Hockey Player)
Kuzkin Cup Hockey
ul Talalikhin vi 28
Moscow 109029, Russia

Myrah, Don (Athlete, Cycler, Olympic
Athlete)
5291 Kentfield Dr
SanJose, CA x CA 95124-5524, USA

Myre, Philippe (Phil) (Athlete, Hockey
Player)
101 Rue Dugas
Joliette, QC J6E 4G7, Canada

Myrick, Bob (Athlete, Baseball Player)
32 Troon
Hattiesburg, MS 39401-8629, USA

Myrick, Daniel (Director)
Artisan Entertainment
2700 Colorado Ave
Santa Monica, CA 90404, USA

Myrin, Arden (Actor)
c/o Steve Caserta *Sanders Armstrong
Caserta*
2120 Colorado Blvd
Suite 120
Santa Monica, CA 90404, USA

Myron, Vicki (Writer)
c/o Staff Member *Grand Central
Publishing*
237 Park Ave
C/O Author Mail: (Author's Name)
New York, NY 10017, USA

Myrow, Brian (Athlete, Baseball Player)
621 Crystal Brook Dr
Saginaw, TX 76179-0939, USA

Myrtle, Chip (Athlete, Football Player)
6010 S Lima Way
Englewood, CO 80111, USA

Mysen, Bjorn O (Misc)
Camegie Institution
5221 Broad Branch Road
Washington, DC 20015, USA

Myslinski, Tom (Athlete, Football Player)
2842 Forest Lake Dr
Westlake, OH 44145, USA

Myss, Caroline (Motivational Speaker)
Transworld Publishers
61-63 Uxbridge Road
London W5 5SA, United Kingdom

Mysterio, Rey (Wrestler)
c/o Kerry Rodgerson *World Wrestling
Entertainment (WWE)*
Titan Towers
1241 E Main St
Stamford, CT 06905-3857, USA

Mystic (Music Group, Musician)
c/o Staff Member *General Entertainment*
1409 East Blvd.
Suite 231
Charlotte, NC 28203, USA

Mystics
The88 Anador St.
Staten Island, NY 10303

Mystikal (Musician)
c/o Staff Member *ICM Partners (ICM-LA)*
10250 Constellation Blvd Fl 7
Los Angeles, CA 90067, USA

Na, Li (Athlete, Tennis Player)
c/o Max Eisenbud *IMG (Cleveland)*
1360 E 9th St
Suite 100
Cleveland, OH 44114, USA

Nabe, Ricky (Actor)
c/o Staff Member *Envision Entertainment*
8840 Wilshire Blvd
3rd Floor
Beverly Hills, CA 90211, USA

Naber, Jofin P (Swimmer)
PO Box 50107
Pasadena, CA 91115, USA

Naber, John (Athlete, Olympic Athlete,
Swimmer)
PNaber And Associates Inc PO Box
50107 O Box 50107
Pasadena, CA 91115-0107, USA

Nabers, Drayton Jr (Business Person)
Protective Life Corp
2801 Highway 280 S
Birmingham, AL 35223, USA

Nabholz, Chris (Athlete, Baseball Player)
2030 W Market St
Pottsville, PA 17901-1917, USA

Nabokov, Evgeni (Athlete, Hockey Player)
5763 Poppy Hills Pl
San Jose, CA 95138-2243, USA

Nabors, Jim (Actor, Musician)
P.O. Box 6364
Honolulu, HI 96816, USA

Nabors, Richard (Athlete, Football Player)
1625 Brighton Ct
Beaumont, TX 77706, USA

Naccarato, Vin (Musician)
Paramount Entertainment
PO Box 12
Far Hills, NJ 07931, USA

Nachamkin, Boris (Athlete, Basketball
Player)
350 E 62nd St
#5J
New York, NY 10021, USA

Nachbaur, Don (Athlete, Hockey Player)
671 Clermont Dr
Richland, WA 99352-9519, USA

Nachmansohn, David (Misc)
560 Riverside Dr
New York, NY 10027, USA

Nacincik, John (Athlete, Basketball Player)
2815 Garrett Rd
White Hall, MD 21161-9737, USA

Nackret, Petra (Stylist)
c/o Staff Member *Ford Models (Miami)*
311 Lincoln Rd
#205
Miami Beach, FL 33139, USA

Nadal, Rafael (Athlete, Tennis Player)
c/o Staff Member *ATP Tour*
201 ATP Tour Blvd
Ponte Vedra Beach, FL 32082-3211, USA

Nada Surf (Music Group)
c/o Staff Member *Paradigm (Monterey)*
404 W Franklin St
Monterey, CA 93940, USA

Nadeau, Jerry (Race Car Driver)
192 Apple Hill Rd.
Troutman, NC 28166-9570, USA

Nadel, Barbara (Writer)
c/o Staff Member *St Martins Press*
Publicity Dept
175 5th Ave
New York, NY 10010, USA

Nadel, Eric (Sportscaster)
10612 De Bercy Ct
Dallas, TX 75229-5331, USA

Nader, Michael (Actor)
28 E 10th St
New York, NY 10003, USA

Nader, Ralph (Activist)
1600 20th St NW
Washington, DC 20009, USA

Nadiadwala, Firoz (Actor, Bollywood)
c/o Jai Khanna *Brillstein Entertainment Partners*
9150 Wilshire Blvd #350
Beverly Hills, CA 90212, USA

Nadiya (Actor, Bollywood)
A Block Door No 23
Anna Nagar
Chennai, TN 600102, INDIA

Nadler, Jerrold (Congressman, Politician)
2334 Ra,yburn HOB
Washington, DC 20515, USA

Nadon, Branden (Actor)
PMG Management
1118 Homer St 228
Vancouver, BC V6B 6L5, CANADA

Nady, Xavier (Athlete, Baseball Player)
11320 Wild Meadow Pl
San Diego, CA 92131-4224, USA

Naehring, Tim (Athlete, Baseball Player)
7300 Pinehurst Dr
Cincinnati, OH 45244-3272, USA

Naeole, Chris (Athlete, Football Player)
1314 Charter Ct E
Jacksonville, FL 32225, USA

Nafziger, Dana A (Athlete, Football Player)
251 El Dorado Way
Pismo Beach, CA 93449, USA

Nagahama, Kazu (Actor)
c/o Staff Member *Ology Entertainment*
9151 Sunset Blvd
West Hollywood, CA 90069, USA

Nagakura, Saburo (Misc)
2-7-13 Higashicho
Kichijoji
Musashino, Tokyo 1800002, JAPAN

Nagano, Kent G
Van Walsum Mgmt
4 Addison Bridge Place
London W14 8XP, UNITED KINGDOM (UK)

Nagao, Tomoaki (Nigo) (Business Person, Producer)
Nowhere Co, Ltd
2-9-9 Sendagaya
Shibuyaku
Tokyo 151-0051, Japan

Nagarjuna (Actor, Bollywood)
29 Kasturi Rangan Rd
Alwarpet
Madras, TN 600018, INDIA

Nagashima, Shigeo (Baseball Player)
3-29-19 Denenchofu
Ohtaku
Tokyo 145, JAPAN

Nagel, Craig (Athlete, Football Player)
222 Woodcrest Dr
Loveland, OH 45140, USA

Nagel, Sidney R (Physicist)
4913 S Kimbark Ave
Chicago, IL 60615-2954, USA

Nagel, Steven R (Astronaut)
16923 Cottonwood Way
Houston, TX 77059, USA

Nagel, Thomas (Misc)
New York University
Law School
40 Washington Square S
New York, NY 10012, USA

Nagelson, Russ (Rusty) (Athlete, Baseball Player)
4 Carriage Ct
Little Rock, AR 72211-2280, USA

Nageotte, Clint (Athlete, Baseball Player)
4700 Morningside Dr
Cleveland, OH 44109-4560, USA

Nagesh (Actor)
127 St Marys Road
Chennai, TN 600 018, INDIA

Naghma (Actor, Bollywood)
23 A Kalpak Aspen 1st Floor
Perry Cross Road Bandra
Bombay, MS 400 050, INDIA

Nagl, Miriam (Athlete, Golfer)
2120 Harbourside Dr
Unit 616
Longboat Key, FL 34228, USA

Nagle, Browning (Athlete, Football Player)
8990 Grovelawn Dr
Germantown, TN 38139-5698, USA

Nagler, Gern (Athlete, Football Player)
73595 Agave Ln
Palm Desert, CA 92260, USA

Nagma (Actor, Bollywood)
43 Iind Street
Navarathna Gardens Ekkaduthangal
Chennai, TN 600017, INDIA

Nagobads, George (Athlete, Hockey Player)
5180 Circle Dr
Minneapolis, MN 55439-1401, USA

Nagra, Parminder (Actor)
c/o Michael Foster *The Rights House (UK)*
Drury House
34-43 Russell St
London WC2B 5HA, UK

Nagy, Charles (Athlete, Baseball Player, Olympic Athlete)
60 Robin Rd
Westbury, NY 11590-1104, USA

Nagy, Ladislav (Athlete, Hockey Player)
10628 E Meadowhill Dr
Scottsdale, AZ 85255-1734, USA

Nagy, Mike (Athlete, Baseball Player)
24 Nial@ra Ln
West Yarmouth, MA 02673-5039, USA

Nagy, Stanislaw Cardinal (Religious Leader)
Priests of Sacred Heart
Via Casale S Piov 20
Rome 00126, ITALY

Nagy, Steve (Athlete, Baseball Player)
2205 NE Ridgewood Dr
Poulsbo, WA 98370-8529, USA

Nahan, Stu (Sportscaster)
11274 Canton Dr
Studio City, CA 91604, USA

Naharin, Ohad (Choreographer)
Dance Theater
Scheldeldoekshaven 60
Gravenhage, EN 2511, NETHERLANDS

Nahorodny, Bill (Athlete, Baseball Player)
1948 Rainbow Dr
Clearwater, FL 33765-3564, USA

Nahorodny, Bill (Athlete, Baseball Player)
1948 Rainbow Dr
Clearwater, FL 33765, USA

Nahrgang, Jim (Athlete, Hockey Player)
18283 Parkshore Dr
Northville, MI 48168-8591, USA

Naifeh, Steven W (Writer)
335 Sumter St SE
Aiken, SC 29801, USA

Nail, Jimmy
76 Oxford St.
London, ENGLAND W1N 0AX

Nailon, Lee (Athlete, Basketball Player)
10013 W Bella Vista St
Wichita, KS 67212-6783, USA

Naimoli, Vincent (Baseball Player)
Tampa Bay Devil Rays
16616 Villalenda De Avila
Tampa, FL 33613-5200, USA

Naipaul, V S (Nobel Prize Laureate)
Aitken & Stone Ltd
29 Fernshaw Road
London SW10 0TG, UNITED KINGDOM (UK)

Nair, Mira (Director)
c/o Staff Member *Mirabai Films*
27 West 24th Street
Suite 403
New York, NY 10010, USA

Naisbitt, John (Writer)
Spittelauer Platz 5A3A
Vienna 1090, AUSTRIA

Naish, Bronwen (Musician)
Moelfre Xwm Pennant
Gamdolbenmaen
Gwunedd
North Wales LL5 9AX, WALES

Najarian, John S (Doctor)
University of Minnesota
Health Center
Surgery Dept
Minneapolis, MN 55455, USA

Najee (Musician)
Associated booking Corp
1995 Broadway
#501
New York, NY 10023, USA

Najera, Eduardo (Basketball Player)
c/o Staff Member *Dallas Mavericks*
2500 Victory Ave
Dallas, TX 75219, USA

Najera, Rick (Actor)
c/o Michelle Grant *Grant Management*
1158 26th St #414
Santa Monica, CA 90403, USA

Najimy, Kathy (Actor, Comedian)
c/o Leigh Brillstein *ICM Partners (ICM-LA)*
10250 Constellation Blvd Fl 7
Los Angeles, CA 90067, USA

Najm, Faheem (T-Pain) (Musician)
c/o Michael Blumstein *Chase Entertainment*
7378 West Atlantic Blvd #250
Margate, FL 33063, USA

Nakajiim, Tadashi (Astronomer)
California Institute of Technology
Astronomy Dept
Pasadena, CA 91125, USA

Nakajima, Tommy (Athlete, Golfer)
c/o Staff Member *IMG (Tokyo)*
8-18 Moto-Akasaka
1-chome, Minato-ku
Tokyo 107, JAPAN

Nakama, Keo (Swimmer)
1344 9th Ave
Honolulu, HI 96816, USA

Nakano, Shinji (Race Car Driver)
Fernandez Racing
6950 Guion Rd. #51
Indianapolis, IN 46268, USA

Nakasone, Yasuhiro (Prime Minister)
3-22-7 Kamikitazawa
Setagayaku
Tokyo, JAPAN

Naked, Bif (Musician)
Crazed Mgmt
PO Box 779
New Hope, PA 18938, USA

Nalder, Eric C (Journalist)
Seattle Times
Editorial Dept
1120 John St
Seattle, WA 98109, USA

Nalen, Tom (Athlete, Football Player)
PO Box 4864
Englewood, CO 80155-4864, USA

Nalick, Anna (Musician)
Lippman Entertainment
23586 Calabasas Rd Ste 208
Calabasas, CA 91302, USA

Nalinikanth (Actor)
413 29th Street
6th Sector
Chennai, TN 600 078, INDIA

Nall, Benita Krista (Actor)
c/o Staff Member *Main Title Entertainment*
8383 Wilshire Blvd
Suite 408
Los Angeles, CA 90211, USA

Nall, N Anita (Swimmer)
PO Box 872505
Tempe, AZ 85287, USA

Nalle, Karen Dotrice (Actor)
12751 Evanston St
Los Angeles, CA 90049, USA

Nam, Leonardo (Actor)
c/o Staff Member *Overbrook Entertainment*
450 N Roxbury Dr
4th Floor
Beverly Hills, CA 90210, USA

Namaliu, Rabbie L (Prime Minister)
PO Box 6655
National Capital District
Boroko, PAPUA NEW GUINEA

Namath, Joe (Actor, Athlete, Football Player)
Joe Namath Camp
P.O. Box 1010
Latham, NY 12110, USA

Nambiar, M N (Actor)
4 6th Street
Gopalapuram
Chennai, TN 600 086, INDIA

Nambu, Yoichiro (Nobel Prize Laureate, Physicist)
University Of Chicago
EFI Box 29 - RI 267
5640 S Ellis Ave
Chicago, IL 60637, USA

Namestnikov, Evgeny (Athlete, Hockey Player)
3110 Bay Front Ct
Waterford, MI 48328-1696, USA

Na-Ming
9903 Santa Monica Blvd. #575
Beverly Hills, CA 90212

Namtchylak, Sainkho (Actor, Composer)
c/o Staff Member *Concerted Efforts*
P.O. Box 440326
Somerville, MA 02144, USA

Nance, John J (Writer)
4512 8th Ave
West Tacorna, WA 98466, USA

Nance, Shane (Athlete, Baseball Player)
3403 Harbour Breeze Ln
Pearland, TX 77584-7958, USA

Nance, Todd (Musician)
Brown Cat Inc
400 Foundary St
Athens, GA 30601, USA

Nancy, Ted L
c/o Daniel Strone *Trident Media Group LLC*
41 Madison Ave
36th Floor
New York, NY 10010, USA

Nankin, Jenna (Stylist)
c/o Staff Member *Workgroup (San Francisco)*
35 Beideman Pl
San Francisco, CA 94115, USA

Nanne, Lou (Athlete, Hockey Player, Olympic Athlete)
6982 Tupa Dr
Minneapolis, MN 55439-1641, USA

Nanni, Gianna
Carmenstr. 12
Zurich, SWITZERLAND CH-8032

Nantais, Rich (Athlete, Hockey Player)
9585 Rue Jourdain
Quebec, QC G2K 1K5, Canada

Nantucket
250 N. Kepler Rd. Deland
FL, CA 33724

Nantz, Jim (Sportscaster)
CBS-TV
Sports Dept
51 W 52nd St
New York, NY 10019, USA

Napier, Hugo
2207 N. Beachwood Dr.
Los Angeles, CA 90068

Napier, James (Actor)
c/o Grahame Dunster *Auckland Actors*
PO Box 56460
Dominion Road
Auckland, NEW ZEALAND

Napier, John (Designer)
MLR Douglas House
16-18 Douglas St
London SW1P 4PB, UNITED KINGDOM (UK)

Napier, Mark (Athlete, Hockey Player)
NHL Alumni Assocation
400 Kipling Ave, 2nd Floor
Attn Executive Director
Etobicoke, ON M8W 5Z5, Canada

Napier, Wilfrid F Cardinal (Religious Leader)
Archbishop's House
154 Gordon Road
Greyville 4023, SOUTH AFRICA

Naples, Al (Athlete, Baseball Player)
99 Nickerson Rd
Orleans, MA 02653-3314, USA

Napoleon, Ed (Athlete, Baseball Player)
1312 73rd St NW
Bradenton, FL 34209-1155, USA

Napoles, Jose (Boxer)
Cerrada De Tizapan 9-303 Ediciov
Codigo Postel
Mexico City 06080, MEXICO

Napoli, Mike (Athlete, Baseball Player)
c/o Staff Member *Los Angeles Dodgers (LA Dodgers)*
1000 Elysian Park Ave
Los Angeles, CA 90012, USA

Naponic, Robert (Athlete, Football Player)
10807 Timberglen Dr
Houston, TX 77024, USA

Naragon, Hal (Athlete, Baseball Player)
1521 Hagey Dr
Barberton, OH 44203-7724, USA

Narain, Nicole (Actor)
8033 Sunset Blvd #224
Hollywood, CA 90046

Naranjo, Monica (Musician)
c/o Staff Member *Sony Music Miami*
605 Lincoln Rd Fl 7
Miami Beach, FL 33139, USA

Narasimhan, V L (Actor)
9-6 L I C Staff Quarters
K K Nagar
Chennai, TN 600 078, INDIA

Nardini, Thomas (Tom) (Actor)
139 Beach Ave
Madison, CT 06443, USA

Narducci, Katherine
2843 Waterbury Ave.
Bronx, NY 10461

Narducci, Tim (Musician)
Artists Group International
9560 Wilshire Blvd
#400
Beverly Hills, CA 90212, USA

Narita, Hiro (Cinematographer)
2262 Magnolia Ave
Petatuma, CA 94952, USA

Narita, Richard
8831 Sunset Blvd. #304
Los Angeles, CA 90069

Narizzano, Silvio (Cas) (Director)
Al Parker
55 Park Lane
London W1Y 3DD, UNITED KINGDOM (UK)

Narron, Jerry (Athlete, Baseball Player, Coach)
304 Ashworth Dr
Goldsboro, NC 27530-5563, USA

Narron, Sam (Athlete, Baseball Player)
101 Mill Pl
Goldsboro, NC 27534-8933, USA

Naruhito (Royalty)
Imperial Palaca
1-1 Chiyoda
Chiyoda-ku
Tokyo, JAPAN

Narveson, Chris (Athlete, Baseball Player)
5525 E Thomas Rd Unit Hl
Phoenix, AZ 85018-8168, USA

Narz, Jack (Television Host)
1906 Beverly Place
Beverly Hills, CA 90210, USA

NAS (Musician)
30 Vintage Ct
McDonough, GA 30253, USA

Nasclemento, Milton (Musician, Songwriter, Writer)
Tribo Producoes
Av A Lombardi 800
Rio de Janeiro 22 640-000, BRAZIL

Naseeruddin, Shah (Actor, Bollywood)
204 Sand Pebbles
Perry X Road Bandra
Mumbai, MS 400050, INDIA

Nash, Charles F (Cotton) (Athlete, Basketball Player)
600 Summershade Cir
Lexington, KY 40502-2723, USA

Nash, David (Artist)
Capel Rhiw Blanau
Flestiniog
Gwynedd Wales LL41 3NT, WALES

Nash, Graham W (Musician, Songwriter, Writer)
709 E. Colorado Blvd.
#220
Pasadena, CA 91101, USA

Nash, Jamia Simone (Actor)
c/o Staff Member *Carson-Adler Agency*
250 West 57 St
Suite 2030
New York, NY 10107, USA

Nash, Jim (Athlete, Baseball Player)
4383 White Surrey Dr NW
Kennesaw, GA 30144-5106, USA

Nash, Joe (Athlete, Football Player)
29 Vermont St
West Roxbury, MA 02132, USA

Nash, John F Jr (Nobel Prize Laureate)
Princeton University
Economics Department
Fine Hall
Princeton, NJ 08544, USA

Nash, Kate (Musician)

Nash, Keisha
344 E. 59th St.
New York, NY 10022

Nash, Kevin (Wrestler)
c/o Andrew Stawiarski *ADS Management*
269 S. Beverly Dr #441
Beverly Hills, CA 90212, USA

Nash, Leigh (Musician)
c/o Staff Member *Paradigm (Monterey)*
404 W Franklin St
Monterey, CA 93940, USA

Nash, Niecy (Actor, Television Host)
19400 Kinzie St
Northridge, CA 91324, USA

Nash, Noreen (Actor)
719 N Maple Dr
Beverly Hills, CA 90210, USA

Nash, Richard
19323 Oxnard St.
Tarzana, CA 91356

Nash, Rick (Athlete, Hockey Player)
c/o Staff Member *Columbus Blue Jackets*
Nationwide Arena
200 W Nationwide Blvd - Suite Level
Columbus, OH 43215, USA

Nash, Robert (Athlete, Basketball Player)
659 Kahiau Loop
Honolulu, HI 96821-2539, USA

Nash, Steve (Athlete, Basketball Player)
c/o Bill Duffy *BDA Sports Management (BDA-CA)*
700 Ygnacio Valley Rd
Suite 330
Walnut Creek, CA 94596, USA

Nash, Terius (The Dream) (Musician)
c/o Staff Member *SMC Europe*
14 Bowling Green Ln
Clerkenwell
London EC1R OBD, UK

Nash, Terius (The-Dream) (Musician)
c/o Staff Member *Island Def Jam Group*
Worldwide Plaza
825 8th Ave Fl 28
New York, NY 10019, USA

Nash, Tyson (Athlete, Hockey Player)
Phoenix Coyotes
6751 N Sunset Blvd Ste 200
Attn: Broadcast Dept
Glendale, AZ 85305-3124, USA

Nash, Tyson (Athlete, Hockey Player)
17751 N 92nd Way
Scottsdale, AZ 85255-6025, USA

Nasland, Markus (Athlete, Hockey Player)
808 Griffiths Way
Vancouver, BC V68 6G1, USA

Naslund, Markus (Athlete, Hockey Player)
Mik
154 Earl St
Kingston, ON K7L 2H2, Canada

Naslund, Mats (Athlete, Hockey Player)
6963 Progressona
Switzerland

Naslund, Ron (Athlete, Hockey Player, Olympic Athlete)
2600 Cheyenne Cir
Hopkins, MN 55305-2309, USA

Nasr, Seyyed Hossein (Misc)
George Washington University
Gelman Library
Washington, DC 20052, USA

Nasreddine, Alain (Athlete, Hockey Player)
35 Brians Pl
Wilkes Barre, PA 18702-7864, USA

Nasser, Jacques A (Business Person)
One Equity Partners
1st National Plaza
Chicago, IL 60607, USA

Nasser M (Actor)
245 Guhan Street
Kamakoti Nagar Valasarawakkam
Chennai, TN 600 087, INDIA

Nastase, Ilie (Tennis Player)
Calea Plevnei 14
Bucarest, HUNGARY

Nastu, Phil (Athlete, Baseball Player)
52 Stratfield Pl
Bridgeport, CT 06606, USA

Nat, Marie-Jose (Actor)
c/o Laurent Gregoire Agence Artistique Adequat
108 rue Reaumur
Paris 75002, France

Natal, Bob (Athlete, Baseball Player)
3913 Cockrill Dr
McKinney, TX 75070-2413, USA

Natali, Vincenzo (Director)
c/o Philip Raskind WME (LA)
9601 Wilshire Blvd Fl 3
Beverly Hills, CA 90210, USA

Natalicio, Diana S (Educator)
University of Texas at El Paso
President's Office
El Paso, TX 79968, USA

Natalie (Musician)
c/o Staff Member Motown Records (NY)
1755 Broadway
7th Floor
New York, NY 10019, USA

Nater, Swen (Athlete, Basketball Player)
4125 248th Ct SE
Issaquah, WA 98029-2189, USA

Nath, Alok (Actor, Bollywood)
901 Skydeck Oshiwara Complex
Off New Link Road Andheri
Mumbai, MS 400061, INDIA

Nathan, Amy (Stylist)
And Inc
99 El Camino Real
Berkeley, CA 94705, USA

Nathan, David G (Physicist)
Dana-Farber Cancer Institute
44 Binney St
Boston, MA 02115, USA

Nathan, Joe (Athlete, Baseball Player)
19066 Vogel Farm Rd
Eden Prairie, MN 55347-4199, USA

Nathan, Joseph A (Business Person)
Compuware Corp
1 Campus Martius
Detroit, MI 48226, USA

Nathan, S R (President)
President's Office
Orchard Road
Istana
Singapore 0922, SINGAPORE

Nathan, Tony C (Athlete, Coach, Football Coach, Football Player)
15110 Dunbarton Pl
Miami Lakes, FL 33016, USA

Nathaniel (Popp), Bishop (Religious Leader)
Romanian Orthodox Episcopate
2522 Grey Tower Road
Jackson, MI 49201, USA

Nathanson, Jeff (Writer)
c/o Staff Member United Talent Agency (UTA)
9336 Civic Center Dr
Beverly Hills, CA 90210, USA

Nathanson, Roy (Musician)
Brad Simon Organization
122 E 57th St
#300
New York, NY 10022, USA

Nathman, John B (Admiral)
Commander Naval Air Force Pacific
NAS North Island
San Diego, CA 92135, USA

Nation, Joey (Athlete, Baseball Player)
2125 N Roff Ave
Oklahoma City, OK 73107-2749, USA

Natividad, Kitten (Actor)
c/o Siouxzan Perry Girlwerks Management
3395 E Camino Rojos
Palm Springs, CA 92262, USA

Naton, Pete (Athlete, Baseball Player)
4136 Split Rock Rd
Camillus, NY 13031-8704, USA

Natowich, Andrew (Athlete, Football Player)
24 Lexington Ave
Brattleboro, VT 05301, USA

Natsios, Andrew (Government Official)
US International Development Agency
320 21st NW
Washington, DC 20523, USA

Natt, Calvin (Athlete, Basketball Player)
25201 E Indore Dr
Aurora, CO 80016-2189, USA

Natter, Robert J (Admiral)
Commander
Atlantic Fleet
Norfolk, VA 23551, USA

Nattiel, Ricky (Athlete, Football Player)
835 NW 119th St
Gainesville, FL 32606, USA

Nattress, Ric (Athlete, Hockey Player)
Stoney Creek Warriors
467 Charlton Ave E
Attn: Coaching Staff
Hamilton, ON L8N 1Z4, Canada

Natural (Musician)
Official International Fan Club
PO Box 5097
Bellingham, WA 98227, USA

Natyshak, Mike (Athlete, Hockey Player)
2005 Mount Vernon Ave
Toledo, OH 43607-1545, USA

Naude, C F Beyers (Religious Leader)
26 Hoylake Road
Greenside 2193, SOUTH AFRICA

Naudet, Jules (Producer)
c/o Staff Member WmE2 (WMA-LA)
1 William Morris Pl
Beverly Hills, CA 90212, USA

Nauert, Paul (Athlete, Baseball Player)
1201 Steeple Run
Lawrenceville, GA 30043-6354, USA

Nauert, Paul (Baseball Player)
1201 Stepple Run
Lawrenceville, GA 30043-6354, USA

Naughton, David (Actor)
4 Via Las Colinas #8
Rancho Mirage, CA 92270, USA

Naughton, James (Actor)
c/o Staff Member Brookside Artists Management (NY)
250 W 57th St
Suite 2303
New York, NY 10107, USA

Naughton, Laurie (Actor)
c/o Bruce Smith OmniPop Talent Group
10700 Ventura Blvd.
2nd Floor
Studio City, CA 91604, USA

Naughton, Naturi (Musician)
c/o Matt Luber Luber Roklin Management
8530 Wilshire Blvd
6th Floor
Beverly Hills, CA 90211, USA

Naulis, Willie (Basketball Player)
Chuck & Willie's Auto Agency
13900 Hawthorne Blvd
Hawthorne, CA 90250, USA

Naulls, Willie (Athlete, Basketball Player)
6501 Orange St Apt 201
Los Angeles, CA 90048-4765, USA

Naulty, Dan (Athlete, Baseball Player)
23705 Via Del Rio
Yorba Linda, CA 92887-2717, USA

Nauman, Bruce L (Artist)
4630 Rising Hill Road
Altadena, CA 91001, USA

Naumenko, Gregg (Athlete, Hockey Player)
991 S Prospect Ave
Elmhurst, IL 60126-5030, USA

Naumoff, Paul (Athlete, Football Player)
932 Mohawk St
Columbus, OH 43206, USA

Naum-Parker, Dorothy (Baseball Player)
2620 Bridlecreek Ln
Galesburg, IL 61401-2136, USA

Nause, Martha (Athlete, Golfer)
13206 Patterson Trail
Minocqua, WI 54548, USA

Nauta, Kate (Actor)
c/o Ben Press Buchwald/Fortitude (LA)
6500 Wilshire Blvd
Suite 2200
Los Angeles, CA 90048, USA

Nava, Daniel (Athlete, Baseball Player)
315 t Francis St
Redwood City, CA 94062-2215, USA

Nava, Gregory (Director)
International Creative Mgmt
8942 Wilshire Blvd
Beverly Hills, CA 90211, USA

Navaira, Emilio (Musician)
c/o Staff Member WmE2 (WMA-LA)
1 William Morris Pl
Beverly Hills, CA 90212, USA

Naval, Deepti (Actor, Bollywood)
603 Oceanic Seven Bungalows
Versova Andheri
Mumbai, MS 400061, INDIA

Navarez, Alfred (Musician)
MPI Talent
9255 Sunset Blvd
#407
Los Angeles, CA 90069, USA

Navarro, Dave (Musician)
c/o Larissa Friend The Spread Group
Prefers to be contacted via email
Los Angeles, CA 90069, USA

Navarro, Dioner (Athlete, Baseball Player)
13243 Pike Lake Dr
Riverview, FL 33579-4039, USA

Navarro, Guillermo J (Cinematographer)
Lyons Sheldon Prosnit Agency
800 S Robertson Blvd
#6
Los Angeles, CA 90035, USA

Navarro, Jaime (Athlete, Baseball Player)
8100 Oak Park Rd
Orlando, FL 32819-3266, USA

Navarro, Juan Carlos (Athlete, Basketball Player)
10545 S Ashglen Cir
Collierville, TN 38107-3660, USA

Navarro, Julio (Athlete, Baseball Player)
10-32 Calle 3 Urb
Santa Rosa
Bayamon, PR 00959-6612, USA

Navarro, Tito (Athlete, Baseball Player)
556 Calle Creuz
Urb Open Land
San Juan, PR 00923-1826, USA

Navas, Bibiana (Actor)
c/o Gabriel Blanco Gabriel Blanco Iglesias (Mexico)
Rio Balsas 35-32
Colonia Cuauhtemoc
DF 06500, Mexico

Navasky, Victor S (Editor, Publisher)
33 W 67th St
New York, NY 10023, USA

Navayne, Kevin (Actor)
c/o Talon Outlaw Outlaw Management Group
9777 Wilshire Blvd
Beverly Hills, CA 90212, USA

Navies, Hannibal (Athlete, Football Player)
2891 Grey Moss Pass
Duluth, GA 30097, USA

Navis, Hannibal (Athlete, Football Player)
4616 Rustling Woods Dr
Denver, NC 28037, USA

Navon, Itzhak (President)
Education & Culture Ministry
Hakiria
Jerusalem, ISRAEL

Navratilova, Martina (Tennis Player)
U.S. Tennis Association
USTA National Headquarters
70 W Red Oak Ln
White Plains, NY 10604-3602, USA

Naylor, Gloria (Writer)
One Way Productions
638 2nd St
Brooklyn, NY 11215, USA

Naymenko, Gregg (Athlete)
2695 E Katella Ave
Anaheim, CA 92803-6177

Nayyar, Kunal (Actor)
c/o Jason Kim *Lovett Management*
1327 Brinkley Ave
Los Angeles, CA 90049, USA

Nazam, Hisham (Government Official)
Ministry of Petroleum & Mineral Resources
Riyadh, SAUDI ARABIA

Nazarbayev, Nursultan A (President)
President's Office
Pl Respublik
Astana 480091, KAZAKHSTAN

Nazarian, Sam (Business Person)
SBE Entertainment
8000 Beverly Blvd
Los Angeles, CA 90048, USA

N Chandra (Bollywood, Director, Filmmaker, Producer)
Ankush 1 Belscot Units Lokhandwala Complex
Andheri Linking Road Andheri
Bombay, MS 400 058, INDIA

N. Cicilline, David (Congressman, Politician)
128 Cannon HOB
Washington, DC 20515, USA

Ndayizeye, Domitien (President)
President's Office
Bujumbura, BURUNDI

Ndegeocello, Me'Shell (Musician)
Monetary Peninsula Artists
509 Hartnell St
Monetary, CA 93940, USA

Ndegeocello, Michelle (Musician)
c/o Staff Member *Paradigm (Monterey)*
404 W Franklin St
Monterey, CA 93940, USA

Ndimira, Pascal Firmin (Prime Minister)
Prime Minister's Office
Bujumbura, BURUNDI

N'Dour, Youssou (Musician)
Konzertagentur Berthold Seliger
Nonnengasse 15
Fulda 36037, GERMANY

N'Dour, Youssou (Musician)
c/o Staff Member *Nonesuch Records*
75 Rockefeller Plz Fl 8
New York, NY 10019, USA

Neagle, Denny (Athlete, Baseball Player)
16254 Sandstone Dr
Morrison, CO 80465, USA

Neal, Blaine (Athlete, Baseball Player)
256 Dowdy Dr
Gibbstown, NJ 08027-1175, USA

Neal, Craig (Athlete, Basketball Player)
9205 Tanoan Dr NE
Albuquerque, NM 87111-5828, USA

Neal, Curley (Athlete, Basketball Player)
1275 Regency Pl
Lake Mary, FL 32746, USA

Neal, Diane (Actor)

Neal, Doris (Athlete, Baseball Player)
477 NW 7th Ave
Webster, FL 33597-4746, USA

Neal, Dylan (Actor)
c/o Sara Schedeen *Metropolitan (MTA)*
4526 Wilshire Blvd
Los Angeles, CA 90010, USA

Neal, Edwin (Actor)
501 W Powell Lane
Austin, TX 78753, USA

Neal, Elise (Actor)
c/o Vincent Cirrincione *Vincent Cirrincione Associates*
1516 N Fairfax Ave
Los Angeles, CA 90046, USA

Neal, Fred (Curly) (Basketball Player)
PO Box 915415
Longwood, FL 32791, USA

Neal, James
803 Medora Dr
Greer, SC 29650-4751, USA

Neal, James F (Attorney, Attorney General, General)
Neal & Harwell
3rd National Bank Building
#800
Nashville, TN 37219, USA

Neal, Lloyd (Athlete, Basketball Player)
905 NE Mariners Loop
Portland, OR 97211-1574, USA

Neal, Lorenzo (Athlete, Football Player)
777 S Orange Ave
Fresno, CA 93702, USA

Neal, Mike (Athlete, Football Player)
c/o Roosevelt Barnes *Maximum Sports Management*
6435 W Jefferson Blvd
#197
Fort Wayne, IN 46804, USA

Neal, Philip M (Business Person)
Avery Dennison Corp
150 N Orange Grove Blvd
Pasadena, CA 91103, USA

Neal, Scott (Actor)
c/o Staff Member *Jonathan Altaras Assoc Ltd*
11 Garrick Street
Covent Garden
London WC2E 9AT, UNITED KINGDOM (UK)

Neal, T Daniel (Dan) (Athlete, Football Player)
711 Homestead Blvd
Louisville, KY 40207, USA

Neale, Gary L (Business Person)
Northern Indiana Service
801 E 86th Ave
Merrillville, IN 46410, USA

Neale, Harry (Athlete, Hockey Player)
224 Quail Hollow Ln
East Amherst, NY 14051-1634, USA

Nealon, Kevin (Actor, Comedian)
c/o Marc Gurvitz *Brillstein Entertainment Partners*
9150 Wilshire Blvd #350
Beverly Hills, CA 90212, USA

Nealy, Eddie (Athlete, Basketball Player)
702 Lightstone Dr
San Antonio, TX 75258-2305, USA

Neame, Christopher (Actor)
Borinstein Oreck Bogart
3172 Dona Susana Dr
Studio City, CA 91604, USA

Near, Holly (Actor, Musician, Songwriter, Writer)
PO Box 236
Ukiah, CA 95482, USA

Nearing, Merna (Baseball Player)
21079 W Good Hope Rd Apt D-1
Lannon, WI 53046-9770, USA

Neary, Martin G J (Musician)
2 Little Cloister
Westminster Abbey
London SW1P 3PL, UNITED KINGDOM (UK)

Neary, Robert (Actor, Director)
c/o Lin Bickelmann *Encore Artists Management*
3815 W Olive Ave
Suite 101
Burbank, CA 91505, USA

Neaton, Pat (Athlete, Hockey Player)
3519 Olde Dominion Dr# 2
Brighton, MI 48114-4942, USA

Nebel, Dorothy Hoyt (Skier)
5340 Balfor Dr
Virginia Beach, VA 23464, USA

Neblett, Carol (Opera Singer)
Sardos Artists
180 W End Ave
New York, NY 10023, USA

Nebout, Claire (Actor)
Artmedia
20 Ave Rapp
Paris 75007, FRANCE

Necciai, Ron (Athlete, Baseball Player)
6261 Overlook Ln
Belle Vernon, PA 15012-3928, USA

Nechaev, Victor (Athlete, Hockey Player)
1806 Twin Palms Dr
San Marino, CA 91108-2555, USA

Nechkov, Anne McLaughlin (Stylist)
559 Fieldstream Blvd
Orlando, FL 32825, USA

Neck, Tommy (Athlete, Football Player)
2107 Marie Pl
Monroe, LA 71201, USA

Neckar, Stanislav (Athlete, Hockey Player)
10255 Waterside Oaks Dr
Tampa, FL 33647-3194, USA

Necker, Stanislav (Athlete, Hockey Player)
10255 Waterside Oaks Dr.
Tampa, FL 33647, USA

Ned, Derrick (Athlete, Football Player)
430 Charles St
Eunice, LA 70535, USA

Nedeljakova, Barbara (Actor)
Beverly Hecht Agency
c/o Robert Depp
3500 W Olive Ave Ste 1180
Burbank, CA 91505, USA

Nedney, Joe (Athlete, Football Player)
121 Lauren Cir
Scotts Valley, CA 95066, USA

Nedomansky, Vaclav (Athlete, Hockey Player)
6600 Beachview Dr Apt 204
Rancho Palos Verdes, CA 90275-5840, USA

Nedorost, Vaclav (Athlete, Hockey Player)
1 Panthers Pkwy
Sunrise, FL 33323, USA

Nedved, Petr (Athlete, Hockey Player)
11230 110th St
Edmonton, AB T5G 3H7, Canada

Needham, Connie (Actor)
2000 Corporate Dr
Apt 202
Ladera Ranch, CA 92694-1109, USA

Needham, Hal (Director)
Laura Lizer Assoc
PO Box 46609
Los Angeles, CA 90046, USA

Needham, James J (Business Person)
97 Coopers Farm Road
#1
Southampton, NY 11968, USA

Needham, Tracey (Actor)
c/o Tony Chargin *Ovation Management*
12028 National Blvd
Los Angeles, CA 90064, USA

Needleman, Jacob (Misc)
841 Wawona Ave
Oakland, CA 94610, USA

Neel, Roy (Politician)
3307 Northampton St NW
Washington, DC 20015-1652, USA

Neel, Troy (Athlete, Baseball Player)
P.O. Box 1582
El Campo, TX 77437-1582, USA

Neelu (Actor)
G-5 Madhuram Flats Ururalagat Kuppam
5th Avenue
Besant Nagar
Chennai, TN 600 090, INDIA

Neely, Bob (Athlete, Hockey Player)
72 Squire Bakers Lane
Markham, ON L3P 3H2, CANADA

Neely, Cam (Athlete, Hockey Player)
Boston Bruins 100 Legends Way Ste 250
Attn Office Of The President
Boston, MA 02114-1389, United States

Neely, Cam (Athlete, Hockey Player)
76 Davison Dr
Lincoln, MA 01773-2216, USA

Neely, Gina (Television Host)
Neely's Bar-b-que
5700 Mt Moriah
Memphis, TN 38115, USA

Neely, Patrick (Pat) (Television Host)
Neely's Bar-b-que
5700 Mt. Moriah
Memphis, TN 38115, USA

Neely, Ralph E (Athlete, Football Player)
6943 Sperry St
Dallas, TX 75214, USA

Neely Jr, Mark E (Historian)
Oxford University Press
198 Madison Ave
New York, NY 10016, USA

Neeman, Cal (Athlete, Baseball Player)
93 Champagne Dr
Lake Saint Louis, MO 63367-1604, USA

Ne'eman, Yuval (Physicist)
Tel-Aviv University
Physics/Astronomy Dept
Tel-Aviv 69978, ISRAEL

Neeson, Liam (Actor)
c/o Alan Nierob *Rogers & Cowan PR (LA)*
Pacific Design Center
8687 Melrose Ave, 7th Floor
West Hollywood, CA 90069, USA

Nef, John U (Historian)
2726 N St NW
Washington, DC 20007, USA

Nef, Sonia (Skier)
Halten 345
Grub 9035, SWITZERLAND

Neff, Bob (Athlete, Football Player)
2 Crestview
Athens, TX 75751, USA

Neff, Francine I (Government Official)
P.O. Box 1498
Pena Blanca, NM 87041-1498, USA

Neff, Lucas (Actor)
c/o Jason Weinberg *Untitled
Entertainment (LA)*
350 S. Beverly Dr #200
Beverly Hills, CA 90212, USA

Neff, Steve (Bowler)
3655 S Sun coast Blvd
Homosassa, FL 34448-2625, USA

Neff, William D (Psychic)
2080 Hideaway Court
Morris, IL 60450, USA

Negishi, Takashi (Economist)
2-10-5-301 Motoazabu
Minatoku
Tokyo 106, JAPAN

Neglshi, Ei-Ishi (Nobel Prize Laureate)
50 Carrington Ct
West Lafayette, IN 47906-8802, USA

Negoesco, Stephen (Coach)
University of San Francisco
Athletic Dept
San Francisco, CA 94117, USA

Negray, Ron (Athlete, Baseball Player)
587 W Nimisila Rd
Akron, OH 44319-4616, USA

Negreanu, Daniel (Actor)
PO Box 416
2251 North Rampart Blvd
Las Vegas, NV 89123, USA

Negron, Chuck (Musician)
c/o Staff Member *Mitch Schneider
Organization (MSO)*
14724 Ventura Blvd #410
Sherman Oaks, CA 91403, USA

Negron, Taylor
8447 Wilshire Blvd. #206
Beverly Hills, CA 90211-3246

Negroponte, John D (Diplomat)
US State Department
2201 C St NW
Washington, DC 20520, USA

Negroponte, Nicholas (Engineer)
69 Mount Vernon St
Boston, MA 02108, USA

Nehamas, Alexander (Misc)
Princeton University
Philosophy Dept
Princeton, NJ 08544, USA

Nehemiah, Renaldo (Athlete, Football
Player)
1751 Pinnacle Dr
Suite 1500
Mc Lean, VA 22102, USA

Neher, Erwin (Nobel Prize Laureate)
Max-Pianck-Institut fur Biophysikalische
Chemie Am Fassberg 11
Goettingen D-37077, GERMANY

Nehmer, Meinhard (Athlete)
Vamkevitz
Altenkirchen 18556, GERMANY

Neibauer, Gary (Athlete, Baseball Player)
146 Delta Ave
Bismarck, ND 58504-6655, USA

Neibhors, William (Athlete, Football
Player)
1904 Chippendale Dr SE
Huntsville, AL 35801, USA

Neid, Silvia (Soccer Player)
Betramstr 18
Frankfurt/Main 60320, GERMANY

Neidert, John (Athlete, Football Player)
4731 Placid Cir
Sarasota, FL 34231, USA

Neidich, Charles (Musician)
Colbert Artists
111 W 57th St
New York, NY 10019, USA

Neidlinger, Jim (Athlete, Baseball Player)
139 Sunset Dr
Burlington, VT 05408-1910, USA

Neiger, Al (Athlete, Baseball Player)
213 Pinehurst Rd
Wilmington, DE 19803-3125, USA

Neil, Andrew F (Editor)
Glenbum Enterprises
PO Box 584
London SW7 3QY, UNITED KINGDOM
(UK)

Neil, Hildegarde (Actor)
Vernon Conway
5 Spring St
London W2 3RA, UNITED KINGDOM
(UK)

Neil, Ray (Baseball Player)
Ethiopian Clowns
250 N Wells Ave Apt 511
Benton Harbor, MI 49022-7735, USA

Neil, Vince (Composer, Musician)
c/o Darren Prince *Prince Marketing
Group*
18 Carillon Cir
Livingston, NJ 07039, USA

Neil, Warden (Stylist)
367 N Laurel Ave
Los Angeles, CA 90048, USA

Neill, Mary Gardner (Director)
Seattle Art Museum
Volunteer Park
Seattle, WA 98112, USA

Neill, Mike (Athlete, Baseball Player,
Olympic Athlete)
17 Cape May Pt
Greensboro, NC 27455-1363, USA

Neill, Noel (Actor)
331 Sage Lane
Santa Monica, CA 90402

Neill, Rolfe (Publisher)
Charlotte News-Observer
600 S Tryon St
Charlotte, NC 28202, USA

Neill, Sam (Actor)
c/o Ann Churchill-Brown *Shanahan
Management*
Level 3 Berman House
Surry Hills 2010, AUSTRALIA

Neill, Ve (Stylist)
306254 Hasley Cyn Rd.
Castaic, CA 91384, USA

Neill, William M (Athlete, Football Player)
34 Gibbs Dr
Wayne, NJ 07470, USA

Neils, Steve (Athlete, Football Player)
1329 Waterford Rd
Woodbury, MN 55125, USA

Neilson, Jim (Athlete, Hockey Player)
907-525 St Mary Ave
Winnipeg, MB R3C 3X3, Canada

Neilson-Bell, Sandra (Swimmer)
3101 Mistyglen Circle
Austin, TX 78746, USA

Nein, Max (Scientist)
1528 Chandler Rd SE
Huntsville, AL 35801-1476, USA

Neinas, Charles M (Chuck) (Misc)
5344 Westridge Dr
Boulder, CO 80301, USA

Neis, Reagan Dale (Actor)
c/o Susan Curtis *Curtis Talent
Management*
9607 Arby Dr
Beverly Hills, CA 90210, USA

Neison, Chuck (Athlete, Baseball Player)
8681 Carriage Hill Draw
Savage, MN 55378, USA

Neizvestny, Ernst I (Artist)
81 Grand St
New York, NY 10013, USA

Nelkin, Stacey
2770 Hutton Dr.
Beverly Hills, CA 90210-1216

Nelligan, Kate (Actor)
c/o Gary Gersh *Innovative Artists (NY)*
235 Park Ave S
7th Floor
New York, NY 10003, USA

Nellis, William J (Physicist)
Lawrence Livermore Laboratory
7000 East St
Livermore, CA 94550, USA

Nellssen, Roelof J (Financier, Government
Official)
PO Box 552
AN Laren 1250, NETHERLANDS

Nelms, Michael (Mike) (Athlete, Football
Player)
11331 Fawn Lake Pkwy
Spotsylvania, VA 22551-4665, USA

Nelsen, Bill (Athlete, Football Player)
13512 Dornoch Dr
Orlando, FL 32828, USA

Nelson
15003 Greenleaf St
Sherman Oaks, CA 91403

Nelson, Al (Athlete, Football Player)
660 Boas St
Apt 918
Harrisburg, PA 17102, USA

Nelson, Andy (Athlete, Football Player)
12251 Manor Rd
Glen Arm, MD 21057, USA

Nelson, Ben (Politician)
9738 Fieldcrest Dr
Omaha, NE 68114-4933, USA

Nelson, Bob (Baseball Player)
Baltimore Orioles
10830 Wallbrook Dr
Dallas, TX 75238-2943, USA

Nelson, Brad (Athlete, Baseball Player)
1405 210th St
Algona, IA 50511, USA

Nelson, Bry (Athlete, Baseball Player)
11 Campden Hill Rd
Sherwood, AR 72120-6536, USA

Nelson, Cailin (Physicist)
Lawrence Livermore Laboratory
7000 East Ave
Livermore, CA 94550, USA

Nelson, Charles L (Athlete, Football
Player)
3028 162nd Pl SE
Mill Creek, WA 98012, USA

Nelson, Charlie (Athlete, Baseball Player,
Olympic Athlete)
11205 Kinsley Street
Eden Prairie, MN 55344-1826, USA

Nelson, Cindy (Athlete, Olympic Athlete,
Skier)
PO Box 1699
0171 Larkspur Lane
Vail, CO 81658-1699, USA

Nelson, Colette (Fitness Expert, Model)
PO Box 1122
Seaford, NY 11783, USA

Nelson, Cordner (Misc)
USA Track & Field
4341 Starlight Dr
Indianapolis, IN 46239, USA

Nelson, Craig Richard (Actor)
Borinstein Oreck Bogart
3172 Dona Susana Dr
Studio City, CA 91604, USA

Nelson, Craig T (Actor)
c/o Connie Tavel *Forward Entertainment*
9255 Sunset Blvd
Suite 805
Los Angeles, CA 90069, USA

Nelson, Darrin (Athlete, Football Player)
215 Marianne Ct
Mountain View, CA 94040, USA

Nelson, Dave (Athlete, Baseball Player)
12213 Clubhouse Dr
Bradenton, FL 34202, USA

Nelson, David (Stylist)
c/o Staff Member *Clutts Agency, The*
1400 Turtle Creek Blvd
#171
Dallas, TX 75207, USA

Nelson, David A (Judge)
US Court of Appeals
Courthouse Building
425 Walnut St
Cincinnati, OH 45202, USA

Nelson, Deborah (Journalist)
Seattle Times
Editorial Dept
1120 John St
Seattle, WA 98109, USA

Nelson, Dennis (Athlete, Football Player)
6098 E 2370 St
Kewanee, Illinois 61443, USA

Nelson, Derrie (Athlete, Football Player)
7790 S Marian Rd
Hastings, NE 68901, USA

Nelson, Diane (Horse Racer)
24 S Howell Ave
Farmingville, NY 11738-1116, USA

Nelson, Dick (Athlete, Baseball Player)
102 N Maple St
Enfield, CT 06082, USA

Nelson, Don
2284 S Kihei Rd
Kihei, HI 96753-8632, USA

Nelson, Donald A (Nellie) (Basketball
Player, Coach)
Dallas Mavericks
2909 Taylor St
Dallas, TX 75226, USA

Nelson, Dorothy W (Judge)
US Court of Appeals
125 S Grand Ave
Pasadena, CA 91105, USA

Nelson, Drew (Actor)
c/o Staff Member *Select Artists Ltd (CA-
Westside Office)*
1138 12th Street
Suite 1
Santa Monica, CA 90403, USA

Nelson, Ed (Athlete, Football Player)
7647 Westlake Rd
Sterlington, LA 71280, USA

Nelson, Gene (Athlete, Baseball Player)
36131 Pine Bluff Loop
Dade City, FL 33525-9527, USA

Nelson, George D (Astronaut)
AAAS Project
1200 New York Ave NW
#100
Washington, DC 20005, USA

Nelson, George D Dr (Astronaut)
1543 Toledo Ct
Bellingham, WA 98229-5375, USA

Nelson, Gunnar
13030 Valleyheart Dr. #105
Studio City, CA 91604

Nelson, Haywood "Butch" (Athlete,
Football Player)
697 Salter Rd
Luverne, AL 36049-5749, USA

Nelson, Jameer (Athlete, Basketball
Player)
c/o Staff Member *Cornerstone
Management*
944 County Line Road
Bryn Mawr, PA 19010, USA

Nelson, James E (Religious Leader)
Baha i Faith
536 Sheridan Road
Wilmette, IL 60091, USA

Nelson, Jamie (Athlete, Baseball Player)
Princeton Devil Rays
1602 Spring Creek Ave
Springdale, AR 72764-7847, USA

Nelson, Janet (Stylist)
311 N Robertson
#777
Beverly Hills, CA 90211, USA

Nelson, Jeff (Athlete, Hockey Player)
249 Simon Rd
Waldoboro, ME 04572-5716, USA

Nelson, Jeff (Athlete, Baseball Player)
5846 Pine Brook Farm Rd
Sykesville, MD 21784-8679, USA

Nelson, Jeff (Athlete, Baseball Player)
323 289th Pl NE
Carnation, WA 98014, USA

Nelson, Jerry E (Astronomer, Physicist)
University of California
Astronomy Dept
Berkeley, CA 94720, USA

Nelson, Jimmy
10404 Greenhaven Parkway
Brecksville, OH 44141-1625

Nelson, Joe (Athlete, Baseball Player)
2407 Azure Cir
West Palm Beach, FL 33410-2521, USA

Nelson, John Allen (Actor)
c/o Cynthia Booth *Global Artists Agency*
6253 Hollywood Blvd
Suite 508
Los Angeles, CA 90028, USA

Nelson, John R (Misc)
1111 Hermann Dr
#19A
Houston, TX 77004, USA

Nelson, John W
Astrid Schoerke
Monckebergallee 41
Hanover 30453, GERMANY

Nelson, Judd (Actor)
c/o Jean-Pierre (JP) Henraux *Henraux
Management*
Prefers to be contacted by telephone
CA, USA

Nelson, Judith (Opera Singer)
2600 Buena Vista Way
Berkeley, CA 94708, USA

Nelson, Karl (Athlete, Football Player)
58 Woodland Rd
Montvale, NJ 07645, USA

Nelson, Kent C (Business Person)
United Parcel Service
55 Glenlake Parkway NE
Atlanta, GA 30328, USA

Nelson, Kirsten (Actor)
c/o Staff Member *Meghan Schumacher
Management*
13351-D Riverside Dr #387
Sherman Oaks, CA 91423, USA

Nelson, Kristin (Stylist)
14918 Dancers Image
San Antonio, TX 78248, USA

Nelson, Larry (Athlete, Golfer)
421 Oakmont Cir SE
Marietta, GA 30067-4819, USA

Nelson, Lee (Athlete, Football Player)
4178 Summit Way
Marietta, GA 30066, USA

Nelson, Lori (Actor)
19558 Pine Valley Ave
Northridge, CA 91326, USA

Nelson, Marilyn Carison (Business Person)
Carlson Companies
Carlson Parkway
PO Box 59159
Minneapolis, MN 55459, USA

Nelson, Mary (Athlete, Baseball Player)
4222 Katrina Ln
San Antonio, TX 78222-2712, USA

Nelson, Matthew
12344 Moorpark St. #4
Studio City, CA 91604

Nelson, Mel (Athlete, Baseball Player)
27420 Fisher St
Highland, CA 92346-3251, USA

Nelson, Prince Rogers (Prince) (Actor,
Director, Musician)
c/o Staff Member *Marshall Arts Ltd*
P.O. Box 66142
London NW1W 8PA, UK

Nelson, Ralph A (Misc)
Carle Foundation Hospital
611 W Park St
Urbana, IL 61801, USA

Nelson, Richard (Baseball Player)
104 Montgomery Ln
Perryville, AR 72126-8114, USA

Nelson, Ricky (Baseball Player)
Seattle Mariners
2599 E Desert Broom Pl
Chandler, AZ 85286-2464, USA

Nelson, Rob (Athlete, Baseball Player)
312 Alta Vista Ave
South Pasadena, CA 91030-3502, USA

Nelson, Roger (Athlete, Baseball Player)
4113 Limerick Dr
Lake Wales, FL 33859-5748, USA

Nelson, Ron (Athlete, Basketball Player)
1550 Eagle Ridge Ln NE
Albuquerque, NM 87122-1187, USA

Nelson, Scott (Athlete, Baseball Player)
811 Overlook Dr
Coshocton, OH 43812-8813, USA

Nelson, Scott (Baseball Player)
811 Overlook Dr
Coshocton, OH 43812-9107, USA

Nelson, Shane (Athlete, Football Player)
559 Carmel Dr
Sandia, TX 78383, USA

Nelson, Terry (Athlete, Football Player)
3393 Highway 51 N
Arkadelphia, AR 71923, USA

Nelson, Tim Blake (Actor, Director)
c/o Amy Guenther *Gateway Management
Company Inc*
860 Via De La Paz
Suite F10
Pacific Palisades, CA 90272, USA

Nelson, Todd (Athlete, Hockey Player)
Oklahoma City Barons
501 N Walker Ave Ste 140
Attn Coaching Staff
Oklahoma City, OK 73102-1233, USA

Nelson, Tracy (Actor)
c/o James Kellem *JKA Talent*
12725 Ventura Blvd
Suite H
Studio City, CA 91604, USA

Nelson, William (Bill) (Politician)
3000 Rocky Point Rd
Malabar, FL 32950-4613, USA

Nelson, Willie (Musician, Songwriter)
12400 St Hwy 71 W
Suite 350
Austin, TX 78738, USA

Nelson Jr, J Bryon (Golfer)
Fairway Ranch
RR 2 Box 5 Litsey Road
Roanoke, TX 76262, USA

Nelson-Walker, Doris (Baseball Player)
7887 N 16th St Unit 129
Phoenix, AZ 85020-4453, USA

Nemchinov, Sergei (Athlete, Hockey
Player)
53 Walker Ave
Rye, NY 10580-1219, USA

Nemcova, Petra (Model)
c/o Michael Samonte *Sunshine, Sachs &
Associates - LA*
8409 Santa Monica Blvd
West Hollywood, CA 90069, USA

Nemec, Corin (Actor)
859 N Hollywood Way
#104
Burbank, CA 91505, USA

Nemechek, Joe (Race Car Driver)
Ginn Racing
128 S. Iredelle Industrial Park
Mooresville, NC 29116, USA

Nemechek, III, Joseph Frank (Race Car
Driver)
128 S. Iredell Industrial Park
Mooresville, NC 28115, USA

Nemelka, Richard (Athlete, Basketball
Player)
6108 S 1300 E
Salt Lake City, UT 84121, USA

Nemeth, Miklos (Prime Minister)
European Reconstruction Bank
1 Exchange Square
London EC2A 2EH, UNITED KINGDOM
(UK)

Nemov, AlekseiRGF
Lujnetskaya Nabereunaya 8
Moscow, RUSSIA 119.270

Nemov, Alexei (Gymnast)
Gymnastics Federation
Lujnetskaya Nabereynaya 8
Moscow 119270, RUSSIA

Nen, Dick (Athlete, Baseball Player)
48 Via Larcaza
Trabuco Canyon, CA 92679-4831, USA

Nen, Robb (Athlete, Baseball Player)
JD Legends Promotions
10808 Foothill Blvd #160-454
Rancho Cucamonga, CA 91730-3889,
USA

Nenez, Clemente (Baseball Player)
6433 Blackberry Pl
Riverside, CA 92505-2205, USA

Nennerman, Richard A (Editor)
PO Box 992
East Brunswick, NJ 08816, USA

Nenninger, Eric (Actor)
c/o Lena Roklin *Luber Roklin
Management*
8530 Wilshire Blvd
6th Floor
Beverly Hills, CA 90211, USA

Nepoleon (Actor)
12/5 Sandilya Apartments Jagathambal
Colony
II Street Royapettah
Chennai, TN 600 014, INDIA

Nepote, Jean (Lawyer)
26 Rue Armengaud
92210 Saint-Cloud
Hauts-de-Seine, FRANCE

N*E*R*D (Music Group)
c/o Staff Member *Paradigm (Monterey)*
404 W Franklin St
Monterey, CA 93940, USA

NERD (Music Group)
c/o Amanda Silverman *42West (NY)*
220 W 42nd St
12th Floor
New York, NY 10036, USA

Nerette, Joseph (Judge, President)
Supreme Court
Chief Justice's Office
Port-au-Prince, HAITI

Neri, Francesca (Actor)
c/o Philip Button *WME (LA)*
9601 Wilshire Blvd Fl 3
Beverly Hills, CA 90210, USA

Neri Vela, Rodolfo Dr (Astronaut)
Playa Copacabana 131
Col Militar Marte, DF 08830, Mexico

Nerl, Manuel (Artist)
greg Kucera Gallery
212 3rd Ave S
Seattle, WA 98104, USA

Nerlove, Marc L (Economist)
University of Maryland
Agricultural/Resource Economics
College Park, MD 20742, USA

Nerl Vela, Rodolfo (Astronaut)
Playa Copacabana 131
Col Marte
Mexico City, DF 08830, MEXICO

Nerman, Maxens (Actor)
Continent II
62, Rue des Grands Champs
75020, PARIS

Nero, Franco ((Actor)
c/o Camilla Fluxman-Pines *Muse Management*
1541 Ocean Ave.
Suite 200
Santa Monica, CA 90401, USA

Nero, Haley (Actor)
c/o Staff Member *Charlie's Talent Agency*
1350 Old Skokie Rd #202
Highland Park, IL 60035, USA

Nero, Peter (Musician)
202 Hidden Acres Lane
Media, PA 19063, USA

Nerud, John (Horse Racer)
19 Pound Hollow Road
Glen Head, NY 11545-2209, USA

Nesbit, Jamar (Athlete, Football Player)
4083 Richmond Park Dr E
Jacksonville, FL 32224, USA

Nesbitt, James (Actor)
c/o Staff Member *Yakety Yak*
8-A Bloomsbury Sq
London WC1A 2NE, UNITED KINGDOM
(UK)

Nesbitt-Wisham, Mary (Athlete, Baseball
Player)
PO Box 194
Hollister, FL 32147-0194, USA

Neserovic, Radoslav (Basketball Player)
San Antonio Spurs
Alamodome
1 SBC Center
San Antonio, TX 78219, USA

Neshek, Pat (Athlete, Baseball Player)
6745 Angeles Dr
Melbourne Beach, FL 32951, USA

Nesher, Avi (Director)
Gersh Agency
232 N Canon Dr
Beverly Hills, CA 90210, USA

Nesic, Alex (Actor)
c/o Staff Member *Principato/Young
Management*
9465 Wilshire Blvd
Suite 430
Beverly Hills, CA 90212, USA

Nesmith, Michael (Mike) (Musician)
Videoranch
8 Harris Court
#C1
Monterey, CA 93940, USA

Nespoli, Paolo (Astronaut)
2011 Dawn Crest Ct
League City, TX 77573-3931, USA

Nespral, Charo (Stylist)
c/o Staff Member *Illusions Management*
129 W 27th St
Penthouse
New York, NY 10001, USA

Nespral, Jackie (Correspondent)
NBC-TV
News Dept
30 Rockefeller Plaza
New York, NY 10112, USA

Ness, Norman F (Scientist)
9 Wilkinson Dr
Landenberg, PA 19350-9359, USA

Ness, Rick (Musician)
Metropolitan Entertainment Group
2 Penn Plaza
#2600
New York, NY 10121, USA

Nessen, Ronald H (Ron) (Politician)
1835 K St NW Ste 805
Washington, DC 20006-1203, USA

Nesterenko, Eric (Athlete, Hockey Player)
PO Box 1025
Vail, CO 81658-102S, USA

Nesterenko, Evgeny Y (Opera Singer)
Fruzenskaya Nab 24 Korp 1
#178
Moscow 119146, RUSSIA

Nestorowicz, Victoria (Actor)
c/o Staff Member *Noble Caplan Abrams*
1260 Yonge St
2nd Floor
Toronto, ON M4T 1W6, Canada

Netanyahu, Benjamin (Politician)
38 Rehou King George
Tel Aviv 61231, Israel

Netherland, Joseph H (Business Person)
FMC Corp
200 E Randolph Dr
Chicago, IL 60601, USA

Netherton, Tom (Musician)
Germantown Performing Arts Centre
1801 Exeter Road
Germantown, TN 38138, USA

Netolicky, Bob (Athlete, Basketball Player)
PO Box 531
Carmel, IN 46082-0531, USA

Netravali, Arun N (Engineer)
10 Byron Court
Westfield, NJ 07090, USA

Nett, Robert B (War Hero)
5417 Kessington Dr
Columbus, GA 31907, USA

Nettles, Doug (Athlete, Football Player)
13105 Quail Creek Ct
Silver Spring, MD 20904, USA

Nettles, Graig (Athlete, Baseball Player)
4255 Parris Dr
Lenoir City, TN 37772-3947, USA

Nettles, Jennifer (Musician)
c/o Gail Gellman *Gail Gellman
Management*
23852 Pacific Coast Highway
Malibu, CA 90265, USA

Nettles, Jim (Athlete, Football Player)
3817 Mandeville Canyon Rd
Los Angeles, CA 90049, USA

Nettles, Jim (Athlete, Baseball Player)
4632 N Darien Dr
Tacoma, WA 98407-1212, USA

Nettles, John (Actor)
Saraband Assoc
265 Liverpool Road
London N1 1LX, UNITED KINGDOM
(UK)

Nettles, Morris (Athlete, Baseball Player)
551 1/2 San Juan Ave
Venice, CA 90291-5643, USA

Neu, Mike (Athlete, Baseball Player)
406 Fraga Ct
Martinez, CA 94553-6812, USA

Neubeck, Francis G (Astronaut)
4702 Arnold Loop
Las Vegas, NV 89115-2370, USA

Neubert, Keith
10000 Santa Monica Blvd. #305
Los Angeles, CA 90067

Neufeld, Elizabeth F (Scientist)
2008 Linda Flora Dr
Los Angeles, CA 90077-1407, USA

Neufeld, Ray (Athlete, Hockey Player)
3919 Henderson Hwy
Winnipeg, MB R2G 1P4, Canada

Neufeld, Ryan (Athlete, Football Player)
625 Spring Hill Dr
Morgan Hill, CA 95037, USA

Neugebauer, Marcia (Physicist)
7519 S Elliot Lane
Tucson, AZ 85747, USA

Neugebauer, Nick (Athlete, Baseball
Player)
101 S Sahuaro Dr
Gilbert, AZ 85233-5927, USA

Neugebauer, Randy (Congressman,
Politician)
1424 Kibgwirth HOB
Washington, DC 20515, USA

Neuharth, Allen H (Publisher)
Freedom Dorum
1101 Wilson Blvd
Arlington, VA 22209, USA

Neuheisel, Richard (Rick) (Athlete,
Coach, Football Coach, Football Player)
3601 Winding Creek Rd
Sacramento, CA 95864, USA

Neumann, Liselotte (Athlete, Golfer)
11003 Muirfield Dr
Rancho Mirage, CA 92270, USA

Neumann, Peter (Athlete, Football Player)
31 Frederick St
St Catharines, ON L2S 2S5, Canada

Neumann, Wolfgang (Opera Singer)
Opera et Concert
Maximilianstr 22
Munich 80539, GERMANY

Neumark, Julie
900 E. First St. #314
Los Angeles, CA 90012

Neumeier, Dan (Athlete, Baseball Player)
N2635 County Road V
Lodi, WI 53555-1568, USA

Neumeier, John (Choreographer)
Hamburg Ballet
54 Caspar-Voght-Str
Hamburg 20535, GERMANY

Neuner, Doris (Athlete)
6024 Innsbruck
AUSTRIA

Neustadt, Richard (Politician)
1010 Memorial Dr
Cambridge, MA 02138-4859, USA

Neuwelt, Edward A (Misc)
Oregon Health Sciences University
Neurology Dept
Portland, OR 97201, USA

Neuwirth, Bebe (Actor)
c/o Risa Shapiro *Schiff Company, The*
9465 Wilshire Blvd
Suite 480
Beverly Hills, CA 90212, USA

Neverett, Tim (Sportscaster)
5730 Rex Norrev Dr
Gibsonia, PA 15044-9720, USA

Nevett, Elijah (Athlete, Football Player)
931 30th St N
Bessemer, AL 35020, USA

Nevil, Bobbie
20 Manchester Sq
London W1M 5AE, ENGLAND

Neville, Aaron (Musician)
c/o Marc Allen *Red Light Management
(VA)*
PO Box 1467
Charlottesville, VA 22902, USA

Neville, Arthel (Correspondent, Television
Host)
1840 Victory Blvd
Glendale, CA 91201, USA

Neville, Bill (Cartoonist)
506 Oakdale Road
Jamestown, NC 27282, USA

Neville, John
506 Oakdale Rd
Jamestown, NC 27282-9214, USA

Neville, John (Actor, Director)
139 Winnett Ave
Toronto, ON M6C 3L7, CANADA

Neville, Katherine (Writer)
PO Box 788
Warrenton, VA 20188, USA

Neville, Robert C (Misc)
Boston University
Theology School
Boston, MA 02215, USA

Neville, Thomas O (Athlete, Football
Player)
P.O. Box 11175
Montgomery, AL 36111, USA

Nevin, Bob (Athlete, Hockey Player)
Soupy's Tavern
Soupy's Tavern 376 Dundas St E
Toronto, ON M5A 2A5, Canada

Nevin, Brooke (Actor)
c/o Suzanne (Sue) Wohl *TalentWorks (LA)*
3500 W Olive Ave
Suite 1400
Burbank, CA 91505, USA

Nevin, Kaleigh (Actor)
3SG Talent Management
c/o Mary Swinton
LL7 45 Charles St E
Toronto, ON M4Y 1S2, CANADA

Nevin, Phil (Athlete, Baseball Player, Olympic Athlete)
18795 Heritage Dr
Poway, CA 92064-6643, USA

Nevins, Claudette (Actor)
Gold Marshak Liedtke
3500 W Olive Ave
#1400
Burbank, CA 91505, USA

Nevins, Sheila (Business Person, Producer)
c/o Staff Member *Home Box Office (HBO-LA)*
2500 Broadway Ste 400
Santa Monica, CA 90404, USA

Nevinson, Nancy
23 Mill Close Fishbourne
Chichester, ENGLAND

Nevitt, Chuck (Athlete, Basketball Player)
3124 Cartwright Dr
Raleigh, NC 27612-2113, USA

Newark, Samantha (Musician)
c/o Arlene Thornton *Arlene Thornton & Associates*
12711 Ventura Blvd
Suite 490
Studio City, CA 91604, USA

Newbern, George (Actor)
c/o Paul Kohner *Kohner Agency, The*
9300 Wilshire Blvd
Suite 555
Beverly Hills, CA 90212, USA

Newberry, Bob (Race Car Driver)
key Prts Racing
5835 Mariaville Rd
Schenectady, NY 12306, USA

Newberry, Jeremy (Athlete, Football Player)
2525 Sunset Rd
Brentwood, CA 94513, USA

Newberry, Thomas (Tom) (Athlete, Football Player)
224 Tarpon St
Tavernier, FL 33070, USA

Newbigging, William (Publisher)
Edmonton Journal
10006 101st St
Edmonton, AB T5J 2S6, CANADA

Newbill, Ivano (Athlete, Basketball Player)
4147 4th Ave
Los Angeles, CA 90008-3901, USA

Newble, Ira
1916 Long Pointe Dr
Bloomfield Hills, MI 48302-0743, USA

Newborn, Ira (Composer)
Vangelos Mgmt
15233 Ventura Blvd
#200
Sherman Oaks, CA 91403, USA

Newbrough, Ashley (Actor)
c/o William Mercer *Thruline Entertainment*
9250 Wilshire Blvd
Ground Fl
Beverly Hills, CA 90212, USA

Newburn, George
PO Box 5617
Beverly Hills, CA 90210

Newcomb, Gerry (Artist)
7029 17th Ave NW
Seattle, WA 98117, USA

Newcomb, Jonathan (Publisher)
35 Pierrepont St
Brooklyn, NY 11201, USA

Newcomb, Mike (Radio Personality)
OnSecondThought
4927 East Palo Brea Ln
Cave Creek, AZ 85331, USA

Newcombe, Don (Athlete, Baseball Player)
c/o Karen Newcombe
Don Newcombe Jr 690 Hahaione St
Honolulu, HI 96825-1060, USA

Newcombe, John (Athlete, Tennis Player)
325 Mission Valley Rd
New Braunfels, TX 78131-0469, USA

Newcomer, Carrie (Musician)
PO Box 5653
Bloomington, IN 47407, USA

New Edition (Music Group)
c/o Amy Malone *GIC Public Relations*
Prefers to be contacted via email or telephone
Los Angeles, CA 90069, USA

Newell, Horner E (Physicist)
2567 Nicky Lane
Alexandria, VA 22311, USA

Newell, James
20519 Rodax St.
Canoga Park, CA 91306

Newell, Mike (Actor, Director, Producer)
c/o Staff Member *50 Cannon Entertainment*
Oxford House
76 Oxford St
London W1D 1BS, UNITED KINGDOM (UK)

Newell, Rick (Athlete, Hockey Player)
5223 N 24th St
Phoenix, AZ 85016-3590, USA

Newell, Tom (Athlete, Baseball Player)
9525 Cordoba St
Sparks, NV 89441-5569, USA

Newfield, Heidi (Musician)
c/o Staff Member *Red Light Management (LA)*
8439 W Sunset Blvd
Suite 2
Los Angeles, CA 90069, USA

Newfield, Marc (Athlete, Baseball Player)
1717 N Los Robles Ave
Pasadena, CA 91104-1051, USA

Newgard, Christopher (Misc)
Southwestern Medical Center
Biochemistry Dept
Dallas, TX 75237, USA

New Grass Revival
PO Box 128037
Nashville, TN 37212

Newhan, David (Athlete, Baseball Player)
2125 Walnut Ln
Vista, CA 92084-7716, USA

Newhan, Ross (Sportscaster)
2678 Harvest Crest Ln
Corona, CA 92881-3572, USA

Newhart, Bob (Actor, Comedian)
420 Amapola Ln
Los Angeles, CA 90077, USA

Newhauser, Don (Athlete, Baseball Player)
321 Sheryl Dr
Deltona, FL 32738-8441, USA

Newhouse, Bob
6847 Truxton
Dallas, TX 75231

Newhouse, Donald E (Publisher)
Advance Publications
950 W Fingerboard Road
Staten Island, NY 10305, USA

Newhouse, Fred
816 Bantry Way
Benicia, CA 94510

Newhouse, Fredrick (Fred) (Athlete, Track Athlete)
3003 Pine Lake Trail
Houston, TX 77068, USA

Newhouse, Robert F (Athlete, Football Player)
6847 Truxton Dr
Dallas, TX 75231, USA

Newhouse Jr, Samuel I (Publisher)
Advance Publications
950 W Fingerboard Road
Staten Island, NY 10305, USA

New Kids on the Block (NKOTB) (Music Group)
c/o Staff Member *Interscope Records (LA) - Main*
2220 Colorado Ave
Santa Monica, CA 90404, USA

Newkirk, Scott (Stylist)
c/o Staff Member *Art Department*
48 Greene St
4th Floor
New York, NY 10013, USA

Newland, Bob (Athlete, Football Player)
3895 Vine Maple St
Eugene, OR 97405, USA

Newlin, Mike (Athlete, Basketball Player)
1414 Horseshoe Dr
Sugar Land, TX 77478-3464, USA

Newman, Al (Athlete, Baseball Player)
Newmie's Rewards
15240 Fairlawn Shores Trl SE
Prior Lake, MN 55372-1940, USA

Newman, Alan (Athlete, Baseball Player)
24 Rice Ln
Dry Prong, LA 71423-8742, USA

Newman, Alec (Actor)
c/o Laina Cohn *Laina Cohn Management*
15066 Sutton St
Sherman Oaks, CA 91403, USA

Newman, Anthony (Conductor, Musician)
I C M Artists
40 W 57th St
New York, NY 10019, USA

Newman, Barry (Actor)
c/o Dick Delson *Dick Delson & Associates*
4520 Bakman Ave
Studio City, CA 91602, USA

Newman, Dan (Athlete, Hockey Player)
192 E County Road
27 RR 1
Cottam, ON NOR 1BO, Canada

Newman, Edward K (Ed) (Athlete, Football Player)
10100 SW 140th St
Miami, FL 33176, USA

Newman, James H (Astronaut)
Naval Post Graduate School
1 University Cir
Attn Nasa Visiting Professor
Monterey, CA 93943-5098, USA

Newman, Jeff (Athlete, Baseball Player, Coach)
10133 N 103rd St
Scottsdale, AZ 85258-4953, USA

Newman, Jimmy C (Musician, Songwriter, Writer)
RR2
Christiana, TN 37037, USA

Newman, Johnny (Athlete, Basketball Player)
Dallas Mavericks
3720 Favero Rd
Henrico, VA 23233-7037, USA

Newman, Jon O (Judge)
US Court of Appeals
450 Main St
Hartford, CT 06103, USA

Newman, Josh (Athlete, Baseball Player)
5909 Canyon Creek Dr
Dublin, OH 43016-7419, USA

Newman, Kevin (Correspondent)
ABC-TV
News Dept
77 W 66th St
New York, NY 10023, USA

Newman, Kyle (Director)
c/o Staff Member *United Talent Agency (UTA)*
9336 Civic Center Dr
Beverly Hills, CA 90210, USA

Newman, Laraine (Actor, Comedian)
c/o Staff Member *TalentWorks (LA)*
3500 W Olive Ave
Suite 1400
Burbank, CA 91505, USA

Newman, Loraine (Comedian)
c/o Staff Member *TalentWorks (LA)*
3500 W Olive Ave
Suite 1400
Burbank, CA 91505, USA

Newman, Nanette (Actor)
Seven Pines Wentworth
Surrey GU25 4QP, UNITED KINGDOM (UK)

Newman, Nell (Business Person)
Newman's Own Organics
246 Post Road East
Westport, CT 06880, USA

Newman, Oscar (Architect)
Community Design Analysis Institute
66 Clover Dr
Great Neck, NY 11021, USA

Newman, Pauline (Judge)
US Court of Appeals
717 Madison Place NW
Washington, DC 20439, USA

Newman, Phyllis (Actor, Musician)
c/o Judy Katz *Judy Katz PR*
250 W 57th St
Suite 1818
New York, NY 10107, USA

Newman, Randy (Musician, Songwriter)
c/o Staff Member *Paradigm (Monterey)*
404 W Franklin St
Monterey, CA 93940, USA

Newman, Ray (Athlete, Baseball Player)
584 Vista Dr
Murrells Inlet, SC 29576-9029, USA

Newman, Rebecca (Stylist)
5 Ridge Dr
Westport, CT 06880, USA

Newman, Ryan (Race Car Driver)
Penske Racing South
316 Jennings Rd.
Statesville, NC 28625-8487, USA

Newman, Ryan (Actor)
c/o Gladys Gonzalez *John Carrabino Management*
5900 Wilshire Blvd Fl 4 #406
Los Angeles, CA 90036, USA

Newman, Terence (Athlete, Football Player)
1 Cowboys Pkwy
Irving, TX 75063, USA

Newman, Thomas (Composer)
c/o Staff Member *Chasen & Company*
8899 Beverly Blvd
Suite 405
Los Angeles, CA 90048, USA

Newman, Thomas (Actor)
c/o Staff Member *Chasen & Company*
8899 Beverly Blvd
Suite 405
Los Angeles, CA 90048, USA

Newmar, Julie (Actor)
204 S Carmelina Ave
Los Angeles, CA 90049, USA

Newmark, Craig
354 Shotwell St
San Francisco, CA 94110-1325, USA

Newmark, Dave (Athlete, Basketball Player)
545 Pierce St
Apt 2301
Albany, CA 94706-1065, USA

New Order (Music Group, Musician)
c/o Staff Member *Warner Bros Records (NY)*
75 Rockefeller Center
New York, NY 10019, USA

New Radicals
c/o Staff Member *MCA Records (LA)*
2220 Colorado Ave
Santa Monica, CA 90404, 310-865-4500

New Rascals, The
PO Box 1821
Ojai, CA 93023

New Riders of the Purple Sage
PO Box 3773
San Rafael, CA 94912-3773

Newsboys (Music Group, Musician)
Sparrow Records
P.O. Box 5010
Brentwood, TN 37024-5010, USA

Newsom, David (Actor)
Innovative Artists
1505 10th St
Santa Monica, CA 90401, USA

Newsom, David D (Diplomat)
500 Crestwood Drive
Apt 2504
Charlottesville, VA 22903-4883, USA

Newsom, Gavin (Politician)
Mayor's Office
City Hall
400 Van Ness Ave
San Francisco, CA 94102, USA

Newsome, Billy (Athlete, Football Player)
P.O. Box 2001
Shreveport, LA 71166-2001, USA

Newsome, Harry (Athlete, Football Player)
531 Manor Rd
Cheraw, SC 29520, USA

Newsome, Ozzie (Athlete, Football Player)
6 Padonia Woods Ct
Cockeysville, MD 21030, USA

Newsome, Timothy A (Athlete, Football Player)
7005 Quartermile Ln
Dallas, TX 75248, USA

Newsome, Vince (Athlete, Football Player)
5308 Woodnote Ln
Columbia, MD 21044, USA

Newson, Warren (Athlete, Baseball Player)
13232 Padre Ave
Fort Worth, TX 76244-4326, USA

New Song (Music Group)
c/o Staff Member *VanLiere-Wilcox*
251 Second Ave S
Franklin, TN 37065, USA

Newsted, Jason (Musician)
205 Alamo View Place
Walnut Creek, CA 94595, USA

Newton, Becki (Actor)
c/o Nicole King *Management 360*
9111 Wilshire Blvd
Beverly Hills, CA 90210, USA

Newton, Ben (Actor)
c/o Staff Member *Sasha Leslie Management*
34 Pember Rd
London NW10 5LS, UNITED KINGDOM

Newton, Bill (Athlete, Basketball Player)
2902 Manitou Park Dr
Rochester, IN 46975-8936, USA

Newton, Cam (Athlete, Football Player, Heisman Trophy Winner)
244-8th Ave W
Melville, SK S0A 2P0, Canada

Newton, Cam (Athlete, Hockey Player)
244-8th Ave W
Melville, SK S0A 2P0, Canada

Newton, Christopher (Director)
22 Prideaux St
Niagara-on-the-Lake, ON L0S 1J0, CANADA

Newton, C M (Athlete, Basketball Player, Coach)
9160 Enterprise Ave NE
Tuscaloosa, AL 35406-1042, USA

Newton, John Haymes (Actor)
c/o Staff Member *Pakula/King & Associates*
9229 Sunset Blvd
Suite 315
Los Angeles, CA 90069, USA

Newton, Jon (Business Person)
American General Corp
2929 Allen Parkway
Houston, TX 77019, USA

Newton, Juice (Musician, Songwriter)
4289 Kerwood Ct
San Diego, CA 92130, USA

Newton, Nate (Athlete, Football Player)
1921 White Oak Clearing
Southlake, TX 76092, USA

Newton, Robert L (Athlete, Football Player)
11500 NE 76th St
Apt A-353
Vancouver, WA 98662, USA

Newton, Roger (Scientist)
Esperion Therapeutics
695 KMS Place
3621 S State St
Ann Arbor, MI 48108, USA

Newton, Thandie (Actor)
c/o Jillian Fowkes *ID Public Relations (ID-LA)*
7060 Hollywood Blvd
8th Floor
Los Angeles, CA 90028, USA

Newton, Tom (Athlete, Football Player)
169 Park Rd
Rochester, NY 14622, USA

Newton, Wayne (Actor, Musician)
3422 Happy Ln
Las Vegas, NV 89120, USA

Newton-John, Olivia (Actor, Musician, Producer)
104 Lighthouse Dr
Jupiter, FL 33460, USA

New York Yankees
Yankee Stadium
161st & River
Bronx, NY 10451, USA

Nex, Kristin (Stylist)
3589 Military Ave
Los Angeles, CA 90034, USA

Ney, Edward N (Business Person, Diplomat)
Burson-Marsteller
230 Park Ave S
New York, NY 10003, USA

Neyelova, Marina M (Actor)
Potapovsky Per 12
Moscow 117333, RUSSIA

Ne-Yo (Musician)
40 Club Ct
Alpharetta, GA 30005, USA

Neyra, Gianella (Actor)
c/o Staff Member *Telefe - Argentina*
Pavon 2444 (C1248AAT)
Buenos Aires, ARGENTINA

Nezelek, Andy (Athlete, Baseball Player)
5707 Long Cove Road
Midlothian, VA 23112-2450, USA

Nezhat, Camran (Misc)
Fertility/Endocrinology Ctr
5555 Peachtree Dunwoody Road NE
Atlanta, GA 30342, USA

Ngata, Haoti (Athlete, Football Player)
c/o Staff Member *Baltimore Ravens*
1 Winning Drive
Owings Mills, MD 21117-4776, USA

Nguema, Tedoro Obiang (President)
President's Office
Malabo
EQUATORIAL GUINEA

Nguyen, Dat (Athlete, Football Player)
3610 Spears Rd
Houston, TX 77066, USA

Nguyen, Dustin (Actor)
1051 S Dunsmuir Ave
Los Angeles, CA 90019, USA

Nguyen, Long (Stylist)
Long Nguyen Photography
Prefers to be contacted
via telephone or email

Nguyen, Navia (Actor)
c/o Michael Greenwald *Buchwald/Fortitude (LA)*
6500 Wilshire Blvd
Suite 2200
Los Angeles, CA 90048, USA

Nguyen, Scotty (Misc)
c/o Staff Member *Poker Royalty, LLC*
10789 W. Twain Ave.
Suite 200
Las Vegas, NV 89135, USA

Nguyen, Thuan "Scotty" (Misc)
6212 Sundown Crest St
Las Vegas, NV 89113-6602, USA

Niarchos, Philip (Philanthropist)
SNF USA, Inc.
645 Madison Ave
Suite 2200
New York, NY 10022, USA

Nicaud, Philippe
104 rue des Sablons
Mareil-Marly, FRANCE 78750

Niccol, Andrew (Director, Producer, Writer)
c/o Richard Green *Creative Artists Agency (CAA-LA)*
2000 Ave Of The Stars
Los Angeles, CA 90067, USA

Nichol, Joseph McGinty (McG) (Musician, Producer, Writer)
c/o Staff Member *Wonderland Sound and Vision*
8739 Sunset Blvd
W Hollywood, CA 90069, USA

Nichol, Scott (Athlete, Hockey Player)
612 Ladyhawk Ln
Victor, NY 14564-9423, USA

Nicholas, Alison (Athlete, Golfer)
Pat Darby The Flat
Badgar Farm House
Badgar near Wolverhampton WV6 7IS, United Kingdom

Nicholas, Denise (Actor)
932 Longwood Ave
Los Angeles, CA 90019, USA

Nicholas, Eric (Writer)
c/o Staff Member *Gersh (LA)*
9465 Wilshire Blvd
Suite 600
Beverly Hills, CA 90212, USA

Nicholas, Henry (Misc)
Hospital & Health Care Union
330 W 42nd St
#1905
New York, NY 10036, USA

Nicholas, J D (Musician)
Management Assoc
1920 Benson Ave
Saint Paul, MN 55116, USA

Nicholas, Peter M (Business Person)
Boston Scientific Corp
1 Boston Scientific Place
Natick, MA 01760, USA

Nicholas, Stephen (Football Player)
c/o Chad Speck *Allegiant Athletic Agency*
35 Market Sq
Suite 201
Knoxville, TN 37902, USA

Nicholas, Thomas Ian (Actor)
Osbrink Talent
4343 Lankershim Blvd
#100
North Hollywood, CA 91602, USA

Nicholas Jr, Nicholas J (Publisher)
Pluggers Inc
1000 SW Broadway
#1850
Portland, OR 97205, USA

Nicholas(Smisko), Bishop (Religious Leader)
American Carpatho
312 Garfield St
Johnstown, PA 15906, USA

Nicholls, Bernie (Athlete, Hockey Player)
17101 Planters Row
Addison, TX 75001-5039, USA

Nicholls, Craig (Musician)
Winterman-Goldstein
17 Holdsworth St
Newton, NSW 2042, AUSTRALIA

Nicholls, Paul (Actor)
c/o Staff Member *IFA Talent Agency*
8730 Sunset Blvd
Suite 490
Los Angeles, CA 90069, USA

Nichols, Austin (Actor)
c/o Joan Green *Joan Green Management*
1836 Courtney Terr
Los Angeles, CA 90046, USA

Nichols, Bobby (Athlete, Golfer)
8681 Glenlyon Ct
Fort Myers, FL 33912-2408, USA

Nichols, Carl (Athlete, Baseball Player)
901 E Artesia Blvd
Compton, CA 90221-5356, USA

Nichols, Dorothy L (Financier)
Farm Credit Administration
1501 Farm Credit Dr
McLean, VA 22102, USA

Nichols, Dr. Michael (Writer)
c/o Staff Member *Guilford Press*
72 Spring St
New York, NY 10012, USA

Nichols, Hamilton J (Athlete, Football Player)
11015 Kirkmead Dr
Houston, TX 77089, USA

Nichols, Joe (Musician)
c/o Larry Murray *Triple 8 Management*
1611 W. 6th St.
Austin, TX 78703, USA

Nichols, John (Writer)
c/o Staff Member *The New Press*
38 Greene St Fl 4
New York, NY 10013, USA

Nichols, Kenwood C (Business Person)
Champion Int'l Corp
1 Champion Plaza
Stamford, CT 06921, USA

Nichols, Kyra (Ballerina)
Peter Diggins Assoc
133 W 71st St
New York, NY 10023, USA

Nichols, Larry (Designer)
Moleculon Research Corp
139 Main St
Cambridge, MA 02142, USA

Nichols, Lorrie (Bowler)
1251 Lexington Dr
Algonquin, IL 60102-2065, USA

Nichols, Marisol (Actor)
c/o Jill Littman *Impression Entertainment*
9229 W Sunset Blvd #700
West Hollywood, CA 90069, USA

Nichols, Mark (Athlete, Football Player)
5905 Penn Station Ln
Bakersfield, CA 93311, USA

Nichols, Mark (Race Car Driver)
Henderson Motosports
566 E. Main St
Abingdon, VA 24210, USA

Nichols, Mike (Comedian, Director)
Friends in Deed Inc
594 Broadway #706
New York, NY 10012, USA

Nichols, Nichelle (Actor)
c/o Jeffrey Leavitt *Leavitt Talent Group*
8255 W Sunset Blvd
West Hollywood, CA 90046, USA

Nichols, Pamela (Stylist)
40 Valley Cir
Mill Valley, CA 94941, USA

Nichols, Peter R (Writer)
Alan Brodie
211 Piccadilly
London W1V 9LD, UNITED KINGDOM (UK)

Nichols, Rachel (Actor)
c/o Peter Kiernan *Management 360*
9111 Wilshire Blvd
Beverly Hills, CA 90210, USA

Nichols, Reid (Athlete, Baseball Player)
Milwaukee Brewers
17547 WEast Wind Ave
Goodyear, AZ 85338-5840, USA

Nichols, Rod (Athlete, Baseball Player)
1570 Elk Trl
Helena, MT 59601-9633, USA

Nichols, Stephen (Actor)
11664 National Blvd
#116
Los Angeles, CA 90064, USA

Nicholson, Bruce
PO Box 2573
Georgetown, SC 29442-2573

Nicholson, Dave (Athlete, Baseball Player)
15316 Lake point Dr
Benton, IL 62812-4676, USA

Nicholson, Don (Dyno) (Race Car Driver)
604 Vista del Playa
Orange, CA 92865, USA

Nicholson, Jack (Actor)
12830/12850/12758 Mulholland Dr
Beverly Hills, CA 90210, USA

Nicholson, Jim (Athlete, Football Player)
91-845 Kauwili St
Ewa Beach, HI 96706, USA

Nicholson, Jim (Government Official, Secretary)
412 Russell Senate Office Building
Washington, DC 20510, USA

Nicholson, Julianne (Actor)
c/o Courtney Kivowitz *Schiff Company, The*
9465 Wilshire Blvd
Suite 480
Beverly Hills, CA 90212, USA

Nicholson, Kathrin
9057-A Nemo St.
W. Hollywood, CA 90069

Nichting, Chris (Athlete, Baseball Player)
7151 Gracely Dr
Cincinnati, OH 45233-1019, USA

Nickelback (Music Group)
c/o John Greenberg *Union Entertainment Group*
1323 Newbury Rd
Suite 104
Thousand Oaks, CA 91320, USA

Nickel Creek (Music Group)
c/o Staff Member *WmE2 (WMA-TN)*
1600 Division St
Suite 300
Nashville, TN 37203, USA

Nickells, Bruce (Horse Racer)
PO Box 5009
Lighthouse Point, FL 33074-5009, USA

Nickens, David (Race Car Driver)
604 Vista del Playa
Orange, CA 92865, USA

Nickerson, Camilla (Stylist)
c/o Staff Member *Art + Commerce*
531 W 25th St # 4
New York, NY 10001, USA

Nickerson, Denice (Actor)
4292 S Salida Way #1
Aurora, CO 80013, USA

Nickerson, Denise (Actor)
c/o Frann Harrison
6853 S. Ivy Way 7-301
Centennial, CO 80112, USA

Nickerson, Hardy O (Athlete, Football Player)
8716 Longview Club Dr
Waxhaw, NC 28173, USA

Nickerson Jr, Donald A (Religious Leader)
Episcopal Church
815 2nd Ave
New York, NY 10017, USA

Nickla, Ed (Athlete, Football Player)
21 Ida Ln
North Babylon, NY 11703, USA

Nicklaus, Gary
112 TPC Blvd.
Ponte Vedra Beach, FL 32082

Nicklaus, Jack (Athlete, Golfer)
11420 Old Harbour Rd
N Palm Beach, FL 33408, USA

Nickle, Doug (Athlete, Baseball Player)
19440 Victoria Ct
Sonoma, CA 95476-3829, USA

Nickles, Don (Politician)
903 Centrillion Dr
Me Lean, VA 22102-1443, USA

Nickolenko, Peter (Scientist)
4950 Winchester Dr
Titusville, FL 32780-6762, USA

Nicks, Carl (Athlete, Basketball Player)
10200 Yosemite Ln
Indianapolis, IN 46234-9821, USA

Nicks, John A W (Misc)
Ice Capades Chalet
13211 Brooks Dr
#A
Baldwin Park, CA 91706, USA

Nicks, Orlando (Athlete, Basketball Player)
10200 Yosemite Ln
Indianapolis, IN 46234-9821, USA

Nicks, Regina (Musician)
Bobby Roberts
909 Meadowlark Lane
Goodlettsville, TN 37072, USA

Nicks, Stevie (Musician, Songwriter)
c/o Liz Rosenberg *Liz Rosenberg Media*
142 W. 57th St
6th Floor
New York, NY 10019, USA

Nickson, Julia (Actor)
Elkins Entertainment
8306 Wilshire Blvd
#438
Beverly Hills, CA 90211, USA

Nickulas, Eric (Athlete, Hockey Player)
616 Huckins Neck Rd
Centerville, MA 02632-1440, USA

Nicol, Steve (Coach, Football Coach)
New England Revolution
CMGI Field
1 Patriot Place
Foxboro, MA 02035, USA

Nicolaou, Kyriacos Costa (Misc)
Scripps Research Institute
10550 N Torrey Pines Road
La Jolla, CA 92037, USA

Nicole
Im Pfarrwittum 1
Nohfelden, GERMANY D-66625

Nicole, Britt (Musician)
c/o Amy Fogleman *Creative Trust, Inc.*
5141 Virginia Way
Suite 320
Brentwood, TN 37027, USA

Nicole, Elizabeth (Stylist)
c/o Staff Member *Zenobia Agency Inc*
PO Box 909
Groveland, CA 95321, USA

Nicole, Kaylan (Adult Film Star)
9800D Topanga Canyon Blvd #3252
Chatsworth, CA 91311, USA

Nicolet, Aurele (Musician)
Hans Ulrich Schmid
Postfach 1617
Hanover 30016, GERMANY

Nicolet, Danielle (Actor)
c/o Lena Roklin *Luber Roklin Management*
8530 Wilshire Blvd
6th Floor
Beverly Hills, CA 90211, USA

Nicoletti Susi
Goethegasse
Vienna, AUSTRIA 1 A-1010

Nicol-Fox, Helen (Athlete, Baseball Player)
432 E Cornell Dr
Tempe, AZ 85283-1908, USA

Nicollier, Claude (Astronaut)
900 N Lake Shore
Dr Apt 2007
Chicago, IL 60611-1521, USA

Nicolson, Graeme (Athlete, Hockey Player)
Village Animal Hospital
PO Box 779
Lakefield, ON K0L 2H0, Canada

Nicolucci, Guy (Writer)
c/o Staff Member *Gersh (LA)*
9465 Wilshire Blvd
Suite 600
Beverly Hills, CA 90212, USA

Nicora, Attilio Cardinal (Religious Leader)
Patrimony of Apostolic See
Palazzo Apostolico
00120, VATICAN CITY

Nicosia, Steve (Athlete, Baseball Player)
190 Northshore Xing
Dallas, GA 30157-1641, USA

Nidetch, Jean (Misc)
9403 Aston Gardens Ct
Parkland, FL 33076-4102, USA

Nieberg, Lars (Misc)
Gestit Waldershausen
Homberg 35315, GERMANY

Nied, David (Athlete, Baseball Player)
211 Masters Ln
Midlothian, TX 76065-7209, USA

Niedenfuer, Tom (Athlete, Baseball Player)
3933 Losillias Dr
Sarasota, FL 34238-4537, USA

Nieder, William H (Bill) (Athlete, Track Athlete)
PO Box 310
Mountain Ranch, CA 95246, USA

Niederhoffer, Victor (Misc)
Niederhoffer Cross Zeckhauser
757 3rd Ave
New York, NY 10017, USA

Niedermayer, Rob (Athlete, Hockey Player)
Titan Sports Management
1105-1009 Expo Blvd
Attn Kevin Epp
Vancouver, BC V6Z 2V9, Canada

Niedermayer, Scott (Athlete, Hockey Player)
Titan Sports Management
1105-1009 Expo Blvd
Attn Kevin Epp
Vancouver, BC V6Z 2V9, Canada

Niedernhuber, Barbara (Athlete)
Schwarzeckstr 58
Ramsau 83486, GERMANY

Niehaus, Dave (Sportscaster)
Seattle Mariners
Safeco Field
PO Box 4100
Seattle, WA 98194, USA

Niehaus, David (Athlete, Baseball Player)
18406 NW Montreux Drive
Issaquah, WA 98027-7817, USA

Niehaus, Lennie (Composer)
Robert Light Agency
6404 Wilshire Blvd
#1225
Los Angeles, CA 90048, USA

Niehaus, Ralph (Athlete, Football Player)
114 Siebenthaler Ave
Cincinnati, OH 45215, USA

Niehaus, Steve (Athlete, Football Player)
114 Siebenthaler Ave
Cincinnati, OH 45215, USA

Niekamp, Jim (Athlete, Hockey Player)
3511 E Cochise Dr
Phoenix, AZ 85028-3924, USA

Niekamp, Ted (Athlete, Hockey Player)
3511 E. Cochise Dr.
Phoenix, AZ 85028, USA

Niekro, Lance (Athlete, Baseball Player)
3822 Cheverly Dr E
Lakeland, FL 33813-1203, USA

Niekro, Phil (Athlete, Baseball Player)
6382 Nichols Rd
Flowery Branch, GA 30542-2619, USA

Niel, Steve (Actor)
c/o Laura Walsh *Central Artists*
3310 W Burbank Blvd #A
Burbank, CA 91505-2230, USA

Nielsen, Brigitte (Actor, Model)
c/o Staff Member *M&G Entertainment*
19360 Rinaldi St
#517
Porter Ranch, CA 91326, USA

Nielsen, Connie (Actor)
c/o Estelle Lasher *Principal Entertainment (NY)*
1964 Westwood Blvd
Suite 400
Los Angeles, CA 90025, USA

Nielsen, Gifford (Athlete, Football Player)
10 Sarahs Cove
Sugar Land, TX 77479, USA

Nielsen, Jeff (Athlete, Hockey Player)
5233 France Ave S
Minneapolis, MN 55410-2038, USA

Nielsen, Jerry (Athlete, Baseball Player)
4631 Kewanee St
Fair Oaks, CA 95628-6219, USA

Nielsen, Lonnie (Athlete, Golfer)
6 Marlwood Ln
Palm Beach Gardens, FL 33418, USA

Nielsen, Rick (Musician)
Monterey Peninsula Artists
509 Hartnell St
Monterey, CA 93940, USA

Nielsen, Scott (Athlete, Baseball Player)
2898 Valley View Ave
Salt Lake City, UT 84117-5550, USA

Niemann, Jeff (Athlete, Baseball Player)
5922 Jason St
Houston, TX 77074-7742, USA

Niemann, Randy (Athlete, Baseball Player)
1585 SW Harbour Isles Cir
Port Saint Lucie, FL 4986-3403, USA

Niemann, Richard (Athlete, Basketball Player)
7911 Stanford Ave
Saint Louis, MO 63130-3613, USA

Niemann-Stirnemann, Gunda (Speed Skater)
Postfach 503
Erfurt 99010, GERMANY

Niemeyer, Paul V (Judge)
US Court of Appeals
101 W Lombard St
Baltimore, MD 21201, USA

Niemi, Lisa (Actor)
c/o Staff Member *Atria Books*
1230 Avenue of the Americas
New York, NY 10020, USA

Niemiec-Konwinski, Dolly (Athlete, Baseball Player)
1821 Spring Meadow Ct SE
Caledonia, MI 49316-9154, USA

Nieminen, Toni (Skier)
Landen Kanava 99
vesijarvenkatu 74
Lahti 15140, FINLAND

Nierman, Leonardo (Artist)
Amsterdam 43 PH
Mexico City 11 DF, MEXICO

Nies, Eric (Actor, Model, Reality TV Star)
c/o Staff Member *Bunim/Murray Productions Inc*
6007 Sepulveda Blvd
Van Nuys, CA 91411, USA

Niese, Jonathon
232 N Wynn Rd
Oregon, OH 43616-1542, USA

Nieson, Chuck (Athlete, Baseball Player)
31923 Trails End Rd
Clinton, MN 56225-5163, USA

Nieto, Adriana (Actor)
c/o Staff Member *Televisa*
Blvd Adolfo Lopez Mateos 232
Colonia San Angel INN
DF CP 01060, MEXICO

Nieto, Tom (Athlete, Baseball Player)
22446 Eagles Watch Dr
Land O Lakes, FL 34639-6759, USA

Nieuwendyk, Joe (Athlete, Hockey Player)
Dallas Stars 2601 Avenue of the Stars Ste 100
Attn: General Manager
Frisco, TX 75034-9016, USA

Nieuwendyk, Joe (Athlete, Hockey Player)
3204 Drexel Dr
Dallas, TX 75205-2913, USA

Nieves, Juan (Athlete, Baseball Player, Coach)
Chicago White Sox
333 W 35th St
Attn: Coaching Staff
Chicago, IL 60616-3696, USA

Nieves, Melvin (Athlete, Baseball Player)
6131 7 Lks W
West End, NC 27376-9320, USA

Nigam, Anjul (Actor)
c/o Lisa DiSante-Frank *DiSante Frank & Company*
10061 Riverside Dr #377
Toluca Lake, CA 91602, USA

Nigam, Sonu (Musician)
c/o Linda Jones *The Mass Appeal*
3940 Laurel Canyon Blvd
Unit 447
Studio City, CA 91604, USA

Nigh, George P (Ex-Governor)
3009 Hackberry Rd
Oklahoma City, OK 73120, USA

Nighswander, Nicholas (Athlete, Football Player)
P.O. Box 46
Burgoon, OH 43407, USA

Nightingale, Maxine
c/o Staff Member *Diva Central Inc*
7510 W Sunset Blvd Ste 1445
Los Angees, CA 90046, USA

Nighy, Bill (Actor)
c/o Chris Andrews *Creative Artists Agency (CAA-LA)*
2000 Ave Of The Stars
Los Angeles, CA 90067, USA

Nigro, Frank (Athlete, Hockey Player)
45 Princeton Terr.
Brampton, ON L6S 3S4, CANADA

Nigro, Lynn (Stylist)
c/o Staff Member *Judy Casey Inc*
114 E 13th St
New York, NY 10003, USA

Nihalani, Govind (Director, Filmmaker, Producer)
139 Aradhana Behind Bhavishya Nidhi
Bandra (E)
Bombay, MS 400 051, INDIA

Niinimaa, Janne (Athlete, Hockey Player)
Thompson, Dorfman, Sweatman
PO Box 639 Stn Main
Attn: Donald Baizley
Winnipeg, MB R3C 2K6, Canada

Niittymaki, Antero (Athlete, Hockey Player)
1184 Nevada Ave
San Jose, CA 95125-3327, USA

Nikkanen, Kurt (Musician)
Columbia Artists Mgmt Inc
165 W 57th St
New York, NY 10019, USA

Nikko (Stylist)
c/o Staff Member *Cloutier Agency*
2632 La Cienega Ave
Los Angeles, CA 90034, USA

Niklas, Jan
Konigsberger Str. 20
Munich, GERMANY D-81927

Niklason, Laura A (Engineer)
Duke University Medical School
Durham, NC 27706, USA

Nikolishin, Andrei (Athlete, Hockey Player)
105 Bloomfield Ave
Hartford, CT 06105, USA

Nilan, Chris (Athlete, Hockey Player)
577 Adams St Unit D
Milton, MA 02186-5636, USA

Niland, John H (Athlete, Football Player)
16058 Chalfont Ct
Dallas, TX 75248, USA

Niles, John (Composer, Musician)
Magic Wing Music
PO Box 222
West Linn, OR 97068, USA

Niles, Nicholas H (Publisher)
Sporting News Publishing Co
1212 N Lindbergh Blvd
Saint Louis, MO 63132, USA

Niles, Prescott (Musician)
Artists & Audience Entertainment
PO Box 35
Pawling, NY 12564, USA

Niles, Thomas M T (Diplomat)
National Defense Hdqs Library
101 C By Dr
Ottawa, ON K1A 0K2, CANADA

Nill, Jim (Athlete, Hockey Player)
20847 Dundee Dr.
Novi, MI 48375, USA

Nill, Jim (Athlete, Hockey Player)
Detroit Red Wings 600 Civic Center Dr
Attn: Asst General Manager
Novi, MI 48375, USA

Nilsen, Reed (Athlete, Football Player)
1078 S 1400 W
Salt Lake City, UT 84104, USA

Nilsmark, Catrin (Athlete, Golfer)
187 Commodore Dr
Jupiter, FL 33477-4007, USA

Nilsson, Dave (Athlete, Baseball Player)
34 Lawnhill Road
Neiang, Queensland, AU 4211, Australia

Nilsson, Inger
Box 12710
Stockholm, SWEDEN 11294

Nilsson, Kent (Athlete, Hockey Player)
9034 Crichton Wood Dr
Orlando, FL 32819-4836, USA

Nilsson, Lennart (Photographer)
Pantheon Books
201 E 50th St
New York, NY 10022, USA

Nilsson, Nils (Athlete, Hockey Player)
Vattugatan 8
Forshaga 667 32, SWEDEN

Nilsson, Ulf (Athlete, Hockey Player)
QBrick AB Sodra Hamnvagen 22
Stockholm S-11541, Sweden

Nimmo, Dirk (Actor)
Michael Whitehall
125 Gloucester Road
London SW7 4TE, UNITED KINGDOM
(UK)

Nimmons, Ernest (Baseball Player)
Indianapolis Clowns
1509 Paine St
Lorain, OH 44052-3253, USA

Nimoy, Leonard (Actor, Director,
Photographer)
c/o Tim Curtis *WME (LA)*
9601 Wilshire Blvd Fl 3
Beverly Hills, CA 90210, USA

Nimphius, Kurt (Athlete, Basketball
Player)
750 Dry Creek Rd
Sedona, AZ 86336-3621, USA

Nimri, Najwa (Actor, Musician)
c/o Staff Member *Kuranda Management*
Santo Angel, 84
Madrid 28043, Spain

Nimziki, Joe (Director)
Paradigm Agency
10100 Santa Monica Blvd
#2500
Los Angeles, CA 90067, USA

Nine Black Alps (Music Group)
c/o Staff Member *Paradigm (Monterey)*
404 W Franklin St
Monterey, CA 93940, USA

Ninedays (Music Group)
c/o Staff Member *Epic Records Group*
550 Madison Ave
22nd Floor
New York, NY 10022, USA

Nine Inch Nails (NIN) (Music Group)
c/o Jim Guerinot *Rebel Waltz Inc*
31652 Second Ave
Laguna Beach, CA 92651, USA

Nininger, Harvey H (Misc)
PO Box 420
Sedona, AZ 86339, USA

Nininger, Susan (Stylist)
c/o Tom Marquardt *ICM Partners
(ICM-LA)*
10250 Constellation Blvd Fl 7
Los Angeles, CA 90067, USA

Ninowski, Jim (Athlete, Football Player)
2715 Melcombe Cir
Apt 302
Troy, MI 48084, USA

Nipar, Yvette (Actor)
Irv Schechter
9300 Wilshire Blvd
#410
Beverly Hills, CA 90212, USA

Nipp, Maury (Athlete, Football Player)
631 E Michelle St
West Covina, CA 91790, USA

Nipper, Al (Athlete, Baseball Player)
401 White Birch Valley Ct
Chesterfield, MO 63017-2457, USA

Nippert, Dustin (Athlete, Baseball Player)
PO Box 8540
Stockton, CA 95208-0540, USA

Nippert, Merlin (Athlete, Baseball Player)
1015 N Michigan Ave
Mangum, OK 73554-1820, USA

Nirenberg, Louis (Mathematician)
221 W 82nd St
New York, NY 10024, USA

Nirmaier, Mary Birch (Aviator)
2500 Rock Quarry Rd
Columbia, MO 65201-4666, USA

Nirmala, Sister (Religious Leader)
Missionaries of Charity
54A Lower Circular Road
Kolkata, WB 700016, INDIA

Nirosha (Actor, Bollywood)
3 Paul Appasamy Street
T Nagar
Chennai, TN 600017, INDIA

Nisbet, Robert A (Activist, Historian)
6131 Purple Aster Lane NE
Albuquerque, NM 87111, USA

Nischwitz, Ron (Athlete, Baseball Player)
6790 Garber Rd
Dayton, OH 45415-1S04, USA

Nish, Wayne
March Restaurant 405
E 58th St
New York, NY 10022-2302, USA

Nish, Wayne (Chef)
March Restaurant 405
E 58th St
New York, NY 10022-2302, USA

Nishimura, Mayumi (Chef)
Clearspring Ltd
19A Acton Park Estate
London W3 7QE, UK

Nishizawa, Junichi (Engineer, Inventor)
Semiconductor Research Institute
Kawauchi
Aobaku
Sendai 9800862, JAPAN

Nishizuka, Yasutomi (Physicist)
Kobe University
7-5-1 Kusunokichochuoki
Kobe 650-0017, JAPAN

Nishkian, Byron (Skier)
150 4th St
#PH
San Francisco, CA 94103, USA

Nispel, Marcus (Director)
c/o Staff Member *WME (LA)*
9601 Wilshire Blvd Fl 3
Beverly Hills, CA 90210, USA

Nissalke, Tom (Basketball Coach, Coach)
3075 Kennedy Dr
Apt 406
Salt Lake City, UT 84108-2200, USA

Nissen, Steve (Doctor)
817 Hanover Road
Gates Mills, OH 44040, USA

Nistico, Lou (Athlete, Hockey Player)
404 Westbury Cres
Thunder Bay, ON P7C 4N4, Canada

Nithya (Actor, Bollywood)
37 Palayakaran Street
Chennai, TN 600024, INDIA

Nitkowski, C J (Athlete, Baseball Player)
205 Townsend Ln
Alpharetta, GA 30004-2553, USA

Nitsirk (Stylist)
c/o Staff Member *Igroup + Ridecreative*
315 W 39th St
#908
New York, NY 10018, USA

Nittmann, David (Artist)
PO Box 19065
Boulder, CO 80308, USA

Nittmo, Bjorn (Athlete, Football Player)
201 E Jefferson St
Phoenix, AZ 85004, USA

Nitty Gritty Dirt Band (Music Group)
c/o Staff Member *Paradigm (Monterey)*
404 W Franklin St
Monterey, CA 93940, USA

Nitz, Leonard (Athlete, Cycler, Olympic
Athlete)
5515 Ruhkala Rd
Rocklin, CA 95677-3117, USA

Nitzkowski, Monte (Athlete, Olympic
Athlete, Swimmer)
7041 Seat Circle
Huntington Beach, CA 92648, USA

Niven, Barbara
Gail Abbott Management
3019 Hollycrest Dr
Los Angeles, CA 90212, USA

Niven, Kip (Actor)
8109 Sagamore Rd
Leawood, KS 66206, USA

Niven, Laurence (Larry) (Writer)
136 El Camino Dr
Beverly Hills, CA 90212-2705, USA

Niven Jr, David (Actor, Producer)
1457 Blue Jay Way
Los Angeles, CA 90069, USA

Nivola, Alessandro (Actor)
c/o William Choi *Management 360*
9111 Wilshire Blvd
Beverly Hills, CA 90210, USA

Niwa, Gail (Musician)
Siegel Artist Mgmt
1416 Hinman Ave
Evanston, IL 60201, USA

Niwano, Nikkyo (Religious Leader)
Rissho Kosel-Kai
2-11-1 Wada Suginamiku
Tokyo 166, JAPAN

Nix, Dyron (Athlete, Basketball Player)
1655 Cutleaf Creek Rd
Sedona, AZ 30017-4140, USA

Nix, Garth (Writer)
Harper Collins
77 - 85 Fulham palace road
London W12 8ER, UNITED KINGDOM

Nix, Jimmy (Race Car Driver)
520 SE 30th #6
Oklahoma City, OK 73129, USA

Nix, John L (Athlete, Football Player)
2278 Lindsey Ct
Fallbrook, CA 92028, USA

Nix, Kent (Athlete, Football Player)
2732 Colonial Pkwy
Fort Worth, TX 76109-1211, USA

Nix, Laynce (Athlete, Baseball Player)
1506 Princeton Ave
Midland, TX 79701-5762, USA

Nix, Matt (Writer)
c/o Staff Member *WME (LA)*
9601 Wilshire Blvd Fl 3
Beverly Hills, CA 90210, USA

Nixey, Troy (Director)
c/o Gary Ungar *Exile Entertainment*
732 El Medio Ave
Pacific Palisades, CA 90272, USA

Nixon, Agnes (Producer, Writer)
774 Conestoga Rd
Bryn Mawr, PA 19010, USA

Nixon, Cynthia (Actor)
c/o Emily Gerson Saines *Brookside Artists
Management (NY)*
250 W 57th St
Suite 2303
New York, NY 10107, USA

Nixon, Derek Lee (Actor, Producer,
Writer)
c/o Staff Member *Mark Robert
Management*
2208 Patricia Ave
Los Angeles, CA 90064, USA

Nixon, Donell (Athlete, Baseball Player)
Seattle Mariners
2681 Mount Olive Rd
Whiteville, NC 28472-6863, USA

Nixon, Jay (Governor)
Office of Governor Jay Nixon
P.O. Box 720
Jefferson City, MO 65102, USA

Nixon, Jeff (Athlete, Football Player)
549 Linwood Ave
Buffalo, NY 14209, USA

Nixon, Kimberley (Actor)
c/o Larry Taube *Principal Entertainment*
(LA)
1964 Westwood Blvd #400
Los Angeles, CA 90025, USA

Nixon, Marni (Actor, Musician)
315 W End Ave #2A
New York, NY 10023, USA

Nixon, Norm (Athlete, Basketball Player)
Nixon and Associates
607 Marguerita Ave
Santa Monica, CA 90402-1919, USA

Nixon, Norman (Athlete, Basketball
Player)
607 Marguerita Ave
Santa Monica, CA 90402, USA

Nixon, Otis (Athlete, Baseball Player)
1000 Montage Way Apt 1814
Atlanta, GA 30341-6071, USA

Nixon, Russ (Athlete, Baseball Player)
4265 N Tee Pee Ln
Las Vegas, NV 89129-2628, USA

Nixon, Sam (Musician)
c/o Staff Member *QVoice*
161 Drury Ln, Covent Garden
3rd Floor
London WC2B 5PN, UK

Nixon, Torran (Athlete, Football Player)
3265 Thorn St
San Diego, CA 92104, USA

Nixon, Trot (Athlete, Baseball Player)
1023 Ocean Ridge Dr
Wilmington, NC 28405, USA

Nixon-Eisenhower, Julie (Politician)
255 Foxall Ln
Berwyn, PA 19312-1843, USA

Niyazov, Saparmurad (President)
President's Office
Karl Marx Str 24
Ashkabad 744017, TURKMENISTAN

Nizhalgal, Raviee (Actor)
4 Sriram Nagar North Street
Chennai, TN 600 018, INDIA

Niziolek, Robert (Athlete, Football Player)
206 W Brome Ave
Lafayette, CO 80026, USA

Niznik, Stephanie (Actor)
c/o Staff Member *Niad Management*
15030 Ventura Boulevard
Bldg 19 Ste 860
Sherman Oaks, CA 91423, USA

Noah, Joakim (Athlete, Basketball Player)
c/o Staff Member *Blackwave Media*
Group
220 West 42nd Street
5th Floor
New York, NY 10036, USA

Noah, John (Athlete, Hockey Player,
Olympic Athlete)
3315 Prairiewood Dr W
Fargo, ND 58103, USA

Noah, Max W (General)
820 Arcturus-on-Potomac
Alexandria, VA 22308, USA

Noah, Trevor (Comedian)
c/o Matthew Blake *Creative Artists*
Agency (CAA-LA)
2000 Ave Of The Stars
Los Angeles, CA 90067, USA

Noah, Yannick (Athlete, Coach, Musician,
Tennis Player)
230 Central Park S
New York, NY 10019, USA

Noakes, Michael (Artist)
146 Hamilton Terrace
Saint John's Wood
London NW8 9UX, UNITED KINGDOM
(UK)

Nobel, Ben (Actor)
c/o Bella Grundy *King Talent (Toronto)*
36 Tiverton Ave
Toronto ON M4M, Canada

Nobilo, Frank (Athlete, Golfer)
10209 Atterbury Ct
Orlando, FL 32827, USA

Nobis, Thomas H (Tommy) Jr (Athlete,
Football Executive, Football Player)
40 S Battery Placa NE
Atlanta, GA 30342, USA

Noble, Adrian K (Director)
Royal Shakespeare Co
Barbican Theater
London EC2Y 8BQ, UNITED KINGDOM
(UK)

Noble, Brandon (Athlete, Football Player)
2154 Ferncroft Ln
Chester Springs, PA 19425, USA

Noble, Brian D (Athlete, Football Player)
2912 Nikki Lee Ct
Green Bay, WI 54313, USA

Noble, James (Actor)
113 Ledgebrook Dr
Norwalk, CT 06854, USA

Noble, John (Actor)
c/o Nicolas Bernheim *Seven Summits*
Pictures & Management
8906 W Olympic Blvd
Ground Floor
Beverly Hills, CA 90211, USA

Noble, Karen (Athlete, Golfer)
36 Edgewood Rd
Chatham, NJ 07928, USA

Noble, Michael
Diva At The Met Restaurant
645 Howe St
Vancouver, BC V6C 2Y9, Canada

Noble, Reginald (Redman) (Musician)
c/o Greg Weiss *Vanguard Management*
Group (NY)
220 5th Ave.
Penthouse West
New York, NY 10001, USA

Noble, Ross (Actor, Comedian)
c/o Staff Member *Real Talent*
Management (UK)
24 Goodge St
London W1T 2QF, UNITED KINGDOM

Noble, Samantha (Actor)
c/o David Rudy *Armada Partners*
815 Moraga Drive
Los Angeles, CA 90049, USA

Noblitt, Niles L (Business Person)
Biomet Inc
Airport Industrial Park
PO Box 587
Warsaw, IN 46581, USA

Noboa, Gustavo (Educator, President)
Palacio de Gobierno
Garcia Moreno, Quito 1043, ECUADOR

Noboa, Junior (Athlete, Baseball Player)
Arizona Diamondbacks
P.O. Box 2095
Attn: Director, Latin American Ops
Phoenix, AZ 85001, USA

Noce, Paul (Athlete, Baseball Player)
942 W Maumee St
Adrian, MI 49221-1916, USA

Nocioni, Andres
2281 Royal Ridge Dr
Northbrook, IL 60062-8608, USA

Nock, George (Athlete, Football Player)
1025 Nine North Dr
Suite H
Alpharetta, GA 30004, USA

Nodell, Mart (Cartoonist)
117 Lake Irene Dr
West Palm Beach, FL 33411, USA

Noel, Alyson (Writer)
14 Monarch Bay Plaza
#186
Monarch Beach, CA 92629, USA

Noel, Chris (Actor)
6815 Lake Avenue
West Palm Beach, FL 33405-4525, USA

Noel, Claude (Athlete, Hockey Player)
4361 Bridgeside Pl
New Albany, OH 43054-7053, USA

Noel, Claude (Athlete, Hockey Player)
Winnipeg Jets 300 Portage Ave
Attn: Coaching Staff
Winnipeg, MB R3C 5S4, Canada

Noel, Don (Race Car Driver)
PO Box 2757
Lake Isabella, CA 93240, USA

Noel, Philip W (Politician)
20403 Wildcat Run Dr
Estero, RI 33928-2014, USA

Nogle, Donald (Athlete, Football Player)
1248 Calle Christopher
Encinitas, CA 92024-5519, United States

Noguchi, Soichi (Astronaut)
100 Cyberonics Blvd
Ste 201
Houston, TX 77058-2074, USA

Noguchi, Thomas (Scientist)
1110 Avoca Ave
Pasadena, CA 91105-3405, USA

Nogulich, Natalia (Actor)
11841 Kiowa Ave #7
Los Angeles, CA 90049

Nogulich, Natalija (Actor)
11841 Kiowa Ave
#7
Los Angeles, CA 90049, USA

Noji, Minae (Actor)
c/o Steven Jensen *Direct Management*
Group
6363 Wilshire Blvd
Suite 115
Los Angeles, CA 90048, USA

Nojima, Minoru (Musician)
John Gingrich Mgmt
PO Box 515
New York, NY 10023, USA

Nokelainen, Petteri (Athlete, Hockey
Player)
c/o Staff Member *Boston Bruins*
TD Banknorth Garden
100 Legends Way, Suite 250
Boston, MA 02114, USA

Nokes, Matt (Athlete, Baseball Player)
2255 Oxford Ave
Cardiff By The Sea, CA 92007-1915, USA

Nolan, Christopher (Writer)
c/o Stuart Manashil *Creative Artists*
Agency (CAA-LA)
2000 Ave Of The Stars
Los Angeles, CA 90067, USA

Nolan, Coleen (Actor)
c/o Staff Member *Urban Associates*
Prefers to be contacted via email or
telephone
London, UK

Nolan, Deanna (Basketball Player)
Detroit Shock
Palace
2 Championship Dr
Auburn Hills, MI 48326, USA

Nolan, Gary (Athlete, Baseball Player)
97 Acacia Ave
Oroville, CA 95966-3658, USA

Nolan, Graham (Cartoonist)
162 Godfrey Terr.
E. Aurora, NY 14052-2040, USA

Nolan, Joe (Athlete, Baseball Player)
9515 Alix Dr
Saint Louis, MO 63123-7101, USA

Nolan, Jonathan (Writer)
c/o Keya Khayatian *United Talent Agency*
(UTA)
9336 Civic Center Dr
Beverly Hills, CA 90210, USA

Nolan, Kathleen (Actor)
c/o Staff Member *House of*
Representatives, The
1434 6th St
Suite 1
Santa Monica, CA 90401, USA

Nolan, Nolan (Athlete, Football Player)
1400 Zillock Rd Ofc
San Benito, TX 78586-9730, USA

Nolan, Owen (Athlete, Hockey Player)
17110 Cooper Hill Dr.
Morgan Hill, CA 95017, USA

Nolan, Simon (Athlete, Hockey Player)
1342 Ruse de la Belle Vue
Cap-Rouge, QC G1Y 2T1, CANADA

Nolan, Ted (Athlete, Coach, Hockey
Player)
269 Queen St. E.
Sault Ste. Marie, ON P6A IY9, Canada

Nolan, Thomas B (Scientist)
2219 California St NW
Washington, DC 20008, USA

Nolan, Tom
1335 N. Ontario St.
Burbank, CA 91505

Nolasco, Amaury (Actor)
c/o Evan Hainey *Untitled Entertainment*
(LA)
350 S. Beverly Dr #200
Beverly Hills, CA 90212, USA

Nolasco, Ricky (Athlete, Baseball Player)
3370 NE 190th St
Apt 1812
Miami, FL 33180-2417, USA

Nold, Dick (Athlete, Baseball Player)
715 Athens St
San Francisco, CA 94112-3513, USA

Nolen, Paul (Athlete, Basketball Player)
480 Pecan Dr
Burleson, TX 76028-6308, USA

Noles, Dickie (Athlete, Baseball Player)
15 Hidden Valley Rd
Aston, PA 19014, USA

Nolet, Simon (Athlete, Hockey Player)
1342 Rue des Grandes-Marees
Quebec, QC G1Y 2Tl, Canada

Nolfi, George (Director)
c/o David Wirtschafter *WME (LA)*
9601 Wilshire Blvd Fl 3
Beverly Hills, CA 90210, USA

Nolin, Gena Lee (Actor)
c/o David Rose *Innovative Artists (LA)*
1505 10th St
Santa Monica, CA 90401, USA

Noll, Chuck (Athlete, Football Coach)
c/o Staff Member *Keppler Associates*
3030 Clarendon Blvd
7th Floor
Arlington, VA 22201, USA

Nolte, Claudia (Government Official)
Mulgarten 28
Ilmenau 98693, GERMANY

Nolte, Eric (Athlete, Baseball Player)
2388S Noelle Ave
Murrieta, CA 92544-2258, USA

Nolte, Nick (Actor, Producer)
c/o Angharad Wood *Tavistock Wood*
Management
32 Tavistock St
London WC2B 5HA, UK

Nolting, Paul F (Religious Leader)
Church of Lutheran Confession
620 E 50th St
Loveland, CO 80538, USA

Nomellini, Leo
520 St. Claire Dr.
Palo Alto, CA 94306-3050

Nomina, Tom (Athlete, Football Player)
731 N County Road 19 E
Loveland, CO 80537, USA

Nomo, Hideo (Athlete, Baseball Player)
11746 Stonehenge Ln
Los Angeles, CA 90077-1302, USA

Nomura, Masayasu (Biologist)
74 Whitman Court
Irvine, CA 92612, USA

Nool, Erki (Athlete, Track Athlete)
Regati 1
Tallinn 11911, ESTONIA

Noonan, Brian (Athlete, Hockey Player)
262 W. Eggleston Ave.
Elmhurst, IL 60126, USA

Noonan, Chris (Director)
c/o Craig Gering *Creative Artists Agency*
(CAA-LA)
2000 Ave Of The Stars
Los Angeles, CA 90067, USA

Noonan, Danny (Athlete, Football Player)
1 Cowboys Pkwy
Irving, TX 75063, USA

Noonan, John T Jr (Judge)
US Court of Appeals
Court Building
95 7th St
San Francisco, CA 94103, USA

Noonan, Karl (Athlete, Football Player)
7149 Oxford Hunt Dr
Stanley, NC 28164, USA

Noonan, Katie (Musician)
c/o Staff Member *The Harbour Agency*
135 Forbes St
Woolloomooloo NSW 2011, Australia

Noonan, Patrick F (Misc)
3553 Hamlet Place
Chevey Chase, MD 20815-4822, USA

Noonan, Peggy (Writer)
Reagan Books
10 E 53rd St
New York, NY 10022, USA

Noonan, Robert W Jr (General)
Deputy Chief of Stafff for Intelligence
HqUSA
Pentagon
Washington, DC 20310, USA

Noone, Kathleen (Actor)
130 W 42nd St
#1804
New York, NY 10036, USA

Noone, Nora Jane (Actor)
c/o Staff Member *Independent Talent*
Group (ITG-UK)
Oxford House
76 Oxford St
London W1D 1BS, UK

Noone, Peter (Actor, Musician)
9265 Robin Lane
Los Angeles, CA 90069, USA

Noor, Queen
Baab al-Salem Palace
Amman, JORDAN

Noor Al-Hussein (Royalty)
Royal Palace
Amman, JORDAN

Norcross, Clayton
951 Galloway St.
Pacific Palisades, CA 90272

Nordbrook, Tim (Athlete, Baseball Player)
14018 Blenheim Rd N
Phoenix, MD 21131-1830, USA

Norden, Tommy (Actor)
34 Bal Bay Dr
Miami, FL 33154, USA

Nordenberg, Mark A (Educator)
University of Pittsburgh
President's Office
Pittsburgh, PA 15261, USA

Nordenstrom, Bjorn (Doctor)
Karolinska Institute
Radiology Dept
Stockholm, SWEDEN

Nordgren, Fred (Athlete, Football Player)
27400 SW Xanthus Ct
Sherwood, OR 97140-7211, USA

Nordhagen, Wayne (Athlete, Baseball
Player)
2S896 Ramillo Way
Valencia, CA 91355-1925, USA

Nordheim, Arne (Composer)
Wergelandsveien 2
Oslo 0167, NORWAY

Nordlander, Mattias (Musician)
MOB Agency
6404 Wilshire Blvd
#505
Los Angeles, CA 90048, USA

Nordli, Odvar (Prime Minister)
Sanveien 4
Ottestad 2312, NORWAY

Nordling, Jeffrey (Actor)
c/o Dan Baron *Agency for the Performing*
Arts (APA-LA)
405 S Beverly Dr
Suite 500
Beverly Hills, CA 90212-4425, USA

Nordmann, Robert (Athlete, Basketball
Player)
631 Sherwood Rd
Williamston, MI 48895-9436, USA

Nordquist, Helen (Athlete, Baseball
Player)
PO Box 474
Alton, NH 03809-0474, USA

Nordquist, Mark (Athlete, Football Player)
3495 Seacrest Dr
Carlsbad, CA 92008, USA

Nordsieck, Kenneth H (Astronaut)
2807 Ridge Rd
Madison, WI 53705-5223, USA

Nordstrom, Christy (Stylist)
1517 NE 107th St
Seattle, WA 98125, USA

Noren, Irv (Athlete, Baseball Player)
3154 Camino Crest Dr
Oceanside, CA 92056-3613, USA

Noren, Lars (Writer)
Ostermalmsgatan 33
Stockholm 11426, SWEDEN

Norgard, Erik C (Athlete, Football Player)
404 Winterthur Way
Littleton, CO 80129, USA

Noriander, John (Basketball Player)
801 9th St N
#102
Virginia, MN 55792, USA

Norick, Lance (Race Car Driver)
6306 S. MacDill Ave. #1724
Tampa, FL 33611, USA

Noriega, Carlos I (Astronaut)
13710 Shadow Falls Court
Houston, TX 77059, USA

Noriega, Carlos L Lt Colonel (Astronaut)
4630 Silhouette Dr
Katy, TX 77493-8099, USA

Noriega, Danny (Musician, Reality TV
Star)

Noriega, Victor (Actor)
c/o Staff Member *Televisa*
Blvd Adolfo Lopez Mateos 232
Colonia San Angel INN
DF CP 01060, MEXICO

Noris, Joe (Athlete, Hockey Player)
1111 Via Carolina
La Jolla, CA 92037-6254, USA

Norman, Chris (Musician)
Denis Vaughan Mgmt
PO Box 28286
London N21 3WT, UNITED KINGDOM
(UK)

Norman, ChrisNL-
Venlo, THE NETHERLANDS 5902 MA

Norman, Dan (Athlete, Baseball Player)
430 McBroom Ave
Barstow, CA 92311-5538, USA

Norman, Edie Jo (Bowler)
3544 Mariner Blvd
Spring Hill, FL 34609-2487, USA

Norman, Fred (Athlete, Baseball Player)
5921 Monnett Rd
Julian, NC 27283-9187, USA

Norman, Greg (Athlete, Golfer)
2041 Vista Pkwy Ste Level
W Palm Beach, FL 33411, USA

Norman, Jessye (Musician)
L'Orchidee
PO Box South
Crugers, NY 10521, USA

Norman, Joe (Athlete, Football Player)
1526 Saunders Dr
Wooster, OH 44691, USA

Norman, Ken (Athlete, Basketball Player)
19020 Kedzie Ave
Homewood, IL 60430-4359, USA

Norman, Les (Athlete, Baseball Player)
1401 Dogwood Dr
Greenwood, MO 64034-8671, USA

Norman, Marsha (Writer)
375 Greenwich St # 700
New York, NY 10013-2376, USA

Norman, Michael (Astronomer, Physicist)
University of California
Astronomy Dept
La Jolla, CA 90293, USA

Norman, Monty (Composer)
PRS
29/33 Berners St
London W1P 4AA, UNITED KINGDOM
(UK)

Norman, Nelson (Athlete, Baseball Player)
6135 Long Key Ln
Boynton Beach, FL 33472-2369, USA

Norman, Pettis (Athlete, Football Player)
1430 Bar Harbor Cir
Dallas, TX 75232, USA

Norman, Steve (Musician)
International Talent Group
729 7th Ave
#1600
New York, NY 10019, USA

Norman, Todd (Athlete, Football Player)
27517 Via Montoya
San Juan Capistrano, CA 92675, USA

Norona, David (Actor)
c/o Staff Member *Kohner Agency, The*
9300 Wilshire Blvd
Suite 555
Beverly Hills, CA 90212, USA

Noronen, Mika (Athlete, Hockey Player)
65 S Autumn Dr
Rochester, NY 14626, USA

Norrena, Fredrik (Athlete, Hockey Player)
1751 Barrington Road
Columbus, OH 43221-3838, USA

Norrington, Roger A C
Camerata Academica Salzburg
Bergstr 22
Salzburg 5020, AUSTRIA

Norris, Aaron (Director, Producer)
C/O Henry Holmes
2450 Colorado Ave Ste 400 E
Santa Monica, CA 90404, USA

Norris, Alan E (Judge)
US Court of Appeals
US Courthouse
85 Marconi Blvd
Columbus, OH 43215, USA

Norris, Chuck (Actor, Producer, Writer)
*National Council On Bible Curriculum In
Public Schools*
Board of Directors
3 Fountain Manor Dr
Greensboro, NC 27405, USA

Norris, Darran (Actor)
c/o Staff Member *ICM Partners (ICM-LA)*
10250 Constellation Blvd Fl 7
Los Angeles, CA 90067, USA

Norris, David Owen (Musician)
Aughton Rise
Collingbourne
Kingston Wilts SN8 3SA, UNITED
KINGDOM (UK)

Norris, Dean (Actor)
c/o Keith Addis *Industry Entertainment
Partners*
955 S Carrillo Dr
Suite 300
Los Angeles, CA 90048, USA

Norris, Duane (Stylist)
c/o Staff Member *Elite Model
Management/Atlanta*
1708 Peachtree St NW
#210
Atlanta, GA 30309, USA

Norris, Dwayne (Athlete, Hockey Player)
850 Eastlake Ct
Oxford, MI 48371-6802, USA

Norris, Jack (Athlete, Hockey Player)
PO Box 323
Delisle, SK SOL OPO, CANADA

Norris, Jim (Athlete, Baseball Player)
6375 Oak Hollow Dr
Burleson, TX 76028-2839, USA

Norris, John (Journalist, Television Host)
c/o Staff Member *MTV News*
1515 Broadway Fl 29
New York, NY 10036, USA

Norris, Martyn (Athlete, Basketball Player)
18943 Crescent Bay Dr
Houston, TX 77094-3329, USA

Norris, Michele (Correspondent)
ABC-TV
News Dept
5010 Creston St
Hyattsville, MD 20781, USA

Norris, Mike (Athlete, Baseball Player)
6228 Ridgemont Dr
Oakland, CA 94619-3725, USA

Norris, Paul J (Business Person)
WR Grace Co
7500 Grace Dr
Columbia, MD 21044, USA

Norris, Terry (Boxer)
Don King Productions
968 Pinehurst Dr
Las Vegas, NV 89109, USA

Norris, Thomas R (General)
33593 E Hayden Lake Rd
Hayden, ID 83835, USA

Norris, Tim (Athlete, Golfer)
1604 Little Kitten Ave
Manhattan, KS 66503-7500, USA

Norris, William A (Judge)
US COurt of Appeals
312 N Springs St
Los Angeles, CA 90012, USA

Norrish, Rod (Athlete, Hockey Player)
3516 Amherst Ave
Dallas, TX 75225-7419, USA

Norseth, Mike (Athlete, Football Player)
9774 Jameson Point Cove
Sandy, UT 84092, USA

North, Andy (Athlete, Golfer)
3289 High Point Rd
Madison, WI 53719-4911, USA

North, Billy (Athlete, Baseball Player)
5523 106th Ave NE
Kirkland, WA 98033-7413, USA

North, Chandra (Model)
c/o Staff Member *Storm Model
Management*
5 Jubilee Pl
1st Floor
London SW3 3TD, UNITED KINGDOM

North, Douglass C (Nobel Prize Laureate)
7569 Homestead Road
Benzonia, MI 49616-9520, USA

North, Heather (Actor)
12996 Galewood St
Studio City, CA 91604-4045, USA

North, Jay (Actor)
290 NE First Ave
Lake Butler, FL 32054, USA

North, J J
PO Box 614
Bloomfield, NJ 07003-0614, USA

North, Lowell (Athlete, Olympic Athlete,
Sailor)
333 San Antonio Ave
San Diego, CA 92106-3546, USA

North, Oliver L (Politician)
c/o Staff Member *Fox News Channel (NY)*
1211 Ave of the Americas
Level C1
New York, NY 10036-8701, USA

North, Peter (Adult Film Star)
c/o Staff Member *Vivid Entertainment*
3599 Cahuenga Blvd #400
Los Angeles, CA 90068, USA

Northam, Jeremy (Actor)
c/o Chris Andrews *Creative Artists Agency
(CAA-LA)*
2000 Ave Of The Stars
Los Angeles, CA 90067, USA

Northcutt, Dennis (Athlete, Football
Player)
13761 S Saxon Lake Dr
Jacksonville, FL 32225, USA

Northey, Scott (Athlete, Baseball Player)
9920 Bankside Dr
Roswell, GA 30076-3735, USA

Northrop, Wayne (Actor)
37900 Road 800
Raymond, CA 93653, USA

Northrup, Wayne
21919 W. Canon Dr.
Topanga, CA 90290

Northrup, MD, Christiane (Writer)
Empowering Women's Wisdom
PO Box 199
Yarmouth, ME 04096

Northtrip, Richard A (Misc)
Cement & Allied Workers Union
2500 Brickdale
Elk Grove Village, IL 60007, USA

Northway, Douglas (Doug) (Swimmer)
3239 E 3rd St
Tucson, AZ 85716, USA

Norton, Brad (Athlete, Hockey Player)
21310 Castillo St
Woodland Hills, CA 91364-4420, USA

Norton, Bryan (Athlete, Golfer)
3816 W 65th St
Mission Hills, KS 66208, USA

Norton, Corin (Actor)
c/o Staff Member *Bruce Heller and
Associates*
3272 Motor Ave Suites F & G
Los Angeles, CA 90039, USA

Norton, Edward (Actor)
c/o Cynthia Swartz *Strategy PR*
220 W 42nd St
12th Floor
New York, NY 10036, USA

Norton, Gale (Politician)
6645 S Quemoy Cir
Aurora, CO 80016-2686, USA

Norton, Graham (Actor)
c/o Melanie Rockcliffe *Troika*
74 Clerkenwell Rd
3rd Floor
London EC1M 5QA, United Kingdom

Norton, Greg (Athlete, Baseball Player)
11130 Eliot Ct
Denver, CO 80234-4682, USA

Norton, James A (Athlete, Football Player)
2550 S Ellsworth Rd
Unit 13
Mesa, AZ 85209, USA

Norton, James C (Athlete, Football Player)
P.O. Box 495997
Garland, TX 75049, USA

Norton, James J (Misc)
Graphic Communications International
1900 L St NW
Washington, DC 20036, USA

Norton, Jeff (Athlete, Hockey Player,
Olympic Athlete)
110 Humphreys Ln
Duxbury, MA 02332-4846, USA

Norton, Jerry (Athlete, Football Player)
6901 Chevy Chase Ave
Dallas, TX 75225, USA

Norton, Peter (Designer)
225 Arizona Ave
#200W
Santa Monica, CA 90401, USA

Norton, Phil (Athlete, Baseball Player)
677 County Road 3772
Queen City, TX 75572-7947, USA

Norton, Richard (Actor)
c/o Ray Cavaleri *Cavaleri & Associates*
178 S Victory Blvd
Suite 205
Burbank, CA 91502, USA

Norton, Rick (Athlete, Football Player)
901 W Mahoney St
Plant City, FL 33563, USA

Norton, Tom (Athlete, Baseball Player)
4900 Southwood Dr
Sheffield Lake, OH 44054-1559, USA

Norton, Virginia (Bowler)
11706 Mindanao St
Cypress, CA 90630-5662, USA

Norton Jr, Ken (Athlete, Coach, Football
Coach, Football Player)
Seattle Seahawks
Coaching Staff
800 Occidental Ave S, Suite 200
Seattle, WA 98134, USA

Norvell, Jay (Athlete, Football Player)
2166 Clinton Ave
Alameda, CA 94501, USA

Norville, Deborah (Journalist)
c/o Rick Hersh *Celebrity Consultants LLC*
3340 Ocean Park Blvd
Suite 1030
Santa Monica, CA 90405, USA

Norvind, Nailea (Actor)
c/o Staff Member *Televisa*
Blvd Adolfo Lopez Mateos 232
Colonia San Angel INN
DF CP 01060, MEXICO

Norwich, Craig (Athlete, Hockey Player)
66 9th St E Unit 2711
Saint Paul, MN 55101-2282, USA

Norwood, Brandy (Actor, Musician)
23463 Park Colombo
Calabasas, CA 91302, USA

Norwood, Jerious (Football Player)
c/o Staff Member *Atlanta Falcons*
4400 Falcon Pkwy
Flowery Branch, GA 30542, USA

Norwood, Lee (Athlete, Hockey Player)
28876 Olson St
Livonia, MI 48150-4038, USA

Norwood, Ray J (Actor, Musician)
c/o Staff Member *Defining Artists Agency*
10 Universal City Plaza
Suite 2000
Universal City, CA 91608, USA

Norwood, Robin (Writer)
c/o Staff Member *Simon & Schuster*
1230 Avenue of the Americas
New York, NY 10020, USA

Norwood, Scott (Athlete, Football Player)
42923 Shelbourne Sq
Chantilly, VA 20152, USA

Norwood, Willie (Athlete, Basketball
Player)
414 W 122nd St
Apt B
Los Angeles, CA 90061-1314, USA

Norwood, Willie (Athlete, Baseball
Player)
225 Gunsmoke Dr
Diamond Bar, CA 91765-1257, USA

Nosbusch, Desiree
Mohrengasse 18
Hohenems, AUSTRIA A-6845

Nosek, Randy (Athlete, Baseball Player)
15485 Knobhill Dr
Linden, MI 48451-8716, USA

Noseworthy, Jack
955 S. Carrillo Dr. #300
Los Angeles, CA 90048

Nossal, Gustav J V (Doctor)
46 Fellows St
Kew, VIC 3101, AUSTRALIA

Nosseck, Noel (Director)
1435 San Ysidro Dr
Beverly Hills, CA 90210, USA

Nossek, Joe (Athlete, Baseball Player)
630 Sunrise Dr
Amherst, OH 44001-1659, USA

Notaro, Phyllis (Bowler)
11123 Maritime Ct
Wellington, FL 33449-8364, USA

Notebaert, Richard (Business Person)
Quest Communications
1801 California St
Denver, CO 80202, USA

Noth, Christopher (Actor)
c/o Nancy Sanders *Sanders Armstrong Caserta*
2120 Colorado Blvd
Suite 120
Santa Monica, CA 90404, USA

Nothstein, Marty (Athlete, Cycler, Olympic Athlete)
1019 Village Round
Allentown, PA 18106-9779, USA

Notkins, Abner L (Scientist)
National Institute of Dental Research
9000 Rockville Pike
Bethesda, MD 20892, USA

Notley, Alice (Writer)
c/o Staff Member *Wesleyan University Press*
215 Long Lane
Middletown, CT 06459, USA

Noto, Lucio A (Business Person)
Mobil Corp
3225 Gallows Road
Fairfax, VA 22037, USA

Nott, John W F (Government Official)
Hillsdown Holdings PLC
32 Hampstead High St
London NW3 1QD, UNITED KINGDOM (UK)

Nott, Tara (Athlete, Olympic Athlete, Weightlifter)
9516 Hayes St
Overland Park, KS 66212-5029, USA

Nottebohm, Andreas (Artist)
Mentzstr 44
Mulheim An Der Ruhr, GERMANY

Nottingham, Don (Athlete, Football Player)
PO Box 459
Belleview, FL 34421-0459, USA

Nottingham, Robert
4348-B Coldwater Canyon
Studio City, CA 91604-5016

Nottle, Ed (Athlete, Baseball Player)
7527 Midway Dr
Evansville, IN 47711-6300, USA

Nouri, Michael (Actor)

Noury, Alain
Soyans s/Crest
, FRANCE 26400

Nouvel, Jean (Architect)
Architectures Jean Nouvel
10 Cite d'Angouleme
Paris 75011, FRANCE

Nova, Heather
Box 3704
London, ENGLAND W4 4ZN

Nova, Nikki (Actor)
4331 E Baseline Road #B105
PO Box 431
Gilbert, AZ 85299, USA

Novack, K J (Business Person)
America Online
22000 AOL Way
Dulles, VA 20166, USA

Novack, William
3 Ashton
Newton, MA 02159

Novak, BJ (Actor, Comedian)
c/o Kevin McLaughlin *Baker Winokur Ryder Public Relations (BWR-LA)*
9100 Wilshire Blvd
Suite 500, West Tower
Beverly Hills, CA 90212, USA

Novak, David C (Business Person)
Tricon Global Restaurants
1441 Gardiner Lane
Louisville, KY 40213, USA

Novak, Jack (Athlete, Football Player)
308 River Chase Ct
Georgetown, TX 78628, USA

Novak, John R (Inventor)
Engelhard Corp
Automotive Emissions Systems
101 Wood Ave
Iselin, NJ 08830, USA

Novak, Kim (Actor)
13777 Agate Rd
Eagle Point, OR 97524, USA

Novak, Michael (Misc)
American Enterprise Institute
1150 17th St NW
Washington, DC 20036, USA

Novak, Pablo (Actor)
c/o Staff Member *Telefe - Argentina*
Pavon 2444 (C1248AAT)
Buenos Aires, ARGENTINA

Novak, Popper Ilona (Swimmer)
II Orso Utca 23
Budapest, HUNGARY

Novakovic, Bojana (Actor)
c/o Suzan Bymel *Management 360*
9111 Wilshire Blvd
Beverly Hills, CA 90210, USA

Novarina, Maurice P J (Architect)
52 Rue Raynouard
Paris 75116, FRANCE

Novelli, William (Misc)
American Association of Retired Persons
601 E St NW
Washington, DC 20049, USA

Novello, Antonia C (Misc)
2700 Virginia Ave NW
#501
Washington, DC 20037, USA

Novello, Antonia Dr (Politician)
1616 Foss Ave
Orlando, FL 32814-6732, USA

Novello, Don
PO Box 245
Fairfax, CA 94930

Novello, Don (Fr Guido Sarducci) (Actor, Comedian)
Elizabeth Rush Agency
82 Cumberland Ave
Verona, NJ 07044-2105, USA

Noveskey, Matt (Musician)
Ashley Talent
2002 Hogback Road
#20
Ann Arbor, MI 48105, USA

Novoa, Rafael (Actor)
c/o Staff Member *TV Caracol*
Calle 76 #11 - 35
Piso 10AA
Bogota DC 26484, COLOMBIA

Novoa, Rafael (Athlete, Baseball Player)
3420 N 47th Way
Phoenix, AZ 85018-6014, USA

Novosel, Michael J (War Hero)
10 Doral Drive
Shalimar, FL 32579-1612, USA

Novoselic, Krist (Activist, Musician)
FairVote
6930 Carroll Ave
Suite 610
Takoma Park, MD 20912, USA

Novoselov, Konstantin (Nobel Prize Laureate)
University of Manchester
Oxford Road Attn: School of Physics
Manchester M13 9PL, United Kingdom

Novoselsky, Brent (Athlete, Football Player)
405 Marvins Way
Buffalo Grove, IL 60089, USA

Novotna, Jana (Tennis Player)
7834 Montvale Way
McLean, VA 22102, USA

Novotny, Dave (Musician)
Helter Skelter Plaza
535 Kings Road
London SW10 0S, UNITED KINGDOM (UK)

Novotny, George (General)
2870 S Townline Rd
Houghton Lake, MI 48629-8290, USA

Nowak, Lisa M (Astronaut)
17123 Parsley Hawthome Court
Houston, TX 77059, USA

Nowak, Lisa M Cdr (Astronaut)
17123 Parsley Hawthorne Ct
Houston, TX 77059-3231, USA

Nowak, Peter (Coach, Soccer Player)
DC United
14120 Newbrook Dr
Chantilly, VA 20151, USA

Nowak, Tim (Athlete, Hockey Player)
7081 Blackberry Ct
Easton, MD 21601-4767, USA

Nowatzke, Tom (Athlete, Football Player)
4335 Diuble Rd
Ann Arbor, MI 48103, USA

Nowell, Peter C (Biologist)
345 Mount Alverno Road
Media, PA 19063, USA

Nowicki, Tom (Actor)
c/o Staff Member *Davis Management*
4111 Lankershim Blvd
Studio City, CA 91602

Nowitzki, Dirk (Athlete, Basketball Player)
10735 Strait Ln
Dallas, TX 75229-5428, USA

Nowra, Louis (Writer)
Level 18 Plaza 11
500 Oxford St
Bondi Junction, NSW 2011, AUSTRALIA

Noxon, Marti (Writer)
c/o Staff Member *WME (LA)*
9601 Wilshire Blvd Fl 3
Beverly Hills, CA 90210, USA

Noyce, Phillip (Director)
c/o Steve Rabineau *United Talent Agency (UTA)*
9336 Civic Center Dr
Beverly Hills, CA 90210, USA

Noyd, R Allen (Religious Leader)
General Council
Christian Church
1294 Rutledge Road
Transfer, PA 16154, USA

Noyes, Albert Jr (Misc)
5102 Fairview Dr
Austin, TX 78731, USA

Noyori, Ryoji (Nobel Prize Laureate)
Nagoya University Research Center for Materials Science
Chikusa, Nagoya 464-8602, JAPAN

Nozieres, Philippe P G F (Physicist)
15 Route d Saint Nizier
Seyssins 38180, FRANCE

Nri, Cyril (Actor)
Bosun House
1 Deer Park Road
Merton
London SW19 3TL, UK

Nsengiyremeye, Dismas (Prime Minister)
Prime Minister's Office
Kigali, RWANDA

Nsibanbi, Apolo (Prime Minister)
Premier's Office
International Conference Center
Kampala, UGANDA

Ntombi (Royalty)
Royal Residence
PO Box 1
Lobamba, SWAZILAND

Ntoutoume, Jean-Francois (Prime Minister)
Prime Minister's Office
BP 546
Libreville, GABON

Nuami, Sheikh Humaid bin Rashid an- (King, Royalty)
Royal Palaca
PO Box 1
Ajman, UNITED ARAB EMIRATES

Nucci, Danny (Actor)
Gold Marshak Liedtke
3500 W Olive Ave
#1400
Burbank, CA 91505, USA

Nucci, Leo (Opera Singer)
I C M Artists
40 W 57th St
New York, NY 10019, USA

Nuckolls, Sara (Stylist)
c/o Staff Member Celestine - CA
1666 20th St
#200-B
Santa Monica, CA 90404, USA

Nugent, Eddie
PO Box 1266
New York, NY 10150-1266

Nugent, Kevin (Athlete, Hockey Player)
86 Glen Dr
New Canaan, CT 06840-3636, USA

Nugent, Nelle (Producer)
Foxboro Entertainment
234 W 44th St #1005
New York, NY 10036, USA

Nugent, Ted (Musician)
4008 W Michigan Ave
Jackson, MI 49202, USA

Nujoma, Sam S (President)
President's Office
State House
Mugabe Ave
Windhoek 9000, NAMIBIA

Numan, Gary (Musician, Songwriter, Writer)
86 Staines Road
Wraysbury
N Staines, Middlesex TW19 5A, UNITED KINGDOM (UK)

Numeroff, Laura Joffe (Writer)
c/o Staff Member HarperCollins Publishers
10 East 53rd St
c/o Author mail, 7th Floor
New York, NY 10022, USA

Numminen, Teppo (Athlete, Hockey Player)
5975 Tipperary Mnr
Clarence Center, NY 14032-9509, USA

Numminen, Teppo (Athlete, Hockey Player)
Buffalo Sabres 1 Seymour H Knox III Plz Ste 1
Attn: Coaching Staff
Buffalo, NY 14203-3096, USA

Nunes, Devin (Congressman, Politician)
1013 Longworth HOB
Washington, DC 20515, USA

Nunez, Abraham (Athlete, Baseball Player)
Pittsburgh Pirates
2863 Post Rock Dr
Tarcon Scrings, FL 34688-7311, USA

Nunez, Chris (Reality TV Star)
c/o Adena Chawke Greenlight Management and Production
13848 Valleyheart Dr
Sherman Oaks, CA 91423, USA

Nunez, Edwin (Athlete, Baseball Player)
2618 E Locust Dr
Chandler, AZ 85286-2721, USA

Nunez, Jorge (Musician)

Nunez, Miguel Angel Jr (Actor)
c/o Patricia (Patty) Woo Patty Woo Management
3500 W Olive Ave #1400
Burbank, CA 91505, USA

Nunez, Oscar (Actor)
c/o Bruce Smith OmniPop Talent Group
10700 Ventura Blvd.
2nd Floor
Studio Clty, CA 91604, USA

Nunez, Victor (Director)
Paul Kohner
9300 Wilshire Blvd
#555
Beverly Hills, CA 90212, USA

Nunez, Vladimir (Athlete, Baseball Player)
2597 Pierce Brennan Ct
Lawrenceville, GA 30043, USA

Nunley, Frank (Athlete, Football Player)
2131 Mulberry Cir
San Jose, CA 95125-4647, USA

Nunley, Jeremy (Athlete, Football Player)
1595 Little Hurricane Rd
Winchester, TN 37398, USA

Nunn, Samuel A (Sam) (Politician)
781 Marietta St NW
Atlanta, GA 30318-5750, USA

Nunn, Teri (Musician)
MOB Agency
6404 Wilshire Blvd
#505
Los Angeles, CA 90048, USA

Nunn, Trevor R (Director)
Royal National Theater
South Bank
London SE1 9PX, UNITED KINGDOM (UK)

Nunnally, Jon (Athlete, Baseball Player)
1380 Old Quarry d
Apt 2
Ringgold, VA 24586-3056, USA

Nunnari, Talmadge (Athlete, Baseball Player)
7101 Joy St
Apt A8
Pensacola, FL 32504-6480, USA

Nunnelee, Alan (Congressman, Politician)
1432 Longworth HOB
Washington, DC 20515, USA

Nunnery, R B (Athlete, Football Player)
3276 Claude Smith Rd
Magnolia, MS 39652, USA

Nurding, Louise (Actor)
42 Colwith Road
London, ENGLAND W6 9EY

Nurse, Paul M (Nobel Prize Laureate)
Clare Hall Laboratories
PO Box 123
Cell Cycle Control Lab
Herts EN6 3LD, England

Nussbaum, Danny (Actor)
Conway Van Gelder RObinson
18-21 Jermyn St
London SW1Y 6NB, UNITED KINGDOM (UK)

Nussbaum, Joe (Actor, Director, Writer)
c/o Adriana Alberghetti WME (LA)
9601 Wilshire Blvd Fl 3
Beverly Hills, CA 90210, USA

Nussbaum, Karen (Misc)
9-5 National Working Women Assn
231 W Wisconsin
#900
Milwaukee, WI 53203, USA

Nussbaum, Martha C (Misc)
University of Chicago
Law School
111 E 60th St
Chicago, IL 60637, USA

Nussiein-Volhard, Christiane (Nobel Prize Laureate)
Max Planck Biology Institute
Spenmannstr 35/Ill
Tubingen 72076, GERMANY

Nusslein-Volhard, Christiane (Nobel Prize Laureate)
Max-Planck Institut fur Entwicklungsbiologie
Spermannstrasse 35/111
Tubingen D-74000, Germany

Nussmeier, Doug (Athlete, Football Player)
28493 SW Meadows Loop
Wilsonville, OR 97070, USA

Nutini, Paolo (Musician)
Atlantic Records UK
Electric Lighting Station
46 Kensington Ct
Londo W8 5DA, UNITED KINGDOM

Nutt, Dennis (Athlete, Basketball Player)
704 Magnolia Dr
Arkadelphia, AR 71923-4109, USA

Nutt, Jim (Artist)
1035 Greenwood Ave
Wilmette, IL 60091, USA

Nutter, Alice (Musician)
Doug Smith Assoc
PO Box 1151
London W3 8ZJ, UNITED KINGDOM (UK)

Nutter, David (Director)
c/o Staff Member Genrebend Productions
233 Wilshire Blvd #400
Santa Monica, CA 90401, USA

Nutting, Ed (Athlete, Football Player)
607 Ashford Pkwy
Atlanta, GA 30338, USA

Nutting, Robert (Sportscaster)
366 Oglebay Dr
Wheeling, WV 26003-1624, USA

Nutting, Wallace H (General)
PO Box 96
Biddeford Pool, ME 04006, USA

Nutzie, Futzie (Artist, Cartoonist)
PO Box 325
Aromas, CA 95004, USA

Nuveman, Stacey (Athlete, Olympic Athlete, Softball Player)
US A Softball Team 2801 NE 50th St
Oklahoma City, OK 73111-7203, USA

Nuwer, Hank (Journalist, Writer)
PO Box 31
Fairlane, IN 46126, USA

Nuyen, France (Actor)
c/o Budd Burton Moss Burton Moss
10533 Strathmore Dr
Los Angeles, CA 90024, USA

Nuzorewa, Abel Tendekayi (Prime Minister)
United African National Council
40 Charter Road
Harare, ZIMBABWE

Nwosu, Julius (Athlete, Basketball Player)
12436 Park Regency P1
Rd Apt 1122
San Antonio, TX 78230-5992, USA

Nyad, Diana (Sportscaster, Swimmer)
Uptown Racquet Club
151 E 86th St
New York, NY 10028, USA

Nyberg, Frederik (Skier)
Kaptensgatan 2C
Froson 832 00, SWEDEN

Nyberg, Karen L (Astronaut)
2518 Lakeside Landing
Seabrook, TX 77586, USA

Nyberg, Karen L Dr (Astronaut)
1848 Lake Landing Dr
League City, TX 77573-7781, USA

Nye, Bill (Scientist)
1319 Dexter Ave N Ste 216
Seattle, WA 98109-3541, USA

Nye, Blaine (Athlete, Football Player)
1200 Bay Laurel Dr
Menlo Park, CA 94025, USA

Nye, Erie (Business Person)
Texas Utilities Co
Energy Plaza
1601 Bryan St
Dallas, TX 75201, USA

Nye, Flora (Stylist)
c/o Staff Member Stockland Martel
343 E 18th St
New York, NY 10003, USA

Nye, Naomi Shihab (Writer)
c/o Staff Member HarperCollins Children's Books
1350 Avenue of The Americas
New York, NY 10019, USA

Nye, Rich (Athlete, Baseball Player)
40W2S7 Seavey Rd
Batavia, IL 60510-9420, USA

Nye, Robert (Writer)
Thomfield
Kingsland
Ballinghassig, County Cork, IRELAND

Nye, Ryan (Athlete, Baseball Player)
3319 Golf Course Dr
Alma, AR 72921-8601, USA

Nyers, Dick (Athlete, Football Player)
4055 N Riverside Dr
Columbus, IN 47203, USA

Nyers, Rezso (Secretary)
Ozgida Utca 22/A
Budapest 1025, HUNGARY

Nygaard, Richard L (Judge)
US Court of Appeals
1st National Bank Building
717 State St
Erie, PA 16501, USA

Nykoluk, Mike (Athlete, Hockey Player)
47 Bennington Dr.
#2
Naples, FL 33942, USA

Nyland, William L (General)
Assistant Commander in Chief HqSMC
2 Navy St
Washington, DC 20380, USA

Nylander, Michael (Athlete, Hockey Player)
726 S Monroe St
Hinsdale, IL 60126-5030, USA

Nylund, Gary (Athlete, Hockey Player)
10-15255 36 Ave
Surrey, BC V3S OY4, Canada

Nyman, Chris (Athlete, Baseball Player)
1700 Happy Creek Rd
Front Royal, VA 22630-6438, USA

Nyman, Jerry (Athlete, Baseball Player)
114 N Parkwood Ln
Pavson, AZ 85541-4357, USA

Nyman, Michael L (Composer, Musician)
Michael Nyman Ltd
PO Box 430
High Wycombe HP13 5QT, UNITED
KINGDOM (UK)

Nyman, Nyls (Athlete, Baseball Player)
P.O. Box 236
Susanville, CA 96130-0236, USA

Nyquist, Ryan (Athlete)
c/o Staff Member *Wasserman Media
Group - Carlsbad*
2052 Corte Del Nogal
150
Carlsbad, CA 92001, USA

Nystrom, Bob (Athlete, Hockey Player)
475 Berry Hill Rd.
Oyster Bay, NY 11771, USA

Nystrom, Eric (Athlete, Hockey Player)
475 Berry Hill Rd.
Oyster Bay, NY 11771, USA

Nystrom, Joakim (Tennis Player)
Torsgatan 194
Skellefteaa 931 00, SWEDEN

Nystrom, Lee (Athlete, Football Player)
18411 Priory Ave
Minnetonka, MN 55345, USA

Nystrom, Lene (Actor)
c/o Staff Member *Lindberg Management*
ST Kongesgade 26-38 1 Sal TV
Copenhagen DK-1264, DENMARK

Nyvell, Vic (Athlete, Football Player)
P.O. Box 159C
Kilgore, TX 75663, USA

N'Zinga, Naila (Stylist)
c/o Staff Member *Stockland Martel*
343 E 18th St
New York, NY 10003, USA

O, Karen (Musician)
Yeah Yeah Yeahs
249 Metropolitan Ave
Brooklyn, NY 11211, USA

Oakenfold, Paul (DJ, Musician)
PO Box 19788
London SW15 2FT, UNITED KINGDOM
(UK)

Oakes, Don (Athlete, Football Player)
101 Aftons Meadow Rd
Vinton, VA 24179, USA

Oakes, James L (Judge)
US Court of Appeals
PO Box 696
Brattleboro, VT 05302, USA

Oakes, Summer Rayne (Model)
59 Grand St
Brooklyn, NY 11211, USA

Oakley, Charles (Athlete, Basketball
Player)
700 Park Regency p1
NE Apt 1105
Antlanta, GA 30326-4211, USA

Oak Ridge Boys (Music Group)
Oak Ridge Boys, Inc.
88 New Shackle Island Rd
Hendersonville, TN 37075, USA

OAR (Music Group)
c/o Dave Roberge *Red Light Management*
(NY)
44 Wall Street
22nd Floor
New York, NY 10005, USA

Oasis
54 Linhope St.
London, ENGLAND NW1 6HL

Oates, Adam (Athlete, Hockey Player)
New Jersey Devils 165 Mulberry St
Attn Coaching Staff
Newark, NJ 07102-3607, USA

Oates, Adam R (Athlete, Hockey Player)
53570 Del Gato Dr
La Quinta, CA 92253-7352, USA

Oates, Bart S (Athlete, Football Player,
Sportscaster)
1 Silverbrook Dr
Morristown, NJ 07960, USA

Oates, John (Musician, Songwriter)
c/o Staff Member *Doyle-Kos
Entertainment*
1 Penn Plz #2107
New York, NY 10119-2107, USA

Oates, Joyce Carol (Writer)
Princeton University
English Dept
Princeton, NJ 08540, USA

Oats, Carleton (Athlete, Football Player)
10605 E Coralbell Ave
Mesa, AZ 85208, USA

Oatway, Devin
10635 Santa Monica Blvd. #130
Los Angeles, CA 90025

Obama, Barack (Politician, President)
The White House
1600 Pennsylvania Ave NW
Washington, DC 20500, USA

Obama, Michelle (First Lady)
The White House
1600 Pennsylvania Ave NW
Washington, DC 20500, USA

Obando, Bravo Miguel Cardinal
(Religious Leader)
Arzobispado
Apartado 3050
Managua, NICARAGUA

Obando, Sherman (Athlete, Baseball
Player)
7037 Coral Cove Dr
Orlando, FL 32818-2866, USA

O'Bannon, Dan (Director)
c/o Staff Member *Agency for the
Performing Arts (APA-LA)*
405 S Beverly Dr
Suite 500
Beverly Hills, CA 90212-4425, USA

O'Bannon, Ed (Basketball Player)
11930 Agnes St
Cerritos, CA 90703, USA

O'Bannon, Ed (Athlete, Basketball Player)
1387 Minuet St
Henderson, NV 89052-6457, USA

O'Bard, Ronnie (Athlete, Football Player)
27121 Puerta del Oro
Mission Viejo, CA 92691, USA

Obasanjo, Olusegun (General, President)
President's Office
State House
Ribadu Road Ikoyi
Lagos, NIGERIA

Obato, Gyo (Architect)
100 N Broadway
Saint Louis, MO 63102-2728, USA

Obee, Duncan (Athlete, Football Player)
4488 283rd St
Toledo, OH 43611, USA

Obeid, Atef (Prime Minister)
Prime Minister's Office
PO Box 191
1 Majlis El-Shaab St
Cairo, EGYPT

Obeidallah, Dean (Comedian)
338 E 70th St #3A
New York, NY 10021, USA

Obeidat, Ahmad Abdul-Majeed (Prime
Minister)
Law & Arbitration Center
PO Box 926544
Amman, JORDAN

Oben, Roman (Athlete, Football Player)
11476 Creekstone Ln
San Diego, CA 92128, USA

Oberding, Mark (Basketball Player)
4131 Cliff Oaks St
San Antonio, TX 78229, USA

Oberg, Margo (Misc)
RR 1 Box 73
Koloa
Kaui, HI 96756, USA

Oberg, Tom (Athlete, Football Player)
280 Avery St
Ashland, OR 97520, USA

Oberholser, Arron (Golfer)
c/o Staff Member *Pro Golfers Association
(PGA) Tour*
112 TPC Blvd
Ponte Vedra Beach, FL 32082, USA

Oberkfell, Ken (Athlete, Baseball Player)
1335 W Welsford Dr
Spring, TX 77386-2599, USA

Oberlin, David W (Government Official)
800 Independence Ave SW
#814
Washington, DC 20591, USA

Obermeyer, Klaus F (Designer, Fashion
Designer)
Sport Obermeyer
115 Atlantic Ave
Aspen, CO 81611, USA

Obermueller, Wes (Athlete, Baseball
Player)
7031 27th Ave
Newhall, IA 52315-9600, USA

Oberoi, Vivek (Actor, Bollywood)
5 Kartar Kunj Golden Beach
Ruia Park Juhu
Mumbai, MS 400 0049, INDIA

O'Berry, Mike (Athlete, Baseball Player)
5977 S Fork Dr
Birmingham, AL 35244-5466, USA

Oberst, Conner
c/o Brian Young *Untitled Entertainment
(LA)*
350 S. Beverly Dr #200
Beverly Hills, CA 90212, USA

Oberst, Conor
Merge Records
PO Box 1235
Chapel Hill, NC 27514-1235, USA

Oberto, Fabricio (Athlete, Basketball
Player)
230 W Superior St
Ste 510
Chicago, IL 60654-3584, USA

O'Boyle, Maureen (Entertainer)
30 Rockefeller Plaza
#820E
New York, NY 10112, USA

Obradors, Jacqueline (Actor)
c/o Todd Eisner *Agency for the
Performing Arts (APA-LA)*
405 S Beverly Dr
Suite 500
Beverly Hills, CA 90212-4425, USA

O'Bradovich, Ed (Athlete, Football Player)
235 N. Smith St
Apt 207
Palatine, IL 60067, USA

Obraztsova, Elena V (Opera Singer)
Bolshoi Theater
Teatralnaya Pl 1
Moscow 103009, RUSSIA

Obregon, Alejandro (Artist)
Apartado Aereo 37
Barranquilla, COLOMBIA

Obregon, Ana (Actor)
Paul Kohner
9300 Wilshire Blvd
#555
Beverly Hills, CA 90212, USA

O'Brian, Hugh (Actor)
Hugh O'Brian Youth Foundation
10880 Wilshire Blvd
#410
Los Angeles, CA 90024, USA

O'Brian, Richard (Actor)
Jonathan Alparas
27 Floral St
London C2E 9DP, UNITED KINGDOM
(UK)

O'Brian-Cooke, Penny (Baseball Player)
307-1335 East 27th St
North Vancouver, BC V7J 1S6, CANADA

O'Brien, Austin (Actor)
Gersh Agency
232 N Canon Dr
Beverly Hills, CA 90210, USA

O'Brien, Bob (Athlete, Baseball Player)
1243 E Jamestown Dr
Fresno, CA 93720-4079, USA

O'Brien, Brian (Physicist)
PO Box 166
Woodstock, CT 06281, USA

O'Brien, Carl (Cubby) (Actor)
2530 Independence Ave
#2J
Bronx, NY 10463, USA

O'Brien, Cathy (Athlete, Track Athlete)
19 Foss Farm Road
Durham, NH 03824, USA

O'Brien, Charlie (Athlete, Baseball Player)
4932 E 38th Pl
Tulsa, OK 74135-5529, USA

O'Brien, Conan (Comedian, Talk Show Host)
1253/1265 Amalfi Dr
Pacific Palisades, CA 90272, USA

O'Brien, Conor Cruise (Diplomat, Writer)
Whitewater
Howth Summit
Dublin, IRELAND

O'Brien, Cubby
2839 N. Surrey Dr.
Carrollton, TX 75004-4800

O'Brien, Dan (Athlete, Baseball Player)
4240Wells Rd
Petersburg, MI 49270-9532, USA

O'Brien, Dan (Athlete, Decathlon Athlete, Olympic Athlete)
9420 N 87th St
Scottsdale, AZ 85258-1901, USA

O'Brien, Dave (Sportscaster)
374 South Rd
#349
R^, NH 03870-2514, USA

O'Brien, David (Athlete, Football Player)
66 Emerson Rd
Watertown, MA 02472, USA

O'Brien, Ed (Musician)
Nasty Little Man
72 Springs St
#1100
New York, NY 10012, USA

O'Brien, Eddie (Athlete, Baseball Player)
522 Alder St
Apt 101
Edmonds, WA 98020-3494, USA

O'Brien, Edna (Writer)
Wylie Agency
52 Knightsbridge
London SW1X 7JP, UNITED KINGDOM
(UK)

O'Brien, Emily (Actor)
c/o Beverly Strong *Strong Management*
9350 Wilshire Blvd
#224
Beverly Hills, CA 90212, USA

O'Brien, G Dennis (Athlete, Hockey Player)
31 Hope St N
Port Hope, ON L1A 2N4, Canada

O'Brien, George H Jr (War Hero)
2001 Douglas St
Midland, TX 79701, USA

O'Brien, Gregory M (Educator)
University of New Orleans
Chancellor's Office
New Orleans, LA 70148, USA

O'Brien, Jim (Athlete, Football Player)
413 Bethany St
Thousand Oaks, CA 91360, USA

O'Brien, Jim (Basketball Player, Coach)
Philadelphia 76er's
1 Union Center
3601 S Broad St
Philadelphia, PA 19148, USA

O'Brien, John (Writer)
2 Columbine Placa
Delran, NJ 08075, USA

O'Brien, Johnny (Athlete, Baseball Player)
2405 N 75th St
Seattle, WA 98103-4959, USA

O'Brien, Keith M P Cardinal (Religious Leader)
Archdiocese
113 Whitehouse Loan
Edinburgh EH9 1BB, SCOTLAND

O'Brien, Kenneth J (Ken) Jr (Athlete, Football Player)
201 Manhattan Ave
Manhattan Beach, CA 90266, USA

O'Brien, Margaret (Actor)
14840 Valerio St
Van Nuys, CA 91405, USA

O'Brien, Mark (Business Person)
Pulte Corp
33 Bloomfield Hills Parkway
Bloomfield Hills, MI 48304, USA

O'Brien, Maureen (Actor)
Kate Feast
Primrose Hill Studios
Fitzroy Road
London NW1 8TR, UNITED KINGDOM
(UK)

O'Brien, Miles (Television Host)
c/o Staff Member *CNN (NY)*
1 Time Warner Center
New York, NY 10019, USA

O'Brien, M Vincent (Coach, Horse Racer)
Ballydoyle House
Cashel
County Tipperary, IRELAND

O'Brien, Pat (Sportscaster, Television Host)
c/o Steven Simon *Prince Marketing Group*
18 Carillon Cir
Livingston, NJ 07039, USA

O'Brien, Pete (Athlete, Baseball Player)
5509 Montclair Dr
Colleyville, TX 76034-5028, USA

O'Brien, Peter
397 Riley St.
Surry Hills, AUSTRALIA NSW 2010

O'Brien, Richard (Composer, Songwriter, Writer)
TimeWarp
1 Elm Grove
Hildenborough
Tonbridge Kent TN11 9HE, UNITED
KINGDOM (UK)

O'Brien, Ron (Coach)
6044 Strafford Oaks Drive
Sebring, FL 33875-4779, USA

O'Brien, Scott (Athlete, Football Player)
12690 Overlook Mountain Dr
Charlotte, NC 28216, USA

O'Brien, Soledad (Correspondent, Television Host)
c/o Eric Ortner *Spivak Management / Laff Mobb Enterprises*
6222 Wilshire Blvd
Suite 240
Los Angeles, CA 90048, USA

O'Brien, Syd (Athlete, Baseball Player)
10189 Hemlock St
Rancho Cucamonga, CA 91730-3023, USA

O'Brien, Thomas H (Financier)
PNC Bank Corp
1 PNC Center
249 5th Ave
Pittsburgh, PA 15222, USA

O'Brien, Thomas M (Financier)
North Side Savings Bank
185 W 23st St
Bronx, NY 10463, USA

O'Brien, Tim (Athlete, Track Athlete)
17 Partride Lane
Boxford, MA 01921, USA

O'Brien, Tina (Actor)
c/o Martin Spencer *Creative Artists Agency (CAA-LA)*
2000 Ave Of The Stars
Los Angeles, CA 90067, USA

O'Brien, Trever (Actor)
c/o Faras Rabadi *Emerald Talent Group*
10 Universal City Plaza
20th Floor
Universal City, CA 91608, USA

O'Brien, Trevor (Actor)
c/o Staff Member *Abrams Artists Agency (LA)*
9200 Sunset Blvd
11th Floor
Los Angeles, CA 90069, USA

O'Brien, W Parry (Athlete, Track Athlete)
3415 Alginet Dr
Encino, CA 91436, USA

O'Bryan, Sean (Actor)
c/o Staff Member *Alan Siegel Entertainment*
345 N Maple Dr
Suite 375
Beverly Hills, CA 90210, USA

Obst, Lynda (Producer)
c/o Staff Member *Lynda Obst Productions*
5555 Melrose Ave #210
Los Angeles, CA 90038

O'Byrne, Ryan (Athlete, Hockey Player)
1262 Beach Dr
Victoria, BC V8S 2N3, Canada

O'Callahan, Jack (Athlete, Hockey Player, Olympic Athlete)
101 Linden Ave.
Glencoe, IL 60022, USA

O'Callahan, John (Athlete, Football Player)
361A La Perle Ln
Costa Mesa, CA 92627, USA

Ocampo Uria, Adriana C (Scientist)
National Aeronautics/Space Administration
300 E St SW
Washington, DC 20456, USA

O'Caroll, Sinead (Musician)
Clintons
55 Drury Lane
Covent Garden
London WC2B 5SQ, UNITED KINGDOM
(UK)

Ocasek, Ric (Musician, Songwriter, Writer)
Elektra Records
75 Rockefeller Plaza
New York, NY 10019, USA

Occhipinti, Andrea (Actor)
Carol Levi Co
Via Giuseppe Pisanelli
Rome 00196, ITALY

Ocean, Billy (Musician)
Laura Jay Enterprises
32 Willesden Lane
London NW6 7ST, UNITED KINGDOM
(UK)

Ocean, Frank (Musician)
c/o Brent Smith *WME (LA)*
9601 Wilshire Blvd Fl 3
Beverly Hills, CA 90210, USA

Ocean Colour Scene (Music Group)
c/o Staff Member *Paradigm (Monterey)*
404 W Franklin St
Monterey, CA 93940, USA

Oceansize (Music Group)
c/o Staff Member *Paradigm (Monterey)*
404 W Franklin St
Monterey, CA 93940, USA

Ochirbat, Punsalmaagiyn (President)
Tengeriin Tsag Co
Olympic St 14
Ulan Bator, MONGOLIA

Ochman, Wieslaw (Opera Singer)
Ul Miaczynska 46B
Warsaw 02-637, POLAND

Ochoa, Alex (Athlete, Baseball Player)
14526 NW 83rd Psge
Hieleah, FL 33016-5726, USA

Ochoa, Ellen (Astronaut)
4515 Sterling Wood Way
Houston, TX 77059-3153, USA

Ochoa, Ellen Dr (Astronaut)
4515 Sterling Wood Way
Houston, TX 77059-3153, USA

Ochoa, Lorena (Golfer)
c/o Staff Member *Ladies Pro Golf Association (LPGA)*
100 International Golf Dr
Daytona Beach, FL 32124-1092, USA

Ochoa, Raymond (Actor)
c/o Robin Spitzer *Origin Talent Agency*
4705 Laurel Canyon #306
Studio City, CA 91607, USA

Ochoa, Ryan (Actor)
c/o Kelly-Marie Smith *Brilliant Public Relations*
6260 W 3rd St
Suite 425
Los Angeles, CA 90036, USA

Ochocinco, Chad (Athlete, Football Player)
c/o Drew Rosenhaus *Rosenhaus Sports Representation*
6400 Allison Road
Miami Beach, FL 33141, USA

Ochowicz, Elli (Athlete, Olympic Athlete, Speed Skater)
945 Hutchinson Ave
Palo Alto, CA 94301-3440, USA

Ochowicz, James (Athlete, Cycler, Olympic Athlete)
945 Hutchinson Ave
Palo Alto, CA 94301-3440, USA

Ochowicz, Sheila Young (Athlete, Olympic Athlete, Speed Skater)
945 Hutchinson Ave
Palo Alto, CA 94301-3440, USA

Ockels, Wubbo (Astronaut)
ESTEC
Postbus 299
Noordwijk, AG 2200, NETHERLANDS

Ockels, Wubbo J Dr (Astronaut)
ESTEC Postbus 299
Code ADM-RE
Noordwijk, NL-2200 Netherlands, USA

O'Connell, Charlie (Actor)
c/o Staff Member *Artistry Management*
340 N. Camden Dr
Suite 302
Beverly Hills, CA 90210, USA

O'Connell, Deirdre (Actor)
c/o Martin Berneman *Precision Entertainment*
6338 Wilshire Blvd
Los Angeles, CA 90048, USA

O'Connell, Jerry (Actor)
c/o Michael Rotenberg *3 Arts Entertainment Inc*
9460 Wilshire Blvd
7th Floor
Beverly Hills, CA 90210, USA

O'Connell, Maura (Musician)
Maura O'Connell Mgmt
4222 Lindawood Ave
Nashville, TN 37215, USA

O'Connell, Mike (Athlete, Hockey Player)
Los Angeles Kings 1111 S Figueroa St Ste 3100
Attn: Pro Development Dept
Los Angeles, CA 90015-1333, USA

O'Connell, Mike (Athlete, Hockey Player)
17 Border St
Cohasset, MA 02025-2020, USA

O'Connell, Patricia (Hitchcock)
3835 E. Thousand Oaks Blvd. #435
Westlake Village, CA 91362

O'Conner, Tom
1 The Stiles Ormskirk
Lancashire, ENGLAND L39 3QG

O'Connolly, James (Director)
61 Edith Grove
London SW10, UNITED KINGDOM (UK)

O'Connolly, James (Astronaut)
1305 Lafayette Dr
Alexandria, VA 22308, USA

O'Connor, Bill (Athlete, Football Player)
1905-40 Richview Rd
Toronto, ON M9A 5C1, Canada

O'Connor, Brian (Athlete, Baseball Player)
3054 Inwood Dr
Cincinnati, OH 45241-3101, USA

O'Connor, Bryan D (Astronaut)
2615 Gadsby Pl
Alexandria, VA 22311-4929, USA

O'Connor, Bryan D Colonel (Astronaut)
1305 Lafayette Dr
Alexandria, VA 22308-1107, USA

O'Connor, Derrick (Actor)
c/o Staff Member *Markham & Froggatt*
4 Windmill St
London W1T 1HZ, UK

O'Connor, Des
23 Eyot Gardens
London, ENGLAND W6 9TR

O'Connor, Edmund F (General)
1169 Ironsides Ave
Melbourne, FL 32940, USA

O'Connor, Frances (Actor)
c/o Staff Member *Creative Artists Agency (CAA-LA)*
2000 Ave Of The Stars
Los Angeles, CA 90067, USA

O'Connor, Gavin (Director)
United Talent Agency
9560 Wilshire Blvd
#500
Beverly Hills, CA 90212, USA

O'Connor, Glynnis (Actor)
c/o Staff Member *Bauman Redanty & Shaul Agency*
5757 Wilshire Blvd
Suite 473
Beverly Hills, CA 90212, USA

O'Connor, Jack (Athlete, Baseball Player)
P.O. Box 430
Yucca Valley, CA 92286-0430, USA

O'Connor, J Dennis (Educator)
Smithsonian Institution
Provost's Office
Washington, DC 20560, USA

O'Connor, Mark (Musician)
CM Mgmt
5749 Lanyan Dr
Woodland Hills, CA 91367, USA

O'Connor, Martin J (Religious Leader)
Palazzo San Carlo
Vatican City 00120, VATICAN CITY

O'Connor, Mary (Athlete, Basketball Player, Olympic Athlete)
60 Romanock Pl
Fairfield, CT 06825-7240, USA

O'Connor, Maryanne (Basketball Player)
60 Romanock Place
Fairfield, CT 06825, USA

O'Connor, Michael (Athlete, Baseball Player)
c/o Staff Member *Washington Nationals*
1500 S Capitol St SE
Washington, DC 20003, USA

O'Connor, Myles (Athlete, Hockey Player)
O'Connors Fine Footwear
1415 1St SW
Calgary, AB T2R OV9, Canada

O'Connor, Patrick (Actor)
c/o Staff Member *Select Artists Ltd (CA-Westside Office)*
1138 12th Street
Suite 1
Santa Monica, CA 90403, USA

O'Connor, Patrick D (Pat) (Director)
International Creative Mgmt
76 Oxford St
London W1N 0AX, UNITED KINGDOM (UK)

O'Connor, Renee (Actor)
c/o Staff Member *Grant Management*
1158 26th St #414
Santa Monica, CA 90403, USA

O'Connor, Sandra Day (Attorney)
United States Supreme Court
11St St NE
PO Box 8795
Washington, DC 20543-0002, USA

O'Connor, Sinead (Musician, Songwriter)
c/o Staff Member *Paradigm (Monterey)*
404 W Franklin St
Monterey, CA 93940, USA

O'Connor, Thom (Artist)
Moss Road
Voorheesville, NY 12186, USA

O'Connor, Tim (Actor)
PO Box 458
Nevada City, CA 95959, USA

O'Connor, Zeke (Athlete, Football Player)
Sir Edmund Hillary Foundation
222 Jarvis St
Toronto, ON M5B 2B8, Canada

O'Conor, John (Musician)
Columbia Artists Mgmt Inc
165 W 57th St
New York, NY 10019, USA

O'Day, Alan (Musician, Songwriter)
c/o Ken Kaufman *Hollywood RPM Entertainment*
4732 Park Granada
Suite 223
Calabasas, CA 91302, USA

O'Day, Aubrey (Musician)
c/o Steven Grossman *Collective*
8383 Wilshire Blvd
Suite 1050
Beverly Hills, CA 90211, USA

O'Day, Darren (Athlete, Baseball Player)
4395 Oakdale Vinii¥KS Cir SE
Smyrna, GA 30080-6982, USA

O'Day, George (Yachtsman)
6 Turtle Lane
Dover, MA 02030, USA

ODB (Musician)
Famous Artists Agency
250 W 57th St
New York, NY 10107, USA

Oddlelfson, Chris (Athlete, Hockey Player)
PO Box 604
Brackendale, BC VON1H, Canada

Oddsson, David (Prime Minister)
Prime Minister's Office
Stjo'maaroshusio
Reykjavik 150, ICELAND

O'Dea, Judith (Actor)
PO Box 3566
Flagstaff, AZ 86003, USA

Odegard, Vickie (Golfer)
112 Ashford Dr
Bridgeport, WV 26330-1138, USA

Odelein, Lyle (Athlete, Hockey Player)
1020 Cherrywood Trail
Coppell, TX 75018, USA

Odelein, Selmar (Athlete, Hockey Player)
Farm
Quill Lake, SK SOA 3WO, Canada

Odeleln, Lyle (Athlete, Hockey Player)
12569 Winding Hollow Ln
Frisco, TX 75033-3497

O'Dell, Billy (Athlete, Baseball Player)
225 Odell Rd
Newberry, SC 29108-9250, USA

Odell, Bob H (Athlete, Coach, Football Coach, Football Player)
911 Stenton Pl
Ocean City, NJ 08226, USA

Odell, Deborah (Actor)
c/o Staff Member *Characters Talent Agency, The (Vancouver)*
1505 W 2nd Ave
#200
Vancouver, BC V6H 3Y4, Canada

O'Dell, Jennifer (Actor)
c/o Scott Hart *Scott Hart Entertainment*
14622 Ventura Blvd
#746
Sherman Oaks, CA 91403, USA

O'Dell, Nancy (Television Host)
c/o Annie Jeeves *Fifteen Minutes (LA)*
8436 W 3rd St
Suite 650
Los Angeles, CA 90048, USA

Odell, Noel E (Mountaineer, Scientist)
5 Dean Court
Cambridge, UNITED KINGDOM (UK)

O'Dell, Stewart (Athlete, Football Player)
3532 State Road 144
Mooresville, IN 46158, USA

O'Dell, Tawni (Writer)
Viking Press
375 Hudson St
New York, NY 10014, USA

O'Dell, Tony
417 Griffith Park Dr.
Burbank, CA 91506

Oden, Beverly (Athlete, Olympic Athlete, Volleyball Player)
4631 Lockhaven Cir
Irvine, CA 92604-2336, USA

Oden, Derrick (Athlete, Football Player)
1805 S Barkley Dr
Mobile, AL 36606, USA

Oden, Greg
c/o Staff Member *BDA Sports Management (BDA-CA)*
700 Ygnacio Valley Rd
Suite 330
Walnut Creek, CA 94596, USA

Oden, Songul (Actor)
c/o Gaye Sokmen *Gaye Sökmen Talent Agency*
Karanfil Caddesi Yolal Sokak Ic
Levent No:3
Istanbul 34330, Turkey

Odenkirk, Bob (Actor)
c/o Tim Sarkes *Brillstein Entertainment Partners*
9150 Wilshire Blvd #350
Beverly Hills, CA 90212, USA

Odermatt, Robert A (Architect)
140 Camino Don Miguel
Orinda, CA 94563, USA

Odessa, Devon (Actor)
c/o Staff Member *Vincent Cirrincione Associates*
1516 N Fairfax Ave
Los Angeles, CA 90046, USA

Odgers, Jeff (Athlete, Hockey Player)
The Farm
Spy Hill, SK 50A 3WO, Canada

Odjig, Daphne (Artist)
102 Foresbrook Place
Penticton, BC V2A 7N4, CANADA

Odjlck, Gino (Athlete, Hockey Player)
Musqueam Golf Academy
3904 51st Ave W
Vancouver, BC V6N 3Wl, Canada

Odom, Cliff (Athlete, Football Player)
6708 Marthas Vineyard Dr
Arlington, TX 76001, USA

Odom, Jason (Athlete, Football Player)
11506 Joshua's Bend Dr
Tampa, FL 33612, USA

Odom, John Lee (Blue Moon) (Athlete, Baseball Player)
10343 Slater Ave
Apt 204
Fountain Valley, CA 92708-4783, USA

Odom, Lamar (Athlete, Basketball Player)
21731 Ventura Blvd
Ste 300
Woodland Hills, CA 91364-1851, USA

Odom, Steve (Athlete, Football Player)
1482 Lincoln St
Berkeley, CA 94702, USA

Odomes, Nathaniel B (Nate) (Athlete, Football Player)
900 Quail Creek Dr
Columbus, GA 31907, USA

Odoms, Riley M (Athlete, Football Player)
834 1/2 Staffordshire Rd
Stafford, TX 77477, USA

O'Donahue, Pat (Athlete, Football Player)
1524 Wheeler Rd
Unit D
Madison, WI 53704, USA

O'Donis, Colby (Musician)
c/o Juliette Harris *It Girl Public Relations*
5301 Beethoven St
Suite 220
Los Angeles, CA 90066, USA

O'Donnell, Andrew (Athlete, Basketball Player)
3310 Lincoln Ave
Allentown, PA 18103-7917, USA

O'Donnell, Annie (Actor)
Capital Artists
6404 Wilshire Blvd
#950
Los Angeles, CA 90048, USA

O'Donnell, Charles (Chuck) (Bowler)
7354 Forest Haven E
Saint Louis, MO 63123, USA

O'Donnell, Chris (Actor)
c/o Jason Weinberg *Untitled Entertainment (LA)*
350 S. Beverly Dr #200
Beverly Hills, CA 90212, USA

O'Donnell, Fred (Athlete, Hockey Player)
690 Carnaby St.
Kingston, ON K7M 5M7, CANADA

O'Donnell, George (Athlete, Baseball Player)
70 Crusaders Rd
Springfield, IL 62704-5207, USA

O'Donnell, James Michael (Baseball Player)
204 N Diamond St
Clifton Heights, PA 33469-2724, USA

O'Donnell, Joe (Athlete, Football Player)
447 Bodley Cres
Milan, MI 48160, USA

O'Donnell, John J (Misc)
Air Line Pilots Assn
1625 Massachusetts Ave NW
Washington, DC 20036, USA

O'Donnell, Keir (Actor)
c/o Tom Parziali *Visionary Entertainment*
1558 N Stanley Ave
Los Angeles, CA 90046, USA

O'Donnell, Lawrence (Producer, Writer)
c/o Ari Emanuel *WME (LA)*
9601 Wilshire Blvd Fl 3
Beverly Hills, CA 90210, USA

O'Donnell, Neil K (Athlete, Football Player)
P.O. Box 403
New Vernon, NJ 07976, USA

O'Donnell, Rosie (Actor, Comedian, Talk Show Host)
c/o Cindi Berger *PMK/BNC Public Relations (PMK-NY)*
622 3rd Ave
8th Floor
New York, NY 10017, USA

O'Donnell, Sean
3550 Sarasota Golf Club Blvd
Sarasota, FL 34240-9318

O'Donnell, William (Bill) (Horse Racer)
569 Penn Estate
East Stroudsburg, PA 18301, USA

O'Donoghue, Colin (Actor)
c/o Jason Barrett *Alchemy Entertainment*
7024 Melrose Ave
Suite 420
Los Angeles, CA 90038, USA

O'Donoghue, Don (Athlete, Hockey Player)

O'Donoghue, John (Athlete, Baseball Player)
5246 Far Oak Cir
Sarasota, FL 34238-3304, USA

O'Donoghue, John (Athlete, Baseball Player)
10107 Summerfield Dr
Denham Springs, LA 70726, USA

O'Donoghue, Neil (Athlete, Football Player)
1118 Flushing Ave
Clearwater, FL 33764, USA

O'Donohue, Jessica (Actor)
c/o Dan Cotoia *Letnom Management*
1776 Broadway
9th Floor
New York, NY 10019, USA

O'Dowd, Anna Mae (Athlete, Baseball Player)
1179 Pelzer Ave
The Villages, FL 32162-8691, USA

O'Dowd, Chris (Actor)
c/o Nick Frenkel *3 Arts Entertainment Inc*
9460 Wilshire Blvd
7th Floor
Beverly Hills, CA 90210, USA

O'Driscoll, Martha (Actor)
22 Indian Creek Island Road
Indian Creek Village, FL 33154, USA

Odrowski, Gerry (Athlete, Hockey Player)
PO Box 126
Trout Creek, Ontario P0H 2L0, Canada

Oduber, Nelson O (Prime Minister)
Movimenti Electoral di Pueblo
Curnana 84
Oranjestad, ARUBA

Oduya, Johnny (Athlete, Hockey Player)
Newport Sports Management
400-201 City Centre Dr
Attn Don Meehan
Mississauga, ON L5B 2T4, Canada

O'Dwyer, Bill
550 Washington St Apt 305
Braintree, MA 02184-5641

Oe, Kenzaburo (Nobel Prize Laureate)
585 Seijo-Machi
Setagayaku
Tokyo, JAPAN

Oechsle, Jennifer (Stylist)
5934 Vicksburg Lane
Indianapolis, IN 46254, USA

Oedekerk, Steve (Actor, Director, Producer, Writer)
O Entertainment
31878 Camino Capistrano
Suite 101
San Juan Capistrano, CA 92675, USA

Oefelein, William A (Astronaut)
1205 Hawkhill Dr
Friendswood, TX 77456, USA

Oefelein, William A Cdr (Astronaut)
Adventure Write
PO Box 113074
Anchorage, AK 99511-3074, USA

Oelkers, Bryan (Athlete, Baseball Player)
3404 Taylor Ave
Bridgeton, MO 63044-3055, USA

Oenish, Dean (Doctor)
Preventive Medical Research Institute
900 Bridgeway
#204
Sausalito, CA 94965, USA

Oester, Ron (Athlete, Baseball Player)
3780 9 MileTobasco Rd
Cincinnati, OH 45255-5232, USA

Oetiker, Phil (Cinematographer)
422 10th St
Brooklyn, NY 11215, USA

Oettinger, Anthony G (Mathematician)
65 Elizabeth Road
Belmont, NY 11215, USA

O'Farrili, Orlando (Athlete, Baseball Player)
Villa Rafael a Herrera Casa A-30
Managua, Nicaragua, USA

O'Farrill, Orlando (Baseball Player)
Philadelphia Stars
Villa Rafaela Herrera Casa A-30
Managua, NICARAGUA

Offerdahl, John A (Athlete, Football Player)
2749 NE 37th Dr
Fort Lauderdale, FL 33308, USA

Offerman, Jose (Athlete, Baseball Player)
10720 Mooroark St
North Hollywood, CA 91602-2723, USA

Offerman, Nick (Actor)
c/o Michelle Benson *42West (NY)*
220 W 42nd St
12th Floor
New York, NY 10036, USA

Office, Rowland (Athlete, Baseball Player)
1028 Lake Glen Way
Sacramento, CA 95822-3224, USA

Offishall, Kardinal (Musician)
c/o Staff Member *MCA Records (LA)*
2220 Colorado Ave
Santa Monica, CA 90404, 310-865-4500

Offspring (Music Group)
c/o Staff Member *Epitaph Records*
2798 Sunset Blvd
Los Angeles, CA 90026, USA

O'Flaherty, Eric (Athlete, Baseball Player)
1100 106th Ave NE
Apt 507
Bellevue, WA 98004-4387, USA

O'Flaherty, Gerry (Athlete, Hockey Player)
5446 Cortez Cres
North Vancouver, BC V7R 4R4, Canada

Of Monaco, Prince Albert II (Politician)
Palouis De Monaco
Boite Postal 518
Monte Carlo 98015, Monaco

Of Monaco, Princess Stephanie (Royalty)
Palais Grimaldi
2 Boulevard De Moulins
Monte Carlo 98015, Monaco

of Wales, Prince Charles (Prince, Royalty)
St. James' Palace
London SW1, UK

of Wessex, HRH Prince Edward (Royalty)
Bagshot Park
Bagshot
Surrey GU19 5PN, UK

Ogato, Sadako (Government Official)
United Nations Office for Refugees
CP 2500
Geneva 2 1211, SWITZERLAND

Ogden, Bud (Athlete, Basketball Player)
3324 S 4th St
Springfield, IL 62703-4619, USA

Ogden, Joanne (Baseball Player)
2001/2 W Cypress St
Glendale, CA 91204-2660, USA

Ogden, Jonathan (Jon) (Athlete, Football Player)
9 Jenner Ct
Owings Mills, MD 21117, USA

Ogden, Margaret (Writer)
4621 N 28th St
Tacoma, WA 98407, USA

Ogden, Ray (Athlete, Football Player)
188 Anderson Dr
Brunswick, GA 31520, USA

Ogea, Chad (Athlete, Baseball Player)
3233 Plantation Ct
Baton Rouge, LA 70820-5753, USA

Ogi, Adolf (President)
Bundesiause-Nord
Kochergasse 10
Berne 3003, SWITZERLAND

Ogier, Bulle (Actor)
Artmedia
20 Ave Rapp
Paris 75007, FRANCE

Ogier, Vivian (Stylist)
c/o Staff Member *Talent Plus*
1222 Lucas Ave
Suite 300
St. Louis, MO 63103, USA

Ogilvie, Brian (Athlete, Hockey Player)
3 MacEwan Meadow Rise NW
Calgary, AB T3K 3Kl, Canada

Ogilvie, Kelvin K (Educator)
Po Box 307
Canning, NS B0P 1X0, CANADA

Ogilvie, Lana (Model)
Company Models
17 Little West 12th St
#333
New York, NY 10014, USA

Ogilvy, Geoff (Golfer)
c/o Staff Member *Pro Golfers Association
(PGA) Tour*
112 TPC Blvd
Ponte Vedra Beach, FL 32082, USA

Ogilvy, Ian (Actor)
Julian Belfarge
46 Albermarle St
London W1X 4PP, UNITED KINGDOM
(UK)

Ogilvy, Ian (Athlete, Hockey Player)
14 New Burlington St.
London W1S 3B, UK

Ogle, Brett (Golfer)
Advantage International
1751 Pinnacle Dr
Ste 1500
Mc Lean, VA 22102-3833, USA

Oglesby, Randy (Actor)

Oglive, Benjamin A (Ben) (Athlete,
Baseball Player)
1012 E Sandpiper Dr
Tempe, AZ 85283, USA

Oglivie, Ben (Athlete, Baseball Player)
1012 E Sandpiper Dr
Tempe, AZ 85283-2021, USA

O'Grady, Gail (Actor)
c/o Alan Iezman *Shelter Entertainment*
9454 Wilshire Blvd.
Suite 715
Beverly Hills, CA 90212, USA

O'Grady, Scott
3519 Wallingford Ave N #2
Seattle, WA 98103-9057, USA

O'Grady, Sean (Boxer)
Adoreable Promotions
PO Box 9
Bay City, MI 48707, USA

Ogrin, David (Athlete, Golfer)
2321 Common St #102
New Braunfels, TX 78130-2453, USA

Ogrodnick, John (Athlete, Hockey Player)
37034 Aldgate Ct
Farmington Hills, MI 48335-5402, USA

Ogunleye, Adewale (Athlete, Football
Player)
19113 NW 23rd Ct
Pembroke Pines, FL 33029, USA

Oh, Sadaharu (Baseball Player)
Fukuoka Dorne Daiei Hawks
6F 2-2-2 Jigyohama
Chuo-Ku Fukouka 810, JAPAN

Oh, Sandra (Actor)
c/o Marsha McManus *Principal
Entertainment (LA)*
1964 Westwood Blvd #400
Los Angeles, CA 90025, USA

Oh, Soon-Teck (Actor)
5091 N Fresno St
Suite 130
Fresno, CA 93710-7617, USA

O?Hagan, Andrew (Editor, Writer)
c/o Staff Member *UNICEF*
Africa House
64-78 Kingsway
London WC2B 6NB, UNITED KINGDOM

O'Hair, Sean (Athlete, Golfer)
c/o Staff Member *Pro Golfers Association
(PGA) Tour*
112 TPC Blvd
Ponte Vedra Beach, FL 32082, USA

O'Halloran, Greg (Athlete, Baseball
Player)
1021 Hedge Dr
Mississauga, ON L4Y 1G3, Canada

O'Hanlon, Bill (Writer)
c/o Staff Member *Loretta Barrett Books,
Inc.*
101 Fifth Ave
11th Floor
New York, NY 10003, USA

O'Hanlon, Francis (Athlete, Basketball
Player)
27 W Wayne Ave
Easton PA, 18042-1662 18042-1662, USA

O'Hara, Catherine (Actor, Comedian)
c/o Marc Gurvitz *Brillstein Entertainment
Partners*
9150 Wilshire Blvd #350
Beverly Hills, CA 90212, USA

O'Hara, David (Actor)
c/o Tammy Rosen *Sanders Armstrong
Caserta*
425 N Robertson Blvd
Los Angeles, CA 90048, USA

O'Hara, Jamie
1025 16th Ave. So. #200
Nashville, TN 37212

O'Hara, Jenny (Actor)
8663 Wonderland Ave
Los Angeles, CA 90046, USA

O'Hara, Kelli (Actor)
c/o Erica Tuchman *One Entertainment
(NY)*
12 W 57th St
Penthouse
New York, NY 10019, USA

O'Hara, Maureen (Actor)
P.O. Box 808
Bantry, Couty Cork, Ireland

O'Hara, Terrence J (Director)
Armstrong/Hirsch
1888 Century Park East
#1800
Los Angeles, CA 90067, USA

O'Hare, Denis (Actor)
c/o Staff Member *Innovative Artists (LA)*
1505 10th St
Santa Monica, CA 90401, USA

Oher, Michael (Athlete, Football Player)
c/o Jimmy Sexton *CAA (Memphis)*
1100 Ridgeway Loop Rd
5th Floor
Memphis, TN 38120, USA

Ohl, Don (Athlete, Basketball Player)
2 E Lockhaven Ct
Edwardsville, IL 62025-3703, USA

Ohlendorf, Ross (Athlete, Baseball Player)
2300 Barton Creek Blvd
Apt 40
Austin, TX 78735-1687, USA

Ohlsson, Garrick (Musician)
International Creative Mgmt
8942 Wilshire Blvd
#219
Beverly Hills, CA 90211, USA

Ohlund, Mattias (Athlete, Hockey Player)
C A A Hockey
204-822 11 Ave SW
Attn J P Barry
Calgary, AB T2R OE5, Canada

Ohman, Jack (Cartoonist, Editor)
Portland Oregonian
Editorial Dept
1320 SW Broadway
Portland, OR 97201, USA

Ohman, Will (Athlete, Baseball Player)
4346 N Desert Oasis Cir
Mesa, AZ 85207-7246, USA

Ohme, Kevin (Athlete, Baseball Player)
806 Starlifter Ln
Valrico, FL 33594-2978, USA

Ohno, Apolo Anton (Athlete, Olympic
Athlete, Speed Skater)
c/o Lee Kernis *Brillstein Entertainment
Partners*
9150 Wilshire Blvd #350
Beverly Hills, CA 90212, USA

Ohoven, Ute-Henriette (Misc)
c/o Staff Member *United Nations
Educational, Scientific and Cultural
Organization (UNESCO)*
7, place de Fontenoy
75352
Paris 07 SP, France

Ohr, Fred (General)
6358 Commonwealth Dr
Loves Park, IL 61111-8657, USA

Ohtani, Monshu Roshin (Religious Leader)
Horikawa-Dori
Hanayachosagaru Shimogyoku
Kyoto 600, JAPAN

O'Hurley, John (Actor)
1710 Monte Cielo Ct
Beverly Hills, CA 90210, USA

Ohyama, Heilchiro (Conductor)
6305 Via Cabrera
La Jolla, CA 92037, USA

Oimeon, Casper (Skier)
540 S Mountain Ave
Ashland, OR 97520, USA

Oistrakh, Igor D (Musician)
Novolesnaya Str 3
Korp 2 #10
Moscow, RUSSIA

Oiter, Bailey (President)
President's Office
Palikia
Pohnepei FM
Kolonia 96941, MICRONESIA

Oja, Kim (Actor)
c/o Staff Member *Gage Group, The (LA)*
14724 Ventura Blvd
Suite 505
Sherman Oaks, CA 91403, USA

Ojala, Kirt (Athlete, Baseball Player)
1902 Forest Lake Dr SE
Grand Rapids, MI 49546-8234, USA

O'Jays, The (Music Group, Musician)
c/o Toby Ludwig *21st Century Artists Inc.*
853 Broadway
Suite 1711
New York, NY 10003, USA

Ojczyk, Cindy (Stylist)
2220 Deer Pass Trail
St Paul, MN 55110, USA

Ojeda, Augie (Athlete, Baseball Player)
5351 W Morgan Pl
Chandler, AZ 85226-8613, USA

Ojeda, Augle (Athlete, Baseball Player)
9402 Dorothy Ave
South Gate, CA 90280, USA

Ojeda, Bob (Athlete, Baseball Player)
20 Somerset Dr
Rumson, NJ 07760-1101, USA

Ojeda, Miguel (Baseball Player)
c/o Staff Member *San Diego Padres*
100 Park Blvd
San Diego, CA 92101, USA

Ojukwu, Chukwuerneka O (General,
President)
Vilaska Lodge
29 Queen's Dr
Ikoyi
Lagos State, NIGERIA

Oka, Masi (Actor, Writer)
c/o Ilan Breil *Mosaic Media Group*
9200 W. Sunset Blvd
10th Floor
Los Angeles, CA 90069, USA

Oka, Takeshi (Misc)
1463 E Park Place
Chicago, IL 60637, USA

Okabe, Noroki (Architect, Engineer)
Kansai Airport
1 Banchi Senshu-Kuko Kita
Izumisanoshi
Osake 549, JAPAN

Okafor, Emeka (Athlete, Basketball Player)
c/o Jeff Schwartz *Excel Sports
Management*
9665 Wilshire Blvd #500
Los Angeles, CA 90212, USA

Okajima, Hideki (Athlete, Baseball Player)
165 Tremont St Unit 1601
Boston, MA 02111-1159, USA

Okamoto, Ayako (Golfer)
22627 Ladeene Ave
Torrance, CA 90505-3438, USA

Okamura, Arthur (Artist)
210 Kale St
Bolinas, CA 94924, USA

Okazake, Kenji (Race Car Driver)
840 Kallin
Long Beach, CA 90815, USA

O'Keefe, Jeremiah J Sr (General)
202 White Blvd
Ocean Springs, MS 39564-5046, USA

O'Keefe, Jodie Lyn (Actor)
c/o Vincent Cirrincione *Vincent
Cirrincione Associates*
1516 N Fairfax Ave
Los Angeles, CA 90046, USA

O'Keefe, Michael (Actor)
c/o Staff Member *Paradigm (LA)*
360 N Crescent Dr
North Bldg
Beverly Hills, CA 90210, USA

O'Keefe, Miles (Actor)
c/o Alexandra Karrys *Divine Management*
117 N Orlando Ave
Los Angeles, CA 90048, USA

O'Keefe, Paul
225 W. 83rd St. #9-5
New York, NY 10027

O'Keefe, Richard (Athlete, Basketball Player)
31 Corte Ortega
Apt 7
Greenbrae, CA 94904-1992, USA

O'Keefe, Sean (Scientist)
43385 Ballantine Pl
Ashburn, VA 20147-5210, USA

O'Keefe, Tommy (Athlete, Basketball Player)
1000 Potomac Ln
Alexandria, VA 22308-2638, USA

Okeniyi, Dayo (Actor)
c/o Kanica Suy *Sweeney Management*
6253 Hollywood Blvd
Suite 201
Los Angeles, CA 90028, USA

Okera (Stylist)
c/o Staff Member *Dossier*
556 S Fair Oaks
#431
Pasadena, CA 91105, USA

Okerlund, Todd (Athlete, Hockey Player, Olympic Athlete)
2950 Dean Pkwy Apt 1104
Minneapolis, MN 55416-4321, USA

Okhotnikoff, Nikolai P (Opera Singer)
Canal Griboedova 109
#13
Saint Petersburg 190068, RUSSIA

Okobi, Chukky (Athlete, Football Player)
600 Georgetowne Ct
Wexford, PA 15090, USA

Okogie, Anthony Olubunmi Cardinal (Religious Leader)
Archdiocese
PO Box 8
19 Catholic Mission St
Lagos, NIGERIA

Okogwu Jr, Patrick (Tinie Tempah) (Musician)
c/o Staff Member *WME (LA)*
9601 Wilshire Blvd Fl 3
Beverly Hills, CA 90210, USA

Okolowicz, Jeff (Musician)
Living Eye Productions
PO Box 12956
Rochester, NY 14612, USA

Okolowicz, Ted (Musician)
Living Eye Productions
PO Box 12956
Rochester, NY 14612, USA

Okonedo, Sophie (Actor)
c/o Pippa Markham *Markham & Froggatt*
4 Windmill St
London W1T 1HZ, UK

Okoniewski, Steve (Athlete, Football Player)
2691 Hillside Heights Dr
Green Bay, WI 54311-6774, USA

O'Koren, Mike (Athlete, Basketball Player)
109 Quaker Rd Mickleton
Mickleton, NJ 08056-1304, USA

Okoye, Amobi (Athlete, Football Player)
2431 Sara Ridge Ln
Katy, TX 77450, USA

Okoye, Christian E (Athlete, Football Player)
10082 Big Pine Dr
Alta Loma, CA 91737, USA

Okposo, Kyle (Athlete, Hockey Player)
4442 Derrymoor Ct
Rosemount, MN 55068-4387

Okrent, Daniel (Sportscaster)
645 W End Ave Apt 12F
New York, NY 10025-7354, USA

Okrie, Len (Athlete, Baseball Player)
2636 Burke Ln
Fayetteville, NC 28306-2629, USA

Okubo, Susumu (Physicist)
1209 East Ave
Rochester, NY 14607, USA

Okuda, Hiroshi (Business Person)
Toyota Motor Corp
1 Toyotacho
Toyota City
Aichi Prefecture 471, JAPAN

Okumura, Tomohiro (Musician)
Jecklin Assoc
2717 Nichols Lane
Davenport, IA 52803, USA

Okun, Daniel A (Engineer)
204 Carol Woods
750 Weaver Dairy Road
Chapel Hill, NC 27514, USA

Okungbowa, Tony (DJ)
1863 Preston Ave
Los Angeles, CA 90026, USA

Okur, Mehmet
1387 Perrys Hollow Rd
Salt Lake City, UT 84103-4263, USA

O'Lachlan, Alex (Actor)
c/o Staff Member *June Cann Management*
73 Jersey Rd
Woollahra 2025, AUSTRALIA

Olah, George A (Nobel Prize Laureate)
2252 Gloaming Way
Beverly Hills, CA 90210-1717, USA

Olajuwon, Hakeem (Athlete, Basketball Player, Olympic Athlete)
1305 N Horseshoe Dr
Sugar Land, TX 77478-3428, USA

Olander, Ed (War Hero)
61 Fox Farms Road
Florence, MA 01062, USA

Olander, Jim (Athlete, Baseball Player)
8421 S Triangle R Ranch Pl
Vail, AZ 85641-8719, USA

Olander, Jimmy (Musician)
Dreamcatcher Artists Mgmt
2908 Poston Ave
Nashville, TN 37203, USA

Olandt, Ken (Actor)
Gold Marshak Liedtke
3500 W Olive Ave
#1400
Burbank, CA 91505, USA

Olay, Ruth (Musician)
3100 Neilson Way
Apt 216
Santa Monica, CA 90405, USA

Olazabel, Jose Maria (Golfer)
Sergio Gomez
Apartado 26
San Sebastian E-20080, SPAIN

Olberding, Mark (Athlete, Basketball Player)
4131 Cliff Oaks St
San Antonio, TX 78229, USA

Olberman, Bob (Athlete, Football Player)
4486 Dobbs Xing
Marietta, GA 30068, USA

Olbermann, Keith (Sportscaster, Television Host)
c/o Michael Price *Price Management*
Prefers to be contacted by telephone
Los Angeles, CA 90069, USA

Olczyk, Ed (Athlete, Hockey Player, Olympic Athlete)
4581 Pamela Ct
Long Grove, IL 60047-5271, USA

Olczyk, Eddie
4581 Pamela Ct
Long Grove, IL 60047-5271

Olczyk, Eddie (Athlete, Hockey Player)
Chicago Blackhawks
1901 W Madison St
Chicago, IL 60612-2459

Old, Lloyd J (Biologist)
Ludwig Institute of Cancer Research
1345 Ave of Americas
New York, NY 10105, USA

Old Crow Medicine Show (Music Group)
c/o Staff Member *Paradigm (Monterey)*
404 W Franklin St
Monterey, CA 93940, USA

Olde, Jeff (Director, Producer)
c/o Staff Member *VH1 Television*
1515 Broadway
New York, NY 10036, USA

Oldenburg, Claes T (Artist)
556 Broome St
New York, NY 10013-1517, USA

Oldenburg, Richard E (Director)
447 E 57th St
New York, NY 10022, USA

Oldendorf, William (Doctor)
University of California
Medical Center
Neurology Dept
Los Angeles, CA 90024, USA

Older, Charles (Chuck) (War Hero)
930 Thayer Ave
Los Angeles, CA 90024, USA

Olderman, Murray (Sportscaster)
832 Inverness Dr
Rancho Mirage, CA 92270-1451, USA

Oldershaw, Kelsey (Actor)
c/o Darren Goldberg *Global Creative*
1051 Cole Ave # B
Los Angeles, CA 90038, USA

Oldfield, Brian (Athlete, Olympic Athlete)
1850 W Hig^land Ave Apt 106
Elgin, IL 60123-5080, USA

Oldfield, Bruce (Designer, Fashion Designer)
27 Beauchamp Place
London SW3, UNITED KINGDOM(UK)

Oldfield, Mike (Actor, Composer, Director)
c/o Staff Member *Air-Edel (UK)*
18 Rodmarton Street
London W1H 3F, United Kingdom

Oldfield, Sally (Musician)
Global Artists Mgmt
Willy-Brandt-Str 39
Erftstadt 50374, GERMANY

Oldham, John (Athlete, Baseball Player)
1845 Anne Way
San Jose, CA 95124-6137, USA

Oldham, John (Athlete, Basketball Player)
2127 Sycamore Dr
Bowling Green, KY 42104-3868, USA

Oldham, Tasha (Director)
c/o Jerry Shandrew *Shandrew Public Relations*
1050 S Stanley Ave
Los Angeles, CA 90019-6634, USA

Oldham, Todd (Designer, Fashion Designer)
c/o Staff Member *Creative Artists Agency (CAA-LA)*
2000 Ave Of The Stars
Los Angeles, CA 90067, USA

Oldis, Bob (Athlete, Baseball Player)
306 Virginia Dr
Iowa City, IA 52245-1639, USA

Oldman, Gary (Actor, Director, Producer)
c/o Douglas Urbanski *Douglas Management Group*
9713 Little Santa Monica Blvd
Beverly Hills, CA 90210, USA

Olds, Bill (Athlete, Football Player)
7414 Pohick Rd
Lorton, VA 22079, USA

Olds, Gabriel (Actor)
c/o Darryl Marshak *Marshak/Zachary Company, The*
8840 Wilshire Blvd
1st Floor
Beverly Hills, CA 90210, USA

Olds, Robin (Athlete, Football Player, War Hero)
P.O. Box 1478
Steamboat Springs, CO 80477, USA

Olds, Sharon (Writer)
New York University
58 W 10 St, Suite 303
Attn: English Department
New York, NY 10011, USA

Olds, Wally (Athlete, Hockey Player, Olympic Athlete)
7343 Colfax Ave S
Minneapolis, MN 55423-3022, USA

Oleary, Dan (Athlete, Football Player)
3300 W 159th St
Cleveland, OH 44111, USA

O'Leary, George (Coach, Football Coach)
Central Florida University
Athletic Dept
Orlando, FL 32918, USA

O'Leary, Hazel R (Secretary)
Energy Department
1000 Independence Ave SW
Washington, DC 20585, USA

O'Leary, John (Athlete, Football Player)
4819 N 160th St
Omaha, NE 68116-8038, USA

O'Leary, John (Actor)
Gage Group
14724 Venture Blvd
#505
Sherman Oaks, CA 91403, USA

O'Leary, Kevin
Audience Relations, CBC
P.O. Box 500
Station A
Toronto, ON M5W 1E6, Canada

O'Leary, Marrissa (Actor)
c/o Staff Member *Select Artists Ltd (CA-Valley Office)*
PO Box 4359
Burbank, CA 91503, USA

O'Leary, Matthew (Actor)
c/o Brian Swardstrom *WME (LA)*
9601 Wilshire Blvd Fl 3
Beverly Hills, CA 90210, USA

O'Leary, Michael (Actor)
38 Prospect Ave
Montclair, NJ 07042, USA

O'Leary, Troy (Athlete, Baseball Player)
1060 W Norwood St
Rialto, CA 92377-8220, USA

O'Leary, William (Actor)
c/o Staff Member *Coast to Coast Talent Group*
3350 Barham Blvd
Los Angeles, CA 90068, USA

Oleg, Deripaska (Business Person)
Basic Element Company
30 Rochdelskaya St
Moscow 123022, Russia

Olejnik, Craig (Actor)
c/o Robert Stein *Robert Stein Management*
PO Box 3797
Beverly Hills, CA 90212, USA

Oleksy, Jozef (Prime Minister)
Ul Wiktorii Wiedenskiej 5 M 4
Warsaw 02-954, POLAND

Olerich, Dave (Athlete, Football Player)
2138 Wellesley St
Palo Alto, CA 94306, USA

Olerud, John (Athlete, Baseball Player)
PO Box 606
Medina, WA 98039-0606, USA

Oleschuk, Bill (Athlete, Hockey Player)
132 Sanderling Rise NW
Calgary, AB T3K 3M7, Canada

Olesz, Rostislav (Athlete, Hockey Player)
201 N Westshore Dr 2801
Chicago, IL 60601-7278

Olevsky, Julian (Musician)
68 Blue Hills Road
Amherst, MA 01002, USA

Oleynick, Frank (Athlete, Basketball Player)
1164 Brooklawn Ave
Bridgeport, CT 06604-1206, USA

Oleynik, Larisa (Actor)
c/o Staff Member *Savage Agency*
6212 Banner Ave
Los Angeles, CA 90038, USA

Oliceira, Ana Cristina (Actor)
c/o Clifford Gilbert-Lurie *Ziffren Brittenham LLP*
1801 Century Park W
Los Angeles, CA 90067, USA

Olin, Ken (Actor)
c/o Staff Member *Creative Artists Agency (CAA-LA)*
2000 Ave Of The Stars
Los Angeles, CA 90067, USA

Olin, Lena (Actor)
c/o Chris Schmidt *Paradigm (LA)*
360 N Crescent Dr
North Bldg
Beverly Hills, CA 90210, USA

Olin, Lina (Actor)
c/o Staff Member *Industry Entertainment Partners*
955 S Carrillo Dr
Suite 300
Los Angeles, CA 90048, USA

Olin, Roxy (Actor)
c/o Katie Mason *Luber Roklin Management*
8530 Wilshire Blvd
6th Floor
Beverly Hills, CA 90211, USA

Olinger, Marilyn (Baseball Player)
6451 Far Hills Ave
Dayton, OH 45459-2725, USA

Olinski, Harry (Athlete, Football Player)
3205 Furman Blvd
Louisville, KY 40220, USA

Oliphant, Patrick B (Cartoonist)
Universal Press Syndicate
4520 Main St
Kansas City, MO 64111, USA

Oliphant, Randall (Business Person)
Barrick Gold Corp
200 Bay St
Toronto, ON M5J 2J3, CANADA

Olitski, Jules (Artist)
PO Box 440
Marlboro, VT 05344, USA

Oliu, Ingrid (Actor)
c/o Staff Member *Cunningham Escott Slevin & Doherty (CESD-LA)*
10635 Santa Monica Blvd
130
Los Angeles, CA 90025, USA

Oliva, L Jay (Educator)
New York University
President's Office
New York, NY 10012, USA

Oliva, Sergio (Misc)
Oliva's Gym
7383 Rogers Ave
Chicago, IL 60626, USA

Oliva, Tony (Athlete, Baseball Player)
Minnesota Twins 1 Twins Way
Attn Alumni Association
Minneapolis, MN 55403-1418, USA

Olivares, Ed (Athlete, Baseball Player)
HC 2 Box 12887
San German, PR 00683, USA

Olivares, Omar (Athlete, Baseball Player)
P.O. Box 1328
San German, PR 00683-1328, USA

Olivares, Ruben (Boxer)
Geno Productions
PO Box 113
Montebello, CA 90640, USA

Olivas, John D (Astronaut)
2618 Sunset Blvd
Houston, TX 77005, USA

Olivas, John D Dr (Astronaut)
595 36th St
Manhattan Beach, CA 90266-3409, USA

Olive, Jason (Actor, Model)
c/o Staff Member *Kazarian Spencer Ruskin & Assoc.*
11969 Ventura Blvd
3rd Floor
Studio City, CA 91604, USA

Olive, John (Athlete, Basketball Player)
8652 Harjoan Ave
San Diego, CA 92123-3445, USA

Oliveira, Elmar (Musician)
Cramer/Marder Artists
3436 Springhill Road
Lafayette, CA 94549, USA

Oliveira, Ray (Stylist)
c/o Staff Member *Jump Management Inc*
17 Little West 12th St
#205-C
New York, NY 10014, USA

Oliver, Al (Athlete, Baseball Player)
PO Box 1466
Portsmouth, OH 45662-1466, USA

Oliver, Albert (Al) (Athlete, Baseball Player)
P.O. Box 1466
Portsmouth, OH 45662, USA

Oliver, Bilal (Musician)
c/o Staff Member *Creative Artists Agency (CAA-LA)*
2000 Ave Of The Stars
Los Angeles, CA 90067, USA

Oliver, Bob (Athlete, Baseball Player)
1716 G St
Rio Linda, CA 95673-4534, USA

Oliver, Christian (Actor)
7211 Mulholland Dr
Los Angeles, CA 90068, USA

Oliver, Clancy (Athlete, Football Player)
233 Springview
Irvine, CA 92620, USA

Oliver, Covey T (Attorney, Attorney General, Diplomat, General)
Ingleton-on-Miles
RR 1 Box 194
Easton, MD 21601, USA

Oliver, Daniel (Government Official)
Heritage Foundation
214 Massachusetts Ave NW
Washington, DC 20002, USA

Oliver, Darren (Athlete, Baseball Player)
1804 Larkspur Ct
Southlake, TX 76092-3572, USA

Oliver, Dave (Athlete, Baseball Player)
1709 Timberlake Cir
Lodi, CA 95242-4283, USA

Oliver, Dean (Race Car Driver)
21386 Notus Road
Greenleaf, ID 83626, USA

Oliver, Hubie (Athlete, Football Player)
136 Blake St
Elyria, OH 44035, USA

Oliver, Jamie (Chef)
Jamie's Kitchen
15 The Brambles
Bishops Storford
Herts CM23 4PX, England

Oliver, Joe (Athlete, Baseball Player)
4137 Bounce Dr
Orlando, FL 32812-8147, USA

Oliver, Kristine (Musician)
349 Stable Rd
Franklin, TN 37069, USA

Oliver, Louis (Athlete, Football Player)
5082 SW 167th Ave
Miramar, FL 33027, USA

Oliver, Mary (Writer)
Molly Malone Cook Agency
PO Box U
Sweet Briar, VA 24595, USA

Oliver, Murray C (Athlete, Hockey Player)
5505 McGuire Rd.
Minneapolis, MN 55439-1342

Oliver, Nate (Athlete, Baseball Player)
4403 Oak Hill Rd
Oakland, CA 94605-4632, USA

Oliver, Pam (Sportscaster)
Fox-TV
Sports Dept
205 W 67th St
New York, NY 10021, USA

Oliver, Ron (Director, Writer)
c/o Mark Itkin *WME (LA)*
9601 Wilshire Blvd Fl 3
Beverly Hills, CA 90210, USA

Oliver, Winslow (Athlete, Football Player)
2027 Summerall Ct
Richmond, TX 77469, USA

Oliveras, Mako (Athlete, Baseball Player)
PO Box 8717
Bayamon, PR 00960-8717, USA

Oliveres, Rubin
PO Box 113
Montebello, CA 90640

Olivia (Musician)
c/o Staff Member *Interscope Records (LA) - Main*
2220 Colorado Ave
Santa Monica, CA 90404, USA

Olivieri, Dawn (Actor)
c/o Joel Stevens *Joel Stevens Entertainment*
5627 Allott Ave
Van Nuys, CA 91401, USA

Olivo, America (Actor)
PO Box 54228
Cincinnati, OH 45254-0228, USA

Olivo, Joey (Boxer)
9628 Poinciana St
Pico Rivera, CA 90660, USA

Olivo, Karen (Actor)
c/o Brian Liebman *Liebman Entertainment*
25 E 21st St #PH
New York, NY 10011-8503, USA

Olivo, Miguel (Athlete, Baseball Player)
10004 Plaza De Oro Dr
Oakdale, CA 95361-9235, USA

Olivor, Jane (Music Group, Musician)
Ed Keane
32 Saint Edwards Road
Boston, MA 02128, USA

Olkewicz, Neal (Athlete, Football Player)
17717 Crystal Spring Ter
Ashton, MD 20861, USA

Olkewicz, Walter (Actor)
Gold Marshak Liedtke
3500 W Olive Ave #1400
Burbank, CA 91505, USA

Ollie, Kevin (Athlete, Basketball Player)
210 Thompson St
South Glastonbury, CT 06073-2915, USA

Ollie, mack (Athlete, Basketball Player)
4023 N Grandview Dr
Peoria, IL 61614-6624, USA

Ollom, Jim (Athlete, Baseball Player)
10916 27th Ave SE
Everett, WA 98208-7807, USA

Olman, Monica (Stylist)
6400 NE 4th Ct
Miami, FL 33138, USA

Olmedo, Alex (Tennis Player)
5067 Woodley Ave
Encino, CA 91436, USA

Olmo, Luis (Athlete, Baseball Player)
620 Calle Jose Ramon Figueroa
San Juan, PR 00907-3928, USA

Olmos, Edward James (Actor)
c/o Matthew DelPiano *Creative Artists Agency (CAA-LA)*
2000 Ave Of The Stars
Los Angeles, CA 90067, USA

Olmstead, Bert
2-1512 High Country Dr NW
High River, AB T1 V 1 V9, Canada

Olmstead, Chris Von Saltza (Athlete, Olympic Athlete, Swimmer)
520 Crocker Rd
Sacramento, CA 95864-5608, USA

Olmstead, Matt (Producer)
c/o Staff Member *ICM Partners (ICM-LA)*
10250 Constellation Blvd Fl 7
Los Angeles, CA 90067, USA

Olmsted, Al (Athlete, Baseball Player)
1008 Pinecone Trl
Florissant, MO 63031-7436, USA

Olmsted, Al (Athlete, Baseball Player)
1008 Pinecone Trl
Florissant, MO 63031, USA

Olmsted, Al
St Louis Cardinals
1008 Pinecone Trl
Florissant, MO 63031-7436, USA

Olney, Claude W (Educator)
Olney 'A' Seminars
PO Box 686
Scottsdale, AZ 85252, USA

O'Loughlin, Alex (Actor, Producer, Writer)
c/o Sarah Caroline Linsten *Linsten Morris Management*
3 Gladstone St
Suite 301
Newtown, New South Wales 2042, Australia

O'Loughlin, Gerald
PO Box 340832
Arleta, CA 91334-0832

O'Loughlin, Gerald S (Actor)
23388 Mulholland Dr
#204
Woodland Hills, CA 91364, USA

Olowaonkandi, Michael (Basketball Player)
c/o Staff Member *Los Angeles Clippers*
1111 South Figueroa Street
Los Angeles, CA 90015, USA

Olowokandi, Michael (Athlete, Basketball Player)
Minnesota Timberwolves
10061 SW 60th CT
Miami, FL 33156-1980, USA

Olsavsky, Bill (Athlete, Football Player)
132 Walnut Ave
Saint Clairsville, OH 43950, USA

Olsavsky, Jerry (Athlete, Football Player)
92 Lake Shore Dr
Youngstown, OH 44511, USA

Olsen, Andrew (Baseball Player)
451 93rd Ave N
Saint Petersburg, FL 33702-3147, USA

Olsen, Andy (Athlete, Baseball Player)
451 93rd Ave N
Saint Petersburg, FL 33702-3147, USA

Olsen, Ashley (Actor)
Dualstar Entertainment Group
3760 Robertson Blvd
Culver City, CA 90067, USA

Olsen, Bud (Athlete, Basketball Player)
1602 Gardiner Ln
Apt 130
Louisville, KY 40205-2761, USA

Olsen, Darryl (Athlete, Hockey Player)
3517 Helen Dr
Magna, UT 84044-2769

Olsen, Elizabeth (Actor)
c/o Rhonda Price *Gersh (NY)*
41 Madison Ave
New York, NY 10010, USA

Olsen, Eric Christian (Actor)
c/o Ellen Meyer *Ellen Meyer Management*
8899 Beverly Blvd
Suite 612
West Hollywood, CA 90048, USA

Olsen, Gregory (Astronaut, Business Person)
Sensors Unlimited
3490 US Route 1
Building 12
Princeton, NJ 08540, USA

Olsen, Kevin (Athlete, Baseball Player)
3353 Dales Dr
Norco, CA 92860-2281, USA

Olsen, Kevin (Ballerina)
Florida Marlins
3353 Dales Dr
Norco, CA 92860-2281, USA

Olsen, Mary-Kate (Actor)
Dualstar Entertainment Group
3760 Robertson Blvd
Culver City, CA 90067, USA

Olsen, Mike (Race Car Driver)
PO Box 427
Main St.
N. Haverhill, NH 03774, USA

Olsen, Olaf (Archaeologist)
Strevelsiovedvej 2
Alro
Oder 8300, DENMARK

Olsen, Paul E (Misc)
Columbia University
Lamont-Doherty Geological Laboratory
New York, NY 10027, USA

Olsen, Phil (Athlete, Football Player)
112 Hitching Post Rd
Bozeman, MT 59715, USA

Olsen, Robert C Jr (Admiral, Educator)
Superintendent's Office
US Coast Guard Academy
New London, CT 06320, USA

Olsen, Scott (Athlete, Baseball Player)
2991 NW 185th St
Unit 1701
Aventura, FL 33180-2904, USA

Olsen, Stanford (Musician, Opera Singer)
c/o Staff Member *Columbia Artists Mgmt Inc*
1790 Broadway Fl 6
New York, NY 10019-1412, USA

Olshwanger, Ron (Photographer)
1447 Meadowside Dr
Saint Louis, MO 63146-4914, USA

Olson, Allen (Politician)
International Joint Commission
324 Mark Ave N Apt 301
Fosston, MN 56542-1024, USA

Olson, Benji (Athlete, Football Player)
2211 Old Natchez Trace
Franklin, TN 37069, USA

Olson, Bree (Adult Film Star)
P.O. Box 10471
Fort Wayne, IN 46852, USA

Olson, Candice (Designer)
Divine Design
2760 Mornington Dr
Atlanta, GA 30327, USA

Olson, Dennis (Athlete, Hockey Player)
521 First AveS
Kenora, ON P9N 1W6, Canada

Olson, Greg (Athlete, Baseball Player)
18592 Saint Mellion Pl
Eden Prairie, MN 55347-3487, USA

Olson, Gregg (Athlete, Baseball Player)
1996 Port Nelson Pl
Newport Beach, CA 92660-6618, USA

Olson, Harold (Athlete, Football Player)
1622 Holly Springs Rd NE
Marietta, GA 30062, USA

Olson, James (Actor)
250 W 57th St #803
New York, NY 10107, USA

Olson, Kaitlin (Actor)
c/o Amy Slomovits *Evolution Entertainment (LA)*
901 N Highland Ave
Los Angeles, CA 90038, USA

Olson, Karl (Athlete, Baseball Player)
P.O. Box 1897
Zephyr Cove, NV 89448, USA

Olson, Lute (Athlete, Basketball Player, Coach)
5831 East Finisterra
Tucson, AZ 85750-1008, USA

Olson, Mancur (Economist)
4316 Claggett Pine Way
University Park, MD 20782, USA

Olson, Mark (Musician, Songwriter, Writer)
Sussman Assoc
1222 16th Ave S #300
Nashville, TN 37212, USA

Olson, Mark (Economist, Government Official)
Federal Reserve Board
20th St & Constitution Ave
Washington, DC 20551, USA

Olson, Nancy (Actor)
945 N Alpine Dr
Beverly Hills, CA 90210, USA

Olson, Peter (Congressman, Politician)
312 Cannon HOB
Washington, DC 20515, USA

Olson, Richard E (Business Person)
Champion Int'l Corp
1 Champion Plaza
Stamford, CT 06921, USA

Olson, Tim (Athlete, Baseball Player)
601 Moss Cliff Cir
McKinney, TX 75071-7629, USA

Olson, Weldon (Athlete, Hockey Player, Olympic Athlete)
2623 Goldenrod Ln
Findlay, OH 45840, USA

Olssen, Lance (Athlete, Football Player)
5222 E Timberwood Dr
Newburgh, IN 47630, USA

Olstead, Renee (Musician)
c/o Beverly Strong *Strong Management*
9350 Wilshire Blvd
#224
Beverly Hills, CA 90212, USA

Olszewski, Jan F (Prime Minister)
Biuro Poselskie
Al Ujazdowskie 13
Warsaw 00-567, POLAND

Olvestad, Jimmie
Magnevagen 1
Nacka 131 46, Sweden

Olwine, Ed (Athlete, Baseball Player)
3419 Jacona Pl
The Villages, FL 32162-6681, USA

Olympia (Music Group, Musician)
c/o Staff Member *Equal Vision Records*
P.O. Box 38202
Albany, NY 12203-8202, USA

Olyphant, Timothy (Actor)
c/o Colton Gramm *Brillstein Entertainment Partners*
9150 Wilshire Blvd #350
Beverly Hills, CA 90212, USA

Omakuchi, Narasimhann (Actor)
24 Vasudevapuram
Besant Road
Chennai, TN 600 005, INDIA

O'Malley, Jim (Athlete, Football Player)
238 S Berryline Cir
Spring, TX 77381, USA

O'Malley, Joe (Athlete, Football Player)
656 Sugar Creek Trl SE
Conyers, GA 30094, USA

O'Malley, Martin (Governor)
100 State Cir
Annapolis, MD 21401, USA

O'Malley, Mike (Actor, Director, Writer)
c/o Peter Principato *Principato/Young Management*
9465 Wilshire Blvd
Suite 430
Beverly Hills, CA 90212, USA

O'Malley, Peter (Baseball Player)
326 S Hudson Ave
Los Angeles, CA 90020, USA

O'Malley, Robert E (General)
PO Box 775
Goldthwaite, TX 76844-0775, USA

O'Malley, Sean Patrick (Religious Leader)
Archdiocese of Boston
2121 Commonwealth Ave
Brighton, MA 02135, USA

O'Malley, Susan (Misc)
Washington Wizards
MCI Centre
601 F St NW
Washington, DC 20004, USA

O'Malley, Thomas D (Business Person)
Tosco Corp
1700 E Putnam Ave
#500
Old Greenwich, CT 06870, USA

O'Malley, Tom (Athlete, Baseball Player)
89 Carriage S.Cl
Montoursville, PA 17754-9112, USA

Oman, Qaboos Bin Said Sultan of
The Palace
Muscat, OMAN

Omar, Chamassi Said (Prime Minister)
Prime Minister's Office
BP 421
Moroni, COMOROS

Omar, Don (Musician)
c/o Christy Haubegger *Creative Artists
Agency (CAA-LA)*
2000 Ave Of The Stars
Los Angeles, CA 90067, USA

O'Mara, Jason (Actor)
c/o Michael (Mike) Jelline *United Talent
Agency (UTA)*
9336 Civic Center Dr
Beverly Hills, CA 90210, USA

O'Mara, Mark (Horse Racer)
629 Laurel Cove Ct Apt 205
Orlando, FL 32825-3220, USA

Omar & The Howlers
PO Box 93
Austin, TX 78767

Omartian, Stormie (Writer)
c/o Staff Member *Harvest House Publisher*
990 Owen Loop North
Eugene, OR 97402, USA

O. Matsui, Doris (Congressman,
Politician)
222 Cannon HOB
Washington, DC 20515, USA

O'Meara, Jo (Actor, Musician)

O'Meara, Mark (Athlete, Golfer)
2000 Auburn Dr #330
Beachwood, OH 44122, USA

O'Meara, Peter (Actor)
c/o Staff Member *ROAR (LA)*
9701 Wilshire Blvd
8th Floor
Los Angeles, CA 90212, USA

OMG Girlz (Music Group, Musician)
c/o Staff Member *Interscope Records (LA)
- Main*
2220 Colorado Ave
Santa Monica, CA 90404, USA

Omidyar, Pierre (Business Person)
eBay
2145 Hamilton Ave
San Jose, CA 95125, USA

Ommanney, Catherine (Reality TV Star)
c/o Staff Member *Bravo (NY)*
30 Rockefeller Plaza
New York, NY 10112, USA

Onanian, Edward (Religious Leader)
Diocese of Armenian Church
630 2nd Ave
New York, NY 10016, USA

Onarati, Peter (Actor)
Liberman Zerman
252 N Larchmont Blvd
Los Angeles, CA 90004, USA

Onassis, Athina (Heir/Heiress)
88 av Foch
Paris, FRANCE F-75116

Ondaatje, Michael (Writer)
Glendon College
English Dept
2275 Bayview
Toronto, ON M4N 3M6, CANADA

Ondetti, Miguel A
79 Hemlock Circle
Princeton, NJ 08540, USA

Ondrasik, John (Musician, Songwriter)
c/o Staff Member *Paradigm (NY)*
360 Park Ave S Fl 16
New York, NY 10010, USA

Ondricek, Miroslav (Cinematographer)
Nad Pomnikem 1
Prague 5, Smichow 15200, CZECH
REPUBLIC

ONeal, Alexander (Musician)
c/o *Eminence Leisure*
18-24 John St
Luton LU1 2JE, UNITED KINGDOM

O'neal, Blair (Athlete, Golfer)
c/o Eddie Smith *Gaylord Sports
Management*
13845 N Northsight Blvd
Suite 200
Scottsdale, AZ 85260, USA

O'Neal, Griffin (Actor)
21368 Pacific Coast Hwy
Malibu, CA 90265, USA

O'Neal, Jamie (Musician, Songwriter,
Writer)
Fitzgerald Hartley
19078 Wedgewood Ave
Nashville, TN 37212, USA

O'Neal, Jermaine (Athlete, Basketball
Player)
c/o Arn Tellem *Wasserman Media Group*
10960 Wilshire Blvd
Suite 2200
Los Angeles, CA 90024, USA

O'Neal, Leslie C (Athlete, Football Player)
5617 Adobe Falls Rd
Apt A
San Diego, CA 92120, USA

O'Neal, Randy (Athlete, Baseball Player)
10015 Honey Tree Ct
Orlando, FL 32836-5937, USA

O'Neal, Ryan (Actor)
21368 Pacific Coast Hwy
Malibu, CA 90265, USA

O'Neal, Shaquille (Athlete, Basketball
Player, Olympic Athlete)
9927 Giffin Ct
Windermere, FL 34786, USA

O'Neal, Shaunie (Actor, Reality TV Star)
c/o Patti Webster *W&W PR*
476 Union Ave
2nd Floor
Middlesex, NJ 08846, USA

O'Neal, Steve (Athlete, Football Player)
2914 Coronado Dr
College Station, TX 77845, USA

O'Neal, Tatum (Actor)
c/o Miles Levy *James/Levy/Jacobson
Management Inc*
3500 W Olive Ave
Suite 1470
Burbank, CA 91505, USA

One Direction (Music Group)
c/o Carrie Gordon *42West (NY)*
220 W 42nd St
12th Floor
New York, NY 10036, USA

One EskimO (Music Group, Musician)
c/o Nick Matthews *Coda Music Agency -
UK*
229 Shoreditch High St
London E1 6PJ, UK

O'Neil, Danny (Stylist)
c/o Staff Member *Artist Untied (LA)*
845 S Mansfield Ave
#1
Los Angeles, CA 90036, USA

O'Neil, Edward W (Athlete, Football
Player)
6691 Aiken Rd
Lockport, NY 14094, USA

O'Neil, Lawrence (Director)
International Creative Mgmt
8942 Wilshire Blvd
#219
Beverly Hills, CA 90211, USA

O'Neil, Ron
10100 Santa Monica Blvd. #2500
Los Angeles, CA 90067

O'Neil, Susie (Athlete, Swimmer)
177 Bridge Road
Richmond, Vic 3121, Australia

O'Neil, Tricia (Actor)
c/o Staff Member *David Shapira &
Associates*
193 N Robertson Blvd
Beverly Hills, CA 90211, USA

O'Neil, Warren (Baseball Player)
Detroit Stars
258 Terrace Park
Rochester, NY 14619-2443, USA

O'Neill, Brian (Athlete, Hockey Player)
2600-1800 Av McGill College
Montreal, QC H3A 3J6, Canada

O'Neill, Ed (Actor)
c/o Marc Gurvitz *Brillstein Entertainment
Partners*
9150 Wilshire Blvd #350
Beverly Hills, CA 90212, USA

O'Neill, Eugene F (Engineer)
394 Dogford Road
Etna, NH 03750-4310, USA

O'Neill, Jennifer (Actor, Model)
Jennifer O'Neill Ministries
1811 Beech Ave
Nashville, TN 37203, USA

O'Neill, Kevin (Athlete, Football Player)
1363 Masters Dr
Metamora, MI 48455, USA

O'Neill, Michael (Actor)
c/o Staff Member *Mitchell K Stubbs &
Assoc (MKS)*
8675 W. Washington Blvd
Suite 203
Culver City, CA 90232, USA

O'Neill, Paul (Athlete, Baseball Player)
7785 Hartford Hill Ln
Cincinnati, OH 45242-4347, USA

O'Neill, Paul H (Politician)
3 Von Lent Place
Pittsburgh, PA 15232-1444, USA

O'Neill, Susan (Susie) (Swimmer)
207 Kent St
#1800
Sydney, NSW 2000, AUSTRALIA

O'Neill, Terence P (Terry) (Photographer)
8 Warwick Ave
London W2 1XB, UNITED KINGDOM
(UK)

O'Neill of Bengarve, O Sylvia (Misc)
NewHam College
Cambridge CB3 9DF, UNITED
KINGDOM (UK)

OneRepublic (Music Group)
c/o Ron Laffitte *Red Light Management
(LA)*
8439 W Sunset Blvd
Suite 2
Los Angeles, CA 90069, USA

Onesti, Larry (Athlete, Football Player)
5476 E James Rd
Bloomington, IN 47408, USA

Onetto, Victoria (Actor)
c/o Staff Member *Telefe - Argentina*
Pavon 2444 (C1248AAT)
Buenos Aires, ARGENTINA

Onkotz, Dennis H (Athlete, Football
Player)
270 Walker Dr
State College, PA 16801, USA

Oñ̃, Tommy (Director)
c/o Staff Member *WmE2 (WMA-LA)*
1 William Morris Pl
Beverly Hills, CA 90212, USA

Ono, Yoko (Artist)
Imagine Peace Tower
1 W 72nd St Apt 1
New York, NY 10023-3414, USA

Onodi, Henrietta (Gymnast)
Gymnastic Federation
Magyar Toma Szovetseg
Budapest 1143, HUNGARY

O'Nora, Brian (Athlete, Baseball Player)
5265 Nashua Dr
Youngstown, OH 44515-5174, USA

O'Nora, Brian (Baseball Player)
4294 Maureen Dr
Youngstown, OH 44511-1014, USA

Onorati, Peter
c/o Kay Liberman *Liberman/Zerman Management*
252 N Larchmont Blvd
Suite 200
Los Angeles, CA 90004, USA

Ontiveros, Steve (Athlete, Baseball Player)
9970 E Charter Oak Rd
Scottsdale, AZ 85260-5138, USA

Ontiveros, Steve (Athlete, Baseball Player)
18061 N 87th Dr
Unit 2127
Peoria, AZ 85382-3073, USA

Ontkean, Michael (Actor)
P.O. Box 51
Kilauea, HI 96754-0051, USA

Onufriyenko, Yuri I (Astronaut, Misc)
Potchta Kosmonavtov
Moskovskoi Oblasti
Syvisdny Goroduk 141160, RUSSIA

Oorvasi (Actor, Bollywood)
117 Solai Krishnan Street
Janaki Nagar
Chennai, TN 600087, INDIA

Oosterhouse, Carter (Television Host)
c/o Robert Flutie *Flutie Entertainment (LA)*
9320 Wilshire Blvd
Suite 202
Beverly Hills, CA 90212, USA

Opalinski-Harrer, Janice (Athlete, Volleyball Player)
Women's Pro Volleyball Assn
3653 Diamond Head Cir
Honolulu, HI 96815, USA

Opasik, Jim (Artist)
1914 Beverly Road
Baltimore, MD 21228, USA

Operator (Music Group)
c/o Staff Member *Agency Group Ltd, The (LA)*
1880 Century Park E
Suite 711
Los Angeles, CA 90067, USA

Opie, John D (Business Person)
General Electric Co
3135 Easton Turnpike
Fairfield, CT 06828, USA

Opik, Ernst J (Astronomer)
University of Maryland
Physics & Astronomy Dept
Colleger Park, MD 20742, USA

Oppegard, Peter (Athlete, Figure Skater, Olympic Athlete)
8 Veranda
Newport Coast, CA 92657-1632, USA

Oppel, Richard A (Editor)
Knight-Ridder
National Press Building
529 14th St NW
Washington, DC 20045, USA

Oppenheim, Irwin (Physicist)
140 Upland Road
Cambridge, MA 02140, USA

Oppenheim-Barnes, Saily (Government Official)
Quietways Highlands
Painswick
Glos, UNITED KINGDOM (UK)

Oppenheimer, Alan
1207 Beverly Green Dr.
Beverly Hills, CA 90212

Oppenheimer, Allan (Actor)
1207 Beverly Green Dr
Beverly Hills, CA 90212, USA

Oppenheimer, Benjamin R (Astronomer)
California Institute of Technology
Astronomy Dept
Pasadena, CA 91125, USA

Oppenheimer, Deborah (Producer)
c/o Staff Member *United Talent Agency (UTA)*
9336 Civic Center Dr
Beverly Hills, CA 90210, USA

Oppewal, Jeannine (Misc)
c/o Barbara Halperin *Gersh (LA)*
9465 Wilshire Blvd
Suite 600
Beverly Hills, CA 90212, USA

O'Pry, Sean (Model)
c/o Staff Member *VNY Model Management*
928 Broadway
Suite 800
New York, NY 10010, USA

Opry, Tonya
1525 E. Noble #160
Visalia, CA 93292

Oquendo, Jose (Athlete, Baseball Player)
13219 Selma Rd
De Soto, MO 63020-5242, USA

O'Quinn, Danny (Race Car Driver)
O'Quinn Motorsports
PO Box 1342
Coeburn, VA 24230, USA

O'Quinn, John M (Attorney, Attorney General, General)
O'Quinn Kerensky McAnich
2300 Lyric Center
440 Louisiana
Houston, TX 77002, USA

O'Quinn, Terry (Actor)
Innovative Artists
1505 10th St
Santa Monica, CA 90401, USA

Oquist, Mike (Athlete, Baseball Player)
1910 Raton Ave
La Junta, CO 81050-3427, USA

Orange, Walter (Clyde) (Music Group, Musician)
Management Assoc
1920 Benson Ave
Saint Paul, MN 55116, USA

Orba, Josephine (Stylist)
111 N Oak Park Ave
Oak Park, IL 60301, USA

Orbach, Raymond L (Educator)
3001 Veazey Terrace NW
Apt 525
Washington, DC 20008-5401, USA

Orban, Bill (Athlete, Hockey Player)
4 Binscarth Cres
Kanata, ON K2L 1S1, Canada

Orbelian, Konstantin A (Composer)
Demirchyan Str 27 #12
Yerevan 3750002, ARMENIA

Orbit, William (Musician)
c/o Staff Member *Creative Artists Agency (CAA-LA)*
2000 Ave Of The Stars
Los Angeles, CA 90067, USA

Orci, Roberto (Producer)
c/o Risa Gertner *Creative Artists Agency (CAA-LA)*
2000 Ave Of The Stars
Los Angeles, CA 90067, USA

Ord, Maren
Frontside Management Group
1187 W 16th Ave
Vancouver V6H 1S8, CANADA

Ord, Robert L (Bob) III (General)
3020 Ribera Road
Carmel, CA 93923, USA

Ordaz, Luis (Athlete, Baseball Player)
Auburn Doubledays 130 N Division St
Attn: Coaching Staff
Auburn, NY 13021-1707, USA

Ordonez, Magglio (Athlete, Baseball Player)
181 Nurmi Dr
Fort Lauderdale, FL 33301-1404, USA

Ordonez, Rey (Athlete, Baseball Player)
1000 SE 9th Ave
Hialeah, FL 33010-5810, USA

Ordovos, Jose M (Scientist)
Tufts University
Nutrition Research Center
Medford, MA 02155, USA

Orduna, Joe (Athlete, Football Player)
15 Grant
Irvine, CA 92620, USA

Ordway, Frederick I III (Writer)
3423 Lookout Dr SE
Huntsville, AL 35801-1020, USA

O'Ree, William E (Willie) (Athlete, Hockey Player)
7961 Anders Cir
La Mesa, CA 91942, USA

O'Regan, Tom (Athlete, Hockey Player)
19 Homestead Park
Needham Heights, MA 02494-1517

O'Reilly, Bill (Television Host)
c/o Staff Member *Fox News Channel (NY)*
1211 Ave of the Americas
Level C1
New York, NY 10036-8701, USA

O'Reilly, Cyril (Actor)
Stone Manners
6500 Wilshire Blvd
#550
Los Angeles, CA 90048, USA

O'Reilly, Sir Anthony J.F. (Business Person)
The O'Reilly Foundation
2 Fitzwilliam Sq
Dublin 2, Ireland

O'Reilly, Terry (Athlete, Coach, Hockey Player)
PO Box 5544
Salisbury, MA 01982, USA

Oremans, Miriam (Tennis Player)
Octagon
1751 Pinnacle Dr #1500
McLean, VA 22102, USA

Orend, Jack R
1808 Van Ness Ave
Hollywood, CA 90028-5674, USA

Orendi, Ron
6323 Salem Park Circle
Mechanicsburg, PA 17055

Orenduff, J Michael (Educator)
New Mexico State University
President's Office
Las Cruces, NM 88003, USA

Orenstein, Andrew (Producer)
c/o Staff Member *United Talent Agency (UTA)*
9336 Civic Center Dr
Beverly Hills, CA 90210, USA

Oreskaband (Music Group)
c/o Staff Member *Paradigm (Monterey)*
404 W Franklin St
Monterey, CA 93940, USA

Oresko, Nicholas (General)
4 Tenakill Park E
Apt 109
Cresskill, NJ 07626-2061, USA

Orgad, Ben-Zion (Composer)
14 Bloch St
Tel-Aviv 64161, ISRAEL

Organ, H Bryan (Artist)
Stables
Marston Trussel near Market Harborough
Leics LE16 9TX, UNITED KINGDOM (UK)

Orgy (Music Group)
c/o Staff Member *Creative Artists Agency (CAA-LA)*
2000 Ave Of The Stars
Los Angeles, CA 90067, USA

Oriard, Michael (Athlete, Football Player)
3010 NW McKinley Dr
Corvallis, OR 97330, USA

Orie, Kevin (Athlete, Baseball Player)
Grubb and Ellis Company 6 PPG
Pl Ste 600
Pittsburgh, PA 15222-5406, USA

Origliasso, Jessica (Actor)
c/o Staff Member *The Harbour Agency*
135 Forbes St
Woolloomooloo NSW 2011, Australia

Origliasso, Lisa (Actor)
c/o Staff Member *The Harbour Agency*
135 Forbes St
Woolloomooloo NSW 2011, Australia

O'Riordan, Dolores (Musician)
c/o Danny Goldberg *Gold Village Entertainment*
37 W 17th St
Suite 7W
New York, NY 10011, USA

Orland, Frank J (Doctor)
519 Jackson Blvd
Forest Park, IL 60130, USA

Orlandi, Oluchi (Model)
c/o Staff Member *Model Africa*
Paramount Place
105 Main Road
Green Point, Cape Town 8001, South Africa

Orlando, Bo (Athlete, Football Player)
1360 Armstrong Rd
Bethlehem, PA 18017, USA

Orlando, Eric (Stylist)
c/o Staff Member *Stockland Martel*
343 E 18th St
New York, NY 10003, USA

Orlando, Gates (Athlete, Hockey Player)
252 Bennington Hills Ct
West Henrietta, NY 14586-9765

Orlando, Geoarge J (Misc)
Distillery Wine & Allied Workers
219 Paterson Ave
Little Falls, NJ 07424, USA

Orlando, Tony (Musician)
c/o David Brokaw *Brokaw Company, The*
9255 Sunset Blvd
Suite 804
Los Angeles, CA 90069, USA

Orleans, Joan (Musician)
PO Box 2596
New York, NY 10009, USA

Orlenko, Oksana (Actor)
c/o Staff Member *Sharp Entertainment*
1515 Broadway
New York, NY 10036, USA

Orlich, Dan (Athlete, Football Player)
1030 Porter Cir
Reno, NV 89509, USA

Orlov, Masha (Stylist)
c/o Staff Member *Rex Agency, The*
6311 Romaine St
Los Angeles, CA 90038, USA

Orlov, Yuri
Cornell Univ.Newman Lab.
Ithaca, NY 14853-5001

Orman, Suze (Business Person,
Correspondent, Writer)
Suze Orman Financial Group
2000 Powell Street #1605
Emeryville, CA 94608, USA

Orme, Stanley (Government Official)
8 Northwood Grove
Sale
Cheshire M33 3DZ, UNITED KINGDOM
(UK)

Ormond, Julia (Actor)
c/o Staff Member *Artists Independent
Management (LA)*
825 Nowita Pl
Venice, CA 90291, USA

Ormond, Paul (Business Person)
Manor Care Inc
333 N Summit St
Toledo, OH 43604, USA

Orms, Barry (Athlete, Basketball Player)
500 N Rossmore Ave #403
Los Angeles, CA 90004-2437, USA

Orndorff, Paul (Athlete, Wrestler)
135 Pamela Ct.
Fayetteville, GA 30214, USA

Ornish, Dean (Doctor, Writer)
Preventative Medicine Research Institue
900 Bridgeway #2
Sausalito, CA 94965, USA

Ornstein, Donald S (Mathematician)
857 Tolman Dr
Stanford, CA 94305, USA

Ornston, David E. (Producer)
Salvatore/Ornston Productions
5650 Camellia Ave
North Hollywood, CA 91601, USA

Oropesa, Eddie (Athlete, Baseball Player)
15757 SW 102nd St
Miami, FL 33196-5420, USA

Orosco, Jesse (Athlete, Baseball Player)
16242 Winecreek Rd
San Diego, CA 92127-3733, USA

Orosz, Tom (Athlete, Football Player)
425 1/2 5th St
Fairport Harbor, OH 44077, USA

O'Rourke, Charles C (Athlete, Football
Player)
220 Bedford St
#A7
Bridgewater, MA 02324, USA

O'Rourke, Charlie (Athlete, Baseball
Player)
15612 N Little Spokane Dr
Spokane, WA 99208-8527, USA

O'Rourke, P.J. (Athlete, Hockey Player)
1 Cherry Lane
Georgetown, MA 02833, USA

O'Rourke, PJ (Actor)
c/o Missy Malkin *Brillstein Entertainment
Partners*
9150 Wilshire Blvd #350
Beverly Hills, CA 90212, USA

O'Rourke, Tom (Actor)
c/o Staff Member *Law & Order: SVU*
100 Universal City Plz
Bldg 2252
Universal City, CA 91608, USA

Orpik, Brooks (Athlete, Hockey Player)
Sports Management
51 Nathaniel Pl
Englewood, NJ 07631-2736, USA

Orr, Christopher (Actor)
c/o Staff Member *3 Arts Entertainment Inc*
9460 Wilshire Blvd
7th Floor
Beverly Hills, CA 90210, USA

Orr, David A (Business Person)
Home Farm House Shackleford
Godalming
Surrey GU8 6AH, UNITED KINGDOM
(UK)

Orr, Gregory (Writer)
University Of Virginia
PO Box 400121
Charlottesville, VA 22904-4121, USA

Orr, James E (Athlete, Football Player)
3104 Glynn Ave
Brunswick, GA 31520, USA

Orr, John (Johnny) (Athlete, Basketball
Player, Coach)
5736 Gallery Court
West Des Moines, IA 50266-6629, USA

Orr, Kay (Politician)
1610 Brent Blvd
Lincoln, NE 68506-1866, USA

Orr, Louis (Athlete, Basketball Player,
Coach)
1333 Pine Valley Drive
Bowling Green, OH 43402-5207, USA

Orr, Pete (Athlete, Baseball Player)
400 Rannie Rd
Newmarket, ON L3X 2N3, Canada

Orr, Terrence S (Dancer)
American Ballet Theatre
890 Broadway
New York, NY 10003, USA

Orr, Terry (Athlete, Football Player)
2710 Kellogg Ave
Dallas, TX 75216, USA

Orrall, Robert Ellis (Musician)
3 E 54th St
#1400
New York, NY 10022, USA

Orr-Cahall, Christina (Director)
Norton Gallery of Art
1451 S Olive Ave
West Palm Beach, FL 33401, USA

Orr-Ewing, Hamish (Business Person)
Fox Mill
Purton near Swindon
Wilts SN5 9EF, UNITED KINGDOM (UK)

Orrico, Stacie (Musician)
c/o Staff Member *Creative Artists Agency
(CAA-LA)*
2000 Ave Of The Stars
Los Angeles, CA 90067, USA

Orr III, James E (Business Person)
UNUMProvident Corp
2211 Congress St
Portland, ME 04122, USA

Orr Jr, James E (Jim) (Athlete, Football
Player)
3104 Glynn Ave
Brunswick, GA 31520, USA

Orser, Brian (Figure Skater)
1600 James Naismith Dr
Gloucester, ON L1B 5N4, CANADA

Orser, Leland (Actor)
c/o Kami Putnam-Heist *Creative Artists
Agency (CAA-LA)*
9601 Wilshire Blvd
3rd Floor
Beverly Hills, CA 90210, USA

Orsin, Raymond (Cartoonist)
Cleveland Plain Dealer
1801 Superior Ave E
Cleveland, OH 44114, USA

Orsini, Myrna J (Artist)
Orsini Studios
4411 N 7th St
Tacoma, WA 98406, USA

Orsino, John (Athlete, Baseball Player)
6141 Terra Mere Cir
Boynton Beach, FL 33437-4920, USA

Orsulak, Joe (Athlete, Baseball Player)
29 Keansburg Rd
Parsippany, NJ 07054-3508, USA

Orta, Jorge (Athlete, Baseball Player)
1201 Heather Hill Cres
Flossmoor, IL 60422-1425, USA

Ortega, Amancio (Business Person)
Edificio Inditex
Industria de Diseno Textil
Avenida de la Diputacion
La Coruna, Arteixo 15142, SPAIN

Ortega, Bill (Athlete, Baseball Player)
4635 NW 95th Ave
Doral, FL 33178-2091, USA

Ortega, Gaspar
38 Branhaven Dr
East Haven, CT 06513

Ortega, Jeannie (Musician)
Hollywood Records
500 S Buena Vista St
Burbank, CA 91521, USA

Ortega, Keith (Athlete, Football Player)
142 Lucille St
Lake Charles, LA 70601, USA

Ortega, Kenny (Actor, Choreographer,
Director, Producer)
c/o Andy Patman *Paradigm (LA)*
360 N Crescent Dr
North Bldg
Beverly Hills, CA 90210, USA

Ortega, Manuel (Actor)
c/o Staff Member *Telefe - Argentina*
Pavon 2444 (C1248AAT)
Buenos Aires, ARGENTINA

Ortega, Phil (Athlete, Baseball Player)
307 Leighton Dr
Ventura, CA 93001-1556, USA

Ortega, Ralph (Athlete, Football Player)
10465 SW 124th St
Miami, FL 33176, USA

Ortega Saavedra, Daniel (President)
Frente Sandinista de Liberacion National
Managua, NICARAGUA

Ortega y Alamino, Jaime Cardinal
(Religious Leader)
Apartado 594
Calle Habana 152
Havana 10100, CUBA

Ortenberg, Arthur (Business Person)
Liz Claiborne Inc
1441 Broadway
New York, NY 10018, USA

Ortenzio, Frank (Athlete, Baseball Player)
2357 Oak Forest Dr
Jacksonville Beach, FL 32250-2942, USA

Orth, Lea Diane (Stylist)
15 W 96th St
#4
New York, NY 10025, USA

Ortiz, Adalberto (Junior) (Athlete,
Baseball Player)
161 Kinchafoonee Creek Rd
Leesburg, GA 31763-4903, USA

Ortiz, Alejo (Actor)
c/o Staff Member *Telefe - Argentina*
Pavon 2444 (C1248AAT)
Buenos Aires, ARGENTINA

Ortiz, Ana (Actor)
c/o Gayle Max *Blue Max Management*
1802 North Kenmore Avenue
Los Angeles, CA 90027, USA

Ortiz, Cristina (Musician)
Harrison/Parrott
12 Penzance Place
London W11 4PA, UNITED KINGDOM
(UK)

Ortiz, David (Athlete, Baseball Player)
278 Peterlynn Dr
Wrightstown, WI 54180-1089, USA

Ortiz, Domingo (Misc)
Brown Cat Inc
400 Foundry St
Athens, GA 30601, USA

Ortiz, Javier (Athlete, Baseball Player)
19520 SW 39th Ct
Miramar, FL 33029-2736, USA

Ortiz, Louis (Baseball Player)
1683 La Verde Dr
San Marcos, CA 92069-5223, USA

Ortiz, Luis (Athlete, Baseball Player)
6408 Rogers Dr
North Richland Hills,
TX 76180-4807-4807, USA

Ortiz, Manuel
1 Hall of Fame Dr.
Canastota, NY 13032

Ortiz, Russ (Athlete, Baseball Player)
4040 E McLellan Rd
Unit 13
Mesa, AZ 85205-3105, USA

Ortiz, Shalim (Actor)
c/o Irene Marie *Irene Marie Management Group*
728 Ocean Drive
Miami Beach, FL 33139, USA

Ortiz, Tito (Athlete, Boxer)
c/o Liam Collopy *Levine Communications Office*
9100 Wilshire Blvd
Suite 540, East Tower
Beverly Hills, CA 90212, USA

Ortiz Jr, Frank V (Diplomat)
4287 W 17th Pl
Yuma, AZ 85364-4829, USA

Ortlieb, Patrick (Skier)
Hotel Montana
Obertech
Lech 6764, AUSTRIA

Ortmann, Charles (Athlete, Football Player)
4 River Birch Ln
Savannah, GA 31411, USA

Ortmeier, Dan (Athlete, Baseball Player)
2121 Fairmont Dr
Flower Mound, TX 75028-4606, USA

Ortmeyer, Jed
1421 S 52nd St
Omaha, NE 68106-2303

Ortner, Bev (Bowler)
Po Box 436
Odebolt, IA 51458-0493, USA

Ortolani, Riz
Via Aurelia km 23 400
Torrimpietra, ITALY I-00050

Orton, Beth (Musician)
c/o Beth Holden-Garland *Untitled Entertainment (LA)*
350 S. Beverly Dr #200
Beverly Hills, CA 90212, USA

Orton, John (Athlete, Baseball Player)
2929 E Dublin St
Gilbert, AZ 85295-0403, USA

Orton, Kyle (Football Player)
c/o Staff Member *Chicago Bears*
1000 Football Dr
Lake Forest, IL 60045, USA

Orton, Randy (Athlete, Wrestler)
c/o Kerry Rodgerson *World Wrestling Entertainment (WWE)*
Titan Towers
1241 E Main St
Stamford, CT 06905-3857, USA

Oruche, Phina (Actor)
c/o Staff Member *Bauman Redanty & Shaul Agency*
5757 Wilshire Blvd
Suite 473
Beverly Hills, CA 90212, USA

Oruviral, Krishna Rao (Actor)
4/1 Vellala Street
Kodambakkam
Chennai, TN 600 024, INDIA

Orvella, Chad (Athlete, Baseball Player)
1205 N 27th Pl
Renton, WA 98056-1472, USA

Orvick, George M (Religious Leader)
Evangelical Lutheran Synod
6 Browns Court
Mankato, MN 56001, USA

Orvis, Herb (Athlete, Football Player)
1475 Abbey Ln
Lafayette, OR 97127, USA

Ory, Meghan (Actor)
c/o Staff Member *Pacific Artists Management*
1285 W Broadway
Suite 685
Vancouver, BC V6H 3X8, Canada

O'Sadnick, Craig (Athlete, Football Player)
10 Huntington Forest Ct E
Saint Charles, MO 63301-0490, USA

Osborn, Danny (Athlete, Baseball Player)
1014 SW Portland St
Seattle, WA 98106-2066, USA

Osborn, David V (Dave) (Athlete, Football Player)
18067 Judicial Way N
Lakeville, MN 55044, USA

Osborn, Jim (Athlete, Football Player)
4 Canyon Ct
Algonquin, IL 60102, USA

Osborn, John Jay
14 Fair Oaks St
San Francisco, CA 94110-2209, USA

Osborn, Kassidy (Musician)
LGB Media
1228 Pineview Lane
Nashville, TN 37211, USA

Osborn, Kelsi (Musician)
LGB Media
1228 Pineview Lane
Nashville, TN 37211, USA

Osborn, Kristyn (Musician, Songwriter, Writer)
LGB Media
1228 Pineview Lane
Nashville, TN 37211, USA

Osborn, William A (Financier)
Northern Trust Corp
50 S LaSalle St
Chicago, IL 60675, USA

Osborne, Barrie M (Director, Producer)
c/o Staff Member *Emerald City Productions*
9777 Wilshire Blvd Ste 550
Beverly Hills, CA 90210, United States

Osborne, Burl (Editor, Publisher)
Dallas Morning News
Editorial Dept
Communications Center
Dallas, TX 75265, USA

Osborne, Burl (Religious Leader)
Salvation Army
799 Bloomfield Ave
Verona, NJ 07044, USA

Osborne, Donovan (Athlete, Baseball Player)
1651 Brightstone Ct
Reno, NV 89521-4049, USA

Osborne, Jeffrey (Musician, Songwriter, Writer)
Entertainment Artists
2409 21st Ave S
#100
Nashville, TN 37212, USA

Osborne, Joan (Musician, Songwriter)
c/o Staff Member *Paradigm (Monterey)*
404 W Franklin St
Monterey, CA 93940, USA

Osborne, Mark (Athlete, Hockey Player)
28 Princess Anne Cres
Etobicoke, ON M9A 2Pl, Canada

Osborne, Mary Pope (Writer)
c/o Staff Member *Random House*
1540 Broadway
New York, NY 10036, USA

Osborne, Richard (Athlete, Football Player)
418 Tango Dr
San Antonio, TX 78216, USA

Osborne, Tom (Athlete, Football Coach, Football Player)
5400 Trotter Rd
Lincoln, NE 68516, USA

Osbourne, Jack (Reality TV Star)
c/o Nicole Perna *Baker Winokur Ryder Public Relations (BWR-LA)*
9100 Wilshire Blvd
Suite 500, West Tower
Beverly Hills, CA 90212, USA

Osbourne, Kelly (Musician)
c/o Staff Member *Sharon Osbourne Management*
9292 Civic Center Dr.
Beverly Hills, CA 90210, USA

Osbourne, Ozzy (Musician, Songwriter)
5535 Dixon Trail Rd
Hidden Hills, CA 91302, USA

Osbourne, Sharon (Business Person, Reality TV Star)
5535 Dixon Trail Rd
Hidden Hills, CA 91302, USA

Osburn, Pat (Athlete, Baseball Player)
208 64th Street Ct NW
Bradenton, FL 34209-1625, USA

Osby, Greg (Musician)
Bridge Agency
35 Clark St
#A5
Brooklyn Heights, NY 11201, USA

O'Scannlain, Diarmuld F (Judge)
US Court of Appeals
Pionner Courthouse
555 SW Yamhill St
Portland, OR 97204, USA

Oscar Scheid, Eusebio Cardinal (Religious Leader)
Archdiocese
Rua Benjamin Constant 23/502
Rio de Janeiro 20241, BRAZIL

Oseary, Guy (Business Person, Producer)
c/o Staff Member *Untitled Entertainment (LA)*
350 S. Beverly Dr #200
Beverly Hills, CA 90212, USA

Osgood, Charlie (Athlete, Baseball Player)
22 S Meadow Rd
Carver, MA 02330-1424, USA

Osgood, Chris (Athlete, Hockey Player)
1445 Penniman Ave
Plymouth, MI 48170-1036, USA

O'Shea, Danny (Athlete, Hockey Player)
7343 Colfax Ave S
Minneapolis, MN 55423-3022

O'Shea, Kevin (Athlete, Hockey Player)

O'Shea, Milo (Actor)
Bancroft Hotel
40 W 72nd St
#17A
New York, NY 10023, USA

O'Shea, Terry (Athlete, Football Player)
1034 Quincy Dr
Greensburg, PA 15601, USA

Osher, John (Business Person)
Maltz Jupiter Theatre
Board of Directors
1001 East Indiantown Rd
Jupiter, FL 33477, USA

Osheroff, Douglas D (Nobel Prize Laureate)
75 Ranch Road
Woodside, CA 94062-4809, USA

Oshima, Nagisa (Director)
Oshima Productions
2-15-7 Arasaka
Minatoku
Tokyo, JAPAN

Oshodin, Willie (Athlete, Football Player)
8134 Murray Hill Dr
Fort Washington, MD 20744, USA

Osiecki, Mark (Athlete, Hockey Player)
7482 New Albany Links Dr
New Albany, OH 43054-6012

Osiecki, Sandy (Athlete, Football Player)
11 Bryan Cir
Seymour, CT 06483, USA

Osik, Keith (Athlete, Baseball Player)
5 Pal Ct
Shoreham, NY 11786-2352, USA

Osima, Nagisa
4-11-5 Kugenuma-Matsugaoka
Fujisawa-Shi, JAPAN 251

Osinski, Dan (Athlete, Baseball Player)
9723 W Amber Trl
Sun City, AZ 85351-1346, USA

Osis, Deborah (Stylist)
c/o Staff Member *Perrella Management*
330 W 38th St Rm 1407
New York, NY 10018, USA

Oslin, K T (Musician)
Moress-Nanas-Hart
704 18th Ave S
Nashville, TN 37203, USA

Osman, Mat (Musician)
Interceptor Enterprises
98 White Lion St
London N1 9PF, UNITED KINGDOM (UK)

Osman, Osman Ahmed (Engineer)
Osman Ahmed Osman Co
34 Adly St
Cairo, EGYPT

Osmar, Dean (Misc)
PO Box 32
Clam Gulch, AK 99568, USA

Osment, Emily (Actor)
c/o Kim Jakwerth *Marleah Leslie & Associates PR*
1645 N Vine St
Suite 712
Los Angeles, CA 90028, USA

Osment, Haley Joel (Actor)
c/o Meredith Fine *Coast to Coast Talent Group*
3350 Barham Blvd
Los Angeles, CA 90068, USA

Osmond, Cliff (Actor, Director)
630 Benvenida Ave
Pacific Palisades, CA 90272, USA

Osmond, Donny (Actor, Musician, Producer)
c/o Eric Gardner *Panacea Entertainment*
13587 Andalusia Dr. East
Camarillo, CA 93012, USA

Osmond, Ken (Actor)
9863 Wornom Ave
Sunland, CA 91040, USA

Osmond, Marie (Actor, Musician)
c/o Allison Garman *Rogers & Cowan PR (LA)*
Pacific Design Center
8687 Melrose Ave, 7th Floor
West Hollywood, CA 90069, USA

Osmond Boys
PO Box 7122
Branson, MO 65615

Osnes, Larry G (Educator)
Hamline University
President's Office
Saint Paul, MN 55104, USA

Osorio, Jorge Federico (Musician)
Columbia Artists Mgmt Inc
165 W 57th St
New York, NY 10019, USA

Osrin, Raymond H (Cartoonist)
Cleveland Plain Dealer
Editorial Dept
1801 Superior E
Cleveland, OH 44114, USA

Oss, Arnold (Athlete, Hockey Player, Olympic Athlete)
25601 N Abajo Dr
Rio Verde, AZ 85263-7219, USA

Ossana, Diana (Producer, Writer)
c/o Adam Shulman *Anonymous Content (LA)*
3531 Hayden Ave
Culver City, CA 90232, USA

Ost, Friedheim (Government Official)
Heiersmauer 59
Paderborn 33098, GERMANY

Ostaseski, Frank (Director)
Zen Hospice Project
273 Page St
San Francisco, CA 94102, USA

Osteen, Claude W (Athlete, Baseball Player)
2313 Duncan Perry Rd
Grand Prairie, TX 75050-2039, USA

Osteen, Darrell (Athlete, Baseball Player)
73901 Cezanne Dr
Palm Desert, CA 92211-4512, USA

Osteen, Joel (Religious Leader, Writer)
Lakwood Church
3700 Southwest Fwy
Houston, TX 77027, USA

Osteen Jr, H M (Financier)
Bankers First Corp
1 10th St
Augusta, GA 30901, USA

Oster, Bill (Athlete, Baseball Player)
56 Little Neck Rd
Centerport, NY 11721-1617, USA

Osterbrock, Donald E
120 Woodside Ave
Santa Cruz, CA 95060-3422, USA

Osterhage, Jeff (Actor)
7309 Santa Barbara St
Carlsbad, CA 92011-4638, USA

Osteroth, Alexander
Steinsdorfstr. 20
Munich, GERMANY 80538

Ostertag, Greg (Athlete, Basketball Player)
7401 Cobblestone Ct
McKinney, TX 75070-5073, USA

Ostheim, Michael (Model)
Louisa Models
Ebersberger Str 9
Munich 81679, USA

Osting, Jimmy (Athlete, Baseball Player)
927 Lakeside Dr
Taylorsville, KY 40071-9271, USA

Ostman, Arnold (Conductor)
Haydn Rawstron
36 Station Road
London SE20 7BQ, UNITED KINGDOM (UK)

Ostos, Javier (Swimmer)
FINA
Isabel La Catolica 13
Desp 401-2
Mexico City 1, DF, MEXICO

Ostriker, Jeremiah P (Physicist)
33 Philip Dr
Princeton, NJ 08540, USA

Ostrom, John H (Misc)
52 Hillhouse Road
Goshen, CT 06756, USA

Ostroski, Gerald (Athlete, Football Player)
6926 E 115th Pl S
Bixby, OK 74008, USA

Ostrosky, Beth (Actor, Model)
c/o Staff Member *Don Buchwald & Associates Inc (NY)*
10 E 44th St
New York, NY 10017

Ostrosky, David (Actor)
c/o Staff Member *Televisa*
Blvd Adolfo Lopez Mateos 232
Colonia San Angel INN
DF CP 01060, MEXICO

Ostrosser, Brian (Athlete, Baseball Player)
27 Chelsea Cres
Stoney Creek, ON L8E 5R7, Canada

Ostrum, Peter (Actor)
6065 Duncan Rd
Glenfield, NY 13343, USA

Ostwald, Martin (Educator)
408 Walnut Lane
Swarthmore, PA 19081, USA

O'Sullevan, Peter J (Sportscaster, Writer)
37 Cranmer Court
London SW3 3HW, UNITED KINGDOM (UK)

O'Sullivan, Charles (General)
8 Pine Tree Pt
North Little Rock, AR 72116-8315, USA

O'Sullivan, Chris (Athlete, Hockey Player)
114 Elmer Rd
Dorchester Center, MA 02124-5034

O'Sullivan, Dan (Athlete, Basketball Player)
33 Cresent Ave
Summit, NJ 07901-1902, USA

O'Sullivan, Gilbert (Musician)
Park Promotions
PO Box 651
Park Road
Oxford OX2 9RB, UNITED KINGDOM (UK)

O'Sullivan, Peter (Editor)
Houston Post
Editorial Dept
4747 Southwest Freeway
Houston, TX 77027, USA

O'Sullivan, Richard (Actor)
Al Mitchell
5 Anglers Lane
Kentish Town
London NW5 3DG, UNITED KINGDOM (UK)

O'Sullivan, Sonia (Athlete, Track Athlete)
Kim McDonald
201 High St
Hampton Hill
Middx TW12 1NL, UNITED KINGDOM (UK)

O' Sullivan, Thaddeus (Director)
c/o Anthony Jones *United Agents*
Drury House
34-43 Russell St
London WC2B 5HA, UK

Osuna, Al (Athlete, Baseball Player)
8256 Via Rosa
Orlando, FL 32836-8789, USA

Osuna, Al (Athlete, Baseball Player)
8256 Via Rosa
Orlando, FL 32836, USA

Osuna, Antonio (Athlete, Baseball Player)
10345 W Olympic Blvd
Los Angeles, CA 90064-2524, USA

Oswald, Mark (Race Car Driver)
Championship Quest Motorsports
237B N. Hollywood Rd.
Houma, LA 70364, USA

Oswald, Mark (Opera Singer)
Herbert Barrett
266 W 37th St
#2000
New York, NY 10018, USA

Oswald, Paul (Athlete, Football Player)
521 Cambridge Ct
Alpharetta, GA 30005, USA

Oswald, Stephen S (Astronaut)
NASA
Johnson Space Center
2101 NASA Road
Houston, TX 77058, USA

Oswald, Stephen S Rear Admiral (Astronaut)
16806 Glenshannon Dr
Houston, TX 77059-5504, USA

Oswalt, Patton (Actor)
c/o Dave Rath *Generate Management*
1545 26th St
Suite 200
Santa Monica, CA 90404, USA

Oswalt, Roy (Athlete, Baseball Player, Olympic Athlete)
PO Box 8
Weir, MS 39772-0008, USA

Oszajca, John (Musician)
Interscope Records
2220 Colorado Ave
Santa Monica, CA 90404, USA

Ota, Tadamichi (Chef)
Nakanobo Zuien 808 Arimamachi Kita-ku
Kobe-shi
Kyogo-ken, japan

Otaka, Tadaaki (Conductor)
Harold Holt
31 Sinclair Road
London W14 0NS, UNITED KINGDOM (UK)

Otanez, Willis (Athlete, Baseball Player)
7904 March Brown Ave
Las Vegas, NV 89149-5101, USA

Otellini, Paul (Business Person)
Intel Corp
2200 Mission College Blvd
Santa Clara, CA 95054, USA

Otep (Musician)
c/o Staff Member *Zen Media Group*
272 Grand St
Suite B
Brooklyn, NY 11211, USA

Oteri, Cheri (Actor, Comedian)
c/o Lori Sale *Paradigm (LA)*
360 N Crescent Dr
North Bldg
Beverly Hills, CA 90210, USA

Otero, Ricky (Athlete, Baseball Player)
126 Calle Sorbona
Urb University Gardens
San Juan, PR 00927, USA

Othenin-Girard, Dominque (Director)
327 Church Lane
Los Angeles, CA 90049, USA

Othick, Trent (Producer)
c/o Staff Member *Creative Artists Agency (CAA-LA)*
2000 Ave Of The Stars
Los Angeles, CA 90067, USA

Otis, Amos J (Athlete, Baseball Player)
8930 Tiger Shale Way
Las Vegas, NV 89123-3132, USA

Otis, Carre (Actor, Model)
c/o Staff Member *Storm Model Management*
5 Jubilee Pl
1st Floor
London SW3 3TD, UNITED KINGDOM

Otis, Glenn K (General)
3401 RR 9
Lake SHore Road
Peru, NY 12972, USA

Otis, James L (Jim) (Athlete, Football Player)
14795 Greenleaf Valley Dr
Chesterfield, MO 63017, USA

Otman, Assed Mohamed (Prime Minister)
Villa Rissani
Route Oued Akrach
Souissi, Rabat, MOROCCO

O'Toole, Annette (Actor)
3202 Club Dr
Los Angeles, CA 90064, USA

O'Toole, Dennis (Denny) (Athlete, Baseball Player)
9105 Royal Oak Ln
Union, KY 41091-8806, USA

O'Toole, Jim (Athlete, Baseball Player)
1010 Lanette Dr
Cincinnati, OH 45230-3616, USA

O'Toole, S Peter (Actor)
c/o Steven Arcieri *Arcieri & Associates Inc*
305 Madison Ave
Suite 2315
New York, NY 10165, USA

O Town
7380 Sand Lake Rd.#350
Orlando, FL 32819

Otstott, Charles P (General)
6152 Pohick Station Dr
Fairfax Station, VA 22039, USA

Otsuka, Akinori (Athlete, Baseball Player)
891 Fairway Dr
Boulder City, NV 89005-3609, USA

Otsuki, Tamayo (Actor)
Patterson Assoc
20318 Hiawatha St
Chatsworth, CA 91311, USA

Ott, Billy (Athlete, Baseball Player)
County Lock 132 W Nyack Way
West Nyack, NY 10993-1339, USA

Ott, Ed (Athlete, Baseball Player)
New Jersey Jackals
1 Hall Dr
Attn: Coaching Staff
Little Falls, NJ 07424, USA

Ott, Ed (Athlete, Baseball Player)
3164 New London Rd
Forest, VA 24551-1814, USA

Ott, Steve (Athlete, Hockey Player)
2758 StClair Rd
Pointe Aux Roches, ON NOR INO,
Canada

Ottaviano, Susan (Stylist)
c/o Staff Member *Ennis*
119 Braintree St
Boston, MA 02134, USA

Otten, Jim (Athlete, Baseball Player)
1417 N Forest
Mesa, AZ 85203-3903, USA

Otten, Mac (Athlete, Basketball Player)
2010 Burroughs Dr
Dayton, NJ 45406-4420, USA

Otter, C.L. (Butch) (Governor)
Office of the Governor
P.O. Box 83720
Boise, ID 83720, USA

Ottey, Merlene
PO Box 120
Indianapolis, IN 46206-0120

Ottey-Page, Merlene (Athlete, Track
Athlete)
Jamaican Olympic Committee
Po Box 544
Kingston 10, JAMAICA

Ottinger, LD (Race Car Driver)
1021 Scarlet Rd
Newport, TN 37821, USA

Otto, August J (Gus) (Athlete, Football
Player)
14411 Open Meadow Ct W
Chesterfield, MO 63017-9627, USA

Otto, Bob (Athlete, Football Player)
1713 Guthrie Dr
Las Vegas, NV 89117, USA

Otto, Dave (Athlete, Baseball Player)
1383 Shady Ln
Wheaton, IL 60187-3722, USA

Otto, Frei (Architect)
Berghalde 19
7250 Leonberg
Warmbroun 71229, GERMANY

Otto, James (Musician)
c/o Dan Anderson *Red Light Management
(Nashville)*
39 Music Square East
Nashville, TN 37203, USA

Otto, James E (Jim) (Athlete, Football
Player)
100 Estates Dr
Auburn, CA 95602, USA

Otto, Joel (Athlete, Hockey Player)
Calgary Hitmen
PO Box 1540 Stn M
Calgary, AB T2P 3B9, T2P 3B9

Otto, Joel (Athlete, Hockey Player,
Olympic Athlete)
77 Sunset Way SE
Calgary, AB T2X 3C1, CANADA

Otto, Kristin (Swimmer)
ZDF Sportedaktion
Postfach 4040
Mainz 55100, GERMANY

Otto, Michael (Business Person)
Spiegel Inc
3500 Lacey Road
Downers Grove, IL 60515, USA

Otto, Miranda (Actor)
Shanahan Mgmt
PO Box 1509
Darlinghurst, NSW 1300, AUSTRALIA

Otto, Sylke (Athlete)
BSD
An der Schiessstatte 4
Berchtesgaden 83471, GERMANY

Otto Jr, A T (Misc)
Railroad Yardmasters Union
1411 Peterson Ave
#201
Park Ridge, IL 60068, USA

Otwell, Ralph M (Editor)
34 knox Circle
Evanston, IL 60201-1912, USA

Ouaido, Nassour Guelengdoussia (Prime
Minister)
Prime Minister's Office
N'Djamena, CHAD

Oubre, Louis (Athlete, Football Player)
11008 Curran Blvd
New Orleans, LA 70127, USA

Ouchi, William G (Educator)
University of California
Graduate Management School
Los Angeles, CA 90024, USA

Oudin, Melanie (Athlete, Tennis Player)
c/o Sam Duvall *Lagardere Unlimited -
(D.C.)*
5335 Wisconsin Ave NW
Suite 850
Washington, DC 20015, USA

Ouedraogo, Gerard Kango (Prime
Minister)
01 BP 347
Ouagadougou, BURKINA FASO

Ouedraogo, Idrissa (Director)
FEPACI
01 BP 2524
Ouagadougou, BURKINA FASO

Ouedraogo, Kdre Desire (Prime Minister)
Prime Minister's Office
Parliament Building
Ouagadougou, BURKINA FASO

Ouellet, Joseph G N Cardinal (Religious
Leader)
Archdiocese
34 Rue de l'Eveche E
CP 730
Rimouski, QC G5L 7C7, CANADA

Ouellette, Dawn (Stylist)
336 E 30th St
#2-A
New York, NY 10016, USA

Ouellette, Gerry (Athlete, Hockey Player)
352 Ch Portage
Grand-Sault/grand Falls, NB E3Z 1M7,
Canada

Ouellette, Phil (Athlete, Baseball Player)
7421 Poppy St
Corona, CA 92881-3739, USA

Ouimet, Ted (Athlete, Hockey Player)
580 Albert St
Strathroy, ON N7G 1W9, Canada

Oureiro, Natalia (Musician)
c/o Staff Member *BMG*
1540 Broadway
New York, NY 10036, USA

Ourisson, Guy (Misc)
10 Rue Geiler
Strasbourg 67000, FRANCE

Our Lady Peace (Music Group)
c/o Eric Lawrence *Coalition Entertainment
Management*
10271 Yonge St
Suite 302
Richmond Hill, Ontario L4C 3B5, Canada

Ousland, Borge (Skier)
Axel Huitfeldts V5
Oslo 1170, NORWAY

Outkast (Music Group)
c/o Charles King *WME (LA)*
9601 Wilshire Blvd Fl 3
Beverly Hills, CA 90210, USA

Outland, Felton (War Hero)
1669 Hwy 158E
Sunbury, NC 27979, USA

Outlar, Jesse (Sportscaster)
1252 Stephens St SW
Lilburn, GA 30047-4354, USA

Outlaw, Charles "bo"
7716 Belvoir Dr
Orlando, FL 32835-8185

Outlaw, Charles (Bo) (Athlete, Basketball
Player)
14815 River Mill
San Antonio, TX 78216, USA

Outlaw, Travis (Athlete, Basketball Player)
c/o Bill Duffy *BDA Sports Management
(BDA-CA)*
700 Ygnacio Valley Rd
Suite 330
Walnut Creek, CA 94596, USA

Outman, Josh (Athlete, Baseball Player)
5273 Seasonbrooks Ln
Imperial, MO 63052-4012, USA

Outman, Tim (Artist)
57101 N Bank Road
McKenzie Bridge, OR 97413, USA

OV7 (Music Group)
c/o Staff Member *Sony Music Miami*
605 Lincoln Rd Fl 7
Miami Beach, FL 33139, USA

Ovchinikov, Vladmir P (Musician)
Manygate
13 Cotswold Mews
30 Battersea Square
London SW11 3RA, UNITED KINGDOM
(UK)

Ovechkin, Alexander (Athlete, Hockey
Player)
1361 Woodside Dr
McLean, VA 22102-1500, USA

Overall, Park (Actor)
1374 Ripley Island Rd
Afton, TN 37616, USA

Overath, Wolfgang
Auf dem Hummerich
Siegburg, GERMANY D-53721

Overbay, Lyle (Athlete, Baseball Player)
107 Captain Ln
Centralia, WA 98531-1614, USA

Overbeck, Carla (Athlete, Olympic
Athlete, Soccer Player)
205 Zapata Ln
Chapel Hill X, Chapel Hill
NC 27517-7742, USA

Overbeek, Jan T G (Misc)
Zweerslaan 35
Bilthoven, HN 3723, NETHERLANDS

Overgard, Robert M (Religious Leader)
Church of Lutheran Brethren
PO Box 655
Fergus Falls, MN 56538, USA

Overgard, William (Cartoonist)
United Feature Syndicate
200 Madison Ave
New York, NY 10016, USA

Overhauser, Chad (Athlete, Football
Player)
8303 North No Pac Expy
Suite 425B
Austin, TX 78759, USA

Overleese, Joanne (Baseball Player)
849 Coach Blvd
La Jolla, CA 92037, USA

Overman, Ion
c/o Staff Member *GVA Talent Agency Inc*
8981 Sunset Blvd.
Suite 101
Los Angeles, CA 90069, USA

Overman, Larry E (Misc)
University of California
Chemistry Dept
Irvine, CA 92717, USA

Overmyer, Amanda (Musician)

Overmyer, Eric (Writer)
c/o Rob Kenneally *Creative Artists Agency
(CAA-LA)*
2000 Ave Of The Stars
Los Angeles, CA 90067, USA

Overstreet, Chord (Actor)
c/o Mara Santino *Luber Roklin
Management*
8530 Wilshire Blvd
6th Floor
Beverly Hills, CA 90211, USA

Overstreet, Paul (Musician, Songwriter, Writer)
White Horse Enterprises
475 Annex Ave
Nashville, TN 37209, USA

Overstreet, Tommy (Musician, Songwriter, Writer)
PO Box 455
Brentwood, TN 37024, USA

Overstreet, Will (Athlete, Football Player)
106 Avondale St
Jackson, MS 39216, USA

Overton, Dolph (General)
709 S Crescent Dr
Smithfield, NC 27577-3841, USA

Overton, Kelly (Actor)
c/o Staff Member *Management 360*
9111 Wilshire Blvd
Beverly Hills, CA 90210, USA

Overton, Rick (Actor)
c/o Staff Member *Sutton Barth & Vennari Inc*
145 S Fairfax
Suite 310
Los Angeles, CA 90036, USA

Overy, Mike (Athlete, Baseball Player)
3010 North 152nd Lane
Goodyear, AZ 85395-8636, USA

Ovitz, Michael S (Business Person)
457 N Rockingham Ave
Los Angeles, CA 90049, USA

Owchar, Dennis (Athlete, Hockey Player)
32 Raeview Dr
Stouffville, ON L4A 7X4, Canada

Owchinko, Bob (Athlete, Baseball Player)
15111 N Hayden Rd # 160-357
Scottsdale, AZ 85260-2581, USA

Owen, Clive (Actor)
c/o Staff Member *42West (NY)*
220 W 42nd St
12th Floor
New York, NY 10036, USA

Owen, Dave (Athlete, Baseball Player)
1921 Fm 3136
Cleburne, TX 76031-8792, USA

Owen, David A L (Government Official)
78 Narrow St
Limehouse
London E14 8BP, UNITED KINGDOM (UK)

Owen, Edwyn (Bob) (Athlete, Hockey Player)
3630 SW Stratford Rd
Topeka, KS 66604, USA

Owen, Glyn (Stylist)
c/o Staff Member *Art Department*
48 Greene St
4th Floor
New York, NY 10013, USA

Owen, Henry (Diplomat)
Brookings Institute
1775 Massachusetts Ave NW
Washington, DC 20036, USA

Owen, Jake (Musician)
c/o Dale Morris *Morris Artists Management*
818 19th Ave S
Nashville, TN 37203, USA

Owen, Larry (Athlete, Baseball Player)
3497 River Narrows Rd
Hilliard, OH 43026-7833, USA

Owen, Michael (Soccer Player)
c/o Staff Member *Newcastle United FC*
Saint James Park
Newcastle-Tyne NE1 4ST, UNITED KINGDOM (UK)

Owen, Michael (Athlete, Soccer Player)
c/o Dan Levy *Wasserman Media Group*
10960 Wilshire Blvd
Suite 2200
Los Angeles, CA 90024, USA

Owen, Randy Y (Musician)
PO Box 529
Fort Payne, AL 35968, USA

Owen, Ray D (Biologist)
1583 Rose Villa St
Pasadena, CA 91106, USA

Owen, Spike (Athlete, Baseball Player)
11211 Musket Rim St
Austin, TX 78738-6613, USA

Owen, Tom (Athlete, Football Player)
P.O. Box 3
Albany, OK 74721, USA

Owens, Al (Baseball Player)
Nashville Elite Giants
63 Bluff Ave
Lagrange, IL 60525-2507, USA

Owens, Billy (Athlete, Basketball Player)
608 Canary Dr
Carlisle, PA 17013-8768, USA

Owens, Brig (Athlete, Football Player)
6902 Lupine Ln
Mc Lean, VA 22101, USA

Owens, Buddy (Athlete, Baseball Player)
63 Bluff Ave
La Grange, IL 60525-2507, USA

Owens, Burgess (Athlete, Football Player)
1430 Telegraph Rd
West Chester, PA 19380, USA

Owens, Charles W (Tinker) (Athlete, Football Player)
2547 McGee Dr
Norman, OK 73072, USA

Owens, Chris (Actor)
c/o Jerry Shandrew *Shandrew Public Relations*
1050 S Stanley Ave
Los Angeles, CA 90019-6634, USA

Owens, Cotton (Race Car Driver)
Cotton Owens Garage
7065 White Ave
Spartanburg, SC 29303, USA

Owens, Craig (Musician)
c/o Staff Member *Equal Vision Records*
P.O. Box 38202
Albany, NY 12203-8202, USA

Owens, Dan (Athlete, Football Player)
280 Selkirk Ln
Duluth, GA 30097, USA

Owens, Darrick (Athlete, Football Player)
610 Cypress St
Raceland, LA 70394, USA

Owens, Eric (Athlete, Baseball Player)
22431 N 54th St
Phoenix, AZ 85054-7210, USA

Owens, Gary (Entertainer)
17856 Via Vallarta
Encino, CA 91316, USA

Owens, Henry (Athlete, Baseball Player)
4944 SW 140th Ct
Miami, FL 33175-4806, USA

Owens, Jackson (Athlete, Baseball Player)
P.O. Box 6046
Decatur, IL 62524-6046, USA

Owens, Jayhawk (Athlete, Baseball Player)
273 Warwick Pl
Castle Pines, CO 80108-8823, USA

Owens, Jim (Athlete, Baseball Player)
1426 Ramada Dr
Houston, TX 77062-5908, USA

Owens, Joe (Athlete, Football Player)
2754 Highway 13 N
Columbia, MS 39429, USA

Owens, Kem (Musician)
c/o Staff Member *The Paradise Group*
PO Box 69451
West Hollywood, CA 90069, USA

Owens, Lorenzo (Musician)
c/o Staff Member *Paradigm (Monterey)*
404 W Franklin St
Monterey, CA 93940, USA

Owens, Luke (Athlete, Football Player)
2970 Richmond Rd
Beachwood, OH 44122, USA

Owens, Mel (Athlete, Football Player)
1230 Market St
Apt 504
San Francisco, CA 94102, USA

Owens, Morris (Athlete, Football Player)
3010 W Yorkshire Dr
Apt 1114
Phoenix, AZ 85027, USA

Owens, Rawleigh C (R C) (Athlete, Football Player)
626 E Yosemite Ave
Manteca, CA 95336, USA

Owens, Rena (Actor, Model)
526 N Larchmont Blvd #201
Los Angeles, CA 90004, USA

Owens, Steve (Athlete, Football Player, Heisman Trophy Winner)
3700 W Robinson St #230
Norman, OK 73072-3639, USA

Owens, Terrell (Athlete, Football Player)
15260 Ventura Blvd #2100
Sherman Oaks, CA 91403-5360, USA

Owens, Terry (Athlete, Football Player)
2524 Poovey Rd SE
Decatur, AL 35603, USA

Owens, Tom (Athlete, Basketball Coach)
19788 Wildwood Dr
West Linn, OR 97068-2252, USA

owens, william (Politician)
14111 Vance Jackson Rd Aot 9306
San Antonio, TX 78249-1999, USA

Owens, William A (Admiral)
510 Lake St S
#B302
Kirkland, WA 98033, USA

Owensby, Earl (Actor)
1056 Old Springs Rd
Shelby, NC 28152, USA

Owings, Jim (Athlete, Football Player)
961 Chestnut St SE Ste 107
Gainesville, GA 30501-6902, USA

Owings, Micah (Athlete, Baseball Player)
2219 Sidney Drve Dr NE
Gainesville GA 30506-1168,
GA 30506-1168, USA

Owings, Richard (Stylist)
c/o Staff Member *De Facto*
41 Union Square West
#1001
New York, NY 10003, USA

Ownbey, Rick (Athlete, Baseball Player)
2166 Via Monserate
Fallbrook, CA 92028-9335, USA

Owsley, Douglas (Misc)
Smithsonian Institute
17th & M Sts NW
Washington, DC 20036, USA

Oxenberg, Catherine (Actor)
c/o Staff Member *Power Entertainment*
9100 Wilshire Blvd #700
Beverly Hills, CA 90212, USA

Oyakawa, Yoshinobu (Yoshi) (Swimmer)
4171 Hutchinson Road
Cincinnati, OH 45248, USA

Oye, Erlend (Musician)
c/o Staff Member *Paradigm (Monterey)*
404 W Franklin St
Monterey, CA 93940, USA

Oz, Amos (Writer)
Ben Gurion University
PO Box 653
Beer-Sheva 84195, ISRAEL

Oz, Dr Mehmet (Correspondent, Doctor, Writer)
30 Rockefeller Plaza
Studio 6A
New York, NY 10112, USA

Oz, Frank R (Director)
c/o David O'Connor *Creative Artists Agency (CAA-LA)*
2000 Ave Of The Stars
Los Angeles, CA 90067, USA

Ozaki, Masashi (Golfer)
Bridgestone Sports
14230 Lochridge Blvd
#G
Covington, GA 30014, USA

Ozawa, Ichiro (Government Official)
Daiichi Giia Kaikan
Nagatacho Chiyodaku
Tokyo 100, JAPAN

Ozbek, Rifat (Designer, Fashion Designer)
Ozbek Ltd
18 Haunch of Venison Yard
London W1Y 1AF, UNITED KINGDOM (UK)

Ozio, David (Bowler)
6110 Barrington Ave
Beaumont, TX 77706-7381, USA

Ozolinsh, Sandis (Athlete, Hockey Player)
701 Golf Club Dr
Castle Rock, CO 80108-8359

Ozomatli (Music Group)
c/o Amy Blackman *Tsunami Entertainment*
2525 Hyperion Ave
Los Angeles, CA 90027, USA

Ozsan, Hal (Actor)
c/o Staff Member *Overbrook Entertainment*
450 N Roxbury Dr
4th Floor
Beverly Hills, CA 90210, USA

Ozzie, Raymond (Ray) (Designer)
33 Harbor St
Manchester-by-the Sea, MA 01944, USA

Paabo, Svante (Director)
Evolutionary Anthropology Inst
Deutscher Platz 6
Leipzig 04103, USA

Paavola, Rodney (Athlete, Hockey Player)
General Delivery
Hancock, MI 49930, USA

Pablo Cruise
PO Box 770850
Orlando, FL 32877

Pacar, Johnny (Actor)
c/o Matt Goldman *Collective*
8383 Wilshire Blvd
Suite 1050
Beverly Hills, CA 90211, USA

Pace, Darrell O (Archer, Athlete, Olympic
Athlete)
4394 Princeton Road
Hamilton, OH 45011, USA

Pace, Dominic (Actor)
c/o Budd Burton Moss *Burton Moss*
10533 Strathmore Dr
Los Angeles, CA 90024, USA

Pace, Judy (Actor)
4139 Cloverdale Ave
Los Angeles, CA 90008, USA

Pace, Justin (Actor)
c/o Todd Justice *Justice & Ponder*
P.O. Box 480033
Los Angeles, CA 90048, USA

Pace, Lee (Actor)
c/o Peter Kiernan *Management 360*
9111 Wilshire Blvd
Beverly Hills, CA 90210, USA

Pace, Leslie (Stylist)
823 N Marion
Oak Park, IL 60302, USA

Pace, Orlando (Athlete, Football Player)
355 Galahad Dr
Saint Charles, MO 63304, USA

Pace, Peter (General)
Vice Chairman
Joint Chiefs of Staff Pentagon
Washington, DC 20318, USA

Pacella, John (Athlete, Baseball Player)
1500 Abbotsford Green Dr
Powell, OH 43065-8938, USA

Pachal, Clayton (Athlete, Hockey Player)
230 Laycoe Cres
Saskatoon, SK S7S lHS, Canada

Pacheco, Abel (President)
Casa Presidencial
Apdo 520-2010
San Jose 1000, COSTA RICA

Pacheco, Ferdie (Sportscaster)
4151 Gate Lane
Miami, FL 33137, USA

Pacheco, Manuel T (Educator)
University of Arizona
President's Office
Tucson, AZ 85721, USA

Pacillo, Pat (Athlete, Baseball Player,
Olympic Athlete)
8 Rocky Glen Way
Lebanon, NJ 08833-4611, USA

Pacino, Al (Actor)
c/o Jeff Berg *ICM Partners (ICM-LA)*
10250 Constellation Blvd Fl 7
Los Angeles, CA 90067, USA

Paciorek, Jim (Athlete, Baseball Player)
9641 E Waters Edge Pl
Tucson, AZ 85749-7901, USA

Paciorek, John (Athlete, Baseball Player)
8400 Huntington Dr
San Gabriel, CA 91775-1154, USA

Paciorek, Tom (Athlete, Baseball Player)
2389 Broad Creek Dr
Stone Mountain, GA 30087-3755, USA

Pacioretty, Max (Athlete, Hockey Player)
589 Oenoke Rdg
New Canaan, CT 06840-3613

Packard, Kelly (Actor, Model)
c/o Michael Valeo *Valeo Entertainment*
8265 Sunset Blvd
Suite 103
Los Angeles, CA 90046, USA

Packard, Scott (Athlete, Baseball Player)
135 Eastview Dr
Horseheads, NY 14845-2548, USA

Packard, Scott (Baseball Player)
135 Eastview Dr
Horseheads, NY 14845-2548, USA

Packer, Billy (Sportscaster)
105 Fescue Dr
Advance, NC 27006, USA

Packer, David (Actor)
c/o Staff Member *Creative Artists Agency
(CAA-LA)*
2000 Ave Of The Stars
Los Angeles, CA 90067, USA

Packer, James (Business Person)
Consolidated Press Holdings
54 Park St
Sydney NSW 2000, AUSTRALIA

Packer Jr, William E. (Producer)
Rainforest Films
323-A Edgewood Ave
Atlanta, GA 30312, USA

Packwocd, Bob (Ex-Senator, Senator)
2201 Wisconsin Ave NW #C-120
Washington, DC 20007-4128, USA

Pacquet, Fernand (Horse Racer)
7563 State Road 7
Lake Worth, FL 33449-6716, USA

Pacquiao, Manny (Athlete, Boxer)
Wild Card Boxing Gym
1123 Vine St
Los Angeles, CA 90038, USA

Pacula, Joanna (Actor)
Chuck Binder
1465 Lindacrest Dr
Beverly Hills, CA 90210, USA

Paczynski, Bohdan (Scientist)
114 Maclean Cir
Princeton, NJ 08540-5623, USA

Padalecki, Jared (Actor)
c/o Daniel Spilo *Industry Entertainment
Partners*
955 S Carrillo Dr
Suite 300
Los Angeles, CA 90048, USA

Padalka, Gennadi I (Cosmonaut)
Potchta Kosmonavtov
Moskovskoi Oblasti
Syvisdny Goroduk 141160, RUSSIA

Paddio, Gerald (Athlete, Basketball
Player)
2801 Crystal Bay Dr
Las Vegas, NV 89117-2235, USA

Paddock, John (Athlete, Hockey Player)
Philadelphia Flyers
3601 S Broad St Ste 2
Philadelphia, PA 19148-5297

Padgett, Jason (Actor)
c/o Staff Member *GVA Talent Agency Inc*
8981 Sunset Blvd.
Suite 101
Los Angeles, CA 90069, USA

Padilla, Douglas (Doug) (Athlete, Track
Athlete)
182 N 555 W
Orem, UT 84057, USA

Padilla, Mikel (Stylist)
c/o Staff Member *Action Agency Stylists*
8424 Santa Monica Blvd
West Hollywood, CA 90069, USA

Padilla, Vicente (Athlete, Baseball Player)
2112 Royal Dominion CT
Arlington, TX 76006-4836, USA

Padjen, Gary (Athlete, Football Player)
9314 Tower Bridge Rd
Apt B
Indianapolis, IN 46240, USA

Padma-Nathan, Harin (Doctor)
1245 16th St
#312
Santa Monica, CA 90404, USA

Padma-Nathan, Harin Dr (Scientist)
1245 16th St Ste 312
Santa Monica, CA 90404-1239, USA

Padmini (Actor, Bollywood)
9 Palot Madhavan Road
Mahalingapuram
Chennai, TN 600034, INDIA

Paek, Jim (Athlete, Hockey Player)
7360 Crystal View Dr SE
Caledonia, MI 49316-7981

Paek, Jim (Athlete, Hockey Player)
Grand Rapids Griffins
130 Fulton St W Ste 111
Grand Rapids, MI 49503-2601

Paepke, Dennis (Athlete, Baseball Player)
4560 Trieste Dr
Carlsbad, CA 92010-3741, USA

Paepke, Jack (Athlete, Baseball Player)
4560 Trieste Dr
Carlsbad, CA 92010-3741, USA

Paes, Leander (Athlete, Tennis Player)
c/o Staff Member *ATP Tour*
201 ATP Tour Blvd
Ponte Vedra Beach, FL 32082-3211, USA

Paetkau, David (Actor)
c/o Martin Berneman *Precision
Entertainment*
6338 Wilshire Blvd
Los Angeles, CA 90048, USA

Paetsch, Nathan (Athlete, Hockey Player)
324 Tennyson Terrace
East Amherst, NY 14051

Paez, Jorge (Maromero) (Boxer)
233 Paulin Ave
Calexico, CA 92231, USA

Paez, Richard A (Judge)
US Appellate Court
Court Building
125 S Grand Ave
Pasadena, CA 91105, USA

Paffrath, Amy (Actor)
c/o Scott Karp *Crystal Sky Pictures*
10203 Santa Monica Blvd
5th Floor
Los Angeles, CA 90067, USA

Pafko, Andrew (Andy) (Athlete, Baseball
Player)
1890 W Glen lord Rd
Stevensville, MI 49127-9560, USA

Pagac, Fred (Athlete, Football Player)
10261 Normandy Crest
Eden Prairie, MN 55347, USA

Pagan, Dave (Athlete, Baseball Player)
504 10th Ave W
Nipawin, SK S0E 1E0, Canada

Pagan, Reo (Baseball Player)
Negro Baseball Leagues
280 Creek View Trl
Fayetteville, GA 30214-7230, USA

Paganelli, Robert P (Diplomat)
331 S Main St
Albion, NY 14411, USA

Page, Alan C (Athlete, Football Player,
Judge)
Page Education Foundation
P.O. Box 581254
Minneapolis, MN 55458, USA

Page, Ashley (Choreographer, Dancer)
Royal Ballet
Covent Garden
Bow St
London WC2E 9DD, UNITED KINGDOM
(UK)

Page, Bettle (Model)
JL Swanson
PO Box 56176
Chicago, IL 60656, USA

Page, Corey (Actor)
Agency for Performing Arts
9200 Sunset Blvd
#900
Los Angeles, CA 90069, USA

Page, David (Artist)
3724 Greenmount Ave
Baltimore, MD 21218, USA

Page, David C (Misc)
Whitehead Institute
9 Cambridge Center
Cambridge, MA 02142, USA

Page, Ellen (Actor)
c/o Kish Igbal *Gary Goddard Agency*
10 St Mary St
Suite 305
Toronto, ON M4Y 1P9, Canada

Page, Erika (Actor)
Progressive Artists Agency
400 S Beverly Dr
#216
Beverly Hills, CA 90212, USA

Page, Genevieve (Actor)
52 Rue de Vaugirard
Paris 75006, FRANCE

Page, Greg (Boxer)
Don King Promotions
968 Pinehurst Dr
Las Vegas, NV 89109, USA

Page, Harrison (Actor)
S D B Partners
1801 Ave of Stars
#902
Los Angeles, CA 90067, USA

Page, Jimmy (Musician)
c/o Staff Member *International Talent Booking*
74A Charlotte St
London W1T 4QJ, UNITED KINGDOM (UK)

Page, Kimberly (Actor)
c/o Staff Member *The Paradise Group*
PO Box 69451
West Hollywood, CA 90069, USA

Page, Larry (Business Person)
Google Inc
1600 Amphitheatre Pkwy
Mountain View, CA 94043-1351, USA

Page, Michael (Misc)
Po Box 229
North Salem, NY 10560, USA

Page, Mike (Athlete, Baseball Player)
599 Briarcliff Dr
Woodruff, SC 29388-2326, USA

Page, Murriel (Basketball Player)
Washington Mystics
MCI Center
601 F St NW
Washington, DC 20004, USA

Page, Oscar C (Educator)
Austin College
President's Office
Sherman, TX 75090, USA

Page, Patti (Actor, Musician)
404 Loma Larga Dr
Solana Beach, CA 92075, USA

Page, Pierre (Athlete, Coach, Hockey Player)
2000 E Gene Autry Way
Anaheim, CA 92806, USA

Page, Robin (Stylist)
c/o Staff Member *Artists by Timothy Priano (CA)*
8447 Wilshire Blvd
#301
Beverly Hills, CA 90211, USA

Page, Sam (Actor)
c/o Lena Roklin *Luber Roklin Management*
8530 Wilshire Blvd
6th Floor
Beverly Hills, CA 90211, USA

Page, Solomon (Athlete, Football Player)
9302 Vista Cir
Irving, TX 75063, USA

Page, Steven (Musician)
c/o Larry Webman *Paradigm (NY)*
360 Park Ave S Fl 16
New York, NY 10010, USA

Page, Tim (Journalist)
Washington Post
Editorial Dept
1150 15th St NW
Washington, DC 20071, USA

Pageau, Paul (Athlete, Hockey Player)
102 Glen hollow Dr
Stoney Creek, ON L8J 3R4, Canada

Pagel, Karl (Athlete, Baseball Player)
2698 N Ellis St
Chandler, AZ 85224-1777, USA

Pagel, Mike (Athlete, Football Player)
11981 Coopers Run
Strongsville, OH 44149, USA

Paget, Debra (Actor)
411 Kari Court
Houston, TX 77024, USA

Pagett, Dana (Athlete, Basketball Player)
120 Yale Ln
Seal Beach, CA 90740-2522, USA

Pagett, Nicola (Actor)
22 Victoria Road
Mortlake
London SW14, UNITED KINGDOM (UK)

Paggi, Nicole (Actor)
c/o Kenneth (Kenny) Goodman *Schiff Company, The*
9465 Wilshire Blvd
Suite 480
Beverly Hills, CA 90212, USA

Paglia, Camile (Writer)
c/o Staff Member *Random House Publicity*
1745 Broadway
New York, NY 10019, USA

Paglia, Camille (Educator, Writer)
University of the Arts
Humanities Dept
320 S Broad St
Philadelphia, PA 19102, USA

Pagliarulo, Michael T (Mike) (Athlete, Baseball Player)
11 Fieldstone Dr
Winchester, MA 01890-3257, USA

Pagliei, Joe (Athlete, Football Player)
7 Pine Ridge Ct
Sewell, NJ 08080, USA

Pagnozzi, Matt (Athlete, Baseball Player)
1710 W Park Ave
Chandler, AZ 85224-9002, USA

Pagnozzi, Thomas A (Tom) (Athlete, Baseball Player)
3288 E Piper Gin
Fayetteville, AR 72703-4394, USA

Pagnucco, Chris (Athlete, Football Player)
937 W Belden Ave
Chicago, IL 60614, USA

Pagonis, William G (General)
202 Smalsitg Road
Evans City, PA 16033-3924, USA

Pahang (Misc)
Istana Abu Bakar
Pekan
Pahang, MALAYSIA

Pahlavi, Ashraf
12 Ave. Montaigne
Paris, FRANCE 75016

Pahlsson, Samuel (Athlete, Hockey Player)
9429 Tartan Ridge Blvd
Dublin, OH 43017-8924

Pahukoa, Jeff (Athlete, Football Player)
20191 Cape Coral Ln
Huntington Beach, CA 92646, USA

Paich, David (Musician)
Fitzgerald-Hartley
34 N Palm St
Ventura, CA 93001, USA

Paiement, Rosaire (Athlete, Hockey Player)
3351 S Palm Aire Dr Apt 301
Pompano Beach, FL 33069-4254

Paiement, Rosey (Athlete, Hockey Player)
4407 W. Atlantis Blvd.
#1209
Pompano Beach, FL 33066, USA

Paiement, Wilf (Athlete, Hockey Player)
1064 Streambank Dr.
Mississaqua, ON L5H 3Z1, Canada

Paige, Betty
PO Box 56176
Chicago, IL 60656

Paige, Colleen (Business Person)
Colleen Paige, LLC
P.O. Box 2061
Kingston, WA 98346, USA

Paige, Elaine (Actor, Musician)
DeWalden Court
85 New Cavendish St
London W1M 7RA, UNITED KINGDOM (UK)

Paige, Janis (Actor)
1700 Rising Glen Road
Los Angeles, CA 90069, USA

Paige, Marcia A (Stylist)
26200 Town Center Dr
#185
Novi, MI 48375, USA

Paige, Peter (Actor)
c/o Suzanne (Sue) Wohl *TalentWorks (LA)*
3500 W Olive Ave
Suite 1400
Burbank, CA 91505, USA

Paige, Rod (Politician, Secretary)
Education Department
14022 Hampton Cove Dr
Houston, TX 77077-2142, USA

Paige, Tarah (Actor)
c/o Michael Henderson *Heresun Management*
4119 West Burbank Blvd.
Burbank, CA 91505, USA

Paik, Kun Woo (Musician)
Worldwide Artists
12 Rosebery
Thomton Heath
Surrey CR7 8PT, UNITED KINGDOM (UK)

Pailes, William A (Astronaut)
411 S Cedar Ridge Cir
Robinson, TX 76706-5681, USA

Pailes, William A Major (Astronaut)
411 S Cedar Ridge Cir
Robinson, TX 76706-5681, USA

Paille, Daniel (Athlete, Hockey Player)
90 Autumn Creek Ln
East Amherst, NY 14051-2918

Paille, Marcel (Athlete, Hockey Player)

Paine, Chris
c/o Eddie Michaels *Insignia Public Relations*
1507 20th St
Santa Monica, CA 90404, USA

Paine, Horner (Athlete, Football Player)
1105 W York Ave
Enid, OK 73703, USA

Paine, John (Musician)
Bob Flick Productions
300 Vine
#14
Seattle, WA 98121, USA

Paintal (Actor, Bollywood, Comedian)
B 103 Sun Swept Lokhandwala Complex
Andheri
Bombay, MS 400 058, INDIA

Painter, John Mark (Musician)
Michael Dixon Mgmt
119 Pebblecreek Road
Franklin, TN 37064, USA

Painter, Lance (Athlete, Baseball Player)
2683 E Pinto Dr
Gilbert, AZ 85296-8934, USA

Paire-Davis, Lavonne (Athlete, Baseball Player)
15847 Marlin Pl
Van Nuys, CA 91406-5019, USA

Paisley, Brad (Musician)
c/o Bill Simmons *Fitzgerald Hartley Co (Nashville)*
1908 Wedgewood Ave
Nashville, TN 37212, USA

Paisley, Ian R K (Politician)
Parsonage
17 Cyprus Ave
Belfast BT5 5NT, NORTHERN IRELAND

Pajaczkowski, Tony (Athlete, Football Player)
2112 Imperial Cir
Naples, FL 34110-1037, USA

Pajaczkowski, Tony (Athlete, Football Player)
35 53rd St
Gulfport, MS 39507-4530, USA

Pak, Charles (Scientist)
University of Texas
Health Sciences Center
Dallas, TX 75235, USA

Pak, Se Ri (Golfer)
8836 Elliotts Court
Orlando, FL 32836, USA

Pakeledinaz, Martin (Designer)
Gersh Agency
232 N Canon Dr
Beverly Hills, CA 90210, USA

Paksas, Rolandus (Prime Minister)
President's Office
Gediminas 53
Vilnius 232026, LITHUANIA

Palacios, Rey (Athlete, Baseball Player)
183 Kings Gate S
Rochester, NY 14617-5439, USA

Palagyi, Mike (Athlete, Baseball Player)
167 14th St
Conneaut, OH 44030-1805, USA

Palahniuk, Chuck (Writer)
c/o Howard Sanders *United Talent Agency (UTA)*
9336 Civic Center Dr
Beverly Hills, CA 90210, USA

Palance, Holly
2753 Roscomare Ave.
Los Angeles, CA 90077

Palast, Greg (Musician)

Palastra Jr, Joseph T (General)
RR 1 Box 267
Myrtle, MO 65778, USA

Palatella, Lou (Athlete, Football Player)
1532 Kennewick Dr
Sunnyvale, CA 94087, USA

Palau, Doug (Producer)
c/o Staff Member *WME (LA)*
9601 Wilshire Blvd Fl 3
Beverly Hills, CA 90210, USA

Palau, Luis (Misc)
1500 NW 167th Place
Beaverton, OR 97006, USA

Palazzari, Doug (Athlete, Hockey Player)
616 Michigan Ave W
Gilbert, MN 55741, USA

Palazzi, Togo (Athlete, Basketball Player)
84 Framingham Rd
Southborough, MA 01772-1206, USA

Paldridge, Curt (Athlete, Football Player)
2820 Country Club Ln
Dekalb, IL 60115, USA

Palekar, Amol (Actor, Bollywood, Director)
Chire Bandee
10th N S Road JVPD Scheme
Mumbai, MS 400049, INDIA

Palelei, Lonnie (Athlete, Football Player)
1808 SW Chief Cir
Blue Springs, MO 64015, USA

Palermo, Olivia (Reality TV Star, Stylist)
c/o Brian Young *Untitled Entertainment (LA)*
350 S. Beverly Dr #200
Beverly Hills, CA 90212, USA

Palermo, Stephen M (Steve) (Athlete, Baseball Player)
5102 West 143rd Terrace
Overland Park, KS 66224-3746, USA

Palermo, Steve (Athlete, Baseball Player)
5102 W 143rd Ter
Overland Park, KS 66224-3746, USA

Palesh, Shirley (Athlete, Baseball Player)
120 Grand Ave Apt 213
Wausau, WI 54403-7202, USA

Paleta, Ludwika (Actor)
c/o Staff Member *Televisa*
Blvd Adolfo Lopez Mateos 232
Colonia San Angel INN
DF CP 01060, MEXICO

Paley, Albert R (Artist)
Paley Studio
25 N Washington St
Rochester, NY 14614, USA

Paley, Grace (Misc)
PO Box 112
Thetford, VT 05074-0112

Palffy, Zigmund (Athlete, Hockey Player)
HK 36 Skalica Clementisova SO
Skalica, 909 01 Slovakia

Palias, Cecile (Actor)
P F D
Drury House
34-43 Russell St
London WC2B 5HA, UNITED KINGDOM (UK)

Palicki, Adrianne (Actor)
c/o Michael Sugar *Anonymous Content (LA)*
3531 Hayden Ave
Culver City, CA 90232, USA

Palin, Bristol (Reality TV Star)
BSMP
711 H St
Suite 620
Anchorage, AK 99501, USA

Palin, Michael (Actor, Writer)
Prominent Palin Productions Ltd.
34 Tavistock Street
London WC2E 7PB, UK

Palin, Sarah (Ex-Governor, Politician)
1140 W Parks Hwy
Wasilla, AK 99654, USA

Pall, Donn (Athlete, Baseball Player)
155 Wellington Dr
Bloomingdale, IL 60108-3012, USA

Pall, Gloria (Actor, Model)
Showgirl Press
12814 Victory Blvd
North Hollywood, CA 91606

Pall, Olga (Skier)
Fahrenweg 28
Absam 6060, AUSTRIA

Palladino, Eric (Actor)
341 N Van Ness Ave
Los Angeles, CA 90004, USA

Palladino, Erik (Actor)
c/o Andrew Tetenbaum *ATA Management*
12 Desbrosses St
New York, NY 10013, USA

Palladino, Vincent (Misc)
National Assn of Postal Supervisors
1727 King St
Alexandria, VA 22314, USA

Pallavi (Actor, Bollywood)
14A Directors Colony
Kodambakkam
Chennai, TN 600024, INDIA

Palli, Anne-Marie (Golfer)
4510 N Alta Haclenda Dr
Phoenix, AZ 85018-2004, USA

Pallone, Dave (Athlete, Baseball Player)
4420 Dickason Ave
Apt 1135
Dallas, TX 80202-1347, USA

Pallone Jr., Frank (Congressman, Politician)
237 Cannon HOB
Washington, DC 20515, USA

Pally, Adam (Actor)
c/o Greg Walter *3 Arts Entertainment Inc*
9460 Wilshire Blvd
7th Floor
Beverly Hills, CA 90210, USA

Palm, Siegfried
Gerhild Baron Mgmt
Dombacher Str 41/III/3
Vienna 1170, AUSTRIA

Palmas, Giorgia (Actor, Model)

Palmateer, Mike (Athlete, Hockey Player)
30 Simmons Cres.
Aurora, ON L4G 6BS, CANADA

Palmaz, Julio (Inventor)
200 Patterson Ave Apt 608
San Antonio, TX 78209-6267, USA

Palmeiro, Orlando (Athlete, Baseball Player)
11991 SW 103rd Ter
Miami, FL 33186-2654, USA

Palmeiro, Rafael C (Athlete, Baseball Player)
5216 Reims Ct
Colleyville, TX 76034-5574, USA

Palmer, Alisa (Actor)
c/o Staff Member *Catch Up Agentur*
Gorzer Strasse 35a
Munchen 81669, Germany

Palmer, Amanda (Musician)
c/o Staff Member *High Road Touring*
751 Bridgeway
3rd Floor
Sausalito, CA 94965, USA

Palmer, Arnold (Athlete, Golfer)
9000 Bay Hill Blvd
Orlando, FL 32819-4831, USA

Palmer, Barbara (Stylist)
805 N Sycamore Ave
Los Angeles, CA 90038, USA

Palmer, Betsy (Actor)
44 W 85th St #2A
New York, NY 10024, USA

Palmer, Brad (Athlete, Hockey Player)
P.O Box 544
Lake Cowichan, BC V0R 2G0, CANADA

Palmer, Bud (Athlete, Basketball Player)
1200 S Flagler Dr
Apt 303
West Palm Beach, FL 33401-6740, USA

Palmer, Carl (Musician)
Asia
9 Hillgate St
London W8 7SP, UNITED KINGDOM (UK)

Palmer, Carson (Athlete, Football Player, Heisman Trophy Winner)
8885 Whisperinhill Dr
Cincinnati, OH 45242-4670, USA

Palmer, C R (Business Person)
Rowan Companies
Transco Tower
2800 Post Oak Blvd
Houston, TX 77056, USA

Palmer, Dave R (Educator, General)
4531 Blue Rldge Dr
Belton, TX 76513, USA

Palmer, David (Athlete, Baseball Player)
5090 Oak Nut Ct
Stone Mountain, GA 30087-3290, USA

Palmer, David (Athlete, Football Player)
527 Carlton Pl
Birmingham, AL 35214, USA

Palmer, Dean (Athlete, Baseball Player)
3907 West Millers Bridge Road
Tallahassee, FL 32312-1054, USA

Palmer, Dean (Athlete, Baseball Player)
3907 W Millers Bridge Rd
Tallahassee, FL 32312, USA

Palmer, Geoffrey (Actor)
c/o Liz Nelson *Conway van Gelder*
8-12 Broadwick St
London W1F 8HW, UK

Palmer, Geoffrey W R (Prime Minister)
63 Roxburgh St
Mount Victoria
Wellington, NEW ZEALAND

Palmer, Gery (Athlete, Football Player)
6411 E Irish Pl
Centennial, CO 80112, USA

Palmer, Gregg (Actor)
5726 Graves Ave.
Encino, CA 91316

Palmer, Jesse (Athlete, Football Player, Reality TV Star)
c/o Staff Member *San Francisco 49ers*
4949 Centennial Blvd
Santa Clara, CA 95054, USA

Palmer, Jim (Athlete, Basketball Player)
4 Route 385
Catskill, NY 12414-5028, USA

Palmer, Jim (Baseball Player, Sportscaster)
2432 Still Forest Rd
Pikesville, MD 21208-3431, USA

Palmer, Keke (Actor)
c/o Annick Oppenheim *Baker Winokur Ryder Public Relations (BWR-LA)*
9100 Wilshire Blvd
Suite 500, West Tower
Beverly Hills, CA 90212, USA

Palmer, Lowell (Athlete, Baseball Player)
P.O. Box 5253
El Dorado Hills, CA 95762-0005, USA

Palmer, Matt (Athlete, Baseball Player)
c/o Staff Member *Los Angeles Dodgers (LA Dodgers)*
1000 Elysian Park Ave
Los Angeles, CA 90012, USA

Palmer, Mitch (Athlete, Football Player)
14420 Cypress Pt
Poway, CA 92064, USA

Palmer, Patsy (Actor)
c/o Staff Member *International Artistes*
Holborn Hall - 4th Floor
London WC1V 7BD, UK

Palmer, Peter (Actor)
216 Kingsway Dr
Temple Terrace, FL 33617, USA

Palmer, Ralph (Baseball Player)
Chicago American Giants
844 48th St SE
Grand Rapids, MI 49508-4718, USA

Palmer, Richard H (Athlete, Football Player)
14420 Cypress Pl
Poway, CA 92064, USA

Palmer, Rob (Athlete, Hockey Player)
3812 Sepulveda Blvd Ste 310
Torrance, CA 90505-2481

Palmer, Sandra (Athlete, Golfer)
498 Peralta Avenue
Long Beach, CA 90803-2218, USA

Palmer, Scott (Athlete, Football Player)
7408 Lady Suzannes Ct
Austin, TX 78729, USA

Palmer, Teresa (Actor)
c/o David Seltzer *Management 360*
9111 Wilshire Blvd
Beverly Hills, CA 90210, USA

Palmer, Vivienne (Stylist)
c/o Staff Member *Celestine - CA*
1666 20th St
#200-B
Santa Monica, CA 90404, USA

Palmer, Walter (Athlete, Basketball Player)
87 South St
Rockport, MA 01966-1924, USA

Palmieri, Eddie (Musician)
Berkeley Agency
2608 9th St
#301
Berkeley, CA 94710, USA

Palmieri, Paul (Religious Leader)
Church of Jesus Christ
6th & Lincoln Sts
Monongahela, PA 15063, USA

Palminteri, Chazz (Actor)
34 Stone Paddock Pl
Bedford, NY 10506, USA

Palmisano, Samuel J (Business Person)
IBM Corp
1 N Castle Dr
Armonk, NY 10504, USA

Palms, John M (Educator)
University of South Carolina
President's Office
Columbia, SC 29208, USA

Palomeque, Lincoln (Actor)
c/o Staff Member *TV Caracol*
Calle 76 #11 - 35
Piso 10AA
Bogota DC 26484, COLOMBIA

Palomino, Carlos (Boxer)
14242 Burbank Blvd
#8
Sherman Oaks, CA 91401, USA

Palone, Dave (Horse Racer)
100 Quarry Rd
Washington, PA 15301-9563, USA

Paltrow, Gwyneth (Actor)
416 Washington St #PH
New York, NY 10013, USA

Paltrow, Jake (Director)
c/o John Lesher *WME (LA)*
9601 Wilshire Blvd Fl 3
Beverly Hills, CA 90210, USA

Palumba, Joe (Athlete, Football Player)
927 Old Garth Rd
Charlottesville, VA 22901, USA

Palys, Stan (Athlete, Baseball Player)
448 Center St
Covington Township, PA 18444-7824,
USA

Pampanini, Sylvana
Via Flaminia 322
Rome, ITALY I-00196

Pampling, Rod (Golfer)
4709 Rangewood Dr
Flower Mound, TX 75028-1695, USA

Pamuk, Orhan (Nobel Prize Laureate)
c/o Staff Member *Farrar, Straus and
Giroux*
18 W 18th St
New York, NY 10011-4607, USA

Pan, Hong (Actor)
Omei Film Studio
Tonghui Menwai
Chengdu City, Sichuan Province, CHINA

Panabaker, Danielle (Actor)
c/o Lainie Sorkin Becky *Management 360*
9111 Wilshire Blvd
Beverly Hills, CA 90210, USA

Panabaker, Kay (Actor)
c/o Lena Roklin *Luber Roklin
Management*
8530 Wilshire Blvd
6th Floor
Beverly Hills, CA 90211, USA

Panafieu, Bernard L A Cardinal (Religious
Leader)
Archdiocese
14 Place du Colonel-Edon
Marseille Cedex 07 13284, FRANCE

Panagaris, Orianthi (Musician)
c/o Sterling McIlwaine *19 Entertainment -
LA*
9000 W Sunset Blvd #1574
West Hollywood, CA 90069, USA

Pancake, Sam (Actor)
c/o Joel King *Pakula/King & Associates*
9229 Sunset Blvd
Suite 315
Los Angeles, CA 90069, USA

Panch, Marvin (Race Car Driver)
1648 Taylor Rd. #406
Port Orange, FL 32128, USA

Pancholi, Aditya (Actor, Bollywood)
Hattes Bungalow
Gandhigram Road Juhu
Mumbai, MS 400049, INDIA

Pancholy, Maulik (Actor)
c/o Staff Member *ROAR (LA)*
9701 Wilshire Blvd
8th Floor
Los Angeles, CA 90212, USA

Panday, Basdeo (Prime Minister)
Premier's Office
Eric Williams Plaza
Port of Spain, TRINIDAD & TOBAGO

Pandey, Chunky (Actor, Bollywood)
1 A/B Monisha Apartments
St Andrews Road Bandra
Mumbai, MS 400050, INDIA

Pandian (Actor)
185/6 Bharatidasan Street
Baskar Colony
Chennai, TN 600 093, INDIA

Pandian, Arun (Actor)
2A Bajaj Apartment
Nandanam
Chennai, TN 600 035, INDIA

Pandiani, Karen (Stylist)
c/o Staff Member *Stockland Martel*
343 E 18th St
New York, NY 10003, USA

Pandolfo, Jay (Athlete, Hockey Player)
Pro-Athletes Management
3 Meadowcroft Rd
Burlington, MA 01803-1019, USA

Panetta, Leon E (Government Official,
Politician)
15 Panetta Road
Carmel Valley, CA 93924-9452, USA

Panettiere, Hayden (Actor)
c/o Emily Gerson Saines *Brookside Artists
Management (NY)*
250 W 57th St
Suite 2303
New York, NY 10107, USA

Pang, Darren (Athlete, Hockey Player)
1009 Mississippi Ave Unit G
Saint Louis, MO 63104-2474

Pang, Darren (Athlete, Hockey Player)
St Louis Blues
1401 Clark Ave
Saint Louis, MO 63103-2700

Pang, May
1619 Third Ave. #9D
New York, NY 10128

Pang, Qing (Figure Skater)
c/o Staff Member *Champions on Ice*
Tom Collins Enterprises Inc
3500 W 80th St
Minneapolis, MN 55431, USA

Panhofer, Walter (Musician)
Erdbergstr 35/9
Vienna 1030, AUSTRIA

Panic, Milan (Business Person, Prime
Minister)
1050 Arden Road
Pasadena, CA 91106, USA

Panic at the Disco (Music Group)
c/o *Fueled by Ramen*
PO Box 1803
Tampa, FL 33601, USA

Panichas, George A (Writer)
PO Box AB
College Park, MD 20741, USA

Panico, Jane (Stylist)
145 E 16th St
New York, NY 10003, USA

Panish, Morton B (Misc)
52 Baldwin Road
Freeport, ME 04032-6485, USA

Panjabi, Archie (Actor)
c/o Angelique ONeil *Angelique ONeil
Enterprises*
200 Riverside Blvd
Suite 401 At Trump Place
New York, NY 10069, USA

Pankewicz, Greg (Athlete, Hockey Player)
209 OakSt
Windsor, CO 80550-5437

Pankey, Irv (Athlete, Football Player)
348 Walker St
Aberdeen, MD 21001, USA

Pankin, Stuart (Actor)
1288 Bienevenda Ave
Pacific Palisades, CA 90272, USA

Pankovits, Jim (Athlete, Baseball Player)
6014 Catalina Dr Unit 115
North Mvrtle Beach, SC 29582-8388,
USA

Pankow, James (Musician)
3874 Puerco Canyon Road
Malibu, CA 90265, USA

Pankow, John (Actor)
Gersh Agency
232 North Canon Dr
Beverly Hills, CA 90210, USA

Panni, Marcello (Composer)
3 Piazza Borghese
Rome 00186, ITALY

Panofsky, Wolfgang K H (Physicist)
25671 Chapin Road
Los Altos Hills, CA 94022, USA

Panos, Joe (Athlete, Football Player)
31010 Chequamegon Dr
Hartland, WI 53029, USA

Panov, Valery M (Ballerina)
Carson Office
119 W 57th St
#903
New York, NY 10019, USA

Panoz, Daniel (Inventor)
5473 Legends Dr
Braselton, GA 30517-4019, USA

Panozzo, Chuck (Musician)
c/o Sterling Bacon *TBA Artist
Management (Atlanta)*
1111 Alderman Dr #285
Alpharetta, GA 30005-5433, USA

Pantaleo, Nancy (Stylist)
c/o Staff Member *Directions USA*
3717-C W Market St
Greensboro, NC 27403, USA

Panteleev, Grigori (Athlete, Hockey
Player)
5 Commonwealth Rd
Natick, MA 01760-1526

Panther, Jim (Athlete, Baseball Player)
7936 Tiger Palm Way
Fort Myers, FL 33966-6447, USA

Pantoja, Arnie (Actor)
c/o Julie Balfour *AKA Talent Agency*
6310 San Vicente Blvd
Suite 200
Los Angeles, CA 90048, USA

Pantoliano, Joe (Joey Pants) (Actor)
c/o Staff Member *WME (LA)*
9601 Wilshire Blvd Fl 3
Beverly Hills, CA 90210, USA

Pantotiano, Joe (Actor)
600 Willow Ave
#3
Hoboken, NJ 07030, USA

Panza dl Blumo, Giuseppe (Misc)
PO Box 3183
Lugano 6901, SWITZERLAND

Paola (Royalty)
Koninklijk Palais
Rue de Brederode
Brussels 1000, BELGIUM

Paolini, Christopher (Writer)
c/o Staff Member *Random House*
1540 Broadway
New York, NY 10036, USA

Paolo, Connor (Actor)
c/o Michael Gagliardo *PMK/BNC Public
Relations (PMK-NY)*
622 3rd Ave
8th Floor
New York, NY 10017, USA

Paolozzi, Eduardo L (President)
107 Dovehouse
London SW3 6JZ, UNITED KINGDOM
(UK)

Paopao, Joe (Athlete, Football Player)
200 University Ave W
Waterloo, ON N2L 3G1, Canada

Papa, Greg (Athlete, Baseball Player)
11 San Andreas Dr
Danville, CA 94506-2035, USA

Papa, John (Athlete, Baseball Player)
275 Mary Ave
Stratford, CT 06614-5329, USA

Papa, Tom (Comedian)
c/o Staff Member *WmE2 (WMA-LA)*
1 William Morris Pl
Beverly Hills, CA 90212, USA

Papach, George (Athlete, Football Player)
5454 S Hohman Ave
Hammond, IN 46320, USA

Papa Doo Run Run
PO Box 255
Cuperino, CA 95015-0255

Papadopoulos, Tassos (President)
Presidential Palace
5 Ioannis Ceridos St
Nicosia, CYPRUS

Papajohn, Michael (Actor)
c/o Monique Moss *Integrated PR*
8060 Melrose Ave
4th Floor
Los Angeles, CA 90046, USA

Papale, Vince (Athlete, Football Player)
2219 S 15th St
Philadelphia, PA 19145, USA

Papamichael, Phedon M
(Cinematographer)
Innovative Artists
1505 10th St
Santa Monica, CA 90401, USA

Papapetrou, Peter (Stylist)
c/o Staff Member *Judy Inc*
1 Yorkville Ave
Toronto ON M4W 1L1, Canada

Papa Roach (Music Group)
c/o Staff Member *10th Street
Entertainment (NY)*
38 W 21st St
Suite 300
New York, NY 10010, USA

Papas, Irene (Actor)
38 Xenokratous St
Athens 106 76, GREECE

Papathanassiou, Aspassia (Actor)
38 Xenokratous St
Athens 106 76, GREECE

Papazian, Marty (Actor)
c/o Lin Bickelmann *Encore Artists
Management*
3815 W Olive Ave
Suite 101
Burbank, CA 91505, USA

Pape, Ken (Athlete, Baseball Player)
2127 Green Creek St
San Antonio, TX 78232-3913, USA

Papelbon, Jonathan (Athlete, Baseball
Player)
127 Wild Mdws
Hattiesburg, MS 39402-8108, USA

Papert, Seymour (Mathematician)
Massachusetts Institute of Technology
20 Ames St
Cambridge, MA 02142, USA

Papi, Stan (Athlete, Baseball Player)
1111 W Sierra Madre Ave
Fresno, CA 93705-0433, USA

Papis, Max (Race Car Driver)
Max Papis Racing
112 Byers Creek Rd
Mooresville, NC 28117, USA

Papit, Johnny (Athlete, Football Player)
29 Sellers Ave
Lexington, VA 24450, USA

Papoose (Musician)
c/o Staff Member *Violator Management*
36 W 25th St
2nd Floor
New York, NY 10010, USA

Pappalardo, Salvatore Cardinal (Religious
Leader)
Arcibescovado
Via Matteo Bonello 2
Palermo 90134, ITALY

Pappano, Antonio
Royal Opera House
Covent Garden
Bow St
London WC2E 9DD, UNITED KINGDOM
(UK)

Pappas, Brenden (Athlete, Golfer)
5770 SW 42nd Place
Ocala, FL 34474-9516, USA

Pappas, Deane (Golfer)
3225 W Orange Country Club Dr
Winter Garden, FL 34787-5304, USA

Pappas, Erik (Athlete, Baseball Player)
10248 S Seeley Ave
Chicago, IL 60643-2631, USA

Pappas, George (Bowler)
21108 Blakely Shores Dr
Cornelius, NC 28031-6606, USA

Pappas, Milt (Athlete, Baseball Player)
502 Highlington Ct
Beecher, IL 60401, USA

Pappas, Stephen (Stylist)
c/o Staff Member *Celestine - CA*
1666 20th St
#200-B
Santa Monica, CA 90404, USA

Pappenheimer, John R (Physicist)
66 Sherman St
#113
Cambridge, MA 02140, USA

Pappin, James J (Jim) (Athlete, Hockey
Player)
44827 Oro Grande Cir
Indian Wells, CA 92210-7412, USA

Paquette, Craig (Athlete, Baseball Player)
16615 5 27th Ave
Phoenix, AZ 85045-2202, USA

Paquette, Julie (Stylist)
c/o Staff Member *Team*
423 W Broadway
4th Floor
Boston, MA 02127, USA

Paquin, Anna (Actor)
c/o JoAnne Colonna *Brillstein
Entertainment Partners*
9150 Wilshire Blvd #350
Beverly Hills, CA 90212, USA

Paquin, Kit (Actor)
c/o Staff Member *Trilogy Talent*
13425 Ventura Blvd
2nd Floor
Sherman Oaks, CA 91423, USA

Paradis, Vanessa (Actor, Model, Musician)
7760 Woodrow Wilson Dr
Los Angeles, CA 90046, USA

Paradise, Bob (Athlete, Hockey Player,
Olympic Athlete)
1303 Beechwood Pl
Saint Paul, MN 55116-2202, USA

Paradise, Dick (Athlete, Hockey Player)

Parado, Alejandra (Actor)
c/o Gabriel Blanco *Gabriel Blanco
Iglesias (Mexico)*
Río Balsas 35-32
Colonia Cuauhtemoc
DF 06500, Mexico

Parahia, Murray (Musician)
I M G Artists
420 W 45th St
New York, NY 10036, USA

Paramore (Music Group, Musician)
c/o Randy Dease *Fly South Music Group*
37 N. Orange Ave.
Suite 790
Orlando, FL 32801, USA

Paraseghian, Ara
51767 Oakbrook Ct
Granger, IN 46539-8731

Parazaider, Walter (Musician)
Front Line Mgmt
8900 Wilshire Blvd
#300
Beverly Hills, CA 90211, USA

Parazynski, Scott E (Astronaut)
2015 Wroxton Road
Houston, TX 77005, USA

Parazynski, Scott E Dr (Astronaut)
2015 Wroxton Rd
Houston, TX 77005-1654, USA

Parcells, Duane C (Bill) (Athlete, Coach,
Football Coach, Football Player)
2 Campion Ln
Saratoga Springs, NY 12866, USA

Parchem, Aaron (Athlete, Figure Skater,
Olympic Athlete)
364 N Vista
Auburn Hills, MI 48326-1446, USA

Pardee, Arthur B (Misc)
15 Buzzards Bay Ave
Woods Hole, MA 02543, USA

Pardee, John P (Jack) (Athlete, Coach,
Football Coach, Football Player)
Hawks Hill Ranch
P.O. Box 272
Gause, TX 77857, USA

Pardes, Herbert (Misc)
15 Claremont Ave
#93
New York, NY 10027, USA

Pardo, Al (Athlete, Baseball Player)
908 Hillary Cir
Lutz, FL 33548-5052, USA

Pardo, Don (Correspondent)
NBC-TV
News Dept
30 Rockefeller Plaza
New York, NY 10112, USA

Pardo, Jimmy (Comedian)
c/o Staff Member *OmniPop Talent Group*
10700 Ventura Blvd.
2nd Floor
Studio Clty, CA 91604, USA

Pardue, Kip (Actor)
c/o Jason Newman *Untitled Entertainment
(LA)*
350 S. Beverly Dr #200
Beverly Hills, CA 90212, USA

Pardue, Wendye (Stylist)
33 Bettswood Rd
Norwalk, CT 06851, USA

Pardus, Dan (Race Car Driver)
Jim & Judie Motorsports
4345 Motorsports Dr.
Concord, NC 28027, USA

Pardy, Adam (Athlete, Hockey Player)
Octagon Sports Management
66 Slater St 23rd Fl
Attn Larry Kelly
Ottawa, ON KlP SHl, Canada

Pare, Jessica (Actor)
c/o Nick Frenkel *3 Arts Entertainment Inc*
9460 Wilshire Blvd
7th Floor
Beverly Hills, CA 90210, USA

Pare, Michael (Actor)
c/o Staff Member *David Shapira &
Associates*
193 N Robertson Blvd
Beverly Hills, CA 90211, USA

Paredes, Marisa (Actor)
Alsira Maroto Garcia
Gran Via 63
#3 Izda
Madrid 28013, SPAIN

Parekh, Asha (Actor, Bollywood)
Azad Road
Juhu
Mumbai, MS 400049, INDIA

Parekh, Kal (Actor)
c/o Jenn Lederer *AFST Management*
350 W 43rd St
Suite 32G
New York, NY 10036, USA

Parent, Bernie (Athlete, Hockey Player)
Offices of Bernie Parent
125 N Route 73
West Berlin, NJ 08091-9225, USA

Parent, Gail
2001 Mandeville Canyon
Los Angeles, CA 90024

Parent, Mark (Athlete, Baseball Player)
8829 Midview Dr
Palo Cedro, CA 96073-8635, USA

Parent, Monique (Actor, Model)
PO Box 3458
Ventura, CA 93006, USA

Parenteau, Pierre-Aiexandr (Athlete,
Hockey Player)
158 Rue de Bresolettes
Boucherville, QC J4B 6M8, Canada

Paret, Peter (Historian, Writer)
Institute for Advanced Studies
Historical Studies School
Princeton, NJ 08540, USA

Paretsky, Sara N (Writer)
5831 S Blackstone Ave
Chicago, IL 60637-1855, USA

Parfit, Derek A (Misc)
All Souls College
Philosophy Dept
Oxford OX1 4AL, UNITED KINGDOM
(UK)

Pargo, Jannero (Athlete, Basketball Player)
3280 Timberwood Ln
Riverwoods, IL 60015-2418

Pargo, Jannero (Athlete, Basketball Player)
3280 Timberwood Ln
Riverwoods, IL 60015-2418, USA

Parham, Gus (Athlete, Football Player)
Taylor Made Office Systems
4294 El Camino Real
Los Altos, CA 94022, USA

Parilla, Jennifer (Athlete, Gymnast,
Olympic Athlete)
21822 Rushford Dr
Lake Forest, CA 92630-6503, USA

Parilla, Lana (Actor)
c/o Liza Anderson *Anderson Group Public Relations*
8060 Melrose Ave Fl 4
Los Angeles, CA 90046, USA

Parillaud, Anne (Actor)
c/o Elisabeth Tanner *ArtMedia*
20 avenue Rapp
Paris 75008, France

Parilli, Vito (Babe) (Athlete, Coach, Football Coach, Football Player)
8060 E Girard Ave
Apt 218
Denver, CO 80231, USA

Paris, Bubba (Athlete, Football Player)
4096 Beacon Pl
Discovery Bay, CA 94505, USA

Paris, Clarke (Race Car Driver)
Crave Racing
PO Box 972
Harvey, LA 70059, USA

Paris, Joel (General)
5775 Medlock Bridge Pkwy
Alpharetta, GA 30022-7319, USA

Paris, Kelly (Athlete, Baseball Player)
1515 Redwood Cir
Thousand Oaks, CA 91360-6336, USA

Paris, Mica (Musician)
Richard Walters
1800 Argyle Ave
#408
Los Angeles, CA 90028, USA

Paris, Twila (Musician, Songwriter, Writer)
Proper Mgmt
PO Box 150867
Nashville, TN 37215, USA

Parise, JP (Athlete, Hockey Player)
1811 Westwood Dr
Faribault, MN 55021-5530

Parise, Louis (Misc)
National Maritime Union
1125 15th St NW
Washington, DC 20005, USA

Parise, Robert L (Basketball Player)
20 Stonybrook Road
#1
Framingham, MA 01702, USA

Parise, Ronald A (Astronaut)
15419 Good Hope Road
Silver Spring, MD 20905, USA

Parise, Vanessa (Actor)
c/o Lara Rosenstock *Lara Rosenstock Management*
8371 Blackburn Ave #1
Los Angeles, CA 90048, USA

Parise, Zach (Athlete, Hockey Player)
c/o Wade Arnott *Newport Sports Management*
201 City Centre Dr
Suite 400
Mississauga, ON L58 2T4, Canada

Parish, Robert (Athlete, Basketball Player)
18730 Peninsula Club Dr
Cornelius, NC 28031-5114, USA

Parish, Sam (General)
5628 Catoctin Ridge Dr
Mount Airy, MD 21771-6010, USA

Parisi, Siobhan
c/o Staff Member *Carry Company, The*
3875 Wilshire Blvd #402
Los Angeles, CA 90010, USA

Parisot, Dean (Director)
c/o Staff Member *3 Arts Entertainment Inc*
9460 Wilshire Blvd
7th Floor
Beverly Hills, CA 90210, USA

Parisse, Annie (Actor)
c/o Stephen Hirsch *Gersh (NY)*
41 Madison Ave
New York, NY 10010, USA

Parizeau, Jacques (Politician)
88 Grand Alle Est
Quebec, PQ G1A 1A2, CANADA

Parizeau, Michel (Athlete, Hockey Player)
250 Rue Chauveau
Drummondville, QC J2C 6L2, Canada

Park, Alyssa (Musician)
Columbia Artists Mgmt Inc
165 W 57th St
New York, NY 10019, USA

Park, Chan Ho (Athlete, Baseball Player)
c/o Team Member *New York Yankees*
Yankee Stadium
161st St & River Ave
Bronx, NY 10451, USA

Park, Charles R (Physicist)
5325 Stanford Dr
Nashville, TN 37215, USA

Park, D Bradford (Brad) (Athlete, Coach, Hockey Player)
100 Legends Way
Suite 250 Attn: Alumni Association
Boston, MA 02114-1389, USA

Park, Ernie (Athlete, Football Player)
3160 Private Road 1101
Clyde, TX 79510, USA

Park, Grace (Actor)
c/o Tyman Stewart *Characters Talent Agency, The (Vancouver)*
1505 W 2nd Ave
#200
Vancouver, BC V6H 3Y4, Canada

Park, Jim (Athlete, Hockey Player)
33 Braeburn Dr
Thornhill, ON L3T 4V2, Canada

Park, Joon (Actor)
c/o Susan Yoo *Susan Yoo*
Prefers to be contacted via telephone
Los Angeles, CA, USA

Park, Linda (Actor)
c/o Ro Diamond *SDB Partners Inc*
1801 Ave of the Stars
Suite 902
Los Angeles, CA 90067, USA

Park, Linkin (Music Group)
c/o Michael Arfin *Artist Group International (NY)*
150 East 58th Street
Fl 19
New York, NY 10155, USA

Park, Merle F (Ballerina)
Royal Ballet School
144 Talgarth Road
London W14 9DE, UNITED KINGDOM (UK)

Park, Nicholas W (Nick) (Animator, Director)
Aardvark Animation
Gas Ferry Road
Bristol B51 6UN, UNITED KINGDOM (UK)

Park, Patrick (Musician)
c/o Staff Member *Red Light Management (LA)*
8439 W Sunset Blvd
Suite 2
Los Angeles, CA 90069, USA

Park, Ray (Actor)
c/o Dino May *Dino May Management*
6362 Hollywood Blvd #422
Hollywood, CA 90028-6323, USA

Park, Reg
Box 1002-Morningside 2057 Sandton
Gauteng, SOUTH AFRICA

Park, Richard (Athlete, Hockey Player)
6416 Vista Pacifica
Rancho Palos Verdes, CA 90275-5896

Park, Steve (Race Car Driver)
261 Indian Trail Rd.
Mooresville, NC 28117-8568, USA

Parke, Evan Dexter (Actor)
c/o Staff Member *McCabe Group, The*
3211 Cahuenga Blvd W Ste 104
Los Angeles, CA 90068, USA

Parkening, Christopher (Musician)
IMG Artists
420 W 45th St
New York, NY 10036, USA

Parker, Ace (Athlete, Baseball Player)
210 Snead Fairway
Portsmouth, VA 23701-1641, USA

Parker, Ace (Athlete, Football Player)
210 Snead Fairway
Portsmouth, VA 23701, USA

Parker, Alan W (Director)
c/o Staff Member *Independent Talent Group (ITG-UK)*
Oxford House
76 Oxford St
London W1D 1BS, UK

Parker, Andrea (Actor)
c/o Dan Baron *Agency for the Performing Arts (APA-LA)*
405 S Beverly Dr
Suite 500
Beverly Hills, CA 90212-4425, USA

Parker, Angie (Stylist)
c/o Staff Member *Mercury Artists*
8460 Higuera St Fl 2
Culver City, CA 90232, USA

Parker, Anthony (Basketball Player)
Orlando Magic
Waterhouse Center
8701 Maitland Summit Blvd
Orlando, FL 32810, USA

Parker, Anthony (Athlete, Football Player)
1054 E Geneva Dr
Tempe, AZ 85282, USA

Parker, Bob (Skier)
408 Camino Don Miguel
Santa Fe, NM 87505, USA

Parker, Brant J (Cartoonist)
901 Glenwood Blvd
Waynesboro, VA 22980, USA

Parker, Bruce C (Biologist)
841 Hutchson Dr
Blackburg, VA 24060, USA

Parker, Caryl Mack (Musician)
Scream Marketing
PO Box 120053
Nashville, TN 37212, USA

Parker, Chris (Actor)
Elstree Centre
Clarendon Road
Borehamwood
Herts WD6 1JF, UK

Parker, Christian (Athlete, Baseball Player)
10101 Mesa Arriba Ave NE
Albuquerque, NM 87111-4962, USA

Parker, Christopher (Actor)
Shepherd Mgmt
13 Radnor Walk
London SW3 4BP, UNITED KINGDOM (UK)

Parker, Clay (Athlete, Baseball Player)
6614 Brickston St
Hixson, TN 37343-2593, USA

Parker, Corey (Actor)
Muse Mgmt
429 Santa Monica Blvd #520
Santa Monica, CA 90401, USA

Parker, Craig (Actor)
c/o Joe Smith *ICM Partners (ICM-LA)*
10250 Constellation Blvd Fl 7
Los Angeles, CA 90067, USA

Parker, Dave (Athlete, Baseball Player)
4038 Oak Tree Ct
Loveland, OH 45140-1090, USA

Parker, Denise (Archer, Athlete, Olympic Athlete)
131 W 4300 N
Ogden, UT 84414-1125, USA

Parker, Eleanor (Actor)
2195 La Paz Way
Palm Springs, CA 92262, USA

Parker, Eugene N (Physicist, Scientist)
1006 Gardner Rd
Flossmoor, IL 60422-1361, USA

Parker, Franklin (Writer)
Western Carolina University
Education & Psychology Dept
Cullowhee, NC 28723, USA

Parker, George M (Misc)
Glass Workers Union
1440 S Byme Road
Toledo, OH 43614, USA

Parker, Georgie (Actor)
c/o Staff Member *Mark Morrissey and Associates*
16 Princess Ave
Rosebery
Sydney NSW 2018, Australia

Parker, Hank Jr (Race Car Driver)
MRO
5555 Concord Pkwy. S. #405
Concord, NC 28027, USA

Parker, Jack Jr (Horse Racer)
38 Lea Ct
Frederica, DE 19946-1985, USA

Parker, Jack Sr (Horse Racer)
127 Roosevelt Ave
Westwood, NJ 07675-2316, USA

Parker, Jameson (Actor)
1604 N. Vista Ave.
Los Angeles, CA 90046, USA

Parker, Jeff (Athlete, Hockey Player)
2018 Riviera Ave S
Lakeland, MN 55043-9419

Parker, Lani Malone (Stylist)
c/o Staff Member *Celestine - CA*
1666 20th St
#200-B
Santa Monica, CA 90404, USA

Parker, Lara (Actor)
PO Box 1254
Topanga, CA 90290, USA

Parker, Larry (Athlete, Football Player)
15903 San Marco Pl
Bakersfield, CA 93314-6650, USA

Parker, Lu
12222 Vance Jackson Rd. #734
San Antonio, TX 78230-5941

Parker, Maceo (Musician)
109 W Newark Ave
Wildwood, NJ 08260-1038

Parker, Mary-Louise (Actor)
c/o Jillian Fowkes *ID Public Relations*
(ID-LA)
7060 Hollywood Blvd
8th Floor
Los Angeles, CA 90028, USA

Parker, Molly (Actor)
c/o Staff Member *Dontanville/Frattaroli*
(D/F)
270 Lafayette St
Suite 402
New York, NY 10012, USA

Parker, Nate (Actor)
c/o Samantha Hill *WKT Public Relations*
(WKT-LA)
9350 Wilshire Blvd
Suite 450
Beverly Hills, CA 90212, USA

Parker, Nathanial
10100 Santa Monica Blvd. #2500
Los Angeles, CA 90067

Parker, Nathaniel (Actor)
Markham & Froggatt
Julian House
4 Windmill St
London W1P 1HF, UNITED KINGDOM
(UK)

Parker, Nicole (Actor)
c/o Mark Rousso *New Wave*
Entertainment (LA)
2660 W Olive Blvd
Burbank, CA 91505, USA

Parker, Nicole Ari (Actor)
c/o Maani Golesorkhi *Bluestone*
Entertainment
9000 Sunset Blvd
Suite 700
Los Angeles, CA 90069, USA

Parker, Noelle
9300 Wilshire Blvd. #555
Beverly Hills, CA 90212

Parker, Oliver
76 Oxford St.
London, ENGLAND W1N 0AX

Parker, Olivia (Photographer)
Robert Klein
38 Newbury St
#400
Boston, MA 02116, USA

Parker, Orlando (Athlete, Football Player)
4402 Chatham Pl
Montgomery, AL 36108, USA

Parker, Paula Jai (Actor)
c/o Leonard Torgan *Collective*
8383 Wilshire Blvd
Suite 1050
Beverly Hills, CA 90211, USA

Parker, Rick (Athlete, Baseball Player)
2641 NE 74th St
Kansas City, MO 64119-5349, USA

Parker, Riddick (Athlete, Football Player)
11226 NE 68th St
Apt 212-B
Kirkland, WA 98033, USA

Parker, Robert (Athlete, Basketball Player)
7947 S Chappel Ave
Chicago, IL 60617-1052, USA

Parker, Robert (Astronaut)
NASA
Johnson Space Center
2101 NASA Rd
Houston, TX 77058, USA

Parker, Robert A Dr (Astronaut)
5316 Godbey Dr
La Canada Flintridee, CA 91011-1833,
USA

Parker, Sarah Jessica (Actor, Producer)
20 E 10th St
New York, NY 10003, USA

Parker, Scott (Athlete, Hockey Player)
1950 W Wolfensberger Ct
Castle Rock, CO 80109-9699

Parker, Scott (Motorcycle Race,
Motorcycle Racer)
6096 Grand Blanc Road
Swartz Creek, MI 48473, USA

Parker, Sean (Business Person)
1 Letterman Dr
Bldg C, Suite 420
San Francisco, CA 94129, USA

Parker, T Jefferson (Writer)
c/o Staff Member *Trident Media Group*
LLC
41 Madison Ave
36th Floor
New York, NY 10010, USA

Parker, Trey (Animator, Writer)
c/o Gabrielle (Gaby) Morgerman *WME*
(LA)
9601 Wilshire Blvd Fl 3
Beverly Hills, CA 90210, USA

Parker, Vaughn (Athlete, Football Player)
2500 6th Ave
Apt 107
San Diego, CA 92103, USA

Parker, Wes (Athlete, Baseball Player)
Los Angeles Dodgers
1000 Elysian Park Ave
Attn: Community Relations Dept
Los Angeles, CA 90090-1111, USA

Parker, Willie (Athlete, Football Player)
9327 Kai Dr
Beach City, TX 77523-2333, USA

Parker-Bowles, Camilla (Royalty)
Clarence House
Stable Yard Gate
London SW1, UNITED KINGDOM (UK)

Parker Jr, Ray (Musician)
c/o Staff Member *Performers of the World*
5657 Wilshire Blvd #280
Los Angeles, CA 90036, USA

Parkhill, Barry (Athlete, Basketball Player)
3429 Cesford Grange
Keswick, VA 22947-9127, USA

Parkhurst, Heather
8383 Wilshire Blvd. #954
Beverly Hills, CA 90211

Parkhurst, Heather Elizabeth (Actor)
8491 Sunset Blvd
#440
West Hollywood, CA 90069, USA

Parkins, Barbara
6399 Wilshire Blvd. #414
Los Angeles, CA 90048

Parkinson, Bradford (Inventor)
2360 Camino Edna
San Luis Obispo, CA 93401-8327, USA

Parkinson, Bradford W (Business Person)
2780 Valley Circle
Meadow Vista, CA 95722, USA

Parkinson, Katherine (Actor)
c/o Sarah McCormick *Curtis Brown*
Group
Haymarket House
28 - 29 Haymarket
London SW1Y 4SP, UNITED KINGDOM

Parkinson, Michael
c/o *PFD*
Drury House
34/43 Russell St
London WC2B 5HA, UNITED KINGDOM

Parkinson, Roger P (Publisher)
Minneapolis Star Tribune
425 Portland Ave
Minneapolis, MN 55488, USA

Parks, Catherine (Actor)
1144 N Vista St #2
W Hollywood, CA 90046, USA

Parks, Cherokee (Athlete, Basketball
Player)
5331 Kadena Garden Ct
North Las Vegas, NV 89031-6605, USA

Parks, Chris (Athlete, Wrestler)
c/o Staff Member *TNA Wrestling*
209 10th Ave S
Suite 302
Nashville, TN 37203, USA

Parks, Dallas (Athlete, Baseball Player)
3353 Pittman Grove Church Rd
Raeford, NC 28376, USA

Parks, David W (Dave) (Athlete, Football
Player)
6629 Southpoint Dr
Dallas, TX 75248, USA

Parks, Derek (Athlete, Baseball Player)
7828 Day Creek Blvd
Act 1214
Rancho Cucamonga, CA 91739-8580,
USA

Parks, Greg (Athlete, Hockey Player)
St Albert Steel 400 Campbell Rd 2nd Fl
St. Albert, AB T8N OR8, Canada

Parks, Maxie (Athlete, Track Athlete)
4545 E Norwich Ave
Fresno, CA 93726, USA

Parks, Michael (Actor)
11684 Ventura Blvd
#476
Studio City, CA 91604, USA

Parks, Michael (Editor)
Los Angeles Times
Editorial Dept
202 W 1st
Los Angeles, CA 90012, USA

Parks, Phaedra (Attorney, Reality TV Star)
c/o Staff Member *Bravo (NY)*
30 Rockefeller Plaza
New York, NY 10112, USA

Parks, Suzan-Lori (Actor, Writer)
c/o Staff Member *Creative Artists Agency*
(CAA-LA)
2000 Ave Of The Stars
Los Angeles, CA 90067, USA

Parks, Van Dyke (Composer)
2141 Layton St
Pasadena, CA 91104-1805, USA

Parks-Young, Barbara (Athlete, Baseball
Player)
5078 Edinboro Ln
Wilmington, NC 28409-8518, USA

Parlavecchio, Chet (Athlete, Football
Player)
211 Brooklake Rd
Florham Park, NJ 07932, USA

Parlen, Megan (Actor)
c/o Staff Member *Cunningham Escott*
Slevin & Doherty (CESD-LA)
10635 Santa Monica Blvd
130
Los Angeles, CA 90025, USA

Parlow, Cindy (Athlete, Olympic Athlete,
Soccer Player)
2611 English Hill Dr
Murfreesboro, TN 37130-1433, USA

Parlow, Sarah (Stylist)
c/o Staff Member *Mark Edward Inc*
325 W 8th St
#1011
New York, NY 10018, USA

Parmalee, Bernie (Athlete, Football
Player)
14695 Heatherton Dr
Granger, IN 46530, USA

Parmenter, Charles S (Misc)
Indiana University
Chemistry Dept
Bloomington, IN 47405, USA

Parmenter, Skip (Athlete, Football Player)
34881 Seagrass Plantation Ln34881
Seagrass Plantation Ln
Dagsboro, DE 19939-3398, USA

Parmet, Philip (Cinematographer)
1080 Hayworth Ave
Los Angeles, CA 90035, USA

Parnell, Bobby (Athlete, Baseball Player)
2265 Barger Rd
Salisbury, NC 28146-5049, USA

Parnell, Chris (Actor)
c/o Jimmy Miller *Mosaic Media Group*
9200 W. Sunset Blvd
10th Floor
Los Angeles, CA 90069, USA

Parnell, Lee Roy (Musician)
PO Box 23451
Nashville, TN 37202, USA

Parnell, LeRoy
PO Box 23451
Nashville, TN 37202

Parnell, Peter (Writer)
c/o Staff Member *United Talent Agency (UTA)*
9336 Civic Center Dr
Beverly Hills, CA 90210, USA

Parnell, Sean (Governor)
Alaska State Capitol Building
P.O. Box 110001
Juneau, AK 99811-0001, USA

Parnevik, Jesper (Golfer)
17553 SE Conch Bar Ave
Jupiter, FL 33469-1709, USA

Parodi, Starr (Musician)
c/o Staff Member *Evolution Music Partners*
1680 N. Vine St.
Hollywood, CA 90028, USA

Paronto, Chad (Athlete, Baseball Player)
617 Benedict Rd
Pittsfield, MA 01201-2899, USA

Parque, Jim (Athlete, Baseball Player, Olympic Athlete)
4109 Crystal Ridge Dr SE
Puyallup, WA 98372-5214, USA

Parque, jim (Athlete, Baseball Player)
3142 Halverson Way
Roseville, CA 95661-4038, USA

Parr, Carolyn Miller (Judge)
US Tax Court
400 2nd St NW
Washington, DC 20217, USA

Parr, Jerry S
4529 38th St NW
Washington, DC 20016, USA

Parr, Ralph S (General, War Hero)
2294 Common St Apt 442
New Braunfels, TX 78130-3586, USA

Parr, Robert G (Misc)
701 Kenmore Road
Chapel Hill, NC 27514, USA

Parr, Todd (Writer)
c/o Staff Member *Suppertime Entertainment*
21300 Oxnard St
Suite 100
Woodland Hills, CA 91367, USA

Parra, Derek (Athlete, Olympic Athlete, Speed Skater)
US Speedskating
14927 Treseder St
Draper, UT 84020-3403, USA

Parra, Manny (Athlete, Baseball Player)
c/o Joe Urbon *Creative Artists Agency (CAA-NY)*
162 Fifth Ave
6th Floor
New York, NY 10010, USA

Parrella, John (Athlete, Football Player)
8161 Regency Dr
Pleasanton, CA 94588, USA

Parrett, Jeff (Athlete, Baseball Player)
722 Seattle Dr
Lexington, KY 40503-2127, USA

Parrett, William (Business Person)
Deloitte Touche Tohmatsu
433 Country Club Road
New Canaan, CT 06840, USA

Parrilla, Lana (Actor)
c/o Pamela Kohl *3 Arts Entertainment Inc*
9460 Wilshire Blvd
7th Floor
Beverly Hills, CA 90210, USA

Parriott, James (Director)
c/o Jamie Mandelbaum *Jackoway Tyerman Wertheimer Austen Mandelbaum Morris & Klein*
1925 Century Park E
22nd Floor
Los Angeles, CA 90067, USA

Parris, Fred (Musician)
Paramount Entertainment
PO Box 12
Far Hills, NJ 07931, USA

Parris, Gary (Athlete, Football Player)
5170 9th St
Vero Beach, FL 32966, USA

Parris, Jonathan (Athlete, Baseball Player)
23127 128th Rd
Springfield Gardens, NY 11413-1310, USA

Parris, Steve (Athlete, Baseball Player)
403 Rookery Ct
Joliet, IL 60431-2820, USA

Parrish, Bernard J (Bernie) (Athlete, Football Player)
140A Torns Creek Rd
Eastanollee, GA 30538, USA

Parrish, Hunter (Actor)
c/o Lainie Sorkin Becky *Management 360*
9111 Wilshire Blvd
Beverly Hills, CA 90210, USA

Parrish, John (Athlete, Baseball Player)
1110 Logan Ln
Narvon, PA 17555-9579, USA

Parrish, Lance M (Athlete, Baseball Player)
c/o Tom Wyroba
PO Box 3308
Melvindale, MI 48122-0308, USA

Parrish, Larry A (Athlete, Baseball Player, Coach)
1269 Blakely Hwy
Fort Gaines, GA 39851-4029, USA

Parrish, Lemar (Athlete, Football Player)
733 Schumate Chapel Rd
Jefferson City, MO 65109, USA

Parrish, Mark (Athlete, Hockey Player, Olympic Athlete)
15525 51st Ave N
Minneapolis, MN 55446-2220, USA

Parro, Dave (Athlete, Hockey Player)
820 3rd Ave
Hershey, PA 17033-1903

Parros, George (Athlete, Hockey Player)
1105 Manhattan Ave
Hermosa Beach, CA 90254, USA

Parros, Peter (Actor)
P.O. Box 3055
West Orange, NJ 07052, USA

Parrot, Andrew
Jonathan Wentworth
10 Fiske Place
#530
Mount Vernon, NY 10550, USA

Parrott, Ian
Abermad nr. Aberystwyth
Dyfed Wales, ENGLAND SY 23 4RS

Parrott, Mike (Athlete, Baseball Player)
PO Box 1264
Lyons, CO 80540-1264, USA

Parry, Craig (Golfer)
5139 Latrobe Dr
Windermere, FL 34786-8916, USA

Parry, Edward (Athlete, Basketball Player)
6152 Benoit Rd
Clay, MI 48001-3302, USA

Parry, Ken (Actor)
c/o Linda Kremer *Billy Marsh Drama Ltd*
20 Garrick St
London WC2E 9BT, UK

Parry, Robert T (Financier)
720 S Colorado Blvd
Suite 290A
Denver, CO 80246-1929, USA

Parry, Vikci (Stylist)
c/o Staff Member *Elite Model Management/Atlanta*
1708 Peachtree St NW
#210
Atlanta, GA 30309, USA

Parseghian, Ara (Coach, Football Coach, Sportscaster)
51767 Oakbridge Court
Granger, IN 46539, USA

Parseghian, Gregory (Business Person)
Federal Home Loan Mortgage
8200 Jones Branch Dr
McLean, VA 22102, USA

Parshall, George W (Misc)
2401 Pennsylvania Avenue
Apt 714
Wilmington, DE 19806-1410, USA

Parsia, Fati (Stylist)
c/o Staff Member *Rex Agency, The*
6311 Romaine St
Los Angeles, CA 90038, USA

Parsky, Gerald L (Attorney, Attorney General, General)
Aurora Capital Partners
1800 Century Park East
Los Angeles, CA 90067, USA

Parsons, Alan (Musician)
c/o Staff Member *Agency Group Ltd, The (NY)*
142 West 57th St
6th Floor
New York, NY 10019, USA

Parsons, Benny (Race Car Driver)
1691 Old Harmony Dr
Concord, NC 28027, USA

Parsons, Bill (Athlete, Baseball Player)
322 Karen Ave Unit 3901
Las Vegas, NV 89109-0453, USA

Parsons, Bob (Athlete, Football Player)
1292 Thorndale Ln
Hawthorn Woods, IL 60047, USA

Parsons, Casey (Athlete, Baseball Player)
17214 E Galactica Ct
Greenacres, WA 99016-7766, USA

Parsons, Craig (Athlete, Hockey Player)
30 Yonge St.
Toronto, ON M5E 1XB, CANADA

Parsons, David (Choreographer)
Parsons Dance Foundation
476 Broadway
New York, NY 10013, USA

Parsons, Estelle (Actor)
924 West End Ave
#T5
New York, NY 10025, USA

Parsons, Jim (Actor)
c/o Marsha McManus *Principal Entertainment (LA)*
1964 Westwood Blvd #400
Los Angeles, CA 90025, USA

Parsons, Johnny (Race Car Driver)
Brian Bollinger CMG
10500 Crosspoint Blvd.
Indianapolis, IN 46356, USA

Parsons, John T (Inventor)
1456 Brigadoon Court
Traverse City, MI 49686, USA

Parsons, Karyn (Actor)
c/o Matthew Lesher *Insight*
1134 S Cloverdale Ave
Los Angeles, CA 90019, USA

Parsons, Nathan (Actor)
c/o Melissa Hirschenson *Innovative Artists (LA)*
1505 10th St
Santa Monica, CA 90401, USA

Parsons, Nicholas (Actor)
Susan Shaper
174/178 N Gower St
London NW1 2NB, UNITED KINGDOM (UK)

Parsons, Phil (Athlete, Race Car Driver)
18801 Coveside Lane
Cornelius, NC 28031-5250, USA

Parsons, Robert (Bob)
Go Daddy
14455 N. Hayden Rd
Suite 219
Scottsdale, AZ 85260, USA

Parsons, Robert K (Aviator)
979 Shalimar Point Dr
Shalimar, FL 32579-1657, USA

Parsons, Tom (Athlete, Baseball Player)
7106 Lorraine Ave NW
North Canton, OH 44720-8832, USA

Parsons-Zipay, Suzanne (Athlete, Baseball Player)
2310 Englewood Rd
Englewood, FL 34223-6333, USA

Part, Arvo (Composer)
Universal Editions
Warwick House
9 Warrick St
London W1R 5RA, UNITED KINGDOM (UK)

Partee, Barbara H (Educator)
50 Hobart Lane
Amherst, MA 01002, USA

Partee, Dennis (Athlete, Football Player)
400 N Bolivar St
Marshall, TX 75670-3311, USA

Parten, Ty (Athlete, Football Player)
41121 N Prosperity Way
Anthem, AZ 85086-1510, USA

Partlow, Hope (Musician)
c/o Staff Member *Virgin Records (NY)*
150 5th Ave
New York, NY 10010, USA

Parton, Dolly (Actor, Musician, Songwriter)
Dollywood Co
2700 Dollywood Parks Blvd
Pigeon Forge, TN 37863, USA

Parton, Stella (Musician)
PO Box 120871
Nashville, TN 37212, USA

Partridge, Derek
96 Broadway Bexley Heath
Kent, ENGLAND DA6 7DE

Partridge, John A (Architect)
20 Old Pye St
Westminster
London SW1, UNITED KINGDOM (UK)

Partridge, Rick (Athlete, Football Player)
707 Reeder Rd
Paramus, NJ 48363-2932, USA

Parvanov, Georgi (President)
President's Office
2 Dondukov Blvd
Sofia 1123, BULGARIA

Pasanella, Giovanni (Architect)
Pasanella & Klein
330 W 42nd St
New York, NY 10036, USA

Pasanella, Marco (Designer)
Pasanella Co
45 W 18th St
New York, NY 10011, USA

Pasarell, Charles (Tennis Player)
78200 Miles Ave
Indian Wells, CA 92210, USA

Pascal, Adam (Actor)
c/o Staff Member *Paradigm (LA)*
360 N Crescent Dr
North Bldg
Beverly Hills, CA 90210, USA

Pascal, Francoise
89 Riverview Gardens
London, ENGLAND SW12 9RA

Pascal, Olivia
Merzstr. 14
Munich, GERMANY D-81679

Paschal, Doug (Athlete, Football Player)
4600 Coburn Ct
Charlotte, NC 28277, USA

Paschall, Bill (Athlete, Baseball Player)
7926 Windspray Dr
Summerfield, NC 27358-9715, USA

Paschall, Jim (Race Car Driver)
RR 2 Box 450
Denton, NC 27239, USA

Paschke, Melanie (Athlete, Track Athlete)
Asseweg 2
Braunschweig 38124, GERMANY

Pasco, Richard (Actor)
Michael Whitehall
125 Gloucester Road
London SW7 4TE, UNITED KINGDOM (UK)

Pascoal, Hermeto (Musician)
Brasil Universo Prod
RVN Vitor Guisard 209
Rio de Janerio 21832, BRAZIL

Pascrell Jr., Bill (Congressman, Politician)
2370 Rayburn HOB
Washington, DC 20515, USA

Pascual, Camilo (Athlete, Baseball Player)
7741 SW 32nd St
Miami, FL 33155-2611, USA

Pascual, Luis (Director)
Theatre de l'Europe
1 Place Paul Claudel
Paris 75006, FRANCE

Pascual, Mercedes (Biologist)
University of Michigan
Ecology & Biology Dept
Ann Arbor, MI 48109, USA

Pascucci, Val (Athlete, Baseball Player)
11163 James Pl
Cerritos, CA 90703-6450, USA

Pasdar, Adrian (Actor)
c/o Leigh Brillstein *ICM Partners (ICM-LA)*
10250 Constellation Blvd Fl 7
Los Angeles, CA 90067, USA

Pashnick, Larry (Athlete, Baseball Player)
506 Highland St
Wyandotte, MI 48192-2433, USA

Pasian, Karina (Musician)
c/o Staff Member *Island Def Jam Group*
Worldwide Plaza
825 8th Ave Fl 28
New York, NY 10019, USA

Pasik, Mario (Actor)
c/o Staff Member *Telefe - Argentina*
Pavon 2444 (C1248AAT)
Buenos Aires, ARGENTINA

Pasillas, Jose (Musician)
c/o Staff Member *ArtistDirect*
9046 Lindblade St
Culver City, CA 90232, USA

Pasin, Dave (Athlete)
787 Holly Oak Dr
Palo Alto, CA 94303-4143

Paskai, Laszio Cardinal (Religious Leader)
Uri Utca 62
Budapest 1014, HUNGARY

Paslawski, Greg (Athlete, Hockey Player)
10 Topping Lane
Des Peres, MO 63133, USA

Pasley, Kevin (Athlete, Baseball Player)
2701 Lancaster Dr
Sun City Center, FL 33573, USA

Pasmore, E J Victor (Artist)
Dar Gamri
Gudja, MALTA

Pasqua, Dan (Athlete, Baseball Player)
10423 Capistrano
Moreno Vally, CA 92557-3036, USA

Pasquale, Edward (Athlete, Hockey Player)
101 Marietta St. NW
#1900
Atlanta, GA 30303, USA

Pasquale, Steven (Actor)
c/o Staff Member *Overbrook Entertainment*
450 N Roxbury Dr
4th Floor
Beverly Hills, CA 90210, USA

Pasqualini, Tony (Actor)
c/o Sandra Joseph *SLJ Management*
833 N Edinburgh Ave Ph 11
Los Angeles, CA 90046, USA

Pasqualoni, Paul (Coach, Football Coach)
Syracuse University
Athletic Dept
Syracuse, NY 13244, USA

Pasquesi, Anthony (Athlete, Football Player)
463 E Clubview Ct
Addison, IL 60101, USA

Pasquesi, David (Actor)
c/o Mark Teitelbaum *Teitelbaum Artists Group*
8840 Wilshire Blvd
3rd Floor
Beverly Hills, CA 90212, USA

Pasquin, John R (Actor, Director, Filmmaker, Producer)
Paradox Productions
801 Tarcuto Way
Los Angeles, CA 90077, USA

Pass, Patrick (Athlete, Football Player)
4 Spruce Pond Rd
Franklin, MA 02038, USA

Passaglia, Martin (Athlete, Basketball Player)
7377 Capay Ave
Orland, CA 95963-9687, USA

Passarelli, Pasquale (Wrestler)
Ander Froschlache 23
Munster 4400, GERMANY

Passer, Ivan (Director)
c/o Staff Member *Innovative Artists (LA)*
1505 10th St
Santa Monica, CA 90401, USA

Passions, The
141 Dunbar Ave.
Fords, NJ 08863

Passman, Elizabeth (Stylist)
927 Noyes St
Evanston, IL 60201, USA

Passmore, Christi (Race Car Driver)
GAP Roofing
Rt. 3
Box 6870
Pryor, OK 74361, USA

Passmore, John A (Misc)
6 Jansz Crescent
Manuka, ACT 2603, AUSTRALIA

Passos, Rosa (Musician)
c/o Staff Member *Concord Music Group, Inc*
900 N. Rohlwing Road
Itasca, IL 60143, USA

Pastan, Linda (Writer)
11710 Beall Mountain Rd
Potomac, MD 20854-1105, USA

Paster, Jessica (Stylist)
c/o Staff Member *Magnet (LA)*
6363 Wilshire Blvd Ste 650
Los Angeles, CA 90048, USA

Pasternak, Michael (Actor)
c/o Craig Wyckoff *Wyckoff and Associates (LA)*
11350 Ventura Blvd
Suite 100
Studio City, CA 91604-3140, USA

Pasternak, Reagan (Actor)
c/o Staff Member *Noble Caplan Abrams*
1260 Yonge St
2nd Floor
Toronto ON M4T 1W6, Canada

Pastor, Ed (Congressman, Politician)
2465 Rayburn HOB
Washington, DC 20515, USA

Pastore, Frank (Athlete, Baseball Player)
1542 Francis Way
Upland, CA 91786-2353, USA

Pastore, Vincent (Actor)
40 Fordham St
Bronx, NY 10464, USA

Pastorini, Darite A (Dan) Jr (Athlete, Football Player)
2703 Stuart Mnr
Houston, TX 77082, USA

Pastornicky, Cliff (Athlete, Baseball Player)
4815 50th Ave W
Bradenton, FL 34210-4907, USA

Pastrana, Arango Andres (President)
Palacio de Narino
Plaza de Bolivar
Carrera 8A
Bogota, DE, COLUMBIA

Pastrana, Travis (Athlete)

Pat, Dunsmore (Athlete, Football Player)
21301 Whispering Dr
Lenexa, KS 66220-3212, USA

Pataki, Governor George E (Ex-Governor, Politician)
Chadbourne & Parke, LLP
1017 Route 9D
Garrison, NY 10524-3636, USA

Pataky, Elsa (Actor)
c/o Carrie Gordon *42West (NY)*
220 W 42nd St
12th Floor
New York, NY 10036, USA

Patane, Giuseppe
Holbeinstr 6
Munich 81679, GERMANY

Pataric, Sebastian (Stylist)
c/o Staff Member *Zenobia Agency Inc*
PO Box 909
Groveland, CA 95321, USA

Patat, Frederic (Misc)
Faculte de Medecine
2 Bis Blvd Tonnelle
Tours Cedex 37032, FRANCE

Pate, Bob (Athlete, Baseball Player)
10447 Sagecrest Dr
Moreno Valley, CA 92557-3036, USA

Pate, Cynthia (Beauty Pageant Winner)
Future Productions
7907 Stafford Trail
Savage, MN 55378-4308, USA

Pate, Jerry (Golfer)
5 Hyde Park Rd
Pensacola, FL 32503-5830, USA

Pate, Rupert (Athlete, Football Player)
428 Shadowbrook Dr
Burlington, NC 27215, USA

Pate, Steve (Golfer)
1034 Brookview Ave
Westlake Village, CA 91361-1623, USA

Patek, Freddie (Athlete, Baseball Player)
5408 NE Wedgewood
Ln
Less Summit, MO 64064-1220, USA

Patekar, Nana (Actor, Bollywood)
304 Sheetal Apna Ghar Society
Samarth Nagar Andheri
Mumbai, MS 400053, INDIA

Patel, Anuradha (Actor, Bollywood)
1001D Abhishek Aptartments
Juhu Versova Road Andheri
Mumbai, MS 400058, INDIA

Patel, C Kumar N (Inventor)
1171 Roberto Lane
Los Angeles, CA 90077, USA

Patel, Dev (Actor)
c/o Sarah Spear *Curtis Brown Ltd*
Hay Market House
28-29 Hay Market
London SW1Y 4SP, UK

Patera, Dennis (Athlete, Football Player)
61535 S Highway 97
Apt 9512
Bend, OR 97702, USA

Patera, George (Athlete, Football Player)
7305 172nd St SW
Edmonds, WA 98026, USA

Patera, John A (Jack) (Athlete, Coach,
Football Coach, Football Player)
82 Osprey Dr
Cle Elum, WA 98922, USA

Patera, Ken (Athlete, Olympic Athlete,
Weightlifter)
6932 Stratford Draw
Saint Paul, MN 55125-2413, USA

Patera, Pavel (Athlete, Hockey Player)
Xcel Enegy Arena
175 Kellogg Blvd W
Saint Paul, MN 55102, USA

Paterra, Greg (Athlete, Football Player)
305 Douglas Ave
Elizabeth, PA 15037, USA

Paterra, Herb (Athlete, Football Player)
3696 Woodmonte Dr
Rochester, MI 48306, USA

Paterson, Bill (Actor)
Kerry Gardner
15 Kensington High St
London W8 5NP, UNITED KINGDOM
(UK)

Paterson, Joe (Athlete, Hockey Player)
49 Sullivan Pl
Lake George, NY 12845-4334

Paterson, Joe (Athlete, Hockey Player)
Adirondack Phantoms
1 Civic Center Plz
Glens Falls, NY 12801-4532

Paterson, Katherine (Writer)
70 Wildersburg Cmn
Barre, VT 05641-9761, USA

Paterson, Rick (Athlete, Hockey Player)
Anaheim Ducks 2695 E Katella Ave
Anaheim, CA 92806-5904

Patey, Doug (Athlete, Hockey Player)
4177 Garnetwood Chase
Mississauga, ON L4W 2H2, Canada

Patey, Larry (Athlete, Hockey Player)
2713 Autumn Run Ct
Chesterfield, MO 63005-7001

Pathon, Jerome (Athlete, Football Player)
4827 Eagles Watch Ln
Indianapolis, IN 46254, USA

Patillo, Maria
6300 Wilshire Blvd. #2110
Los Angeles, CA 90048

Patinkin, Mandy (Actor, Musician)
c/o Iris Grossman *ICM Partners (ICM-LA)*
10250 Constellation Blvd Fl 7
Los Angeles, CA 90067, USA

Patitz, Tatjana (Model)
c/o Gordon Rael *JV Entertainment*
5455 Wilshire Blvd #2114
Los Angeles, CA 90036, USA

Patkau, John (Architect)
Patkau Architects
560 Beaty St
#L110
Vancouver, BC V6B 2L3, CANADA

Paton, Nikki (Stylist)
c/o Staff Member *Independent NY*
15 E 30th St #401
New York, NY 10016, USA

Patrese, Ricardo (Race Car Driver)
Via Umberto 1
Padova 35100, ITALY

Patriarco, Earie (Opera Singer)
I C M Artists
40 W 57th St
New York, NY 10019, USA

Patric, Jason (Actor, Producer)
c/o Michael Nilon *Kritzer Levine Wilkins
Entertainment (KLWG)*
11872 La Grange Ave
1st Floor
Los Angeles, CA 90025, USA

Patrick, Bronswell (Athlete, Baseball
Player)
3202 Morton Ln
Greenville, NC 27834-4930, USA

Patrick, Craig (Athlete, Coach, Hockey
Player)
113 Royston Rd
Pittsburgh, PA 15238-2311, USA

Patrick, Danica (Race Car Driver)
Danica Racing
12985 N. 119th St.
Scottsdale, AZ 85259-2735, USA

Patrick, Deval (Governor)
State House, Office of the Governor
Room 280
Boston, MA 02133, USA

Patrick, Frank (Athlete, Football Player)
9800 W Old Cheney Rd
Denton, NE 68339, USA

Patrick, Glenn (Athlete, Hockey Player)
14 Gordon Ave
Dallas, PA 18612-1113

Patrick, Ian (Actor)
c/o Monique Moss *Integrated PR*
9025 Wilshire Blvd
Suite 400
Beverly Hills, CA 90211, USA

Patrick, James (Athlete, Hockey Player)
5024 Red Tail Run
Buffalo, NY 14221-4176

Patrick, James (Athlete, Hockey Player)
Buffalo Sabres
1 Seymour H Knox III Plz Ste 1
Buffalo, NY 14203-3096

Patrick, John (Writer)
PO Box 2386 Fortuna Mill Estate
Charlotte Amalie, VI 00801, USA

Patrick, Marcus (Actor)
c/o Staff Member *Gar Lester Agency*
11026 Ventura Blvd
Suite 10
Studio city, CA 91602, USA

Patrick, Mary Anthony
56 Copsterhill Rd.Oldham
Manchester, ENGLAND

Patrick, Nicholas J M (Astronaut)
10811 Oak Creek St
Houston, TX 77024-3016, USA

Patrick, Pat (Misc)
Patrick Racing
8431 Green Town Road
#400
Indianapolis, IN 46234, USA

Patrick, Richard (Musician)
c/o Jamie Talbot *Sanctuary Artist
Management*
8750 Wilshire Blvd Ste 200
Beverly Hills, CA 90211, USA

Patrick, Robert (Actor, Producer)
c/o Susan Patricola *Patricola Lust PR*
9171 Wilshire Blvd
Suite 441
Beverly Hills, CA 90210, USA

Patrick, Robert (Race Car Driver)
Patrick Racing
Box 3366
College Station
Fredericksburg, VA 22402, USA

Patrick, Ruth (Educator)
Academy of Natural Sciences
19th & Parkway
Philadelphia, PA 19103, USA

Patrick, Steve (Athlete, Hockey Player)
Patrick Realty Ltd
2003 Portage Ave
Winnipeg, MB R3J OK3, Canada

Patrick, Tera (Adult Film Star)
14813 Huston St
Van Nuys, CA 91403, USA

Patrick, Thomas M (Business Person)
Peoples Energy Corp
130 E Randolph Dr
Chicago, IL 60601, USA

Patrick, Tom
Heimeranstr. 51
Munich, GERMANY D-80339

Patridge, Audrina (Actor, Reality TV Star)
c/o David (Dave) Fleming *Mosaic Media
Group*
9200 W. Sunset Blvd
10th Floor
Los Angeles, CA 90069, USA

Patrone, Shana
209 10th Ave. S. #229
Nashville, TN 37230

Patten, Joel (Athlete, Football Player)
13415 Marble Rock Dr
Chantilly, VA 20151, USA

Patten of Barnes, Christopher F
(Government Official)
The House Of Lords
London SW1A OPW, UK

Patterson, Bob (Athlete, Baseball Player)
1093 7th Street Blvd SE
Hickory, NC 28602-4342, USA

Patterson, Carly (Athlete, Gymnast,
Olympic Athlete)
3401 Therodunn Dr
Plano, TX 75023-6007, USA

Patterson, Colin (Athlete, Hockey Player)
128-2100 13th St. S.
Cranbrook, BC V1C 7J5, Canada

Patterson, Corey (Athlete, Baseball Player)
1115 Gordon Combs Rd NW
Marietta, GA 30064-1225, USA

Patterson, Danny (Athlete, Baseball
Player)
13944 E Yucca St
Scottsdale, AZ 85259-4638, USA

Patterson, Daryl (Athlete, Baseball Player)
20145 Tollhouse Rd
Clovis, CA 93619-9760, USA

Patterson, Dave (Athlete, Baseball Player)
8425 Evanston Ave
Raytown, MO 64138-3346, USA

Patterson, Dennis (Athlete, Hockey
Player)
46808 Glengarry Blvd
Canton, MI 48188-3056

Patterson, Don (Athlete, Football Player)
1558 Halisport Lake Dr NW
Kennesaw, GA 30152, USA

Patterson, Elvis V (Athlete, Football
Player)
3939 Alberta St
Houston, TX 77021, USA

Patterson, Francine G (Penny) (Misc)
Gorilla Foudation
PO Box 620-640
Woodside, CA 94062, USA

Patterson, Gary (Cartoonist)
Patterson International
25208 Malibu Rd
Malibu, CA 90265-4635, USA

Patterson, Gil (Athlete, Baseball Player)
16124 Pebblebrook Dr
Tampa, FL 33624-1035, USA

Patterson, James (Business Person, Writer)
James Patterson Entertainment
10 Red Horse Hill Rd
Sharon, CT 06069, USA

Patterson, Jarrod (Athlete, Baseball
Player)
405 6th St N
Clanton, AL 35045-2823, USA

Patterson, Jeff (Athlete, Baseball Player)
27825 Tamara Dr
Yorba Linda, CA 92887-5843, USA

Patterson, John (Athlete, Baseball Player)
2659 E Jade Pl
Chandler, AZ 85286-2697, USA

Patterson, John (Athlete, Baseball Player)
2709 Country Club Dr
Orange, TX 77630, USA

Patterson, John M (Ex-Governor)
Court of Judiciary
P.O. Box 30155
Montgomery, AL 36103, USA

Patterson, Katerine (Writer)
70 Wildersburgh Common
Barre, VT 05641, USA

Patterson, Ken (Athlete, Baseball Player)
9100 Aspen Dr
Woodway, TX 76712-8771, USA

Patterson, Lorna (Actor)
23852 Pacific Coast Highway #355
Malibu, CA 90265, USA

Patterson, Marne (Actor)
c/o Matthew Lesher *Insight*
1134 S Cloverdale Ave
Los Angeles, CA 90019, USA

Patterson, Marnette (Actor)
c/o Matthew Lesher *Insight*
1134 S Cloverdale Ave
Los Angeles, CA 90019, USA

Patterson, Melody (Actor)
MILLER SPECIALTIES
141 Sunny Lane
Branson West, MO 65737, USA

Patterson, Michael (Financier)
JP Morgan Chase
270 Park Ave
New York, NY 10017, USA

Patterson, Mike (Athlete, Baseball Player)
19306 Chamblee Ave
Cerritos, CA 90703-6751, USA

Patterson, Neva
2498 Mandeville Canyon Rd.
Los Angeles, CA 90049

Patterson, Percival J (Prime Minister)
Prime Minister's Office
1 Devon Road
PO Box 272
Kingston 6, JAMAICA

Patterson, Reggie (Athlete, Baseball Player)
7748 S Crest Trl
Bessemer, AL 35022-4337, USA

Patterson, Richard North (Writer)
PO Box 183
West Tisbury, MA 02575, USA

Patterson, Robert M (General, War Hero)
907 Ironwood Dr
Henderson, KY 42420, USA

Patterson, Ross (Actor)
c/o Gina Hoffman *Baker Winokur Ryder Public Relations (BWR-LA)*
9100 Wilshire Blvd
Suite 500, West Tower
Beverly Hills, CA 90212, USA

Patterson, Scott (Athlete, Baseball Player)
148 Tall MaPle Ct
Freeburg, IL 62243-4078, USA

Patterson, Scott (Actor)
c/o Laina Cohn *Laina Cohn Management*
15066 Sutton St
Sherman Oaks, CA 91403, USA

Patterson, Shawn (Athlete, Football Player)
15711 E Avenida Del Ville Ct
Chandler, AZ 85249, USA

Patterson, Suzanne (Stylist)
13226 Grand Junction Dr
Fairfax, VA 22033-1328, USA

Patterson, Todd (Race Car Driver)
Todd Racing
PO Box 338
920 Industrial Rd.
Augusta, KS 67010, USA

Patterson, Willie (Baseball Player)
New York Cubans
409 Tuscaloosa Ave SW Apt 7
Birmingham, AL 35211-1457, USA

Patterson, Worthy (Athlete, Basketball Player)
2091 Kerwood Ave
Los Angeles, CA 90025-6006, USA

Pattillo, Charles (General)
11514 Little Bay Harbor Way
Spotsylvania, VA 22551-8901, USA

Pattillo, Cuthbert A (General)
4440 Grattan Price Dr Apt 1
Harrisonburg, VA 22801-2360, USA

Pattillo, Linda (Correspondent)
Cable News Network
News Dept
820 1st St NE
Washington, DC 20002, USA

Pattin, Marty (Athlete, Baseball Player)
3401 Sweetgrass Ct
Lawrence, KS 66049-4245, USA

Pattinson, Robert (Actor)
c/o Nick Frenkel *3 Arts Entertainment Inc*
9460 Wilshire Blvd
7th Floor
Beverly Hills, CA 90210, USA

Pattison, Mark (Athlete, Football Player)
3828 48th Ave NE
Seattle, WA 98105, USA

Patton, Donovan (Actor)
c/o Staff Member *Glasser/Black Management*
283 Cedarhurst Ave
Cedarhurst, NY 11516, USA

Patton, Eric (Athlete, Football Player)
23732 San Esteban Dr
Mission Viejo, CA 92691-3346, USA

Patton, Marvcus (Athlete, Football Player)
12994 Wyckland Dr
Clifton, VA 20124, USA

Patton, Mel (Athlete, Olympic Athlete, Track Athlete)
2312 Via Del Aguagate
Fallbrook, CA 92028, USA

Patton, Melvin (Mel) (Athlete, Track Athlete)
2312 Via Del Aguagate
Fallbrook, CA 92028, USA

Patton, Paula (Actor, Director)
c/o Melissa Stone *42West (LA)*
11400 W Olympic Blvd
Suite 1100
Los Angeles, CA 90064, USA

Patton, Tom (Athlete, Baseball Player)
577 Daisy Dr
New Holland, PA 17557-8708, USA

Patton, Troy (Athlete, Baseball Player)
c/o Staff Member *Baltimore Orioles*
333 W Camden St
Baltimore, MD 21201, USA

Patton, Virginia (Actor)
2205 Melrose Ave
Ann Arbor, MI 48104, USA

Patton, Will (Actor)
c/o Kate Edwards *Grand View Management*
578 Washington Blvd #688
Marina del Rey, CA 90292, USA

Patty, Edward
14 Ave. de Jurigoz
Lausanne, SWITZERLAND 1006

Patty, J Edward (Budge) (Tennis Player)
La Mame
14 Ave de Jurigoz
Lausanne 1006, SWITZERLAND

Patty, Sandi (Musician)
5701 NW 163rd Terr
Edmond, OK 73013, USA

Patu, Saul (Athlete, Football Player)
10234 Renton Ave S
Seattle, WA 98178, USA

Patulski, Walter G (Walt) (Athlete, Football Player)
420 Kimber Rd
Syracuse, NY 13224, USA

Patzaichin, Ivan (Athlete)
SC Sportiv Unirea Tricolor
Soseaua Stefan Cel Mare 9
Bucharest, ROMANIA

Patzak, PeterJosef
Schottlgasse 23
Klosterneuburg, AUSTRIA A-3400

Patzakis, Michele (Opera Singer)
Kunstleragentur Raab & Bohrn
Plandengasse 7
Vienna 1010, AUSTRIA

Pauk, Gyorgy (Musician)
27 Armitage Road
London NW11, UNITED KINGDOM (UK)

Paukner, Catherine (Stylist)
328 Mountain Rd
Wilton, CT 06897, USA

Paul, Aaron (Actor)
c/o Loch Powell *Leverage Management*
3030 Pennsylvania Ave
Santa Monica, CA 90404, USA

Paul, Adrian (Actor, Director, Producer)
c/o David (Dave) Fleming *Mosaic Media Group*
9200 W. Sunset Blvd
10th Floor
Los Angeles, CA 90069, USA

Paul, Alan (Music Group, Musician)
Columbia/CBS Records
1801 Century Park West
Los Angeles, CA 90067, USA

Paul, Alexandra (Actor)
c/o Chuck Binder *Binder & Associates*
1465 Lindacrest Dr
Beverly Hills, CA 90210, USA

Paul, Billy (Musician)
8215 Winthrop St
Philadelphia, PA 19136, USA

Paul, Chris (Athlete, Basketball Player)
c/o Chris Chambers *The Chamber Group*
416 West 13th St
Suite 105
New York, NY 10014, USA

Paul, Christi (Correspondent)
Cable News Network
News Dept
1050 Techwood Dr NW
Atlanta, GA 30318, USA

Paul, Don Michael (Actor, Director)

Paul, Emily (Actor)
c/o Simon Millar *Rumble Media*
1620 Broadway
Santa Monica, CA 90403, USA

Paul, Henry (Music Group, Musician)
Vector Mgmt
1607 17th Ave S
Nashville, TN 37212, USA

Paul, Jarrad (Actor)
c/o JC Spink *Benderspink*
5870 W Jefferson Blvd
Studio E
Los Angeles, CA 90016, USA

Paul, John Michael (Actor)

Paul, Josh (Athlete, Baseball Player)
28751 Win dover St
Wesley Chapel, FL 33545-4378, USA

Paul, Markus (Athlete, Football Player)
P.O. Box 423041
Kissimmee, FL 34742, USA

Paul, Mike (Athlete, Baseball Player)
5121 N Circulo Sobrio
Tucson, AZ 85718-6037, USA

Paul, Robert (Figure Skater)
10675 Rochester Ave
Los Angeles, CA 90024, USA

Paul, Ron (Congressman, Politician)
979-285-0231
122 West Way
Suite 301
Jackson, TX 77566, USA

Paul, Vinnie (Musician)
Concrete Mgmt
361 W Broadway #200
New York, NY 10013, USA

Paul, Whitney (Athlete, Football Player)
6802 Thornwild Rd
Missouri City, TX 77489-2649, USA

Paul, Wolfgang (Soccer Player)
Postfach 1324
Olsberg-Bigge 59939, GERMANY

Paul, Xavier (Athlete, Baseball Player)
2637 5th St
Slidell, LA 70458-4105, USA

Paula, Alejandro F (Jandi) (Prime Minister)
Primier's Office
Fort Amsterdam 17
Willemstad, NETHERLANDS ANTILLES

Paul & Paula
7251 Lowell Dr. #200
Overland Park, KS 66204

Paulauskas, Arturas (President)
President's Office
Gediminas 53
Vilnius 232026, LITHUANIA

Pauley, David (Athlete, Baseball Player)
19839 N 45th Ave
Glendale, AZ 85308-7389, USA

Pauley, Jane (Journalist)
14 Governors Island
Branford, CT 06405, USA

Paulino, Felipe (Athlete, Baseball Player)
12312 Evening Bav Dr
Pearland, TX 77584-8827, USA

Paulino, Ronny (Athlete, Baseball Player)
129 Cardinal Cir
Pittsburgh, PA 15237-1067, USA

Paul Jr, John (Race Car Driver)
44 Musdogee Rd.
Atlanta, GA 30305, USA

Paulk, Charlie (Athlete, Basketball Player)
5750 Friars Rd Apt 102
San Diego, CA 92110-1833, USA

Paulk, Jeff (Athlete, Football Player)
7751 S Bonarden Ln
Tempe, AZ 85284, USA

Paulo (DJ)
c/o Staff Member *Diva Central Inc*
7510 W Sunset Blvd Ste 1445
Los Angees, CA 90046, USA

Pauls, Raymond (Composer, Music
Group, Musician)
Veidenbaum Str 41/43 #26
Riga 226001, LATVIA

Paulsen, Erik (Congressman, Politician)
127 Cannon HOB
Washington, DC 20515, USA

Paulsen, Robert (Rob) (Artist, Voice Over
Artist)
c/o Staff Member *Sutton Barth & Vennari
Inc*
145 S Fairfax
Suite 310
Los Angeles, CA 90036, USA

Paulson, Brandon (Athlete, Olympic
Athlete, Wrestler)
4165 120th Ave NW
Minneapolis, MN 55433-1611, USA

Paulson, Carl (Golfer)
8211 Tibet Butler Dr
Windermere, FL 34786-5614, USA

Paulson, Dainard (Athlete, Football
Player)
700 W Goodlander Rd
Selah, WA 98942, USA

Paulson, Dennis (Golfer)
1721 Aryana Dr
Encinitas, CA 92024-1282, USA

Paulson, Richard L (Business Person)
Potlatch Corp
601 W Riverside Ave
Spokane, WA 99201, USA

Paulson, Sarah (Actor)
c/o Judy Hofflund *Hofflund/Polone*
9465 Wilshire Blvd #420
Beverly Hills, CA 90212, USA

Paultz, Billy (Athlete, Basketball Player)
1941 Waters Edge Ln
Seabrook, TX 77586-2598, USA

Paulusma, Polly (Musician)
c/o Staff Member *Paradigm (Monterey)*
404 W Franklin St
Monterey, CA 93940, USA

Paup, Bryce E (Athlete, Football Player)
4300 Oak Ridge Cir
De Pere, WI 54115-8327, USA

Pausini, Laura (Musician)
c/o Staff Member *Creative Artists Agency
(CAA-LA)*
2000 Ave Of The Stars
Los Angeles, CA 90067, USA

Pavan, Marisa (Actor)
4 Allee des Brouillards
Paris 75018, FRANCE

Pavano, Carl (Athlete, Baseball Player)
110 Playa Rienta Way
Apt 23C
Palm Beach Gardens, FL 33418, USA

Pavelich, Mark (Athlete, Hockey Player,
Olympic Athlete)
19 E Norwood Shores
Lutsen, MN 55612, USA

Pavelich, Marty (Athlete, Hockey Player)
PO Box 160448
Big Sky, MT 59716-0448

Pavelich, Matt (Athlete, Hockey Player)
3485 Everts Ave
Windsor, ON N9E 2V9, UCanada

Pavelka, Jake (Reality TV Star)
c/o Janice Lee *Entertainment Fusion
Group*
7080 Hollywood Blvd
Suite 903
Los Angeles, CA 90028, USA

Pavelski, Joe (Athlete, Hockey Player)
1486 Hicks Ave
San Jose, CA 95125-3821

Paven, Corey
2515 McKinney #930 Box 10
Dallas, TX 75201

Paver, Michelle (Writer)
ILRM LLC
186 Bickenhall Mansions
London W1U 6BX, UNITED KINGDOM

Pavese, Jim (Athlete, Hockey Player)
65 Whittier Dr
Kings Park, NY 11754-2339

Pavia, Joe (Horse Racer)
1600 SW 3rd St
Pompano Beach, FL 33069-3102, USA

Pavia, Ria
3500 W. Olive Ave. #1400
Burbank, CA 91505

Pavin, Corey (Golfer)
4332 Gilbert Ave
Dallas, TX 75219-2908, USA

Pavlas, David (Dave) (Athlete, Baseball
Player)
P.O. Box 1224
Shiner, TX 77984-1224, USA

Pavletic, Viaiko (President)
Presidential Palace
Pantovcak 241
Zagreb 10000, CROATIA

Pavletich, Don (Athlete, Baseball Player)
13645 Adelaide Ln
Brookfield, WI 53005-4965, USA

Pavlick, Greg (Athlete, Baseball Player)
936 Pinellas Bavwav
S Unit TH8
Saint Petersburg, FL 33715-2158, USA

Pavlik, Kelly (Boxer)
Top Rank Inc
3908 Howard Hughes Pkwy #580
Las Vegas, NV 89109, USA

Pavlik, Roger (Athlete, Baseball Player)
622 Beaver Bend Rd
Houston, TX 77037-2004, USA

Pavlovic, Aleksandar (Basketball Player)
Utah Jazz
Delta Center
301 W South Temple
Salt Lake City, UT 84101, USA

Pavlow, Muriel
2 Conduit St.
London, ENGLAND W1R 9TG

Pawelczyk, James A Dr (Astronaut)
2047 Pine Cliff Rd
State College, PA 16801-2405, USA

Pawelczyk, James A (Jim) (Astronaut)
NASA
Johnson Space Center
2101 NASA Road
Houston, TX 77058, USA

Pawlenty, Tim (Politician)
4117 Countrvview Dr
Saint Paul, MN 55123-3948, USA

Pawloski, Stan (Athlete, Baseball Player)
413 Maryjoe Way
Warrington, PA 18976-1695, USA

Pawlowski, John (Athlete, Baseball Player)
257 Mill Branch Way
North Augusta, SC 29860-8622, USA

Pawuk, Mark (Race Car Driver)
PO Box 535
Richfield, OH 44286, USA

Paxman, Jeremy
56 Wood Lane
London, ENGLAND W12 7RJ

Paxon, L William (Bill) (Misc)
Akin Gump Strauss Hauer Feld
1333 New Hampshire NW
Washington, DC 20036, USA

Paxson, Jim (Athlete, Basketball Player)
8500 N Senero Tres M
Paradise Valley, AZ 45409-1130, USA

Paxson, Jim (Athlete, Basketball Player)
3225 Southdale Dr
Apt 1
Dayton, OH 45409-1130, USA

Paxson, John (Athlete, Basketball Player,
Misc)
125 Boardman Ct
Lake Bluff, IL 60044, USA

Paxson, Melanie (Actor)
c/o Staff Member *Brady Brannon & Rich*
5670 Wilshire Blvd
Suite 820
Los Angeles, CA 90036, USA

Paxton, Bill (Actor)
c/o Jillian Fowkes *ID Public Relations
(ID-LA)*
7060 Hollywood Blvd
8th Floor
Los Angeles, CA 90028, USA

Paxton, John (Editor)
Saint Martin's Press
175 5th Ave
New York, NY 10010, USA

Paxton, Mike (Athlete, Baseball Player)
1145 S Indian Wells Dr
Collierville, TN 38017-3667, USA

Paxton, Sara (Actor)
c/o TJ Stein *Stein Entertainment Group*
1351 N Crescent Heights Blvd #312
West Hollywood, CA 90046, USA

Paxton, Tom (Music Group, Musician,
Songwriter, Writer)
Fleming Tamulevich Assoc
733 N Main St
Ann Arbor, MI 48104, USA

Payer, Serge
2343 Lorraine St RR 1
Rockland, ON K4K 1K7, Canada

Payette, Jean (Athlete, Hockey Player)
512 Bathurst Ave
Ottawa, ON K1G OX5, Canada

Payette, Julie (Astronaut)
Space Agency
12175 Shenandoah Rd
Middletown, CA 95461-7707, USA

Paymer, David (Actor)
327 19th St
Santa Monica, CA 90402, USA

Payne, Alexander (Actor, Director,
Producer)
c/o Craig Gering *Creative Artists Agency
(CAA-LA)*
2000 Ave Of The Stars
Los Angeles, CA 90067, USA

Payne, Allen (Actor)
c/o Tom Harrison *Diverse Talent Group*
9911 W Pico Blvd Ste 340W
Los Angeles, CA 90035, USA

Payne, Anthony E (Composer)
2 Wilton Square
London N1 3DL, UNITED KINGDOM
(UK)

Payne, Barbara (Athlete, Baseball Player)
15897 W Desert Meadow Dr
Surprise, AZ 85374-5636, USA

Payne, Bruce (Actor)
c/o Gordon Gilbertson *Gilbertson
Management*
1334 3rd St Promenade #201
Santa Monica, CA 90401, USA

Payne, David N (Engineer)
Southampton University
Highfield
Southampton SO17 1BJ, UNITED
KINGDOM (UK)

Payne, Davis (Athlete, Hockey Player)
16406 Wilson Creek Ct
Chesterfield, MO 63005-4566

Payne, Dougie (Musician)
Wildlife Entertainment
21 Heathmans Road
London SW6 4TJ, UNITED KINGDOM
(UK)

Payne, Freda (Music Group, Musician)
c/o Staff Member *Diva Central Inc*
7510 W Sunset Blvd Ste 1445
Los Angees, CA 90046, USA

Payne, Frederick (General)
19 Seville Dr
Rancho Mirage, CA 92270-3850, USA

Payne, Greg (Model)
c/o Staff Member *Why Not Model Agency*
via Zenale 9
Milano 20123, Italy

Payne, Harry C (Educator)
Williams College
President's Office
Williamstown, MA 01267, USA

Payne, Henry (Cartoonist, Editor)
Detroit News
Editorial Dept
615 W Lafayette
Detroit, MI 48226, USA

Payne, Julie (Actor)
c/o Staff Member *Pakula/King &
Associates*
9229 Sunset Blvd
Suite 315
Los Angeles, CA 90069, USA

Payne, Keith (General, War Hero)
2 Saint Bee's Ave
Bucasia, QLD 4740, AUSTRALIA

Payne, Kenny (Athlete, Basketball Player)
1968 General Warfield Way
Lexington, KY 40505^4836, USA

Payne, Kherington (Actor)
c/o Staff Member *Luber Roklin Management*
8530 Wilshire Blvd
6th Floor
Beverly Hills, CA 90211, USA

Payne, Ladell (Educator)
Randolph-Macon College
President's Office
Ashland, VA 23005, USA

Payne, Rod (Athlete, Football Player)
9622 Stonemasters Dr
Loveland, OH 45140, USA

Payne, Roger S (Biologist, Misc)
191 Western Road
Lincoln, MA 01773, USA

Payne, Scherrie-
433 N. Camden Dr. #400
Beverly Hills, CA 90210

Payne, Seth (Athlete, Football Player)
5004 Chestnut St
Bellaire, TX 77401, USA

Payne, Steve (Athlete, Hockey Player)
N6497 County Rd N
Beldenville, WI 54003-4903

Payne, Tom (Actor)
c/o Beth Holden-Garland *Untitled Entertainment (LA)*
350 S. Beverly Dr #200
Beverly Hills, CA 90212, USA

Payne, Waylon (Actor, Musician)
c/o Ben Feigin *Anonymous Content (LA)*
3531 Hayden Ave
Culver City, CA 90232, USA

Paynter, Kent (Athlete, Hockey Player)
RR 1
Richmond, PE COB 1 YO, Canada

Paynter, Kristen (Stylist)
c/o Staff Member *Montana Artists Agency*
9150 Wilshire Blvd Ste 100
Beverly Hills, CA 90212, USA

Pays, Amanda (Actor)
11955 Addison St
Valley Village, CA 91607, USA

Payton, Benjamin F (Educator)
Tuskegee Institute
President's Office
Tuskegee, AL 36088, USA

Payton, Christian (Actor)
c/o Staff Member *WmE2 (WMA-LA)*
1 William Morris Pl
Beverly Hills, CA 90212, USA

Payton, Eddie (Athlete, Football Player)
118 Woodland Hills Blvd
Madison, MS 39110, USA

Payton, Gary (Athlete, Basketball Player, Olympic Athlete)
1114 Post Ave
Seattle, WA 98101-2915, USA

Payton, Gary E (Astronaut)
10140 Community Lane
Fairfax Station, VA 22039, USA

Payton, Gary E Colonel (Astronaut)
2367 Diamond Creek Dr
Colorado Springs, CO 80921-2916, USA

Payton, James (Actor)
c/o Staff Member *Debbie Edler Management Ltd.*
Little Friars Cottage
Lombard St
Eynsham, Oxon OX29 4HT, UK

Payton, Jay (Athlete, Baseball Player)
2002 Wild Waters Dr
Raleigh, NC 27614-7636, USA

Payton, JoMarie (Actor)
c/o Gar Lester *Gar Lester Agency*
11026 Ventura Blvd
Suite 10
Studio city, CA 91602, USA

payton, khary (Actor)
c/o Theodore B Gekis *Gekis Management*
4217 Verdugo View Dr
Los Angeles, CA 90065-4317, USA

Payton, Nicholas (Musician)
Management Ark
116 Village Blvd #200
Princeton, NJ 08540, USA

Payton, Sean (Football Player)
Chicago Bears
Dallas Cowboys 1 Cowboys Pkwy Attn: Coaching Staff
Irving, TX 75063-4945, USA

Pazienda, Vinnie
64 Waterman Ave.
Cranston, RI 02910

Pazienza, Vinny (Boxer)
c/o Darren Prince *Prince Marketing Group*
18 Carillon Cir
Livingston, NJ 07039, USA

Pazik, Mike (Athlete, Baseball Player)
8413 Comanche Ct
Bethesda, MD 20817-4533, USA

Pazos, Anthony (Stylist)
648 North Doheny Dr
West Hollywood, CA 90069, USA

P. Bilbray, Brian (Congressman, Politician)
2410 Rayburn HOB
Washington, DC 20515, USA

PC Quest
PO Box 720423
Norman, OK 73070-4310

P. Duffy, Sean (Congressman, Politician)
1208 Longworth HOB
Washington, DC 20515, USA

Peace, Terry (Actor)
PO Box 74
Allison Park, PA 15101, USA

Peace, Warren (Baseball Player)
Newark Eagles
27921 NC Highway 903
Robersonville, NC 27871-8904, USA

Peaches and Herb (Music Group)
c/o Staff Member *Universal Attractions*
135 W 26th St
12 Floor
New York, NY 10001, USA

Peacock, Andrew S (Government Official)
30 Monomeath Ave
Canterbury, VIC 3126, AUSTRALIA

Peacocke, Arthur R (Misc)
Society of Ordained Scientists
St Mark's Rectory
11 Summer
Augusta, ME 04330, USA

Peacosh, Gene (Athlete, Hockey Player)
915 9th St S
Cranbrook, BC VlC 1R8, Canada

Peake, Don (Musician)
c/o Mike Rosen *Working Artists Agency*
13525 Ventura Blvd
Sherman Oaks, CA

Peake, James B (General)
Sergeon General US Army
5109 Leesburg Pike
Falls Church, VA 22041, USA

Peake, Pat (Athlete, Hockey Player)
327 Hecht Dr
Madison Heights, MI 48071-2890

Peaker, E J (Actor)
4935 Densmore Ave
Encino, CA 91436, USA

Peaks, Pandora (Adult Film Star)
Photo Clubs
6011-201 Winterpointe Dr
Raleigh, NC 27606, USA

Pear, Dave (Athlete, Football Player)
3126 199th Ave SE
Sammamish, WA 98075, USA

Pearce, Colby (Athlete, Cycler, Olympic Athlete)
755 Hawthorn Ave
Boulder, CO 80304-2139, USA

Pearce, Frank (Business Person)
Blizzard Entertainment
P.O. Box 18979
Irvine, CA 92623, USA

Pearce, Guy (Actor)
c/o Ann Churchill-Brown *Shanahan Management*
Level 3 Berman House
Surry Hills 2010, AUSTRALIA

Pearce, Jacqueline (Actor)
Rhubarb Personal Mgmt
6 Langley St #41
London WC2H 9JA, UNITED KINGDOM (UK)

Pearce, Josh (Athlete, Baseball Player)
2607 Draper Rd
Yakima, WA 98903-9216, USA

Pearce, Richard I (Director)
240 Bentley Cir
Los Angeles, CA 90049, USA

Pearce, Stevan (Congressman, Politician)
2432 Rayburn HOB
Washington, DC 20515, USA

Pearce, Steve (Athlete, Baseball Player)
7109 Twelve Oaks Dr
Lakeland, FL 33813, USA

Pearcy, James W (Athlete, Football Player)
P.O. Box 609
Cobbs Creek, VA 23035, USA

Pearl, Barry (Actor)
c/o Staff Member *Coolwaters Productions*
10061 Riverside Dr.
Box 531
Toluca Lake, CA 91602, USA

Pearl Jam (Music Group)
c/o Kelly Curtis *Curtis Management*
1900 S. Corgiat Dr.
Seattle, WA 98108, USA

Pearlman, Rhea (Actor)
c/o Stan Rosenfield *Stan Rosenfield & Associates*
2029 Century Park E
Suite 1190
Los Angeles, CA 90067, USA

Pearlman, Steve
c/o Sean Freidin *ICM Partners (ICM-LA)*
10250 Constellation Blvd Fl 7
Los Angeles, CA 90067, USA

Pearlman, Zack (Actor)
c/o Paul Young *Principato/Young Management*
9465 Wilshire Blvd
Suite 430
Beverly Hills, CA 90212, USA

Pearlstein, Philip (Artist)
361 W 36th St
New York, NY 10018, USA

Pearlstine, Norman (Writer)
c/o Lynn Nesbit *Janklow & Nesbit Associates*
445 Park Ave
New York, NY 10022, USA

Pears, David F (Misc)
7 Sandford Road
Littlemore
Oxford OX4 4PU, UNITED KINGDOM (UK)

Pearson, Albie (Athlete, Baseball Player)
55473 Oakhill
La Quinta, CA 92253-4730, USA

Pearson, Barry (Athlete, Football Player)
85 Westledge Rd
West Simsbury, CT 06092, USA

Pearson, Corey (Actor)
c/o Colton Gramm *Brillstein Entertainment Partners*
9150 Wilshire Blvd #350
Beverly Hills, CA 90212, USA

Pearson, David (Race Car Driver)
290 Burnett Rd.
Spartanburg, SC 29303-5934, USA

Pearson, Drew (Athlete, Football Player)
3721 Mt Vernon Way
Plano, TX 75025, USA

Pearson, Durk
PO Box 1067
Hollywood, FL 33022

Pearson, Jason (Athlete, Baseball Player)
2373 Sunset Dr
Freeport, IL 61032-8348, USA

Pearson, Jayice (Athlete, Football Player)
721 SW Winterhill Ln
Less Summit, MO 64081-2676, USA

Pearson, Larry (Race Car Driver)
Buckshot Racing
182 Belue Rd.
Spartanburg, SC 29303, USA

Pearson, Lindell (Athlete, Football Player)
5512 NW 114th St
Oklahoma City, OK 73162, USA

Pearson, Malina (Stylist)
c/o Staff Member *Faucher Artists*
636 Broadway #1218
New York, NY 10012, USA

Pearson, Mel (Athlete, Hockey Player)

Pearson, Preston (Athlete, Football Player)
9104 Moss Farm Ln
Dallas, TX 75243, USA

Pearson, Rob (Athlete, Hockey Player)
15 Belleview Crt
Courtice, ON LIE 1J1, Canada

Pearson, Scott (Athlete, Hockey Player)
114 Lauren Ln
Brunswick, GA 31525-9579

Pearson, Terry (Athlete, Baseball Player)
3010 Wisteria Ln
Northport, AL 35473-8165, USA

Pearson-Tesseine, Dolly (Baseball Player)
1510A Canterbury Trl
Mount Pleasant, MI 48858-4002, USA

Peart, Neil (Musician)
c/o Staff Member *SRO Management*
189 Carlton St
Toronto, ON M5A 2K7, Canada

Pease, Patsy (Actor)
15432 Hartland St
Van Nuys, CA 91406

Peasgood, Julie (Actor)
c/o Staff Member *NCI Management Ltd*
51 Queen Ann Street
Floor 2
London W1G 9HS, UNITED KINGDOM
(UK)

Peatros, Maurice (Athlete, Baseball
Player)
Homestead Grays
8633 Copper Mine Ave
Las Vegas, NV 89129-7630, USA

Peavy, Jake (Athlete, Baseball Player)
c/o Staff Member *Chicago White Sox*
U.S. Cellular Field
333 Wes 35th St
Chicago, IL 60616, USA

Peay, Francis (Athlete, Football Player)
7351 Overbrook Dr
St Louis, MO 63121-2533, USA

Peca, Michael (Athlete, Hockey Player)
46 Golden Pheasant Dr
Getzville, NY 14068-1461

Peca, Michael (Athlete, Hockey Player)
Buffalo Junior Sabres
1615 Amherst Manor Dr
Williamsville, NY 14221-2040

Peck, Austin (Actor)
The Michael Bruno Group Los Angeles
13576 Cheltenham Dr
Sherman Oaks, CA 91423, USA

Peck, Ethan (Actor)
c/o Stephanie Ritz *WME (LA)*
9601 Wilshire Blvd Fl 3
Beverly Hills, CA 90210, USA

Peck, J Eddie (Actor)
28354 Linda Vista St
Canyon Country, CA 91387, USA

Peck, Josh (Actor)
c/o Sam Maydew *Collective*
8383 Wilshire Blvd
Suite 1050
Beverly Hills, CA 90211, USA

Peck, Richard (Writer)
c/o Staff Member *Scholastic Entertainment*
557 Broadway
New York, NY 10012, USA

Peck, Tom (Race Car Driver)
Peckie's Auto Body Repair
417 E North St
McConnellsburg, PA 17233, USA

Pecota, Bill (Athlete, Baseball Player)
332 NE Warrington Ct
Lees Summit, MO 64064-1605, USA

Pedersen, Allen (Athlete, Hockey Player)
2261 Fieldcrest Dr.
Colorado Springs, CO 80921-4000, USA

Pedersen, Tilly Scott (Actor)
c/o George Englund *George Englund Jr
Management*
11661 San Vicente Blvd
#609
Los Angeles, CA 90049, USA

Pederson, Barry (Athlete, Hockey Player)
16 Cutting Rd
Swampscott, MA 01907-1602, USA

Pederson, Barry (Athlete, Hockey Player)
Boston Bruins
100 Legends Way Ste 250
Boston, MA 02114-1389

Pederson, Denis (Athlete, Hockey Player)
PO Box 31721
Pitt Meadows, BC V3Y 2H1, Canada

Pederson, Mark (Athlete, Hockey Player)
151 Equestrian Ln
Kalispell, MT 59901-8050

Pederson, Stu (Athlete, Baseball Player)
45 Alannah Ct
Palo Alto, CA 94303-3009, USA

Pederson, Tom (Athlete, Hockey Player)
Ice Oasis Ice Skating Rink 3140 Bay Rd
Redwood City, CA 94063-3907

Pedre, Jorge (Athlete, Baseball Player)
7894 Bellflower Dr
Buena Park, CA 90620-2208, USA

Pedregon, Frank (Race Car Driver)
6174 Cabernet Place
Alta Loma, CA 91766, USA

Pedriaue, Al (Athlete, Baseball Player)
10382 E Oakbrook St
Tucson, AZ 85747-5967, USA

Pedrigue, Al (Athlete, Baseball Player)
10382 E Oakbrook St
Tucson, AZ 85747, USA

Pedrique, Al (Athlete, Baseball Player,
Coach)
10382 E Oakbrook St
Tucson, AZ 85747, USA

Pedroia, Dustin (Athlete, Baseball Player)
c/o Seth Levinson *A.C.E.S*
188 Montague St
#6
Brooklyn 11201, USA

Peebles, Danny (Athlete, Football Player)
12205 Fieldmist Dr
Raleigh, NC 27614, USA

Peebles, P J (Scientist)
24 Markham Rd
Princeton, NJ 08540-5348, USA

Peek, Richard (Athlete, Basketball Player)
15631 State Highway 31 W
Tyler, TX 75709-3335, USA

Peeler, Anthony (Athlete, Basketball
Player)
4502 E 48th St
Kansas City, MO 64130-2?31, USA

Peeples, George (Athlete, Basketball
Player)
1032 Loma Lisa Ln
Arcadia, CA 91006-2218, USA

Peeples, Nathaniel (Athlete, Baseball
Player)
Kansas City Monarchs
536 Lipford St
Memphis, TN 38112-2934, USA

Peeples, Nia (Actor)
c/o Staff Member *Stone Manners Salners
Agency (LA)*
9911 W Pico Blvd Ste 1400
Los Angeles, CA 90035, USA

Peet, Amanda (Actor)
c/o Eric Kranzler *Management 360*
9111 Wilshire Blvd
Beverly Hills, CA 90210, USA

Peet, Lizzie (Actor)
952 Maltman Avenue
Suite 108
Los Angeles, CA 90026, USA

Peete, Calvin (Golfer)
128 Garden Gate Dr
Ponte Vedra Beach, FL 32082-3668, USA

Peete, Rodney (Athlete, Football Player,
Television Host)
4848 Encino Ave
Encino, CA 91316, USA

Peeters, Pete (Athlete, Hockey Player)
Anaheim Ducks 2695 E Katella Ave
Anaheim, CA 92806-5904

Peeters, Pete (Athlete)
farm
Namao, AB TOA 2NO, Canada

Peets, Brian (Athlete, Football Player)
5361 Auburn Blvd
Sacramento, CA 95841, USA

Pegg, Simon (Actor)
c/o Dawn Sedgwick *Dawn Sedgwick
Management*
3 Goodwins Ct
Covent Garden
London WC2N 4LL, United Kingdom

Pegler, Luke (Actor)
c/o Will Ward *ROAR (LA)*
9701 Wilshire Blvd
8th Floor
Los Angeles, CA 90212, USA

Pegram, Erric (Athlete, Football Player)
5913 Sterling Trl
McKinney, TX 75071-8028, USA

Peguero, Julio (Athlete, Baseball Player)
1500 State Road 1
Socorro, NM 87801-5093, USA

Pegues, Steve (Athlete, Baseball Player)
362 Presidents Dr
Pontotoc, MS 38863-2322, USA

Peguese, Willis (Athlete, Football Player)
Hialeah-Miami Lakes High School
7977 W 12th Ave
Hialeah, FL 33014, USA

Pei, I M (Architect)
Pei Cobb Freed & Partners
11 Sutton Pl
New York, NY 10022-2406, USA

Peil, Mary Beth (Actor)
c/o Lindsay Porter *Gersh (NY)*
41 Madison Ave
New York, NY 10010, USA

Peirce, Kimberly (Director, Producer,
Writer)
c/o Staff Member *Creative Artists Agency
(CAA-LA)*
2000 Ave Of The Stars
Los Angeles, CA 90067, USA

Peirse, Sarah (Actor)
c/o Dallas Smith *United Agents*
12-26 Lexington St
London W1F OLE, UK

Peirsol, Aaron (Athlete, Olympic Athlete,
Swimmer)
4110 Shoal Creek Blvd
Austin, TX 78756-3517, USA

Peirson, John (Athlete, Hockey Player)
3 Steepletree Ln
Wayland, MA 01778-3912

Peizerat, Gwendal (Figure Skater)
c/o Staff Member *Champions on Ice*
Tom Collins Enterprises Inc
3500 W 80th St
Minneapolis, MN 55431, USA

Pelaez, Alex (Athlete, Baseball Player)
1501 Oleander Ave
Chula Vista, CA 91911-5623, USA

Peldon, Ashley (Actor)
c/o Pamela Wagner *Metropolitan (MTA)*
4526 Wilshire Blvd
Los Angeles, CA 90010, USA

Peldon, Courtney (Actor)
c/o Steve Rodriguez *McGowan
Management*
8733 W Sunset Blvd
Suite 103
West Hollywood, CA 90069, USA

Pele (Athlete, Soccer Player)
Rua Riachuelo 121-3
Andar-Fones 34-1633/35
Santos SP, Brazil

Pelfrey, Mike (Athlete, Baseball Player)
13406 E Windham St
Wichita, KS 67230-7915, USA

Pelfrey, Raymond (Athlete, Football
Player)
1301 Summit St
Portsmouth, OH 45662, USA

Peli, Oren (Director)
c/o Staff Member *Creative Artists Agency
(CAA-LA)*
2000 Ave Of The Stars
Los Angeles, CA 90067, USA

Pelikan, Lisa (Actor)
c/o Peter Giagni *Premier Talent Group*
4370 Tujunga Avenue
Suite 110
Studio City, CA 91604, USA

Pell, Claybourne (Ex-Senator, Senator)
45 Ledge Road
Newport, RI 02840-4257, USA

Pellegrini, Margaret (Actor)
5018 N. 61st Ave.
Glendale, AZ 85301, USA

Pellegrini, Robert
1731 Route 9
Unit 97
Ocean View, NJ 08230-1388

Pellegrino, Mark (Actor)
c/o Mary Ellen Mulcahy *Framework Entertainment (LA)*
9057 Nemo St
Suite C
West Hollywood, CA 90069, USA

Pellerin, Scott (Athlete, Hockey Player)
10 Dunraven Rd.
Windham, NH 03087-1263

Pelletier, Bronson (Actor)
c/o Staff Member *Carrier Talent Management*
#705-1080 Howe St.
Vancouver BC V6Z 2T1, CANADA

Pelletier, Bruno (Musician)
c/o Staff Member *Agence Ginette Achim, Inc.*
1053 rue Laurier Ouest
Outremont, QC H2V 2L2, Canada

Pelletier, Jean-Marc (Athlete, Hockey Player)
83 Canterbury Cir
East Longmeadow, MA 01028-5705

Pelletier, Lysa (Stylist)
c/o Staff Member *Team*
423 W Broadway
4th Floor
Boston, MA 02127, USA

Pelletier, Marcel (Athlete, Hockey Player)
2129 Old Marlton Pike
Cherry Hill, NJ 08003-1302

Pelley, Scott (Correspondent)
c/o Staff Member *ABC News*
77 W 66th St
3rd Floor
New York, NY 10023, USA

Pellington, Mark (Director, Producer)
c/o Staff Member *3 Arts Entertainment Inc*
9460 Wilshire Blvd
7th Floor
Beverly Hills, CA 90210, USA

Pellow, Kit (Athlete, Baseball Player)
1229 W Bluegrass Rd
Nixa, MO 65714-8058, USA

Pellow, Marti (Musician)
c/o Staff Member *Solo Agency Ltd (UK)*
55 Fulham High St
2nd Floor
London SW6 3JJ, United Kingdom

Pelluer, Steve (Athlete, Football Player)
1306 177th Ave NE
Bellevue, WA 98008, USA

Peloffy, Andre (Athlete, Hockey Player)
P.O. Box 2382
Morehead City, NC 28557-2382

Pelosi, Nancy (Congressman, Politician)
235 Cannon HOB
Washington, DC 20515, USA

Pelphrey, Tom (Actor)
c/o Cyrena Esposito *Cyrena Esposito Management*
437 West 48th Street
Suite D
New York, NY 10036, USA

Peltier, Dan (Athlete, Baseball Player)
1643 Oak Hill Dr
Hastings, MN 55033-5000, USA

Peltier, Leonard (Writer)
c/o Staff Member *St Martins Press*
Publicity Dept
175 5th Ave
New York, NY 10010, USA

Peltonen, Ville (Athlete, Hockey Player)
12210 NW 71st St.
Parkland, FL 33076, USA

Peltz, Nicola (Actor)
c/o Cynthia Pett-Dante *Brillstein Entertainment Partners*
9150 Wilshire Blvd #350
Beverly Hills, CA 90212, USA

Peluce, Meeno (Actor)
2445 Metzler Dr.
Los Angeles, CA 90031, USA

Peluso, Mike (Athlete, Hockey Player)
6111 Magnolia Dr
Bismarck, ND 58503-9311

Peluso, Mike (Athlete, Hockey Player)
3616 W Fuller St
Edina, MN 55410-2362

Pelyk, Mike (Athlete, Hockey Player)
56-385 The East Mall
Toronto, ON M9B 6J4, Canada

Pelzer, Dave (Writer)
Box 1846
Rancho Mirage, CA 92270-1081

Pember, Dave (Athlete, Baseball Player)
1013 Sandy Springs Rd NW
Huntsville, AL 35806-2411, USA

Pemberton, Brock (Athlete, Baseball Player)
1402 N Elm St
Owasso, OK 74055-4926, USA

Pemberton, Rudy (Athlete, Baseball Player)
P.O. Box 602
Imperial, PA 15126-0602, USA

Pempengco, Charice (Musician)
c/o Liz Rosenberg *Liz Rosenberg Media*
142 W. 57th St
6th Floor
New York, NY 10019, USA

Pena, Alejandro (Athlete, Baseball Player)
12635 Etris Rd
Roswell, GA 30075-1039, USA

Pena, Brayan (Athlete, Baseball Player)
14217 SW 102nd St
Miami, FL 33186-6970, USA

Pena, Carlos (Athlete, Baseball Player)
8157 Via Bella Notte
Orlando, FL 32836-7705, USA

Pena, Carlos (Musician)
c/o Glenn Hughes III *Gem Entertainment Group*
10701 Wilshire Blvd.
Ste. 1202
Los Angeles, CA 90024, USA

Peña, Elizabeth (Actor, Director)
c/o Staff Member *Rugolo Entertainment*
195 S Beverly Dr
Suite 400
Beverly Hills, CA 90212, USA

Pena, Federico (Politician)
362 Detroit St Unit A
Denver, CO 80206-4377, USA

Pena, Federico Secy
3517 Sterling Ave
Alexandria, VA 22304, USA

Pena, Geronimo (Athlete, Baseball Player)
Dominican Republic
KM 17 7 Pista Duarte
Los Alcarrizos
USA

Pena, Hipolito (Athlete, Baseball Player)
11412 Park Blvd
Seminole, FL 33772-4620, USA

Pena, Jim (Athlete, Baseball Player)
3228 E Silverwood Dr
Phoenix, AZ 85048-7257, USA

Pena, Juan (Athlete, Baseball Player)
5356 SW 133rd Ave
Miramir, FL 33027-6304, USA

Pena, Michael (Actor)
c/o Eric Kranzler *Management 360*
9111 Wilshire Blvd
Beverly Hills, CA 90210, USA

Pena, Orlando (Athlete, Baseball Player)
1750 W 46th St
Apt 416
Hialeah, FL 33012-2884, USA

Pena, Ramiro (Athlete, Baseball Player)
c/o Team Member *New York Yankees*
Yankee Stadium
161st St & River Ave
Bronx, NY 10451, USA

Pena, Robert (Athlete, Football Player)
77 John Parker Rd
East Falmouth, MA 02536, USA

Pena, Tony (Athlete, Baseball Player, Coach)
New York Yankees
161st Street and River Avenue
Attn: Coaching Staff
Bronx, NY 10451-2100, USA

Pena, Willy Mo (Athlete, Baseball Player)
27520 Breakers Dr
Wesle'y' Chapel, FL 33544-6667, USA

Pena, Wily Mo (Athlete, Baseball Player)
27520 Breakers Dr
Wesley Chapel, FL 33544, USA

Penaranda, Jairo (Athlete, Football Player)
2023 Lloyd Center
Portland, OR 97232, USA

Pence, Hunter (Athlete, Baseball Player)
25344 FM 2100 Rd
Huffman, TX 78758-3548, USA

Pence, Mike (Congressman, Politician)
100 Cannon HOB
Washington, DC 20515, USA

Penchion, Bob (Athlete, Football Player)
315 County Road 266
Town Creek, AL 35672, USA

Pender, Jerry Lee (Athlete, Basketball Player)
382 Chrystal Way
Rocky Mount, NC 27801-9323, USA

Pender, Mel (Athlete, Olympic Athlete, Track Athlete)
2330 Goodwood Blvd SE
Smyrna, GA 30080-8207, USA

Pendleton, Austin
155 E. 76th St.
New York, NY 10021

Pendleton, Karen (Actor)
7328 N Fruit Ave
Fresno, CA 93711, USA

Pendleton, Terry (Athlete, Baseball Player)
2998 Grey Moss Pass
Duluth, GA 30078-7782, USA

Penfold, James (Model)
c/o Staff Member *DNA Model Management*
555 W 25th St
New York, NY 10001, USA

Penghlis, Thaao (Actor)
c/o Christopher Barrett *Metropolitan (MTA)*
4526 Wilshire Blvd
Los Angeles, CA 90010, USA

Pengilly, Kirk (Musician)
The Eye Foundation
94-98 Chalmers Street
Surry Hills, NSW 2010, Australia

Penguins, The
24210 E. Fork Rd. #9
Azusa, CA 91702

Penhaligon, Susan
109 Jermyn St
London, ENGLAND SW1

Penhall, Bruce (Race Car Driver)
PO Box 5625
Norco, CA 92860, USA

Peniche, Arturo (Actor)
c/o Staff Member *Televisa*
Blvd Adolfo Lopez Mateos 232
Colonia San Angel INN
DF CP 01060, MEXICO

Peniche, Kari Ann (Actor)
c/o Ted Maier *Maier Management*
9025 Wilshire Blvd.
Suite 450
Beverly Hills, CA 90211, USA

Penick, Trevor (Musician)
Trans Continental Records
7380 Sand Lake Road
#350
Orlando, FL 32819, USA

Penikett, Tahmoh (Actor)
c/o Robert Stein *Robert Stein Management*
PO Box 3797
Beverly Hills, CA 90212, USA

Peniston, Ce Ce
250 W. 57th St. #821
New York, NY 10107

Peniston, CeCe (Musician)
c/o Staff Member *Diva Central Inc*
7510 W Sunset Blvd Ste 1445
Los Angees, CA 90046, USA

Penky, Joseph F (Engineer)
Purdue University
Chemical Engineering Dept
West Lafayette, IN 47907, USA

Penn, Chris (Athlete, Football Player)
P.O. Box 123
S Coffeyville, OK 74072, USA

Penn, Hayden (Athlete, Baseball Player)
9150 Canyon Park Ter
Santee, CA 92071-4733, USA

Penn, Jesse (Athlete, Football Player)
8420 Wildcreek Dr
Plano, TX 75025, USA

Penn, Kal (Actor, Producer)
c/o Daniel Spilo *Industry Entertainment Partners*
955 S Carrillo Dr
Suite 300
Los Angeles, CA 90048, USA

Penn, Michael (Musician)
c/o Staff Member *Kraft-Engel Management*
15233 Ventura Blvd
Suite 200
Sherman Oaks, CA 91403, USA

Penn, Sean (Actor, Director)
c/o Mara Buxbaum *ID PR (LA)*
7060 Hollywood Blvd
8th Floor
Los Angeles, CA 90028, USA

Penn, Shannon (Athlete, Baseball Player)
1548 Jonathan Ave
#2
Cincinnati, OH 45206-1340, USA

Penna, Angel (Horse Racer)
17 Chestnut H
Roslyn, NY 11576-2821, USA

Pennacchio, Len A (Misc)
Stanford University
Human Genome Center
Stanford, CA 94305, USA

Penn & Teller (Comedian, Magician)
c/o Glenn Alai *Star Price Productions*
3555 West Reno Ave #L
Las Vegas, NV 89118, USA

Pennebaker, Ed (Artist)
428 County Road 9351
Green Forest, AR 72638, USA

Pennell, Larry
15516 Sunset Blvd. #101
Pacific Palisades, CA 90272

Penner, Dustin (Athlete, Hockey Player)
The Sports Corporation
2735-10088 102 Ave NW
Attn Rich Winter
Edmonton, AB TSJ 2Z1, Canada

Penner, Jonathan (Actor)
c/o Staff Member *Modus Entertainment*
8569 Holloway Dr
Apt 1
West Hollywood, CA 90069-6918, USA

Penner, Stanford S (Engineer)
5912 Avenida Chamnez
La Jolla, CA 92037, USA

Penney, Rick
1901 75th St SE
Everett, WA 98203-6843, USA

Penney, Steve (Athlete, Hockey Player)
155 rue Notre Dame St.
Saint-Ferreoi-Les-Neiges, QC GOA 3RO, CANADA

Penniman, Michael (Mika) (Musician)
c/o Jbeau Lewis *Creative Artists Agency (CAA-LA)*
2000 Ave Of The Stars
Los Angeles, CA 90067, USA

Penniman, Micheal (Mika) (Musician)
c/o Jbeau Lewis *Creative Artists Agency (CAA-LA)*
2000 Ave Of The Stars
Los Angeles, CA 90067, USA

Pennington, Ann
701 N. Oakhurst Dr.
Beverly Hills, CA 90210

Pennington, Art (Athlete, Baseball Player)
Chicago American Giants
922 5th St SE Apt E5
Cedar Rapids, IA 52401-2440, USA

Pennington, Brad (Athlete, Baseball Player)
7220 E State Road 160
Salem, IN 47167-7856, USA

Pennington, Chad (Athlete, Football Player)
c/o Team Member *New York Jets*
1 Jets Dr
Florham Park, NJ 07932, USA

Pennington, Cliff (Athlete, Hockey Player)
9960 5th St N Aot 203
Saint Petersburg, FL 33702-2200

Pennington, Granvil "Al" (Scientist)
11326 Sagetrail Dr
Houston, TX 77089-4418, USA

Pennington, Janice (Actor, Model)
PO Box 11402
Beverly Hills, CA 90213, USA

Pennington, Julia
PO Box 5617
Beverly Hills, CA 90210

Pennington, Michael (Actor)
Marmont Mgmt
Langham House
302/8 Regent St
London W1R 5AL, UNITED KINGDOM (UK)

Pennington, T Durwood (Athlete, Football Player)
480 Peninsula Rd
Gainesville, GA 30506, USA

Pennington, Ty (Actor)
2554 Lincoln Blvd
#660
Venice, CA 90291, USA

Pennison, Jay (Athlete, Football Player)
3007 W Autumn Run Cir
Sugar Land, TX 77479, USA

Pennock, Chris (Actor)
25150 1/2 Malibu Road
Malibu, CA 90265, USA

Pennock of Norton, Raymond (Business Person)
Morgan Grenfell Group
23 Great Winchester St
London EC2P 2AX, UNITED KINGDOM (UK)

Pennv, Brad (Athlete, Baseball Player)
25071 Abercrombie Ln
Calabasas, CA 91302-2360, USA

Penny, Brad (Athlete, Baseball Player)
25071 Abercrombie Ln
Calabasas, CA 91302, USA

Penny, Brad (Athlete, Baseball Player)
25071 Abercrombie Ln
Calabasas, CA 91302-2360, USA

Penny, Joe (Actor)
c/o Staff Member *Geddes Agency, The*
8430 Santa Monica Blvd
Suite 200
Los Angeles, CA 90069, USA

Penny, Roger P (Business Person)
Bethlehem Steel
1170 8th Ave
Bethlehem, PA 18016, USA

Penny, Sudney (Actor)
Baker/Winokur/Ryder
9100 Wilshire Blvd
#600
Beverly Hills, CA 90212, USA

Penny, Sydney (Actor)
c/o Bob McGowan *McGowan Management*
8733 W Sunset Blvd
Suite 103
West Hollywood, CA 90069, USA

Pennyfeather, Will (Athlete, Baseball Player)
333 Rector St
Apt 6D
Perth Amboy, NJ 08861-4277, USA

Penny's
3220 Altura #106
La Crescenta, CA 91214

Pennywell, Carlos (Athlete, Football Player)
3729 Clover Dr
Arcadia, LA 71001, USA

Pennywell, Robert (Athlete, Football Player)
1523 Staring Ln
Baton Rouge, LA 70810, USA

Penot, Jacques
9 rue de l'Isly
Paris, FRANCE F-75008

Penrose, Craig R (Athlete, Football Player)
1609 Camino Way
Woodland, CA 95695, USA

Penske, Roger (Race Car Driver)
Penske Racing
2555 Telegraph Rd.
Bloomfield Hills, MI 48302-0954, USA

Pensky, Robert (Writer)
Boston University 236 Bay State Rd Attn English Dept
Boston, MA 02215-1403, USA

Pentecost, Del (Actor)
c/o Staff Member *Paradigm (LA)*
360 N Crescent Dr
North Bldg
Beverly Hills, CA 90210, USA

Penthouse Pets
277 Park Ave
New York, NY 10172-0003

Pentland, Alex P (Scientist)
Massachusetts Institute of Technology
Media Laboratory
Cambridge, MA 02139, USA

Pentland, Jeff (Athlete, Baseball Player)
1032 N Cherry
Mesa, AZ 85201-3208, USA

Pentz, Gene (Athlete, Baseball Player)
207 Rainbow Dr
Johnstown, PA 15904, USA

Penzias, Arno A (Nobel Prize Laureate)
AT & T Bell Laboratories
AT & T Bell Labs 600 Mountain Ave
New Providence, NJ 07974-2070, USA

People, Village (Music Group, Musician)
c/o Staff Member *WmE2 (WMA-LA)*
1 William Morris Pl
Beverly Hills, CA 90212, USA

Peoples, John (Physicist)
Fermi Nat Acceleration Lab
CDF Collaboration
PO Box 500
Batavia, IL 60510, USA

Pepin, Jacques (Chef)
214 Durham Rd
Madison, CT 06443, USA

Pepitone, Joseph A (Joe) (Athlete, Baseball Player)
101 W Shore Dr
Massapequa, NY 11758, USA

Peplinski, Jim (Athlete, Hockey Player)
Peplinski's Leasemaster
212 Meridian Rd NE
Calgary, AB T2A 2N6, Canada

Peplowski, Mike (Athlete, Basketball Player)
4110 Harris Rd
Williamston, MI 48895-9149, USA

Peppas, June (Athlete, Baseball Player)
1700 NE Indian River Dr #302
Jensen Beach, FL 34957-5860, USA

Pepper, Barry (Actor)
c/o Nancy Mccarty Iannios *Nancy Iannois Public Relations*
P.O. Box 430
Signal Mountain, TN 37377-0430, USA

Pepper, Cynthia (Actor)
219 Friendly Ct
Henderson, NV 89052

Pepper, Don (Athlete, Baseball Player)
7 Beckenham Ln
Greenville, SC 43068-9328, USA

Pepper, Dottle (Golfer)
108 Micco Cir
Jupiter, FL 33458-7730, USA

Pepper, Laurin (Athlete, Baseball Player)
8932 Davis St
Oecan Springs, MS 39564, USA

Peppers, Julius (Athlete, Football Player)
173 Rehoboth Ln
Mooresville, NC 28117, USA

Peppler, Mary Jo (Athlete, Volleyball Player)
Bridge Volleyball Club
2390 Boswell Rd
Suite 400
Chula Vista, CA 91414, USA

Perabo, Piper (Actor)
c/o Tina Thor *TMT Entertainment Group*
648 Broadway
Suite 1002
New York, NY 10012, USA

Perak, Sultan of (King)
Sultan's Palace
Istana Bukit Serene
Kula Lumpur, MALAYSIA

Perakis, Nicos
Isabellastr. 19
Munich, GERMANY D-80798

Peralta, Jhonny (Athlete, Baseball Player)
27940 Berringer Run
Westlake, OH 44145-3063, USA

Peralta, Ricardo (Astronaut)
Ingeneria Instituto
Ciudad Universitaria
Mexico City, DF 04510, MEXICO

Peranoski, Ron (Baseball Player)
Los Angeles Dodgers
3805 Indian River Dr E
Vero Beach, FL 32963-1404, USA

Perayra, Marianela (Television Host)
c/o Michael (Mike) Esterman
Esterman.Com, LLC
Prefers to be contacted via email
MD, USA

Peraza, Alejandro (Stylist)
c/o Staff Member *Mercury Artists*
8460 Higuera St Fl 2
Culver City, CA 90232, USA

Percival, Lance (Actor)
PVA 2 High St
Westbury-on-Trim
Bristol BS9 3DU, UNITED KINGDOM
(UK)

Percival, Mac (Athlete, Football Player)
6710 Flowermound Dr
Sugar Land, TX 77479, USA

Percival, Troy E (Athlete, Baseball Player)
2127 Century Ave
Riverside, CA 92506-4653, USA

Perconte, Jack (Athlete, Baseball Player)
6197 Hinterlong Ct
Lisle, IL 60532-2818, USA

Percy, James (General)
1100 Fruitdale Dr Apt 55
Grants Pass, OR 97527-5085, USA

Perdue, Bev (Governor)
Office of the Governor
20301 Mail Service Center
Raleigh, NC 27699-0301, USA

Perdue, Sonny (Governor, Politician)
217 Houston Drive
Bonaire, GA 31005, USA

Perdue, Will (Athlete, Basketball Player)
6310 Innisbrook Dr
Prospect, KY 40059-9223, USA

Perec, Marie-Jose (Athlete, Track Athlete)
Federacion d'Athletisme
10 Rue du Fg Poissonniere
Paris 75480, FRANCE

Peregrym, Missy (Actor)
c/o Jai Khanna *Brillstein Entertainment Partners*
9150 Wilshire Blvd #350
Beverly Hills, CA 90212, USA

Perek, Lubos (Astronomer)
Astronomical Institute
Budecska 6
Prague 2, CZECH REPUBLIC

Perelman, Ronald O (Business Person)
MacAndrews & Forbes
35 East 62nd St
New York, NY 10021, USA

Perelman, Vadim (Director)
c/o Simon Millar *Rumble Media*
1620 Broadway
Santa Monica, CA 90403, USA

Perenyi, Miklos (Musician)
Erdoalja Utca 1/B
Budapest 1037, HUNGARY

Peres, Shimon (Nobel Prize Laureate)
Aenot Law House
8 Shaul Hamelech Blvd
Tel Aviv 64733, ISRAEL

Peres, Shimon (Politician)
Amot Low House 8 Shaul Hamelech Blvd
Tel Aviv 64733, Israel

Peretokin, Mark (Dancer)
Bolshoi Theater
Teatralnaya Pl 1
Moscow 103009, RUSSIA

Perez, Atanasio (Athlete, Baseball Player)
1717 North Bayshore Dr
Miami, FL 33132, USA

Perez, Chris (Musician)
Big FD Entertainment
301 Arizona Ave
#200
Santa Monica, CA 90401, USA

Perez, Danny (Athlete, Baseball Player)
10511 Cuesta Brava Ln
El Paso, TX 79935-2210, USA

Perez, Dick (Artist)
P.O. Box 503
Wayne, PA 19087, USA

Perez, Eddie (Athlete, Baseball Player)
615 Rose Creek Cir
Duluth, GA 30518-6721, USA

Perez, Eduardo (Athlete, Baseball Player)
113 Calle Las Flores
San Juan, PR 00911-2298, USA

Perez, George (Athlete, Baseball Player)
711 S Old Stage Rd
Cave Junction, OR 97523-9362, USA

Perez, Hugo (Soccer Player)
22018 Newbridge Dr
Lake Forest, CA 92630, USA

Perez, Luiz (Louie) (Musician)
Gold Mountain
3575 Cahuenga Blvd W
#450
Los Angeles, CA 90068, USA

Perez, Manny (Actor, Producer, Writer)
c/o Scott Zimmerman *Evolution Entertainment (LA)*
901 N Highland Ave
Los Angeles, CA 90038, USA

Perez, Marty (Athlete, Baseball Player)
30 Willowick Dr
Lithonia, GA 30038-1722, USA

Perez, Melido (Athlete, Baseball Player)
Nigua KM 21 1/2
Santo Domingo, Dominican Republic

Perez, Mike (Athlete, Baseball Player)
800 Kylewood Pl
Ballwin, MO 63021-4796, USA

Perez, Neifi (Athlete, Baseball Player)
43515 Blacksmith SQ Apt 106
Ashburn, VA 20147-4637, USA

Perez, Odalis A (Baseball Player)
Los Angeles Dodgers
Stadium
1000 Elysian Park Ave
Los Angeles, CA 90012, USA

Perez, Oliver (Baseball Player)
c/o Scott Boras *Boras Corporation*
18 Corporate Plaza
Newport Beach, CA 92660, USA

Perez, Pascual (Athlete, Baseball Player)
Salvador Cucurulo #105
Santiago, Dominican Republic

Perez, Rosie (Actor, Producer)
c/o Jon Rubinstein *Authentic Talent and Literary Management*
45 Main St
Suite 1004
Brooklyn, NY 11201, USA

Perez, Scott (Cartoonist)
DC Comics
1700 Broadway
New York, NY 10019, USA

Perez, Timothy Paul (Actor)
Badgley Connor Talent
9229 Sunset Blvd
#311
Los Angeles, CA 90069, USA

Perez, Tony (Athlete, Baseball Player, Coach)
1717 N Bayshore Dr #A-2735
Miami, FL 33132-1180, USA

Perez, Vincent (Actor)
c/o Staff Member *ArtMedia*
20 avenue Rapp
Paris 75008, France

Perez, Yorkis (Athlete, Baseball Player)
3303 Potter St
Philadelphia, PA 19134-1404, USA

Perez-Brown, Maria (Producer)
c/o Staff Member *WmE2 (WMA-LA)*
1 William Morris Pl
Beverly Hills, CA 90212, USA

Perezchica, Tony (Athlete, Baseball Player)
79220 Victoria Dr
La Quinta, CA 92253-4274, USA

Perez de Cuellar, Javier (General, Secretary)
Avenida A Miro Quesada
Lima 1071, PERU

Perez de Tagle, Anna Maria (Actor)
c/o Beverly Strong *Strong Management*
3532 Hayden Ave
Culver City, CA 90232, USA

Perez de Tagle, Anna Marie (Actor)
c/o Beverly Strong *Strong Management*
3532 Hayden Ave
Culver City, CA 90232, USA

Perez Esquivel, Adolfo (Nobel Prize Laureate)
Servicio Paz y Justicia
Piedras 730
Buenos Aires 1070, ARGENTINA

Perez Fernandez, Pedro (Government Official)
PSOE
Ferraz 68 y 70
Madrid 28008, SPAIN

Perez Limon, Iyari (Actor)
c/o Mitchell Stubbs *Mitchell K Stubbs & Assoc (MKS)*
8675 W. Washington Blvd
Suite 203
Culver City, CA 90232, USA

Pergine, John (Athlete, Football Player)
5 Jody Dr
Plymouth Meeting, PA 19462, USA

Perick, Christof (Conductor)
Kaylor Mgmt
130 W 57th St
#8G
New York, NY 10019, USA

Perillo, Gregory (Artist)
2 Blackwell Rd
Nesconset, NY 11767-2802, USA

Perino, Dana (Television Host)
611 Pennsylvania Ave. SE
#312
Washington, DC 20003, USA

Perishers, The (Music Group)
c/o Staff Member *Paradigm (Monterey)*
404 W Franklin St
Monterey, CA 93940, USA

Perisho, Matt (Athlete, Baseball Player)
1462 W Cardinal Way
Chandler, AZ 85286-4379, USA

Periyar, Dasan (Actor)
30 Muthaiappa Street
Shenoy Nagar
Chennai, TN 600 030, INDIA

Perkins, Broderick (Athlete, Baseball Player)
5367 San Vincente Blvd
Apt 237
Los Angeles, CA 91977-6509, USA

Perkins, Bruce (Athlete, Football Player)
19014 E Ryan Rd
Queen Creek, AZ 85242-6877, USA

Perkins, Cecil (Athlete, Baseball Player)
711 Cushwa Rd
Martinsburg, WV 25403-1228, USA

Perkins, Dan (Athlete, Baseball Player)
1509 Kenan St NW
Wilson, NC 33158-2043, USA

Perkins, David D (Biologist)
367 S Baywood Ave
San Jose, CA 95128-5123, USA

Perkins, Edward J (Diplomat)
State Department
2201 C St NW
Washington, DC 20520, USA

Perkins, Elvis (Musician)
c/o Staff Member *Paradigm (Monterey)*
404 W Franklin St
Monterey, CA 93940, USA

Perkins, Elizabeth (Actor)
c/o Leslie Siebert *Gersh (LA)*
9465 Wilshire Blvd
Suite 600
Beverly Hills, CA 90212, USA

Perkins, Emily (Actor)
c/o Tyman Stewart *Characters Talent Agency, The (Vancouver)*
8 Elm St
2nd Floor
Toronto, ON M5G 1G7, Canada

Perkins, Glen (Athlete, Baseball Player)
18401 Lake Forest Dr
Lakeville, MN 55044, USA

Perkins, John (Writer)
c/o Paul Fedorko *Trident Media Group LLC*
41 Madison Ave
36th Floor
New York, NY 10010, USA

Perkins, John M (Activist)
1655 Saint Charles St
Jackson, MS 39209, USA

Perkins, Kathleen Rose (Actor)
c/o Devon Jackson *Trademark Talent*
4758 Allott Avenue
Sherman Oaks, CA 91423-2403, USA

Perkins, Kendrick (Athlete, Basketball Player)
8522 Haven Trl
#1
Tomball, TX 77375-2650, USA

Perkins, Lucian (Journalist, Photographer)
3103 17th St NW
Washington, DC 20010-2701, USA

Perkins, Millie (Actor)
2511 Canyon Dr
Los Angeles, CA 90068, USA

Perkins, Oz
7720 Sunset Blvd.
Los Angeles, CA 90046

Perkins, Ross (Athlete, Hockey Player)
4-400 Jim Common Dr
Sherwood Park, AB T8H OKS, Canada

Perkins, Sam (Athlete, Basketball Player)
14901 Bellbrook Dr
Dallas, TX 75254-7673, USA

Perkins, Tex (Musician)
Stack/Polydor Records
70 Universal City Plaza
Universal City, CA 91608, USA

Perkins, Warren (Athlete, Basketball Player)
717 Fairfield Ave
Gretna, LA 70056-7625, USA

Perkins, W Ray (Athlete, Coach, Football Coach, Football Player)
57 Honors Ln
Hattiesburg, MS 39402, USA

Perkoff, Gerald T (Doctor)
1300 Torrey Pines Dr
Columbia, MO 65203, USA

Perkowski, Harry (Athlete, Baseball Player)
211 McGinnis St
Beckley, WV 25801-5725, USA

Perks, Craig (Golfer)
321 Thibodeaux Dr
Lafayette, LA 70503-4444, USA

Perl, Frank J (Cinematographer)
5020 Biloxi Ave
North Hollywood, CA 91601, USA

Perl, Martin L (Nobel Prize Laureate)
3737 El Centro Ave
Palo Alto, CA 94306-2642, USA

Perle, George (Composer)
Queens College
Music Dept
Flushing, NY 11367, USA

Perles, George (Athlete, Football Coach, Football Player)
6153 W Longview Dr
East Lansing, MI 48823, USA

Perley, James (Misc)
American Assn of University Professors
1012 14th St NW
Washington, DC 20005, USA

Perlich, Max (Actor)
c/o Staff Member *Metropolitan (MTA)*
4526 Wilshire Blvd
Los Angeles, CA 90010, USA

Perlick-Keating, Edythe (Baseball Player)
3051 S Palm Aire Dr Bldg 34
Pompano Beach, FL 33069-4277, USA

Perlini, Fred (Athlete, Hockey Player)
409 Albert St W
Sault Ste. Marie, ON P6A 1C2, Canada

Perlman, Itzhak (Conductor, Musician)
c/o Wray Armstrong *IMG Artists Worldwide (UK)*
The Light Box
111 Power Road
London W4 5PY, United Kingdom

Perlman, Jon (Athlete, Baseball Player)
3225 Bryn Mawr Dr
Dallas, TX 75225-7646, USA

Perlman, Lawrence (Business Person)
Ceridian Corp
3311 E Old Shakopee Road
Minneapolis, MN 55425, USA

Perlman, Phil
439 S. Catalina Ave. #102
Pasadena, CA 91106

Perlman, Rhea (Actor, Producer)
1028 Ridgedale Dr
Beverly Hills, CA 90210, USA

Perlman, Ron (Actor)
4025 Cromwell Ave
Los Angeles, CA 90027, USA

Perlmutter, Ed (Congressman, Politician)
1221 Longworth HOB
Washington, DC 20515, USA

Perlmutter, Saul (Nobel Prize Laureate)
127 Poplar St
Berkeley, CA 94708-1325, USA

Perlozzo, Sam (Athlete, Baseball Player, Coach)
18101 Emerald Bay St
Tampa, FL 33647-3316, USA

Perls, Tom (Misc)
2 Harrington Lane
Weston, MA 02493, USA

Pernandez, Mervyn (Athlete, Football Player)
1546 Morning Star Dr
Morgan Hill, CA 95037, USA

Perner, Wolfgang (Athlete)
Schildlehen 29
ramsau-D 8972, AUSTRIA

Pernice Jr, Tom (Golfer)
c/o Staff Member *Pro Golfers Association (PGA) Tour*
112 TPC Blvd
Ponte Vedra Beach, FL 32082, USA

Pero, Perry R (Financier)
Northern Trust Corp
50 S La Salle St
Chicago, IL 60675, USA

Peron, Isabelita Martinez de (President)
Moreto 3
Los Jeronimos
Madrid 28014, SPAIN

Perot, Henry Ross (Aviator)
PO Box 269014
Plano, TX 75026-9014, USA

Perot, Pete (Athlete, Football Player)
2401 Hillside Rd
Ruston, LA 71270, USA

Perot, Ross H (Business Person)
c/o Staff Member *Perot Group*
2300 W Plano Pkwy
Plano, TX 75075, USA

Perot Jr, Henry Ross (Business Person)
c/o Staff Member *Perot Group*
2300 W Plano Pkwy
Plano, TX 75075, USA

Perranoski, Ron (Athlete, Baseball Player)
4800 Hwy A1A #307
Vero Beach, FL 32963-1230, USA

Perreau, Gigi (Actor)
5841 Cantaloupe Ave
Van Nuys, CA 91401, USA

Perreault, Bob (Athlete, Hockey Player)

Perreault, Gilbert (Athlete, Hockey Player)
4 Rue de la Serenite
Victoriaville, QC G6S 1J4, Canada

Perreault, Gilbert (Gil) (Athlete, Hockey Player)
Buffalo Sabres
1 Seymour H Knox III Plz Ste 1
Buffalo, NY 14203-3096

Perreault, Yanic (Athlete, Hockey Player)
1565 Rue Malouin
Sherbrooke, QC JIJ 3CS, Canada

Perret, Christine (Stylist)
c/o Staff Member *O'Gorman/Schramm Represents, Inc*
642 Washington St
#1-A
New York, NY 10014, USA

Perret, Craig (Horse Racer)
4149 Palomar Blvd
Lexington, KY 40513-1316, USA

Perretta, Ralph (Athlete, Football Player)
1305 Calle Scott
Encinitas, CA 92024, USA

Perrette, Pauley (Actor)
c/o Steven Jang *SDB Partners Inc*
1801 Ave of the Stars
Suite 902
Los Angeles, CA 90067, USA

Perrier, Mireille (Actor)
Cineart
36 Rue de Ponthieu
Paris 75008, FRANCE

Perriman, Brett (Athlete, Football Player)
P.O. Box 83337
Conyers, GA 30013, USA

Perrin, Benny (Athlete, Football Player)
2509 Burningtree Dr SE
Decatur, AL 35603, USA

Perrin, Eric (Athlete, Hockey Player)
111 Forsyth Trl
Canton, GA 30114-5519

Perrin, Lonnie (Athlete, Football Player)
7809 Green St
Clinton, MD 20735, USA

Perrin, Philippe (Astronaut)
11923 Mighty Redwood Dr
Houston, TX 77059, USA

Perrin, Philippe Colonel (Astronaut)
11923 Mighty Redwood Dr
Houston, TX 77059-5542, USA

Perrine, Valerie (Actor)
c/o Staff Member *Bensky Entertainment*
15030 Ventura Blvd
Suite 343
Sherman Oaks, CA 91403, USA

Perrineau Jr, Harold (Harry) (Actor, Producer)
c/o Stacy Abrams *Abrams Entertainment*
5225 Wilshire Blvd #515
Suite 515
Los Angeles, CA 90036, USA

Perron, Jean (Coach)
5 Thomas Mellon Circle
San Francisco, CA 94134, USA

Perroni, Maite (Actor)
c/o Staff Member *Televisa S.A. de C.V.*
Av. Vasco de Quirroga 2000
DF 01210, Mexico

Perrotta, Tom (Writer)
Saint Martin's Press
175 5th Ave
New York, NY 10010, USA

Perry, Alex (Designer)
Alex Perry
Level 1, 60 Riley St
East Sydney NSW 2010, Australia

Perry, Anne (Writer)
Turn Vawr
Seafield Postmahomack
Rosshire IV20 1RE, SCOTLAND

Perry, Barbara
6926 La Presa Dr.
Los Angeles, CA 90068

Perry, Barry W (Business Person)
Engelhard Corp
101 Wood Ave
Iselin, NJ 08830, USA

Perry, Bob (Athlete, Baseball Player)
445 Fox Chase Vig
New Bern, NC 28562-2819, USA

Perry, Chan (Athlete, Baseball Player)
788 NE County Road 353
Mayo, FL 32066-5450, USA

Perry, Chris (Athlete, Golfer)
170 Valley Run Dr
Powell, OH 43065-9454, USA

Perry, Chris (Athlete, Football Player)
c/o Eugene Parker *Maximum Sports Management*
6435 W Jefferson Blvd
#197
Fort Wayne, IN 46804, USA

Perry, Darren (Athlete, Football Player)
6451 Pinehurst Ln
Mason, OH 45040, USA

Perry, Ed (Athlete, Football Player)
1583 SW 161st Ave
Pembroke Piners, FL 33027, USA

Perry, Elliott (Athlete, Basketball Player)
3306 Darby Dan Cv
Germantown, TN 38138, USA

Perry, Felton (Actor)
PO Box 931359
Los Angeles, CA 90093, USA

Perry, Gaylord (Athlete, Baseball Player)
P.O. Box 489
Spruce Pine, NC 28777-0489, USA

Perry, Gerald (Athlete, Baseball Player)
1348 Waterford Green Close
Marietta, GA 30068-2919, USA

Perry, Gerald (Athlete, Football Player)
2940 Dell Dr
Columbia, SC 29209, USA

Perry, Gerald E (Athlete, Football Player)
336 5th St
Manhattan Beach, CA 90266, USA

Perry, Herb (Athlete, Baseball Player)
978 N Fletcher Ave
Mayo, FL 32066-4506, USA

Perry, Ira (Stylist)
c/o Staff Member *Axis Models & Talent*
P.O. Box 367
Ringwood, NJ 07456-0367, USA

Perry, Jeff (Actor)
c/o Marsha McManus *Principal
Entertainment (LA)*
1964 Westwood Blvd #400
Los Angeles, CA 90025, USA

Perry, Jim (Athlete, Baseball Player)
155 Printers Ln
New London, NC 28127-8104, USA

Perry, Joe (Musician, Songwriter)
c/o Daniel Weiner *Paradigm (Monterey)*
404 W Franklin St
Monterey, CA 93940, USA

Perry, John Bennett (Actor)
Judy Schoen
606 N Larchmont Blvd
#309
Los Angeles, CA 90004, USA

Perry, John R (Misc)
Stanford University
Language & Information Study Center
Stanford, CA 94305, USA

Perry, Katy (Musician)
8159 Hollywood Blvd
West Hollywood, CA 90069, USA

Perry, Kenny (Golfer)
418 Quail Ridge Rd
Franklin, KY 42134-9650, USA

Perry, Leon (Athlete, Football Player)
RR 1 Box 195A
Gloster, MS 39638, USA

Perry, Linda (Musician, Producer)
Custard Records
8939 1/2 Santa Monica
West Hollywood, CA 90069, USa

Perry, Luke (Actor)
c/o Arnold Robinson *Rogers & Cowan PR
(LA)*
Pacific Design Center
8687 Melrose Ave, 7th Floor
West Hollywood, CA 90069, USA

Perry, Matthew (Actor)
c/o Lisa Kasteler *WKT Public Relations
(WKT-LA)*
9350 Wilshire Blvd
Suite 450
Beverly Hills, CA 90212, USA

Perry, Michael Dean (Athlete, Football
Player)
P.O. Box 221771
Charlotte, NC 28222, USA

Perry, Nickolas (Director, Editor, Writer)
c/o Staff Member *WmE2 (WMA-LA)*
1 William Morris Pl
Beverly Hills, CA 90212, USA

Perry, Pat (Athlete, Baseball Player)
1115 W Franklin St
Taylorville, IL 62568-2037, USA

Perry, Rachel (Actor)
c/o Staff Member *Envision Entertainment*
8840 Wilshire Blvd
3rd Floor
Beverly Hills, CA 90211, USA

Perry, Richard (Musician, Producer)
1575 Carla Ridge
Beverly Hills, CA 90210, USA

Perry, Rick (Governor, Politician)
1010 Colorado St
Austin, TX 78701-2334, USA

Perry, Robert P (Biologist)
1808 Bustleton Pike
Churchville, PA 18966, USA

Perry, Rod (Athlete, Football Player)
P.O. Box 532551
Indianapolis, IN 46253, USA

Perry, Ruth (Prime Minister)
Prime Minister's Office
Capitol Hill
Monrovia, LIBERIA

Perry, Ryan (Athlete, Baseball Player)
12360 N Feather Song Ave
Marana, AZ 85658-4697, USA

Perry, Scott (Athlete, Football Player)
3708 S Dolphin St
San Pedro, CA 90731, USA

Perry, Steve (Musician)
c/o Lee Phillips *Manatt Phelps & Phillips
LLP*
11355 W Olympic Blvd
Los Angeles, CA 90064, USA

Perry, Steve (Director, Producer)
c/o Staff Member *DH1 Studios*
8730 Sunset Blvd Fl 6
West Hollywood, CA 90069, USA

Perry, Todd (Athlete, Football Player)
13805 Brittle Rd
Alpharetta, GA 30004, USA

Perry, Tyler (Actor, Director, Producer,
Writer)
2025 Garraux Rd NW
Atlanta, GA 30327, USA

Perry, Vernon (Athlete, Football Player)
P.O. Box 842201
Houston, TX 77284, USA

Perry, William (Politician)
620 Sand Hill Rd Apt 421E
Palo Alto, CA 94304-2079, USA

Perry, William (Refrigerator) (Athlete,
Football Player)
349 Kershaw St NE
Aiken, SC 29801, USA

Perry, Wilmont (Athlete, Football Player)
1757 W River Rd
Franklinton, NC 27525, USA

Perry, Yvonne (Actor)
As World Turns Show
CBS-TV
524 W 57th St
New York, NY 10019, USA

Perryman, Jill
4 Hillside Crescent
Gooseberry Hill, AUSTRALIA 6076 W
Aus

Perryman, Jim (Athlete, Football Player)
2345 Southwood Dr
Pittsburgh, PA 15241, USA

Perryman, Robert (Athlete, Football
Player)
P.O. Box 8543
Haverhill, MA 01835, USA

Perschy, Maria
Maxingstr. 30
Vienna, AUSTRIA 1130

Persoff, Nahemiah (Actor)
5670 Moonstone Beach Dr
Cambria, CA 93428, USA

Persoff, Nehemiah (Actor)
5670 Moonstone Beach Dr.
Cambria, CA 93428, USA

Person, Chuck (Athlete, Basketball Player)
2301 S Garfield Dr
Inidianapolis, IN 46203-4218, USA

Person, Clayton (Scientist)
15349 Columbia Ave
White Rock, BC V4B 1J8, Canada

Person, Robert (Athlete, Baseball Player)
25 Bellerive Acres
Saint Louis, MO 63121-4328, USA

Person, Wesley (Athlete, Basketball
Player)
P.O. Box 481
Brantley, AL 36009-0481, USA

Persons, Peter (Golfer)
1153 Saint Andrews Dr
Macon, GA 31210, USA

Persson, Goeran (Prime Minister)
Statsradsberedningen
Rosenbad 4
Stockholm 103 33, SWEDEN

Persson, Nina (Musician)
Motor SE
Gotabergs Gatan 2
Gothenburg 400 14, SWEDEN

Persson, Ricard (Athlete, Hockey Player)
Thompson, Dorfman, Sweatman
PO Box 639 Stn Main
Attn: Donald Baizley
Winnipeg, MB R3C 2K6, Canada

Persson, Stefan (Business Person)
Sverige H & M Hennes & Mauritz AB
Sverigekontoret
Stockholm SE-106 38, SWEDEN

Persuaders, The
225 W. 57th St. #500
New York, NY 10019

Pertucceli, Valeria (Actor)
c/o Staff Member *Telefe - Argentina*
Pavon 2444 (C1248AAT)
Buenos Aires, ARGENTINA

Pertwee, Bill
25 Whitehall
London, ENGLAND SW1A 2BS

Peruzovic, Josip (Actor, Wrestler)
c/o Nick Cordasco *Prince Marketing
Group*
18 Carillon Cir
Livingston, NJ 07039, USA

Pervical, Troy (Baseball Player)
California Angels
2127 Century Ave
Riverside, CA 92506-4653, USA

Perzanowski, Stan (Athlete, Baseball
Player)
10908 Wheat Rd
New Park, PA 17352-9563, USA

Perzigian, Jerry (Producer, Writer)
c/o Joseph Cohen *Creative Artists Agency
(CAA-LA)*
2000 Ave Of The Stars
Los Angeles, CA 90067, USA

Pescatelli, Tammy (Actor)
c/o Douglas Edley *Gersh (LA)*
9465 Wilshire Blvd
Suite 600
Beverly Hills, CA 90212, USA

Pesce, P J (Director, Writer)
c/o Jordan Bayer *Original Artists (LA)*
9465 Wilshire Blvd Ste 870
Beverly Hills, CA 90212, USA

Pesch, Doro & Warlock
Box 8721
Dusseldorf 1, GERMANY D-(W) 4000

Pesci, Joe (Actor)
c/o Jay Julien *Jay Julien Management*
Prefers to be contacted via telephone
New York, NY 10036, USA

Pescow, Donna (Actor)
8267 Paseo Canyon Dr
Malibu, CA 90265, USA

Pesek, Libor (Conductor)
I M G Artists
Media House
3 Burlington Lane
London W4 2TH, UNITED KINGDOM
(UK)

Pesi, Gino Anthony (Actor)
c/o Loch Powell *Leverage Management*
3030 Pennsylvania Ave
Santa Monica, CA 90404, USA

Pesonen, Richard (Athlete, Football
Player)
765 Pine Hills Pl
The Village, FL 32162, USA

Pestana, Simon (Actor)
c/o Staff Member *Telefe - Argentina*
Pavon 2444 (C1248AAT)
Buenos Aires, ARGENTINA

Pestano, Vinnie (Athlete, Baseball Player)
6058 E Silverspur Trl
Anaheim, CA 92807-4728, USA

Pestka, Sidney (Misc)
Robert Wood Johnson Medical School
675 Hoes Lane
Piscataway, NJ 08854, USA

Pesut, George (Athlete, Hockey Player)
1008-415 Michigan St
Victoria, BC V8V 1R8, Canada

Petagine, Roberto (Athlete, Baseball
Player)
1098 Hunting Lodge Dr
Miami Springs, FL 33166-5754, USA

Petcka, Joe (Actor)
c/o Marta Michaud *Cinematic
Management*
249 1/2 E 13th St
New York, NY 10003, USA

Peter, Philipp (Race Car Driver)
Dorricott Racing
29103 Arnold Dr.
Sonoma, CA 95476, USA

Peter, Valentine J (Educator, Religious
Leader)
Father Flanagan's Boys Home
Boys Town, NE 68010, USA

Peterdi, Gabor (Artist)
108 Highland Ave
Norwalk, CT 06853, USA

Peterek, Jeff (Athlete, Baseball Player)
8073 Elm Valley Rd
Three Oaks, MI 49120-8738, USA

Peter II, Edward C (General)
4 Herons Nest
Savannah, GA 31410-3332, USA

Peterman, Melissa (Actor, Producer)
c/o Staff Member *Agency for the Performing Arts (APA-LA)*
405 S Beverly Dr
Suite 500
Beverly Hills, CA 90212-4425, USA

Peter Paul & Mary (Music Group, Musician)
121 Mt. Herman Way
Ocean Grove, NJ 07756-1443

Peters, Andrew (Athlete, Hockey Player)
107 Huntington Ct
Buffalo, NY 14221, USA

Peters, Andy (Television Host)
c/o Staff Member *BBC Artist Mail*
PO Box 1116
Belfast BT2 7AJ, United Kingdom

Peters, Anthony L (Tony) (Athlete, Football Player)
2402 Boston St
Muskogee, OK 74401, USA

Peters, Barbara (Director)
1118 Magnolia Blvd
North Hollywood, CA 91601, USA

Peters, Bernadette (Actor, Musician)
c/o Jeff Hunter *WME (WMA-NY)*
1325 Ave of the Americas
New York, NY 10019, USA

Peters, Bob (Coach)
Bernidji State University
Athletic Dept
Bernidji, MN 56601, USA

Peters, Caleigh (Musician)
c/o Siri Garber *Platform Public Relations*
2666 N Beachwood Dr
Los Angeles, CA 90068, USA

Peters, Charlie (Writer)
c/o Todd Feldman *Creative Artists Agency (CAA-LA)*
2000 Ave Of The Stars
Los Angeles, CA 90067, USA

Peters, Chris (Athlete, Baseball Player)
613 Chessbriar Dr
Bethel Park, PA 15102-1531, USA

Peters, Clarke (Actor)
c/o Staff Member *Writers and Artists Group Intl (NY)*
360 Park Ave #16
New York, NY 10022-5909, USA

Peters, Dan (Musician)
Legends of 21st Century
7 Trinity Row
Florence, MA 01062, USA

Peters, Emmitt (Dog Sled Racer)
General Delivery
Ruby, AK 99768, USA

Peters, Even (Actor)
c/o Megan Silverman *WME (LA)*
9601 Wilshire Blvd Fl 3
Beverly Hills, CA 90210, USA

Peters, Garry (Athlete, Hockey Player)
3020 Eastview
Saskatoon, SK S7J 3J2, Canada

Peters, Gary (Athlete, Baseball Player)
7121 N Serenoa Dr
Sarasota, FL 34241-9271, USA

Peters, Gordon
20 Elm Tree Ave.
Ester Surrey, ENGLAND

Peters, Gretchen (Musician, Songwriter, Writer)
Gretchen Peters Management
PO Box 331242
Nashville, TN 37203, USA

Peters, Hank (Baseball Player)
3407 S Ocean Blvd APt 8D
Highland Beach, FL 33487-4714, USA

Peters, Jason (Athlete, Football Player)
11611 Secretariat Dr
Walton, NE 68461, USA

Peters, Jim (Athlete, Hockey Player)
1455 Santolina Ct
San Jacinto, CA 92582-6200

Peters, Kate (Stylist)
2121 E 7th Pl
#201
Los Angeles, CA 90021, USA

Peters, Maria Liberia (Prime Minister)
Prime Minister's Office
Fort Amsterdam
Willemstad, NETHERLANDS ANTILLES

Peters, Marjorie (Athlete, Baseball Player)
4081 S 122nd St
Greenfield, WI 53228-1823, USA

Peters, Mary (Athlete, Track Athlete)
Willowtree Cottage
River Road
Dunmurray, Belfast, NORTHERN IRLAND

Peters, Mike (Cartoonist)
PO Box 957
Bradenton, FL 34206, USA

Peters, Ray (Athlete, Baseball Player)
11013 Southerland Dr
Denton, TX 76207-8687, USA

Peters, Rick (Actor)
c/o Patricia (Patty) Woo *Patty Woo Management*
8906 W Olympic Blvd
Beverly Hills, CA 90211, USA

Peters, Rick (Athlete, Baseball Player)
43977 W Junioer Ave
Maricopa, AZ 85138-4072, USA

Peters, Roberta (Actor, Opera Singer)
19356 Cedar Glen Dr
Boca Raton, FL 33434, USA

Peters, Russell (Actor)
c/o Paul Canterna *Seven Summits Pictures & Management*
8906 W Olympic Blvd
Ground Floor
Beverly Hills, CA 90211, USA

Peters, Steve (Athlete, Hockey Player)
1021 Golfview Rd
Peterborough, ON K9J 7W2, Canada

Peters, Steve (Athlete, Baseball Player)
1524 SW 123rd St
Oklahoma CIty, OK 73170, USA

Peters, Timothy (Race Car Driver)
BHR
PO Box 1708
Mt Juliet, TN 37121, USA

Peters, Tom (Business Person)
Tom Peters Group
555 Hamilton Avenue
Palo Alto, CA 94301, USA

Peters, Volney (Athlete, Football Player)
325 Lancaster Rd
Walnut Creek, CA 94595, USA

Petersdorf, Robert G (Physicist)
8001 Sand Point Way NE
#C71
Seattle, WA 98115, USA

Petersen, Byron (Scientist)
University of Pittsburgh
Medical Center
Pittsburgh, PA 15260, USA

Petersen, Chris (Athlete, Baseball Player)
242 Timberland Ave
Longwood, FL 32750-6159, USA

Petersen, Jan (Government Official)
Utenriksdepatementet
Postboks 8114 Dep
Oslo 0032, NORWAY

petersen, jim (Athlete, Basketball Player)
14794 Summer Oaks Dr
Wayzata, MN 55391-2230, USA

Petersen, Kurt (Athlete, Football Player)
5520 Linmore Ln
Plano, TX 75093, USA

Petersen, Loy (Athlete, Basketball Player)
475 NE Meadowlark Ln
Madras, OR 97741-9063, USA

Petersen, Melvin (Athlete, Basketball Player)
2896 Evergreen Ln
Aurora, IL 60502-6303, USA

Petersen, Niels Helveg (Government Official)
Drosselvej 72
Frederiksberg 2000, DENMARK

Petersen, Pat
1634 Veteran Ave.
Los Angeles, CA 90025

Petersen, Patty (Actor)
60 Kennedy St
Camarillo, CA 93010, USA

Petersen, Robert E (Publisher)
Petersen Publishing Co
6420 Wilshire Blvd
#100
Los Angeles, CA 90048, USA

Petersen, Stewart
Box 64
Cokeville, WY 83114

Petersen, Ted (Athlete, Football Player)
323 Ridge Point Cir
Apt 32A
Bridgeville, PA 15017, USA

petersen, Toby (Athlete, Hockey Player)
3105 Milton Ave
Dallas, TX 75205-1449

Petersen, William L (Actor, Producer)
c/o Staff Member *High Horse Films*
25135 Anza Dr
Stage 5
Santa Clarita, CA 91355, USA

Petersen, Wolfgang (Director)
c/o Staff Member *Radiant Productions*
914 Montana Ave Fl 2
Santa Monica, CA 90403, USA

Petersmark, Brett (Athlete, Football Player)
2082 Pennsbury Ln
Hanover Park, IL 60133, USA

Peterson, Adam (Athlete, Baseball Player)
5610 NE 33rd Ave
Vancouver, WA 98663-1414, USA

Peterson, Adrian (Athlete, Football Player)
1087 Mount Vernon Dr
Grayslake, IL 60030, USA

Peterson, Anthony (Boxer)
c/o Staff Member *Top Rank Inc.*
3908 Howard Hughes Pkwy
#580
Las Vegas, NV 89109, USA

Peterson, Anthony (Athlete, Football Player)
1974 Montrose Dr
Atlanta, GA 30344, USA

Peterson, Ben (Athlete, Olympic Athlete, Wrestler)
205 Dewey Ave
Watertown, WI 53094-3915, USA

Peterson, Brent (Athlete, Hockey Player)
724 Glen Oaks Dr
Franklin, TN 37067-1345

Peterson, Buzz (Coach)
University of Tennessee
Athletic Dept
Knoxville, TN 37996, USA

Peterson, Cal (Athlete, Football Player)
22646 Ingomar St
Canoga Park, CA 91304, USA

Peterson, David C (Journalist, Photographer)
4805 Pinehurst Court
Pleasant Hill, IA 50327-0959, USA

Peterson, Debbi (Musician)
Bangles Mall
1341 Fullerton Ave
Box 180
Chicago, IL 60614, USA

Peterson, Donald H
427 Pebblebrook
Seabrook, TX 77588, USA

Peterson, Donald H Colonel (Astronaut)
427 Pebblebrook Dr
El lago, TX 77586-6012, USA

Peterson, Donald R (Astronaut)
Aerospace Operations Consultants
427 Pebblebrook Dr
Seabrook, TX 77586, USA

Peterson, Elly (Activist)
1515 M St NW
Washington, DC 20005, USA

Peterson, Forrest J (Misc)
17 Collins Meadow Dr
Georgetown, SC 29440, USA

Peterson, Fritz (Athlete, Baseball Player)
P.O. Box 802
Dubuque, IA 61025-0137, USA

Peterson, Harding (Hardy) (Athlete, Baseball Player)
2822 Sherbrooke Ln
Apt C
Palm Harbor, FL 34684-2545, USA

Peterson, Jessie Lee (Radio Personality, Television Host)
PO Box 35090
Los Angeles, California 90035, USA

Peterson, John (Wrestler)
457 19th Ave
Comstock, WI 54826, USA

Peterson, Kyle (Athlete, Baseball Player)
13253 Hamilton St
Omaha, NE 68154-5293, USA

Peterson, Larry (Race Car Driver)
Bales Motorsports
PO Box 4098
107 Bennett St.
Sidney, OH 45365, USA

Peterson, Lars (Doctor)
Sahlgrenska University Hospital
Surgery Dept
Goteborg 413 45, SWEDEN

Peterson, Maggie
3310 W. Warm Springs Rd.
Las Vegas, NV 89118

peterson, melvin (Athlete, Basketball
Player)
2896 Evergreen Ln
Aurora, IL 60502-6303, USA

Peterson, Michael (Athlete, Football
Player)
P.O. Box 904
Alachua, FL 32616, USA

Peterson, Mike (Athlete, Olympic Athlete,
Rower)
7321 Elbow Ln
Philadelphia, PA 19119-2810, USA

Peterson, Morris (Athlete, Basketball
Player)
909 Lafayette St Apt 12
New Orleans, LA 70113-1041, USA

Peterson, Patrick (Athlete, Baseball
Player)
c/o Patrick William Lawlor *Galaxy Sports*
811 E. Hillsboro Blvd.
Deerfield Beach, FL 33441, USA

Peterson, Paul E (Scientist)
5 Midland Road
Wellesley, MA 05482, USA

Peterson, Peter G (Politician)
Blackstone Group 345 Park Ave Bsmt LB4
New York, NY 10154-3001, USA

Peterson, Peter G (Business Person,
Financier, Secretary)
Blackstone Group
345 Park Ave
New York, NY 10154, USA

Peterson, Seth (Actor)
3424 Blair Dr
Los Angeles, CA 90068, USA

Peterson, Steven (Architect)
Peterson/Littenberg Architecture
131 E 66th St
New York, NY 10021, USA

Peterson, Todd (Athlete, Football Player)
3249 Chatham Rd NW
Atlanta, GA 30305, USA

Peterson, Vicki (Musician)
Bangles Mall
1341 W Fullerton Ave
Box 180
Chicago, IL 60614, USA

Peterson, William (Actor)
c/o Steve Dontanville *Circle of Confusion*
(NY)
107-23 71st Rd #300
Forest Hills, NY 11375, USA

Peterson, William W (Athlete, Football
Player)
13536 Mijo Ln
Lakeside, CA 92040, USA

Peterson-Fox, Betty Jean (Athlete,
Baseball Player)
PO Box 280 110 E North St
Wyanet, IL 61379-0280, USA

Peterson-Parker, Katie (Golfer)
527 Henkel Cir
Winter Park, FL 32789-5127, USA

Pete Stark, Fortney (Congressman,
Politician)
239 Cannon HOB
Washington, DC 20515, USA

Petherbridge, Edward (Actor)
Jonathan Altaras
13 Shorts Gardens
London WC2H 9AT, UNITED KINGDOM
(UK)

Petievich, Gerald (Producer, Writer)
c/o Brian Lipson *WME (LA)*
9601 Wilshire Blvd Fl 3
Beverly Hills, CA 90210, USA

Petit, Michel (Athlete, Hockey Player)
129 Latches Lane
Media, PA 19063-5309

Petit, Philippe (Misc)
Cathedral of Saint John the Devine
1047 Amsterdam Ave
New York, NY 10025, USA

Petitbon, John (Athlete, Football Player)
3804 N Labarre Rd
Metairie, LA 70002, USA

Petitbon, Richie (Athlete, Football Coach,
Football Player)
9628 Percussion Way
Vienna, VA 22182, USA

Petitgout, Luke (Athlete, Football Player)
267 Prospect St
Ridgewood, NJ 07450, USA

Petke, Mike (Soccer Player)
DC United
14120 Newbrook Dr
Chantilly, VA 20151, USA

Petkovic, Andrea (Athlete, Tennis Player)
c/o Staff Member *Women's Tennis
Association (WTA (US))*
One Progress Plaza
Ste 1500
St Petersburg, FL 33701, USA

Petkovsek, Mark (Athlete, Baseball Player)
5575 Duff St
Beaumont, TX 77706-6307, USA

Peto, Richard (Misc)
Radcliffe Infirmary
Harkness Building
Oxford, ON OX2 6HE, UNITED
KINGDOM (UK)

Petra, Yvon (Tennis Player)
Residence du Prieure
Saint Germain en Laye 78100, FRANCE

Petraeus, David (General)
Central Intelligence Agency
Director's Office
Washington, DC 20505, USA

Petraglia, Johnny (Bowler)
25 Turn bridge Ct
Jackson, NJ 08527-6412, USA

Petralli, Geno (Athlete, Baseball Player)
119 Laser Ln
Weatherford, TX 76087-4006, USA

Petras, Ernestine (Athlete, Baseball Player)
5 Greenwood Ave
Haskell, NJ 07420-1417, USA

Petrassi, Gottfredovia
Ferdinando di Savola 3
Rome, ITALY 00196

Petree, Andy (Race Car Driver)
Petree Racing
908 Upward Rd.
Box 325
East Flat Rock, NC 28131, USA

Petrenko, Victor (Figure Skater)
c/o Staff Member *Champions on Ice*
Tom Collins Enterprises Inc
3500 W 80th St
Minneapolis, MN 55431, USA

Petrenko, Viktor (Figure Skater)
International Skating Center
PO Box 577
Sinsbury, CT 06070, USA

Petrey, Dan
1808 Cartlen Dr.
Placentia, CA 92670

Petri, Michala (Musician)
Nordskraenten 3
Kokkedal 2980, DENMARK

Petri, Nina (Actor)
Agentur Carola Studlar
Agnesstr 47
Munich 80798, GERMANY

Petrich, Bob (Athlete, Football Player)
1391 Silverberry Ct
El Cajon, CA 92019, USA

Petrick, Ben (Athlete, Baseball Player)
1553 NE Jackson School Rd
Hillsboro, OR 97124-2425, USA

Petrick, Billy (Athlete, Baseball Player)
103 Hickorv Ln
Morris, IL 60450-1627, USA

Petrie, Donald (Director)
c/o Alan Gasmer *Alan Gasmer
Management Company*
10877 Wilshire Blvd.
Suite 603
Los Angeles, CA 90024, USA

Petrie, Geoff (Athlete, Basketball Player)
3675 Holly Hill Ln
Loomis, CA 95650-8818, USA

Petrocelli, Americo P (Rico) (Athlete,
Baseball Player)
37 Green Heron Ln
Nashua, NH 03062-2239, USA

Petrocelli, Daniel (Attorney, Attorney
General, General)
Mitchell Silverberg Krupp
11377 W Olympic Blvd
Los Angeles, CA 90064, USA

Petrone, Rocco A (Engineer)
1329 Granvia Atlamira
Palos Verdes Estates, CA 90274, USA

Petrone, Shana (Musician)
Creative Artists Agency
3310 W End Ave
#500
Nashville, TN 37203, USA

Petrone, Shana (Musician)
c/o Staff Member *Creative Artists Agency
(CAA-TN)*
3310 West End Ave
5th Floor
Nashville, TN 37203, USA

Petroni, Michael (Director)
United Talent Agency
9560 Wilshire Blvd
#500
Beverly Hills, CA 90212, USA

Petronio, Stephen (Choreographer,
Dancer)
95 Saint Marks Place
New York, NY 10019, USA

Petroske, John (Athlete, Hockey Player)
Po Box 366
Side Lake, MN 55781, USA

Petrov, Andrei P (Composer)
Petrovskaya Str 42
#75
Saint Petersburg 197046, RUSSIA

Petrovic, Tim (Golfer)
12708 Tradition Dr
Dade City, FL 33525-8275, USA

Petrovicky, Robert (Athlete, Hockey
Player)
20944 Island Sound Cir Unit 106
Estero, FL 33928-8996

Petrovicky, Ronald (Athlete, Hockey
Player)
4768 Strom Pl
Prince George, BC V2M 7E4, Canada

Petrovics, Emil (Composer)
Attila Utca 29
Budapest 1013, HUNDARY

Petrovsky, Daniel J (General)
Commanding General
UN Command Korea
APO, AE 96343, USA

Petrucci, John (Musician)
c/o Staff Member *Agency Group Ltd, The
(LA)*
1880 Century Park E
Suite 711
Los Angeles, CA 90067, USA

Petry, Dan (Athlete, Baseball Player)
30715 Mystic Forest Dr
Farmington Hills, MI 48331-110, USA

Petry, Dan (Athlete, Baseball Player)
30715 Mystic Forest Dr
Farmington Hills, MI 48331, USA

Petryna-Mullins, Doreen (Athlete,
Baseball Player)
1104 Somonauk St
Sycamore, IL 60178-2521, USA

Pet Shop Boys (Music Group)
c/o Staff Member *Creative Artists Agency
(CAA-LA)*
2000 Ave Of The Stars
Los Angeles, CA 90067, USA

Petsko, Gregory A (Misc)
8 Jason Road
Belmont, MA 02478, USA

Pett, Joel (Cartoonist)
Lexington Herald-Leader
1010 New Circle Road NW
Lexington, KY 40511, USA

Pettee, Roger (Athlete, Football Player)
210 S Obrien St
Tampa, FL 33609, USA

Pettengill, Gordon H (Physicist)
Massachusetts Institute of Technology
Space Research Ctr
Cambridge, MA 02139, USA

Petter, Noel (Stylist)
1716 Hillside Dr
Glendale, CA 91208-2559, USA

Petterson, Donald K (Diplomat)
American Embassy Khartoum
#63900
APO, AE 09829, USA

Pettersson, Carl (Athlete, Golfer)
2208 Oak Lawn Way
Wake Forest, NC 27587-4700, USA

Pettibon, Raymond (Artist)
Michael Kohn Gallery
920 Colorado Ave
Santa Monica, CA 90401, USA

Pettibon, Richard A (Richie) (Athlete,
Football Player)
9628 Percussion Way
Vienna, VA 22182, USA

Pettibone, Jay (Athlete, Baseball Player)
5112 Via Marcos
Yorba Linda, CA 92887-2530, USA

Pettie, Jim (Athlete, Hockey Player)
81 Kirk Rd
Rochester, NY 14612-3301

Petties, Neal (Athlete, Football Player)
767 Jewell Dr
San Diego, CA 92113, USA

Pettiet, Christopher
9255 Sunset Blvd. #620
Los Angeles, CA 90069

Pettiford, Valarie
c/o Jeff Morrone *Jeff Morrone
Entertainment*
9350 Wilshire Blvd
Suite 224
Beverly Hills, CA 90212, USA

Pettigrew, Gary (Athlete, Football Player)
1107 W 33rd Ave
Spokane, WA 99203, USA

Pettigrew, L Eudora (Educator)
State University of New York
President's Office
Old Westbury, NY 11568, USA

Pettijohn, Francis J (Misc)
11630 Glen Arm Road
#V51
Glen Arm, MD 21057, USA

Pettinato, Rachelle (Actor)
c/o Staff Member *Select Artists Ltd (CA-
Westside Office)*
1138 12th Street
Suite 1
Santa Monica, CA 90403, USA

Pettinger, Matt (Athlete, Hockey Player)
3075 Eastdowne Rd
Victoria, BC V8R SSl, Canada

Pettini, Joe (Athlete, Baseball Player)
112 Logan Ct
Bethany, WV 26032-2016, USA

Pettis, Gary (Athlete, Baseball Player)
3129 Crestline Ct
Antioch, CA 92673-3658, USA

Pettis, Madison (Actor)
c/o Alissa Vradenburg *Untitled
Entertainment (LA)*
350 S. Beverly Dr #200
Beverly Hills, CA 90212, USA

Pettis, Madsion (Actor)
c/o Alissa Vradenburg *Untitled
Entertainment (LA)*
350 S. Beverly Dr #200
Beverly Hills, CA 90212, USA

Pettit, Bob (Athlete, Basketball Player)
7 Garden Ln
New Orleans, LA 70124-1024, USA

Pettit, Donald R (Astronaut)
2014 Country Ridge Dr
Houston, TX 77062-3636, USA

Pettit, Paul (Athlete, Baseball Player)
928 Sarazen St
Hemet, CA 92543-8057, USA

Pettit Jr, Robert L (Bob) (Basketball
Player)
7 Garden Lane
New Orleans, LA 70124, USA

Pettitte, Andy (Athlete, Baseball Player)
c/o Team Member *New York Yankees*
Yankee Stadium
161st St & River Ave
Bronx, NY 10451, USA

Pettway, Kenneth (Athlete, Football
Player)
2631 Via Verona
Lancaster, CA 9353S-2853, USA

Petty, Kyle (Race Car Driver)
Petty Enterprises
112 Byers Cfoeek Rd.
Mooresville, NC 28117, USA

Petty, Lori (Actor)
c/o Mark J. Holder *Zero Gravity
Management*
1531 14th. St
Santa Monica, CA 90404, USA

Petty, Maurice (Race Car Driver)
248 Branson Mill Rd
Randleman, NC 27317-8007, USA

Petty, Richard (Race Car Driver)
Richard Petty Museum
142 Academy St.
Randleman, NC 22737, USA

Petty, Tom (Musician, Songwriter)
c/o Staff Member *Warner Bros Records
(LA)*
P.O. Box 6868
Burbank, CA 91510, USA

Pettyfer, Alex (Actor)
c/o Simon Halls *Slate Public Relations*
9000 Sunset Blvd #915
West Hollywood, CA 90069, USA

Pettyiohn, Adam (Athlete, Baseball Player)
4626 W Addisy_n
Visalia, CA 93291-9150, USA

Pettyjohn, Adam (Athlete, Baseball Player)
717 Westwood Dr
Exeter, CA 93221, USA

Petzschler, Horst (General)
411 Elpyco St
Wichita, KS 67218-1525, USA

Petzy, Paul Angelo (Stylist)
c/o Staff Member *Ennis*
119 Braintree St
Boston, MA 02134, USA

Pevec, Katja (Actor)
c/o Anne Woodward *ROAR (LA)*
9701 Wilshire Blvd
8th Floor
Los Angeles, CA 90212, USA

Pevey, Marty (Athlete, Baseball Player)
158 Nightwind Trce
Acworth, GA 30101-5981, USA

Peviani, Bob (Athlete, Football Player)
25262 Northrup Dr
Laguna Hills, CA 92653, USA

Peyroux, Madeline (Musician, Songwriter,
Writer)
Bumstead Productions
PO Box 158
Station E
Toronto, ON M6H 4E2, CANADA

Peyton, Brad (Director)
c/o Staff Member *WME (LA)*
9601 Wilshire Blvd Fl 3
Beverly Hills, CA 90210, USA

Peyton of Yeovil, John W W
(Government Official)
Old Malt House
Hinton Saint George
Somerset TA17 8SE, UNITED KINGDOM
(UK)

Pezzano, Chuck (Writer)
27 Mountainside Terrace
Clifton, NJ 07013, USA

Pezzano, Chuck (Bowler)
27 Mountainside Ter
Clifton, NJ 07013-1107, USA

Pfaff, Judy (Artist)
Holly Solomon Gallery
175 E 79th St
#2B
New York, NY 10021, USA

Pfann, George R (Athlete, Coach, Football
Coach, Football Player)
120 Warwick Pl
Ithaca, NY 14850, USA

Pfeiffer, Dedee (Actor, Model)
c/o David Rose *Innovative Artists (LA)*
1505 10th St
Santa Monica, CA 90401, USA

Pfeiffer, Doug (Editor)
Po Box 1806
Big Bear Lake, CA 92315, USA

Pfeiffer, Michelle (Actor)
c/o Jessica Kolstad *WKT Public Relations
(WKT-LA)*
9350 Wilshire Blvd
Suite 450
Beverly Hills, CA 90212, USA

Pfeiffer, Norman (Architect)
Hardy Holzman Pfeiffer
811 W 7th St
Los Angeles, CA 90017, USA

Pfeil, Bobby (Athlete, Baseball Player)
2358 Pheasant Run Cir
Stockton, CA 95207-5210, USA

Pfeil, Mark (Golfer)
2565 Chelsea Rd
Palos Verdes Estates, CA 90274-4309,
USA

Pfister, Dan (Athlete, Baseball Player)
1436 NW 9th St
Dania, FL 33004-2332, USA

Pflug, Jo Ann (Actor)
P.O. Box 3292
Jupiter, FL 33469-1004, USA

P. Frelinghuysen, Rodney (Congressman,
Politician)
2369 Rayburn HOB
Washington, DC 20515, USA

Pfund, Lee (Athlete, Baseball Player)
130 Windsor Park Dr
Apt C214
Carol Stream, IL 60188-1998, USA

Pfund, Randy (Basketball Coach, Coach)
1015 E Sunrise Blvd #559
Apt 1206
Ft Lauderdale, FL 33304-2850, USA

P. Gibson, Christopher (Chris)
(Congressman, Politician)
502 Cannon HOB
Washington, DC 20515, USA

Phair, Liz (Actor, Musician, Songwriter)
c/o Jason Weinberg *Untitled
Entertainment (LA)*
350 S. Beverly Dr #200
Beverly Hills, CA 90212, USA

Phair, Lyle (Athlete, Hockey Player)
16256 Winchester Dr
Northville, MI 48168-2347

Pham, Tuan (Cosmonaut)
4C-1000-Soc Son
Hanoi, VIETNAM

Pham Dinh Tung, Paul J Cardinal
(Religious Leader)
Archdiocese
Toa Tong Giam Muc
Pho Nha Chung
Hanoi 40, VIETNAM

Pham Minh Man, Jean-Baptiste Cardinal
(Religious Leader)
Toa Tonggiam Muc
180 Nguyen Dink Chieu
Thanh-Pho Ho Chi Minh, VIETNAM

Phan, Dat (Actor, Comedian)
c/o Gayle Divine *Divine Management*
3822 Latrobe St
Los Angeles, CA 90031

Phan, Van Khai (Prime Minister)
Prime Minister's Office
Hoang Hoa Thum St
Hanoi, VIETNAM

Phaneuf, Al (Athlete, Football Player)
5376 Pepper Brush Cv
Apopka, FL 32703-1971, USA

Phaneuf, Dion (Athlete, Hockey Player)
Newport Sports Management
400-201 City Centre Dr
Attn Don Meehan
Mississauga, ON LSB 2T4, Canada

Phaneuf, Jean-Luc (Athlete, Hockey
Player)
230 Rue Chagall
Le Gardeur, QC JSZ 4Kl, Canada

Phantog (Mountaineer)
Wuxi Sports & Physical Culture Comm
Jiagnsu, CHINA

Phegley, Roger (Athlete, Basketball Player)
43 Timberlane Dr
Morton, IL 61550-1146, USA

Pheil, Anna (Actor)
c/o Scott Zimmerman *Evolution
Entertainment (LA)*
901 N Highland Ave
Los Angeles, CA 90038, USA

Phelan, Jack (Athlete, Basketball Player)
5504 Country Lakes Trl
Sarasota, FL 34243, USA

Phelan, Jim (Athlete, Basketball Player)
16579 Old Emmitsburg Rd
Emmitsburg, MD 21727, USA

Phelos, Travis (Athlete, Baseball Player)
PO Box 336
Wheaton, MO 64874-0336, USA

Phelps, Brian
1265 Coldwater Canyon Dr.
Beverly Hills, CA 90210

Phelps, Doug (Musician)
Mitchell Fox Mgmt
212 3rd Ave N
#301
Nashville, TN 37201, USA

Phelps, Edmund S (Economist)
45 E 89th St
New York, NY 10128, USA

Phelps, Edmund S (Nobel Prize Laureate)
45 E 89th St Apt 28B
New York, NY 10128-1230, USA

Phelps, James (Actor)
JOP Project
PO Box 9765
Coldfield
Sutton B75 5XB, UNITED KINGDOM
(UK)

Phelps, Jaycie (Athlete, Gymnast, Olympic Athlete)
Cincinnati Gymnastics
3635 Woodridge Blvd
Fairfield, OH 45014, USA

Phelps, Josh (Athlete, Baseball Player)
1503 Regal Mist Loop
Trinity, FL 34655-4974, USA

Phelps, Kelly Joe (Athlete, Football Player)
Fleming/Tamulevich Assoc
8782 Brooks Creek Dr Apt 1516
Cincinnati, OH 45249-3001, USA

Phelps, Ken (Athlete, Baseball Player)
6030 E Foothill Dr N
Paradise Valley, AZ 85253-3070, USA

Phelps, Michael (Athlete, Olympic Athlete, Swimmer)
967 Fell St
Baltimore, MD 21231-3505, USA

Phelps, Michael (Scientist)
UCLA School Of Medicine PO Box
951735 Attn Dept of Molecular Pharma
Los Angeles, CA 90095-1735, USA

Phelps, Oliver (Actor)
c/o Staff Member *JOP Project*
PO Box 9765
Sutton Coldfield B75 5XB, United Kingdom

Phelps, Richard (Athlete)
c/o Staff Member *ESPN (Main)*
ESPN Plaza
935 Middle St
Bristol, CT 06010-1001, USA

Phelps, Richard F (Digger) (Coach)
ESPN-TV
Sports Dept
ESPN Plaza 935 Middle St
Bristol, CT 06010, USA

Phelps, Tommy (Athlete, Baseball Player)
4418 Pawnee Path
Valrico, FL 33594-5529, USA

Phelps, Travis (Athlete, Baseball Player)
P.O. Box 336
Wheaton, MO 64874, USA

Phelps Jr, Ashton (Publisher)
New Orleans Times-Picayune
3800 Howard Ave
New Orleans, LA 70125, USA

Phenix, Perry Lee (Athlete, Football Player)
4849 Frankford Rd
Apt 715
Dallas, TX 75287, USA

Phifer, Mekhi (Actor)
c/o Emily Gerson Saines *Brookside Artists Management (NY)*
250 W 57th St
Suite 2303
New York, NY 10107, USA

Phifer, Roman Z (Athlete, Football Player)
P.O. Box 83215
Los Angeles, CA 90083, USA

Philaret, Patriarch (Religious Leader)
10 Osvobozdeniya St
Minsk 22004, BELARUS

Philbin, Gerry (Athlete, Football Player)
9976 Marsala Way
Delray Beach, FL 33446-9727, USA

Philbin, Joy
101 W. 67th St. #51A
New York, NY 10023-5953

Philbin, Regis (Television Host)
101 West 67th St
Apt 51A
New York, NY 10023, USA

Philbrick, Denise (Golfer)
5364 Carnegie loop
Livermore, CA 94550-7136, USA

Philcox, Todd (Athlete, Football Player)
1201 1st St N
Apt 703
Jacksonville Beach, FL 32250, USA

Philip (Prince)
Buckingham Palace
London SW1A 1AA, UNITED KINGDOM
(UK)

Philip, HRH Prince
Buckingham Palace
London, ENGLAND SW1

Philip, Primate (Religious Leader)
Antiochian Orthodox Christian Church
358 Mountain Road
Englewood, NJ 07631, USA

Philipp, Stephanie (Model)
Agentur Margit de la Berg
Icking-Isartal 82057, GERMANY

Philippoussis, Mark (Tennis Player)
Octagon
1751 Pinnacle Dr
#1500
McLean, VA 22102, USA

Philipps, Elizabeth (Busy) (Actor)
c/o Steven Levy *Framework Entertainment (LA)*
9057 Nemo St
Suite C
West Hollywood, CA 90069, USA

Philips, brandon (Athlete, Baseball Player)
586 Rowland Rd
Stone Mountain, GA 30083-4573, USA

Philips, Chuck (Journalist)
Los Angeles Times
Editorial Dept
202 W 1st St
Los Angeles, CA 90212, USA

Philips, Emo (Actor)
c/o Staff Member *OmniPop Talent Group*
10700 Ventura Blvd.
2nd Floor
Studio City, CA 91604, USA

Philips, Gina (Actor)
c/o Erik Kritzer *Kritzer Levine Wilkins Entertainment (KLWG)*
11872 La Grange Ave
1st Floor
Los Angeles, CA 90025, USA

Philips, Jeanne (Writer)

Phillios, Jason (Athlete, Baseball Player)
7111 Defranzo Loop
Fort George G Meade, MD 20755-4053, USA

Phillipoff, Harold (Athlete, Hockey Player)
446 Harrison St
Sumas, WA 98295-9613, USA

Phillippe, Ryan (Actor)
c/o David Schiff *The Schiff Company*
9107 Wilshire Blvd #600
Beverly Hills, CA 90210-5519, USA

Phillips, Anthony (Musician, Songwriter, Writer)
Solo Agency
55 Fulham High St
London SW6 3JJ, UNITED KINGDOM
(UK)

Phillips, Bijou (Actor, Model, Musician)
c/o Jennifer Merlino *Untitled Entertainment (LA)*
350 S. Beverly Dr #200
Beverly Hills, CA 90212, USA

Phillips, Bill (Writer)
High Point Media LLC
10100 Santa Monica Blvd Ste 1300
Los Angeles, CA 90067, USA

Phillips, Bobbie (Actor)
The Kelly Agency
3001 Heavenly Ridge St
Thousand Oaks, CA 91362, USA

Phillips, Brandon (Athlete, Baseball Player)
586 Rowland Rd
Stone Mountain, GA 30083, USA

Phillips, Bum (Athlete, Football Coach, Football Player)
2981 S Riverdale Ln
Goliad, TX 77963, USA

Phillips, Caryl (Writer)
Amherst College
English Dept
Amherst, MA 01002, USA

Phillips, Chris (Athlete, Hockey Player)
C A A Hockey
204-822 11 Ave SW
Attn J P Barry
Calgary, AB T2R OES, Canada

Phillips, Chynna (Actor, Musician)
1007 Montana Avenue
#230
Santa Monica, CA 90403, USA

Phillips, Davey (Athlete, Baseball Player)
12 Upper Whitmoor Dr
Weldon Springs, MO 63304-0541, USA

Phillips, Davey (Baseball Player)
12 Upper Whitmoor Dr
Saint Charles, MO 63304-0541, USA

Phillips, Eddie (Athlete, Baseball Player)
1323 S Oak Run Pl
Springfield, MO 32055-3241, USA

Phillips, Eddie Lee (Athlete, Basketball Player)
800 McCary St SW
Birmingham, AL 35211, USA

Phillips, Emo (Comedian)
Harbour Agency
63 William St
#300
East Sydney, NSW 1022, AUSTRALIA

Phillips, Ethan (Actor)
4212 McFarlane Ave
Burbank, CA 91505, USA

Phillips, Gary (Athlete, Basketball Player)
729 Country Club Dr
Kerrville, TX 94538-2618, USA

Phillips, Gene (Athlete, Basketball Player)
4630 Eldon Run
San Antonio, TX 78230-3520, USA

Phillips, Gersha (Designer)
c/o Staff Member *Paradigm (LA)*
360 N Crescent Dr
North Bldg
Beverly Hills, CA 90210, USA

Phillips, Glasgow (Director)
c/o Brett Hansen *United Talent Agency (UTA)*
9336 Civic Center Dr
Beverly Hills, CA 90210, USA

Phillips, Graham (Actor)
c/o Dannielle Thomas *Untitled Entertainment (LA)*
350 S. Beverly Dr #200
Beverly Hills, CA 90212, USA

Phillips, Grant Lee (Musician)
c/o Staff Member *Paradigm (Monterey)*
404 W Franklin St
Monterey, CA 93940, USA

Phillips, Howard (Misc)
Conservative Caucus
47 West St
Boston, MA 02111, USA

Phillips, Jack (Athlete, Baseball Player)
721 May Rd
Potsdam, NY 13676, USA

Phillips, James (Red) (Athlete, Football Player)
1948 Wicker Point Rd
Alexander City, AL 35010, USA

Phillips, Jason (Athlete, Football Player)
3001 North Boulevard
Richmond, VA 23230, USA

Phillips, Jason (Athlete, Baseball Player)
265 Katie Ln
Montoursville, PA 17754, USA

Phillips, Jason (Athlete, Baseball Player)
1777 Tara Way
San Marcos, CA 92078, USA

Phillips, Jeffrey
8436 W. Third St. #740
Los Angeles, CA 90048-4100

Phillips, Jess (Athlete, Football Player)
2820 San Antonio St
Beaumont, TX 77085, USA

Phillips, Jim (Athlete, Football Player)
67 Lakeview Dr
Unit 10D
Alexander City, AL 35010, USA

Phillips, Joe (Athlete, Football Player)
425 Barker Ave
Oregon City, OR 97045, USA

Phillips, John (Coach)
University of Tulsa
Athletic Dept
Tulsa, OK 74104, USA

Phillips, John L (Astronaut)
4422 Cedar Ridge Trail
Houston, TX 77059, USA

Phillips, John L Dr (Astronaut)
154 Canoe Cove Ln
Sandpoint, ID 83864-7968, USA

Phillips, Joseph C
8730 Sunset Blvd #480
Los Angeles, CA 90069, USA

Phillips, J R (Athlete, Baseball Player)
22410 N 74th Ln
Glendale, AZ 85351-3663, USA

Phillips, Julianne (Actor)
2227 Mandeville Canyon Road
Los Angeles, CA 90049, USA

Phillips, Kevin (Actor)
c/o Todd Eisner *Agency for the
Performing Arts (APA-LA)*
405 S Beverly Dr
Suite 500
Beverly Hills, CA 90212-4425, USA

Phillips, Kim (Stylist)
c/o Staff Member *Elite Model
Management/Atlanta*
1708 Peachtree St NW
#210
Atlanta, GA 30309, USA

Phillips, Kirk (Athlete, Football Player)
2103 E Alma Ave
Sherman, TX 75090, USA

Phillips, Lawrence (Athlete, Football
Player)
PO Box 4430
Lancaster, CA 93539-4430, USA

Phillips, Leslie (Actor)
Storm Artists Mgmt
47 Brewer St
London W1R 3FD, UNITED KINGDOM
(UK)

Phillips, Lou Diamond (Actor)
c/o JB Roberts *Thruline Entertainment*
9250 Wilshire Blvd
Ground Fl
Beverly Hills, CA 90212, USA

Phillips, Loyd (Athlete, Football Player)
General Delivery
Springdale, AR 72764, USA

Phillips, Mackenzie (Actor)
c/o Geneva Bray *GVA Talent Agency Inc*
8981 Sunset Blvd.
Suite 101
Los Angeles, CA 90069, USA

Phillips, Mel (Athlete, Football Player)
6368 Milk Wagon Ln
Miami Lakes, FL 33014, USA

Phillips, Michelie (Actor, Musician)
c/o Marc Chancer *Origin Talent Agency*
4705 Laurel Canyon #306
Studio City, CA 91607, USA

Phillips, Michelle (Actor)
c/o Merritt Blake *The Blake Agency*
23441 Malibu Colony Rd
Malibu, CA 90265, USA

Phillips, Mike (Athlete, Baseball Player)
3322 Ridgefield St
Irving, TX 75062-4157, USA

Phillips, Norma (Activist)
Mothers Against Drunk Driving
PO Box 819100
Dallas, TX 75381, USA

Phillips, Owen M (Engineer)
462 Heron Point
Chestertown, MD 21620-1681, USA

Phillips, Paul (Athlete, Baseball Player)
507 N Mine Ave
Demopolis, AL 36732-2021, USA

Phillips, Peter C B (Economist)
P.O. Box 208281
New Haven, CT 06520-8281, USA

Phillips, Phillip (Musician)
c/o Staff Member *19 Entertainment - LA*
9000 W Sunset Blvd #1574
West Hollywood, CA 90069, USA

Phillips, Princess Zara (Royalty)
Gatcombe Park
Minchinhampton
Stroud GL6 9AT, United Kingdom

Phillips, Richard (Captain)
211 River Rd
Underhill, VT 05489-9417, USA

Phillips, Ricky (Musician)
c/o Sterling Bacon *TBA Artist
Management (Atlanta)*
1111 Alderman Dr #285
Alpharetta, GA 30005-5433, USA

Phillips, Sam (Musician, Songwriter,
Writer)
Prager & Fenton
12424 Wilshire Blvd
#1000
Los Angeles, CA 90025, USA

Phillips, Scott (Musician)
Agency Group
1776 Broadway
#430
New York, NY 10019, USA

Phillips, Sean
153 Petherton Rd. Highbury
London, ENGLAND N5 2RS

Phillips, Shaun (Athlete, Football Player)
c/o Staff Member *EAG Sports
Management*
12910 Agustin Pl
Playa Vista, CA 90094, USA

Phillips, Sian (Actor)
8 Alexa Court
78 Lexham Gardens
London, ENGLAND W8 6JL, UNITED
KINGDOM (UK)

Phillips, steve (Sportscaster)
148 Mather St
Wilton, CT 06897-5011, USA

Phillips, Stone (Correspondent)
c/o Staff Member *Dateline NBC*
NBC News
30 Rockefeller Plz
New York, NY 10112, USA

Phillips, Stu (Musician)
654 Long Hollow Pike
Goodlettsville, TN 37072, USA

Phillips, Susan M (Financier, Government
Official)
Federal Reserve Board
20th St & Constitution NW
Washington, DC 20551, USA

Phillips, Tari (Basketball Player)
New York Liberty
Madison Square Garden
2 Penn Plaza
New York, NY 10121, USA

Phillips, Taylor (Athlete, Baseball Player)
594 Mein Mitchell Rd
Hiram, GA 30141-5810, USA

Phillips, Ted (Business Person, Football
Executive)
125 Ellis Ave
Libertyville, IL 60048-1957, USA

Phillips, Teresa (Basketball Player, Coach)
Tennessee State University
Athletic Dept
Nashville, TN 37209, USA

Phillips, Todd (Actor, Director, Producer,
Writer)
c/o Todd Feldman *Creative Artists Agency
(CAA-LA)*
2000 Ave Of The Stars
Los Angeles, CA 90067, USA

Phillips, Tony (Athlete, Baseball Player)
13341 E Cochise Rd
Scottsdale, AZ 85259-5442, USA

Phillips, Wade (Athlete, Coach, Football
Coach, Football Player)
6115 Norway Rd
Dallas, TX 75230, USA

Phillips, Warren H (Publisher)
Bridge Works Publications
PO Box 1798
Bridgehampton, NY 11932, USA

Phillips, William D (Nobel Prize Laureate)
13409 Chestnut Oak Dr
Gaithersburg, MD 20878-3541, USA

Phillips-Bannister, Kristie (Gymnast)
KPAC Gymnastics
2809 Amity Hill Rd
Statesville, NC 28010, USA

Phillips, Craig, and Dean (Musician)
c/o Staff Member *INO Records*
210 Jamestown Park
Suite 100
Brentwood, TN 37027, USA

Phillips Jr, J Dixon (Judge)
US Court of Appeals
100 Europa Dr
Chapel Hill, NC 27517, USA

Phillopusis, Mark (Tennis Player)
c/o Staff Member *Octagon (VA)*
1751 Pinnacle Dr #1500
McLean, VA 22102, USA

Philyaw, Charles (Athlete, Football Player)
3929 Eileen Ln
Shreveport, LA 71109, USA

Philyaw, Dino (Athlete, Football Player)
3164 Arrowhead St
Eugene, OR 97404, USA

Phinney, Davis (Athlete, Cycler, Olympic
Athlete)
470 Juniper Ave
Boulder, CO 80304-1716, USA

Phipps, Martin (Composer)
c/o Darrell Alexander *Cool Music Ltd*
1A Fishers Ln
Chiswick
London W4 1RX, England

Phipps, Michael E (Mike) (Athlete,
Football Player)
2748 NE 25th St
Lighthouse Point, FL 33064, USA

Phipps, Ogden M (Horse Racer)
1486 N Lake Way
Palm Beach, FL 33480-3031, USA

Phipps, Sam
2346 Walgrove Ave
Los Angeles, CA 90066

Phish (Music Group)
c/o Patrick Jordan *Red Light Management
(VA)*
44 Wall Street
22nd Floor
New York, NY 10005, USA

Phoebus, Thomas H (Tom) (Athlete,
Baseball Player)
2822 SW Lakemont Pl
Palm City, FL 34990-6094, USA

Phoenix, Beth (Wrestler)
c/o Kerry Rodgerson *World Wrestling
Entertainment (WWE)*
Titan Towers
1241 E Main St
Stamford, CT 06905-3857, USA

Phoenix, Joaquin (Actor)
c/o Jenni Weinman *Patricola Lust PR*
9171 Wilshire Blvd
Suite 441
Beverly Hills, CA 90210, USA

Phoenix, Rain (Actor)
c/o Josh Taylor *Val's Artist Management*
259 W 30th St
15th Floor
New York, NY 10001, USA

Phoenix, Steve (Athlete, Baseball Player)
11212 Horizon Hills Dr
El Cajon, CA 92020-8231, USA

Phoenix, Summer (Actor)
2054 Laughlin Park Dr
Los Angeles, CA 90027, USA

Physioc, Steve (Sportscaster)
32923 Brookseed Dr
Trabuco Canyon, CA 92679-4318

Pianalto, Sandra (Financier)
Federal Reserve Bank
1455 E 6th St
Cleveland, OH 44144, USA

Piano, Renzo (Architect, Nobel Prize
Laureate)
Renzo Piano Building Workshop
Via Rubens 29
Genoa 16158, ITALY

Piatkowski, Eric (Athlete, Basketball
Player)
9211 N 46th St
Phoenix, AZ 68130-2834, USA

Piatkowski, Walt (Athlete, Basketball
Player)
2453 Broadmoor Ct
Rapid City, SD 57702-8335, USA

Piatt, Adam (Athlete, Baseball Player)
1808 SE 37th Ter
Cape Coral, FL 33904-5036, USA

Piatt, Doug (Athlete, Baseball Player)
29 L St
Beaver, PA 15009, USA

Piazza, Mike (Athlete, Baseball Player)
1401 W 27th St
Miami Beach, FL 33140-4208, USA

Piazza, Vincent (Actor)
c/o Rhonda Price *Gersh (NY)*
41 Madison Ave
New York, NY 10010, USA

Picard, Alexandre (Athlete, Hockey Player)
Arena
200 W Nationwide Blvd
Columbus, OH 43215, USA

Picard, Geoffrey (Athlete, Olympic Athlete, Rower)
2020 W Lake Blvd
Tahoe City, CA 96145, USA

Picard, Robert (Athlete, Hockey Player)
4718 Grand Cvpress Cir N
Coconut Creek, FL 33073-2337

Picard, Roger (Athlete, Hockey Player)
733 Rue de Perce
Repentigny, QC J6A 7JS, Canada

Picardo, Robert (Actor, Writer)
c/o Peter Young *Sovereign Talent Group*
8421 Wilshire Blvd
Suite 200
Beverly Hills, CA 90211, USA

Picasso, Paloma (Actor, Designer)
Paloma Picasso & Cie.
41 Rue Martre
Clichy 92117, France

Picatto, Alexandra (Actor)
c/o Kari Estrin *Paradigm (LA)*
360 N Crescent Dr
North Bldg
Beverly Hills, CA 90210, USA

Piccard, Bertrand (Misc)
Media Impact
Rue de Lausanne 42
Geneva 1201, SWITZERLAND

Piccard, Jacques E J (Scientist)
Place d'Armes
Cully 1096, SWITZERLAND

Piccard, Noel
3636 Wilmington St
St. Louis, MO 63116, USA

Picciolo, Rob (Athlete, Baseball Player)
11773 Invierno Dr
San Diego, CA 92124-2814, USA

Picco, Giandomenico
1 United Nations Plaza
New York, NY 10017

Piccoli, Camille (Actor)
Cineart
36 Rue de Ponthieu
Paris 75008, FRANCE

Piccoli, Michel (Actor)
11 Rue des Lions Saint Paul
Paris 75004, FRANCE

Piccone, Lou (Athlete, Football Player)
49 S Youngs Rd
Williamsville, NY 14221, USA

Piccone, Robin (Designer, Fashion Designer)
Piccone Apparel Corp
1424 Washington Blvd
Venice, CA 90291, USA

Piccuito, Paul E (Stylist)
16 Olmstead Pl
East Norwalk, CT 06855-1318, USA

Pichardo, Hipolito (Athlete, Baseball Player)
21218 Saint Andrews Blvd
Apt 305
Boca Raton, FL 33433-2435, USA

Pichette, Dave (Athlete, Hockey Player)
4751 Rue Escoffier
Quebec, QC GIY 3J4, Canada

Pichler, David (Athlete, Diver, Olympic Athlete)
9346 SW 1st St
Plantation, FL 33324-2449, USA

Pichler, Joseph A (Business Person)
Kroger Co
1014 Vine St
Cincinnati, OH 45202, USA

Pichlikova, Lenka (Actor)
101 Knickerbocker
Stamford, CT 06907, USA

Pick, Amelie (Actor)
Artmedia
20 Ave Rapp
Paris 75007, FRANCE

Pickard, Nancy (Writer)
7258 Mastin Street
Shawnee, KS 66203-4606, USA

Pickel, William (Bill) (Athlete, Football Player)
9 Autumn Ridge Rd
South Salem, NY 10590, USA

Pickens, Bruce (Athlete, Football Player)
2811 Wickeford Mill Dr
Buford, GA 30519, USA

Pickens, Carl M (Athlete, Football Player)
623 Terrace Ave
Murphy, NC 28906, USA

Pickens, Jo Ann (Opera Singer)
Norman McCann Artists
56 Lawrie Park Gardens
London SE26 6XJ, UNITED KINGDOM (UK)

Pickens, Robert (Athlete, Football Player)
6701 S Crandon Ave
Apt 21B
Chicago, IL 60649, USA

Pickens, T Boone
8117 Preston Rd Ste 260
Dallas, TX 75225-6321, USA

Pickens Jr, James (Actor)
c/o Staff Member *Grey's Anatomy*
500 S Buena Vista St
Burbank, CA 91521, USA

Pickering, Byron (Artist)
6919 NE Highland Dr
Lincoln City, OR 97367, USA

Pickering, Calvin (Baseball Player)
Baltimore Orioles
201 Tanglewood Pl Apt 305
Tampa, FL 92604-2811, USA

Pickering, Donald
Back Court Manor House
Eastleach Glos, ENGLAND

Pickering, Jeff (Cartoonist)
c/o Staff Member *King Features Syndication*
300 W 57th St
15th Floor
New York, NY 10019-5238, USA

Pickering, Thomas R (Business Person, Diplomat)
2318 Kimbro Street
Alexandria, VA 22307, USA

Pickett, Cecil "Ricky" (Athlete, Baseball Player)
110 Wagon Wheel Rd
Willow Park, TX 76087-3135, USA

Pickett, Cindy (Actor)
c/o Andrew Howard *Incognito Management*
9440 Santa Monica Blvd #302
Beverly Hills, CA 90210, USA

Pickett, Jay
24801 Eilat St.
Woodland Hills, CA 91367-1036

Pickett, Rex
c/o Daniel Strone *Trident Media Group LLC*
41 Madison Ave
36th Floor
New York, NY 10010, USA

Pickett, Ricky (Athlete, Baseball Player)
1017 Wood Ridge Dr
Azle, TX 76020, USA

Pickett, Ryan (Athlete, Football Player)
901 N Broadway
Saint Louis, MO 63101, USA

Picketts, Hal (Athlete, Hockey Player)
410 Miles St
Asquith, SK SOK OJO, Canada

Pickford, Kevin (Athlete, Baseball Player)
6006 N Harcourt Dr
Coeur D Alene, ID 83815-8473, USA

Pickford, Mary Foundation
9171 Wilshire Blvd. #512
Beverly Hills, CA 90210

Pickitt, John L (General)
38 Sunrise Point Road
Lake Wylie, SC 29710, USA

Pickler, John M (General)
Director Army Staff
HqUSA Pentagon
Washington, DC 20310, USA

Pickler, Kellie (Musician, Reality TV Star)
c/o Larry Fitzgerald *Fitzgerald Hartley Co (Nashville)*
1908 Wedgewood Ave
Nashville, TN 37212, USA

Pickles, Christina (Actor)
137 S Westgate Ave
Los Angeles, CA 90049, USA

Pickles, Vivian
91 Regent St.
London, ENGLAND W1R 8RU

Pickren, Bradley (Actor)
c/o Philip Marcus *Clear Talent Group (LA)*
10950 Ventura Blvd
Studio City, CA 91604, USA

Pickren, Spencer (Actor)
c/o Philip Marcus *Clear Talent Group (LA)*
10950 Ventura Blvd
Studio City, CA 91604, USA

Pickup, Ronald
54 Crouch Hall Rd.
London, ENGLAND N8 8HG

Pickus, Karen (Stylist)
175 W 76th St
New York, NY 10023, USA

Pico, Jeff (Athlete, Baseball Player)
3291 Grape Way
Chico, CA 95973-9622, USA

Picone, Mario (Athlete, Baseball Player)
8876 Bay 16th St
Brooklyn, NY 11214-5902, USA

Picou, James (Horse Racer)
8961 S Hollybrook Blvd Apt 104
Pembroke Pines, FL 33025-1313, USA

Picoult, Jodi (Writer)
38 Goodfellow Rd
Hanover, NH 03755, USA

Pictor, Bruce (Musician)
Variety Artists
1924 Spring St
Paso Robles, CA 93446, USA

Pidgeon, Rebecca (Actor)
Julian Belfarge
46 Albermarle St
London W1X 4PP, UNITED KINGDOM (UK)

Piech, Ferdinand (Business Person)
Volkswagenwerk AG
Braunschweiger Str 63
Schwulper 38179, GERMANY

Piedmont, Matt (Director, Producer, Writer)
c/o Simon Millar *Rumble Media*
1620 Broadway
Santa Monica, CA 90403, USA

Pied Pipers, The
25 Cobble Creek Dr. RD #1 Box 91
Tannersville, PA 18372

Piedra, Jorge (Athlete, Baseball Player)
5608 Fairfax Dr
Frisco, TX 76262-4824, USA

Piekarski, Julie (Actor)
Phoenix Productions
#301-100 Donwood Drive
Winnipeg, MB R2G 0W1, CANADA

Pienaar, Jacobus F (Misc)
Rugby Football Union
PO Box 99
Newlands, 7725, SOUTH AFRICA

Piene, Otto (Artist)
383 Old Ayer Road
Groton, MA 01450, USA

Pierce, Adrienne (Musician)
c/o Staff Member *Paradigm (Monterey)*
404 W Franklin St
Monterey, CA 93940, USA

Pierce, Antonio (Athlete, Football Player, Sportscaster)
c/o Andy Elkin *Creative Artists Agency (CAA-LA)*
2000 Ave Of The Stars
Los Angeles, CA 90067, USA

Pierce, Chester M (Psychic)
17 Prince St
Jamaica Plain, MA 02130, USA

Pierce, David Hyde (Actor)
c/o Cara Tripicchio *WKT Public Relations (WKT-LA)*
9350 Wilshire Blvd
Suite 450
Beverly Hills, CA 90212, USA

Pierce, Ed (Athlete, Baseball Player)
543 Crestview Dr
Glendora, CA 91741-2851, USA

Pierce, Jack (Athlete, Baseball Player)
1002 Cortez St
Laredo, TX 78040, USA

Pierce, Jeff (Athlete, Baseball Player)
1046 Lantern Ln
Circle Pines, MN 55014-1335, USA

Pierce, Jeffrey (Actor)
c/o Gary Pearl *Pearl Pictures & Management*
10956 Weyburn Ave #200
Los Angeles, CA 90024, USA

Pierce, Jill (Actor)
Extreme Team Productions
15941 S Harlem
#319
Tinley Park, IL 60477, USA

Pierce, John (Musician)
c/o Staff Member *Paradigm (Monterey)*
404 W Franklin St
Monterey, CA 93940, USA

Pierce, Jonathan (Musician)
Muse Assoc
330 Franklin Road
#135-8
Brentwood, TN 37027, USA

Pierce, Lincoln (Cartoonist)
United Feature Syndicate
200 Madison Ave
New York, NY 10016, USA

Pierce, Paul (Athlete, Basketball Player)
79 Winter St
Lincoln, MA 01773-3502, USA

Pierce, Randy (Athlete, Hockey Player)
178 Five Arches Dr RR 3
Pakenham, ON K0A 2X0, Canada

Pierce, Ron (Horse Racer)
PO Box 361
Clarksburg, NJ 08510-0361, USA

Pierce, Stack (Actor)
Haeggstrom Office
11288 Ventura Blvd
#620
Studio City, CA 91604, USA

Pierce, Tamora (Writer)
612 Westcott St
Syracuse, NY 13210-2536, USA

Pierce, Tony (Athlete, Baseball Player)
6119 Brittany Ct
Columbus, GA 31909-4247, USA

Pierce, Wendell (Actor)
c/o Staff Member *Paradigm (LA)*
360 N Crescent Dr
North Bldg
Beverly Hills, CA 90210, USA

Pierce, W William (Billy) (Athlete, Baseball Player)
1321 Baileys Crossing Dr
Lemont, IL 60439, USA

Pierce-Roberts, Tony (Cinematographer)
1 Princes Garden
London W5 1SD, UNITED KINGDOM (UK)

Pierces, The (Music Group)
c/o Staff Member *Paradigm (Monterey)*
404 W Franklin St
Monterey, CA 93940, USA

Pierce The Veil (Music Group, Musician)
c/o Staff Member *Equal Vision Records*
P.O. Box 38202
Albany, NY 12203-8202, USA

Piercy, Marge (Writer)
PO Box 1473
Wellfleet, MA 02667, USA

Pieri, Damon (Athlete, Football Player)
1120 West Tuckey Lane
Phoenix, AZ 85013-1049, USA

Pierpoint, Eric (Actor)
2199 Topanga Skyline Dr
Topanga, CA 90290, USA

Pierre, Andrew J (Scientist)
Carnegie Endowment for Peace
1779 Massachusetts NW
Washington, DC 20036, USA

Pierre, Juan (Athlete, Baseball Player)
6148 NW 65th Ter
Parkland, FL 33067-1553, USA

Pierre of Normandy, Abbe (Activist, Religious Leader)
La Halte d'Emmaus
Esteville 76690, FRANCE

Piers, Julie (Golfer)
5019 SW Hammock Creek Dr
Palm City, FL 34990-7909, USA

Piersall, James A (Jimmy) (Athlete, Baseball Player)
1105 Oakview Dr
Wheaton, IL 60187-3026, USA

Piersoll, Chris (Athlete, Baseball Player)
4417 Groveland Ave
Sarasota, FL 34231, USA

Pierson, Geoff (Actor)
Ambrosio/Mortimer
165 W 46th St
New York, NY 10036, USA

Pierson, John (Athlete, Hockey Player)
3 Steepletree
Wayland, MA 01178, USA

Pierson, Kate (Musician)
Direct Management Group
947 N La Cienega Blvd
#2
Los Angeles, CA 90069, USA

Pierson, Pete (Athlete, Football Player)
19130 Beckett Dr
Odessa, FL 33556, USA

Pierzynski, Anthony J (AJ) (Athlete, Baseball Player)
2139 N Clifton Ave
Chicago, IL 60614-4115, USA

Pieterse, Sasha (Actor)
c/o Ryan Martin *Agency for the Performing Arts (APA-LA)*
405 S Beverly Dr
Suite 500
Beverly Hills, CA 90212-4425, USA

Pietkiewicz, Stan (Athlete, Basketball Player)
2213 Venetian Way
Winter Park, Fl 32789-1215, USA

Pietrangeli, Nicola (Tennis Player)
Via Eustachio Manfredi
Rome 15, ITALY

Pietrangelo, Frank (Athlete, Hockey Player)
6371 Maretta Dr
Niagara Falls, ON L2J 4H7, Canada

Pietrus, Mickael (Basketball Player)
Golden State Warriors
1001 Broadway
Oakland, CA 94607, USA

Pietrus, Mikael
13420 Bonica Way
Windermere, FL 34786-5701, USA

Pietruski Jr, John M (Business Person)
27 Paddock Lane
Colts Neck, NJ 07722, USA

Pietrzak, Jim (Athlete, Football Player)
9800 4th St N
Suite 400
Saint Petersburg, FL 33702, USA

Pietrzykowski, Zbigniew (Boxer)
Ul Gomicza 5
Bielsko-Blata 43-409, POLAND

Pietsch, Barbara (Stylist)
126 Powell Lane
Upper Darby, PA 19082, USA

Pietz, Amy (Actor)
c/o Scott Howard *Howard Entertainment*
10850 Wilshire Blvd
Suite 1260
Los Angeles, CA 90024, USA

Pifferini, Bob Sr (Athlete, Football Player)
4160 Jade St
Spc 65
Capitola, CA 95010, USA

Pigford, Eva (Model, Reality TV Star)
c/o Joseph Babineaux *Perspective Public Relations*
9107 Wilshire Blvd
Suite 450
Beverly Hills, CA 90210, USA

Pigford, Eva (Marcille) (Actor, Model)
c/o Joseph (Joe) Rice *Abrams Artists Agency (LA)*
9200 Sunset Blvd
11th Floor
Los Angeles, CA 90069, USA

Piggott, Lester K (Jockey)
Beech Tree House
Tostock Bury Saint Edmonds
Suffolk 1P20 9NY, UNITED KINGDOM (UK)

Pignatano, Joe (Athlete, Baseball Player)
150 78th St
Brooklyn, NY 11209-2914, USA

Pignatiello, Carmen (Athlete, Baseball Player)
4087 Milford Ln
Aurora, IL 60504-2059, USA

Pignatiellp, Carmen (Athlete, Baseball Player)
4087 Milford Ln
Aurora, IL 60504, USA

Pi-Gonzalez, Amaury (Sportscaster)
4940 Adagio Ct
Fremont, CA 94538-3201, USA

Pigott, Mark C (Business Person)
PACCAR Inc
777 106th Ave NE
Bellevue, WA 98004, USA

Pigott, Sebastian (Actor)
c/o Andrew Edwards *Wishlab*
2225-A Hyperion Ave
Los Angeles, CA 90027, USA

Pigott-Smith, Tim (Actor)
P F D Drury House
34-43 Russell St
London WC2B 5HA, UNITED KINGDOM (UK)

Pikaizen, Viktor A (Musician)
Chekhova Str 31/22
#37
Moscow, RUSSIA

Pike, Deborah (Stylist)
341 Scottswood Rd
Riverside, IL 60546, USA

Pike, Gary (Musician)
10031 Benares Place
Sun Valley, CA 91352, USA

Pike, Jim (Musician)
MPI Talent Agency
9255 Sunset Blvd
#407
Los Angeles, CA 90069, USA

Pike, Rosamund (Actor)
c/o Dallas Smith *United Agents*
12-26 Lexington St
London W1F OLE, UK

Pike, Rosamund (Actor)
c/o Shelley Browning *Magnolia Entertainment (LA)*
9595 Wilshire Blvd
Suite 601
Beverly Hills, CA 90212, USA

Pikser, Jeremy (Actor)
c/o Margaret Riley *Brillstein Entertainment Partners*
9150 Wilshire Blvd #350
Beverly Hills, CA 90212, USA

Pilarczyk, Daniel E (Religious Leader)
100 E 8th St
Cincinnati, OH 45202, USA

Pileggi, Mitch (Actor)
c/o Joel King *Pakula/King & Associates*
9229 Sunset Blvd
Suite 315
Los Angeles, CA 90069, USA

Pilic, Nicki (Tennis Player)
DTB
Otto-Fleck-Schneise 8
Frankfurt/Maim 60528, GERMANY

Piligian, Craig (Producer)
c/o Staff Member *WmE2 (WMA-LA)*
1 William Morris Pl
Beverly Hills, CA 90212, USA

Pilkey, Dav (Writer)
Scholastic Press
555 Broadway
New York, NY 10012, USA

Pilkey, Dave (Writer)
7406 Summer Trail Dr
Sugarland, TX 77479, USA

Pilkis, Simon J (Physicist)
State University of New York
Health Sciences Center
Stony Brook, NY 11794, USA

Pill, Alison (Actor)
c/o Joanna (Joanie) Burstein *Burstein Company, The*
15304 Sunset Blvd
suite 208
Pacific Palisades, CA 90272, USA

Pilla, Anthony M (Religious Leader)
Catholic Bishops National Conference
3211 4th St
Washington, DC 20017, USA

Pillath, Roger (Athlete, Football Player)
N3623 Lepinsky Rd
Peshtigo, WI 54157, USA

Piller, Zach (Athlete, Football Player)
3907 Dunleer Ct
Tallahassee, FL 32309, USA

Pillers, Lawrence (Athlete, Football Player)
4305 Handing Moss Rd
Jackson, MS 39206, USA

Pilliod Jr, Charles J (Business Person, Diplomat)
494 Saint Andrews Dr
Akron, OH 44303, USA

Pillow, Ray (Musician)
900 Harpeth Trace Dr
Nashville, TN 37221, USA

Pilon, Rich (Athlete, Hockey Player)
RR 8 LCD Main
Saskatoon, SK S7K 1M2, Canada

Pilotdrift (Music Group)
c/o Staff Member *Paradigm (Monterey)*
404 W Franklin St
Monterey, CA 93940, USA

Pilote, Pierre P (Athlete, Hockey Player)
Hockey Hall of Fame Brookfield Place
30 Yonge St
Toronto, ON MSE 1X8, CANADA

Pilska, Paul (Opera Singer)
George M Martynuk
352 7th Ave
New York, NY 10001, USA

Pimenta, Simon Ignatius Cardinal (Religious Leader)
Archbishop's House
21 Nathalal Parekh Marg
Mumbai, MS 400 039, INDIA

Pimental, Nancy (Actor, Writer)
c/o Staff Member *WME (LA)*
9601 Wilshire Blvd Fl 3
Beverly Hills, CA 90210, USA

Pinal, Silvia
Av. de las Fuentas 629 Pedregal de San Angel
Mexico DF, MEXICO

Pincay, Laffit (Horse Racer)
719 Carriage House Dr
Arcadia, CA 91006-2010, USA

Pinchak, Jimmy (Jax) (Actor)
c/o Staff Member *Agency for the Performing Arts (APA-LA)*
405 S Beverly Dr
Suite 500
Beverly Hills, CA 90212-4425, USA

Pinchot, Bronson (Actor)
10061 Riverside Dr
Toluca Lake, CA 91602, USA

Pinckney, Ed (Athlete, Basketball Player)
3350 SW 27th Ave
Apt 1202
Miami, FL 33133-5326, USA

Pinckney, Sandra (Chef, Television Host)
c/o Staff Member *Food Network, The*
1180 Ave of the Americas Fl 11
New York, NY 10036, USA

Pinder, Cyril (Athlete, Football Player)
7137 S Luella Ave
Chicago, IL 60649, USA

Pinder, Gary (Athlete, Hockey Player)
320 39 Ave SW
Calgary, AB T2S 0W7, Canada

Pinder, Gerry (Athlete, Hockey Player)
320 39th Ave. SW
Calgary, AB T2S 0W7, Canada

Pinder, Michael (Mike) (Misc)
Moody Blues
53-55 High St
Cobham
Surrey KT11 3DP, UNITED KINGDOM (UK)

Pine, Chris (Actor)
c/o John Carrabino *John Carrabino Management*
5900 Wilshire Blvd Fl 4 #406
Los Angeles, CA 90036, USA

Pine, Courtney (Musician)
Elizabeth Rush Agency
100 Park St
#4
Montclair, NJ 07042, USA

Pine, Phillip (Actor)
3972 Acapulco Ave
Las Vegas, NV 89121-6104, USA

Pine, Robert (Actor)
4212 Ben Ave
Studio City, CA 91604, USA

Pineau-Valencienne, Didler (Business Person)
Schneider
64/70 J Baptiste Clement
Boulogne-Billancourt 92646, FRANCE

Pineda, Salvador (Actor)
c/o Staff Member *TV Azteca*
Periferico Sur 4121
Colonia Fuentes del Pedregal
DF CP 14141, Mexico

Pinero, Joel (Athlete, Baseball Player)
9406 Lake Washington Blvd NE
Bellevue, WA 98004, USA

Pines, Alexander (Misc)
University of California
Chemistry Dept
Hildebrand Hall
Berkeley, CA 94720, USA

Pinette, John
c/o Staff Member *ICM Partners (ICM-LA)*
10250 Constellation Blvd Fl 7
Los Angeles, CA 90067, USA

Pingel, John S (Athlete, Football Player)
80 Celestial Way
Apt 203
Juno Beach, FL 33408, USA

Pinger, Mark (Swimmer)
5201 Orduna Dr
#6
Coral Gables, FL 33146, USA

Ping Lu, Kun (Misc)
Beth Israel Deaconess Medical Center
3300 Brookline Ave
Boston, MA 02215, USA

Pingree, Chellie (Congressman, Politician)
1318 Longworth HOB
Washington, DC 20515, USA

Piniella, Louis V (Lou) (Athlete, Baseball Player, Coach)
1005 Taray De Avila
Tampa, FL 33613-1099, USA

Pink, Steve
c/o Gabrielle (Gaby) Morgerman *WME (LA)*
9601 Wilshire Blvd Fl 3
Beverly Hills, CA 90210, USA

Pinkel, Donald P (Misc)
275 Martene Dr
San Luis Obispo, CA 93405, USA

Pinkel, Gary (Coach, Football Coach)
University of Missouri
Athletic Dept
Columbia, MO 64211, USA

Pinker, Steven (Scientist, Writer)
Harvard, FAS Department Of Psychology
William James Hall 970
33 Kirland St
Cambridge, MA 02138, USA

Pinkett, Allen (Athlete, Football Player)
2026 Tuam St
Houston, TX 77004-1349, USA

Pinkett Smith, Jada (Actor, Producer, Writer)
c/o Miguel Melendez *Overbrook Entertainment*
450 N Roxbury Dr
4th Floor
Beverly Hills, CA 90210, USA

Pink Floyd (Music Group, Musician)
370 City Rd. Islington
London EC1V 2QA, UK

Pinkham Jr, Daniel R (Composer)
150 Chilton St
Cambridge, MA 02138, USA

Pinkins, Tonya (Actor)
Innovative Artists
1505 10th St
Santa Monica, CA 90401, USA

Pink (P!nk) (Musician)
6902 Wildlife Rd
Malibu, CA 90265, USA

Pinkston, Rob (Actor)
c/o Staff Member *Mark Robert Management*
2208 Patricia Ave
Los Angeles, CA 90064, USA

Pinkston, Ryan (Actor)
c/o Staff Member *Morra Brezner Steinberg & Tenenbaum (MBST) Entertainment*
345 N Maple Dr
Suite 200
Beverly Hills, CA 90210, USA

Pinkston, Todd (Athlete, Football Player)
1 Novacare Way
Philadelphia, PA 19145, USA

Pinmonkey (Music Group)
c/o Staff Member *WmE2 (WMA-TN)*
1600 Division St
Suite 300
Nashville, TN 37203, USA

Pinner, Artose (Athlete, Football Player)
102 Big Blue Ct
Hopkinsville, KY 42240, USA

Pinney, Ray (Athlete, Football Player)
6529B NE Windermere Rd
Seattle, WA 98105, USA

Pinnock, Trevor (Conductor, Musician)
35 Gloucester Crescent
London NW1 7DL, UNITED KINGDOM (UK)

Pino, Danny (Actor)
c/o Geordie Frey *GEF Entertainment*
122 N Clark Dr
Suite 401
Los Angeles, CA 90048, USA

Pinone, John (Athlete, Basketball Player)
108 Riverview Rd
Glastonbury, CT 06033-3140, USA

Pinos, Carmen (Architect)
Av Diagonal 490
#3/2
Barcelona 08006, SPAIN

Pinsent, Gordon (Actor)
c/o Steve Lovett *Lovett Management*
1327 Brinkley Ave
Los Angeles, CA 90049, USA

Pinsky, Dr. Drew (Doctor, Reality TV Star, Television Host)
2050 Huntington Dr #D
S Pasadena, CA 91030, USA

Pinsky, Robert N (Writer)
Boston University
Boston University 236 Bay State Rd Attn English Dept
Boston, MA 02215-1403, USA

Pinson, Julie (Actor)
13576 Cheltenham Dr
Sherman Oaks, CA 91423, USA

Pinson, Vada
710 31st St.
Oakland, CA 94609

Pintauro, Danny (Actor)
c/o Arnold M Preston *Preston Entertainment Inc*
8033 Sunset Blvd #7250
Los Angeles, CA 90046, USA

Pintilie, Lucian (Director)
44 Mihail Kogalniceanu Blvd
Bucharest, ROMANIA

Pinto, Freida (Actor)
c/o Staff Member *Performers Management*
258 E 3rd St #B
Vancouver BC V7W 1E7, CANADA

Pintscher, Matthias (Composer)
Van Walsum Mgmt
4 Addison Bridge Place
London W14 8XP, UNITED KINGDOM (UK)

Piotrowski, Tom (Athlete, Basketball Player)
80 Clarks Landing Rd
Port Republic, NJ 08241-9741, USA

Piovanelli, Silvano Cardinal (Religious Leader)
Piazzi S Giovanni 3
Florence 50129, ITALY

Piper, Billie (Actor)
c/o Staff Member *Rights House, The*
Drury House
34-43 Russell St
London WC2B 5HA, UK

Piper, Jacki (Actor)
Lengford Assoc
17 Westfields Ave
Barnes
London SW13 0AT, UNITED KINGDOM
(UK)

Piper, Rowdy Roddy (Actor, Athlete, Wrestler)
Flying Noodles Inc.
Roderic Toombs
13110 SW Whitmore Rd
Hillosboro, OR 97123, USA

Pipes, Leah (Actor)
c/o Jason Newman *Untitled Entertainment (LA)*
350 S. Beverly Dr #200
Beverly Hills, CA 90212, USA

Pipes, R Byron (Educator)
Po Box 1147
Hudson, OH 44236, USA

Pipettes, The (Music Group)
c/o Staff Member *Paradigm (Monterey)*
404 W Franklin St
Monterey, CA 93940, USA

Pippen, Scottie (Basketball Player, Olympic Athlete)
2571 Del Lago Dr
Fort Lauderdale, FL 33316-2303, USA

Pippig, Uta (Athlete, Olympic Athlete, Track Athlete)
Postfach 1249
Straus berg, D 15331, USA

Piquet, Nelson (Race Car Driver)
Autodromo
SEN/CDPM
Rua da Gasolina #01
Brasilia, DF 7007-400, BRAZIL

Pirae, Marcus Jean (Actor)
c/o Tom Parziali *Visionary Entertainment*
1558 N Stanley Ave
Los Angeles, CA 90046, USA

Piraro, Dan (Cartoonist)
United Feature Syndicate
200 Madison Ave
New York, NY 10016, USA

Pirates of the Mississippi
Box 17087
Nashville, TN 37217

Pirelli, Leopoldo (Business Person)
Via Gaetano Negri 10
Milan 20123, ITALY

Pires, Alexandre (Musician)
c/o Staff Member *BMG*
1540 Broadway
New York, NY 10036, USA

Pires, Mary Joao (Musician)
Columbia Artists Mgmt Inc
165 W 57th St
New York, NY 10019, USA

Pires, Pedro V R (General, Prime Minister)
PAICV
CP 22
Praia
Santiago, CAPE VERDE

Pires de Miranda, Pedro (Government Official)
Avenida da India 10
Lisbon 1300, PORTUGAL

Pirie, Lockwood (Athlete, Olympic Athlete, Sailor)
5644 Ravenspur Dr Apt 319
Rancho Palos Verdes, CA 90275-3585, USA

Pirkl, Greg (Athlete, Baseball Player)
6822 Emerald Bay Ln
Indianapolis, IN 46237-5063, USA

Pirner, Dave (Musician, Songwriter, Writer)
Monterey Peninsula Artists
509 Hartnell St
Monterey, CA 93940, USA

Piro, Stephanie (Cartoonist)
Po Box 605
Hampton, NH 03843, USA

Pirok, Pauline (Athlete, Baseball Player)
13636 86th Ave
Orland Park, IL 60462-1612, USA

Pirri, Jim
9300 Wilshire Blvd. #555
Beverly Hills, CA 90212

Pirtle, Gerry (Athlete, Baseball Player)
30306 E 59th St
Broken Arrow, OK 74014-8434, USA

Pirus, Alex (Athlete, Hockey Player)
15W222 Concord St
Elmhurst, IL 60126-5326

Pisanos, Steve (General)
17717 Fonticello Way
San Diego, CA 92128-1848, USA

Pisarcik, Joe (Athlete, Football Player)
27 Compass Cir
Mount Laurel, NJ 08054, USA

Pisarkiewicz, Steve (Athlete, Football Player)
10442 Carlson Cir
Clermont, FL 34711, USA

Pischetsrider, Bernd (Business Person)
Bayerishe Motoren Werke
Petuelring 130
Munich 80788, GERMANY

Pisciotta, Marc (Athlete, Baseball Player)
867 Village Greene NW
Marietta, GA 30064, USA

Piscopo, Joe (Actor, Comedian)

Piskula, Grace (Athlete, Baseball Player)
415 Cherry Hill Dr
Racine, WI 53406-3523, USA

pissarides, Christopher (Nobel Prize Laureate)
ch-ondon Scho()) of Economics Houghton Street Attn: Norman So_snow Chair in Economics
London wC2A 2AE, England

Pister, Karl S (Educator)
University of California
Chancellor's Office
Santa Cruz, CA 95064, USA

Pistone, Tom (Race Car Driver)
7858 Old Concord Rd.
Charlotte, NC 28213, USA

Pitbull (Musician)
c/o Michael Becker *Imprint Entertainment*
100 Universal City Plaza
Bungalow #7152
Universal City, CA 91608, USA

Pitchford, Dean
1701 Queens Rd
Los Angeles, CA 90069

Pitcock, Joan (Golfer)
341 E Lester Ave
Fresno, CA 93720-1615, USA

Pithart, Petr (Government Official)
Senate
Vakdstejnske Nam 4
Prague 118 11, CZECH REPUBLIC

Pitillo, Maria (Actor)
c/o Jonathan Howard *Innovative Artists (LA)*
1505 10th St
Santa Monica, CA 90401, USA

Pitino, Rick (Basketball Coach, Coach)
214 Mockingbird Gardens Drive
Louisville, KY 40207, USA

Pitlick, Lance (Athlete, Hockey Player)
5010 Shenandoah Ln N
Minneapolis, MN 55446-2120

Pitlock, Skip (Athlete, Baseball Player)
215 Prospect St
Seguin, TX 78155, USA

Pitman, Jennifer S (Race Car Driver)
Weathercock House
Upper Lamboum Hungerford
Berks RG17 8QT, UNITED KINGDOM
(UK)

Pitoc, John Paul (Actor)
c/o Amy Slomovits *Evolution Entertainment (LA)*
9320 Wilshire Blvd
Suite 202
Beverly Hills, CA 90212, USA

Pitoc, J P
1836 Courtney Terr
Los Angeles, CA 90046, USA

Pitou, Penny
100 Potter Hill Rd
Gilford, NH 03249-6802, USA

Pitou Zimmerman, Penny (Skier)
560 Sanborn Road
Sanbornton, NH 03269, USA

Pitt, Brad (Actor)
c/o Cynthia Pett-Dante *Brillstein Entertainment Partners*
9150 Wilshire Blvd #350
Beverly Hills, CA 90212, USA

Pitt, Eugene (Musician)
Paramount Entertainment
PO Box 12
Far Hills, NJ 07931, USA

Pitt, Michael (Actor)
c/o Jason Weinberg *Untitled Entertainment (LA)*
350 S. Beverly Dr #200
Beverly Hills, CA 90212, USA

Pitt, William
9 rue Jean Mermoz
Paris, FRANCE F-75008

Pittaro, Chris (Athlete, Baseball Player)
42 Pintinalli Dr
Trenton, NJ 08619-1558, USA

Pittenger, Mark F (Scientist)
Osrins Therapeutics
2001 Aliceanna St
Baltimore, MD 21231, USA

Pittis, Domenic (Athlete, Hockey Player)
5243 Barron Dr NW
Calgarv, AB T2L 1T7, Canada

Pittman, Charles (Athlete, Basketball Player)
16286 N 29th Dr
Phoenix, AZ 85053-3004, USA

Pittman, Danny (Football Player)
New York Giants
University of Wyoming Attn: Alumni Association
Laramie, WY 82071, USA

Pittman, Joe (Athlete, Baseball Player)
809 McKinnon Dr
Columbus, GA 31907-6508, USA

Pittman, R F (Publisher)
Tampa Tribune
202 S Parker St
Tampa, FL 33606, USA

Pittman, Richard A (General, War Hero)
-^ Pittman, Richard 1217 Chaparral Way
Stockton, CA 95209-1413, USA

Pittman, Sheldon (Race Car Driver)
Morgan McClure Racing
26502 Newbanks
Abingdon, VA 24210, USA

Pittman Jr, James A (Misc)
5 Ridge Dr
Birmingham, AL 35213, USA

Pitts, Chester (Athlete, Football Player)
c/o Staff Member *EAG Sports Management*
12910 Agustin Pl
Playa Vista, CA 90094, USA

Pitts, Frank (Athlete, Football Player)
8249 S Laredo Ave
Baton Rouge, LA 70811, USA

Pitts, Gaylen (Athlete, Baseball Player)
214 Rocky Bluff Ln
Mountain Home, AR 72653-7186, USA

Pitts, Greg
c/o Amy Slomovits *Evolution Entertainment (LA)*
9320 Wilshire Blvd
Suite 202
Beverly Hills, CA 90212, USA

Pitts, Hugh (Athlete, Football Player)
3612 Short St
Greenville, TX 75401, USA

Pitts, Jacob (Actor)
c/o Robert Stein *Robert Stein Management*
PO Box 3797
Beverly Hills, CA 90212, USA

Pitts, John (Athlete, Football Player)
4899 W Tyson St
Chandler, AZ 85226, USA

Pitts, Robert (R C) (Athlete, Basketball Player)
12655 E Milburn Ave
Baton Rouge, LA 70815, USA

Pitts, Ron (Athlete, Football Player)
3811 Davids Rd
Agoura Hills, CA 91301, USA

Pitts, Ron (Sportscaster)
Fox TV
Sports Dept
205 W 67th St
New York, NY 10021, USA

Pitts, Tyrone S (Religious Leader)
Progressive National Baptist Convention
601 50th St NE
Washington, DC 20019, USA

Pittsley, Jim (Athlete, Baseball Player)
102 Dixon Ave
Du Bols, PA 15801-1215, USA

Pivec, Dave (Athlete, Football Player)
1288 Fenwick Garth
Arnold, MD 21012, USA

Piven, Jeremy (Actor)
c/o Jon Rubinstein *Authentic Talent and Literary Management*
45 Main St
Suite 1004
Brooklyn, NY 11201, USA

Pivonka, Michal (Athlete, Hockey Player)
8312 Grand Estuary Trl Unit 102
Bradenton, FL 34212-4264

Pixies (Music Group, Musician)
c/o John Branigan *WME (LA)*
9601 Wilshire Blvd Fl 3
Beverly Hills, CA 90210, USA

Piza, Arthur Luiz de (Artist)
16 Rue Dauphine
Paris 75006, FRANCE

Pizarro, Artur (Musician)
c/o Staff Member *Musicians Corporate Management*
PO Box 825
Highland, NY 12528, USA

Pizarro, Juan (Athlete, Baseball Player)
2262 Ave Borinquen
San Juan, PR 00915-4421, USA

Piziou, Peter
16 Belsize Park
London, ENGLAND NW3 4ES

Pizzarelli, John (Musician)
c/o Staff Member *Challenge Records International*
Noorderweg 68
Hilversum 1221 AB, The Netherlands

Pizzo, Angelo (Director, Producer, Writer)
c/o David Greenblatt *Greenlit*
1800 N Highland Ave
Suite 500
Los Angeles, CA 90028, USA

PJ & Duncan
PO Box 122Ashford
Kent, ENGLAND TN27 9BZ

Pjetray, Brittany (Beauty Pageant Winner)
641 Hollylake Rd
Aiken, SC 29803, USA

Place, Marcella (Athlete, Hockey Player, Olympic Athlete)
141 Meadow View Rd
Orinda, CA 94563-3250, USA

Place, Mary Kay (Actor)
c/o Staff Member *Gersh (LA)*
9465 Wilshire Blvd
Suite 600
Beverly Hills, CA 90212, USA

Placebo (Music Group)
Elevator Lady Ltd
4 South Street
Epsom
Surrey KT18 7PF, UNITED KINGDOM

Plachta, Leonard E (Educator)
Central Michigan University
President's Office
Mount Pleasant, MI 48859, USA

Placido, Michele
. 5200 via San Cornelia
Formello-RM, ITALY 00060

Pladson, Gordon (Gordie) (Athlete, Baseball Player)
19087 87a Ave
Surrey, BC V4N 3G5, Canada

Plager, Bob (Athlete, Hockey Player)
St Louis Blues
1401 Clark Ave
Saint Louis, MO 63103-2700

Plager, Robert B (Bob) (Athlete, Coach, Hockey Player)
362 Branchport Dr
Chesterfied, MO 63017-2902

Plager, S Jay (Judge)
US Court of Appeals
7171 Madison Place NW
Washington, DC 20439, USA

Plainic, Zoran (Basketball Player)
New Jersey Nets
390 Murray Hill Parkway
East Rutherford, NJ 07073, USA

Plain White T's (Music Group)
c/o Sharrin Summers *Hollywood Records*
500 S Buena Vista St
Burbank, CA 91521, USA

Plakson, Suzie (Actor)
302 N La Brea Ave
#363
Los Angeles, CA 90036, USA

plamondon, Gerry (Athlete, Hockey Player)
450 Rue de Montreal
Sherbrooke, QC J 1H 1E5, Canada

Plana, Tony (Actor)
c/o Todd Eisner *Agency for the Performing Arts (APA-LA)*
405 S Beverly Dr
Suite 500
Beverly Hills, CA 90212-4425, USA

Plan B (Music Group)
c/o Staff Member *Paradigm (Monterey)*
404 W Franklin St
Monterey, CA 93940, USA

Planchon, Roger (Director, Writer)
Teatre National Populaire
8 Pl Lazare Goujon
Villeurbanne 69627, FRANCE

Plank, Doug (Athlete, Football Player)
12622 E Paradise Dr
Scottsdale, AZ 85259, USA

Plank, Ed (Eddie) (Athlete, Baseball Player)
1353 Leawood Rd
Englewood, FL 34223-1714, USA

Plank, Kevin (Business Person)
Under Armour, Inc.
1020 Hull St
Suite 300
Baltimore, MD 21230, USA

Plank, Raymond (Business Person)
Apache Corp
2000 Post Oak Blvd
Houston, TX 77056, USA

Plano, Richard J (Physicist)
PO Box 5306
Sommerset, NJ 08875, USA

Plant, Robert (Musician, Songwriter)
c/o Rod MacSween *International Talent Booking*
74A Charlotte St
London W1T 4QJ, UNITED KINGDOM (UK)

Plante, Bruce (Cartoonist)
Chattanooga Times
Editorial Dept
100 E 11th St #400
Chattanooga, TN 37402, USA

Plante, Cam (Athlete, Hockey Player)
36 Frobisher Cres
Brandon, MB R7A 5B9, Canada

Plante, Dan (Athlete, Hockey Player)
5 Gillingham Ct
Algonquin, IL 60102-6285

Plante, Derek (Athlete, Hockey Player)
5325 Roosevelt Dr
Hermantown, MN 55811-3679

Plante, Jacques (Athlete, Hockey Player)

Plante, Pierre (Athlete, Hockey Player)
25 Rue Ewing
Salaberry-De-Valleyfield, QC J6S 2X8, Canada

Plante, Tyler (Athlete, Hockey Player)
36 Frobisher Cres
Brandon, MB R7A 5B9, Canada

Plante, William M (Correspondent)
CBS-TV
News Dept
2020 M St NW
Washington, DC 20036, USA

Plantenberg, Erik (Athlete, Baseball Player)
1846 Creekside Dr NE
Owatonna, MN 55060-3973, USA

Plantery, Mark (Athlete, Hockey Player)
ON182 Alexander Dr
Geneva, IL 60134-6001

Plantier, Phil (Athlete, Baseball Player)
San Diego Padres PO Box 122000 Attn Coaching Staf
San Diego, CA 92112-2000, USA

Plantu (Cartoonist)
Le Monde
Editorial Dept
21 Bis Rue Claude Bernard
Paris 75005, FRANCE

Planutis, Jerry (Athlete, Football Player)
3776 Stadium Dr
Bridgman, MI 49106, USA

Plaskett, Thomas G (Business Person)
5215 N O'Connor Blvd
#1070
Irving, TX 75039, USA

Plater-Zyberk, Elizabeth M (Architect)
Duany & Plater-Zyberk Architects
1023 SW 25th Ave
Miami, FL 33135, USA

Platini, Michel
90 av. des Champs-Elysees
Paris, FRANCE F-75008

Platinli, Michel (Soccer Player)
World Cup Organization
17-21 Ave Gen Mangin
Paris Cedex 75024, FRANCE

Platinum Blonde
Box 1223 Sta. F
Toronto, CANADA Ont.M4Y 2T

Platon, Nicolas (Archaeologist)
Leof Alexandras 126
Athens 11471, GREECE

Platov, Yevgeni (Dancer)
Connecticut Skating Center
300 Alumni Road
Newington, CT 06111, USA

Platt, David (Soccer Player)
FourFourTwo
52 Victoria Street
McMahons Point NSW 2060, AUSTRALIA

Platt, Howard (Actor)
9200 Sunset Blvd #1130
Los Angeles, CA 90069, USA

Platt, Kenneth A (Doctor)
11435 Quivas Way
Westminster, CO 80234, USA

Platt, Lewis E (Lew) (Business Person)
Hewlett-Packard Co
3000 Hanover St
Palo Alto, CA 94304, USA

Platt, Nicholas (Diplomat)
131 E 69th St
New York, NY 10021, USA

Platt, Oliver (Actor, Producer)
c/o Tamar Salup *I/D PR (NY)*
150 W 30th St
19th Floor
New York, NY 10001, USA

Platters
2756 N. Green Valley Parkway #449
Las Vegas, NV 89014-2100

Platts, Todd (Congressman, Politician)
2455 Rayburn HOB
Washington, DC 20515, USA

Plavinsky, Dmitri P (Artist)
Arbat Str 51
Kotp 2 #97
Moscow 121002, RUSSIA

Plavsic, Adrien (Athlete, Hockey Player)
Lausanne Hockey Club SA
Case Postale 171
Lausanne 1000, Switzerland

Playboy Playmates
2112 Broadway
Santa Monica, CA 90404-2912

Player, Gary J (Athlete, Golfer)
11390 North Jog Road
Suite 100
Palm Beach Gardens, FL 33418-1755, USA

Player, Scott (Athlete, Football Player)
1583 W Saltsage Dr
Phoenix, AZ 85045, USA

Playfair, Jim (Athlete, Hockey Player)
Phoenix Coyotes
6751 N Sunset Blvd Ste 200
Glendale, AZ 85305-3124

Playfair, Jim (Athlete, Hockey Player)
200-99 Station St
Saint John, NB E2L 4X4, Canada

Playfair, Larry (Athlete, Hockey Player)
724 Ransom Rd.
Grand Island, NY 14072-1464

Playfair, Larry (Athlete, Hockey Player)
Buffalo Sabres
1 Seymour H Knox III Plz Ste 1
Buffalo, NY 14203-3096

Plaza, Aubrey (Actor)
c/o Greg Walter *3 Arts Entertainment Inc*
9460 Wilshire Blvd
7th Floor
Beverly Hills, CA 90210, USA

The Celebrity Black Book 2013

Pleasant, Anthony (Athlete, Football Player)
17249 Connor Quay Ct
Cornelius, NC 28031, USA

Pleasant, Reggie (Athlete, Football Player)
8270 Milford Plantation Rd
Pinewood, SC 29125, USA

Pleau, Larry (Athlete, Hockey Player, Olympic Athlete)
650 Spyglass Summit Dr
Chesterfield, MO 63017-2143

Pleau, Larry (Athlete, Hockey Player)
St Louis Blues
1401 Clark Ave
Saint Louis, MO 63103-2700

Pleis, Bill (Athlete, Baseball Player)
11 Palomino Ridge Ct
Lake Saint Louis, MO 63367-2162, USA

Plemons, Jesse (Actor)
c/o Staff Member *Simmons & Scott Entertainment*
4110 W. Burbank Blvd.
Burbank, CA 91505, USA

Plenty, Patty
1350 E. Flamingo Rd. #150
Las Vegas, NV 89118

Plesac, Dan (Athlete, Baseball Player)
Major League Basebal Network 40 Hartz Way Ste 1
Attn On Air PPrsonality secaucus,
NJ 07094-2403, USA

Pleshette, John (Actor)
2643 Creston Dr
Los Angeles, CA 90068, USA

Pless, Rance (Athlete, Baseball Player)
5528 Asheville Hwy
Greeneville, TN 37743-2287, USA

Pletcher, Eidon (Cartoonist)
210 Canberra Court
Slidell, LA 70458, USA

Pletnev, Mikhail V (Musician)
Starpkonyushenny Per 33
#16
Moscow, RUSSIA

Plett, Willi (Athlete, Hockey Player)
125 Riding Trail Ct
Roswell, GA 30075-1759

Plews, Herb (Athlete, Baseball Player)
350 Ponca Pl
Boulder, CO 80303-3876, USA

Plimpton, Calvin H (Doctor)
Downstate Medical Center
450 Clarkson Ave
Brooklyn, NY 11203, USA

Plimpton, Martha (Actor)
c/o Jill Littman *Impression Entertainment*
9229 W Sunset Blvd #700
West Hollywood, CA 90069, USA

Plisetskaya, Maiya M (Ballerina)
Tverskaya 25/9
#31
Moscow 103050, RUSSIA

Plodinec, Tim (Athlete, Baseball Player)
23251 Gilmore St
West Hills, CA 91307-3427, USA

Ploeger, Kurt (Athlete, Football Player)
304 2nd Ave SW
Pipestone, MN 56164, USA

Ploen, Ken (Athlete, Football Player)
178 Shoreline Dr
Winnipeg, MB R3P 2E8, Canada

Plotkin, Stanley A (Musician)
3940 Delancey St
Philadelphia, PA 19104, USA

Plott, Charles R (Economist)
881 El Campo Dr
Pasadena, CA 91107, USA

Plouffe, Trevor (Baseball Player)
11437 Vineland Ct
Porter Ranch, CA 91326-4178

Plough, Thomas (Educator)
North Dakota State University
President's Office
Fargo, ND 58105, USA

Plowden, David (Photographer, Writer)
3005 W Logan Blvd Apt 4
Chicago, IL 60647-1786, USA

Plowright, Joan A (Opera Singer)
83 Saint Mark's Ave
Salisbury
Wilts SP1 3DW, UNITED KINGDOM (UK)

Plowright, Joan A (Actor)
Malthouse
Horsham Road Ashurst Steying
West Sussex BN44 3AR, UNITED KINGDOM (UK)

Pluhar, Erika
Huschkagasse 5
Vienna, AUSTRIA A-1190

Plum, Milton R (Milt) (Athlete, Football Player)
1104 Oakside Ct
Raleigh, NC 27609, USA

Plum, Ted (Athlete, Football Player)
17 Laurel Hill Dr
Cherry Hill, NJ 08003, USA

Plumb, Eve (Actor)
c/o Mark Measures *Abrams Artists Agency (LA)*
9200 Sunset Blvd
11th Floor
Los Angeles, CA 90069, USA

plumb, Ron (Athlete, Hockey Player)
975 Auden Park Dr
Kingston, ON K7M 7T9, Canada

Plumer, Patricia (PattiSue) (Athlete, Track Athlete)
USA Track & Field
4341 Starlight Dr
Indianapolis, IN 46239, USA

Plummer, Amanda (Actor)
c/o Perry Zimel *Oscars Abrams Zimel & Associates, Inc. (OAZ)*
438 Queen St E
Toronto ON M5A 1T4, CANADA

Plummer, Bill (Athlete, Baseball Player, Coach)
52171 Sageway Dr
Redding, CA 96003-9384, USA

Plummer, Christopher (Actor, Musician)
49 Wampum Hill Road
Suite 480
Weston, CT 06883, USA

Plummer, Garry (Athlete, Basketball Player)
2119 Arthur Ave
Belmont, CA 94002-1660, USA

Plummer, Gary (Athlete, Basketball Player)
87 Rock Harbor Ln
Foster City, CA 94404, USA

Plummer, Gary (Athlete, Football Player)
10374 Rue Chamberry
San Diego, CA 92131, USA

Plummer, Glenn (Actor)
c/o Brian Wilkins *Kritzer Levine Wilkins Entertainment (KLWG)*
11872 La Grange Ave
1st Floor
Los Angeles, CA 90025, USA

Plummer, Scotty
909 Parkview Ave.
Lodi, CA 95240

Plummer, Stephen B (General)
Deputy to Assistant Secretary
HqUSAF Pentagon
Washington, DC 20330, USA

Plunk, Eric (Athlete, Baseball Player)
9500 Pats Point Dr
Corona, CA 92883-5068, USA

Plunkett, Jim (Athlete, Football Player, Heisman Trophy Winner)
51 Kilroy Way
Atherton, CA 94027-5405, USA

Plunkett, Maryann
10 E. 44th St.
New York, NY 10017

Plunkett, Warren (Athlete, Football Player)
25150 N Windy Walk Dr
Unit 30
Scottsdale, AZ 85255, USA

Plushenko, Evgeni (Figure Skater)
c/o Staff Member *Champions on Ice*
Tom Collins Enterprises Inc
3500 W 80th St
Minneapolis, MN 55431, USA

Plus One (Music Group)
c/o Teresa Davis *Paradigm (Nashville)*
124 12th Ave S
Suite 410
Nashville, TN 37203, USA

Ply, Bobby (Athlete, Football Player)
8616 Ash Ave
Raytown, MO 64138, USA

Plympton, Jeff (Athlete, Baseball Player)
8 Robin St
Plainville, MA 02762-1522, USA

Plyushch, Ivan S (Misc)
Verkhovna Rada
M Hrushevskoho 5
Kiev 252019, UKRAINE

P. McGovern, James (Congressman, Politician)
438 Cannon HOB
Washington, DC 20515, USA

P. McKeon, Howard H (Congressman, Politician)
2184 Rayburn HOB
Washington, DC 20515, USA

PM Dawn (Music Group)
Raw Shack
857 Atlantic Avenue
#5
Brokklyn, NY 11238, USA

P. Moran, James (Congressman, Politician)
2239 Rayburn HOF
Washington, DC 20515, USA

Poapst, Steve (Athlete, Hockey Player)
502 Kelly Ct
Lombard, IL 60148-3115

Poapst, Steve (Athlete, Hockey Player)
Rockford Icehogs
300 Elm St
Rockford, IL 61101-1238

Pochman, Owen (Athlete, Football Player)
7405 91st Ave SE
Mercer Island, WA 98040, USA

Pochmara, Brian (Athlete, Hockey Player)
18854 Monica Dr
Clinton Township, MI 48036-4204

Pocklington, Peter H (Misc)
Edmonton Oilers
11230 110th St
Edmonton, AB T5G 3H7, CANADA

Pocoroba, Biff (Athlete, Baseball Player)
3445 Broxton Mill Way
Snellville, GA 30039-4441, USA

Pocza, Harvie (Athlete, Hockey Player)
135 Sun Harbour Close SE
Calgary, AB T2X 3C4, Canada

POD (Music Group)
c/o Staff Member *Paradigm (Monterey)*
404 W Franklin St
Monterey, CA 93940, USA

Podein, Shjon (Athlete, Hockey Player)
4350 Browndale Ave
Minneapolis, MN 55424-1012

Podell, Eyal (Actor)
c/o Samantha Crisp *Kohner Agency, The*
9300 Wilshire Blvd
Suite 555
Beverly Hills, CA 90212, USA

Podesta, John (Government Official)
White House
1600 Pennsylvania Ave NW
Washington, DC 20500, USA

Podesta, Rosanna
Via Bartolomeo Ammannati 8
Rome, ITALY I-00197

Podesta, Rossana (Actor)
Via Bartolomeo Ammanatti 8
Rome 00187, ITALY

Podeswa, Jeremy (Director, Writer)
c/o Jennifer Levine *Untitled Entertainment (LA)*
350 S. Beverly Dr #200
Beverly Hills, CA 90212, USA

Podewell, Cathy (Actor)
17328 S Crest Dr
Los Angeles, CA 90035, USA

Podkopayeva, Lilia
Rue des Oeuches 10
Moutier, SWITZERLAND CP 350 374

Podloski, Ray (Athlete, Hockey Player)
1622 Kerr Rd NW
Sumas, WA 98295-9613, USA

Podolak, Edward J (Ed) (Athlete, Football Player)
2227 Emma Rd
Basalt, CO 81621, USA

Podollan, Jason (Athlete, Hockey Player)
430 Niblick Crt
Vernon, BC V1H 1 V6, Canada

Podolski, Lukas (Soccer Player)
Norbert Pflippen
Heinz-Nixdorf-Straøe 33
Mönchengladbach 41179, GERMANY

Podres, Johnny (Athlete, Baseball Player)
1 Colonial Ct
Queensbury, NY 12804, USA

Podsednik, Scott (Athlete, Baseball Player)
c/o Staff Member *Chicago White Sox*
U.S. Cellular Field
333 Wes 35th St
Chicago, IL 60616, USA

Poe, Gregory (Designer, Fashion
Designer)
Dutch Courage
1950 S Santa Fe Ave
Los Angeles, CA 90021, USA

Poe, Johnnie (Athlete, Football Player)
924 Donald F McHenry Pl
East Saint Louis, IL 62201, USA

Poe, Richard
10 Prospect Park SW #17
Brooklyn, NY 11215-5937

Poe, Ted (Congressman, Politician)
320 Cannon HOB
Washington, DC 20515, USA

Poehler, Amy (Actor, Comedian)
c/o David (Dave) Becky *3 Arts
Entertainment Inc*
9460 Wilshire Blvd
7th Floor
Beverly Hills, CA 90210, USA

Poepping, Mike (Athlete, Baseball Player)
13047 230th Ave
Pierz, MN 56364, USA

Poesy, Clemence (Actor)
c/o Hylda Queally *Creative Artists Agency
(CAA-LA)*
2000 Ave Of The Stars
Los Angeles, CA 90067, USA

Poff, John (Athlete, Baseball Player)
2786 Mishler Rd
Mio, MI 48647-9505, USA

Pogorelich, Ivo (Musician)
Kantor Concert Mgmt
67 Teignmouth Road
London NW2 4EA, UNITED KINGDOM
(UK)

Pogrebin, Letty Cottin (Activist, Editor,
Writer)
33 W 67th St
New York, NY 10023, USA

Pogue, David (Correspondent)
c/o Staff Member *CNBC*
900 Sylvan Ave
Englewood Cliffs, NJ 07632, USA

Pogue, Donald W (Judge)
IS International Trade Court
1 Federal Plaza
New York, NY 10278, USA

Pogue, William Colonel (Astronaut)
709 Greenwood Way
Bentonville, AR 72712-7906, USA

Pogue, William R (Astronaut)
4 Cromer Dr
Bella Vista, AR 72115, USA

Pohl, Dan (Golfer)
3424 E Suncrest Ct
Phoenix, AZ 85044-3506, USA

Pohl, Don (Golfer)
3424 E Suncrest Court
Phoenix, AZ 85044, USA

Pohl, Frederick (Writer)
855 S. Harvard Dr.
Palatine, IL 60067-7026, USA

Pohl, Johnny (Athlete, Hockey Player)
10812 Falling Water Ln Unit G
Saint Paul, MN 55129-5267

Pohlad, Carl (Baseball Player, Business
Person)
c/o Staff Member *Minnesota Twins*
Metrodome
34 Kirby Punkett Place
Minneapolis, MN 55412, USA

Pohn, Carol (Stylist)
2259 N Wayne St
Chicago, IL 60614, USA

Poimboeuf, Lance (Athlete, Football
Player)
309 Fairfield Dr
Thibodaux, LA 70301, USA

Poindexter, Anthony (Athlete, Football
Player)
RR 3 Box 128
Forest, VA 24551, USA

Poindexter, Buster (Musician)
c/o Nina Nisenholtz *N2N Entertainment*
1230 Montana Ave
Suite 203
Santa Monica, CA 90403, USA

Poindexter, Christian H (Business Person)
Constellation Energy Group
39 W Lexington St
Baltimore, MD 21201, USA

Poindexter, John M
10 Barrington Fare
Rockville, MD 20850-3001, USA

Pointer, Aaron (Baseball Player)
Houston Colt .45's
4902 N Scenic View Ln
Tacoma, WA 98407-1365, USA

Pointer, Aaron (Athlete, Baseball Player)
4902 N Scenic View Ln
Tacoma, WA 98407, USA

Pointer, Anita (Musician)
12060 Crest Ct
Beverly Hills, CA 90210, USA

Pointer, Bonnie (Musician)
T-Best Talent Agency
508 Honey Lake Court
Danville, CA 94506, USA

Pointer, Priscilla (Actor)
c/o Staff Member *WmE2 (WMA-LA)*
1 William Morris Pl
Beverly Hills, CA 90212, USA

Pointer, Priscilla (Musician)
213 16th St
Santa Monica, CA 90402, USA

Point of Grace (Music Group)
c/o David Breen *The Breen Agency*
25 Music Sq W
Nashville, TN 37203, USA

Poirier, Anne
32 rue Lenine
Ivry, FRANCE F-94200

Poirier, Mark (Writer)
c/o Rowena Arguelles *Creative Artists
Agency (CAA-LA)*
2000 Ave Of The Stars
Los Angeles, CA 90067, USA

Poirier, Patrick
32 rue Lenine
Ivry, FRANCE F-94200

Poitier, Sidney (Actor)
1718 Angelo Dr
Beverly Hills, CA 90210, USA

Polaha, Kristoffer (Actor)
c/o Paul Rosicker *Gersh (LA)*
9465 Wilshire Blvd
Suite 600
Beverly Hills, CA 90212, USA

Polamalu, Troy (Athlete, Football Player)
1761 Colgate Cir
La Jolla, CA 92037-6910, USA

Polanco, Placido (Athlete, Baseball Player)
8950 SW 63rd Ct
Miami, FL 33156-1830, USA

Polano, Nick (Athlete, Hockey Player)
16981 Birchwood Dr
Northville, MI 48168-4422, USA

Polanski, Roman (Director)
c/o Jeff Berg *ICM Partners (ICM-LA)*
10250 Constellation Blvd Fl 7
Los Angeles, CA 90067, USA

Polansky, Abraham
135 S. McCarty Dr.#4
Beverly Hills, CA 90212

Polansky, Mark (Astronaut)
2010 Hillside Oak Lane
Houston, TX 77062-3642, USA

Polanyi, John C (Nobel Prize Laureate)
142 Collier St
Toronto, ON M4W 1M3, CANADA

Polchinski, Joseph G (Physicist)
University of California
Physics Institute
Santa Barbara, CA 93106, USA

Polcovich, Kevin (Athlete, Baseball Player)
3 Beardsley St
Auburn, NY 13021-2809, USA

Poldberg, Brian
1119 Cachelin Dr
Carter Lake, IA 51510-1233

Pole, Dick (Athlete, Baseball Player)
5124 Marsh Field Ln
Sarasota, FL 34235-7014, USA

Poledouris, Basil (Composer)
Kraft-Benjamin-Engel
15233 Ventura Blvd
#200
Sherman Oaks, CA 91403, USA

Polee, Dwayne (Athlete, Basketball
Player)
1169 E 60th St
Los Angeles, CA 90001-1117, USA

Poleshchuk, Alexander F (Cosmonaut)
Potchta Kosmonavtov Moskovskoi Oblasti
Syvisdny Goroduk 141160, RUSSIA

Poletiek, Noah (Actor)
c/o Staff Member *Protege Entertainment*
710 E. Angeleno Ave
Burbank, CA 91501, USA

Poletto, Severino Cardinal (Religious
Leader)
Via Arcivescovado 12
Torino 10121, ITALY

Polic, Henry II (Actor)
Sutton Barth Vennari
145 S Fairfax Ave
#310
Los Angeles, CA 90036, USA

Police, The (Music Group)
194 Kensington Park Rd.
London, ENGLAND W11 2ES, UNITED
KINGDOM

Polich, Mike (Athlete, Hockey Player)
825 3rd St NE
Osseo, MN 55369-1409

Polish, Mark (Actor, Producer, Writer)
c/o Sean Elliott *WME (LA)*
9601 Wilshire Blvd Fl 3
Beverly Hills, CA 90210, USA

Polish, Michael (Director)
Endeavor Talent Agency
9701 Wilshire Blvd
#1000
Beverly Hills, CA 90212, USA

Polishchuk, Oleksiy (Figure Skater)
c/o Staff Member *Champions on Ice*
Tom Collins Enterprises Inc
3500 W 80th St
Minneapolis, MN 55431, USA

Politis, Irene (Stylist)
201 E 21st St
#4-C
New York, NY 10010, USA

Polito, Jon (Actor)
c/o Mary Ellen Mulcahy *Framework
Entertainment (LA)*
9057 Nemo St
Suite C
West Hollywood, CA 90069, USA

Politte, Cliff (Athlete, Baseball Player)
6306 Sprig Oak Ct
Apt C
Saint Louis, MO 63128-4336, USA

Politz, Henry A (Judge)
US Court of Appeals
500 Fannin St
Shreveport, LA 71101, USA

Politzer, Hugh David (Nobel Prize
Laureate)
California Institute Of Technology
1145 Linda Vista Ave
Pasadena, CA 91103-2751, USA

Poliziani, Dan (Athlete, Hockey Player)
5611 W Lake Rd
Conesus, NY 14435-9322

Polizzi, Nicole (Snooki) (Reality TV Star)
c/o Stacey Wechsler *Hired Gun Publicity*
250 W 19th St
15F
New York, NY 10011, USA

Polk, Steven R (General)
Vice Commander
Pacific Air Forces
Hickam Air Force Base, HI 96853, USA

Polke, Sigmar (Artist)
Michael Werner
4 E 77th St
#200
New York, NY 10021, USA

Polkinghome, John C (Physicist)
Queen's College
Cambridge University
Cambridge CB3 9ET, UNITED KINGDOM
(UK)

Polla, Dennis L (Engineer)
University of Minnesota
Electrical Engineering Dept
Minneapolis, MN 55455, USA

Pollack, Andrea (Swimmer)
SSV
Postfach 420140
Kassel 34070, GERMANY

Pollack, Daniel (Musician)
University of Southern California
Music Dept
Los Angeles, CA 90089, USA

Pollack, Frank (Athlete, Football Player)
4027 Austin Meadow Dr
Sugar Land, TX 77479, USA

Pollack, Jim (Actor)
Ericka Wain
1418 N Highland Ave
#102
Los Angeles, CA 90028, USA

Pollack, Joseph (Misc)
Insurance Workers Union
1017 12th St NW
Washington, DC 20005, USA

Pollack, Kevin (Actor)
c/o Annett Wolf *WKT Public Relations
(WKT-LA)*
9350 Wilshire Blvd
Suite 450
Beverly Hills, CA 90212, USA

Pollack, Sam (Misc)
6811 Monkland Ave
Montreal, QC H4B 1J2, CANADA

Pollak, Kevin (Actor, Comedian)
Calm Down Productions
1360 N Crescent Heights Blvd
Los Angeles, CA 90046, USA

Pollan, Tracy (Actor)
c/o Bob Gersh *Gersh (LA)*
9465 Wilshire Blvd
Suite 600
Beverly Hills, CA 90212, USA

Pollard, Bob (Athlete, Football Player)
8987 Washington Blvd
Beaumont, TX 77707, USA

Pollard, Frank (Athlete, Football Player)
1526 N 12th St
Waco, TX 76707, USA

Pollard, Marcus (Athlete, Football Player)
2991 Cameo Dr
Carmel, IN 46032, USA

Pollard, Michael J (Actor)
520 S Burnside Ave
#12A
Los Angeles, CA 90036, USA

Pollard, Scot (Athlete, Basketball Player)
10389 Windemere
Carmel, IN 46032-8594, USA

Pollard, Sue (Su) (Actor)
c/o Staff Member *Noel Gay Artists*
19 Denmark St
London WC2H 8NA, United Kingdom

Pollard, Tiffany (New York) (Actor,
Reality TV Star)
c/o Chuck Binder *Binder & Associates*
1465 Lindacrest Dr
Beverly Hills, CA 90210, USA

Pollari, Joey (Actor)
c/o Nancy Kremer *Nancy Kremer
Management*
4545 Morse Ave
Studio City, CA 91604, USA

Polle, David R (Misc)
Nashville Predators
501 Broadway
Nashville, TN 37203, USA

Polle, Norman R (Bud) (Athlete, Coach,
Hockey Player)
1509-2004 Fullerton Ave
North Vancouver, BC V7P 3G8, Canada

Pollen, Arabella R H (Designer, Fashion
Designer)
Canham Mews
#8 Canham Road
London W3 7SR, UNITED KINGDOM
(UK)

Polley, Dale (Ballerina)
New York Yankees
107 Redding Rd
Georgetown, KY 40324-1078, USA

Polley, Dale (Athlete, Baseball Player)
107 Redding Rd
Georgetown, KY 40324, USA

Polley, Sarah (Actor, Director, Writer)
c/o Frank Frattaroli *Circle of Confusion
(NY)*
270 Lafayette St
Suite 402
New York, NY 10012, USA

Pollini, Maurizio (Musician)
RESIA
Via Manzoni 31
Milan 20120, ITALY

Pollitt-Deschaine, Alice (Athlete, Baseball
Player)
9140 Silver Strand Rd
Levering, MI 49755-9103, USA

Pollock, Alex J (Business Person)
Federal Home Loan Bank
111 E Wacker Dr
Chicago, IL 60601, USA

Pollock, Michael P (Admiral)
Ivy House
Churchstoke Montgomery
Powys SY15 6DU, WALES

polndexter, john (General)
10 Barrington Fare
Rockville, MD 20850-3001, USA

Polo, Ana Maria (Actor)
c/o Staff Member *Telemundo*
2470 West 8th Avenue
Hialeah, FL 33010, USA

Polo, Teri (Actor)
c/o Bob McGowan *McGowan
Management*
8733 W Sunset Blvd
Suite 103
West Hollywood, CA 90069, USA

Polo, Terri (Actor)
c/o Staff Member *United Talent Agency
(UTA)*
9336 Civic Center Dr
Beverly Hills, CA 90210, USA

Polofsky, Gordon (Athlete, Football
Player)
8815 Gatwick Dr
Concord, TN 37922, USA

Polone, Gavin (Producer)
c/o Staff Member *WME (LA)*
9601 Wilshire Blvd Fl 3
Beverly Hills, CA 90210, USA

Poloni, John (Athlete, Baseball Player)
1714 Polo Club Dr
Tarpon Springs, FL 34689-8013, USA

Polonich, Dennis (Athlete, Hockey Player)
70 Varsity Estates Close NW
Calgary, AB T3B 5J, Canada

Poloujadoff, Michel E (Engineer)
8 Rue Roches
Buthiers 77760, FRANCE

Polow Da Don (Musician)
c/o Laura Wright *Avid Exposure*
8721 W Sunset Blvd
Suite P3
West Hollywood, CA 90069, USA

Polowski, Larry (Athlete, Football Player)
365 E Brookhollow Dr
Boise, ID 83706, USA

Polozkova, Lidia P (Speed Skater)
Solianka Str 14/2
Moscow 109240, RUSSIA

Polshak, James Stewart (Architect)
James Polshak Partners
320 W 134th St
#800
New York, NY 10030, USA

Polson, John (Actor)
c/o Robyn Gardiner *RGM Artist Group*
64-76 Kippax St
Level 2, Suite 202 & 206
Surry Hills, NSW 2010, Australia

Polson, Ralph (Athlete, Basketball Player)
3846 S Eagle Ln
Spokane Valley, WA 99206, USA

Polyakov, Valeri V (Cosmonaut)
Health Ministry
Choroshevskoye Chaussee 76A
Moscow 123007, RUSSIA

Polynice, Olden (Athlete, Basketball
Player)
PO Box 220339
Newhall, CA 91322-0339, USA

Polyphonic Spree, The (Music Group)
c/o Staff Member *Paradigm (Monterey)*
404 W Franklin St
Monterey, CA 93940, USA

Pomers, Scarlett
c/o Rhonda Boudreaux *Rhonda
Boudreaux Publicity*
Prefers to be contacted via telephone
Oakland, CA 900, USA

Pominville, Jason (Athlete, Hockey Player)
9123 Curry Ln
Clarence Center, NY 14032-9505

Pommier, Jean-Bernard (Musician)
2 Chemin des Cotes de Montmoiret
Lausanne 1012, SWITZERLAND

Pomodora, Arnaldo (Artist)
Via Vigevano 5
Milan 20144, ITALY

Pompedda, Mario Francesco Cardinal
(Religious Leader)
Palazzo della Cancelleria
Plazza della Cancelleria 1
Rome 00186, ITALY

Pompeo, Ellen (Actor)
c/o Judy Hofflund *Hofflund/Polone*
9465 Wilshire Blvd #420
Beverly Hills, CA 90212, USA

Pompeo, Mike (Congressman, Politician)
107 Cannon HOB
Washington, DC 20515, USA

Ponazecki, Joe (Actor)
Don Buchwald
10 E 44th St
New York, NY 10017, USA

Ponce, Carlos (Musician)
c/o Staff Member *WmE2 (WMA-LA)*
1 William Morris Pl
Beverly Hills, CA 90212, USA

Ponce, Carlos (Athlete, Baseball Player)
590 Kingsbury Ct
Wellington, FL 33414-3919, USA

Ponce, Enrile Juan (Government Official)
2305 Morado St
Dasmarinas Village Makati
Metro Manila, PHILLIPPINES

Ponce, LuAnne (Actor)
Gold Marshak Liedtke
3500 W Olive Ave
#1400
Burbank, CA 91505, USA

Ponce, Walter (Musician)
Columbia Artists Mgmt Inc
165 W 57th St
New York, NY 10019, USA

Poncino, Larry (Athlete, Baseball Player)
2954 N Calle Ladera
Tucson, AZ 85715-3202, USA

Poncino, Larry (Baseball Player)
2954 N Calle Ladera
Tucson, AZ 85715-3202, USA

Pond, Lennie (Race Car Driver)
4301 Coronado Dr.
Chester, VA 23831, USA

Pond, Matt (Musician)
c/o Staff Member *Paradigm (Monterey)*
404 W Franklin St
Monterey, CA 93940, USA

Ponder, Christian (Football Player)
c/o Pat Dye Jr *SportsTrust Advisors - GA*
3340 Peachtree Rd NE
16th Floor
Atlanta, GA 30326, USA

Ponder, Dave (Athlete, Football Player)
1818 Sandalwood Ln
Grapevine, TX 76051, USA

Pondexter, Cliff (Athlete, Basketball
Player)
1135 W Stuart Ave
Fresno, CA 93711, USA

Pondexterok, Cliff
1135 W Stuart Ave
Fresno, CA 93711-2040, USA

Ponikarovsky, Alexei (Athlete, Hockey
Player)
645 29th St
Manhattan Beach, CA 90266-2232

Pons, B Stanley (Misc)
University of Utah
Chemistry Dept
Eyring Building
Salt Lake City, UT 84112, USA

Pons, Juan (Opera Singer)
Herbert Breslin
119 W 57th St
#1505
New York, NY 10019, USA

Ponson, Sidney (Athlete, Baseball Player)
443 Hendricks Isle Slip 2
Fort Lauderdale, FL 33301-5740, USA

Pontes, Marcos (Astronaut)
16807 Soaring Forest Dr
Houston, TX 77059, USA

Pontes, Marcos Major (Astronaut)
16807 Soaring Forest Dr
Houston, TX 77059-4002, USA

Ponti, Cario (Producer)
Palazzo Colonna
1 Piazza d'Ara Coell 1
Rome, ITALY

Ponti, Michael (Musician)
Heubergstr 32
Eschenlohe 83565, GERMANY

Pontius, Chris (Actor, Writer)
c/o Beth Holden-Garland *Untitled Entertainment (LA)*
350 S. Beverly Dr #200
Beverly Hills, CA 90212, USA

Pontois, Noella-Chantal (Ballerina)
25 Rue de Maubeuge
Paris 75009, FRANCE

Ponty, Jean-Luc (Composer, Musician)
c/o Staff Member *Paradigm (NY)*
360 Park Ave S Fl 16
New York, NY 10010, USA

Pony, Trick (Music Group)
c/o Staff Member *Creative Artists Agency (CAA-TN)*
3310 West End Ave
5th Floor
Nashville, TN 37203, USA

Ponzini, Anthony (Actor)
Gold Marshak Liedtke
3500 W Olive Ave
#1400
Burbank, CA 91505, USA

Ponzo, Rosemary (Stylist)
181 7th Ave
#3-B
New York, NY 10011, USA

Pooja, Bhatt (Actor, Bollywood)
601 Kyle More Apartments
Behind Mehboob Studios Bandra(W)
Mumbai, MS 400050, INDIA

Pook, Chris (Race Car Driver)
Championship Auto Racing
5350 Lakeview Parkway S Dr
Indianapolis, IN 46268, USA

Pool, David (Athlete, Football Player)
460 Vista Glen Dr
Cincinnati, OH 45246, USA

Pool, John L (Doctor)
4104 Corbin Hall Lane
Fredericksburg, VA 22408-9534, USA

Pool, Tilman (General)
232 Warrenton Dr
Houston, TX 77024-6226, USA

Poole, Bob (Athlete, Football Player)
7802 Shadyvilla Ln
Houston, TX 77055, USA

Poole, Brian (Musician)
67 Tower Drive
Neath Hill
Milton Keynes MK14 6JX, UNITED KINGDOM (UK)

Poole, David J (Artist)
Trinity Flint Bam
Weston Lane
Petersfield Hants GU32 3NN, UNITED KINGDOM (UK)

Poole, George B (Athlete, Football Player)
P.O. Box 278
Gloster, MS 39638, USA

Poole, Jim (Athlete, Baseball Player)
605 Falls Lake Dr
Alpharetta, GA 30022-8059, USA

Poole, Keith (Athlete, Football Player)
2027 E Teakwood Pl
Chandler, AZ 85249-3508, USA

Poole, Larry (Athlete, Football Player)
15803 Sea Oats Pl
Tampa, FL 33624, USA

Poole, Nathan (Athlete, Football Player)
8686 Longwood St
San Diego, CA 92126, USA

Poole, Oliver (Athlete, Football Player)
P.O. Box 184
Gloster, MS 39638, USA

Poole, Tyrone (Athlete, Football Player)
3415 Rivers Call Blvd
Atlanta, GA 30339, USA

Poole, William (Government Official)
Federal Reserve Bank
411 Locust St
Saint Louis, MO 63102, USA

Pooley, Don (Athlete, Golfer)
5251 N Camino Sumo
Tucson, AZ 857186047, USA

Pooley, Paul (Athlete, Hockey Player)
51029 Broken Wood Ct
Grange, IN 46530-4816

Poons, Larry (Artist)
PO Box 115
Islamorada, FL 33036, USA

Poornam, Viswanatha (Actor)
7 Lodi Khan Street
T Nagar
Chennai, TN 600 017, INDIA

Poots, Imogen (Actor)
c/o Ted Schachter *Schachter Entertainment*
1157 S Beverly Dr Fl 2
Los Angeles, CA 90035, USA

Pop, Iggy (Actor, Composer, Musician, Songwriter)
c/o Marsha Vlasic *ICM Partners (ICM-LA)*
10250 Constellation Blvd Fl 7
Los Angeles, CA 90067, USA

Popcorn, Faith (Journalist)
Brain Reserve
1 Dag Hammarskjold Plaza
885 Second Avenue Fl 16
New York, NY 10017-2201, USA

Pope, Bucky (Athlete, Football Player)
7 Bunker Hill Dr
Washington Crossing, PA 18977, USA

Pope, Carly (Actor, Producer)
c/o Ben Levine *Kritzer Levine Wilkins Entertainment (KLWG)*
11872 La Grange Ave
1st Floor
Los Angeles, CA 90025, USA

Pope, Eddie (Soccer Player)
New York/New Jersey MetroStars
1 Harmon Plaza
#300
Secaucus, NJ 07094, USA

Pope, Edwin (Sportscaster)
Miami Herald Editorial Dept
Miami Herald 1 Herald Plaza
Miami, FL 33132-1693, USA

Pope, Everett P (War Hero)
Medal of Honor Society
40 Patriots Point Rd
Mt Pleasant, SC 29464, USA

Pope, Marguez P (Athlete, Football Player)
P.O. Box 470487
San Francisco, CA 94147, USA

Pope, Marquez (Athlete, Football Player)
110 Avila St
San Francisco, CA 94123, USA

Pope, Monsanto (Athlete, Football Player)
312 13th St NW
Apt 10
Charlottesville, VA 22903, USA

Pope, Odeon (Musician)
Brad Simon Organization
122 E 57th St
#300
New York, NY 10022, USA

Pope, Rosie (Reality TV Star)
Rosie Pope Maternity
18 E 41st St
Suite 1702
New York, NY 10017, USA

Pope, Willie (Baseball Player)
Homestead Grays
7616 Bennett St
Pittsburgh, PA 15208-1602, USA

Popeil, Ron (Business Person, Inventor)
192 Monte Cielo Dr
Beverly Hills, CA 90210, USA

Popein, Larry (Athlete, Hockey Player)
80-650 Harrington Rd
Kamloops, BC V2B 6T7

popfinger, Bill (Horse Racer)
2395 NE 28th St
Lighthouse Point, FL 33064-8235, USA

popfinger, Frank (Horse Racer)
52 Cambridge Ave
Garden City, NY 11530-5125, USA

Popiel, Jan (Athlete, Hockey Player)
17214 Lakeway Park
Tomball, TX 77375-8398, USA

Popiel, Poul P (Athlete, Hockey Player)
2501 Peppermill Ridge Dr
Chesterfield, MO 63005-6707

Poplawski, Joe (Athlete, Football Player)
8-3421 Portage_^ve
Winnipeg, MB R3K 2C9, Canada

Popoff, A Jay (Musician)
Sepetys Entertainment
1223 Wilshire Blvd
#804
Santa Monica, CA 90403, USA

Popoff, Frank P (Business Person)
Dow Chemical
2030 Dow Center
Midland, MI 48674, USA

Popov, Aleksandr (Swimmer)
Swimming Assn
Sports House
Maitland Road #7
Hackett 2602, AUSTRALIA

Popov, Leonid I (Cosmonaut)
Potchta Kosmonavtov Moskovskoi Oblasti
Syvisdny Goroduk 141160, RUSSIA

Popovac, Gwynn (Artist)
17270 Robin Ridge
Sonora, CA 95370, USA

Popovic, Mark (Athlete, Hockey Player)
30 New Mountain Rd
Stoney Creek, ON L8G 2R7, Canada

Popovich, Gregg (Athlete, Basketball Player, Coach)
41 Vineyard Dr
San Antonio, TX 93711-2040, USA

Popovich, Milt (Athlete, Football Player)
810 N Hoback St
Helena, MT 59601, USA

Popovich, Paul (Athlete, Baseball Player)
2604 Woodlawn Rd
Northbrook, IL 60062, USA

Popowich, Paul (Actor)
c/o Mark Schumacher *Schumacher Management*
1122 San Vicente Blvd.
Santa Monica, CA 90402, USA

Popp, Nathaniel (Religious Leader)
Romanian Orthodox Episcopate
PO Box 309
Grass Lake, MI 49240, USA

Poppe, Nils
Fredriksdale Theaterin Domsten
Helsingborg, SWEDEN 25590

Popper, John (Musician)
c/o Staff Member *ArtistDirect*
9046 Lindblade St
Culver City, CA 90232, USA

Popplewell, Anna (Actor)
c/o Staff Member *Sasha Leslie Management*
34 Pember Rd
London NW10 5LS, UNITED KINGDOM

Popson, Dave (Athlete, Basketball Player)
82 Fall St
Ashley, PA 18706-2709, USA

Poquette, Ben (Athlete, Basketball Player)
17917 N Shore Estates Rd
Spring Lake, MI 78257-1236, USA

Poquette, Tom (Baseball Player)
3411 RidgewayDr
Eau Claire, WI 54701-8142

Poquette, Tom (Athlete, Baseball Player)
3411 Ridgeway Dr
Eau Claire, WI 54701, USA

Porcaro, Jeff
5247 Twin Oaks Rd.
Hidden Hills, CA 91302

Porcaro, Steve (Composer)
13596 Contour Dr
Sherman Oaks, CA 91423, USA

Porcaro, Steve (Musician)
Fitzgeraid-Hartley
34 N Palm St
Ventura, CA 93001, USA

Porcello, Rick (Baseball Player)
PO Box 27
Oldwick, NJ 08858-0027

Porch, Colleen (Actor)
c/o Vincent Cirrincione *Vincent
Cirrincione Associates*
1516 N Fairfax Ave
Los Angeles, CA 90046, USA

Porcher, Robert (Athlete, Football Player)
PO Box 691464
Orlando, FL 32869-1464, USA

Porfilio, John C (Judge)
US Court of Appeals
1919 Stout St
Denver, CO 80294, USA

Porizkova, Paulina (Actor, Model)
c/o Heather Reynolds *One Entertainment*
(NY)
12 W 57th St
Penthouse
New York, NY 10019, USA

Pork Tornado (Music Group)
c/o Staff Member *Paradigm (Monterey)*
404 W Franklin St
Monterey, CA 93940, USA

Porras, German (Director)
c/o Staff Member *Gabriel Blanco Iglesias*
(Colombia)
Dg 127A #20-36
Conjunto Plenitud, Apto 132
Bogota, Colombia

Porretta, Matthew (Actor)
Damage Mgmt
10 Southwick Mews
London W2, UNITED KINGDOM (UK)

Port, Chris (Athlete, Football Player)
452 Walnut St
New Orleans, LA 70118, USA

Port, Michael (Sportscaster)
61 Presidential Dr
Southborough, MA 01772-1126, USA

Port, Whitney (Reality TV Star)
c/o Nicole Perez-Krueger *PMK/BNC
Public Relations (PMK-LA)*
8687 Melrose Ave Fl 8
West Hollywood, CA 90069, USA

Portale, Carl (Publisher)
Elle Magazine
Hachette Filipacchi
1633 Broadway
New York, NY 10019, USA

Porteous, Peter
Glencot Parkside Cheam
Surrey, ENGLAND SM3 8BS

Porter, Adina (Actor)
c/o Heidi Ifft *Bamboo Management*
17 Bucaneer Street
Marina del Rey, CA 90292, USA

Porter, Alan (Athlete, Baseball Player)
993 Browning Pl
Warminster, PA 18974-3807, USA

Porter, Andrew (Athlete, Baseball Player)
4881 Linscott Place
Apt 1
Los Angeles, CA 90016-5422, USA

Porter, Billy (Musician)
c/o Staff Member *Gersh (LA)*
9465 Wilshire Blvd
Suite 600
Beverly Hills, CA 90212, USA

Porter, Bob (Athlete, Baseball Player)
771 Pueblo Ave
Napa, CA 94558-3546, USA

Porter, Chuck (Athlete, Baseball Player)
9321 Snyder Ln
Perry Hall, MD 21128-9414, USA

Porter, Colin (Athlete, Baseball Player)
245 E Sunburst Cir
Tucson, AZ 85704-7325, USA

Porter, Dan (Athlete, Baseball Player)
40275 Colony Dr
Murrieta, CA 92562-5514, USA

Porter, Daryl (Athlete, Football Player)
9053 W Sunrise Blvd
Plantation, FL 33322, USA

Porter, David H (Educator)
Skidmore College
President's Office
Saratoga Springs, NY 12866, USA

Porter, Doug (Athlete, Football Player)
PO Box 588
Grambling, LA 71245-0588, USA

Porter, Gail (Actor)
c/o Staff Member *Yakety Yak*
8-A Bloomsbury Sq
London WC1A 2NE, UNITED KINGDOM
(UK)

Porter, Gary (Misc)
c/o Staff Member *Feld Entertainment, Inc.*
8607 Westwood Center Dr.
Vienna, VA 22182, USA

Porter, Gregory (Actor)
c/o Staff Member *Wehmann Models/
Talent Inc*
1128 Harmon Pl
Suite 202
minneapolis, MN 55403, USA

Porter, Gregory (Musician)
c/o Paul Ewing *Wingsmusic
Entertainment, Inc*
Prefers to be contacted via email or
telephone
NY, USA

Porter, Jack (Athlete, Football Player)
1027 County Road 1530
Rush Springs, OK 73082, USA

Porter, Jay (Athlete, Baseball Player)
9677 Heather Cir W
Palm Beach Gardens, FL 33410-5467,
USA

Porter, Jean (Actor)
200 Glenwood Cir
Apt 717
Monterey, CA 93940-6750, USA

Porter, Jody (Musician)
MOB Agency
6404 Wilshire Blvd
#505
Los Angeles, CA 90048, USA

Porter, Joey (Athlete, Football Player)
c/o Staff Member *Pittsburgh Steelers*
3400 S Water St
Pittsburgh, PA 15203-2349, USA

Porter, Kalan (Musician, Reality TV Star)
c/o Joanne Setterington *BMG Canada Inc*
190 Liberty St #100
Toronto, ON M6K3L5, CANADA

Porter, Lee (Athlete, Golfer)
1604 Birch Ln
Greensboro, NC 27408-6500, USA

Porter, Marina Oswald
1850 WFM Rd. 550
Rockwall, TX 75087

Porter, Marquis (Bo) (Athlete, Baseball
Player)
Washington Nationals 1500 S Capitol St
SE Attn: Coachr
Washington, DC 20003-3599, USA

Porter, Randy (Race Car Driver)
Laughlin Racing
113 Pride Dr.
Simpsonville, SC 29681-3241, USA

Porter, Rick
943 Hartzell St.
Pacific Palisades, CA 90272

Porter, Ricky (Athlete, Football Player)
5800 Airline Dr
Metairie, LA 70003, USA

Porter, Rufus (Athlete, Football Player)
20403 Amberlight Ln
Katy, TX 77450, USA

Porter, Scott (Actor)
c/o Staff Member *Brillstein Entertainment
Partners*
9150 Wilshire Blvd #350
Beverly Hills, CA 90212, USA

Porter, Terry (Basketball Player, Coach)
Milwaukee Bucks
Bradley Center
1001 N 4th St
Milwaukee, WI 53203, USA

Porter, Tracy (Athlete, Football Player)
c/o Roosevelt Barnes *Maximum Sports
Management*
6435 W Jefferson Blvd
#197
Fort Wayne, IN 46804, USA

Porterfield, Ellary Hume (Actor)
c/o Marv Dauer *Marv Dauer Management*
11661 San Vicente Blvd
Suite 104
Los Angeles, CA 90049, USA

Porterfield, Garry (Athlete, Football
Player)
7621 S Harvard Pl
Tulsa, OK 74136, USA

Porter-King, Mary Bea (Golfer)
6412 Kalama Rd
Kapaa, HI 96746-8633, USA

Portes, Richard D (Economist)
Economic Policy Centre
90-98 Goswell Road
London EC1V 7RR, UNITED KINGDOM
(UK)

Portilla, Jose (Athlete, Football Player)
3520 Mystic Dr
Buford, GA 30519, USA

Portillo, Alfonso (President)
President's Office
Palacio Nacional
Guatemala City, GUATEMALA

Portis, Charles (Writer)
7417 Kingwood Road
Little Rock, AR 72207, USA

Portis, Clinton (Athlete, Football Player)
7409 Georgetown Pike
McLean, VA 22102, USA

Portisch, Lajos (Misc)
Chess Federation
Nephadsereg Utca 10
Budapest 1055, HUNGARY

Portishead (Music Group)
c/o Staff Member *High Road Touring*
751 Bridgeway
3rd Floor
Sausalito, CA 94965, USA

Portland, Rene (Coach)
Pennsylvania State University
Greenberg Complex
University Park, PA 16802, USA

Portman, Natalie (Actor)
c/o Aleen Keshishian *Brillstein
Entertainment Partners*
9150 Wilshire Blvd #350
Beverly Hills, CA 90212, USA

Portman, Rachel (Composer)
PRS
29/33 Berners St
London W1P 4AA, UNITED KINGDOM
(UK)

Portman, Robert (Athlete, Basketball
Player)
2107 Cedar St
San Carlos, CA 27278-7382, USA

Porto, James (Photographer)
601 W 26th St
#1321
New York, NY 10001, USA

Portugal, Mark (Athlete, Baseball Player)
67 Serpentine Rd
Warren, RI 02885-1812, USA

Portugal. The Man (Music Group,
Musician)
c/o Matt Hickey *High Road Touring*
751 Bridgeway
3rd Floor
Sausalito, CA 94965, USA

Portwich, Ramona (Athlete)
KC Limmer
Stockhardweg 3
Hanover 30453, GERMANY

Porvari, Jukka (Athlete, Hockey Player)
Pohjola Vahinkovakuutus Oy
Ostoreskontra
E1 Lapinmaentie 1
Pohjola Fl-00013, Finland

Poryes, Michael (Producer, Writer)
c/o Debbee Klein *Paradigm (LA)*
360 N Crescent Dr
North Bldg
Beverly Hills, CA 90210, USA

Porzio, Mike (Athlete, Baseball Player)
P.O. Box 2242
Westport, CT 06880-0242, USA

Posa, Victor (Athlete, Hockey Player)
8170 Burleigh Rd
Grand Blanc, MI 48439, CANADA

Posada, Jorge (Baseball Player)
9335 Salada St
Coral Gables, FL 33156-2333

Posada, Jorge (Athlete, Baseball Player)
300 E 77th St
Apt 11B
New York, NY 10075, USA

Posada, Leo (Athlete, Baseball Player)
8200 Grand Canal Dr
Miani, FL 33144-3538, USA

Posavad, Mike (Athlete, Hockey Player)
Compass Flooring
6390 Kestrel Rd
Mississauga, ON LST 1Z3, Canada

Poschl, Hanno
Singerstr. 13/15
Vienna, AUSTRIA 1010

Pose, Scott (Athlete, Baseball Player)
1216 Kintail Dr
Raleigh, NC 27613-8121, USA

Posehn, Brian (Comedian)
c/o Dave Rath *Generate Management*
1545 26th St
Suite 200
Santa Monica, CA 90404, USA

Posen, Zac (Designer)
c/o Susan Posen
115 Spring St
New York, NY 10012, USA

Poses, Frederic M (Business Person)
AlliedSignal Inc
PO Box 4000
Morristown, NJ 07962, USA

Posey, Bill (Congressman, Politician)
120 Cannon HOB
Washington, DC 20515, USA

Posey, Buster (Athlete, Baseball Player)
137 Leland Ferrell Dr
Leesburg, GA 31763, USA

Posey, Gerald (Buster) (Athlete, Baseball Player)
137 Leland Ferrell Dr
Leesburg, GA 31763-4559, USA

Posey, James (Athlete, Basketball Player)
4671 E 153rd St
Cleveland, OH 44128-3014, USA

Posey, Parker (Actor)
c/o Frank Frattaroli *Circle of Confusion (NY)*
270 Lafayette St
Suite 402
New York, NY 10012, USA

Posey, Sam (Race Car Driver)
Low Road
Sharon, CT 06069, USA

Posey, Tyler Garcia (Actor)
c/o Sarah Shyn *3 Arts Entertainment Inc*
9460 Wilshire Blvd
7th Floor
Beverly Hills, CA 90210, USA

Posner, Mike (Musician)
c/o Jamie Abzug *Sony/RCA Records*
550 Madison Ave
New York, NY 10022, USA

Posner, Richard A (Judge)
US Court of Appeals
219 S Dearborn St
Chicago, IL 60604, USA

Posner, Vladimir
1125 16th St. NW
Washington, DC 20036

Posokhin, Mikhail M (Architect)
Mosproyekt-2
2 Brestskaya Str 5
Moscow 123056, RUSSIA

Post, Avery D (Religious Leader)
80 Lyme Road
Apt 246
hanover, NH 03755-1246, USA

Post, Markie (Actor)
c/o Staff Member *Insight*
1134 S Cloverdale Ave
Los Angeles, CA 90019, USA

Post, Mike (Composer)
Mike Post Productions
1007 W Olive Ave
Burbank, CA 91506, USA

Post, Richard (Athlete, Football Player)
1812 Rickey Canyon Rd
Rice, WA 99167, USA

Post, Sandra (Golfer)
Ladies Pro Golf Assn
100 International Golf Dr
Daytona Beach, FL 32124, USA

Post, Ted (Director)
Norman Blumenthal
11030 Santa Monica Blvd
Los Angeles, CA 90025, USA

Post, William (Business Person)
Pinnacle West Capital
400 E Van Buren St
PO Box 52132
Phoenix, AZ 85072, USA

Postaer, Staffan (Writer)
c/o David Krintzman *Morris, Yorn, Barnes, Levine, Krintzman, Rubenstein and Kohner*
2000 Ave of the Stars
3rd Floor, North Tower
Los Angeles, CA 90067, USA

Postell, Lavor (Athlete, Basketball Player)
2008 Murray Hill Ln
Albany, GA 31707-3262, USA

Postema, Pam (Baseball Player)
171 Garver Rd
Mansfield, OH 44903-9056, USA

Poster, Steve (Cinematographer)
Smith/Gosnell/Nicholson
PO Box 1156
Studio City, CA 91614, USA

Post III, Glen F (Business Person)
Centurytel Inc
100 Century Park Dr
Monroe, LA 71203, USA

Postlewait, Kathy (Golfer)
111 Saint Johns Landing Dr
Winter Springs, FL 32708-6501, USA

Postman, Marc (Astronomer)
3303 Lightfoot Dr
Pikesville, MD 21208, USA

Postrel, Virginia (Writer)
c/o Staff Member *Simon & Schuster*
1230 Avenue of the Americas
New York, NY 10020, USA

Pote, Lou (Athlete, Baseball Player)
10601 Orchard Ln
Chicago Ridge, IL 60415-1864, USA

Poteat, Hank (Athlete, Football Player)
4107 Buxmont Rd
Marlton, NJ 08053, USA

Potente, Franka (Actor)
c/o Ashley Franklin *Thruline Entertainment*
8383 Wilshire Blvd
Suite 1050
Beverly Hills, CA 90211, USA

Pothan, Pratap (Actor)
8-C Peninsula Apartments
Tailers Road Kilpauk
Chennai, TN 600 010, INDIA

Pothier, Brian (Athlete, Hockey Player)
437 Neck Rd
Rochester, MA 02770-1709, USA

Poti, Tom (Athlete, Hockey Player, Olympic Athlete)
2 Honey Locust Ln
Sandwich, MA 02563-2700

Potrykus, Ingo (Scientist)
Eidgenossische Tech Hochshule
Plant Sci Dept
Zurich 8093, SWITZERLAND

Potter, Carol
c/o Staff Member *Pakula/King & Associates*
9229 Sunset Blvd
Suite 315
Los Angeles, CA 90069, USA

Potter, Chris (Actor, Director)
c/o Gayle Abrams *Oscars Abrams Zimel & Associates, Inc. (OAZ)*
438 Queen St E
Toronto ON M5A 1T4, CANADA

Potter, Chris (Musician)
c/o Louise Holland *Vision Arts Management*
16 Clint Finger Rd
Saugerties, NY 12477, USA

Potter, Cindy
1189 Ragley Hall Rd. NE
Atlanta, GA 30319

Potter, Cynthia (Athlete, Diver, Olympic Athlete)
2628 Winding Ln NE
Atlanta, GA 30319-3232, USA

Potter, Cynthia (Cindy) (Sportscaster, Swimmer)
1188 Ragley Hall Road NE
Atlanta, GA 30319, USA

Potter, Dan M (Religious Leader)
21 Forest Dr
Albany, NY 12205, USA

Potter, Huntington (Scientist)
Harvard Medical School
25 Shattuck St
Boston, MA 02115, USA

Potter, John (Government Official)
US Postal Service
475 L'Enfant Plaza SW
Washington, DC 20260, USA

Potter, Lauren (Actor)
c/o Patrick Welborn *Kazarian Spencer Ruskin & Assoc.*
11969 Ventura Blvd
3rd Floor
Studio City, CA 91604, USA

Potter, Mike (Race Car Driver)
1318 E. Lakeview Dr.
Johnson City, TN 37801, USA

Potter, Mike (Athlete, Baseball Player)
21582 Archer Cir
Huntington Beach, CA 92646-8017, USA

Potter, Monica (Actor)
c/o Christian Donatelli *Schiff Company, The*
9465 Wilshire Blvd
Suite 480
Beverly Hills, CA 90212, USA

Potter, Nelson (Business Person)
Fleetwood Enterprises
3125 Myers St
Riverside, CA 92503, USA

Potter, Philip A (Religious Leader)
3A York Castle Ave
Kingston 6, JAMAICA

Potter, Ryan (Actor)
c/o Karen Renna *Talent Company, The*
P.O. Box 4227
Burbank, CA 91503, USA

Potter, Scott (Athlete, Baseball Player)
1637 Cordova Ave
Daytona Beach, FL 32117-1708, USA

Potter, Scott (Athlete, Baseball Player)
1637 Cordova Avenue
Daytona Beach, FL 32117-1708, USA

Potter, Steve (Athlete, Football Player)
750 SE 7th Ave
Pompano Beach, FL 33060, USA

Potter, William (Scientist)
1000 Henderson Rd NW
Huntsville, AL 35816-3512, USA

Pottinger, Stanley (Writer)
c/o Staff Member *St Martins Press*
Publicity Dept
175 5th Ave
New York, NY 10010, USA

Pottruck, David S (Financier)
Charles Schwab Co
101 Montgomery St
San Francisco, CA 94104, USA

Potts, Annie (Actor, Producer)
16 S Oakland Ave
Pasadena, CA 91101, USA

Potts, Cliff (Actor)
PO Box 131
Topanga, CA 90290, USA

Potts, Erwin (Business Person)
McClatchy Newspapers
2100
Sacramento, CA 95816, USA

Potts, MC
818 18th Ave. So.
Nashville, TN 37203

Potts, Mike (Athlete, Baseball Player)
60418th St
Butner, NC 27509-2001, USA

Potts, Roosevelt (Athlete, Football Player)
2800 Crystal St
Apt J-4
Anderson, IN 46012, USA

Potts, Sarah-Jane (Actor)
c/o Staff Member *Anonymous Content (LA)*
3531 Hayden Ave
Culver City, CA 90232, USA

Potts, Tony (Television Host)
c/o Access Hollywood *KNBC (LA)*
3000 W Alameda Ave
Burbank, CA 91523, USA

Potvin, Denis (Athlete, Hockey Player)
Ottawa Senators
110-1000 Palladium Dr
Ottawa, ON K2V IAS, Canada

Potvin, Denis (Athlete, Hockey Player)
6820 NW 101st Ter
Parkland, FL 33076-2921, USA

Potvin, Felix (Athlete, Hockey Player)
40 Grove St.
#430
Wellesley, MA 02482, USA

Potvin, Jean R (Athlete, Hockey Player)
24 Longwood Dr.
Huntington, NY 11746-4716

Poudrier, Daniel (Athlete, Hockey Player)
189 rue Sainte-Marguerite Street N
Thetford Mines, QC G6H 4T6, Canada

Pough, Ernest (Athlete, Football Player)
2141 Buckman St
Jacksonville, FL 32206, USA

Pouke (Stylist)
Prefers to be contacted
via telephone or email
San Francisco, CA, USA

Poul, Alan (Producer)
c/o Andrew Cannava *United Talent
Agency (UTA)*
9336 Civic Center Dr
Beverly Hills, CA 90210, USA

Poulin, Dave (Athlete, Hockey Player)
Toronto Maple Leafs
400-40 Bay St
Toronto, ON M5J 2X2, Canada

Poulin, Dave (Athlete, Coach, Hockey
Player)
16771 Orchard Ridge Ct.
Granger, IN 46530-5916

Poulin, Rene (Horse Racer)
147 Alden St
Wallington, NJ 07057-1433, USA

Poullain, Frankie (Musician)
c/o Sue Whitehouse *Whitehouse
Management*
PO Box 43829
London NW6 3PJ, UNITED KINGDOM

Poulsen, Ken (Athlete, Baseball Player)
P.O. Box 1699
Oakhurst, CA 93644-1699, USA

Poulson, Josh (Actor)
c/o Staff Member *WME (LA)*
9601 Wilshire Blvd Fl 3
Beverly Hills, CA 90210, USA

Poulter, Ian (Athlete, Golfer)
9791 Covent Garden Dr
Orlando, FL 32827, USA

Pouncey, Mike (Football Player)
c/o Joel Segal *Lagardere Unlimited - NY*
845 UN Plaza
New York, NY 10017, USA

Pound, Ralston (General)
3800 Shamrock Dr
Charlotte, NC 28215-3220, USA

Pound, Richard W D (Misc)
87 Arlington Ave
Westmount, QC H3Y 2W5, CANADA

Pound, The Dog
8942 Wilshire Blvd.
Beverly Hills, CA 90211

Pounder, CCH (Actor)
c/o Richard Hoffman *Warren Cowan &
Associates PR*
8899 Beverly Blvd #919
Los Angeles, CA 90048, USA

Poundstone, Paula (Actor, Comedian)
c/o William (Bill) Sobel *Edelstein Laird &
Sobel*
9255 Sunset Blvd
Suite 800
Los Angeles, CA 90069

Poupard, Paul Cardinal (Religious Leader)
Pontificium Consilium Pro Dialogo
00120, VATICAN CITY

Pousette, Lena (Actor)
Atkins Assoc
8040 Ventura Canyon Ave
Panorama City, CA 91402, USA

Poussaint, Alvin F (Educator)
Judge Baker Guidance Center
295 Longwood Ave
Boston, MA 02115, USA

Povich, Maury (Journalist)
The Maury Show
1 W 72nd St Apt 4
New York, NY 10023-3414, USA

Povitsky, Esther (Little Esther) (Comedian,
Internet Star)
c/o Lee Kernis *Brillstein Entertainment
Partners*
9150 Wilshire Blvd #350
Beverly Hills, CA 90212, USA

Powe, Karl (Athlete, Football Player)
P.O. Box 13293
Mobile, AL 36663, USA

Powell, A J Philip (Architect)
16 Little Boltons
London SW10, UNITED KINGDOM (UK)

Powell, Alonzo (Athlete, Baseball Player)
Tacoma Rainiers 2502 S Tyler St Attn:
Coaching Staff
Tacoma, WA 98405-1051, USA

Powell, Andre (Athlete, Football Player)
N50W16962 Maple Crest Ln
Menomonee Falls, WI 53051, USA

Powell, Art (Athlete, Football Player)
25221 Via Lido
Laguna Niguel, CA 92677, USA

Powell, Arthur (Art) (Athlete, Football
Player)
25221 Via Lido
Laguna Niguel, CA 92677, USA

Powell, Brittany
145 S. Fairfax Ave. #310
Los Angeles, CA 90036

Powell, Brittney (Actor, Model)
c/o Mike Eistenstadt *Amsel, Eisenstadt &
Frazier Talent Agency (AEF)*
5055 Wilshire Blvd
Suite 860
Los Angeles, CA 90036-6108, USA

Powell, Cecil (Nobel Prize Laureate,
Physicist)
220 Villa Verde Dr SE
Rio Rancho, NM 87124-1341, USA

Powell, Charley (Athlete, Football Player)
4119 Aralia Rd
Altadena, CA 91001, USA

Powell, Cincy (Athlete, Basketball Player)
2541 Brookside Dr
Irving, TX 75063-3173, USA

Powell, Clifton (Actor)
c/o Christopher Black *Opus Entertainment*
5225 Wilshire Blvd #905
Los Angeles, CA 90036, USA

Powell, Colin (Politician)
1317 Ballantrae Farm Dr
McLean, VA 22101-3028, USA

Powell, Cristen (Race Car Driver)
3072 Patricia Ave
Los Angeles, CA 90064, USA

Powell, Dante (Athlete, Baseball Player)
5715 E Walton St
Long Beach, CA 90815-1325, USA

Powell, Dennis (Athlete, Baseball Player)
1743 Eastgate Ave
Upland, CA 91784-9211, USA

Powell, Dick (Athlete, Baseball Player)
2864 Hunt Valley Drive
Glenwood, MD 21738-9639, USA

Powell, Drew (Actor)
c/o Billy Miller *Billy Miller Management*
8322 Ridpath Dr
Los Angeles, CA 90046, USA

Powell, Dwane (Cartoonist)
PO Box 191
Raleigh, NC 27602-9150, USA

Powell, Hosken (Athlete, Baseball Player)
1289 Tamara Dr
Pensacola, FL 32504-6642, USA

Powell, James R (Inventor)
Plus Ultra Technologies
25 E Loop Road
Stony Brook, NY 11790, USA

Powell, Jane (Actor)
150 W End Ave #26C
New York, NY 10023, USA

Powell, Jay (Athlete, Baseball Player)
155 Butler Dr
Ridgeland, MS 39157-9779, USA

Powell, Jeremy (Athlete, Baseball Player)
3022 W Summit Walk Ct
Anthem, AZ 85086-1012, USA

Powell, Jesse (Musician)
c/o Staff Member *Pyramid Entertainment
Group*
377 Rector Pl #21A
New York, NY 10280-1439, USA

Powell, John (Athlete, Olympic Athlete)
5545 Sobb Ave
Las Vegas, NV 89118-3422, USA

Powell, John G (Athlete, Track Athlete)
John Powell Assoc
10445 Mary Ave
Cupertino, CA 95014, USA

Powell, John W (Boog) (Athlete, Baseball
Player)
Boog's Barbeque
333 W Camden St
Baltimore, MD 21201, USA

Powell, Landon (Athlete, Baseball Player)
104 Meyers Dr
Greenville, SC 29605-1923, USA

Powell, Lawrence (General)
17270 Devonshire St
Northridge, CA 91325-1541, USA

Powell, Leroy (Athlete, Baseball Player)
PO Box 4036
Muscle Shoals, AL 35662-4036, USA

Powell, Marvin (Athlete, Football Player)
5441 8th Ave
Los Angeles, CA 90043, USA

Powell, Michael K (Government Official)
Federal Communications Commission
1919 M St NW
Washington, DC 20036, USA

Powell, Michael (Mike) (Athlete, Track
Athlete)
Team Powell
PO Box 8000-354
Alta Loma, CA 91701, USA

Powell, Mike
1751 Pinnacle Dr. #1500
McLean, VA 22102-3833

Powell, Monroe (Musician)
Personality Presents
880 E Sahara Ave
#101
Las Vegas, NV 89104, USA

Powell, Nicole (Basketball Player)
Charlotte Sting
100 Hive Dr
Charlotte, NC 28217, USA

Powell, Paul (Athlete, Baseball Player)
5254 E Enrose St
Mesa, AZ 85205-5484, USA

Powell, Randolph
2644 Highland Ave.
Santa Monica, CA 90405

Powell, Robert (Actor)
10 Pond Place
London W12 7RJ, UNITED KINGDOM
(UK)

Powell, Ross (Athlete, Baseball Player)
605 Bristlewood Dr
McKinney, TX 75070-8361, USA

Powell, Sandy (Designer)
London Mgmt
2-4 Noel St
London W1V 3RB, UNITED KINGDOM
(UK)

Powell, Susan (Actor)
6333 Bryn Mawr Dr
Los Angeles, CA 90068, USA

Powell, Ted (Athlete, Football Player)
308 Hodder Ln
Henrico, VA 23075-2510, USA

Powell, William (Baseball Player)
Birmingham Black Barons
5516 Avenue I
Birmingham, AL 35208-3011, USA

Powell III, Earl A (Rusty) (Misc)
National Gallery of Art
Constitution Ave & 4th St NW
Washington, DC 20565, USA

Powell Jr, D Duane (Cartoonist)
215 S McDowell St
Raleigh, NC 27601, USA

Power, Cat (Actor, Composer, Musician)

Power, Dave (Actor)
c/o Steven Siebert *Lighthouse
Entertainment*
9220 W Sunset Blvd Ste 200
West Hollywood, CA 90069, USA

Power, J D (Dave) (Business Person)
J D Power Associates
2625 Townsgate Road
Westlake Village, CA 91361, USA

Power, Romina(Brindise)
I-72020 Cellino
San Marco, ITALY

Power, Taryn (Actor)
522 1/2 S Main St
Viroqua, WI 54665, USA

Power, Ted (Athlete, Baseball Player)
Louisville Bats 401 E Main St Attn:
Coaching Staf
Louseville, K 40707-1110, USA

Power, Udana
1962 Beachwood Dr. #202
Los Angeles, CA 90068

Powers, Alexandra (Actor)
United Talent Agency
9560 Wilshire Blvd
#500
Beverly Hills, CA 90212, USA

Powers, Clyde (Athlete, Football Player)
17 S Point Ct
Bluffton, SC 29910-6132, USA

Powers, James B (Religious Leader)
American Baptist Assn
4605 N State Line
Texarkana, TX 75503, USA

Powers, Jeff (Athlete)
USA Water Polo
2124 Main Street
Suite 210
Huntington Beach, CA 92648, USA

Powers, Ross (Athlete, Olympic Athlete,
Snowboarder)
PO Box 186
Londonderry, VT 05148-0186, USA

Powers, Stefanie (Actor)
c/o Alexandra McLean *McLean-Williams
Management*
Gainsborough House
81 Oxford St
London W1D 2EU, UK

Powers, Stephanie (Actor)
c/o Staff Member *McLean-Williams
Management*
Gainsborough House
81 Oxford St
London W1D 2EU, UK

Powers, Warren (Athlete, Football Player)
3909 Lausanne Rd
Randallstown, MD 21133, USA

Powers, Warren A (Athlete, Football
Player)
14742 Thornbird Manor Pkwy
Chesterfield, MO 63017, USA

Powis, Lynn (Athlete, Hockey Player)
2669 S Columbine St
Denver, CO 80210-6441

Powis, Lynn (Athlete, Hockey Player)
23 Lombard Cres
St. Albert, AB T8N 3Nl, Canada

Powlus, Ron (Athlete, Football Player)
1012 Ruthann Dr
Berwick, PA 18603, USA

Powter, Daniel (Musician)
c/o Staff Member *Paradigm (Monterey)*
404 W Franklin St
Monterey, CA 93940, USA

Poynter, Dougie (Musician)
c/o Staff Member *Universal Music Group
(UMG - LA)*
2220 Colorado Ave
Santa Monica, CA 90404, USA

Poza, Jorge (Actor)
c/o Staff Member *Televisa*
Blvd Adolfo Lopez Mateos 232
Colonia San Angel INN
DF CP 01060, MEXICO

Pozderac, Phil (Athlete, Football Player)
2193 Carmel Dr
Carroliton, TX 75006, USA

Pozdnykova, Tatyana (Athlete, Track
Athlete)
4151 NW 43rd St
Gainesville, FL 32606, USA

Pozsgay, Imre (Government Official)
Parliament Buildings
Kossuth Lajos Ter 1
Budapest 1055, HUNGARY

Prabhu (Actor)
16 Chevaliea Sivaji Ganesan Salai
T Nagar
Chennai, TN 600 017, INDIA

Prada, Aura Helena (Actor)
c/o Gabriel Blanco *Gabriel Blanco
Iglesias (Mexico)*
Rio Balsas 35-32
Colonia Cuauhtemoc
DF 06500, Mexico

Prada, Miuccia (Designer, Fashion
Designer)
Prada SPA
Via Andrea Maffei 2
Milan 20154, ITALY

Prado, Edgar (Horse Racer)
c/o Staff Member *HarperCollins Publishers*
10 East 53rd St
c/o Author mail, 7th Floor
New York, NY 10022, USA

Praed, Michael
11500 W. Olympic Blvd. #510
Los Angeles, CA 90064

Prager, Dennis (Radio Personality)
c/o Staff Member *Creators Syndicate*
5777 W Century Blvd #700
Los Angeles, CA 90045, USA

Prall, Willie (Athlete, Baseball Player)
3 Pheasant Run
Kinnelon, NJ 07405-3022, USA

Pran (Actor, Bollywood)
25 Union Park
Khar
Bombay, MS 400 052, INDIA

Prance, Ghilean T (Misc)
Kew Royal Botanic Gardens
Richmond
Surrey TW9 3AE, UNITED KINGDOM
(UK)

Prange, Laurie
1519 Sargent Pl.
Los Angeles, CA 90026

Pranger, Chris (Athlete, Hockey Player)
345 S Hinchman Ave
Haddonfield, NJ 08033-3716

Prangley, Chris
c/o Jeff Morrone *Jeff Morrone
Entertainment*
9350 Wilshire Blvd
Suite 224
Beverly Hills, CA 90212, USA

Prappas, Ted (Race Car Driver)
3072 Patricia Ave.
Los Angeles, CA 90064, USA

Pras (Musician)
DAS Communications
83 Riverside Dr
New York, NY 10024, USA

Prasanna (Actor)
C4 Cauvery Apartments
14 Brindavanam Street
Chennai, TN 600 004, INDIA

Prashanth (Actor)
No 40 North Usman Road
Thiagaraja Nagar
Chennai, TN 600 017, INDIA

Pratchett, Terry (Writer)
Colin Smythe
P.O. Box 6
Gerrards Cross
Bucks SL9 8XA, UNITED KINGDOM (UK)

Prater, Luther D (General)
355 S Orange Grove Ave
Los Angeles, CA 90036-3103, USA

Prather, Joan (Actor)
31647 Sea Level Dr
Malibu, CA 90265, USA

Pratiwi, Sudarmono (Astronaut)
Jalan Pegangsaan
Timur
Jakarta 16, INDONESIA

Pratt, Andy (Athlete, Baseball Player)
1244 Gardenia Ln
Prescott, AZ 86305-6749, USA

Pratt, Awadagin (Musician)
Cramer/Marder Artists
3436 Springhill Road
Lafayette, CA 94549, USA

Pratt, Chris (Actor)
c/o Jimmy Miller *Mosaic Media Group*
9200 W. Sunset Blvd
10th Floor
Los Angeles, CA 90069, USA

Pratt, Deborah (Actor, Producer, Writer)
c/o Staff Member *Hirsch Wallerstein
Hayum Matlof & Fishman*
10100 Santa Monica Blvd
23rd Floor
Los Angeles, CA 90067, USA

Pratt, Heidi Montag (Musician, Reality TV
Star)
c/o Spencer Pratt *Innovator Management*
8899 Beverly Boulevard
Suite 622
Los Angeles, CA 90048, USA

Pratt, Judson
8745 Oak Park Ave.
Northridge, CA 91325

Pratt, Kelly (Athlete, Hockey Player)
23 Lombard Cres
St. Albert, AB T8N 3Nl, Canada

Pratt, Keri Lynn (Actor)
c/o Steve Caserta *Sanders Armstrong
Caserta*
2120 Colorado Blvd
Suite 120
Santa Monica, CA 90404, USA

Pratt, Kyla (Actor)
c/o Judy Landis *Landis-Simon Productions
Talent Management*
625 E. Thousand Oaks Blvd #279
Thousand Oaks, CA 91362, USA

Pratt, Kyle (Actor)
c/o Staff Member *Acme Talent & Literary
(LA)*
1400 Atlantic Ave
Suite 274
Long Beach, CA 90814, USA

Pratt, Mary (Athlete, Baseball Player)
1000 Southern Artery
Apt 219
Quincy, MA 02169-8500, USA

Pratt, Michael (Athlete, Basketball Player)
3211 Chipaway Ct
Floyds Knobs, IN 40245-4190, USA

Pratt, Nolan (Athlete, Hockey Player)
Springfield Falcons
45 Falcons Way
Springfield, MA 01103-1742

Pratt, Robert (Athlete, Football Player)
320 Greenway Ln
Richmond, VA 23226, USA

Pratt, Roger (Cinematographer)
10 Nightingale Lane
Hornsey
London N8 7QU, UNITED KINGDOM
(UK)

Pratt, Spencer (Reality TV Star)
c/o Adam Gelvan *WME (LA)*
9601 Wilshire Blvd Fl 3
Beverly Hills, CA 90210, USA

Pratt, Stephanie (Reality TV Star)
c/o Leslie Allan-Rice *Leslie Allan-Rice
Management*
1007 Maybrook Dr
Beverly Hills, CA 90210, USA

Pratt, Susan C (Actor)
7 Old Pound Rd
Pound Ridge, NY 10576, USA

Pratt, Todd (Athlete, Baseball Player)
5950 Dorset Bridge Rd
Douglasville, GA 30135-6014, USA

Pratt, Tracy (Athlete, Hockey Player)
1705-15038 101 Ave
Surrey, BC V3R ON2, Canada

Pratt, Vicky
1930 Yonge St. #1155 Toronto
CANADA, CA Ont. M4A 1

Pratt, Victoria (Actor)
c/o Gordon Gilbertson *Gilbertson
Management*
1334 3rd St Promenade #201
Santa Monica, CA 90401, USA

Preate Jr, Ernest D (Attorney, Attorney
General, General, Government Official)
Attorney General's Office
4th & Walnut
Harrisburg, PA 17120, USA

Prebola, Gene (Athlete, Football Player)
24 Hayward Rd
Sparta, NJ 07871, USA

Precourt, Charles J (Astronaut)
1960 Shoshone Dr
Ogden, UT 84403-4655, USA

Precourt, Charles J Colonel (Astronaut)
1960 Shoshone Dr
Ogden, UT 84403-4655, USA

Predock, Antoine (Architect)
Antoine Predock Architect
300 12th St
Northwest Albuquerque, NM 87102, USA

Preece, Steve (Athlete, Football Player)
2723 NW Monte Vista Ter
Portland, OR 97210, USA

Preer Jr, John R (Biologist)
1414 E Maxwell Lane
Bloomington, IN 47401, USA

Pregenzer, John (Athlete, Baseball Player)
6316 104th StE
Puyallup, WA 98373-4127, USA

Pregerson, Harry (Judge)
US Court of Appeals
21800 Oxnard St
Woodland Hills, CA 91367, USA

Pregulman, Merv (Athlete, Football Player)
44 S Crest Rd
Chattanooga, TN 37404, USA

Preissing, Tom (Athlete, Hockey Player)
1590 Little Raven St Unit 601
Denver, CO 80202-6183

Prejean, Carrie (Beauty Pageant Winner)
14945 Via La Senda
Del Mar, CA 92014, USA

Prejean, Helen Sister (Writer)
317 Bonnabel Blvd
Metairie, LA 70005-3740, USA

Prejean, Patrick
B5 135 Poissonniere
Paris, FRANCE F-75002

Preki (Soccer Player)
Kansas City Wizards
2 Arrowhead Dr
Kansas City, MO 64129, USA

Premice, Josephine
755 West End Ave.
New York, NY 10023

Premji, Ajij (Business Person)
Wipro Technologies
Doddakannelli
Sarjapur Rd
Bangalore 560 035, India

Prendergast, John (Writer)
c/o Joe Veltre *Gersh (NY)*
41 Madison Ave
New York, NY 10010, USA

Prentice, Dean S (Athlete, Hockey Player)
350 Doon Valley Drive
Kitchener, ON N2P 2M9, Canada

Prentiss, Lee
122 Middlesex St.
London, ENGLAND E1 7HY

Prentiss, Paula (Actor, Comedian)
719 Foothill Road
Beverly Hills, CA 90210, USA

Prepon, Laura (Actor)
c/o Paul Brown *New Wave Entertainment (LA)*
2660 W Olive Blvd
Burbank, CA 91505, USA

Presar, Barbara (Stylist)
622 E 20th St
#7-D
New York, NY 10009, USA

Prescott, Edward (Nobel Prize Laureate)
2308 Lake Pl
Minneapolis, MN 55405-2472, USA

Prescott, John L (Government Official)
365 Saltshouse Road
Sutton-on-Hull
North Humberside, UNITED KINGDOM (UK)

Prescott, Jon (Actor)
c/o Miles Levy *James/Levy/Jacobson Management Inc*
3500 W Olive Ave
Suite 1470
Burbank, CA 91505, USA

Presko, Joe (Athlete, Baseball Player)
1612 NE 77th Terr
Kansas City, MO 64118-1939, USA

Presle, Micheline (Actor)
6 Rue Antoine Dubois
Paris 75006, FRANCE

Presley, Alex (Baseball Player)
10000 Ferry Creek Dr
Shreveport, LA 71106-8406, USA

Presley, Brian (Actor)
c/o Nikki Joel *ICM Partners (ICM-LA)*
10250 Constellation Blvd Fl 7
Los Angeles, CA 90067, USA

Presley, Jim (Athlete, Baseball Player)
Baltimore Orioles 333 W Camden St Attn: Coaching
Baltimore, MD 21201-2496, USA

Presley, Lisa-Marie (Musician)
c/o Staff Member *XIX Entertainment*
35-37 Parkgate Rd
32/33 Ransomes Dock
London SW11 4NP, UNITED KINGDOM (UK)

Presley, Priscilla (Actor, Producer, Writer)
c/o Susan Haber *Haber Entertainment*
434 S Canon Dr
Suite 204
Beverly Hills, CA 90212, USA

Presley, Reg (Musician)
Stan Green
PO Box 4
Dartmouth
Devon TQ6 0YD, UNITED KINGDOM (UK)

Presley, Richard (Musician)
c/o Staff Member *WmE2 (WMA-LA)*
1 William Morris Pl
Beverly Hills, CA 90212, USA

Presley, Wayne (Athlete, Hockey Player)
1339 Kingsway Dr
Highland, MI 48356-1165

Press, Bill (Correspondent)
Cable News Network
News Dept
1050 Techwood Dr NW
Atlanta, GA 30318, USA

Press, Frank (Physicist)
2500 Virginia Ave
#616
Washington, DC 20037, USA

Pressel, Morgan (Golfer)
9266 Legare St
Boca Raton, FL 33434, USA

Pressey, Paul (Athlete, Basketball Player, Coach)
782 Haddonstone Cir
Lake Mary, FL 75975-5129, USA

Pressler, H Paul (Attorney, Attorney General, General, Judge)
3711 San Felipe St
#9J
Houston, TX 77027, USA

Pressler, Larry L (Politician)
2812 Davis Ave
Alexandria, VA 22302-2507, USA

Pressler, Menahem M J (Musician)
Melvin Kaplan
115 College St
Burlington, VT 05401, USA

Pressley, Dominic (Athlete, Basketball Player)
1406 Whopping Ct
Upper Marlboro, MD 20774-7086, USA

Pressley, Harold (Athlete, Basketball Player)
6470 Matheny Way
Citrus Heights, CA 95621-4839, USA

Pressley, Paul (Athlete, Basketball Player)
Pressliz Inc
600 County Road 4694
Timpson, TX 75975, USA

Pressley, Robert (Race Car Driver)
6 Forestdale Dr
Ashville, NC 28803, USA

Pressly, Jaime (Actor)
c/o Andrea Pett-Joseph *Brillstein Entertainment Partners*
9150 Wilshire Blvd #350
Beverly Hills, CA 90212, USA

Pressman, Edward R (Producer)
Edward Pressman Films
130 El Camino Dr
Beverly Hills, CA 90212, USA

Pressman, Lawrence (Actor)
15033 Encanto Dr
Sherman Oaks, CA 91403, USA

Pressman, Michael (Actor, Director, Producer)
c/o Judy Hofflund *Hofflund/Polone*
9465 Wilshire Blvd #420
Beverly Hills, CA 90212, USA

Pressman, Sally (Actor)
c/o Staff Member *Abrams Artists Agency (LA)*
9200 Sunset Blvd
11th Floor
Los Angeles, CA 90069, USA

Presswood, Hank (Athlete, Baseball Player)
1445 W 71st Pl
Chicago, IL 60636-3961, USA

Presswood, Henry (Baseball Player)
Cincinnati Buckeyes
1445 W 71st Pl
Chicago, IL 60636-3961, USA

Presta, Peter (DJ)
c/o Len Evans *Project Publicity*
312 West 53rd St
Suite 202
New York, NY 10019, USA

Prestel, Jim (Athlete, Football Player)
6150 N Hurricane Ct
Parker, CO 80134, USA

Preston, Carrie (Actor)
c/o Steve Caserta *Sanders Armstrong Caserta*
2120 Colorado Blvd
Suite 120
Santa Monica, CA 90404, USA

Preston, Cynthia (Actor)
c/o Charles Silver *Silver Massetti & Szatmary (SMS) Talent Inc*
8383 Wilshire Blvd
Suite 230
Beverly Hills, CA 90211, USA

Preston, Duncan
46 Hilltop House Hornsey Lane
London, ENGLAND N6 5NW

Preston, J A (Actor)
Paradigm Agency
10100 Santa Monica Blvd
#2500
Los Angeles, CA 90067, USA

Preston, Johhny
PO Box 1875
Gretna, LA 70054

Preston, Kelly (Actor)
c/o Michelle Pesce *WKT Public Relations (WKT-LA)*
9350 Wilshire Blvd
Suite 450
Beverly Hills, CA 90212, USA

Preston, Ray (Athlete, Football Player)
12885 Prairie Dog Ave
San Diego, CA 92129, USA

Preston, Simon J (Musician)
Little Hardwick
Langton Green Tunbridge Wells
Kent TN3 0EY, UNITED KINGDOM (UK)

Preston-Campbell, Brian (Stylist)
214 N Henry St
#2
Brooklyn, NY 11222, USA

Prestridge, Luke (Athlete, Football Player)
17802 Island Spring Ln
Tomball, TX 77377-8155, USA

Pretre, Georges (Conductor)
Chateau de Vaudricourt
A Naves
Par Casters 81100, FRANCE

Pretti, Kim Healy (Stylist)
c/o Celebrity Stylist *Zenobia Agency Inc*
PO Box 909
Groveland, CA 95321, USA

Prettyman, Tristan (Musician)
c/o Staff Member *Paradigm (Monterey)*
404 W Franklin St
Monterey, CA 93940, USA

Pretty Ricky (Music Group)
c/o Staff Member *Atlantic Records (NY)*
1290 Ave of the Americas
New York, NY 10104

Preus, David W (Religious Leader)
2481 Como Ave
Saint Paul, MN 55108, USA

Previte, Richard (Business Person)
Advanced Micro Devices
1 AMD Place
PO Box 3453
Sunnyvale, CA 94088, USA

Prevost, Josette (Actor)
Tisherman Agency
6767 Forest Lawn Dr
#101
Los Angeles, CA 90068, USA

Prew, William A (Business Person, Swimmer)
30600 Telegraph Road
#3110
Bingham Farms, MI 48025, USA

Pribilinec, Jozef (Athlete, Track Athlete)
Moyzesova 75
Lutila 966 22, SLOVAKIA

Price, AJ (Athlete, Basketball Player)
c/o Jeff Schwartz *Excel Sports Management*
9665 Wilshire Blvd #500
Los Angeles, CA 90212, USA

Price, Alan (Musician, Songwriter, Writer)
Lustig Talent
PO Box 770850
Orlando, FL 32877, USA

Price, Antony (Designer, Fashion Designer)
468 Kings Road
London SW1, UNITED KINGDOM (UK)

Price, Brent (Athlete, Basketball Player)
1111 W Wynona Ave
Enid, OK 73703-6909, USA

price, Bryan (Baseball Player, Coach)
10987 N 122nd Street
Scottsdale, AZ 85259

Price, Charles W (Athlete, Football Player)
3712 43rd St
Lubbock, TX 79413-3036, USA

Price, David (Baseball Player)
450 Knights Run Ave Unit 1004
Tampa, FL 33602-5806

Price, Elex (Athlete, Football Player)
2833 Newport St
Jackson, MS 39213, USA

Price, Ferne (Baseball Player)
720 E Mary Ln
Terre Haute, IN 47802-4617, USA

Price, Frank (Misc)
Price Entertainment
2425 Olympic Blvd
Santa Monica, CA 90404, USA

Price, Frederick K C (Religious Leader)
Crenshaw Christian Church
7901 S Vermont Ave
Los Angeles, CA 90044, USA

Price, George C (Prime Minister)
House of Representatives
Belmopan, BELIZE

Price, Hillary (Cartoonist)
221 Pine St
#4G3
Florence, MA 01062, USA

Price, James G (Doctor)
12205 Mohawk Road
Leawood, KS 66209, USA

Price, Jim (Athlete, Baseball Player)
Detroit Tigers 2100 Woodward Ave Attn Broadcast
Detroit, MI 48201-3474, USA

Price, Joe (Athlete, Baseball Player)
1874 Arabian Ct
Hebron, KY 41048-8436, USA

Price, Katie (Jordan) (Actor, Model)
Pricey Media
P.O. Box 5036
Argus House, Crowhurst Road
Brighton, East Sussex BN1 8AR, UK

Price, Kelly (Musician)
JL Ent
18653 Ventura Blvd
#340
Tarzana, CA 91356, USA

Price, Larry C (Photographer)
930 South Garfield Street
Denver, CO 80209-5006, USA

Price, Lindsay (Actor)
c/o Leslie Sloane *Baker Winokur Ryder Public Relations BWR (BWR-NY)*
292 Madison Ave
12th Floor
New York, NY 10017, USA

Price, Lloyd (Musician, Songwriter, Writer)
95 Horseshoe Hill Road
Pound Ridge, NY 10576, USA

Price, Lonny (Actor)
c/o Joy Gorman *Anonymous Content (LA)*
3531 Hayden Ave
Culver City, CA 90232, USA

Price, Marc (Actor)
8444 Magnolia Dr
Los Angeles, CA 90046, USA

Price, Marvin (Athlete, Baseball Player)
Chicago American Giants
12136 S Princeton Ave
Chicago, IL 60628-6516, USA

Price, Megyn (Actor)
c/o Leslie Allan-Rice *Leslie Allan-Rice Management*
1007 Maybrook Dr
Beverly Hills, CA 90210, USA

Price, Mike (Athlete, Basketball Player)
4415 Thornleigh Dr
Inidianapolis, IN 46226-2165, USA

Price, Mike (Coach, Football Coach)
University of Texas
Athletic Dept
El Paso, TX 79968, USA

Price, Mitchell (Athlete, Football Player)
3935 Thousand Oaks Dr
Apt 1506
San Antonio, TX 78217, USA

Price, Molly (Actor)
c/o Stephen Hirsch *Gersh (NY)*
41 Madison Ave
New York, NY 10010, USA

Price, M V Leontyne (Opera Singer)
9 Van Dam St
New York, NY 10003, USA

Price, Nick (Golfer)
Nick Price Group Inc
900 S US Highway #1 Ste #5
Jupiter, FL 33477, USA

Price, Noel (Athlete, Hockey Player)
21 Windeyer Crescent
Kanata, ON K2K 2P6, Canada

Price, Paul B (Physicist)
1056 Overlook Road
Berkeley, CA 94708, USA

Price, Peerless (Athlete, Football Player)
5658 Legends Club Cir
Braselton, GA 30517, USA

Price, Phoebe (Actor)
c/o Staff Member *Bernstein Entertainment*
12581 Venice #204
Los Angeles, CA 90066, USA

Price, Randy (Stylist)
c/o Staff Member *Independent Artists*
448 E Riverdale Ave
Orange, CA 92865, USA

Price, Ray (Musician)
P.O. Box 1986
Mt. Pleasant, TX 75456, USA

Price, S H (Publisher)
Newsweek Inc
251 W 57th St
New York, NY 10019, USA

Price, Steven (Athlete, Hockey Player)
Stable 26 Inc
180 King St S #300
Waterloo, ON N2J 1P8, CANADA

Price, Terry (Athlete, Football Player)
59 Fieldstone Dr
South Glastonbury, CT 06073, USA

Price, Tom (Congressman, Politician)
403 Cannon HOB
Washington, DC 20515, USA

Price, Vanessa (Stylist)
c/o Staff Member *Rex Agency, The*
6311 Romaine St
Los Angeles, CA 90038, USA

Price, Willard D
PO Box 2783
Laguna Hills, CA 92654, USA

Price, W Mark (Basketball Player)
Georgia Institute of Technology
Athletic Dept
Atlanta, GA 30332, USA

Price-Bunch, Ashil (Golfer)
1629 Country Club Dr
Morristown, TN 37814-3316, USA

Prichard, Peter S (Editor)
USA Today
Editorial Dept
1000 Wilson Blvd
Arlington, VA 22209, USA

Priddy, Bob (Athlete, Baseball Player)
136 Shingiss St
Apt 214
Mc Kees Rocks, PA 15136-5500, USA

Priddy, Bob (Athlete, Basketball Player)
Lazy Arrow Ranch
P.O. Box 3169
Boys Ranch, TX 79010, USA

Priddy, Nancy (Actor)
11223 Sunshine Terrace
Studio City, CA 91604, USA

Pride, Charley (Baseball Player)
Memphis Red Sox
PO Box 670507
Dallas, TX 75367-0507, USA

Pride, Charlie (Musician)
CECCA Productions
PO Box 670507
Dallas, TX 75367, USA

Pride, Curtis (Athlete, Baseball Player)
1288 Lake Breeze Dr
Wellington, FL 33414-7953, USA

Pride, Dicky (Golfer)
PO Box 844
Windermere, FL 34786-0844, USA

Pride, Lynn (Basketball Player)
Minnesota Lynx
Target Center
600 1st Ave N
Minneapolis, MN 55403, USA

Pride, Mack (Baseball Player)
Kansas City Monarchs
3305 Pierce St
Wheatridge, CO 80033-6333, USA

Pridemore, Tom (Athlete, Football Player)
3935 Poplar Springs Rd
Gainesville, GA 30507, USA

Pridie, Jason (Baseball Player)
4475 E Campbell Ct
Gilbert, AX 85234-7643

Pridy, Todd (Athlete, Baseball Player)
3430 Scenic Dr
Napa, CA 94558-4239, USA

Priesand, Sally J (Religious Leader)
10 Wedgewood Circle
Eatontown, NJ 07724, USA

Priest, Eddie (Athlete, Baseball Player)
445 Ballard Rd
Altoona, AL 35952-6227, USA

Priest, Judas (Music Group, Musician)
c/o Troy Blakely *Agency for the Performing Arts (APA-LA)*
405 S Beverly Dr
Suite 500
Beverly Hills, CA 90212-4425, USA

Priest, Maxi (Musician)
Virgin Records
150 5th Ave
New York, NY 10011, USA

Priest, Steve (Musician)
DCM International
296 Nether St
Finchley
London N3 1RJ, UNITED KINGDOM (UK)

Priestlay, Ken (Athlete, Hockey Player)
5438 Crescent Dr
Delta, BC V4K 2C9, Canada

Priestley, Jason (Actor, Race Car Driver)
c/o JB Roberts *Thruline Entertainment*
9250 Wilshire Blvd
Ground Fl
Beverly Hills, CA 90212, USA

Priestley, Jr, Thomas (Director, Photographer)
c/o Jay Gilbert *Broder Webb Chervin Silbermann Agency, The (BWCS)*
10250 Constellation Blvd
Los Angeles, CA 90067-6200, USA

Prieto, Ariel (Athlete, Baseball Player)
Vermont Lake Monsters 1 King Street
Ferry Dock Attn
Burlimrton, VT 05401, USA

Prieto, Chris (Athlete, Baseball Player)
Eugene Emeralds PO Box 10911 Attn:
Coaching Staff
eugene, OR 7440-7Q11, USA

Prieto, Rodrigo (Cinematographer)
2926 Nicada Dr
Los Angeles, CA 90077, USA

Primack, Joel R (Astronomer)
University of California
Astronomy Dept
Santa Cruz, CA 95064, USA

Primatesta, Raul Francisco Cardinal
(Religious Leader)
Arzobispado
Ave H Irigoyen 98
Cordoba 5000, ARGENTINA

Primeau, Keith (Athlete, Hockey Player)
2 Danforth Dr
Voorhees, NJ 08043-3947

Primeau, Wayne (Athlete, Hockey Player)
Durham Fury
595 Wentworth St E
Oshawa, ON LIH 3V8, Canada

Primeaux, Brian (Stylist)
32 Thompson St
#6
New York, NY 10013, USA

Primrose, Neil (Musician)
Wildlife Entertainment
21 Heathmans Road
London SW6 4TJ, UNITED KINGDOM
(UK)

Primus, Barry (Actor)
2735 Creston Dr.
Los Angeles, CA 90068

Prince, Angel (Dancer)
Prince Dance
P.O. Box 1991
Honokaa, HI 96727, USA

Prince, Charles (Chuck) (Financier)
Citigroup Inc
399 Park Ave
New York, NY 10022, USA

Prince, Clayton
3500 W. Olive Ave. #1400
Burbank, CA 91505

Prince, Don (Athlete, Baseball Player)
11143 James B White Hwy S
Whiteville, NC 28472, USA

Prince, Don (Baseball Player)
11143 James B White Hwy S
Whiteville, NC 28472-6419, USA

Prince, Faith (Actor, Musician)
Innovative Artists
1505 10th St
Santa Monica, CA 90401, USA

Prince, Harold S (Hal) (Director,
Producer)
Harold Prince Organization
10 Rockefeller Plz #1104
New York, NY 10020, USA

Prince, Jonathan
526 N. Camden Dr.
Beverly Hills, CA 90210

Prince, Karim
3313 1/2 Barham Blvd.
Los Angeles, CA 90068

Prince, Larry L (Business Person)
Genuine Parts Co
2999 Circle 75 Parkway
Atlanta, GA 30339, USA

Prince, Tayshaun (Athlete, Basketball
Player)
5550 Leeds Ct
Oakland Township, MI 90220-4814, USA

Prince, Tom (Athlete, Baseball Player)
6816 10th Ave NW
Bradenton, FL 34209-1209, USA

Prince-Bythewood, Gina (Director,
Producer, Writer)
c/o Ava DuVernay The DuVernay Agency
Prefers to be contact via telephone or
email
Los Angeles, CA 90069, USA

Prince Harry (Prince, Royalty)
St. James Palace
London SW1A 1BS, UK

Prince Jr, Gregory S (Educator)
Hampshire College
President's Office
Amherst, MA 01002, USA

Princess Ann Claire (Actor, Musician,
Royalty)
c/o Staff Member Love Is In The Heir
E! Entertainment Television
5750 Wilshire Blvd
Los Angeles, CA 90036, USA

Princess Beatrice (Royalty)
Buckingham Palace
London SW1A 1AA, United Kingdom

Princess Eugenie (Royalty)
Buckingham Palace
London SW1A 1AA, United Kingdom

Principal, Victoria (Actor, Business
Person, Producer)
c/o Alan lezman Shelter Entertainment
9454 Wilshire Blvd.
Suite 715
Beverly Hills, CA 90212, USA

Principe, Dom (Athlete, Football Player)
300 N Highway A1A
Apt E303
Jupiter, FL 33477, USA

Principi, Anthony (Politician)
Veteran Affairs Department
24710 New Post Rd
Saint Michaels, MD 21663-2308, USA

Prine, Andrew (Actor)
3364 Longridge Ave
Sherman Oaks, CA 91423, USA

Prine, John (Musician, Songwriter, Writer)
Al Bunetta Mgmt
33 Music Square W
#102B
Nashville, TN 37203, USA

Pringle, Joan (Actor)
Gold Marshak Liedtke
3500 W Olive Ave
#1400
Burbank, CA 91505, USA

Pringley, Mike (Athlete, Football Player)
6344 Mimosa Cir
Tucker, GA 30084-1946, USA

Prinosil, David (Athlete)
TC Wolfsberg
Am Schanzl 3
Amberg 92224, GERMANY

Prinz, Bret (Athlete, Baseball Player)
15471 N 88th Ave
Peoria, AZ 85382-3789, USA

Prinze Jr, Freddie (Actor)
c/o Aleen Keshishian Brillstein
Entertainment Partners
9150 Wilshire Blvd #350
Beverly Hills, CA 90212, USA

Prinzi, Frank (Cinematographer)
571 W 113th St
#24
New York, NY 10025, USA

Prioleau, Pierson (Athlete, Football Player)
2221 Santee River Rd
Alvin, SC 29479, USA

Prior, Anthony (Athlete, Football Player)
3861 Lofton Pl
Riverside, CA 92501, USA

Prior, Maddy (Musician)
Park Promotions
PO Box 651
Park Road
Oxford OX2 9RB, UNITED KINGDOM
(UK)

Prior, Mark (Athlete, Baseball Player)
4340 Altamirano Wav
San Diego, CA 92103-1004, USA

Prior of Brampton, James M L
(Government Official)
36 Morpeth Mansions
London SW1, UNITED KINGDOM (UK)

Priory, Richard B (Business Person)
Duke Energy Co
526 S Church St
Charlotte, NC 28202, USA

Pritchard, Barry (Musician)
Lustig Talent
PO Box 770850
Orlando, FL 32877, USA

Pritchard, Buddy (Athlete, Baseball
Player)
507 E Sunny Hills Rd
Fullerton, CA 92835-1357, USA

Pritchard, David E (Physicist)
Massachusetts Institute of Technology
Physics Dept
Cambridge, MA 02139, USA

Pritchard, Kevin (Athlete, Basketball
Player)
10492 Mission Park Ave
Las Vegas, NV 89135-1047, USA

Pritchard, Michael (Athlete, Football
Player)
1041 Collingtree St
Las Vegas, NV 89145, USA

Pritchard, Ron (Athlete, Football Player)
495 E Coconino Dr
Chandler, AZ 85249-5302, USA

Pritchett, Chris (Athlete, Baseball Player)
959 Fir Tree Pl
Carlsbad, CA 92011-3926, USA

Pritchett, Kelvin (Athlete, Football Player)
4765 Guilford Forest Dr SW
Atlanta, GA 30331, USA

Pritchett, Matt (Cartoonist)
London Daily Telegraph
181 Marsh Wall
London E14 9SR, UNITED KINGDOM
(UK)

Pritchett, Sir Victor
12 Regent's Park Terrace
London, ENGLAND NW1

Pritchett, Stanley (Athlete, Football
Player)
523 Monteagle Trce
Stone Mountain, GA 30087, USA

Pritchett, Wes (Athlete, Football Player)
1194 Brookgate Way NE
Atlanta, GA 30319, USA

Pritha, Saratha (Actor, Bollywood)
2 1st Main Road
West Shenoy Nagar
Chennai, TN 600030, INDIA

Prithiveeraj (Bablu) (Actor)
146 Anna Nagar (West)
Chennai, TN 600 040, INDIA

Pritikin, Greg (Director)
c/o Staff Member Anonymous Content
(LA)
3531 Hayden Ave
Culver City, CA 90232, USA

Pritkin, Roland I (Doctor)
4128 Grove Ave
Stickney, IL 60402, USA

Pritko, Steve (Athlete, Football Player)
328 Chanticlair Dr
Apex, NC 27502, USA

Prix, Wolf (Architect)
Coop Himmelblau
3526 Beethoven St
Los Angeles, CA 90066, USA

Probst, Jeff (Game Show Host, Reality TV
Star, Television Host)
3171 Brookdale Rd
Studio City, CA 91604, USA

Proceviat, Dick (Athlete, Hockey Player)
56078 Rocky Plains Road
Whitemouth, MB ROE 2GO, Canada

Prochazka, Martin (Athlete, Hockey
Player)
40 Bay St
Toronto, ON M5J 2K2, Canada

Prochnow, Jurgen (Actor)
c/o Staff Member ICM Partners (ICM-LA)
10250 Constellation Blvd Fl 7
Los Angeles, CA 90067, USA

Prock, Markus (Athlete)
6142 Mieders
AUSTRIA

Proclaimers, The (Music Group)
c/o Staff Member A.S.S. Concerts &
Promotion GMBH
Rahlstedter Str. 92 A
Hamburg 22149, Germany

Procol Harum
195 Sandycombe Rd.
Kew, ENGLAND TW9 2EW

Procter, Emily (Actor)
c/o Brad Slater WME (LA)
9601 Wilshire Blvd Fl 3
Beverly Hills, CA 90210, USA

Proctor, Charles N (Skier)
100 Lockwood Lane
#238
Scotts Valley, CA 95066, USA

Proctor, David (Baseball Player)
Bowman
5517 SW 23rd St
Topeka, KS 66614-1727, USA

Proctor, James (Jim) (Athlete, Baseball
Player)
2 Westmoreland Pl
Saint Louis, MO 63108-1228, USA

Proctor, Scott (Athlete, Baseball Player)
428 NE Bavberrv Ln
Jensen Beach, FL 34957-4612, USA

Prodi, Romano (Prime Minister)
European Communities Commission
200 Rue de la Loi
Brussels, BELGIUM

Prodigy (Music Group)
c/o Staff Member *Maverick Recording Co (LA)*
3300 Warner Blvd
Burbank, CA 91505-4632, USA

P. Roe, David (Congressman, Politician)
419 Cannon HOB
Washington, DC 20515, USA

Proehl, Ricky (Athlete, Football Player)
3504 Bromley Wood Ln
Greensboro, NC 27410, USA

Professor, Griff (Actor, Musician)
c/o Staff Member *WmE2 (WMA-LA)*
1 William Morris Pl
Beverly Hills, CA 90212, USA

Profit, Gene (Athlete, Football Player)
6116 Nightshade Ct
Rockville, MD 20852, USA

Profit, Mel (Athlete, Football Player)
PO Box 4155
Redondo Beach, CA 90277-1750, USA

Project 86 (Music Group)
c/o Staff Member *Paradigm (Monterey)*
404 W Franklin St
Monterey, CA 93940, USA

Prokhorov, Mikhail (Business Person)
P.O. Box 55
Moscow 129626, Russia

Prokop, Matt (Actor)
c/o Margot Menzel *Evolution Entertainment (LA)*
9111 Wilshire Blvd
Beverly Hills, CA 90210, USA

Prokopec, Luke (Athlete, Baseball Player)
178 18th St
Renmark, SA 5341, Australia

Proly, Mike (Athlete, Baseball Player)
112 Country Mist Dr
Greer, SC 29651-1919, USA

Promisel-Ryan, Shelley (Stylist)
230Sunridge St
Playa del Rey, CA 90293, USA

Pronger, Chris (Athlete, Hockey Player)
Newport Sports Management
400-201 City Centre Dr
Attn Don Meehan
Mississauga, ON L5B 2T4, Canada

Pronger, Sean (Athlete, Hockey Player)
321 Costa Mesa St
Costa Mesa, CA 92627-2307

Pronites, Diane (Stylist)
1767 N 1220 East Rd
Gilman, IL 60938-6106, USA

Pronovost, Claude (Athlete, Hockey Player)
268 388e Av
Saint-Hippolyte, QC J8A 3A2, Canada

Pronovost, Jean (Athlete, Hockey Player)
Hockey Ministries International
7-1100 Av des Canadiens-De-Montreal
Montreal, QC H3B 2S2, Canada

Pronovost, R Marcel (Athlete, Hockey Player)
4620 Dall Ct.
Windsor, ON N9G 2M8, Canada

Proops, Greg (Actor)
c/o Lee Kernis *Brillstein Entertainment Partners*
9150 Wilshire Blvd #350
Beverly Hills, CA 90212, USA

Prophet, Billy (Musician)
Paramount Entertainment
PO Box 12
far Hills, NJ 07931, USA

Prophet, Elizabeth Clare (Religious Leader)
Church Universal & Triumphant
Box A
Livingston, MT 59047, USA

Prophet, Ronnie
1227 Saxon Dr.
CA, TN 37215

Propp, Brian (Athlete, Hockey Player)
2320 Riverton Rd
Cinnaminson, NJ 08077-3719

Props, Rene (Actor)
Agency for Performing Arts
9200 Sunset Blvd
#900
Los Angeles, CA 90069, USA

Prospal, Vaclav (Athlete, Hockey Player)
4401 N Federal Hwy #201
Boca Raton, FL 33431-5164, USA

Prospal, Vactav (Athlete, Hockey Player)
Ice Palace
401 Channelside Dr
Tampa, FL 33602, USA

Prosper, Sandra (Actor)
c/o Staff Member *Mitchell K Stubbs & Assoc (MKS)*
8675 W. Washington Blvd
Suite 203
Culver City, CA 90232, USA

Prosser, C Ladd (Misc)
101 W Windsor Road
#2106
Urbana, IL 61802, USA

Prosser, Robert (Religious Leader)
Cumberland Presbyterian Church
1978 Union Ave
Memphis, TN 38104, USA

Prost, Alain M P (Race Car Driver)
Prost-Grand-Prix
7 Ave Eugene Freyssinet
Guyancourt 78286, FRANCE

Prost, Sharon (Judge)
US Court of Appeals
717 Madison Place NW
Washington, DC 20439, USA

Protopopov, Oleg (Figure Skater)
Chalet Hubel
Grindelwald 3818, SWITZERLAND

Proulx, Brooklynn (Actor)
c/o Christopher Rockwell *Global Creative*
1051 Cole Ave # B
Los Angeles, CA 90038, USA

Proulx, E Annie (Writer)
c/o Staff Member *The Sayle Literary Agency*
1 Petersfield
Cambridge CB1 1BB, UK

Prout, Bob (Athlete, Football Player)
23102 N Shepard Rd
Chillicothe, IL 61523, USA

Prout, Brian (Musician)
Oreamcatcher Artists Mgmt
2908 Poston Ave
Nashville, TN 37203, USA

Prout, Kirsten (Actor)
c/o Allan Grifka *Alchemy Entertainment*
7024 Melrose Ave
Suite 420
Los Angeles, CA 90038, USA

Proval, David (Actor)
c/o Andrew Howard *Incognito Management*
9440 Santa Monica Blvd #302
Beverly Hills, CA 90210, USA

Provence, Andrew (Athlete, Football Player)
224 Providence Rd
Fayetteville, GA 30215, USA

Provenza, Paul (Actor)
c/o Peter Golden *Golden Entertainment West*
10921 Wilshire Blvd
Los Angeles, CA 90024, United States

Provenzano, Chris (Director, Writer)
c/o David Ginsberg *Insight*
1134 S Cloverdale Ave
Los Angeles, CA 90019, USA

Provost, Jon
627 Montclair Dr
Santa Rosa, CA 95409

Prowse, David (Actor)
c/o Nick Cordasco *Prince Marketing Group*
18 Carillon Cir
Livingston, NJ 07039, USA

Proyas, Alex (Director)
International Creative Mgmt
8942 Wilshire Blvd
#219
Beverly Hills, CA 90211, USA

Prpic, Joel (Athlete, Hockey Player)
2586 South Shore Rd
Sudbury, ON P3G 1M3, Canada

Prudden, Bonnie (Misc)
PO Box 65240
Tucson, AZ 85728, USA

Prudhomme, Don (Race Car Driver)
1232 Distribution Way
Vista, CA 92081, USA

Prudhomme, Paul (Chef)
527 Mandeville St
New Orleans, LA 70117-8627, USA

Pruett, Harold
8904 Wonderland Ave.
Los Angeles, CA 90046

Pruett, Jeanne (Musician, Songwriter)
Joe Taylor Artists Agency
PO Box 279
Williamstown, NJ 37068, USA

Pruett, Scott (Race Car Driver)
Rocket Sports
3400 West Rd.
East Lansing, MI 48823, USA

Pruitt, Gregory D (Greg) (Athlete, Football Player)
13851 Larchmere Blvd
Cleveland, OH 44120, USA

Pruitt, James (Athlete, Football Player)
P.O. Box 244483
Boynton Beach, FL 33424, USA

Pruitt, Jason (Baseball Player)
Topps
320 Clark Drive Apt 101
Summerfield, NC 27358, USA

Pruitt, Jordan (Musician)
c/o Thor Bradwell *WME (LA)*
9601 Wilshire Blvd Fl 3
Beverly Hills, CA 90210, USA

Pruitt, Ron (Athlete, Baseball Player)
3632 Turnberry Dr
Medina, OH 44256-6827, USA

Pruitt, Toni (Stylist)
c/o Staff Member *Celestine - CA*
1666 20th St
#200-B
Santa Monica, CA 90404, USA

Pruitt Jr, Basil A (Doctor)
US Army Institute of Surgical Research
Fort Sam Houston, TX 78234, USA

Prunariu, Dumitru D (Cosmonaut)
Str Sf Spiridon 12
#4
Bucharest 70231, ROMANIA

Prunskiene, Kazimiera (Politician)
Lithuanian-European Institute
Vilnius St 45-13
Vilnius 2001, LITHUANIA

Prusiner, Stanley B (Nobel Prize Laureate)
University of California
Biochemistry Dept
San Francisco, CA 94143-0001, USA

Prust, Brandon (Athlete, Hockey Player)
Newport Sports Management
400-201 City Centre Dr
Attn Don Meehan
Mississauga, ON L5B 2T4, Canada

Pryce, Jonathan (Actor, Musician)
46 Albermarle St
London, ENGLAND W1X 4PP, UK

Pryce, Travor (Athlete, Football Player)
13655 E Broncos Pkwy
Englewood, CO 80112, USA

Prydz, Eric (DJ)
c/o Simon Clarkson *WmE2 (WMA-UK)*
103 New Oxford St
London WC1A 1DD, UK

Pryor, Chris (Athlete, Hockey Player)
6877 Macbeth Ct
Saint Paul, MN 55125-2409

Pryor, Chris (Athlete, Hockey Player)
Philadelphia Flyers
3601 S Broad St Ste 2
Philadelohia, PA 19148-5297

Pryor, David H (Politician)
712 S 61/2 St
Paragould, AR 72450-5005, USA

Pryor, Greg (Athlete, Baseball Player)
9726 W 115th Ter
Overland Park, KS 66210-2927, USA

Pryor, Hubert (Editor, Publisher)
3560 S Ocean Blvd
#607
Palm Beach, FL 33480, USA

Pryor, Kelli (Writer)
c/o Andrea Simon *Andrea Simon Entertainment*
4230 Woodman Avenue
Sherman Oaks, CA 91423, USA

Pryor, Mark (Politician)
5511 Stonewall Rd
Little Rock, AR 72207-4527, USA

Pryor, Nicholas (Actor)
116 Inlet Ct
Hampstead, NC 28443, USA

Pryor, Peter P (Editor)
Daily Variety
Editorial Dept
5700 Wilshire Blvd #120
Los Angeles, CA 90036, USA

Pryor, Rain (Actor, Producer)
2809 Saint Paul St #2
Baltimore, MD 21218-4312, USA

Prystai, Metro (Athlete, Hockey Player)
77 Crestwood Cres
Yorkton, SK S3N 2P2, Canada

Przybilla, Joel (Athlete, Basketball Player)
104 Oakview Cir
Monticello, MN 97062-6044, USA

Psaltis, Jim (Athlete, Football Player)
23115 Samuel St
Apt 23
Torrance, CA 90505, USA

P. Sarbanes, John (Congressman)
2444 Rayburn HOB
Washington, DC 20515, USA

PSY (Musician)
c/o Scooter Braun *Island Def Jam Group*
Worldwide Plaza
825 8th Ave Fl 28
New York, NY 10019, USA

Psycho, Les (Musician)
c/o Staff Member *Agency Group Ltd, The (NY)*
142 West 57th St
6th Floor
New York, NY 10019, USA

Ptacek, Bob (Athlete, Football Player)
648 Deptford Ave
Dayton, OH 45429, USA

Ptacek, Louis (Misc)
University of Utah
Howard Hughes Institute
Salt Lake City, UT 84112, USA

Ptak, Frank (Business Person)
Illinois Tool Works
3600 W Lake Ave
Glenview, IL 60025, USA

Ptashne, Mark S (Misc)
Harvard University
Biochemistry Dept
Cambridge, MA 02138, USA

Public Enemy (Music Group, Musician)
c/o Walter F. Leaphart Jr *Creamworks*
8391 Beverly Blvd.
Suite 352
Los Angeles, CA 90048, USA

Pucci, Ben (Athlete, Football Player)
8502 Timber West St
San Antonio, TX 78250, USA

Pucci, Bert (Publisher)
Los Angeles Magazine
1888 Century Park East
Los Angeles, CA 90067, USA

Puck, Wolfgang (Chef)
805 N Sierra Dr
Beverly Hills, CA 90210-2644, USA

Puckett, Gary (Musician, Songwriter, Writer)
10710 Seminole Blvd
#3
Largo, FL 33778, USA

Puemer, John P (Publisher)
Chicago Tribune
435 N Michigan Ave
Chicago, IL 60611, USA

Puenzo, Luis A (Director)
Cinematografia Nacional Instituto
Lima 319
Buenos Aires 1073, ARGENTINA

Puerner, John P (Publisher)
Los Angeles Times
Editorial Dept
202 W 1st St
Los Angeles, CA 90012, USA

Puett, Tommy (Actor)
16621 Cerulean Court
Chino Hills, CA 91709, USA

Puetz, Garry (Athlete, Football Player)
1779 Robinson Rd
Dahlonega, GA 30533, USA

Puffer, Brandon (Athlete, Baseball Player)
1546 Havnie Bnd
Round Rock, TX 78665-1216, USA

Pugacheva, Alia B (Musician)
State Variety Theater
Bersenevskaya Nab 20/2
Moscow 109072, RUSSIA

Pugh, Daniel Patrick (Dan Patrick) (Sportscaster)
c/o Staff Member *Simon & Schuster*
1230 Avenue of the Americas
New York, NY 10020, USA

Pugh, Larry (Football Player)
RR 4
New Castle, PA 16101, USA

Pugh, Lewis Gordon (Sportscaster)
c/o Staff Member *WmE2 (WMA-LA)*
1 William Morris Pl
Beverly Hills, CA 90212, USA

Pugh, Tim (Athlete, Baseball Player)
7906 N 125th East Cir
Owasso, OK 74055-3539, USA

Pugh, Willard E. (Actor)
c/o Shirley Wilson *Shirley Wilson Agency*
5410 Wilshire Blvd #806
Los Angeles
CA 90036, USA

Pugh Jr, Jethro (Athlete, Football Player)
329 E Colorado Blvd
Apt 505
Dallas, TX 75203-1257, USA

Pugliese, Charles (Producer)
c/o Staff Member *Killer Films (US)*
526 W 26th St
Rm 715
New York, NY 10001-5524, USA

Pugsley, Don (Actor)
c/o Hazel Shallon *Shallon Star Management*
14320 Ventura Blvd #624
Sherman Oaks, CA 91423, USA

Puhl, Terry (Athlete, Baseball Player)
918 Gondola St
Sugar Land, TX 77478-3414, USA

Puig, Rich (Athlete, Baseball Player)
4216 Mill Valle_yCt
Tampa, FL 33618-7430, USA

Pujats, Janis Cardinal (Religious Leader)
Metropolijas Jurija
Maza Pils lela 2/A
Riga 1050, LATVIA

Pujol, Laetitia (Ballerina)
Paris Opera Ballet
Place de l'Opera
Paris 75009, FRANCE

Pujol I Soley, Jordi (Politician)
Generalitat Palau
Placa Sant Jaume S/N
Barcelona 2, SPAIN

Pujols, Albert (Athlete, Baseball Player)
102 Grand Meridien Frst
Chesterfield, MO 63005-4980, USA

Pujols, Luis B (Athlete, Baseball Player, Coach)
2 Townsend St Aot 2-613
San Francisco, CA 94107-2061, USA

Pulcini, Robert (Director)
c/o Staff Member *Creative Artists Agency (CAA-LA)*
2000 Ave Of The Stars
Los Angeles, CA 90067, USA

Puleo, Charlie (Athlete, Baseball Player)
3202 Miser Station Rd
Louisville, TN 37777-3604, USA

Pulford, Robert J (Bob) (Athlete, Hockey Player)
78 Coventry Rd.
Northfield, IL 60093-3117

Pulido, Carlos (Athlete, Baseball Player)
55 SE 6th St Apt 2001
Miami, FL 33131-2564, USA

Puljic, Vinko Cardinal (Religious Leader)
Nadbiskupski Ordinarijat
Kaptol 7
Sarajevo 71000, BOSNIA HERZEGOVINA

Pulkkinen, David (Athlete, Hockey Player)
5095 Croatia Rd
Sudbury, ON P3G 1L5, Canada

Pullard, Anthony (Athlete, Basketball Player)
3518 Monroe St
Lake Charles, LA 70607-3204, USA

Pullen, Melanie Clark (Actor)
c/o Staff Member *Julian Belfrage & Associates*
9 Argyll St
3rd Floor
London W1F 7TG, UK

Pulli, Frank (Baseball Player)
1981Downing Pl
Palm Harbor, FL 34683-5727, USA

Pulliam, Harvey (Athlete, Baseball Player)
1111 James Donlon Blvd Aot 2064
Antioch, CA 94509-7034, USA

Pulliam, Keshia Knight (Actor)
PO Box 866
Teaneck, NJ 07666, USA

Pullman, Bill (Actor, Director)
c/o Staff Member *One Talent Management*
9220 Sunset Blvd
Los Angeles, CA 90069, USA

Pullman, Philip (Writer)
24 Templar Road
Oxford OX2 8LT, UNITED KINGDOM (UK)

Pulman, Bill (Actor, Director, Producer)
c/o Graciella Sanchez *One Talent Management*
9220 Sunset Blvd
Los Angeles, CA 90069, USA

Pulp (Music Group)
c/o Staff Member *Paradigm (Monterey)*
404 W Franklin St
Monterey, CA 93940, USA

Pulsipher, Bill (Athlete, Baseball Player)
1986 SW Certosa Rd
Port Saint Lucie, FL 34953-1393, USA

Pulver, Liselotte (Actor)
Villa Bip
Kanton Vaudois
Perroy 1166, SWITZERLAND

Pumpkins, Penelope (Adult Film Star)
1247 14th St #104
Santa Monica, CA 90404, USA

Pumple, Rich (Athlete, Hockey Player)
51 Monmouth St
Riverside, RI 02915-1467, USA

Punch, Lucy (Actor)
c/o Christian Donatelli *Schiff Company, The*
9465 Wilshire Blvd
Suite 480
Beverly Hills, CA 90212, USA

Punk, Daft (Composer, Writer)
c/o Staff Member *Primary Talent International (UK)*
The Primary Building
10-11 Jockeys Fields
London WC1R 4BN, UK

Punsley, Bernard (Actor)
1415 Granvia Altemeia
Palos Verdes Estates, CA 90274, USA

Punto, Nick (Athlete, Baseball Player)
19550 N Grayhawk Dr
Unit 1122
Scottsdale, AZ 85255-3986, USA

Puppa, Daren (Athlete, Hockey Player)
4526 Chevel Blvd.
Lutz, FL 33558-5331

Puppies, The
15476 NW 77th Ct. #286
Miami Lakes, FL 33016

Pupunu, Alfred (Athlete, Football Player)
13343 Akagi Ln
Draper, UT 84020, USA

Purcell, Dominic (Actor)
c/o Beth Holden-Garland *Untitled Entertainment (LA)*
350 S. Beverly Dr #200
Beverly Hills, CA 90212, USA

Purcell, Herman (Athlete, Baseball Player)
Cleveland Buckeyes
1031 Cass Ave SE
Grand Rapids, MI 49507-1119, USA

Purcell, James N (Government Official)
6 Chateau-Banquet
Geneva 1202, SWITZERLAND

Purcell, Lee (Actor)
11101 Provence Lane
Tujunga, CA 91042, USA

Purcell, Patrick B (Publisher)
Boston Herald
1 Herald St
Boston, MA 02118, USA

Purcell, Philip J (Financier)
Morgan Stanley Co
1585 Broadway
New York, NY 10036, USA

Purcell, Sarah (Actor)
6525 Esplanade St
Playa del Rey, CA 90293, USA

Purcell, William (Physicist)
Northwestern University
Astrophysics Dept
Evanston, IL 60208, USA

Purcey, David (Athlete, Baseball Player)
4339 Highlander Dr
Dallas, TX 75287-6842, USA

Purdee, Nathan (Actor)
56 W 66th St
New York, NY 10023, USA

Purdin, John (Athlete, Baseball Player)
4942 Southgate Pkwy
Myrtle Beach, SC 29579, USA

Purdom, Edmund (Actor)
Via Isonzo 42/C
Rome 00198, ITALY

Purdy, Alfred (Writer)
Harbour Publishing
PO Box 219
Madeira Park, BC V0N 2H0, CANADA

Purdy, Ted (Athlete, Golfer)
5600 N 4th St
Phoenix, AZ 85012-1305, USA

Purefoy, James (Actor)
c/o JoAnne Colonna *Brillstein*
Entertainment Partners
9150 Wilshire Blvd #350
Beverly Hills, CA 90212, USA

Pure Reason Revolution (Music Group)
c/o Staff Member *Paradigm (Monterey)*
404 W Franklin St
Monterey, CA 93940, USA

Puri, Om (Actor)
703 Trishul II Seven Bangalows
Versova Andheri
Bombay, MS 400 061, INDIA

Purim, Flora (Musician)
A Train Mgmt
PO Box 29242
Oakland, CA 94604, USA

Purinton, Dale (Athlete, Hockey Player)
2045 Cowichan Bay Rd
Cowichan Bay, BC V0R 1N1, Canada

Purinton, Dale (Athlete, Hockey Player)
Cowichan Valley Capitals
2687 James St
Duncan, BC V9L2X5, Canada

Purkey, Bob (Athlete, Baseball Player)
5559 Steeplechase Ct
Bethel Park, PA 15102, USA

Purl, Linda (Actor)

Purnell, Ella (Actor)
c/o Oriana Elia *Rights House, The*
Drury House
34-43 Russell St
London WC2B 5HA, UK

Purpura, Dominick P (Scientist)
Albert Einstein College of Medicine
1300 Morris Park Ave
Bronx, NY 10461, USA

Purpura, Tim (Baseball Player)
9156 Waterash Ln N
Pinellas Park, FL 33782-4325, USA

Purtzer, Tom (Golfer)
9828 E Desert Cove Ave
Scottsdale, AZ 85260-6220, USA

Purves, William (Financier)
87 Chester Square
London SW1W 9HT, UNITED KINGDOM
(UK)

Purvis, Jeff (Race Car Driver)
1157 Dunbat Cove Rd.
Clarksville, TN 37043, USA

Puryear, Martin (Artist)
Nancy Drysdale Gallery
700 New Hampshire Ave NW
#917
Washington, DC 20037, USA

Pushelberg, Glenn (Designer)
Yabu Pushelberg
55 Booth Ave
Toronto, ON M4M 2M3, CANADA

Pushor, Jamie (Athlete, Hockey Player)
29 Jay Rd W
Lake George, NY 12845-4426

Pushor, Jamie
29 Jay Rd W
Lake George, NY 12845-4426

Puskaric, Joseph (Athlete, Baseball Player)
201 West Dr N
Apt 63
Marshall, MI 49068, USA

Puskarioc, Joseph (Baseball Player)
429 35th St
Mc Keesport, PA 15132-7226, USA

Pussycat Dolls (Music Group)
c/o Staff Member *WmE2 (WMA-LA)*
1 William Morris Pl
Beverly Hills, CA 90212, USA

Pustari, Rit (Race Car Driver)
Pustari-Goodrich Racing
4 Taft #82
S Norwalk, CT 06854, USA

Pustovyi, Yarolslav Dr (Astronaut)
Nasa Johnson Space Center 2101 Nasa
Pkwy Bldg 4
Houston, TX 77058-3607, USA

Putch, John (Actor)
3972 Sunswept Dr
Studio City, CA 91604, USA

Putilin, Nikolai G (Opera Singer)
Mariinsky Theater
Teatralnaya Square 1
Saint Petersburg 190000, RUSSIA

Putin, Vladimir (Politician)
The State
Office of the Prime Minister
Krelim
Moscow 103073, Russia

Putin, Vladimir V (President)
President's Office
Kremlin
Staraya Pl 4
Moscow 103132, RUSSIA

Putman, Earl (Athlete, Football Player)
P.O. Box 18091
Munds Park, AZ 86017-8091, USA

Putman, Ed (Athlete, Baseball Player)
P.O. Box 3366
Mesquite, NV 89024-3366, USA

Putman, Pat (Baseball Player)
Texas Rangers
2311 Carrell Rd
Fort Myers, FL 33901-8012, USA

Putnam, David (Actor, Producer)
c/o Staff Member *Enigma Productions*
429 Santa Monica Blvd #700
Santa Monica, CA 90401, USA

Putnam, Duane (Athlete, Football Player)
1545 Magnolia Ave
Ontario, CA 91762, USA

Putnam, Hilary W (Misc)
116 Winchester Road
Arlington, MA 02474, USA

Putnam, Pat (Athlete, Baseball Player)
4040 Staley Rd
Fort Myers, FL 33905-6410, USA

Putti, Frank (Athlete, Baseball Player)
1981 Downing Pl
Palm Harbor, FL 34683, USA

Puttnam, David T (Producer)
Engima Productions
29A Tufton St
London SW1P 3QL, UNITED KINGDOM
(UK)

Putz, J J (Athlete, Baseball Player)
2425 NE IvY Way
Issaauah, WA 98029-7621, USA

Putzier, Jeb (Athlete, Football Player)
5305 Pocahontas St
Bellaire, TX 77401, USA

Puyana, Rafael (Musician)
88 Rue de Grenelle
Paris 75007, FRANCE

Puz, Craig A (Astronaut)
S313 Devils Head Cir
Golden, CO 80403-2066, USA

Pyatt, Nelaon (Athlete, Hockey Player)
1680 Arthur St W
Thunder Bay, ON P7K IA8, Canada

Pyavko, Vladislav I (Opera Singer)
Bryusov Per 2/14
#27
Moscow 103009, RUSSIA

Pyburn, Jack (Athlete, Football Player)
1197 Peachtree St NE
Suite 533A
Atlanta, GA 30361, USA

Pye, Eddie (Athlete, Baseball Player)
307 Polk St
Columbia, TN 338401-4453, USA

Pye, William B (Artist)
43 Hambalt Road
Clapham
London SW4 9EQ, UNITED KINGDOM
(UK)

Pyeatt, John (Johnny) (Athlete, Football
Player)
18374 E Via De Palmas
Queen Creek, AZ 85242, USA

Pyecha, John (Athlete, Baseball Player)
107 Nottingham Dr
Chapel Hill, NC 27517-6569, USA

Pyfrom, Shawn (Actor)
c/o Eric Podwall *Podwall Entertainment*
710 N Orlando Ave
Loft 203
Los Angeles, CA 90069, USA

Pygram, Wayne (Actor)
c/o Bob Knotek *McCann - Knotek*
Associates
8539 Sunset Blvd
Suite 4-136
Los Angeles, CA 90069, USA

Pyle, Andy (Musician)
Larry Page
29 Ruston Mews
London W11 1RB, UNITED KINGDOM
(UK)

Pyle, Michael J (Mike) (Athlete, Football
Player)
2436 Saranac Ct
Glenview, IL 60025, USA

Pyle, Missi (Actor)
c/o Mel McKeon *McKeon-Myones*
Management
3500 Olive Ave
Suite 770
Burbank, CA 91505, USA

Pyle, Missy (Actor)
Paradigm Agency
10100 Santa Monica Blvd
#2500
Los Angeles, CA 90067, USA

Pyle, Palmer (Athlete, Football Player)
2487 Potter Rd E
Traverse City, MI 49686, USA

Pym of Sandy, Francis L (Government
Official)
Everton Park
Sandy
Beds SG19 2DE, UNITED KINGDOM
(UK)

Pyne, George F (Athlete, Football Player)
123 Congress St
Milford, MA 01757, USA

Pyne, Natasha (Actor)
Kate Feast
Primrose Hill Studios
Fitzroy Road
London NW1 8TR, UNITED KINGDOM
(UK)

Pyne, Stephen J (Historian, Writer)
Arizona State University
History Dept
Tempe, AZ 85287, USA

Pyott, David E I (Business Person)
Allergan Inc
2525 Dupont St
Irvine, CA 92612, USA

Pyper-Ferguson, John (Actor)
c/o Adena Chawke *Greenlight*
Management and Production
13848 Valleyheart Dr
Sherman Oaks, CA 91423, USA

Python, Monty
34 Thistlewaite Rd.
London, ENGLAND E5 0QQ

Pyznarski, Tim (Athlete, Baseball Player)
10716 Austin Ave
Chicago Ridge, IL 60415-2224, USA

Q, Maggie (Actor)
c/o Andrew Ooi *Echelon Talent*
Management
3674 Oxford St
Vancouver BC V5K 1P3, Canada

Qabas ibn Sa'id al Sa'id (King)
Royal Palace
PO Box 252
Muscat, OMAN

Qaiyum, Gregory (GQ) (Actor)
c/o Sandra Joseph *SLJ Management*
833 N Edinburgh Ave Ph 11
Los Angeles, CA 90046, USA

Qarase, Laisenia (Prime Minister)
Prime Minister's Office
6 Berkeley Crescent
Suva
VITI LEVU, FIJI

Qasimi, Sheikh Saqr bin Muhammad al
(President)
Ruler's Palace
Ras Al Khaimah
UNITED ARAB EMIRATES

Qasimi, Sheikh Sultan bin Muhammad al
(President)
Ruler's Palace
Sharjah, UNITED ARAB EMIRATES

Qi, Shu (Actor)
c/o Steve Chasman *Current Entertainment*
9378 Wilshire Blvd
Sutie 210
Beverly Hills, CA 90212, USA

Qin, Shaobo (Actor)
c/o Don Hughes *IAI Presentations*
PO Box 4
Pismo Beach, CA 93448, USA

Q-Tip (Actor, Producer)
c/o Staff Member *Violator Management*
36 W 25th St
2nd Floor
New York, NY 10010, USA

Quackenbush, Bill
54 Danielle Ct.
Lawrenceville, NJ 08848-1452

Quackenbush, Max (Athlete, Hockey
Player)
476 Lockvlew Rd
Fall River, NS B2T IJI, Canada

Quade, John (Actor)
Alex Brewis
12429 Laurel Terrace Dr
Studio City, CA 91604, USA

Quade, Mike (Athlete, Baseball Player)
823 Hadleigh Pass
Westfield, IN 46074-5900, USA

Quaerna, Jerry (Athlete, Football Player)
1211 Pheasant Ct
Lake Geneva, WI 53147, USA

Quaid, Dennis (Actor)
c/o Cara Tripicchio *WKT Public Relations
(WKT-LA)*
9350 Wilshire Blvd
Suite 450
Beverly Hills, CA 90212, USA

Quaid, Jack (Actor)
c/o Tony Lipp *Anonymous Content (LA)*
3531 Hayden Ave
Culver City, CA 90232, USA

Quaid, Randy (Actor)
P.O. Box 17372
Beverly Hills, CA 90209, USA

Quaintance, Rachel (Comedian)
c/o Staff Member *OmniPop Talent Group*
10700 Ventura Blvd.
2nd Floor
Studio Clty, CA 91604, USA

Qualife, Pete (Musician)
Larry Page
29 Ruston Mews
London W11 1RB, UNITED KINGDOM
(UK)

Qualls, Chad (Athlete, Baseball Player)
8416 Big View Dr
Austin, TX 78730-1534, USA

Qualls, DJ (Actor)
c/o Staff Member *Principato/Young
Management*
9465 Wilshire Blvd
Suite 430
Beverly Hills, CA 90212, USA

Qualls, Jim (Athlete, Baseball Player)
410 N County Road 950
Sutter, IL 62373-5021, USA

Qualters, Tom (Athlete, Baseball Player)
235 Mallard Rd
Somerset, PA 15501-7023, USA

Quan, Samantha (Actor)
c/o Vincent Cirrincione *Vincent
Cirrincione Associates*
1516 N Fairfax Ave
Los Angeles, CA 90046, USA

Quance, Kristine (Athlete, Olympic
Athlete, Swimmer)
1320 Moncada Dr
Glendale, CA 91207-1832, USA

Quandt, Richard E (Economist)
162 Springdale Road
Princeton, NJ 08540, USA

Quann, Megan (Athlete, Olympic Athlete,
Swimmer)
3516 109th Street Ct NW
Gig Harbor, WA 98332-8991, USA

Quanstrom, Nissa (Stylist)
c/o Staff Member *Artist Untied (LA)*
845 S Mansfield Ave
#1
Los Angeles, CA 90036, USA

Quant, Mary (Designer, Fashion Designer)
Mary Quant Ltd
3 Ives St
London SW3 2NE, UNITED KINGDOM
(UK)

Quantrill, Paul (Athlete, Baseball Player)
334 E Lake Rd
Palm Harbor, FL 34685-2427, USA

Quarashi (Musician)
c/o Staff Member *Creative Artists Agency
(CAA-LA)*
2000 Ave Of The Stars
Los Angeles, CA 90067, USA

Quaresma, Rhonda Lee (Misc)
PO Box 22033
Kingston, ON K7M 8S5, CANADA

Quarles, Shelton (Athlete, Football Player)
17019 Candeleda De Avila
Tampa, FL 33613, USA

Quarrie, Donald (Don) (Athlete, Track
Athlete)
Jamaican Amateur Athletic Assn
PO Box 272
Kingston 5, JAMAICA

Quarshie, Hugh (Actor)
PO Box 20092
London NW2 6FJ, UNITED KINGDOM
(UK)

Quarterflash
5410 SW MacAdam Ave. #280
Portland, OR 97201

Quastel, J Hirsch (Biologist, Scientist)
4585 Langara Ave
Vancouver, BC V6R 1C9, CANADA

Quasthoff, Thomas (Musician)
Cramer/Marser Artists
3436 Springhill Road
Lafayette, CA 94549, USA

Quate, Calvin F (Scientist)
340 Princeton Road
Menlo Park, CA 94025-5220, USA

Quatro, Suzi (Musician, Songwriter,
Writer)
Jive
4 Pasteur Courtyard Whittle Road
Corby
Norths, FL NN17 5DX, UNITED
KINGDOM (UK)

Quayle, Anna (Actor)
CDA
47 Courtfield Road
London, ENGLAND SW7 4DB, UNITED
KINGDOM (UK)

Quayle, Benjamin (Congressman,
Politician)
1419 Longworth HOB
Washington, DC 20515, USA

Quayle, Dan (Politician)
c/o Laura Minter
6224 N 61st Pl
Paradise Valley, AZ 85253-4212, USA

Quayle, Jenny (Actor)
c/o Staff Member *Michelle Braidman
Assoc*
Lower John St Fl 3 #10/11
London W1F 9EB, UNITED KINGDOM
(UK)

Qubein, Nido (Business Person)
Creative Services Inc
PO Box 6008
806 Westchester Dr
High Point, NC 27262, USA

Quddus (Television Host)
c/o Michael (Mike) Esterman
Esterman.Com, LLC
Prefers to be contacted via email
MD, USA

Queen (Music Group, Musician)
16-A High Street Barnes
London SW13 9LW, UK

Queen, Ida (Musician)
Traditional Arts Services
16045 36th Ave NE
Lake Forest Park, WA 98155, USA

Queen, Jeff (Athlete, Football Player)
1367 Temple Heights Dr
Oceanside, CA 92056, USA

Queen, Konga (Actor, Wrestler)
PO Box 5050
Carson, CA 90749, USA

Queen Elizabeth II (Royalty)
Buckingham Palace
London SW1A 1AA, UNITED KINGDOM
(UK)

Queen Rania (Royalty)
Royal Palace
Amman, JORDAN

Queens of the Stone Age (Music Group)
c/o Staff Member *Creative Artists Agency
(CAA-LA)*
2000 Ave Of The Stars
Los Angeles, CA 90067, USA

Queensryche (Music Group)
c/o Staff Member *Monterey International
(Chicago)*
200 W Superior
Suite 202
Chicago, IL 60610, USA

Queffelec, Anne (Musician)
15 Ave Corneille
Maisons-Laffittle 78600, FRANCE

Queler, Eve (Conductor)
Opera Orchestra of New York
239 W 72nd St
#2R
New York, NY 10023, USA

Quellmatz, Udo (Athlete)
Friedhofstr 10
Omgolstandt 85049, GERMANY

Queloz, Didier (Astronomer)
University of Geneva
Geneva Observatory
Geneva, SWITZERLAND

Quenneville, Joel (Athlete, Hockey Player)
Chicago Blackhawks
1901 W Madison St
Chicago, IL 60612-2459

Quenneville, Joel (Athlete, Coach,
Hockey Player)
835 S Park Ave
Hinsdale, IL 60521-4569

Quentin, Carlos (Athlete, Baseball Player)
17887 Old Winemaster Way
Poway, CA 92064, USA

Quenzrd, Nathalie (Actor)
Cineart
36 Rue de Ponthieu
Paris 75008, FRANCE

Query, Jeff (Athlete, Football Player)
93 Woodlily Pl
Spring, TX 77382-1254, USA

Quester, Hugues (Actor)
Cineart
36 Rue de Ponthieu
Paris 75008, FRANCE

Questlove (Musician)
Motown Records
6255 Sunset Blvd
Los Angeles, CA 90028, USA

Questrom, Allen I (Business Person)
J C Penney Co
6501 Legacy Dr
Plano, TX 75024, USA

Quezada, Milly (Musician)
c/o Staff Member *Sony Music Miami*
605 Lincoln Rd Fl 7
Miami Beach, FL 33139, USA

Quezada Toruno, Rodolfo Cardinal
(Religious Leader)
Archdiocese
7A Avenida 6-21
Zona 1
Guatemala City 01001, GUATEMALA

Quick, Clarence E (Musician, Songwriter,
Writer)
376 Quincy St
Brroklyn, NY 11216, USA

Quick, Diana (Actor)
39 Seymour Walk
London SW10, UNITED KINGDOM (UK)

Quick, James E (Jim) (Actor)
PO Box 12760
Scottsdale, AZ 85267, USA

Quick, Jim (Athlete, Baseball Player)
6061 Keeble Ln
Camino, CA 95709-9100, USA

Quick, Jonathan (Athlete, Hockey Player)
c/o Staff Member *Los Angeles Kings*
1111 S. Figueroa St
Suite 3100
Los Angeles, CA 90015, USA

Quick, Michael A (Mike) (Athlete,
Football Player)
13 Slab Branch Rd
Marlton, NJ 08053, USA

Quick, Rebecca (Talk Show Host)
Squawk Box
900 Sylvan Ave
Englewood Cliffs, NJ 07632, USA

Quick, Richard (Coach, Swimmer)
Stanford University
Athletic Dept
Stanford, CA 94305, USA

Quicksilver (Music Group)
c/o Staff Member *Paradigm (Monterey)*
404 W Franklin St
Monterey, CA 93940, USA

Quie, Al (Politician)
4209 Christy Ln
Minnetonka, MN 55345-3001, USA

Quie, Albert H (Al) (Ex-Governor)
4209 Christy Ln
Minnetonka, MN 55345, USA

Quiel, Norwald (General)
6761 Camino Del Prado
Carlsbad, CA 92011-3313, USA

Quiet Riot
2002 Hogback Rd. #20
Ann Arbor, MI 48105

Quigley, Austin E (Educator)
Columbia College
President's Office
New York, NY 10027, USA

Quigley, Dana (Golfer)
Crestwood Country Club
90 Wheeler St
Rehoboth, MA 02769, USA

Quigley, Donald (General)
464 James Way Apt 226
Marion, OH 43302-7820, USA

Quigley, Linnea (Actor)
2608-1 N. Ocean Blvd
#126
Pompano Beach, FL 33062, USA

Quigley, Mike (Congressman, Politician)
3742 W Irving Park Rd
Chicago, IL 60618, USA

Quigley, Philip J (Phil) (Business Person)
Pacific Telesis Group
130 Keamy St
San Francisco, CA 94108, USA

Quik, D J (Musician)
International Creative Mgmt
8942 Wilshire Blvd
#219
Beverly Hills, CA 90211, USA

Quilici, Frank (Athlete, Baseball Player,
Coach)
3413 E 126th St
Burnsville, MN 55337-3440, USA

Quill, Leonard W (Financier)
Wilmington Trust Corp
Rodney Square N
1100 N Market St
Wilmington, DE 19801, USA

Quill, Timothy E (Activist)
University of Rochester
Medical & Dentistry School
Rochester, NY 14642, USA

Quillan, Frederick (Fred) (Athlete,
Football Player)
2924 Bailey Ln
Eugene, OR 97401, USA

Quinaz, Victor (Director)
c/o Chad Hamilton *Anonymous Content
(LA)*
3531 Hayden Ave
Culver City, CA 90232, USA

Quindlen, Anna (Writer)
New York Times 229 W 43rd St
New York, NY 10036-3913, USA

Quinlan, Kathleen (Actor)
P.O. Box 6728
Malibu, CA 90264, USA

Quinlan, Maeve (Actor)
c/o Staff Member *Main Title Entertainment*
8383 Wilshire Blvd
Suite 408
Los Angeles, CA 90211, USA

Quinlan, Maive
1123 N. Flores St.
W. Hollywood, CA 90069

Quinlan, Robb (Athlete, Baseball Player)
5875 Ueland Ln N
Minneapolis, MN 55446-4535, USA

Quinlan, Sally (Golfer)
325 E Sola St #89
Santa Barbara, CA 93101, USA

Quinlan, Tom (Athlete, Baseball Player)
1061 Sterling St S
Saint Paul, MN 55119-5972, USA

Quinlan, William D (Bill) (Athlete,
Football Player)
393 Mount Vernon St
Lawrence, MA 01843, USA

Quinn, Aidan (Actor)
c/o Peg Donegan *Framework
Entertainment (LA)*
9057 Nemo St
Suite C
West Hollywood, CA 90069, USA

Quinn, Aileen (Actor)
c/o Corey Smith *Gemini Entertainment*
P.O. Box 1772
New York, NY 10101, USA

Quinn, Brady (Athlete, Football Player)
c/o Team Member *Cleveland Browns*
76 Lou Groza Blvd
Berea, OH 44017, USA

Quinn, Brandon (Actor)
c/o Ben Feigin *Anonymous Content (LA)*
3531 Hayden Ave
Culver City, CA 90232, USA

Quinn, Brian (Coach, Soccer Player)
San Jose Earthquakes
3550 Stevens Creek Blvd
#200
San Jose, CA 95117, USA

Quinn, Chris
13000 SW 92nd Ave
Apt B311, FL 33176-5756, USA

Quinn, Colin (Actor, Comedian)
c/o Staff Member *Agency for the
Performing Arts (APA-LA)*
405 S Beverly Dr
Suite 500
Beverly Hills, CA 90212-4425, USA

Quinn, Colleen (Actor)
Bauman Assoc
5750 Wilshire Blvd
#473
Los Angeles, CA 90036, USA

Quinn, Dan (Athlete, Hockey Player)
3150 San Michele Dr
Palm Beach Gardens, FL 33418-6702

Quinn, Danny (Actor)
c/o Michael Greenwald *Buchwald/
Fortitude (LA)*
6500 Wilshire Blvd
Suite 2200
Los Angeles, CA 90048, USA

Quinn, David W (Business Person)
Centex Corp
2728 N Harwood
Dallas, TX 75201, USA

Quinn, DeClan (Cinematographer)
22 Cherry Ave
Cornwall on Hudson, NY 12520, USA

Quinn, Ed (Actor)
c/o Staff Member *Burstein Company, The*
15304 Sunset Blvd
suite 208
Pacific Palisades, CA 90272, USA

Quinn, Freddy
Am Pfeilshof 35
Hamburg, GERMANY D-22393

Quinn, Glenn (Actor)
Sanders Armstrong Management
2120 Colorado Blvd #120
Santa Monica, CA 90404, USA

Quinn, Jane Bryant (Journalist)
Newsweek Magazine
Editorial Dept
251 W 57th St
New York, NY 10019, USA

Quinn, Jim (Misc)
675 S Sierra Ave
#32
Solana Beach, CA 92075, USA

Quinn, John A (Engineer)
275 E Wynnewood Road
Merion Station, PA 19066, USA

Quinn, John C (Editor)
365 S Atlantic Ave
Cocoa Beach, FL 32931, USA

Quinn, Mark (Athlete, Baseball Player)
1013 S Dancove Dr
West Covina, CA 91791-3720, USA

Quinn, Martha (Actor, Model)
11684 Ventura Blvd #453
Studio City, CA 91604, USA

Quinn, Mike (Athlete, Football Player)
10703 Del Monte Dr
Houston, TX 77042, USA

Quinn, Molly (Actor)
c/o Ellen Meyer *Ellen Meyer Management*
8899 Beverly Blvd
Suite 612
West Hollywood, CA 90048, USA

Quinn, Pat (Governor)
Office of the Governor
207 State House
Springfield, IL 62706, USA

Quinn, Pat (Athlete, Coach, Hockey
Player)
Edmonton Oilers
11230 110 St NW
Edmonton, AB T5G 3H7, Canada

Quinn, Patricia (Actor)
Jonathan Altaras Associates
11 Garrick Street
London WC2E 9AR, United Kingdom

Quinn, Robert (Football Player)
c/o Carl Carey *Champion Pro Consulting
Group*
3547 Ruth St
Houston, TX 77004, USA

Quinn, Sally (Journalist)
3014 N St NW
Washington, DC 20007-3404, USA

Quinn, Stephen (Athlete, Football Player)
RR 1 Box 163
Mount Sterling, IL 62353, USA

Quinnett, Brian (Athlete, Basketball
Player)
862 Indian Hills Dr
Moscow, ID 83843-9373, USA

Quinney, Ken (Athlete, Hockey Player)
3638 Starbright Ln
Las Vegas, NV 89147-6524

Quinones, John (Correspondent)
c/o Staff Member *ABC News*
77 W 66th St
3rd Floor
New York, NY 10023, USA

Quinones, Luis (Athlete, Baseball Player)
5821 Calle San Bruno
Urb Santa Teresita
Ponce, PR 00730-4443, USA

Quinones, Rey (Athlete, Baseball Player)
216 Calle Ronda Villa Andalucia
San Juan, PR 00926-2351, USA

Quint, Deron (Athlete, Hockey Player)
21154 N 36th Pl
Phoenix, AZ 85050-8386

Quintal, Stephane (Athlete, Hockey
Player)
1356A La Fontaine
Montreal, QC H2L 1T5, Canada

Quintana, Chela (Golfer)
Ladies Pro Golf Assn
100 International Golf Dr
Daytona Beach, FL 32124, USA

Quintanilla, Omar (Athlete, Baseball
Player)
12457 Paseo De Arco Ct
El Paso, TX 79928-5669, USA

Quintero, Humberto
12201 Mossy Trail Ct
Pearland, TX 77584-4558, USA

Quintin, J F (Athlete, Hockey Player)
6821 Oak St
Kansas City, MO 64113-2476

Quinto, Zachary (Actor)
c/o Jason Weinberg *Untitled Entertainment (LA)*
350 S. Beverly Dr #200
Beverly Hills, CA 90212, USA

Quirico, Rafael (Athlete, Baseball Player)
2901 N Dale Mabry Hwy #2103
Tampa, FL 33607, USA

Quiring, Frederic (Actor)
Cineart
36 Rue de Ponthieu
Paris 75008, FRANCE

Quirk, Art (Athlete, Baseball Player)
2 Ensign Ln
Stonington, CT 06378-2944, USA

Quirk, James P (Jamie) (Athlete, Baseball Player)
Houston Astros 501 Crawford St Ste 400
Attn: Coaching Staff
Houston, TX 77002-2113, USA

Quirk, Michael J (War Hero)
1700 Kit Lane
Navarre, FL 32566, USA

Quiroga, Elena (Writer)
Agencia Balcells
Diagonal 580
Barcelona 08021, SPAIN

Quiroga, Jorge (Tuto) (President)
President's Office
Palacio de Gobierno
Plaza Murllia
La Paz, BOLIVIA

Quist, Janet (Model)
13446 Poway Road
#239
Poway, CA 92064, USA

Quitones, John (Correspondent)
ABC-TV
News Dept
77 W 66th St
New York, NY 10023, USA

Quivar, Florence (Opera Singer)
Columbia Artists Mgmt Inc
165 W 57th St
New York, NY 10019, USA

Quivers, Robin (Actor, Entertainer, Radio Personality, Talk Show Host)
c/o Staff Member *Buchwald/Fortitude (LA)*
6500 Wilshire Blvd
Suite 2200
Los Angeles, CA 90048, USA

Qulgley, Brett (Golfer)
127 Sandpiper Cir
Jupiter, FL 33477-8434, USA

Qulgley, Dana (Golfer)
2670 Tecumseh Dr
West Palm Beach, FL 33409-7421, USA

Quon, Di (Actor)
c/o Loch Powell *Leverage Management*
3030 Pennsylvania Ave
Santa Monica, CA 90404, USA

Quon, Erin (Stylist)
544 Central Ave
San Francisco, CA 94117-1313, USA

Qureia, Ahmed (Prime Minister)
Prime Minister's Office
Gara City
Gaza Strip
Palestine, ISRAEL

R

Raab, Chris (Actor)
c/o Staff Member *Haber Entertainment*
434 S Canon Dr
Suite 204
Beverly Hills, CA 90212, USA

Raab, Marc (Athlete, Football Player)
8500 Sea Pines Pl
McKinney, TX 75070, USA

Raab, Stefan (Musician)
c/o Staff Member *Allendorf Riehl GmbH*
Kaesenstrasse 17
Koeln D-50677, Germany

Raabe, Brian (Athlete, Baseball Player)
38760 Kost Trl
North Branch, MN 55056-6722, USA

Raabe, Max (Opera Singer)
Klimperkasten
Thuyring 63
Berlin 12101, GERMANY

Raakhee (Actor, Bollywood)
Muktangan Sarojini Naidu Road
Santacruz
Bombay, MS 400 054, INDIA

Raaurn, Gustav (Skier)
PO Box 700
Mercer Island, WA 98040, USA

Raba, Robert (Athlete, Football Player)
16066 Acre St
North Hills, CA 91343, USA

Rabb, John (Athlete, Baseball Player)
8614 Hoocer Ave
Los Angeles, CA 90002-1143, USA

Rabe, Charlie (Athlete, Baseball Player)
6059 E Sierra Blanca St
Mesa, AZ 85215-7753, USA

Rabe, Josh (Athlete, Baseball Player)
Quincy University 1800 College Ave
Attn: Mens Baseball Head Coa
Quincy, IL 62301-2610, USA

Rabe, Lily (Actor)
c/o Peg Donegan *Framework Entertainment (LA)*
9057 Nemo St
Suite C
West Hollywood, CA 90069, USA

Rabe, Pamela (Actor)
Shanahan Mgmt
PO Box 1509
Darlinghurst, NSW 1300, AUSTRALIA

Rabelo, Mike (Athlete, Baseball Player)
5813 N 17th St
Tampa, FL 33610-4308, USA

Rabensteiner, Robert (Stylist)
c/o Staff Member *Michele Filomeno New York LLC*
515 Greenwich St Ste 503
New York, NY 10013, USA

Rabin, Trevor (Composer)
Kraft-Benjamin-Engel
15233 Ventura Blvd
#200
Sherman Oaks, CA 91403, USA

Rabinovitch, Benton S (Misc)
12530 42nd Ave NE
Seattle, WA 98125, USA

Rabinowitz, Dorothy (Journalist)
Wall Street Journal
Editorial Dept
200 Liberty St
New York, NY 10281, USA

Rabinowitz, Harry (Composer, Conductor)
11 Mead Road
Cranleigh
Surrey GU6 7BG, UNITED KINGDOM (UK)

Rabinowitz, Jesse C (Misc)
University of California
Molecular & Cell Biology Dept
Berkeley, CA 94720, USA

Rabkin, Mitchell T (Doctor)
Beth Israel Deaconess Medical Center
330 Brookline Ave
Boston, MA 02215, USA

Raburn, Ryan (Athlete, Baseball Player)
PO Box 304
Balm, FL 33503-0304, USA

Raby, Stuart (Physicist)
Ohio State University
Physics Dept
Columbus, OH 43210, USA

Racan, Ivica (Prime Minister)
Prime Minister's Office
Jordanovac 71
Zagreb 41000, CROATIA

Racette, Patricia (Opera Singer)
Columbia Artists Mgmt Inc
165 W 57th St
New York, NY 10019, USA

Rachal, Latorio (Athlete, Football Player)
3266 Golden Ave
Long Beach, CA 90806, USA

Rachin, Julian (Musician)
Columbia Artists Mgmt Inc
165 W 57th St
New York, NY 10019, USA

Rachins, Alan (Actor)
c/o Mark Teitelbaum *Teitelbaum Artists Group*
8840 Wilshire Blvd
3rd Floor
Beverly Hills, CA 90212, USA

Racicot, Jody (Actor)
c/o Jamie Levitt *Lauren Levitt & Associates Inc*
1525 W 8th St 3rd Fl
Vancouver V6J 1T5, British Columbia

Racicot, Marc F (Politician)
28013 Swan Cove Dr
Bigfork, MT 59911-7846, USA

Racicot, Pierre (Athlete, Hockey Player)
828 Hampton Ct
Weston, FL 33326-2917

Racine, Bruce (Athlete, Hockey Player)
35 S Ridge Meadows Ln
Troy, MO 63379-6306

Racine, Jean (Athlete, Bobsledder, Olympic Athlete)
14515 S 29th Cir
Bellevue, NE 68123-4776, USA

Racine, Yves (Athlete, Hockey Player)
Arizona Capital Inc
1515 Av StJean Baptiste
Quebec, QC G2E SE2, Canada

Rackers, Neil (Athlete, Football Player)
945 Shady Path Ct
Saint Peters, MO 63376, USA

Rackley, David (Athlete, Baseball Player)
7009 Almeda Rd Apt 236
Houston, TX 77054-2177, USA

Rackley, Derek (Athlete, Football Player)
5659 Legends Club Cir
Braselton, GA 30517, USA

Rackley, Luther (Athlete, Basketball Player)
36 W 128th St
Apt 2
New York, NY 10027-2106, USA

Rackley, Marv (Athlete, Baseball Player)
512 S Bibb St
Westminster, SC 29693-2134, USA

Raczka, Mike (Athlete, Baseball Player)
72 Foley Dr
Southington, CT 06489-4400, USA

Radachowsky, George (Athlete, Football Player)
87 Merrimac St
Danbury, CT 06810, USA

Radcliffe, Daniel (Actor)
c/o Scott Boute *Scott Boute Publicity*
529 W 42nd St
Apt 5A
New York, NY 10036, USA

Raddatz, Carl
Stalluponer Allee 54
Berlin, GERMANY 14055

Rade, John (Athlete, Football Player)
611 Deertrail Dr
Hailey, ID 83333-8731, USA

Rademacher, Bill (Athlete, Football Player)
5409 Maple Ridge
Haslett, MI 48840, USA

Rademacher, Ingo (Actor)
S D B Partners
1801 Ave of Stars
#902
Los Angeles, CA 90067, USA

Rademacher, Pete (Athlete, Boxer, Olympic Athlete)
5585 River Styx Rd.
Medina, OH 44256, USA

Rademacher, T Peter (Pete) (Boxer)
5585 River Styx Road
Medina, OH 44256, USA

Rader, Dave (Athlete, Baseball Player)
2660 Sunset Hls
Escondido, CA 92025-7850, USA

Rader, Douglas L (Doug) (Athlete, Baseball Player, Coach)
P.O. Box 2768
Stuart, FL 34995-2768, USA

Rader, Randall R (Judge)
US Appeals Court
717 Madison Place NW
Washington, DC 20439, USA

Rader, Stanley
360 Waverly Dr.
Pasadena, CA 91105

Radford, Mark (Athlete, Basketball Player)
5160 NE Wistaria Dr
Portland, OR 97212-2432, USA

Radford, Michael (Director)
38 Rickering Mews
London W2 5AD, UNITED KINGDOM
(UK)

Radford, Wayne (Athlete, Basketball
Player)
4660 Running Brook Ter
Greenwood, IN 46143-9254, USA

Radha Ravi (Actor)
23 Poes Road
Teynampet
Chennai, TN 600 018, INDIA

Radhika (Actor, Bollywood)
3 Paul Appasamy Street
Abhirampuram
Chennai, TN 600018, INDIA

Radigan, Terry (Musician, Songwriter)
Frank Callan Corp
209 10th Ave S #322
Nashville, TN 37203, USA

Radin, Joshua
c/o Debbie Wilson *Wilspro Management*
P.O. Box 9
Point Pleasant, NY 10001, USA

Radinsky, Scott (Athlete, Baseball Player)
1605 E Hillcrest Dr
Unit B
Thousand Oaks, CA 91362-2647, USA

Radiohead (Music Group)
c/o Staff Member *XL Recordings*
1 Codrington Mews
London W11 2EH, UNITED KINGDOM

Radisic, Zivko (President)
President's Office
Marsala Titz 7
Sarajevo 71000, BOSNIA &
HERZEGOVINA

Radison, Dan (Athlete, Baseball Player)
116 SE 20th Ave
Deerfield Beach, FL 33441-4521, USA

Radke, Brad W (Athlete, Baseball Player)
125 18th St
Belleair Beach, FL 33786-3313, USA

Radko, Christopher (Artist)
PO Box 536
Elmsford, NY 10523, USA

Radloff, Wayne (Athlete, Football Player)
106 Wedgefield Dr
Hilton Head Island, SC 29926, USA

Radlosky, Rob (Athlete, Baseball Player)
1219 W Broward St
Lantana, FL 33462-3013, USA

Radmanovich, Ryan (Athlete, Baseball
Player)
25 Ware Ave
West Hartford, CT 06119-1532, USA

Radner, Roy (Economist)
30711 Overlook Run
Buena Vista, CO 81211, USA

Radnor, Josh (Actor)
c/o Carrie Byalick *I/D PR (NY)*
150 W 30th St
19th Floor
New York, NY 10001, USA

Radojevic, Danilo (Dancer)
American Ballet Theatre
890 Broadway
New York, NY 10003, USA

Radosevich, George (Athlete, Football
Player)
414 Shaffer Ave
Elizabeth, PA 15037, USA

Radovich, Frank (Athlete, Basketball
Player)
121 Lakewood Dr
Statesboro, GA 30458, USA

Radtke, Sheilah (Stylist)
c/o Staff Member *Page.214*
3303 Lee Pkwy
#205
Dallas, TX 75219, USA

Raduege Jr, Harry D (General)
Director
Defense Information Systems Agency
Arlington, VA 22204, USA

Radwanski, George (Editor)
Toronto Star
Editorial Dept
1 Yonge St
Toronto, ON M5E 1E6, CANADA

Rady, Michael (Actor)
c/o Kasra Ajir *Station3*
1051 Cole Av
Culver City, CA 90038, USA

Radziwill, Lee (Misc)
c/o Staff Member *Assouline Publishing,
Inc.*
601 W 26th St
18th Floor
New York, NY 10001, USA

Rae, Cassidy (Actor)
SDB Partners Inc
c/o Ro Diamond
1801 Avenue of the Stars #902
Los Angeles, CA 90067, USA

Rae, Charlotte (Actor)
10790 Wilshire Blvd
#903
Los Angeles, CA 90024, USA

Rae, Emily (Actor)
c/o Pamela Kohl *3 Arts Entertainment Inc*
9460 Wilshire Blvd
7th Floor
Beverly Hills, CA 90210, USA

Rae, Fiona (Artist)
The Royal Academy of Arts
Burlington House
Piccadilly
London W1J 0BD, UK

Rae, Mike (Athlete, Football Player)
18541 Auburn Ave
Santa Ana, CA 92705, USA

Rae, Patricia (Actor)

Rae, Robert K (Bob) (Politician)
Goodman Phillips Vineberg
250 Yonge St
Toronto, ON M5B 2M6, CANADA

Rae, Savannah Paige
c/o Sarah Shyn *3 Arts Entertainment Inc*
9460 Wilshire Blvd
7th Floor
Beverly Hills, CA 90210, USA

Raekwon (Musician)
c/o Drew Elliot *Universal Media Artists*
8255 W Sunset Blvd
Los Angeles, CA 90046, USA

Raether, Hal (Athlete, Baseball Player)
6105 Lincoln Dr
Apt 133
Minneapolis, MN 55436-1619, USA

Rae Westley, Jennifer (Actor)
c/o Staff Member *da Vinci Talent*
919 Marie Anne Est
Montreal QC H2J 2B2, CANADA

Rafalski, Brian (Athlete, Hockey Player,
Olympic Athlete)
20 Holton Lane
Essex Falls, NJ 07021-1709, USA

Rafelson, Bob (Director)
1543 Dog Team Road
1022 Palm Ave. #3
New Haven, VT 05472, USA

Raffarin, Jean-Pierre (Prime Minister)
Sénat
15 Rue De Vaugirard
Cedex 06
Paris F-75291, FRANCE

Rafferty, Thomas M (Tom) (Athlete,
Football Player)
1526 Mount Galead Rd
Roanoke, TX 76262-7358, USA

Raffo, Al (Athlete, Baseball Player)
330 Pleasant View Cir
Jasper, TN 37347-7242, USA

Rafikov, Mars Z (Cosmonaut)
Ul M Gorkova 59
KV 44
Almaty 480 002, KAZAKHSTAN

Rafko, Kaye Lani Rae
4932 Frary Lane
Monroe, MI 48161

Rafsanjani, Hashemi (Ex-President,
President)
Ali Shariati Ave
Tehran, IRAN

Rafsanjani, Hojatoleslam H (President)
*Expediency Council of Islamic Order
Majlis*
Teheran, IRAN

Rafshoon, Gerald
3028 Q St. NW
Washington, DC 20006

Rafter, Patrick (Tennis Player)
PO Box 1235
North Sydney, NSW 2059, AUSTRALIA

Raftery, Erin (Actor)
c/o Rachel Rothman *Rothman / Patino /
Andres Entertainment*
4370 Tujunga Ave
Suite 120
Studio City, CA 91604, USA

Raftery, S Frank (Misc)
Painters & Allied Trades Union
1750 New York Ave NW
Washington, DC 20006, USA

Ragan, Dave (Athlete, Golfer)
Dave Ragan Inc
PO Box 1131
Harrisburg, NC 28075, USA

Ragan, David (Race Car Driver)
c/o Staff Member *NASCAR*
1801 Speedway Blvd
Daytona Beach, FL 32015, USA

Ragavendar (Actor)
2-C Palace View Apartments
788 Santhome High Road
Chennai, TN 600 028, INDIA

Rage Against The Machine (Music Group,
Musician)
c/o Staff Member *Columbia Records UK*
Bedford House
69-79 Fulham High St
London SW6 3JW, United Kingdom

Rager, Roger (Race Car Driver)
1680 64th Street SW
Pequot Lakes, MN 56472, USA

Raggi, Florencia (Actor)
c/o Staff Member *Telefe - Argentina*
Pavon 2444 (C1248AAT)
Buenos Aires, ARGENTINA

Raggio, Brady (Athlete, Baseball Player)
10653 Rue D Azur
Reno, NV 89511-4308, USA

Raggio, Lisa
9300 Wilshire Blvd. #410
Beverly Hills, CA 90212

Raghavan, V S (Actor)
6 School View Road
Mandavelli
Chennai, TN 600 028, INDIA

Raghavi (Actor, Bollywood)
18 Crescent Park Road
T Nagar
Chennai, TN 600017, INDIA

Raghuvaran (Actor)
D-1 Ist Floor Anandsree Apartments
32 Hindi Prachar Saba Street
Chennai, TN 600 017, INDIA

Ragin, Derek Lee (Opera Singer)
Colbert Artists
111 W 57th St
New York, NY 10019, USA

Ragin, John S (Actor)
5706 Briarcliff Road
Los Angeles, CA 90068, USA

Raglan, Herb (Athlete, Hockey Player)
1206 Cabot St
Peterborough, ON K9H 6W9, CANADA

Ragland, Tom (Athlete, Baseball Player)
20201 Greenlawn St
Detroit, MI 48221-1187, USA

Raglin, Floyd (Athlete, Football Player)
2701 Alister Ave
Tustin, CA 92782, USA

Ragnarsson, Marcus (Athlete, Hockey
Player)
Hallonstigen 2
Bjorklinge, S-74030 Sweden

Ragnone, Teresa (Stylist)
5679 SE International Way
Portland, OR 97222, USA

Rago, Pablo (Actor)
c/o Staff Member *Telefe - Argentina*
Pavon 2444 (C1248AAT)
Buenos Aires, ARGENTINA

Ragogna, Mike (Musician, Producer)
3975 Meier St #201
Los Angeles, CA 90066, USA

Ragsdale, William (Actor)
Innovative Artists
1505 10th St
Santa Monica, CA 90401, USA

Rahal, Bashar (Actor)
c/o Victor (Viktor) Kruglov *Victor Kruglov
Talent Management*
7461 Beverly Blvd Ste 403
Los Angeles, CA 90036, USA

Rahal, Bobby
PO Box 429
New Albany, OH 43054-0429

Rahal, Robert W (Bobby) (Race Car
Driver)
Team Rahal Racing
5 New Albany Farms Road
New Albany, OH 43054, USA

Rahel (Stylist)
c/o Staff Member *L'Agence*
5901-C Peachtree Dunwoody Rd
#60
Atlanta, GA 30328, USA

Rahlves, Daron (Athlete, Olympic Athlete,
Skier)
11655 Mount Rose View Dr
Truckee, CA 96161, USA

Rahm, Kevin (Actor)
3 Arts Entertainment
9460 Wilshire Blvd
#700
Beverly Hills, CA 90212, USA

Rahman, A.R. (Bollywood, Composer)
c/o Sam Schwartz *Gorfaine/Schwartz
Agency Inc*
4111 W Alameda Ave
Suite 509
Burbank, CA 91505, USA

Rahman, Hamida Betty (Stylist)
2329 NE Clackamas St
Portland, OR 97232, USA

Rahman Khan, Ataur (Prime Minister)
Bangladesh Jatiya League
500 A Dhanmondi R/A
Road 7
Dhaka, BANGLADESH

Rahner, Robert (Horse Racer)
5 Catalina Ln
Selden, NY 11784-1775, USA

Rahul, Roy (Actor, Bollywood)
502 Gildar Villa
17 Master Vinayak X Road Bandra
Mumbai, MS 400050, INDIA

Rahyel, Bobby (Race Car Driver)
934 Crescent Blvd.
Glenellyn, IL 60137, USA

Rahzel (Musician)
c/o Staff Member *Agency Group Ltd, The
(NY)*
142 West 57th St
6th Floor
New York, NY 10019, USA

Rai, Aishwarya (Actor, Bollywood,
Dancer)
402 Ramalaxmi Nowas
16th Road Khar(W)
Mumbai, MS 400054, India

Rai, Rajeev (Bollywood, Director,
Filmmaker, Producer)
22 Sonmarg Nepean Sea Road
Bombay, MS 400 006, INDIA

Rai, Rajiv (Bollywood, Director, Producer)
B-11 Commerce Center
Tardeo
Mumbai, MS 400034, INDIA

Raible, Steve (Athlete, Football Player)
2721 1st Ave
Apt 1002
Seattle, WA 98424, USA

Raich, Benjamin (Athlete, Skier)
Ferienhof Raich
Leins 12
Arzl im Pitztal- Tirol A-6471, Austria

Raich, Eric (Athlete, Baseball Player)
3963 Edward Dr
Brunswick, OH 44212-1509, USA

Raichle, Marcus E (Doctor)
Washington University
Medical School
Neurology Dept
Saint Louis, MO 63130, USA

Raider-Wexler, Victor (Actor)
c/o Lorraine Berglund *Lorraine Berglund
Management*
11537 Hesby St.
North Hollywood, CA 91601, USA

Raiken, Sherwin (Athlete, Basketball
Player)
2400 McClellan Blvd
Apt 120B
Pennsauken, NJ 08109, USA

Raikkonen, Kimi (Race Car Driver)
c/o Staff Member *Formula Management
Ltd*
PO Box 222
Borehamwood
Herts WD6 3FJ, United Kingdom

Railsback, Steve (Actor)
11684 Ventura Blvd
#581
Studio City, CA 91604, USA

Raimi, Sam (Writer)
c/o Richard Lovett *Creative Artists Agency
(CAA-LA)*
2000 Ave Of The Stars
Los Angeles, CA 90067, USA

Raimi, Ted (Director, Producer)

Raimond, Jean-Bernard (Government
Official)
Servier SA
22 Rue Garnier
Neuilly-sur-Seine 92200, FRANCE

Raimondi, Ben (Athlete, Football Player)
5 Grandview Dr
Holmdel, NJ 07733, USA

Raimondi, Ruggero (Opera Singer)
M Gromof
140 Bis Rue Lecourbe
Paris 75015, USA

Rain, Misty
Box 67
Lakewood, CA 90714

Rain, Steve (Athlete, Baseball Player)
20320 E Crestline Dr
Walnut, CA 91789-4605, USA

Raine, Craig A (Writer)
New College
English Dept
Oxford OX1 3BN, UNITED KINGDOM
(UK)

Raine, Gillian
13 Billing Rd.
London, ENGLAND SW10

Rainer, Luise (Actor)
54 Eaton Square
London SW1, UNITED KINGDOM (UK)

Rainer, Wali (Athlete, Football Player)
4715 Monaco Dr
Sandston, VA 23150, USA

Raines, Cristina
6399 Wilshire Blvd. #414
Los Angeles, CA 90048

Raines, Franklin D (Financier,
Government Official)
Federal National Mortgage Assn
3900 Wisconsin Ave NW
Washington, DC 20016, USA

Raines, Mike (Athlete, Football Player)
112 Lupine Dr
Jacksonville, FL 32259, USA

Raines, Tim (Athlete, Baseball Player)
1242 Saint Albans Loop
Lake Mary, FL 32746-1978, USA

Raines, Tony (Race Car Driver)
Front Row Motorsports
3536 Denver Dr.
Denver, NC 28037, USA

Rainey, Chuck (Athlete, Baseball Player)
6484 Del Cerro Blvd
San Diego, CA 92120-4804, USA

Rainey, Matt (Journalist)
Star-Ledger
Editorial Dept
1 Star-Ledge Plaza
Newark, NJ 07102, USA

Rains, Dan (Athlete, Football Player)
2509 Wigwam Rd
Aliquippa, PA 15001, USA

Rains, Luce (Actor, Producer)
c/o Andrew Stawiarski *ADS Management*
269 S. Beverly Dr #441
Beverly Hills, CA 90212, USA

Rainwater, G L (Business Person)
Ameren Corp
1901 Chouteau Ave
Saint Louis, MO 63103, USA

Rainwater, Gregg (Actor)
PO Box 291836
Los Angeles, CA 90029, USA

Rainwater, Marvin (Musician)
36968 295th St
Aitkin, MN 56431, USA

Raisa, Francia (Actor)
c/o Faras Rabadi *Emerald Talent Group*
10 Universal City Plaza
20th Floor
Universal City, CA 91608, USA

Raisman, Aly (Athlete, Gymnast, Olympic
Athlete)
Brestyan's American Gymnastics Club
13 Ray Ave
Burlington, MA 01803, USA

Raitt, Bonnie L (Musician, Songwriter,
Writer)
c/o Staff Member *Paradigm (Monterey)*
404 W Franklin St
Monterey, CA 93940, USA

Raj, Prakash (Actor)
183 Bharathidasan Street
Baskar Colony Virugambakka
Chennai, TN 600 092, INDIA

Raja (Actor)
6 Ranjith Road
Kotturpuram
Chennai, TN 600 085, INDIA

Rajasulochana (Actor, Bollywood)
70 G N Chetty Road
T Nagar
Chennai, TN 600017, INDIA

Rajat, Kapoor (Actor, Bollywood)
Unit No 140 Andheri Indl Est
Off Veera Desai Road Andheri (W)
Mumbai, MS 400053, INDIA

Rajeev (Actor)
12/V Ambedkar Street Gandhi Nagar
Saligramam
Chennai, TN 600 093, INDIA

Rajeevi (Actor, Bollywood)
32 Raman Street
T Nagar
Chennai, TN 600017, INDIA

Rajendran, S S (Actor)
3/3 Eldams Road
Chennai, TN 600 018, INDIA

Rajesh (Actor)
7 Kannappa Salai
Ashok Nagar
Chennai, TN 600 083, INDIA

Rajinikanth (Actor)
18 Raghava Veera Ave
Poes Garden
Chennai, TN 600 086, INDIA

Rajisich, Dave (Athlete, Baseball Player)
1605 N Main St
Flagstaff, AZ 86004-4917, USA

Rajkiran (Actor, Bollywood)
145/5 North Boag Road
T Nagar
Chennai, TN 600017, INDIA

Rajkumar, Puru (Actor, Bollywood)
57 Worli Sea Face
Worli
Mumbai, MS 400018, INDIA

Rajna, Thomas (Composer, Musician)
10 Wyndover Road
Claremont
Cape 7700, SOUTH AFRICA

Rajnikant (Actor, Bollywood)
18 Ragava Veera Avenue
Poes Garden
Madras, TN 600 086, INDIA

Rajsich, Dave (Athlete, Baseball Player)
1605 N Main St
Flagstaff, AZ 86004, USA

Rajsich, Gary (Athlete, Baseball Player)
6510 Charleston Dr
Colleyville, TX 76034-5670, USA

Rajskub, Mary Lynn (Actor, Writer)
c/o Christie Smith *Mosaic Media Group*
9200 W. Sunset Blvd
10th Floor
Los Angeles, CA 90069, USA

Rajtar, John (Stylist)
5032 17th Ave
South Minneapolis, MN 55417, USA

Rakers, Aaron (Athlete, Baseball Player)
553 W 3rd St
Trenton, IL 62293-1013, USA

Rakers, Jason (Athlete, Baseball Player)
547 Hickory Hollow Dr
Canfield, OH 44406-1052, USA

Rakestraw, Larry (Athlete, Football Player)
2462 Welford Ct
Suwanee, GA 30024, USA

Rakestraw, Wilbur (Race Car Driver)
2609 Marietta Hwy.
Dallas, GA 39157, USA

Rakhmonov, Emomali (President)
President's Office
Supreme Soviet
Dushanbe, TAJIKISTAN

Raki, Laya (Actor)
Atkins Assoc
8040 Ventura Canyon Ave
Panorama City, CA 91402, USA

Rakim (Musician)
Padell Nadell Fine Wineberger
156 W 56th St
#400
New York, NY 10019, USA

Rakoczy, Gregg (Athlete, Football Player)
8709 Hidden Green Ln
Tampa, FL 33647, USA

Rakos, Shawn (Athlete, Baseball Player)
23405 Fiske Road E
Orting, WA 98360, USA

Rakowski, Mieczyslaw F (Prime Minister)
Miesiecznik Dzis
Ul Poznanska 3
Warsaw 00-680, POLAND

Rales, Steven M (Business Person, Producer)
c/o Staff Member *Indian Paintbrush*
2308 Broadway
Santa Monica, CA 90405, USA

Rall, J Edward (Doctor)
3947 Baltimore St
Kensington, MD 20895, USA

Rall, Roberta (Stylist)
38 France St
Norwalk, CT 06851-3820, USA

Rall, Ted (Cartoonist)
Chronicle Features
901 Mission St
San Francisco, CA 94103, USA

Rall, Tommy (Dancer)
777 Enchanted Way
Pacific Palisades, CA 90272, USA

Ralph, Christopher (Actor)
c/o Rich Kaplan *Noble Caplan Abrams*
1260 Yonge St
2nd Floor
Toronto ON M4T 1W6, Canada

Ralph, Jim (Athlete, Hockey Player)
439 Hollandview Trail
Aurora, ON L4G 7MG, Canada

Ralston, Bob (Actor)
17027 Tennyson Pl.
Granada Hills, CA 91344-1225

Ralston, Dennis (Tennis Player)
2005 San Vicente Dr
Concord, CA 94519, USA

Ralston, John R (Athlete, Coach, Football Coach, Football Player)
8245 Claret Ct
San Jose, CA 95135, USA

Ralston, Steve (Soccer Player)
New England Revolution
CMGI Field
1 Patriot Place
Foxboro, MA 02035, USA

Ram, C Venkata (Doctor)
Texas Southwestern Medical Center
5323 Harry Hines Blvd
Dallas, TX 75390, USA

Ramage, Rob (Athlete, Hockey Player)
16127 Wilson Manor Dr
Chesterfield, MO 63005-4583, USA

Ramahata, Victor (Prime Minister)
PO Box 6004
Antanarivo 101, MADAGASCAR

Rama IX (King)
Chitralada Villa
Bangkok, THAILAND

Ramakrishnan, Venkatraman (Nobel Prize Laureate)
144 Branch St
Scituate, MA 02066-2554, USA

Ramamurthy, Sendhil (Actor)
c/o Mary Erickson *Levine Okwu Erickson Management*
6363 Wilshire Blvd
Suite 300
Los Angeles, CA 90048, USA

Raman, Priya (Actor, Bollywood)
Plot No 69
Part II VGP Sea View Palavakkam
Chennai, TN 600041, INDIA

Raman, Ragha (Actor, Bollywood)
Flat 202 II Floor
167 Eldams Road Teynampet
Chennai, TN 600018, INDIA

Ramani, Karthik (Engineer)
3421 Crawford St
West Lafayette, IN 47906, USA

Ramaphosa, M Cyril (Government Official)
New Africa Investments
PO Box 782922
Sandton 2416, SOUTH AFRICA

Ramarajan (Actor)
1 Ramakrishna Street
T Nagar
Chennai, TN 600 017, INDIA

Rama Rau, Santha (Writer)
496 Leedsville Road
Amenia, NY 12501, USA

Ramasami, V. K. (Actor, Bollywood)
26 Tilak Street
T Nagar
Chennai, TN 600017, INDIA

Ramazzotti, Eros (Musician)
Via Vittoria Colonna
Milan, ITALY I-20149

Ramba (Actor, Bollywood)
184 Bharathidasan Salai
Baskaran Colony Saligramam
Chennai, TN 600092, INDIA

Ramba (Actor)
44/1 Navaneethammal Street
Saligramam
Chennai, TN 600 093, INDIA

Rambahadur, Limbu (War Hero)
Box 420
Bandar Seri Begawan
Negara Brunei Darussalam, BRUNEI

Rambert, Charles J J (Architect)
179 Rue de Courcelles
Paris 75017, FRANCE

Rambin, Leven (Actor)
c/o Rhonda Price *Gersh (NY)*
41 Madison Ave
New York, NY 10010, USA

Rambis, Kurt (Athlete, Basketball Player)
20 Chatham
Manhattan Beach, CA 90266-7225, USA

Rambis, Kurt (Athlete, Basketball Player, Coach)
20 Chatham
Manhattan Beach, CA 90266, USA

Rambo, David L (Religious Leader)
Christian & Missionary Alliance
PO Box 35000
Colorado Springs, CO 80935, USA

Rambo, John (Athlete, Track Athlete)
1847 Myrtle Ave
Long Beach, CA 90806, USA

Rambola, Tony (Musician)
c/o Staff Member *WmE2 (WMA-LA)*
1 William Morris Pl
Beverly Hills, CA 90212, USA

Ramey, Louis (Actor, Comedian)
Top Draw Entertainment
108-39 Union Tpke
Forest Hills, NY 11375, USA

Ramey, Samuel E (Opera Singer)
320 Central Park West
New York, NY 10025, USA

Ramgoolam, Navinchandra (Prime Minister)
85 Sir Seewilsagur Ramgoolam St
Port Louis, MAURITIUS

Ramgoolam, Seewosagur (Prime Minister)
85 Desforges St
Port Louis, MAURITIUS

Ramini, TJ (Actor)
c/o Joel King *Pakula/King & Associates*
9229 Sunset Blvd
Suite 315
Los Angeles, CA 90069, USA

Ramirez, Alex (Athlete, Baseball Player)
P.O. Box 880
Winter Haven, FL 33882, USA

Ramirez, Allan (Athlete, Baseball Player)
8 Line Drive Rd
Victoria, TX 77905-5414, USA

Ramirez, Aramis (Athlete, Baseball Player)
1440 N Lake Shore Dr
Apt 10EG
Chicago, IL 60610-1626, USA

Ramirez, Carolina (Actor)
c/o Gabriel Blanco *Gabriel Blanco Iglesias (Mexico)*
Rio Balsas 35-32
Colonia Cuauhtemoc
DF 06500, Mexico

Ramirez, Cierra (Actor)
c/o Thomas Richards *Corsa Agency, The*
11704 Wilshire Blvd #204
Los Angeles, CA 90025, USA

Ramirez, Dania (Actor, Producer)
c/o Jeff Morrone *Jeff Morrone Entertainment*
9350 Wilshire Blvd
Suite 224
Beverly Hills, CA 90212, USA

Ramirez, Edgar (Actor)
c/o Leslie Sloane *Baker Winokur Ryder Public Relations BWR (BWR-NY)*
292 Madison Ave
12th Floor
New York, NY 10017, USA

Ramirez, Efren (Actor)
c/o Staff Member *James/Levy/Jacobson Management Inc*
3500 W Olive Ave
Suite 1470
Burbank, CA 91505, USA

Ramirez, Erasmo (Athlete, Baseball Player)
3605 S Parton St
Santa Ana, CA 92707-4824, USA

Ramirez, Hanley (Athlete, Baseball Player)
2903 Lake Ridge Ln
Weston, FL 33332-2505, USA

Ramirez, Horacio (Athlete, Baseball Player)
6424 Queens Court Trce
Mableton, GA 30126-7227, USA

Ramirez, Manny (Athlete, Baseball Player)
13737 NW 18th Ct
Pembroke Pines, FL 33028-2602, USA

Ramirez, Mario (Athlete, Baseball Player)
HC 3 Box 14107
Yauco, PR 00698, USA

Ramirez, Michael P (Mike) (Cartoonist)
Los Angeles Times
Editorial Dept
202 W 1st St
Los Angeles, CA 90012, USA

Ramirez, Milt (Athlete, Baseball Player)
7 Calle Tulio Larrinaga
Urb Ramirez De Arellano
Mayaguez, PR 00682-2447, USA

Ramirez, Pedro J (Editor)
El Mundo
Calle Pradillo 42
Madrid 28002, SPAIN

Ramirez, Rafael (Baseball Player)
5701 NW 3rd St
Miami, FL 33126-4705, USA

Ramirez, Raul (Tennis Player)
Avenida Ruiz
65 Sur Ensenada
Baja California, MEXICO

Ramirez, RaulAvenida Ruiz
65 Sur Ensenada
Baja, California MEXICO

Ramirez, Sara (Actor)
c/o Staff Member *Mitchell K Stubbs & Assoc (MKS)*
8675 W. Washington Blvd
Suite 203
Culver City, CA 90232, USA

Ramirez, Twiggy (Musician)
c/o Staff Member *Mitch Schneider Organization (MSO)*
14724 Ventura Blvd #410
Sherman Oaks, CA 91403, USA

Ramirez Vazquez, Pedro (Architect)
Ave de la Fuentes 170
Mexico City, DF 01900, MEXICO

Ramis, Harold (Actor, Director)
160 Euclid Ave
Glencoe, IL 60022, USA

Ramm, Haley (Actor)
c/o Wendi Niad *Niad Management*
15030 Ventura Boulevard
Bldg 19 Ste 860
Sherman Oaks, CA 91423, USA

Rammstein (Music Group, Musician)
c/o Staff Member *Pilgrim Management*
Postfach 540 101
Berlin 10042, Germany

Ramo, Simon (Business Person)
9200 Sunset Blvd #401
W Hollywood, CA 90069, USA

Ramon, Haim (Government Official)
Knesset
Jerusalem 91010, ISRAEL

Ramone, Phil (Musician)
c/o Staff Member *Gorfaine/Schwartz
Agency Inc*
4111 W Alameda Ave
Suite 509
Burbank, CA 91505, USA

Ramones, The (Music Group)
c/o Gary Kurfirst *Kurfirst/Blackwell
Management*
601 W 26th St
Fl 11
New York, NY 10001

Ramon Gaspar, Henderson (Athlete,
Baseball Player)
205 Cedar Run Dr
Douglassville, PA 19518-8707, USA

Ramos, Bobby (Athlete, Baseball Player)
15109 SW 62nd St
Miami, FL 33193-2735, USA

Ramos, Cesar (Athlete, Baseball Player)
8371 Tele11raoh Rd
Pico Rivera, CA 90660-4928, USA

Ramos, Constance (Connie) (Actor,
Reality TV Star)
c/o Staff Member *Extreme Makeover:
Home Edition*
Endemol Entertainment USA
9225 Sunset Blvd #1100
Los Angeles, CA 90069, USA

Ramos, Diego (Actor)
c/o Gabriel Blanco *Gabriel Blanco
Iglesias (Mexico)*
Rio Balsas 35-32
Colonia Cuauhtemoc
DF 06500, Mexico

Ramos, Domingo (Athlete, Baseball
Player)
Carr Duarte KM 8 1/2 Licey Al Medio
Santiago, Dominican Republic

Ramos, Fidel (President)
Malacanang Palace
Manila, PHILIPPINES

Ramos, John (Athlete, Baseball Player)
4214 W Leona St
Tampa, FL 33629-7714, USA

Ramos, Jorge (Actor)
c/o Staff Member *Univision*
605 3rd St. Fl12
New York, NY 10158, USA

Ramos, Ken (Athlete, Baseball Player)
9 lronbrid11e Ln
Pueblo, CO 81001-1303, USA

Ramos, Mario (Athlete, Baseball Player)
20228 Mustang Island Cir
Pflugerville, TX 78660-7720, USA

Ramos, Mel (Artist)
5941 Ocean View Dr
Oakland, CA 94618, USA

Ramos, Monica (Musician)
MNW Records Group
PO Box 535
Taby 183 25, SWEDEN

Ramos, Nathalia (Actor)
c/o Loch Powell *Leverage Management*
3030 Pennsylvania Ave
Santa Monica, CA 90404, USA

Ramos, Pedro (Athlete, Baseball Player)
6637 W 22nd Ln
Hialeah, FL 33016-3916, USA

Ramos, Sarah (Actor)
c/o Staff Member *Abrams Artists Agency
(LA)*
9200 Sunset Blvd
11th Floor
Los Angeles, CA 90069, USA

Ramos, Tab (Athlete, Soccer Player)
Tab Ramos Soccer Programs
17 Blair Rd
Aberdeen, NJ 07747, USA

Ramos-Horta, Jose (Nobel Prize Laureate)
East Timor Relief Association PO Box
1102
Parramatta DSW 2124, australia

Rampling, Charlotte (Actor)
c/o Elisabeth Tanner *ArtMedia*
20 avenue Rapp
Paris 75008, France

Ramsay, Anne
c/o Todd Eisner *Agency for the
Performing Arts (APA)-LA)*
405 S Beverly Dr
Suite 500
Beverly Hills, CA 90212-4425, USA

Ramsay, Bruce
9150 Wilshire Blvd. #350
Beverly Hills, CA 90212-3427

Ramsay, Craig (Athlete, Coach, Hockey
Player)
10602 Plantation Bay Dr
Tampa, FL 33647-3319

Ramsay, Craig (Athlete, Hockey Player)
Florida Panthers
1 Panther Pkwy
Sunrise, FL 33323-5315

Ramsay, Gordon (Chef)
Gordon Ramsay Holding Ltd
1 Catherine Place
London sw1e6dx

Ramsay, Jack (Basketball Coach, Coach,
Sportscaster)
11118 Gulf Shore Dr
Apt 904
Naples, FL 34108-1731, USA

Ramsay, Keshu (Director, Filmmaker,
Producer)
Maharaja Surajmal 'C'
New Versova Link Road Andheri
Bombay, MS 400 058, INDIA

Ramsay, Laymon (Baseball Player)
Chicago American Giants
2417 Princeton Ave SW
Birmingham, AL 35211-3144, USA

Ramsay, Lynne (Cinematographer,
Director, Writer)
c/o Jon Rubinstein *Authentic Talent and
Literary Management*
45 Main St
Suite 1004
Brooklyn, NY 11201, USA

Ramsay, Robert (Athlete, Baseball Player)
6097 N La Rochelle Dr
Coeur D Alene, ID 83815-9802, USA

Ramsay, Tana (Chef, Writer)
c/o Staff Member *HarperCollins Publishers*
10 East 53rd St
c/o Author mail, 7th Floor
New York, NY 10022, USA

Ramsay, Wayne (Athlete, Hockey Player)
Oak River, MB R0K 1T0, Canada

Ramsbottom, Nancy (Golfer)
2216 Parkers Hill Dr
Maidens, VA 23102, USA

Ramsey, Bill (Athlete, Baseball Player)
6301 Village Grove Dr
Memphis, TN 38115, USA

Ramsey, Boniface (Writer)
c/o Staff Member *New City Press*
202 Comforter Blvd
Hyde Park, NY 12538, USA

Ramsey, Cal (Athlete, Basketball Player)
New York University
181 Mercer St Office
New York, NY 10012-1501, USA

Ramsey, Chuck (Athlete, Football Player)
17519 Marvel Rd
Lenior City, TN 37772, USA

Ramsey, David (Actor)
c/o Staff Member *Agency for the
Performing Arts (APA-LA)*
405 S Beverly Dr
Suite 500
Beverly Hills, CA 90212-4425, USA

Ramsey, Derrick (Athlete, Football Player)
1801 Barwick Dr
Lexington, KY 40505, USA

Ramsey, Fernando (Athlete, Baseball
Player)
2501 Sandy Trl
Keller, TX 76248-8490, USA

Ramsey, Frank (Athlete, Basketball Player,
Coach)
PO Box 363
Madisonville, KY 42431-0007, USA

Ramsey, Gerrard (Athlete, Football Player)
4102 US Highway 411 S
Maryville, TN 37801, USA

Ramsey, John (Misc)
Campaign Headquarters
PO Box 243
Cheboygan, MI 49721-0243, USA

Ramsey, Laura (Actor)
c/o Michael Nilon *Kritzer Levine Wilkins
Entertainment (KLWG)*
11872 La Grange Ave
1st Floor
Los Angeles, CA 90025, USA

Ramsey, Logan
12923 Killion St.
Van Nuys, CA 91401

Ramsey, Marion (Actor)
c/o Aine Leicht *Horror & Hilarity*
Prefers to be contacted via telephone
Los Angeles, CA 90067, USA

Ramsey, Mary (Musician)
Agency for Performing Arts
9200 Sunset Blvd
#900
Los Angeles, CA 90069, USA

Ramsey, Michael (Mike) (Athlete, Hockey
Player)
445 W 79th St
Chanhassen, MN 55317, USA

Ramsey, Mike (Athlete, Hockey Player,
Olympic Athlete)
6362 Oxbow Bnd
Chanhassen, MN 55317-9109

Ramsey, Mike (Athlete, Baseball Player)
P.O. Box 262
Harlem, GA 30814-0262, USA

Ramsey, Mike (Athlete, Baseball Player)
11564 92nd Way
Largo, FL 33773-4606, USA

Ramsey, Nate (Athlete, Football Player)
1938 Cambridge St
Philadelphia, PA 19130, USA

Ramsey, Ray (Athlete, Basketball Player)
1721 N Albany St
Springfield, IL 62702-3122, USA

Ramsey, Rick (Stylist)
c/o Staff Member *Ken Barboza Associates*
115 W 30th St Rm 203
New York, NY 10001, USA

Ramsey, Tom (Athlete, Football Player)
5435 E Otero Dr
Centennial, CO 80122, USA

Ramsey, Wayne (Athlete, Hockey Player)
NW17-14-21
Oak River, MB ROK ITO, Canada

Ramsey, Wes (Actor)
c/o Robert Attermann *Abrams Artists
Agency (LA)*
9200 Sunset Blvd
11th Floor
Los Angeles, CA 90069, USA

Ramsey, William E (Admiral)
825 Bayshore Dr
Pensacola, FL 32507, USA

Ramson, Eason (Athlete, Football Player)
1000 Claudia Ct
Apt 39
Antioch, CA 94509, USA

Ran, Shulamit (Composer)
University of Chicago
Music Dept
5845 S Ellis Ave
Chicago, IL 60637, USA

Rana, Ashutosh (Actor, Bollywood)
23 Bharat Petroleum Colony
Aziz Baug Chembur
Mumbai, MS 400074, INDIA

Ranaut, Kangna (Actor)
c/o Staff Member *Viaan Media
Consultants*
8/c, Morya House, Veera Industrial Estate
Off New Link Road, Andheri
Mumbai 400 053, India

Rancic, Bill (Business Person, Reality TV
Star)
12218 Octagon St
Los Angeles, CA 90049, USA

Rancic, Giuliana (Actor, Reality TV Star,
Television Host)
12218 Octagon St
Los Angeles, CA 90049, USA

Rancid (Music Group, Musician)
c/o Staff Member *Leave Home Booking*
1400 S. Foothill Dr
Suite 34
Salt Lake City, UT 84108, USA

Rand, Marvin (Photographer)
Marvin Rand Assoc
1310 Abbot Kinney Blvd
Venice, CA 90291, USA

Rand, Reese Mary (Athlete, Track Athlete)
6650 Los Gatos
Atascadero, CA 93422, USA

Rand, Robert W (Educator)
Good Samaritan Hospital
Neurosciences Institute
Los Angeles, CA 90017, USA

Randa, Joe (Athlete, Baseball Player)
6436 Ensley Ln
Mission Hills, KS 66208-1932, USA

Randall, Alice (Writer)
c/o Staff Member *Houghton Mifflin
Company (Trade Division)*
222 Berkeley St
Adult Editorial, 8th Floor
Boston, MA 02116-3764, USA

Randall, Anne (Model)
10526 W Tropicana Cir
Sun City, AZ 85351, USA

Randall, Bob (Athlete, Baseball Player)
2105 Hillview Dr
Manhattan, KS 66502-1942, USA

Randall, Carolyn D (Judge)
US Court of Appeals
515 Rusk St
Houston, TX 77002, USA

Randall, Claire (Religious Leader)
10015 West Royal Oak Road
Apt 1214
Sun City, AZ 85351-6116, USA

Randall, Frankie (Boxer)
355 Fish Hatchery Road
#02
Morristown, TN 37813, USA

Randall, James (Sap) (Athlete, Baseball
Player)
158 Heather Ln
Ruston, LA 71270-1165, USA

Randall, Jon (Musician)
Joe's Garage
4405 Belmont Park Terrace
Nashville, TN 37215, USA

Randall, Josh (Actor)
I F A Talent Agency
8730 Sunset Blvd
#490
Los Angeles, CA 90069, USA

Randall, Kikkan (Athlete, Olympic
Athlete, Track Athlete)
8601 Pioneer Dr
Anchorage, AK 99504-4215, USA

Randall, Mark (Athlete, Basketball Player)
10476 Lynx Bay
Lone Tree, CO 80124-9549, USA

Randall, Maurice (Race Car Driver)
426 Sumpter St.
Box 606
Charlotte, MI 48813, USA

Randall, Rebel (Actor)
PO Box 1405
Riverside, CA 92502-1405, USA

Randall, Scott (Athlete, Baseball Player)
7290 Julynn Rd
Colorado Springs, CO 80919-5035, USA

Randall, Theresa (Stylist)
c/o Staff Member *The Docherty Agency -
OH*
2044 Euclid Ave
Cleveland, OH 44115, USA

Randall, Tom (Athlete, Football Player)
2521 Park Vista Cir
Ames, IA 50014, USA

Randall Johnson, Nicole (Actor)
c/o Paul Brown *New Wave Entertainment
(LA)*
2660 W Olive Blvd
Burbank, CA 91505, USA

Randazzo, Barbara (Stylist)
619 SPruce Dr
Hollbrook, NY 11741, USA

Randazzo, Mike (Actor, Talk Show Host)
c/o Mike Randazzo
3469 West Stones Crossing Road
Greenwood, IN 46143-8564, USA

Randazzo, Tony (Athlete, Baseball Player)
2462 Los Alamos Ct
Las Crusces, NM 88011-1657, USA

Randi, James (Misc)
2941 Fairview Park Dr Ste 105
Falls Church, VA 22042-4526, USA

Randie, John (Athlete, Football Player)
P.O. Box 489
Harrisonburg, VA 22803, USA

Randle, Betsy
9300 Wilshire Blvd. #555
Beverly Hills, CA 90212

Randle, Ervin (Athlete, Football Player)
900 Spring Creek Dr
Grapevine, TX 76051-8269, USA

Randle, John (Football Player)
c/o Staff Member *Seattle Seahawks*
12 Seahawks Way
Renton, WA 98056, USA

Randle, Lenny (Athlete, Baseball Player)
39461 Cozumel Ct
Murrieta, CA 92563-2552, USA

Randle, Lynda (Musician)
5565 NW Barry Road
PO Box 236
Kansas City, MO 64154, USA

Randle, Tate (Athlete, Football Player)
495 Koebig Rd
Seguin, TX 78155, USA

Randle, Theresa (Actor)
c/o Jason Priluck *Agency Group Ltd, The
(LA)*
1880 Century Park E
Suite 711
Los Angeles, CA 90067, USA

Randle, Ulmo (Sonny) (Athlete, Football
Player)
P.O. Box 487
Harrisonburg, VA 22803, USA

Randolph, Alvin (Athlete, Football Player)
319 Roble Ave
Redwood City, CA 94061, USA

Randolph, A Raymond (Judge)
US Court of Appeals
333 Constitution NW
Washington, DC 20001, USA

Randolph, Carl (Musician)
David Levin Mgmt
200 W 57th St
#308
New York, NY 10019, USA

Randolph, Jackson H (Business Person)
Cinergy Corp
139 E 4th St
Cincinnati, OH 45202, USA

Randolph, Jay (Baseball Player)
12021 Charter Oak Pkwy
Saint Louis, MO 63146-5207, USA

Randolph, Joyce (Actor)
295 Central Park W. #18-A
New York, NY 10024

Randolph, Judson G (Doctor)
111 Michigan Ave NW
Washington, DC 20010, USA

Randolph, Robert (Musician)
c/o Coran Capshaw *Red Light
Management (VA)*
PO Box 1467
Charlottesville, VA 22902, USA

Randolph, Sam (Golfer)
1305 Briar Ridge Dr
Keller, TX 76248-8376, USA

Randolph, Stephen (Athlete, Baseball
Player)
3706 Apache Forest Dr
Austin, TX 78739-4418, USA

Randolph, Willie L (Athlete, Baseball
Player, Coach)
715 Jenney Trl
Franklin Lakes, NJ 07417-2907, USA

Randolph, Zach (Athlete, Basketball
Player)
c/o Staff Member *Memphis Grizzlies*
191 Beale St
Memphis, TN 38103, USA

Randrup, Michael (Misc)
10 Fairlawn Road
Lythamst Annes
Lancashire FY8 5PT, UNITED KINGDOM
(UK)

Rands, Bernard (Composer)
Harvard University
Music Dept
Cambridge, MA 02138, USA

Randy, Duncan (Athlete, Football Player)
4240 Foster Dr
Des Moines, IA 50312-2542, USA

Randy Rogers Band (Music Group,
Musician)
c/o Joey Lee *WmE2 (WMA-TN)*
1600 Division St
Suite 300
Nashville, TN 37203, USA

Raney, Catherine (Athlete, Olympic
Athlete, Speed Skater)
5800 Chaseview Rd
Nashville, TN 37221-4115, USA

Ranganathan, Suman (Actor, Bollywood)
Gilder Building
Turner Road Bandra
Mumbai, MS 400050, INDIA

Rangel, Charles B (Politician)
74 W. 132nd St.
New York, NY 10037-3313

Ranger, Bruce (Horse Racer)
2205 S Cypress Bend Dr Apt 705
Pompano Beach, FL 33069-4459, USA

Ranger, Doug (Songwriter, Writer)
New Frontier Mgmt
1921 Broadway
Nashville, TN 37203, USA

Ranger, Paul (Athlete, Hockey Player)
58 Henderson Dr
Whitby, ON L1N 7Y5, CANADA

Ranheim, Paul (Athlete, Hockey Player)
12128 N Reflection Ridge Dr
Oro Valley, AZ 85755-0837

Rani (Actor, Bollywood)
Anubhav Apts
Arunachalam Road
Chennai, TN 600083, INDIA

Ranieri, George (Athlete, Hockey Player)
217 Wimpole St SS 1
Mitchell, ON N0K 1N0, Canada

Ranis, Gustav (Economist)
7 Mulberry Road
Woodbridge, CT 06525, USA

Ranjani (Actor, Bollywood)
78/a Moubrews Road
Alwarpet
Chennai, TN 600018, INDIA

Ranjeet (Actor, Bollywood)
14 Silver Beach A B Nair Road
Juhu
Bombay, MS 400 049, INDIA

Ranki, Dezso (Musician)
OrdogoromLejto 11/B
Budapest 1112, HUNGARY

Rankin, Chris (Actor)
c/o Staff Member *Ken McReddie Ltd*
11 Connaught Pl
London W2 2ET, UNITED KINGDOM

Rankin, Ian (Writer)
c/o Staff Member *St Martins Press*
Publicity Dept
175 5th Ave
New York, NY 10010, USA

Rankin, Judy (Golfer)
2715 Racquet Club Dr
Midland, TX 79705-7432, USA

Rankin, Kenny (Musician, Songwriter)
c/o Staff Member *Variety Artists
International Inc*
793 Higuera Street
Suite 6
San Luis, CA 93401-0500, USA

Rankin, Kevin (Actor)
c/o Dominic Friesen *Bridge and Tunnel
Communications*
9157 Sunset Blvd.
West Hollywood, CA 90069, USA

Rankin, Robert (General)
83 Stone Dr
Brevard, NC 28712-7677, USA

Rankin, Rose (Stylist)
223 Brees Blvd
San Antonio, TX 78209, USA

Rankine, Terry (Architect)
Cambridge Seven Assoc
1050 Massachusetts Ave
Cambridge, MA 02138, USA

Rankin Jr, Alfred M (Business Person)
NACCO Industries
5875 Landerbrook Dr
Mayfield Heights, OH 44124, USA

Ranks, Shabba (Musician)
c/o Clifton Dillon *Shang Artist Management*
222 N.E. 27th St
Miami, FL 33137, USA

Ransdell, Gary (Educator)
Western Kentucky University
President's Office
Bowling Green, KY 42101, USA

Ransey, Kelvin (Athlete, Basketball Player)
3195 Monterey Dr
Tupelo, MS 38801-6817, USA

Ransom, Cody (Athlete, Baseball Player)
3146 E Boston St
Gilbert, AZ 85295-1458, USA

Ransom, Derrick (Athlete, Football Player)
6521 Sparrowood Ct
Indianapolis, IN 46236, USA

Ransom, Jeff (Athlete, Baseball Player)
2131 Curtis St
Berkeley, CA 94702-1815, USA

Ransome, Prunella
59 Frith St.
London, ENGLAND W1

Ransone, James (Actor)
c/o Kimberlin Dalehite *Magnolia Entertainment (LA)*
9595 Wilshire Blvd
Suite 601
Beverly Hills, CA 90212, USA

Rao, Ashok (Actor)
28 17th Cross Malleswaram
Bangalore, KA, INDIA

Rao, Calyampudi R (Mathematician)
826 W Aaron Dr
State College, PA 16803, USA

Rao, C N Ramchandra (Misc)
JNC President's House
Indian Science Institute
Bangalore, KA 560012, INDIA

Rao, T Rama (Actor, Bollywood, Director, Filmmaker, Producer)
No 14 1st Balaji Street Balaji Avenue
T Nagar
Madras, TN 600 017, INDIA

Raoul, Dale (Actor)
c/o Staff Member *JC Robbins Management*
113 S Kilkea Dr
Los Angeles, CA 90048, USA

Rapace, Noomi (Actor)
c/o Shelley Browning *Magnolia Entertainment (LA)*
9595 Wilshire Blvd
Suite 601
Beverly Hills, CA 90212, USA

Rapada, Clay (Athlete, Baseball Player)
37224 Summerglen Ave
Murrieta, CA 92563-5070, USA

Rapaport, Michael (Actor)
c/o Suzan Bymel *Management 360*
9111 Wilshire Blvd
Beverly Hills, CA 90210, USA

Raper, Kenneth B (Misc)
602 N Segoe Road
Madison, WI 53705, USA

Raphael (Actor)
Kaduri Agency
16125 NE 18th Ave
North Miami Beach, FL 33162, USA

Raphael, Fredric M (Writer)
Largadeile
Saint Lauraent la Vallee
Belves 24170, FRANCE

Raphael, June Diane (Actor, Writer)
c/o Jon Rubinstein *Authentic Talent and Literary Management*
45 Main St
Suite 1004
Brooklyn, NY 11201, USA

Raphael, Sally Jessy (Journalist)
616 Quaker Hill Rd
Pawling, NY 12564-3321, USA

Rapoport, Anatol (Scientist)
38 Wychwood Pk
Toronto, ON M6G 2V5, Canada

Raposo, Greg (Musician)
PO Box 434
Glen Head, NY 11545

Rapp, Anthony (Actor)
c/o Elise Konialian *Untitled Entertainment (NY)*
322 8th Ave #601
New York, NY 10001-6715, USA

Rapp, Pat (Athlete, Baseball Player)
2554 Pete Seay Rd
Sulphur, LA 70663-9377, USA

Rapp, Vern (Athlete, Baseball Player, Coach)
1559 Redwing Ln
Broomfield, CO 80020-0614, USA

Rappa, Tamara (Stylist)
c/o Staff Member *Exclusive Artists Mgmt*
7700 Sunset Blvd
#205
Los Angeles, CA 90046, USA

Rappaport, Sheeri (Actor)
c/o Paul Greenstone *Paul Greenstone Entertainment*
3008 Sorrelwood Dr
San Ramon, CA 94582-5008, USA

Rappeneau, Jean-Paul (Director)
24 Rue Henri Barbusse
Paris 75005, FRANCE

Rapping 4-Tay (Musician)
Richard Walters
1800 Argyle Ave
#408
Los Angeles, CA 90028, USA

Rappuoli, Rino (Scientist)
Sclavo Research Center
Via Fiorentina 1
Siena 53100, ITALY

Rapuano, Ed (Athlete, Baseball Player)
10815 Japonia Ct
Boca Raton, FL 33498-4839, USA

Rapuano, Ed (Baseball Player)
10815 Japonica Ct
Boca Raton, FL 33498-4839, USA

Rare, Vanessa (Actor)
c/o Staff Member *Auckland Actors*
PO Box 56460
Dominion Road
Auckland, NEW ZEALAND

Rarick, Cindy (Golfer)
1625 N Via Dorado
Tucson, AZ 85715-4724, USA

Rarick, Heather (Scientist)
2701 Moss Ct
Seabrook, TX 77586-2835, USA

Rasa Don (Musician)
William Morris Agency
1325 Ave of Americas
New York, NY 10019, USA

Rasby, Walter (Athlete, Football Player)
6413 Brookbury Ct
Charlotte, NC 28226, USA

Rascal, Dizzee (Musician)
c/o Peter Elliot *Primary Talent International (UK)*
The Primary Building
10-11 Jockeys Fields
London WC1R 4BN, UK

Rascal Flatts (Music Group)
c/o Jake Basden *Big Machine Records*
1219 16th Ave South
Nashville, TN 37212, USA

Rasche, David (Actor)
c/o Brian Liebman *Liebman Entertainment*
25 E 21st St #PH
New York, NY 10011-8503, USA

Raschke, Kaylynn (Stylist)
PO Box 392 Times Square Station
New York, NY 10108, USA

Rascoe, Robert (Bobby) (Athlete, Basketball Player)
523 Sumpter Ave
Bowling Green, KY 42101-3750, USA

Rascon, Alfred V (General)
10397 Derby Dr
Laurel, MD 20723-5743, USA

Rash, Jim
c/o Jeff Morrone *Jeff Morrone Entertainment*
9350 Wilshire Blvd
Suite 224
Beverly Hills, CA 90212, USA

Rash, Steve (Director)
c/o Staff Member *Gersh (LA)*
9465 Wilshire Blvd
Suite 600
Beverly Hills, CA 90212, USA

Rashad, Ahmad (Athlete, Football Player)
13220 Verdun Dr
Palm Beach Gardens, FL 33410, USA

Rashad, Phylicia (Actor)
c/o Johnnie Planco *Parseghian Planco LLC*
322 8th Ave
Suite 601
New York, NY 10001, USA

Rasheeda (Musician)
c/o Staff Member *ICM Partners (ICM-LA)*
10250 Constellation Blvd Fl 7
Los Angeles, CA 90067, USA

Rashid, Karim (Designer)
357 W 17th St
New York, NY 10011, USA

Rashnikov, Viktor (Business Person)
Magnitogorsk Iron and Steel Works
92 Kirov St
Magnitogorsk, Chelyabinsk
region 455002, Russia

Rasi (Actor, Bollywood)
28B Main Road
Zakkaria Colony Saligramam
Chennai, TN 600094, INDIA

Rask, Tuuka (Athlete, Hockey Player)
19 Pier 7 Unit 19
Charlestown, MA 02129-4225

Raskin, Alex (Journalist)
Los Angeles Times
Editorial Dept
202 W 1st St
Los Angeles, CA 90012, USA

Rasley, Rocky (Athlete, Football Player)
1918 S Mills Ave
Apt 4
Lodi, CA 95242, USA

Rasmus, Colby (Athlete, Baseball Player)
3110 Newsome Rd
Phenix CitY, AL 36870-2827, USA

Rasmussen, Anders Fogh (Prime Minister)
prins Jorgens Gard 11
Copenhagen K 2000, DENMARK

Rasmussen, Blair (Athlete, Basketball Player)
3258 74th Ave SE
Mercer Island, WA 98040-3419, USA

Rasmussen, Dennis (Athlete, Baseball Player)
PO Box 547341
Orlando, FL 32854-7341, USA

Rasmussen, Eric (Athlete, Baseball Player)
237 SW 45th St
Cape Coral, FL 33914-5907, USA

Rasmussen, Erik (Athlete, Hockey Player)
16705 50th Ct N
Minneapolis, MN 55446-4532

Rasmussen, Eris (Athlete, Baseball Player)
237 SW 45th St
Cape Coral, FL 33914, USA

Rasmussen, Gerry (Cartoonist)
9352 64 Ave NW
Edmonton, AB T6E OH9, Canada

Rasmussen, Poul Nyrup (Prime Minister)
Aliegade 6A
Frederiksberg 2000, DENMARK

Rasmussen, Randy (Athlete, Football Player)
3990 114th Ln NW
Coon Rapids, MN 55433, USA

Rasmussen, Randy (Athlete, Football Player)
81 Grumman Hill Rd
Wilton, CT 06897, USA

Rasmussen, Wayne (Athlete, Football Player)
9000 E Maple St
Brandon, SD 57005, USA

Rasner, Darrell (Athlete, Baseball Player)
Tohoku Rakuten Golden Eagles 2-11-6
Miyagino
Miyagino-ku Sendai-shi
Mivagi-ken 983-0045, Japan

Raspberry, William J (Journalist)
Washington Post
Editorial Dept
1150 15th St NW
Washington, DC 20071, USA

Rassas, Nick (Athlete, Football Player)
P.O. Box 227
Moose, WY 83012, USA

Rasuk, Victor (Actor)
c/o Katherine Atkinson *Washington Square Arts (LA)*
1041 N Formosa Ave
The Lot Writers Bldg, Room 305
West Hollywood, CA 90046, USA

Ratchford, Jeremy (Actor)
Paradigm Agency
10100 Santa Monica Blvd
#2500
Los Angeles, CA 90067, USA

Ratchuk, Peter (Athlete, Hockey Player)
218 Ruskin Rd
Buffalo, NY 14226-4256

Ratcliffe, John A (Astronomer)
193 Huntingdon Road
Cambridge CB3 0DL, UNITED
KINGDOM (UK)

Ratelle, Jean (Athlete, Hockey Player)
1200 Salem St.
#111
Lynnfield, MA 01940-1595

Rath, Fred (Athlete, Baseball Player)
7308 Pelican Island Dr
Tampa, FL 33634-7470, USA

Rath, Gary (Athlete, Baseball Player)
15433 Meadow Brook Ct
Gulfoort, MS 39503-9465, USA

Rath, Meaghan (Actor)
Rosenthal Mercer Hamou Talent
2101 St. Laurent Blvd
Montreal, QC H2X 2T5, CANADA

Rathbone, Jackson (Actor)
c/o Pat Cutler *Cutler Management*
13043 Sunset Blvd
Los Angeles, CA 90049, USA

Rather, Bo (Athlete, Football Player)
7728 La Jessica Cir
Kalamazoo, MI 49009, USA

Rather, Dan (Journalist)
Dan Rather Reports
45 E 80th St Apt 26A
New York, NY 10075-0189, USA

Rathje, Mike (Athlete, Hockey Player)
14850 Blossom Hill Rd
Los Gatos, CA 95032-4901

Rathke, Henrich K M H (Religious Leader)
Schleifmuhlenweg 11
Schwering 19061, GERMANY

Rathman, Tom (Athlete, Football Player)
222 Republic Dr
Allen Park, MI 48101-3650, USA

Rathmann, Jim (Race Car Driver)
800 S. Harbor City Blvd.
Melbourne, FL 32901, USA

Rathnam, Mani (Bollywood, Director)
3 First Cross Road
Venus Colony
Alwarpet, Madras 600018, INDIA

Rathwell, Jake (Athlete, Hockey Player)
15 Outlook
Temiscaming, QC JOZ 3RO, Canada

Ratican, Tim (Race Car Driver)
TNT Motorsports
929 Jacaranda Dr.
Lady Lake, FL 32159, USA

Ratigan, Brian (Athlete, Football Player)
743 26th St
Manhattan Beach, CA 90266, USA

Ratkowski, Ray (Athlete, Football Player)
P.O. Box 2736
Hyannis, MA 02601, USA

Ratleff, Ed (Athlete, Basketball Player,
Olympic Athlete)
4202 Paseo De Oro
Cypress, CA 90630-3420, USA

Ratley, Sarah Gorelick (Aviator)
4100 W 95th St
Prairie Village, KS 66207-2703, USA

Ratliff, Don (Athlete, Football Player)
9048 Bay Hill Rd
Orlando, FL 32819, USA

Ratliff, Gene (Athlete, Baseball Player)
315 Southern Walk Cir
Gray, GA 31032-4528, USA

Ratliff, Jon (Athlete, Baseball Player)
289 Boughton Hill Rd
Honeoye Falls, NY 14472-9706, USA

Ratliff, Theo (Athlete, Basketball Player)
118e Mount Paran Rd NW
Atlanta, GA 30327-3702, USA

Ratliffe, Paul (Athlete, Baseball Player)
78 Campton Pl
Laguna Niguel, CA 92677-4734, USA

Ratner, Brett (Director)
c/o Richard Lovett *Creative Artists Agency
(CAA-LA)*
2000 Ave Of The Stars
Los Angeles, CA 90067, USA

Ratner, Ellen (Actor, Radio Personality)
c/o Judy Orbach *Judy O Productions*
6136 Glen Holly
Hollywood, CA 90068, USA

Ratner, Mark A (Misc)
615 Greenleaf Ave
Glencoe, IL 60022, USA

Ratnoff, Oscar D (Doctor)
1801 Chestnut Hills Dr
Cleveland, OH 44106, USA

Rato, Rodrigo (Government Official)
International Monetary Fund
700 19th St NW
Washington, DC 20431, USA

Ratser, Dmitri (Musician)
Naxim Gershunoff
1401 NE 9th St
#38
Fort Lauderdale, FL 33304, USA

Ratsiraka, Didier (Admiral, President)
President's Office
Iavoloha
Antananarivo, MADAGASCAR

Ratt (Music Group)
WBS, Inc
11684 Ventura Blvd #675
Studio City, CA 91604, USA

Rattner, Steven (Business Person)
Quadrangle Group LLC
375 Park Ave
New York, NY 10152, USA

Ratushinskaya, Irina B (Writer)
Vargius Publishing House
Kuzakova Str 18
Moscow 107005, RUSSIA

Ratzenberger, John (Actor)
Shelter Entertainment
9255 Sunset Blvd
#1010
Los Angeles, CA 90069, USA

Ratzer, Steve (Athlete, Baseball Player)
5746 Deer Flag Dr
Lakeland, FL 33811-2001, USA

Ratzinger, Joseph A Cardinal (Religious
Leader)
Palazzo del S Uffizio II
Rome 00193, ITALY

Rau, Doug (Athlete, Baseball Player)
1615 Treasure Oaks Dr
Katy, TX 77450-5088, USA

Rau, Doug (Athlete, Baseball Player)
1615 Treasure Oaks Dr
Katy, TX 77450, USA

Rauch, Bob (Athlete, Baseball Player)
3350 W Pepperwood Loop
Tucson, AZ 85742-9389, USA

Rauch, Jon (Athlete, Baseball Player,
Olympic Athlete)
14081 N Old Forest Trl
Oro Valley, AZ 85755-5789, USA

Rauch, Siegfried (Actor)
c/o Gabriele Frederking *Alexander
Agency*
Lamontstrasse 9
Munich D-81679, GERMANY

Raudman, Bob (Athlete, Baseball Player)
PO Box 8675
Jackson, WY 83002-8675, USA

Raudman, Craig (Race Car Driver)
Dave Reed Racing/AMI
6145-F Northbelt Parkway
Norcross, GA 30071, USA

Rauner-Harrington, Helen (Baseball
Player)
2027 Kentucky Ave
Fort Wayne, IN 46805-4442, USA

Raup, David M (Musician)
RR1 Box 168Y
Washington Island, WI 54246, USA

Rauschenberg, Robert (Artist)
381 Lafayette Street
New York, NY 10003, USA

Rausse, Errol (Athlete, Hockey Player)
338 Rosslare Dr
Arnold, MD 21012-3014

Rautins, Andy (Athlete, Basketball Player)
c/o Bill Duffy *BDA Sports Management
(BDA-CA)*
700 Ygnacio Valley Rd
Suite 330
Walnut Creek, CA 94596, USA

Rautins, Leo (Athlete, Basketball Player)
202 Litchfield Dr
Syracuse, NY 13224-2023, USA

Rautio, Nina (Opera Singer)
Herbert Breslin
119 W 57th St
#1505
New York, NY 10019, USA

Rautzhan, Lance (Athlete, Baseball Player)
2472 Covington Dr
Myrtle Beach, SC 29579-3123, USA

Raval, Manish (Composer, Musician)
c/o Staff Member *Aperture Music*
P.O. Box 90010
Pasadena, CA 91109, USA

Ravalec, Blanche (Actor)
Babette Pouget
6 Square Villaret de Joyeuse
Paris 75017, FRANCE

Ravali (Actor, Bollywood)
159 Thirupathi Nagar
Valasaravakkam
Chennai, TN 600087, INDIA

Ravalomanana, Marc (President)
President's Office
Iavoloha
Antananarivo, MADAGASCAR

Raveena, Tondon (Actor, Bollywood)
Nippon Society
Juhu Church
Mumbai, MS 400049, INDIA

Raven, Eddy (Musician, Songwriter,
Writer)
Great American Talent
PO Box 2476
Hendersonville, TN 37077, USA

Raven, Marion (Musician)
c/o Frank Cimler *10th Street
Entertainment (LA)*
700 San Vicente Blvd
Suite G410
West Hollywood, CA 90069, USA

Raven, Peter H (Scientist)
Missouri Botanical Garden
17143 Hidden Valley Frst
Eureka, MO 63025-2367, USA

Ravensberg, Robert (Athlete, Football
Player)
636 Sherwood Dr
Saint Louis, MO 63119, USA

Raver, Kim (Actor)
c/o David (Dave) Fleming *Mosaic Media
Group*
9200 W. Sunset Blvd
10th Floor
Los Angeles, CA 90069, USA

Raver, Lorna

Ravitch, Diane S (Historian)
New York University
Press Building
Washington Place
New York, NY 10003, USA

Ravlich, Matt (Athlete, Hockey Player)
15 Appletree Ln
Dalton, MA 01226-1351

Ravony, Francisque (Prime Minister)
Union des Forces Vivas Democratiques
Antananarivo, MADAGASCAR

Ravotti, Eric (Athlete, Football Player)
6000 Christopher Wren Dr
Apt 117
Wexford, PA 15090, USA

Rawail, Rahul (Bollywood, Director,
Filmmaker, Producer)
B103 Kailash Juhu Church Road
Juhu
Bombay, MS 400 049, INDIA

Rawal, Paresh (Actor, Bollywood,
Comedian)
11 Sea Breeze Apartments 12th Road
JVPD Scheme
Bombay, MS 400 049, INDIA

Rawat, Navi (Actor)
c/o Jai Khanna *Brillstein Entertainment
Partners*
9150 Wilshire Blvd #350
Beverly Hills, CA 90212, USA

Rawi, Raad (Actor)
c/o Ken McReddie *Ken McReddie Ltd*
11 Connaught Pl
London W2 2ET, UNITED KINGDOM

Rawis, Betsy (Golfer)
501 Country Club Dr
Wilmington, DE 19803-2430, USA

Rawley, Shane (Athlete, Baseball Player)
4587 Cherrybark Ct
Sarasota, FL 34241-9213, USA

Rawlings, Adrian (Actor)
Ken McReddie Ltd
91 Regent St
London W1R 7TB, ENGLAND

Rawlings, Pat (Artist)
2200 Space Park Dr
Suite 200
Houston, TX 77058, USA

Rawlins, V Lane (Educator)
Washington State University
President's Office
Pullman, WA 99164, USA

Rawlinson, Chris (Athlete, Olympic
Athlete)
Trafford Athletic Club
Longford Park Stadium
Ryebank Road
Chorlton Cum Hardy, Manchester M21
9TA, UNITED KINGDOM

Rawlinson of Ewell, Peter A G
(Government Official)
Wardour Castle
Tisbury
Wilts SP3 6RH, UNITED KINGDOM (UK)

Rawls, Betsy (Athlete, Golfer)
501 Country Club Sr
Wilmington, DE 19803, USA

Rawls, Elizabeth E (Betsy) (Golfer)
501 Country Club Dr
Wilmington, DE 19803, USA

Rawls, Sam (Cartoonist)
*c/o Staff Member King Features
Syndication*
300 W 57th St
15th Floor
New York, NY 10019-5238, USA

Rawson, Anna (Athlete, Golfer, Model)
*c/o Jeff Chilcoat Sterling Sports
Management, LLC*
7650 Rivers Edge Dr
Suite 100
Columbus, OH 43235, USA

Ray, Amy (Musician, Songwriter)
c/o Staff Member High Road Touring
751 Bridgeway
3rd Floor
Sausalito, CA 94965, USA

Ray, Bobby (B.o.B.) (Musician)
2352 Old Ivey Walk
Stone Mountain, GA 30087, USA

Ray, Chris (Athlete, Baseball Player)
15311 Winding Creek Dr
Tampa, FL 33613-1217, USA

Ray, Darrol (Athlete, Football Player)
13000 Doriath Way
Oklahoma, OK 73170, USA

Ray, David (Athlete, Football Player)
6962 Bridgewater Dr
Huntington Beach, CA 92647, USA

Ray, Dipierro (Athlete, Football Player)
10542 Fremont Pike
Apt 256
Perrysburg, OH 43551-3367, USA

Ray, Ear (Athlete, Basketball Player)
446 N Lowell St
Casper, WY 82601, USA

Ray, Earl (Athlete, Basketball Player)
446 N Lowell St
Casper, WY 82601-2147, USA

Ray, Eddie (Athlete, Football Player)
5319 Avondale Dr
Sugarland, TX 77479, USA

Ray, Edward J (Educator)
Oregon State University
President's Office
Corvallis, OR 97331, USA

Ray, Frankie (Actor)

Ray, Fred Olen (Director)
PO Box 3563
Van Nuys, CA 91407, USA

Ray, Greg (Race Car Driver)
Access Motorsports
8227 Northwest Blvd #300
Indianapolis, IN 46278, USA

Ray, James Arthur (Business Person)
James Ray International
5927 Balfour Ct Ste 104
Carlsbad, CA 92008, USA

Ray, Jimmy (Musician)
Nineteen Music/Mgmt
35-37 Parkgate Road
London SW11 4NP, UNITED KINGDOM
(UK)

Ray, John (Athlete, Football Player)
10 Ranger Ln
Charleston, WV 25309, USA

Ray, Johnny (Athlete, Baseball Player)
12470 S 432
Chouteau, OK 74337-6097, USA

Ray, Ken (Athlete, Baseball Player)
8952 W Electra Ln
Peoria, AZ 85383-1404, USA

Ray, Larry (Athlete, Baseball Player)
26 Masters Place Cv
Maumelle, AR 72113-7018, USA

Ray, Lisa (Actor)
*c/o Dannielle Thomas Untitled
Entertainment (LA)*
350 S. Beverly Dr #200
Beverly Hills, CA 90212, USA

Ray, Marguerite (Actor)
1329 N Vista
#106
Los Angeles, CA 90046, USA

Ray, Rachael (Chef, Talk Show Host)
c/o Charlie Dougiello The Door
246 Withers St
1B
Brooklyn, NY 11211, USA

Ray, Rob (Athlete, Hockey Player)
289 Sausalito Dr
East Amherst, NY 14051-1472

Ray, Rob (Athlete, Hockey Player)
Buffalo Sabres
1 Seymour H Knox III Plz Ste 1
Buffalo, NY 14203-3096

Ray, Robert D (Ex-Governor)
114 SW 51st St
Des Moines, IA 50312, USA

Ray, Ronald E (General)
2670 Saint Andrews Blvd
Tarpon Springs, FL 34688-6339, USA

Ray, Sugar (Music Group)
c/o Staff Member Pinnacle Entertainment
30 Glenn St
White Plains, NY 10603, USA

Ray, Terry (Athlete, Football Player)
42559 Angel Wing Way
Ashburn, VA 20148, USA

Ray, Vanessa (Actor)
c/o Randi Goldstein Gersh (NY)
41 Madison Ave
New York, NY 10010, USA

Raybon, Marty (Musician)
Hallmark Direction
15 Music Square W
Nashville, TN 37203, USA

Raycroft, Andrew (Hockey Player)
c/o Staff Member Toronto Maple Leafs
Air Canada Centre
400-40 Bay St
Toronto, ON M5J 2X2, Canada

rayder, franki (Model)
Why Not
via Zenale, 9
Milano 20123, Italy

Raydon, Curt (Athlete, Baseball Player)
P.O. Box 5124
Jasper, TX 75951-7701, USA

Raye, Collin (Musician)
*c/o Dave Fowler Nashville Artist
Management*
Prefers to be contacted via telephone
Nashville, TN, USA

Raye, Lisa (Actor)
c/o Susan Haber Haber Entertainment
434 S Canon Dr
Suite 204
Beverly Hills, CA 90212, USA

Rayford, Floyd (Athlete, Baseball Player)
11701 Pointe Cir
Fort Meyers, FL 33908-2161, USA

Rayhal, Bobby
934a Crescent Blvd.
Glenellyn, IL 60137

Rayl, James (Athlete, Basketball Player)
58 Rideout Rd
Hollis, NH 03049-6110, USA

Raymer, Cory (Athlete, Football Player)
46629 Hampshire Station Dr
Sterling, VA 20165, USA

Raymer, Greg (Misc)
2622 Village Manor Way
Raleigh, NC 27614-8097, USA

Raymo, Maureen (Misc)
Boston University
Geology Dept
Boston, MA 02215, USA

Raymond, Claude (Athlete, Baseball
Player)
3 Rue de la Citiere
Saint-Jean-Sur-Richelieu, QC J2W 1B8,
Canada

Raymond, Corey (Athlete, Football Player)
106 Carter St
New Iberia, LA 70560, USA

Raymond, Craig (Athlete, Basketball
Player)
4617 N 265 E
Provo, UT 84604-5403

Raymond, Gary (Actor)
*c/o Staff Member Scott Marshall Partners
Ltd*
15 Little Portland St
2nd Floor
London W1W 8BW, UK

Raymond, Guy (Actor)
550 Erskine Dr
Pacific Palisades, CA 90272, USA

Raymond, Jeff (Actor)
8687 Melrose Avenue
West Hollywood, CA 90069-5701, USA

Raymond, Kenneth N (Misc)
University of California
Chemistry Dept
Berkeley, CA 94720, USA

Raymond, Lee R (Business Person)
Exxon Corp
5959 Las Colinas Blvd
Irving, TX 75039, USA

Raymond, Lisa (Tennis Player)
Octagon
1751 Pinnacle Dr
#1500
McLean, VA 22102, USA

Raymond, Mason (Athlete, Hockey Player)
RR 2 Stn Main
Cochrane, AB T4C 1A2, Canada

Raymond, Paula (Actor)
PO Box 86
Beverly Hills, CA 90213, USA

Raymond, Usher (Dancer, Musician)
4065 Merriweather Woods
Alpharetta, GA 30022, USA

Raymonde, Tania (Actor)
*c/o Katie Rhodes Untitled Entertainment
(LA)*
350 S. Beverly Dr #200
Beverly Hills, CA 90212, USA

Raymund, Monica (Actor)
c/o Kyle Luker The Group Entertainment
115 West 29th Street
#1102
New York, NY 10001, USA

Rayner, Chuck
116-5710 201st St.
Langley, CANADA BC V3A 8A6

Ray Newman, Jaime (Actor)
*c/o Joanna (Joanie) Burstein Burstein
Company, The*
15304 Sunset Blvd
suite 208
Pacific Palisades, CA 90272, USA

Raynis, Richard (Producer)
*c/o Staff Member Creative Artists Agency
(CAA-LA)*
2000 Ave Of The Stars
Los Angeles, CA 90067, USA

Raynor, Bruce (Politician)
Unite
275 7th Ave
New York, NY 10001, USA

Raynr, David (Actor, Director, Producer)
c/o Simon Millar Rumble Media
1620 Broadway
Santa Monica, CA 90403, USA

Raz, Kavi (Actor)
c/o Staff Member Almond Talent Agency
8217 Beverly Blvd.
Suite 8
West Hollywood, CA 90048, USA

Raza, S Atiq (Business Person)
Advanced Micro Devices
1 AMD Place
Sunnyvale, CA 94085, USA

Razanamasy, Guy (Prime Minister)
Prime Minister's Office
Mahazoarivo
Antananarivo, MADAGASCAR

Raz B (Actor, Musician)
c/o Michael (Mike) Esterman
Esterman.Com, LLC
Prefers to be contacted via email
MD, USA

Razborov, A A (Mathematician)
Princeton University
Mathematics Dept
Princeton, NJ 08540, USA

Raziano, Barry (Athlete, Baseball Player)
1315 4th St
Kenner, LA 70062-7311, USA

Razorlight (Music Group)
Universal Music Operations
364-366 Kensington High St
London W14 8NS, UNITED KINGDOM

R. Carter, John (Congressman, Politician)
409 Cannon HOB
Washington, DC 20515, USA

R. Conseco, Francisco (Congressman, Politician)
1339 Longworth HOB
Washington, DC 20515, USA

Re, Giovanni Battsti Cardinal (Religious Leader)
Palazzo delle Congregazioni
Piazza Pio XII #10
Rome 00193, ITALY

Rea, Connie (Athlete, Basketball Player)
13 Marina Dr
Winter Haven, FL 33881-9710, USA

Rea, Stephen (Actor, Writer)
c/o Sue Leibman *Barking Dog Entertainment*
609 Greenwich St
6th Floor
New York, NY 10014, USA

Read, Amy (Golfer)
7622 Fall Creek Bend
Humble, TX 77396-3460, USA

Read, James (Actor)
c/o Staff Member *Pakula/King & Associates*
9229 Sunset Blvd
Suite 315
Los Angeles, CA 90069, USA

Read, Nicolas (Actor)
c/o Carlo Capomazza *Capocom Entertainment*
8970 Norma Pl
Los Angeles, CA 90069, USA

Read, Richard (Journalist)
Portland Oregonian
Editorial Dept
1320 SW Broadway
Portland, OR 97201, USA

Read, Sister Joel (Educator)
Alvermo College
President's Office
PO Box 343922
Milwaukee, WI 53234, USA

Readdy, William F (Bill) (Astronaut)
NASA
Johnson Space Center
2101 NASA Road
Houston, TX 77058, USA

Readdy, William F Captain (Astronaut)
1818 S Lynn St
Arlington, VA 22202-1619, USA

Reading, John (Musician)
14321 Draft Horse Lane
Wellington, Fl 33414-1020, USA

Read-Martin, Dolly
30765 Pacific Coast Hwy. #103
Malibu, CA 90265-3643

Ready, Randy (Athlete, Baseball Player)
4410 Enfield Dr
Dallas, TX 75220-6406, USA

Reagan, Bernice Johnson (Musician)
American University
History Dept
Washington, DC 20016, USA

Reagan, Michael
The Michael Reagan
P.O. Box 6061-405
Sherman Oaks, CA 91412, USA

Reagan, Nancy (Politician)
10880 Wilshire Blvd
#870
Los Angeles, CA 90024, USA

Reagan, Ron (Journalist)
2612 28th Ave. W.
Seattle, WA 98199-3320, USA

Reagins, Tony (Baseball Player)
18934 Secretariat Way
Yorba Linda, CA 92886-2672, USA

Reagor, Montae (Athlete, Football Player)
1511 Drexel Dr
Waxahachie, TX 75165, USA

Real, Roxanne (Musician)
Headline Talent
1650 Broadway
#508
New York, NY 10019, USA

Real, Terrence (Writer)
Real Relational Solutions
754 Massachusetts Ave
Arlington, MA 02476, USA

Reality, Maxim (Musician)
Midi Mgmt
Jenkins Lane
Great Hallinsbury
Essex CM22 7QL, UNITED KINGDOM (UK)

Ream, Charles (Athlete, Football Player)
1412 Snowmass Rd
Columbus, OH 43235, USA

Reames, Britt (Athlete, Baseball Player)
806 Dalton Rd
Seneca, SC 29678-3722, USA

Reamon, Tommy (Athlete, Football Player)
709 Galahad Dr
Newport News, VA 23608, USA

Reams, Leroy (Athlete, Baseball Player)
6140 E 17th St
Oakland, CA 94621-4108, USA

Reardon, Jeff (Athlete, Baseball Player)
5 Marlwood Ln
Palm Beach Gardens, FL 33418-6805, USA

Reardon, John (Actor)
c/o Courtney Kivowitz *Schiff Company, The*
9465 Wilshire Blvd
Suite 480
Beverly Hills, CA 90212, USA

Reardon, Ken (Athlete, Hockey Player)
568 Grosvenor Ave.
WestmOtint, PQ H3Y 4Z3, CANADA

Reardon, Kerry (Stylist)
The Agency
580 Broadway
Suite 500
New York, NY 10012, USA

Reaser, Elizabeth (Actor)
c/o Perri Kipperman *Kipperman Management*
420 West End Avenue
Suite 1G
New York, NY 10024, USA

Reason, Rex (Actor)
Roadside Productions
20105 Rhapsody Road
Walnut Creek, CA 91789, USA

Reason, Rhodes (Actor)
PO Box 503
Gladstone, OR 97027, USA

Reasoner, Marty (Athlete, Hockey Player)
5250 Winlane Dr
Bloomfield Hills, MI 48302-2960

Reasons, Gary P (Athlete, Football Player)
17029 Hardwood Pl
Edmond, OK 73012, USA

reaugh, daryl (Athlete, Hockey Player)
3400 Saint Johns Dr
Dallas, TX 75205-2906

Reaugh, Daryl (Athlete, Hockey Player)
Dallas Stars
2601 Avenue of the Stars Ste 100
Frisco, TX 75034-9016

Reaume, Marc (Athlete, Hockey Player)
2991 Laurler Dr.
Windsor, ON N9J IL7, Canada

Reaux, Angelina (Opera Singer)
Herbert Breslin
119 W 57th St
#1505
New York, NY 10019, USA

Reaves, Ken (Athlete, Football Player)
413 Oakside Dr SW
Atlanta, GA 30331, USA

Reaves, Shawn (Actor)
c/o Claudia Black *Glasser/Black Management*
283 Cedarhurst Ave
Cedarhurst, NY 11516, USA

Reaves, Stephanie (Race Car Driver)
Rapid Motorsports Inc
PO Box 55
Bar Mills, ME 04004, USA

Reaves, T Johnson (John) (Athlete, Coach, Football Coach, Football Player)
5716 Bayshore Blvd
Tampa, FL 33611, USA

Reaves, Willard (Athlete, Football Player)
150 Wallingford Cres
Winnipeg, MB R3P II5, Canada

Reavis, Dave (Athlete, Football Player)
5495 S Newport Cir
Greenwood Village, CO 80111, USA

Reavis, Phil (Athlete, Olympic Athlete)
41 School St
Somerville, MA 02143-1721, USA

Rebagliati, Ross
One Erieview Plaza #1300
Cleveland, OH 44114

Rebardo, Joe (Musician)
Billy Paul Mgmt
8215 Winthrop St
Philadelphia, PA 19136, USA

Rebekah (Musician)
Int'l Talent Booking
27A Floral St
#300
London WC2E 9DQ, UNITED KINGDOM (UK)

Rebel Emergency (Music Group)
c/o Staff Member *Paradigm (Monterey)*
404 W Franklin St
Monterey, CA 93940, USA

Reberger, Frank (Athlete, Baseball Player)
439 Sunset View Ln
Hope, ID 83836-9845, USA

Rebhorn, James (Actor)
145 West 45th St
#1204
New York, NY 10036, USA

Reboulet, Jeff (Athlete, Baseball Player)
Horizon Wealth Management
8280 YMCA Plaza Dr
Bldg 5
Baton Rouge, LA 70810-0927, USA

Rebowe, Rusty (Athlete, Football Player)
656 Pine St
Norco, LA 70079, USA

Rebraca, Zeljko (Athlete, Basketball Player)
1550 8th St
Manhattan Beach, CA 90266-6351, USA

Recari, Beatriz (Athlete, Golfer)
c/o Staff Member *Ladies Pro Golf Association (LPGA)*
100 International Golf Dr
Daytona Beach, FL 32124-1092, USA

Recasner, Eldridge (Athlete, Basketball Player)
6159 164th Ave SE
Bellevue, WA 98006-5613, USA

Recchi, Mark (Athlete, Hockey Player)
The Orr Hockey Group
PO Box 290836
Charlestown, MA 02129-0215, USA

Recher, Dave (Athlete, Football Player)
970 E Devon Dr
Gilbert, AZ 85296, USA

Rechichar, Albert (Bert) (Athlete, Football Player)
141 W McClain Rd
Belle Vernon, PA 15012, USA

Rechter, Yacov (Architect)
150 Arlozorov St
Tel Aviv 62098, ISRAEL

Reckell, Peter (Actor)
c/o Staff Member *Rebel Entertainment Partners*
5700 Wilshire Blvd
Suite 456
Los Angeles, CA 90036, USA

Reckless Kelly (Music Group)
c/o Staff Member *Paradigm (Monterey)*
404 W Franklin St
Monterey, CA 93940, USA

Records, Max (Actor)
c/o Ara Keshishian *Creative Artists Agency (CAA-LA)*
2000 Ave Of The Stars
Los Angeles, CA 90067, USA

Rector, Jeff (Actor)
10748 Aqua Vista St
North Hollywood, CA 91602, USA

Rector, Milton G (Misc)
National Council on Crime & Delinquency
288 Monroe
River Edge, NJ 07661, USA

Red Alert, Kool DJ (Musician)
c/o Staff Member *Violator Management*
36 W 25th St
2nd Floor
New York, NY 10010, USA

Redbone, Leon (Musician)
Red Shark Inc
2169 Aquetong Road
New Hope, PA 18938, USA

Redd, Michael (Athlete, Basketball Player)
2 Crescent Pond
New Albany, OH 43054-9081, USA

Redden, Barry (Athlete, Football Player)
22503 Diamond Shore Ct
Katy, TX 77450, USA

Redden, Wade (Athlete, Hockey Player)
Newport Sports Management
400-201 City Centre Dr
Attn Don Meehan
Mississauga, ON LSB 2T4, Canada

Reddick, Cat (Athlete, Olympic Athlete, Soccer Player)
2620 Altadena Rd
Vestavia, AL 35243-4500, USA

Reddick, Eldon "Pokey" (Athlete, Hockey Player)
7794 Briana Renee Way
Las Vegas, NV 89123-0447

Reddick, Josh (Athlete, Baseball Player)
97 Drew Dr
Guyton, GA 31312-4867, USA

Reddicliffe, Steven (Editor)
TV Guide Magazine
Editorial Dept
100 Matsonford Road
Radnor, PA 19080, USA

Redding, Juli
PO Box 1806
, Beverly Hills 90212

Redding, Tim (Athlete, Baseball Player)
8882 Souire Trl
Bellevue, MI 49021-9566, USA

Reddout, Frank (Athlete, Basketball Player)
379 Niblick Cir
Winter Haven, FL 33881-9572, USA

Reddy, D Raj (Scientist)
Robotics Institute
Carnegie-Mellon University
Pittsburgh, PA 15213, USA

Reddy, Helen (Musician)
c/o Staff Member *T-Best Talent Agency*
508 Honey Lake Court
Danville, CA 94506, USA

Redfern, Pete (Athlete, Baseball Player)
12516 Haddon Ave
Sylmar, CA 91342-3636, USA

Redfield, James (Actor, Producer, Writer)
c/o Hampton Roads Publishing
1125 Stoney Ridge Road
Charlottesville, VA 22902, USA

Redfield, Joe (Athlete, Baseball Player)
307 Glenview Cir
Woodway, TX 76712-3141, USA

Redford, Blair (Actor)
c/o Matt Fletcher *Greene & Associates*
1901 Avenue Of The Stars Ste 130
Los Angeles, CA 90067, USA

Redford, Jamie (Producer)
c/o Jim Ehrich *Rothman Brecher Kim*
9250 Wilshire Blvd #PHB
Beverly Hills, CA 90212-3346, USA

Redford, Paul (Producer, Writer)
c/o Cori Wellins *WME (LA)*
9601 Wilshire Blvd Fl 3
Beverly Hills, CA 90210, USA

Redford, Robert (Actor, Director)
c/o Staff Member *The Sundance Institute*
8530 Wilshire Blvd.
3rd Floor
Beverly Hills, CA 90211, USA

Redgrave, Corin (Actor)
Kate Feast
Primrose Hill Studios
Fitzroy Road
London NW1 8TR, UNITED KINGDOM (UK)

Redgrave, Jemma (Actor)
Conway Van Gelder Robinson
18-21 Jermyn St
London SW1Y 6NB, UNITED KINGDOM (UK)

Redgrave, Vanessa (Actor)
c/o Nicole Caruso *Wolf Kasteler Van Iden & Associates (NY)*
584 Broadway
Suite 310
New York, NY 10012, USA

Red-Horse, Valerie (Actor, Director, Producer, Writer)
c/o Staff Member *Suite A Management Talent & Literary Agency*
120 El Camino Dr
Suite 202
Beverly Hills, CA 90212, USA

Red Hot Chili Peppers (Music Group)
c/o Cliff Burnstein *Q Prime Inc*
729 7th Ave
16th Floor
New York, NY 10019, USA

Redick, JJ (Athlete, Basketball Player)
315 E New England Ave Unit 13
Winter Park, FL 32789-4477, USA

Reding, Juli (Actor)
PO Box 1806
Beverly Hills, CA 90213, USA

Redman, Amanda (Actor)
c/o Staff Member *Lip Service Casting Ltd*
60-66 Wardour St
London W1F 0TA, UK

Redman, Brian (Race Car Driver)
10945 Scott Hill Rd.
Jacksonville, FL 32217, USA

Redman, Dewey (Composer, Musician)
Joel Chriss
300 Mercer St
#3J
New York, NY 10003, USA

Redman, Joshua (Composer, Musician)
Wilkins Mgmt
323 Broadway
Cambridge, MA 02139, USA

Redman, Joshua (Race Car Driver)
Wilkins Management
323 Broadway
Cambridge, MA 02139, USA

Redman, Julian "Tike" (Athlete, Baseball Player)
W155N6984 Amberlelgh Cir
Menomonee Falls, WI 53051-5088, USA

Redman, Magdalen (Athlete, Baseball Player)
N7780 Vicksburg Way Apt D
Oconomowoc, WI 53066-2016, USA

Redman, Mark (Athlete, Baseball Player)
6818 E 109th St
Tulsa, OK 74133-7153, USA

Redman, Michele (Golfer)
3410 Queensland Ln N
Minneapolis, MN 55447-1153, USA

Redman, Prentice (Athlete, Baseball Player)
1831 Boulder Springs
Dr Apt K
Saint louis, MO 63146-3953, USA

Redman, Susle (Golfer)
137 SW Sarasota Ave
Port Saint Lucle, FL 34952, USA

Redmann, Teal (Actor)
c/o Amy Abell *Glick Agency*
1505 10th St
Santa Monica, CA 90401, USA

Redmayne, Eddie (Actor)
c/o Gene Parseghian *Parseghian Planco LLC*
322 8th Ave
Suite 601
New York, NY 10001, USA

Redmon, Glenn (Athlete, Baseball Player)
PO Box 2171
Riverview, FL 33568-2171, USA

Redmond, Craig (Athlete, Hockey Player)
10332 McEachern St
Maple Ridge, BC V2W OB2, Canada

Redmond, Marge (Actor)
Abrams Artists
9200 Sunset Blvd
#1125
Los Angeles, CA 90069, USA

Redmond, Markus (Actor)
c/o Staff Member *Gersh (LA)*
9465 Wilshire Blvd
Suite 600
Beverly Hills, CA 90212, USA

Redmond, Marlon (Athlete, Basketball Player)
441 Oak St
San Francisco, CA 94102-5609, USA

Redmond, Michael E (Mickey) (Athlete, Hockey Player)
30699 Harlincin Ct
Franklin, MI 48025-1521, USA

Redmond, Mickey (Athlete, Hockey Player)
Detroit Red Wings
600 Civic Center Dr
Detroit, MI 48226-4419

Redmond, Mike (Athlete, Baseball Player)
13506 S Bluegrouse Ln
Spokane, WA 99224-8523, USA

Redmond, Rudy (Athlete, Football Player)
17091 Melrose St
Southfield, MI 48075, USA

Redmond, Wayne (Athlete, Baseball Player)
18061 Sussex St
Detroit, MI 48235-2835, USA

Rednikova, Yekaterina (Actor)
c/o Larry Hummel
358 North Gardner St
Los Angeles, CA 90036, USA

Redpath, Jean (Musician)
Sunny Knowe
Promenade
Leven, Fife, SCOTLAND

Redquest, Greg (Athlete, Hockey Player)
16 Hall St RR 1
Phelpston, ON LOL 2KO, Canada

Redstone, Summer M (Business Person)
Viacom Inc
1515 Broadway
New York, NY 10036, USA

Redstone, Sumner (Misc)
c/o Staff Member *Viacom Entertainment Group*
5555 Melrose Ave
Los Angeles, CA 90038

Redus, Gary (Athlete, Baseball Player)
2202 Mallard Ln SE
Decatur, AL 35601-6759, USA

Redwine, Jarvis J (Athlete, Football Player)
2707 W 79th St
Inglewood, CA 90305, USA

Redwine, Tim
3518 Cahuenga Blvd. W. #200
Los Angeles, CA 90068

Reece, Beasley (Athlete, Football Player, Sportscaster)
17 Stirling Way
Lunberton, NJ 08048, USA

Reece, Bob (Athlete, Baseball Player)
3106 Castlewood Cir
Pollock Pines, CA 95726-9522, USA

Reece, Carmen (Musician)
c/o Mark Feist *Real MF Ltd*
22425 Ventura Blvd
#179
Woodland Hills, CA 91364, USA

Reece, Carole (Stylist)
c/o Staff Member *Talent Plus*
1222 Lucas Ave
Suite 300
St. Louis, MO 63103, USA

Reece, Daniel (Danny) (Athlete, Football Player)
5519 S Corning Ave
Los Angeles, CA 90056, USA

Reece, Dave (Athlete, Hockey Player)
138 Peaked Rock Rd
Wakefield, RI 02879-2384

Reece, Gabrielle (Gabby) (Athlete, Model, Volleyball Player)
c/o Lisa Shotland *Creative Artists Agency (CAA-LA)*
2000 Ave Of The Stars
Los Angeles, CA 90067, USA

Reece, John (Athlete, Football Player)
5927 Cape Hatteras Dr
Houston, TX 77041, USA

Reece, Maynard (Artist)
5315 Robertson Dr
Des Moines, IA 50312-2133, USA

Reece, Thomas L (Business Person)
Dover Corp
280 Park Ave
New York, NY 10017, USA

Reed, Alvin (Athlete, Football Player)
3910 Abbeywood Dr
Pearland, TX 77584-4943, USA

Reed, Alyson (Actor)
c/o Christopher Black *Opus Entertainment*
5225 Wilshire Blvd #905
Los Angeles, CA 90036, USA

Reed, Andre D (Athlete, Football Player)
16 Gypsy Ln
East Aurora, NY 14052, USA

Reed, Ben
c/o Staff Member *AKA Talent Agency*
6310 San Vicente Blvd
Suite 200
Los Angeles, CA 90048, USA

Reed, Bob (Athlete, Baseball Player)
42519 Lake Hospitality Ln
Altoona, FL 32702-9584, USA

Reed, Bruce (Writer)
c/o Staff Member *Public Affairs Books*
1094 Flex Dr
Jackson, TN 38301, USA

Reed, Chad (Motorcycle Racer)
c/o Staff Member *Rockstar Makita Suzuki Factory Racing*
P.O. Box 27740
Las Vegas, NV 89126, USA

Reed, Crystal (Actor)
c/o Staff Member *Main Title Entertainment*
8383 Wilshire Blvd
Suite 408
Los Angeles, CA 90211, USA

Reed, Darren (Athlete, Baseball Player)
8101 Santa Ana Rd
Ventura, CA 93001-9723, USA

Reed, Diana (Beauty Pageant Winner)
c/o Judy Sawkins
PO Box 25
Bettendorf, IA 52722, USA

Reed, Dizzy (Musician)
c/o Joel Miller *Albion Entertainment*
24331 Hatteras St.
Woodland Hills, CA 91367, USA

Reed, Ed (Athlete, Football Player)
1 Winning Dr
Owings Mills, MD 21117, USA

Reed, Eddie (Athlete, Baseball Player)
Memphis Red Sox
708 8th Ave S
Great Falls, MT 59405-2052, USA

Reed, Eric (Musician)
Joel Chriss
300 Mercer St
#3J
New York, NY 10003, USA

Reed, Hub (Athlete, Basketball Player)
46601 Garretts Lake Rd
Shawnee, OK 74804-9494, USA

Reed, Jack (Athlete, Baseball Player)
PO Box 97
Silver City, MS 39166, USA

Reed, Jeff (Athlete, Baseball Player)
17688 Sylvan Hill Road
Elizabethton, TN 37643, USA

Reed, Jeremy (Athlete, Baseball Player)
4819 N 35th St
Phoenix, AZ 85018-3476, USA

Reed, Jerry (Athlete, Baseball Player)
13964 106th Ave
Largo, FL 33774-4543, USA

Reed, Jim (Race Car Driver)
8 Cutler La ne
Garrison, NY 10524, USA

Reed, Jody (Athlete, Baseball Player)
19153 E Briarwood Dr
Centennial, CO 80016-2161, USA

Reed, Joe (Athlete, Football Player)
106 Whitechapel Ct
Cedar Park, TX 78613-3219, USA

Reed, Johnny (Musician)
Jackson Artists
7251 Lowell Dr
#200
Overland Park, KS 66204, USA

Reed, John S (Financier)
Citigroup Inc
399 Park Ave
New York, NY 10022, USA

Reed, Josh (Athlete, Football Player)
124 Allegro Ave
Duson, LA 70529, USA

Reed, Keith (Athlete, Baseball Player)
513A S Main St
Rolesville, NC 27571-9666, USA

Reed, Kira
PO Box 251255
Los Angeles, CA 90025

Reed, Lou (Actor, Composer, Musician, Songwriter)
c/o Tom Sarig *Esther Creative Group*
27 W 24th St
Suite 404
New York, NY 10010, USA

Reed, Margaret
524 W. 57th St. #5330
New York, NY 10019

Reed, Mark A (Doctor)
Yale University
Electrical Engineering Dept
PO Box 2157
New Haven, CT 06520, USA

Reed, Nikki (Actor, Producer, Writer)
c/o Amy Zvi *Thruline Entertainment*
9250 Wilshire Blvd
Ground Fl
Beverly Hills, CA 90212, USA

Reed, Oscar (Athlete, Football Player)
700 Elizabeth Ln
Minneapolis, MN 55411, USA

Reed, Pamela (Actor)
Innovative Artists
1505 10th St
Santa Monica, CA 90401, USA

Reed, Peyton (Actor, Director, Producer)
c/o Staff Member *Moxie Pictures*
2644 30th St
Santa Monica, CA 90405, USA

Reed, Priscilla (Musician)
153 Rue De Grande
Brentwood, TN 37027, USA

Reed, Rex (Journalist)
Dakota Hotel
1 W 72nd St Apt 86
New York, NY 10023-3425, USA

Reed, Richard A (Rick) (Baseball Player)
Pittsburgh Pirates
86 Private Drive 8323
Proctorville, OH 45669-7914, USA

Reed, Richard J (Misc)
University of Washington
Atmospheric Sciences Dept
Seattle, WA 98195, USA

Reed, Rick (Athlete, Baseball Player)
4938 Crestone Way
Rochester, MI 48306, USA

Reed, Rick (Athlete, Baseball Player)
9604 State Route 7
Unit 7
Proctorville, OH 45669, ISA

Reed, Robert (Athlete, Football Player)
21 Wells S
Saratoga Springs, NY 12866, USA

Reed, Ronald L (Ron) (Athlete, Baseball Player, Basketball Player)
2613 Cliffview Dr SW
Lilburn, GA 30047-4794, USA

Reed, Royce (Actor)
c/o Dominic Friesen *Bridge and Tunnel Communications*
9157 Sunset Blvd.
West Hollywood, CA 90069, USA

Reed, Shanna (Actor)
1327 Brinkley Ave
Los Angeles, CA 90049, USA

Reed, Steve (Athlete, Baseball Player)
5335 Pine Ridge Rd
Golden, CO 80403-8030, USA

Reed, Thomas C (Government Official)
Quaker Hill Development Corp
PO Box 2240
Healdsburg, CA 95448, USA

Reed, Tom (Congressman, Politician)
1037 Longworth HOB
Washington, DC 20515, USA

Reed, Tony (Athlete, Football Player)
14068 Mount Tabor Rd
Odessa, MO 64076-7109, USA

Reed, Walter
3400 Paul Sweet Rd. #B-209
Santa Cruz, CA 95065

Reed, Willis (Athlete, Basketball Player, Football Player)
PO Box 1779
Ruston, LA 71273-1779, USA

Reed Jr, Alan
3455 Laurelvale Dr
Studio City, CA 91604, USA

Reeds, Mark (Athlete, Hockey Player)
7823 Cardinal Ridge Ct
Saint Louis, MO 63119, USA

Reeds, Mark (Athlete, Hockey Player)
Ottawa Senators
110-1000 Palladium Dr
Ottawa, ON K2V IAS, Canada

Reedus, Norman (Actor, Model)
c/o Staff Member *ROAR (LA)*
9701 Wilshire Blvd
8th Floor
Los Angeles, CA 90212, USA

Reehl, Robert (Race Car Driver)
13434 Lambert Rd.
Whittier, CA 90603, USA

Reekie, Joe (Athlete, Hockey Player)
1421 Gilbert Rd
Arnold, MD 21012-2539

Reel & Reel
Box 480 High Wycombe
Bucks., ENGLAND PH12 4LH

Reep, Jon (Actor, Comedian)
c/o Kara Welker *Generate Management*
1545 26th St
Suite 200
Santa Monica, CA 90404, USA

Rees, Andrew (Opera Singer)
Van Walsum Mgmt
4 Addison Bridge Place
London W14 8XP, UNITED KINGDOM (UK)

Rees, Angharad (Actor)
James Sharkey
21 Golden Square
London W1R 3PA, UNITED KINGDOM (UK)

Rees, Dai (Designer, Fashion Designer)
c/o Staff Member *Dai Rees*
6 Blackstock Mews
Blackstock Road
London, England N42BT, United Kingdom

Rees, Eberhard (Physicist)
69 Revere Way
Huntsville, AL 35801, USA

Rees, Jed (Actor)
c/o Staff Member *Elizabeth Hodgson Management Group*
1688 Cypress St
Suite 405
Vancouver, BC V6J 5J1, Canada

Rees, John (Musician)
TPA
PO Box 124
Round Corner, NSW 2158, USA

Rees, Martin J (Astronomer)
King's College
Astronomy Institute
Cambridge CB2 1ST, UNITED KINGDOM (UK)

Rees, Martin Sir (Scientist)
320 Red Feather Ln
Brentwood, TN 37027-4771, USA

Rees, Mina (Mathematician)
301 E 66th St
New York, NY 10021, USA

Rees, Norma S (Educator)
California State University
President's Office
Hayward, CA 94542, USA

Rees, Roger (Actor)
Innovative Artists
1505 10th St
Santa Monica, CA 90401, USA

Reese, Brian Adrian (Cassidy) (Musician)
c/o Greg Cohen *Amalgam Management*
705 Town Blvd NE #510
Atlanta, GA 30318-3082, USA

Reese, Calvin (Pokey) (Athlete, Baseball Player)
12416 Sylvan Oak Way
Charlotte, NC 28273-4728, USA

Reese, Della (Actor, Musician)
c/o Lynda Bensky *Bensky Entertainment*
15030 Ventura Blvd
Suite 343
Sherman Oaks, CA 91403, USA

Reese, Eddie (Coach, Swimmer)
University of Texas
Athletic Dept
Austin, TX 78712, USA

Reese, Guy (Athlete, Football Player)
2409 Cardinal Way
McKinney, TX 75070-5966, USA

Reese, Izell (Athlete, Football Player)
4037 Thessa Cove NE
Roswell, GA 30075, USA

Reese, Jeff (Athlete, Hockey Player)
697 Maple Ave
Haddonfield, NJ 08033-1146

Reese, Kevin (Athlete, Baseball Player)
1221 Willow St
San Diego, CA 92106-2538, USA

Reese, Rich (Athlete, Baseball Player)
P.O. Box 2339
Carefree, AZ 85377-2339, USA

Reese, Steve (Athlete, Football Player)
1146 Parkwood Trc
Stone Mountain, GA 30083, USA

Reeser, Autumn (Actor)
c/o Staff Member *Kritzer Levine Wilkins Entertainment (KLWG)*
11872 La Grange Ave
1st Floor
Los Angeles, CA 90025, USA

Reeser, Morgan (Athlete, Olympic Athlete, Sailor)
1948 Coral Gardens Dr
Wilton Manors, FL 33306-1334, USA

Reeser, Robert (Horse Racer)
139 Barksdale Ct
Milford, DE 19963-4174, USA

Rees-Jones, Trevor
Oswestry
Shropshire, ENGLAND

Rees Jr, Clifford H (Ted) (General)
1620 Mayflower Court
#B414
Winter Park, FL 32792, USA

Rees-Mogg of Hinton Bleweet, William (Publisher)
3 Smith Square
London SW1, UNITED KINGDOM (UK)

Reeves, Bryant (Athlete, Basketball Player)
116458 S 4710 Rd
Muldrow, OK 74948-6882, USA

Reeves, Dan (Athlete, Football Player)
785 W Conway Dr NW
Atlanta, GA 30327, USA

Reeves, Diane
PO Box 66
Englishtown, NJ 07726

Reeves, Dianne (Musician)
Po Box 66
Englishtown, NJ 07726, USA

Reeves, Julie
PO Box 300
Russell, KY 41169

Reeves, Keanu (Actor)
c/o Erwin Stoff *3 Arts Entertainment Inc*
9460 Wilshire Blvd
7th Floor
Beverly Hills, CA 90210, USA

Reeves, Khalid (Athlete, Basketball Player)
11519 140th St
Jamaica, NY 11436-1018, USA

Reeves, Martha (Musician)
1300 E Lafayette St #1211
Detroit, MI 48207, USA

Reeves, Melissa
6520 Platt Ave. #634
West Hills, CA 91307-3218

Reeves, Perrey (Actor)
2101 Broadview Terrace
Los Angeles, CA 90068, USA

Reeves, Randy (General)
300 W Redbud Ln
Lancaster, TX 75146-3128, USA

Reeves, Richard (Misc)
Universal Press Syndicate
4520 Main St
Kansas City, MO 64111, USA

Reeves, Rodrick (Stylist)
c/o Staff Member *Ford Models (Chicago)*
311 W Superior St
Chicago, IL 60654, USA

Reeves, Ronna
5114 Albert Dr.
Brentwood, TN 37021

Reeves, Sarah Gore (Stylist)
c/o Staff Member *Art House Management*
1548 16th St
Santa Monica, CA 90404, USA

Reeves, Saskia (Actor)
Markham & Froggatt
Julian House
4 Windmill St
London W1P 1HF, UNITED KINGDOM (UK)

Reeves, Scott (Actor)
6520 Platt Ave
#634
West Hills, CA 91307, USA

Reeves, Stevie (Race Car Driver)
CAA Performance Group
218 Chestnut Ave.
Kannapolis, NC 28081, USA

Reeves, Teri (Actor)
c/o Paul Brown *New Wave Entertainment (LA)*
2660 W Olive Blvd
Burbank, CA 91505, USA

Reeves, Walter (Athlete, Football Player)
5013 Lincoln Oaks Dr S
Apt 1805
Fort Worth, TX 76132-2250, USA

Refaeli, Bar (Actor, Model)
c/o Scott Lipps *One Model Management*
42 Bond St
2nd Floor
New york, NY 10012, USA

Reffner, Bryan (Race Car Driver)
Phelon Motors
3980 Richland Ave.
Aiken, SC 29801, USA

Regaibuto, Joe (Actor)
724 24th St
Santa Monica, CA 90402, USA

Regalado, Rudy (Athlete, Baseball Player)
P.O. Box 475
Borrego Springs, CA 92004-0475, USA

Regalbuto, Joe
724 24th St.
Santa Monica, CA 90402

Regan, Brian (Actor, Comedian)
c/o Staff Member *WME (LA)*
9601 Wilshire Blvd Fl 3
Beverly Hills, CA 90210, USA

Regan, Bridget (Actor)
c/o Staff Member *TMT Entertainment Group*
648 Broadway
Suite 1002
New York, NY 10012, USA

Regan, Chris (Writer)
c/o Staff Member *Gersh (LA)*
9465 Wilshire Blvd
Suite 600
Beverly Hills, CA 90212, USA

Regan, Donald T
240 McLaws Cir #142
Williamsburg, VA 23185, USA

Regan, Gerald A (Government Official)
PO Box 828
Station B
Ottawa, ON K1P 5P9, CANADA

Regan, Judith (Talk Show Host, Writer)
c/o Staff Member *Regan Media*
10100 Santa Monica Blvd
10th Fl
Santa Monica, CA 90067, USA

Regan, Larry (Athlete, Hockey Player)
260 Metcalfe #39
Ottawa, ON K2P 1R6, CANADA

Regan, Laura (Actor)
c/o Staff Member *TMT Entertainment Group*
648 Broadway
Suite 1002
New York, NY 10012, USA

Regan, Phil (Athlete, Baseball Player, Coach)
1687 SW Harbour Isles Cir #6
Port St Lucie, FL 34986-3405, USA

Regas, Karen (Stylist)
3573 Linden Lane
Coconut Grove, FL 33133-5614, USA

Regazzoni, Clay (Race Car Driver)
Via Monzoni 13
Lugano 6900, SWITZERLAND

Regehr, Duncan (Actor)
2501 Main St
Santa Monica, CA 90405, USA

Regen, Elizabeth (Actor)
c/o Mark Measures *Abrams Artists Agency (LA)*
9200 Sunset Blvd
11th Floor
Los Angeles, CA 90069, USA

Reger, John (Athlete, Football Player)
9919 SW 42nd Rd
Gainesville, FL 32608-7103, USA

Reger, Nate (Writer)
c/o Staff Member *ICM Partners (ICM-LA)*
10250 Constellation Blvd Fl 7
Los Angeles, CA 90067, USA

Reggiani, Serge (Actor, Musician)
Charley Marouani
4 Ave Hoche
Paris 75008, FRANCE

Reggio, Godfrey (Director)
Regional Education Institute
PO Box 2404
Santa Fe, NM 87504, USA

Reghanti, Noel (Stylist)
c/o Staff Member *Artist Untied (LA)*
845 S Mansfield Ave
#1
Los Angeles, CA 90036, USA

Reghi, Mike (Baseball Player)
9344 Saybrook Dr
North Ridgeville, OH 44039-8748, USA

Regier, Darcy (Athlete, Hockey Player)
8362 Black Walnut Dr.
E. Elmhurst, NY 14051-1561

Regier, Darcy (Athlete, Hockey Player)
Buffalo Sabres
1 Seymour H Knox III Plz Ste 1
Buffalo, NY 14203-3096

Regilio, Nick (Athlete, Baseball Player)
6505 Raham Ct
Port Orange, FL 32128-6069, USA

Regina, Paul
2911 Canna St.
Thousand Oaks, CA 91360-1718

Regine (Business Person)
502 Park Ave
New York, NY 10022, USA

Regis, John (Athlete, Track Athlete)
67 Fairby Road
London SE12, UNITED KINGDOM (UK)

Register, Steven (Athlete, Baseball Player)
698 Hunter Ct
Auburn, AL 36832-5403, USA

Regner, Tom (Athlete, Football Player)
2231 Big Trail Cir
Reno, NV 89521, USA

Regnier, Charles (Actor, Director)
Neherstr 7
Munich 81675, GERMANY

Rehberg, Denny (Congressman, Politician)
2448 Rayburn HOB
Washington, DC 20515, USA

Rehberg, Scott (Athlete, Football Player)
1153 Thistle Ln
Lebanon, OH 45036-7788, USA

Rehder, Tom (Athlete, Football Player)
730 Monarch Ln
Nipomo, CA 93444, USA

Rehm, Diane (Radio Personality)
c/o Staff Member *National Public Radio (NPR)*
635 Massachusetts Ave NW
Washington, DC 20001, USA

Rehm, Fred (Athlete, Basketball Player)
19340A Stonehedge Dr
Brookfield, WI 53045-3665, USA

Rehm, Jack D (Publisher)
19 Neponset Ave
#9A
Old Saybrook, CT 06475, USA

Rehm Jr, Daniel R (War Hero)
1043 Del Norte St
Houston, TX 77018, USA

Rehn, Trista (Reality TV Star)
42 Meadow Dr
Vail, CO 81657, USA

Rehr, Frank (Cartoonist)
United Feature Syndicate
200 Madison Ave
New York, NY 10016, USA

Rehrer-Carteaux, Rita (Athlete, Baseball Player)
3210 Kenwood Ave
Fort Wayne, IN 46805-2932, USA

Reich, Charles A (Educator, Lawyer)
Crown Publishers
225 Park Ave S
New York, NY 10003, USA

Reich, Doris (Stylist)
882 Carroll St
Brooklyn, NY 11215, USA

Reich, Frank M (Athlete, Football Player)
12551 Glendurgan Dr
Carmel, IN 46032-8314, USA

Reich, Jason (Writer)
c/o Staff Member *Kaplan Stahler Agency*
8383 Wilshire Blvd
Suite 923
Beverly Hills, CA 90211, USA

Reich, John (Director)
724 Bohemia Parkway
Sayville, NY 11782, USA

Reich, Robert (Politician)
1230 Bonita Ave
Berkeley, CA 94709-1923, USA

Reich, Steve M (Composer)
Nonesuch Records
75 Rockefeller Plaza
New York, NY 10019, USA

Reichard, Daniel
c/o Jeff Morrone *Jeff Morrone Entertainment*
9350 Wilshire Blvd
Suite 224
Beverly Hills, CA 90212, USA

Reichardt, Rick (Athlete, Baseball Player)
2605 NW 90th Ter
Gainesville, FL 32606-6742, USA

Reichel, Robert (Athlete, Hockey Player)
Lesni 391
Litvinov, ON 436 01, Czech Republic

Reichenbach, Mike (Athlete, Football Player)
2230 Cloverly Cir
Jamison, PA 18929, USA

Reichert, Bill (Race Car Driver)
Bar's Leak Racing
203 S. Gould St.
Owosso, MI 48887, USA

Reichert, Dan (Athlete, Baseball Player)
6620 Glass Ridge Dr
Lincoln, NE 68526-9752, USA

Reichert, Jack F (Business Person)
580 Douglas Dr
Lake Forest, IL 60045, USA

Reichert, Tanja (Actor)
Pacific Artists
1404-510 W Hastings St
Vancouver, BC V6B 1L8, CANADA

Reichl, Ruth M (Editor)
Gourmet Magazine
Editorial Dept
4 Times Square
New York, NY 10036, USA

Reichman, Fred (Artist)
1235 Stanyan St
San Francisco, CA 94117, USA

Reichow, Garet N (Athlete, Football Player)
P.O. Box 822
Tesuque, NM 87574-0822, USA

Reichs, Kathy (Writer)
c/o Jennifer Rudolph Walsh *WME (WMA-NY)*
1325 Ave of the Americas
New York, NY 10019, USA

Reid, Andy (Coach, Football Coach)
Philadelphia Eagles
1215 Page Ter
Villanova, 19085-2132 19145, USA

Reid, Antonio (L.A.) (Producer)
836 Sagg Main St
Sagaponack, NY 11962, USA

Reid, Brandon (Athlete, Hockey Player)
21 Place du Champagne
Kirkland, QC H9H SJ4, Canada

Reid, Christopher (Actor)
c/o Rod Baron *Baron Entertainment*
13848 Ventura Blvd
Suite A
Sherman Oaks, CA 91423-3654

Reid, Daphne (Actor)
New Millenium
1 New Millenium Dr
Petersburg, VA 23805, USA

Reid, Dave (Athlete, Hockey Player)
1522 Hawkswood Dr RR 1
Ennismore, ON KOL ITD, Canada

Reid, Dave (Athlete, Hockey Player)
Peterborough Petes
151 Lansdowne St W
Peterborough, ON K9J 1Y4, Canada

Reid, Don S (Musician, Songwriter, Writer)
American Major Talent
8747 Highway 304
Hernando, MS 38632, USA

Reid, Dorice (Athlete, Baseball Player)
1165 Via Santa Paulo
Vista, CA 92081-6332, USA

Reid, Douglas (Race Car Driver)
Doug Reid Racing
1217 - 24th Ave.
Hueytown, AL 35023, USA

Reid, Elliott
11201 Ventura Blvd
Studio City, CA 91604-3136, USA

Reid, Harold (Musician, Songwriter, Writer)
1004 E Beverly St
Staunton, VA 24401, USA

Reid, Harry (Politician)
1155 23rd St NW Apt 2E
Washington, DC 20037-3302, USA

Reid, Jesse (Athlete, Baseball Player)
2641 Carey Station Rd
Greensboro, GA 30642, USA

Reid, Joe (Athlete, Football Player)
651 Shady Hollow St
Houston, TX 77056, USA

Reid, J R (Athlete, Basketball Player)
121 Cemetary St
Chester, SC 29706-1620, USA

Reid, Michael B (Mike) (Athlete, Composer, Football Player)
825 Overton Ln
Nashville, TN 37220, USA

Reid, Michael Eric (Actor)
c/o Rita Berger *Rita B Management*
10063 Riverside Dr
#2763
Toluca Lake, CA 91602, USA

Reid, Mike (Golfer)
935 E 80 N
Orem, UT 84097-4978, USA

Reid, Mike (Athlete, Football Player)
P.O. Box 362
Pacolet, SC 29372, USA

Reid, Norman R (Misc)
50 Brabourne Rise
Park Langley Beckenham
Kent, UNITED KINGDOM (UK)

Reid, Odgen R (Diplomat, Journalist)
Ophir Hill
Purchase, NY 10577, USA

Reid, Ogden
Ophir Hill
Purchase, NY 10577

Reid, Scott (Athlete, Baseball Player)
10827 S 26th Ave
Phoenix, AZ 85041-9630, USA

Reid, Stephen E (Steve) (Athlete, Doctor, Football Player)
1784 Locust St
Des Plaines, IL 60018, USA

Reid, Tara (Actor)
c/o Darris Hatch *Daris Hatch Management*
10027 Rossbury Pl
Los Angeles, CA 90064-4825, USA

Reid, Tim (Actor, Director)
New Millenium
1 New Millenium Dr
Petersburg, VA 23805, USA

Reid, Tom (Athlete, Hockey Player)
603 Hawthorne Woods Dr
Saint Paul, MN 55123-3052

Reid, Tom (Athlete, Hockey Player)
Minnesota Wild 317 Washington St
Saint Paul, MN 55102-1667

Reid, William (General)
Cranford Ferntower Place Crieff
Perthshire PH7 3DD, England

Reid, William J (Athlete, Football Player)
315 Ramona St
Palo Alto, CA 94301, USA

Reierson, Dave (Athlete, Hockey Player)
99 Grand Ave
Grand Haven, MI 49417-2408

Reifsnyder, Robert H (Bob) (Athlete, Football Player)
4 Helm Ct
Berlin, MD 21811, USA

Reightler, Kenneth S Captain (Astronaut)
1602 Honeysuckle Ridge Ct
Annapolis, MD 21401-6425, USA

Reightler Jr, Kenneth S (Astronaut)
1602 Honeysuckle Ridge Court
Annapolis, MD 21401, USA

Reihner, George (Athlete, Football Player)
1010 Electric St
Scranton, PA 18509, USA

Reil, Shannen
Murray State University
Po Box 661
W Van Lear, KY 41295, USA

Reilly, Gabrielle (Model)
PO Box 3145
Shawnee, KS 66203, USA

Reilly, Jennifer
345 N. Maple Dr. #397
Beverly Hills, CA 90210

Reilly, John (Actor)
c/o Peter Young *Sovereign Talent Group*
8421 Wilshire Blvd
Suite 200
Beverly Hills, CA 90211, USA

Reilly, John C (Actor)
c/o Peg Donegan *Framework Entertainment (LA)*
9057 Nemo St
Suite C
West Hollywood, CA 90069, USA

Reilly, Kevin (Athlete, Football Player)
Webster Farms
521 Rothbury Rd
Wilmington, DE 119803-2439, USA

Reilly, Mike (Athlete, Baseball Player)
131 Smithfield Rd
Battle Creek, MI 49015-3545, USA

Reilly, Mike (Athlete, Football Player)
708 Loretto Ct
Dubuque, IA 52003, USA

Reilly, Rick (Writer)
236 Cook St
Denver, CO 80206, USA

Reilly, William K (Government Official)
Stanford University
International Studies Institute
Stanford, CA 94305, USA

Reilly II, James F (Astronaut)
15903 Lake Lodge Dr
Houston, TX 77062-4745, USA

Reimer, Dennis Gen (General)
2602 N Brandywine St
Arlington, VA 22207-2719, USA

Reimer, Dennis J (Denny) (General)
MIPT
PO Box 889
Oklahoma City, OK 73101, us3

Reimer, James (Athlete, Hockey Player)
PO Box 508
Arborg, MB ROC OAO, Canada

Reimer, Kevin (Athlete, Baseball Player)
1797 W 28th Ave Apt 250
Apache Junction, AZ 85120-9504, USA

Reimer, Roland (Religious Leader)
mennonite Brethren Churches Conference
8000 W 21st St N
Wichita, KS 67205, USA

Reimers, Bruce (Athlete, Football Player)
2206 W River Dr
Humboldt, IA 50548, USA

Reimold, Nolan (Athlete, Baseball Player)
10 Callahan Rd
Greenville, PA 16125-9629, USA

Rein, Andrew (Athlete, Olympic Athlete, Wrestler)
31 Acorn Dr
Hawthorn Woods, IL 60047-7408, USA

Rein, Andrew (Athlete, Olympic Athlete, Wrestler)
31 Acorn Dr
Hawthorn Woods, IL 60047-7408, United States

Reina (Musician)
c/o Staff Member *Diva Central Inc*
7510 W Sunset Blvd Ste 1445
Los Angees, CA 90046, USA

Reincke, Heinz
Hof 38
Mondsee, AUSTRIA A-5310

Reineck, Thomas (Athlete)
Graf-Bernadotte-Str 4
Essen 45133, GERMANY

Reineke, Chad (Athlete, Baseball Player)
1904 Tanelewood Dr
Defiance, OH 43512-3638, USA

Reiner, Carl (Actor, Director)
c/o Staff Member *Clear Productions*
9171 Wilshire Blvd
#350
Beverly Hills, CA 90210, USA

Reiner, ex-DA Ira
1290 Sunset Plaza Dr.
Los Angeles, CA 90069

Reiner, John (Cartoonist)
Parade Magazine
30 Nathan Hale Dr Apt 71B
Huntington, NY 11743-7034, USA

Reiner, Rob (Actor, Director)
23704 Malibu Colony Rd
Malibu, CA 90265, USA

Reinfeldt, Mike (Athlete, Football Player)
1204 Waterstone Blvd
Franklin, TN 37069, USA

Reinhard, Bill (Athlete, Football Player)
43683 Old Troon Ct
Indio, CA 92201, USA

Reinhardt, Doug (Athlete, Baseball Player, Reality TV Star)
c/o Liza Anderson *Anderson Group Public Relations*
8060 Melrose Ave Fl 4
Los Angeles, CA 90046, USA

Reinhardt, John E (Diplomat)
3154 Gracefield Road
Apt 417
Silver Spring, MD 20904-0808, USA

Reinhardt, Stephen R (Judge)
US Court of Appeals
312 N Spring St
Los Angeles, CA 90012, USA

Reinhart, Haley (Musician, Reality TV Star)
Alex Theatre
216 N. Brand Blvd
Glendale, CA 91206, USA

Reinhart, Paul (Athlete, Hockey Player)
2911 Altamont Cres
West Vancouver, BC V7V 3B9, Canada

Reinharz, Jehuda (Educator)
Brandeis University
President's Office
Waltham, MA 02254, USA

Reinhold, Judge (Actor, Director)
c/o Tiffany Kuzon *Evolution Entertainment (LA)*
901 N Highland Ave
Los Angeles, CA 90038, USA

Reininger, Travis (Athlete, Baseball Player)
3470 Hottman St
Brighton, CO 80601-3424, USA

Reinking, Ann (Actor, Dancer, Director)
International Creative Mgmt
40 W 57th St
#1800
New York, NY 10019, USA

Reinprecht, Steven (Athlete, Hockey Player)
45 S Garfield St
Denver, CO 80209-3115

Reinsdorf, Jerry (Baseball Player)
Chicago White Sox
40 E Elm St
Chicago, IL 60611-1016, USA

Reirden, Todd (Athlete, Hockey Player)
45 S Garfield St
Denver, CO 80209-3115

Reirden, Todd (Athlete, Hockey Player)
Pittsburgh Penguins
66 Mario Lemieux Pl Ste 2
Pittsburgh, PA 15219-3504

Reis, Tommy (Athlete, Baseball Player)
15456 SW 15th Terrace Rd
Ocala, FL 34473, USA

Reise, Leo (Athlete, Hockey Player)
27 Cumming Crt
Ancaster, ON L9G 1 V4, Canada

Reiser, Jerry (Architect)
28 S Washington Ave
Dobbs Ferry, NY 10522, USA

Reiser, Paul (Actor, Producer)
c/o Mark Rousso *New Wave Entertainment (LA)*
2660 W Olive Blvd
Burbank, CA 91505, USA

Reiser, Robbie (Race Car Driver)
Reiser Motorsports
142 Pointe End Dr.
Mooresville, NC 28117-7303, USA

Reiser, Rock
9014 Melrose Ave.
W. Hollywood, CA 90069-5610

Reisman, Garrett E (Astronaut)
1715 Hedgecroft Dr
Seabrook, TX 77586, USA

Reisman, GarrettE Dr (Astronaut)
Spacex 1 Rocket Rd Attn: Engineeril¥g_ Dept, Astronaut Safety
Hawthorne, CA 90250-6844, USA

Reiss, Howard (Misc)
16656 Oldham St
Encino, CA 91436, USA

Reisz, Michael (Actor)
c/o Staff Member *WmE2 (WMA-LA)*
1 William Morris Pl
Beverly Hills, CA 90212, USA

Reiter, Mario (Skier)
Hauselweg 5
Rankweil 6830, AUSTRIA

Reiter, Thomas (Astronaut)
Europe Astronaut Center
European Space Centre I EAC Linder
Hohe Postfach 90 60 96
Koln D-51147, GERMANY

Reith, Brian (Athlete, Baseball Player)
9706 54th Ct E
Parrish, FL 34219-4440, USA

Reitherman, Bruce (Cinematographer, Producer, Writer)
c/o Staff Member *Pandion Enterprises, Inc.*
2287 Whitney Ave
Summerland, CA 93067, USA

Reitman, Ivan (Director, Producer)
900 Cold Springs Road
Montecito, CA 93108, USA

Reitman, Jason (Director)
c/o BeBe Lerner *ID Public Relations (ID-LA)*
7060 Hollywood Blvd
8th Floor
Los Angeles, CA 90028, USA

Reitman, Joe (Actor)
c/o Suzanne (Sue) Wohl *TalentWorks (LA)*
3500 W Olive Ave
Suite 1400
Burbank, CA 91505, USA

Reitsma, Chris (Athlete, Baseball Player)
6050 Jim Davis Rd
Parrish, FL 34219-9363, USA

Reitz, Bruce (Doctor)
Johns Hopkins Hospital
600 N Wolfe St
Baltimore, MD 21287, USA

Reitz, Ken (Athlete, Baseball Player)
1704 Carbine Ln
Saint Charles, MO 63303-1104, USA

ReK (Artist)
Rek's World
PO Box 1484
Southampton, PA 18966, USA

Rekar, Bryan (Athlete, Baseball Player)
4326 Waterville Ave
Wesley Chapel, FL 33543-7037, USA

Reklow, Jesse (Cartoonist)
2415 College Ave
#20
Berkeley, CA 94704, USA

Relaford, Desmond (Athlete, Baseball Player)
12483 Highview Dr
Jacksonville, FL 32225-5725, USA

Relch, Steve (Baseball Player)
US Olympic Team
28 Scofield Hill Rd
Washington Depot, CT 06794-1012, USA

Reld, Andy (Athlete, Football Coach, Football Player)
1215 Page Ter
Villanova, PA 19085, USA

Relient K (Music Group, Musician)
c/o Kevin Spellman *Vector Management (LA)*
1100 Glendon Ave.
Suite 2000
Los Angeles, CA 90024, USA

Reliford, Charlie (Athlete, Baseball Player)
1509 Cypress St
Ashland, KY 41101-3624, USA

Reliford, Charlie (Baseball Player)
1509 Cypress St
Ashland, KY 41101-3624, USA

Rell, M Jodi (Politician)
18 Andover Ct
Brookfield, CT 06804-2715, USA

Rellford, Richard (Athlete, Basketball Player)
28 Balfour Rd W
Palm Beach Gardens, FL 33418-7e9e, USA

Relman, Arnold S (Doctor, Editor)
New England Journal of Medicine
860 Winter St
#2
Waltham, MA 02451, USA

R E M (Music Group)
170 College Ave
Athens, GA 30601, US

Remar, James (Actor)
409 N Camden Dr
#202
Beverly Hills, CA 90210, USA

Rembert, Johnny (Athlete, Football Player)
2564 Willow Creek Dr
Orange Park, FL 32003-8375, USA

Remedios, Alberto T (Opera Singer)
21 Lanhill Road
London W9 2BS, UNITED KINGDOM (UK)

Remek, Vladimir (Cosmonaut)
Veletrzni 17
Prague 7 17000, CZECH REPUBLIC

Remigino, Lindy (Athlete, Olympic Athlete, Track Athlete)
22 Paris Lane
Newington, CT 06111-1628, USA

Remington, Deborah W (Artist)
309 W Broadway
New York, NY 10013, USA

Remini, Leah (Actor)
P.O. Box 15669
North Hollywood, CA 91615, USA

Remlinger, Mike (Athlete, Baseball Player)
18331 N 93rd Way
Scottsdale, AZ 85255-6048, USA

Remmen, Larry (Horse Racer)
319 Marshall St
Ridgewood, NJ 07450-3320, USA

Remmen, Ray (Horse Racer)
PO Box446
Lodi, NJ 07644-0446, USA

Remmerswaal, Win (Athlete, Baseball Player)
Doktor Van Praag St 16
Wassenaar, Holland

Remmert, Dennis (Athlete, Football Player)
3933 Briarwood Dr
Cedar Falls, IA 50613, USA

Remnick, David (Writer)
c/o Robert (Bob) Bookman *Creative Artists Agency (CAA-LA)*
2000 Ave Of The Stars
Los Angeles, CA 90067, USA

Remnick, David J (Editor, Writer)
257 W 86th St
#11A
New York, NY 10024, USA

Remo, Ken
121 S. Orange Dr.
Los Angeles, CA 90036

Rempt, Rodney (Admiral, Educator)
Superintendent
US Naval Academy
Annapolis, MD 21402, USA

Remy, Gerald P (Jerry) (Athlete, Baseball Player)
1403 Wisteria Way
Wayland, MA 01778-2850, USA

Renard, Mercedes (Actor)
c/o Evan Hainey *Untitled Entertainment (LA)*
350 S. Beverly Dr #200
Beverly Hills, CA 90212, USA

Renaud, Line (Musician)
5 Rue du Bois-de-Boulogne
Paris 75116, FRANCE

Renaud, Mark (Athlete, Hockey Player)
11788 Tecumseh Rd E
Windsor, ON N8N 1L7, Canada

Renault, Dennis (Cartoonist)
Sacramento Bee
Editorial Dept
21st & Q Sts
Sacramento, CA 95852, USA

Renbourn, John (Musician)
Folklore Inc
1671 Appian Way
Santa Monica, CA 90401, USA

Rencher, Terrence (Athlete, Basketball Player)
2001 S Mo Pac Expy
Apt 924
Austin, TX 78746-7579, USA

Rendall, Mark (Actor)
c/o Staff Member *Artist Management Inc*
464 King St E
Toronto ON M5A 1L7, CANADA

Rendell, Edward (Politician)
3425 Warden Dr
Philadelphia, PA 19129-1417, USA

Rendell, Majorie O (Judge)
US Court of Appeals
US Courthouse
601 Market St
Philadelphia, PA 19106, USA

Rendell, Ruth
Nusstead's Polstead Suffolk
Colchester, ENGLAND CO6 5DN

Rendell of Barbergh, Ruth B (Writer)
Nussteads Polstead
Suffolk
Colchester CO6 5DN, UNITED KINGDOM (UK)

Rene, Chris
c/o Staff Member *FanManager, LLC*
15335 Morrison St.
Suite 325
Sherman Oaks, CA 91403, USA

Rene, France-Albert (President)
President's Office
State House
Victoria
Mahe, SEYCHELLES

Reneau, Daniel D (Educator)
Louisiana Tech University
President's Office
Ruston, LA 71272, USA

Renfrew, Royce (Scientist)
2719 Raven Falls Ln
Friendswood, TX 77546-6075, USA

Renfrew of Kaimsthorn, Andrew C (Archaeologist)
McDonald Archaeological Institute
Downing St
Cambridge CB2 3ER, UNITED KINGDOM (UK)

Renfro, Leonard (Athlete, Football Player)
8893 E 24th Pl #103
Denver, CO 80238, USA

Renfro, Mike (Athlete, Football Player)
P.O. Box 93073
Southlake, TX 76092-1073, USA

Renfroe, Jay (Producer)
c/o Staff Member *Renegade 83 Entertainment*
5700 Wilshire Blvd
6th Floor
Los Angeles, CA 90036, USA

Renfroe, Laddie (Athlete, Baseball Player)
236 Hickory Ln
Batesville, MS 38606-9339, USA

Rengel, Mike (Athlete, Football Player)
1982 Montane Dr E
Golden, CO 80401, USA

Renger, Annemarie (Government Official)
Bundestag
Bundestag
Platz der Republik 1
Berlin 11011, GERMANY

Renick, Rick (Athlete, Baseball Player)
7320 Hawkins Rd
Sarasota, FL 34241-9375, USA

Renier, Jeremie (Actor)
Artmedia
20 Ave Rapp
Paris 75007, FRANCE

Renis, Tony (Musician)
Ischia Global
501 Deep Valley Dr.
1st Floor
Palos Verdes Peninsula, CA 90274, USA

Renk, Silke (Athlete, Track Athlete)
Erhard-Hubner-Str 13
Halle/S 06132, GERMANY

Renken, Henry (General)
Inter-Prove Inc 228 N Jackson St
Glendale, CA 91206-4337, USA

Renko, Steven (Steve) (Athlete, Baseball Player)
15812 W 136th St
Olathe, KS 66062-5310, USA

Renn, Crystal (Model)
c/o Staff Member *Ford Models (NY)*
238 E 4th St
New York, NY 10009, USA

Renna, Bill (Athlete, Baseball Player)
1476 Lesher Ct
San Jose, CA 95125-3936, USA

Renna, Eugene A (Business Person)
Mobil Corp
3225 Gallows Road
Fairfax, VA 22037, USA

Renna, Patrick (Actor)
c/o Staff Member *Talent Company, The*
P.O. Box 4227
Burbank, CA 91503, USA

Renne, Paul (Misc)
Berkeley Geochronology Center
2445 Ridge Road
Berkeley, CA 94709, USA

Rennebohm, J Fred (Religious Leader)
Congregational Christian Churches Assn
PO Box 1620
Oak Creek, MI 53154, USA

Rennebohm, J Fred (Misc)
Holbeinstr 58
Berlin 12203, GERMANY

Renner, Jeremy (Actor)
c/o Beth Holden-Garland *Untitled Entertainment (LA)*
350 S. Beverly Dr #200
Beverly Hills, CA 90212, USA

Rennert, Dutch (Athlete, Baseball Player)
2560 46th Rd
Vero Beach, FL 32966-2053, USA

Rennert, Dutch (Baseball Player)
Walkers Glen 2560 46th Rd
Vero Beach, FL 32966-2053, USA

Rennert, Gunther (Director, Opera Singer)
Holbeinstr 58
Berlin 12203, GERMANY

Renni, Gino (Actor)
c/o Staff Member *Telefe - Argentina*
Pavon 2444 (C1248AAT)
Buenos Aires, ARGENTINA

Reno, Jack
PO Box 1001
Florence, KY 41042

Reno, Janet (Politician)
11200 N Kendall Dr
Miami, FL 33176-1108, USA

Reno, Jean (Actor)
c/o Amy Guenther *Gateway Management Company Inc*
860 Via De La Paz
Suite F10
Pacific Palisades, CA 90272, USA

Reno, William H (General)
2706 S Ives St
Arlington, VA 22202, USA

Renoth, Heidi (Skier)
Lercheckerweg 23
Berchtesgaden 83471, GERMANY

Rensberger, Scott (Journalist)
914 7th St NE
Washington, DC 20002-3612, USA

Renteria, Edgar (Athlete, Baseball Player)
6633 Allison Rd
Miami, FL 33141, USA

Renteria, Rich (Athlete, Baseball Player)
930 Pacific Hills Pt
Apt B103
Colorado Springs, CO 80906, USA

Renteria, Rick (Athlete, Baseball Player)
1700 S Arabv Dr Apt 72
Palm Springs, CA 92264-6816, USA

Rentie, Caesar (Athlete, Football Player)
7614 Fallen Antler Pl
Arlington, TX 76002-4320, USA

Rentmeester, Co (Photographer)
PO Box 1562
West Hampton Beach, NY 11978-7562, USA

Renton of Mount Harry, R Timothy (Government Official)
House of Lords
Westminster
London SW1A 0PW, UNITED KINGDOM (UK)

Rentzel, Lance (Athlete, Football Player)
12104 Monument Dr
Apt 354
Fairfax, VA 22033, USA

Rentzepis, Peter M (Misc)
University of California
Chemistry Dept
Irvine, CA 92717, USA

Renucci, Robin
64 rue Condorcet
Paris, FRANCE 75009

Renvall, Johan (Dancer)
American Ballet Theatre
890 Broadway
New York, NY 10003, USA

Renyi, Thomas A (Financier)
Bank of New York
1 Wall St
New York, NY 10286, USA

Repeta, Nina (Actor)
Gage Group
14724 Ventura Blvd
Suite 505
Los Angeles, CA 91403, USA

Repin, Vadim V (Musician)
Eckholdtweg 2A
Lubeck 23566, GERMANY

Repko, Jason (Athlete, Baseball Player)
93005 E Chelsea Rd
Kennewick, WA 99338-8906, USA

Repoz, Roger (Athlete, Baseball Player)
930 Whitewater Dr
Fullerton, CA 92833-2194, USA

Rerych, Stephen (Athlete, Olympic Athlete, Swimmer)
1142 Ridgewood Dr
Point Pleasant, WV 25550-3578, USA

Resch, Alexander (Athlete)
BSD
An der Schiessstatte 4
Berchtesgaden 83471, GERMANY

Resch, Chico (Athlete, Hockey Player)
P.O. Box 207
1171 Dahler Ave
Emily, MN 56447, USA

Resch, Glenn "Chico" (Athlete, Hockey Player)
607 8th St
Lyndhurst, NJ 07071-3105

Resch, Glenn "Chico" (Athlete, Hockey Player)
New Jersey Devils
165 Mulberry St
Newark, NJ 07102-3607

Rescher, Nicholas (Misc)
1033 Milton Street
Pittsburgh, PA 15218-1228, USA

Resnais, Alain (Director)
70 Rue des Plantes
Paris 75014, FRANCE

Resnik, Regina (Opera Singer)
American Guild of Musical Arts
1430 Broadway
New York, NY 10018, USA

Resop, Chris (Athlete, Baseball Player)
2152 Harlans Run
Naples, FL 34105-8518, USA

Resor, Helen (Athlete, Hockey Player, Olympic Athlete)
22 N Stanwich Rd
Greenwich, CT 06831-2841, USA

Ressler, Glenn E (Athlete, Football Player)
1524 Woodcreek Dr
Mechanicsburg, PA 17055, USA

Ressler, Robert
PO Box 187
Spotsylvania, VA 22553

Restani, Jane A (Judge)
US Court of International Trade
1 Federal Plaza
New York, NY 10278, USA

Restless Heart (Music Group)
c/o Staff Member *Agency for the Performing Arts (APA-Nashville)*
3017 Poston Ave
Nashville, TN 37203

Reston, James (Journalist)
4714 Hunt Ave
Chevy Chase, MD 20815-5423, USA

Restovich, Michael (Athlete, Baseball Player)
710 11th St SW
Rochester, MN 55902-6339, USA

Reswick, James B (Engineer)
1834 Calf Mountain Road
Crozet, VA 22932, USA

Retherford, Dave (Athlete, Football Player)
68 Pine Lake Dr NW
Atlanta, GA 30327-4934, USA

Retore, Guy (Director)
Theatre de l'Est Parislen
159 Ave Gambetta
Paris 75020, FRANCE

Rettenmund, Merv (Athlete, Baseball Player)
655 India St
Unit 123
San Diego, CA 92101-6738, USA

Retton, Mary Lou (Athlete, Gymnast)
110 Kennywood Dr
Fairmont, WV 26554-8358, USA

Rettondini, Francesca (Actor)
c/o Staff Member *C.D.A. Studio Di Nardo*
Via Cavour
Rome 00184, Italy

Retzer, Ken (Athlete, Baseball Player)
8445 Las Vegas Blvd S #1137
Las Vegas, NV 8912-1674, USA

Retzer, Otto W (Director)
Justinus-Kerner-Str 10
Munich 80686, GERMANY

Retzlaff, Palmer (Pete) (Athlete, Football Player)
669 New Rd
Gilbertsville, PA 19525, USA

Reuben, Gloria (Actor)
c/o Staff Member *Untitled Entertainment (LA)*
350 S. Beverly Dr #200
Beverly Hills, CA 90212, USA

Reubens, Paul (Actor, Comedian)
PO Box 29373
Los Angeles, CA 90029, USA

Reukauf, Timothy (Stylist)
c/o Staff Member *Marek & Associates Inc*
508 W 26th St
#12-C
New York, NY 10001, USA

Reuschel, Paul (Athlete, Baseball Player)
1143 Stacy Ln
Macomb, IL 61455-2646, USA

Reuschel, Ricky E (Rick) (Athlete, Baseball Player)
P.O. Box 143
Renfrew, PA 16053-0143, USA

Reuss, Jerry (Athlete, Baseball Player)
Los Angeles Dodgers
1000 Elysian Park Ave
Attn: Broadcast Dept
Los Angeles, CA 90090-1112, USA

Reusser, Ken L (War Hero)
17345 SW Reusser Court
Aloha, OR 97007, USA

Reutemann, Carlos
San Martin 3233
Santa Fe, ARGENTINA

Reuten, Thekla (Actor)
c/o Paula Rosenberg *ICA Talent*
818 12th Street Ste 9
Santa Monica, CA 90403, USA

Reuter, Edzard (Business Person)
Daimler-benz AG
Postfach 800230
Stuttgart 70546, GERMANY

Reutershan, Randy (Athlete, Football Player)
4 Indian Field Ct
Mahwah, NJ 07430, USA

Reutersward, Carl Fredrik (Artist)
6 Rue Montilieu
Bussigny/Lausanne 1030, SWITZERLAND

Reutimann, David (Race Car Driver)
6910 Wire Road
Zephyrhills, FL 33542, USA

Revathi (Actor, Bollywood)
7 1st Crescent Road
GandhiNagar Adyar
Chennai, TN 600020, INDIA

Reveiz, Fuad (Athlete, Football Player)
2160 Lakeside Centre Way
Suite 250
Knoxville, TN 37922, USA

Revell, Graeme (Composer)
APRA
PO Box 567
Crow's Nest, NSW 2065, AUSTRALIA

Revenig, Todd (Athlete, Baseball Player)
2412 E Prescott Pl
Chandler, AZ 85249-2946, USA

Revere, Ben (Athlete, Baseball Player)
108 White Oak Dr
Richmond, KY 40475-8619, USA

Revere, Paul (Musician)
Paradise Artists
108 E Matilija St
Ojai, CA 93023, USA

Reverho, Christine (Actor)
Artmedia
20 Ave Rapp
Paris 75007, FRANCE

Revering, Dave (Athlete, Baseball Player)
1063 Crows Wing Way
Ivins, UT 84738-6364, USA

Revill, Clive (Actor)
15029 Encanto Dr
Sherman Oaks, CA 91403, USA

Revolution Mother (Music Group, Musician)
c/o Staff Member *Velvet Hammer*
9014 Melrose Ave
Los Angeles, CA 90069, USA

Revs, The (Music Group)
c/o Staff Member *Paradigm (Monterey)*
404 W Franklin St
Monterey, CA 93940, USA

Rex (Musician)
Concrete Mgmt
361 W Broadway
#200
New York, NY 10013, USA

Rex, Simon (Sebastian) (Actor, Television Host)
c/o Katie Mason *Luber Roklin Management*
8530 Wilshire Blvd
6th Floor
Beverly Hills, CA 90211, USA

Rey, Paola (Actor)
c/o Gabriel Blanco *Gabriel Blanco Iglesias (Mexico)*
Rio Balsas 35-32
Colonia Cuauhtemoc
DF 06500, Mexico

Rey, Reynaldo (Actor, Comedian, Writer)
Starwil Talent
433 N Camden Dr
#400
Beverly Hills, CA 90210, USA

Reyburn, Daniel (Athlete, Baseball Player)
514 Maplegrove
Franklin, TN 37064-5124, USA

Reyes, Anthony (Athlete, Baseball Player)
8929 Watson Ave
Whittier, CA 90605-2035, USA

Reyes, Carlos (Athlete, Baseball Player)
7205 N Cortez Ave
Tampa, FL 33614-2638, USA

reyes, Jo-Jo (Athlete, Baseball Player)
9554 Paradise Pl
Riverside, CA 92508-8007, USA

Reyes, Jose (Athlete, Baseball Player)
24 Stone Hill Dr S
Manhasset, NY 11030-4426, USA

Reyes, Judy (Actor)
c/o Leonard Torgan *Collective*
8383 Wilshire Blvd
Suite 1050
Beverly Hills, CA 90211, USA

Reyes, Lalo (Actor)
c/o Paul Uvanitte *ProActive Management Group (PMG)*
10944 Bluffside Dr
Suite 213
Studio City, CA 91604, USA

Reyes, Sandra (Actor)
c/o Staff Member *TV Caracol*
Calle 76 #11 - 35
Piso 10AA
Bogota DC 26484, COLOMBIA

Reyes, Senen (Sen Dog) (Actor, Composer, Musician)
c/o Randy Cabrera *Brass Artists & Associates*
9025 Wilshire Blvd
Suite 400
Beverly Hills, CA 90211, USA

Reyes, Silvestre (Congressman, Politician)
2210 Rayburn HOB
Washington, DC 20515, USA

Reyes Jr, Ernie
12561 Willard St
N Hollywood, CA 91605, USA

Reymundo, Alex (Comedian)
c/o Alex D'Andrea *Edmonds Management*
1635 N Cahuenga Blvd Fl 5
Los Angeles, CA 90028, USA

Reynold, Catherine B (Business Person)
Catherine B Reynolds Foundation
PO Box 11346
McLean, VA 22102, USA

Reynolds, Alastair (Writer)
P F D Drury House
34-43 Russell St
London WC2B 5HA, UNITED KINGDOM (UK)

Reynolds, Albert (Prime Minister)
Mount Carmel House
Dublin Road
Longford, IRELAND

Reynolds, Anna (Opera Singer)
Peesten 9
Kasendorf 95359, GERMANY

Reynolds, Archie (Athlete, Baseball Player)
1828 Pinecrest Dr
Tyler, TX 75701-5006, USA

Reynolds, Bob (Athlete, Baseball Player)
21035 40th Pl S
Unit K1
Seatac, WA 98198-4293, USA

Reynolds, Burt (Actor, Director)
c/o Erik Kritzer *Kritzer Levine Wilkins Entertainment (KLWG)*
11872 La Grange Ave
1st Floor
Los Angeles, CA 90025, USA

Reynolds, Craig (Athlete, Baseball Player)
4210 Hidden links Ct
Kingwood, TX 77339-5308, USA

Reynolds, David S (Historian, Writer)
16 Linden Lane
Old Westbury, NY 11568, USA

Reynolds, Debbie (Actor, Musician)
6514 Lankershim Blvd
N Hollywood, CA 91606, USA

Reynolds, Don (Athlete, Baseball Player)
6035 NE 35th Pl
Portland, OR 97211-7358, USA

Reynolds, Ed (Athlete, Football Player)
173 Moyer Rd
Stoneville, NC 27048, USA

Reynolds, Gene (Actor, Producer)
2034 Castilian Dr
Los Angeles, CA 90068, USA

Reynolds, Glenn F (Inventor)
242 Edgewood Ave
Westfield, NJ 07090, USA

Reynolds, Harold (Athlete, Baseball Player)
2890 NW Angelica Dr
Corvallis, OR 97330-3619, USA

Reynolds, Harry (Butch) (Athlete, Track Athlete)
Advantage International
1025 Thomas Jefferson NW
#450
Washington, DC 20007, USA

Reynolds, Jack (Athlete, Football Player)
11480 SW 102nd St
Miami, FL 33176, USA

Reynolds, Jamai (Athlete, Football Player)
P.O. Box 10628
Green Bay, WI 54307, USA

Reynolds, Jamal (Athlete, Football Player)
31 Sellers Dr
q
Crawfordville, FL 32327-0595, USA

Reynolds, James (Baseball Player)
708 Highpoint Dr
Rocky Hill, CT 06067-1088, USA

Reynolds, James (Actor)
1925 Hanscom Dr
South Pasadena, CA 91030, USA

Reynolds, Jerry O (Coach)
Sacramento Kings
Arco Arena
1 Sports Parkway
Sacramento, CA 95834, USA

Reynolds, Jim (Athlete, Baseball Player)
708 Highpoint Dr
Rocky Hill, CT 06067-1088, USA

Reynolds, John R (Educator, Physicist)
University of California
Physics Dept
Berkeley, CA 94720, USA

Reynolds, Ken (Athlete, Baseball Player)
182 Greenwood St
Marlborough, MA 01752-3307, USA

Reynolds, Kevin (Director, Writer)
c/o Mike Simpson *WME (LA)*
9601 Wilshire Blvd Fl 3
Beverly Hills, CA 90210, USA

Reynolds, Mark (Athlete, Baseball Player)
10960 Wilshire Blvd Fl 5
Los Angeles, CA 90024-3708, USA

Reynolds, Patti
PO Box 530
Fontana, WI 53125

Reynolds, Rachel (Actor, Model)
c/o Staff Member *Price Is Right, The*
2700 Colorado Ave Fl 4
Santa Monica, CA 90404, USA

Reynolds, Randolph N (Business Person)
Reynolds Metal Co
6601 Broad St
PO Box 27003
Richmond, VA 23261, USA

Reynolds, Richard V (General)
Commander Aeronautical Systems
Wright-Patterson Air Force Base,
OH 45433, USA

Reynolds, Ricky (Athlete, Football Player)
18032 Java Isle Dr
Tampa, FL 33647-2708, USA

Reynolds, Robert (Musician)
AristoMedia
1620 16th Ave S
Nashville, TN 37212, USA

Reynolds, Ronn (Athlete, Baseball Player)
1410 N Armour St
Wichita, KS 67206-1128, USA

Reynolds, Roxy (Actor)
c/o Staff Member *Sosincere Entertainment*
2054 Nostrand Ave Apt 4F
Brooklyn, NY 11210, USA

Reynolds, Ryan (Actor)
c/o Meredith O'Sullivan *42West (LA)*
11400 W Olympic Blvd
Suite 1100
Los Angeles, CA 90064, USA

Reynolds, Shane (Athlete, Baseball Player)
3540 Maranatha Dr
Sugarland, TX 77479-9666, USA

Reynolds, Sheldon (Musician)
Great Scott Productions
137 N Wetherly Dr
#403
Los Angeles, CA 90048, USA

Reynolds, Tom (Athlete, Baseball Player)
640 Jinks Crossing Rd
Bainbridge, GA 39819-1334, USA

Reynolds Booth, Nancy (Skier)
3197 Padaro Lane
Carpinteria, CA 93013, USA

Reynolds Jr, Thomas A (Lawyer)
Winston & Strawn
1 First National Plaza
45 W Wacker Dr
Chicago, IL 60601, USA

Reynoso, Armando (Athlete, Baseball Player)
PO Box 442
Scottsdale, AZ 85252-0442, USA

Reza, Yasmina (Actor, Writer)
Marta Andras
14 Rue des Sablons
Paris 75116, FRANCE

Rezendes, Dave (Race Car Driver)
3 Sammy's Lane
Assonat, MA 02102, USA

Reznor, Trent (Musician)
c/o Marc Geiger *WME (LA)*
9601 Wilshire Blvd Fl 3
Beverly Hills, CA 90210, USA

Rhames, Ving (Actor)
c/o Steven Muller *Innovative Artists (LA)*
1505 10th St
Santa Monica, CA 90401, USA

Rhea, Caroline (Actor, Comedian)
c/o Jonathan Howard *Innovative Artists (LA)*
1505 10th St
Santa Monica, CA 90401, USA

Rheams, Leonta (Athlete, Football Player)
1712 W Jackson St
Tyler, TX 75701, USA

Rheaume, Manon (Athlete, Hockey Player)
Manon Rheaume Foundation
PO Box 701816
Plymouth, MI 48170-0971

Rheinecker, John (Athlete, Baseball Player)
100 Jefferson Dr
Waterloo, IL 62298-1551, USA

Rhett, Alicia (Actor)
PO Box 700
Charleston, SC 29402-0700, USA

Rhett, Errict (Athlete, Football Player)
6 NW 108th Ter
Plantation, FL 33324, USA

Rhimes, Shonda (Actor, Producer, Writer)
Shondaland
4151 Prospect Ave
Los Feliz Tower 4th Fl
Los Angeles, CA 90027, USA

Rhind-Tutt, Julian (Actor)
c/o Staff Member *The Rights House (UK)*
Drury House
34-43 Russell St
London WC2B 5HA, UK

Rhine, Kendall (Athlete, Baseball Player)
624e State Route 127 N
Alto Pass, IL 629e5-323e, USA

Rhinehart, Coby (Athlete, Football Player)
3206 Walker Dr
Richardson, TX 75082-2451, USA

Rhines, Peter B (Oceanographer)
5753 61st Ave NE
Seattle, WA 98105, USA

Rhine Sr, Kendall (Athlete, Basketball Player)
6240 State Route 127 N
Alto Pass, IL 62905, USA

Rhiness, Brad (Athlete, Hockey Player)
4 St. Lawrence Pl
Cobourg, ON K9A 4G8, Canada

Rhino, Randy (Athlete, Football Player)
5750 Vinings Retreat Way SW
Mableton, GA 30126-2578, USA

Rhoades, George
1478 Mecklenburg Rd
Ithaca, NY 14850-9301, USA

Rhoades, Kerry (Football Player)
c/o Team Member *New York Jets*
1 Jets Dr
Florham Park, NJ 07932, USA

Rhoades, Lisa (Stylist)
c/o Staff Member *Perrella Management*
330 W 38th St Rm 1407
New York, NY 10018, USA

Rhoads, George (Artist)
1478 Mecklenburg Road
Ithaca, NY 14850, USA

Rhoads, James B (Misc)
1300 Fox Run Trail
Platte City, MO 64079, USA

Rhoda, Hilary (Model)
c/o Staff Member *IMG*
304 Park Ave S Fl 12
New York, NY 10010, USA

Rhode, Kim (Athlete, Olympic Athlete, Shooter)
11640 Hemlock St
El Monte, CA 91732, USA

Rhoden, Rick (Athlete, Baseball Player)
1253 Killarney Dr
Ormond Beach, FL 32174, USA

Rhodes, Arthur (Athlete, Baseball Player)
14114 Phoenix Rd
Phoenix, MD 21131-1020, USA

Rhodes, Cynthia (Actor, Dancer)
15260 Ventura Blvd
#2100
Sherman Oaks, CA 91403, USA

Rhodes, Damian (Athlete, Hockey Player)
22309 N 36th St
Phoenix, AZ 85050-7399

Rhodes, Donnelly (Actor)
Gold Marshak Liedtke
3500 W Olive Ave
#1400
Burbank, CA 91505, USA

Rhodes, Eugene (Athlete, Basketball Player)
132 N Peterson Ave
Apt 7
Louisville, KY 4e2e6-234e, USA

Rhodes, Frank H T (Educator)
Cornell University
Geology Dept
Snee Hall
Ithaca, NY 14853, USA

Rhodes, Harry (Athlete, Baseball Player)
7207 S Evans Ave
Chicago, IL 60619-1224, USA

Rhodes, Jan (Stylist)
106 Dolores St
San Francisco, CA 94110-4907, USA

Rhodes, Karl (Athlete, Baseball Player)
8507 Hidden Hollow Ct
Missouri City, TX 77459-7514, USA

Rhodes, Lou (Musician)
c/o Staff Member *Paradigm (Monterey)*
404 W Franklin St
Monterey, CA 93940, USA

Rhodes, Mark (Musician)
c/o Staff Member *QVoice*
161 Drury Ln, Covent Garden
3rd Floor
London WC2B 5PN, UK

Rhodes, Nick (Musician)
DD Productions
93A Westbourne Park Villas
London W2 5ED, UNITED KINGDOM

Rhodes, Philip (Musician)
William Morris Agency
2100 W End Ave
#1000
Nashville, TN 37203, USA

Rhodes, Ray (Athlete, Coach, Football Coach, Football Player)
1507 Juliet Dr
Allen, TX 75013-5816, USA

Rhodes, Richard L (Writer)
Janklow & Nesbit
445 Park Ave
#1300
New York, NY 10022, USA

Rhodes, Rodrick (Athlete, Basketball Player)
P.O. Box 17704
Sugar Land, TX 77496-77e4, USA

Rhodes, Tom (Actor, Comedian, Writer)
c/o Staff Member *WmE2 (WMA-LA)*
1 William Morris Pl
Beverly Hills, CA 90212, USA

Rhodes, Zandra (Designer, Fashion Designer)
79-85 Bermondsey St
London SE1 3XF, UNITED KINGDOM (UK)

Rhomberg, Kevin (Athlete, Baseball Player)
9692 Executive Ct
Mentor, OH 44060-8721, USA

Rhome, Gerald B (Jerry) (Athlete, Coach, Football Coach, Football Player)
3883 Morning Meadow Ln
Buford, GA 30519, USA

Rhome, Earriest C (Ernie) (Athlete, Football Player)
3603 Potomac Ave
Texarkana, TX 75503-3519, USA

Rhone, Sylvia (Business Person)
Elektra Entertainment Group
75 Rockefeller Plaza
15th Floor
New York, NY 10019

Rhude, Kellan (Actor)
c/o Staff Member *Diverse Talent Group*
9911 W Pico Blvd Ste 340W
Los Angeles, CA 90035, USA

Rhyan, Dick (Golfer)
111 Camp Dr
Georgetown, TX 78628-4874, USA

Rhymer, Don (Writer)
c/o David Kramer *United Talent Agency (UTA)*
9336 Civic Center Dr
Beverly Hills, CA 90210, USA

Rhymes, Busta (Musician)
c/o Staff Member *Violator Management*
36 W 25th St
2nd Floor
New York, NY 10010, USA

Rhymes, Buster (Athlete, Football Player)
17120 NW 37th Ave
Carol City, FL 33056, USA

Rhymes, Will (Athlete, Baseball Player)
6914 9th Ct E
Sarasota, FL 34243-1211, USA

Rhys, Matthew (Actor)
c/o Suzan Bymel *Management 360*
9111 Wilshire Blvd
Beverly Hills, CA 90210, USA

Rhys, Paul (Actor)
Gersh Agency
232 N Canon Dr
Beverly Hills, CA 90210, USA

Rhys, Phillip (Actor)
c/o Joe Vance *Domain Talent*
9229 Sunset Boulevard
Suite 710
Los Angeles, CA 90069, USA

Rhys-Davies, John (Actor)
3428 Oak Glen Dr
Los Angeles, CA 90068, USA

Rhys-Jones, HRH Sophie (Duchess of Wessex)
Bagshot Park
Surrey, ENGLAND GUl9 5PN

Rhys-Meyers, Jonathan (Actor)
c/o Stacy O'Neil *Brillstein Entertainment Partners*
9150 Wilshire Blvd #350
Beverly Hills, CA 90212, USA

Rhythm Syndicate
6255 Sunset Blvd. #2100
Los Angeles, CA 90028

Ribant, Dennis (Athlete, Baseball Player)
46 Sidra Cv
Newport Coast, CA 92657-2115, USA

Ribas Reig, Oscar (Government Official)
Governmental Offices
Andorra la Vella, ANDORRA

Ribble, Pat (Athlete, Hockey Player)
23 Cheyenne Ct.
Learnington, ON N8H SE3, CANADA

Ribbs, Willy (Race Car Driver)
Craftsman
1801 W. Speedway Blvd.
Daytona Beach, FL 32114, USA

Ribeau, Sidney A (Educator)
Bowling Green State University
President's Office
Bowling Green, OH 43403, USA

Ribeiro, Alfonso (Actor)
c/o Konrad Leh *Creative Talent Group*
1900 Avenue of the Stars
Suite 2475
Los Angeles, CA 90067, USA

Ribeiro, Andre (Race Car Driver)
4192 Weaver Ct.
Hilliard, OH 43026, USA

Ribeiro, Ignacio (Designer, Fashion Designer)
Clements Ribejro Ltd
48 S Molton St
London W1X 1HE, UNITED KINGDOM (UK)

Ribeiro, Mike (Athlete, Hockey Player)
5609 Monterey Dr
Frisco, TX 75034-4076

Ribisi, Giovanni (Actor)
c/o Eric Kranzler *Management 360*
9111 Wilshire Blvd
Beverly Hills, CA 90210, USA

Ribisi, Marissa (Actor)
4121 Wilshire Blvd
#415
Los Angeles, CA 90010, USA

Ribot, Mark (Composer, Musician)
c/o Staff Member *Concerted Efforts*
P.O. Box 440326
Somerville, MA 02144, USA

Riboud, Marc (Photographer)
Magnum Photos 151 W 25th St Fl 5
New York, NY 10001-7257, USA

Ricard, Alan (Athlete, Football Player)
10306 Ripple Lake Dr
Houston, TX 77065-4087, USA

Ricardo, Benny (Athlete, Football Player)
3012 Harding Way
Costa Mesa, CA 92626, USA

Ricardo Y Alberto (Music Group)
c/o Staff Member *Sony Music Miami*
605 Lincoln Rd Fl 7
Miami Beach, FL 33139, USA

Ricca, John (Athlete, Football Player)
4 Fairfax Ct Apt 22
Chevy Chase, MD 20815-6522, USA

Riccelli, Frank (Athlete, Baseball Player)
P.O. Box 2102
Syracuse, NY 13220-2102, USA

Ricci, Christina (Actor)
c/o David Seltzer *Management 360*
9111 Wilshire Blvd
Beverly Hills, CA 90210, USA

Ricci, Chuck (Athlete, Baseball Player)
110 Moonlight Dr
Greencastle, PA 17225-1059, USA

Ricci, Mike (Athlete, Hockey Player)
286 Mountain Laurel Ln
Los Gatos, CA 95032-5740

Ricci, Mike (Athlete, Hockey Player)
San Jose Sharks
525 W Santa Clara St
SanJose, CA 95113-1500

Ricciarelli, Katia (Opera Singer)
Via Magellana 2
Corsica 20097, ITALY

Rice, Alex (Actor)
c/o Staff Member *Artist Representation Company, The*
1147 S Big Island Rd
RR 1
Demorestville ON K0K 1W0, CANADA

Rice, Andy (Athlete, Football Player)
801 N Main St
Hallettsville, TX 77964, USA

Rice, Anne (Writer)
9 Monte Carlo Dr
Kenner, LA 70065-2028, USA

Rice, Bobby G
505 Canton Pass
Madison, TN 37115, USA

Rice, Buddy (Race Car Driver)
Team Rahal
4601 Lyman Dr
Hilliard, OH 43026, USA

Rice, Christopher (Writer)
1239 First St
New Orleans, LA 70730, USA

Rice, Condoleezza (Government Official)
Stanford University
Freeman Spogli Institute For International Studies
616 Serra St C100
Stanford, CA 94305-6010, USA

Rice, Damien (Musician)
c/o Staff Member *Paradigm (Monterey)*
404 W Franklin St
Monterey, CA 93940, USA

Rice, Elizabeth (Actor)
c/o Steven Warren *Hansen, Jacobson, Teller, Hoberman, Newman, Warren & Richman*
450 N Roxbury Dr
8th Floor
Beverly Hills, CA 90210, USA

Rice, Gene D (Religious Leader)
Church of God
PO Box 2430
Cleveland, TN 37320, USA

Rice, Gigi (Actor)
14951 Alva Dr
Pacific Palisades, CA 90272, USA

Rice, Glen
9492 Doral Blvd
Miami, FL 33178

Rice, Glen (Athlete, Basketball Player)
13621 Deering Ba_y_ Dr
Apt 304
Coral Gables, FL 33158-2845, USA

Rice, Glenn (Athlete, Basketball Player)
4835 SW 82nd St
Miami, FL 33143, USA

Rice, James E (Jim) (Athlete, Baseball Player)
35 Bobby Jones Dr
Andover, MA 01810-2880, USA

Rice, James R (Geophysicist, Physicist)
Harvard University
Applied Science Division
Cambridge, MA 02138, USA

Rice, Jerry (Athlete, Football Player)
c/o Jim Steiner *CAA - St. Louis*
222 S Central Ave
Suite 1008
St Louis, MO 63105, USA

Rice, John (Athlete, Baseball Player)
2666 E 73rd St
Apt 12W
Chicago, IL 60649, USA

Rice, John (Baseball Player)
2666 E 73rd St Apt 12W
Chicago, IL 60649-2732, USA

Rice, Ken (Athlete, Football Player)
10619 Big Canoe
Big Canoe, GA 30143, USA

Rice, Larry (Race Car Driver)
1150 Forest
Brownsburg, IN 46112, USA

Rice, Norman B (Politician)
Mayor's Office
Municipal Building
600 4th Ave
Seattle, WA 98104, USA

Rice, Pat (Athlete, Baseball Player)
4090 Zurich Dr
Colorado Springs, CO 80920-7521, USA

Rice, Regina (Actor, Producer)
c/o Staff Member *Temptation Management*
1010 S Robertson Blvd
Suite 2
Los Angeles, CA 90035, USA

Rice, Ron (Athlete, Football Player)
22880 Twyckingham Way
Southfield, MI 48034, USA

Rice, Simeon (Athlete, Football Player)
371 Channelside Walk Way Unit 401
Tampa, FL 33602-6767, USA

Rice, Stuart A (Misc)
5517 S Kimbark Ave
Chicago, IL 60637, USA

Rice, Thomas M (Physicist)
Theoretische Physik
ETH-Hoggerberg
Zurich, 8093, SWITZERLAND

Rice, Tim (Musician)
Chiltens
France-Hill Dr Camberley
Surrey GU153-30A, UNITED KINGDOM (UK)

Rice, Tony (Athlete, Football Player)
PO Box 6455
South Bend, IN 46660-6455, USA

Rice-Hughes, Donna
PO Box 888
Fairfax, VA 22030

Rich, Adam (Actor)
4814 Lemona Ave
Sherman Oaks, CA 91403, USA

Rich, Alexander (Misc)
2 Walnut Ave
Cambridge, MA 02140, USA

Rich, Allan (Actor)
225 E 57th St
New York, NY 10022, USA

Rich, Christopher (Actor)
Bresler Kelly Assoc
11500 W Olympic Blvd
#510
Los Angeles, CA 90064, USA

Rich, Claude
18 Chemin de la Butte
Orgeval, FRANCE F-78630

Rich, Clayton (Doctor)
University of Oklahoma
Health Services Center
Oklahoma City, OK 73190, USA

Rich, Denise (Musician)
IGD Music & Media
785 5th Avenue
New York, NY 10022-1012

Rich, Elaine
500 S. Sepulveda Blvd
Los Angeles, CA 90049-3540

Rich, John (Musician)
c/o Dale Morris *Morris Artists Management*
818 19th Ave S
Nashville, TN 37203, USA

Rich, Katie
10100 Santa Monica Blvd. #2490
Los Angeles, CA 90067

Rich, Matty
9560 Wilshire Blvd. #500
Beverly Hills, CA 90212

Rich, Mike (Writer)

Rich, Randy (Athlete, Baseball Player)
9421 Eagle Springs Ct
Roseville, CA 95747-6316, USA

Rich, Richie (Fashion Designer)
MAC Cosmetics
575 Broadway 2nd Fl
New York, NY 10012, USA

Rich, Tony (Musician)
Prestige
220 E 23rd St
#303
New York, NY 10010, USA

Richard, Chris (Athlete, Baseball Player)
11389 Ironwood Rd
San Diego, CA 92131-1916, USA

Richard, Clayton (Athlete, Baseball Player)
3551 Eisenhower Rd
Lafayette, IN 47905-4108, USA

Richard, Cliff (Musician)
Harley House
Portsmouth Road Box 46C
Esher
Surrey KT10 9AA, UK

Richard, Deb (Golfer)
125 Hidden Cove Ln
Ponte Vedra Beach, FL 32082-2154, USA

Richard, Henri (Athlete, Hockey Player)
Montreal Canadiens
1275 Rue Saint-Antoine 0
Montreal, QC H3C SL2, Canada

Richard, Henri (Athlete, Hockey Player)
905-4300 Place de Cageux
Ile Paton Laval, QC H7W 4Z3, Canada

Richard, Ivor S (Government Official)
11 South Square
Gray's Inn
London WC1R 5EU, UNITED KINGDOM (UK)

Richard, James Rodney (J R) (Athlete, Baseball Player)
5615 Chimney Rock Rd
Apt 338
Houston, TX 77081, USA

Richard, J R (Athlete, Baseball Player)
Mary Olive Baptist Church
2804 McGowen St
Attn Associate Pastor
Houston, TX 77004-1658, USA

Richard, Lee (Athlete, Baseball Player)
1621 14th St
POrt Arthur, TX 77640-4482, USA

Richard, Pierre
6 rue de Vieux-Moulin
Droue-sur-Drouette, FRANCE 28230

Richard, Ruth (Athlete, Baseball Player)
880 Allentown Rd
Sellersville, PA 18960-1000, USA

Richard III, Oliver G (Business Person)
Columbia Energy Group
200 Civic Center Dr
Columbus, OH 43215, USA

Richards, Ariana (Actor)
Don Buchwald
6500 Wilshire Blvd
#3300
Los Angeles, CA 90048, USA

Richards, Bob (Athlete, Olympic Athlete, Track Athlete)
PO Box 134
Santo, TX 76472-0134, USA

Richards, Bob (Doctor)
1616 Estates Dr
Waco, TX 76712, USA

Richards, Bobby (Athlete, Football Player)
2881 Fairplay Rd
Rutledge, GA 30663, USA

Richards, Brad (Athlete, Hockey Player)
101 Warren St Apt 3150
New York, NY 10007-1375

Richards, Charles (Writer)
c/o David Hahn *Planned Television Arts*
1110 2nd Ave
New York, NY 10022, USA

Richards, Curvin (Athlete, Football Player)
11000 Gatesden Dr
Apt 1311
Tomball, TX 77377, USA

Richards, Dakota Blue (Actor)
c/o Sue Latimer *Artists Rights Group (ARG)*
4 Great Portland St
London W1W 8PA, UNITED KINGDOM (UK)

Richards, David R (Athlete, Football Player)
4209 San Carlos St
Dallas, TX 75205, USA

Richards, DeLeon (Actor)
c/o Staff Member *Britto Agency PR*
234 W 56th St
Penthouse
New York, NY 10019, USA

Richards, Denise (Actor)
c/o Ame Van Iden *PMK/BNC Public Relations (PMK-LA)*
8687 Melrose Ave Fl 8
West Hollywood, CA 90069, USA

Richards, Duane (Athlete, Baseball Player)
P.O. Box 54
Palestine, OH 45352-0054, USA

Richards, Emelie
PO Box 7052
Arlington, VA 22207

Richards, Evan
1800 Ave. of the Stars #400
Los Angeles, CA 90067

Richards, Fred (Athlete, Baseball Player)
1760 Dodge Dr NW
Warren, OH 44485-1823, USA

Richards, Frederic M (Misc)
69 Andrews Road
Guilford, CT 06437, USA

Richards, Garrett (Athlete, Baseball Player)
5812 Country Club Dr
Edmond, OK 73025-2741, USA

Richards, Gene (Athlete, Baseball Player)
1468 Normandv Dr
Chula Vista, CA 91913-3903, USA

Richards, Golden (Athlete, Football Player)
7274 Winesap Ct
Salt Lake City, UT 84121, USA

Richards, Howard (Athlete, Football Player)
PSC 98 Box 30
APO, AE 09830, USA

Richards, I Vivian A (Viv) (Cricketer)
West Indian Cricket Board
PO Box 616
Saint John's, ANTIGUA & BARBUDA

Richards, James B (Athlete, Football Player)
733 Vanderbilt Ave
Virginia Beach, VA 23451, USA

Richards, Jasmine (Actor)
c/o Staff Member *Noble Caplan Abrams*
1260 Yonge St
2nd Floor
Toronto, ON M4T 1W6, Canada

Richards, J August (Actor)
PO Box 99
China Spring, TX 76633, USA

Richards, J R (Musician)
William Morris Agency
1325 Ave of Americas
New York, NY 10019, USA

Richards, Keith (Musician)
c/o Kenneth Kleinberg *Kleinberg Lange Cuddy & Klein LLP*
2049 Century Park E
Suite 3180
Los Angeles, CA 90067, USA

Richards, Kim (Actor, Reality TV Star)
c/o Bette Smith *Bette Smith Management*
499 N Canon Dr
Beverly Hills, CA 90210, USA

Richards, Kyle (Actor, Reality TV Star)
c/o Bette Smith *Bette Smith Management*
499 N Canon Dr
Beverly Hills, CA 90210, USA

Richards, Lou
2467 Brighton Dr. #2-B
Valencia, CA 91355

Richards, Mark (Misc)
755 Hunter St
Newcastle, NSW 2302, AUSTRALIA

Richards, Michael (Actor, Comedian)
c/o Staff Member *Untitled Entertainment (NY)*
322 8th Ave #601
New York, NY 10001-6715, USA

Richards, Paul G (Misc)
Lamont-Doherty Geological Observatory
Palisades, NY 10964, USA

Richards, Paul W (Astronaut)
NASA
605 First St
Annapolis, MD 21403-3321, USA

Richards, Renee (Tennis Player)
1604 Union St
San Francisco, CA 94123, USA

Richards, Rex E (Misc)
13 Woodstock Close
Oxford OX2 8DB, UNITED KINGDOM (UK)

Richards, Richard N (Astronaut)
NASA
Johnson Space Center
2101 NASA Road
Houston, TX 77058, USA

Richards, Richard N Captain (Astronaut)
3317 Las Palmas St
Houston, TX 77027-6345, USA

Richards, Robert E (Bob) (Athlete, Track Athlete)
1616 Estates Dr
Waco, TX 76712, USA

Richards, Rosemary Elam (Stylist)
60 Ross Ave
#1
San Anselmo, CA 94960-2832, USA

Richards, Rusty (Athlete, Baseball Player)
2606 Thompson Crossing Dr
Richmond, TX 77406-6932, USA

Richards, Sanya (Athlete, Olympic Athlete)
c/o Lowell Taub *Creative Artists Agency (CAA-NY)*
162 Fifth Ave
6th Floor
New York, NY 10010, USA

Richards, Stephanie (Actor)
H David Moss
733 Seward St
#PH
Los Angeles, CA 90038, USA

Richards, Todd (Athlete, Hockey Player)
5208 107th Ave N
Minneapolis, MN 55443-5902

Richards, Todd (Athlete, Hockey Player)
Columbus Blue Jackets
200 W Nationwide Blvd Unit 1
Columbus, OH 43215-2564

Richards, Viv (Cricketer)
c/o Staff Member *West Indies Cricket Club*
PO Box 616
St John's, ANTIGUA

Richards, Warren J
PO Box 2496
Salt Lake City, UT 84110, USA

Richardson, Al (Athlete, Football Player)
3003 Mary Ashley Ct SE
Conyers, GA 30013, USA

Richardson, Andrew (Stylist)
c/o Staff Member *Streeters*
560 Broadway
Suite 203
New York, NY 10012, 212-219-9566

Richardson, Ashley (Model)
c/o Staff Member *Ford Models (NY)*
238 E 4th St
New York, NY 10009, USA

Richardson, Bill (Politician)
1058 Encantado Dr
Santa Fe, NM 87501-1086, USA

Richardson, Bucky (Athlete, Football
Player)
9015 Stones Throw Ln
Missouri City, TX 77459-2990, USA

Richardson, Cameron (Actor)
c/o Staff Member *United Talent Agency
(UTA)*
9336 Civic Center Dr
Beverly Hills, CA 90210, USA

Richardson, Cheryl (Actor)
749 Fair Oaks Dr
Alamo, CA 94507, USA

Richardson, Cliff (Athlete, Basketball
Player)
6236 Radiance Blvd E
#2
Tacoma, WA 98424, USA

Richardson, Clint (Athlete, Basketball
Player)
12e7 9th Ave NW
Puyallup, WA 98371-4e25, USA

Richardson, Damien (Athlete, Football
Player)
1300 E Cromwell Ave
Apt 102
Fresno, CA 93720-2628, USA

Richardson, Dan (Musician)
c/o Staff Member *Agency Group Ltd, The
(NY)*
142 West 57th St
6th Floor
New York, NY 10019, USA

Richardson, Dave (Athlete, Hockey
Player)
62 Agissing Dr.
Winnipeg, MB R3T 2K7, CANADA

Richardson, Donna (Misc)
Anchor Bay Entertainment
500 Kirts Blvd
Troy, MI 48084, USA

Richardson, Dot (Athlete, Olympic
Athlete, Softball Player)
1120 W Lakeshore Dr
Clermont, FL 34711-2936, USA

Richardson, Earl (Educator)
Morgan State University
President's Office
Baltimore, MD 21239, USA

Richardson, Eliot
1100 Crest Lane
McLean, VA 22101

Richardson, Eric (Athlete, Football Player)
509 Ely Blvd S
Petaluma, CA 94954, USA

Richardson, Gloster (Athlete, Football
Player)
9143 S Euclid Ave
Chicago, IL 60617, USA

Richardson, Gordie (Athlete, Baseball
Player)
23 Saint Paul Church Rd
Colquitt, GA 39837-6829, USA

Richardson, Gordon W H (Financier)
Morgan Stanley
25 Cabot Square
Canary Wharf
London E14 4QA, UNITED KINGDOM
(UK)

Richardson, Grady (Athlete, Football
Player)
3633 Mentone Ave Apt 203
Los Angeles, CA 90034-5659, USA

Richardson, Greg (Boxer)
382 Camden Ave
Youngstown, OH 44505, USA

Richardson, Hamilton (Tennis Player)
870 United Nations Plaza
New York, NY 10017, USA

Richardson, Huey (Athlete, Football
Player)
161 W 16th St Apt 17A
New York, NY 10011-6207, USA

Richardson, Jack (Artist)
12171 Sunset Ave
Grass Valley, CA 95945, USA

Richardson, Jake (Actor)
c/o Meredith Fine *Coast to Coast Talent
Group*
3350 Barham Blvd
Los Angeles, CA 90068, USA

Richardson, Jason (Athlete, Basketball
Player)
c/o Dan Fegan *Lagardere Unlimited - (LA)*
10866 Wilshire Blvd
Los Angeles, CA 90024, USA

Richardson, Jay (Athlete, Football Player)
c/o Eugene Parker *Maximum Sports
Management*
6435 W Jefferson Blvd
#197
Fort Wayne, IN 46804, USA

Richardson, Jeff (Athlete, Baseball Player)
47 Kuester Lk
Grand Island, NE 68801-8609, USA

Richardson, Jeffrey (Jeff) (Athlete,
Baseball Player)
11779 W Fordson Dr
Marana, AZ 85653-7722, USA

Richardson, Jerome "Pooh" (Athlete,
Basketball Player)
23434 Sherman Way
West Hills, CA 91307-1426, USA

Richardson, Jerry (Business Person,
Football Executive)
6245 N Shore Dr A14
Nebo, NC 28761-8604, USA

Richardson, Joely (Actor)
c/o Charles Finch *Finch & Partners*
Top Floor
29-37 Heddon St
London W1B 4BR, UNITED KINGDOM

Richardson, John (Athlete, Football
Player)
3053 Eagles Claw Ave
Thousand Oaks, CA 91362-1771, USA

Richardson, John T (Educator)
2233 N Kenmore Ave
Chicago, IL 60614, USA

Richardson, Ken (Athlete, Hockey Player)
Hockey Heritage North
PO Box 156 Stn Main
Kirkland Lake, ON P2N 3M6, Canada

Richardson, Kevin Michael (Actor)
c/o David Ginsberg *Insight*
1134 S Cloverdale Ave
Los Angeles, CA 90019, USA

Richardson, Kristin (Actor)
c/o Brady McKay *Flutie Entertainment
(LA)*
9320 Wilshire Blvd
Suite 202
Beverly Hills, CA 90212, USA

Richardson, LaTanya (Actor, Producer)
c/o Staff Member *Paradigm (LA)*
360 N Crescent Dr
North Bldg
Beverly Hills, CA 90210, USA

Richardson, Laura (Congressman,
Politician)
1330 Longworth HOB
Washington, DC 20515, USA

Richardson, Leo (Actor)
c/o Lou Coulson *Lou Coulson Agency*
37 Berwick St
1st Floor
London W1F 8RS, UNITED KINGDOM
(UK)

Richardson, Linda (Opera Singer)
Van Walsum Mgmt
4 Addison Bridge Place
London W14 8XP, UNITED KINGDOM
(UK)

Richardson, Luke (Athlete, Hockey Player)
Ottawa Senators
110-1000 Palladium Dr
Ottawa, ON K2V IAS, Canada

Richardson, Michael Ray (Athlete,
Basketball Player)
121 N Elk Ct
Aurora, CO 80018-1599, USA

Richardson, Mike (Producer)
c/o Staff Member *Dark Horse
Entertainment*
1438 N Gower St
Box 23 Bldg 28 #200
Hollywood, CA 90028, USA

Richardson, Mike (Athlete, Football
Player)
1619 W Caldwell St
Compton, CA 90220, USA

Richardson, Mike (Athlete, Football
Player)
7310 Covewood Dr
Garland, TX 75044-2624, USA

Richardson, Miranda (Actor)
Kerry Gardner Mgmt
7 Saint George's Square
London SW1V 2HX, UNITED KINGDOM
(UK)

Richardson, Nolan (Coach)
2539 E Joyce St
Fayetteville, AR 72703, USA

Richardson, Patricia (Actor)
c/o Jonathan Howard *Innovative Artists
(LA)*
1505 10th St
Santa Monica, CA 90401, USA

Richardson, Quentin (Basketball Player)
Los Angeles Clippers
Staples Center
1111 S Figueroa St
Los Angeles, CA 90015, USA

Richardson, Robert (Race Car Driver)
R3 Motorsports
3685 Hwy. 152 W.
Chi na Grove, SC 28023, USA

Richardson, Robert (Cinematographer)
c/o Spyros Skouras *The Skouras Agency*
1149 Third Street Fl 3
Santa Monica, CA 90403, USA

Richardson, Robert C (Nobel Prize
Laureate)
4 Hunter Lane
Ithaca, NY 14850, USA

Richardson, Robert C (Bobby) (Athlete,
Baseball Player)
47 Adams Ave
Sumter, SC 29150-4037, USA

Richardson, Sam (Artist)
4121 Sequoyah Road
Oakland, CA 94605, USA

Richardson, Terry (Athlete, Hockey
Player)
3598 Rosemary Heights Cres
Surrey, BC V3S OP2, Canada

Richardson, W Franklyn (Religious
Leader)
National Baptist Convention
52 S 6th Ave
Mount Vernon, NY 10550, USA

Richardson, Willam C (Educator)
W K Kellogg Foundation
1 Michigan Ave E
Battle Creek, MI 49017, USA

Richardson, Willie (Athlete, Football
Player)
5928 Waverly Dr
Jackson, MS 39206, USA

Richardson of Lee, John S (Doctor)
Windcutter
Lee
North Devon EX34 8LW, UNITED
KINGDOM (UK)

Richardson-Whitfield, Salli (Actor)
c/o Craig Dorfman *Frontline Management*
5670 Wilshire Blvd.
Suite 1370
Los Angeles, CA 90036, USA

Richardt, Mike (Athlete, Baseball Player)
3236 W Western Ave
Fresno, CA 93722-4843, USA

Richer, Stephane (Athlete, Hockey Player)
Club de Golf Montpelier
440 Ave. Stephanie Richter
Montpelier, QC J0V 1MO, CANADA

Richert, Nate (Actor)
c/o Iris Burton *Iris Burton Agency*
10100 Santa Monica Blvd Ste 1300
Los Angeles, CA 90067, USA

Richert, Pete (Athlete, Baseball Player)
80 La Cerra Dr
Rancho Mirage, CA 92270-3811, USA

Richeson, Ray (Athlete, Football Player)
1348 Willoughby Rd
Birmingham, AL 35216, USA

Richey, Cliff (Tennis Player)
2936 Cumberland Dr
San Angelo, TX 76904, USA

Richey, Jennifer (Actor)
c/o Staff Member *Cunningham Escott Slevin & Doherty (CESD-LA)*
10635 Santa Monica Blvd
130
Los Angeles, CA 90025, USA

Richey, Nancy (Tennis Player)
2936 Cumberland Dr
San Angelo, TX 76904, USA

Richey, Wade (Athlete, Football Player)
PO Box 775
Carencro, LA 70520-0775, USA

Richie, Lionel (Musician, Songwriter)
Lionel Richie Productions, Inc.
2850 Ocean Park Boulevard
Suite 300
Santa Monica, CA 90405, USA

Richie, Michele (Stylist)
2521 Lincoln Ave
Miami, FL 33133, USA

Richie, Nicole (Heir/Heiress, Reality TV Star)
c/o Michael Baum *Impression Entertainment*
9229 W Sunset Blvd #700
West Hollywood, CA 90069, USA

Richie, Rob (Athlete, Baseball Player)
1835 Meadowvale Way
Sparks, NV 89431-2949, USA

Richie, Shane (Actor)
c/o Phil Dale *Qdos Entertainment*
8 King St
Covent Garden
London WC2 8HN, UNITED KINGDOM

Riching, Julian (Actor)
c/o Staff Member *Gary Goddard Agency*
10 St Mary St
Suite 305
Toronto, ON M4Y 1P9, Canada

Richman, Adam (Television Host)
c/o Eileen Stringer *Rain Management Group (RMG)*
10850 Wilshire Blvd
Suite 1260
Los Angeles, CA 90024, USA

Richman, Caryn (Actor)
1805 Via Arribe
Palos Verdes Estates, CA 90274, USA

Richman, Jonathan (Actor, Musician)
High Road
751 Bridgeway
#300
Sausalito, CA 94965, USA

Richman, Peter Mark (Actor)
5114 Del Moreno Dr
Woodland Hills, CA 91364, USA

Richmond, Branscombe (Actor)
5706 Calvin Ave
Tarzana, CA 91356, USA

Richmond, Mitch (Athlete, Basketball Player, Olympic Athlete)
25374 Prado De La Felicidad
Calabasas, CA 91302-3649, USA

Richmond, Steve (Athlete, Hockey Player)
21290 W Pepper Dr
Lake Zurich, IL 60047-8046

Richmond, Steve (Athlete, Hockey Player)
Washington Capitals
627 N Glebe Rd Ste 850
Arlington, VA 22203-2144

Richmond, Tequan (Actor)
c/o Temple Poteat *AMP Live Entertainment*
3727 W. Magnolia Blvd
446
Burbank, CA 91505, USA

Richt, Mark (Coach, Football Coach)
University of Georgia
Athletic Dept
PO Box 1472
Athens, GA 30603, USA

Richter, Al (Athlete, Baseball Player)
3810 Atlantic Ave
Apt 703
Virginia Beach, VA 23451-2736, USA

Richter, Andy (Actor, Comedian)
c/o Tim Sarkes *Brillstein Entertainment Partners*
9150 Wilshire Blvd #350
Beverly Hills, CA 90212, USA

Richter, Barry (Athlete, Hockey Player, Olympic Athlete)
PO Box 259408
Madison, WI 53725-9408, USA

Richter, Burton (Nobel Prize Laureate)
Stanford University
620 Sand Hill Rd Apt 206C
Palo Alto, CA 94304-2091, USA

Richter, Dave (Athlete, Hockey Player)
16910 Trenton Ln
Eden Prairie, MN 55347-3377

Richter, Frank (Athlete, Football Player)
734 Creekside Dr
Leesburg, GA 31763-4804, USA

Richter, Gerhard (Artist)
Bismarckstr 50
Cologne 50672, GERMANY

Richter, Hans
In der Wasserschopp 43
Heppenheim, GERMANY D-64646

Richter, James A (Jim) (Athlete, Football Player)
8620 Bournemouth Dr
Raleigh, NC 27615, USA

Richter, Jason James (Actor)
United Talent Agency
9560 Wilshire Blvd
#500
Beverly Hills, CA 90212, USA

Richter, John (Athlete, Basketball Player)
2740 Narcissa Rd
Plymouth Meeting, PA 19462, USA

Richter, Les (Race Car Driver)
c/o Staff Member *NASCAR*
1801 Speedway Blvd
Daytona Beach, FL 32015, USA

Richter, Mike (Athlete, Hockey Player, Olympic Athlete)
61 Cutler Rd
Greenwich, CT 06831-2508

Richter, Pat V (Athlete, Football Executive, Football Player)
833 Kings Way
Madison, WI 53704, USA

Richwine, Maria (Actor)
Abrams-Rubaloff Lawrence
8075 W 3rd St
#303
Los Angeles, CA 90048, USA

Rickards, Ashley (Actor)
c/o Ben Levine *Kritzer Levine Wilkins Entertainment (KLWG)*
11872 La Grange Ave
1st Floor
Los Angeles, CA 90025, USA

Ricker, Robert S (Religious Leader)
Baptists Conference
2002 Arlington Heights Road
Arlington Heights, IL 60005, USA

Ricketts, Dave (Athlete, Baseball Player)
12860 Polo Parc Dr
Saint Louis, MO 63146, USA

Ricketts, Jeff (Actor)

Ricketts, Tom (Athlete, Football Player)
720 Warrendale Bayne Rd
Wexford, PA 60091-2811, USA

Rickey, Dixon (Athlete, Football Player)
908 Country Creek Ln
Red Oak, TX 75154, USA

Rickles, Don (Actor, Comedian)
10249 Century Woods Dr
Los Angeles, CA 90067, USA

Rickman, Alan (Actor, Producer)
c/o Judy Hofflund *Hofflund/Polone*
9465 Wilshire Blvd #420
Beverly Hills, CA 90212, USA

Rickon-Mitchell, Kelly (Athlete, Olympic Athlete, Rower)
3120 Goldsmith St
San Diego, CA 92106-1419, USA

Ricks, Lawrence (Athlete, Football Player)
6417 Timbermill Way
Reynoldsburg, OH 43068-4327, USA

Ricks, Mikhael (Athlete, Football Player)
5024 Lincoln St
Hollywood, FL 33021-5256, USA

Rico, Alfredo (Fred) (Athlete, Baseball Player)
7720 Ensign Ave
Sun Valley, CA 91352-4451, USA

Ricoeur, Paul (Misc)
18 Rue Henri Marrou
Chatenay Malabry 92290, FRANCE

Rida, Flo (Musician)
c/o Nick Carcaterra *Susan Blond Inc (NY)*
50 W 57th St
14th Floor
New York, NY 10019, USA

Ridder, P Anthony (Business Person, Publisher)
Knight-Ridder Inc
50 W San Fernando St
San Jose, CA 95113, USA

Riddick, Frank A Jr (Physicist)
1923 Octavia St
New Orleans, LA 70115, USA

Riddick, Steve (Athlete, Olympic Athlete, Track Athlete)
Petersburg F C I PO Box 1000 #07533-010
Petersburg, VA 23804-1000, USA

Riddiford, Lynn M (Biologist)
40733 Manor House Road
Leesburg, VA 20175-6517, USA

Riddleberger, Denny (Athlete, Baseball Player)
35785 Hunter Ave
Westland, MI 48185-6669, USA

Riddles, Libby (Dog Sled Racer)
PO Box 15253
Fritz Creek, AK 99603, USA

Riddoch, Greg (Athlete, Baseball Player, Coach)
703 Windflower Dr
Longmont, CO 80504-2770, USA

Rider, Amy (Actor)
c/o Amy Slomovits *Evolution Entertainment (LA)*
9320 Wilshire Blvd
Suite 202
Beverly Hills, CA 90212, USA

Rider, Isiah
PO Box 121R
Montchanin, DE 19710, USA

Rider, Isiah (J R) (Athlete, Basketball Player)
P.O. Box 121R
Montchanin, DE 19710, USA

Riders In The Sky
38 Music Sq. E. #300
Nashville, TN 37203

Riders of the Purple Sage
PO Box 1987
Studio City, CA 91604

Ridge, Houston (Athlete, Football Player)
7027 Benson Ave
San Diego, CA 92114, USA

Ridge, Thomas (Politician)
5315 Woodlawn Ave
Chevv Chase, MD 20815-6635, USA

Ridgeley, Andrew (Musician)
8800 Sunset Blvd
#401
Los Angeles, CA 90069, USA

Ridgeway, Angle (Golfer)
c/o Staff Member *Pro Golfers Association (PGA) Tour*
112 TPC Blvd
Ponte Vedra Beach, FL 32082, USA

Ridgeway, Frank (Cartoonist)
c/o Staff Member *King Features Syndication*
300 W 57th St
15th Floor
New York, NY 10019-5238, USA

Ridgle, Elston (Athlete, Football Player)
5317 Wilkinson Ave
Studio City, CA 91607, USA

Ridgley, Bob (Actor)
20th Century Artists
4605 Lankershim Blvd
#305
North Hollywood, CA 91602, USA

Ridgway, Brunilde S (Archaeologist)
Bryn Mawr College
Archaeology Dept
Bryn Mawr, PA 19010, USA

Ridgway, Dave (Athlete, Football Player)
5875 W State Highway 250
Paris Crossing, IN 47270-9785, USA

Ridgway, Jeff (Athlete, Baseball Player)
9041 Parlor Dr
Ladson, SC 29456-5528, USA

Ridings, Holly (Scientist)
18506 Kingstown Ct
Houston, TX 77058-4211, USA

Ridings, Tag (Athlete, Golfer)
2040 Bantry Drive
Roanoke, TX 76262-9001, USA

Ridker, Paul (Doctor)
Brigham & Women's Hospital
75 Francis St
Boston, MA 02115, USA

Ridlehuber, Preston (Athlete, Football
Player)
720 Serramonte Dr
Marietta, GA 30068, USA

Ridley, Curt (Athlete, Hockey Player)
722 E Grubb Dr
Mesquite, TX 75149-7502

Ridley, John (Director, Producer, Writer)
c/o Nancy Josephson *WME (LA)*
9601 Wilshire Blvd Fl 3
Beverly Hills, CA 90210, USA

Ridley, Mike (Athlete, Hockey Player)
Home Run Sports
20 de la Seigneurie Blvd
Winnipeg, MB R3X OE9, CANADA

Ridlon, James A (Athlete, Football Player)
8006 E Lake Rd
Cazenovia, NY 13035, USA

Ridnour, Luke (Basketball Player)
Seattle SuperSonics
351 Elliot Ave W
#500
Seattle, WA 98119, USA

Ridzik, Steve (Athlete, Baseball Player)
7008 11th Ave W
Bradenton, FL 34209, USA

Riedel, Lars (Athlete, Track Athlete)
LAC Chemnitz
Reichenhainer Str 154
Chemnitz 09125, GERMANY

Riedlbauch, Vaclav (Composer)
Revolucni 6
Prague 1 110 00, CZECH REPUBLIC

Riedling, John (Athlete, Baseball Player)
2118 Homestead Ln
Franklin, TN 37064-1177, USA

Riegel, Eden (Actor, Musician)
c/o Leigh Brillstein *ICM Partners (ICM-LA)*
10250 Constellation Blvd Fl 7
Los Angeles, CA 90067, USA

Rieger, Max (Skier)
Innsbrucker Str 12
Mittenwald 82481, GERMANY

Riegert, Peter (Actor)
c/o John S Kelly *Bresler Kelly &
Associates*
11500 W Olympic Blvd
Suite 510
Los Angeles, CA 90064, USA

Riegger, John (Golfer)
768 Tossa De Mar Ave
Henderson, NV 89015-6536, USA

Riegle, Bruce (Horse Racer)
300 W Main St
Greenville, OH 45331-1432, USA

Riegle, Gene (Coach, Horse Racer)
818 Chestnut Cir
Greenville, OH 45331-1075, USA

Riegle Jr, Donald W (Business Person, Ex-
Senator, Senator)
APCO Worldwide
700 12th St NW
Suite 800
Washington, DC 20005, USA

Riehle, Richard (Actor)
Abrams Artists
9200 Sunset Blvd
#1125
Los Angeles, CA 90069, USA

Rieker, Rich (Athlete, Baseball Player)
1223 Grey Fox Run
Weldon Spring, MO 63304-0307, USA

Rieker, Richard (Baseball Player)
5337 Foxshire Ct
Orlando, FL 32819-3824, USA

Riendeau, Vincent (Athlete, Hockey
Player)
6105 Suitor Ch
Waterville, QC J0B 3H0, Canada

Rienstra, John (Athlete, Football Player)
5056 Briscoglen Dr
Colorado Springs, CO 80906, USA

Riepe, James S (Business Person)
T Rowe Price Assoc
100 E Pratt St
Baltimore, MD 21202, USA

Ries, Christopher D (Artist)
Keelersburg Road
Tunkhannock, PA 18657, USA

Riesch, Maria (Athlete, Skier)
Postfach 1728
Garmisch Partenkirchen 82457,
Germany

Riesenberg, Doug (Athlete, Football
Player)
25068 Starr Creek Rd
Corvallis, OR 97333, USA

Riesgo, Nikco (Damon) (Athlete, Baseball
Player)
29625 Bermuda Ln
Southfield, MI 48076-1663, USA

Riesgraf, Beth (Actor)
c/o Matthew Lesher *Insight*
1134 S Cloverdale Ave
Los Angeles, CA 90019, USA

Riess, Adam (Astronomer, Physicist)
Space Telescope Science Institute
3700 San Martin Dr
Baltimore, MD 21218, USA

Riess, Adam (Nobel Prize Laureate)
7100 Sheffield Rd
Baltimore, MD 21212-1629, USA

Riessen, Marty (Tennis Player)
PO Box 5444
Santa Barbara, CA 93150, USA

Ries-Zillmer, Ruth (Baseball Player)
133 Adeline St
Walworth, WI 53184-9522, USA

Rieu, Andre (Musician)
Polygram Holland
Mozartlaan 25
Hilversum, CM 1217, NETHERLANDS

Rieves, Charles (Athlete, Football Player)
3107 Long Bay Ct
Houston, TX 77059, USA

Rieves, Charley (Athlete, Football Player)
3107 Long Bay Ct
Houston, TX 77059-3720, USA

Rife, Rikki
520 Washington Blvd. #924
Marina del Rey, CA 90292-5442

Riff
PO Box 7257
Paterson, NJ 07509

Rifkin, Adam (Actor, Director, Writer)
c/o Simon Millar *Rumble Media*
1620 Broadway
Santa Monica, CA 90403, USA

Rifkin, Jeremy (Activist, Writer)
1660 L St NW
#216
Washington, DC 20036, USA

Rifkin, Ron (Actor, Musician)
c/o Marcia Hurwitz *Innovative Artists (LA)*
1505 10th St
Santa Monica, CA 90401, USA

Rifkind, Joshua (Conductor, Musician)
100 Montgomery St
Cambridge, MA 02140, USA

Rigali, Justin F Cardinal (Religious Leader)
Archdiocese
222 N 17th St
Philadelphia, PA 19103, USA

Rigazio, Donald (Athlete, Hockey Player,
Olympic Athlete)
8514 Cheffield Dr
Louisville, KY 40222-5665, USA

Rigby, Alden (General)
266 Lago Vista Cir
Bountiful, UT 84010-1821, USA

Rigby, Amy (Musician, Songwriter, Writer)
Press Network
1229 17th Ave S
Nashville, TN 37212, USA

Rigby, Brad (Athlete, Baseball Player)
1317 Ballentyne Pl
Apopka, FL 32703-6870, USA

Rigby, Cathy (Athlete, Gymnast, Olympic
Athlete)
110 E Wilshire Ave #200
Fullerton, CA 92832-1956, USA

Rigby, Jean P (Opera Singer)
Harold Holt
31 Sinclair Road
London W14 0NS, UNITED KINGDOM
(UK)

Rigby, Paul (Cartoonist)
119 Monterey Pointe Dr
West Palm Beach, FL 33418, USA

Rigby, Randall Jr (General)
Deputy CG
US Army Training/Doctrine Command
Fort Monroe, VA 23651, USA

Rigdon, Paul (Athlete, Baseball Player)
9231 Coxwell Ct
Jacksonville, FL 32221, USA

Rigg, Diana (Actor)
Chichester Festival Theatre
Oaklands Park
Chichester
West Sussex PO19 6AP, UK

Rigg, Rebecca (Actor)
June Cann Mgmt
110 Queen St
Woollahra, NSW 2025, AUSTRALIA

Riggan, Jerrod (Athlete, Baseball Player)
P.O. Box 1019
Brewster, WA 98812-1019, USA

Riggans, Shawn (Athlete, Baseball Player)
5700 Hancock Rd
Southwest Ranches, FL 33330-3006, USA

Riggin, Dennis (Athlete, Hockey Player)
244 Goderich St.
Kincardine, ON N2Z 2K5, CANADA

Riggin, Pat (Athlete, Hockey Player)
112 Fairlane Ave.
London, ON N6K 3E6, Canada

Riggins, Mark (Athlete, Baseball Player)
101 Arbor Dr
Murray, KY 42071-6835, USA

Riggio, Dominic (Athlete, Football Player)
4621 Mandalay Ave
Royal Oak, MI 48073-1623, USA

Riggio, Leonard (Business Person)
Barnes & Noble Inc
122 5th Ave
New York, NY 10011, USA

Riggle, Bob (Athlete, Football Player)
55 Waynesburg Rd
Washington, PA 15301, USA

Riggle, Rob (Actor)
c/o Peter Principato *Principato/Young
Management*
9465 Wilshire Blvd
Suite 430
Beverly Hills, CA 90212, USA

Riggleman, James D (Jim) (Athlete,
Baseball Player, Coach)
14950 Gulf Blvd
Apt 1003
Madeira Beach, FL 33708-2047, USA

Riggs, Adam (Athlete, Baseball Player)
26 Pebble Hollow Ct
Spring, TX 77381-4803, USA

Riggs, Chandler (Actor)
c/o Joanna (Joanie) Burstein *Burstein
Company, The*
15304 Sunset Blvd
suite 208
Pacific Palisades, CA 90272, USA

Riggs, Gerald (Athlete, Football Player)
1810 Verona Dr
Chattanooga, TN 37421-3064, USA

Riggs, Gerald (Athlete, Football Player)
2574 Bright Ct
Decatur, GA 30034, USA

Riggs, Jim (Athlete, Football Player)
15 Dellany Ct
Greer, SC 29651-6857, USA

Riggs, Lorrin A (Misc)
80 Lyme Road
#104
Hanover, NH 03755, USA

Riggs, Scott (Race Car Driver)
MBV/MB2 Motorsports
7065 Zephr Pl NW
Concord, NC 29028, USA

Riggs, Thron (Athlete, Football Player)
2645 E Southern Ave
Apt 496
Tempe, AZ 85282-7797, USA

Righetti, Amanda (Actor, Producer)
c/o David (Dave) Fleming *Mosaic Media
Group*
9200 W. Sunset Blvd
10th Floor
Los Angeles, CA 90069, USA

Righetti, David A (Dave) (Athlete, Baseball Player)
552 Magdalena Ave
Los Altos Hills, CA 94024-5233, USA

Righteous Bros (Music Group)
c/o Staff Member *WmE2 (WMA-LA)*
1 William Morris Pl
Beverly Hills, CA 90212, USA

Rightnowar, Ron (Athlete, Baseball Player)
8926 Stonybrook Blvd
Sylvania, OH 43560-8906, USA

Rights, Graham H (Religious Leader)
Moravian Church Southern Province
459 S Church St
Winston Salem, NC 27101, USA

Right Said Fred
PO Box 891135
Edam, NETHERLANDS ZJ

Rigoli, Joe (Athlete, Baseball Player)
117 Metro Trl
Hocatcong, NJ 07843-1554, USA

Rigsbee, Shani (Actor, Bollywood)
c/o Staff Member *Cherokee Productions*
8491 Sunset Blvd #277
Los Angeles, CA 90069, USA

Rigsby, Donald (Musician)
Donald Rigsby Group, Inc
31959 Amverlea Rd
Dade City, FL 33523, USA

Rihanna (Musician)
932 Rivas Canyon Rd
Pacific Palisades, CA 90272, USA

Rijker, Lucia (Actor)
c/o Harlan Werner *Sports Placement Service*
330 W 11th St
Suite 105
Los Angeles, CA 90015, USA

Rijo, Jose (Athlete, Baseball Player)
2127 Brickell Ave
Apt 2101
Miami, FL 33129-2146, USA

Rikaart, Greg (Actor)
c/o Kyle Fritz *Kyle Fritz Management*
6325 Heather Dr
Los Angeles, CA 90068, USA

Riker, Albert J (Misc)
2760 E 8th St
Tucson, AZ 85716, USA

Riker, Robin (Actor)
c/o Staff Member *Buchwald/Fortitude (LA)*
6500 Wilshire Blvd
Suite 2200
Los Angeles, CA 90048, USA

Riker, Tom (Athlete, Basketball Player)
600 Fines Creek Rd
Clyde, NC 28721-9183, USA

Riklis, Meshulam (Business Person)
Riklis Family Corp
2901 Las Vegas Blvd S
Las Vegas, NV 89109, USA

Riles, Ernest (Athlete, Baseball Player)
221 Asante Dr
Ellenwood, GA 30294-3187, USA

Riley, Amber (Actor)
c/o Nicki Fioravante *PMK/BNC - LA*
8687 Melrose Ave
8th Floor
West Hollywood, CA 90069, USA

Riley, Bill (Athlete, Hockey Player)
286 Buckingham Ave
Riverview, NB E1B 2P2, Canada

Riley, Boots (Musician)
c/o Danny Goldberg *Gold Village Entertainment*
37 W 17th St
Suite 7W
New York, NY 10011, USA

Riley, Bridget L (Artist)
Mayor Rowan Gallery
31A Bruton Place
London W1X 7A8, UNITED KINGDOM (UK)

Riley, Chris (Golfer)
2289 Surrey Meadows Ave
Henderson, NV 89052-2335, USA

Riley, Elaine (Actor)
405 N Bay Front
Newport Beach, CA 92262, USA

Riley, Eric (Athlete, Basketball Player)
6601 Sands Point Dr
Apt 4
Houston, TX 77e74-3731, USA

Riley, Forbes (Actor)
c/o Staff Member *Cohen Entertainment*
964 Hancock Ave
Suite 305
West Hollywood, CA 90069, USA

Riley, George (Athlete, Baseball Player)
451 Basket Rd
Oley, PA 19547-9245, USA

Riley, Gerald (Jerry) (Dog Sled Racer)
General Delivery
Nenana, AK 99760, USA

Riley, H John Jr (Business Person)
Cooper Industries
600 Travis
Houston, TX 77002, USA

Riley, Jack (Athlete, Hockey Player, Olympic Athlete)
PO Box 1302
Marstone Mills, MA 02648-5302

Riley, Jack (Actor)
c/o Staff Member *House of Representatives, The*
1434 6th St
Suite 1
Santa Monica, CA 90401, USA

Riley, James (Athlete, Football Player)
2201 Cardinal Dr
Edmond, OK 73013, USA

Riley, James C (General)
Commanding General
V Corps
APO, AE 09079, USA

Riley, Jeannie (Musician)
1003 Lakeview Dr
Brenham, TX 77833, USA

Riley, Ken (Athlete, Football Player)
1865 E Gibbons St
Bartow, FL 33830, USA

Riley, Kim Manske (Stylist)
3802 Ridge Manor Cr
Kingswood, TX 77345-1216, USA

Riley, Madison (Actor)
c/o Mona Loring *MLC PR*
7080 Hollywood Blvd
Suite 903
Los Angeles, CA 90028, USA

Riley, Matt (Athlete, Baseball Player)
6 Kirra Ct
Aliso Vieio, AZ 92656-4276, USA

Riley, Michael
9200 Sunset Blvd. #900
Los Angeles, CA 90069

Riley, Mike (Coach, Football Coach)
Oregon State University
Athletic Dept
Corvallis, OR 97331, USA

Riley, Pat (Athlete, Basketball Coach, Basketball Player, Coach)
800 S Pointe Dr #B
Miami Beach, FL 33139-7163, USA

Riley, Raven (Actor)
Evil Motion Pictures
Prefers to be contacted via email
Phoenix, AZ 85066, USA

Riley, Richard D (Misc)
16 Boathouse Road
Laconia, NH 03246, USA

Riley, Robert (Politician)
742 County Road 5
Ashland, AL 36251-5533, USA

Riley, Ruth (Athlete)
3777 Lapeer Rd
Auburn Hills, MI 48326-1733

Riley, Sam (Actor)
c/o Angharad Wood *Tavistock Wood Management*
32 Tavistock St
London WC2B 5HA, UK

Riley, Steve (Athlete, Football Player)
7 Via Cancion
San Clemente, CA 92673, USA

Riley, Talulah (Actor)
c/o Laura Symons *Premier PR (UK)*
91 Berwick St
London W1F 0NE, UK

Riley, Teddy (Musician, Songwriter)
Future Enterprise Records
70 Universal City Plaza
Universal City, CA 91608, USA

Riley, Terry M (Composer, Musician)
Shri Moonshine Ranch
13699 Moonshire Road
Camptonville, CA 95922, USA

Riley, Victor (Athlete, Football Player)
136 Sandy Oak Ln
Gaston, SC 29053, USA

Riley, William Jay (Judge)
US Court of Appeals
Federal Bldg
PO Box 307
Omaha, NE 68101, USA

Rilling, Helmuth
Int'l Bach Academy
Johann-Sebastian-Bach-Platz
Stuttgart 70178, GERMANY

Rimando, Nick (Soccer Player)
DC United
RFK Stadium
2400 East Capitol St, SE
Washington, DC 20003, USA

Rimer, Jeff (Sportscaster)
9916 Morris Drive
Dublin, OH 43017-8859, USA

Rimes, LeAnn (Musician)
c/o Mark Hartley *Fitzgerald-Hartley*
34 N Palms St
Suite 100
Ventura, CA 93001, USA

Rimington, Dave (Athlete, Football Player)
222 Riverside Dr #11-D
New York, NY 10025, USA

Rimington, Stella (Government Official)
PO Box 1604
London SW1P 1XB, UNITED KINGDOM (UK)

Rimmel, James E (Religious Leader)
Evangetical Presbyterian Church
26049 Five Mile Road
Detroit, MI 48239, USA

Rinaldi, Kathy (Tennis Player)
Advantage International
1025 Thomas Jefferson NW
#450
Washington, DC 20007, USA

Rinaldi, Rich (Athlete, Basketball Player)
1117 Perry Ln
Collegeville, PA 19426-1e67, USA

Rinaldo, Benjamin (Skier)
Ski World
2680 Buena Park Dr
North Hollywood, CA 91604, USA

Rincon, Andy (Athlete, Baseball Player)
5425 Los Toros Ave
Pico Rivera, CA 90660-3038, USA

Rincon, Juan (Athlete, Baseball Player)
5150 Lincoln Dr
Minneapolis, MN 55436-1010, USA

Rincon, Ricardo (Baseball Player)
c/o Staff Member *Oakland Athletics*
7000 Coliseum Way
Oakland, CA 94621, USA

Rinearson, Peter M (Journalist)
Seattle Times
Editorial Dept
1120 John St
Seattle, WA 98109, USA

Rineer, Jeff (Athlete, Baseball Player)
325 W Charlotte St
Millersville, PA 17551-9515, USA

Rinehart, Kenneth (Misc)
University of Illinois
Chemistry Dept
Urbana, IL 61801, USA

Rines, Robert H (Inventor)
17 Ripley Road
Belmont, MA 02478, USA

Ring, Bob (Athlete, Hockey Player)
28 St Simons Dr
Bluffton, SC 29910-6151

Ring, Royce (Athlete, Baseball Player)
2860 Aber St
San Diego, CA 92117-2422, USA

Ringadoo, Veerasamy (President)
Corner of Farquhar & Sir Celicourt
Antelme Sts
Quatre-Bornes, MAURITIUS

Ringenberg, Margaret (Aviator)
14406 Sunrise Ct
Leo, IN 46765-9515, USA

Ringer, Jenifer (Ballerina)
c/o Staff Member *New York City Ballet*
New York State Theater
20 Lincoln Center
New York, NY 10023, USA

Ringer, Robert J (Motivational Speaker, Writer)
c/o Staff Member *The Harry Walker Agency*
355 Lexington Ave
21st Floor
New York, NY 10017, USA

Ringolsby, Tracy (Baseball Player)
1526 Fox Chase Rd
Cheyenne, WY 82009-8396, USA

Ringwald, Molly (Actor)
217 E 85th St #18
New York, NY 10028, USA

Rini, Mary (Athlete, Baseball Player)
37592 Charter Oaks Blvd
Clinton Township, MI 48036-2422, USA

Rinker, Larry (Golfer)
1615 Woodland Ave
Winter Park, FL 32789-2774, USA

Rinna, Lisa (Actor)
3007 Lake Glen Dr
Beverly Hills, CA 90210, USA

Rinne, Pekka (Athlete, Hockey Player)
Puckagency LLC
555 Pleasantville Rd Ste 210N
Attn Jay Grossman
Briarcliff Manor, NY 10510-1900, USA

Rinser, Luise
via di Marino 49
Rocca di Papa, ITALY I-00040

Rintoul, David
91 Regent St.
London, ENGLAND W1R 7TB

Rintoul, Steve (Golfer)
17506 Osprey Manor Way
Lithia, FL 33547-5044, USA

Rintzler, Marius A (Opera Singer)
Friedingstr 18
Dusseldorf 40625, GERMANY

Riopelle, Howard "Rip" (Athlete, Hockey Player)
4 Beechmont Crt
Gloucester, ON KlB 4Bl, Canada

Riordan, Marjorie
1833 Pelham Ave.
Los Angeles, CA 90025

Riordan, Mike (Athlete, Basketball Player)
Riordan's Saloon
14e Inwood Rd
Stevensville, MD 21666-3969, USA

Riordan, Richard J (Politician)
Bingham McCutchen
355 S Grand Ave
Suite 4400
Los Angeles, CA 90005, USA

Rios, Alberto (Writer)
Arizona State University
English Dept
Tempe, AZ 85287, USA

Rios, Alexis (Baseball Player)
Yale Field
252 Derby Ave
West Haven, CT 06516, USA

Rios, Armando (Athlete, Baseball Player)
790 Ridenhour Cir
Orlando, FL 32809-7158, USA

Rios, Brandon (Boxer)
c/o Staff Member *Top Rank Inc.*
3908 Howard Hughes Pkwy
#580
Las Vegas, NV 89109, USA

Rios, Danny (Athlete, Baseball Player)
2523 W 9th Ln
Hialeah, FL 33010-1225, USA

Rios, Emily (Actor)
c/o Staff Member *Kass & Stokes Management*
9229 Sunset Blvd
Suite 504
Los Angeles, CA 90069, USA

Rios, Marcelo (Tennis Player)
Int'l Mgmt Group
Via Augusta 200
#400
Barcelona 08021, SPAIN

Rios, Osvaldo (Actor)
c/o Staff Member *TV Caracol*
Calle 76 #11 - 35
Piso 10AA
Bogota DC 26484, COLOMBIA

Riotta, Vincent (Actor)
c/o Staff Member *Scott Marshall Partners Ltd*
15 Little Portland St
2nd Floor
London W1W 8BW, UK

Rioux, Gerry (Athlete, Hockey Player)
213 Grosvenor
Iroquois Falls A, ON POK 1GO, Canada

Ripa, Kelly (Actor)
Live
WABC-TV
7 Lincoln Sq Floor 5
New York, NY 10023, USA

Ripert, Eric (Chef)
Le Bernardin
787 7th Ave
New York, NY 10019, USA

Ripken, Billy (Athlete, Baseball Player)
Major League Basebal Network
900 Mount Soma Ct
Fallston, MD 21047-1935, USA

Ripken Jr, Cal (Athlete, Baseball Player)
Cal Ripken Foundation
1427 Clarkview Rd
Suite 100
Baltimore, MD 21209-0030, USA

Ripley, Alexandra (Writer)
24 Ripley St
Newport News, VA 23603-1305, USA

Ripley, Alexandra
24 Ripley St
Newport News, VA 23603-1305, USA

Ripley, Alice (Actor, Musician)
c/o Staff Member *Douglas Gorman Rothacker & Wilhelm Inc*
1501 Broadway
Suite 703
New York, NY 10036, USA

Ripley, Allen (Athlete, Baseball Player)
50 Dunham St
Attleboro, MA 02703-3052, USA

Rippelmeyer, Ray (Athlete, Baseball Player)
104 Eagle Ct
Waterloo, IL 62298-3158, USA

Rippey, Rodney Allan (Actor)
3941 Veselich Ave
#4-251
Los Angeles, CA 90039, USA

Rippey, Rodney Allen
3939 Veselich Ave. #351
Los Angeles, CA 90039-1435

Ripple, Kenneth F (Judge)
US Court of Appeals
204 S Main St
South Bend, IN 46601, USA

Rippley, Steve (Athlete, Baseball Player)
3900 Galt Ocean Dr
Apt 1406
Fort Lauderdale, FL 33308-6606, USA

Rippley, Steve (Baseball Player)
3900 Galt Ocean Dr Apt 1406
Fort Lauderdale, FL 33308-6606, USA

Ris, Hans (Biologist)
2116 Madison Street
Madison, WI 53711-2132, USA

Riseborough, Andrea (Actor)
c/o Ciara Parkes *Public Eye Communications*
535 Kings Rd
Suite 313 Plaza
London SW10 0SZ, United Kingdom

Risebrough, Doug (Athlete, Coach, Hockey Player)
5809 Schaefer Rd
Minneapolis, MN 55436-1115

Risen, Arnie (Athlete, Basketball Player)
3217 Bremerton Rd
Cleveland, OH 44124-5346, USA

Risher, Alan (Athlete, Football Player)
15814 Chantilly Ave
Baton Rouge, LA 70817, USA

Risien, Cody L (Athlete, Football Player)
12060 Lake Ave
Apt 401
Lakewood, OH 44107-1865, USA

Risinger, Earlene (Baseball Player)
334 Aurora St SE
Grand Rapids, MI 49507-9178, USA

Risk, Thomas N (Financier)
10 Belford Place
Edinburgh EH4 3DH, SCOTLAND

Riske, Alison (Athlete, Tennis Player)
c/o Staff Member *Women's Tennis Association (WTA (US))*
One Progress Plaza
Ste 1500
St Petersburg, FL 33701, USA

Riske, David (Athlete, Baseball Player)
2771 Culloden Ave
Henderson, NV 89044-0233, USA

Risley, Bill (Athlete, Baseball Player)
1160 Prim Rose Cir
Greenwood, AR 72936-3066, USA

Risner, Robinson (General)
118 Meadow Ln
Bridgewater, VA 22812-1759, USA

Risney, Jodee (Stylist)
3234 Maplethorpe Lane
Soquel, CA 95073-2917, USA

Rison, Andre (Athlete, Football Player)
6293 N Jennings Rd
Royal Oak, MI 48073-1623, USA

Rispoli, Michael (Actor)
c/o Staff Member *Gersh (LA)*
9465 Wilshire Blvd
Suite 600
Beverly Hills, CA 90212, USA

Rissling, Gary (Athlete, Hockey Player)
717 Paige Cir
Bel Air, MD 21014, USA

Rissmiller, Pat (Athlete, Hockey Player)
276 Brackett St Apt 2R
Portland, ME 04102-3239

Rissmiller, Ray (Athlete, Football Player)
114 Iken Cir
Goose Creek, SC 29445, USA

Rist, Robbie
PO Box 867
Woodland Hills, CA 91365

Ristorucci, Lisa (Actor)
Progressive Artists Agency
400 S Beverly Dr
#216
Beverly Hills, CA 90212, USA

Ritch, Michael (Race Car Driver)
David & Wright Motorsports
2730 Zion Church Rd.
Concord, NC 28025-7027, USA

Ritcher, James A (Jim) (Athlete, Football Player)
8620 Boumemouth Dr
Raleigh, NC 27615, USA

Ritchie, Daniel L (Educator, Television Host)
University of Denver
Chancellor's Office
Denver, CO 80208, USA

Ritchie, Guy (Director, Producer, Writer)
c/o Cindy Guagenti *Baker Winokur Ryder Public Relations (BWR-LA)*
9100 Wilshire Blvd
Suite 500, West Tower
Beverly Hills, CA 90212, USA

Ritchie, Ian (Architect)
110 Three Colt St
London E14 8A2, UNITED KINGDOM (UK)

Ritchie, Jay (Athlete, Baseball Player)
8275 Highway 52
Rockwell, NC 28138-8545, USA

Ritchie, Jill (Actor)
c/o Staff Member *Rugolo Entertainment*
195 S Beverly Dr
Suite 400
Beverly Hills, CA 90212, USA

Ritchie, Jim (Artist)
Mark Hotel
19 E 82nd St
New York, NY 10028-0302, USA

Ritchie, John H (Architect)
Mount Heswall
Wirral L60 4RD, UNITED KINGDOM (UK)

Ritchie, Jon (Football Player)
c/o Staff Member *Philadelphia Eagles*
1 NovaCare Way
Philadelphia, PA 19145, USA

Ritchie, Steven (General)
PO Box 1942
Monument, CO 80132-1942, USA

Ritchie, Todd (Athlete, Baseball Player)
114 Hulan Dr
Kerens, TX 75144-6046, USA

Ritchie, Wally (Athlete, Baseball Player)
417 Robert Cir
Santa Clara, UT 84765-5617, USA

Ritchie Family, The
4100 W. Flagler St. #B-2
Miami, FL 33134

Ritchson, Alan (Actor)
c/o Gayle Divine *Divine Management*
3822 Latrobe St
Los Angeles, CA 90031

Ritenour, Lee (Composer, Musician)
11808 Dorothy St
#108
Los Angeles, CA 90049, USA

Ritger, Dick (Bowler)
804 Valley View Dr
River Falls, WI 54022-2724, USA

Rittenhouse, Lenore (Golfer)
295 Bellhaven Dr
Carthage, NC 28327-7133, USA

Ritter, C Dowd (Financier)
AmSouth Bancorp
AmSouth Sonat Tower
1900 5th Ave N
Birmingham, AL 35203, USA

Ritter, Huntley (Actor, Producer)
c/o Sheila Wenzel *Innovative Artists (LA)*
1505 10th St
Santa Monica, CA 90401, USA

Ritter, Jason (Actor)
c/o Joanna (Joanie) Burstein *Burstein Company, The*
15304 Sunset Blvd
suite 208
Pacific Palisades, CA 90272, USA

Ritter, Krysten (Actor)
c/o Nancy Sanders *Sanders Armstrong Caserta*
2120 Colorado Blvd
Suite 120
Santa Monica, CA 90404, USA

Ritter, Lawrence (Baseball Player)
424 W End Ave Apt 6D
New York, NY 10024-5777, USA

Ritter, Paul (Actor)
c/o Lou Coulson *Lou Coulson Agency*
37 Berwick St
1st Floor
London W1F 8RS, UNITED KINGDOM (UK)

Ritter, Reggie (Athlete, Baseball Player)
1564 Estep Rd
Donaldson, AR 71941-8987, USA

Rittinger, Al (Athlete, Hockey Player)
5423 Wallace Ave
Delta, BC V4M 3V4, Canada

Ritts, Jim (Golfer, Television Host)
Ladies Pro Golf Assn
100 International Golf Dr
Daytona Beach, FL 32124, USA

Rittwage, Jim (Athlete, Baseball Player)
23931 Columbus Rd
Bedford, OH 44146-2969, USA

Ritz, David
c/o Daniel Strone *Trident Media Group LLC*
41 Madison Ave
36th Floor
New York, NY 10010, USA

Ritz, Kevin (Athlete, Baseball Player)
836 N 6th St
Cambridge, OH 43725-1400, USA

Ritzenhaler, Henry Leon
1617 Pearson Rd.
Paradise, CA 95969

Ritzman, Alice (Golfer)
614 S Foys Lake Dr
Kalispell, MT 59901, USA

riutta, bruce (Athlete, Hockey Player, Olympic Athlete)
1243 Sunny Creek Dr
Green Bay, WI 54313-5884, USA

Riutta, Ernest R (Admiral)
Commander
US Coast Guard Pacific
Coast Guard Island
Alameda, CA 94501, USA

Riva, Diana Maria (Actor)
c/o Amy Guenther *Gateway Management Company Inc*
860 Via De La Paz
Suite F10
Pacific Palisades, CA 90272, USA

Riva, Emmanuelle
37 rue de la Harpe
Paris, FRANCE F-75005

Rivaldo (Soccer Player)
AC Milan
Via Turati 3
Milan 20221, ITALY

Rivard, Bob (Athlete, Hockey Player)
882 Chapel Rd
Peterborough, ON K9H 7M3, Canada

Rivas, Daniel Louis (Actor)
c/o Paul Santana *Agency for the Performing Arts (APA-LA)*
405 S Beverly Dr
Suite 500
Beverly Hills, CA 90212-4425, USA

Rivas, Gonzalo (Actor)
c/o Staff Member *Televisa*
Blvd Adolfo Lopez Mateos 232
Colonia San Angel INN
DF CP 01060, MEXICO

Rivas Montaño, Hanna (Actor)
c/o Staff Member *Televisa*
Blvd Adolfo Lopez Mateos 232
Colonia San Angel INN
DF CP 01060, MEXICO

Rivera, Alex (Baseball Player)
21228 Shell Valley Rd
Edmonds, WA 98026-7346, USA

Rivera, Ana Liz (Actor)
c/o Staff Member *Televisa*
Blvd Adolfo Lopez Mateos 232
Colonia San Angel INN
DF CP 01060, MEXICO

Rivera, Angelica (Actor)
c/o Staff Member *Televisa*
Blvd Adolfo Lopez Mateos 232
Colonia San Angel INN
DF CP 01060, MEXICO

Rivera, Chita (Actor, Dancer, Musician)
c/o Staff Member *WmE2 (WMA-LA)*
1 William Morris Pl
Beverly Hills, CA 90212, USA

Rivera, David (Congressman, Politician)
417 Cannon HOB
Washington, DC 20515, USA

Rivera, Emilio (Actor)
4637 W Willow Crest Ave
Toluca Lake, CA 91602, USA

Rivera, Geraldo (Journalist, Television Host)
c/o Jim Griffin *Paradigm (NY)*
360 Park Ave S Fl 16
New York, NY 10010, USA

Rivera, Jerry (Musician)
c/o Staff Member *BMG*
1540 Broadway
New York, NY 10036, USA

Rivera, Jim (Athlete, Baseball Player)
2311 Abbey Dr
Apt 7
Fort Wayne, IN 46835-3150, USA

Rivera, Jose (Producer, Writer)
c/o Rick Berg *Code Entertainment*
9229 Sunset Blvd #615
Los Angeles, CA 90069, USA

Rivera, Juan (Athlete, Baseball Player)
c/o Staff Member *Los Angeles Dodgers (LA Dodgers)*
1000 Elysian Park Ave
Los Angeles, CA 90012, USA

Rivera, Luis (Athlete, Baseball Player)
16 Calle Lazaro Ramos
Cidra, PR 00739-3424, USA

Rivera, Lupillo (Music Group)
c/o Staff Member *Sony Music Miami*
605 Lincoln Rd Fl 7
Miami Beach, FL 33139, USA

Rivera, Mariano (Athlete, Baseball Player)
147 Anderson Hill Rd
Purchase, NY 10577-2007, USA

Rivera, Maxwell (Musician)
c/o Staff Member *Shore Fire Media*
32 Court St
16th Floor
Brooklyn, NY 11201, USA

Rivera, Mike (Athlete, Baseball Player)
2814 Harwood Ct
Kissimmee, FL 34744-8416, USA

Rivera, Naya (Actor)
c/o Sharyn Berg *Sharyn Talent Management*
P.O. Box 18033
Encino, CA 91416, USA

Rivera, Ron (Athlete, Football Player)
14420 Rancho Del Prado Trail
San Diego, CA 92127, USA

Rivera, Ximena Sarinana (Musician)
c/o Staff Member *Warner Bros Music*
4000 Warner Blvd
Burbank, CA 91522

Rivera Carrera, Norberto Cardinal (Religious Leader)
Curia Arzobispal
Aptdo Postal 24-4-33
Mexico City, DF 06700, MEXICO

Rivera-Drew, Malaya (Actor)
8777 Lookout Mountain Ave
Los Angeles, CA 90046, USA

Rivero, Jorge (Actor)
H David Moss
733 Seward St
#PH
Los Angeles, CA 90038, USA

Rivers, David (Athlete, Basketball Player)
10509 Greensprings Dr
Tampa, FL 33626-1724, USA

Rivers, Glenn "Doc" (Athlete, Basketball Player)
5 Isle of SicilY
Winter Park, FL 32789-1505, USA

Rivers, Glenn (Doc) (Athlete, Basketball Coach, Basketball Player, Coach)
5 Isle of Sicily
Winter Park, FL 32789-1505, USA

Rivers, Jamie (Athlete, Hockey Player)
2754 Farriers Lane
Gloucester, ON KIT 1X8, Canada

Rivers, Jamie (Athlete, Football Player)
4006 Lindell Blvd
Saint Louis, MO 63108, USA

Rivers, Joan (Comedian, Producer)
Joan Rivers Worldwide Enterprises
P.O. Box 1150
F.D.R. Station
New York, NY 10150, USA

Rivers, Johnny (Musician, Songwriter, Writer)
3141 Coldwater Canyon Lane
Beverly Hills, CA 90210, USA

Rivers, Marcellus (Athlete, Football Player)
12003 Eden Ln
Frisco, TX 75034-1146, USA

Rivers, Melissa (Talk Show Host)
c/o Larry Thompson *Larry A Thompson Organization*
9663 Santa Monica Blvd
Suite 801
Beverly Hills, CA 90210, USA

Rivers, Mickey (Athlete, Baseball Player)
M D M Sports Marketing
218 Washington Ave Apt C14
Attn: David Ratner
Cedarhurst, NY 11516-1510, USA

Rivers, Philip (Athlete, Football Player)
4020 Murphy Canyon Rd
San Diego, CA 92123, USA

Rivers, Reggie (Athlete, Football Player)
5003 E Weaver Pl
Centennial, CO 80121, USA

Rivers, Shawn (Athlete, Hockey Player)
1962 Queensdale Ave
Gloucester, ON KIT IKI, Canada

Rivers, Wayne (Athlete, Hockey Player)
2821 San Ardo Way
Belmont, CA 94002-1341

Riverside, Vincent
c/o Melanie Sharp *Sharp Talent*
117 N Orlando Ave
Los Angeles, CA 90048, USA

Rives, Don (Athlete, Football Player)
603 E Garfield Ave
Morton, TX 79346, USA

Rivest, Ronald (Scientist)
Massachusetts Institute of Technology
Cambridge, MA 02139, USA

Rivet, Craig (Athlete, Hockey Player)
Newport Sports Management
400-201 City Centre Dr
Attn Don Meehan
Mississauga, ON LSB 2T4, Canada

Rivette, Jacques (Director)
20 Blvd de la Bastille
Paris 75012, FRANCE

Riviere, Marie (Actor, Director)
c/o Staff Member *Dominique Sarais
Agence Artistique*
37 rue du Port a l'Anglais
Alfortville 94140, France

Rivlin, Alice M (Government Official)
2842 Chesterfield Place
Washington, DC 20008, USA

Rizzle Kicks (Music Group)
c/o Staff Member *Sony Music
Entertainment Germany*
Neumarkter Str. 28
Muenchen 81673, Germany

Rizzo, Jack (Athlete, Football Player)
1105 Forest Trails Dr
Castle Rock, CO 80108, USA

Rizzo, Jerry (Athlete, Basketball Player)
2548 126th St
Apt 1
Flushing, NY 11354, USA

Rizzo, Joe (Horse Racer)
5 Berkshire Dr
Howell, NJ 07731-2355, USA

Rizzo, Joe (Athlete, Football Player)
6131 Dorsett Pl
Wilmington, NC 28403, USA

Rizzo, John R (Athlete, Football Player)
1105 Forest Trails Dr
Castle Rock, CO 80108, USA

Rizzo, Patti (Golfer)
2455 Provence Circle
Weston, FL 33327, USA

Rizzo, Rizzo (DJ)
c/o Len Evans *Project Publicity*
312 West 53rd St
Suite 202
New York, NY 10019, USA

Rizzo, Rob (Race Car Driver)
Rizzo Racing
700 Main St.
East Greenwich, RI 02838, USA

Rizzo, Todd (Athlete, Baseball Player)
7 Williamsburg Ct
Sewell, NJ 08080-3230, USA

Rizzo-Depardon, Patti (Golfer)
1008 SE 5th Ct
Ft Lauderdale, FL 33301-3004, USA

Rizzotti, Jennifer (Basketball Player, Coach)
University of Hartford
Athletic Dept
West Hartford, CT 06117, USA

Rizzs, Rick (Sportscaster)
4008 243rd Pl SE
issaauah, WA 98029-7586

Rizzuto, Garth (Athlete, Hockey Player)
JO Ced(lr Bowl Cres RR 4
Fernie, BC V0B 1M4, Canada

R. Keating, William (Congressman, Politician)
315 Cannon HOB
Washington, DC 20515, USA

R. Labrador, Raul (Congressman, Politician)
1523 Longworth HOB
Washington, DC 20515, USA

R. Langevin, James (Congressman, Politician)
109 Cannon HOB
Washington, DC 20515, USA

Rlchardson, Robert (Nobel Prize Laureate)
4 Hunter Ln
Ithaca, NY 14850-9662, USA

R M A, Bharathimohan (Actor)
31/8 Madley Lind Street
T Nagar
Chennai, TN 600 017, INDIA

Roa, Joe (Athlete, Baseball Player)
677 E Brickley Ave
Hazel Park, MI 48030-1270, USA

Roa Bastos, Augusto (Writer)
Berutti 2828
Martinez
Buenos Aires, ARGENTINA

Roach, Andy (Athlete, Hockey Player)
PO Box488
Mattawan, MI 49071-0488

Roach, Jason (Athlete, Baseball Player)
12295 SE Birkdale Run
Jupiter, FL 33469-1746, USA

Roach, Jay (Director, Producer, Writer)
c/o Staff Member *Everyman Pictures*
3000 W Olympic Blvd
Suite 1500
Santa Monica, CA 90404, USA

Roach, John (Athlete, Football Player)
4101 San Carlos St
Dallas, TX 75205, USA

Roach, Mel (Athlete, Baseball Player)
4131 Southaven Rd
Richmond, VA 23235-1026, USA

Roache, Linus (Actor)
c/o Staff Member *WME (LA)*
9601 Wilshire Blvd Fl 3
Beverly Hills, CA 90210, USA

Roaches, Carl (Athlete, Football Player)
1314 Twining Oaks Ln
Missouri City, TX 77489, USA

Roaf, William L (Willie) (Athlete, Football Player)
1900 E 38th Ave
Pine Bluff, AR 71601, USA

Roan, Michael (Athlete, Football Player)
11275 Green Valley Rd
Sebastopol, CA 95472, USA

Roan, Oscar (Athlete, Football Player)
9 Pringle Ln
Rockwall, TX 75087, USA

Roark, Terry P (Educator)
1752 Edward Dr
Laramie, WY 82072, USA

Roarke, Mike (Athlete, Baseball Player)
940 Quaker Ln Apt 2302
East Greenwich, RI 02818-5085, USA

Roath, Stephen D (Business Person)
Longs Drug Stores
141 N Civic Dr
Walnut Creek, CA 94596, USA

Robach, Amy (Correspondent)

Robards, Jake (Actor)
c/o Staff Member *Don Buchwald &
Associates Inc (NY)*
10 E 44th St
New York, NY 10017

Robards, Sam (Actor)
Rigberg Roberts Rugolo
1180 S Beverly Dr
#601
Los Angeles, CA 90035, USA

Robb, Annasophia (Actor)
c/o Alissa Vradenburg *Untitled
Entertainment (LA)*
350 S. Beverly Dr #200
Beverly Hills, CA 90212, USA

Robb, Charles (Politician)
612 Chain Bridge Rd
Me Lean, VA 22101-1810, USA

Robb, David (Actor)
c/o Staff Member *Emptage Hallett*
14 Rathbone Pl
London W1T 1HT, UNITED KINGDOM
(UK)

Robb, Doug (Musician)

Robb, Lynda Bird Johnson (Misc)
612 Chain Bridge Rd.
McLean, VA 22101, USA

Robb, Lynda Johnson (Politician)
612 Chain Bridge Rd
Me Lean, VA 22101-1810, USA

Robb, Riddick (Athlete, Football Player)
101 Hearthstone Dr
Woodstock, GA 30189-5263, USA

Robb, Walter L (Business Person, Inventor)
1358 Ruffner Road
Niskayuna, NY 12309, USA

Robbers on High Street (Music Group)
c/o Staff Member *Paradigm (Monterey)*
404 W Franklin St
Monterey, CA 93940, USA

Robbie, Margot (Actor)
c/o Chris Huvane *Management 360*
9111 Wilshire Blvd
Beverly Hills, CA 90210, USA

Robbie, Timothy J (Tim) (Football Executive)
Miami Dolphins
7500 SW 30th St
Davie, FL 33314, USA

Robbins, Amy (Actor)
c/o Staff Member *Artists Rights Group
(ARG)*
4 Great Portland St
London W1W 8PA, UNITED KINGDOM
(UK)

Robbins, Anthony (Tony) (Motivational Speaker, Writer)
Robbins Research International Inc
9888 Carroll Center Rd #100
San Diego, CA 92126, USA

Robbins, Austin (Athlete, Football Player)
4627 Hilltop Ter SE
Washington, DC 20019, USA

Robbins, Barret (Athlete, Football Player)
26186 Shadow Rock Ln
Valencia, CA 91381, USA

Robbins, Brian (Director)
c/o Staff Member *Tollin/Robbins
Management*
4130 Cahuenga Blvd
Unit 305
Toluca Lake, CA 91602, USA

Robbins, Bruce (Athlete, Baseball Player)
13023 E 239th St
Noblesville, IN 46060-6988, USA

Robbins, Deanna (Actor)
630 N Keystone St
Burbank, CA 91506, USA

Robbins, Doug (Athlete, Baseball Player, Olympic Athlete)
7655 W Randolph County Line
Williamsburg, IN 47393-9500, USA

Robbins, Jake (Athlete, Baseball Player)
14208 Castle Abbey Ln
Charlotte, NC 28277-1612, USA

Robbins, Jane (Actor)
Scott Marshall Mgmt
44 Perry Road
London W3 7NA, UNITED KINGDOM
(UK)

Robbins, John (Writer)
c/o Staff Member *Red Wheel / Weiser
/Conari*
65 Parker St
Suite 7
Newburyport, MA 01950, USA

Robbins, Kelly (Golfer)
1025 Lincoln Dr
Weidman, MI 48893-9365, USA

Robbins, Lizz (Model)
c/o Michael (Mike) Esterman
Esterman.Com, LLC
Prefers to be contacted via email
MD, USA

Robbins, Randy (Athlete, Football Player)
1131 E Valle Vista Dr
Nogales, AZ 85621, USA

Robbins, Tim (Actor, Director)
c/o Jen Turner *Wolf Kasteler Van Iden &
Associates (NY)*
584 Broadway
Suite 310
New York, NY 10012, USA

Robbins, Tom (Writer)
PO Box 338
La Conner, WA 98257, USA

Robbins, Tootie (Athlete, Football Player)
6712 W Shannon St
Chandler, AZ 85226-1669, USA

Robelot, Jane (Correspondent)
CBS-TV
News Dept
51 W 52nd St
New York, NY 10019, USA

Robens of Woldingham, Alfred (Educator, Government Official)
2 Laleham Abbey
Staines, Middx TW18 1SZ, UNITED
KINGDOM (UK)

Roberge, Bert (Athlete, Baseball Player)
267 Sunderland Dr
Auburn, ME 04210-9232, USA

Roberson, Antoinette (Musician)
c/o Staff Member *Diva Central Inc*
7510 W Sunset Blvd Ste 1445
Los Angees, CA 90046, USA

Roberson, Chris (Athlete, Baseball Player)
10626 Liberty Bell Dr
Tampa, FL 33647-3656, USA

Roberson, Irvin (Bo) (Athlete, Football
Player, Track Athlete)
820 N Raymond Ave
Apt 47
Pasadena, CA 91103, USA

Roberson, James (Athlete, Football Player)
417 LaBarre Ct
Saint Johns, FL 32259, USA

Roberson, James W (Cinematographer)
PO Box 121013
Big Bear Lake, CA 92315, USA

Roberson, Kevin (Athlete, Baseball Player)
1565 E North Port Rd
Decatur, IL 62526-2823, USA

Roberson, Rick (Athlete, Basketball
Player)
635 W West Ave
Fullerton, CA 92832-2120, USA

Roberson, Sid (Athlete, Baseball Player)
1625 Felch Ave
Jacksonville, FL 32207-5404, USA

Robert, Jacques F (Attorney, Attorney
General, General)
14 Villa Saint-Georges
Antony 92160, FRANCE

Robert, Rene (Athlete, Hockey Player)
1400 Majestic Woods Dr
Grand Island, NY 14072-1180, CANADA

Roberto, Phil (Athlete, Hockey Player)
5238 Ottawa Ave
Niagara Falls, ON L2E 4Y8, Canada

Roberts, Alfredo (Athlete, Football Player)
20406 Donegal Ln
Strongsville, OH 44149, USA

Roberts, Allene (Actor)
7703 Carlton Dr SW
Huntsville, AL 35802, USA

Roberts, Bernard (Musician)
Uwchlaw'r Coed
Llanbedr
Gwynedd LL45 2NA, WALES

Roberts, Bert C Jr (Business Person)
MCI WorldCom Inc
500 Clinton Dr
Clinton, MS 39056, USA

Roberts, Beverly
30912 Ariana Lane
Laguna Niguel, CA 92677

Roberts, Beverly (Actor)
30912 Ariana Lane
Laguna Niguel, CA 92677, USA

Roberts, Brad (Musician)
Macklam Feldman Mgmt
1505 W 2nd Ave
#200
Vancouver, BC V6H 3Y4, CANADA

Roberts, Bret (Actor)
c/o Scott Karp *Crystal Sky Pictures*
10203 Santa Monica Blvd
5th Floor
Los Angeles, CA 90067, USA

Roberts, Brian (Athlete, Baseball Player)
4712 Higel Ave
Sarasota, FL 34242-1208, USA

Roberts, Brian L (Business Person)
Comcast
1500 Market St Fl #33E
Philadelphia, PA 19102, USA

Roberts, Bruce (Musician, Songwriter,
Writer)
c/o Staff Member *Gorfaine/Schwartz
Agency Inc*
4111 W Alameda Ave
Suite 509
Burbank, CA 91505, USA

Roberts, Cecil (Misc)
United Mine Workers
8315 Lee Highway
#500
Fairfax, VA 22031, USA

Roberts, Cokie (Correspondent)
5315 Bradley Blvd
Bethesda, MD 20814, USA

Roberts, Cokie (Journalist)
5315 Bradley Blvd
Bethesda, MD 20814-1244, USA

Roberts, Dale (Athlete, Baseball Player)
206 Berry Ave
Versailles, KY 40383, USA

Roberts, Dallas (Actor)
c/o Marnie Briskin *Circle of Confusion
(NY)*
107-23 71st Rd #300
Forest Hills, NY 11375, USA

Roberts, Danny (Reality TV Star)
c/o Staff Member *Heffner Management*
80 Vine St.
Suite 203
Seattle, WA 98121, USA

Roberts, Dave (Athlete, Baseball Player)
6937 Laurel Valley Dr
Fort Worth, TX 76132-4461, USA

Roberts, Dave (Athlete, Baseball Player)
San Diego Padres
PO Box 122000
Attn Coaching Staff
San Diego, CA 92112-2000, USA

Roberts, Dave (Athlete, Baseball Player)
1208 Crestview Dr
Cardiff By The Sea, CA 92007-1400, USA

Roberts, Dave (Athlete, Baseball Player)
9705 Sam Bass Trl
Fort Worth, TX 76244-6092, USA

Roberts, David (Athlete, Hockey Player)
Telemus Capital Partners
110 Miller Ave Ste 300, MI 48104-1305

Roberts, David (Dave) (Athlete, Track
Athlete)
14310 SW 73rd Ave
Archer, FL 32618, USA

Roberts, Dee (Artist)
2012 N 19th St
Boise, ID 83702, USA

Roberts, Doris (Actor)
6225 Quebec Dr
Los Angeles, CA 90068, USA

Roberts, Doug (Athlete, Hockey Player)
PO Box 1011
Old Lyme, CT 06371-0999, USA

Roberts, Emma (Actor)
c/o David Sweeney *Sweeney
Management*
6253 Hollywood Blvd
Suite 201
Los Angeles, CA 90028, USA

Roberts, Eric (Actor)
c/o Mark Teitelbaum *Teitelbaum Artists
Group*
8840 Wilshire Blvd
3rd Floor
Beverly Hills, CA 90212, USA

Roberts, Fred (Athlete, Basketball Player)
463 Knight Cir
Alpine, UT 84004-1259, USA

Roberts, Gary (Athlete, Hockey Player)
12348 NW 69th Ct
Parkland, FL 33076-3334

Roberts, Gordie (Athlete, Hockey Player)
7812 Bush Lake Dr
Minneapolis, MN 55438-3200, USA

Roberts, Gordon R (General)
1844 Horseshoe Bend Rd
Erwin, NC 28339-8566, USA

Roberts, Grant (Athlete, Baseball Player)
1299 Vista Captain Dr
El Cajon, CA 92020-1343, USA

Roberts, Gregory David (Writer)
c/o Staff Member *United Talent Agency
(UTA)*
9336 Civic Center Dr
Beverly Hills, CA 90210, USA

Roberts, Jake (Actor, Writer)
Box 3859
Stamford, CT 06905

Roberts, James A (Jim) (Athlete, Coach,
Hockey Player)
137 Ridgecrest Dr
Chesterfield, MO 63017-2653

Roberts, J D (Athlete, Football Coach,
Football Player)
6708 Trevi Ct
Oklahoma City, OK 73116, USA

Roberts, Jim (Athlete, Hockey Player)
PO Box 732
Markdale, ON NOC 1HO, Canada

Roberts, Joe (Athlete, Basketball Player)
10975 Elvessa St
Oakland, CA 94605-5511, USA

Roberts, John (Director)
c/o Staff Member *Independent Talent
Group (ITG-UK)*
Oxford House
76 Oxford St
London W1D 1BS, UK

Roberts, John (Judge)
US Supreme Court
1st St NE
Washington, DC 20543, USA

Roberts, John D (Misc)
California Institute of Technology
Chemistry Dept
Pasadena, CA 91125, USA

Roberts, John D (J D) (Athlete, Coach,
Football Player)
6708 Trevi Ct
Oklahoma City, OK 73116, USA

Roberts, Julia (Actor)
c/o Marcy Engleman *Engelman &
Company*
156 Fifth Ave #
Suite 711
New York, NY 10010, USA

Roberts, Julie (Musician)
c/o Staff Member *Creative Artists Agency
(CAA-LA)*
2000 Ave Of The Stars
Los Angeles, CA 90067, USA

Roberts, Kenny (Motorcycle Race,
Motorcycle Racer)
KR Marketing
419 Medina Road
Medina, OH 44256, USA

Roberts, Larry (Race Car Driver)
MR Motorsports
PO Box 194
Novi, MI 48376, USA

Roberts, Lawrence G (Scientist)
Caspian Networks
170 Baytech Dr
San Jose, CA 95134, USA

Roberts, Leon (Athlete, Baseball Player)
4711 Chapel Springs Ct
Arlington, TX 76017-1204, USA

Roberts, Leonard (Business Person)
Tandy Corp
100 Throckmorton St
Fort Worth, TX 76102, USA

Roberts, Leonard (Athlete, Baseball
Player)
1027 Waterford Dr
Dallas, TX 75218, USA

Roberts, Leonard (Actor)
c/o Lena Roklin *Luber Roklin
Management*
8530 Wilshire Blvd
6th Floor
Beverly Hills, CA 90211, USA

Roberts, Leon "Bip" (Athlete, Baseball
Player)
3569 Rosincress Dr
San Ramon, CA 94582-5078, USA

Roberts, Leon (Bip) (Athlete, Baseball
Player)
3569 Rosincress Dr
San Ramon, CA 94582, USA

Roberts, Loren (Athlete, Golfer)
8429 Orchard Hill Drive
Germantown, TN 38138-6297, USA

Roberts, Louie
2401 12th Ave. So.
Nashville, TN 37203

Roberts, Lynn
42 Vespers Way
Okatie, SC 29909-6216, USA

Roberts, Marcus (Musician)
Columbia Artists Mgmt Inc
165 W 57th St
New York, NY 10019, USA

Roberts, Marvin (Athlete, Basketball
Player)
6202 Carriage Gate Ln SE
Mableton, GA 30126-7714, USA

Roberts, M Brigitte (Writer)
Atkins & Stone
29 Fernshaw Road
London SW10 0TG, UNITED KINGDOM
(UK)

Roberts, Mica (Musician)
c/o Curt Motley *Paradigm (Nashville)*
124 12th Ave S
Suite 410
Nashville, TN 37203, USA

Roberts, Michael D (Actor)
c/o Staff Member *Talent Company, The*
P.O. Box 4227
Burbank, CA 91503, USA

Roberts, Nora (Writer)
19239 Burnside Bridge Road
Keedysville, MD 21756, USA

Roberts, Pat (Politician)
2203 Whiteoaks Dr
Alexandria, VA 22306-2436, USA

Roberts, Paul H (Mathematician)
PO Box 951567
Los Angeles, CA 90095, USA

Roberts, Rachel (Actor, Model)
c/o Staff Member *Models 1*
12 Macklin St
Covent Gardens
London WC2B 5SZ, UK

Roberts, Ralph J (Business Person)
Comcast Corp
1500 Market St
Philadelphia, PA 19102, USA

Roberts, Randy (Actor)
Ryan Artists, Inc
c/o Mary Dangerfield
239 NW 13th Ave Ste 215
Portland, OR 97209, USA

Roberts, Randy (Actor)
14220 Winterset Dr
Greenwell Springs, LA 70739, USA

Roberts, Randy (Actor)
Attn: Renee Amaireh
14220 Winterset Dr
Greenwell Springs, LA 70739, USA

Roberts, Richard J (Nobel Prize Laureate)
New England Biolabs
New England Biolabs 240 County Rd
Ipswich, MA 01938-2723, USA

Roberts, Rick
9150 Wilshire Blvd. #350
Beverly Hills, CA 90212-3427

Roberts, R Michael (Scientist)
2213 Hominy Branch Court
Columbia, MO 65201, USA

Roberts, Robin (Sportscaster, Television Host)
c/o Staff Member *Good Morning America (NY)*
ABC
147 Columbus Ave Fl 6
New York, NY 10023, USA

Roberts, Rodney (Race Car Driver)
MR Motorsports
PO Box 92826
Lakeland, FL 33804, USA

Roberts, Ryan (Athlete, Baseball Player)
6017 Avalon St
North Richland Hills, TX 76180-5593, USA

Roberts, Shawn (Actor)
c/o Staff Member *Christopher Wright Management*
3207 Winnie Dr
Los Angeles, CA 90068, USA

Roberts, Stanley (Athlete, Basketball Player)
1192 Congaree Rd
Hopkins, SC 29061-9704, USA

Roberts, Steven
5315 Bradley Blvd.
Bethesda, MD 20814

Roberts, Tanya (Actor)
c/o Jay Schwartz *Jay D Schwartz & Associates*
3151 Cahuenga Blvd W
Suite 220
Los Angeles, CA 90068, USA

Roberts, Thomas (Journalist, Television Host)
c/o Staff Member *MSNBC*
30 Rockfeller Plz
New York, NY 10112, USA

Roberts, Tiffany (Athlete, Olympic Athlete, Soccer Player)
2772 Ascot Dr
San Ramon, CA 94583-2504, USA

Roberts, Tim (Athlete, Football Player)
3930 Minnow Rd
Rex, GA 30273, USA

Roberts, Tony (Actor)
970 Park Ave
#8N
New York, NY 10028, USA

Roberts, Trish (Athlete, Basketball Player, Olympic Athlete)
218 Carver Dr
Monroe, GA 30655-1814, USA

Roberts, Vicki (Actor)
c/o Arthur Andelson *Kismet Talent Agency*
3435 Ocean Park Blvd.
Suite 107
Santa Monica, CA 90405, USA

Roberts, Walter (Athlete, Football Player)
268 Kenbrook Cir
San Jose, CA 95111, USA

Roberts, Willa (Stylist)
319 Stratford Rd
Brooklyn, NY 11218-4315, USA

Roberts, William H (Athlete, Football Player)
18520 NW 67th Ave
Apt 141
Hialeah, FL 33015, USA

Roberts, Willie (Athlete, Baseball Player)
11476 Emuness Rd
Jacksonville, FL 32218, USA

Roberts, Willis (Athlete, Baseball Player)
11478 Vera Dr
Jacksonville, FL 32218, USA

Roberts, Xavier (Business Person, Designer)
PO Box 1438
Cleveland, GA 30528, USA

Robertson, Alvin (Athlete, Basketball Player, Olympic Athlete)
6515 Amber Oak
San Antonio, TX 78249-1586, USA

Robertson, Andre (Athlete, Baseball Player)
2229 Cross Ln
Orange, TX 77630-2561, USA

Robertson, Belinda (Designer, Fashion Designer)
BR Cashmere
22 Palmerston Place
Edinburgh EH12 5AL, SCOTLAND

Robertson, Bob (Athlete, Football Player)
411 Belle Monti Ct
Aptos, CA 95003, USA

Robertson, Bob (Athlete, Baseball Player)
10015 Shinnamon Dr SW
Cumberland, MD 21502-6149, USA

Robertson, Brittany (Britt) (Actor)
c/o Francis Okwu *Zero Gravity Management*
6363 Wilshire Blvd
Suite 300
Los Angeles, CA 90048, USA

Robertson, Connor (Athlete, Baseball Player)
2201 Champions Cir
Franklin, TN 37064-2870, USA

Robertson, Dale (Actor)
PO Box 850707
Yukon, OK 73085, USA

Robertson, Daryl (Athlete, Baseball Player)
52 Princeton Dr
Midvale, UT 84047-7514, USA

Robertson, David (Athlete, Baseball Player)
c/o Team Member *New York Yankees*
Yankee Stadium
161st St & River Ave
Bronx, NY 10451, USA

Robertson, Davis (Dancer)
Joffrey Ballet
70 E Lake St
#1300
Chicago, IL 60601, USA

Robertson, DeWayne (Athlete, Football Player)
1000 Fulton Ave
Hempstead, NY 11550, USA

Robertson, Don (Athlete, Baseball Player)
5715 W Monte Vista Rd
Phoenix, AZ 85035-3626, USA

Robertson, Geordie (Athlete, Hockey Player)
1 Scarborough Park
Rochester, NY 14625-1363

Robertson, Gordon (Religious Leader, Television Host)
c/o 700 Club *Christian Broadcasting Network (CBN)*
977 Centerville Tpke
Virginia Beach, VA 23464, USA

Robertson, Isiah (Athlete, Football Player)
P.O. Box 1405
Mabank, TX 75147, USA

Robertson, Jenny (Actor)
Shelter Entertainment
9255 Sunset Blvd
#1010
Los Angeles, CA 90069, USA

Robertson, Jerry (Race Car Driver)
Quick Time Motorsports
124 N. 325 W. #58-6
Hurricane, UT 84737, USA

Robertson, Jim (Athlete, Baseball Player)
2515 109th Ave SE
Bellevue, WA 98004-7331, USA

Robertson, Kathleen (Actor)
c/o Staff Member *Jeff Morrone Entertainment*
9350 Wilshire Blvd
Suite 224
Beverly Hills, CA 90212, USA

Robertson, Kimmy (Actor)
Commercials Unlimited
8383 Wilshire Blvd
#850
Beverly Hills, CA 90211, USA

Robertson, Korie
The Duck Commander
117 Kings Ln
Monrow, LA 71292, USA

Robertson, Leslie E (Engineer)
Robertson Fowler Assoc
211 E 46th St
New York, NY 10017, USA

Robertson, Lisa
1365 Enterprise Dr.
West Chester, PA 18380

Robertson, Marcus A (Athlete, Football Player)
3218 Cypress Point Dr
Missouri City, TX 77459, USA

Robertson, Mike (Athlete, Baseball Player)
2626 E Viking Rd
Las Vegas, NV 89121-4114, USA

Robertson, Nate (Athlete, Baseball Player)
7918 W 53rd St N
Maize, KS 67101-9185, USA

Robertson, Oscar (Athlete, Basketball Player, Olympic Athlete)
621 Tusculum Ave
Cincinnati, OH 45226-1771, USA

Robertson, Pat (Religious Leader, Television Host)
PO Box 64303
Virginia Beach, VA 23467, USA

Robertson, Phil (Reality TV Star)
c/o Staff Member *Gurney Productions*
8929 S. Sepulveda Blvd
Suite 510
Los Angeles, CA 90045, USA

Robertson, Rich (Athlete, Baseball Player)
32202 Sandwedge Dr
Waller, TX 77484, USA

Robertson, Rich (Athlete, Baseball Player)
1201 Crescent Ter
Sunnyvale, CA 94087-2855, USA

Robertson, Robbie (Musician, Songwriter, Writer)
323 14th St
Santa Monica, CA 90402, USA

Robes, Ernest C (Bill) (Skier)
3 Mile Road
Etna, NH 03750, USA

Robey, Rick (Athlete, Basketball Player)
15129 Chestnut Ridge Cir
Louisville, KY 40245-5291, USA

Robidas, Stephane (Athlete, Hockey Player)
3216 Wellshire Ct
Plano, TX 75093-3458

Robidoux, Billy Joe (Athlete, Baseball Player)
2 King George Dr
Ware, MA 01082-9799, USA

Robidoux, Florent (Athlete, Hockey Player)
5 Pearce Dr
Marden, MB R6M 1R2, CANADA

Robie, Jarod (Race Car Driver)
Robie Racing
232 Chester Rd.
Candia, NH 03034, USA

Robinowitz, Joseph R (Editor, Publisher)
TV Guide Magazine
Editorial Dept
100 Matsonford Road
Radnor, PA 19080, USA

Robins, Lee N (Scientist)
Washington University
Medical School
Psychiatry Dept
Saint Louis, MO 63110, USA

Robins, Oliver (Actor, Director)
c/o Dawn Goodson *Genius Talent Management*
342 1/2 N Genesee Ave
Los, CA 90036, USA

Robinson, Aldrick (Athlete, Football Player)
c/o Jordan Woy *Willis and Woy Management*
3030 Olive St #520
Dallas, TX 75219, USA

Robinson, Alexia
3500 W. Olive #920
Burbank, CA 91505

Robinson, Alicia (Stylist)
c/o Staff Member *Ford Models (Chicago)*
311 W Superior St
Chicago, IL 60654, USA

Robinson, Andrea (Actor)
c/o Alan Saffron *Saffron Management*
9171 Wilshire Blvd #441
Beverly Hills, CA 90210, USA

Robinson, Andrew (Actor)
2671 Byron Place
Los Angeles, CA 90046, USA

Robinson, Ann (Actor)
1357 Elysian Park Dr
Los Angeles, CA 90026, USA

Robinson, Arthur H (Misc)
7707 N Brookline Dr
#302
Madison, WI 53719, USA

Robinson, Bo (Athlete, Football Player)
P.O. Box 2323
Coppell, TX 75019, USA

Robinson, Brooks (Athlete, Baseball Player)
P.O. Box 1168
Baltimore, MD 21203-1168, USA

Robinson, Bruce (Director)
c/o Rand Holston *Creative Artists Agency (CAA-LA)*
2000 Ave Of The Stars
Los Angeles, CA 90067, USA

Robinson, Bruce (Athlete, Baseball Player)
1310 Dellcrest Ln
La Jolla, CA 92037-5207, USA

Robinson, Bumper (Actor)
c/o David Altman *Altman Greenfield & Selvaggi*
200 Park Avenue S #8
New York, NY 10003, United States

Robinson, Cary (Stylist)
c/o Staff Member *Karlee Artist Management*
2658 Griffith Park Blvd
#171
Los Angeles, CA 90039, USA

Robinson, Charles
10000 Santa Monica Blvd. #305
Los Angeles, CA 90067

Robinson, Charles Knox
10637 Burbank Blvd.
No. Hollywood, CA 91601

Robinson, Chip (Race Car Driver)
PO Box 476
Oldwick, NJ 08858, USA

Robinson, Chris (Musician)

Robinson, Chris (Director)
c/o Peter Safran *The Safran Company*
8748 Holloway Dr
Los Angeles, CA 90069, USA

Robinson, Christina (Actor)
c/o Bill Perlman *New Talent Management*
PO Box 2939
Beverly Hills, CA 90213, USA

Robinson, Clarence (Arnie) (Athlete, Track Athlete)
2904 Ocean View Blvd
San Diego, CA 92113, USA

Robinson, Cliff (Athlete, Basketball Player)
98 S Bardsbrook Cir
Spring, TX 77382-2858, USA

Robinson, Clifford (Athlete, Basketball Player)
702 Sandia Pl
Franklin Lakes, NJ 07417-2120, USA

Robinson, Craig (Athlete, Baseball Player)
648 Picketts Mill Dr
Shreveport, LA 71115-3862, USA

Robinson, Craig (Actor)
c/o Mark Schulman *3 Arts Entertainment Inc*
9460 Wilshire Blvd
7th Floor
Beverly Hills, CA 90210, USA

Robinson, Daniel (Baseball Player)
10889 Dauphine St
Shreveport, LA 71106-8524, USA

Robinson, Dave (Athlete, Baseball Player)
6140 Camino Del Rincon
San Diego, CA 92120-3112, USA

Robinson, David (Athlete, Basketball Player)
PO Box 691207
San Antonio, TX 78269-1207, USA

Robinson, David M (Athlete, Basketball Player)
Ship Mates, Inc.
24165 IH-I O West
San Antonio, TX 78257, USA

Robinson, Dawn (Actor, Musician)
c/o Jonathan Clardy *CN Publicity*
9107 Wilshire Blvd
Suite 450
Beverly Hills, CA 90210, USA

Robinson, Dewey (Athlete, Baseball Player)
1388 Cottonwood Trl
Sarasota, FL 34232-3437, USA

Robinson, Don (Athlete, Baseball Player)
1215 86th Ct NW
Bradenton, FL 34209-9307, USA

Robinson, Doug (Athlete, Hockey Player)
6 Tiffany Crt
St Catharines, ON L2M 7N3, Canada

Robinson, Dwight P (Financier)
Government National Mortgage Assn
451 7th St SW
Washington, DC 20410, USA

Robinson, Earl (Athlete, Baseball Player)
6895 Oakwood Dr
Oakland, CA 94611, USA

Robinson, Eddie (Athlete, Baseball Player)
6104 Cholla Dr
Fort Worth, TX 76112-1105, USA

Robinson, Elizabeth
12706 E. Pacific Circle #202
Aurora, CO 80014

Robinson, Emily (Musician)
c/o Staff Member *Creative Artists Agency (CAA-LA)*
2000 Ave Of The Stars
Los Angeles, CA 90067, USA

Robinson, Emily Erwin (Athlete, Football Player)
4400 Falcon Pkwy
Flowery Branch, GA 30542, USA

Robinson, Fatima
Fatima
8306 Wilshire Blvd
PMB 833
Beverly Hills, CA 90211, USA

Robinson, Floyd (Athlete, Baseball Player)
P.O. Box 152419
San Diego, CA 92195-2419, USA

Robinson, Flynn (Athlete, Basketball Player)
11875 Manor Dr
Apt 1
Hawthorne, CA 90250-2950, USA

Robinson, Frank (Athlete, Baseball Player, Coach)
15557 Aqua Verde Dr
Los Angeles, CA 90077-1503, USA

Robinson, Frank (Athlete, Football Player)
15401 E Wyoming Dr
Unit C
Aurora, CO 80017, USA

Robinson, Gerald (Athlete, Football Player)
4708 Scarborough Pl
Stone Mountain, GA 30087, USA

Robinson, Glenn (Basketball Player, Coach)
Franklin & Marshall College
Athletic Dept
Lancaster, PA 17604, USA

Robinson, Jackie (Athlete, Basketball Player)
10595 Riva Grande Ct
Las Vegas, NV 89135-2455, USA

Robinson, Jacob (Baseball Player)
Chicago American Giants
1300 Giddings Ave SE
Grand Rapids, MI 49506-3216, USA

Robinson, James (Baseball Player)
Philadelphia Stars
65 W 96th St Apt 22G
New York, NY 10025-6533, USA

Robinson, Janice (Musician)
c/o Staff Member *Diva Central Inc*
7510 W Sunset Blvd Ste 1445
Los Angees, CA 90046, USA

Robinson, Jay (Actor)
13757 Milbank Ave
Sherman Oaks, CA 91403, USA

Robinson, Jeff (Athlete, Baseball Player)
27 Weber Ln
Trabuco Canyon, CA 92679-5235, USA

Robinson, Jeff (Athlete, Baseball Player)
5317 W 158th Pl
Overland Park, KS 66224, USA

Robinson, Jerry (Athlete, Football Player)
1408 Fairoaks Ct
Merced, CA 95340, USA

Robinson, John A (Athlete, Coach, Football Coach, Football Player)
6991 Goldstone Rd
Carlsbad, CA 92009-1711, USA

Robinson, Johnny N (Athlete, Football Player)
3209 S Grand St
Monroe, LA 71202, USA

Robinson, Julie Anne (Director)
c/o Leslie Maskin *United Talent Agency (UTA)*
9336 Civic Center Dr
Beverly Hills, CA 90210, USA

Robinson, Keith (Actor)
c/o Staff Member *Stone Manners Salners Agency (LA)*
9911 W Pico Blvd Ste 1400
Los Angeles, CA 90035, USA

Robinson, Keith (Musician)
c/o Staff Member *Paradigm (NY)*
360 Park Ave S Fl 16
New York, NY 10010, USA

Robinson, Kenneth (Government Official)
12 Grove Terrace
London NW5, UNITED KINGDOM (UK)

Robinson, Kerry (Athlete, Baseball Player)
133 Vlasis Dr
Ballwin, MO 63011-3055, USA

Robinson, Kim Stanley (Writer)
c/o Vince Gerardis *Grok! Studio*
Prefers to be contacted via email or telephone
Los Angeles, CA, USA

Robinson, Koren (Athlete, Football Player)
12 Henry Ave
Belmont, NC 28012, USA

Robinson, Larry (Athlete, Coach, Hockey Player)
10709 Winding Stream Way_
Bradenton, FL 34212-5255

Robinson, Larry (Athlete, Hockey Player)
New Jersey Devils
165 Mulberry St
Newark, NJ 07102-3607

Robinson, Laura (Actor)
Henderson/Hogan
8285 W Sunset Blvd
#1
West Hollywood, CA 90046, USA

Robinson, Leon (Leon) (Actor, Producer)
c/o Leo Bozzuto *HYPHENATE*
9701 Wilshire Blvd.
10th floor
Beverly Hills, CA 90212, USA

Robinson, Leroy
1183 Broad Rd
Tignall, GA 30668-1205, USA

Robinson, Madeleine
63 av. de Chillon
Territet-Veytaux, SWITZERLAN D1820

Robinson, Marcus (Athlete, Football
Player)
P.O. Box 1924
Fort Valley, GA 31030, USA

Robinson, Mark (Athlete, Football Player)
303 Pennsylvania Ave
Palm Harbor, FL 32223, USA

Robinson, Mary (Ex-President, Politician)
United Nations Headquarters Office of
Human Rights
Geneva CH-1211, Switzerland

Robinson, Matt (Athlete, Football Player)
12374 Mandarin Rd
Jacksonville, FL 32223, USA

Robinson, Moe (Athlete, Hockey Player)
3811 Gregoire Rd
Russell, ON K4R 1E5, Canada

Robinson, Nichole (Actor)
c/o Tiffany Kuzon *Evolution Entertainment
(LA)*
901 N Highland Ave
Los Angeles, CA 90038, USA

Robinson, Oliver (Athlete, Basketball
Player)
9640 Eastpointe Cir
Birmingham, AL 35217-5202, USA

Robinson, Patrick (Athlete, Football
Player)
Cincinnati Bengals
3875 N Advantage Way Dr
Apt 104
Memphis, TN 38128, USA

Robinson, Patrick (Designer, Fashion
Designer)
Gap
1 Harrison Street
San Francisco, CA 94105, USA

Robinson, Paul (Athlete, Football Player)
1303 W 26th St
Safford, AZ 85546, USA

Robinson, Rachel (Baseball Player)
The Jackie Robinson Foundation
75 Varick St Fl 2
New York, NY 10013, USA

Robinson, Rachel (Misc)
Jackie Robinson Foundation 75 Varick St
Frnt 2
New York, NY 10013-1947, USA

Robinson, Rafael (Athlete, Football Player)
6203 Wynbrook Dr
Randolph, NJ 07869, USA

Robinson, Randall
1744 R St .NW
Washington, DC 20009

Robinson, Rich (Musician)
c/o Staff Member *Paradigm (Monterey)*
404 W Franklin St
Monterey, CA 93940, USA

Robinson, Richard D (Dave) (Athlete,
Football Player)
406 S Rose Blvd
Akron, OH 44320, USA

Robinson, Rob (Athlete, Hockey Player)
23466 Greening Dr
Novi, MI 48375-3225

Robinson, Robinson (Director)
c/o Peter Safran *The Safran Company*
8748 Holloway Dr
Los Angeles, CA 90069, USA

Robinson, Ron (Athlete, Baseball Player)
3128 E Race Ave
Visalia, CA 93292-6858, USA

Robinson, Ronnie (Athlete, Basketball
Player)
4169 S Germantown Rd
Memphis, TN 38125-2624, USA

Robinson, Roxanne (Stylist)
c/o Staff Member *Jed Root Inc*
61-A Walker St
New York, NY 10013, USA

Robinson, Rumeal (Athlete, Basketball
Player)
3645 Brushy Wood Dr
Loganville, GA 30052-5481, USA

Robinson, Sam (Athlete, Basketball Player)
130 W Harcourt St
Long Beach, CA 90805-2124, USA

Robinson, Sammy (Baseball Player)
Detroit Stars
503 Umatilla St SE
Grand Rapids, MI 49507-1218, USA

Robinson, Sandra Dee (Actor)
c/o Vincent Cirrincione *Vincent
Cirrincione Associates*
1516 N Fairfax Ave
Los Angeles, CA 90046, USA

Robinson, Shaun (Correspondent)
c/o Susan Haber *Haber Entertainment*
434 S Canon Dr
Suite 204
Beverly Hills, CA 90212, USA

Robinson, Shawna (Race Car Driver)
Shawna Robinson Racing
PO Box 1858
New Smyrna Beach, FL 32168, USA

Robinson, Shelton (Athlete, Football
Player)
18725 20th Dr SE
Bothell, WA 98012, USA

Robinson, Stephen K (Astronaut)
2405 Airline Dr
Friendswood, TX 77546-5509, USA

Robinson, Ted (Sportscaster)
c/o Lou Oppenheim *Headline Media
Management*
888 7th Ave #503
New York, NY 10106, USA

Robinson, Tony (Actor, Producer, Writer)
c/o Staff Member *Jeremy Hicks Associates*
114-115 Tottenham Court Rd
London W1T 5AH, UK

Robinson, Trayvon (Athlete, Baseball
Player)
1455 W 97th St
Los Angeles, CA 90047-3934, USA

Robinson, T Wayne
PO Box 249
McConnellsburg, PA 17233, USA

Robinson, V Gene (Religious Leader)
Saint Paul's Church
21 Centre St
Concord, NH 03301, USA

Robinson, Wendy Raquel (Actor)
c/o Patricia (Patty) Woo *Patty Woo
Management*
8906 W Olympic Blvd
Beverly Hills, CA 90211, USA

Robinson, Wilbert (Athlete, Basketball
Player)
2124 Bedell Rd
Grand Island, NY 14072-1652, USA

Robinson, William (Smokey) (Musician,
Producer, Songwriter, Writer)
Smokey Robinson Foundation
385 S Lemon Ave
Suite E181
Walnut, CA 91789, USA

Robinson, Zuleikha (Actor)
c/o Daniel Spilo *Industry Entertainment
Partners*
955 S Carrillo Dr
Suite 300
Los Angeles, CA 90048, USA

Robinson of Woolwich, John (Religious
Leader)
Trinity College
Cambridge CB2 1TQ, UNITED
KINGDOM (UK)

Robinson-Peete, Holly (Actor)
4848 Encino Ave
Encino, CA 91316, USA

Robisch, Dave (Athlete, Basketball Player)
1401 Guemes Ct
Springfield, IL 62702-6400, USA

Robiskie, Terry (Athlete, Football Player)
40 River Mountain Dr
Moreland Hills, OH 44022, USA

Robison, Bruce (Musician, Songwriter,
Writer)
Artists Envoy Agency
1016 16th Ave S
#101
Nashville, TN 37212, USA

Robison, Charlie (Musician, Songwriter)
c/o Staff Member *Paradigm (Monterey)*
404 W Franklin St
Monterey, CA 93940, USA

Robison, Paula (Musician)
18 Allison Ave
Staten Island, NY 10306, USA

Robison, Tommy (Athlete, Football Player)
3614 Misty Woods Cir
Milton, FL 32571-8388, USA

Robitaille, Luc (Athlete, Hockey Player)
370 25th St
Santa Monica, CA 90402-2522

Robitaille, Luc (Athlete, Hockey Player)
Los Angeles Kings
1111 S Figueroa St Ste 3100
Los Angeles, CA 90015-1333

Robitaille, Mike (Athlete, Hockey Player)
Buffalo Sabres
1 Seymour H Knox III Plz Ste 1
Buffalo, NY 14203-3096

Robl, Harold (Athlete, Football Player)
W1089 County Road C
Gleason, WI 54435, USA

Robles, Jorge (Actor)
c/o Staff Member *Televisa*
Blvd Adolfo Lopez Mateos 232
Colonia San Angel INN
DF CP 01060, MEXICO

Robles, Marisa (Musician)
38 Luttrll Ave
London SW15 6PE, UNITED KINGDOM
(UK)

Robles, Mike (Producer)
ICM
8942 Wilshire Blvd
Beverly Hills, CA 90212

Roboz, Zsuzsi (Artist)
6 Bryanston Court
George St
London W1H 7HA, UNITED KINGDOM
(UK)

Robson, Bryan (Soccer Player)
Middlesbrough FC
Riverside Stadium
Midds
Cleveland TS3 6RS, UNITED KINGDOM
(UK)

Robson, Tom (Athlete, Baseball Player)
8902 E Hercules Ct
Sun Lakes, AZ 85248-9005, USA

Robson, Wade (Choreographer)
c/o Andrew Jacobs *McDonald/Selznick
Assoc (MSA)*
1611A N El Centro Ave
Hollywood, CA 90028, USA

Robuchon, Joel (Chef)
Societe de Gestion Culinaire
67 Blvd du Gen M Valin
Paris 75015, FRANCE

Robuck, Nicolas (Nic) (Actor)
c/o Margot Menzel *Evolution
Entertainment (LA)*
901 N Highland Ave
Los Angeles, CA 90038, USA

Roby, Martha (Congressman, Politician)
414 Cannon HOB
Washington, DC 20515, USA

Robyn (Musician)
Lifeline
73C Saint Charles Square
London W10 6EJ, UNITED KINGDOM
(UK)

Rocard, Michel L L (Prime Minister)
Hotel de Ville
63 Rue M Berteaux
Conflans-Sainte-Honorine 78700,
FRANCE

Rocca, Constantino (Golfer)
Golf Products International
5719 Lake Lindero Dr
Agoura Hills, CA 91301, USA

Rocca, Costentino (Golfer)
Golf Projects International
5719 Lake Lindero Dr
Agoura Hills, CA 91301-1413, USA

Rocca, Mo (Correspondent)
c/o Don Epstein *Greater Talent Network
Inc*
437 Fifth Ave
7th Floor
New York, NY 10016, USA

Rocca, Peter (Swimmer)
534 Hazel Ave
San Bruno, CA 94066, USA

Rocco, Alex (Actor)
c/o Staff Member *Bresler Kelly &
Associates*
11500 W Olympic Blvd
Suite 510
Los Angeles, CA 90064, USA

Rocco, Rinaldo (Actor)
Carol Levi Co
Via Giuseppe Pisanelli
Rome 00196, ITALY

Rocha, Coco (Musician)
c/o Christina Neuman *Full Picture (NY)*
915 Broadway
20th Floor
New York, NY 10010, USA

Rocha, Enrique (Actor)
c/o Staff Member *Televisa*
Blvd Adolfo Lopez Mateos 232
Colonia San Angel INN
DF CP 01060, MEXICO

Rocha, John (Designer, Fashion Designer)
12-13 Temple Ln
Dublin 2, IRELAND

Rocha, Kali (Actor)
c/o Katie Rhodes *Untitled Entertainment (LA)*
350 S. Beverly Dr #200
Beverly Hills, CA 90212, USA

Roche, Alden (Athlete, Football Player)
1082 Farragut St
New Orleans, LA 70114, USA

Roche, Anthony D (Tony) (Tennis Player)
5 Kapiti St
Saint Ives, NSW 2075, AUSTRALIA

Roche, Brian (Athlete, Football Player)
1358 Oak Tree Cir
Chino Hills, CA 91709, USA

Roche, E Kevin (Architect)
Roche Dinkeloo Assoc
20 Davis St
Hamden, CT 06517, USA

Roche, George A (Financier)
T Rowe Price Assoc
100 E Pratt St
Baltimore, MD 21202, USA

Roche, James G (Secretary)
Air Force Department
Secretary's Office
Pentagon
Washington, DC 20310, USA

Roche, John (Athlete, Basketball Player)
191 Clayton Ln
Unit 303
Denver, CO 80206-5679, USA

Rochefort, Jean (Actor)
Le Chene Rogneaux
Grosvre 078125, FRANCE

Rochefort, Leon (Athlete, Hockey Player)
1661 Notre-Dame St E
Trois-Rivieres, QC G8T 4J9, Canada

Rochefort, Normand (Athlete, Hockey Player)
7704 Camminare Dr
Sarasota, FL 34238-4777

Rochester, Paul (Athlete, Football Player)
218 Evans Dr
Jacksonville, FL 32250, USA

Rochford, Mike (Athlete, Baseball Player)
926 N 0 St
Lake Worth, FL 33460-2746, USA

Rochon, Debbie (Actor)
PO Box 1299
New York, NY 10009

Rochon, Frank (Athlete, Hockey Player)
1753 Signature Pl
Wilmington, NC 28405-4131, USA

Rochon, Lela (Actor)
3332 Clerendon Rd
Beverly Hills, CA 90210, USA

Rock (Actor, Wrestler)
World Wrestling Entertainment
Titan Towers
1241 E Main St
Stamford, CT 06902, USA

Rock, Angela (Athlete, Volleyball Player)
University of California - SB
Athletic Dept
1210 Cheadle Hall
Santa Barbara, CA 93106, USA

Rock, Chris (Actor, Comedian, Director, Producer)
c/o Leslie Sloane *Baker Winokur Ryder Public Relations BWR (BWR-NY)*
292 Madison Ave
12th Floor
New York, NY 10017, USA

Rock, Pete
Reach Global
3500 Rose Crest Ln
Fairfax, VA 22033, USA

Rock, Tony (Comedian)
c/o Staff Member *New Wave Entertainment (LA)*
2660 W Olive Blvd
Burbank, CA 91505, USA

Rock, Walt (Athlete, Football Player)
1030 Highams Ct
Woodbridge, VA 22191, USA

Rockburne, Dorothea G (Artist)
140 Grand St
New York, NY 10013, USA

Rock City (Music Group, Musician)
c/o Noel Palm *Element Talent Agency*
3211 Cahuenga Blvd W Ste 104
Los Angeles, CA 90068, USA

Rockefeller, David (Financier)
146 East 65th St & Lexington Ave
New York, NY 10021, USA

Rockefeller, Happy (Governor, Politician, Vice President)
812 5th Ave
New York, NY 10065-7253, USA

Rockefeller, Jay (Governor, Politician)
2121 Park Rd NW
Washington, DC 20010-1049, USA

Rockefeller, Laurance S (Misc)
Rockefeller Bros Fund
30 Rockefeller Plaza
#5600
New York, NY 10112, USA

Rockefeller, Sharon Percy
1940 Shepherd St NW
Washington, DC 20011

Rocker, David (Athlete, Football Player)
465 Belle Dr
Fayetteville, GA 30214, USA

Rocker, John (Athlete, Baseball Player)
1223 Manor Oaks Ct
Atlanta, GA 30338-2756, USA

Rockett, Pat (Athlete, Baseball Player)
17107 Eagle Hollow Dr
San Antonio, TX 78248-1553, USA

Rockett, Rikki (Musician)
c/o Staff Member *HK Management (LA)*
10866 Wilshire Blvd Ste 200
Los Angeles, CA 90024, USA

Rockford, Jim (Athlete, Football Player)
1829 Camden St
Springfield, IL 62702, USA

Rockwell, Martha (Coach, Skier)
Dartmouth College
PO Box 9
Hanover, NH 03755, USA

Rockwell, Nancy (Athlete, Baseball Player)
54658 County Road 101
Elkhart, IN 46514-8967, USA

Rockwell, Robert
18428 Coastline Dr.
Malibu, CA 90265

Rockwell, Sam (Actor)
c/o Liz Mahoney *ID Public Relations (ID-LA)*
7060 Hollywood Blvd
8th Floor
Los Angeles, CA 90028, USA

Rockwood, Marcia (Editor)
Reader's Digest
Editorial Dept
PO Box 100
Pleasantville, NY 10572, USA

Rodan, Jay (Actor)
c/o Staff Member *WmE2 (WMA-LA)*
1 William Morris Pl
Beverly Hills, CA 90212, USA

Rodas, Rich (Athlete, Baseball Player)
6877 Bergano Pl
Rancho Cucamonga, CA 91701-8606, USA

Rodata, Antonio (Scientist)
European Space Agency 8-10 rue Mario-Nikis Attn: Director Generals Office
Paris F-75738, France

Roday, James (Actor, Writer)
c/o Larry Taube *Principal Entertainment (LA)*
1964 Westwood Blvd #400
Los Angeles, CA 90025, USA

Rodd, Marcia (Actor)
11738 Moorpark St
#C
Studio City, CA 91604, USA

Roddam, Franc (Director)
William Morris Agency
52/53 Poland Place
London W1F 7LX, UNITED KINGDOM (UK)

Roddick, Andy (Athlete, Tennis Player)
140 Shermans Mill Dr
Ingram, TX 78025, USA

Rodenhauser, Mark (Athlete, Football Player)
1451 Charlotte Hwy
York, SC 29745, USA

Rodenheiser, Richard "Dick" (Athlete, Hockey Player)
285 Babcock St.
Boston, MA 02215, USA

Rodenhiser, Dick (Athlete, Hockey Player, Olympic Athlete)
186 State St
Framingham, MA 01702-2462, USA

Roder, Mirro (Athlete, Football Player)
181 Herrick Rd
Riverside, IL 60546, USA

Roderick, Brande (Actor, Model)
c/o Shannon Barr *Shannon Barr Public Relations*
1600 Rosecrans Ave
Media Center Bldg. 7, 4th Floor
Manhattan Beach, CA 90266-3708, USA

Rodgers, Aaron (Athlete, Football Player)
2360 Crown Pointe Blvd
Suamico, WI 54173, USA

Rodgers, Anton
The White House Lower Basildon
Berkshire, ENGLAND

Rodgers, Bill (Athlete, Olympic Athlete, Track Athlete)
Bill Rodgers Running Center 1 N Market St Ste 353
Boston, MA 02109-6244, USA

Rodgers, Del (Athlete, Football Player)
3112 Yosemite Park Way
Elk Grove, CA 95758, USA

Rodgers, Derrick (Athlete, Football Player)
5550 SW 192nd Ter
Southwest Ranches, FL 33332, USA

Rodgers, Jimmie (Musician)
42230 Sandy Bay Road
Bermuda Dunes, CA 92203-1394, USA

Rodgers, Jimmy (Basketball Coach, Coach)
4995 Marsh Turtle Trail
Unit 101
Estero, FL 33928, USA

Rodgers, Johnny (Athlete, Football Player, Heisman Trophy Winner)
PO Box 11172
Omaha, NE 68111-0172, USA

Rodgers, Michael (Actor)
c/o Adam Levine *Levine Okwu Erickson Management*
9601 Wilshire Blvd
3rd Floor
Beverly Hills, CA 90210, USA

Rodgers, Paul (Musician)
Work Hard PR
19D Pinhold Road
London SW16 5GD, United Kingdom

Rodgers, Phil (Golfer)
Eddle Elias Enterprises
4067 N Shore Dr
Akron, OH 44333-8305, USA

Rodgers, Robert "Buck" (Athlete, Baseball Player)
5181 W Knoll Dr
Yorba Linda, CA 92886-4338, USA

Rodgers, Robert (Buck) (Athlete, Baseball Player, Coach)
5181 W Knoll Dr
Yorba Linda, CA 92886, USA

Rodgers, Roscoe (Horse Racer)
7834 N Music Mountain Ln
Prescott Valley, AZ 86315-9085, USA

Rodgers-Cromartie, Dominique (Athlete, Football Player)
c/o Eugene Parker *Maximum Sports Management*
6435 W Jefferson Blvd
#197
Fort Wayne, IN 46804, USA

Rodin, Judith S (Educator)
35 Hillhouse Ave
New Haven, CT 06511, USA

Rodina, Irina (Athlete)
13243 Fiji Way #7
Marina del Rey, CA 90392, USA

Rodman, Dennis (Athlete, Basketball Player)
Rodman Group
4910 Campus Dr
Newport Beach, CA 92660-2119, USA

Rodman, Judy (Musician, Songwriter)
308 Cody Hill Pl
Nashville, TN 37211, USA

Rodrigue, George (Artist)
P.O. Box 51227
Lafayette, LA 70505, USA

Rodrigues, Bienvenido (Athlete, Baseball Player)
PO Box42
Santa Isabel, PR 00757-0042, USA

Rodrigues, Blenvenido (Baseball Player)
Chicago American Giants
PO Box 42
Santa Isabel, PR 00757-0042, USA

Rodrigues, Darryl (Stylist)
c/o Staff Member *Jed Root Inc*
61-A Walker St
New York, NY 10013, USA

Rodriguez, Adam (Actor)
c/o Melissa Stone *42West (LA)*
11400 W Olympic Blvd
Suite 1100
Los Angeles, CA 90064, USA

Rodriguez, Alex (Athlete, Baseball Player)
4358 N Bay Rd
Miami, FL 33140-2855, USA

Rodriguez, Anthony (Golfer)
13602 Summer Glen Dr
San Antonio, TX 78247-3510, USA

Rodriguez, Carlos (Athlete, Baseball Player)
7562 Burgstresser Ct
Canal Winchester, OH 43110-8432, USA

Rodriguez, Eddie (Athlete, Baseball Player)
4320 N Elias St
Mesa, AZ 85215-7740, USA

Rodriguez, Eduardo (President)
President's Office
Palacio de Gobierno
Plaza Murilla
La Paz, BOLIVIA

Rodriguez, Edwin (Athlete, Baseball Player)
7901 30th Ave N
Saint Petersburg, FL 33710-1151, USA

Rodriguez, Ellie (Athlete, Baseball Player)
Astro Melia 1787 Mansiones De Rio Piedras
SanJuan, PR 00926, USA

Rodriguez, Francisco (Athlete, Baseball Player)
c/o Staff Member *New York Mets*
Shea Stadium
123-01 Roosevelt Avenue
Flushing, NY 11368-1699, USA

Rodriguez, Freddy (Actor)
c/o Robbie Kass *Kass & Stokes Management*
9229 Sunset Blvd
Suite 504
Los Angeles, CA 90069, USA

Rodriguez, Freddy (Actor)
c/o Staff Member *Kass & Stokes Management*
9229 Sunset Blvd
Suite 504
Los Angeles, CA 90069, USA

Rodriguez, Genesis (Actor)
c/o Ivan De Paz *DePaz Management*
2011 N Vermont Ave.
Los Angeles, CA 90027, USA

Rodriguez, Geoffrey (Stylist)
c/o Staff Member *Mercury Artists*
8460 Higuera St Fl 2
Culver City, CA 90232, USA

Rodriguez, Henry (Athlete, Baseball Player)
295 Wadworth Ave
Apt 3F
New York, NY 10040-4416, USA

Rodriguez, Ivan (Pudge) (Athlete, Baseball Player)
15530 SW 70th Terr
Miami, FL 33193, USA

Rodriguez, Jai (Actor, Television Host)
c/o Michael Einfeld *Michael Einfeld Management*
10630 Moorpark Ave.
Ste. 101
Toluca Lake, CA 91602, USA

Rodriguez, Javier (Actor)
c/o Staff Member *Select Artists Ltd (CA-Valley Office)*
PO Box 4359
Burbank, CA 91503, USA

Rodriguez, Jesse (Stylist)
c/o Staff Member *Arlene Wilson Management*
807 N Jefferson St
#200
Milwaukee, WI 53202, USA

Rodriguez, Johnny
PO Box 23162
Nashville, TN 37202

Rodriguez, Jose Luis (El Puma) (Musician)
c/o Staff Member *BMG*
1540 Broadway
New York, NY 10036, USA

Rodriguez, Juan (Chi Chi) (Athlete)
Eddie Elias Enterprises
3916 Clock Pointe Trail #101
Stow, OH 44224

Rodriguez, Maggie (Anchor)
c/o Staff Member *CBS News Productions*
524 W 57th St
8th Floor
New York, NY 10019, USA

Rodriguez, Michelle (Actor)
c/o Jason Weinberg *Untitled Entertainment (LA)*
350 S. Beverly Dr #200
Beverly Hills, CA 90212, USA

Rodriguez, Paul (Actor)
c/o Staff Member *ICM Partners (ICM-LA)*
10250 Constellation Blvd Fl 7
Los Angeles, CA 90067, USA

Rodriguez, Raini (Actor)
c/o Susan Osser *Susan Osser Talent Company*
Prefers to be contacted via telephone and email
Los Angeles, CA, USA

Rodriguez, Ramon (Actor)
c/o Allan Grifka *Alchemy Entertainment*
7024 Melrose Ave
Suite 420
Los Angeles, CA 90038, USA

Rodriguez, Rich (Athlete, Baseball Player)
231 Village Commons Blvd Unit 27
Camarillo, CA 93012-7819, USA

Rodriguez, Rick (Athlete, Baseball Player)
Oakland Athletics 7000 Coliseum Way
Ste 3 Attn Coaching Staff
oakland, CA 94621-1992, USA

Rodriguez, Rico (Actor)
c/o Traci Harper *Harper PR*
3940 Laurel Canyon Blvd #1010
Studio City, CA 91604, USA

Rodriguez, Robert (Director, Producer)
c/o Robert Newman *WME (LA)*
9601 Wilshire Blvd Fl 3
Beverly Hills, CA 90210, USA

Rodriguez, Steve (Athlete, Baseball Player)
28905 Bardell Dr
Agoura Hills, CA 91301-2133, USA

Rodriguez, Vic (Athlete, Baseball Player)
631 SE 9th Pl
Cape Coral, FL 33990-2950, USA

Rodriguez, Wandy (Athlete, Baseball Player)
2501 Still Bay St
Pearland, TX 77584-8289, USA

Rodriquez, La Mala (Musician)
c/o Staff Member *Zona Bruta Discos S.L.*
C Clemente Fernandez 56 Local Izda
Madrid 28011, Spain

Rodriquez, Paul (Skateboarder)
Plan B Skateboards
121 Waterworks Way
Suite 100
Irvine, CA 92618, USA

Roe, Billy (Race Car Driver)
9595 E Sunnyside Drive
Scottsdale, AZ 85260, USA

Roe, Elwin (Preacher) (Athlete, Baseball Player)
204 Wildwood Ter
West Plains, MO 65775, USA

Roe, Rocky (Athlete, Baseball Player)
2033 Stefano Ct
Mount Dora, FL 32757-6511, USA

Roe, Tommy
PO Box 26037
Minneapolis, MN 55426

Roebuck, Daniel (Actor)
c/o Leslie Allan-Rice *Leslie Allan-Rice Management*
1007 Maybrook Dr
Beverly Hills, CA 90210, USA

Roebuck, Ed (Athlete, Baseball Player)
3434 Warwood Rd
Lakewood, CA 90712-3751, USA

Roedel, Herb (Athlete, Football Player)
4810 201st St
Flushing, NY 11364, USA

Roeg, Nicolas
14 Courtnell St
London, ENGLAND W2 5BX

Roelofs, Wendell (Scientist)
4 Crescence Dr
Geneva, NY 14456-1302, USA

Roemer, Charles "Buddy" (Governor, Politician)
1437 Nashville Ave
New Orleans, LA 70115-4349, USA

Roemer, Sarah (Actor, Model)
c/o Staff Member *Luber Roklin Management*
8530 Wilshire Blvd
6th Floor
Beverly Hills, CA 90211, USA

Roenick, Jeremy (Athlete, Hockey Player, Olympic Athlete)
Roenicklife LLC
8912 E Pinnacle Peak Rd #F9-661
Scottsdale, AZ 85255, USA

Roenicke, Gary (Athlete, Baseball Player)
11023 Rough and Ready Rd
Rough and Ready, CA 95975-9750, USA

Roenicke, Josh (Athlete, Baseball Player)
8130 Santa Rosa Ct
Sarasota, FL 34243-3000, USA

Roenicke, Ron (Athlete, Baseball Player)
787 Avenida Salvador
San Clemente, CA 92672-2369, USA

Roeper, Lindsey
Palms Playboy Club
4321 W Flamingo Rd
Las Vegas, NV 89103, USA

Roerig, Zach (Actor)
c/o Loch Powell *Leverage Management*
3030 Pennsylvania Ave
Santa Monica, CA 90404, USA

Roesler, Mike (Athlete, Baseball Player)
12033 Fallen Leaf Ct
Fort Wayne, IN 46845-8992, USA

Roessler, Pat (Athlete, Baseball Player)
4910 Hidden Oaks Trl
Sarasota, FL 34232-3040, USA

Roethlisberger, Ben (Athlete, Football Player)
c/o Ryan Tollner *REP 1 Sports Group*
2 Corporate Park
Suite 106
Irvine, CA 92606, USA

Roethlisberger, Fred (Athlete, Gymnast, Olympic Athlete)
W9920 710th Ave
River Falls, WI 54022-4017, USA

Roffe-Barker, Melanie (Director)
c/o Staff Member *Don Capo Entertainment*
Ste 5 South Bank Terrace
Surbiton
Surrey KT6 6DG, UNITED KINGDOM (UK)

Roffe-Barker, Nigel (Director, Producer, Writer)
c/o Staff Member *Don Capo Entertainment*
Ste 5 South Bank Terrace
Surbiton
Surrey KT6 6DG, UNITED KINGDOM (UK)

Roffe-Steinrotter, Diann (Athlete, Olympic Athlete, Skier)
248 N 29th St
Camp Hill, PA 17011-2904, USA

Rogan, Joe (Comedian)
c/o Ivo Fischer *WME (LA)*
9601 Wilshire Blvd Fl 3
Beverly Hills, CA 90210, USA

Rogan, Markus (Athlete, Swimmer)
Oesterreichischer Schwimmverband
Engerthstrasse 267-269
Wien 1020, Austria

Rogas, Dan (Athlete, Football Player)
2352 Evalon St
Beaumont, TX 77702, USA

Rogen, Seth (Actor)
c/o Marsha McManus Principal
Entertainment (LA)
1964 Westwood Blvd #400
Los Angeles, CA 90025, USA

Roger, Elena (Musician)
c/o Bill Butler Industry Entertainment
Partners
955 S Carrillo Dr
Suite 300
Los Angeles, CA 90048, USA

Roger, John (Religious Leader)
John Roger Foundation
2101 Wilshire Blvd
Santa Monica, CA 90403, USA

Rogers, Bill (Golfer)
710 Patterson Ave
San Antonio, TX 78209-5637, USA

Rogers, Brendan (Athlete, Football Player)
RBC Dominion Securities
800-1 Lombard Pl
Winnipeg, MB R3B0Y2, Canada

Rogers, Chad (Business Person, Reality TV
Star)
Hilton & Hyland
250 N Canon Dr
Beverly Hills, CA 90210, USA

Rogers, Dennis (Athlete)
c/o Staff Member Big Machine Media
780 3rd Ave
15th Floor
New York, NY 10017, USA

Rogers, Gene (Misc)
P.O. Box 3537
McAlester, OK 74502-3637, USA

Rogers, George (Athlete, Football Player,
Heisman Trophy Winner)
1007 Lofty Pine Dr
Columbia, SC 29212, USA

Rogers, Greg (Writer)
614 Big Hill Cir
McAlester, OK 74501-2591, USA

Rogers, Harold (Congressman, Politician)
2406 Rayburn HOB
Washington, DC 20515, USA

Rogers, Jackie (Race Car Driver)
5731 Camellia Lane
Wilmington, NC 28409, USA

Rogers, Jane
1485 S. Beverly Dr. #8
Los Angeles, CA 90035

Rogers, Jimmy (Athlete, Baseball Player)
7235 S Janet St Trlr 10
Oklahoma City, OK 73150-7426, USA

Rogers, Joy
4141 W. Kling St. #3
Burbank, CA 91505-3309

Rogers, Kenny (Athlete, Baseball Player)
1730 Ottinger Rd
Roanoke, TX 76262-7367, USA

Rogers, Kenny (Musician)
1730 Ottinger Rd
Roanoke, TX 76262, USA

Rogers, Kenny (Photographer)
RR 1 Box 100
Colbert, GA 30628, USA

Rogers, Kevin (Athlete, Baseball Player)
604 Douglas Ave
Cleveland, MS 38732-2026, USA

Rogers, Lamarr (Baseball Player)
1240 Spring Green Ln
Burnsville, MN 55306-6413, USA

Rogers, Melody
2051 Nichols Canyon Rd.
Los Angeles, CA 90046

Rogers, Mike (Congressman, Politician)
324 Cannon HOB
Washington, DC 20515, USA

Rogers, Mike (General)
5348 Calle Real Apt D
Santa Barbara, CA 93111-1675, USA

Rogers, Mike (Athlete, Hockey Player)
63 Calling Horse Estate
Calgary, AB T3Z 1H4, Canada

Rogers, Mike (Athlete, Hockey Player)
Calgary Flames
PO Box 1540
Calgary, AB T2P 3B9, Canada

Rogers, Mimi (Actor)
c/o Staff Member Millbrook Farm
Productions
11693 San Vicente Blvd #241
Los Angeles, CA 90049, USA

Rogers, Paul (Actor)
9 Hillside Gardens
London, ENGLAND N6 5SU, United
Kingdom

Rogers, Reg (Actor)
c/o Staff Member Brookside Artists
Management (NY)
250 W 57th St
Suite 2303
New York, NY 10107, USA

Rogers, Shorty
PO Box 1711
Bellingham, WA 98227

Rogers, Stephen D (Steve) (Baseball
Player)
3746 S Madison Ave
Tulsa, OK 74105, USA

Rogers, Steve (Athlete, Baseball Player)
2 Lenape Ln
Princeton Junction, NJ 08550-1817, USA

Rogers, Suzanne (Actor)
11266 Canton Dr
Studio City, CA 91604, USA

Rogers, Tracy (Athlete, Football Player)
1011 Tam O Shanter Dr
Bakersfield, CA 93309, USA

Rogers, Wayne (Actor)
11828 La Grange Ave
Los Angeles, CA 90025, USA

Roges, Al (Athlete, Basketball Player)
6217 Scenic Ave
Los Angeles, CA 90068-2914, USA

Rogge, Jacques (Misc)
Int'l Olympic Committee
Chateau de Vidy
Lausanne 1007, SWITZERLAND

Roggeman, Tom (Athlete, Football Player)
51267 Pembridge Ct
Granger, IN 46530, USA

Roggenburk, Garry (Athlete, Baseball
Player)
33550 Streamview Dr
Avon, OH 44011-2597, USA

Roggin, Fred
3000 W. Alameda Ave.
Burbank, CA 91523

Rogiani, Elisabetta (Stylist)
7466 Beverly Blvd
Los Angeles, CA 90036, USA

Rogin, Gilbert L (Editor)
21 W 10th St
#5A
New York, NY 10011, USA

Rogodzinski, Mike (Athlete, Baseball
Player)
1 Emlyn Ct
Clementon, NJ 08021-4871, USA

Rogoff, Ilan (Musician)
Apdo 1098
Palma de Mallorca 07080, SPAIN

Rogow, Stan (Producer)
c/o Staff Member ICM Partners (ICM-LA)
10250 Constellation Blvd Fl 7
Los Angeles, CA 90067, USA

Rogue Wave (Music Group)
c/o Staff Member Paradigm (Monterey)
404 W Franklin St
Monterey, CA 93940, USA

Rohan, Margo (Stylist)
c/o Staff Member Halley Resources
37 W 20th St
#603
New York, NY 10011, USA

Rohatgi, Payal (Actor, Bollywood)
c/o Bunty Bahl Carving Dreams
Entertainment
304-305, Oberoi Chambers II
B Wing, Off New Link Road, Andheri
West
Mumbai 400053, INDIA

Rohde, Bruce (Business Person)
ConAgra Inc
1 ConAgra Dr
Omaha, NE 68102, USA

Rohde, Dave (Athlete, Baseball Player)
1707 Port Barmouth Pl
Newport Beach, CA 92660-5314, USA

Rohde, David (Journalist)
229 W 43rd St
New York, NY 10036-3913, USA

Rohde, Kristen (Actor)
c/o Staff Member Gersh (LA)
9465 Wilshire Blvd
Suite 600
Beverly Hills, CA 90212, USA

Rohde, Len (Athlete, Football Player)
324 Alta Vista Ave
Los Altos, CA 94022, USA

Rohde, Lisa (Athlete, Olympic Athlete,
Rower)
9807 Whitethorn Dr
Charlotte, NC 28277-9029, USA

Rohini (Actor, Bollywood)
D-1 Ist Floor Anandsree Apartments
32 Hindi Prachara Saba Street
Chennai, TN 600017, INDIA

Rohlander, Uta (Athlete, Track Athlete)
Liebigstr 9
Leuna 06237, GERMANY

Rohlinger, Ryan (Athlete, Baseball Player)
2100 Canary St
West Bend, WI 53090-2764, USA

Rohloff, Jon (Athlete, Hockey Player)
40057 County Road 242
Cohasset, MN 55721-8819

Rohloff, Kenneth (Athlete, Basketball
Player)
206 Cedar Ln
Atlantic Beach, NC 28512-5747, USA

Rohloff, Todd (Athlete, Hockey Player)
309 W Avenue C
Bismarck, ND 58501-3418

Rohm, Elisabeth (Actor)
c/o Katie Mason Luber Roklin
Management
8530 Wilshire Blvd
6th Floor
Beverly Hills, CA 90211, USA

Rohm, Elizabeth (Actor)
c/o Katie Mason Luber Roklin
Management
8530 Wilshire Blvd
6th Floor
Beverly Hills, CA 90211, USA

Rohn, Dan (Athlete, Baseball Player)
2406 Arthur Ct
Traverse City, MI 49685-7411, USA

Rohner, Clayton (Actor)
6924 Treasure Trail
Los Angeles, CA 90068

Rohner, Georges (Artist)
Galerie Framond
3 Rue des Saints Peres
Paris 75006, FRANCE

Rohr, Bill (Athlete, Baseball Player)
67545 S Lae:una Dr
Cathedral City, CA 92234-7487, USA

Rohr, James E (Financier)
PNC Bank Corp
1 PNC Plaza
249 5th Ave
Pittsburgh, PA 15222, USA

Rohr, Les (Athlete, Baseball Player)
1508 Wicks Ln
Billings, MT 59105-4412, USA

Rohrbacher, Dana (Congressman,
Politician)
2300 Rayburn HOB
Washington, DC 20515, USA

Rohrer, Heinrich (Nobel Prize Laureate)
IBM Research Laboratory
IBM Research Lab Saumerstrasse 4
Ruschilkon, CH 8803, SWITZERLAND

Rohrer, Jeff (Athlete, Football Player)
3201 Executive Cir
Dallas, TX 75234, USA

Rohrmeier, Dan (Athlete, Baseball Player)
1029 Ede:etree Ln
Cincinnati, OH 45238-4318, USA

Roig, Tony (Athlete, Baseball Player)
24125 E Lakeridge Dr
Liberty Lake, WA 99019, USA

Roitman, Esther (Stylist)
c/o Staff Member Walter Schupfer
Management Corp
413 W 14th St
3rd Floor
New York, NY 10014, USA

Roiz, Sasha (Actor)
c/o Pearl Hanan *Pearl Hanan Management*
7775 Sunset Blvd
Suite 118
Los Angeles, CA 90046, USA

Roizman, Bernard (Biologist)
5555 S Everett Ave
Chicago, IL 60637, USA

Roizman, Owen (Cinematographer)
17533 Magnolia Blvd
Encino, CA 91316, USA

Roja (Actor)
12 43rd Street
6th Avenue Ashok Nagar
Chennai, TN 600 083, INDIA

Roja (Actor, Bollywood)
8 Saravana Mudali Street
T.Nagar
Chennai, TN 600017, INDIA

Rojas, Euky (Athlete, Baseball Player)
14777 SW 80th St
Miami, FL 33193-1515, USA

Rojas, Geoffrey (Prince Royce) (Musician)
c/o Staff Member *WmE2 (WMA-Miami)*
119 Washington Ave
Suite 400
Miami, FL 33139, USA

Rojas, Goffrey (Prince Royal) (Musician)
c/o Michael Vega *WmE2 (WMA-Miami)*
119 Washington Ave
Suite 400
Miami, FL 33139, USA

Rojas, Mel (Athlete, Baseball Player)
15645 Collins Ave
Apt 802
North Miami Beach, FL 33160, USA

Rojas, Nydia (Musician)
Silverlight Entertainment
9171 Wilshire Blvd
#426
Beverly Hills, CA 90210, USA

Rojas, Octavio R (Cookie) (Athlete, Baseball Player, Coach)
19195 Mystic Pointe Dr
Apt 3002
Aventura, FL 33180-4505, USA

Rojcewicz, Susan (Athlete, Basketball Player, Olympic Athlete)
16360 Blackie Rd
Salinas, CA 93907-8855, USA

Rojeski, Shawn (Athlete, Olympic Athlete)
510 11th St NW
Chisholm, MN 55719-1157, USA

Rojo, Ana Patricia (Actor)
c/o Staff Member *Televisa*
Blvd Adolfo Lopez Mateos 232
Colonia San Angel INN
DF CP 01060, MEXICO

Rojo, Gustavo (Actor)
c/o Staff Member *Televisa*
Blvd Adolfo Lopez Mateos 232
Colonia San Angel INN
DF CP 01060, MEXICO

Roker, Al (Correspondent, Television Host)
c/o Staff Member *Today Show, The*
30 Rockefeller Plz
New York, NY 10112, USA

Rokita, Todd (Congressman, Politician)
236 Cannon HOB
Washington, DC 20515, USA

Rokk, Marika
Mozartstr. 15
Baden, AUSTRIA A-2500

Rokke, Ervin J (General)
810 Dolan Drive
Monument, CO 80132-2219, USA

Roland, Ed (Musician, Songwriter, Writer)
Spivak Entertainment
11845 W Olympic Blvd
#1125
Los Angeles, CA 90064, USA

Roland, Jim (Athlete, Baseball Player)
1802 Arbor Way Dr
Shelby, NC 28150, USA

Roland, Joan (Stylist)
370 E 76th St
#A-201
New York, NY 10021, USA

Roland, Johnny E (Athlete, Coach, Football Player)
8701 S Hardy Dr
Tempe, AZ 85284, USA

Rolandi, Gianna (Opera Singer)
Columbia Artists Mgmt Inc
165 W 57th St
New York, NY 10019, USA

Rolen, Scott (Athlete, Baseball Player)
721 Kev Rovale Dr
Holmes Beach, FL 34217-1231, USA

Roleson, Dwayne (Athlete, Hockey Player)
705 Nelson St
Port Dover, ON N0A 1N2, Canada

Roles-Williams, Barbara (Athlete, Figure Skater, Olympic Athlete)
3790 Leisure Lane
Las Vegas, NV 89103, USA

Rolfe, Dale (Athlete, Hockey Player)
365 Hughson St
Gravenhurst, ON P1P 1G8, Canada

Rolfe, Johnson Anthony (Opera Singer)
I C M Artists
40 W 57th St
New York, NY 10019, USA

Rolison, Nathan (Nate) (Athlete, Baseball Player)
118 County Road 3709
Enterorise, MS 39330-7803, USA

Rolle, Butch (Athlete, Football Player)
17822 NW 15th St
Pembroke Pines, FL 33029, USA

Roller, Becky (Stylist)
801 S Chester St
Park Ridge, IL 60068-4614, USA

Roller, David E (Athlete, Football Player)
1404 Bristol Pkwy
Alpharetta, GA 30022, USA

Rollin, Betty (Correspondent, Writer)
67 Park Ave
New York, NY 10016, USA

Rolling Stones (Music Group)
c/o Fran Curtis *Rogers & Cowan PR (LA)*
Pacific Design Center
8687 Melrose Ave, 7th Floor
West Hollywood, CA 90069, USA

Rollins, Ed
c/o Staff Member *WmE2 (WMA-LA)*
1 William Morris Pl
Beverly Hills, CA 90212, USA

Rollins, Henry (Musician, Songwriter)
c/o Tiffany Kuzon *Evolution Entertainment (LA)*
901 N Highland Ave
Los Angeles, CA 90038, USA

Rollins, Jerry (Athlete, Hockey Player)
14062 Caminito Vistana
San Diego, CA 92130-3719, USA

Rollins, Jimmy (Athlete, Baseball Player)
120 Fox Chase Ct
Swedesboro, NJ 08085-3043, USA

Rollins, John (Golfer)
8703 Playground Court
Richmond, VA 23237, USA

Rollins, Kenneth (Athlete, Basketball Player, Olympic Athlete)
1497 N County Road 175 W
Greencastle, IN 46135-9239, USA

Rollins, Phil (Athlete, Basketball Player)
221 Norbourne Blvd
Louisville, KY 40207, USA

Rollins, Rich (Athlete, Baseball Player)
4146 Evergreen Ln
Richfield, OH 44286-9592, USA

Rollins, Rose (Actor)
c/o David Sweeney *Sweeney Management*
6253 Hollywood Blvd
Suite 201
Los Angeles, CA 90028, USA

Rollins, Sonny (Composer, Musician)
c/o Ted Kurland *Ted Kurland Associates*
173 Brighton Ave
Boston, MA 02134, USA

Rollins, Wayne (Tree) (Athlete, Basketball Player, Coach)
PO Box 1209
Apopka, FL 32704-1209, USA

Rolls, Damian (Athlete, Baseball Player)
11112 Shadybrook Dr
Tamoa, FL 33625-5708, USA

Roloff, Matt
23985 Grossen Rd.
Hillsboro, OR 97124

Roloson, Dwayne (Athlete, Hockey Player)
Global Hockey Consultants
175 Federal St Ste 1325
Attn Mark Witkin
Boston, MA 02110-2221, USA

Rolston, Brian (Athlete, Hockey Player, Olympic Athlete)
Sports Consulting Group
65 Monroe Ave Ste D
Pittsford, NY 14534-1318, USA

Rolston, Holmes III (Misc)
Colorado State University
Philosophy Dept
Fort Collins, CO 80523, USA

Rolston, Matthew (Photographer)
Venus Entertainment
3630 Eastham Dr
Culver City, CA 90232, USA

Roman, Bill (Athlete, Baseball Player)
1720 Yale Ct
Lake Forest, IL 60045-5117, USA

Roman, Dan (Baseball Player)
10313 Arran Ct
Huntersville, NC 28078-7021, USA

Roman, John (Athlete, Football Player)
13 Mendham Rd
Bernardsville, NJ 07924, USA

Roman, Joseph (Misc)
Glass & Ceramic Workers Union
556 E Town St
Columbus, OH 43215, USA

Roman, Kevin (Stylist)
c/o Staff Member *Ford Models (Chicago)*
311 W Superior St
Chicago, IL 60654, USA

Roman, Lauren
170 Flanders Drakestown Rd.
Flanders, NJ 07036-9736

Roman, Petre (Prime Minister)
Str Gogol 2
Sector 1
Bucharest, ROMANIA

Roman, Phil
10635 Riverside Dr.
Toluca Lake, CA 91602

Romanchych, Larry (Athlete, Hockey Player)
3989 206A St
Langley, BC V3A 7 A8, Canada

Romanek, Mark (Director)
c/o Staff Member *Creative Artists Agency (CAA-LA)*
2000 Ave Of The Stars
Los Angeles, CA 90067, USA

Romanenko, Roman Y (Cosmonaut)
Polchta Kosmonavtov
Moskovskoi Oblasti
Syvisdny Goroduk 141160, RUSSIA

Romanenko, Yuri V (Cosmonaut)
Polchta Kosmonavtov
Moskovskoi Oblasti
Syvisdny Goroduk 141160, RUSSIA

Romanetti, Ray (Horse Racer)
227 S Spring Valley Rd
Canonsburg, PA 15317-2823, USA

Roman Holiday
Box 475
London, ENGLAND

Romanick, Ron (Athlete, Baseball Player)
17108 E Kingstree Blvd Apt 1
Fountain Hills, AZ 85268-5556, USA

Romaniszyn, Jim (Athlete, Football Player)
619 Amy Lee Cir
Port Orange, FL 32127, USA

Romano, Christy Carlson (Actor)
c/o Staff Member *Global Artists Agency*
6253 Hollywood Blvd
Suite 508
Los Angeles, CA 90028, USA

Romano, Jason (Athlete, Baseball Player)
1411 Willow Oak Cir
Bradenton, FL 34209-7822, USA

Romano, John (Misc)
212 Valley Road
Merion Station, PA 19066, USA

Romano, Johnny (Athlete, Baseball Player)
160 W Pago Pago Dr
Naples, FL 34113-8616, USA

Romano, Larry (Actor)
Gold Marshak Liedtke
3500 W Olive Ave
#1400
Burbank, CA 91505, USA

Romano, Mike (Athlete, Baseball Player)
1202 N Lee Rd
Covington, LA 70433-1738, USA

Romano, Pete (Cinematographer)
HydroFlex Inc
5335 McConnell Ave
Los Angeles, CA 90066, USA

Romano, Ray (Actor, Comedian, Producer, Writer)
5225 Encino Ave
Encino, CA 91316, USA

Romano, Roberta (Attorney, Educator)
Yale University
Law School
127 Wall St
New Haven, CT 06520, USA

Romano, Roberto (Athlete, Hockey Player)
S865 Rue Brossard
Saint-Leonard, QC HlT 3R6, Canada

Romano, Rocco (Athlete, Football Player)
Calgary Stampeders
1817 Crowchild Trail NW
Calgary, AB T2M4R6, Canada

Romano, Tom (Athlete, Baseball Player)
1266 Penora St
Depew, NY 14043-4512, USA

Romano, Umberto (Artist)
162 E 83rd St
New York, NY 10028, USA

Romanos, John J (Jack) Jr (Publisher)
Pocket Books
1230 Ave of Americas
New York, NY 10020, USA

Romanov, Pyotr V (Government Official)
Communist Party
Bolshoy Komsomlsky Per 8/7
Moscow 10100, RUSSIA

Romanov, Stephanie (Actor)
c/o Staff Member *Diverse Talent Group*
9911 W Pico Blvd Ste 340W
Los Angeles, CA 90035, USA

Romanowski, Bill (Athlete, Football Player)
3706 Mount Diablo Blvd.
Suite 200
Lafayette, CA 94549, USA

Romansky, Monroe J (Doctor)
5600 Wisconsin Ave
Chevy Chase, MD 20815, USA

Romantics, The
1924 Spring St.
Paso Robles, CA 93446

Romanus, Richard (Actor)
Chasin Agency
8899 Beverly Blvd
#716
Los Angeles, CA 90048, USA

Romanus, Robert (Actor)
c/o Melanie Sharp *Sharp Talent*
117 N Orlando Ave
Los Angeles, CA 90048, USA

Roman Waugh, Ric (Director)
2967 E 3rd St
Los Angeles, CA 90033, USA

Romar, Lorenzo (Athlete, Basketball Player)
4408 164th Ln SE
Issaquah, WA 98027-9046, USA

Romario (Soccer Player)
Fluminense FC
Rua Alvaro Chaves 41
Rio de Janiero 22231-200, BRAZIL

Romashin, Anatoliy V (Actor)
Vspolny Per 16 Korp 1
#60
Moscow 103101, RUSSIA

Romatowski, Jenny (Athlete, Baseball Player)
678 Channing Dr
Palm Harbor, FL 34684-3911, USA

Rombough, Doug (Athlete, Hockey Player)
10434 Sunrise Lakes Blvd Apt 303
Sunrise, FL 33322-S961

Romby, Bob (Baseball Player)
Baltimore Elite Giants
38 Holman Mill Rd
Cumberland, VA 23040-2804, USA

Rome, Jim (Actor)
c/o Jeffrey Jacobs *Creative Artists Agency (CAA-LA)*
2000 Ave Of The Stars
Los Angeles, CA 90067, USA

Rome, Jim (Sportscaster)
3801 Marfield Ave
Tarzana, CA 91356-5812, USA

Rome, Stan (Athlete, Football Player)
4489 Green Island Rd
Valdosta, GA 31602, USA

Romelfanger, Charles (Misc)
Pattern Makers League
4106 34th Ave
Moline, IL 61265, USA

Romer, Roy R (Ex-Governor, Politician)
Strong American Schools
4861 County Road 43
Bailev, CO 80421-1138, USA

Romer, Suzanne F C (Prime Minister)
Prime Minister's Office
Willemstad, Curacao, NETHERLANDS ANTILLES

Romero, Celino (Musician)
Columbia Artists Mgmt Inc
165 W 57th St
New York, NY 10019, USA

Romero, Danny Jr (Boxer)
800 Salida Sandia SW
Albuquerque, NM 87105, USA

Romero, Ed (Athlete, Baseball Player)
1380 Wood Row Way
Wellington, FL 33414-9082, USA

Romero, George
c/o Staff Member *Gersh (LA)*
9465 Wilshire Blvd
Suite 600
Beverly Hills, CA 90212, USA

Romero, Gus (Stylist)
c/o Celebrity Stylist *Oliver Piro Inc*
725 Riverside Dr Apt 3A
New York, NY 10031, USA

Romero, J.C (Athlete, Baseball Player)
140 Augusta Ct
Fairhope, AL 36532-6352, USA

Romero, Mandy (Athlete, Baseball Player)
19280 SW 216th St
Miami, FL 33170-1214, USA

Romero, Ned (Actor)
19438 Lassen Ave
Northridge, CA 91324, USA

Romero, Patricia (Stylist)
c/o Staff Member *Perrella Management*
330 W 38th St Rm 1407
New York, NY 10018, USA

Romero, Randy (Horse Racer)
1019 Kaliste Sa loom Rd Aot 955
Lafayette, LA 70508-4936, USA

Romero, Richard (Actor)
c/o Staff Member *Select Artists Ltd (CA-Valley Office)*
PO Box 4359
Burbank, CA 91503, USA

Romijn, Rebecca (Actor, Model)
c/o Molly Madden *3 Arts Entertainment Inc*
9460 Wilshire Blvd
7th Floor
Beverly Hills, CA 90210, USA

Romine, Alton (Athlete, Football Player)
286 Highway 79
Phil Campbell, AL 35581, USA

Romine, Andrew (Athlete, Baseball Player)
22701 Fernwood St
Lake Forest, CA 92630-3612, USA

romine, Austin (Athlete, Baseball Player)
22701 Fernwood St
Lake Forest, CA 92630-3612, USA

Romine, Kevin (Athlete, Baseball Player)
22701 Fernwood St
Lake Forest, CA 92630-3612, USA

Romine, Paul (Race Car Driver)
Aerolite Racing
3645 Developer's Rd.
Indianapolis, IN 46227, United States

Rominger, Kent V (Astronaut)
2714 Bridgeport Avenue
Salt Lake City, UT 84121-5603, USA

Rominger, Kent V Captain (Astronaut)
2714 Bridgeport Ave
Salt Lake City, UT 84121-5603, USA

Rominski, Dale (Athlete, Hockey Player)
32043 Staman Ct
Farmington Hills, Ml 48336-1861

Romita Sr., John (Artist, Cartoonist)
11301 Olympic Blvd.
#587
Los Angeles, CA 90064, USA

Rommel, Ex-Mayor Manfred (Politician)
Eduard-Steinle-Str 60
Stuttgart D-70619, GERMANY

Rommelaere-Manning, Martha (Baseball Player)
503-3252 Glasgow Ave
Victoria, BC V8X 1M2, CANADA

Romney, Ann (Politician)
Mitt Romney for President Inc
19 Greensbrook Way
Belmont, MA 02478, USA

Romney, Mitt (Business Person, Politician)
Romney For President Inc
19 Greensbrook Way
Belmont, MA 02478-1126, USA

Romo, Daniela (Actor)
c/o Staff Member *Televisa*
Blvd Adolfo Lopez Mateos 232
Colonia San Angel INN
DF CP 01060, MEXICO

Romo, Sergio (Athlete, Baseball Player)
9738 E Idaho Ave
Mesa, AZ 85209-7071, USA

Romo, Tony (Athlete, Football Player)
c/o Tom Condon *CAA - St. Louis*
222 S Central Ave
Suite 1008
St Louis, MO 63105, USA

Ron, Duncan (Athlete, Football Player)
500 N Fountain Ave
Springfield, OH 45504-2539, USA

Ron, Moo-hyun (President)
President's Office
Chong Wa Dae
1 Sejong-no
Seoul, SOUTH KOREA

Ronaldo, Cristiano (Athlete, Soccer Player)
c/o Jorge Mendes *Gestifute (Porto)*
Praceta Do Bom Sucesso 61
Salas 706/7/8
Porto 4150-146, Portugal

Ronan, Ed (Athlete, Hockey Player)
70 Jefferson Rd.
Franklin, MA 02038-3363

Ronan, Len (Athlete, Hockey Player)
2006 SW Eastwood Ave.
Gresham, OR 97068, USA

Ronan, Marc (Athlete, Baseball Player)
5603 Chadwick Dr
Rogers, AR 72758-8223, USA

Ronan, Saoirse (Actor)
c/o Staff Member *Creative Artists Agency (CAA-LA)*
2000 Ave Of The Stars
Los Angeles, CA 90067, USA

Ronan, William J (Engineer)
525 S Flagler Dr
West Palm Beach, FL 33401, USA

Rondeau, Pete (Race Car Driver)
PO Box 1918
Biddeford, ME 04005, USA

Rondo, Rajon (Athlete, Basketball Player)
c/o Bill Duffy *BDA Sports Management (BDA-CA)*
700 Ygnacio Valley Rd
Suite 330
Walnut Creek, CA 94596, USA

Rondon, Gilberto (Gil) (Athlete, Baseball Player)
357 N Oak St Apt A
Orange, CA 92867-7737, USA

Ronettes, The
855 E. Twain #123411
Las Vegas, NV 89109

Roney, Matt (Athlete, Baseball Player)
1809 Nighthawk Ct
Edmond, OK 73034-6110, USA

Roney, Paul H (Judge)
US Court of Appeals
100 1st Ave S
Saint Petersburg, FL 33701, USA

Ronney, Paul D (Astronaut)
613 Ranchito Road
Monrovia, CA 91016, USA

Ronney, Paul D Dr (Astronaut)
613 Ranchito Rd
Monrovia, CA 91016-3733, USA

Ronning, Cliff (Athlete, Hockey Player)
317 Washington St.
St. Paul, MN 55102, USA

Ronningen, Jon (Wrestler)
Mellomasveien 132
Trollasen 1414, NORWAY

Rono, Peter (Athlete, Track Athlete)
Mount Saint Mary's College
Athletic Dept
Emmitsburg, MD 21727, USA

Ronson, Len (Athlete, Hockey Player)
2006 SW Eastwood Ave
Gresham, OR 97080-57S1

Ronson, Mark (Musician)
c/o Staff Member *Red Ink (Germany)*
Schlegelstr. 26b
Berlin 10115, Germany

Ronson, Samantha (DJ, Musician)
3012 Bentley Ct
Santa Monica, CA 90405, USA

Ronstadt, Linda (Musician)
c/o Sheldon (Shelly) Schultz *Trident
Media Group LLC*
41 Madison Ave
36th Floor
New York, NY 10010, USA

Ronty, Paul (Athlete, Hockey Player)
2300 Commonwealth Ave Apt 3-4
Auburndale, MA 02466-1796

Roocroft, Amanda (Opera Singer)
Ingpen & Williams
26 Wadham Road
London SW15 2LR, UNITED KINGDOM
(UK)

Roof, Gene (Athlete, Baseball Player)
175 Spring Valley Dr
Paducah, KY 42003-8894, USA

Roof, Michael (Actor)
c/o Staff Member *3 Arts Entertainment Inc*
9460 Wilshire Blvd
7th Floor
Beverly Hills, CA 90210, USA

Roof, Phil (Athlete, Baseball Player)
1301 Pillar Chase
Paducah, KY 42001-6137, USA

Rook, Jerry (Athlete, Basketball Player)
Route 9 Box 124L
Jonesboro, AR 72404, USA

Rook, Susan (Correspondent)
Cable News Network
News Dept
1050 Techwood Dr NW
Atlanta, GA 30318, USA

Rooker, Jim (Athlete, Baseball Player)
2378 Windchime Dr
Jacksonville, FL 32224-2016, USA

Rooker, Michael (Actor)
8330 Mcgroarty St
Sunland, CA 91040, USA

Roomes, Rolando (Athlete, Baseball
Player)
11520 E Pratt Ave
Mesa, AZ 85212-1949, USA

Roomful of Blues (Music Group,
Musician)
c/o Staff Member *Concerted Efforts*
P.O. Box 440326
Somerville, MA 02144, USA

Rooney, Art (Horse Racer)
1190 Washington Rd
Pittsburgh, PA 15228-1817, USA

Rooney, Dan (Football Executive)
940 N Lincoln Ave
Pittsburgh, PA 15233, USA

Rooney, Jim (Soccer Player)
New England Revolution
CMGI Field
1 Patriot Place
Foxboro, MA 02035, USA

Rooney, Joe Don (Musician)
LGB Media
1228 Pineview Lane
Nashville, TN 37211, USA

Rooney, Kevin (Actor)
c/o Staff Member *Emptage Hallett*
14 Rathbone Pl
London W1T 1HT, UNITED KINGDOM
(UK)

Rooney, Mickey (Actor, Director, Writer)
1400 Red Sail Cir
Westlake Village, CA 91361, USA

Rooney, Pat (Athlete, Baseball Player)
4825 Lighthouse Dr
Racine, WI 53402-2666, USA

Rooney, Patrick W (Business Person)
Cooper Tire & Rubber Co
Lima & Western Aves
Findlay, OH 45840, USA

Rooney, Steve (Athlete, Hockey Player)
5 Helen Dr
Canton, MA 02021-2404

Rooney, Timothy (Horse Racer)
810 Central Park Ave
Yonkers, NY 10704, USA

Rooney, Wayne (Soccer Player)
c/o Staff Member *Ian Monk Associates*
2 Station Rd
Gerrards Cross
Buckinghamshire SL9 8EL, UK

Rooney II, Art (Business Person, Football
Executive)
1300 Inverness Ave
Pittsburgh, PA 15217-1156, USA

Roop, Richard (Business Person)
Bottom Line Results Inc
743 Goldhills Pl S #239
Woodland Park, CO 80863-1101, USA

Roopenian, Mark (Athlete, Football
Player)
358 Charles River Rd
Watertown, MA 02472, USA

Rooper, Jemima (Actor)
c/o Staff Member *Conway van Gelder*
8-12 Broadwick St
London W1F 8HW, UK

Roos, Don (Actor, Producer)
c/o Steve Rabineau *United Talent Agency
(UTA)*
9336 Civic Center Dr
Beverly Hills, CA 90210, USA

Rooster (Music Group)
c/o Staff Member *BMG*
1540 Broadway
New York, NY 10036, USA

Rooster, The Red
PO Box 3859
Stamford, CT 06905

Root, Bill (Athlete, Hockey Player)
33 Hamilton Hall Dr
Markham, ON L3P 3L5, Canada

Root, Bonnie (Actor)
c/o Tracy Steinsapir *Main Title
Entertainment*
8383 Wilshire Blvd
Suite 408
Los Angeles, CA 90211, USA

Root, Stephen (Steven) (Actor)
c/o Jai Khanna *Brillstein Entertainment
Partners*
9150 Wilshire Blvd #350
Beverly Hills, CA 90212, USA

Roots, Melvin H (Misc)
Plasters & Cement Workers Union
1125 17th St NW
Washington, DC 20036, USA

Roots, The (Music Group)
c/o Cara Lewis *Creative Artists Agency
(CAA-LA)*
1325 Ave of the Americas
New York, NY 10019, USA

Roper, Dee Dee (Spinderella) (Musician)
Nest Plateau Records
1650 Broadway
#1130
New York, NY 10019, USA

Roper, John (Athlete, Football Player)
4213 Alice St
Houston, TX 77021, USA

Roper, John (Athlete, Baseball Player)
519 John Roper Ave
Raeford, NC 28376-2211, USA

Rorem, Ned (Composer, Writer)
PO Box 764
Nantucket, MA 02554, USA

Rorty, Richard M (Misc)
402 Peacock Dr
Charlottesville, VA 22903, USA

Rosa, John (Educator, General)
Citadel
President's Office
Charleston, SC 06520, USA

Rosa, Robi Draco (Composer, Musician,
Producer)
Tanner Mainstain Assoc
10866 Wilshire Blvd
#10000
Los Angeles, CA 90024, USA

Rosa, Rosa
6640 Sunset Blvd. #110
Los Angeles, CA 90028

Rosado, Eduardo (Opera Singer)
Calle 3
Ave Cupules 112A Col G Giberes
Menda, Yucatan 97070, MEXICO

Rosales, Adam (Athlete, Baseball Player)
1900 Woodland Ave
Park Ridge, IL 60068-1911, USA

Rosales, Jenny (Athlete, Golfer)
265 S Vine St
Anaheim, CA 92805-4128, USA

Rosales, Leo
952 N Ardmore Ave Apt 7
Los Angeles, CA 90029-3389, USA

Rosamund, John
4 Dean's Yard
London, ENGLAND SW1P

Rosand, David (Historian)
560 Riverside Dr
New York, NY 10027, USA

Rosario, Jimmy (Athlete, Baseball Player)
PO Box 9020739
San Juan, PR 00902-0739, USA

Rosario, Mel (Athlete, Baseball Player)
205 Round Tree Ct
Egg Harbor Township, NJ 08234-7910,
USA

Rosario, Santiago (Athlete, Baseball
Player)
Kansas City A's
PO Box 561238
Guayanilla, PR 00656-3238, USA

Rosas, Cesar (Musician, Songwriter,
Writer)
Monterey International
200 W Superior
#202
Chicago, IL 60610, USA

Rosato, Cristina (Actor)
c/o Sandy Martinez *Martinez Creative
Management*
7012 St Laurent Blvd
Suite 200
Montreal, QC H2S 3E2, Canada

Rosato, Genesia (Ballerina)
Royal Ballet
Covent Garden
Bow St
London WC2E 9DD, UNITED KINGDOM
(UK)

Rosato, Tony (Actor, Writer)
c/o Staff Member *Don Capo
Entertainment*
Ste 5 South Bank Terrace
Surbiton
Surrey KT6 6DG, UNITED KINGDOM
(UK)

Rosberg, Keke (Race Car Driver)
7 Rue Gabian
Monte Carlo 9800, MONACO

Rosburg, Bob (Golfer)
49425 Avenida Club La Quinta
La Quinta, CA 92253-2703, USA

Roschkov, Victor (Cartoonist, Editor)
Toronto Star
Editorial Dept
1 Yonge St
Toronto, ON M5E 1E5, CANADA

Rose, Adam (Actor)
c/o Steven Siebert *Lighthouse
Entertainment*
9220 W Sunset Blvd Ste 200
West Hollywood, CA 90069, USA

Rose, Amber (Actor)
30 Virginia Ln
Canonsburg, PA 15317, USA

Rose, Anika Noni (Actor)
c/o David Williams *David Williams
Management*
9614 Olympic Blvd
Suite F
Beverly Hills, CA 90212, USA

Rose, Axl (Musician, Songwriter, Writer)
5055 Latigo Canyon Rd
Malibu, CA 90265, USA

Rose, Barry (Athlete, Football Player)
1761 W White Ash Dr
Balsam Lake, WI 54810, USA

Rose, Bernard (Director, Producer, Writer)
c/o Jenne Casarotto *Casarotto Ramsay & Associates Ltd (UK)*
Waverley House
7-12 Noel St
London W1F 8GQ, UK

Rose, Bobby (Athlete, Baseball Player)
2713 Highview Dr
Bullhead City, AZ 86429-5928, USA

Rose, Brian (Athlete, Baseball Player)
5 Ashland St
South Dartmouth, MA 02748-3211, USA

Rose, Carol (Attorney, Educator)
Yale University
Law School
127 Wall St
New Haven, CT 06520, USA

Rose, Charles (Charlie) (Television Host)
Charlie Rose Inc
2100 Crystal Dr.
Arlington, VA 22202, USA

Rose, Charlie (Journalist)
499 Park Ave FilS
New York, NY 10022-1240, USA

Rose, Chris (Television Host)
c/o Staff Member *Best Damned Sports Show Period, The*
Fox Sports Net
10201 W Pico Blvd
Los Angeles, CA 90035, USA

Rose, Clarence (Golfer)
405 Walnut Creek Dr
Goldsboro, NC 27534-8995, USA

Rose, Cristine (Actor)
c/o Staff Member *Silver Massetti & Szatmary (SMS) Talent Inc*
8383 Wilshire Blvd
Suite 230
Beverly Hills, CA 90211, USA

Rose, Derrick (Athlete, Basketball Player)
c/o BJ Armstrong *Wasserman Media Group*
10960 Wilshire Blvd
Suite 2200
Los Angeles, CA 90024, USA

Rose, Don (Athlete, Baseball Player)
16254 Palomino Mesa Way
San Diego, CA 92127-4445, USA

Rose, Donovan (Athlete, Football Player)
103 Lenox Ct
Yorktown, VA 23693, USA

Rose, Emily (Actor)
c/o Connie Tavel *Forward Entertainment*
9255 Sunset Blvd
Suite 805
Los Angeles, CA 90069, USA

Rose, Felipe (Musician)
1 Vanada Dr
Neptune, NJ 07753, USA

Rose, Franklin (General)
6004 Mineola Ct
Springfield, VA 22152-1232, USA

Rose, George (Athlete, Football Player)
712 Indian Mound Rd
Brunswick, GA 31525, USA

Rose, H Michael (General)
Coldstream Guards
Wellington Barracks
London SW1E 6HQ, UNITED KINGDOM (UK)

Rose, Howie (Baseball Player)
5 Turret Ln
Woodbury, NY 11797-1021, USA

Rose, Irwin A. (Nobel Prize Laureate)
The University of California
14900 1st Ave NE Apt 230
Shoreline, WA 98155-6813, USA

Rose, Jalen (Athlete, Basketball Player)
4512 Orchard Trail Ct
Orchard Lake, MI 48324-3039, USA

Rose, Jamie (Actor)
c/o Staff Member *Marshak/Zachary Company, The*
8840 Wilshire Blvd
1st Floor
Beverly Hills, CA 90210, USA

Rose, Jessica (Actor)
c/o Brad Marks *Apoko Group*
1550 17th St
Santa Monica, CA 90404-3402, USA

Rose, Joe (Athlete, Football Player)
3293 SW 138th Way
Davie, FL 33330, USA

Rose, John (Cartoonist)
95 Laurel St
Harrisonburg, VA 22801-2732, USA

Rose, Justin (Golfer)
c/o Staff Member *Pro Golfers Assoc of America (PGA)*
112 TPC Blvd
Ponte Vedra Beach, FL 32082-3077, USA

Rose, Katy (Musician)
c/o Staff Member *Paradigm (Monterey)*
404 W Franklin St
Monterey, CA 93940, USA

Rose, Ken (Athlete, Football Player)
1736 Bronzewood Ct
Thousand Oaks, CA 91320, USA

Rose, Lee (Director, Producer)
c/o Staff Member *Broder Webb Chervin Silbermann Agency, The (BWCS)*
10250 Constellation Blvd
Los Angeles, CA 90067-6200, USA

Rose, Lucy (Musician)
c/o Staff Member *ICM Partners (ICM-LA)*
10250 Constellation Blvd Fl 7
Los Angeles, CA 90067, USA

Rose, Malik (Athlete, Basketball Player)
1318 Greystone Rdg
San Antonio, TX 78258-4406, USA

Rose, Marie (Actor)
6916 Chisholm Ave
Van Nuys, CA 91406, USA

Rose, Matthew (Business Person)
Burlington North/Santa Fe
2650 Lou Menk Dr
Fort Worth, TX 76131, USA

Rose, Mauri (Race Car Driver)
International Motorsports
PO Box 1018
Tallaldega, AL 35160, USA

Rose, Monica (Stylist)
c/o Staff Member *Rex Agency, The*
6311 Romaine St
Los Angeles, CA 90038, USA

Rose, Pete (Athlete, Baseball Player, Coach)
13348 Chandler Blvd
Sherman Oaks, CA 91401-5323, USA

Rose, Peter H (Business Person)
Krytek Corp
2 Centennial Dr
Peabody, MA 01960, USA

Rose, Richard (Scientist)
Bennochy
1 E Abercromby St
Helensburgh, Dunbartonshire G84 7SP, SCOTLAND

Rose, Shayna (Actor)
Rough Diamond Productions
C/O Bill Kravitz
1424 N Kings Rd
Los Angeles, CA 90069, USA

Rose, Sherrie (Actor, Model)
1758 Laurel Canyon Blvd
Los Angeles, CA 90046, USA

Roseau, Maurice E D (Engineer)
144 Bis Ave du General Leclerc
Sceaux 92330, FRANCE

Rosecrans, James (Athlete, Football Player)
210 Houston Ave
Syracuse, NY 13224, USA

Rosegarten, Rory (Producer)
c/o Staff Member *WmE2 (WMA-LA)*
1 William Morris Pl
Beverly Hills, CA 90212, USA

Rose Jr, Pete (Athlete, Baseball Player)
3921 Legendary Ridge Ln
Cleves, OH 45002, USA

Rosell, Janet (Stylist)
c/o Staff Member *Clutts Agency, The*
1400 Turtle Creek Blvd
#171
Dallas, TX 75207, USA

Roselle, David P (Educator)
14 Laurel Ridge Lane
Wilmington, DE 19807-1322, USA

Roselli, Bob (Athlete, Baseball Player)
100 Clydesdale Way
Roseville, CA 95678, USA

Rosello, Dave (Athlete, Baseball Player)
160 Calle La Paz
Urb Bo Paris
Mayaguez, PR 00680, USA

Rosema, Roger (Athlete, Football Player)
6081 Champagne Ct SE
Grand Rapids, MI 49546, USA

Roseman, Saul (Scientist)
8206 Cranwood Court
Baltimore, MD 21208, USA

Rosemont, Romy (Actor)
c/o Tracy Steinsapir *Main Title Entertainment*
8383 Wilshire Blvd
Suite 408
Los Angeles, CA 90211, USA

Rosen, Albert (Al) (Conductor)
Corbett Arts Mgmt
2101 California St
#2
San Francisco, CA 94115, USA

Rosen, Albert L (Al) (Athlete, Baseball Player)
15 Mayfair Dr
Rancho Mirage, CA 92270-2586, USA

Rosen, Beatrice (Actor)
c/o Staff Member *Inspire Entertainment*
315 7th Ave
Suite 17E
New York, NY 10001, USA

Rosen, Harold A (Engineer, Inventor)
Rosen Electrical Equipment
8226 E Whittier Blvd
Pico Rivera, CA 90660, USA

Rosen, Jeneffer Jones (Stylist)
255 Shrader St
#8
San Francisco, CA 94117, USA

Rosen, Milton W (Engineer, Physicist)
5610 Alta Vista Road
Bethesda, MD 20817, USA

Rosen, Nathaniel (Musician)
4555 Henry Hudson Parkway
#1110
Bronx, NY 10471, USA

Rosen, Sam (Actor)
c/o Staff Member *Brookside Artists Management (NY)*
250 W 57th St
Suite 2303
New York, NY 10107, USA

Rosenbaum, Edward E (Physicist)
333 NW 23rd St
Potland, OR 97210, USA

Rosenbaum, Glen (Architect, Baseball Player)
3759 W 1050 S
Union Mills, IN 46382-9762, USA

Rosenbaum, Michael (Actor)
c/o Jason Newman *Untitled Entertainment (LA)*
350 S. Beverly Dr #200
Beverly Hills, CA 90212, USA

Rosenberg, Alan
PO Box 5617
Beverly Hills, CA 90210

Rosenberg, Alyse (Producer)
c/o Staff Member *The Alpern Group*
15645 Royal Oak Road
Encino, CA 91436, USA

Rosenberg, Craig (Director, Writer)
c/o Staff Member *Firm, The*
2049 Century Park E #2550
Los Angeles, CA 90067, USA

Rosenberg, Gabrielle (Stylist)
17 Downing St
New York, NY 10014, USA

Rosenberg, Howard (Misc)
5859 Larboard Lane
Agoura Hills, CA 91301, USA

Rosenberg, Joel C (Writer)
Beverly Rykerd Public Relations
C/O Beverly Rykerd
PO Box 88180
Colorado Springs, CO 80908, USA

Rosenberg, Michael (Producer)
c/o Staff Member *Imagine Films Entertainment*
1925 Century Park E
Los Angeles, CA 90067, USA

Rosenberg, Pierre M (Director)
Musee du Louvre
34-36 Quai du Louvre
Paris 75068, FRANCE

Rosenberg, Scott (Writer)
c/o David O'Connor *Creative Artists Agency (CAA-LA)*
2000 Ave Of The Stars
Los Angeles, CA 90067, USA

Rosenberg, Sena (Stylist)
c/o Staff Member *Fifty8 Artists*
58 W Huron St
Chicago, IL 60610, USA

Rosenberg, Steve (Athlete, Baseball Player)
2430 NE 35th St
Lighthouse Point, FL 33064-8155, USA

Rosenberg, Steven A (Doctor)
10104 Iron Gate Road
Potomac, MD 20854, USA

Rosenberg, Stuart (Director)
1984 Coldwater Canyon Dr
Beverly Hills, CA 90210, USA

Rosenberg, Tina (Writer)
New School for Social Research
World Policy Institute
New York, NY 10011, USA

Rosenblath, Marshall N (Physicist)
2311 Via Siena
La Jolla, CA 92037, USA

Rosenblatt, Dana (Boxer)
30 Cleveland Road
Chestnut Hill, MA 02467-1417, USA

Rosenbluth, Leonard (Lennie) (Athlete, Basketball Player)
123 Priestly Creek Dr
Chapel Hill, NC 27514-5432, USA

Rosenbohm, Jim (Baseball Player)
9513 Bedford Ave
Omaha, NE 68134-4607, USA

Rosenburg, Saul A (Doctor)
Stanford University
Oncology Division
Stanford, CA 94305, USA

Rosendahl, Heidemarie (Heide) (Athlete, Track Athlete)
Burscheider Str 426
Leverkusen 51381, GERMANY

Rosenfeld, Arnold S (Editor)
Cox Newspapers
PO Box 105720
Atlanta, GA 30348, USA

Rosenfeld, Isadore (Physicist)
Warner Books
1271 Ave of Americas
New York, NY 10020, USA

Rosenfels, Sage (Athlete, Football Player)
110 Ferndale St
Bellaire, TX 77401, USA

Rosenfelt, David (Writer)
c/o Staff Member *St Martins Press*
Publicity Dept
175 5th Ave
New York, NY 10010, USA

Rosenfield, John Max (Educator)
165 Chestnut Road
Brookline, MA 02445-7592, USA

Rosengarten, David (Writer)
PO Box 20459
New York, NY 10025, USA

Rosenman, Howard (Producer)
c/o Staff Member *Marshak/Zachary Company, The*
8840 Wilshire Blvd
1st Floor
Beverly Hills, CA 90210, USA

Rosenmeyer, Grant (Actor)
c/o Staff Member *DreamWorks SKG*
1000 Flower St
Glendale, CA 91201, USA

Rosenn, Max (Judge)
US Court of Appeals
US Courthouse
197 S Main St
Wilkes Barre, PA 18701, USA

Rosenquist, James A (Artist)
P.O. Box 4
Aripeka, FL 34679-0004, USA

Rosenstein, Samuel M (Judge)
US Court of International Trade
2200 S Ocean Lane
Fort Lauderdale, FL 33316, USA

Rosenthal, Albert J (Attorney, Attorney General, Educator, General)
15 Oak Way
Scarsdale, NY 10583, USA

Rosenthal, A M (Journalist)
New York Times 229 W 43rd St Attn Editorial Dept
New York, NY 10036-3913, USA

Rosenthal, Amy Krouse (Writer)
Crown Publishing Group
1745 Broadway
New York, NY 10019, USA

Rosenthal, David S (Director, Writer)
1801 Century Park E #2160
Los Angeles, CA 90067

Rosenthal, Dick (Athlete, Basketball Player)
169 Lake Forest Cir
Apt 201
Niles, MI 49210, USA

Rosenthal, Howard L (Scientist)
Princeton University
Politics Dept
Princeton, NJ 08544, USA

Rosenthal, Jane (Producer)
c/o Staff Member *Tribeca Productions*
375 Greenwich St Fl 8
New York, NY 10013, USA

Rosenthal, Mark D (Writer)
c/o Tom Strickler *WME (LA)*
9601 Wilshire Blvd Fl 3
Beverly Hills, CA 90210, USA

Rosenthal, Mike (Athlete, Football Player)
6112 Every Sail Path
Clarksville, MD 21029, USA

Rosenthal, Philip (Producer)
c/o Adam Berkowitz *Creative Artists Agency (CAA-LA)*
2000 Ave Of The Stars
Los Angeles, CA 90067, USA

Rosenthal, Richard L (Rick) (Director, Producer)
c/o Staff Member *Whitewater Films*
11264 La Grange Ave
Los Angeles, CA 90025-5514, USA

Rosenthal, Robert J (Editor)
Philadelphia Inquirer
Editorial Dept
400 N Broad St
Philadelphia, PA 19130, USA

Rosenthal, Sean (Athlete, Volleyball Player)
USA Volleyball
715 South Circle Drive
Colorado Springs, CO 80910, USA

Rosenthal, Tony (Artist)
173 E 73rd St
New York, NY 10021, USA

Rosenthal, Wayne (Athlete, Baseball Player)
10224 Allamanda Blvd
Palm Beach Gardens, FL 33410-5206, USA

Rosenzweig, Barney (Producer)
2311 Fisher Island Dr
Miami Beach, FL 33109, USA

Rosenzweig, Mark R (Misc)
University of California
Psychology Dept
Tolman Hall
Berkeley, CA 94720, USA

Rosenzweig, Robert M (Educator)
1462 Dana Ave
Palo Alto, CA 94301, USA

Roses, Allen D (Doctor)
Duke University
Medical Center
Bryan Research Center
Durham, NC 27706, USA

Rosewall, Ken (Tennis Player)
Turramurra
111 Pentacost Ave
Sydney, NSW 2074, AUSTRALIA

Rosewoman, Michele (Musician)
Abby Hoffer
223 1/2 E 48th St
New York, NY 10017, USA

Roshan, Hrithik (Actor, Bollywood)
c/o Jai Khanna *Brillstein Entertainment Partners*
9150 Wilshire Blvd #350
Beverly Hills, CA 90212, USA

Roshan, Rakesh (Actor, Bollywood, Director, Producer)
c/o Asal Masomi *Asal Masomi Public Relations*
6320 Canoga Ave
Suite 1513
WoodlandHills, CA 91367, USA

Rosi, Francesco
Via Gregoriana 36
Rome, ITALY 1-00187

Rosin, Walter L (Religious Leader)
Lutheran Church Missouri Synod
1333 S Kirkwood Road
Saint Louis, MO 63122, USA

Rosinski, Edward J (Inventor)
2305 Arnold Ave
Yorkville, NY 13495, USA

Roskill of Newtown, Eustace W (Judge)
New Court
Temple
London EC4, UNITED KINGDOM (UK)

Roskos, John (Athlete, Baseball Player)
P.O. Box 45514
Rio Rancho, NM 87174-5514, USA

Ros-Lehtinen, Ileana (Congressman, Politician)
2206 Rayburn HOB
Washington, DC 20515, USA

Rosman, Mackenzie (Actor)
c/o Kanica Suy *Sweeney Management*
6253 Hollywood Blvd
Suite 201
Los Angeles, CA 90028, USA

Rosner, Robert (Astronomer)
4950 S Greenwood Ave
Chicago, IL 60615, USA

Rosnes, Renee (Musician)
Integrity Talent
PO Box 961
Burlington, MA 01803, USA

Ross, Al (Cartoonist)
2185 Bolton St
Bronx, NY 10462-1367, USA

Ross, Anne (Stylist)
4640 Vantage Ave
Valley Village, CA 91607, USA

Ross, Ben (Director)
United Talent Agency
9560 Wilshire Blvd
#500
Beverly Hills, CA 90212, USA

Ross, Betsy (Sportscaster)
ESPN-TV
Sports Dept
ESPN Plaza 935 Middle St
Bristol, CT 06010, USA

Ross, Bob (Athlete, Baseball Player)
862 Bergamo Ave
San Jacinto, CA 92583-2967, USA

Ross, Brian (Correspondent)
c/o Staff Member *ABC News*
77 W 66th St
3rd Floor
New York, NY 10023, USA

Ross, Charlotte (Actor)
c/o Paul Santana *Agency for the Performing Arts (APA-LA)*
405 S Beverly Dr
Suite 500
Beverly Hills, CA 90212-4425, USA

Ross, Chelcie (Actor)
c/o Staff Member *Geddes Agency, The*
8430 Santa Monica Blvd
Suite 200
Los Angeles, CA 90069, USA

Ross, Cody (Athlete, Baseball Player)
21469 N 83rd St
Scottsdale, AZ 85255-6473, USA

Ross, Dave (Athlete, Baseball Player)
2604 Antietam Trl
Tallahassee, FL 32312, USA

Ross, David (Architect, Baseball Player)
2548 Halleck Ln
Tallahassee, FL 32312-7566, USA

Ross, David A (Director)
Whitney Museum of American Art
945 Madison Ave
New York, NY 10021, USA

Ross, Dennis (Congressman, Politician)
404 Cannon HOB
Washington, DC 20515, USA

Ross, Diana (Actor, Musician)
c/o Whitney Tancred *Sunshine, Sachs & Associates - LA*
8409 Santa Monica Blvd
West Hollywood, CA 90069, USA

Ross, Don (Athlete)
PO Box 981
Venice, CA 90294, USA

Ross, Donald R (Judge)
US Court of Appeals
Federal Building
PO Box 307
Omaha, NE 68101, USA

Ross, Douglas T (Scientist)
Softech Inc
2 Highwood Dr
#200
Tewksbury, MA 01876, USA

Ross, Emma (Stylist)
c/o Staff Member *Michele Karpe*
11959 Woodbridge St
Studio City, CA 91604, USA

Ross, Evan (Actor)
c/o Adam Griffin *Kritzer Levine Wilkins Entertainment (KLWG)*
11872 La Grange Ave
1st Floor
Los Angeles, CA 90025, USA

Ross, Fairbanks Anne (Swimmer)
10 Grandview Ave
Troy, NY 12180, USA

Ross, Gary (Director, Producer, Writer)
c/o Staff Member *Larger Than Life Productions*
100 Universal City Plz
Bldg 5138
Universal City, CA 91608, USA

Ross, Gary (Athlete, Baseball Player)
1729 Cuadro Vis
San Marcos, CA 92078-2102, USA

Ross, George (Business Person, Reality TV Star)
c/o Staff Member *The Apprentice*
The Trump Co
725 Fifth Ave
New York, NY 10022, USA

Ross, Heather (Musician)
HER Productions
6736 Breezy Palm Drive
Riverview, FL 33578-8802, USA

Ross, Ian M (Engineer)
5 Blackpoint Road
Horseshoe
Rumson, NJ 07760, USA

Ross, Jeffrey (Actor, Comedian)
c/o Amy Zvi *Thruline Entertainment*
9250 Wilshire Blvd
Ground Fl
Beverly Hills, CA 90212, USA

Ross, Jerry L (Astronaut)
NASA
Johnson Space Center
2101 NASA Road
Houston, TX 77058, USA

Ross, Jerry L Colonel (Astronaut)
301 Gleneagles Dr
Friendswood, TX 77546-5634, USA

Ross, Jim (Athlete, Wrestler)
605 Shadow View Court
Norman, OK 73072-4827, USA

Ross, Jimmy D (General)
4981 Maple Glen Road
Lake Forest, FL 32771, USA

Ross, John (Misc)
620 Sand Hill Rd
Apt 405E
Palo Alto, CA 94304-2078, USA

Ross, Jonathan (Actor)
c/o Staff Member *Off The Kerb Productions*
Hammer House, 3rd Fl
113-117 Wardour St
London W1F 0UN, UK

Ross, Jonathon (Actor, Producer, Writer)
Talking Concepts
19 Bird Street
Lichfield, Staffordshire WS13 6PW,
UNITED KINGDOM

Ross, Karie (Sportscaster)
ESPN-TV
Sports Dept
ESPN Plaza 935 Middle St
Bristol, CT 06010, USA

Ross, Katharine
33050 Pacific Coast Hwy
Malibu, CA 90265

Ross, Katherine (Actor)
33050 Pacific Coast Highway
Malibu, CA 90265, USA

Ross, Kevin (Athlete, Football Player)
146 High St
Woodbury, NJ 08096, USA

Ross, Lonny (Actor)
c/o Ashley Franklin *Thruline Entertainment*
9250 Wilshire Blvd
Ground Fl
Beverly Hills, CA 90212, USA

Ross, Louis (Athlete, Football Player)
4283 Booker St
Orlando, FL 32811, USA

Ross, Marion (Actor)
4230 Natoma
Woodland Hills, CA 91364, USA

Ross, Mark (Athlete, Baseball Player)
1747 N Wild Hyacinth Dr
Tucson, AZ 85715-5912, USA

Ross, Mike (Congressman, Politician)
2436 Rayburn H(:)B
Washington, DC 20515, USA

Ross, Rick (Musician)
c/o Drew Elliot *Universal Media Artists*
8222 Melrose Ave
Suite 203
Los Angeles, CA 90048, USA

Ross, Robert J (Bobby) (Coach, Football Coach)
US Millitary Academy
Athletic Dept
West Point, NY 10996, USA

Ross, Ryan (Actor)
c/o Staff Member *Vincent Cirrincione Associates*
1516 N Fairfax Ave
Los Angeles, CA 90046, USA

Ross, Scott (Athlete, Football Player)
303 Lake View Dr
Unit D
Montgomery, TX 77356, USA

Ross, Stan
1410 N. Gardner
Los Angeles, CA 90046

Ross, Tracee Ellis (Actor)
c/o Janean Glover *Screen Partners*
9663 Santa Monica Blvd #639
Beverly Hills, CA 90210, USA

Ross, Wilburn K (General)
819 Haskell St
Dupont, WA 98327-9017, USA

Ross, Willie (Athlete, Football Player)
1100 S Hamilton Ave
Chicago, IL 60612, USA

Ross, Yolanda (Actor)
c/o Brian Liebman *Liebman Entertainment*
25 E 21st St #PH
New York, NY 10011-8503, USA

Rossdale, Gavin (Actor, Musician)
c/o Cynthia Pett-Dante *Brillstein Entertainment Partners*
9150 Wilshire Blvd #350
Beverly Hills, CA 90212, USA

Rosselli, Jimmy
344 Paterson Plank Rd
Jersey City, NJ 07307

Rosselli, Joe (Athlete, Baseball Player)
6231 Le Sage Ave
Woodland Hills, CA 91367-1327, USA

Rossellini, Isabella (Actor)
c/o Staff Member *D'Management Group*
13 Via Forcella
Milano 20144, Italy

Rossen, Carol
1119 23rd St. #8
Santa Monica, CA 90403

Rossen, Daniel (Musician)
c/o Sam Kirby *WME (WMA-NY)*
1325 Ave of the Americas
New York, NY 10019, USA

Rosser, Ronald (General)
36 James Street
Roseville, OH 43777-1228, USA

Rosset, Ricardo (Race Car Driver)
Minardi Italia
Via Spallanzani 21
Faenza 48081, ITALY

Rossi, Alice (Scientist)
34 Stagecoach Rd
Amherst, MA 01002, USA

Rossi, Gretchen (Reality TV Star)
c/o Marki Costello *Creative Management Entertainment Group (CMEG)*
2050 S Bundy Dr
Suite 280
Los Angeles, CA 90025, USA

Rossi, Luigi Francis (Shorty) (Actor)
Shorty's Pit Bull Rescue
12405 Venice Blvd
Suite 7
Los Angeles, CA 90066, USA

Rossi, Tony (Ray) (Actor)
c/o Kristene Wallis *Wallis Agency*
210 N Pass Ave
Suite 205
Burbank, CA 915053989, USA

Rossi, Valentino (Motorcycle Racer)
Yamaha Motor Europe N.V.
Koolhovenlaan 101
1119 NC 1119 NC, The Netherlands

Rossio, Terry (Writer)
c/o Brian Siberell *Creative Artists Agency (CAA-LA)*
2000 Ave Of The Stars
Los Angeles, CA 90067, USA

Rossovich, Rick
PO Box 5617
Beverly Hills, CA 90210

Rossovich, Tim (Athlete, Football Player)
19811 Wildwood West Dr
Penn Valley, CA 95946, USA

Rossum, Allen (Athlete, Football Player)
2520 Johnson Dr
Mesquite, TX 75181, USA

Rossum, Emmy (Actor, Musician)
c/o Christian Donatelli *Schiff Company, The*
9465 Wilshire Blvd
Suite 480
Beverly Hills, CA 90212, USA

Rossy, Rico (Athlete, Baseball Player)
A7 Calle Atenas Repto Flamingo
Bayamon, PR 00959-4928, USA

Rostosky, Pete (Athlete, Football Player)
637 E McMurray Rd
Canonsburg, PA 15317, USA

Rostow, Walt
1 Wildwind Point
Austin, TX 78746

Rota, Darcy (Athlete, Hockey Player)
2510 Ashurst Ave
Coquitlam, BC V3K 5T4, Canada

Rota, Randy (Athlete, Hockey Player)
78 Bestwick Dr
Kamloops, BC V2C 6P7, Canada

Rotblatt, Marv (Athlete, Baseball Player)
8975 W Golf Rd #1010
Niles, IL 60714-5846, USA

Rote, Kyle
24700 Deepwater Pt. Dr. #14
St. Michaels, MD 21663

Rote, Tobin
7590 Lighthouse Rd
Port Hope, MI 48468-9760

Rote Jr, Kyle
6075 Poplar Ave #920
Memphis, TN 38119-4717, USA

Rotem, Jonathan (J.R.) (Producer)
c/o Zach Katz *Beluga Heights Management*
5225 Wilshire Blvd Ste 336
Los Angeles, CA 90036, USA

Roth, Andrea (Actor)
c/o Staff Member *Levine Okwu Erickson Management*
6363 Wilshire Blvd
Suite 300
Los Angeles, CA 90048, USA

Roth, Arnold (Cartoonist)
9 Ebony Ct
Brooklyn, NY 11229-5939, USA

Roth, David Lee (Musician)
c/o Garry Buck *Monterey International*
P.O. Box 297
Carmel-by-the-Sea, CA 93921, USA

Roth, Doug (Athlete, Basketball Player)
9975 Spillway Cir
Apt 201
Cordova, TN 38016-7152, USA

Roth, Ed (Race Car Driver)
The Rat Fink
377 E. 100th North
Manti, UT 84642, USA

Roth, Eli (Producer, Writer)
c/o Simon Halls *Slate Public Relations*
9000 Sunset Blvd #915
West Hollywood, CA 90069, USA

Roth, Ellaine (Baseball Player)
872 Goguac St W
Springfield, MI 49015-1737, USA

Roth, Eric (Writer)
c/o Staff Member *Creative Artists Agency
(CAA-LA)*
2000 Ave Of The Stars
Los Angeles, CA 90067, USA

Roth, Matt
PO Box 5617
Beverly Hills, CA 90210

Roth, Philip (Writer)
c/o Andrew Wylie *The Andrew Wylie
Agency*
250 W 57th St
Suite 2114
New York, NY 10107, USA

Roth, Rachel (Actor)
c/o Justine Hunt *Hines and Hunt
Entertainment*
1213 W Magnolia Blvd
Burbank, CA 91506, USA

Roth, Tim (Actor)
c/o Pippa Markham *Markham & Froggatt*
4 Windmill St
London W1T 1HZ, UK

Rothemund, Marc (Director)
c/o Daniel J Talbot *ICM Partners (ICM-LA)*
10250 Constellation Blvd Fl 7
Los Angeles, CA 90067, USA

Rothenberg, Irv (Athlete, Basketball
Player)
6600 Capistrano Beach Trl
Delray Beach, FL 33446, USA

Rothery, Teryl (Actor)
c/o Staff Member *Twenty First Century
Artists*
501 - 825 Granville St
Vancouver BC V6Z 1K9, CANADA

Rothman, John
9229 Sunset Blvd. #710
Los Angeles, CA 90069

Rothman, Les (Athlete, Basketball Player)
11854 Fountainside Cir
Boynton Beach, FL 33437-4923, USA

Rothrock, Cynthia
20670 Callon Drive
Topanga, CA 90290-3712

Rothschild, Larry (Athlete, Baseball
Player, Coach)
4508 W Culbreath Ave
Tampa, FL 33609-4206, USA

Rothstein, Ron (Athlete, Basketball Coach,
Basketball Player, Coach)
60 Edgewater Drive
Apt 4E
Coral Gables, FL 33133, USA

Rotimi (Actor, Dancer, Musician)
c/o Staff Member *WME (LA)*
9601 Wilshire Blvd Fl 3
Beverly Hills, CA 90210, USA

Rottino, Vinny (Athlete, Baseball Player)
4939 Crystal Spg
Racine, WI 53406-1526, USA

Rotunno, Giuseppe
Via Crescenzio 58
Rome, ITALY 00193

Rouen, Amy Van Dyken (Athlete,
Olympic Athlete, Swimmer)
19447 N 84th St
Scottsdale, AZ 85255, USA

Rouen, Tom (Athlete, Football Player)
19947 N 84th St
Scottsdale, AZ 85255, USA

Roughan, Howard (Writer)
c/o Jennifer Rudolph Walsh *WME
(WMA-NY)*
1325 Ave of the Americas
New York, NY 10019, USA

Rougier, Michael (Photographer)
RR 3
Vergennes, VT 05491, USA

Rougier, Michael
RR 3
Vergennes, VT 05491, USA

Rouillard, Richard
11750 Sunset Blvd. #117
Los Angeles, CA 90049

Roulston, Tom (Athlete, Hockey Player)
6814 E. 25th St. Ct. N.
Wichita, KS 67226, USA

Roumel, Katie (Producer)
c/o Staff Member *Killer Films (US)*
526 W 26th St
Rm 715
New York, NY 10001-5524, USA

Roundfield, Dan (Athlete, Basketball
Player)
340 Spring Lake Ter
Roswell, GA 30076-3234, USA

Rounds, Lil (Musician)

Rounds, Michael (Governor, Politician)
2418 Whispering Shores Dr
Fort Pierre, SD 57532-2403, USA

Roundtree, Raleigh (Athlete, Football
Player)
2001 Roosevelt Dr
Augusta, GA 30904, USA

Roundtree, Richard (Actor)
7120 Hayvenhurst Ave.
#409
Van Nuys, CA 91406, USA

Rounsaville, Gene (Athlete, Baseball
Player)
537 Red Rome Ln
Brentwood, CA 94513-2689, USA

Rountree, Mary (Athlete, Baseball Player)
8204 NW 80th St
Tamarac, FL 33321, USA

Rourke, Jim (Athlete, Football Player)
466 Plymouth St
Abington, MA 02351, USA

Rourke, Mickey (Actor)
1203 Washington Ave
Miami Beach, FL 33139, USA

Rouse, Bob (Athlete, Hockey Player)
19135 74th Ave.
RR #15
Surrey, BC V4N 3G5, CANADA

Rouse, Curtis (Athlete, Football Player)
301 Hampshire Ct
Clarksville, TN 37043, USA

Rouse, Irving (Misc)
509 Rockavon Road
Narberth, PA 19072-2318, USA

Rouse, Jeff (Athlete, Olympic Athlete,
Swimmer)
600 Sharon Park Dr #B208
Menlo Park, CA 94025-6989, USA

Rouse, mike (Athlete, Baseball Player)
30055 Monteras St
Laguna Niguel, CA 92677-8822, USA

Rouse, Mitch (Actor)
c/o David (Dave) Becky *3 Arts
Entertainment Inc*
9460 Wilshire Blvd
7th Floor
Beverly Hills, CA 90210, USA

Rousey, Ronda (Athlete, Olympic Athlete,
Wrestler)
c/o Staff Member *WmE2 (WMA-LA)*
1 William Morris Pl
Beverly Hills, CA 90212, USA

Roush, Jack (Race Car Driver)
Roush Racing
122 Knob Hill Road
Mooresville, NC 28115, USA

Rouson, Lee (Athlete, Football Player)
20 Main St
Flanders, NJ 07836, USA

Rousseau, Bobby (Athlete, Hockey Player)
580 Ch du Golf
Louisville, QC J5V 2L4, CANADA

Rousseau, Dune (Athlete, Hockey Player)
261 Stradford St
Winnipeg, MB R2Y 2El, Canada

Rousseau, Guy (Athlete, Hockey Player)
124 Av. Maitland
Point-Claire, PQ H9R 3X4, CANADA

Roussel, Dominic (Athlete, Hockey
Player)
Ecole De Hockey Co-Jean
58 Rue des Tourterelles
Attn: Coaching Staff
Blainville, QC J7C 5T6, CANADA

Roussel, Tom (Athlete, Football Player)
13 Heron Ln
Mandeville, LA 70471, USA

Roussell, Thierry
Villa Crystal
St. Moritz, SWITZERLAND CH-7500

Rousset, Christophe (Musician)
Trawick Artists
1926 Broadway
New York, NY 10023, USA

Roustabouts, The
PO Box 25371
Charlotte, NC 28212

Routh, Brandon (Actor)
c/o Stewart Strunk *Main Title
Entertainment*
8383 Wilshire Blvd
Suite 408
Los Angeles, CA 90211, USA

Routledge, Alison (Actor)
Marmont Mgmt
Langham House
302/8 Regent St
London W1R 5AL, UNITED KINGDOM
(UK)

Routledge, Patricia (Actor)
6 King George Gardens
Chichester
W Sussex PO19 6LB, UK

Roux, Albert H (Chef)
Le Gavroche
43 Upper Brook St
London W1Y 1PF, UNITED KINGDOM
(UK)

Roux, Jean-Louis (Actor, Director)
4145 Blueridge Crescent
#2
Montreal, QC H3H 1S7, CANADA

Roux, Michel A (Chef)
Le Gavroche
43 Upper Brook St
London W1K 7QR, UK

Rove, Karl (Government Official)
1111 New Hampshire Ave NW #600
Washington, DC 20036-1532, USA

Rovick, Sheriff John
3531 Clifton Pl.
Glendale, CA 91206

Rowan, Carl T
3116 Fessenden St NW
Washington, DC 20008, USA

Rowan, Kelly (Actor, Producer)
c/o British Reece *PMK/BNC Public
Relations (PMK-LA)*
8687 Melrose Ave Fl 8
West Hollywood, CA 90069, USA

Rowand, Aaron (Athlete, Baseball Player)
34 Meadowhawk Ln
Las Vegas, NV 89135-5201, USA

Rowden, William H (Admiral)
1306 Dehlgren Avenue SE
Washington Navy Yard
Washington, DC 20374-5055, USA

Rowdon, Wade (Athlete, Baseball Player)
230 Crooked Tree Trl
Deland, FL 32724-3426, USA

Rowe, Alan
8 Sherwood Close
London, ENGLAND SW13

Rowe, Bob (Athlete, Football Player)
2564 Viola Gill Ln
Grover, MO 63040-1165, USA

Rowe, Brad (Actor, Producer, Writer)
1327 Brinkley Ave
Los Angeles, CA 90049, USA

Rowe, Dave (Athlete, Football Player)
330 W Presnell St
Apt 43
Asheboro, NC 27203, USA

Rowe, John W (Business Person)
Unicom Corp
10 S Dearborn St
Chicago, IL 60603, USA

Rowe, John W (Business Person)
Aetna Inc
151 Farmington Ave
Hartford, CT 06156, USA

Rowe, Ken (Athlete, Baseball Player)
347 Princeton Dr
Dallas, GA 30157-0853, USA

Rowe, Maggie (Comedian)
c/o Staff Member *ICM Partners (ICM-LA)*
10250 Constellation Blvd Fl 7
Los Angeles, CA 90067, USA

Rowe, Mike (Television Host)
c/o Scott Agostini *WME (LA)*
9601 Wilshire Blvd Fl 3
Beverly Hills, CA 90210, USA

Rowe, Misty (Actor)
2193 River Road
Egg Harbor Cay, NJ 08215, USA

Rowe, Nicolas
52 Shaftesbury Ave
London, ENGLAND WlV 7DE

Rowe, Patrick (Athlete, Football Player)
6259 Alderley St
San Diego, CA 92114, USA

Rowe, Ray (Athlete, Football Player)
11443 Westonhill Dr
San Diego, CA 92126, USA

Rowe, Red
79 Margarita
Camarillo Springs, CA 93010

Rowe, Sandra M (Editor)
Portland Oregonian
Editorial Dept
1320 SW Broadway
Portland, OR 97201, USA

rowe, Tom (Athlete, Hockey Player)
38 Holly Hill Dr
Amherst, NH 03031-1627

Rowe-Jackson, Debbie
435 N. Roxbury Dr.
Beverly Hills, CA 90210

Rowell, Victoria (Actor)
c/o Tracy Christian *Buchwald/Fortitude (LA)*
6500 Wilshire Blvd
Suite 2200
Los Angeles, CA 90048, USA

Rowland, Betty (Dancer)
125 N Barrington Ave
#103
Los Angeles, CA 90049, USA

Rowland, Brad (Athlete, Football Player)
552 Rosebud Dr N
Lombard, IL 60148, USA

Rowland, Dave
PO Box 121089
Nashville, TN 37212

Rowland, Derrick (Athlete, Basketball Player)
3 Island View Rd
Cohoes, NY 12047-4929, USA

Rowland, Gord (Athlete, Football Player)
198 Harris Blvd
Winnipeg, MB R3J3PS, Canada

Rowland, James A (General)
17 Pindari Ave
Mosman, NSW 2088, AUSTRALIA

Rowland, J David (Business Person)
National Westminster Bank
41 Lothbury
London EC2P 2BP, UNITED KINGDOM (UK)

Rowland, John (Governor, Politician)
98 Leonard Rd
Middlebury, CT 06762-3603, USA

Rowland, John W (Misc)
Amalgamated Transit Union
5025 Wisconsin Ave NW
Washington, DC 20016, USA

Rowland, Justin (Athlete, Football Player)
1919 NW Loop 410
Suite 200
San Antonio, TX 78213, USA

Rowland, Kelly (Musician)
c/o Steven Grossman *Collective*
8383 Wilshire Blvd
Suite 1050
Beverly Hills, CA 90211, USA

Rowland, Landon H (Business Person)
Kansas City Southern
PO Box 219335
Kansas City, MO 64121, USA

Rowland, Mike (Athlete, Baseball Player)
12104 E Mescal St
Scottsdale, AZ 85259-4230, USA

Rowland, Rich (Athlete, Baseball Player)
91 Clark Ave
Cloverdale, CA 9542S-3918, USA

Rowland, Rodney (Actor, Model)
Booh Schut
11350 Ventura Blvd
#206
Studio City, CA 91604, USA

Rowland, Troy (Producer)
c/o Susan Curtis *Curtis Talent Management*
9607 Arby Dr
Beverly Hills, CA 90210, USA

Rowlands, Gena (Actor)
c/o Lou Pitt *Pitt Group, The*
9465 Wilshire Blvd
Suite 420
Beverly Hills, CA 90212, USA

Rowlands, Patsy
265 Liverpool Rd.
London, ENGLAND N1 1LX

Rowlands, Sherry
5055 Seminary Rd
Alexandria, VA 22311

Rowley, Cynthia (Designer, Fashion Designer)
c/o Staff Member *IMG*
304 Park Ave S Fl 12
New York, NY 10010, USA

Rowley, Denise (Stylist)
PO Box 146
White Sulpher Springs, NY 12787, USA

Rowley, Elwood R (Athlete, Football Player)
712 Southwick Ave
Clayton, NC 27527, USA

Rowley, Janet D (Physicist)
5310 S University Ave
Chicago, IL 60615, USA

Rowling, JK (Writer)
c/o Staff Member *Christopher Little Literary Agency*
10 Eel Brook Studios
London SW6 4PS, UNITED KINGDOM

Rowlinson, John S (Misc)
12 Pullens Field
Headington OX3 0BU, UNITED KINGDOM (UK)

Rowny, Edward L (General)
6200 Oregon Avenue NW
Apt 345
Washington, DC 20015-1542, USA

Rowse, Darren (Internet Star)
PO BOX 1295
North Fitzroy, Victoria 3068, AUSTRALIA

Rowser, John (Athlete, Football Player)
17564 Alta Vista Dr
Southfield, MI 48075, USA

Roxborough, Charlene (Stylist)
c/o Staff Member *Mercury Artists*
8460 Higuera St Fl 2
Culver City, CA 90232, USA

Roxburgh, Richard (Actor, Music Group)
c/o Eric Kranzler *Management 360*
9111 Wilshire Blvd
Beverly Hills, CA 90210, USA

Roxette (Music Group)
c/o Staff Member *D&D Management*
Drottning Gatan 55
Stockholm 11121, Sweden

Roxton, Steve
6 Thornton Rd. Leytonstone
London, ENGLAND E11

Roy (Misc)
Beyond Belief
1639 N Valley Dr
Las Vegas, NV 89108, USA

Roy, Andre (Athlete, Hockey Player)
17352 Emerlad Chase Drive
Tampa, FL 33647-3517, USA

Roy, Aruna (Activist)
PUCL
81 Sahayoga apartments
Mayur Vihar - I
Delhi 110 091, India

Roy, Arundhati (Writer)
c/o Kimberly Witherspoon *Inkwell Management*
521 Fifth Ave
New York, NY 10175, USA

Roy, Brandon (Athlete, Basketball Player)
c/o Arn Tellem *Wasserman Media Group*
10960 Wilshire Blvd
Suite 2200
Los Angeles, CA 90024, USA

Roy, Deep (Actor)
c/o Victor (Viktor) Kruglov *Victor Kruglov Talent Management*
7461 Beverly Blvd Ste 403
Los Angeles, CA 90036, USA

Roy, Derek (Athlete, Hockey Player)
100 Rivermist Dr
Buffalo, NY 14202-4300

Roy, Drew (Actor)
c/o Matt Luber *Luber Roklin Management*
8530 Wilshire Blvd
6th Floor
Beverly Hills, CA 90211, USA

Roy, James D (Financier)
Federal Hone Loan Bank
601 Grant St
Pittsburgh, PA 15219, USA

Roy, Jean-Pierre (Athlete, Baseball Player)
407 Rue Des Harfangs
Saint-Nicolas, QC G7A 3H4, Canada

Roy, John (Actor, Comedian)
c/o Gabrielle Krengel *Domain Talent*
9229 Sunset Boulevard
Suite 710
Los Angeles, CA 90069, USA

Roy, Patricia (Athlete, Baseball Player)
201 E Am key Way
Carmel, IN 46032-5170, USA

Roy, Patrick (Athlete, Hockey Player)
201 Ch de la Plage-Saint-Laurent
Quebec, QC G1Y 1W6, Canada

Roy, Pierre (Athlete, Hockey Player)
120-145 King Edward St
Coquitlam, BC V3K 6M2, Canada

Roy, Rachel (Fashion Designer)
The Jones Group Inc
180 Rittenhouse Cir
Bristol, PA 19007, USA

Roy, Reena (Actor, Bollywood)
Pam Villa D'Monte Park Road
Bandra
Bombay, MS 400 050, INDIA

Roy, Stephane (Race Car Driver)
Hammerhead Racing
7026 E. Aster Dr.
Scottsdale, AZ 85254, USA

Royal, Billy Joe (Musician, Songwriter, Writer)
1306 Patterson Street
Morehead City, NC 28557-4100, USA

Royale, Maureen (Stylist)
c/o Staff Member *Marilyn's Inc*
601 Norwalk St
Greensboro, NC 27407, USA

Royals, Mark (Athlete, Football Player)
9921 Menander Wood Ct
Odessa, FL 33556, USA

Royals, Reggie (Athlete, Basketball Player)
P.O. Box 742
Tulsa, OK 74101, USA

Roybal-Allard, Lucille (Congressman, Politician)
2330 Rayburn HOB
Washington, DC 20515, USA

Royce, Kenneth
3 Abbott's Close Andover
Hants., ENGLAND SP11 7NP

Royce, Mike (Comedian)
c/o Staff Member *United Talent Agency (UTA)*
9336 Civic Center Dr
Beverly Hills, CA 90210, USA

Roye, Orpheus (Athlete, Football Player)
26403 Primrose Ln
Westlake, OH 44145, USA

Royer, Stan (Athlete, Baseball Player)
9301 Christopher Lake Dr
Columbia, IL 62236-3458, USA

Roylance, Juanita (Baseball Player)
PO Box 282
Lorida, FL 33857-0282, USA

Roylance, Pamela
221 S. Gale Dr. #403
Beverly Hills, CA 90211

Royo, Sanchez Aristides (President)
Morgan & Morgan
PO Box 1824
Panama City 1, PANAMA

Royster, Jeron K (Jerry) (Athlete, Baseball Player, Coach)
36000 Portofino Cir Apt 114
Palm Beach Gardens, FL 33418-1284, USA

Royster, Mazio (Athlete, Football Player)
7348 Crimson Dr
Highland, CA 92346, USA

Royster, Willie (Athlete, Baseball Player)
229 55th St NE
Washington, DC 20019-6737, USA

Rozalla (Musician)
c/o Staff Member *Diva Central Inc*
7510 W Sunset Blvd Ste 1445
Los Angees, CA 90046, USA

Rozanov, Evgeny G (Architect)
Int'l Architecture Academy
Bolshara Dmitrovka 24
Moscow 103284, RUSSIA

Rozelle, Pete (Athlete, Football Player)
23800 Valley Oak Ct
Newhall, CA 91321-3746, USA

Rozema, Dave (Athlete, Baseball Player)
1560 N Renaud Rd
Grosse Pointe Woods, MI 48236-1763,
USA

Rozhdestvensky, Gennady N
Victor Hochhauser Ltd
4 Oak Hill Way
London NW3, UNITED KINGDOM (UK)

Rozier, Clifford (Athlete, Basketball
Player)
P.O. Box 1194
Palmetto, FL 34220-1194, USA

Rozier, Mike (Athlete, Football Player,
Heisman Trophy Winner)
9 Hidden Hollow Ln
Sicklerville, NJ 08081-3910, USA

Roznovsky, Vic (Athlete, Baseball Player)
266 W Bluff Ave
Fresno, CA 93711-6930, USA

Rozon, Tim (Actor)
c/o Pearl Hanan *Pearl Hanan
Management*
7775 Sunset Blvd
Suite 118
Los Angeles, CA 90046, USA

Rozsival, Michal (Athlete, Hockey Player)
The Sports Corporation
2735-10088 102 Ave NW
Attn Rich Winter
Edmonton, AB TSJ 2ZI, Canada

Rozumek, Dave (Athlete, Football Player)
18 Old Rockingham Rd
Salem, NH 03079, USA

Rozzell, Aubrey (Athlete, Football Player)
P.O. Box 844
Quitman, MS 39355, USA

R Pandiarajan (Actor)
18 Sivasailam Street
T Nagar
Chennai, TN 600 017, INDIA

R Partheepan (Actor)
Veerappa Nagar
Chennai, TN 600 093, INDIA

R. Pierluisi, Pedro (Congressman,
Politician)
1213 Longworth HOB
Washington, DC 20515, USA

R. Pitts, Joseph (Congressman, Politician)
420 Carmon HOB
Washington, DC 20515, USA

R. Rothman, Stevan (Congressman,
Politician)
2303 Rayburn HOB
Washington, DC 20515, USA

R. Rothman, Steven (Congressman,
Politician)
2303 Rayburn HOB
Washington, DC 20515, USA

R. Royce, Edward (Congressman,
Politician)
2185 Rayburn HOB
Washington, DC 20515, USA

R. Tipton, Scott (Congressman, Politician)
218 Cannon HOB
Washington, DC 20515, USA

R. Turner, Michael (Congressman,
Politician)
2454 Rayburn HOB
Washington, DC 20515, USA

Ruah, Daniela (Actor)
c/o Rhonda Price *Gersh (NY)*
41 Madison Ave
New York, NY 10010, USA

Rubalcaba, Gonzalo (Musician)
Eardrums Music
5930 NW 201st St
Miami, FL 33105, USA

Rubbia, Carlo (Nobel Prize Laureate)
CERN
Organisation Europeenne pour la
Recherche Nucleaire EP Division
Geneva CH-1211, SWITZERLAND

Rubel, Fran (Director, Producer)
c/o Staff Member *Kuzui Enterprises*
8225 Santa Monica Blvd
West Hollywood, CA 90046, USA

Ruben, Joseph P (Joe) (Director)
250 W 57th St
#1905
New York, NY 10107, USA

Rubens, Larry (Athlete, Football Player)
12213 Ansley Ct
Knoxville, TN 37922, USA

Rubenstein, Ann (Correspondent)
NBC-TV
News Dept
30 Rockefeller Plaza
New York, NY 10112, USA

Rubenstein, David (Business Person)
Carlyle Group
1001 Pennsylvania Ave NW
Washington, DC 20004, USA

Rubenstein, Edward (Physicist)
Stanford University Medical School
Surgery Dept
Stanford, CA 94305, USA

Ruberto, Sonny (Athlete, Baseball Player)
207 Ambridge ct Apt
204
Chesterfield, MO 63017-9506, USA

Rubiano, Saenz Pedro Cardinal (Religious
Leader)
Arzubispado
Carrera 7A N 10-20
Santafe de Bogota, DC 1, COLOMBIA

Rubick, Rob (Athlete, Football Player)
1571 Stonewood Dr
Lapeer, MI 48446, USA

Rubik, Erno (Inventor)
Rublik Erno
Rubik Studios Varosmajor Utca 74
Budapest 1122, HUNGARY

Rubin, Amy (Actor)
Hervey/Grimes
PO Box 64249
Los Angeles, CA 90064, USA

Rubin, Benjamin A (Inventor)
1329 173rd St
Hazel Crest, IL 60429, USA

Rubin, Chanda (Athlete, Olympic Athlete,
Tennis Player)
708 So. St. Antoine St.
Lafayette, LA 70501, USA

Rubin, Chandra (Tennis Player)
708 S Saint Antoine St
Lafayette, LA 70501, USA

Rubin, Ellis (Lawyer)
4141 NE 2nd Ave
#203A
Miami, FL 33137, USA

Rubin, Gloria (Actor)
c/o Leigh Brillstein *ICM Partners (ICM-LA)*
10250 Constellation Blvd Fl 7
Los Angeles, CA 90067, USA

Rubin, Harry (Biologist)
University of California
Molecular Biology Dept
Berkeley, CA 94720, USA

Rubin, Leigh (Cartoonist)
Creators Syndicate
5777 W Century Blvd
#700
Los Angeles, CA 90045, USA

Rubin, Louis D Jr (Writer)
702 Ginghoul Road
Chapel Hill, NC 27514, USA

Rubin, Rick (Musician, Producer)
c/o Staff Member *American Recordings*
3300 Warner Blvd
Burbank, CA 91505, USA

Rubin, Robert (Misc)
Massachusetts General Hospital
32 Fruit St
Boston, MA 02114, USA

Rubin, Robert E (Financier, Politician,
Secretary)
Citigroup Inc
911 Park Ave
New York, NY 10075-0337, USA

Rubin, Theodore I (Misc)
219 E 62nd St
New York, NY 10021, USA

Rubin, Tibor (General)
5442 Marietta Ave
Garden Grove, CA 92845-2339, USA

Rubin, Vanessa (Musician)
Joel Chriss
300 Mercer St
#3J
New York, NY 10003, USA

Rubin, Vera C (Astronomer)
Carnegie Institution
5241 Broad Branch Road NW
Washington, DC 20015, USA

Rubin, William (Misc)
Museum of Modern Art
11 W 53rd St
New York, NY 10019, USA

Rubinek, Saul (Actor)
Gersh Agency
232 North Canon Dr
Beverly Hills, CA 90210, USA

Rubinfeld, Daniel (Attorney, Educator)
University of California
Law School
Boalt Hall
Berkeley, CA 94720, USA

Rubino, Frank A (Lawyer)
2601 S Bayshore Dr
Miami, FL 33133, USA

Rubinoff, Ira (Biologist)
Smithsonian Tropical Research Institute
Unit 0848
APO, AA 34002, USA

Rubinoff, Marla (Actor)
c/o Staff Member *John Glenn Harding
Management*
7004 Oakwood Ave
Los Angeles, CA 90036, USA

Rubins, Kathleen Dr (Astronaut)
19220 Space Center Blvd Apt 623
Houston, TX 77058-3748, USA

Rubinstein, John (Actor)
4417 Leydon Ave
Woodland Hills, CA 91364, USA

Rubinstein, Zeida (Actor)
The Agency
1800 Ave of Stars
#400
Los Angeles, CA 90067, USA

Rubin-Vega, Daphne (Actor)
c/o Jeremy Katz *Katz Company, The*
1674 Broadway
7th Floor
New York, NY 10019, USA

Rubio, Marco (Senator)
B40A Dirksen Senate Office Bldg
Washington, DC 20510, USA

Rubio, Maria
2238Blvd. Adolfo Lopez Mateo 5
Placopac San Angel
Mexico DF, MEXICO 01040

Rubio, Paulina (Musician)
c/o Rick Canny *Sanctuary Artist
Management*
8750 Wilshire Blvd Ste 200
Beverly Hills, CA 90211, USA

Ruby & The Romantics
1650 Broadway #508
New York, NY 10119-6833

Rucchin, Steve (Athlete, Hockey Player)
614 Acacia Ave
Corona Del Mar, CA 92625-1907

Rucci, Todd (Athlete, Football Player)
5 Southview Ln
Lititz, PA 17543, USA

Ruccolo, Richard (Actor)
ER Talent
301 W 53rd St
#4K
New York, NY 10019, USA

Ruch, Charles (Educator)
Boise State University
President's Office
Boise, ID 83725, USA

Rucinski, Mike (Athlete, Hockey Player)
5175 Pinetum Trl
Brighton, MI 48114-9076

Rucinski, Mike (Athlete, Hockey Player)
11980 Cape Cod Ln
Huntley, IL 60142-8168

Rucinsky, Martin (Athlete, Hockey Player)
800 Griffiths Way
Vancouver, BC V6B 6G1, Canada

Ruck, Alan (Actor)
c/o Lisa Lieberman *Innovative Artists (NY)*
235 Park Ave S
7th Floor
New York, NY 10003, USA

Rucka, Leo (Athlete, Football Player)
814 Crosby Dayton Rd
Crosby, TX 77532, USA

Ruckelshaus, William D (Business Person, Government Official, Politician)
PO Box 76
Median, WA 98039-0076, USA

Ruckenstein, Eli (Engineer)
755 Renaissance Drive
Apt 203
Buffalo, NY 14221-8046, USA

Rucker, Anja (Athlete, Track Athlete)
TUS Jena
Wollnitzer Str 42
Jena 07749, GERMANY

Rucker, Darius (Musician)
c/o Scott McGhee *McGhee Entertainment*
8730 Sunset Blvd
Suite 175
Los Angeles, CA 90069, USA

Rucker, Dave (Athlete, Baseball Player)
18602 Piper Pl
Yorba Linda, CA 92886-2559, USA

Rucker, Michael (Athlete, Football Player)
5971 Rolling Ridge Dr
Kannapolis, NC 28081, USA

Rucker, Reggie (Athlete, Football Player)
26300 Village Ln
Apt 303
Beachwood, OH 44122, USA

Rucker, Reginald J (Reggie) (Athlete, Football Player)
3128 Richmond Rd
Beachwood, OH 44122, USA

Rudbottom, Roy R Jr (Diplomat)
7831 Park Lane
#213A
Dallas, TX 75225, USA

Rudd, Delaney (Athlete, Basketball Player)
422 Chesham Dr
Kernersville, NC 27284, USA

Rudd, Dwayne (Athlete, Football Player)
P.O. Box 273309
Boca Raton, FL 33427, USA

Rudd, John (Athlete, Basketball Player)
4440 Sweet Bay Dr
Lake Charles, LA 70611, USA

Rudd, Kevin (Prime Minister)
Parliament House
Canberra ACT 2600, AUSTRALIA

Rudd, Paul (Actor)
c/o Aleen Keshishian *Brillstein Entertainment Partners*
9150 Wilshire Blvd #350
Beverly Hills, CA 90212, USA

Rudd, Ricky (Race Car Driver)
Entertainment Market
124 Summerville Dr.
Mooresville, NC 28115, USA

Rudd, Xavier (Musician)
c/o Staff Member *Paradigm (Monterey)*
404 W Franklin St
Monterey, CA 93940, USA

Ruddell, George (General)
3723 Fifteen Mile Rd
The Dalles, OR 97058-9622, USA

Ruddle, Francis H (Biologist)
Yale University
Biology Dept
New Heaven, CT 06511, USA

Ruddock, Donovan (Razor) (Boxer)
7379 NW 34th St
Lauderhill, FL 33319, USA

Ruddy, Al
1601 Clearview Dr.
Beverly Hills, CA 90210

Ruddy, Albert (Producer)
1601 Clearview Dr
Beverly Hills, CA 90210, USA

Ruddy, Tim (Athlete, Football Player)
3885 Vale View Ln
Mead, CO 80542, USA

Rude, Jim (Stylist)
935 Alpine Dr
Janesville, WI 53546, USA

Rudel, Julius
101 Central Park West
#11A
New York, NY 10023, USA

Rudenstine, Neil L (Educator)
41 Armour Road
Princeton, NJ 08540, USA

Ruder, Bill
1731 Stillwater Cir
1731 Stillwater Cir, TN 37027-8645, USA

Ruder, David S (Educator, Government Official)
Baker & McKenzie
1 Prudential Plaza
130 E Randolph Dr
Chicago, IL 60601, USA

Rudi, Joseph O (Joe) (Athlete, Baseball Player)
PO Box425
Baker City, OR 97814-0425, USA

Rudie, Evelyn (Actor)
Santa Monica Playhouse
7514 Hollywood Blvd
Los Angeles, CA 90046, USA

Rudin, Scott (Filmmaker, Producer)
Scott Rudin Productions
120 W 45th St
New York, NY 10036, USA

Rudis-Bestudik, Mary (Baseball Player)
4333 Deeboyar Ave
Lakewood, CA 90712-3703, USA

Rudnay, Jack (Athlete, Football Player)
7219 Whipperwill Rd
Versailles, MO 65084, USA

Rudner, Rita (Actor, Comedian)
c/o Staff Member *ICM Partners (ICM-LA)*
10250 Constellation Blvd Fl 7
Los Angeles, CA 90067, USA

Rudnick, Paul (Writer)
c/o Robert (Bob) Bookman *Creative Artists Agency (CAA-LA)*
2000 Ave Of The Stars
Los Angeles, CA 90067, USA

Rudnick, Tim (Athlete, Football Player)
7311 N Octavia Ave
Chicago, IL 60631, USA

Rudolph, Alan
15760 Ventura Blvd. #16
Encino, CA 91436

Rudolph, Alan S (Director)
International Creative Mgmt
8942 Wilshire Blvd
#219
Beverly Hills, CA 90211, USA

Rudolph, Ben (Athlete, Football Player)
561 E General Gorgas Dr
Mobile, AL 36617, USA

Rudolph, Coleman (Athlete, Football Player)
412 Billings Farm Ln
Canton, GA 30115, USA

Rudolph, Council (Athlete, Football Player)
8310 Lago Vista Dr
Tampa, FL 33614, USA

Rudolph, Frederick (Historian)
234 Ide Road
Williamstown, MA 01267, USA

Rudolph, Ken (Athlete, Baseball Player)
1317 W Sands Ct
Gilbert, AZ 85233-6637, USA

Rudolph, Larry (Producer)
c/o Staff Member *ReignDeer Entertainment*
100 Glendon Ave
Suite 1100
Los Angeles, CA 90024, USA

Rudolph, Maya (Actor)
4900 Casa Dr
Tarzana, CA 91356, USA

Rudometkin, John (Athlete, Basketball Player)
6181 Wise Rd
Newcastle, CA 95658, USA

Rudzinski, Paul (Athlete, Football Player)
3216 Delahaut St
Green Bay, WI 54301, USA

Rudzinski, Witold (Composer)
Ul Narbutta 50 m 6
Warsaw 02-541, POLAND

Rue, Sara (Actor)
c/o Alan David *Alan David Management*
8840 Wilshire Blvd
Suite 200
Beverly Hills, CA 90211, USA

Ruebel, Matt (Athlete, Baseball Player)
7509 W Augusta Blvd
Yorktown, IN 47396-9354, USA

Ruegamer, Grey (Athlete, Football Player)
P.O. Box 70155
Las Vegas, NV 89170, USA

Ruehe, Volker (Government Official)
Bundesministerium Der Verteidigunj
Hardthoehe
Honn 53125, GERMANY

Ruehl, Mercedes (Actor)
c/o Jonathan Howard *Innovative Artists (LA)*
1505 10th St
Santa Monica, CA 90401, USA

Ruel, Claude (Athlete, Hockey Player)
102-1450 Rue Beauharnois
Longueuil, QC J4M 1X2, Canada

Ruelas, Gabriel (Gabe) (Athlete, Boxer)
1119 S Hudson Ave
Los Angeles, CA 90019-1807, USA

Ruell, Aaron (Actor, Director, Writer)
c/o Staff Member *Brillstein Entertainment Partners*
9150 Wilshire Blvd #350
Beverly Hills, CA 90212, USA

Ruelle, David P (Mathematician)
1 Ave Charles-Cormar
Bures-sur-Yvette 91440, FRANCE

Rueter, Kirk (Athlete, Baseball Player)
46 Pheasant Ridge Ct
Nashville, IL 62263-5845, USA

Ruether, Mike (Athlete, Football Player)
23014 Gardner Dr
Alpharetta, GA 30004, USA

Ruether, Rosemary R (Misc)
530 Mayflower Road
Claremont, CA 91711, USA

Ruettgers, Ken (Athlete, Football Player)
16897 Golden Stone Dr
Sisters, OR 97759, USA

Ruettgers, Michael C (Business Person)
ECM Corp
35 Parkway Dr
Hopkinton, MA 01748, USA

Ruettiger, Daniel (Rudy) (Athlete, Football Player)
12 Highland Creek Dr
Henderson, NV 28052-6609, USA

Ruff, Howard J (Economist, Writer)
PO Box 441
Orem, UT 84059, USA

Ruff, Lindy (Athlete, Hockey Player)
Buffalo Sabres
1 Seymour H Knox III Plz Ste 1
Buffalo, NY 14203-3096

Ruff, Lindy (Athlete, Coach, Hockey Player)
5006 Winding Ln
Clarence, NY 14031-1500, USA

Ruffalo, Mark (Actor)
c/o Jessica Kolstad *WKT Public Relations (WKT-LA)*
9350 Wilshire Blvd
Suite 450
Beverly Hills, CA 90212, USA

Ruffcorn, Scott (Athlete, Baseball Player)
2137 Barton Hills Dr
Austin, TX 78704-4659, USA

Ruffin, Bruce (Athlete, Baseball Player)
3410 Pawnee Pass S
Austin, TX 78738-1709, USA

Ruffin, Jimmy
102 Ryder's Lane
East Brunswick, NJ 08816

Ruffin, Johnny (Athlete, Baseball Player)
4229 Trumpworth Ct
Valrico, FL 33596-8494, USA

Ruffini, Attilio (Government Official)
Camera dei Deputati
Via della Missione 10
Rome 00187, ITALY

Ruffner, Barry (Athlete, Football Player)
134 Frogtown Rd
New Alexandria, PA 15670-3080, USA

Ruffner, Paul (Athlete, Basketball Player)
4508 Brookshire Dr
Provo, UT 84604-5245, USA

Ruffo, Victoria (Actor)
c/o Staff Member *Televisa*
Blvd Adolfo Lopez Mateos 232
Colonia San Angel INN
DF CP 01060, MEXICO

Rufus
7250 Beverly Blvd. #200
Los Angeles, CA 90036

Ruge, John A (Cartoonist)
240 Nronxville Road
#B4
Bronxville, NY 10708, USA

Ruggiano, Justin (Athlete, Baseball Player)
2710 Capstone Way
Rockwall, TX 75032-6836, USA

Ruggiero, Adamo (Actor)
c/o Shari Quallenberg *AMI Artist
Management*
464 King St E
Toronto, ON M5A 1L7, Canada

Ruggiero, Angela (Athlete, Hockey Player,
Olympic Athlete)
Shade Global
10 E 40th St Fl 48
New York, NY 10016-0301, USA

Ruggiero, John (Stylist)
c/o Staff Member *Mercury Artists*
8460 Higuera St Fl 2
Culver City, CA 90232, USA

Ruhman, Chris (Athlete, Football Player)
13206 Vinery Ct
Cypress, TX 77429, USA

Ruivivar, Anthony Michael (Actor)
c/o Nick Collins *Gersh (LA)*
9465 Wilshire Blvd
Suite 600
Beverly Hills, CA 90212, USA

Ruiz, Chico (Athlete, Baseball Player)
267 Calle Tapia
SanJuan, PR 00912-4201, USA

Ruiz, John (Boxer)
John Ruiz Inc
P.O. Box 2581
Taunton, MA 02780, USA

Ruiz, Jose Carlos (Actor)
c/o Staff Member *Televisa*
Blvd Adolfo Lopez Mateos 232
Colonia San Angel INN
DF CP 01060, MEXICO

Ruiz, Rodrigo (Actor)
c/o Staff Member *Televisa*
Blvd Adolfo Lopez Mateos 232
Colonia San Angel INN
DF CP 01060, MEXICO

Rukavina, Terry (Baseball Player)
6676 Washington Cir
Franklin, OH 45005-5521, USA

Ruklick, Joe (Athlete, Basketball Player)
1300 Central St
Apt 302
Evanston, IL 60201-1678, USA

Ruland, Jeff (Athlete, Basketball Player)
38 Glen Lake Dr
Medford, NJ 08055-3104, USA

Rule, Bob (Athlete, Basketball Player)
4303 Kansas Ave
Riverside, CA 92507-5153, USA

Rule, Gordon (Athlete, Football Player)
716 Manchester Rd
Neenah, WI 54956, USA

Rulin, Olesya (Actor)
c/o Brian Medavoy *Medavoy
Management*
10203 Santa Monica Blvd
Suite 400
Los Angeles, CA 90067, USA

Rulli, Sebastian (Actor)
c/o Gabriel Blanco *Gabriel Blanco
Iglesias (Mexico)*
Rio Balsas 35-32
Colonia Cuauhtemoc
DF 06500, Mexico

Rullo, Jerry (Athlete, Basketball Player)
3ee Brookline Blvd
Havertown, PA 19083-3923, USA

Rumble, Darren (Athlete, Hockey Player)
Seattle Thunderbirds
625 W James St
Kent, WA 98032-4406

Rumer (Music Group, Musician)
c/o Christian Bernhardt *Agency Group
Ltd, The (LA)*
1880 Century Park East
Los Angeles, CA 90067, USA

Rummells, Dave (Golfer)
1820 Harbor Blvd
Kissimmee, FL 34744-6623, USA

Rumsey, Janet (Athlete, Baseball Player)
7830 West County Road 80 North
Greensburg, IN 47240-7910, USA

Rumsfeld, Donald (Business Person)
1718 M. Street, NW 366
Washington, DC 20036, USA

Runager, Max (Athlete, Football Player)
P.O. Box 37971
Rock Hill, SC 29732, USA

Runco, Mario Lt Cmdr (Astronaut)
207 Lakeshore Dr
Seabrook, TX 77586-6128, USA

Rundgren, Todd (Musician)
c/o Staff Member *Agency Group Ltd, The
(NY)*
142 West 57th St
6th Floor
New York, NY 10019, USA

Rundles, Rich (Athlete, Baseball Player)
2103 Creekside Way
Jefferson City, TN 37760-1707, USA

Rundqvist, Thomas (Athlete, Hockey
Player)
Slobacksvagen 3
Hammaro 66341, Sweden

Runga, Bic (Musician)
c/o Staff Member *Paradigm (Monterey)*
404 W Franklin St
Monterey, CA 93940, USA

Runge, Brian (Athlete, Baseball Player)
1333 Via Isidro
Oceanside, CA 92021-8826, USA

Runge, Brian (Athlete, Baseball Player)
1333 Via Isidro
Oceanside, CA 92056-5629, USA

Runge, Paul (Athlete, Baseball Player)
8225 E County Dr
El Cajon, CA 92021-8826, USA

Runge, Paul (Athlete, Baseball Player)
1719 W Community Dr
Jupiter, FL 33458-8218, USA

Runnells, Tom (Athlete, Baseball Player,
Coach)
6045 Settlers Ridge Cir
Sylvania, OH 43560-9474, USA

Runnels, Terri (Model, Wrestler)
11520 NW 8th Ln
Gainesville, FL 32086, USA

RunningWolf, Myrton (Actor)
c/o Tracey Mapes *Imperium 7 Talent
Agency*
5455 Wilshire Blvd
Suite 1706
Los Angeles, CA 90036, USA

Runrig (Music Group)
c/o Staff Member *Sony Music
Entertainment Germany*
Neumarkter Str. 28
Muenchen 81673, Germany

Runte, Dan (Misc)
BIGFOOT 4x4, Inc.
6311 N Lindbergh Blvd
Hazelwood, MO 63042-2876, USA

Runyan, Jon (Congressman, Politician)
1239 Longworth HOB
Washington, DC 20515, USA

Runyan, Jon (Athlete, Football Player)
262 Mount Laurel Rd
Mount Laurel, NJ 08054, USA

Runyan, Marla (Athlete, Olympic Athlete,
Track Athlete)
5135 Center Way
Eugene, OR 97405-4673, USA

Runyan, Sean (Athlete, Baseball Player)
1958 Bermuda Pointe Dr
Haines City, FL 33844-2413, USA

Runyon, Jennifer (Actor)
5922 SW Amberwood Ave
Corvalis, OR 97333, USA

Ruotsalainen, Reijo (Athlete, Hockey
Player)
Jukurit Mikkeli Raviradantie 1
Mikkeli 50100, Finland

RuPaul (Actor, Model, Musician)
RuCo Inc
332 Bleecker St
#F-22
New York, NY 10014, USA

Rupe, Josh (Athlete, Baseball Player)
225 Arrowfield Rd
Virginia Beach, VA 23454-4300, USA

Rupe, Ryan (Athlete, Baseball Player)
5338 Pine Wood Hills Ct
Spring, TX 77386-3801, USA

Rupp, Debra Jo (Actor)
c/o Staff Member *Christopher Wright
Management*
3207 Winnie Dr
Los Angeles, CA 90068, USA

Rupp, Duane (Athlete, Hockey Player)
2446 McMonagle Ave
Pittsburgh, PA 15216-2705, USA

Rupp, Michael (Athlete, Hockey Player)
1936 Medford Sq
Hilliard, OH 43026-2219

Ruppe, Ing H 0 (Scientist)
Technische Universitat Munchen Richard-
Wagner-Str 18
Munich D-80333, GERMANY

Ruppersberger, C. A. (Congressman,
Politician)
2453 Rayburn HOB
Washington, DC 20515, USA

Ruprecht, Tom (Writer)
c/o Staff Member *3 Arts Entertainment Inc*
9460 Wilshire Blvd
7th Floor
Beverly Hills, CA 90210, USA

Rusch, Glendon (Athlete, Baseball Player)
6428 Chaffee St
Tujunga, CA 91042-2811, USA

Rusch, Kristine Kathryn (Writer)
PO Box 479
Lincoln City, OR 97367-0479, USA

Ruscha, Edward (Artist)
1840 Carla Rdg
Beverly Hills, CA 90210-1914, USA

Ruse, Michael Dr (Scientist)
651 E 6th Ave
Tallahassee, FL 32303-6305, USA

Rusedski, Greg (Tennis Player)
G-Force
PO Box 57
Caernarfon LL55 4WL, UNITED
KINGDOM

Rush (Music Group)
c/o Staff Member *Artist Group
International (NY)*
150 East 58th Street
Fl 19
New York, NY 10155, USA

Rush, Barbara (Actor)
1709 Tropical Avenue
Beverly Hills, CA 90210, USA

Rush, Cathy (Athlete, Basketball Player)
2433 Linden Dr
Havertown, PA 19083-1651, USA

Rush, Deborah (Actor)
c/o Rhonda Price *Gersh (NY)*
41 Madison Ave
New York, NY 10010, USA

Rush, Geoffrey (Actor)
c/o Stan Rosenfield *Stan Rosenfield &
Associates*
2029 Century Park E
Suite 1190
Los Angeles, CA 90067, USA

Rush, Ian (Athlete, Football Player)
McDonald's Sport Ambassadors
McDonald's Restaurants Ltd:
11 - 59 High Rd, East Finchley
London N2 8AW, UK

Rush, Jennifer (Musician)
c/o Staff Member *Armin Rahn Agency and
Management*
Dreimuehlenstr. 7
Muenchen 80469, Germany

Rush, Jerry (Athlete, Football Player)
17536 Oak Dr
Detroit, MI 48221, USA

Rush, Joshua (Actor)
c/o Susan Curtis *Curtis Talent
Management*
9607 Arby Dr
Beverly Hills, CA 90210, USA

Rush, Kareem (Athlete, Basketball Player)
2805 E 62nd St
Kansas City, MO 64130-3745, USA

Rush, Mathew (Adult Film Star)
c/o Staff Member *Diva Central Inc*
7510 W Sunset Blvd Ste 1445
Los Angees, CA 90046, USA

Rush, Matthew (Actor, Adult Film Star)
c/o Staff Member *Diva Central Inc*
7510 W Sunset Blvd Ste 1445
Los Angees, CA 90046, USA

Rush, Merrilee (Musician)
21458 NE Redmond Fall City Rd
Redmond, WA 98053, USA

Rush, Robert J (Athlete, Football Player)
8201 Scruggs Dr
Germantown, TN 38138, USA

Rush, Rudy (Comedian)
c/o Staff Member *ICM Partners (ICM-LA)*
10250 Constellation Blvd Fl 7
Los Angeles, CA 90067, USA

Rush, Sarah (Actor)
c/o Staff Member *Acme Talent & Literary (LA)*
1400 Atlantic Ave
Suite 274
Long Beach, CA 90814, USA

Rush, Tom (Musician)
Maple Hill Productions Inc
PO Box 1570
Wilson, WY 83014-1570, USA

Rushdie, A Salman (Writer)
Wylie Agency
Deborah Rodgers Ltd 49 Blenhiem Crescent
London Wll, England

Rushen, Patrice
PO Box 6278
Altadena, CA 91003, USA

Rushford, Jim (Athlete, Baseball Player)
11069 Caminito Alegra
San Diego, CA 92131-3504, USA

Rushing, Marion (Athlete, Football Player)
358 Bathon Dr
Pinckneyville, IL 62274, USA

Ruskin, Scott (Athlete, Baseball Player)
387 Saint Johns Golf Dr
Saint Augustine, FL 32092-1082, USA

Ruskowski, Terry (Athlete, Hockey Player)
2542 Silent Shore Ct
Richmond, TX 77406-1814, USA

Rusler, Robert
c/o Staff Member *Ellis Talent Group*
4705 Laurel Canyon Blvd
Suite 300
Valley Village, CA 91607, USA

Russ, Steve (Athlete, Football Player)
602 Charlesgate Cir
East Amherst, New York 14051, USA

Russ, Tim (Actor, Director)
7336 Santa Monica Blvd #711
W Hollywood, CA 90046, USA

Russell, Adam (Athlete, Baseball Player)
627 Mariner Vlg
Huron, OH 44839-1004, USA

Russell, Andy (Athlete, Football Player)
625 Liberty Ave #3100
Pittsburgh, PA 15222-3115, USA

Russell, Betsy (Actor)
c/o Mark Burg *Evolution Entertainment (LA)*
901 N Highland Ave
Los Angeles, CA 90038, USA

Russell, Bill (Athlete, Basketball Player, Olympic Athlete)
9415 SE 52nd St
Mercer Island, WA 98040-4723, USA

Russell, Bill (Athlete, Baseball Player, Coach)
27982 Red Pine Ct
Valencia, CA 91354-1888, USA

Russell, Bing
229 E. Gainsborough Rd.
Thousand Oaks, CA 91360

Russell, Bob (Athlete, Hockey Player)
World Hockey Centre
123-16715 Yonge St
Attn: Presidents Office
Newmarket, ON L3X 1X4, Canada

Russell, Brenda (Actor, Musician)
c/o Seth Keller *SKM Artist Management*
PO Box 25906
Los Angeles, CA 90025, USA

Russell, Brian (Athlete, Football Player)
15310 SE 80th St
Newcastle, MA 98059, USA

Russell, Bryon
455e E Thousand Oaks Blvd Ste 1ee
Westlake Village, CA 91362-3824, USA

Russell, Cam (Athlete, Hockey Player)
Halifax Mooseheads
5284 Duke St
Halifax, NS B3J 3L2, Canada

Russell, Cameron (Model)
c/o Staff Member *Elite Model Management (UK)*
40-42 Parker St
London WC2B 5PQ, United Kingdom

Russell, Campy (Athlete, Basketball Player)
66 Earlmoor Blvd
Pontiac, MI 48341-2816, USA

Russell, Cazzie (Athlete, Basketball Player)
Savannah College of Art and Design
Live Oak Community Church
425 W Montgomery Xrd
Savannah, GA 31406-3310, USA

Russell, Chuck (Director)
c/o Robert Stein *Paradigm (LA)*
360 N Crescent Dr
North Bldg
Beverly Hills, CA 90210, USA

Russell, Dana (Stylist)
c/o Staff Member *Ford Models (Chicago)*
311 W Superior St
Chicago, IL 60654, USA

Russell, David O (Actor, Director, Producer)
c/o Cynthia Swartz *Strategy PR*
535 8th Ave
20th Floor
New York, NY 10018, USA

Russell, Fred (Sportscaster)
226 Ensworth Pl
Nashville, TN 37205-1922, USA

Russell, JaMarcus (Athlete, Football Player)
2325 River Forest Dr
Mobile, AL 36605, USA

Russell, James (Athlete, Baseball Player)
2325 Oak Knoll Dr
Colleyville, TX 76034-4478, USA

Russell, Jeannie (Actor)
101923 Riverside Dr
N Hollywood, CA 91602, USA

Russell, Jeff (Athlete, Baseball Player)
2325 Oak Knoll Dr
Colleyville, TX 76034-4478, USA

Russell, John (Athlete, Baseball Player, Coach)
8004 Grand Estuary
Trl Unit 103
Bradenton, FL 34212-4256, USA

Russell, Johnny
Box Drawer 37
Hendersonville, TN 37077

Russell, Ken (Football Player)
c/o Staff Member *Detroit Lions*
222 Republic Dr
Allen Park, MI 48101, USA

Russell, Ken (Director)
c/o Staff Member *Independent Talent Group (ITG-UK)*
Oxford House
76 Oxford St
London W1D 1BS, UK

Russell, Keri (Actor)
c/o Joanna (Joanie) Burstein *Burstein Company, The*
15304 Sunset Blvd
suite 208
Pacific Palisades, CA 90272, USA

Russell, Kimberly
11617 Laurelwood Dr
Studio City, CA 91604-3818

Russell, Kurt (Actor, Producer, Writer)
c/o Michael Cooper *Creative Artists Agency (CAA-LA)*
2000 Ave Of The Stars
Los Angeles, CA 90067, USA

Russell, Leon (Musician)
Leon Russell Records
PO Box 58095
Nashville, TN 37205, USA

Russell, Leonard (Athlete, Football Player)
497 Saint Louis Ave
Apt 102
Long Beach, CA 90814, USA

Russell, Liane (Scientist)
130 Tabor Rd
Oak Ridge, TN 37830-5537, USA

Russell, Lynne (Anchor, Designer)
Benevento Lampshade Co
Lynne Russell Unlimited Inc
880 Marietta Hwy #630-273
Roswell, GA 30075

Russell, Mark
3201 33rd Pl .NW
Washington, DC 20008

Russell, Mark (Politician)
PO Box 9904
Washington, DC 20016-8904, USA

Russell, Phil (Athlete, Hockey Player)
590 Wind Drift Ln
Spring Lake, MI 49456-2168

Russell, Rubin (Athlete, Basketball Player)
P.O. Bix 542742
Grand Prairie, TX 75054-2742, USA

Russell, T E
8271 Melrose Ave #110
Los Angeles, CA 90046, USA

Russell, Theresa (Actor)
c/o Scott Zimmerman *Evolution Entertainment (LA)*
901 N Highland Ave
Los Angeles, CA 90038, USA

Russell, Twan (Athlete, Football Player)
11201 NW 8th St
Plantation, FL 33325, USA

Russell, Victoria (Actor)
c/o Staff Member *Wizzo and Company*
47 Beak St
London W1F 9SE, UK

Russell, William (Actor)
Kate Feast
Primrose Hill Studios
Fitzroy Road
London NW1 8TR, UNITED KINGDOM (UK)

Russell, Willy (Writer)
W R Ltd 43 Canning Street
London L87NN, England

Russell, Willy
W R Ltd 43 Canning Street
London L87NN, England

Russert, Luke (Correspondent)
c/o Staff Member *NBC Nightly News*
30 Rockefeller Plz #300S
New York, NY 10112, USA

Russhon, Chris (Stylist)
1531 E Stphens Dr
Tempe, AZ 85283, USA

Russi, Bernhard
6490 Andermatt
, SWITZERLAND

Russo, Deanna (Actor)
c/o Staff Member *Paradigm (LA)*
360 N Crescent Dr
North Bldg
Beverly Hills, CA 90210, USA

Russo, Gia (Stylist)
c/o Staff Member *Celestine - CA*
1666 20th St
#200-B
Santa Monica, CA 90404, USA

Russo, James (Actor)
c/o Staff Member *United Talent Agency (UTA)*
9336 Civic Center Dr
Beverly Hills, CA 90210, USA

Russo, Joe (Director, Producer, Writer)
c/o Staff Member *United Talent Agency (UTA)*
9336 Civic Center Dr
Beverly Hills, CA 90210, USA

Russo, John
218 Euclid Ave.
Glassport, PA 15045-1331

Russo, Patricia (Business Person)
Lucent Technologies Inc
600 Mountain Ave
New Providence, NJ 07974, USA

Russo, Rene (Actor, Model)
c/o John Crosby *Crosby/Spilo Management*
1310 N Spaulding Ave
Los Angeles, CA 90046, USA

Rust, Rod (Athlete, Football Coach, Football Player)
1 W 13th St
Ocean City, NJ 08226, USA

Rusteck, Dick (Athlete, Baseball Player)
6302 N 87th St
Scottsdale, AZ 85250-5712, USA

Rutan, Dick (Aviator)
2833 Delmar Ave
Mojave, CA 93501-1113, USA

Rutan, Elbert L (Burt) (Designer)
14329 Rutan Road
Mojave, CA 93501, USA

Rutan, Richard G (Dick) (Designer)
2833 Delmar Ave
Mojave, CA 93501, USA

Rutgens, Joe (Athlete, Football Player)
227 W Devlin St
Spring Valley, IL 61362, USA

Ruth, Lauren (Cartoonist)
PO Box 200206
New Heaven, CT 06520, USA

Ruth, Mike (Athlete, Football Player)
85 Jenkins Rd
Andover, MA 01810, USA

Rutherford, Jim (Athlete, Hockey Player)
Carolina Hurricanes
1400 Edwards Mill Rd
Raleigh, NC 27607-3624

Rutherford, Jim (Athlete, Hockey Player)
2521 Sharon View
Raleigh, NC 27614-6813, USA

Rutherford, Johnny (Athlete, Baseball
Player)
765 Briar Hill Ln
Bloomfield Hills, MI 48304-1443, USA

Rutherford, Johnny (Race Car Driver)
4919 Black Oak Lane
Fort Worth, TX 76114

Rutherford, Kelly (Actor)
c/o Katie Mason *Luber Roklin
Management*
8530 Wilshire Blvd
6th Floor
Beverly Hills, CA 90211, USA

Rutherford, Mike (Musician)
Solo Agency
55 Fulham High St
London SW6 3JJ, UNITED KINGDOM
(UK)

Rutherfurd, Emily (Actor)
c/o Chris Schmidt *Paradigm (LA)*
360 N Crescent Dr
North Bldg
Beverly Hills, CA 90210, USA

Ruthven, Dick (Athlete, Baseball Player)
13480 Providence Lake Dr
Alpharetta, GA 30004-7510, USA

Rutigliano, Sam (Athlete, Coach, Football
Coach, Football Player)
9671 Metcalf Rd
Willoughby, OH 44094, USA

Rutkowski, Ed (Athlete, Football Player)
47 Brenton Ln
Hamburg, NY 14075, USA

Rutland, Reggie (Athlete, Football Player)
4265 Jailette Rd
Atlanta, GA 30349, USA

Rutledge, Jeffrey R (Jeff) (Athlete, Coach,
Football Coach, Football Player)
6102 W Gary Dr
Chandler, AZ 85226, USA

Rutledge, Johnny (Athlete, Football
Player)
948 SW Avenue J
Belle Glade, FL 33430, USA

Rutledge, Wayne (Athlete)

Rutschman, Adolph (Ad) (Coach, Football
Coach)
2142 NW Pinehurst Dr
McMinnville, OR 97128, USA

Ruttan, Susan (Actor)
c/o Christopher Black *Opus Entertainment*
5225 Wilshire Blvd #905
Los Angeles, CA 90036, USA

Rutten, Bas (Actor, Athlete, Wrestler)
c/o Chandra Keyes *Jeff Sussman
Management*
15374 Dickens St
2nd Floor
Sherman Oaks, CA 91403

Rutter, Artur (Chef)
Chez Sylvia 15-6-101 HiRashi Honcho
HiRashi Kurume-shi, Tokyo, japan

Rutter, John M (Composer)
Old Lacey's
Saint John's Church
Duxford, Cambridge, UNITED KINGDOM
(UK)

Ruttgers, Jurgen (Government Official)
BM fur Bildung/Technologie
Heinemannstr 2
Bonn 53175, GERMANY

Rutting, Barbara
Sommerholz 30
Neumarkt, AUSTRIA 5202

Ruttman, Joe (Race Car Driver)
c/o Staff Member *NASCAR*
1801 Speedway Blvd
Daytona Beach, FL 32015, USA

Ruud, Sigmund (Skier)
Kirkeveien 57
Oslo 3, NORWAY

Ruud, Tom (Athlete, Football Player)
1821 S 33rd St
Lincoln, NE 68506, USA

Ruuska, Percy Sylvia (Swimmer)
4216 College View Way
Carmichael, CA 95608, USA

Ruusuvuori, Aarno E (Architect)
Annankalu 15 B 10
Helsinki 12 00120, UNITED KINGDOM
(UK)

Ruutel, Arnold (President)
Koidula Str 3-5
Tallinn 0010, ESTONIA

Ruwe, Robert P (Judge)
US Tax Court
400 2nd St NW
Washington, DC 20217, USA

Ruzek, Roger (Athlete, Football Player)
921 Warwick St
Bedford, TX 76022, USA

Ruzicka, Vladimir (Athlete, Hockey
Player)
17 Highland Ct
Needham, MA 02492, USA

R. Wolf, Frank (Congressman, Politician)
241 Cannon HOB
Washington, DC 20515, USA

Ryal, Mark (Athlete, Baseball Player)
204 E UniversitY Dr
Auburn, AL 36832-6703, USA

Ryal, Rusty (Athlete, Baseball Player)
204 E University D
Auburn, Al 36832-6703, USA

Ryan, Amy (Actor)
c/o Jennifer Wiley *Framework
Entertainment (NY)*
129 W 27th St Fl 12
New York, NY 10001, USA

Ryan, Arthur F (Business Person)
Prudential Insurance
Prudential Plaza
751 Broad St
Newark, NJ 07102, USA

Ryan, B J (Athlete, Baseball Player)
4014 Wisteria Ln
Benton, LA 71006, USA

Ryan, B J (Athlete, Baseball Player)
1211 Perdenalas Trl
Westlake, TX 6262-4820, USA

Ryan, Blanchard (Actor)
c/o Staff Member *Jeff Morrone
Entertainment*
9350 Wilshire Blvd
Suite 224
Beverly Hills, CA 90212, USA

Ryan, Bobby (Athlete, Hockey Player)
c/o Donald Meehan *Newport Sports
Management*
201 City Centre Dr
Suite 400
Mississauga, ON L58 2T4, Canada

Ryan, Buddy (Athlete, Football Coach,
Football Player)
819 Abingdon Ln
Shelbyville, KY 40065, USA

Ryan, Dave (Musician)
c/o Staff Member *Agency Group Ltd, The
(NY)*
142 West 57th St
6th Floor
New York, NY 10019, USA

Ryan, Debbie (Actor)
c/o Staff Member *Kritzer Levine Wilkins
Entertainment (KLWG)*
11872 La Grange Ave
1st Floor
Los Angeles, CA 90025, USA

Ryan, Debble (Comedian)
University of Virginia
Athletic Dept
PO Box 3785
Charlottesville, VA 22903, USA

Ryan, Debby (Actor)
c/o Jennifer Patredis *Innovative Artists (LA)*
10635 Santa Monica Blvd
130
Los Angeles, CA 90025, USA

Ryan, Dusty (Athlete, Baseball Player)
3906 Menton Ct
Merced, CA 95348-9537, USA

Ryan, Ed (Horse Racer)
PO Box 6249
Freehold, NJ 07728-6249, USA

Ryan, Fran
4204 Woodland
Burbank, CA 91505

Ryan, Frank (Athlete, Football Player)
P.O. Box 185
Grafton, VT 05146, USA

Ryan, Jay (Athlete, Baseball Player)
1232 Rocky River Rd W
Charlotte, NC 28213-5034, USA

Ryan, Jeri (Actor)
c/o David Lust *Rogers & Cowan PR (LA)*
9171 Wilshire Blvd
Suite 441
Beverly Hills, CA 90210, USA

Ryan, Ken (Athlete, Football Player)
45 Tanager Rd
Seekonk, MA 02771, USA

Ryan, Ken (Athlete, Baseball Player)
45 Tanager Rd
Seekonk, MA 02771-2707, USA

Ryan, Lee (Actor)
c/o Jack Gilardi *ICM Partners (ICM-LA)*
10250 Constellation Blvd Fl 7
Los Angeles, CA 90067, USA

Ryan, Lisa Dean (Actor)
c/o Staff Member *Pakula/King &
Associates*
9229 Sunset Blvd
Suite 315
Los Angeles, CA 90069, USA

Ryan, Marisa (Actor)
c/o Bob McGowan *McGowan
Management*
8733 W Sunset Blvd
Suite 103
West Hollywood, CA 90069, USA

Ryan, Mark (Actor)
c/o Staff Member *Starfish PR*
PO Box 7000-54
Redondo Beach, CA 90277, USA

Ryan, Max (Actor)
c/o Erik Kritzer *Kritzer Levine Wilkins
Entertainment (KLWG)*
11872 La Grange Ave
1st Floor
Los Angeles, CA 90025, USA

Ryan, Meg (Actor)
c/o Stephen Huvane *Slate Public
Relations*
9000 Sunset Blvd #915
West Hollywood, CA 90069, USA

Ryan, Michael (Athlete, Baseball Player)
521 Water St
Indiana, PA 15701-1927, USA

Ryan, Michelle (Actor)
c/o Philip Grenz *ICM Partners (ICM-LA)*
9601 Wilshire Blvd Fl 3
Beverly Hills, CA 90210, USA

Ryan, Mike (Athlete, Baseball Player)
592 Stoneham Rd
Wolfeboro, NH 03894-4711, USA

Ryan, Mitchell (Actor)
30355 Mulholland Dr
Cornell, CA 91301, USA

Ryan, Nolan (Athlete, Baseball Player)
The Nolan Ryan Foundation
2925 S Bvpass 35
Alvin, TX 77511-4721, USA

Ryan, Norbert R Jr (Admiral)
Cheif of Naval Porsonnel
2 Navy St
Washington, DC 20370, USA

Ryan, Pat (Athlete, Football Player)
6930 Old Kent Dr
Knoxville, TN 37919, USA

Ryan, Patrick G (Business Person)
Aon Corp
200 East Randolf St
Chicago, IL 60601, USA

Ryan, Paul (Congressman, Politician)
20 South Main St
Suite 10
Janesville, WI 53545, USA

Ryan, Rex (Athlete, Football Coach)
c/o David Dunn *Athletes First, LLC*
9140 Irvine Center Dr
Irvine, CA 92618, USA

Ryan, Rob (Athlete, Baseball Player)
12402 N Division St
Spokane, WA 99218-1930, USA

Ryan, Roz (Actor)
c/o Staff Member *Gage Group, The (LA)*
14724 Ventura Blvd
Suite 505
Sherman Oaks, CA 91403, USA

Ryan, Ryan (Actor)
c/o Staff Member *Warner Bros Television Production*
4000 Warner Blvd
Burbank, CA 91522-0001

Ryan, Sharon (Stylist)
c/o Staff Member *Halley Resources*
37 W 20th St
#603
New York, NY 10011, USA

Ryan, Shawn (Producer)
c/o Staff Member *ICM Partners (ICM-LA)*
10250 Constellation Blvd Fl 7
Los Angeles, CA 90067, USA

Ryan, Thomas M (Business Person)
CVS Corp
1 CVS Dr
Woonsocket, RI 02895, USA

Ryan, Tim (Congressman, Politician)
1421 Longworth HOB
Washington, DC 20515, USA

Ryan, Tim E (Athlete, Football Player)
1159 Calle Ventura
San Jose, CA 95120, USA

Ryan, Timothy T (Tim) (Athlete, Football Player)
4901 Sugar Creek Dr
Evansville, IN 47715, USA

Ryan, Tom K (Cartoonist)
North American Syndicate
235 E 45th St
New York, NY 10017, USA

Ryans, Larry (Athlete, Football Player)
110 Brookfield Dr
Greenwood, SC 29646, USA

Ryazanov, Eldar A (Director)
Bolshoi Tishinski Per 12 #70
Moscow 123557, RUSSIA

Rybak, Alexander (Musician)
c/o Staff Member *Lionheart International AB*
P.O. Box 11108
Nytorgsgatan 40 A
Stockholm SE-10061, Sweden

Rybkin, Ivan (Government Official)
National Security Council
4 Staraya Poischad
Moscow 103073, RUSSIA

Rybska, Agnieszka (Music Group, Musician)
RPM Music Productions
130 W 57th St #9D
New York, NY 10019, USA

Rychel, Warren (Athlete, Hockey Player)
Windsor Spitfires
8787 McHugh St
Windsor, ON N8S OA1, Canada

Rychlec, Tom (Athlete, Football Player)
71 Round Hill Rd
Southington, CT 06489, USA

Ryckman, Billy (Athlete, Football Player)
513 Doucet Rd
Lafayette, LA 70503, USA

rycroft, Mark (Athlete, Hockey Player)
2746 S Grant St
Englewood, CO 80113-1611

Rycroft, Melissa (Actor)
c/o Susan Madore *Guttman Associates*
118 S Beverly Dr
Suite 201
Beverly Hills, CA 90212, USA

Ryczek, Dan (Athlete, Football Player)
3714 Monitor Pl
Olney, MD 20832, USA

Ryczek, Paul (Athlete, Football Player)
9335 Scott Rd
Roswell, GA 30076, USA

Rydal, Emma (Actor)
c/o Lucy Brazier *The Rights House (UK)*
Drury House
34-43 Russell St
London WC2B 5HA, UK

Rydalch, Ron (Athlete, Football Player)
500 E Durfee
Grantsville, UT 84029, USA

Rydell, Bobby (Actor, Music Group, Musician)
917 Bryn Mawr Ave
Narberth, PA 19072, USA

Rydell, Christopher (Actor)
911 N Sweetzer #C
Los Angeles, CA 90069, USA

Rydell, Mark (Director)
Concourse Productions
3110 Main St #220
Santa Monica, CA 90405, USA

Ryder, JoJo (Actor, Producer, Writer)
c/o Staff Member *Untouchable J Productions*
9300 Civic Center Dr
#202
Beverly Hills, CA 90210, USA

Ryder, Lisa (Actor)
c/o Deb Dillistone *Red Management*
100 W. Pender St
Sun Tower, 7th Floor
Vancouver, BC V6B 1R8, Canada

Ryder, Michael (Athlete, Hockey Player)
c/o Staff Member *Boston Bruins*
TD Banknorth Garden
100 Legends Way, Suite 250
Boston, MA 02114, USA

Ryder, Mitch (Music Group, Musician)
Entertainment Services Int'l
6400 Pleasant Park Dr
Chanhassen, MN 55317, USA

Ryder, Nick (Athlete, Football Player)
14 Ridgeway
Goshen, NY 10924, USA

Ryder, Thomas O (Publisher)
Reader's Digest Assn
PO Box 100
Pleasantville, NY 10572, USA

Ryder, Winona (Actor)
c/o Mara Buxbaum *ID PR (LA)*
7060 Hollywood Blvd
8th Floor
Los Angeles, CA 90028, USA

Ryders, Ruff (Music Group)
c/o Staff Member *Universal Attractions*
135 W 26th St
12 Floor
New York, NY 10001, USA

Rydman, Blaine (Athlete, Hockey Player)
132 Wintergreen Rd
Winston Salem, NC 27107-1754, USA

Rydze, Richard (Athlete, Diver, Olympic Athlete)
915 Penn Ave Apt 1011
Pittsburgh, PA 15222-3831, USA

Ryerson, Ann
935 Gayley Ave.
Los Angeles, CA 90024

Ryerson, Gary (Athlete, Baseball Player)
1059 Terrace Crst
El Cajon, CA 92019-3129, USA

Ryff, Frankie
2055 McGraw
Bronx, NY 10462

Rykiel, Sonia F (Designer, Fashion Designer)
175 Blvd Saint Germain
Paris 75006, FRANCE

Ryknow (Musician)
c/o Staff Member *Agency Group Ltd, The (NY)*
142 West 57th St
6th Floor
New York, NY 10019, USA

Rylan, Marcy (Actor)
c/o Marnie Sparer *Innovative Artists (LA)*
1505 10th St
Santa Monica, CA 90401, USA

Rylance, Mark (Actor, Director)
Shakespeare's Globe
Southwark
London SE1, UNITED KINGDOM (UK)

Ryman, Robert T (Artist)
17 W 16th St
New York, NY 10011-6301, USA

Rymer, Charlie (Golfer)
1450 Spartan Ln
Athens, GA 30606-5326, USA

Rymsha, Andy (Athlete, Hockey Player)
8124 Huntington Rd
Huntington Woods, MI 48070-1654

Rynkiewicz, Mariusz (Artist, Misc)
12401 Alexander Road
Everett, WA 98204, USA

Rypdal, Terje (Musician)
PJP as
Utragata 16
Voss 5700, NORWAY

Rypien, Mark (Race Car Driver)
8718 Statesville Rd.
Charlotte, NC 28269, USA

Rysanek, Leony
Altenbeuren, GERMANY D-88682

Ryumin, Valery V (Astronaut, Misc)
Potchta Kosmonavtov
Moskovskoi Oblasti
Syvsdny Goroduk 141160, RUSSIA

Ryun, Jim (Athlete, Olympic Athlete, Track Athlete)
132 D St SE
Washington, DC 20003-1810, USA

Ryzhkov, Nikolai I (Misc)
State Duma
Okhotny Ryad 1
Moscow 103009, RUSSIA

RZA (Artist, Director, Musician)
c/o Holly Shakoor *42West (LA)*
11400 W Olympic Blvd
Suite 1100
Los Angeles, CA 90064, USA

Rzepczvnski, Marc (Athlete, Baseball Player)
5415 Christooher Dr
Yorba Linda, CA 92887-5851, USA

Rzeznik, Johnny (Musician)
c/o Staff Member *WmE2 (WMA-LA)*
1 William Morris Pl
Beverly Hills, CA 90212, USA

S, Kimberley
c/o Staff Member *Diva Central Inc*
7510 W Sunset Blvd Ste 1445
Los Angees, CA 90046, USA

S, Kimberly (DJ)
c/o Len Evans *Project Publicity*
312 West 53rd St
Suite 202
New York, NY 10019, USA

s, Mel (Athlete, Baseball Player)
RR 1 Box 97
West Columbia, WV 25287-8692, USA

Saad, Mindy (Stylist)
c/o Staff Member *Art House Management*
1548 16th St
Santa Monica, CA 90404, USA

Saadiq, Raphael (Musician)
c/o Marty Diamond *Paradigm (NY)*
360 Park Ave S Fl 16
New York, NY 10010, USA

Saakashvili, Mikhail (President)
President's Office
Rustaveli Prosp 29
Tbilsi 380008, GEORGIA

Saalfeld, Kelly (Athlete, Football Player)
761 N 153rd Ave
Omaha, NE 68154, USA

Saar, Bettye (Artist)
8074 Willow Glen Road
Los Angeles, CA 90046, USA

Saari, Roy A (Swimmer)
PO Box 7086
Mommoth Lakes, CA 93546, USA

Saarloos, Kirk (Athlete, Baseball Player)
8608 E Sunnywalk Ln
Anaheim, CA 92808-1689, USA

Saatchi, Charles (Business Person)
M&C Saatchi
36 Golden Square
London W1R 4EE, UNITED KINGDOM (UK)

Saatchi, Maurice (Business Person)
36 Golden Square
London W1R 4EE, UNITED KINGDOM (UK)

Sabah (Stylist)
6267 Bay Club Dr
#3
Fort Lauderdale, FL 33308, USA

Sabah, Sheikh Saad al-Abdullah al-Salem (Prime Minister, Prince)
Prime Minister's Office
PO Box 4
Safat
Kuwait City 13001, KUWAIT

Saban, Haim (Producer)
c/o Staff Member *Saban Entertainment*
10100 Santa Monica Blvd
26th Floor
Los Angeles, CA 90067, USA

Saban, Nick (Athlete, Football Coach, Football Player)
1549 Sharlo Ave
Baton Rouge, LA 70820, USA

Sabara, Daryl (Actor)
c/o Katie Rhodes *Untitled Entertainment (LA)*
350 S. Beverly Dr #200
Beverly Hills, CA 90212, USA

Sabathia, CC (Athlete, Baseball Player)
c/o Scott Parker *Legacy Sports Group*
500 Newport Center Dr
Suite 800
Newport Beach, GA 92660, USA

Sabatini, Gabriela (Tennis Player)
c/o Staff Member *Women's Tennis Association (WTA (UK))*
Palliser House
Palliser Rd
London W149EB, UK

Sabatino, Joe (Actor)
c/o Melanie Sharp *Sharp Talent*
117 N Orlando Ave
Los Angeles, CA 90048, USA

Sabatino, Michael (Actor)
13538 Valleyheart Dr
Sherman Oaks, CA 91423, USA

Sabato Jr, Antonio (Actor, Model)
c/o Tracy Steinsapir *Main Title Entertainment*
8383 Wilshire Blvd
Suite 408
Los Angeles, CA 90211, USA

Sabb, Dwayne (Athlete, Football Player)
26 Marie Rd
Fords, NJ 08863, USA

Sabbah, Michel (Religious Leader)
Latin Patriarch Office
PO Box 14152
Jerusalem, ISRAEL

Sabbatini, Rory (Athlete, Golfer)
9472 Sagrada Park
Fort Worth, TX 76126-1915, USA

Sabean, Brian (Baseball Player)
12 Solana Ct
Belmont, Cl\ 94nn2-36?, USA

Sabel, Erik (Athlete, Baseball Player)
3113 N 400 W
West Lafayette, IN 47906, USA

Sabella, Ernie (Actor, Artist, Voice Over Artist)
c/o Staff Member *Gage Group, The (LA)*
14724 Ventura Blvd
Suite 505
Sherman Oaks, CA 91403, USA

Sabelle (Music Group, Musician, Songwriter, Writer)
Sarmast Entertainment
241 W 36th St #2R
New York, NY 10018, USA

Saberhagen, Bret W (Athlete, Baseball Player)
Make a Difference Foundation
22817 Ventura Blvd
Suite 474
Woodland Hills, CA 91364-1202, USA

Sabetzki, Gunther (Athlete, Hockey Player)
30 Yonge St.
Toronto, ON M5E 1XB, Canada

Sabihy, Kyle (Actor)
c/o Dino May *Dino May Management*
6362 Hollywood Blvd #422
Hollywood, CA 90028-6323, USA

Sabiston Jr, David C (Doctor)
622 Cedar Club Circle
Chapel Hill, NC 27517-7215, USA

Sablan, Gregorio (Congressman, Politician)
423 Cannon HOB
Washington, DC 20515, USA

Sabo, Christopher A (Chris) (Athlete, Baseball Player)
7455 Stonemeadow Ln
Monteomerv, OH 45242-6305, USA

Sabo-Dusanko, Julie (Baseball Player)
7702 E Doubletree Ranch Rd Ste 150
Scottsdale, AZ 85258-2130, USA

Sabourin, Bob (Athlete, Hockey Player)
7400 Hogan Rd Apt 219
Jacksonville, FL 32216-1608

Sabourin, Gary (Athlete, Hockey Player)
54 Holland Ave
Chatham, ON N7M 2C7, Canada

Sabourin, Ken
728 White Oaks Ave
Catonsville, MD 21228-5868

Sabourin, Ken (Athlete, Hockey Player)
Washington Capitals
627 N Glebe Rd Ste 850, Arlington VA, 22203-2144

Sabuda, Robert (Writer)
155 West 72nd Street # 401
New York, NY 10023, USA

Saca, Elias Antonio (President)
Casa Presidencial Avda Cuba
Barrosan Jacinto
San Salvador, El SALVADOR

Sacchi, Robert
203 N. Gramercy Pl
Los Angeles, CA 90004

Sacco, Albert Dr (Astronaut)
101 Shane Way Unit 5
Laconia, NH 03246-1685, USA

Sacco, David (Athlete, Hockey Player, Olympic Athlete)
3 Bishop Ln
Middleton, MA 01949-1697, USA

Sacco, Joe (Athlete, Hockey Player)
Colorado Avalanche
1000 Chopper Cir
Denver, CO 80204-5805

Sacco, Joe (Athlete, Hockey Player, Olympic Athlete)
c/o Staff Member *Fantagraphics Books*
7563 Lake City Way
Seattle, WA 98115, USA

Sacco, Michael (Misc)
Seafarers International Union
5201 Auth Way
Suitland, MO 20746, USA

Saccomanno, Mark
8200 neely Dr apt 139
Austin, TX 78759-8556, USA

Saccone, Viviana (Actor)
c/o Staff Member *Telefe - Argentina*
Pavon 2444 (C1248AAT)
Buenos Aires, ARGENTINA

Sachdev, Asha (Actor, Bollywood)
18B Sunset Heights
59 Pali Hill Bandra
Mumbai, MS 40050, INDIA

Sachenbacher, Evi (Skier)
WSV Reit im Winkl
Rthausplatz 1
Reit im Winkl 83242, GERMANY

Sachin (Actor, Bollywood, Director, Filmmaker)
B609 Pearl Apartments 33 Swami Samarth Nagar
Cross Road No 3 Andheri
Bombay, MS 400 058, INDIA

Sachs, Andrew (Actor)
Richard Stone
2 Henrietta St
London WC2E 8PS, UNITED KINGDOM (UK)

Sachs, Gunter
101 E. 63rd St.
New York, NY 10021

Sachs, Jeffrey D (Economist)
The Earth Institute, Columbia University
405 Low Library, MC 4335
535 W 116th St
New York, NY 10027, USA

Sachs, Richard (Doctor)
6 Saint Ronan Terr
New Haven, CT 06511, USA

Sachs, William (Director)
3739 Montuso Place
Encino, CA 91436, USA

Sachu (Actor, Bollywood)
78 Sairam Colony
Alwarpet
Chennai, TN 600018, INDIA

Sack, Kevin (Journalist)
Los Angeles Times
Editorial Dept
202 W 1st St
Los Angeles, CA 90012, USA

Sack, Steve (Cartoonist)
Minneapolis Star-Tribune
425 Portland Ave
Minneapolis, MN 55488, USA

Sackheim, Daniel (Director, Editor, Producer)
c/o Chris Simonian *Creative Artists Agency (CAA-LA)*
2000 Ave Of The Stars
Los Angeles, CA 90067, USA

Sackhoff, Katee (Actor)
c/o Leland LaBarre *Bleu, An Entertainment Company*
5225 Wilshire Blvd
Suite 701
Los Angeles, CA 90036, USA

Sackinsky, Brian (Athlete, Baseball Player)
8 Valley Forge Rd
Shrewsbury, MA 01545-1553, USA

Sacks, Greg (Race Car Driver)
6092 Sabal Creek Blvd
Port Orange, FL 32128, USA

Sacks, Jonathan H (Religious Leader)
735 High Road
London N12 0US, UNITED KINGDOM (UK)

Sacks, Oliver W (Doctor, Writer)
2 Horatio St #3G
New York, NY 10014-1638, USA

Sackton, Frank (General)
7814 E Northland Dr
Scottsdale, AZ 85251-1635, USA

Sacramone, Alicia (Athlete, Gymnast, Olympic Athlete)
c/o Staff Member *USA Gymnastics*
Pan American Plz #300
201 S Capitol Ave
Indianapolis, IN 46225, USA

Sadanah, Kamal (Actor, Bollywood)
Jal Kamal Plot 202
23rd Road Bandra
Mumbai, MS 400050, INDIA

Sadat, Jehan El- (Activist)
University of Maryland
Int'l Development Center
College Park, MD 20742, USA

Sadat, Madame Jehan
NW2310 Decatur Pl.
Washington, DC 20008

Sadecki, Raymond M (Ray) (Athlete, Baseball Player)
4237 E Clovis Ave
Mesa, AZ 85206-1945, USA

Sadek, Mike (Athlete, Baseball Player)
6741 Quartz Mine Rd
Mountain Ranch, CA 95246-9748, USA

Sadik, Nafis (Government Official)
United Nations Population Fund
220 E 42nd St
New York, NY 10017, USA

Sadler, Billy
236llnverness Dr
Pensacola, FL 32503-5049, USA

Sadler, Carl (Athlete, Baseball Player)
2280 NW Bailey Grade Rd
Greenville, FL 32331-4500, USA

Sadler, Donnie (Athlete, Baseball Player)
802 Sadler Rd
Valley Mills, Tx 76689-4499, USA

Sadler, Elliott (Race Car Driver)
Gillette/Evernham
160 Munday Rd
Statesville, NC 28677, USA

Sadler, Hermie (Race Car Driver)
PO Box 32
Endoria, VA 23847, USA

Sadler, Ray (Athlete, Baseball Player)
4423 Lake Shore Dr
Waco, TX 76710-1448, USA

Sadler, William (Actor)
c/o James Suskin *James Suskin Management*
2 Charlton St Ste 5K
New York, NY 10014, USA

Sadoski, Thomas (Actor)
c/o Howard Axel *TMT Entertainment Group*
648 Broadway
Suite 1002
New York, NY 10012, USA

Sadoulet, Bernard (Astronomer)
2824 Forest Ave
Berkeley, CA 94705, USA

Sadowski, Bob (Athlete, Baseball Player)
26 Barrington Ct
Sharpsburg, GA 30277, USA

Sadowski, Bob (Athlete, Baseball Player)
1465 Creekside Dr
High Ridge, MO 63049-1314, USA

Sadowski, Jim (Athlete, Baseball Player)
537 Fieldcrest Dr
Pittsburgh, PA 15209-1211, USA

Sadowski, Jonathan (Actor)
c/o Susan Yoo *Susan Yoo*
Prefers to be contacted via telephone
Los Angeles, CA, USA

Sadowsky, Clint (Athlete, Baseball Player)
2801 Tropicana Ave
Norman, OK 73071-1711, USA

Saenz, Chris (Athlete, Baseball Player)
7919 N Rondure Loop
Tucson, AZ 85743-7413, USA

Saenz, Olmedo
Aminta Burgos Amado 2027
Chitre Herrera, Panama, USA

Safdie, Moshe (Architect)
100 Rev Nazareno Properzi Way
Somerville, MA 02143, USA

Safer, Morley (Journalist)
c/o 60 Minutes *CBS News Productions*
524 W 57th St
8th Floor
New York, NY 10019, USA

Saferight, Harry (Baseball Player)
2321 Wadebridge Rd
Midlothian, VA 23113-3839, USA

Saffell, Tom (Athlete, Baseball Player)
1503 Clower Creek Dr
Apt Ha262
Sarasota, FL 34231-1911, USA

Saffiotti, Umberto (Doctor)
5114 Wissioming Road
Bathesda, MD 20816, USA

Safin, Marat (Tennis Player)
TC Weiden am Postkeller
Schirmitzer Weg
Weiden 92637, GERMANY

Safina, Alessandro (Opera Singer)
Interscope Records
2220 Colorado Ave
Santa Monica, CA 90404, USA

Safina, Carl (Scientist)
National Audubon Society
700 Broadway
New York, NY 10003-9536, USA

Safina, Dinara (Athlete, Tennis Player)
c/o Staff Member *Women's Tennis Association (WTA (US))*
One Progress Plaza
Ste 1500
St Petersburg, FL 33701, USA

Safka, Melanie (Musician)
Two Story Records, Inc
53 Baymont St
Clearwater, FL 33767-1705, USA

Safran Foer, Jonathan (Writer)
c/o Geoffrey Sanford *Rabineau Wachter & Sanford Literary*
522 Wilshire Blvd Ste L
Santa Monica, CA 90401, USA

Safuto, Dominick (Randy) (Music Group, Musician)
PO Box 656507
Fresh Meadows, NY 11365, USA

Safuto, Frank (Music Group, Musician)
PO Box 656507
Fresh Meadows, NY 11365, USA

Sagal, Jean (Actor)
Progressive Artists Agency
400 S Beverly Dr #216
Beverly Hills, CA 90212, USA

Sagal, Katey (Actor)
c/o Belle Zwerdling *B and B Management*
1041 N Formosa Ave
Formosa Bldg Rm. 194
W Hollywood, CA 90046, USA

Sagal, Liz (Actor)
c/o Staff Member *Gersh (LA)*
9465 Wilshire Blvd
Suite 600
Beverly Hills, CA 90212, USA

Sagan, Carl (Astronomer, Writer)
Carl Sagan Productions, Inc
7165 Sunset Blvd
Los Angeles, CA 90046-4417, USA

Saganiuk, Rocky (Athlete, Hockey Player)
12909 Norwich St
Plainfield, IL 60585-7908

Sagansky, Jeff
145 Ocean Ave.
Santa Monica, CA 90402

Sagar, Ramanand (Actor, Director, Filmmaker, Producer)
Natraj Studios 194 M V Road
Andheri (E)
Bombay, MS 400 069, INDIA

Sagdeev, Roald Z (Physicist)
Space Research Institute
Profsoyuznaya 84/32
Moscow B485 11780, RUSSIA

Sage, Halston (Actor)
c/o Nick Styne *Creative Artists Agency (CAA-LA)*
2000 Ave Of The Stars
Los Angeles, CA 90067, USA

Sage, William (Actor)
Gersh Agency
232 N Canon Dr
Beverly Hills, CA 90210, USA

Sagebrecht, Marianne (Actor)
Kaulbachstr 61
Ruckgeb
Munich 80539, GERMANY

Sagely, Floyd (Athlete, Football Player)
181 Wildflower Pl
Edwards, CO 81362, USA

Sagemiller, Melissa (Actor)
c/o Leslie Siebert *Gersh (LA)*
9465 Wilshire Blvd
Suite 600
Beverly Hills, CA 90212, USA

Sager, A J (Athlete, Baseball Player)
10310 Belmont Meadows Ln
errysburg, OH 43551-6403, USA

Sager, Carole Bayer (Musician, Songwriter)
10761 Bellagio Road
Los Angeles, CA 90077, USA

Sagers, Rand (Stylist)
c/o Celebrity Stylist *Oliver Piro Inc*
725 Riverside Dr Apt 3A
New York, NY 10031, USA

Saget, Bob (Actor)
c/o Daniel (Danny) Sussman *Brillstein Entertainment Partners*
9150 Wilshire Blvd #350
Beverly Hills, CA 90212, USA

Saglio, Laura (Actor)
Cineart
36 Rue de Ponthieu
Paris 75008, FRANCE

Sagmoen, Marc (Athlete, Baseball Player)
19715 1st Pl SW
Normandy Park, WA 98166-4007, USA

Sagnier, Ludivine (Actor)
c/o Jon Rubinstein *Authentic Talent and Literary Management*
45 Main St
Suite 1004
Brooklyn, NY 11201, USA

Sagona, Katie (Actor)
Wilhelmina Creative Mgmt
300 Park Ave S #200
New York, NY 10010, USA

Sahagun, Elena (Actor)
Artists Agency
1180 S Beverly Dr #301
Los Angeles, CA 90035, USA

Sahara Hotnights (Music Group)
c/o Staff Member *Paradigm (Monterey)*
404 W Franklin St
Monterey, CA 93940, USA

Sahgal, Ajay (Actor, Producer, Writer)
c/o Nicole Clemens *ICM Partners (ICM-LA)*
10250 Constellation Blvd Fl 7
Los Angeles, CA 90067, USA

Sahgal, Nayantara (Writer)
181B Rajpur Road
Dehra Dun, Uttar Pradesh 248009, INDIA

Sahi, Deepa (Actor, Bollywood)
466 Laxmi Bhuvan Sardar Patel Road
Mumbai, MS 400004, INDIA

Sahl, Mort (Actor, Comedian)
1441 3rd Ave #12-C
New York, NY 10028, USA

Sahm, Hans-Werner (Artist)
Zur Wasserburg 7
Bidingen
Schwab, GERMANY

Said, Boris (Race Car Driver)
32675 Schoolcraft Rd
Livonia, MI 48150, USA

Said III, Boris (Race Car Driver)
441 Victory Rd.
Winchester, VA 22602, USA

Saidock, Tom (Athlete, Football Player)
20316 Old Colony Rd
Dearborn Heights, MI 48127, USA

Sailer, Anton (Toni) (Skier)
Gundhabing 19
Kitzbuhl 6370, AUSTRIA

Sailer, Toni
Gundhabing 19
Kitzbuhel, AUSTRIA A-6370

Sailors, Kenny (Ken) (Athlete, Basketball Player)
571e Howe Ln
Laramie, WY 82070-8935, USA

Saimes, George (Athlete, Football Executive, Football Player)
2307 Beechmoor Dr NW
North Canton, OH 44720, USA

Sain, Johnny
2 So. 707 Ave. Latour
Oakbrook, IL 60521

Saindon, Pat (Athlete, Football Player)
105 King Arthur Pl
Alabaster, AL 35007, USA

Sainsbury of Preston Candover, John D (Business Person)
J Sainsbury PLC
Stamford House
Stamford St
London SE1 9LL, UNITED KINGDOM (UK)

Sainsbury of Turville, David J (Business Person)
4 Charterhouse Mews
Charterhouse Square
London EC1M 6BB, UNITED KINGDOM (UK)

Saint, Crosbie E (General)
1116 N Pitt St
Alexandria, VA 22314, USA

Saint, Eva Marie (Actor)
c/o Joel Dean *TalentWorks (LA)*
3500 W Olive Ave
Suite 1400
Burbank, CA 91505, USA

Saint, Silva (Adult Film Star)
c/o Staff Member *Atlas Multimedia Inc*
9005 Eton Ave Ste C
Canoga Park, CA 91304-1743, USA

Saint, Sylvia
Suze.net
26500 W Agoura Rd #389
Calabasas, CA 91302

Sainte-Marie, Buffy (Musician, Songwriter)
RR 1 Box 368
Kapaa, HI 96746, USA

Saint James, Sara
289 So. Robertson Blvd. #259
Beverly Hills, CA 90212

Saint James, Susan (Actor)

Sainz, Salvador (Actor, Director)
Ave Prat de la Riba 43
Reus (Tarragona) 43201, SPAIN

Saipe, Mike (Athlete, Baseball Player)
4191 Combe Way
San Diego, CA 92122-2511, USA

Sajak, Pat (Game Show Host)
c/o Staff Member *PAT Productions*
10202 W Washington Blvd
Robert Young Bldg., Suite 2000
Culver City, CA 90232, USA

Sajawal, Aziz (Actor, Bollywood, Director, Filmmaker)
S303 Sameer Society JP Road
Seven Bungalows Andheri
Mumbai, MS 400058, INDIA

Sajko, Kristina (Model)
Karin Models
6 W 14th St #300
New York, NY 10011, USA

Sakai, Hiroyuki (Chef)
La Rochelle 2-15-1 Shibuya Toho
Seimei Building Shibuya-ku
Tokyo, USA

Sakamoto, Ryoichi (Composer)
Columbia Artists Mgmt Inc
165 W 57th St
New York, NY 10019, USA

Sakamoto, Soichi (Coach, Swimmer)
768 McCully St
Honolulu, HI 96826, USA

Sakamura, Ken (Inventor)
University of Tokyo
Information Science Dept
Tokyo, JAPAN

Sakata, Lenn (Athlete, Baseball Player)
San Jose Giants
6770 Hawaii Kai Dr Apt 609
Honolulu, HI 96825-1529, USA

Sakata, Theresa Kemper (Stylist)
12515 Portada Pl
San Diego, CA 92130, USA

Sakato, George T (General)
8369 Katherine Way
Denver, CO 80221-4613, USA

Sakharov, Alik (Cinematographer)
6050 Boulevard E #4D
West New York, NJ 07093, USA

Sakic, Joe (Athlete, Hockey Player)
Thompson, Dorfman, Sweatman
PO Box 639 Stn Main
Attn: Donald Baizley
Winnipeg, MB R3C 2K6, Canada

Sakmann, Bert (Nobel Prize Laureate)
Max-Planck Institut furrschu Medizinische
Forschung Jahnstrasse 29
Heidelberg 69120, GERMANY

Saks, Gene (Actor, Director)
International Creative Mgmt
40 W 57th St #1800
New York, NY 10019, USA

Sakshaug, Eugene C (Engineer)
18 Grove Ave
Pittsfield, MA 01201, USA

Sala, Edoardo (Actor)
Carol Levi Co
Via Giuseppe Pisanelli
Rome 00196, ITALY

Sala, Oskar
Leistikowstr. 5
Berlin, GERMANY 14050

Sala, Richard (Cartoonist)
3131 College Ave
Berkeley, CA 94705, USA

Salaam, Abdul (Athlete, Football Player)
11153 Embassy Dr
Cincinnati, OH 45240, USA

Salaam, Ephraim (Athlete, Football Player)
c/o Staff Member *EAG Sports Management*
12910 Agustin Pl
Playa Vista, CA 90094, USA

Salaam, Rashaan (Athlete, Football Player, Heisman Trophy Winner)
8132 Brookhaven Rd
San Diego, CA 92114, USA

Salac, Joe
2205 Avenue Colisee Quebec
PQ, CANADA GIL 4W7

Salad Hassan, Abdikassim (President)
President's Office
People's Palace
Mogadishu, SOMALIA

Salahi, Michaele (Reality TV Star)
c/o Staff Member *Bravo (NY)*
30 Rockefeller Plaza
New York, NY 10112, USA

Salamanca & Garcia (Writer)
c/o Gabriel Blanco *Gabriel Blanco Iglesias (Mexico)*
Rio Balsas 35-32
Colonia Cuauhtemoc
DF 06500, Mexico

Salanda, Zoe (Actor)
c/o Andrea Pett-Joseph *Brillstein Entertainment Partners*
9150 Wilshire Blvd #350
Beverly Hills, CA 90212, USA

Salans, Lester B (Doctor)
Sandoz Research Institute
RR 10
Hanover, NJ 07936, USA

Salas, Mark (Athlete, Baseball Player)
1302 6th St SE
Ruskin, FL 33570-5308, USA

Salata, Paul (Athlete, Football Player)
3723 Birch St
Apt 11
Newport Beach, CA 92660, USA

Salazar, Alberto (Athlete, Olympic Athlete, Track Athlete)
Nike Inc 1 SW Bowerman Dr
Beaverton, OR 97005-0979, USA

Salazar, Arion (Musician)
Eric Godtland Mgmt
5715 Claremont Ave #C
Oakland, CA 94618, USA

Salazar, Eliseo (Race Car Driver)
701 S. Girls School Rd.
Indianapolis, IN 46231, USA

Salazar, Luis (Athlete, Baseball Player)
20808 Cabrillo Way
Boca Raton, FL 33428-1201, USA

Saldana, Theresa (Actor)
c/o Staff Member *Leavitt Talent Group*
8255 W Sunset Blvd
West Hollywood, CA 90046, USA

Saldana, Zoe (Actor)
2320 St George St
Los Angeles, CA 90027, USA

Saldanha, Carlos (Animator, Director)
c/o Staff Member *Blue Sky Studios*
44 South Broadway Fl 17
White Plains, NY 10601, USA

Saldarini, Giovanni Cardinal (Religious Leader)
Archdiocese of Turin
Via dell'Archivescovado 12
Turin 10121, ITALY

Saldi, Jay (Athlete, Football Player)
303 Donley Ct
Southlake, TX 76092, USA

Sale, Jamie (Dancer)
12116 NW 128th St
Edmonton, AB T5L 1C3, CANADA

Saleaumua, Dan (Athlete, Football Player)
8234 Marshall Dr
Overland Park, KS 66214, USA

Saleen, Steve
Saleen Inc.
76 Fairbanks
Irvine, California 92618-1602, USA

Saleh, Ali Abdullah (General, President)
President's Office
Zubairy St
Sana'a, YEMEN ARAB REPUBLIC

Salem, Dahlia (Actor)
c/o Robert (Rob) Gomez *Precision Entertainment*
6338 Wilshire Blvd
Los Angeles, CA 90048, USA

Salem, Harvey (Athlete, Football Player)
25 Menlo Pl
Berkeley, CA 94707, USA

Salem, Marc (Actor, Comedian)

Salemi, Sam (Athlete, Football Player)
2971 Delaware Ave
Kenmore, NY 14217, USA

Salenger, Meredith (Actor)
c/o Scott Zimmerman *Evolution Entertainment (LA)*
901 N Highland Ave
Los Angeles, CA 90038, USA

Salerno-Sonnenberg, Nadja (Musician)
Columbia Artists Mgmt Inc
165 W 57th St
New York, NY 10019, USA

Sales, Eugenio de Araujo Cardinal (Religious Leader)
Palacio Sao Joaquim
Rua Gloria 446
Rio de Janeiro RJ 20241-150, BRAZIL

Sales, Nykesha (Basketball Player)
Connecticut Sun
Mohegan Sun Arena
Uncasville, CT 06382, USA

Saleski, Don (Athlete, Hockey Player)
1800 N. Ridley Creek. Rd.
Media, PA 19063-4529, USA

Salgado, Michael (Musician)
c/o Staff Member *Sony Music Miami*
605 Lincoln Rd Fl 7
Miami Beach, FL 33139, USA

Salgado, Sabastiano R (Photographer)
Instituto Terra
Fazenda Bulcao
Minas Gerais, BRAZIL

Saliba, Metropolitan Primate Philip (Religious Leader)
Antiochian Orthodox Christian Diocese
358 Mountain Road
Englewood, NJ 07631, USA

Saliers, Emily (Musician, Songwriter, Writer)
Russell Carter Artist Mgmt
315 Ponce de Leon Ave #755
Decatur, GA 30030, USA

Salim, Salim Ahmed (Prime Minister)
Organization of African Unity
PO Box 3243
Addis Ababa, ETHIOPIA

Salinas, Carmen (Actor)
c/o Staff Member *Televisa*
Blvd Adolfo Lopez Mateos 232
Colonia San Angel INN
DF CP 01060, MEXICO

Salinas, Dixie Carter (Producer)
TNA Wrestling, LLC
209 10th Ave South
Suite 302
Nashville, TN 37210, USA

Salinas, Jorge (Actor)
c/o Staff Member *Televisa*
Blvd Adolfo Lopez Mateos 232
Colonia San Angel INN
DF CP 01060, MEXICO

Salinas, Maria Elena (Actor)
c/o Staff Member *Univision*
605 3rd St. Fl12
New York, NY 10158, USA

Salinas, Nora (Actor)
c/o Staff Member *Televisa*
Blvd Adolfo Lopez Mateos 232
Colonia San Angel INN
DF CP 01060, MEXICO

Salinger, Amy (Stylist)
c/o Staff Member *Arlene Wilson Management*
807 N Jefferson St
#200
Milwaukee, WI 53202, USA

Salinger, Diane (Actor)
c/o Robert Depp *Beverly Hecht Agency*
3500 W Olive Ave
Suite 1180
Burbank, CA 91505, USA

Salinger, Emmanuel (Actor)
Cineart
36 Rue de Ponthieu
Paris 75008, FRANCE

Salinger, Matt (Actor)
Bresler Kelly Assoc
11500 W Olympic Blvd #510
Los Angeles, CA 90064, USA

Salisbury, Benjamin (Actor)
c/o Staff Member *ICA Talent*
818 12th Street Ste 9
Santa Monica, CA 90403, USA

Salisbury, Sean (Athlete, Football Player)
5823 Brushy Creek Trl
Dallas, TX 75252, USA

Salise, Steve (Congressman, Politician)
429 Cannon HOB
Washington, DC 20515, USA

Salkeld, Roger (Athlete, Baseball Player)
27824 Ridgegrove Dr
Santa Clarita, CA 91350-1747, USA

Salkind, Ilya (Producer)
Pinewood Studios
Iverheath
Iver
Bucks SL0 0NH, UNITED KINGDOM
(UK)

Sall, John (Misc)
201 Vineyard Ln
Cary, NC 27513-3067, USA

Salle, David (Artist)
Larry Gagosian Gallery
980 Madison Ave #PH
New York, NY 10021, USA

Salles, Gualter (Race Car Driver)
Dale Coyne Racing
13400 Budier Rd
Plainfield, IL 60544, United States

Salles, Walter (Director, Producer)
c/o Staff Member *WME (LA)*
9601 Wilshire Blvd Fl 3
Beverly Hills, CA 90210, USA

Salley, John (Athlete, Basketball Player, Television Host)
Black Folk Entertainment
Salley Foundation
1ees2 Shana Way
Elk Grove, CA 95757-5956, USA

Sallinen, Aulis H (Composer)
Runneberginkatu 37A
Helsinki 10 00100, FINLAND

Salling, Mark (Actor)
c/o Jason Solomon *Full Circle Management*
4932 Lankershim Blvd
Suite 202
North Hollywood, CA 91601, USA

Sallis, Peter (Actor)
Jonathan Altaras
13 Shorts Gardens
London WC2H 9AT, UNITED KINGDOM (UK)

Sally, Jerome (Athlete, Football Player)
4107 Roxbury Ct
Columbia, MO 65203, USA

Salminen, Matti (Opera Singer)
Mariedi Anders Artists
535 El Camino del Mar
San Francisco, CA 94121, USA

Salming, Borje (Athlete, Hockey Player)
Borje SalminE and Company
Box 45438
Stockholm S-10431, Sweden

Salmon, Brad (Athlete, Baseball Player)
11102 Herschel Loop
Daphne, AL 36526-6648, USA

Salmon, Colin (Actor)
Markham & Froggatt
Julian House
4 Windmill St
London W1P 1HF, UNITED KINGDOM (UK)

Salmon, Tim (Athlete, Baseball Player)
6061 E Sunnyside Dr
Scottsdale, AZ 85254-4977, USA

Salmons, John (Basketball Player)
Philadelphia 76ers
909 Waverly Rd
Bryn Mawr, PA 190l0-1930, USA

Salo, Mika (Race Car Driver)
TWI Formula One
Leafield
Whitney
Oxon OX8 5PF, UNITED KINGDOM (UK)

Salo, Mike (Race Car Driver)
Sauber Racing
Wildbachstr. 9
Hinwil, SWITZERLAND

Salo, Tommy (Athlete, Hockey Player)
Leksands IF Ishockey
Box 118
Leksand, S-79323 Sweden

Salome, Angel (Athlete, Baseball Player)
2153 Amsterdam Ave Apt 15
New York, NY 10032-2530, USA

Salomon, Mikael (Cinematographer)
PO Box 2230
Los Angeles, CA 90078, USA

Salomon, Sandy (Actor)
Cineart
36 Rue de Ponthieu
Paris 75008, FRANCE

Salonen, Brian (Athlete, Football Player)
2801 S Russell St
Suite 33
Missoula, MT 59801, USA

Salonen, Esa-Pekka (Composer)
Los Angeles Philharmonic
Music Center
135 N Grand Ave
Los Angeles, CA 90012, USA

Salonga, Lea (Actor, Musician)
c/o Staff Member *Agency Group Ltd, The (UK)*
361-373 City Rd
London EC1V 1PQ, UK

Salopek, Paul (Journalist)
Chicago Tribune
Editorial Dept
435 N Michigan Ave
Chicago, IL 60611, USA

Salpeter, Edwin E (Scientist)
116 Westbourne Lane
Ithaca, NY 14850-2414, USA

Salt, Jennifer (Actor)
3742 Sheridge Dr
Sherman Oaks, CA 91403-5005, USA

Saltalamacchia, Jarrod (Athlete, Baseball Player)
12688 Headwater Cir
Wellington, FL 33414-4908, USA

Salter, Bryant (Athlete, Football Player)
16810 SW 88th Ct
Palmetto Bay, FL 33157, USA

Salter, Hans
3658 Woodhill Canyon
Studio City, CA 91604

Saltpeter, Edwin E (Misc)
Cornell University
Physical Sciences Dept
Ithaca, NJ 14853, USA

Saltykov, Aleksey A (Director)
Institute Mosfilmosvsky
Per 4A #104
Moscow 119285, RUSSIA

Saltykov, Boris G (Economist, Government Official)
Bryusov Per 11
Moscow 103009, RUSSIA

Salva, Victor (Director)
c/o Staff Member *Gersh (LA)*
9465 Wilshire Blvd
Suite 600
Beverly Hills, CA 90212, USA

Salvador, Bryce (Athlete, Hockey Player)
1059 Lawrence Ave
Westfield, NJ 07090-3740

Salvador, Henri
6 place Vendome
Paris, FRANCE 75001

Salvadori, Al (Athlete, Basketball Player)
787 Lindsay Rd
Carnegie, PA 15106-3845, USA

Salvail, Eve (DJ)
c/o Len Evans *Project Publicity*
312 West 53rd St
Suite 202
New York, NY 10019, USA

Salvatore, Adamo (Musician)
Tonight Music S.A.
Avenue Louise 522
Bruxelles 1050, BELGIUM

Salvatore, Robert Anthony (R.A.) (Writer)
c/o Staff Member *Random House*
1540 Broadway
New York, NY 10036, USA

Salvay, Bennett (Composer, Musician)
c/o Staff Member *Gorfaine/Schwartz Agency Inc*
4111 W Alameda Ave
Suite 509
Burbank, CA 91505, USA

Salvian, Dave (Athlete, Hockey Player)
4451 Breckongate Crt
Burlington, ON L7L OB2, Canada

Salvino, Carmen (Bowler)
65 Stevens Dr
Schaumburg, IL 60173-2176, USA

Samaras, Lucas (Artist, Photographer)
Pace Gallery
32 E 57th St
New York, NY 10022, USA

Samardzija, Jeff (Athlete, Baseball Player)
3351 N Southoort Ave
Chicago, IL 60657-1440, USA

Samberg, Andy (Actor)
c/o Staff Member *Mosaic Media Group*
9200 W. Sunset Blvd
10th Floor
Los Angeles, CA 90069, USA

Sambito, Joe (Athlete, Baseball Player)
23 Modesto
Irvine, CA 92602-0929, USA

Sambora, Richie (Music Group, Musician, Songwriter)
c/o Chris Goodman *Outside Organisation, The*
Butler House
177-178 Tottenham Court Rd
London W1T 7NY, UNITED KINGDOM (UK)

Samcoff, Ed (Athlete, Baseball Player)
8153 Maderia Port Ln
Fair Oaks, CA 95628-2833, USA

Samford, Ron (Athlete, Baseball Player)
2174 Kessler Ct
Dallas, TX 75208-2948, USA

Samios, Nicholas P (Misc, Physicist)
Brookhaven National Laboratory
Directors's Office
2 Center St
Upton, NY 11973, USA

Samis, Phil
1509 Rue Sherbrooke O
Montreal, CANADA QC H3G 1M1

Sammartino, Bruno (Wrestler)
413 Goldsmith Road
Pittsburgh, PA 15237-3723, USA

Sammie (Actor)
c/o Staff Member *Green Light Talent Agency*
P.O. Box 3172
Beverly Hills, CA 90212, USA

Sammons, Clint (Athlete, Baseball Player)
732 King Sword Ct SE
Mableton, GA 30126-6437, USA

Samms, Emma (Actor)
2934 1/2 N Beverly Glen Circle #417
Los Angeles, CA 90077, USA

Sammy, Sugar (Actor)
c/o Jodi Lieberman *Parallel Entertainment*
9420 Wilshire Blvd #250
Beverly Hills, CA 90212, USA

Samoilova, Tatiana Y (Actor)
Spiridonyevsky Per 8/11
Moscow 103104, RUSSIA

Samotsvetov, Anatoly (Athlete, Hockey Player)
501 Broadway
Nashville, TN 37203, USA

Sampaio, Jorge (President)
President's Office
Palacio de Belem
Lisbon 1300, PORTUGAL

Sampen, Bill (Athlete, Baseball Player)
11 Carnaby Ct
Brownsburg, IN 46112-8834, USA

Sample, Billy (Athlete, Baseball Player)
10 Pascack Rd
Township of Washington, NJ 07676-5116, USA

Sample, Joe (Musician)
1255 5th Ave #7J
New York, NY 10029-3848, USA

Sample, Steven B (Educator)
University of Southern California
President's Office
Los Angeles, CA 90089, USA

Samples, Keith (Director, Producer, Writer)
c/o Rob Kenneally *Creative Artists Agency (CAA-LA)*
2000 Ave Of The Stars
Los Angeles, CA 90067, USA

Sampleton, Lawrence (Athlete, Football Player)
2900 Bunny Run
Austin, TX 78746, USA

Sampras, Pete (Athlete, Olympic Athlete, Tennis Player)
2552 Via Anita
Palos Verdes Estates, CA 90274-1011

Sampson, Benj (Athlete, Baseball Player)
8312 Flat Rock Ct
North Richland Hills, TX 76180-8471, USA

Sampson, Chris (Athlete, Baseball Player)
13703 Elm Shores Dr
Houston, TX 77044-5615, USA

Sampson, Gary (Athlete, Hockey Player, Olympic Athlete)
Alaska Sportsman's Lodge PO Box 231985
Anchorage, AK 99523-1985, USA

Sampson, Greg (Athlete, Football Player)
3286 Highland Dr
Carlsbad, CA 92008, USA

Sampson, Kelvin (Basketball Player, Coach)
University of Oklahoma
Lloyd Noble Complex
Norman, OK 73019, USA

Sampson, Linda (Stylist)
827 Ursulines
New Orleans, LA 70116, USA

Sampson, Ralph L Jr (Athlete, Basketball Player, Coach)
530 Myrtle St
Harrisonburg, VA 22802-4725, USA

Sampson, Robert (Actor)
20th Century Artists
4605 Lankershim Blvd #305
North Hollywood, CA 91602, USA

Sams, Dean (Musician)
c/o Staff Member *Borman Entertainment (TN)*
4322 Harding Pike #429
Nashville, TN 37205, USA

Sams, Doris (Athlete, Baseball Player)
2405 Alberta Dr
Knoxville, TN 37920-4701, USA

Sams, Jeffrey D (Actor)
c/o Toni Benson *Third Hill Entertainment*
195 S Beverly Dr
Suite 400
Beverly Hills, CA 90212, USA

Sams, Judy (Golfer)
2603 Wells Ave
Sarasota, FL 34232-3954, USA

Sams, Russell (Actor)
c/o Jon Simmons *Simmons & Scott Entertainment*
4110 W. Burbank Blvd.
Burbank, CA 91505, USA

Samson, Savanna (Adult Film Star)
c/o Natalie Oliveras
118 Fullerton St #149
New York, NY 10038, USA

Samsonov, Sergei (Athlete, Hockey Player)
2896 Croftshire Ct
Rochester, MI 48306-4925

Sam the Sham (Musician)
6123 Old Brunswick Road
Arlington, TN 38002, USA

Samuel, Amado (Athlete, Baseball Player)
1931 Yale Dr
Louisville, KY 40205-2038, USA

Samuel, Juan (Athlete, Baseball Player)
19712 Maddelena Cir
Fort Myers, FL 33967-0537, USA

Samuel, Skinner (Politician)
111ndian Hill Rd
Winnetka, IL 60093-3923, USA

Samuel, Xavier (Actor)
c/o David Seltzer *Management 360*
9111 Wilshire Blvd
Beverly Hills, CA 90210, USA

Samuels, Chris (Athlete, Football Player)
18303 Oakhampton Dr
Houston, TX 77084, USA

Samuels, Dale (Athlete, Football Player)
7625 Highway X
Three Lakes, WI 54562, USA

Samuels, Jack (Athlete, Baseball Player)
16040 Leffingwell Rd
Apt 25
Whittier, CA 90603, USA

Samuels, Jack (Athlete, Baseball Player)
16040 Leffingwell Rd #25
Whittler, CA 90603-3120, USA

Samuels, Roger (Athlete, Baseball Player)
4865 Tampico Way
San Jose, CA 95118-2348, USA

Samuels, Ron
PO Box 1690
Rancho Mirage, CA 92270-1058

Samuels, Skyler (Actor)
c/o Aleen Keshishian *Brillstein Entertainment Partners*
9150 Wilshire Blvd #350
Beverly Hills, CA 90212, USA

Samuels, Stephanie (Stylist)
5008 N Leavitt St
Chicago, IL 60625, USA

Samuelson, Joan Benoit (Athlete, Olympic Athlete, Track Athlete)
95 Lower Flying Point Rd
Freeport, ME 04032, USA

Samuelson, Kjell (Athlete, Hockey Player)
7 Knottingham Dr.
Voorhees, NJ 08043, USA

Samuelson, Pamela (Attorney, Attorney General, General)
University of California
Center for Law/Technology
Berkeley, CA 94720, USA

Samuelsson, Bengt I (Nobel Prize Laureate)
Karolinska Institute Solnavagen 1
Department of Medical Biochemistry
Stockholm 171 77, SWEDEN

Samuelsson, Kjell (Athlete, Hockey Player)
10 Simsbury Dr
Voorhees, NJ 08043-3949, USA

Samuelsson, Marcus (Chef, Reality TV Star)
c/o Andrew Chason *The Legacy Agency*
230 Park Ave
Suite 851
New York, NY 10169, USA

Samuelsson, Mikael (Athlete, Hockey Player)
Puckagency LLC
555 Pleasantville Rd Ste 210N
Attn Rick Komarow
Briarcliff Manor, NY 10510-1900, USA

Samuelsson, Ulf (Athlete, Hockey Player)
19175 N. 95th Pl.
Scottsdale, AZ 85222, USA

Samyn, Jean-Luc (Horse Racer)
57 Shore Rd
Manhasset, NY 11030-1323, USA

Sanabria, Marilyn (Actor)
c/o Laura Walsh *Central Artists*
3310 W Burbank Blvd #A
Burbank, CA 91505-2230, USA

Sanada, Hiroyuki (Actor)
c/o William Choi *Management 360*
9111 Wilshire Blvd
Beverly Hills, CA 90210, USA

San Basilio, Paloma (Music Group)
c/o Staff Member *Sony Music Miami*
605 Lincoln Rd Fl 7
Miami Beach, FL 33139, USA

Sanborn, David (Musician)
c/o Staff Member *ICM Partners (ICM-LA)*
10250 Constellation Blvd Fl 7
Los Angeles, CA 90067, USA

Sanches, Brian (Athlete, Baseball Player)
903 N 31st St
Nederland, TX 77627-6706, USA

Sanches, Stacy (Model)
c/o Staff Member *Playboy Productions*
2706 Media Center Drive
Los Angles, CA 90065, USA

Sanchez, Aaron (Chef)
c/o Andrew Chason *The Legacy Agency*
230 Park Ave
Suite 851
New York, NY 10169, USA

Sanchez, Alex (Athlete, Baseball Player)
1400 Mellissa Cir
Antioch, CA 94509-6301, USA

Sanchez, Duaner (Athlete, Baseball Player)
56748 Eastvue Dr
Osceola, IN 46561, USA

Sanchez, Eduardo (Director)
c/o Staff Member *Elements Entertainment*
312 W 5th St Apt 815
Los Angeles, CA 90013, USA

Sanchez, Emilio (Tennis Player)
Sabiono de Avena 28
Barcelona 46, SPAIN

Sanchez, Emma (Stylist)
c/o Staff Member *Marek & Associates Inc*
508 W 26th St
#12-C
New York, NY 10001, USA

Sanchez, Evet (Stylist)
c/o Staff Member *Fred Segal Beauty*
PO Box 5304
Beverly Hills, CA 90209, USA

Sanchez, Freddy (Athlete, Baseball Player)
2494 E Cloud Dr
Chandler, AZ 85249-3777, USA

Sanchez, Gaby (Athlete, Baseball Player)
5621 SW 130th Pl
Miami, FL 33183-1207, USA

Sanchez, Humberto (Athlete, Baseball Player)
1064 Glen raven Ln
Clermont, FL 34711-9011, USA

Sanchez, Israel (Athlete, Baseball Player)
5444 N Spaulding Ave
Chicago, IL 60625-4608, USA

Sanchez, Jessica (Musician)
c/o Staff Member *19 Entertainment - LA*
9000 W Sunset Blvd #1574
West Hollywood, CA 90069, USA

Sanchez, Jose T Cardinal (Religious Leader)
Via Rusticucci 13
Rome 00193, ITALY

Sanchez, Juan (Pepe) (Basketball Player)
c/o Staff Member *Detroit Pistons*
2 Championship Dr
Auburn Hills, MI 48326, USA

Sanchez, Kiele (Actor)
c/o Daniel Spilo *Industry Entertainment Partners*
955 S Carrillo Dr
Suite 300
Los Angeles, CA 90048, USA

Sanchez, Linda (Congressman, Politician)
2423 Rayburn HOB
Washington, DC 20515, USA

Sanchez, Loretta (Congressman, Politician)
1114 Longworth HOB
Washington, DC 20515, USA

Sanchez, Lupe (Athlete, Football Player)
29070 Road 68
Visalia, CA 93277, USA

Sanchez, Marco (Actor)
c/o Steve Himber *Steve Himber Entertainment*
211 S Beverly Dr #601
Beverly Hills, CA 90212, USA

Sanchez, Mark (Athlete, Football Player)
c/o David Dunn *Athletes First, LLC*
9140 Irvine Center Dr
Irvine, CA 92618, USA

Sanchez, Monika (Actor)
c/o Gabriel Blanco *Gabriel Blanco Iglesias (Mexico)*
Rio Balsas 35-32
Colonia Cuauhtemoc
DF 06500, Mexico

Sanchez, Oscar Arias (Nobel Prize Laureate)
Arias Foundation for Peace Aoartado
8-6410-1000
San Jose, USA

Sanchez, Pepe (Director)
c/o Staff Member *Gabriel Blanco Iglesias (Colombia)*
Dg 127A #20-36
Conjunto Plenitud, Apto 132
Bogota, Colombia

Sanchez, Rey (Athlete, Baseball Player)
788 Calle Pampero
Urb Country Club
San Juan, PR 00924-1772, USA

Sanchez, Rick (Correspondent, Journalist)
c/o Staff Member *CNN (Atlanta)*
One CNN Center
PO Box 105366
Atlanta, GA 30303, USA

Sanchez, Roselyn (Actor)
c/o Lena Roklin *Luber Roklin Management*
8530 Wilshire Blvd
6th Floor
Beverly Hills, CA 90211, USA

Sanchez Azuara, Rocio (Actor)
c/o Staff Member *TV Azteca*
Periferico Sur 4121
Colonia Fuentes del Pedregal
DF CP 14141, Mexico

Sanchez Gijon, Aitana (Actor)
Alsira Garcia Maroto
Gran Via 63 #3
Izda
Madrid 28013, SPAIN

Sanchez-Vicario, Arantxa (Tennis Player)
Sabino de Arana 28 #6-1A
Barcelona 08028, SPAIN

Sanctus Real (Music Group, Musician)
c/o Dan Spencer *Flat-Out Management*
1800 Blair Blvd
Nashville, TN 37212, USA

Sand, Paul (Actor)
Paradigm Agency
10100 Santa Monica Blvd #2500
Los Angeles, CA 90067, USA

Sand, Shauna
c/o Staff Member *Acme Talent & Literary (LA)*
1400 Atlantic Ave
Suite 274
Long Beach, CA 90814, USA

Sand, Todd (Figure Skater)
2973 Harbor Blvd #468
Costa Mesa, CA 92626, USA

Sanda, Dominique
201 rue du Faubourg St. Honore
Paris, FRANCE F-75008

Sandage, Allan (Scientist)
8319 Josard Rd
San Gabriel, CA 91775-1003, USA

Sandbeck, Cal (Athlete, Hockey Player)
PO Box 129
La Veta, CO 81055-0129, USA

Sandberg, Jared (Athlete, Baseball Player)
4275 NE 125th St
Seattle, WA 98125-4635, USA

Sandberg, Ryne (Athlete, Baseball Player)
26 Biltmore Est
Phoenix, AZ 85016-2823, USA

Sande, Emeli (Musician)
c/o Nick Matthews *Coda Music Agency - UK*
229 Shoreditch High St
London E1 6PJ, UK

Sandelin, Scott (Athlete, Hockey Player)
4880 Adrian Ln
Hermantown, MN 55811-3904

Sandeno, Kaitlin (Athlete, Olympic Athlete, Swimmer)
c/o Staff Member *Premier Management Group (PMG Sports)*
115 Crescent Commons Dr Ste 250
Cary, NC 27518, USA

Sander, Casey
c/o Jeffrey Leavitt *Leavitt Talent Group*
8255 W Sunset Blvd
West Hollywood, CA 90046, USA

Sander, Ian (Producer)
c/o Staff Member *WmE2 (WMA-LA)*
1 William Morris Pl
Beverly Hills, CA 90212, USA

Sander, Mark (Athlete, Football Player)
4930 NW 83rd Ave
Lauderhill, FL 33351, USA

Sanderman, Bill (Athlete, Football Player)
Tahoma Meadows Bed & Breakfast
P.O. Box 203
Homewood, CA 96141, USA

Sanders, Anthony (Athlete, Baseball Player)
7881 E McGee Mountain Rd
Tucson, AZ 85750-7406, USA

Sanders, Barry (Athlete, Football Player, Heisman Trophy Winner)
PO Box 3079
Farmington Hills, MI 48333-3079, USA

Sanders, Beverly (Actor)
12218 Morrison St
Valley Village, CA 91607, USA

Sanders, Bill (Cartoonist)
PO Box 661
Milwaukee, WI 53201, USA

Sanders, Bobby (Baseball Player)
Birmingham Black Barons
24799 Lake Shore Blvd Apt 712
Euclid, OH 44123-4246, USA

Sanders, Charles A (Charlie) (Athlete, Coach, Football Coach, Football Player)
3418 Palm Aire Ct
Rochester Hills, MI 48309, USA

Sanders, Chris (Director)
c/o Rob Carlson *WME (LA)*
9601 Wilshire Blvd Fl 3
Beverly Hills, CA 90210, USA

Sanders, Christoph (Actor)
c/o Beverly Strong *Strong Management*
3532 Hayden Ave
Culver City, CA 90232, USA

Sanders, Daryl (Athlete, Football Player)
9220 Shawnee Trl
Powell, OH 43065, USA

Sanders, David (Athlete, Baseball Player)
10411 S Ellen St
Mulvane, KS 67110-9374, USA

Sanders, Deion (Athlete, Baseball Player)
1280 N Preston Rd
PrOStler, TX 75078-8798, USA

Sanders, Doug (Golfer)
8828 Sandringham Dr
Houston, TX 77024-5819, USA

Sanders, Eric D (Athlete, Football Player)
9325 Tailey Cir
Duluth, GA 30097, USA

Sanders, James (Baseball Player)
Kansas City Monarchs
1001 43rd Pl
Birmingham, AL 35208-1402, USA

Sanders, Jay O (Actor)
165 W 46th St
#409
New York, NY 10036, USA

Sanders, Jeff (Athlete, Basketball Player)
PO Box 374
South Holland, IL 60473-0374, USA

Sanders, John (Athlete, Baseball Player)
3004 Cheshire Ct
Woodstock, GA 30189-6690, USA

Sanders, John M (Athlete, Football Player)
520 Old Whitfield Rd
Pearl, MS 39208, USA

Sanders, Jonathan (Jon) (Yachtsman)
28 Portland St
Redlands, WA 6009, AUSTRALIA

Sanders, Ken (Athlete, Baseball Player)
12141 Parkview Ln
Hales Corners, WI 53130-2341, USA

Sanders, Mariene (Correspondent)
WNET-TV
News Dept
356 W 58th St
New York, NY 10019, USA

Sanders, Marlene
175 Riverside Dr.
New York, NY 10024

Sanders, Orban (Athlete, Football Player)
3520 NW Ferris Ave
Lawton, OK 73505, USA

Sanders, Pharoah (Musician)
Joel Chriss
300 Mercer St #3J
New York, NY 10003, USA

Sanders, Pilar (Actor)
c/o Staff Member *Kim Dawson Agency, The*
1645 Stemmons Fwy
Suite B
Dallas, TX 75207, USA

Sanders, Reggie
122 Vista Del Mar Ln Unit 102
Myrtle Beach, SC 29572-8148, USA

Sanders, Robert J (Athlete, Football Player)
412 Homestead Ave
Metairie, LA 70005, USA

Sanders, Rupert (Director)
c/o Guymon Casady *Management 360*
9111 Wilshire Blvd
Beverly Hills, CA 90210, USA

Sanders, Scott G (Athlete, Baseball Player)
315 Belmont Dr
Thibodaux, LA 70301-2908, USA

Sanders, Summer (Athlete, Olympic Athlete, Swimmer)
731 Martingale Ln
Park City, UT 84098-7559, USA

Sanders, Thomas (Athlete, Football Player)
72 S Flore Pkwy
Vernon Hills, IL 60061, USA

Sanders, Thomas "Satch" (Athlete, Basketball Player, Misc)
PO Box 505
Sturbridge, MA 01566-0505, USA

Sanders, W J (Jerry) III (Business Person)
Advanced Micro Devices
1 AMD Place
PO Box 3453
Sunnyvale, CA 94088, USA

Sanderson, Cael (Wrestler)
Steve Sanderson
1380 Valley Hills Blvd
Heber City, UT 84032, USA

Sanderson, Derek (Athlete, Hockey Player)
Howland Captital Management
75 Federal St Ste 1100
Boston, MA 02110-1911, USA

Sanderson, Geoff (Athlete, Hockey Player)
New York Islanders
1255 Hempstead Tpke
Uniondale, NY 11553-1200, USA

Sanderson, Nikki (Actor)
c/o Coronation Sreet
Granada Studios, Quay St
Manchester M60 9EA, UNITED KINGDOM

Sanderson, Peter (Artist)
1105 Shell Gate Plaza
Alameda, CA 94501, USA

Sanderson, Reggie (Athlete, Football Player)
160 Mara Ave
Ventura, CA 93004, USA

Sanderson, Scott (Athlete, Baseball Player)
945 Newcastle Dr
Lake Forest, IL 60045-4928, USA

Sanderson, Theresa (Tessa) (Athlete, Track Athlete)
Tee-Dee Promotion
Atles Center
Oxgate Lane
London NW2 7HU, UNITED KINGDOM (UK)

Sanderson, William (Actor)
c/o Lori DeWaal *Lori DeWaal & Associates PR*
7080 Hollywood Blvd
Suite 515
Los Angeles, CA 90028, USA

Sandeson, William S (Cartoonist, Editor)
2230 Muskoday Pass
Fort Wayne, IN 46809-1428, USA

Sandford, Ed (Athlete, Hockey Player)
18 Clearwater St
Winchester, MA 01890-4011

Sandiford, L Erskine (Prime Minister)
Hillvista
Porters
Saint James, BARBADOS

Sandin, Bill (Inventor)
University of Illinois
Electronic Visualization Lab
Chicago, IL 60607, USA

Sandit, Tom (Athlete)
540 S Ashland Ave
La Grange, IL 60525-2811

Sandlak, Jim (Athlete, Hockey Player)
74 Green Hedge Lane
London, ON N6H 5A6, Canada

Sandler, Adam (Actor, Comedian)
c/o Sandy Wernick *Brillstein Entertainment Partners*
9150 Wilshire Blvd #350
Beverly Hills, CA 90212, USA

Sandler, Elliott (Race Car Driver)
Cox Marketing
149-B Rolling Hills Rd.
Mooresville, NC 28117, USA

Sandler, Herbert M (Financier)
Golden West Financial
1901 Harrison St
Oakland, CA 94612, USA

Sandlock, Mike (Athlete, Baseball Player)
81 Bible St
Cos Cob, BT 06807-2109, USA

Sandlund, Debra (Actor)
Innovative Artists
1505 10th St
Santa Monica, CA 90401, USA

Sandman, Cindy (Stylist)
c/o Staff Member *Barbara Laurie Photographers*
152 Madison Ave
#1803
New York, NY 10016, USA

Sandoval, Arturo (Musician)
4706 Granada Blvd
Coral Gables, FL 33146-1250, USA

Sandoval, Brian (Governor)
State Capitol
101 N. Carson Street
Carson City, NV 89701, USA

Sandoval, Hope (Music Group, Musician)
Rough Trade Mgmt
66 Golbarne Road
London W10 5PS, UNITED KINGDOM (UK)

Sandoval, Miguel (Actor)
Paradigm Agency
10100 Santa Monica Blvd #2500
Los Ageles, CA 90067, USA

Sandoval, Sonny (Musician)
East West America Records
75 Rockefeller Plaza
New York, NY 10019, USA

Sandoval Iniguez, Juan Cardinal
(Religious Leader)
Morelos 244
San Pedro Tlaquepaque 45500, MEXICO

Sandow, Nick (Actor)
c/o Tina Thor *TMT Entertainment Group*
648 Broadway
Suite 1002
New York, NY 10012, USA

Sandre, Didier (Actor)
Agents Associes Beaume
201 Faubourg Saint Honore
Paris 75008, FRANCE

Sandrelli, Stefania (Actor)
TNA
Viale Parioli 41
Rome 00197, ITALY

Sandrich, Jay (Director)
c/o Staff Member *Creative Artists Agency
(CAA-LA)*
2000 Ave Of The Stars
Los Angeles, CA 90067, USA

Sands, Charlie (Athlete, Baseball Player)
4740 Stratford Ct
Apt 1603
Naples, FL 34105-6689, USA

Sands, Jerry (Athlete, Baseball Player)
121 Christian St
Clayton, NC 27527-7519, USA

Sands, Julian (Actor)
1287 Ozeta Terrace
Los Ageles, CA 90069, USA

Sands, Tommy (Actor, Musician)
Green Linnet
916 19th Ave S
Nashville, TN 37212, USA

Sands-Ferguson, Sarah Jane (Athlete,
Baseball Player)
338 Rohrsburg Rd
Orangeville, PA 17859-9108, USA

Sandstrom, Sven (Financier)
AES Corporation
4300 Wilson Blvd
11th Floor
Arlington, VA 22203, USA

Sandt, Tommy (Athlete, Baseball Player)
4207 Harvey Way
Lake Oswego, OR 97035-3412, USA

Sandusky, Alexander B (Alex) (Athlete,
Football Player)
22 Floral Ave
Key West, FL 33040, USA

Sandusky, Mike (Athlete, Football Player)
2786 Amberwood Ct
Naples, FL 34120, USA

Sandvoss, Steve (Actor)
c/o Joan Hyler *Hyler Management*
20 Ocean Park Blvd
Suite 25
Santa Monica, CA 90405, USA

Sandy, Baby (Sandra Magee)
6846 Haywood
Tujunga, CA 91042

Sandy, Gary (Actor)
PO Box 818
Cynthiana, KY 41031, USA

Sandy B (Musician)
Atlantic Entertainment Group
2922 Atlantic Ave #200
Atlantic City, NJ 08401, USA

Sandy Jr, Alomar (Baseball Player)
4635 Prestwick Xing
Westlake, OH 44145, USA

Sanford, Chance (Athlete, Baseball Player)
15028 Bardwell Ln
Frisco, TX 75035-0412, USA

Sanford, Ed (Athlete, Hockey Player)
18 Clearwater Rd
Winchester, MA 01890-4011

Sanford, Jack
2300 Presidential Way
West Palm Beach, FL 33401

Sanford, Jennifer S (Misc)
1725 Atlantic Ave
Sullivan's Island, SC 29482, USA

Sanford, Leo (Athlete, Football Player)
3044 Gorton Rd
Shreveport, LA 71119, USA

Sanford, Lucius M (Athlete, Football
Player)
8745 Carriage Hills Dr
Columbia, MD 21046, USA

Sanford, Mark (Politician)
800 Richland St
Columbia, SC 29201-2327, USA

Sanford, Meredith (Athlete)
2800 Highway 389
Starkville, MS 39759-8379

Sanford, Mo (Athlete, Baseball Player)
2800 Highway 389
Starkville, MS 39759-8379, USA

Sanford, Richard M (Rick) (Athlete,
Football Player)
335 Lemonts Rd
Chapin, SC 29036, USA

Sanford, Ron (Athlete, Basketball Player)
3129 Santana Ln
Plano, TX 75023-3630, USA

Sangalo, Ivete (Musician)
Concerti e Produzioni S.r.l.
via Bonafous, 6
Torino 10123, Italy

Sangare, Oumou (Actor, Composer,
Musician)
c/o Staff Member *Concerted Efforts*
P.O. Box 440326
Somerville, MA 02144, USA

Sangavi (Actor, Bollywood)
20 4th Street
Dr. Subraya Nagar Kodambakkam
Chennai, TN 600024, INDIA

Sangeetha (Actor, Bollywood)
26A Brindavan Apartments
Karumari Amman Koil Street Vadapalani
Chennai, TN 600026, INDIA

Sanger, David J (Musician)
Old Wesleyan Chapel
Embleton Near Cockermouth
Cumbria CA13 9YA, UNITED KINGDOM
(UK)

Sanger, Frederick (Nobel Prize Laureate)
Far Leys Fen Lane
Swaffham Bulbeck
Cambridge, UNITED KINGDOM (UK)

Sanger, Stephan W (Business Person)
General Mills Inc
1 General Mills Blvd
PO Box 1113
Minneapolis, MN 55440, USA

SanGiacomo, Laura (Actor)
c/o Staff Member *Rugolo Entertainment*
195 S Beverly Dr
Suite 400
Beverly Hills, CA 90212, USA

Sangster, Thomas (Actor)
c/o Duncan Millership *WME (LA)*
9601 Wilshire Blvd Fl 3
Beverly Hills, CA 90210, USA

Sangueli, Andrei (Prime Minister)
Parliament House
Prosp 105
Kishineau 277073, MOLDOVA

Sanguillen, Manny (Athlete, Baseball
Player)
2838 SW 4th St
Boynton Beach, FL 33435-7902, USA

Sanguinetti Cairolo, Julio Maria
(President)
Partido Colorado
Andres Martinez Trueba 1271
Montevideo, URUGUAY

Sanjukta, Singh (Actor, Bollywood)
4th Floor Mona Apts
Breach Candy
Mumbai, MS 400036, INDIA

Sannes, Amy (Athlete, Olympic Athlete,
Speed Skater)
143 W Pleasant Lake Rd
Saint Paul, MN 55127-2630, USA

Sano, Roya A (Religious Leader)
United Methodist Church
PO Box 320
Nashville, TN 37202, USA

Sanobar, Kabir (Actor, Bollywood)
402 Karan Building Yari Road
Versova Andheri (W)
Mumbai, MS 400061, INDIA

Sansom, Bruce (Ballerina)
c/o Staff Member *Royal Ballet*
Covent Garden
Bow St
London WC2E 9DD, UK

Sansom, Chip (Cartoonist)
United Media PO Box 5610
Cincinnati, OH 45201-5610, USA

Sant, Alfred (Prime Minister)
National Labor Center
Mills End Road
Hannum, MALTA

Santamaria, Eduardo (Actor)
c/o Gabriel Blanco *Gabriel Blanco
Iglesias (Mexico)*
Rio Balsas 35-32
Colonia Cuauhtemoc
DF 06500, Mexico

Santana, Ava (Actor)
c/o Claudia Speicher *New Orleans Talent
Agency*
1347 Magazine St
New Orleans, LA 70124, USA

Santana, Carlos (Musician, Songwriter)
Santana Management
121 Jordan St
Ran Rafael, CA 94901, USA

Santana, Johan (Athlete, Baseball Player)
10471 Via Lombardia Ct
Miromar Lakes, FL 33913-7782, USA

Santana, Juelz (Musician)
c/o Staff Member *Island Def Jam Group*
Worldwide Plaza
825 8th Ave Fl 28
New York, NY 10019, USA

Santana, Manuel (Tennis Player)
International Tennis Hall of Fame
194 Bellevue Ave
Newport, RI 02840, USA

Santana, Maria (Stylist)
c/o Staff Member *Ray Brown Represents*
601 W 26th St
#1310
New York, NY 10001, USA

Santana, Rafael (Athlete, Baseball Player)
3220 SE 1st Ave
Cape Coral, FL 33904-4103, USA

Santangelo, F P (Athlete, Baseball Player)
3602 Rocky Ridge Way
El Dorado Hills, CA 95762-4432, USA

Santaolalla, Gustavo (Musician)
c/o Robert Messinger *First Artists
Management*
4764 Park Granada
Suite 210
Calabasas, CA 91302, USA

Santa Rosa, Gilberto (Musician)
c/o Staff Member *Richard De La Font
Agency*
3808 W South Park Blvd
Broken Arrow, OK 74011, USA

Santer, Jacques (Misc)
69 Rue J P Huberty
1742, LUXEMBOURG

Santerre, Andy (Race Car Driver)
5254 Pitt Rd. So.
Harrisburg, NC 28075, United States

Santiago (Stylist)
339 W 48th St
New York, NY 10036, USA

Santiago, Benito R (Athlete, Baseball
Player)
610 W Las Olas Blvd Apt 1212W
Fort Lauderdale, FL 33312-7129, USA

Santiago, Carlos (Baseball Player)
New York Cubans
7 Calle Archilla Cabrera
Mayaguez, PR 00680-3302, USA

Santiago, Daniel (Basketball Player)
c/o Staff Member *Phoenix Suns*
201 East Jefferson Street
Phoenix, AZ 85004, USA

Santiago, Danny (Stylist)
c/o Staff Member *Blink Management*
421 Washington Ave
#202
Miami Beach, FL 33139, USA

Santiago, Eddie (Musician)
c/o Staff Member *Sony Music Miami*
605 Lincoln Rd Fl 7
Miami Beach, FL 33139, USA

Santiago, Jose (Athlete, Baseball Player)
690 Calle Cesar Gonzalez Apt 2108
SanJuan, PR 00918-3906, USA

Santiago, Ray (Actor)
c/o Scott Zimmerman *Evolution Entertainment (LA)*
901 N Highland Ave
Los Angeles, CA 90038, USA

Santiago, Rodiney (Model, Reality TV Star)
c/o Staff Member *Mega Models (Miami)*
420 Lincoln Rd #408
Miami, FL 33139, USA

Santiago, Tessie (Actor)
c/o Craig Shapiro *ICM Partners (ICM-LA)*
10250 Constellation Blvd Fl 7
Los Angeles, CA 90067, USA

Santiago, Victor (Nore) (Musician)
c/o Staff Member *Violator Management*
36 W 25th St
2nd Floor
New York, NY 10010, USA

Santiago-Hudson, Ruben (Actor)
c/o Vincent Cirrincione *Vincent Cirrincione Associates*
1516 N Fairfax Ave
Los Angeles, CA 90046, USA

Santini, Geo (Director)
c/o Kieran Maguire *The Arlook Group*
205 S Beverly Dr
Suite 209
Beverly Hills, CA 90212, USA

Santo & Johnny
217 Edgewood Ave.
Clearwater, FL 34615

Santo Domingo, Rafael (Athlete, Baseball Player)
P.O. Box 21
Orocovis, PR 00720-0021, USA

Santorelli, Frank (Actor)
c/o Mitch Smelkinson *Stone, Meyer, Genow, Smelkinson and Binder*
9665 Wilshire Blvd
Suite 500
Beverly Hills, CA 90212, USA

Santorini, Al (Athlete, Baseball Player)
9 Daniele Dr
Ocean, NJ 07712-7910, USA

Santorini, AL (Athlete, Baseball Player)
100 Wescott Dr
Clemson, SC 29631, USA

Santorini, Paul E (Engineer, Physicist)
PO Box 49
Athens, GREECE

Santoro, Nicoletta (Stylist)
c/o Staff Member *Art + Commerce*
531 W 25th St # 4
New York, NY 10001, USA

Santoro, Rodrigo (Actor)
c/o Aleen Keshishian *Brillstein Entertainment Partners*
9150 Wilshire Blvd #350
Beverly Hills, CA 90212, USA

Santorum, Rick (Politician)
PO Box 609
Great Falls, VA 22066-0609, USA

Santos, Al (Actor)
c/o Staff Member *Buchwald/Fortitude (LA)*
6500 Wilshire Blvd
Suite 2200
Los Angeles, CA 90048, USA

Santos, Anthony (Romeo) (Musician)
c/o John Reilly *Rogers & Cowan PR (LA)*
Pacific Design Center
8687 Melrose Ave, 7th Floor
West Hollywood, CA 90069, USA

Santos, Bruno (Model)
c/o Staff Member *Why Not Model Agency*
via Zenale 9
Milano 20123, Italy

Santos, Carlos (Comedian)
c/o Staff Member *WmE2 (WMA-LA)*
1 William Morris Pl
Beverly Hills, CA 90212, USA

Santos, Joe (Actor)
c/o Mike Eistenstadt *Amsel, Eisenstadt & Frazier Talent Agency (AEF)*
5055 Wilshire Blvd
Suite 860
Los Angeles, CA 90036-6108, USA

Santos, Jose (Horse Racer)
1055 Papaya St
Hollywood, FL 33019-4842, USA

Santos, Omir (Athlete, Baseball Player)
2252 Viehman Trl
Kissimmee, FL 34746-2211, USA

Santos, Rey-Phillip (Actor)
c/o Staff Member *Dramatic Artists Agency*
103 W. Alameda Ave
Suite 139
Burbank, CA 91502, USA

Santos, Rick (Race Car Driver)
S&S Automotive
14127 Washington Ave.
San Leandro, CA 94578, USA

Santos, Sergio (Athlete, Baseball Player)
746 Cienaga Dr
Fullerton, CA 92835-1224, USA

Santos de Oliveira, Alessandra (Basketball Player)
Washington Mystics
MCI Center
601 F St NW
Washington, DC 20004, USA

Santovenia, Nelson (Athlete, Baseball Player)
14642 SW 141st Ct
Miami, FL 33186-7260, USA

Sanz, Alejandro (Musician, Songwriter)
c/o Javier Martin *RLM*
420 Lincoln Rd #285
Miami Beach, FL 33139, USA

Sanz, Horatio (Actor)
c/o David (Dave) Becky *3 Arts Entertainment Inc*
9460 Wilshire Blvd
7th Floor
Beverly Hills, CA 90210, USA.

Saper, Clifford (Doctor)
Beth Israel Hospital
Neurology Dept
330 Brookline Ave
Boston, MA 02215, USA

Saperstein, David (Director, Producer, Writer)
c/o Staff Member *Fran Saperstein Organization*
Marina del Rey, CA 90292, USA

Sapienza, Al
10474 Santa Monica Blvd. #380
W. Los Angeles, CA 90025

Sapienza, Americo (Athlete, Football Player)
6 Forenza Rd
Peabody, MA 01960, USA

Sapir, Tamir (Misc)
384 5th Ave Fl 7
New York, NY 10018-8166, USA

Saplenza, Al (Actor)
PO Box 691240
West Hollywood, CA 90069, USA

Saporta, Gabe (Musician)
c/o Staff Member *Fueled By Ramen*
PO Box 1803
Tampa, FL 33601, USA

Sapp, Bob (Actor)
c/o Blake Bandy *Kritzer Levine Wilkins Entertainment (KLWG)*
11872 La Grange Ave
1st Floor
Los Angeles, CA 90025, USA

Sapp, Carolyn
1840 41st Ave. #102-227
Capitola, CA 95010-2513

Sapp, Theron (Athlete, Football Player)
892 N Belair Rd
Evans, GA 30809, USA

Sapp, Warren (Athlete, Football Player)
c/o Drew Rosenhaus *Rosenhaus Sports Representation*
6400 Allison Road
Miami Beach, FL 33141, USA

Sappleton, Wayne (Athlete, Basketball Player)
8040 N Nob Hill Rd
Apt 205
Tamarac, FL 33321-7410, USA

Saprykin, Oleg (Athlete, Hockey Player)
15802 N 71st St Unit 301
Scottsdale, AZ 85254-7107

Sara, Mia (Actor)
c/o Andy Freedman *Andrew J Freedman Personal Management*
20 Ironsides St #18
Marina del Rey, CA 90292, USA

Saracco, Joe (Stylist)
4642 E 26th St
Tucson, AZ 85711, USA

Sarachan, Dave (Coach, Soccer Player)
Chicago Fire
980 N Michigan Ave #1998
Chicago, IL 60611, USA

Sarafian, Richard C (Actor, Director, Writer)
c/o Staff Member *Leavitt Talent Group*
8255 W Sunset Blvd
West Hollywood, CA 90046, USA

Sarafin, Michael (Scientist)
425 8th St NW Apt 630
Washington, DC 20004-2113, USA

Sarah, Duchess of York
Birch Hall
Windlesham Surrey, ENGLAND GU2O 6BN

Sarahyba, Daniella (Model)
c/o Staff Member *IMG Models (NY)*
304 Park Ave S
12th Floor
New York, NY 10010, USA

Saraiva Martins, Jose Cardinal (Religious Leader)
Via Pancrazio Pfeiffer 10
Rome 00193, ITALY

Saralegui, Cristina (Correspondent)
c/o Staff Member *Creative Artists Agency (CAA-LA)*
2000 Ave Of The Stars
Los Angeles, CA 90067, USA

Sarandon, Chris (Actor)
c/o Miles Levy *James/Levy/Jacobson Management Inc*
3500 W Olive Ave
Suite 1470
Burbank, CA 91505, USA

Sarandon, Susan (Actor, Producer)
c/o Meredith Wechter *ICM Partners (ICM-LA)*
10250 Constellation Blvd Fl 7
Los Angeles, CA 90067, USA

Saranya (Actor, Bollywood)
17A Rajaram Directors Colony
Kodambakkam
Chennai, TN 600024, INDIA

Saraste, Jukka-Pekka
Van Walsum Mgmt
4 Addison Bridge Place
London W14 8XP, UNITED KINGDOM (UK)

Sarazen-Smith, Dorothy (Baseball Player)
4774 Eagle Crest Dr
Madison, WI 53704-6426, USA

Sarbanes, Paul (Politician)
320 Suffolk Rd
Baltimore, MD 21218-2521, USA

Sarcev, Ursula
PO Box 25738
Los Angeles, CA 90025

Sardinha, Bronson (Athlete, Baseball Player)
156 Kuulei Rd
Kailua, HI 96734-2718, USA

Sardinha, Dane (Athlete, Baseball Player)
156 Kuulei Rd
Lailua, HI 96734-2718, USA

Sare, Chris
21100 Erwin St.
Woodland Hills, CA 91367

Sarfate, Dennis (Athlete, Baseball Player)
78 w Powell Way
Chandler, AZ 85248-5210, USA

Sarfatl, Alain (Architect)
28 Rue Barbet du Jouy
Paris 75007, FRANCE

Sargent, Ben (Cartoonist, Editor)
Austin American-Statesman
166 E Riverside Dr
Austin, TX 78704, USA

Sargent, Fran
3208 SE Brae mar Way
Port Saint Lucie, FL 34952-6034, USA

Sargent, Gary (Athlete, Hockey Player)
9624 Power Dam Rd NE
Bemidji, MN 56601-7414

Sargent, Joseph (Director, Producer)
27432 Latigo Bay View Dr
Malibu, CA 90265, USA

Sargent, Nikki (Stylist)
c/o Staff Member *Celestine - CA*
1666 20th St
#200-B
Santa Monica, CA 90404, USA

Sargent, Ronald L (Business Person)
Staples Inc
PO Box 9265
Framingham, MA 01701, USA

Sargent, Wallace
400 S Berkeley Ave
Pasadena, CA 91107-5062, USA

Sargeson, Alan M (Misc)
National University
Chemistry Dept
Canberra, ACT 0200, AUSTRALIA

Sari, Gabriela (Actor)
c/o Staff Member *Telefe - Argentina*
Pavon 2444 (C1248AAT)
Buenos Aires, ARGENTINA

Sarich, Cory (Athlete, Hockey Player)
19322 Autumn Woods Avenue
Tampa, FL 33647-3249, USA

Sarif, Shamim (Actor, Director, Writer)
Enlightenment Productions
77 Cheyne Court
London SW3 5TT, United Kingdom

Saritha (Actor, Bollywood)
Karthik Apartments III Floor, No.46,
Vijayaraghava Road
T. Nagar
Chennai, TN 600017, INDIA

Sark, Eari (Athlete, Football Player)
8656 W Bowling Green Ln NW
Lancaster, OH 43130-7857, USA

Sarkisian, Alex (Athlete, Football Player)
1604 E 142nd St
East Chicago, IN 46312, USA

Sarkozy, Nicolas (President)
c/o UMP
55 Rue La Boetie
Paris 75384, FRANCE

Sarmiento, Manny (Athlete, Baseball Player)
14904 Southfork Dr
Tampa, FL 33624-2322, USA

Sarna, Craig (Athlete, Hockey Player)
1375 Brown Rd S
Wayzata, MN 55391, USA

Sarne, Tanya (Designer, Fashion Designer)
Ghost
Chapel 263 Kensal Road
London W10 5DB, UNITED KINGDOM
(UK)

Sarner, Craig (Athlete, Hockey Player,
Olympic Athlete)
1375 Brown Rd S
Wayzata, MN 55391-9316, USA

Sarni, Vincent A (Baseball Player, Misc)
Pittsburgh Pirates
PNC Park
115 Federal St
Pittsburgh, PA 15212, USA

Sarnoff, Liz (Actor)
c/o Staff Member *Creative Artists Agency
(CAA-LA)*
2000 Ave Of The Stars
Los Angeles, CA 90067, USA

Sarnoff, William (Publisher)
Warner Publishing Inc
1325 Ave of Americas
New York, NY 10019, USA

Sarojadevi (Actor, Bollywood)
351 4th Main Road
Sadasivanagar
Bangalore, KA 560080, INDIA

Sarosi, Imre (Coach, Swimmer)
1033 Bp Harrer Dal Utca 4
HUNGARY

Sarra, Joe (Stylist)
c/o Staff Member *Elite Model
Management/Atlanta*
1708 Peachtree St NW
#210
Atlanta, GA 30309, USA

Sarratt, Charles (Athlete, Football Player)
5812 Oak Tree Rd
Edmond, OK 73003, USA

Sarrazin, Dick (Athlete, Hockey Player)
3391 Ch des Grives
la Conception, QC J0T 1M0, Canada

Sarsgaard, Peter (Actor)
c/o Jon Rubinstein *Authentic Talent and
Literary Management*
45 Main St
Suite 1004
Brooklyn, NY 11201, USA

Sartain, Gailard (Actor)
c/o Michael Livingston *Leavitt Talent
Group*
8255 W Sunset Blvd
West Hollywood, CA 90046, USA

Sartzetakis, Christos (President)
Presidential Palace
7 Vas Georgiou B
Odos Zalokosta 10
Athens, GREECE

Sarver, Bruce (Race Car Driver)
Bruce Sarver Racing
4550 Coffee Rd. #1-A 192
Bakersfield, CA 93308, USA

Sarver, Michael (Musician)

Sarzo, Rudy
1155 N. La Cienega Blvd. #506
Los Angeles, CA 90069

Sasaki, Kazuhiro (Baseball Player)
Seattle Mariners
Safeco Field
PO Box 4100
Seattle, WA 98194, USA

Sasaki, Norio (Coach)
Japan Football Association
3-10-15 Hongo
Bunkyo-ku
Tokyo 113-0033, Japan

Sasdy, Peter (Director)
Cleves
21 Matham Rd E
Molesey
Surrey KT8 0SX, ENGLAND

Sasikala (Actor, Bollywood)
D-10 Parsan Apartments
204 T.T.K. Road Alwarpet
Chennai, TN 600018, INDIA

Saskamoose, Fred (Athlete, Hockey
Player)
Sandy Lake Indian Res.
Canwood, SK S0J 0K0, CANADA

Sassano, C E (Business Person)
Bausch & Lomb
1 Bausch & Lomb Place
Rochester, NY 14604, USA

Sassard, Jacqueline
54 av. Montaigne
Paris, FRANCE F-75008

Sasselov, Dimitar (Astronomer)
Harvard-Smithsonian Astrophysics Center
60 Garden St
Cambridge, MA 02138, USA

Sasser, Clarence E (General)
13414 FM 521
Rosharon, TX 77583-6608, USA

Sasser, Grant (Athlete, Hockey Player)
1949 SE Orient Dr
Gresham, OR 97080-7228

Sasser, Jason (Athlete, Basketball Player)
4211 Tiffany Trl
Grand Prairie, TX 75052-2823, USA

Sasser, Mackey (Athlete, Baseball Player)
19 Harrington Ln
Dothan, AL 36305-9732, USA

Sasser, Rob (Athlete, Baseball Player)
1004 Delta River Way
Knightdale, NC 27545-7326, USA

Sasso, Will (Actor, Comedian)
c/o Staff Member *Lord Mucker
Entertainment*
839 E Orange Grove Ave
Burbank, CA 91501, USA

Sasson, Debra (Opera Singer)
Erlenhaupstr 10
Bensheim 64625, GERMANY

Sasson, Steven (Inventor)
12 Carefree Ln
Hilton, NY 14468-9326, USA

Sassoon, David (Designer, Fashion
Designer)
Bellville Sassoon
18 Culford Gardens
London SW3 2ST, UNITED KINGDOM
(UK)

Sassoon Adams, Beverly (Model)
848 Oso Ave
Canoga Park, CA 91306, USA

Sassou-Nguesso, Denis (President)
President's Office
Brazzaville, CONGO REPUBLIC

Sastre, Ines (Actor)
c/o Brad Schenck *Paradigm (LA)*
360 N Crescent Dr
North Bldg
Beverly Hills, CA 90210, USA

Satan, Miroslav (Athlete, Hockey Player)
46 Kettlepond Rd
Jericho, NY 11753-1158

Satanowski, Robert (Conductor)
Ul Madalinskiego 50/52 m 1
Warsaw 02-581, POLAND

Satcher, David (Misc)
Kaiser Family Foundation
2400 Sand Hill Road
Menlo Park, CA 94025, USA

Satcher, Dr L Robert (Astronaut)
5510 S Rice Ave Apt 131
Houston, TX 77081-2132, USA

Satcher, Leslie (Music Group, Musician,
Songwriter, Writer)
Warner Bros Records
3300 Warner Blvd
Burbank, CA 91505, USA

Satchwell, Brooke (Actor)
Darren Gray Management
2 Marston Lane
Portsmouth
Hampshire, England PO3 5TW

Sather, Glen (Athlete, Coach, Hockey
Player)
77380 Vista Rosa
La Quinta, CA 92253-2586, Canada

Sather, Glen (Athlete, Hockey Player)
New York Rangers
2 Penn Plz Fl 22, New York NY, 10121-
2299

Sathiyaraj (Actor)
13-A Pirakathambal Street
Chennai, TN 600 034, INDIA

Sato, Kazuo (Economist)
300 E 71st St #15H
New York, NY 10021, USA

Satra, Sonia (Actor)
Innovative Artists
1505 10th St
Santa Monica, CA 90401, USA

Satre, Philip G (Business Person)
Harrah's Entertainment
1023 Cherry Road
Memphis, TN 38117, USA

Satriani, Joe (Musician)
c/o Staff Member *Solo Agency Ltd (UK)*
55 Fulham High St
2nd Floor
London SW6 3JJ, United Kingdom

Satriano, Tom (Athlete, Baseball Player)
5320 Otis Ave
Tarzana, CA 91356-4214, USA

Satterfield, Paul (Actor)
PO Box 6945
Beverly Hills, CA 90212, USA

Satterwhite, AL (Photographer)
446 Linnie Canal
Venice, CA 90291-4622, USA

Satterwhite, Howard (Athlete, Football
Player)
3418 Action Ln
San Antonio, TX 78210, USA

Satturno, William (Archaeologist)
University of New Hampshire
Archaelogy Dept
Durham, NH 03824, USA

Saturday, Jeff (Athlete, Football Player)
2437 Londonberry Blvd
Carmel, IN 46032, USA

Saubert, Jean M (Skier)
147 Harbor Heights Blvd
Bigfork, MT 59911, USA

Saucier, Frank (Athlete, Baseball Player)
1615 S Bryan St
Apt 9
Amarillo, TX 79102-2326, USA

Saucier, Kevin (Athlete, Baseball Player)
2316 Silversides Loop
Pensacola, FL 32526-1509, USA

Saud, Prince Sultan Bin Abdulaziz al
(Government Official)
Defense Ministry
PO Box 26731
Airport Road
Riyadh 11165, SAUDI ARABIA

Saudek, Jan (Photographer)
Blodkova 6
Prague 3 130 00, CZECH REPUBLIC

Sauderbeck, Scott (Athlete, Baseball Player)
3919 Riverview Blvd
Bradenton, FL 34209, USA

Sauer, Craig (Athlete, Football Player)
6926 Pagenkopf Rd
Maple Plain, MN 55359, USA

Sauer, George H Jr (Athlete, Football Player)
4775 Smoketalk Ln
Westerville, OH 43081-4428, USA

Sauer, Kurt (Athlete, Hockey Player)
7610 E Rose Garden Ln
Scottsdale, AZ 85255-4789

Sauer, Louis (Architect)
3472 Marlowe St
Montreal, QC H4A 2L7, CANADA

Sauer, Richard J (Educator)
National 4-H Council
7100 Connecticut Ave
Bethesda, MD 20815, USA

Sauerbeck, Scott (Athlete, Baseball Player)
1818 4th St W
Palmetto, FL 34221-4304, USA

Sauerlander, Willibald P W (Historian)
Zentralinstitut fyr Kunstgeschichte
Meiserstr 10
Munich 80333, GERMANY

Sauers, Gene (Golfer)
9 Judsons Ct
Savannah, GA 31410, USA

Saul, April (Journalist)
Philadelphia Inquirer
Editorial Dept
400 N Broad St
Philadelphia, PA 19130, USA

Saul, Bernard (Misc)
1 Quincy St
Chevy Chase, MD 20815-4226, USA

Saul, Frank "Pep"
23 Queensbridge Dr
East Hanover, NJ 07936-3563, USA

Saul, Jim (Athlete, Baseball Player)
2405 Osborne St
Bristol, VA 24201-2322, USA

Saul, John
Robin Straus
229 E 79th St
New York, NY 10021

Saul, John (Writer)
Grade A Entertainment
368 North La Cienega Blvd
Los Angeles, CA 90048, USA

Saul, John W III (Writer)
The Firm
9100 Wilshire Blvd #100W
Beverly Hills, CA 90210, USA

Saul, Ralph S (Business Person)
1400 Waverly Road
Apt B145
Gladwyne, PA 19035-1264, USA

Saul, Stephanie (Journalist)
Newsday
Editorial Dept
235 Pinelawn Road
Melville, NY 11747, USA

Sauli, Daniel (Actor)
c/o James Suskin *James Suskin Management*
2 Charlton St Ste 5K
New York, NY 10014, USA

Sauls, Don (Religious Leader)
Pentecostal Free Will Baptist Church
PO Box 1568
Dunn, NC 28335, USA

Saulters, Glynn (Athlete, Basketball Player, Olympic Athlete)
240 Country Ln
Quitman, LA 71268-1226, USA

Saum, Sherri (Actor)
c/o Christian Donatelli *Schiff Company, The*
9465 Wilshire Blvd
Suite 480
Beverly Hills, CA 90212, USA

Saunders, Bernie (Athlete, Hockey Player)
150 Pinecrest Dr Hastings On
Hudson, NY 10706-3702

Saunders, Dennis (Athlete, Baseball Player)
2854 Rosewood St
Trenton, MI 48183-3602, USA

Saunders, Doug (Athlete, Baseball Player)
10580 Parkington Ln
Unit A
Littleton, CO 80126-6748, USA

Saunders, Doug
43 Saint Kitts
Dana Point, CA 92629

Saunders, George (Writer)
Random House
1745 Broadway #B1
New York, NY 10019, USA

Saunders, George L Jr (Attorney, Attorney General, General)
179 E Lake Shore Dr
Chicago, IL 60611, USA

Saunders, Jennifer (Actor)
c/o Maureen Vincent *United Agents*
12-26 Lexington St
London W1F OLE, UK

Saunders, Joe (Athlete, Baseball Player)
1415 E Grand Canyon Dr
Chandler, AZ 85249-5456, USA

Saunders, John (Cartoonist)
c/o Staff Member *King Features Syndication*
300 W 57th St
15th Floor
New York, NY 10019-5238, USA

Saunders, John (Sportscaster)
ESPN-TV
Sports Dept
ESPN Plaza 935 Middle St
Bristol, CT 06010, USA

Saunders, John R (Race Car Driver)
Watkins Glen Speedway
PO Box 500F
Watkins Glen, NY 14891, USA

Saunders, Lori (Actor)
Lori's Friends
99 La Vuelta Road
Santa Barbara, CA 93108, USA

Saunders, Phillip (Flip) (Basketball Coach, Coach)
395 Calamus Cir
Hamel, MN 55340-9228, USA

Saunders, Rachel (Beauty Pageant Winner)
203 Bocage Drive
Dothan, AL 36303-2944, USA

Saunders, Tony (Athlete, Baseball Player)
1067 Vena Ln
Pasadena, MD 21122-1861, USA

Saunders, Townsend (Athlete, Olympic Athlete, Wrestler)
733 Chantilly Dr
Sierra Vista, AZ 85635, USA

Saura, Carlos (Director)
Antonio Duran
Calle Arturo Soria 52
#Edif 2 1-5A
Madrid 28027, SPAIN

Sauter, Jay (Race Car Driver)
4l5-D River Hwy
Box 278
Mooresville, NC 28115, USA

Sauter, Johnny (Race Car Driver)
Richard Childress Racing
236 Industrial Dr.
Welcome, NC 27374, USA

Sauve, Marie-Amelie (Stylist)
c/o Staff Member *Management + Artists + Organization*
330 W 38th St
#1401
New York, NY 10018, USA

Sauve, Robert (Bob) (Athlete, Hockey Player)
803-3080 Boul le Carrefour
Laval, QC H7T 2R5, Canada

Sauveur, Rich (Athlete, Baseball Player)
3312 47th Ave E
Bradenton, FL 34203-3947, USA

Sauvion, Mariann (Stylist)
309 E 108th St
#2-H
New York, NY 10029, USA

Savage, Adam (Television Host)
Behr Abramson Kaller
9701 Wilshire Blvd Ste 800
Beverly Hills, CA 90212, USA

Savage, Andrea (Actor, Producer, Writer)
c/o Julie Darmody *Mosaic Media Group*
9200 W. Sunset Blvd
10th Floor
Los Angeles, CA 90069, USA

Savage, Ann (Actor)
1541 N Hayworth Ave #203
Los Angeles, CA 90046, USA

Savage, Ben (Actor)
c/o Staff Member *Abrams Artists Agency (LA)*
9200 Sunset Blvd
11th Floor
Los Angeles, CA 90069, USA

Savage, Bob (Athlete, Baseball Player)
95 Raycrest Dr
Randolph, NH 03593-5213, USA

Savage, Brian (Athlete, Hockey Player)
8030 E Whistling Wind Way
Scottsdale, AZ 85255-6480, USA

Savage, Chad (Adult Film Star)
c/o Staff Member *Diva Central Inc*
7510 W Sunset Blvd Ste 1445
Los Angees, CA 90046, USA

Savage, Chantay (Music Group, Musician)
Famous Artists Agency
250 W 57th St
New York, NY 10107, USA

Savage, Dan (Writer)
It Gets Better Project
8023 Beverly Blvd. #191
Los Angeles, CA 90048, USA

Savage, Don (Athlete, Basketball Player)
53 Park Edge # IE
Berkeley Heights, NJ 07922-1281, USA

Savage, Fred (Actor)
c/o Andy Elkin *Creative Artists Agency (CAA-LA)*
2000 Ave Of The Stars
Los Angeles, CA 90067, USA

Savage, Herschel (Adult Film Star)
c/o Staff Member *Vivid Entertainment*
3599 Cahuenga Blvd #400
Los Angeles, CA 90068, USA

Savage, Jack (Athlete, Baseball Player)
9920 White Blossom Blvd
Louisville, KY 40241-4163, USA

Savage, John (Actor)
5584 Bonneville Road
Hidden Hills, CA 91302, USA

Savage, Michael (Radio Personality)
110 Pacific Ave
Box 135
San Francisco, CA 94111, USA

Savage, Reggie (Athlete, Hockey Player)
2000 Harbour Gates Dr Apt 7
Annapolis, MD 21401-2286

Savage, Rick (Musician)
c/o Rod MacSween *International Talent Booking*
74A Charlotte St
London W1T 4QJ, UNITED KINGDOM (UK)

Savage, Stephanie (Producer, Writer)
c/o Staff Member *Wonderland Sound and Vision*
8739 Sunset Blvd
W Hollywood, CA 90069, USA

Savage, Ted (Athlete, Baseball Player)
1510 Mallard Landing Ct
Chesterfield, MO 63017-5588, USA

Savage, Tracie
6212 Banner Ave.
Los Angeles, CA 90038

Saval, Dany
131 rue de l'Universite
Paris, FRANCE 75007

Savant, Doug (Actor)
c/o Kay Liberman *Liberman/Zerman Management*
252 N Larchmont Blvd
Suite 200
Los Angeles, CA 90004, USA

Savard, Denis (Athlete, Hockey Player)
8307 Regency Ct
Toronto, ON M5E 1X8, CANADA

Savard, Marc (Athlete, Hockey Player)
c/o Staff Member *Boston Bruins*
TD Banknorth Garden
100 Legends Way, Suite 250
Boston, MA 02114, USA

Savard, Serge A (Athlete, Hockey Player)
1790 Ch du Golf
RR 1
Saint Bruno, QC J3V 4P6, Canada

Savary, Jerome (Director)
Theatre National de Chaillot
1 Place du Trocadero
Paris 75116, FRANCE

Savchenko, Arkadly M (Opera Singer)
8-358 Storozhovskaya Str
Minsk 220002, BELARUS

Save Ferris (Music Group)
c/o Staff Member *Epic Records Group*
550 Madison Ave
22nd Floor
New York, NY 10022, USA

Saveleva, Lyudmila M (Actor)
Tverskaya Str 19
#76
Moscow 103050, RUSSIA

Saverine, Bob (Athlete, Baseball Player)
228 Slice Dr
Stamford, CT 06907-1137, USA

Saverson, Henry (Baseball Player)
Detroit Stars
1726 Benjamin Ave NE
Grand Rapids, MI 49505-5434, USA

Saves the Day (Music Group)
c/o Richard Egan *Hard 8 Management*
1100 Glendon Ave
Suite 1100
Los Angeles, CA 90024, USA

Savident, John (Actor)
c/o Staff Member *Coronation Street*
Granada Television
Quay Street
Manchester M60 9EA, UNITED
KINGDOM (UK)

Savidge, Jennifer (Actor)
c/o Staff Member *TalentWorks (LA)*
3500 W Olive Ave
Suite 1400
Burbank, CA 91505, USA

Savile, David
28 Colomb St.
London, ENGLAND SW10 9EW

Saville, Curtis (Misc)
RFD Box 44
West Charleston, VT 05872, USA

Saville, Fleur (Actor)
c/o Staff Member *Auckland Actors*
PO Box 56460
Dominion Road
Auckland, NEW ZEALAND

Saville, Kathleen (Misc)
RFD Box 44
West Charleston, VT 05872, USA

Saving Jane (Music Group)
9423 Old Forest Lane
Loveland, Ohio 45140, USA

Savini, Tom
311 Taylor St.
Pittsburgh, PA 15224

Savinykh, Viktor P (Misc)
Moscow State University
Gorochovskii 4
Moscow 103064, RUSSIA

Savitskaya, Svetalana Y (Misc)
Russian Association
Khovanskaya Str 3
Moscow 129515, RUSSIA

Savitt, Dick
19 E. 80th St.
New York, NY 10021-0109

Savitt, Richard (Dick) (Tennis Player)
19 E 80th St
New York, NY 10021, USA

Savoie, Matt (Athlete, Figure Skater,
Olympic Athlete)
1026 N Maplewood Ave
Peoria, IL 61606-1034, USA

Savoretti, Jack (Musician)
c/o Michael Moses *Baker Winokur Ryder
Public Relations (BWR-LA)*
9100 Wilshire Blvd
Suite 500, West Tower
Beverly Hills, CA 90212, USA

Savoy, Gene
643 Ralston St.
Reno, NV 89503

Savoy, Guy (Chef)
101 Blvd Pereire
Paris 75017, FRANCE

Savransky, Moe (Athlete, Baseball Player)
128 Dorset D
Boca Raton, FL 33434-3076, USA

Savre, Danielle (Actor)
c/o Adam Griffin *Kritzer Levine Wilkins
Entertainment (KLWG)*
11872 La Grange Ave
1st Floor
Los Angeles, CA 90025, USA

Sawa, Devon (Actor)
c/o Brian Wilkins *Kritzer Levine Wilkins
Entertainment (KLWG)*
11872 La Grange Ave
1st Floor
Los Angeles, CA 90025, USA

Sawalha, Julia (Actor)
P F D
Drury House
34-43 Russell St
London WC2B 5HA, UNITED KINGDOM
(UK)

Sawalha, Nadia (Talk Show Host)
BBC
Broadcasting House
Portland Place
London, UK W1A 1AA

Sawallisch, Wolfgang (Conductor,
Musician)
Hinterm Bichi 2
Grassau 83224, GERMANY

Sawyer, Alan (Athlete, Basketball Player)
117 San Juan Dr
Sequim, WA 98382-9326, USA

Sawyer, Amos (President)
President's Office
Executive Mansion
PO Box 9001
Monrovia, LIBERIA

Sawyer, Charles H (Misc)
466 Tuallitan Road
Los Angeles, CA 90049, USA

Sawyer, Daine (Correspondent)
147 Columbus Ave #300
New York, NY 10023, USA

Sawyer, Diane (Journalist)
77 West 66 St.
New York, NY 10023-6201, USA

Sawyer, Elton (Race Car Driver)
Akins Motorsports
185 McKenzie Road
Mooresville, NC 28115, USA

Sawyer, Forrest (Correspondent)
NBC-TV
News Dept
30 Rockefeller Plaza
New York, NY 10112, USA

Sawyer, James L (Misc)
Leather Workers Union
11 Peabody Square
Peabody, MA 01960, USA

Sawyer, John (Athlete, Football Player)
23637 Sunnyside Ln
Zachary, LA 70791, USA

Sawyer, Ken (Athlete, Football Player)
667 Violet Ave
Lot 36
Hyde Park, NY 12538, USA

Sawyer, Kevin (Athlete, Hockey Player)
519 S Lucille Ct
Spokane Valley, WA 99216-0827, USA

Sawyer, Mary Jane (Stylist)
c/o Staff Member *Ennis*
119 Braintree St
Boston, MA 02134, USA

Sawyer, Paul (Race Car Driver)
Richmond International Raceway
PO Box 9257
Richmond, VA 23227, USA

Sawyer, Rick (Athlete, Baseball Player)
1201 Calle Extrano
Bakersfield, CA 93309-7116, USA

Sawyer, Robert E (Religious Leader)
Moravian Church Southern Province
459 S Church St
Winston Salem, NC 27101, USA

Sawyer, Talance (Athlete, Football Player)
6150 Brookhaven Dr
Bastrop, LA 71220, USA

Sawyer Brown (Music Group)
c/o Staff Member *Paradigm (Nashville)*
124 12th Ave S
Suite 410
Nashville, TN 37203, USA

Sax, Dave (Athlete, Baseball Player)
3352 Eaton Dr
Roseville, CA 95661-7907, USA

Sax, Steve (Athlete, Baseball Player)
201 Wesley Ct
Roseville, CA 95661-7913, USA

Saxe, Adrian (Artist)
4835 N Figueroa St
Los Angeles, CA 90042, USA

Saxon, David S (Physicist)
1008 Hilts Ave
Los Angeles, CA 90024, USA

Saxon, Edward (Producer)
c/o Staff Member *Creative Artists Agency
(CAA-LA)*
2000 Ave Of The Stars
Los Angeles, CA 90067, USA

Saxon, James E (Athlete, Football Player)
RR 3 Box 34X
Beaufort, SC 29906, USA

Saxon, James E (Jimmy) (Athlete, Football
Player)
1 Mulberry Ln
Austin, TX 78746, USA

Saxon, John (Actor)
2432 Banyan Dr
Los Angeles, CA 90049, USA

Saxon, Mike (Athlete, Football Player)
660 W Peninsula Dr
Coppell, TX 75019, USA

Saxton, Brian (Athlete, Football Player)
3604 Tudor Dr
Pompton Plains, NJ 07444, USA

Saxton, Jimmy (Athlete, Football Player)
1 Mulberry Ln
Austin, TX 78746, USA

Saxton, Johnny (Boxer)
Crystal Palms
1710 4th Ave N
Lake Worth, FL 33460, USA

Saxton, Shirley Childress (Music Group,
Musician)
Sweet Honey Agency
PO Box 600099
Newtonville, MA 02460, USA

Say, Peggy
438 Lake Shore Dr.
Cadiz, KY 42211

Sayed, Mostafa Amr El (Misc)
579 Westover Dr NW
Atlanta, GA 30305, USA

Sayer, Leo (Music Group, Musician,
Songwriter, Writer)
Mission Control
Business Center
Lower Road
London SE16 2XB, UNITED KINGDOM
(UK)

Sayers, E Roger (Educator)
University of Alabama
President's Office
Tuscaloosa, AL 35487, USA

Sayers, Gale (Athlete, Football Player)
1313 N Ritchie Ct
Apt 407
Chicago, IL 60610, USA

Saykally, Richard J (Misc)
University of California
Chemistry Dept
Latimer Hall
Berkeley, CA 94720, USA

Sayles, John (Director)
210 13th St
Hoboken, NJ 07030, USA

Saylor, Edward (General)
14010 99th Ave E
Puyallup, WA 98373-2509, USA

Sayre, Anne
1268 E. 14th St.
Brooklyn, NY 11230

Sbarge, Raphael (Actor)
c/o Tracy Steinsapir *Main Title
Entertainment*
8383 Wilshire Blvd
Suite 408
Los Angeles, CA 90211, USA

Sbranti, Ron (Athlete, Football Player)
2925 Roosevelt Ln
Antioch, CA 94509, USA

Scaasi, Arnold (Designer, Fashion Designer)
16 E 52nd St
New York, NY 10022, USA

Scacchi, Greta (Actor)
c/o Susan Smith *Susan Smith Company, The*
1344 N Wetherly Dr
Los Angeles, CA 90069-1817, USA

Scaduto, Al (Cartoonist)
571 Swanson Crest
Milford, CT 06461-2735, USA

Scadyac, Tom (Director)
c/o Staff Member *Creative Artists Agency (CAA-LA)*
2000 Ave Of The Stars
Los Angeles, CA 90067, USA

Scafa, Bob (Baseball Player)
US Olympic Team
2090 Milton Ave
Park Ridge, IL 60068-2320, USA

Scaggs, Boz (Musician)
9460 Wilshire Blvd. #310
Beverly Hills, CA 90212

Scaggs, William R (Boz) (Music Group, Musician, Songwriter, Writer)
c/o Staff Member *HK Management (LA)*
10866 Wilshire Blvd Ste 200
Los Angeles, CA 90024, USA

Scagliotti-Smith, Allison (Actor)
c/o Staff Member *Osbrink Talent Agency*
4343 Lankershim Blvd
Suite 100
Universal City, CA 91602, USA

Scalabrine, Brian
1513 Griffin Ave
Enumclaw, WA 98022-2827, USA

Scales, Bobby (Athlete, Baseball Player)
3547 Archgate Ct
AlPharetta, GA 30004-0635, USA

Scales, Charlie (Athlete, Football Player)
4035 Vistaview St
West Mifflin, PA 15122, USA

Scales, DeWayne
8505 Sikorski Ln
Dallas, TX 75228-5446, USA

Scales, Dwight (Athlete, Football Player)
6112 Rosevelt Cir NW
Huntsville, AL 35810, USA

Scales, Greg (Athlete, Football Player)
4118 Carnation Dr
Winston Salem, NC 27105, USA

Scales, Hurles (Athlete, Football Player)
600 N Adams St
Amarillo, TX 79107, USA

Scales, Prunella (Actor)
Conway Van Gelder Robinson
18-21 Jermyn St
London SW1Y 6NB, UNITED KINGDOM (UK)

Scalia, Antonin (Attorney)
6713 Wemberly Way
Me Lean, VA 22101-1529, USA

Scalia, Jack (Actor)
c/o Alan Ellsweig *Shadow Entertainment*
10 Universal City Plz
20th Floor
Universal City, CA 91608, USA

Scalia, Pietro (Actor, Director, Editor, Producer)
c/o Spyros Skouras *The Skouras Agency*
1149 Third Street Fl 3
Santa Monica, CA 90403, USA

Scalians, Bret (Musician)
Media Five Entertainment
3005 Brodhead Read #170
Bethlehem, PA 18020, USA

Scalzitti, Will (Baseball Player)
19321 SW 61st St
Ft Lauderdale, FL 33332-3354, USA

Scalzo, Tony (Musician)
c/o Staff Member *Russell Carter Artist Management*
567 Ralph McGill Blvd NE
Atlanta, GA 30312-1110, USA

Scaminace, Joseph M (Business Person)
Sherwin-Williams Co
101 W Prospect Ave
Cleveland, OH 44115, USA

Scamurra, Peter (Athlete, Hockey Player)
15 Guinevere Ct
Getzville, NY 14068-1194

Scancarelli, Jim (Cartoonist)
Mark J Cohen
PO Box 1892
Santa Rosa, CA 95402, USA

Scandiuzzi, Roberto (Opera Singer)
Opera et Concert
Maximilianstr 22
Munich 80539, GERMANY

Scanga, Italo (Artist)
7127 Olivetas
La Jolla, CA 92037, USA

Scanlan, Bob (Athlete, Baseball Player)
12400 Montecito Rd
Apt 315
Seal Beach, CA 90740-2733, USA

Scanlan, Hugh P S (Misc)
23 Seven Stones Dr
Broadstairs
Kent, UNITED KINGDOM (UK)

Scanlon, Pat (Athlete, Baseball Player)
7400 Portland Ave
Minneapolis, MN 55423-4343, USA

Scapinello, Ray (Athlete, Hockey Player)
Hockey Hall of Fame
Brookfield Place 30 Yonge St
Toronto, ON M5E 1X8, Canada

Scarbath, John C (Jack) (Athlete, Football Player)
736 Calvert Rd
Rising Sun, MD 21911, USA

Scarber, Sam (Athlete, Football Player)
12209 Crewe St
North Hollywood, CA 91605, USA

Scarbery, Randy (Athlete, Baseball Player)
5010 E Lewis Ave
Fresno, CA 93727-2418, USA

Scarborough, Joe (Congressman, Television Host)
c/o Staff Member *HarperCollins Publishers*
10 East 53rd St
c/o Author mail, 7th Floor
New York, NY 10022, USA

Scarborough, Jon (Television Host)

Scarbrough, W Carl (Misc)
Furniture Workers Union
1910 Airlane Dr
Nashville, TN 37210, USA

Scarce, Mac (Athlete, Baseball Player)
1010 Richmond Glen Cir
Alpharetta, GA 30004-8216, USA

Scardelletti, Robert A (Misc)
Transportation Communications Union
3 Research Place
Rockville, MD 20850, USA

Scardino, Albert J (Journalist)
19 Empire House
Thurloe Place
London SW7 2RU, UNITED KINGDOM (UK)

Scarf, Herbert E (Economist)
88 Blake Road
Hamden, CT 06517, USA

Scarf, Maggie (Writer)
c/o Camille McDuffie *Goldberg McDuffie Communications*
444 Madison Ave
Suite 3300
New York, NY 10022, USA

Scarface (Musician)
c/o Staff Member *American Talent Agency*
248 W 35th St
Suite 501
New York, NY 10001, USA

Scarfe, Gerald A (Cartoonist)
10 Cheyne Walk
London SW3, UNITED KINGDOM (UK)

Scarfe, Jonathan
4739 Lankershim Blvd.
No. Hollywood, CA 91602-1803

Scargill, Arthur (Misc)
National Union of Mineworkers
2 Huddersfield Road
Barnsley, UNITED KINGDOM (UK)

Scarpati, Joseph H (Athlete, Football Player)
32 Lexington Cir
Marlton, NJ 08053, USA

Scarpelli, Glenn (Actor)
300 Mountain Shadows Dr
Sedona, AZ 86336, USA

Scarpitto, Bob (Athlete, Football Player)
123 White Oak Ln
Carmel Valley, CA 93924-9650, USA

Scarry, Mike (Athlete, Football Player)
7430 Lake Breeze Dr
Apt 104
Fort Myers, FL 33907, USA

Scarsone, Steve (Athlete, Baseball Player)
3935 E Rough Rdr Rd
Unit 1158
Phoenix, AZ 85050-7356, USA

Scarwid, Diana (Actor)
PO Box 3614
Savannah, GA 31414, USA

Scatchard, Dave (Athlete, Hockey Player)
215 Orchard Valley Dr
Harriman, TN 37748-4698

Scates, Al (Coach, Volleyball Player)
UCLA
Athletic Dept - Volleyball
J.D. Morgan Center, P.O. Box 24044
Los Angeles, CA 90024, USA

Scattini, Monica (Actor)
Carol Levi Co
Via Giuseppe Pisanelli
Rome 00196, ITALY

Scelba-Shorte, Mercedes (Reality TV Star)
c/o Staff Member *Ty Ty Baby Productions*
8346 W Third St #650
Los Angeles, CA 90048, USA

Scelzi, Gary (Race Car Driver)
Alen Johnson Racing
2772 S. Cherry Ave.
Fresno, CA 93106, USA

Schaaf, Fred (Athlete, Baseball Player)
2782 Countryside Blvd Apt 3
Clearwater, FL 33761-3646, USA

Schaaf-Behle, Petra
Am Rodeland 22
Willingen, GERMANY D-34508

Schaal, Paul (Athlete, Baseball Player)
68-1962 Puu Nui St
Waikoloa, HI 96738-5238, USA

Schaal, Richard (Actor)
612 Gulf Blvd #9
Indian Rocks Beach, FL 33785, USA

Schaal, Wendy (Actor)
Gage Group
14724 Ventura Blvd #505
Shreman Oaks, CA 91403, USA

Schaap, Dick
77 W. 66th St.
New York, NY 10023

Schabarum, Pete (Athlete, Football Player)
46170 E Eldorado Dr
Indian Wells, CA 92210, USA

Schacher, Mel (Musician)
Lustig Talent
PO Box 770850
Orlando, FL 32877, USA

Schachman, Howard K (Biologist)
University of California
Molecular Biology Dept
Berkeley, CA 94720, USA

Schachnow, Eddie (Stylist)
c/o Staff Member *Celestine - CA*
1666 20th St
#200-B
Santa Monica, CA 90404, USA

Schacht, Henry B (Business Person)
Lucent Technologies Inc
600 Mountain Ave
New Providence, NJ 07974, USA

Schachter, Blanche (Baseball Player)
163 W 18th St Apt 3A
New York, NY 10011, USA

Schachter, Steven (Director, Writer)
c/o Staff Member *Ken Gross Management*
12135 Stanwood Dr
Los Angeles, CA 90066, USA

Schachter Sisters
182-06 Midland Park Blvd.
Jamaica Estates, NY 11432

Schacker, Hal (Athlete, Baseball Player)
4609 N Matanzas Ave
Tampa, FL 33614-6652, USA

Schade, Frank (Athlete, Basketball Player)
825 Nicolet Ave
Oshkosh, WI 5490l-1635, USA

Schade, Molly (Actor)
c/o Aron Giannini *Collective*
8383 Wilshire Blvd
Suite 1050
Beverly Hills, CA 90211, USA

Schadler, Ben
808 Bauer Dr
San Carlos, CA 94070-3614, USA

Schadler, Jay (Correspondent)
c/o Staff Member *Primetime*
147 Columbus Ave
New York, NY 10023, USA

Schadt, James P (Publisher)
Reader's Digest Assn
Reader's Digest Road
Pleasantville, NY 10570, USA

Schaech, Johnathon (Actor, Producer, Writer)
c/o Eli Selden *Anonymous Content (LA)*
3531 Hayden Ave
Culver City, CA 90232, USA

Schaefer, Bob (Athlete, Baseball Player, Coach)
9070 Old Hickory Cir
Fort Myers, FL 33912-6844, USA

Schaefer, Don (Athlete, Football Player)
286 Birch Pkwy
Wyckoff, NJ 07481, USA

Schaefer, Ernst J (Scientist)
Tufts University
Nutrition Research Center
Medford, MA 02155, USA

Schaefer, George A Jr (Financier)
Fifth Third Bancorp
38 Fountain Square Plaza
Cincinnati, OH 45263, USA

Schaefer, Henry F III (Misc)
University of Georgia
Computational Quantum Chemistry Center
Athens, GA 30602, USA

Schaefer, Jeff (Athlete, Baseball Player)
2110 Woodbend Trl
Fort Mill, SC 29708-8343, USA

Schaefer, Roberto (Cinematographer)
Innovative Artists
1505 10th St
Santa Monica, CA 90401, USA

Schaefer, Yvonne Maria (Actor, Producer)
YMC Films
343 E 76th St
New York, NY 10021, USA

Schaeffer, Billy
7 Ames Pl
Huntington Station, NY 11746-4701, USA

Schaeffer, Danny (Athlete, Baseball Player)
Round Rock Express
3400 E Palm Valley Blvd
Attn: Coaching Staff
Round Rock, TX 78665, USA

Schaeffer, Eric (Actor, Director)
c/o Norman Aladjem *Levity Entertainment Group*
360 N Crescent Dr
North Bldg
Beverly Hills, CA 90210, USA

Schaeffer, George
1040 Woodland Dr.
Beverly Hills, CA 90210

Schaeffer, Leonard (Business Person)
WellPoint Health Networks
1 Wellpoint Way
Westlake Village, CA 91362, USA

Schaeffer, Mark (Athlete, Baseball Player)
18261 Parthenia St
Northridge, CA 91325-3303, USA

Schaefzel, John R (Writer)
2 Bay Tree Lane
Bethesda, MD 20816, USA

Schafer, Edward (Politician)
4426 Carrie Rose Ln S
Fargo, ND 58104-6818, USA

Schafer, Jordan (Athlete, Baseball Player)
80 Pine Forest Dr
Haines City, FL 33844-9710, USA

Schaffel, Lewis (Basketball Player, Misc)
Miami Heat
American Airlines Arena
601 Biscayne Blvd
Miami, FL 33132, USA

Schaffer, Akiva (Director, Editor, Writer)
c/o Staff Member *Mosaic Media Group*
9200 W. Sunset Blvd
10th Floor
Los Angeles, CA 90069, USA

Schaffer, Eric (Music Group, Musician)
Kennedy Center for Performing Arts
Washington, DC 20011, USA

Schaffer, Jimmie (Athlete, Baseball Player)
655 Birch Ter
Coopersburg, PA 18036-2407, USA

Schaffermoth, Joe (Athlete, Baseball Player)
20 Marion Ave
Berkeley Heights, NJ 07922, USA

Schaffernoth, Joe (Athlete, Baseball Player)
20 Marion Ave
Berkeley Heights, NJ 07922-1260, USA

Schafrath, Dick (Athlete, Football Player)
704 Ashland Dr
Mansfield, OH 44905, USA

Schalder, Ben (Athlete, Basketball Player)
808 Bauer Dr
San Carlos, CA 94070, USA

Schall, Alvin A (Football Coach, Football Player)
US Appeals Court
717 Madison Place NW
Washington, DC 20439, USA

Schall, Benny (Athlete, Basketball Player)
4305 Robinhood Ln
Toldeo, OH 43623-2537, USA

Schall, Gene (Athlete, Baseball Player)
1582 Bromley Dr
Harleysville, PA 19438-3056, USA

Schaller, Cliff (Athlete, Baseball Player)
1978 3847 Powner Rd
Cincinnati, OH 45248-2918, USA

Schaller, George B (Biologist)
90 Sentry Hill Road
Roxbury, CT 06783, USA

Schaller, Willie (Soccer Player)
3283 S Indiana St
Lakewood, CO 80228, USA

Schallert, William (Actor)
Distinguished Character
14920 Ramos Pl
Pacific Palisades, CA 90272, USA

Schallock, Art (Athlete, Baseball Player)
749 Crocus Dr
Sonoma, CA 95476-8325, USA

Schally, Andrew V (Nobel Prize Laureate)
3801 Collins Avenue
Miami Beach, FL 33140-3705, USA

Schama, Simon M (Historian, Writer)
Minda de Gunzburg European Studies Center
Adolphus Hall
Cambridge, MA 02138, USA

Schamehorn, Kevin (Athlete, Hockey Player)
5536 Stoney_ Brook Rd
Kalamazoo, MI 49009-7703

Schanberg, Sydney H (Journalist)
PO Box 236
Rifton, NY 12471-0236, USA

Schank, Roger C (Doctor, Scientist)
Northwestern University
Learning Sciences Institute
Evanston, IL 60201, USA

Schankweiler, Scott (Athlete, Football Player)
11 Bartley Ct
Nottingham, MD 21236, USA

Schanz, Heidi (Actor)
Gersh Agency
232 N Canon Dr
Beverly Hills, CA 90210, USA

Schapansky, Glen (Athlete, Football Player)
PO Box 215
Woodlands, MB ROC 3HO, Canada

Schapker, Alison (Producer, Writer)
c/o Ilan Breil *Mosaic Media Group*
9200 W. Sunset Blvd
10th Floor
Los Angeles, CA 90069, USA

Schapp, Dick (Sportscaster)
ESPN-TV
Sports Dept
ESPN Plaza 935 Middle St
Bristol, CT 06010, USA

Schar, Dwight (Business Person)
NVR Inc
7601 Lewinsville Rd #300
McLean, VA 22102, USA

Scharansky, Natan (Activist, Scientist)
Trade & Industry Ministry
30 Rehov Agron
Jerusalem 91002, ISRAEL

Scharar, Erich (Athlete)
Grutstrasse 63
Herrliberg 8074, SWITZERLAND

Scharf, Ted (Athlete, Hockey Player)
50 Westmount Rd N
Waterloo, ON N2L 2R5, Canada

Scharping, Rudolf (Government Official)
Wilhelmstr 5
Lahnstein 56112, GERMANY

Schattinger, Jeff (Athlete, Baseball Player)
P.O. Box 134
Lake Arrowhead, CA 92352-0134, USA

Schatz, Albert (Biologist)
Rutgers University
Research/Endowment Foundation
New Brunswick, NJ 08903, USA

Schatz, Donny (Race Car Driver)
Schatz Motorsports
4510 19th Ave. SW
Fargo, ND 58103, USA

Schatz, Gottfried (Biologist, Misc)
Basle University
Klingelbergstr 70
Basle 4056, SWITZERLAND

Schatz, Howard (Photographer)
435 W Broadway #2
New York, NY 10012, USA

Schatzberg, Jerry N (Director)
c/o Staff Member *ICM Partners (ICM-LA)*
10250 Constellation Blvd Fl 7
Los Angeles, CA 90067, USA

Schatzeder, Dan (Athlete, Baseball Player)
186 River Mist Dr
Oswego, IL 60543-8358, USA

Schatzman, Evry (Physicist)
11 Rue de l'Église
Domplerre
Maignelay-Montigny 60420, FRANCE

Schaudt, Martin (Athlete, Horse Racer)
Gerhardstr 10/2
Albstadt 72461, GERMANY

Schaufuss, Peter (Ballerina, Director)
Papoutsis Representation
18 Sundial Ave
London SE25 4BX, UNITED KINGDOM (UK)

Schaum, Greg (Athlete, Football Player)
4303 Piney Park Rd
Perry Hall, MD 21128, USA

Schauman, Wilhelm (Athlete, Golfer)
c/o Jim Lehrman *SFX Golf*
36855 W Main St Ste 200
Purcellville, VA 20132, USA

Schayes, Danny (Athlete, Basketball Player)
7035 E Berneil Dr
Paradise Valley, AZ 85253-1944, USA

Schayes, Dolph (Athlete, Basketball Player)
200 Polk St
Denver, CO 80239, USA

Schayes, Wendy Lucero (Athlete, Diver, Olympic Athlete)
7035 E Berneil Dr
Paradise Valley, AZ 85253-1944, Usa

Schechkter, Tomas (Race Car Driver)
5101 Decatur Blvd #P
Indianapolis, IN 46241-9528, USA

Scheck, Barry (Attorney, Attorney General, Educator, General)
Yeshiva University
Law School
55 5th Ave
New York, NY 10003, USA

Scheckter, Jody D (Race Car Driver)
39 Ave Princess Grace
Monte Carlo, MONACO

Scheckter, Tomas (Race Car Driver)
11412 Divers Cove Ct.
Indianapolis, IN 46236-8601, USA

Schecter, Leroy (Business Person)
12 Indian Creek Dr
Indian Creek Village, FL 33154, USA

Schecter, Wendy (Stylist)
20 W 27th St
#2
New York, NY 10001, USA

Schectman, Ossie (Athlete, Basketball Player)
101 Canter Ct
Goshen, NY 10924-8930, USA

Schedeen, Anne (Actor)
c/o Tom Markley *Metropolitan Talent Agency*
7020 La Presa Dr
Los Angeles, CA 90068, USA

Scheer-Demme, Amanda (Business Person, Producer)
c/o Staff Member *Thrive Music*
1024 N Orange Dr
Los Angeles, CA 90038, USA

Scheffer, Aaron (Athlete, Baseball Player)
1351 Sharon St
Westland, MI 48186-5044, USA

Scheffer, Victor B (Biologist)
14806 SE 54th St
Bellevue, WA 98006, USA

Scheffler, Israel (Misc)
Harvard University
Larsen Hall
Cambridge, MA 02138, USA

Scheffler, Tony (Football Player)
c/o Staff Member *Denver Broncos*
13655 E Broncos Pkwy
Englewood, CO 80112, USA

Schefft, Jen (Reality TV Star)
3650 Magnolia Ave
Chicago, IL 60613, USA

Scheib, Carl (Athlete, Baseball Player)
2922 Old Ranch Rd
San Antonio, TX 78217-5858, USA

Scheibel, Arnold B (Doctor)
16231 Morrison St
Encino, CA 91436, USA

Scheid, Rich (Athlete, Baseball Player)
402 Grant Ave
Hightstown, NJ 08520-4100, USA

Scheimer, Lou (Producer)
18918 La Montana Pl
Tarzana, CA 91356-4819, USA

Schein, Philip S (Doctor)
6212 Robinwood Road
Bethesda, MD 20817, USA

Scheinblum, Richie (Athlete, Baseball Player)
1308 Woodstock Dr
Palm Harbor, FL 34684-2246, USA

Schekman, Randy W (Scientist)
Howard Hughes Institute
4000 Jones Bridge Road
Chevy Chase, MD 20815, USA

Schell, Catherine (Actor)
Postfach 800504
Cologne 51005, GERMANY

Schell, Jonathan (Journalist)
Newsday
Editorial Dept
235 Pinelawn Road
Melville, NY 11747, USA

Schell, Jozef S (Biologist, Scientist)
College de France
11 Pl Marcelin-Berthelot
Paris Cedex 05 75231, FRANCE

Schell, Maximilian (Actor)
16501 Ventura Blvd
Suite 304
Encino, CA 91436-2067, USA

Schell, Maximillian (Actor, Director, Writer)
c/o Staff Member *The Blake Agency*
23441 Malibu Colony Rd
Malibu, CA 90265, USA

Schell, Ronnie
Angel City Talent
4741 Laurel Canyon Blvd
#101
Valley Village, CA 91607, USA

Schellen, Mark (Athlete, Football Player)
320 Shorewood Ln
Waterloo, NE 68069-9717, USA

Schellenbach, Kate (Musician)
Metropolitan Entertainment
2 Penn Plaza #2600
New York, NY 10121, USA

Schellenberg, August (Actor)
Gold Marshak Liedtke
3500 W Olive Ave #1400
Burbank, CA 91505, USA

Schellhase, Dave (Athlete, Basketball Player)
862 Walnut Rdg E
Logansport, IN 46947-3965, USA

Schelling, Gunther F K (Engineer)
Graz University
Rechbauerstr 12
Graz 8010, AUSTRIA

Schelling, Thomas C (Economist)
University of Maryland
Economics Dept
College Park, MD 20742, USA

Schellman, John A (Misc)
65 W 30th Ave #508
Eugene, OR 97405, USA

Schelmerding, Kirk (Race Car Driver)
Childress Racing
PO Box 1189
Industrial Dr
Welcome, NC 27374, USA

Schemansky, Norbert (Athlete, Olympic Athlete, Weightlifter)
24826 New York St
Dearborn, MI 48124, USA

Schembechler, Bo
1904 Boulder Dr.
Ann Arbor, MI 48104

Schembechler, Glenn E (Bo) Jr (Athlete, Coach, Football Player)
1904 Boulder Dr
Ann Arbor, MI 48104, USA

Schemling, Bill
PO Box 11308
Portland, OR 97211-0308

Schenert, Turk (Athlete, Football Player)
239 Willow Ave
Pompton Lakes, NJ 07442, USA

Schenk, Franziska (Speed Skater)
DSEG
Mensinger Str 68
Munich 80992, GERMANY

Schenkenberg, Markus (Actor, Model)
c/o Maury DiMauro *Innovative Artists (LA)*
235 Park Ave S
10th Floor
New York, NY 10003, USA

Schenker, Dr Eran (Astronaut)
PO Box 4572
Jerusalem, USA

Schenker, Nathan (Athlete, Football Player)
26400 George Zeiger Dr
Apt 116
Beachwood, OH 44122, USA

Schenkkan, Robert F (Writer)
Dramatist Guild
1501 Broadway #701
New York, NY 10036, USA

Schenkman, Eric (Musician)
DAS Communications
84 Riverside Dr
New York, NY 10024, USA

Schepisi, Fred (Director)
c/o Staff Member *WmE2 (WMA-LA)*
1 William Morris Pl
Beverly Hills, CA 90212, USA

Schepisl, Frederic A (Director)
Film House
159 Eastern Road
South Melbourne, VIC 3205, AUSTRALIA

Scherbo, Vitali (Gymnast)
8308 Aqua Spray Ave
Las Vegas, NV 89128, USA

Scherbo, Vitaly
8308 Aqua Spray Ave
Las Vegas, NV 89128-7432

Scherega, Harold A (Misc)
212 Homestead Terrace
Ithaca, NY 14850, USA

Scherer, Bernard (Athlete, Football Player)
P.O. Box 5201
Carmel by the Sea, CA 93921, USA

Scherer, Lee (Scientist)
10606 Falcon Rim Pt
San Diego, CA 92131-2309, USA

Scherfig, Lone (Director)
c/o Jodi Shields *Casarotto Ramsay & Associates Ltd (UK)*
Waverley House
7-12 Noel St
London W1F 8GQ, UK

Scherman, Fred (Athlete, Baseball Player)
7454 S Tipp Cowlesville Rd
Tipp City, OH 45371-8351, USA

Scherrer, Bill (Athlete, Baseball Player)
4155 E Rockledge Rd
Phoenix, AZ 85044-6770, USA

Scherrer, Jean-Louis (Designer, Fashion Designer)
51 Ave du Montaigne
Paris 75008, FRANCE

Scherza, Chuck (Athlete, Hockey Player)
51 Manistee St
Pawtucket, RI 02861

Scherzer, Max (Athlete, Baseball Player)
534 Glenfield Ridge Ct
Chesterfield, MO 63017-2782, USA

Scherzinger, Nicole (Actor, Musician)
c/o British Reece *PMK/BNC Public Relations (PMK-LA)*
8687 Melrose Ave Fl 8
West Hollywood, CA 90069, USA

Scheuer, Paul J (Misc)
3271 Melemele Place
Honolulu, HI 96822, USA

Scheufelen, Klaus (Scientist)
Im Buchs 1
Lenningen, Germany

Scheuring, Paul (Director)
c/o Adam Berkowitz *Creative Artists Agency (CAA-LA)*
2000 Ave Of The Stars
Los Angeles, CA 90067, USA

Scheve, Carin (Stylist)
c/o Staff Member *ESP (London)*
63 Charlotte St.
1st Floor
London W11 4PG, UK

Schevill, James (Writer)
1309 Oxford St
Berkeley, CA 94709, USA

Schiavo, Mary (Activist, Government Official)
Ohio State University
Public Policy Dept
Columbus, OH 43210, USA

Schickel, Richard (Critic, Writer)
9051 Dicks St
Los Angeles, CA 90069, USA

Schickele, Peter (Comedian, Composer)
International Creative Mgmt
40 W 57th St #1800
New York, NY 10019, USA

Schiebeler, Kurt (Aviator)
Lotsenstrasse 7 Solingen

Schiebold, Hans (Artist)
13705 SW 118th Court
Tigard, OR 97223, USA

Schieffer, Bob (Journalist)
Cbs News
2020 Main St NW
Washington, DC 20036-3304, USA

Schierholtz, Nate (Athlete, Baseball Player)
7500 E Deer Valley Rd
Unit 118
Scottsdale, AZ 85255-4867, USA

Schiff, Andras (Musician)
Shirley Kirshbaum
711 W End Ave #5KN
New York, NY 10025, USA

Schiff, Heinrich (Musician)
Astrid Schoerke
Monckegergallee 41
Hannover 30453, GERMANY

Schiff, John J Jr (Financier)
Cincinnati Financial Corp
6200 S Gilmore Road
Fairfield, OH 45014, USA

Schiff, Mark (Actor, Comedian)
Gail Stocker Presents
1025 N Kings Road #113
Los Angeles, CA 90069, USA

Schiff, Richard (Actor, Director)
c/o Michael Garnett *Leverage Management*
3030 Pennsylvania Ave
Santa Monica, CA 90404, USA

Schiff, Robin (Writer)
c/o Staff Member *Broder Webb Chervin Silbermann Agency, The (BWCS)*
10250 Constellation Blvd
Los Angeles, CA 90067-6200, USA

Schiffer, Claudia (Model)
Räuberstege 22
Rheinberg 47495, Germany

Schiffer, Eric (Writer)
6965 El Camino Real #105
PMB 517
Carlsbad, CA 92009

Schiffer, Menahem M (Mathematician)
6404 Ruffin Road
Chevy Chase, MD 20815, USA

Schiffer, Michael (Writer)
c/o Greg Weiss *Vanguard Management Group (NY)*
220 5th Ave.
Penthouse West
New York, NY 10001, USA

Schiffner, Travis (Actor)
c/o Staff Member *Bohemia Group*
1680 Vine St Ste 216
Los Angeles, CA 90028, USA

Schifrin, Lalo (Composer)
710 N Hillcrest Road
Beverly Hills, CA 90210, USA

schilebener, Andy (Athlete, Hockey Player)
1980 Sliver pines Cres
Orleans, ON K1 W 1J7, Canada

Schiller, Harvey W (Misc)
Turner Sports
1050 Techwood Dr NW
Atlanta, GA 30318, USA

Schiller, Lawrence J (Director, Writer)
5430 Oakdale Ave
Woodland Hills, CA 91364, USA

Schilling, Chuck (Athlete, Baseball Player)
907 Caroline Ct
New Bern, NC 28560-1804, USA

Schilling, C Thomas (Nobel Prize Laureate)
4506 Wetherill Rd
Bethesda, MD 20816-1814, USA

Schilling, Curtis (Curt) M (Athlete, Baseball Player)
7 Woodridge Rd
Medfield, MA 02052-2526, USA

Schilling, Peter
Geiselgasteigstr. 76
Munich, GERMANY 81545

Schilling, William
626 N. Valley St.
Burbank, CA 91505

Schimberg, Henry R (Business Person)
Coca-Cola Enterprises
2500 Windy Ridge Parkway
Atlanta, GA 30339, USA

Schimberni, Mario (Business Person)
Armando Curcio Editore SpA
Via IV Novembre
Rome 00187, ITALY

Schimmel, Paul R (Biologist, Misc)
Scripps Research Institute
10550 N Torrey Pines Road
La Jolla, CA 92037, USA

Schindelholz, Lorenz (Athlete)
Hardstr 184
Herbetswil 4715, SWITZERLAND

Schindler, Steve (Athlete, Football Player)
6109 Willow Springs Dr
Morrison, CO 80465, USA

Schinkel, Kenneth (Ken) (Athlete, Hockey Player)
19927 Beaulieu Ct
Fort Myers, FL 33908, USA

Schino, Dominic (Producer)
c/o Staff Member *Magic Touch Records*
12-15 36th Avenue
#4-E
Long Island City, NY 11106, USA

Schipper, Ron (Coach, Football Coach)
1088 Fountain View Circle
Unit 1
Holland, MI 49423-5620, USA

Schiraldi, Calvin (Athlete, Baseball Player)
9108 Tweed Berwick Dr
Austin, TX 78750-3554, USA

Schirinowskij, Wladimir
Sokolnitscheskij wal 38-114
Moscow, RUSSIA 107113

Schirmacher, Carolyn (Stylist)
3307 SW Dosch Rd
Portland, OR 97239, USA

Schirripa, Steve (Actor)
c/o Brad Stokes *Kass & Stokes Management*
9229 Sunset Blvd
Suite 504
Los Angeles, CA 90069, USA

Schisgal, Murray J (Writer)
International Creative Mgmt
40 W 57th St #1800
New York, NY 10019, USA

Schissler, Les (Bowler)
3060 E Bridge St Lot 20
Brighton, CO 80601-2718, USA

Schlafly, Phyllis (Activist)
68 Fairmont Ave
Alton, IL 62002, USA

Schlag, Edward W (Misc)
Osterwaldstr 91
Munich 80805, GERMANY

Schlamme, Thomas (Actor)
c/o Rosalie Swedlin *Anonymous Content (LA)*
3531 Hayden Ave
Culver City, CA 90232, USA

Schlatmann, Gert Jan
Oostzeedijk Gen 39a
Rotterdam, HOLLAND NL 3062 WK

Schlatter, Charlie (Actor)
638 Lindero Canyon Road #322
Oak Park, CA 91377, USA

Schlatter, George
400 Robert Lane
Beverly Hills, CA 90210

Schleech, Russ (Misc)
21634 Paseo Maravia
Mission Viejo, CA 92962, USA

Schlegel, Ernie (Bowler)
13300 SE Angus St
Vancouver, WA 98683-6694, USA

Schlegel, Hans W (Astronaut)
European Astronaut Centre
Postfach 906058
Cologne 51140, GERMANY

Schlegel, John P (Educator)
University of San Francisco
President's Office
San Francisco, CA 94117, USA

Schleinzer, Markus (Director)

Schleinzer, Markus (Director)
c/o Doug MacLaren *ICM Partners (ICM-LA)*
10250 Constellation Blvd Fl 7
Los Angeles, CA 90067, USA

Schleper, Sarah (Athlete, Olympic Athlete)
595 Stone Creek Drive
Avon, CO 81620, usa

Schlereth, Daniel (Athlete, Baseball Player)
9479 S Shadow Hill Cir
Lone Tree, CO 80124-5484, USA

Schlereth, Mark (Athlete, Football Player)
c/o Lou Oppenheim *Headline Media Management*
888 7th Ave #503
New York, NY 10106, USA

Schlesinger, Adam (Music Group, Musician, Songwriter, Writer)
MOB Agency
6404 Wilshire Blvd #505
Los Angeles, CA 90048, USA

Schlesinger, Bill (Athlete, Baseball Player)
4230 Glenway Ave
Apt 2
Deer Park, OH 45236-3646, USA

Schlesinger, Cory (Athlete, Football Player)
36 Bradford Ct
Dearborn, MI 48126, USA

Schlesinger, Iliza (Comedian)
c/o Staff Member *Gersh (LA)*
9465 Wilshire Blvd
Suite 600
Beverly Hills, CA 90212, USA

Schlesinger, James (Politician)
The Mitre Corporation
7515 Colshire Dr Attn: Chairman's Office
Mclean, VA 22102-7538, USA

Schlesinger, James R (Secretary)
Georgetown University
1800 K St NW #400
Washington, DC 20006, USA

Schlesinger, Rudy (Athlete, Baseball Player)
5708 Abelia Ct
Cincinnati, OH 45213, USA

Schlessinger, Laura (Radio Personality, Writer)
P.O. Box 8120
Van Nuys, CA 91409, USA

Schleyer, Paul Von R (Misc)
Frederich-Alexander-Universtat
Henkestr 41
Erlangen 91469, GERMANY

Schlichting, Travis (Athlete, Baseball Player)
2202 Parkland Cv
Round Rock, TX 78681-4086, USA

Schlichtmann, Jan (Attorney, Attorney General, General)
359 Hale St
Beverly Farms, MA 01915, USA

Schlidt, Rudolf (Scientist)
3104 Panorama Dr SE
Huntsville, AL 35801-1108

Schlitter, Brian (Athlete, Baseball Player)
912 S Greenwood Ave
Park Ridge, IL 60068-4544, USA

Schlondorff, Volker (Director)
Studio Babelsberg
Postfach 900361
Potsdam 14439, GERMANY

Schlopy, Erik (Athlete, Olympic Athlete, Skier)
731 Martingale Ln
Park City, UT 84098-7559, USA

Schloredt, Robert S (Bob) (Athlete, Football Player)
1827 N 167th St
Shoreline, WA 98133, USA

Schlossberg, Edwin (Writer)
The John F Kennedy Presidential Library & Museum
Columbia Point
New York, NY 02125

Schlossberg, Katie (Actor)
Talent Group
6300 Wilshire Blvd #2100
Los Angeles, CA 90048, USA

Schlossberg, Katie (Actor)
Talent Group
5670 Wilshire Blvd
#820
Los Angeles, CA 90036, USA

Schlosser, Eric (Writer)
c/o Staff Member *Houghton Mifflin*
215 Park Ave S
New York, NY 10003, USA

Schlueter, Dale (Athlete, Basketball Player)
15555 SW Harcourt Ter
Portland, OR 97224-5234, USA

Schluter, Poul H (Politician)
Frederiksberg Allee 66
Frederiksberg C 1820, DENMARK

Schmack, Brian (Athlete, Baseball Player)
504 E Wye Mesa
Brookings, SD 57006-4534, USA

Schmautz, Bobby (Athlete, Hockey Player)
19866 N 90th Ave
Peoria, AZ 85382-8678, USA

Schmelz, Al (Athlete, Baseball Player)
7406 E Camino Rayo De Luz
Scottsdale, AZ 85266-4295, USA

Schmelz, Al (Athlete, Baseball Player)
7406 E Camino Rayo De Luz
Scottsdale, AZ 85266, USA

Schmemann, Serge (Journalist)
New York Times 229 W 43rd St
Attn Editorial Dept
New York, NY 10036-3913, USA

Schmid, Dave
17173 Rayen St.
Northridge, CA 91325-2908

Schmid, Kyle (Actor)
c/o Norbert Abrams *Noble Caplan Abrams*
1260 Yonge St
2nd Floor
Toronto ON M4T 1W6, Canada

Schmid, Rudi (Misc)
211 Woodland Road
Kentfield, CA 94904, USA

Schmid, Sigi (Coach, Soccer Player)
Los Angeles Galaxy
1010 Rose Bowl Dr
Pasadena, CA 91103, USA

Schmidgall, Jennifer (Athlete, Hockey Player, Olympic Athlete)
3640 Wooddale Ave S
Unit 103
Minneapolis, MN 55416, USA

Schmidly, David J (Educator)
Texas Tech University
President's Office
Lubbock, TX 79409, USA

Schmidt, Andreas (Opera Singer)
Fossredder 51
Hamburg 22359, GERMANY

Schmidt, Benno C Jr (Educator)
Edison Project
375 Park Ave
New York, NY 10152, USA

Schmidt, Bob (Athlete, Football Player)
10005 Sky View Way
Apt 2106
Fort Myers, FL 33913, USA

Schmidt, Bob (Athlete, Baseball Player)
9 Hardwood Dr
Saint Charles, MO 63303-5942, USA

Schmidt, Brian (Nobel Prize Laureate)
The Australian National University
Via Cotter Road
Weston Creek ACT, USA

Schmidt, Curt (Athlete, Baseball Player)
4025 Clara Ln
Billings, MT 59105-5659, USA

Schmidt, Dave (Athlete, Baseball Player)
26636 Portales Ln
Mission Viejo, CA 92691-5122, USA

Schmidt, Dave (Athlete, Baseball Player)
7172 N Serenoa Dr
Sarasota, FL 34241-9270, USA

Schmidt, Eric E (Business Person, Engineer)
c/o Staff Member *Google Inc*
1600 Ampitheatre Pkwy
Mountain View, CA 94043, USA

Schmidt, Freddy (Athlete, Baseball Player)
128 Constitution Ave
Wind Gap, PA 18091-1119, USA

Schmidt, Hank (Athlete, Football Player)
4641 Mission Bell Ln
La Mesa, CA 91941, USA

Schmidt, Harald (Athlete, Track Athlete)
Schulstr 11
Hasselroth 63594, GERMANY

Schmidt, Helmut (Politician)
Neuberger Weg 80
Hamburg 22419, GERMANY

Schmidt, Jason (Athlete, Baseball Player)
6539 E Cheney Dr
Paradise Valley, AZ 85253-3511, USA

Schmidt, Jean (Congressman, Politician)
2464 Rayburn HOB
Washington, DC 20515, USA

Schmidt, Jeff (Athlete, Baseball Player)
1028 Seminole Hwy
Madison, WI 53711-3021, USA

Schmidt, Joseph P (Joe) (Athlete, Football Coach, Football Player)
226 Norcliff Dr
Bloomfield Hills, MI 48302, USA

Schmidt, Kathryn (Kate) (Athlete, Track Athlete)
1008 Dexter St
Los Angeles, CA 90042, USA

Schmidt, Kendall (Musician)
c/o David Eisenberg *Protege Entertainment*
710 E. Angeleno Ave
Burbank, CA 91501, USA

Schmidt, Kenneth (Actor)
c/o Staff Member *Coast to Coast Talent Group*
3350 Barham Blvd
Los Angeles, CA 90068, USA

Schmidt, Kevin (Actor)
c/o David Eisenberg *Protege Entertainment*
710 E. Angeleno Ave
Burbank, CA 91501, USA

Schmidt, Maarten
California Institue Of Technology 1200 E California Blvd Dept 105-24
Pasadena, CA 91125-0001, USA

Schmidt, Mike (Athlete, Baseball Player)
c/o Staff Member *National Baseball Hall of Fame*
P.O. Box 590
Cooperstown, NY 13326, USA

Schmidt, Milton C (Milt) (Athlete, Hockey Player)
10 Longwood Dr #376
Westwood, MA 02090-1144, USA

Schmidt, Ole (Composer, Conductor)
Puggaardsgade 17
Copenhagen 1573, DENMARK

Schmidt, Richard (Doctor)
University of Pennsylvania
3400 Spruce St
Philadelphia, PA 19104, USA

Schmidt, Roy (Athlete, Football Player)
1844 Highpoint Rd
Snellville, GA 30078, USA

Schmidt, Sam (Race Car Driver)
Treadway Racing
6017 W. 7lst St.
Indianapolis, IN 46278, USA

Schmidt, Stephanie (Stylist)
2901 4th St
#318
Sanata Monica, CA 90405, USA

Schmidt, Steve (Race Car Driver)
Schmidt Racing
8405 E 30th St
Indianapolis, IN 46219, USA

Schmidt, Terry (Athlete, Football Player)
2 Stone River Dr
Asheville, NC 28804, USA

Schmidt, William (Bill) (Athlete, Track Athlete)
1809 Devonwood Court
Knoxville, TN 37922, USA

Schmidt, Wolfgang (Athlete, Track Athlete)
Birkheckenstr 116B
Stuttgart 70599, GERMANY

Schmidt, Wolfgang (Opera Singer)
Kunstleragentur Raab & Bohm
Plankengasse 7
Vienna 1010, AUSTRIA

Schmidtmer, Christiane (Actor, Model)
Postfach 120617
Heidelberg 69067, GERMANY

Schmidt-Nielsen, Knut (Doctor)
Kuke University
Zoology Dept
Durham, NC 27706, USA

Schmidtt, Harrison (Ex-Senator, Senator)
PO Box 90730
Albuquerque, NM 87199-0730, USA

Schmidt-Weitzman, Violet (Athlete, Baseball Player)
225 S Mill St
Mishawaka, IN 46544-2002, USA

Schmiege, Marilyn (Opera Singer)
Opera et Concert
Maximilianstr 22
Munich 80539, GERMANY

Schmiegel, Klaus K (Inventor)
4507 Stoughton Dr
Indianapolis, IN 46226-3127, USA

Schmiesing, Joe (Athlete, Football Player)
19460 County 2
Sauk Centre, MN 56378, USA

Schmit, Timothy B (Musician)
William Morris Agency
1325 Ave of Americas
New York, NY 10019, USA

Schmitt, Dr H Harrison (Astronaut)
PO Box90730
Albuquerque, NM 87199-0730, USA

Schmitt, Harrison H (Jack) (Astronaut, Ex-Senator)
PO Box 90730
Albuquerque, NM 87199, USA

Schmitt, John (Athlete, Football Player)
2 Mayflower Rd
Glen Head, NY 11545, USA

Schmitt, Martin (Skier)
Muhleschweg 4
VA-Tannehim 78052, GERMANY

Schmock, Jonathan (Actor)
c/o Judy Orbach *Judy O Productions*
6136 Glen Holly
Hollywood, CA 90068, USA

Schmoeller, David (Director)
3910 Woodhill Ave
Las Vegas, NV 89121, USA

Schmoll, Steve (Athlete, Baseball Player)
4758 Chastain Dr
Melbourne, FL 32940-1274, USA

Schnabel, Julian (Artist, Director)
c/o Bart Walker *ICM Partners (ICM-LA)*
555 W 25th St
4th Floor
New York, NY 10001, USA

Schnabel, Marco (Director)
c/o Staff Member *3 Arts Entertainment Inc*
9460 Wilshire Blvd
7th Floor
Beverly Hills, CA 90210, USA

Schnackenberg, Roy L (Artist)
1919 N Orchard St
Chicago, IL 60614, USA

Schnarch, David (Writer)
c/o Staff Member *HarperCollins Publishers*
10 East 53rd St
c/o Author mail, 7th Floor
New York, NY 10022, USA

Schnarre, Monika (Actor, Model)
Alex Stevens
137 N Larchmont #259
Los Angeles, CA 90004, USA

Schnebli, Dolf (Architect)
Sudstr 45
Zurich 8008, SWITZERLAND

Schneck, Dave (Athlete, Baseball Player)
3891 Lehigh Dr
Northampton, PA 18067-9771, USA

Schneck, Mike (Athlete, Football Player)
110 Three Degree Rd
Allison Park, PA 15101, USA

Schneider, Andrew (Journalist)
c/o Richard Weitz *WME (LA)*
9601 Wilshire Blvd Fl 3
Beverly Hills, CA 90210, USA

Schneider, Bernd (Race Car Driver)
Team AMG Mercedes
Daimlerstr 1
Affalterbach 71563, GERMANY

Schneider, Bob (Musician)
c/o Paul Nugent *Rainmaker Artists*
10925 Estate Ln
Suite 124
Dallas, TX 75238, USA

Schneider, Brian (Athlete, Baseball Player)
130 Playa Rienta Way
Palm Beach Gardens, FL 33418-6210, USA

Schneider, Cory (Athlete, Hockey Player)
12 Preston Ct
Swampscott, MA 01907-1650

Schneider, Dan (Producer, Writer)
c/o Staff Member *WME (LA)*
9601 Wilshire Blvd Fl 3
Beverly Hills, CA 90210, USA

Schneider, Dan (Athlete, Baseball Player)
P.O. Box 2421
Tubac, AZ 85646-2421, USA

Schneider, Fred (Musician, Songwriter)
c/o Staff Member *Direct Management Group*
947 N La Cienega Blvd
Suite G
Los Angeles, CA 90069, USA

Schneider, Helen (Musician)
c/o Staff Member *UD Promotion*
Uwe Darkow
Hauptstr. 64-66
Essen-Kettwig 45219, Germany

Schneider, Helge (Actor)
Helge Schneider Enterprises
Schloßstr. 33
Mülheim/Ruhr D-45468, Germany

Schneider, Howie (Cartoonist)
United Feature Syndicate
200 Madison Ave
New York, NY 10016, USA

Schneider, Jeff (Athlete, Baseball Player)
268 Pin Oak Dr
Geneseo, IL 61254-1944, USA

Schneider, John (Actor, Musician)
c/o Staff Member *The Michael Gursey Company*
1482 E Valley Rd
Suite 112
Santa Barbara, CA 93108, USA

Schneider, Mathieu (Athlete, Hockey Player)
1311 6th St
Manhattan Beach, CA 90266-6041, USA

Schneider, Max (Actor)
c/o Jeff Golenberg *Collective*
8383 Wilshire Blvd
Suite 1050
Beverly Hills, CA 90211, USA

Schneider, Paul (Actor)
c/o Jillian Fowkes *ID Public Relations (ID-LA)*
7060 Hollywood Blvd
8th Floor
Los Angeles, CA 90028, USA

Schneider, Rob (Actor, Comedian, Producer, Writer)
c/o Lisa Blum *New Wave Entertainment (LA)*
2660 W Olive Blvd
Burbank, CA 91505, USA

Schneider, T Edward (Aviator)
1004 Shady Maple Cir
Ocoee, FL 34761-3418, USA

Schneider, Vreni (Skier)
Dorf
Elm 8767, SWITZERLAND

Schneider, William "Buzz" (Athlete, Hockey Player)
5656 Turtle Lake Rd
Saint Paul, MN 55126-4769, USA

Schneider, William (Buzz) (Athlete, Hockey Player, Olympic Athlete)
5656 Turtle Lake Rd
Saint Paul, MN 55126-4769, USA

Schneider, William G (Misc)
National Research Council
65 Whitemart Dr #2
Ottawa, ON K1L 8J9, CANADA

Schneiderman, David A (Editor, Publisher)
Village Voice
President's Office
36 Cooper Square
New York, NY 10003, USA

Schneiderman, Leon (Musician)
The Alliance for Democracy
P.O. Box 540115
Waltham, MA 02454, USA

Schnelker, Bob (Coach)
Philadelphia Eagles
85 Silver Oaks Cir #6102
Naples, FL 34119-4665, USA

Schnelldorfer, Manfred (Figure Skater)
Seydlitzstr 55
Munich 80993, GERMANY

Schnellenberger, Howard (Athlete, Coach, Football Coach, Football Player)
5109 N Ocean Blvd
Apt G
Ocean Ridge, FL 33435, USA

Schnetzer, Ben (Actor)
c/o Rhonda Price *Gersh (NY)*
41 Madison Ave
New York, NY 10010, USA

Schnetzer, Stephen (Actor)
c/o Matthew Sullivan *Sullivan Talent Group*
305 W 105th St #3B
New York, NY 10025, USA

Schnitker, Mike (Athlete, Football Player)
P.O. Box 968
Conifer, CO 80433, USA

Schnittker, Richard (Dick) (Athlete, Basketball Player)
203 E Las Granadas
Green Valley, AZ 85614-2233, USA

Schobel, Frank (Actor, Musician)
Wielandstrasse 6
Berlin D-12623, Germany

Schochet, Bob (Cartoonist)
6 Sunset Road
Highland Mills, NY 10930, USA

Schock, Aaron (Congressman, Politician)
328 'Cannon HOB
Washington, DC 20515, USA

Schock, Gina (Musician)
PO Box 720160
San Francisco, CA 94172-0160, USA

Schock, Ron (Athlete, Hockey Player)
1360 Whalen Rd
Penfield, NY 14526-1918, USA

Schockemohle, Alwin (Horse Racer)
Munsterlandstr 51
Muhlen 49439, GERMANY

Schoeffling, Michael (Actor)
413 Crestmont
Newfoundland, PA 18445, USA

Schoelen, Jill (Actor)
Gold Marshak Liedtke
3500 W Olive Ave #1400
Burbank, CA 91505, USA

Schoen, Gerry (Athlete, Baseball Player)
13 Santa Fe
Prescott, AZ 86305-5068, USA

Schoen, Max H (Doctor)
123 Wallfleet Cir
Folsom, CA 95630-6541, USA

Schoen, Tom (Athlete, Football Player)
437 W Belmont Ave
Apt 13
Chicago, IL 60657, USA

Schoenbaechler, Andreas (Skier)
Muhlrustistr 2
Affoltern a A 8910, SWITZERLAND

Schoenberg, Marv (Stylist)
878 West End Ave
#10-A
New York, NY 10025-4955, USA

Schoenborn, Christoph Cardinal (Religious Leader)
Wollzeile 2
Vienna 1010, AUSTRIA

Schoendienst, Red (Athlete, Baseball Player, Coach)
1105 Jo Carr Dr
Chesterfield, MO 63017-8401, USA

Schoene, Russ (Athlete, Basketball Player)
1136 205th Ave NE
Sammamish, WA 98074-6654, USA

Schoeneweis, Scott (Athlete, Baseball Player)
14420 E Kern Ct
Fountain Hills, AZ 85268-6383, USA

Schoenfeld, Jim (Athlete, Coach, Hockey Player)
45 W 60th St Apt 18D
New York, NY 10023-7944

Schoenfeld, Jim (Athlete, Hockey Player)
New York Rangers
2 Penn Plz Fl 22
New York, NY 10121-2299

Schoenfield, Al (Athlete, Swimmer)
75 Santa Rosa St
San Luis Obispo, CA 93405-1819, USA

Schoenfield, Dana (Swimmer)
7734 Lakeview Trail
Orange, CA 92869, USA

Schoenke, Raymond F (Athlete, Football Player)
21151 Woodfield Rd
Laytonsville, MD 20882, USA

Schoffer, Nicolas (Artist)
Villa Des Arts
15 Rue Hegesippe-Moreau
Paris 75018, FRANCE

Schofield, Annabel (Actor)
Special Artists Agency
345 N Maple Dr #302
Beverly Hills, CA 90210, USA

Schofield, Dick (Athlete, Baseball Player)
17703 Gardenview Place Ct
Glencoe, MO 63038-1495, USA

Schofield, Dwight (Athlete, Hockey Player)
9024 Cardinal Ter
Saint Louis, MO 63144-1103

Schofield, John (Actor, Producer)
c/o Pete Franciosa *United Talent Agency (UTA)*
9336 Civic Center Dr
Beverly Hills, CA 90210, USA

Schofield, Phillip
56 Wood Lane
London, ENGLAND W12 7RJ

Scholder, Fritz (Artist)
118 Cattletrack Road
Scottsdale, AZ 85251, USA

Scholes, Clarke (Athlete, Olympic Athlete, Swimmer)
20671 Wedgewood Dr
Grosse Pointe Woods, MI 48236-1560, USA

Scholes, Myron S (Nobel Prize Laureate)
34 Stern Ln
Atherton, CA 94027-5423, USA

Schollander, Don (Athlete, Olympic Athlete, Swimmer)
3576 Lakeview Blvd
Lake Oswego, OR 97035, USA

Schollander, Donald A (Don) (Swimmer)
3576 Lakeview Blvd
Lake Oswego, OR 97035, USA

Scholten, Jim (Music Group, Musician)
Sawyer Brown Inc
5200 Old Harding Road
Franklin, TN 37064, USA

Scholtz, Bob (Athlete, Football Player)
6721 S 71st East Ave
Tulsa, OK 74133, USA

Scholtz, Bruce (Athlete, Football Player)
6607 Cypress Point N
Austin, TX 78746-7104, USA

Scholz, Rupert (Government Official)
Postfach 1328
Bonn 1 5300, GERMANY

Scholz, Tom (Musician)
c/o Gail Parenteau *Parenteau Guidance*
132 East 35th St #3J
New York, NY 10016, USA

Schomberg, A Thomas (Artist)
4923 S Snowberry Lane
Evergreen, CO 80439, USA

Schon, Jan Hendrik (Inventor)
Lucent Technology Bell Laboratory
600 Mountain Ave
New Providence, NJ 07974, USA

Schon, Kyra (Actor)
930 N Sheridan Ave
Pittsburgh, PA 15206, USA

Schon, Neal (Musician)
c/o Staff Member *WmE2 (WMA-LA)*
1 William Morris Pl
Beverly Hills, CA 90212, USA

Schon, Neil (Musician)
c/o Staff Member *WmE2 (WMA-LA)*
1 William Morris Pl
Beverly Hills, CA 90212, USA

Schone, Lydia
2020 Broadway
Santa Monica, CA 90404

Schoneberger, Barbara (Correspondent)
Kick Media AG
Eifelstrasse 31
Koln 50677, Germany

Schonhuber, Franz (Correspondent)
Europaburo
Fraunhoferstr 23
Munich 80469, GERMANY

Schoofs, Mark (Journalist)
Village Voice
Editorial Dept
32 Cooper Square
New York, NY 10003, USA

Schooler, Mike (Athlete, Baseball Player)
519 N Buttonwood St
Anaheim, CA 92805-2226, USA

Schoolnik, Gary (Biologist)
Stanford University
Medical School
Microbiology Dept
Stanford, CA 94305, USA

Schools, Dave (Musician)
Brown Cat Inc
400 Foundry St
Athens, GA 30601, USA

Schoomaker, Peter J (Pete) (General)
Chief of Staff HqUSA
Pentagon
Washington, DC 20310, USA

Schoon, Milton (Athlete, Basketball Player)
1218 Blaine Ave
Janesville, WI 52545-1834, USA

Schoonmaker, Jerry (Athlete, Baseball Player)
8343 Schreiber Dr
Munster, IN 46321-1829, USA

Schopf, J William (Biologist)
University of California
Study of Evolution Center
Los Angeles, CA 90024, USA

Schorer, Jane (Journalist)
Des Moines Register
Editorial Dept
PO Box 957
Des Moines, IA 50304, USA

Schorr, Bill (Cartoonist)
United Feature Syndicate
200 Madison Ave
New York, NY 10016, USA

Schott, Stephen (Baseball Player)
Oakland A's
12330 Hilltop Dr
Los Altos Hills, CA 94024-5218, USA

Schott, Steve (Baseball Player)
12330 Hilltop Dr
Los Altos Hil, CA

Schotte, Jan P Cardinal (Religious Leader)
Sinodo Dei Vescovi
00120, VATICAN CITY

Schottenheimer, Marty (Athlete, Football
Coach, Football Player)
19825 Northcove Rd
Suite B
Cornelius, NC 28031, USA

Schou, Mogens (Doctor)
Aarhus University
Institute of Psychiatry
Aarhus, DENMARK

Schourek, Pete (Athlete, Baseball Player)
14917 Cub Run Park Dr
Centreville, VA 20120-1234, USA

Schowalter, Edward R Jr (War Hero)
913 Bibb Ave #312
Auburn, AL 36830, USA

Schrader, Ken (Race Car Driver)
Ken Schrader Racing Incorporated
PO Box 5430
Concord, NC 28027, USA

Schrader, Kurt (Congressman, Politician)
314 Cannon HOB
Washington, DC 20515, USA

Schrader, Maria (Actor)
c/o Joel Kleinman *Baier/Kleinman
International*
3575 Cahuenga Blvd W #500
Los Angeles, CA 90068, USA

Schrader, Paul (Actor, Director, Writer)
c/o Johnnie Planco *Parseghian Planco LLC*
322 8th Ave
Suite 601
New York, NY 10001, USA

Schram, Bitty (Actor)
c/o Robert Marsala *Wishlab*
2225-A Hyperion Ave
Los Angeles, CA 90027, USA

Schram, Jessy (Actor)
c/o Brian Wilkins *Kritzer Levine Wilkins
Entertainment (KLWG)*
11872 La Grange Ave
1st Floor
Los Angeles, CA 90025, USA

Schramka, Paul (Athlete, Baseball Player)
W180N9923 Riversbend Cir W
Germantown, WI 53022-4656, USA

Schramm, David (Actor)
3521 Berry Dr
Studio City, CA 91604, USA

Schranz, Karl (Skier)
Hotel Garni
Saint Anton 6580, AUSTRIA

Schreder, Sabina (Stylist)
c/o Staff Member *Walter Schupfer
Management Corp*
413 W 14th St
3rd Floor
New York, NY 10014, USA

Schreiber, Adam (Athlete, Football Player)
2520 River Summit Dr
Duluth, GA 30097, USA

Schreiber, Avery
6399 Wilshire Blvd. #414
Los Angeles, CA 90048

Schreiber, Larry (Athlete, Football Player)
388 Albion Ave
Woodside, CA 94062, USA

Schreiber, Liev (Actor)
c/o Jason Weinberg *Untitled
Entertainment (LA)*
350 S. Beverly Dr #200
Beverly Hills, CA 90212, USA

Schreiber, Martin J (Ex-Governor)
2700 S Shore Dr
#B
Milwaukee, WI 53207, USA

Schreiber, Ted (Athlete, Baseball Player)
116 Nantucket Is
Centerville, GA 31028-8547, USA

Schreler, Peter (Conductor, Opera Singer)
Calberlastr 13
Dresdon 01326, GERMANY

Schremmer, Patty (Golfer)
714 Siesta Key Cir
Sarasota, FL 34242-1250, USA

Schremp, Bob (Athlete, Football Player)
P.O. Box 584
Bellflower, CA 90707, USA

Schremp, Rob (Athlete, Hockey Player)
303 Phillips St
Fulton, NY 13069-1514

Schrempf, Detlef (Athlete, Basketball
Player, Olympic Athlete)
9735 NE 1st St
Bellevue, WA 98004-5413, USA

Schrempp, Jurgen E (Business Person)
Daimler-Chrysler AG
Plieningerstra
Stuttgart 70546, GERMANY

Schrenk, Steve (Athlete, Baseball Player)
2547 Oakboro Ln
Charlotte, NC 28214-6900, USA

Schreyer, Cindy (Golfer)
18 Cottage Dr
Newman, GA 30265-5513, USA

Schreyer, Edward R (Ex-Governor)
3069 Henderson Hwy
Winnipeg, MB R2E 0H9, Canada

Schrieber, Paul (Athlete, Baseball Player)
9715 E Gary Rd
Scottsdale, AZ 85260-6225, USA

Schrieffer, John R (Nobel Prize Laureate)
4061 Rodgers St
West Palm Beach, FL 33410-5967, USA

Schrier, Eric W (Editor)
Reader's Digest
Editorial Dept
PO Box 100
Pleasantville, NY 10572, USA

Schriesheim, Alan (Misc)
1440 N Lake Shore Dr #31AC
Chicago, IL 60610, USA

Schrimshaw, Nevin S (Doctor)
Sandwich Notch Farm
Thompton, NH 03223, USA

Schriner, David
3216 Upland Pl. NW Calgary
Alb., CANADA

Schrock, Richard R (Nobel Prize Laureate)
15 Cabot St
Winchester, MA 01890-3501, USA

Schroder, Bob (Athlete, Baseball Player)
2810 Jefferson Dr
Hattiesburg, MS 39402-2047, USA

Schroder, Chris (Athlete, Baseball Player)
2710 W Oklahoma Ave
Guthrie, OK 73044-6314, USA

Schroder, Ernst A (Actor)
Podere Montalto
Castellina In Chianti
Siena 53011, ITALY

Schroder, Gerhard
Bundeskanzleramt
Berlin, GERMANY 11012

Schroder, Jochen
Postfach 10 23 46
Bochum, GERMANY D-44723

Schroder, Ricky (Actor)
c/o Rebecca (Becca) Kovacik *Hofflund/
Polone*
9465 Wilshire Blvd #420
Beverly Hills, CA 90212, USA

Schroeder, Barbet (Director, Producer)
8033 W Sunset Blvd #51
West Hollywood, CA 90046, USA

Schroeder, Bill (Athlete, Baseball Player)
S75W17724 Harbor Cir
Muskego, WI 53150-9182, USA

Schroeder, Carly (Actor)
c/o Beverly Strong *Strong Management*
9350 Wilshire Blvd
#224
Beverly Hills, CA 90212, USA

Schroeder, Dorsey (Race Car Driver)
RR #1
Box 943
Osage Beach, MO 65065, USA

Schroeder, Gene (Athlete, Football Player)
788 Eastbrook Ln
Crown Point, IN 46307, USA

Schroeder, Gerhard (Misc)
Bundeskanzlerant
Willy-Brandt-Str 1
Berlin 10557, GERMANY

Schroeder, Jay (Athlete, Football Player)
1849 S Paragon Dr
St George, UT 04790, USA

Schroeder, Jeret (Race Car Driver)
529 Old Mill Rd.
Millersville, MD 21108-1327, USA

Schroeder, Jim (Bowler)
3 Greenhaven Terrace
Tonawanda, NY 14150-5503, USA

Schroeder, John (Athlete, Golfer)
PO Box 2768
Del Mar, CA 92014-5768, USA

Schroeder, John H (Educator)
University of Wisconsin
Chancellor's Office
Milwaukee, WI 53211, USA

Schroeder, Kenneth L (Business Person)
KLA-Tencor Corp
160 Rio Robles
San Jose, CA 95134, USA

Schroeder, Lisa Golden (Stylist)
39 Apple Orchard Rd
St Paul, MN 55110, USA

Schroeder, Manfred R (Physicist)
Rieswartenweg 8
Gottingen 37073, GERMANY

Schroeder, Mary M (Judge)
US Court of Appeals
230 N 1st Ave
Phoenix, AZ 85025, USA

Schroeder, Patricia S (Politician)
c/o Staff Member *21st Century Speakers*
1352 Lake Rd
Gouldsboro, PA 18424, USA

Schroeder, Paul W (Writer)
University of Illinois
History Dept
810 S Wright St
Urbana, IL 61801, USA

Schroeder, Steven A (Doctor, Misc)
10 Paseo Mirasol
Bel Tiburon, CA 94920, USA

Schroeder, Terry (Athlete, Coach)
4901 Lewis Road
Agoura Hills, CA 91301, USA

Schroedter, Katherine (Stylist)
88 W Schiller
#204
Chicago, IL 60610, USA

Schroll, William (Athlete, Football Player)
1640 Oakley Dr
Baton Rouge, LA 70806, USA

Schrom, Ken (Athlete, Baseball Player)
1002 Black Diamond Ct
Portland, TX 78374-4162, USA

Schroy, Ken (Athlete, Football Player)
79 Russell Rd
Garden City, NY 11530, USA

Schruefer, John J (Doctor)
Georgetown University Hospital
Ob-Gyn Dept
Washington, DC 20007, USA

Schu, Rick (Athlete, Baseball Player)
2013 Driftwood Cir
El Dorado Hills, CA 95762-3744, USA

Schuba, Beatrice (Trixi) (Figure Skater)
Giorgengasse 2/1/8
Vienna 1190, AUSTRIA

Schubb, Mark
9744 Wilshire Blvd. #308
Beverly Hills, CA 90212

Schubert, Eric (Athlete, Football Player)
722 Homestead Ave
Maybrook, NY 12543, USA

Schubert, Mark (Coach, Swimmer)
PO Box 479
Surfside, CA 90743, USA

Schubert, Richard F (Misc)
6615 Madison McLean Dr
McLean, VA 22101, USA

Schubert, Steve (Athlete, Football Player)
7 Douglas Dr
Candia, NH 03034, USA

Schuck, Anett (Athlete)
Defoestry 6A
Leipzig 04159, GERMANY

Schuck, John (Actor)
1501 Broadway #703
New York, NY 10036, USA

Schueler, Jon R (Artist)
40 W 22nd St
New York, NY 10010, USA

Schueler, Ron (Athlete, Baseball Player)
3108 E San Juan Ave
Phoenix, AZ 85016-3725, USA

Schuenke, Donald J (Business Person)
Nortel Networks Corp
8200 Dixie Road
Brampton, ON L6T 5P6, CANADA

Schuerholz, John (Baseball Player)
Atlanta Braves
1025 Royal Dr
Canonsburg, PA 15317-5004, USA

Schuessel, Wolfgang (Misc)
Chancellor's Office
Ballhausplatz 2
Vienna 1014, AUSTRIA

Schuessler, Jack (Business Person)
Wendy's International
4288 W Dublin-Granville Road
Dublin, OH 43017, USA

Schuffenhauer, Bill (Athlete, Bobsledder, Olympic Athlete)
2888 Marilyn Dr
Ogden, UT 84403-0462, USA

Schuh, Harry F (Athlete, Football Player)
2309 Massey Rd
Memphis, TN 38119, USA

Schuh, Jeff (Athlete, Football Player)
5550 Vagabond Ln N
Minneapolis, MN 38119, USA

Schuhmacher, John (Athlete, Football Player)
6000 Reims Rd
Apt 3006
Houston, TX 77036, USA

Schul, Bob (Athlete, Olympic Athlete, Track Athlete)
320 Wisteria Dr
Dayton, OH 45419, USA

Schuldt, Travis (Actor)
c/o Robert Marsala *Wishlab*
2225-A Hyperion Ave
Los Angeles, CA 90027, USA

Schuler, Carolyn (Swimmer)
26552 Via del Sol
Mission Viejo, CA 92691, USA

Schuler, Dave (Athlete, Baseball Player)
17210 Chatham St
Lewes, DE 19958-7229, USA

Schulhofer, Scotty (Misc)
PO Box 1581
Waynesville, NC 28786, USA

Schull, Rebecca (Actor)
Writers & Artists
8383 Wilshire Blve #550
Beverly Hills, CA 90211, USA

Schuller, Grete (Artist)
8 Barstow Road #7G
Great Neck, NY 11021, USA

Schuller, Gunther (Composer, Conductor)
Margun Music
167 Dudley Road
Newton Center, MA 02459, USA

Schuller, Robert (Religious Leader)
Crystal Cathedral Ministries
12141 Lewis St
Garden Grove, CA 92840, USA

Schullstrom, Erik (Athlete, Baseball Player)
1425 Court St
Alameda, CA 94501-3145, USA

Schulman, Ariel (Director)
c/o Rowena Arguelles *Creative Artists Agency (CAA-LA)*
2000 Ave Of The Stars
Los Angeles, CA 90067, USA

Schult, Art (Athlete, Baseball Player)
9225 SW 90th St
Ocala, FL 34481-8485, USA

Schult, Jurgen (Athlete, Track Athlete)
Drosselweg 6
Leuna 19069, GERMANY

Schulte, Greg (Baseball Player)
Arizona Diamondbacks
20723 N 56th Ave
Glendale, AZ 85308-6276, USA

Schulte, Paxton (Athlete, Hockey Player)
RR 1
Onoway, AB TOE 1VO, Canada

Schulte, Richard (Athlete, Football Player)
1216 N Kenneth Pl
Chandler, AZ 85226, USA

Schulters, Lance (Athlete, Football Player)
594 Grant Ave
Roselle, NJ 07203, USA

Schultz, Axel (Boxer)
Axel Schultz Mgmt
Kloetzrstr 15
Riesa 01587, GERMANY

Schultz, Barney (Athlete, Baseball Player)
790 Woodlane Rd
Beverly, NJ 08010, USA

Schultz, Bill (Athlete, Football Player)
10302 Lakeland Dr
Fishers, IN 46038, USA

Schultz, Boomer (Race Car Driver)
Schultz Sports Marketing
PO Box 8648
So. Lake Tahoe, CA 96158, USA

Schultz, Buddy (Athlete, Baseball Player)
5629 E Thunderbird Rd
Scottsdale, AZ 85254-3741, USA

Schultz, Dave (Athlete, Hockey Player)
505 Alpine Ct
Mays Landing, NJ 08330-2213, USA

Schultz, Dave (Race Car Driver)
2365 Lazy River Lane
Fort Myers, FL 33905, USA

Schultz, Dean (Financier)
Federal Home Laon Bank
1079 Hutchinson Road
Walnut Creek, CA 94598, USA

Schultz, Dwight (Actor)
Borinstein Oreck Bogart
3172 Dona Susana Dr
Studio City, CA 91604, USA

Schultz, Ed (Radio Personality)
The Ed Schultz Show
417 38th St. SW
Suite F
Fargo, ND 58103-2312, USA

Schultz, Frederick H (Government Official)
PO Box 1200
Jacksonville, FL 32201, USA

Schultz, George (Athlete, Baseball Player)
400 Fern Brook Ln # 218
Mount Laurel, NJ 08054-9542, USA

Schultz, Howard (Business Person)
Starbucks Corp
2401 Utah Ave S
Seattle, WA 98134, USA

Schultz, John (Athlete, Football Player)
503 Skyline Dr
Vestal, NY 13850, USA

Schultz, John (Director)
c/o Staff Member *Creative Artists Agency (CAA-LA)*
2000 Ave Of The Stars
Los Angeles, CA 90067, USA

Schultz, Kirki (Stylist)
5007 Dupont Ave
South Minneapolis, MN 55419, USA

Schultz, Kurt (Athlete, Football Player)
5075 Rockledge Dr
Clarence, NY 14031, USA

Schultz, Michael A (Director)
Chrystalite Productions
PO Box 1940
Santa Monica, CA 90406, USA

Schultz, Mitch (Stylist)
c/o Staff Member *Ford Models (Chicago)*
311 W Superior St
Chicago, IL 60654, USA

Schultz, Nick (Athlete, Hockey Player)
201 Downey St
Strasbourg, SK SOG 4VO, Canada

Schultz, Peter C (Inventor)
Heraeus Amersil Inc
3473 Satellite Blvd #300
Duluth, GA 30096, USA

Schultz, Peter G (Misc)
Salk Research Institute
10550 N Torrey Pine Road
La Jolla, CA 92037, USA

Schultz, Richard D (Misc)
US Olympic Committee
1 Olympia Plaza
Colorado Springs, CO 80909, USA

Schultze, Charles L (Government Official)
Brookings Institute
1775 Massachusetts Ave NW
Washington, DC 20036, USA

Schulz, Axel
Zehmeplatz 10
Frankfurt/Oder, GERMANY D-15230

Schulz, Jeff (Athlete, Baseball Player)
1167 S Stockwell Rd
Evansville, IN 47714-0749, USA

Schulz, Jody (Athlete, Football Player)
222 Schulz Ln
Chester, MD 21619, USA

Schulz, Kurt (Athlete, Football Player)
5075 Rockledge Dr
Clarence, NY 14031, USA

Schulz, William (Editor)
Reader's Digest
Editorial Dept
PO Box 100
Pleasantville, NY 10572, USA

Schulze, Don (Athlete, Baseball Player)
1851 N Brinton Ave
Dixon, IL 61021-8262, USA

Schulze, Matt (Actor)
c/o David Gardner *Principato/Young Management*
9465 Wilshire Blvd
Suite 430
Beverly Hills, CA 90212, USA

Schulze, Paul (Actor)
c/o Staff Member *Kyle Fritz Management*
6325 Heather Dr
Los Angeles, CA 90068, USA

Schulze, Richard M (Business Person)
Best Buy Co
7601 Penn Ave S
Minneapolis, MN 55423, USA

Schumacher, Gregg (Athlete, Football Player)
104 Surfview Dr
Apt 2108
Palm Coast, FL 32137, USA

Schumacher, Joel (Director)
Greenfield & Selvaggi
11766 Wilshire Blvd #1610
Los Angeles, CA 90025, USA

Schumacher, Kelly (Basketball Player)
Indiana Fever
Conseco Fieldhouse
125 S Pennsylvania
Indianapolis, IN 46204, USA

Schumacher, Kurt (Athlete, Football Player)
673 Northfield Ln
Harleysville, PA 19438, USA

Schumacher, Michael (Race Car Driver)
Mercedes Grand Prix
Via Ascari 55-57
Maranello 40153, ITALY

Schumacher, Ralf (Race Car Driver)
Weber Mgmt
Wentage
Oxfordshire OX12.0DQ, UNITED KINGDOM (UK)

Schumacher, Tony (Race Car Driver)
PO Box 308
1134 Uufflems Le
Chateau, SWITZERLAND

Schumaker, Jared (Skip) (Athlete, Baseball Player)
6 Illuminata Ln
Ladera Ranch, CA 92694, USA

Schuman, Allan L (Business Person)
Ecolab Inc
Ecolab Center
370 Wabasha St N
Saint Paul, MN 55102, USA

Schuman, Melissa (Actor)
c/o Staff Member *Kazarian Spencer Ruskin & Assoc.*
11969 Ventura Blvd
3rd Floor
Studio City, CA 91604, USA

Schuman, Tom (Musician)
PO Box 435
Highland Mills, NY 10930, USA

Schumann, Jochen (Yachtsman)
Birkenstr 88
Penzberg 48336, GERMANY

Schumann, Ralf (Misc)
Steomach 22
Stockheim 97640, GERMANY

Schumer, Charles (Politician)
9 Prospect Park W Apt IOB
Brooklyn, NY 11215-1741, USA

Schur, Michael (Writer)
c/o Staff Member *3 Arts Entertainment Inc*
9460 Wilshire Blvd
7th Floor
Beverly Hills, CA 90210, USA

Schurig, Roger (Athlete, Basketball Player)
1031 Brookside
Greensboro, GA 30642-6814, USA

Schurman, M F (Athlete, Hockey Player)
301 Beaver St
Summerside, PE C1N 2A2, Canada

Schurmann, Petra (Swimmer)
Max-Emanuel-Str 7
Starnberg 82319, GERMANY

Schurr, Harry W (War Hero)
Cleverland Cavaliers
1178 Davis Dr
Fairborn, OH 45324-4122, USA

Schurr, Wayne (Athlete, Baseball Player)
10030W 500 S
Hudson, IN 46747-9705, USA

Schurr, Wayne (Athlete, Baseball Player)
10030 W 500 S
Hudson, IN 46747, USA

Schussler Florenza, Elisabeth (Writer)
Notre Dame University
Theology Dept
Notre Dame, IN 46556, USA

Schuster, Rudolf (President)
President's Office
Nam Slobody 1
Bratislava 91370, SLOVAKIA

Schute, Anja
Parkstr. 37
Erfstadt, GERMANY D-50374

Schutt, Rod (Athlete, Hockey Player)
1450 Gennings St
Sudbury, ON P3E 6J2, Canada

Schutz, Carl (Athlete, Baseball Player)
P.O. Box 162
French Settlement, LA 70733-0162, USA

Schutz, Klaus (Government Official)
9 Konstanzerstr
Berlin 10707, GERMANY

Schutz, Stephen (Artist)
Blue Mountain Arts Inc
PO Box 4549
Boulder, CO 80306, USA

Schutz, Susan Polis (Writer)
Blue Mountain Arts Inc
PO Box 4549
Boulder, CO 80306, USA

Schuur, Diane (Music Group, Musician)
Paul Canter Enterprises
33042 Ocean Ridge
Dana Point, CA 92629, USA

Schwab, Charles (Misc)
PO Box 620070
Redwood City, CA 94062-0070, USA

Schwab, Corey (Athlete, Hockey Player)
20633 76th Ave SE
Snohomish, WA 98296-5169

Schwab, Corey (Athlete, Hockey Player)
San Jose Sharks
525 W Santa Clara St
SanJose, CA 95113-1500

Schwab, John J (Doctor)
6217 Innes Trace Road
Louisville, KY 40222, USA

Schwabe, Mike (Athlete, Baseball Player)
13341 Presidio Pl
Tustin, CA 92782-9105, USA

Schwall, Don (Athlete, Baseball Player)
741 Wolverine Rd
Mason, MI 15044-7425, USA

Schwantz, Jim (Athlete, Football Player)
1047 W Chatham Dr
Palatine, IL 60067, USA

Schwarthoff, Florian (Athlete, Track Athlete)
Fischweiher 51
Heppenheim 64646, GERMANY

Schwartz, Debbie (Stylist)
c/o Staff Member *Axis Models & Talent*
P.O. Box 367
Ringwood, NJ 07456-0367, USA

Schwartz, Don (Athlete, Football Player)
19410 NE Redmond Rd
Redmond, WA 98053, USA

Schwartz, Jacob T (Scientist)
New York University
Courant Math Sciences Institute
New York, NY 10012, USA

Schwartz, Josh (Producer, Writer)
3556 Lowry Rd
Los Angeles, CA 90027, USA

Schwartz, Kevin (Race Car Driver)
606A Performance Rd.
Mooresville, NC 28115, USA

Schwartz, Lloyd (Journalist)
27 Pennsylvania Ave
Somerville, MA 02145, USA

Schwartz, Maxime (Misc)
Institut Pasteur
25-28 Rue du Docteur-Roux
Paris Cedex 15 75724, FRANCE

Schwartz, Melvin (Nobel Prize Laureate)
PO Box 5068
Ketchum, ID 83340, USA

Schwartz, Neil
3044 Pearl Harbor Dr
Las Vegas, NV 89117, USA

Schwartz, Neil J (Actor)
3044 Pearl Harbor Dr
Las Vegas, NV 89117, USA

Schwartz, Norton A (General)
Commander
11th Air Force
Elmendorf Air Force Base, AK 99506, USA

Schwartz, Randy (Athlete, Baseball Player)
757 El Rancho Dr
El Cajon, CA 92019-1141, USA

Schwartz, Stephen L (Composer, Music Group, Musician, Songwriter, Writer)
Chaplin Entertainment
545 8th Ave
#14
New York, NY 10018, USA

Schwartz, Thomas A (General)
Commander
United Nations Command/US Forces Korea
APO, AP 96205, USA

Schwartzman, Jason (Actor)
c/o Matthew Labov *Forefront Media*
8500 Melrose Ave Ste 205
West Hollywood, CA 90069, USA

Schwartzman, Robert (Actor)
c/o Joanne Wiles *ICM Partners (ICM-LA)*
10250 Constellation Blvd Fl 7
Los Angeles, CA 90067, USA

Schwarz, Gerard R (Conductor)
New York Chamber Symphony
1395 Lexington Ave
New York, NY 10128, USA

Schwarz, Hanna (Opera Singer)
Opera et Concert
Maximilianstr 22
Munich 80539, GERMANY

Schwarz, Jeff (Athlete, Baseball Player)
912 Club Dr
Palm Beach Gardens, FL 33418-7065, USA

Schwarz, John H (Physicist)
California Institute of Technology
Physics Dept
Pasadena, CA 91125, USA

Schwarzbein, Diana (Doctor, Writer)
Health Communications
3201 SW 15th St
Deerfield Beach, FL 33442, USA

Schwarzenegger, Arnold (Politician)
c/o Josh Lieberman *Creative Artists Agency (CAA-LA)*
2000 Ave Of The Stars
Los Angeles, CA 90067, USA

Schwarzkopf, Norman (General)
Black Summit
302 Knights Run Ave
Suite 900
Tampa, FL 33602, USA

Schwarzman, Stephen (Steve) (Business Person)
The Blackstone Group
345 Park Ave
New York, NY 10154, USA

Schwarzman, Steve (Business Person)
Blackstone Group
345 Park Ave
New York, NY 10154, USA

Schwarz-Shilling, Christian (Government Official)
Post-Telecomm Ministry
Heinrich-von-Stephanstr 1
Bonn 53175, GERMANY

Schwebel, Stephen M (Judge)
PO Box 356
Woodstock, VT 05091, USA

Schwedes, Gerhard (Athlete, Football Player)
P.O. Box 570
Clayton, NY 13624, USA

Schwedes, Scott (Athlete, Football Player)
6871 Claret Cir
Fayetteville, NY 13066, USA

Schweickart, Russell L (Astronaut)
7218 Swansong Way
Bethesda, MD 20817-1271, USA

Schweig, Eric (Actor)
Prime Talent
PO Box 5163
Vancouver, BC V7B 1M4, CANADA

Schweiger, Til (Actor, Director, Producer)
barefoot films
Saarbrueckerstrasse 36
Berlin 10405, Germany

Schweighofer, Matthias (Actor)
c/o Cecile Felsenberg *UBBA*
6 rue de Braque
Paris 75003, France

Schweiker, Richard S (Politician)
8890 Windy Ridge Way
McLean, VA 22102-1558, USA

Schweikert, David (Congressman, Politician)
1205 Longworth HOB
Washington, DC 20515, USA

Schweikert, J E (Religious Leader)
Old Roman Catholic Church
4200 N Kedvale Ave
Chicago, IL 60641, USA

Schweikhard, G William (Aviator)
804 E 8th St
Georgetown, TX 7862-6034, USA

Schweinsteiger, Bastian (Soccer Player)
FC Bayern Munich
Attention Bastian Schweinsteiger
Säbener Strasse 51
Munich 81547, GERMANY

Schweitz, John (Athlete, Basketball Player)
813 Smith Dr
Florence, SC 29501-5979, USA

Schweitzer, Brian (Governor)
Office of the Governor, Montana State Capitol Bldg.
P.O. Box 200801
Helena, MT 59620-0801, USA

Schwertsik, Kurt (Composer)
Doblinger Music
Dorotheerhgasse 10
Vienna 1011, AUSTRIA

Schwery, Henry Cardinal (Religious Leader)
Bishoporic of Sion
CP 2068
Sion 2 1950, SWITZERLAND

Schwimmer, David (Actor)
c/o Eric Kranzler *Management 360*
9111 Wilshire Blvd
Beverly Hills, CA 90210, USA

Schwimmer, Lacey-Mae (Actor)
c/o Ben Russo *EMC / Bowery*
8145 Santa Monica Blvd
Suite 200
West Hollywood, CA 90046, USA

Schwinden, Ted (Ex-Governor)
18811 North 19th Avenue
Apt. 3022
Phoenix, AZ 85027-5283, USA

Schwitters, Roy F (Physicist)
1718 Cromwell Hill
Austin, TX 78703, USA

Schygulla, Hanna (Actor)
ZBF Agentur
Leopoldstr 19
Munich 80802, GERMANY

Schypinski, Jerry (Athlete, Baseball Player)
28014 Shadowood Ln
Harrison Township, MI 48045-2246, USA

Scialfa, Patty (Music Group, Musician)
c/o Staff Member *Sony Music International*
550 Madison Ave
New York, NY 10022-3211, USA

Sciambi, Jon (Baseball Player)
540 West Ave Apt 1813

Sciarra, John M (Athlete, Football Player)
4420 Woodleigh Ln
Flintridge, CA 91011, USA

Sciascia, Leonardo
Viale Scaduto 10/B
Palermo, ITALY 1-90144

Scifres, Steve (Athlete, Football Player)
2026 Northglen Dr
Colorado Springs, CO 80909, USA

Sciole, Jennifer (Actor, Producer)
c/o Steve Honig *Honig Company, The*
4804 Laurel Canyon Blvd.
#828
Studio City, CA 91607, USA

Scioli, Brad (Football Player)
Indianapolis Colts
5433 Bay Harbor Dr
Indianapolis, IN 46254-4510, USA

Sciorra, Annabella (Actor)
c/o Staff Member *Dontanville/Frattaroli (D/F)*
270 Lafayette St
Suite 402
New York, NY 10012, USA

Scioscia, Michael L (Mike) (Athlete, Baseball Player, Coach)
1915 Falling Star Ave
Westlake Village, CA 91362-5284, USA

Scirica, Anthony J (Judge)
US Court of Appeals
US Courthouse
601 Market St
Philadelphia, PA 19106, USA

Scissor Sisters (Music Group)
c/o Darin Harmon *3D Management*
1901 Main St
3rd Floor
Santa Monica, CA 90405, USA

Sciutto, Nellie (Actor)
c/o Ted Schachter *Schachter Entertainment*
1157 S Beverly Dr Fl 2
Los Angeles, CA 90035, USA

S Club 7 (Music Group)
c/o Staff Member *Creative Artists Agency (CAA-LA)*
2000 Ave Of The Stars
Los Angeles, CA 90067, USA

Scodelario, Kaya (Actor)
c/o Kate Staddon *Curtis Brown Group*
Haymarket House
28 - 29 Haymarket
London SW1Y 4SP, UNITED KINGDOM

Scofield, Dean
12304 Santa Monica Blvd. #104
Los Angeles, CA 90025

Scofield, Dino (Actor)
3330 Barham Blvd #103
Los Angeles, CA 90068, USA

Scofield, John (Musician)
Ted Kurland
173 Brighton Ave
Boston, MA 02134, USA

Scofield, Paul (Actor)
Gables
Balcombe
Sussex RH17 6ND, UNITED KINGDOM (UK)

Scofield, Richard M (Dick) (General)
3251 Country Club Pkwy
Castle Rock, CO 80108-9078, USA

Scoggins, Matt (Swimmer)
4900 Calhoun Canyon Loop
Austin, TX 78735, USA

Scoggins, Tracy (Actor)
c/o Staff Member *Bette Smith Management*
499 N Canon Dr
Beverly Hills, CA 90210, USA

Scola, Angelo Cardinal (Religious Leader)
Archdiocese
S Marco 320/A
Venezia 30124, ITALY

Scola, Ettore (Director)
Via Bertoloni 1/E
Rome 00197, ITALY

Scola, Luis
11801 Sea Shadow Bnd
Pearland, TX 77584-6807, USA

Scolari, Luiz Felipe (Football Coach)
FC Bunyodkor
3 Beruniy St
Shaykhontohur District
Tashkent, Uzbekistan

Scolari, Peter (Actor)
c/o Staff Member *Peter Strain & Associates Inc (LA)*
5455 Wilshire Blvd
Suite 1812
Los Angeles, CA 90036-4368, USA

Scollay, Gabrielle (Actor)
c/o Fleur Griffin *Mark Morrissey and Associates*
16 Princess Ave
Rosebery
Sydney NSW 2018, Australia

Scolnick, Edward M (Doctor, Scientist)
1201 Magnolia Drive
Wayland, MA 01778-2848, USA

Scolnik, Glenn (Athlete, Football Player)
301 Willowgate Dr
Indianapolis, IN 46260, USA

Sconiers, Daryl (Athlete, Baseball Player)
15985 Hibiscus St
Fontana, CA 92336-0504, USA

Scooters, The
15190 Encanto Dr.
Sherman Oaks, CA 91403

Scorpions (Music Group)
Musikproduktions- Und Verlags GmbH
Bohlenweg 8
Langenhagen 30835, Germany

Scorsese, Martin (Director)
c/o Rick Yorn *LBI Entertainment*
2000 Avenue of the Stars
3rd Floor, North Tower
Los Angeles, CA 90067, USA

Scorsese, Nicolette (Actor)
c/o Gregory (Greg) Mayo *Orange Grove Group, The*
12178 Ventura Blvd #205
Studio City, CA 91604, USA

Scorupco, Izabella (Actor, Model, Music Group, Musician)
c/o Anne Woodward *ROAR (LA)*
9701 Wilshire Blvd
8th Floor
Los Angeles, CA 90212, USA

Scott, Adam (Actor)
c/o Danielle Thomas *Untitled Entertainment (LA)*
350 S. Beverly Dr #200
Beverly Hills, CA 90212, USA

Scott, Adam (Golfer)
c/o Staff Member *Pro Golfers Assoc of America (PGA)*
112 TPC Blvd
Ponte Vedra Beach, FL 32082-3077, USA

Scott, Alvin (Athlete, Basketball Player)
5786 W Townley Ave
Glendale, AZ 85302-4612, USA

Scott, Andy (Musician)
DCM International
296 Nether St
Finchley
London N3 1RJ, UNITED KINGDOM (UK)

Scott, Arthur (Athlete, Football Player)
209 Lincoln Ave
Conshohocken, PA 19428, USA

Scott, Ashley (Actor)
c/o Mary Putnam Greene *MPG Management*
9150 Wilshire Blvd
Suite 350
Beverly Hills, CA 90212, USA

Scott, Austin (Congressman, Politician)
516 Cannon HOB
Washington, DC 20515, USA

Scott, Bo (Athlete, Football Player)
1301 Fountain Ln
Apt 1
Columbus, OH 43213, USA

Scott, Bobby (Athlete, Football Player)
801 McKinley Pointe Ln
Knoxville, TN 37922, USA

Scott, Byron (Athlete, Basketball Player, Coach)
668 Euclid Ave Unit 527
Cleveland, OH 44114-3014, USA

Scott, Camilla
23773 Via Canon #201
Newhall, CA 91321

Scott, Campbell (Actor)
c/o Clifford Stevens *Paradigm (NY)*
360 Park Ave S Fl 16
New York, NY 10010, USA

Scott, Captain E Winston (Astronaut)
Florida Institute Of Technology
150 W University_ Blvd Attn Dean Cllg of Aeronautics
Melbourne, FL 32901-6975, USA

Scott, Carlos (Athlete, Football Player)
RR 1 Box 346
Hempstead, TX 77445, USA

Scott, Chad (Athlete, Football Player)
18526 Reliant Dr
Gaithersburg, MD 20879, USA

Scott, Chuck (Athlete, Football Player)
875 Landover Xing
Suwanee, GA 30024, USA

Scott, Clarence (Athlete, Football Player)
3-17-6 NishiAzabu Regency
Apt 202
Minato-ku, Tokyo, Japan

Scott, Clarence (Athlete, Football Player)
216 Sisson Ave NE
Atlanta, GA 30317, USA

Scott, Clyde L (Smackover) (Athlete, Football Player, Track Athlete)
12840 Rivercrest Dr
Little Rock, AR 72212, USA

Scott, Colonel David (Astronaut)
Scott Science And Technology Inc
6033 W Century Blvd Ste 400
Los Angeles, CA 90045-6416, USA

Scott, Coltin
195 S. Beverly Dr. #400
Beverly Hills, CA 90212-3044

Scott, Dale (Athlete, Baseball Player)
1283 SW Cardinell Dr
Portland, OR 97201, USA

Scott, Dale (Baseball Player)
1283 SW Cardinell Dr
Portland, OR 97201-3114, USA

Scott, Dale (Athlete, Baseball Player)
1283 SW Cardinell Dr
Portland, OR 97201-3114, USA

Scott, Darnay (Athlete, Football Player)
13151 Scabard Pl
San Diego, CA 92128, USA

Scott, Darryl (Athlete, Baseball Player)
4026 E Hamblin Dr
Phoenix, AZ 85255-5421, USA

Scott, Dave (Athlete, Football Player)
3151 Robindale Rd
Decatur, GA 30034, USA

Scott, David (Congressman, Politician)
225 Cannon HOB
Washington, DC 20515, USA

Scott, David
1300-B Manhattan Ave.
Manhattan Beach, CA 90266

Scott, David R (Astronaut)
Merces
VC Johnson
30 Hackamore Lane #1
Bell Canyon, CA 91307, USA

Scott, Dennis (Athlete, Basketball Player)
9832 Laurel Valley Dr
Windermere, FL 34786-8911, USA

Scott, Dick (Athlete, Baseball Player)
166 Sunset Ln
Cairo, GA 39828-6737, USA

Scott, Dick (Athlete, Baseball Player)
7399 E Cortez Rd
Scottsdale, AZ 85260, USA

Scott, Donnie (Athlete, Baseball Player)
6042 114th Ter
Pinellas Park, FL 33782-2018, USA

Scott, Donovan (Actor)
Talent Group
6300 Wilshire Blvd #2100
Los Angeles, CA 90048, USA

Scott, Dougray (Actor)
c/o Staff Member *Dontanville/Frattaroli (D/F)*
270 Lafayette St
Suite 402
New York, NY 10012, USA

Scott, Dragos (Athlete, Football Player)
1750 Pacific Beach Dr
San Diego, CA 92109, USA

Scott, Edward (Politician)
4508 Greenbreeze Ln
Fuquay Varina, NC 27526-6864, USA

Scott, Edward (Baseball Player)
Indianapolis Clowns
720 Kesserine Pass
Mobile, AL 36609-6430, USA

Scott, Eric
11934 River Grove Ct
. Moorpark, CA 93021

Scott, Freddie (Musician)
Headline Talent
1650 Broadway #508
New York, NY 10019, USA

Scott, Freddie L (Athlete, Football Player)
P.O. Box 197
Coahoma, MS 38617, USA

Scott, Gary (Athlete, Baseball Player)
25 W Elm St
Apt 47
Greenwich, CT 06830-2802, USA

Scott, Gavin (Writer)
c/o Jordan Bayer *Original Artists (LA)*
9465 Wilshire Blvd Ste 870
Beverly Hills, CA 90212, USA

Scott, Geoffrey
1126 Hollywood Way #203-A
Burbank, CA 91505

Scott, George (Athlete, Baseball Player)
1316 Goodrich St
Greenville, MS 38701-6130, USA

Scott, Gloria Dean Randle (Educator)
Bennett College
President's Office
Greensboro, NC 27401, USA

Scott, Herbert (Athlete, Football Player)
605 Rawhide Ct
Plano, TX 75023, USA

Scott, H Lee Jr (Business Person)
Wal-Mart Stores
702 SW 8th St
Bentonville, AR 72712, USA

Scott, Jack (Music Group, Musician, Songwriter, Writer)
34039 Coachwood Dr
Sterling Heights, MI 48312, USA

Scott, Jacob E (Jake) Jr (Athlete, Football Player)
P.O. Box 857
Hanalei, HI 96714, USA

Scott, James (Actor)
c/o Sandra Siegal *Siegal Company, The*
9025 Wilshire Blvd #400
Beverly Hills, CA 90211, USA

Scott, James (Athlete, Football Player)
10127 Chisholm Trl
Dallas, TX 75243, USA

Scott, Jill (Actor, Musician)
c/o Sherlen Archibald *The Chamber Group*
416 West 13th St
Suite 105
New York, NY 10014, USA

Scott, Jimmy (Music Group, Musician)
J's Way Jazz
175 Prospect St #20D
East Orange, NJ 07017, ITALY

scott, joe b (Athlete, Baseball Player)
1749 Netherwood Ave
Memphis, TN 38114-1932, USA

Scott, John (Composer, Musician)
c/o Otto Vavrin II *SMC Artists*
4400 Coldwater Canyon Ave #127
Studio City, CA 91604, USA

Scott, John (Athlete, Football Player)
1583 N Ellen Ave
Decatur, IL 62526, USA

Scott, John (Athlete, Baseball Player)
917 S Pearl Ave
Compton, CA 90221-4320, USA

Scott, Josey (Music Group, Musician)
Helter Skelter
Plaza
535 Kings Road
London SW10 0S, UNITED KINGDOM (UK)

Scott, Judson
10000 Santa Monica Blvd. #305
Los Angeles, CA 90067, USA

Scott, Kathryn Leigh (Actor)
3236 Bennett Dr
Los Angeles, CA 90068, USA

Scott, Kevin B (Athlete, Football Player)
2335 Cascade St
Milpitas, CA 95035, USA

Scott, Klea (Actor)
c/o Staff Member *Wyckoff and Associates (LA)*
11350 Ventura Blvd
Suite 100
Studio City, CA 91604-3140, USA

Scott, Lary R (Business Person)
Carolina Freight Corp
PO Box 1000
Cherryville, NC 28021, USA

Scott, Lew (Athlete, Football Player)
4 Osprey Ct
Streamwood, IL 60107, USA

Scott, Lindsay (Athlete, Football Player)
214 N Troupe St
Valdosta, GA 31601, USA

Scott, Lizabeth (Actor)
8277 Hollywood Blvd
West Hollywood, CA 90069, USA

Scott, Lorna (Actor)
c/o Staff Member *Kjar and Associates*
10153 1/2 Riverside Drive
Toluca Lake, CA 91602, USA

Scott, Luke (Athlete, Baseball Player)
1245 Arredondo Grant Rd
De Leon Springs, FL 32130-0039, USA

Scott, L'Wren (Fashion Designer, Stylist)
L'Wren Scott
58/63 Tuxedo Ter
Hollywood, CA 90068, USA

Scott, Melody Thomas (Actor)
12068 Crest Court
Beverly Hills, CA 90210, USA

Scott, Michael W (Mike) (Athlete, Baseball Player)
28355 Chat Dr
Laguna Niguel, CA 92677-1384, USA

Scott, Patricia (Athlete, Baseball Player)
320 Edwards Ave
Walton, KY 41094-1096, USA

Scott, Paul (Writer)
33 Drumsheugh Gardens
Edinburgh, SCOTLAND

Scott, Pippa (Actor)
10850 Wilshire Blvd #250
Los Angeles, CA 90024, USA

Scott, Randy (Athlete, Football Player)
1440 Woodland Lake Dr
Snellville, GA 30078, USA

Scott, Ray (Basketball Player, Coach)
Colonial Life Insurance
33200 Schoolcraft Road
Livonia, MI 48150, USA

Scott, Reppert (Athlete, Football Player)
3133 N Bass Lake Rd
Eagle River, WI 54521-9150, USA

Scott, Richard U (Dick) (Athlete, Football Player)
3369 Upland Ct
Adamstown, MD 21710, USA

Scott, Rick (Governor)
Office of Governor Rick Scott
State of Florida, The Capitol
400 S. Monroe St.
Tallahassee, FL 32399, USA

Scott, Ridley (Director)
c/o Simon Halls *Slate Public Relations*
9000 Sunset Blvd #915
West Hollywood, CA 90069, USA

Scott, Robert (Baseball Player)
New York Black Yankees
236 W Grand St
Eliabeth, NJ 07202-1284, USA

Scott, Robert L Jr (War Hero, Writer)
PO Box 2469
Warner Robins, GA 31099, USA

Scott, Rodney (Athlete, Baseball Player)
4206 Priscilla Ave
Indianapolis, IN 46226-3334, USA

Scott, Ron (Athlete, Hockey Player)
8822 Madeleine Dr
Baldwinsville, NY 13027-8916

Scott, Russell J (Aviator)
364 Lynn Cove Rd
Asheville, NC 28804-1915, USA

Scott, Sean (Athlete, Football Player)
3217 Boise St
Berkeley, CA 94702, USA

Scott, Seann William (Actor, Producer)
c/o Christina Papadopoulos *Baker Winokur Ryder Public Relations BWR (BWR-NY)*
292 Madison Ave
12th Floor
New York, NY 10017, USA

Scott, Shelby (Misc)
American Federation of TV/Radio Artists
260 Madison Ave
New York, NY 10016, USA

Scott, Stephanie (Stylist)
1208 S Genesee Ave
Los Angeles, CA 90019, USA

Scott, Stephen (Musician)
Bridge Agency
35 Clark St #A5
Brooklyn Heights, NY 11201, USA

Scott, Steven M (Steve) (Athlete, Track Athlete)
4106 La Portalada Dr
Carlsbad, CA 92008, USA

Scott, Stuart
c/o Staff Member *ESPN (Main)*
ESPN Plaza
935 Middle St
Bristol, CT 06010-1001, USA

Scott, Thomas C (Tom) (Athlete, Football Player)
3259 Kirkwood Ct
Keswick, VA 22947, USA

Scott, Tighe (Race Car Driver)
RD #1 - Box 1847
First St.
Saylorsburg, PA 18353, United States

Scott, Tim (Congressman, Politician)
1117 Longwortij HOB
Washington, DC 20515, USA

Scott, Tim (Athlete, Baseball Player)
956 W Julia Way
Hanford, CA 93230-8552, USA

Scott, Todd (Athlete, Football Player)
5605 Avenue P
Galveston, TX 77551, USA

Scott, Tom (Athlete, Football Player)
1012 Peed Dr
Apt 8
Greenville, NC 27834, USA

Scott, Tom (Athlete, Football Player)
3359 Kirkwood Ct
Keswick, VA 22947, USA

Scott, Tom (Musician)
Performers of the World
8901 Melrose Ave #200
West Hollywood, CA 90069, USA

Scott, Tom Everett (Actor)
c/o John Carrabino *John Carrabino Management*
5900 Wilshire Blvd Fl 4 #406
Los Angeles, CA 90036, USA

Scott, Tony (Athlete, Baseball Player)
156 Oakwood Ave
Spartanburg, SC 29306-5342, USA

Scott, Walter (Athlete, Football Player)
1991 Edgefield Rd
Trenton, SC 29847, USA

Scott, Willard (Television Host)
c/o Staff Member *NBC Universal (NY)*
30 Rockefeller Plaza
New York, NY 10112, USA

Scott, Willard W Jr (Educator, General)
9115 McNair Dr
Alexandria, VA 22309, USA

Scott, William (Politician)
9229 Arlington Blvd Apt 250
Fairfax, VA 22031-2543, USA

Scott, William Lee
c/o Daniel Spilo *Industry Entertainment Partners*
955 S Carrillo Dr
Suite 300
Los Angeles, CA 90048, USA

Scott, Willie (Athlete, Football Player)
1123 Long St
Newberry, SC 29108, USA

Scott, Winston E (Astronaut)
PO Box 1192
Cape Canaveral, FL 32920, USA

Scott, W Richard (Misc)
940 Lathrop Place
Stanford, CA 94305, USA

Scott Brown, Denise (Architect)
Venturi Scott Brown Assoc
4236 Main St
Philadelphia, PA 19127, USA

Scott-Brown, Denise (Architect)
Venturi Scott Brown Assoc
4236 Main St
Philadelphia, PA 19127, USA

Scotti, Benjamin (Athlete, Football Player)
715 N Beverly Dr
Beverly Hills, CA 90210, USA

Scotti, Nick (Actor, Musician)
c/o Elise Konialian *Untitled Entertainment (NY)*
322 8th Ave #601
New York, NY 10001-6715, USA

Scott Kay, Dominic (Actor)
c/o Rich Hueners *Paradigm (LA)*
360 N Crescent Dr
North Bldg
Beverly Hills, CA 90210, USA

Scotto, Renata (Opera Singer)
c/o Staff Member *Opera Et Concert*
37, rue de la Chaussée d'Antin
Paris F-75009, France

Scotto, Rosanna (Correspondent)
WNYW TV
205 E. 67th St
New York, NY 10021, USA

Scottoline, Lisa (Writer)
Harper Collins Publishers
10 E 53rd St
New York, NY 10022, USA

Scott Thomas, Kristin (Actor)
c/o Mara Buxbaum *ID PR (LA)*
7060 Hollywood Blvd
8th Floor
Los Angeles, CA 90028, USA

Scotty K (DJ)
c/o Staff Member *Diva Central Inc*
7510 W Sunset Blvd Ste 1445
Los Angees, CA 90046, USA

Scouler, Angela (Actor)
Daly Gagan
60 Old Brompton Road
London SW7 3LQ, UNITED KINGDOM
(UK)

Scovell, Nell (Producer)
c/o Staff Member *WmE2 (WMA-LA)*
1 William Morris Pl
Beverly Hills, CA 90212, USA

Scoville, Darrel (Athlete, Hockey Player)
18 Landmark Rd
Scarborough, ME 04074-8482

Scowcroft, Brent (Politician)
350 Park Ave #2600
New York, NY 10022-6022, USA

Scrafford, Kirk (Athlete, Football Player)
19400 US Highway 93 N
Florence, MT 59833, USA

Scranton, Jim (Athlete, Baseball Player)
27519 Hammack Ave
Perris, CA 92570-7071, USA

Scranton, Nancy (Golfer)
15820 Sanctuary Dr
Tampa, FL 33647-1075, USA

Scranton, William (Politician)
Council Of American Ambassadors
PO Box 116
Dalton, PA 18414-0116, USA

Scratch (Artist, Musician)
William Morris Agency
1325 Ave of Americas
New York, NY 10019, USA

Scream3 (Music Group)
c/o Staff Member *Wind-up Records*
72 Madison Ave Fl 8
New York, NY 10016, USA

Scremin, Claudio (Athlete, Hockey Player)
84 Littlebrook Ln
Eliot, ME 03903-1512

Scribner, Bucky (Athlete, Football Player)
512 Georgina Ave
Santa Monica, CA 90402, USA

Scribner, Rick (Race Car Driver)
8904 Amerigo Ave
Orangevale, CA 95662, USA

Scrimm, Angus (Actor)
PO Box 5193
North Hollywood, CA 91616, USA

Scrimshaw, Nevin S (Doctor)
Sandwich Mountain Farm
PO Box 330
Campton, NH 03223, USA

Scripps, Charles E (Publisher)
10 Grandin Lane
Cincinnati, OH 45208, USA

S. Critz, Mark (Congressman, Politician)
1022 Longworth HOB
Washington, DC 20515, USA

Scrivener, Chuck (Athlete, Baseball Player)
1766 Hazel St
Birmingham, MI 48009-6892, USA

Scriver, Charles (Scientist)
232 Av Strathearn N
Montreal-Ouest, Canada

Scroggins, Tracy (Athlete, Football Player)
2026 Willow Leaf Dr
Rochester Hills, MI 48309, USA

Scruggs, Eugene (Baseball Player)
Detroit Stars
618 Dawson Ter NW
Huntsville, AL 35811-1782, USA

Scruggs, Randy (Musician)
McLachlan Scruggs
2821 Bransford Ave
Nashville, TN 37204, USA

Scruggs, Tony (Athlete, Baseball Player)
11621 Braddock Dr
Apt 17
Culver City, CA 90230-5175, USA

Scudamore, Peter (Jockey)
Mucky Cottage Grangehill
Naunton Cheltenham
Glos GL54 3AY, UNITED KINGDOM
(UK)

Scudder, Scott (Athlete, Baseball Player)
943 Farm Road 1499
Paris, TX 75473-4345, USA

Scuderi, Rob (Athlete, Hockey Player)
Sports Consulting Group
65 Monroe Ave Ste D
Pittsford, NY 14534-1318, USA

Scudero, Joe (Athlete, Football Player)
11811 Mandy Ln
Manassas, VA 20112, USA

Scully, John (Athlete, Football Player)
3500 Bankview Dr
Joliet, IL 60431, USA

Scully, Sean P (Artist)
Timothy Taylor Gallery
1 Bruton Place
London W1X 7AB, UNITED KINGDOM
(UK)

Scully, Vin (Sportscaster)
c/o Staff Member *Los Angeles Dodgers (LA Dodgers)*
1000 Elysian Park Ave
Los Angeles, CA 90012, USA

Scully-Power, Paul D (Astronaut)
Civil Aviation Safety Authority
Box 2005
Canberra, ACT 2600, AUSTRALIA

Sculthorpe, Peter J (Composer)
91 Holdsworth St
Woollahra, NSW 2025, AUSTRALIA

Scurry, Briana (Athlete, Olympic Athlete, Soccer Player)
11610 137th Ave N
Dayton, MN 55327-9730, USA

Scurti, John (Actor)
c/o Jennifer Konawal *Gersh (NY)*
41 Madison Ave
New York, NY 10010, USA

Scutaro, Marco (Athlete, Baseball Player)
19877 E Country Club Dr
Apt 3503
Miami, FL 33178-2804, USA

Scutt, Der (Architect)
Der Scutt Architect
44 W 28th St
New York, NY 10001, USA

Sczurek, Stan (Athlete, Football Player)
689 Beaver Ridge Trl
Broadview Heights, OH 44147, USA

Sea, Daniela (Actor)
c/o Hannah Roth *Buchwald/Fortitude (LA)*
6500 Wilshire Blvd
Suite 2200
Los Angeles, CA 90048, USA

Seabol, Scott (Athlete, Baseball Player)
427 Cedar Dr
Elizabeth, PA 15037-2167, USA

Seabra, Verissimo Correia (General, President)
President's Office
Bissau, GUINEA-BISSAU

Seabron, Malcolm (Athlete, Football Player)
10418 Cliffwood Dr
Houston, TX 77035, USA

Seabrook, Andrea (Correspondent)
c/o Staff Member *National Public Radio (NPR)*
635 Massachusetts Ave NW
Washington, DC 20001, USA

Seabrook, Brent (Athlete, Hockey Player)
3323 N Hoyne Ave
Chicago, IL 60618-6243

Seacrest, Ryan (Producer, Radio Personality, Television Host)
c/o Melissa Stone *42West (LA)*
11400 W Olympic Blvd
Suite 1100
Los Angeles, CA 90064, USA

Seaforth Hayes, Susan (Actor)
4528 Beck Ave N
Hollywood, CA 91602, USA

Seaga, Edward P G (Prime Minister)
24-26 Grenada Crescent
New Kingston
Kingston 5, JAMAICA

Seagal, Steven (Actor)
c/o Alix Gucovsky *Special Artists Agency*
9465 Wilshire Blvd #820
Beverly Hills, CA 90212, USA

Seagrave, Jocelyn (Actor)
c/o Gregg Steiner *Perspective Film*
15030 Ventura Blvd
Sherman Oaks, CA 91403, USA

Seagraves, Ralph (Race Car Driver)
RR 10 Box 413
Winston Salem, NC 27127, USA

Seagren, Bob (Athlete, Olympic Athlete, Track Athlete)
International City Racing
3000 Pacific Ave
Attn: CEO
Long Beach, CA 90806-1356, USA

Seagrove, Jenny (Actor)
Marmont Mgmt
Langham House
302/8 Regent St
London W1R 5AL, UNITED KINGDOM
(UK)

Seal (Musician)
c/o Mitch Rose *Creative Artists Agency (CAA-LA)*
2000 Ave Of The Stars
Los Angeles, CA 90067, USA

Seal, Paul (Athlete, Football Player)
21599 Hidden Rivers Dr N
Southfield, MI 48075, USA

Seale, John C (Cinematographer)
Mirisch Agency
1801 Century Park E
Los Angeles, CA 90067, USA

Seale, Johnnie (Athlete, Baseball Player)
1941 County Road 207
Durango, CO 81301-7700, USA

Seale, Sam (Athlete, Football Player)
1818 Da Gama Ct
Escondido, CA 92026, USA

Sealey, Tom (Athlete, Basketball Player)
316 Fountain Ave
Brooklyn, NY 11208, USA

Seals, Brady
2100 West End Ave. #1000
Nashville, TN 37203

Seals, Bruce (Athlete, Basketball Player)
115 Prospect St
Ashland, MA 01721-2249, USA

Seals, George (Athlete, Football Player)
1101 1st St
Unit 204
Coronado, CA 92118, USA

Seals, Ray (Athlete, Football Player)
664 NW Shaw Glen
Lake City, FL 32055, USA

Seals & Croft (Music Group)
c/o Staff Member *4STAR Entertainment LLC*
1675 York Ave
Ste 32C
New York, NY 10128, USA

Sealy, Tom (Athlete, Basketball Player)
387 Classon Ave
Brooklyn, NY 11238-1307, USA

Seaman, Christopher (Conductor)
25 Westfield Dr
Glasgow G52 2SG, SCOTLAND

Seaman, David (Soccer Player)
Arsenal London
Avenell Road
Highbury
London N5 1BU, UNITED KINGDOM
(UK)

Seaman, Kim (Athlete, Baseball Player)
4900 Main St
Moss Point, MS 39567-6707, USA

Sean, Jay (Musician)
c/o David Zedeck *Creative Artists Agency
(CAA-NY)*
162 Fifth Ave
6th Floor
New York, NY 10010, USA

Sean, SeanMahan (Athlete, Football
Player)
4202 E 116th Pl
Tulsa, OK 74137-6120, USA

Seanez, Rudy (Athlete, Baseball Player)
1422 McCabe Cove Rd
El Centro, CA 92243-9741, USA

Searage, Ray (Athlete, Baseball Player)
9737 Pine Lake Trl
Saint Petersburg, FL 33716-3146, USA

Searchers, The
2514 Build America Dr.
Hampton, VA 22666

Searcy, Leon (Athlete, Football Player)
3841 Biggin Church Rd
Jacksonville, FL 32224, USA

Searcy, Nick (Actor)
c/o Joseph (Joe) Rice *Abrams Artists
Agency (LA)*
9200 Sunset Blvd
11th Floor
Los Angeles, CA 90069, USA

Searcy, Steve (Athlete, Baseball Player)
5112 Gouffon Rd
Knoxville, TN 37918-9319, USA

Searcy, Steve (Athlete, Baseball Player)
5112 Gouffon Rd
Knoxville, TN 37918, USA

Searfoss, Colonel A Richard (Astronaut)
25101 Bear Valley Rd
Tehachapi, CA 93561-8311, USA

Searfoss, Richard A (Astronaut)
24480 Silver Creek Way
Tehachapi, CA 93561, USA

Searle, Jackie
7214 Chestwood Dr.
Tujunga, CA 91042

Searle, John R (Misc)
109 Yosemite Road
Berkeley, CA 94707, USA

Searle, Ronald (Animator, Cartoonist)
Elaine McMahon Agency
PO Box 1062
Bayonne, NJ 07002, USA

Searles, Kyle (Actor)
c/o Loch Powell *Leverage Management*
3030 Pennsylvania Ave
Santa Monica, CA 90404, USA

Sears, Brian (Horse Racer)
83 Osprey Ct
Secaucus, NJ 07094-2934, USA

Sears, Jay (Horse Racer)
750 NW 30th Ave Apt A
Delray Beach, FL 33445-2077, USA

Sears, Ken (Athlete, Basketball Player)
40 Cutter Dr
Watsonville, CA 95076-2229, USA

Sears, Paul B (Misc)
17 Las Milpas
Taos, NM 87571, USA

Sears, Todd (Athlete, Baseball Player)
513 NW Chapel Dr
Ankeny, IA 50023-1420, USA

Sears, Dr, William
34761 Doheny Place
Capistrano Beach, CA 92624

Sease, Marvin
Malaco Music Group
PO Box 9287
Jackson, MS 39286-9287, USA

Seaver, Tom (Athlete, Baseball Player)
1761 Diamond Mountain Rd
Calistoga, CA 94515-9672, USA

Seaward, Tracey (Producer)
c/o Staff Member *ICM Partners (ICM-LA)*
10250 Constellation Blvd Fl 7
Los Angeles, CA 90067, USA

Seaward, Tracy (Producer)
c/o Staff Member *Independent Talent
Group (ITG-UK)*
Oxford House
76 Oxford St
London W1D 1BS, UK

Seay, Bobby (Athlete, Baseball Player,
Olympic Athlete)
1591 Oak Cir N
Sarasota, FL 34232-3478, USA

Seay, Laura (Actor)
c/o Susan Smith *Susan Smith Company,
The*
1344 N Wetherly Dr
Los Angeles, CA 90069-1817, USA

Seay, Mark (Athlete, Football Player)
2866 Muscupiabe Dr
San Bernardino, CA 92405, USA

Seay, Virgil (Athlete, Football Player)
5611 Fort Corloran Dr
Burke, VA 22015, USA

Sebaldt, Maria
Geranienstr. 3
Grunwald, GERMANY D-82031

Sebastian (Stylist)
c/o Staff Member *Ford Models (Chicago)*
311 W Superior St
Chicago, IL 60654, USA

Sebastian, Cuthbert (General,
Government Official, Governor)
Governor General's House
6 Canyon St
Basseterre, Saint Kitts & Nevis

Sebastian, John (Musician)
Lustig Talent
PO Box 770850
Orlando, FL 32877, USA

Sebastiani, Sergio Cardinal (Religious
Leader)
Palazzo delle Congregazioni
Lardo del Colonnato 3
Rome 00193, ITALY

Sebbah, Kate (Stylist)
c/o Staff Member *Streeters*
560 Broadway
Suite 203
New York, NY 10012, 212-219-9566

Sebelius, Kathleen (Politician)
224 SW Greenwood Ave
Topeka, KS 66606-1228, USA

Sebesky, Don (Musician)
c/o Staff Member *Bennett Morgan &
Associates*
1022 Route 376
Wappingers Falls, NY 12590, USA

Sebestyen, Marta (Music Group,
Musician)
Konzertgentur Berthold Seliger
Nonnengasse 15
Fulda 36037, GERMANY

Sebold, Alice (Writer)
c/o Staff Member *Steven Barclay Agency*
12 Western Ave
Petaluma, CA 94952, USA

Sebra, Bob (Athlete, Baseball Player)
20 Misners Trl
Ormond Beach, FL 32174-8531, USA

Secada, Jon (Musician)
c/o Susan Haber *Haber Entertainment*
434 S Canon Dr
Suite 204
Beverly Hills, CA 90212, USA

Seck, Idrissa (Prime Minister)
Prime Minister's Office
Ave Leopold Sedar Senghor
Dakar, SENEGAL

Secor, Kyle (Actor)
Brillstein/Grey
9150 Wilshire Blvd #350
Beverly Hills, CA 90212, USA

Secord, Al (Athlete, Hockey Player)
950 Ginger St
Southlake, TX 76092-6063

Secord, John (Music Group, Musician)
Making Texas Music
Old Putnam Bank Building
PO Box 1013
Putnam, TX 76469, USA

Secord, Richard (Politician)
Thermal Imaging
108 Windlake Ct
Niceville, FL 32578-4804, USA

Secrest, Charles (Baseball Player)
215 Orchard Grove Ave
Lewistown, PA 17044-7509, USA

Secret GardenContinental AS, Marcus
Thranesgate 2b
Oslo, NORWAY 0473

Secrets, No (Music Group)
Official International Fan Club
PO Box 5247
Bellingham, WA 98227, USA

Secrist, Don (Athlete, Baseball Player)
5851 Park Rd
Pinckneyville, IL 62832-3738, USA

Secules, Scott (Athlete, Football Player)
1007 Hawkins Wood Ln
Midlothian, VA 23114-4577, USA

Secunda, Andrew (Writer)
c/o Staff Member *United Talent Agency
(UTA)*
9336 Civic Center Dr
Beverly Hills, CA 90210, USA

Seda, Jon (Actor)
c/o Staff Member *Anthem Entertainment*
9595 Wilshire Blvd
Suite 900
Los Angeles, CA 90212-2509, USA

Sedaka, Neil (Musician)
Sedaka Music
201 E 66th St #3N
New York, NY 10021, USA

Sedar, Ed (Athlete, Baseball Player)
8 SLake Ave
Third Lake, IL 60030-8431, USA

Sedaris, Amy (Actor)
c/o Sarah Fargo *Paradigm (NY)*
360 Park Ave S Fl 16
New York, NY 10010, USA

Sedaris, David (Comedian, Writer)
c/o Staff Member *Little, Brown & Co.*
237 Park Ave
15th Floor
New York, NY 10017, USA

Seddon, Dr Rhea M (Astronaut)
1709 Shagbark Trl
Murfreesboro, TN 37130-1136, USA

Seddon, Margaret Rhea (Astronaut)
1709 Shagbark Trail
Murfreesboro, TN 37130, USA

Seddon, M Rhea
1709 Shagbark Trail
Murfreesboro, TN 37130, USA

Sedelmaier, Joe (Cartoonist)
Sedelmaier Film Productions
858 W Armitage Ave #267
Chicago, IL 60614-4370, USA

Sedgman, Frank (Tennis Player)
28 Bolton Ave
Hampton, VIC 3188, AUSTRALIA

Sedgwick, Bill (Race Car Driver)
33056 Acklins Ave.
Acton, CA 93510, USA

Sedgwick, Kyra (Actor)
2800 Glendowe Ave
Los Angeles, CA 90027, USA

Sedgworth, Bill
1811 Volusia Ave.
Daytona Beach, FL 32015

Sedin, Daniel (Athlete, Hockey Player)
C A A Hockey
204-822 11 Ave SW
Attn J P Barry
Calgary, AB T2R OES, Canada

Sedin, Henrik (Athlete, Hockey Player)
C A A Hockey
204-822 11 Ave SW
Attn J P Barry
Calgary, AB T2R OES, Canada

Sedlacek, Shawn (Athlete, Baseball Player)
11008 W 131st St
Overland Park, KS 66213, USA

Sedlbauer, Ron (Athlete, Hockey Player)
3021 Woodland Park Dr
Burlington, ON L7N 1K8, Canada

Sedney, Jules (Prime Minister)
Maystreet 24
Paramaribo, SARINAME

Sedoris, Chris (Athlete, Football Player)
7500 Turner Ridge Rd
Crestwood, KY 40014, USA

Seduction (Music Group)
c/o Staff Member *Diva Central Inc*
7510 W Sunset Blvd Ste 1445
Los Angees, CA 90046, USA

Sedykh, Yuri G (Athlete, Track Athlete)
Russian Light Athletics Federation
Luzhnetskaya Nab 8
Moscow, RUSSIA

See, Carolyn (Writer)
17339 Tramonto Dr #303
Pacific Palisades, CA 90272, USA

See, Larry (Athlete, Baseball Player)
1913 W Remington Dr
Chandler, AZ 85286-6231, USA

See, Marshall (Athlete, Basketball Player)
1138 S Canal Cir
Camp Verde, AZ 86322, USA

Seear, Beatrice N S (Government Official)
189B Kennington Road
London SE11 6ST, UNITED KINGDOM
(UK)

Seebold, Bill (Race Car Driver)
Motorsports HOF
PO Box 193
Novi, MI 48316-0194, USA

Seed, Huckleberry (Misc)
391 Crestview Dr
Mount Charleston, NV 89124-9229, USA

Seegal, Denise (Business Person)
Liz Claiborne Inc
1441 Broadway
New York, NY 10018, USA

Seeger, Michael
PO Box 1592
Lexington, VA 24450

Seeger, Mike (Composer, Musician)
c/o Staff Member *Forklore Productions*
1671 Appian Way
Santa Monica, CA 90401-3292, USA

Seeger, Pete (Musician, Songwriter)
PO Box 431
Duchess Junction
Beacon, NY 12508, USA

Seehorn, Rhea (Actor)
c/o Randi Ross *Wyckoff and Associates
(LA)*
11350 Ventura Blvd
Suite 100
Studio City, CA 91604-3140, USA

Seelbach, Chris (Athlete, Baseball Player)
347 Greenwood Dr
Hilton Head Island, SC 29928-3126, USA

Seelbach, Chuck (Athlete, Baseball Player)
13800 airhill Rd
Apt 501
Cleveland, OH 60467-8769, USA

Seelenfreund, Alan (Business Person)
McKesson HBOC Inc
1 Post St
San Francisco, CA 94104, USA

Seeler, Uwe (Soccer Player)
HSV
Rothenbaumchaussee 125
Hamburg 20149, GERMANY

Seeley, Andrew (Actor, Musician)
c/o Ellen Drantch-Billet *EDB Management*
1953 Barry Ave
Los Angeles, CA 90025-5381, USA

Seeling, Angelle (Motorcycle Race,
Motorcycle Racer)
Star Performance Suzuki Racing Team
PO Box 1241
Americus, GA 31709, USA

Seely, Jeannie (Music Group, Musician,
Songwriter, Writer)
c/o Staff Member *Tessier-Marsh Talent*
505 Canton Pass
Madison, TN 37115, USA

Seelye, Talcott W (Diplomat)
5510 Pembroke Road
Bethesda, MD 20817, USA

Seema (Actor, Bollywood)
25 Madhavan Nair Road
Mahalingapuram
Chennai, TN 600034, INDIA

Seether (Music Group)
c/o Staff Member *Wind-up Records*
72 Madison Ave Fl 8
New York, NY 10016, USA

Sefcik, Kevin (Athlete, Baseball Player)
16921 Steeplechase Pkwy
Orland Park, IL 60467-8769, USA

Seffrin, John R (Misc)
American Cancer Society
1599 Clifton Road NE
Atlanta, GA 30329, USA

Sefolosha, Thabo (Athlete, Basketball
Player)
910 Colony Dr
Salisbury, MD 21804-8758, USA

Sega, Dr M Ronald
1700 W Plum St Apt 54B
Fort Collins, CO 80521-3802, USA

Segal, Fred (Designer, Fashion Designer)
Fred Segal Jeans
8100 Melrose Ave
Los Angeles, CA 90046, USA

Segal, George (Horse Racer)
US Trotting Association
750 Michigan Ave
Columbus, OH 43215-1191, USA

Segal, George (Actor)
c/o Abe Hoch *A Management*
9107 Wilshire Blvd.
Suite 650
Beverly Hills, CA 90210, USA

Segal, Jonathan
PO Box 3059
Tel Aviv, ISRAEL 61030

Segal, Michael
27 Cyprus Ave Finchley
London, ENGLAND N3 1SS

Segal, Peter (Director, Producer, Writer)
c/o Adam Kanter *Creative Artists Agency
(CAA-LA)*
2000 Ave Of The Stars
Los Angeles, CA 90067, USA

Segal, Uri
MA Artists Mgmt
28 Sheffield Terrace
London W8 7NA, UNITED KINGDOM
(UK)

Segall, Pamela (Actor)
c/o Staff Member *Meghan Schumacher
Management*
13351-D Riverside Dr #387
Sherman Oaks, CA 91423, USA

Seganti, Paolo (Actor)
PFD
Drury House
34-43 Russell St
London W8 7NA, UNITED KINGDOM
(UK)

Ségara, Hélène (Musician)
c/o Staff Member *BG Productions*
10, rue Damrémont
Paris 75918, France

Segel, Jason (Actor, Producer)
c/o Stacy Abrams *Abrams Entertainment*
5225 Wilshire Blvd #515
Suite 515
Los Angeles, CA 90036, USA

Segelke, Herman (Athlete, Baseball
Player)
1833 Kern Mountain Way
Antioch, CA 94531-2513, USA

Seger, Bob (Musician, Songwriter)
c/o Staff Member *Creative Artists Agency
(CAA-LA)*
2000 Ave Of The Stars
Los Angeles, CA 90067, USA

Seger, Shea (Music Group, Musician)
Helter Skelter
Plaza
535 Kings Road
London SW10 0S, UNITED KINGDOM
(UK)

Segerstam, Leif S (Composer)
Garvey & Ivor
59 Lansdowne Place
Hove BN3 1FL, UNITED KINGDOM (UK)

Segreti, Donald (Politician)
387 Timber Ridge Dr
Bartlett, IL 60103-6605, USA

Segrist, Kal (Athlete, Baseball Player)
3813 55th St
Lubbock, TX 79413-4619, USA

Segui, David V (Athlete, Baseball Player)
2740 N 131st St
Kansas, KS 66109-3365, USA

Segui, Diego P (Athlete, Baseball Player)
13421 Leavenworth Rd
Kansas City, KS 66109-3351, USA

Seguignol, Fernando (Athlete, Baseball
Player)
3517 Turenne W^y
Wellin_gton, FL 33449-8061, USA

Seguin, Tyler (Athlete, Hockey Player)
17 Ferncastle Cres
Brampton, ON L7A 3P2, Canada

Segura, Francisco (Pancho) (Tennis
Player)
Rancho La Costa Hotel & Spa
7690 Camino Real
Carlsbad, CA 92009, USA

Segura, Pancho
. La Costa Hotel
Costa Del Mar Rd, Carlsbad 92009

Seguso, Robert (Athlete, Olympic Athlete,
Tennis Player)
3904 Bayside Ct
Bradenton, FL 34210-4107, USA

Sehorn, Jason (Athlete, Football Player)
5314 Round Meadow Rd
Hidden Hills, CA 91302, USA

Seibel, Phil (Athlete, Baseball Player)
351 Woodland Dr
Driftwood, TX 85251-5082, USA

Seibert, Kurt (Athlete, Baseball Player)
95 Amberwood Cir
Irmo, SC 29063-7942, USA

Seibou, Ali (General, President)
Chairman's Office
National Orientation Higher Council
Niamey, NIGER

Seidel, Frederick (Writer)
c/o Staff Member *Farrar, Straus and
Giroux*
18 W 18th St
New York, NY 10011-4607, USA

Seidel, Guenter (Athlete, Horse Racer,
Olympic Athlete)
2108 Oxford Ave
Cardiff By The Sea, CA 92007-1820, USA

Seidel, Kelly
8441 Balboa Blvd. #36
Northridge, CA 91325

Seidel, Martie (Music Group, Musician)
Senior Mgmt
9465 Wilshire Blvd
Beverly Hills, CA 90212, USA

Seidelman, Susan (Director)
Michael Shedler
225 W 34th St #1012
New York, NY 10122, USA

Seidenberg, Dennis (Athlete, Hockey
Player)
20073 N 85th Pl
Scottsdale, AZ 85255-6301

Seidenberg, Ivan G (Business Person)
Bell Atlantic Corp
1095 Ave of Americas
New York, NY 10036, USA

Seidler, David (Writer)
c/o Jeff Aghassi *Jeff Aghassi Management*
2810 S. Bedford St.
Los Angeles, CA 90034, USA

Seidman, L William (Business Person,
Government Official)
1025 Connecticut Ave NW #800
Washington, DC 20036, USA

Seifert, Bill (Race Car Driver)
17007 Jettson Rd
Cornelius, NC 28031, United States

Seifert, George G (Athlete, Coach,
Football Coach, Football Player,
Sportscaster)
1276 Estate Dr
Los Altos, CA 94024, USA

Seifert, Mike (Athlete, Football Player)
1605 E Bristlecone Dr
Hartland, WI 53029, USA

Seifert, Mike (Athlete, Football Player)
5610N Lac Verde Cir
Green Lake, WI 54941, USA

Seigenthaler, John L (Television Host)

Seigner, Emmanuelle (Actor)
Artmedia
20 Ave Rapp
Paris 75007, FRANCE

Seigner, Mathilde (Actor)
Artmedia
20 Ave Rapp
Paris 75007, FRANCE

Seignoret, Clarence H A (President)
24 Cork St
Roseau, DOMINICA

Seiheimer, Rick (Athlete, Baseball Player)
401 Hickory Hollow Ln
Brenham, TX 77833, USA

Seikaly, Rony (Athlete, Basketball Player)
400 Alton Rd Apt 3201
Miami Beach, FL 33139-6756, USA

Seilacher, Adolf (Geophysicist, Physicist)
Yale University
Geology/Geophysics Laboratory
New Haven, CT 06520, USA

Seilheimer, Rick (Athlete, Baseball Player)
401 Hickory Hollow Ln
Brenham, TX 77833-9240, USA

Seiling, Ric (Athlete, Hockey Player)
71 Christina Dr
North Chili, NY 14514-9754

Seiling, Rod (Athlete, Hockey Player)
Ontario Racing Commission
400-10 Carlson Crt
Toronto, ON M9W 6L2, Canada

Seinfeld, Evan (Actor, Adult Film Star, Musician)
14813 Huston St
Van Nuys, CA 91403, USA

Seinfeld, Jerry (Actor, Comedian)
c/o George Shapiro *Shapiro/West & Associates*
141 El Camino Dr #205
Beverly Hills, CA 90212, USA

Seinfeld, Jessica (Chef)
2971 Bellmore Ave
Bellmore, NY 11710, USA

Seinfeld, John H (Engineer)
363 Patrician Way
Pasadena, CA 91105, USA

Seiple, Larry (Athlete, Football Player)
1361 W Golfview Dr
Pembroke Pines, FL 33026, USA

Seitz, Frederick (Educator, Politician)
Rockefeller University
Physics Dept
1230 York Ave
New York, NY 10021, USA

Seitz, Raymond G H (Diplomat)
Lehman Brothers International
1 Broadgate
London EC2M 7HA, UNITED KINGDOM (UK)

Seitzer, Kevin (Athlete, Baseball Player)
Mac-N-Seitz
13705 Holmes Rd
Kansas City, MO 66224-4211, USA

Seiwald, Robert J (Inventor)
59 Burnside Ave
San Francisco, CA 94131-2904, USA

Seixas, E Victor (Vic) Jr (Tennis Player)
8 Harbor Point Dr #207
Mill Valley, CA 94941, USA

Seixas, Vic
8 Harbor Point Dr. #207
Mill Valley, CA 94941

Seizinger, Katja (Skier)
Rudolf-Epp-Str 48
Eberbach 69412, GERMANY

Seka
1122 White Rock
Dixon, IL 60121

Sela, Michael (Doctor, Misc)
Weizmann Science Institute
Immunology Dept
Rehovot 76100, ISRAEL

Selanne, Teemu (Athlete, Hockey Player)
Thompson, Dorfman, Sweatman
PO Box 639 Stn Main
Attn: Donald Baizley
Winnipeg, MB R3C 2K6, Canada

Selby, Bill (Athlete, Baseball Player)
228 Eunice Bonner Rd
Waynesboro, MS 38637-9064, USA

Selby, Brit (Athlete, Hockey Player)
174 Divadale Dr
East York, ON M4G 2P6, Canada

Selby, David (Actor)
International Creative Mgmt
8942 Wilshire Blvd #219
Beverly Hills, CA 90211, USA

Selby, Philip (Composer)
Hill Cottage
Via 1 Maggio 93
Rignano Flaminio
Rome 00068, ITALY

Seldes, Marian (Actor)
c/o Clifford Stevens *Paradigm (NY)*
360 Park Ave S Fl 16
New York, NY 10010, USA

Seldin, Donald W (Doctor)
Texas Southwestern Medical Center
5323 Harry Hines Blvd
Dallas, TX 75390, USA

Sele, Aaron H (Athlete, Baseball Player)
11 Honors Dr
Newport Beach, CA 92660-42900, USA

Seles, Monica (Athlete, Olympic Athlete, Tennis Player)
2895 Dick Wilson Dr
Sarasota, FL 34240, USA

Seley, Jason (Artist)
Cornell University
Art Dept
Ithaca, NY 14853, USA

Self, Bill (Athlete, Basketball Player, Coach)
Bill Self's Assists Foundation
1651 Naismith Dr
Lawrence, KS 66045, USA

Self, Steve (Athlete, Hockey Player)
744 River Rd S
Peterborough, ON K9J 1E8, Canada

Self, Todd (Athlete, Baseball Player)
10238 Cardiff Dr
Keithville, LA 71111-6352, USA

Selfridge, Andy (Athlete, Football Player)
3400 Dunscroft Ct
Keswick, VA 22947, USA

Selig, Bud (Baseball Player, Misc)
Baseball Commissioner's Office
1480 E Standish Pl
Bayside, WI 53217-1958, USA

Seliger, Mark (Photographer)
Little Brown
3 Center Plaza
Boston, MA 02108, USA

Seligman, Martin E P (Doctor)
University of Pennsylvania
Psychology Dept
Philadelphia, PA 19104, USA

Selig-Prieb, Wendy (Baseball Player)
Milwaukee Brewers
6620 N Lake Dr
Milwaukee, WI 53217-4245, USA

Selivanov, Alexander (Athlete, Hockey Player)
1379 80th St S
Saint Petersburg, FL 33707-2722

Selkirk, George N (Government Official)
Rose Lawn Coppice
Wimborne
Dorset, UNITED KINGDOM (UK)

Selkoe, Dennis J (Doctor)
Brigham & Women's Hospital
221 Longwood Ave
Boston, MA 02115, USA

Selldorf, Annabelle (Architect)
Selldorf Architects
62 White St
New York, NY 10013, USA

Selleca, Connie (Actor)
c/o Chuck Binder *Binder & Associates*
1465 Lindacrest Dr
Beverly Hills, CA 90210, USA

Selleck, Tom (Actor, Producer, Writer)
c/o Bettye McCartt *Agency for Artists*
9939 Robbins Dr
Beverly Hills, CA 90212, USA

Seller, Peg (Coach, Swimmer)
72 Monkswood Crescent
Newmarket, ON L3Y 2K1, CANADA

Sellers, Brad (Athlete, Basketball Player)
682 Arbor Way
Aurora, OH 44202-9113, USA

Sellers, Franklin (Religious Leader)
Reformed Episcopal Church
2001 Frederick Road
Baltimore, MD 21228, USA

Sellers, Goldie (Athlete, Football Player)
13425 Braun Rd
Golden, CO 80401, USA

Sellers, Jeff (Athlete, Baseball Player)
833 S 224th Ln
Buckeye, AZ 29640-7692, USA

Sellers, Justin (Athlete, Baseball Player)
Double Diamond Sports Management
7640 NW 79th Ave Apt L8
Tamarac, Fl 3321-2868, USA

Sellers, Larry (Actor)
c/o Vaughn Hart *Vaughn Hart & Associates*
12304 Santa Monica Blvd
Suite 111
Los Angeles, CA 90025-2586, USA

Sellers, Michael (Actor, Producer, Writer)
c/o Staff Member *Quantum Entertainment*
209 E Alameda Ave #203
Burbank, CA 91502-2674, USA

Sellers, Mike (Athlete, Football Player)
7526 Totten ham Dr
White Plains, MD 20695-4437, USA

Sellers, Piers J (Astronaut)
16011 Craighurst Dr
Houston, TX 77059-6424, USA

Sellers, Robert (Writer)
c/o Staff Member *Pollinger Limited*
9 Staple Inn
Holborn
London WC1V 7QH, UK

Sellers, Ron F (Athlete, Football Player)
137 Via Paradisio
Palm Beach Gardens, FL 33418, USA

Sellers, Shane (Horse Racer)
326 Orange Ave
Lake Arthur, LA 70549-4428, USA

Sellers, Victoria
1927 Vista Del Mar Ave.
Hollywood, CA 90068

Sellick, Phyllis (Musician)
Beverly House
29A Ranelagh Ave
Barnes SW13 0BN, UNITED KINGDOM (UK)

Sells, Dave (Athlete, Baseball Player)
700 Blue Ridge Ln
Vacaville, CA 95688-2023, USA

Selmon, Dewey W (Athlete, Football Player)
2725 S Berry Rd
Norman, OK 73072, USA

Selmon, Lucious (Athlete, Coach, Football Player)
1 AllTell Stadium Pl
Jacksonville, FL 32202, USA

Selten, Reinhard (Nobel Prize Laureate)
Hardtweg 23
Konigswinter, Germany D-53639, USA

Selten, Reinhard (Nobel Prize Laureate)
Hardtweg 23
Konigswinter 53639, GERMANY

Seltz, Rolland (Basketball Player)
3328 Oswego Heights Road
Shoreview, MN 55126, USA

Seltz, Rollie (Athlete, Basketball Player)
3328 Owasso Heights Rd
Saint Paul, MN 55126-4149, USA

Seltzer, David (Director, Producer, Writer)
c/o Dan Aloni *WmE2 (WMA-LA)*
1 William Morris Pl
Beverly Hills, CA 90212, USA

Selverstone, Katy (Actor)
c/o Jason Priluck *Agency Group Ltd, The (LA)*
1880 Century Park E
Suite 711
Los Angeles, CA 90067, USA

Selvy, Frank (Athlete, Baseball Player)
125 Mount Vista Ave
Greenville, sc 29605-1120, USA

Selvy, Franklin D (Frank) (Athlete, Basketball Player)
18 Oglethrope Ln
Hilton Head Island, SC 29926, USA

Selway, Phil (Musician)
8017 Fareholm Dr
Los Angeles, CA 90046, USA

Selwood, Brad (Athlete, Hockey Player)
77 Colonel Wayling Blvd
Sharon, ON LOG 1VO, Canada

Selwyn, Zach (Actor)
c/o Kenneth (Kenny) Goodman *Schiff Company, The*
9465 Wilshire Blvd
Suite 480
Beverly Hills, CA 90212, USA

Selya, Bruce M (Judge)
US Court of Appeals
US Courthouse
Providence, RI 02903, USA

Selzer, Richard (Doctor, Writer)
6 Saint Ronan Terrace
New Haven, CT 06511, USA

Selznick, Albie
2800 Nielsen Way
Santa Monica, CA 90405-4025

Selznick, Brian (Writer)
c/o Jason Dravis *Monteiro Rose Dravis Agency*
4370 Tujunga
Suite 145
Studio City, CA 91604, USA

Semak, Alexander (Athlete, Hockey Player)
305 W 13th St Apt 1J
New York, NY 10014-1223

Semak, Michael W (Photographer)
1796 Spruce Hill Road
Pickering, ON L1V 1S4, CANADA

Sembello, Michael (Musician, Songwriter)
105 Shad Row #B
Piermont, NY 10968, USA

Sember, Mike (Athlete, Baseball Player)
285 S Country Club Blvd
Boca Raton, FL 33487-2326, USA

Sembier, Melvin F (Diplomat)
Sembler Co
5858 Central Ave
Saint Petersburgh, FL 33707, USA

Semchuk, Thomas "Brandy" (Athlete, Hockey Player)
1242 E Champlain Dr Apt 201
Fresno, CA 93720-5071

Semel, David (Director)
c/o Staff Member *3 Arts Entertainment Inc*
9460 Wilshire Blvd
7th Floor
Beverly Hills, CA 90210, USA

Semel, Terry (Business Person)
Yahoo! Inc
701 First Ave
Sunnyvale, CA 94089, USA

Semenova, Juliana (Basketball Player)
Zalalela 4-35
Riga 1010, LATVIA

Semenyaka, Lyudmila (Ballerina)
Bolshoi Theater
Teatralnaya Pl 1
Moscow 103009, RUSSIA

Semin, Alexander (Athlete, Hockey Player)
3133 N Piedmont St
Arlington, VA 22207-5330

Seminara, Frank (Athlete, Baseball Player)
8029 Harbor View Ter
Brooklyn, NY 11209-2822, USA

Semiz, Teata (Bowler)
27 Burnside Pl
Haskell, NJ 07420-1003, USA

Semiz, Teata (Bowler)
3131 Kennedy Blvd
North Bergen, NJ 07047, USA

Semizorova, Nina L (Ballerina)
2 Zhukovskaya St
#8
Moscow, RUSSIA

Semjonova, Uljana (Athlete, Basketball Player)
Zalaiela 4-35
Riga 1010, Latvia

Semkow, Jerzy G
Ul Dynasy 6 m 1
Warsaw 00-354, POLAND

Semler, Dean (Cinematographer, Director)
4260 Arcola Ave
Toluca Lake, CA 91602, USA

Semmelrogge, Martin
Terhallestr. II
Munich, GERMANY D-81545

Sempe, Jean-Jacques (Cartoonist)
4 rue de Moulin-Vert
Paris, France F-75014, USA

Sempe, Jean-Jacques (Cartoonist)
Editions Denoel
9 Rue du Cherche-Midi
Paris 75006, FRANCE

Semproch, Ray (Athlete, Baseball Player)
4220 Buechner Ave
Cleveland, OH 44109-5035, USA

Semyonov, Vladilen G (Ballerina)
15/17-504 Roubinshteina St
Saint Petersburg 191002, RUSSIA

sen, Amartya (Nobel Prize Laureate)
Trinity College Attn: Economics Dept
Cambridge, England CB2 1 TQ, USA

Sen, Amartya K (Nobel Prize Laureate)
Trinity College
Economics Dept
Cambridge CB2 1TP, UNITED KINGDOM (UK)

Sen, Moon Moon (Actor)
Ruia Park Flat No 62 'B'
Juhu
Bombay, MS 400 049, INDIA

Sen, Mrinal (Director)
4E Motilal Nehru Road
Culcutta 700029, INDIA

Sen, Riya (Actor, Bollywood)
62-B Ruia Park
Juhu
Mumbai, MS 400049, INDIA

Sen, Sushmita (Actor, Bollywood)
6th Floor Beach Queen
Yari Road Versova Andheri (W)
Mumbai, MS 400061, INDIA

Sena, Dominic (Director)
c/o Robert Newman *WME (LA)*
9601 Wilshire Blvd Fl 3
Beverly Hills, CA 90210, USA

Sena, Suzanne
6310 San Vicente Blvd. #200
Los Angeles, CA 90048

Sendel, Lorri (Stylist)
c/o Staff Member *AFG Management*
Pier 62
Chelsea Piers #203
New York, NY 10011, USA

Sendel, Peter (Athlete)
Zallaer Str 9
Oberhof 98599, GERMANY

Sendel, Sergio (Actor)
c/o Staff Member *Televisa*
Blvd Adolfo Lopez Mateos 232
Colonia San Angel INN
DF CP 01060, MEXICO

Senderens, Alain (Chef)
Restaurant Lucas Carton
9 Place de la Madeleine
Paris 75008, FRANCE

Sendlein, Robin (Athlete, Football Player)
14737 E Mark Ln
Scottsdale, AZ 85262, USA

Senff, Dina (Nida) (Swimmer)
DW Coutuner-Senff
Praam 122
Amstelveen 1186 TL, NETERLANDS

Senior, Peter (Golfer)
c/o Staff Member *Pro Golfers Association (PGA) Tour*
112 TPC Blvd
Ponte Vedra Beach, FL 32082, USA

Senn, Adam (Model)
c/o Staff Member *NEXT*
188 rue de Rivoli
Paris 75001, FRANCE

Senneker, Bob (Race Car Driver)
PO Box 140984
Grand Rapids, MI 49514, USA

Sennett, Susan (Actor)
1201 Oak Ave
Manhattan Beach, CA 90266, USA

Sennewald, Robert W (General)
212 Wolfe Street
Alexandria, VA 22314-3858, USA

Senser, Joe (Athlete, Football Player)
Joe Senser's Sports Grill
4217 W 80th St
Bloomington, MN 55437, USA

Sensiba, Dave (Race Car Driver)
Throop Motorsports Racing
2775 Horseshoe Dr.
Grandville, MI 49418, USA

Sensibaugh, Mike (Athlete, Football Player)
18414 Woodlands Terrace Dr
Glencoe, MO 63038, USA

Senske, Sara (Race Car Driver)
Lynx Racing
5806 Saloma Ave.
Van Nuys, CA 91411, USA

Sentelle, David B (Judge)
US Court of Appeals
333 Constitution Ave NW
Washington, DC 20001, USA

Senter, Marc (Actor)
c/o Jennifer Shoucair Weaver *S/W Pr Shop*
142 S Cresent Dr
Beverly Hills, CA 90212, USA

Sentes, Rick (Athlete, Hockey Player)
2166 Abbott St
Kelowna, BC V1 Y 1C7, Canada

Seoane, Manny (Athlete, Baseball Player)
8912 Southbay Dr
Tampa, FL 33603-2826, USA

Seow, Yit Kin (Musician)
8 North Terrace
London SW3 2BA, UNITED KINGDOM (UK)

Sepe, Crescenzio Cardinal (Religious Leader)
Piazza della Citta Leonina 9
Rome 00193, ITALY

Seper, Zeynep (Beauty Pageant Winner)
Rue de Dilbeeck 200
Brussels B-1082, BELGIUM

Seppa, Jyrki (Athlete, Hockey Player)
Vetiex Oy Silvolantie 3
Kerimaki, 58410, Finland

Septimus, Jake (Producer)
c/o Staff Member *Creative Artists Agency (CAA-LA)*
2000 Ave Of The Stars
Los Angeles, CA 90067, USA

Sepulveda, Charlie (Musician)
Ralph Mercado Mgmt
568 Broadway #608
New York, NY 10012, USA

Sequeira, Luis (Biologist, Scientist)
10 Appomattox Court
Madison, WI 53705, USA

Serafini, Dan (Athlete, Baseball Player)
430 Alamosa Dr
Sparks, NV 89441-8583, USA

Serafini, Ron (Athlete, Hockey Player)
Morgan and Milzow Realty
25 S Main St
Clarkston, MI 48346-1525, USA

Serafini, Tito A (Biologist)
University of California
Neurobiology Dept
San Francisco, CA 94143, USA

Serafinowitz, Peter (Actor, Producer, Writer)
c/o Peter Principato *Principato/Young Management*
9465 Wilshire Blvd
Suite 430
Beverly Hills, CA 90212, USA

Serano, Greg (Actor)
c/o Erik Kritzer *Kritzer Levine Wilkins Entertainment (KLWG)*
11872 La Grange Ave
1st Floor
Los Angeles, CA 90025, USA

Seraphin, Oliver (Prime Minister)
44 Green's Lane
Goodwill, DOMINICA

Serbedzija, Rade (Actor)
P F D
Drury House 34-43 Russell St
London WC2B 5HA, UNITED KINGDOM (UK)

Serebrier, Jose (Composer)
20 Queensgate Gardens
London SW7 5LZ, UNITED KINGDOM (UK)

Serebrov, Alexander A (Misc)
Potchta Kosmonavtov
Moskovskoi Oblasti
Syvisdny Goroduk 141160, RUSSIA

Serembus, John (Misc)
Upholsterers Union
25 N 4th St
Philadelphia, PA 19106, USA

Serendipity Singers, The (Music Group)
349 S Main Street
Wauconda, IL 60084-1966

Sereno, Paul (Scientist)
University of Chicago
Paleontology Dept
Chicago, IL 60537, USA

Seresin, Michael (Cinematographer)
59 North Wharf Road
London W2 1LA, UNITED KINGDOM (UK)

Sereys, Jacques
84 bd. Malesherbes
Paris, FRANCE F-75008

Sergei, Ivan (Actor)
c/o Joanna (Joanie) Burstein *Burstein Company, The*
15304 Sunset Blvd
suite 208
Pacific Palisades, CA 90272, USA

Serig, Jennifer (Designer, Fashion Designer)
c/o Staff Member *Perception Public Relations LLC*
3940 Laurel Canyon Blvd
Suite 169
Studio City, CA 91604, USA

Seriki, Hakeem (Chamillionaire) (Musician)
c/o Sara Ramaker *Paradigm (LA)*
360 N Crescent Dr
North Bldg
Beverly Hills, CA 90210, USA

Serious, Yahoo (Actor)
12/33 E Crescent St
McMahons Point, NSW 2060, AUSTRALIA

Serkin, Peter A (Musician)
Manne Music College
150 W 85th St
New York, NY 10024, USA

Serkis, Andy (Actor)
c/o Larry Taube *Principal Entertainment (LA)*
1964 Westwood Blvd #400
Los Angeles, CA 90025, USA

Serlemitsos, Peter J (Astronomer)
BBXRT Project
Goddard Space Flight Center
Greenbelt, MD 20771, USA

Serlenga, Nikki (Athlete, Olympic Athlete, Soccer Player)
1489 Hawthorne Ave NW
Atlanta, GA 30309-2229, USA

Sermon, Eric (Musician)
Richard Walters
1800 Argyle Ave
#408
Los Angeles, CA 90028, USA

Serna, Assumpta (Actor)
8306 Wilshire Blvd #438
Beverly Hills, CA 90211, USA

Serna, Diego (Soccer Player)
Los Angeles Galaxy
1010 Rose Bowl Dr
Pasadena, CA 91103, USA

Serna, Paul (Athlete, Baseball Player)
32421 Outrigger Way
Laguna Niguel, CA 92656-3329, USA

Serna, Pepe (Actor)
127 Ruby Ave
Newport Beach, CA 92662, USA

Serota, Nicholas A (Director)
Tate Gallery
Millbank
London SW1P 4RG, UNITED KINGDOM (UK)

Serowik, Jeff (Athlete, Hockey Player)
371 Davisville Rd
East Falmouth, MA 02536-7085

Serpa, Joseph (Stylist)
c/o Staff Member *Ennis*
119 Braintree St
Boston, MA 02134, USA

Serra, Eduardo (Cinematographer)
c/o Staff Member *United Talent Agency (UTA)*
9336 Civic Center Dr
Beverly Hills, CA 90210, USA

Serra, Pablo (Writer)
c/o Gabriel Blanco *Gabriel Blanco Iglesias (Mexico)*
Rio Balsas 35-32
Colonia Cuauhtemoc
DF 06500, Mexico

Serra, Richard (Artist)
173 Duane St
New York, NY 10013, USA

Serrano, Jimmy (Athlete, Baseball Player)
2943 E Erika Ct
Grand Junction, CO 81504-6963, USA

Serrano, Juan (Musician)
Prince/SF Productions
1450 Southgate Ave #206
Daly City, CA 94015, USA

Serrano, Nestor (Actor)
c/o Danielle Galiana-Allman *InnerAct Entertainment*
141 Barrington Ave #E
Los Angeles, CA 90049, USA

Serratos, Christian (Actor)
c/o Katie Rhodes *Untitled Entertainment (LA)*
350 S. Beverly Dr #200
Beverly Hills, CA 90212, USA

Serrauot, Michel
201 rue Du Faubourg-St.-Honore
Paris, FRANCE F-75008

Serre, Jean-Pierre (Mathematician)
6 Ave de Montespan
Paris 75116, FRANCE

Serreau, Coline (Director)
Artmedia
20 Ave Rapp
Paris 75007, FRANCE

Serrin, James B (Mathematician)
4422 Dupont Ave S
Minneapolis, MN 55409, USA

Serum, Gary (Athlete, Baseball Player)
10525 Hidden Oaks Ln N
Champlin, MN 55316-3045, USA

Servais, Scott (Athlete, Baseball Player, Olympic Athlete)
4409 Triple Eagle Trl
Larkspur, CO 80118-5744, USA

Servan-Schreiber, Jean-Claude (Journalist)
147 Bis Rue d'Alesia
Paris 75014, FRANCE

Server, Josh (Actor)
c/o Mike Eistenstadt *Amsel, Eisenstadt & Frazier Talent Agency (AEF)*
5055 Wilshire Blvd
Suite 860
Los Angeles, CA 90036-6108, USA

Servia, Oriol (Race Car Driver)
PWR Racing
4001 Methanol Lane
Indianapolis, IN 46268, USA

Service, Scott (Athlete, Baseball Player)
7959 Gaines Rd
Cincinnati, OH 45252-2122, USA

Serviss, Tom (Athlete, Hockey Player)
184 Comus Pl
Kelowna, BC V1V 1N2, Canada

Sesa, Moses (General)
Box 42, GIZO
Western Province, Solomon, Islands

Sesame Street
1 Lincoln Plaza
New York, NY 10022

Sessions, Jeff (Politician)
208 Justice Ct NE Apt A
Washington, DC 20002-5788, USA

Sessions, John
4 Windmill St.
London, ENGLAND W1P 1HF

Sessions, Pete (Congressman, Politician)
2233 Rayburn HOB
Washington, DC 20515, USA

Sessions, Ronnie (Musician)
540 Gunson Ridge Rd
Cumberland City, TN 37050, USA

Sessions, William (Politician)
3920 Argyle Ter NW
Washington, DC 20011-5329, USA

Sessions, William S (Judge)
112 E Pecan #2900
San Antonio, TX 78205, USA

Sessler, Gerhard M (Inventor)
Fichtestrasse 30B
Darmstadt, Germany D-64285, USA

Sessler, Gerhard M (Inventor)
Fichtenstra 30B
Darmstadt 64285, GERMANY

Setari, Robert (Actor)
c/o Patty Stevens *Vessel Entertainment*
10989 Bluffside Dr #3210
Studio City, CA 91604

Seter, Mordecai (Composer)
1 Kamy St
Ramat Aviv
Tel-Aviv, ISRAEL

Seth, Joshua (Actor)
c/o Staff Member *Sutton Barth & Vennari Inc*
145 S Fairfax
Suite 310
Los Angeles, CA 90036, USA

Seth, Oliver (Judge)
US Court of Appeals
PO Box 1
Santa Fe, NM 87504, USA

Seth, Vikram (Writer)
Phoenix House
Orion House
5 Upper St
London WC2H 9EA, UNITED KINGDOM (UK)

Sethi, Parmeet (Actor, Bollywood)
702/B-1 Sundervan
Off Lokhandwala Road Andheri (W)
Mumbai, MS 400053, INDIA

Setlow, Richard B (Biologist)
4 Beachland Ave
East Quogue, NY 11942, USA

Settle, John (Athlete, Football Player)
2626 Placid St
Fitchburg, WI 53711, USA

Settle, Matthew (Actor)
c/o Jeb Brandon *Kritzer Levine Wilkins Entertainment (KLWG)*
11872 La Grange Ave
1st Floor
Los Angeles, CA 90025, USA

Settles, Sandra (Stylist)
423 27th St
San Francisco, CA 94131-1916, USA

Settles, Tawambi (Athlete, Football Player)
4204 Rogers Rd
Chattanooga, TN 37411, USA

Setzer, Brian (Music Group, Musician)
c/o Staff Member *WmE2 (WMA-LA)*
1 William Morris Pl
Beverly Hills, CA 90212, USA

Setzer, Dennis (Race Car Driver)
PO Box 665
Dawsonville, GA 30534-0476, USA

Setziol, LeRoy I (Roy) (Artist)
30450 Moriah Lane
Sheridan, OR 97378, USA

Setzler, Steve (Athlete, Football Player)
1S767 Hemlock Ct
Saint Paul, MN 55124-7145, USA

Seubert, Rich (Athlete, Football Player)
D1891 County Road C
Stratford, WI 54484, USA

Seurer, Frank (Athlete, Football Player)
16168 S Brookfield St
Olathe, KS 66062, USA

Sevani, Adam (Actor)
c/o Christian Donatelli *Schiff Company, The*
9465 Wilshire Blvd
Suite 480
Beverly Hills, CA 90212, USA

Sevastyanov, Vitayi I (Misc)
Potchta Kosmonavtov
Moskovskoi Oblasti
Syvisdny Goroduk 141160, RUSSIA

Sevcik, Jaroslav (Athlete, Hockey Player)
New Bridge Academy
Attn: Hockey Instructor
409 Glendale Dr
Lower Sacville, NS B4C 2T6, CANADA

Sevcik, John (Athlete, Baseball Player)
10107 Shinnecock Hills Dr
Austin, TX 78747-1318, USA

Sevendust (Music Group)
c/o Staff Member *TVT Records*
23 E 4th St
3rd Floor
New York, NY 10003, USA

Severance, Joan (Actor)
c/o Steven Jensen *Independent Group, The*
6363 Wilshire Blvd
Suite 115
Los Angeles, CA 90048, USA

Severeid, Suzanne (Actor, Model)
PO Box 4171
Malibu, CA 90264, USA

Severinsen, Al (Athlete, Baseball Player)
133 Warren Ave
Mystic, CT 06355, USA

Severinsen, Carl H (Doc) (Musician)
11812 San Vicente Blvd
Suite 200
Los Angeles, CA 90049-6622, USA

Severson, Jeff (Athlete, Football Player)
20625 Sierra Elena
Murrieta, CA 92562, USA

Severson, Kimberly (Athlete, Horse Racer, Olympic Athlete)
631 Dobby Creek Rd
Scottsville, VA 24590-3026, USA

Severson, Rich (Athlete, Baseball Player)
1036 N 145th Cir
Omaha, NE 68154-1108, USA

Severyn, Brent (Athlete, Hockey Player)
4521 Ave bury Dr
Plano, TX 75024-7358

Sevier, Corey (Actor)
c/o Sheila Wenzel *Innovative Artists (LA)*
1505 10th St
Santa Monica, CA 90401, USA

Sevigny, Chloe (Actor)
c/o Daniel (Danny) Sussman *Brillstein Entertainment Partners*
9150 Wilshire Blvd #350
Beverly Hills, CA 90212, USA

Sevilla, Carmen
Plaza de Pablo Ruiz Picasso s/n Torre
Picasso Planto 36
Madrid, SPAIN 2800

Sevsec, Pedro (Actor)
c/o Staff Member *Telemundo*
2470 West 8th Avenue
Hialeah, FL 33010, USA

Sevy, Jeff (Athlete, Football Player)
P.O. Box 2177
Loomis, CA 95650, USA

Seward, George C (Attorney, Attorney General, General)
Seward & Kissel
1 Battery Park Plaza
New York, NY 10004, USA

Sewell, George (Actor)
Peter Charlesworth
68 Old Brompton Road
London SW7 3LQ, UNITED KINGDOM (UK)

Sewell, Rufus (Actor)
c/o Gene Parseghian *Parseghian Planco LLC*
322 8th Ave
Suite 601
New York, NY 10001, USA

Sewell, Steve (Athlete, Football Player)
15918 E Crestridge Pl
Centennial, CO 80015, USA

Sewell, Terri (Congressman, Politician)
1133 Longworth HOB
Washington, DC 20515, USA

Seweryn, Andrzej (Actor)
Comedie Francaise
Place Colette
Paris 75001, FRANCE

Sex Pistols
c/o Mitch Schneider *Mitch Schneider Organization (MSO)*
14724 Ventura Blvd #410
Sherman Oaks, CA 91403, USA

Sexsmith, Ron (Musician)
c/o Staff Member *Paradigm (Monterey)*
404 W Franklin St
Monterey, CA 93940, USA

Sexson, Richie (Athlete, Baseball Player)
6539 170th Pl SE
Bellevue, WA 98642-9260, USA

Sexto, Camilo (Musician)
c/o Staff Member *BMG*
1540 Broadway
New York, NY 10036, USA

Sexton, Brent (Actor)
c/o Staff Member *Greene & Associates*
1901 Avenue Of The Stars Ste 130
Los Angeles, CA 90067, USA

Sexton, Charlie (Musician)
Courage Artists
310 Water St
#201
Vancouver, BC V6B 1B6, CANADA

Sexton, Chris (Athlete, Baseball Player)
7030 Baytowne Dr
Cincinnati, OH 45247-5097, USA

Sexton, Dan (Athlete, Hockey Player)
7683 133rd St W
Apple Valley, MN 55124-7617

Sexton, Jimmy (Athlete, Baseball Player)
2680 Baxter Rd
Wilmer, AL 36587-8225, USA

Sexton, John (Photographer)
291 Calle De Los Agrinemsors
Carmel Valley, CA 93924-9725, USA

Sexton III, Brendan (Actor)
c/o Staff Member *Gersh (LA)*
9465 Wilshire Blvd
Suite 600
Beverly Hills, CA 90212, USA

Seydoux, Geraldine (Biologist)
Johns Hopkins University
Molecular Biology Dept
Baltimore, MD 21218, USA

Seydoux, Lea (Actor)
c/o Dallas Smith *United Agents*
12-26 Lexington St
London W1F OLE, UK

Seyferth, Dietmar (Misc)
Massachusetts Institute of Technology
Chemistry Dept
Cambridge, MA 02139, USA

Seyfried, Amanda (Actor)
3140 Tighlman St #B
PMB 216
Allentown, PA 18104, USA

Seyfried, Gordon (Athlete, Baseball Player)
56428 Lowe Ave
Yucca Valley, CA 92284-1740, USA

Seyler, Athene (Actor)
Coach House
26 Upper Mall Hammersmith
London W8, UNITED KINGDOM (UK)

Seymour, Cara (Actor)
c/o Vanessa Pereira *Artists Independent Management (LA)*
825 Nowita Pl
Venice, CA 90291, USA

Seymour, Caroline (Actor)
Langford Assoc
17 Westfields Ave
London SW13 0AT, UNITED KINGDOM (UK)

Seymour, Carolyn (Actor)
Chasin Agency
8899 Beverly Blvd #716
Los Angeles, CA 90048, USA

Seymour, Jane (Actor, Producer)
c/o Susan Madore *Guttman Associates*
118 S Beverly Dr
Suite 201
Beverly Hills, CA 90212, USA

Seymour, John (Senator)
77655 Iroquois Dr
Indian Wells, CA 92210-6130, USA

Seymour, John (Politician)
77655 Iroquois Dr
Indian Wells, CA 92210-6130, USA

Seymour, Lynn (Ballerina)
Artistes in Action
16 Balderton St
London W1Y 1TF, UNITED KINGDOM (UK)

Seymour, Paul (Athlete, Football Player)
4188 Shoals Dr
Okemos, MI 48864, USA

Seymour, Paul C (Athlete, Football Player)
4188 Shoals Dr
Okemos, MI 48864, USA

Seymour, Richard (Athlete, Football Player)
c/o Eugene Parker *Maximum Sports Management*
6435 W Jefferson Blvd
#197
Fort Wayne, IN 46804, USA

Seymour, Stephanie (Model)
c/o Peg Donegan *Framework Entertainment (LA)*
9057 Nemo St
Suite C
West Hollywood, CA 90069, USA

Seymour, Stephanie K (Judge)
US Court of Appeals
US Courthouse
333 W 4th St
Tulsa, OK 74103, USA

Seymour, Terri (Actor)
c/o Ivo Fischer *WME (LA)*
9601 Wilshire Blvd Fl 3
Beverly Hills, CA 90210, USA

Seynhaeve, Ingrid
111 E. 22nd St. #200
New York, NY 10010

Sezer, Ahmet Necdet (President)
President's Office
Cumhurbaskanlgl Kosku
Cankaya
Ankara, TURKEY

Sfar, Rachid (Prime Minister)
278 Ave de Tervuren
Brussels 1150, BELGIUM

Sfeir, Nasrallah Pierre Cardinal (Religious Leader)
Patriarcat Maronite
Bkerke, LEBANON

Sgouros, Dimitris (Musician)
Tompazi 28 Str
Piraeus 18537, GREECE

Shaback, Nick (Athlete, Basketball Player)
3019 49th St
Apt 2N
Astoria, NY 11103-1315, USA

Shabala, Adam (Athlete, Baseball Player)
6 M St
Streator, IL 60647-7088, USA

Shack, Edward S P (Eddie) (Athlete, Hockey Player)
508 Fairlawn Ave
North York, ON M5M 1V2, Canada

Shack, William A (Misc)
2597 Hilgard Ave
Berkeley, CA 94709, USA

Shackelford, Brian (Athlete, Baseball Player)
2812 N Birch St
McAlester, OK 74501-2412, USA

Shackelford, Don (Athlete, Football Player)
P.O. Box 1468
Lansdale, PA 19446, USA

shackelford, ray (Athlete, Baseball Player)
716 El Toro Rd
Ojai, CA 93023-1756, USA

Shackelford, Ted (Actor)
12305 Valley Heart Dr
Studio City, CA 91604, USA

Shackleford, Brian (Athlete, Baseball Player)
2812 N Birch St
McAlester, OK 74501, USA

Shackleford, Charles (Athlete, Basketball Player)
107 E Peyton Ave Apt 5H
Kinston, NC 28501-4375, USA

Shackleton, Simon (Elite Force) (Musician)
c/o Staff Member *Beatport*
2399 Blake St
Suite 170
Denver, CO 80205, USA

Shackouls, Bobby S (Business Person)
Burlington Resources
5051 Westheimer
Houston, TX 77056, USA

Shadic-Campbell, Lillian (Athlete, Baseball Player)
61 Bloody Hill Rd
Craryville, NY 12521-5101, USA

Shadow (DJ)
Quannum Projects LLC
690 Fifth St #208
San Francisco, CA 94107, USA

Shadyac, Tom (Director)
c/o Dan Aloni *WmE2 (WMA-LA)*
1 William Morris Pl
Beverly Hills, CA 90212, USA

Shaeffer, william (General)
1865 Paseo Del Oro
Colorado Springs, CO 80904-1698, USA

Shafer, Martin (Business Person)
c/o Staff Member *Castle Rock Entertainment*
335 North Maple Dr
Suite 135
Beverly Hills, CA 90210-3867, USA

Shafer, Matthew (Uncle Kracker) (Music Group, Musician)
c/o Jeff Kwatinetz *Prospect Park*
2049 Century Park East
Suite 2550
Century City, CA 90067, USA

Shafer, R Donald (Religious Leader)
Brethren in Christ Church
PO Box 290
Grantham, PA 17027, USA

Shaffer, Akiva (Director, Writer)
c/o Staff Member *Mosaic Media Group*
9200 W. Sunset Blvd
10th Floor
Los Angeles, CA 90069, USA

Shaffer, Atticus (Actor)
c/o Linda Defilippo *D.C. Talent Management*
Prefers to be contacted via email or telephone
Los Angeles, CA 90069, USA

Shaffer, David H (Publisher)
MacMillan
175 5th Ave
New York, NY 10010, USA

Shaffer, Lee (Athlete, Basketball Player)
3822 Nottaway Rd
Durham, NC 27707-5421, USA

Shaffer, Paul (Musician)
Worldwide Pants
Ed Sullivan Theatre
1697 Broadway
New York, NY 10019, USA

Shaffer, Peter (Writer)
Lantz
200 W 57th St
Ste. 503
New York, NY 10019, USA

Shafsky, Janet (Stylist)
3920 O'Malley Rd
Anchorage, AK 99507, USA

Shagari, Alhaji Shehu Usman Aliu (President)
22 Shehu Crescent
PO Box 162 Adarawa
Sokoto State, NIGERIA

Shaggy (Radio Personality)
c/o Staff Member *WPKX*
1331 Main St Fl 4
Springfield, MA 01103, USA

Shah, Idries (Writer)
AP Watt Ltd
26/28 Bedford Row
London WC1R 4HL, UNITED KINGDOM (UK)

Shah, Kiran (Actor)
c/o Michael Henderson *Heresun Management*
4119 West Burbank Blvd.
Burbank, CA 91505, USA

Shah, Satish (Actor, Bollywood, Comedian)
30A Anand Nagar
Forjeet Street
Bombay, MS 400 036, INDIA

Shahan, Gil (Musician)
ICM Artists
40 W 57th St
New York, NY 10019, USA

Shahans, Shirley Bridges (Race Car Driver)
1400 Colorado St.
Boulder City, NV 89005, USA

Shaheen, Jeanne (Politician)
73 Perkins Rd
Madbury, NH 03823-7612, USA

Shahi, Sarah (Actor)
c/o Laura Myones *McKeon-Myones Management*
3500 Olive Ave
Suite 770
Burbank, CA 91505, USA

Shahidi, Yara (Actor)
c/o Laura Ackerman *Persona PR*
8075 W 3rd St
Suite 500
Los Angeles, CA 90048, USA

Shaiman, Marc (Composer)
8476 Brier Dr
West Hollywood, CA 90046, USA

Shakar, Martin (Actor)
118 37th St
New York, NY 10016, USA

Shake, Christi (Model)
Starr Entertainment
2518 Lodge Forest Dr
Baltimore, MD 21219, USA

Shakes, Paul (Athlete, Hockey Player)
RR4
Stayner, ON LOM 1SO, Canada

Shakespeare, Frank J Jr (Diplomat, Television Host)
303 Coast Blvd
La Jolla, CA 92037, USA

Shakira (Musician)
c/o Ceci Kurzman *Nexus Management Group*
220 W 42nd St
#4
New York, NY 10036, USA

Shakur, Kula
39-A Gramercy Park N. #1-C
New York, NY 10010

Shakurov, Sergei K (Actor)
Bibliotechnava Str 27
#94
Moscow 109544, RUSSIA

Shalala, Donna (Politician)
8565 Old Cutler Rd
Coral Gables, FL 33143-6217, USA

Shalala, Donna (Secretary)
University of Miami
President's Office
Coral Gables, FL 33124, USA

Shalamar
707 18th Ave. So.
Nashville, TN 37203

Shales, Thomas W (Journalist)
Washington Post
Editorial Dept
1150 15th St NW
Washington, DC 20071, USA

Shales, Tom
1650 Kirby Rd.
McLean, VA 22101

Shalets, Victoria (Actor)
c/o Angharad Wood *Tavistock Wood Management*
32 Tavistock St
London WC2B 5HA, UK

Shalhoub, Tony (Actor)
c/o Mary Goldberg *Mary Goldberg Management*
4158 Grand Ave
Ojai, CA 93023, USA

Shal-Houd, Tony
9560 Wilshire Blvd. #516
Beverly Hills, CA 90212

Shalim (Musician)
c/o Staff Member *Sony Music Miami*
605 Lincoln Rd Fl 7
Miami Beach, FL 33139, USA

Shalit, Gene (Critic)
NBC-TV
News Dept
30 Rockefeller Plaza
New York, NY 10112, USA

Shallow, Parvati (Reality TV Star)
c/o Ken Jacobson *Ken Jacobson Management*
Preferred to be contacted by phone or email
Los Angeles, CA 91367, USA

Shamir, Yitzhak (Prime Minister)
Beit Amot Mishpat
8 Shaul Hamelech Blvd
Tel Aviv 64733, ISRAEL

Shamrock, Ken (Actor, Athlete, Wrestler)
c/o Staff Member *UFC*
P.O. Box 26959
Las Vegas, NV 89126-0959, USA

Shamsky, Art (Athlete, Baseball Player)
P.O. Box 1400
New York, NY 10163-1400, USA

Shanahan, Brendan (Athlete, Hockey Player)
47 Saquatucket Bluffs Rd
Harwich Port, MA 02646-2510

Shanahan, Greg (Athlete, Baseball Player)
3883 E Street
Eureka, CA 95503, USA

Shanahan, Mike (Athlete, Coach, Football Coach, Football Player)
20 Cherry Hill Farm Dr
Englewood, CO 80113, USA

Shanahan, Sean (Athlete, Hockey Player)
121 Glen Rd
Toronto, ON M4W 2W1, Canada

Shand, David (Athlete, Hockey Player)
307 N Harris St
Saline, MI 48176-1225

Shand, Remy (Music Group, Musician, Songwriter, Writer)
Universal Records
2550 Victoria Park
Toronto, ON M2J 4A2, CANADA

Shandling, Garry (Actor, Comedian)
c/o Ari Emanuel *WME (LA)*
9601 Wilshire Blvd Fl 3
Beverly Hills, CA 90210, USA

Shandrowsky, Alex (Misc)
Marine Engineer Beneficial Assn
444 N Capitol St NW
Washington, DC 20001, USA

Shane, Bob (Music Group, Musician)
9410 S 46th St
Phoenix, AZ 85044, USA

Shangri-La's, The
27 L'Ambiance Ct
Bardonia, NY 10954

Shanice (Musician)
Richard Walters
1800 Argyle Ave #408
Los Angeles, CA 90028, USA

Shank, Harvey (Athlete, Baseball Player)
201 E Jefferson St
Phoenix, AZ 85004-2412, USA

Shank, Michael (Race Car Driver)
Michael Shank Racing
1386 Fields Ave.
Columbus, OH 43211, USA

Shank, Roger C (Scientist)
Northwestern University
Learning Sciences Institute
Evanston, IL 60201, USA

Shanker, Ravi (Composer, Musician)
17 Warden Court
Gowalia Tank Road
Bonbay 36, INDIA

Shankle, Joel (Athlete, Olympic Athlete, Track Athlete)
16181 Berryvale Ln
Culpeper, VA 22701-5530, USA

Shankley, Amelia
2-4 Noel St.
London, ENGLAND W1V 3RB

Shankman, Adam (Choreographer, Director)
c/o BeBe Lerner *ID Public Relations (ID-LA)*
7060 Hollywood Blvd
8th Floor
Los Angeles, CA 90028, USA

Shanks, Michael (Actor, Director, Writer)
c/o Jay Schwartz *Jay D Schwartz & Associates*
3151 Cahuenga Blvd W
Suite 220
Los Angeles, CA 90068, USA

Shan Kuo-Hsi, Paul Cardinal (Religious Leader)
Bishop's House
125 Szu-Wie 3rd Road
Kaohsiung 80203, TAIWAN

Shanley, Jim (Athlete, Football Player)
4 Brookside Dr
Apt D
Walla Walla, WA 99362, USA

Shanley, John Patrick (Director, Writer)
c/o Staff Member *Creative Artists Agency (CAA-LA)*
2000 Ave Of The Stars
Los Angeles, CA 90067, USA

Shannon (Music Group, Musician)
Big Mgmt
226 5th Ave
New York, NY 10001, USA

Shannon (Musician)
c/o Staff Member *Diva Central Inc*
7510 W Sunset Blvd Ste 1445
Los Angees, CA 90046, USA

Shannon, Carver (Athlete, Football Player)
6005 S La Cienega Blvd
Los Angeles, CA 90056, USA

Shannon, Darrin (Athlete, Hockey Player)
Cia rica
23 Victoria St W
Alliston, ON L9R 1S9, Canada

Shannon, Darryl (Athlete, Hockey Player)
18 Landings Dr
Buffalo, NY 14228-1479

Shannon, Mem (Musician, Songwriter)
1048 Hesper Ave
Mateaire, LA 70005-1552, USA

Shannon, Michael (Actor)
c/o Bryna Rifkin *ID PR (LA)*
7060 Hollywood Blvd
8th Floor
Los Angeles, CA 90028, USA

Shannon, Michael E (Business Person)
Ecolab Inc
Ecolab Center
370 Wabasha St N
Saint Paul, MN 55102, USA

Shannon, Mike (Athlete, Baseball Player)
Mike Shannon's Steaks And Seafood
3104 Southwick Dr
Saint Charles, MO 63301-1191, USA

Shannon, Molly (Actor, Comedian)
c/o Steven Levy *Framework Entertainment (LA)*
9057 Nemo St
Suite C
West Hollywood, CA 90069, USA

Shannon, Polly (Actor)
c/o Richard Caplan *Noble Caplan Abrams*
1260 Yonge St
2nd Floor
Toronto, ON M4T 1W6, Canada

Shannon, Randy (Athlete, Football Player)
7420 SW 107th Ave
Apt 7-207
Miami, FL 33173, USA

Shannon, Vicellous (Actor)
c/o Tony Chargin *Ovation Management*
12028 National Blvd
Los Angeles, CA 90064, USA

Shantz, Robert C (Bobby) (Athlete, Baseball Player)
152 E Mount Pleasant Ave
Ambler, PA 19002-4209, USA

Shanze, Michael
Fichtenweg 8
Feldafing, GERMANY D-82340

Shapar, Howard K (Government Official)
PO Box 30242
Bethesda, MD 20824-0242, USA

Shaparo, Cara (Stylist)
c/o Staff Member *Artists by Timothy Priano (CA)*
8447 Wilshire Blvd
#301
Beverly Hills, CA 90211, USA

Shapiro, Ascher H (Engineer)
111 Perkins St
Jamaica Plain, MA 02130, USA

Shapiro, Dani (Writer)
Random House
1745 Broadway
#B1
New York, NY 10019, USA

Shapiro, Debbie (Actor)
Agency for Performing Arts
9200 Sunset Blvd
#900
Los Angeles, CA 90069, USA

Shapiro, Harold T (Educator)
10 Campbelton Circle
Princeton, NJ 08540, USA

Shapiro, Irwin I (Physicist)
17 Lantern Lane
Lexington, MA 02421, USA

Shapiro, James (Doctor)
University of Alberta
114th St & 89th Ave
Edmonton T6G 2M7, CANADA

Shapiro, Jim (Actor)
Legislative Office Building Room 4028
Hartford, CT 06106 -1591, USA

Shapiro, Joel E (Artist)
Pace Gallery
32 E 57th St
New York, NY 10022, USA

Shapiro, Karl (Writer)
211 W 106th St Apt 11C
New York, NY 10025-3688, USA

Shapiro, Kevin (Stylist)
c/o Staff Member *Montana Artists Agency*
9150 Wilshire Blvd Ste 100
Beverly Hills, CA 90212, USA

Shapiro, Lorraine (Stylist)
7416 Waring Ave
Los Angeles, CA 90046, USA

Shapiro, Mark (Commentator)
70 Winding River Trl
Chagrin Falls, OH 44022-3607, USA

Shapiro, Mary L (Government Official)
Securities & Exchange Commission
450 5th St NW
Washington, DC 20001, USA

Shapiro, Maurice M (Physicist)
5809 Nicholson Lane
#801
Rockville, MD 20852, USA

Shapiro, Mel (Writer)
University of California
Theater Film/TV Dept
Los Angeles, CA 90024, USA

Shapiro, Neal (Horse Racer)
296 Sharon Rd
Trenton, NJ 08691, USA

Shapiro, Richard & Esther
617 N. Alta Dr.
Beverly Hills, CA 90210

Shapiro, Robert
2590 Wallingford Dr
Beverly Hills, CA 90210-1073, USA

Shapiro, Robert (Lawyer)
Christensen, Glaser, Fink, Jacobs, Glaser, Weil and Shapiro
10250 Constellation Blvd.
19th Floor
Los Angeles, CA 90067, USA

Shapley, Lloyd S (Economist, Mathematician)
University of California
Economics Dept
Los Angeles, CA 90024, USA

Shapley, Willis (Scientist)
4000 Cathedral Ave NW Apt 512B
Washington, DC 20016-5224, USA

Sharapova, Maria (Athlete, Tennis Player)
c/o Max Eisenbud *IMG (Cleveland)*
1360 E 9th St
Suite 100
Cleveland, OH 44114, USA

Share, Charlie (Athlete, Baseball Player)
12922 Twin Meadows Ct
Saint Louis, MO 63146-1803, USA

Share, Charlie (Chuck) (Athlete, Basketball Player)
12922 Twin Meadows Ct
Saint Louis, MO 63146, USA

Sharif, Omar (Actor)
BP 41
Bougival
Yvelines 78380, FRANCE

Sharipov, Salizhan S (Astronaut)
Lyotchik Cosmonavt Yuri Gagarin
Cosmonaut Training Center 141160
Zvezdny Gorodok
Moskovskoi Oblasti Pot, Russia, USA

Sharipov, Sallzhan S (Cosmonaut)
Potchta Kosmonavtov
Moskovskoi Oblasti
Syvisdny Goroduk 141160, RUSSIA

Sharkey, Ed (Athlete, Football Player)
3615 Russell Rd
Centralia, WA 98531, USA

Sharkey, Jack (Writer)
39927 Chippewa Cir
Murrieta, CA 92562-4109, USA

Sharma, Barbara (Actor)
PO Box 29125
Los Angeles, CA 90029, USA

Sharma, Chris (Athlete)
c/o Staff Member *Sanuk Climbing Team*
9600 Toledo Way
Irvine, CA 92618, USA

Sharma, Kawal (Actor, Bollywood)
A 502 Janak Deep Seven Bangalows
Versova Andheri
Bombay, MS 400 049, INDIA

Sharma, Rakesh (Cosmonaut)
Hindustan Aeronautics
Bangalore, KA 560037, INDIA

Sharma, Robin (Motivational Speaker, Writer)
Sharma Leadership International
92B Scollard St.
2nd Floor
Toronto, ON M5R 1G2, Canada

Sharma, Suraj (Actor)
c/o Jennifer Plante *SLATE Public Relations - NY*
307 7th Ave
Suite 2401
New York, NY 10001, USA

Sharman, Bill (Athlete, Basketball Player)
138 Paseo De Gracia
Redondo Beach, CA 90277-5803, USA

Sharman, Helen (Cosmonaut)
12 Stratton Court
Adelaide Road Surbiton
Surrey, UNITED KINGDOM (UK)

Sharman, Jim (Director)
M&L
49 Daringhurst St
Kings Cross, NSW 2100, AUSTRALIA

Sharmila (Actor, Bollywood)
5 Narsimhan 1st CrossStreet
B.N. Reddy Road T.Nagar
Chennai, TN 600017, INDIA

Sharmili (Actor, Bollywood)
5/A, Karnan Street
SVT Maligai Rangarajapuram
Chennai, TN 600024, INDIA

Sharockman, Ed (Athlete, Football Player)
8955 Thomas Ln
Woodbury, MN 55125, USA

Sharon, Dick (Athlete, Baseball Player)
1143 N 31st St
Billings, MT 59101-0132, USA

Sharp, Bill (Athlete, Baseball Player)
2244 Thornwood Ave
Wilmette, IL 60091-1454, USA

Sharp, Dee Dee (Musician)
William W Witherspoon Esq.
c/o Dione LaRue
125 Union Ave PO Box 7
Lakehurst, NJ 33322, USA

Sharp, Don
80 Castelnau
London, ENGLAND SW13 9EX

Sharp, Kevin (Musician)
Rising Star
1415 River Landing Way
Woodstock, GA 30188, USA

Sharp, Lesley
76 Oxford St.
London, ENGLAND WlN OAX

Sharp, Leslie (Actor)
International Creative Mgmt
8942 Wilshire Blvd
#219
Beverly Hills, CA 90211, USA

Sharp, Linda K (Coach)
Phoenix Mercury
American West Arena
201 E Jefferson St
Phoenix, AZ 85004, USA

Sharp, Marsha (Coach)
Texas Tech University
Athletic Dept
Lubbock, TX 79409, USA

Sharp, Mitchell W (Government Official)
33 Monkland Ave
Ottawa, ON K1S 1Y8, CANADA

Sharp, Phillip A (Nobel Prize Laureate)
36 Fairmont Ave
Newton, MA 02458-2506, USA

Sharp, Phillip A (Nobel Prize Laureate)
36 Fairmont Ave
Newton, MA 02458, USA

Sharp, Preston (Actor, Reality TV Star)
c/o Staff Member *Extreme Makeover: Home Edition*
Endemol Entertainment USA
9225 Sunset Blvd #1100
Los Angeles, CA 90069, USA

Sharp, Richard L (Business Person)
Circuit City Group
9950 Maryland Dr
Richmond, VA 23233, USA

Sharp, Scott (Race Car Driver)
Fernandez Racing
6950 Guion Rd.
#51
Indianapolis, IN 46278, United States

Sharpe, Luis (Athlete, Football Player)
Arizona State Prison
PO Box 3939 - Kingman
DOC #122301
Kingman, AZ 86402, USA

Sharpe, Rochelle P (Journalist)
94 Dudley St
#2
Brookline, MA 02445-5937, USA

Sharpe, Shannon (Athlete, Football Player)
867 Carlton Rdg NE
Atlanta, GA 30342, USA

Sharpe, Sterling (Athlete, Football Player)
81 Running Fox Rd
Columbia, SC 29223, USA

Sharpe, Thomas R (Tom) (Writer)
38 Tunwells Lane
Great Shelford
Cambridge CB2 5LJ, UNITED KINGDOM
(UK)

Sharpe, william (Nobel Prize Laureate)
PO Box 610
Los Altos, CA 94023-0610, USA

Sharpe, William F (Nobel Prize Laureate)
P.O. Box 610
Los Altos, CA 94023-0610, USA

Sharper, Darren (Athlete, Football Player)
11613 Hevereley Ct
Glen Allen, VA 23059, USA

Sharper, Jamie (Athlete, Football Player)
11613 Hevereley Ct
Glen Allen, VA 23059, USA

Sharples, Jeff (Athlete, Hockey Player)
2504 Mahaila Cir
Henderson, NV 89074-5909

Sharples, Scott (Athlete, Hockey Player)
50 Rockel iff Landng NW
Calgary, AB T3G SZ6, Canada

Sharpless, Barry (Nobel Prize Laureate)
Scripps Research Institute 10550 N Torrey
Pines Rd
La Jolla, CA 92037-1000, USA

sharpless, Josh (Athlete, Baseball Player)
206 Mountain Dr
Carnegie, PA 15106-2266, USA

Sharpless, K Barry (Nobel Prize Laureate)
Scripps Research Institute
10650 Torrey Pines Road
La Jolla, CA 92037, USA

Sharpley, Glen (Athlete, Hockey Player)
Sharpley Sports
536 Highland St
Haliburton, ON K0M 1S0, CANADA

Sharpton, Al (Activist, Religious Leader)
National Action Network
106 W 145th St
Harlem, NY 10039, USA

Sharqi, Sheikh Hamad bin Muhammad al
(President)
Royal Palace
Emiri Court
PO Box 1
Fujairah, UNITED ARAB EMIRATES

Sharvani, Isha (Actor, Bollywood)
c/o Bunty Bahl *Carving Dreams
Entertainment*
304-305, Oberoi Chambers II
B Wing, Off New Link Road, Andheri
West
Mumbai 400053, INDIA

Shasky, John (Athlete, Basketball Player)
1755 S Benson Rd
Frankfort, KY 40601-7649, USA

Shatalov, Vladimir A (Cosmonaut)
Potchta Kosmonavtov
Moskovskoi Oblasti
Syvisdny Goroduk 141160, RUSSIA

Shatkin, Aaron J (Biologist)
Center for Advanced Biotechnology
679 Hoes Lane
Piscataway, NJ 08854, USA

Shatner, Melanie (Actor)
Henderson/Hogan
8285 W Sunset Blvd
#1
West Hollywood, CA 90046, USA

Shatner, William (Actor)
c/o Larry Thompson *Larry A Thompson
Organization*
9663 Santa Monica Blvd
Suite 801
Beverly Hills, CA 90210, USA

Shatraw, David
c/o Staff Member *Stone Manners Salners
Agency (LA)*
9911 W Pico Blvd Ste 1400
Los Angeles, CA 90035, USA

Shattuck, Kim (Musician)
International Creative Mgmt
40 W 57th St
#1800
New York, NY 10019, USA

Shattuck, Molly (Reality TV Star)
c/o Staff Member *Fox Broadasting
Company*
PO Box 900
Beverly Hills, CA 90213

Shattuck, Shari (Actor, Writer)
4142 Big Tujunga Canyon Road
Tujunga, California 91242

Shaud, Grant (Actor)
8738 Appian Way
Los Angeles, CA 90046, USA

Shaud, John A (General)
Air Force Aid Society
1745 Jefferson Davis Highway
#202
Arlington, VA 22202, USA

Shaughnessy, Charles (Actor)
c/o Staff Member *Marshak/Zachary
Company, The*
8840 Wilshire Blvd
1st Floor
Beverly Hills, CA 90210, USA

Shaunessy, Scott (Athlete, Hockey Player)
1 Treetop Ln
Duxbury, MA 02332-4123

Shave, Jon (Athlete, Baseball Player)
851 Parkview Pl W
Fernandina Beach, FL 32034-4633, USA

Shavelson, Mel
11947 Sunshine Terrace
No. Hollywood, CA 91602

Shaver, Billy Joe (Musician, Songwriter,
Writer)
435 N Martell Ave
Los Angeles, CA 90036, USA

Shaver, Helen (Actor)
Innovative Artists
1505 10th St
Santa Monica, CA 90401, USA

Shaver, Jeff (Athlete, Baseball Player)
9651 E Clinton St
Scottsdale, AZ 85260-6209, USA

Shavers, Ernie (Boxer)
30 Doreen Ave Moretown Wirral
Merseyside CH46 6DN, UNITED
KINGDOM (UK)

Shavick, James (Actor, Director, Producer,
Writer)

Shaw, Bernard (Journalist)
17 Pine Ave
Takoma Park, MD 20912-4677, USA

Shaw, Bernard (Correspondent)
7526 Heatherton Ln
Potomac, MD 20854, USA

Shaw, Brad (Athlete, Hockey Player)
St Louis Blues
1401 Clark Ave
Saint Louis, MO 63103-2700

Shaw, Brad (Athlete, Hockey Player)
1866 Braumton Court
Chesterfield, MO 63017-8027

Shaw, Brewster H Colonel (Astronaut)
3519 Rice Blvd
Houston, TX 77005-2937, USA

Shaw, Bryant (Athlete, Football Player)
13832 Far Hills Ln
Dallas, TX 75240-3737, USA

Shaw, Carolyn Hagner (Publisher)
Social Register
2620 P St NW
Washington, DC 20007, USA

Shaw, David (Athlete, Hockey Player)
105 Belfair Rd
Irmo, SC 29063, USA

Shaw, Dennis (Athlete, Football Player)
14844 Priscilla St
San Diego, CA 92129-1525, USA

Shaw, Don (Athlete, Baseball Player)
857 Waterford Villas Dr
Lake Saint Louis, MO 63367-2574, USA

Shaw, Eric (Athlete, Football Player)
3450 Wallingford Ct
Lexington, KY 40503-4332, USA

Shaw, Fiona (Actor)
International Creative Mgmt
76 Oxford St
London W1N 0AX, UNITED KINGDOM
(UK)

Shaw, Jeffrey L (Jeff) (Athlete, Baseball
Player)
1215 Storybrook Dr
Washington Court House,
OH 43160-2608, USA

Shaw, Jim (Athlete, Hockey Player)
266 Churchill Dr
Saskatoon, SK S7K 3Y7, Canada

Shaw, John H (Geophysicist, Physicist)
Harvard University
Geophysics Dept
Cambridge, MA 02138, USA

Shaw, Kenneth A (Educator)
Syracuse University
President's Office
Syracuse, NY 13244, USA

Shaw, Kim (Actor)
c/o Marilyn Glasser *Glasser/Black
Management*
283 Cedarhurst Ave
Cedarhurst, NY 11516, USA

Shaw, Lindsey (Actor)
c/o Pat Cutler *Cutler Management*
13043 Sunset Blvd
Los Angeles, CA 90049, USA

Shaw, Mariena (Musician)
Berkeley Agency
2608 9th St
Berkeley, CA 94710, USA

Shaw, Martin (Actor)
36 - 40 Glasshouse St
London W1B 5DL, UNITED KINGDOM
(UK)

Shaw, Pete (Athlete, Football Player)
25052 Pappas Rd
Ramona, CA 92065, USA

Shaw, Robert (Athlete, Football Player)
4013 Centenary Ave
Dallas, TX 75225, USA

Shaw, Robert (Athlete, Football Player)
487 Old Coach Rd
Apt D
Westerville, OH 43081, USA

Shaw, Run Run (Producer)
Shaw House
Lot 220 Clear Water Bar Road
Kowloon, Hong Kong, CHINA

Shaw, Scott (Photographer)
20771 Lake Rd
Rocky River, OH 44116-1335, USA

Shaw, Scott (Journalist)
20771 Lake Road
Cleveland, OH 44116, USA

Shaw, Sedrick (Athlete, Football Player)
1007 Waller St
Austin, TX 78702, USA

Shaw, Stan (Actor)
Innovative Artists
1505 10th St
Santa Monica, CA 90401, USA

Shaw, Tim
5315 River Ave.
Newport Beach, CA 92663

Shaw, Timothy A (Tim) (Swimmer)
5315 River Ave
Newport Beach, CA 92663, USA

Shaw, Todd (Too Short) (Musician)
c/o David Weintraub *DWE Talent*
Prefers to be contacted via telephone
CA, USA

Shaw, Tommy (Musician, Songwriter,
Writer)
c/o Sterling Bacon *TBA Artist
Management (Atlanta)*
1111 Alderman Dr #285
Alpharetta, GA 30005-5433, USA

Shaw, Victoria (Musician, Songwriter,
Writer)
P.O. Box 58175
Nashville, TN 37205, USA

Shaw, Vinessa (Actor)
Industry Entertainment
955 Carillo Dr
#300
Los Angeles, CA 90048, USA

Shaw, Wayne (Athlete, Football Player)
625 12th St E
LexingtonSaskatoon, SK S7N OH3,
Canada

Shaw, William L (Billy) (Athlete, Football
Player)
3427 Old Rothell Rd
Toccoa, GA 30577, USA

Shaw Jr, Brewster H (Astronaut)
3519 Rice Blvd
Houston, TX 77005-2937, USA

Shawkat, Alia (Actor, Producer)
c/o Michelle Theodat *Kipperman
Management*
420 West End Avenue
Suite 1G
New York, NY 10024, USA

Shawn, Wallace (Actor, Writer)
c/o Christopher Black *Opus Entertainment*
5225 Wilshire Blvd #905
Los Angeles, CA 90036, USA

Shawyer, David
16 Rylett Rd.
London, ENGLAND W12

Shay, Art (Photographer)
618 Indian Hill Rd
Deerfield, IL 60015-4047, USA

Shay, Jerry (Athlete, Football Player)
81 E Shasta St
Chula Vista, CA 91910, USA

Shaye, Lin (Actor)
Paul Kohner
9300 Wilshire Blvd
#555
Beverly Hills, CA 90212, USA

Shaye, Skyler (Actor)
c/o Dorothy Koster *Crystal Sky/Artists Only Management*
10203 Santa Monica Blvd
5th Floor
Los Angeles, CA 90067, USA

Shchedrin, Rodion K (Composer)
Tverskaya St
#31
Moscow 103050, RUSSIA

Shea, Charity (Actor)
c/o Scott Karp *Crystal Sky Pictures*
10203 Santa Monica Blvd
5th Floor
Los Angeles, CA 90067, USA

Shea, Dan (Actor)
c/o Staff Member *Talent Plus*
1222 Lucas Ave
Suite 300
St. Louis, MO 63103, USA

Shea, Eric (Actor)
27710 Jubilee Run Road
Pearblossom, CA 93553, USA

Shea, George Beverly
1300 Harmon Pl.
Minneapolis, MN 55403

Shea, Jere (Actor)
SMS Talent
8730 Sunset Blvd
#440
Los Angeles, CA 90069, USA

Shea, John (Actor)
Mutant X
40 Carl Hall Road
Toronto, ON M3K 2B8, CANADA

Shea, Joseph F (Scientist)
15 Dogwood Road
Weston, MA 02493, USA

Shea, Judith (Artist)
Barbara Krakow Gallery
10 Newbury St
Boston, MA 02116, USA

Shea, Katt (Actor)
International Creative Mgmt
8942 Wilshire Blvd
#219
Beverly Hills, CA 90211, USA

Shea, Pat (Athlete, Football Player)
1175 Evergreen Dr
Encinitas, CA 92024, USA

Shea, Robert M (General)
Director Cmd Control Communications
HqUSMC 2 Navy St
Washington, DC 20380, USA

Shea, Steve (Athlete, Baseball Player)
1 Shepherds Ln
North Hampton, NH 03862-2133, USA

Shea, Terry (Coach, Football Coach)
San Jose State University
Athletic Dept
San Jose, CA 95192, USA

Sheaffer, Danny (Athlete, Baseball Player)
165 Savannah Ln
Mount Airy, NC 27030-8688, USA

Shealy, Ryan (Athlete, Baseball Player)
2168 NE 63rd Ct
Fort Lauderdale, FL 33308-1335, USA

Shear, Jules (Actor, Musician, Songwriter, Writer)
c/o Staff Member *Concerted Efforts*
P.O. Box 440326
Somerville, MA 02144, USA

Shear, Rhonda (Actor, Comedian, Model)
J Cast Productions
2550 Greenvalley Rd
Los Angeles, CA 90046, USA

Sheard, Kiera Kiki (Musician)
c/o Staff Member *EMI Gospel*
PO Box 5085
Brentwood, TN 37024-5085, USA

Shearer, Al (Actor, Reality TV Star)

Shearer, Alan (Soccer Player)
Newcastle United FC
Saint James Park
Newcastle-Tyne NE1 4ST, UNITED KINGDOM (UK)

Shearer, Bob (Golfer)
International Management Group
281 Clarence Street
2nd Floor
Sydney, NSW 2000, AUSTRALIA

Shearer, Harry (Actor, Comedian)
c/o Melanie Greene *Affirmative Entertainment*
425 N Robertson Blvd
Los Angeles, CA 90048, USA

Shearer, Peter M (Geophysicist, Physicist)
Scripps Oceanography Institute
Geophysics Dept
La Jolla, CA 92093, USA

Shearer, S Bradford (Brad) (Athlete, Football Player)
1909B Lakeshore Dr
Apt B
Austin, TX 78746, USA

Shearin, Joe (Athlete, Football Player)
3533 Stanford Ave
Dallas, TX 75225, USA

Shearmur, Edward (Ed) (Composer, Musician)
c/o Staff Member *Gorfaine/Schwartz Agency Inc*
4111 W Alameda Ave
Suite 509
Burbank, CA 91505, USA

Shearn, Tom (Athlete, Baseball Player)
20429 Rita Blanca Cir
Pflugerville, TX 78660-7752, USA

Shears, Jake (Musician)
c/o Staff Member *Paradigm (NY)*
360 Park Ave S Fl 16
New York, NY 10010, USA

Shears, Larry (Athlete, Football Player)
355 Cam mel St
Mobile, AL 36610-3529, USA

Shearsmith, Reece (Actor)
c/o Lorraine Hamilton *Hamilton Hodell Ltd*
66-68 Margaret St Fl 5
London W1W 8SR, UK

Shechtman, Daniel (Nobel Prize Laureate)
Israel Institute ofTechnology Tecnion City
Attn: Materials Engineering Dept
Haifa, Israe 32000, USA

Sheckler, Ryan (Actor, Skateboarder)
c/o Nick Styne *Creative Artists Agency (CAA-LA)*
2000 Ave Of The Stars
Los Angeles, CA 90067, USA

Shedd, Kenny (Athlete, Football Player)
1928 Tiago Pass Way
Antioch, CA 94531, USA

Shedden, Doug (Athlete, Hockey Player)
7 E Main St
Stony Point, NY 10980-1615

Sheedy, Ally (Actor)
c/o Bill Veloric *Innovative Artists (NY)*
235 Park Ave S
7th Floor
New York, NY 10003, USA

Sheehan, Doug (Actor)
Innovative Artists
1505 10th St
Santa Monica, CA 90401, USA

Sheehan, Jeremiah J (Business Person)
Reynolds Metals Co
6601 Broad St
PO Box 27003
Richmond, VA 23261, USA

Sheehan, Neil (Journalist)
4505 Klingle St NW
Washington, Dc 20016-3580, USA

Sheehan, Neil (Journalist)
4505 Klingle St NW
Washington, DC 20016, USA

Sheehan, Patrick (Golfer)
2913 Ashton Ter
Oviedo, FL 32765-7949, USA

Sheehan, Patty (Golfer)
c/o Staff Member *Ladies Pro Golf Association (LPGA)*
100 International Golf Dr
Daytona Beach, FL 32124-1092, USA

Sheehan, Susan (Writer)
4505 Klingle St NW
Washington, DC 20016, USA

Sheehy, Neil (Athlete, Hockey Player)
Sheehy Hockey LLC
900 2nd AveS Ste 1650
Minneapolis, MN 55402-5359

Sheehy, Tim (Athlete, Hockey Player, Olympic Athlete)
Sheehy Hockey LLC 4 Boswell Lane
Southborough, MA 01772-1763, USA

Sheelor, Willie (Baseball Player)
Chicago American Giants
152 Beaumont Ave
Kannapolis, NC 28083-6501, USA

Sheen, Charles (Actor)
Jeffrey Ballard
4814 Lemara Ave
Sherman Oaks, CA 91403, USA

Sheen, Charlie (Actor)
Mail Man Inc
4570 Van Nuys Blvd #306
Sherman Oaks, CA 91403, USA

Sheen, Martin (Actor)
c/o Steve Rohr *Lexicon Public Relations*
1901 Ave of the Stars
2nd Floor
Los Angeles, CA 90067, USA

Sheen, Michael (Actor, Producer)
c/o Tammy Rosen *Sanders Armstrong Caserta*
425 N Robertson Blvd
Los Angeles, CA 90048, USA

Sheen, Ramon
6916 Dume Dr.
Malibu, CA 90265

Sheer, Ireen
Yachthof B-22
Waldeck, GERMANY D-34513

Sheeran, Ed (Musician)
c/o Staff Member *Paradigm (NY)*
360 Park Ave S Fl 16
New York, NY 10010, USA

Sheerer, Gary (Athlete)
1557 Country Club Dr
Los Altos Hills, CA 94024, USA

Sheets, Andy (Athlete, Baseball Player)
104 Villaggio Dr
Lafayette, LA 70508-6795, USA

Sheets, Ben (Athlete, Baseball Player, Olympic Athlete)
105 E Shore Rd
Monroe, LA 71203-8857, USA

Sheets, Larry (Athlete, Baseball Player)
1411 Chippendale Rd
Lutherville Timonium, MD 21093-1608, USA

Sheffer, Craig (Actor)
5699 Kanan Dr
#275
Agoura, CA 91301, USA

Sheffield, Fred (Athlete, Basketball Player)
11664 McDougall
Tustin, CA 92782-3345, USA

Sheffield, Gary A (Athlete, Baseball Player)
922 Anchorage Rd
Tampa, FL 33602-5754, USA

Sheffield, Johnny
834 1st Ave.
Chula Vista, CA 91911

Sheffield, Lois (Athlete, Baseball Player)
227 Jones St
Wellington, OH 44090-1062, USA

Sheffield, Tony (Baseball Player)
PO Box 164
Tullahoma, TN 37388-0164, USA

Sheffield, William J (Bill) (Ex-Governor)
P.O. Box 911476
Anchorage, AK 99509, USA

Shefft, Jen (Reality TV Star)
c/o Michael (Mike) Esterman
Esterman.Com, LLC
Prefers to be contacted via email
MD, USA

Shehee, Rashaan (Athlete, Football Player)
6120 Bay Club Ct
Bakersfield, CA 93312, USA

Sheibler, Jim
PO Box 60
Venice, CA 90294

Sheik, Duncan (Musician, Songwriter, Writer)
Nonesuch Records
75 Rockefeller Plaza
New York, NY 10019, USA

Sheikh, Farooque (Actor, Bollywood)
Rafi Mansion 28th Road
Bandra
Mumbai, MS 400050, INDIA

Sheila E (Musician)
Ofoove Ent
1005 N Alfred St
#2
West Hollywood, CA 90069, USA

Sheindlin, Judith (Judge Judy) (Judge, Television Host)
Big Ticket Television
c/o KTLA Studios
5800 Sunset Blvd
Hollywood, CA 90028, USA

Sheiner, David S (Actor)
1827 Veteran Ave
#19
Los Angeles, CA 90025, USA

Sheinfeld, David (Composer)
112 Ash Way
San Rafael, CA 94903, USA

Shelby, Carol (Race Car Driver)
19020 Anelo Ave
Gardena, CA 90248

Shelby, John (Athlete, Baseball Player)
2232 Broadhead Pl
Lexington, KY 40515-1147, USA

Shelby, Mark (Composer, Musician)
Thomas Cassidy
11761 E Speedway Blvd
Tucson, AZ 85748, USA

Shelby, Richard (Politician)
1414 High Forest Dr N
Tuscaloosa, AL 35406-2152, USA

Sheldon, Bob (Athlete, Baseball Player)
3013 River Lakes Dr
Whitefish, MT 59937-7801, USA

Sheldon, Jack (Musician)
7095 Hollywood Blvd
#617
Los Angeles, CA 90028, USA

Sheldon, Rollie (Athlete, Baseball Player)
614 NE Coronado Ave
Lees Summit, MO 64063-2522, USA

Sheldon, Scott (Athlete, Baseball Player)
5202 Blue Cypress Ln
League CitY, TX 77573-6240, USA

Shell, Arthur (Art) (Athlete, Coach, Football Coach, Football Player)
4319 Rilea Way
Oakland, CA 94605, USA

Shell, Donnie (Athlete, Football Player)
2945 Shandon Rd
Rock Hill, SC 29730, USA

Shell, Todd (Athlete, Football Player)
4222 E McLellan Cir
Unit 15
Mesa, AZ 85205, USA

Shellen, Stephen (Actor)
3655 St. Laurent
#205
Montreal, Quebec HX 2V5, Canada

Shellenback, Jim (Athlete, Baseball Player)
10627 Dreamy Ln
Parker, AZ 85344-7576, USA

Shellenbeck, Jim (Athlete, Baseball Player)
10627 Dreamy Ln
Parker, AZ 85344, USA

Shelley, Barbara (Actor)
Ken McReddie
91 Regent St
London W1R 7TB, UNITED KINGDOM (UK)

Shelley, Carole (Actor)
c/o Steve Stone *Cornerstone Talent Agency*
37 W 20th St
New York, NY 10011, USA

Shelley, Howard G (Conductor, Musician)
38 Cholmeley Park
London N6 5ER, UNITED KINGDOM (UK)

Shelley, Jody (Athlete, Hockey Player)
211 Chestnut St
Haddonfield, NJ 08033-1814

Shelley, Rachel (Actor)
c/o Kesha Williams *Affirmative Entertainment*
425 N Robertson Blvd
Los Angeles, CA 90048, USA

Shelly, Randy (Actor)
c/o Ellen Gilbert *Abrams Artists Agency (LA)*
9200 Sunset Blvd
11th Floor
Los Angeles, CA 90069, USA

Shelmerdine, Kirk (Race Car Driver)
Kirk Shelmerdine Racing
PO Box 1133
Welcome, NC 27374, United States

Shelton, Abigail (Actor)
Dale Garrick
8831 Sunset Blvd
#402
Los Angeles, CA 90069, USA

Shelton, Angela V (Comedian)
c/o Staff Member *Gekis Management*
4217 Verdugo View Dr
Los Angeles, CA 90065-4317, USA

Shelton, Ben (Athlete, Baseball Player)
1192 Clarence Ave Unit 11
Oak Park, IL 60304-2169, USA

Shelton, Blake (Musician)
c/o Julie Colbert *WME (LA)*
9601 Wilshire Blvd Fl 3
Beverly Hills, CA 90210, USA

Shelton, Chris (Athlete, Baseball Player)
6382 Shady Grove Cir
Salt Lake City, UT 84121-6508, USA

Shelton, Craig (Athlete, Basketball Player)
8618 Leslie Ave
Glenarden, MD 20706-1528, USA

Shelton, Deborah (Actor)
c/o Marc Bass *Beacon Talent Agency*
170 Apple Ridge Rd
Woodcliff, NJ 07677, USA

Shelton, Derek (Athlete, Baseball Player)
203 46th Ave St
Pete Beach, FL 33706-2575, USA

Shelton, L J (Athlete, Football Player)
650 Carrotwood Ter
Plantation, FL 33324, USA

Shelton, Lonnie (Athlete, Basketball Player)
3883 Union Ave Apt 5
Bakersfield, CA 93305-2444, USA

Shelton, Marley (Actor)
c/o Jason Weinberg *Untitled Entertainment (LA)*
350 S. Beverly Dr #200
Beverly Hills, CA 90212, USA

Shelton, Richard (Athlete, Football Player)
6367 Raw Hyde Trl N
Jacksonville, FL 32210, USA

Shelton, Ricky Van (Musician, Songwriter)
PO Box 111
Woodlawn, VA 24381, USA

Shelton, Ronald W (Director)
c/o Staff Member *WmE2 (WMA-LA)*
1 William Morris Pl
Beverly Hills, CA 90212, USA

Shelton, Samantha (Actor)
c/o Staff Member *Innovative Artists (LA)*
1505 10th St
Santa Monica, CA 90401, USA

Shelton, William E (Educator)
Eastern Michigan University
President's Office
Ypsilanti, MI 48197, USA

Shemin, Robert (Business Person, Writer)
Robert Shemin Inc
c/o PREIG
7965 S 700 E
Sandy, UT 84070, USA

Shen, Parry (Actor)
c/o Staff Member *Lichtman/Salners Company*
12216 Moorpark St
Studio City, CA 91604, USA

Shenandoah (Music Group)
P.O. Box 680956
Franklin, TN 37068, USA

Shenandoh, Joanne (Musician, Songwriter, Writer)
Oneida Nation Territory
PO Box 450
Oneida, NY 13421, USA

Shenkman, Ben (Actor)
2 Charlton St Apt 5K
New York, NY 10014, USA

Shepard, Dax (Actor, Reality TV Star, Writer)
c/o Staff Member *Baker Winokur Ryder Public Relations (BWR-LA)*
9100 Wilshire Blvd
Suite 500, West Tower
Beverly Hills, CA 90212, USA

Shepard, Devon (Producer, Writer)
c/o Staff Member *Agency for the Performing Arts (APA-LA)*
405 S Beverly Dr
Suite 500
Beverly Hills, CA 90212-4425, USA

Shepard, Jean (Musician)
Billy Deaton Talent
1214 16th Ave S
Nashville, TN 37212, USA

Shepard, Judy (Activist)
The Matthew Shepard Foundation
301 Thelma Dr #512
Casper, WY 82609, USA

Shepard, Kenny Wayne (Musician)
c/o Staff Member *Richard De La Font Agency*
3808 W South Park Blvd
Broken Arrow, OK 74011, USA

Shepard, Kiki (Actor)
c/o Staff Member *Cunningham Escott Slevin & Doherty (CESD-LA)*
10635 Santa Monica Blvd
130
Los Angeles, CA 90025, USA

Shepard, Roger N (Psychic)
5775 Montclair Ave
Marysville, CA 95901, USA

Shepard, Samuel (Sam) (Actor, Writer)
c/o Judy Boals *Judy Boals*
307 W. 38th St.
#812
New York, NY 10018, USA

Shepard, Sara (Writer)
c/o Andy McNicol *WME (WMA-NY)*
1325 Ave of the Americas
New York, NY 10019, USA

Shepard, Vonda (Actor, Musician, Songwriter)
1114 Harvard St
Santa Monica, CA 90403, USA

Sheperd, Ben (Musician)
Susan Silver Mgmt
6523 California Ave SW
#348
Seattle, WA 98136, USA

Sheperd, Elizabeth (Actor)
London Mgmt
2-4 Noel St
London W1V 3RB, UNITED KINGDOM (UK)

Sheperd, Morgan (Race Car Driver)
57 Rhody Creek Loop
Stuart, VA 24171, USA

Shephard, Gillian P (Government Official)
House of Commons
Westminster
London SW1A 0AA, UNITED KINGDOM (UK)

Shepherd, Chris (Director, Writer)
c/o Staff Member *Slinky Pictures*
Old Truman Brewery
91 Brick Ln
London E16 QN, UNITED KINGDOM (UK)

Shepherd, Cybill (Actor)
c/o Judy Hofflund *Hofflund/Polone*
9465 Wilshire Blvd #420
Beverly Hills, CA 90212, USA

Shepherd, Gannon (Athlete, Football Player)
5818 Alvaton Ct
Norcross, GA 30092, USA

Shepherd, Keith (Athlete, Baseball Player)
2201 Parnell Ave
Ft Wayne, IN 46805-3338, USA

Shepherd, Morgan (Race Car Driver)
PO Box 623
Conover, NC 28612, USA

Shepherd, Ron (Athlete, Baseball Player)
5821 Fm 349
Kilgore, TX 75662-6905, USA

Shepherd, Sherri (Actor, Comedian, Talk Show Host)
c/o Staff Member *View, The*
320 W 66th St
New York, NY 10023-6338, USA

Shepherd, Sherrie (Cartoonist)
United Feature Syndicate
200 Madison Ave
New York, NY 10016, USA

Shepherd, William M (Astronaut)
18623 Prince William Lane
Houston, TX 77058, USA

Shepherd, William M Captain (Astronaut)
2853 Wood Duck Dr
Virginia Beach, VA 23456-4463, USA

Shepis, Tiffany (Actor)
c/o Michael J Roberts *D-Mentd Entertainment*
Prefers to be contact via email or telephone
Wilmington, NC, USA

Sheppard, Delia (Actor, Model)
4795 South Sandhill Road
Suite 9
Las Vegas, NV 89121, USA

Sheppard, Gregg (Athlete, Hockey Player)
2521 Blue Jay Cres
North Battleford, SK S9A 3Z3, Canada

Sheppard, Jonathan (Misc)
287 Lamborn Town Road
West Grove, PA 19390, USA

Sheppard, Julian (Comedian)
c/o Staff Member *Gersh (LA)*
9465 Wilshire Blvd
Suite 600
Beverly Hills, CA 90212, USA

Sheppard, Mike (Coach, Football Coach)
University of New Mexico
Athletic Dept
Albuquerque, NM 87131, USA

Sheppard, Ray (Athlete, Hockey Player)
Cornwall Colts
100 Water St E
Cornwall, ON K6H 6G4, Canada

Sheppard, Ray (Athlete, Hockey Player)
19110 Fox Landing Dr.
Boca Raton, FL 33434-5156

Sheppard, William Morgan (Actor)
c/o Bri Franchot *Franchot Management*
P.O. Box 48890A
Los Angeles, CA 90048, USA

Sheps, Cecil G (Biologist)
388 Carolina Meadows Villa
Chapel Hill, NC 27517, USA

Sher, Antony (Actor)
Conway Van Gelder Robinson
18-21 Jermyn St
London SW1Y 6NB, UNITED KINGDOM (UK)

Sher, Eden (Actor)
c/o Adam Griffin *Kritzer Levine Wilkins Entertainment (KLWG)*
11872 La Grange Ave
1st Floor
Los Angeles, CA 90025, USA

Shera, Mark (Actor)
PO Box 15717
Beverly Hills, CA 90209, USA

Sherba, John (Musician)
Kronos Quartet
1235 9th Ave
San Francisco, CA 94122, USA

Sherbedgia, Rade (Actor)
Innovative Artists
1505 10th St
Santa Monica, CA 90401, USA

Sherer, Dave (Athlete, Football Player)
4212 Colgate Ave
Dallas, TX 75225, USA

Sherffius, John (Cartoonist)
Saint Louis Post Dispatch
Editorial Dept
900 N Tucker
Saint Louis, MO 63101, USA

Sheridan, Bonnie (Musician)
c/o Mike Eistenstadt *Amsel, Eisenstadt & Frazier Talent Agency (AEF)*
5055 Wilshire Blvd
Suite 860
Los Angeles, CA 90036-6108, USA

Sheridan, Bonnie Bramlett (Actor, Musician)
18011 Martha St
Encino, CA 91316, USA

Sheridan, Dave C (Actor, Writer)
c/o Kara Welker *Generate Management*
1545 26th St
Suite 200
Santa Monica, CA 90404, USA

Sheridan, Dinah (Actor)
International Creative Mgmt
76 Oxford St
London W1N 0AX, UNITED KINGDOM (UK)

Sheridan, Jamey (Actor)
c/o Scott Schachter *United Talent Agency (UTA)*
9336 Civic Center Dr
Beverly Hills, CA 90210, USA

Sheridan, Jim (Actor, Director, Producer, Writer)
Hell's Kitchen International Ltd.
21 Mespil Rd.
Dublin 4, Ireland

Sheridan, Lisa (Actor)
c/o Joanna (Joanie) Burstein *Burstein Company, The*
15304 Sunset Blvd
suite 208
Pacific Palisades, CA 90272, USA

Sheridan, Liz (Actor)
11333 Moorpark #427
West Hollywood, CA 91602

Sheridan, Neill (Athlete, Baseball Player)
150 Chaucer Ct
Pleasant Hill, CA 94523-4104, USA

Sheridan, Nicole (Adult Film Star)
c/o Staff Member *Atlas Multimedia Inc*
9005 Eton Ave Ste C
Canoga Park, CA 91304-1743, USA

Sheridan, Nicollette (Actor)
c/o Nicole Perna *Baker Winokur Ryder Public Relations (BWR-LA)*
9100 Wilshire Blvd
Suite 500, West Tower
Beverly Hills, CA 90212, USA

Sheridan, Pat (Athlete, Baseball Player)
31654 Taft St
Wayne, MI 48184-2234, USA

Sheridan, Rondell (Actor)
Gail Stocker Presents
1025 N Kings Road
#113
Los Angeles, CA 90069, USA

Sheridan, Tony (Musician)
Gems
PO Box 1031
Montrose, CA 91021, USA

Sheriff, Haja (Actor)
20/1 Desikar Street
Chennai, TN 600 026, INDIA

Sherk, Jerry M (Athlete, Football Player)
1819 Bel Air Ter
Encinitas, CA 92024, USA

Sherk, Kathy (Golfer)
Canadian Golf Hall of Fame
1333 Dorval Dr
Oakville, ON L6M 4G2, CANADA

Sherlock, Glenn (Athlete, Baseball Player)
5905 E Beryl Ave
Paradise Valley, AZ 85253-1105, USA

Sherlock, Nancy J (Astronaut)
2003 Morning Tide Ln
League City, TX 77573-6640, USA

Sherlock, Nancy J (Astronaut)
NASA
Johnson Space Center
2101 NASA Road
Houston, TX 77058, USA

Sherlock-Currie, Nancy
2101 NASA Rd
Houston, TX 77058, USA

Sherman, Allie (Athlete, Football Coach, Football Player)
136 E 55th St
Apt 12H
New York, NY 10022, USA

Sherman, Bobby (Actor, Musician)
1870 Sunset Plaza Dr
Los Angeles, CA 90069, USA

Sherman, Brad (Congressman, Politician)
2242 Rayburn HOB
Washington, DC 20515, USA

Sherman, Brent (Race Car Driver)
Atkins Motorsports
222 Raceway Dr.
Mooresvile, NC 28117-6510, USA

Sherman, Cindy (Photographer)
Metro Pictures
519 W 24th St
New York, NY 10011, USA

Sherman, Darrell (Athlete, Baseball Player)
12622 Memorial Way Apt 1144
Moreno Valley, CA 92553-7542, USA

Sherman, Edgar A (Coach, Football Coach)
681 Nancy Lane
Newark, OH 43055, USA

Sherman, Heath (Athlete, Football Player)
RR 1 Box 290
Wharton, TX 77488, USA

Sherman, Mike (Athlete, Coach, Football Coach, Football Player)
2739 Talbott St
Houston, TX 77005, USA

Sherman, Richard M (Composer, Musician)
PO Box 17740
Beverly Hills, CA 90209, USA

Sherman, Rod (Football Player)
Oakland Raiders
3410 Mira Vista Cir
San Jose, CA 95132-3123, USA

Sherman, Saul (Athlete, Football Player)
175 E Delaware Pl
Apt 6410
Chicago, IL 60611, USA

Sherman-Palladino, Amy (Director, Producer, Writer)
c/o Staff Member *Creative Artists Agency (CAA-LA)*
2000 Ave Of The Stars
Los Angeles, CA 90067, USA

Shernoff, William M (Attorney, Attorney General, General)
600 S Indian Hill Road
Claremont, CA 91711, USA

Sherod, Edmund (Athlete, Basketball Player)
519 Montvale Ave
Richmond, VA 23222-3020, USA

Shero-Witiuk, Doris (Athlete, Baseball Player)
11821 N Hemlock St
Spokane, WA 99218-2718, USA

Sherrard, Michael W (Mike) (Athlete, Football Player)
5661 Colony Dr
Agoura Hills, CA 91301-2217, USA

Sherrill, Dennis (Athlete, Baseball Player)
1691 Tolley Ter SE
Palm Bay, FL 32909-8831, USA

Sherrill, George (Athlete, Baseball Player)
1442 E Vine Meadow Cir
Salt Lake City, UT 84121-1785, USA

Sherrill, Jackie W (Coach, Football Coach)
Mississippi State University
Athletic Dept
Mississippi State, MS 39762, USA

Sherrill, Tim (Athlete, Baseball Player)
P.O. Box 812
Harrison, AR 72602-0812, USA

Sherrin, Edward G (Ned) (Director)
4 Cornwall Mansions
Ashburnham Road
London SW10 0PE, UNITED KINGDOM (UK)

Sherrington, Georgina (Actor)
c/o Staff Member *JGM*
15 Lexham Mews
London W8 6JW, UNITED KINGDOM (UK)

Sherrit, Jim (Athlete, Hockey Player)
7 Dancy Dr
Orillia, ON L3V 7M1, Canada

Sherrod, Derek (Football Player)
c/o Adisa P. Bakari *Dow Lohnes PLLC*
1200 New Hampshire Ave, NW
Suite 800
Washington, DC 20036, USA

Sherry, Norm (Athlete, Baseball Player, Coach)
4383 Nobel Dr
Unit 89
San Diego, CA 92122-1575, USA

Sherry, Paul H (Religious Leader)
United Church of Christ
700 Prospect Ave
Cleveland, OH 44115, USA

Sherven, Gord (Athlete, Hockey Player)
184 Hampshire Grove NW
Calgary, AB T3A SB3, Canada

Sherwin, Tim (Athlete, Football Player)
6 Mill Rd
Latham, NY 12110, USA

Sherwood, Brad (Actor, Producer)
c/o Erik Kritzer *Kritzer Levine Wilkins
Entertainment (KLWG)*
11872 La Grange Ave
1st Floor
Los Angeles, CA 90025, USA

Sheshadri, Meenakshi (Actor, Bollywood)
601 Sheshadri Moonbeam
Union Park Khar (W)
Mumbai, MS 400052, INDIA

Shesol, Jeff (Cartoonist)
Creators Syndicate
5777 W Century Blvd
#700
Los Angeles, CA 90045, USA

Shestakova, Tatyana B (Actor)
Maly Drama Theatre
Rubinstein St 18
Saint Petersburgh, RUSSIA

Shetty, Reshma (Actor)
c/o Smith (Stevie) Stephanie *Station3*
1051 Cole Av
Culver City, CA 90038, USA

Shetty, Shilpa (Actor, Bollywood)
12 Dev Darshan
262 St Anthony Road Chembur
Mumbai, MS 400071, INDIA

Shetty, Sunil (Actor, Bollywood)
18/B Prithvi Apartments
Altamont Road
Mumbai, MS 400026, INDIA

Shevardnadze, eduard (Politician)
Plekhanova 103
Tbilisi 880064, Georgia

Shevchenko, Arkady N (Politician)
Alfred Knopf/Ballantine/Fawcett Publishers
201 East 50th Street
New York, NY 10022

Shi, David E (Educator)
Furman University
President's Office
Greenville, SC 29613, USA

Shicoff, Neil (Opera Singer)
Opera et Concert
Maximilianstr 22
Munich 80539, GERMANY

Shields, Ben (Actor)
10965 Fruitland Drive
Suite 102
Studio City, CA 91604, USA

Shields, Beth K (Stylist)
3001 Carob St
Newport Beach, CA 92660-3216, USA

Shields, Billy (Athlete, Football Player)
12701 Treeridge Ter
Poway, CA 92064, USA

Shields, Brooke (Actor, Model)
Christa Inc
9200 Sunset Blvd
Suite 600
Los Angeles, CA 90069, USA

Shields, Carol (Writer)
103-407 Swift St
Victoria, BC V8W 1S2, Canada

Shields, Carol
103-407 Swift St
Victoria, BC V8W 1S2, Canada

Shields, James (Athlete, Baseball Player)
3042 Leanne Ct
Clearwater, FL 33759-1425, USA

Shields, Lebron (Athlete, Football Player)
1405 82nd Ave Lot 31
Vero Beach, FL 32966, USA

Shields, Perry (Judge)
US Tax Court
400 2nd St NW
Washington, DC 20217, USA

Shields, Robert (Misc)
Robert Shields Designs
PO Box 10024
Sedona, AZ 86339, USA

Shields, Samona (Samantha Strong) (Adult
Film Star)
3324 Castle Heights Ave
Los Angeles, CA 90034, USA

Shields, Scott (Athlete, Football Player)
16139 Pine Valley Dr
Northville, MI 48168-9655, USA

Shields, Steve (Athlete, Baseball Player)
4969 Leonard Dr
Gadsden, AL 35903-4638, USA

Shields, Steve (Athlete, Hockey Player)
123 E Balboa Blvd
Newport Beach, CA 92661-1117

Shields, Steve (Athlete, Hockey Player)
Michigan Tech University Athletics
1400 Townsend Dr
Houghton, MI 49931-1295

Shields, Tommy (Athlete, Baseball Player)
518 N Elm St
Lititz, PA 17543-1312, USA

Shields, Tyler (Cinematographer)
c/o Eric Podwall *Podwall Entertainment*
710 N Orlando Ave
Loft 203
Los Angeles, CA 90069, USA

Shields, Will H (Athlete, Football Player)
13125 W 127th Pl
Overland Park, KS 66213, USA

Shiell, Jason (Athlete, Baseball Player)
301 Sting Ray Ct
Guyton, GA 31312-6592, USA

Shiely, John S (Business Person)
Briggs & Stratton
PO Box 702
Milwaukee, WI 53201, USA

Shifflett, Garland (Athlete, Baseball
Player)
1095 Cody St
Lakewood, CO 80215-4818, USA

Shifflett, Steve (Athlete, Baseball Player)
24004 E 172nd St
Pleasant Hill, MO 64080-7582, USA

Shifty, Shellshock (Musician)
Q Prime
729 7th Ave
#1600
New York, NY 10019, USA

Shigeta, James (Actor)
10635 Santa Monica Blvd
#130
Los Angeles, CA 90025, USA

Shih, Wen Yann (Actor)
c/o Vincent Cirrincione *Vincent
Cirrincione Associates*
1516 N Fairfax Ave
Los Angeles, CA 90046, USA

Shikler, Aaron (Artist)
44 W 77th St
New York, NY 10024, USA

Shiley, Newhouse Jean (Athlete, Track
Athlete)
1100 Sunnybrae Ave
Chatsworth, CA 91311, USA

Shilling, Curt (Baseball Player)
c/o Staff Member *Boston Red Sox*
4 Yawkey Way
Boston, MA 02215, USA

Shilton, Justin (Actor)
c/o Staff Member *Magnolia Entertainment
(LA)*
9595 Wilshire Blvd
Suite 601
Beverly Hills, CA 90212, USA

Shilton, Peter (Soccer Player)
Hubbards Cottage
Bentley Lane
Maxstoke near Coleshill B46 2QR,
UNITED KINGDOM (UK)

Shima, Masatoshi (Engineer)
Shima Co
260 Tsurumaki
Omika Haramachishi
Fukushima 975-0049, JAPAN

Shimada, Yoko
7245 Hillside Ave. #415
Los Angeles, CA 90046

Shimell, William (Opera Singer)
I M G Artists
3 Burlington Lane
Chiswick
London W4 2TH, UNITED KINGDOM
(UK)

Shimer, Brian (Athlete, Bobsledder,
Olympic Athlete)
2613 Lakeview Dr
Naples, FL 34112-5872, USA

Shimerman, Armin (Actor)
Innovative Artists
1505 10th St
Santa Monica, CA 90401, USA

Shimkis, Joanna
9255 Doheny Rd.
Los Angeles, CA 90069-3201

Shimkus, Joanna (Actor)
c/o Staff Member *Creative Artists Agency
(CAA-LA)*
2000 Ave Of The Stars
Los Angeles, CA 90067, USA

Shimkus, John (Congressman, Politician)
2452 Rayburn HOB
Washington, DC 20515, USA

Shimmerman, Armin (Actor)
c/o Staff Member *Innovative Artists (LA)*
1505 10th St
Santa Monica, CA 90401, USA

Shimomura, Osamu (Nobel Prize
Laureate)
324 Sippewissett Rd
Falmouth, MA 02540-2210, USA

Shimono, Sab (Actor)
12711 Ventura Blvd
#440
Studio City, CA 91604, USA

Shin, Yong Moon (Biologist)
National University
Sillimdong
Gwanakgu
Seoul 151-742, SOUTH KOREA

Shinall, Zak (Athlete, Baseball Player)
16605 Sell Cir
Huntington Beach, CA 92649-3299, USA

Shindle, Kate
2 Ocean Way #1000
Atlantic City, NJ 08401-4163

Shinefield, Henry R (Misc)
2240 Hyde St
#2
San Francisco, CA 94109, USA

Shiner, Dick (Athlete, Football Player)
19 Fox Trl
Gettysburg, PA 17325, USA

Shines, Anthony (Razor) (Athlete,
Baseball Player)
11508 Herb Cv
Austin, TX 78750-3671, USA

Shinko (Stylist)
c/o Staff Member *Rex Agency, The*
6311 Romaine St
Los Angeles, CA 90038, USA

Shinn, Christopher (Comedian)
c/o Staff Member *Gersh (LA)*
9465 Wilshire Blvd
Suite 600
Beverly Hills, CA 90212, USA

Shinn, George (Business Person)
New Orleans/Oklahoma City Hornets
Oklahoma Tower
210 Park Ave Ste 1850
Oklahoma City, OK 73102, USA

Shinners, John (Athlete, Football Player)
N120W1495 Freistadt Road
Germantown, WI 53022, USA

Shinoda, Mike (Musician)
Artist Group International
9560 Wilshire Blvd
#400
Beverly Hills, CA 90212, USA

Shinske, Rich (Athlete, Hockey Player)
531 Pearkes Rd
Victoria, BC V9C 2L6, Canada

Shiny Toy Guns (Music Group)
c/o Staff Member *Paradigm (Monterey)*
404 W Franklin St
Monterey, CA 93940, USA

Shipanoff, Dave (Athlete, Baseball Player)
3 Salina Dr
St Albert, AB T8N 0L1, Canada

Shipka, Kiernan (Actor)
c/o Alexandra Crotin *42West (LA)*
11400 W Olympic Blvd
Suite 1100
Los Angeles, CA 90064, USA

Shipler, David K (Journalist)
4005 Thornapple St
Bethesda, MD 20815, USA

Shipley, Craig (Athlete, Baseball Player)
Boston Red Sox
4 Yawkey Way
Attn: V.P. Scouting Dept
Boston, MA 02215, USA

Shipley, Jenny (Politician)
Parliament Buildings
Wellington, New Zealand

Shipley, Joe (Athlete, Baseball Player)
23 Park Dr
Saint Charles, MO 63303, USA

Shipley, Joe (Athlete, Baseball Player)
23 Park
Dr Saint Charles, MO 63303-3607

Shipley, Julie (Race Car Driver)
M&S Management
13904 Fiji Way
#242
Marina del Rey, CA 90292, USA

Shipley, Walter V (Financier)
Chase Manhattan Corp
270 Park Ave
New York, NY 10017, USA

Shipman, Clarie (Correspondent)
ABC-TV
News Dept
77 W 66th St
New York, NY 10017, USA

Shipman, Kim (Golfer)
239 Texas Dr
Lindale, TX 75771-5030, USA

Shipp, E R (Misc)
New York Daily News
Editorial Dept
220 E 42nd St
New York, NY 10017, USA

Shipp, Jackie (Athlete, Football Player)
3117 Trails Ct
Norman, OK 73072, USA

Shipp, Jerry (Athlete, Basketball Player, Olympic Athlete)
P.O. Box 370
Kingston, OK 73439-0370, USA

Shipp, John Wesley (Actor)
c/o Janette Anderson *Janette Anderson Entertainment*
9682 Via Torino
Burbank, CA 91504, USA

Shipp, William (Athlete, Football Player)
3920 Camellia Dr
Mobile, AL 36693, USA

Shirakawa, Hideki (Nobel Prize Laureate)
University of Tsukuba
Chemistry Dept
Sakura-Mura
Ibaraki 305, JAPAN

Shirakawa, hideki (Nobel Prize Laureate)
University ofTsukuba Institute of Materials
Sciences Sakura-Mura
Ibaraki, Japan 305, USA

Shirayanagi, Peter Seiichi Cardinal (Religious Leader)
Archbishop's House
3-16-15 Sekiguchi
Bunkyoku
Tokyo 112, JAPAN

Shire, David L (Composer)
19 Ludlow Ave
Palisades, NY 10964, USA

Shire, Talia (Actor, Director)
10730 Beliagio Rd
Los Angeles, CA 90077, USA

Shirelles, The
PO Box 100
Clifton, NJ 07011

Shires, Jim (Athlete, Hockey Player)
24141 Fairway Ln
Trabuco Canyon, CA 92679-4184

Shirk, Gary (Athlete, Football Player)
5419 Silchester Ln
Charlotte, NC 28215, USA

Shirley, Bart (Athlete, Baseball Player)
5757 S Staples St
Apt 4208
Corpus Christi, TX 78414-6088, USA

Shirley, Bob (Athlete, Baseball Player)
761 W 13th St
Tulsa, OK 74127-9162, USA

Shirley, Caroline (Stylist)
c/o Staff Member *Ennis*
119 Braintree St
Boston, MA 02134, USA

Shirley, George I (Opera Singer)
University of Michigan
Music School
Ann Arbor, MI 48109, USA

Shirley, J Dallas (Referee)
5324 Pommel Dr
Mount Airy, MD 21771, USA

Shirley, Steve (Athlete, Baseball Player)
9200 James Pl NE
Albuquerque, NM 87111-3323, USA

Shirley-Quirk, John S (Opera Singer)
6062 Red Clover Lane
Clarksville, MD 21029, USA

Shirodkar, Shilpa (Actor, Bollywood)
Venkatesh Vihar
4th Floor 7th Road Khar
Mumbai, MS 400050, INDIA

Shirton, Glen (Athlete, Hockey Player)
5 Ziraldo Rd
St Catharines, ON L2N 6S6, Canada

Shiver, Sanders (Athlete, Football Player)
9217 Christo Ct
Owings Mills, MD 21117, USA

Shivers, Roy (Athlete, Football Player)
2067 Hidden Hollow Ln
Henderson, NV 89012, USA

Shivpuri, Himani (Actor)
16A/24 PGM Colony Poonam Nagar
Mahakali Caves Road Andheri (E)
Bombay, MS 400 093, INDIA

Shivpuri, Ritu (Actor, Bollywood)
12 Poonam 29/30 Pali Hill Union Bank
Khar
Bombay, MS 400 052, INDIA

Shlaudeman, Harry W (Diplomat)
7006 Pebble Beach Way
San Luis Obispo, CA 93401, USA

Shlomi, Vince (Offer) (Director)
1680 Michigan Ave
Suite 700
Miami Beach, FL 33139, USA

Shlyapina, Galina A (Ballerina)
Bolshoi Theater
Teatralnaya Pl 1
Moscow 103009, RUSSIA

Shmyr, John (Athlete, Hockey Player)
140 Nonquon Rd
Oshawa, ON L1G 3S5, Canada

Shmyr, Paul (Athlete, Hockey Player)

Shnayerson, Robert B (Editor)
118 Riverside Dr
New York, NY 10024, USA

Shoals, Roger (Athlete, Football Player)
365 Righters Mill Rd
Gladwyne, PA 19035, USA

Shobana (Actor, Bollywood)
77/5 Gulmohar Avenue
Velachery High Road
Chennai, TN 600032, INDIA

Shobana, Maganadhi (Actor, Bollywood)
A P 198
16th Street 2nd Sector
Chennai, TN 600078, INDIA

Shobert, Bubba (Race Car Driver)
8905 153rd St
Wolfforth, TX 79382, USA

Shocked, Michelle (Musician)
Skyline Music
28 Union St
Whitefield, NH 03598, USA

Shockey, Jeremy (Athlete, Football Player)
c/o Traci Harper *Harper PR*
3940 Laurel Canyon Blvd #1010
Studio City, CA 91604, USA

Shockley, Costen (Athlete, Baseball Player)
403 Wilson St
Georgetown, DE 19947, USA

Shockley, Costen
403 Wilson St
Georgetown, DE 19947-2340, USA

Shockley, Jeremy (Football Player)
New York Giants
Giants Stadium
East Rutherford, NJ 07073, USA

Shockley, William (Actor)
6345 Balboa Blvd
#375
Encino, CA 91316, USA

Shoebottom, Bruce (Athlete, Hockey Player)
40 Woodfield Dr
Scarborough, ME 04074-8437

Shoecraft, John A (Misc)
Shoecraft Contracting Co
7430 E Stetson Dr
Scottsdale, AZ 85251, USA

Shoeffling, Michael
PO Box 2563
Canyon Country, CA 91351

Shoemaker, Bill
250 W. Main St. #1820
Lexington, KY 40502-1733

Shoemaker, carolyn (Scientist)
US Geological Survey 2255 N Gemini Dr
Flagstaff, AZ 86001-1637, USA

Shoemaker, Carolyn S (Astronomer)
Lowell Observatory
1400 W Mars Hill Road
Flagstaff, AZ 86001, USA

Shoemaker, Craig (Actor)
c/o Staff Member *Osbrink Talent Agency*
4343 Lankershim Blvd
Suite 100
Universal City, CA 91602, USA

Shoemaker, John (Race Car Driver)
American Eagle Racing
3305 Horseshoe Dr.
Sacramento, CA 95821, USA

Shoemaker, Robert M (General)
PO Box 768
Belton, TX 76513, USA

Shoemaker, Sydney S (Misc)
104 Northway Road
Ithaca, NY 14850, USA

Shoemate, C Richard (Business Person)
Bestfoods
International Plaza
700 Sylvan Ave
Englewood Cliffs, NJ 07632, USA

Shofner, Delbert M (Del) (Athlete, Football Player)
1665 Del Mar Ave
San Marino, CA 91108, USA

Shofner, James (Jim) (Athlete, Football Coach, Football Player)
9620 Champions Dr
Granbury, TX 76049, USA

Shoji, Dave (Coach)
University of Hawaii
Athletic Dept
Hilo, HI 96720, USA

Shonekan, Ernest A O (President)
12 Alexander Ave
Ikoyi
Lagos, NIGERIA

Shonin, Georgi S (Cosmonaut, General)
Potchta Kosmonavtov
Moskovskoi Oblasti
Syvisdny Goroduk 141160, RUSSIA

Shoop, Ron
PO Box 92
Rural Valley, PA 16249

Shopay, Tom (Athlete, Baseball Player)
10145 NW 19th St
Doral, FL 33156-3165, USA

Shope, Allan (Architect)
Shope Reno Wharton
18 W Putnam Ave
Greenwich, CT 06830, USA

Shoppach, Kelly (Athlete, Baseball Player)
15358 Briarcrest Cir
Fort Myers, FL 76112-1066, USA

Shor, Anya (Stylist)
c/o Staff Member *Judy Inc*
1 Yorkville Ave
Toronto ON M4W 1L1, Canada

Shore, David (Producer, Writer)
c/o Lawrence Shuman *Shuman Company*
3815 Hughes Ave
4th Floor
Culver City, CA 90232, USA

Shore, Howard (Actor, Composer, Musician)
c/o Staff Member *Columbia Artists Mgmt Inc*
1790 Broadway Fl 6
New York, NY 10019-1412, USA

Shore, Pauly (Actor, Comedian)
c/o Staff Member *Landing Patch Productions*
8491 sunset Blvd #700
Hollywood, CA 90069, USA

Shore, Roberta
PO Box 71639
Salt Lake City, UT 84171-0639

Shores, Del (Writer)
Del Shores Productions
13636 Ventura Blvd #218
Sherman Oaks, CA 91423, USA

Shorr, Lonnie
707 18th Ave. So.
Nashville, TN 37203

Short, Bill (Athlete, Baseball Player)
2975 57th St
Sarasota, FL 34243-2434, USA

Short, Brandon (Athlete, Football Player)
1717 Sumac St
McKeesport, PA 15132, USA

Short, Columbus (Actor)
c/o Colton Gramm *Brillstein Entertainment Partners*
9150 Wilshire Blvd #350
Beverly Hills, CA 90212, USA

Short, Eugene (Athlete, Basketball Player)
8111 Fondren Lake Dr
Houston, TX 77071, USA

Short, Martin (Actor, Comedian, Musician)
15907 Alcima Ave
Pacific Palisades, CA 90272, USA

Short, Nigel (Misc)
Daily Telegraph
Peterborough Court
Marsh Wall
London E14, UNITED KINGDOM (UK)

Short, Purvis (Athlete, Basketball Player)
8111 Fondren Lake Dr
Houston, TX 77071-3610, USA

Short, Rick (Athlete, Baseball Player)
3021 Forsythe Ct
Peoria, IL 61614-1119, USA

Short, Thomas C (Misc)
Theatrical Stage Employees Alliance
1515 Broadway
New York, NY 10036, USA

Shorter, Frank (Athlete, Olympic Athlete, Track Athlete)
558 Utica Court
Boulder, CO 80304, USA

Shorter, Wayne (Composer, Musician)
International Music Network
278 S Main St
#400
Gloucester, MA 01930, USA

Shorthill, Richard W (Engineer)
University of Utah
Mechanical Engineering Dept
Salt Lake City, UT 84112, USA

Shortridge, Stephen (Actor)
3304 E Sky Harbor Dr
Coeur d'Alene, ID 83814, USA

Shortridge, Steve (Actor)
1707 Clearview Dr
Beverly Hills, CA 90210, USA

Shorts, Peter (Athlete, Football Player)
810 S Cedar Point Dr
Anaheim, CA 92808, USA

Shostakovich, Maxim D (Musician)
PO Box 273
Jordanville, NY 13361, USA

Shou, Robin (Actor)
Paradigm Agency
10100 Santa Monica Blvd
#2500
Los Angeles, CA 90067, USA

Shouse, Brian (Athlete, Baseball Player)
1616 Magnolia
Washington, IL 61615-8879, USA

Shouse, Dexter (Athlete, Basketball Player)
4523 E Rhonda Dr
Phoenix, AZ 85018, USA

Shout Out Louds (Music Group)
c/o Staff Member *Paradigm (Monterey)*
404 W Franklin St
Monterey, CA 93940, USA

Show, Frida (Actor)
c/o Kim Matuka *Online Talent Group*
Prefers to be contacted via email or telephone
Los Angeles, CA 90069, USA

Show, Grant (Actor)
c/o Heather Reynolds *One Entertainment (NY)*
12 W 57th St
Penthouse
New York, NY 10019, USA

Showalter III, William N (Buck) (Athlete, Baseball Player, Coach)
9736 Hathaway St
Dallas, TX 75220-2114, USA

Showder, Lisa (Race Car Driver)
1650 E. Golf Rd.
Schaumburg, IL 60196, USA

Shower, Kathy (Actor, Model)
Provenca 23 1-1
Barcelona, SPAIN

Shraner, Kim (Actor)
c/o Robyn Friedman *Artist Management Inc*
464 King St E
Toronto ON M5A 1L7, CANADA

Shreve, Anita (Writer)

Shreve, Susan R (Writer)
3506 35th Street NW
Washington, DC 20016-3114, USA

Shribman, David M (Journalist)
Boston Globe
Editorial Dept
1130 Connecticut Ave NW
Washington, DC 20036, USA

Shrider, Richard (Athlete, Basketball Player)
6666 Morning Sun Rd
Osford, OH 45056-8843, USA

Shrimpton, Jean (Actor, Model)
Abbey Hotel Penzance
Cornwall, UNITED KINGDOM (UK)

Shriner, Kin (Actor)
Don Buchwald
6500 Wilshire Blvd
#2200
Los Angeles, CA 90048, USA

Shriner, Wil (Entertainer)
5313 Quakertown Ave
Woodland Hills, CA 91364, USA

Shriver, Anthony
100 SE 2nd St. #1990
Miami, FL 33131

Shriver, Bobby
501 Colorado Ave. #200
Santa Monica, CA 90401

Shriver, Duward F (Scientist)
1100 Colfax St
Evanston, IL 60201, USA

Shriver, Loren J (Astronaut)
108 Charleston St
Friendswood, TX 77456, USA

shriver, Loren J Colonel (Astronaut)
108 Charleston St
Friendswood, TX 77546-4928, USA

Shriver, Maria (Journalist)
3110 Main St Ste 300
Santa Monica, CA 90405-5354, USA

Shriver, Maria (Correspondent, Television Host)
3110 Main St
#300
Santa Monica, CA 90405, USA

Shriver, Mark Kennedy
10015 Carter Rd
Bethesda, MD 20817

Shriver, Pam (Athlete, Olympic Athlete, Tennis Player)
c/o Jill Smoller *WME (LA)*
9601 Wilshire Blvd Fl 3
Beverly Hills, CA 90210, USA

Shriver, R
1325 G St NW
Washington, DC 20005, USA

Shriver, Timothy (Philanthropist)
Special Olympics
1133 19th Street NW
Washington, DC 20036-3604, USA

Shroff, Jackie (Actor, Bollywood)
1302 Le Pepeyon
Mount Mary Road Bandra
Mumbai, MS 400050, INDIA

Shrontz, Frank A (Business Person)
2949 81st Place
#P
Mercer Island, WA 98040, USA

Shroud, Johnathan (Writer)
Laura Cecil Literary Agency
17 Alwyne Villas
London N1 2HG, UNITED KINGDOM

Shrowder, Lisa (Race Car Driver)
1650 E Golf Road
Schaumburg, IL 60196, USA

Shroyer, Sonny (Actor)
12725 Ventura Blvd
#F
Studio City, CA 91604, USA

Shtalenkov, Mikhail (Athlete, Hockey Player)
7 Faenza
Newport Coast, CA 92657-1602

Shtokolov, Boris T (Opera Singer)
Mariinsky Theater
Teatralnaya Pl 1
Saint Petersburg, RUSSIA

Shuart, James M (Educator)
Hofstra University
President's Office
Hempstead, NY 11550, USA

Shuba, George (Athlete, Baseball Player)
3421 Bentwillow Ln
Youngstown, OH 44511-2502, USA

Shubin, Neil H (Biologist)
Harvard University
Biology Dept
Cambridge, MA 02138, USA

Shuchuk, Gary (Athlete, Hockey Player)
5713 Lancashier Ct
Fitchburg, WI 53711-6504

Shue, Andrew (Actor)
c/o Jimmy Darmody *Creative Artists Agency (CAA-LA)*
2000 Ave Of The Stars
Los Angeles, CA 90067, USA

Shue, Elisabeth (Actor)
c/o David Seltzer *Management 360*
9111 Wilshire Blvd
Beverly Hills, CA 90210, USA

Shue, Gene (Athlete, Basketball Player, Coach)
4338 Redwood Ave
Apt 303
Marina del Rey, CA 90292-7648, USA

Shuey, Paul (Athlete, Baseball Player)
5252 Mill Dam Rd
Wake Forest, NC 27587-6386, USA

Shugart, Alan F (Inventor)
Seagate Technologies
920 Disc Dr
Scotts Valley, CA 95066, USA

Shugart, Clyde (Athlete, Football Player)
6368 Heronwalk Dr
Gulf Breeze, FL 32563, USA

Shugarts, Bret (Athlete, Football Player)
18823 Forest Bend Creek Way
Spring, TX 77379, USA

Shuken, Ettie Benjamin (Stylist)
c/o Staff Member *Judy Inc*
1 Yorkville Ave
Toronto ON M4W 1L1, Canada

Shukovsky, Joel (Writer)
Shukovsky-English Ent
4024 Radford Ave
Studio City, CA 91604, USA

Shula, David D (Dave) (Athlete, Coach, Football Coach, Football Player)
10805 Indian Trl
Cooper City, FL 33328, USA

Shula, Don (Athlete, Coach, Football Coach, Football Player)
16 Indian Creek Dr
Indian Creek Village, FL 33154, USA

Shula, Mike (Athlete, Coach, Football Coach, Football Player)
13754 Bromley Point Dr
Jacksonville, FL 32225, USA

Shuler, Heath (Athlete, Football Player)
Shuler Real Estate
8550 Kingston Pike
Knoxville, TN 37919, USA

Shuler, Joseph Heath (Congressman, Politician)
229 69,non HOB
Washington, DC 20515, USA

Shuler, Mickey C (Athlete, Football Player)
332 Belle Vista Dr
Marysville, PA 17053, USA

Shuler Jr, Ellie G (Buck) (General)
32 Willow Way W
Alexander City, AL 35010, USA

Shulgin, Alexander (Scientist)
1483 Shulgin Road
Lafayette, CA 94549, USA

Shulman, Lawrence E (Scientist)
3726 Tudor Arms Ave
Baltimore, MD 21211, USA

Shulman, Robert G (Biologist)
333 Cedar St
New Haven, CT 06510, USA

Shulock, John (Athlete, Baseball Player)
4180 5th St SW
Vero Beach, FL 32968-3909, USA

Shulock, John (Baseball Player)
4180 5th St SW
Vero Beach, FL 32968-3909, USA

Shultz, George (Politician)
776 Dolores St
Stanford, CA 94305-8428, USA

Shultz, George P (Politician, Secretary)
Hoover Institute
Stanford University
Stanford, CA 94305, USA

Shumaker, Anthony (Athlete, Baseball
Player)
2213 Jefferson Rd
Paducah, KY 42001-3108, USA

Shumaker, John W (Educator)
University of Louisville
President's Office
Louisville, KY 40292, USA

Shuman-Juransinski, Amy (Baseball
Player)
424 Douglass St
Wyomissing, PA 19610-2906, USA

Shumate, John (Athlete, Basketball Player,
Coach)
16406 S 12th Pl
Phoenix, AZ 85048-4045, USA

Shumate, Rachel (Actor)
c/o Sean Fay *Kritzer Levine Wilkins
Entertainment (KLWG)*
11872 La Grange Ave
1st Floor
Los Angeles, CA 90025, USA

Shum Jr., Harry (Actor)
c/o Marissa Upchurch *Triniti Management*
12400 Ventura Blvd
#668
Studio City, CA 91604, USA

Shumlin, Peter (Governor, Politician)
Pavilion Office Bldg
109 State St Fl 5
Montpelier, VT 05609, USA

Shumpert, Terry (Athlete, Baseball Player)
8432 Fairview Ct
Lone Tree, CO 80124, USA

Shust, Aaron (Musician)
c/o Mitch White *Moose Management*
Prefers to be contacted via telephone
Nashville, TN, USA

Shuster, Bill (Congressman, Politician)
204 Cannon HOB
Washington, DC 20515, USa

Shutan, Jan (Actor)
3115 Deep Canyon Dr
Beverly Hills, CA 90210, USA

Shutt, Byron (Athlete, Hockey Player)
29723 Lake Rd
Bay Village, OH 44140-1277, USA

Shutt, Steve (Athlete, Coach, Hockey
Player)
137 Easton Cir
Fairhope, AL 36532-6344

Shuttleworth, Mark (Astronaut)
HBD Ventura Capital
PO Box 1159
Durbanville 7551, SOUTH AFRICA

Shuttz, George P
776 Dolores St
Stanford, CA 94305, USA

Shut Up Stella (Music Group)
c/o Staff Member *Paradigm (Monterey)*
404 W Franklin St
Monterey, CA 93940, USA

Shy, Les (Athlete, Football Player)
1777 W Crystal Ln #556
Mt Prospect, IL 60056-5437, USA

Shyamalan, M Night (Director, Producer,
Writer)
c/o Staff Member *Night Chronicles*
c/o Media Rights Capital
1800 Century Park East
Los Angles, CA 90067, USA

Shydner, Ritch (Comedian)
c/o Staff Member *Agency for the
Performing Arts (APA-LA)*
405 S Beverly Dr
Suite 500
Beverly Hills, CA 90212-4425, USA

Shyer, Charles R (Director, Writer)
227 N Glenroy Ave
Los Angeles, CA 90049, USA

Shys, The (Music Group)
c/o Staff Member *Paradigm (Monterey)*
404 W Franklin St
Monterey, CA 93940, USA

Sia, Beau (Actor)
c/o Staff Member *Creative Artists Agency
(CAA-LA)*
2000 Ave Of The Stars
Los Angeles, CA 90067, USA

Siana (Model)
PO Box 4957
Virginia Beach, VA 23454

Sias, John B (Publisher)
Chronicle Publishing Co
901 Mission St
San Francisco, CA 94103, USA

Sibbett, Jane (Actor)
c/o John Carrabino *John Carrabino
Management*
5900 Wilshire Blvd Fl 4 #406
Los Angeles, CA 90036, USA

Sibert, Sam (Athlete, Basketball Player)
3604 Yachtclub Dr
Arlington, TX 76016, USA

Sibley, Antoinette (Ballerina)
Royal Dancing Academy
36 Battersea Square
London SW11 3LT, UNITED KINGDOM
(UK)

Sibley, David (Actor)
c/o Staff Member *Select Artists Ltd (CA-
Westside Office)*
1138 12th Street
Suite 1
Santa Monica, CA 90403, USA

Sibley, Marilyn (Stylist)
c/o Staff Member *Clutts Agency, The*
1400 Turtle Creek Blvd
#171
Dallas, TX 75207, USA

Sibley, Mark (Athlete, Basketball Player)
334 E McKenna Ct
Elmhurst, IL 60126, USA

Sicard, Pedro (Actor)
c/o Gabriel Blanco *Gabriel Blanco
Iglesias (Mexico)*
Rio Balsas 35-32
Colonia Cuauhtemoc
DF 06500, Mexico

Sichting, Jerry (Basketball Player)
3190 Country Club Road
Martinsville, IN 46151, USA

Sicinski, Bob (Athlete, Hockey Player)
1741 Pengilley Pl
Mississauga, ON L5J 4R8, Canada

Siddall, Joe (Athlete, Baseball Player)
2785 Sierra Dr
Windsor, ON N9E 2Y9, Canada

Siddig, Alexander (Actor)
c/o Pippa Markham *Markham & Froggatt*
4 Windmill St
London W1T 1HZ, UK

Siddiqui, Aamera (Actor)
c/o Staff Member *NUTS*
820 N Lilac Dr
Suite 101
Golden Valley, MN 55422, USA

Siddiqui, Farouge (Director, Filmmaker)
16/24 Old Collector Compound
Malvani Colony Gate No 5 Malad
Bombay, MS 400 095, INDIA

Siddons, Anne (Writer)
60 Church St
Charleston, SC 29401-2558, USA

Siddons, Anne R (Writer)
767 Vermont Road
Atlanta, GA 30319, USA

Siddons, Ann Rivers (Writer)
60 Church St
Charleston, SC 29401

Sidenbladh, Goran (Architect)
Narvagen 23
Stockholm 114 60, SWEDEN

Sider, Harvey R (Religious Leader)
Brethren in Christ Church
PO Box 290
Grantham, PA 17027, USA

Sidewalk Prophets (Music Group,
Musician)
c/o Scott Bickell *Brickhouse Entertainment*
106 Mission Court
Suite 1202
Franklin, TN 37067, USA

Sidgmore, John (Business Person)
WorldCom
500 Clinton Center Dr
Clinton, MS 39056, USA

Sidibe, Gabourey (Gabby) (Actor)
c/o Jill Kaplan *Principal Entertainment
(NY)*
130 W 42nd St
Suite 614
New York, NY 10036, USA

Sidime, Lamine (Prime Minister)
Prime Minister's Office
Conakry, GUINEA

Sidlin, Murry (Conductor)
Catholic University
Music School
Washington, DC 20064, USA

Sidney, Dainon (Athlete, Football Player)
605 Lakemeade Pl
Old Hickory, TN 37138, USA

Sidney, Rice (Athlete, Football Player)
11931 Tiffany Ln
Eden Prairie, MN 55344-5384, USA

Sidor, Susan (Stylist)
361 E 50th St
New York, NY 10022, USA

Sidorkiewicz, Peter (Athlete, Hockey
Player)
1056 Swiss Hts
Oshawa, ON L1K 3B4, Canada

Sidran, Ben (Race Car Driver)
Go Jazz
PO Box 2023
Madison, WI 53101, USA

Sidransky, David (Doctor, Scientist)
Baylor Medical Center
1200 Moursand Ave
Houston, TX 77030, USA

Siebel, Jennifer (Actor, Producer)
Girl's Club Entertainment
San Francisco, CA, USA

Sieber, Christopher (Actor)
c/o Richard Fisher *Abrams Artists Agency
(NY)*
275 Seventh Ave
26th Floor
New York, NY 10001, USA

Siebern, Norm (Athlete, Baseball Player)
2006 Palo Alto Ave
Lady Lake, FL 34119-1505, USA

Siebert, Paul (Athlete, Baseball Player)
1711 Acker St
Orlando, FL 32837-6588, USA

Siebert, Sonny
2583 Brush Creek
St. Louis, MO 63129-5601, USA

Siebert, Wilfred C (Sonny) (Athlete,
Baseball Player)
2555 Brush Creek Rd
Saint Louis, MO 63129, USA

Siebler, Dwight (Athlete, Baseball Player)
11565 S 204th St
Gretna, NE 68028-7974, USA

Siebold, Pete
Scaled Composites LLC 1624 Flight Line
Attn: Director of Flight Operations
Mojave, CA 93501-1663, USA

Sieck, Robert (Scientist)
6990 Hinsdale Dr
Melbourne, FL 32940-6644, USA

Siega, Marcos (Director)
c/o Staff Member *WME (LA)*
9601 Wilshire Blvd Fl 3
Beverly Hills, CA 90210, USA

Siegal, Bernard (Writer)
61 0x Bow Ln
Woodbridge, CT 06525-1525

Siegal, Jay (Music Group, Musician)
Brothers Mgmt
141 Dunbar Ave
Fords, NJ 08863, USA

Siegal, John (Football Player)
Chicago Bears
Harvey's Bt
Harveys Lake, PA 18618, USA

Siegbahn, Kai M B (Nobel Prize Laureate)
University of Uppasala
Physics Institute
Box 530
Uppasala 75 121, SWEDEN

Siegel, Barry (Journalist)
Los Angeles Times
Editorial Dept
202 W 1st St
Los Angeles, CA 90012, USA

Siegel, Bernie (Doctor, Writer)
61 Oxbow Lane
Woodbridge, CT 06525, USA

Siegel, Eric (Actor)
c/o Mickey Berman *United Talent Agency (UTA)*
9336 Civic Center Dr
Beverly Hills, CA 90210, USA

Siegel, Herbert J (Business Person)
Chris-Craft Industries
767 5th Ave
New York, NY 10153, USA

Siegel, Ira T (Publisher)
16589 Senterra Dr
Delray Beach, FL 33484, USA

Siegel, Jake (Actor)
c/o Staff Member *JC Robbins Management*
113 S Kilkea Dr
Los Angeles, CA 90048, USA

Siegel, Janis (Musician)
International Creative Mgmt
40 W 57th St #1800
New York, NY 10019, USA

Siegel, L Pendleton (Business Person)
Potlatch Corp
601 W Riverside Ave
Spokane, WA 99201, USA

Siegel, Norman (Attorney)
Committee for Norman Siegel
260 Madison Ave
New York, NY 10016, USA

Siegel, Robert C (Correspondent)
c/o Gregory McKnight *Creative Artists Agency (CAA-LA)*
2000 Ave Of The Stars
Los Angeles, CA 90067, USA

Siegel, Ron (Chef)
Charles Nob Hill 1250 Jones St
San Francisco, CA 94109-4261, USA

Siegert, Wayne (Athlete, Football Player)
401 E 4th St
Pana, IL 62557, USA

Siegfried And (&) Roy (Magician)
Mirage Hotel & Casino
3400 Las Vegas Blvd
Las Vegas, NV 89109, USA

Siekevitz, Philip (Biologist)
290 W End Ave
New York, NY 10023, USA

Siemaszko, Casey (Actor)
Gersh Agency
232 N Canon Dr
Beverly Hills, CA 90210, USA

Siemaszko, Nina (Actor)
c/o David Rose *Innovative Artists (LA)*
1505 10th St
Santa Monica, CA 90401, USA

Sieminski, Chuck (Athlete, Football Player)
5000 Village Way
Apt 406
Marcus Hook, PA 19061, USA

Siemon, Jeffrey G (Jeff) (Athlete, Football Player)
5401 Londonderry Rd
Edina, MN 55436, USA

Sienkiewicz, Troy (Athlete, Football Player)
186 Darcy Ave
Goose Creek, SC 29445-6664, USA

Sierchio, Tom (Actor, Writer)
c/o Alan Gasmer *Alan Gasmer Management Company*
10877 Wilshire Blvd.
Suite 603
Los Angeles, CA 90024, USA

Siering, Lauri (Swimmer)
3829 Rotterdam Ave
Modesto, CA 95356, USA

Sierra, Jessica (Musician)
c/o Network Solutions
PO Box 447
Herndon, VA 20172-0447, USA

Sierra, Pedro (Athlete, Baseball Player)
Indianapolis Clowns
3708 Lehigh Ct
Mays Landing, NJ 08330-3249, USA

Sierra, Ruben A (Athlete, Baseball Player)
12355 SW 51st St
Miami, FL 33175, USA

Sierra, Rubin
Ed 25 #2501 Jardines Selles
Rio Piedras, PR 00924

Siers, Kevin (Cartoonist, Editor)
Charlotte Observer
Editorial Dept
600 S Tryon St
Charlotte, NC 28202, USA

Sievers, Eric (Athlete, Football Player)
11550 Great Falls Way
Great Falls, VA 22066, USA

Sievers, Gary (Actor)
c/o Staff Member *Dani's Agency*
434 E Southern Ave
Tempe, AZ 85282, USA

Sievers, Roy E (Athlete, Baseball Player)
11505 Bellefontaine Rd
Saint Louis, MO 63138-1706, USA

Sieverts, Thomas C W (Architect)
Buschstr 20
Bonn 53113, GERMANY

Siff, Maggie (Actor)
c/o James Suskin *James Suskin Management*
2 Charlton St Ste 5K
New York, NY 10014, USA

Sifford, Charlie (Athlete, Golfer)
7540 Sanctuary Cir
Brecksville, OH 44141-3195, USA

Sific, Mokdad (Prime Minister)
Prime Minister's Office
Government Palais
Al-Moradia
Algiers, ALGERIA

Sigalet, Jordan (Athlete, Hockey Player)
PO Box 3454 Stn LCD 1
Langley, BC V3A 4R8, Canada

Sigel, Beanie (Musician)
International Creative Mgmt
8942 Wilshire Blvd
#219
Beverly Hills, CA 90211, USA

Sigel, Jay (Golfer)
1284 Farm Rd
Berwyn, PA 19312-2000, USA

Sigel, Tom (Cinematographer)
International Creative Mgmt
8942 Wilshire Blvd #219
Beverly Hills, CA 90211, USA

Sigholtz, Bob
5425 Shirley Ave.
Tarzana, CA 91356

Sigler, Jamie-Lynn (Actor)
c/o Glenn Gulino *G2 Entertainment LLC*
1 Columbus Pl #S-25E
New York, NY 10019, USA

Sigman, Stan (Business Person)
Cingular Creative Mgmt
5565 Glenridge Connector
Atlanta, GA 30342, USA

Sigur Ros (Music Group)
c/o Staff Member *Paradigm (Monterey)*
404 W Franklin St
Monterey, CA 93940, USA

Sigwart, Ulrich (Doctor)
Centre Hospitalier Universitaire Vaudois
Lausanne, SWITZERLAND

Siilasvuo, Ensio (General)
Castrenikatu 6A17
Helsinki 53 00530, FINLAND

Sikahema, Vai (Athlete, Football Player)
28 Abington Rd
Mount Laurel, NJ 08054, USA

Sikes, Alfred C (Government Official)
3214 Kirwans Neck Road
Church Creek, MD 21622, USA

Sikes, Cynthia (Actor)
250 N Delfern
Los Angeles, CA 90077, USA

Sikharulidze, Anton (Figure Skater)
Ice House Skating Rink
111 Midtown Bridge Approach
Hackensack, NJ 07601, USA

Sikich, Mike P (Athlete, Football Player)
702 Tudor Dr
Janesville, WI 53546, USA

Sikking, James B (Actor)
258 S Carmelina Ave
Los Angeles, CA 90049, USA

Siklenka, Mike (Athlete, Hockey Player)
Farm
Meadow Lake, SK S9X 1 T8, Canada

Sikma, Jack (Athlete, Basketball Player)
9125 NE 21st Pl
Clyde Hill, WA 98004-2437, USA

Sikora, Joe (Actor)
c/o Myrna Jacoby *MJ Management*
130 W 57th St
Suite 11A
New York, NY 10019, USA

Sikora, Nicole (Athlete, Golfer)
Westchester Golf Range
701 Dobbs Ferry Rd
White Plains, NY 10607, USA

Sikorski, Brian (Athlete, Baseball Player)
17930 Wexford St
Roseville, MI 48066-4630, USA

Silas, James (Athlete, Basketball Player)
6800 Thistle Hill Way
Austin, TX 78754-5800, USA

Silas, Paul (Athlete, Basketball Player, Coach)
2463 Peninsula Shores Ct
Denver, NC 28037-7655, USA

Silatolu, Ratu Timoci (Prime Minister)
Prime Minister's Office
6 Berkeley Crescent
Suva
Viti Levu, FIJI

Silberling, Bradley (Brad) (Director, Producer)
c/o Staff Member *Reveal Entertainment*
310 North Stanley Avenue
Los Angeles, CA 90036, USA

Silberman, Laurence H (Diplomat, Judge)
US Court of Appeals
3rd & Constitution NW
Washington, DC 20001, USA

Silbermann, Jake (Actor)
c/o Robyn Ziegler *Robyn Ziegler Management*
143 W 29th St Ste 1103
New York, NY 10001, USA

Silberstein, Diane Wichard (Publisher)
New Yorker Magazine
Publisher's Office
4 Times Square
New York, NY 10036, USA

Silbey, Robert J (Misc)
Massachusetts Institute of Technology
Chemistry Dept
Cambridge, MA 02139, USA

Sileo, Dan (Athlete, Football Player)
46 Woodland Dr #203
Vero Beach, FL 32962, USA

Silia, Felix (Actor)
8927 Snowden Ave
Arleta, CA 91331, USA

Silja, Anja (Opera Singer)
Colbert Artists
111 W 57th St
New York, NY 10019, USA

Silk (Artist, Musician)
c/o Staff Member *Faa*
250 West 57th Street
New York, NY 10107, USA

Silk, Dave (Athlete, Hockey Player, Olympic Athlete)
PO Box 130
Minot, MA 02055-0130

Silla, Felix
8927 Snowden Ave.
Arleta, CA 91331

Sillas, Karen (Actor)
PO Box 725
Wading River, NY 11792, USA

Siller, Eugenio (Actor)
c/o Tom Harrison *Diverse Talent Group*
9911 W Pico Blvd Ste 340W
Los Angeles, CA 90035, USA

Silliman, Ron (Writer)
262 Orchard Rd
Paoli, PA 19301-1116, USA

Sillinger, Mike (Athlete, Hockey Player)
419-4009 Harbour Landing Dr
Regina, SK S4W OE3, Canada

Sillinger, Mike (Athlete, Hockey Player)
Edmonton Oilers
11230 110 St NW
Edmonton, AB TSG 3H7, Canada

Sills, Douglas (Actor, Musician)
Gold Marshak Liedike
3500 W Olive Ave
#1400
Burbank, CA 91505, USA

Sills, Stephen (Architect, Designer)
Sills Huniford Assoc
30 E 67th St
New York, NY 10021, USA

Siltala, Mike (Athlete, Hockey Player)
1693 Ruscombe Close
Mississauga, ON LSJ 1Y4, Canada

Silva, Adele (Actor, Model)
c/o Staff Member *McLean-Williams Management*
Gainsborough House
81 Oxford St
London W1D 2EU, UK

Silva, Anderson (Athlete, Wrestler)
c/o Staff Member *Black House Team Nogueira*
7550 Miramar Rd
Suite 330
San Diego, CA 92126, USA

Silva, Daniel (Writer)
3512 Winfield Lane NW
Washington, DC 20007

Silva, Gilberto (Football Player)
Arsenal Stadium
Highbury
London N5 1BU, ENGLAND

Silva, Henry (Actor)
8747 Clifton Way #305
Beverly Hills, CA 90211, USA

Silva, Jackie (Athlete, Volleyball Player)
Jackie Sports and Marketing
Prefers to be contacted via email or telephone

Silva, Jason (Television Host)
c/o Rob Levy *Untitled Entertainment (LA)*
350 S. Beverly Dr #200
Beverly Hills, CA 90212, USA

Silva, Jose (Stylist)
c/o Staff Member *Directions USA*
3717-C W Market St
Greensboro, NC 27403, USA

Silva, Jose (Athlete, Baseball Player)
401 Pappan Dr
Imperial, PA 15126-1192, USA

Silva, Tom (Entertainer)
This Old House Show
PO Box 2284
South Burlington, VT 05407, USA

Silva, Zack (Actor)
Valeo Entertainment
c/o Michael Dean Valeo
8265 Sunset Blvd Ste 103
Los Angeles, CA 90046, USA

Silver, Beverly (Stylist)
4 E 36th St
#5-R
New York, NY 10016, USA

Silver, Edward J (Religious Leader)
Bible Way Church
5118 Clarendon Road
Brooklyn, NY 11203, USA

Silver, Harvey (Actor)
c/o Staff Member *Anonymous Content (LA)*
3531 Hayden Ave
Culver City, CA 90232, USA

Silver, Horace (Composer, Musician)
Bridge Agency
35 Clark St #A5
Brooklyn, NY 11201, USA

Silver, Jeffrey (Producer)
c/o Staff Member *Outlaw Productions*
9350 Civic Center Dr #100
Beverly Hills, CA 90210-3629, USA

Silver, Joan Macklin (Director)
Silverfilm Productions
510 Park Ave #9B
New York, NY 10022, USA

Silver, Joel (Producer)
c/o Staff Member *Silver Pictures*
4000 Warner Blvd
Bldg 90
Burbank, CA 91522

Silver, Michael B
9229 Sunset Blvd #315
Los Angeles, CA 90069, USA

Silver, Pamela (Stylist)
c/o Staff Member *Lachapelle Representation Ltd*
420 E 54th St
#14-F
New York, NY 10022, USA

Silver, Robert S (Engineer)
Oakbank
Breadalbane St
Tobermory, Isle of Mull, SCOTLAND

Silver, Spencer (Inventor)
378 Summit Ave Apt C
Saint Paul, MN 55102-2166, USA

Silvera, Charlie (Athlete, Baseball Player)
1240 Manzanita Dr
Milbrae, CA 94030-2934, USA

Silverberg, Robert (Writer)
c/o Tom Doherty Associates, LLC
175 Fifth Ave
New York, NY 10010, USA

Silverbush, Lori (Actor)
c/o Brantley Brown *Schachter Entertainment*
1157 S Beverly Dr Fl 2
Los Angeles, CA 90035, USA

Silverchair
Box 15
Merewether, AUSTRALIA NSW 2291

Silverio, Luis (Athlete, Baseball Player)
3130 NW 89th Ter
Kansas City, MO 33076-1825, USA

Silverman, Al (Publisher)
411 E 53rd St
16H
New York, NY 10022, USA

Silverman, Barry G (Judge)
US Court of Appeals
230 N 1st St
Phoenix, AZ 85025, USA

Silverman, Benjamin (Producer)
c/o Staff Member *NBC Universal (LA)*
100 Universal City Plz
Universal City, CA 91608, USA

Silverman, Fred
1642 Mandeville Canyon
Los Angeles, CA 90049

Silverman, Henry R (Business Person)
Cendant Corp
9 W 57th St
New York, NY 10019, USA

Silverman, Jerry (Horse Racer)
3888 Meadow Ln
Hollywood, FL 33021-2645, USA

Silverman, Jonathan (Actor)
c/o Beth Holden-Garland *Untitled Entertainment (LA)*
350 S. Beverly Dr #200
Beverly Hills, CA 90212, USA

Silverman, Sarah (Actor, Comedian)
c/o Amy Zvi *Thruline Entertainment*
9250 Wilshire Blvd
Ground Fl
Beverly Hills, CA 90212, USA

Silvers, Robert (Artist)
Henry Holt
115 W 18th St
New York, NY 10011, USA

Silverstein, Elliott (Director)
Gersh Agency
232 N Canon Dr
Beverly Hills, CA 90210, USA

Silverstein, Joseph H (Conductor, Musician)
Utah Symphony Orchestra
123 W South Temple
Salt Lake City, UT 84101, USA

Silverstone, Alicia (Actor)
c/o Jason Weinberg *Untitled Entertainment (LA)*
350 S. Beverly Dr #200
Beverly Hills, CA 90212, USA

Silverstone, Ben (Actor)
c/o Staff Member *London Management*
2-4 Noel St
London W1V 3RB, UNITED KINGDOM (UK)

Silversun Pickups (Music Group, Musician)
c/o Cliff Burnstein *Q Prime Inc*
729 7th Ave
16th Floor
New York, NY 10019, USA

Silvestre, Armando
Cerro Macultepec 273Col. Campestre Churubusco
Mexico DF, MEXICO

Silvestri, Alan A (Composer, Musician)
c/o Staff Member *Gorfaine/Schwartz Agency Inc*
4111 W Alameda Ave
Suite 509
Burbank, CA 91505, USA

Silvestri, Dave (Athlete, Baseball Player, Olympic Athlete)
1888 Schoettler Valley Dr
Chesterfield, MO 63017-5141, USA

Silvestrini, Achille Cardinal (Religious Leader)
Oriental Churches Congregation
Via Conciliazione 34
Rome 00193, ITALY

Silvia (Royalty)
Kungliga Slottet
Stottsbacken
Stockholm 111 30, SWEDEN

Silvstedt, Victoria (Actor, Model)
c/o Liza Anderson *Anderson Group Public Relations*
8060 Melrose Ave Fl 4
Los Angeles, CA 90046, USA

Sim, Gerald (Actor)
Associated Internationl Mgmt
7 Great Russell St
London W1D 1BS, UNITED KINGDOM (UK)

Sim, Jonathan (Athlete, Hockey Player)
104 Willow Ave
New Glasgow, NS B2H lZS, Canada

Sim, Sheila
Old Friars Richmond Greene
Surrey, ENGLAND

Simanek, Robert E (War Hero)
25194 Westmoreland Dr
Farmington Hills, MI 48336, USA

Simanek, Robert E (General)
25194 Westmoreland Dr
Farmington Hills, MI 48336-1270, USA

Simas, Bill (Athlete, Baseball Player)
6084 Millerton Rd
Friant, CA 93720-5633, USA

Simcoe, Anthony (Actor)
c/o Pauline Lee *International Casting Service & Associates*
2/218 Crown St (via Kings Lane)
Darlinghurst NSW 2010, Australia

Sime, Dave (Athlete, Olympic Athlete, Track Athlete)
9140 Bay Dr
Surfside, FL 33154-3112, USA

Simeoni, Sara (Athlete, Track Athlete)
Via Castello Rivoli Veronese
Verona 37010, ITALY

Simeon II (King, Prime Minister)
Prime Minister's Office
1 Dondukov Blvd
Sofia 1000, BULGARIA

Simhan, Meera (Actor)
Bamboo Management
C/O Heidi L Ifft
17 Buccaneer St
Marina Del Rey, CA 90292, USA

Simic, Charles (Writer)
PO Box 192
Strafford, NH 03884, USA

Simic, Charles (Writer)
PO Box 192
Strafford, NH 03884-0192, USA

Simien, Tracy (Athlete, Football Player)
3219 Sumac Dr
Pearland, TX 77584-8069, USA

Simien, Wayne (Basketball Player)
c/o Staff Member *Miami Heat*
1 SE 3rd Avenue
Suite 2300
Miami, FL 33131, USA

Simitis, Costas (Prime Minister)
35 Akadanuas St
Athens 106 72, GREECE

Simkin, Margery (Misc)
CSA
606 N. Larchmont Blvd
4-B
Los Angeles, CA 90004, USA

Simkus, Arnold (Athlete, Football Player)
4248 Chicago Rd
Warren, MI 48092, USA

Simmel, Johannes Mario
Bohlgutsch 3
Zug, SWITZERLAND CH-6300

Simmer, Charles (Athlete, Hockey Player)
70 Couplee View
SW
Calgary, AB T3H 5J7, Canada

Simmer, Charlie (Athlete, Hockey Player)
70 Coulee View SW
Calgary, AB T3H 5J6, Canada

Simmer, Charlie (Athlete, Hockey Player)
Calgary Flames
PO Box 1540 Stn M
Calgary, AB T2P3B9, Canada

Simmonds, Kennedy A (Prime Minister)
PO Box 167
Earle Mome Development
Basseterre, SAINT KITTS & NEVIS

Simmonds, Sara (Actor)
c/o Steven Jensen *Independent Group, The*
6363 Wilshire Blvd
Suite 115
Los Angeles, CA 90048, USA

Simmons, Arthur (Baseball Player)
Kansas City Monarchs
27 158th Pl Apt 2W
Calumet, IL 60409-4945, USA

Simmons, Bob (Athlete, Football Player)
16040 Chalfont Cir
Dallas, TX 75248, USA

Simmons, Brian (Athlete, Football Player)
9240 Liberty Hill Ct
Cincinnati, OH 45242, USA

Simmons, Brian (Athlete, Baseball Player)
226 Village Dr
Canonsburg, PA 15317-2367, USA

Simmons, Canary (Athlete, Football Player)
13531 Lyndonville Dr
Houston, TX 77041-4804, USA

Simmons, Chelan (Actor)
c/o Staff Member *Pacific Artists Management*
1285 W Broadway
Suite 685
Vancouver, BC V6H 3X8, Canada

Simmons, Curtis T (Curt) (Athlete, Baseball Player)
200 Park Rd
Ambler, PA 19002-1121, USA

Simmons, Dan (Writer)
c/o Michael Prevett *The Gotham Group Inc*
9255 Sunset Blvd
Suite 515
Los Angeles, CA 90069, USA

Simmons, Earl (DMX) (Actor, Musician)
c/o Staff Member *J Mike Management & Entertainment*
9107 Wilshire Blvd
Suite 450
Beverly Hills, CA 90210, USA

Simmons, Ed (Athlete, Football Player)
P.O. Box 6632
Kennewick, WA 99336, USA

Simmons, Gary (Athlete, Hockey Player)
2624 Inverness Dr.
Lake HavasU City, AZ 86404-1373

Simmons, Gene (Business Person, Musician, Reality TV Star)
PO Box 16075
Beverly Hills, CA 90210, USA

Simmons, Grant (Athlete, Basketball Player)
7274 E Costilla Pl
Centennial, CO 80112, USA

Simmons, Harold (Business Person)
Simmons Biomedical Research Building
6000 Harry Hines Blvd #NB2.300
Dallas, TX 75235-5303, USA

Simmons, Henry (Actor)
c/o Jason Shapiro *United Talent Agency (UTA)*
9336 Civic Center Dr
Beverly Hills, CA 90210, USA

Simmons, Hubert (Baseball Player)
Baltimore Elite Giants
3247 Sonia Trl
Ellicott City, MD 21043-3273, USA

Simmons, Jaason (Actor)
Gilbertson & Kincaid Mgmt
1330 4th ST
Santa Monica, CA 90401, USA

Simmons, Jason (Athlete, Football Player)
2828 Spring St
Pittsburgh, PA 15210, USA

Simmons, Jeff (Race Car Driver)
Team Green
7615 Zionsville Rd.
Indianapolis, IN 46268-2174, USA

Simmons, Jerry (Athlete, Football Player)
2233 S King Dr
Chicago, IL 60616, USA

Simmons, JK (Actor)
c/o Stephen Hirsh *Gersh (NY)*
41 Madison Ave
New York, NY 10010, USA

Simmons, Johnny (Actor)
c/o Mimi DiTrani *Schiff Company, The*
9465 Wilshire Blvd
Suite 480
Beverly Hills, CA 90212, USA

Simmons, Joseph (Rev Run) (Actor, Producer)
Rush Philanthropic Arts Foundation
512 Seventh Avenue
43rd Floor
New York, New York 10018, USA

Simmons, Kimora Lee (Designer, Fashion Designer)
c/o Staff Member *Phat Fashions LLC*
512 Seventh Ave
New York, NY 10018, USA

Simmons, Lionel (Athlete, Basketball Player)
108 Wellesley Ct
Mount Laurel, NJ 08054-5133, USA

Simmons, Lionel J (Athlete, Basketball Player)
108 Wellesley Ct
Mount Laurel, NJ 08054, USA

Simmons, Lon (Sportscaster)
10 Wailea Ekolu Pl J\pt 1707
Kihei, HI 96753-9505, USA

Simmons, Nelson (Athlete)
4445 Rosebud Ln Apt B
La Mesa, CA 91941-6255, USA

Simmons, Richard (Actor, Fitness Expert, Producer)
c/o Rick Hersh *Celebrity Consultants LLC*
3340 Ocean Park Blvd
Suite 1030
Santa Monica, CA 90405, USA

Simmons, Richard D (Publisher)
Int'l Herald Tribune
181 Ave Charles de Gaulie
Neuilly 92521, FRANCE

Simmons, Richard P (Business Person)
Allegheny Teledyne
1000 6 PPG Place
Pittsburgh, PA 15222, USA

Simmons, Russell (Producer)
Simmons-Lathan Media Group
6100 Wilshire Blvd
Suite 1111
Los Angeles, CA 90048, USA

Simmons, Ruth (Educator)
Brown University
President's Office
Providence, RI 02912, USA

Simmons, Shadia (Actor)
265 GA Hwy 30 West
Americus, GA 31709, USA

Simmons, Stacey (Athlete, Football Player)
1780 Harbor Dr
Clearwater, FL 33755, USA

Simmons, Tabitha (Stylist)
c/o Staff Member *Streeters*
560 Broadway
Suite 203
New York, NY 10012, 212-219-9566

Simmons, Ted L (Athlete, Baseball Player)
P.O. Box 26
Chesterfield, MO 63006, USA

Simmons, Todd (Baseball Player)
39778 Pinedale Way
Murrieta, CA 92562-6719, USA

Simmons, Tony (Athlete, Football Player)
366 Grand Ave
Apt 319
Oakland, CA 94610, USA

Simmons, Vanessa (Model)
c/o Staff Member *Ford Models (LA)*
9200 Sunset Blvd #805
West Hollywood, CA 90069, USA

Simmons, Victor (Athlete, Football Player)
P.O. Box 2992
Chicago, IL 60690, USA

Simms, Chris (Football Player)
c/o Team Member *Tampa Bay Buccaneers*
1 Bucaneer Pl
Tampa, FL 33607, USA

Simms, Joan (Actor)
MGA
Southbank House
Black Prince Road
London SE1 7SJ, UNITED KINGDOM (UK)

Simms, Julie (Stylist)
1800 S Hobart Blvd
Los Angeles, CA 90006, USA

Simms, Larry (Actor)
1043 Keeho Marina
Honolulu, HI 96819, USA

Simms, Mike (Athlete, Baseball Player)
118 Via Monte Picayo
San Clemente, CA 76092-0111, USA

Simms, Molly (Actor)
c/o Alissa Vradenburg *Untitled Entertainment (LA)*
350 S. Beverly Dr #200
Beverly Hills, CA 90212, USA

Simms, Philip (Phil) (Athlete, Football Player, Sportscaster)
930 Old Mill Rd
Franklin Lakes, NJ 07417, USA

Simms, Primate George Otto (Religious Leader)
62 Cypress Grove Road
Dublin 6, IRELAND

Simo, Brian (Race Car Driver)
28033 Arnold Rd.
EC-2
Sonoma, CA 95476, USA

Simollardes, Drew (Musician)
David Levin Mgmt
200 W 57th St
#308
New York, NY 10019, USA

Simon, Bob (Correspondent)
c/o 60 Minutes *CBS News Productions*
524 W 57th St
8th Floor
New York, NY 10019, USA

Simon, Carly (Composer, Musician)
c/o Larry Ciancia *Ciancia Management*
5419 Evergreen Heights Dr
Evergreen, CO 80439, USA

Simon, Chris (Athlete, Hockey Player)
702 Foch St
Williston Park, NY 11596, Canada

Simon, Corey (Athlete, Football Player)
9010 Winged Foot Dr
Tallahassee, FL 32312-4000, USA

Simon, Daniella (Designer)
Daniella Fashions, Inc
315 W 70th St
Apt 8i
New York, NY 10023, USA

Simon, David (Actor, Producer, Writer)
c/o Staff Member *Creative Artists Agency (CAA-LA)*
2000 Ave Of The Stars
Los Angeles, CA 90067, USA

Simon, Dick (Race Car Driver)
Dick Simon Racing
24896 Sea Crest Dr.
Dana Point, CA 92829, USA

Simon, George W (Astronaut)
PO Box 62
Sunspot, NM 88349, USA

Simon, James (Athlete, Football Player)
8501 SW 103rd Ave
Gainesville, FL 32608, USA

Simon, Josette (Actor)
Conway Van Gelder Robinson
18-21 Jermyn St
London SW1Y 6NB, UNITED KINGDOM (UK)

Simon, Neil (Writer)
c/o Staff Member *WmE2 (WMA-LA)*
1 William Morris Pl
Beverly Hills, CA 90212, USA

Simon, Neil (Writer)
465 Park Ave Apt 14D
New York, NY 10022-1943, USA

Simon, Paul (Musician, Songwriter)

Simon, Roger M (Writer)
Baltimore Sun
Editorial Dept
1627 K St NW
Washington, DC 20006, USA

Simon, Salem (Athlete, Football Player)
2245 Sheridan Rd
Evanston, IL 60201, USA

Simon, Sam
c/o Gary Cosay *United Talent Agency (UTA)*
9336 Civic Center Dr
Beverly Hills, CA 90210, USA

Simon, Scott (Correspondent)
NBC-TV
News Dept
30 Rockefeller Plaza
New York, NY 10112, USA

Simon, Todd (Athlete, Hockey Player)
Morrell Wine Bar and Cafe
1 Rockefeller Plz
New York, NY 10020-2003

Simon, White (Stylist)
c/o Staff Member *Rex Agency, The*
6311 Romaine St
Los Angeles, CA 90038, USA

Simone, Albert J (Educator)
Rochester Institute of Technology
President's Office
Rochester, NY 14623, USA

Simoneau, Mark (Athlete, Football Player)
17 Waterview Dr
Sicklerville, NJ 08081, USA

Simoneau, Yves (Director, Producer, Writer)
c/o Adam Levine *Levine Okwu Erickson Management*
9601 Wilshire Blvd
3rd Floor
Beverly Hills, CA 90210, USA

Simonetti, Frank (Athlete, Hockey Player)
33 Perkins St
Stoneham, MA 02180-4345

Simonini, Edward (Ed) (Athlete, Football Player)
3825 E 66th St
Tulsa, OK 74136, USA

Simonis, Adrianus J Cardinal (Religious Leader)
Aartbisdom
BP 14019 Maliebaan
Utrecht, SB 3508, NETHERLANDS

Simonon, Paul (Musician)
Clash
268 Camden Rd
London NW1, UNITED KINGDOM

Simonov, Yuriy I (Conductor)
Moscow Conservatory
Gertsema St 13
Moscow, RUSSIA

Simons, Doug (Athlete, Baseball Player)
1988 Mount Olive Rd
Lookout Mountain, GA 30750-4746, USA

Simons, Elwyn L (Misc)
Duke University
Primate Center
3705 Erwin Road
Durham, NC 27705, USA

Simons, James (Producer)
c/o Staff Member *Paradigm (LA)*
360 N Crescent Dr
North Bldg
Beverly Hills, CA 90210, USA

Simons, Lawrence B (Government Official)
Powell Goldstein Frazier
1001 Pennsylvania Ave NW
Washington, DC 20004, USA

Simonsen, Renee (Actor, Model)
c/o Staff Member *Ford Models (NY)*
238 E 4th St
New York, NY 10009, USA

Simonsen, Rob (Composer, Musician)
c/o Neil Kohan *Greenspan Artist Management*
8760 W Sunset Blvd
West Hollywood, CA 90069, USA

Simonson, Dave (Athlete, Football Player)
408 1st St SW
Austin, MN 55912, USA

Simontacchi, Jason (Athlete, Baseball Player)
6924 Birdie Ln
Saint Louis, MO 63129-5408, USA

Simpkins, Dickey (Athlete, Basketball Player)
6104 St Andrews Way
Hixson, TN 37343-3284, USA

Simple Kid (Music Group)
c/o Staff Member *Paradigm (Monterey)*
404 W Franklin St
Monterey, CA 93940, USA

Simple Plan (Music Group)
c/o Staff Member *Creative Artists Agency (CAA-LA)*
2000 Ave Of The Stars
Los Angeles, CA 90067, USA

Simpson, Alan (Politician)
1201 Sunshine Ave
Cody, WY 82414-4228, USA

Simpson, Alan (Educator)
Yellow Gate Farm
Little Compton, RI 02837, USA

Simpson, Alan K (Senator)
1201 Sunshine Ave
PO Box 270
Cody, WY 82414, USA

Simpson, Arnelle
11661 San Vicente Blvd. #632
Los Angeles, CA 90049

Simpson, Bill (Athlete, Football Player)
5732 Huntley Ave
Garden Grove, CA 92845, USA

Simpson, Bobby (Athlete, Hockey Player)
4779 Limestone Ln NW
Acworth, GA 30102-6484

Simpson, Carl (Athlete, Football Player)
12106 Parkview Ln
Alpharetta, GA 30005, USA

Simpson, Carole (Correspondent)
ABC-TV
News Dept
77 W 66th St
New York, NY 10023, USA

Simpson, Charles R (Judge)
US Tax Court
400 2nd St NW
Washington, DC 20217, USA

Simpson, Cody (Musician)
P.O. Box 1766
Studio City, CA 91614, USA

Simpson, Craig (Athlete, Hockey Player)
CBC TV
PO Box 500 Stn A 5H100
Toronto, ON M5W lEG, Canada

Simpson, Dick (Athlete, Baseball Player)
P.O. Box 3593
Culver City, CA 90231-3593, USA

Simpson, Duke (Athlete, Baseball Player)
3821 Park Dr
El Dorado Hills, CA 95762-4568, USA

Simpson, Geoffrey (Cinematographer)
PO Box 3194
Bellevue Hills, NSW 2023, AUSTRALIA

Simpson, Herbert (Athlete, Baseball Player)
Birmingham Black Barons
1462 Farragut St
New Orleans, LA 70114-2818, USA

Simpson, Jason
11661 San Vicente Blvd. #632
Los Angeles, CA 90049

Simpson, Jessica (Musician)
9555 Lime Orchard Rd
Beverly Hills, CA 90210, USA

Simpson, Jimmi (Actor)
c/o Staff Member *ROAR (LA)*
9701 Wilshire Blvd
8th Floor
Los Angeles, CA 90212, USA

Simpson, Joanne G (Scientist)
NASA/GSFC
Mail Code 912
Earth Sciences Center
Greenbelt, MD 20771, USA

Simpson, Joe (Athlete, Baseball Player)
4681 Jefferson Township Ln
Marietta, GA 30066-1737, USA

Simpson, Joe (Producer)
3830 Hayvenhurst Dr
Encino, CA 91436, USA

Simpson, John (Horse Racer)
51 High Rock Rd N
Hanover, PA 17331-9454, USA

Simpson, Juliene (Athlete, Basketball Player, Olympic Athlete)
PO Box 1267
Stroudsburg, PA 18360-4267, USA

Simpson, Juliene Brazinski (Athlete, Basketball Player)
P.O. Box 1267
Stroudsburg, PA 18360, USA

Simpson, Keith (Athlete, Football Player)
20710 Castle Bend Dr
Katy, TX 77450, USA

Simpson, OJ (Actor, Athlete, Football Player, Heisman Trophy Winner, Sportscaster)
Lovelock Correctional Facility
1200 Prison Rd
#1027820
Lovelock, NV 89419-5110, USA

Simpson, Ralph (Athlete, Basketball Player)
5185 Fraser St
Denver, CO 80239-6065, USA

Simpson, Reid (Athlete, Hockey Player)
340 W Superior St Apt 1210
Chicago, IL 60654-6190

Simpson, Scott (Athlete, Golfer)
15778 Paseo Hermosa
Poway, CA 92064-2164, USA

Simpson, Stern Carol (Misc)
American Assn of University Professors
1012 14th St NW
Washington, DC 20005, USA

Simpson, Suzi (Actor, Model)
24338 El Toro Road
#E315
Laguna Woods, CA 92653, USA

Simpson, Terry (Coach)
Anaheim Mighty Ducks
2000 E Gene Autry Way
Anaheim, CA 92806, USA

Simpson, Todd (Athlete, Hockey Player)
Royal Lepage Kelowna
1-1890 Cooper Rd
Kelowna, BC Vl Y 8B7, Canada

Simpson, Wayne K (Athlete, Baseball Player)
330 E Collamer Dr
Carson, CA 90746-1139, USA

Simpson, Webb (Athlete, Golfer)
c/o Thomas Parker *GPR Sports Management*
11715 Spinnaker Way
Hollywood, FL 33026, USA

Simpson, William (Writer)
c/o Staff Member *HarperCollins Publishers*
10 East 53rd St
c/o Author mail, 7th Floor
New York, NY 10022, USA

Simpson Sr, John F (Race Car Driver)
Mount Morris Star Route
Waynesburg, PA 15370, USA

Simpson-Wentz, Ashlee (Actor, Musician)
c/o Joe Simpson *JT Entertainment*
1453 3rd Street Promenade Ste 320
Santa Monica, CA 90401, USA

Simpy Red (Music Group)
c/o Staff Member *Lee & Thompson*
4 Gee's Ct
St Christopher's Place
London W1U 1JD, UK

Simran (Actor)
C/o Hotel Residency
Thyagaraya Nagar
Chennai, TN 600 017, INDIA

Sims, Al (Athlete, Hockey Player)
4215 Winding Way Dr
Fort Wayne, IN 46835-1466

Sims, Barry (Athlete, Football Player)
3578 Rosincress Dr
San Ramon, CA 94582, USA

Sims, Billy R (Athlete, Football Player)
P.O. Box 3147
Coppell, TX 75019, USA

Sims, Darryl (Athlete, Football Player)
P.O. Box 379
Mc Farland, WI 53558, USA

Sims, Duane "Duke" (Athlete, Baseball Player)
10509 Shoalhaven Dr
Las Vegas, NV 89134-7425, USA

Sims, Duane (Duke) (Athlete, Baseball Player)
10509 Shoalhaven Dr
Las Vegas, NV 89134, USA

Sims, Greg (Athlete, Baseball Player)
6700 Rancho Pico Way
Sacramento, CA 95828-1325, USA

Sims, Heath (Athlete, Olympic Athlete, Wrestler)
1027 Pearl St
La Jolla, CA 92037-5162, USA

Sims, Joan
17 Esmond Ct.Thackery St.
London, ENGLAND WE 5HB

Sims, Keith (Athlete, Football Player)
2920 Luckle Rd
Weston, FL 33331, USA

Sims, Ken (Athlete, Football Player)
4898 Converse Ave
East Saint Louis, IL 62207, USA

Sims, Kenneth W (Athlete, Football Player)
P.O. Box 236
Kosse, TX 76653, USA

Sims, Molly (Actor)
c/o Alissa Vradenburg *Untitled Entertainment (LA)*
350 S. Beverly Dr #200
Beverly Hills, CA 90212, USA

Sims, Robert (Athlete, Basketball Player)
915 Highland Ave
Apt 3
Duarte, CA 91010, USA

Sin, Jaime L Cardinal (Religious Leader)
121 Arzobispo St Entramuros
PO Box 132
Manila 10099, PHILIPPINES

Sinatra, Nancy (Actor, Musician)
c/o Thomas De Lorenzo *SmartPR*
8033 Sunset Blvd
Suite 1033
Los Angeles, CA 90046, USA

Sinatra, Ray
1234 S. 8th Pl.
Las Vegas, NV 89104

Sinatra Jr, Frank (Musician)
c/o Seth Shomes *Day After Day Productions*
436 1st St
Suite 102
Solvang, CA 93436, USA

Sinatro, Matt (Athlete, Baseball Player)
2619 239th Ave SE
Sammamish, WA 98075-9442, USA

Sinbad (Actor, Comedian)
c/o Linda Jones *The Mass Appeal*
3940 Laurel Canyon Blvd
Unit 447
Studio City, CA 91604, USA

Sinceno, Kaseem (Athlete, Football Player)
168B Bradford Ct
Mount Laurel, NJ 08054, USA

Sinceros
25 Buliver St.Shephard's Bush
London, ENGLAND W12 8AR

Sinclair, Cameron (Architect, Business Person)
Architecture for Humanity
848 Folsom
Suite 201
San Francisco, CA 94107-1173, USA

Sinclair, Clive M (Inventor)
Sinclair Research
7 York Central
70 York Way
London N1 9AG, UNITED KINGDOM (UK)

Sinclair, Harry (Director, Writer)
c/o Ken Kamins *ICM Partners (ICM-LA)*
10250 Constellation Blvd Fl 7
Los Angeles, CA 90067, USA

Sinclair, Joshua (Actor, Director, Producer, Writer)
c/o Staff Member *Sun Gateway Entertainment*
Taubenheimstr 30
70372, GERMANY

Sinclair, Michael (Athlete, Football Player)
14215 Heidi Oaks Ln
Humble, TX 77396, USA

Sinclair, Reggie
10 Golf Club Crt
Rothesay, NB E2H 2Pl, Canada

Sindelar, Jerry
213 Prospect Hill Rd
Horseheads, NY 14845

Sindelar, Joan (Baseball Player)
504 W Sunland Ave
Phoenix, AZ 85041-4822, USA

Sindelar, Joey (Golfer)
18 Prospect Rdg
Horseheads, NY 14845-7988, USA

Sinden, Donald A (Actor)
Rats Castle
Isle of Oxney
Kent TN30 7HX, UNITED KINGDOM (UK)

Sinden, Harry (Athlete, Hockey Player)
9 Olde Village Dr
Winchester, MA 01890-2213

Sinden, Harry (Athlete, Hockey Player)
Boston Bruins
100 Legends Way Ste 250
Boston, MA 02114-1389

Sinegal, James (Business Person)
Costco Wholesale Corp
999 Lake Dr
Issaquah, WA 98027, USA

Sing, Daniel (Actor)
c/o Kathryn Rawlings *Kathryn Rawlings Actors Agency*
4/28 Williamson Ave.
Grey Lynn
Auckland, New Zealand

Singer, Bryan (Director)
c/o Staff Member *Bad Hat Harry Productions*
4000 Warner Blvd
Bldg 81 #200
Burbank, CA 91522, USA

Singer, Isadore (Scientist)
989 Hill Rd
Boxborough, MA 01719-1011, USA

Singer, Isadore M (Mathematician)
Massachusetts Institute of Technology
Mathematics Dept
Cambridge, MA 02139, USA

Singer, Lori (Actor)
Chuck Binder
1465 Linda Crest Dr
Beverly Hills, CA 90210, USA

Singer, Marc (Actor)
11218 Canton Dr
Studio City, CA 91604, USA

Singer, Maxine F (Educator)
5410 39th St NW
Washington, DC 20015, USA

Singer, Peter A D (Misc)
Princeton University
Human Values Center
Princeton, NJ 08544, USA

Singer, Ramona (Designer, Reality TV Star)
c/o Staff Member *Bravo (NY)*
30 Rockefeller Plaza
New York, NY 10112, USA

Singer, S Fred (Physicist)
4084 University Dr
#101
Fairfax, VA 22030, USA

Singer, William R (Bill) (Athlete, Baseball Player)
1119 Mallard Marsh Dr
Osprey, FL 34229-6810, USA

Singh, Amrita (Actor, Bollywood)
Bungalow 5
Lokhandwala Complex Andheri Link Road
Mumbai, MS 400058, INDIA

Singh, Archana Puran (Actor, Bollywood)
G426 Anjali Apartments
Seven Bungalows Anheri
Mumbai, MS 400061, INDIA

Singh, Bipin (Choreographer, Dancer)
Manipuri Nartanalaya
15A Bipin Pal Road
Kolkata, WB 700026, INDIA

Singh, Chandrachur (Actor, Bollywood)
6th Floor Oakland Park
Off Lokhandwala Complex Versova
Mumbai, MS 400049, INDIA

Singh, Manmohan (Prime Minister)
Premier's Office
South Block
Safdarjung Road
New Delhi, Delhi 110011, INDIA

Singh, Sukhmander (Engineer)
Santa Clara University
Civil Engineering Dept
Santa Clara, CA 95053, USA

Singh, Tjinder (Musician)
Legends of 21st Century
7 Trinity Row
Florence, MA 01062, USA

Singh, Vijay (Golfer)
1275 Ponte Vedra Blvd
Ponte Vedra Beach, FL 32082-4402, USA

Singh, Vishwanath Pratap (Prime Minister)
1 Teen Murti Marg
New Delhi, ND 110001, INDIA

Singh, Yuvraj (Athlete, Cricketer)
c/o Staff Member *Board of Control for Cricket in India*
Cricket Centre" Wankhede Stadium
'D' Road, Churchgate
Mumbai 400 020, India

Singletary, Daryl
1000 18th Ave. So.
Nashville, TN 37212

Singletary, Michael (Mike) (Athlete, Football Player)
14982 Sobey Rd
Saratoga, CA 95070, USA

Singletary, Tony (Director)
c/o Staff Member *Agency for the Performing Arts (APA-LA)*
405 S Beverly Dr
Suite 500
Beverly Hills, CA 90212-4425, USA

Singleton, Chris (Athlete, Baseball Player)
2038 Town Manor Dr
Dacula, GA 30019-3247, USA

Singleton, Chris (Athlete, Football Player)
42599 W Sunland Dr
Maricopa, AZ 85238-1630, USA

Singleton, Duane (Athlete, Baseball Player)
191 Macdonogh St
Brooklyn, NY 11216-2507, USA

Singleton, Isaac (Actor)
c/o Jason Mellerstig *Artist International Management (LA)*
9595 Wilshire Blvd Fl 9
Los Angeles, CA 90212, USA

Singleton, John D (Director, Producer, Writer)
c/o Staff Member *Creative Artists Agency (CAA-LA)*
2000 Ave Of The Stars
Los Angeles, CA 90067, USA

Singleton, Kenneth W (Kenny) (Athlete, Baseball Player)
10 Sparks Farm Rd
Sparks Glencoe, MD 21152-9300, USA

Singleton, Margie (Musician)
PO Box 567
Hendersonville, TN 37077, USA

Sinha, Mala (Actor)
8 Turner Road
Bandra
Bombay, MS 400 050, INDIA

Sinha, Shatrughan (Actor, Bollywood, Politician)
104 Green Star Apts Rizvi Complex
Sherly Rajan Road Bandra
Bombay, MS 400 050, INDIA

Sinisalo, Ilkka (Athlete, Hockey Player)
6221 Main St
Voorhees, NJ 08043-4629

Sinise, Gary (Actor)
c/o Marc Gurvitz *Brillstein Entertainment Partners*
9150 Wilshire Blvd #350
Beverly Hills, CA 90212, USA

Sinn, Pearl (Golfer)
132 21st Pl
Manhattan Beach, CA 90266-4402, USA

Sinner, George (Politician)
1013rd St N
Moorhead, MN 56560-1952, USA

Sinner, George A (Ex-Governor)
101 3rd St N
Moorhead, MN 56560, USA

Sinnott, John (Athlete, Football Player)
9 Primrose Ln
North Providence, RI 02904, USA

Sinton, Nell (Artist)
484 Lake Park Ave
#189
Oakland, CA 94610, USA

Sinyavskaya, Tamara I (Opera Singer)
Kunstleragentur Raab & Bohm
Plankengasse 7
Vienna 1010, AUSTRIA

Siouxsie & The Banshees
1325 Ave. of the Americas
New York, NY 10019

Siouzsie, Sioux (Musician)
Helter Skelter
Plaza
535 Kings Road
London SW10 0S, UNITED KINGDOM
(UK)

Sipchen, Bob (Journalist)
Los Angeles Times
Editorial Dept
202 W 1st St
Los Angeles, CA 90012, USA

Sipe, Brian W (Athlete, Football Player)
17 East H St
Encinitas, CA 92024, USA

Siphandon, Khamtay (General, President)
President's Office
Vientiane, LAOS

Sipin, John (Athlete, Baseball Player)
455 Ponza Ln
Soquel, CA 95073-9528, USA

Sipinen, Arto K (Architect)
Arkkitehtitoimistro Arto Sipinen Ky
Ahertajantie 3
Espoo 02100, FINLAND

Sipos, Shaun (Actor)
c/o Sheila Wenzel *Innovative Artists (LA)*
1505 10th St
Santa Monica, CA 90401, USA

Sipp, Tony (Athlete, Baseball Player)
3976 River Pine Drive
Moss Point, MS 39563, USA

Sippy, G P (Actor)
3/G Naaz Building
Lamington Road
Bombay, MS 400 004, INDIA

Sippy, Raj (Bollywood, Director,
Filmmaker, Producer)
101 Jal Tarang Kishore Kumar Ganguly
Marg
Juhu Tara Road
Bombay, MS 400 049, INDIA

Sippy, Ramesh (Bollywood, Director,
Filmmaker, Producer)
379 Sathe House 14th Road
Khar
Bombay, MS 400 052, INDIA

Sippy Cups, The (Music Group)
c/o Staff Member *Paradigm (Monterey)*
404 W Franklin St
Monterey, CA 93940, USA

Siragusa, Tony (Athlete, Football Player)
349 Ashwood Ave
Kenilworth, NJ 07033, USA

Sir Douglas Quintet
59 Parsons St.
Newtonville, MA 02160

Siren, Heikki (Architect)
Tiirasaarentie 35
Heisinki 00200, FINLAND

Siren, Katri A H (Architect)
Tiirasaarentie 35
Heisinki 00200, FINLAND

Sires, Albin (Congressman, Politician)
2342 Rayburn HOB
Washington, DC 20515, USA

Sirgo, Otto (Actor)
c/o Staff Member *Televisa*
Blvd Adolfo Lopez Mateos 232
Colonia San Angel INN
DF CP 01060, MEXICO

Sirhan, Sirhan
#B21014Corcoran State Prison Box 8800
Corcoran, CA 93212

Siriano, Christian (Designer, Reality TV
Star)
260 W 35th St
New York, NY 10001, USA

Sirico, Tony (Actor)
c/o Bob McGowan *McGowan
Management*
8733 W Sunset Blvd
Suite 103
West Hollywood, CA 90069, USA

Sirikit (Royalty)
Chritrada Villa
Bangkok, THAILAND

Siri Singh Sahib (Religious Leader)
Sikh
PO Box 351149
Los Angeles, CA 90035, USA

Sir Mix-a-lot (Musician)
c/o Eva Arthur *Universal Attractions*
135 W 26th St
12 Floor
New York, NY 10001, USA

Sirmon, Peter (Athlete, Football Player)
5255 McGavock Rd
Brentwood, TN 37027, USA

Sirotka, Mike (Athlete, Baseball Player)
20704 N 90th Pl Unit 1005
Scottsdale, AZ 85255-9135, USA

Sirtis, Marina (Actor)
c/o Alan Saffron *Saffron Management*
9171 Wilshire Blvd #441
Beverly Hills, CA 90210, USA

Sisco, Andrew (Athlete, Baseball Player)
25324 176th Ave SE
Covington, WA 98042-6709, USA

Sisco, Joseph J (Engineer, Government
Official)
2702 Parkview Drive
Riva, MD 21140-1017, USA

Sisco, Steve (Athlete, Baseball Player)
630 San Doval Pl
Thousand Oaks, CA 91360-1314, USA

Sisemore, Jerald G (Jerry) (Athlete,
Football Player)
17301 Whipporwill Trl
Leander, TX 78645, USA

Sisk, Bradford (Producer)
c/o Staff Member *Bankable Productions*
226 W 26th St
4th Floor
New York, NY 10001-6700, USA

Sisk, Doug (Athlete, Baseball Player)
3610 42nd Ave NE
Tacoma, WA 98422-2480, USA

Sisk, John (Athlete, Football Player)
7814 W Wisconsin Ave
Wauwatosa, WI 53213, USA

Sisk, Tommie (Athlete, Baseball Player)
164 E 4635 N
Provo, UT 84604-5447, USA

Siskin, Aaron (Photographer)
15 Elmway St
Providence, RI 02906-4709, USA

Sisko, David (Race Car Driver)
2125 Lindon Hwy
Hohenwald, TN 38462, USA

Sislen, Myrna (Musician)
Lindy Martin Mgmt
5 Lob Lolly Court
Pinehurst, NC 28374, USA

Sisqo (Musician)
c/o Jason Priluck *Agency Group Ltd, The
(LA)*
1880 Century Park E
Suite 711
Los Angeles, CA 90067, USA

Sissel (Musician)
Stageway Impressario
Skuteviksboder 11
Bergen 5035, NORWAY

Sissel, George A (Business Person)
Ball Corp
10 Longs Peak Dr
Broomfield, CO 80021, USA

Sissi (Actor)
c/o Staff Member *Univision*
605 3rd St. Fl12
New York, NY 10158, USA

Sisson, Doug (Athlete, Baseball Player)
1821 Matts Ln
Watkinsville, GA 30677-4862, USA

Sisson, Scott (Athlete, Football Player)
902 Ravenwood Way
Canton, GA 30115, USA

Sissons, Kimber (Actor)
412 Amaz Dr
#204
Los Angeles, CA 90048, USA

Sister, Max (Designer, Fashion Designer)
Mount Everest Centre for Buddhist Studies
Kathmandu, NEPAL

Sister Hazel (Music Group)
c/o Staff Member *Sixthman*
83 Walton St
Atlanta, GA 30303, USA

Sister Sledge (Music Group)
c/o Staff Member *Tony Denton
Promotions Limited (UK)*
P.O. Box 2839
London W1K 5LE, United Kingdom

Sisters of Mercy
28 Kensington Church St.
London, ENGLAND W8 4EP

Sisto, Jeremy (Actor)
c/o Christina Papadopoulos *Baker
Winokur Ryder Public Relations BWR
(BWR-NY)*
292 Madison Ave
12th Floor
New York, NY 10017, USA

Sistrunk, Manny (Athlete, Football Player)
1601 Jarvis Ave
Oxon Hill, MD 20745, USA

Sistrunk, Otis (Athlete, Football Player)
P.O. Box 372
Dupont, WA 98327, USA

Sites, Brian (Actor)
c/o Staff Member *Innovative Artists (LA)*
1505 10th St
Santa Monica, CA 90401, USA

Sites, James W (Producer)
American Legion Magazine
700 N Pennsylvania St
Indianapolis, IN 46204, USA

Sithara (Actor, Bollywood)
556 I Floor
2nd Block 2nd Cross R T Nagar
Bangalore, KA 560032, INDIA

Sitkovetsky, Dmitry (Musician)
Columbia Artists Mgmt Inc
165 W 57th St
New York, NY 10019, USA

Sitter, Charles R (Business Person)
Exxon Corp
5959 Las Collinas Blvd
Irving, TX 75039, USA

Sittler, Darrell (Athlete, Hockey Player)
84 Buttonwood Ct
East Amherst, NY 14051, USA

Sittler, Darryl (Athlete, Hockey Player)
171 Glengarry Ave
Toronto, ON M5M IEI, Canada

Sittler, Darryl (Athlete, Hockey Player)
Toronto Maple Leafs
400-40 Bay St
Toronto, ON M5J 2X2, Canada

Sittler, Walter (Actor)
Agentur Heppeler
Seinstr 54
Munich 81667, GERMANY

Sitton, Charles (Athlete, Basketball Player)
3035 SW Homesteader Rd
West Linn, OR 97068-9612, USA

Sivad, Darryl (Actor)
c/o Staff Member *Leavitt Talent Group*
8255 W Sunset Blvd
West Hollywood, CA 90046, USA

Sivam, Peeli (Actor)
43 Parthasarathy Pettai
II Street
Chennai, TN 600 086, INDIA

Sivan, Santosh (Cinematographer,
Director, Writer)
c/o Staff Member *Paradigm (LA)*
360 N Crescent Dr
North Bldg
Beverly Hills, CA 90210, USA

Sivaranjani (Ooha) (Actor, Bollywood)
7 Vivekananda Nagar
Nesapakkam
Chennai, TN 600092, INDIA

Siwy, Jim (Athlete, Baseball Player)
6919 April Wind Ave
Las Vegas, NV 89131-0119, USA

Six Shooter
PO Box 53
Portland, TN 37148

Sixthman (Music Group, Musician)
158 Moreland Avenue SE
Atlanta, GA 30316-1676, USA

Sixx
9255 Sunset Blvd. #200
Los Angeles, CA 90069-3309

Sixx, Nikki (Musician)
Royal Underground
2532 White Rd
Irvine, CA 92614, USA

Siza, Alvaro (Architect)
Oporto University
Architecture School
Oporto, PORTUGAL

Sizemore, Grady (Athlete, Baseball
Player)
1951 W 26th St Aot 512
Cleveland, OH 44113-3467, USA

Sizemore, Marge
1951 Bottlebrush Dr
Melbourne, FL 32935-4783, USA

Sizemore, Matt (Adult Film Star)
c/o Staff Member *Diva Central Inc*
7510 W Sunset Blvd Ste 1445
Los Angees, CA 90046, USA

Sizemore, Ted (Athlete, Baseball Player)
14030 Conway Rd
Chesterfield, MO 63017-3402, USA

Sizemore, Tom (Educator)
Brown University
Essential Schools Coalition
Providence, RI 02912, USA

Sizemore, Tom (Actor)
c/o Staff Member *Evolution Entertainment*
(LA)
901 N Highland Ave
Los Angeles, CA 90038, USA

Sizova, Alla I (Ballerina)
Universal Ballet School
4301 Harewood Road NE
Washington, DC 20017, USA

S Jayaram (Actor)
7-Majestic Terrace 48 Arcot Road
Saligramam
Chennai, TN 600 098, INDIA

Sjoberg, Lars-Erik (Athlete, Hockey
Player)

Sjoberg, Patrik (Athlete, Track Athlete)
Hokegatan 17
Goteberg 416 66, SWEDEN

Sjodin, Tommy (Athlete, Hockey Player)
Karlvagen 2
Gavle, 80266 Sweden

Sjostrom, Fredrik (Athlete, Hockey Player)
18362 N 94th Pl
Scottsdale, AZ 85255-6001

Skaalen, Jim (Athlete, Baseball Player)
2608 El Aguila Ln
Carlsbad, CA 92009-4332, USA

Skabo, Paul
262 Santa Rosa Ave
Sausalito, CA 94965-2037, USA

Skaggs, Dave (Athlete, Baseball Player)
11131 Arlington Ave
Riverside, CA 92505-2148, USA

Skaggs, Jim (Athlete, Football Player)
421 Falcon Ridge Rd
Ellensburg, WA 98926, USA

Skaggs, Ricky (Actor, Musician)
c/o Bobby Cudd *Paradigm (Nashville)*
124 12th Ave S
Suite 410
Nashville, TN 37203, USA

Skah, Khalid (Athlete, Track Athlete)
Boite Postale 2577
Fez, MOROCCO

Skala, Brian T (Actor)
c/o Staff Member *Osbrink Talent Agency*
4343 Lankershim Blvd
Suite 100
Universal City, CA 91602, USA

Skalde, Jarred (Athlete, Hockey Player)
602 E Livingston St
Orlando, FL 32803-5618

Skalski, Joe (Athlete, Baseball Player)
15546 Drexel Ave
Dolton, IL 60419-2750, USA

Skarda, Randy (Athlete, Hockey Player)
26885 Noble Rd
Excelsior, MN 55331-8239

Skarsgard, Alexander (Actor)
5699 Holly Oak Dr
Los Angeles, CA 90068, USA

Skarsgard, J Stellan (Actor)
Hogersgatan 40
Stockholm 118 26, SWEDEN

Skarsgard, Stellan
Hogbergsgatan 40 II
Stockholm, SWEDEN S-118 26

Skarsten, Rachel (Actor)
c/o Steve Lovett *Lovett Management*
1327 Brinkley Ave
Los Angeles, CA 90049, USA

Skaugstad, Daryle (Athlete, Football
Player)
17216 NE 195th St
Woodinville, WA 98072, USA

Skaugstad, Dave (Athlete, Baseball Player)
16222 Monterey Ln
Spc 274
Huntington Beach, CA 92649-2248, USA

Skayskal, Wayne
PO Box 191
Tampa, FL 33601

Skeels, Mark (Baseball Player)
1835 Hilton Head Rd
El Cajon, CA 92019-4472, USA

Skeen, Archie (Baseball Player)
2685 N 4275 W
Ogden, UT 84404-9074, USA

Skeet, DJ Skeet (DJ)
c/o Ron Laffitte *Red Light Management*
(LA)
8439 W Sunset Blvd
Suite 2
Los Angeles, CA 90069, USA

Skeeters, The (Music Group)
c/o Staff Member *Paradigm (Monterey)*
404 W Franklin St
Monterey, CA 93940, USA

Skeggs, Leonard T Jr (Misc)
10212 Blair Lane
Kirtland, OH 44094, USA

Skeie, Andris (Prime Minister)
Prime Minister's Office
Brivibus Bulv 36
Riga, PDP 226170, LATVIA

Skelton, Byron G (Judge)
US Court of Appeals
717 Madison Ave NW
Washington, DC 20439, USA

Skelton, Mike (Writer)
c/o Jon Huddle *United Talent Agency*
(UTA)
9336 Civic Center Dr
Beverly Hills, CA 90210, USA

Skerritt, Tom (Actor)
c/o Amy Weiss *Brillstein Entertainment*
Partners
9150 Wilshire Blvd #350
Beverly Hills, CA 90212, USA

Skibbie, Lawrence F (General)
2309 S Queen St
Arlington, VA 22202, USA

Skibinski, Joe (Athlete, Football Player)
1912 Pine St
Peru, IL 61354, USA

Skibniewska, Halina (Architect)
Wydzlat Architektury Politechniki
Ul Koszykowa 55
Warsaw 00-659, POLAND

Skidmore, Paul (Athlete, Hockey Player)
469W 760 N
Santaquin, UT 84655-5545

Skidmore, Roe (Athlete, Baseball Player)
964 E Marlin Dr
Decatur, IL 62521-5549, USA

Skid Row (Music Group)
720 Palisades Ave
Englewood Cliffs, NJ 07632, USA

Skiles, Scott (Athlete, Basketball Player)
3975 S Inverness Farm Rd
Bloomington, IN 47401-9190, USA

Skillets (Music Group, Musician)
c/o Staff Member *Q Management Group*
P.O. Box 273
Franklin, TN 37065, USA

Skillman-Hull, Melanie (Archer, Athlete,
Olympic Athlete)
907 Carsonia Ave
Reading, PA 19606-1203, USA

Skinner, Al (Athlete, Basketball Player)
145 Great Plains Ave
Wellesley, MA 02482-7211, USA

Skinner, Frank (Actor, Comedian)
P.O. Box 168
London, England W10 6WH, UK

Skinner, Jane (Anchor)
c/o Staff Member *Fox News Channel (NY)*
1211 Ave of the Americas
Level C1
New York, NY 10036-8701, USA

Skinner, Jeff (Athlete, Hockey Player)
c/o Darren Ferris *The Orr Hockey Group*
- MA
P.O. Box 290836
Charlestown, MA 02129, USA

Skinner, Joel P (Athlete, Baseball Player,
Coach)
275 Pamilla Cir
Avon Lake, OH 44012-1973, USA

Skinner, Jonty (Coach, Swimmer)
University of Alabama
Athletic Dept
Tuscaloosa, AL 35487, USA

Skinner, Larry (Athlete, Hockey Player)
Nexient Learning
1600 Scott St Tower B 3rd Floor
Ottawa, ON KlY 4N7, Canada

Skinner, Mike (Race Car Driver)
Mike Skinner Enterprises
3685 Hwy
152 W
China Grove, NC 28023, USA

Skinner, Robert R (Bob) (Athlete, Baseball
Player, Coach)
1576 Diamond St
San Diego, CA 92109-3050, USA

Skinner, Samuel K (Business Person,
Secretary)
Commonwealth Edison
1 First National Plaza
PO Box 767
Chicago, IL 60690, USA

Skinner, Sonny (Golfer)
114 Northlake Dr
Sylvester, GA 31791-3909, USA

Skinner, Val (Golfer)
44 Bridge Ave
Bay Head, NJ 08742-4747, USA

Skinny Puppy (Music Group, Musician)
c/o Jeremy Holgersen *Agency Group Ltd,*
The (NY)
142 West 57th St
6th Floor
New York, NY 10019, USA

Skizas, Lou (Athlete, Baseball Player)
2101 W White St
Apt 118
Champaign, IL 61821-7203, USA

Skjelbreid, Ann-Elen (Athlete)
5640 Eikelandsosen
NORWAY

Skladany, John (Athlete, Football Player)
541 Wilmington Cir
Oviedo, FL 32765-6988

Skladany, Thomas E (Tom) (Athlete,
Football Player)
6666 Highland Lakes Pl
Westerville, OH 43082, USA

Sklvorecky, Josef (Writer)
Erindale College
English Dept
Toronto, ON M5S 1A5, CANADA

Skok, Craig (Athlete, Baseball Player)
981 Slash Pine Way
Lawrenceville, GA 30043-3465, USA

Skol, Michael (Diplomat)
PO Box 596
Dennis, MA 02638, USA

Skolimowski, Jerzy (Director)
Film Polski
Ul Mazowiecka 6/8
Warsaw 00-048, POLAND

Skoll, Jeff (Business Person, Producer)
Skoll Foundation
250 University Av #200
Palo Alto, CA 94301, USA

Skolnick, Mark H (Scientist)
University of Utah
Medical Center
Genetics Dept
Salt Lake City, UT 84112, USA

Skoog, Meyer (Whitey) (Athlete,
Basketball Player, Coach)
1545 Aspen Dr
Saint Peter, MN 56082, USA

Skoog, Myer (Athlete, Baseball Player)
1302 W Traverse Rd Apt 203
Saint Peter, MN 56082-1748, USA

Skopil Jr, Otto R (Judge)
US Court of Appeals
Pionner Courthouse
555 SW Yamhill St
Portland, OR 97204, USA

Skorodenski, Warren (Athlete, Hockey
Player)
161 MacEwan Ridge Cir NW
Calgary, AB T3K 3W3, Canada

Skoronski, Bob (Athlete, Football Player)
3907 Signature Dr
Middleton, WI 53562, USA

Skorupan, John P (Athlete, Football
Player)
142 Crossing RIdge Trl
Cranberry Township, PA 16066, USA

Skotheim, Robert A (Misc)
2120 Place Road
Port Angeles, WA 98363, USA

Skou, Jens (Nobel Prize Laureate)
Risslundvei 9
Risskon, DK 8240, Denmark

Skou, Jens C (Nobel Prize Laureate)
Rislundvej 9
Risskov 8240, DENMARK

Skoula, Martin (Athlete, Hockey Player)
2441 Sheridan AveS
Minneapolis, MN 55405-2341

Skouras, Thanos (Economist)
8 Chlois St
Athens 145 62, GREECE

Skov, Glen (Athlete, Hockey Player)
3898 Timber Ridge Ct
Palm Harbor, FL 34685-3127

Skovhus, Bo (Opera Singer)
Balmer & Dixon Mgmt
Granitweg 2
Zurich 8006, SWITZERLAND

Skowron, Moose (Baseball Player)
1118 Beachcomber Dr.
Schaumburg, IL 60193

Skrebneski, Victor (Photographer)
1350 N LaSalle Dr
Chicago, IL 60610, USA

Skrepcinski, Denice (Stylist)
5 Spring Ct
Edgewood, NM 87015, USA

Skrepenak, Greg (Athlete, Football Player)
Hyders Total Fitnbess Center
400 Middle Rd
Nanticoke, PA 18634, USA

Skribble (DJ)
c/o Len Evans *Project Publicity*
312 West 53rd St
Suite 202
New York, NY 10019, USA

Skriko, Petri (Athlete, Hockey Player)
Kirjatyontekijankatu 4 A 3
Helsinki, 00170 Finland

Skrillex (DJ, Musician)
c/o Ryan Downey *Blood Company*
PO Box 46851
Hollywood, CA 90046, USA

Skrmetta, Matt (Athlete, Baseball Player)
527 Siena Ct
Satellite Beach, FL 32937-2991, USA

Skrovan, Steve (Comedian)
c/o Staff Member *WmE2 (WMA-LA)*
1 William Morris Pl
Beverly Hills, CA 90212, USA

Skrowaczewski, Stanislaw (Composer)
Minnesota Symphony
1111 Nicollet Mail
Minneapolis, MN 55403, USA

Skrudland, Brian (Athlete, Hockey Player)
Florida Panthers
1 Panther Pkwy
Sunrise, FL 33323-5315

Skrudland, Brian (Athlete, Hockey Player)
3225 7 St SW
Calgary, AB T2T 2X8, Canada

Skrypnk, Metropolitan Mstyslav S
(Religious Leader)
Ukranian Orthodox Church
PO Box 445
South Bound Brook, NJ 08880, USA

Skube, Bob (Athlete, Baseball Player)
7135 W Foothill Dr
Glendale, AZ 85310-5817, USA

Skufca, Scott (Race Car Driver)
5903 Reynolds Rd.
Menttor, OH 44060, USA

Skuza, Dean (Race Car Driver)
650 Ken Mar Industrial Parkway
Broadview Heights, OH 44147, USA

Sky, Jennifer (Actor)
12533 Woodgreen
Los Angeles, CA 90066, USA

Sky, Nina (Music Group, Musician)
c/o Tammy Brook *FYI Public Relations*
174 5th Ave
Suite 404
New York, NY 10010, USA

Skye, Azura (Actor)
c/o Brian Wilkins *Kritzer Levine Wilkins
Entertainment (KLWG)*
11872 La Grange Ave
1st Floor
Los Angeles, CA 90025, USA

Skye, Britney (Adult Film Star)
Sin City Video
9155-9161 Derring Ave
Chatsworth, CA 91304, USA

Skye, Ione (Actor)
c/o Mike Packenham *Concrete
Entertainment*
468 North Camden Drive
#200
Beverly HIlls, CA 90210, USA

Sky Eats Airplane (Music Group,
Musician)
c/o Brigitte Wright *Brigitte Wright
Management*
1674 Broadway
3rd Floor
New York, NY 10019, USA

Skyrms, Brian (Misc)
University of California
Philosophy Dept
Irvine, CA 92717, USA

Slaby, Lou (Athlete, Football Player)
6 Elder Pl
Denville, NJ 07834, USA

Slack, Reggie (Athlete, Football Player)
5973 Queen St
Milton, FL 32570, USA

Slack, Reggie
6653 Walker St
Milton, FL 32570-6672, USA

Slade, Bernard N (Writer)
345 N Saltair Ave
Los Angeles, CA 90049, USA

Slade, Chris (Athlete, Football Player)
4810 Ivy Rodge Dr SE
Unit 201
Smyrna, GA 30080, USA

Slade, Chris (Musician)
11 Leominster Road
Morden
Surrey SA4 6HN, UNITED KINGDOM
(UK)

Slade, David (Director)
c/o Keith Redmon *Anonymous Content
(LA)*
3531 Hayden Ave
Culver City, CA 90232, USA

Slade, Jeff (Athlete, Basketball Player)
5354 Farmington Rd
Toledo, OH 43623-2636, USA

Slade, Mark (Actor)
38 Joppa Road
Worcester, MA 01602, USA

Slagle, James R
13630 Barryknoll Lane
Houston, TX 77079, USA

Slagle, Roger (Athlete, Baseball Player)
7560 George Nash Rd
White House, TN 37188-5101, USA

Slagle, Tim (Race Car Driver)
2824-E Door Ave.
Fairfax, VA 22031, USA

Slaney, John (Athlete, Hockey Player)
11 Hunts Point Rd
Cape Elizabeth, ME 04107-2926

Slaney, John (Athlete, Hockey Player)
Portland Pirates
94 FreeSt
Portland, ME 04101-3920

Slaney, Mary Decker (Athlete, Olympic
Athlete, Track Athlete)
87141 Kellmore Street
Eugene, OR 97402-9128, USA

Slash (Musician)
P.O. Box 57593
Sherman Oaks, CA 91403, USA

Slaten, Doug (Athlete, Baseball Player)
233 Rennie Ave
Venice, CA 90291-2645, USA

Slater, Bob (Baseball Player)
4322 Avenida Rio Del Oro
Yorba Linda, CA 92886-3011, USA

Slater, Christian (Actor)
c/o Jason Newman *Untitled Entertainment
(LA)*
350 S. Beverly Dr #200
Beverly Hills, CA 90212, USA

Slater, Helen (Actor)
c/o Lisa DiSante-Frank *DiSante Frank &
Company*
10061 Riverside Dr #377
Toluca Lake, CA 91602, USA

Slater, Jackie (Athlete, Football Player)
P.O. Box 6411
Orange, CA 92863, USA

Slater, Jock C K (John) (Admiral)
Naval Secretary
Victory Bldg
HM Naval Base
Portsmouth PO1 3LS, UNITED
KINGDOM (UK)

Slater, Kelly (Actor, Athlete)
Quiksilver Inc
15202 Graham St
Huntington Beach, CA 92649, USA

Slater, Mark (Athlete, Football Player)
10545 Rome Ave
Young America, MN 55397, USA

Slater, Ryan
3500 W. Olive Ave. #1400
Burbank, CA 91505

Slater, Suzanne
10000 Riverside Dr. #10
Toluca Lake, CA 91602

Slatkin, Leonard E (Conductor, Musician)
c/o Staff Member *Askonas Holt Ltd*
Lincoln House
300 High Holborn
London WC1V 7JH, UK

Slaton, Jim (Athlete, Baseball Player)
4082 N Arbor Ln
Buckeye, AZ 85396-3603, USA

Slaton, Mike (Athlete, Football Player)
7691 Park Village Rd
San Diego, CA 92129, USA

Slaton, Tony (Athlete, Football Player)
122 E Childs Ave
Merced, CA 95340, USA

Slattery, John M (Actor)
c/o Chris Kanarick *ID Public Relations
(ID-NY)*
8409 Santa Monica Blvd
West Hollywood, CA 90069, USA

Slattvik, Simon (Athlete)
Bankgata 22
Lillehammer 2600, NORWAY

Slaught, Don (Athlete, Baseball Player)
27 Middleridge Ln S
Rolling Hills, CA 90274-4055, USA

Slaughter (Music Group)
c/o Staff Member *Artist Representation &
Management*
1257 Arcade St
St Paul, MN 55106

Slaughter, Frank (Doctor)
Box 14 Ortega Station
Jacksonville, FL 32210, USA

Slaughter, J Mack (Actor)
c/o Jeff Golenberg *Collective*
8383 Wilshire Blvd
Suite 1050
Beverly Hills, CA 90211, USA

Slaughter, John B (Educator)
Occidental College
President's Office
Los Angeles, CA 90041, USA

Slaughter, Mickey (Athlete, Football Player)
1402 Mesa Ave
Ruston, LA 71270, USA

Slaughter, Stering (Athlete, Baseball Player)
742 E Avenida Sierra Madre
Gilbert, AZ 85296, USA

Slaughter, Sterling (Athlete, Baseball Player)
742 E Avenida Sierra Madre
Gilbert, AZ 85296-1108, USA

Slaughter, Webster (Athlete, Football Player)
3706 Rory Ct
Missouri City, TX 77459, USA

Slavin, Randall (Actor)
Gold Marshak Liedtke
3500 W Olive Ave
#1400
Burbank, CA 91505, USA

Slavitt, David R (Writer)
35 West St
#5
Cambridge, MA 02139, USA

Slay, Brandon (Wrestler)
6155 Lehman Ave
Colorado Springs, CO 80918, USA

Slayback, Bill (Athlete, Baseball Player)
25710 Armstrong Cir Unit E
Stevenson Ranch, CA 91381-2336, USA

Slayton, Bobby (Comedian)
c/o Sherry Marsh *Marsh Entertainment*
12444 Ventura Blvd #203
Studio City, CA 91604, USA

Sleater, Lou (Athlete, Baseball Player)
12 Bandon Ct
Unit 102
Lutherville Timonium, MD 21093, USA

Sledd, William L (Internet Star)
PO Box 3714
Paducah, KY 42002-3714, USA

Sledge, Kathy (Musician)
c/o Staff Member *Webster & Associates PR*
3573 Couchville Pike
Hermitage, TN 37076, USA

Sledge, Leroy (Athlete, Football Player)
6036 Golden Gate Cir
Dallas, TX 75241, USA

Sledge, Percy (Musician)
c/o Terry Shields
9430 Palmetto Ln
Shreveport, LA 71118, USA

Sledge, Termel (Athlete, Baseball Player)
30041 Medford Pl
Castaic, CA 91384, USA

Sledge, Terrmel (Athlete, Baseball Player)
30041 Medford Pl
Castaic, CA 91384-4565, USA

Sleep, Mike (Athlete, Hockey Player)
249 Fairbank Cres
Thunder Bay, ON P7B 5M1, Canada

Sleep, Wayne (Actor, Choreographer, Dancer)
996 N Player Ave
Eagle, ID 83616, us

Sleepy Jackson, The (Music Group)
c/o Staff Member *Paradigm (Monterey)*
404 W Franklin St
Monterey, CA 93940, USA

Slegr, Jiri (Athlete, Hockey Player)
U Cfsaskych lazni 7
Teplice 415 01, Czech Republic

Slegr, Jirl (Athlete, Hockey Player)
1 Fleet Center
Boston, MA 02114, USA

Sleigher, Louis (Athlete, Hockey Player)
250 Rte du President-Kennedy
Levis, QC G6V 9J6, Canada

Slezak, Erika (Actor)
International Creative Mgmt
40 W 57th St
#1800
New York, NY 10019, USA

Slice, Kimbo (Athlete, Wrestler)
c/o Raphael Berko *Media Artists Group (LA)*
8255 W Sunset Blvd
Los Angeles, CA 90046, USA

Slichter, Charles P (Physicist)
61 Chestnut Court
Champaign, IL 61822, USA

Slichter, Jacob (Musician)
Monterey Peninsula Artists
509 Hartnell St
Monterey, CA 93940, USA

Slick, Grace (Musician, Songwriter)
5956 Kanan Dume Rd
Malibu, CA 90265, USA

Slick, Rick (Musician)
Famous Artists Agency
250 W 57th St
New York, NY 10107, USA

Slider, Rac (Athlete, Baseball Player)
123 County Road 3306
De Kalb, TX 75559-4342, USA

Sliger, Bernard F (Educator)
3341 E Lakeshore Dr
Tallahassee, FL 32312, USA

Slightly Stoopid (Music Group)
c/o Jon Phillips *Silverback Professional Artist Management*
9469 Jefferson Blvd
Suite 101
Culver City, CA 90232, USA

Slim Helu, Carlos (Business Person)
Telmex
Porque Via 198
Cuahtemoc CP
Mexico City, DF 06599, MEXICO

Slipknot (Musician)
c/o Staff Member *Agency Group Ltd, The (NY)*
142 West 57th St
6th Floor
New York, NY 10019, USA

Sliwa, Curtis
215 E 96th St
New York, NY 10128-3835, USA

Sliwiak, Dina (Stylist)
c/o Staff Member *Montana Artists Agency*
9150 Wilshire Blvd Ste 100
Beverly Hills, CA 90212, USA

Sliwinska, Edyta (Dancer, Reality TV Star)
c/o Bob Knotek *McCann - Knotek Associates*
8539 Sunset Blvd
Suite 4-136
Los Angeles, CA 90069, USA

Sloan (Music Group)
c/o Staff Member *Paradigm (Monterey)*
404 W Franklin St
Monterey, CA 93940, USA

Sloan, Amy (Actor)
c/o Marion Campbell *TalentWorks (LA)*
3500 W Olive Ave
Suite 1400
Burbank, CA 91505, USA

Sloan, David (Athlete, Football Player)
10898 E Butherus Dr
Scottsdale, AZ 85255-1848, USA

Sloan, Ed (Musician)
216 Lincoln Street
West Columbia, SC 29170, USA

Sloan, Gerald E (Jerry) (Basketball Player, Coach)
300 S Washington St
McLeansboro, IL 62859, USA

Sloan, Holly Goldberg (Director)
Sanford-Beckett-Skouras
1015 Gayley Ave
#300
Los Angeles, CA 90024, USA

Sloan, Jerry (Athlete, Basketball Player)
5583 W 13680 S
Herriman, UT 84096-1713, USA

Sloan, Michael (Actor, Producer)
c/o Mickey Freiberg *Acme Talent & Literary (LA)*
1400 Atlantic Ave
Suite 274
Long Beach, CA 90814, USA

Sloan, P F (Musician, Songwriter, Writer)
All the Best
PO Box 164
Cedarhurst, NY 11516, USA

Sloan, Stephen C (Steve) (Coach, Football Coach, Football Player)
University of Central Florida
Athletic Dept
Orlando, FL 32816, USA

Sloan, Tod (Athlete, Hockey Player)
11 Hedge Rd RR 2
Sutton West, ON LOE IRO, Canada

Sloane, Carol (Musician)
Magi Productions
705 Centre St
#300
Boston, MA 02130, USA

Sloane, Hilary (Stylist)
1616 Fremont Ave
South Pasadena, CA 91030, USA

Sloane, Jeremy Major (General)
12243 E Cortez Dr
Scottsdale, AZ 85259-3310, USA

Sloane, Lindsay (Actor)
c/o Ron West *Thruline Entertainment*
9250 Wilshire Blvd
Ground Fl
Beverly Hills, CA 90212, USA

Sloan Jr, Robert B (Educator)
Bayor University
President's Office
Waco, TX 76798, USA

Sloat, Micah (Actor)
c/o Alex Cole *Elevate Entertainment*
10100 Santa Monica Blvd.
Suite 300
Los Angeles, CA 90067, USA

Sloatman, Lala
11917 Vose St.
No. Hollywood, CA 91605

Slobodyanik, Alexander (Musician)
Columbia Artists Mgmt Inc
165 W 57th St
New York, NY 10019, USA

Slocombe, Douglas (Cinematographer)
London Mgmt
2-4 Noel St
London W1V 3RB, UNITED KINGDOM (UK)

Slocum, Brian (Athlete, Baseball Player)
81 Rose Ave
Eastchester, NY 10709-3835, USA

Slocum, Heath (Golfer)
5640 Keystone Rd
Pensacola, FL 32504-8416, USA

Slocum, Ron (Athlete, Baseball Player)
35080 Chandler Ave Spc 28
Calimesa, CA 92320-1927, USA

Slocumb, Heathcliff (Heath) (Athlete, Baseball Player)
1045 Arthur St
Uniondale, NY 11553-3103, USA

Slon, Steve (Editor)
AARP Magazine
601 E St NW
Washington, DC 20049, USA

Slonimsky, Sergey M (Composer)
9 Kanal Griboedova
#97
Saint Petersburg, RUSSIA

Slosburg, Phil (Athlete, Football Player)
201 Glen Ln
Elkins Park, PA 19027, USA

Slotnick, Joey (Actor)
Gersh Agency
232 N Canon Dr
Beverly Hills, CA 90210, USA

Slotnick, Mortimer H (Artist)
43 Amherst Dr
New Rochelle, NY 10804, USA

Slotnick, R Nathan (Doctor)
825 Fairfax Ave
Norfolk, VA 23507, USA

Slovan, Eric (Comedian)
c/o Staff Member *WmE2 (WMA-LA)*
1 William Morris Pl
Beverly Hills, CA 90212, USA

Slover, Karl (Actor)
504 Firetower Road
Dublin, GA 31021-2642, USA

Slovin, Eric (Writer)
c/o Staff Member *Principato/Young Management*
9465 Wilshire Blvd
Suite 430
Beverly Hills, CA 90212, USA

Sloviter, Dolores K (Judge)
US Court of Appeals
US Courthouse
601 Market St
Philadelphia, PA 19106, USA

Slowes, Charles (Baseball Player, Sportscaster)
Tampa Bay Devil Rays
3936 Mimosa Pl
Palm Harbor, FL 34685-3674, USA

Slowey, Kevin (Athlete, Baseball Player)
1748 Quigg Dr
Pittsburgh, PA 15241-2023, USA

Sloyan, James (Actor)
920 Kagawa St
Pacific Palisades, CA 90272, USA

Sluby, Tom (Athlete, Basketball Player)
39 Poplar St
Ramsey, NJ 07446, USA

Sluman, Jeff (Golfer)
808 McKinley Ln
Hinsdale, IL 60521-4831, USA

Slusarski, Joe (Athlete, Baseball Player, Olympic Athlete)
11 Rodelle Roods Dr
Weldon Springs, MO 63304-7875, USA

Slutskaya, Irina (Figure Skater)
c/o Staff Member *Champions on Ice*
Tom Collins Enterprises Inc
3500 W 80th St
Minneapolis, MN 55431, USA

Slutsky, Lorie A (Misc)
New York Community Trust
2 Park Ave
New York, NY 10016, USA

Slyman, Darin (Stylist)
c/o Staff Member *Talent Plus*
1222 Lucas Ave
Suite 300
St. Louis, MO 63103, USA

Smaby, Matt (Athlete, Hockey Player)
5037 Newton AveS
Minneapolis, MN 55419-1027

Smagala, Stan (Athlete, Football Player)
13155 Meadow Hill Ln
Lemont, IL 60439, USA

Smagorinsky, Joseph (Misc)
72 Gabriel Court
Hillsborough, NJ 08844, USA

Smail, Doug (Athlete, Hockey Player)
23550 Pondview Pl.
Golden, CO 80401-9353

Smajstria, Craig (Athlete, Baseball Player)
4606 Honey Creek Ct
Pearland, TX 77584, USA

Smajstrla, Craig (Athlete, Baseball Player)
4606 Honev Creek Ct
Pearland, TX 77584-1285, USA

Smale, Stephen (Mathematician)
68 Highgate Road
Kensington, CA 94707, USA

Small, Aaron (Athlete, Baseball Player)
775 Loudon Road
Loudon, TN 37774-6705, USA

Small, Jim (Athlete, Baseball Player)
7960 Island Ct
Stanwood, MI 49346-8920, USA

Small, Lawrence W (Financier)
Smithsonian Institution
1000 Jefferson Dr SW
Washington, DC 20560, USA

Small, Mark (Athlete, Baseball Player)
10605 229th Pl SW
Edmonds, WA 98020-6151, USA

Small, Mary
165 W. 66th St.
New York, NY 10023

Small, Marya (Actor)
CL Inc
843 N Sycamore Ave
Los Angeles, CA 90038, USA

Small, Torrance (Athlete, Football Player)
66 Chateau Mouton Dr
Kenner, LA 70065, USA

Small, William N (Admiral)
1605 Bluecher Court
Verginia Beach, VA 23454, USA

Smalley, Roy (Athlete, Baseball Player)
6319 Timber Trl
Minneapolis, MN 55439-1049, USA

Smallwood, Dwana (Dancer)
Alvin Ailey American Dance Foundation
211 W 61st St #300
New York, NY 10023, USA

Smallwood, Richard (Music Group, Musician)
Sierra Mgmt
1035 Bates Court
Hendersonville, TN 37075, USA

Smart, Amy (Actor)
c/o Jennifer Merlino *Untitled Entertainment (LA)*
350 S. Beverly Dr #200
Beverly Hills, CA 90212, USA

Smart, Erinn (Athlete, Olympic Athlete)
201 S 18th St Apt 301
Philadelphia, PA 19103-5920, USA

Smart, J D (Athlete, Baseball Player)
1325 Lost Creek Blvd
Austin, TX 78746-6331, USA

Smart, Jean (Actor)
17351 Rancho St
Encino, CA 91316, USA

Smart, Keeth (Athlete, Fencer, Olympic Athlete)
415 Argyle Rd Apt 6F
Brooklyn, NY 11218-5419, USA

Smart, Keith (Athlete, Basketball Player, Coach)
5306 Asterwood Dr
Dublin, CA 94S68-7718, USA

Smart, Pamela
#93G0356 Bedford Hills Corr. Fac.
Bedford Hills, NY 10507-2496

Smashing Pumpkins (Music Group)
c/o Staff Member *Creative Artists Agency (CAA-LA)*
2000 Ave Of The Stars
Los Angeles, CA 90067, USA

Smash Mouth (Music Group, Musician)
c/o Staff Member *Creative Artists Agency (CAA-LA)*
2000 Ave Of The Stars
Los Angeles, CA 90067, USA

Smeal, Eleanor C (Activist)
900 N Stafford St #1217
Arlington, VA 22203, USA

Smear, Steve (Athlete, Football Player)
1701 Tree House Ct
Annapolis, MD 21401-6539, USA

Smeaton, Bruce
585 Nepean Hwy. Carrum
Victoria, AUSTRALIA 3197

Smedley, Geoffrey (Artist)
RR 3
Gambier Island
Gibsons, BC V0N 1V0, CANADA

Smedsmo, Dale (Athlete, Hockey Player)
609 3rd St NE
Roseau, MN 56751-1201, USA

Smedvig, Rolf (Musician)
Columbia Artists Mgmt Inc
165 W 57th St
New York, NY 10019, USA

Smeenge, Joel (Athlete, Football Player)
9148 Sugarland Dr
Jacksonville, FL 32256, USA

Smehlik, Richard (Athlete, Hockey Player)
8824 Hearthstone Dr
East Amherst, NY 14051-2354

Smerek, Don (Athlete, Football Player)
1298 Valhalla Dr
Denver, DC 28037-5503, USA

Smerlas, Fred (Athlete, Football Player)
11 Saddle Ridge Rd
Sudbury, MA 01776, USA

Smid, Ladislav (Athlete, Hockey Player)
2000 E Gene Autry Way
Anaheim, CA 92806, USA

Smigel, Irwin (Doctor)
Smigel Research
635 Madison Ave
New York, NY 10022, USA

Smigel, Robert (Actor, Writer)
c/o Staff Member *Creative Artists Agency (CAA-LA)*
2000 Ave Of The Stars
Los Angeles, CA 90067, USA

Smigelsky, Dave (Athlete, Football Player)
4332 Nesting Pl
Oakwood, GA 30566, USA

Smiley, Don (Baseball Player)
10539 NW lOth St
Plantation, FL 33322-6546, USA

Smiley, Don (Baseball Player, President)
Florida Marlins
3233 Huntington
Weston, FL 33332-1820, USA

Smiley, Jane (Writer)
235 El Caminito Rd
Carmel Valley, CA 93924-9636, USA

Smiley, Jane (Writer)
c/o Lynn Pleshette *Lynn Pleshette Literary Agency*
2700 N. Beachwood Dr.
Los Angeles, CA 90068, USA

Smiley, John (Athlete, Baseball Player)
208 W 3rd Ave
Collegeville, PA 19426-2212, USA

Smiley, Justin (Athlete, Football Player)
2771 Regatta Way
Tuscaloosa, AL 35406, USA

Smiley, Rickey (Comedian)
c/o Kevin Wasson *Breakwind Entertainment*
P.O. Box 59784
Birmingham, AL 35259-9784, USA

Smiley, Tavis (Radio Personality, Television Host)
The Tavis Smiley Show
4401 Sunset Blvd
Los Angeles, CA 90027, USA

Smiley, Tommie B (Athlete, Football Player)
5340 Timberline Ln
Beaumont, TX 77706, USA

S. Miller, Candice (Congressman, Politician)
1034 Longworth HOB
Washington, DC 20515, USA

Smirnoff, Karina (Dancer)
c/o Staff Member *Continuum Entertainment*
303 Park Ave S
Suite 1220
New York, NY 10010, USA

Smirnoff, Yakov (Actor, Comedian)
c/o Staff Member *Richard De La Font Agency*
3808 W South Park Blvd
Broken Arrow, OK 74011, USA

Smirnov, Nikolai I (Admiral)
Ministry of Defense
4 Staraya Pl
Moscow 103073, RUSSIA

Smith, Adam (Congressman, Politician)
2402 Rayburn HOB
Washington, DC 20515, USa

Smith, Adrian (Congressman, Politician)
503 CanoonHOB
Washington, DC 20515, USA

Smith, Adrian (Musician)
Chipster Entertainment
1976 E High St #101
Pottstown, PA 19464, USA

Smith, Adrian (Athlete, Basketball Player, Olympic Athlete)
2829 Saddleback Dr
Cincinnati, OH 4S244-3914, USA

Smith, Al (Athlete, Hockey Player)

Smith, Akili (Athlete, Football Player)
PO Box 95
Jamul, CA 91935-0095, USA

Smith, Al (Athlete, Football Player)
15 Pembroke St
Sugar Land, TX 77479, USA

Smith, Al (Athlete, Basketball Player)
308 S Sterling Ave
Peoria, IL 61604, USA

Smith, Aldon (Football Player)
c/o Tom Condon *CAA - St. Louis*
222 S Central Ave
Suite 1008
St Louis, MO 63105, USA

Smith, Alexander J C (Financier)
Marsh & McLennan Co
1166 Ave of Americas
New York, NY 10036, USA

Smith, Alexis (Artist)
215 Windward Ave
Venice, CA 90291, USA

Smith, Alice (Musician)
c/o Staff Member *Paradigm (Monterey)*
404 W Franklin St
Monterey, CA 93940, USA

Smith, Allison (Actor)
Innovative Artists
1505 10th St
Santa Monica, CA 90401, USA

Smith, Amber (Actor, Model)
c/o Jerry Shandrew *Shandrew Public Relations*
1050 S Stanley Ave
Los Angeles, CA 90019-6634, USA

Smith, Amy J (Stylist)
611 Main St
#A
Sausalito, CA 94965, USA

Smith, Ann (Athlete, Tennis Player)
3737 Cole Ave
Apt 110
Dallas, TX 75204-1594, USA

Smith, Anna Deavere (Actor, Producer, Writer)
c/o Johnnie Planco *Parseghian Planco LLC*
322 8th Ave
Suite 601
New York, NY 10001, USA

Smith, Anthony (Athlete, Football Player)
P.O. Box 573
Fontana, CA 92334, USA

Smith, Anthony W (Educator)
PO Box 573
Fontana, CA 92334-0573, USA

Smith, Antowain (Athlete, Football Player)
2121 Hepburn St
Apt 917
Houston, TX 77054, USA

Smith, April (Writer)
427 7th St
Santa Monica, CA 90402, USA

Smith, Art (Chef)
c/o Staff Member *Premier Management Group (PMG Sports)*
115 Crescent Commons Dr Ste 250
Cary, NC 27518, USA

Smith, Arthur (Producer)
A. Smith and Company Properties
9911 W Pico Blvd
Suite 250
Los Angeles, CA 90035, USA

Smith, Arthur K Jr (Educator)
5346 Mcculloch Circle
Houston, TX 77056, USA

Smith, Artie (Athlete, Football Player)
3809 W 68th St
Stillwater, OK 74074, USA

Smith, Barbara (Business Person)
B. Smith Enterprises
1120 Ave of the Americas Fl 4
New York, NY 10036, USA

Smith, Barry (Athlete, Football Player)
2837 Voltz Ln
Knoxville, TN 37914-9796, USA

Smith, Barty (Athlete, Football Player)
2290 Dabney Rd
Richmond, VA 23230, USA

Smith, Beau (Cartoonist)
Flying Fist Ranch
PO Box 706
Ceredo, WV 25507, USA

Smith, Ben (Cartoonist)
c/o Staff Member *King Features Syndication*
300 W 57th St
15th Floor
New York, NY 10019-5238, USA

Smith, Ben (Athlete, Hockey Player, Olympic Athlete)
47 Norwood Hts
Gloucester, MA 01930, USA

Smith, Ben (Athlete, Football Player)
1127 Riverbend Club Dr SE
Atlanta, GA 30339, USA

Smith, Bennett W (Religious Leader)
Progressive National Baptist Convention
601 50th St NE
Washington, DC 20019, USA

Smith, Bernie (Athlete, Baseball Player)
P.O. Box 513
Lutcher, LA 70071-0513, USA

Smith, Bill (Athlete, Football Player)
19 Woodcrest Dr
Lexington, NC 27295, USA

Smith, Bill (Athlete, Hockey Player)
New York Islanders
1255 Hempstead Tpke
Uniondale, NY 11553-1200

Smith, Billy (Athlete, Hockey Player)
8356 Quail Meadow Way
West Palm Beach, FL 33412, USA

Smith, Billy (Athlete, Baseball Player)
333 Rolling Hills Dr
Conroe, TX 77304-1280, USA

Smith, Billy (Athlete, Baseball Player)
5304 Vicksburg Dr
Arlington, TX 76017, USA

Smith, Billy Ray Jr (Athlete, Football Player)
XX Sports Radio
6160 Cornerstone Ct E #100
San Diego, CA 92121, USA

Smith, Bob (Golfer)
PO Box 6511
Ventura, CA 93006, USA

Smith, Bob (Athlete, Baseball Player)
221 Hackberry Ln
Aiken, SC 29803-2733, USA

Smith, Bobby (Athlete, Hockey Player)
10800 E Cactus Rd
#46
Scottdale, AZ 85259, USA

Smith, Bobby (Athlete, Baseball Player)
2822 60th Ave
Oakland, CA 94605, USA

Smith, Bobby Gene (Athlete, Baseball Player)
1267 Tucker Road
Unit 15
Hood River, OR 97031-8601, USA

Smith, Brad (Musician)
Shapiro Co
9229 Sunset Blvd
#607
Los Angeles, CA 90069, USA

Smith, Brad (Athlete, Hockey Player)
Colorado Avalanche
1000 Chopper Cir
Denver, CO 80204-5805

Smith, Brent (Athlete, Football Player)
258 Ridgewood Dr
Pontotoc, MS 38863, USA

Smith, Brian (Athlete, Baseball Player)
203 Bo Howard Rd
Toney, AL 35773-9235, USA

Smith, Brian D (Athlete, Hockey Player)

Smith, Brick (Athlete, Baseball Player)
4743 Amity Pl
Charlotte, NC 28212-5305, USA

Smith, Brooke (Actor)
c/o Sue Leibman *Barking Dog Entertainment*
609 Greenwich St
6th Floor
New York, NY 10014, USA

Smith, Bruce W (Director)
c/o Staff Member *Jambalaya Studio*
111 N Maryland Ave #300
Glendale, CA 92206, USA

Smith, Bryn (Athlete, Baseball Player)
1239 Highway 1
Santa Maria, CA 93455-5909, USA

Smith, Calvin (Athlete, Track Athlete)
16703 Sheffield Park Dr
Lutz, FL 33549, USA

Smith, Carl R (General)
2345 S Queen St
Arlington, VA 22202, USA

Smith, Carolyn Renee
PO Box. 813
No. Hollywood, CA 91603

Smith, Chad (Musician)
c/o Peter Mensch *Q Prime South*
729 Seventh Ave
16th Floor
New York, NY 10019, USA

Smith, Charles (Athlete, Basketball Player)
P.O.Box 433
Cedar Grove, NJ 07009-0433, USA

Smith, Charles Martin (Actor, Director)
c/o David Saunders *Agency for the Performing Arts (APA-LA)*
405 S Beverly Dr
Suite 500
Beverly Hills, CA 90212-4425, USA

Smith, Charlie E (Athlete, Football Player)
1906 Crescent Dr
Monroe, LA 71202, USA

Smith, Charlie H (Athlete, Football Player)
14074 Skyline Blvd
Oakland, CA 94619, USA

Smith, Chelsi
335 E. San Augustine St.
Deer Park, TX 77536-4127

Smith, Chris (Golfer)
208 S Bellerive Dr
Peru, IN 46970-8060, USA

Smith, Chris (Athlete, Baseball Player)
4206 Dawn Ln
Oceanside, CA 92056-4716, USA

Smith, Chris M (Athlete, Football Player)
1424 Martway Cir
Apt A
Olathe, KS 66061, USA

Smith, Chuck (Athlete, Football Player)
1155 Havenbrook Ct
Suwanee, GA 30024, USA

Smith, Chuck (Athlete, Baseball Player)
1300 Saint Charles Pl Apt 810
Pembroke Pines, FL 33026-3340, USA

Smith, Clifford (Method Man) (Musician, Television Host)
c/o Shauna Garr *Smart Girl Productions*
8335 Sunset Blvd
Suite 222
West Hollywood, CA 90069, USA

Smith, Clinton J (Clint) (Athlete, Hockey Player)
501-1919 Bellview Ave
West Vancouver, BC V7V 1B7, Canada

Smith, Colleen (Actor)
c/o Mark Scroggs *David Shapira & Associates*
193 N Robertson Blvd
Beverly Hills, CA 90211, USA

Smith, Connie (Music Group, Musician)
Gurley Co
1204B Cedar Lane
Nashville, TN 37212, USA

Smith, Cotter (Actor)
15332 Antioch St #800
Pacific Palisades, CA 90272, USA

Smith, Dallas (Athlete, Hockey Player)
4390 SW 107th Ave Apt 4
Beaverton, OR 97005-3192

Smith, Dan (Athlete, Baseball Player)
715 N Carbon St
Girard, KS 66743, USA

Smith, Daniel E. (Actor)
c/o Worthy Patterson *Evolution Entertainment (LA)*
901 N Highland Ave
Los Angeles, CA 90038, USA

Smith, Danny (Actor)
c/o Lisa Harrison *WME (LA)*
9601 Wilshire Blvd Fl 3
Beverly Hills, CA 90210, USA

Smith, Dante (Mos Def) (Actor, Musician)
c/o Linda Carbone *Press Here Publicity*
138 W. 25th St
9th Floor
New York, NY 10001, USA

Smith, Darden (Music Group, Musician, Songwriter, Writer)
AGF Entertainment
30 W 21st St #700
New York, NY 10010, USA

Smith, Darrin (Athlete, Football Player)
7395 NW 19th Ct
Hollywood, FL 33024, USA

Smith, Daryl (Athlete, Football Player)
1636 Norton Hill Dr
Jacksonville, FL 32225, USA

Smith, Daryl (Athlete, Baseball Player)
3 Sunny Mills Ct
Randallstown, MD 21133-4449, USA

Smith, Dave (Athlete, Baseball Player)
16330 Jersey Dr
Jersey Village, TX 77040-2020, USA

Smith, Dave (Athlete, Football Player)
7906 W 116th Ter
Overland Park, KS 66210, USA

Smith, Dave (Athlete, Football Player)
650 S 13th St
Apt 123-20
Indiana, PA 15701, USA

Smith, D Brooks (Judge)
US Court of Appeals
Penn Traffic Bldg
319 Washington St
Johnstown, PA 15901, USA

Smith, Dean (Athlete, Basketball Player)
105 Fox Run
Chapel Hill, NC 27516-0608, USA

Smith, Dean E (Athlete, Basketball Player, Coach)
University of North Carolina
P.O. Box 2126
Chapel Hill, NC 27515, USA

Smith, Delia (Actor, Chef, Writer)
Delia Online
PO Box 1124
Knaphill GU21 9AA, United Kingdom

Smith, Dennis (Athlete, Football Player)
2450 Achilles Dr
Los Angeles, CA 90046, USA

Smith, Derek (Athlete, Football Player)
4949 Centennial Blvd
Santa Clara, CA 95054, USA

Smith, Derek (Athlete, Hockey Player)
201 Bramblewood Ln
East Amherst, NY 14051-2228

Smith, Dick (Athlete, Coach, Swimmer)
P.O. Box 1831
Dewey, AZ 86327-1831, USA

Smith, Dick (Athlete, Baseball Player)
1926 Norwood Ln
State College, PA 16803-1326, USA

Smith, Dick (Athlete, Baseball Player)
2615 Gates Rd
Lincolnton, NC 28092, USA

Smith, Dick (Athlete, Baseball Player)
6850 Downing Rd
Spc 35
Central Point, OR 97502, USA

Smith, Dick (Business Person)
Dick Smith Foods
10 Cassola Pl
Penrith 2750, Australia

Smith, Dick (Athlete, Football Player)
5718 Chillum Pl NE
Washington, DC 20011-2528, USA

Smith, D J (Athlete, Hockey Player)
Windsor Spitfires
8787 McHugh St
Windsor, ON N8S 0Al, Canada

Smith, Donald L (Athlete, Football Player)
3338 Pineview Dr
Holiday, FL 34691, USA

Smith, Doug (Athlete, Basketball Player)
25482 Pennsylvania Ave
Novi, MI 48375, USA

Smith, Doug (Coach, Football Coach, Football Player)
University of Southern California
Heritage Hall
Los Angeles, CA 90089, USA

Smith, Doug (Athlete, Football Player)
25661 Pacific Crest Dr
Mission Viejo, CA 92692, USA

Smith, Doug (Athlete, Hockey Player)
PO Box 276
Woodlawn, ON K0A 3M0, CANADA

Smith, Douglas (Doug) (Actor)
c/o Beverly Strong *Strong Management*
3532 Hayden Ave
Culver City, CA 90232, USA

Smith, Dr. Robin (Writer)
210 W Rittenhouse Sq
Suite 408
Philadelphia, PA 19103, USA

Smith, Dwight (Athlete, Baseball Player)
P.O. Box 98
Varnville, SC 29944-0098, USA

Smith, Earl (Athlete, Baseball Player)
2764 N Leonard Ave
Fresno, CA 93737-9720, USA

Smith, Elliot (Athlete, Football Player)
1343 Cadillac Dr
Jackson, MS 39213, USA

Smith, Elmore (Athlete, Basketball Player)
PO Box 24147S
Cleveland, OH 44124-847S, USA

Smith, Emil L (Biologist, Physicist)
University of California
Medical School
Los Angeles, CA 90024, USA

Smith, Emmitt (Athlete, Football Player)
15001 Winnwood Rd
Dallas, TX 75254, USA

Smith, Eric (Race Car Driver)
Southtown Motorsports
1701 W. Washington St.
Bloomington, IL 61701, USA

Smith, Eugene (Baseball Player)
Cincinnati Buckeyes
8337 Flora Ave
Vinita Park, MO 63114-6203, USA

Smith, F Dean (Athlete, Track Athlete)
PO Box 71
Breckenridge, TX 76424, USA

Smith, Floyd (Athlete, Hockey Player)
138 Stonehenge Dr
Orchard Park, NY 14127-2845

Smith, Forry
3500 W. Olive #1400
Burbank, CA 91505

Smith, Frankie (Athlete, Football Player)
620 N Grayson St
Groesbeck, TX 76642, USA

Smith, Frederick W (Business Person)
FDX Corp
942 S Shady Grove Road
Memphis, TN 38120, USA

Smith, Garfield (Athlete, Basketball Player)
2006 Idylwild Ct
Richmond, KY 4047S-3606, USA

Smith, Gary (Athlete, Hockey Player)
Villa Cortina
4451 Albert St #102
Burnaby, BC V5C 2G4, Canada

Smith, G E
24 Thorndike St
Cambridge, MA 02141-1882, USA

Smith, G Elaine (Religious Leader)
American Baptist Churches USA
PO Box 851
Valley Forge, PA 19482, USA

Smith, Geoff (Athlete, Hockey Player)
42-1525 Westside Rd S
Kelowna, BC VlZ 3Y3, Canada

Smith, George (Cartoonist)
Universal Press Syndicate
4520 Main St
Kansas City, MO 64111, USA

Smith, George E. (Nobel Prize Laureate)
Bell Labs
600 Mountain Ave
Murray Hill, NJ 07974-0636, USA

Smith, Gerald (Misc)
World Tennis Assn
133 1st St NE
Saint Petersburg, FL 33701, USA

Smith, Gerald C (Government Official)
2425 Tracy Place NW
Washington, DC 20008, USA

Smith, Gord (Athlete, Hockey Player)
6 Carriage Dr.
West Haven, CT 06516-5514

Smith, Gordon (Politician)
8611 Country Club Dr
Bethesda, MD 20817-4579, USA

Smith, Greg (Athlete, Baseball Player)
27435 Hanes Rd E
Davenport, WA 99122-9443, USA

Smith, Greg (Athlete, Hockey Player)
909 56th St W
Billings, MT 59106-2240

Smith, Greg (Athlete, Basketball Player)
9930 SW Lumbee Ln
Tualatin, OR 97062-73SS, USA

Smith, Gregory (Actor, Producer)
c/o JJ Harris *One Talent Management*
9220 Sunset Blvd
Los Angeles, CA 90069, USA

Smith, Gregory White (Writer)
129 1st Ave SW
Aiken, SC 29801, USA

Smith, Guy (Race Car Driver)
Tasman Motorsports
4192 Weaver Ct.
Hilliard, OH 43206, USA

Smith, Hal (Athlete, Football Player)
P.O. Box 570517
Tarzana, CA 91357, USA

Smith, Hal (Athlete, Baseball Player)
637 Houston St
Columbus, TX 78934-2618, USA

Smith, Hamilton (Nobel Prize Laureate)
13607 Hanover Pike
Reisterstown, MD 21136-4520, USA

Smith, Hamilton O (Nobel Prize Laureate)
13607 Hanover Road
Reisterstown, MD 21136, USA

Smith, Harry (Correspondent)
c/o Staff Member *Early Show, The* (NY)
524 W 57th St
New York, NY 10019, USA

Smith, Harry (Bowler)
580 E Cuyahoga Falls Ave
Akron, OH 44310, USA

Smith, Harry E (Black Jack) (Athlete, Coach, Football Coach, Football Player)
805 Leawood Ter
Columbia, MO 65203, USA

Smith, Hedrick L (Journalist)
4204 Rasemary St
Chevy Chase, MD 20815, USA

Smith, Helen (Athlete, Baseball Player)
1600 Westbrook Ave
Apt 436
Richmond, VA 23227-3318, USA

Smith, Hillary B
8730 Sunset Blvd #480
Los Angeles, CA 90069, USA

Smith, Hunter (Athlete, Football Player)
9601 East 300 S
Zionsville, IN 46077, USA

Smith, Ivor (Architect)
Station Officer's House
Prawle Pointe Kingsbridge
Devon TQ7 2BX, UNITED KINGDOM
(UK)

Smith, Jack (Athlete, Baseball Player)
250 Doubles Dr
Covington, GA 30016-1736, USA

Smith, Jackie L (Athlete, Football Player)
1566 Walpole Dr
Chesterfield, MO 63017, USA

Smith, Jaclyn (Actor)
10398 W Sunset Blvd
Los Angeles, CA 90049, USA

Smith, Jacob (Actor)
c/o Elaine Lively *Elaine Entertainment*
Prefers to be contacted via telephone
Northridge, CA 91324, USA

Smith, Jaden (Actor)
c/o Miguel Melendez *Overbrook Entertainment*
450 N Roxbury Dr
4th Floor
Beverly Hills, CA 90210, USA

Smith, James (Bonecrusher) (Boxer)
355 Keith Hills Road
Lillington, NC 27546, USA

Smith, Jamie Renee (Actor)
c/o Pam Grimes *Hervey/Grimes Talent Agency*
10561 Missouri Ave
Suite 2
Los Angeles, CA 90025, USA

Smith, Jason V (Athlete, Basketball Player)
c/o Mark Bartelstein *Priority Sports & Entertainment - Chicago*
312 N La Salle
Suite 650
Chicago, IL 60610, USA

Smith, J D (Athlete, Football Player)
1615 County Road 204
Richland Springs, TX 76871, USA

Smith, J D Jr (Athlete, Football Player)
3332 Florida St
Oakland, CA 94602, USA

Smith, Jean (Baseball Player)
5351 S Lake Shore Dr
Harbor Springs, MI 49740-9109, USA

Smith, Jean Kennedy (Misc)
The Kennedy Center
2700 F Street, NW
Washington, DC 20566, USA

Smith, Jennifer M (Prime Minister)
Premier's Office
Cabinet Building
105 Front St
Hamilton, HM 12, BERMUDA

Smith, Jermaine (Athlete, Football Player)
1345 12th St
Augusta, GA 30901, USA

Smith, Jerry (Judge)
US Court of Appeals
515 Rusk Ave
Houston, TX 77002, USA

Smith, Jim (Athlete, Football Player)
2639 Round Table Blvd
Lewisville, TX 75056-5723, USA

Smith, Jim (Athlete, Baseball Player)
1730 S Arroyo Ln
Gilbert, AZ 85295-4815, USA

Smith, Jim Field (Actor, Director)
c/o Trevor Engelson *Underground Management*
447 S. Highland Ave.
Los Angeles, CA 90036, USA

Smith, Jimmy Lee (Athlete, Football Player)
1302 Charter Ct E
Jacksonville, FL 32225, USA

Smith, Jim Ray (Athlete, Football Player)
7049 Cliffbrook Dr
Dallas, TX 75254, USA

Smith, Joe (Basketball Player)
7639 Leafwood Dr
Norfolk, VA 23518, USA

Smith, John (Race Car Driver)
5611 Hwy. 81 North
Williamston, SC 29697, USA

Smith, John (Actor)
c/o Alan Ellsweig *Shadow Entertainment*
10 Universal City Plz
20th Floor
Universal City, CA 91608, USA

Smith, John L (Coach, Football Coach)
Michigan State University
Daugherty Field House
East Lansing, MI 48824, USA

Smith, John M (Athlete, Football Player)
184 Centre St
Dover, MA 02030, USA

Smith, John W (Wrestler)
5315 S Sangre Road
Stillwater, OK 74074, USA

Smith, josh (Scientist)
University Of Pennsylvania
3320 Smith Walk# 240
Philadelphia, PA 19104-6316, USA

Smith, Josh (Misc)
University of Pennsylvania
240 S 33rd St
Philadelphia, PA 19104, USA

Smith, J Robert (Athlete, Football Player)
6102 Timberlake Ct
Flower Mound, TX 75022, USA

Smith, J T (Athlete, Football Player)
10110 Planters Row
Frisco, TX 75034-0255, USA

Smith, Justin (Athlete, Football Player)
5045 Rollman Estates Dr
Cincinnati, OH 45236, USA

Smith, Karin
2300 Palisades St
Los Osos, CA 93402

Smith, Kathy (Misc)
PO Box 491433
Los Angeles, CA 90049, USA

Smith, Katie (Athlete, Basketball Player, Olympic Athlete)
2494 Farleigh Rd
Columbus, OH 43221-2618, USA

Smith, Kayla (Stylist)
663 W 2575
North Clinton, UT 84015, USA

Smith, Keith (Athlete, Baseball Player)
5823 13th St E
Bradenton, FL 34203-6819, USA

Smith, Keith (Athlete, Baseball Player)
15711 Ada St
Canyon Country, CA 91387, USA

Smith, Kellita (Actor)
c/o Lynn Jeter *Lynn Jeter & Associates*
3699 Wilshire Blvd #850
Los Angeles, CA 90010, USA

Smith, Ken (Athlete, Baseball Player)
Bluff City Jaguar 6335 Wheel Cv Attn Sales Dept
Memobis, TN 38119-8244, USA

Smith, Ken (Architect)
80 Warren St
#28
New York, NY 10007, USA

Smith, Kenneth L (Athlete, Baseball Player, Football Player)
313 Ellen Dr
Deer Park, TX 77536-3534, USA

Smith, Kenny (Sportscaster)
c/o Staff Member *Octagon Home Office*
1751 Pinnacle Dr
15th Floor
McLean, VA 22102, USA

Smith, Kerr (Actor, Director)
c/o Steven Kavovit *Thruline Entertainment*
9250 Wilshire Blvd
Ground Fl
Beverly Hills, CA 90212, USA

Smith, Kevin (Actor, Director, Producer, Writer)
c/o Tony Angellotti *Angellotti Company*
12423 Ventura Ct
Studio City, CA 91604, USA

Smith, Kevin (Athlete, Football Player)
7001 Parkwood Blvd
Apt 3204
Plano, TX 75024-7176, USA

Smith, Kim (Actor)
c/o Staff Member *Clipse Management*
279 W main St
Dallas, TX 75034, USA

Smith, Kurtwood (Actor)
c/o Kelly Garner *Pop Art Management*
P.O. Box 55363
Sherman Oaks, CA 91413, USA

Smith, Labradford (Athlete, Basketball Player)
410 Thompson Dr
Bay City, TX 77414-7910, USA

Smith, Lamar (Congressman, Politician)
2409 Rayburn HOB
Washington, DC 20515, USA

Smith, Lance (Athlete, Football Player)
14907 Rocky Top Dr
Huntersville, NC 28078-2648, USA

Smith, Larry (Athlete, Football Player)
3601 Bayshore Blvd
Tampa, FL 33629, USA

Smith, Larry (Athlete, Basketball Player)
1767 Lakeside Dr
Vicksburg, MS 39180-9369, USA

Smith, Lauren Lee (Actor)
c/o Kim Callahan *Industry Entertainment Partners*
955 S Carrillo Dr
Suite 300
Los Angeles, CA 90048, USA

Smith, Laury (Stylist)
c/o Staff Member *Mercury Artists*
8460 Higuera St Fl 2
Culver City, CA 90232, USA

Smith, Laverne (Athlete, Football Player)
2122 N Homestead St
Wichita, KS 67208, USA

Smith, Lawrence Leighton
Louisville Symphony
611 W Main St
Louisville, KY 40202, USA

Smith, Lee (Athlete, Baseball Player)
P.O. Box 399
Castor, LA 71016-0399, USA

Smith, Lee A (Baseball Player)
Atlanta Braves
2124 Highway 507
Castor, LA 71016-4069, USA

Smith, Leonard P (Athlete, Football Player)
18053 Creek Hollow Rd
Baton Rouge, LA 70817, USA

Smith, Leslie (General)
1700 Tice Valley Blvd Apt 417
Walnut Creek, CA 94595-1645, USA

Smith, Lewis
8271 Melrose Ave. #110
Los Angeles, CA 90046

Smith, Liz (Journalist)
160 E 38th St Apt 33C
New York, NY 10016-2615, USA

Smith, Liz (Writer)
160 E 38th St
New York, NY 10016, USA

Smith, Lois (Actor)
c/o Steve Stone *Cornerstone Talent Agency*
37 W 20th St
New York, NY 10011, USA

Smith, Lonnie (Athlete, Baseball Player)
145 Wesley Forest Dr
Fayetteville, GA 30214-1094, USA

Smith, Loren A (Judge)
US Claims Court
717 Madison Place NW
Washington, DC 20439, USA

Smith, Louise (Race Car Driver)
International Motorsports
PO Box 1018
Talladega, AL 77024-5012, USA

Smith, Lovie (Athlete, Coach, Football Coach, Football Player)
1000 Football Dr
Lake Forest, IL 60045, USA

Smith, Madeline (Actor)
Joan Gray
Sunbury Island
Sunbury on Thames
Middx, UNITED KINGDOM (UK)

Smith, Maggie (Actor)
c/o Toni Howard *ICM Partners (ICM-LA)*
10250 Constellation Blvd Fl 7
Los Angeles, CA 90067, USA

Smith, Malcolm (Race Car Driver)
Motorsports HOF
PO Box 194
Novi, MI 48376-0194, USA

Smith, Margaret (Producer, Writer)
c/o Gail Stocker *Gail Stocker Presents*
1025 N Kings Rd #113
Los Angeles, CA 90069, USA

Smith, Margo (Musician, Songwriter, Writer)
Tristar Enterprises Inc
PO Box 3367
Brentwood, TN 37024-3367, USA

Smith, Marilynn (Golfer)
3784 N 162nd Ln
Goodyear, AZ 85338-8017, USA

Smith, Mark (Athlete, Hockey Player)
Ayla Boutique
381 E Campbell Ave
Campbell, CA 95008-2013

Smith, Mark (Athlete, Baseball Player)
907 Forest Green Rd
Reedville, VA 22539-3577, USA

Smith, Mark (Athlete, Baseball Player)
1312 Elmhurst Ln
Flower Mound, TX 75028-3847, USA

Smith, Marquis (Athlete, Football Player)
843 51st St
San Diego, CA 92114, USA

Smith, Martha (Actor, Model)
9690 Heather Road
Beverly Hills, CA 90210, USA

Smith, Marvel (Athlete, Football Player)
30 Waterfront Dr
Pittsburgh, PA 15222, USA

Smith, Marvin (Smitty) (Musician)
Joel Chriss
300 Mercer St
#3J
New York, NY 10003, USA

Smith, Matt (Actor)
c/o Michael Duff *Troika*
74 Clerkenwell Rd
3rd Floor
London EC1M 5QA, United Kingdom

Smith, Melanie (Actor)
Innovative Artists
1505 10th St
Santa Monica, CA 90401, USA

Smith, Michael (Athlete, Basketball Player)
PO Box 91912
Washington, DC 20090-1912, USA

Smith, Michael Bailey (Actor)
c/o Alexandra Karrys *Divine Management*
117 N Orlando Ave
Los Angeles, CA 90048, USA

Smith, Michael W (Musician, Songwriter, Writer)
c/o Staff Member *Creative Artists Agency (CAA-TN)*
3310 West End Ave
5th Floor
Nashville, TN 37203, USA

Smith, Mike (Race Car Driver)
Paul Smith Racing
800 NE 3rd St.
Boynton Beach, FL 33435, USA

Smith, Mike (Athlete, Football Player)
619 Feamster Dr
Houston, TX 77022, USA

Smith, Mike (Misc)
Names Project Foundation
310 Townsend St
San Francisco, CA 94107, USA

Smith, Mike (Athlete, Baseball Player)
3226 Livingston Rd
Jackson, MS 39213-6106, USA

Smith, Mike (Athlete, Baseball Player)
3226 Livingston Rd
Jackson, MS 39213, USA

Smith, Mike (Athlete, Baseball Player)
6 Willett Pond Rd
Westwood, MA 02090, USA

Smith, Mike (Athlete, Baseball Player)
7605 Antique Oak St
Live Oak, TX 78233, USA

Smith, Mike (Cartoonist)
Las Vegas Sun
Editorial Dept
2275 Corporate Circle Dr
Henderson, NV 89074, USA

Smith, Mike (Horse Racer)
3445 NE 210th St
Miami, Fl 33180-3587, USA

Smith, Mindy (Musician, Songwriter, Writer)
Vanguard Records
2700 Pennsylvania Ave
Santa Monica, CA 90404, USA

Smith, Mitchell (Race Car Driver)
Mitchell Smith Racing
4834 West 200 South
Anderson, IN 46011, USA

Smith, Moishe (Artist)
Utah State University
Art Dept
Logan, UT 84322, USA

Smith, Monika (Actor)
c/o David Gardner *Principato/Young Management*
9465 Wilshire Blvd
Suite 430
Beverly Hills, CA 90212, USA

Smith, Myron (Athlete, Football Player)
6604 Sandgate Dr
Arlington, TX 76002-5549, USA

Smith, Nate (Athlete, Baseball Player)
6365 Tahoe Dr
Atlanta, GA 30349-4052, USA

Smith, Neil (Athlete, Football Player)
9423 Nail Ave
Overland Park, KS 66207-2529, USA

Smith, Nicholas (Actor)
Michelle Braidman
10/11 Lower John St
London, ENGLAND W1R 3PE, UNITED KINGDOM (UK)

Smith, Noland (Athlete, Football Player)
4338 Watkins Dr
Jackson, MS 39206, USA

Smith, O C
1650 Broadway #508
New York, NY 10019, USA

Smith, O Guinn (Athlete, Track Athlete)
1 Hawthorne Place
Apt 3P
Boston, MA 02114-2304, USA

Smith, Orin R (Business Person)
Engelhard Corp
101 Wood Ave S
Iselin, NJ 08830, USA

Smith, Orlando (Tubby) (Coach)
University of Kentucky
Athletic Dept
Lexington, KY 40536, USA

Smith, Osborne E (Ozzie) (Athlete, Baseball Player)
201 Kendall Bluff Ct
Chesterfield, MO 63017-2158, USA

Smith, Otis (Athlete, Basketball Player)
607 Applewood Ave
Altamonte Springs, FL 32714-7301, USA

Smith, Patti (Musician, Songwriter)
Primary Talent International Ltd
2-12 Pentonville Road
5th Fl
Sausalito, London N1 9PL, UNITED KINGDOM

Smith, Paul (Athlete, Baseball Player)
711 Trevino Ln
Conroe, TX 77302-3835, USA

Smith, Paul B (Designer, Fashion Designer)
Paul Smith Ltd
41/44 Floral St
Covent Garden
London WC2E 9DG, UNITED KINGDOM (UK)

Smith, Pete (Athlete, Baseball Player)
10030 Halstead Dr
Suwanee, GA 30024, USA

Smith, Pete (Athlete, Baseball Player)
3512 Dixon Ln
The Villages, FL 32162-7150, USA

Smith, Putter (Actor)
1414 Lyndon St
Pasadena, CA 91030, USA

Smith, Quincy (Baseball Player)
Cleveland Buckeyes
715 S 14th St
Terre Haute, IN 47807-4920, USA

Smith, Quinn (Actor)
1738 N Whitley Ave
Hollywood, CA 90028

Smith, Rachel (Beauty Pageant Winner)

Smith, Ralph (Athlete, Football Player)
P.O. Box 1406
McComb, MS 39649, USA

Smith, Ralph (Cartoonist)
c/o Staff Member *King Features Syndication*
300 W 57th St
15th Floor
New York, NY 10019-5238, USA

Smith, Randy (Baseball Player)
7941 E Via De Luna Dr
Scottsdale, AZ 85255-4113, USA

Smith, Ray (Athlete, Baseball Player)
17183 Poblano Ct
San Diego, CA 92127-1431, USA

Smith, Ray E (Religious Leader)
Open Bible Standard Churches
2020 Bell Ave
Des Moines, IA 50315, USA

Smith, Raymond W (Business Person, Financier)
Rothschild North America
1251 Ave of Americas
New York, NY 10020, USA

Smith, RD (Race Car Driver)
Congdon Racing
4500 Turnberry Ct
Concord, NC 28027, USA

Smith, Regan (Race Car Driver)
Furniture Row Racing
4000 Forest St
Denver, CO 80216, USA

Smith, Reggie (Athlete, Basketball Player)
6975 Claywood Way
San Jose, CA 9S120-2241, USA

Smith, Reggie (Athlete, Baseball Player)
Reggie Smith Baseball Center
16161Ventura Blvd Ste 775
Encino, CA 91436-2522, USA

Smith, Remy (Remy Ma) (Musician)
c/o Staff Member *ReachGlobal Music Publishing*
4201 Burbank Blvd
Burbank, CA 91505, USA

Smith, Renee Felice (Actor)
c/o Hannah Roth *Buchwald/Fortitude (LA)*
6500 Wilshire Blvd
Suite 2200
Los Angeles, CA 90048, USA

Smith, Rex (Actor)
16986 Encino Hills Dr
Encino, CA 91436, USA

Smith, Richard A (Publisher)
Harcourt general
275 Washington St
Newton, MA 02458, USA

Smith, Richard M (Editor)
Newsweek Magazine
Editorial Dept
251 W 57th St
New York, NY 10019, USA

Smith, Rick (Athlete, Hockey Player)
RR 1
Perth Road, ON K0H 2L0, Canada

Smith, Rickie (Race Car Driver)
Rt 3 Box 19
Kirby Rd
King, NC 27021, USA

Smith, Rico (Athlete, Football Player)
8976 Foothill Blvd
Unit B7-389
Rancho Cucamonga, CA 91730, USA

Smith, Riley (Actor)
c/o Mark Armstrong *Sanders Armstrong Caserta*
2120 Colorado Blvd
Suite 120
Santa Monica, CA 90404, USA

Smith, R Jackson (Swimmer)
122 Palmers Hill Road
#3101
Stamford, CT 06902, USA

Smith, Robert (Musician)
c/o Staff Member *Geffen Records*
9126 Sunset Blvd
West Hollywood, CA 90069, USA

Smith, Robert (Athlete, Baseball Player)
1274 Norman Rd
Colton, CA 92324-1713, USA

Smith, Robert B (Athlete, Football Player)
1012 S Royal St
Bogalusa, LA 70427, USA

Smith, Robert C (Editor)
TV Guide Magazine
Editorial Dept
100 Matsonford Road
Radnor, PA 19080, USA

Smith, Robert C (Bob) (Senator)
9012 Rocky Lake Circle
Sarasota, FL 34238-4008, USA

Smith, Robert Gray (Graysmith) (Cartoonist)
San Francisco Chronicle
901 Mission St
San Francisco, CA 94103, USA

Smith, Robert L (Athlete, Football Player)
426 Cape Lookout Dr
Corpus Christi, TX 78412, USA

Smith, Robert S (Athlete, Football Player)
5668 Harrison Ave
Maple Heights, OH 44137, USA

Smith, Robyn (Jockey)
1155 San Ysidro Dr
Beverly Hills, CA 90210, USA

Smith, Rod (Athlete, Football Player)
821 W 4th St
Charlotte, NC 28202, USA

Smith, Roger (Actor)
2707 Benedict Canyon Dr
Beverly Hills, CA 90210, USA

Smith, Roger Guenveur (Actor, Writer)
Luna Ray Films
2018 North Vine Street
Los Angeles, CA 90068, USA

Smith, Rogers
PO Box 2907
Mammoth Lakes, CA 93546-2907, USA

Smith, Rolland (Correspondent)
CBS-TV
News Dept
524 W 57th St
New York, NY 10019, USA

Smith, Ron (Race Car Driver)
14933 175th Pl SE
Renton, WA 98059, USA

Smith, Ron (Athlete, Football Player)
1804 Park Ave
Richmond, VA 23220, USA

Smith, Ron (Athlete, Football Player)
266 York St
Trussville, AL 35173, USA

Smith, Ronnie Ray (Athlete, Track Athlete)
752 W Athens Blvd
Los Angeles, CA 90044, USA

Smith, Roy (Athlete, Baseball Player)
472 Gramatan Ave
Apt G2
Mount Vernon, NY 10552-2940, USA

Smith, Roy (Athlete, Baseball Player)
908 Woodbridge Ct
Safety Harbor, FL 34695, USA

Smith, Russell (Musician)
LC Media
PO Box 965
Antioch, TN 37011, USA

Smith, Sam (Athlete, Basketball Player)
5790 Cedar Bay Dr
Millington, TN 38053, USA

Smith, Sarah Christine (Actor)
c/o Staff Member *Hervey/Grimes Talent Agency*
10561 Missouri Ave
Suite 2
Los Angeles, CA 90025, USA

Smith, Seth (Athlete, Baseball Player)
101 Elizabeth Dr
Brandon, MS 39042-6501, USA

Smith, Shawnee (Actor)
c/o Brian Wilkins *Kritzer Levine Wilkins Entertainment (KLWG)*
11872 La Grange Ave
1st Floor
Los Angeles, CA 90025, USA

Smith, Shelley (Actor)
4184 Colfax Ave
Studio City, CA 90212, USA

Smith, Sherman (Athlete, Football Player)
1421 Primose Ln
Franklin, TN 37064, USA

Smith, Shevin (Athlete, Football Player)
10110 Farmingdale Pl
Tampa, FL 33624, USA

Smith, Sid (Athlete, Football Player)
1939 Melody Ln
Richmond, TX 77469, USA

Smith, Sinjin (Athlete, Volleyball Player)
Beach Volleyball Camps
P.O. Box 1714
Pacific Palisades, CA 90272, USA

Smith, Skip (Race Car Driver)
2143-C Statesville Blvd #117
Salisbury, NC 28147, USA

Smith, Sonny (Baseball Player)
Chicago American Giants
3549 N College Ave
Indianapolis, IN 46205-3733, USA

Smith, Stan
194 Bellevue Ave.
Newport, RI 02840-3515

Smith, Stanley (Race Car Driver)
1740 Rd #39
Chelsea, AL 35043, USA

Smith, Stanley R (Stan) (Tennis Player)
ProServe
1101 Woodrow Wilson Blvd
#1800
Arlington, VA 22209, USA

Smith, Stephen A (Correspondent, Radio Personality)
c/o Staff Member *WmE2 (WMA-LA)*
1 William Morris Pl
Beverly Hills, CA 90212, USA

Smith, Steve (Producer)
c/o Staff Member *Hall Webber*
1200 Bay St
Suite 400
Toronto, ON M5R 2A5, Canada

Smith, Steve (Race Car Driver)
Steve Smith Racing
PO Box 266
Princeton, NC 27589, USA

Smith, Steve (Athlete, Hockey Player)
Edmonton Oilers
11230 110 St NW
Edmonton, AB T5G 3H7, Canada

Smith, Steve (Athlete, Baseball Player, Olympic Athlete)
240 W Escalones
San Clemente, CA 92024-5455, USA

Smith, Steven D (Steve) (Basketball Player)
c/o Staff Member *Charlotte Bobcats*
333 E Trade St
Charlotte, NC 28202-2331, USA

Smith, Steven L (Astronaut)
15728 Lake Lodge Dr
Houston, TX 77062, USA

Smith, Steve Smith (Athlete, Olympic Athlete)
Del Mar Realty 222 Avenida Del Mar
San Clemente, CA 92672-4094, USA

Smith, Susan
Leath Correctional Institution
Leath Correctional Institution
2809 Airport Rd
Greenwood, SC 29649

Smith, Taran (Actor)
Full Circle Mgmt
12665 Kling St
North Hollywood, CA 91604, USA

Smith, Tasha (Actor)
c/o Staff Member *Luber Roklin Management*
8530 Wilshire Blvd
6th Floor
Beverly Hills, CA 90211, USA

Smith, Terry (Sportscaster)
12 Cleome St
Ladera Ranch, CA 92694-0858, USA

Smith, Thomas (Athlete, Football Player)
RR 1 Box 198
Gates, NC 27937, USA

Smith, Tommie (Athlete, Olympic Athlete, Track Athlete)
1800 Lilburn Stone Mountain Rd
Stone Mountain, GA 30087, USA

Smith, Tommy (Athlete, Baseball Player)
1299 E Cannon Ave
Albermarle, NC 28001-4360, USA

Smith, Tony (Athlete, Football Player)
P.O. Box 480234
Charlotte, NC 28269, USA

Smith, Tony (Athlete, Basketball Player)
2645 N 40th St
Milwaukee, WI 53210-2505, USA

Smith, Travian (Athlete, Football Player)
13941 County Road 2167D
Tatum, TX 75691, USA

Smith, Travis (Athlete, Baseball Player)
1865 Cherry St
Clarkston, WA 99403-8717, USA

Smith, Troy (Athlete, Football Player, Heisman Trophy Winner)
c/o Staff Member *Baltimore Ravens*
1 Winning Drive
Owings Mills, MD 21117-4776, USA

Smith, Tyron (Football Player)
c/o Joe Panos *Lock Metz Milanovic LLC*
6900 E. Camelback
Suite 600
Scottsdale, AZ 85251, USA

Smith, Vern (Athlete, Hockey Player)
15 Meadowlark Dr
East Longmeadow, MA 01028-3173

Smith, Vernice (Athlete, Football Player)
4347 Arajo Ct
Orlando, FL 32812, USA

Smith, Vernon L (Nobel Prize Laureate)
801 North Monroe Street
Apt 501
Arlington, VA 22311-5055, USA

Smith, Vernon L (Nobel Prize Laureate)
6020 N Pontatoc Rd
Tucson, AZ 85718-4323, USA

Smith, Vince (Musician)
Process Talent Management
439 Wiley Ave
Franklin, PA 16323, USA

Smith, Wallace B (Religious Leader)
Reorganized Church of Latter Day Saints
PO Box 1059
Independence, MO 64051, USA

Smith, Walter (Designer, Engineer)
Microsoft Corp
1 Microsoft Way
Redmond, WA 98052, USA

Smith, Walter H F (Oceanographer)
Nat'l Oceanic/Atmospheric Administration
Commerce Dept
Washington, DC 20230, USA

Smith, Walter S
11301 Cielo Pl
Santa Ana, Ca 92705-2435, USA

Smith, Wayne (Athlete, Football Player)
7730 S Bishop St
Chicago, IL 60620, USA

Smith, Wilbur (Writer)
Charles Pick Constituency
3 Bryanston Place
#3
London W1H 7FN, UNITED KINGDOM (UK)

Smith, Will (Actor, Musician, Producer)
c/o James Lassiter *Overbook Entertainment*
450 N Roxbury Dr
4th Floor
Beverly Hills, CA 90210, USA

Smith, William (Actor)
3202 Anacapa St
Santa Barbara, CA 93105, USA

Smith, William (Stylist)
80 Cranberry St
#12-K
Brooklyn Heights, NY 11201, USA

Smith, William A. (Athlete, Basketball Player)
4379 Tami Ln
Central Point, OR 97S02-104e, USA

Smith, William D (Admiral)
7025 Fairway Oaks
Fayetteville, PA 17222, USA

Smith, William Jay (Writer)
62 Luther Shaw Road
RR 1 Box 151
Cummington, MA 01026, USA

Smith, William Y (General)
6541 Brooks Place
Falls Church, VA 22044, USA

Smith, Willie (Football Player)
Baltimore Ravens
Ravens Stadium
11001 Russell St
Baltimore, MD 21230, USA

Smith, Willie (Athlete, Baseball Player)
1330 E 68th St
Savannah, GA 31404-5718, USA

Smith, Willow (Actor)
c/o Miguel Melendez *Overbrook Entertainment*
450 N Roxbury Dr
4th Floor
Beverly Hills, CA 90210, USA

Smith, W Lawrence (Athlete, Football Player)
3601 Bayshore Blvd
Tampa, FL 33629, USA

Smith, Wyatt (Athlete, Hockey Player)
17465 46th Ave N
Minneapolis, MN 55446-1957

Smith, Yeardley (Actor)
c/o Meredith O'Sullivan *42West (LA)*
11400 W Olympic Blvd
Suite 1100
Los Angeles, CA 90064, USA

Smith, Zadie (Writer)
Random House
1745 Broadway
#B1
New York, NY 10019, USA

Smith, Zane (Athlete, Baseball Player)
420 Windship Pl NW
Atlanta, GA 30327-4967, USA

Smithberg, Roger (Athlete, Baseball Player)
988 Glenmore Ln
Elgin, IL 60124-2303, USA

Smith Court, Margaret (Tennis Player)
21 Lewanna Way
City Beach
Perth, WA 6010, AUSTRALIA

Smitherman, Stephen (Athlete, Baseball Player)
HC 74 Box 240-10
Hartshorne, OK 74502-1890, USA

Smithers, Jan (Actor)
c/o Staff Member *Innovative Artists (LA)*
1505 10th St
Santa Monica, CA 90401, USA

Smithers, William (Actor)
2202 Anacapa St.
Santa Barbara, CA 93105, USA

Smithies, Oliver (Misc)
318 Urnstead Dr
Chapel Hill, NC 27516, USA

Smithies, Oliver (Nobel Prize Laureate)
318 Umstead Dr
Chapel Hill, Nc 27516-1809, USA

Smith III, Earl (J.R.) (Athlete, Basketball Player)
c/o Shawn Zanotti *Exact Publicity Sports PR & Marketing*
One S. Dearborn
Suite 2100
Chicago, IL 60603, USA

Smith Jr, John F (Jack) (Business Person)
General Motors Corp
100 Renaissance Center
Detroit, MI 48243, USA

Smith Jr, Lonnie Liston (Musician)
Associated Booking Corp
1995 Broadway
#501
New York, NY 10023, USA

Smith Jr, William R (Lawyer)
1 Harbour Place
PO Box 3239
Tampa, FL 33601, USA

Smith-McCulloch, Colleen (Athlete, Baseball Player)
228 20th Ave W
Vancouver, BC V5Y 2C6, CANADA

Smith-McPhee, Sianoa (Actor)
c/o Kenneth (Kenny) Goodman *Schiff Company, The*
9465 Wilshire Blvd
Suite 480
Beverly Hills, CA 90212, USA

Smith Osborne, Madolyn (Actor)
United Talent Agency
9560 Wilshire Blvd #500
Beverly Hills, CA 90212, USA

Smithson, Carly (Musician)

Smithson, Mike (Athlete, Baseball Player)
2540 Swan Creek Rd
Centerville, TN 37033-4374, USA

Smithson, Ryan (Writer)
c/o Staff Member *HarperCollins Publishers*
10 East 53rd St
c/o Author mail, 7th Floor
New York, NY 10022, USA

Smit-McPhee, Kodi (Actor)
c/o Kenneth (Kenny) Goodman *Schiff Company, The*
9465 Wilshire Blvd
Suite 480
Beverly Hills, CA 90212, USA

Smitrovich, Bill (Actor)
c/o Steven Siebert *Lighthouse Entertainment*
9220 W Sunset Blvd Ste 200
West Hollywood, CA 90069, USA

Smits, Jimmy (Actor)
c/o Daniel (Danny) Sussman *Brillstein Entertainment Partners*
9150 Wilshire Blvd #350
Beverly Hills, CA 90212, USA

Smits, Rik (Athlete, Basketball Player)
8346 E 550 S
Zionsville, IN 46077-8610, USA

Smogolski, Henry R (Financier)
Northwestern Savings & Loan
2300 N Western Ave
Chicago, IL 60647, USA

Smolan, Rick (Artist, Photographer)
Workman Publishers
225 Varick St Fl 9
New York, NY 10014-4381, USA

Smoler, Carol (Stylist)
1825 N Sedgwick St
Chicago, IL 60614, USA

Smolinski, Bryan (Athlete, Hockey Player)
4869 Stoneleigh Rd
Bloomfield Hills, MI 48302-2171

Smolinski, Mark (Athlete, Football Player)
3300 Country Club Rd
Petoskey, MI 49770, USA

Smolka, James W (Misc)
PO Box 2123
Lancaster, CA 93539, USA

Smolka, James W Ltcol
PO Box 2123
Lancaster, CA 93539-2123, USA

Smollett, Jurnee (Actor)
c/o Jon Leshay *Storefront Entertainment*
647 N Martel Ave
Suite 102
Los Angeles, CA 90036, USA

Smoltz, John A (Athlete, Baseball Player)
700 Foxhollow Run
Alpharetta, GA 30302-4064, USA

Smoot, Fred (Football Player)
c/o Staff Member *Washington Redskins*
21300 Redskin Park Dr
Ashburn, VA 20147, USA

Smoot, George (Nobel Prize Laureate)
10 Panoramic Way
Berkeley, CA 94704-1828, USA

Smoot III, George F. (Nobel Prize Laureate, Physicist)
University Of California SSL
LBL Bldg 50/5005
Berkeley, CA 94720, USA

Smoove, J.B. (Actor, Writer)
c/o Staff Member *Rain Management Group (RMG)*
1631 21st St
Santa Monica, CA 90404, USA

Smothers, Dick (Actor, Comedian)
c/o Staff Member *WmE2 (WMA-LA)*
1 William Morris Pl
Beverly Hills, CA 90212, USA

Smothers, Tom (Actor, Comedian)
PO Box 759
Kenwood, CA 95452, USA

Smothers Brothers, The (Comedian)
c/o Staff Member *WmE2 (WMA-LA)*
1 William Morris Pl
Beverly Hills, CA 90212, USA

Smrek, Peter (Athlete, Hockey Player)
J Mazura 14/52
Martin 1, 036 01 Slovakia

Smrke, John (Athlete, Hockey Player)
4 Brooks Rd
Ajax, ON LlS 6G3, Canada

Smuin, Michael (Ballerina, Choreographer)
Smuin Ballets
1314 34th Ave
San Francisco, CA 94122, USA

Smulders, Cobie (Actor)
c/o Staff Member *ROAR (LA)*
9701 Wilshire Blvd
8th Floor
Los Angeles, CA 90212, USA

Smurfit, Victoria (Actor)
c/o Richard Cook *WME (LA)*
9601 Wilshire Blvd Fl 3
Beverly Hills, CA 90210, USA

S. Murphy, Christopher (Congressman, Politician)
412 Cannon HOB
Washington, DC 20515, USA

Smyl, Stan (Athlete, Hockey Player)
Vancouver Canucks
800 Griffiths Way
Vancouver, BC V6B 6Gl, Canada

Smyl, Stan (Athlete, Hockey Player)
4730 The Glen
West Vancouver, BC V7S 3C3, Canada

Smyth, Charles P (Misc)
245 Prospect Ave
Princeton, NJ 08540, USA

Smyth, Craig H (Historian)
Po Box 39
Cresskill, NJ 07626, USA

Smyth, Greg (Athlete, Hockey Player)
62 Carrick Dr
St. John's, NL AlA 4N7, Canada

Smyth, Joe (Music Group, Musician)
Sawyer Brown Inc
5200 Old Harding Road
Franklin, TN 37064, USA

Smyth, Kevin (Athlete, Hockey Player)
4881 Key St
Blaine, WA 98230-7000

Smyth, Patty (Musician)
23712 Malibu Colony Road
Malibu, CA 90265, USA

Smyth, Randy (Yachtsman)
17136 Bluewater Lane
Huntington Beach, CA 92649, USA

Smyth, Ryan (Athlete, Hockey Player)
Chance Restaurant
2550-10155 102 St NW
Edmonton, AB T5J 4G8, Canada

Smyth, Ryan (Athlete, Hockey Player)
52314th St
Manhattan Beach, CA 90266-4836

Smyth, Steve (Athlete, Baseball Player)
44005 Northgate Ave
Temecula, CA 92592-3000, YSA

Smythe, Marcus (Actor)
c/o Bob Waters *Bob Waters Agency*
9301 Wilshire Blvd
Suite 300
Beverly Hills, CA 90210, USA

Snapp, Helen
800 SW 142nd Ave Apt 212
Pembroke Pines, Fl 33027-1571, USA

Snare, Ryan (Athlete, Baseball Player)
2671 Derby Walk NE
Atlanta, GA 30319-3657, USA

Snarr, Trevor (Actor)
c/o Elizabeth Knight *KnightStar Multimedia*
PO Box 893
Lehi, UT 84043, USA

Snead, Esix (Athlete, Baseball Player)
1332 42nd St
Orlando, FL 32839-1276, USA

Snead, Jesse Caryle (J C) (Golfer)
PO Box 782170
Wichita, KS 67278, USA

Snead, Norman B (Norm) (Athlete, Football Player)
508 Veranda Way
Apt C204
Naples, FL 34104, USA

Snead, W T Sr (Religious Leader)
Baptist Convention Missionary
1404 E Firestone Blvd
Los Angeles, CA 90001, USA

Sneaker Pimps (Music Group)
c/o Staff Member *Paradigm (Monterey)*
404 W Franklin St
Monterey, CA 93940, USA

Snedden, Stephen (Actor)
c/o Don Carroll *Don Carroll Management*
14211 Hatteras St.
Sherman Oaks, CA 91401, USA

Sneddon, Bob (Athlete, Football Player)
901 E 1140 S
Ogden, UT 84404, USA

Snedeker, Brandt (Golfer)
704 Arkland Pl
Nashville, TN 37215, USA

Sneed, Ed (Golfer)
4155 Nottinghill Gate Rd
Columbus, OH 43220-3942, USA

Sneed, Floyd (Musician)
McKenzie Accountancy
5171 Caliente St #134
Las Vegas, NV 89119, USA

Sneed, Joseph T (Judge)
US Court of Appeals
Court Building
95 7th St
San Francisco, CA 94103, USA

Snelder, Richard L (Diplomat)
211 Central Park West
New York, NY 10024, USA

Snell, Chris (Athlete, Hockey Player)
883 Peggoty Cir
Oshawa, ON LlK 2G6, Canada

Snell, Esmond E (Misc)
819 Tempted Ways Drive
Longmont, CO 80504-8467, USA

Snell, Ian (Athlete, Baseball Player)
90 Beechwood Ave
Dover, DE 34202-5844, USA

Snell, Matthews (Matt) (Athlete, Football Player)
S C I Limited Inc
175 Clendenny Ave
Jersey City, NJ 07304, USA

Snell, Nate (Athlete, Baseball Player)
7299 Old State Rd
Holly Hill, SC 29033-4010, USA

Snell, Peter (Athlete, Olympic Athlete, Track Athlete)
6452 Dunston Lane
Dallas, TX 75214, USA

Snell, Ray (Athlete, Football Player)
10306 Councils Way
Tampa, FL 33617, USA

Snelling, Chris (Athlete, Baseball Player)
18122 Rhodes Lake Rd E
Bonney Lake, WA 98391, USA

Snepsts, Harold (Athlete, Hockey Player)
5623 Highfield Dr
Burnaby, BC V5B 1E4, Canada

Sneva, Jerry (Race Car Driver)
2652 East 35th Street
Spokane, WA 99203, USA

Sneva, Tom (Race Car Driver)
3301 E. Valley Vista Lane
Paradise Valley, AZ 85253, USA

Sniadecki, Jim (Athlete, Football Player)
3267 Congressional Cir
Fairfield, CA 94534, USA

Snicket, Lemony (Writer)
Harper Collins Publishers
10 E 53rd St
new York, NY 10022, USA

Snider, Dee (Musician)
Pooch
9511 Weldon Circle #316
Fort Lauderdale, FL 33321, USA

Snider, Edward M (Ed) (Athlete, Hockey Player)
P.O. Box 25088
Phildelphia, PA 19147-0288

Snider, George (Race Car Driver)
7404 Lucille Avenue
Bakersfield, CA 93308, USA

Snider, Mike (Musician)
P.O. Box 610
Gleason, TN 38229, USA

Snider, R Michael (Scientist)
Pfizer Pharmaceuticals
Eastern Point Road
Groton, CT 06340, USA

Snider, Todd (Music Group, Musician, Songwriter, Writer)
Al Bunneta Mgmt
33 Music Square W #102B
Nashville, TN 37203, USA

Snider, Travis (Athlete, Baseball Player)
3116 164th St SW #603
Lynnwood, WA 98087, USA

Snider, Van (Athlete, Baseball Player)
1615 Windsor Dr
Cleveland, OH 44124-3616, USA

Snipes, Wesley (Actor)
c/o David Schiff *The Schiff Company*
9107 Wilshire Blvd #600
Beverly Hills, CA 90210-5519, USA

Snipscheer, Fred (Athlete, Hockey Player)
13404 Macaw Way
Carmel, IN 46033, USA

Snitker, Brian (Athlete, Baseball Player)
3148 Pine Needle Ct SW
Lilburn, GA 30047-1972, USA

Snitzer, Herb (Photographer)
4619 Alcazar Way S
Saint Petersburg, FL 33712-4209, USA

Snitzier, Larry (Musician)
Lindy Martin Mgmt
5 Lob Lolly Court
Pinehurst, NC 28374, USA

Snodgrass, William (Writer)
3061 Hughes Rd
Erieville, Ny 13061-4128, USA

Snodgrass, William D (Writer)
3061 Hughes Road
Erieville, NY 13061, USA

Snook, Frank (Athlete, Baseball Player)
2580 Elysium Ave
Eugene, OR 97401-7441, USA

Snopek, Chris (Athlete, Baseball Player)
103 Bradford Dr
Cynrhiana, KY 39110-8468, USA

Snow (Artist, Musician, Songwriter, Writer)
Hype Music
2076 Sherobee Road #510
Mississauga, ON L5A 4C4, CANADA

Snow, Al (Race Car Driver)
1227 W. Leland Avenue
Lima, OH 45805, USA

Snow, Brittany (Actor)
c/o Marcel Pariseau *True Public Relations*
6725 W Sunset Blvd #470
Los Angeles, CA 90028-7180, USA

Snow, DeShawn (Reality TV Star)
c/o Abbey MacDonald *New Wave Entertainment (LA)*
2660 W Olive Blvd
Burbank, CA 91505, USA

Snow, Eric (Athlete, Basketball Player)
311S Manor Bridge Dr
Alpharetta, GA 30004-8821, USA

Snow, Garth (Athlete, Hockey Player)
New York Islanders
1255 Hempstead Tpke
Uniondale, NY 11553-1200

Snow, Garth (Athlete, Hockey Player, Olympic Athlete)
4 Weeping Willow Ct
Glen Head, NY 11545-2420

Snow, Gene (Race Car Driver)
5719 Airport Freeway
Ft. Worth, TX 76117, USA

Snow, John (Politician)
122 Tempsford Ln
Richmond, VA 23226-2319, USA

Snow, John W (Secretary)
Treasury Department
1500 Pennsylvania Ave NW
Washington, DC 20220, USA

Snow, Jon (Actor)
c/o Staff Member *Knight Ayton Management*
35 Great James St
London WC1N 3HB, UK

Snow, J T (Athlete, Baseball Player)
15 Bridle Ct
Hillsborough, CA 94010-7451, USA

Snow, Justin (Athlete, Football Player)
1826 Milford St
Carmel, IN 46032, USA

Snow, Kate (Television Host)
c/o Staff Member *Good Morning America (NY)*
ABC
147 Columbus Ave Fl 6
New York, NY 10023, USA

Snow, Mark (Composer, Musician)
c/o Staff Member *Robert Urband & Associates*
8981 W Sunset Blvd #311
W Hollywood, CA 90069-1881, USA

Snow, Percy L (Football Player)
Kansas City Chiefs
2010 48th St NE
Canton, OH 44705-3082, USA

Snow, Randy (Athlete, Olympic Athlete)
105 E High St
Terrell, TX 75160-2660, USA

Snow, Richard F (Editor)
American Heritage Magazine
Editorial Dept
60 5th Ave
New York, NY 10011, USA

Snowden, Alison (Director, Writer)
c/o Melissa Myers *WME (LA)*
9601 Wilshire Blvd Fl 3
Beverly Hills, CA 90210, USA

Snowden, Earl of (A C R Armstrong-Jones) (Photographer)
22 Launceston Place
London W8 5RL, UNITED KINGDOM (UK)

Snowden, Lisa (Model)
c/o Marki Costello *Creative Management Entertainment Group (CMEG)*
2050 S Bundy Dr
Suite 280
Los Angeles, CA 90025, USA

Snowden, Lord (Photographer)
22 Launceston Place
London, W1 England, USA

Snowdon, Lisa (Actor)
c/o Marki Costello *Creative Management Entertainment Group (CMEG)*
2050 S Bundy Dr
Suite 280
Los Angeles, CA 90025, USA

Snowdon, Lord
22 Launceston Pl
London, ENGLAND W1

Snowe, Olympia (Politician)
337 Foreside Rd
Falmouth, ME 04105-1431, USA

Snow Patrol (Music Group)
c/o Staff Member *Paradigm (Monterey)*
404 W Franklin St
Monterey, CA 93940, USA

Snuggerud, Dave (Athlete, Hockey Player, Olympic Athlete)
968 Bavaria Hills Terr
Chaska, MN 55318, USA

Snuka, Jimmy (Superfly) (Actor, Wrestler)
647 Pacific Ave
Atco, NJ 08004-2117

Snvder, Kyle (Athlete, Baseball Player)
1869 Upper CoveTer
Sarasota, FL 34231-5437, USA

Snyder, Allan W (Scientist)
National University
Optical Science Center
Canberra, ACT 2601, AUSTRALIA

Snyder, Ben (Comedian)
c/o Staff Member *Gersh (LA)*
9465 Wilshire Blvd
Suite 600
Beverly Hills, CA 90212, USA

Snyder, Bill (Coach, Football Coach)
Kansas State University
Athletic Dept
Manhattan, KS 66506, USA

Snyder, Brian (Athlete, Baseball Player)
14834 Wood Home Rd
Centreville, VA 20120-1546, USA

Snyder, Chris (Athlete, Baseball Player)
4921 W Electra Ln
Glendale, AZ 85310-3838, USA

Snyder, Cory (Athlete, Baseball Player, Olympic Athlete)
468 N Loafer Dr
Payson, UT 84651-4535, USA

Snyder, Daniel (Football Executive)
c/o Staff Member *Washington Redskins*
21300 Redskin Park Dr
Ashburn, VA 20147, USA

Snyder, Dick (Athlete, Basketball Player)
4621 E Mockingbird Ln
Paradise Valley, AZ 85253-2420, USA

Snyder, Dylan Riley (Actor)
c/o Alexandra Heller *Persona PR*
8840 Wilshire Blvd
Suite 212
Beverly Hills, CA 90211, USA

Snyder, Earl (Athlete, Baseball Player)
58 Diamond Ave
Plainville, CT 06062-2904, USA

Snyder, Evan (Doctor)
Harvard Medical School
25 Shattuck St
Boston, MA 02115, USA

Snyder, Fonda (Actor)
c/o Staff Member *WmE2 (WMA-LA)*
1 William Morris Pl
Beverly Hills, CA 90212, USA

Snyder, Gary (Writer)
18442 MacNab Cypress Rd
Nevada City, CA 95959-8504, USA

Snyder, Gary S (Writer)
18442 MacNab Cypress Road
Nevada City, CA 95959, USA

Snyder, James (Actor)
c/o Brad Schenck *Paradigm (LA)*
360 N Crescent Dr
North Bldg
Beverly Hills, CA 90210, USA

Snyder, Jerry (Athlete, Baseball Player)
29603 Imperial Creek Dr
Tomball, TX 77586-2632, USA

Snyder, Jim (Athlete, Baseball Player, Coach)
7516 Dunbridge Dr
Odessa, FL 33556, USA

Snyder, Jim (Athlete, Baseball Player)
7516 Dunbridge Dr
Odessa, FL 33556-2270, USA

Snyder, John (Athlete, Baseball Player)
17729 W Port Royale Ln
Surprise, AZ 85388-7593, USA

Snyder, Joshua (Actor)
c/o Staff Member *Main Title Entertainment*
8383 Wilshire Blvd
Suite 408
Los Angeles, CA 90211, USA

Snyder, Kyle (Athlete, Baseball Player)
1869 Upper Cove Ter
Sarasota, FL 34231, USA

Snyder, Liza (Actor)
c/o Susan Smith *Susan Smith Company, The*
1344 N Wetherly Dr
Los Angeles, CA 90069-1817, USA

Snyder, Loren (Athlete, Football Player)
7727 Via Cortona
San Diego, CA 92127-3824, USA

Snyder, Rick (Governor)
P.O. Box 30013
Lansing, MI 48909, USA

Snyder, Russ (Athlete, Baseball Player)
P.O. Box 264
Nelson, NE 68961-0264, USA

Snyder, Solomon H (Doctor)
3801 Canterbury Road #1001
Baltimore, MD 21218, USA

Snyder, Suzanne (Actor)
Premiere Artists Agency
1875 Century Park E #2250
Los Angeles, CA 90067, USA

Snyder, Todd (Race Car Driver)
Brian Stewart Racing
P.O. Box 251
L.P.O.
Niagara Falls, NY 14304, usa

Snyder, Todd (Football Player)
Atlanta Falcons
850 S Valley Ln
Palatine, IL 60067-7185, USA

Snyder, William (Journalist)
508 Young St
Dallas, TX 75202, USA

Snyder, William (Photographer)
508 Young St
Dallas, TX 75202-4808, USA

Snyder, William D (Journalist, Photographer)
Dallas Morning News
Communivations Center
Editorial Dept
Dallas, TX 75265, USA

Snyder, Zack (Director, Writer)
c/o Todd Feldman *Creative Artists Agency (CAA-LA)*
2000 Ave Of The Stars
Los Angeles, CA 90067, USA

Snyderman, Nancy (Doctor, Entertainer)
Leading Authorities Inc
1220 L St
NW Ste 850
Washington, DC 20005, USA

So, Linda (Model)
6130 W Tropicana Blvd #280
Las Vegas, NV 89103

Soares, Mario A N L (President)
Rue Dr Joao Soares #2-3
Lisbon 1600, PORTUGAL

Soares, Jr., John (Race Car Driver)
4004 Dyer Road
Livermore, CA 94550, USA

Sobchuk, Dennis (Athlete, Hockey Player)
37300 N Tom Darlington Rd #N
Carefree, AZ 85377, USA

Sobchuk, Gene (Athlete, Hockey Player)
Farm
Milestone, SK SOG 3LO, Canada

Sobel, Barry
9000 Sunset Blvd. #1200
Los Angeles, CA 90069

Sobers, Garfield S (Gary) (Cricketer)
Cricket Board
9 Appleblossom
Petit Valley
Diego Martin, TRINIDAD

Sobers, Rickey (Athlete, Basketball Player)
6530 Annie Oakley Dr
Apt 1414
Henderson, NV 89014, USA

Sobers, Ricky
6S3e Annie Oakley Dr Apt 1414
Henderson, NV 89014-2171, USA

Sobieski, Leelee (Actor)
c/o Shelley Browning *Magnolia Entertainment (LA)*
9595 Wilshire Blvd
Suite 601
Beverly Hills, CA 90212, USA

Sobkowiak, Scott (Athlete, Baseball Player)
817 Symphony Dr
Aurora, IL 60516-3743, USA

Soble, Ron (Actor)
Tyler Kjar
4637 Willowcrest Ave
North Hollywood, CA 91602, USA

Sobule, Jill (Musician, Songwriter, Writer)
c/o Jonny (Jon) Podell *Podell Talent Agency LLC*
22 W 21st St
9th Floor
New York, NY 10010, USA

Socha, Lauren (Actor)
c/o Nicola Van Gelder *Conway van Gelder*
8-12 Broadwick St
London W1F 8HW, UK

Socha, Michael (Actor)
c/o Saskia Mulder *Ken McReddie Ltd*
11 Connaught Pl
London W2 2ET, UNITED KINGDOM

Sochor, James (Jim) (Coach, Football Coach)
1018 Kent Dr
Davis, CA 95616, USA

Social Distortion (Music Group, Musician)
c/o Jim Guerinot *Rebel Waltz Inc*
31652 Second Ave
Laguna Beach, CA 92651, USA

Society, Honor (Music Group, Musician)
c/o Staff Member *Walt Disney Music*
500 S Buena Vista Street
Animation 2E16
Burbank, CA 91521-1759

Socolofsky, Shelley (Artist)
3285 Sumac Dr S
Salem, OR 97302, USA

Sodano, Angelo Cardinal (Religious Leader)
Office of Secretary of State
Palazzo Apostolico
00120, VATICAN CITY

Soderbaum, Kristina
St.-Jakobs-platz 10 D-
Munich, GERMANY 80331

Soderberg, E Loren (Photographer)
PO Box 313
Sausalito, CA 94966, USA

Soderbergh, Steven (Director, Producer)
c/o Michael Sugar *Anonymous Content (LA)*
3531 Hayden Ave
Culver City, CA 90232, USA

Soderholm, Eric (Athlete, Baseball Player)
10S360 Hampshire Ln
Willowbrook, IL 60527-6018, USA

Soderstrom, Elizabeth
19 Jersbyvagen
Lidingo, SWEDEN 181-42

Soderstrom, Steve (Athlete, Baseball Player)
301 N Faith Home Rd
Turlock, CA 95380-9458, USA

Soderstrom, Tommy (Athlete, Hockey Player)
Oxelvagen 41
Alta, 13832 Sweden

Sodowsky, Client (Athlete, Baseball Player)
2801 Tropicana Ave
Norman, OK 73071, USA

Soetaert, Doug (Athlete, Hockey Player)
13006 66th Ave SE
Snohomish, WA 98296-8997

Sofaer, Abraham D (Lawyer)
120 Bryant St
Palo Alto, CA 94301, USA

Sofer, Rena (Actor)
c/o Nancy Iannios *Nancy Iannios PR*
PO Box 430
Signal Mountain, TN 37377, USA

Soff, Ray (Athlete, Baseball Player)
146 Drew Ave
Deerfield, MI 49228-1274, USA

Soffer, Jesse Lee (Actor)
c/o Marnie Sparer *Innovative Artists (LA)*
1505 10th St
Santa Monica, CA 90401, USA

Sofield, Rick (Athlete, Baseball Player)
18811 Big Cypress Dr
Jupiter, FL 29909-6085, USA

Sofie von Otter, Anne (Musician)
c/o Staff Member *ICM Partners (ICM-LA)*
10250 Constellation Blvd Fl 7
Los Angeles, CA 90067, USA

Softley, Iain (Director)
32A Camaby St
London, W1V 1PA UNITED KINGDOM

Sogard, Eric (Athlete, Baseball Player)
15039 N 19th Way
Phoenix, AZ 85022-3904, USA

Sohmer, Steve
2625 Larmar Rd.
Los Angeles, CA 90068

Sohn, Sonja (Actor)
c/o James Suskin *James Suskin Management*
2 Charlton St Ste 5K
New York, NY 10014, USA

Sohn Kee-Chung (Athlete, Track Athlete)
Korean Olympic Committee
International PO Box 1106
Seoul, SOUTH KOREA

Sojo, Luis (Athlete, Baseball Player)
17647 SW 20th St
Miramar, FL 33558-9701, USA

Soklosky, Bing (Cinematographer)
4654 Cartwright Ave
Toluca Lake, CA 91602, USA

Sokol, Marilyn (Actor)
24 W 40th St #1700
New York, NY 10018, USA

Sokoloff, Louis (Misc)
National Mental Health Institute
9000 Rockville Pike
Bethesda, MD 20892, USA

Sokoloff, Marla (Actor)
The Firm
9100 Wilshire Blvd #100W
Beverly Hills, CA 90210, USA

Sokolosky, John (Football Player)
Detroit Lions
13240 Leech Dr
Sterling Heights, MI 48312-3253, USA

Sokolov, Grigory L (Musician)
Trawick Artists
1926 Broadway
New York, NY 10023, USA

Sokolove, James G (Lawyer)
1 Boston Place
Boston, MA 02108, USA

Sokomanu, A George (President)
Mele Village
PO Box 1319
Port Villa, VANUATU

Sokurov, Alexander N (Director)
Smolenskaya Nab 4 #222
Saint Petersburg 199048, RUSSIA

Solana Madariaga, Javier (Government Official)
European Union Foreign Office
Rue de la Loi
Brussels 1048, BELGIUM

Solano, Jose (Actor)
c/o Staff Member *Stephany Hurkos Management*
11935 Kling St
Valley Village, CA 91607, USA

Solars, Stephen
241 Dover St.
Brooklyn, NY 11235

Solberg, Magnar (Athlete)
Stabellvn 60
Trondheim 7000, NORWAY

Solder, Nate (Football Player)
c/o David Dunn *Athletes First, LLC*
9140 Irvine Center Dr
Irvine, CA 92618, USA

Soleil, Stella (Music Group, Musician)
Kurfirst/Blackwell
350 W End Ave #1A
New York, NY 10024, USA

Soleri, Paolo (Architect)
Cosanti Foundation
6433 Doubletree Road
Scottsdale, AZ 85253, USA

Soles, Pamela Jayne (PJ) (Actor)
c/o Bill Philputt *Re-Evolution*
Prefers to be contacted via telephone
Los Angeles Area, CA 90069, USA

Solh, Rashid (Prime Minister)
Chambre of Deputes
Place de l'Etoile
Beirut, LABANON

Solheim, Ken (Athlete, Hockey Player)
44 Shaw Crescent SW
Medicine Hat, AB T1B 3Y6, CANADA

Solich, Frank (Coach, Football Coach)
University of Nebraska
Athletic Dept
Lincoln, NE 68588, USA

Solinger, Bob (Athlete, Hockey Player)
65-101 Grove Dr
Spruce Grove, AB T7X 3H7, Canada

Solis, Alex (Horse Racer)
2241 Redwood Dr
Glendora, CA 91741-6421, USA

Solis, Christina
9300 Wilshire Blvd. #555
Beverly Hills, CA 90212

Sollscher, Goran (Musician)
Kunstleragentur Raab & Bohm
Plankengasse 7
Vienna 1010, AUSTRIA

Solo, Hope (Athlete, Olympic Athlete, Soccer Player)
5837 115th Pl NE
Kirkland, WA 98033-8708, USA

Soloman, Anthony M (Financier)
535 Park Ave
New York, NY 10021, USA

Soloman, Freddie (Football Player)
803 Turtle River Court
Plant City, FL 33567, USA

Soloman, Richard
1550 M St NW Ste 700
Washington, DC 20005-1703, USA

Solomon, Ariel (Football Player)
Pittsburgh Steelers
3142 5th St
Boulder, CO 80304-2504, USA

Solomon, Arthur K (Physicist)
27 Cragie St
Cambridge, MA 02138, USA

Solomon, Bruce
3518 Cahuenga Blvd. W. #316
Los Angeles, CA 90068

Solomon, David (Director)
c/o Cori Wellins *WME (LA)*
9601 Wilshire Blvd Fl 3
Beverly Hills, CA 90210, USA

Solomon, David H (Scientist)
3640 Dragonfly Dr #202
Thousand Oaks, CA 91360-8445, USA

Solomon, Ed (Writer)
c/o Todd Feldman *Creative Artists Agency
(CAA-LA)*
2000 Ave Of The Stars
Los Angeles, CA 90067, USA

Solomon, Edward I (Misc)
Stanford University
Chemistry Dept
Stanford, CA 94305, USA

Solomon, Harold (Tennis Player)
Int'l Mgmt Group
1 Erieview Plaza
1360 E 9th St #1300
Cleveland, OH 44114, USA

Solomon, Jesse (Football Player)
Minnesota Vikings
205 W Bunker St
Madison, FL 32340-2309, USA

Solomon, Richard H (Diplomat,
Politician, Scientist)
US Institute for Peace
1200 17th St NW
#200
Washington, DC 20036, USA

Solomon, Sophie (Musician)
c/o Staff Member *Paradigm (Monterey)*
404 W Franklin St
Monterey, CA 93940, USA

Solomon, Stacey (Musician, Reality TV
Star)
c/o Staff Member *Max Clifford Associates*
Moss House
15-16 Brooks Mews
Mayfair, London W1K 4DS, UK

Solomon, Susan (Misc)
National Oceanic & Atmospheric Admin
325 Broadway
Boulder, CO 80305, USA

Solomon, Yonty (Musician)
56 Canonbury Park N
London N1 2JT, UNITED KINGDOM (UK)

Solondz, Todd (Director, Writer)
Industry Entertainment
955 Carillo Dr
#300
Los Angeles, CA 90048, USA

Solovey, Sam (Actor)
c/o Staff Member *Ruth Webb Enterprises*
10580 Des Moines Ave
Northridge, CA 91326, USA

Soloviyev, Vladimir A (Cosmonaut)
Khovanskaya Ui D 3
Kv 28
Moscow 129515, RUSSIA

Solovyev, Anatoli Y (Cosmonaut)
Potchta Kosmonavtov
Moskovskoi Oblasti
Syvisdny Goroduk 141160, RUSSIA

Solovyev, Sergei A (Director, Writer)
Akademika Pilyugina Str 8
Korp 1 #330
Moscow 11393, RUSSIA

Solow, Robert (Nobel Prize Laureate)
1010 Waltham St Apt 328
Lexington, MA 02421-8057, USA

Solow, Robert M (Nobel Prize Laureate)
528 Lewis Wharf
Boston, MA 02110, USA

Soloway, Jill (Producer)
c/o Staff Member *ICM Partners (ICM-LA)*
10250 Constellation Blvd Fl 7
Los Angeles, CA 90067, USA

Solt, Ron (Football Player)
Indianapolis Colts
1200 Thornhurst Rd
Wilkes Barre, PA 18702-8212, USA

Soltan, Jerzy (Architect)
6 Shady Hill Square
Cambridge, MA 02138, USA

Soltau, Gordie (Football Player)
San Francisco 49ers
1290 Sharon Park Dr Apt 50
Mento Park, CA 94025-7038, USA

Soltau, Gordon (Gordy) (Football Player)
1290 Sharon Park Dr
Mento Park, CA 94025, USA

Soltau, Gordy
1111 Hamilton Ave
Palo Alto, CA 94301

Soluna (Music Group)
c/o Staff Member *Creative Artists Agency
(CAA-LA)*
2000 Ave Of The Stars
Los Angeles, CA 90067, USA

Solymosi, Zoltan (Dancer)
Royal Ballet
Covent GArden
Bow St
London WC2E 9DD, UNITED KINGDOM
(UK)

Solyom, Janos P (Musician)
Norr Malarstrand 54
VII
Stockholm 11220, SWEDEN

Solzhenitsyn, Ignat (Musician)
Columbia Artists Mgmt Inc
165 W 57th St
New York, NY 10019, USA

Somare, Michael T (Prime Minister)
Assembly House
Karan
Murik Lakes
East Sepik, PAPUA NEW GUINEA

Sombrotto, Vincent R (Misc)
National Letter Carriers Assn
100 Indiana Ave NW
Washington, DC 20001, USA

Somerhalder, Ian (Actor)
c/o Alissa Vradenburg *Untitled
Entertainment (LA)*
350 S. Beverly Dr #200
Beverly Hills, CA 90212, USA

Somers, Gwen (Actor, Model)
Alice Fries Agency
1927 Vista Del Mar Ave
Los Angeles, CA 90068, USA

Somers, Suzanne (Actor)
Port Charley Productions
23677 Calabasas Rd.
#663
Calabasas, CA 91302, USA

Somerset, Willie (Athlete, Basketball
Player)
6441 Oak View Dr
Harrisburg, PA 17112-1889, USA

Somerville, Bonnie (Actor)
c/o Staff Member *McKeon-Myones
Management*
3500 Olive Ave
Suite 770
Burbank, CA 91505, USA

Something Corporate (Music Group)
c/o Staff Member *Agency for the
Performing Arts (APA-LA)*
405 S Beverly Dr
Suite 500
Beverly Hills, CA 90212-4425, USA

Sommars, Julie (Actor)
7272 Outlook Cove Dr
Los Angeles, CA 90068, USA

Sommaruga, Cornelio (Misc)
International Red Cross
19 Ave de la Paix
Genoa 1202, SWITZERLAND

Sommer, Elke (Actor)
Atzelaberger Str 46
Marloffstein D-91080, GERMANY

Sommer, Rich (Actor)
c/o Staff Member *Davis Spylios
Management*
244 West 54th Street #707
New York, NY 10019

Sommer, Roy (Athlete, Hockey Player)
65 Roman Dr
Shrewsbury, MA 01545-5819

Sommer, Roy (Athlete, Hockey Player)
Worcester Sharks
50 Foster St
Worcester, MA 01608-1305

Sommerfeld, Kent (Sportscaster)
Milwaukee Brewers
13935 W Maria Dr
New Berlin, WI 53151-6891, USA

Sommers, Denny (Athlete, Baseball
Player)
210 W Bath St Apt 133
Hortonville, WI 54944-9459, USA

Sommers, Gordon L (Religious Leader)
Moravian Church Northem Province
1021 Center St
bethlehem, PA 18018, USA

Sommers, Joanie (Musician)
Xentel
900 SE 3rd Ave
#201
Fort Lauderdale, FL 33316, USA

Sommers, Stephen (Director, Producer,
Writer)
c/o Stuart Rosenthal *Bloom Hergott
Diemer Rosenthal Laviolette & Feldman*
150 S Rodeo Dr Fl 3
Beverly Hills, CA 90212, USA

Sommore (Comedian)
c/o Staff Member *ICM Partners (ICM-LA)*
10250 Constellation Blvd Fl 7
Los Angeles, CA 90067, USA

Somogyi, Jennie R (Ballerina)
c/o Staff Member *New York City Ballet*
New York State Theater
20 Lincoln Center
New York, NY 10023, USA

Somogyi, Jozsef (Artist)
Marton Utca 3/5
Budapest 1038, HUNGARY

Somorjai, Gabor A (Misc)
665 San Luis Road
Berkeley, CA 94707, USA

Sondeckis, Saulls (Conductor)
Ciurlionio 28
Vilnius, LITHUANIA

Sondheim, Stephen (Composer, Musician)
246 E 49th St
New York, NY 10017, USA

Sondrini, Joe (Athlete, Baseball Player)
16712 Stockland Court
Huntersville, NC 28078-6438, USA

Song, Brenda (Actor)
c/o Richard Konigsberg *RKM*
400 N Mansfield Ave
Los Angeles, CA 90036, USA

Song, Xiaodong (Misc)
Columbia University
Lamont-Doherty Earth Observatory
New York, NY 10027, USA

Songaila, Antoinette (Astronomer)
University of Hawaii
Astronomy Dept
Honolulu, HI 96822, USA

Songaila, Darius
141 S Longfellow Ln
Mooresville, NC 28117-7116, USA

Songin, Tom (Athlete, Hockey Player)
70 Cascade Ter
Walpole, MA 02081-3239, USA

Songz, Trey (Musician)
c/o Dana Sims *ICM Partners (ICM-LA)*
10250 Constellation Blvd Fl 7
Los Angeles, CA 90067, USA

Soni, Jimmy (Journalist, Writer)
c/o Staff Member *Huffington Post*
675 Sixth Ave
New York, NY 10010, USA

Soni, Rebecca (Athlete, Swimmer)
c/o Staff Member *USA Swimming
Association*
1 Olympic Plz
Colorado Springs, CO 80909-5770, USA

Sonja (Royalty)
Det Kongelige Slott
Drammensveien 1
Oslo 0010, NORWAY

Sonmor, Glen (Athlete, Hockey Player)
2301 Vtllase Ln Apt 214
MInneapolis, MN 55431-5815, USA

Sonnanstine, Andy (Athlete, Baseball Player)
526 Reimer Rd
Wadsworth, OH 33707-3832, USA

Sonnenfeld, Barry (Director)
c/o Richard Lovett *Creative Artists Agency (CAA-LA)*
2000 Ave Of The Stars
Los Angeles, CA 90067, USA

Sonnenschein, Hugo F (Educator)
University of Chicago
President's Office
Chicago, IL 60637, USA

Sonnenschein, Klaus
Breisgauer Str. 15a
Berlin, GERMANY D-14129

Sonnier, Jo-El (Musician)
Entertainment Artists
2409 21st Ave S
#100
Nashville, TN 37212, USA

Sonsini, Larry W (Lawyer)
Wilson Sonsini Goodrich Rosati
650 Page Mill Road
Palo Alto, CA 94304, USA

Sons of the Desert (Music Group)
c/o Staff Member *WmE2 (WMA-TN)*
1600 Division St
Suite 300
Nashville, TN 37203, USA

Sons of the Pioneers
117 Berms Circle 45 #4
Branson, MO 65616-3744

Sonus Quartet (Music Group, Musician)
Prefers to be contacted via telephone or email

Sonzero, Jim (Writer)
c/o Andrew Cannava *United Talent Agency (UTA)*
9336 Civic Center Dr
Beverly Hills, CA 90210, USA

Sood, Veena (Actor, Producer)
c/o Robyn Friedman *Artist Management Inc*
464 King St E
Toronto ON M5A 1L7, CANADA

Soo Hoo, Hayward (Actor)
1411 Solar Dr
Monterey Park, CA 91754, USA

Soomekh, Bahar (Actor)
c/o Paul Kohner *Kohner Agency, The*
9300 Wilshire Blvd
Suite 555
Beverly Hills, CA 90212, USA

Sopel, Brent (Athlete, Hockey Player)
5506 S Park Ave
Hinsdale, IL 60521-5019, USA

Sophia (Royalty)
Palacio de la Zarzuela
Madrid 28071, SPAIN

Sopko, Michael D (Business Person)
Inco Ltd
145 King St W
Toronto, ON M5H 4B7, CANADA

Sopkovic, Kay (Athlete, Baseball Player)
6540 W Butler Dr
Unit 62
Glendale, AZ 85302-4313, USA

Sorbo, Kevin (Actor)
c/o Sherry Marsh *Marsh Entertainment*
12444 Ventura Blvd #203
Studio City, CA 91604, USA

Sorel, Edward (Artist)
156 Franklin St
New York, NY 10013, USA

Sorel, Jean (Actor)
Cineart
36 Rue de Ponthieu
Paris 75008, FRANCE

Sorel, Louise (Actor)
10808 Lindbrook Dr
Los Angeles, CA 90024, USA

Sorel, Ted (Actor)
c/o Staff Member *Kerin-Goldberg Associates*
155 E 55th St #5D
New York, NY 10022, USA

Sorensen, Jacki F (Misc)
Jacki's Inc
129 1/2 N Woodland Blvd
#5
Deland, FL 32720, USA

Sorensen, Lary (Athlete, Baseball Player)
42515 Northville Place Dr
Apt 406
Northville, MI 49321-9149, USA

Sorensen, Nick (Football Player)
St Louis Rams
305 Grandview Dr
Blacksburg, VA 24060-6222, USA

Sorensen, Zach (Athlete, Baseball Player)
1322 S 2670 E
Saint George, UT 84790-6197, USA

Sorenson, Heidi (Actor, Model)
Shelly & Pierce
13775A Mono Way #220
Sonora, CA 95370, USA

Sorenson, Reed (Race Car Driver)
Richard Petty Motorsports
320 Aviation Dr.
Mooresville, NC 28677, USA

Sorenson, Theodore
1285 Ave. of the Americas
New York, NY 10019

Sorenson, Zach (Athlete, Baseball Player)
2690 E 1400 South Cir
Saint George, UT 84790, USA

Sorenstam, Annika (Golfer)
c/o Staff Member *IMG (Cleveland)*
1360 E 9th St
Suite 100
Cleveland, OH 44114, USA

Sorenstam, Charlotta (Golfer)
c/o Patrick Levine
1411 Whitman Ct
Anthem, AZ 85086, USA

Sorey, Revie (Football Player)
Chicago Bears
485 Saint Moritz Dr
Glen Ellyn, IL 60137-4320, USA

Sorgers, Jana (Athlete)
Potsdamer RG
An Der Pirschheide
Potsdam 14471, GERMANY

Sorgi, Jim (Athlete, Football Player)
72 Holloway Blvd
Brownsburg, Indiana 46112, USA

Soria, Oscar (Sportscaster)
111 E Beth Dr
Phoenix, AZ 85042-7657, USA

Soriano, Alfonso G (Baseball Player)
Texas Rangers
1000 Ballpark Way
Arlington, TX 60611-3954, USA

Soriano, Rafael (Athlete, Baseball Player)
6820 81st Dr NE
Marysville, WA 30328-7256, USA

Sorkin, Aaron (Producer, Writer)
c/o Rick Rosen *WME (LA)*
9601 Wilshire Blvd Fl 3
Beverly Hills, CA 90210, USA

Sorkin, Andrew Ross (Correspondent)
c/o Staff Member *The New York Times Company*
229 W 43rd St
New York, NY 10036, USA

Sorkin, Arleen (Actor)
623 S Beverly Glen Blvd
Los Angeles, CA 90024, USA

Sorlie, Donald M (Aviator)
14612 44th Ave NW
Gig Harbor, WA 98332-9048, USA

Sorokin, Peter P (Physicist)
5 Ashwood Road
South Salem, NY 10590, USA

Soros, Alexander (Philanthropist)
Jewish Funds for Justice
330 7th Ave
Suite 1902
New York, NY 10001, USA

Soros, George (Business Person, Financier)
Soros Fund Mgmt
888 7th Ave #3300
New York, NY 10106, USA

Soroya, Princess
Ave. Montaigne
Paris, FRANCE 75008

Sorrentino, Mike (The Situation) (Reality TV Star)
MPS Management
4400 Route 9 S
Suite 1000
Freehold, NJ 07728, USA

Sorrento, Paul (Athlete, Baseball Player)
5918 Mont Blanc Pl NW
Issaquah, WA 98027-7859, USA

Sorrento, Paul A (Baseball Player)
5918 Mont Blance Place NW
Issaquah, WA 98027, USA

Sorsa, T Kalevi (Prime Minister)
Hakaniemenranta 16D
Helsinki 00530, FINLAND

Sorte, Maria (Actor)
c/o Staff Member *Televisa*
Blvd Adolfo Lopez Mateos 232
Colonia San Angel INN
DF CP 01060, MEXICO

Sortun, Henrik (Athlete, Football Player)
6708 16th Ave NW
Seattle, WA 98117-5513, USA

Sorum, Matt (Musician)
c/o Todd Cameron *Abrams Artists Agency (LA)*
9200 Sunset Blvd
11th Floor
Los Angeles, CA 90069, USA

Sorvino, Mira (Actor)
c/o Jason Weinberg *Untitled Entertainment (LA)*
350 S. Beverly Dr #200
Beverly Hills, CA 90212, USA

Sorvino, Paul (Actor)
c/o Steven Muller *Innovative Artists (LA)*
1505 10th St
Santa Monica, CA 90401, USA

Sosa, Elias (Athlete, Baseball Player)
3126 Summerfield Ridge Ln
Matthews, NC 28105-8509, USA

Sosa, Samuel (Sammy) (Athlete, Baseball Player)
Chicago Cubs
1060 W Addison St, Suite 1
Attn: Alumni Association
Chicago, IL 33160-5212, USA

Sosenka, Don (Race Car Driver)
Mr Magoo
P.O. Box 679
Spring Branch, TX 78070, USA

So Solid Crew (Music Group)
c/o Staff Member *Mission Control Artists Agency*
Unit 3 City Business Centre
St Olav's Court, Lower Road
London SE16 2XB, UNITED KINGDOM (UK)

Sospiri, Vincenzo (Race Car Driver)
Dan Gurney's All American Racing
2334 S. Broadway
Santa Ana, CA 92707, USA

Sossamon, Lou (Athlete, Football Player)
6308 Exum Drive
West Columbia, SC 29169-7184, USA

Sossamon, Shannyn (Actor)
c/o Oren Segal *Management Production Entertainment (MPE)*
9229 Sunset Blvd.
Suite 301
West Hollywood, CA 90069, USA

Soter, Paul (Comedian)
c/o Staff Member *United Talent Agency (UTA)*
9336 Civic Center Dr
Beverly Hills, CA 90210, USA

Sotin, Hans (Opera Singer)
Schulheide 10
Bendestorf 21227, GERMANY

Sotirhos, Michael A (Diplomat)
American Embassy
A Leoforos Vassilissis Sofias 91
Athens 106 60, GREECE

Sotkilava, Zurab L (Opera Singer)
Bolshoi Theater
Teatralnaya Pi 1
Moscow 103009, RUSSIA

Soto, Gabriel (Actor)
c/o Staff Member *Televisa*
Blvd Adolfo Lopez Mateos 232
Colonia San Angel INN
DF CP 01060, MEXICO

Soto, Geovany (Athlete, Baseball Player)
6319 Perch Creek Dr
Houston, TX 77049, USA

Soto, Mario M (Athlete, Baseball Player)
6319 Perch Creek Dr
Houston, TX 77049, USA

Soto, Talisa (Actor)
c/o Peg Donegan *Framework Entertainment (LA)*
9057 Nemo St
Suite C
West Hollywood, CA 90069, USA

Sotomayor, Antonio (Artist)
3 LeRoy Place
San Francisco, CA 94109, USA

Sotomayor, Nancy (Stylist)
430 W 24th St
#9-F
New York, NY 10011, USA

Sotomayor Sanabria, Javier (Athlete, Track Athlete)
Int'l Mgmt Group
1 Erieview Plaza
1360 E 9th St #1300
Cleveland, OH 44114, USA

Sottsass Jr, Ettore (Designer)
Via Manzoni 14
Milan 20121, ITALY

Souch, Carolyn (Stylist)
c/o Staff Member *Judy Inc*
1 Yorkville Ave
Toronto ON M4W 1L1, Canada

Soucy, Christian (Athlete, Hockey Player)
274 Wildflower Cir
Williston, VT 05495-9391, USA

Souders, Cecil (Football Player)
Detroit Lions
1803 Channingway Court E
Reynoldsburg, OH 43068, USA

Soul, David (Actor, Musician)
Innovative Artists
1505 10th St
Santa Monica, CA 90401, USA

Soulages, Pierre (Artist)
18 Rue des Trois-Portes
Paris 75005, FRANCE

Soul Asylum (Music Group, Musician)
955 S. Carrillo Dr. #300
Los Angeles, CA 90048, USA

SoulDecision (Music Group)
c/o Staff Member *Bruce Allen Talent*
425 Carrall St
Suite 500
Vancouver, BC V6B 6E3, Canada

Soul II Soul (Music Group)
c/o Staff Member *Profile Artists Agency*
Unit 10, J Block
Tower Bridge Business Complex, 110 Clements Road
London SE16 4DG, United Kingdom

Sound Tribe Sector 9 (Music Group)
c/o Staff Member *Paradigm (Monterey)*
404 W Franklin St
Monterey, CA 93940, USA

Souray, Sheldon (Athlete, Hockey Player)
27927 Pacific Coast Hwy
Malibu, CA 90265-4326, USA

Sousa, Mauricio de (Cartoonist)
Mauricio de Sousa Producoes
Rua do Curtume 745
Sao Paulo SP, BRAZIL

Soutar, Dave (Bowler)
6910 Chickasaw Falls Ave
Bradenton, FL 34203-7874, USA

Soutar, Judy (Bowler)
3914 102nd Place N
Clearwater, FL 33762-S404, USA

Soutendijk, Renee (Actor)
Marion Rosenberg
PO Box 69826
West Hollywood, CA 90069, USA

Souter, David H (Attorney)
US Supreme Court
214 Hopkins Green Rd
Contoocook, NH 03229-2611, USA

South, Mike
PO Box 1288
Tucker, GA 30084

Southam, James (Athlete, Olympic Athlete, Track Athlete)
18230 Norway Dr
Anchorage, AK 99516-6033, USA

Southcott, Susan (Stylist)
12313 Culver Dr
Culver CIty, CA 90230, USA

Souther, J D (Musician, Songwriter, Writer)
8263 Hollywood Dr
Los Angeles, CA 90069, USA

Southerland, Ron (Race Car Driver)
7416 East Palo Verde Drive
Scottsdale, AZ 85253, USA

Southerland II, Steve (Congressman, Politician)
1229 Longworth HOB
Washington, DC 20515, USA

Southern, Silas (Eddie) (Athlete, Track Athlete)
2006 Custer Pkwy
Richardson, TX 75080-3403, USA

Southern Belles
11150 W. Olympic Blvd. #1100
Los Angeles, CA 90064

Southworth, Bill (Athlete, Baseball Player)
320 Dobbin Rd
Saint Louis, MO 63119-4515, USA

Southworth, Carrie (Actor)
c/o Van Johnson *Van Johnson Company*
350 S. Beverly Dr.
Suite 200
Beverly Hills, CA 90212, USA

Souza, Mark (Athlete, Baseball Player)
10001 Woodcreek Oaks Blvd
Apt 817
Roseville, CA 95747-5811, USA

Sova, Peter M (Cinematographer)
1492 Roses Brook Road
South Kortright, NY 13842, USA

Sovereign, Lady (Musician)
c/o Staff Member *Paradigm (Monterey)*
404 W Franklin St
Monterey, CA 93940, USA

Sovern, Michael I (Educator)
Columbia University
Law School
435 W 116th St
New York, NY 10027, USA

Sovey, William P (Business Person)
Newell Co
20 E Milwaukee St #212
Janesville, WI 53545, USA

Sovran, Gino (Athlete, Basketball Player)
2669 Cheswick Dr
Troy, MI 48084-1069, USA

Soward, R J (Football Player)
Jacksonville Jaguars
7660 Chipwood Ln
Jacksonville, FL 32256-2338, USA

Sowell, Arnold (Arnie) (Athlete, Track Athlete)
1647 Waterstone Lane
#1
Charlotte, NC 28262, USA

Sowell, Thomas (Economist)
Stanford University
Hoover Institution
Stanford, CA 94305, USA

Sowells, Rich (Football Player)
New York Jets
6711 McCullum Rd
Missouri City, TX 77489-3430, USA

Sowers, Barbara (Athlete, Baseball Player)
5601 Duncan Rd Lot 199
Punta Gorda, FL 33982-4762, USA

Sowers, Jeremy (Athlete, Baseball Player)
43793 APache Wells Ter
Leesburg, VA 20176-7423, USA

Soyer, David (Musician)
PO Box 307
Brattleboro, VT 05302, USA

Soyinka, Wale (Nobel Prize Laureate)
PO Box 935
Obeokuta Ogun State, Nigeria

Soyinka, Wole (Nobel Prize Laureate)
University of Nevada
Creative Writing Dept
Las Vegas, NV 89154, USA

Soyster, Harry E (General)
4706 Duncan Dr
Annandale, VA 22003, USA

Spaak, Catherine
Viale Parioli 59
Rome, ITALY 00197

Spacek, Jaroslav (Athlete, Hockey Player)
6301 OspreyTer
Coconut Creek, FL 33073-2624, USA

Spacek, Sissy (Actor)
Beau Val Farm
P.O. Box 22
Cobham, VA 22947, USA

Spacey, Kevin (Actor, Producer)
c/o Joanne Horowitz *Joanne Horowitz Management*
9350 Wilshire Blvd #224
Beverly Hills, CA 90212, USA

Spaddky, Boris V (Misc)
State Committee for Sports
Skatertny Pereulok 4
Moscow, RUSSIA

Spade, David (Actor, Comedian)
c/o Marc Gurvitz *Brillstein Entertainment Partners*
9150 Wilshire Blvd #350
Beverly Hills, CA 90212, USA

Spade, Kate (Designer, Fashion Designer)
Public Relations Dept
48 W 25th St Fl 4
New York, NY 10010, USA

Spader, James (Actor)
254 S. Windsor Blvd
Los Angeles, CA 90004, USA

Spafford, Eugene (Educator)
Purdue University
Education Research Center
West Lafayette, IN 47907, USA

Spagnardi, Darren (Athlete, Baseball Player)
2364 W Center Street Ext
Lexington, NC 27295-5943, USA

Spagnola, John S (Football Player)
Philadelphia Eagles
414 Hillbrook Road
Bryn Mawr, PA 19010-3634, USA

Spahn, Ryan (Actor)
c/o Ann Kelly *Ann Kelly Management*
245 W 51st St
Suite 411
New York, NY 10019, USA

Spahr, Charles E (Business Person)
800 Beach Road
Vero Beach, FL 32963, USA

Spain, Douglas (Actor)
Innovative Artists
1505 10th St
Santa Monica, CA 90401, USA

Spain, Gary (Stylist)
c/o Staff Member *Clutts Agency, The*
1400 Turtle Creek Blvd
#171
Dallas, TX 75207, USA

Spalding, Esperanza (Musician)
c/o Daniel Florestano *Montuno Productions*
C/ Rosselló 248, 5º - 2ª
Barcelona 08008, Spain

Spalding, Leslie (Athlete, Golfer)
1055 O'Malley Drive
Billings, MT 59102-2524, USA

Spali, Timothy (Actor)
Markham & Froggatt
Julian House
4 Windmill St
London W1P 1HF, UNITED KINGDOM (UK)

Spall, Timothy (Actor)
c/o Laura Berwick *Hofflund/Polone*
9465 Wilshire Blvd #420
Beverly Hills, CA 90212, USA

Spanarkel, Jim (Athlete, Basketball Player)
436 Edgewood Pl
Rutherford, NJ 07070-2662, USA

Spanger, Amy (Actor)
c/o Maureen Taran *New Wave Entertainment (LA)*
2660 W Olive Blvd
Burbank, CA 91505, USA

Spangler, Al (Athlete, Baseball Player)
27202 Afton Way
Huffman, TX 77336-3601, USA

Spangler, Al (Athlete, Baseball Player)
27202 Afton Way
Huffman, TX 77336, USA

Spang-McCook, Laurette (Actor)
4154 Colbath Ave
Sherman Oaks, CA 91423, USA

Spanhel, Martin (Athlete, Hockey Player)
1017 Starlight Ln
Westerville, OH 43082-7092, USA

Spani, Gary (Football Player)
Kansas City Chiefs
3920 NE Sequoia St
Lees Summit, MO 64064-1574, USA

Spanic, Gabriela (Actor)
c/o Staff Member *Televisa*
Blvd Adolfo Lopez Mateos 232
Colonia San Angel INN
DF CP 01060, MEXICO

Spanjers, Martin (Actor)
c/o Sommer Smith *Innovative Artists (LA)*
1505 10th St
Santa Monica, CA 90401, USA

Spano, Joe (Actor)
EC Assoc
10315 Woodley Ave
#110
Granada Hills, CA 91344, USA

Spano, Nick (Actor)
c/o Justin Evans *The Independent Group*
6363 Wilshire Blvd
Suite 115
Los Angeles, CA 90048, USA

Spano, Robert (Musician)
c/o Staff Member *ICM Partners (ICM-LA)*
10250 Constellation Blvd Fl 7
Los Angeles, CA 90067, USA

Spano, Vincent (Actor)
c/o Jo Kincaid *Gilbertson Management*
1334 3rd St Promenade #201
Santa Monica, CA 90401, USA

Spanos, Alex (Football Executive)
1533 W Lincoln Rd
Stockton, CA 95207-2447, USA

Spanoulis, Vassilis (Athlete, Basketball
Player)
c/o Jeff Schwartz *Excel Sports
Management*
9665 Wilshire Blvd #500
Los Angeles, CA 90212, USA

Spanswick, Bill (Athlete, Baseball Player)
1200 Commonwealth Cir
Apt 202
Naples, FL 34116-6631, USA

Sparks
106 N. Buffalo St. #200
Warsaw, IN 46580

Sparks, Dana (Actor)
VOX
5670 Wilshire Blvd
#820
Los Angeles, CA 90036, USA

Sparks, Daniel (Athlete, Basketball Player)
2396 N Bruceville Rd
Vincennes, IN 47591-9698, USA

Sparks, Hal (Actor, Comedian, Musician,
Producer)
c/o Alison Leslie *Marleah Leslie &
Associates PR*
1645 N Vine St
Suite 712
Los Angeles, CA 90028, USA

Sparks, Hayley
5757 Wilshire Blvd. #512
Los Angeles, CA 90036

Sparks, Jeff (Athlete, Baseball Player)
714 W 42nd St
Houston, TX 77018-4429, USA

Sparks, Joe (Athlete, Baseball Player)
3915 E Cholla S
Phoenix, AZ 85028-2116, USA

Sparks, Jordin (Musician)
c/o Brian Manning *Creative Artists Agency
(CAA-LA)*
2000 Ave Of The Stars
Los Angeles, CA 90067, USA

Sparks, Kylie (Actor)
c/o Myrna Lieberman *Myrna Lieberman
Management*
3001 Hollyridge Drive
Hollywood, CA 90068, USA

Sparks, Mike (Referee)
c/o Staff Member *World Wrestling
Entertainment (WWE)*
Titan Towers
1241 E Main St
Stamford, CT 06905-3857, USA

Sparks, Nicholas (Writer)
c/o Theresa Park *Park Literary*
270 Lafayette St
Suite 1504
New York, NY 10012, USA

Sparks, Phillippi (Football Player)
Green Bay Packers
3315 W Walter Way
Phoenix, AZ 85027-1084, USA

Sparks, Stephanie (Golfer)
48 Redwood Ln
Wheeling, WV 26003-4854, USA

Sparks, Steve (Athlete, Baseball Player)
4019 Colony Oaks Dr
Sugar Land, TX 77479-2420, USA

Sparks, Steve (Athlete, Baseball Player)
23378 Wilson Dr
Loxley, AL 36551, USA

Sparlis, Alexander (Al) (Football Player)
Green Bay Packers
HC 4 Box 243
Porterville, CA 93257-9706, USA

Sparrow, Guy (Athlete, Basketball Player)
1709 McCulloch Blvd S
Lake Havasu City, AZ 86406-8847, USA

Sparrow, Rory (Athlete, Basketball Player)
111 Valley Rd
Montclair, NJ 07042-2322, USA

Sparv, Camilla (Actor)
1500 Ocean Dr #602
Miami Beach, FL 33139, USA

Sparxxx, Bubba (Musician)
c/o Staff Member *Paradigm (Monterey)*
404 W Franklin St
Monterey, CA 93940, USA

Spassky, Boris
Skatertny Pereulok 5
Moscow, CA RUSSIA

Speake, Bob (Athlete, Baseball Player)
4742 SW Urish Rd
Topeka, KS 66610-9758, USA

Speakes, Larry (Politician)
924 McKnight Rd
Cleveland, MS 38732-9753, USA

Speakman, Jeff (Actor)
7868 Milliken Ave
Rancho Cucamonga, CA 91730, USA

Speakman-Pitt, William (War Hero)
Victoria Cross Assn
Old Admiralty Building
London SW1A 2BL, UNITED KINGDOM
(UK)

Speaks, Ruben L (Religious Leader)
African Methodist Episcopal Zion Church
PO Box 32843
Charlotte, NC 28232, USA

Spear, Kristin (Stylist)
c/o Staff Member *Zenobia Agency Inc*
PO Box 909
Groveland, CA 95321, USA

Spear, Laurinda H (Architect)
Arquitectonica International
550 Brickell Ave
#200
Miami, FL 33131, USA

Spearman, Alvin (Athlete, Baseball Player)
635 E 49th St #3
Chicago, IL 60615, USA

Spearritt, Hannah (Actor, Musician)
c/o Jeb Brandon *Kritzer Levine Wilkins
Entertainment (KLWG)*
11872 La Grange Ave
1st Floor
Los Angeles, CA 90025, USA

Spears, Aries (Actor)
c/o Staff Member *AKA Talent Agency*
6310 San Vicente Blvd
Suite 200
Los Angeles, CA 90048, USA

Spears, Billie Jo (Musician)
PO Box 23470
Nashville, TN 37202, USA

Spears, Britney (Dancer, Musician)
398 W Stafford Rd
Thousand Oaks, CA 91361, USA

Spears, Eddie (Actor)
c/o Jennie Saks *NASS Talent Management*
2212 Lea Ave
Bozeman, MT 59715, USA

Spears, Ernest (Athlete, Football Player)
201 50th Ave #24K
Long Island City, NY 11101-5782, USA

Spears, Jamie Lynn (Actor)
c/o Nick Styne *Creative Artists Agency
(CAA-LA)*
2000 Ave Of The Stars
Los Angeles, CA 90067, USA

Spears, Lynne (Educator, Writer)
c/o Staff Member *Thomas Nelson Inc*
Author Mail
PO Box 141000
Nashville, TN 37214, USA

Spears, Marcus (Athlete, Football Player)
10402 Reading Road
Richmond, TX 77469-7330, USA

Spears, Peter (Actor)
c/o Jaclyn Travers *Creative Artists Agency
(CAA-LA)*
2000 Ave Of The Stars
Los Angeles, CA 90067, USA

Spears, Randy (Adult Film Star)
c/o Staff Member *Wicked Pictures*
9040 Eton Ave
Canoga Park, CA 91304, USA

Spears, William D (Football Player)
63 Waterbridge Place
Ponte Vedra Beach, FL 32082, USA

Specht, Greg (Athlete, Football Player)
8650 SW Woodside Dr
Portland, OR 97225-1742, USA

Speck, Cliff (Athlete, Baseball Player)
823 S Nueva Vista Dr
Palm Springs, CA 92264-3425, USA

Speck, Fred (Athlete, Hockey Player)

Specter, Arlen (Politician)
4109 Timber Ln
Philadelphia, PA 19129-5525, USA

Specter, Rachel (Actor)
c/o Adam Griffin *Kritzer Levine Wilkins
Entertainment (KLWG)*
11872 La Grange Ave
1st Floor
Los Angeles, CA 90025, USA

Spector, Phil (Business Person,
Songwriter, Writer)
686 S Arroyo Parkway #175
Pasadena, CA 91105, USA

Spector, Ronnie (Musician)
c/o Barry Dickins *International Talent
Booking*
74A Charlotte St
London W1T 4QJ, UNITED KINGDOM
(UK)

Speech (Artist, Musician)
William Morris Agency
1325 Ave of Americas
New York, NY 10019, USA

Speed, Grant (Artist)
139 S 400 E
Lindon, UT 84042-2120, USA

Speed, Horace (Athlete, Baseball Player)
6821 State Boulevard Ext
Meridian, MS 39305, USA

Speed, Lake (Race Car Driver)
c/o Staff Member *NASCAR*
1801 Speedway Blvd
Daytona Beach, FL 32015, USA

Speed, Lizz (Producer)
c/o Staff Member *Jackoway Tyerman
Wertheimer Austen Mandelbaum Morris
& Klein*
1925 Century Park E
22nd Floor
Los Angeles, CA 90067, USA

Speedman, Scott (Actor)
c/o Frank Frattaroli *Circle of Confusion
(NY)*
270 Lafayette St
Suite 402
New York, NY 10012, USA

Speedwagon, REO (Music Group,
Musician)
c/o Keith Naisbitt *Agency Group Ltd, The
(LA)*
1880 Century Park E
Suite 711
Los Angeles, CA 90067, USA

Speer, Bill (Athlete, Hockey Player)

Speer, Del (Football Player)
Cleveland Browns
17620 NW 40th Ave
Opa Locka, FL 33055-3864, USA

Speer, Hugo (Actor)
c/o Fiona McLoughlin *Independent Talent
Group (ITG-UK)*
Oxford House
76 Oxford St
London W1D 1BS, UK

Speers, Ted (Athlete, Hockey Player)
61515 Brookway Dr
South Lyon, MI 48178, USA

Spehr, Tim (Athlete, Baseball Player)
8524 Briargrove Dr
Woodway, TX 76712, USA

Speier, Chris (Athlete, Baseball Player)
3102 N Manor Dr W
Phoenix, AZ 91302-2970, USA

Speier, Jackie (Congressman, Politician)
211 Cannon HOB
Washington, DC 20515, USA

Speier, Justin (Athlete, Baseball Player)
9405 S 51st St
Phoenix, AZ 92625-2425, USA

Speier, Ryan (Athlete, Baseball Player)
15450 FM 1325 APt 1724
Austin, TX 78728-2841, USA

Speight, Derrick (Producer)
c/o Staff Member *Screen Door Entertainment*
15223 Burbank Blvd
Sherman Oaks, CA 91411, USA

Speight, Lester (Rasta) (Actor)
c/o Staff Member *WME (LA)*
9601 Wilshire Blvd Fl 3
Beverly Hills, CA 90210, USA

Speigner, Levale (Athlete, Baseball Player)
1041 Bond St
Thomasville, GA 31757-0221, USA

Speir, Chris
6114 E. Montecito
Scottsdale, AZ 85251

Speiser, Jerry (Musician)
TPA
PO Box 124
Round Corner, NSW, AUSTRALIA

Spektor, Regina (Actor, Musician)
c/o Ron Shapiro *Ron Shapiro Management & Consulting*
135 W 26th St
Suite 4A
New York, NY 10001, USA

Spelke, Elizabeth S (Doctor)
Harvard University
Psychology Dept
Cambridge, MA 02138, USA

Spelling, Candy (Actor)
c/o Kevin Sasaki *Kevin Sasaki Public Relations & Media Counsel*
8491 Sunset Blvd
Suite 224
Los Angeles, CA 90069, USA

Spelling, Randy (Actor)
c/o Staff Member *Innovative Artists (LA)*
1505 10th St
Santa Monica, CA 90401, USA

Spelling, Tori (Actor)
c/o Meghan Prophet *PMK/BNC Public Relations (PMK-LA)*
8687 Melrose Ave Fl 8
West Hollywood, CA 90069, USA

Spellman, Alonzo R (Football Player)
Chicago Bears
1300 Marigold Way
Pflugerville, TX 78660-4137, USA

Spellman, John D (Ex-Governor)
Carney Stephenson Badley
Columbia Center
701 5th Ave.
Seattle, WA 98104, USA

Spelvin, Georgina
3121 Ledgewood Dr
Hollywood, CA 90068

Spence, A Michael (Nobel Prize Laureate)
768 Mayfield Ave
Stanford, CA 94305-1044, USA

Spence, Blake (Athlete, Football Player)
14005 SW Teal Blvd #D
Beaverton, OR 97008, USA

Spence, Bob (Athlete, Baseball Player)
3081 Bonita Woods Dr
Bonita, CA 91902-2020, USA

Spence, Bruce (Actor)
c/o Imogen Johnson *Johnson and Laird Management*
P.O. Box 78340
Grey Lynn Auckland 1245, New Zealand

Spence, Dave (Misc)
Horseshores Union
RR 2 Box 71C
Englishtown, NJ 07726, USA

Spence, Gerry (Attorney)
PO Box 548
Jackson, WY 83001, USA

Spence, Jonathan D (Historian, Writer)
691 Forest Road
West Haven, CT 06516, USA

Spence, Sebastian (Actor)
c/o Lesa Kirk *Open Entertainment*
1051. N Cole Ave
Suite B
Los Angeles, CA 90038, USA

Spencer, Abigail (Actor)
c/o Jon Rubinstein *Authentic Talent and Literary Management*
45 Main St
Suite 1004
Brooklyn, NY 11201, USA

Spencer, Andre (Athlete, Basketball Player)
1315 W Gage Ave
Los Angeles, CA 90044-2733, USA

Spencer, Anthony (Athlete, Football Player)
c/o Eugene Parker *Maximum Sports Management*
6435 W Jefferson Blvd
#197
Fort Wayne, IN 46804, USA

Spencer, Bud (Actor)
Mistral Film Group
Via Archmede 24
Rome 00187, ITALY

Spencer, Chaske (Actor)
c/o Staff Member *Josselyne Herman & Associates*
345 East 56th Street #3B
New York, NY 10022, USA

Spencer, Chris (Actor)
c/o Julia Buchwald *Buchwald/Fortitude (LA)*
6500 Wilshire Blvd
Suite 2200
Los Angeles, CA 90048, USA

Spencer, Dale (General)
1885 Silver Oak Way
Hemet, CA 92545-7741, USA

Spencer, Danielle (Actor)
c/o Martin Bedford *Bedford & Pearce Management Martin Bedford*
2/263-269 Alfred St N
North Sydney NSW 2060, Australia

Spencer, Darryl (Athlete, Football Player)
1473 Beechfern Drive
Melbourne, FL 32935-5989, USA

Spencer, Daryl (Athlete, Baseball Player)
2740 S Larkin St
Wichita, KS 67216-1258, USA

Spencer, Earl Charles (Government Official)
The Stables
Althorp
Northampton NN7 4HQ, UNITED KINGDOM (UK)

Spencer, Elizabeth (Writer)
402 Longleaf Dr
Chapel Hill, NC 27517, USA

Spencer, Elmore (Athlete, Basketball Player)
2770 Foxlair Trl
Atlanta, GA 30349-4436, USA

Spencer, Felton (Athlete, Basketball Player)
4102 Nicholas Roy Ct
Prospect, KY 40059-8209, USA

Spencer, Frank Cole (Doctor, Educator)
560 1st Ave
New York, NY 10016, USA

Spencer, Freddie (Race Car Driver)
Freddie Specer's
7055 Speedway Blvd.
#E-106
Las Vegas, NV 89115, USA

Spencer, GC (Race Car Driver)
698 Pickens Bridge Road
Gray, TN 37615, USA

Spencer, George (Athlete, Baseball Player)
8160 Hickory Ave
Galena, OH 43021-8508, USA

Spencer, Jesse (Actor)
c/o Jason Weinberg *Untitled Entertainment (LA)*
350 S. Beverly Dr #200
Beverly Hills, CA 90212, USA

Spencer, Jimmy (Race Car Driver)
160 Gasoline Alley
Mooresville, NC 28115, USA

Spencer, Jimmy (Football Player)
5331 Talavero Pl
Parker, CO 80134, USA

Spencer, John (Athlete, Misc)
17 Knowles St
Radcliffe
Lancs M26 0DN, UNITED KINGDOM (UK)

Spencer, J Robert (Actor)
c/o Nyle Brenner *Brenner Management*
9171 Wilshire Blvd #441
Beverly Hills, CA 90210, USA

Spencer, Lara (Television Host)
c/o Jonathan Rosen *WME (WMA-NY)*
1325 Ave of the Americas
New York, NY 10019, USA

Spencer, Irv (Athlete, Hockey Player)

Spencer, Marc (Radio Personality)
c/o Staff Member *WPKX*
1331 Main St Fl 4
Springfield, MA 01103, USA

Spencer, Maurice (Football Player)
St Louis Cardinals
61 W 62nd St
New York, NY 10023-7015, USA

Spencer, Melvin J (Attorney, Attorney General, General, Religious Leader)
5910 N Shawnee Ave
Oklahoma City, OK 73112, USA

Spencer, Octavia (Actor)
c/o Melissa Kates *Viewpoint Inc*
8820 Wilshire Blvd.
Suite 220
Beverly Hills, CA 90211, USA

Spencer, Roderick
602 Bay St.
Santa Monica, CA 90405

Spencer, Sean (Athlete, Baseball Player)
3584 E Calistoga Ct
Port Orchard, WA 98366-4084, USA

Spencer, Shane (Athlete, Baseball Player)
2858 Manzanita View Rd
Alpine, CA 91901-3988, USA

Spencer, Stan (Athlete, Baseball Player)
3100 NE 188th St
Ridgefield, WA 98642-9515, USA

Spencer, Susan (Correspondent)
CBS-TV
News Dept
2020 M St NW
Washington, DC 20036, USA

Spencer, Timothy (Tim) (Football Player)
San Diego Chargers
1435 Sherborne Lane
Powell, OH 43065-7604, USA

Spencer, Tom (Athlete, Baseball Player)
2021 E Conner Stra
Tucson, AZ 85719-3206, USA

Spencer, Tracie (Musician)
Rogers & Cowan
6340 Breckenridge Run
Rex, GA 30273, USA

Spencer, Willie (Football Player)
Minnesota Vikings
1109 Johnson St SE
Massillon, OH 44646-8266, USA

Spencer-Churchill, Victor
6 Cumberland Geo. St.
London, ENGLAND W1

Spencer-Devlin, Muffin (Golfer)
1278 Glenneyre St Apt 155
Laguna Beach, CA 92651-3103, USA

Spender, Percy C (Judge)
Headingley House
11 Wellington St Woolhara
Sydney, NSW 2025, AUSTRAILIA

Spenn, Fred (Athlete, Baseball Player)
5201 Desoto Rd
Sarasota, FL 34235-3607, USA

Sperber Carter, Paula (Bowler)
9895 SW 96th St
Miami, FL 33176, USA

Spergel, David (Misc)
Princeton University
Astrophysicist Dept
Princeton, NJ 08544, USA

Sperling, Gene (Government Official, Politician)
National Economic Council
1600 Pennsylvania Ave NW
Washington, DC 20506, USA

Spero, Nancy
530 La Guardia Place
New York, NY 10012, USA

Sperring, Rob (Athlete, Baseball Player)
13302 Chriswood Dr
Cypress, TX 77429, USA

Spevack, Jason (Actor)
c/o Dana Wdrick Fletcher *Coast to Coast Talent Group*
3350 Barham Blvd
Los Angeles, CA 90068, USA

Speyrer, Cotton (Football Player)
Baltimore Colts
7905 San Felipe Blvd Apt 117
Austin, TX 78729-7638, USA

Spezza, Jason (Athlete, Hockey Player)
The Orr Hockey Group
PO Box 290836
Charlestown, MA 02129-0215, USA

Spheeris, Penelope (Director)
PO Box 1128
Studio City, CA 91614, USA

Spice 1 (Artist, Musician)
JL Entertainment
18653 Ventura Blvd #340
Tarzana, CA 91356, USA

Spice Girls (Music Group)
35 Parkgate Rd. #32 Ransome Dock
London, ENGLAND SW11 4NP

Spicer, Bob (Athlete, Baseball Player)
423 McPhee Dr
Fayetteville, NC 28305, USA

Spicer III, William E (Physicist)
620 Sand Hill Rd
Apt 305E
Palo Alto, CA 94304-2610, USA

SPider Loc (Musician)
c/o Staff Member *Interscope Records (NY)*
1755 Broadway
New York, NY 10019, USA

Spidia, Vladimir (Prime Minister)
Kancelar Presidenta Republiky
Hradecek
Prague 1 119 08, CZECH REPUBLIC

Spiegel, Henry W (Economist)
6848 Nashville Road
Lanham Seabrook, MD 20706, USA

Spiegelman, Art (Writer)
c/o Staff Member *Steven Barclay Agency*
12 Western Ave
Petaluma, CA 94952, USA

Spieier, Patrick (Baseball Player)
6635 S 108th Ave
Omaha, NE 68137-4733, USA

Spielberg, David (Actor)
10537 Cushdon Ave
Los Angeles, CA 90064, USA

Spielberg, Steven (Director, Producer)
1513 Amalfi Dr
Pacific Palisades, CA 90272, USA

Spieler, Patrick (Athlete, Baseball Player)
6635 S 108th Ave
Omaha, NE 68138-6018, USA

Spielman, Chris (Athlete, Football Player, Sportscaster)
OSU 336 LLC
Attn: Carry Billy
PO Box 342
Powell, OH 43065, USA

Spier, Peter E (Artist)
PO Box 566
Shoreham, NY 11786, USA

Spier, Wolfgang
Kaiserdamm 98
Berlin, GERMANY 14057

Spiers, Bill (Athlete, Baseball Player)
9233 Old State Rd
Cameron, SC 29030-8129, USA

Spiers, Judi
1-3 Charlotte St.
London, ENGLAND W1P 1HD

Spiers, Ronald I (Diplomat)
1176 Middletown Road
South Londonderry, VT 05155, USA

Spies, Joshua (Artist)
PO Box 90
Watertown, SD 57201-0090, USA

Spiezio, Ed (Athlete, Baseball Player)
2027 Taller Rd
Morris, IL 60450-8913, USA

Spiezio, Scott (Athlete, Baseball Player)
2027 Taller Rd
Morris, IL 60450-8789, USA

Spikes, Cameron (Football Player)
St Louis Rams
3001 Fraternity Row # 132
College Station, TX 77845-6504, USA

Spikes, Charlie (Athlete, Baseball Player)
531 N Border Dr
Bogalusa, LA 70427-3307, USA

Spikes, Jack E (Football Player)
Dallas Texans
9537 Highland View Dr
Dallas, TX 75238-1025, USA

Spikes, Takeo (Athlete, Football Player)
5005 Heatherwood Court
Roswell, GA 30075-2285, USA

Spilborghs, Ryan (Athlete, Baseball Player)
2220 Elise Way
Santa Barbara, CA 80205-2290, USA

Spilde, Jenna (Model, Reality TV Star)
c/o Staff Member *The Sports Illustrated Fresh Faces Competition*
NBC Entertainment
3000 W Alameda Ave #5366
Burbank, CA 91523, USA

Spilker, Angela
425 N. Oakhurst Dr.
Beverly Hills, CA 90210

Spiller, Michael A (Cinematographer)
2418 Roscornare Road
Los Angeles, CA 90077, USA

Spillner, Dan (Athlete, Baseball Player)
18505 SE Newport Way
Unit C113
Issaquah, WA 98027-9032, USA

Spilman, Harry (Athlete, Baseball Player)
4423 Saint Phillips Rd S
Mount Vernon, IN 47620-9629, USA

Spin Doctors, The (Music Group)
c/o Staff Member *Paradigm (Monterey)*
404 W Franklin St
Monterey, CA 93940, USA

Spindt, Capp (Inventor)
SRI International
333 Ravenswood Ave
Menlo Park, CA 94025, USA

Spinella, Stephen (Actor)
c/o Staff Member *Innovative Artists (LA)*
1505 10th St
Santa Monica, CA 90401, USA

Spinelli, Jerry (Writer)
331 Melvin Rd
Phoenixville, PA 19460, USA

Spinelli, Paul (Photographer)
6701 Center Dr W Ste 1111
Los Angeles, CA 90045-1552, USA

Spiner, Brent (Actor)
c/o Rebecca (Becca) Kovacik *Hofflund/Polone*
9465 Wilshire Blvd #420
Beverly Hills, CA 90212, USA

Spinetta, Jean-Cyril (Business Person)
Group Air France
45 Rue de Paris
Roissy CDG Cedex 95747, FRANCE

Spinks, Michael (Athlete, Boxer, Olympic Athlete)
Butch Lewis Productions
925 Centre Rd
Wilmington, DE 19807, USA

Spinks, Scipio (Athlete, Baseball Player)
11422 Rock Bridge Ln
Sugar Land, TX 77498-0923, USA

Spinney, Caroll (Actor)
940 Brickyard Rd
Woodstock, CT 06281, USA

Spinotti, Dante (Cinematographer)
Smith/Gosnell/Nicholson
PO Box 1156
Studio City, CA 91614, USA

Spires, Greg (Football Player)
New England Patriots
175 Centre St # 520
Quincy, MA 02169-8600, USA

Spiro, Jordana (Actor)
c/o Larry Taube *Principal Entertainment (LA)*
1964 Westwood Blvd #400
Los Angeles, CA 90025, USA

Spiro, Lev L (Director)
c/o Staff Member *WME (LA)*
9601 Wilshire Blvd Fl 3
Beverly Hills, CA 90210, USA

Spirtas, Kevin (Actor)
c/o Robert Baird *Baird Artists Management*
P.O. Box 5016
Station A
Toronto, ON M5W 1N4, Canada

Spittka, Marko (Athlete)
Judo Club 90
Zielona-Gora-Str 9
Frankfurt/Ober 15230, GERMANY

Spitz, Mark (Athlete, Olympic Athlete, Swimmer)
c/o Staff Member *Premier Management Group (PMG Sports)*
115 Crescent Commons Dr Ste 250
Cary, NC 27518, USA

Spitzer, Eliot (Ex-Governor, Talk Show Host)
985 5th Ave.
New York, NY 10075-0142, USA

Spitzer, Robert (Doctor, Psychic)
Columbia University
Psychiatry School
New York, NY 10027, USA

Spivakov, Vladmir T (Musician)
Vspolny Per 17
#14
Moscow, RUSSIA

Spivey, Junior (Athlete, Baseball Player)
4140 S Ambrosia Dr
Chandler, AZ 85248-4804, USA

Spivey, Sebron (Football Player)
Dallas Cowboys
435 Capitol View Dr
Columbus, OH 43203-1037, USA

Splatt, Rachel (Race Car Driver)
12629 N Tatum Blvd
#184
Phoenix, AZ 85032, USA

Splatt, Rachelle (Race Car Driver)
12629 N. Tatum Blvd.
#184
Phoenix, AZ 85032, USA

Split Ends
136 New Kings Rd.
London, ENGLAND SW6

Spoelstra, Erik (Coach)
c/o Howard Nuchow *CAA Sports (LA)*
2000 Avenue of the Stars
Los Angeles, CA 90067, USA

Spoiler, The
3615 W. Waters Box 110
Tampa, FL 33614

Spoliaric, Paul (Athlete, Baseball Player)
545 Gramiak Rd
KelownaBC V1X 1K4, BC V1X
1K4 Canada, USA

Spoljario, Paul (Baseball Player)
Toronto Blue Jays
13261 N 73rd Ave
Peoria, AZ 85381-6054, USA

Sponable, Jess M (Astronaut)
Universal Space Lines 1501 Quail St Ste 102
Newport Beach, CA 92660-2726, USA

Sponenburgh, Mark (Artist)
5562 NW Pacific Coast Highway
Seal Rock, OR 97376, USA

Spong, Annie (Stylist)
c/o Staff Member *Cloutier Agency*
2632 La Cienega Ave
Los Angeles, CA 90034, USA

Spong, John S (Religious Leader)
24 Puddingdtone Road
Morris Plains, NJ 07950, USA

Spooner, John (Financier, Writer)
Houghton Mifflin
222 Berkeley St
#700
Boston, MA 02116, USA

Spooneybarger, Tim (Athlete, Baseball Player)
4109 Bamboo Dr
Pensacola, FL 32526-8783, USA

Spork, Shirley (Golfer)
73010 Somera Rd
Palm Desert, CA 92260-6032, USA

Sporkin, Stanley (Government Official, Judge)
US District Court
Courthouse
3rd & Constitution NW
Washington, DC 20001, USA

Sporleder, Gregory (Actor)
c/o Julia Buchwald *Buchwald/Fortitude (LA)*
6500 Wilshire Blvd
Suite 2200
Los Angeles, CA 90048, USA

Sposa, Mike (Golfer)
8317 Old Town Dr
Tampa, FL 33647-3335, USA

Spottiswoode, Roger (Director)
c/o Staff Member *ICM Partners (ICM-LA)*
10250 Constellation Blvd Fl 7
Los Angeles, CA 90067, USA

Spottsville, Ray (Baseball Player)
Houston Eagles
PO Box 591
Colfax, LA 71417-0591, USA

Spound, Michael (Actor)
James/Levy/Jacobson
3500 W Olive Ave
#1470
Burbank, CA 91505, USA

Spradlin, Danny (Football Player)
Dallas Cowboys
1011 Laurie St
Maryville, TN 37803-6731, USA

Spradlin, Jerry (Athlete, Baseball Player)
2824 E Diana Ave
Anaheim, CA 90717-2024, USA

Spradling, Charlie (Actor)
c/o Staff Member *Don Buchwald & Associates Inc (NY)*
10 E 44th St
New York, NY 10017

Spragan, Donnie (Football Player)
Denver Broncos
312 Riviera Dr
Union City, CA 94587-3722, USA

Sprague, Ed (Athlete, Olympic Athlete, Swimmer)
4677 Pine Valley Cir
Stockton, CA 95219, USA

Sprague, Ed (Athlete, Baseball Player)
19015 N Davis Rd
Lodi, CA 95242-9203, USA

Sprague, Jack (Race Car Driver)
X-Press Motorsports
610 Performance Rd.
Mooresville, NC 28117, USA

Spratlan, Lewis (Composer)
Amherst College
Music Dept
Amherst, MA 01002, USA

Sprayberry, Dylan (Actor)
c/o Laura Pallas *Pallas Management*
5301 Bellaire Ave
Valley Vilage, CA 91607, US

Sprayberry, James M (General)
426 Holiday Dr
Titus, AL 36080-2520, USA

Spreitler, Taylor (Actor)
c/o Cameron Curtis *Curtis Talent Management*
9607 Arby Dr
Beverly Hills, CA 90210, USA

Sprewell, Latrell (Athlete, Basketball Player)
850 W Dean Rd
Milwaukee, WI 53217-2527, USA

Spriggs, George (Athlete, Baseball Player)
77A W Bay Front Rd
Lothian, MD 20711-9711, USA

Spriggs, Larry (Athlete, Basketball Player)
7870 Boeing Ave
Los Angeles, CA 90045-142, USA

Spring, Dan (Athlete, Hockey Player)
2005 Canyon St
Creston, BC VOB 1G5, Canada

Spring, Don (Athlete, Hockey Player)
Spring Fuel Distributors
2780 Acland Rd
Kelowna, BC V1X 7X1, Canada

Spring, Frank (Athlete, Hockey Player)
638 Upper Ottawa St
Hamilton, ON L8T 3T5, CANADA

Spring, Jack (Athlete, Baseball Player)
P.O. Box 118
Colbert, WA 99005-0118, USA

Spring, Sherwood C (Astronaut)
8244 Native Violet Drive
Lorton, VA 22079-5664, USA

Spring, Sherwood C Colonel (Astronaut)
2116 McDonough Ln
San Diego, CA 92106-6087, USA

Springer, Dennis (Athlete, Baseball Player)
1060 W Windsor Ct
Hanford, CA 93230^6572, USA

Springer, Jerry (Journalist)
454 N Columbus Dr# 200
Chicago, IL 60611-5807, USA

Springer, Michael (Golfer)
1482 E Forest Oaks Dr
Fresno, CA 93720, USA

Springer, Mike (Golfer)
1482 E Forest Oaks Dr
Fresno, CA 93720-3443, USA

Springer, Robert C (Astronaut)
202 Village Dr
Sheffield, AL 35660, USA

Springer, Robert C Colonel (Astronaut)
202 Village Cir
Sheffield, AL 35660-5632, USA

Springer, Russ (Athlete, Baseball Player)
PO Box 185
4357 Highway 8
Pollock, LA 71467-0185, USA

Springer, Steve (Athlete, Baseball Player)
6962 Caria Cir
Huntington Beach, CA 92647-4315, USA

Springfield, Marty (Athlete, Baseball Player)
5164 Flciker Field Cir
Sarasota, FL 34231, USA

Springfield, Rick (Actor, Musician)
30635 La Sonora Dr
Malibu, CA 90265, USA

Springgs, Marcus (Football Player)
Buffalo Bills
830 Regal St
Houston, TX 77034-1231, USA

Springs, Alice (Photographer)
7 Ave Saint-Ramon #T1008
Monte Carlo, MONACO

Springs, Kirk (Football Player)
New York Jets
4925 Paddock Rd
Cincinnati, OH 45237-5548, USA

Springs, Shawn (Football Player)
Washington Redskins
21300 Redskin Park Dr
Ashburn, VA 20147, USA

Springsteen, Bruce (Musician, Songwriter)
36/40 Bellevue Ave
Rumson, NJ 07760, USA

Springsteen, Pamela (Actor, Photographer)
c/o Caryn Weiss *Weiss Artists*
6311 Romaine St #7234
Los Angeles, CA 90038, USA

Sprinkel, Beryl W (Government Official)
20140 Saint Andrews Dr
Olympia Fields, IL 60461, USA

Sprinkel, Patrick (Stylist)
c/o Staff Member *Zenobia Agency Inc*
PO Box 909
Groveland, CA 95321, USA

Sprinkle, Edward A (Ed) (Football Player)
Chicago Bears
3 Saint Moritz Dr
Palos Park, IL 60464-3146, USA

Sprotte, Jimmy (Football Player)
Cincinnati Bengals
2163 E Palmcroft Dr
Tempe, AZ 85282-3062, USA

Sprouse, Cole (Actor)
c/o Megan Moss Pachon *ID Public Relations (ID-LA)*
7060 Hollywood Blvd
8th Floor
Los Angeles, CA 90028, USA

Sprouse, Dylan (Actor)
c/o Megan Moss Pachon *ID Public Relations (ID-LA)*
7060 Hollywood Blvd
8th Floor
Los Angeles, CA 90028, USA

Sprouse, James M (Judge)
US Court of Appeals
PO Box 401
122 N Court St
Lewisburg, WV 24901, USA

Sprout, Bob (Athlete, Baseball Player)
227 County Road 740
Enterprise, AL 32159-2294, USA

Sprowl, Bobby (Athlete, Baseball Player)
4711 Leeward Ave
Northport, AL 35473-1934, USA

Spruce, Andy (Athlete, Hockey Player)
12 Rathgar St
London, ON N5Z 1Y4, Canada

Spurgeon, Jay (Athlete, Baseball Player)
212 Hartsdale Rd
Rochester, NY 14622-2007, USA

Spurling, Chris (Athlete, Baseball Player)
27247 Copper Ridge Dr
Wesley Chapel, FL 37188-5431, USA

Spurlock, Morgan (Actor)
c/o Richard Arlook *The Arlook Group*
205 S Beverly Dr
Suite 209
Beverly Hills, CA 90212, USA

Spurrier, Paul
Beccles Rd. 47
Lowestoft/Norfolk, ENGLAND

Spurrier, Steve (Athlete, Coach, Football Coach, Football Player, Heisman Trophy Winner)
126 Beaver Ridge Dr
Elgin, SC 29045, USA

Spurrior, Stephen O (Steve) (Coach, Football Player)
17050 Silver Charm Place
Leesburg, VA 20176, USA

Spuzich, Sandra (Golfer)
Ladies Pro Golf Assn
100 International Gold Dr
Daytona Beach, FL 32124, USA

Spyro Gyro
200 W. Superior #202
Chicago, IL 60610, USA

Squierek, Jack (Football Player)
4051 Vezbar Dr
Seven Hills, OH 44131, USA

Squirek, Jack (Football Player)
Los Angeles Raiders
4051 Vezber Dr
Seven Hills, OH 44131-6233, USA

Squires, Mike (Athlete, Baseball Player)
9548 Autumnwood Cir
Kalamazoo, MI 49009-9385, USA

Squirrel Nut Zippers
2756 N. Green Valley Parkway #449
Las Vegas, CA 89014-2100

Squyres, Steven Dr (Scientist)
Cornell University 428 Space Science
Bldg Department Of Astronomy
Ithaca, NY 14853, USA

Squyres, Steven W (Scientist)
Cornell University
Planetary Science Dept
Ithaca, NY 14853, USA

Sranowski, Wally
Mill Rd.
Toronto, CANADA Ont M9C 1Y

Srb, Adrian M (Misc)
411 Cayuga Heights Road
Ithaca, NY 14850, USA

Sri Chinmoy (Religious Leader)
85-45 Sri Chinmoy St
Jamaica, NY 11432, USA

Sridevi (Actor, Bollywood)
1 Bishop Wallers South Avenue
C I T Colony
Chennai, TN 600004, INDIA

Sridevi (Actor, Bollywood)
Green Acres
7 Bungalows Lokhandwala Complex
Andheri(W)
Mumbai, 400058 MS, INDIA

Sripriya (Actor, Bollywood)
10 Muthu Pandian Avenue
Santhome
Chennai, TN 600004, INDIA

Srividhya (Actor, Bollywood)
22 North Street
Sriram Nagar
Chennai, TN 600018, INDIA

St, Clair Carl
Pacific Symphony Orchestra
1231 E Dyer Road
Santa Ana, CA 92705, USA

Staab, Rebecca (Actor)
Don Buchwald
6500 Wilshire Blvd
#2200
Los Angeles, CA 90048, USA

Staal, Eric (Athlete, Hockey Player)
The Orr Hockey Group
PO Box 290836
Charlestown, MA 02129-0215, USA

Staal, Jordan (Athlete, Hockey Player)
Candy Mountain Dr RR 6
Thunder Bay, ON P7C 5N5, Canada

Staal, Marc (Athlete, Hockey Player)
Candy Mountain Dr RR 6
Thunder Bay, ON P7C 5N5, Canada

Staats, Dewavne (Sportscaster)
1170 Gulf Blvd Apt 1601
Clearwater Beach, FL 33767-2785, USA

Staats, Dewayne (Baseball Player, Sportscaster)
Tampa Bay Devil Rays
1170 Gulf Blvd Apt 1601
Clearwater Beach, FL 33767-2785, USA

Stabenow, Deborah (Politician)
238 9th St SE
Washington, DC 20003-2111, USA

Stabile, Nick
c/o Staff Member *Diverse Talent Group*
9911 W Pico Blvd Ste 340W
Los Angeles, CA 90035, USA

Stablein, George (Athlete, Baseball Player)
2903 Penman
Tustin, CA 92782-3314, USA

Stabler, Ken
260 N. Joachim St.
Mobile, AL 36603

Stabler, Ken M (Kenny) (Football Player)
260 N Joachim St
Mobile, AL 36603, USA

Stables, Kelly (Actor)
c/o Kurt Patino *Rothman / Patino / Andres Entertainment*
4370 Tujunga Ave
Suite 120
Studio City, CA 91604, USA

Stacey, Caitlin (Actor)
21 Esmond Rd
London W4 1JG, UNITED KINGDOM

Stacey, Siran (Football Player)
Philadelphia Eagles
PO Box 131
Hartford, AL 36344-0131, USA

Stacey Q (Actor, Music Group, Musician)
641 S Palm St #D
La Habra, CA 90631, USA

Stack, Brian (Writer)
c/o Staff Member *3 Arts Entertainment Inc*
9460 Wilshire Blvd
7th Floor
Beverly Hills, CA 90210, USA

Stack, Rosemarie (Actor)
10375 Wilshire Blvd #1B
Los Angeles, CA 90024, USA

Stack, Timothy
10635 Santa Monica Blvd. #130
Los Angeles, CA 90025

Stackhouse, Charles (Football Player)
New York Giants
240 Shady Grove St
Marion, AR 72364-9412, USA

Stackhouse, Jerry (Athlete, Basketball Player)
S266 Settles Bridge Rd
Suwanee, GA 30024-769S, USA

Stackhouse, Ron (Athlete, Hockey Player)
RR 2
Haliburton, ON KOM 1SO, Canada

Stackpole, H C (Hank) (General)
Asia-Pacific Security Studies Center
2058 Maluhia Road
Honolulu, HI 96815, USA

Stacom, Kevin (Athlete, Basketball Player)
14 Florida Ave
Jamestown, RI 02835-1548, USA

Stacy, Billy (Football Player)
Chicago Cardinals
400 Colonial Cir
Starkville, MS 39759-4214, USA

Stacy, Hollis (Golfer)
9400 W 10th Ave
Lakewood, CO 80215-4700, USA

Stacy, James (Actor)
478 Severn Ave
Tampa, FL 33606, USA

Stadlen, Lewis J. (Actor)
c/o Staff Member *Access Talent Voice Overs*
171 Madison Avenue
Suite 900
New York, NY 10016

Stadler, Craig (Golfer)
113 Elk Xing
Evergreen, CO 80439-4114, USA

Stadler, Sergei V (Musician)
Kaiserstr 43
Munich 80801, GERMANY

Stadtman, Earl R (Misc)
16907 Redland Road
Derwood, MD 20855, USA

Stadtman, Thressa C (Misc)
16907 Redland Road
Derwood, MD 20855, USA

Staehle, Marv (Athlete, Baseball Player)
19421 Cromwell Ct
Apt 208
Fort Myers, FL 33912-0386, USA

Staff, Kathy
17 Maple Mews
London, ENGLAND NW6

Staffieri, Joe (Football Player)
Philadelphia Eagles
6825 Polo Fields Pkwy
Cumming, GA 30040-5731, USA

Stafford, Ben (Horse Racer)
22 Glen Dr
Voorhees, NJ 08043-1404, USA

Stafford, Jerry (Baseball Player)
2316 Catalina Cir Apt 276
Oceanside, CA 92056-5395, USA

Stafford, Jim (Musician, Songwriter)
1 Stafford Pl
Branson, MO 65616, USA

Stafford, John R (Business Person)
American Home Products
5 Giralda Farms
Madison, NJ 07940, USA

Stafford, Matthew (Athlete, Football Player)
c/o Tom Condon *CAA - St. Louis*
222 S Central Ave
Suite 1008
St Louis, MO 63105, USA

Stafford, Michelle (Actor)
c/o Marlan Willardson *MWPR*
10153 Riverside Drive
#157
Toluca Lake, CA 91602, USA

Stafford, Nancy (Actor)
PO Box 11807
Marina del Rey, CA 90295, USA

Stafford, Steve (Actor)
Studio Wings, Inc.
855 Aviation Dr
Camarillo, CA 93010, USA

Stafford, Thomas
1006 Cameron St
Alexandria, VA 22314-2427

Stafford, Thomas P (Astronaut, General)
AVD
PO Box 604
Glenn Dale, MD 20769, USA

Stafford, Thomas P Lt Gen (Astronaut)
1006 N Royal St
Alexandria, VA 22314-1530, USA

Stageman-Roberts, Donna (Athlete, Baseball Player)
1831 Jerome Pl
Helena, MT 59601-4735, USA

Staggers, Jon (Football Player)
Pittsburgh Steelers
3835 Oakes Dr
Hayward, CA 94542-1720, USA

Staggs, Jeff (Football Player)
San Diego Chargers
4641 Jeri Way
El Cajon, CA 92020-8329, USA

Staggs, Steve (Athlete, Baseball Player)
4021 Kent St
Norman, OK 73072-4020, USA

Stagliano, John
14141 Covello St.
Van Nuys, CA 91405

Stagus, Gus (Coach, Swimmer)
University of Michigan
Athletic Dept
Ann Arbor, MI 48104, USA

Stahl, Jerry (Actor, Writer)
c/o Staff Member *United Talent Agency (UTA)*
9336 Civic Center Dr
Beverly Hills, CA 90210, USA

Stahl, Larry (Athlete, Baseball Player)
1506 E Main St # A
Belleville, IL 62221, USA

Stahl, Lesley (Journalist)
c/o Staff Member *WmE2 (WMA-LA)*
1 William Morris Pl
Beverly Hills, CA 90212, USA

Stahl, Leslie (Actor)
c/o Staff Member *WmE2 (WMA-LA)*
1 William Morris Pl
Beverly Hills, CA 90212, USA

Stahl, Lisa (Actor)
Don Buchwald
6500 Wilshire Blvd #2200
Los Angeles, CA 90048, USA

Stahl, Nick (Actor)
c/o Sean Fay *Kritzer Levine Wilkins Entertainment (KLWG)*
11872 La Grange Ave
1st Floor
Los Angeles, CA 90025, USA

Stahl, Norman H (Judge)
US Appeals Court
McCormack Federal Building
Boston, MA 02109, USA

Stahler, Jeff (Cartoonist, Editor)
Cincinnati Post
Editorial Dept
125 E Court St
Cincinnati, OH 45202, USA

Stahley, Adele (Baseball Player)
3700 SE Jennings Rd Apt 214W
Port St Lucie, FL 34952-7780, USA

Stahoviak, Scott (Athlete, Baseball Player)
507 Balmoral Cr
Grayslake, IL 60030-9303, USA

Stai, Brendon (Football Player)
Pittsburgh Steelers
1431 Teal Trce
Pittsburgh, PA 15237-3848, USA

Staib, David P (Astronaut)
6905 Vantage Dr
Alexandria, VA 22306-1245, USA

Staiger, Roy (Athlete, Baseball Player)
1233 Tyler Dr
Lebanon, MO 65536, USA

Staind (Music Group)
c/o Staff Member *Mitch Schneider Organization (MSO)*
14724 Ventura Blvd #410
Sherman Oaks, CA 91403, USA

Staios, Steve (Athlete, Hockey Player)
1213 Newbridge Tree NE
Atlanta, GA 30319-4549, USA

Stairs, Matt (Athlete, Baseball Player)
76 Skyline Rd
Bangor, ME 04401-2156, USA

Staite, Jewel (Actor)
c/o Nils Larsen *Principato/Young Management*
312 W 5th St Apt 815
Los Angeles, CA 90013, USA

Stajan, Matthew (Athlete, Hockey Player)
Newport Sports Management
400-201 City Centre Dr
Attn Don Meehan
Mississauga, ON LSB 2T4, Canada

Stajola, Enzo
Piazza Augusto Albini 5
Rome, ITALY I-00154

Stalcup, Jerry (Football Player)
Los Angeles Rams
1023 Westchester Dr
Rockford, IL 61107-3442, USA

Staley, Alan "Red" (Athlete, Hockey Player)
600-337 6th Ave N
Saskatoon, SK S7K 2S4, Canada

Staley, Bill (Football Player)
Cincinnati Bengals
9210 Todd Rd
Potter Valley, CA 95469-9727, USA

Staley, Dawn (Athlete, Basketball Player, Olympic Athlete)
Dawn Staley Foundation
1224 Glenwood Rd
Columbia, SC 29204-3351, USA

Staley, Dawn M (Basketball Player, Coach)
1228 Callowhill St #603
Philadelphia, PA 19123, USA

Staley, Jerry (Athlete)
2517 NE 100th St
Vancouver, WA 98686

Staley, Joan (Actor)
24516 Windsor Dr
#B
Valencia, CA 91355, USA

Staley, Lex (Radio Personality)
c/o Staff Member *The Lex & Terry Morning Radio Network*
11700 Central Pkwy
Jacksonville, FL 32224, USA

Staley, Matthew R (Actor, Musician)
PO Box 590
New York, NY 10108-0590, USA

Staley, Walter (Athlete, Hockey Player)
214 Teal Lake Rd
Mexico, MO 65265, USA

Stallard, Tracy (Athlete, Baseball Player)
P.O. Box 905
Wise, VA 24293-0905, USA

Staller, Ilona 'Cicciolina' (Adult Film Star, Politician)
Via Cassia 1818
Rome I-00123, ITALY

Stallings, Gene (Athlete, Football Coach, Football Player)
6508 County Road 43200
Powderly, TX 75473, USA

Stallings, Larry (Football Player)
St Louis Cardinals
207 S Mason Road
Saint Louis, MO 63141-8026, USA

Stallings, Matthew Davey (Race Car Driver)
632 Wears Valley Road
Pigeon Forge, TN 37883, USA

Stallone, Frank (Actor, Musician)
c/o Staff Member *Noris Media Management*
Postfach 2117
Fürth 90711, Germany

Stallone, Jackie (Actor)
P.O. Box 491550
Los Angeles, CA 90049, USA

Stallone, Sylvester (Actor, Director, Producer)
c/o Michelle Bega *Rogers & Cowan PR (LA)*
Pacific Design Center
8687 Melrose Ave, 7th Floor
West Hollywood, CA 90069, USA

Stalls, David (Football Player)
Dallas Cowboys
2100 Stout St
Denver, CO 80205-2827, USA

Stallworth, Bud (Athlete, Basketball Player)
14 Westwood Rd
Lawrence, KS 66044-4560, USA

Stallworth, Dave (Athlete, Basketball Player)
4400 N Rushwood St
Wichita, KS 67226-1475, USA

Stallworth, Donte (Athlete, Football Player)
6 Arvis Court
Sacramento, California 95835, USA

Stallworth, Johnny L (John) (Athlete, Football Player)
302 Osman Drive
Madison, AL 35756-3499, USA

Stallworth, Ron (Football Player)
New York Jets
1834 Parkview Dr S
Montgomery, AL 36117-7701, USA

Stalmaster, Lynn
12400 Wilshire Blvd. #920
Los Angeles, CA 90025

Stam, Jessica (Model)
c/o Staff Member *IMG*
304 Park Ave S Fl 12
New York, NY 10010, USA

Stam, Katie (Beauty Pageant Winner)
The Miss America Organization
222 New Rd
Suite 700
Linwood, NJ 08221, USA

Stamatopoulos, Dino (Writer)
c/o Greg Cavic *Creative Artists Agency (CAA-LA)*
2000 Ave Of The Stars
Los Angeles, CA 90067, USA

Stamberg, Josh (Actor)
c/o James Suskin *James Suskin Management*
2 Charlton St Ste 5K
New York, NY 10014, USA

Stamkos, Steven (Athlete, Hockey Player)
Newport Sports Management
400-201 City Centre Dr
Attn Don Meehan
Mississauga, ON L5B 2T4, Canada

Stamler, Jonathan (Misc)
Duke University
Medical Center
Hematology Dept
Durham, NC 27708, USA

Stamler, Lorne (Athlete, Hockey Player)
1011 Orca Ct
Holiday, FL 34691-9817, USA

Stamm, Michael (Mike) (Athlete, Swimmer)
23 Wildwood Rd
Orinda, CA 94563, USA

Stammen, Craig (Athlete, Baseball Player)
13235 State Route 127
Rossburg, OH 45362-9505, USA

Stamos, John (Actor, Musician)
c/o Daniel (Danny) Sussman *Brillstein Entertainment Partners*
9150 Wilshire Blvd #350
Beverly Hills, CA 90212, USA

Stamos, Theodoros (Artist)
37 W 83rd St
New York, NY 10024, USA

Stamp, Terence (Actor)
c/o Beth Holden-Garland *Untitled Entertainment (LA)*
350 S. Beverly Dr #200
Beverly Hills, CA 90212, USA

Stamps, Sylvester (Athlete, Football Player)
Atlanta Falcons
951 Royal Oak Dr
Jackson, MS 39209, USA

Stams, Frank (Football Player)
Los Angeles Rams
2870 Marcia Blvd
Cuyahoga Falls, OH 44223-1146, USA

Stan, Jason (Musician)
Visions Casting Agency Pty Ltd
Level 6/3 Bowen Crs
Victoria, Melbourne 3000, AUSTRALIA

Stan, Sebastian (Actor)
c/o Emily Gerson Saines *Brookside Artists Management (NY)*
250 W 57th St
Suite 2303
New York, NY 10107, USA

Stanat, Dug (Artist)
46828 Bradley St
Fremont, CA 94534, USA

Stanback, Haskel (Football Player)
Atlanta Falcons
1530 Kingston Dr
Kannapolis, NC 28083-9280, USA

Stanchfield, Darby (Actor)
c/o Michael Smith *Principal Entertainment (LA)*
1964 Westwood Blvd #400
Los Angeles, CA 90025, USA

Standal, Barb (Stylist)
4115 Juneau Lane
Plymouth, MN 55446, USA

Standhardt, Kenneth (Artist)
620 Elmwood Dr
Eugene, OR 97401, USA

Standing, George (Athlete, Hockey Player)
34 Cliff Ave
Huntsville, ON P1H 1G1, Canada

Standing, John (Actor)
International Creative Mgmt
76 Oxford St
London W1N 0AX, UNITED KINGDOM (UK)

Standly, Mike (Golfer)
2306 Columbia Cir
League City, TX 77573-7622, USA

Standridge, Billy (Race Car Driver)
1521 Sulphur Springs Road
Shelby, NC 28152, USA

Standridge, Jason (Athlete, Baseball Player)
6228 Cardinal Dr
Pinson, AL 35126-3492, USA

Stanek, Al (Athlete, Baseball Player)
96 Allyn St
Holyoke, MA 01040, USA

Stanfel, Richard (Dick) (Coach, Football Player)
Detroit Lions
1104 Juniper Parkway
Libertyville, IL 60048-3543, USA

Stanfield, Fred (Athlete, Hockey Player)
59 Cheshire Lane
East Amherst, NY 14051, USA

Stanfield, Jack (Athlete, Hockey Player)
5715 Logan Lane
Houston, TX 77007, United States

Stanfield, Kevin (Athlete, Baseball Player)
7565 Newcomb St
San Bernardino, CA 92410-4333, USA

Stanfill, Dennis
908 Oak Grove Ave.
San Marino, CA 91108

Stanfill, William T (Bill) (Athlete, Football Player)
3117 Wisteria Ct
Albany, GA 31721, USA

Stanford, Aaron (Actor)
c/o Lainie Sorkin Becky *Management 360*
9111 Wilshire Blvd
Beverly Hills, CA 90210, USA

Stanford, Angela (Golfer)
6225 Pecan Orchard Ct
Ft Worth, TX 76179, USA

Stanford, Jason (Athlete, Baseball Player)
4505 W Mesquital Del Oro
Tucson, AZ 85742-9704, USA

Stang, Peter J (Misc)
University of Utah
Chemistry Dept
Salt Lake City, UT 84112, USA

Stangassinger, Thomas (Skier)
Hofgasse 19
Durenberg-Hallein 5422, AUSTRIA

Stange, Lee (Athlete, Baseball Player)
436 Dolphin St
Melbourne Beach, FL 32951-2916, USA

Stange, Maya (Actor)
c/o Lindy King *United Agents*
12-26 Lexington St
London W1F OLE, UK

Stangel, Eric (Producer, Writer)
c/o Staff Member *3 Arts Entertainment Inc*
9460 Wilshire Blvd
7th Floor
Beverly Hills, CA 90210, USA

Stangel, Justin (Producer, Writer)
c/o Staff Member *3 Arts Entertainment Inc*
9460 Wilshire Blvd
7th Floor
Beverly Hills, CA 90210, USA

Stanger, Patti (Business Person, Reality TV Star)
c/o Lance Klein *WME (LA)*
9601 Wilshire Blvd Fl 3
Beverly Hills, CA 90210, USA

Stanhouse, Don (Athlete, Baseball Player)
4 Creekmere Dr
Roanoke, TX 76262-9755, USA

Stanicek, Pete (Athlete, Baseball Player)
525 Wilson St
Downers Grove, IL 60515-3845, USA

Stanicek, Steve (Athlete, Baseball Player)
16354 Lanfear Dr
Lockport, IL 60441-4747, USA

Stanich, George (Athlete, Olympic Athlete)
15816 Marigold Ave
Gardena, CA 90249-4837, USA

Stanifer, Rob (Athlete, Baseball Player)
10618 Park Place Dr
Largo, FL 33774-4632, USA

Stanis, Bernadette (Actor)
Sheba Media Group
c/o Vanessa Morman
11152 Westheimer Rd #299
Houston, TX 77042, USA

Stanka, Joe (Athlete, Baseball Player)
32718 Weymouth Ct
Fulshear, TX 77441-4164, USA

Stankalla, Stefan (Skier)
Furstenstr 14
Gramisch-Partenkirchen 82467, GERMANY

Stankavage, Scott (Football Player)
Denver Broncos
3843 Somerset Dr
Durham, NC 27707-5016, USA

Stankiewicz, Andy (Athlete, Baseball Player)
9729 Wren Bluff Dr
San Diego, CA 85234-8209, USA

Stankiewicz, Myron (Athlete, Hockey Player)
53 Tynedale Ave
London, ON N6H SP6, Canada

Stankovic, Borislav (Boris) (Athlete, Basketball Player, Misc)
P.O. Box 7005
Munich D-81479, Germany

Stankowski, Paul (Athlete, Golfer)
4713 Rangewood Dr
Flower Mound, TX 75028-1695, USA

Stanlch, George (Athlete, Basketball Player, Track Athlete)
15816 Marigold Ave
Gardena, CA 90249, USA

Stanler, John W (Misc)
Coutts & Co
440 Strand
London SC2R 0QS, UNITED KINGDOM (UK)

Stanley, Allan H (Athlete, Hockey Player)
RR 3
Fennelon Falls, ON K0M 1N0, Canada

Stanley, Bob (Athlete, Baseball Player)
30 Tansv Ave
Stratham, NH 03885-2288, USA

Stanley, Bob (Athlete, Baseball Player)
30 Tansy Ave
Stratham, NH 03885, USA

Stanley, Chad (Athlete, Football Player)
17496 US Highway 69 S
Tyler, Texas 75703, USA

Stanley, Christopher (Actor)
c/o Dan Baron *Agency for the Performing Arts (APA-LA)*
405 S Beverly Dr
Suite 500
Beverly Hills, CA 90212-4425, USA

Stanley, Daryl (Athlete, Hockey Player)
PO Box 164
Balmoral, MB ROC OHO, Canada

Stanley, Frank (Cinematographer)
Po Box 2230
Los Angeles, CA 90078, USA

Stanley, Fred (Athlete, Baseball Player)
2109 Winthrop Mill Rd
Argyle, TX 76226-2103, USA

Stanley, Israel (Football Player)
New Orleans Saints
3850 S Miner St
Milwaukee, WI 53221-1250, USA

Stanley, James (Producer)
c/o Staff Member *United Talent Agency (UTA)*
9336 Civic Center Dr
Beverly Hills, CA 90210, USA

Stanley, Marianne Crawford (Coach)
New York Liberty
Madison Square Garden
2 Penn Plaza
New York, NY 10121, USA

Stanley, Marlanne Crawford (Basketball Player, Coach)
Washington Mystics
MCI Center
601 F St NW
Washington, DC 20004, USA

Stanley, Mickey (Athlete, Baseball Player)
6370 CunninghamLake Rd
Lake Rd, Brighton 48116-5222, Brighton

Stanley, Mike (Athlete, Baseball Player)
1108 NE 10th Ave
Fort Lauderdale, FL 33304-2115, USA

Stanley, Paul (Musician)
c/o Doc McGhee *McGhee Entertainment*
8730 Sunset Blvd
Suite 175
Los Angeles, CA 90069, USA

Stanley, Ralph (Music Group, Musician)
Press Office
2607 Westwood Dr
Nashville, TN 37204, USA

Stanley, Richard (Athlete, Football Player)
4248 S FM 2869
Hawkins, TX 75765-5300, USA

Stanley, Steven M (Misc)
4308 Folly Quarter Road
Ellicott City, MD 21042-1424, USA

Stanley, Walter (Athlete, Football Player)
23977 East Alamo Place
Aurora, CO 80016-4247, USA

Stanowski, Wally (Athlete, Hockey Player)
227 Mill Rd
Toronto, ON M9C 1Y3, Canada

Stansberry, Craig (Athlete, Baseball Player)
3433 Adirondack Ln
Frisco, TX 75033-1398, U S A

Stansbury, Terence
901 N Franklin St # 2
Wilmington, DE 19806-4529, USA

Stansbury, Terrace (Athlete, Basketball Player)
901 N Franklin St
#2
Wilmington, DE 19806, USA

Stansfield, Claire
9300 Wilshire Blvd. #555
Beverly Hills, CA 90212

Stansfield, Lisa (Music Group, Musician, Songwriter, Writer)
PO Box 59
Ashwell
Herts SG7 5NG, UNITED KINGDOM (UK)

Stansfield Smith, Colin (Architect)
Three Ministers House
76 High St Winchester
Hants SO23 8UL, UNITED KINGDOM (UK)

Stansky, Peter D L (Historian)
375 Pinehill Road
Hillsborough, CA 94010, USA

Stantis, Scott (Cartoonist, Editor)
Birmingham News
Editorial Dept
2200 4th Ave N
Birmingham, AL 35203, USA

Stanton, Andrew (Animator, Director, Writer)
Pixar
1200 Park Ave
Emeryville, CA 94608, USA

Stanton, Frank N (Misc)
25 W 52nd St
New York, NY 10019, USA

Stanton, Harry Dean (Actor)
14527 Mulholland Dr
Los Angeles, CA 90077, USA

Stanton, Jeff (Race Car Driver)
1137 Athens Road
Sherwood, MI 49089, USA

Stanton, Leroy (Athlete, Baseball Player)
1751 N Norwood Ln
Florence, SC 29506-6901, U S A

Stanton, Mike (Athlete, Baseball Player)
3801 E Van Buren St
Phoenix, AZ 98282-7090, USA

Stanton, Molly (Actor)
c/o Rick Kurtzman *Creative Artists Agency (CAA-LA)*
2000 Ave Of The Stars
Los Angeles, CA 90067, USA

Stanton, Paul (Athlete, Hockey Player)
2150 Sheepshead Dr
Naples, FL 34102, USA

Stanton, Phil (Entertainer)
Blue Man Group
Luxor Hotel
3900 Las Vegas Blvd S
Las Vegas, NV 89119, USA

Stapf, David (Business Person)
c/o Staff Member *CBS Paramount Network Television*
CBS Studios
4024 Radford Ave
Studio City, CA 91604, USA

Stapinski, Helene (Writer)
Saint Martin's Press
175 5th Ave
New York, NY 10010, USA

Staples, Mavis (Music Group, Musician)
PO Box 498360
Chicago, IL 60649, USA

Staple Singers, The
PO Box 170429
San Francisco, CA 94117

Stapleton, Dave (Athlete, Baseball Player)
51 N Bayview St
Fairhope, AL 36527-8690, USA

Stapleton, Dave (Athlete, Baseball Player)
418 S Galaxy Dr
Chandler, AZ 85226

Stapleton, Jacinta (Actor)
c/o Stacey Testro *Stacey Testro International*
8265 Sunset Blvd #102
Los Angeles, CA 90046, USA

Stapleton, Jean (Actor)
155 W 68th St
Spt 29C
New York, NY 10023, USA

Stapleton, Kevin (Actor)
Gersh Agency
232 N Canon Dr
Beverly Hills, CA 90210, USA

Stapleton, Mike (Athlete, Hockey Player)
PO Box 1896
Sault Sainte Marie, MI 49783-7896, USA

Stapleton, Oliver (Cinematographer)
MacCorkindale & Holton
1640 5th St #205
Santa Monica, CA 90401, USA

Stapleton, Parish (Stylist)
c/o Staff Member *Independent Artists*
448 E Riverdale Ave
Orange, CA 92865, USA

Stapleton, Pat (Athlete, Hockey Player)
623 Saulsbury St
Strathroy, ON N7G 3R4, Canada

Stapleton, Sullivan (Actor)
c/o Esther Chang *WME (LA)*
9601 Wilshire Blvd Fl 3
Beverly Hills, CA 90210, USA

Stapleton, Walter K (Judge)
US Court of Appeals
Federal Building
844 N King St
Wilmington, DE 19801, USA

Stapp, Scott (Musician)
c/o Staff Member *Wind-up Records*
72 Madison Ave Fl 8
New York, NY 10016, USA

Star, Darren (Doctor, Producer, Writer)
c/o Tracey Jacobs *United Talent Agency (UTA)*
9336 Civic Center Dr
Beverly Hills, CA 90210, USA

Star, Marilyn (Adult Film Star)
1521 Alton Rd #369
Miami Beach, FL 33139, USA

Star, Ryan (Musician)
c/o Michael (Mike) Esterman *Esterman.Com, LLC*
Prefers to be contacted via email
MD, USA

Starbird, Kate (Basketball Player)
Indiana Fever
Conseco Fieldhouse
125 S Pennsylvania
Indianapolis, IN 46204, USA

Starbuck, Jo Jo (Athlete, Figure Skater, Olympic Athlete)
33 Pomeroy Road
Madison, NJ 07940, USA

Starch, Ken (Football Player)
Green Bay Packers
603 E Hillcrest Dr
Verona, WI 53593-1517, USA

Starck, Philippe (Architect, Designer)
3 Rue Faisans
Shiltigheim 67300, FRANCE

Starfield, Barbara H (Doctor)
Johns Hopkins University
Hygiene School
624 N Broadway
Baltimore, MD 21205, USA

Stargell, Tony (Athlete, Football Player)
131 Jenny Rd
Grantville, GA 30220-2134, USA

Starikov, Sergei (Athlete, Hockey Player)
209 Green brook Rd
Green Brook, NJ 08812-2205, USA

Stark, Chad (Football Player)
Seattle Seahawks
3316 46th Ave SW
Fargo, ND 58104-6655, USA

Stark, Collin (Actor)
c/o Peter Himberger *Impact Artists Group LLC*
42 Hamilton Ter
New York, NY 10031, USA

Stark, Dennis (Athlete, Baseball Player)
213 N Elm St
Edgerton, OH 43517-9672, USA

Stark, Don (Actor)
c/o Tom Harrison *Diverse Talent Group*
9911 W Pico Blvd Ste 340W
Los Angeles, CA 90035, USA

Stark, Freya M (Writer)
Via Canova
Asolo
Treviso, ITALY

Stark, Graham (Actor)
International Creative Mgmt
76 Oxford St
London W1N 0AX, UNITED KINGDOM
(UK)

Stark, Koo (Actor)
Rebecca Blond
52 Shaftesbury Ave
London W1V 7DE, UNITED KINGDOM
(UK)

Stark, Matt (Athlete, Baseball Player)
721 Shirehampton Dr
Las Vegas, NV 85249-9683, USA

Stark, Melissa (Correspondent,
Sportscaster)
NBC-TV
News Dept
30 Rockefeller Plaza
New York, NY 10112, USA

Stark, Nathan J (Lawyer)
4000 Cathedral Ave NW #132
Washington, DC 20016, USA

Stark, Rohn T (Football Player)
Baltimore Colts
PO Box 10067
Lahaina, HI 96761-0067, USA

Starke, Anthony (Actor)
c/o Staff Member *Paradigm (LA)*
360 N Crescent Dr
North Bldg
Beverly Hills, CA 90210, USA

Starker, James
1241 Winfield Rd.
Bloomington, IN 47401

Starker, Janos (Musician)
1241 Winfield Road
Bloomington, IN 47401, USA

Starkey, Jason (Athlete, Football Player)
1525 Washington Avenue
#1
Huntington, WV 25704-1520, USA

Starks, Duane (Football Player)
Baltimore Ravens
811 NW 199th St
Miami, FL 33169-2847, USA

Starks, John (Athlete, Basketball Player)
P.O. Box 8146
Stamford, CT 06905-8146, USA

Starks, Max (Athlete, Football Player)
c/o Eugene Parker *Maximum Sports
Management*
6435 W Jefferson Blvd
#197
Fort Wayne, IN 46804, USA

Starkweather, Gary K (Engineer)
10274 Parkwood Dr #7
Cupertino, CA 95014, USA

Starling, Carol (Stylist)
702 Tennessee St
San Francisco, CA 94107, USA

Starling, James D (General)
3581 Joshua Rd
Shingle Springs, CA 95682-9478, USA

Starn, Douglas (Photographer)
Stux Gallery
163 Mercer St #1
New York, NY 10012, USA

Starn, Mike (Photographer)
Stux Gallery
163 Mercer St #1
New York, NY 10012, USA

Starner, Shelby (Music Group, Musician)
Morebam Music
30 Hillcrest Ave
Morristown, NJ 07960, USA

Starnes, John G (Football Player)
Atlanta Falcons
8826 Shade Tree
San Antonio, TX 78254-6821, USA

Staroba, Paul (Football Player)
Cleveland Browns
9235 McWain Rd
Grand Blanc, MI 48439-8006, USA

Starr, Albert (Doctor)
5050 SW Patton Road
Portland, OR 97221, USA

Starr, Bart (Athlete, Football Coach,
Football Player)
Healthcare Realty Services
2647 Rocky Ridge Ln
Birmingham, AL 35216, USA

Starr, Beau (Actor)
c/o Geneva Bray *GVA Talent Agency Inc*
8981 Sunset Blvd.
Suite 101
Los Angeles, CA 90069, USA

Starr, Brenda K (Music Group, Musician)
Brothers Mgmt
141 Dunbar Ave
Fords, NJ 08863, USA

Starr, Chauncey (Engineer)
95 Stern Lane
Atherton, CA 94027, USA

Starr, David (Race Car Driver)
Boys Will Be Boys Racing
610 Performance Rd
Mooresville, NC 28115, USA

Starr, Dick (Athlete, Baseball Player)
613 N Crescent Dr
Kittanning, PA 16201-2214, USA

Starr, Fredro (Actor, Artist, Musician)
c/o Keith Brown *KBiz Entertainment*
6938 Laurel Canyon Blvd
Suite 214
North Hollywood, CA 91605, USA

Starr, Garrison (Musician)
c/o Staff Member *MCT Management*
520 8th Ave Rm 2205
New York, NY 10018, USA

Starr, Kay (Music Group, Musician)
Ira Okun Entertainment
708 Palisades Dr
Pacific Palisades, CA 90272, USA

Starr, Keith (Athlete, Basketball Player)
1S83 Graystone Canyon Ave
Las Vegas, NV 89183-6309, USA

Starr, Kenneth (Government Official,
Judge)
Pepperdine Law School
24255 Pacific Coast Highway
Malibu, CA 90263, USA

Starr, Leonard (Cartoonist)
Tribune Media Services
319 Bayberry Ln
Westport, CT 06880-1314, USA

Starr, Martin (Actor)
c/o Ben Feigin *Anonymous Content (LA)*
3531 Hayden Ave
Culver City, CA 90232, USA

Starr, Paul E (Misc)
Princeton University
Sociology Dept
Green Hall
Princeton, NJ 08544, USA

Starr, Randy (Music Group, Musician,
Songwriter, Writer)
DDS
230 Park Ave
New York, NY 10169, USA

Starr, Ringo (Actor, Musician)
918 N Hillcrest Rd
Beverly Hills, CA 90210, USA

Starr, Steve (Journalist, Photographer)
720 Arcadia Place
Colorado Springs, CO 80903, USA

Starr, Steven (Photographer)
720 Arcadia Pl
Colorado SPrings, CO 80903-2813, USA

Starrette, Herm (Athlete, Baseball Player)
103 Howard Pond Loop
Statesville, NC 28625-2280, USA

Starring, Stephen (Football Player)
New England Patriots
6120 W Tropicana Ave Ste A 16
Las Vegas, NV 89103-4697, USA

Star Sailor (Musician)
c/o Staff Member *Solo Agency Ltd (UK)*
55 Fulham High St
2nd Floor
London SW6 3JJ, United Kingdom

Starsailor (Music Group)
c/o Staff Member *Paradigm (Monterey)*
404 W Franklin St
Monterey, CA 93940, USA

Starship
9850 Sandalfoot Blvd. #458
Boca Raton, FL 33428

Starting Line (Music Group)
c/o Staff Member *Virgin Records (NY)*
150 5th Ave
New York, NY 10010, USA

Starzewski, Tomasz (Designer, Fashion
Designer)
House of Tomasz Trarzewski
15-17 Pont St
London SW1X 9EH, UNITED KINGDOM
(UK)

Starzl, Thomas (Scientist)
4320 Centre Ave
Pittsburgh, PA 15213-1403, USA

Stasey, Caitlin (Actor)
c/o Shelley Browning *Magnolia
Entertainment (LA)*
9595 Wilshire Blvd
Suite 601
Beverly Hills, CA 90212, USA

Stashwick, Todd (Actor)
c/o Staff Member *Meghan Schumacher
Management*
13351-D Riverside Dr #387
Sherman Oaks, CA 91423, USA

Stasiuk, Vic (Athlete, Hockey Player)
7 Canyon Gdns W
Lethbridge, AB T1K 6V1, Canada

Stassforth, Bowen (Athlete, Olympic
Athlete, Swimmer)
26203 Birchfield Ave
Rancho Palos Verdes, CA 90275-1719,
USA

Stastny, Anton (Athlete, Hockey Player)
Rte De Broye 45
Prilly 1030, Switzerland

Stastny, Marian (Athlete, Hockey Player)
Club de Golf Marian Stastny
537 Rte Marie-Victorin
Saint-Nicolas, QC G7A 2X6, Canada

Stastny, Paul (Athlete, Hockey Player)
465 South Mason Road
St. Louis, MO 63141-8519, USA

Stastny, Peter (Athlete, Hockey Player)
465 S Mason Rd
Saint Louis, MO 63141, USA

Stastny, Yan (Athlete, Hockey Player)
465 S Mason Rd
Saint Louis, MO 63141-8519, USA

Staszak, Ray (Athlete, Hockey Player)
8273 96th Ct S
Boynton Beach, FL 33472-4405, USA

Stata, Raymond S (Business Person)
Analog Devices Inc
1 Technology Way
Norwood, MA 02062, USA

Staten, Vince (Writer)
9323 Loch Lea Ln
Louisville, KY 40291-1477, USA

Statham, Jason (Actor)
c/o Steve Chasman *Current Entertainment*
9378 Wilshire Blvd
Sutie 210
Beverly Hills, CA 90212, USA

Static, Wayne (Musician)
Andy Gould Mgmt
9100 Wilshire Blvd #400W
Beverly Hills, CA 90212, USA

Statler Brothers (Music Group)
The Statler Brothers, LLC
PO Box 2703
Staunton, VA 24402-2703, USA

Staton, Aaron (Actor)
c/o Carol Goll *ICM Partners (ICM-LA)*
10250 Constellation Blvd Fl 7
Los Angeles, CA 90067, USA

Staton, Candi (Music Group, Musician)
Capital Entertainment
1201 N St NW #A5
Washington, DC 20005, USA

Staton, Dave (Athlete, Baseball Player)
2175 Arnold Dr
Rocklin, CA 95765-5901, USA

Staton, Joe (Athlete, Baseball Player)
2929 76th Ave SE
Apt 201
Mercer Island, WA 98040-2715, USA

Staton, Leroy (Athlete, Baseball Player)
1751 N Norwood Ln
Florence, SC 29506, USA

Staton, Mike (Athlete, Baseball Player)
19602 Indigo Lake Rd
Magnolia, TX 77355, USA

Status Quo (Music Group, Musician)
c/o Simon Porter *Duroc Media Ltd.*
Riverside House
10-12 Victoria Road
Uxbridge, Middlesex UB8 2TW, UK

Staub, Chelsea (Actor)
c/o Margot Menzel *Evolution Entertainment (LA)*
9111 Wilshire Blvd
Beverly Hills, CA 90210, USA

Staub, Daniel J (Rusty) (Athlete, Baseball Player)
WWOR-Radio
9 Broadcast Plaza
Secaucus, NJ 33401-5767, USA

Staub, Danielle (Reality TV Star)
c/o Jeffre Phillips *Ja-Tail Enterprises*
8306 Wilshire Blvd.
Suite 528
Beverly Hills, CA 90211, USA

Staubach, Roger (Athlete, Football Player, Heisman Trophy Winner)
Roger Staubach Foundation
5601 Dallas Pkwy #400
Addison, TX 75001, USA

Staubach, Scott (Football Player)
New Orleans Saints
6701 Miwok Ct
Bakersfield, CA 93309-3436, USA

Stauber, Liz (Actor)
c/o Sally Ware *Gersh (NY)*
41 Madison Ave
New York, NY 10010, USA

Stauber, Robb (Athlete, Hockey Player)
Stauber's Goal Crease
7401A Washington AveS
Minneapolis, MN 55439, USA

Stauffer, Tim (Athlete, Baseball Player)
2790 Bellezza Dr
San Diego, CA 92007-2432, USA

Stauffer, William A (Bill) (Athlete, Basketball Player)
913 Shoal Creek Place
Wilmington, NC 28405-5211, USA

Staunton, Imelda (Actor)
P F D
Drury House
34-43 Russell St
London WC2B 5HA, UNITED KINGDOM (UK)

Staurovsky, Jason (Football Player)
St Louis Cardinals
4822 E 87th Pl
Tulsa, OK 74137-2825, USA

Stause, Chrishell (Actor)
c/o Staff Member *Rooster Films*
5225 Wilshire Blvd
Suite 701
Los Angeles, CA 90036, USA

Stautberg, Gerald (Athlete, Football Player)
3200 Park Rd
Monkton, MD 21111, USA

Staveley, William D M (Admiral)
Thames Health Authority
40 Eastbourne Terrace
London W2 3QR, UNITED KINGDOM (UK)

Stavinoha, Nick (Athlete, Baseball Player)
30606 N Hollv Oaks Cir
Magnolia, TX 77355-5733, USA

Stavropoulos, William S (Business Person)
Dow Chemical
2030 Dow Center
Midland, MI 48674, USA

Stayskal, Wayne (Cartoonist, Editor)
Tampa Tribune
Editorial Dept
200 S Parker St
Tampa, FL 33606, USA

Staysniak, Joseph A (Joe) (Football Player)
Buffalo Bills
4094 Forest Dr
Brownsburg, IN 46112-8672, USA

St. Clair, Jessica (Actor)
c/o Christie Smith *Mosaic Media Group*
9200 W. Sunset Blvd
10th Floor
Los Angeles, CA 90069, USA

St Clair, Mike (Football Player)
Cleveland Browns
1606 Birchwood Ave
Cincinnati, OH 45224-2002, USA

St Clair, Robert B (Bob) (Athlete, Football Player)
3312 Parker Hill Rd
Saratoga, CA 95070, USA

St Claire, Randy (Athlete, Baseball Player)
7117 State Route 8
Brant Lake, NY 12815, USA

StClaire, Randy (Athlete, Baseball Player)
7117 State Route 8
Brant Lake, NY 12815-2234, USA

St. Croix, Rick (Athlete, Hockey Player)
27 Brigantine Bay
Winnipeg, MB R3P 1R1, CANADA

Stead, Eugene A Jr (Doctor)
5113 Townsville Road
Bullock, NC 27507, USA

Steadman, Alison (Actor)
P F D
Drury House
34-43 Russell St
London WC2B 5HA, UNITED KINGDOM (UK)

Steadman, J Richard (Doctor)
Steadman Hawkins Clinic
181 W Meadows Dr #400
Vail, CO 81657, USA

Steadman, Mark (Writer)
450 Pin-du-Lac Dr
Central, SC 29630, USA

Steadman, Ralph I (Cartoonist)
Old Loose Court
Loose Valley Maidstone
Kent ME15 9SE, UNITED KINGDOM (UK)

Steadman, Robert L (Cinematographer)
15925 Temecula St
Pacific Palisades, CA 90272, USA

Steall, Ben (Horse Racer)
1289 Brampton Cv
Wellington, FL 33414-8984, USA

Stearns, Cheryl (Misc)
613 Saddlebred Lane
Raeford, NC 28376, USA

Stearns, Cliff (Congressman, Politician)
2306 Rayburn HOB
Washington, DC 20515, USA

Stearns, Jeff
9200 Sunset Blvd. #1130
Los Angeles, CA 90069

Stearns, John (Athlete, Baseball Player)
Columbus Clippers 1155 W Mound St
Columbus, OH 34986-3405, USA

Stebbins, Richard (Athlete, Olympic Athlete, Track Athlete)
10675 Gramercy Pl Unit 317
Columbia, MD 21044-3027, USA

Stecher, Renate Meissner- (Athlete, Track Athlete)
Haydnstr 11
#526/38
Jena 07749, GERMANY

Stecher, Theodore P (Astronomer)
UIT Project
Goddard Space Flight Center
Greenbelt, MD 20771, USA

Stechschulte, Gene (Athlete, Baseball Player)
206 Wellington Pl
Findlav, OH 45840-8303, USA

Steckel, David (Athlete, Hockey Player)
1516 Jefferson St
West Bend, WI 53090-1343, USA

Steckel, Les (Athlete, Football Coach, Football Player)
9152 Saddlebow Dr
Brentwood, TN 37027, USA

Steckler, Ray Dennis (Director)
2375 E Tropicana Ave
Las Vegas, NV 89119, USA

Steck-Weiss, Elma (Athlete, Baseball Player)
12543 W Skyview Dr
Sun City West, AZ 85375-5168, USA

Steding, Katy (Athlete, Basketball Player, Olympic Athlete)
21625 SW 100th Dr
Tualatin, OR 97062-8581, USA

Steeb, Carl-Uwe
18 chemin des Jardillets
Hauterive, SWITZERLAND CH-2068

Steed, Joel (Football Player)
Pittsburgh Steelers
2639 Holly St
Denver, CO 80207-3229, USA

Steege, Deb (Stylist)
c/o Staff Member *Help Me Rhonda*
541 10th St NW #294
Atlanta, GA 30318, USA

Steel, Amy (Actor)
Innovative Artists
1505 10th St
Santa Monica, CA 90401, USA

Steel, David M S (Government Official)
Aikwood Tower
Ettrick Bridge
Selkirkshire, SCOTLAND

Steel, John (Musician)
Lustig Talent
PO Box 770850
Orlando, FL 32877, USA

Steele, Alex (Actor)
c/o Alvina Roman *Roman Empire Management*
Prefers to be contacted via telephone or email
Los Angeles, CA 90210, USA

Steele, Allan (Actor)
c/o Staff Member *Baumgarten Management*
11925 Wilshire Blvd
Suite 310
Los Angeles, CA 90025, USA

Steele, Barbara (Actor)
2460 Benedict Canyon
Beverly Hills, CA 90210, USA

Steele, Billy (DJ)
c/o Len Evans *Project Publicity*
312 West 53rd St
Suite 202
New York, NY 10019, USA

Steele, Brian (Actor)
c/o Joan Vento-Hall *Law Offices of Joan Vento-Hall, The*
10250 Constellation Blvd Fl 19
Los Angeles, CA 90067, USA

Steele, Cassie (Actor)
c/o Staff Member *Noble Caplan Abrams*
1260 Yonge St
2nd Floor
Toronto ON M4T 1W6, Canada

Steele, Danielle (Writer)
2080 Washington St
San Francisco, CA 94109, USA

Steele, Dave (Race Car Driver)
Team Sabco
114 Meadow Hill Circle
Mooresville, NC 28115, USA

Steele, Glen (Football Player)
Cincinnati Bengals
303 E 5th St
Ligonier, IN 46767-2205, USA

Steele, Joshua (Flux Pavilion) (DJ, Producer)
Circus Records
Corner Chambers
590A Kingsbury Rd
Birmingham B24 9ND, UK

Steele, Joyce (Athlete, Baseball Player)
627 Sr4010
Mehoopany, PA 18629-8841, USA

Steele, Larry (Athlete, Basketball Player)
27448 NW Saint Helens Rd Slip 470
Slip 25
Scappoose, OR 97056-3233, USA

Steele, Michael (Politician)
Republican National Committee
310 First St
Washington, DC 20003, USA

Steele, Michael (Musician)
Bangles Mall
1341 W Fullerton Ave
Box 180
Chicago, IL 60614, USA

Steele, Nick (Stylist)
c/o Celebrity Stylist *Oliver Piro Inc*
725 Riverside Dr Apt 3A
New York, NY 10031, USA

Steele, Richard (Boxer, Referee)
2438 Antler Point Dr
Henderson, NV 89074, USA

Steele, Robert (Football Player)
Dallas Cowboys
813 Burning Tree Ct SE
Marietta, GA 30067-4719, USA

Steele, Shelby (Writer)
San Jose State University
English Dept
San Jose, CA 95192, USA

Steele, Tim (Race Car Driver)
24th Avenue
Marne, MI 49435, USA

Steele, Tommy (Actor, Musician)
IMG
Media House
3 Burlington Lane
London W4 2TH, UNITED KINGDOM
(UK)

Steele, William M (Mike) (General)
Commanding General
Combined Arms Center
Fort Leavenworth, KS 66207, USA

Steel Magnolia (Music Group, Musician)
c/o Staff Member *Big Machine Records*
1219 16th Ave South
Nashville, TN 37212, USA

Steels, Jim (Athlete, Baseball Player)
1654 Via Rico
Santa Maria, CA 93454-2609, USA

Steely Dan (Music Group)
c/o Barry Dickins *International Talent Booking*
74A Charlotte St
London W1T 4QJ, UNITED KINGDOM
(UK)

Steen, Alexander (Athlete, Hockey Player)
352 Ries Bend Road
Ballwin, MO 63021-3902, USA

Steen, Anders (Athlete, Hockey Player)
Farjestadsvagen 85
Karlstad S-65465, Sweden

Steen, Jessica (Actor)
Innovative Artists
1505 10th St
Santa Monica, CA 90401, USA

Steen, Thomas (Athlete, Hockey Player)
Winnipeg City Council
510 Main St
Winnipeg, MB R3B 1B9, Canada

Steenburgen, Mary (Actor)
656 Moreno Ave
Los Angeles, CA 90049, USA

Steenstra, Ken (Athlete, Baseball Player)
1228 Pheasant Ct
Liberty, MO 64068, USA

Steenstra, Kennie (Athlete, Baseball Player)
1228 Pheasant Ct
Liberty, MO 64068-8464, USA

Steeples, Eddie (Actor)
c/o Staff Member *LRB Publicity*
2206 Rockefeller Lane Suite #1
Redondo Beach, CA 90278, USA

Steer, Rachel (Athlete, Biathlete, Olympic Athlete)
11480 Mountain Lake Dr
Anchorage, AK 99516-1881, USA

Steere, Richard (Football Player)
Philadelphia Eagles
1810 Fox Bridge Ct
Fallbrook, CA 92028-8745, USA

Steers, Burr (Director)
c/o Shawn Simon *Anonymous Content (LA)*
3531 Hayden Ave
Culver City, CA 90232, USA

Steevens, Morrie (Athlete, Baseball Player)
14465 Cadillac Dr
San Antonio, TX 78248-1001, USA

Stefan, Greg (Athlete, Hockey Player)
37648 Baywood Dr
Unit 33
Farmington Hills, MI 48335, USA

Stefan, Patrik (Athlete, Hockey Player)
1450 Bluebird Cany_on Dr
Laguna Beach, CA 92651-3007, USA

Stefani, Gwen (Fashion Designer, Musician, Songwriter)
c/o Jim Guerinot *Rebel Waltz Inc*
31652 Second Ave
Laguna Beach, CA 92651, USA

Stefanich, Jim (Bowler)
1444 Corla Bell Drive
Joliet, IL 60435-3979, USA

Stefanik, Mlke (Race Car Driver)
106 Pierremount Avenue
New Britain, CT 06053, USA

Stefanski, Bud (Athlete, Hockey Player)
RR 1
Buckhorn, ON KOL 1JO, Canada

Stefanson, Leslie (Actor)
c/o Andy Cohen *Gersh (LA)*
10250 Constellation Blvd Fl 7
Los Angeles, CA 90067, USA

Stefanyshyn-Piper, Heidemarie M (Astronaut)
3722 W Pine Brook Way
Houston, TX 77059, USA

Stefanyshyn-Piper, Heidemarie M Cdr (Astronaut)
6875 Rolling Creek Way
Alexandria, VA 22315-6122, USA

Stefero, John (Athlete, Baseball Player)
6239 Chestnut Oak Ln
Linthicum Heights, MD 21090-2148, USA

Steffen, Dave (Baseball Player)
30531 Maple View Ln
Flat Rock, MI 48134-2744, USA

Steffen, Jim (Football Player)
Detroit Lions
1440 Westway
Arnold, MD 21012-2428, USA

Steffes, Kent (Athlete, Volleyball Player)
14675 Titus St
Panorama City, CA 91402, USA

Stefy (Music Group)
Wind-up Records
72 Madison Avenue 8th Fl
New York, NY 10016, USA

Stegall, Keith (Musician)
c/o Staff Member *Sony Music Nashville*
8 Music Sq W
Nashville, TN 37203, USA

Stegall, Milt (Athlete, Football Player)
51 Springside Dr SE
Atlanta, GA 303S4-2145, USA

Stegent, Larry (Football Player)
St Louis Cardinals
1177 West Loop S # 525
Houston, TX 77027-9006, USA

Steger, Joseph A (Educator)
University of Cincinnati
President's Office
Cincinnati, OH 45221, USA

Steger, Michael (Actor)
c/o Staff Member *Marianne Daniels & Associates*
8491 Sunset Blvd #416
Los Angeles, CA 90036, USA

Steger, Will (Misc)
International Arctic Project
990 3rd St E
Saint Paul, MN 55106, USA

Stegman, Dave (Athlete, Baseball Player)
3234 Simmons Dr
Grove City, OH 43123-1835, USA

Stegman, Millie (Actor)
c/o Staff Member *Telefe - Argentina*
Pavon 2444 (C1248AAT)
Buenos Aires, ARGENTINA

Stehlin, Savannah (Actor)
c/o Sharon Lane *Lane Management Group*
13017 Woodbridge St
Studio City, CA 91604, USA

Steiger, Ueli (Cinematographer)
2222 Kenilworth Ave
Los Angeles, CA 90039, USA

Stein, Ben (Actor, Comedian, Producer, Writer)
602 N Crescent Dr
Beverly Hills, CA 90210, USA

Stein, Bill (Athlete, Baseball Player)
13713 Tajamar St
Corpus Christi, TX 76244-6345, USA

Stein, Blake (Athlete, Baseball Player)
115 Formosa Dr
Brandon, MS 39047-8789, USA

Stein, Bob (Basketball Player, Misc)
Minnesota Timberwolves
Target Center
600 1st Ave N
Minneapolis, MN 55403, USA

Stein, Carolyn (Stylist)
1901 S Oak Haven Circle
Miami, FL 33179, USA

Stein, Chris (Musician)
Shore Fire Media
32 Court St #1600
Brooklyn, NY 11201, USA

Stein, Ed (Cartoonist, Editor)
Rocky Mountain News
Editorial Dept
400 W Colfax Ave
Denver, CO 80204, USA

Stein, Elias M (Mathematician)
132 Dodds Lane
Princeton, NJ 08540, USA

Stein, Garth (Writer)
c/o Staff Member *HarperCollins Publishers*
10 East 53rd St
c/o Author mail, 7th Floor
New York, NY 10022, USA

Stein, Gilbert (Gil) (Athlete, Hockey Player)
650 5th Ave
Apt 3300
New York, NY 10019, USA

Stein, Irving (Writer)
8708 Ridgeway Ave
Skokie, IL 60076-2214, USA

Stein, James (Business Person)
Fluor Corp
3353 Michelson Dr
Irvine, CA 92612, USA

Stein, Mark (Music Group, Musician)
Future Vision
280 Riverside Dr #12L
New York, NY 10025, USA

Stein, Pamela Jean
2112 Broadway
Santa Monica, CA 90404-2912

Stein, Robert (Editor)
McCall's Magazine
Editorial Dept
375 Lexington Ave
New York, NY 10017, USA

Steinauer, Orlando (Athlete, Football Player)
2378 Highcroft Rd
Oakville, ON L6M 4Y6, Canada

Steinbach, Alice (Journalist)
Baltimore Sun
Editorial Dept
501 N Calvert St
Baltimore, MD 21202, USA

Steinbach, Terry (Athlete, Baseball Player)
Terry Steinbach Scholarship Fund
PO Box 181
Hamel, MN 55340-0181, USA

Steinberg, Leigh (Attorney, Attorney General, General)
Steinberg Moorad Dunn
660 Newport Center Dr #1000
Newport Beach, CA 92660, USA

Steinberg, Paul (Cartoonist)
New Yorker Magazine
Editorial Dept
4 Times Square
New York, NY 10036, USA

Steinberg, Ruth (Stylist)
PO Box 5242
Santa Monica, CA 90409, USA

Steinberg, Tristam (Stylist)
c/o Staff Member *Koko Represents*
166 Geary St
#1007
San Francisco, CA 94108, USA

Steinberger, Jack (Nobel Prize Laureate)
25 Chemin des Merles
1213 Onex
Geneva, SWITZERLAND

Steinbrenner, Hal (Baseball Player)
4926 Andros Dr
Tampa, FL 33629-4802, USA

Steinbrenner, Hank (Baseball Player)
402 Saint Andrews
Dr Belleair, FL 33756-1935, USA

Steindler, Mary-Helen (Stylist)
2725 N Hermitage Ave
Chicago, IL 60614, USA

Steindorff, Scott (Producer, Writer)
c/o Staff Member *Stone Village Entertainment*
9200 Sunset Blvd #520
Los Angeles, CA 90069, USA

Steinem, Gloria (Journalist, Writer)
118 E 73rd St
New York, NY 10021, USA

Steiner, Andre (Athlete)
Bismarckstr 4
Berlin 14109, GERMANY

Steiner, Charley (Sportscaster)
867 S Bund_y_Dr
Los Al¥Reles, CA 90049-5216, USA

Steiner, George (Writer)
32 Barrow Road
Cambridge, UNITED KINGDOM (UK)

Steiner, Mel (Baseball Player)
11296 Linda Way
Los Alamitos, CA 90720-3918, USA

Steiner, Paul (Cartoonist)
Washington Times
3600 New York Ave NE
Washington, DC 20002, USA

Steiner, Peter (Cartoonist)
New Yorker Magazine
Editorial Dept
4 Times Square
New York, NY 10036, USA

Steiner, Rebel (Athlete, Football Player)
112 Aaronvale Circle
Birmingham, AL 35242-7353, USA

Steiner, Reed (Producer)
c/o Staff Member *WmE2 (WMA-LA)*
1 William Morris Pl
Beverly Hills, CA 90212, USA

Steines, Mark (Television Host)
c/o Staff Member *Entertainment Tonight (ET)*
4024 Radford Ave.
Studio City, CA 91604, USA

Steinfeld, Hailee (Actor)
c/o Doug Wald *Anonymous Content (LA)*
3531 Hayden Ave
Culver City, CA 90232, USA

Steinfeld, Jake (Actor, Athlete, Wrestler)
622 Toyopa Dr.
Pacific Palisades, CA 90272-4471

Steinfield, Jake (Actor, Misc, Wrestler)
622 Toyopa Dr
Pacific Palisades, CA 90272, USA

Steinfort, Fred (Athlete, Football Player)
P.O. Box 24981
Denver, CO 80224-0981, USA

Steinhardt, Arnold (Musician)
Herbert Barrett
266 W 37th St #2000
New York, NY 10018, USA

Steinhardt, Gillian (Stylist)
c/o Staff Member *Judy Inc*
1 Yorkville Ave
Toronto ON M4W 1L1, Canada

Steinhardt, Paul J (Physicist)
1000 Cedargrove Road
Wynnewood, PA 19096, USA

Steinhardt, Richard (Biologist)
University of California
Biology Dept
Berkeley, CA 94720, USA

Steinhauer, Sherri (Golfer)
5010 Hammersley Rd
Madison, WI 53711-2616, USA

Steinkraus, William (Athlete, Olympic Athlete)
PO B40 Great Is
Darien, CT 06820, USA

Steinkuhler, Dean E (Football Player)
Houston Oilers
1135 Oak St
Syracuse, NE 68446-9483, USA

Steinman, Jim (Songwriter, Writer)
DAS Communications
83 Riverside Dr
New York, NY 10024, USA

Steinmetz, Richard (Actor)
c/o Staff Member *Personal Management Company*
425 N Robertson Dr
Los Angeles, CA 90048, USA

Steinsaltz, Adin (Religious Leader)
Israel Talmudic Publications Institute
PO Box 1458
Jerusalem, ISRAEL

Steinseifer Bates, Carrie (Swimmer)
9309 Benzon Dr
Pleasanton, CA 94588, USA

Steirer, Ricky (Athlete, Baseball Player)
1015 Haverhill Rd
Baltimore, MD 1229-5115, USA

Steitz, Joan A (Scientist)
45 Prospect Hill Road
Branford, CT 06405-5711, USA

Steitz, Thomas (Nobel Prize Laureate)
45 Prospect Hill Rd
Branford, CT 06405-5711, USA

Stela, Annie (Musician)
c/o Staff Member *Paradigm (Monterey)*
404 W Franklin St
Monterey, CA 93940, USA

Stella, Frank (Artist)
17 Jones St
New York, NY 10014-4131, USA

Stella, Martina (Actor)
c/o Daniela di Santo *Moviement*
Via P Cavallini 24
Rome 00193, ITALY

Stelle, Kellogg S (Physicist)
Imperial College
Prince Consort Road
London SW7 2BZ, UNITED KINGDOM (UK)

Stelmaszek, Rick (Athlete, Baseball Player)
2734 E 97th St
Chicago, IL 60617-4928, USA

Stember, Jeff (Athlete, Baseball Player)
9517 E Altadena Ave
Scottsdale, AZ 85260-5865, USA

Stemie, Steve (Athlete, Baseball Player)
4011 Weatherby Way
New Albany, IN 47150, USA

Stemkowski, Peter (Athlete, Hockey Player)
146 Albany Blvd Apt 21C
Atlantic Beach, NY 11509-1207, USA

Stemle, Steve (Athlete, Baseball Player)
927 St Johns Church Rd NE
Lanesville, IN 47136, USA

Stempel, Herbert (Misc)
10510 66th Ave Apt 3G
Forest Hills, NY 11375-2103, USA

Stempniak, Lee (Athlete, Hockey Player)
4469 Clinton St
Buffalo, NY 14224-1700, USA

Stemrick, Greg (Football Player)
Houston Oilers
1012 Matthews Dr
Cincinnati, OH 45215-1804, USA

Stenberg, Amandla (Actor)
c/o Mimi DiTrani *Schiff Company, The*
9465 Wilshire Blvd
Suite 480
Beverly Hills, CA 90212, USA

Stenberg, Brigitta
11484th St. #116
Santa Monica, CA 90403

Stenders, Kriv (Director)
c/o Staff Member *HLA Management*
PO Box 1536
Strawberry Hills 2012, AUSTRALIA

Stenger, Brian (Football Player)
Pittsburgh Steelers
7921 Kellogg Creek Dr
Mentor, OH 44060-7111, USA

Stenhouse, Dave (Athlete, Baseball Player)
20 Hayward St
Cranston, RI 02910-2701, USA

Stenhouse, Mike (Athlete, Baseball Player)
70 Woodbury Rd
Cranston, RI 33027-1628, USA

Stenko, Paul (Football Player)
New York Giants
414 Martzville Rd
Berwick, PA 18603-5642, USA

Stenlund, Vern (Athlete, Hockey Player)
1220 Cabana Rd W
Windsor, ON N9G 1B7, Canada

Stenmark, Ingemar (Skier)
Residence l'Annonciade
17 Av de l'Anncenciade
Monte Carlo 98000, MONACO

Stennett, Rennie (Athlete, Baseball Player)
6519 Boticelli Dr
Lake Worth, FL 33467, USA

Stensrud, Mike (Football Player)
Houston Oilers
304 S Winnebago St
Lake Mills, IA 50450-1637, USA

Stenstrom, Steve (Athlete, Football Player)
1845 Bay Laurel Drive
Menlo Park, California 94025, USA

Stepanova, Maria (Basketball Player)
Phoenix Mercury
American West Arena
201 E Jefferson St
Phoenix, AZ 85004, USA

Stepashin, Sergei V (General, Prime Minister)
Government of Russia
Kasnopresneskaya Embankment 2
Moscow 103274, RUSSIA

Stephanapoulous, Constantinos (Politician)
President of the Hellenic Rej:>ublic
Athens, Greece

Stephanie (Royalty)
Maison Clos St Martin
Saint Remy de Provence, FRANCE

Stephanopolous, Constantine (Costis) (President)
Presidential Palace
7 Vas Georgiou B
Odos Zalokosta 10
Athens, GREECE

Stephanopoulos, George (Politician)
c/o Staff Member *ABC News*
77 W 66th St
3rd Floor
New York, NY 10023, USA

Stephanson, Ken (Athlete, Hockey Player)
6 Heron Road Box 1491
Gimli, MB ROC 1BO, Canada

Stephen, Buzz (Athlete, Baseball Player)
15512 Sycamore St
Porterville, CA 93257-2594, USA

Stephen, Scott (Athlete, Football Player)
5931 Howell Dr #25
La Mesa, CA 91942-3853, USA

Stephens, Darryl (Actor)
c/o Staff Member *Noah's Arc*
75 Charles Rowen House
Merlin Street
London WC1X OEJ, UNITED KINGDOM

Stephens, Everette (Athlete, Basketball Player)
1347 Adams Ave
Saint Charles, IL 60174-3307, USA

Stephens, Gene (Athlete, Baseball Player)
6504 Circo Dr
Granbury, TX 71201-4710, USA

Stephens, Hal (Football Player)
Detroit Lions
221 W Virginia St
Rocky Mount, NC 27804-4939, USA

Stephens, Jamain (Athlete, Football Player)
105 West 6th Street
Tabor City, North Carolina 28463, USA

Stephens, James
8271 Melrose Ave. #110
Los Angeles, CA 90046

Stephens, Janaya (Actor)
c/o Penny Noble *Noble Caplan Abrams*
1260 Yonge St
2nd Floor
Toronto ON M4T 1W6, Canada

Stephens, John (Athlete, Baseball Player)
1325 Oak Point Ct
Venice, FL 34292-1635, USA

Stephens, John (Athlete, Football Player)
P.O. Box 496
Shreveport, LA 71107-7407, USA

Stephens, Laraine
10800 Chalon Rd.
Los Angeles, CA 90077

Stephens, Ray (Athlete, Baseball Player)
1065 Council Rd NE
Charleston, TN 37310-6232, USA

Stephens, Robert (Business Person)
Adaptec Inc
691 S Milpitas Blvd
Milpitas, CA 95035, USA

Stephens, Santo (Football Player)
Kansas City Chiefs
1205 Winding Meadows Rd
Rockledge, FL 32955-8404, USA

Stephens, Stanley (Politician)
210 Columba Ln
Kalispell, MT 59901-2601, USA

Stephens, Toby (Actor)
c/o Simon Halls *Slate Public Relations*
9000 Sunset Blvd #915
West Hollywood, CA 90069, USA

Stephens, Tom (Football Player)
Boston Patriots
69 Orchard Rd
Swampscott, MA 01907-2349, USA

Stephenson, Bob (Athlete, Hockey Player)
8 Tufts Cres
Outlook, SK SOL 2ND, Canada

Stephenson, Debra
2 Henrietta St.
London, ENGLAND WC2E 8PS

Stephenson, Dwight E (Football Player)
Miami Dolphins
4785 Tree Fern Dr
Delray Beach, FL 33445-7025, USA

Stephenson, Earl (Athlete, Baseball Player)
4043 Zacks Mill Rd
Angier, NC 27501-7185, USA

Stephenson, Garrett (Athlete, Baseball Player)
947 W State St
Eagle, ID 83616-4807, USA

Stephenson, Gordon (Architect)
55/14 Albert St
Claremont, WA 6010, AUSTRALIA

Stephenson, John (Athlete, Baseball Player)
7 Mauroner Dr
Hammond, LA 70401-1728, USA

Stephenson, John (Actor, Voice Over Artist)
c/o Staff Member *ICM Partners (ICM-LA)*
10250 Constellation Blvd Fl 7
Los Angeles, CA 90067, USA

Stephenson, Kay (Athlete, Football Player)
310 Plantation Hill Rd
Gulf Breeze, FL 32561, USA

Stephenson, Pamela (Actor)
Tickety-Boo Ltd.
2 Triq Il-Barriera
Balzen BZN 06, Malta

Stephenson, Phil (Athlete, Baseball Player)
1307 Hancock St
Dodge City, KS 67801-3451, USA

Stepp, Craig
6310 San Vicente Blvd. #520
Los Angeles, CA 90048

Steppe, Brook (Athlete, Basketball Player)
3486 Clare Cottage Trce SW
Marietta, GA 30008-6075, USA

Steppenwolf (John Kay)
108 E. Matilija
Ojai, CA 93023

Steptoe, Jack (Football Player)
San Francisco 49ers
40855 Sandy Gale Ln Apt C
Palm Desert, CA 92211-7232, USA

Steranko, Jim (Cartoonist)
PO Box 974
Reading, PA 19603, USA

Steranko, Jim (Cartoonist)
PO Box 974
Reading, PA 19603-0974, USA

Sterban, Richard (Musician)
125 Bluegrass Cir
Hendersonville, TN 37075, USA

Stereo Fuse (Music Group)
c/o Staff Member *Wind-up Records*
72 Madison Ave Fl 8
New York, NY 10016, USA

Stereo MC's (Music Group)
c/o Staff Member *Paradigm (Monterey)*
404 W Franklin St
Monterey, CA 93940, USA

Stereophonics (Music Group)
c/o Staff Member *Nettwerk Management (Canada)*
1850 W Second Ave
Vancouver BC V6J 4R3, CANADA

Sterger, Jenn (Model, Television Host)
PO Box 2642
Lutz, FL 33548-2642, USA

Sterkel, Jill (Athlete, Olympic Athlete, Swimmer)
2206 Heritage Well Ln
Pflugerville, TX 78660-2968, USA

Sterling, Annette (Music Group, Musician)
Soundedge Personal Mgmt
332 Southdown Road
Lloyd Harbor, NY 11743, USA

Sterling, Ashleigh (Actor)
10 Silkleaf
Irvine, CA 92614, USA

Sterling, John (Sportscaster)
440 Russell Ave
Edgewater, NJ 07020-3134, USA

Sterling, Mindy (Actor)
7307 Melrose Ave
Los Angeles, CA 90046, USA

Sterling, Nici (Adult Film Star)
c/o Staff Member *Atlas Multimedia Inc*
9005 Eton Ave Ste C
Canoga Park, CA 91304-1743, USA

Sterling, Rachel (Actor)
c/o Leland LaBarre *Bleu, An Entertainment Company*
5225 Wilshire Blvd
Suite 701
Los Angeles, CA 90036, USA

Sterling, Randy (Athlete, Baseball Player)
2516 Linda Ave
Key West, FL 33040-5114, USA

Sterling, Tisha (Actor)
PO Box 788
Ketchum, ID 83340, USA

Stern, Adam (Athlete, Baseball Player)
40 Summit Ave
London, ON N6H 4S3 Canada, USA

Stern, Andrew L (Misc)
Service Employees International Union
1313 L St NW
Washington, DC 20005, USA

Stern, Bert (Photographer)
330 E 39th St
New York, NY 10016-2135, USA

Stern, Daniel (Actor)
PO Box 6788
Malibu, CA 90264, USA

Stern, David J (Basketball Player, Misc)
National Basketball Assn
Olympic Tower
122 E 55th St
New York, NY 10022, USA

Stern, Dawn (Actor)
c/o Holly Shelton *Precision Entertainment*
6338 Wilshire Blvd
Los Angeles, CA 90048, USA

Stern, Ellen (Stylist)
6231 SW 116th Pl
Miami, FL 33173, USA

Stern, Fritz R (Historian)
15 Claremont Ave
New York, NY 10027, USA

Stern, Gardner (Producer, Writer)
c/o Rick Rosen *WME (LA)*
9601 Wilshire Blvd Fl 3
Beverly Hills, CA 90210, USA

Stern, Gary H (Financier, Government Official)
Federal Reserve Bank
PO Box 291
Minneapolis, MN 55480, USA

Stern, Howard (Radio Personality, Talk Show Host)
The Howard Stern Show
Sirius Satellite Radio
1221 Avenue of the Americas
New York, NY 10020, USA

Stern, Howard K (Attorney, Reality TV Star)
c/o Staff Member *E! Entertainment Television (LA)*
5750 Wilshire Blvd
Los Angeles, CA 90036, USA

Stern, Joseph (Actor, Producer)
c/o Chris Simonian *Creative Artists Agency (CAA-LA)*
2000 Ave Of The Stars
Los Angeles, CA 90067, USA

Stern, Michael (Mike) (Musician)
Tropix International
163 3rd Ave #206
New York, NY 10003, USA

Stern, Richard G (Writer)
University of Chicago
English Dept
Chicago, IL 60637, USA

Stern, Robert A M (Architect)
Robert A M Stern Architects
460 W 34th St
New York, NY 10001, USA

Stern, Shoshannah (Actor)
c/o David Ginsberg *Insight*
1134 S Cloverdale Ave
Los Angeles, CA 90019, USA

Sternberg, Stuart (Baseball Player)
85 Bellevue Ave
Rve, NY 10580-1840, USA

Sternberg, Thomas (Business Person)
Staples Inc
PO Box 9265
Framingham, MA 01701, USA

Sternecky, Neal (Cartoonist)
52 Bluebird Lane
Naperville, IL 60565-1347, USA

Sterner, Ulf (Athlete, Hockey Player)
Grava-Rud 761
Karlstad 655 9', Sweden

Sternhagen, Frances (Actor)
152 Sutton Manor Road
New Rochelle, NY 10801, USA

Sternin, Joshua (Actor)
c/o Staff Member *ICM Partners (ICM-LA)*
10250 Constellation Blvd Fl 7
Los Angeles, CA 90067, USA

Sternoff, Miriam (Stylist)
c/o Celebrity Stylist *Oliver Piro Inc*
725 Riverside Dr Apt 3A
New York, NY 10031, USA

Sterrett, Samuel B (Judge)
US Tax Court
400 2nd St NW
Washington, DC 20217, USA

Stetson, Mark (Designer, Special Effects Designer)
c/o Staff Member *ICM Partners (ICM-LA)*
10250 Constellation Blvd Fl 7
Los Angeles, CA 90067, USA

Stetter, Karl (Biologist)
Universtat Regensburg
Universitatsstr 31
Regensburg 93053, GERMANY

Stetter, Mitch (Athlete, Baseball Player)
3120 N Marigold Dr
Phoenix, AZ 85018-6741, USA

Steuert-Armstrong, Beverly (Athlete, Baseball Player)
211 Cathi Ln
Kernersville, NC 27284-9363, USA

Steussie, Todd E (Athlete, Football Player)
34535 Emigrant Trail
Shingletown, CA 96088-9342, USA

Steve, Rehage (Athlete, Football Player)
2632 Montana Ave
Metairie, LA 70003-5246, USA

Steve Miller Band (Music Group)
c/o Staff Member *Paradigm (Nashville)*
124 12th Ave S
Suite 410
Nashville, TN 37203, USA

Stevens, Amber (Actor)
c/o Robert Enriquez *Red Baron Management*
1600 Rosecrans Ave
Bldg 7 Fl 4
Long Beach, CA 90266, USA

Stevens, Andrew (Actor)
Irv Schechter
9300 Wilshire Blvd #410
Beverly Hills, CA 90212, USA

Stevens, April (Music Group, Musician)
19530 Superior St
Northridge, CA 91324, USA

Stevens, Bob (Producer)
c/o Staff Member *United Talent Agency (UTA)*
9336 Civic Center Dr
Beverly Hills, CA 90210, USA

Stevens, Brinke (Actor, Athlete)
PO Box 7112
Van Nuys, CA 91409-7112, USA

Stevens, Cat
Steinhauser Str. 3
Munich, GERMANY 81677

Stevens, Cat (Yusef Islam) (Music Group, Musician, Songwriter, Writer)
Ariola Steinhauser Str 3
Munich 81667, USA

Stevens, Chuck (Photographer)
PO Box 422782
San Francisco, CA 94142, USA

Stevens, Chuck (Athlete, Baseball Player)
12591 George Reyburn Rd
Garden Grove, CA 92845-2404, USA

Stevens, Connie (Actor, Music Group, Musician)
243 Delfern Dr
Los Angeles, CA 90077, USA

Stevens, Courtenay J (Actor)
c/o Caldwell Jeffery
943 Queen St E2nd fl
Toronto, ON M4M 1J6, CANADA

Stevens, Dave (Athlete, Baseball Player)
2630 Candlewood Way
La Habra, CA 90631-6203, USA

Stevens, Dirk (Race Car Driver)
P.O. Box 1197
Huntersville, NC 28078, USA

Stevens, Dodie (Musician)
c/o Jim Wagner *American Management*
19948 Mayall St
Chatsworth, CA 91311, USA

Stevens, Earl (E-40) (Musician)
c/o Staff Member *Warner Bros Records (LA)*
P.O. Box 6868
Burbank, CA 91510, USA

Stevens, Eileen (Activist)
126 Marion St
Sayville, NY 11782, USA

Stevens, Eric Sheffer (Actor)
c/o Greg Weiss *Vanguard Management Group (NY)*
220 5th Ave.
Penthouse West
New York, NY 10001, USA

Stevens, Fisher (Actor)
329 N Orange Grove
Los Angeles, CA 90036, USA

Stevens, Gary (Horse Racer)
1308 Isleworth Dr
Louisville, KY 40245-5252, USA

Stevens, George Jr (Producer)
New Liberty Productions
John F Kennedy Center
Washington, DC 20566, USA

Stevens, Howard (Athlete, Football Player)
834 St Catherines Dr
Wake Forest, NC 27587-6639, USA

Stevens, Jeremy (Actor, Producer, Writer)
c/o Staff Member *WmE2 (WMA-LA)*
1 William Morris Pl
Beverly Hills, CA 90212, USA

Stevens, Jerramy (Athlete, Football Player)
10047 Main Street
Apt 515
Bellevue, Washington 98004, USA

Stevens, John (Athlete, Hockey Player)
Los Angeles Kings
1111 S Figueroa St Ste 3100
Attn Coaching Staff
Los Angeles, CA 90015-1333, USA

Stevens, John Paul (Attorney)
US Supreme Court
United States Supreme Court 11st St NE
Washington, DC 20543-0002, USA

Stevens, Katie (Musician)
c/o Simon Fuller *XIX Entertainment*
35-37 Parkgate Rd
32/33 Ransomes Dock
London SW11 4NP, UNITED KINGDOM (UK)

Stevens, Kenneth N (Engineer)
15298 SE Oregon Trail Dr
Clackamas, OR 97015, USA

Stevens, Kevin (Athlete, Hockey Player, Olympic Athlete)
37 Hawkins Pl
Duxbury, MA 02332, USA

Stevens, Laraine
10800 Chalon Rd.
Los Angeles, CA 90077

Stevens, Lee (Athlete, Baseball Player)
9157 Buck Hill Dr
Littleton, CO 80126-5042, USA

Stevens, Mick
PO Box 344
West Tisbury, MA 02575-0344

Stevens, Rachel (Actor, Musician)
c/o Kat Gosling *Finch & Partners*
Top Floor
29-37 Heddon St
London W1B 4BR, UNITED KINGDOM

Stevens, Ray (Musician, Songwriter)
1707 Grand Ave
Nashville, TN 37212, USA

Stevens, Richard (Football Player)
Philadelphia Eagles
4100 Cimmaron Trl
Granbury, TX 76049-5252, USA

Stevens, Richie (Race Car Driver)
Richie Stevens Fan Club
9600 Chief Hwy.
New Orleans, LA 70127, USA

Stevens, Rise (Opera Singer)
930 5th Ave
New York, NY 10021, USA

Stevens, Robert B (Educator)
Covington/Burling
Leconfield House
Curzon St
London W1Y 8AS, UNITED KINGDOM (UK)

Stevens, Robert J (Business Person)
Lockheed Martin Corp
6801 Rockledge Dr
Bethesda, MD 20817, USA

Stevens, Rogers (Musician)
Shapiro Co
9229 Sunset Blvd #607
Los Angeles, CA 90069, USA

Stevens, Ronnie (Actor)
Caroline Dawson
125 Gloucester Road
London SW7 4IE, UNITED KINGDOM (UK)

Stevens, Scott (Athlete, Hockey Player)
280 Spook Hollow Rd
Far Hills, NJ 07931-2707, USA

Stevens, Scott (Athlete, Hockey Player)
New Jersey Devils
165 Mulberry St
Attn Special Assignment Coach
Newark, NJ 07102-3607, USA

Stevens, Shadoe (Radio Personality)
2934 N. Beverly Glen Circle #399
Los Angeles, CA 90077, USA

Stevens, Shakin' (Music Group, Musician)
c/o Ed Stringfellow *Agency Group Ltd, The (UK)*
361-373 City Rd
London EC1V 1PQ, UK

Stevens, Stella (Actor, Model)
2180 Coldwater Canyon Dr
Beverly Hills, CA 90210, USA

Stevens, Steve (Musician)
c/o Staff Member *J H Cohn LLP*
720 Palisade Ave
Englewood Cliffs, NJ 07632, USA

Stevens, Steven (Actor)
Stevens Group
3518 Cahuenga Blvd W
Los Angeles, CA 90068, USA

Stevens, Sufjan (Musician)
c/o Ali Hedrick *Billions Corporation, The*
833 W Chicago Ave
Suite 101
Chicago, IL 60622-5497, USA

Stevens, Tony (Musician)
Lustig Talent
PO Box 770850
Orlando, FL 32877, USA

Stevens, Warren (Actor)
14155 Magnolia Blvd #27
Sherman Oaks, CA 91423, USA

Stevens, William S (Football Player)
Green Bay Packers
PO Box 221320
El Paso, TX 79913-4320, USA

Stevenson, Adlai
20 N Clark St Ste 750
Chicago, IL 60602-4116, USA

Stevenson, Cynthia (Actor)
c/o Elizabeth Much *Much and House Public Relations*
8075 W 3rd St
Suite 500
Los Angeles, CA 90048, USA

Stevenson, DeShawn (Basketball Player)
Utah Jazz
1348 Lake Whitney Dr
301 W South Temple
Windermere, FL 34786-6072, USA

Stevenson, James (Actor)
c/o Melissa Prophet *Melissa Prophet Management*
Prefers to be contacted by telephone
CA, USA

Stevenson, Jeremy (Athlete, Hockey Player)
7899 W 6 Mile Rd
Brimley, MI 49715-9281, USA

Stevenson, Juliet (Actor)
68 Pall Mall
London SW1Y 5ES, UNITED KINGDOM (UK)

Stevenson, Parker (Actor)
c/o Laina Cohn *Laina Cohn Management*
15066 Sutton St
Sherman Oaks, CA 91403, USA

Stevenson, Ray (Actor)
c/o Liz Nelson *Conway van Gelder*
8-12 Broadwick St
London W1F 8HW, UK

Stevenson, Rosemary (Athlete, Baseball Player)
19123 120th Ave
Nunica, MI 49448-9460, USA

Stevenson, Shayne (Athlete, Hockey Player)
33 Glendower Cres
Keswick, ON L4P OAS, Canada

Stevenson, Turner (Athlete, Hockey Player)
5623 245th Ave NE
Redmond, WA 98053, USA

Stevenson, Venetia (Actor)
1403 Keys Crossing Dr NE
Atlanta, GA 30319, USA

Steverson, Todd (Athlete, Baseball Player)
109 W Glenhaven Dr
Phoenix, AZ 85045-0717, USA

Steward, Robert L
2864 S Circle Dr #800
Colorado Springs, CO 80906, USA

Stewart, Al (Music Group, Musician, Songwriter, Writer)
Chapman & Co
14011 Ventura Blvd #405
Sherman Oaks, CA 91423, USA

Stewart, Alana (Actor)
c/o Arnold Robinson *Rogers & Cowan PR (LA)*
Pacific Design Center
8687 Melrose Ave, 7th Floor
West Hollywood, CA 90069, USA

Stewart, Alec (Cricketer)
Surrey County Cricket Club
Kennington Oval
London SE11 5SS, UNITED KINGDOM (UK)

Stewart, Alexandra
37 Ave. de la Dame Blanche
Fontenay-Bois, FRANCE 94120

Stewart, Amy (Actor)
c/o Lisa DiSante-Frank *DiSante Frank & Company*
10061 Riverside Dr #377
Toluca Lake, CA 91602, USA

Stewart, Andy (Athlete, Baseball Player)
641 Geddes St
Wilmington, DE 19805-3718, USA

Stewart, Bill (Musician)
Blue Note Records
6920 Sunset Blvd
Los Angeles, CA 90028, USA

Stewart, Bill (Athlete, Hockey Player)
7175 McColl Dr
Niagara Falls, ON L2J 1G7, Canada

Stewart, Bill (Athlete, Baseball Player)
44842 Aspen Ridge Dr
Northville, MI 48168-4435, USA

Stewart, Blair (Athlete, Hockey Player)
1604 Cotten ham Ln
Virginia Beach, VA 23454-6406, USA

Stewart, Bob (Athlete, Hockey Player)
16756 Kehrs Mill Estates Dr
Chesterfield, MO 63005-6526, USA

Stewart, Boo Boo (Actor)
c/o Staff Member *Osbrink Talent Agency*
4343 Lankershim Blvd
Suite 100
Universal City, CA 91602, USA

Stewart, BooBoo (Actor)
c/o Siri Garber *Platform Public Relations*
2666 N Beachwood Dr
Los Angeles, CA 90068, USA

Stewart, Cam (Athlete, Hockey Player)
2929 Buffalo Speedwa_y Unit 218
Houston, TX 77098-1719, USA

Stewart, Catherine Mary (Actor)
350 DuPont St
Toronto, ON M5R 1Z9, Canada

Stewart, Danica (Actor)
c/o Terrance Hines *Hines and Hunt Entertainment*
1213 W Magnolia Blvd
Burbank, CA 91506, USA

Stewart, Dave (Composer, Musician, Producer)
c/o Allison Elbl *ID PR (LA)*
7060 Hollywood Blvd
8th Floor
Los Angeles, CA 90028, USA

Stewart, Dave (Athlete, Baseball Player)
17762 Vineyard Ln
Powny, CA 92064-1061, USA

Stewart, David K (Dave) (Baseball Player)
Los Angeles Dodgers
17762 Vineyeard Lane
Poway, CA 92064-1061, USA

Stewart, Elizabeth (Stylist)
c/o Staff Member *Cloutier Agency*
2632 La Cienega Ave
Los Angeles, CA 90034, USA

Stewart, Fivel (Actor)
c/o Siri Garber *Platform Public Relations*
2666 N Beachwood Dr
Los Angeles, CA 90068, USA

Stewart, Freddie
4862 Excelente Dr.
Woodland Hills, CA 91364

Stewart, French (Actor)
c/o J.C. (JC) Robbins *JC Robbins Management*
113 S Kilkea Dr
Los Angeles, CA 90048, USA

Stewart, Ian (Government Official)
House of Commons
Westminster
London SW1A 0AA, UNITED KINGDOM (UK)

Stewart, Jackie (Race Car Driver)
The British Racing Drivers Club
24 Rte. de Divonne
Nyon 1260, SWITZERLAND

Stewart, James B (Journalist)
Wall Street Journal
Editorial Dept
200 Liberty St
New York, NY 10281, USA

Stewart, James C (War Hero)
8793 Grape Wagon Circle
San Jose, CA 95135, USA

Stewart, Jermaine (Music Group, Musician)
Richard Walters
1800 Argyle Ave #408
Los Angeles, CA 90028, USA

Stewart, Jim (Athlete, Hockey Player)
57 Lincoln St
Spencer, MA 01562-1623, USA

Stewart, Jimmy (Athlete, Baseball Player)
15644 Eastbourn Dr
Odessa, FL 33556, USA

Stewart, Jimmy (Athlete, Baseball Player)
15644 Eastbourn Dr
Odessa, FL 33556-2850, USA

Stewart, John (Athlete, Hockey Player)
1085 Southlake Cv
Birmingham, AL 35244-3283, USA

Stewart, John A (Athlete, Hockey Player)
16424 Grenwich Ter
Eden Prairie, MN 55346-1421, USA

Stewart, Jon (Actor, Comedian, Television Host)
The Daily Show with Jon Stewart
604 W 52nd St
New York, NY 10019, USA

Stewart, Josh (Actor)
c/o Lena Roklin *Luber Roklin Management*
8530 Wilshire Blvd
6th Floor
Beverly Hills, CA 90211, USA

Stewart, Josh (Athlete, Baseball Player)
182 Stewart Ln
Ledbetter, KY 42058-9549, USA

Stewart, Kimberly (Actor, Model)
c/o Kenya Knight *Nous Model Management*
117 N Robertson Blvd
Los Angeles, CA 90048, USA

Stewart, Kordell (Athlete, Football Player)
2045 Caladium Way
Roswell, GA 30075, USA

Stewart, Kristen (Actor)
1963 De Mille Dr
Los Angeles, CA 90027, USA

Stewart, Ian (Athlete, Baseball Player)
12 Ocaso Dr
Asheville, NC 28806-8202, USA

Stewart, Lisa (Actor, Producer)
c/o Staff Member *Vinyl Films*
5555 Melrose Ave
Los Angeles, CA 90038-3989, USA

Stewart, Lisa (Musician)
Friedman & LaRosa
1344 Lexington Ave
New York, NY 10128, USA

Stewart, Martha (Business Person, Television Host, Writer)
48 Girdle Ridge Rd
Katonah, NY 10536, USA

Stewart, Mary (Writer)
House of Letterawe
Lock Awe
Argyll PA33 1AH, SCOTLAND

Stewart, Maxine (Actor)
180 Comanche
Topanga, CA 90290-4426, USA

Stewart, Mel (Athlete, Olympic Athlete, Swimmer)
7308 Seneca Falls Loop
Austin, TX 78739-2216, USA

Stewart, Melvin Jr (Swimmer)
c/o Scott Karp *Crystal Sky Pictures*
10203 Santa Monica Blvd
5th Floor
Los Angeles, CA 90067, USA

Stewart, Michael
6234 Louise Cove Dr
Windermere, FL 34786-8941, USA

Stewart, Michael (Football Player)
Los Angeles Rams
717 Palo Verde St
Bakersfield, CA 93309-1863, USA

Stewart, Natalie (Musician, Songwriter, Writer)
DreamWorks Records
9268 W 3rd St
Beverly Hills, CA 90210, USA

Stewart, Norman (Athlete, Basketball Player)
University of Missouri
3201 Westcrest Circle
Columbia, MO 65203, USA

Stewart, Norman W (Stylist)
c/o Staff Member *Zenobia Agency Inc*
PO Box 909
Groveland, CA 95321, USA

Stewart, Patrick (Actor, Director, Producer)
288 7th St #3
Brooklyn, NY 11215, USA

Stewart, Paul (Athlete, Hockey Player)
16 Bridgeview Cir
Walpole, MA 02081-3766, USA

Stewart, Paul Anthony (Actor)
c/o Paul Reisman *Abrams Artists Agency (NY)*
275 Seventh Ave
26th Floor
New York, NY 10001, USA

Stewart, Peggy (Actor)
PO Box 2468
N Hollywood, CA 91602-1878, USA

Stewart, Potter (Judge)
US Court of Appeals
US Courthouse
100 E 5th St
Cincinnati, OH 45202, USA

Stewart, Ralph (Athlete, Hockey Player)
175 Sherwood Dr
Thunder Bay, ON P7B 6Ll, Canada

Stewart, Ray (Golfer)
2777 Dehavilland Place
Abbotsford, BC V2T 5E2, CANADA

Stewart, Robert L (Astronaut, General)
815 Sun Valley Dr
Woodland Park, CO 80863, USA

Stewart, Robert L Brig Gen (Astronaut)
815 Sun Valley Dr
Woodland Park, CO 80863-7729, USA

Stewart, Rod (Actor, Musician)
1435 S Ocean Blvd
Palm Beach, FL 33480, USA

Stewart, Ryan (Football Player)
Detroit Lions
2715 Owens Ave SW
Marietta, GA 30064-4253, USA

Stewart, Sammy (Athlete, Baseball Player)
Craggy Correctional Center
P.O. Box 399 #0390745
Asheville, NC 28814-0089, USA

Stewart, Scott (Athlete, Baseball Player)
5243 Hickory Knoll Ln
Mount Holly, NC 28120-9344, USA

Stewart, Scott (Actor)
c/o Jeff Okin *Anonymous Content (LA)*
3531 Hayden Ave
Culver City, CA 90232, USA

Stewart, Shannon (Athlete, Baseball Player)
14348 SW 156th Ave
Miami, FL 33196-6072, USA

Stewart, Shannon H (Athlete, Baseball Player)
14348 SW 156th Avenue
Miami, FL 33196-6072, USA

Stewart, Steve (Football Player)
Atlanta Falcons
1161 Jeans Ln
Amery, WI 54001-5109, USA

Stewart, Thomas J Jr (Opera Singer)
Columbia Artists Mgmt Inc
165 W 57th St
New York, NY 10019, USA

Stewart, Tonea (Actor)
Alabama State University
Theater Arts Dept
Montgomery, AL 36101, USA

Stewart, Tony (Race Car Driver)
Tony Stewart Racing
6001 Haas Way
Kannapolis, NC 28081, USA

Stewart, Tyler (Musician)
Nettwerk Mgmt
8730 Wilshire Blvd #304
Beverly Hills, CA 90211, USA

Stewart, Will Foster (Actor)
8730 Santa Monica Blvd #1
Los Angeles, CA 90069, USA

Stewart-Hardway, Donna (Actor)
PO Box 777
Pinch, WV 25156, USA

Steyn, Mark (Writer)
Mark Steyn Enterprises Inc
P.O. Box 30
Woodsville, NH 03785, USA

Stezer, Philip (Musician)
I M G Artists
3 Burlington Lane
Chiswick
London W4 2TH, UNITED KINGDOM (UK)

St Florian, Friedrich G (Architect)
Rhode Island School of Design
Architecture Dept
Providence, RI 02903, USA

St George, William R (Admiral)
862 San Antonio Place
San Diego, CA 92106, USA

Stich, Michael (Tennis Player)
Ernst-Barlach-Str 44
Elmshom 25336, GERMANY

Sticht, J Paul (Business Person)
11732 Lake House Court
North Palm Beach, FL 33408, USA

Stickel, Fred A (Publisher)
Portland Oregonian
1320 SW Broadway
Portland, OR 97201, USA

Stickle, Leon (Athlete, Hockey Player)
National Hockey League
SO Bay Street 11th Floor
Toronto, ON MSJ 2X8, Canada

Stickler, Alfons M Cardinal (Religious Leader)
Piazza del S Uffizio 11
Rome 00193, ITALY

Stickles, Montford (Monty) (Football Player)
San Francisco 49ers
1363 3rd Ave
San Francisco, CA 94122-2718, USA

Stickles, Ted (Swimmer)
1142 Sharynwood Dr
Baton Rouge, LA 70808, USA

Stidham, Howard (Athlete, Football Player)
185 Beil Drive West
Winchester, TN 37398-5401, USA

Stidham, Phil (Athlete, Baseball Player)
5025 Malabar Blvd
Melbourne Beach, FL 32951-3268, USA

Stieb, David (Dave) A (Athlete, Baseball Player)
3375 Corey Dr
Reno, NV 89509-3991, USA

Stieber, Tamar (Journalist)
Albuquerque Journal
Editorial Dept
7777 Jefferson NE
Albuquerque, NM 87109, USA

Stiefel, Ethan (Ballerina)
American Ballet Theatre
890 Broadway
New York, NY 10003, USA

Stiegler, Josef (Pepi) (Skier)
PO Box 290
Teton Village, WY 83025, USA

Stiegler, Resi (Athlete, Olympic Athlete, Skier)
PO Box 1150
Wilson, WY 83014-1150, USA

Stienburg, Trevor (Athlete, Hockey Player)
2376 Connaught Ave
Halifax, NS B3L 2Z4, Canada

Stienke, Jim (Football Player)
Cleveland Browns
4707 Interlachen Ln
Austin, TX 78747-1457, USA

Stiers, David Ogden (Actor)
c/o Staff Member *Mitchell K Stubbs & Assoc (MKS)*
8675 W. Washington Blvd
Suite 203
Culver City, CA 90232, USA

Stieve, Terry (Athlete, Football Player)
1407 Vail Pl
Saint Louis, MO 63104-2570, USA

Stigers, Curtis (Actor, Musician)
Shore Fire Media
32 Court St 16th Fl
Brooklyn, NY 11201, USA

Stigler, George (Nobel Prize Laureate)
2621 Brassie Ave
Flossmoor, IL 60422-1819, USA

Stiglitz, Joseph E (Nobel Prize Laureate)
Columbia University
International Affairs Building
New York, NY 10027-7235, USA

Stigman, Dick (Athlete, Baseball Player)
12914 5th Ave S
Burnsville, MN 55337-3504, USA

Stigwood, Robert C (Producer)
Barton Manor
Whippingham
East Cowes
Isle of Wight PO32 6LB, UNITED KINGDOM (UK)

Stiles, Darron (Athlete, Golfer)
130 Wild Turkey Run
Pinehurst, NC 28374, USA

Stiles, Jackie (Basketball Player)
Patrick J Stiles
115 E Hamilton
Claflin, KS 67525, USA

Stiles, Julia (Actor)
c/o Jason Weinberg *Untitled Entertainment (LA)*
350 S. Beverly Dr #200
Beverly Hills, CA 90212, USA

Stiles, Ryan (Actor, Comedian)
c/o Kay Liberman *Liberman/Zerman Management*
252 N Larchmont Blvd
Suite 200
Los Angeles, CA 90004, USA

Stiles, Tony (Athlete, Hockey Player)
Calgary Police Service
133 6 Ave SE
Attn Tactical Unit
Calgary, AB T2G 4Zl, Canada

Stilgoe, Richard (Songwriter, Writer)
Noel Gray Artists
24 Denmark St
London WC2H 8NJ, UNITED KINGDOM (UK)

Still, Arthur B (Art) (Athlete, Football Player)
9813 Betsy Ross Ct
Liberty, MO 64068-8418, USA

Still, Bryan (Football Player)
San Diego Chargers
3812 Brennan Robert Pl
Glen Allen, VA 23060-2505, USA

Still, Ken (Golfer)
1210 Princeton St
Fircrest, WA 98466-6035, USA

Still, Ray (Conductor, Musician)
7101 Bay Front Drive
Apt 514
Annapolis, MD 21403-3753, USA

Still, Susan L (Astronaut)
NASA
Johnson Space Center
2101 NASA Road
Houston, TX 77058, USA

Still, William C Jr (Misc)
Columbia University
Chemistry Dept
New York, NY 10027, USA

Stiller, Ben (Actor, Comedian, Director)
c/o Kelly Bush *ID PR (LA)*
7060 Hollywood Blvd
8th Floor
Los Angeles, CA 90028, USA

Stiller, Jerry (Actor, Comedian)
c/o Pearl Wexler *Kohner Agency, The*
9300 Wilshire Blvd
Suite 555
Beverly Hills, CA 90212, USA

Stiller, Stephen (Music Group, Musician)
17525 Ventura Blvd #210
Encino, CA 91316, USA

Stillman, Cory (Athlete, Hockey Player)
Florida Panthers 1 Panther Pkwy
Attn: Player Development Dept
Sunrise, FL 33323-5315, USA

Stillman, Denise (Stylist)
PO Box 7692 Laguna
Niguel, CA 92607-7692, USA

Stillman, Royle (Athlete, Baseball Player)
580 JB Ct
Glenwood Springs, CO 81601-8733, USA

Stillman, Whit (Director)
International Creative Mgmt
8942 Wilshire Blvd
#219
Beverly Hills, CA 90211, USA

Stills, Chris (Musician)
Atlantic Records
9229 Sunset Blvd
#900
Los Angeles, CA 90069, USA

Stills, Ken (Football Player)
Green Bay Packers
647 Michael St
Oceanside, CA 92057-3505, USA

Stills, Stephen (Musician)
c/o Marsha Vlasic *ICM Partners (ICM-LA)*
10250 Constellation Blvd Fl 7
Los Angeles, CA 90067, USA

Stills, The (Music Group)
c/o Staff Member *Paradigm (Monterey)*
404 W Franklin St
Monterey, CA 93940, USA

Stillwagon, Jim (Athlete, Football Player)
890 Gate house Ln
Columbus, OH 43235-1734, United States

Stillwagon, Jim R (Football Player)
3999 Parkway Lane
Hilliard, OH 43026, USA

Stillwell, Kurt (Athlete, Baseball Player)
1105 Lassen View Dr
Westwood, CA 96137-9537, USA

Stillwell, Richard D (Opera Singer)
1969 Rockingham St
McLean, VA 22101, USA

Stillwell, Ron (Athlete, Baseball Player)
1105 Lassen View Dr
Westwood, CA 96137-9537, USA

Stilson, Jeff (Producer)
c/o Staff Member *Creative Artists Agency (CAA-LA)*
2000 Ave Of The Stars
Los Angeles, CA 90067, USA

Stilwell, Victoria (Television Host)
c/o Cristina Dennstedt *Sarah Hall Productions Inc*
670 Broadway
Suite 504
New York, NY 10012, USA

Stinchcomb, Matt (Athlete, Football Player)
312 Bradford Way
Peachtree City, GA 30269-2311, USA

Stincic, Thomas (Football Player)
Dallas Cowboys
2121 E Oasis St
Mesa, AZ 85213-9743, USA

Stine, Richard (Cartoonist)
PO Box 348 Hansville WA 98340-0348
Hansville, WA 98340-0348, USA

Stine, Robert L (R L) (Writer)
Scholastic Book Services
555 Broadway
New York, NY 10012, USA

Stine, Robert (RL) (Writer)
225 W 71st St
New York, NY 10023, USA

Sting (Actor, Musician, Producer)
c/o Kathy Schenker *KSM Inc.*
1776 Broadway
Suite 2205
New York, NY 10019, USA

Sting, Charlotte (Athlete, Basketball Player)
333 East Trade Street
Charlotte, NC 28202-2331, USA

Stinnett, Kelly (Athlete, Baseball Player)
6840 E Portia St
Mesa, AZ 85207-1558, USA

Stinson, Bob (Athlete, Baseball Player)
1309 Bando Ln
The Villages, FL 32162-0115, USA

Stipanovich, Steve (Athlete, Basketball Player)
409 Conway Wold Byway
Saint Louis, MO 63141-8637, USA

Stipe, Michael (Musician)
Single Cell Pictures
1016 North Palm Ave
West Hollywood, CA 90069, USA

Stiritz, William P (Business Person)
Ralston Purina Co
Checkerboard Square
Saint Louis, MO 63164, USA

Stirling, Rachel (Actor)
c/o Staff Member *Management Inc*
2032 Pinehurst Rd
Los Angeles, CA 90068

Stirling, Steve (Athlete, Coach, Hockey Player)
118 Sassamon Ave
Milton, MA 02186-5828, USA

Stirvins, Alex (Athlete, Basketball Player)
11330 N Sundown Dr
Scottsdale, AZ 85260, USA

Stith, Bryant (Athlete, Basketball Player)
20697 Governor Harrison Pkwy
Freeman, VA 23856-2451, USA

Stith, Samuel (Athlete, Basketball Player)
36 Madison St NE
Washington, DC 20011-2352, USA

Stith, Thomas (Athlete, Basketball Player)
105 Overlook Dr
Farmingville, NY 11738, USA

Stivers, Steve (Congressman, Politician)
1007 Longworth HOB
Washington, DC 20515, USa

Stivrins, Alex
11330 N Sundown Dr
Scottsdale, AZ 85260-5538, USA

St James, James (Jimmy) (Actor, Radio Personality)
The Real Jimmy Hollywood
7510 Sunset Blvd #333
Hollywood, CA 90046, USA

St. James, Lyn (Race Car Driver)
57-D Gasoline Alley
Indianapolis, IN 46222, USA

St. James, Rebecca (Musician)
c/o Staff Member *Smallbone Management*
P.O. Box 1524
Franklin, TN 37064, USA

St Jean, Garry (Basketball Player, Coach)
Golden State Warriors
1001 Broadway
Oakland, CA 94607, USA

St Jean, Len (Football Player)
Boston Patriots
32 Ledgebrook Ave
Stoughton, MA 02072-1054, USA

St John, Andrew (Actor)
c/o Loch Powell *Leverage Management*
3030 Pennsylvania Ave
Santa Monica, CA 90404, USA

St John, Gina (Actor, Television Host)
Howard Talent West
10657 Riverside Dr
Toluca Lake, CA 91602, USA

St John, Jill (Actor)
c/o Staff Member *Borinstein Oreck Bogart Agency*
8271 Melrose Ave
Suite 110
Los Angeles, CA 90046, USA

St John, Kristoff (Actor)
c/o Steve Rohr *Lexicon Public Relations*
1901 Ave of the Stars
2nd Floor
Los Angeles, CA 90067, USA

St John, Lara (Musician)
Columbia Artists Mgmt Inc
165 W 57th St
New York, NY 10019, USA

St John, Mia (Boxer)
c/o Staff Member *Amsel, Eisenstadt & Frazier Talent Agency (AEF)*
5055 Wilshire Blvd
Suite 860
Los Angeles, CA 90036-6108, USA

St John of Fawsley, Norman A F
(Government Official)
Old Rectory Preston Capes
Daventry
Northants NN11 6TE, UNITED KINGDOM (UK)

St Laurent, Andre (Athlete, Hockey Player)
947 Rue Riverview
Otterburn Park, QC J3H 1Zl, Canada

St Laurent, Dollard (Athlete, Hockey Player)
Les Tours Angrignons
6662 Rue Saint-Denis
Montreal, QC H2S 2R9, Canada

St Louis, Martin (Athlete, Hockey Player)
18145 Longwater Run Dr
Tampa, FL 33647-2212, USA

St. Marseille, Frank (Athlete, Hockey Player)
RR #4
Ashton, ON KOA 1BO, CANADA

Stoa, Ryan (Athlete, Hockey Player)
9634 12th Avenue Cir
Bloomington, MN 55425-2510, USA

Stobart, John (Artist)
613/4 Bat Club Dr
Fort Lauderdale, FL 33308, USA

Stock, Barbara (Actor)
22532 Margarita Dr
Woodland Hills, CA 91364-4030, USA

Stock, Mark (Football Player)
Pittsburgh Steelers
9344 Crest Hill Rd
Marshall, VA 20115-3017, USA

Stock, P J (Athlete, Hockey Player)
Team 990
1310 Greene Ave Suite 300
Montreal, QC H3Z 2BS, Canada

Stock, Wes (Athlete, Baseball Player)
P.O. Box 1309
Allyn, WA 98524-1309, USA

Stockdale, Charlotte (Stylist)
c/o Staff Member *Camilla Lowther Managment (CLM Represents)*
30-32 Ericsson Pl
New York, NY 10013, USA

Stockdale, Gretchen
520 Washington Blvd. #248
Marina del Rey, CA 90292

Stockdale, James
Hoover Inst
Stanford, CA 94305-6010, USA

Stockemer, Ralph (Athlete, Football Player)
4001 Madison Circle
Plano, TX 75023-5910, USA

Stocker, Kevin (Athlete, Baseball Player)
1204 N Murray Ln
Liberty Lake, WA 99019-7555, USA

Stocker-Bottazzi, Jeanette (Athlete, Baseball Player)
1440 W Walnut St Apt 811
Allentown, PA 18102-4445, USA

Stockham, Benjamin (Actor)
c/o Beverly Strong *Strong Management*
9350 Wilshire Blvd
#224
Beverly Hills, CA 90212, USA

Stockhausen, Karl-Heinz
Stockhausen-Verlag
Kuerten, GERMANY D-51515

Stockhausen, Karlheinz (Composer)
Stockhausen-Vertag
Kurten 51515, GERMANY

Stockman, David (Politician)
Blackstone Group
150 Greenfield Rd
Winter Haven, FL 33884-1306, USA

Stockman, Phil (Athlete, Baseball Player)
2013 Red Oak Rd
Norcross, GA 30071-3819, USA

Stockman, Shawn (Music Group, Musician)
c/o Steve C Smith *Creative Talent Management Group (CTMG)*
433 N Camden Dr
Suite 600
Beverly Hills, CA 90210, USA

Stockmayer, Walter H (Doctor, Misc)
Willey Hill
Norwich, VT 05055, USA

Stockton, Dave K (Golfer)
222 Escondido Dr
Redlands, CA 92373, USA

Stockton, David (Golfer)
222 Escondido Dr
Redlands, CA 92373-7215, USA

Stockton, David Jr (Golfer)
10 Carrera Pl
Rancho Mirage, CA 92270-3227, USA

Stockton, Dick (Sportscaster)
2519 NW 59th St
Boca Raton, FL 33496-2224, USA

Stockton, John (Athlete, Basketball Player)
The Warehouse
538 W Sumner Ave
Spokane, WA 99204-3738, USA

Stockton, Richard L (Dick) (Tennis Player)
715 Stadium Dr
San Antonio, TX 78212, USA

Stockwell, Dean (Actor)
95723 Highway 99 W
Junction City, OR 97448, USA

Stockwell, Jeff (Writer)
c/o Staff Member *United Talent Agency (UTA)*
9336 Civic Center Dr
Beverly Hills, CA 90210, USA

Stockwell, John (Actor)
United Talent Agency
9560 Wilshire Blvd #500
Beverly Hills, CA 90212, USA

Stoddard, Bob (Athlete, Baseball Player)
15760 Sunnyside Ave
Morgan Hill, CA 95037-5331, USA

Stoddard, Brandon
241 N. Glenroy Ave.
Los Angeles, CA 90049

Stoddard, Jack (Athlete, Hockey Player)
27-4275 Millcroft Park Dr
Burlington, ON ON L7M 4L9, Canada

Stoddard, Tim (Athlete, Baseball Player)
104 Hawthorne Dr
Twin Lakes, WI 53181-9564, USA

Stofa, John (Football Player)
Miami Dolphins
7344 Jefferson Meadows Dr
Blacklick, OH 43004-9813, USA

Stoffer, Karen (Race Car Driver)
1408 Industrial Way
Unit 16
Gardnerville, NV 89410, USA

Stoicheff, Boris P (Physicist)
66 Collier St #6B
Toronto, ON M4W 1L9, CANADA

Stoitchkov, Hristo (Soccer Player)
DC United
14120 Newbrook Dr
Chantilly, VA 20151, USA

Stojakovic, Peja
501 Gibson Dr Apt 424
Roseville, CA 95678-6501, USA

Stojko, Elvis (Figure Skater)
Mentor Marketing
2 Saint Clair Ave E
Toronto, ON M4T 2T, CANADA

Stokes, Brian (Athlete, Baseball Player)
12140 66th Ave
Seminole, FL 33772-6122, USA

Stokes, Chris (Business Person, Director, Musician)
c/o Staff Member *Tobin & Associates PR*
4929 Wilshire Blvd #245
Los Angeles, CA 90010-3859, USA

Stokes, Fred (Football Player)
Los Angeles Rams
735 Mosleytown Rd
Tarrytown, GA 30470-4052, USA

Stokes, Greg (Athlete, Basketball Player)
2505 Plymouth St
Marion, IA 52302-5609, USA

Stokes, Jesse (Football Player)
Denver Broncos
5810 Cayuga Dr
San Antonio, TX 78228-4325, USA

Stokes, John (General)
351 Windermere Blvd Apt 411
Alexandria, LA 71303-2658, USA

Stokes, Sims (Football Player)
Dallas Cowboys
1011 Wind Ridge Cir
Duncanville, TX 75137-3741, USA

Stokes of Leyland, Donald G (Business Person)
2 Branksome Cliff
Westminster Road Poole
Dorset BH13 6JW, UNITED KINGDOM (UK)

Stokkan, Bill (Race Car Driver)
Championship Auto Racing
5350 Lakeview Parkway S Dr
Indianapolis, IN 46268, USA

Stokley, Brandon (Athlete, Football Player)
12479 Autumn Gate Way
Carmel, Indiana 46033, USA

Stoklos, Randy (Athlete, Volleyball Player)
Beach Volleyball Camps
P.O. Box 1714
Pacific Palisades, CA 90272, USA

Stole, Mink (Actor)
635 Colorado Ave #3B
Baltimore, MD 21210-2135, USA

Stolhandske, Tom (Football Player)
San Francisco 49ers
2531 Old Orchard Ln
San Antonio, TX 78230-4610, USA

Stolhanske, Erik (Comedian)
c/o Staff Member *United Talent Agency (UTA)*
9336 Civic Center Dr
Beverly Hills, CA 90210, USA

Stoll, Jarrett (Athlete, Hockey Player)
2021 Monterey Blvd
Hermosa Beach, CA 90254-2913, USA

Stolle, Frederick S (Tennis Player)
Turnberry Isle Yacht & Racquet Club
19735 Turnberry Way
Miami, FL 33180, USA

Stoller, Mike (Composer)
Leiber/Stoller Entertainment
9000 W Sunset Blvd
West Hollywood, CA 90069, USA

Stoller, Nicholas (Director)

Stollery, David (Actor)
3203 Bern Court
Laguna Beach, CA 92651, USA

Stolley, Paul D (Doctor)
10205 Wincopin Circle
Apt 312
Columbia, MD 21044-3435, USA

Stolley, Richard B (Editor)
Time Inc
Time-Life Building
Rockefeller Center
New York, NY 10020, USA

Stolojan, Theodor (Prime Minister)
World Bank
1818 H St NW
Washington, DC 20433, USA

Stolper, Pinchas (Religious Leader)
Orthodox Jewish Congregations Union
11 Broadway
New York, NY 10004, USA

Stoltenberg, Bryan (Football Player)
San Diego Chargers
3207 W Farmington Ln
Sugar Land, TX 77479-1883, USA

Stoltz, Eric (Actor, Director, Producer)
c/o Helen Sugland *Landmark Artists*
4116 W Magnolia Blvd
Suite 101
Burbank, CA 91505, USA

Stoltz, Roland (Athlete, Hockey Player)
Lillgatan 16
Skelleftea S-93154, Sweden

Stoltzfus, Levi (Horse Racer)
234A N Harvest Rd
Ronks, PA 17572-9727, USA

Stolze, Lena (Actor)
Agentur Carola Studlar
Neuroeder Str 1C
Planegg 82152, GERMANY

Stomare, Peter
1129 N. Poinsettia Dr.
W. Hollywood, CA 90046

Stone, Albert L (Race Car Driver)
700 Central Ave
PO Box 8427
Louisville, KY 40208, USA

Stone, Andrew L (Director)
2132 Century Park Lane #212
Los Angeles, CA 90067, USA

Stone, Angie (Musician)
c/o Reina King *Paradigm (LA)*
360 N Crescent Dr
North Bldg
Beverly Hills, CA 90210, USA

Stone, Benjamin (Actor)
c/o Mara Santino *Luber Roklin Management*
8530 Wilshire Blvd
6th Floor
Beverly Hills, CA 90211, USA

Stone, Brock(randy) (Scientist)
4726 Pine Heather Ct
Houston, TX 77059-3293, USA

Stone, Curtis (Chef, Television Host)
c/o Todd Jacobs *WME (LA)*
9601 Wilshire Blvd Fl 3
Beverly Hills, CA 90210, USA

Stone, Dean (Athlete, Baseball Player)
213 13th St
Silvis, IL 61282-1267, USA

Stone, Debbie (Stylist)
c/o Staff Member *Independent NY*
15 E 30th St #401
New York, NY 10016, USA

Stone, Dee Wallace (Actor)
c/o Laura Pallas *Pallas Management*
5301 Bellaire Ave
Valley Vilage, CA 91607, US

Stone, Doug (Musician)
PO Box 943
Springfield, TN 37172

Stone, Eddie (Adult Film Star)
c/o Staff Member *Diva Central Inc*
7510 W Sunset Blvd Ste 1445
Los Angees, CA 90046, USA

Stone, Edward C (Scientist)
Jet Propulsion Laboratory
1227 Arden Rd
Pasadena, CA 91106-4135, USA

Stone, Emma (Actor)
1853 Noel Pl
Beverly Hills, CA 90210, USA

Stone, Fred (Artist)
Equinart Inc 5911 Colodny Dr
Agoura Hills, CA 91301-1841, USA

Stone, Gene (Athlete, Baseball Player)
6897 Highway 262 SE
Othello, WA 99344-9761, USA

Stone, George H (Athlete, Baseball Player)
1304 Fairfield Dr
Ruston, LA 71270-3540, USA

Stone, Jack (Football Player)
Dallas Texans
16125 Crestridge Ave
Sonora, CA 95370-8752, USA

Stone, Jack (Religious Leader)
Church of Nazarene
6401 Paseo
Kansas City, MO 64131, USA

Stone, Jeff (Athlete, Baseball Player)
69 County Highway 244
Portageville, MO 63873-9587, USA

Stone, Jennifer (Actor)
c/o Laura Ackerman *Persona PR*
8075 W 3rd St
Suite 500
Los Angeles, CA 90048, USA

Stone, Joss (Musician, Songwriter)
c/o Patrick Confrey *Sunshine, Sachs & Associates*
149 Fifth Ave
7th Floor
New York, NY 10010, USA

Stone, Ken (Football Player)
Buffalo Bills
1158 Jason Way
West Palm Beach, FL 33406-5255, USA

Stone, Lara (Model)
c/o Staff Member *IMG World (NY)*
420 W 45th St
New York, NY 10036, USA

Stone, Matt (Animator, Writer)
c/o Mike Simpson *WME (LA)*
9601 Wilshire Blvd Fl 3
Beverly Hills, CA 90210, USA

Stone, Michael (Athlete, Football Player)
c/o Eugene Parker *Maximum Sports Management*
6435 W Jefferson Blvd
#197
Fort Wayne, IN 46804, USA

Stone, Nicole (Athlete, Olympic Athlete, Skier)
5272 Heather Ln
Park City, UT 84098-5967, USA

Stone, Nikki (Skier)
Podium Enterprises
PO Box 680-332
Park City, UT 84068, USA

Stone, Oliver (Actor, Director, Producer, Writer)
c/o Emily Lowe *Rubenstein Associates Inc*
1345 Avenue of the Americas
30th Floor
New York, NY 10105, USA

Stone, Richard (Politician)
4508 Foxhall Cres NW
Washington, DC 20007-1055, USA

Stone, Ricky (Athlete, Baseball Player)
6494 Lakeview Ct
Hamilton, OH 45011-8139, USA

Stone, Rob
8033 Sunset Blvd. #450
Los Angeles, CA 90046

Stone, Robert A (Writer)
Donadio & Ashworth
121 W 27th St #704
New York, NY 10001, USA

Stone, Robert B. (Writer)
Editorial Diana
Sand Not. 24, North Building
Former-Estate Guadalupe
Chimalistac, Mexico

Stone, Roger D (Politician)
34 W 88th St
New York, NY 10024, USA

Stone, Ron (Athlete, Baseball Player)
11720 NW Lovejoy St
Portland, OR 97229-5028, USA

Stone, Sammy
PO Box 2825
Port Arthur, TX 77642

Stone, Sharon (Actor)
c/o Chuck Binder *Binder & Associates*
1465 Lindacrest Dr
Beverly Hills, CA 90210, USA

Stone, Steve (Athlete, Baseball Player, Sportscaster)
9261 N 128th Way
Scottsdale, AZ 85259-6233, USA

Stone, William J (Football Player)
Baltimore Colts
618 Woodland Knolls Rd
Metamora, IL 61548-9429, USA

Stonebreaker, Mike (Football Player)
Chicago Bears
3300 Delaware Ave Apt A
Kenner, LA 70065-3689, USA

Stonecipher, David A (Financier)
Jefferson-Pilot Corp
100 N Greene St
Greensboro, NC 27401, USA

Stonecipher, Harry C (Business Person)
Boeing Co
PO Box 3707
Seattle, WA 98124, USA

Stone Foxes, The (Music Group, Musician)
c/o Rob Weldon *Wingman Music*
Prefers to be contacted by email or telephone
CA, USA

Stone III, Charles (Actor, Director, Writer)
c/o Barbara Dreyfus *United Talent Agency (UTA)*
9336 Civic Center Dr
Beverly Hills, CA 90210, USA

Stoneman, Bill (Athlete, Baseball Player)
2519 N San Miguel Dr
Orange, CA 92867-8604, USA

Stoner, Alyson (Musician)
c/o Cindy Osbrink *Osbrink Talent Agency*
4343 Lankershim Blvd
Suite 100
Universal City, CA 91602, USA

Stoner, Bob (Race Car Driver)
Vapor Racing
10785 Oakland Dr.
Portage, MI 49024, USA

Stoner, Sherri (Actor, Producer, Writer)
c/o Tom Strickler *WME (LA)*
9601 Wilshire Blvd Fl 3
Beverly Hills, CA 90210, USA

Stoner, Tobi (Athlete, Baseball Player)
2532 Raintree Dr Unit P299
Fort Collins, CO 80526-8100, USA

Stone-Richards, Lucille (Athlete, Baseball Player)
17 Stonemeadow Dr
Bridgewater, MA 02324-1995, USA

Stones
4790 Irvine Blvd. #105
Irvine, CA 92720-1998

Stones, Dwight E (Athlete, Olympic Athlete)
27472 Portola Pkwy Ste 205
Foothill Ranch, CA 92620, USA

Stonesifer, Don (Football Player)
Chicago Cardinals
1502 Canbury Ct Apt C1
Wheeling, IL 60090-6974, USA

Stonesipher, Don (Football Player)
1502 Canberry Court
Wheeling, IL 60090, USA

Stone Sour (Music Group)
c/o Cory Brennan *Sanctuary Artist Management (NY)*
75 9th Ave
New York, NY 10011, USA

Stonestreet, Eric (Actor)
c/o Suzanne (Sue) Wohl *TalentWorks (LA)*
3500 W Olive Ave
Suite 1400
Burbank, CA 91505, USA

Stone Temple Pilots (Music Group)
c/o Rod MacSween *International Talent Booking*
74A Charlotte St
London W1T 4QJ, UNITED KINGDOM (UK)

Stookey, Donald (Inventor)
100 Hahnemann Trl Apt 229
Pittsford, NY 14534-2352, USA

Stookey, Paul (Music Group, Musician, Songwriter, Writer)
Newworld
RR 175
South Blue Hill Falls, ME 04615, USA

Stoops, Bob (Coach, Football Coach)
University of Oklahoma
Athletic Dept
108 Brooks St
Norman, OK 73069, USA

Stoops, Jim (Athlete, Baseball Player)
205 Foster Dr
Oswego, IL 60543-4053, USA

Stoops, Mike (Coach, Football Coach)
Arizona State University
Athletic Dept
Tempe, AZ 85287, USA

Stopanovich, Steve (Athlete, Basketball Player)
14 Ridgecreek
Saint Louis, MO 63141, USA

Stopel, Terry (Football Player)
Chicago Bears
804 Saddlebrook Dr S
Bedford, TX 76021-5360, USA

Stoppard, Tom (Writer)
P F D
Peters Fraser and Dunlop Group 504/506
The Chambers Chelsea
London SW10 OXF, England

Storaro, Vittorio (Cinematographer)
Via Divino Amore 2
Frattocchie Merino 00040, ITALY

Storch, Larry (Actor)
330 W End Ave #17F
New York, NY 10023, USA

Storch, Scott (Producer)
c/o Tracy Christian *Buchwald/Fortitude (LA)*
6500 Wilshire Blvd
Suite 2200
Los Angeles, CA 90048, USA

Storer, Chris (Stylist)
c/o Staff Member *Judy Inc*
1 Yorkville Ave
Toronto ON M4W 1L1, Canada

Storey, David M (Writer)
2 Lyndhurst Gardens
London NW3, UNITED KINGDOM (UK)

Storey, June
338 Morgan Pl.
Vista, CA 92083-8018

Storey, Lisa (Stylist)
c/o Staff Member *Independent NY*
15 E 30th St #401
New York, NY 10016, USA

Storey, Meredith (Stylist)
c/o Staff Member *Clutts Agency, The*
1400 Turtle Creek Blvd
#171
Dallas, TX 75207, USA

Stori, Moneca (Actor)
c/o Elena Kirschner *Lucas Talent Inc*
100 W. Pender St
Sun Tower, 7th Floor
Vancouver, BC V6B 1R8, Canada

Stork, Gilbert (Scientist)
188 Chestnut St
Englewood Cliffs, NJ 07632-1908, USA

Stork, Jeff (Athlete, Coach, Volleyball Player)
California State University Northridge
Athletic Dept
18111 Nordhoff St
Northridge, CA 91330, USA

Stork, Travis (Doctor, Talk Show Host)
The Doctors
5555 Melrose Ave
Mae West Building, Second Floor
Los Angeles, CA 90038, USA

Storke, Adam (Actor)
c/o Marc Epstein *Marc Epstein Entertainment*
108 Breeze Ave
Venice, CA 90291, USA

Storm, Avery (Musician)
c/o Staff Member *Derrty Entertainment*
9648 Olive Blvd
#230
St. Louis, MO 63132, USA

Storm, Crystal
2139 University Dr. #297
Coral Springs, FL 33071

Storm, Hannah (Correspondent, Sportscaster)
c/o Staff Member *ESPN (Main)*
ESPN Plaza
935 Middle St
Bristol, CT 06010-1001, USA

Storm, Jim
13576 Cheltenham Dr.
Sherman Oaks, CA 91423

Storm, Jim (Athlete, Hockey Player)
2609 Harvest Hill Dr
Brighton, MI 48114-8299, USA

Storm, Lauren (Actor)
c/o Staff Member *Aquarius Public Relations*
5320 Sylmar Ave
Sherman Oaks, CA 91401, USA

Storm, Tempest (Dancer)
3905 Cambridge St
Unit 3
Las Vegas, NV 89119-7402, USA

Stormare, Peter (Actor)
c/o Jeff Golenberg *Collective*
8383 Wilshire Blvd
Suite 1050
Beverly Hills, CA 90211, USA

Stormer, Horst L (Nobel Prize Laureate)
20 E 9th St #14P
New York, NY 10003-5944, USA

Storms, Kirsten (Actor)
c/o Nils Larsen *Principato/Young Management*
312 W 5th St Apt 815
Los Angeles, CA 90013, USA

Storr, Jamie (Athlete, Hockey Player)
Jamie Storr Goalie School
650 N Sepulveda Blvd
Los Angeles, CA 90049-2108, USA

Storraro, Vittorio (Cinematographer)
c/o Paul Hook *ICM Partners (ICM-LA)*
10250 Constellation Blvd Fl 7
Los Angeles, CA 90067, USA

Story, Tim (Director)
c/o Staff Member *WmE2 (WMA-LA)*
1 William Morris Pl
Beverly Hills, CA 90212, USA

Story, Winston (Actor)
c/o Brian McCabe *Venture IAB*
3211 Cahuenga Blvd W Ste 104
Los Angeles, CA 90068, USA

Storz, Erik (Football Player)
Jacksonville Jaguars
114 Andrea Dr
Rockaway, NJ 07866-3702, USA

Stossel, John (Journalist)
c/o Staff Member *NS Bienstock Inc*
250 W 57th St
Suite 333
New York, NY 10107, USA

Stott, Kathryn L (Musician)
Mire House
West Martor near Skipton
Yorks BD23 3UQ, UNITED KINGDOM (UK)

Stott, Nicole P (Astronaut)
NASA
2007 Golden Bay Ln
League City, TX 77573-3968, USA

Stottlemyre, Melvin L (Mel) (Athlete, Baseball Player)
3314 Meadowlark Dr
Lewiston, ID 83501-8609, USA

Stottlemyre, Todd (Athlete, Baseball Player)
6918 E Bronco Dr
Paradise Valley, AZ 85253-3123, USA

Stottlemyre Jr, Mel (Athlete, Baseball Player)
26004 SE 27th St
Sammamish, WA 98075-9140, USA

Stotts, Terry (Athlete, Basketball Coach, Basketball Player, Coach)
7639 Tralee Way
Bradenton, FL 34202-6010, USA

Stoudamire, Damon (Athlete, Basketball Player)
c/o Lon Rosen *Lagardere Unlimited - (D.C.)*
5335 Wisconsin Ave NW
Suite 850
Washington, DC 20015, USA

Stoudemire, Amare (Athlete, Basketball Player)
c/o Happy Walters *Immortal Sports*
12200 Olympic Blvd #400
Los Angeles, CA 90064, USA

Stouder, Sharon M (Swimmer)
144 Loucks Ave
Los Altos, CA 94022, USA

Stoudt, Bud (Bowler)
431 Lehman St
Lebanon, PA 17046-3639, USA

Stoudt, Cliff (Football Player)
Pittsburgh Steelers
326 Doe Run Circle
Henderson, NV 89012-2701, USA

Stouffer, Kelly (Football Player)
Seattle Seahawks
HC 81 Box 55
Rushville, NE 69360-9729, USA

Stoughton, Blaine (Athlete, Hockey Player)
8770 Ashbrook Dr
West Chester, OH 45069-3350, USA

Stovall, Da Rond (Athlete, Baseball Player)
1107 Goelz Dr
East Saint Louis, IL 62203-1917, USA

Stovall, Jerry L (Football Player)
St Louis Cardinals
417 Highland Trace Dr #D
Baton Rouge, LA 70810-5062, USA

Stove, Betty (Tennis Player)
Advantage International
1025 Thomas Jeffferson NW #450
Washington, DC 20007, USA

Stover, George (Actor)
PO Box 10005
Baltimore, MD 21285, USA

Stover, Irwin Russ Juno (Athlete, Swimmer)
512 Lanai Circle
Union City, CA 94587, USA

Stover, Jeff (Athlete, Football Player)
260 Cohasset Road
Suite 190
Chico, CA 95926-2282, USA

Stover, Matt (Football Player)
Cleveland Browns
10024 Rustleleaf Dr
Dallas, TX 75238-2143, USA

Stover, Scott (Scientist)
4382 Parnell Dr
Mercersburg, PA 17236-9607, USA

Stover, Stewart (Football Player)
Dallas Texans
9334 La Highway 82
Abbeville, LA 70510-2356, USA

Stowe, David H Jr (Business Person)
Deere Co
John Deere Road
Moline, IL 61265, USA

Stowe, Hal (Athlete, Baseball Player)
1361 Union New Hope Rd
Gastonia, NC 28056-8574, USA

Stowe, Madeleine (Actor)
c/o Cynthia Pett-Dante *Brillstein Entertainment Partners*
9150 Wilshire Blvd #350
Beverly Hills, CA 90212, USA

Stowe, Medeleine (Actor)
United Talent Agency
9560 Wilshire Blvd #500
Beverly Hills, CA 90212, USA

Stowe, Otto (Football Player)
Miami Dolphins
546 Mills Way
Goleta, CA 93117-4021, USA

Stowers, Chris (Athlete, Baseball Player)
3773 Wakefield Hall Sg SE
Smyrna, GA 30080-4917, USA

Stowers, Tommie (Football Player)
New Orleans Saints
2435 NW Valley View Dr
Lees Summit, MO 64081-1977, USA

Stoyanov, Krasimir M (Misc)
Potchta Kosmonavtov
Moskovskoi Oblasti
Syvisdny Goroduk 141160, RUSSIA

Stoyanovich, Peter (Pete) (Athlete, Football Player)
18185 Parkshore Drive
Northville, MI 48168-8591, USA

St Patrick, Mathew (Actor)
c/o Todd Eisner *Agency for the Performing Arts (APA-LA)*
405 S Beverly Dr
Suite 500
Beverly Hills, CA 90212-4425, USA

St Patrick, Matthew (Actor)
c/o Staff Member *Untitled Entertainment (LA)*
350 S. Beverly Dr #200
Beverly Hills, CA 90212, USA

St. Pierre, Georges (Athlete)
c/o Staff Member *Creative Artists Agency (CAA-LA)*
2000 Ave Of The Stars
Los Angeles, CA 90067, USA

Stracey, John (Boxer)
Van Laeken 4
Norsey Road Billericay
Essex CM11 2AD, UNITED KINGDOM (UK)

Strachan, Gordon (Politician)
PO Box 3747
Park City, UT 84060-3747, USA

Strachan, Mike (Football Player)
New Orleans Saints
PO Box 642007
Kenner, LA 70064-2007, USA

Strachan, Rod (Athlete, Olympic Athlete, Swimmer)
11632 Ranch Hill
Santa Ana, CA 92705, USA

Strachan, Steve (Football Player)
Oakland Raiders
46 Crimson Rd
Billerica, MA 01821-5420, USA

Strachan, Tyaon (Athlete, Hockey Player)
5550 Flint Creek Ave
Dublin, OH 43016-9645, USA

Straczynski, J Michael (Actor)
c/o Chris Harbert *Creative Artists Agency (CAA-LA)*
2000 Ave Of The Stars
Los Angeles, CA 90067, USA

Strader, Cam (Athlete, Race Car Driver)
10974 Hertiage Green Drive
Cornelius, NC 28031-7407, USA

Stradlin, Izzy (Musician)
Big FD Entertainment
301 Arizona Ave #200
Santa Monica, CA 90401, USA

Stradling, Harry A Jr (Cinematographer)
3664 Avenida Callada
Calabasas, CA 91302, USA

Strahan, Michael (Athlete, Football Player)
62 8th St. #A
Hermosa Beach, CA 90254, USA

Strahler, Mike (Athlete, Baseball Player)
8 Canyon Draw
Alamogordo, NM 88310-3613, USA

Strahovski, Yvonne (Actor)
1603 Tower Grove Dr
Beverly Hills, CA 90210, USA

Straight, Bering (Music Group)
c/o Staff Member *Creative Artists Agency (CAA-TN)*
3310 West End Ave
5th Floor
Nashville, TN 37203, USA

Strain, Joe (Athlete, Baseball Player)
8668 E Otero Cir
Centennial, CO 80112-3351, USA

Strain, Julie (Actor, Model)
Cooking with Mama
8491 Sunset Blvd
Suite 1850
West Hollywood, CA 90069, USA

Strain, Sammy (Music Group, Musician)
Associated Booking Corp
1995 Broadway #501
New York, NY 10023, USA

Strait, Bob (Race Car Driver)
Carnes-Miller Motorsports
12515 Kened
Elbert, CO 80106, USA

Strait, Donald (General)
6 Burning Tree Place
Jackson Springs, NC 27281-9756, USA

Strait, George (Musician)
c/o Staff Member *Erv Woolsey Agency, The*
1000 18th Ave S
Nashville, TN 37212, USA

Strait, Steven (Actor)
c/o Chris Andrews *Creative Artists Agency (CAA-LA)*
2000 Ave Of The Stars
Los Angeles, CA 90067, USA

Straka, Martin (Athlete, Hockey Player)
HC Plzen Stefanikovo namesti. 1
Pl zen 301 33, Czech Republic

Straker, Lee (Athlete, Baseball Player)
Philadelphia Phillies
1 Citizens Bank Way
Attn: Venezulan Baseball Academy
Philadelphia, PA 19148, USA

Strampe, Bob (Athlete, Baseball Player)
19210 W LAnce Hill Rd
Cheney, WA 99004-7907, USA

Strampe, Bob (Bowler)
31029 Louise Ct
Warren, MI 48088-2005, USA

Stranahan, Frank (Golfer)
8400 Heritage Club Dr
W Palm Beach, FL 33412, USA

Strand, Mark (Writer)
5825 S Dorchester Ave Apt 9W
Chicago, IL 60637-1701, USA

Strand, Robin (Actor)
4118 Elmer Ave
North Hollywood, CA 91602, USA

Strane, John (War Hero)
18230 Mirasol Dr
San Diego, CA 92128, USA

Strang, Deborah (Actor)
Henderson/Hogan
8285 W Sunset Blvd #1
West Hollywood, CA 90046, USA

Strang, William G (Mathematician)
7 Southgate Road
Wellesley, MA 02181, USA

Strange, Doug (Athlete, Baseball Player)
435 Heights Dr
Gibsonia, PA 15044-6032, USA

Strange, Pat (Athlete, Baseball Player)
156 Mill St
Springfield, MA 01108-1022, USA

Strange, Sarah (Actor)
c/o Ryan Martin *Agency for the Performing Arts (APA-LA)*
405 S Beverly Dr
Suite 500
Beverly Hills, CA 90212-4425, USA

Strange Boys, The (Music Group)
c/o Staff Member *Paradigm (Monterey)*
404 W Franklin St
Monterey, CA 93940, USA

Strange-Hansen, Martin (Actor)
c/o Staff Member *Gersh (LA)*
9465 Wilshire Blvd
Suite 600
Beverly Hills, CA 90212, USA

Stransky, Bob (Football Player)
Denver Broncos
5970 W Colgate Pl
Denver, CO 80227-3814, USA

Strasburg, Stephen (Athlete, Baseball Player)
7511 Blue Lake Dr
San Diego, CA 92119-3010, USA

Strasser, Teresa (Comedian, Television Host)
c/o Staff Member *OmniPop Talent Group*
10700 Ventura Blvd.
2nd Floor
Studio Clty, CA 91604, USA

Strasser, Todd (Writer)
PO Box 859
Larchmont, NY 10538-0859, USA

Strassman, Marcia (Actor)
4024 Dixie Canyon Ave
Sherman Oaks, CA 91423, USA

Stratas, Teresa (Opera Singer)
Vincent Farrell Assoc
481 8th Ave #340
New York, NY 10001, USA

Strate, Gord (Athlete, Hockey Player)
10711106 Ave
Fort St. John, BC V1J SP1, Canada

Strathairn, David (Actor)
Ryan Entertainment
c/o Madeline Ryan
461 South Ogden Dr
Los Angeles, CA 90036, USA

Stratham, Jason (Actor)
International Creative Mgmt
8942 Wilshire Blvd #219
Beverly Hills, CA 90211, USA

Strathiam, David (Actor)
United Talent Agency
9560 Wilshire Blvd #500
Beverly Hills, CA 90212, USA

Stratton, Dan
65 Broadway
Suite 504
New York, New York 10006, USA

Stratton, Frederick P Jr (Business Person)
Briggs & Stratton
PO Box 702
Milwaukee, WI 53201, USA

Stratton, Mike (Football Player)
Buffalo Bills
2611 Shoreline Rd
Knoxville, TN 37932-1724, USA

Stratus, Trish (Wrestler)
Stratus Enterprises, Inc
5468 Dundas St West
#579
Toronto, ON M9B 6E3, CANADA

Straub, Peter (Writer)
53 W. 85th St.
New York, NY 10024-4132, USA

Straub, Peter F (Writer)
53 W 85th St
New York, NY 10024, USA

Straus, Robert (Scientist)
656 Raintree Road
Lexington, KY 40502, USA

Strauss, Neil (Writer)
8491 Sunset Blvd
#348
West Hollywood, CA 90069, USA

Strauss, Peter (Actor)
Wolf/Kasteller
335 n Maple Dr
#351
Beverly Hills, CA 90210, USA

Strauss, Robert S (Diplomat, Politician)
Akin Gump Strauss Hauer Feld
1700 Pacific Ave
#4100
Dallas, TX 75201, USA

Strauss-Schulson, Todd (Director)
c/o Christie Smith *Mosaic Media Group*
9200 W. Sunset Blvd
10th Floor
Los Angeles, CA 90069, USA

Straw, John W (Jack) (Government Official)
House of Commons
Westminster
London SW1A 0AA, UNITED KINGDOM (UK)

Straw, Syd (Musician)
c/o Staff Member *Agency Group Ltd, The (NY)*
142 West 57th St
6th Floor
New York, NY 10019, USA

Strawberry, Darryl E (Athlete, Baseball Player)
Strawberry's Sports Grill
1802 Sterling Oaks Dr
Saint Peters, MO 63376-1187, USA

Strawberry, D J (Athlete, Basketball Player)
943 Bellevue St
Cape Girardeau, MO 63701-5401, USA

Strawberry Blondes
Box 33 Pontypool
Gwent, ENGLAND NP4 6YU

Stray Cats (Music Group, Musician)
c/o Dave Kaplan *Dave Kaplan Management*
1126 S Coast Hwy
Suite 101
Encinitas, CA 92024, USA

Strayhorn, Les (Football Player)
Dallas Cowboys
109 Sir Richard Ln
Chapel Hill, NC 27517-5531, USA

Streater, Sonja (Stylist)
c/o Staff Member *Celestine - CA*
1666 20th St
#200-B
Santa Monica, CA 90404, USA

Streep, Meryl (Actor)
c/o Michelle Benson *42West (NY)*
220 W 42nd St
12th Floor
New York, NY 10036, USA

Street, Huston (Athlete, Baseball Player)
8300 Big View Dr
Austin, TX 78730-1520, USA

Street, John (Politician)
Mayor's Office
City Hall
23 N Juniper St
Philadelphia, PA 19107, USA

Street, Picabo (Athlete, Olympic Athlete, Skier)
PO Box 321
Hailey, ID 83333, USA

Street, Rebecca (Actor)
19 W 69th St
Apt 101
New York, NY 10023-4751, USA

Streeter, George (Athlete, Football Player)
35 Brentwood Place
Fort Thomas, KY 41075-2446, USA

Streetman, Ben G (Engineer)
3915 Glengarry Dr
Austin, TX 78731, USA

Streiber, Whitley (Writer)
c/o Paul Canterna *Seven Summits Pictures & Management*
8906 W Olympic Blvd
Ground Floor
Beverly Hills, CA 90211, USA

Streisand, Barbra (Actor, Director, Musician, Producer)
c/o Martin Erlichman *Martin Erlichman Associates*
5670 Wilshire Blvd #2400
Los Angeles, CA 90036

Streit, Clarence K (Journalist)
2853 Ontario Road NW
Washington, DC 20009, USA

Streit, Mark (Athlete, Hockey Player)
C A A Sports
2000 Avenue of the Stars
Fl 3
Los Angeles, CA 90067-4704, USA

Streitwieser Jr, Andrew (Misc)
University of California
Chemistry Dept
berkeley, CA 94720, USA

Strekalov, Gennadi M (Cosmonaut)
Federation Peace Committee
36 Mira Prospekt
Moscow 129090, RUSSIA

Stremme, David (Race Car Driver)
Penske Racing
200 Penske Way
Mooresville, NC 28115, USA

Strenger, Rich (Football Player)
Detroit Lions
1064 Arbroak Way
Lake Orion, MI 48362-2500, USA

Streuli, Wait (Athlete, Baseball Player)
1107 Westminster Dr
Greensboro, NC 27410, USA

Streuli, Walt (Athlete, Baseball Player)
1107 Westminster Dr
Greensboro, NC 27410-4545, USA

Stricker, Bill (Athlete, Basketball Player)
2930 Driftwood Pl
Apt 70
Stockton, CA 95219-8027, USA

Stricker, Steve (Athlete, Golfer)
5804 North Sherman Avenue
Madison, WI 53704-2147, USA

Strickland, Donald (Athlete, Football Player)
1110 Gilman Avenue
San Francisco, California 94124, USA

Strickland, Gail (Actor)
14732 Oracle Place
Pacific Palisades, CA 90272, USA

Strickland, Jim (Athlete, Baseball Player)
2139 Equestrian Rd
Paso Robles, CA 93446-4149, USA

Strickland, KaDee (Actor)
c/o Jason Trawick *WME (LA)*
9601 Wilshire Blvd Fl 3
Beverly Hills, CA 90210, USA

Strickland, Rod (Athlete, Basketball Player)
14401 Darren Ct
Bowie, MD 40503-2216, USA

Strickland, Scott (Athlete, Baseball Player)
415 Enchanted River Rd
Spring, TX 77388-5981, USA

Stricklin, Hut (Race Car Driver)
9990 Caldwell Rd.
Mt. Ulla, NC 28125, USA

Strieber, Whitley (Writer)
c/o Staff Member *Gersh (LA)*
9465 Wilshire Blvd
Suite 600
Beverly Hills, CA 90212, USA

Striker, Jake (Athlete, Baseball Player)
1963 SE Gregory Dr
Dallas, OR 97338-2746, USA

Stringer, Howard (Business Person)
Sony Corporation of America
Sony Drive
Park Ridge, NJ 07656, USA

Stringer, Rob (Business Person)
c/o Staff Member *Epic Records Group*
550 Madison Ave
22nd Floor
New York, NY 10022, USA

Stringer, Vivian (Athlete, Basketball Coach)
6 Lavender Dr
Princeton, NJ 08540-9448, USA

Stringert, Hal (Football Player)
San Diego Chargers
1711 Dole St Apt 603
Honolulu, HI 96822-4946, USA

Stringfield, Sherry (Actor)
c/o Leanne Coronel *Coronel Group*
1100 Glendon Ave
17th Floor
Los Angeles, CA 90046, USA

Stritch, Elaine (Actor, Musician)
c/o Staff Member *ICM Partners (ICM-LA)*
10250 Constellation Blvd Fl 7
Los Angeles, CA 90067, USA

Strittmatter, Mark (Athlete, Baseball Player)
6533 Dutch Creek St
Highlands Ranch, CO 80130-3859, USA

Strobel, Eric (Athlete, Hockey Player, Olympic Athlete)
6617 129th St W
Saint Paul, MN 55124, USA

Stroble, Bobby (Golfer)
526 W 2nd Ave
Albany, GA 31701-2205, USA

Strock, Donald J (Don) (Coach, Football Coach, Football Player)
Miami Dolphins
1512 Passion Vine Circle
Weston, FL 33326-3656, USA

Strode, Lester (Athlete, Baseball Player)
2523 Trenton Sta
Saint Charles, MO 63303-2913, USA

Strohmayer, John (Athlete, Baseball Player)
4379 Wild Flower Way
Redding, CA 96001-3776, USA

Strohmayer, Tod (Astronomer)
Goddard Space Flight Center
NASA/GSFC
Greenbelt, MD 20771, USA

Strolz, Hubert (Skier)
6767 Warth 19
AUSTRIA

Strom, Brent (Athlete, Baseball Player)
2202 N Catalina Vista Loop
Tucson, AZ 85749-7908, USA

Strom, Brock T (Football Player)
4301 W 110th St
Leawood, KS 66211, USA

Strom, Karin (Stylist)
150 Polkville Rd
Columbia, NJ 07832, USA

Strom, Rick (Football Player)
Pittsburgh Steelers
8905 Moor Park Run
Duluth, GA 30097-6622, USA

Stroma, Freddie (Actor)
c/o Danny Mancini *Affirmative Entertainment*
425 N Robertson Blvd
Los Angeles, CA 90048, USA

Stroman, Susan (Director)
c/o Leslee Dart *42West (NY)*
220 W 42nd St
12th Floor
New York, NY 10036, USA

Stromberg, Mike (Football Player)
New York Jets
PO Box 1510
Shelter Island, NY 11964-1510, USA

Strominger, Jack L (Misc)
Dana Faber Cancer Institute
Biochemistry Dept
44 Binney St
Boston, MA 02115, USA

Stronach, Belinda (Business Person)
Magna International
600 Wilshire Dr
Troy, MI 48084, USA

Strong, Brenda (Actor)
c/o Kay Liberman *Liberman/Zerman Management*
252 N Larchmont Blvd
Suite 200
Los Angeles, CA 90004, USA

Strong, Danny (Actor, Producer, Writer)
c/o Staff Member *The Gotham Group Inc*
9255 Sunset Blvd
Suite 515
Los Angeles, CA 90069, USA

Strong, Derek (Athlete, Basketball Player)
5434 Hillcrest Dr
Los Angeles, CA 90293-8716, USA

Strong, Jamal (Athlete, Baseball Player)
12635 Versaille St
Victorville, CA 92394-9568, USA

Strong, Jeremy (Actor)
c/o Meredith Wechter *ICM Partners (ICM-LA)*
10250 Constellation Blvd Fl 7
Los Angeles, CA 90067, USA

Strong, Jim (Football Player)
San Francisco 49ers
9303 Oxted Ln
Spring, TX 77379-6621, USA

Strong, Joe (Athlete, Baseball Player)
1340 Corcoran Ave
Vallejo, CA 94589-1878, USA

Strong, Johnny (Actor)
c/o Beverly Strong *Strong Management*
9350 Wilshire Blvd
#224
Beverly Hills, CA 90212, USA

Strong, Ken (Athlete, Hockey Player)
1100 Birchview Ave
Oakville, ON L6J 6N3, Canada

Strong, Mack (Football Player)
c/o Staff Member *Maxx Sports & Entertainment*
546 Fifth Ave Fl 6
New York, NY 10036, USA

Strong, Mark (Actor)
c/o Pippa Markham *Markham & Froggatt*
4 Windmill St
London W1T 1HZ, UK

Strong, Maurice F (Government Official)
255 Consummers Road
#401
Toronto, ON M2J 5B6, CANADA

Strong, Rider (Actor)
c/o Ellen Meyer *Ellen Meyer Management*
8899 Beverly Blvd
Suite 612
West Hollywood, CA 90048, USA

Strong, Tara (Actor)
c/o Jeff Danis *Danis, Panaro, Nist (DPN)*
9201 W Olympic Blvd
Beverly Hills, CA 90212, USA

Strongin-Weiss, Randy (Stylist)
10 Bittersweet Ct
Centerport, NY 11721, USA

Stroock, Daniel W (Mathematician)
55 Frost St
Cambridge, MA 02140, USA

Strossen, Nadine (Politician)
57 Worth St
New York, NY 10013-2926, USA

Strother, Dora Dougherty (Aviator)
16208 Bonneville Dr
Tampa, FL 33624-1113, USA

Stroud, Carlos (Misc)
Rockefeller University
Physics Dept
1230 York Ave
Cambridge, MA 02138, USA

Stroud, Don (Actor)
500 Lunalilo Home Rd #16A
Honolulu, HI 96825-1718, USA

Stroud, Les (Cinematographer, Director, Writer)
c/o Staff Member *Les Stroud Productions Inc.*
1235 Deerhurst Dr
Huntsville, Ontario P1H 2E8, Canada

Stroud, Morris (Athlete, Football Player)
11214 College Ave
Kansas City, MO 64137-2221, USA

Stroughter, Steve (Athlete, Baseball Player)
247 E Ashland Ave
Visalia, CA 93277-6702, USA

Stroup, Jessica (Actor)
c/o Erica Tarin *ID Public Relations (ID-LA)*
7060 Hollywood Blvd
8th Floor
Los Angeles, CA 90028, USA

Stroup Jr, Theodore G (Ted) (General)
2085 Hopewood Dr
Falls Church, VA 22043, USA

Strouse, Charles (Composer)
171 W 57th St
New York, NY 10019, USA

Strube, Juergen F (Business Person)
BASF Corp
Carl-Bosch Str 38
Ludwigshafen 67063, GERMANY

Struber, Larry (Producer)
c/o Staff Member *WmE2 (WMA-LA)*
1 William Morris Pl
Beverly Hills, CA 90212, USA

Struchkova, Raisa S (Ballerina)
Sovetskiy Ballet
Tverskaya 22B
Moscow 103050, RUSSIA

Struck, Heinz G (Scientist)
2304 Oakwood Ave NW
Huntsville, AL 35810-4408, USA

Strudwick, Suzanne (Golfer)
5500 Crestwood Dr
Knoxville, TN 37914-5108, USA

Struever, Stuart M (Misc)
200 Sheridan Road
Evanston, IL 60208, USA

Strug, Kerri (Athlete, Gymnast, Olympic Athlete)
1099 1st St
Coronado, CA 92118-1357, USA

Strugnell, John (Misc)
Harvard University
Divinity School
45 Francis Ave
Cambridge, MA 02138, USA

Strus, Lusia (Actor)
c/o Staff Member *Steve Himber Entertainment*
211 S Beverly Dr #601
Beverly Hills, CA 90212, USA

Struthers, Sally (Actor)
c/o Vincent Cirrincione *Vincent Cirrincione Associates*
1516 N Fairfax Ave
Los Angeles, CA 90046, USA

Struycken, Carel (Actor)
1665 E Mountain St
Pasadena, CA 91104, USA

Stryker, Bradley (Actor)
c/o Staff Member *House of Representatives, The*
1434 6th St
Suite 1
Santa Monica, CA 90401, USA

Strykert, Ron (Musician)
TPA
PO Box 124
Round Corner, NSW 2158, AUSTRALIA

Stuart, Brad (Athlete, Hockey Player)
C A A Sports
2000 Avenue of the Stars
Fl 3
Los Angeles, CA 90067-4704, USA

Stuart, Eric (Actor, Musician)
330 Carroll Street
Brooklyn, NY 11231, USA

Stuart, Jason (Actor, Comedian)
c/o Bonny Dore *Bonny Dore Management*
8530 Wilshire Blvd #400
Beverly Hills, CA 90211

Stuart, Katie (Actor)
c/o Russ Mortensen *Pacific Artists Management*
1285 W Broadway
Suite 685
Vancouver, BC V6H 3X8, Canada

Stuart, Katie (Actor)
c/o Blaine Greenberg *Speak Softly Legal Management*
13540 Ventura Blvd
Sherman Oaks, CA 91423, USA

Stuart, Lyle (Publisher)
1530 Palisade Ave
#6L
Fort Lee, NJ 07024, USA

Stuart, Mark (Athlete, Hockey Player)
6320 Oak Meadow Lane N.
Rochester, MN 55901, USA

Stuart, Marty (Musician, Songwriter)
c/o Staff Member *Paradigm (Monterey)*
404 W Franklin St
Monterey, CA 93940, USA

Stuart, Maxine (Actor)
S D B Partners
1801 Ave of Stars
#902
Los Angeles, CA 90067, USA

Stuart, Roy (Athlete, Football Player)
6800 S Granite Ave
Apt 339
Tulsa, OK 74136-7043, USA

Stubbins Jr, Hugh Asher (Architect)
6110 N Ocean Blvd
Boynton Beach, FL 33435, USA

Stubblefield, Dana W (Athlete, Football Player)
5226 Pisa Ct
San Jose, CA 95138-2122, USA

Stubblefield, Marga (Golfer)
PO Box 140
Kailua, HI 96734, USA

Stubblefield, Mickey (Athlete, Baseball Player)
Kansas City Monarchs
:4870 Seldon Way SE
Smyrna, GA 30080-9266, USA

Stubbs, Franklin (Athlete, Baseball Player)
13706 Mockingbird Dr
Prospect, KY 40059-9026, USA

Stubbs, Imogen M (Actor)
International Creative Mgmt
76 Oxford St
London W1N 0AX, UNITED KINGDOM (UK)

Stubing, Larry (Moose) (Athlete, Baseball Player, Coach)
10821 Laconia Dr
Villa Park, CA 92861-6408, USA

Stuck, Hans-Joachim (Race Car Driver)
Harmstatt 3
Ellmau/Tirol 6352, AUSTRIA

Stuckey, Henry (Athlete, Football Player)
3615 Winchester Avenue
Atlantic City, New Jersey 08401, USA

Stuckey, James (Jim) (Football Player)
San Francisco 49ers
2044 Egret Lane
Charleston, SC 29414-5302, USA

Stuckey, Joe (Stylist)
c/o Staff Member *L'Agence*
5901-C Peachtree Dunwoody Rd
#60
Atlanta, GA 30328, USA

Stuckey, Rodney (Athlete, Basketball Player)
c/o Steve Banks *Banks Sports Ventures*
1126 17th Ave
Seattle, WA 98122-4645, USA

Studaway, Mark (Football Player)
Houston Oilers
4524 Saint Honore Dr
Memphis, TN 38116-2012, USA

Studdard, Ruben (Musician)
c/o Cara Lewis *Creative Artists Agency (CAA-LA)*
1325 Ave of the Americas
New York, NY 10019, USA

Studdard, Vern (Football Player)
New York Jets
11449 Tara Blvd
Lovejoy, GA 30250, USA

Studer, Cheryl (Opera Singer)
Columbia Artists Mgmt Inc
165 W 57th St
New York, NY 10019, USA

Studi, Wes (Actor)
c/o Nevin Dolcefino *Innovative Artists (LA)*
1505 10th St
Santa Monica, CA 90401, USA

Studnicka-Caden, Mary Lou (Athlete, Baseball Player)
29 Mazarron Dr
Hot Springs Village, AR 71909-5827, USA

Studnicki-Caden, Mary Lou (Baseball Player)
29 Mazarron Dr
Hot Springs Village, AR 71909-5827, USA

Studstill, Patrick L (Pat) (Football Player)
Detroit Lions
2235 Linda Flora Dr
Los Angeles, CA 90077-1410, USA

Studt, Amy (Musician)

Studwell, Scott (Football Player)
Minnesota Vikings
10415 Brown Farm Cir
Eden Prairie, MN 55347-4926, USA

Stuffel, Paul (Athlete, Baseball Player)
25786 Buttercup Ct
Bonita Springs, FL 34135-9407, USA

Stuhlbarg, Michael (Actor)
c/o Lisa Loosemore *Viking Entertainment*
445 W 23rd St
Suite 1A
New York, NY 10011, USA

Stuhr, Jerzy (Actor, Director)
Graffutu Ltd
Ul SW Gertrudy 5
Cracow 31-107, POLAND

Stuhr-Thompsen, Beverly (Athlete, Baseball Player)
6379 N Muscatel Ave
San Gabriel, CA 91775-1843, USA

Stuhr-Thompson, Beverly (Baseball Player)
6379 N Muscatel Ave
San Gabriel, CA 91775-1843, USA

Stukes, Charles (Football Player)
Baltimore Colts
2040 Bishop St
Petersbug, VA 23805-2220, USA

Stull, Everett (Athlete, Baseball Player)
1667 Fieldgreen Overlook
Stone Mountain, GA 30088-3112, USA

Stults, Eric (Athlete, Baseball Player)
13810 Ranier Dr
Middlebury, IN 46540-8786, USA

Stults, Geoff (Actor)
c/o Ashley Franklin *Thruline Entertainment*
8383 Wilshire Blvd
Suite 1050
Beverly Hills, CA 90211, USA

Stults, George (Actor)
c/o Staff Member *Bleu, An Entertainment Company*
5225 Wilshire Blvd
Suite 701
Los Angeles, CA 90036, USA

Stump, David (Cinematographer)
HFWD Creative Representation
394 E Glaucus St
Encinitas, CA 92024, USA

Stump, Gene (Athlete, Basketball Player)
1418 Coral Ave
Vero Beach, FL 32803-6514, USA

Stump, Jim (Athlete, Baseball Player)
7432 Creekside Dr
Lansing, MI 48917-9693, USA

Stump, Patrick (Musician)
c/o Staff Member *Fueled By Ramen*
PO Box 1803
Tampa, FL 33601, USA

Stumpel, Jozef (Athlete, Hockey Player)
12057 NW 69th Court
Parkland, FL 33076-3335, USA

Stumpf, Kenneth E (General)
16528 State Highway 131
Tomah, WI 54660-6803, USA

Stumpf, Paul K (Misc)
1515 Shasta Dr
Apt 2219
Davis, CA 95616-6683, USA

Stumps, Kathy (Actor)
c/o Staff Member *Gersh (LA)*
9465 Wilshire Blvd
Suite 600
Beverly Hills, CA 90212, USA

Stunyo-Korpak, Jeanne (Athlete, Diver, Olympic Athlete)
1435 Almagre Peak Dr
Colorado Springs, CO 80921-3659, USA

Stuper, John (Athlete, Baseball Player)
38 Lake St
Hamden, CT 06517-2315, USA

Stura, Paul (Stylist)
c/o Staff Member *Katy Barker Agency Inc*
6606 10th Ave Apt 3R
Brooklyn, NY 11219, USA

Sturckow, Frederick W (Rick) (Astronaut)
RR 2 Box 14
Dickinson, TX 77539, USA

Sturckow, Frederick W "Rick" Lt Colonel (Astronaut)
7118 FM 517 Rd W
Dickinson, TX 77539-8751, USA

Sturgeon, Bob
3903 Lewis Ave.
Long Beach, CA 90807

Sturgess, Jim (Actor)
c/o Jodi Gottlieb *Independent Public Relations*
7060 Hollywood Blvd
8th Floor
Los Angeles, CA 90028, USA

Sturgess, Shannon (Actor)
1223 Wilshire Blvd
#577
Santa Monica, CA 90403, USA

Sturm, Jerry (Football Player)
Denver Broncos
3 Niblick Ln
Littleton, CO 80123-6621, USA

Sturm, John F (Misc)
Newspaper Assn of America
1921 Gallows Road
#4
Vienna, VA 22182, USA

Sturm, Marco (Athlete, Hockey Player)
500 Atlantic Ave Unit 14P
Boston, MA 02210-2245, USA

Sturm, Yfke (Model)
c/o Staff Member *Storm Model Management*
5 Jubilee Pl
1st Floor
London SW3 3TD, UNITED KINGDOM

Sturman, Eugene (Artist)
1108 W Washington Blvd
Venice, CA 90291, USA

Sturmer, Christina (Musician)
Postfach 113
Wien A-1218, Austria

Sturr, Jimmy (Musician)
United Polka Artists
PO Box 1
Florida, NY 10921, USA

Sturridge, Charles (Director)
PFD
Drury House
34-43 Russell St
London WC2B 5HA, UNITED KINGDOM (UK)

Sturridge, Tom (Actor)
c/o Sarah Spear *Curtis Brown Ltd*
Hay Market House
28-29 Hay Market
London SW1Y 4SP, UK

Sturt, Fred (Football Player)
Washington Redskins
120 N Berkey Southern Rd
Swanton, OH 43558-8907, USA

Sturtevant, Julian M (Misc)
14025 3rd Ave
NW
Seattle, WA 98177, USA

Sturtze, Tanyon (Athlete, Baseball Player)
7 E Lake St
Worcester, MA 01604-1315, USA

Sturza, Ion (Prime Minister)
Premier's Office
Piaca Maril Atuner Nacional
Chishinev 277033, MOLDOVA

Stutter, Jason (Director, Producer, Writer)
c/o Simon Millar *Rumble Media*
1620 Broadway
Santa Monica, CA 90403, USA

Stuttering John (Radio Personality)
c/o Staff Member *Howard Stern Show*
Sirius Satellite Radio
1221 Avenue of the Americas
New York, NY 10020, USA

Stutzman, Martin (Congressman, Politician)
1728 Longworth HOB
Washington, DC 20515, USA

Stutzmann, Nathalie (Opera Singer)
Herbert Breslin
119 W 57th St
#1505
New York, NY 10019, USA

Styler, Kara
PO Box 8002
Honolulu, HI 96820

Styler, Trudie (Actor, Director, Producer)
c/o Staff Member *Xingu Films*
12 Cleveland Row
St James
London SW1A 1DH, UNITED KINGDOM (UK)

Styles, Harry (Musician)
Erskine House
Spaniards Road
Hamstead, London NW3 7JJ, UNITED KINGDOM

Styles, Stephanie (Stylist)
622 Washington St
#2-A
New York, NY 10014, USA

Stynes, Chris (Athlete, Baseball Player)
1980 NE 7th St
Suite 106
Deerfield Beach, FL 33441-3778, USA

Styx (Music Group, Musician)
c/o Keith Naisbitt *Agency Group Ltd, The (LA)*
1880 Century Park E
Suite 711
Los Angeles, CA 90067, USA

Suarez, Carlos (Actor)
c/o Staff Member *Televisa*
Blvd Adolfo Lopez Mateos 232
Colonia San Angel INN
DF CP 01060, MEXICO

Suarez, Ken (Athlete, Baseball Player)
6000 Forest Ln
Fort Worth, TX 76112-1060, USA

Suarez Gomez, Hector (Actor)
c/o Gabriel Blanco *Gabriel Blanco Iglesias (Mexico)*
Rio Balsas 35-32
Colonia Cuauhtemoc
DF 06500, Mexico

Suarez Gonzalez, Adolfo (Prime Minister)
Sagasta
33
Madrid 4, SPAIN

Suarez Rivera, Adolfo A Cardinal (Religious Leader)
Apartado Postal 7
Loma Larga 2429 Sierra Madre
Monterrey 64000, MEXICO

Suau, Anthony (Photographer)
Denver Post
Denver Post PO Box 1709
Denver, CO 80201-1709, USA

Suazo, Chloe (Actor)
c/o Cindy Osbrink *Osbrink Talent Agency*
4343 Lankershim Blvd
Suite 100
Universal City, CA 91602, USA

Subhash, B (Actor, Bollywood)
1 Coelho House
Juhu Tara Road Juhu
Mumbai, MS 400049, INDIA

Sublime (Music Group, Musician)
c/o Jon Phillips *Silverback Professional Artist Management*
9469 Jefferson Blvd
Suite 101
Culver City, CA 90232, USA

Subotnick, Morton L (Composer)
25 Minetta Lane
#4B
New York, NY 10012, USA

Subways, The (Music Group)
c/o Staff Member *Paradigm (Monterey)*
404 W Franklin St
Monterey, CA 93940, USA

Such, Alec John (Musician)
Bon Jovi Mgmt
248 W 17th St
#501
New York, NY 10011, USA

Such, Dick (Athlete, Baseball Player)
7614 Divot Dr
Sanford, NC 27332-8804, USA

Sucherman, Todd (Musician)
c/o Sterling Bacon *TBA Artist Management (Atlanta)*
1111 Alderman Dr #285
Alpharetta, GA 30005-5433, USA

Suchet, David (Actor, Producer)
c/o Sarah Jackson *Seven Summits Pictures & Management*
8906 W Olympic Blvd
Ground Floor
Beverly Hills, CA 90211, USA

Suchocka, Hanna (Prime Minister)
Urzad Rady Ministrow
Al Ujazdowskie 1/3
Warsaw 00-567, POLAND

Suci, Robert (Football Player)
Houston Oilers
2341 Morton Ave
Flint, MI 48507-4445, USA

Sudakis, Bill (Athlete, Baseball Player)
81150 Avenida Graneros
Indio, CA 92203-7894, USA

Sudan, Madhu (Scientist)
81 Benton Road
Somerville, MA 02143, USA

Sudduth, Jill (Athlete, Swimmer)
9917 Calabasas Avenue
Las Vegas, NV 89117, USA

Sudduth, Skipp (Actor)
c/o Heather Reynolds *One Entertainment (NY)*
12 W 57th St
Penthouse
New York, NY 10019, USA

Sudduth-Smith, Jill (Athlete, Olympic Athlete, Swimmer)
7615 Kiva Dr
Austin, TX 78749-2915, USA

Sudeikis, Jason (Actor, Comedian)
c/o Geoff Cheddy *Brillstein Entertainment Partners*
9150 Wilshire Blvd #350
Beverly Hills, CA 90212, USA

Sudersham, Ennackel (Physicist)
University of Texas
Physics Dept
Austin, TX 78713, USA

Sudharmono (General, Government Official)
Senopati St 44B
Jakarta Selatan, INDONESIA

Sudol, Alison (Actor, Musician)
c/o Julie Colbert *WME (LA)*
9601 Wilshire Blvd Fl 3
Beverly Hills, CA 90210, USA

Suede
PO Box 3431
London, ENGLAND N1 7LW

Suerth, Herbert (General)
2850 West Rd
Wavzata, MN 55391-2749, USA

Sues, Alan (Actor)
9014 Dorrington Ave
West Hollywood, CA 90048, USA

Suess, Hans E (Misc)
University of California
Chemistry Dept
La Jolla, CA 92093, USA

Suganya (Actor, Bollywood)
4/5 Oorur Alcot
5thAvenue Besant Nagar
Chennai, TN 600090, INDIA

Sugar, Alan (Business Person, Reality TV Star)
Amstrad Plc
Brentwood House
169 Kings Rd
Brentwood, Essex CM14 4EF, UK

Sugar, Leo T (Football Player)
Chicago Cardinals
7161 Golden Eagle Court
#1012
Fort Myers, FL 33912-1708, USA

Sugarcult (Actor)
Kio Novina Management & Booking
545 N Rossmore Ave
#3
Los Angeles, CA 90004

Sugarland (Music Group)
c/o Staff Member *Gail Gellman Management*
23852 Pacific Coast Highway
Malibu, CA 90265, USA

Sugarman, Burt (Producer)
Giant Group
9440 Santa Monica Blvd
#407
Beverly Hills, CA 90210, USA

Sugarman, Joseph (Joe) (Business Person, Writer)
Blublocker Corp
3350 Palm Center Dr
Las Vegas, NV 89103, USA

Sugarman, Josh (Activist)
1650 Harvard St NW
Washington, DC 20009, USA

Sugg, Diana K (Journalist)
Baltimore Sun
Editorial Dept
501 N Calvert St
Baltimore, MD 21202, USA

Suggs, M Louise (Golfer)
424 Royal Crescent Court
Saint Augustine, FL 32092, USA

Suggs, Shafer (Athlete, Football Player)
12849 Barrow Ln
Plainfield, IL 60585-4214, USA

Suggs, Terrell (Athlete, Football Player)
Baltimore Ravens
Ravens Stadium
11001 Russell St
Baltimore, MD 21230, USA

Suggs, Walt (Football Player)
Houston Oilers
11105 Bradyville Pike
Readyville, TN 37149-4513, USA

Suh, Ndamukong (Athlete, Football Player)
c/o Roosevelt Barnes *Maximum Sports Management*
6435 W Jefferson Blvd
#197
Fort Wayne, IN 46804, USA

Suharto, Mohamed (General, President)
8 Jalan Cendana
Jakarta, INDONESIA

suharto, Mohammed (Politician)
8 Jalan Cendana
Jakarta, Indonesia

Suhey, Matthew J (Matt) (Football Player)
Chicago Bears
550 Carriage Way
Deerfield, IL 60015-4535, USA

Suhl, Harry (Physicist)
University of California
Physics Dept
9500 Gilman Dr
La Jolla, CA 92093, USA

Suhonen, Alpo (Coach)
Chicago Blackhawks
United Center
1901 W Madison St
Chicago, IL 60612, USA

Suhor, Yvonne (Actor)
J Michael Bloom
233 Park Ave S
#1000
New York, NY 10003, USA

Suhrheinrich, Richard F (Judge)
US Court of Appeals
315 W Allegan
Lansing, MI 48933, USA

Suhrstedt, Timothy (Cinematographer)
Gersh Agency
232 N Canon Dr
Beverly Hills, CA 90210, USA

Suitner, Otmar
Platanestr 13
Berlin-Niederschonhausen 13156,
GERMANY

Suits, Julia (Cartoonist)
Creators Syndicate
5777 W Century Blvd
#700
Los Angeles, CA 90045, USA

Sukla, Ed (Athlete, Baseball Player)
16 Perch
Irvine, CA 92604-3688, USA

Sukova, Helena (Tennis Player)
1 Ave Grande Bretagne
Monte Carlo, MONACO

Sukowa, Barbara (Actor)
Artmedia
20 Ave Rapp
Paris 75007, FRANCE

Sukselainen, Vieno J (Prime Minister)
Palvattarenpolku 2
Tapiola 02100, FINALND

Sulaiman, Jose (Misc)
World Boxing Council
Genova 33
Colonia Juarez
Cuahtetemoc 0660, MEXICO

Sularz, Guy (Athlete, Baseball Player)
10818 N 83rd St
Scottsdale, AZ 85260-6550, USa

Suleman, Nadya (Octomom) (Reality TV Star)
2051 Madonna Ln
La Habra, CA 90631, USA

Suleymanoglu, Naim (Wrestler)
Olympic Committee
Sisli
Buyukdere Cad 18 Tankaya
Istanbul, TURKEY

Sulin, Suzanne (Stylist)
c/o Staff Member *Ford Models (Chicago)*
311 W Superior St
Chicago, IL 60654, USA

Suliotis, Elena (Opera Singer)
Villa il Poderino
Via Incontri
Florence 38, ITALY

Sulkin, Gregg (Actor)
c/o Danielle Allman-Del *D2 Management*
141 S. Barrington Ave
Los Angeles, CA 90049, USA

Sulliman, Doug (Athlete, Hockey Player)
117454 N 100th Pl
Scottsdale, AZ 85255, USA

Sullivan, Brian (Athlete, Hockey Player)
392 E Beach Rd
Charlestown, RI 02813-1311, USA

Sullivan, Charlotte (Actor)
c/o Evan Hainey *Untitled Entertainment (LA)*
350 S. Beverly Dr #200
Beverly Hills, CA 90212, USA

Sullivan, Chip (Golfer)
49 Homestead Cir
Troutville, VA 24175-6995, USA

Sullivan, CHris (Football Player)
New England Patriots
64 Wagon Wheel Rd
North Attleboro, MA 02760-3576, USA

Sullivan, Cory (Athlete, Baseball Player)
1214 S Ogden St
Denver, CO 80210, USA

Sullivan, Dan (Football Player)
Baltimore Colts
25 Algonquin Ave
Andover, MA 01810-5527, USA

Sullivan, Daniel (Producer, Writer)
c/o Alan Wertheimer *Jackoway Tyerman Wertheimer Austen Mandelbaum Morris & Klein*
1925 Century Park E
22nd Floor
Los Angeles, CA 90067, USA

Sullivan, Danny (Race Car Driver)
4042 Ormond Rd.
Louisville, KY 40207, USA

Sullivan, Dennis P (Mathematician)
Queens College
Mathematics Dept
33 W 42nd St #308
New York, NY 10036, USA

Sullivan, Erik Per (Actor)
c/o Suzanne Smith *Suzanne Smith Management*
451 Greenwich St #500
New York, NY 10103, USA

Sullivan, Frank (Athlete, Baseball Player)
PO Box 1873
Lihue, HI 96766-5873, USA

Sullivan, Franklin L (Frank) (Athlete, Baseball Player)
P.O. Box 1873
Lihue, HI 96766, USA

Sullivan, George (Football Player)
Boston Yanks
41 Howard St
Norwood, MA 02062-2323, USA

Sullivan, George "Red" (Athlete, Hockey Player)
RR 2
Indian River, ON K0L 2B0, Canada

Sullivan, Greg (Musician)
David Levin Mgmt
200 W 57th St
#308
New York, NY 10019, USA

Sullivan, James V Colonel (Aviator)
5513 Belmont Ct
Stansbury Park, UT 84074-8131, USA

Sullivan, Jazmine (Musician)
c/o Daniel Kim *WME (LA)*
9601 Wilshire Blvd Fl 3
Beverly Hills, CA 90210, USA

Sullivan, John (Athlete, Baseball Player)
24 Highland Ave
Dansville, NY 14437-1648, USA

Sullivan, John (Congressman, Politician)
434 Cannon HOB
Washington, DC 20515, USA

Sullivan, Julie (Stylist)
c/o Staff Member *Artist Agency, THE (NY)*
230 W 55th St #29D
New York, NY 10019

Sullivan, Kathleen (Journalist)
1025 N Kings Road
#202
West Hollywood, CA 90069-6008, USA

Sullivan, Kathryn D (Astronaut)
795 Old Oak Trace
Columbus, OH 43235, USA

Sullivan, Kathryn D Dr (Astronaut)
795 Old Oak Tree
Columbus, OH 43235-1761, USA

Sullivan, Kevin (Journalist)
Washington Post
Editorial Dept
1150 15th St NW
Washington, DC 20071, USA

Sullivan, Kevin Rodney (Actor, Director, Producer, Writer)
c/o Arnold Robinson *Rogers & Cowan PR (LA)*
Pacific Design Center
8687 Melrose Ave, 7th Floor
West Hollywood, CA 90069, USA

Sullivan, Louis (Politician)
Morehouse College
5287 N Powers Ferry Rd NW
Atlanta, GA 30327-4666, USA

Sullivan, Marc (Athlete, Baseball Player)
2038 W 1st St
Suite 100
Fort Myers, FL 33901-3109, USA

Sullivan, Michael J (Mike) (Politician)
Rothgerber, Johnson, & Lyons
1124 S Durbin St
Casper, WY 82601-4328, USA

Sullivan, Mike (Athlete, Coach, Hockey Player)
256 Washington St
Duxbury, MA 02332-4548, USA

Sullivan, Mike (Athlete, Football Player)
Cleveland Brown
76 Lou Groza Blvd
Attn: Coaching Staff
Berea, OH 44017, USA

Sullivan, Nicole (Actor)
c/o Jonathan Howard *Innovative Artists (LA)*
1505 10th St
Santa Monica, CA 90401, USA

Sullivan, Pat (Coach, Football Coach, Football Player, Heisman Trophy Winner)
1717 Indian Creek Dr
Vestavia, AL 35243-1745, USA

Sullivan, Peter (Athlete, Hockey Player)
316 Fairway Rd
Regina, SK S4Y 1JS, Canada

Sullivan, Phil (Football Player)
New York Jets
4113 Rollingwood Ct
Jacksonville, FL 32257-7665, USA

Sullivan, Russ (Athlete, Baseball Player)
1701 Hill N Dale St
Fredericksburg, VA 22405, USA

Sullivan, Scott (Athlete, Baseball Player)
1649 Mayfair Ct
Auburn, AL 36830-2128, USA

Sullivan, Steve (Athlete, Hockey Player)
5536 Iron Gate Dr
Franklin, TN 37069-7238, USA

Sullivan, Susan (Actor)
c/o Staff Member *Paradigm (LA)*
360 N Crescent Dr
North Bldg
Beverly Hills, CA 90210, USA

Sullivan, Tim (Director)
Agency for Performing Arts
9200 Sunset Blvd
#900
Los Angeles, CA 90069, USA

Sullivan, Timothy J (Educator)
College of William & Mary
President's Office
Williamsburg, VA 23187, USA

Sullivan, Tom (Actor, Writer)
c/o Chris Ridenhour *Evolution Entertainment (LA)*
901 N Highland Ave
Los Angeles, CA 90038, USA

Sullivan, William J (Educator)
Seattle University
President's Office
Seattle, WA 98122, USA

Sullivan Jr, Brendan V (Lawyer)
Williams & Connolly
725 12th St NW
Washington, DC 20005, USA

Sullivan Jr, Brendon V
725 12th St NW
Washington, DC 20005, USA

Sulston, John E (Nobel Prize Laureate)
The Sanger Centre Wellcome Trust
Genome Campus Hinxton
Cambridge CB10 1SA, England

Sultan, Altoon (Artist)
PO Box 2
Groton, VT 05046, USA

Sultan, Donald K (Artist)
19 E 70th St
New York, NY 10021, USA

Sultan of Brunei
Bandar Seri
Begawan, BRUNEI

Sultanov, Alexel (Musician)
Columbia Artists Mgmt Inc
165 W 57th St
New York, NY 10019, USA

Sultan Salman, Abdulaziz Al-Saud
(Astronaut)
PO Box 18368
Riyadh 11415, SAUDI ARABIA

Sultonov, Outkir T (Prime Minister)
Prime Minister's Office
Mustarilik 5
Tashkent 70008, UZBEKISTAN

Sum 41 (Music Group)
c/o Ron Laffitte *Red Light Management (LA)*
8439 W Sunset Blvd
Suite 2
Los Angeles, CA 90069, USA

Suman, Shekhar (Actor, Bollywood, Comedian, Talk Show Host)
1 Krishna Apartments 168 Sher-E-Punjab Colony
Mahakali Caves Road Andheri (E)
Bombay, MS 400 093, INDIA

Sumaye, Frederick T (Prime Minister)
Prime Minister's Office
PO Box 980
Dodoma, TANZANIA

Sumerfelt, Josh
6550 Yucca #310
Los Angeles, CA 90028

Sumika, Aya (Actor)
c/o Jill Littman *Impression Entertainment*
9229 W Sunset Blvd #700
West Hollywood, CA 90069, USA

Sumino, Naoko (Astronaut)
NASDA
Tsukuba Space Center
2-1-1 Sengen Tukubashi
Ibaraka 305, JAPAN

Summer, Cree (Actor)
Monterey Peninsula Artists
509 Hartnell St
Monterey, CA 93940, USA

Summerall, Pat (Sportscaster)
Detroit Lions
710 S White Chapel Blvd
Southlake, TX 76092-7319, USA

Summer-Francks, Cree
PO Box 5617
Beverly Hills, CA 90210

Summerhays, Bob (Athlete, Football Player)
12345 SE 91st Avenue
Summerfield, FL 34491-8251, USA

Summerhays, Boyd (Athlete, Golfer)
297 Frontier Rd
Farmington, UT 84025-2616, USA

Summerleigh, George A (Pat) (Football Player)
710 S White Chapel Blvd
Southlake, TX 76092, USA

Summers, Andy (Musician)
1111 San Vicente Blvd
Santa Monica, CA 90402, USA

Summers, Carol (Artist)
2817 Smith Grade
Santa Cruz, CA 95060, USA

Summers, Champ (Athlete, Baseball Player)
13708 SW 111th Ave
Dunnellon, FL 34432-8797, USA

Summers, Dana (Cartoonist)
Orlando Sentinel
Editorial Dept
633 N Orange Ave
Orlando, FL 32801, USA

Summers, Henry (Stylist)
69 Edgewood Ave
Clifton, NJ 07012, USA

Summers, Isabel (Stylist)
300 Mercer St
#9-H
New York, NY 10003, USA

Summers, Jerry (Musician)
American Promotions
2011 Ferry Ave
#U19
Camden, NJ 08104, USA

Summers, Lawrence (Politician)
Harvard University
5409 Falmouth Rd
Bethesda, MD 20816-2918, USA

Summers, Marc (Actor, Chef, Director, Producer, Television Host)
c/o Staff Member *Marc Summers Productions*
23705 Vanowen Street
Suite 105
Canoga Park, CA 91307-3030, USA

Summers, Tara (Actor)
c/o Lena Roklin *Luber Roklin Management*
8530 Wilshire Blvd
6th Floor
Beverly Hills, CA 90211, USA

Summers, Wilbur (Football Player)
Detroit Lions
PO Box 72734
Louisville, KY 40272-0734, USA

Summers, Yale (Actor)
c/o Staff Member *Screen Actors Guild (SAG-LA)*
5757 Wilshire Blvd
Los Angeles, CA 90036, USA

Summitt, Pat (Athlete, Basketball Player, Olympic Athlete)
3720 River Trace Ln
Knoxville, TN 37920-7118, USA

Sumner, Peter (Actor)
15/71 Avenue Road
Mosman 2088, AUSTRALIA

Sumner, Walt (Football Player)
Cleveland Browns
PO Box 112
Ocilla, GA 31774-0112, USA

Sumners, Rosalynn (Athlete, Figure Skater, Olympic Athlete)
7815 115th Pl NE
Kirkland, WA 98033-6710, USA

Sumpter, Jeremy (Actor)
c/o Mark Robert *Mark Robert Management*
2208 Patricia Ave
Los Angeles, CA 90064, USA

Sumpter, Tony (Football Player)
Chicago Rockets
702 S Gray St
Stillwater, OK 74074-4331, USA

Sundance, Robert (Activist)
California Indian Alcoholism Commission
225 W 8th St
Los Angeles, CA 90014, USA

Sun Dao Lin (Actor, Director)
Shanghai Film Studio
595 Tsao Hsi North Road
Shanghai 200030, CHINA

Sunday, Gabriel (Actor)
c/o Judy Savage *Savage Agency*
6212 Banner Ave
Los Angeles, CA 90038, USA

Sundberg, Jim (Athlete, Baseball Player)
2308 Newforest Ct
Arlington, TX 76017-2638, USA

Sunde, Milt (Football Player)
Minnesota Vikings
6008 W 104th St
Bloomington, MN 55438-1826, USA

Sunderland, Zac (Athlete)
1710 N. Moorpark Road
#212
Thousand Oaks, CA 91360, USA

Sundhage, Pia (Coach)
U.S. Soccer Federation
Women's National Team
1801 S. Prairie Ave.
Chicago, IL 60616, USA

Sundin, Gordie (Athlete, Baseball Player)
28132 Goby Trl
Bonita Springs, FL 34135-8469, USA

Sundin, Mats (Athlete, Hockey Player)
C A A Hockey
204-822 11 Ave SW
Attn J P Barry
Calgary, AB T2R OES, Canada

Sundstrom, Peter (Athlete, Hockey Player)
Bygardesvagen 32
Malmo 21621, Sweden

Sundvold, Jon (Athlete, Basketball Player)
2700 Westbrook Way
Columbia, MO 65203-5221, USA

Sung, Elizabeth (Actor)
GVA Talent
9229 Sunset Blvd
#320
Los Angeles, CA 90069, USA

Sunjata, Daniel (Actor)
c/o Meg Mortimer *Principal Entertainment (NY)*
130 W 42nd St
Suite 614
New York, NY 10036, USA

Sunshine, Caroline (Actor)
c/o Reg Reg Askew *Fly Guy Management*
1 W 34th St #201
New York, NY 10016, USA

Sunshine Underground, The (Music Group)
c/o Staff Member *Paradigm (Monterey)*
404 W Franklin St
Monterey, CA 93940, USA

Sununu, John E (Politician)
49 Linden Rd
Hampton Falls, NH 03844-2035, USA

Sunyaev, Rashid A (Scientist)
Russian Academy of Sciences
Profsoyuznaya St 84/32 Space Research Institute
Moscow 117810, Russia

Suomi, Al (Athlete, Hockey Player)
5847 Sunset Ave
La Grange Highlands, IL 60525-7118, USA

Superdrag (Music Group)
c/o Staff Member *Paradigm (Monterey)*
404 W Franklin St
Monterey, CA 93940, USA

Supergrass (Music Group)
c/o Staff Member *Paradigm (Monterey)*
404 W Franklin St
Monterey, CA 93940, USA

Supernaw, Kywin (Football Player)
Detroit Lions
1123 Clairborne Ct
Indianapolis, IN 46280-1100, USA

Supertramp
16530 Ventura Blvd. #201
Encino, CA 91436

Suplee, Ethan (Actor)
Don Buchwald
6500 Wilshire Blvd
#2200
Los Angeles, CA 90048, USA

Suppan, Jeff (Athlete, Baseball Player)
25315 Prado De La Felicidad
Calabasas, CA 91302-3651, USA

Suppes, Patrick (Psychic)
678 Mirada Ave
Stanford, CA 94305, USA

Supremes, The (Music Group)
PO Box 1821
Ojai, CA 93024

Suquia Goicoechea, Angel Cardinal
(Religious Leader)
El Cardenal Arxobispo
San Justo 2
Madrid 28074, SPAIN

Sura, Bob (Basketball Player)
Atlanta Hawks
190 Marietta St SW
Atlanta, GA 77019-1845, USA

Sure, Al B (Musician)
c/o Staff Member *ICM Partners (ICM-LA)*
10250 Constellation Blvd Fl 7
Los Angeles, CA 90067, USA

Surhoff, BJ (Athlete, Baseball Player,
Olympic Athlete)
2205 Pine Hill Farms Ln
Cockeysville, MD 21030-1023, USA

Surhoff, Rick (Athlete, Baseball Player)
1839 White Oak Dr
Reading, PA 19608-9468, USA

Surin, Bruny (Athlete, Track Athlete)
PO Box 2
Succ Saint Michel
Montreal, QC H2A 3L8, CANADA

Surkowski-Delmonico, Lee (Athlete,
Baseball Player)
10 Via Las Colinas Apt 1
Rancho Mirage, CA 92270-6015, USA

Surkowski-Deyotte, Anne (Athlete,
Baseball Player)
632 Southwind Dr
Kelowna, BC V1W 3G1, CANADA

Surma, Damian (Athlete, Hockey Player)
1057 Emmons Blvd
Lincoln Park, MI 48146-4240, USA

Surman, Jamie (Stylist)
c/o Staff Member *Jed Root Inc*
61-A Walker St
New York, NY 10013, USA

Surratt, Al (Baseball Player)
Kansas City Monarchs
3448 E 54th St
Kansas City, MO 64130-4027, USA

Sursok, Tammin (Actor)
c/o David Gardner *Principato/Young
Management*
9465 Wilshire Blvd
Suite 430
Beverly Hills, CA 90212, USA

Surtain, Patrick (Athlete, Football Player)
14557 Sherwood Road
Overland Park, KS 66224-9807, USA

Surtees, John (Race Car Driver)
Team Surtees
P.O. Box 1018
Talladega, AL 35161, USA

Survivor
PO Box 1821
Ojai, CA 93024

Susa, Conrad (Composer)
433 Eureka St
San Francisco, CA 94114, USA

Susana, Marta (Actor)
c/o Staff Member *Univision*
605 3rd St. Fl12
New York, NY 10158, USA

Susanka, Sarah (Architect, Writer)
c/o Suzanne Fedoruk *Fedoruk &
Associates*
P.O. Box 43298
Minneapolis, MN 55423, USA

Suschitzky, J Peter (Cinematographer)
13 priory Road
London NW6 4NN, UNITED KINGDOM
(UK)

Suschitzky, Wolfgang (Cinematographer)
Douglas House
6 Maida Ave #11
London W2 1TG, UNITED KINGDOM
(UK)

Susclick, Kenneth S (Misc)
University of Illinois
Chemistry Dept
Champaign, IL 61820, USA

Susco, Stephen (Producer, Writer)
c/o Chris Ridenhour *Evolution
Entertainment (LA)*
901 N Highland Ave
Los Angeles, CA 90038, USA

Susi, Carol Ann (Actor)
846 N Sweetzer Ave
Los Angeles, CA 90069, USA

Susman, Todd (Actor)
Pakula/King
9229 Sunset Blvd
#315
Los Angeles, CA 90069, USA

Sussin, Christen (Actor)
c/o Elizabeth Much *Much and House
Public Relations*
8075 W 3rd St
Suite 500
Los Angeles, CA 90048, USA

Sussman, Adam (Writer)
c/o Staff Member *McKuin Frankel
Whitehead*
141 El Camino Dr
Suite 100
Beverly Hills, CA 90212, USA

Sussman, Kevin (Actor)
c/o Jill McGrath *The Group Entertainment*
275 Seventh Ave
26th Floor
New York, NY 10001, USA

Sussman, Susan
927 Noyes St.
Evanston, IL 60201

Sutcliffe, David (Actor)
c/o Robert Stein *Robert Stein Management*
PO Box 3797
Beverly Hills, CA 90212, USA

Sutcliffe, Richard L (Rick) (Athlete,
Baseball Player)
616 NE Seabrook Ct
Lees Summit, MO 64064-1261, USA

Suter, Bob (Athlete, Hockey Player,
Olympic Athlete)
2961 Waubesa Ave
Madison, WI 53711, USA

Suter, Gary (Athlete, Hockey Player,
Olympic Athlete)
2128 County Road D
Lac Du Flambeau, WI 54538-9726, USA

Suter, Ryan (Athlete, Hockey Player)
1554 Shining Ore Dr
Brentwood, TN 37027-2218, USA

Sutera, Paul
11365 Ventura Blvd. #100
Studio City, CA 91604-7403

Sutherin, Don (Athlete, Football Player)
1043 Cayuga Trl SW
Hartville, OH 44632-9488, USA

Sutherland, Bill (Athlete, Hockey Player)
41-472 Templeton Ave
Winnipeg, MB R2V 4Y8, Canada

Sutherland, Bill (Actor)
c/o Staff Member *Select Artists Ltd (CA-
Westside Office)*
1138 12th Street
Suite 1
Santa Monica, CA 90403, USA

Sutherland, Darrell (Athlete, Baseball
Player)
1011 NW Jeffrey Pl
Beaverton, OR 97006-6335, USA

Sutherland, David (Golfer)
5431 Tree Side Dr
Carmichael, CA 95608, USA

Sutherland, Donald (Actor, Musician,
Producer, Writer)
c/o Allen Eichhorn *PMK/BNC Public
Relations (PMK-NY)*
622 3rd Ave
8th Floor
New York, NY 10017, USA

Sutherland, Doug (Football Player)
New Orleans Saints
511 Kenilworth Ave
Duluth, MN 55803-2113, USA

Sutherland, Gary (Athlete, Baseball
Player)
338 Oakcliff Rd
Monrovia, CA 91016-1823, USA

Sutherland, Kevin (Golfer)
1230 Carter Rd
Sacramento, CA 95864-5328, USA

Sutherland, Kiefer (Actor, Director,
Producer)
c/o Suzan Bymel *Management 360*
9111 Wilshire Blvd
Beverly Hills, CA 90210, USA

Sutherland, Kristine (Actor)
c/o Staff Member *Silver Massetti &
Szatmary (SMS) Talent Inc*
8383 Wilshire Blvd
Suite 230
Beverly Hills, CA 90211, USA

Sutherland, Leo (Athlete, Baseball Player)
12082 Nieta Dr
Garden Grove, CA 92840-3524, USA

Sutherland, Peter D (Government
Official)
68 Eglinton Road
Dublin 4, IRELAND

Sutherland, Shirley (Athlete, Baseball
Player)
9613 Ritter Dr
Machesney Park, IL 61115-1759, USA

Sutherland, Steve (Athlete, Hockey
Player)
275 Av Wilfrid-Laurier
Quebec, QC G1R 2K8, Canada

Sutherland, Thomas
229 Columbine Ct.
Ft. Collins, CO 80521

Sutko, Glenn (Athlete, Baseball Player)
4475 Settles Bridge Rd
Suwanee, GA 30024-1981, USA

Sutkus, Mary (Stylist)
720 Limedale Lane
Florissant, MO 63031, USA

Sutor, George (Athlete, Basketball Player)
29840 State Highway 27
Holcombe, WI 54745-8798, USA

Sutorius, James
14014 Milbank St. #1
Sherman Oaks, CA 91423

Sutter, Brent (Athlete, Coach, Hockey
Player)
PO Box 545
Viking, AB T0B 4N0, Canada

Sutter, Brent (Athlete, Hockey Player)
Calgary Flames PO Box 1540 Stn M
Attn: Coaching Staff
Calgary, AB T2P 3B9, Canada

Sutter, Brian (Athlete, Coach, Hockey
Player)
PO Box 545
Viking, AB T0B 4N0, Canada

Sutter, Bruce (Athlete, Baseball Player)
59 Waterside Dr SE
Cartersville, GA 30121-6615, USA

Sutter, Darryl (Athlete, Coach, Hockey
Player)
P.O. Box 1540
Station M
Calgary, AB T2P 3B9, Canada

Sutter, Duane (Athlete, Hockey Player)
3703 High Pine Dr
Coral Springs, FL 33065, USA

Sutter, Eddie (Football Player)
Cleveland Browns
5104 N Bevalon Pl
Peoria, IL 61614-4606, USA

Sutter, Rich (Athlete, Hockey Player)
Sutter Ice 1920 17 St
Coaldale, AB T1M 1M1, Canada

Sutter, Ron (Athlete, Hockey Player)
44 Chaparral Cove SE
Calgary, AB T2X 3L4, Canada

Sutter, Ryan (Football Player)
Carolina Panthers
2405 Rollingwood Dr
Fort Collins, CO 80525-1943, USA

Sutter, Trista (Reality TV Star)
42 W Meadow Dr
Vail, Colorado 81657, USA

Sutterluty, Elizabeth (Actor)
Cineart
36 Rue de Ponthleu
Paris 75008, FRANCE

Suttle, Dane (Athlete, Basketball Player)
138 W 69th St
Los Angeles, CA 90003-1824, USA

Sutton, Andy (Athlete, Hockey Player)
491 Peachtree Battle Ave NW
Atlanta, GA 30305-4062, USA

Sutton, Betty (Congressman, Politician)
1519 Longworth HOB
Washington, DC 20515, USA

Sutton, Daron (Baseball Player)
8645 E Chervl Dr
Scottsdale, AZ 85258-1435, USA

Sutton, Don (Athlete, Baseball Player)
611 Riverlawn Ct
Atlanta, GA 30339-2993, USA

Sutton, Drew (Athlete, Baseball Player)
1600 Birch mont Ln
Keller, TX 76248-8221, USA

Sutton, Greg (Athlete, Basketball Player)
P.O. Box 1801
Edmond, OK 73083-8101, USA

Sutton, Hal (Golfer)
909 Trabue St
Shreveport, LA 71106-1114, USA

Sutton, Joe (Football Player)
Philadelphia Eagles
508 44th Ave E Lot K48
Bradenton, FL 34203-7526, USA

Sutton, John (Athlete, Baseball Player)
536 Blueberry Blvd
Dallas, TX 75217-4201, USA

Sutton, Kelly (Race Car Driver)
8410 Streamview Dr
#G
Huntsville, TN 28070, USA

Sutton, Ken (Athlete, Hockey Player)
223 Oakfern Way SW
Calgary, AB T2V 4K2, Canada

Sutton, Larry (Athlete, Baseball Player)
14209 Woodward St
Overland Park, KS 66223-2561, USA

Sutton, Michael (Actor)
Somers Teitelbaum David
8840 Wilshire Blvd
#200
Beverly Hills, CA 90211, USA

Sutton, Percy E (Politician)
10 W 135th St
New York, NY 10037, USA

Sutton, Randi (Stylist)
7 Victoria Falls Dr
Mirage, CA 92270, USA

Sutton, Ricky (Football Player)
Pittsburgh Steelers
1112 To Lani Farm Rd
Stone Mountain, GA 30083-5364, USA

Suu Kyi, Aung San (Nobel Prize Laureate)
54 University Ave
Yangon 11181, Myanmar

Suvadova, Silvia (Actor)
c/o Michael Henderson *Heresun Management*
4119 West Burbank Blvd.
Burbank, CA 91505, USA

Suvalatsumi (Actor)
58 2nd Street Venkatesh Nagar
Virugambakkam
Chennai, TN 600 092, INDIA

Suvaluxmi (Actor, Bollywood)
Matri Aasis 22/1/1/1 Monohar Pukur Road
PO Rash Behari Avenue
Kolkata, WB 700029, INDIA

Suvari, Mena (Actor)
c/o Jason Barrett *Alchemy Entertainment*
7024 Melrose Ave
Suite 420
Los Angeles, CA 90038, USA

Suwa, Gen (Misc)
University of California
Human Evolutionary Science Lab
Berkeley, CA 94720, USA

Suwyn, Mark A (Business Person)
Louisiana-Pacific Corp
111 SW 5th Ave
Portland, OR 97204, USA

Suzman, Janet (Actor)
Faircroft
11 Keats Grove
Hampstead
London NW3, UNITED KINGDOM (UK)

Suzor, Mark (Athlete, Hockey Player)
1639 Hillcrest Dr
Sheridan, WY 82801-3242, USA

Suzuki, David (Scientist)
David Suzuki Foundation
2211 W 4th Ave
Suite 219
Vancouver, BC V6K 4S2, CANADA

Suzuki, Ichiro (Athlete, Baseball Player)
4101 185th Pl SE
Issaquah, WA 98027, USA

Suzuki, Kurt (Athlete, Baseball Player)
5111 Steveann St
Torrance, CA 90503-5359, USA

Suzuki, Mac (Athlete, Baseball Player)
5122 E Shea Blvd Unit 1164
Scottsdale, AZ 85254-4677, USA

Suzuki, Pat
343 E. 30th St
New York, NY 10016

Suzuki, Robert (Educator)
California State University
President's Office
Bakersfield, CA 93311, USA

Suzy (Writer)
18 E 68th St
#1B
New York, NY 10021, USA

Svankmajer, Jan (Director)
Ceminska 5
Prague 1 118 00, CZECH REPUBLIC

Svare, Harland (Athlete, Coach, Football Coach, Football Player)
6773 Turnstone Ave
Castle Rock, Colorado 80104, USA

Svatos, Marek (Athlete, Hockey Player)
10322 Bluffmont Dr
Lone Tree, CO 80124-5579, USA

Svehla, Robert (Athlete, Hockey Player)
Dukla Trencin Hockey Club Povaszka 34
Attn: President's Office
Trencin 91101, Slovakia

Svejkovsky, Jaroslav "Yogi" (Athlete, Hockey Player)
184 Kilarney Pl
Point Roberts, WA 98281-9518, USA

Svenden, Birgitta (Musician)
Ulf Tomqvist
Sankt Eriksgatan 100
Stockholm 113 31, SWEDEN

Svendsen, George (Football Player)
163 Wayzata Blvd W
#315
Wayzata, MN 55391, USA

Svendsen, Louise A (Misc)
16 Park Ave
New York, NY 10016, USA

Sveningsson, Magnus (Musician)
Motor SE
Gotabergs Gatan 2
Gothenburg 400 14, SWEDEN

Svenson, Bo (Actor)
312 Bellino Dr
Pacific Palisades, CA 90272, USA

Svensson, Leif (Athlete, Hockey Player)
Lisselbyvagan 39
Leksand S-79333, Sweden

Svensson, Peter (Musician, Songwriter, Writer)
Motor SE
Gotabergs Gatan 2
Gothenburg 400 14, SWEDEN

Sverak, Jan (Director)
PO Box 33
Prague 515 155 00, CZECH REPUBLIC

Sveum, Dale (Athlete, Baseball Player)
13483 E Estrella Ave
Scottsdale, AZ 85259-5417, USA

Svihus, Bob (Football Player)
Oakland Raiders
23000 Guidotti Dr
Salinas, CA 93908-1022, USA

Svitov, Alexander (Athlete, Hockey Player)
Puckagency LLC
555 Pleasantville Rd Ste 210N
Attn Jay Grossman
Briarcliff Manor, NY 10510-1900, USA

Svoboda, Petr (Athlete, Hockey Player)
Sport rust Associates International 818
18th St Unit F
Santa Monica, CA 90403-1935, USA

Swaby, Don (Actor)
c/o Staff Member *Stone Manners Salners Agency (LA)*
9911 W Pico Blvd Ste 1400
Los Angeles, CA 90035, USA

Swaby, Donn (Actor)
c/o Don Carroll *Don Carroll Management*
14211 Hatteras St.
Sherman Oaks, CA 91401, USA

Swados, Elizabeth A (Composer, Writer)
360 Central Park West
#16G
New York, NY 10025, USA

Swagerty, Jane (Swimmer)
9128 N 70th St
Paradise Valley, AZ 85253, USA

Swagerty, Keith (Athlete, Basketball Player)
22232 17th Ave SE
Suite 205
Bothell, WA 98021-7411, USA

Swaggart, Jimmy L (Misc)
PO Box 262550
Baton Rouge, LA 70826, USA

Swaggert, Jimmy
8912 World Ministry Ave
Baton Rouge, LA 70810

Swaggerty, Bill (Athlete, Baseball Player)
116 S Forney Ave
Hanover, PA 17331-3711, USA

Swail, Julie (Athlete, Coach)
University of California
Athletic Dept
Irvine, CA 92697, USA

Swaim, Caskey
1605 N. Cahuenga Blvd. #202
Los Angeles, CA 90028

Swain, Brennan (Athlete)
c/o Jerry Shandrew *Shandrew Public Relations*
1050 S Stanley Ave
Los Angeles, CA 90019-6634, USA

Swain, Chelse (Actor)
c/o Staff Member *Identity Talent Agency (ID)*
9107 Wilshire Blvd
Suite 500
Beverly Hills, CA 90210, USA

Swain, Dominique (Actor)
c/o Michael Garnett *Leverage Management*
3030 Pennsylvania Ave
Santa Monica, CA 90404, USA

Swain, Garry (Athlete, Hockey Player)
PO Box 729
West Simsbury, CT 06092-0729, USA

Swain, John (Football Player)
Minnesota Vikings
409 E 135th St
Burnsville, MN 55337-4019, USA

Swaminathan, Monkombu S (Scientist)
MS Swaminathan Foundation
3 Cross St
Taramani
Chennai, TN 600113, INDIA

Swan, Billy (Musician, Songwriter, Writer)
Muirhead Mgmt
202 Fulham Road
Chelsea
London SW10 9PJ, UNITED KINGDOM (UK)

Swan, Craig (Athlete, Baseball Player)
296 Sound Beach Ave
Old Greenwich, CT 06870-1626, USA

Swan, John W D (President)
Swan Building
26 Victoria St
Hamilton HM12, BERMUDA

Swan, Michael (Actor)
13576 Cheltenham Dr
Sherman Oaks, CA 91423, USA

Swan, Richard G (Mathematician)
700 Melrose Ave
#M3
Winter Park, FL 32789, USA

Swan, Serinda (Actor)
c/o Alex Cole *Elevate Entertainment*
10100 Santa Monica Blvd.
Suite 300
Los Angeles, CA 90067, USA

Swanagon, Mary Lou (Baseball Player)
2193 E Amarillo Way
Palm Springs, CA 92264-8637, USA

Swanepoel, Candice (Model)
c/o Staff Member *MC2 Israel*
26 Hayarkon St
2nd Floor
Tel Aviv 68011, Israel

Swank, Hilary (Actor)
c/o Kim Hodgert *Creative Artists Agency (CAA-LA)*
2000 Ave Of The Stars
Los Angeles, CA 90067, USA

Swanke, Karl (Football Player)
Green Bay Packers
4 Butternut Ct
Essex Junction, VT 05452-3959, USA

Swann, Lynn C (Athlete, Football Player, Sportscaster)
506 Hegner Way #2
Sewickley, PA 15143, USA

Swann, Pedro (Athlete, Baseball Player)
9 Westbury Dr
New Castle, DE 19720-8812, USA

Swanson, August G (Physicist)
3146 Portage Bay Place E
#H
Seattle, WA 98102, USA

Swanson, Jackie (Actor)
15155 Albright St
Pacific Palisades, CA 90272, USA

Swanson, John (Race Car Driver)
235-237 Main St.
Maynard, MA 01754, USA

Swanson, Judith (Actor)
Persona Mgmt
40 E 9th St
New York, NY 10003, USA

Swanson, Kristy (Actor, Model)
c/o Leo Bozzuto *HYPHENATE*
9701 Wilshire Blvd.
10th floor
Beverly Hills, CA 90212, USA

Swanson, Red (Athlete, Baseball Player)
1139 Chippenham Dr
Baton Rouge, LA 70808-5694, USA

Swanson, Stan (Athlete, Baseball Player)
688 Bass Ln
Corvallis, MT 59828-9739, USA

Swanson, Steven R (Astronomer)
16403 Bougainville Lane
Friendswood, TX 77546, USA

Swanson, Steven R Dr (Astronaut)
1414 Blueberry Ln
Friendswood, TX 77546-5213, USA

Swarbrick, George (Athlete, Hockey Player)
14918 Ridgeview Dr
Plattsmouth, NE 68048-8798, USA

Sward, Melinda (Actor)
c/o Sheila Wenzel *Innovative Artists (LA)*
1505 10th St
Santa Monica, CA 90401, USA

Swardson, Nick (Actor, Musician)
c/o Tim Sarkes *Brillstein Entertainment Partners*
9150 Wilshire Blvd #350
Beverly Hills, CA 90212, USA

Swarn, George (Football Player)
Cleveland Browns
442 Daisy St
Mansfield, OH 44903-1305, USA

Swaroop, Shikha (Actor, Bollywood)
13/14 Atmanand Saraswat Colony
Santacruz
Mumbai, MS 400054, INDIA

Swarovski, Fiona (Business Person)
Unterhirzinger Hof
Kitzbuhel 6370, Austria

Swartwoudt, Gregg (Football Player)
New York Giants
202 Anderson Rd
Esko, MN 55733-9413, USA

Swartz, Jacob T (Scientist)
New York University
251 Mercer St
New York, NY 10012, USA

Swartzbaugh, Dave (Athlete, Baseball Player)
113 Orchard St
Middletown, OH 45044-4920, USA

Swatek, Barret (Actor)
c/o Tammy Rosen *Sanders Armstrong Caserta*
425 N Robertson Blvd
Los Angeles, CA 90048, USA

Swathi (Actor, Bollywood)
Flat No 4-42
47th Street 9thAvenue Ashok Nagar
Chennai, TN 600083, INDIA

Swatland, Richard (Football Player)
Houston Oilers
178 Club Rd
Stamford, CT 06905-2120, USA

Sway (Television Host)
c/o Staff Member *Music Television (MTV) Networks (NY)*
1515 Broadway
New York, NY 10036, USA

Swayne, Harry (Football Player)
Tampa Bay Buccaneers
956 Cheswick Dr
Gurnee, IL 60031-5600, USA

Swayze, Don
247 S. Beverly Dr. #102
Beverly Hills, CA 90212

Swearingen, John E Jr (Business Person)
1420 Lake Shore Dr
Chicago, IL 60610, USA

Sweat, Keith (Musician, Songwriter)
c/o Michael Irving *Emancipated Talent*
215 Clinton St
Brooklyn, NY 11201, USA

Sweat, Lynn (Artist)
29 Bantry Rd
Simsbury, CT 06070-3192, USA

Swedberg, Heidi (Actor)
c/o Staff Member *Marathon Entertainment*
8060 Melrose #400
Los Angeles, CA 90046

Swedish House Mafia (DJ, Music Group)
c/o Sara Newkirk *WME (LA)*
9601 Wilshire Blvd Fl 3
Beverly Hills, CA 90210, USA

Swedlin, Rosalie (Producer)
c/o Staff Member *Jackoway Tyerman Wertheimer Austen Mandelbaum Morris & Klein*
1925 Century Park E
22nd Floor
Los Angeles, CA 90067, USA

Sweeney, Alison (Actor)
c/o Elissa Leeds-Fickman *Reel Talent Management*
P.O. Box 491035
Los Angeles, CA 90049, USA

Sweeney, Bob (Athlete, Hockey Player)
110 Brookview Dr
North Andover, MA 01845-3253, USA

Sweeney, Brian (Athlete, Baseball Player)
111 Old Coach Rd
Clifton Park, NY 12065-7618, USA

Sweeney, Calvin (Athlete, Football Player)
4120 Olympiad Dr
Los Angeles, CA 90043, USA

Sweeney, D B (Actor)
c/o Staff Member *Lighthouse Entertainment*
9220 W Sunset Blvd Ste 200
West Hollywood, CA 90069, USA

Sweeney, Don (Athlete, Hockey Player)
10 Munroe Rd
Lexington, MA 02421-7812, USA

Sweeney, Don (Athlete, Hockey Player)
Boston Bruins 100 Legends Way Ste 250
Attn: Asst General Manager
Boston, MA 02114-1389, USA

Sweeney, John J (Politician)
AFL-CIO
1750 New York Ave NW
Washington, DC 20006, USA

Sweeney, Julia (Actor, Comedian)
c/o Staff Member *WME (LA)*
9601 Wilshire Blvd Fl 3
Beverly Hills, CA 90210, USA

Sweeney, Kevin (Athlete, Football Player)
12401 N Via Tuscania Ave
Clovis, CA 93611, USA

Sweeney, Mark (Athlete, Baseball Player)
9299 E Hillery Way
Scottsdale, AZ 85260, USA

Sweeney, Michael J (Mike) (Athlete, Baseball Player)
2802 E Tam 0 Shanter Ct
Ontario, CA 91761-7423, USA

Sweeney, Pepper
1930 Century Park W. #403
Los Angeles, CA 90067

Sweeney, Ryan (Athlete, Baseball Player)
6941 Waterview Dr SW
Cedar Raoids, IA 52404-7749, USA

Sweeney, Sunny (Musician)
c/o Staff Member *WmE2 (WMA-TN)*
1600 Division St
Suite 300
Nashville, TN 37203, USA

Sweeney, Terry (Actor, Comedian, Writer)
c/o Staff Member *Creative Artists Agency (CAA-LA)*
2000 Ave Of The Stars
Los Angeles, CA 90067, USA

Sweeney, Tim (Athlete, Hockey Player)
47 Ledgewood Dr
Hanover, MA 02339-1329, USA

Sweeney, Walter F (Walt) (Athlete, Football Player)
5832 Kantor Court
San Diego, CA 92122-3832, USA

Sweet, Don (Athlete, Football Player)
5-20751 87 Ave
Langley, BC V1M 2X3, Canada

Sweet, Joe (Athlete, Football Player)
1503 NE 89th Ct
Vancouver, WA 98664, USA

Sweet, Matthew (Musician, Songwriter, Writer)
Russell Carter Artists Mgmt
315 W Ponce De Leon Ave
#755
Decatur, GA 30030, USA

Sweet, Rachel (Producer)
c/o Staff Member *WME (LA)*
9601 Wilshire Blvd Fl 3
Beverly Hills, CA 90210, USA

Sweet, Rick (Athlete, Baseball Player)
1503 NE 89th Ct
Vancouver, WA 98664-6413, USA

Sweet, Sharon (Opera Singer)
Columbia Artists Mgmt Inc
165 W 57th St
New York, NY 10019, USA

Sweet, Shay (Adult Film Star)
c/o Staff Member *Atlas Multimedia Inc*
9005 Eton Ave Ste C
Canoga Park, CA 91304-1743, USA

Sweeten, Madylin (Actor)
c/o Dino May *Dino May Management*
6362 Hollywood Blvd #422
Hollywood, CA 90028-6323, USA

Sweethearts of the Rodeo
5101 Overton Rd.
Nashville, TN 37220

Sweetin, Jodie (Actor)
c/o Staff Member *Savage Agency*
6212 Banner Ave
Los Angeles, CA 90038, USA

Sweetlin, Jodie
6212 Banner Ave.
Los Angeles, CA 90038

Sweetman, Julie (Stylist)
c/o Staff Member *Artist Agency, THE (NY)*
230 W 55th St #29D
New York, NY 10019

Sweetney, Mike (Basketball Player)
New York Knicks
Madison Square Garden
2 Penn Plaza
New York, NY 10121, USA

Swensen, Joseph A (Composer, Conductor)
c/o Victoria Rowsell *Victoria Rowsell Artist Management Ltd*
34 Addington Sq
London SE5 7LB, UK

Swenson, August
1702 Azores Dr.
Pflugerville, TX 78880

Swenson, Cal (Athlete, Hockey Player)
Box 92 Site 310 RR 3
Stony Plain, AB AB T7Z 1X3, Canada

Swenson, Eliza (Actor, Musician)
Ad Astra Management
5118 Vineland Ave #102
North Hollywood, CA 91601, USA

Swenson, Inga (Actor, Musician)
3351 Halderman St
Los Angeles, CA 90066, USA

Swenson, Rick (Dog Sled Racer)
PO Box 16205
Two Rivers, AK 99716, USA

Swenson, Robert C (Bob) (Athlete, Football Player)
910 Cypress Ln
Louisville, CO 80027, USA

Swenson, Ruth Ann (Opera Singer)
Columbia Artists Mgmt Inc
165 W 57th St
New York, NY 10019, USA

Swensson, Earl S (Architect)
Earl Swensson Assoc
2100 W End Ave
#1200
Nashville, TN 37203, USA

Swerling Jr, Jo
25745 Vista Verde Dr
Calabasas, CA 91302-2165, USA

Swick, Mike (Athlete)
c/o Staff Member *Zinkin Entertainment & Sports Management*
5 River Park Pl W
Suite 203
Fresno, CA 93720, USA

Swiczinsky, Helmut (Architect)
Coop Himmelblau
Seilerstatte 16/11A
Vienna 81010, AUSTRIA

Swider, Larry (Athlete, Football Player)
1903 W 93rd Ave
Crown Point, IN 46307, USA

Swienton, Gregory T (Business Person)
Ryder System Inc
3600 NW 82nd Ave
Miami, FL 33166, USA

Swierc, Carl
Carl Swierc
Houston, TX 77018-1209, USA

Swierc, Carl (Athlete, Football Player)
Carl Swierc
Houston, TX 77018-1209, USA

Swift, Billy (Athlete, Baseball Player)
5880 E Sapphire Ln
Paradise Valley, AZ 85253-2200, USA

Swift, Clive (Actor)
Roxane Vacca Mgmt
8 Silver Place
London W1R 3LJ, UNITED KINGDOM
(UK)

Swift, Doug (Athlete, Football Player)
265 S 25th St
Philadelphia, PA 19103, USA

Swift, Graham C (Writer)
AP Watt
20 John St
London WC1N 2DR, UNITED KINGDOM
(UK)

Swift, Harley (Athlete, Basketball Player)
357 Cliffside Dr
Kingsport, TN 37660-7161, USA

Swift, Hewson H (Biologist)
University of Chicago
Cell Biology Dept
Chicago, IL 60637, USA

Swift, Stephanie (Adult Film Star)
P.O. Box 9864
Canoga Park, CA 91309-0864, USA

Swift, Stephen J (Judge)
US Tax Court
400 2nd St NW
Washington, DC 20217, USA

Swift, Stromile (Athlete, Basketball Player)
1111 Lincoln Rd
FL 4
Miami Beach, FL 38125-1705, USA

Swift, Taylor (Musician)
c/o Jake Basden *Big Machine Records*
1219 16th Ave South
Nashville, TN 37212, USA

Swilley, Dennis (Athlete, Football Player)
1020 Gruene River Dr
New Braunfels, TX 78132, USA

S. Wilson, Frederica (Congressman, Politician)
208 Cannon HOB
Washington, DC 20515, USA

Swindell, F Gregory (Greg) (Athlete, Baseball Player)
6213 Terwilliger Way
Houston, TX 77057-2803, USA

Swindell, Jeff (Race Car Driver)
TW Racing
1921 W. 4th St.
Marion, IN 46952, USA

Swindell, Sammy (Race Car Driver)
7540 Bartlett Corporate Cove
Bartlett, TN 38133, USA

Swindells, William Jr (Business Person)
Williamette Industries
1300 SW 5th Ave
Portland, OR 97201, USA

Swindle, Orson
500 University Ave. #309
Honolulu, HI 96826

Swindle, RJ (Athlete, Baseball Player)
9382 Ayscough Rd
Summerville, SC 29485-8677, USA

Swindoll, Luci (Writer)
Thomas Nelson, Inc
PO Box 141000
Nashville, TN 37214, USA

Swinford, Wayne (Athlete, Football Player)
100 Beacham Dr
Athens, GA 30606, USA

Swingfly
c/o Staff Member *United Stage Artist*
Box 11029
Stockholm S-10061, Sweden

Swingle, Paul (Athlete, Baseball Player)
6844 S Whetstone Pl
Chandler, AZ 85249-9149, USA

Swingley, Doug (Dog Sled Racer)
General Delivery
Lincoln, MT 59634, USA

Swing Out Sister
132 Liverpool Rd Islington
London, ENGLAND N1 1LA

Swink, James E (Jim) (Athlete, Football Player)
723 Euclid Ave
Rusk, TX 75785-1919, USA

Swinney, Clovis
963 N Patrick St
Jonesboro, AR 72401-8161, USA

Swinny, Wayne (Musician)
Helter Skelter Plaza
535 Kings Road
London SW10 0S, UNITED KINGDOM
(UK)

Swinson, Aaron (Athlete, Basketball Player)
1004 Longley Cove
Heathrow, FL 32746-1921, USA

Swinton, Tilda (Actor)
c/o Christian Hodell *Hamilton Hodell Ltd*
66-68 Margaret St Fl 5
London W1W 8SR, UK

Swisher, Carl C (Misc)
Institute of Human Origins
1288 9th St
Berkeley, CA 94710, USA

Swisher, Nick (Athlete, Baseball Player)
c/o Team Member *New York Yankees*
Yankee Stadium
161st St & River Ave
Bronx, NY 10451, USA

Swisher, Steve (Athlete, Baseball Player)
432 60th St
Vienna, WV 26105-8091, USA

Swisshelm, Ann (Athlete, Olympic Athlete)
855 W Erie St Apt 106
Chicago, IL 60642-5948, USA

Swisten, Amanda (Actor)
c/o Staff Member *WNWN Media*
348 S. Hauser Blvd #PH414
Los Angeles, CA 90036, USA

Swistowicz, Mike (Athlete, Football Player)
2519 S Drake Ave
Chicago, IL 60623, USA

Swit, Loretta (Actor)
310 Tahiti Way #103
Marina Del Rey, CA 90292, USA

Switchfoot (Music Group)
c/o Staff Member *Red Light Management (LA)*
8439 W Sunset Blvd
Suite 2
Los Angeles, CA 90069, USA

Switzer, Barry (Athlete, Coach, Football Coach, Football Player)
700 W Timberdell Rd
Norman, OK 73072, USA

Switzer, Barry (Basketball Player)
PO Box 43021
Lubbock, TX 79409, USA

Switzer, Jon (Athlete, Baseball Player)
3915 Oakmont Blvd
Austin, TX 78731-6048, USA

Switzer, Veryl (Athlete, Football Player)
1412 Wreath Ave
Manhattan, KS 66503, USA

Swoboda, Ron (Athlete, Baseball Player)
315 Alonzo St
New Orleans, LA 70115-2119, USA

Swoopes, Sheryl (Athlete, Basketball Player, Olympic Athlete)
14110 Scarborough Fair St
Houston, TX 77077-1820, USA

Swope, Tracy Brooks
8730 Sunset Blvd. #480
Los Angeles, CA 90069

Sword, Sam (Athlete, Football Player)
2781 San Leandro Blvd
San Leandro, CA 94578, USA

SWV
6464 Sunset Blvd. #610
Hollywood, CA 90028-8013

Swygert, H Patrick (Educator)
Howard University
President's Office
Washington, DC 20059, USA

Syal, Meera (Actor)
c/o Dallas Smith *United Agents*
12-26 Lexington St
London W1F OLE, UK

Syberberg, Hans-Jurgen (Director)
Genter Str 15A
Munich 80805, GERMANY

Sybil (Musician)
Mission Control
Business Center
Lower Road
London SE16 2XB, UNITED KINGDOM
(UK)

Sydney, Harry (Athlete, Football Player)
2025 Argonne St
Green Bay, WI 54304, USA

sydor, Darryl (Athlete, Hockey Player)
3358 Windmill Curv
Saint Paul, MN 55129-6708, USA

Sydor, Darryl
Minnesota Wild 317 Washington St
Attn Coaching Staff
Saint Paul, MN 55102-1667, USA

Sykes, Bob (Athlete, Baseball Player)
1451 County Road 900 E
Carmi, IL 62821, USA

Sykes, Eric (Actor)
Norma Farnes
9 Orme Court
London W2 4RL, UNITED KINGDOM
(UK)

Sykes, Eugene (Gene) (Athlete, Football Player)
8155 Jefferson Hwy
Apt 903
Baton Rouge, LA 70809, USA

Sykes, Lynn R (Geophysicist, Physicist)
RR 1 Box 248
100 Washington Spring Road
Palisades, NY 10964, USA

Sykes, Melanie (Actor)
c/o Staff Member *Money Management*
22 Noel Street
London W1f 8GS, United Kingdom

Sykes, Peter (Director)
International Creative Mgmt
76 Oxford St
London W1N 0AX, UNITED KINGDOM
(UK)

Sykes, Phil (Athlete, Hockey Player)
1486 Brooke Ct
Hastings, MN 55033-3266, USA

Sykes, Wanda (Actor, Comedian)
c/o Danica Smith *PMK/BNC Public Relations (PMK-LA)*
8687 Melrose Ave Fl 8
West Hollywood, CA 90069, USA

Sykora, Michal (Athlete, Hockey Player)
Tepleho 2034
Pardubice 530 02, Czech Republic

Sylbert, Anthea (Designer)
13949 Ventura Blvd
#309
Oaks, CA 91423, USA

Sylver, Marshall (Misc)
1027 S. Rainbow Blvd Ste 281
Las Vegas, NV 89145, USA

Sylvester, Chuck (Horse Racer)
PO Box 1066
Williamstown, NJ 08094-5066, USA

Sylvester, Dean (Athlete, Hockey Player)
51 Upland Rd
Plympton, MA 02367-1602, USA

Sylvester, George H (General)
4571 Conicville Road
Mount Jackson, VA 22842, USA

Sylvester, Harold (Actor)
International Creative Mgmt
8942 Wilshire Blvd
#219
Beverly Hills, CA 90211, USA

Sylvester, Michael (Opera Singer)
Columbia Artists Mgmt Inc
165 W 57th St
New York, NY 10019, USA

Sylvester, Steven P (Athlete, Football Player)
10425 Londonderry Ct
Cincinnati, OH 45242, USA

Sylvestri, Don (Athlete, Hockey Player)
327-1758 LaSalle Blvd
Sudbury, ON P3A 5W4, Canada

Sylvia (Musician)
So Much More Media
PO Box 120426
Nashville, TN 37212, USA

Symington, Fife (Politician)
1700 W Washington St
Phoenix, AZ 85007-2812, USA

Symmonds, Nick (Athlete, Olympic Athlete, Track Athlete)
c/o Staff Member Total Sports Management
115 Beechnut St #D3
Johnson City, TN 37601, USA

Symms, Steven (Politician)
43527 Butler Pl
Leesburg, VA 20176-7428, USA

Symone, Raven (Actor)
c/o Todd Diener Collective
8383 Wilshire Blvd
Suite 1050
Beverly Hills, CA 90211, USA

Symonette, Josh (Athlete, Football Player)
4923 Forrest Run
Lithonia, GA 30038, USA

Symons, Bill (Athlete, Football Player)
235 Wilton Dr Attn
Bolton, ON L7E 4W6, Canada

Syms, Sylvia (Actor)
Barry Brown
47 West Square
London SE11 4SP, UNITED KINGDOM (UK)

Synkowski, Judy (Stylist)
305 E 76th St
#2-D
New York, NY 10021, USA

Sypek, Ryan (Actor)
c/o Leonard Torgan Collective
8383 Wilshire Blvd
Suite 1050
Beverly Hills, CA 90211, USA

Syreeta
6255 Sunset Blvd. #1800
Los Angeles, CA 90028

Syron, Richard F (Financier, Government Official)
Genzyme
500 Kendall St
Cambridge, MA 02142, USA

System of a Down (Music Group)
c/o David Benveniste Velvet Hammer
9014 Melrose Ave
Los Angeles, CA 90069, USA

Sytsma, John F (Politician)
Locomotive Engineers Brotherhood
1370 Ontario Ave
Cleveland, OH 44113, USA

Syvret, Dave (Athlete, Hockey Player)
17 Binkly Cres
Waterdown, ON L0R 2H0, Canada

Szabo, Istvan (Director)
Objektiv Fil Studio-MAFILM
Rona Utca 174
Budapest 1149, HUNGARY

Szajda, Pawel (Actor)
c/o Staff Member Stone Manners Salners Agency (LA)
9911 W Pico Blvd Ste 1400
Los Angeles, CA 90035, USA

Szarabajka, Keith (Actor)
c/o Staff Member Bauman Redanty & Shaul Agency
5757 Wilshire Blvd
Suite 473
Beverly Hills, CA 90212, USA

Szczerbiak, Wally (Athlete, Basketball Player, Sportscaster)
c/o Jim Ornstein WME (WMA-NY)
1325 Ave of the Americas
New York, NY 10019, USA

Szczerbiak, Walt (Wally) (Athlete, Basketball Player)
20 Peabody Rd
Cold Spring Harbor, NY 11724-1714, USA

Szegedy, Todd (Race Car Driver)
13 Mallory Hill Rd.
Ridgefield, CT 06877, USA

Szekely, Eva (Swimmer)
Szepvolgyi Utca 4/B
Budapest 1025, HUNGARY

Szekessy, Karen (Photographer)
Haynstr 2
Hamburg 20249, GERMANY

Szep, Paul M (Cartoonist)
10610 Andrew Ln
Seminole, FL 33777-1223, USA

Szewczenki, Tanya (Figure Skater)
Niederbeerbacher Str 10
Muhital 64367, GERMANY

Szigmond, Vilmos (Cinematographer)
PO Box 2230
Los Angeles, CA 90078, USA

Szmanda, Eric (Actor)
c/o Michael Gruber After Dark Management Group
Prefers to be contacted via telephone
Los Angeles, CA 90069, USA

Szohr, Jessica (Actor)
c/o Lena Roklin Luber Roklin Management
8530 Wilshire Blvd
6th Floor
Beverly Hills, CA 90211, USA

Szoka, Edmund C Cardinal (Religious Leader)
Prefecture for Economic Affairs
Vatican City 00120, VATICAN CITY

Szostak, Jack W. (Nobel Prize Laureate)
Massachusetts General Hospital
390 Marlborough St
Boston, MA 02115-1502, USA

Szotkiewicz, Ken (Athlete, Baseball Player)
849 Dusky SapCt
Griffin, GA 30223-5994, USA

Szott, David (Athlete, Football Player)
11 Manor Dr
Morristown, NJ 07960, USA

Szuminski, Jason (Athlete, Baseball Player)
1766 Jackson St
San Francisco, CA 94109-2918, USA

Szura, Joe (Athlete, Hockey Player)

Szymanski, Jim (Athlete, Football Player)
541 Riverwalk Dr
Mason, MI 48854, USA

Szymanski, Richard (Dick) (Athlete, Football Player)
5270 Forest Edge Ct
Lake Forest, FL 32771, USA

Tabachnik, Michel (Composer, Conductor)
Garvey & Ivor
59 Lansdowne Place
Hove BN3 1FL, UNITED KINGDOM (UK)

Tabackin, Lewis B (Lew) (Musician)
38 W 94th St
New York, NY 10025, USA

Tabai, Ieremia T (President)
South Pacific Forum Secretariat
Ratu Su Kuna Rd
GPO Box 856
Suva, FIJI

Tabak, Zan (Athlete, Basketball Player)
Saint Joseph Girona Basketball Team
Av Josep Tarradellas 22-24
Girona 17007, SPAIN

Tabaka, Jeff (Athlete, Baseball Player)
1481 Norview Dr
Clinton, OH 44216-8804, USA

Tabakov, Oleg P (Actor, Director)
Chemysherskogo 39
#3
Moscow 103062, RUSSIA

Tabaksblat, Morris (Business Person)
Unilever NV
Weena 455
Rotterdam, DK 3000, NETHERLANDS

Tabaracci, Rick (Athlete, Hockey Player)
7771 Westhills Trl
Park City, UT 84098-6262, USA

Tabassum (Actor, Bollywood, Talk Show Host, Television Host)
11A Pooja Apartments Master Vinayak Road
Bandra
Bombay, MS 400 050, INDIA

Tabb, Jerry (Athlete, Baseball Player)
7819 Gable Bridge Ln
Richmond, TX 77407-5586, USA

Taber, Catherine (Actor)
c/o Staff Member Charles Riley
7122 Beverly Blvd
Suite F
Los Angeles, CA 90036, USA

Tabitha, Masentle (Royalty)
Royal Palace
PO Box 524
Maseru, LESOTHO

Tabler, Pat (Athlete, Baseball Player, Sportscaster)
Toronto Blue Jays
1 Blue Jays Way, Suite 3200
Attn: Broadcast Dept
Toronto, ON M5V 1J1, Canada

Tabois, Sean (Stylist)
c/o Staff Member Stockland Martel
343 E 18th St
New York, NY 10003, USA

Tabone, Anton (President)
33 Carmel St
Slierna, MALTA

Tabor, David (Physicist)
8 Rutherford Road
Cambridge CB2 2HH, UNITED KINGDOM (UK)

Tabor, Greg (Athlete, Baseball Player)
29317 Whalebone Way
Hayward, CA 94544-6427, USA

Tabor, Herbert (Scientist)
National Institute of Health
8 Center Dr
Bethesda, MD 20892, USA

Tabor, Paul (Athlete, Football Player)
3308 Riverwalk Dr
Norman, OK 73072, USA

Tabor, Phil (Athlete, Football Player)
806 Wood N Creek Rd
Ardmore, OK 73401, USA

Tabori, Kristoffer (Actor)
International Artists
235 Regent St
London W1R 8AX, USA

Tabori, Laszlo (Athlete, Track Athlete)
2221 W Olive Ave
Burbank, CA 91506, USA

Tabu (Actor, Bollywood)
Anukool 2nd Floor
7 Bungalows Versova Andheri (W)
Mumbai, MS 400058, INDIA

Taccone, Jorma (Writer)
c/o Julie Darmody Mosaic Media Group
9200 W. Sunset Blvd
10th Floor
Los Angeles, CA 90069, USA

Tacha, Deanell R (Judge)
US Court of Appeals
4830 W 15th St
Lawrence, KS 66049, USA

Tackett, Jeffrey (Jeff) (Athlete, Baseball Player)
1574 Frazier St
Camarillo, CA 93012-4431, USA

Taco (Musician)
8124 W 3rd St
#204
Los Angeles, CA 90048, USA

Tada, Joni Eareckson (Writer)
Joni And Friends headquarters
Po Box 3333
Agoura Hills, CA 91376-3333, USA

Tadic, Boris (President)
President's Office
Nemanjina 11
Belgrade 11000, SERBIA

Taeger, Ralph
5619 Mother Lode
Placerville, CA 95667

Taff, Russ
PO Box 570815
Tarzana, CA 91357-0815

Taffe, Jeff (Athlete, Hockey Player)
1455 Truax Cir
Hastings, MN 55033-2476, USA

Taffoni, Joe (Athlete, Football Player)
103 Pine Valley Dr
Medford, NJ 08055, USA

Tafone, Phil (Horse Racer)
419 Star St
East Meadow, NY 11554-3308, USA

Tafoya, Michele (Sportscaster)
CBS-TV
Sports Dept
51 W 52nd St
New York, NY 10019, USA

Tafoya, Michele (Sportscaster)
c/o Staff Member *ESPN (Main)*
ESPN Plaza
935 Middle St
Bristol, CT 06010-1001, USA

Taft, John
5224 Oaklawn Ave
Minneapolis, MN 55424-1307, USA

Taft, Reed (Athlete, Football Player)
1101 Atlanta St
Hattiesburg, MS 39401-1454, USA

Taft, Robert (Politician)
2933 Lower Bellbrook Rd
Spring Valley, OH 45370-8761, USA

Taft, William H IV (Government Official)
1001 Pennsylvania Ave NW
Washington, DC 20004, USA

Taft, William Howard (Politician)
PO Box 227
Lorton, VA 22199-0227, USA

Tagawa, Cary-Hiroyuki (Actor)
c/o Joseph (Joe) Rice *Abrams Artists Agency (LA)*
9200 Sunset Blvd
11th Floor
Los Angeles, CA 90069, USA

Tagge, Jerry (Athlete, Football Player)
15033 Patterson Cir
Omaha, NE 68137, USA

Taghmaoui, Said (Actor)
c/o Leonard Torgan *Collective*
8383 Wilshire Blvd
Suite 1050
Beverly Hills, CA 90211, USA

Tagliabue, Paul (Business Person, Football Executive)
4149 Parkglen Ct NW
Washington, DC 20007-2137, USA

Taglianetti, Peter (Athlete, Hockey Player)
67 Merion Ct
Bridgeville, PA 15017, USA

Taglianetti, Peter (Athlete, Hockey Player)
67 Bayhill Dr
Bridgeville, PA 15017-1088, USA

Tagliani, Alex (Race Car Driver)
Players//Forsythe Racing
7321 Georgetown Rd.
Indianapolis, IN 46268, USA

Taguchi, So (Athlete, Baseball Player)
12931 Twin Meadows Ct
Saint Louis, MO 63146-1803, USA

Tahil, Dalip (Actor, Bollywood)
19 Deepali St Cyril Road
Bandra
Mumbai, MS 400050, INDIA

Tahir, Faran (Actor)

Tai, Kobe (Adult Film Star)
c/o Staff Member *Atlas Multimedia Inc*
9005 Eton Ave Ste C
Canoga Park, CA 91304-1743, USA

Taichman, Tamara (Stylist)
c/o Staff Member *Marek & Associates Inc*
508 W 26th St
#12-C
New York, NY 10001, USA

Tailes, Devin Star (Dev) (Musician)
c/o Jenn Tolman *Paradigm (LA)*
360 N Crescent Dr
North Bldg
Beverly Hills, CA 90210, USA

Taillibert, Roger R (Architect)
163 Rue de la Ponpe
Paris 75116, FRANCE

Tait, John (Athlete, Football Player)
876 E Tyson Ct
Gilbert, AZ 85296, USA

Tait, John E (Business Person)
Penn Mutual Life
Independence Square
Philadelphia, PA 19172, USA

Tait, Tristan (Actor)
Paradigm Agency
10100 Santa Monica Blvd
#2500
Los Angeles, CA 90067, USA

Taittinger, Jean (Business Person)
58 Blvd Gouvion
Saint-Cyr
Paris 75017, FRANCE

Tak, Saawan Kumar (Bollywood, Director, Filmmaker, Producer)
A/11 Dakshina Park 10th Road
Juhu
Bombay, MS 400 049, INDIA

Taka, Miiko
14560 Round Valley Dr.
Sherman Oaks, CA 91403

Takac, Robby (Musician)
c/o Staff Member *Atlas/Third Rail Entertainment*
9200 Sunset Blvd
Floor 10
Los Angeles, CA 90069, USA

Takacs, Tibor (Director)
IP
104 Richview Ave
Toronto, ON M5P 3E9, CANADA

Takacs-Nagy, Gabor (Musician)
Case Postale 196
Collonge-Bellerive 1245, SWITZERLAND

Takagi, Tora (Race Car Driver)
Nakajima Planing
1-3-10 Higuishi
Shivuya-ku
Tokyo 150-0011, JAPAN

Takahashi, Joseph S (Scientist)
Northwestern University
Neurobiology Dept
2153 N Campus Dr
Evanston, IL 60208, USA

Takahashi, Michiaki (Scientist)
Osaka University
Microbe Diseases Research Institute
Osaka, JAPAN

Takamatsu, Shin (Architect)
Shin Takamatsu Assoc
195 Jobodaiincho Takeda
Kyoto, JAPAN

Take 6 (Music Group, Musician)
c/o Staff Member *Agency for the Performing Arts (APA-LA)*
405 S Beverly Dr
Suite 500
Beverly Hills, CA 90212-4425, USA

Takei, George (Actor)
c/o Michael Greenwald *Buchwald/Fortitude (LA)*
6500 Wilshire Blvd
Suite 2200
Los Angeles, CA 90048, USA

Takenouchi, Naoko (Artist)
Kathleen Gaffney
Art Glass Int'l
PO Box 58922
Renton, WA 98058, USA

Take That
69-79 Fulham High St.
London, ENGLAND SW6 3JW

Takeuchi, Esther (Inventor)
38 San Rafael Ct
East Amherst, NY 14051-2233, USA

Takezawa, Kyoko (Musician)
I C M Artists
40 W 57th St
New York, NY 10019, USA

Takko, Kari (Athlete, Hockey Player)
Dallas Stars 2601 Avenue ofthe Stars Ste 100
Attn Dir European Scouting
Frisco, TX 75034-9016, USA

Takle, Darien (Actor)
c/o Staff Member *Robert Bruce Agency*
218 Richmond Rd
Grey Lynn
Auckland 2, New Zealand

Takter, Jimmy (Horse Racer)
1079 Old York Rd
East Windsor, NJ 08520-4710, USA

Tal, Alona (Actor)
c/o Laura Myones *McKeon-Myones Management*
3500 Olive Ave
Suite 770
Burbank, CA 91505, USA

Talafous, Dean (Athlete, Hockey Player)
2418 Foxglove Cir
Hudson, WI 54016-8251, USA

Talalay, Paul (Scientist)
5512 Boxhill Lane
Baltimore, MD 21210, USA

Talalay, Rachel (Director)
1047 Grant St
Santa Monica, CA 90405, USA

Talamini, Robert (Athlete, Football Player)
3577 Cave Creek Mnr
Las Cruces, NM 88011-4015, USA

Talancon, Ana Claudia (Actor)
c/o Carlos Carreras *Agency for the Performing Arts (APA-LA)*
360 N Crescent Dr
North Bldg
Beverly Hills, CA 90210, USA

Talavera, Tracee (Gymnast)
1761 Fisher Dr
Concord, CA 94520, USA

Talbert, Billy (Athlete)
194 Bellevue Avenue
Newport, RI 02840, USA

Talbert, Diron (Athlete, Football Player)
3803 B F Terry Blvd
Rosenberg, TX 77471, USA

Talbert, Don (Athlete, Football Player)
P.O. Box 261
3027 Highway 123
Richmond, TX 77406, USA

Talbot, Bob (Athlete, Baseball Player)
608 W Kaweah Ave
Visalia, CA 93277-2510, USA

Talbot, Dale (Baseball Player)
Chicago Cubs
608 W Kaweah Ave
Visalia, CA 93277-2510, USA

Talbot, Diron V (Athlete, Football Player)
3803 B F Terry Blvd
Rosenberg, TX 77471, USA

Talbot, Don (Coach, Swimmer)
Sports Federation
333 River Road
Vanier
Ottawa, ON K1L 8B9, CANADA

Talbot, Fred (Athlete, Baseball Player)
7701 Lunceford Ln
Falls Church, VA 22043-1207, USA

Talbot, Joby (Composer, Musician)
c/o Catherine Manners *Manners McDade Artist Management*
46 Copperfield St
London SE1 0DY, UK

Talbot, Maxime (Athlete, Hockey Player)
111 Bellevue Ave
Pittsburgh, PA 15229-1705, USA

Talbot, Mitch (Athlete, Baseball Player)
1138 Brook St
Cedar Citv, UT 84721-6340, USA

Talbot, Nita (Actor)
3420 Merrimac Road
Los Angeles, CA 90049, USA

Talbot, Susan (Actor)
Media Artists Group
6300 Wilshire Blvd
#1470
Los Angeles, CA 90048, USA

Talbott, Gloria (Actor)
2066 Montecito Dr
Glendale, CA 91208, USA

Talbott, John H (Doctor)
Commodore Club
177 Ocean Lane Dr
Key Biscayne, FL 33149, USA

Talbott, John R (Writer)
c/o Staff Member *St Martins Press*
Publicity Dept
175 5th Ave
New York, NY 10010, USA

Talbott, Michael (Actor)
2011 Euclid Ave
Waverly, IA 50677-9700, USA

Talbott, Strobe (Journalist)
State Department
2201 C St NW
Washington, DC 20520, USA

Talent, James (Politician)
1470 Country Lake Estates Dr
Chesterfield, MO 63005-4347, USA

Talese, Gay (Writer)
154 E Atlantic Blvd
Ocean City, NJ 08226-4511, USA

Taliaferro, George (Athlete, Football Player)
2708 Olcott Blvd
Bloonington, IN 47401, USA

Taliaferro, Mike (Athlete, Football Player)
7332 Oakbluff Dr
Dallas, TX 75254, USA

Talla (DJ)
c/o Staff Member *Diva Central Inc*
7510 W Sunset Blvd Ste 1445
Los Angees, CA 90046, USA

Tallackson, Barry (Athlete, Hockey Player)
10011 Colorado Ave N
Minneapolis, MN 55445-2363, USA

Tallas, George (Race Car Driver)
21st Century Racing
5245 Crooked Mountain Ct.
Las Vegas, NV 89129, USA

Tallas, Rob
Florida Panthers 1 Panther Pkwy
Attn: Coaching Staff
Sunrise, FL 33323-5315, USA

Tallas, Rob (Athlete, Hockey Player)
1844 Classic Drive
Coral Springs, FL 33071-7753, USA

Tallchief, Maria (Dancer)
48 Prospect
Highland Park, IL 60035, USA

Tallet, Brian (Athlete, Baseball Player)
3167 McClendon Ct
Baton Rouge, LA 70810-8376, USA

Talley, Darryl V (Athlete, Football Player)
8713 Lake Tibet Ct
Orlando, FL 32836, USA

Talley, Gary (Musician)
Horizon Mgmt
PO Box 8770
Endwell, NJ 13762, USA

Talley, Joel E (War Hero)
20 Lakeshore Dr
Shalimar, FL 32579, USA

Talley, Stan (Athlete, Football Player)
24241 Porto Cristo
Dana Point, CA 92629, USA

Tallinder, Henrik (Athlete, Hockey Player)
40 Maple Ave
Madison, NJ 07940-2618, USA

Tallman, Patricia (Actor)
PMB 2161
1801 E Tropicana
#9
Las Vegas, NV 89119, USA

Tallman, Richard C (Judge)
US Court of Appeals
US Courthouse
1010 5th Ave
Seattle, WA 98104, USA

Tallon, Dale (Athlete, Hockey Player)
1480 Ocean Dr Apt 3H
Vero Beach, FL 32963-5345, USA

Tallon, Dale
Florida Panthers 1 Panther Pkwy
Attn: General Manager
Sunrise, FL 33323-5315, USA

Talor, Vanessa
11271 Ventura Blvd. #396
Studio City, CA 91604

Talore, Brandy (Adult Film Star)
P.O. Box 253
Findlay, OH 45840, USA

Talsania, Tiku (Actor, Bollywood)
22-A Shruti Yashudham Enclave
Filmcity Rd Goregaon (E)
Mumbai, MS 400053, INDIA

Talton, Tim (Athlete, Baseball Player)
130 Hardy Talton Rd NW
Pikeville, NC 27863-8601, USA

Tam, Amy (Stylist)
c/o Staff Member *L'Agence*
5901-C Peachtree Dunwoody Rd
#60
Atlanta, GA 30328, USA

Tam, Jeffrey (Jeff) (Athlete, Baseball Player)
5255 Pina Vista Dr
Melbourne, FL 32934-7897, USA

Tamahori, Lee W (Director)
International Creative Mgmt
8942 Wilshire Blvd
#219
Beverly Hills, CA 90211, USA

Tamargo, John (Athlete, Baseball Player)
19018 Fern Meadow Loop
Lutz, FL 33558-4000, USA

Tamaro, Janet (Journalist)
c/o Rob Kenneally *Creative Artists Agency (CAA-LA)*
2000 Ave Of The Stars
Los Angeles, CA 90067, USA

Tamayo, Mendez Amaldo (Cosmonaut)
Calle 16
#504 C/5A y 7MA
Miramar, Ciudad Havana 11300, CUBA

Tambellini, Roger (Athlete, Golfer)
32531 North Scottsdale Road
Suite 105
Scottsdale, AZ 85266-1519, USA

Tambellini, Steve (Athlete, Hockey Player)
Edmonton Oilers 11230 110 St NW
Attn General Manager
Edmonton, AB T5G 3H7, Canada

Tamberino, Paul (Referee)
349 Homeland Southway
Baltimore, MD 21212, USA

Tambiah, Stanley J (Misc)
Harvard University
Anthropology Dept
Cambridge, MA 02138, USA

Tamblyn, Amber (Actor)
c/o Joan Hyler *Hyler Management*
20 Ocean Park Blvd
Suite 25
Santa Monica, CA 90405, USA

Tamblyn, Russ (Actor, Dancer)
2310 6th St #2
Santa Monica, CA 90405, USA

Tambone, Jeanne D (Stylist)
9 Lauri Lane
Middlesex, NJ 08846, USA

Tambor, Jeffrey (Actor)
c/o Leslie Siebert *Gersh (LA)*
9465 Wilshire Blvd
Suite 600
Beverly Hills, CA 90212, USA

Tamburello, Ben (Athlete, Football Player)
4385 Milner Rd W
Birmingham, AL 35242, USA

Tamer, Chris (Athlete, Hockey Player)
4215 Cornwell Ln
Whitmore Lake, MI 48189-9771, USA

Tamke, George W (Business Person)
Emerson Electric Co
PO Box 4100
Saint Louis, MO 63136, USA

Tamm, Peter (Publisher)
Elbchaussee 277
Hamburg 22605, GERMANY

Tamm, Ralph (Athlete, Football Player)
2670 Atlantic Ave
Bensalem, PA 19020, USA

Tan, Amy (Writer)
c/o Staff Member *Steven Barclay Agency*
12 Western Ave
Petaluma, CA 94952, USA

Tan, Dun (Composer)
Columbia University
Arts School
Dodge Hall
New York, NY 10027, USA

Tan, Elaine (Actor)
CAM
19 Denmark Street
London WC2H 8NA, UNITED KINGDOM (UK)

Tan, Melvyn (Musician)
Valerie Barber Mgmt
4 Winsley St
#305
London W1N 7AR, UNITED KINGDOM (UK)

Tan, Phillip (Actor)
c/o Michael Henderson *Heresun Management*
4119 West Burbank Blvd.
Burbank, CA 91505, USA

Tanabe, David (Athlete, Hockey Player)
2321 Fieldstone Curv
Saint Paul, MN 55129-6218, USA

Tanaev, Nikoly (Prime Minister)
Prime Minister's Office
Ul Perromayskaya 57
Bishkek, KYRGYZSTAN

Tanaka, Koichi (Nobel Prize Laureate)
Shimadzu Corp
1 Nishinokyo-Kuwabaracho
Nakagoku
Kyoto 604-8511, JAPAN

Tanaka, Machiko (Stylist)
2378 Silver Ridge Ave
Los Angeles, CA 90039, USA

Tanaka, Shoji (Physicist)
Superconductivity Laboratory
1-10-13 Shinonome
Kotoku
Tokyo 135, JAPAN

Tanana, Frank (Athlete, Baseball Player)
28492 Harwich Dr
Farmington Hills, MI 48334-4281, USA

Tancill, Chris (Athlete, Hockey Player)
14 Kingswood Cir
Verona, WI 53593-7921, USA

Tancredo, Tom (Politician)
15342 W Iliff Dr
Lakewood, CO 80228, USA

Tandon, Raveena (Actor, Bollywood)
Tandon House Nippon Society
Juhu Church
Mumbai, MS 400049, INDIA

Tandon, Ravi (Bollywood, Director, Filmmaker, Producer)
B/58 Ravi Kiran
New Linking Road
Bombay, MS 400 058, INDIA

Tanford, Charles (Doctor)
Tarlswood
Back Lane
Easingwold, York YO6 3BG, UNITED KINGDOM (UK)

Tang, David (Designer)
Shanghai Tang
Guangdong Investment Tower 23rd Floor
148 Connaught Road Central
Central Hong Kong, HONG KONG

Tang, Felicia (Race Car Driver)
9461 Charleville Blvd.
#352
Beverly Hills, CA 90212, USA

Tangerine Dream
PO Box 29242
Oakland, CA 94604

Tanguay, Alex (Athlete, Hockey Player)
Jandec Inc
803-3080 Le Carrefour Blvd
Attn Robert Sauve
Laval, QC H7T 2R5, Canada

Tani, Daniel M (Astronaut)
14827 Sparkling Bay Ln
Houston, TX 77062-2325, USA

Taniguchi, Tadatsugu (Biologist)
University of Osaka
Molecular & Cellular Biology Dept
Osaka, JAPAN

Tanka, Aiko (Model)
PO Box 1025
Beverly Hills, CA 90213, USA

Tankersley, Dennis (Athlete, Baseball Player)
1032 Pearview Dr
Saint Peters, MO 63376-2269, USA

Tankersley, Taylor (Athlete, Baseball Player)
853 Chartier Ct
Asheboro, NC 27205-0545, USA

Tankian, Serj (Musician)
c/o David Holmes *3D Management*
1901 Main St
3rd Floor
Santa Monica, CA 90405, USA

Tanksley, Steven D (Scientist)
Cornell University
Plant Genetics Dept
Emerson Hall
Ithaca, NY 14853, USA

Tannahill, Don (Athlete, Hockey Player)
10113 Lakeview Dr
Rancho Mirage, CA 92270-1474, USA

Tannen, Steve (Athlete, Football Player)
735 N Niagara St
Burbank, CA 91505, USA

Tannenwald, Theodore Jr (Judge)
US Tax Court
400 2nd St NW
Washington, DC 20217, USA

Tanner, Alain (Director)
Chemin Point-du-Jour 12
Geneva 1202, SWITZERLAND

Tanner, Barron (Athlete, Football Player)
7556 W Oregon Ave
Glendale, AZ 85303, USA

Tanner, Bruce (Athlete, Baseball Player)
324 Hearthstone Dr
New Castle, PA 16105-1374, USA

Tanner, John (Athlete, Hockey Player)
Hewlett Packard 101-5150 Spectrum Way
Mississauga, ON L4W SGl, Canada

Tanner, Joseph R (Astronaut)
800 Nelson Park Ln
Longmont, CO 80503-7688, USA

Tanning, Dorothea (Artist)
40 5th Ave
New York, NY 10011-8843, USA

Tannous, Afif I (Government Official)
6912 Oak Court
Annandale, VA 22003, USA

Tantaros, Andrea (Television Host)
c/o Staff Member *Keppler Associates*
3030 Clarendon Blvd
7th Floor
Arlington, VA 22201, USA

Tanti, Tony (Athlete, Hockey Player)
Tanti Interiors 121-2323 Boundarv Rd
Vancouver, BC VSM 4V8, Canada

Tanuja (Actor, Bollywood)
14 Usha Kiran 15
M L Dhahanukar Marg
Mumbai, MS 400026, INDIA

Tanumafili, Malietoa II (President)
Government House
Valima, Apia, SAMOA

Tanzi, Vito (Economist)
5912 Walhondine Road
Bethesda, MD 20816, USA

Taormina, Sheila (Athlete, Olympic
Athlete, Swimmer)
16087 Riverside St
Livonia, MI 48154-2460, USA

Tapani, Kevin (Athlete, Baseball Player)
781 Ferndale Rd N
Wayzata, MN 55391-1010, USA

Tape, Gerald F (Physicist)
9707 Old Georgetown Road
#2518
Bethesda, MD 20814, USA

Tapert, Robert (Director, Producer,
Writer)
c/o Staff Member *Renaissance Pictures /
Ghost House Pictures*
315 S Beverly Dr
Suite 216
Beverly Hills, CA 90212, USA

Tapes N Tapes (Music Group)
c/o Staff Member *Paradigm (Monterey)*
404 W Franklin St
Monterey, CA 93940, USA

Tapia, Roberto (Musician)
c/o Staff Member *Universal Music Group
(UMG - LA)*
2220 Colorado Ave
Santa Monica, CA 90404, USA

Tapp, James (General)
5202 Keystone Creek Ct
Fort Collins, CO 80528-8556, USA

Tappan V, Alfredo (Director)
c/o Gabriel Blanco *Gabriel Blanco
Iglesias (Mexico)*
Rio Balsas 35-32
Colonia Cuauhtemoc
DF 06500, Mexico

Tapper, Brad (Athlete, Hockey Player)
8132 Bibiana Way Apt 103
Fort Myers, FL 33912-9022, USA

Tapper, Brad (Athlete, Hockey Player)
Florida Everblades 11000 Everblades
Pkwy
Attn: Coaching Staff
louebec, QC GIG 3Z8, Canada

Tapping, Amanda (Actor)
c/o Staff Member *Stargate SG-1*
MGM
10250 Constellation Blvd
Los Angeles, CA 90067, USA

Tapply, William G. (Writer)
c/o Staff Member *St Martins Press*
Publicity Dept
175 5th Ave
New York, NY 10010, USA

Tapscott, Mark
5663 Ruthwood Dr.
Calabasas, CA 91302

Tarand, Andres (Prime Minister)
Riigikogu
Lossi Plats 1A
Tallinn 10130, ESTONIA

Tarango, Jeff (Athlete, Olympic Athlete,
Tennis Player)
1166 Longfellow Dr
Manhattan Beach, CA 90266-6848, USA

Tarantina, Brian (Actor)
c/o Staff Member *Cunningham Escott
Slevin & Doherty (CESD-LA)*
10635 Santa Monica Blvd
130
Los Angeles, CA 90025, USA

Tarantino, Quentin (Actor, Director,
Producer, Writer)
c/o Mike Simpson *WME (LA)*
9601 Wilshire Blvd Fl 3
Beverly Hills, CA 90210, USA

Taranu, Cornel (Composer, Conductor)
Str Nicolae Iorga
Ckuj-Napoca 3400, ROMANIA

Tarasco, Tony (Athlete, Baseball Player)
3528 Maplewood Ave
Los Angeles, CA 90066-3020, USA

Tarasova, Tatiana (Coach, Figure Skater)
Connecticut Skating Center
300 Alumni Road
Newington, CT 06111, USA

Tarasovic, George (Athlete, Football
Player)
1503 Michael Dr
Pittsburgh, PA 15227, USA

Tarbuck, Jimmy (Comedian)
c/o Staff Member *International Artistes*
Holborn Hall - 4th Floor
London WC1V 7BD, UK

Tardif, Patrice (Athlete, Hockey Player)
1472 Rue Michel Louvain
Thetford Mines, QC G6G 7S8, Canada

Tardiff, Marc (Athlete, Hockey Player)
Charlesbourg Toyota 16070 Boul Henri-
Bourassa
Quebec, QC G1G 3Z8, Canada

Tardits, Richard (Athlete, Football Player)
3590 Round Bottom Rd
Cincinnati, OH 45244, USA

Tarjan, Robert E (Mathematician)
4 Constitution Hl E
Princeton, NJ 08540, USA

Tarkan (Musician)
c/o Staff Member *Mydonose Productions*
No 22 K 14
Park Plaza Eski Buyukdere Cad
Maslak, Istanbul, Turkey

Tarkanian, Jerry (Basketball Coach,
Coach)
4767 Ocean Blvd
Unit 1005
San Diego, CA 92109, USA

Tarkenton, Fran (Athlete, Business Person,
Football Player)
3340 Peachtree Rd NE
Apt 2570
Atlanta, GA 30326, USA

Tarle, Jim (Athlete, Football Player)
2125 Willesdon Dr E
Jacksonville, FL 32246, USA

Tarmichael, Stephen (Stylist)
P.O. Box 1121
Palm Springs, CA 92263-1121, USA

Tarnasky, Nick (Athlete, Hockey Player)
6010 Interba¥' Blvd
Tampa, FL 33611-4745, USA

Tarpey, Erin
77 W. 66th St.
New York, NY 10023

Tarpley, Ron (Athlete, Basketball Player)
819 Foxridge Dr
Arlington, TX 76017, USA

Tarpley, Roy (Athlete, Basketball Player)
819 Foxridge Dr
Arlington, TX 76017-6451, USA

Tarr, Curtis W (Business Person,
Government Official)
Intermet Corp
5445 Corporate Dr
#200
Troy, MI 48098, USA

Tarrant, Chris (Game Show Host)
c/o Staff Member *Who Wants to Be a
Millionaire*
30 W 67th St
New York, NY 10023

Tarr Jr, Robert J (Publisher)
58 River Marsh Ln
Johns Island, SC 29455-5202, USA

Tarses, Matt (Producer)
c/o Staff Member *WME (LA)*
9601 Wilshire Blvd Fl 3
Beverly Hills, CA 90210, USA

Tartabull, Danilio (Dan) (Athlete, Baseball
Player)
8200 Redlands St
Apt 112
Playa Del Rey, CA 90293, USA

Tartabull, Danny (Athlete, Baseball
Player)
28990 Oak Creek Ln Apt 1611
Agoura Hills, CA 91301-6437, USA

Tartabull, Jose (Athlete, Baseball Player)
1658 W 72nd St
Hialeah, FL 33014-4443, USA

Tartaglia, John (Actor, Producer, Writer)
Shrek, The Musical
Broadway Theatre
1681 Broadway
New York, NY 10019, USA

Tartakovsky, Genndy (Director, Producer,
Writer)
c/o Staff Member *WmE2 (WMA-LA)*
1 William Morris Pl
Beverly Hills, CA 90212, USA

Tarter, Jill (Astronomer, Physicist)
Seti Institute Research Center
2035 Mountain View
Mountain View, CA 94043, USA

Tarver, Antonio (Athlete, Boxer, Olympic
Athlete)
3959 Van Dyke Rd
Lutz, FL 33558-8025, USA

Tarver, John (Athlete, Football Player)
12056 SE Mount Scott Blvd
Happy Valley, OR 97086-6939, USA

Tarver, Laschelle (Athlete, Baseball
Player)
4410 N Emerson Ave
Fresno, CA 93705-1203, USA

Tarzier, Carol (Artist)
1217 32nd St
Oakland, CA 94608, USA

Tasby, Willie (Athlete, Baseball Player)
1210 E Renfro St
Plant City, FL 33563-5850, USA

Taschner, Jack (Athlete, Baseball Player)
2170 Hidden Creek Rd
Neenah, WI 54956-8916, USA

Tashima, A Wallace (Judge)
US Court of Appeals
125 S Grand Ave
Pasadena, CA 91105, USA

Tasker, Steven J (Steve) (Athlete, Football
Player, Sportscaster)
16 Gypsy Ln
East Aurora, NY 14052, USA

Tata, Joe E (Actor)
c/o Jeffrey Leavitt *Leavitt Talent Group*
8255 W Sunset Blvd
West Hollywood, CA 90046, USA

Tata, Jordan (Athlete, Baseball Player)
709 Sunfish St
Lakeway, TX 78734-4409, USA

Tata, Ratan (Business Person)
Tata
Bombay House
24 Homi Mody St
Mumbai 400 001, India

Tata, Terry (Athlete, Baseball Player)
23 Stonegate Cir
Cheshire, CT 06410-3461, USA

Tata, Terry (Athlete, Baseball Player)
23 Stonegate Circle
Cheshire, CT 06410-3461, USA

Tatar, Jerome F (Business Person)
Mead Corp
Courthouse Plaza N
Dayton, OH 45463, USA

Tatarek, Bob (Athlete, Football Player)
5829 Southhall Rd
Birmingham, AL 35213, USA

Tataryn, Dave (Athlete, Hockey Player)
27 Fairway Crt
Shanty Bay, ON L0L 2L0, Canada

Tataurangi, Phil (Golfer)
5204 Glen Heather Dr
Flower Mound, TX 75028-6035, USA

Tatchell, Spence (Athlete, Hockey Player)
176-1995 Burtch Rd
Kelowna, BC V1Y 4B4, Canada

Tate, Albert Jr (Judge)
US Court of Appeals
600 Camp St
New Orleans, LA 70130, USA

Tate, Bruce (Musician)
David Harris Enterprises
24210 E Fork Road
#9
Azusa, CA 91702, USA

Tate, Catherine (Actor, Writer)
BBC Broadcasting House
c/o Doctor Who
Cardiff CF5 2YQ, United Kingdom

Tate, David (Athlete, Football Player)
3481 S Blackhawk Way
Aurora, CO 80014, USA

Tate, Frank (Boxer)
12731 Water Oak Dr
Missouri City, TX 77489, USA

Tate, James (Writer)
PO Box 9668
North Amherst, MA 01059-9668, USA

Tate, Jeffrey P
English Chamber Orchestra
2 Coningsby Road
London W5 4HR, UNITED KINGDOM
(UK)

Tate, Kevin
6834 Hollywood Blvd. #303
Hollywood, CA 90028-6175

Tate, Lahmard (Actor)
c/o Rob D'Avola *Rob DAvola &
Associates*
9107 Wilshire Blvd #450
Beverly Hills, CA 90210, USA

Tate, Larena
4116 W. Magnolia Blvd. #101
Burbank, CA 91505-2700

Tate, Larenz (Actor)
c/o Thea Ellis *Fifteen Minutes (LA)*
8436 W 3rd St
Suite 650
Los Angeles, CA 90048, USA

Tate, Lee (Athlete, Baseball Player)
6905 Pratt St
Omaha, NE 68104-2528, USA

Tate, Randy (Politician)
Chrsitian Coalition
100 Centerville Tumpike
Virginia Beach, VA 23463, USA

Tate, Randy (Athlete, Baseball Player)
106 King St
Muscle Shoals, AL 35661-3698, USA

Tate, Stu (Athlete, Baseball Player)
1436 Nocoseka Trl Apt N1
Anniston, AL 36207-6739, USA

Tatel, David S (Judge)
US Court of Appeals
333 Constitution Ave NW
Washington, DC 20001, USA

Tatiana (Model)
c/o Staff Member *Ford Models (NY)*
238 E 4th St
New York, NY 10009, USA

Tatlitug, Kivanc (Actor)
c/o Gaye Sokmen *Gaye Sökmen Talent
Agency*
Karanfil Caddesi Yolal Sokak Ic
Levent No:3
Istanbul 34330, Turkey

Tatrai, Vilmos (Musician)
R Wallenberg Utca 4
Budapest XIII 1136, HUNGARY

TATU (Music Group)
c/o Robert Hayes *Sound Management*
1525 S Winchester Blvd
San Jose, CA 95128, USA

Tatum, Bradford
1505 10th St.
Santa Monica, CA 90401

Tatum, Channing (Actor)
c/o William Choi *Management 360*
9111 Wilshire Blvd
Beverly Hills, CA 90210, USA

Tatum, Craig (Athlete, Baseball Player)
105 Morrell Cir
Hattiesburg, MS 39402-8142, USA

Tatum, Earl (Athlete, Basketball Player)
2300 W Skyline Rd
Milwaukee, WI 53209-2176, USA

Tatum, Jim (Athlete, Baseball Player)
7433 Indian Wells Cv
Lone Tree, CO 80124-4207, USA

Tatum, Ken (Athlete, Baseball Player)
19 Oakdale Dr
Montevallo, AL 35115-5435, USA

Tatum, Kinnon (Athlete, Football Player)
4109 Knollwood Dr
Fayetteville, NC 28304, USA

Tatupu, Lofa (Athlete, Football Player)
5817 106th Ave NE
Bellevue, WA 98033, USA

Taube, Sven-Bertil
113Cheyne Walk
London, ENGLAND SWl0 OES

Taubensee, Ed (Athlete, Baseball Player)
2234 Fountain Key Cir
Windermere, FL 34786-5804, USA

Taubman, A Alfred (Business Person)
Taubman Co
200 E Long Lake Road
Bloomfield Hills, MI 48304, USA

Taupin, Bernie (Musician, Songwriter,
Writer)
2905 Roundup Road
Santa Ynez, CA 93460, USA

Tauran, Jean-Louis Cardinal (Religious
Leader)
Palazzo Apostolico
Vatican City 00120, VATICAN CITY

Taurasi, Diana (Basketball Player)
c/o Staff Member *Phoenix Mercury*
201 E Jefferson St
Phoenix, AZ 85004, USA

Taurel, Sidney (Business Person)
Eli Lilly Co
Lilly Corporate Center
Indianapolis, IN 46285, USA

Tausch, Terry (Athlete, Football Player)
2804 Ryder Ct
Plano, TX 75093, USA

Tauscher, Hansjorg (Skier)
Schwand 7
Oberstdorf 87561, GERMANY

Tauscher, Mark (Athlete, Football Player)
2245 Red Tail Gin
De Pere, WI 54115, USA

Tauskey, Mary (Athlete, Horse Racer,
Olympic Athlete)
6 Morris Rd
Ambler, PA 19002-5407, USA

Taussig, Don (Athlete, Baseball Player)
1111 Ocean Dunes Cir
Jupiter, FL 33477-9128, USA

Tautalatasi, Junior (Athlete, Football
Player)
1032 Eagle Avenue
Apt A
Alameda, CA 94501, USA

Tautolo, Terry (Athlete, Football Player)
5713 E Huntdale St
Long Beach, CA 90808, USA

Tautou, Audrey (Actor)
c/o Claire Blondel *ArtMedia*
20 avenue Rapp
Paris 75008, France

Tauziat, Nathalie (Tennis Player)
Federation de Tennis
1 Ave Gordon Bennett
Paris 75016, FRANCE

Tavard, Georges H (Misc)
330 Market St
Brighton, MA 02135, USA

Tavare, Jay (Actor)
c/o Paul Greenstone *Paul Greenstone
Entertainment*
3008 Sorrelwood Dr
San Ramon, CA 94582-5008, USA

Tavares, Alex (Athlete, Baseball Player)
Calle 7B #18
Reparto Perello Santiago, Dominican
Republic

Tavares, John (Athlete, Hockey Player)
c/o Pat Brisson *Creative Artists Agency
(CAA-LA)*
2000 Ave Of The Stars
Los Angeles, CA 90067, USA

Tavarez, Christopher (Actor, Football
Player)
c/o Staff Member *Ella Bee*
Prefers to be contacted by telephone or
email
Atlanta, GA, USA

Tavarez, Julian (Athlete, Baseball Player)
1108 Fireside Trl
Broadview Heights, OH 44147-3625,
USA

Tavener, John K (Composer)
Chester Music
8-9 Firth St
London W1V 5TZ, UNITED KINGDOM
(UK)

Taveras, Willy (Athlete, Baseball Player)
6014 Floyd St
Houston, TX 77584-8289, USA

Taverner, Sonia (Ballerina)
PO Box 129
Stony Plain, AB, CANADA

Tavernier, Bertrand R M (Director)
Little Bear Productions
7-9 Rue Arthur Groussler
Paris 75010, FRANCE

Taviani, Paolo (Director)
Instituto Luce SPA
Via Tuscolana 1055
Rome 00173, ITALY

Taviani, Vittorio (Director)
Instituto Luce SPA
Via Tuscolana 1055
Rome 00173, ITALY

Taxier, Arthur (Actor)
Pakula/King
9229 Sunset Blvd
#315
Los Angeles, CA 90069, USA

Taya, Maawiya Ould Sid'Ahmed
(President)
President's Office
Boite Postale 184
Nouakchott, MAURITANIA

Taylor, Aaron (Athlete, Baseball Player)
13649 Winstanley Way
San Diego, CA 92130-1412, USA

Taylor, Alphonso (Athlete, Football
Player)
254 W Trenton Ave
Apt 314B
Morrisville, PA 19067, USA

Taylor, Andy (Musician)
DD Productions
93A Westbourne Park Villas
London W2 5ED, UNITED KINGDOM
(UK)

Taylor, Anthony (Athlete, Basketball
Player)
5300 Parkview Dr
Apt 1093
Lake Oswego, OR 97035-8728, USA

Taylor, Arthur R (Business Person,
Educator)
Muhlenburg College
President's Office
Allentown, PA 18104, USA

Taylor, Ben (Football Player)

Taylor, Benedict
4 Great Queen St.
London, ENGLAND WC28 5DG

Taylor, Billy (Athlete, Baseball Player)
201 Washington Pl
Thomasville, GA 31792-4785, USA

Taylor, Billy (Athlete, Football Player)
3 Greenwich Dr
Apt 86
Jersey City, NJ 07305, USA

Taylor, Bob (Athlete, Baseball Player)
27 Sunnybrook Rd
Springfield, MA 01119-2209, USA

Taylor, Bobby "The Chief"
Tampa Bay Lightning 401 Channelside Dr
Attn Broadcast Dept
Tamoa, FL 33602-5400, USA

Taylor, Bobby "The Chief" (Athlete,
Hockey Player)
3912 Americana Dr
Tampa, FL 33634-7405, USA

Taylor, Brian (Athlete, Basketball Player)
3622 Green Vista Dr
Encino, CA 91436-4038, USA

Taylor, Brien (Baseball Player)
147 Brien Taylor Ln
Beaufort, NC 28516-6664, USA

Taylor, Bruce (Athlete, Baseball Player)
8 Highland Park Rd
Rutland, MA 01543-1742, USA

Taylor, Bruce L. (Athlete, Football Player)
10324 Pontofino Cir
Trinity, FL 34655, USA

Taylor, Buck (Actor)
1305 Clyde Dr
Marrero, LA 70072, USA

Taylor, Carl (Athlete, Baseball Player)
2356 Riveria Dr
Sarasota, FL 34232-3522, USA

Taylor, Carl E (Physicist)
Bittersweet Acres
1201 Hollins Lane
Baltimore, MD 21209, USA

Taylor, Cecil P (Composer, Musician)
Joel Chriss
300 Mercer St
#3J
New York, NY 10003, USA

Taylor, Chad (Musician)
Freedman & Smith
1790 Broadway
#131
New York, NY 10019, USA

Taylor, Charles R (Charley) (Athlete,
Football Executive, Football Player)
12023 Center Ln
Reston, VA 20191, USA

Taylor, Chris (Athlete, Hockey Player)
24 WHam Cir
North Chili, NY 14514-9762

Taylor, Chris (Athlete, Hockey Player)
Rochester Americans
1 War Memorial Sq Ste 228
Rochester, NY 14614-2192

Taylor, Christian (Actor)
c/o Staff Member *KST Productions*
5543 Edmondson Pike # 1
Nashville, TN 37211-5808, USA

Taylor, Christine (Actor)
c/o Kimberlin Dalehite *Magnolia
Entertainment (LA)*
9595 Wilshire Blvd
Suite 601
Beverly Hills, CA 90212, USA

Taylor, Christy (Race Car Driver)
10990 Massachusetts Ave.
#3
Los Angeles, CA 90024, USA

Taylor, Christy (Actor)
10990 Massachusetts Ave
#3
Los Angeles, CA 90024, USA

Taylor, Cindy (Actor)
c/o Allee Newhoff *Elite Model
Management*
119 Washington Ave
Suite 501
Miami Beach, FL 33139, USA

Taylor, Clarice (Actor)
380 Elkwood Terrace
Englewood, NJ 07631, USA

Taylor, Cordell (Athlete, Football Player)
1825 Chaswood Park Dr
Marietta, GA 30066, USA

Taylor, Corey (Musician)
c/o Staff Member *Agency Group Ltd, The
(LA)*
1880 Century Park E
Suite 711
Los Angeles, CA 90067, USA

Taylor, Dana (Actor)
100 S Sunrise Way
#468
Palm Springs, CA 92262, USA

Taylor, Dave (Athlete, Hockey Player)
18920 Pasadero Dr
Tarzana, CA 91356-5122, USA

Taylor, David (Writer)
c/o Author Mail *Bantam-Dell Publishing
(NY)*
1745 Broadway
New York, NY 10019, USA

Taylor, David (Athlete, Football Player)
304 Paddington Rd
Baltimore, MD 21212, USA

Taylor, Delores (Actor)
PO Box 840
Moorpark, CA 93020, USA

Taylor, Dennis (Race Car Driver)
1255 N. Tustin Ave.
Anaheim, CA 92807, USA

Taylor, Dorn (Athlete, Baseball Player)
405 Avenue D
Horsham, PA 19044, USA

Taylor, Doug (Race Car Driver)
6630 Denver Industrial Park Blvd.
Denver, NC 28092, USA

Taylor, Dwight (Athlete, Baseball Player)
5163 Queen Mary Ln
Jackson, MS 39209-3141, USA

Taylor, Ed (Athlete, Football Player)
2901 Clarke Rd
Memphis, TN 38115, USA

Taylor, Eric (Artist)
13 Tredgold Ave
Branhope near Leeds
West Yorkshire LS16 9BS, UNITED
KINGDOM (UK)

Taylor, Eunice (Baseball Player)
955 Carroll Ln
Mount Dora, FL 32757-3726, USA

Taylor, Femi (Actor)
Paul Telford Mgmt
23 Noel St
London W1V 3RD, UNITED KINGDOM
(UK)

Taylor, Fred (Athlete, Football Player)
7975 Monterey Bay Dr
Jacksonville, FL 32256, USA

Taylor, Gary (Athlete, Baseball Player)
995 Beaumont Rd
Highland, MI 48356-3202, USA

Taylor, Gilbert (Cinematographer)
Cinematography Society
11 Croft
Gerrards Cross
Bucks SL9 9E, UNITED KINGDOM (UK)

Taylor, Glen (Basketball Player)
Minnesota Timberwolves
Target Center
600 1st Ave N
Minneapolis, MN 55403, USA

taylor, Graham (Athlete, Baseball Player)
2705 Vera Cruz Dr
Villa Hills, KY 41017-1070, USA

Taylor, Harry (Athlete, Baseball Player)
2125 Cooks Ln
Fort Worth, TX 76120-5301, USA

Taylor, Henry S (Writer)
1120 Aqua Vista Dr NW
Gig Harbor, WA 98335-1536, USA

Taylor, Holland (Actor)
c/o Bob Gersh *Gersh (LA)*
9465 Wilshire Blvd
Suite 600
Beverly Hills, CA 90212, USA

Taylor, Hosea (Athlete, Football Player)
208 Bobby St
Longview, TX 75602-3804, USA

Taylor, Jack (Business Person)
Enterprise Rent-A-Car
600 Corporate Park Dr
St Louis, MO 63105, USA

Taylor, Jackie Lynn (Actor)
PO Box 3182
Citrus Heights, CA 95611, USA

Taylor, James (Musician, Songwriter)
15 Muddy Cove Rd
Chilmark, MA 02535, USA

Taylor, James A (General)
PO Box 284
Trinity Center, CA 96091-0284, USA

Taylor, James Arnold (Actor, Voice Over
Artist)
c/o Pat Brady *Cunningham Escott Slevin
& Doherty (CESD-LA)*
10635 Santa Monica Blvd
130
Los Angeles, CA 90025, USA

Taylor, James C (Jim) (Athlete, Football
Player)
7840 Walden Rd
Baton Rouge, LA 70808, USA

Taylor, Jason (Athlete, Football Player)
2980 Paddock Rd
Weston, FL 33331, USA

Taylor, Jason (Rugby Player)
Parramatta Eels
PO BOX 2666
North Parramatta, NSW 1750,
AUSTRALIA

Taylor, Jay (Business Person)
Placer Dorne Inc
1600-1055 Dunsmuir St
Vancouver, BC V7X 1P1, CANADA

Taylor, Jayceon (The Game) (Musician)
c/o Staff Member *Czar Entertainment*
11 W 25th St
Suite 300
New York, NY 10010, USA

Taylor, Jeff (Race Car Driver)
2017 E. 5th St.
Lumberton, NC 28358, USA

Taylor, Jennifer Bini (Actor)
c/o Brad Warshaw *Brad Warshaw*
P.O. Box 931332
Los Angeles, CA 90093, USA

Taylor, J Herbert (Biologist)
110 Wood Road
#H210
Los Gatos, CA 95030, USA

Taylor, Jim (Writer)
c/o Staff Member *WmE2 (WMA-LA)*
1 William Morris Pl
Beverly Hills, CA 90212, USA

Taylor, Jonathan (Producer)
c/o Staff Member *United Talent Agency
(UTA)*
9336 Civic Center Dr
Beverly Hills, CA 90210, USA

Taylor, Joseph H Jr (Nobel Prize Laureate)
PO Box 708
Princeton, NJ 08542-0708, USA

Taylor, Josh (Actor)
4151 Vanalden Ave
Tarzana, CA 91356-5527, USA

Taylor, J T (Musician)
Famous Artists Agency
250 W 57th St
New York, NY 10107, USA

Taylor, Judson H (Educator)
State University of New York College
President's Office
Cortland, NY 13045, USA

Taylor, Karen (Comedian)
c/o Staff Member *Avalon Management*
4A Exmoor St
London W10 6BD, UK

Taylor, Kerry (Athlete, Baseball Player)
1705 331/2 St S
Moorhead, MN 56560-3945, USA

Taylor, Kim (Musician)
c/o Staff Member *Paradigm (Monterey)*
404 W Franklin St
Monterey, CA 93940, USA

Taylor, Kitrick L (Athlete, Football Player)
18215 Foothill Blvd
Apt 94
Fontana, CA 92335, USA

Taylor, Lance J (Economist)
PO Box 378
Old County Road
Washington, DC 04574, USA

Taylor, Lauriston S (Physicist)
10450 Lottsford Road
#1-5
Bowle, MD 20721, USA

Taylor, Lawrence (Athlete, Football
Player)
2850 Lost Lakes Way
Powder Springs, GA 30127, USA

Taylor, Lee (Stylist)
c/o Staff Member *Directions USA*
3717-C W Market St
Greensboro, NC 27403, USA

Taylor, Lili (Actor)
c/o Staff Member *Dontanville/Frattaroli
(D/F)*
270 Lafayette St
Suite 402
New York, NY 10012, USA

Taylor, Lionel (Athlete, Coach, Football Coach, Football Player)
201 Pinnacle Dr SE
Apt 3614
Rio Rancho, NM 87124-0458, USA

Taylor, Livingston (Musician)
Fat City Artists
1906 Chet Atkins Place
#502
Nashville, TN 37212, USA

Taylor, Marianne (Actor)
Jack Scagnatti
5118 Vineland Ave
#102
North Hollywood, CA 91601, USA

Taylor, Mark (Athlete, Hockey Player)
110-5620 152 St
Surrey, BC V3S 3K2, CANADA

Taylor, Mark L (Actor)
7919 Norton Ave
West Hollywood, CA 90046, USA

Taylor, Maurice (Basketball Player)
Houston Rockets
Toyota Center
2 E Greenway Plaza
Houston, TX 77046, USA

Taylor, Meldrick (Athlete, Boxer, Olympic Athlete)
2736 W Lehigh Ave
Philadelphia, PA 19132-3128, USA

Taylor, Meshach (Actor)
c/o Gordon Gilbertson *Gilbertson Management*
1334 3rd St Promenade #201
Santa Monica, CA 90401, USA

Taylor, Michael (Athlete, Football Player)
5014 Crane St
Detroit, MI 48213, USA

Taylor, Mick (Musician)
Jacobson & Colin
60 Madison Ave #1026
New York, NY 10010-1666, USA

Taylor, Mike (Athlete, Football Player)
19632 Quiet Bay Ln
Huntington Beach, CA 92648, USA

Taylor, Natascha (Actor)
c/o Staff Member *ICM Partners (ICM-LA)*
10250 Constellation Blvd Fl 7
Los Angeles, CA 90067, USA

Taylor, Niki (Actor, Model)
c/o Lou Taylor *Tri Star Sports & Entertainment Group*
215 Ward Cir
Suite 200
Brentwood, TN 37027, USA

Taylor, Noah (Actor)
June Cann Mgmt
110 Quenn St
Woolahra, NSW 2025, AUSTRALIA

Taylor, Ollie (Athlete, Basketball Player)
4008 Spring Garden Dr
Pearland, TX 77584-9308, USA

Taylor, Otis (Athlete, Football Player)
6608 Woodson Rd
Raytown, MO 64133, USA

Taylor, Paul B (Choreographer, Dancer)
Paul Taylor Dance Co
552 Broadway
New York, NY 10012, USA

Taylor, Penny (Basketball Player)
Cleveland Rockers
Gund Arena
1 Center Court
Cleveland, OH 44115, USA

Taylor, Phil (Football Player)
c/o Peter Schaffer *All Pro Sports and Entertainment*
36 Steele St
Suite 100
Denver, CO 80206, USA

Taylor, Priscilla (Actor, Model)
c/o Staff Member *Crystal Sky Pictures*
10203 Santa Monica Blvd
5th Floor
Los Angeles, CA 90067, USA

Taylor, Rachael (Actor)
c/o Annett Wolf *WKT Public Relations (WKT-LA)*
9350 Wilshire Blvd
Suite 450
Beverly Hills, CA 90212, USA

Taylor, Reggie (Athlete, Baseball Player)
828 Havird St
Newberry, SC 29108, USA

Taylor, Reggie
828 Havird St
Newberry, SC 29108-3727, USA

Taylor, Regina (Actor)
8048 Dusenberg Ct
Sacramento, CA 95828-5834, USA

Taylor, Renee (Actor)
613 N Arden Dr
#309
Beverly Hills, CA 90210, USA

Taylor, Richard E (Nobel Prize Laureate)
757 Mayfield Ave
Stanford, CA 94305-1043, USA

Taylor, Rip (Actor, Comedian)
1133 N Clark St
Los Angeles, CA 90069, USA

Taylor, Rod (Actor)
2375 Bowmont Dr
Beverly Hills, CA 90210, USA

Taylor, Roger (Musician)
c/o Staff Member *DD Productions*
93A Westbourne Park Villas
London W2 5ED, UNITED KINGDOM (UK)

Taylor, Roger (Tennis Player)
39 Newstead Way
Wimbledon SW19, UNITED KINGDOM (UK)

Taylor, Roland (Athlete, Basketball Player)
3812 Homewood Ave
Ashtabula, OH 44004-5939, USA

Taylor, Ron (Athlete, Baseball Player)
SC Cooper Sports Medical Clinic
600 University Ave
Toronto, ON M5G 1X5, CANADA

Taylor, Roosevelt (Athlete, Football Player)
7331 Ebbtide Dr
New Orleans, LA 70126, USA

Taylor, Sam (Sammy) (Athlete, Baseball Player)
248 N 74th St
East Saint Louis, IL 62203-2411, USA

Taylor, Sandra (Actor, Model)
c/o Craig Wyckoff *Wyckoff and Associates (LA)*
11350 Ventura Blvd
Suite 100
Studio City, CA 91604-3140, USA

Taylor, Scott (Athlete, Baseball Player)
1349 N Forestview Ct
Wichita, KS 67235-7033, USA

Taylor, Stephen Monroe (Actor)
c/o Staff Member *Main Title Entertainment*
8383 Wilshire Blvd
Suite 408
Los Angeles, CA 90211, USA

Taylor, Susan L. (Editor)
National Cares Mentoring Movement
408 W. 58th St
New York, NY 10019, USA

Taylor, Tamara (Actor)
3704 Sheridge Dr
Sherman Oaks, CA 91403, USA

Taylor, Tate (Director)
c/o John Norris *Artists and Directors Cooperative*
1041 N Formosa Ave
Writers Building Suite 8
West Hollywood, CA 90046, USA

Taylor, Ted (Athlete, Hockey Player)
PO Box 244
Oak Lake, MB ROM 1PO, Canada

Taylor, Terry (Athlete, Baseball Player)
743 W Walnut Ave
Crestview, FL 32536-3919, USA

Taylor, Tim (Athlete, Hockey Player)
Hockey Training Above
353 McCarthy Rd PO Box 818
Stratford, ON NSA 7S7, Canada

Taylor, Tommy (Athlete, Baseball Player)
Kansas City Monarchs
524 Whitehall St
Jackson, TN 38301-5535, USA

Taylor, Tony (Athlete, Baseball Player)
8415 NW 165th Ter
Hialeah, FL 33016-6137, USA

Taylor, Tracy (Stylist)
c/o Staff Member *Kramer + Kramer*
156 5th Ave#420
New York, NY 10010, USA

Taylor, TW (Race Car Driver)
22909 Airpark Dr.
Petersburg, VA 23803, USA

Taylor, Vaughn (Golfer)
2536 Queens Ct
Grovetown, GA 30813, USA

Taylor, Wade (Athlete, Baseball Player)
6 Sleepy Hollow Cv
Longwood, FL 32750-3845, USA

Taylor, Wayne (Race Car Driver)
501 N. Orlando Ave.
#313-189
Winter Park, FL 32789, USA

Taylor, Wilson H (Business Person)
CIGNA Corp
1 Liberty Place
1650 Market St
Philadelphia, PA 19192, USA

Taylor-Compton, Scout (Actor)
c/o Nicki Fioravante *PMK/BNC - LA*
8687 Melrose Ave
8th Floor
West Hollywood, CA 90069, USA

Taylor-Cotter, Eliza (Actor)
c/o Staff Member *Nickelodeon UK*
PO Box 6425
LONDON W1A 6UR, UNITED KINGDOM

Taylor-Grauman, Joan
9920 Robin Dr.
Los Angeles, CA 90069

Taylor-Lukin, Norna (Baseball Player)
7934 W Maple Grove Rd
Andrews, IN 46702-9518, USA

Taylor-Taylor, Courtney (Musician)
Monqui Records
PO Box 5908
Portland, OR 97228, USA

Taylor-Young, Leigh (Actor)
11300 W Olympic Blvd
#610
Los Angeles, CA 90064, USA

Taymor, Julie (Director, Producer, Writer)
c/o Bart Walker *ICM Partners (ICM-LA)*
555 W 25th St
4th Floor
New York, NY 10001, USA

Tchaikovsky, Aleksandr V (Composer, Musician)
Leningradsky Prosp 14
#4
Moscow 125040, RUSSIA

Tcherkassky, Marianna (Ballerina)
American Ballet Theatre
890 Broadway
New York, NY 10003, USA

Teaff, Grant (Coach, Football Coach)
8265 Forest Ridge Dr
Waco, TX 76712, USA

Teagarden, Taylor (Baseball Player)
2007 Bluestem Ln
Carrollton, TX 75007-5313

Teagle, Terry (Athlete, Basketball Player)
2111 Heatherwood Dr
Missouri City, TX 77489-3277, USA

Teague, George (Athlete, Football Player)
6561 Meadow Lark Dr
Montgomery, AL 36116, USA

Teague, Kerry (Race Car Driver)
3110 Roberta Road
Concord, NC 28027, United States

Teague, Lewis
2190 N. Beverly Glen Blvd.
Los Angeles, CA 90077

Teague, Marshall (Actor)
c/o Richard Lewis *Geddes Agency, The*
8430 Santa Monica Blvd
Suite 200
Los Angeles, CA 90069, USA

Teahen, Mark (Athlete, Baseball Player)
8610 E Via Del Sol Dr
Scottsdale, AZ 85255-5253, USA

Teal, Jeff (Athlete, Hockey Player)
1840 Wood Duck Ln
Excelsior, MN 55331-6507

Teal, Jim F (Athlete, Football Player)
38444 Kingsway Ct
Farmington Hills, MI 48331, USA

Teal, Jimmy D (Athlete, Football Player)
2636 Spring Branch Rd
Mesquite, TX 75181, USA

Teal, Willie (Athlete, Football Player)
1322 Westchester Dr
Baton Rouge, LA 70810, USA

Tea Leaf Green (Music Group)
c/o Staff Member *Paradigm (Monterey)*
404 W Franklin St
Monterey, CA 93940, USA

Teannaki, Teatao (President)
President's Office
PO Box 68
Bairiki
Tarawa Atoll, KIRBATI

Tearry, Larry (Athlete, Football Player)
1334 Kienast Dr
Fayetteville, NC 28314, USA

Tears For Fears (Music Group)
c/o Staff Member *Creative Artists Agency*
(CAA-LA)
2000 Ave Of The Stars
Los Angeles, CA 90067, USA

Teasdale, Kathryn (Race Car Driver)
P.O. Box 4950
Pinehurst, NC 28374, USA

Teasley, Nikki (Basketball Player)
Los Angeles Sparks
Staples Center
1111 S Figueroa St
Los Angeles, CA 90015, USA

Teasley, Ron (Athlete, Baseball Player)
New York Cubans
19317 Coyle St
Detroit, MI 48235-2039, USA

Tebbit of Chingford, Norman B
(Government Official)
House of Lords
Westminsiter
London SW1A 0PW, UNITED KINGDOM
(UK)

Tebbutt, Arthur R (Mathematician)
1511 Pelican Point Dr
Sarasota, FL 34231, USA

Tebow, Tim (Athlete, Football Player,
Heisman Trophy Winner)
9200 Otis Rd
Jacksonville, FL 32220-2946, USA

Techine, Andre J F (Director)
Artmedia
20 Ave Rapp
Paris 75007, FRANCE

Tedeschi, Susan (Musician)
Blue Sky Artists
761 Washington Ave N
Minneapolis, MN 55401, USA

Tedford, Travis (Actor)
c/o Staff Member *Acme Talent & Literary*
(LA)
1400 Atlantic Ave
Suite 274
Long Beach, CA 90814, USA

Teed, Dick (Athlete, Baseball Player)
45 Taylor St
Windsor, CT 06095-2437, USA

Teegarden, Aimee (Actor)
c/o Tara Friedlander *ID PR (LA)*
7060 Hollywood Blvd
8th Floor
Los Angeles, CA 90028, USA

Teela, Jeremy (Athlete, Biathlete, Olympic
Athlete)
PO Box 681240
Park City, UT 84068-1240, USA

Teerlinck, John (Athlete, Football Player)
9713 Bay Hill Dr
Lone Tree, CO 80124, USA

Teeter, Mike (Athlete, Football Player)
4393 E Mount Garfield Rd
Fruitport, MI 49415, USA

Teevens, Buddy (Coach, Football Coach)
Stanford University
Athletic Dept
Stanford, CA 94395, USA

Tefkin, Blair (Actor)
Lucie Gamelon
8022 Sunset Blvd #4049
Los Angeles, CA 90046, USA

Tegan and Sara (Music Group)
c/o Staff Member *Paquin Entertainment*
(Winnipeg)
395 Notre Dame Ave
Winnipeg MT R3B 1R2, CANADA

Tegart Dalton, Judy (Tennis Player)
72 Grange Road
Toorak, VIC 3412, AUSTRALIA

Teglianetti, Peter (Athlete, Hockey Player)
67 Bayhill Dr.
Bridgeville, PA 15017, USA

Teich, Kim (Stylist)
c/o Staff Member *Team*
423 W Broadway
4th Floor
Boston, MA 02127, USA

Teich, Malvin C (Engineer)
Boston University
Electrical/Computer Engineering Dept
Boston, MA 02215, USA

Teichner, Helmut (Skier)
4250 Marine Dr
#2101
Chicago, IL 60613, USA

Teillet-Schick, Yolande (Baseball Player)
1016 Chevrier Blvd Ft Garry
Winnipeg, MB R3T 1X9, CANADA

Teitel, Robert (Producer)
c/o Staff Member *Creative Artists Agency*
(CAA-LA)
2000 Ave Of The Stars
Los Angeles, CA 90067, USA

Teitelbaum, Philip (Doctor)
University of Florida
Psychology Dept
Gainesville, FL 32611, USA

Teitell, Conrad L (Lawyer)
16 Marlow Court
Riverside, CT 06878, USA

Teitler, William (Producer)
c/o Staff Member *ICM Partners (ICM-LA)*
10250 Constellation Blvd Fl 7
Los Angeles, CA 90067, USA

Teixeira, Mark (Athlete, Baseball Player)
2220 King Fisher Dr
Westlake, TX 76262-4815

Tejada, Miguel O M (Athlete, Baseball
Player)
3013 NE 20th C
Ft Lauderdale, FL 33305-1807, USA

Tejeda, Robinson (Baseball Player)
45 Appletree Ln Apt D
Old Bridge, NJ 08857-4586

Tejera, Michael (Athlete, Baseball Player)
14271 SW 18th St
Miami, FL 33175-7062, USA

Te Kanawa, Kiri (Opera Singer)
Jules Haelliger Impressario
Postfach 4113
Lucerne 6002, SWITZERLAND

Tekulve, Kenton C (Kent) (Athlete,
Baseball Player)
350 Fruitwood Dr
Bethel Park, PA 15102-1008, USA

Telemaco, Amaury (Athlete, Baseball
Player)
830 S Webster Ave
Scranton, PA 18505, USA

Telfer, Paul (Actor)
c/o Michael Greenwald *Buchwald/*
Fortitude (LA)
6500 Wilshire Blvd
Suite 2200
Los Angeles, CA 90048, USA

Telford, Anthony (Athlete, Baseball
Player)
9109 Cypress Keep Ln
Odessa, FL 33556-3150, USA

Telford, Jennifer (Stylist)
c/o Staff Member *Zenobia Agency Inc*
PO Box 909
Groveland, CA 95321, USA

Telgdi, Valentine L (Physicist)
Eidgenossosche Technische Hochschule
Houggerberg
Zurich, SWITZERLAND

Telgheder, David (Athlete, Baseball
Player)
50 Orchard Crest Dr
Westtown, NY 10998-3425, USA

Tellem, Nancy (Business Person)
c/o Staff Member *CBS Paramount*
International Television
7800 Beverly Blvd
Los Angeles, CA 90036, USA

Teller (Actor, Comedian, Magician)
7570 Gary Ave
Las Vegas, NV 89178, USA

Teller, Edward (Doctor)
Box 808
Livermore, CA 94550, USA

Telles, Rick (Director, Producer)
c/o Josh Levenbrown *Agency for the*
Performing Arts (APA-LA)
405 S Beverly Dr
Suite 500
Beverly Hills, CA 90212-4425, USA

Tellez, Steve (Actor)
c/o Staff Member *Innovative Artists (LA)*
1505 10th St
Santa Monica, CA 90401, USA

Tellman, Tom (Athlete, Baseball Player)
271 Yankee Bush Rd
Warren, PA 16365, USA

Tellmann, Tom (Baseball Player)
1021 Yankee Bush Rd
Warren, PA 16365-8536, USA

Tellqvist, Mikael (Athlete, Hockey Player)
7932 E Feathersong Ln
Scottsdale, AZ 85255-6418

Telnaes, Ann (Cartoonist)
Tribune Media Services
435 N Michigan Ave
#1500
Chicago, IL 60611, USA

Teltscher, Eliot (Coach, Tennis Player)
Pepperdine University
Athletic Dept
Malibu, CA 90265, USA

Teltschik, John (Athlete, Football Player)
9624 Nathan Way
Plano, TX 75025-5896, USA

Telushkin, Rabbi Joseph (Writer)
2316 Delaware Ave #266
Ste 4-B
Buffalo, NY 14216-2687, USA

Telymonde, Louis (Horse Racer)
190 Biabou Dr
Toms River, NJ 08757-3731, USA

Temchen, Sybil (Actor)
c/o Staff Member *Untitled Entertainment*
(LA)
350 S. Beverly Dr #200
Beverly Hills, CA 90212, USA

Temesvari, Andrea (Tennis Player)
ProServe
1101 Woodrow Wilson Blvd
#1800
Arlington, VA 22209, USA

Temirkanov, Yuri K
State Philharmonia
Mikhailovskaya 2
Saint Petersburg, RUSSIA

Temko, Allan B (Journalist)
San Francisco Chronicle
Editorial Dept
901 Mission
San Francisco, CA 94103, USA

Temp, Jim (Athlete, Football Player)
311 Roselawn Blvd
Green Bay, WI 54301, USA

Tempero, Bill (Race Car Driver)
915 Turman Dr.
Collins, CO 80525, USA

Temple, Collins (Athlete, Basketball
Player)
2614 Dalrymple Dr
Baton Rouge, LA 70808, USA

Temple, Collis (Athlete, Basketball Player)
1974 San Antonio Spurs
2614 Dalrvmole DrBaton Rouge,
LA 70808-2038

Temple, Josh (Television Host)
c/o Steven Neibert *Imperium 7 Talent*
Agency
5455 Wilshire Blvd
Suite 1706
Los Angeles, CA 90036, USA

Temple, Juno (Actor)
c/o Jessica Kolstad *WKT Public Relations*
(WKT-LA)
9350 Wilshire Blvd
Suite 450
Beverly Hills, CA 90212, USA

Temple, Lew (Actor)
c/o Peter Young *Sovereign Talent Group*
8421 Wilshire Blvd
Suite 200
Beverly Hills, CA 90211, USA

Temple Black, Shirley (Actor, Musician)
O'Melveny & Myers
400 S Hope St
Los Angeles, CA 90071, USA

Temple-Black, Shirley (Politician)
115 Lakeview Dr
Woodside, CA 94062-1124, USA

Templeman, Simon (Voice Over Artist)
305 15th St
Santa Monica, CA 90402, USA

Templeman of White Lackington, Sydney W (Judge)
Manor Heath
Know Hill Woking
Surrey GU22 7HL, UNITED KINGDOM (UK)

Templeton, Ben (Cartoonist)
Tribune Media Services
435 N Michigan Ave
#1500
Chicago, IL 60611, USA

Templeton, Garry L (Athlete, Baseball Player)
13552 Del Poniente Rd
Poway, CA 92064-2230, USA

Templeton, John M (Financier)
Lyford Cay Club
Box N7776
Nassau, BAHAMAS

Tempo, Nino (Actor)
9255 Doheny Rd #2504
W Hollywood, CA 90069

Temptations, The (Music Group)
c/o Steve Levine *ICM Partners (ICM-LA)*
10250 Constellation Blvd Fl 7
Los Angeles, CA 90067, USA

Tena, Natalia (Actor)
c/o Sarah Spear *Curtis Brown Ltd*
Hay Market House
28-29 Hay Market
London SW1Y 4SP, UK

Tenace, F Gene (Athlete, Baseball Player, Coach)
2650 Cliff Hawk Ct
Redmond, OR 97756-7301, USA

Tendulkar, Priya (Actor, Bollywood)
1 Anookul Apartments Harminder Singh Marg
Seven Bangalows Versova Andheri
Bombay, MS 400 061, INDIA

Tengbom, Anders (Architect)
Kornhaminstorg 6
Stockholm 11127, SWEDEN

Teng-Hui, Lee (President)
Chaehshou Hall Chung King South Rd.
Taipei 10728, TAIWAN

Tennant, Andy (Actor, Director, Writer)
c/o Eddie Michaels *Insignia Public Relations*
1507 20th St
Santa Monica, CA 90404, USA

Tennant, David (Actor)
c/o Billy Lazarus *United Talent Agency (UTA)*
9336 Civic Center Dr
Beverly Hills, CA 90210, USA

Tennant, Stella (Model)
Select Model Mgmt
Archer House
43 King St
London WC2E 8RJ, UNITED KINGDOM (UK)

Tennant, Veronica (Ballerina)
National Ballet of Canada
157 King St E
Toronto, ON M5C 1G9, CANADA

Tennant, Victoria (Actor)
PO Box 929
Beverly Hills, CA 90213, USA

Ten Napel, Garth (Athlete, Football Player)
P.O. Box 26
Carmen, ID 83462, USA

Tenney, Jon (Actor)
c/o Brian Wilkins *Kritzer Levine Wilkins Entertainment (KLWG)*
11872 La Grange Ave
1st Floor
Los Angeles, CA 90025, USA

Tennille, Toni (Actor, Musician)
4225 W Latham Cir
Prescott, AZ 86305, USA

Tennison, Chalee (Musician)
Tanasi Entertainment
1204 17th Ave S
Nashville, TN 37212, USA

Tennon, Julius (Actor)
c/o Jim Kelly *Charles Talent Agency*
11950 Ventura Blvd #3
Studio City, CA 91604, USA

Tennyson, Brian (Athlete, Golfer)
2775 Mesa Verde Dr E #P114
Costa Mesa, CA 92626-5008, USA

Tenorio, Pedro P (Ex-Governor)
P.O. Box 567
Saipan, MP 96950, USA

Tensi, Steve (Athlete, Football Player)
300 Flannery Fork Rd
Blowing Rock, NC 28605, USA

Tenth Avenue North (Musician)
c/o Staff Member *Reunion Records*
Provident Music Group / Sony BMG
741 Cool Springs Blvd
Franklin, TN 37067, USA

Tenuta, Judy (Actor, Comedian)
13504 Contour Dr
Sherman Oaks, CA 91423, USA

Tepedino, Frank (Athlete, Baseball Player)
2 Pear Ct
Saint James, NY 11780-2143, USA

Tepper, Lou (Coach, Football Coach)
University of Illinois
Assembly Hall
Champaign, IL 61820, USA

Tepper, Stephen (Athlete, Hockey Player)
35 Brook St
Shrewsbury, MA 01545-4804

Tequila (Nguyen), Tila (Model, Reality TV Star)
Til's Hot Spot
1603 Cloverfield #420
Santa Monica, CA 90404, USA

Teran, Arlet (Actor)
c/o Gabriel Blanco *Gabriel Blanco Iglesias (Mexico)*
Rio Balsas 35-32
Colonia Cuauhtemoc
DF 06500, Mexico

Teraoka, Masami (Artist)
41-048 Kaulu St
Waimanalo, HI 96795, USA

TerBlanche, Esta (Actor)
c/o Chris Schmidt *Paradigm (LA)*
360 N Crescent Dr
North Bldg
Beverly Hills, CA 90210, USA

Terentyeva, Nina N (Opera Singer)
Bolshoi Theater
Teatralnaya Pl 1
Moscow 103009, RUSSIA

Tereschenko, Sergei A (Prime Minister)
Prime Minister's Office
Dom Pravieelstra
Alma-Ata 148008, KAZAKHSTAN

Tereshinski, Joe (Athlete, Football Player)
6508 Millwood Rd
Bethesda, MD 20817, USA

Tereshkova, Valentina V (Cosmonaut)
Int'l Co-operation Assn
Vozdvizhenka Str 14-18
Moscow 103885, RUSSIA

Tergesen, Lee (Actor)
Gersh Agency
232 N Canon Dr
Beverly Hills, CA 90210, USA

Ter Horst, Jerald F (Government Official, Journalist)
7815 Evening Lane
Alexandria, VA 22306, USA

Terlecki, Bob (Athlete, Baseball Player)
113 Shady Brook Dr
Langhorne, PA 19047-8028, USA

Terlecky, Greg (Athlete, Baseball Player)
2130 Camino Laurel
San Clemente, CA 92673-5650, USA

Terlesky, John (Actor)
14229 Dickens
#5
Sherman Oaks, CA 91423, USA

Termeer, Henricus A (Business Person)
Genzyme Corp
1 Kendall Square
Cambridge, MA 02139, USA

Terminator X (Musician)
c/o Staff Member *WmE2 (WMA-LA)*
1 William Morris Pl
Beverly Hills, CA 90212, USA

Termo, Leonard (Actor)
Baumgarten/Prophet
1041 N Formosa Ave
#200
West Hollywood, CA 90046, USA

Ter-Petrosyan, Levon A (President)
Marshal Baghramjan Prospect 19
Yerevan 375016, ARMENIA

Terpko, Jeff (Athlete, Baseball Player)
3546 Riverside Dr
Sayre, PA 18840-7864, USA

Terrani, Lucia Valenti
Via Venti Settembre 72
Padova, ITALY I-35122

Terranova, Joe (Musician)
Joe Taylor Mgmt
PO Box 279
Williamstown, NJ 08094-0279, USA

Terranova, Phil (Boxer)
30 Bogardus Place
New York, NY 10040, USA

terraro, Dave (Bowler)
672 E Chester St
Kingston, NY 12401-1742, USA

Terrasson, Jacky (Musician)
Joel Chriss
300 Mercer St
#3J
New York, NY 10003, USA

Terrazas Sandoval, Julio Cardinal (Religious Leader)
Arzobispado Casilla 25
Calle Ingavi 49
Santa Cruz, BOLIVIA

Terrell, David (Athlete, Football Player)
43628 Cather Ct
Ashburn, VA 20147, USA

Terrell, Ernie
11136 So. Parnell
Chicago, IL 60628

Terrell, Ira (Athlete, Basketball Player)
1327 Fernwood Ave
Dallas, TX 75216-1265, USA

Terrell, Jerry (Athlete, Baseball Player)
1301 NE Sunny Creek Ln
Blue Springs, MO 64014-2041, USA

Terrell, Pat (Athlete, Football Player)
40 Hidden Lake Dr
Burr Ridge, IL 60527-8371, USA

Terrell, Walt (Athlete, Baseball Player)
1304 Oxley Ct
Union, KY 41091-7145, USA

Terreri, Chris (Athlete, Hockey Player)
New Jersey Devils
165 Mulberry St, Newark NJ, 07102-3607

Terreri, Chris (Athlete, Hockey Player, Olympic Athlete)
120 Lake Dr
Mountain Lakes, NJ 07046-1646

Terrero, Jessy (Director, Producer)
c/o Charles King *WME (LA)*
9601 Wilshire Blvd Fl 3
Beverly Hills, CA 90210, USA

Terrile, Richard (Scientist)
2121 E Woodlyn Road
Pasadena, CA 91104-3334, USA

Terrio, Deney (Dancer, Entertainer)
Paramount Entertainment
PO Box 12
Far Hills, NJ 07931, USA

Terrion, Greg (Athlete, Hockey Player)
Terri on Esso Service Ltd
PO Box 428
Marmora, ON K0K 2M0, Canada

Terris, Malcolm
14 England's Lane
London, ENGLAND NW3

Terry, Chuck (Athlete, Basketball Player)
11 Ravenna
Irvine, CA 92614-5329, USA

Terry, Clark (Musician)
4720 S Beech Street
Pine Bluff, AR 71603-7327, USA

Terry, Claude (Athlete, Basketball Player)
4621 Via Fiori
Modesto, CA 95357-0658, USA

Terry, Hilda (Cartoonist)
8 Henderson Place
New York, NY 10028, USA

Terry, Jason (Basketball Player)
Atlanta Hawks
190 Marietta St SW
Atlanta, GA 30342-2183, USA

Terry, John (Soccer Player)
The FA
25 Soho Square
London W1D 4FA, UNITED KINGDOM

Terry, John Q (Architect)
Old Exchange Dedham
Colchester
Essex CO7 6HA, UNITED KINGDOM
(UK)

Terry, Lee (Congressman, Politician)
2331 Rayburn HOB
Washington, DC 20515, USA

Terry, Megan D (Writer)
2309 Hansom Blvd
Omaha, NE 68105, USA

Terry, Nat (Athlete, Football Player)
3003 W Palmetto St
Tampa, FL 33607, USA

Terry, Nigel (Actor)
c/o Staff Member *BBC Artist Mail*
PO Box 1116
Belfast BT2 7AJ, United Kingdom

Terry, Ralph W (Athlete, Baseball Player)
801 Park St
Larned, KS 67550-2632, USA

Terry, Randall A (Activist)
Operation Rescue National
PO Box 360221
Melbourne, FL 32936, USA

Terry, Richard E (Business Person)
Peoples Energy Corp
130 E Randolph Dr
Chicago, IL 60601, USA

Terry, Rick (Athlete, Football Player)
109 Highgate Ln
Lexington, NC 27292, USA

Terry, Ruth (Actor, Musician)
622 Hospitality Dr
Rancho Mirage, CA 92270, USA

Terry, Scott (Athlete, Baseball Player)
4943 Montford Dr
Saint Louis, MO 63128-3134, USA

Terry, Tony (Musician)
Richard Walters
1800 Argyle Ave
#408
Los Angeles, CA 90028, USA

Terwilliger, Wayne (Athlete, Baseball
Player)
1909 Clear Creek Dr
Weatherford, TX 76087-3802, USA

Terzian, Jacques (Artist)
PO Box 883753
San Francisco, CA 94188, USA

Terzopoulos, Demetri (Scientist)
815 Stradella Rd
Los Angeles, CA 90077-3309, USA

Tesh, John (Composer, Entertainer,
Musician)
PO Box 6010
Sherman Oaks, CA 91413, USA

Tesher, Howard (Horse Racer)
525 E 72nd St Apt 22B
New York, NY 10021-9607, USA

Teske, Rachel (Golfer)
c/o Staff Member *Pro Golfers Association
(PGA) Tour*
112 TPC Blvd
Ponte Vedra Beach, FL 32082, USA

Tesori, Kathleen (Fitness Expert, Model)
1934 Willow Wood Ln
S Ogden, UT 84403, USA

Tess, John (Business Person)
Heritage
123 NW Second Avenue
Suite 200
Portland, OR 97209

Tessier, Orval (Athlete, Hockey Player)
412 Fifth St E
Cornwall, ON K6H 2M2, Canada

Tessler-Lavigne, Marc (Doctor)
361 Ridgeway Road
Woodside, CA 94062, USA

Tessmer, Jay (Athlete, Baseball Player)
2359 Livingston Bridge Rd
Norman Park, GA 1771-4258, USA

Testa, M David (Financier)
T Rowe Price Assoc
100 E Pratt St
Baltimore, MD 21202, USA

Testa, Nick (Athlete, Baseball Player)
1 Consulate Dr Apt 2L
Tuckahoe, NY 10707-2432, USA

Testaverde, Vinny (Athlete, Football
Player, Heisman Trophy Winner)
17122 Gunn Hwy
Odessa, FL 33556-1909, USA

Tester, Hans
6310 San Vicente Blvd. #401
Los Angeles, CA 90048

Testerman, Don (Athlete, Football Player)
3101 Bridges St
Morehead City, NC 28557, USA

Testi, Fabio
Via Francesco Siacci 38
Rome, ITALY I-00197

Testl, Fabio (Actor)
Via Siacci 38
Rome 00197, ITALY

Testone, Elise (Musician)
c/o Staff Member *19 Entertainment - LA*
9000 W Sunset Blvd #1574
West Hollywood, CA 90069, USA

Tetarenko, Joey (Athlete, Hockey Player)
5307 Chelsea Fair Ln
Spring, TX 77379-6244

Teteak, Deral (Athlete, Football Player)
9458 S County Road G
Suring, WI 54174, USA

Teter, Hannah (Athlete, Olympic Athlete,
Snowboarder)
1554 Plumas Cir
South Lake Tahoe, CA 96150-4822, USA

Tetley, Glen (Choreographer, Director)
15 W 9th St
New York, NY 10011, USA

Tetrault, Roger E (Business Person)
McDermott International
1450 Polydras St
New Orleans, LA 70112, USA

Tetro-Atkinson, Barbara (Athlete, Baseball
Player)
7110 Cross Creek Blvd
Louisville, KY 40228-1305, USA

Tettamanzi, Dlonigi Cardinal (Religious
Leader)
Arclvescovado
Plazza Matteotti 4
Genoa 16123, ITALY

Tettleton, Mickey (Athlete, Baseball
Player)
346 W Franklin Rd
Norman, OK 73069-8105, USA

Tetzlaff, Christian (Musician)
Shuman Assoc
120 W 58th St
#80
New York, NY 10019, USA

Teufel, Tim (Athlete, Baseball Player)
PO Box 3517
Jupiter, FL 33469-1009, USA

Teut, Nate (Athlete, Baseball Player)
2010 Sugar Creek D
Waukee, IA 50263-8093, USA

Teutul Sr, Paul (Reality TV Star,
Television Host)
c/o Sean Perry *WME (LA)*
9601 Wilshire Blvd Fl 3
Beverly Hills, CA 90210, USA

Tewell, Doug (Athlete, Golfer)
11414 Waters Welling Way
Edmond, OK 73013-0455, USA

Tewes, Lauren (Actor)
c/o Staff Member *The Actor's Group
Talent and Literary Agency*
3400 Beacon Ave South
Seattle, CA 98144, USA

Tewkesbury, Joan F (Director, Writer)
c/o Staff Member *Creative Artists Agency
(CAA-LA)*
2000 Ave Of The Stars
Los Angeles, CA 90067, USA

Tewksbury, Bob (Athlete, Baseball Player)
55 Mount Vernon St
Somersworth, NH 03878-2642, USA

Tewksbury, Mark
2380 Pierre Depuy Ave
Montreal, CANADA PQ H3C 3R4

Tews, Andreas (Boxer)
Hamburger Allee 1
Schwerin 19063, GERMANY

Texada, Tia (Actor)
c/o Staff Member *Rogers & Cowan PR
(LA)*
Pacific Design Center
8687 Melrose Ave, 7th Floor
West Hollywood, CA 90069, USA

Tezak-Papesh, Virginia (Athlete, Baseball
Player)
1400 Clement St
Jollet, IL 60435-4209, USA

Thabu (Actor, Bollywood)
Ankul II Floor
7 Bungalows Andheri West
Mumbai, MS 400054, INDIA

Thacker, Brian M (General)
11413 Monterey Dr
Wheaton, MD 20902-2657, USA

Thacker, Tom (Athlete, Basketball Player)
3655 Dogwood Ln
Cincinnati, OH 45213-2601, USA

Thackery, Jimmy (Musician)
Mongrel Music
743 Center Blvd
Fairfax, CA 94930, USA

Thaddeus, Patrick (Physicist)
58 Garfield St
Cambridge, MA 02138, USA

Thagard, Norman E (Astronaut, Physicist)
502 N Ride
Tallahassee, FL 32303, USA

Thagard, Norman E Dr (Astronaut)
502 N Ride
Tallahassee, FL 32303-5127, USA

Thain, John (Financier)
New York Stock Exchange
11 Wall St
New York, NY 10005, USA

Thaksin, Shinawatra (Prime Minister)
Premier's Office
Govt House
Luke Road
Bangkok 10300/2, THAILAND

Thal, Eric (Actor)
c/o Phillip Carlson *Carlson Menashe
Agency*
149 Fifth avenue
Suite 1204
New York, NY 10010

Thalheimer, Mona (Stylist)
Mona Thalheimer & Co
630 Washington Ave
Santa Monica, CA 90403, USA

Thalia (Actor, Musician)
c/o Staff Member *WmE2 (WMA-LA)*
1 William Morris Pl
Beverly Hills, CA 90212, USA

Thames, Marcus (Athlete, Baseball Player)
72 Overview Rd
Starkville, MS 39759-6489, USA

Than, Shwe (General, Prime Minister)
Prime Minister's Office
Theinbyu Road
Botahtaung
Yangon, MYANMAR

Thani, Sheikh Hamad bin Khalifa al
(Royalty)
Royal Palace
PO Box 923
Dohar, QATAR

Thapa, Surya Bahadur (Prime Minister)
Tangal
Kathmandu, NEPAL

Tharp, Twyla (Choreographer, Dancer)
Twyla Tharp Productions
336 Central Park W
#17B
New York, NY 10025, USA

Tharpe, Larry (Athlete, Football Player)
3665 Greenbriar Rd E
Macon, GA 31204, USA

Thatcher, David (General)
440 Dearborn Ave
Missoula, MT 59801-8033, USA

Thatcher, Joe (Athlete, Baseball Player)
310 Ruddell Dr
Kokomo, IN 46901-4249, USA

Thatcher, Margaret (Politician)
11 Dutwich Gate
Dulwich
London SE12, UNITED KINGDOM (UK)

Thatcher, Roland (Golfer)
18 Flowertuft Ct
Springs, TX 77380-1529, USA

Thaxton, Galand (Athlete, Football Player)
1571 N 22nd St
Laramie, WY 82072, USA

Thaxton, James (Athlete, Football Player)
4319 Deergrove Rd
Memphis, TN 38141, USA

Thayer, Bill (Misc)
PO Box 233
Snohomish, WA 98291, USA

Thayer, Brynn (Actor)
c/o Steven Neibert *Imperium 7 Talent Agency*
5455 Wilshire Blvd
Suite 1706
Los Angeles, CA 90036, USA

Thayer, Dale
9611 Woodlawn Dr
Huntington Beach, CA 92646-3635

Thayer, Greg (Athlete, Baseball Player)
1000 3rd St N
Sauk Rapids, MN 56379-2417, USA

Thayer, Helen (Skier)
PO Box 233
Snohomish, WA 98291, USA

Thayer, Maria (Actor)
c/o Barry McPherson *Agency for the Performing Arts (APA-LA)*
405 S Beverly Dr
Suite 500
Beverly Hills, CA 90212-4425, USA

Thayer, Tom (Athlete, Football Player)
330 W Diversey Pkwy
Apt 2303
Chicago, IL 60657, USA

Thayer, Tommy (Musician)
PO Box 7147
Thousand Oaks, CA 91359, USA

Thayer, W Paul (Business Person, Government Official)
10200 Hollow Way
Dallas, TX 75229, USA

The Academy Is (Music Group)
c/o Bob McLynn *Crush Management*
60-62 E 11th St
7th Floor
New York, NY 10003, USA

The Band Perry (Music Group, Musician)
c/o Jake Basden *Big Machine Records*
1219 16th Ave South
Nashville, TN 37212, USA

The Beach Boys (Music Group)
c/o Elliott Lott *Boulder Creek Entertainment*
P.O. Box 91002
San Diego, CA 92191, USA

Theberge, Greg (Athlete, Hockey Player)
31 Edgar
Sundridge, ON P0A 1Z0, Canada

Theberge, James D (Diplomat)
4462 Cathedral Ave NW
Washington, DC 20016, USA

The Bronx (Music Group)
c/o Jonathan Daniel *Crush Management*
60-62 E 11th St
7th Floor
New York, NY 10003, USA

The Color Fred (Music Group, Musician)
c/o Matt Galle *Paradigm (NY)*
360 Park Ave S Fl 16
New York, NY 10010, USA

The Darkness (Music Group)
c/o Sue Whitehouse *Whitehouse Management*
PO Box 43829
London NW6 3PJ, UNITED KINGDOM

The Dear & Departed (Music Group, Musician)
c/o Stephen Looker *Knives Out Management*
P.O. Box 480519
Los Angeles, CA 90048, USA

The Decemberists (Music Group)
c/o Ron Laffitte *Red Light Management (LA)*
8439 W Sunset Blvd
Suite 2
Los Angeles, CA 90069, USA

Thedford, Marcello (Actor)
c/o J.C. (JC) Robbins *JC Robbins Management*
113 S Kilkea Dr
Los Angeles, CA 90048, USA

The Expendables (Music Group, Musician)
c/o Jon Phillips *Silverback Professional Artist Management*
9469 Jefferson Blvd
Suite 101
Culver City, CA 90232, USA

The Fabulous Thunderbirds (Music Group)
c/o Patrick McAuliff *Monterey International (Chicago)*
200 W Superior
Suite 202
Chicago, IL 60610, USA

The Fall of Troy (Music Group)
c/o David Benveniste *Velvet Hammer*
9014 Melrose Ave
Los Angeles, CA 90069, USA

The Fray (Music Group)
c/o Joseph Carozza *Epic Records Group*
550 Madison Ave
22nd Floor
New York, NY 10022, USA

The Godfathers (Music Group, Musician)
c/o Matt Suhar *Tantrum Management*
3341 W. Berteau Ave
Chicago, IL 60618, USA

The Good The Bad & The Queen (Music Group)
c/o Staff Member *Paradigm (Monterey)*
404 W Franklin St
Monterey, CA 93940, USA

The Great Khali (Writer)
c/o Kerry Rodgerson *World Wrestling Entertainment (WWE)*
Titan Towers
1241 E Main St
Stamford, CT 06905-3857, USA

Theile, David (Swimmer)
84 Woodville St
Hendea
Brisbane, QLD 4011, AUSTRALIA

The Imponderables (Music Group, Musician)
c/o Monique Moss *Integrated PR*
8060 Melrose Ave
4th Floor
Los Angeles, CA 90046, USA

The Insult Comic Dog, Triumph (Actor, Comedian)
c/o Staff Member *Creative Artists Agency (CAA-LA)*
2000 Ave Of The Stars
Los Angeles, CA 90067, USA

Theis, Dave (Athlete, Baseball Player)
7250 Lewis Ridge Pkwy
Apt 206
Minneapolis, MN 55439, USA

Theismann, Joe (Athlete, Football Player)
21495 Ridgetop Cir Ste 304A
Sterling, VA 20166-6512, USA

Theismann, Joseph R (Joe) (Athlete, Football Player, Sportscaster)
P.O. Box 186
Leesburg, PA 20178, USA

Theiss, Duane (Athlete, Baseball Player)
66 Juniper Ave
Westerville, OH 43081-1700, USA

The Jets (Music Group)
c/o Staff Member *Lustig Talent Enterprises Inc*
PO Box 770850
Orlando, FL 32877, USA

The Jonas Brothers (Music Group)
c/o Staff Member *Hollywood Records*
500 S Buena Vista St
Burbank, CA 91521, USA

The Killers (Music Group)
c/o Staff Member *Island Records*
825 Eighth Ave
New York, NY 10019, USA

Thelan, Jodi
8428-C Melrose Pl.
Los Angeles, CA 90069

The Lonely Island (Music Group)
c/o Staff Member *Silva Artist Management (SAM)*
722 Seward St
Los Angeles, CA 90038, USA

Thelven, Michael (Athlete, Hockey Player)
TSS AB PO Box 7296
Taby 18714, Sweden

The Maine (Music Group)
Fearless Records
13772 Goldenwest St #545
Westminster, CA 92683, USA

Themmen, Paris (Actor)
2109 S. Wilbur Ave
Walla Walla, WA 99362, USA

The Moody Blues (Music Group, Musician)
c/o Ivy Stewart *Threshold Recording Co. Ltd.*
53 High St
Cobham KT11 3DP, UK

The National (Music Group)
c/o Dawn Berger *Post Hoc Management*
320 7th Ave #145
Brooklyn, NY 11215, USA

The Neptunes (Musician, Producer)
c/o Staff Member *Star Trak Entertainment*
1755 Broadway
3rd Floor
New York, NY 10019, USA

Theobald, Ron (Athlete, Baseball Player)
319 Jacaranda Pl
Fullerton, CA 92832-1434, USA

Theodorakis, Mikis (Composer)
Epifanous 1
Akropolis
Athens, GREECE

Theodore, Donna
10000 Santa Monica Blvd. #305
Los Angeles, CA 90067

Theodore, George (Athlete, Baseball Player)
1388 Princeton Ave
Salt Lake City, UT 84105-1921, USA

Theodore, Jose (Athlete, Hockey Player)
Newport Sports Management
400-201 City Centre Dr
Attn Don Meehan
Mississauga, ON L5B 2T4, Canada

Theodorescu, Monica (Athlete)
Gestit Lindenhof
Sassenberg 48336, GERMANY

Theodorou, Susie (Stylist)
c/o Staff Member *Jean Conlon*
461 Broome St
New York, NY 10013, USA

Theodosakis, Jason (Doctor, Writer)
Saint Martin's Press
175 5th Ave
New York, NY 10010, USA

Theodosius, Primate Metropolitian (Religious Leader)
Orthodox Church in America
PO Box 675 RR 25A
Syosset, NY 11791, USA

The Offspring (Music Group, Musician)
c/o Jim Guerinot *Rebel Waltz Inc*
31652 Second Ave
Laguna Beach, CA 92651, USA

Theofiledes, Harry (Athlete, Football Player)
17806 Carrollwood Dr
Dallas, TX 75252, USA

Theo Paphitis, Theo Paphitis (Business Person)
Ryman House , Savoy Rd
Crewe
Cheshire CW1 6NA, UK

The Pointer Sisters (Music Group, Musician)
c/o Konrad Leh *Creative Talent Group*
1900 Avenue of the Stars
Suite 2475
Los Angeles, CA 90067, USA

The Pretenders (Music Group)
c/o Staff Member *WmE2 (WMA-LA)*
1 William Morris Pl
Beverly Hills, CA 90212, USA

The Priests (Music Group, Musician)
Bishop's House
Lisbreen, 73 Somerton Rd
Belfast BT15 4DE, Ireland

The Prize Fighter Inferno (Music Group, Musician)
c/o Blaze James *Black Sheep Fellowship*
6255 Sunset Blvd
Suite 910
Los Angeles, CA 90028, USA

The Rasmus (Music Group)
c/o Staff Member *Playground Music Scandinavia*
Box 3171
Malmö s-200 22, SWEDEN

Therefore I Am (Music Group, Musician)
c/o Cody DeLong *Kenmore Agency, The*
59 Park St
2nd Floor
Beverly, MA 01915, USA

Therien, Chris (Athlete, Hockey Player)
15 Milford Dr
Marlton, NJ 08053-5408

Therien, Chris (Athlete, Hockey Player)
Philadelphia Flyers
3601 S Broad St Ste 2
Philadelphia, PA 19148-5297

Theriot, Ryan (Athlete, Baseball Player)
241 Granville Ct
Baton Rouge, LA 70810-4860, USA

The Rockers
PO Box 3859
Stamford, CT 06905

Theron, Charlize (Actor, Model)
c/o Elyse Scherz *WME (LA)*
9601 Wilshire Blvd Fl 3
Beverly Hills, CA 90210, USA

Theroux, Justin (Actor)
c/o Nick Frenkel *3 Arts Entertainment Inc*
9460 Wilshire Blvd
7th Floor
Beverly Hills, CA 90210, USA

Theroux, Louis (Television Host)
c/o Staff Member *BBC Artist Mail*
PO Box 1116
Belfast BT2 7AJ, United Kingdom

Theroux, Paul E (Writer)
35 Elsynge Road
London SW18 2NR, UNITED KINGDOM
(UK)

Therrien, Gaston (Athlete, Hockey Player)
RDS 300-1755 Boul Rene-Levesque E
Montreal, QC H2K 4P6, Canada

Therrien, Michel (Athlete, Hockey Player)
3800 Hillcrest Dr Apt 1204
Hollywood, FL 33021-7940

The Saturdays (Music Group, Musician)
c/o Staff Member *Polydor Records*
364-366 Kensington High St
London W14 8NS, UK

The Saw Doctors (Music Group)
Saw Doctors Office
3 St Mary's Terrace
Galway, IRELAND

The Script (Music Group, Musician)
c/o Cindi Berger *PMK/BNC Public Relations (PMK-NY)*
622 3rd Ave
8th Floor
New York, NY 10017, USA

The Snake The Cross The Crown (Music Group, Musician)
c/o Staff Member *Equal Vision Records*
P.O. Box 38202
Albany, NY 12203-8202, USA

The The (Music Group)
c/o Staff Member *Paradigm (Monterey)*
404 W Franklin St
Monterey, CA 93940, USA

Theuriau, Melissa (Television Host)
Beaugard
4 Sente Des Robertines
Chanteloup-les-Vignes 78570, FRANCE

Theus, Reggie (Athlete, Basketball Player)
2364 Tuscan Hills Ln
Las Cruces, NM 88011, USA

The Vaccines (Music Group, Musician)
c/o Staff Member *Paradigm (NY)*
360 Park Ave S Fl 16
New York, NY 10010, USA

The Veronicas (Music Group, Musician)
c/o Staff Member *Wilhelmina Dan Agency*
KimBrough Office Tower
1503 Union Avenue, Suite 211
Memphis, TN 38014, USA

The Weeknd (Musician)
c/o Staff Member *Atlanta Got Sole*
Prefers to be contacted by telephone
Atlanta, GA, USA

The Wiggles (Music Group, Musician)
The Wiggles Office
P.O. Box 7873
Baulkham Hills, BC NSW 2153, Australia

Thewlis, David (Actor)
c/o Staff Member *United Talent Agency (UTA)*
9336 Civic Center Dr
Beverly Hills, CA 90210, USA

The Yellowjackets (Music Group)
Axis Artist Management Inc
9715 Belmar Ave
Northridge, CA 91324, USA

Theys, Didier (Race Car Driver)
5773 North 78th Place
Scottsdale, AZ 85259, USA

Thiandoum, Hyacinthe Cardinal (Religious Leader)
Archeveche
Ave Jean XXIII
Dakar 1908, SENEGAL

Thibaud, Todd (Musician)
c/o Staff Member *Paradigm (Monterey)*
404 W Franklin St
Monterey, CA 93940, USA

Thibaudet, Jean-Yves (Musician)
3601 Griffith Park Blvd
Los Angeles, CA 90027, USA

Thibault, Charles (Doctor)
4 Place Jussieu
Paris 75005, FRANCE

Thibault, Jocelyn (Athlete, Hockey Player)
550 Ch du Domaine RR 5
Saint-Denis-De-Brompton, QC J0B 2P0,
Canada

Thibeaux, Peter (Athlete, Basketball Player)
2036 Paradise Dr
Apt 2
Belvedere Tiburon, CA 94920, USA

Thibert, Jim (Athlete, Football Player)
1365 County Road L
Swanton, OH 43558, USA

Thibiant, Aida (Designer, Fashion Designer)
Institut de Beaute
449 N Canon Dr
Beverly Hills, CA 90210, USA

Thibodeaux, Keith (Actor)
5372 Jamaica Dr
Jackson, MS 39211-4057, USA

Thicke, Alan (Actor)
10505 Sarah St
Toluca Lake, CA 91602, USA

Thicke, Robin (Musician)
1568 Blue Jay Way
Los Angeles, CA 90069, USA

Thiebaud, Wayne (Artist)
1617 7th Ave
Sacramento, CA 95818-3803, USA

Thieben, Bill (Athlete, Basketball Player)
225 Jayne Ave
Patchogue, NY 11772, USA

Thiedemann, Fritz (Misc)
Ostreherweg 28
Heide 25746, GERMANY

Thiel, Bert (Athlete, Baseball Player)
W11077 County Road D
Marion, WI 54950-9068, USA

Thiel, Peter (Business Person)
The Thiel Foundation
1 Letterman Dr
Bldg C, Suite 400
San Francisco, CA 94117, USA

Thiele, Gerhard P J (Astronaut)
ESA/EAC
Linder Hohe
Cologne 51147, GERMANY

Thiele, Gerhard P J Dr (Astronaut)
European Space Policy Institute
Schwarzenbergplatz 6 Attn: Resident
Fellow
Wien 1030, Austria

Thielemann, Ray C (R C) (Athlete, Football Player)
210 Rose Meadow Ln
Alpharetta, GA 30005, USA

Thielemans, Jean B (Toots) (Musician)
Peter Levinson Communications
2575 Palisade Ave
#11H
Bronx, NY 10463, USA

Thielen, Gunter (Business Person)
Bertelsmann AG
Carl-Bertelsmann-Str 270
Guetersloh 33311, GERMANY

Thiemann, Charles Lee (Financier)
Federal Home Loan Bank
PO Box 598
Cincinnati, OH 45201, USA

Thieme, Paul (Misc)
Tubingen University
Wilhelmstr 7
Tubingen 72074, GERMANY

Thier, Samuel O (Educator, Physicist)
99-20 Florence St
#4B
Chestnut Hill, MA 02467, USA

Thieriot, Max (Actor)
c/o Ruth Bernstein *Viewpoint Inc*
8820 Wilshire Blvd.
Suite 220
Beverly Hills, CA 90211, USA

Thierry, John F (Athlete, Football Player)
1431 Federal Rd
Opelousas, LA 70570, USA

Thies, Dave (Baseball Player)
35737 Tympani Cir
Palm Desert, CA 92211-3067

Thies, Jake (Athlete, Baseball Player)
4 Cornflower Ct
Florissant, MO 63033-6530, USA

Thiessen, Tiffani (Actor)
c/o Jai Khanna *Brillstein Entertainment Partners*
9150 Wilshire Blvd #350
Beverly Hills, CA 90212, USA

Thievery Corporation (Music Group, Musician)
c/o Sandee Fenton *Fresh and Clean Media*
12701 Venice Blvd.
Los Angeles, CA 90066, USA

Thiffault, Leo (Athlete, Hockey Player)
2001 Paquin Rte RR 1
Herouxville, QC G0X 1J0, Canada

Thigpen, Bobby (Athlete, Baseball Player)
Winston-Salem Dash 926 Brookstown
Ave Attn: Coaching
Winston Salem, NC 27101-3625, USA

Thigpen, Curtis (Athlete, Baseball Player)
1405 W 51st St
Austin, TX 78756-2607, USA

Thile, Chris (Actor, Musician)
c/o Staff Member *IMG Artists Worldwide (NY)*
825 Seventh Ave
New York, NY 10019, USA

Thimmesch, Nicholas (Journalist)
6301 Broad Branch Road
Chevy Chase, MD 20815, USA

Thinnes, Roy (Actor)
952 Peekskill Hollow Rd
Putnam Valley, NY 10579, USA

Third Day (Music Group)
c/o Staff Member *Red Light Management (LA)*
8439 W Sunset Blvd
Suite 2
Los Angeles, CA 90069, USA

Third Eye Blind (Music Group)
c/o Carla Parisi *Kid Logic*
156 Liberty St
#12
Little Ferry, NJ 07643, USA

Third World (Music Group)
Lion Entertainment
P.O. Box 5231
Hollywood, FL 33083, USA

Thirlby, Olivia (Actor)
c/o William Choi *Management 360*
9111 Wilshire Blvd
Beverly Hills, CA 90210, USA

Thirsk, Robert (Astronaut)
Candian Institutes of Health Research
160 Elgin St Fl 9
Attn: VP - Public Government & Institute
Affairs
Ottawa, ON K1A 0W9, CANADA

Thirty (30) Seconds to Mars (Music Group, Musician)
c/o Irving Azoff *Azoff Music Management/ Front Line*
1100 Glendon Ave
Los Angeles, CA 90024, USA

This Time Next Year (Music Group, Musician)
c/o Staff Member *Equal Vision Records*
P.O. Box 38202
Albany, NY 12203-8202, USA

Thobe, J J (Athlete, Baseball Player)
902 Grovemont St
Santa Ana, CA 92706-2046, USA

Thobe, Tom (Baseball Player)
21661 Brookhurst St APt 175
Huntington Beach, CA 92646-8122

Thode, Henry G (Scientist)
McMaster University
Nuclear Research Dept
Hamilton, ON L8S 4M1, CANADA

Thoenen, Dick (Athlete, Baseball Player)
862 Smith St
Harrisburg, OR 97446-9505, USA

Thom, Sandi (Musician)
c/o Staff Member Paradigm (Monterey)
404 W Franklin St
Monterey, CA 93940, USA

Thoma, Dieter (Skier)
Am Rossleberg 35
Hinterzarten 79856, GERMANY

Thoma, Georg (Skier)
Bisten 6
Hinterzarten 79856, GERMANY

Thoma, Tyrus
32 Wellesley Cir
Northbrook, IL 60062-1137, USA

Thomalla, Georg (Actor)
Hans Nefer
Bad Gastein 5640, AUSTRIA

Thomas, Aaron (Athlete, Football Player)
2906 NW Golf Course Dr S
Bend, OR 97701, USA

Thomas, Adalius (Athlete, Football Player)
1 Willow Bend Dr
Hattiesburg, MS 39402, USA

Thomas, Alex (Actor)
c/o Staff Member Identity Talent Agency
(ID)
9107 Wilshire Blvd
Suite 500
Beverly Hills, CA 90210, USA

Thomas, Andrew S W (Andy) (Astronaut)
NASA
Johnson Space Center
2101 NASA Road
Houston, TX 77058, USA

Thomas, AndrewS W Dr (Astronaut)
2421 Clopper St
Seabrook, TX 77586-3738, USA

Thomas, Aurelius (Athlete, Football
Player)
P.O. Box 91157
Columbus, OH 43209, USA

Thomas, Barbara S (Government Official)
News International
1 Virginia St
London E1 9XY, UNITED KINGDOM
(UK)

Thomas, Ben (Athlete, Football Player)
2155 Herndon St
AUburn, AL 36830, USA

Thomas, Betty (Actor, Director, Producer)
c/o Bryan Lourd Creative Artists Agency
(CAA-LA)
2000 Ave Of The Stars
Los Angeles, CA 90067, USA

Thomas, Billy M (General)
2387 Spanish Oak Terrace
Colorado Springs, CO 80920, USA

Thomas, B J (Musician, Songwriter,
Writer)
Gloria Thomas
1324 Crownhill Dr
Arlington, TX 76012, USA

Thomas, BJ (Musician)
c/o Staff Member Gloria Thomas Inc
1424 Crownhill Drive
Arlington, TX 76012, USA

Thomas, Blair (Athlete, Football Player)
401 Gulph Ridge Dr
King of Prussia, PA 19406, USA

Thomas, Broderick (Athlete, Football
Player)
14442 Junction Place Dr
Houton, TX 77045-6562, USA

Thomas, Bruce (Actor)
c/o Jerry Shandrew Shandrew Public
Relations
1050 S Stanley Ave
Los Angeles, CA 90019-6634, USA

Thomas, Calvin (Athlete, Football Player)
908 Manchester Ave
Westchester, IL 60154, USA

Thomas, Carl (Athlete, Baseball Player)
7910 E Camelback Rd Unit 202
Scottsdale, AZ 85251-8609, USA

Thomas, Carl (Musician)
c/o Staff Member Red Entertainment
Agency
505 8th Ave
Suite 1004
New York, NY 10018, USA

Thomas, Carotine Bedell (Physicist)
2401 Calvert St NW
#504
Washington, DC 20008, USA

Thomas, Charles (Athlete, Baseball Player)
137 Black Oak Dr
Asheville, NC 28804-1835, USA

Thomas, Chris (Musician)
Associated Booking Corp
1995 Broadway
#501
New York, NY 10023, USA

Thomas, Chuck (Athlete, Football Player)
2201 Purple Majesty Ct
Las Vegas, NV 89117, USA

Thomas, Clarence (Attorney)
US Supreme Court
United States Supreme Court 11st St NE
Washington, DC 20543-0002, USA

Thomas, Clendon (Athlete, Football
Player)
7508 Rumsey Rd
Oklahoma City, OK 73132, USA

Thomas, Clete (Athlete, Baseball Player)
802 Wyoming Ave
Lynn Haven, FL 32444-1963

Thomas, Craig (Actor)
Granada Television
Quay Street
Manchester M60 9EA, UK

Thomas, Cy (Athlete, Hockey Player)
2216 33 St SW
Calgary, AB T3E 2T1, Canada

Thomas, Damien
31 Kensington Church St.
London, ENGLAND W8 4LL

Thomas, Dave (Comedian)
c/o David Boxerbaum Agency for the
Performing Arts (APA-LA)
405 S Beverly Dr
Suite 500
Beverly Hills, CA 90212-4425, USA

Thomas, Dave G (Athlete, Football Player)
2127 Brickell Ave
Apt 3404
Miami, FL 33129, USA

Thomas, David (Musician)
74 Hyde Vale
Greenwich
London SE10 8HP, UNITED KINGDOM
(UK)

Thomas, David (Business Person)
Thomson Corp
Metro Center
1 Station Pl
Stanford, CT 06902, USA

Thomas, David (Athlete, Football Player)
c/o Staff Member New England Patriots
1 Patriot Pl
Foxboro, MA 02035-1388, USA

Thomas, Debi (Athlete, Figure Skater,
Olympic Athlete)
2601 Windward Blvd
Champaign, IL 61821-6963, USA

Thomas, Debra J (Deb) (Figure Skater)
Mentor Mgmt
202 S Michigan St
#810
South Bend, IN 46601, USA

Thomas, Dennis (DT) (Musician)
c/o Staff Member Pyramid Entertainment
Group
377 Rector Pl #21A
New York, NY 10280-1439, USA

Thomas, Derrel (Athlete, Baseball Player)
112 JuniQ.erhill Ln
Riverside, CA 92506-6217, USA

Thomas, Dominic R (Religious Leader)
Church of Jesus Christ
6th & Lincoln Sts
Monongahela, PA 15063, USA

Thomas, Donald A (Astronaut)
1029 Hart Rd
Towson, MD 21286-1630, USA

Thomas, Donald A Dr (Astronaut)
1029 Hart Rd
Towson, MD 21286-1630, USA

Thomas, Donald Michael (D M) (Writer)
Coach House
Rashleigh Vale Tregolls Rd
Truro, Cornwall TR1 1TJ, UNITED
KINGDOM (UK)

Thomas, Doug (Athlete, Football Player)
11220 NE 53rd St
Kirkland, WA 98033, USA

Thomas, Duane (Athlete, Football Player)
P.O. Box 862
Del Mar, CA 92014, USA

Thomas, Earl (Athlete, Football Player)
1000 Farrah Ln
Apt 825
Stafford, TX 77477-6046, USA

Thomas, Earlie (Athlete, Football Player)
P.O. Box 1445
Laporte, CO 80535, USA

Thomas, Eddie Kaye (Actor)
c/o Greg Clark Untitled Entertainment
(LA)
350 S. Beverly Dr #200
Beverly Hills, CA 90212, USA

Thomas, E Donall (Nobel Prize Laureate)
Fred Hutchinson Cancer Research Center
PO Box 19024
Seattle, WA 98109-1024, USA

Thomas, Elizabeth Marshall (Writer)
80 E Mountain Road
Petersborough, NH 03458, USA

Thomas, Emmitt (Athlete, Football Player)
5318 Harbury Cove
Suwanee, GA 30024, USA

Thomas, Ernest (Actor)
Coast to Coast Talent
3350 Barham Blvd
Los Angeles, CA 90068, USA

Thomas, Etan (Athlete, Basketball Player)
c/o Arn Tellem Wasserman Media Group
10960 Wilshire Blvd
Suite 2200
Los Angeles, CA 90024, USA

Thomas, Evan (Writer)
c/o Staff Member Public Affairs Books
1094 Flex Dr
Jackson, TN 38301, USA

Thomas, Frank J (Athlete, Baseball Player)
118 Doray Dr
Pittsburgh, PA 15237-3681, USA

Thomas, Fred (Government Official,
Lawyer)
Metropolitan Police Dept
300 Indiana Ave NW
Washington, DC 20001, USA

Thomas, Gareth (Engineer)
University of California
Materials Science Dept
Berkeley, CA 94720, USA

Thomas, Gareth (Actor)
c/o Staff Member Julian Belfrage &
Associates
9 Argyll St
3rd Floor
London W1F 7TG, UK

Thomas, George (Athlete, Baseball Player)
5804 Ivrea Dr
Sarasota, FL 34238-4730

Thomas, Gorman (Athlete, Baseball
Player)
W331S5179 Hood Pkwy
North Prairie, WI 53153-9719, USA

Thomas, Heather (Actor)
c/o Larry Kennar Code Entertainment
9229 Sunset Blvd #615
Los Angeles, CA 90069, USA

Thomas, Heidi (Actor)

Thomas, Helen (Journalist)
2501 Calvert St NW
Washington, DC 20008-2604, USA

Thomas, Henry (Actor)
c/o Colton Gramm Brillstein
Entertainment Partners
9150 Wilshire Blvd #350
Beverly Hills, CA 90212, USA

Thomas, Henry L Jr (Athlete, Football
Player)
16811 Southern Oaks Dr
Houston, TX 77068, USA

Thomas, Henry W (Writer)
3214 Warder St NW
Washington, DC 20010-2521, USA

Thomas, Hollis (Athlete, Football Player)
920 Yeadon Ave
Lansdowne, PA 19050, USA

Thomas, Irma (Musician)
c/o Staff Member *Concerted Efforts*
P.O. Box 440326
Somerville, MA 02144, USA

Thomas, Irving (Athlete, Basketball Player)
5117 Lakosee Ct
Orlando, FL 32818-8330, USA

Thomas, Isaac (Athlete, Football Player)
510 Grady Ln
Cedar Hill, TX 75104, USA

Thomas, Jabe (Race Car Driver)
850 Mountainview Dr.
Christiansburg, VA 24073, USA

Thomas, Jack Ward (Biologist,
Government Official)
University of Montana
Biology Dept
Missoula, MT 59812, USA

Thomas, Jake (Actor)
c/o Connie Tavel *Forward Entertainment*
9255 Sunset Blvd
Suite 805
Los Angeles, CA 90069, USA

Thomas, Jay (Actor)
c/o Christine Holder *Zero Gravity
Management (II)*
9255 Sunset Blvd
Suite 1010
Los Angeles, CA 90069, USA

Thomas, Jean (Artist)
1427 Summit Road
Berkeley, CA 94708, USA

Thomas, Jeremy (Filmmaker, Producer)
Recorded Picture Co
8-12 Broadwick St
London W1V 1FH, UNITED KINGDOM
(UK)

Thomas, Joe L (Musician)
c/o Staff Member *Kedar Entertainment*
21 W 39th St
6th Floor
New York, NY 10018, USA

Thomas, Joey (Athlete, Football Player)
c/o Eugene Parker *Maximum Sports
Management*
6435 W Jefferson Blvd
#197
Fort Wayne, IN 46804, USA

Thomas, John (Basketball Player)
Toronto Raptors
Air Canada Center
40 Bay St
Toronto, ON M5J 2N8, CANADA

Thomas, John (Athlete, Olympic Athlete)
51 Mulberry St
Brockton, MA 02302, USA

Thomas, John (Bud) (Athlete, Baseball
Player)
2475 Woodland Dr
Sedalia, MO 65301-8915, USA

Thomas, John M (Scientist)
Royal Institution
21 Albemarle St
London W1X 4BS, UNITED KINGDOM
(UK)

Thomas, Johnny (Athlete, Football Player)
1818 Darby Ln
Fresno, TX 77545, USA

Thomas, Jonathan Taylor (Actor)
c/o Abby Bluestone *Innovative Artists (LA)*
1505 10th St
Santa Monica, CA 90401, USA

Thomas, J T (Athlete, Football Player)
408 Arden Dr
Monroeville, PA 15146, USA

Thomas, Khleo (Actor)
c/o Staff Member *Beverly Hecht Agency*
3500 W Olive Ave
Suite 1180
Burbank, CA 91505, USA

Thomas, Kleo (Musician)

Thomas, Kurt (Athlete, Gymnast, Olympic
Athlete)
4421 Hidden Hill Rd
Norman, OK 73072-2899, USA

Thomas, Kurt (Athlete, Basketball Player)
1826 Brook Terrace Trl
Dallas, TX 75232-3708, USA

Thomas, Lamar (Athlete, Football Player)
2907 NW 9th Pl
Gainesville, FL 32605, USA

Thomas, Larry (Athlete, Baseball Player)
3825 Graham Ln
Eight Mile, AL 36613-2306, USA

Thomas, Larry (Actor)
c/o Dora Whitaker *Whitaker Agency, The*
4924 Vineland Avenue
N Hollywood, CA 91601, USA

Thomas, LaToya (Basketball Player)
San Antonio Silver Stars
1 SBC Center
San Antonio, TX 78219, USA

Thomas, Lavale (Athlete, Football Player)
2626 Northwoods Lake Ct
Duluth, GA 30096, USA

Thomas, Lee (Athlete, Baseball Player)
14260 Manderleigh Woods Dr
Chesterfield, MO 63017-8051, USA

Thomas, Mark A (Athlete, Football Player)
556 Hillsboro St
Monticello, GA 31064, USA

Thomas, Marlo (Actor)
120/122 Beachside Ave
Westport, CT 06880, USA

Thomas, Mary (Musician)
Superstars Unlimited
PO Box 371371
Las Vegas, NV 89137, USA

Thomas, Mava Lee (Athlete, Baseball
Player)
9163 SE 48th Court Rd
Ocala, FL 34480-4203, USA

Thomas, Merilisa (Stylist)
84912 Sunset Blvd
#262
Los Angeles, CA 90069, USA

Thomas, Michael Tilson (Conductor,
Musician)
San Francisco Symphony
Davies Symphony Hall
San Francisco, CA 94102, USA

Thomas, Michelle Rene (Actor)
Agency for Performing Arts
9200 Sunset Blvd #900
Los Angeles, CA 90069

Thomas, Mike (Athlete, Baseball Player)
4808 Gregory Cir
Jonesboro, AR 72401, USA

Thomas, Mike (Athlete, Football Player)
P.O. Box 446
Missouri City, TX 77459, USA

Thomas, Norris (Athlete, Football Player)
4510 Chippewa Ave
Pascagoula, MS 39581, USA

Thomas, Pamela (Business Person)
c/o Staff Member *CNBC*
900 Sylvan Ave
Englewood Cliffs, NJ 07632, USA

Thomas, Pat (Athlete, Football Player)
612 Middle Cove Dr
Plano, TX 75023, USA

Thomas, Philip Michael (Actor)
PO Box 3714
Brooklyn, NY 11202, USA

Thomas, Ralph (Athlete, Football Player)
3270 Alum Creek Ct
Reno, NV 89509, USA

Thomas, Randy (Athlete, Football Player)
2945 Jones St
Apt 4
Atlanta, GA 30344, USA

Thomas, Ray (Nobel Prize Laureate)
Insight Mgmt
1222 16th Ave S
#300
Nashville, TN 37212, USA

Thomas, Reg (Athlete, Hockey Player)
7245 Colonel Talbot Rd
London, ON N6L 1H9, Canada

Thomas, Reginald
18 Belgrave Mews West
London, ENGLAND SW1X 8HT

Thomas, Richard (Actor)
c/o Emily Gerson Saines *Brookside Artists
Management (NY)*
250 W 57th St
Suite 2303
New York, NY 10107, USA

Thomas, Ricky (Athlete, Football Player)
4621 Melbourne Rd
Indianapolis, IN 46228, USA

Thomas, Rob (Musician, Songwriter)
c/o Michael Lippman *Lippman
Entertainment*
23586 Calabasas Road
Suite 208
Calabasas, CA 91302, USA

Thomas, Rob (Director, Producer, Writer)
c/o Ari Greenburg *WME (LA)*
9601 Wilshire Blvd Fl 3
Beverly Hills, CA 90210, USA

Thomas, Robb (Athlete, Football Player)
179 NW Outlook Vista Dr
Bend, OR 97701, USA

Thomas, Robert D (Publisher)
223 Mariomi Road
New Canaan, CT 06840, USA

Thomas, Robert L (Athlete, Football
Player)
2810 W Slauson Ave
Apt 5
Los Angeles, CA 90043, USA

Thomas, Robert R (Athlete, Football
Player)
970 Ridgewood Dr
West Chicago, IL 60185, USA

Thomas, Robin (Actor)
c/o Staff Member *Marshak/Zachary
Company, The*
8840 Wilshire Blvd
1st Floor
Beverly Hills, CA 90210, USA

Thomas, Ross (Actor)
c/o Bryan Bukowski *Simmons & Scott
Entertainment*
4110 W. Burbank Blvd.
Burbank, CA 91505, USA

Thomas, Roy (Athlete, Baseball Player)
3825 Tribute Cir E
Tacoma, WA 98424-3797, USA

Thomas, Rozonda (Chili) (Musician)
1971 E Gate Dr
Stone Mountain, GA 30087, USA

Thomas, Scott (Athlete, Hockey Player)
49 Redspire Way
East Amherst, NY 14051-1675

Thomas, Sean Patrick (Actor)
c/o Karen Samfilippo *Image Management
PR*
1810 14th St
Suite 205
Santa Monica, CA 90404, USA

Thomas, Serena Scott (Actor)
S M S Talent
8730 Sunset Blvd
#440
Los Angeles, CA 90069, USA

Thomas, Stan (Athlete, Baseball Player)
10827 159th Ct NE
Redmond, WA 98052-2691, USA

Thomas, Stayve (Slim Thug) (Musician)
c/o Wes Stevens *Vox*
6420 Wilshire Blvd Ste 1080
Los Angeles, CA 90048, USA

Thomas, Steve (Athlete, Hockey Player)
Plain and Simple
289 Bering Ave
Toronto, ON M8Z 3A5, Canada

Thomas, Steve (Entertainer)
This Old House Show
PO Box 2284
South Burlington, VT 05407, USA

Thomas, Taylor Lea (Designer,
Entertainer)
c/o Staff Member *Elite Soiree*
1221 Brickell Avenue
Suite 800
Miami, FL 33131, USA

Thomas, Ted (Business Person)
C/O Jones & Trevor Marketing
234 Willard St Ste
Cocoa, FL 32922, USA

Thomas, Thurman L (Athlete, Football
Player)
240 Pound Rd
Elma, NY 14059, USA

Thomas, Tim (Athlete, Hockey Player)
PO Box 2160
Peabody, MA 01960-7160

Thomas, Tony (Actor, Producer)
Witt/Thomas/Harris Productions
11901 Santa Monica Blvd #596
West Los Angeles, CA 90025, USA

Thomas, Tra (Athlete, Football Player)
1 Novacare Way
Philadelphia, PA 19145, USA

Thomas, Wayne (Athlete, Hockey Player)
San Jose Sharks 525 W Santa Clara St
San Jose, CA 95113-1500

Thomas, William H Jr (Athlete, Football
Player)
2401 Echo Dr
Amarillo, TX 79107, USA

Thomas, William J (Athlete, Football
Player)
16 Russell St
Waltham, MA 02453, USA

Thomas, Zach (Athlete, Football Player)
1051 NW 122nd Ave
Planation, FL 33323, USA

Thomaselli, Rich (Athlete, Football Player)
96A Seneca St
Weirton, WV 26062, USA

Thomas III, Isiah L (Athlete, Basketball
Player)
1 Azalea Cir
Purchase, NY l0577-1131, USA

Thomas III, Leon (Actor)
c/o Bryan Leder *Management 101*
11271 Ventura Blvd
#102
Studio City, CA 91604, USA

Thomas Jr, Frank E (Athlete, Baseball
Player)
1540 Villa Rica Dr
Henderson, NV 89052-4050, USA

Thomas Jr, James (Athlete, Basketball
Player)
4499 Willow Hill Rd
Portal, GA 30450-5344, USA

Thomas of Swynnerton, Hugh S
(Historian)
Well House
Sudbourne, Suffolk, UNITED KINGDOM
(UK)

Thomason, Bob (Athlete, Football Player)
2645 Bucknell Ave
Charlotte, NC 28207, USA

Thomason, CJ (Actor)
c/o Staff Member *Robert Stein
Management*
PO Box 3797
Beverly Hills, CA 90212, USA

Thomason, Erskine (Athlete, Baseball
Player)
932 Dial Pl
Laurens, SC 29360-8850, USA

Thomason, Harry (Producer)
c/o Staff Member *Mozark Productions*
4024 Radford Ave
Bldg 5 #104
Studio City, CA 91604, USA

Thomason, Harry Z (Producer)
10732 Riverside Dr
North Hollywood, CA 91602, USA

Thomason, Marsha (Actor)
c/o Kesha Williams *Affirmative
Entertainment*
425 N Robertson Blvd
Los Angeles, CA 90048, USA

Thomassin, Florence (Actor)
Artmedia
20 Ave Rapp
Paris 75007, FRANCE

Thomasson, Gary (Athlete, Baseball
Player)
8300 N 53rd St
Paradise Valley, AZ 85253-2512, USA

Thome, James H (Jim) (Athlete, Baseball
Player)
125 E 8th St
Hinsdale, IL 60521-4520, USA

Thomerson, Tim (Actor)
2635 28th St
#14
Santa Monica, CA 90405, USA

Thomlinson, Dave (Athlete, Hockey
Player)
52 Kenilworth Cres St.
Albert, AB T8N 7G3, Canada

Thomlinson, John (Baseball Player)
Negro Baseball Leagues
2351 Beach Way SW
Atlanta, GA 30310-1005, USA

Thomopoulos, Anthony (Business Person)
10727 Wilshire Blvd
#1602
Los Angeles, CA 90024, USA

Thomopoulos, Tony
1280 Stone Canyon Rd.
Los Angeles, CA 90077-2920

Thompson, Ahmir-Khalib (Musician)
c/o Sara Ramaker *Paradigm (LA)*
360 N Crescent Dr
North Bldg
Beverly Hills, CA 90210, USA

Thompson, Andrea (Actor)
Dayton Milrad Cho Management
8306 Wilshire Blvd #56
Beverly Hills, CA 90211, USA

Thompson, Andy (Athlete, Baseball
Player)
1405 Bavshore Blvd
Tampa, FL 33606-3001, USA

Thompson, Anthony (Coach, Football
Coach, Football Player)
Indiana University
Athletic Dept
Bloomington, IN 47405, USA

Thompson, Arland (Athlete, Football
Player)
6692 S Routt St
Littleton, CO 80127-4962, USA

Thompson, Aundra (Athlete, Football
Player)
12060 Galva Dr
Dallas, TX 75243, USA

Thompson, Barbara (Athlete, Baseball
Player)
1721 Edgebrook Dr
Rockford, IL 61107-1320, USA

Thompson, Bennie (Athlete, Football
Player)
Baltimore Ravens
11001 Russell St
Baltimore, MD 21230, USA

Thompson, Billy (Athlete, Basketball
Player)
10678 Palm Spring Dr
Boca Raton, FL 33428-4125, USA

Thompson, Bobby (Athlete, Football
Player)
23600 Lahser Rd
Southfield, MI 48034, USA

Thompson, Brent (Athlete, Hockey Player)
Bridgeport Sound Tigers
600 Main St Ste 1
Bridgeport, CT 06604-5106

Thompson, Brian
1010 Olive Lane
La Canada, CA 91011

Thompson, Brooks (Athlete, Basketball
Player)
29222 Oakview Rdg
Boerne, TX 78015-4457, USA

Thompson, Caroline W (Director,
Producer, Writer)
c/o Brian Sher *Category 5 Entertainment*
10250 Constellation Blvd
7th Floor
Los Angeles, CA 90067, USA

Thompson, Christopher (Astronomer)
University of North Carolina
Astrophysics Dept
Chapel Hill, NC 27599, USA

Thompson, Cornelius (Athlete, Basketball
Player)
207 Lamentation Dr
Berlin, CT 06037-3727, USA

Thompson, Craig (Athlete, Football
Player)
913 C St
Hartsville, SC 29550, USA

Thompson, Daley (Athlete)
1 Church Row Wandsworth Plain
London, ENGLAND SW18 1ES

Thompson, Darrell (Athlete, Football
Player)
4220 Oakview Ln N
Plymouth, MN 55442, USA

Thompson, David O (Athlete, Basketball
Player)
USA

Thompson, David W (Scientist)
Orbital Science Corp
21839 Atlantic Blvd
Sterling, VA 20166, USA

Thompson, Derek (Athlete, Baseball
Player)
3212 Pine Shadow Dr
Land O Lakes, FL 34639-4516, USA

Thompson, Donnell (Athlete, Football
Player)
1302 Village Crossing Dr
Chapel Hill, NC 27517, USA

Thompson, Edward K (Editor)
Rock Ledge Farm
RR 8 Box 350 Union Valley Road
Mahopac, NY 10541, USA

Thompson, Edward T (Editor)
11 Cotswold Dr
North Salem, NY 10560, USA

Thompson, Emma (Actor)
c/o Catherine Olim *PMK/BNC Public
Relations (PMK-LA)*
8687 Melrose Ave Fl 8
West Hollywood, CA 90069, USA

Thompson, Ernest
Rt. #1 Box 3248
Ashland, NH 03217

Thompson, Errol (Athlete, Hockey Player)
20 Nevada Crt
Summerside, PEI C1N 6A8, Canada

Thompson, F M (Daley) (Athlete, Track
Athlete)
Olympic Assn
1 Wadsworth Plain
London SW18 1EH, UNITED KINGDOM
(UK)

Thompson, Fred dalton (Politician)
1287 Ballantrae Farm Dr
Me Lean, VA 22101-3027, USA

Thompson, Gary (Basketball Player)
2531 Park Vista Circle
Arnes, IA 50014, USA

Thompson, Gary Scott (Producer, Writer)
c/o Rob Carlson *WME (LA)*
9601 Wilshire Blvd Fl 3
Beverly Hills, CA 90210, USA

Thompson, Gina (Musician)
Richard Walters
1800 Argyle Ave
#408
Los Angeles, CA 90028, USA

Thompson, G Kennedy (Financier)
First Union Corp
1 First Union Center
Charlotte, NC 28288, USA

Thompson, Glenn (Congressman,
Politician)
124 Cannon HOB
Washington, DC 20515, USA

Thompson, G Ralph (Religious Leader)
Seventh-Day Adventists
12501 Old Columbia Pike
Silver Spring, MD 20904, USA

Thompson, Hank (Musician, Songwriter,
Writer)
2000 Vista Road
Roanoke, TX 76262, USA

Thompson, Hilarie
13202 Weddington St.
Van Nuys, CA 91401

Thompson, Hugh L (Educator)
Washburn University
President's Office
Topeka, KS 66621, USA

Thompson, Ian
44 Perryn Rd
London, ENGLAND W3 7NA

Thompson, Jack (Athlete, Football Player)
2507 29th Ave W
Seattle, WA 98199, USA

Thompson, Jack (Actor)
June Cann Mgmt
110 Queen St
Woollahra, NSW 2025, AUSTRALIA

Thompson, Jack E (Business Person)
Homestake Mining Co
650 California St
San Francisco, CA 94108, USA

Thompson, James B Jr (Misc)
1010 Waltham St
#F1
Lexington, MA 02421, USA

Thompson, James R (Jim) Jr (Politician)
Winston & Strawn
Winston And Strawn LLP 35 W Wacker
Dr Ste 4200
Chicago, IL 60601-1695, USA

Thompson, James R Jr (Misc)
416 Randolph Ave SE
Huntsville, AL 35801, USA

Thompson, Jason (Athlete, Baseball Player)
10359 Trillium Dr
Las Vegas, NV 89135-4055, USA

Thompson, Jason (Actor)
c/o Ryan Daly *Zero Gravity Management*
1531 14th. St
Santa Monica, CA 90404, USA

Thompson, Jason D (Athlete, Baseball Player)
4056 Summerfield Dr
Troy, MI 48085-7033, USA

Thompson, Jennifer (Jenny) (Swimmer)
USA Swimming
1 Olympia Plaza
Colorado Springs, CO 80909, USA

Thompson, Jenny
One Olympic Plaza
Colorado Springs, CO 80909-5770

Thompson, Jill (Cartoonist)
DC Comics
1700 Broadway
New York, NY 10019, USA

Thompson, J Lee
9595 Lime Orchard Rd
Beverly Hills, CA 90210, USA

Thompson, John (Athlete, Basketball Player, Olympic Athlete)
Basketball Hall of Fame
1000 Hall of Fame Ave Ste 100
Springfield, MA 01105-2545, USA

Thompson, Justin (Athlete, Baseball Player)
37111 Edgewater Dr
Pinehurst, TX 77362-1936, USA

Thompson, Kenan (Actor)
c/o Michael Goldman *Michael Goldman Management*
7471 Melrose Ave
Suites 10 and 11
Los Angeles, CA 90046, USA

Thompson, Kenneth L (Scientist)
AT & T Bell Lucent Laboratory
366 Ridge Rd
Watchung, NJ 07069-5432, USA

Thompson, Kevin (Athlete, Basketball Player)
9808 Wesm_ark Dr
Benbrook, TX 76126-3125, USA

Thompson, Lasalle (Athlete, Basketball Player)
399 Du Bois Ave
Sacramento, CA 95747-6328, USA

Thompson, Laura Ann (Stylist)
c/o Staff Member *Zenobia Agency Inc*
PO Box 909
Groveland, CA 95321, USA

Thompson, Lea (Actor)
c/o Lisa Lieberman *Innovative Artists (NY)*
235 Park Ave S
7th Floor
New York, NY 10003, USA

Thompson, Leonard (Athlete, Football Player)
5534 W Glenrosa Ave
Phoenix, AZ 85031, USA

Thompson, Leonard (Golfer)
9010 Marsh View Ct
Ponte Vedra Beach, FL 32082-1928, USA

Thompson, Leroy (Athlete, Football Player)
5005 Princess Ann Ct
Knoxville, TN 37918, USA

Thompson, Linda (Actor)
25254 Eldorado Meadows Road
Hidden Hills, CA 91302, USA

Thompson, Linda (Musician)
High Road
751 Bridgeway
#300
Sausalito, CA 94965, USA

Thompson, Lonnie (Scientist)
Ohio State University
Geology Dept
Columbus, OH 43210, USA

Thompson, Mark (Athlete, Baseball Player)
2600 Chandler Dr Apt 1311
Bowling Green, KY 42104-6235, USA

Thompson, Martel (Stylist)
c/o Staff Member *Montana Artists Agency*
9150 Wilshire Blvd Ste 100
Beverly Hills, CA 90212, USA

Thompson, Marty (Athlete, Football Player)
1290 Lone Star Ct
Calimesa, CA 92320, USA

Thompson, Mike (Athlete, Baseball Player)
7565 Turner Dr
Denver, CO 80221-3432, USA

Thompson, Mike (Congressman, Politician)
231 Cannon HOB
Washington, DC 20515, USA

Thompson, Mike (Cartoonist, Editor)
Detroit Free Press
Editorial Dept
600 W Fort St
Detroit, MI 48226, USA

Thompson, Milt (Athlete, Baseball Player)
P.O. Box 663
Williamstown, NJ 08094-0663, USA

Thompson, Morgan
c/o Jeff Morrone *Jeff Morrone Entertainment*
9350 Wilshire Blvd
Suite 224
Beverly Hills, CA 90212, USA

Thompson, Mychal (Athlete, Basketball Player)
11 Paverstone Ln
Ladera Ranch, CA 92694-0454, USA

Thompson, Norm (Athlete, Football Player)
P.O. Box 4552
Hayward, CA 94540, USA

Thompson, Obadele (Athlete, Track Athlete)
Amateur Athletics Assn
PO Box 46
Bridgetown, BARBADOS

Thompson, Paul (Athlete, Basketball Player)
3422 N 40th St
Milwaukee, WI 53216-3637, USA

Thompson, Paul H (Educator)
Weber State University
President's Office
Ogden, UT 84408, USA

Thompson, Ray (Athlete, Football Player)
1501 N Johnson St
Apt A208
New Orleans, LA 70116, USA

Thompson, Raynoch (Athlete, Football Player)
1739 2nd St
New Orleans, LA 70113, USA

Thompson, Reece (Actor)
c/o Vickie Petronio *Play Management*
807 Powell St
Suite 220
Vancouver V6A 1H7, CANADA

Thompson, Reyna (Athlete, Football Player)
1502 NW 183rd Ter
Pembroke Pines, FL 33029, USA

Thompson, Rich (Athlete, Baseball Player)
7 Chambers Ct
Huntington Station, NY 11746-2620, USA

Thompson, Rich (Athlete, Baseball Player)
47 Murray St
Binghamton, NY 13905-4522, USA

Thompson, Richard (Musician, Songwriter, Writer)
Elizabeth Rush Agency
100 Park St
#4
Montclair, NJ 07042, USA

Thompson, Richard K (Religious Leader)
African Methodist Episcopal Zion Church
PO Box 32843
Charlotte, NC 28232, USA

Thompson, Ricky (Athlete, Football Player)
815 Woodland West Dr
Waco, TX 76712, USA

Thompson, Robert (Athlete, Football Player)
Deerfield Beach High School
910 SW 15th St
Deerfield Beach, FL 33441, USA

Thompson, Robert G K (General)
Pitcott House
Winsford Minehead
Somerset, UNITED KINGDOM (UK)

Thompson, Robert L (Athlete, Football Player)
10712 S 7th Ave
Inglewood, CA 90303, USA

Thompson, Robert R (Robby) (Athlete, Baseball Player)
Seattle Mariners PO Box 4100 Attn Coaching Staff
Seattle, WA 9R1Q4-fl1nn, USA

Thompson, Rocky (Athlete, Hockey Player)
Oklahoma City Barons
501 N Walker Ave Ste 140
Oklahoma City, OK 73102-1233

Thompson, Ryan (Athlete, Baseball Player)
2153 Fullerton Dr
Indianapolis, IN 46214-2130, USA

Thompson, Sarah (Actor)
c/o Gerry Harrington *Brillstein Entertainment Partners*
9150 Wilshire Blvd #350
Beverly Hills, CA 90212, USA

Thompson, Scot (Athlete, Baseball Player)
6142 Penn Dr
Butler, PA 16002-0406, USA

Thompson, Scottie (Actor)
c/o Mary Putnam Greene *MPG Management*
1136 Roxbury Drive
Los Angeles, CA 90035, USA

Thompson, Shawn
5319 Biloxi Ave.
No. Hollywood, CA 91601

Thompson, Sophie (Actor)
Jonathan Altaras
13 Shorts Gardens
London WC2H 9AT, UNITED KINGDOM (UK)

Thompson, Soren (Athlete, Fencer, Olympic Athlete)
12777 Monterey Cypress Way
San Diego, CA 92130-2426, USA

Thompson, Starley L (Scientist)
National Atmospheric Research Center
PO Box 3000
Boulder, CO 80307, USA

Thompson, Steve M (Athlete, Football Player)
11115 Vernon Rd
Lake Stevens, WA 98258, USA

Thompson, Sue (Musician)
Curb Entertainment
3907 W Alameda Ave
#200
Burbank, CA 91505, USA

Thompson, Susanna
PO Box 15717
Beverly Hills, CA 90209-1717

Thompson, Tara (Actor)
c/o Staff Member *Innovative Artists (LA)*
1505 10th St
Santa Monica, CA 90401, USA

Thompson, Ted (Athlete, Football Player)
Green Bay Packers
P.O. Box 10628
Director Of Player Personnel
Green Bay, WI 54307, USA

Thompson, Tessa (Actor)
c/o Siri Garber *Platform Public Relations*
2666 N Beachwood Dr
Los Angeles, CA 90068, USA

Thompson, Tim (Athlete, Baseball Player)
536 Summit Dr
Lewistown, PA 17044-1252, USA

Thompson, Tommy (Politician)
1313 Manassas Trail
Madison, WI 53718-8243, USA

Thompson, Tommy G (Secretary)
Health/Human Service Department
200 Independence SW
Washington, DC 20201, USA

Thompson, Weegie (Athlete, Football Player)
14501 Felbridge Way
Midlothian, VA 23113, USA

Thompson, Wilbur (Moose) (Athlete, Track Athlete)
11372 Martha Ann
Los Alamitos, CA 90720, USA

Thompson, William A (Athlete, Football Player)
14616 E Hawaii Pl
Aurora, CO 80012-5747, USA

Thompson, William P (Religious Leader)
World Council of Churches
475 Riverside Dr
New York, NY 10115, USA

Thompson-Griffin, Viola (Athlete,
Baseball Player)
232 Guthrie Rd
Belton, SC 29627-8900, USA

Thompson Square (Music Group,
Musician)
c/o Staff Member *WmE2 (WMA-TN)*
1600 Division St
Suite 300
Nashville, TN 37203, USA

Thompson Twins
9 Eccleston St.
London, ENGLAND SW1W 9LX

Thoms, Art (Athlete, Football Player)
90 Goodfellow Dr
Moraga, CA 94556, USA

Thoms, Tracie (Actor)
c/o Ted Schachter *Schachter
Entertainment*
1157 S Beverly Dr Fl 2
Los Angeles, CA 90035, USA

Thomsen, Cecilie (Actor)
c/o Staff Member *Special Artists Agency*
9465 Wilshire Blvd #820
Beverly Hills, CA 90212, USA

Thomsen, Mary Sue (Stylist)
8 Oak Pl
Belvedere, CA 94920, USA

Thomsen, Ulrich (Actor)
Paradigm Agency
10100 Santa Monica Blvd
#2500
Los Angeles, CA 90067, USA

Thomson, Anna (Actor)
Innovative Artists
1505 10th St
Santa Monica, CA 90401, USA

Thomson, Brian E (Designer)
5 Little Dowling St
Paddington, NSW 2021, AUSTRALIA

Thomson, Cyndi (Musician)
The Firm
9100 Wilshire Blvd
#100W
Beverly Hills, CA 90210, USA

Thomson, David (Business Person)
The Thomson Corporation
Metro Center
1 Station Place
Stamford, CT 06902, USA

Thomson, Dorrie
3349 Cahuenga Blvd. W. #2
Los Angeles, CA 90068

Thomson, Floyd (Athlete, Hockey Player)
GD
Dunchurch, ON POA 1GO, Canada

Thomson, Gordon (Actor)
3914 Fredonia Dr
Los Angeles, CA 90068, USA

Thomson, H C (Hank) (Misc)
PO Box 38
Mullet Lake, MI 49761, USA

Thomson, James A (Biologist)
University of Wisconsin
Medical School
Biology Dept
Madison, WI 53706, USA

Thomson, Jim (Athlete, Hockey Player)
18 Blackbird Cres
Richmond Hill, ON L4E 4B3, Canada

Thomson, John (Athlete, Baseball Player)
1414 E Kent Dr
Sulphur, LA 70663-5017, USA

Thomson, June (Correspondent)
KNBC-TV
News Dept
3000 W Alameda Ave
Burbank, CA 91523, USA

Thomson, Peter (Golfer)
44 Mathoura Street
Toorak, VIC 3142, AUSTRALIA

Thomson, Rob (Athlete, Baseball Player)
17428 Equestrian Trl
Odessa, FL 33556-1846, USA

Thomson, Scott (DJ)
c/o Staff Member *Sharp Talent*
117 N Orlando Ave
Los Angeles, CA 90048, USA

Thon, Dickie (Athlete, Baseball Player)
C17 Calle Lirio Del Mar
Urb Dorado Del Mar
Dorado, PR 00646-2126, USA

Thon, Olaf (Activist)
FC Schalke 04
Postfach 200861
Gelsenkirchen 45843, GERMANY

Thone, Charles (Ex-Governor)
Erickson & Sederstrom
301 S 13th St
Suite 400
Lincoln, NE 68508, USA

Thoni, Gustav (Coach, Skier)
39026 Prato Allo
Stelvio-Prao, BZ, ITALY

T Hooft, Gerardus (Nobel Prize Laureate)
Leuvenlaan 4
Postbus 80.195
Utrecht 3508, NETHERLANDS

Thor, Brad (Writer)
c/o Staff Member *Sanford J Greenburger
Associates Inc*
55 Fifth Avenue
New York, NY 10003, USA

Thora (Actor)
CunninghamEscottDipene
10635 Santa Monica Blvd
#130
Los Angeles, CA 90025, USA

Thorburn, Christine (Athlete, Cycler,
Olympic Athlete)
141 Mimosa Way
Portola Valley, CA 94028-7429, USA

Thorell, Clarke (Actor)
Bauman, Redanty & Shaul Agency
5757 Wilshire Blvd #473
Los Angeles, CA 90036

Thoren, Skip (Athlete, Basketball Player)
330 Buckland Trce
Louisville, KY 40245-4272, USA

Thorin, Christopher (Musician)
Shapiro Co
9229 Sunset Blvd
#607
Los Angeles, CA 90069, USA

Thorman, Scott (Athlete, Baseball Player)
561 Trico Dr
Cambridge, ON N3H SM8, Canada

Thormodsgard, Paul (Athlete, Baseball
Player)
7752 E Rose Ln
Scottsdale, AZ 85249-4724, USA

Thorn, Gaston (Prime Minister)
1 Rue de la Forge
Luxembourg, LUXEMBOURG

Thorn, Paul (Musician)
c/o Staff Member *Paradigm (Monterey)*
404 W Franklin St
Monterey, CA 93940, USA

Thorn, Rod (Athlete, Basketball Player)
20 Loewen Ct
Rye, NY 34110-2756, USA

Thorn, Tracey (Musician)
JFD Mgmt
Acklam Worshops
10 Acklam Road
London W10 5QZ, UNITED KINGDOM
(UK)

Thornberry, Mac (Congressman,
Politician)
2209 Rayburn HOB
Washington, DC 20515, USA

Thornbladh, Robert (Athlete, Football
Player)
3775 Bradford Square Dr
Ann Arbor, MI 48103, USA

Thornburgh, Richard (Dick) (Politician)
2540 Massachusetts Ave NW Ste 405
Washington, DC 20008-2843, USA

Thornburgh, Richard L (Dick) (Ex-
Governor)
1601 K Street NW
Washington, DC 20006, USA

Thornbury, Tom (Athlete, Hockey Player)
PO Box 262
Woodville, ON KOM 2TO, Canada

Thorne, Bella (Actor)
c/o Adam Griffin *Kritzer Levine Wilkins
Entertainment (KLWG)*
11872 La Grange Ave
1st Floor
Los Angeles, CA 90025, USA

Thorne, Callie (Actor)
c/o Lindsay Porter *Gersh (NY)*
41 Madison Ave
New York, NY 10010, USA

Thorne, Dyanne (Actor)
5192 Placentia Pkwy
Las Vegas, NV 89118, USA

Thorne, Frank (Cartoonist)
1967 Grenville Road
Scotch Plains, NJ 07076-2907, USA

Thorne, Gary (Correspondent)
ABC-TV
Sports Dept
77 W 66th St
New York, NY 10023, USA

Thorne, Kip S (Physicist)
California Institute of Technology
Physics Dept
Pasadena, CA 91125, USA

Thorne, Remy (Actor)
c/o Adam Griffin *Kritzer Levine Wilkins
Entertainment (KLWG)*
11872 La Grange Ave
1st Floor
Los Angeles, CA 90025, USA

Thornell, Jack R (Photographer)
3421 Tennessee Ave
Kenner, LA 70065-3826, USA

Thorne-Smith, Courtney (Actor, Model)
c/o Staff Member *IMPR (Image
Management PR)*
357 S Robertson Blvd.
Beverly Hills, CA 90211, USA

Thornhill, Arthur H Jr (Publisher)
50 S School St
Portsmouth, NH 03801, USA

Thornhill, Josh (Athlete, Football Player)
1580 Haddon Hall Dr
Holt, MI 48842, USA

Thornhill, Leeroy (Dancer)
Midi Mgmt
Jenkins Lane
Great Hallinsburry, Essex CM22 9QL,
UNITED KINGDOM (UK)

Thornhill, Lisa (Actor)
208-11 Anin St
Bedford Nova
Scotia B4A 4E3, CANADA

Thornton, Andre (Athlete, Baseball Player)
P.O. Box 395
Chagrin Falls, OH 44022-0395, USA

Thornton, Billy Bob (Actor, Director)
c/o Geyer Kosinski *Media Talent Group*
9200 Sunset Blvd
Suite 550
Los Angeles, CA 90069, USA

Thornton, Bob (Athlete, Basketball Player)
27865 Espinoza
Mission Viejo, CA 92692-2151, USA

Thornton, Bruce (Athlete, Football Player)
3117 Hazlewood Ct
Bedford, TX 76021, USA

Thornton, Dick (Athlete, Football Player)
5022 P Burgos Street Suite 11
Makati City, Metro Manila, USA

Thornton, Frank (Actor)
David Daly
586A King Road
London SW6 2DX, UNITED KINGDOM
(UK)

Thornton, George (Athlete, Football
Player)
2830 Marti Ln
Montgomery, AL 36116, USA

Thornton, James (Athlete, Football Player)
1010 Fuller Rd
Gurnee, IL 60031, USA

Thornton, Joe (Athlete, Hockey Player)
c/o Staff Member *San Jose Sharks*
525 W Santa Clara St
San Jose, CA 95113, USA

Thornton, John (Athlete, Football Player)
6192 Otoole Ln
Mount Morris, MI 48458, USA

Thornton, John (Athlete, Football Player)
7340 Indian Hill Rd
Cincinnati, OH 45243, USA

Thornton, Kalen (Athlete, Football Player)
c/o Eugene Parker *Maximum Sports
Management*
6435 W Jefferson Blvd
#197
Fort Wayne, IN 46804, USA

Thornton, Kathryn C (Astronaut)
100 Bedford Place
Charlottesville, VA 22903, USA

Thornton, Kathryn C Dr (Astronaut)
100 Bedford Pl
Charlottesville, VA 22903-4622, USA

Thornton, Lou (Athlete, Baseball Player)
725 Henderson Rd
Hope Hull, AL 36043-4429, USA

Thornton, Matt (Athlete, Baseball Player)
9820 W Eagle Talon Trl
Peoria, AZ 85383-2926, USA

Thornton, Melody (Musician)
c/o Page Jeter *Entertainment Fusion Group*
8899 Beverly Blvd
Suite 412
West Hollywood, CA 90046, USA

Thornton, Michael (General)
16856 Falcon Sound Dr
Montgomery, TX 77356-8386, USA

Thornton, Otis (Athlete, Baseball Player)
4312 Avenue L
Birmingham, AL 35208-1812, USA

Thornton, Scott (Athlete, Hockey Player)
Indestri Gvm 23 Stewart Rd
Collingwood, ON L9Y4M7, Canada

Thornton, Shawn (Athlete, Hockey Player)
12 Sackville St
Unit 2
Charlestown, MA 02129-1923, USA

Thornton, Sidney (Athlete, Football Player)
748 Royal St
Natchitoches, LA 71457, USA

Thornton, Sigrid (Actor)
International Casting Services
147 King St
Sydney, NSW 2000, AUSTRALIA

Thornton, Terrence (Pusha T) (Musician)
c/o Mitch Blackman *ICM Partners (ICM-NY)*
730 Fifth Ave
New York, NY 10019, USA

Thornton, Tiffany (Actor)
c/o Nikki Pederson *Nikki Pederson Talent*
Prefers to be contacted via telephone or email
The Woodlands, TX, USA

Thornton, William E (Astronaut)
7640 Pimilco Lane
Boerne, TX 78015, USA

Thornton, William E Dr (Astronaut)
2501 Monterey St
Sarasota, FL 34231-5275, USA

Thornton, Zach (Soccer Player)
Chicago Fire
980 N Michigan Ave
#1998
Chicago, IL 60611, USA

Thorogood, George (Musician)
Michael Donahue Mgmt
PO Box 807
Lewisburg, VA 24901, USA

Thorp, Amanda (Actor)

Thorpe, Alexis (Actor)
c/o Marv Dauer *Marv Dauer Management*
11661 San Vicente Blvd
Suite 104
Los Angeles, CA 90049, USA

Thorpe, Ian (Swimmer)
PO Box 427
Milsons Point, NSW 2061, AUSTRALIA

Thorpe, James (Director)
20 Loeffler Road
#T320
Bloomfield, CT 06002, USA

Thorpe, Jeremy J (Government Official)
2 Orme Square
Bayswater
London W2, UNITED KINGDOM (UK)

Thorpe, Jim (Golfer)
138 Harston Ct
Lake Mary, FL 32746, USA

Thorpe, Otis (Athlete, Basketball Player)
632 Casper Ave
W Palm Beach, FL 33413-1227, USA

Thorsell, William (Editor)
Toronto Globe & Mail
444 Front St W
Toronto, ON M5V 2S9, CANADA

Thorsness, Leo K (General)
239 Watterson Way
Madison, AL 35756-6426, USA

Thorson, Celeste (Producer, Writer)
c/o Alex Fox *Cunningham Escott Slevin & Doherty (CESD-LA)*
10635 Santa Monica Blvd
130
Los Angeles, CA 90025, USA

Thorson, Linda (Actor)
S M S Talent
8730 Sunset Blvd
#440
Los Angeles, CA 90069, USA

Those, Tom (Athlete, Baseball Player)
740 W Mingus Ave
Apt 1012E
Cottonwood, AZ 86326, USA

Thousand Foot Krutch (Music Group)
Tooth & Nail Records
PO Box 12698
Seattle, WA 98111, USA

Thout, Pierre
6606 Patrick Ct.
Centreville, VA 21020

Thranhardt, Carlo
Brauweilerstr. 14
Koln, GERMANY D-50859

Thrash, James (Athlete, Football Player)
16005 Hampton Rd
Hamilton, VA 20158, USA

Threadgill, Henry L (Composer, Musician)
Joel Chriss
300 Mercer St
#3J
New York, NY 10003, USA

Threats, Jabbar (Athlete, Football Player)
2015 Miracle Mile
Springfield, OH 45503, USA

Threatt, Sedale (Athlete, Basketball Player)
8400 E Dixileta Dr
Unit 191
Scottsdale, AZ 85266, USA

Three 6 Mafia (Music Group, Musician)
c/o Jennifer Wilson *Entertainment Fusion Group*
8899 Beverly Blvd
Suite 412
West Hollywood, CA 90046, USA

Three Days Grace (Music Group, Musician)
c/o Cliff Burnstein *Q Prime Inc*
729 Seventh Ave
16th Floor
New York, NY 10019, USA

Three Degrees
19 The Willows Maidenhead Rd.
Windsor Berkshire, ENGLAND

Three Dog Night

Threets, Erick (Athlete, Baseball Player)
2080 Vintage Ln
Livermore, CA 94550-8202, USA

Threlfall, David (Actor)
c/o Staff Member *James Sharkey Assoc*
15 Golden Sq Fl 3
London W1R 3PA, UNITED KINGDOM (UK)

Threshie, R David Jr (Publisher)
Orange County Register
625 N Grand Ave
Santa Ana, CA 92701, USA

Thrice (Music Group)
c/o Staff Member *Nick Ben-Meir CPA*
652 N Doheny Dr
West Hollywood, CA 90069, USA

Thrift, Cliff (Athlete, Football Player)
705 Trisha Ln
Norman, OK 73072, USA

Throne, Malachi (Actor)
11805 Mayfield Ave
#306
Los Angeles, CA 90049, USA

Throop, George (Athlete, Baseball Player)
239 Windwood Ln
Sierra Madre, CA 91024-2677, USA

Thrower, Jim (Athlete, Football Player)
17421 Pontchartrain Blvd
Detroit, MI 48203, USA

Throwing Muses (Composer, Musician)
c/o Staff Member *Concerted Efforts*
P.O. Box 440326
Somerville, MA 02144, USA

Thumann, Chad (Writer)

Thunman, Nils R (Admiral)
1516 S Willemore Ave
Springfield, IL 62704, USA

Thuot, Pierre
21700 Atlantic Blvd.
Dulles, VA 21066

Thuot, Pierre J (Astronaut)
6606 Patrick Court
Centreville, VA 20120, USA

Thuot, Pierre J Captain (Astronaut)
22897 Thornbury Dr
Hollywood, MD 20636-4228, USA

Thurlby, Tom (Athlete, Hockey Player)
158 Welborne Ave
Kingston, ON K7M 4E9, Canada

Thurlow, Steve (Athlete, Football Player)
198 Shore Rd
Old Greenwich, CT 06870, USA

Thurm, Maren (Actor)
ZBF Agentur
Ordensmeisterstr 15-16
Berlin 12099, GERMANY

Thurman, Annie (Actor)
c/o Tina Treadwell *Treadwell Entertainment*
1327 W Valleyheart Dr
Burbank, CA 91506, USA

Thurman, Corey (Athlete, Baseball Player)
713 S Duke St
York, PA 17401-3113, USA

Thurman, Dennis L (Athlete, Football Player)
4501 Eli Dr
Apt G
Owings Mill, MD 21117-3798, USA

Thurman, Gary (Athlete, Baseball Player)
225 W 32nd St
Indianapolis, IN 46208-4603, USA

Thurman, Mike (Athlete, Baseball Player)
1360 7th St
West Linn, OR 97068-4718, USA

Thurman, Uma (Actor, Producer)
c/o Jason Weinberg *Untitled Entertainment (LA)*
350 S. Beverly Dr #200
Beverly Hills, CA 90212, USA

Thurman, William E (General)
10 Firestone Dr
Pinehurst, NC 28374, USA

Thurmond, Mark (Athlete, Baseball Player)
1614 Kings Castle Dr
Katy, TX 77450-4300, USA

Thurmond, Nate (Athlete, Basketball Player)
5094 Diamond Heights Blvd #B
San Francisco, CA 94131-1653, USA

Thurow, Lester C (Economist)
Massachusetts Institute of Technology
Economics Dept
Cambridge, MA 02139, USA

Thursday (Music Group)
c/o Staff Member *Island Records*
825 Eighth Ave
New York, NY 10019, USA

Thurston, Frederick C (Fuzzy) (Athlete, Football Player)
E1462 Grandview Rd
Waupaca, WI 54981, USA

Thurston, Joe (Athlete, Baseball Player)
9024 Paso Robles Way
Elk Grove, CA 95758-6131, USA

Thwaites, Brenton (Actor)
c/o Daniel Spilo *Industry Entertainment Partners*
955 S Carrillo Dr
Suite 300
Los Angeles, CA 90048, USA

Thwaites, David (General)
483 Old Orchard Cir
Millersville, MD 21108-2010, USA

Thyer, Mario (Athlete, Hockey Player)
170 Silver Rd
Bangor, ME 04401-5829

Thyne, TJ (Actor)
4715 Camellia Ave
N Hollywood, CA 91602, USA

Thyssen, Greta (Actor)
444 E 82nd St
New York, NY 10028, USA

Tian, Jiyun (Government Official)
Vice President's Office
State Council
Beijing, CHINA

Tiant, Luis (Athlete, Baseball Player)
24 Southwood Dr
Southborough, MA 01772-1976, USA

Tibbets, Paul W
5574 Knollwood Dr
Columbus, OH 43227, USA

Tibbets, Paul W Jr (War Hero)
5574 Knollwood Dr
Columbus, OH 43232, USA

Tibbetts, Billy (Athlete, Hockey Player)
79 Jericho Rd
Scituate, MA 02066-4809

Tibbs, Jay (Athlete, Baseball Player)
905 Smith Rd
Oneonta, AL 35121-7181, USA

Tice, George A (Photographer)
581 Kings Highway E
Atlantic Hills, NJ 07716-2326, USA

Tice, John (Athlete, Football Player)
1004 Bartlett Loop
Apt B
West Point, NY 10996, USA

Tice, Michael P (Mike) (Athlete, Football
Coach, Football Player)
2114 Gail Ave
Apt A
Jacksonville Beach, FL 32250, USA

Tichenor, Todd (Athlete, Baseball Player)
504 David Ave
Holcomb, KS 67851-9771, USA

Tichmarsh, Alan (Actor, Writer)
c/o Staff Member *Arlington Enterprises Ltd*
1-3 Charlotte St
London W1P 1HD, UNITED KINGDOM
(UK)

Tichnor, Alan (Religious Leader)
*United Synagogues of Conservative
Judaism*
155 5th Ave
New York, NY 10010, USA

Tichy, Milan (Athlete, Hockey Player)
2413 NW 7th St
Boynton Beach, FL 33426-8783

Tickner, Charles (Athlete, Figure Skater,
Olympic Athlete)
1826 Dolphin Ct
Discovery Bay, CA 94505-9362, USA

Ticotin, Rachel (Actor)
c/o Staff Member *Stone Manners Salners
Agency (LA)*
9911 W Pico Blvd Ste 1400
Los Angeles, CA 90035, USA

Tiddy, Kim (Actor)
Bosun House
1 Deer Park Rd
Merton
London SW19 9TL, ENGLAND

Tidey, Alec (Athlete, Hockey Player)
1877 Marine Dr
N Vancouver, BC V7P 1V5, CANADA

Tidrow, Dick (Athlete, Baseball Player)
324 NE Warrington Ct
Lees Summit, MO 64064-1605, USA

Tidwell, Moody R III (Judge)
US Claims Court
717 Madison Place NW
Washington, DC 20439, USA

Tiefenbach, Dov (Actor)
c/o Staff Member *Bauman Redanty &
Shaul Agency*
5757 Wilshire Blvd
Suite 473
Beverly Hills, CA 90212, USA

Tiefenthaler, Verfe (Athlete, Baseball
Player)
1852 Quint Ave
Carroll, IA 51401, USA

Tiefenthaler, Verle (Athlete, Baseball
Player)
1852 Quint Ave
Carroll, IA 51401-3567, USA

Tiegs, Cheryl (Model, Television Host)
9663 Santa Monica Blvd #339
Beverly Hills, CA 90210, USA

Tieman, Dan (Athlete, Basketball Player)
8 Janet Dr
Taylor Mill, KY 41015-1731, USA

Tiernan, Andrew (Actor)
c/o Paula Rosenberg *ICA Talent*
818 12th Street Ste 9
Santa Monica, CA 90403, USA

Tierney, Maura (Actor)
c/o Christina Papadopoulos *Baker
Winokur Ryder Public Relations BWR
(BWR-NY)*
292 Madison Ave
12th Floor
New York, NY 10017, USA

Tiesto (DJ, Musician)
c/o Josh Neuman *The Ascot Club*
55 Washington St
Suite 658
Brooklyn, NY 11201, USA

Tiffany (Musician)
c/o Charlie Davis *Paradise Artists*
P.O. Box 1821
Ojai, CA 93024-1821, USA

Tiffee, Terry (Athlete, Baseball Player)
2620 Calico Creek Dr
North Little Rock, AR 72116-7638, USA

Tiffin, Pamela (Actor)
15 W 67th St
New York, NY 10023, USA

Tiger, Lionel (Scientist)
248 W 23rd St
#400
New York, NY 10011, USA

Tigerman, Stanley (Architect)
Tigerman McCurry Architect
444 N Walls St
Chicago, IL 60610, USA

Tighe, Kevin (Actor)
c/o Joanna (Joanie) Burstein *Burstein
Company, The*
15304 Sunset Blvd
suite 208
Pacific Palisades, CA 90272, USA

Tikkanen, Esa (Athlete, Hockey Player)
Curtiusstr 2
Essen 45144, Germany

Tilberg, Tasha (Model)
c/o Staff Member *Next (LA)*
8447 Wilshire Boulevard, Suite 301
erly Hills, CA 90211, USA

Tilford, Terrell (Actor)
c/o Staff Member *Silver Massetti &
Szatmary (SMS) Talent Inc*
8383 Wilshire Blvd
Suite 230
Beverly Hills, CA 90211, USA

Tilghman, Shirley M C (Biologist,
Educator)
Princeton University
President's Office
Princeton, NJ 08544, USA

Tilker, Ewald (Athlete)
2767 40th Ave
San Francisco, CA 94116, USA

Till, Brian (Race Car Driver)
19 Lake Dr.
Plainfield, IL 60544, USA

Till, Lucas (Actor)
c/o Ellen Meyer *Ellen Meyer Management*
8899 Beverly Blvd
Suite 612
West Hollywood, CA 90048, USA

Tilleman, Mike (Athlete, Football Player)
180 County Road 800 NW
Havre, MT 59501, USA

Tiller, Chris (Athlete, Baseball Player)
604 Morningside
Bullard, Tx 75757-5181, USA

Tiller, Joe (Coach, Football Coach)
Purdue University
Athletic Dept
W Lafayette, IN 47907, USA

Tiller, Nadja (Actor)
Via Tamporiva 26
Castagnola 6976, SWITZERLAND

Tilley, Patrick L (Pat) (Athlete, Coach,
Football Coach, Football Player)
P.O. Box 4523
Shreveport, LA 71134, USA

Tilley, Tom (Athlete, Hockey Player)
14724 Maple St
Overland Park, KS 66223-1216

Tillis, Mel (Musician, Songwriter, Writer)
P.O. Box 305
Silver Springs, FL 34489-0305, USA

Tillis, Pam (Musician, Songwriter)
Fitzgerald Hartley Co
1908 Wedgewood Ave
Nashville, TN 37212, USA

Tillison, Ed (Athlete, Football Player)
38504 James Crosby Rd
Pearl River, LA 70452, USA

Tillman, Andre (Athlete, Football Player)
P.O. Box 743204
Dallas, TX 75374-3204, USA

Tillman, Kerry Rusty (Athlete, Baseball
Player)
35119th St
Atlantic Beach, FL 32233-4540, USA

Tillman, Lewis (Athlete, Football Player)
P.O. Box 166
Madison, MS 39130, USA

Tillman, Robert L (Business Person)
Lowe's Companies
1605 Curtis Bridge Road
Wilkesboro, NC 28697, USA

Tillman, Rusty (Athlete, Baseball Player)
8711 Newton Rd
Apt 61
Jacksonville, FL 32216, USA

Tillman Jr, George (Director, Producer,
Writer)
State Street Pictures
10201 West Pico Blvd
Bldg 52, Room 123
Los Angeles, CA 90064, USA

Tillotson, Johnny (Musician)
American Mgmt
19948 Mayall St
Chatsworth, CA 91311, USA

Tilly, Jennifer (Actor)
c/o Sue Leibman *Barking Dog
Entertainment*
609 Greenwich St
6th Floor
New York, NY 10014, USA

Tilly, Meg (Actor)
c/o Staff Member *IFA Talent Agency*
8730 Sunset Blvd
Suite 490
Los Angeles, CA 90069, USA

Tilson, Joseph (Joe) (Artist)
2 Brook Street Mansions
41 Davies St
London W1Y 1FJ, UNITED KINGDOM
(UK)

Tilton, Charlene (Actor)
c/o Staff Member *Bohemia Group*
1680 Vine St Ste 216
Los Angeles, CA 90028, USA

Tilton, Charline (Actor)
c/o Staff Member *Bohemia Group*
1680 Vine St Ste 216
Los Angeles, CA 90028, USA

Tilton, Glenn F (Business Person)
UAL Corp
1200 E Algonquin Road
Arlington Heights, IL 60005, USA

Tilton, Robert (Misc)
Robert Tilton Ministries
PO Box 819000
Dallas, TX 75381, USA

Timberlake, Gary (Athlete, Baseball
Player)
14016 Waters Edge Dr
Louisville, KY 40245-5250, USA

Timberlake, George (Athlete, Football
Player)
13880 Canoe Brook Dr
Apt 4D
Seal Beach, CA 90740, USA

Timberlake, Justin (Actor, Musician,
Producer)
c/o Rick Yorn *LBI Entertainment*
2000 Avenue of the Stars
3rd Floor, North Tower
Los Angeles, CA 90067, USA

Timberlake, Robert W (Bob) (Athlete,
Football Player)
2219 E Jarvis St
Milwaukee, WI 53211, USA

Timchal, Cindy (Coach)
University of Maryland
Athletic Dept
College Park, MD 20742, USA

Times, Ken (Athlete, Football Player)
2603 S Sanford Ave
Sanford, FL 32773, USA

Timken, William R Jr (Business Person)
Timken Co
1835 Dueber Ave SW
Canton, OH 44706, USA

Timlin, Mike (Athlete, Baseball Player)
355 High Ridge Way
Castle Pines, CO 80108-3422, USA

Timme, Robert (Architect)
Taft Architects
2370 Rice Blvd
#112
Houston, TX 77005, USA

Timmerman, Adam (Athlete, Football Player)
6209 Mid Rivers Mall Dr
Saint Peters, MO 63304, USA

Timmermann, Tom (Athlete, Baseball Player)
197 Coyote Ct
Pinckney, MI 48169-8022, USA

Timmermann, Ulf (Athlete, Track Athlete)
Conrad Blenkle Str 34
Berlin 1055, GERMANY

Timmins, Call (Actor)
The Agency
1800 Ave of Stars
#400
Los Angeles, CA 90067, USA

Timmons, Harold
PO Box 140571
Nashville, TN 37214

Timmons, Jeff (Musician)
DAS Communications
83 Riverside Dr
New York, NY 10024, USA

Timmons, Margo (Musician)
Macklam Feldman Mgmt
1505 W 2nd Ave
#200
Vancouver, BC V6H 3Y4, CANADA

Timmons, Michael (Musician, Songwriter, Writer)
Macklam Feldman Mgmt
1505 W 2nd Ave
#200
Vancouver, BC V6H 3Y4, CANADA

Timmons, Ozzie (Athlete, Baseball Player)
4901 S 83rd St
Tampa, FL 33619-7101, USA

Timmons, Peter (Musician)
Macklam Feldman Mgmt
1505 W 2nd Ave
#200
Vancouver, BC V6H 3Y4, CANADA

Timmons, Tim (Athlete, Baseball Player)
5055 Johnstown Rd
New Albany, OH 43054-9578, USA

Timmons, Tim (Athlete, Baseball Player)
P.O. Box 574
New Albany, OH 43054, USA

Timofeev, Valeri (Artist)
464 Blue Mountain Lake
East Stroudsburg, PA 18301, USA

Timofeyeva, Nina V (Ballerina)
Bolshoi Theater
Teatralnaya Pl 1
Moscow 103009, RUSSIA

Timonen, Kimmo (Athlete, Hockey Player)
125 Upland Way
Haddonfield, NJ 08033-3603, USA

Timpner, Clay (Athlete, Baseball Player)
3847 Shaftbury Pl
Oviedo, FL 32765-9311, USA

Timpson, Michael D (Athlete, Football Player)
4722 Saint Simon Dr
Coconut Creek, FL 33073, USA

Tina, Fasano-Cucci (Stylist)
3286 Polo Pl
Bronx, NY 10465, USA

Tindermans, Leo (Prime Minister)
Jan Verbertiel 24
Edegem 2520, BELGIUM

Tindle, David (Astronaut)
Redfern Gallery
20 Cork St
London W1, UNITED KINGDOM (UK)

Ting, Samuel C C (Nobel Prize Laureate)
15 Moon Hill Rd
Lexington, MA 02421-6112, USA

Tingelhoff, Mick (Athlete, Football Player)
20517 Kalmeadow Ct
Lakeville, MN 55044, USA

Tingle, Scott D Cmdr (Astronaut)
2106 Bayou Cove Ln
League City, TX 77573-3248, USA

Tinglehoff, H Michael (Mick) (Athlete, Football Player)
19288 Judicial Rd
Prior Lake, MN 55372, USA

Tingley, Leeann (Beauty Pageant Winner)
Miss Rhode Island Pageant
PO Box 3509
Cranston, RI 02910, USA

Tingley, Ron (Athlete, Baseball Player)
349 Omni Dr
Sparks, NV 89441-7295, USA

Ting Tings, The (Music Group)

Tinker, Grant (Business Person)
531 Barnaby Rd
Los Angeles, CA 90077, USA

Tinkham, Michael (Physicist)
98 Rutledge Road
Belmont, MA 02478, USA

Tinoco, Joe
118 N. Keeler
Olathe, KS 66061

Tinordi, Mark (Athlete, Hockey Player)
545 Devonshire Ct
Severna Park, MD 21146-1001, Canada

Tinsley, Bruce (Cartoonist, Editor)
c/o Staff Member *King Features Syndication*
300 W 57th St
15th Floor
New York, NY 10019-5238, USA

Tinsley, George (Athlete, Basketball Player)
The Tinsley Group
P.O. Box 1442
Auburndale, FL 33823, USA

Tinsley, Jackson B (Jack) (Editor)
Fort Worth Star-Telegram
Editorial Dept
400 W 7th St
Fort Worth, TX 76102, USA

Tinsley, Jamaal (Basketball Player)
Indiana Pacers
Conseco Fieldhouse
125 S Pennsylvania
Indianapolis, IN 46253-2417, USA

Tinsley, Lee (Athlete, Baseball Player)
237 Tenor St
Shelbyville, KY 40065-9255, USA

Tinsley, Scott (Athlete, Football Player)
26852 Sommerset Ln
Lake Forest, CA 92630, USA

Tint, Francine (Stylist)
1 University Pl
Penthouse 22-B
New York, NY 10003, USA

Tin Tin, Rin
PO Box 27
Crockett, TX 75835

Tiomkin, Jon (Athlete, Fencer, Olympic Athlete)
254 Adams Rd
Hewlett, NY 11557-2741, USA

tipper, Ed (General)
1245 S Pennsylvania St
Denver, CO 80210-1532, USA

Tippet, Andre B (Athlete, Football Player)
17 Knob Hill St
Sharon, MA 02067, USA

Tippett, Dave (Athlete, Hockey Player)
Phoenix Coyotes
6751 N Sunset Blvd Ste 200
Glendale, AZ 85305-3124

Tippett, Dave (Athlete, Coach, Hockey Player)
19468 N lOlst St
Scottsdale, AZ 85255-3779

Tippett, Sir Michael
48 Great Marborough St.
London, ENGLAND W1V 2BN

Tippin, Aaron (Musician, Songwriter)
Tip Top Entertainment
PO Box 41689
Nashville, TN 37204, USA

Tippins, Ken (Athlete, Football Player)
RR 2 Box 173
Adel, GA 31620, USA

Tipton, Daniel (Religious Leader)
Churches of Christ in Christian Union
PO Box 30
Circleville, OH 43113, USA

Tipton, Dave L (Athlete, Football Player)
915 Bonneville Way
Sunnyvale, CA 94087, USA

Tiriac, Ion (Coach, Tennis Player)
Blvd. D'Italie 44
Monte Carlo, MONACO

Tirico, Mike (Sportscaster)
ABC-TV
Sports Dept
77 W 66th St
New York, NY 10023, USA

Tirimo, Martino (Musician)
1 Romeyn Road
London SW16 2NU, UNITED KINGDOM (UK)

Tirole, Jean M (Economist)
Institut D'Economie Industrielle
Toulouse, FRANCE

Tisch, James S (Business Person)
Loews Corp
667 Madison Ave
New York, NY 10021, USA

Tisch, Joan (Misc)
3 TimberTrl
Rye, NY 10580-1934, USA

Tisch, Preston R (Business Person, Government Official)
Loews Corp
667 Madison Ave
New York, NY 10021, USA

Tisch, Steve (Writer)
1162 Tower Road
Beverly Hills, CA 90210, USA

Tischinski, Tom (Athlete, Baseball Player)
9905 N Donnelly Ave
Kansas City, MO 64157-7861, USA

Tischiski, Tom (Athlete, Baseball Player)
9905 N Donnelly Ave
Kansas City, MO 64157, USA

Tisdale, Ashley (Actor)
4314 Mariota Ave
Toluca Lake, CA 91602, USA

Tisdale, Jennifer (Actor)
c/o Bill Perlman *New Talent Management*
PO Box 2939
Beverly Hills, CA 90213, USA

Tishby, Noa (Actor)
c/o Bob McGowan *McGowan Management*
8733 W Sunset Blvd
Suite 103
West Hollywood, CA 90069, USA

Tisser, Orna (Stylist)
c/o Staff Member *Celestine - CA*
1666 20th St
#200-B
Santa Monica, CA 90404, USA

Titanic, Morris (Athlete, Hockey Player)
120 Cambrook Row
Buffalo, NY 14221-5228

Titanic Historical Society
PO Box 51053
Indian Orchard, MA 01151

Titchmarsh, Alan (Talk Show Host)
Alan Titchmarsh Products
New Mills
Slad Rd
Stroud, Gloucestershire Engl GL5 1RN, UNITED KINGDOM (UK)

Titensor, Glen (Athlete, Football Player)
729 Montrose Ct
Flower Mound, TX 75022, USA

Tito, Dennis (Astronaut)
1800 Alta Mura Road
Pacific Palisades, CA 90272, USA

Tito, Teburoro (President)
President's Office
Tarawa, KIRIBATI

Titone, Jackie (Actor)
c/o Staff Member *WME (LA)*
9601 Wilshire Blvd Fl 3
Beverly Hills, CA 90210, USA

Titov, German (Athlete, Hockey Player)
246 Slopeview Dr SW
Calgary, AB T3H 4GS, Canada

Titov, Vladimir
3 Hovanskaya Str. 8
Moscow, RUSSIA 129515

Titov, Vladimir G (Cosmonaut)
Potcha Kosmonavtov
Moskovskoi Oblasti
Syvisdny Goroduk 141160, RUSSIA

Titov, Yuri E (Gymnast)
Kolokolnikov Per 6
#19
Moscow 103045, RUSSUA

Tits, Jacques L (Mathematician)
12 Rue du Moulin des Pres
Paris 75013, FRANCE

Tittle, Y A (Athlete, Football Player)
1890 N Shoreline Blvd
2nd Floor
Mountain View, CA 94043, USA

Tittle, Yelberton A (Y A) (Athlete,
Football Player)
2500 E Camino Real
Palo Alto, CA 94306, USA

Titus, Christopher (Writer)
c/o Max Burgos *Agency for the
Performing Arts (APA-LA)*
8383 Wilshire Blvd
Suite 1050
Beverly Hills, CA 90211, USA

Titus-Carmel, Gerard (Artist)
La Grand Maison
Oulchy Le Chateau 02210, FRANCE

Tixby, Dexter (Musician)
David Harris Enterprises
24210 E Fork Road
#9
Azusa, CA 91702, USA

Tizard, Catherine A (Ex-Governor)
12A Wallace St
Herne Bay, Auckland 1, New Zealand

Tiziani, Mario (Athlete, Golfer)
c/o Jim Lehrman *SFX Golf*
36855 W Main St Ste 200
Purcellville, VA 20132, USA

Tizon, Albert (Journalist)
Seattle Times
Editorial Dept
1120 John St
Seattle, WA 98109, USA

Tizzio, Thomas R Sr (Business Person)
American Int'l Group
70 Pine St
New York, NY 10270, USA

Tjeknavorian, Loris-Zare (Composer,
Conductor)
State Philharmonia
Mashtotsi Prospekt 46
Yerevan, ARMENIA

Tjoflat, Gerald B (Judge)
US Court of Appeals
311 W Monroe St
Jacksonville, FL 32202, USA

Tkachuk, Keith (Athlete, Hockey Player,
Olympic Athlete)
Pro-Athletes Management
2 Center Plz Ste 420
Boston, MA 02108-1929, USA

Tkaczuk, Daniel (Athlete, Hockey Player)
iHockey Trainer 172 Dunlop St W Unit A
Barrie, ON L4N 1B3, Canada

Tkaczuk, Ivan (Religious Leader)
Ukrainian Orthodox Church
3 Davenport Ave
#2A
New-Rochelle, NY 10805, USA

Tkaczuk, Walter R (Walt) (Athlete,
Hockey Player)
River Valley Golf and Country Club RR 3
Lakeside, ON N0M 2G0, Canada

T. King, Peter (Congressman, Politician)
339 Cannon HOB
Washington, DC 20515, USA

TLC (Music Group)
c/o Staff Member *Creative Artists Agency
(CAA-LA)*
2000 Ave Of The Stars
Los Angeles, CA 90067, USA

T. McCaul, Michael (Congressman,
Politician)
131 Cannon HOB
Washington, DC 20515, USA

TNA Wrestling (Wrestler)
c/o Staff Member *Paradigm (Monterey)*
404 W Franklin St
Monterey, CA 93940, USA

To, Tony (Director, Producer)
*Studios International / Ensemble
Development*
3000 West Olympic Blvd
Suite 2405
Santa Monica, CA 90404, USA

Toale, Will (Actor)
c/o Jennifer Wiley *Framework
Entertainment (NY)*
129 W 27th St Fl 12
New York, NY 10001, USA

Toback, James (Director)
International Creative Mgmt
8942 Wilshire Blvd
#219
Beverly Hills, CA 90211, USA

Tobeck, Robbie (Athlete, Football Player)
2018 Newport Way NW
Issaquah, WA 98027, USA

Tober, Ronnie (Business Person)
C/O Jan Jochems
Tober Jochems VOF
Stadskade 258
Apeldoorn 7311 XV, NETHERLANDS

Tobey, James (Actor)
Paradigm Agency
10100 Santa Monica Blvd
#2500
Los Angeles, CA 90067, USA

Tobian, GAry M (Misc)
9171 Belted Kingfisher Road
Blaine, WA 98230, USA

Tobias, Andrew (Business Person, Writer)
787 NE 71 St.
Miami, FL 33138, USA

Tobias, Oliver (Actor)
Gavin Barker Assoc
2D Wimpole St
London W1G 0EB, UNITED KINGDOM
(UK)

Tobias, Phillip V (Scientist)
Witwatersrand University
7 York Road
Johannesburg 2193, SOUTH AFRICA

Tobias, Randall L (Business Person)
Eli Lilly Co
Lilly Corporate Center
Indianapolis, IN 46285, USA

Tobias, Robert M (Misc)
National Treasury Employees Union
901 E St NW
Washington, DC 20004, USA

Tobias, Stephen C (Business Person)
Norfolk Southern Corp
3 Commercial Place
Norfolk, VA 23510, USA

Tobik, Dave (Athlete, Baseball Player)
848 Chancellor Heights Dr
Ballwin, MO 63011-3580, USA

Tobin, Don (Cartoonist)
12312 Ranchwood Road
Santa Ana, CA 92705-3349, USA

Tobin, Vince (Athlete, Coach, Football
Coach, Football Player)
15997 W Monterrey Way
Goodyear, AZ 85395, USA

Tobolowsky, Stephen (Actor, Director,
Writer)
c/o Steven Levy *Framework Entertainment
(LA)*
9057 Nemo St
Suite C
West Hollywood, CA 90069, USA

Toburen, Nelson (Athlete, Football Player)
1007 Village Dr
Pittsburg, KS 66762, USA

Tobymac (Musician)
c/o Staff Member *True Artist Management*
227 3rd Ave
North Franklin, TN 37064, USa

Toca, Jorge (Athlete, Baseball Player)
7940 NW 167th Ter
Hialeah, FL 33016-3424, USA

Tocchet, Rick (Athlete, Hockey Player)
PO Box 13563
Pittsburgh, PA 15243-0563, USA

Toczyska, Stefania (Opera Singer)
Columbia Artists Mgmt Inc
165 W 57th St
New York, NY 10019, USA

Todd, Anne E (Actor)
2419 Oregon St
Berkeley, CA 94705, USA

Todd, Hallie (Actor)
Ann Morgan Guilbert
550 Erskine Dr
Pacific Palisades, CA 90272, USA

Todd, Jackson (Athlete, Baseball Player)
8958 E 76th St
Tulsa, OK 74133-4406, USA

Todd, James R (Jim) (Athlete, Baseball
Player)
21639 Hill Gail Way
Parker, CO 80138-7249, USA

Todd, Jeanine (Stylist)
360 W 22nd St
New York, NY 10011, USA

Todd, Josh (Musician)
The Firm
9100 Wilshire Blvd
#100W
Beverly Hills, CA 90210, USA

Todd, Kate (Actor)
c/o Robert Lanni *Coalition Entertainment
Management*
10271 Yonge St
Suite 302
Richmond Hill, Ontario L4C 3B5, Canada

Todd, Kendra (Business Person, Reality
TV Star)
C/O Eric Hanson
Letnom Management
423 W 55th St 2nd Fl
New York, NY 10019, USA

Todd, Kevin (Athlete, Hockey Player)
15 Narla Ln
Utica, NY 13501-5560

Todd, Mark (Horse Racer)
PO Box 507
Cambridge, NEW ZEALAND

Todd, Rachel (Actor)
6310 San Vicente Blvd
#520
Los Angeles, CA 90048, USA

Todd, Richard (Football Player)
New York Jets
PO Box 471
Shelfield, AL 35660-0471, USA

Todd, Tony (Actor)
c/o Jeff Goldberg *Jeff Goldberg
Management*
817 Monte Leon Dr
Beverly Hills, CA 90210, USA

Todd, Trisha (Actor)
c/o Staff Member *Henry Downey Talent
Management*
4045 Vineland Ave #538
Studio City, CA 91604, USA

Todd, Virgil H (Religious Leader)
Memphis Theological
168 E Parkway S
Memphis, TN 38104, USA

Todorov, Stanko (Prime Minister)
Narodno Sobranie
Sofia, BULGARIA

Todorovsky, Piotr Y (Director)
Vernadskogo Prospect 70A
#23
Moscow 117454, RUSSIA

Todosey, Jordan (Actor)
c/o Amanda Rosenthal *Amanda Rosenthal
Talent Agency*
543 Richmond St W
Suite 123
Toronto, ON M5V 1Y6, Canada

Toennies, Jan Peter (Physicist)
Ewaldstr 7
Gottingen 37075, GERMANY

Toerzs, Gregor (Actor)
c/o Beate Wolgast *Die Agenten*
Auguststraße 34
Berlin 10119, Germany

Toews, Jeffrey M (Jeff) (Athlete, Football
Player)
11924 SW 44th St
Davie, FL 33330, USA

Toews, Jonathan (Athlete, Hockey Player)
c/o Pat Brisson *Creative Artists Agency
(CAA-LA)*
2000 Ave Of The Stars
Los Angeles, CA 90067, USA

Toews, Loren (Athlete, Football Player)
165 Hawthorne Ave
Los Altos, CA 94022, USA

Tofani, Loretta A (Journalist)
Philadelphia Inquirer
Editorial Dept
400 N Broad St
Philadelphia, PA 19130, USA

Toffler, Alvin (Writer)
Randon House
1745 Broadway
#B1
New York, NY 10019, USA

Toffoli, Brian (Stylist)
c/o Staff Member *Cloutier Agency*
2632 La Cienega Ave
Los Angeles, CA 90034, USA

Toft, Rod (Bowler)
1120 Cryan Trl N
Stillwater, MN 55082-1887, USA

Tognini, Michel (Cosmonaut)
5413 Newcastle St
Bellaire, TX 77401, USA

Tognini, Michel Brig Gen (Astronaut)
15 ter rue des Tourelles
L'Hay-les-Roses F-94240, France

Tognoni, Gina (Actor)
c/o Marnie Sparer *Innovative Artists (LA)*
1505 10th St
Santa Monica, CA 90401, USA

Togo, Jonathan (Actor)
c/o Cynthia Shelton-Droke *Sweet Mud Group*
648 Broadway #1002
New York, NY 10012, USA

Togunde, Victor (Actor)
c/o Staff Member *GVA Talent Agency Inc*
8981 Sunset Blvd.
Suite 101
Los Angeles, CA 90069, USA

Toguri, Iva (General)
218 W Main St
West Dundee, IL 60118-2019, USA

Tointon, Kara (Actor)
c/o Staff Member *RKM Communications*
4 New Burlington St
5th Floor
London W1S 2JG, UK

Tokarev, Valeri I (Cosmonaut)
Potcha Kosmonavtov
Moskovskoi Oblasti
Syvisdny Goroduk 141160, RUSSIA

Tokes, Laszlo (Politician, Religious Leader)
Calvin Str 1
Oradea 3700, ROMANIA

Tokio Hotel (Music Group, Musician)
c/o Staff Member *Universal Music Deutschland*
Stralauer Allee 1
Berlin 10245, Germany

Tokody, Ilona (Opera Singer)
Hungarian State Opera
Andrassy Utca 22
Budapest 1062, HUNGARY

Tolan, Peter (Actor, Director, Producer, Writer)

Tolan, Robert (Bobby) (Athlete, Baseball Player)
804 Woodstock St
Bellaire, TX 77401-4716, USA

Tolar, Kevin (Athlete, Baseball Player)
3738 Greentree Cir
Panama City, FL 32405-6624, USA

Tolbert, Berlinda (Actor)
c/o Staff Member *Pallas Management*
5301 Bellaire Ave
Valley Vilage, CA 91607, US

Tolbert, Jim (Athlete, Football Player)
2435 Corinna Ct
San Diego, CA 92105, USA

Tolbert, Ray (Athlete, Basketball Player)
2205 Crestwood Dr
Anderson, IN 46016-2751, USA

Tolbert, Tom (Athlete, Basketball Player)
368 Creedon Cir
Alameda, CA 94502-7793, USA

Tolbert, Tony L (Athlete, Football Player)
475 S White Chapel Blvd
Southlake, TX 76092, USA

Toldeo, Esteban (Golfer)
135 Spring Vly
Irvine, CA 92602-0919, USA

Toledo, Alejandro (President)
Palacio de Gobierno S/N
Plaza de Armas S/N
Lima 1, PERU

Tolentino, Jose (Athlete, Baseball Player)
26711 Caceres Cir
Mission Viejo, CA 92691-5503, USA

Toler, Ken (Athlete, Football Player)
2064 Brecon Dr
Jackson, MS 39211, USA

Toles, Alvin (Athlete, Football Player)
106 Todd Creek Pl
Forsyth, GA 31029, USA

Toles, Ted (Athlete, Baseball Player)
250 Tod Ave NW Apt 305
Warren, OH 44485-2950, USA

Toles, Thomas G (Tom) (Cartoonist, Editor)
4625 46th St NW
Washington, DC 20016, USA

Tolins, Jonathan (Writer)
c/o Cori Wellins *WME (LA)*
9601 Wilshire Blvd Fl 3
Beverly Hills, CA 90210, USA

Toliver, Freddie (Athlete, Baseball Player)
674 Medical Center Dr
San Bernardino, CA 92411-2520, USA

Toliver, Jerry (Mad Man) (Race Car Driver)
7402 Mount Joy #A
Huntington Beach, CA 92648, USA

Tolkan, James (Actor)
Paradigm Agency
10100 Santa Monica Blvd
#2500
Los Angeles, CA 90067, USA

Tollberg, Brian (Athlete, Baseball Player)
2104 39th St W
Bradenton, FL 34205-1334, USA

Tolle, Eckhart (Writer)
Eckhart Teachings
P.O. Box 93661 Nelson Park RPO
Vancouver, BC V6E 4L7, CANADA

Tollefsen, Ole-Kristian (Athlete, Hockey Player)
250 Daniel Burnham Square
#702
Columbus, OH 43215 2693, USA

Tollerod, Siri (Model)
c/o Staff Member *Modelwerk Modelagentur GmbH*
Rothenbaum Chaussee 1
Hamburg 20148, Germany

Tolles, Tommy (Golfer)
c/o Staff Member *Pro Golfers Association (PGA) Tour*
112 TPC Blvd
Ponte Vedra Beach, FL 32082, USA

Tolleson, Steve (Athlete, Baseball Player)
313 Mossvcup Oak Ct
Spartanburg, SC 29306-6627, USA

Tolleson, Wayne (Athlete, Baseball Player)
313 Mossycup Oak Ct
Spartanburg, SC 29306-6627, USA

Tollin, Michael (Director, Producer, Writer)
c/o Staff Member *Tollin/Robbins Management*
4130 Cahuenga Blvd
Unit 305
Toluca Lake, CA 91602, USA

Tolliver, Billy Joe (Athlete, Football Player)
9837 Neesonwood Dr
Shreveport, LA 71106, USA

Tolman, Tim (Athlete, Baseball Player)
11425 N Ingot Loop
Tucson, AZ 85737-9450, USA

Tolsky, Susan (Actor)
10815 Acama St
North Hollywood, CA 91602, USA

Tolson, Billy
2710 N. Stemmons Frwy. #700
Dallas, TX 75207

Tolson, Byron (Athlete, Basketball Player)
4012 N Orchard St
Tacoma, WA 98407-4215, USA

Tom, Braatz (Athlete, Football Player)
3131 NE 55th Ct
Fort Lauderdale, FL 33308, USA

Tom, David
3033 Vista Crest
Los Angeles, CA 90068

Tom, Dimmick (Athlete, Football Player)
204 Broadmoor Blvd
Lafayette, LA 70503, USA

Tom, Duniven (Athlete, Football Player)
503 Seis Lagos Trl
Wylie, TX 75098-8228, USA

Tom, Heather (Actor)
c/o Staff Member *Michael Einfeld Management*
10630 Moorpark Ave.
Ste. 101
Toluca Lake, CA 91602, USA

Tom, Kiana (Actor, Fitness Expert)
KT Productions
555 North El Camino Real
Suite A401
San Clemente, CA 92672, USA

Tom, Lauren (Actor)
c/o Kelly Garner *Pop Art Management*
P.O. Box 55363
Sherman Oaks, CA 91413, USA

Tom, Logan (Athlete, Olympic Athlete, Volleyball Player)
2001 E 21st St Unit 136
Signal Hill, CA 90755-5960, USA

Tom, Nicholle (Actor)
c/o Michael Einfeld *Michael Einfeld Management*
10630 Moorpark Ave.
Ste. 101
Toluca Lake, CA 91602, USA

Tom, Nicolle
3033 Vista Crest
Los Angeles, CA 90068

Toma, David (Writer)
PO Box 854
Clark, NJ 07066-0854, USA

Tomaini, Amadeo (Athlete, Football Player)
3750 Oakhill Dr
Titusville, FL 32780, USA

Tomaino, Jamie (The Jet) (Race Car Driver)
Impact Motorsports
6610 Hudspeth
Harrisburg, NC 28075, USA

Tomalty, Glenn (Athlete, Hockey Player)
GE Capital Rail Services
Attn: Senior Account Manager
2100-530 8th Ave SW
Calgary, AB T2P 3S8, CANADA

Tomanek, Dick (Athlete, Baseball Player)
165 Duff Dr
Avon Lake, OH 44012-1234, USA

Tomanovich, Dara
8016 Willow Glen Rd.
Los Angeles, CA 90046

Tomas, Hildi Santo (Actor, Television Host)
741 Parkside Trail
Marietta, GA 30064, USA

Tomasetti, Louis (Athlete, Football Player)
100 Powell St
Old Forge, PA 18518, USA

Tomasevicz, Curt (Athlete, Bobsledder, Olympic Athlete)
2 Jarecki Lk
Columbus, NE 68601-9404, USA

Tomasik, Kathleen (Director)
c/o David Krintzman *Morris, Yorn, Barnes, Levine, Krintzman, Rubenstein and Kohner*
2000 Ave of the Stars
3rd Floor, North Tower
Los Angeles, CA 90067, USA

Tomasina Keough, Jeana (Reality TV Star)
c/o Patrick Hughes *Hughes Capital Entertainment*
22817 Ventura Blvd
#471
Woodland Hills, CA 91364, USA

Tomasson, Helgi (Ballerina, Director)
San Francisco Ballet
455 Franklin St
San Francisco, CA 94102, USA

Tomba, Alberto (Skier)
Castel dei Britti
Bologna 40100, ITALY

Tomberlin, Andy (Athlete, Baseball Player)
7411 Crooked Creek Church Rd
Monroe, NC 28110-8283, USA

Tomberlin, Pat (Athlete, Football Player)
891 Arthur Moore Dr
Green Cove Springs, FL 32043, USA

Tomblin, Earl Ray (Governor)
State Capitol Bldg
Charleston, WV 25305, USA

Tombs, Tina (Golfer)
1916 E Medlock Dr
Phoenix, AZ 85016, USA

Tomczak, Mike (Athlete, Football Player)
400 Broad St #106
Sewickley, PA 15143-1500, USA

Tomei, Concetta (Actor)
765 Linda Flora Dr
Los Angeles, CA 90049, USA

Tomei, Marisa (Actor)
c/o Jason Weinberg *Untitled
Entertainment (LA)*
350 S. Beverly Dr #200
Beverly Hills, CA 90212, USA

Tomel, Marisa (Actor)
Three Arts Entertainment
9460 Wilshire Blvd
#700
Beverly Hills, CA 90212, USA

Tomey, Dick (Coach, Football Coach)
San Francisco 49ers
4949 Centennial Blvd
Santa Clara, CA 95054, USA

Tomfohrde, Heinn F (Business Person)
GAF Corp
1361 Alps Road
Wayne, NJ 07470, USA

Tomich, Jared (Athlete, Football Player)
2222 Red River Dr
Schereville, IN 46375, USA

Tomita, Stan (Photographer)
2439 Saint Louis Dr
Honolulu, HI 96816, USA

Tomita, Tamlyn (Actor)
c/o Nancy Moon-Broadstreet *Geddes
Agency, The*
8430 Santa Monica Blvd
Suite 200
Los Angeles, CA 90069, USA

Tomjanovich, Rudolph (Rudy) (Athlete,
Basketball Player, Coach)
19 West Ln
Houston, TX 77019-1007, USA

Tom Jr, Layne (Actor)
3838 Humboldt Dr
Huntington Beach, CA 92649, USA

Tomko, Brett (Athlete, Baseball Player)
14008 Lake Poway Rd
Poway, CA 92064-1421, USA

Tomko, Jozef Cardinal (Religious Leader)
Villa Betania
Via Urbano VIII-16
Rome 00165, ITALY

Tomlak, Mike (Athlete, Hockey Player)
2200 Bordeaux Cres
Thunder Bay, ON P7K 1C2, Canada

Tomlin, Chris (Musician)
c/o Shelley Giglio *Six Steps Records*
P.O. Box 5
Roswell, GA 30077, USA

Tomlin, Dave (Athlete, Baseball Player)
2020 Clayton Pike
Manchester, OH 45144-9429, USA

Tomlin, Lily (Actor, Comedian)
c/o Jennifer Allen *Viewpoint Inc*
8820 Wilshire Blvd.
Suite 220
Beverly Hills, CA 90211, USA

Tomlin, Mike (Athlete, Football Coach,
Football Player)
1224 Shady Ave
Pittsburgh, PA 15232, USA

Tomlin, Randy (Athlete, Baseball Player)
153 Ridgeview Ln
Madison Heights, VA 24572-6037, USA

Tomlinson, Charles (Writer)
Bristol University
English Dept
Bristol BS8 1TH, UNITED KINGDOM
(UK)

Tomlinson, Dave (Athlete, Hockey Player)
Vancouver Canucks
800 Griffiths Way
vancouver, BC V6B 6Gl, Canada

Tomlinson, John (Opera Singer)
Music International
13 Ardilaun Road
Highbury
London N5 2QR, UNITED KINGDOM
(UK)

Tomlinson, LaDainian (Football Player)
c/o Tom Condon *Creative Artists Agency
(CAA-LA)*
2000 Ave Of The Stars
Los Angeles, CA 90067, USA

Tomlinson, Louis (Musician)
c/o Nick Styne *Creative Artists Agency
(CAA-LA)*
2000 Ave Of The Stars
Los Angeles, CA 90067, USA

Tomlinson, Mel A (Ballerina)
790 Riverside Dr
#6B
New York, NY 10032, USA

Tommy Tutone (Music Group, Musician)
c/o Jake Hooker *Hook Entertainment*
26033 Mulholland Hwy
Malibu, CA 91302, USA

Tomowa-Sintow, Anna (Opera Singer)
Columbia Artists Mgmt Inc
165 W 57th St
New York, NY 10019, USA

Tompkins, Allie (Baseball Player)
Pittsburgh Crawfords
931 1/2 Clarissa St
Pittsburgh, PA 15219-5705, USA

Tompkins, Angel (Actor)
Hurkos
11935 Kling St
#10
Valley Village, CA 91607, USA

Tompkins, Barry (Sportscaster)
PO Box 8
Ross, CA 94957-0008, USA

Tompkins, Dariene (Actor)
15413 Hall Road
#230
Macomb, MI 48044, USA

Tompkins, Ron (Athlete, Baseball Player)
25072 Leucadia St
Unit G
Laguna Niguel, CA 92677-7598, USA

Tompkins, Susie (Designer, Fashion
Designer)
2500 Steiner St
#PH
San Francisco, CA 94115, USA

Toms, David (Golfer)
6606 Gilbert Dr
Shreveport, LA 71106-2300, USA

Toms, Tommy (Athlete, Baseball Player)
126 Leadbetter Rd
Wayne, ME 04284-3144, USA

Tom Scholz (Music Group, Musician)
c/o Gail Parenteau *Parenteau Guidance*
132 East 35th St #3J
New York, NY 10016, USA

Tomsco, George (Musician)
Fireballs Entertainment
1224 Cottonwood
Raton, NM 87740, USA

Tomsic, Dubravka (Musician)
Trawick Artists
1926 Broadway
New York, NY 10023, USA

Tomsic, Ronald (Athlete, Basketball
Player, Olympic Athlete)
22 Twilight Blf
Newport Coast, CA 92657-2126, USA

Toneff, Robert (Bob) (Athlete, Football
Player)
18 Dutch Valley Ln
San Anselmo, CA 94960, USA

Tonegawa, Susumu (Nobel Prize Laureate)
Massachusetts Institute of Technology
101 Chestnut Hill Rd
Chestnut Hill, MA 02467-1309, USA

Tonelli, John (Athlete, Hockey Player)
4 Vincent Ln
Armonk, NY 10504-1245

Tone Loc (Musician)
c/o Bobby Bessone *Entertainment Artists*
2409 21st Ave S #100
Nashville, TN 37212, USA

Toner, Mike (Journalist)
Atlanta Journal-Constitution
Editorial Dept
72 Marietta
Atlanta, GA 30303, USA

Toner Jr, Ed (Athlete, Football Player)
12 Preston Ct
Swampscott, MA 01907, USA

Toner Sr, Ed (Athlete, Football Player)
225 Ocean St
Lynn, MA 01902, USA

Toney, Andrew (Athlete, Basketball
Player)
1044 Villa Rica Ct #A
Birmingtham, AL 35204-2726, USA

Toney, Sedric (Athlete, Basketball Player)
3831 Sweetwater Dr
Brecksville, OH 44141-4102, USA

Tong, Jian (Figure Skater)
c/o Staff Member *Champions on Ice*
Tom Collins Enterprises Inc
3500 W 80th St
Minneapolis, MN 55431, USA

Tong, Pete (DJ, Musician)
c/o Joel Zimmerman *WME (WMA-NY)*
1325 Ave of the Americas
New York, NY 10019, USA

Tong, Stanley (Director)
c/o Ramses Ishak *United Talent Agency
(UTA)*
9336 Civic Center Dr
Beverly Hills, CA 90210, USA

Tongue, Marco (Athlete, Football Player)
8051 Winding Wood Rd
Glen Burnie, MD 21061, USA

Tonic (Music Group)
Tonic Tonic
652 North Doheny Drive
Los Angeles, CA 90069

Tonini, Ersilio Cardinal (Religious Leader)
Via Santa Teresa 8
Ravenna 48100, ITALY

Tonioli, Bruno (Actor)
c/o Duncan Heath *Independent Talent
Group (ITG-UK)*
Oxford House
76 Oxford St
London W1D 1BS, UK

Tonis, Mike (Athlete, Baseball Player)
9231 Bella Vista Pl
Elk Grove, CA 95624-2152, USA

Tonkin, Phoebe (Actor)
c/o Matt Andrews *Marquee Management*
The Gatehouse
188 Oxford St Studio B
Paddington NSW 2021, Australia

Tonko, Paul (Congressman, Politician)
422 Cannon HOB
Washington, DC 20515, USA

Tonkovich, Andy (Athlete, Basketball
Player)
2400 Forest Dr
Apt 210
Inverness, FL 34453-3705, USA

Tonnema, Pat (Stylist)
24551/2 Cheremoya Ave
Los Angeles, CA 90068, USA

Tony! Toni! Tone!
1995 Broadway #501
New York, NY 10023

Too, Slim (Musician)
New Frontier Mgmt
1921 Broadway
Nashville, TN 37203, USA

Tookey, Tim (Athlete, Hockey Player)
21008 W Ridge Rd
Buckeye, AZ 85396-1590

Tool (Music Group)
Tool Dissectional
2311 Empire Ave
Burbank, CA 91504, USA

Toole, Tara (Stylist)
c/o Staff Member *Crews*
828 Clemont Dr
Atlanta, GA 30306, USA

Toolson, Andy (Athlete, Basketball Player)
722 Ranch Dr
Alpine, UT 84004-1971, USA

Toomay, John (Athlete, Basketball Player)
7103 Primrose Way
Carlsbad, CA 92011, USA

Toomay, Pat (Athlete, Football Player)
5603 Gaudalupe Trl NW
Albuquerque, NM 87107-5423, USA

Toomer, Amani (Athlete, Football Player)
25 Regency Pl
Weehawken, NJ 07086, USA

Toomey, Bill (Athlete, Decathlon Athlete,
Olympic Athlete)
98 Full Cir
Davis, CA 95618-5439, USA

Toomey, Sean (Athlete, Hockey Player)
1741 Saunders Ave
Saint Paul, MN 55116-2432

Toomey, Toomey (Cartoonist, Writer)
Andrews & McMeel
4520 Main Street
Kansas City, MO 64111, USA

Toomin Straus, Amy (Writer)
c/o Staff Member *United Talent Agency (UTA)*
9336 Civic Center Dr
Beverly Hills, CA 90210, USA

Toon, Al (Athlete, Football Player)
4915 Champions Run
Middleton, WI 53562, USA

Tootoo, Jardin (Athlete, Hockey Player)
2600 Hillsboro Pike Apt 359
Nashville, TN 37212-5666

Tootoosis, Gordon (Actor)
c/o Staff Member *Artist Representation Company, The*
1147 S Big Island Rd
RR 1
Demorestville ON K0K 1W0, CANADA

Toots & The Maytals (Music Group)
c/o Staff Member *WME (WMA-NY)*
1325 Ave of the Americas
New York, NY 10019, USA

Top, Carrot (Actor, Comedian)
11 Isle of Sicily
Winter Park, FL 32789, USA

Toploader (Music Group)
c/o Staff Member *Helter Skelter (UK)*
535 Kings Rd
The Plaza
London SW10 0SZ, UNITED KINGDOM (UK)

Topol, Chaim (Actor)
22 Vale Court Maidville
London W9 1RT, UNITED KINGDOM (UK)

Topor, Ted (Athlete, Football Player)
2840 Condit St
Highland, IN 46322, USA

Toporowski, Shayne (Athlete, Hockey Player)
26 Creston St.
Worcester, MA 01604-2814

Topp, Robert (Athlete, Football Player)
10351 Douglas Ave
Plainwell, MI 49080, USA

Topper, John (Musician)
Monterey Peninsula Artists
509 Hartnell St
Monterey, CA 93940, USA

Toppin, Rupe (Athlete, Baseball Player)
P.O. Box 25724
Miami, FL 33102-5724, USA

Topping, Marshall (Race Car Driver)
2950 Randolph Avenue
Costa Mesa, CA 92626, USA

Topping, Seymour (Editor)
5 Heathcote Road
Scarsdale, NY 10583, USA

Toppo, Telesphore P Cardinal (Religious Leader)
Archdiocese
PO Box 5
Purulia Road
Ranchi, Jharkhand 834001, INDIA

Toradze, Alexander (Musician)
Columbia Artists Mgmt Inc
165 W 57th St
New York, NY 10019, USA

Torborg, Jeff (Athlete, Baseball Player, Coach)
47 Railroad Ave
Manahawkin, NJ 08050-3932, USA

Torcato, Tony (Athlete, Baseball Player)
9934 SE Talbert St
Clackamas, OR 97015-9638, USA

Torchett, John (Athlete, Hockey Player)
14 Crows Nest Ln
Marshfield, MA 02050-3161

Torchetti, John (Athlete, Hockey Player)
Houston Aeros
5300 Memorial Dr
Houston, TX 77007-8200

Torczon, Laverne J (Athlete, Football Player)
6472 Country Club Dr
Columbus, NE 68601, USA

Toregas, Wyatt (Athlete, Baseball Player)
1461 Brown St
Akron, OH 44301-2302, USA

Torgensen, Paul E (Educator)
Virginia Polytechnic Institute
President's Office
Blacksburg, VA 24061, USA

Torgeson, Lavern (Athlete, Football Player)
17672 Gainsford Ln
Huntington Beach, CA 92649, USA

Tork, Peter (Musician)
614 Wormwood Hill Rd
Mansfield Center, CT 06250, USA

Torkelson, Eric (Athlete, Football Player)
1196 Pleasant Valley Dr
Oneida, WI 54155, USA

Torkildsen, Justin
7800 Beverly Blvd. #3371
Los Angeles, CA 90036

Torme, Daisy (Actor)
c/o Steven Neibert *Imperium 7 Talent Agency*
5455 Wilshire Blvd
Suite 1706
Los Angeles, CA 90036, USA

Torme, Steve March (Actor, Musician)
c/o Mark Lourie *Skyline Music*
28 Union St
Whitefield, NH 03598, USA

Tormohlen, Gene (Athlete, Basketball Player)
2248 Walker Dr
Lawrenceville, GA 30043-2472, USA

Torn, Rip (Actor)
c/o Alan Somers *Pure Arts Entertainment*
1925 Century Park East
Suite 2320
Los Angeles, CA 90067, USA

Tornatore, Giuseppe (Director)
c/o Staff Member *Marco Patrizi*
Viale Giuseppe Mazzini, 11
Roma 00195, Italy

Torok, Mitchell (Musician)
5100 Weaver Rd #702
Lake Charles, LA 70605, USA

Torp, Niels A (Architect)
Industrigaten 59
PO Box 5387
Oslo 0304, NORWAY

Torrance, Sam (Golfer)
Carnegie Sports
The Glassmill
Battersea Bridge Rd
London SW11 3BZ, UNITED KINGDOM (UK)

Torrance, Thomas F (Educator, Religious Leader)
37 Braid Farm Road
Edinburgh EH10 6LE, SCOTLAND

Torre, Frank (Athlete, Baseball Player)
13901 Palm Grove Pl
West Palm Beach, FL 33418-6977, USA

Torre, Joe (Athlete, Baseball Player, Coach)
20 Lawrence Ln
Harrison, NY 10528-1108, USA

Torre, Jose Maria (Actor)
c/o Staff Member *Televisa*
Blvd Adolfo Lopez Mateos 232
Colonia San Angel INN
DF CP 01060, MEXICO

Torre, Steve (Horse Racer)
240 Court Pl Apt B
Brick, NJ 08723, USA

Torrealba, Yorvit (Athlete, Baseball Player)
3801 S Ocean Dr
Apt 15F
Hollywood, FL 33019-2901, USA

Torrence, Gwendolyn (Gwen) (Athlete, Track Athlete)
Gold Medal Mgmt
1750 14th St
Boulder, CO 80302, USA

Torrens, David (Actor)
c/o Gabriel Blanco *Gabriel Blanco Iglesias (Mexico)*
Rio Balsas 35-32
Colonia Cuauhtemoc
DF 06500, Mexico

Torres, Dara (Athlete, Olympic Athlete, Swimmer)
c/o Staff Member *Premier Management Group (PMG Sports)*
115 Crescent Commons Dr Ste 250
Cary, NC 27518, USA

Torres, Diego (Actor)
c/o Jon Simmons *Simmons & Scott Entertainment*
4110 W. Burbank Blvd.
Burbank, CA 91505, USA

Torres, Felix (Athlete, Baseball Player)
HC 1 Box 6424
Santa Isabel, PR 00757-9777, USA

Torres, Gina (Actor)
c/o Christopher Barrett *Metropolitan (MTA)*
4526 Wilshire Blvd
Los Angeles, CA 90010, USA

Torres, Harold (Musician)
Brothers Mgmt
141 Dunbar Ave
Fords, NJ 08863, USA

Torres, Hector (Athlete, Baseball Player)
662 Lexington St
Dunedin, FL 34698-8405, USA

Torres, Jacques (Chef, Television Host)
c/o Staff Member *Food Network, The*
1180 Ave of the Americas Fl 11
New York, NY 10036, USA

Torres, Jose (Boxer)
364B Greenwich St
#B
New York, NY 10013, USA

Torres, Oscar (Athlete, Basketball Player)
c/o Michael Esola *WME (LA)*
9601 Wilshire Blvd Fl 3
Beverly Hills, CA 90210, USA

Torres, Raffi (Athlete, Hockey Player)
59 Eakin Mill Rd
Markham, ON T5G 3H7, Canada

Torres, Rusty (Athlete, Baseball Player)
250 N Cedar St
Massapequa, NY 11758-2822, USA

Torres, Salomon (Athlete, Baseball Player)
101 Crimson Dr
Pittsburgh, PA 15237-1069, USA

Torres, Tia Maria (Reality TV Star)
Villalobos Rescue Center
P.O. Box 1544
Canyon Country, CA 91386, USA

Torres, Tico (Musician)
Bon Jovi Mgmt
248 W 17th St
#501
New York, NY 10011, USA

Torres, Tommy (Musician)
c/o Staff Member *Sony Music Miami*
605 Lincoln Rd Fl 7
Miami Beach, FL 33139, USA

Torretta, Gino (Athlete, Football Player, Heisman Trophy Winner)
3000 Groves Edge Ln
Waxhaw, NC 28173-8291, USA

Torrey, Bill (Misc)
2740 Clubhouse Pointe
West Palm Beach, FL 33409, USA

Torrey, Rich (Cartoonist)
c/o Staff Member *King Features Syndication*
300 W 57th St
15th Floor
New York, NY 10019-5238, USA

Torrez, Mike (Athlete, Baseball Player)
1015 Frances Ct
Naperville, IL 60563-3370, USA

Torricelli, Robert (Politician)
PO Box 229
Rosemont, NJ 08556-0229, USA

Torriero, Talan (Actor)
c/o Scott Karp *Crystal Sky Pictures*
10203 Santa Monica Blvd
5th Floor
Los Angeles, CA 90067, USA

Torrijos, Martin (President)
Palacio Presidencial
Valija 50
Panama City 1, PANAMA

Torrini, Emiliana (Musician)
c/o Staff Member *Paradigm (Monterey)*
404 W Franklin St
Monterey, CA 93940, USA

Torruella, Juan R (Judge)
US Court of Appeals
150 Ave Carlos Chardon
#119
San Juan, PR 00918, USA

Torry, Guy (Actor, Comedian)
c/o Janean Glover *Screen Partners*
9663 Santa Monica Blvd #639
Beverly Hills, CA 90210, USA

Torry, Joe (Comedian)
c/o Staff Member *WmE2 (WMA-LA)*
1 William Morris Pl
Beverly Hills, CA 90212, USA

Torteller, Yan Pascal (Musician)
MA de Valmalete
Building Gaceau
11 Ave Delcasse
Paris 75635, FRANCE

Torti, Robert (Actor)
5722 Ranchito Ave
Van Nuys, CA 91401, USA

Tortorella, John (Athlete, Coach, Hockey Player)
108 3rd Ave St Pete
Beach, FL 33706-4306, USA

Tortorella, Nico (Actor)
c/o Brian Wilkins *Kritzer Levine Wilkins Entertainment (KLWG)*
11872 La Grange Ave
1st Floor
Los Angeles, CA 90025, USA

Tortorici, Nick (Stylist)
c/o Staff Member *Solo Artists*
2148 Federal Ave
Los Angeles, CA 90025, USA

Torv, Anna
c/o Christine Tripicchio *WKT Public Relations (WKT-LA)*
9350 Wilshire Blvd
Suite 450
Beverly Hills, CA 90212, USA

Torvaids, Linus (Designer)
Transmeta Corp
3990 Freedom Circle
Santa Clara, CA 95054, USA

Torvalds, Linus (Designer, Engineer)
Open Source Development Labs
12725 SW Millikan Way
Beaverton, OR 97005, USA

Torve, Kelvin (Athlete, Baseball Player)
18701 Hammock Ln
Davidson, NC 28036-8836, USA

Torvill, Jayne (Dancer)
Sue Young
PO Box 32
Heathfield, East Sussex TN21 0BW,
UNITED KINGDOM (UK)

Tosca, Carlos (Athlete, Baseball Player, Coach)
PO Box 3623
Brandon, FL 33509-3623, USA

Toscano, Andrew (Horse Racer)
PO Box 34
Verbank, NY 12585-0034, USA

Toscano, Harry (Golfer)
3209 Mercer Rd
New Castle, PA 16105-5311, USA

Toscano, Linda (Horse Racer)
49 Euretta Ave
Freehold, NJ 07728-2631, USA

Tosh, Daniel (Comedian)
c/o Staff Member *Mosaic Media Group*
9200 W. Sunset Blvd
10th Floor
Los Angeles, CA 90069, USA

Toski, Bob (Golfer)
20914 Hamaca Ct
Boca Raton, FL 33433-2716, USA

Tostenson, Laura (Stylist)
c/o Staff Member *Page.214*
3303 Lee Pkwy
#205
Dallas, TX 75219, USA

Totenberg, Nina (Correspondent)
National Public Radio
News Dept
615 Main Ave NW
Washington, DC 20024, USA

Toth, Tom (Athlete, Football Player)
13723 Lindsay Dr
Orland Park, IL 60462, USA

Toth, Zollie (Athlete, Football Player)
1612 Hideaway Ct
Baton Rouge, LA 70806, USA

Totmianina, Tatyana (Figure Skater)
c/o Staff Member *Champions on Ice*
Tom Collins Enterprises Inc
3500 W 80th St
Minneapolis, MN 55431, USA

Totten, Robert (Director)
PO Box 7180
Big Bear Lake, CA 92315, USA

Totter, Audrey (Actor)
Motion Picture Country Home
23388 Mulholland Dr
Woodland Hills, CA 91364, USA

Totushek, John B (Admiral)
Commander
Naval Reserve Force HqUSN
Pentagon
Washington, DC 20350, USA

Toulouse, Gerard (Physicist)
Laboratoire de Physique de l'ENS
24 Rue Lhomond
Paris 75231, FRANCE

Tountas, Pete (Bowler)
10100 N Calle del Camero
Tucson, AZ 85737-9516, USA

Touraine, Jean-Louis (Biologist)
Edouard-Herriot Hopital
Place d'Arsonval
Lyons Cedex 03 69437, FRANCE

Toure, Younoussi (Prime Minister)
Union Economique/Monetaire
01 BP 543
Quagadougou 01, Burkina Faso, MALI

Tournier, Michel (Writer)
Le Presbytree Choisel
Chevreuse 78460, FRANCE

Toussaint, Allen (Composer, Musician)
272 Abalon Ct
New Orleans, LA 70114, USA

Toussaint, Beth (Actor)
c/o Staff Member *Buchwald/Fortitude (LA)*
6500 Wilshire Blvd
Suite 2200
Los Angeles, CA 90048, USA

Toussaint, Lorraine (Actor)
c/o Jonathan Howard *Innovative Artists (LA)*
1505 10th St
Santa Monica, CA 90401, USA

Tovar, Lupita
1527 N. Tigertail Rd
Los Angeles, CA 90049

Tovar, Steven E (Steve) (Athlete, Football Player)
1026 Brower Rd
Lima, OH 45801, USA

Tovoli, Luciano (Cinematographer)
United Talent Agency
9560 Wilshire Blvd
#500
Beverly Hills, CA 90212, USA

Towe, Monte (Athlete, Basketball Player, Coach)
3616 Dade St
Raleigh, NC 37130-8423, USA

Tower, Joan P (Composer)
Bard College
Music Dept
Annandale-on-Hudson, NY 12504, USA

Tower, Keith (Athlete, Basketball Player)
12530 Aldershot Ln
Windermere, FL 34786-6610, USA

Tower, Rob (Race Car Driver)
TBE Inc
33 Patton St.
Fitchburg, MA 01420, USA

Tower of Power (Music Group, Musician)
c/o Staff Member *CT Creative Talent GmbH*
Koepenicker Strasse 48/49
Berlin 10179, GERMANY

Towers, Constance (Actor)
c/o Staff Member *Stone Manners Salners Agency (LA)*
9911 W Pico Blvd Ste 1400
Los Angeles, CA 90035, USA

Towers, Josh (Athlete, Baseball Player)
1033 Crescent Falls St
Henderson, NV 89011-2506, USA

Towers, Kevin (Baseball Player)
5580 La Jolla Blvd
La Jolla, CA 92037-7651, USA

Towery, Blackie (Athlete, Basketball Player)
314 W Carlisle St
Marion, KY 42064-1506, USA

Towle, Stephen R (Steve) (Athlete, Football Player)
609 NE Lake Pointe Dr
Lees Summit, MO 64064, USA

Towles, J R (Athlete, Baseball Player)
13806 Lowell Ave
Tomball, TX 77377-7218, USA

Towles, Tom (Actor)
c/o Craig Dorfman *Frontline Management*
5670 Wilshire Blvd.
Suite 1370
Los Angeles, CA 90036, USA

Towne, Katharine (Actor)
United Talent Agency
9560 Wilshire Blvd
#500
Beverly Hills, CA 90212, USA

Towne, Robert (Writer)
1417 San Remo Dr
Pacific Palisades, CA 90272, USA

Towner, Ralph N (Musician)
Ted Kurtland
173 Brighton Ave
Boston, MA 02134, USA

Townes, Charles H (Nobel Prize Laureate)
1850 Alice St Apt 713
Oakland, CA 94612-4114, USA

Townes, Linton (Athlete, Basketball Player)
P.O. Box 254
Luray, VA 22835-0254, USA

Townes, Willie (Athlete, Football Player)
5714 Logancraft Dr
Dallas, TX 75227, USA

Towns, Bobby (Athlete, Football Player)
1351 Jennings Mill Rd
Unit A
Bogart, GA 30622, USA

Towns, Edolphus (Congressman, Politician)
2232 Rayburn HOB
Washington, DC 20515, USA

Towns, Morris (Athlete, Football Player)
7102 Rustling Oaks Dr
Richmond, TX 77469, USA

Townsell, Jo Jo (Athlete, Football Player)
1857 Borda Way
Gardnerville, NV 89410, USA

Townsend, Andre (Athlete, Football Player)
6206 Providence Club Dr
Mableton, GA 30126, USA

Townsend, Colleen (Actor)
645 E Champlain Dr #150
Fresno, CA 93730, USA

Townsend, John W Jr (Scientist)
6532 79th St
Cabin John, MD 20818-1201, USA

Townsend, Raymond (Athlete, Basketball Player)
5160 Caibari Knls
San Jose, CA 995135-1327, USA

Townsend, Robert (Actor, Director, Producer, Writer)
c/o Jeff Witjas *Agency for the Performing Arts (APA-LA)*
405 S Beverly Dr
Suite 500
Beverly Hills, CA 90212-4425, USA

Townsend, Roscoe (Religious Leader)
Evangelical Friends
2018 Maple St
Wichita, KS 67213, USA

Townsend, Stuart (Actor)
c/o Vanessa Pereira *Artists Independent Management (LA)*
825 Nowita Pl
Venice, CA 90291, USA

Townsend, Tammy (Actor)
c/o Marni Goldman *Abrams Artists Agency (LA)*
9200 Sunset Blvd
11th Floor
Los Angeles, CA 90069, USA

Townsend, Wade (Athlete, Baseball Player)
Columbus Catfish
PO Box 2744
Columbus, GA 31902, USA

Townshend, Graeme (Athlete, Hockey Player)
169 Bradley St
Saco, ME 04072, USA

Townshend, Peter D B (Musician, Songwriter, Writer)
4 Friars Ln
Richmond, Surrey TW9 1NL, UK

Toya (Musician)

Toyoda, Akio (Business Person)
Toyota
1 Toyota-Cho
Toyota City
Aichi 471-8571, Japan

Toyoda, Shoichiro (Business Person)
Keidanren
1-9-4 Ohtemachi
Chuyodaku
Tokyo 100, JAPAN

Tozzi, Tahyna (Actor)
c/o Elise Konialian *Untitled Entertainment (NY)*
322 8th Ave #601
New York, NY 10001-6715, USA

Tozzi, Umberto
Heussweg 25
Hamburg, GERMANY D-20255

T Pain (Musician)
c/o Staff Member *Jive Records*
550 Madison Ave
New York, NY 10022-3211, USA

Traa (Musician)
East West America Records
75 Rockefeller Plaza
New York, NY 10019, USA

Traber, Billy (Athlete, Baseball Player)
836 Lomita St
El Segundo, CA 90245-2541, USA

Traber, Jim (Athlete, Baseball Player)
1917 Rosebrook
Norman, OK 73072-3104, USA

Trabert, Tony (Actor)
115 Knotty Pine Trail
Ponte Vedra, FL 32082

Tracewski, Dick (Athlete, Baseball Player, Coach)
5 Flora Dr
Peckville, PA 18452-1004, USA

Trachsel, Stephen P (Steve) (Athlete, Baseball Player)
18750 Heritage Dr
Poway, CA 92064-6643, USA

Trachta, Jeff (Actor)
PO Box 124
Skyforest, CA 92385-0124, USA

Trachte, Don (Cartoonist)
c/o Staff Member *King Features Syndication*
300 W 57th St
15th Floor
New York, NY 10019-5238, USA

Trachtenberg, Lyle
18619 Collins St. #F-7
Tarzana, CA 91356

Trachtenberg, Michelle (Actor)
c/o Peg Donegan *Framework Entertainment (LA)*
9057 Nemo St
Suite C
West Hollywood, CA 90069, USA

Trachtenberg, Stephen J (Educator)
George Washington University
President's Office
Washington, DC 20052, USA

Track, Emma (Stylist)
c/o Staff Member *Photogenics Media*
8549 Higuera St
Building B
Culver City, CA 90232, USA

Tracy, Andy (Athlete, Baseball Player)
2226 Park Cir
Lewis Center, OH 43035-6052, USA

Tracy, Brian (Business Person, Writer)
Brian Tracy International
462 Stevens Ave #202
Solana Beach, CA 92075, USA

Tracy, Chad (Athlete, Baseball Player)
9422 Sir Huon Ln
Waxhaw, NC 28173-0112, USA

Tracy, James E (Jim) (Athlete, Baseball Player, Coach)
9191 E Harvard Ave
Denver, CO 80231-3843, USA

Tracy, Jeanie (Musician)
c/o Staff Member *Diva Central Inc*
7510 W Sunset Blvd Ste 1445
Los Angees, CA 90046, USA

Tracy, Keegan Connor (Actor)
c/o Deb Dillistone *Red Management*
100 W. Pender St
Sun Tower, 7th Floor
Vancouver, BC V6B 1R8, Canada

Tracy, Michael C (Dancer, Director)
Pilobolus Dance Theater
PO Box 388
Washington Depot, CT 06794, USA

Tracy, Paul (Race Car Driver)
Hogan Penske Racing
9700 Highridge
Las Vegas, NV 89134, USA

Trader, Larry (Athlete, Hockey Player)
105 Sufian Rd
Pembroke, ON K8A 6W6, Canada

Trafficant, James (Politician)
125 Market St.
Youngstown, OH 45503-1780

Trafton, Stephanie Brown (Athlete, Track Athlete)
c/o Staff Member *USA Track & Field*
132 E Washington St
Suite 800
Indianapolis, IN 46204, USA

Trager, Milton (Doctor)
Trager Institute
3800 Park East Dr
#100
Beachwood, OH 44122, USA

Trager, William (Biologist)
Rockefeller University
Parasitology Lab
1230 York Ave
New York, NY 10021, USA

Traill, Phil (Director)
c/o Rosalie Swedlin *Anonymous Content (LA)*
3531 Hayden Ave
Culver City, CA 90232, USA

Train (Music Group, Musician)
c/o Jonathan Daniel *Crush Management*
60-62 E 11th St
7th Floor
New York, NY 10003, USA

Train, Harry D II (Admiral)
401 College Place
#10
Norfolk, VA 23510, USA

Trainor, Bernard E (General)
46874 Grissom Street
Sterling, VA 20165-3574, USA

Trainor, Jerry (Actor)
c/o Staff Member *Burstein Company, The*
15304 Sunset Blvd
suite 208
Pacific Palisades, CA 90272, USA

Trainor, Mary Ellen (Actor)
c/o Staff Member *Creative Artists Agency (CAA-LA)*
2000 Ave Of The Stars
Los Angeles, CA 90067, USA

T Rajendar (Actor)
33 Hindi Prachar Sabha Road
T Nagar
Chennai, TN 600 017, INDIA

Trammell, Alan (Athlete, Baseball Player, Coach)
5852 Box Canvon Rd
La Jolla, CA 92037-7405, USA

Trammell, Sam (Actor)
c/o Gene Parseghian *Parseghian Planco LLC*
322 8th Ave
Suite 601
New York, NY 10001, USA

Trammell, Terry (Doctor)
Orthopedics-Indianapolis
1801 N Senate Blvd
#200
Indianapolis, IN 46202, USA

Trammell, Thomas (Bubba) (Athlete, Baseball Player)
4672 NW 114th Ave
Apt 310
Doral, FL 33178-4825, USA

Tramps, The
102 Ryders Lane
East Brunswick, NJ 08816

Tran, Duc Luong (President)
President's Office
Hoang Hoa Tham St
St Hanoi, VIETNAM

Tran, Huy K (Stylist)
c/o Staff Member *Artist Untied (LA)*
845 S Mansfield Ave
#1
Los Angeles, CA 90036, USA

Tranelli, Deborah (Actor, Musician)
c/o Staff Member *Image Entertainment*
20525 Nordhoff St #200
Chatsworth, CA 91311, USA

Trang, Thuy
209 N. Kenilworth Ave
Glendale, CA 91203

Trani, Eugene P (Educator)
Virginia Commonwealth University
President's Office
Richmond, VA 23284, USA

Traore, Rokia (Actor, Composer)
c/o Staff Member *Concerted Efforts*
P.O. Box 440326
Somerville, MA 02144, USA

Trapani, Gina (Internet Star)

Trapp, John (Athlete, Basketball Player)
1836 Remembrance Hill St
Las Vegas, NV 48203-5218, USA

Trask, Emma (Stylist)
c/o Staff Member *Mercury Artists*
8460 Higuera St Fl 2
Culver City, CA 90232, USA

Trask, Stephen (Composer)
c/o Brice Gaeta *Broder Webb Chervin Silbermann Agency, The (BWCS)*
10250 Constellation Blvd
Los Angeles, CA 90067-6200, USA

Trask, Thomas E (Religious Leader)
Assemblies of God
1445 Boonville Ave
Springfield, MO 65802, USA

Traub, Charles (Photographer)
39 E 10th St
New York, NY 10003, USA

Traue, Antje (Actor)
c/o Staff Member *Anthem Entertainment*
9595 Wilshire Blvd
Suite 900
Los Angeles, CA 90212-2509, USA

Trauth, AJ (Actor)
c/o Felicia Sager *Sager Management*
260 S Beverly Dr
Suite 205
Beverly Hills, CA 90212, USA

Trautmann, Richard (Athlete)
Horemansstr 29
Munich 80636, GERMANY

Trautwein, John (Athlete, Baseball Player)
882 Beach Rd
Sanibel, FL 33957-6907, USA

Trautwig, Al (Sportscaster)
ABC-TV
Sports Dept
77 W 66th St
New York, NY 10023, USA

Travanti, Daniel J (Actor)
1077 Melody Road
Lake Forest, IL 60045, USA

Travers, Bill (Athlete, Baseball Player)
10 Shoreline Dr
Foxboro, MA 02035-1115, USA

Travers, Pat (Musician)
ARM
1257 Arcade St
Saint Paul, MN 55106, USA

Travis (Music Group)
c/o Staff Member *MCT Management*
520 8th Ave Rm 2205
New York, NY 10018, USA

Travis, Kylie (Actor, Model)
1196 Summit Dr
Beverly Hills, CA 90210, USA

Travis, Mack (Athlete, Football Player)
605 Holland Ave
Las Vegas, NV 89106, USA

Travis, Nancy (Actor, Producer)
c/o Adena Chawke *Greenlight Management and Production*
13848 Valleyheart Dr
Sherman Oaks, CA 91423, USA

Travis, Randy (Musician, Songwriter)
Travis Management
P.O. Box 121712
Nashville, TN 37212, USA

Travis, Stacey (Actor)
c/o Brian Alexander *Essential Talent Management*
6399 Wilshire Blvd
Suite 401
Los Angeles, CA 90048, USA

Traviss, Adrienne (Stylist)
c/o Staff Member *Judy Inc*
1 Yorkville Ave
Toronto ON M4W 1L1, Canada

Travolta, Ellen (Actor)
6470 E Sunnyside Rd
Coeur D Alene, ID 83814-9503, USA

Travolta, Joey (Actor)
c/o Staff Member *Stephany Hurkos Management*
11935 Kling St
Valley Village, CA 91607, USA

Travolta, John (Actor)
Jumbolair Estates
1401 NE 77th St
Ocala, FL 34479, USA

Traya, Misti (Actor)
c/o Darren Goldberg *Global Creative*
1051 Cole Ave # B
Los Angeles, CA 90038, USA

Trayham, Jerry (Athlete, Football Player)
6606 S Tomaker Ln
Spokane, WA 99223, USA

Traylor, B Keith (Athlete, Football Player)
1000 Football Dr
Lake Forest, IL 60045, USA

Traylor, Keith (Athlete, Football Player)
11043 S 4317
Chouteau, OK 74337, USA

Traylor, Susan (Actor)
Propaganda Films Mgmt
1741 Ivar Ave
Los Angeles, CA 90028, USA

Traynham, Wade (Athlete, Football Player)
P.O. Box 176
Wake, VA 23176, USA

Traynor, Jay (Musician)
Jet Music
17 Pauline Court
Rensselaer, NY 12144, USA

Traynowicz, Mark (Athlete, Football Player)
8000 Alimark Ln
Lincoln, NE 68516, USA

Treach (Musician)
International Creative Mgmt
8942 Wilshire Blvd
#219
Beverly Hills, CA 90211, USA

Treacy, Carolyn (Athlete, Biathlete, Olympic Athlete)
145 Sylvan St
Malden, MA 02148-1723, USA

Treacy, Philip (Designer, Fashion Designer)
Philip Treacy Ltd
69 Elizabeth St
London SW1W 9PJ, UNITED KINGDOM (UK)

Treadaway, John (Athlete, Football Player)
3140 N 83rd Ave
Phoenix, AZ 85033, USA

Treadway, Edward A (Politician)
Elevator Constructors Union
5565 Sterret Place
Columbia, MD 21044, USA

Treadway, James C Jr (Government Official)
Laurel Ledge Farm
Croton Lake Road
RR 4
Mount Kisco, NY 10549, USA

Treadway, Jeff (Athlete, Baseball Player)
8812 Estes Rd
Macon, GA 31220-5649, USA

Treadway, Kenneth (Misc)
Phillips Petroluem Co
Adams Building
Bartlesville, OK 74003, USA

Treadway, Nick (Athlete, Baseball Player)
1442 Bishop Dr
Troy, MO 63379-3336, USA

Treadway, Ty (Actor)
c/o Frank Gonzales *The Agency (CA)*
3711 Ocean Front Walk #1
Marina del Rey, CA 90292-5705, USA

Treadwell, David (Athlete, Football Player)
5445 Dtc Pkey
Suite 800
Greenwood Village, CO 80111, USA

Treanor, Matt (Athlete, Baseball Player)
1440 Coral Ridge Dr
Coral Springs, FL 33071-5433, USA

Trebek, Alex (Game Show Host)
10202 W Washington Blvd
Culver City, CA 90232, USA

Trebelhorn, Thomas L (Tom) (Athlete, Baseball Player, Coach)
7753 E Montebello Ave
Scottsdale, AZ 85250-6165, USA

Trebi, Dan (Athlete, Hockey Player)
8551 Big Woods Ln
Eden Prairie, MN 55347-5361

Trebunskaya, Anna (Dancer, Reality TV Star)
c/o Staff Member *American Broadcasting Company (ABC LA)*
500 S Buena Vista St
Burbank, CA 91521-4551, USA

Tree, Michael (Musician)
45 E 89th St
New York, NY 10128, USA

Trefilov, Andrei
Calgary Flames
PO Box 1540
Station M
Calgary, AB T2P 3B9, CANADA

Trejo, Danny (Actor)
c/o Gloria Hinojosa *Amsel, Eisenstadt & Frazier Talent Agency (AEF)*
5055 Wilshire Blvd
Suite 860
Los Angeles, CA 90036-6108, USA

Trelford, Donald G (Editor)
15 Fowler Road
London N1 2EA, UNITED KINGDOM (UK)

Tremblay, Brent (Athlete, Hockey Player)
671 Ski Club Rd
North Bay, ON p1B 7R5, Canada

Tremblay, Gilles (Athlete, Hockey Player)
104-218 Rue Notre-Dame
Repentigny, QC J6A 7E1, Canada

Tremblay, Mario (Athlete, Coach, Hockey Player)
RDS - Le Reseau des Sports
1755 Boul Rene Levesque-Est
Clifton, NJ Q7012-1867, CANADA

Tremblay, Michel (Writer)
294 Carre Saint Louis
#5E
Montreal, QC H2X 1A4, CANADA

Tremblay, Yannick (Athlete, Hockey Player)
9911 Carrington Ln
Alpharetta, GA 30022-8527

Trembley, Dave (Athlete, Baseball Player, Coach)
Baltimore Orioles
3145 S Atlantic Ave
APt 601
Davtona Beach Shores, FL 32118-6273, USA

Tremel, Bill (Athlete, Baseball Player)
315 E 23rd Ave
Altoona, PA 16601-4002, USA

Tremie, Chris (Athlete, Baseball Player)
484 Marion Ln
New Waverly, TX 77358-4S04, USA

Tremie, Chris (Athlete, Baseball Player)
Akron Aeros 300 S Main St
Attn: Managers Office
Akron, OH 44308-1204, USA

Tremko, Anne
10100 Santa Monica Blvd. #2500
Los Angeles, CA 90067

Tremlett, David R (Artist)
Broadlawns
Chipperfield Road
Bovingdon, Herts, UNITED KINGDOM (UK)

Tremont, Ray C (Religious Leader)
Volunteers of America
3939 N Causeway Blvd
#400
Metairie, LA 70002, USA

Trenary, Jill (Athlete, Figure Skater, Olympic Athlete)
4115 Stone Manor Hts
Colorado Springs, CO 80906-5799, USA

Trendy, Bobby (Designer)
c/o Darryl Marshak *Marshak/Zachary Company, The*
8840 Wilshire Blvd
1st Floor
Beverly Hills, CA 90210, USA

Trenhaile, John
4 Wailands Crescent Lewes
E. Sussex, ENGLAND BNT 2QT

Treniers, The
520 N. Camden Dr.
Beverly Hills, CA 90210

Trent, Buck (Musician)
Buck Trent Breakfast Theater
118 Hampshire Drive
Branson, MO 65616, USA

Trent, Gary (Athlete, Basketball Player)
1150 Northwood Cir
New Albany, OH 43054-9056, USA

Trenyce (Reality TV Star)
c/o Staff Member *Diva Central Inc*
7510 W Sunset Blvd Ste 1445
Los Angees, CA 90046, USA

Treschev, Sergei Y (Cosmonaut)
Potchta Kosmonavtov
Moskovskoi Oblasti
Syvisdny Goroduk 141160, RUSSIA

Trese, Adam (Actor)
c/o Staff Member *Robert Stein Management*
PO Box 3797
Beverly Hills, CA 90212, USA

Tressel, Jim (Coach, Football Coach)
Ohio State University
Athletic Dept
Columbus, OH 43210, USA

Trestman, Marc (Football Player)
Minnesota Vikings
Arizona Cardinals PO Box 888 Attn:
Coaching Staff
Phoenix, AZ 85001-0888, USA

Tresvant, John (Athlete, Basketball Player)
14814 61st Dr SE
Snohomish, WA 98296-4221, USA

Tretiak, Vladislav (Athlete, Hockey Player)
1925 Birch Rd
Northbrook, IL 60062-5911

Tretlak, Vladislav (Athlete, Coach, Hockey Player)
94 Festival Dr
Toronto, ON M2R 3V1, Canada

Tretyak, Ivan (General)
Ministry of Defense
34 Manerezhnaya M Thoreza
Moscow, RUSSIA

Treu, Adam (Athlete, Football Player)
556 Creedon Cir
Alameda, CA 94502, USA

Treuel, Ralph (Athlete, Baseball Player)
15 Middleton Rd
Wolfeboro, NH 03894-4421, USA

Trevanian (Writer)
Jove Books
Berkeley Publishing Group
375 Hudson St
New York, NY 10014, USA

Trevelyan, Edward (Athlete, Olympic Athlete, Sailor)
25028 Maplewood Dr
Saint Michaels, MD 21663-2753, USA

Trever, John (Cartoonist, Editor)
Albuquerque Journal
Editorial Dept
717 Silver Ave SW
Albuquerque, NM 87102, USA

Treves, Frederick
5 St. Catherine's Mews Milner St.
London, ENGLAND SW3 2PX

Trevi, Gloria (Musician)
Leisil Entertainment
Avenida Parque 67 Napoles
Mexico City, DF 03810, MEXICO

Trevino, Alex (Athlete, Baseball Player)
P.O. Box 288
Houston, TX 77001-0288, USA

Trevino, Lee (Golfer)
4906 Park Ln
Dallas, TX 75220, USA

Trevino, Michael (Actor)
c/o Lena Roklin *Luber Roklin Management*
8530 Wilshire Blvd
6th Floor
Beverly Hills, CA 90211, USA

Trevino, Rick (Musician)
William Morris Agency
2100 W End Ave
#1000
Nashville, TN 37203, USA

Trevor, Linden (Athlete, Hockey Player)
1362 23 St SE
Medicine Hat, AB TlA 2C9, Canada

Trevor, William (Writer)
P F D
Drury House
34-43 Russell St
London WC2B 5HA, UNITED KINGDOM
(UK)

Triandos, C Gus (Athlete, Baseball Player)
P.O. Box 5642
San Jose, CA 95150-S642, USA

Trias, Jasmine (Musician)

Tribbett, Tye (Musician)
c/o Staff Member *Sony Music International*
550 Madison Ave
New York, NY 10022-3211, USA

Tribe, Laurence H (Attorney, Attorney General, Educator, General)
Harvard University
Law School
Griswold Hall
Cambridge, MA 02138, USA

Trible, Paul S Jr (Politician)
Christopher Newport University
Christopher_l\(_e^_p_ort University
50_Shoe_L_rl_^
Newport News, VA 23606-2998, USA

Trice, Obie (Musician)
BME Recordings
2144 Hills Ave NW
D2
Atlanta, GA 30318, USA

Trichter, Judd
10264 Rochester Ave
Los Angeles, CA 90024-5331

Trick, Cheap (Music Group, Musician)
c/o Dave Frey *Red Light Management (VA)*
PO Box 1467
Charlottesville, VA 22902, USA

Trickett, Libby (Athlete, Swimmer)
c/o Staff Member *International Quarterback*
12 Ross St
Brisbane
Newstead QLD 4006, Australia

Trickey, Paula
PO Box 261098
Encino, CA 91426

Trickle, Dick (Race Car Driver)
Donlavey Racing
5415 Vesuvius-Furnace Rd.
Iron Station, NC 28080, USA

Trickside (Music Group)
c/o Staff Member *Wind-up Records*
72 Madison Ave Fl 8
New York, NY 10016, USA

Triffle, Carol (Director)
Imago Theater
17 SE 8th Ave
Portland, OR 97214, USA

Trigg, Alex (Baseball Player)
Detroit Stars
900 Turner Ln
Shreveport, LA 71106-4528, USA

Trigger, Sarah (Actor)
Paradigm Agency
10100 Santa Monica Blvd
#2500
Los Angeles, CA 90067, USA

Triggs, Trini
3178 Allen Marthaville Rd.
Robeline, LA 71469

Trillin, Calvin M (Writer)
New Yorker Magazine
Editorial Dept
4 times Square
New York, NY 10036, USA

Trillo, Manny (Athlete, Baseball Player)
Calle 724 Ave 3AM Ed. Everest #14
Maracaibo, Venezuela

Trimble, David (Nobel Prize Laureate)
Ulster Unionists Party 3 Glendale Street
Belfast BT12 5AE, NORTHERN IRELAND

Trimble, Solomon (Actor)
c/o Kaili Canfield *Arthouse Talent and Literary*
107 SE Washington St.
Suite 156
Portland, OR 97214, USA

Trimble, Vance H (Editor)
25 Oakhurst St
Wewoka, OK 74884, USA

Trimble, Vivian (Musician)
Metropolitan Entertainment
2 Penn Plaza
#2600
New York, NY 10121, USA

Trimper, Tim (Athlete, Hockey Player)
1028 Broughton Lane
New market, ON L3X 2L7, Canada

Trina (Musician)
c/o Staff Member *Pyramid Entertainment Group*
377 Rector Pl #21A
New York, NY 10280-1439, USA

Trineer, Connor (Actor)
c/o Gregg A Klein *Abrams Artists Agency (LA)*
9200 Sunset Blvd
11th Floor
Los Angeles, CA 90069, USA

Trinh, Eugene (Astronaut)
NASA Headquarters
300 E St SW
Washington, DC 20546, USA

Trinh, Eugene H Dr (Astronaut)
3549 Kelton Ave
Los Angeles, CA 90034-5505, USA

Trinidad, Felix (Tito) (Boxer)
RR 6 Box 11479
Rio Piedras, PR 00926, USA

Trinkaus, Erik (Biologist)
Washington University
Paleontology Dept
Saint Louis, MO 63130, USA

Trinneer, Connor (Actor)
c/o Staff Member *Abrams Artists Agency (LA)*
9200 Sunset Blvd
11th Floor
Los Angeles, CA 90069, USA

Trintignant, Jean-Louis (Actor)
Artmedia
20 Ave Rapp
Paris 75007, FRANCE

Triola, Michelle
23215 Mariposa De Oro
Malibu, CA 90265

Triplet, Kirk (Golfer)
8141 E Overlook Dr
Scottsdale, AZ 85255, USA

Triplett, Bill (Athlete, Football Player)
222 Beachwood Dr
Youngstown, OH 44505, USA

Triplett, Kirk (Golfer)
8141 E Overlook Dr
Scottsdale, AZ 85255-6481, USA

Triplett, Wally (Athlete, Football Player)
4250 Fullerton St
Detroit, MI 48238, USA

Tripp, Linda
27285 Boyce Mill Rd.
Greensboro, MD 21639

Tripp, Valerie (Writer)
Pleasant Company Publications
PO Box 620991
Middleton, WI 53562-0991, USA

Trippi, Charles L (Charlie) (Athlete, Football Player)
125 Riverhill Ct
Athens, GA 30606, USA

Tripplehorn, Jeanne (Actor)
c/o Cynthia Pett-Dante *Brillstein Entertainment Partners*
9150 Wilshire Blvd #350
Beverly Hills, CA 90212, USA

Tripplett, Larry (Athlete, Football Player)
5324 Overdale Dr
Los Angeles, CA 90043, USA

Triptow, Dick (Athlete, Basketball Player)
325 Birkdale Rd
Lake Bluff, IL 60044-2334, USA

Tripucka, Kelly (Athlete, Basketball Player)
14 Devon Rd
Boonton, NJ 07005-9305, USA

Tritt, Travis (Actor, Musician)
c/o Duke Cooper *Quantum Management*
5340 Forest Acres Dr
Nashville, TN 37220, USA

Trivanovich, Cristina (Stylist)
c/o Staff Member *Creative Talent Columbus*
5864 Nike Dr
Hilliard, OH 43026, USA

Trivium (Music Group)
c/o Staff Member *Roadrunner Records Inc*
902 Broadway Fl 8
New York, NY 10010, USA

Trixter
210 Westfield Ave
Clark, NJ 07066

Trlicek, Rick (Athlete, Baseball Player)
P.O. Box 1109
La Grange, TX 78945-1109, USA

Troche, Rose (Actor, Director, Producer, Writer)
c/o Staff Member *Gersh (NY)*
41 Madison Ave
New York, NY 10010, USA

Troedson, Rich (Athlete, Baseball Player)
899 Bowen Ave
San Jose, CA 95123-5303, USA

Troegel, Butch (Athlete, Football Player)
230 Norcross St
Bossier City, LA 71111-6046, USA

Troger, Christian-Alexander (Swimmer)
I Muncher SC
Josefstr 26
Deisenhofen 82941, GERMANY

Troisgros, Pierre E R (Business Person)
Place Jean Troisgros
Roanne 42300, FRANCE

Troitskaya, Natalia L (Opera Singer)
Klostergasse 37
Vienna 1170, AUSTRIA

Troliope, Joanna (Writer)
P F D
Drury House
34-43 Russell St
London WC2B 5HA, UNITED KINGDOM
(UK)

Trombley, Mike (Athlete, Baseball Player)
2 Hilltop Park
Wilbraham, MA 01095-1753, USA

Trondheim, Lewis (Artist)
c/o Staff Member *Fantagraphics Books*
7563 Lake City Way
Seattle, WA 98115, USA

Trone, Roland (Don) (Musician)
Mars Talent
27 L'Ambiance Court
Bardonia, NY 10954, USA

Tronnier, Ellen (Athlete, Baseball Player)
PO Box 255
Palmyra, WI 53156-0255, USA

Trosch, Gene (Athlete, Football Player)
6393 Oak Tree Dr
Mc Calla, AL 35111, USA

Trosky, Hal (Athlete, Baseball Player)
1414 Curtis Bridge Rd NE
Swisher, IA 52338-9588, USA

Trosper, Jennifer Harris (Scientist)
Jet Propulsion Laboratory
4800 Oak Grove Dr
Pasadena, CA 91109, USA

Trost, Barry M (Scientist)
24510 Amigos Court
Los Altos Hills, CA 94024, USA

Trost, Carlisle A H (Admiral)
11 Compromise St
Annapolis, MD 21401, USA

Trott, Stephen S (Judge)
US Court of Appeals
US Courthouse
550 W Fort St
Boise, ID 83724, USA

Trotter, Deedee (Athlete, Olympic Athlete, Track Athlete)
9900 Brannigan Cir
Knoxville, TN 37923-1965, USA

Trottier, Bryan J (Athlete, Coach, Hockey Player)
504 Bluegrass Dr
Canonsburg, PA 15317-4949

Trottier, Guy (Athlete, Hockey Player)
1003 Hazel Ave
Englewood, OH 45322-2426

Trottier, Rocky (Athlete, Hockey Player)
9562 International Dr
Indianapolis, IN 46268-3267

Trotz, Barry (Athlete, Hockey Player)
9001 Demery Ct
Brentwood, TN 37027-3300

Trotz, Barry (Athlete, Hockey Player)
Nashville Predators
501 Broadway
Nashville, TN 37203-3980

Trouble, Valli (Musician)
Q Prime
729 7th Ave
#1600
New York, NY 10019, USA

Troup, Bill (Athlete, Football Player)
4 Quail Wood Ct
Parkton, MD 21120, USA

Troup, Franklin (General)
2318 Woodcliff Rd SE
Huntsville, AL 35801-1472, USA

Troup, Guppy (Bowler)
60 Dwayne Dr
Taylorsville, NC 28681-8243, USA

Troup, Tom
8829 Ashcroft Ave.
Los Angeles, CA 90048

Troupe, Tom (Actor)
8829 Ashcroft Ave
West Hollywood, CA 90048, USA

Trousdale, Chris (Actor, Musician)
c/o Staff Member *Adonis Productions*
175 Skillman St
Brooklyn, NY 11205, USA

Trout, David (Athlete, Football Player)
408 Paddock Ct
Sewell, NJ 08080, USA

Trout, Steve (Athlete, Baseball Player)
P.O. Box 1155
Tinley Park, IL 60477-7955, USA

Troutt, William E (Educator)
Belmont University
President's Office
Nashville, TN 37212, USA

Trova, Ernest T (Artist)
6 Laylon Terrace
Saint Louis, MO 63124, USA

Trowbridge, Alexander B Jr (Secretary)
1823 23rd St NW
Washington, DC 20008, USA

Trower, Robin (Musician)
Stardust Enterprises
4600 Franklin Ave
Los Angeles, CA 90027, USA

Troxel, Gary
11471 Earle Dr
Nount Vernon, WA 98273, USA

Troxell, Melanie (Race Car Driver)
201 S. George St.
Decatur, MI 49045, USA

Troy, Cowboy (Musician)
919 Sam Johnson Rd
Columbia, TN 38401, USA

Troy, Drake (Athlete, Football Player)
20103 Desert Forest Dr
Ashburn, VA 20147-3179, USA

Troy, Mike (Athlete, Olympic Athlete, Swimmer)
21187 E Alyssa Rd
Queen Creek, AZ 85142-6558, USA

Troyat, Henri (Writer)
Academie Francaise
23 Quai de Conti
Paris 75006, FRANCE

Troyer, Maynard (Race Car Driver)
4555 Lyell Road
Rochester, NY 14606, United States

Troyer, Verne (Actor)
c/o Elaina Bertnolli *Fonolli Management*
11218 Osborne St
Lakeview Terrace, CA 91342, USA

Truax, Billy (Athlete, Football Player)
735 Ruth Ave
Gulfport, MS 39501, USA

Truax, Dalton (Athlete, Football Player)
77 Chateau Magdelaine Dr
Kenner, LA 70065, USA

Truax, Mike (Athlete, Football Player)
5925 Cleveland Pl
Metairie, LA 70003-1047, USA

Truby, Chris (Athlete, Baseball Player)
12244 Silverado Dr
Fishers, IN 46037-8328, USA

Truby, Chris (Athlete, Baseball Player)
Lakewood Blueclaws 2 Stadium Way
Attn: Managers Office
Lakewood, NL 08701-4536

Trucco, Michael (Actor)
McKeon-Myones
3500 Olive Ave Ste 770
Burbank, CA 91505, USA

Trucks, Virgil (Athlete, Baseball Player)
1016 Waterford Trl
Calera, AL 35040-7613, USA

Trudeau, Garry (Cartoonist)
14 Governors Island
Branford, CT 06405, USA

Trudeau, Jack F (Athlete, Football Player)
9150 Timberwolf Ln
Zionsville, IN 46077, USA

Trudeau, Paul (Stylist)
c/o Staff Member *Team*
423 W Broadway
4th Floor
Boston, MA 02127, USA

True, Rachel (Actor)
c/o Lorrie Bartlett *ICM Partners (ICM-LA)*
10250 Constellation Blvd Fl 7
Los Angeles, CA 90067, USA

Trueco, Michael (Actor)
c/o Staff Member *Raw Talent Management*
545 Veterans Ave
Los Angeles, CA 90024, USA

Truesdale, Yanic (Actor)
c/o Danielle Allman-Del *D2 Management*
141 S. Barrington Ave
Los Angeles, CA 90049, USA

True Vibe (Music Group)
c/o Staff Member *Creative Artists Agency (CAA-LA)*
2000 Ave Of The Stars
Los Angeles, CA 90067, USA

Truex Jr, Martin (Race Car Driver)
c/o Staff Member *Michael Waltrip Racing*
20310 Chartwell Center Dr.
Cornelius, NC 28031, USA

Trufant, Marcus (Athlete, Football Player)
11220 NE 53rd St
Kirkland, WA 98033, USA

Truhill, Jerri (Aviator)
1431 Lamp Post Ln
Richardson, TX 75080-5723, USA

Truhitte, Dan
4630 Sapp Rd.
Concord, NC 28027

Truhitte, Daniel (Actor)
4630 Sapp Rd
Concord, NC 28025, USA

Truitt, Anne D (Artist)
29 Boutonville Road
South Salem, NY 10007-2705, USA

Truitt, Ansley (Athlete, Basketball Player)
18601 Cairo Ave
Carson, CA 90746, USA

Truitt, Olanda (Athlete, Football Player)
1901 16th Way N
Bessemer, AL 35020, USA

Trujillo, Chadwick (Astronomer)
California Institute of Technology
Astronomy Dept
Pasadena, CA 91125, USA

Trujillo, J J (Athlete, Baseball Player)
1329 York Ave
Corous Christi, TX 78415-4337, USA

Trujillo, J J (Athlete, Baseball Player)
1329 York Ave
Corpus Christi, TX 78415, USA

Trujillo, Mike (Athlete, Baseball Player)
16373 6475 Rd
Montrose, CO 81403-8578, USA

Trujillo, Solomon D (Business Person)
US West Inc
1801 California St
Denver, CO 80202, USA

Trull, Don (Athlete, Football Player)
16435 Elmwood Point Ln
Sugar Land, TX 77478, USA

Trulli, Jarno (Race Car Driver)
Jordan Grand Prix
Buckingham Rd.
Silverstone
Norhants NN12 9TJ, UNITED KINGDOM (UK)

Truly, Richard N (Admiral, Astronaut)
2340 Juniper Court
Golden, CO 80401-8087, USA

Truly, Richard Radm (Scientist)
2340 Juniper Ct
Golden, CO 80401-8087, USA

Truman, Dan (Musician)
Dreamcatcher Artists Mgmt
2908 Poston Ave
Nashville, TN 37203, USA

Truman, James (Editor)
Conde Nast Publications
Editorial Dept
4 Times Square
New York, NY 10036, USA

Trumbo, Karen (Actor)
c/o Staff Member *Creative Artists Management (OR)*
909 SW Saint Clair Avenue
Portland, OR 97205-1330, USA

Trumbo, Mark (Athlete, Baseball Player)
1801 E Katella Ave
Apt 4131
Anaheim, CA 92805-6672, USA

Trumka, Richard L (Politician)
AFL-CIO
1750 New York Ave NW
Washington, DC 20006, USA

Trump, Blaine
166 Ave of the Americas
New York, NY 10013, USA

Trump, Donald (Business Person, Misc, Reality TV Star)
c/o Staff Member *Trump Organization*
725 Fifth Ave
New York, NY 10022, USA

Trump, Ivana (Business Person, Misc, Model)
10 E 64th St
New York, NY 10065-7212, USA

Trump, Ivanka (Business Person, Heir/Heiress)
Ivanka Trump Flagship Boutique
109 Mercer St
New York, NY 10012, USA

Trump, Melania (Model)
c/o Marc Beckman *Designers Management Agency*
446 Broadway Fl4
New York, NY 10013, USA

Trumpy, Robert T (Bob) Jr (Athlete, Football Player, Sportscaster)
75 Oak St
Cincinnati, OH 45246, USA

Trundy, Natalie (Actor)
2109 S Wilbur Ave
Walla Walla, WA 99362, USA

Truran, James W Jr (Physicist)
210 Wysteria Dr
Olympia Fields, IL 60461, USA

Truscott, Lucian K IV (Writer)
Avon/William Morrow
1350 Ave of Americas
New York, NY 10019, USA

Truth, Hurts (Actor, Songwriter, Writer)
Aftermath/Interscope Records
2220 Colorado Ave
Santa Monica, CA 90404, USA

Truvillion, Eric (Athlete, Football Player)
10436 Saint Tropez Pl
Tampa, FL 33615, USA

Truvillion, Tobias (Actor)
c/o Kim Matuka *Online Talent Group*
Prefers to be contacted via email or telephone
Los Angeles, CA 90069, USA

Tryba, Ted (Athlete, Golfer)
6321 Cheryl St
Orlando, FL 32819-7511, USA

Tryon, Ty (Golfer)
8713 The Esplanade #1
Orlando, FL 32836, USA

Tsai, Cheryl (Actor)
c/o Jason Solomon *Full Circle Management*
4932 Lankershim Blvd
Suite 202
North Hollywood, CA 91601, USA

Tsai, Sue (Stylist)
c/o Staff Member *Exclusive Artists Mgmt*
7700 Sunset Blvd
#205
Los Angeles, CA 90046, USA

Tsakalidis, Iakovos (Jake) (Basketball Player)
Memphis Grizzlies
175 Toyota Plaza
#150
Memphis, TN 85253-1922, USA

Tsamis, George (Athlete, Baseball Player)
12 Sweetbriar Ct
Colchester, CT 06415-1887, USA

Tsamis, George (Athlete, Baseball Player)
St Paul Saints 1771 Energy Park Dr
Attn Managers Office
Saint Paul, MN 55108-2720

Tsang, Bion (Musician)
Columbia Artists Mgmt Inc
165 W 57th St
New York, NY 10019, USA

Tsantiris, Len (Football Player)
University of Connecticut
Athletic Dept
Storrs Mansfield, CT, USA

Tsao, I Fu (Engineer)
University of Michigan
Chemical Engineering Dept
Ann Arbor, MI 48109, USA

Tschechowa, Vera (Actor)
c/o Ute Nicolai *Agentur Ute Nicolai*
Gosslerstrasse 2
Berlin 12161, Germany

Tschida, Tim (Baseball Player)
274 15 1/2 Ave
Turtle Lake, WI 54889-8825, USA

Tschida, Tim (Athlete, Baseball Player)
274 15 1/2 Ave
Turtle Lake, WI 54889-8825, USA

T. Schilling, Robert (Congressman, Politician)
507 Cannon HOB
Washington, DC 20515, USA

Tschogl, John (Athlete, Basketball Player)
295 Shirley St
Chula Vista, CA 9191e-ll0l, USA

Tschumi, Bernard (Architect)
7 Rue Pecquay
Paris 75004, FRANCE

Tseng, Yani (Athlete, Golfer)
c/o Jay Burton *IMG (Cleveland)*
1360 E 9th St
Suite 100
Cleveland, OH 44114, USA

Tsibliyev, Vasili V (Cosmonaut)
Potchta Kosmonavtov
Moskovskoi Oblasti
Syvisdny Goroduk 141160, RUSSIA

Tsien, Roger (Nobel Prize Laureate)
2665 Idle Hour Ln
La Jolla, CA 92037-1123, USA

Tsioropoulos, Lou (Athlete, Basketball Player)
2404 Chattesworth Ln
Louisville, KY 40242-2852, USA

Tsitouris, John (Athlete, Baseball Player)
5207 Austin Rd
Monroe, NC 28112-7948, USA

Tskitishvili, Nikoloz (Basketball Player)
Denver Nuggets
Pepsi Center
1000 Chopper Circle
Denver, CO 80204, USA

Tsongas, Niki (Congressman, Politician)
1607 Longworth HOB
Washington, DC 20515, USA

Tsoucalas, Nicholas (Judge)
US Court of International Trade
1 Federal Plaza
New York, NY 10278, USA

Tsu, Irene (Actor)
c/o Richard A. Castleberry *Castleberry Talent*
636 Acanto St.
Suite 205
Los Angeles, CA 90049, USA

Tsui, Daniel C (Nobel Prize Laureate)
53 College Rd W
Princeton, NJ 08540-5049, USA

Tsui, Lap-Chee (Biologist)
Sick Children Hospital
555 University Ave
Toronto, ON M5G 1X8, CANADA

Tsui, Lap-Chee Dr (Scientist)
Hospital for Sick Children 555 University Ave
Toronto, ON M5G 1X8, CANADA

Tsukasa, Helene (Stylist)
2100 Federal Ave
Los Angeles, CA 90025, USA

Tu, Francesca (Actor)
c/o Staff Member *Agentur Jovanovic*
Theresienstrasse 124
Munchen 80333, Germany

Tuanku, Salehuddin Abdul Aziz Shah (King, Royalty)
Sultan's Palace
Istana Bukit Serene
Kuala Lumpur 50502, MALAYSIA

Tuaolo, Esera (Athlete, Football Player)
6520 Promontory Dr
Eden Prairie, MN 55346, USA

Tubbs, Billy (Coach)
Lamar University
Athletic Dept
Beaumont, TX 77710, USA

Tubbs, Greg (Athlete, Baseball Player)
833 Clay Ave
Cookeville, TN 38501-2261, USA

Tubbs, Winfred (Athlete, Football Player)
RR 1 Box 800
Oakwood, TX 75855, USA

Tubert, Marcelo (Actor)
c/o Staff Member *Richard Schwartz Management*
2934-1/2 Beverly Glen Cir #107
Los Angeles, CA 90077, USA

Tuberville, Tommy (Coach, Football Coach)
Aubum University
Athletic Dept
Aubum University, AL 36849, USA

Tubiola, Nicole (Actor)
c/o Charlton Blackburne *A Management*
9107 Wilshire Blvd.
Suite 650
Beverly Hills, CA 90210, USA

Tucci, Michael (Actor)
1425 Irving Ave
Glendale, CA 91201, USA

Tucci, Roberto Cardinal (Religious Leader)
Palazzo Pio
Piazza Pia 3
Rome 00193, ITALY

Tucci, Stanley (Actor, Director)
c/o Jennifer Plante *SLATE Public Relations - NY*
307 7th Ave
Suite 2401
New York, NY 10001, USA

Tuchman, Maurice (Misc)
150 E 57th St
#PH 1A
New York, NY 10022, USA

Tuck, Gary (Athlete, Baseball Player)
2196 Grandma Barnes Rd
Nashville, IN 47448-8880, USA

Tuck, Hillary (Actor)
c/o Justin Evans *The Independent Group*
6363 Wilshire Blvd
Suite 115
Los Angeles, CA 90048, USA

Tuck, Jessica (Actor)
Brett Adams
448 W 44th St
New York, NY 10036, USA

Tucker, Barbara (Musician)
c/o Staff Member *Diva Central Inc*
7510 W Sunset Blvd Ste 1445
Los Angees, CA 90046, USA

Tucker, Bill (Boxer)
26126 Meadowcrest Blvd
Huntington Woods, MI 48070, USA

Tucker, Bill (Bowler)
26126 Meadowcrest Blvd
Huntington Woods, MI 48070-1534, USA

Tucker, Bob (Athlete, Football Player)
8 Hunter Rd
Hazleton, PA 18201, USA

Tucker, Charles (Aviator)
3435 Buckingham Dr
San Jose, CA 95118-1509, USA

Tucker, Chris (Actor, Comedian)
c/o Tracy Krammer *Toltec Artists*
7674 Woodrow Wilson Dr
Los Angeles, CA 90046-1252, USA

Tucker, Corin (Musician)
Legends of 21st Century
7 Trinity ROw
Florence, MA 01062, USA

Tucker, Darcy (Athlete, Hockey Player)
Turning Point Sports Management
102 W Main St #301
Auburn, WA 98001, USA

Tucker, Eddie (Athlete, Baseball Player)
2216 Red Maple Ln
Dawsonville, GA 30534, USA

Tucker, Elizabeth (Athlete, Baseball Player)
4037 N Fremont Ave
Tucson, AZ 85719-1065, USA

Tucker, Jason (Athlete, Football Player)
620 Remington Park
Robinson, TX 76706, USA

Tucker, Jerry (Actor)
788 St Anns Ave
Copiague, NY 11726, USA

Tucker, Jim
1781 Linden Cv
Saint Paul, MN 5511e-6202

Tucker, John (Athlete, Hockey Player)
19833 Michigan Ave
Odessa, FL 33556-4237

Tucker, Jonathan (Actor)
8265 Sunset Blvd #201
Los Angeles, CA 90064, USA

Tucker, Marshall Band (Music Group)
c/o Ron Rainey *Ron Rainey Management Inc.*
315 South Beverly Dr.
Suite 300
Beverly Hills, CA 90212, USa

Tucker, Michael (Actor, Producer)
P.O. Box 843
Santa Ynez, CA 93460-0843, USA

Tucker, Michael (Athlete, Baseball Player, Olympic Athlete)
407 Maple Ave N
Lehigh Acres, FL 33972-4001, USA

Tucker, Paul (Musician)
c/o Staff Member *Kitchenware Management*
The Stables
St. Thomas Street
Newcastle Upon Tyne NE1 4LE, UK

Tucker, Rex (Athlete, Football Player)
2300 Culpeper Dr
Midland, TX 79705, USA

Tucker, Robin (Stylist)
9120 Beverlywood St
Los Angeles, CA 90034, USA

Tucker, Ryan (Athlete, Football Player)
c/o Team Member *Cleveland Browns*
76 Lou Groza Blvd
Berea, OH 44017, USA

Tucker, Tanya (Musician)
c/o Staff Member *Webster & Associates PR*
3573 Couchville Pike
Hermitage, TN 37076, USA

Tucker, T J (Athlete, Baseball Player)
6616 Ridge Top Dr
New Port Richey, FL 34655-5614, USA

Tucker, Tony (Boxer)
Club Prana
1619 7th Ave
Ybor City
Tampa, FL 33605, USA

Tucker, Travis (Athlete, Football Player)
1568 Lee Terrace Dr
Wickliffe, OH 44092, USA

Tucker, Trent (Athlete, Basketball Player)
433 River St
Minneapolis, MN 5540l-2515, USA

Tucker, Wendell (Athlete, Football Player)
2042 E 171st Pl
South Holland, IL 60473, USA

Tucker, William E (Educator)
Texas Christian University
Chancellor's Office
Fort Worth, TX 76129, USA

Tucker, Y Arnold (Athlete, Football Player)
P.O. Box 514
Hilbert, WI 54129, USA

Tuckwell, Barry E
13140 Fountain Head Road
Hagerstown, MD 21742, USA

Tudor, John (Athlete, Baseball Player)
5 Nathan Ln
Middleton, MA 01949-1531, USA

Tudor, Rob (Athlete, Hockey Player)
2 Drake Landing Rd
Okotoks, AB TlS 2M2, Canada

Tudyk, Alan (Actor)
c/o Nick Collins *Gersh (LA)*
9465 Wilshire Blvd
Suite 600
Beverly Hills, CA 90212, USA

Tuero, Esteban (Race Car Driver)
Minardi Italia
via Spallanzani 21
Faenza 48081, ITALY

Tueting, Sarah (Athlete, Hockey Player, Olympic Athlete)
488 Ash St
Winnetka, IL 60093, USA

Tufts, Bob (Athlete, Baseball Player)
6738 108th St
Apt A27
Forest Hills, NY 11375-2358, USA

Tuggle, Anthony (Athlete, Football Player)
12345 Plymouth Dr
Baton Rouge, LA 70807, USA

Tuggle, Jessie (Athlete, Football Player)
540 Avala Ct
Alpharetta, GA 30022, USA

Tugnutt, Ron (Athlete, Hockey Player)
2427 Julia's Creek Rd RR 2
Lakefield, ON KOL 2HO, Canada

Tugnutt, Ron (Athlete, Hockey Player)
Peterborough Petes
151 Lansdowne St W
Peterborough, ON K9J 1Y4, Canada

Tuiasosopo, Marques (Athlete, Football Player)
5569 Gold Creek Dr
Castro Valley, CA 94552, USA

Tuiasosopo, Peter Navy (Actor)
c/o Harold Gray *Shirley Wilson Agency*
5410 Wilshire Blvd #806
Los Angeles
CA 90036, USA

Tuibahadur, Pun (War Hero)
Victoria Cross Assn
Old Admiralty Building
London SW1A 2BL, UNITED KINGDOM
(UK)

Tuilaepa, Sailele Maljelegaio (Prime Minister)
Prime Minister's Office
PO Box 193
Apia, SAMOA

Tuinei, Tom (Athlete, Football Player)
714 Kihapai Pl
Apt B2
Kailua, HI 96734, USA

Tuininga, Heidi (Stylist)
c/o Staff Member *Zenobia Agency Inc*
PO Box 909
Groveland, CA 95321, USA

Tuipala, Joe (Athlete, Football Player)
43845 Thornberry Sq
Unit 103
Leesburg, VA 20176, USA

Tull, Thomas (Producer)
Legendary Pictures
4000 Warner Blvd.
Bldg 76
Burbank, CA 91522, ISA

Tullis, Willie (Athlete, Football Player)
10018 Knoboak Dr
Apt 4
Houston, TX 77080, USA

Tully, Darrow (Publisher)
9862 Bridgeton Dr
Tampa, FL 33626, USA

Tully, Susan (Actor, Director)
c/o Bryn Newton *Saraband Associates*
265 Liverpool Rd
London N1 1LX, UNITED KINGDOM
(UK)

Tulonen, Reino (Race Car Driver)
113 Summit St.
Fitchburg, MA 01420, USA

Tulowitzki, Troy (Athlete, Baseball Player)
Colorado Rockies Foundation 2001 Blake St
Unit A
Denver, CO 80205-2060, USA

Tulving, Endel (Misc)
45 Baby Point Crescent
York, ON M6S 2B7, CANADA

Tulving, Endel Dr (Scientist)
45 Baby_ Point Cres
York, ON M6S 2B7, CANADA

Tumi, Christian W Cardinal (Religious Leader)
Archveche
BP 179
Douala, CAMEROON

Tumpane, John (Athlete, Baseball Player)
9900 S 55th Court Apt 3M
Oak Lawn, IL 60453, USA

Tumulty, Tom (Athlete, Football Player)
167 Woodside Ln
Verona, PA 15147, USA

Tune, Tommy (Actor, Dancer)
222 Park Ave S #12C
New York, NY 10003-1508, USA

Tung, Chee-Hwa (Misc)
Asia Pacific Finance Tower
3 Garden Road
Hong Kong, CHINA

Tunie, Tamara (Actor)
c/o Jean-Pierre (JP) Henraux *Henraux Management*
Prefers to be contacted by telephone
CA, USA

Tunnell, Denise (Stylist)
c/o Staff Member *Help Me Rhonda*
541 10th St NW #294
Atlanta, GA 30318, USA

Tunnell, Janice (Stylist)
c/o Staff Member *Help Me Rhonda*
541 10th St NW #294
Atlanta, GA 30318, USA

Tunnell, Lee (Athlete, Baseball Player)
6000 Kingsbridge Dr
Oklahoma City, OK 73162-3208, USA

Tunney, John V (Politician, Senator)
1819 Ocean Ave
Santa Monica, CA 90401-3215, USA

Tunney, Robin (Actor)
c/o Joan Hyler *Hyler Management*
20 Ocean Park Blvd
Suite 25
Santa Monica, CA 90405, USA

Tupa, Thomas J (Tom) (Athlete, Football Player)
5921 Fawn Ln
Brecksville, OH 44141, USA

Tupman, Matt (Athlete, Baseball Player)
3 Lincoln St
Concord, NH 03301-2404, USA

Tupouto'a (Prince)
Royal Palace
PO Box 6
Nuku'alofa, TONGA

Tupper, James (Actor)
c/o Jason Weinberg *Untitled Entertainment (LA)*
350 S. Beverly Dr #200
Beverly Hills, CA 90212, USA

Tupper, Jeff (Athlete, Football Player)
3263 W 164th Ter
Stilwell, KS 66085, USA

Turang, Brian (Athlete, Baseball Player)
3014 McNab Ave
Long Beach, CA 90808-4002, USA

Turco, Marty (Athlete, Hockey Player)
3616 Wolcott Dr
Flower Mound, TX 75028-8712

Turco, Paige (Actor)
c/o Rhonda Price *Gersh (NY)*
41 Madison Ave
New York, NY 10010, USA

Turco, Richard P (Scientist)
R&D Assoc
4340 Admiralty Way
Marina del Rey, CA 90292, USA

Turcotte, Alfie (Athlete, Hockey Player)
816 Hawk Dr
Wolverine Lake, Ml 48390-3011

Turcotte, Darren (Athlete, Hockey Player)
North Bay Skyhawks Hockey Club
100 Chippewa St W
North Bav, ON P1B 6G2, Canada

Turcotte, Donald L (Don) (Geophysicist, Physicist)
27104 Middle Golf Dr
El Macero, CA 95618, USA

Turcotte, Jean-Claude Cardinal (Religious Leader)
1071 Rue de la Cathedrale
Montreal, QC H2B 2V4, CANADA

Turcotte, Mel (Horse Racer)
4260 NW 12th St
Coconut Creek, FL 33066-1506, USA

Turcotte, Ron (Horse Racer, Jockey)
PO Box 215
Van Buren, ME 04785-0215, USA

Tureaud, Lawrence (Mr T) (Actor)
c/o Barry M. Greenberg *Celebrity Connection*
2208 Patricia Avenue
Los Angeles, CA 90064-2318, USA

Turek, Roman (Athlete, Hockey Player)
The Sports Corporation
10088 102 Ave NW Twr 2735 TO
Edmonton, AB T5J 2Z1, Canada

Turgeon, Pierre (Athlete, Hockey Player)
1075 E Oxford Ln
Englewood, CO 80113-4822

Turiaf, Ronny (Athlete, Basketball Player)
c/o Mark Bartelstein *Priority Sports & Entertainment - Chicago*
312 N La Salle
Suite 650
Chicago, IL 60610, USA

Turin Brakes (Music Group)
c/o Staff Member *Paradigm (Monterey)*
404 W Franklin St
Monterey, CA 93940, USA

Turk, Brian (Actor)
c/o Staff Member *House of Representatives, The*
1434 6th St
Suite 1
Santa Monica, CA 90401, USA

Turk, Godwin (Athlete, Football Player)
1303 Magnolia Cir
Orange, TX 77632, USA

Turk, Stephen (Cartoonist)
927 Westbourne Dr
Los Angeles, CA 90069-4113, USA

Turkel, Ann (Actor)
c/o Mark Baintree *Brian Baintree Agency*
4 West 58th St
New York, NY 10019, USA

Turkoglu, Hidayet (Hedo) (Athlete, Basketball Player)
100 S Eola Dr
Unit 1603
Orlando, FL 32801, USA

Turkson, Peter K A Cardinal (Religious Leader)
Archdiocese
PO Box 112
Cape Coast, GHANA

Turley, Bob (Athlete, Baseball Player)
3284 Chipping Wood Ct
Alpharetta, GA 30004-4305, USA

Turley, Kyle (Football Player)
c/o Staff Member *St Louis Rams*
1 Rams Way
Earth City, MO 63045, USA

Turley, Robert L (Bob) (Athlete, Baseball Player)
Po Box 659
Morganton, GA 30560, USA

Turlik, Gordon (Athlete, Hockey Player)
3618 E Garnet Ave
Spokane, WA 99217-6916

Turlington, Christy (Model)
c/o Lisa Jacobson *United Talent Agency (UTA)*
9336 Civic Center Dr
Beverly Hills, CA 90210, USA

Turman, Glynn (Actor, Director, Musician)
48421 Three Points Rd
Lake Hughes, CA 93532, USA

Turnage, Mark-Anthony (Composer)
Schott Co
Great Marlborough St
London W1V 2BN, UNITED KINGDOM
(UK)

Turnbow, Derrick (Athlete, Baseball Player)
2224 Brienz Vallev Dr
Franklin, TN 37064-1401, USA

Turnbow, Scot (Baseball Player)
Anaheim Angels
404 Newbary Ct
Franklin, TN 37069-1848, USA

Turnbull, Alistair (Stylist)
c/o Staff Member *Pat Bates & Associates*
300 W 12th St
New York, NY 10014, USA

Turnbull, David (Physicist)
29 Concord Ave
#715
Cambridge, MA 02138, USA

Turnbull, Ian (Athlete, Hockey Player)
23930 Ocean Ave Apt 154
Torrance, CA 90505-5880

Turnbull, Perry (Athlete, Hockey Player)
2186 Cedar Forest Court
Chesterfield, MO 63017-7201

Turnbull, Wendy (Tennis Player)
822 Boylston Dt
#203
Chestnut Hill, MA 02467, USA

Turner, Aiden (Actor)
c/o Marnie Sparer *Innovative Artists (LA)*
1505 10th St
Santa Monica, CA 90401, USA

Turner, Bake (Athlete, Football Player)
P.O. Box 277
Alpine, TX 79831, USA

Turner, Betty Stagg (Aviator)
PO Box 20197
Columbus, OH 43220-0197, USA

Turner, Bree (Actor)
c/o Jai Khanna *Brillstein Entertainment Partners*
9150 Wilshire Blvd #350
Beverly Hills, CA 90212, USA

Turner, Cathy (Speed Skater)
251 East Ave
Hilton, NY 14468, USA

Turner, Cecil (Athlete, Football Player)
2717 Dog Leg Trl
McKinney, TX 75069, USA

Turner, Chris (Athlete, Baseball Player)
28SS3 N Quarry Dr
Elberta, AL 36530-5792, USA

Turner, Dean (Athlete, Hockey Player)
26900 Captains Ln
Franklin, MI 48025-1717

Turner, Debbye (Doctor)
PO Box 12450
St. Louis, MO 63132-0150, USA

Turner, Edwin L (Physicist)
Princeton University
Astrophysical Sciences Dept
Princeton, NJ 08544, USA

Turner, Elston (Athlete, Basketball Player)
23 Commanders Cv
Missouri City, TX 77459-6517, USA

Turner, Floyd (Athlete, Football Player)
9626 Garden Row Dr
Sugar Land, TX 77478, USA

Turner, Fred (Race Car Driver)
107 Brush Road
Greensboro, NC 27409, USA

Turner, Fred L (Business Person)
McDonald Corp
McDonald's Plaza
1 Kroc Dr
Oak Brook, IL 60523, USA

Turner, Gideon (Actor)
c/o Staff Member *Ken McReddie Ltd*
11 Connaught Pl
London W2 2ET, UNITED KINGDOM

Turner, Glenn (Business Person)
P.O. Box 952608
Lake Mary, FL 32795-2608, USA

Turner, Grant
PO Box 414
Brentwood, TN 37027

Turner, Guinevere (Actor)
Gersh Agency
41 Madison Ave
#3300
New York, NY 10010, USA

Turner, Hamp (Athlete, Football Player)
430172 Milledge Ter
Athens, GA 30605, USA

Turner, Herschel (Athlete, Football Player)
16622 Equestrian Ln
Chesterfield, MO 49505-7702, USA

Turner, Hersh (Athlete, Basketball Player)
1706 Lamberton Creek Ct NE
Grand Rapids, MI 49505, USA

Turner, Jackie Lee (Athlete, Basketball Player)
2402 H St
Bedford, IN 47421-5122, USA

Turner, James A (Jim) (Athlete, Football Player)
14155 W 59th Pl
Arvada, CO 80004, USA

Turner, James Jr (Business Person)
General Dynamics
3190 Fairview Park Dr
Falls Church, VA 22042, USA

Turner, James T (Judge)
US Claims Court
717 Madison Place NW
Washington, DC 20439, USA

Turner, Janine (Actor, Model)
c/o Tiffany Smith *Binder & Associates*
1465 Lindacrest Dr
Beverly Hills, CA 90210, USA

Turner, Jeff
1590 Woodland Ave
Winter Park, FL 32789-2773, USA

Turner, Jerry (Athlete, Baseball Player)
1935 18th St
Apt B
Santa Monica, CA 90404-4732, USA

Turner, Jesse
1502 N. 5th St.
Boise, ID 83702-3703

Turner, Jim (Actor)
c/o Margrit Polak *Margrit Polak Management*
1954 Hillhurst Ave
Suite 405
Los Angeles, CA 90027, USA

Turner, John (Athlete, Football Player)
3217 Cedar Ave S
Minneapolis, MN 55407, USA

Turner, John N (Prime Minister)
27 Dunice Road
Toronto, ON M4V 2W4, CANADA

Turner, Josh (Musician)
c/o Staff Member *Modern Management*
1625 Broadway Fl 6
Nashville, TN 37203, USA

Turner, Karri (Actor)
Premiere Artists Agency
1875 Century Park E
#2250
Los Angeles, CA 90067, USA

Turner, Kathleen (Actor)
c/o Alan Nierob *Rogers & Cowan PR (LA)*
Pacific Design Center
8687 Melrose Ave, 7th Floor
West Hollywood, CA 90069, USA

Turner, Keena (Athlete, Coach, Football Coach, Football Player)
8200 W Erb Way
Tracy, CA 95304, USA

Turner, Ken (Athlete, Baseball Player)
P.O. Box 252
San Marcos, CA 92079-0252, USA

Turner, Kenneth (Race Car Driver)
957 South Trade St.
Tyron, SC 28782, USA

Turner, Kevin (Athlete, Football Player)
414 Shady Nook Dr
Deatsville, AL 36022, USA

Turner, Kriss (Producer)
c/o Staff Member *WmE2 (WMA-LA)*
1 William Morris Pl
Beverly Hills, CA 90212, USA

Turner, Kristin (Stylist)
c/o Staff Member *Perrella Management*
330 W 38th St Rm 1407
New York, NY 10018, USA

Turner, Kristopher (Actor)
c/o Shelley Browning *Magnolia Entertainment (LA)*
9595 Wilshire Blvd
Suite 601
Beverly Hills, CA 90212, USA

Turner, Lane (Musician)
c/o Staff Member *Paradigm (Monterey)*
404 W Franklin St
Monterey, CA 93940, USA

Turner, Lowri (Actor)
c/o Staff Member *Noel Gay Artists*
19 Denmark St
London WC2H 8NA, United Kingdom

Turner, Marcus (Athlete, Football Player)
5032 Meadow Wood Ave
Lakewood, CA 90712, USA

Turner, Matt (Athlete, Baseball Player)
829 Della Dr
Lexington, KY 40504-2319, USA

Turner, Maurice (Athlete, Football Player)
3558 Tiffany Ln
Shoreview, MN 55126, USA

Turner, Michael (Football Player)
c/o Staff Member *Atlanta Falcons*
4400 Falcon Pkwy
Flowery Branch, GA 30542, USA

Turner, Morrie (Cartoonist)
127 Touchstone Pl
West Sacramento, CA 95691-4612, USA

Turner, Norv (Athlete, Coach, Football Coach, Football Player)
1256 Rose Ln
Lafayette, CA 94549, USA

Turner, Odessa (Athlete, Football Player)
1416 Perry Ave
Bastrop, LA 71220, USA

Turner, Pete (Photographer)
PO Box 203
Wainscott, NY 11975-0203, USA

Turner, Richard (Athlete, Football Player)
408 Piney Oak Dr
Norman, OK 73072, USA

Turner, Ryan (Baseball Player)
1221 Shafter St
San Mateo, CA 94402-2901, USA

Turner, Shane (Athlete, Baseball Player)
3032 Van Reed Rd
Reading, PA 19608-1037, USA

Turner, Shelly N (Stylist)
232 President St
#3-L
Brooklyn, NY 11231, USA

Turner, Sherri (Athlete, Golfer)
P.O. Box 26
Yale, OK 74085-0026, USA

Turner, Stacie (Business Person, Reality TV Star)
c/o Staff Member *Bravo (NY)*
30 Rockefeller Plaza
New York, NY 10112, USA

Turner, Stansfield
488 River Bend Rd
Great Falls, VA 22066-4016, USA

Turner, Ted (Business Person, Producer)
Turner Foundation
133 Luckie St, NW
2nd Floor
Atlanta, GA 30303, USA

Turner, Thomas (Athlete, Baseball Player)
4817 Delhi Arnheim Rd
Georgetown, OH 45121-8229, USA

Turner, Tina (Musician)
c/o Steven Manzano *RDWM America*
1158 26th St
Suite 564
Santa Monica, CA 90403, USA

Turner, Tyrin (Actor)
c/o David Saunders *Agency for the Performing Arts (APA-LA)*
405 S Beverly Dr
Suite 500
Beverly Hills, CA 90212-4425, USA

Turner, Vernon (Athlete, Football Player)
86 Crosshill St
Staten Island, NY 10301, USA

Turner, William (Athlete, Basketball Player)
3271 Wisteria Tree St
Las Vegas, NV 89135-1787, USA

Turnesa, Jim (Golfer)
24 Poplar St
Elmsford, NY 10523-3726, USA

Turnesa, Mike (Golfer)
c/o Staff Member *Pro Golfers Association (PGA) Tour*
112 TPC Blvd
Ponte Vedra Beach, FL 32082, USA

Turnesa, Willie (Golfer)
41 Sheraton Dr
Poughkeepsie, NY 12601-5629, USA

Turney, Maura
PO Box 5617
Beverly Hills, CA 90210

Turnley, David (Photographer)
Detroit Free Press 600 W Fort St
Detroit, MI 48226-3198, USA

Turow, Scott (Writer)
c/o Robert (Bob) Bookman *Creative Artists Agency (CAA-LA)*
2000 Ave Of The Stars
Los Angeles, CA 90067, USA

Turpin, Miles (Athlete, Football Player)
8444 Wildflower Pl
Lone Tree, CO 80124, USA

Turris, Kyle (Athlete, Hockey Player)
19820 N 84th St
Scottsdale, AZ 85255-3964

Turteltaub, Jon (Director)
Junction Entertainment
500 South Buena Vista St
Animation Building Ste 1B
Burbank, CA 91521, USA

Turtles, The
PO Box 1821
Ojai, CA 93024

Turturro, Aida (Actor)
c/o Peg Donegan *Framework Entertainment (LA)*
9057 Nemo St
Suite C
West Hollywood, CA 90069, USA

Turturro, John (Actor)
c/o Bart Walker *ICM Partners (ICM-LA)*
555 W 25th St
4th Floor
New York, NY 10001, USA

Turturro, Nicholas (Actor)
c/o Staff Member *Agency for the Performing Arts (APA-LA)*
405 S Beverly Dr
Suite 500
Beverly Hills, CA 90212-4425, USA

Turturro, Nick (Actor)
c/o Adam Griffin *Kritzer Levine Wilkins Entertainment (KLWG)*
11872 La Grange Ave
1st Floor
Los Angeles, CA 90025, USA

Tush, Bill
1 City CNN Center Box 105366
Atlanta, GA 30348-5366

Tushingham, Rita
4 Kingly St
London, ENGLAND W1R 5LF

Tuso, Gena (Stylist)
c/o Celebrity Stylist *Cloutier Agency*
2632 La Cienega Ave
Los Angeles, CA 90034, USA

Tuten, Rick (Athlete, Football Player)
1146 SE 15th St
Ocala, FL 34471, USA

Tutera, David (Reality TV Star)
c/o Eda Kalkay *EKPR*
470 7th Ave
11th Floor
New York, NY 10018, USA

Tutin, Dame Dorothy
13 St. Martin's Rd.
London, ENGLAND SW9 0SP

Tutson, Tom (Athlete, Football Player)
6655 Poplar Grove Way
Stone Mountain, GA 30087, USA

Tutt, Brian (Athlete, Hockey Player)
PO Box 306
Evansburg, AB TOE OTO, Canada

Tuttle, Matthew Chal (Stylist)
2304 Fortune Ln
Greensboro, NC 27408, USA

Tuttle, Perry (Athlete, Football Player)
14224 King Eider Dr
Charlotte, NC 28273, USA

Tuttle, Steve (Athlete, Hockey Player)
928 Belfair Rd.
Bellevue, WA 85255-3964

Tutu, Desmond (Religious Leader)
PO Box 1092
Milnerton, Cape Town 7435, SOUTH AFRICA

Tutu, Desmond (Nobel Prize Laureate)
Bishopscourt
Claremont Cape 7700, South Africa

Tuzzolino, Tony (Athlete, Hockey Player)
4466 Sunflower Cir Apt 39
Clarkston, MI 48346-4956

Tverdovsky, Oleg (Athlete, Hockey Player)
8850 E Garden View Dr
Anaheim, CA 92808-1677

Tvrdon, Roman (Athlete, Hockey Player)
Mierova 1435/53
Galanta, 924 01 Slovakia

Twain, Shania (Actor, Musician)
c/o Peter Mensch *Q Prime South*
729 Seventh Ave
16th Floor
New York, NY 10019, USA

Twardzik, Dave (Athlete, Basketball Player)
2139 Alaqua Lakes Blvd
Longwood, FL 32703-7853, USA

Tway, Bob (Golfer)
6300 Oak Heritage Trl
Edmond, OK 73003-2766, USA

Tweed, Shannon (Actor, Model, Reality TV Star)
c/o Danielle Allman-Del *D2 Management*
141 S. Barrington Ave
Los Angeles, CA 90049, USA

Tweeden, Leeann (Actor, Model, Sportscaster)
c/o Jon Orlando *WNWN Media*
348 S. Hauser Blvd #PH414
Los Angeles, CA 90036, USA

Tweet, Rodney (Athlete, Football Player)
2096 Placita De Vida
Santa Fe, NM 87505, USA

Twigg, Rebecca (Athlete, Cycler, Olympic Athlete)
7001 Old Redmond Rd Apt E318
Redmond, WA 98052-4293, USA

Twiggs, Greg (Golfer)
c/o Staff Member *Pro Golfers Association (PGA) Tour*
112 TPC Blvd
Ponte Vedra Beach, FL 32082, USA

Twilight Singers (Music Group)
c/o Staff Member *Paradigm (Monterey)*
404 W Franklin St
Monterey, CA 93940, USA

Twilley, Howard J Jr (Athlete, Football Player)
3109 S Columbia Cir
Tulsa, OK 74105, USA

Twilly, Dwight
PO Box 1821
Ojai, CA 93024

Twist, Tony (Athlete, Hockey Player)
63 Nordic Ln
Defiance, MO 63341-2332

Twista (Actor, Musician)
c/o Staff Member *Violator Management*
36 W 25th St
2nd Floor
New York, NY 10010, USA

Twitty, Howard (Golfer)
8007 E Mercer Ln
Scottsdale, AZ 85260-6563, USA

Twitty, Jeff (Athlete, Baseball Player)
812 Willow Cove Road
Chapin, SC 29036-8733, USA

Twohy, David (Actor)
c/o John Burnham *ICM Partners (ICM-LA)*
10250 Constellation Blvd Fl 7
Los Angeles, CA 90067, USA

Twohy, Mike (Cartoonist)
605 Beloit Ave
Kensington, CA 94708, USA

Twohy, Robert (Cartoonist)
New Yorker Magazine
Editorial Dept
4 Times Square
New York, NY 10036, USA

Twyford, Dwan (Business Person)
Millionaire Mindset Collection
15 Gramercy Park S #3
New York, NY 10003, USA

Twyman, Jack (Athlete, Basketball Player)
8955 Indian Ridge Ln
Cincinnati, OH 45243-374e, USA

Tydings, Joseph D (Politician, Senator)
2705 Pocock Road
Monkton, MD 21111-2311, USA

Tyers, Kathy (Writer)
Martha Millard Agency
204 Park Ave
Madison, NJ 07940, USA

Tyga (Musician)
c/o Nick Storch *ICM Partners (ICM-NY)*
730 Fifth Ave
New York, NY 10019, USA

Tykwer, Tom (Actor, Composer, Director, Producer, Writer)
X-Filme Creative Pool
Kurfürstenstrasse 57
Berlin 10785, Germany

Tyler, Aisha (Actor, Comedian)
c/o Jordan Tilzer *ROAR (LA)*
9701 Wilshire Blvd
8th Floor
Los Angeles, CA 90212, USA

Tyler, Anne (Writer)
c/o Staff Member *Random House Publicity*
1745 Broadway
New York, NY 10019, USA

Tyler, B J
1994 Philadelphia 76ers
Port Arthur, TX 77640-4483, USA

Tyler, Bonnie (Musician, Songwriter)
c/o Andrew Leighton *Leighton Pope Organization*
8 Glenthorpe Mews
115A Glenthorpe Road
London W6 0LJ, UNITED KINGDOM (UK)

Tyler, Brian (Race Car Driver)
4410 West Alva St.
Tampa, FL 33614, USA

Tyler, Cory
9955 Balboa Blvd.
Northridge, CA 91325

Tyler, Harold R Jr (Attorney, Attorney General, General)
Patterson Belknap Webb Tyler
30 Rockefeller Plaza
New York, NY 10112, USA

Tyler, James Michael (Actor)
c/o Craig Mobbs *AKA Talent Agency*
6310 San Vicente Blvd
Suite 200
Los Angeles, CA 90048, USA

Tyler, Jess (Radio Personality)
c/o Staff Member *WPKX*
1331 Main St Fl 4
Springfield, MA 01103, USA

Tyler, Karmyn (Actor, Musician)
c/o Staff Member *BMI (LA)*
8730 Sunset Blvd Fl 3
Los Angeles, CA 90069

Tyler, Liv (Actor)
255 W 11th St
New York, NY 10014, USA

Tyler, Maurice (Athlete, Football Player)
7066 Whitfield Dr
Riverdale, GA 30296, USA

Tyler, Mia (Actor)
c/o Staff Member *Core/Lapides Lear Entertainment*
14724 Ventura Blvd.
Penthouse
Sherman Oaks, CA 91403, USA

Tyler, Nikki
4F So. Main St. PMB 307
West Bridgewater, MA 02379

Tyler, Richard (Designer, Fashion Designer)
c/o Staff Member *Richard Tyler*
525 Mission St
S Pasadena, CA 91030-3035, USA

Tyler, Robert (Actor)
Innovative Artists
1505 10th St
Santa Monica, CA 90401, USA

Tyler, Steven (Musician, Songwriter)
c/o Irving Azoff *Azoff Music Management/ Front Line*
1100 Glendon Ave
Los Angeles, CA 90024, USA

Tyler, Terry (Athlete, Basketball Player)
6500 Tauton Rd NW
Albuquerque, NM 87120-2e61, USA

Tyler, Wendell A (Athlete, Football Player)
4083 W Avenue L
Apt 294
Quartz Hill, CA 93536, USA

Tyler, Willie
1650 Broadway #705
New York, NY 10019

Tylo, Hunter (Actor)
11684 Ventura Blvd. #910
Studio City, CA 91604-2613

Tylo, Michael (Actor)
11684 Ventura Blvd
#910
Studio City, CA 91604, USA

Tylo, Noa (DJ)
c/o Len Evans *Project Publicity*
312 West 53rd St
Suite 202
New York, NY 10019, USA

Tylski, Richard (Athlete, Football Player)
5456 Tierra Verde Ln
Jacksonville, FL 32258, USA

Tynan, Ronan (Musician)
c/o Lynnette Crouse *CMI Entertainment*
925 E. 9th St
Port Angeles, WA 98362, USA

Tyne, George
1449 Benedict Canyon
Beverly Hills, CA 90210

Tyner, Charles (Actor)
Dade/Schultz
6442 Coldwater Canyon Ave
#206
Valley Green, CA 91606, USA

Tyner, Jason (Athlete, Baseball Player)
5535 Sul Ross Ln
Beaumont, TX 77706-3435, USA

Tyner, Tray (Athlete, Golfer)
208 Plantation Path
Boerne, TX 78006-3879, USA

Type O Negative (Music Group)
c/o Staff Member *Helter Skelter (UK)*
535 Kings Rd
The Plaza
London SW10 0SZ, UNITED KINGDOM
(UK)

Tyree, David (Athlete, Football Player)
15 Fox Hill Dr
Wayne, NJ 07470, USA

Tyrell, Steve (Musician)
c/o Staff Member *WmE2 (WMA-LA)*
1 William Morris Pl
Beverly Hills, CA 90212, USA

Tyrone, Jim (Athlete, Baseball Player)
1115 Park Vista Dr #703
Arlington, TX 76012-2341, USA

Tyrone, Wayne (Athlete, Baseball Player)
505 Tish Cir
Apt 404
Arlington, TX 76006-3549, USA

Tyronn, Lue
2926 Montessouri St
Las Vegas, NV 89117-3152

Tyrrell, Genevieve (Stylist)
c/o Staff Member *Montana Artists Agency*
9150 Wilshire Blvd Ste 100
Beverly Hills, CA 90212, USA

Tyrrell, Tim (Athlete, Football Player)
17 Fallstone Dr
Streamwood, IL 60107, USA

Tysoe, Ronald W (Business Person)
Federated Department Stores
151 W 34th Ave
New York, NY 10001, USA

Tyson, Cathy (Actor)
P F D Drury House
34-43 Russell St
London WC2B 5HA, UNITED KINGDOM
(UK)

Tyson, Cicely (Actor)
c/o Staff Member *WmE2 (WMA-LA)*
1 William Morris Pl
Beverly Hills, CA 90212, USA

Tyson, Dick (Athlete, Football Player)
3835 N 67th St
Kansas City, KS 66104, USA

Tyson, Ian (Musician)
Richard Flohil Assoc
60 McGill St
Toronto, ON M5B 1H2, CANADA

Tyson, Laura D'Andrea (Politician)
National Economic Council 1600
Pennsylvania Ave NW
Washington, DC 20500-0003, USA

Tyson, Mike (Athlete, Baseball Player)
479 Thunderhead Canyon Dr
Ballwin, MO 63011-1736, USA

Tyson, Mike (Athlete, Boxer)
c/o Harlan Werner *Sports Placement Service*
330 W 11th St
Suite 105
Los Angeles, CA 90015, USA

Tyson, Neil de Grasse (Physicist)
Hayden Planetarium
W 81st St & Central Park
New York, NY 10024, USA

Tyson, Richard (Actor)
c/o Staff Member *Cunningham Escott Slevin & Doherty (CESD-LA)*
10635 Santa Monica Blvd
130
Los Angeles, CA 90025, USA

Tyurin, Mikhail (Cosmonaut)
Potcha Kosmonavtov
Moskovskoi Oblasti
Syvisdny Goroduk 141160, RUSSIA

Tyus, Wyomia (Athlete, Olympic Athlete, Track Athlete)
1102 Keniston Ave
Los Angeles, CA 90019, USA

Tyutin, Fedor (Athlete, Hockey Player)
3444 Rockpointe Court
Columbus, OH 43221-4948

Tzadua, Paulos Cardinal (Religious Leader)
PO Box 2141
Addis Abeba, ETHIOPIA

U2 (Musician)
c/o Keryn Kalpan *Principle Management*
250 W 57th St
Suite 2120
New York, NY 10107, USA

UB 40
Kensal House 553-579 Harrow Rd.
London, ENGLAND W10 4RH

UB40 (Music Group)
c/o Staff Member *International Talent Booking (ITB - UK)*
27A Floral St Fl 3
Covent Garden
London WC2E 9, UNITED KINGDOM

Ubach, Alanna (Actor)
c/o Staff Member *Margrit Polak Management*
1954 Hillhurst Ave
Suite 405
Los Angeles, CA 90027, USA

Uberroth, Peter (Baseball Player)
Baseball Commissioner's Office
184 Emerald Bay
Laguna Beach, CA 92651-1209, USA

Ubriaco, Gene (Athlete, Hockey Player)
Chicago Wolves
2301 Ravine Way
Glenview, IL 60025-7627

Ubriaco, Gene (Athlete, Coach, Hockey Player)
Chicago Wolves
621 Winston Dr
Melrose Park, IL 60160-2350

Uchida, Irene A (Scientist)
20 North Shore Blvd W
Burlington, ON L7T 1A1, CANADA

Uchida, Irene Dr (Scientist)
20 North Shore Blvd W
Burlington, ON L7T 1A1, CANADA

Uchida, Mitsuko (Musician)
Arts Management Group
1133 Broadway
#1025
New York, NY 10010, USA

Udenio, Fabiana (Actor)
Michael Slessinger
8730 Sunset Blvd
#220W
Los Angeles, CA 90069, USA

Uderzo, Albert
26 av. Victor Hugo
Paris, FRANCE F-75116

Udhas, Pankaj (Musician)
Velvet Voices
20-A, Vijay Chambers
Opp Dreamlead Cinema, Tribhuvan Rd
Mumbai 400 004, India

Udoka, Ime
PO Box 4e8e2
Portland, OR 97240-0802, USA

Udrih, Beno (Athlete, Basketball Player)
825 N Prospect Ave Unit 23e2
Milwaukee, WI 53202-3966

Udvar-Hazy, Steven (Misc)
67 Beverly Park
Beverly Hills, CA 90210-1542, USA

Udvari, Frank (Athlete, Hockey Player)
6 WillowSt
Waterloo, ON N2J 4S3, CANADA

Udvati, Frank (Athlete, Hockey Player)
6 Willow St.
Waterloo, ON N2J 4S3, CANADA

Udy, Helene (Actor)
Sterling/Winters
10877 Wilshire Blvd
#15
Los Angeles, CA 90024, USA

Ueberroth, John A (Business Person)
Preferred Hotel Group
311 South Wacker Drive
Suite 1900
Chicago, IL 60606-6620, USA

Ueberroth, Peter (Baseball Player)
184 Emerald Bay
Laguna Beach, CA 92651-1209

Ueberroth, Peter V (Misc)
Doubletree Hotels Corp
755 Crossover Lane
Memphis, TN 38117, USA

Uecker, Bob (Athlete, Baseball Player, Sportscaster)
c/o Deborah Miller *Shelter Entertainment*
9454 Wilshire Blvd.
Suite 715
Beverly Hills, CA 90212, USA

Uecker, Gunther (Artist)
Dusseldorfer Str 29A
Dusseldorf 40545, GERMANY

Uecker, Keith (Athlete, Football Player)
1230 Sunset View Dr
Akron, OH 44313, USA

Uehara, Koji (Athlete, Baseball Player)
c/o Staff Member *SFX Sports Management*
5335 Wisconsin Ave NW #850
Washington, DC 20015, USA

Uelses, John (Athlete, Track Athlete)
30660 Rolling Hills Dr
Valley Center, CA 92082, USA

Uelsmann, Jerry N (Photographer)
5701 SW 17th Dr
Gainesville, FL 32608-5365, USA

Ueltschi, Albert L (Business Person)
Flight Safety Int'l
Marine Air Terminal
LaGuardia Airport
Flushing, NY 11371, USA

Ufland, Len (Actor, Director)
4400 Hillcreat Dr
#901
Hollywood, FL 33021, USA

UFO
10 Sutherland
London, ENGLAND W9 24Q

Uggams, Leslie (Actor, Musician)
c/o Philip Adelman *Gage Group, The (NY)*
450 7th Ave
Suite 1809
New York, NY 10123, USA

Uggla, Dan (Athlete, Baseball Player)
3325 Piedmont Rd NE #3201
Atlanta, GA 30305, USA

Ughi, Uto (Musician)
Cannareggio 4990/E
Venice 30121, ITALY

U-God (Artist)
Famous Artists Agency
250 W 57th St
New York, NY 10107, USA

Ugueto, Luis (Athlete, Baseball Player)
21915 NE 85th St
Redmond, WA 98053-2204, USA

Uhalt, Alfred H Capt (Aviator)
2533 Shalimar Dr
Colorado Springs, CO 80915-1030, USA

Uh Huh Her (Music Group)
c/o Staff Member *Paradigm (Monterey)*
404 W Franklin St
Monterey, CA 93940, USA

Uhl, George (Biologist)
Johns Hopkins University
Medical Center
Genetics Dept
Baltimore, MD 21218, USA

Uhl, Petr (Activist)
Anglicka 8
Prague 2 120 00, CZECH REPUBLIC

Uhlenbeck, Karen K (Mathematician)
University of Texas
Mathematics Dept
Austin, TX 78712, USA

Uhlenhake, Jeffrey (Athlete, Football Player)
1304 Normandy Dr
Newark, OH 43055, USA

Uhlig, Anneliese
1519 Escalona Dr.
Santa Cruz, CA 95060

Uhry, Alfred F (Writer)
Marshall Purdy
226 W 47th St Ste 900
New York, NY 10036-1413, USA

Ujdur, Jerry (Athlete, Baseball Player)
112 Riveness Rd
Duluth, MN 55811-2873, USA

Ukropina, James R (Attorney, Attorney General, Business Person, General)
O'Melveny & Myers
400 S Hope St
Los Angeles, CA 90071, USA

Ulene, Art (Doctor)
6511 Moore Dr
Los Angeles, CA 90048-5325, USA

Ulevich, Neal (Journalist, Photographer)
11954 Glencoe Dr
Thornton, CO 80233-1895, USA

Ulion, Gretchen (Athlete, Hockey Player)
22181 Toro Hills Dr
Salinas, CA 93908, USA

Ulion-Silverman, Gretchen (Athlete, Hockey Player, Olympic Athlete)
505 Westledge Dr
Torrington, CT 06790-4490, USA

Ullger, Scott (Athlete, Baseball Player)
Minnesota Twins 1 Twins Way Attn
Coaching Staff
Minniapollis, MN 55403-1418, USA

Ulliel, Gaspard (Actor)
c/o Brinda Bhatt *Innovative Artists (LA)*
9560 Wilshire Blvd
5th Floor
Beverly Hills, CA 90212, USA

Ullman, Norman V A (Norm) (Athlete, Hockey Player)
819-25 Austin Dr
Markham, ON L3R 8H4, Canada

Ullman, Ricky (Actor)
c/o Terry Saperstein *Nani/Saperstein Management*
481 8th Ave #1575
New York, NY 10001, USA

Ullman, Tracey (Actor, Comedian)
c/o Brian Swardstrom *WME (LA)*
9601 Wilshire Blvd Fl 3
Beverly Hills, CA 90210, USA

Ullmann, Liv J (Actor)
Hafrsfjordgata 7
Oslo N-0273, Norway

Ulloa, Christina (Actor)
c/o Michael Greenwald *Buchwald/Fortitude (LA)*
6500 Wilshire Blvd
Suite 2200
Los Angeles, CA 90048, USA

Ullsten, Ola (Prime Minister)
Folkpartiet
PO Box 6508
Stockholm 11383, SWEDEN

Ulmar, Bin Hassan (Musician)
Agency Group
1775 Broadway
#433
New York, NY 10019, USA

Ulmer, Arthur (Athlete, Football Player)
1133 Lloyd Dr
F0rest Park, GA 30297, USA

Ulmer, John (Athlete, Football Player)
3050 Aries Pl
Burnaby, BC V3J7E9, Canada

Ulmer, Kristen (Athlete)
3671 Willow Canyon Dr
Salt Lake City, UT 84121, USA

Ulmer, Layne (Athlete, Hockey Player)
2024 Foley Dr
North Battleford, SK S9A 3G9, Canada

Ulrich, Henry (Admiral)
Commander
Naval Striking Force Central Europe & 6th Fleet
FPO, AE 09609, USA

Ulrich, Kim Johnston (Actor)
S D B Partners
1801 Ave of Stars
#902
Los Angeles, CA 90067, USA

Ulrich, Lars (Musician)
Q Prime Inc
729 7th Ave
#1600
New York, NY 10019, USA

Ulrich, Laurel T (Historian)
University of New Hampshire
History Dept
Durham, NH 03824, USA

Ulrich, Robert (Business Person)
Target Corporation
1000 Nicollet Mall
Minneapolis, MN 55403-2467

Ulrich, Robert J (Business Person)
Daytone Hudson
1000 Nicollet Mall
Minneapolis, MN 55403, USA

Ulrich, Skeet (Actor)
c/o Andrea Pett-Joseph *Brillstein Entertainment Partners*
9150 Wilshire Blvd #350
Beverly Hills, CA 90212, USA

Ulrich, Thomas (Boxer)
Brunsbutteler Damm 29
Berlin 13581, GERMANY

Ultang, Don (Photographer)
3500 Lower West Branch Rd # 121
Iowa City, IA 52245-4106, USA

Ultra, Nate (Musician)
Peach Bisquit
451 Washington Ave
#5A
Brooklyn, NY 11238, USA

Ulufa'alu, Bartholomew (Prime Minister)
Premier's Office
Legakiki Ridge
Honiara
Guadacanal, SOLOMON ISLANDS

Ulusu, Bulent (Admiral, Prime Minister)
Ciftehavuzlar Yesilbahar 50K 8/27
Kadikoy/Istanbul, TURKEY

Ulvaeus, Bjorn (Composer, Musician)
Gorel Hanser
Sodra Brobanken 41A
Skeppsholmen
Stockholm 11149, SWEDEN

Ulvang, Vegard (Skier)
Fiellveien 53
Kirkenes 9900, NORWAY

Ulyanov, Mikhail A (Actor, Director)
Theater Vakhtango
26 Arbat
Moscow 121002, RUSSIA

Umana, Christina (Actor)
c/o Staff Member *TV Caracol*
Calle 76 #11 - 35
Piso 10AA
Bogota DC 26484, COLOMBIA

Umbach, Arnie (Athlete, Baseball Player)
760 Moores Mill Rd
Auburn, AL 36830-6032, USA

Umbarger, Jim (Athlete, Baseball Player)
3909 W Harmont Dr
Phoenix, AZ 85051-5721, USA

Umberger, Andy (Actor)
c/o Claire Miller *Bauman Redanty & Shaul Agency*
5757 Wilshire Blvd
Suite 473
Beverly Hills, CA 90212, USA

Umberger, RJ (Athlete, Hockey Player)
1616 Woodland Hall Dr
Delaware, OH 43015, USA

Umbers, Mark (Actor)
c/o Nick Frenkel *3 Arts Entertainment Inc*
9460 Wilshire Blvd
7th Floor
Beverly Hills, CA 90210, USA

Umermoto, Nanako (Architect)
118 E 59th St
New York, NY 10022, USA

Umphlett, Tommy (Athlete, Baseball Player)
104 Berkley Rd
Ahoskie, NC 27910-9575, USA

Umphrey's McGee (Music Group)
c/o Staff Member *Paradigm (Monterey)*
404 W Franklin St
Monterey, CA 93940, USA

Umrao, Singh (War Hero)
Victoria Cross Assn
Old Admirally Building
London SW1A 2BL, UNITED KINGDOM (UK)

Umrigar, Jeannine (Stylist)
c/o Staff Member *Stockland Martel*
343 E 18th St
New York, NY 10003, USA

Unanue, Emil R (Misc)
Washington University
Medical School
Pathology Dept
Saint Louis, MO 63110, USA

Underhill, Barbara (Figure Skater)
c/o Staff Member *Guelph Storm Hockey Club*
55 Wyndham St N
Guelph, ON N1H 7T8, Canada

Underhill, Matt (Athlete, Hockey Player)
29 Draper St
Medford, MA 02155, USA

Underwood, Blair (Actor)
c/o Ron West *Thruline Entertainment*
9250 Wilshire Blvd
Ground Fl
Beverly Hills, CA 90212, USA

Underwood, Carrie (Musician)
c/o Ann Edulblute *XIX Entertainment - LA*
9000 W Sunset Blvd
Penthouse
Los Angeles, CA 90069, USA

Underwood, Cecil (Politician)
1578 Kanawha Blvd E Apt 1C
Charleston, WV 25311-2459, USA

Underwood, Jacob (Musician)
Trans Continental Records
7380 Sand Lake Road
#350
Orlando, FL 32819, USA

Underwood, Jay (Actor)
6100 Wilshire Blvd
#1170
Los Angeles, CA 90048, USA

Underwood, Matthew (Sportscaster)
c/o Glenn Hughes III *Gem Entertainment Group*
10701 Wilshire Blvd.
Ste. 1202
Los Angeles, CA 90024, USA

Underwood, Olen (Athlete, Football Player)
302 N Main St
Conroe, TX 77301, USA

Underwood, Pat (Athlete, Baseball Player)
708 Riverview Dr
Kokomo, IN 46901-7024, USA

Underwood, Ron (Director)
United Talent Agency
9560 Wilshire Blvd
#500
Beverly Hills, CA 90212, USA

Underwood, Sarah Jean (Actor)
c/o Matt Cohen *IAG Entertainment & Sports*
5189 Argonne Ct
San Diego, CA 92117, USA

Underwood, Scott (Musician)
Jon Landua
80 Mason St
Greenwich, CT 06830, USA

Underwood, Sheryl (Actor)
c/o Staff Member *Universal Attractions*
135 W 26th St
12 Floor
New York, NY 10001, USA

Ungaro, Emanuel M (Designer, Fashion Designer)
2 Ave du Montaigne
Paris 75008, FRANCE

Ungaro, Susan Kelliher (Editor)
Family Circle Magazine
Editorial Dept
375 Lexington Ave
New York, NY 10017, USA

Unger, Billy (Actor)
c/o Matt Luber *Luber Roklin Management*
8530 Wilshire Blvd
6th Floor
Beverly Hills, CA 90211, USA

Unger, Brian (Television Host)
c/o Staff Member *Extra (LA)*
Telepictures Productions
1840 Victory Blvd
Glendale, CA 91201, USA

Unger, Brian
5750 Wilshire Blvd.
Los Angeles, CA 90036

Unger, Deborah Kara (Actor)
c/o Sarah Jackson *Seven Summits Pictures
& Management*
8906 W Olympic Blvd
Ground Floor
Beverly Hills, CA 90211, USA

Unger, Garry D (Athlete, Hockey Player)
Banff Hockey Academy
PO Box 2242
Banff, AB T1L1B9, Canada

Unger, Jim (Cartoonist)
Universal Press Syndicate
4520 Main St
Kansas City, MO 64111, USA

Unger, Leonard (Diplomat)
31 Amherst Road
Belmont, MA 02478, USA

Ungers, Oswald M (Architect)
Belvederestr 60
Cologne 50933, GERMANY

Union, Gabrielle (Actor)
c/o Jeff Morrone *Jeff Morrone
Entertainment*
9350 Wilshire Blvd
Suite 224
Beverly Hills, CA 90212, USA

Union, Sarah (Actor)
c/o Jason Barrett *Alchemy Entertainment*
7024 Melrose Ave
Suite 420
Los Angeles, CA 90038, USA

Unkefer, Ronald A (Business Person)
Good Guys Inc
1600 Harbor Bay Parkway
Alameda, CA 94502, USA

Uno, Osamu (Business Person)
1-46 Showacho
Hamadera Sakai
Osaka 592, JAPAN

Unroe, Tim (Athlete, Baseball Player)
2719 S Joplin
Mesa, AZ 85209-2508, USA

Unruh, James A (Business Person)
5426 E Morrison Ln
Paradise Valley, AZ 85253, USA

Unseld, Wes (Athlete, Basketball Player,
Coach)
2210 Cedar Circle Dr
Catonsville, MD 21228-3747, USA

Unser, Al (Race Car Driver)
7625 Central N.W
Albuquerque, NM 87121, USA

Unser, Bobby (Misc, Race Car Driver)
7700 Central SW
Albuquerque, NM 87121-2113, USA

Unser, Del (Athlete, Baseball Player)
33516 N 79th Way
Scottsdale, AZ 85266-4244, USA

Unser, Johnny (Race Car Driver)
19 Lake Drive
Plainfield, IL 60594, United States

Unser Jr, Al (Race Car Driver)
Galles Racing
130 Lomas Blvd
Albuquerque, NM 87102, USA

Unutoa, Morris (Athlete, Football Player)
821B Country Club Pkwy
Mount Laurel, NJ 08054, USA

Upatnieks, Juris (Engineer)
Applied Optics
2662 valley Dr
Ann Arbor, MI 48103, USA

Upbin, Lori (Stylist)
37 Greenacres Ave
Scarsdale, NY 10583, USA

Upchurch, Rickie (Rick) (Athlete, Football
Player)
463 Hagens Aly
Mesquite, NV 89027, USA

Upham, Dr Steadman (Educator)
University of Tulsa
President's Office
Tulsa, OK 74104, USA

Upham, John (Athlete, Baseball Player)
1502 Pierre Ave
Windsor, ON N8X 4P5, Canada

Upham, Misty (Actor)
c/o Molly Conners *Rogues Gallery*
20 Clinton St
Suite C-7
New York, NY 10002, USA

Uphoff-Becker, Nicole (Horse Racer)
Freiherr-von-Lanen-Str 15
Warendorf 48231, GERMANY

Upshaw, Marv (Athlete, Football Player)
3851 Madrone Ave
Oakland, CA 94619, USA

Upshaw, Regan (Athlete, Football Player)
21300 Redskin Park Dr
Ashburn, VA 20147, USA

Upshaw, Willie (Athlete, Baseball Player)
Bridgeport Bluefish 500 Main St Attn:
Managers Office
Bridgeport, CT 06604-5136, USA

Upton, Arthur C (Physicist)
250 East Alameda Street
Apt 636
Santa Fe, NM 87501-6205, USA

Upton, Fred (Congressman, Politician)
2183 Rayburn HOB
Washington, DC 20515, USA

Upton, Justin (Athlete, Baseball Player)
7275 N Scottsdale Rd Unit 1017
Scottsdale, AZ 85253-2616, USA

Upton, Kate (Model)
c/o Lisa Benson *IMG Models (NY)*
304 Park Ave S
12th Floor
New York, NY 10010, USA

Upton, Melvin "B J" (Athlete, Baseball
Player)
1428 Harbour Walk Rd
Tampa, FL 33602-5971, USA

Upton, Melvin (B J) (Athlete, Baseball
Player)
1428 Harbour Walk Rd
Tampa, FL 33602, USA

Urb, Johann (Actor)
c/o Lena Roklin *Luber Roklin
Management*
8530 Wilshire Blvd
6th Floor
Beverly Hills, CA 90211, USA

Urban, Karl (Actor)
c/o Jennifer Rawlings *Principato/Young
Management*
9465 Wilshire Blvd
Suite 430
Beverly Hills, CA 90212, USA

Urban, Keith (Musician)
9579 Lime Orchard Dr
Beverly Hills, CA 90210, USA

Urban, Thomas N (Business Person)
Pioneer Hi-Bred Int'l
Capital Square
400 Locust St
Des Moines, IA 50309, USA

Urban, Tim (Musician)
c/o Simon Fuller *XIX Entertainment*
35-37 Parkgate Rd
32/33 Ransomes Dock
London SW11 4NP, UNITED KINGDOM
(UK)

Urbanchek, Jon (Coach)
University of Michigan
Athletic Dept
Ann Arbor, MI 48109, USA

Urbanek, Karel (President)
Kvetna 54
Brno, CZECHOSLOVAKIA

Urbani, Luca Dr (Astronaut)
18290 Upper Bay Rd
Houston, TX 77058-4122, USA

Urbani, Tom (Athlete, Baseball Player)
3347 Corinthian Ln
Auburn, CA 95603-9066, USA

Urbano, Mike (Musician)
c/o Staff Member *Creative Artists Agency
(CAA-LA)*
2000 Ave Of The Stars
Los Angeles, CA 90067, USA

Urbanova, Eva (Opera Singer)
National Theater
Narodni Divadlo
Prague 1, CZECH REPUBLIC

Urbanski, Douglas (Actor, Producer,
Writer)
Douglas Management Group (
9713 Little Santa Monica Blvd
Suite 218
Beverly Hills, CA 90210, USA

Urbina, Ugueth U (Athlete, Baseball
Player)
Venezuela

Urch, Scott (Athlete, Football Player)
645 Foxboro Dr
Avon, IN 46123, USA

Ure, Midge (Musician)
#8 Glenthome 115A Glenhome
Hammersm
London W6 0LJ, UNITED KINGDOM
(UK)

Urenda, Herman (Athlete, Football Player)
225 Upton Pyne Dr
Brentwood, CA 94513, USA

Uresti, Omar (Golfer)
2503 Pebble Beach Dr
Austin, TX 78747-1618, USA

Urguhart, Lawrence M (Business Person)
English China Clays
Business Park
Theale
Reading RG7 4SA, UNITED KINGDOM
(UK)

Uribe, Diane (Actor)
23874 Via Jacara
Valencia, CA 91355, USA

Uribe, Juan (Athlete, Baseball Player)
1817 Micanopy Ave
Miami, FL 33133-3329, USA

Urich, Justin (Actor)
Talent Group
5670 Wilshire Blvd
#820
Los Angeles, CA 90036, USA

Urie, Brendon (Musician)
c/o Staff Member *Fueled By Ramen*
PO Box 1803
Tampa, FL 33601, USA

Urie, Michael (Actor)
7135 Hollywood Blvd #1002
Los Angeles, CA 90046, USA

Urkal, Oklay (Boxer)
Bautzener Str 4
Berlin 10829, GERMANY

Urlacher, Brian (Football Player)
c/o Staff Member *Chicago Bears*
1000 Football Dr
Lake Forest, IL 60045, USA

Urmanov, Aleksei (Figure Skater)
Union of Skaters
Luzhnetskaya Nab 8
Moscow 119871, RUSSIA

Urmanov, Alexei
Luzhnetskaya nab. 8
Moscow, RUSSIA 119871

Urmson, Claire (Model)
c/o Staff Member *Ford Models (NY)*
238 E 4th St
New York, NY 10009, USA

Urness, Ted (Athlete, Football Player)
PO Box 267
Rose Valley, SK SOE 1MO, Canada

Urquhart, Brian E (Diplomat)
Howard Farms
Jerusalem Road
Tyringham, MA 01264, USA

Urrea, John (Athlete, Baseball Player)
75 E 24th St
Upland, CA 91784-8353, USA

Urseth, Bonnie (Actor)
c/o Staff Member *Gage Group, The (LA)*
14724 Ventura Blvd
Suite 505
Sherman Oaks, CA 91403, USA

Urshan, Nathaniel A (Religious Leader)
United Pentecostal Church International
8855 Dunn Road
Hazelwood, MO 63042, USA

Ursi, Corrado Cardinal (Religious Leader)
Via Capodimonte 13
Naples 80136, ITALY

Usachyov, Yuri V (Cosmonaut)
Potcha Kosmonavtov
Moskovskoi Oblasti
Syvisdny Goroduk 141160, RUSSIA

Usaher (Actor, Artist)
J Pat Mgmt
3996 Pleasantville Road
#104A
Dovaville, GA 30340, USA

Used, The (Music Group)
c/o Staff Member Freeze Artist
Management
27783 Hidden Trail Rd
Laguna Hills, CA 92653

Usery, William J Jr (Politician, Secretary)
1101 S Arlington Ridge Road
Arlington, VA 22202-1928, USA

Usher, Bob (Athlete, Baseball Player)
1022 N 5th St
San Jose, CA 95112-4413, USA

Usher, Paul (Actor)
c/o Staff Member Qdos Entertainment
8 King St
Covent Garden
London WC2 8HN, UNITED KINGDOM

Usher, Thomas J (Business Person)
USX Corp
600 Grant St
Pittsburgh, PA 15219, USA

Ushkowitz, Jenna (Actor)
c/o Jill Fritzo PMK/BNC Public Relations
(PMK-NY)
622 3rd Ave
8th Floor
New York, NY 10017, USA

Uslan, Michael (Producer, Writer)
Branded Entertainment
333 Crestmont Road
Cedar Grove, NJ 07009, USA

Usova, Maya (Figure Skater)
Connecticut Skating Center
300 Alumni Road
Newington, CT 06111, USA

Ustorf, Stefan (Athlete, Hockey Player)
8502 Waynesboro Way
Waynesville, OH 45068-7720

Ustvolskaya, Galina I (Composer)
Prospect Gagarina 27
#72
Saint Petersburg 196135, RUSSIA

Ut, Nick (Photographer)
Associated Press
Associated Press 221 S Figueroa St Ste
300 Attn Photo Dept
Los Angeles, CA 90012-2553, USA

Utay, William (Actor)
c/o Staff Member Days of Our Lives
3000 W Alameda Ave
Burbank, CA 91523, USA

Uteem, Cassam (President)
President's Office
Le Redult
Port Louis, MAURITIUS

Utley, Adrian (Musician)
Fruit
Saga Centre
326 Kensal Road
London W10 5BZ, UNITED KINGDOM
(UK)

Utley, Chase (Athlete, Baseball Player)
210 W Washington Sa APt 12SW
Philadelphia, PA 19106-3579, USA

Utley, Garrick (Correspondent)
ABC-TV
News Dept
8 Carburton St
London W1P 7DT, UNITED KINGDOM
(UK)

Utley, Mike (Athlete, Football Player)
P.O. Box 349
Orondo, WA 98843, USA

Utley, Stan (Golfer)
20701 N Scottsdale Rd
107-619
Scottsdale, AZ 85255-6413, USA

Utsman, Thomas E (Scientist)
56 Country Club Rd
Cocoa Beach, FL 32931-2002, USA

Utt, Ben (Athlete, Football Player)
3378 Habersham Rd NW
Atlanta, GA 30305, USA

Utzon, Jorn (Architect)
General Delivery
Hellebaek 3150, DENMARK

Uyeda, Seiya (Geophysicist, Physicist)
2-39-6 Daizawa
Setagayaku
Tokyo 113, JAPAN

Uzawa, Hirofumi (Economist)
Higashi 1-3-6 Hoya
Tokyo, JAPAN

v, Avram
Technion 1 Efron Street PO Box 9697
Haifa, Israel 31096, USA

V, Michael (Stylist)
c/o Staff Member Koko Represents
166 Geary St
#1007
San Francisco, CA 94108, USA

Vaamonde, Lisa (Stylist)
c/o Staff Member Team
423 W Broadway
4th Floor
Boston, MA 02127, USA

Vaca, Joselito (Soccer Player)
Dallas Burn
14800 Quorum Dr
#300
Dallas, TX 75254, USA

Vacano, Jost (Cinematographer)
Leoprechtingstr 18
Munich 81739, GERMANY

Vacanti, Charles A (Doctor)
Massachusetts University Med Center
Anesthesiology Dept
Worcester, MA 02139, USA

Vacariou, Nicolae (Prime Minister)
Romanian Senate
Piata Revolutiei
Bucharest 71243, ROMANIA

Vacariu, Alina (Model)
c/o Staff Member Elite Model
Management - Los Angeles
345 N Maple Dr
Suite 176
Beverly Hills, CA 90210, USA

Vaccaro, Brenda (Actor)
c/o Stephen (Steve) LaManna Innovative
Artists (LA)
1505 10th St
Santa Monica, CA 90401, USA

Vacendak, Steve (Athlete, Basketball
Player)
608 Gaston St
Suite 100
Raleigh, NC 27603, USA

Vachon, Christine (Producer)
c/o Staff Member Killer Films (US)
526 W 26th St
Rm 715
New York, NY 10001-5524, USA

Vachon, Louis-Albert Cardinal (Religious
Leader)
Seminaire de Quebec
1 Rue des Remparts
Quebec, QC G1R 5LY, CANADA

Vachon, Nicholas (Athlete, Hockey
Player)
1926 Curtis Ave Apt B
Redondo Beach, CA 90278-2313

Vachon, Paul (Wrestler)
RR 4
Mansonville, QC J0E 1X0, CANADA

Vachon, Rogatien R (Rogie) (Athlete,
Coach, Hockey Player)
2228 Glyndon Ave
Venice, CA 90291-4043

Vachon, Rogie (Athlete, Hockey Player)
Los Angeles Kings
1111 S Figueroa St Ste 3100
Los Angeles, CA 90015-1333

Vack, Peter (Actor)
c/o Raina Seides Baker Winokur Ryder
Public Relations BWR (BWR-NY)
292 Madison Ave
12th Floor
New York, NY 10017, USA

Vactor, Ted (Athlete, Football Player)
11504 Channing Dr
Wheaton, MD 20902, USA

Vadivukkarasi (Actor, Bollywood)
49/1A Sadulla Street
Chennai, TN 600017, INDIA

Vadnais, Carol (Athlete, Hockey Player)
Proulx, Vadnais and Associes
955 Rue Bergar
Laval, QC H7L 4Z6, CANADA

Vadsaria, Dilshad (Actor)
c/o Staff Member Kass & Stokes
Management
9229 Sunset Blvd
Suite 504
Los Angeles, CA 90069, USA

Vaduva, Leontina (Opera Singer)
Luisa Petrov
Glaburgstr 95
Frankfurt 60318, GERMANY

Vaea of Houma, Baron (Prime Minister)
Prime Minister's Office
Nuku'alofa, TONGA

Vagelos, P Roy (Biologist, Business
Person)
1 Crossroads Dr
500 Building A
Bedminster, NJ 07921, USA

Vaglica, Jim (Actor)
c/o Lisa Lobel Boston Casting Inc
129 Braintree St
Suite 107
Boston, MA 02134, USA

Vago, Constantin (Misc)
University of Sciences
Place Eugene Bataillon
Montpellier 34095, FRANCE

Vahi, Tiit (Prime Minister)
Coalition Party Eesti Koonderakond
Kuhlbarsi 1
Tallinn 0104, ESTONIA

Vai, Steve (Musician)
c/o Ruta Seopetys Sepetys Entertainment
Group
5543 Edmonton Pike
Suite 8A
Nashville, TN 37211, USA

Vaic, Lubomir (Athlete, Hockey Player)
Jeronymova 37 I 577
Liberic 46007, Czech Republic

Vaidisova, Nicole (Tennis Player)
c/o Staff Member IMG (Cleveland)
1360 E 9th St
Suite 100
Cleveland, OH 44114, USA

Vaidya, Daya (Actor)
c/o Rob D'Avola Rob DAvola &
Associates
9107 Wilshire Blvd. #405
Beverly Hills, CA 90210, USA

Vaidyanathan, Aparna (Actor, Bollywood)
520 19th Cross 14th Main
Benasankari 2nd Stage
Bangalore, KA 560070, INDIA

Vail, Eric (Athlete, Hockey Player)
10055 Piney Ridge Walk
Alpharetta, GA 30022-5065

Vail, Justina (Actor)
651 N Kilkea Dr
Los Angeles, CA 90048, USA

Vail, Mike (Athlete, Baseball Player)
2348 Aztec Ruin Way
Henderson, NV 89044-4496, USA

Vail, Thomas (Editor)
Cleveland Plain Dealer
Editorial Dept
1801 Superior
Cleveland, OH 44114, USA

Vails, Nelson (Athlete, Cycler, Olympic
Athlete)
7914 Tanager Ln
Indianapolis, IN 46256-1720, USA

Vaishnavi (Actor, Bollywood)
2 Sambandam Street
G N Chetty Road
Chennai, TN 600017, INDIA

Vaive, Rick (Athlete, Hockey Player)
574 Blenheim Cres
Oakville, ON L6J 6P6, Canada

Vajiralongkorn (Prince)
Royal Residence
Chirtalad a Villa
Bangkok, THAILAND

Vajna, Andrew (Andy) (Filmmaker,
Producer)
c/o Staff Member C-2 Pictures
2308 Broadway
Santa Monica, CA 90404, USA

Vajpayee, Atal Bihari (Prime Minister)
6 Raisina Road
New Delhi, Delhi 110011, INDIA

Valabik, Boris (Athlete, Hockey Player)
13 South Ave SE
Atlanta, GA 30315, USA

Valance, Holly (Musician)
c/o Andrew Edwards *Wishlab*
2225-A Hyperion Ave
Los Angeles, CA 90027, USA

Valandrey, Charlotte (Athlete, Football Player)
c/o Staff Member *ArtMedia*
20 avenue Rapp
Paris 75008, France

Valar, Paul (Skier)
34 Hubertus Ring
Franconia, NH 03580, USA

Valastro, Buddy (Chef)
Carlos Bakery
95 Washington St
Hoboken, NJ 07030, USA

Valbuena, Gary (Athlete, Football Player)
5040 Breckenridge Ave
Banning, CA 92220-7140, USA

Valderrama, Carlos (Soccer Player)
Colorado Rapids
555 17th St
#3350
Denver, CO 80202, USA

Valderrama, Wilmer (Actor)
c/o Glenn Rigberg *HYPHENATE*
9701 Wilshire Blvd.
10th floor
Beverly Hills, CA 90212, USA

Valdes, Ismael (Athlete, Baseball Player)
13732 SW 285th St
Homestead, FL 33033-5708, USA

Valdes, Jesus (Chucho) (Musician)
IMN
278 Main St
Gloucester, MA 01930, USA

Valdes, Marc (Athlete, Baseball Player)
Binghamton Mets PO Box 598 Attn:
Coaching Staff
binghamton, NY 13902-0598, USA

Valdes, Mark (Athlete, Baseball Player)
7519 Paula Dr
Tampa, FL 33615, USA

Valdes, Maximiano (Conductor)
Cramer/Marder Artists
3436 Springhill Road
Lafayette, CA 94549, USA

Valdespino, Sandy (Athlete, Baseball Player)
434 SE 3rd St
Dania, FL 33004-4014, USA

Valdes-Rodriguez, Alisa (Writer)
c/o Staff Member *Greater Talent Network Inc*
437 Fifth Ave
7th Floor
New York, NY 10016, USA

Valdez, Ismael (Athlete, Baseball Player)
4001 26th St
Vero Beach, FL 32960, USA

Valdez, Luis (Writer)
El Teatro Capesino
705 4th St
San Juan Bautista, CA 95045, USA

Valdivielso, Jose (Athlete, Baseball Player)
14 Rita Dr
Mount Sinai, NY 11766-2215, USA

Vale, Angelica (Actor)
c/o Staff Member *Televisa*
Blvd Adolfo Lopez Mateos 232
Colonia San Angel INN
DF CP 01060, MEXICO

Vale, Jerry (Musician)
40960 Glenmore Dr
Palm Desert, CA 92260, USA

Vale, Tina (Musician)
DreamWorks Records
9268 W 3rd St
Beverly Hills, CA 90210, USA

Vale, Virginia
4039 Edenhurst Ave
Los Angeles, CA 90039-1469

Valek, Vladimir (Conductor)
Na Vapennem 6
Prague 4 140 00, CZECH REPUBLIC

Valen, Nancy (Actor)
c/o Michael Livingston *Leavitt Talent Group*
8255 W Sunset Blvd
West Hollywood, CA 90046, USA

Valencia, Danny (Athlete, Baseball Player)
2289 NW 36th S
Boca Raton, FL 33431-5417, USA

Valensi, Nick (Musician)
c/o Staff Member *MVO Ltd*
307 Seventh Ave #807
New York, NY 10001, USA

Valent, Eric (Athlete, Baseball Player)
107 Lengle Ave
Wernersville, PA 19565-1331, USA

Valente, Catarina (Musician)
Villa Corallo Via ai Ronci
Bissone 6816, SWITZERLAND

Valente, Caterina (Musician)
ERAKI Entertainment
Casella Postale 91
6976 Castagnola
SWITZERLAND

Valenti, Carl M (Publisher)
Information Services
Dow Jones Telerate
200 Liberty St
New York, NY 10281, USA

Valentin, Barbara (Actor)
Hans-Sachs-Str 22
Munich 80469, GERMANY

Valentin, Dave (Musician)
Turi's Music Enterprises
103 Westwood Dr
Miami Springs, FL 33166, USA

Valentin, John (Athlete, Baseball Player)
Albuquerque Isotopes 1601 Avenida
Cesar Chavez SE
Albauauguergue, NM 87106-3930, USA

Valentin, Jose (Athlete, Baseball Player)
Fort Wayne Tincaps 1301 Ewing Street
Attn: Managers Office
wayne, IN 46802, USA

Valentine, Bill (Baseball Player)
15 Blue Ridge Cir
Little Rock, AR 72207-1901, USA

Valentine, Bill (Athlete, Baseball Player)
15 Blue Ridge Cir
Little Rock, AR 72207-1901, USA

Valentine, Bobby (Athlete, Baseball Player, Coach)
48 Chestnut Woods Rd
Redding, CT 06896-1819, USA

Valentine, Brooke (Musician)
c/o Staff Member *Virgin Records (NY)*
150 5th Ave
New York, NY 10010, USA

Valentine, Chris (Athlete, Hockey Player)
Freedom 55 Financial
1223 Michael St Suite 300
Ottawa, ON K1J 7T2, Canada

Valentine, Dan (Business Person)
C-Cube Microsystems
1551 McCarthy Blvd
Milpitas, CA 95035, USA

Valentine, Darnell (Athlete, Basketball Player, Olympic Athlete)
7546 SW Ashford St
Portland, OR 97224-6629, USA

Valentine, Donald T (Business Person)
Network Appliance Inc
495 E Java Dr
Sunnyvale, CA 94089, USA

Valentine, Ellis (Athlete, Baseball Player)
2708 Bridgemaker Dr
Grand Prairie, TX 75054-7262, USA

Valentine, Fred (Athlete, Baseball Player)
4838 Blagden Ave NW
Washington, DC 20011-3716, USA

Valentine, Gary (Actor, Comedian)
c/o Staff Member *Anonymous Content (LA)*
3531 Hayden Ave
Culver City, CA 90232, USA

Valentine, James (Musician)
c/o Staff Member *Creative Artists Agency (CAA-LA)*
2000 Ave Of The Stars
Los Angeles, CA 90067, USA

Valentine, James W (Biologist)
1351 Glendale Ave
Berkeley, CA 94708, USA

Valentine, Joe (Athlete, Baseball Player)
4168 Chiffon Ln
North Port, FL 34287-3236, USA

Valentine, Karen (Actor)
PO Box 1410
Washington Depot, CT 06793, USA

Valentine, Kym (Actor)
Julie Torrance Management
P O Box 463
Elwood, Victoria 3184, AUSTRALIA

Valentine, Raymond C (Misc)
University of California
Plant Growth Laboratory
Davis, CA 95616, USA

Valentine, Scott (Actor)
17465 Flanders St
Granada Hills, CA 91344, USA

Valentine, Stacy (Adult Film Star)
200 W Houston St
New York, NY 10014, USA

Valentine, Steve (Actor)
c/o Nicholas Bogner *Affirmative Entertainment*
425 N Robertson Dr
Los Angeles, CA 90048, USA

Valentine, Victoria
PO Box 12324
La Crescenta, CA 91224

Valentine, William N (Doctor)
2128 Quail Point Circle
Medford, OR 97504, USA

Valentine, Zack (Athlete, Football Player)
162 Harvest Rd
Swedesboro, NJ 08085, USA

Valentinetti, Vito (Athlete, Baseball Player)
271 Summit Ave
Mount Vernon, NY 10552-3309, USA

Valentino, Bobby (Musician)
c/o Staff Member *Island Def Jam Group*
Worldwide Plaza
825 8th Ave Fl 28
New York, NY 10019, USA

Valentino, Kristen (Stylist)
c/o Staff Member *Crews*
828 Clemont Dr
Atlanta, GA 30306, USA

valenzuela, Benny (Athlete, Baseball Player)
Bahia San Esteban #267
Sur Los Mochis
Sinaloa, Mexico, USA

Valenzuela, Fernando (Athlete, Baseball Player)
2123 N Beachwood Dr
Los Angeles, CA 90068-3403, USA

valera, Julio (Athlete, Baseball Player)
685 Urb Colinas
Verdes D4
San Sebastian, PR 00685, USA

Valeriani, Richard G (Correspondent)
23 Island View Dr
Sherman, CT 06784, USA

Valetta, Amber (Model)
c/o Daniel Spilo *Industry Entertainment Partners*
955 S Carrillo Dr
Suite 300
Los Angeles, CA 90048, USA

Valiant, Leslie G (Scientist)
50 Tyler Road
Belmont, MA 02478, USA

Valicevic, Rob (Athlete, Hockey Player)
54666 Sassafras Dr
Shelby Township, MI 48315-6902

Valiee, Bert L (Doctor)
300 Boyksti St
#712
Boston, MA 02116, USA

Valiquette, Jack (Athlete, Hockey Player)
28 Peacock Lane
Barrie, ON L4N 3R8, Canada

Valk, Garry (Athlete, Hockey Player)
681 Baycrest Dr
North Vancouver, BC V7G 1N7, Canada

Valle, Aurora (Actor)
c/o Staff Member *TV Azteca*
Periferico Sur 4121
Colonia Fuentes del Pedregal
DF CP 14141, Mexico

Valle, Dave (Athlete, Baseball Player)
2260 95th Ave NE
Clyde Hill, WA 98004-2516, USA

Valle, Hector (Athlete, Baseball Player)
HC 2 Box 19813
Cabo Rojo, PR 00623-9240, USA

Vallely, James (Jim) (Writer)
c/o Staff Member *Creative Artists Agency (CAA-LA)*
2000 Ave Of The Stars
Los Angeles, CA 90067, USA

Vallely, John (Athlete, Basketball Player)
2042 Commodore Rd
Newport Beach, CA 92660-4306, USA

Valletta, Amber (Actor, Model)
c/o Lee Daniels *Lee Daniels Entertainment*
315 W 36th St Fl 10
New York, NY 10037, USA

Valley, Mark (Actor)
c/o Christine Tripicchio *WKT Public Relations (WKT-LA)*
9350 Wilshire Blvd
Suite 450
Beverly Hills, CA 90212, USA

Vallez, Emilio (Football Player)
Chicago Bears
General Delivery
Polvadera, NM 87828-9999, USA

Valli, Frankie (Musician)
5603 Winton Ct
Calabasas, CA 91302, USA

Vallien, Bertil (Artist)
Roleks Vall
93 Visby
 621, SWEDEN

Vallina, Dea (Stylist)
14521 Crossway Ct
Chesterfield, MO 63017, USA

Vallone, Raf
Viale R. Bacone 14
Rome, ITALY

Valmon, Andrew (Athlete, Olympic Athlete, Track Athlete)
16403 Danforth Ct
Rockville, MD 20853-3278, USA

Valo, Ville (Musician)
HIM
P.O. Box 194
Helsinki FIN-00121, Finland

Valot, Daniel L (Business Person)
Total Petroleum
900 19th St
Denver, CO 80202, USA

Valtman, Edmund S (Cartoonist, Editor)
9 Rundelane
Bloomfield, CT 06002-1522, USA

Valverde, Jose (Athlete, Baseball Player)
773 W Raven Dr
Chandler, AZ 85286-4484, USA

Valverde, Rawley
15207 Magnolia #106
Sherman Oaks, CA 91403

Van, Allen (Athlete, Hockey Player)
4890 Ashley Ln
Unit 206
Inver Grove Heights, MN 55077, USA

Van, Joey
48607 Presidential Dr. #2.
Macomb Twp, MI 48044

VanAllen, James A (Physicist)
5 Woodland Mounds Road
RFD 6
Iowa City, IA 52245, USA

VanAllen, Richard (Opera Singer)
18 Octavia St
London SW11 3DN, UNITED KINGDOM (UK)

Van Allsburg, Chris (Writer)
c/o Houghton Mifflin Children's Books
222 Berkeley St 8th Fl
Boston, MA 02116, USA

VanAlmsick, Franziska (Franzi) (Swimmer)
Eichhom
Bizetstr 1
Berlin 13088, GERMANY

VanAmerongen, Jerry (Cartoonist)
2533 Washburn Ave S
MinneaQolis, MN 55416-4350, USA

Van Ark, Joan (Actor)
4556 Dundee Dr
Los Angeles, CA 90027, USA

VanArsdale, Dick (Athlete, Basketball Player)
6028 E Calle Tuberia
Scottsdale, AZ 85251-4229, USA

VanArsdale, Tom (Athlete, Basketball Player)
7510 N Eucalyptus Dr
Paradise Valley, AZ 85253-3319, USA

Vanasse, Karine (Actor)
c/o Lainie Sorkin Becky *Management 360*
9111 Wilshire Blvd
Beverly Hills, CA 90210, USA

VanAuken, John A (Misc)
Canadian Tennis Technology
PO Box 1538
Sydney, NS B1P 6R7, CANADA

VanBasten, Marco (Soccer Player)
AC Milan
Via Turati 3
Milan 20121, ITALY

Van Benschoten, John (Athlete, Baseball Player)
5918 Milburne Dr
Milford, OH 45150-4101, USA

VanBerg, John C (Jack) (Coach)
420 Fair Hill Dr
#1
Elkton, MD 21921, USA

Vanbiesbrouck, John (Athlete, Hockey Player, Olympic Athlete)
67960 Campground Rd
Washington, MI 48095-1217, USA

Van Boxmeer, John (Athlete, Hockey Player)
8033 E Santa Cruz Ave
Orange, CA 92869-5652

Van Brabant, Ozzie (Athlete, Baseball Player)
5389 William Dr
Lexington, MI 48450-8864, USA

Van Breda Kolff, Jan (Athlete, Basketball Player)
1102 French Town Ln
Franklin, TN 37067-4666, USA

Van Buren, Abigail (Journalist)
PO Box 69440
West Hollywood, CA 90069-0440, USA

Van Buren, Ebert (Athlete, Football Player)
2100 Highway 165 S
Monroe, LA 71202, USA

Van Buren, Jermaine (Athlete, Baseball Player)
557 Acree Ln
Columbus, OH 43228-8907, USA

Van Burkleo, Ty (Athlete, Baseball Player)
19681 Rabon Valley Rd
Grass Valley, CA 95949-8166, USA

VanCamp, Emily (Actor)
c/o Marc Hamou *Thruline Entertainment*
9250 Wilshire Blvd
Ground Fl
Beverly Hills, CA 90212, USA

Vance, Cory (Athlete, Baseball Player)
1321 Surrey Rd
Vandalia, OH 45377-1646, USA

Vance, Courtney B (Actor, Producer)
4710 Hillard Ave
La Canada Flintridge, CA 91011, USA

Vance, Cyrus
425 Lexington Ave.
New York, NY 10017

Vance, Ellis (Athlete, Basketball Player)
6 Carriage Way
Champaign, IL 61821-5119, USA

Vance, Eric (Athlete, Football Player)
17613 Archland Pass Rd
Lutz, FL 33558, USA

Vance, Judy (Stylist)
720 S Stone Ave
La Grange, IL 60525, USA

Vance, Kenny (Musician)
PO Box 116
Fort Tilden, NY 11695, USA

Vance, Robert S (Judge)
US Court of Appeals
1800 5th Ave N
Birmingham, AL 35203, USA

Vance, Sandy (Athlete, Baseball Player)
5863 Chelton Dr
Oakland, CA 94611-2423, USA

VanCitters, Robert L (Psychic)
University of Washington
Medical School
Physiology Dept
Seattle, WA 98815, USA

VanClief, D G (Race Car Driver)
Breeders Cup Ltd
2525 Harrodsburg Road
Lexington, KY 40504, USA

van Clse, Edward (Scientist)
15710 Bowsprit Ln
Houston, TX 77062-4518, USA

VanCulin, Samuel (Religious Leader)
All Hallows Church
43 Trinity Square
London EC3N 4DJ, UNITED KINGDOM (UK)

VanDam, Jose (Opera Singer)
Zurich Artists
Rutistr 52
Zurich, Gockhausen 8044, SWITZERLAND

Van Dam, Rob (Actor)
c/o Staff Member *Coast to Coast Talent Group*
3350 Barham Blvd
Los Angeles, CA 90068, USA

Van Damme, Jean-Claude (Actor)
Jean Claude Van Damme Foundation
4502 Wood St
Erie, PA 16509-1839, USA

Vande Berg, Ed (Athlete, Baseball Player)
4903 S Meadows Pl
Chandler, AZ 85248-5460, USA

Vande Hei, Mark T Lt Colonel (Astronaut)
1831 Raintree Cir
El Lago, TX 77586-5930, USA

Vande Hei, Mark T Ltcolonel (Astronaut)
1831 Raintree Cir
El Lago, TX 77586-5930, USA

Vandeman, George
1600 Waverly Rd.
San Marino, CA 91108

VandenBerg, Lodewijk (Astronaut)
Constellation Technology Corp
7887 Bryan Dairy Road
#100
Largo, FL 33777, USA

Van Den Berg, Lodewijk Dr (Astronaut)
9658 Leeward Ave
Largo, FL 33773-4423, USA

VandenBergh, M A (Business Person)
Royal Dutch Petroleum
30 Van Bylandtlaan
Hague, HR 2596, NETHERLANDS

Vanden Bosch, Kyle (Athlete, Football Player)
25 Governors Way
Brentwood, TN 37027-8926, USA

VandenBussche, Ryan (Athlete, Hockey Player)
Tri-County Pros Hockey School
150 Oak St Unit 14
Simcoe, ON N3Y 5M5, Canada

VanDenHoogenband, Pieter (Athlete, Swimmer)
PO Box 302
Amhem, AH 6800, NETHERLANDS

Vander, Jagt Guy (Misc)
Baker & Hostetler
1050 Connecticut Ave NW
Washington, DC 20036, USA

Vander, Musetta (Actor)
c/o Jeff Goldberg *Jeff Goldberg Management*
817 Monte Leon Dr
Beverly Hills, CA 90210, USA

Van Der Beek, James (Actor)
c/o Daniel (Danny) Sussman *Brillstein Entertainment Partners*
9150 Wilshire Blvd #350
Beverly Hills, CA 90212, USA

Vanderbeek, Matt (Athlete, Football Player)
4 Monstad St
Aliso Viejo, CA 95656, USA

Vanderberg Shaw, Helen (Coach)
Heaven's Fitness
301 14th St NW
Calgary, AB T2N 2A1, CANADA

Vanderbilt, Gloria (Writer)
c/o Staff Member *HarperCollins Publishers*
10 East 53rd St
c/o Author mail, 7th Floor
New York, NY 10022, USA

Vanderbundt, Skip (Athlete, Football Player)
4225 Los Coches Way
Sacramento, CA 95864, USA

Van Derbur, Marilyn (Actor)
195 S Dahlia St
Denver, CO 80246, USA

Vanderbush, Carin Cone (Athlete, Olympic Athlete, Swimmer)
47 Rose Dr
Highland Falls, NY 10928-4310, USA

Vandergriff Jr, Bob (Race Car Driver)
845 McFarland Rd.
Alpharetta, GA 30201, USA

Vanderhoef, Larry N (Educator)
University of California
President's Office
Davis, CA 95616, USA

Vanderkaay, Peter (Athlete, Olympic Athlete, Swimmer)
5787 Brewster Rd
Rochester, MI 48306-2317, USA

Vanderkelen, Ron (Athlete, Football Player)
5300 Vernon Ave S
Apt 102
Edina, MN 55436, USA

Vanderlip-Ozburn, Dolly (Athlete, Baseball Player)
N2844 Smith Valley Rd RR2
La Crosse, WI 54601-2935, USA

Vanderloo, Mark (Model)
Wilhelmina Models
300 Park Ave S
#200
New York, NY 10010, USA

Vandermeer, Jim (Athlete, Hockey Player)
17967 N 95th St
Scottsdale, AZ 85255-6086

Van Der Meer, Johnny
4005 Leona Ave.
Tampa, FL 33606

Vandermeersch, Bernard (Misc)
University of Bordeaux
Anthropology Dept
Bordeaux, FRANCE

Van Der Perren, Kevin (Figure Skater)
Emily Bruines
Dr W Drees laan 35
Goes 4463 XE, NETHERLANDS

Van der Pol, Anneliese (Actor, Musician)
c/o Victoria Morris *Kazarian Spencer Ruskin & Assoc.*
11969 Ventura Blvd
3rd Floor
Studio City, CA 91604, USA

Vanderpump, Lisa (Business Person, Reality TV Star)
c/o Bette Smith *Bette Smith Management*
499 N Canon Dr
Beverly Hills, CA 90210, USA

Vandersea, Phil (Athlete, Football Player)
34 Hunting Ave
Shrewsbury, MA 01545, USA

Vanderveen, Loet (Artist)
Lime Creek 5
Big Sur, CA 93920, USA

VanDerveer, Tara (Athlete, Basketball Player, Olympic Athlete)
1036 Cascade Dr
Menlo Park, CA 94025-6629, USA

Vandervoort, Laura (Actor)
c/o Staff Member *Levine Okwu Erickson Management*
6363 Wilshire Blvd
Suite 300
Los Angeles, CA 90048, USA

Vander Wal, John (Athlete, Baseball Player)
5142 Abbeydale Dr SE
Grand Rapids, MI 49546-7565, USA

VandeSande, Theo A (Cinematographer)
2337 High Oak Dr
Los Angeles, CA 90068, USA

Van Devere, Trish (Actor)
7036 Grasswood Ave
Malibu, CA 90265-4247, USA

Vandeweghe, Coco (Athlete, Tennis Player)
c/o Staff Member *Women's Tennis Association (WTA (UK))*
Palliser House
Palliser Rd
London W149EB, UK

Vandeweghe, Ernie (Athlete, Basketball Player)
2109 E 9th Ave
Denver, CO 91316-4424, USA

Vandeweghe, Kiki (Athlete, Basketball Player)
c/o Staff Member *Denver Nuggets*
1000 Chopper Cir
Denver, CO 80204, USA

VandeWetering, John E (Educator)
17 Cricket Hill Dr
Pittsford, NY 14534, USA

Van Dien, Casper (Actor)
c/o Barry McPherson *Agency for the Performing Arts (APA-LA)*
405 S Beverly Dr
Suite 500
Beverly Hills, CA 90212-4425, USA

Vandis, Titos
1930 Century Park W. #303
Los Angeles, CA 90067

Van Doren, Charles (Misc)
3 Bradford Rd
West Cornwall, CT 06796, USA

Van Doren, Mamie (Actor)
3419 Via Lido #184
Newport Beach, CA 92663, USA

Van Dusen, Fred (Athlete, Baseball Player)
319 N Rowan Ave
Los Angeles, CA 90063-2323, USA

Van Dusen, Granville
10974 Alta View Dr.
Studio City, CA 91604

VanDusen, Granville (Actor)
10974 Alta View Dr
Studio City, CA 91604, USA

Van Dyk, Paul (DJ, Musician)
c/o Joel Zimmerman *WME (WMA-NY)*
1325 Ave of the Americas
New York, NY 10019, USA

Van Dyke, Barry (Actor)
27800 Blythdale Rd
Agoura, CA 91301, USA

Van Dyke, Bruce (Athlete, Football Player)
143 Lakeview Dr
Mc Murray, PA 15317, USA

Van Dyke, Dick (Actor)
23215 Mariposa De Oro
Malibu, CA 90265, USA

Van Dyke, Jerry (Actor)
503 Jonah Ln
Malvern, AR 72104, USA

Van Dyke, Leroy
Rt. 1 Box 271
Smithton, MO 65350

VanDyke, Philip (Actor)
1464 Madera Rd #108N
Simi Valley, CA 93065, USA

Van Eeghen, Mark (Athlete, Football Player)
90 Woodstock Ln
Cranston, RI 02920, USA

Van Egmond, Tim (Athlete, Baseball Player)
8839 Callaway Rd
Gay, GA 30218-1817, USA

Vanek, Thomas (Athlete, Hockey Player)
9131 Curry Ln
Clarence CenterClarence CenterClarence Center, NY 14032-9505

Van Eman, Charles
12304 Santa Monica Blvd. #104
Los Angeles, CA 90025

Van Ert, Sondra (Athlete, Olympic Athlete, Snowboarder)
PO Box 671
Northport, WA 99157-0671, USA

Van Every, Jonathan (Athlete, Baseball Player)
555 Dixton Dr
Brandon, MS 39047-8125, USA

Van Exel, Nick (Athlete, Basketball Player)
3102 Noble Lakes Ln
Houston, TX 77082, USA

Van Galder, Don (Athlete, Football Player)
1611 Giles St
Austin, TX 78722-1242, USA

Van Galder, Tim (Athlete, Football Player)
11851 Charlemagne Dr
Maryland Heights, MO 63043, USA

Vangelis (Musician)
c/o Staff Member *Robert Urband & Associates*
8981 W Sunset Blvd #311
W Hollywood, CA 90069-1881, USA

Vangen, Scott D (Astronaut)
Nasa Johnson Space Center 2101 Nasa Pkwy Bldg 4
Houston, TX 77058-3607, USA

Van Gorder, Dave (Athlete, Baseball Player)
212 Black Eagle Ave
Henderson, NV 89002-9234, USA

Van Gorkum, Harry (Actor)
2552 Dearborn Drive
Los Angeles, CA 90068, USA

Van Gundy, Jeff (Sportscaster)
c/o Staff Member *WmE2 (WMA-LA)*
1 William Morris Pl
Beverly Hills, CA 90212, USA

Van Gundy, Stan (Basketball Coach, Coach)
329 Turtle Trl
Lake Mary, FL 32746-3619, USA

Van Halen (Music Group)
c/o Irving Azoff *Azoff Music Management/ Front Line*
1100 Glendon Ave
Los Angeles, CA 90024, USA

Van Halen, Alex (Musician)
c/o Irving Azoff *Azoff Music Management/ Front Line*
1100 Glendon Ave
Los Angeles, CA 90024, USA

Van Halen, Eddie (Musician)
10100 Santa Monica Blvd
#2460
Los Angeles, CA 90067, USA

Van Hekken, Andy (Athlete, Baseball Player)
4742 64th St
Holland, MI 49423-8980, USA

Van Heusen, Billy (Athlete, Football Player)
835 Hudson St
Denver, CO 80220, USA

Van Hoften, James D Dr (Astronaut)
131 Camelia Ln
Lafayette, CA 94549-2733, USA

Van Hollen, Chris (Congressman, Politician)
51 Monroe St
Suite 507
Rockville, MD 20850, USA

Van Hollen, Chris (Congressman, Politician)
1707 Longworth HOB
Washington, DC 20515, USA

Van Holt, Brian (Actor)
c/o Brad Schenck *Paradigm (LA)*
360 N Crescent Dr
North Bldg
Beverly Hills, CA 90210, USA

VanHorn, Buddy (Director)
4409 Ponca Ave
Toluca Lake, CA 91602, USA

Van Horn, Doug (Athlete, Football Player)
149 Feronia Way
Rutherford, NJ 07070, USA

Van Horn, Kelly (Producer, Writer)
c/o Staff Member *Mirisch Agency*
8840 Wilshire Blvd
Suite 100
Beverly Hills, CA 90211, USA

Van Horn, Patrick
9200 Sunset Blvd. #1130
Los Angeles, CA 90069

Van Horne, Dave (Sportscaster)
202 Bent Tree Dr
Palm Beach Gardens, FL 33418-3401, USA

Van Horne, Keith (Football Player)
c/o Staff Member *Dallas Mavericks*
2500 Victory Ave
Dallas, TX 75219, USA

Van Houten, Leslie
#W13378 Bed #1B314U CA Inst. for Women16756 Chino Corona
Frontera, CA 91720

Vanilla Fudge
141 Dunbar Ave.
Fords, NJ 08863

Van Impe, Ed (Athlete, Hockey Player)
Philadelphia Flyers Alumni Association
PO Box 302
Cherry Hill, NJ 08003, USA

van Johnson, Rodney (Actor)
c/o Staff Member *Passions*
4024 Radford Ave
Studio City, CA 91604, USA

Van Kemp, Merete
10000 Santa Monica Blvd. #305
Los Angeles, CA 90067

Van Kempen, Simon (Reality TV Star)
c/o Staff Member *Bravo (NY)*
30 Rockefeller Plaza
New York, NY 10112, USA

Van Keulen, Isabelle (Musician)
c/o Staff Member *Columbia Artists Mgmt Inc*
1790 Broadway Fl 6
New York, NY 10019-1412, USA

Van Kirk, Theodore (General)
1440 Parkview Blvd
Stone Mountain, GA 30087-6721, USA

Van Landingham, William (Athlete, Baseball Player)
3023 Old Hillsboro Rd
Franklin, TN 37064, USA

Van Landingham, William (Athlete, Baseball Player)
3023 Old Hillsboro Rd
Franklin, TN 37064-9544, USA

Vann, Marc (Actor)
c/o Staff Member *McCabe Group, The*
3211 Cahuenga Blvd W Ste 104
Los Angeles, CA 90068, USA

Vannelli, Gino
6118 SW Nevada Ct
Portland, OR 97219, USA

Vanner, Sue
26 Wellesley Rd. Cheswick
London, ENGLAND W4 4BN

van Nistelrooy, Ruud (Soccer Player)
c/o Staff Member *Manchester United PLC*
Sir Matt Busby Way
Old Trafford
Manchester M160RA, UNITED KINGDOM

Van Note, Jeff (Athlete, Football Player)
345 Hollyberry Dr
Roswell, GA 30076, USA

Van Ornum, John (Athlete, Baseball Player)
PO Box 26808
Fresno, CA 93729-6808, USA

Vanous, Lucky (Actor, Model)
28345 La Calenta Mission
Vlejo, CA 92692, USA

Vanover, Larry (Baseball Player)
801 Glenn Ct
Owensboro, KY 42303-0520, USA

Vanover, Larry (Athlete, Baseball Player)
3037 Sterling Ct
Owensboro, KY 42303-6393, USA

Vanover, Tamarick (Athlete, Football Player)
703 NW Wilson St
Lake City, FL 32055, USA

Vanoy, Vern (Athlete, Football Player)
3710 E 51st St
Apt 409
Kansas City, MO 64130, USA

Van Patten, Dick (Actor)
c/o Daniel Bernstein *Bernstein Entertainment*
12581 Venice #204
Los Angeles, CA 90066, USA

Van Patten, James
14411 Riverside Dr. #15
Sherman Oaks, CA 91423

Van Patten, Joyce
c/o Staff Member *Silver Massetti & Szatmary (SMS) Talent Inc*
8383 Wilshire Blvd
Suite 230
Beverly Hills, CA 90211, USA

Van Patten, Nels
14411 Riverside Dr. #18
Sherman Oaks, CA 91423

Van Patten, Tim (Actor, Director, Writer)
c/o Jeffrey Jacobs *Creative Artists Agency (CAA-LA)*
2000 Ave Of The Stars
Los Angeles, CA 90067, USA

Van Patten, Timothy
13920 Magnolia Blvd
Sherman Oaks, CA 91423

Van Patten, Vincent
13926 Magnolia Blvd
Sherman Oaks, CA 91423-1230

Van Peebles, Mario (Actor, Director, Producer)
c/o Vincent Cirrincione *Vincent Cirrincione Associates*
1516 N Fairfax Ave
Los Angeles, CA 90046, USA

Van Peebles, Melvin (Writer)
353 W 56th St Apt 10F
New York, NY 10019-3777, USA

Van Pelt, Alex (Athlete, Football Player)
7209 Quaker Rd
Orchard Park, NY 14127, USA

Van Pelt, Bo (Athlete, Golfer)
c/o Jim Lehrman *SFX Golf*
36855 W Main St Ste 200
Purcellville, VA 20132, USA

Van Pelt, Erika (Musician)
c/o Staff Member *19 Entertainment - LA*
9000 W Sunset Blvd #1574
West Hollywood, CA 90069, USA

Van Pier, Andre
P.O. Box 555
New York, New York 10156, USA

Van Poppel, Todd (Athlete, Baseball Player)
340 Springfield Bnd
Argyle, TX 76226-6848, USA

Van Praagh, James (Actor, Producer, Writer)
Spiritual Horizons
PO Box 60517
Pasadena, CA 91116, USA

Van Raaphorst, Dick (Athlete, Football Player)
720 Devon Ct
San Diego, CA 92109, USA

Van Ryn, Ben (Athlete, Baseball Player)
8911 Saddle Trl
San Antonio, TX 78255-2371, USA

Van Ryn, Mike (Athlete, Hockey Player)
Houston Aeros
5300 Memorial Dr
Houston, TX 77007-8200

Van Ryn, Mike (Athlete, Hockey Player)
17681 SW 54th Street
Southwest Ranches, FL 33331-2308

Van Sant, Doug G (Director)
c/o Gabrielle (Gaby) Morgerman *WME (LA)*
9601 Wilshire Blvd Fl 3
Beverly Hills, CA 90210, USA

Van Sant, Gus (Actor, Director, Producer, Writer)
c/o Gabrielle (Gaby) Morgerman *WME (LA)*
9601 Wilshire Blvd Fl 3
Beverly Hills, CA 90210, USA

VanSanten, Shantel (Actor)
c/o Loch Powell *Leverage Management*
3030 Pennsylvania Ave
Santa Monica, CA 90404, USA

Van Sant-Machado, Helene (Baseball Player)
1221 Marlon Ave
San Bernardino, CA 92407-1217, USA

Vansina, Jan M J (Historian)
2810 Ridge Rd
Madison, WI 53705, USA

Vanska, Osmo
Minnesota Symphony
Orchestra Hall
1111 Nicollet Mall
Minneapolis, MN 55403, USA

Van Slyke, Andy (Athlete, Baseball Player)
710 S Price Rd
Saint Louis, MO 63124-1867, USA

Van Susteren, Greta (Television Host)
c/o Staff Member *Fox News Channel (NY)*
1211 Ave of the Americas
Level C1
New York, NY 10036-8701, USA

Van Valkenberg, Pete (Athlete, Football Player)
3072 Ninebark Cir
Saint George, UT 84790, USA

Van Valkenburgh, Deborah
2025 Stanley Hills Dr
Los Angeles, CA 90046

VanValkenburgh, Deborah (Actor)
Gaye West
PO Box 1515
Studio City, CA 91614, USA

Van Varenberg, Kristopher (Actor)
c/o Jack Gilardi *ICM Partners (ICM-LA)*
10250 Constellation Blvd Fl 7
Los Angeles, CA 90067, USA

Vanvieren, Pete (Baseball Player, Sportscaster)
Atlanta Braves
12260 Magnolia Cir
Alpharetta, GA 30005-7234, USA

Van Vleet, Michael (Baseball Player)
118 Dreamfield Dr
Battle Creek, MI 49014-7846, USA

Van Vleet, Michael (Athlete, Baseball Player)
8462 Grapevine Cir
Mattawan, MI 49071-8433, USA

Van Vooren, Monique
165 E. 66th St.
New York, NY 10021

Van Wageningen, Yorick (Actor)
c/o Staff Member *Nine Yards Entertainment*
8530 Wilshire Blvd Fl 5
Beverly Hills, CA 90211, USA

Van Wagner, James (Athlete, Football Player)
5246 N Royal Dr
Traverse City, MI 49684, USA

Van Wieren, Pete (Baseball Player)
12260 Magnolia Cir
Alpharetta, GA 30005-7234, usa

Van Winkle, Travis (Actor)
c/o Scott Fish *Vital Management Group (VMG)*
5225 Wilshire Blvd #303
Los Angeles, CA 90036, USA

Van Wormer, Steve (Actor)
c/o Staff Member *Innovative Artists (LA)*
1505 10th St
Santa Monica, CA 90401, USA

Van Zandt, Caitlin (Actor)
Persona Management
40 E 9th St #11J
New York, NY 10003, USA

Van Zandt, Steven (Actor)
c/o Staff Member *Renegade Nation Holdings*
434 Sixth Avenue
Suite 6R
New York, NY 10011, USA

Van Zant, Donnie (Musician)
c/o Staff Member *Vector Management*
P.O. Box 120479
Nashville, TN 37212, USA

Vanzant, Iyanla (Television Host, Writer)
c/o Jerome Martin *Jerome Martin Management*
1655 N Cherokee Ave
2nd Floor
Hollywood, CA 90028, USA

Van Zee, Margie (Stylist)
17207 E Rand Dr
Fountain Hills, AZ 85268, USA

Van Zeeland, Kathy (Designer)
VZI Investment Corp
1359 Broadway
21st Floor
New York, NY 10018, USA

Vapors, The
44 Valmoral Dr. Woking
Surrey, ENGLAND

Varada, Vaclav (Athlete, Hockey Player)
9042 Stonebriar Dr.
Clarence Center, NY 14032

Varda, Agnes (Director)
Cine-Tamaris
86 Rue Daguerre
Paris 75014, FRANCE

Vardalos, Nia (Actor)
c/o Peter Safran *The Safran Company*
8748 Holloway Dr
Los Angeles, CA 90069, USA

Vardell, Tommy (Athlete, Football Player)
2424 E Ruby Hill Dr
Pleasanton, CA 94565, USA

Varela, Leonor (Actor)
c/o Adam Griffin *Kritzer Levine Wilkins Entertainment (KLWG)*
11872 La Grange Ave
1st Floor
Los Angeles, CA 90025, USA

Varga, Imre (Artist)
Bartha Utca 1
Budapest XII, HUNGARY

Vargas, Elizabeth (Television Host)
c/o Staff Member *ABC News*
77 W 66th St
3rd Floor
New York, NY 10023, USA

Vargas, Jacob (Actor)
c/o Matt Luber *Luber Roklin Management*
8530 Wilshire Blvd
6th Floor
Beverly Hills, CA 90211, USA

Vargas, Jason (Athlete, Baseball Player)
14775 Keota Ln
Apple Valley, CA 92307-5137, USA

Vargas, Jay R (General)
12466 Thombrush Court
San Diego, CA 92131-2251, USA

Vargas, Ramon (Opera Singer)
Columbia Artists Mgmt Inc
165 W 57th St
New York, NY 10019, USA

Vargas, Roberto (Baseball Player)
Chicago American Giants
Urb Runoz Rivera 24 Calle Brizaida
Guaynabo, PR 00969-3529, USA

Vargas, Valentina (Actor)
5 Rue Norvins
Paris 75018, FRANCE

Vargo, Ed (Athlete, Baseball Player)
101 Freedom Rd
Butler, PA 16001, USA

Vargo, Larry (Athlete, Football Player)
23337 S Colonial Ct
Saint Clair Shores, MI 48080, USA

Vargo, Tim (Business Person)
AutoZone Inc
123 S Front St
Memphis, TN 38103, USA

Varian, Hal R (Economist)
576 Del Amigo Rd
Danville, CA 94526-3215, USA

Varitek, Jason (Athlete, Baseball Player)
c/o Scott Boras *Boras Corporation*
18 Corporate Plaza
Newport Beach, CA 92660, USA

Varkonyi, Robert (Misc)
6Willow Ln
Great Neck, NY 11023-1139, USA

Varlamov, Sergei (Athlete, Hockey Player)
213 Germain St
Saint John, NB E2L 2G5, Canada

Varma, Indira (Actor)
c/o Tammy Rosen *Sanders Armstrong Caserta*
425 N Robertson Blvd
Los Angeles, CA 90048, USA

Varmus, Harold E (Nobel Prize Laureate)
Memorial Sloan-Kettering Cancer Center
1 Gracie Sq Apt 1E
New York, NY 10028-8001, USA

Varnado, Victor (Actor, Comedian)
New York Comedy Consultants
1600 Broadway #410
New York, NY 10019, USA

Varney, Pete (Athlete, Baseball Player)
14 Juniper Ridge Rd
Acton, MA 01720-2213, USA

Varo, Marton (Artist)
Phillips Gallery
PO Box 5807
Carmel, CA 93921, USA

Varone, Phil (Musician)
c/o Barbara Papageorge *Barbara Papageorge Publicity*
790 Amsterdam Ave
New York, NY 10025, USA

Varoni, Miguel (Actor)
c/o Oswaldo Pisfil *NCM Productions*
10770 NW 66 Th Street Suite 512
Miami, FL 33178, USA

Varrela, Leonor (Actor)
c/o Mimi DiTrani *Schiff Company, The*
9465 Wilshire Blvd
Suite 480
Beverly Hills, CA 90212, USA

Varrichione, Frank (Athlete, Football Player)
4118 Jefferson Pl
Bellingham, MA 02019-6305, USA

Varrichone, Frank (Athlete, Football Player)
RR 72 Box 319
Alton, NJ 03809, USA

Varshavsky, Alexander (Biologist)
California Institute of Technology
Cell Biology Dept
Pasadena, CA 91125, USA

Varsho, Gary (Athlete, Baseball Player, Coach)
11921 Starr Rd
Chili, WI 54420-9502, USA

Vartan, Michael (Actor)
c/o Stephen Hanks *Stephen Hanks Management*
252 N Larchmont Blvd #200
Los Angeles, CA 90004, USA

Vartan, Sylvie (Musician)
Scotti
706 N Beverly Dr
Beverly Hills, CA 90210, USA

Varty, Keith (Designer, Fashion Designer)
Bosco di San Francesco #6
Sirolo, ITALY

Varvatos, John (Designer, Fashion Designer)
John Varvatos
315 Bowery
New York, NY 10003, USA

Vasarely, Victor
83 rue aux Religues
Annet-sur-Marne, FRANCE F-77410

Vasary, Tamas (Musician)
9 Village Road
London N3, UNITED KINGDOM (UK)

Vasilak, Peg (Stylist)
5544 N Glenwood Ave
Chicago, IL 60640-1235, USA

Vasile, Radu (Prime Minister)
Premier's Office
Piata Vicotriel 1
Bucharest 71201, ROMANIA

Vasilyev, Vladimir V (Ballerina, Dancer)
Bolshoi Theater
Teatralnaya Pl 1
Moscow 103009, RUSSIA

Vaske, Dennis (Athlete, Hockey Player)
9236 Dunmore Dr
Orland Park, IL 60462-1152

Vasquez, Juan F (Judge)
US Tax Court
400 2nd St NW
Washington, DC 20217, USA

Vasquez, Junior (DJ, Musician)
Junior Vasquez Music
647 9th Ave #3
New York, NY 10003, USA

Vasquez, LaLa (Television Host)
c/o Stephanie Simon *Untitled Entertainment (LA)*
350 S. Beverly Dr #200
Beverly Hills, CA 90212, USA

Vasquez, Rana Mario (Publisher)
El Sol de Mexico
Guillermo Prieto 7
Mexico City, DF, MEXICO

Vasquez, Randy
10600 Holman Ave. #1
Los Angeles, CA 90024

Vasquez, Virgil (Athlete, Baseball Player)
32 Saint Francis Way
Santa Barbara, CA 93105-2552, USA

Vass, Irene (Stylist)
270 Park Ave
#8-D
New York, NY 10010, USA

Vass, Zita (Actor)
c/o Kim Matuka *Online Talent Group*
Prefers to be contacted via email or telephone
Los Angeles, CA 90069, USA

Vasser, Jimmy (Race Car Driver)
8605 Robinson Ridge Dr.
Las Vegas, NV 89117, USA

Vassey, Liz (Actor)
c/o Nevin Dolcefino *Innovative Artists (LA)*
1505 10th St
Santa Monica, CA 90401, USA

Vassilieva, Sofia (Actor)
c/o Jason Trawick *WME (LA)*
9601 Wilshire Blvd Fl 3
Beverly Hills, CA 90210, USA

Vassillou, George V (President)
PO Box 874
21 Academiou Ave
Aglandjia, Nicosia, CYPRUS

Vasu, P (Actor, Bollywood)
25 D Tilak Street
T Nagar
Chennai, TN 600017, INDIA

Vaswani, Vivek (Actor, Bollywood)
141 142 Dalamal Park
Cuffe Parade
Bombay, MS 400 005, INDIA

Vasys, Arunas (Athlete, Football Player)
2525 Hanford Ln
Aurora, IL 60504, USA

Vasyuchenko, Yuri (Ballerina, Dancer)
Bolshoi Theater
Teatralnaya Pl 1
Moscow 103009, RUSSIA

Vasyutin, Vladimir V (Cricketer)
Potcha Kosmonavtov
Moskovskoi Oblasti
Syvisdny Goroduk 141160, RUSSIA

Vataha, Randy (Athlete, Football Player)
36 Longmeadow Rd
Lincoln, MA 01773, USA

Vatcher, Jim (Athlete, Baseball Player)
16039 Northfield St
Pacific Palisades, CA 90272-4261, USA

Vatterott, Charles (Athlete, Football Player)
3708 W Pine Orchard Dr
Pearland, TX 77581, USA

Vaughan, Charlie (Athlete, Baseball Player)
5717 Brazilwood Ct
Harlingen, TX 78552-2027, USA

Vaughan, Denis E (Musician)
c/o Staff Member *Schofer/Gold Agency*
51 Riverside Dr
New York, NY 10024, USA

Vaughan, Greg (Actor)
c/o Alex Cole *Elevate Entertainment*
10100 Santa Monica Blvd.
Suite 300
Los Angeles, CA 90067, USA

Vaughan, Jimmie (Musician)
c/o Staff Member *Monterey International (Chicago)*
200 W Superior
Suite 202
Chicago, IL 60610, USA

Vaughan, Martha (Biologist)
11608 W Hill Dr
Rockville, MD 20852, USA

Vaughan, Peter (Actor)
International Creative Mgmt
76 Oxford St
London W1N 0AX, UNITED KINGDOM (UK)

Vaughan, Stoll (Musician)
c/o Staff Member *Paradigm (Monterey)*
404 W Franklin St
Monterey, CA 93940, USA

Vaughn, Bruce (Golfer)
5615 N Monroe St
Hutchinson, KS 67502-3251, USA

Vaughn, Charles (Athlete, Basketball Player)
P.O. Box 95
Cairo, IL 62914-0095, USA

Vaughn, Countess (Actor)
c/o Staff Member *Amsel, Eisenstadt & Frazier Talent Agency (AEF)*
5055 Wilshire Blvd
Suite 860
Los Angeles, CA 90036-6108, USA

Vaughn, Damian (Athlete, Football Player)
423 Danvers Ct
Orrville, OH 44667, USA

Vaughn, David (Basketball Player)
New Jersey Nets
390 Murray Hill Parkway
East Rutherford, NJ 07073, USA

Vaughn, Dewayne (Athlete, Baseball Player)
5501 NW 37th St
Warr Acres, OK 73122-2210, USA

Vaughn, Gregory L (Greg) (Athlete, Baseball Player)
10830 Sheldon Woods Way
Elk Grove, CA 95624-9630, USA

Vaughn, Jacque (Basketball Player)
Atlanta Hawks
190 Marietta St SW
Atlanta, GA 66049-7845, USA

Vaughn, Jimmie (Musician)
Mark I Mgmt
PO Box 29480
Austin, TX 78755, USA

Vaughn, John H (Johnny) (Athlete, Coach, Football Player)
Highway 6 W
Oxford, MS 38655, USA

Vaughn, Jonathan S (Jon) (Athlete, Football Player)
224 N US HIghway 67
Florissant, MO 63031-5904, USA

Vaughn, Kip (Baseball Player)
1820 Wildbrook Ct Apt C
Concord, CA 94521-1464, USA

Vaughn, Linda (Race Car Driver)
PO Box 352
Newville, PA 17241, USA

Vaughn, Matthew (Actor, Director)
c/o Naren Desai *Brillstein Entertainment Partners*
9150 Wilshire Blvd #350
Beverly Hills, CA 90212, USA

Vaughn, Maurice (Mo) (Athlete, Baseball Player)
Omni New York LLC 1 Dag
Hammarskjold Plz Bsmt C
NewYork, NY 10017-2201, USA

Vaughn, Ned (Actor)
James/Levy/Jacobson
3500 W Olive Ave
#920
Burbank, CA 91505, USA

Vaughn, Robert (Actor)
PO Box 2071
Los Angeles, CA 90028, USA

Vaughn, Terri J (Actor)
c/o Sandra Siegal *Siegal Company, The*
9025 Wilshire Blvd #400
Beverly Hills, CA 90211, USA

Vaughn, Thomas R (Athlete, Football Player)
860 E Linda Ln
Gilbert, AZ 85234, USA

Vaughn, Vince (Actor)
c/o Alan Nierob *Rogers & Cowan PR (LA)*
Pacific Design Center
8687 Melrose Ave, 7th Floor
West Hollywood, CA 90069, USA

Vaught, Loy (Athlete, Basketball Player)
1289 Perkins Ave NE
Grand Rapids, MI 49505-5625, USA

Vaugier, Emmanuelle (Actor)
c/o David (Dave) Fleming *Mosaic Media Group*
9200 W. Sunset Blvd
10th Floor
Los Angeles, CA 90069, USA

Vavra, Joe (Athlete, Baseball Player)
E4640 483rd Ave
Menomonie, WI 54751-5481, USA

Vayda, Brandon Michael (Actor)
c/o Omar Mayet *Gel Entertainment*
9255 W Sunset Blvd #803
Los Angeles, CA 90069, USA

Vaydik, Greg (Athlete, Hockey Player)
3211 Wessex Cir
Richardson, TX 75082-3113

Vaynerchuk, Gary (Business Person, Writer)
c/o Staff Member *Vaynermedia*
586 Morris Ave
Springfield, NJ 07081, USA

Vaziri, Khosrow (Wrestler)
c/o Eric Simms *ESS Promotions*
P.O. Box 52
Marlboro, NJ 07746, USA

Vazquez, Armondo (Baseball Player)
Indianapolis Clowns
160 W 85th St Apt 1K
New York, NY 10024-4410, USA

Vazquez, Javier (Athlete, Baseball Player)
1441 S Prairie Ave
Chicago, IL 60605-2886, USA

Vazquez, LaLa (Actor)
c/o Shannon Barr *Shannon Barr Public Relations*
1600 Rosecrans Ave
Media Center Bldg. 7, 4th Floor
Manhattan Beach, CA 90266-3708, USA

Vazquez, Yul (Actor)
c/o Sarah Fargo *Paradigm (NY)*
360 Park Ave S Fl 16
New York, NY 10010, USA

Veal, Coot (Athlete, Baseball Player)
238 Stonegables Dr
Gray, GA 31032-5526, USA

Veal, Donnie (Athlete, Baseball Player)
13032 E Powell Pl
Chandler, AZ 85249-2000, USA

Veale, Robert A (Bob) (Athlete, Baseball Player)
2833 Bush Blvd
Birmingham, AL 35208-2227, USA

Veals, Elton (Athlete, Football Player)
2981 Joyce Dr
Baton Rouge, LA 70814, USA

Veasey, Josephine (Opera Singer)
5 Meadow Biew
Whitechurch
Hunts RG28 7BL, UNITED KINGDOM (UK)

Vecchione, Mike (Scientist)
Nat'l Oceanic/Atmosphere Admin
14th & Constitution
Washington, DC 20230, USA

Vecsei, Eva H (Architect)
Vecsei Architects
1425 Rue du Fort
Montreal, QC H3H 2C2, CANADA

Vedder, Eddie (Musician)
c/o Kelly Curtis *Curtis Management*
1900 S. Corgiat Dr.
Seattle, WA 98108, USA

Vee, Bobby (Musician, Songwriter, Writer)
The Bobby Vee Connection
St Ives
Eden Road
Gordon, Berwickshire TD3 6JT, Scotland

Veerapha, P S (Actor, Bollywood)
Porur
Chennai, TN 600116, INDIA

Vega, Alexa (Actor, Musician)
S D B Partners
1801 Ave of Stars
#902
Los Angeles, CA 90067, USA

Vega, Antonio (Stylist)
c/o Staff Member *Zenobia Agency Inc*
PO Box 909
Groveland, CA 95321, USA

Vega, Makenzie (Actor)
c/o Ro Diamond *SDB Partners Inc*
1801 Ave of the Stars
Suite 902
Los Angeles, CA 90067, USA

Vega, Paz (Actor)
c/o Scott Henderson *WME (LA)*
9601 Wilshire Blvd Fl 3
Beverly Hills, CA 90210, USA

Vega, Suzanne (Musician)
c/o Staff Member *WME (WMA-NY)*
1325 Ave of the Americas
New York, NY 10019, USA

Vega 4 (Music Group)
c/o Staff Member *Paradigm (Monterey)*
404 W Franklin St
Monterey, CA 93940, USA

Vegas, Dirty (Music Group)
c/o Staff Member *Creative Artists Agency (CAA-LA)*
2000 Ave Of The Stars
Los Angeles, CA 90067, USA

Veil, Simone (Government Official)
11 Place Vauban
Paris 75007, FRANCE

Veils, The (Music Group)
c/o Staff Member *Paradigm (Monterey)*
404 W Franklin St
Monterey, CA 93940, USA

Veingrad, Alan (Athlete, Football Player)
614 SE 26th Ave
Fort Lauderdale, FL 33301, USA

Veisor, Mike (Athlete, Hockey Player)
16091 W Lakepoint Ct
Prairieville, LA 70769-4980

Veitch, Darren (Athlete, Hockey Player)
3603 E Utopia Rd
Phoenix, AZ 85050-3927

Vejar, Chico (Boxer)
56 Glenbrook Road
#3214
Stamford, CT 06902, USA

Vejtasa, Stanley W (Swede) (General)
1649 Summit Lane
Escondido, CA 92025-7535, USA

Velaquez, Nydia M. (Congressman, Politician)
266 Broadway
Suite 201
Brooklyn, NY 11211, USA

Velarde, Randy (Athlete, Baseball Player)
4902 Thames Ct
Midland, TX 79705-1796, USA

Velasquez, Cain (Athlete)
c/o Bob Cook *Zinkin Entertainment & Sports Management*
5 River Park Pl W
Suite 203
Fresno, CA 93720, USA

Velasquez, Guillermo (Athlete, Baseball Player)
13842 Clear Trail Ln
Houston, TX 77034-2158, USA

Velasquez, Jaci (Musician)
Jaci Inc
PO Box 3568
Brentwood, TN 37024, USA

Velasquez, Jorge
770 Allerton Ave.
Bronx, NY 10467

Velasquez, Jorge L Jr (Jockey)
770 Allerton Ave
Bronx, NY 10467, USA

Velasquez, Patricia (Actor, Model)
c/o Staff Member *Principal Entertainment (LA)*
1964 Westwood Blvd #400
Los Angeles, CA 90025, USA

Velazquez, Freddie (Athlete, Baseball Player)
Dominican Republic
Jose Amado Soler No. 70
Santo Domingo, USA

Velazquez, Freddie (Athlete, Baseball Player)
Jose Amado Soler No. 70
Santo Domingo, Dominican Republic

Velazquez, Gil (Athlete, Baseball Player)
9424 Wakashan Ave
Las Vegas, NV 89149-0501, USA

Velazquez, John (Horse Racer)
133 Avon Pl
West Hempstead, NY 11552-1703, USA

Velazquez, Nadine (Actor, Model)
c/o Courtney Kivowitz *Schiff Company, The*
9465 Wilshire Blvd
Suite 480
Beverly Hills, CA 90212, USA

Velez, Eddie (Actor)
c/o Staff Member *Stone Manners Salners Agency (LA)*
9911 W Pico Blvd Ste 1400
Los Angeles, CA 90035, USA

Velez, Fermin (Race Car Driver)
701 S. Girls School Rd.
Indianapolis, IN 46231, USA

Velez, Gloria (Model)
c/o Michael (Mike) Esterman
Esterman.Com, LLC
Prefers to be contacted via email
MD, USA

Velez, Lauren (Actor)
c/o Staff Member *Gersh (LA)*
9465 Wilshire Blvd
Suite 600
Beverly Hills, CA 90212, USA

Velez, Lisa Lisa (Musician)
c/o Staff Member *WmE2 (WMA-LA)*
1 William Morris Pl
Beverly Hills, CA 90212, USA

Velez, Mia (Stylist)
c/o Staff Member *Blink Management*
421 Washington Ave
#202
Miami Beach, FL 33139, USA

Velez, Otto (Baseball Player)
33 Villas de Cambalache
Rio Grande, PR 00966, USA

Velez-Mitchell, Jane (Actor, Correspondent)
c/o Staff Member *NS Bienstock Inc*
250 W 57th St
Suite 333
New York, NY 10107, USA

Velga, Carlos A Wahnon de C (Prime Minister)
Prime Minister's Office
Varzea CP 16
Praia, Santiago, CAPE VERDE

Velikhov, Yevgeni P (Physicist)
Kurchatovskiy Institute
Kurchatova Pl 1
Moscow 12182, RUSSIA

Velischek, Randy (Athlete, Hockey Player)
126 Ch du Lac Quenouville
Vai-Des-Lacs, QC J0T 2P0, Canada

Vel Johnson, Reginald (Actor)
DGRW
1501 Broadway
Suite 703
New York, NY 10036

Veljohnson, Reginald (Actor)
9637 Allenwood Dr
Los Angeles, CA 90046, USA

Vella, John (Athlete, Football Player)
1890 Saint George Rd
Danville, CA 94526, USA

Vellucci, Mike (Athlete, Hockey Player)
17302 Cameron Dr
Northville, MI 48168-3212

Veloso, Caetano (Musician, Songwriter, Writer)
Natasha Records/Shows
Rua Marquis Sao Vincente
Rio de Janiero, BRAZIL

Veltman, Martinus J G (Nobel Prize Laureate)
Sachubertiaan 15
Bilthoven 3723, NETHERLANDS

Velvet, Jimmy
PO Box 808
Lititz, PA 17543

Velvet Revolver (Music Group)
c/o Staff Member *RCA Records (LA)*
8750 Wilshire Blvd Fl 2
Beverly Hills, CA 90211, USA

Vemtrone, Raymond (Athlete, Hockey Player)
c/o Staff Member *Boston Bruins*
TD Banknorth Garden
100 Legends Way, Suite 250
Boston, MA 02114, USA

Venable, Mac (Athlete, Baseball Player)
107 Clark St
San Rafael, CA 94901, USA

Venable, Max (Athlete, Baseball Player, Coach)
107 Clark St
San Rafael, CA 94901-3604, USA

Venable, will (Athlete, Baseball Player)
107 Clark St
San Rafael, CA 94901-3604, USA

Venables, Terry F (Coach, Football Coach)
Terry Venables Holdings
213 Putney Bridge Road
London SW15 2NY, UNITED KINGDOM (UK)

Venafro, Mike (Athlete, Baseball Player)
15151 Whimbrel Ct
Fort Myers, FL 33908-1900, USA

Venasky, Vic (Athlete, Hockey Player)
4307 W 234th Pl
Torrance, CA 90505-4506

Venditti, Antonello
Via Zara 12
Rome, ITALY

Vendt, Erik (Athlete, Olympic Athlete, Swimmer)
22 Anchorage Rd
North Falmouth, MA 02S56-2216, USA

Veneruzzo, Gary (Athlete, Hockey Player)
185 Fans haw St
Thunder Bay, ON P7C 5T7, Canada

Venet, Bernar (Artist)
533 Canal St
New York, NY 10013, USA

Veneziale, Mike (Baseball Player)
110 Cloverdale Ln
Williamstown, NJ 08094-2341, USA

Vengerov, Maxim (Musician)
Lies Askonas
6 Henrietta St
London WC2E 8LA, UNITED KINGDOM (UK)

Venita, Carla (Musician)
3087 James Rd
Memphis, TN 38128, USA

Venitucci, Michele (Actor)
Carol Levi Co
Vla Giuseppe Pisanelli
Rome 00196, ITALY

Venkataraman, Prof. G. (Physicist)
Ex Vice Chancellor
Sri Sathya Sai Institute of Higher Learning
Prashantinilayam, Anantapur Dist.
A.P. 515 134, India

Venniraadai, Murthy (Actor, Bollywood)
44 4th Main Road
Kottur Garden
Chennai, TN 600085, INDIA

Venora, Diane (Actor)
Innovative Artists
1505 10th St
Santa Monica, CA 90401, USA

Venter, J Craig Dr (Scientist)
1718 Nordic Hill Cir
Silver Spring, MD 20906-5949, USA

Ventimiglia, John (Actor)
c/o Stacy Abrams *Abrams Entertainment*
5225 Wilshire Blvd #515
Suite 515
Los Angeles, CA 90036, USA

Ventimiglia, John
9150 Wilshire Blvd. #350
Beverly Hills, CA 90212

Ventimiglia, Milo (Actor)
c/o Jason Heyman *Creative Artists Agency (CAA-LA)*
2000 Ave Of The Stars
Los Angeles, CA 90067, USA

Ventimilia, Jeffrey (Actor)
c/o Staff Member *ICM Partners (ICM-LA)*
10250 Constellation Blvd Fl 7
Los Angeles, CA 90067, USA

Vento, Mike (Athlete, Baseball Player)
7142 Kendall Heath Way
Land O Lakes, FL 34637-7554, USA

Ventresca, Vincent (Actor)
Mindel/Donigan
9057 Nemo St
#C
West Hollywood, CA 90069, USA

Ventrone, Raymond (Athlete, Football Player)
c/o Staff Member *New England Patriots*
1 Patriot Pl
Foxboro, MA 02035-1388, USA

Ventura, Cassandra (Cassie) (Musician)
c/o Tommy Mottola *Mottola Company, The*
745 5th Ave #800
New York, NY 10151, USA

Ventura, Jesse (Politician, Talk Show Host)
c/o Barry Bloom *Braverman/Bloom Company*
14320 Ventura Blvd
Suite 632
Sherman Oaks, CA 91423, USA

Ventura, Robin (Athlete, Baseball Player)
1088 Newsom Springs Rd
Arroyo Grande, CA 93420-3618, USA

Ventura, Robin M (Baseball Player)
106 Dingletown Road
Greenwich, CT 06830, USA

Ventura-Manina, Virginia (Baseball Player)
PO Box 2306
Garfield, NJ 07026-4306, USA

Venturella, Michelle (Athlete, Olympic Athlete, Softball Player)
Iowa University Softball
219 Carver Hawkeye Arena
Iowa City, IA 52242-1020, USA

Ventures, The (Music Group)
11761 E Speedway Blvd
Tucson, AZ 85748-2017, USA

Venturi, Ken (Golfer)
161 Waterford Circle
Rancho Mirage, CA 92270, USA

Venturi, Rick (Athlete, Football Coach, Football Player)
1935 Sumter Ridge Ct
Chesterfield, MO 63017, USA

Venturini, Bill (Race Car Driver)
7621 Texas Trail
Boca Raton, FL 33487, USA

Venturini, Tisha (Athlete, Olympic Athlete, Soccer Player)
7101 Del Rio Dr
Modesto, CA 95356-9643, USA

Venus Hum (Music Group)
c/o Staff Member *Paradigm (Monterey)*
404 W Franklin St
Monterey, CA 93940, USA

Vera, Audry (Actor)
c/o Staff Member *Televisa*
Blvd Adolfo Lopez Mateos 232
Colonia San Angel INN
DF CP 01060, MEXICO

Veras, Quilvio (Athlete, Baseball Player)
4244 Vineyard Cir
Weston, FL 33332-2153, USA

Verastegui, Eduardo (Producer)
c/o Staff Member *Rain Management Group (RMG)*
1631 21st St
Santa Monica, CA 90404, USA

Verba, Ross (Athlete, Football Player)
3066 Arden Pl
St Paul, MN 55129, USA

Verbanic, Joe (Athlete, Baseball Player)
Chris Potter Sports 9722 Groffs Mill Dr
Mill Dr Ste 107
Owings Mills, MD 21117-6341, USA

Verbeek, Lotte (Actor)
c/o Lindsay Galin *Rogers & Cowan PR (NY)*
Prefers to be contacted via telephone and email
New York, NY, USA

Verbeek, Pat (Athlete, Hockey Player)
Tampa Bay Lightning
401 Channelside Dr
Tampa, FL 33602-5400

Verbeek, Pat (Athlete, Hockey Player)
Verbeek Farm RR 1
Wyoming, ON N0N lTD, Canada

Verbinski, Gore (Director, Producer)
c/o Dave Morrison *Anonymous Content (LA)*
3531 Hayden Ave
Culver City, CA 90232, USA

Verble, Gene (Athlete, Baseball Player)
633 Camrose Cir NE
Concord, NC 28025-3280, USA

Verboom, Hanna (Actor)
c/o Greg Siegel *WME (LA)*
9601 Wilshire Blvd Fl 3
Beverly Hills, CA 90210, USA

Verchota, Phil (Athlete, Hockey Player, Olympic Athlete)
PO Box 1181
Bemidji, MN 56619, USA

Verdi, Robert (Stylist, Television Host)
c/o Jeff Googel *WME (WMA-NY)*
1325 Ave of the Americas
New York, NY 10019, USA

Verdin, Clarence (Athlete, Football Player)
6221 Eastover Dr
New Orleans, LA 70128, USA

Verdugo, Elena
PO Box 2048
Chula Vista, CA 92012

Vereen, Ben (Actor, Dancer, Musician)
The Cooper Company
729 Seventh Ave
New York, NY 10019, USA

Vereen, Carl (Athlete, Football Player)
140 Connemara Rd
Roswell, GA 30075, USA

Veres, Dave (Athlete, Baseball Player)
871 Diamond Ridge Cir
Castle Rock, CO 80108-7812, USA

Veres, Randy (Athlete, Baseball Player)
9213 W Frank Ave
Peoria, AZ 85382-5364, USA

Vergara, Sofia (Actor, Musician)
c/o Evan Hainey *Untitled Entertainment (LA)*
350 S. Beverly Dr #200
Beverly Hills, CA 90212, USA

Verhoeven, John (Athlete, Baseball Player)
20805 Paseo De La Rambla
Yorba Linda, CA 92887-2429, USA

Verhoeven, Lis
Merzstrasse 14
Munich, GERMANY D-81679

Verhoeven, Paul (Director, Writer)
c/o Staff Member *Marion Rosenberg Office, The*
PO Box 69826
Los Angeles, CA 90069-0826, USA

Verhoeven, Peter (Athlete, Basketball Player)
12722 Fargo Ave
Hanford, CA 93230-9645, USA

Verica, Tom (Actor)
c/o Laura Fogelman *Independent Artists Agency*
9601 Wilshire Blvd.
Suite 750
Beverly Hills, CA 90210, USA

Veris, Garin (Athlete, Football Player)
23 Nichols Ave
Newmarket, NH 03857, USA

Verlander, Justin (Athlete, Baseball Player)
744 Grasslands Village Cir
Lakeland, FL 33803-5480, USA

Verma, Deven (Actor, Bollywood)
7B Todiwala Road
Pune, MS 400041, INDIA

Vermeil, Dick (Athlete, Coach, Football Coach, Football Player)
775 Fairview Rd
Coatesville, PA 19320, USA

Vermette, Antoine (Athlete, Hockey Player)
2475 Sherwin Rd
Columbus, OH 43221-3621

Vermette, Mark (Athlete, Hockey Player)
235 Hammell Road
Red Lake, ON POV 2MO, Canada

Vermilyea, Jamie (Athlete, Baseball Player)
7051 E Calle Arandas
Tucson, AZ 85750-2563, USA

Vernarsky, Kris (Athlete, Hockey Player)
24323 Tallman Ave
Warren, MI 48089-1847, USA

Vernon, Conrad (Actor)
c/o Ilan Breil *Mosaic Media Group*
9200 W. Sunset Blvd
10th Floor
Los Angeles, CA 90069, USA

Vernon, Kate (Actor)
c/o Staff Member *Shelter Entertainment*
9454 Wilshire Blvd.
Suite 715
Beverly Hills, CA 90212, USA

Vernon Jr, Gary Wayne (Gary Levox) (Musician)
c/o Staff Member *Lyric Street Records*
1100 Demonbreun Street
Suite 100
Nashville, TN 37203, USA

Veroni, Craig (Actor)
c/o Staff Member *Muse Artists Management*
401-207 W Hastings St
Vancouver, BC V6B 1H7, Canada

Verplank, Scott (Athlete, Golfer)
1850 W Waterloo Rd
Edmond, OK 73025-1801, USA

Ver Ploeg, Marcia (Stylist)
c/o Staff Member *VP Communications*
22 Gladbrook Rd
Pittsford, NY 14534, USA

Verraros, Jim (Musician)
PO Box 99
West Dundee, IL 60118

Verreos, Nick (Fashion Designer)
NIKOLAKI DESIGN
530 Molino St
Suite 108
Los Angeles, CA 90013-2275, USA

Verret, Claude (Athlete, Hockey Player)
Ligue Majeure de Hockey Olympique CP
88218 Succ Vai-Belair
Quebec, QC G3J 1Y9, Canada

Versace, Donatella (Designer, Fashion Designer)
Gianni Versace SPA
Via Manzoni 38
Milan 20121, ITALY

Verser, David (Athlete, Football Player)
2600 SW Arvonia Pl
Topeka, KS 66614, USA

Versini, Marie
23 res. Elysses 78170 La Celle-St Cloud, FRANCE

Verstappen, Jos (Race Car Driver)
Arrows Grand Prix
Leafield Tech. Centre
Oakland Pl. OX8 5PF, UNITED KINGDOM (UK)

Versteeg, Kris (Athlete, Hockey Player)
Thunder Creek Management
453-230 22nd St E
Attn David Kaye
Saskatoon, SK S7K OE9, Canada

Vertical Horizon (Music Group)
c/o Staff Member *Paradigm (Monterey)*
404 W Franklin St
Monterey, CA 93940, USA

Veruca Salt (Music Group)
Veruca Salt/Louise Post
P.O. Box 291105
Los Angeles, CA 90027, USA

Verveen, Arie (Actor)
c/o Scott Karp *Crystal Sky Pictures*
10203 Santa Monica Blvd
5th Floor
Los Angeles, CA 90067, USA

Verve Pipe, The (Music Group)
c/o Staff Member *Paradigm (Monterey)*
404 W Franklin St
Monterey, CA 93940, USA

Ververgaert, Dennis (Athlete, Hockey Player)
34484 Stoneleigh Ave
Abbotsford, BC V2S 8N5, Canada

Verve, The (Music Group)
c/o Staff Member *Paradigm (Monterey)*
404 W Franklin St
Monterey, CA 93940, USA

Verwey, Bob (Golfer)
I M G
1360 E 9th St
Ste 100
Cleveland, OH 44114, USA

Veryzer, Tom (Athlete, Baseball Player)
41 Union Ave
Islip, NY 11751-3919, USA

Verzi, Linda (Stylist)
2913 Payton Rd
Atlanta, GA 30345, USA

Vesey, Jim (Athlete, Hockey Player)
11 Ellwood St
Charlestown, MA 02129-3809

Vessey, Tricia (Actor)
c/o Staff Member *Brillstein Entertainment Partners*
9150 Wilshire Blvd #350
Beverly Hills, CA 90212, USA

Vest, Jake (Cartoonist)
PO Box 350757
Grand Island, FL 32735-0757, USA

Vest, R Lamar (Religious Leader)
Church of God
PO Box 2430
Cleveland, TN 37320, USA

Vestal, David (Photographer)
PO Box 309
Bethlehem, CT 06751-0309, USA

Veters, Michael (Race Car Driver)
Black Stallion Racing
9950 Downsville Pike
Hagerstown, MD 21740, USA

Vetri, Victoria (Actor)
7045 Hawthorn Ave
#206
Los Angeles, CA 90028, USA

Vetrov, Aleksandr (Ballerina, Dancer)
Bolshoi Theater
Teatralnaya Pl 1
Moscow 103009, RUSSIA

Vettel, Sebastian (Race Car Driver)
Postfach 1479
Heppenheim D-64632, Germany

Vetter, Jack (Athlete, Football Player)
312 N Grand St
McPherson, KS 67460, USA

Vettori, Ernst (Skier)
Fohrenweg 1
Absam, Eichat 6060, AUSTRIA

Vettrus, Richard J (Religious Leader)
Church of Lutheran Brethren
707 Crestview Dr
West Union, IA 52175, USA

Vey, Michelle (Stylist)
c/o Staff Member *Arlene Wilson Management*
807 N Jefferson St
#200
Milwaukee, WI 53202, USA

Veysey, Sid (Athlete, Hockey Player)
178 Ridgevale Dr.
Bedford, NS B4A 3S7, Canada

Vez, El
3322 Hamilton Way
Los Angeles, CA 90026-2112

V Gopalakrishnan (Actor)
11D4 Habibullah Road
T Nagar
Chennai, TN 600 017, INDIA

V. Gutterrez, Luis (Congressman, Politician)
2266 Rayburn HOB
Washington, DC 20515, USA

Viaene, David (Athlete, Football Player)
W9859 School Rd
Hortonville, WI 54944, USA

Vial, Dennis (Athlete, Hockey Player)
Aqua Valley Water Co Ltd
6998 Highway 1 Unit 4
Coldbrook, NS B4R 1B6, Canada

Vian, Sissy (Stylist)
c/o Staff Member *Michele Filomeno New York LLC*
515 Greenwich St Ste 503
New York, NY 10013, USA

Viardo, Vladimir V (Musician)
457 Piedmont Rd
Cresskill, NJ 07626, USA

Vichitra (Actor, Bollywood)
821 Jeevanandam Salai
Chennai, TN 600078, INDIA

Viciedo, Dayan (Athlete, Baseball Player)
1001 Brickell Bay Dr
Fl 9
Miami, FL 33131-4937, USA

Vicius, Nicole (Actor)
c/o Mimi DiTrani *Schiff Company, The*
9465 Wilshire Blvd
Suite 480
Beverly Hills, CA 90212, USA

Vick, Michael (Athlete, Football Player)
c/o Rick French *French/West/Vaughan*
185 Madison Ave
Suite 401
New York, NY 10016, USA

Vick, Roger (Athlete, Football Player)
12919 Windfern Rd
Apt 1902
Houston, TX 77064-3068, USA

Vickaryous, Scott (Actor)
c/o Staff Member *Artists Only Management*
10203 Santa Monica Blvd
Los Angeles, CA 90067, USA

Vickers, Brian (Race Car Driver)
BLV Motorsports
42 High Tech Blvd
Thomasville, NC 27360, USA

Vickers, Jonathan S (Jon) (Opera Singer)
Collingtree
18 Riddells Bay Road
Warwick WK 04, BERMUDA

Vickers, Kipp (Athlete, Football Player)
3224 Acacia Dr
Indianapolis, IN 46214, USA

Vickers, Steve (Athlete, Hockey Player)
- 238 Zokol Dr
Aurora, ON L4G OC2, Canada

Vickers, Steve (Athlete, Hockey Player)
209 Washington Ave
Batavia, NY 14020, USA

Vickrey, Robert (Artist)
10 Crvstal Lake Dr
Orleans, MA 02653, USA

Victor, James
1944 N. Whitley Ave. #306
Los Angeles, CA 90036

Victoria (Royalty)
Royal Palace
Kung Slottet
Stottsbacken
Stockholm 11130, SWEDEN

Victorino, Shane (Athlete, Baseball Player)
1997 Alcova Ridlle Dr
Las Vegas, NV 89135-1551, USA

Victorin (Ursache), Archbishop (Religious Leader)
Romanian Orthodox Church
19959 Riopelle St
Detroit, MI 48203, USA

Vida Blue (Music Group)
c/o Staff Member *Paradigm (Monterey)*
404 W Franklin St
Monterey, CA 93940, USA

Vidal, Christina (Actor)
c/o Bob McGowan *McGowan Management*
8733 W Sunset Blvd
Suite 103
West Hollywood, CA 90069, USA

Vidal, Deborah (Golfer)
2033 Paramount Dr
Los Angeles, CA 90068-3120, USA

Vidal, Jean-Pierre (Skier)
Ski Federation
50 Rue de Marquisats
BP 51
Annecy Cedex 74011, FRANCE

Vidal, Lisa (Actor)
c/o Bob McGowan *McGowan Management*
8733 W Sunset Blvd
Suite 103
West Hollywood, CA 90069, USA

Vidal, Raquel (Stylist)
c/o Staff Member *Anyway Productions*
870 Avenue of the Americas
New York, NY 10001, USA

Vidal, Ricardo J Cardinal (Religious Leader)
Chancery
PO Box 52
Cebu City 6401, PHILIPINES

Vidal, Rodrigo (Actor)
c/o Staff Member *Televisa*
Blvd Adolfo Lopez Mateos 232
Colonia San Angel INN
DF CP 01060, MEXICO

Vidali, Lynn (Swimmer)
14750 Mosegard
Morgan Hills, CA 95037, USA

Vider, Ricky (Stylist)
c/o Staff Member *Walter Schupfer Management Corp*
413 W 14th St
3rd Floor
New York, NY 10014, USA

Vidmar, Peter (Athlete, Gymnast, Olympic Athlete)
18 Downfield Way
Trabuco Canyon, CA 92679-5004, USA

Vidrine, David M (Astronaut)
12821 N Meadview Way
Oro Val lev, AZ 85755-6635, USA

Vidro, Jose A C (Athlete, Baseball Player)
PO Box 385
Sabana Grande, PR 00637-0385, USA

Vie, Richard C (Business Person)
PO Box 191
Lake Forest, IL 60045, USA

Viehboeck, Franz (Cosmonaut)
Brunnerbergstr 3021
Perchtoldsdorf 2380, AUSTRIA

Vieillard, Roger (Artist)
7 Rue de l'Estrapade
Paris 75005, FRANCE

Vieira, Meredith (Game Show Host, Television Host)
Meredith Vieira Productions
888 Seventh Ave
New York, NY 10106, USA

Vieira, Patrick (Soccer Player)
Juventus FC
Corso Galileo Ferraris 32
Turin 10128, ITALY

Vieluf, Vince (Actor)
c/o Tammy Rosen *Sanders Armstrong Caserta*
425 N Robertson Blvd
Los Angeles, CA 90048, USA

Vien, Dominique (Stylist)
c/o Staff Member *Judy Inc*
1 Yorkville Ave
Toronto ON M4W 1L1, Canada

Viener, John (Actor)
c/o Kevin Crotty *ICM Partners (ICM-LA)*
10250 Constellation Blvd Fl 7
Los Angeles, CA 90067, USA

Viera, Joey
4253 Navajo Ave.
No. Hollywood, CA 91602

Viereck, Peter (Writer)
1346 Murrell Ave
Columbus, OH 43212, USA

Viertel, Peter Wyhergut
7250 Klosters
Grisons, SWITZERLAND

Vieth, Michelle (Actor)
c/o Staff Member *Televisa*
Blvd Adolfo Lopez Mateos 232
Colonia San Angel INN
DF CP 01060, MEXICO

View, The (Music Group)
c/o Staff Member *Paradigm (Monterey)*
404 W Franklin St
Monterey, CA 93940, USA

Vieyra, Veronica (Actor)
c/o Staff Member *Telefe - Argentina*
Pavon 2444 (C1248AAT)
Buenos Aires, ARGENTINA

Vig, Butch (Musician)
c/o Staff Member *Borman Entertainment (TN)*
4322 Harding Pike #429
Nashville, TN 37205, USA

Vigman, Gillian (Actor)
c/o Jeanne Newman *Hansen, Jacobson, Teller, Hoberman, Newman, Warren & Richman*
450 N Roxbury Dr
8th Floor
Beverly Hills, CA 90210, USA

Vigneault, Alain (Athlete, Coach, Hockey Player)
Vancouver Canucks 800 Griffiths Way
Attn: Coaching Staff
Vancouver, BC V6B 6Gl, Canada

Vigneron, Thierry (Athlete, Track Athlete)
Adidas USA
5675 N Blackstock Road
Spartanburg, SC 29303, USA

Vignesh (Actor, Bollywood)
AP 210 9th Street
2nd Sector
Chennai, TN 600078, INDIA

Vigoda, Abe (Actor)
c/o Staff Member *Cunningham Escott Slevin & Doherty (CESD-LA)*
10635 Santa Monica Blvd
130
Los Angeles, CA 90025, USA

Vigorito, Tommy (Athlete, Football Player)
19 Garden Pl
Pompton Plains, NJ 07444-1409, USA

Viguerie, Richard
7777 Leesburg Pike
Falls Church, VA 22043

Vijay, S A (Actor, Bollywood)
64 Kaveri Street
Saligramam
Chennai, TN 600093, INDIA

Vijayakanth (Actor, Bollywood)
54 Kannambal Street
Kannapiran Colony Saligramam
Chennai, TN 600093, INDIA

Vijaya K R (Actor, Bollywood)
9 Raman Street
Chennai, TN 600018, INDIA

Vijayakumar, Manjula (Actor, Bollywood)
236 & 237 8th Street
Asthalakshmi Nagar
Chennai, TN 600116, INDIA

Vila, Bob (Actor, Producer, Television Host)
Vila Ventures
162 Fifth Ave, Suite 901
Attn: Agnieszka
New York, NY 10010, USA

Vilanch, Bruce (Comedian, Writer)
c/o Joan Hyler *Hyler Management*
20 Ocean Park Blvd
Suite 25
Santa Monica, CA 90405, USA

Vilanich, Bruce (Comedian)
c/o Staff Member *WmE2 (WMA-LA)*
1 William Morris Pl
Beverly Hills, CA 90212, USA

Vilar, Tracy (Actor)
c/o Doug Wald *Anonymous Content (LA)*
3531 Hayden Ave
Culver City, CA 90232, USA

Vilas, Guillermo
86 av. Foch F-75116
Paris, FRANCE

Vilasuso, Jordi (Actor)
c/o Jeb Brandon *Kritzer Levine Wilkins Entertainment (KLWG)*
11872 La Grange Ave
1st Floor
Los Angeles, CA 90025, USA

Vilasuso, Jordie (Actor)
c/o Staff Member *Innovative Artists (LA)*
1505 10th St
Santa Monica, CA 90401, USA

Vilella, Edward
905 Lincoln Blvd.
Miami, FL 33139

Vilgraln, Claude (Athlete, Hockey Player)
Playworks 85 Douglasdale Cres SE
Calgary, AB T2Z 3B3, Canada

Viljoen, Marais (President)
PO Box 5555
Pretoria 0001, SOUTH AFRICA

Villa, Aston (Athlete, Soccer Player)
Aston Villa FC
Villa Park
Birmingham B6 6HE, UK

Villacis, Eduardo (Athlete, Baseball Player, Coach)
Casper Rockies
P.O. Box 1293
Attn: Coaching Staff
Casper, WY 82602, USA

Villacorta (Stylist)
c/o Staff Member *Action Agency Stylists*
8424 Santa Monica Blvd
West Hollywood, CA 90069, USA

Villa-Cryan, Marge (Athlete, Baseball Player)
16305 Summershade Dr
La Mirada, CA 90638-2742, USA

Villafuerte, Brandon (Athlete, Baseball Player)
P.O. Box 188
North Bridgton, ME 04057-0188, USA

Villalon, Jade Valerie (Musician)
c/o Staff Member *Universal Records*
825 8th Avenue
New York, NY 10019, USA

Villano, Mike (Baseball Player)
Bowman
1041 South Dr
Mt Pleasant, MI 48858-2856, USA

Villanueva, Carlos (Athlete)
c/o Staff Member *SFX Sports Management*
5335 Wisconsin Ave NW #850
Washington, DC 20015, USA

Villanueva, Charlie (Athlete, Basketball Player)
c/o Jeff Schwartz *Excel Sports Management*
9665 Wilshire Blvd #500
Los Angeles, CA 90212, USA

Villanueva, Danny (Athlete, Football Player)
P.O. Box 258
Somis, CA 93066, USA

Villapiano, Phillip J (Phil) (Athlete, Football Player)
21 Riverside Dr
Rumson, NJ 07760, USA

Villaraigosa, Antonio (Politician)
City of Los Angeles
200 N Spring St #303
Los Angeles, CA 90012, USA

Villari, Guy (Musician)
293 Airport Road
Liberty, NY 12754, USA

Villarrial, Chris (Athlete, Football Player)
254 Hidden Meadow Ln
Ebensburg, PA 15931, USA

Villarroel, Vernoica (Opera Singer)
Columbia Artists Mgmt Inc
165 W 57th St
New York, NY 10019, USA

Villegas, Camilo (Athlete, Golfer)
c/o Staff Member *IMG Miami*
Miami, FL, USA

Villella, Edward J (Ballerina, Choreographer)
Miami City Ballet
2200 Liberty Ave
Miami Beach, FL 33139, USA

Villemure, Gilles (Athlete, Hockey Player)
38 Grey Ln
Levittown, NV 11756-4498, USA

Villeneuve, Jacques (Race Car Driver)
British American Racing
PO Box 5014
Brackley
Northamptonshire NN13 7YY, UNITED
KINGDOM (UK)

Villet, Grey (Photographer)
General Delivery
Shushan, NY 12873-9999, USA

Villiers, Christopher (Actor)
c/o Staff Member *Katie Threlfall
Associates*
2A Gladstone Rd
London SW19 1QT, UNITED KINGDOM
(UK)

Villone, Ron (Athlete, Baseball Player)
3 Schnidler Ct
Upper Saddle River, NJ 07458-2363, USA

Viloria, Brian (Boxer)

Vilsack, Thomas (Politician)
2229 Bancroft Pl NW Apt 101
Washington, DC 20008-4026, USA

Viltz, Theo (Athlete, Football Player)
2729 E De Soto St
Long Beach, CA 90814, USA

Vimond, Paul M (Architect)
91 Ave Niel
Paris 75017, USA

Vina, Fernando (Athlete, Baseball Player)
11703 Colony Rd
Galt, CA 95632-8547, USA

Vinatieri, Adam (Athlete, Football Player)
12850 Horseferry Rd
Carmel, IN 46032, USA

Vince, Pruitt Taylor (Actor)
c/o Joanna (Joanie) Burstein *Burstein
Company, The*
15304 Sunset Blvd
suite 208
Pacific Palisades, CA 90272, USA

Vince, Taylor (Misc)
20160 NW 9th Dr
Pembroke Pines, FL 33029, USA

Vincelette, Dan (Athlete, Hockey Player)
1345 Rue Bernier RR 3
Acton Vale, QC J0H lAO, Canada

Vincent, Brooke (Actor)
c/o Staff Member *Laine Management*
Laine House
131 victoria road
Salford M6 8LF, UNITED KINGDOM

Vincent, Cerina (Actor)
c/o Adam Seid *Bohemia Group*
1680 Vine St Ste 216
Los Angeles, CA 90028, USA

Vincent, Christian (Actor)
c/o Staff Member *Noah's Arc*
75 Charles Rowen House
Merlin Street
London WC1X OEJ, UNITED KINGDOM

Vincent, Fay (Athlete, Baseball Player)
290 Harbor Drive
Stamford, CT 32963-3702, USA

Vincent, Jan-Michael (Actor, Producer)
c/o Staff Member *Genesis Creations*
Contact through website
unknown, CA 00000, USA

Vincent, Jay (Athlete, Basketball Player)
P.O. Box 27459
Lansing, MI 48823-6722, USA

Vincent, June
1541 Via Entrada del Lago
Lake San Marcos, CA 92069

Vincent, Marjorie
1325 Boardwalk
Atlantic City, NJ 08401

Vincent, Rhonda (Musician)
c/o Scott Clayton *Creative Artists Agency
(CAA-TN)*
3310 West End Ave
5th Floor
Nashville, TN 37203, USA

Vincent, Richard F (Misc)
House of Lords
Westminster
London SW1A 0PW, UNITED KINGDOM
(UK)

Vincent, Rick (Musician, Songwriter,
Writer)
Carter Career Mgmt
1028 18th Ave S
#B
Nashville, TN 37212, USA

Vincent, Sam (Athlete, Basketball Player)
6727 Fairway Cove Dr
Orlando, FL 32835, USA

Vincent, Troy (Athlete, Football Player)
18900 Longhouse Pl
Leesburg, VA 20176, USA

Vincent, Virginia (Actor)
1001 Hammond St
Los Angeles, CA 90069, USA

Vinci, Charles (Athlete, Olympic Athlete,
Weightlifter)
10915 Burns Ave
Elyria, OH 44035-7515, USA

Vinci, Vince (Horse Racer)
9 Summit Dr
Denville, NJ 07834-2312, USA

Vincz, Melanie (Actor)
2212 Earle Court
Redondo Beach, CA 90278, USA

Vineetha (Actor, Bollywood)
Flat No 3B Chandrika Apartments
5 & 6 Ashok Avenue Directors Colony
Kodambakkam
Chennai, TN 600024, INDIA

Vinegrad, Kat (Stylist)
c/o Staff Member *Photogenics Media*
8549 Higuera St
Building B
Culver City, CA 90232, USA

Vines, C Jerry (Religious Leader)
First Baptist Church
124 W Ashley St
Jacksonville, FL 32202, USA

Vines, Ellsworth
4680 Irvine Blvd. #203
Irvine, CA 92620

Vines, Mark (Athlete, Hockey Player)
75 Hazelglen Dr
Kitchener, ON N2M 2E2, Canada

Vines, The (Music Group)
c/o Rick Roskin *Creative Artists Agency
(CAA-LA)*
2000 Ave Of The Stars
Los Angeles, CA 90067, USA

Vineyard, Dave (Athlete, Baseball Player)
1850 Tariff Rd
Left Hand, WV 25251-9542, USA

Vineyard, Merriwell (General)
1803 Brewton Ct
Wilmington, NC 28403-5372, USA

Vinge, Vernor (Writer)
Tom Doherty Associates, LLC
175 Fifth Ave
New York, NY 10010, USA

Vining, David (Doctor, Scientist)
1955 Greenberry Road
Baltimore, MD 21209-4555, USA

Vining, Ken (Athlete, Baseball Player)
517 Mount Elon Church
Rd
Hopkins, SC 29061-8666, USA

Vinith, R (Actor, Bollywood)
Flat G 1
68 Halls Road Kilpauk
Chennai, TN 600010, INDIA

Vinnie (Artist, Music Group)
International Creative Mgmt
8942 Wilshire Blvd #219
Beverly Hills, CA 90211, USA

Vinogradov, Oleg M (Ballerina)
Mariinsky Theater
Teatralnaya Square 1
Saint Petersburg 190000, RUSSIA

Vinoly, Rafael (Architect)
1016 5th Ave
New York, NY 10028, USA

Vinothini (Actor, Bollywood)
3 Alagar Perumal Koil Street
Chennai, TN 600026, INDIA

Vinson, Charlie (Athlete, Baseball Player)
3821 Walters Ln
District Heights, MD 20747-3943, USA

Vinson, Fernandus (Athlete, Football
Player)
6572 Glenwood Ave
Apt 221
Raleigh, NC 27612, USA

Vinson, Fred (Athlete, Basketball Player)
13701 Marina Pointe Dr
Apt 304
Marina Del Rey, CA 90302-1426, USA

Vinson, Fred (Athlete, Football Player)
11220 NE 53rd St
Kirkland, WA 98033, USA

Vinson, James S (Educator)
University of Evansville
President's Office
Evansville, IN 47722, USA

Vint, Jesse
10637 Burbank Blvd
No. Hollywood, CA 91601

Vint, Jesse Lee III (Actor)
Film Artists
13563 1/2 Ventura Blvd #200
Sherman Oaks, CA 91423, USA

Vinton, Bobby (Musician)
c/o Staff Member *MPI Talent Agency*
1801 Avenue of the Stars
Suite 1420
Los Angeles, CA 90067, USA

Vinton, Will (Animator, Cartoonist,
Director, Producer)
c/o Rob Kenneally *Creative Artists Agency
(CAA-LA)*
2000 Ave Of The Stars
Los Angeles, CA 90067, USA

Viola, Bill (Artist)
282 Granada Ave
Long Beach, CA 90803, USA

Viola, Frank
844 Sweetwater Island Circle
Longwood, FL 32779-2345

Viola, Frank J Jr (Athlete, Baseball Player)
9868 Kilgore Rd
Orlando, FL 32836-5708, USA

Viola, Lisa (Dancer)
Paul Taylor Dance Co
552 Broadway
New York, NY 10012, USA

Violent Femmes (Music Group)
15030 Ventura Blvd #710
Sherman Oaks, CA 91403, USA

Violetta-Kunkel, Karen (Athlete, Baseball
Player)
904 Garfield Ave
Marquette, MI 49855-3214, USA

Violette, Chris (Actor)
c/o Staff Member *Power Rangers SPD*
500 South Buena Vista St
Burbank, CA 91521, USA

Vipond, Pete (Athlete, Hockey Player)
69 Admiral Drive
Fenelon Falls, ON K0M lN0, Canada

Virata, Cesar E (Prime Minister)
63 E Maya Dr
Quezon City, PHILIPPINES

Virden, Claude (Athlete, Basketball
Player)
337 Fernwood Dr
Akron, OH 44320-231, USA

Virdon, William C (Bill) (Athlete, Baseball
Player, Coach)
1311 E River Rd
Springfield, MO 65804-7901, USA

Viren, Lasse (Athlete, Track Athlete)
Suomen Urhellulirto Ry
Box 25202
Helsinki 25 00250, FINLAND

Virgil Jr, Ozzie (Athlete, Baseball Player)
4316 W Mescal St
Glendale, AZ 85310-3724, USA

Virgil Sr, Ozzie (Athlete, Baseball Player)
5444 W Creedance Blvd
Glendale, AZ 85310-3724, Dominican
Republic

Virgins, The (Music Group)
c/o Staff Member *Paradigm (Monterey)*
404 W Franklin St
Monterey, CA 93940, USA

Virts, Terry W Jr (Astronaut)
1904 Edgewater Court
Friendswood, TX 77546, USA

Virts, Terry W Major (Astronaut)
1904 Edgewater Dr
Friendswood, TX 77546-7845, USA

Virtue, Doreen (Writer)
Angel Therapy
PO Box 5100
Carlsbad, CA 92018

Virtue, Frank (Musician)
8309 Rising Sun Ave
Philadelphia, PA 19111, USA

Virtue, Thomas (Tom) (Actor)
c/o Staff Member *Gage Group, The (LA)*
14724 Ventura Blvd
Suite 505
Sherman Oaks, CA 91403, USA

Virzaladze, Elizo K (Music Group, Musician)
Moscow Conservatory
Bolshaya Nikitskaya Str 13
Moscow, RUSSIA

Vis, Anthony (Religious Leader)
Reformed Church in America
475 Riverside Dr
New York, NY 10115, USA

Viscardi, Johnston Catherine (Publisher)
Mirabella Magazine
200 Madison Ave
New York, NY 10016, USA

Visclosky, Pete (Congressman, Politician)
7895 Broadway
Suite A
Merrillville, IN 46410, USA

Visconti, Tony (Musician, Producer)
c/o Joe D'Ambrosio *Joe D'Ambrosio Management Inc*
STAR Mgmt. Group
1311 Mamaroneck Ave #220
White Plains, NY 10605-5222, USA

Visculo, Sal
6491 Ivarene Ave.
Los Angeles, CA 90068

Viscuso, Sal (Actor)
6491 Ivarene Ave
Los Angeles, CA 90068, USA

Vise, David A (Journalist)
Washington Post
Editorial Dept
1150 15th St NW
Washingon, DC 20071, USA

Vishnevski, Vitali (Athlete, Hockey Player)
International Sports Advisors
878 Ridge View Way
Franklin Lakes, NJ 07417-1524, USA

Vishnyova, Diana V (Ballerina)
Maninsky Theater
Teatralnaya Square 1
Saint Petersburg 190000, RUSSIA

Visitor, Nana (Actor)
c/o Staff Member *Diverse Talent Group*
9911 W Pico Blvd Ste 340W
Los Angeles, CA 90035, USA

Visnjic, Goran (Actor)
c/o Elyse Scherz *WME (LA)*
9601 Wilshire Blvd Fl 3
Beverly Hills, CA 90210, USA

Visnovsky, Lubomir (Athlete, Hockey Player)
15319th St
Manhattan Beach, CA 90266-6126, USA

Viso, Michel (Misc)
7 Domaine Chateau-Gaillard
Maison-d' Alfort 94700, FRANCE

Visscher, Maurice B (Doctor)
120 Melbourne Ave SE
Minneapolis, MN 55414, USA

Visser, Lesley (Sportscaster)
c/o Staff Member *CBS Television*
51 W 52nd St
New York, NY 10019, USA

Visu (Actor, Bollywood)
11 Agastheya Nagar
Kilpaul Garden
Chennai, TN 600012, INDIA

Viswanathan, Padma
213 N Summit Ave
Fayetteville, AR 72701, USA

Vitale, Dick (Athlete, Basketball Player, Coach, Sportscaster)
7810 Mathern Court
Lakewood Ranch, FL 34202-2592, USA

Vitale, Joe (Business Person, Writer)
The Vitale Estate
121 Canyon Gap Rd
Wimberley, TX 78676, USA

Vitale, Tony (Actor, Director, Writer)
c/o Staff Member *Hansen, Jacobson, Teller, Hoberman, Newman, Warren & Richman*
450 N Roxbury Dr
8th Floor
Beverly Hills, CA 90210, USA

Vitamin-C (Actor, Musician)
c/o Carter Cohn *ICM Partners (ICM-LA)*
10250 Constellation Blvd Fl 7
Los Angeles, CA 90067, USA

Viterbi, Andrew J (Engineer, Scientist)
QUALCOMM Inc
5775 Morehouse Dr
San Diego, CA 92121, USA

Vitez, Michael (Journalist)
Philadelphia Inquirer
Editorial Dept
400 N Broad St
Philadelphia, PA 19130, USA

Vitiello, Joe (Athlete, Baseball Player)
13615 Old El Camino Real
San Diego, CA 92130-3088, USA

Vitiello, Sandro (Athlete, Football Player)
9 Dwight Cir
Commack, NY 11725, USA

Vitko, Joe (Athlete, Baseball Player)
1853 Frankstown Rd Apt 1
Johnstown, PA 15902-4504, USA

Vito, Don (Producer)
606 Treecrest Pkwy
Decatur, GA 30035, USA

Vitolo, Dennis (Race Car Driver)
Payton-Coyne Racing
13400 Budler Rd
Plainfield, IL 60544, USA

Vitousek, Peter M (Misc)
Stanford University
Biological Science Dept
Stanford, CT 94305, USA

Vitrano, Bob (Horse Racer)
16 Farnworth Close
Freehold, NJ 07728-3852, USA

Vitti, Monica (Actor)
IPC
Via F Siacci 38
Rome 00197, ITALY

Vittori, Roberto (Astronaut)
Europe Astronaut Center
520 N Iowa Ave
League City, TX 77573-2356, Italy

Vitukhnovskaya, Alina A (Writer)
Leningradskoye Shosse 80 #89
Moscow 125565, RUSSIA

Vivas, Juan Carlos (Actor)
c/o Gabriel Blanco *Gabriel Blanco Iglesias (Mexico)*
Rio Balsas 35-32
Colonia Cuauhtemoc
DF 06500, Mexico

Vivek (Actor, Bollywood)
9 Subhiksha Apts
5 Tank Street U.I. Colony
Chennai, TN 600024, INDIA

Viviano, Joseph P (Business Person)
Hershey Foods Corp
100 Crystal A Dr
Hershey, PA 17033, USA

Vizcaino, Jose (Athlete, Baseball Player)
5976 Germaine Ln
La Jolla, CA 92037-7430, USA

Vizquel, Omar E (Athlete, Baseball Player)
2704 212th Ave SE
Sammamish, WA 98075-7167, USA

V. Johnson, Timothy (Congressman, Politician)
8426 Porter Ln
Alexandria, VA 22308-2139, USA

Vlacil, Frantisek (Director)
Cinska 5
Prague 6 160 00, CZECH REPUBLIC

Vladeck, Judith P (Attorney, Attorney General, General)
Vladeck Waidman Elias Engelhard
1501 Broadway
New York, NY 10036, USA

Vladimir, Potanin (Business Person, Politician)
Interros
40 Bolshaya Yakimanka St
Moscow 119049, Russia

Vlady, Marina (Actor)
10 Ave de Marivaux
Mission Lafitte 78800, FRANCE

Vlardo, Vladimir V (Musician)
457 Piedmont Road
Cresskill, NJ 07626, USA

Vlasak, Tomas (Athlete, Hockey Player)
Stefanikovo nam. 1
Pi zen 30133, Czech Republic

Vlasic, Mark (Athlete, Football Player)
12809 Catalina St
Leawood, KS 66209, USA

Vlassic, Robert
1910 Rothmor Rd.
Bloomfield, MI 48304

Vlk, Miloslav Cardinal (Religious Leader)
Arcibiskupstvi
Hradcanske Nam 16/56
Prague 1 119 02, CZECH REPUBLIC

V M T Chaarllee (Actor)
Plot No 11 Kamarajar Nagar
II Street Sathya Gardens Saligramam
Chennai, TN 600 093, INDIA

Voce, Gary (Athlete, Basketball Player)
25912 147th Ave
Rosendale, NY 11422-3321, USA

Vodianova, Natalia (Model)
c/o Staff Member *DNA Model Management*
555 W 25th St
New York, NY 10001, USA

Voevodsky, Vladimir (Mathematician)
22 Earle Lane
Princeton, NJ 08540, USA

Vogel, Bob (Athlete, Football Player)
2065 N Galena Rd
Sunbury, OH 43074, USA

Vogel, Dariene (Actor)
Michael Slessinger
8730 Sunset Blvd #220W
Los Angeles, CA 90069, USA

Vogel, Darlene (Actor)
c/o Staff Member *The Paradise Group*
PO Box 69451
West Hollywood, CA 90069, USA

Vogel, Hans-Jochen (Government Official)
Stresemanstr 6
Bonn-Bad Godesberg 53123, GERMANY

Vogel, Mark (Composer)
c/o Staff Member *Gorfaine/Schwartz Agency Inc*
4111 W Alameda Ave
Suite 509
Burbank, CA 91505, USA

Vogel, Matt (Athlete, Olympic Athlete, Swimmer)
6863 Maplecrest Rd
Fort Wayne, IN 46835-1864, USA

Vogel, Mike (Actor)
c/o Geordie Frey *GEF Entertainment*
122 N Clark Dr
Suite 401
Los Angeles, CA 90048, USA

Vogel, Mitch (Actor)
3335 Honeysuckle Ave
Palmdale, CA 93550, USA

Vogelsong, Ryan (Athlete, Baseball Player)
637 W Jardin Dr
CasaGrande, AZ 85122-5117, USA

Vogelstein, Bert (Doctor, Scientist)
Johns Hopkins University
Medical School
Oncology Center
Baltimore, MD 21218, USA

Vogler, Karl Michael
Auweg 8
Seehausen, GERMANY D-82418

Vogler, Tim (Athlete, Football Player)
6710 Woodland Dr
Hamburg, NY 14075, USA

Vogt, Lars (Musician)
c/o Staff Member *ICM Partners (ICM-NY)*
730 Fifth Ave
New York, NY 10019, USA

Vogt, Paul (Actor)
c/o Judy Coppage *Coppage Company, The*
5411 Camellia Ave
North Hollywood, CA 91601, USA

Vogt, Peter K (Misc, Scientist)
LA County/USC Medical School
2011 Zonal Ave
Los Angeles, CA 90089, USA

Vogt, Rochus E (Astronomer, Physicist)
California Institute of Technology
Bridge Laboratory
Pasadena, CA 91125, USA

Vogtli, Jillian (Athlete, Olympic Athlete, Skier)
PO Box 683153
Park City, UT 84068-3153, USA

Vogts, Hans-Hubert (Berti) (Soccer Player)
Mozartweg 2
Korschenbroich 41352, GERMANY

Voight, Jon (Actor, Producer, Writer)
c/o Brian Medavoy *Medavoy Management*
10203 Santa Monica Blvd
Suite 400
Los Angeles, CA 90067, USA

Voight, Karen (Fitness Expert)
Entertaining Fitness, Inc
827 Chautauqua Blvd
Pacific Palisades, CA 90272-3802, USA

Voight, Stu (Athlete, Football Player)
8832 Hunters Way
Apple Valley, MN 55124, USA

Voigt, Cynthia (Writer)
Atheneum 866 3rd Ave
New York, NY 10022-6221, USA

Voigt, Jack (Athlete, Baseball Player)
1759 Bayshore Rd
Nokomis, FL 34275-1413, USA

Voinovich, George (Ex-Governor, Politician, Senator)
17820 Rosecliff Rd
Cleveland, OH 44119-1346, USA

Voisard, Mark (Baseball Player)
222 Meadowlane Dr
Sidney, OH 45365-7000, USA

Vokoun, Tomas (Athlete, Hockey Player)
6685 NW 122nd Avnue
Parkland, FL 33076-3325, USA

Volberding, Paul (Scientist)
General Hospital AIDS Activities Dept
995 Potrero Ave
San Francisco, CA 94110, USA

Volcan, Mickey (Athlete, Hockey Player)
10716 69 St NW
Edmonton, AB T6A 2Tl, Canada

Volchenkov, Anton (Athlete, Hockey Player)
Puckagency LLC
555 Pleasantville Rd Ste 210N
Attn Jay Grossman
Briarcliff Manor, NY 10510-1900, USA

Volcker, Paul (Politician)
151 E 79th St
New York, NY 10075-0417, USA

Voldstad, John (Actor)
24812 Van Owen St
West Hills, CA 91300, USA

Volek, Billy (Athlete, Football Player)
14544 Millards Rd
Poway, CA 92064-5036, USA

Volek, David (Athlete, Hockey Player)
5 Blue Sky Ct
Huntington, NY 11743-2901, USA

Volibracht, Michaele (Artist, Designer, Fashion Designer)
General Delivery
Safety Harbor, FL 34695, USA

Volk, Igor P (Misc)
Potchta Kosmonavtov
Moskovskoi Oblasti
Syvisdny Gorodukl 141160, RUSSIA

Volk, Patricia (Writer)
Gloria Loomis
133 E 35th St
New York, NY 10016, USA

Volk, Phil (Musician)
Paradise Artists
108 E Matilija St
Ojai, CA 93023, USA

Volk, Richard R (Rick) (Athlete, Football Player)
15860 Irish Ave
Monkton, MD 21111, USA

Volker, Sandra (Swimmer)
DESG
Mensingen Str 68
Munich 80992, GERMANY

Volkert, Stephan (Athlete)
Semmelweisstr 42
Cologne 51061, GERMANY

Volkov, Aleksandr A (Misc)
Potchta Kosmonavtov
Moskovskoi Oblasti
Syvisdny Goroduk 141160, RUSSIA

Volkov, Alexander (Athlete, Basketball Player)
1413 Waterford Green Dr
Marietta, GA 30068-29l0, USA

Voll, Rich (Actor)

Vollebak, Knut (Government Official)
Royal Norwegian Embassy
2720 34th St NW
Washington, DC 20008, USA

Vollenweider, Andreas (Musician)
Sempacher Str 16
Zurich 8032, SWITZERLAND

Vollmer, Dana (Athlete, Olympic Athlete, Swimmer)
4002 Laramie Dr
Granbury, TX 76049-7224, USA

Volmar, Doug (Athlete, Hockey Player, Olympic Athlete)
19 Eliot St
Framingham, MA 01702-6403, USA

Volodos, Arcadl (Musician)
Columbia Artists Mgmt Inc
165 W 57th St
New York, NY 10019, USA

Voloshin, Valeri (Cosmonaut)
Potchta Kosmonavtov
Moskovskoi Oblasti
Syvisdny Goroduk 141160, RUSSIA

Volstad, Chris (Athlete, Baseball Player)
11774 Hemlock St
Palm Beach Gardens, FL 33410-2637, USA

Volstad, John (Actor)
c/o Brandon Pender *Ithaca Entertainment Media Group*
P.O. Box 1880
Studio City, CA 91614-0880, USA

Voltaggio, Vic (Baseball Player)
1049 Florian Way
Spring Hill, FL 34609-9021, USA

VOltaggio, Vic (Athlete, Baseball Player)
1049 Florian Way
Spring Hill, FL 34609-9021, USA

Voltz, Jeanne (Stylist)
305 W 98th St
New York, NY 10025, USA

Volynov, Boris V (Misc)
Potchta Kosmonavtov
Moskovskoi Oblasti
Syvisdny Goroduk 141160, RUSSIA

Volz, Wilbur (Athlete, Football Player)
35 Seminary Hill
Apt C-31
West Lebanon, NH 03784, USA

Volz, Wolfgang (Actor)
Konstanzer Strasse 8
Berlin D-10707, Germany

Von Bargen, Daniel (Actor)
c/o Mitchell Stubbs *Mitchell K Stubbs & Assoc (MKS)*
8675 W. Washington Blvd
Suite 203
Culver City, CA 90232, USA

Von Daniken, Eric (Writer)
Chalet Aelpli
Beatenberg 3803, Switzerland

Vonderau, Kathryn (Athlete, Baseball Player)
7224 Hawthorn Avenue NE
Albuquerque, NM 87113-2084, USA

von Detten, Erik (Actor)
c/o Elissa Leeds-Fickman *Reel Talent Management*
P.O. Box 491035
Los Angeles, CA 90049, USA

von Dohlen, Lenny (Actor)
c/o Martin Gage *Gage Group, The (LA)*
14724 Ventura Blvd
Suite 505
Sherman Oaks, CA 91403, USA

VonDohnanyi, Christoph (Conductor)
Cleveland Orchestra
Severance Hall
Cleveland, OH 44106, USA

Von Drachenberg, Katherine (Artist, Reality TV Star)
High Voltage Tattoo
1259 N. La Brea Ave
West Hollywood, CA 90038, USA

Von Erich, Jaret (Actor, Musician)
c/o Linda Kordek *Agency Group Ltd, The (LA)*
1880 Century Park E
Suite 711
Los Angeles, CA 90067, USA

VonErich, Waldo (Wrestler)
Columbia Sports Med Center
9-145 Columbia W
Waterloo, ON N2L 3L2, CANADA

VonEschenbach, Andrew (Doctor)
National Cancer Institute
9000 Rockville Pike
Bethesda, MD 20892, USA

Von Frankenstein, Clement (Actor)
c/o Staff Member *Matt Sherman Management*
7510 W Sunset Blvd
Suite 1413
Los Angeles, CA 90046, USA

Von Furstenberg, Betsy (Actor)
230 Central Park W.
New York, NY 10024, USA

VonFurstenberg, Betsy (Actor)
230 Central Park West
New York, NY 10024, USA

Von Furstenberg, Diane (Fashion Designer)
444 W 14th St
New York, NY 10014-1004, USA

VonFurstenberg, Egon (Designer, Fashion Designer)
50 E 72nd St
New York, NY 10021, USA

VonGarnier, Katja (Director, Writer)
c/o John Campisi *Creative Artists Agency (CAA-LA)*
2000 Ave Of The Stars
Los Angeles, CA 90067, USA

Vongerichten, Jean-Georges (Chef)
Jean-Georges Enterprises, LLC
19 Greene St
New York, NY 10012, USA

VonGerkan, Meinhard (Architect)
Elbchaussee 139
Hamburg 22763, GERMANY

VonGrunigen, Michael (Skier)
Chalet Sunneblick
Schonried 3778, SWITZERLAND

Vo Nguyen Giap (General)
Dang Cong San Vietnam
1C Blvd Hoang Van Thu
Hanoi, VIETNAM

VonHippel, Peter H (Misc)
1900 Crest Dr
Eugene, OR 97405, USA

Von Hoff, Bruce (Athlete, Baseball Player)
5289 6th PIS
Gulfoort, FL 33707-2501, USA

Von Hohenzollern, Maja Synke (Prince, Princess)
c/o Joerg Bobsin
11605 West Pico Boulevard, #200
Los Angeles, CA 90064, USA

VonKlitzing, Klaus (Nobel Prize Laureate)
Max Planck Institute
Max-Planck Institut Heisenbergstrasse 1
Postfach 800665
Stuttgart D-70506, GERMANY

VonMehren, Arthur T (Attorney, Attorney General, Educator, General)
68 Sparks St
Cambridge, MA 02138, USA

VonMehren, Arthur T (Attorney, Attorney General, General)
925 Park Ave
New York, NY 10028, USA

Vonn, Lindsey (Athlete, Skier)
c/o Staff Member *US Ski And Snowboard Association*
Box 199
Park City, UT 84060, USA

Vonnegut Jr, Kurt (Writer)
Seven Stories Press
140 Watts Street
New York, NY 10013, USA

Von Nieda, Stanley "Whitey
lle5 James Buchanan Dr
Elizabethtown, PA 17022-3169, USA

Von Nieda, Whitey (Athlete, Basketball Player)
1105 James Buchanan Dr
Elizabethtown, PA 17022, USA

Vonoelhoffen, Kimo (Athlete, Football Player)
1503 Scarlet Oak Dr
Wexford, PA 15090, USA

Von Ohlen, Dave (Athlete, Baseball Player)
653 Windmill Ave
West Babylon, NY 11704-4403, USA

Vonohlen, Dave (Baseball Player)
St Louis Cardinals
74 Elizabeth St
Floral Park, NY 11001-2129, USA

Vonoimoana, Eric
715 S. Circle Dr.
Colorado Springs, CO 80910

VonOtter, Anne Sofie (Opera Singer)
I C M Aritsts
40 W 57th St
New York, NY 10019, USA

Von Oy, Jenna (Actor)
19 Saddle Ridge Rd.
Newtown, CT 06470-2417, USA

VonOy, Jenna (Actor)
19 Saddle Ridge Road
Newtown, CT 06470, USA

von Pfetten, Stefanie (Actor)
c/o Marina D'Amico *Precision Entertainment*
6338 Wilshire Blvd
Los Angeles, CA 90048, USA

VonPierer, Heinrich (Business Person)
Seimens AG
Wittelsbacherplatz 2
Munich 80333, GERMANY

Von Pragenau, Georg (Scientist)
3509 Mae Dr SE
Huntsville, AL 35801-6120, USA

Von Puttkamer, Jesco
Nasa Headquarters 300 ESt SW MS Ml
Washington, DC 20546-0005, USA

VonQuast, Veronika (Actor)
ZBF Agentur
Leopoldstr 19
Munich 80802, GERMANY

VonRunkle, Theodora (Designer, Fashion Designer)
8805 Lookout Mountain Road
Los Angeles, CA 90046, USA

VonSaltza Olmstead, S Christine (Chris) (Swimmer)
7060 Fairway Place
Carmel, CA 93923, USA

Von Schamann, Uwe (Athlete, Football Player)
P.O. Box 5562
Norman, OK 73070, USA

Von Scherler Mayer, Daisy (Director)
c/o Keith Addis *Industry Entertainment Partners*
955 S Carrillo Dr
Suite 300
Los Angeles, CA 90048, USA

Vonsonn, Andrew (Athlete, Football Player)
P.O. Box 791538
Paia, HI 96779, USA

Von Stade, Frederica (Opera Singer)
1200 San Antonio Ave
Alameda, CA 94501, USA

VonStrateen, Frans (Artist)
Samuel Muller Plein 17C
Rotterdam 3023, DENMARK

Von Sydow, Max (Actor)
c/o Staff Member *United Talent Agency (UTA)*
9336 Civic Center Dr
Beverly Hills, CA 90210, USA

Von Teese, Dita (Dancer, Model)
PO Box 1760
Eagle, ID 83616, USA

Von Tiesenhausen, Georg (Scientist)
1800 Nixon Ave NE
Huntsville, AL 35811-2210, USA

von Trier, Lars (Director, Writer)
c/o Staff Member *Jeff Morrone Entertainment*
9350 Wilshire Blvd
Suite 224
Beverly Hills, CA 90212, USA

von Weizsacker, Carl
Alpenstr. 15
Socking, GERMANY D-82319

VonWeizsacker, Carl Friedrich (Misc)
Aplenstr 15
Socking 82319, GERMANY

von Weizsacker, Richard (Ex-President, President)
Meisenstr 6
Berlin D-14195, GERMANY

VonWeizsacker, Richard (President)
Meisenstr 6
Berlin 14195, GERMANY

von Wietersheim, Sharon
Leopoldstr. 19
Munich, GERMANY D-80802

Voog, Ana (Music Group, Musician, Songwriter, Writer)
MCA Records
1755 Broadway
New York, NY 10019, USA

Voorhees, John J (Doctor)
3965 Waldenwood Dr
Ann Arbor, MI 48105, USA

Voorhies, Lark (Actor)
10635 Santa Monica Blvd #130
Los Angeles, CA 90025, USA

Voorman, Klaus (Artist)
K & K Galleries Grindelalla 182
Hamburg D-20144, Germany

Vopat, Jan (Athlete, Hockey Player)
Skalni 426
Litvinov 3 436 01, Czech Republic

Vorgan, Gigi (Actor)
3637 Stone Canyon
Sherman Oaks, CA 91403, USA

Vorhies, Lark (Actor)
c/o Geoff Cheddy *Brillstein Entertainment Partners*
9150 Wilshire Blvd #350
Beverly Hills, CA 90212, USA

Voris, Roy M (Butch) (Misc)
14563 Fruitvale Avenue
Saratoga, CA 95070-6152, USA

Voronin, Vladimir (President)
President's Office
23 Nicolae lorge Str
Chishinev 277033, MOLDOVA

Voronina, Irina (Model)
7119 Sunset Blvd
Box 293
Los Angeles, CA 90046, USA

Vos, Rich (Actor, Comedian)
c/o Jason Steinberg *Steinberg Talent Management Group*
1560 Broadway #405
New York, NY 10036, US

Vosberg, Ed (Athlete, Baseball Player)
7839 E Marquise Dr
Tucson, AZ 85715-3774, USA

Voser, Peter (Business Person)
Shell U.K. Limited
Shell Centre
London SE1 7NA, UK

Voskuhl, Jake
4356 E Selena Dr
Phoenix, AZ 85050-430, USA

Vosloo, Arnold (Actor)
c/o James (Jim) Gosnell *Agency for the Performing Arts (APA-LA)*
405 S Beverly Dr
Suite 500
Beverly Hills, CA 90212-4425, USA

Voss, Bill (Athlete, Baseball Player)
10625 E Oak Creek Trl
Cornville, AZ 86325-5824, USA

Voss, Brian (Bowler)
1635 Old 41 Hwy NW Ste 112
Kennesaw, GA 30152-4481, USA

Voss, James S (Astronaut)
4207 Indian Sunrise Court
Houston, TX 77059, USA

Voss, James S Colonel (Astronaut)
4207 Indian Sunrise Ct
Houston, TX 77059-5533, USA

Votaw, Ty (Golfer)
Ladies Pro Golf Assn
100 International Golf Dr
Daytona Beach, FL 32124, USA

Voth, Julia (Actor)
c/o Alex Fox *Cunningham Escott Slevin & Doherty (CESD-LA)*
10635 Santa Monica Blvd
130
Los Angeles, CA 90025, USA

Votto, Joey (Athlete, Baseball Player)
c/o Staff Member *Cincinnati Reds*
Great American Ball Park
100 Main St
Cincinnati, OH 45202-4109, USA

Vouyer, Vince (Adult Film Star)
Vouyer Media Inc
9020 Eton Ave #G
Canoga Park, CA 91304, USA

Vowell, Sarah (Actor, Writer)
c/o Staff Member *Steven Barclay Agency*
12 Western Ave
Petaluma, CA 94952, USA

Voyce, Inez (Athlete, Baseball Player)
2107 Ashland Ave
Santa Monica, CA 90405-6025, USA

Voyles, Brad (Athlete, Baseball Player)
314 East Ave
Casco, WI 54205-9679, USA

Voytek, Edward (Athlete, Football Player)
2111 NW 13th St
Blue Springs, MO 64015, USA

Vraa, Sanna (Actor, Model)
Irv Schechter
9300 Wilshire Blvd #410
Beverly Hills, CA 90212, USA

Vrabel, Mike (Athlete, Football Player)
8552 Misty Woods Cir
Powell, OH 43065, USA

Vrabel, Mike (Athlete, Football Player)
74 Concerto Ct
North Easton, MA 02356, USA

Vraciu, Alexander (Alex) (General)
309 Merrille Place
Danville, CA 94526-4315, USA

Vranes, Danny (Athlete, Basketball Player, Olympic Athlete)
6480 Canyon Ranch Rd
Salt Lake City, UT 84121-6366, USA

Vranes, Slavko (Basketball Player)
c/o Staff Member *Portland Trail Blazers*
1 Center Court
Sutie 200
Portland, OR 97227, USA

Vranitzky, Franz
Ballhausplatz 2
Vienna, AUSTRIA 1015

Vuarnet, Jean (Skier)
Chalet Squaw Peak
Auoriaz 74110, FRANCE

Vuckovich, Peter D (Pete) (Athlete, Baseball Player)
86 Leonard St
Johnstown, PA 15902-1234, USA

Vujtek, Vladimir (Athlete, Hockey Player)
Mexico- 813
Vresina 74285, Czech Republic

Vukota, Mick (Athlete, Hockey Player)
PO Box 3213 7 Peases Point Rd
Edgartown, MA 02539-3213, USA

Vukovich, George (Athlete, Baseball Player)
305 W Calle Gota
Sahuarita, AZ 85629-7845, USA

Vulkovich, Frances (Athlete, Baseball Player)
258 W 28th St
Holland, MI 49423-4939, USA

Vullo, Jennifer (Stylist)
c/o Staff Member *Crews*
828 Clemont Dr
Atlanta, GA 30306, USA

Vullo, Maria T (Attorney)
LLP L, Weiss, Rifkind, Warton & Garrison,
Ll 1285 Avenue of the Americas
New York, NY 10019-6031, USA

Vuono, Carl E (General)
5796 Westchester St
Alexandria, VA 22310, USA

Vyent, Louise (Model)
Pauline's Talent Corp
379 W Broadway #502
New York, NY 10012, USA

W, Kristine (Musician)
c/o Staff Member *Diva Central Inc*
7510 W Sunset Blvd Ste 1445
Los Angees, CA 90046, USA

Waadataar, Paar (Musician)
Banada Mgmt
11 Elvaston Place #300
London SW 7 5QC, UNITED KINGDOM (UK)

Waalkes, Otto
Papenhuder Str. 61
Hamburg, GERMANY D-22087

Wach, Caitlin (Actor)
c/o David Brownstein *Art Work*
Entertainment
5900 Wilshire Blvd #2150
Los Angeles, CA 90036, USA

Wachowski, Andy (Director, Producer,
Writer)
c/o Lawrence Mattis *Circle of Confusion*
(NY)
107-23 71st Rd #300
Forest Hills, NY 11375, USA

Wachowski, Larry (Director, Producer,
Writer)
c/o Lawrence Mattis *Circle of Confusion*
(NY)
107-23 71st Rd #300
Forest Hills, NY 11375, USA

Wachs, Caitlin (Actor)
c/o Shelley Browning *Magnolia*
Entertainment (LA)
9595 Wilshire Blvd
Suite 601
Beverly Hills, CA 90212, USA

Wachtel, Christine (Athlete, Track
Athlete)
Rostock Sports Club
Rostock
Mecklenburg-Vorpommoem, GERMANY

Wachter, Anita (Skier)
Gantschierstr 579
Schruns 6780, AUSTRIA

Wacksman, Sara (Stylist)
c/o Staff Member *Apostrophe (NY)*
527 W 29th St
New York, NY 10001, USA

Waddell, Charles (Athlete, Football
Player)
3600 Bon Rea Dr
Charlotte, NC 28226, USA

Waddell, Don (Athlete, Hockey Player)
2554 Thurleston Ln
Duluth, GA 30097-7474, USA

Waddell, Ernest (Actor)
c/o Bob McGowan *McGowan*
Management
8733 W Sunset Blvd
Suite 103
West Hollywood, CA 90069, USA

Waddell, Jason (Athlete, Baseball Player)
3574 Gwinnett Dr
Riverside, CA 92503-5013, USA

Waddell, John Henry (Artist)
Star Route 2273
Oak Creek Village Road
Cornville, AZ 86325, USA

Waddell, Justine (Actor)
International Creative Mgmt
8942 Wilshire Blvd #219
Beverly Hills, CA 90211, USA

Waddell, Tom (Athlete, Baseball Player)
10171 E Achi St
Tucson, AZ 85748-1803, USA

Waddell-Wyatt, Helen (Athlete, Baseball
Player)
7714 Deerfield Rd
Loves Park, IL 61111-3218, USA

Waddington, Steven (Actor)
Julian Belfrage Associates
Adam House
14 New Burlington Street
London W1S 3BQ, UNITED KINGDOM
(UK)

Waddle, Tom (Athlete, Football Player)
1260 W Kennicott Dr
Lake Forest, IL 60045, USA

Waddy, Billy (Athlete, Football Player)
2838 Highway 88
Minneapolis, MN 55418, USA

Wade, Abdoulaye (President)
President's Office
Ave Roume
Dakar BPI 168, SENEGAL

Wade, Adam (Musician)
118 E 25th St #600
New York, NY 10010, USA

Wade, Charlie (Athlete, Football Player)
3109 E Raines Rd
Memphis, TN 38118, USA

Wade, Cory (Athlete, Baseball Player)
c/o Staff Member *Los Angeles Dodgers*
(LA Dodgers)
1000 Elysian Park Ave
Los Angeles, CA 90012, USA

Wade, Dwyane (Athlete, Basketball
Player)
c/o Leon Rose *CAA - NJ*
4300 Haddenfield Rd
Suite 309
Pennsauken, NJ 08109, USA

Wade, Dwyane (Athlete, Basketball
Player)
c/o Henry Thomas *CAA Sports (LA)*
2000 Avenue of the Stars
Los Angeles, CA 90067, USA

Wade, Ed (Athlete, Baseball Player)
169 Pitman Downer Rd
Sewell, NJ 08080-1878, USA

Wade, Ed (Actor)
436 SW 50th Avenue
Pratt, KS 67212-7731, USA

Wade, Edgar L (Religious Leader)
4466 Elvis Presley Blvd
#222
Memphis, TN 38116, USA

Wade, Gale (Athlete, Baseball Player)
4809 Granada Blvd
Sebring, FL 33872-1531, USA

Wade, Jason (Musician)
DreamWorks Records
9268 W 3rd St
Beverly Hills, CA 90210, USA

Wade, Kevin (Writer)
c/o David Lonner *Oasis Media Group*
8730 W. Sunset Blvd
Suite 700
Los Angeles, CA 90036, USA

Wade, Mark (Athlete, Basketball Player)
405 S Centre St
Apt 37
San Pedro, CA 90731-2732, USA

Wade, Russell
47-287 W. Eldorado Dr.
Indian Wells, CA 92260

Wade, Sonny (Athlete, Football Player)
943 Jones Ridge Rd
Axton, VA 24054-2888, USA

Wade, Terrell (Athlete, Baseball Player)
6380 Dinkins Mill Rd
Rembert, SC 29128-9789, USA

Wade, Todd (Athlete, Football Player)
217 Hendricks Isle
Apt 302
Fort Lauderdale, FL 33301, USA

Wade, Tom (Athlete, Football Player)
3309 Oak Knoll Dr
Tyler, TX 75707, USA

Wade, Virginia (Tennis Player)
Sharstead Court
Sittingbourne
Kent, UNITED KINGDOM (UK)

Wade, William J (Bill) Jr (Athlete,
Football Player)
7740 Buffalo Rd
Nashville, TN 37221, USA

Wadhams, Wayne (Musician)
73 Hemenway
Boston, MA 02115, USA

Wadhawan, Avinash (Actor, Bollywood)
305 Skyway Shastri Nagar
Off J P Road Andheri
Mumbai, MS 400058, INDIA

Wadkins, Bobby (Golfer)
204 Kinloch Rd
Manakin Sabot, VA 23103, USA

Wadkins, Lanny (Golfer)
6002 Kettering Ct
Dallas, TX 75248-2137, USA

Wadsworth, Andre (Athlete, Football
Player)
14003 N 99th Way
Scottsdale, AZ 85260-8851, USA

Wadsworth, Charles W (Musician)
PO Box 157
Charleston, SC 29402, USA

Wadsworth, Fred (Golfer)
823 Bryon Rd
Columbia, SC 29209-2303, USA

Waechter, Doug (Athlete, Baseball Player)
4590 13th WayNE
Saint Petersburg, FL 33703-5324, USA

Waelsch, Salome G (Doctor, Scientist)
90 Morningside Dr
New York, NY 10027, USA

Wafer, Von (Athlete, Basketball Player)
2503 Dallas St
Houston, TX 77003-3605, USA

Wages, Harmon (Athlete, Football Player)
1846 Margaret St
Apt 3C
Jacksonville, FL 32204, USA

Wages, Robert E (Misc)
Oil Chemical Atomic Workers
International Union
PO Box 2812
Denver, CO 80201, USA

Wages, William (Cinematographer)
Innovative Artists
1505 10th St
Santa Monica, CA 90401, USA

Waggoner, Bashie (Stylist)
6333 Monterey Rd
Los Angeles, CA 90042, USA

Waggoner, Lyle (Actor)
1124 Oak Mirage Place
Westlake Village, CA 91362, USA

Waggoner, Paul E (Misc)
314 Vineyard Point Road
Guilford, CT 06437, USA

Wagner, Alex (Journalist)
c/o Staff Member *MSNBC*
30 Rockfeller Plz
New York, NY 10112, USA

Wagner, Allison (Athlete, Olympic
Athlete, Swimmer)
912 NW 45th Ter
Gainesville, FL 32605-4590

Wagner, Amanda
PO Box 1294
Los Alamos, NM 87544-1294

Wagner, Bret (Baseball Player)
US Olympic Team Bowman
489 Ridge Rd
Lewisberry, PA 17339-9308, USA

Wagner, Bruce (Writer)
United Talent Agency
9560 Wilshire Blvd #500
Beverly Hills, CA 90212, USA

Wagner, Bryan (Athlete, Football Player)
6020 Arlyne Ln
Medina, OH 44256, USA

Wagner, Chuck (Actor, Musician)
1200 Maldonado Dr
Pensacola Beach, FL 32561, USA

Wagner, Dajuan (Basketball Player)
Cleveland Cavaliers
Gund Arena
1 Center Court
Cleveland, OH 08086-2233, USA

Wagner, Fred (Cartoonist)
c/o Staff Member *King Features*
Syndication
300 W 57th St
15th Floor
New York, NY 10019-5238, USA

Wagner, Gary (Athlete, Baseball Player)
1707 Northbrook Ct
Seymour, IN 47274-4801, USA

Wagner, Harold A (Business Person)
Air Products & Chemicals
7201 Hamilton Blvd
Allentown, PA 18195, USA

Wagner, Hermann (Scientist)
116 Madison Ave
Madison, AL 35758-8539, USA

Wagner, Jack (Actor, Musician)
314 Waverly Place Ct
Chesterfield, MO 63017, USA

Wagner, Jane
PO Box 27700
Los Angeles, CA 90027

Wagner, Jill (Actor)
c/o Jeff Golenberg *Collective*
8383 Wilshire Blvd
Suite 1050
Beverly Hills, CA 90211, USA

Wagner, John (Cartoonist)
Hallmark Cards
Shoebox Division
101 McDonald Dr
Lawrence, KS 66044, USA

Wagner, Katey (Actor)
1500 Old Oak Rd
Los Angeles, CA 90049, USA

Wagner, Katie (Actor, Television Host)
c/o Staff Member *TV Guide Channel*
7140 S Lewis Ave
Tulsa, OK 74136, USA

Wagner, Lindsay (Actor)
Bartels Co
PO Box 57593
Sherman Oaks, CA 91413, USA

Wagner, Lou (Actor)
21224 Celtic St
Chatsworth, CA 91311, USA

Wagner, Louis C Jr (General)
6336 Manchester Way
Alexandria, VA 22304-3534, USA

Wagner, Maggie (Actor)
Stephany Hurkos Management
11935 Kling St #10
Valley Village, CA 91607, USA

Wagner, Mark (Athlete, Baseball Player)
1838 Willow Arms Dr
Ashtabula, OH 44004-7810, USA

Wagner, Matt (Cartoonist)
DC Comics
1700 Broadway
New York, NY 10019, USA

Wagner, Matt (Athlete, Baseball Player)
1112 Lilac Ln
Cedar Falls, IA 50613-5342, USA

Wagner, Melinda (Composer)
Theodore Presser
588 N Gulph Road
King of Prussia, PA 19406, USA

Wagner, Michael R (Mike) (Athlete,
Football Player)
203 East Cherry Dr
Mars, PA 16046, USA

Wagner, Mike (Athlete, Football Player)
2607 Lakeview Way
Plant City, FL 33566, USA

Wagner, Natasha Gregson (Actor)
c/o Amy Guenther *Gateway Management
Company Inc*
860 Via De La Paz
Suite F10
Pacific Palisades, CA 90272, USA

Wagner, Paul (Athlete, Baseball Player)
N1960 State Road 67
Neosho, WI 53059-9723, USA

Wagner, Paula (Producer)
Chestnut Ridge Productions
3000 Olympic Blvd
Bldg 1 #2515
Santa Monica, CA 90404, USA

Wagner, Philip M (Writer)
32 Montgomery St
Boston, MA 02116, USA

Wagner, Phillip (Athlete, Basketball
Player)
328 Glenloch Ln
Stockbridge, GA 30281, USA

Wagner, Robert (Actor)
c/o Chuck Binder *Binder & Associates*
1465 Lindacrest Dr
Beverly Hills, CA 90210, USA

Wagner, Robin S A (Designer)
Robin Wagner Studio
890 Broadway
New York, NY 10003, USA

Wagner, Roy H (Actor, Director)
c/o Lisa Helsing Lenhoff *Lenhoff &
Lenhoff*
830 Palm Ave
West Hollywood, CA 90069

Wagner, Ryan (Athlete, Baseball Player)
59 County Road 311
Yoakum, TX 77995-6014, USA

Wagner, William E (Billy) (Athlete,
Baseball Player)
5066 Jones Mill Rd
Crozet, VA 22932-2610, USA

Wagoner, Dan (Choreographer, Dancer)
Contemporary Dance Theater
17 Duke's Road
London WC1H 9AB, UNITED KINGDOM
(UK)

Wagoner, Dan (Athlete, Football Player)
714 Carriage Hill Rd
Simpsonville, SC 29681, USA

Wagoner, David R (Writer)
5416 154th Place SW
Edmonds, WA 98026, USA

Wagoner, G Richard (Business Person)
General Motors Corp
100 Renaissance Center
Detroit, MI 48243, USA

Wagoner, Harold E (Architect)
331 Lindsey Dr
Berwyn, PA 19312, USA

Wagstaff, Patricia (Aviator)
1417 Sadler Rd
Fernandina Beach, FL 32034-0301, USA

Wahl, Deborah (Stylist)
4010 Band Shell Ct
Chesapeake Beach, MD 20732, USA

Wahl, Ken (Actor)
c/o Susan Balistocky *Law Offices of Sysan
Balistocky*
1901 Avenue of the Stars
Suite 1900
Los Angeles, CA 90067, USA

Wahlberg, Donnie (Actor, Musician)
c/o Jonathan Baruch *Rain Management
Group (RMG)*
1631 21st St
Santa Monica, CA 90404, USA

Wahlberg, Mark (Actor, Model, Musician)
c/o Stephen (Steve) Levinson *Leverage
Management*
3030 Pennsylvania Ave
Santa Monica, CA 90404, USA

Wahle, Mike (Athlete, Football Player)
914 Laurie Dr
Madison, WI 53711, USA

Wahlgren, Olof G C (Editor)
Nicoloviusgatan 5B
Malmo 217 57, SWEDEN

Wahlquist, Heather (Actor)
c/o Troy Begnaud *Evolution Entertainment
(LA)*
901 N Highland Ave
Los Angeles, CA 90038, USA

Wahlstrom, Becky (Actor)
c/o Rob D'Avola *Rob DAvola &
Associates*
9107 Wilshire Blvd #450
Beverly Hills, CA 90210, USA

Wahlstrom, Jarl H (Religious Leader)
Borgstrominkuja 1A10
Helsinki 84 00840, FINLAND

Waigel, Theodor (Government Official)
Oberrohr
Ursberg 86513, GERMANY

Waihee, John D III (Politician)
733 Ulumaika St
Honolulu, HI 96813-5109, USA

Wain, Bea (Musician)
9955 Durant Dr #305
Beverly Hills, CA 90212, USA

Wainhouse, Dave (Athlete, Baseball
Player)
6101 85th Pl SE
Mercer Island, WA 98040-4916, USA

Wainscott, Loyd (Athlete, Football Player)
401 Tarpey Rd
Texas City, TX 77591, USA

Wainwright, Adam (Athlete, Baseball
Player)
2100 Brook Hill Ct
Chesterfield, MO 63017-7941, USA

Wainwright, James (Actor)
Lew Sherrell
937 N Sinova
Mesa, AZ 85205, USA

Wainwright, Loudon (Actor)
c/o Harriet Sternberg *Harriet Sternberg
Management*
4530 Gloria Ave
Encino, CA 91436, USA

Wainwright, Loudon III (Musician,
Songwriter, Writer)
Teddy Wainwright
521 SW Halpatiokee St
Stuart, FL 34994, USA

Wainwright, Rufus (Musician)
c/o Barry Taylor *MCT Management*
520 8th Ave Rm 2205
New York, NY 10018, USA

Wainwright, Rupert (Director)
c/o Staff Member *United Talent Agency
(UTA)*
9336 Civic Center Dr
Beverly Hills, CA 90210, USA

Waite, Jimmy (Athlete, Hockey Player)
Chicoutimi Sagueneens
643 Rue Begin
Attn: Coaching Staff
Chicoutimi, QC G7H 4N7, Canada

Waite, John (Musician, Songwriter,
Writer)
506 Walt Whitman Rd
Melville, NY 11747, USA

Waite, Liam
c/o Staff Member *Gersh (LA)*
9465 Wilshire Blvd
Suite 600
Beverly Hills, CA 90212, USA

Waite, Ralph (Actor)
73317 Ironwood St
Palm Desert, CA 92260, USA

Waite, Terence H (Terry) (Religious
Leader)
Wheelrights Green Harvest
Bury Saint Demunds
Suffolk IP29 4DH, UNITED KINGDOM
(UK)

Waite, Terry (Politician)
Wheelrights The Green Hartest Burv St
Edmunds
Suffolk IP29 4DH, England

Waiters, Granville (Athlete, Basketball
Player)
481 Oakwood Ave
Columbis, OH 43110-8082, USA

Waiters, Van (Athlete, Football Player)
6021 NW 201st Ln
Hialeah, FL 33015, USA

Waitley, Denis (Writer)
The Waitley Institute
P.O. Box 197
Rancho Santa Fe, CA 92067, USA

Waitley, Denis (Business Person)
The Waitley Institute
PO Box 197
Rancho Santa Fe, CA 92067, USA

Waits, Rick (Athlete, Baseball Player)
PO Box 1001
Patagonia, AZ 85624-1001, USA

Waits, Tom (Music Group, Musician,
Songwriter, Writer)
c/o Adam Isaacs *WME (LA)*
9601 Wilshire Blvd Fl 3
Beverly Hills, CA 90210, USA

Waitt, Theodore W (Ted) (Business
Person)
Gateway Inc
7565 Irvine Center Drive
Irvine, CA 92618, USA

Waitz, Richard H (Cinematographer)
405 Zenith Ave
Lafayette, CO 80026, USA

Wajda, Andrezei
u1 Jezefa Hauke Boska 14
Warsaw, POLAND 01-540

Wajda, Andrzej (Director)
Ul Konopnickiej 26
Cracow 30-302, POLAND

Wakaluk, Darcy (Athlete, Hockey Player)
Calgary Hitmen
PO Box 1540 Stn M
Attn: Coaching Staff
Calgary, AB T2P 3B9, Canada

Wakamatsu, Don (Athlete, Baseball
Player)
8740 Ramblewood Ct
Keller, TX 76248-0361, USA

Wakasugi, Hiroshi
Astrid Schoerke
Monckebergallee 41
Hanover 30453, GERMANY

Wakata, Koichi (Astronaut)
NASA
13507 Country Green Ct
Houston, TX 77059-3558, USA

Wakefield, Abbey-May (Actor)
c/o Simon Millar *Rumble Media*
1620 Broadway
Santa Monica, CA 90403, USA

Wakefield, Andre (Athlete, Basketball
Player)
320 Wisconsin Ave
Apt 519
Oak Park, IL 60302-3459, USA

Wakefield, Bill (Athlete, Baseball Player)
1 Baypoint Village Dr
San Rafael, CA 94901-8409, USA

Wakefield, Cameron (Actor)
c/o Simon Millar *Rumble Media*
1620 Broadway
Santa Monica, CA 90403, USA

Wakefield, Rhys (Actor)
c/o Darren Statt *Creative Artists Agency (CAA-LA)*
2000 Ave Of The Stars
Los Angeles, CA 90067, USA

Wakefield, Tim (Athlete, Baseball Player)
241 Lansing Island Dr
Indian Harbour Beach, FL 32937-5102, USA

Wakeham of Maldon, John (Government Official)
House of Lords
Westminster
London SW1A 0PW, UNITED KINGDOM (UK)

Wakeland, Chris (Athlete, Baseball Player)
60997 Luttrell Ln
Saint Helens, OR 97051-9126, USA

Wakeley, Amanda (Designer, Fashion Designer)
79-91 New Kings Road
London SW6 4SQ, UNITED KINGDOM (UK)

Wakely, Ernie (Athlete, Hockey Player)
11052 E Roundup Dr
Dewey, AZ 86327-5411, USA

Wakeman, Frederic E Jr (Historian)
702 Gonzalez Dr
San Francisco, CA 94132, USA

Wakeman, Rick (Musician, Songwriter, Writer)
Bajonor House
2 Bridge St Peel
Isle of Man, UNITED KINGDOM (UK)

Waknin, Deborah (Stylist)
c/o Staff Member *Photogenics Media*
8549 Higuera St
Building B
Culver City, CA 90232, USA

Wako, Gabriel Zubeir Cardinal (Religious Leader)
Archdiocese
PO Box 49
Khartoum, SUDAN

Wakoski, Diane (Writer)
607 Division St
East Lansing, MI 48823, USA

Walackas, Augie (Race Car Driver)
255 Plymouth St.
Whitman, MA 02382, USA

Walbeck, Matt (Athlete, Baseball Player)
8216 Olive Ave
Fair Oaks, CA 95628-7623, USA

Walberg, Mark L. (Actor, Television Host)
c/o Staff Member *WME (LA)*
9601 Wilshire Blvd Fl 3
Beverly Hills, CA 90210, USA

Walberg, Tim (Congressman, Politician)
418 Cannon HOB
Washington, DC 20515, USA

Walby, Chris (Athlete, Football Player)
22 Serenity Cove
Winnipeg, MB R2G 2P7, CANADA

Walcott, Derek (Nobel Prize Laureate)
c/o Staff Member *Farrar, Straus and Giroux*
18 W 18th St
New York, NY 10011-4607, USA

Walcott, Gregory (Actor)
22246 Saticoy St
Canoga Park, CA 91303, USA

Walcott, Jennifer (Model)
4400 N Scottsdale Rd Ste 9
Scottsdale, AZ 85251-3331, USA

Walcutt, John (Actor)
c/o Staff Member *MC Talent Management*
4821 Lankershim Blvd #F329
N Hollywood, CA 91601, USA

Walczak, Mark (Athlete, Football Player)
P.O. Box 372
Scottsdale, AZ 85252-0372, USA

Wald, Charles F (General)
Deputy CofS for Air/Space Operations
HqUSAF Pentaton
Washington, DC 20330, USA

Wald, Jeff (Producer)
c/o Jeff Wald *Jeff Wald Entertainment*
3000 W Olympic Blvd
Bldg 2 #1400
Santa Monica, CA 90404, USA

Wald, Patricia M (Judge)
US Court of Appeals
3rd & Constitution NW
Washington, DC 20001, USA

Waldegrave, William (Government Official)
66 Palace Gardens Terrace
London W8 4RR, UNITED KINGDOM (UK)

Waldemore, Stan (Athlete, Football Player)
P.O. Box 611
New Vernon, NJ 07976, USA

Walden, Greg (Congressman, Politician)
2182 Rayburn HOB
Washington, DC 20515, USA

Walden, Robert (Actor)
415 East 54th St #24C
New York, NY 10022, USA

Walden, Robert E (Bobby) (Athlete, Football Player)
1403 E Douglas Dr
Bainbridge, GA 39819, USA

Walden, Ronnie (Athlete, Baseball Player)
1007 Autumn Way
Blanchard, OK 73010, USA

Walder, Katie
c/o Jeff Morrone *Jeff Morrone Entertainment*
9350 Wilshire Blvd
Suite 224
Beverly Hills, CA 90212, USA

Waldheim, Kurt (President)
1 Lobkowitz Platz
Vienna 1010, AUSTRIA

Waldhorn, Gary (Actor)
London Mgmt
2-4 Noel St
London W1V 3RB, UNITED KINGDOM (UK)

Waldie, Marc (Athlete, Volleyball Player)
Murray Lampert Construction
3545 Camino Del Rio South
Suite C
San Diego, CA 92108, USA

Waldman, Suzyn (Sportscaster)
8 Foster Ct
Croton On Hudson, NY 10520-3303, USA

Waldner, Jan-Ove (Athlete, Tennis Player)
Banda
Skiulstagatan 1O
Eskilstuna 632 29, SWEDEN

Waldo, Janet
15735 Royal Oak Rd
Encino, CA 91316

Waldorf, Duffy (Golfer)
17100 Halsted St
Northridge, CA 91325, USA

Waldorf, Julie (Stylist)
c/o Staff Member *Fred Segal Beauty*
PO Box 5304
Beverly Hills, CA 90209, USA

Waldron, Jeremy J (Educator)
1061 Keith Ave
Berkeley, CA 94708, USA

Wales, Ross (Swimmer)
2730 Walsh Road
Cincinnati, OH 45208, USA

Walesa, Lech (Politician)
Polskistr 53
Gdansk-Oiiwa, POLAND

Waletrs, David (Politician)
RR 2
Watts, OK 74964, USA

Walewander, Jim (Athlete, Baseball Player)
6149 Loch Raven Dr
Me Lean, VA 22101-3131, USA

Walger, Sonya (Actor)
c/o Jon Rubinstein *Authentic Talent and Literary Management*
45 Main St
Suite 1004
Brooklyn, NY 11201, USA

Walheim, Rex J (Astronaut)
142 Hidden Lake Dr
League City, TX 77573, USA

Walheim, Rex J Lt Colonel (Astronaut)
142 Hidden Lake Dr
League City, TX 77573-6976, USA

Walia, Sonu (Actor, Bollywood)
20 The Anchorage Juhu-Versova Link Road
Andheri(W)
Bombay, MS 400 058, INDIA

Walik, Billy (Athlete, Football Player)
P.O. Box 10712
Bainbridge Island, WA 98110, USA

Walk, Bob (Athlete, Baseball Player)
2494 Shadowbrook Dr
Wexford, PA 15090-7982, USA

Walk, Neal (Athlete, Basketball Player)
6030 N 11th Ave
Phoenix, AZ 85013-1415, USA

Walkabouts, The
PO Box 360524
Berlin, GERMANY 10975

Walken, Christopher (Actor)
c/o Mara Buxbaum *ID PR (LA)*
7060 Hollywood Blvd
8th Floor
Los Angeles, CA 90028, USA

Walker, Adam (Athlete, Football Player)
915 Brookline Way
Alpharetta, GA 30022, USA

Walker, Alan (Misc)
Johns Hopkins
Medical School
Cell Biology/Anatomy Dept
Baltimore, MD 21205, USA

Walker, Alice M (Writer)
PO Box 378
Philo, CA 95466, USA

Walker, Ally (Actor)
c/o Katie Mason *Luber Roklin Management*
8530 Wilshire Blvd
6th Floor
Beverly Hills, CA 90211, USA

Walker, Anetia
19551 Turtle Ridge Lane
Northridge, CA 91326-3808

Walker, Ann (Actor)
c/o Pam Ellis *Ellis Talent Group*
4705 Laurel Canyon Blvd
Suite 300
Valley Village, CA 91607, USA

Walker, Antoine (Athlete, Basketball Player)
3950 Wood Ave
Miami, FL 60654-3495, USA

Walker, Arnetia (Actor)
19551 Turtle Ridge Lane
Northridge, CA 91326, USA

Walker, Benjamin (Actor)
c/o Cara Tripicchio *WKT Public Relations (WKT-LA)*
9350 Wilshire Blvd
Suite 450
Beverly Hills, CA 90212, USA

Walker, B J (Financier)
First Union Corp
1 First Union Center
Charlotte, NC 28288, USA

Walker, Bree
3347 Tareco Dr.
Los Angeles, CA 90068

Walker, Brian (Cartoonist)
c/o Staff Member *King Features Syndication*
300 W 57th St
15th Floor
New York, NY 10019-5238, USA

Walker, Bruce (Athlete, Football Player)
279 Eastlawn St
Detroit, MI 48215, USA

Walker, Butch (Musician)
c/o Jonathan Daniel *Crush Management*
60-62 E 11th St
7th Floor
New York, NY 10003, USA

Walker, Caroline (Actor)
c/o Staff Member *Badgley-Connor-King*
9229 Sunset Blvd.
Suite 311
Los Angeles, CA 90069, USA

Walker, Charles D (Astronaut)
Boeing Co
12771 N Morgan Ranch Rd
Oro Valley, AZ 85755-6767, USA

Walker, Charls E (Economist)
9426 Thrush Lane
Potomac, MD 20854-3991, USA

Walker, Chet (Athlete, Basketball Player)
P.O. Box 9451
Marina Del Rey, CA 90069-1514, USA

Walker, Chico (Athlete, Baseball Player)
6 Athena Ct
Tinley Park, IL 60477-4815, USA

Walker, Chris (Actor)
Roll Kruger
121 Gloucester Place
London W1H 3PJ, UNITED KINGDOM
(UK)

Walker, Chuck (Athlete, Football Player)
1613 Tradd Ct
Chesterfield, MO 63017, USA

Walker, Clarence "Foots (Athlete,
Basketball Player)
706 NE Hunters Rd
Blue Springs, MO 64014-6530, USA

Walker, Clay (Musician)
c/o Liza Prijate *Susan Blond Inc (NY)*
50 W 57th St
14th Floor
New York, NY 10019, USA

Walker, Cleo (Athlete, Football Player)
512 Tecumseh Dr
Shepherdsville, KY 40165, USA

Walker, Clint (Actor)
101 W. Mcknight Way
B-202
Grass Valley, CA 95949, USA

Walker, Darnell (Athlete, Football Player)
2636 Columbus St
Muskogee, OK 74401, USA

Walker, Darrell (Athlete, Basketball
Player, Coach)
16122 Patriot Dr
Little Rock, AR 72212-2669, USA

Walker, David (Government Official)
General Accounting Office
441 G St NW
Washington, DC 20548, USA

Walker, Denard (Athlete, Football Player)
17214 Lechlade Ln
Dallas, TX 75252-4208, USA

Walker, Derek (Architect)
2 General Sage Dr
Santa Fe, NM 87505, USA

Walker, Derrick (Race Car Driver)
Walker Racing
147 Midland Rd Royston
Bamsley
S York S71 4B1, UNITED KINGDOM
(UK)

Walker, Dewayne (Athlete, Football
Player)
2364 Tuscan Hills Ln
Las Cruces, NM 88011-4105, USA

Walker, Dreama (Actor)
c/o Randi Goldstein *Gersh (NY)*
41 Madison Ave
New York, NY 10010, USA

Walker, Duane (Athlete, Baseball Player)
2509 Georgia Ave
Deer Park, TX 77536-4732, USA

Walker, Dwight (Athlete, Football Player)
221 N Laurel St
Apt B
Metairie, LA 70003, USA

Walker, Eamonn (Actor)
c/o Scott Schachter *United Talent Agency
(UTA)*
9336 Civic Center Dr
Beverly Hills, CA 90210, USA

Walker, Fiona (Writer)
c/o Susan Fletcher *Hodder & Stoughton
Limited*
338 Euston Rd
London NW1 3BH, UK

Walker, George T Jr (Composer)
323 Grove St
Montclair, NJ 07042, USA

Walker, Glen (Athlete, Football Player)
5592 Nelson St
Cypress, CA 90630, USA

Walker, Greg (Athlete, Baseball Player)
530 N Lake Shore Dr
Apt 1009
Chicago, IL 60611-7426, USA

Walker, Greg (Cartoonist)
c/o Staff Member *King Features
Syndication*
300 W 57th St
15th Floor
New York, NY 10019-5238, USA

Walker, Harry
RR #2Box 145
Leeds, AL 35094

Walker, Herschel (Athlete, Football
Player, Heisman Trophy Winner)
2210 King Fisher Dr
Westlake, TX 76262-4815, USA

Walker, Hezekiah (Musician)
c/o Staff Member *The Alliance Agency*
1035 Bates Ct.
Hendersonville, TN 37075, USA

Walker, Howard (Athlete, Hockey Player)
PO Box 254
Wembley, AB T0H 3S0, Canada

Walker, Hugh (Baseball Player)
Bowman
24 Georgeann Dr
Jacksonville, AR 72076-5352, USA

Walker, Jackie (Athlete, Football Player)
13014 N Dale Mabry Hwy #120
Tampa, FL 33618, USA

Walker, James E (Educator)
Middle Tennessee State University
President's Office
Murfreesboro, TN 37132, USA

Walker, James L (Jimmy) (Misc)
Fireman & Oilers Brotherhood
1100 Circle 75 Parkway
Atlanta, GA 30339, USA

Walker, Jamie (Athlete, Baseball Player)
11450 W 187th St
Spring Hill, KS 66083-7593, USA

Walker, Jason (Musician)
c/o Len Evans *Project Publicity*
312 West 53rd St
Suite 202
New York, NY 10019, USA

Walker, Javon (Athlete, Football Player)
7375 Talon Trl
Parker, CO 80138, USA

Walker, Jeff (Athlete, Football Player)
3712 Ringgold Rd
Apt 204
Chattanooga, TN 37412, USA

Walker, Jerry (Athlete, Baseball Player)
2015 Collins Blvd
Ada, OK 74820, USA

Walker, Jerry Jeff (Musician, Songwriter)
Tried & True Music
PO Box 39
Austin, TX 78767, USA

Walker, Jimmie (J J) (Actor, Comedian)
c/o Wes Stevens *Vox*
6420 Wilshire Blvd Ste 1080
Los Angeles, CA 90048, USA

Walker, Joe Louis (Musician)
Rick Bates Mgmt
714 Brookside Lane
Sierra Madre, CA 91024, USA

Walker, John (Athlete, Track Athlete)
Jeffs Road
RD Papatoetoe, NEW ZEALAND

Walker, John (Nobel Prize Laureate)
MRC Molecular Biology Laboratory
Medical Research Center Council
Laboratory of Molecular BiologyHills
Road
London CB2 2QH, UNITED KINGDOM
(UK)

Walker, Johnny (Athlete, Baseball Player)
Raleigh Tigers
718 Franklin St SE
Grand Rapids, MI 49507-1307, USA

Walker, Junior
141 Dunbar Ave.
Fords, NJ 08863

Walker, Kenny (Athlete, Basketball Player)
7235 Darsena
Grand Prairie, TX 75054-6508, USA

Walker, Kenyatta (Athlete, Football
Player)
14813 Tudor Chase Dr
Tampa, FL 33626, USA

Walker, Kevin (Athlete, Baseball Player)
759 Chestnut Ave
Holtville, CA 92250-1410, USA

Walker, Kurt (Athlete, Hockey Player)
196 N Wesley Chapel Rd
Eatonton, GA 31024-6047, USA

Walker, Larry (Athlete, Baseball Player)
1667 Flagler Pkwy
West Palm Beach, FL 334111-1874, USA

Walker, Leslie David (Actor)
13952 Hartsook St
Sherman Oaks, CA 91423, USA

Walker, Luke (Athlete, Baseball Player)
316 Loma Linda St
Wake Village, TX 75501-8638, USA

Walker, Malcolm (Athlete, Football
Player)
7140 Winterwood Ln
Dallas, TX 75248, USA

Walker, Marquis (Athlete, Football Player)
17576 Cherrylawn St
Detroit, MI 48221, USA

Walker, Mickey (Athlete, Football Player)
22828 S Maple Point Rd
Pickford, MI 49774, USA

Walker, Mike (Athlete, Baseball Player)
23195 Tankersley Rd
Brooksville, FL 34601-4818, USA

Walker, Mike (Athlete, Baseball Player)
24616 Marks Rd
Splendora, TX 77372, USA

Walker, Mort (Cartoonist)
61 Studio Court
Stamford, CT 06903-4724, USA

Walker, Nicholas
1900 Ave. of the Stars #1640
Los Angeles, CA 90067

Walker, Olene (Politician)
3135 Jacob Hamblin Dr
Saint George, UT 84790-7807, USA

Walker, Paul (Actor)
c/o Matt Luber *Luber Roklin Management*
8530 Wilshire Blvd
6th Floor
Beverly Hills, CA 90211, USA

Walker, Paul L (Religious Leader)
Church of God
PO Box 2430
Cleveland, TN 37320, USA

Walker, Pete (Athlete, Baseball Player)
2 White Oak Ln
Quaker Hill, CT 06375-1045, USA

Walker, Peter (Director)
23 Bentick St
London W1, UNITED KINGDOM (UK)

Walker, Phillip (Athlete, Basketball Player)
720 E Phil Ellena St
Philadelphia, PA 19119, USA

Walker, Polly (Actor)
c/o Jon Rubinstein *Authentic Talent and
Literary Management*
45 Main St
Suite 1004
Brooklyn, NY 11201, USA

Walker, Rick (Athlete, Football Player)
906 Winstead St
Great Falls, VA 22066, USA

Walker, Robert M (Physicist)
1 Brookings Dr #CB1105
Saint Louis, MO 63130, USA

Walker, Roger N (Architect)
8 Brougham St
Mount Victoria
Wellington, NEW ZEALAND

Walker, Ronald C (Publisher)
Smithsonian Magazine
900 Jefferson Dr SW
Washington, DC 20560, USA

Walker, Sammy (Athlete, Football Player)
1031 Kings Row
Mc Kinney, TX 75069, USA

Walker, Sandra (Opera Singer)
Columbia Artists Mgmt Inc
165 W 57th St
New York, NY 10019, USA

Walker, Sarah E B (Opera Singer)
152 Inchmery Road
London SE6 1DF, UNITED KINGDOM
(UK)

Walker, Scott (Director)
c/o Michael Esola *WME (LA)*
9601 Wilshire Blvd Fl 3
Beverly Hills, CA 90210, USA

Walker, Scott (Governor, Politician)
State Capitol
PO Box 7863
Madison, WI 53702, USA

Walker, Shannon Dr (Astronaut)
2421 Clopper St
Seabrook, TX 77586-3738, USA

Walker, Todd (Athlete, Baseball Player)
212 Madonna Dr
Benton, LA 71006-4217, USA

Walker, Tom (Athlete, Baseball Player)
817 Whippoorwill Hill Rd
Gibsonia, PA 15044-8985, USA

Walker, Tony (Athlete, Baseball Player)
2030 Goldenrod Ln
San Ramon, CA 94582-5543, USA

Walker, Tyler (Race Car Driver)
222 Raceway Dr.
Mooresville, NC 28117, United States

Walker, Tyler (Athlete, Baseball Player)
400 Sansome St
San Francisco, CA 94111, USA

Walker, Val Joe (Athlete, Football Player)
3857 S Versailles Ave
Dallas, TX 75209, USA

Walker, Wally (Athlete, Basketball Player)
154 Lombard St
Apt 58
San Francisco, CA 94111-1125, USA

Walker, Wayne (Athlete, Football Player)
2033 White Pine Ln
Boise, ID 83706, USA

Walker, Wesley D (Athlete, Football Player)
P.O. Box 20438
Huntington Station, NY 11746, USA

Walker, William D (Business Person)
Tektronix Inc
26600 Sourtwest Parkway
Wilsonville, OR 97070, USA

Walker Jr, Robert (Actor)
TOPS
23410 Civic Center Way #C-1
Malibu, CA 90265, USA

Walker of Worchester, Peter E
(Government Official)
Abbots Morton Manor
Grooms Hill Abbots Morton
Worc WR7 4LT, UNITED KINGDOM
(UK)

Walkom, Stephen (Athlete, Hockey Player)
1709 Wheatland Dr
Coraopolis, PA 15108-9208, USA

Wall, Bob (Athlete, Hockey Player)
1203 Canuck Trail RR 5
Minden, ON K0M 2Al, Canada

Wall, Brian A (Artist)
306 Lombard St
San Francisco, CA 94133, USA

Wall, Carolyn (Publisher)
Newsweek Magazine
251 W 57th St
New York, NY 10019, USA

Wall, David (Ballerina)
Royal Ballet
Covent Garden
Bow St
London WC2E 9DD, UNITED KINGDOM
(UK)

Wall, Donne (Athlete, Baseball Player)
116 River Breeze Way
Saint Louis, MO 63129, USA

Wall, Frederick T (Athlete, Football Player)
2044 Kerwood Ave
Los Angeles, CA 90025-6007, USA

Wall, John (Athlete, Basketball Player)
c/o Dan Fegan *Lagardere Unlimited - (LA)*
10866 Wilshire Blvd
Los Angeles, CA 90024, USA

Wall, John F (General)
507 Hanover St
Fredericksburg, VA 22401, USA

Wall, Lindsay (Hockey Player)
University of Minnesota
Athletic Dept
Minneapolis, MN 55455, USA

Wall, Paul (Musician)
c/o Drew Elliot *Universal Media Artists*
8255 W Sunset Blvd
Los Angeles, CA 90046, USA

Wall, Shana (Actor)
c/o Elizabeth Much *Much and House Public Relations*
8075 W 3rd St
Suite 500
Los Angeles, CA 90048, USA

Wall, Stan (Athlete, Baseball Player)
9907 E 80th St
Raytown, MO 64138, USA

Wallace, Aaron (Athlete, Football Player)
612 Gardenia St
Desoto, TX 75115, USA

Wallace, Andy (Race Car Driver)
Childress-Howard Motorsports
PO Box 889
Denver, 28037 USA, USA

Wallace, Anthony F C (Misc)
University of Pennsylvania
Anthropology Dept
Philadelphia, PA 19014, USA

Wallace, Aria (Actor)
c/o DebraLynn Findon *Discover Inc Management*
11425 Moorpark St
Studio City, CA 91602, USA

Wallace, Barron Steven (Steve) (Athlete, Football Player)
305 Heards Ferry Rd
Atlanta, GA 30328, USA

Wallace, Ben (Basketball Player)
c/o Staff Member *Chicago Bulls*
1901 W Madision St
Chicago, IL 60612, USA

Wallace, B J (Athlete, Baseball Player, Olympic Athlete)
12775 River Creek Dr
Fairhope, AL 36532-6501, USA

Wallace, Bob (Athlete, Football Player)
44111 N 43rd Dr
New River, AZ 85087-5956, USA

Wallace, Bruce (Doctor, Scientist)
940 McBryde Dr
Blacksburg, VA 24060, USA

Wallace, Carol (Editor)
People Magazine
Editorial Dept
Time-Life Building
New York, NY 10020, USA

Wallace, Cathy (Stylist)
PO Box 140725
Irving, TX 75014-0725, USA

Wallace, Chris (Correspondent)
c/o Staff Member *ABC News*
77 W 66th St
3rd Floor
New York, NY 10023, USA

Wallace, Christopher (Chris)
(Correspondent)
Fox-TV
News Dept
205 E 67th St
New York, NY 10021, USA

Wallace, Clifford J (Judge)
US Court of Appeals
940 Front St
San Diego, CA 92101, USA

Wallace, Cooper (Athlete, Football Player)
c/o Chad Speck *Allegiant Athletic Agency*
35 Market Sq
Suite 201
Knoxville, TN 37902, USA

Wallace, Craig K (Doctor)
National Institutes of Health
9000 Rockville Pike
Bethesda, MD 20892, USA

Wallace, Dave (Athlete, Baseball Player)
82 Whipple Brook Rd
Wrenthan, MA 02093-2512, USA

Wallace, Derek (Athlete, Baseball Player)
4250 SE Boxleaf Pl
Stuart, FL 34997-2253, USA

Wallace, Don (Actor)
c/o Staff Member *Silver Massetti & Szatmary (SMS) Talent Inc*
8383 Wilshire Blvd
Suite 230
Beverly Hills, CA 90211, USA

Wallace, Don (Athlete, Baseball Player)
23 Kris Ln
Manitou Springs, CO 80829-2709, USA

Wallace, George (Musician)
c/o Staff Member *Paradigm (Monterey)*
404 W Franklin St
Monterey, CA 93940, USA

Wallace, Gerald (Athlete, Basketball Player)
8381 Providence Rd
Charlotte, NC 28277-9753, USA

Wallace, Jane (Entertainer)
Cosgrove-Meurer Productions
4303 W Verdugo Ave
Burbank, CA 91505, USA

Wallace, Jeff (Athlete, Baseball Player)
235 Crawford St
Beckley, WV 25801-5633, USA

Wallace, Jennifer (Stylist)
c/o Staff Member *Fred Segal Beauty*
PO Box 5304
Beverly Hills, CA 90209, USA

Wallace, Julie T (Actor)
Annette Stone
9 Newburgh St
London W1V 1LH, UNITED KINGDOM
(UK)

Wallace, Kenny (Race Car Driver)
8995 Harrjs Rd.
Concord, NC 28027-8670, USA

Wallace, Laurie
PO Box 3023
Guttenberg, NJ 07093

Wallace, Marcia (Actor)
c/o Sandie Schnarr *AVOTalent Agency*
5670 Wilshire Blvd.
Suite 1930
Los Angeles, CA 90036, USA

Wallace, Mike (Race Car Driver)
Morgan-McClure Racing
26502 Newbanks Rd.
Abington, VA 24210, USA

Wallace, Mike (Athlete, Baseball Player)
12483 Elk Run Rd
Midland, VA 22728-2316, USA

Wallace, Randall (Actor, Director, Producer, Writer)
c/o Staff Member *Wheelhouse, The*
15464 Ventura Blvd
Sherman Oaks, CA 91403-3002

Wallace, Rasheed (Athlete, Basketball Player)
1979 Arthurs Way
Rochester Hills, MI 48306-3363, USA

Wallace, Ray (Athlete, Football Player)
2480 Port Kembla Dr
Mount Juliet, TN 37122, USA

Wallace, Rheagan (Actor)
c/o Linda McAlister *Linda McAlister Talent*
100 Oak Ln
Waxahachie, TX 75167-8412, USA

Wallace, Rodney (Athlete, Football Player)
20566 E Maplewood Pl
Centennial, CO 80016, USA

Wallace, Roger (Athlete, Football Player)
408 N Oakland St
Urbana, OH 43078, USA

Wallace, Rusty (Race Car Driver)
149 Knob Hill Rd
Mooresville, NC 28117, USA

Wallace, Steve (Race Car Driver)
c/o Staff Member *Rusty Wallace Racing, LLC*
149 Knob Hill Rd
Mooresville, NC 28117, USA

Wallace, Tommy Lee (Director)
Innovative Artists
1505 10th St
Santa Monica, CA 90401, USA

Wallace, Will (Actor)
c/o Andrew Stawiarski *ADS Management*
269 S. Beverly Dr #441
Beverly Hills, CA 90212, USA

Wallace, William (General)
Commanding General
V Corps
APO, AE 09079, USA

Wallach, Eli (Director)
140 Riverside Dr #19E
New York, NY 10024, USA

Wallach, Evan J (Judge)
US International Trade Court
1 Federal Plaza
New York, NY 10278, USA

Wallach, Tim (Athlete, Baseball Player)
21750 Deveron Cv
Yorba Linda, CA 92887-2662, USA

Wallack, Anna (Stylist)
c/o Staff Member *Team*
423 W Broadway
4th Floor
Boston, MA 02127, USA

Wallechinsky, David (Writer)
c/o Staff Member *HarperCollins Publishers*
10 East 53rd St
c/o Author mail, 7th Floor
New York, NY 10022, USA

Wallem, Linda (Actor, Producer)
c/o Staff Member *Creative Artists Agency (CAA-LA)*
2000 Ave Of The Stars
Los Angeles, CA 90067, USA

Wallenberg, Raoul Committee
823 UN Plaza 8th Flr.
New York, NY 10017

Wallendas, The Great
138 Frog Hollow Rd
Churchville, PA 18966

Waller, Dwight (Athlete, Basketball Player)
1038 S Brookside Dr
Gallatin, TN 37066-5612, USA

Waller, Jamie (Athlete, Basketball Player)
904 Owens Ave
South Boston, VA 24592-3728, USA

Waller, Jo (Stylist)
18 E 18th St
#5-E
New York, NY 10003, USA

Waller, Michael (Editor)
Hartford Courant Co
285 Broad St
Hartford, CT 06115, USA

Waller, Peter
7 Passage St. owley
Cornwall, ENGLAND PL23 IDE

Waller, Robert (Writer)
12 Old Harper Rd
Harpe, TX 78631-5255, USA

Waller, Ron (Athlete, Football Player)
900 Concord Rd
Seaford, DE 19973, USA

Waller, Ty (Athlete, Baseball Player)
16963 Silver Crest Dr
San Diego, CA 92127, USA

Waller, Tye (Athlete, Baseball Player)
16963 Silver Crest Dr
San Diego, CA 92127-2816, USA

Waller, William L (Ex-Governor)
Waller and Waller
220 S President St
Jackson, MS 39201, USA

Wallerstein, Ralph G (Misc)
3447 Clay St
San Francisco, CA 94118, USA

Wallflowers, The (Music Group)
c/o Rick Roskin *Creative Artists Agency (CAA-LA)*
2000 Ave Of The Stars
Los Angeles, CA 90067, USA

Walliams, David (Actor, Producer, Writer)
c/o Kevin McLaughlin *Baker Winokur Ryder Public Relations (BWR-LA)*
9100 Wilshire Blvd
Suite 500, West Tower
Beverly Hills, CA 90212, USA

Wallin, Niclas (Athlete, Hockey Player)
244 Johnson Ave
Los Gatos, CA 95030-6218, USA

Walling, Camryn (Actor)
c/o Staff Member *Abrams Artists Agency (LA)*
9200 Sunset Blvd
11th Floor
Los Angeles, CA 90069, USA

Walling, Cheves T (Misc)
214 Rivermead Road
Peterborough, NH 03458-1745, USA

Walling, Denny (Athlete, Baseball Player)
P.O. Box 1312
Waynesboro, VA 22980-0902, USA

Wallis, Annabelle (Actor)
c/o Craig Schneider *Pinnacle Public Relations*
8265 Sunset Blvd
Suite 201
Los Angeles, CA 90064, USA

Wallis, Joe (Athlete, Baseball Player)
PO Box 2284
Saint Louis, MO 63109-0284, USA

Wallis, Kevin (Horse Racer)
2874 NE 33rd St
Lighthouse Point, FL 33064-8551, USA

Wallis, Shani (Actor)
P.O. Box 3604
Dana Point, CA 92629, USA

Walliser, Maria (Skier)
Selfwingert
Malans 7208, SWITZERLAND

Wallner, Hakan (Horse Racer)
PO Box 3153
Pompano Beach, FL 33072-3153, USA

Walls, Denise (Nee-C) (Musician, Songwriter, Writer)
2113 South Ave
Youngstown, OH 44502, USA

Walls, Everson C (Athlete, Football Player)
4812 Portrait Ln
Plano, TX 75024, USA

Walls, Herkie (Athlete, Football Player)
1002 Cherrywood Dr
Garland, TX 75040, USA

Walls, Jeannette (Writer)
c/o Staff Member *Keppler Associates*
3030 Clarendon Blvd
7th Floor
Arlington, VA 22201, USA

Walls, Lenny (Athlete, Football Player)
2800 Bush St
San Francisco, CA 94115, USA

Walls, Wesley (Athlete, Football Player)
8711 Lake Challis Ln
Charlotte, NC 28226, USA

Walmsley, Jon (Actor)
217 Grand Ave
Apt 5
Long Beach, CA 90803-6135, USA

Walpot, Heike (Astronaut)
DLR
Abt Raumflugbetrieb
Cologne 51170, GERMANY

Walrond, Les (Athlete, Baseball Player)
5170 Hickory Hollow Pkwy Unit 262
Antioch, TN 37013-3062, USA

Walser, Derrick (Athlete, Hockey Player)
592 Lorne St
New Glasgow, NS B2H 4L3, Canada

Walser, Don (Musician, Songwriter, Writer)
Nancy Fly Agency
6618 Wolfcreek Pass
Austin, TX 78749, USA

Walser, Martin
Zum Hecht 36
Uberlingen, GERMANY D-88662

Walsh, Addie (Writer)
c/o Staff Member *WmE2 (WMA-LA)*
1 William Morris Pl
Beverly Hills, CA 90212, USA

Walsh, Amanda (Actor)
c/o Laina Cohn *Laina Cohn Management*
15066 Sutton St
Sherman Oaks, CA 91403, USA

Walsh, Arthur
12360 Riverside Dr.
No. Hollywood, CA 91607

Walsh, Bradley (Actor)
c/o Debi Allen *Debi Allen Associates*
22 Torrington Pl
London WC1E 7HP, UK

Walsh, Catherine (Stylist)
3800 Overdale Dr
Columbus, OH 43220, USA

Walsh, Chris (Athlete, Football Player)
4834 N 74th St
Scottsdale, AZ 85251, USA

Walsh, Dave (Athlete, Baseball Player)
500 Concord Ln
Edmond, OK 73003-6127, USA

Walsh, David M (Cinematographer)
15436 Valley Vista Blvd
Sherman Oaks, CA 91403, USA

Walsh, Diana Chapman (Educator)
Wellesley College
President's Office
Wellesley, MA 02181, USA

Walsh, Don (Athlete, Swimmer)
International Maritime Inc
14758 Sitkum Lane
Myrtle Point, OR 97458, USA

Walsh, Donnie (Basketball Coach, Coach)
5625 Audubon Ridge Ln
Indianapolis, IN 46250-2320, USA

Walsh, Dylan (Actor)
c/o Bob McGowan *McGowan Management*
8733 W Sunset Blvd
Suite 103
West Hollywood, CA 90069, USA

Walsh, Frances (Fran) (Producer, Writer)
c/o Staff Member *WingNut Films*
PO Box 15-208
Miramar
Wellington 6003, NEW ZEALAND

Walsh, Gwynyth (Actor)
c/o Staff Member *Characters Talent Agency, The (Vancouver)*
1505 W 2nd Ave
#200
Vancouver, BC V6H 3Y4, Canada

Walsh, Joe (Musician, Songwriter)
400 Porter St
Easton, PA 18042-1726, USA

Walsh, Joe (Congressman, Politician)
432 Cannon HOB
Washington, DC 20515, USA

Walsh, John (Television Host)
c/o Sean Perry *WME (LA)*
9601 Wilshire Blvd Fl 3
Beverly Hills, CA 90210, USA

Walsh, Kate (Actor)
c/o Justin Grey Stone *Untitled Entertainment (LA)*
350 S. Beverly Dr #200
Beverly Hills, CA 90212, USA

Walsh, Kerri (Athlete, Volleyball Player)
c/o Ryan Morgan *MAG Sports Agency*
451 Los Gatos Blvd #103
Los Gatos, CA 95032, USA

Walsh, Kimberley (Actor, Musician)
c/o Staff Member *Artists Rights Group (ARG)*
4 Great Portland St
London W1W 8PA, UNITED KINGDOM (UK)

Walsh, Lawrence E (Attorney, Attorney General, General, Government Official)
1902 Bedford St
Nichols Hills, OK 73116, USA

Walsh, Louis (Actor)
c/o Staff Member *Hackford Jones PR*
19 Nassau St
London W1W 7AF, UK

Walsh, Maiara (Actor)
c/o Staff Member *Mattie Management*
1438 N Gower St #57
Los Angeles, CA 90028-8358, USA

Walsh, Martin (Misc)
National Organization on Disability
910 16th St NW
Washington, DC 20006, USA

Walsh, Matt (Comedian)
c/o Staff Member *United Talent Agency (UTA)*
9336 Civic Center Dr
Beverly Hills, CA 90210, USA

Walsh, M Emmet (Actor)
4173 Motor Ave
Culver City, CA 90232, USA

Walsh, M. Emmett (Actor)
c/o Sandra Joseph *SLJ Management*
833 N Edinburgh Ave Ph 11
Los Angeles, CA 90046, USA

Walsh, Mike (Athlete, Hockey Player)
29 North Street
Andover, NH 03216, USA

Walsh, Patrick C (Doctor)
Johns Hopkins University
Brady Urological Institute
Baltimore, MD 21205, USA

Walsh, Peter (Designer)
Peter Walsh Design
15030 Ventura Blvd #19-881
Sherman Oaks, CA 91403, USA

Walsh, Sheila (Musician, Writer)
PO Box 150783
Nashville, TN 37215, USA

Walsh, Shelia (Musician, Writer)
P.O. Box 1516
Celina, TX 75009-1516, USA

Walsh, Stephen J (Steve) (Athlete, Football Player)
339 Flamigo Dr
West Palm Beach, FL 33401, USA

Walsh, Steve
Box 6 Wickford
Essex, ENGLAND SS12 9D0

Walsh, Sydney (Actor)
Innovative Artists
1505 10th St
Santa Monica, CA 90401, USA

Walsh, Tom (Artist)
PO Box 133
Philomath, OR 97370, USA

Walsh, Ward (Athlete, Football Player)
1658 W Carson St
Suite C
Torrance, CA 90501, USA

Walshe, Tommy (Actor, Television Host)
c/o Staff Member *Arlington Enterprises Ltd*
1-3 Charlotte St
London W1P 1HD, UNITED KINGDOM
(UK)

Walske, Steven (Business Person)
Parametric Technology
140 Kendrick St
Needham Heights, MA 02494, USA

Walsman, Leanna (Actor)
c/o Chris Andrews *Creative Artists Agency*
(CAA-LA)
2000 Ave Of The Stars
Los Angeles, CA 90067, USA

Walte, Grant (Golfer)
9380 S Magnolia Ave
Ocala, FL 34476-7535, USA

Walter, Dr Ulrich (Astronaut)
IBM Deutschland Entwicklung Abtig 8515
Schonaicherstrasse 220
Boblingen D-71032, Germany

Walter, Gene (Athlete, Baseball Player)
1901 Fairway Dr
La Grange, KY 40031, USA

Walter, Harriet (Actor)
c/o Jeremy Conway *Conway van Gelder*
8-12 Broadwick St
London W1F 8HW, UK

Walter, Jessica (Actor)
c/o Sandra Chang *Anonymous Content*
(LA)
955 S Carrillo Dr
Suite 300
Los Angeles, CA 90048, USA

Walter, Joe (Athlete, Football Player)
4136 Binley Dr
Richardson, TX 75082, USA

Walter, Lisa Ann (Actor)
c/o Mel McKeon *McKeon-Myones*
Management
3500 Olive Ave
Suite 770
Burbank, CA 91505, USA

Walter, Michael (Athlete, Football Player)
6900 SW Knollwood St
Tualatin, OR 97062, USA

Walter, Mike (Athlete, Football Player)
6900 SW Knollwood St
Tualatin, OR 97062, USA

Walter, Paul H L (Misc)
3 Benedictine Retreat
Savannah, GA 31411, USA

Walter, Robert D (Business Person)
Cardinal Health
7000 Cardinal Place
Dublin, OH 43017, USA

Walter, Ryan (Athlete, Hockey Player)
19633 8 Av
Langley, BC V2Z lWl, Canada

Walter, Tracey (Actor)
257 N Rexford Dr
Beverly Hills, CA 90210, USA

Walter, Ulrich (Astronaut)
IBM Germany
Schonaicherstr 220
Boblingen 71032, GERMANY

Walters, Barbara (Journalist, Talk Show
Host)
944 5th Ave
New York, NY 10021-2656, USA

Walters, Charles (Director)
23922 De Ville Way #A
Malibu, CA 90265, USA

Walters, Charlie (Athlete, Baseball Player)
1717 Sutton Ln
Saint Paul, MN 55118-3717, USA

Walters, Dan (Athlete, Baseball Player)
Physically Unable To Sign Autographs

Walters, David (Politician)
RR 2
Watts, OK 74964, USA

Walters, Donna (Stylist)
6611 W 62nd St
Mission, KS 66202, USA

Walters, Harry N (Government Official)
DHC Holdings Corp
125 Thomas Dale
Williamsburg, VA 23185, USA

Walters, Hugh
15 Christchurch Ave
London, ENGLAND NW6 7QP

Walters, Jamie (Actor, Musician)
4702 Ethel Ave
Sherman Oaks, CA 91423, USA

Walters, Julie (Actor)
c/o Tom Burke *ICM Partners (ICM-LA)*
10250 Constellation Blvd Fl 7
Los Angeles, CA 90067, USA

Walters, Lisa (Athlete, Golfer)
211 South Westland Avenue
Unit 2
Tampa, FL 33606-1721, USA

Walters, Melora (Actor)
c/o Staff Member *Platform Public*
Relations
2666 N Beachwood Dr
Los Angeles, CA 90068, USA

Walters, Michael (Stylist)
10 Circle Way
MillValley, CA 94941, USA

Walters, Mike (Athlete, Baseball Player)
79070 Desert Stream Dr
La Quinta, CA 92253-4295, USA

Walters, Peter I (Business Person)
22 Hill St
London W1X 7FU, UNITED KINGDOM
(UK)

Walters, Phil (Race Car Driver)
23 Sycamore
Homosassa, FL 32646, USA

Walters, PJ (Athlete, Baseball Player)
29476 Oakstone Dr E
Daphne, AL 36526-5602, USA

Walters, Rex (Athlete, Basketball Player)
21602 W 99th St
Lenexz, KS 94121-2445, USA

Walters, Roger T (Architect)
46 Princess Road
London NW1 8JL, UNITED KINGDOM
(UK)

Walters, Scot (Race Car Driver)
Brewco Motorsports
P.O. Box 37
321 W. Reservoir
Central City, KY 42330, USA

Walters, Stan (Athlete, Football Player)
10 lcklingham Wood
Sewell, NJ 08080, USA

Walters, Susan (Actor)
c/o Gabrielle Krengel *Domain Talent*
9229 Sunset Boulevard
Suite 710
Los Angeles, CA 90069, USA

Walters, Tom (Athlete, Football Player)
8 Heritage Ln
Magnolia, TX 77354, USA

Walters, Tome H Jr (General)
Defense Security Cooperation Agency
1111 Davis Highway
Arlington, VA 22202, USA

Walterschield, Len (Athlete, Football
Player)
2312 I Rd
Grand Junction, CO 81505, USA

Walther, Herbert (Physicist)
Egenhoferstr 7A
Munich 81243, GERMANY

Walther, Paul (Athlete, Basketball Player)
6555 Riverside Dr NW
Atlanta, GA 313328-27135, USA

Walton, Alice (Business Person)
Wal-Mart Stores
702 SW 8th St
Bentonville, AR 72716, USA

Walton, Anna (Actor)
c/o Rupert Fowler *ID Public Relations*
Pall Mall Deposit 124-128 Barlby Rd
Unit 27A
London W10 6BL, UK

Walton, Anthony J (Tony) (Designer)
International Creative Mgmt
40 W 57th St #1800
New York, NY 10019, USA

Walton, Bennie (Baseball Player)
188 S Palm Villas Way
Lake Worth, FL 33461-1084, USA

Walton, Bill (Athlete, Basketball Player,
Sportscaster)
1010 Myrtle Way
San Diego, CA 92103-5123, USA

Walton, Bruce (Athlete, Baseball Player)
10704 Sunset Canvon Dr
Bakersfield, CA 93311-2746, USA

Walton, Cedar A Jr (Musician)
Bridge Agency
35 Clark St #A5
Brooklyn Heights, NY 11201, USA

Walton, Christy (Business Person)
Wal-Mart Stores
702 SW 8th St
Bentonville, AR 72716, USA

Walton, Danny (Athlete, Baseball Player)
P.O. Box 296
Huntsville, UT 84317-0296, USA

Walton, David (Actor)
c/o Nick Collins *Gersh (LA)*
9465 Wilshire Blvd
Suite 600
Beverly Hills, CA 90212, USA

Walton, Jerome (Athlete, Baseball Player)
4500 Shannon Blvd Sot 8C
Union City, GA 30291-2425, USA

Walton, Jess (Actor)
c/o Staff Member *Stone Manners Salners*
Agency (LA)
9911 W Pico Blvd Ste 1400
Los Angeles, CA 90035, USA

Walton, Jim (Business Person)
The Walton Family Foundation
P.O. Box 2030
Bentonville, AR 72712, USA

Walton, John (Athlete, Football Player)
401 New York Ave
Elizabeth City, NC 27909, USA

Walton, Joseph (Joe) (Athlete, Coach,
Football Coach, Football Player)
8 Windy Crest Dr
Beaver Falls, PA 15010, USA

Walton, Lawrence (Athlete, Football
Player)
8636 N 96th Ln
Peoria, IL 85345-7759, USA

Walton, Luke (Athlete, Basketball Player)
1613 Gates Ave
Manhattan Beach, CA 913266-71328,
USA

Walton, Mike (Athlete, Hockey Player)
RE/MAX Realty
102B-45 Bramalea Rd
Brampton, ON L6T 2W4, Canada

Walton, Reggie (Athlete, Baseball Player)
1142 S Curson Ave
Los Angeles, CA 90019-6611, USA

Walton, Robin (Golfer)
8404 SW 50th Ln
Gainesville, FL 32608-4307, USA

Walton, S Robson (Rob) (Business Person)
Wal-Mart Stores
702 SW 8th St
Bentonville, AR 72716, USA

Walton, Whip (Athlete, Football Player)
5662 Weatherstone Ct
San Diego, CA 92130, USA

Waltrip, Darrell (Race Car Driver)
110 Deerfield
Franklin, TN 37064, USA

Waltrip, Michael (Race Car Driver)
Michael Waltrip Racing
8566 Dog Leg Rd.
Sherrills Ford, NC 28673-7723, USA

Waltrip, Robert L (Business Person)
Service Corp International
1929 Allen Parkway
Houston, TX 77019, USA

Waltz, Christoph (Actor)
c/o Craig Bankey *WKT Public Relations*
(WKT-LA)
9350 Wilshire Blvd
Suite 450
Beverly Hills, CA 90212, USA

Waltz, Lisa (Actor)
c/o Donald Spradlin *Essential Talent*
Management
6399 Wilshire Blvd
Suite 401
Los Angeles, CA 90048, USA

Waltz, Rich (Sportscaster)
1429 NW 127th Ave
Coral SPrimzs, FL 33071-5447, USA

Walz, Carl E (Astronaut)
129 Lake Point Dr
League City, TX 77573, USA

Walz, Carl E Col (Astronaut)
15506 Eagle Tavern Ln
Centreville, VA 20120-3701, USA

Walz, Wes (Athlete, Hockey Player)
10435 Raleigh Rd
Saint Paul, MN 55129-4202, USA

Walz, Zach (Athlete, Football Player)
6270 E Wilshire Dr
Scottsdale, AZ 85257, USA

Wamala, Emmanuel Cardinal (Religious Leader)
PO Box 14125
Mengo
Kampala, UGANDA

Wambach, Abby (Athlete, Olympic Athlete, Soccer Player)
446 Monterey Blvd Apt H2
Hermosa Beach, CA 90254-4575, USA

Wambaugh, Joseph (Writer)
30 Linda Isle
Newport Beach, CA 92660-7206, USA

Wambold, Richard L (Business Person)
Pactiv Corp
1900 W Field Court
Lake Forest, IL 60045, USA

Wamsley, Rick (Athlete, Hockey Player)
1171 Wildhorse Meadows Drive
Chesterfield, MO 63005, USA

Wan, James (Director)
c/o Stacey Testro Stacey Testro International
8265 Sunset Blvd #102
Los Angeles, CA 90046, USA

Wan, Li (Government Official)
State Council
People's Congress
Tian An Men Square
Beijing, CHINA

Wanamaker, Zoe (Actor)
Conway Van Gelder Robinson
18-21 Jermyn St
London SW1Y 6NB, UNITED KINGDOM (UK)

Wandrey, Ralph (General)
632 Silver Springs Cir
Cottonwood, AZ 86326-4484, USA

Wang, Alexander (Fashion Designer)
Alexander Wang Inc
386 Broadway
3rd Floor
New York, NY 10013, USA

Wang, Garrett (Actor)
501 E Del Mar Blvd #310
Pasadena, CA 91101-3613, USA

Wang, Hannah
c/o Staff Member Nickelodeon UK
PO Box 6425
LONDON W1A 6UR, UNITED KINGDOM

Wang, Henry Y (Engineer)
University of Michigan
Chemical Engineering Dept
Ann Arbor, MI 48109, USA

Wang, Jida (Artist)
7612 35th Ave #3E
Jackson Heights, NY 11372, USA

Wang, Junxia (Athlete, Track Athlete)
Athletic Assn
9 Tlyuguan Road
Chongwen District
Beijing 10061, CHINA

Wang, Taylor G (Astronaut, Physicist)
4999 Tyne Ridge Ct
Nashville, TN 37220-1531, USA

Wang, Tian-Ren (Artist)
Shaanxi Sculpture Institute
Longshoucun
Xi'am
Shaanxi 710016, CHINA

Wang, Vera (Designer, Fashion Designer)
Vera Wang Bridal House
225 W 39th St #1000
New York, NY 10018, USA

Wang, Wayne (Director)
1888 Century Park E
#1888
Los Angeles, CA 90067, USA

Wang, Zhen-Yi (Doctor, Scientist)
Hopital de Shanghai
Rul Jin Road 11
Shanghai 200025, CHINA

Wangchuck, Dasho Jigme Khesar Namgyal (Prince)
Royal Palace
Tashichhodzong
Thimpu, BHUTAN

Wangchuck, Jigme Singye (King)
Royal Palace
Tashichhodzong
Thimpu, BHUTAN

Wang Zhl Zhi (Basketball Player)
Miami Heat
American Airlines Arena
601 Biscayne Blvd
Miami, FL 33132, USA

Wanner, H Eric (Misc)
Russell Sage Foundation
112 E 64th St
New York, NY 10021, USA

Wannsdedt, David R (Dave) (Coach, Football Coach)
12600 N Stonebrook Circle
Davie, FL 33330, USA

Wannstedt, David R (Dave) (Athlete, Coach, Football Coach, Football Player)
151 Rock Haven Ln
Pittsburgh, PA 15228, USA

Wansel, Dexter (Musician)
Walt Reeder Productions
PO Box 27641
Philadelphia, PA 19118, USA

Wanted, The (Music Group)
c/o Scooter Braun Island Def Jam Group
Worldwide Plaza
825 8th Ave Fl 28
New York, NY 10019, USA

Wanzer, Bobby (Athlete, Basketball Player)
28 Greenwood Park
Pittsford, NY 14534-2965, USA

Waples, Keith (Horse Racer)
PO Box 632
Durham, ON N0G 1R0, CANADA

Waples, Ron (Horse Racer)
7 Mill RunW
Hightstown, NJ 08520-3021, USA

Wapner, Joseph (Joe) (Attorney)
2388 Century Hill
Los Angeles, CA 90067-3514, USA

Wapnick, Steve (Athlete, Baseball Player)
5934 Woodcliffe Dr
Windsor, CO 80550-8025, USA

Wappel, Gord (Athlete, Hockey Player)
5544 Kartusch PI
Regina, SK S4X 4Kl, Canada

War
250 W. 57th St. #407
New York, NY 10019-3202

Warbeck, Stephen (Composer)
c/o Staff Member Soundtrack Music Assoc
1460 4th St
Suite 308
Santa Monica, CA 90401, USA

Warburton, Patrick (Actor)
c/o James Weir Anderson Group Public Relations
8060 Melrose Ave Fl 4
Los Angeles, CA 90046, USA

Ward, Aaron (Athlete, Hockey Player)
112 Ronsard Ln
Cary, NC 27511-6019, USA

Ward, Anita (Musician)
c/o Staff Member Diva Central Inc
7510 W Sunset Blvd Ste 1445
Los Angees, CA 90046, USA

Ward, Bert (Actor)
c/o Wes Stevens Vox
6420 Wilshire Blvd Ste 1080
Los Angeles, CA 90048, USA

Ward, Bryan (Athlete, Baseball Player)
140 Bannock Ct
East Dundee, IL 60118-1626, USA

Ward, Cam (Athlete, Hockey Player)
501 Regency Dr
Sherwood Park, AB T8A SN2, Canada

Ward, Charlie (Athlete, Basketball Player, Football Player, Heisman Trophy Winner)
3717 Drake St
Houston, TX 7713135-1117, USA

Ward, Chris (Athlete, Baseball Player)
12858 Williams Ranch Rd
Moorpark, CA 93021-2109, USA

Ward, Chris (Athlete, Football Player)
1920 Sylvan Ridge Dr SW
Atlanta, GA 30310, USA

Ward, Christopher L (Chris) (Athlete, Football Player)
P.O. Box 1365
Inglewood, CA 90308, USA

Ward, Colby (Athlete, Baseball Player)
1508 Hobble Creek Dr
Springville, UT 84663-2890, USA

Ward, Colin (Athlete, Baseball Player)
1220 E Commerce Ave
Gilbert, AZ 85234-4856, USA

Ward, Dale (Musician)
A Crosse the World
PO Box 23066
London W11 3FR, UNITED KINGDOM (UK)

Ward, Daryle (Athlete, Baseball Player)
18073 Granite Ave
Riverside, CA 92508, USA

Ward, David (Opera Singer)
1 Kennedy Crescent
Lake Wanaka, NEW ZEALAND

Ward, Dedric (Athlete, Football Player)
3435 N 45th St
Phoenix, AZ 85018, USA

Ward, Dixon (Athlete, Hockey Player)
Okanagan Hockey School
201-853 Eckhardt Ave W
Attn: Vice President's Office
Penticton, BC V2A 9C4, Canada

Ward, Don (Athlete, Hockey Player)
3013 22nd Ave W
Seattle, WA 98199-2918, USA

Ward, Ed (Athlete, Hockey Player)
9150 Weathervane Trl
Galesburg, MI 49053-9777, USA

Ward, Fred (Actor)
c/o Ben Levine Kritzer Levine Wilkins Entertainment (KLWG)
11872 La Grange Ave
1st Floor
Los Angeles, CA 90025, USA

Ward, Gary (Athlete, Baseball Player)
18073 Granite Ave
Riverside, CA 92508-9777, USA

Ward, Gemma (Actor, Model)
c/o Staff Member Caliber Media Company
9229 W Sunset Blvd Ste 705
West Hollywood, CA 90069, USA

Ward, Gerry (Athlete, Basketball Player)
14 Comstock Ct
Ridgefield, CT 136877-5826, USA

Ward, Hines (Athlete, Football Player)
6215 Riverside Dr NW
Sandy Springs, GA 30328, USA

Ward, Jason (Athlete, Hockey Player)
133 Emerald Hill Way
Valrico, FL 33594-5027

Ward, Jeff (Race Car Driver)
AJ Foyt Racing
64l5 Toledo St.
Houston, TX 77008, USA

Ward, Joe (Athlete, Hockey Player)
2218 199th St SW
Lynnwood, WA 98036-7014, USA

Ward, Joel (Athlete, Hockey Player)
Cooney Management
220 Boylston St Apt 1202
Boston, MA 02116-3950, USA

Ward, John (Athlete, Football Player)
9501 Sllver Lake Dr
Oakahoma City, OK 73162, USA

Ward, John F (Business Person)
Russell Corp
755 Lee St
Alexander City, AL 35010, USA

Ward, John Milton (Educator)
20 Follen St
Cambridge, MA 02138, USA

Ward, Jonathan (Actor)
Auckland Actors
Po Box 56460
Dominion Road
Auckland 1030, NEW ZELAND

Ward, Jon P (Business Person)
RR Donnelley & Sons
77 W Wacker Dr
Chicago, IL 60601, USA

Ward, Kevin (Athlete, Baseball Player)
160 F Ave
Coronado, CA 92118-1212, USA

Ward, Lala (Actor)
London Mgmt
2-4 Noel St
London W1V 3RB, UNITED KINGDOM
(UK)

Ward, Maggie Hill (Stylist)
24317 Glyndon Ave
Venice, CA 90291, USA

Ward, Mary (Actor)
Melbourne Artists
643 Saint Kilda Road
Melbourne, VIC 3004, AUSTRALIA

Ward, Mary B (Actor)
Innovative Artists
1505 10th St
Santa Monica, CA 90401, USA

Ward, Megan (Actor)
PO Box 481219
Los Angeles, CA 90036, USA

Ward, Michael P (Doctor, Mountaineer)
Saint Andrews's Hospital
Bow St
London E3 3NT, UNITED KINGDOM
(UK)

Ward, Micky (Athlete, Boxer)
c/o Nick Cordasco *Prince Marketing Group*
18 Carillon Cir
Livingston, NJ 07039, USA

Ward, Pete (Athlete, Baseball Player)
575 G Ave
Lake Oswego, OR 97034-2272, USA

Ward, Preston (Athlete, Baseball Player)
4371 De Silva Pl
Las Vegas, NV 89121-5347, USA

Ward, Rachel (Actor)
c/o Kate Richter *HLA Management*
PO Box 1536
Strawberry Hills 2012, AUSTRALIA

Ward, R Duane (Athlete, Baseball Player)
PO Box 312 361 S Camino Del Rio
Durango, CO 81302-0312, USA

Ward, Robert (Composer, Musician)
2701 Pickett Road #4022
Durham, NC 27705, USA

Ward, Robert R (Bob) (Athlete, Football Player)
P.O. Box 535
Riva, MD 21140, USA

Ward, Ronald L (Ron) (Athlete, Hockey Player)
3178 W 140th St
Cleveland, OH 44111, USA

Ward, Sela (Actor)
1492 Stone Canyon Rd
Los Angeles, CA 90077, USA

Ward, Simon (Actor)
Shepherd & Ford
13 Radner Walk
London SW3 4BP, UNITED KINGDOM
(UK)

Ward, Sterling (Religious Leader)
Brethren Church
524 College Ave
Ashland, OH 44805, USA

Ward, Susan (Actor)
c/o Staff Member *Agency Group Ltd, The (LA)*
1880 Century Park E
Suite 711
Los Angeles, CA 90067, USA

Ward, Turner M (Athlete, Baseball Player)
232 Autumn Dr
Saraland, AL 36571-2619, USA

Ward, Vincent (Director)
PO Box 423
Kings Cross
Sydney, NSW 2011, AUSTRALIA

Ward, Wendy (Golfer)
12845 Sassin Station Road N
Edwall, WA 99008-9564, USA

Ward, Zach (Actor)
Diverse Talent Group
1875 Century Park E
#2250
Los Angeles, CA 90067, USA

Warden, John (Attorney, Attorney General, General)
Sullivan & Cromwell
125 Broad St
New York, NY 10004, USA

Warden, Jon (Athlete, Baseball Player)
6575 Oasis Dr
Loveland, OH 45140-5817, USA

Wardlaw, Kim McLane (Judge)
US Court of Appeals
125 S Grand Ave
Pasadena, CA 91105, USA

Wardle, Curt (Athlete, Baseball Player)
13900 Pheasant Knoll Ln
Moreno Valley, CA 92553-5330, USA

Ware, Andre (Athlete, Football Player, Heisman Trophy Winner)
3910 Wood Park
Sugar Land, TX 77479, USA

Ware, Chris (Artist)
c/o Staff Member *Fantagraphics Books*
7563 Lake City Way
Seattle, WA 98115, USA

Ware, Clyde (Director, Producer, Writer)
5142 Clinton Street
Los Angeles, CA 90004-1661, USA

Ware, DeMarcus (Athlete, Football Player)
c/o Bill Johnson *SportsTrust Advisors - GA*
3340 Peachtree Rd NE Fl 16
Atlanta, GA 30326, USA

Ware, Derek (Athlete, Football Player)
4426 E Desert Willow Rd
Phoenix, AZ 85044, USA

Ware, Jeff (Athlete, Baseball Player)
2560 Mulberry Loop
Virginia Beach, VA 23456-7818, USA

Warfield, Eric (Athlete, Football Player)
718 Meadows Rd
Texarkana, AR 71854, USA

Warfield, Paul D (Athlete, Football Player)
16 Normandy Way
Rancho Mirage, CA 92270, USA

Wargo, Tom (Athlete, Golfer)
2801 Putter Dr
Centralia, IL 62801-6183, USA

Warhola, James (Writer)
56 Walkers Hl
Tivoli, NY 12583-5806, USA

Warhols, James (Writer)
PO Box 748
Rhinebeck, NY 12572, USA

Warhop, George (Athlete, Football Coach, Football Player)
4767 Hill Top View Pl
San Jose, CA 95138, USA

Wariner, Steve (Musician, Songwriter, Writer)
Steve Wariner Productions
PO Box 1647
Franklin, TN 37065, USA

Waring, Amanda
8 Chester Close Queens Ride
Barnes, ENGLAND

Waring, Richard
1 Chester Close Queens Ride
London, ENGLAND SW13 OJE

Waring, Todd (Actor)
Artists Agency
1180 S Beverly Dr #301
Los Angeles, CA 90035, USA

Wark, Robert R (Misc)
Huntington Library & Art Gallery
1151 Oxford Road
San Marino, CA 91108, USA

Warlick, Ernie (Athlete, Football Player)
121 Presidents Walk
Buffalo, NY 14221, USA

Warlock, Billy (Actor)
c/o Staff Member *Peter Strain & Associates Inc (LA)*
5455 Wilshire Blvd
Suite 1812
Los Angeles, CA 90036-4368, USA

Warmenhoven, Daniel (Business Person)
Network Appliance Inc
495 E Java Dr
Sunnyvale, CA 94089, USA

Warmerdam, Cornelius
3976 N. 1st St.
Fresno, CA 93726

Warne, Jim (Athlete, Football Player)
5850 Hardy Ave
Apt 112
San Diego, CA 92115, USA

Warnecke, John Carl (Architect)
300 Broadway St
San Francisco, CA 94133, USA

Warnecke, Mark (Swimmer)
Am Schichtmeister 100
Witten 58453, GERMANY

Warner, Amelia (Actor)
c/o Jon Rubinstein *Authentic Talent and Literary Management*
45 Main St
Suite 1004
Brooklyn, NY 11201, USA

Warner, Charley (Athlete, Football Player)
1890 Rena St
Beaumont, TX 77705, USA

Warner, Chris (Cartoonist)
Dark House Publishing
10956 SE Main St
Portland, OR 97216, USA

Warner, Cornell (Athlete, Basketball Player)
2479 Glen Meadow Ln
Escondido, CA 921327-28113, USA

Warner, Curt (Athlete, Football Player)
10811 SE Mill Plain Blvd
Vancouver, WA 98664, USA

Warner, Dan (Actor)
c/o Staff Member *Players Talent Agency*
7700 W Sunset Blvd #1
Los Angeles, CA 90046-3913, USA

Warner, David (Actor)
Julian Belfarge
46 Albermarle St
London W1X 4PP, UNITED KINGDOM
(UK)

Warner, Douglas A III (Financier)
JP Morgan Chase
270 Park Ave
New York, NY 10017, USA

Warner, Jack (Athlete, Baseball Player)
5938 W Calle Lejos
Glendale, AZ 85310-35'05, USA

Warner, Jackie (Fitness Expert, Reality TV Star)
Sky Sport & Spa
8500 Wilshire Blvd
Beverly Hills, CA 90212, USA

Warner, Jackie (Athlete, Baseball Player)
19136 Us Highway 18
Apple Valley, CA 92307-2507, USA

Warner, Jane
166 Ditching Rd.
Brighton, CA BN1 6JA EN

Warner, John (Politician)
2011 Fort Dr
Alexandria, VA 22307-1133, USA

Warner, Julie (Actor, Director, Producer)
c/o Nevin Dolcefino *Innovative Artists (LA)*
1505 10th St
Santa Monica, CA 90401, USA

Warner, Kirk (Athlete, Football Player)
409 5th St SE
Cochran, GA 31014, USA

Warner, Kurt (Athlete, Football Player)
10105 E Via Linda
Suite 103
Scottsdale, AZ 85258, USA

Warner, Malcolm Jamal (Actor)
c/o Adam Griffin *Kritzer Levine Wilkins Entertainment (KLWG)*
11872 La Grange Ave
1st Floor
Los Angeles, CA 90025, USA

Warner, Margaret (Correspondent)
News Hour Show
2700 S Quincy St
Arlington, VA 22206, USA

Warner, Mark (Politician)
1227 King St
Alexandria, VA 22314, USA

Warner, T C (Actor)
S D B Partners
1801 Ave of Stars #902
Los Angeles, CA 90067, USA

Warner, Todd (Artist)
8799 Boyne City Road
Charlevoix, MI 49720, USA

Warner, Tom (Producer)
Carsey-Warner Productions
4024 Radford Ave
Building 3
Studio City, CA 91604, USA

Warner, Ty (Designer)
Ty Inc
PO Box 5377
Oak Brook, IL 60522, USA

Warner, William W (Writer)
2243 47th St NW
Washington, DC 20007, USA

Warnes, Jennifer (Musician, Songwriter, Writer)
Donald Miller
12746 Kling St
Studio City, CA 91604, USA

Warnke, Paul
5037 Garfield St. NW
Washington, DC 20016

Warnock, John (Business Person)
Adobe Systems
345 Park Ave
San Jose, CA 95110, USA

Warren, Cash (Producer)
1913 N Beverly Dr
Beverly Hills, CA 90210, USA

Warren, Chris (Athlete, Football Player)
Seattle Seahawks
13707 Black Spruce Way
Chantilly, VA 20151, USA

Warren, Cicero (Athlete, Baseball Player)
Homestead Grays
119 Brookwood St
East Orange, NJ 07018-2317, USA

Warren, Diane (Musician, Songwriter)
Realsongs
6363 Sunset Blvd #810
Los Angeles, CA 90028, USA

Warren, Don (Athlete, Football Player)
Centerville High School
6001 Union Mill Rd
Attn: Athletic Dept
Clifton, VA 20124, USA

Warren, Estalia (Actor, Model)
AGS
200 Park Ave #800
New York, NY 10036, USA

Warren, Estella (Actor, Model)
c/o Stephanie Simon *Untitled Entertainment (LA)*
350 S. Beverly Dr #200
Beverly Hills, CA 90212, USA

Warren, Fran (Musician)
Richard Barz
21 Cobble Creek Dr
Tannersville, PA 18372, USA

Warren, Frank (Internet Star)
13345 Copper Ridge Rd
Germantown 20874, USA

Warren, Frederick M (Architect)
65 Cambridge Terrace
Christchurch 1, NEW ZEALAND

Warren, Gerard (Football Player)
c/o Staff Member *Denver Broncos*
13655 E Broncos Pkwy
Englewood, CO 80112, USA

Warren, Gloria (Actor, Musician)
16872 Bosque Dr
Encino, CA 91436, USA

Warren, Jennifer (Actor)
1675 Old Oak Road
Los Angeles, CA 90049, USA

Warren, John Robin (Nobel Prize Laureate)
Royal Perth Hospital
178 Lake Street
Perth WA 6000, Australia

Warren, Karle (Actor)
c/o Justine Hunt *Hines and Hunt Entertainment*
1213 W Magnolia Blvd
Burbank, CA 91506, USA

Warren, Kenneth S (Doctor, Scientist)
Picower Medical Research Institute
350 Community Dr
Manhasset, NY 11030, USA

Warren, Kiersten (Actor)
c/o Staff Member *Mitchell K Stubbs & Assoc (MKS)*
8675 W. Washington Blvd
Suite 203
Culver City, CA 90232, USA

Warren, L D (Cartoonist, Editor)
1815 William Howard Taft Road #203
Cincinnati, OH 45206, USA

Warren, Lesley Ann (Actor)
c/o Staff Member *Untitled Entertainment (LA)*
350 S. Beverly Dr #200
Beverly Hills, CA 90212, USA

Warren, Martina (Adult Film Star)
Penthouse Pets
8675 W Washington Blvd #203
Culver City, CA 90232, USA

Warren, Michael
11500 W. Olympic Blvd #510
Los Angeles, CA 90064, USA

Warren, Michael (Mike) (Actor, Basketball Player)
21216 Escondido St
Woodland Hills, CA 91364, USA

Warren, Mike (Athlete, Baseball Player)
12281 Diane St
Garden Grove, CA 92840-3224, USA

Warren, Neil Clark
eHarmony
c/o Eharmony.com
P.O. Box 60157
Pasadena, CA 91116, USA

Warren, Rick (Religious Leader, Writer)
Saddleback Church
1 Saddleback Pkwy
Lake Forest, CA 92630, USA

Warren, Robert (Athlete, Basketball Player)
989 Hardin Wadesboro Rd
Hardin, KY 42048, USA

Warren, Ron (Athlete, Baseball Player)
Detroit Stars
4025 Paddock Rd Apt 401
Cincinnati, OH 45229-1635, USA

Warren, Rosanna (Writer)
11 Robinwood Ave
Needham, MA 02492, USA

Warren, Sahron (Actor)
c/o Kathryn Boole *Studio Talent Group*
1328 12th Street
Santa Monica, CA 90401, United states

Warren, Thomas L (Misc)
National Wildlife Federation
11100 Wildlife Center Dr
Reston, VA 20190, USA

Warren, Tom (Athlete)
2393 La Marque St
San Diego, CA 92109, USA

Warren, Ty (Athlete, Football Player)
c/o Staff Member *New England Patriots*
1 Patriot Pl
Foxboro, MA 02035-1388, USA

Warren Brothers
PO Box 120479
Nashville, TN 37212, USA

Warren Brothers, The (Music Group)
c/o Staff Member *Creative Artists Agency (CAA-TN)*
3310 West End Ave
5th Floor
Nashville, TN 37203, USA

Warrener, Rhett (Athlete, Hockey Player)
761 W Ferry St
Buffalo, NY 14222-1618, USA

Warren G (Artist, Music Group, Musician)
Richard Walters
1800 Argyle Ave #408
Los Angeles, CA 90028, USA

Warren-Green, Christopher (Conductor, Musician)
Columbia Artists Mgmt Inc
165 W 57th St
New York, NY 10019, USA

Warren Jr, Christopher C (Chris) (Athlete, Football Player)
1020 W Casino Rd
Everett, WA 98204, USA

Warrenskjold, Dorothy
165 W. 57th St.
New York, NY 10019

Warrick, Peter (Athlete, Football Player)
4305 17th St E
Ellenton, FL 34222, USA

Warriner, Todd (Athlete, Hockey Player)
Blenheim Blades
PO Box 1775
Attn: Coaching Staff
Blenheim, ON N0P IAO, Canada

Warrington, Clint (Horse Racer)
69 Oakcrest Ln
Westampton, NJ 08060-5729, USA

Warrington, Steve (Horse Racer)
31926 Lambson Forest Rd
Galena, MD 21635-1523, USA

Warrington, Walter (Horse Racer)
31930 Lambson Forest Rd
Galena, MD 21635-1523, USA

Warsi, Arshad (Actor, Bollywood)
Kohinoor Apartments 503 Yari Road
Versova Andheri
Mumbai, MS 400061, INDIA

Warthen, Dan (Athlete, Baseball Player)
3933 SW Wapato Ave
Portland, OR 97239-1412, USA

Warwick, Carl (Athlete, Baseball Player)
14102 Bonney Brier Dr
Houston, TX 77069-1324, USA

Warwick, Dionne (Musician)
c/o Kevin Sasaki *Kevin Sasaki Public Relations & Media Counsel*
8491 Sunset Blvd
Suite 224
Los Angeles, CA 90069, USA

Warwick, Lonnie (Athlete, Football Player)
828 Main St
Mount Hope, WV 25880, USA

Warzeka, Ron (Athlete, Football Player)
424 McEwen Dr
Belgrade, MT 59714, USA

Was, Don (Composer, Musician)
10984 Bellagio Road
Los Angeles, CA 90077, USA

Wasdin, John (Athlete, Baseball Player)
2676 Riverport DrS
Jacksonville, FL 32223-7115, USA

Wash, Martha (Musician)
c/o Staff Member *Diva Central Inc*
7510 W Sunset Blvd Ste 1445
Los Angees, CA 90046, USA

Washbrook, Johnny (Actor)
66 RR 1
Edgartown, MA 02539, USA

Washburn, Abigail (Musician)
c/o Staff Member *Paradigm (Monterey)*
404 W Franklin St
Monterey, CA 93940, USA

Washburn, Barbara (Misc)
1010 Waltham Street
Apt D327
Lexington, MA 02421-8063, USA

Washburn, Beverly (Actor)
2561 Olivia Heights Avenue
Henderson, NV 89052-7130, USA

Washburn, Greg (Athlete, Baseball Player)
1685 E Stellon St
Diamond, IL 60416-6028, USA

Washburn, Jarrod M (Athlete, Baseball Player)
10003 Olinger Road
Webster, WI 54893-7435, USA

Washburn, Ray C (Athlete, Baseball Player)
1103 N 49th St
Seattle, WA 98103-6630, USA

Washburn Jr, H Bradford (Misc)
1010 Waltham Street
Apt D237
Lexington, MA 02421, USA

Washetz, Joel A (Stylist)
1435 12th St
Key West, FL 33040, USA

Washington, Algernod Lanier (Plies) (Musician)
c/o Cara Donatto *Atlantic Records (LA)*
3400 W Olive Ave
2nd Floor
Burbank, CA 91505, USA

Washington, Alonzo (Cartoonist)
Omega 7
PO Box 171046
Kansas City, KS 66117, USA

Washington, Baby (Musician)
Headline Talent
1650 Broadway #508
New York, NY 10019, USA

Washington, Chris (Athlete, Football Player)
2823 Lloyd St
San Diego, CA 92117, USA

Washington, Claudell (Athlete, Baseball Player)
4081 Clayton Rd
Apt 227
Concord, CA 94521-2615, USA

Washington, Denzel (Actor)
c/o Alan Nierob *Rogers & Cowan PR (LA)*
Pacific Design Center
8687 Melrose Ave, 7th Floor
West Hollywood, CA 90069, USA

Washington, Dewayne (Athlete, Football Player)
6205 Rocky Creek Way
Wake Forest, NC 27587, USA

Washington, Don
8 Thurston Dr
Upper Marlboro, MD 213774-1426, USA

Washington, Dwayne (Pearl) (Basketball Player)
206 Grenadier Dr #206C
Liverpool, NY 13090, USA

Washington, Eugene (Gene) (Athlete, Football Player)
2725 N Jewell Ln
Plymouth, MN 55447, USA

Washington, Evelyn Ashford (Athlete, Olympic Athlete, Track Athlete)
1804 12th St Apt 12
Riverside, CA 92507-5359, USA

Washington, Gene A (Athlete, Football Player)
10521 Bellagio Rd
Los Angeles, CA 90077, USA

Washington, Hayma (Producer)
c/o Lindsay Williams *The Gotham Group Inc*
9255 Sunset Blvd
Suite 515
Los Angeles, CA 90069, USA

Washington, Herb (Athlete, Baseball Player)
640 Saddlebrook Dr
Youngstown, OH 44512-4781, USA

Washington, Isaiah (Actor)
c/o Vincent Cirrincione *Vincent Cirrincione Associates*
1516 N Fairfax Ave
Los Angeles, CA 90046, USA

Washington, Jascha (Actor)
c/o Staff Member *House of Representatives, The*
1434 6th St
Suite 1
Santa Monica, CA 90401, USA

Washington, Jim (Athlete, Basketball Player)
1108 Cardinal Way SW
Atlanta, GA 30311, USA

Washington, Joe (Athlete, Football Player)
434 E 42nd Pl
Chicago, IL 60653, USA

Washington, Joe (Athlete, Football Player)
4 Treadwell Ct
Lutherville Timonium, MD 21093, USA

Washington, Joe D (Athlete, Football Player)
2350 W Joppa Rd
Lutherville, MD 21093, USA

Washington, Keith (Athlete, Football Player)
548 Parkview Dr
Grand Prairie, TX 75052, USA

Washington, Kelley (Athlete, Football Player)
c/o Chad Speck *Allegiant Athletic Agency*
35 Market Sq
Suite 201
Knoxville, TN 37902, USA

Washington, Kermit (Athlete, Basketball Player)
7208 NE Hazel Dell Ave
Vancouver, WA 913274-34137, USA

Washington, Kerry (Actor)
c/o Kathy Atkinson *Washington Square Arts (LA)*
1041 N Formosa Ave
The Lot Writers Bldg, Room 305
West Hollywood, CA 90046, USA

Washington, Larue (Athlete, Baseball Player)
6323 Reseda Blvd
Unit 16
Tarzana, CA 91335-6981, USA

Washington, Lionel (Athlete, Football Player)
1873 Horseshoe Ln
De Pere, WI 54115, USA

Washington, MaliVai (Tennis Player)
5 S Roscoe Blvd
Ponte Vedra Beach, FL 32082, USA

Washington, Marcus (Athlete, Football Player)
2196 Wedgewood Ct
Auburn, AL 36830, USA

Washington, Mickey (Athlete, Football Player)
9420 Riggs St
Beaumont, TX 77707, USA

Washington, Mike L (Athlete, Football Player)
3235 Hernon Rd
Montgomery, AL 36106, USA

Washington, Richard (Athlete, Basketball Player)
4606 SE Logus Rd
Portland, OR 97222-51513, USA

Washington, Rico (Athlete, Baseball Player)
2050 Old Clinton Rd
Macon, GA 31211-1064, USA

Washington, Ron (Athlete, Baseball Player)
2406 Copper Ridge Rd
Arlington, TX 76006-2726, USA

Washington, Ron (Athlete, Baseball Player, Coach)
7365 Perth St
New Orleans, LA 70126, USA

Washington, Ronnie (Athlete, Football Player)
2204 Burg Jones Ln
Monroe, LA 71202, USA

Washington, Russ (Athlete, Football Player)
9060 Gramercy Dr
San Diego, CA 92123, USA

Washington, Sam (Athlete, Football Player)
7111 Cumberland Pl
Tampa, FL 33617, USA

Washington, Ted (Athlete, Football Player)
P.O. Box 434
Waxhaw, NC 28173, USA

Washington, Theodore (Ted) (Athlete, Football Player)
3522 E 26th Ave
Tampa, FL 33605, USA

Washington, U L (Athlete, Baseball Player)
PO Box 164
Stringtown, OK 74569-0164 Wasi, USA

Washington, U L (Athlete, Baseball Player)
PO Box 164
Stringtown, OK 74569-0164, USA

Washington, U L (Athlete, Baseball Player)
P.O. Box 164
Stringtown, OK 74569, USA

Washington, Wilson (Athlete, Basketball Player)
2625 Mapleton Ave
Norfolk, VA 235134-3717, USA

Wasikowska, Mia (Actor)
c/o Christine Tripicchio *WKT Public Relations (WKT-LA)*
9350 Wilshire Blvd
Suite 450
Beverly Hills, CA 90212, USA

Wasilewski, Paul Thomas (Paul Wesley) (Actor)
c/o Susan Calogerakis *Thruline Entertainment*
9250 Wilshire Blvd
Ground Fl
Beverly Hills, CA 90212, USA

Wasim, Akram (Cricketer)
Lancashire Cricket Club
Old Trafford
Manchester M16 0PX, UNITED KINGDOM (UK)

Wasinger, Mark (Athlete, Baseball Player)
303 S Seneca St
Witchia, KS 67213-5539, USA

Waskiewicz, Jim (Athlete, Football Player)
4360 Nelson Dr
Broomfield, CO 80023, USA

Waskow, Thomas C (General)
Commander
US Forces Japan & 5th Air Force Unit 5068
APO, AP 96328, USA

Waslewski, Gary (Athlete, Baseball Player)
1799 E Terrestrial Pl
Tucson, AZ 85737-3469, USA

Wasmeier, Markus (Athlete, Skier)
D&F Academy
Shanghaiallee 9
Hamburg D-20457, Germany

Wass, Ted (Actor)

Wasserburg, Gerald J (Geophysicist, Physicist, Scientist)
PO Box 2959
Florence, OR 97439-0167, USA

Wasserman, Allan (Actor)
c/o Judy Orbach *Judy O Productions*
6136 Glen Holly
Hollywood, CA 90068, USA

Wasserman, Dale (Writer)
Casa Blanca Estates
#37
Paradise Valley, AZ 95253, USA

Wasserman, Dan (Cartoonist, Editor)
Boston Globe
Editorial Dept
135 William Morrissey Blvd
Dorchester, MA 02125, USA

Wasserman, Kevin (Noodles) (Musician)
c/o Staff Member *Sugaroo! LLC*
3650 Helms Ave
Culver City, CA 90232, USA

Wasserman, Lew
911 N. Foothill Rd.
Beverly Hills, CA 90210

Wasserman, Lisa (Stylist)
1420 W Oceanfront
#2
Newport Beach, CA 92661, USA

Wasserman, Rob (Musician)
Leslie Wiener Financial Services
PO Box 245
Sausalito, CA 94966, USA

Wasserman, Robert H (Doctor)
Cornell University
Veterinary Medicine College
Ithaca, NY 14853, USA

Wasserman Schultz, Debbie (Congressman, Politician)
118 Cannon HOB
Washington, DC 20515, USA

Wasserstein, Bruce (Business Person)
Lazard
30 Rockefeller Plz
New York, NY 10020, USA

Wasserstein, Wendy (Writer)
c/o Robert (Bob) Bookman *Creative Artists Agency (CAA-LA)*
2000 Ave Of The Stars
Los Angeles, CA 90067, USA

Wasson, Erin (Model)
I M G Models
304 Park Ave S #1200
New York, NY 10010, USA

Waszgis, B J (Athlete, Baseball Player)
2708 Dover Ln
Albany, GA 31721, USA

Waszgis, BJ (Athlete, Baseball Player)
2708 Dover Ln
Albany, GA 31721-1583, USA

Watanabe, Gedde
1632 Westerly Terr
Los Angeles, CA 90026-1234

Watanabe, Ken (Actor)
c/o Will Ward *ROAR (LA)*
9701 Wilshire Blvd
8th Floor
Los Angeles, CA 90212, USA

Watanabe, Milio (Scientist)
Nippon Electric Co
Computer Labs
5-33-1 Shiba
Tokyo, JAPAN

Watanabe, Sadao (Musician)
International Music Network
278 S Main St #400
Gloucester, MA 01930, USA

Waterboys
3 Monmouth Rd.
London, ENGLAND W2

Waterbury, Steve (Athlete, Baseball Player)
710 N Garfield St
Marion, IL 62959-3429, USA

Waterhouse, Matthew (Actor)
Boyce
1 Kingsway House
Albion Rd
London N16 0TA, UNITED KINGDOM
(UK)

Waterman, Denis
D&J Arlon
Pinewood Studios
Iverheath
Iver SL0 0NH, UNITED KINGDOM (UK)

Waterman, Felicity (Actor)
P.O. Box 234
Elk, CA 95432-0234, USA

Waterman, Michael (Mathematician)
University of Southern California
Mathematics Dept
Los Angeles, CA 90089, USA

Waters, Alice (Chef)
Chez Panisse
1517 Shattuck Ave
Berkeley, CA 94709, USA

Waters, Brian (Athlete, Football Player)
1417 Wolf Dr
DeSoto, TX 75115, USA

Waters, Charles T (Charlie) (Athlete,
Coach, Football Coach, Football Player)
9305 Moss Trl
Dallas, TX 75231, USA

Waters, Crystal (Musician)
270 Lafayette St #602
New York, NY 10012, USA

Waters, Derek (Actor)
c/o Naomi Odenkirk *Odenkirk Provissiero
Entertainment*
Raleigh Studios
650 N. Bronson Ave, Bldg. B145
Los Angeles, CA 90004, USA

Waters, Frank (Muddy) (Coach, Football
Coach)
4850 Gratiot Road
No. 2D
Saginaw, MI 48638-6202, USA

Waters, John (Director)
c/o Steven Trachtenbroit *Big Hassle
Media*
40 Exchange Pl #1900
New York, NY 10005, USA

Waters, John B (Government Official)
405 Burridge Waters Edge
Sevierville, TN 37862, USA

Waters, Lou (Correspondent)
Cable News Network
News Dept
1050 Techwood Dr NW
Atlanta, GA 30318, USA

Waters, Mark (Director)
c/o Robert (Bob) Bookman *Creative Artists
Agency (CAA-LA)*
2000 Ave Of The Stars
Los Angeles, CA 90067, USA

Waters, Maxine (Congressman, Politician)
2344 Rayburn HOB
Washington, DC 20515, USA

Waters, Richard (Publisher)
13919 Woods Run Ct
Centreville, VA 20121-3078, USA

Waters, Roger (Musician)
157 E 61st St #5
New York, NY 10065, USA

Waterston, James (Actor)
c/o Beth Colt *Gateway Management
Company Inc*
860 Via De La Paz
Suite F10
Pacific Palisades, CA 90272, USA

Waterston, Katherine (Actor)
c/o Allison Band *Gersh (LA)*
9465 Wilshire Blvd
Suite 600
Beverly Hills, CA 90212, USA

Waterston, Robert (Biologist)
Washington University Medical School
Biology Dept
Saint Louis, MO 63130, USA

Waterston, Sam (Actor)
c/o Keith Addis *Industry Entertainment
Partners*
955 S Carrillo Dr
Suite 300
Los Angeles, CA 90048, USA

Wathan, Dusty (Athlete, Baseball Player)
1132 Turnbridge Rd
Charlotte, NC 28226-5862, USA

Wathan, John D (Athlete, Baseball Player,
Coach)
1354 NE Todd George Rd
Lees Summit, MO 64086-5337, USA

Watkins, Bob (Athlete, Baseball Player)
4417 W 58th Pl
Los Angeles, CA 90043-3409, USA

Watkins, Bobby (Athlete, Football Player)
1112 Devonshire Dr
Desoto, TX 75115, USA

Watkins, Carlene (Actor)
104 Fremont Place W
Los Angeles, CA 90005, USA

Watkins, Danny (Football Player)
c/o Joe Panos *Lock Metz Milanovic LLC*
6900 E. Camelback
Suite 600
Scottsdale, AZ 85251, USA

Watkins, Dave (Athlete, Baseball Player)
506 Ridgewood Rd
Louisville, KY 40207-1325, USA

Watkins, Dean A (Business Person,
Inventor)
Watkins-Johnson Co
401 River Oaks Parkway
San Jose, CA 95134, USA

Watkins, Lloyd I (Economist)
PO Box 111
Bloomington, IL 61702, USA

Watkins, Marilyn
217 No. San Marino Ave
San Gabriel, CA 91775

Watkins, Michaela (Actor, Comedian)
c/o Amy Slomovits *Evolution
Entertainment (LA)*
9320 Wilshire Blvd
Suite 202
Beverly Hills, CA 90212, USA

Watkins, Michelle (Actor)
Capital Artists
6404 Wilshire Blvd
#950
Los Angeles, CA 90048, USA

Watkins, Pat (Athlete, Baseball Player)
1205 Fowler Dr
Garner, NC 27529-4420, USA

Watkins, Rhonda (Stylist)
4007 Huntingdon Dr
Minnetonka, MN 55305, USA

Watkins, Robert A (Athlete, Football
Player)
6 White Alder Way
South Dartmouth, MA 02748, USA

Watkins, Scott (Athlete, Baseball Player)
14660 W 18th St S
Sand Springs, OK 74063-4405, USA

Watkins, Steve (Athlete, Baseball Player)
3408 Evanston Ave
Lubbock, TX 79407-4039, USA

Watkins, Tasker (Judge, War Hero)
5 Pump Court
Middle Temple
London EC4, UNITED KINGDOM (UK)

Watkins, Tionne (T-Boz) (Artist, Musician)
c/o Jack Iannaci *Brass Artists & Associates*
9025 Wilshire Blvd
Suite 400
Beverly Hills, CA 90211, USA

Watkins, Tommy (Athlete, Baseball
Player)
Beloit Snappers
PO Box 8S5
Attn: Coaching Staff Beloit
Beloit, WI 53512-0855, USA

Watkins, Tuc (Actor)
c/o Brad Warshaw *Brad Warshaw*
P.O. Box 931332
Los Angeles, CA 90093, USA

Watkins, William D (Business Person)
Seagate Technology
920 Disc Dr
Scotts Valley, CA 95066, USA

Watkinson of Working, Harold A
(Government Official)
Tyma House
Bosham near Chichester
Sussex, UNITED KINGDOM (UK)

Watley, Jody (Musician)
Baker Winokur Rider
9100 Wilshire Blvd #600
Beverly Hills, CA 90212, USA

Watling, Deborah
183 Trevelyan Rd
London, ENGLAND SW17 9LW

Watling, Leonor (Actor)
c/o Staff Member *WME (LA)*
9601 Wilshire Blvd Fl 3
Beverly Hills, CA 90210, USA

Watlington, Neal (Athlete, Baseball
Player)
P.O. Box 418
Yanceyville, NC 27379-0418, USA

Watney, Heidi (Baseball Player)
160 Boylston St Apt 2362
Chestnut Hill, MA 02467-2017, U S A

Watney, Nick (Athlete, Golfer)
c/o Staff Member *Gaylord Sports
Management*
13845 N Northsight Blvd
Suite 200
Scottsdale, AZ 85260, USA

Watrin, Ray (Athlete, Football Player)
5 Downey Bay
Okotoks, AB T1S 1H7, Canada

Watros, Cynthia (Actor)
c/o Marsha McManus *Principal
Entertainment (LA)*
1964 Westwood Blvd #400
Los Angeles, CA 90025, USA

Watrous, Cynthia (Actor)
c/o Staff Member *Innovative Artists (LA)*
1505 10th St
Santa Monica, CA 90401, USA

Watson, A J (Engineer, Race Car Driver)
5420 Crawfordsville Road
Indianapolis, IN 46224, USA

Watson, Alberta (Actor)
c/o Staff Member *Cathy Atkinson*
2629 Main Street
PMB 129
Santa Monica, CA 90405, USA

Watson, Albert M (Photographer)
777 Washington St
New York, NY 10014, USA

Watson, Alexander F (Diplomat)
Nature Conservancy International
4245 Fairfax Dr #100
Arlington, VA 22203, USA

Watson, Allen (Athlete, Baseball Player)
6144 65th St
Middle Village, NY 11379-1027, USA

Watson, Angela (Actor)
c/o Tom Chasin *Chasin Agency, The*
8899 Beverly Blvd
Suite 716
Los Angeles, CA 90048-2449, USA

Watson, Barry (Actor)
c/o Ruth Bernstein *Viewpoint Inc*
8820 Wilshire Blvd.
Suite 220
Beverly Hills, CA 90211, USA

Watson, Benjamin (Athlete, Football
Player)
c/o Staff Member *New England Patriots*
1 Patriot Pl
Foxboro, MA 02035-1388, USA

Watson, Bill (Athlete, Hockey Player)
1725 Vermilion Rd
Duluth, MN 55803-2508, USA

Watson, Bob (Athlete, Baseball Player)
9319 Montridge Dr
Houston, TX 77080-5429, USA

Watson, Brandon (Athlete, Baseball
Player)
22273 Del Valle St
Woodland Hills, CA 91364-1516, USA

Watson, Bryan (Athlete, Hockey Player)
400 Madison St
Alexandria, VA 22314-1755, USA

Watson, Bubba (Athlete, Golfer)
c/o Jens Beck *Pro-Sport Management*
8355 E Hartford Dr
Suite 105
Scottsdale, AZ 85255-2533, USA

Watson, Cecil J (Doctor)
Abbott Northwestern Hospital
2727 Chicago Ave
Minneapolis, MN 55407, USA

Watson, Dale (Musician)
Crowley Artist Mgmt
602 Wayside Dr
Wimberley, TX 78676, USA

Watson, Dave (Athlete, Hockey Player)
1431 Pinecraft Dr
Winston Salem, NC 27104-1351, USA

Watson, Denis (Athlete, Golfer)
14209 Evans Rd
Pacific Palisades, CA 90272, USA

Watson, Elizabeth M (Judge)
Houston Police Department
Chief's Office
1200 Travis St
Houston, TX 77002, USA

Watson, Emily (Actor)
c/o George Freeman *WME (LA)*
9601 Wilshire Blvd Fl 3
Beverly Hills, CA 90210, USA

Watson, Emma (Actor)
c/o Jodi Gottlieb *Independent Public Relations*
7060 Hollywood Blvd
8th Floor
Los Angeles, CA 90028, USA

Watson, Florene Miller (Aviator)
1602 Primrose Ln
Borger, TX 79007-6446, USA

Watson, Gene (Musician)
Bobby Roberts
909 Meadowlark Lane
Goodlettsville, TN 37072, USA

Watson, James D (Nobel Prize Laureate)
1 Bungtown Rd
Cold Spring Harbor, NY 11724-2209, USA

Watson, Jamie (Athlete, Basketball Player)
P.O. Box 761
Elm City, NC 27822-13761, USA

Watson, Jim (Athlete, Hockey Player)
8190 W Deer Valley Rd Ste 104
Peoria, AZ 85382-2126, USA

Watson, Jim (Athlete, Hockey Player)
1702 Coventry Ln
Glen Mills, PA 19342, USA

Watson, Joe (Athlete, Hockey Player)
220 Park Pl
Media, PA 19063-2045, USA

Watson, Kenneth M (Oceanographer, Physicist)
8515 Costa Verde Blvd #2008
San Diego, CA 92122, USA

Watson, Mark (Athlete, Baseball Player)
555 Spender Trce
Atlanta, GA 30350-5017, USA

Watson, Martha (Athlete, Olympic Athlete)
5509 Royal Vista Lane
Las Vegas, NV 89149, USA

Watson, Matt (Athlete, Baseball Player)
636 Quail Crk
Manheim, PA 17545-8770, USA

Watson, Max P Jr (Business Person)
BMC Software
2101 CityWest Blvd
Houston, TX 77042, USA

Watson, Mills (Actor)
PO Box 600
Talent, OR 97540, USA

Watson, Pamela (Stylist)
c/o Staff Member *The Montgomery Group*
210 W 29th St
#6
New York, NY 10001, USA

Watson, Paul (Misc)
Sea Shepherd Conservation Society
Po Box 2616
Friday Harbor, WA 98250, USA

Watson, Paul (Journalist, Photographer)
Toronto Star
Editorial Dept
1 Yonge St
Toronto, ON M5E 1E6, CANADA

Watson, Polly Jo (Misc)
Washington University
Anthropology Dept
Saint Louis, MO 63130, USA

Watson, Robert (Athlete, Basketball Player)
1625 Sherwood Dr
Owensboro, KY 42301, USA

Watson, Robert A (Religious Leader)
Salvation Army
615 Slaters Lane
Alexandria, VA 22314, USA

Watson, Robert M (Bobby) Jr (Musician)
Split Second Timing
11 Ridge Road
Chappaqua, NY 10514, USA

Watson, Russell (Musician)
Box 806
Manchester M60 2XS, UNITED KINGDOM (UK)

Watson, Sheri (Stylist)
4440 Ambrose Ave
#110
Los Angeles, CA 90027, USA

Watson, Stephen E (Business Person)
Dayton Hudson
1000 Nicollet Mall
Minneapolis, MN 55403, USA

Watson, Stephen R (Athlete, Football Player)
4675 S Vine Way
Englewood, CO 80113, USA

Watson, Thomas S (Tom) (Athlete, Golfer)
16104 Riggs Rd
Stilwell, KS 66085, USA

Watson, Tim (Athlete, Football Player)
113 Crestwood Dr
RR 13
Fort Valley, GA 31030, USA

Watson, Wayne (Musician)
TBA Artist Mgmt
300 10th Ave S
Nashville, TN 37203, USA

Watson, Whit (Sportscaster)
810 N Phelps Ave
Winter Park, FL 32789-2759, USA

Watson-Johnson, Vernee (Actor)
Gage Group
14724 Ventura Blvd #505
Sherman Oaks, CA 91403, USA

Watson Jr, Jack H (Government Official)
Long Aldridge Norman
1900 K St NW
Washington, DC 20006, USA

Watson Richardson, Lillian (Pockey) (Swimmer)
4960 Maunalani Circle
Honolulu, HI 96816, USA

Watt, Ben (Musician, Songwriter, Writer)
JFD Mgmt
Acklam Workshops
10 Acklam Road
London W10 5QZ, UNITED KINGDOM (UK)

Watt, Eddie (Athlete, Baseball Player)
940 Locust St
North Bend, NE 68649-4543, USA

Watt, James (Politician)
1558 Calle Encantado
Wickenburg, AZ 85390-3132, USA

Watt, Jim (Athlete, Hockey Player)
52 Amy Lane
Esko, MN 55733-9566, USA

Watt, J.J. (Football Player)
c/o Tom Condon *CAA - St. Louis*
222 S Central Ave
Suite 1008
St Louis, MO 63105, USA

Watt, Mike (Musician)
c/o Staff Member *Agency Group Ltd, The (NY)*
142 West 57th St
6th Floor
New York, NY 10019, USA

Watt, Mike (Athlete, Hockey Player)
N84W27677 Twin Pines Cir
Hartland, WI 53029-8572, USA

Watt, Tom (Athlete, Coach, Hockey Player)
P.O. Box 1540
Station M
Calgary, AB T2P 3B9, Canada

Wattelet, Frank (Athlete, Football Player)
4 Deer Run Dr
Joplin, MO 64804, USA

Wattenberg, Ben J (Television Host)
Think Tank with Ben Wattenberg
4455 Connecticut Ave NW #C100
Washington, DC 20036, USA

Watters, Bill (Correspondent)
c/o Staff Member *Landmark Sport Group*
1 City Centre Dr
Suite 605
Mississauga, Ontario L5B 1M2, Canada

Watters, Richard J (Rickie) (Athlete, Football Player)
11100 NE 8th St
Apt 600
Bellevue, WA 98004, USA

Watters, Ricky (Athlete, Football Player)
8815 Conroy-Windermere Rd
#332
Orlando, FL 32835, USA

Watters, Tim (Athlete, Hockey Player)
219 E Oregon Ave
Phoenix, AZ 85012-1435, USA

Watterson, John B (Brett) (Astronaut)
2508 Via Anacapa
Palos Verdes Estates, CA 90274, USA

Wattle, Dave (Athlete, Olympic Athlete, Track Athlete)
9245 Forest Hill Ln
Germantown, TN 38139-7906, USA

Wattles, Stan (Race Car Driver)
2391 Old Dixie Hwy
Riviera Beach, FL 33404, USA

Wattleton, A Faye (Entertainer)
Fischer-Ross Agency
250 W 57th St
New York, NY 10107, USA

Watts, Andre (Musician)
205 W 57th St
New York, NY 10019, USA

Watts, Brian (Athlete, Hockey Player)
1300 Via Coronel
Palos Verdes Estates, CA 90274-1938, USA

Watts, Brian (Athlete, Golfer)
1701 Wisteria Way
Westlake, TX 76262-9083, USA

Watts, Charles (General)
4500 Alamance St
Baytown, TX 77521-3054, USA

Watts, Charles R (Charlie) (Musician)
Halsdon Farm
Dolton Winkleigh
Devon EX19 8RF, UK

Watts, D Henry (Business Person)
Norfolk Southern Corp
3 Commercial Place
Norfolk, VA 23510, USA

Watts, Donald (Athlete, Basketball Player)
51315 256th Ave NE
Redmond, WA 981353-85135, USA

Watts, Ernest J (Ernie) (Musician)
DeLeon Artists
4031 Panama Court
Piedmont, CA 94611, USA

Watts, Ernie (Designer, Director)
International Creative Mgmt
40 W 57th St #1800
New York, NY 10019, USA

Watts, Helen J (Opera Singer)
Rock House Wallis
Ambleston Haverford-West
Dyfed SA62 5RA, WALES

Watts, J C (Politician)
J C Watts Companies 600 13th St NW Ste 790
Washington, DC 20005-3021, USA

Watts, JC (Athlete, Football Player)
3512 Rose Crest Ln
Fairfax, VA 22033-1636, USA

Watts, Kristi (Religious Leader, Television Host)
c/o 700 Club *Christian Broadcasting Network (CBN)*
977 Centerville Tpke
Virginia Beach, VA 23464, USA

Watts, Naomi (Actor)
c/o Jason Weinberg *Untitled Entertainment (LA)*
350 S. Beverly Dr #200
Beverly Hills, CA 90212, USA

Watts, Quincy (Athlete, Track Athlete)
First Team Marketing
PO Box 67581
Los Angeles, CA 90067, USA

Watts, Robert (Athlete, Football Player)
99 Villa Dr
San Pablo, CA 94806, USA

Watts, Ronald (Athlete, Basketball Player)
11800 Sunset Hills Rd
Apt 908
Reston, VA 213815-7504, USA

Watts III, Claudius E (Educator, General)
Citadel
President's Office
Charleston, SC 29409, USA

Waugh, John S (Misc)
Massachusetts Institute of Technology
Chemistry Dept
Cambridge, MA 02139, USA

Waugh, Stephen (Steve) (Cricketer)
Octagon
1751 Pinnacle Dr #1500
McLean, VA 22102, USA

Wawryshyn-Moroz, Evelyn (Athlete, Baseball Player)
139 Royal Ave
Winnipeg, MB R2V 1H5, CANADA

Wax, Ruby (Actor, Comedian)
c/o Nicola Richardson *QVoice*
161 Drury Ln, Covent Garden
3rd Floor
London WC2B 5PN, UK

Waxenberg, Alan M (Publisher)
Good Housekeeping Magazine
959 8th Ave
New York, NY 10019, USA

Waxman, Henry (Congressman, Politician)
2204 Rayburn HOB
Washington, DC 20515, USA

Waxman, Keoni (Director, Writer)
c/o Jeff Okin *Anonymous Content (LA)*
3531 Hayden Ave
Culver City, CA 90232, USA

Wayans, Damien Dante (Actor, Director, Producer)
c/o Kim Dixon *Dominion3*
6464 W Sunset Blvd
Suite 740
Los Angeles, CA 90028, USA

Wayans, Damon (Actor)
c/o Kim Dixon *Dominion3*
6464 W Sunset Blvd
Suite 740
Los Angeles, CA 90028, USA

Wayans, Keenen Ivory (Actor, Director, Producer)
Defenders of the Faith
6959 Dume Dr
Malibu, CA 90265, USA

Wayans, Kim (Actor)
c/o Staff Member *Wayans Brothers Entertainment*
8730 W Sunset Blvd #290
W Hollywood, CA 90069, USA

Wayans, Marlon (Actor, Comedian)
c/o Lisa Blum *New Wave Entertainment (LA)*
8569 Holloway Dr
Apt 1
West Hollywood, CA 90069-6918, USA

Wayans, Shawn (Actor)
c/o Staff Member *Wayans Brothers Entertainment*
8730 W Sunset Blvd #290
W Hollywood, CA 90069, USA

Wayans Jr, Damon (Actor)
c/o Cecy Galvan *Bleu Entertainment*
10750 Palms Blvd #108
Los Angeles, CA 90034, USA

Wayda, Stephen (Photographer)
Playboy Magazine
Reader Service
680 N Lake Shore Dr
Chicago, IL 60611, USA

Wayne, Fredd
117 Strand St.
Santa Monica, CA 90405

Wayne, Gary (Athlete, Baseball Player)
5762 W Asbury Pl
Lakewood, CA 80227-2550, USA

wayne, Hale (Scientist)
904 Applewood Dr
Friendswood, TX 77546-5201, USA

Wayne, Jeff (Composer)
Lyndhurst Green St
Shenley
Hertfordshire WD7 9BD, UK

Wayne, Jimmy (Musician)
Big Machine Music
1219 16th Avenue S
Nashville, TN 37212, USA

Wayne, John (Bowler)
5018 S Barley Ct
Gilbert, AZ 95234, USA

Wayne, Justin (Athlete, Baseball Player)
302 Muirfield Ct
Jupiter, FL 33458-8060, USA

Wayne, Nathaniel (Athlete, Football Player)
2878 Grey Moss Pass
Duluth, GA 30097, USA

Wayne, Patrick (Actor)
10502 Whipple St
Toluca Lake, CA 91602, USA

Wayne, Reggie (Athlete, Football Player)
7001 W 56th St
Indianapolis, IN 46254, USA

Wayt, Russell (Athlete, Football Player)
600 E Tuttle Rd
White Oak, TX 75693, USA

Wazed, Sheik Hasina (Prime Minister)
Sere-e Bangla Nagar
Gono Bhaban
Sher-e-Banglanagar
Dakar, BANGLADESH

Wazniak, Steve (Business Person, Inventor)
16400 Blackberry Hill Road
Los Gatos, California 95030, USA

W. Boustany Jr., Charles (Congressman, Politician)
1431 Longworth HOB
Washington, DC 20515, USA

W. Dent, Charles (Congressman, Politician)
1009 Longworth HOB
Washington, DC 20515, USA

Weah, George (Soccer Player)
AC Milan
Via Turati 3
Milan 20221, ITALY

Wearstler, Kelly (Writer)
c/o Staff Member *HarperCollins Publishers*
10 East 53rd St
c/o Author mail, 7th Floor
New York, NY 10022, USA

Weatherill, B Bruce (Government Official)
Emmets House
Ide Hill
Kent TN14 6BA, UNITED KINGDOM (UK)

Weatherly, Gerald (Athlete, Football Player)
506 1/2 E Clayton St
Cuero, TX 77954, USA

Weatherly, Jim (Athlete, Football Player)
23679 Calabasas Rd
Apt 558
Calabasas, CA 91302, USA

Weatherly, Michael (Actor)
c/o Jai Khanna *Brillstein Entertainment Partners*
9150 Wilshire Blvd #350
Beverly Hills, CA 90212, USA

Weatherly, Shwan (Actor, Beauty Pageant Winner)
135 N Westgate Ave
Los Angeles, CA 90049, USA

Weathers, Carl (Athlete, Football Player)
2228 Walnut Ave
Venice, CA 90291, USA

Weathers, Carl (Actor)
c/o Mark Measures *Abrams Artists Agency (LA)*
9200 Sunset Blvd
11th Floor
Los Angeles, CA 90069, USA

Weathers, Dave (Athlete, Baseball Player)
979 Lexington Hwy
Loretto, TN 38469-2732, USA

Weatherspoon, Cephus (Athlete, Football Player)
5322 W Henderson Pl
Santa Ana, CA 92704, USA

Weatherspoon, Clarence (Athlete, Basketball Player)
P.O. Box 117
Crawford, MS 39743, USA

Weatherspoon, Teresa G (Basketball Player)
Los Angeles Sparks
Staples Center
1111 S Figueroa St
Los Angeles, CA 90015, USA

Weatherwax, Bob
16133 Soledad Canyon Rd.
Canyon Country, CA 91351

Weatherwax, Jim (Athlete, Football Player)
636 Cucharas Mountain Dr
Livermore, CO 80536, USA

Weaver, Delores (Business Person, Football Executive)
6120 San Jose Blvd W
Jacksonville, FL 32217-2345, USA

Weaver, Dewitt (Athlete, Golfer)
5640 Golf Club Dr
Braselton, GA 30517, USA

Weaver, Earl (Athlete, Baseball Player, Coach)
501 Cypress Pointe Dr W
Pembroke Pines, FL 33027-1356, USA

Weaver, Eric (Athlete, Baseball Player)
2641 Weaver Rd
Illopolis, IL 62539-3640, USA

Weaver, Fritz (Actor)
161 W 75th St
New York, NY 10023, USA

Weaver, Gary (Athlete, Football Player)
3496 Arden Rd
Hayward, CA 94545, USA

Weaver, Herman (Athlete, Football Player)
8105 Hamilton Mill Dr
Chattanooga, TN 37421, USA

Weaver, Jacki (Actor)
c/o Alex Cole *Elevate Entertainment*
10100 Santa Monica Blvd.
Suite 300
Los Angeles, CA 90067, USA

Weaver, James (Race Car Driver)
165 Smith St.
Bougbkeepsie, NY 12601, United States

Weaver, Jason (Actor)
c/o Lisa Chance *Kyle Avery Public Relations*
1107 Fair Oaks Ave #321
S Pasadena, CA 91030, USA

Weaver, Jed (Athlete, Football Player)
696 E 16th Ave
Eugene, OR 97401, USA

Weaver, Jeff (Athlete, Baseball Player, Olympic Athlete)
1740 Classic Rose Ct
Westlake Village, CA 91362-5134, USA

Weaver, Jered (Athlete, Baseball Player)
c/o Staff Member *Los Angeles Dodgers (LA Dodgers)*
1000 Elysian Park Ave
Los Angeles, CA 90012, USA

Weaver, Jim (Athlete, Baseball Player)
6916 8th Ave W
Bradenton, FL 34209-3416, USA

Weaver, Jim (Athlete, Baseball Player)
626 Prince George Dr
Lancaster, PA 17601-8802, USA

Weaver, John (Athlete, Football Player)
520 E Ward St
Versailles, OH 45380, USA

Weaver, John (Race Car Driver)
Dream Weaver Family Racing
9246 E. Lacey Blvd.
Hanford, CA 93230, USA

Weaver, Michael (Actor)
c/o Siri Garber *Platform Public Relations*
2666 N Beachwood Dr
Los Angeles, CA 90068, USA

Weaver, Reg (Misc)
National Education Assn
1201 16th St NW
Washington, DC 20036, USA

Weaver, Roger (Athlete, Baseball Player)
65 Moyer St
Canajoharie, NY 13317-1430, USA

Weaver, Rufus (Inventor)
77 Adelaide St
New London, CT 06320, USA

Weaver, Sigourney (Actor)
c/o Michelle Benson *42West (NY)*
220 W 42nd St
12th Floor
New York, NY 10036, USA

Weaver, Warren E (Misc)
7607 Horsepen Road
Richmond, VA 23229, USA

Weaver, Wayne (Business Person, Football Executive)
6120 San Jose Blvd W
Jacksonville, FL 32217-2345, USA

Weaving, Hugo (Actor)
c/o Ann Churchill-Brown *Shanahan Management*
Level 3 Berman House
Surry Hills 2010, AUSTRALIA

Weaving, Ryan (Stylist)
c/o Staff Member *Judy Inc*
1 Yorkville Ave
Toronto ON M4W 1L1, Canada

Webb, Brandon (Athlete, Baseball Player)
8750 Tipton Ross Rd
Ashland, KY 41102-8920, USA

Webb, Charley (Actor)
c/o Staff Member *Emmerdale Yorkshire Television*
Yorkshire Television Centre
Leeds
West Yorkshire LS3 1JS, UK

Webb, Chloe (Actor)
PO Box 2824
Venice, CA 90294, USA

Webb, Christiaan (Musician, Songwriter, Writer)
SuperVision Mgmt
109B Regents Park Road
London NW1 8UR, UNITED KINGDOM (UK)

Webb, Hank (Athlete, Baseball Player)
4527 Lake Valencia Blvd W
Palm Harbor, FL 34684-3920, USA

Webb, James R (Jimmy) (Athlete, Football Player)
1319 S Prairie Flower Rd
Turlock, CA 95380, USA

Webb, Jeff (Athlete, Basketball Player)
8011 Fm 621
Martindale, TX 78655-2521, USA

Webb, Justin (Musician, Songwriter, Writer)
SuperVision Mgmt
109B Regents Park Road
London NW1 8UR, UNITED KINGDOM (UK)

Webb, Karrie (Athlete, Golfer)
725 Presidential Dr
Boynton Beach, FL 33435, USA

Webb, Lee (Religious Leader, Television Host)
c/o 700 Club *Christian Broadcasting Network (CBN)*
977 Centerville Tpke
Virginia Beach, VA 23464, USA

Webb, Lucy (Actor, Comedian)
1360 N Crescent Heights #38
West Hollywood, CA 90046, USA

Webb, Marc (Director)
c/o Michael Sugar *Anonymous Content (LA)*
3531 Hayden Ave
Culver City, CA 90232, USA

Webb, Morgan (Actor)
c/o Andrea Ross *Creative Artists Agency (CAA-LA)*
2000 Ave Of The Stars
Los Angeles, CA 90067, USA

Webb, Richmond J (Athlete, Football Player)
4120 Humphrey Dr
Dallas, TX 75216, USA

Webb, Russell (Athlete)
611 Knob Hill Ave
Redondo Beach, CA 90277-4255, USA

Webb, Sonny (Baseball Player)
Negro Baseball Leagues
3194 Jordan Rd
Pleasant Plain, OH 45162-9238, USA

Webb, Spud (Athlete, Basketball Player)
1453 Mosslake Dr
Desoto, TX 75115-7713, USA

Webb, Steve (Athlete, Hockey Player)
27 Barberry Ln
Center Moriches, NY 11934-1410, USA

Webb, Tamilee (Athlete)
7031 Calle Portone
Rancho Santa Fe, CA 92091-0262, USA

Webb, Veronica (Actor, Model)
c/o Rae Ruff *Don Buchwald & Associates Inc (NY)*
10 E 44th St
New York, NY 10017

Webb, Wayne (Bowler)
5850 Freeport Blvd
Sacramento, CA 95822-3505, USA

Webb, Wellington E (Misc)
Mayor's Office
City-County Building
1437 Bannock St
Denver, CO 80202, USA

Webb, William H (Business Person)
Altria Group
120 Park Ave
New York, NY 10017, USA

Webber, Andrew Lloyd (Composer, Musician, Producer)
c/o Staff Member *The Really Useful Group*
22 Tower St
London WC2H 9NS, UNITED KINGDOM (UK)

Webber, Chris (Sportscaster)
c/o Andy Elkin *Creative Artists Agency (CAA-LA)*
2000 Ave Of The Stars
Los Angeles, CA 90067, USA

Webber, Julian Lloyd (Musician)
Columbia Artists Mgmt Inc
165 W 57th St
New York, NY 10019, USA

Webber, Mark (Actor)
c/o Abby Bluestone *Innovative Artists (LA)*
1505 10th St
Santa Monica, CA 90401, USA

Webber, Mayce (Athlete, Basketball Player)
21731 Ventura Blvd Ste 31313
Woodland Hills, CA 91364-1851, USA

Webber, Tristan (Designer, Fashion Designer)
Brower Lewis
74 Gloucester Place
London W1H 3HN, UNITED KINGDOM (UK)

Webby, Chris
c/o Jesse Kirschbaum *New Universal Entertainment Agency*
1115 Broadway Fl 12
New York, NY 10010, USA

Weber, Amy (Actor)
c/o Staff Member *Select Artists Ltd (CA-Westside Office)*
1138 12th Street
Suite 1
Santa Monica, CA 90403, USA

Weber, Arnold R (Educator)
Northwestern University
Chancellor's Office
Evanston, IL 60208, USA

Weber, Ben (Actor)
c/o Amy Guenther *Gateway Management Company Inc*
860 Via De La Paz
Suite F10
Pacific Palisades, CA 90272, USA

Weber, Ben (Athlete, Baseball Player)
5550 Baird St
Groves, TX 77619-3231, USA

Weber, Bruce (Coach)
University of Illinois
Athletic Dept
Assembly Hall
Champaign, IL 61820, USA

Weber, Bruce (Photographer)
Robert Miller Gallery
526 W 26th St #10A
New York, NY 10001, USA

Weber, Charlie (Actor)
c/o Bernard Kira *Vanguard Management Group*
8060 Melrose Ave
4th Floor
Los Angeles, CA 90046, USA

Weber, Chuck (Athlete, Football Player)
12740 CObblestone Creek Rd
Poway, CA 92064-3508, USA

Weber, Eberhard (Composer, Musician)
Ted Kurland
173 Brighton Ave
Boston, MA 02134, USA

Weber, Eugen J (Historian)
11579 Sunset Blvd
Los Angeles, CA 90049, USA

Weber, George B (Misc)
Chemin Moise-Duboule 19
Geneva 1209, SWITZERLAND

Weber, Jack (Actor)
Gersh Agency
232 N Canon Dr
Beverly Hills, CA 90210, USA

Weber, Jake (Actor)
c/o Staff Member *Gersh (LA)*
9465 Wilshire Blvd
Suite 600
Beverly Hills, CA 90212, USA

Weber, Leyna Juliet
c/o Staff Member *Atlas Talent Agency Inc*
36 W 44th St
New York, NY 10036, USA

Weber, Mary E (Astronaut)
14 Hawkview St
Portola Valley, CA 94028, USA

Weber, Mary Ellen Dr (Astronaut)
14 Hawkview St
Portola Valley, CA 94028-8037, USA

Weber, Neil (Athlete, Baseball Player)
1 Morning Vw
Irvine, CA 92603-3716, USA

Weber, Peter D (Pete) (Bowler)
10500 Saint Xavier Lane
Saint Ann, MO 63074, USA

Weber, Robert M (Bob) (Cartoonist)
New Yorker Magazine
Editorial Dept
4 Times Square
New York, NY 10036, USA

Weber, Shea (Athlete, Hockey Player)
4527 Yancey Dr
Nashville, TN 37215-4115, USA

Weber, Stephen L (Educator)
State University of New York
President's Office
Oswego, NY 13126, USA

Weber, Steven (Actor)
c/o Daniel (Danny) Sussman *Brillstein Entertainment Partners*
9150 Wilshire Blvd #350
Beverly Hills, CA 90212, USA

Weber, Vin (Misc)
Empower America
1776 I St NW
Washington, DC 20006, USA

Weber Jr, Bob (Cartoonist)
c/o Staff Member *King Features Syndication*
300 W 57th St
15th Floor
New York, NY 10019-5238, USA

Webre, Septime (Choreographer)
Washington Ballet
3515 Wisconsin Ave NW
Washington, DC 20016, USA

Webster, Ben (Horse Racer)
452 Oak Haven Dr
Altamonte Springs, FL 32701-6318, USA

Webster, Corey (Athlete, Football Player)
c/o Jimmy Sexton *CAA (Memphis)*
1100 Ridgeway Loop Rd
5th Floor
Memphis, TN 38120, USA

Webster, Cornell (Athlete, Football Player)
4575 Palm Ave
Apt H
Riverside, CA 92501, USA

Webster, Daniel (Congressman, Politician)
1039 Longworth HOB
Washington, DC 20515, USA

Webster, Jason (Athlete, Football Player)
c/o Staff Member *New England Patriots*
1 Patriot Pl
Foxboro, MA 02035-1388, USA

Webster, Jeff (Athlete, Basketball Player)
10405 SE 15th St
Oklahoma City, OK 731313-5714, USA

Webster, Larry (Athlete, Football Player)
12 Oakridge Ct
Elkton, MD 21921, USA

Webster, Lenny (Athlete, Baseball Player)
6211 Bridgeport Dr
Charlotte, NC 28215-2319, USA

Webster, Mitch (Athlete, Baseball Player)
3120 NE 91st Ter
Kansas City, MO 64156-1071, USA

Webster, Ramon (Athlete, Baseball Player)
PO Box 6-5790
ElDorado, Panama, USA

Webster, Ray (Athlete, Baseball Player)
311 5th St
Marysville, CA 95901-5714, USA

Webster, R Howard (Baseball Player, Publisher)
Toronto Globe & Mail
444 Front St W
Toronto, ON M5V 2S9, CANADA

Webster, Robert D (Bob) (Athlete, Swimmer)
269 Hacienda Carmel
Carmel, CA 93923-7947, USA

Webster, Tom (Athlete, Coach, Hockey Player)
1750 Longfellow Dr
Canton, MI 48187, USA

Webster, Victor (Actor)
c/o Courtney Kivowitz *Schiff Company, The*
9465 Wilshire Blvd
Suite 480
Beverly Hills, CA 90212, USA

Webster, William H (Government Official, Politician)
4777 Dexter St NW
Washington, DC 20007-1060, USA

We Came As Romans (Music Group, Musician)
c/o Matthew Stewart *Outerloop Management*
2200 Clarendon Blvd
Suite 1400
Arlington, VA 22201, USA

Wechsler, Nick (Actor)
c/o Benjamin Tappan *Tappan Entertainment*
8324 Fountain Ave
Suite C
Los Angeles, CA 90069, USA

Wecht, Cyril H
5420 Darlington Rd
Pittsburgh, PA 15217, USA

Weck, Peter
Bambauer Keplerstr. 2
Munich, GERMANY D-81679

Wecker, Andreas (Gymnast)
Am Dorfplatz 1
Klein-Ziethen 16766, GERMANY

Weddington, Mike (Athlete, Football Player)
237 Sycamore Grove St
Simi Valley, TX 93605-7342, USA

Weddington, Sarah R (Attorney)
709 W 14th St
Austin, TX 78701-1707, USA

Weddle-Hines, Mary (Athlete, Baseball Player)
329 Park Hill Rd
Corbin, KY 40701-2583, USA

Wedeen, Kelsey (Actor)
c/o Staff Member *Select Artists Ltd (CA-Westside Office)*
1138 12th Street
Suite 1
Santa Monica, CA 90403, USA

Wedel, Dieter (Director)
Tonndorfer Strand 2
Hamburg 22045, GERMANY

Weder, Gustav (Athlete)
Haltenstr 2
Stachen/TG, SWITZERLAND

Wedge, Chris (Actor, Director, Writer)
c/o Staff Member *Blue Sky Studios*
44 South Broadway Fl 17
White Plains, NY 10601, USA

Wedge, Eric M (Athlete, Baseball Player, Coach)
8285 SE 82nd St
Mercer Island, WA 98040-5653, USA

Wedgeworth, Ann (Actor)
70 Riverside Dr
New York, NY 10024, USA

Wedman, Scott (Athlete, Basketball Player)
7912 NW Scenic Dr
Kansas City, MO 64152-164, USA

Weed, Kent (Director, Producer, Writer)
c/o Staff Member *Arthur Smith & Co*
1811 Centinela Ave
Santa Monica, CA 90404, USA

Weed, Maurice James (Composer, Musician)
308 Overlook Road #55
Asheville, NC 28803, USA

Weege, Reinhold (Producer)
2035 Via Don Berito
La Jolla, CA 92037, USA

Weekend Players (Music Group)
c/o Staff Member *Paradigm (Monterey)*
404 W Franklin St
Monterey, CA 93940, USA

Weekes, Kevin (Athlete, Hockey Player)
251 Yonge St Suite 8 887
Richmond Hill, ON L4C 9T3, Canada

Weekley, Thomas (Boo) (Athlete, Golfer)
2555 New York St
Jay, FL 32565, USA

Weeks, Claire
11048 Chimineas Ave
Northridge, CA 91326

Weeks, John D (Misc)
15301 Watergate Road
Silver Spring, MD 20905, USA

Weeks, John R (Architect)
39 Jackson's Lane
Highgate
London N6 5SR, UNITED KINGDOM (UK)

Weeks, Michelle
c/o Staff Member *Diva Central Inc*
7510 W Sunset Blvd Ste 1445
Los Angees, CA 90046, USA

Weeks, Rickie (Athlete, Baseball Player)
353 Woldunn Cir
Lake Mary, FL 32746-3942, USA

Weeks, Rollo (Actor)
Artists Independent Network
270 Lafayette St #402
New York, NY 212-343-0069, 212-343-3216

Weeks, Rosey (Baseball Player)
1290 Menna St
Jacksonville, FL 32205-8330, USA

Weeks, Steve (Athlete, Hockey Player)
8210 Woodiron Dr
Duluth, GA 30097-3753, USA

Ween (Music Group, Musician)
ATTN: Mickey Melchiondo
P.O. Box 324
New Hope, PA 18938, USA

Weezer (Music Group)
c/o Don Muller *WME (LA)*
9601 Wilshire Blvd Fl 3
Beverly Hills, CA 90210, USA

Wefald, Jon (Educator)
Kansas State University
President's Office
Manhattan, KS 66506, USA

Wegener, Mike (Athlete, Baseball Player)
1507 Bennett Rd
Madison, OH 44057-1415, USA

Weger, Mike (Athlete, Football Player)
825 Markwood Dr
Oxford, MI 48370, USA

Wegman, Bill (Athlete, Baseball Player)
20521 Heather Ct
Lawrenceburg, IN 47025-9396, USA

Wegman, Marie (Baseball Player)
4158 Westwood Northern Blvd
Cincinnati, OH 45211-2444, USA

Wegman, William G (Artist, Photographer)
239 W 18th St
New York, NY 10011, USA

Wegner, Hans J (Designer)
Tinglevej 17
Gentofte 2820, DENMARK

Wegner, Mark (Baseball Player)
3215 Stevenson St
Plant City, FL 33566-1084, USA

Wegner, Mark (Athlete, Baseball Player)
2607 Lakeview Way
Plant City, FL 33566-6774, USA

Wehling, Ulrich (Athlete)
Skiverband
Hubertusstr 1
Munich 81477, GERMANY

Wehner, John (Athlete, Baseball Player)
105 Averys Way
Cranberry Twp, PA 16066-3303, USA

Wehr, Dick (Athlete, Basketball Player)
4425 Thomas Dr
Unit 813A
Panama City, FL 3131333-46134, USA

Wehrli, Roger R (Athlete, Football Player)
46 Fox Meadows Ct
Saint Charles, MO 63303, USA

Wehrmeister, Dave (Athlete, Baseball Player)
4216 Dubhe Ct
Concord, CA 94521-1820, USA

Wei, Dan-Wen (Musician)
Columbia Artists Mgmt Inc
165 W 57th St
New York, NY 10019, USA

Wei, James (Engineer)
571 Lake St
Princeton, NJ 08540, USA

Weibel, Robert (Doctor)
University of Pennsylvania
Med School
Pediatrics Dept
Philadelphia, PA 19104, USA

Weibring, D A (Athlete, Golfer)
5865 Versailles Ave
Frisco, TX 75034, USA

Weich, Gillian (Musician)
DS Mgmt
1017 16th Ave S
Nashville, TN 37212, USA

Weicker, Lowell P Jr (Ex-Governor, Ex-Senator, Politician)
Trust for America's Health
PO Box 877
Old Lym, CT 06371-0877, USA

Weickgenannt, Bob (Race Car Driver)
B&B Racing
8835-M Columbia 100 Parkway
Columbia, MD 21045, USA

Weida, Johnny (Educator, General)
Superintendent
US Air Force Academy
Colorado Springs, CO 80840, USA

Weide, Bob (Director)
Wahyaduck Productions
4804 Laurel Canyon Bl.
PMB 502
North Hollywood, CA 91607, USA

Weide, Robert B (Director, Producer)
c/o Jonathan Brandstein *Morra Brezner Steinberg & Tenenbaum (MBST) Entertainment*
345 N Maple Dr
Suite 200
Beverly Hills, CA 90210, USA

Weidemann, Jakob (Artist)
Ringsveen
Lillehammer 2600, NORWAY

Weidenbaum, Murray L (Economist, Government Official)
6231 Rosebury Ave
Saint Louis, MO 63105, USA

Weidenfeld of Chelsea, Arthur G (Publisher)
9 Chelsea Embankment
London SW3 4LE, UNITED KINGDOM (UK)

Weider, Betty (Actor)
131 S Hudson Ave
Los Angeles, CA 90004, USA

Weider, Joe (Publisher)
Weider Health & Fitness
21100 Erwin St
Woodland Hills, CA 91367, USA

Weidinger, Christine (Opera Singer)
John J Miller
801 W 181st St #20
New York, NY 10033, USA

Weidlinger, Paul (Engineer)
Weidlinger Assoc
375 Hudson Ave
New York, NY 10014, USA

Weidner, Bert (Athlete, Football Player)
517 NW 106th Ave
Plantation, FL 33324, USA

Weidner, Brant (Athlete, Basketball Player)
1111 Colfax St
Evanston, IL 6132131-26113, USA

Weigel, Dana (Scientist)
2728 Villa Pisa Ln
League City, TX 77573-3292

Weigel, Teri (Adult Film Star)
Lisa Ann's Talent Mgmt
4924 Balboa Blvd
Castaic, CA 91310, USA

Weigert, Robin (Actor)
c/o Staff Member *Frontline Management*
5670 Wilshire Blvd.
Suite 1370
Los Angeles, CA 90036, USA

Weight, Doug (Athlete, Hockey Player, Olympic Athlete)
72 Feeks Ln
Locust Valley, NY 11560-2022, USA

Weihenmayer, Erik (Mountaineer)
682 Partridge Circle
Golden, CO 80403, USA

Weikel, M Keith (Business Person)
Manor Care Inc
333 N Summit St
Toledo, OH 43604, USA

Weikl, Bernd (Opera Singer)
Ulf Torgvist
Sankt Eriksgatan 100
Stockholm 113 31, SWEDEN

Weil, Andrew (Doctor, Writer)
c/o Richard S. Pine *Inkwell Management*
521 Fifth Ave
New York, NY 10175, USA

Weil, Bruno (Composer, Conductor)
Kaylor Mgmt
130 W 57th St #8G
New York, NY 10019, USA

Weil, Cynthia (Musician, Songwriter)
c/o Staff Member *Gorfaine/Schwartz Agency Inc*
4111 W Alameda Ave
Suite 509
Burbank, CA 91505, USA

Weil, Frank A (Misc)
Smithsonian Institution
900 Jefferson Dr SW
Washington, DC 20560, USA

Weil, Jeri (Actor)
11564 Kling St #N
Hollywood, CA 91602, USA

Weil, Liza (Actor)
c/o Kim Hodgert *Creative Artists Agency (CAA-LA)*
2000 Ave Of The Stars
Los Angeles, CA 90067, USA

Weiland, Scott (Musician, Songwriter)
c/o Andrea Pett-Joseph *Brillstein Entertainment Partners*
9150 Wilshire Blvd #350
Beverly Hills, CA 90212, USA

Weill, Claudia B (Director)
2800 Seattle Dr
Los Angeles, CA 90046, USA

Weill, Dave (Athlete, Olympic Athlete)
120 Mountain Spring Ave
San Francisco, CA 94114-2120, USA

Weill, Sanford I (Sandy) (Business Person)
Citigroup Inc
399 Park Ave
New York, NY 10022, USA

Weinbach, Arthur F (Business Person)
Automatic Data Processing
1 ADP Blvd
Roseland, NJ 07068, USA

Weinbach, Lawrence A (Business Person)
Unisys Corp
Unisys Way
Blue Bell, PA 19424, USA

Weinberg, Mike (Actor)
c/o Elissa Leeds-Fickman *Reel Talent Management*
P.O. Box 491035
Los Angeles, CA 90049, USA

Weinberg, Rebecca (Stylist)
c/o Staff Member *Judy Casey Inc*
114 E 13th St
New York, NY 10003, USA

Weinberg, Robert A (Doctor, Scientist)
Whitehead Institute
9 Cambridge Center
Cambridge, MA 02142, USA

Weinberg, Steven (Nobel Prize Laureate)
University of Texas
Physics Dept
2613 Wichita St
Austin, TX 78712, USA

Weinberger, Caspar (Publisher, Secretary)
Rogers & Wells
2001 K St NW
Washington, DC 20006, USA

Weinbrecht, Donna (Athlete, Olympic Athlete, Skier)
177 High Crest Dr
West Milford, NJ 07480, USA

Weiner, Art E (Athlete, Football Player)
404 Kimberly Dr
Greensboro, NC 27408, USA

Weiner, Eric (Producer, Writer)
c/o Staff Member *ICM Partners (ICM-LA)*
10250 Constellation Blvd Fl 7
Los Angeles, CA 90067, USA

Weiner, Gerry (Government Official)
40 Fredmir St
Dollard-des-Ormeaux, PQ H9A 2R3, CANADA

Weiner, Matthew (Producer)
c/o Ted Miller *Creative Artists Agency (CAA-LA)*
2000 Ave Of The Stars
Los Angeles, CA 90067, USA

Weiner, Timothy E (Tim) (Journalist)
New York Times
Editorial Dept
1627 I St NW
Washington, DC 20006, USA

Weiner-Davis, Michele (Writer)
c/o Staff Member *21st Century Speakers*
1352 Lake Rd
Gouldsboro, PA 18424, USA

Weingarten, David M (Architect)
Ace Architects
330 2nd St
Oakland, CA 94607, USA

Weingarten, Reid (Attorney, Attorney General, General)
Steptoe & Johnson
4603 Harrison St
Chevy Chase, MD 20815, USA

Weinhandl, Mattias (Athlete, Hockey Player)
Puckagency LLC
555 Pleasantville Rd Ste 210N
Attn Jay Grossman
Briarcliff Manor, NY 10510-1900, USA

Weinke, Chris (Athlete, Football Player, Heisman Trophy Winner)
John Madden Football Academy
Attn: Directors Office
5500 34th St W
Bradenton, FL 34210, USA

Weinman, Roz (Producer)
c/o Staff Member *Wolf Films Inc (LA)*
100 Universal City Plz
Bldg 2252
Universal City, CA 91608-1085, USA

Weinrich, Eric (Athlete, Hockey Player, Olympic Athlete)
337 Sea Meadows Ln
Yarmouth, ME 04096-5556, USA

Weinstein, Bob (Business Person, Producer)
c/o Staff Member *Weinstein Company, The*
345 Hudson St
13th Floor
New York, NY 10014, USA

Weinstein, Diane Gilbert (Judge)
US Court of Claims
717 Madison Place NW
Washington, DC 20439, USA

Weinstein, Eric
c/o Staff Member *Home Box Office (HBO-LA)*
2500 Broadway Ste 400
Santa Monica, CA 90404, USA

Weinstein, Harvey (Actor, Business Person, Director, Producer)
c/o Staff Member *Weinstein Company, The*
345 Hudson St
13th Floor
New York, NY 10014, USA

Weinstein, Jack B (Judge)
US District Court
US Courthouse
225 Cadman Plaza E
Brooklyn, NY 11201, USA

Weinstein, Sidney T (General)
11936 Holly Branch Court
Great Falls, VA 22066, USA

Weintraub, Carl
10390 Santa Monica Blvd. #300
Los Angeles, CA 90025

Weintraub, Jerry (Producer)
27740 Pacific Coast Highway
Malibu, CA 90265, USA

Weir, Amanda (Athlete, Olympic Athlete, Swimmer)
765 Barongate Dr
Lawrenceville, GA 30044-6079, USA

Weir, Arabella (Actor)
c/o Staff Member *Lip Service Casting Ltd*
60-66 Wardour St
London W1F 0TA, UK

Weir, Bill (Correspondent)
c/o Staff Member *Good Morning America (NY)*
ABC
147 Columbus Ave Fl 6
New York, NY 10023, USA

Weir, Bob (Musician)
c/o John Scher *Metropolitan Entertainment Group*
2 Penn Plaza, 26th Floor
New York, NY 10121, USA

Weir, Gillian C (Musician)
78 Robin Way
Tilehurst
Berks RG3 5SW, UNITED KINGDOM (UK)

Weir, Glen (Athlete, Football Player)
40 Maxwell Cres
London, ON N5X 1Z1, Canada

Weir, Johnny (Athlete, Figure Skater)
c/o Tara Modlin *Fireworks Sorts Marketing*
475 Park Ave S Fl 6
New York, NY 10016, USA

Weir, Judith (Composer)
Chester Music
8/9 Frith St
London W1V 5TZ, UNITED KINGDOM (UK)

Weir, Kenneth W Gen (Aviator)
12122 SE Skyline Dr
Santa Ana, CA 92705-3150, USA

Weir, Mike (Athlete, Golfer)
2960 Oberland Rd
Sandy, UT 84092-7128, USA

Weir, Peter (Director)
Salt Pan Films
PO Box 29
Palm Beach, NSW 2108, AUSTRALIA

Weir, Stephanie (Actor)
c/o Dan Baron *Agency for the Performing Arts (APA-LA)*
405 S Beverly Dr
Suite 500
Beverly Hills, CA 90212-4425, USA

Weir, Wally (Athlete, Hockey Player)
448 Lakeshore Rd
Beaconsfield, QC H9W 4J5, Canada

Weirs, Peter (Director)
c/o Staff Member *Anonymous Content (LA)*
3531 Hayden Ave
Culver City, CA 90232, USA

Weis, Al (Athlete, Baseball Player)
902 S Poplar Ave
Elmhurst, IL 60126-4547, USA

Weis, Charlie (Athlete, Coach, Football Coach, Football Player)
50905 Fox Trl
Rail # T-5
Granger, IN 46530, USA

Weis, Heidelinde
Schleissheimer Str. 207
Munich, GERMANY D-80809

Weis, Joseph F Jr (Judge)
US Court of Appeals
US Courthouse
700 Grant St
Pittsburgh, PA 15219, USA

Weis, Lianne (Stylist)
c/o Staff Member *Sally Bjornsen Represents*
2008 3rd Ave
North Seattle, WA 98109, USA

Weis, Scott (Race Car Driver)
Wiseguys/Weis Racing
5401 Lakeside Ave.
Richmond, VA 23228, USA

Weisacosky, Ed (Athlete, Football Player)
15321 Lawrence 2090
Mount Vernon, MO 65712, USA

Weisberg, Ruth (Artist)
11452 W Washington Blvd
Los Angeles, CA 90066, USA

Weisberg, Tim (Musician)
c/o Staff Member *Pyramid Entertainment Group*
377 Rector Pl #21A
New York, NY 10280-1439, USA

Weisburg, Alyssa (Producer)
c/o Staff Member *Casting Society of America*
606 N Larchmont Blvd
#4B
Los Angeles, CA 90004, USA

Weiser-Most, Franz (Conductor)
Van Walsum Mgmt
4 Addison Bridge Place
London W14 8XP, UNITED KINGDOM
(UK)

Weishoff, Paula (Athlete, Olympic Athlete, Volleyball Player)
20021 Colgate Cir
Huntington Beach, CA 92646-4913, USA

Weishuhn, Clayton (Athlete, Football Player)
4521 Kropala Rd
San Angelo, TX 76905, USA

Weiskrantz, Lawrence (Doctor)
Oxford University
Experimental Psychology Dept
Oxford OX1 3UD, UNITED KINGDOM
(UK)

Weisman, Annie (Comedian)
c/o Staff Member *Gersh (LA)*
9465 Wilshire Blvd
Suite 600
Beverly Hills, CA 90212, USA

Weisman, Kevin (Actor)
c/o Holly Lebed *Holly Lebed Personal Management*
10535 Wilshire Boulevard
Suite 808
Los Angeles, CA 90024, USA

Weisman, Sam (Actor, Director)
United Talent Agency
9560 Wilshire Blvd
#500
Beverly Hills, CA 90212, USA

Weisner, Maurice F (Admiral)
3000 Steeplechase
Alpharetta, GA 30004-1443, USA

Weiss, Barry (Reality TV Star)
Storage Wars
C/O Original Production
308 W Verdugo Ave
Burbank, CA 91502, USA

Weiss, Brian L (Writer)
c/o Staff Member *WmE2 (WMA-LA)*
1 William Morris Pl
Beverly Hills, CA 90212, USA

Weiss, Frank (Athlete, Football Player)
729 Fairfax Dr
Salinas, CA 93901, USA

Weiss, Gary (Athlete, Baseball Player)
1700 Weiss Ln
Brenham, TX 77833-7063, USA

Weiss, Glenn (Director)
c/o Staff Member *WmE2 (WMA-LA)*
1 William Morris Pl
Beverly Hills, CA 90212, USA

Weiss, Heinz
Rosskopfstr. 10
Grunwald, GERMANY D-82031

Weiss, Janet (Musician)
Legends of 21st Century
7 Trinity Row
Florence, MA 01062, USA

Weiss, Julie (Designer)
International Creative Mgmt
8942 Wilshire Blvd
#219
Beverly Hills, CA 90211, USA

Weiss, Karen (Athlete, Golfer)
1135 Raymond Avenue
Saint Paul, MN 55108-1922, USA

Weiss, Kirsten Kjaer (Stylist)
c/o Staff Member *Independent NY*
15 E 30th St #401
New York, NY 10016, USA

Weiss, Margaret (Writer)
TSR
PO Box 707
Renton, WA 98057, USA

Weiss, Melvyn I (Attorney, Attorney General, General)
Milberg Weiss Bershad
1 Pennsylvania Plaza
New York, NY 10119, USA

Weiss, Michael (Figure Skater)
PO Box 12311
Burke, VA 22009, USA

Weiss, Michael T (Actor, Director)
c/o Robert Stein *Robert Stein Management*
PO Box 3797
Beverly Hills, CA 90212, USA

Weiss, Morry (Business Person)
American Greetings Corp
1 American Road
Cleveland, OH 44144, USA

Weiss, Roberta (Actor)
Sarnoff Co
3500 W Olive Ave #300
Burbank, CA 91505, USA

Weiss, Robert W (Bob) (Athlete, Basketball Player, Coach)
1600 Windermere Dr E
Seattle, WA 98112-3749, USA

Weiss, Shaun
c/o Jeff Morrone *Jeff Morrone Entertainment*
9350 Wilshire Blvd
Suite 224
Beverly Hills, CA 90212, USA

Weiss, Stephen (Athlete, Hockey Player)
899 NW 123rd Drive
Coral Springs, FL 33071-5039, USA

Weiss, Walter W (Walt) (Athlete, Baseball Player)
1275 Castle Pointe Dr
Castle Rock, CO 80104-3258, USA

Weissenhofer, Ron (Athlete, Football Player)
16156 Seneca Lake Cir
Crest Hill, IL 60435, USA

Weissflog, Jens (Skier)
Markt 2
Kurort Oberweisenthal 09484, GERMANY

Weissman, Irving L (Biologist, Doctor)
Stanford University
Pathology Dept
Beckman Center
Stanford, CA 94305, USA

Weissman, Robert (Business Person)
IMS Health Inc
1499 Post Road
Fairfield, CT 06824, USA

Weissman, Steven (Artist)
c/o Staff Member *Fantagraphics Books*
7563 Lake City Way
Seattle, WA 98115, USA

Weisz, Martin (Director)
c/o Doreen Wilcox Little *Anonymous Content (LA)*
3531 Hayden Ave
Culver City, CA 90232, USA

Weisz, Paul B (Engineer, Physicist)
University of Pennsylvania
Bio-Engineering Dept
Philadelphia, PA 19104, USA

Weisz, Rachel (Actor)
c/o Stacy O'Neil *Brillstein Entertainment Partners*
9150 Wilshire Blvd #350
Beverly Hills, CA 90212, USA

Weithaas, Antje (Musician)
Harrison/Parrott
12 Penzance Place
London W11 4PA, UNITED KINGDOM
(UK)

Weitz, Bruce (Actor)
18826 Erwin St
Tarzana, CA 91335, USA

Weitz, Chris (Actor, Director, Writer)
c/o David Lubliner *WmE2 (WMA-LA)*
1 William Morris Pl
Beverly Hills, CA 90212, USA

Weitz, Paul (Director, Writer)
Depth of Field
1424 Second St. Fl 3
Santa Monica, CA 90401, USA

Weitz, Paul J (Astronaut)
3086 N Tam Oshanter Dr
Flagstaff, AZ 86004-7405, USA

Weitzenberg, Charles B (Athlete, Olympic Athlete, Water Polo Player)
1699 Happy Valley Rd
Santa Rosa, CA 95409-4000, USA

Weitzman, Howard (Attorney, Attorney General, General)
Katten Muchin Zavis Weitzman
1999 Ave of Stars #1400
Los Angeles, CA 90067, USA

Weitzman, Rick (Athlete, Basketball Player)
76 Birch St
Peabody, MA 1319613-21359, USA

Weixler, Jess (Actor)
c/o Rhonda Price *Gersh (NY)*
41 Madison Ave
New York, NY 10010, USA

Wejbe, Jolean (Actor)
c/o Bob McGowan *McGowan Management*
8733 W Sunset Blvd
Suite 103
West Hollywood, CA 90069, USA

Wek, Alek (Model)
c/o Staff Member *IMG*
304 Park Ave S Fl 12
New York, NY 10010, USA

Welbourn, John (Athlete, Football Player)
3301 Palos Verdes Dr N
Palos Verdes Estates, CA 90274, USA

Welbring, D A (Golfer)
c/o Staff Member *Pro Golfers Association (PGA) Tour*
112 TPC Blvd
Ponte Vedra Beach, FL 32082, USA

Welch, Brian (Head) (Musician)
4025 E. Chandler Blvd
Suite 70-B3
Phoenix, AZ 85048, USA

Welch, Claxton (Athlete, Football Player)
9721 SE Ankeny St
Portland, OR 97216, USA

Welch, Darrell (General)
102 El Rancho Way
San Antonio, TX 78209-2116, USA

Welch, Florence (Musician)
c/o Mairead Nash *LuvLuvLuv Management*
106 Leonard St Fl 1
London EC2A 4RH, UNITED KINGDOM
(UK)

Welch, Gillian (Musician)
c/o Peter Mensch *Q Prime South*
729 Seventh Ave
16th Floor
New York, NY 10019, USA

Welch, Herb (Athlete, Football Player)
999 La Senda
Santa Barbara, CA 93105, USA

Welch, Jack (Astronomer)
University of California
Electrical Engineering Dept
Berkeley, CA 94720, USA

Welch, Jack (Business Person)
Jack Welch Management Institute
Strayer University Office of the General Counsel
2303 Dulles Station Blvd. #6C
Herndon, VA 20171, USA

Welch, Justin (Musician)
CMO Mgmt
Ransomes Dock
35037 Parkgate Road
London SW11 4NP, UNITED KINGDOM
(UK)

Welch, Lenny (Musician)
Brothers Mgmt
141 Dunbar Ave
Fords, NJ 08863, USA

Welch, Michael (Actor)
c/o Susan Curtis *Curtis Talent Management*
9607 Arby Dr
Beverly Hills, CA 90210, USA

Welch, Mike (Athlete, Baseball Player)
3 Inca Dr
Nashua, NH 03063-3544, USA

Welch, Milt (Athlete, Baseball Player)
818 Jannette Ct
Springfield, OR 97477-3694, USA

Welch, Peter
1404 Longworth HOB
Washington, DC 20515, USA

Welch, Raquel (Actor)
9903 Santa Monica Blvd
Suite 514
Beverly Hills, CA 90212, USA

Welch, Robert L (Bob) (Athlete, Baseball Player)
13452 E Desert Trl
Scottsdale, AZ 85259-2247, USA

Welch, Tahnee (Actor, Model)
PO Box 823
Beverly Hills, CA 90213, USA

Welchel, Don (Athlete, Baseball Player)
21518 Patton Ave
Lago Wista, TX 78645-6770, USA

Welch Jr, John F (Business Person)
General Electric Co
3135 Easton Turnpike
Fairfield, CT 06828, USA

Weld, Susan (Tuesday) (Actor)
c/o Alexa Pagonas *Michael Black Management*
9701 Wilshire Blvd
10th Floor
Beverly Hills, CA 90212, USA

Weld, William (Ex-Governor, Politician)
120 Zaccheus Mead Ln
Greenwich, CT 06831-3751, USA

Weldon, Ann (Actor)
c/o Staff Member *Sutton Barth & Vennari Inc*
145 S Fairfax
Suite 310
Los Angeles, CA 90036, USA

Weldon, Fay (Writer)
Casorotto Ramsay
National House
62/66 Wardour
London W1V 3HP, UNITED KINGDOM (UK)

Weldon, Joan (Actor)
67 E 78th St
New York, NY 10021, USA

Weldon, W Casey (Athlete, Football Player)
380 Castleton Cir
Tallahassee, FL 32312, USA

Welk, Lawrence (Actor)
841 N St Elena St
Gilbert, AZ 85231, USA

Welk, Tanya (Actor)
9633 La Tuna Canyon Rd
Sun Valley, CA 91352, USA

Welke, Tim (Athlete, Baseball Player)
7790 Doubletree Ct
Kalamazoo, MI 49009-9771, USA

Welke, William (Bill) (Athlete, Baseball Player)
54 Country Hls
Marshall, MI 49068-9674, USA

Welker, Frank (Actor)
c/o Staff Member *Cunningham Escott Slevin & Doherty (CESD-LA)*
10635 Santa Monica Blvd
130
Los Angeles, CA 90025, USA

Welker, Wes (Athlete, Football Player)
251 SW 87th Terr
Plantation, FL 33324-2602, USA

Welland, Colin (Actor, Writer)
Peter Charlesworth
68 Old Brompton Road
London SW7 3LQ, UNITED KINGDOM (UK)

Wellborn, Joe (Athlete, Football Player)
803 Paulus St
Schulenburg, TX 78956, USA

Wellemeyer, Todd (Athlete, Baseball Player)
8402 Westover Dr
Prospect, KY 40059-9497, USA

Weller, Freddie (Musician, Songwriter, Writer)
Ace Productions
PO Box 428
Portland, TN 37148, USA

Weller, Paul (Musician)
c/o Staff Member *Variety Artists International Inc*
793 Higuera Street
Suite 6
San Luis, CA 93401-0500, USA

Weller, Peter (Actor)
c/o Bill Treusch *Bill Treusch Management*
853 7th Ave Suite 9A
New York, NY 10019, USA

Weller, Rene (Boxer)
Hirsauerstrasse 50
Pforzheim D-75180, Germany

Weller, Robb (Television Host)
4249 Beck Ave.
Studio City, CA 91604, USA

Weller, Watter (Musician)
Doblinger Hauptstr 40
Vienna 1190, AUSTRIA

Wellford, Harry W (Judge)
US Court of Appeals
Federal Building
167 N Main St
Memphis, TN 38103, USA

Welling, Tom (Actor, Director)
c/o Simon Halls *Slate Public Relations*
9000 Sunset Blvd #915
West Hollywood, CA 90069, USA

Wellman, Brad (Athlete, Baseball Player)
733 Graham Ct
Danville, CA 94526-4326, USA

Wellman, Gary (Athlete, Football Player)
1638 Wellington Pl
Westlake Village, CA 91361, USA

Wellman Jr, William (Actor)
15935 Meadowcrest Rd
Sherman Oaks, CA 91403, USA

Wells, Annie (Journalist, Photographer)
Press Democrat
Editorial Dept
427 Mendocino Ave
Santa Rosa, CA 95401-6385, USA

Wells, Audrey (Director, Writer)
c/o David Lonner *Oasis Media Group*
8730 W. Sunset Blvd
Suite 700
Los Angeles, CA 90036, USA

Wells, Bob (Athlete, Baseball Player)
154 Wilcox Rd
Cowiche, WA 98923-9775, USA

Wells, Carole (Actor)
c/o Staff Member *Burton Moss*
10533 Strathmore Dr
Los Angeles, CA 90024, USA

Wells, Casper (Athlete, Baseball Player)
252 Guv Park Ave
Amsterdam, NY 12010-2333, USA

Wells, Charles (Athlete, Baseball Player)
Philadelphia Stars
1035 Beaver Creek Dr
Duncanville, TX 75137-3731, USA

Wells, Chris (Athlete, Hockey Player)
PO Box 880883
Boca Raton, FL 33488-0883, USA

Wells, Claudia (Actor)
c/o Staff Member *Privilege Talent Agency*
PO Box 260860
Encino, CA 91426-0860, USA

Wells, Cory (Musician)
Three Dog Night
Business Office
PO Box 96597
Las Vegas, NV 89193, USA

Wells, Dan (Actor)
c/o Jon Simmons *Simmons & Scott Entertainment*
4110 W. Burbank Blvd.
Burbank, CA 91505, USA

Wells, David (Dave) (Athlete, Baseball Player)
16956 Laurel Hill Ln
Unit 197
San Diego, CA 92127-6869, USA

Wells, Dawn (Actor)
c/o Wes Stevens *Vox*
6420 Wilshire Blvd Ste 1080
Los Angeles, CA 90048, USA

Wells, Dean (Athlete, Football Player)
1146 Copperfield Dr
Georgetown, IN 47122, USA

Wells, Gawen D (Bonzi) (Basketball Player)
c/o Staff Member *Sacramento Kings*
1 Sports Parkway
Sacramento, CA 95834

Wells, Greg (Athlete, Baseball Player)
1 Sterling Ct
Cartersville, GA 30120-6469, USA

Wells, Harold (Athlete, Football Player)
2315 New Bern Ave
Raleigh, NC 27610, USA

Wells, Jane (Correspondent)
c/o Staff Member *CNBC*
900 Sylvan Ave
Englewood Cliffs, NJ 07632, USA

Wells, Jay (Athlete, Hockey Player)
990 Keg Lane
Paris, ON N3L 3E2, Canada

Wells, Jay (Athlete, Hockey Player)
Barrie Colts 555 Bayview Dr
Attn Coaching Staff
Barrie, ON L4N 8Y2, Canada

Wells, Joel (Athlete, Football Player)
11 Flicker Pt
Greenville, SC 29609, USA

Wells, John (Producer)
c/o Staff Member *John Wells Productions*
4000 Warner Blvd
Bldg 1
Burbank, CA 91522, USA

Wells, Kip (Athlete, Baseball Player)
12891 Westbrook Dr
Tyler, TX 75704-2460, USA

Wells, Kitty (Musician)
240 Old Hickory Rd
Madison, TN 37115, USA

Wells, Llewellyn (Producer)
c/o Wayne Fitterman *United Talent Agency (UTA)*
9336 Civic Center Dr
Beverly Hills, CA 90210, USA

Wells, Mark (Athlete, Hockey Player, Olympic Athlete)
2341 Union Rd #132
W Seneca, NY 14224-1469, USA

Wells, Norman (Athlete, Football Player)
600 Lakes Edge Dr
Oxford, MI 48371, USA

Wells, Patricia (Journalist)
Harper Collins Publishers
10 E 53rd St
New York, NY 10022, USA

Wells, Terry (Athlete, Football Player)
25036 Polktown Rd
Lucedale, MS 39452, USA

Wells, Terry (Athlete, Baseball Player)
110 Seymour Creek Dr
Cary, NC 27519-5870, USA

Wells, Thelma (Writer)
1934 Lanark Ave
Dallas, TX 75203-4523, USA

Wells, Theodore V (Attorney)
Paul, Weiss, Rifkind, Warton & Garrison, LLC 1285 Avenue ofthe Americas
New York, NY 10019-6031, USA

Wells, Thomas B (Judge)
US Tax Court
400 2nd St NW
Washington, DC 20217, USA

Wells, Vernon (Athlete, Baseball Player)
1400 Fountain Grass Ct
Westlake, TX 76262-9032, USA

Wells, Warren (Athlete, Football Player)
1399 Pipkin St
Beaumont, TX 77705, USA

Wells, Wayne (Athlete, Olympic Athlete, Wrestler)
PO Box 69
Arcadia, OK 73007-0069, USA

Wells-Hawkes, Sharlene (Beauty Pageant Winner)
77 W Lund Ln
Centerville, UT 84014, USA

Welp, Christian (Athlete, Basketball Player)
10235 Central Valley Rd NW
Poulsbo, WA 981321-7264, USA

Welser-Most, Franz (Conductor)
Cleveland Symphony
Severance Hall
11001 Euclid Ave
Cleveland, OH 44106, USA

Welsh, Chris (Athlete, Baseball Player)
12640 Huey Ln
Walton, KY 41094-9511, USA

Welsh, Irvine (Writer)
c/o Laura Hassan *Random House Group Limited*
The Book Service Limited
20 Vauxhall Bridge Road
London SW1V 2SA, United Kingdom

Welsh, Moray M (Musician)
28 Somerfield Ave
Queens Park
London NW6 6JY, UNITED KINGDOM (UK)

Welsh, Stephanie (Journalist, Photographer)
PO Box 277
Wayne, ME 04284-0277, USA

Welsom, Elleen (Journalist)
Albuquerque Tribune
Editorial Dept
7777 Jefferson NE
Albuquerque, NM 87109, USA

Welsome-Martin, Eileen (Journalist,
Photographer)
2040 Locust St
Denver, CO 80207-3941, USA

Welteroth, Dick (Athlete, Baseball Player)
122 Eldred St
Williamsport, PA 17701-3434, USA

Welti, Lisa (Actor)
c/o Staff Member *Select Artists Ltd (CA-
Westside Office)*
1138 12th Street
Suite 1
Santa Monica, CA 90403, USA

Welty, John D (Educator)
4411 N Van Ness Blvd
Fresno, CA 93704, USA

Wen, Jinbao (Prime Minister)
Premier's Office
Zhonganahai
Beijing, CHINA

Wendeii-Pohl, Krissy (Athlete, Hockey
Player, Olympic Athlete)
10812 Falling Water Ln Unit G
Saint Paul, MN 55129-5267, USA

Wendell, Krissy (Hockey Player)
University of Minnesota
Athletic Dept
Minneapolis, MN 55455, USA

Wendell, Martin (Athlete, Football Player)
405 W Olive Ave
Prospect Heights, IL 60070, USA

Wendell, Ryan (Athlete, Football Player)
c/o Staff Member *New England Patriots*
1 Patriot Pl
Foxboro, MA 02035-1388, USA

Wendell, Steven "Turk" (Athlete, Baseball
Player)
11245 Palmer Divide Ave
Larkspur, CO 80118-5009, USA

Wendelstedt, Harry (Athlete, Baseball
Player)
88 S Saint Andrews Dr
Ormond Beach, FL 32174-3857, USA

Wendelstedt, Hunter (Athlete, Baseball
Player)
101 Howthorne Hollow Dr
Madisonville, LA 70447-9340, USA

Wenden, Michael (Swimmer)
Palm Beach Currmbin Center
Thrower Dr
Palm Beach Queens, AUSTRALIA

Wenders, Wim (Director)
Road Movies Filmproduton
Clausewitzstra 4
Berlin 10629, GERMANY

Wendkos, Gina (Writer)
c/o Staff Member *Industry Entertainment
Partners*
955 S Carrillo Dr
Suite 300
Los Angeles, CA 90048, USA

Wendorf, Edward (General)
2076 Springs of Life Ct
Spring Valley, CA 91977-3467, USA

Wendt, George (Actor)
3856 Vantage Ave
Studio City, CA 91604, USA

Wenge, Ralph (Correspondent)
Cable News Network
News Dept
1050 Techwood Dr NW
Atlanta, GA 30318, USA

Wenger, Arsene (Coach)
Arsenal Football Club
Highbury House
75 Drayton Park
London N5 1BU, UNITED KINGDOM

Wengert, Don (Athlete, Baseball Player)
13100 Cedarwood Ave
Clive, IA 50325-8568, USA

Wenglikowski, Alan (Athlete, Football
Player)
422 Lake Ave
Franklin, OH 45005, USA

Wengren, Mike (Musician)
c/o Staff Member *Mitch Schneider
Organization (MSO)*
14724 Ventura Blvd #410
Sherman Oaks, CA 91403, USA

Wenham, David (Actor, Producer)
c/o Julie Curran *Shanahan Management*
Level 3, Berman House
91 Campbell St
Surry Hills NSW 2010, Australia

Wenner, Jann (Journalist)
37 W 70th St
New York, NY 10023-4502, USA

Wenner, Jann S (Publisher)
Wenner Media
1290 Ave of the Americas
New York, NY 10104, USA

Wennington, Bill (Athlete, Basketball
Player)
1085 Oak Grove Ln
Lake Forest, IL 601345-1629, USA

Wensink, John (Athlete, Hockey Player)
29311 Bidwell Creek Rd
Fredericktown, MO 63645-8900, USA

Wenstrom, Matt (Athlete, Basketball
Player)
15714 Blanco Trail Ln
Cypress, TX 77429-4618, USA

Went, Joseph J (General)
9204 Kristin Lane
Fairfax, VA 22032, USA

Wente, Jean R (Business Person)
California State Automobile Assn
PO Box 422940
San Francisco, CA 94142, USA

Wente, Jr., Bob (Race Car Driver)
59 Windam Place Dr.
St. Charles, MO 63304, USA

Wentworth, Alexandra (Ali) (Actor,
Comedian)
c/o Rhonda Price *Gersh (NY)*
41 Madison Ave
New York, NY 10010, USA

Wentz, Pete (Musician)
c/o Nick Styne *Creative Artists Agency
(CAA-LA)*
2000 Ave Of The Stars
Los Angeles, CA 90067, USA

Wenz, Fred (Athlete, Baseball Player)
1 Circle Dr
Branchburg, NJ 08876-3905, USA

Wenzel, Andreas (Skier)
Oberhul 151
Liechtenstein-Gamprin, LIECHENSTEIN

Wenzel, Hanni Weirather- (Skier)
Fanalwegle 4
Schaan 9494, LIECHENSTEIN

Wenzell, Margaret (Athlete, Baseball
Player)
78287 Brookhaven Ln
Palm Desert, CA 92211-2735, USA

Wenzell, Marge (Baseball Player)
78287 Brookhaven Ln
Palm Desert, CA 92211-2735, USA

Wepner, Chuck (Boxer)
153 Ave E
Bayonne, NJ 07002, USA

Wepper, Fritz (Actor)
c/o Staff Member *NDF*
Joseph-Dollinger-Bogen 26
München 80807, Germany

Werbach, Adam (Misc)
Sierra Club
85 2nd St #200
San Francisco, CA 94105, USA

Werbowy, Daria (Model)
c/o Staff Member *IMG*
304 Park Ave S Fl 12
New York, NY 10010, USA

Werdann, Robert (Athlete, Basketball
Player)
4739 40th St
Apt 5F
Sunnyside, NY 11104-403S, USA

Werhas, Johnny (Athlete, Baseball Player)
23705 Via Del Rio
Yorba Linda, CA 92887-2717, USA

Werkheiser, Devon (Actor)
c/o Cameron Curtis *Curtis Talent
Management*
9607 Arby Dr
Beverly Hills, CA 90210, USA

Werley, George (Athlete, Baseball Player)
15415 Elk Ridge Ln
Chesterfield, MO 63017-5309, USA

Werner, Anna (Correspondent)
KHOU
News Department
1945 Allan Parkway
Houston, TX 77019, USA

Werner, Clyde (Athlete, Football Player)
3009 Islandview Ct
Gig Harbor, WA 98335, USA

Werner, Don (Athlete, Baseball Player)
2204 Briarwood Blvd
Arlington, TX 76013-3316, USA

Werner, Marianne (Athlete, Track Athlete)
Gauseland 2A
Dortmund 44227, GERMANY

Werner, Michael (Misc)
Michael Werner Ltd
21 E 67th St
New York, NY 10021, USA

Werner, Roger L Jr (Television Host)
Prime Sports Ventures
10000 Santa Monica Blvd
Los Angeles, CA 90067, USA

Werner, Tom (Producer)
c/o Staff Member *Carsey-Werner-
Mandabach*
16027 Ventura Blvd
6th Floor
Encino, CA 91436, USA

Wersching, Annie (Actor)
c/o Tara Friedlander *ID PR (LA)*
7060 Hollywood Blvd
8th Floor
Los Angeles, CA 90028, USA

Wersching, Raimund (Ray) (Athlete,
Football Player)
18 Buttercup Ln
San Carlos, CA 94070, USA

Wert, Don (Athlete, Baseball Player)
341 Smithville Rd
New Providence, PA 17560-9729, USA

Werth, Dennis (Athlete, Baseball Player)
2505 Tartan Way
Springfield, IL 62711-6755, USA

Werth, Isabell (Horse Racer)
Winterswicker Feld 4
Rheinberg 47495, USA

Werth, Jayson (Athlete, Baseball Player)
2713 Tartan way
Springfield, IL 62711-6717, USA

Wertheim, Jorge (Misc)
UNESCO
Director's Office
UN Plaza
New York, NY 10017, USA

Wertheimer, Fredric M (Misc)
3502 Macomb St NW
Washington, DC 20016, USA

Wertheimer, Linda (Correspondent)
National Public Radio
News Dept
2025 M St NW
Washington, DC 20036, USA

Werthein, Julio
c/o Staff Member *United Nations
Educational, Scientific and Cultural
Organization (UNESCO)*
7, place de Fontenoy
75352
Paris 07 SP, France

Wertimer, Ned (Actor)
Acme Talent
4727 Wilshire Blvd #333
Los Angeles, CA 90010, USA

Wertmuller, Lina (Director)
Piazza Clotilde
Rome 00196, ITALY

Wertz, Bill (Athlete, Baseball Player)
26514 Mingo Dr
Perrysburg, OH 43551-5437, USA

Wescott, Scott (Athlete, Snowboarder)
c/o Ben Morrill *Octagon*
2 Union St
Suite 300
Portland, ME 04101, USA

Wescott, William (General)
1038 N Ambrosia
Mesa, AZ 85205-5820, USA

Wesker, Arnold (Writer)
37 Ashley Road
London N19 3AG, UNITED KINGDOM
(UK)

Wesley, Blake (Athlete, Hockey Player)
Okanagan Hockey Schools
201-853 Eckhardt Ave W
Attn: Senior Director of Hockey
Operations
Penticton, BC V2A 9C4, Canada

Wesley, Dante (Athlete, Football Player)
104 Fawn Cv
White Hall, AR 71602, USA

Wesley, David (Athlete, Basketball Player)
2S06 Baywater Canyon Dr
Pearland, TX 77S84-4310, USA

Wesley, Glen (Athlete, Hockey Player)
5305 Newstead Manor Ln
Raleigh, NC 27606-9515, USA

Wesley, Glen (Athlete, Hockey Player)
Carolina Hurricanes
1400 Edwards Mill Rd
^ir Defenseman Development
Raleigh, NC 27607-3624, USA

Wesley, James (Musician)
c/o Staff Member *Broken Bow Records*
209 10th Ave S, Suite 230
Cummins Station
Nashville, TN 37203, USA

Wesley, Norman (Business Person)
Fortune Brands Inc
300 Tower Parkway
Lincolnshire, IL 60069, USA

Wesley, Paul (Actor)
c/o Susan Calogerakis *Thruline Entertainment*
9250 Wilshire Blvd
Ground Fl
Beverly Hills, CA 90212, USA

Wesley, Rutina (Actor)
c/o Holly Shakoor *42West (LA)*
11400 W Olympic Blvd
Suite 1100
Los Angeles, CA 90064, USA

Wesley, Walt (Athlete, Basketball Player)
6417 Scott Ln
Fort Myers, FL 33966-4713, USA

WesleySmith, Michael (Actor)
c/o Staff Member *Sharon Power Management*
Pope Street
Camborne, Wellington, New Zealand

Wessinger, Jim (Athlete, Baseball Player)
4275 Altair Crse
Liverpool, NY 13090-2230, USA

Wessling, John (Actor, Comedian)
c/o Nick Nuciforo *Creative Artists Agency (CAA-LA)*
2000 Ave Of The Stars
Los Angeles, CA 90067, USA

Wesson, Barry (Athlete, Baseball Player)
36 Shore Dr NE
Brookhaven, MS 39601-8756, USA

West, Adam (Actor)
PO Box 3477
Ketchum, ID 83340, USA

West, Billy (Artist, Voice Over Artist)
c/o Jeff Danis *Danis, Panaro, Nist (DPN)*
9201 W Olympic Blvd
Beverly Hills, CA 90212, USA

West, Bob (Athlete, Football Player)
3915 Boston Ave
San Diego, CA 92113, USA

West, Chandra
c/o Staff Member *Industry Entertainment Partners*
955 S Carrillo Dr
Suite 300
Los Angeles, CA 90048, USA

West, Cornel (Activist)
Harvard University
Afro American Studies Dept
Cambridge, MA 02138, USA

West, David (Athlete, Baseball Player)
1242 SW Sea hawk Way
Palm City, FL 34990-4246, USA

West, David (Basketball Player)
New Orleans Homets
New Orleans Arena
1501 Girod St
New Orleans, LA 70113, USA

West, David (Athlete, Baseball Player)
1242 SW Seahawk Way
Palm City, FL 34990, USA

West, Delonte (Athlete, Basketball Player)
c/o Aaron Goodwin *Goodwin Sports Management*
Prefers to be contacted via email or telephone
Seattle, WA, USA

West, Dominic (Actor, Director)
c/o Angharad Wood *Tavistock Wood Management*
32 Tavistock St
London WC2B 5HA, UK

West, Doug (Athlete, Basketball Player)
Villanova University see E Lancaster Ave
Attn Basketball Coaching Staff
Villanova, PA 1908S-1478, USA

West, Ed (Athlete, Football Player)
1930 Ma Lee Dr
Moody, AL 35004, USA

West, Ernest E (General, War Hero)
912 Adams Ave
Wurtland, KY 41144-1504, USA

West, Jake (Misc)
International Assn of Iron Workers
1750 New York Ave NW
Washington, DC 20006, USA

West, James (Inventor)
724 Berkeley Ave
Plainfield, NJ 07062-2010, USA

West, Jeff (Athlete, Football Player)
12376 Adair Creek Way NE
Redmond, WA 98053, USA

West, Jerry (Athlete, Basketball Player, Olympic Athlete)
Golden State Warriors
Attn: Executive Board
1011 Broadway
Oakland, CA 94607-4027, USA

West, Joe (Athlete, Baseball Player)
17531 Cobblestone Ln Ln
Clermont, FL 34711-5906, USA

West, Joel (Model)
William Morris Agency
1325 Ave of Americas
New York, NY 10019, USA

West, John B (Scientist)
9626 Blackgold Rd
La Jolla, CA 92037, USA

West, Jon Fredric (Opera Singer)
Opera et Concert
Maximillianstr 22
Munich 80539, GERMANY

West, Kanye (Actor, Musician, Producer)
c/o Michael Green *Collective*
8383 Wilshire Blvd
Suite 1050
Beverly Hills, CA 90211, USA

West, Leslie (Musician)
James Faith Entertainment
318 Wynne Lane
Port Jefferson, NY 11777, USA

West, Lizzie (Musician)
Warner Bors Records
3300 Warner Blvd
Burbank, CA 91505, USA

West, Lori (Golfer)
2110 Augusta Dr SE
Marietta, GA 30067-8215, USA

West, Lyle (Athlete, Football Player)
719 1st Street SE
Moultrie, GA 31768, USA

West, Mario
390 Vine Mountain Way
Mableton, GA 30126-72SS, USA

West, Mario (Athlete, Basketball Player)
390 Vine Mountain Way
Mableton, GA 30126-72SS, USA

West, Mark (Athlete, Basketball Player)
644 Old Wagner Rd
Petersburg, VA 23805, USA

West, Matthew (Musician)
c/o Mandy Parsons *Savvy Media Solutions*
133 Holiday Ct
Franklin, TN 37067, USA

West, Nathan (Actor)
c/o Jason Egenberg *United Talent Agency (UTA)*
9336 Civic Center Dr
Beverly Hills, CA 90210, USA

West, Paula (Musician)
PO Box 2142
San Francisco, CA 94126, USA

West, Peter
4708 Largo Way
Las Vegas, NV 89121

West, Price (Athlete, Baseball Player)
Raleigh Tigers
3540 Mill Point Dr SE
Grand Rapids, MI 49512-9337, USA

West, Red (Actor)
c/o Anne Geddes *Geddes Agency, The*
8430 Santa Monica Blvd
Suite 200
Los Angeles, CA 90069, USA

West, Richard L (War Hero)
6341 Crosswoods Drive
Falls Church, VA 22044-1209, USA

West, Roland (Athlete, Basketball Player)
7464 Shaker Run Ln
Wesy Chester, OH 4S069-6301, USA

West, Ronnie (Athlete, Football Player)
P.O. Box 110
Pineview, GA 31071, USA

West, Sam
34-43 Russell
London, ENGLAND WC2B 5HA

West, Samuel (Actor)
P F D
Drury House
34-43 Russell St
London WC2B 5HA, UNITED KINGDOM (UK)

West, Shane (Actor)
c/o Matt Luber *Luber Roklin Management*
8530 Wilshire Blvd
6th Floor
Beverly Hills, CA 90211, USA

West, Simon (Director)
c/o Staff Member *Simon West Productions*
5555 Melrose Ave
Dressing Room Building 109
Los Angeles, CA 90038, USA

West, Timothy L (Actor)
Gavin Barker Assoc
2D Wimpote St
London W1G 0EB, UNITED KINGDOM (UK)

West, Troy (Athlete, Football Player)
725 N Greenberry Ave
West Covina, CA 91790, USA

West, Willie (Athlete, Football Player)
P.O. Box 50430
Eugene, OR 97405, USA

Westbrook, Bryant (Athlete, Football Player)
310 S 4th St
Unit 1710
Phoenix, AZ 85004-2472, USA

Westbrook, Erinn (Actor)
c/o Tina Treadwell *Treadwell Entertainment*
1327 W Valleyheart Dr
Burbank, CA 91506, USA

Westbrook, Jake (Athlete, Baseball Player)
PO Box 574
Danielsville, GA 30633-0574, USA

Westbrook, Marie (Actor)

Westbrook, Michael (Athlete, Football Player)
1585 Oregon Trl
Elk Grove, IL 60007, USA

Westbrook, Peter (Athlete, Fencer, Olympic Athlete)
209 W 123rd St
New York, NY 10027-5429, USA

Westbrook, Russell (Athlete, Basketball Player)
c/o Arn Tellem *Wasserman Media Group*
10960 Wilshire Blvd
Suite 2200
Los Angeles, CA 90024, USA

Westbrooks, Greg (Athlete, Football Player)
3832 10th Avenue Pl
Moline, IL 61265, USA

Westcott, Seth (Athlete, Snowboarder)
c/o Staff Member *US Ski And Snowboard Association*
Box 199
Park City, UT 84060, USA

Westenhoefer, Suzanne (Actor, Comedian)
100 South 4th Street
Los Angeles, California 90046

Westenra, Hayley (Actor)
c/o Staff Member *Decca Music Group Limited*
347-353 Chiswick High Rd
London W4 4HS, UNITED KINGDOM

Wester, Travis (Actor)
c/o Abby Bluestone *Innovative Artists (LA)*
1505 10th St
Santa Monica, CA 90401, USA

Westerberg, Paul (Musician, Songwriter)
c/o Staff Member *WmE2 (WMA-LA)*
1 William Morris Pl
Beverly Hills, CA 90212, USA

Westerfield, Putney (Publisher)
10 Green View Lane
Hillsborough, CA 94010, USA

Westerman-Austin, Helen (Baseball Player)
1837 Stonehenge Rd
Springfield, IL 62702-3244, USA

Western, Johnny (Musician)
19 E 16th Ave
Hutchinson, KS 67501, USA

Western Underground (Music Group)
c/o Staff Member *Paradigm (Monterey)*
404 W Franklin St
Monterey, CA 93940, USA

Westfall, Ed (Athlete, Hockey Player)
PO Box 39
Locust Valley, NY 11560

Westfall, V Edward (Ed) (Athlete, Hockey Player)
699 Hillside Ave
New Hyde Park, NY 11040, USA

Westfeldt, Jennifer (Actor)
c/o Courtney Kivowitz *Schiff Company, The*
9465 Wilshire Blvd
Suite 480
Beverly Hills, CA 90212, USA

Westfield, Ernest (Athlete, Baseball Player)
PO Box 7091
Champaign, IL 61826-7091, USA

Westhead, Barb (Golfer)
9820 E Thompson Peak
Pkwy Unit 707
Scottsdale, AZ 85255-6656, USA

Westhead, Paul (Athlete, Basketball Coach, Basketball Player, Coach)
2217 Via Alamitos
Palos Verdes Estates, CA 90274, USA

Westheimer, Doctor Ruth (Doctor)
c/o Staff Member *Cunningham Escott Slevin & Doherty (CESD-LA)*
10635 Santa Monica Blvd
130
Los Angeles, CA 90025, USA

Westheimer, Gerald (Doctor, Misc)
582 Santa Barbara Road
Berkeley, CA 94707, USA

Westheimer, Ruth (Scientist)
900 W 190th St Apt 100
New York, NY 10040-3665, USA

West Jr, Togo D (General, Secretary)
922 N Cameron Ave
Winston Salem, NC 27101-3316, USA

Westlake, Wally (Athlete, Baseball Player)
3800 61st St
Sacramento, CA 95820-2421, USA

Westlife (Music Group, Musician)
c/o Staff Member *Solo Agency Ltd (UK)*
55 Fulham High St
2nd Floor
London SW6 3JJ, United Kingdom

Westling, Jon (Educator)
285 Goddard Ave
Brookline, MA 02445, USA

Westling, Wayde (Stylist)
c/o Staff Member *Celestine - CA*
1666 20th St
#200-B
Santa Monica, CA 90404, USA

Westmore, McKenzie (Actor)
3904 Laurel Canyon Blvd
#766
Studio City, CA 91604, USA

Westmoreland, Dick (Athlete, Football Player)
5601 Sea Reef Pl
San Diego, CA 92154, USA

Westmoreland, James (Actor)
8019 1/2 W Norton Ave
West Hollywood, CA 90046, USA

Westmoreland, Lynn (Congressman, Politician)
2433 Rayburn HOB
Washington, DC 20515, USA

Weston, Celia (Actor)
c/o Staff Member *Innovative Artists (LA)*
1505 10th St
Santa Monica, CA 90401, USA

Weston, David
123-A Grosvenor Rd.
London, ENGLAND SW1

Weston, Jeff (Athlete, Football Player)
7235 Alakoko St
Honolulu, HI 96825, USA

Weston, J Fred (Educator)
258 Tavistock Ave
Los Angeles, CA 90049, USA

Weston, Kim (Musician)
Powerplay
5434 W Sample Road
PMB 533
Pompano Beach, FL 33073, USA

Weston, Mickey (Athlete, Baseball Player)
2702 Elsenhower Ave
Valparaiso, IN 46383-3273, USA

Weston, P John (Government Official)
13 Denbigh Gardens
Richmond
Surrey TW10 6EN, UNITED KINGDOM (UK)

Weston, Randolph (Randy) (Musician)
PO Box 749
Maplewood, NJ 07040, USA

Weston, Wesley (Lil' Flip) (Musician)
c/o Staff Member *Sony Music Entertainment*
555 Madison Avenue
New York, NY 10022-3211, USA

Westphal, Paul D (Athlete, Basketball Player, Coach)
1424 Granvia Altamira
Palos Verdes Estates, CA 90274-2131, USA

Westwick, Ed (Actor)
c/o Melanie Greene *Affirmative Entertainment*
425 N Robertson Blvd
Los Angeles, CA 90048, USA

Westwood, Lee (Athlete, Golfer)
c/o Andrew "Chubby" Chandler *International Sports Management Ltd (ISM UK)*
Cherry Tree Farm
Cherry Tree Lane
Rostherne, Cheshire WA14 3RZ, UNITED KINGDOM

Westwood, Vivienne (Designer, Fashion Designer)
Westwood Studios
9-15 Elcho St
London SW11 4AU, UNITED KINGDOM (UK)

We The Kings (Musician)
c/o Staff Member *Ozone Entertainment*
60-62 E. 11th St
7th Floor
New York, NY 10003, USA

Wetherbee, James D (Astronaut)
710 Huntercrest St
Seabrook, TX 77586, USA

Wetherbee, James D Captain (Astronaut)
3818 Trailstone Ln
Katy, TX 77494-2472, USA

Wetherby, Jeff (Athlete, Baseball Player)
28410 Great Bend Pl
Wesley Chapel, FL 33543-5726, USA

Wetherell, T R (Educator)
Florida State University
Athletic Dept
Tallahassee, FL 32306, USA

Wetherill, George W (Geophysicist, Physicist)
Camergie Institution
Terrestrial Magnetism Dept
Washington, DC 20015, USA

Wethington, Charles T Jr (Educator)
2926 Four Pines Dr
Lexington, KY 40502, USA

Wetnight, Ryan S (Athlete, Football Player)
3156 Griffon Ct
Simi Valley, CA 93065, USA

Wetoska, Robert (Athlete, Football Player)
1295 Forest Glen Dr S
Winnetka, IL 60093, USA

Wetteland, John (Athlete, Baseball Player)
1229 Kentucky Derby Dr
Argyle, TX 76226-7005, USA

Wetter, Friedrich Cardinal (Religious Leader)
Kardinal-Faulhaber-Str 7
Munich 80333, GERMANY

Wetterich, Brett (Athlete, Golfer)
149 Morning Dew Cir
Jupiter, FL 33458, USA

Wettig, Patricia (Actor)
c/o Lori Jonas *Jonas Public Relations*
240 26th St
Suite 3
Santa Monica, CA 90402, USA

Wetton, John (Musician)
Entourage Talent
133 W 25th St #500
New York, NY 10001, USA

Wetzel, Carl (Athlete, Hockey Player)
609 4th St.
#477
Gaylord, MN 55334, USA

Wetzel, Gary G (General, War Hero)
PO Box 84
Oak Creek, WI 53154-0084, USA

Wetzel, John (Athlete, Basketball Player, Coach)
13011 N Sunrise Canyon Ln
Marana, AZ 8S6S8-403S, USA

Wetzel, Robert L (General)
1425 Dartmouth Road
Columbus, GA 31904, USA

Wetzel, Rosemarie
111 E. 22nd St. #200
New York, NY 10010

Wever, Stefan (Athlete, Baseball Player)
7 Corte Los Sombras
Greenbrae, CA 94904-1149, USA

Wexler, Anne (Government Official)
1317 F St NW #600
Washington, DC 20004, USA

Wexler, Haskell (Cinematographer)
1247 Lincoln Blvd #585
Santa Monica, CA 90401, USA

Wexner, Leslie H (Business Person)
Limited Inc
3 Limited Parkway
PO Box 16000
Columbus, OH 43216, USA

Weyerhaeuser, George (Business Person)
Weyerhaeuser Co
33663 32nd Ave S
Federal Ave, WA 98023, USA

Whalen, Dorothy (Baseball Player)
8315 125th St
Kew Gardens, NY 11415-2705, USA

Whalen, Jim (Athlete, Football Player)
9 Wauketa Rd
Gloucester, MA 01930, USA

Whalen, Laurence J (Judge)
US Tax Court
400 2nd St NW
Washington, DC 20217, USA

Whalen, Lindsay (Basketball Player)
Connecticut Sun
Mohegan Sun Arena
Uncasville, CT 06382, USA

Whalen, Sara (Athlete, Olympic Athlete, Soccer Player)
10 Francis Dr
Greenlawn, NY 11740-2504, USA

Whaley, Frank (Actor)
c/o Staff Member *Shelter Entertainment*
9454 Wilshire Blvd.
Suite 715
Beverly Hills, CA 90212, USA

Whaley, Joanne (Actor)
c/o Staff Member *Creative Artists Agency (CAA-LA)*
2000 Ave Of The Stars
Los Angeles, CA 90067, USA

Whalin, Justin (Actor)
c/o Deborah Miller *Shelter Entertainment*
9454 Wilshire Blvd.
Suite 715
Beverly Hills, CA 90212, USA

Whalley, Joanne (Actor)
c/o Louisa Spring *Louisa Spring Management*
Prefers to be contacted via telephone
Venice, CA 90016, USA

Whalum, Kirk (Musician)
Cole Classic Mgmt
PO Box 231
Canoga Park, CA 91305, USA

Whang, Suzanne (Actor)
c/o Staff Member *Kragen & Company*
14039 Aubrey Rd
Beverly Hills, CA 90210-1062, USA

Whannell, Leigh (Actor, Writer)
c/o Stacey Testro *Stacey Testro International*
8265 Sunset Blvd #102
Los Angeles, CA 90046, USA

W. Hanorable, Colleen (Congressman, Politician)
238 Cannon HOB
Washington, DC 20515, USA

Wharram, Ken (Athlete, Hockey Player)
382 Aubrey St
North Bay, ON P1B 6H9, Canada

Wharton, Bernard (Architect)
Shope Reno Wharton
18 W Putnam Ave
Greenwich, CT 06830, USA

Whatley, Ennis (Athlete, Basketball Player)
P.O. Box 43
Highland, MD 20777-0043, USA

Wheatley, E H (Publisher)
Vancouver Sun
2250 Granville St
Vancouver, BC V6H 3G2, CANADA

Wheatley, Terrence (Athlete, Football Player)
c/o Staff Member *New England Patriots*
1 Patriot Pl
Foxboro, MA 02035-1388, USA

Wheatley, Tyrone (Athlete, Football Player)
20730 Westhampton St
Oak Park, MI 48237, USA

Wheaton, David (Tennis Player)
20045 Cottagewood Ave
Excelsior, MN 55331, USA

Wheaton, Kenny (Athlete, Football Player)
6427 S 21st Pl
Phoenix, AZ 85042, USA

Wheaton, Wil (Actor)
c/o Christopher Black *Opus Entertainment*
5225 Wilshire Blvd #905
Los Angeles, CA 90036, USA

Wheatus (Music Group)
c/o Robert Hollingsworth *So Called Management*
1055 Homer St #1006
Vancouver, BC V6B 1G3, CANADA

Whedon, Joss (Director, Producer, Writer)
c/o Chris Harbert *Creative Artists Agency (CAA-LA)*
2000 Ave Of The Stars
Los Angeles, CA 90067, USA

Wheeler, Blake (Athlete, Hockey Player)
c/o Staff Member *Boston Bruins*
TD Banknorth Garden
100 Legends Way, Suite 250
Boston, MA 02114, USA

Wheeler, Charles F (Cinematographer)
79125 Jack Rabbit Trail
La Quinta, CA 92253, USA

Wheeler, Cheryl (Musician, Songwriter, Writer)
Morningstar Mgmt
PO Box 1770
Hendersonville, TN 37077, USA

Wheeler, Chris (Sportscaster)
302 Saint Andrews Pl
Blue Bell, PA 19422-1290, USA

Wheeler, Clinton (Athlete, Basketball Player)
199 Scenic View Ln
Stone Mountain, GA 30087-6222, USA

Wheeler, Daniel (Dan) (Athlete, Baseball Player)
215 Harrison Ave
Belleair Beach, FL 33786-3619, USA

Wheeler, Daniel S (Editor)
American Legion Magazine
700 N Pennsylvania St
Indianapolis, IN 46204, USA

Wheeler, Dwight (Athlete, Football Player)
2124 Blair Blvd
Nashville, TN 37212, USA

Wheeler, Ellen
13576 Cheltenham Dr
Sherman Oaks, CA 91423

Wheeler, H Anthony (Architect)
Hawthornbank House
Dean Village
Edinburgh EH4 3BH, SCOTLAND

Wheeler, John (Actor)
Levin Agency
8484 Wilshire Blvd #745
Beverly Hills, CA 90211, USA

Wheeler, Joni (Stylist)
2803 Woodlawn Dr
Nashville, TN 37215, USA

Wheeler, Maggie (Actor)
c/o Belle Zwerdling *B and B Management*
1041 N Formosa Ave
West Hollywood, CA 90046, USA

Wheeler, Margaret
4950 Cahuenga Blvd.
No. Hollywood, CA 91607

Wheeler, Mark (Athlete, Football Player)
101 Meadowridge Cove
San Marcos, TX 78666, USA

Wheelock, Douglas H Lt Colonel (Astronaut)
PO Box 580408
Houston, TX 77258-0408, USA

Wheelock, Gary (Athlete, Baseball Player)
3724 N Springfield St
Buckeye, AZ 85396-3537, USA

Whelan, Bill (Composer)
Sony Records
2100 Colorado Ave
Santa Monica, CA 90404, USA

Whelan, Jill (Actor)
c/o Staff Member *Scott Stander & Associates*
13701 Riverside Dr
Suite 201
Sherman Oaks, CA 91423, USA

Whelan, Julia (Actor)
c/o Tracy Brennan *Creative Artists Agency (CAA-LA)*
2000 Ave Of The Stars
Los Angeles, CA 90067, USA

Whelan, Nicky (Actor)
c/o Justin Grey Stone *Untitled Entertainment (LA)*
350 S. Beverly Dr #200
Beverly Hills, CA 90212, USA

Whelan, Wendy (Ballerina)
New York City Ballet
Lincoln Center Plaza
New York, NY 10023, USA

Whelchel, Lisa (Actor)
8221 Navisota Dr
Lantana, TX 76226, USA

Wheless, Jamy (Animator)
405 Fair St
Pefaluma, CA 94952, USA

Whelpley, John (Actor)
c/o Staff Member *Lenhoff & Lenhoff*
830 Palm Ave
West Hollywood, CA 90069

Whibley, Deryck (Musician)
15445 Varden St
Sherman Oaks, CA 91403-3815, USA

Whicker, Alan D (Correspondent)
Le Gallais Chambers
Saint Helier
Jersey, UNITED KINGDOM (UK)

Whigham, Larry (Athlete, Football Player)
6110 Midway Rd
Raymond, MS 39154, USA

Whigham, Shea (Actor)
c/o Larry Taube *Principal Entertainment (LA)*
1964 Westwood Blvd #400
Los Angeles, CA 90025, USA

Whillock, Jack (Athlete, Baseball Player)
2118 River Ridge Rd
Arlington, TX 76017-2758, USA

Whinnery, Barbara (Actor)
Baier/Kleinman
3575 Cahuenga Blvd #500
Los Angeles, CA 90068, USA

Whinnery, John R (Engineer)
1804 Wales Dr
Walnut Creek, CA 94595, USA

Whipple Jr, Allen (Race Car Driver)
GAS Motorsports
Route 11 & 103 Newport Rd.
Claremont, NH 03743, USA

Whirry, Shannon (Actor)
Shapiro-Lichtman
8827 Beverly Blvd
Los Angeles, CA 90048, USA

Whisenant, Matt (Athlete, Baseball Player)
1035 Fairview Dr
La Canada Flintridge, CA 91011-2351, USA

Whisenhunt, Ken (Athlete, Football Player)
1511 W Grand Canyon Dr
Chandler, AZ 85248, USA

Whisenton, Larry (Athlete, Baseball Player)
524 Main St
Canton, MS 39046-3208, USA

Whishaw, Anthony (Artist)
7A Albert Place
Victoria Road
London W8 5PD, UNITED KINGDOM (UK)

Whishaw, Ben (Actor)
c/o Clair Dobbs *Public Eye Communications*
535 Kings Rd
Suite 313 Plaza
London SW10 0SZ, United Kingdom

Whiskey Myers (Music Group, Musician)
c/o Joey Lee *WmE2 (WMA-TN)*
1600 Division St
Suite 300
Nashville, TN 37203, USA

Whisler, J Steven (Business Person)
Phelps Dodge Corp
1 N Central Ave
Phoenix, AZ 85004, USA

Whisler, Randy (Athlete, Baseball Player)
6920 Hilvard Ct
Klamath Falls, OR 97603-9620, USA

Whisler, Wes (Athlete, Baseball Player)
15029 Midland Ln
Noblesville, IN 46062-4637, USA

Whisman, Greg (Athlete, Golfer)
1908 129th Pl SE
Everett, WA 98208, USA

Whistle, Rob (Athlete, Hockey Player)
154 King Lane
Hampton, ON L0B IJO, Canada

Whiston, Don (Athlete, Hockey Player, Olympic Athlete)
2 Jeffreys Neck
Ipswich, MA 01938, USA

Whitacre, Edward E Jr (Business Person)
SBC Communications
175 E Houston
San Antonio, TX 78205, USA

Whitaker, Alaina (Musician)
PO Box 703165
Tulsa, OK 74170-3165, USA

Whitaker, Denzel (Actor)
c/o Brad Slater *WME (LA)*
9601 Wilshire Blvd Fl 3
Beverly Hills, CA 90210, USA

Whitaker, Ed (Race Car Driver)
923 Wagner Road
Bristol, VA 24201, USA

Whitaker, Forest (Actor, Director, Producer)
3036 Beckman Rd/3040 Munro Cir
Los Angeles, CA 90068, USA

Whitaker, Jack (Sportscaster)
American Sportscasters Association 225
Broadway Fl 20
New York, NY 10007-3001, USA

Whitaker, Johnny
4924 Vineland Ave.
No. Hollywood, CA 9l60l

Whitaker, Louis R (Lou) Jr (Athlete, Baseball Player)
17 Brownstone Ln
Greensboro, NC 27410-5145, USA

Whitaker, Mark (Editor)
Newsweek Magazine
Editorial Dept
251 W 57th St
New York, NY 10019, USA

Whitaker, Meade (Judge)
US Tax Court
400 2nd St NW
Washington, DC 20217, USA

Whitaker, Pernell (Athlete, Boxer, Olympic Athlete)
3808 Cranberry Court
Virginia Beach, VA 23456, USA

Whitaker, Robert (Writer)
c/o Staff Member *Park Literary*
270 Lafayette St
Suite 1504
New York, NY 10012, USA

Whitaker, Roger
1730 Tree Blvd. #2
St. Augustine, FL 32086

Whitaker, Steve (Athlete, Baseball Player)
900 SE 6th Ct
Fort Lauderdale, FL 33301-3018, USA

Whitaker, William (Athlete, Football Player)
Lake Road 135
Gravois Mills, MO 65037, USA

Whitbank, Ben (Baseball Player)
203 Apollo Ln
Milton, DE 19968-9781, USA

Whitbread, Fatima (Athlete, Track Athlete)
Chafford Information Ctr
Elozabeth Road
Grays
Essex RM16 6QZ, UNITED KINGDOM (UK)

Whitby, Bill (Athlete, Baseball Player)
13926 Huntersville Concord Rd
Huntersville, NC 28078-6262, USA

Whitcomb, Bob (Race Car Driver)
Whitcomb Racing
9201 Garrison Road
Charlotte, NC 28278, USA

Whitcomb, Edgar D (Ex-Governor)
3905 Highwater Rd.
Cannelton, IN 47520, USA

Whitcomb, Ian (Musician, Songwriter, Writer)
PO Box 451
Altadena, CA 91003, USA

Whitcomb, Richard T (Inventor)
119 Tide Mill Lane
Hampton, VA 23666, USA

White, Adrian (Athlete, Football Player)
686 Allen Ln
Orange Park, FL 32073, USA

White, Alan (Musician)
Ignition Mgmt
54 Linhope St
London NW1 6HL, UNITED KINGDOM (UK)

White, Albert (Baseball Player)
St Louis Browns
32 Jessana Hts
Colorado Springs, CO 80906-7902, USA

White, Andre (Athlete, Football Player)
5122 Hunters Luck
Stone Mountain, GA 30088, USA

White, Anna
9950 Durant Dr. #402
Beverly Hills, CA 90212

White, Ben (Horse Racer)
452 Oak Haven Dr
Altamonte Springs, FL 32701-6318, USA

White, Betty (Actor, Comedian)
PO Box 491965
Los Angeles, CA 90049, USA

White, Bill (Athlete, Hockey Player)
3-21 Ben lamond Ave
Toronto, ON M4E 1Y8, Canada

White, Bob W (Athlete, Football Player)
763D Espada Dr
El Paso, TX 79912, USA

White, Bradley
8730 Sunset Blvd. #480
Los Angeles, CA 90069

White, Brain (Athlete, Hockey Player)
3 Godlclc Rd
Burltnaton, MA 01803-1007, USA

White, Brian (Actor)
c/o Lena Roklin *Luber Roklin Management*
8530 Wilshire Blvd
6th Floor
Beverly Hills, CA 90211, USA

White, Brooke (Musician)
c/o Rick Canny *Sanctuary Artist Management*
8750 Wilshire Blvd Ste 200
Beverly Hills, CA 90211, USA

White, Bryan (Musician, Songwriter, Writer)
Holly Co
3415 W End Ave #101G
Nashville, TN 37203, USA

White, Charles (Athlete, Football Player, Heisman Trophy Winner)
31841 Via Faisan
Trabuco Canyon, CA 92679-4182, USA

White, Cheryl (Musician)
Hallmark Direction
713 18th Ave S
Nashville, TN 37203, USA

White, Chris (Musician)
Lustig Talent
PO Box 770850
Orlando, FL 32877, USA

White, Colin (Athlete, Hockey Player)
1221 Crosstns Way
Wayne, NJ 07470-4738, USA

White, Dana (Business Person)
Zuffa LLC
2960 W Sahara
Suite 200
Las Vegas, NV 89102, USA

White, Danny (Athlete, Coach, Football Player)
111 S Saint Joseph St
South Bend, IN 46601, USA

White, Dean (Producer)
c/o Sean Freidin *ICM Partners (ICM-LA)*
10250 Constellation Blvd Fl 7
Los Angeles, CA 90067, USA

White, Derrick (Athlete, Baseball Player)
3524 Derby Shire Cir
Windsor Mill, MD 21244-3624, USA

White, Devon M (Athlete, Baseball Player)
6440 E Sierra Vista Dr
Paradise Valley, AZ 85253-4351, USA

White, DeVoreaux
4505 Santa Rosalia Dr
Los Angeles, CA 90008

White, Diz (Actor)
203 N Plymouth Blvd
Los Angeles, CA 90004, USA

White, Donna (Athlete, Golfer)
200 Caribe Ct
Greenacres, FL 33413, USA

White, Dwayne (Athlete, Football Player)
1916 Dickinson St
Philadelphia, PA 19146, USA

White, Ed
1225 Grand View Dr.
Berkeley, CA 94705-1629

White, Ed (Athlete, Football Player)
P.O. Box 1437
Julian, CA 92036, USA

White, Edit (Stylist)
2155 W Tourhy Ave
Chicago, IL 60645, USA

White, Edmund (Writer)
185 Nassau St
Room 224
Princeton, NJ 08544, USA

White, Edward A (Ed) (Athlete, Football Player)
P.O. Box 1437
Julian, CA 92036, USA

White, Eric (Athlete, Basketball Player)
1945 Bush St
Apt K
San Francisco, CA 9411S-3226, USA

White, Eugene (Baseball Player)
Chicago American Giants
4166 Lockhart Dr N
Jacksonville, FL 32209-1928, USA

White, Frank (Athlete, Baseball Player)
PO Box 573
Blue Springs, MO 64013-0573, USA

White, Gabe (Athlete, Baseball Player)
1571 Lakeview Dr
Sebring, FL 33870-7940, USA

White, Gerald (Athlete, Football Player)
Halo Creative Concepts
1501 Halo Dr
Troy, MI 48084, USA

White, Gilbert F (Misc)
624 Pearl St #302
Boulder, CO 80302, USA

White, Glodean (Musician)
8000 Oceaus Dr
Los Angeles, CA 90046, USA

White, Hubie (Athlete, Basketball Player)
101 E Gowen Ave
Philadelphia, PA 19119-1613, USA

White, Jack (Musician)
c/o Staff Member *WmE2 (WMA-LA)*
1 William Morris Pl
Beverly Hills, CA 90212, USA

White, Jahidi (Athlete, Basketball Player)
c/o Staff Member *Washington Wizards*
601 F Street NW
Washington, DC 20071, USA

White, Jaleel (Actor)
c/o Joy Tom *Imperium 7 Talent Agency*
5455 Wilshire Blvd
Suite 1706
Los Angeles, CA 90036, USA

White, James
7529 Franklin Ave
Los Angeles, CA 90046-2241

White, James B (Attorney, Attorney General, Educator, General)
1606 Morton Ave
Ann Arbor, MI 48104, USA

White, James C (Athlete, Football Player)
14430 Andrea Way Ln
Houston, TX 77083-7712, USA

White, James (Whirlwind) (Misc)
c/o Staff Member *Peller Artistes Limited*
39 Princes Ave
London N3 2DA, UK

White, Jamie (Radio Personality)
c/o Staff Member *Star 98.7 FM*
3400 W Olive AVe #550
Burbank, CA 91505, USA

White, Jan (Athlete, Football Player)
6507 Burkwood Dr
Clayton, OH 45315, USA

White, Jason (Athlete, Football Player, Heisman Trophy Winner)
3203 Stone Dr
Tuttle, OK 73089-7972, USA

White, Jeremy Allen (Actor)
c/o Jillian Fowkes *ID Public Relations (ID-LA)*
7060 Hollywood Blvd
8th Floor
Los Angeles, CA 90028, USA

White, Jeris (Athlete, Football Player)
P.O. Box 3031
Frederick, MD 21705, USA

White, Jerry (Athlete, Baseball Player)
581 Glen Drive
San Leandro, CA 94577-2900, USA

White, Jessica (Model)
c/o Staff Member *IMG*
304 Park Ave S Fl 12
New York, NY 10010, USA

White, John (Photographer)
Chicago Sun-Times 350 N Orleans St
Fl10
Chicago, IL, USA

White, Jonah (Business Person)
Billy Bob Teeth, Inc.
Rt. 100, P.O. Box 389
Hardin, IL 62047, USA

White, Joseph (Jo Jo) (Athlete, Basketball Player)
2 Mansfield Road
Middleton, MA 01949-ISIS, USA

White, Joy Lynn (Musician)
Buddy Lee
38 Music Square E #300
Nashville, TN 37203, USA

White, Judith M (Biologist)
University of San Francisco
Biology Dept
San Francisco, CA 94117, USA

White, Julie (Actor)
c/o Staff Member *Steve Himber Entertainment*
211 S Beverly Dr #601
Beverly Hills, CA 90212, USA

White, Karyn (Musician)
Warner Bors Records
3300 Warner Blvd
Burbank, CA 91505, USA

White, Kate (Editor)
Cosmopolitan Magazine
Editorial Dept
224 W 57th St
New York, NY 10019, USA

White, Lan (Athlete, Hockey Player)
310 Cedar Cres
Steinbach, MB RSG OKS, Canada

White, Lari (Actor)
c/o Staff Member *WmE2 (WMA-LA)*
1 William Morris Pl
Beverly Hills, CA 90212, USA

White, Larri (Musician, Songwriter, Writer)
Carter Career Mgmt
1028 18th Ave S #B
Nashville, TN 37212, USA

White, Larry (Athlete, Baseball Player)
19053 N 37th Pl
Phoenix, AZ 85050-2699, USA

White, Lee (Athlete, Football Player)
600 Langtry Dr
Las Vegas, NV 89107, USA

White, Leon (Athlete, Football Player)
11033 Paseo Castanada
La Mesa, CA 91941, USA

White, Lorenzo (Athlete, Football Player)
3450 NW 7th St
Fort Lauderdale, FL 33311, USA

White, L Robert (Bob) (Athlete, Football Player)
1044 Grouse Way
Venice, FL 34285, USA

White, Marco P (Chef)
The Restaurant
66 Knightsbridge
London SW1X 7LA, UNITED KINGDOM (UK)

White, Marilyn (Athlete, Track Athlete)
9605 6th Ave
Inglewood, CA 90305, USA

White, Mark (Musician)
DAS Communications
84 Riverside Dr
New York, NY 10024, USA

White, Marsh (Athlete, Football Player)
7502 Bayhill Dr
Rowlett, TX 75088, USA

White, Martha G (Publisher)
London Free Press
369 York St
London, ON N6A 4G1, CANADA

White, Mary Anne (Scientist)
30 Burnt Log Cres
Etobicoke, ON M9C 2J8, CANADA

White, Matt (Athlete, Baseball Player)
1853 Old Route 9
Windsor, MA 01270-9397, USA

White, Meg (Music Group, Musician)
Jack White Productions
Muenchner Str 45
Unterfoehring 85774, GERMANY

White, Michael Jai (Actor)
c/o Craig Baumgarten *Baumgarten Management*
11925 Wilshire Blvd
Suite 310
Los Angeles, CA 90025, USA

White, Michael S (Producer)
48 Dean St
London W1V 5HL, UNITED KINGDOM (UK)

White, Mike (Athlete, Baseball Player)
26438 S Jardin Dr
Sun Lakes, AZ 85248-7114, USA

White, Mike (Athlete, Coach, Football Coach, Football Player)
115 Grand Canal
Newport Beach, CA 92662, USA

White, Mike (Actor)
c/o Staff Member *Black and White Productions*
100 Universal City Plaza
Bldg 4113
Universal City, CA 91608, USA

White, Miles D (Business Person)
Abbott Laboratories
100 Abbott Park Road
Abbott Park, IL 60064, USA

White, Myron (Athlete, Baseball Player)
3201 S Deegan Dr
Santa Ana, CA 92704-6614, USA

White, Nera (Athlete, Basketball Player)
RR 3 Box 165
Lafayette, TN 37083, USA

White, Paula (Religious Leader, Television Host, Writer)
Paula White Ministries
PO Box 25151
Tampa, FL 33622, USA

White, Persia (Actor)
c/o Staff Member *Acme Talent & Literary (LA)*
1400 Atlantic Ave
Suite 274
Long Beach, CA 90814, USA

White, Peter (Actor)
S M S Talant
8730 Sunset Blvd #440
Los Angeles, CA 90069, USA

White, Randy L (Athlete, Football Player)
Randy White's HOF BBQ
9225 Preston Rd.
Frisco, TX 75034, USA

White, Raymond P Jr (Doctor)
1506 Velma Road
Chapel Hill, NC 27514, USA

White, Reggie (Athlete, Football Player)
3631 Washington Ave
Baltimore, MD 21244, USA

White, Rex (Race Car Driver)
P.O. Box 1422
Forest Park, GA 30298, USA

White, Ric (Stylist)
c/o Staff Member *Judy Inc*
1 Yorkville Ave
Toronto ON M4W 1L1, Canada

White, Rick (Athlete, Baseball Player)
2860 Windy Ridge Dr
Springfield, OH 45502-7230, USA

White, Robert A (Athlete, Football Player)
11 Jackson St
Jefferson, MA 01522, USA

White, Robert M (Misc)
Somerset House II
5610 Wisconsin Ave #1506
Bethesda, MD 20815, USA

White, Robert M II (Journalist)
4871 Glenbrook Road NW
Washington, DC 20016, USA

White, Rodney (Basketball Player)
Denver Nuggets
Pepsi Center
1000 Chopper Circle
Denver, CO 80204, USA

White, Ron (Actor, Comedian, Writer)
c/o John MacDonald *MacDonald-Murray Management*
11846 Ventura Blvd Ste 202
Studio City, CA 91604-2620, USA

White, Ron (Actor, Comedian)
c/o Michael Blakey *Electra Star Management*
9229 Sunset Blvd #415
Los Angeles, CA 90069, USA

White, Rondell (Athlete, Baseball Player)
11111 Pine Lodge Trl
Davie, FL 33328-7317, USA

White, Rory (Athlete, Basketball Player)
S303 32nd St S
Fargo, NO S8104-6743, USA

White, RoseDenville Hall
62 Ducks Hill Rd. Northwood
Middlesex, ENGLAND HA6 2SB

White, Roy (Athlete, Baseball Player)
M D M Sports Marketing
218 Washington Ave Apt C14
Attn:David Ratner
Cedarhurst, NY 11516-1510, USA

White, Roy H (Baseball Player)
1001 2nd St
Sacramento, CA 95814, USA

White, Russell (Athlete, Football Player)
17450 Vanowen St
Unit 4
Van Nuys, CA 91406, USA

White, Sammy (Athlete, Football Player)
102 Margaret Dr
Monroe, LA 71203, USA

White, Sharon
380 Forest Retreat
Hendersonville, TN 37075

White, Shaun (Athlete, Snowboarder)
c/o Staff Member *US Ski And Snowboard Association*
Box 199
Park City, UT 84060, USA

White, Sheldon (Athlete, Football Player)
P.O. Box 622
Novi, MI 48376, USA

White, Sherman (Athlete, Football Player)
2710 Summerland Rd
Aromas, CA 95004, USA

White, Shernan E (Sherm) (Athlete, Football Player)
P.O. Box 1856
Pebble Beach, CA 93953, USA

White, Stan (Athlete, Football Player)
10716 Pot Spring Rd
Cockeysville, MD 21030, USA

White, Stephen (Writer)
Penguin Books
375 Hudson St
New York, NY 10014, USA

White, Steve (Athlete, Football Player)
11928 Middlebury Dr
Tampa, FL 33626, USA

White, Steven A (Admiral, Business Person)
4 Mount Royal Ave 3420
Marlborough, MA 01752-1961, USA

White, Sue (Stylist)
218 Forbes Ave
San Rafael, CA 94901, USA

White, Timothy D (Misc)
University of California
Hiuman Evolutionary Studies Lab
Berkeley, CA 94720, USA

White, Todd (Athlete, Hockey Player)
16 Charlesworth Ct
Kanata, ON K2K 3L5, CANADA

White, Tony
224 Durham St
New Westminster, BC V3L 1X3, Canada

White, Tony (Athlete, Basketball Player)
1213 Holston Park Rd
Knoxville, TN 37914-S733, USA

White, Tony L (Business Person)
PE Corp
710 Bridgeport Ave
Shelton, CT 06484, USA

White, Vanna (Entertainer, Model)
c/o Staff Member *PAT Productions*
10202 W Washington Blvd
Robert Young Bldg., Suite 2000
Culver City, CA 90232, USA

White, Verdine (Musician)
c/o Staff Member *Atlas/Third Rail Entertainment*
9200 Sunset Blvd
Floor 10
Los Angeles, CA 90069, USA

White, Walter (Athlete, Football Player)
504 NW 44th Ter
Kansas City, MO 64116, USA

White, Wilford (Athlete, Football Player)
30A S Macdonald
Mesa, AZ 85210, USA

White, Willard W (Opera Singer)
10 Montague Ave
London SE4 1YP, UNITED KINGDOM (UK)

White, William (Athlete, Football Player)
4619 Sandwich Ct
Dublin, OH 43016, USA

White, William B (Bill) (Athlete, Baseball Player)
PO Box 199
Upper Black Eddy, PA 18972-0199, USA

White, Willye B (Athlete, Track Athlete)
5882 S Ensenada St
Aurora, CO 80015-5110, USA

Whited, Ed (Athlete, Baseball Player)
Po Box 34
Carmel, IN 46082-0034, USA

Whitefield, A D (Athlete, Football Player)
807 Tangle Way Ct
Cedar Hill, TX 75104, USA

Whitehead, Alfred K (Misc)
International Assn of Fire Fighters
1750 New York Ave NW
Washintgon, DC 20006, USA

Whitehead, Barb (Athlete, Golfer)
9820 E Thompson Peak Pkwy
Unit 707
Scottsdale, AZ 85255, USA

Whitehead, Bud (Athlete, Football Player)
5438 N Brooks Ave
Fresno, CA 93711, USA

Whitehead, Cindy (Stylist)
2804 Ingleside Dr
Hermosa Beach, CA 90254, USA

Whitehead, Geoffrey
81 Shaftesbury Ave.
London, ENGLAND W1

Whitehead, George W (Mathematician)
299 Cambridge Street
Unit 424
Winchester, MA 01890-2392, USA

Whitehead, Jerome (Athlete, Basketball Player)
1543 Merritt Dr
El Cajon, CA 92020-7847, USA

Whitehead, John C (Financier, Government Official)
131 Old Chester Road
Essex Fells, NJ 07021, USA

Whitehead, John C (Scientist)
Brookings Institute
1775 Massachusetts Ave NW
Washington, DC 20036, USA

Whitehead, Kimberly (Race Car Driver)
Miss Dirt Motorsports
P.O. Box 206
Sussex, NJ 07461, USA

Whitehead, Lorne (Inventor)
3015 12th Ave W
Vancouver, BC V6K 2R4, CANADA

Whitehead, Lorne A (Scientist)
3015 12th Ave W
Vancouver, BC V6K 2R4, CANADA

Whitehead, Nicholas (Stylist)
c/o Staff Member *Rex Agency, The*
6311 Romaine St
Los Angeles, CA 90038, USA

Whitehead, Paxton (Actor)
c/o Robert Attermann *Abrams Artists Agency (LA)*
9200 Sunset Blvd
11th Floor
Los Angeles, CA 90069, USA

Whitehead, Richard F (Admiral)
American Cage & Machine Co
135 S LaSalle St
Chicago, IL 60674, USA

Whitehead, Steven (Stylist)
c/o Staff Member *Artists by Timothy Priano (NY)*
15 Watts St
6th Floor
New York, NY 10013, USA

Whitehouse, Len (Athlete, Baseball Player)
300 Shore Rd
Burlington, VT 05408-2632, USA

Whitehurst, C David (Athlete, Football Player)
11010 Linbrook Ln
Duluth, GA 30097, USA

White Jr, Josh (Musician)
23625 Ripple Creek
Novi, MI 48375, USA

Whitelaw, Billie (Actor)
Rose Cottage Plum St
Glensford
Suffolk CO10 7PX, UNITED KINGDOM
(UK)

Whitemore, Hugh (Writer)
c/o Staff Member *Creative Artists Agency (CAA-LA)*
2000 Ave Of The Stars
Los Angeles, CA 90067, USA

Whitemore, Willet F Jr (Doctor, Scientist)
2 Hawthorne Lane
Plandome, NY 11030, USA

Whiten, Mark (Athlete, Baseball Player)
5810 Jefferson Park Dr
Tampa, FL 33625-3313, USA

Whiten, Richard (Actor)
247 S Beverly Dr
#102
Beverly Hills, CA 90212, USA

White of Rhymney, Eirene L (Government Official)
64 Vandon Court
Petty France
London SW1H 9HF, UNITED KINGDOM
(UK)

Whiteread, Rachel (Artist)
Anthony d'Offay
22 Dering St
London W1R 9AA, UNITED KINGDOM
(UK)

White's
PO Box 2158
Hendersonville, TN 37075

Whitesell, Emily (Producer, Writer)
c/o Staff Member *WME (LA)*
9601 Wilshire Blvd Fl 3
Beverly Hills, CA 90210, USA

Whitesell, Josh (Athlete, Baseball Player)
1719 Deanna Way
Redlands, CA 92374-4716, USA

Whitesell, Sean (Actor, Producer)
c/o Staff Member *United Talent Agency (UTA)*
9336 Civic Center Dr
Beverly Hills, CA 90210, USA

Whiteside, Eli (Athlete, Baseball Player)
414 S Central Ave
New Albany, MS 38652, USA

Whiteside, Matt (Athlete, Baseball Player)
255 Palisades Ridge Ct
Eureka, MO 63025-3706, USA

Whiteside, Sean (Athlete, Baseball Player)
3506 N Hills Dr
Haleyville, AL 35565-6746, USA

Whiteside, Sean (Athlete, Baseball Player)
654 W Olymoic Pl APt 501
Seattle, WA 98119-3698, USA

Whitesides, George (Scientist)
124 Grasmere St
Newton, MA 02458-2235, USA

Whitesides, George M (Misc)
124 Grasmere St
Newton, MA 02458, USA

Whitesnake (Music Group)
c/o Rod MacSween *International Talent Booking*
74A Charlotte St
London W1T 4QJ, UNITED KINGDOM
(UK)

White Stripes, The (Music Group, Musician)
c/o Ian Montone *Monotone Inc.*
820 Seward St
Los Angeles, CA 90028, USA

Whitfield, Annelie (Actor)
c/o Catriona Ribon *The Rights House (UK)*
Drury House
34-43 Russell St
London WC2B 5HA, UK

Whitfield, Dondre T (Actor)
c/o Sheree Cohen *Kohner Agency, The*
9300 Wilshire Blvd
Suite 555
Beverly Hills, CA 90212, USA

Whitfield, Ed (Congressman, Politician)
2368 Rayburn HOB
Washington, DC 20515, USA

Whitfield, Fred (Athlete, Baseball Player)
2532 Fairview Rd
Gadsden, AL 35904-3102, USA

Whitfield, Karen (Stylist)
854 Katella St
Laguna Beach, CA 92651, USA

Whitfield, Lynn (Actor)
c/o Staff Member *Innovative Artists (LA)*
1505 10th St
Santa Monica, CA 90401, USA

Whitfield, Mal (Athlete, Olympic Athlete, Track Athlete)
1322 28th St SE
Washington, DC 20020-3647, USA

Whitfield, Sheree (Designer, Reality TV Star)
c/o Staff Member *Bravo (NY)*
30 Rockefeller Plaza
New York, NY 10112, USA

Whitfield, Terry (Athlete, Baseball Player)
849 Clearfield Dr
Millbrae, CA 94030-2148, USA

Whitfield, Trent (Athlete, Hockey Player)
207 Red Chimney Dr
Warwick, RI 02886-9320, USA

Whitford, Brad (Musician)
12811 Ninebark Trl
Charlotte, NC 28278-6837, USA

Whitford, Bradley (Actor)
c/o Adena Chawke *Greenlight Management and Production*
13848 Valleyheart Dr
Sherman Oaks, CA 91423, USA

Whiting, Leonard
7 Leicester Pl.
London, ENGLAND WC2H 7BP

Whitlam, Gough (Prime Minister)
Westfiel Towers
100 William St
Sydney, NSW 2001, AUSTRALIA

Whitley, Keith Society
Box 222
Sandy Hook, KY 41171

Whitley, Kim E (Actor, Producer)
c/o Judy Apperson *Morra Brezner Steinberg & Tenenbaum (MBST) Entertainment*
345 N Maple Dr
Suite 200
Beverly Hills, CA 90210, USA

Whitley, Kym (Actor, Producer)
c/o Adam Williamson *Thruline Entertainment*
9250 Wilshire Blvd
Ground Fl
Beverly Hills, CA 90212, USA

Whitlock, Bod (Athlete, Hockey Player)
Whitlock Insurance Services
1403 Bay Ave
Trail, BC V1R 4A9, Canada

Whitlow, Bob (Athlete, Football Player)
315 W Gordon Pike Trl
Bloomington, IN 47403, USA

Whitman, Kari (Actor, Model)
1155 N La Cienega Blvd #104
West Hollywood, CA 90069, USA

Whitman, Kenedy (Stylist)
157 E J
St Benicia, CA 94510, USA

Whitman, Mae (Actor)
c/o Daniel Spilo *Industry Entertainment Partners*
955 S Carrillo Dr
Suite 300
Los Angeles, CA 90048, USA

Whitman, Marina Von Neumann (Economist)
University of Michigan
Public Policy School
Ann Arbor, MI 48109, USA

Whitman, Meg (Business Person)
eBay
2145 Hamilton Ave
San Jose, CA 95125, USA

Whitman, Meg (Misc)
24 Edge Rd
Atherton, CA 94027-2226, USA

Whitman, Slim (Musician)
3830 Old Jennings Road
Middleburg, FL 32068, USA

Whitman, Stuart (Actor)
749 San Ysidro Road
Santa Barbara, CA 93108, USA

Whitmer, Dan (Athlete, Baseball Player)
823 Robinhood Ln
Redlands, CA 92373-6665, USA

Whitmire, Steve (Actor)

Whitmore, Darrell (Athlete, Baseball Player)
301 E 15th St
Front Royal, VA 22630-4112, USA

Whitmore, Kay (Athlete, Hockey Player)
National Hockey League
50 Bay Street 11th Floor
Attn: Director of Goaltender Eauioment
Toronto, ON M5J 2X8, Canada

Whitmyer, Nat (Athlete, Football Player)
5305 W Goldenwood Dr
Inglewood, CA 90302, USA

Whitney, Ashley (Athlete, Olympic Athlete, Swimmer)
124 Hearthstone Manor Cir
Brentwood, TN 37027, USA

Whitney, CeCe (Actor)
1145 Barham Dr #217
San Marcos, CA 92078, USA

Whitney, David (Athlete, Baseball Player)
Kansas City Monarchs
2178 Popps Ferry Rd
Biloxi, MS 39532-4233, USA

Whitney, Jane (Entertainer)
5 TV Place
Needham, MA 02494, USA

Whitney, Ray (Athlete, Hockey Player)
2908 Spaldwick Ct.
Raleigh, NC 27613-5471, USA

Whitney, Russ (Business Person, Misc)
Whitney Education Group Inc
1612 Cape Coral Pkwy
Cape Coral, FL 33904, USA

Whitney, Ryan (Athlete, Hockey Player)
179 Edward Foster Rd
Scituate, MA 02066-4342, USA

Whitney-Dearfield, Norma (Athlete,
Baseball Player)
1803 Delaware Ave
White Oak, PA 15131-1660, USA

Whitney-Lee, Grace (Actor)
PO Box 79
Coarsegold, CA 93614, USA

Whitsett, Vivicca (Actor)
c/o Karin Olsen *Amazon PR*
269 S Beverly Dr #750
Beverly Hills, CA 90212, USA

Whitson, Ed (Athlete, Baseball Player)
10473 MacKenzie Way
Dublin, OH 43017-8775, USA

Whitson, Peggy A (Astronaut)
306 Lakeview Circle
Seabrook, TX 77586, USA

Whitson, Peggy A Dr (Astronaut)
306 Lakeview Cir
El Lago, TX 77586-5846, USA

Whitt, Ernie (Athlete, Baseball Player)
37370 Moravian Dr
Clinton Township, MI 48036-3604, USA

Whittaker, James (Jim) (Mountaineer)
2023 E Sims Way #277
Port Townsend, WA 98368, USA

Whittaker, Roger (Musician, Songwriter,
Writer)
BML Mgmt
426 Marsh Point Circle
Saint Augustine, FL 32080, USA

Whitted, Alvis (Athlete, Football Player)
6107 Bent Oak Dr
Durham, NC 27705, USA

Whittinghill, Dick
11310 Valley Spring Lane
Toluca Lake, CA 91602

Whittington, Art (Athlete, Football Player)
6709 La Tijera Blvd
Apt 190
Los Angeles, CA 90045, USA

Whittington, Bill (Race Car Driver)
1881 West State Rd 84
Ft. Lauderdale, FL 33315, USA

Whittington, C L (Athlete, Football Player)
2332 Galilee Rd
Apt 121
Hallsville, TX 75650, USA

Whittington, Dale (Race Car Driver)
1881 West State Rd 84
Ft. Lauderdale, FL 33315, USA

Whittington, Don (Race Car Driver)
1881 W. State Road 84
Ft Lauderdale, FL 33315, USA

Whittington, Michael S (Athlete, Football
Player)
4246 Turtle Mound Rd
Melbourne, FL 32934, USA

Whittle, Ricky (Athlete, Football Player)
514 Tulare St
Fresno, CA 93706, USA

Whitw, Shelbe (Philanthropist)
*The Shelby White-Leon Levy Program for
Archaeological Publications*
6 Divinity Avenue
Cambridge, Massachuetts 02138, USA

Whitwam, David R (Business Person)
Whirlpool Corp
2000 N State St
RR 63
Benton Harbor, MI 49022, USA

Whitwell, Mike (Athlete, Football Player)
P.O. Box 6
Cotulla, TX 78014, USA

Whitworth, Johnny
c/o Lena Roklin *Luber Roklin
Management*
8530 Wilshire Blvd
6th Floor
Beverly Hills, CA 90211, USA

Whitworth, Kathy
5990 Lindenshire Lane #101
Dallas, TX 75230-2726

Whitworth, Kathy (Athlete, Golfer)
1735 Mistletoe Dr
Flower Mound, TX 75022, USA

Wholey, Dennis (Television Host)
Dennis Wholey Enterprises
1333 H St NW
Washington, DC 20005-4704, USA

Whoppers, Wendy (Actor)
c/o Staff Member *Wow Entertainment Inc*
8362 Pines Blvd #296
Pembroke Pines, FL 33024, USA

Whyte, Kenneth (Writer)
c/o Staff Member *Counterpoint*
2117 4th St
Suite D
Berkeley, CA 94710, USA

Whyte, Sandra (Athlete, Hockey Player,
Olympic Athlete)
81 Golden Hills Rd
Saugus, MA 01906, USA

Whyte, Sean (Athlete, Hockey Player)
600 W Grove Pkwy #1026
Mesa, AZ 85283, USA

WI, Charlie (Athlete, Golfer)
9400 Burnet Ave
Unit 109
North Hills, CA 91343, USA

Wiberg, Kenneth B (Misc)
160 Carmalt Road
Hamden, CT 06517, USA

Wiberg, Pernilla (Skier)
Katterunsvagen 32
Norrkopping 60 210, SWEDEN

Wick, Charles Z (Government Official)
US Information Agency
400 C St SW
Washington, DC 20024, USA

Wick, Douglas (Producer)
c/o David O'Connor *Creative Artists
Agency (CAA-LA)*
2000 Ave Of The Stars
Los Angeles, CA 90067, USA

Wickander, Kevin (Athlete, Baseball
Player)
4319 W Banff Ln
Glendale, AZ 85306-3601, USA

Wicker, Floyd (Athlete, Baseball Player)
1758 W Greensboro Chapel Hill Rd
Snow Camp, NC 27349-9544, USA

Wicker, tom (Writer)
PO Box 361
Rochese, VT 05767-0361

Wickersham, Dave (Athlete, Baseball
Player)
25340 Quivira Rd
Louisburg, KS 66053-5204, USA

Wickert, Tom (Athlete, Football Player)
3717 Beach Dr SW
Seattle, WA 98116, USA

Wickham, Daniel (Athlete, Baseball
Player)
3221 E Mountain Vista Dr
Phoenix, AZ 85048-5802, USA

Wickham, John (General)
13500 N Rancho Vistoso Blvd Apt 519
Oro Valley, AZ 85755-5967, USA

Wickham, John A Jr (General)
13590 N Fawnbrooke Dr
Tucson, AZ 85737, USA

Wicki-Fink, Agnes (Actor)
Weisgerberstr 2
Munich 80805, GERMANY

Wickman, Robert J (Bob) (Athlete,
Baseball Player)
6568 Cheyenne Dr
Abrams, WI 54101-9434, USA

Wicks, Ben (Cartoonist, Editor)
38 Yorkville Ave
Toronto, ON M4W 1L5, CANADA

Wicks, Chuck (Musician)
c/o Staff Member *Webster & Associates
PR*
3573 Couchville Pike
Hermitage, TN 37076, USA

Wicks, Ron (Athlete, Hockey Player)
4 Mclaughlin Rd S
Brampton, ON L6Y 3B2, Canada

Wicks, Sidney (Athlete, Basketball Player)
112 Great Oak Dr
Hampstead, CA 28443-2142, USA

Wicks, Sue (Basketball Player)
New York Liberty
Madison Square Garden
2 Penn Plaza
New York, NY 10121, USA

Wicoff, Erika (Athlete, Golfer)
7815 Four leaf Drive
Greenville, IN 47124-9524, USA

Widby, G Ronald (Ron) (Athlete,
Basketball Player, Football Player)
542 Mahler Rd
Wichita Falls, TX 76310-0326, USA

Widdoes, Kathleen (Actor)
24 E 11th St
New York, NY 10003, USA

Widdoes, Kathleen (Actor)
"As the World Turns" Show
CBS-TV
524 W 57th St 5330
New York, NY 10019, USA

Widdrington, Peter N T (Business Person)
Laidlaw Inc
3221 N Service Road
Burlington, ON L7R 3Y8, CANADA

Widell, Dave (Athlete, Football Player)
13050 Wexford Hollow Rd N
Jacksonville, FL 32224, USA

Widell, Doug (Athlete, Football Player)
870 21st St
Vero Beach, FL 32960, USA

Wideman, Dennis (Athlete, Hockey
Player)
26 Stillman St Apt 5-2
Boston, MA 02113-1695, USA

Wideman, John Edgar (Writer)
University of Massachusetts
Englesh Dept
Amherst, MA 01003, USA

Widener, Jeff (Photographer)
818 S King St Apt 2007
Honolulu, HI 96813-3033, USA

Widener Jr, H Emroy (Judge)
PO Box 1689
Bristol, VA 24203-1689, USA

Widenhouse, Bill (Race Car Driver)
P.O. Box 34
Highway 601
Midland, NC 28107, USA

Widenhouse, Dink (Race Car Driver)
693 Warren St. NE
Concord, NC 28025, USA

Widger, Chris (Athlete, Baseball Player)
95 Fort Mott Rd
Pennsville, NJ 08070-2839, USA

Widjaja, David (Stylist)
c/o Staff Member *Frame Representatives*
275 West St
New York, NY 10013, USA

Widman, Herbert (Herb) (Athlete,
Swimmer)
844 Monarch Circle
San Jose, CA 95138, USA

Widmer, Corey (Athlete, Football Player)
2640 Lake Shore Dr
Unit 2508
West Palm Beach, FL 33404, USA

Widmer, Jason (Athlete, Hockey Player)
PO Box 55289
Lexington, KY 40555-5289, USA

Widnall, Sheila (General)
Massachusetts Institute Of Technology 77
Massachusetts Ave# 33207
Cambridge, MA 02139-4301, USA

Widom, Benjamin (Misc)
204 The Parkway
Ithaca, NY 14850, USA

Wie, Michelle (Athlete, Golfer)
17217 Leal Ave
Cerritos, CA 90703, USA

Wieand, Ted (Athlete, Baseball Player)
216 S Walnut St
Slatington, PA 18080-2026, USA

Wiebe, Mark (Athlete, Golfer)
4123 S Elkhart St
Aurora, CO 80014-8100, USA

Wiebe, Susanne (Designer, Fashion
Designer)
Amalienstr 39
Munich 80799, GERMANY

Wieber, Jordyn (Athlete, Gymnast,
Olympic Athlete)
Twistars Gymnastics
9410 Davis Highway
Dimondale, MI 48821, USA

Wiedemann, Josef (Architect)
Im Eichgeholz 11
Munich 80997, GERMANY

Wiedenbauer, Tom (Athlete, Baseball Player)
1460 Kilrush Dr
Ormond Beach, FL 32174-2882, USA

Wiedlin, Jane (Musician)
420 S. San Pedro St. #612
Los Angeles, CA 90013, USA

Wiedorfer, Paul J (General)
3210 Chesley Ave
Parkville, MD 21234-7816, USA

Wiegart, Zach (Athlete, Football Player)
3747 Saltmeadow Ct S
Jacksonville, FL 32224, USA

Wiegert, Zach (Athlete, Football Player)
919 N 264th St
Waterloo, NE 68069-6207, USA

Wieghaus, Tom (Athlete, Baseball Player)
9724 E 8000N Rd
Grant Park, IL 60940-5364, USA

Wiegmann, Casey (Athlete, Football Player)
30051 N Waukegan Rd
North Chicago, IL 60064, USA

Wiehl, Christopher (Actor)
c/o Staff Member *Gersh (LA)*
9465 Wilshire Blvd
Suite 600
Beverly Hills, CA 90212, USA

Wielicki, Krzysztof (Mountaineer)
Ul A Frycza Modrzewskiego 21
Tychy 43-100, POLAND

Wieman, Carl E (Nobel Prize Laureate)
University of Colorado
University Of Colorado Campus# 440
Boulder, CO 80309-0001, USA

Wiemer, Jason (Athlete, Hockey Player)
428-5201 Dalhousie Dr NW
Calgary, AB T3A 5Y7, CANADA

Wiemer, Jim
152 Country Ln
Rochester, NY 14626-3308, USA

Wiener, Amy (Stylist)
2026 County Road
1503
Athens, TX 75751-5635, USA

Wiener, Jacques L Jr (Judge)
US Court of Appeals
Federal Buliding
500 Fannin St
Shreveport, LA 71101, USA

Wier, Murray (Athlete, Basketball Player, Coach)
118 Goodwater St
Georgetown, TX 78633-4Ses, USA

Wieschaus, Eric (Nobel Prize Laureate)
11 Pelham St
Princeton, NJ 08540-5314, USA

Wiese, John P (Judge)
US Claims Court
717 Madison Place NW
Washington, DC 20439, USA

Wiesel, Elie (Nobel Prize Laureate, Writer)
Boston University
555 Madison Ave Fl 20
New York, NY 10022-3301, USA

Wiesel, Torsten (Nobel Prize Laureate)
Rockefeller University 1230 York Ave
New York, NY 10065-6399, USA

Wiesen, Bernard (Director)
Weisgerberstr 2
Munich 80805, GERMANY

Wiesenhahn, Robert (Athlete, Basketball Player)
3315 Hickorycreek Dr
Cincinnati, OH 4S244-2S33, USA

Wiesler, Bob (Athlete, Baseball Player)
2325 Indiancup Dr
Florissant, MO 63033-1736, USA

Wiesner, Kenneth (Athlete, Olympic Athlete)
3601 Meta Lake Road
Eagle River, WI 54521, USA

Wiest, Dianne (Actor)
230 West 79th St
New York, NY 10024, USA

Wieters, Matt (Athlete, Baseball Player)
4703 Hunters Run
Sarasota, FL 34241-9200, USA

Wigger, Lones (Athlete, Olympic Athlete, Shooter)
630 Wuthering Heights Dr
Colorado Springs, CO 80921-2533, USA

Wiggin, Paul (Athlete, Coach, Football Coach, Football Player)
5013 Ridge Rd
Edina, MN 55436, USA

Wiggins, Al (Athlete, Olympic Athlete, Swimmer)
167 Chancery Ln
Ligonier, PA 15658-1286, USA

Wiggins, Audrey (Musician)
William Morris Agency
2100 W End Ave #1000
Nashville, TN 37203, USA

Wiggins, Candice (Athlete, Basketball Player)
BDA Sports Management
700 Ygnacio Valley Rd
Suite 330
Walnut Creek, CA 94596, USA

Wiggins, Jermaine (Athlete, Football Player)
403 Overlook Dr
Beckley, WV 25801, USA

Wiggins, John (Musician)
William Morris Agency
2100 W End Ave #1000
Nashville, TN 37203, USA

Wiggins, Mitchell (Athlete, Basketball Player)
P.O. Box 5072
Kinston, NC 28S03-S072, USA

Wiggins, Scott (Athlete, Baseball Player)
17 N Crescent Ave
Fort Thomas, KY 41075-2109, USA

Wigginton, Ty (Athlete, Baseball Player)
120 Manitoba Ln
Mooresville, NC 28117-5822, USA

Wigglesworth, Marian McKean (Skier)
General Delivery
Wilson, WY 83014, USA

Wiggs, Susan (Writer)
PO Box 4469
Rolling Bay, WA 98061, USA

Wight, Paul (Big Show) (Athlete, Wrestler)
c/o Staff Member *World Wrestling Entertainment (WWE)*
Titan Towers
1241 E Main St
Stamford, CT 06905-3857, USA

Wightman, Arthur S (Mathematician, Physicist)
16 Balsam Lane
Princeton, NJ 08540, USA

Wightman, Donald E (Misc)
Utility Workers Union
815 16th Ave NW
Washington, DC 20006, USA

Wigiser, Margaret (Athlete, Baseball Player)
7101 SE Quincy Ter
Hobe Sound, FL 33455-7357, USA

Wigle, Ernest D (Doctor)
101 College St
Toronto, ON M56 1L7, CANADA

Wihtol, Sandy (Athlete, Baseball Player)
496 1st St #200
Los Altos, CA 94022-3678, USA

Wiig, Kristen (Actor)
c/o Naomi Odenkirk *Odenkirk Provissiero Entertainment*
Raleigh Studios
650 N. Bronson Ave, Bldg. B145
Los Angeles, CA 90004, USA

Wiik, Sven (Skier)
PO Box 774484
Steamboat Springs, CO 80477, USA

Wijdenbosch, Jules A (President)
Presidential Palace
Onafhankelikheidsplein 1
Paramaribo, SURINAME

Wiklund, Stefan (Stylist)
c/o Staff Member *Halley Resources*
37 W 20th St
#603
New York, NY 10011, USA

Wilander, Mats (Tennis Player)
Einar Wilander
Vickervagen 2
Vaxjo 352 53, SWEDEN

Wilber, Doreen V H (Athlete)
1401 W Lincoln Way
Jefferson, IA 50129, USA

Wilborn, Ted (Athlete, Baseball Player)
6671 Pocket Rd
Sacramento, CA 95831-1904, USA

Wilbraham, John H G (Musician)
9 D Cuthbert St
Wells
Somerset BA5 2AW, UNITED KINGDOM (UK)

Wilbur, John (Athlete, Football Player)
P.O. Box 10002
Honolulu, HI 96816-0002, USA

Wilbur, Richard C (Judge)
US Tax Court
400 2nd St NW
Washington, DC 20217, USA

Wilbur, Richard P (Writer)
88 Dodswell Road
Cummington, MA 01026-9705, USA

Wilbur, Richard S (Doctor)
985 Hawthome Place
Lake Forest, IL 60045, USA

Wilburn, J R (Athlete, Football Player)
2211 Chalkwell Dr
Midlothian, VA 23113, USA

Wilburn, Ken (Athlete, Basketball Player)
17 E Meyran Ave
Somers Point, NJ 08244, USA

Wilburn Brothers
Box 50
Goodlettsville, TN 37072-0050, USA

Wilby, James (Actor)
William Morris Agency
52/53 Poland Place
London W1F 7KX, UNITED KINGDOM (UK)

Wilcher, Mary (Actor)
c/o Staff Member *Levine Management*
9028 W Sunset Blvd #PH1
Los Angeles, CA 90069, USA

Wilcox, Barry (Athlete, Hockey Player)
18859 86 Ave
Surrey, BC V4N 6E3, Canada

Wilcox, Chris (Athlete, Basketball Player)
c/o Jeff Schwartz *Excel Sports Management*
9665 Wilshire Blvd #500
Los Angeles, CA 90212, USA

Wilcox, Christopher (Editor)
Reader's Digest Magazine
Reader's Digest Road
Pleasantville, NY 10570, USA

Wilcox, David (Composer, Music Group, Musician, Songwriter, Writer)
c/o Staff Member *Concerted Efforts*
P.O. Box 440326
Somerville, MA 02144, USA

Wilcox, Davie (Dave) (Athlete, Football Player)
94471 Willamette Dr
Junction City, OR 97448, USA

Wilcox, John (Athlete, Football Player)
82038 S Fork Walla Walla River Rd
Milton, OR 97862, USA

Wilcox, Larry (Actor)
10 Appaloosa Lane
Bell Canyon, CA 91307, USA

Wilcox, Lisa (Actor)
Stone Manners
6500 Wilshire Blvd #550
Los Angeles, CA 90048, USA

Wilcox, Milt (Athlete, Baseball Player)
10064 Vernon Ave
Huntington Woods, MI 48070, USA

Wilcox, Shannon (Actor)
1753 Centinela Ave #A
Santa Monica, CA 90404, USA

Wilcutt, Terence W (Terry) (Astronaut)
1216 Red Wing Dr
Freindswood, TX 77546, USA

Wilcutt, Terrence W Colonel (Astronaut)
1216 Red Wing Dr
Friendswood, TX 77546-5888, USA

Wilczek, Frank (Nobel Prize Laureate)
Massachusetts Inst. Of Technology
4 Wyman Rd
Cambridge, MA 02138-2218, USA

Wild, Rebecca (Actor, Model)
PO Box 1074
Westerville, OH 43086, USA

Wilde, Abby
c/o Ileane Rusch *Superior Talent Agency*
11712 Moorpark Street
Suite 209
Studio City, CA 91604, USA

Wilde, Kim (Musician, Songwriter, Writer)
Dance Crazy Mgmt
294-296 Nether St
Finchley
Lake Forest N31 RJ, UNITED KINGDOM
(UK)

Wilde, Olivia (Actor)
c/o Jason Weinberg *Untitled Entertainment (LA)*
350 S. Beverly Dr #200
Beverly Hills, CA 90212, USA

Wilde, Patricia (Artist, Ballerina, Director)
Pittsburgh Ballet Theater
2900 Liberty Ave
Pittsburgh, PA 15201, USA

Wilder, Alan (Musician)
Reach Media
295 Greenwich St #109
New York, NY 10007, USA

Wilder, Bert (Athlete, Football Player)
501 Willow View Dr
Greensboro, NC 27455, USA

Wilder, Don (Cartoonist)
North American Syndicate
235 E 45th St
New York, NY 10017, USA

Wilder, Gene (Actor, Director, Writer)
476 Scofieldtown Rd
Stamford, CT 06903, USA

Wilder, James (Actor)
Stone Manners
6500 Wilshire Blvd
#550
Los Angeles, CA 90048, USA

Wilder, L Douglas (Politician)
2805 E Wevburn Rd
Richmond, VA 23235-3257, USA

Wilder, Sharon (Athlete, Golfer)
72730 Homestead Rd
Palm Desert, CA 92260, USA

Wilder, Yvonne
11836 Hesby St.
No. Hollywood, CA 91607

Wilding, Anna (Actor)
c/o Staff Member *Carpe Diem Films LLC*
9663 Santa Monica Blvd # 557
Beverly Hills, CA 90210, USA

Wilding, Norman (Race Car Driver)
Double A Racing
2644 Michigan Ave.
#E, Kissimmee FL, 34744

Wildman, George (Cartoonist)
1640 Shepard Ave
Hamden, CT 06518, USA

Wildman, Valerie (Actor)
110 Hurricane St #305
Marina del Rey, CA 90292, USA

Wildmon, Donald (Activist)
National Federation of Decency
PO Box 1398
Tupelo, MS 38802, USA

Wild Orchid
PO Box 90370
City of Industry, CA 91715-0370

Wild Orchid (Music Group)
c/o Staff Member *Diva Central Inc*
7510 W Sunset Blvd Ste 1445
Los Angees, CA 90046, USA

Wilds, Tristan (Actor)
c/o Elise Koseff *J Mitchell Management*
440 Park Ave S
New York, NY 10016, USA

Wiles, Andrew J (Mathematician)
Princeton University
Mathematics Dept
Princeton, NJ 08544, USA

Wiles, Jason (Actor)
c/o Joanne Wiles *ICM Partners (ICM-LA)*
10250 Constellation Blvd Fl 7
Los Angeles, CA 90067, USA

Wiles, Randy (Athlete, Baseball Player)
3716 Lake Catherine Dr
Harvey, LA 70058-5509, USA

Wiley, Enloe Steve (Baseball Player)
Negro Baseball Leagues
1222 Cedar St
Clarksville, TN 37040-3515, USA

Wiley, Lee (Musician)
Country Crossroads
7787 Monterey St
Gilroy, CA 95020, USA

Wiley, Marcellus (Athlete, Football Player)
P.O. Box 83070
Los Angeles, CA 90083, USA

Wiley, Mark (Athlete, Baseball Player)
22273 Vista Lago Dr
Boca Raton, FL 33428-4765, USA

Wiley, Michael (Athlete, Basketball Player)
2461 Elm Ave
Apt 2
Long Beach, CA 90806-3142, USA

Wiley, Michael E (Business Person)
Atlantic Richfield Co
333 S Hope St
Los Angeles, CA 90071, USA

Wiley, Morlan (Athlete, Basketball Player)
2S21 Fallview Ln
Carrollton, TX 75007-1934, USA

Wiley, Morlon (Athlete, Basketball Player)
1967 Legacy Cove Dr
Maitland, FL 32751, USA

Wiley, William T (Artist)
PO Box 1105
Woodacre, CA 94973-1105, USA

Wiley-Sears, Janet (Baseball Player)
19629 Gilmer St
South Bend, IN 46614-5605, USA

Wilfong, Rob (Athlete, Baseball Player)
126 Maverick Dr
San Dimas, CA 91773-1127, USA

Wilford, John Noble Jr (Journalist)
232 W 10th St
New York, NY 10014-2976, USA

Wilfork, Vince (Athlete, Football Player)
c/o Staff Member *New England Patriots*
1 Patriot Pl
Foxboro, MA 02035-1388, USA

Wilheim, Jim (Athlete, Baseball Player)
348 Laurel Way
Mill Valley, CA 94941, USA

Wilhelm, David (General)
5865 N Placita Del Conde
Tucson, AZ 85718-4330, USA

Wilhelm, Erik (Athlete, Football Player)
6452 SE Division St
Portland, OR 97206-1278, USA

Wilhelm, Jim (Athlete, Baseball Player)
348 Laurel Way
Mill Valley, CA 94941-4046, USA

Wilhelm, John W (Misc)
Hotel & Restaurant Employees Union
1219 28th St NW
Washington, DC 20007, USA

Wilhelm, Kati (Athlete)
SC Motor Zella-Mehlis
Bierbachstr 68
Zella-Mehlis 98544, USA

Wilhite, Jonathan (Athlete, Football Player)
c/o Staff Member *New England Patriots*
1 Patriot Pl
Foxboro, MA 02035-1388, USA

Wilhoite, Kathleen
PO Box 5617
Beverly Hills, CA 90210

Wilk, Brad (Musician)
GAS Entertainment
8935 Lindblade St
Culver City, CA 90232, USA

Wilk, Vic (Athlete, Golfer)
1350 N Town Center Dr
Unit 2082
Las Vegas, NV 89144, USA

Wilkening, Laurel L (Educator)
University of California
Chancellor's Office
Irvine, CA 92717, USA

Wilkens, Lanny
2660 Peachtree Rd. W #39F
Atlanta, GA 30305-3683

Wilkens, Lenny (Athlete, Basketball Coach, Basketball Player, Coach)
3429 Evergreen Point Rd
Medina, WA 98039-1022, USA

Wilkerson, Bob (Bobby) (Athlete, Basketball Player)
PO Box 74S3
Upper Marlboro, MD 20792-74S3, USA

Wilkerson, Brad (Athlete, Baseball Player, Olympic Athlete)
5640 Native Dancer Rd S
Palm Beach Gardens, FL 33418-7732, USA

Wilkerson, Bruce (Athlete, Football Player)
2013 Breakers Pt
Knoxville, TN 37922, USA

Wilkerson, Curtis (Athlete, Baseball Player)
P.O. Box 182993
Arlington, TX 76096-2993, USA

Wilkerson, Doug (Athlete, Football Player)
P.O. Box 7090
Rancho Santa Fe, CA 92067, USA

Wilkerson, Muhammad (Football Player)
c/o Chad Wiestling *Integrated Sports Management*
2120 Texas Ave
Suite 2204
Houston, TX 77003, USA

Wilkerson, Tim (Race Car Driver)
Demand Flow Racing
2901 Stevenson Dr.
Springfield, IL 62703, USA

Wilkes, Donna
16228 Maplegrove St
La Puente, CA 91744

Wilkes, Glenn (Basketball Player, Coach)
Stetson University
Athletic Dept
Campus Box 8359
DeLand, FL 32720, USA

Wilkes, Jamal (Athlete, Basketball Player)
7846 W 81st St
Playa del Rey, CA 90293-7911, USA

Wilkes, Jimmy (Baseball Player)
Newark Eagles
26-C Oakhill Drive
Brantford, ON N3T 1R1, CANADA

Wilkes, Reggie (Athlete, Football Player)
6912 Wissahickon Ave
Philadelphia, PA 19119, USA

Wilkie, Bob (Athlete, Hockey Player)
303 S Forge Rd
Palmyra, PA 17078-2613, USA

Wilkie, Chris (Musician)
Primary Talent Int'l
2-12 Petonville Road
London N1 9PL, UNITED KINGDOM
(UK)

Wilkie, David (Swimmer)
Oaklands Queens Hill
Ascot
Berkshire, UNITED KINGDOM (UK)

Wilkie, David (Athlete, Hockey Player)
9008 N 155th St
Bennington, NE 68007-8090, USA

Wilkin, Richard E (Religious Leader)
Winebrenner Theological Seminary
950 N Main St
Findlay, OH 45840, USA

Wilkins, Damien
10490 Bent Tree Vw
Duluth, GA 30097-4423, USA

Wilkins, Dean (Athlete, Baseball Player)
10974 Tobago Rd
San Diego, CA 92126-2040, USA

Wilkins, Dominique (Athlete, Basketball Player)
4415 Felix Way SE
Smyrna, GA 30082-4700, USA

Wilkins, Donna (Athlete, Golfer)
3617 Bancroft Main NW
Kennesaw, GA 30144-6011, USA

Wilkins, Eddie Lee (Athlete, Basketball Player)
304S Mockingbird Ln
Atlanta, GA 30344-S679, USA

Wilkins, Eric (Athlete, Baseball Player)
1650 W Joshua Ln
Meridian, ID 83642-6194, USA

Wilkins, Laisha (Actor)
c/o Staff Member *Televisa*
Blvd Adolfo Lopez Mateos 232
Colonia San Angel INN
DF CP 01060, MEXICO

Wilkins, Mac (Athlete, Olympic Athlete, Track Athlete)
1915 NW Columbine Ln
Portland, OR 97229-9173, USA

Wilkins, Marc (Athlete, Baseball Player)
1636 State Route 314 N
Mansfield, OH 44903-7405, USA

Wilkins, Mardell (Athlete, Golfer)
26982 Durango Ln
Mission Viejo, CA 92691, USA

Wilkins, Rick (Athlete, Baseball Player)
12766 Longview Dr W
Jacksonville, FL 32223-2620, USA

Wilkins, Roger (Journalist)
George Mason University
207 East Building
Fairfax, VA 22030, USA

Wilkins, William W Jr (Judge)
US Court of Appeals
PO Box 10857
Greenville, SC 29603, USA

Wilkins Myrick, Sue (Congressman, Politician)
230 Cannon HOB
Washington, DC 20515, USA

Wilkinson, Adrienne (Actor)
9157 Sunset Blvd
#215
W. Hollywood, CA 90069, USA

Wilkinson, Amanda (Music Group, Musician)
Fitzgerald-Hartley
1908 Wedgewood Ave
Nashville, TN 37212, USA

Wilkinson, Bill (Athlete, Baseball Player)
3738 Yuhas Ave
Helena, MT 59602-7404, USA

Wilkinson, Bruce (Writer)
Global Vision Resources
6400 Atlantic Blvd
Norcross, GA 30071, USA

Wilkinson, Dale (Athlete, Basketball Player)
3045 Goldfield Dr
Pocatello, ID 83201-2778, USA

Wilkinson, Dan (Athlete, Football Player)
222 Republic Dr
Allen Park, MI 48101, USA

Wilkinson, Geoffrey (Nobel Prize Laureate)
Imperial College
Chemistry Dept
London SW7 2AY, UNITED KINGDOM (UK)

Wilkinson, J Harvie III (Judge)
US Court of Appeals
255 W Main St
Charlottesville, VA 22902, USA

Wilkinson, Jonathan (Jonny) (Athlete, Soccer Player)
c/o Staff Member *Newcastle Falcons RFC*
Kingston Park
Brunton Rd, Kenton Bank Foot
Newcastle NE138AF, UK

Wilkinson, Joseph B Jr (Admiral)
340 Chesapeake Dr
Great Falls, VA 22066, USA

Wilkinson, June (Actor, Model)
4060 E Grenora Way
Long Beach, CA 90815-2613, USA

Wilkinson, Kendra (Model, Reality TV Star)
c/o Liza Anderson *Anderson Group Public Relations*
8060 Melrose Ave Fl 4
Los Angeles, CA 90046, USA

Wilkinson, Laura (Athlete, Diver, Olympic Athlete)
PO Box 131961
Spring, TX 77393-1961, USA

Wilkinson, Neil
PO Box 57
Sherwood, OR 97140-0057, USA

Wilkinson, Signe (Cartoonist, Editor)
Philadelphia Daily News
Editorial Dept
400 N Broad
Philadelphia, PA 19130, USA

Wilkinson, Steve (Musician)
Fitzgerald Hartley
1908 Wedgewood Ave
Nashville, TN 37212, USA

Wilkinson, Tom (Actor)
c/o Larry Taube *Principal Entertainment (LA)*
1964 Westwood Blvd #400
Los Angeles, CA 90025, USA

Wilkinson, Tyler (Musician)
Fritzgerald Hartley
1908 Wedgewood Ave
Nashville, TN 37212, USA

Wilks, Jim (Athlete, Football Player)
4314 Leaflock Ln
Katy, TX 77450, USA

Will, George (Writer)
9 Grafton St
Chevy Chase, MD 20815, USA

Will, George (Journalist)
9 Grafton St
Chew Chase, MD 20815-3427, USA

Willard, Fred (Actor, Comedian)
c/o Glenn Schwartz *Glenn Schwartz Company*
4046 Declaration Ave
Calabasas, CA 91302, USA

Willard, Jerry (Athlete, Baseball Player)
1421 Kumquat Pl
Oxnard, CA 93036-6219, USA

Willard, Kenneth H (Ken) (Athlete, Football Player)
3071 Viewpoint Rd
Midlothian, VA 23113, USA

Willard, Rod (Athlete, Hockey Player)
7736 Arboretum Dr Apt 108
Charlotte, NC 28270-0348

Willcocks, David V (Musician)
13 Grange Road
Cambridge CB3 9AS, UNITED KINGDOM (UK)

Willcox, Toyah (Actor)
c/o Staff Member *Roseman Organisation, The*
51 Queen Anne St
London W1G 9HS, UK

Willebrands, Johannes Cardinal (Religious Leader)
Council for Promoting Christian Unity
Via dell'Erba I
Rome 00120, ITALY

Willem-Alexander (Prince)
Huis ten Bosch
Hague, NETHERLANDS

Willerth, Jeffrey
6615 W. Tamarack Ave.
Sun Valley, CA 91352

Willet, E Crosby (Artist)
Willet Stained Glass Studios
811 E Cayuga St
Philadelphia, PA 19124, USA

Willets, Kathy (Actor)
3251 Spanish River Dr
Pompano Beach, FL 33062

Willett, Chad
PO Box 5617
Beverly Hills, CA 90210

Willett, Malcolm (Cartoonist)
Universal Press Syndicate
4520 Main St
Kansas City, MO 64111, USA

Willett, Walter (Doctor, Scientist)
Harvard Medical School
25 Shattuck St
Boston, MA 02115, USA

Willette, Jo Ann
9300 Wilshire Blvd. #400
Beverly Hills, CA 90212

Willey, Cary (Athlete, Baseball Player)
P.O. Box 64
Cherryfield, ME 04622, USA

Willey, Kathleen
2642 New Timer Way
Powhattan, VA 23139-5320

Will-Halpin, Maggie (Athlete, Golfer)
12423 Carnoustie Ln
Richmond, VA 23236, USA

Willhite, Gerald (Athlete, Football Player)
10464 Cliff Ct
Rancho Cordova, CA 95670, USA

Willhite, Kevin (Athlete, Football Player)
9784 W Taron Dr
Elk Grove, CA 95758, USA

Will.I.Am (Musician)
c/o Jeffrey Jacobs *Creative Artists Agency (CAA-LA)*
2000 Ave Of The Stars
Los Angeles, CA 90067, USA

William (Prince)
Clarence House
Stable Yard Gate
London SW1, UNITED KINGDOM (UK)

William, David (Actor, Director)
194 Langarth St E
London, ON N6C 1Z5, CANADA

William, Edward (Religious Leader)
Bible Way Church
5118 Clarendon Road
Brooklyn, NY 11203, USA

William, Prince (Duke of Cambridge) (Prince, Royalty)
St James Palace
London SW1A 1BS, UNITED KINGDOM

Williams, Adrian (Basketball Player)
Phoenix Mercury
American West Arena
201 E Jefferson St
Phoenix, AZ 85004, USA

Williams, Aeneas D (Athlete, Football Player)
746 High Hampton Rd
Saint Louis, MO 63124, USA

Williams, Al (Athlete, Baseball Player)
3428 E Shore Rd
Miramar, FL 33023-4978, USA

Williams, Al (Athlete, Basketball Player)
2809 S 36th St
Fort Smith, AR 72903, USA

Williams, Alfred H (Athlete, Football Player)
Sportsradio 950 The Fan
7800 E Orchard Rd
Suite 400
Greenwood Village, CO 80111, USA

Williams, Allison (Actor)
c/o Lindsay Galin *Rogers & Cowan PR (NY)*
919 Third Ave
18th Floor
New York, NY 10022, USA

Williams, Alvin (Basketball Player)
Toronto Raptors
Air Canada Center
40 Bay St
Toronto, ON M5J 2N8, CANADA

Williams, Anson (Actor)
c/o Art Rutter *Shapiro-Lichtman Talent Agency*
1333 Beverly Green Drive
Los Angeles, CA 90035-1018, USA

Williams, Anthony A (Politician)
Mayor's Office
District Building
14th & E Sts NW
Washington, DC 20004, USA

Williams, Ashley (Actor)
c/o Lena Roklin *Luber Roklin Management*
8530 Wilshire Blvd
6th Floor
Beverly Hills, CA 90211, USA

Williams, Barbara (Actor)
Innovative Artists
1505 10th St
Santa Monica, CA 90401, USA

Williams, Barry (Actor, Musician)
c/o Staff Member *Good Guy Entertainment*
3733 Oakfield Dr
Sherman Oaks, CA 91423, USA

Williams, Bernabe (Bernie) (Athlete, Baseball Player)
180114th St Unit 210
Oakland, CA 94607-1564, USA

Williams, Bernard (Athlete, Football Player)
1570 Waverly Ave
Memphis, TN 38106, USA

Williams, Bernie (Athlete, Baseball Player)
5 Hallock Pl
Armonk, NY 10504-1131, USA

Williams, Bert (Actor)
Susan Nathe
8281 Melrose Ave
#200
Los Angeles, CA 90046, USA

Williams, Betty (Nobel Prize Laureate)
PO Box 725
Valparaiso, FL 32580-0725, NORTHERN IRELAND

Williams, Billy (Athlete, Baseball Player)
3227 Randolph Ave
Oakland, CA 94602-1539, USA

Williams, Billy (Athlete, Baseball Player)
586 Prince Edward Rd
Glen Ellyn, IL 60137-6711, USA

Williams, Billy (Cinematographer)
Coah House
Hawkshill Place Esher
Surrey KT10 9HY, UNITED KINGDOM
(UK)

Williams, Billy Dee (Actor)
c/o Bradley Kramer *Kramer Management*
5699 Kanan Rd #275
Agoura Hills, CA 91301, USA

Williams, Bob A (Athlete, Football Player)
602 Stone Bam Rd
Towson, MD 21286, USA

Williams, Branden (Actor)
c/o Staff Member *Edward Horowitz*
1155 N. La Cienega Blvd.
Suite 203
West Hollywood, CA 90069, USA

Williams, Brian (Athlete, Football Player)
1725 Charleston Ln
Waconia, MN 55387, USA

Williams, Brian (Athlete, Football Player)
5319 Lyoncrest Ct
Dallas, TX 75287, USA

Williams, Brian (Athlete, Baseball Player)
2409 Colt Ln
Crowley, TX 76036-4703, USA

Williams, Brian (Correspondent,
Television Host)
c/o Staff Member *NBC Nightly News*
30 Rockefeller Plz #300S
New York, NY 10112, USA

Williams, Bruce (Entertainer)
P.O. Box 2095
Elfers, FL 34680-2095, USA

Williams, Bruce (General)
3125 Mulberry D^S
Salem, OR 97302-5912, USA

Williams, Bryan (Baby) (Musician)
c/o Staff Member *Universal Music Group
(UMG - LA)*
2220 Colorado Ave
Santa Monica, CA 90404, USA

Williams, Buck (Athlete, Basketball
Player)
9219 Fox Meadow Ln
Potomac, MD 20854-4619, USA

Williams, Calvin (Athlete, Football Player)
5032 Yellowood Ave
Baltimore, MD 21209, USA

Williams, Cara (Actor)
Dann
9903 Santa Monica Blvd
#606
Beverly Hills, CA 90212, USA

Williams, Carlton (Athlete, Football
Player)
5 Pinegate Ct
Peachtree City, GA 30269, USA

Williams, Carnell (Cadillac) (Football
Player)
c/o Jim Steiner *CAA - St. Louis*
222 S Central Ave
Suite 1008
St Louis, MO 63105, USA

Williams, Charlie (Athlete, Football
Player)
2607 Encina
Irving, TX 75038, USA

Williams, Charlie (Athlete, Baseball
Player)
44 Frederick Ave
Port Orange, FL 32127-8628, USA

Williams, Charlie (Athlete, Basketball
Player)
374 S Belvoir Blvd
Cleveland, OH 44121-2349, USA

Williams, Chris (Athlete, Football Player)
2851 E Nunneley Rd
Gilbert, AZ 85296, USA

Williams, Chris (Actor)
c/o Carolyn Govers *Artist Management*
1119 Colorado Ave
Suite 12
Santa Monica, CA 90401, USA

Williams, Chris A (Athlete, Football
Player)
2800 Christopher Blvd
Hamburg, NY 14075, USA

Williams, Christopher (Musician)
c/o Ken Maldonado *Zia Artists*
506 Fort Washington Ave, 1H
New York, NY 10033, USA

Williams, Christy (Artist)
PO Box 849
Lopez Island, WA 98261, USA

Williams, Cindy (Actor)
c/o Staff Member *Bette Smith
Management*
499 N Canon Dr
Beverly Hills, CA 90210, USA

Williams, C K (Writer)
Princeton University
English Dept
Princeton, NJ 08544, USA

Williams, Clarence (Journalist)
Los Angeles Times
Los Angeles Times 145 S Spring St
Los Angeles, CA 90012-3601, USA

Williams, Cliff (Musician)
11 Leominster Road
Morden
Surrey SA4 6HN, UNITED KINGDOM
(UK)

Williams, Clyde (Athlete, Football Player)
9754 Highway 79
Bethany, LA 71007, USA

Williams, Clyde (Baseball Player)
Cleveland Buckeyes
17135 San Juan Dr
Detroit, MI 48221-2622, USA

Williams, Colleen (Correspondent)
KNBC-TV
News Dept
3000 W Alameda Ave
Burbank, CA 91523, USA

Williams, Cress (Actor)
c/o Marni Rosenzweig *Abrams Artists
Agency (LA)*
9200 Sunset Blvd
11th Floor
Los Angeles, CA 90069, USA

Williams, Curtis (Musician)
Neal Hollander Agency
9966 Majorca Place
Boca Raton, FL 33434, USA

Williams, Cynda (Actor)
Innovative Artists
1505 10th St.
Santa Monica, CA 90401, USA

Williams, Dafydd R (David) (Astronaut)
NASA
Johnson Space Center
2101 NASA Road
Houston, TX 77058, USA

Williams, Dallas (Athlete, Baseball Player)
7638 Allenwood Cir
Indianapolis, IN 46268-4738, USA

Williams, Dana (Athlete, Baseball Player)
121 Arlene Dr
North Versailles, PA 15137-2432, USA

Williams, Dana (Musician)
Dreamcatcher Artists Mgmt
2908 Poston Ave
Nashville, TN 37203, USA

Williams, Daniel (General)
Governor General's Office
Botanical Gardens
Saint George's, GRENADA

Williams, Danny (Boxer)
c/o Frank Warren *Sports Network*
Centurion House
Bircherley Green
Hertford HERTS SG14 1AP, UNITED
KINGDOM

Williams, Darnell (Actor)
Stone Manners
6500 Wilshire Blvd
#550
Los Angeles, CA 90048, USA

Williams, Darryl (Athlete, Football Player)
7351 Peppertree Cir S
Davie, FL 33314, USA

Williams, Darryl
Vancouver Canucks
800 Griffiths Way
Attn: Coaching Staff
Vancouver, BC V6B 6G1, Canada

Williams, Dave (Athlete, Baseball Player)
157 Carter Ln
Camden, DE 19934-1212, USA

Williams, David (Athlete, Football Player)
30201 Redtree Dr
Leesburg, FL 34748, USA

Williams, David (Athlete, Football Player)
30826 Tanoa Rd
Evergreen, CO 80439, USA

Williams, David (Athlete, Hockey Player)
5 Barn Swallow Ln
Duxbury, MA 02332-3628, USA

Williams, David (Athlete, Football Player)
109 E Oxford St
Valley Stream, NY 11580, USA

Williams, Davida (Actor)
c/o Marvet Britto *Britto Agency PR*
234 W 56th St
Penthouse
New York, NY 10019, USA

Williams, David G T (Educator)
Emmanuel College
Cambridge CB2 3AP, UNITED
KINGDOM (UK)

Williams, David W (Athlete, Football
Player)
108 E Oxford St
Valley Stream, NY 11580, USA

Williams, Delvin (Athlete, Football Player)
173 Sierra Vista Ave
Apt 11
Mountain View, CA 94043, USA

Williams, Deniece (Musician)
Green Light Talent Agency
PO Box 3172
Beverly Hills, CA 90212, USA

Williams, Deren (Athlete, Basketball
Player)
6190 Murdoch Woods Pl
Salt Lake City, UT 84121-2206, USA

Williams, Deron (Athlete, Basketball
Player)
c/o Bob McClaren *McClaren Sports*
1401 McKinney
Suite 2222
Houston, TX 77010, USA

Williams, Derwin (Athlete, Football
Player)
12014 Windermere Crossing Cir
Winter Garden, FL 34787, USA

Williams, Dick
3680 Madrid St.
Las Vegas, NV 89121

Williams, Don (Athlete, Basketball Player)
6109 Rosedale Dr
Hyattsville, MD 20782-2296, USA

Williams, Don (Athlete, Baseball Player)
5597 Greene Road 125
Paragould, AR 72450-9020, USA

Williams, Don (Musician, Songwriter)
2000 Neptune Rd #A
Ashland City, TN 37015, USA

Williams, Donald E (Astronaut)
Science Applications Int'l
2200 Space Park Dr
#200
Houston, TX 77058, USA

Williams, Donald E Captain (Astronaut)
16430 Larkfield Dr
Houston, TX 77059-5415, USA

Williams, Donald "Spin" (Athlete, Baseball
Player)
240 Shoute Division
El Dorado, AR 71730-8984, USA

Williams, Doug (Comedian)
c/o James Kellem *JKA Talent*
12725 Ventura Blvd
Suite H
Studio City, CA 91604, USA

Williams, Douglas L (Doug) (Athlete,
Coach, Football Coach, Football Player)
10120 Lemon Rd
Zachary, LA 70791, USA

Williams, Dudley (Dancer)
Alvin Alley American Dance Foundation
211 W 61st St
#300
New York, NY 10023, USA

Williams, Earl (Athlete, Baseball Player)
61 Winston Dr
Somerset, NJ 08873-2333, USA

Williams, Easy (Actor)
Judy Schoen
606 N Larchmont Blvd
#309
Los Angeles, CA 90004, USA

Williams, Ed (Athlete, Football Player)
521 Royal Ave
Oklahoma City, OK 73130, USA

Williams, Eddie (Athlete, Baseball Player)
22809 Boxwood Ln
Santa Clarita, CA 91390-4155, USA

Williams, Edy (Actor, Model)
PO Box 6325
Woodland Hills, CA 91365, USA

Williams, Eli (Baseball Player)
St Louis Stars
214 Thomas Ct NW
Ft Walton Beach, FL 32548-4139, USA

Williams, Ellery (Athlete, Football Player)
1987 Wimbledon Pl
Los Altos, CA 94024, USA

Williams, Elmo (Director, Producer)
1249 Iris St
Brookings, OR 97415, USA

Williams, Eric (Football Player)
c/o Staff Member *Pittsburgh Steelers*
3400 S Water St
Pittsburgh, PA 15203-2349, USA

Williams, Eric (Football Player)
c/o Staff Member *Saint Louis Cardinals (St Louis Cardinals)*
700 Clark Ave
St Louis, MO 63102, USA

Williams, Eric (Basketball Player)
c/o Staff Member *Toronto Raptors*
400-40 Bay St
Toronto, Ontario M5J 2X2, Canada

Williams, Eric M (Athlete, Football Player)
13330 Noel Rd
Apt 825
Dallas, TX 75240-5092, USA

Williams, Erik (Athlete, Football Player)
1 Wortham Ct
Bear, DE 19701, USA

Williams, Ernie (Athlete, Football Player)
45 Oakwood Dr
Chapel Hill, NC 27517, USA

Williams, Erwin (Athlete, Football Player)
33 Manly St
Portsmouth, VA 23702, USA

Williams, Esther (Actor, Swimmer)
9377 Readcrest Dr
Beverly Hills, CA 90210, USA

Williams, E Virginia (Choreographer, Director)
Boston Ballet
19 Clarendon St
Boston, MA 02116, USA

Williams, Frank (Basketball Player)
New York Knicks
Madison Square Garden
2 Penn Plaza
New York, NY 10121, USA

Williams, Freeman (Athlete, Basketball Player)
450 W 41st Pl
Los Angeles, CA 90037-2119, USA

Williams, Gary (Basketball Player, Coach)
University of Maryland
Athletic Dept
College Park, MD 20742, USA

Williams, Gary Anthony (Actor)
c/o Staff Member *Innovative Artists (LA)*
1505 10th St
Santa Monica, CA 90401, USA

Williams, George (Athlete, Baseball Player)
N5250 County Road M
West Salem, WI 54669-9202, USA

Williams, Gerald (Athlete, Baseball Player)
17011 Candeleda De Avila
Tampa, FL 33613-5213, USA

Williams, Gerald (Athlete, Football Player)
9613 Callis Ct
Harrisburg, NC 28075, USA

Williams, Gerri (Stylist)
c/o Staff Member *Marnie Rose Agency*
37 Lower Shad
Pound Ridge, NY 10576, USA

Williams, Gluyas (Cartoonist)
New Yorker Magazine
Editorial Dept
4 Times Square
New York, NY 10036, USA

Williams, Greg (Actor)
1680 Vine St
#604
Los Angeles, CA 90028, USA

Williams, Gregg (Athlete, Coach, Football Coach, Football Player)
16897 Bold Venture Dr
Leesburg, VA 20176, USA

Williams, Gregory Alan (Actor)
c/o Staff Member *Pakula/King & Associates*
9229 Sunset Blvd
Suite 315
Los Angeles, CA 90069, USA

Williams, Gus (Athlete, Basketball Player)
P.O. Box 262
Mount Vernon, NY 10552, USA

Williams, Hal (Actor)
Marter
PO Box 14227
Palm Desert, CA 92255, USA

Williams, Harland (Actor)
c/o Jeff Witjas *Agency for the Performing Arts (APA-LA)*
405 S Beverly Dr
Suite 500
Beverly Hills, CA 90212-4425, USA

Williams, Harold M (Misc)
J Paul Getty Museum
Getty Center
1200 Getty Center Dr
Los Angeles, CA 90049, USA

Williams, Hayley (Musician)
c/o Mark Mercado *Fly South Music Group*
37 N. Orange Ave.
Suite 790
Orlando, FL 32801, USA

Williams, Herb (Athlete, Basketball Coach, Basketball Player, Coach)
67 Revonah Cir
Stamford, CT 0690S-4026, USA

Williams, Hershel W (War Hero)
3450 Wire Branch Road
Ona, WV 25545, USA

Williams, Hershel W (General)
3450 Wire Branch Rd
Ona, WV 25545-9513, USA

Williams, Howard E (Howie) (Basketball Player)
1940 Hamilton Lane
Carmel, CA 46032, USA

Williams, Howard L (Howie) (Athlete, Football Player)
4731 Proctor Ave
Oakland, CA 94618, USA

Williams, Hype (Actor, Director, Producer)
c/o Staff Member *Creative Artists Agency (CAA-LA)*
2000 Ave Of The Stars
Los Angeles, CA 90067, USA

Williams, Ivy (Writer)
Mediachase
834 N Harper Ave
Los Angeles, CA 90046, USA

Williams, Jaimie (Actor)
1019 Kane Concourse
#202
Bay Harbour Islands, FL 33154, USA

Williams, Jamal (Athlete, Football Player)
4020 Murphy Canyon Rd
San Diego, CA 92123, USA

Williams, James A (General)
8928 Maurice Lane
Annandale, VA 22003, USA

Williams, James A (Froggy) (Athlete, Football Player)
296 Sugarberry Cir
Houston, TX 77024, USA

Williams, James D (Admiral)
1111A N Stuart St
Arlington, VA 22201, USA

Williams, James F (Jimy) (Athlete, Baseball Player, Coach)
1506 S Evergreen Ave
Clearwater, FL 33756-2263, USA

Williams, James "Fly"
682 Ralph Ave Apt 2E
Brooklyn, NY 11212-38S3, USA

Williams, James (Fly) (Athlete, Basketball Player)
672 Ralph Ave
Apt 4A
Brooklyn, NY 11212, USA

Williams, James O (Athlete, Football Player)
330 S Western Ave
Lake Forest, IL 60045, USA

Williams, Jason (Athlete, Basketball Player)
6103 Louise Cove Dr
Windermere, FL 34786-8939, USA

Williams, Jason (Athlete, Hockey Player)
Newport Sports Management
400-201 City Centre Dr
Attn Wade Arnott
Mississauga, ON L5B 2T4, Canada

Williams, Jay (Athlete, Football Player)
1503 Alydar Ct
Waxhaw, NC 28173, USA

Williams, Jay (Basketball Player)
Chicago Bulls
United Center
1901 W Madison St
Chicago, IL 60612, USA

Williams, Jayson (Basketball Player, Sportscaster)
NBC-TV
Sports Dept
30 Rockefeller Plaza
New York, NY 10112, USA

Williams, Jeff (Athlete, Football Player)
9710 15th Ave NW
Seattle, WA 98117, USA

Williams, Jeffrey N (Astronaut)
4918 Cross Creek Ln
League City, TX 77573-6267, USA

Williams, Jeffrey N Colonel (Astronaut)
4918 Cross Creek Ln
League City, TX 77573-6267, USA

Williams, Jennifer (Reality TV Star)
Flirty Girl Fitness
PO Box 8349
Van Nuys, CA 91409, USA

Williams, Jerome (Athlete, Basketball Player)
c/o Staff Member *Toronto Raptors*
400-40 Bay St
Toronto, Ontario M5J 2X2, Canada

Williams, Jerrol (Athlete, Football Player)
13741 Allied Rd
Chester, VA 23836-6441, USA

Williams, Jesse (Actor)
c/o Staff Member *ROAR (LA)*
9701 Wilshire Blvd
8th Floor
Los Angeles, CA 90212, USA

Williams, Jessica (Musician)
c/o Staff Member *Diva Central Inc*
7510 W Sunset Blvd Ste 1445
Los Angees, CA 90046, USA

Williams, Jim (Athlete, Baseball Player)
16 Stone Pne
Aliso Viejo, CA 92656-2132, USA

Williams, Jimmy (Athlete, Baseball Player, Coach)
4 Old Sound Rd
Joppa, MD 21085-4525, USA

Williams, JoBeth (Actor)
c/o Staff Member *Innovative Artists (LA)*
1505 10th St
Santa Monica, CA 90401, USA

Williams, Jody (Nobel Prize Laureate)
115 Earls Way
Putney, VT 05346-8692, USA

Williams, Joel (Athlete, Football Player)
1515 Penn Ave
Apt 305
Wilkinsburg, PA 15221, USA

Williams, John (Composer, Musician)
Askonas Holt Ltd
27 Chancery Lane
London WC2A 1PF, UNITED KINGDOM (UK)

Williams, John A (Writer)
693 Forest Ave
Teaneck, NJ 07666, USA

Williams, John T (Composer, Conductor, Musician)
c/o Staff Member *Chasen & Company*
8899 Beverly Blvd
Suite 405
Los Angeles, CA 90048, USA

Williams, John T (Actor, Composer)
c/o Staff Member *Gorfaine/Schwartz Agency Inc*
4111 W Alameda Ave
Suite 509
Burbank, CA 91505, USA

Williams, Joseph R (Publisher)
Memphis Commercial Appeal
495 Union Ave
Memphis, TN 38103, USA

Williams, Juan (Correspondent)
c/o 21st Century Speakers
Box 1422
Gouldsboro, Pennsylvania 18424, USA

Williams, Justin (Athlete, Hockey Player)
7 Hart Ln
Ventnor City, NJ 08406-1215, USA

Williams, Kameelah (Musician)
c/o Staff Member *Creative Artists Agency*
(CAA-LA)
2000 Ave Of The Stars
Los Angeles, CA 90067, USA

Williams, Karen (Comedian)
HaHA Institute
P.O. Box 32147
Cleveland, Ohio 44132, USA

Williams, Karl (Athlete, Football Player)
6502 Falcon St
Rowlett, TX 75089, USA

Williams, Katt (Actor, Comedian)
c/o Staff Member *Collective*
8383 Wilshire Blvd
Suite 1050
Beverly Hills, CA 90211, USA

Williams, Keith (Athlete, Baseball Player)
1756 N Avignon Ln
Clovis, CA 93619-3799, USA

Williams, Kelli (Actor, Musician)
c/o John Carrabino *John Carrabino*
Management
5900 Wilshire Blvd Fl 4 #406
Los Angeles, CA 90036, USA

Williams, Ken (Athlete, Baseball Player)
6430 E Sierra Vista Dr
Paradise Valley, AZ 85253321___, USA

Williams, Kevin (Athlete, Football Player)
2201 Wembley Downs Dr
Arlington, TX 76017, USA

Williams, Kevin (Athlete, Basketball
Player)
1102 Blake Ave # 2
Brooklyn, NY 11208-3634, USA

Williams, Kevin (Athlete, Football Player)
9520 Viking Dr
Eden Prairie, MN 55344, USA

Williams, Kiely Alexis (Actor, Director,
Musician)
c/o Laurie Pozmantier *WME (LA)*
9601 Wilshire Blvd Fl 3
Beverly Hills, CA 90210, USA

Williams, Kim (Athlete, Golfer)
34350 Tuscany Ave
Sorrento, Fl 32776, USA

Williams, Kimberly (Actor, Producer)
c/o Michael Nilon *Kritzer Levine Wilkins*
Entertainment (KLWG)
2000 Ave Of The Stars
Los Angeles, CA 90067, USA

Williams, Kimberly Kevon (Actor)
c/o TJ Stein *Stein Entertainment Group*
1351 N Crescent Heights Blvd #312
West Hollywood, CA 90046, USA

Williams, Lauryn (Athlete, Track Athlete)
PO Box 8008
Gray, TN 37615, USA

Williams, Lee E (Athlete, Football Player)
11651 NW 4th St
Plantation, FL 33325, USA

Williams, Leona (Musician)
Leona Williams Enterprises
PO Box 777
Vienna, MO 65582, USA

Williams, Lewis T (Scientist)
Howard Hughes Medical Institute
5323 Harry Hines Blvd
Dallas, TX 75390, USA

Williams, Lucinda (Musician, Songwriter)
c/o Paul Fenn *Asgard Promotions*
125 Parkway
London NW1 7PS, United Kingdom

Williams, Lynn R (Misc)
Harvard University
Politics Institute
79 Kennedy St
Cambridge, MA 02138, USA

Williams, Madieu (Athlete, Football
Player)
12750 Gladys Retreat Cir
Bowie, MD 20720, USA

Williams, Maiya (Producer)
c/o Staff Member *Principal Entertainment*
(LA)
1964 Westwood Blvd #400
Los Angeles, CA 90025, USA

Williams, Malinda (Actor)
c/o Staff Member *Leverage Management*
3030 Pennsylvania Ave
Santa Monica, CA 90404, USA

Williams, Mark (Athlete, Baseball Player)
1453 Trumansburg Rd
Ithaca, NY 14850-9530, USA

Williams, Mark (Bowler)
Professional Bowlers Assn
719 2nd Ave
#701
Seattle, WA 98104, USA

Williams, Mary Alice (Correspondent)
c/o Staff Member *CBS News Productions*
524 W 57th St
8th Floor
New York, NY 10019, USA

Williams, Mason (Composer, Musician)
13479 SE Lost Lake Drive
Prineville, OR 97754-8487, USA

Williams, Matt (Athlete, Baseball Player)
205 Tearose Ln
Lake Jackson, TX 77566-6043, USA

Williams, Matt (Athlete, Baseball Player)
4400 N Scottsdale Rd
381
Scottsdale, AZ 85251-3331, USA

Williams, Matt (Writer)
Zeiderman
211 E 48th St
New York, NY 10017, USA

Williams, Maurice (Musician)
Willis Blume Agency, The
PO Box 509
Orangeburg, SC 29116-0509, USA

Williams, Maurice J (Misc)
Overseas Development Council
1875 Connecticut Ave NW
Washington, DC 20009, USA

Williams, Merriwether (Producer)
c/o Bruce Gellman *Felker, Toczek,*
Gellman, Suddleson
10880 Wilshire Blvd
Suite 2070
Los Angeles, CA 90024, USA

Williams, Michael (Athlete, Basketball
Player)
1005 Lakeridge Ct
Colleyville, TX 76034-2825, USA

Williams, Michael D (Mike) (Athlete,
Baseball Player)
302 Horseshoe Farm Rdd
Pembroke, VA 24136-3478, USA

Williams, Michael J (General)
Assistant Commander in Chief
HqUSMC 2 Navy St
Washington, DC 20380, USA

Williams, Michael Kenneth (Actor)
c/o Tracy Christian *Buchwald/Fortitude*
(LA)
6500 Wilshire Blvd
Suite 2200
Los Angeles, CA 90048, USA

Williams, Michael L (Actor)
Julian Belfarge
46 Albermarle St
London W1X 4PP, UNITED KINGDOM
(UK)

Williams, Micheal (Basketball Player)
1415 Reynoldston Lane
Dallas, TX 75232, USA

Williams, Michelle (Musician)
c/o Matthew Knowles *Music World*
Entertainment
1384 Broadway #2200
New York, NY 10018, USA

Williams, Michelle (Actor, Director,
Producer, Writer)
c/o Frank Frattaroli *Circle of Confusion*
(NY)
270 Lafayette St
Suite 402
New York, NY 10012, USA

Williams, Mike (Athlete, Football Player)
2152 NW 74th Ave
Hollywood, FL 33024, USA

Williams, Mike (Athlete, Football Player)
1 Bills Dr
Orchard Park, NY 14127, USA

Williams, Mikell (Athlete, Football Player)
222 W Edwards St
Covington, LA 70433, USA

Williams, Mitch (Athlete, Baseball Player)
67 Highbridge Blvd
Medford, NJ 08055-3341, USA

Williams, Montel B (Actor, Producer, Talk
Show Host)
c/o Jonathan Franks *Lucid Public*
Relations
3867 Grand View Blvd
2nd Floor
Los Angeles, CA 90066, USA

Williams, Natalie (Basketball Player)
Indiana Fever
Conseco Fieldhouse
125 S Pennsylvania
Indianapolis, IN 46204, USA

Williams, Natashia (Actor)
c/o Teresa Valente *Beverly Hecht Agency*
3500 W Olive Ave
Suite 1180
Burbank, CA 91505, USA

Williams, Nate (Athlete, Basketball Player)
132 Stanmore Cir
Vallejo, CA 94591-6859, USA

Williams, Nick (Athlete, Football Player)
21760 Parklane St
Farmington Hills, MI 48335, USA

Williams, O L (Religious Leader)
United Free Will Baptist Church
1101 University St
Kinston, NC 28501, USA

Williams, Oliver (Athlete, Football Player)
11924 Daleside Ave
Hawthorne, CA 90250, USA

Williams, Olivia (Actor)
c/o Risa Shapiro *Schiff Company, The*
9465 Wilshire Blvd
Suite 480
Beverly Hills, CA 90212, USA

Williams, Parker (Adult Film Star)
c/o Staff Member *Diva Central Inc*
7510 W Sunset Blvd Ste 1445
Los Angees, CA 90046, USA

Williams, Pat (Football Player)
DVA Brand Communications
c/o Danielle Gibbs
1968 W Adams Blvd Ste 205
Los Angeles, CA 90018, USA

Williams, Patrick (Musician)
3156 Mandeville Canyon Road
Los Angeles, CA 90049, USA

Williams, Paul (Writer)
c/o Chris Fenton *H2F Entertainment*
644 N Cherokee Ave
Los Angeles, CA 90004, USA

Williams, Perry (Athlete, Football Player)
273 Old Laurinburg Rd
Hamlet, NC 28345, USA

Williams, Perry (Athlete, Football Player)
480 Canyon Oaks Dr
Apt A
Oakland, CA 94605, USA

Williams, Pete (Writer)
c/o Chris Fenton *H2F Entertainment*
644 N Cherokee Ave
Los Angeles, CA 90004, USA

Williams, Pharrell (Actor, Composer)
c/o David Schiff *The Schiff Company*
9465 Wilshire Blvd
Suite 480
Beverly Hills, CA 90212, USA

Williams, Phillip L (Publisher)
Los Angeles Times
Editorial Dept
202 W 1st St
Los Angeles, CA 90012, USA

Williams, Prince Charles (Boxer)
Boxing Ministry
3675 Polley Dr
Austintown, OH 44515, USA

Williams, Randy (Athlete, Baseball Player)
610 Reynaldo St
Dickinson, TX 77539-6123, USA

Williams, Randy (Athlete, Track Athlete)
5655 N Marty Ave
#204
Fresno, CA 93711, USA

Williams, Reggie (Athlete, Baseball Player)
9300 Clearstone Cv
Collierville, TN 38017-9414, USA

Williams, Reggie (Athlete, Baseball Player)
920 E Estates Blvd Apt E
Charleston, SC 29414-5455, USA

Williams, Reggie (Athlete, Basketball Player)
2016 Calloway St
Temple Hills, MD 20748-4354, USA

Williams, Reginald (Reggie) (Athlete, Football Player)
503 Jennifer Ln
Windermere, FL 34786, USA

Williams, Reuben (Baseball Player)
Chicago American Giants
PO Box 3982
Winter Haven, FL 33885-3982, USA

Williams, Richard (Cartoonist)
138 Royal College Street
London, NWl OTA, England

Williams, Rick (Athlete, Baseball Player, Coach)
1217 Wessmith Way
Madera, CA 93638-1854, USA

Williams, Ricky (Athlete, Football Player)
c/o Drew Rosenhaus *Rosenhaus Sports Representation*
6400 Allison Road
Miami Beach, FL 33141, USA

Williams, R J
1505 10th St
Santa Monica, CA 90401, USA

Williams, Robbie (Musician)
c/o Josie Cliff *IE Music Ltd*
111 Frithville Gardens
Shepherds Bush
London W12 7JQ, UNITED KINGDOM (UK)

Williams, Robert (Baseball Player)
Newark Eagles
6233 Delancey St
Philadelphia, PA 19143-1019, USA

Williams, Robert (Artist)
c/o Staff Member *Fantagraphics Books*
7563 Lake City Way
Seattle, WA 98115, USA

Williams, Robert A (Athlete, Football Player)
602 Stone Barn Rd
Towson, MD 21286, USA

Williams, Robert C (Athlete, Football Player)
347 Walnut Grove Ln
Coppell, TX 75019, USA

Williams, Robert Cary
c/o Staff Member *Robert Cary Williams*
5 Claremont Villas, Southampton Way
Camberwell
London, England 8E4 96W, United Kingdom

Williams, Robert J (Ben) (Athlete, Football Player)
5961 Huntview Dr
Jackson, MS 39206, USA

Williams, Robert (Meek Mill) (Musician)
c/o Staff Member *Warner Bros Records (LA)*
P.O. Box 6868
Burbank, CA 91510, USA

Williams, Robin (Actor, Comedian)
1 Blackfield Dr #409
Tiburon, CA 94920, USA

Williams, Roderick (Opera Singer)
Van Walsum Mgmt
4 Addison Bridge Place
London W14 8XP, UNITED KINGDOM (UK)

Williams, Rodney (Athlete, Football Player)
44520 15th St E
Unit 3
Lancaster, CA 93535, USA

Williams, Roland (Athlete, Football Player)
5671 Wrenwyck Pl
Weldon Spring, MO 63304, USA

Williams, Rosel (Athlete, Baseball Player)
Birmingham Black Barons
PO Box 442
Ninety Six, SC 29666-0442, USA

Williams, Roshumba (Model)
c/o Gail Parenteau *Parenteau Guidance*
132 East 35th St #3J
New York, NY 10016, USA

Williams, Rowan (Religious Leader)
Lambert Palace
London SE1 9JU, UNITED KINGDOM (UK)

Williams, Roy (Athlete, Football Player)
1 Cowboys Pkwy
Irving, TX 75063, USA

Williams, Sam (Athlete, Football Player)
28960 Westfield St
Livonia, MI 48150, USA

Williams, Sam (Athlete, Basketball Player)
9751 W Teresa Ln
Milwaukee, WI 53224-4651, USA

Williams, Sam B (Inventor)
Williams International
2280 W Maple Road
Walled Lake, MI 48390, USA

Williams, Samuel (Athlete, Basketball Player)
6116 S Verdun Ave
Los Angeles, CA 90043-3632, USA

Williams, Scott (Athlete, Football Player)
284 Heathrow Dr
Riverdale, GA 30274, USA

Williams, Scott (Basketball Player)
Phoenix Suns
8217 N Coconino Rd
Paradise Valley, AZ 85253-8104, USA

Williams, Sean
4399 Whitmore Ln
Fairfield, OH 45014-8553, USA

Williams, Serena (Athlete, Olympic Athlete, Tennis Player)
1201 Stone Canyon Rd
Los Angeles, CA 90077, USA

Williams, Shad (Athlete, Baseball Player)
4682 E Cornell Ave
Fresno, CA 93703-1607, USA

Williams, Shammond (Athlete, Basketball Player)
200 Gardner Cir
Chapel Hill, NC 27516-8373, USA

Williams, Shaun (Athlete, Football Player)
11738 Gruen St
Lake View Terrace, CA 91342, USA

Williams, Sherman (Athlete, Football Player)
119 Patricia Ave
Prichard, AL 36610, USA

Williams, Sidney (Athlete, Football Player)
1044 W 82nd St
Los Angeles, CA 90044, USA

Williams, Simon (Actor)
Rebecca Blond Assoc
69A Kings Road
London SW3 4NX, UNITED KINGDOM (UK)

Williams, Stanley W (Stan) (Athlete, Baseball Player)
4702 Hayter Ave
Lakewood, CA 90712-3509, USA

Williams, Stepfret (Athlete, Football Player)
913 S Talton St
Minden, LA 71055, USA

Williams, Stephanie E (Actor)
S M S Talent
8730 Sunset Blvd
#440
Los Angeles, CA 90069, USA

Williams, Stephen (Misc)
1017 Foothills Trail
Santa Fe, NM 87505, USA

Williams, Stephen F (Judge)
US Court of Appeals
333 Constitution NW
Washington, DC 20001, USA

Williams, Steven (Actor)
Geddes Agency
8430 Santa Monica Blvd
#200
West Hollywood, CA 90069, USA

Williams, Sunita L (Astronomer)
16140 Seahorse Dr
Houston, TX 77062-6218, USA

Williams, Sun ita L Cdr (Astronaut)
1522 Festival Dr
Houston, TX 77062-4526, USA

Williams, Tamika (Basketball Player)
Minnesota Lunx
Target Center
600 1st Ave N
Minneapolis, MN 55403, USA

Williams, Tank (Athlete, Football Player)
c/o Staff Member *New England Patriots*
1 Patriot Pl
Foxboro, MA 02035-1388, USA

Williams, Tavares "Monty"
316 Darrington Blvd
Metairie, LA 70005-3816, USA

Williams, Tavares (Monty) (Athlete, Basketball Player)
316 Darrington Blvd
Metairie, LA 70005-3816, USA

Williams, Terrie (Biologist)
University of California
Biology Dept
Santa Cruz, CA 95064, USA

Williams, Terry (Musician)
Damage Mgmt
16 Lambton Place
London W11 2SH, UNITED KINGDOM (UK)

Williams, Terry Tempest
Brandt & Brandt Literary Agency
1501 Broadway
New York, NY 10036

Williams, Thomas S Cardinal (Religious Leader)
Viard
21 Eccleston Hill Po Box 198
Wellington 1, NEW ZELAND

Williams, Todd (Actor)
c/o Steve Caserta *Sanders Armstrong Caserta*
2120 Colorado Blvd
Suite 120
Santa Monica, CA 90404, USA

Williams, Todd (Athlete, Baseball Player)
16707 Whispering Glen Dr
Lutz, FL 33558-4960, USA

Williams, Tom (Athlete, Hockey Player)
2411 Princess Ave
Windsor, ON N8T 1 V2, Canada

Williams, Tony (Athlete, Football Player)
1321 W Liberty Dr
Wheaton, IL 60187, USA

Williams, Tonya Lee (Actor)
Artists Agency
1180 S Beverly Dr
#301
Los Angeles, CA 90035, USA

Williams, Treat (Actor)
c/o Melanie Greene *Affirmative Entertainment*
425 N Robertson Blvd
Los Angeles, CA 90048, USA

Williams, Trent (Athlete, Football Player)
c/o Eugene Parker *Maximum Sports Management*
6435 W Jefferson Blvd
#197
Fort Wayne, IN 46804, USA

Williams, Tyler James (Actor)
c/o Staff Member *Osbrink Talent Agency*
4343 Lankershim Blvd
Suite 100
Universal City, CA 91602, USA

Williams, Tyrone (Athlete, Football Player)
9516 Valley Ranch Pkwy E Apt 1024
Irving, TX 75063, USA

Williams, Ulis (Athlete, Track Athlete)
2511 29th St
Santa Monica, CA 90405, USA

Williams, Van (Athlete, Football Player)
1804 Parkwood Ln
Apt 26
Johnson City, TN 37604, USA

Williams, Van (Actor)
Pierce & Shelly
612 Lighthouse Ave
#220
Pacific Grove, CA 93950, USA

Williams, Vanessa (Actor, Musician)
c/o Geordie Frey *GEF Entertainment*
122 N Clark Dr
Suite 401
Los Angeles, CA 90048, USA

Williams, Venus (Athlete, Olympic Athlete, Tennis Player)
313 Grand Key Ter
Palm Beach Gardens, FL 33418-4628, USA

Williams, Victoria (Musician, Songwriter, Writer)
PO Box 342
Joshua Tree, CA 92252, USA

Williams, Victor L (Actor, Musician)

Williams, Virginia (Actor)
c/o Lisa Blum *New Wave Entertainment (LA)*
8569 Holloway Dr
Apt 1
West Hollywood, CA 90069-6918, USA

Williams, Wade (Actor, Director, Producer, Writer)
c/o Stacey Bock-McLaughlin *Principal Entertainment (LA)*
1964 Westwood Blvd #400
Los Angeles, CA 90025, USA

Williams, Walt (Athlete, Baseball Player)
2417 Monterey St
Brownwood, TX 76801-7808, USA

Williams, Walt (Athlete, Basketball Player)
3240 Beaumont St
Temple Hills, MD 20748-4541, USA

Williams, Walter (Athlete, Baseball Player)
Newark Eagles
15700 Good Hope Rd
Silver Spring, MD 20905-4034, USA

Williams, Walter (Musician)
Associated Booking Corp
1995 Broadway
#501
New York, NY 10023, USA

Williams, Walter E. (Economist, Writer)
George Mason University
333 Enterprise Hall
Department of Economics MSN 3G4
Fairfax, Virginia 22030-4444, USA

Williams, Warren "Butch" (Athlete, Hockey Player)
518 N. 15th Ave. E.
Duluth, MN 55812-1237, USA

Williams, W Clyde (Religious Leader)
Christian Methodist Episcopal Church
4466 E Presley Blvd
Memphis, TN 38116, USA

Williams, Wendy (Radio Personality, Talk Show Host)
Talk WW Productions
The Wendy Williams Show
433 West 53rd St
New York, NY 10019, USA

Williams, Wendy Lian (Swimmer)
Advantage International
1025 Thomas Jefferson NW
#450
Washington, DC 20007, USA

Williams, William (Stylist)
c/o Staff Member *Rex Agency, The*
6311 Romaine St
Los Angeles, CA 90038, USA

Williams, William A (Astronaut)
Environmental Protection Agency
200 SW 35th St
Corvallis, OR 97333, USA

Williams, Willie (Athlete, Football Player)
4928 Country Club Dr
Mesquite, TX 75150, USA

Williams, Willie (Athlete, Football Player)
1402 Forest Edge Ct
Wexford, PA 15090, USA

Williams, Willie (Baseball Player)
Newark Eagles
2729 20th St
Saratoga, FL 34234-7807, USA

Williams, Woody (Athlete, Baseball Player)
5110 Newpoint Dr
Fresno, TX 77545-9212, USA

Williams & Ree
PO Box 163
Hendersonville, TN 37077

Williams Brothers (Music Group, Musician)
c/o Staff Member *Universal Attractions*
135 W 26th St
12 Floor
New York, NY 10001, USA

Williams III, Clarance (Actor)
c/o Staff Member *Abrams Artists Agency (LA)*
9200 Sunset Blvd
11th Floor
Los Angeles, CA 90069, USA

Williams III, James (Fly) (Actor)
c/o Margaret Matuka *Schuller Talent Agency*
276 Fifth Ave
Suite 206
New York, NY 10001, USA

Williams III, Shelton Hank (Musician)
c/o Mitch Schneider *Mitch Schneider Organization (MSO)*
14724 Ventura Blvd #410
Sherman Oaks, CA 91403, USA

Williams Jr, Ernest H (Writer)
c/o Staff Member *Oxford University Press*
Great Clarendon Street
Oxford OX2 6DP, UNITED KINGDOM

Williams Jr, Hank (Actor, Musician, Songwriter)
P.O. Box 40929
Nashville, TN 37204, USA

Williams Jr, Redford B (Misc)
Duke University
Medical School
Box 3708
Durham, NC 27706, USA

Williams Jr, Walter Ray (Bowler)
303 SE 17th St # 309-171
Ocala, FL 34471-4421, USA

Williams Jr, Warren (Athlete, Football Player)
1935 Pauldo St
Fort Myers, FL 33916, USA

Williams of Crosby, Shirley V T B (Government Official)
House of Lords
Westminster
London SW1A 0PW, UNITED KINGDOM (UK)

Williams of Elvel, Charles C P (Government Official)
48 Thurloe Square
London SW7 2SX, UNITED KINGDOM (UK)

Williamson, Antone (Athlete, Baseball Player)
9419 S Stanley Pl
Tempe, AZ 85284-4109, USA

Williamson, Corliss (Basketball Player)
c/o Staff Member *Sacramento Kings*
1 Sports Parkway
Sacramento, CA 95834

Williamson, Cris (Musician)
Bird Ankles Music
PO Box 30067
Seattle, Washington 98113, USA

Williamson, Fred (Actor, Athlete, Football Player)
c/o Stephany Hurkos *Stephany Hurkos Management*
11935 Kling St
Valley Village, CA 91607, USA

Williamson, Jay (Athlete, Golfer)
24 Clermont Ln
Saint Louis, MO 63124-1346, USA

Williamson, Joe (Stylist)
c/o Staff Member *Arends, Frank Inc*
216 W 18th St
#703-B
New York, NY 10011, USA

Williamson, Keith A (Misc)
National Westminster Bank
Fakenham
Norfolk, UNITED KINGDOM (UK)

Williamson, Kerry (Writer)
c/o Staff Member *Gersh (LA)*
9465 Wilshire Blvd
Suite 600
Beverly Hills, CA 90212, USA

Williamson, Kevin (Director, Producer, Writer)
c/o Staff Member *Outerbanks Entertainment*
9000 Sunset Blvd #1001
Los Angeles, CA 90069, USA

Williamson, Marianne (Radio Personality, Writer)
PO Box 2428
Nipomo, CA 93444, USA

Williamson, Mark (Athlete, Baseball Player)
1260 Hidden Mountain Dr
El Cajon, CA 92019-3639, USA

Williamson, Michael (Writer)
10400 Hutting Place
Silver Spring, MO 20902, USA

Williamson, Michael (Journalist)
Washington Post
10400 Hutting Pl
Silver Spring, MD 20902-4952, USA

Williamson, Mykelti (Actor)
c/o Jim Hess *Hess Entertainment*
360 N Crescent Dr
North Bldg
Beverly Hills, CA 90210, USA

Williamson, Oliver E (Economist, Nobel Prize Laureate)
University of California
170 Tamalpais Rd
Berkeley, CA 94708-1947, USA

Williamson, Richard (Athlete, Football Coach, Football Player)
5137 Morrowick Rd
Charlotte, NC 29226, USA

Williamson, Scott (Athlete, Baseball Player)
21563 Fox Rd
Guilford, IN 47022-9706, USA

Williamson, Shaun (Actor)
McIntosh Rae Management
Thornton House
Thornton Road
London SW19 4NG, ENGLAND

Williamson Jr, Samuel R (Educator)
University of the South
President's Office
Sewanee, TN 37375, USA

Willie, Reid
2690 Hunters Point Dr
Wexford, PA 15090-7991, USA

Williford, Duncan (Athlete, Basketball Player)
3703 Westfield St
High Point, NC 27265, USA

Williford, Vann (Athlete, Basketball Player)
4455 Fair Oaks Ln
High Point, NC 27265-8705, USA

Willig, Matt (Athlete, Football Player)
4241 Prado De Los Pajaros
Calabasas, CA 91302-3619, USA

Willingham, Josh (Athlete, Baseball Player)
108 Cascade Dr
Florence, AL 35633-7621, USA

Willingham, Larry (Athlete, Football Player)
983 West Lagoon Ave
Gulf Shores, AL 36542, USA

Willingham, Tyrone (Coach, Football Coach)
University of Washington
Athletic Dept
Seattle, WA 98195, USA

Willis, Bruce (Actor)
c/o Paul Bloch *Rogers & Cowan PR (LA)*
Pacific Design Center
8687 Melrose Ave, 7th Floor
West Hollywood, CA 90069, USA

Willis, Carl (Athlete, Baseball Player)
6811 Lipscomb Dr
Durham, NC 27712-9292, USA

Willis, Connie (Voice Over Artist)
Brevard Talent Group
301 E Pine St Ste 175
Orlando, FL 32801, USA

Willis, Dale (Athlete, Baseball Player)
3415 Hayes Bayou Dr
Ruskin, FL 33570-6157, USA

Willis, Dave (Writer)
c/o Staff Member *WmE2 (WMA-LA)*
1 William Morris Pl
Beverly Hills, CA 90212, USA

Willis, Dontrelle (Athlete, Baseball Player)
9820 E Thompson Peak Pkwy Unit 726
Scottsdale, AZ 85255-6657, USA

Willis, Fred (Athlete, Football Player)
31 Blithewood Ave
Apt 601
Worcester, MA 01604, USA

Willis, Garrett (Athlete, Golfer)
628 Mountain Pass Ln
Knoxville, TN 37923, USA

Willis, Gordon (Cinematographer)
11849 W Olympic Blvd
#100
Los Angeles, CA 90064, USA

Willis, Jim (Artist)
5323 SW 53rd Court
Portland, OR 97221, USA

Willis, Jim (Athlete, Baseball Player)
P.O. Box 35
Boyce, LA 71409-0035, USA

Willis, Katherine (Actor)
c/o Heather Collier *Collier Talent Agency*
2313 Lake Austin Blvd
Suite 103
Austin, TX 78703, USA

Willis, Keith (Athlete, Football Player)
116 Coffeeberry Ct
Garner, NC 27529, USA

Willis, Kelly (Musician)
c/o Staff Member *Davis McLarty Agency*
708 South Lamar
Suite D
Austin, TX 78704, USA

Willis, Kevin A (Athlete, Basketball Player)
1481 Jones Rd
Roswell, GA 30075-2723, USA

Willis, Mark (Musician)
c/o Staff Member *WmE2 (WMA-TN)*
1600 Division St
Suite 300
Nashville, TN 37203, USA

Willis, Mike (Athlete, Baseball Player)
6234 Taggart St
Houston, TX 77007-2051, USA

Willis, Mitch (Athlete, Football Player)
1398 Fairhaven Dr
Mansfield, TX 76063-3765, USA

Willis, Nadine (Model)
c/o Staff Member *New York Model Management*
596 Broadway #701
New York, NY 10012, USA

Willis, Patrick (Athlete, Football Player)
c/o Denise White *EAG Sports Management*
12910 Agustin Pl
Playa Vista, CA 90094, USA

Willis, Pete (Musician)
Q Prime Mgmt
729 7th Ave
#1400
New York, NY 10019, USA

Willis, Peter Tom (Athlete, Football Player)
P.O. Box 237
Morris, AL 35116, USA

Willis, Rumer (Actor)
c/o Jennifer Merlino *Untitled Entertainment (LA)*
350 S. Beverly Dr #200
Beverly Hills, CA 90212, USA

Willison, Mike (Musician)
Metropolitan Entertainment Group
2 Penn Plaza
#2600
New York, NY 10121, USA

Willman, David (Journalist)
Los Angeles Times
Editorial Dept
202 W 1st St
Los Angeles, CA 90012, USA

Willmon, Trent (Musician)
Hallmark Direction Company
c/o Shelia Shipley Biddy
713 18th Ave S
Nashville, TN 37203, USA

Willms, Andre (Athlete)
Rennebogen 94
Magdeburg 39130, GERMANY

Willoch, Kare I (Prime Minister)
Fr Nansens V 17
Lysaker 1324, NORWAY

Willoughby, Bill (Basketball Player)
350 W Englewood Ave
Englewood, NJ 07631, USA

Willoughby, Jim (Athlete, Baseball Player)
P.O. Box 707
Eufaula, OK 74432-0707, USA

Wills, Dave (Sportscaster)
PO Box 4057
Eatonton, GA 31024-4057, U S A

Wills, Elliott (Bump) (Athlete, Baseball Player)
Central Valley High School
821 S Sullivan Rd
Spokane Valley, WA 99037, USA

Wills, Garry (Historian, Writer)
Northwestern University
History Dept
Evanston, IL 60201, USA

Wills, Maurice M (Maury) (Athlete, Baseball Player, Coach)
M & R Sports Marketing
5 Dalton Valley Dr
Saint Peters, MO 63376-7720, USA

Wills, Rick (Musician)
Hard to Handle Mgmt
16501 Ventura Blvd
#602
Encino, CA 91436, USA

Wills, Ted (Athlete, Baseball Player)
10585 E Duckpoint Way
Clovis, CA 93619-4629, USA

Willson, Don (Athlete, Hockey Player)
1303 Rendezvous Dr
Windsor, ON N8P 1K7, Canada

Willson, John (Business Person)
Placer Dome Inc
1600-1055 Dunsmuir St
Vancouver, BC V7X 1P1, CANADA

Will to Power (Music Group)
c/o Staff Member *Diva Central Inc*
7510 W Sunset Blvd Ste 1445
Los Angees, CA 90046, USA

Willumstad, Robert (Financier)
Brysam Global Partners
277 Park Ave
35th Floor
New York, NY 10172, USA

Wilmarth, Dick (Misc)
1111 F St
Anchorage, AK 99501, USA

Wilmer, Douglas (Actor)
Julian Belfarge
46 Albermarle St
London W1X 4PP, UNITED KINGDOM (UK)

Wilmer, Harry A (Psychic)
Texas Health Science Center
Psychiatric Dept
San Antonio, TX 78284, USA

Wilmes, Gary (Actor)
c/o Ruthanne Secunda *United Talent Agency (UTA)*
9336 Civic Center Dr
Beverly Hills, CA 90210, USA

Wilmet, Paul (Athlete, Baseball Player)
P.O. Box 330074
Nashville, TN 37203-8135, USA

Wilmore, Barry E (Astronaut)
3002 Bryant Ln
Webster, TX 77598-6011, USA

Wilmore, Barry E Cdr (Astronaut)
3002 Bryant Ln
Webster, TX 77598-6011, USA

Wilmsmeyer, Klaus (Athlete, Football Player)
1509 Bellingham Ct
Louisville, KY 40245, USA

Wilmut, Ian (Misc)
Roslin Institute
Roslin Bio Centre
Midlothian EH25 9PS, SCOTLAND

Wilmut, Ian (Scientist)
Roslin Institute Development & Reproduction Dept
Midlothian, EH25 9PS, Scotland

Wilpers, John J (General)
10701 Kenilworth Ave
Garrett Park, MD 20896-1502, USA

Wilpon, Fred (Baseball Player)
New York Mets
100 Sheep Ln
Locust Valley, NY 11560-1115, USA

Wilson, Adrian (Athlete, Football Player)
c/o Eugene Parker *Maximum Sports Management*
6435 W Jefferson Blvd
#197
Fort Wayne, IN 46804, USA

Wilson, Al (Athlete, Football Player)
3445 Stratford Rd NE #3901
Atlanta, GA 30326, USA

Wilson, Alexander G (Sandy) (Composer, Writer)
2 Southwell Gardens
#4
London SW7 4SB, UNITED KINGDOM (UK)

Wilson, Alexandra (Actor)
c/o Staff Member *GVA Talent Agency Inc*
8981 Sunset Blvd.
Suite 101
Los Angeles, CA 90069, USA

Wilson, Allan B (Biologist)
University of California
Molecular Biology Dept
Berkeley, CA 94724, USA

Wilson, A N (Writer)
21 Arlington Road
London NW1 7ER, UNITED KINGDOM (UK)

Wilson, Ann (Actor, Musician)
c/o Carol Peters *Peters Management Syndicate*
P.O. Box 1710
Topanga, CA 90290, USA

Wilson, Behn (Athlete, Hockey Player)
955 Bolender Dr.
Delray Beach, FL 33483-4970, USA

Wilson, Ben (Athlete, Football Player)
702 Maple St
Crossett, AR 71635-3520, USA

Wilson, Bill (Athlete, Baseball Player)
132 Wickenbv Ct
Roseville, CA 95661-4044, USA

Wilson, Blaine (Athlete, Gymnast, Olympic Athlete)
7441 Murrayfield Dr
Columbus, OH 43085-1739, USA

Wilson, Blenda J (Educator)
California State University
President's Office
Northridge, CA 91330, USA

Wilson, Bob (Athlete, Baseball Player)
806 Cabot Ln
Madison, WI 53711-2810, USA

Wilson, Brian (Athlete, Basketball Player)
1201 Hummingbird Hill Rd
Chapel Hill, NC 27517-7791, USA

Wilson, Brian (Musician, Songwriter)
c/o Jean Sievers *CO5 Media*
2271 Cheremoya Ave
Los Angeles, CA 90068, USA

Wilson, Brian (Athlete, Baseball Player)
741 S Banning Cir
Mesa, AZ 85206-4104, USA

Wilson, Brian Anthony (Actor)
Bernard Liebhaber
352 7th Ave
New York, NY 10001, USA

Wilson, Carey (Athlete, Hockey Player)
85 Jean Louis Rd
Winnipeg, MB R2N 4A9, CANADA

Wilson, Carnie (Musician)
c/o Terry Anzaldo *Good Guy Entertainment*
3733 Oakfield Dr
Sherman Oaks, CA 91423, USA

Wilson, Casey (Actor)
c/o Staff Member *Odenkirk Provissiero Entertainment*
Raleigh Studios
650 N. Bronson Ave, Bldg. B145
Los Angeles, CA 90004, USA

Wilson, C A S John (Architect)
John Wilson Assoc
27 Horsell Road
London N5 1XL, UNITED KINGDOM (UK)

Wilson, Cassandra (Musician)
Dream Street Mgmt
4346 Redwood Ave
#307
Marina del Rey, CA 90292, USA

Wilson, Chandra (Actor)
c/o Staff Member *Station3*
1051 Cole Av
Culver City, CA 90038, USA

Wilson, Charles (Athlete, Football Player)
5444 Calder Dr
Tallahassee, FL 32317, USA

Wilson, Charlie (Musician)
c/o Carlos Keyes *Red Entertainment Agency*
505 8th Ave
Suite 1004
New York, NY 10018, USA

Wilson, Cherilyn (Actor)
c/o Jon Simmons *Simmons & Scott Entertainment*
4110 W. Burbank Blvd.
Burbank, CA 91505, USA

Wilson, Chris (Musician)
c/o Staff Member *Fein Music*
81 Pondfield Rd
Bronxville, NY 10708, USA

Wilson, Cindy (Musician)
Direct Management Group
947 N La Cienega Blvd
#2
Los Angeles, CA 90069, USA

Wilson, Colin H (Writer)
Tetherdown Trewallock Lane
Gorran Haven
Cornwall, UNITED KINGDOM (UK)

Wilson, Craig (Misc)
1423 Lake Blvd
David, CA 95616, USA

Wilson, Craig (Athlete, Baseball Player)
461 S Brent St
Ventura, CA 93003-4706, USA

Wilson, Craig (Athlete, Baseball Player)
3427 E Tere St
Phoenix, AZ 85044-3625, USA

Wilson, Dan (Musician, Songwriter, Writer)
Monterey Peninsula Artists
509 Hartnell St
Monterey, CA 93940, USA

Wilson, Daniel A (Dan) (Athlete, Baseball Player)
2161 E Interlaken Blvd
Seattle, WA 98112-3432, USA

Wilson, Daniel H (Writer)
c/o Linda Chester *Linda Chester Literary Agency*
630 Fifth Ave #2036
Rockefeller Center
New York, NY 10111, USA

Wilson, Dave (Athlete, Football Player)
4301 San Rufino Ct
Yorba Linda, CA 92886, USA

Wilson, Dean (Athlete, Golfer)
10914 Iris Canyon Ln
Las Vegas, NV 89135-1719, USA

Wilson, De'Angelo (Actor)
c/o Staff Member *Overbrook Entertainment*
450 N Roxbury Dr
4th Floor
Beverly Hills, CA 90210, USA

Wilson, Debra (Actor)
c/o Joan Rosenberg *Joan Rosenberg & Assoc Ltd*
3 Adam St
New York, NY 11001, USA

Wilson, Desi (Athlete, Baseball Player)
8 Janet Ln
Glen Cove, NY 11542-2809, USA

Wilson, Desire (Race Car Driver)
4197 Serenade Rd
Castle Rock, CO 80104, USA

Wilson, Don The Dragon
178 S. Victory Blvd. #205
Burbank, CA 91502-2881

Wilson, Dorien (Actor)
c/o Susie Tobin *Peter Strain & Associates Inc (LA)*
5455 Wilshire Blvd
Suite 1812
Los Angeles, CA 90036-4368, USA

Wilson, Doug (Athlete, Hockey Player)
5620 Country Club Pkwy
San Jose, CA 95138-2220, USA

Wilson, Doug (Athlete, Hockey Player)
San Jose Sharks
525 W Santa Clara St
Attn: General Manager
SanJose, CA 95113-1500, USA

Wilson, Duane (Athlete, Baseball Player)
1945 N Porter Ave
Apt A54
Wichita, KS 67203, USA

Wilson, Dune (Athlete, Hockey Player)
PO Box 28
Rossland, BC V0G 1 Y0, Canada

Wilson, Earl (Athlete, Football Player)
1510 W Riverside Dr
Atlantic City, NJ 08401, USA

Wilson, Earle L (Religious Leader)
Wesleyan Church
PO Box 50434
Indianapolis, IN 46250, USA

Wilson, Edward (Scientist)
Museum Of Comparative Zoology 26 Oxford St
Cambridge, MA 02138-2902, USA

Wilson, Edward O (Writer)
Harvard University
Department of Organismic and Evolutionary Biology
Cambridge, MA 02138, USA

Wilson, Elizabeth (Actor)
c/o Staff Member *Paradigm (NY)*
360 Park Ave S Fl 16
New York, NY 10010, USA

Wilson, Eric C T (War Hero)
Woodside Cottage
Stowell Sherborne
Dorset, UNITED KINGDOM (UK)

Wilson, Eugene (Skier)
25775 Ranchview Lane N
#1
Plymouth, MN 55447, USA

Wilson, F Paul (Writer)
1933 State Route 35 Ste 337
Wall Township, NJ 07719-3502, USA

Wilson, F Perry (Engineer)
225 N 56th St
#217
Lincoln, NE 68504, USA

Wilson, Frank (Race Car Driver)
North Carlonia Motor Speedway
PO Box 500
Rockingham, NC 28380, USA

Wilson, Gahan (Cartoonist)
New Yorker Magazine
PO Box 1558
Sag Harbor, NY 11963-0057, USA

Wilson, Gale (Race Car Driver)
203 Northmont Dr.
Statesville, NC 28677, USA

Wilson, Gary (Athlete, Baseball Player)
327 40th St
Sacramento, CA 95819-2027, USA

Wilson, Gary (Athlete, Baseball Player)
713 Ouachita 64
Camden, AR 71701-9616, USA

Wilson, George (Athlete, Basketball Player, Olympic Athlete)
151 Twin Lakes Dr
Fairfield, OH 45014-5257, USA

Wilson, Georges (Director)
Moulin de Vilgris
Rambouillet 78120, FRANCE

Wilson, Gerald S (Composer, Musician)
4625 Brynhurst Ave
Los Angeles, CA 90043, USA

Wilson, Glenn (Athlete, Baseball Player)
300 Tara Park
Conroe, TX 77302-37S6, USA

wilson, Gord (Athlete, Hockey Player)
Ottawa Senators
110-1000 Palladium Dr
Attn: Broadcast Dept
Ottawa, ON K2V IAS, Canada

Wilson, Gretchen (Musician)
c/o Staff Member *WmE2 (WMA-LA)*
1 William Morris Pl
Beverly Hills, CA 90212, USA

Wilson, Harry (Athlete, Football Player)
2600 N Lawrence St
Apt 307
Philadelphia, PA 19133, USA

Wilson, Harry C (Religious Leader)
Wesleyan Church Int'l Center
6060 Castleway West Dr
Indianapolis, IN 46250, USA

Wilson, Hugh (Director, Producer, Writer)
c/o Staff Member *ICM Partners (ICM-LA)*
10250 Constellation Blvd Fl 7
Los Angeles, CA 90067, USA

Wilson, Jack (Athlete, Baseball Player)
365 E Avenida De los Arboles
Thousand Oaks, CA 91360-2975, USA

Wilson, James (Athlete, Football Player)
4688 NW Falling Creek Rd
Lake City, FL 32055, USA

Wilson, James B (Admiral)
321 Crosslands Drive
Kennett Square, PA 19348-2007, USA

Wilson, James M (Misc)
University of Pennsylvania
Med Center
Genetics Dept
Philadelphia, PA 19104, USA

Wilson, Jane (Artist)
317 W 83rd St Apt 2E
New York, NY 10024-4804, USA

Wilson, Janet (Stylist)
1644 Summit Lake Blvd
Akron, OH 44314, USA

Wilson, J C (Athlete, Football Player)
4785 Young Rd
Waldorf, MD 20601, USA

Wilson, J C (Athlete, Football Player)
13410 Buchanan Dr
Fort Washington, MD 20744, USA

Wilson, Jean D (Doctor)
Texas Southwestern Medical Center
5323 Harry Hines Blvd
Dallas, TX 75390, USA

Wilson, Jeannie (Actor)
General Delivery
Ketchum, ID 83340, USA

Wilson, Jennifer
1947 Lakeshore Dr.
Branson, MO 65616

Wilson, Jerry (Athlete, Football Player)
2117 Mountainview Dr
Birmingham, AL 35216, USA

Wilson, Jerry (Athlete, Football Player)
4272 Ironwood Ct
Weston, FL 33331, USA

Wilson, Jim (Athlete, Baseball Player)
8112 NW Bacon Rd
Vancouver, WA 98665-6634, USA

Wilson, Joe (Congressman, Politician)
2229 Rayburn HOB
Washington, DC 20515, USA

Wilson, Joe (Athlete, Football Player)
328 Valley View Ln
Chester Springs, PA 19425, USA

Wilson, John (Athlete, Hockey Player)
4024 Old Dominion Dr.
West Bloomfield Hills, MI 48323, USA

Wilson, Josh (Athlete, Baseball Player)
2304 Cramden Rd
Pittsbur11h, PA 15241-2438, USA

Wilson, J Tylee (Business Person)
PO Box 2057
Ponte Vedra Beach, FL 32004, USA

Wilson, Julie (Actor, Musician)
415 W 55th St
New York, NY 10019, USA

Wilson, Justin (Musician)
David Levin Mgmt
200 W 57th St
#308
New York, NY 10019, USA

Wilson, Kenneth G (Nobel Prize Laureate)
Ohio State University
Ohio State U Physics Dept 174 W 18th Ave
Columbus, OH 43210-1106, USA

Wilson, Kim (Musician)
Ricci Assoc
28205 Agoura Road
Agoura Hills, CA 91301, USA

Wilson, Kris (Athlete, Baseball Player)
P.O. Box 15
Chillicothe, MO 64601-0015, USA

Wilson, Kristen (Actor)
c/o Norman Aladjem *Levity Entertainment Group*
360 N Crescent Dr
North Bldg
Beverly Hills, CA 90210, USA

Wilson, Lambert (Actor)
c/o Estelle Lasher *Principal Entertainment (NY)*
1964 Westwood Blvd
Suite 400
Los Angeles, CA 90025, USA

Wilson, Landon (Athlete, Hockey Player)
127 Tennyson Pl
Coppell, TX 75019-5364

Wilson, Lawrence F (Larry) (Athlete, Football Player)
11834 N Blackheath Rd
Scottsdale, AZ 85254, USA

Wilson, Luke (Actor)
c/o Mara Buxbaum *ID PR (LA)*
7060 Hollywood Blvd
8th Floor
Los Angeles, CA 90028, USA

Wilson, Mara (Actor)
c/o Bonnie Liedtke *Principato/Young Management*
9465 Wilshire Blvd
Suite 430
Beverly Hills, CA 90212, USA

Wilson, Marc (Athlete, Football Player)
18020 157th Ave NE
Woodinville, WA 98072, USA

Wilson, Marc D (Athlete, Football Player)
113113 Mount Wallace Ct
Alta Loma, CA 91737, USA

Wilson, Marie
6 Oakdale
Irvine, CA 92604

Wilson, Mark (Athlete, Golfer)
N41W27751 Ishnala Trl
Pewaukee, WI 53072-2140, USA

Wilson, Marty (Musician)
c/o Staff Member *VocalPoint*
25 Denmark St Fl 1
London WC2H 8NJ, UNITED KINGDOM (UK)

Wilson, Max (Race Car Driver)
Minardi Team Spa
Via Spallanzani 21
Faenza 48018, ITALY

Wilson, Melanie (Actor)
Irv Schechter
9300 Wilshire Blvd
#410
Beverly Hills, CA 90212, USA

Wilson, Michael G (Producer)
c/o Staff Member *Danjaq*
2400 Colorado Ave
Suite 310
Santa Monica, CA 90404, USA

Wilson, Michael H (Government Official)
Industry & Science Dept
235 Queen's St
Ottawa, ON K1A OH5, CANADA

Wilson, Michael (Tack) (Athlete, Baseball Player)
768 Forest St Aot 6
Roswell, GA 30075-6527, USA

Wilson, Mike (Athlete, Hockey Player)
4647 Lake Charles Dr
Independence, OH 44131-6062, USA

Wilson, Mike D (Athlete, Football Player)
1967 Litchfield Ave
Dayton, OH 45406, USA

Wilson, Mike R (Athlete, Football Player)
2908 N Poinsettia Ave
Manhattan Beach, CA 90266, USA

wilson, Mitch (Athlete, Hockey Player)
PO Box 343
Brinnon, WA 98320-0343, USA

Wilson, Mookie (Athlete, Baseball Player)
1111 Heyward Wilson Rd
Eastover, SC 29044-9627, USA

wilson, Murray (Athlete, Hockey Player)
Wilson Consulting
432-410 Bank St
Ottawa, ON K2P 1 Y8, Canada

Wilson, Nancy (Actor, Composer, Musician)
c/o Carol Peters *Peters Management Syndicate*
P.O. Box 1710
Topanga, CA 90290, USA

Wilson, Natalie (Stylist)
8950 W Olympic Blvd
#299
Beverly Hills, CA 90211, USA

Wilson, Neal C (Religious Leader)
Seventh-Day Adventists
12501 Old Columbus Pike
Silver Spring, MD 20904, USA

Wilson, Neil (Athlete, Baseball Player)
4300 Highway 412 W
Lexington, TN 38351-5423, USA

Wilson, Nemiah (Athlete, Football Player)
11000 E Idaho Pl
Aurora, CO 80012, USA

Wilson, Nigel (Athlete, Baseball Player)
35 Sabbe Cres
Ajax, ON L1T 4E3, Canada

Wilson, Olin C (Astronomer)
1508 Circa del Lago
B110
San Marcos, CA 92069, USA

Wilson, Othell (Athlete, Basketball Player)
3413 Caledonia Cir
Woodbridge, VA 22192-1069, USA

Wilson, Otis (Athlete, Football Player)
7B W 15th St
Chicago, IL 60605, USA

Wilson, Owen (Actor)
947 23rd St
Santa Monica, CA 90403, USA

Wilson, Patrick (Actor, Musician)
c/o Jennifer Plante *SLATE Public Relations - NY*
307 7th Ave
Suite 2401
New York, NY 10001, USA

Wilson, Patti (Stylist)
c/o Staff Member *Management + Artists + Organization*
330 W 38th St
#1401
New York, NY 10018, USA

Wilson, Paul (Athlete, Baseball Player)
949 Lenmore Ct
Orlando, FL 32812-1980, USA

Wilson, Peta (Actor)
c/o Gordon Gilbertson *Gilbertson Management*
1334 3rd St Promenade #201
Santa Monica, CA 90401, USA

Wilson, Pete (Governor, Politician)
2700 Monte MarTer
Los Angeles, CA 90064-3408, USA

Wilson, Preston (Athlete, Baseball Player)
136 Paloma Dr
Coral Gables, FL 33143-6545, USA

Wilson, Rainn (Actor)
5683 Colony Dr
Agoura Hills, CA 91301, USA

Wilson, Ralph C (Business Person, Football Executive)
Buffalo Bills
99 Kercheval Ave
Grosse Pointe Farms, MI 48236-3618, USA

Wilson, Rebel (Actor)
c/o Daniel Weiner *Paradigm (Monterey)*
9100 Wilshire Blvd
Suite 500, West Tower
Beverly Hills, CA 90212, USA

Wilson, Red (Athlete, Baseball Player)
806 Cabot Ln
Madison, WI 53711, USA

Wilson, Reinard (Athlete, Football Player)
2595 NW 49th Ave
Apt 108
Laud Lakes, FL 33313, USA

Wilson, Rick (Race Car Driver)
PO Box 304
Mulberry, FL 33860-0304, USA

Wilson, Rick (Athlete, Coach, Hockey Player)
1624 Reno Run
Lewisville, TX 75077-7522, USA

Wilson, Rick (Athlete, Basketball Player)
535 E Ormsby Ave
Louisville, KY 40203-2620, USA

Wilson, Ricky (Athlete, Basketball Player)
8007 Oat Ridge Ct
Bowie, MD 20715-4620, USA

Wilson, Rik (Athlete, Hockey Player)
12076 Manchester Rd
Saint Louis, MO 63131-4401, USA

Wilson, Rita (Actor)
c/o Heidi Schaeffer *PMK/BNC Public Relations (PMK-LA)*
8687 Melrose Ave Fl 8
West Hollywood, CA 90069, USA

Wilson, Robert Charles (Writer)
Tom Doherty Associates, LLC
175 Fifth Ave
New York, NY 10011, USA

Wilson, Robert E (Bobby) (Athlete, Football Player)
1034 Liberty Park Dr
Apt 408R
Austin, TX 78746, USA

Wilson, Robert M (Actor)
RW Work
131 Varick St
#908
New York, NY 10013, USA

Wilson, Robert N (Business Person)
Johnson & Johnson
1 Johnson & Johnson Plaza
New Brunswick, NJ 08933, USA

Wilson, Robert W (Nobel Prize Laureate)
38 Cole Ct
Dumont, NJ 07628-1007, USA

Wilson, Robin (Musician)
William Morris Agency
2100 W End Ave
#1000
Nashville, TN 37203, USA

Wilson, Roger (Actor)
c/o Staff Member *Joel Stevens Entertainment*
5627 Allott Ave
Van Nuys, CA 91401, USA

Wilson, Ron (Athlete, Coach, Hockey Player)
17 Middleton Gardens Pl
Bluffton, SC 29910-4954, USA

Wilson, Ron (Athlete, Hockey Player)
Toronto Maple Leafs 400-40 Bay St
Attn: Coaching Staff
Toronto, ON M5J 2X2, Canada

Wilson, Ruth (Actor)
c/o Jason Weinberg *Untitled Entertainment (LA)*
350 S. Beverly Dr #200
Beverly Hills, CA 90212, USA

Wilson, Ryan (Actor)
c/o Cindy Osbrink *Osbrink Talent Agency*
4343 Lankershim Blvd
Suite 100
Universal City, CA 91602, USA

Wilson, Samuel W (Educator, General)
Hampden-Sydney College
President's Office
Hampden-Sydney, VA 23943, USA

Wilson, Scott
PO Box 5617
Beverly Hills, CA 90210

Wilson, Sherlee (Actor)
c/o Staff Member *Cunningham Escott Slevin & Doherty (CESD-LA)*
10635 Santa Monica Blvd
130
Los Angeles, CA 90025, USA

Wilson, Sophie (Stylist)
c/o Staff Member *Directions USA*
3717-C W Market St
Greensboro, NC 27403, USA

Wilson, Stephanie D (Astronaut)
14910 Hollydale Dr
Houston, TX 77062, USA

Wilson, Stephen (Athlete, Basketball Player)
71 S Jones Creek Ln
Pine, CO 80470-9675, USA

Wilson, Steve (Athlete, Football Player)
3503 Brymore Ct
Pearland, TX 77584, USA

Wilson, Steve (Athlete, Baseball Player)
23-1041 Comox St
Vancouver, BC V6E 1K1, Canada

Wilson, Stuart (Actor)
c/o Staff Member *Curtis Brown Group*
Haymarket House
28 - 29 Haymarket
London SW1Y 4SP, UNITED KINGDOM

Wilson, Thomas L (Athlete, Football Player)
4342 Oakdale Pl
Pittsburg, CA 94565, USA

Wilson, Thomas (Tom) F (Actor)
c/o Alex Murray *McDonald-Murray Management*
11846 Ventura Blvd Ste 202
Studio City, CA 91604, USA

Wilson, Tom (Athlete, Baseball Player)
2771 Holiday Dr
Lake Havasu City, AZ 86403-6079, USA

Wilson, Torrie (Model, Wrestler)
c/o Staff Member *Good Guy Entertainment*
3733 Oakfield Dr
Sherman Oaks, CA 91423, USA

Wilson, Trevor (Athlete, Basketball Player)
824 15th St
Hermosa Beach, CA 90254-3202, USA

Wilson, Trevor (Athlete, Baseball Player)
11857 White Ln
Oregon City, OR 97045-5716, USA

Wilson, Troy (Athlete, Football Player)
14213 W 138th Pl
Olathe, KS 66062, USA

Wilson, Vance (Athlete, Baseball Player)
6368 Elizabeth Ave
Springdale, AR 72762-4234, USA

Wilson, Wade (Athlete, Football Player)
6126 Mimosa Ln
Dallas, TX 75230, USA

Wilson, Wayne (Athlete, Football Player)
5430 Lynx Ln
Apt 152
Columbia, MD 21044, USA

Wilson, William (Athlete, Basketball
Player)
130 Belmont St
Englewood, NJ 07631-1502, USA

Wilson, William J (Activist)
Harvard University
Kennedy Government School
Cambridge, MA 02138, USA

Wilson, Willie (Athlete, Baseball Player)
Willie Wilson Baseball Foundation PO
Box 34665
kansas city, MO 64116-1065, USA

Wilson, Woody (Cartoonist)
c/o Staff Member *King Features
Syndication*
300 W 57th St
15th Floor
New York, NY 10019-5238, USA

Wilson David, Mackenzie (Director)
Lifeboat House
Castletown
Isle of Man IM9 1LD, UNITED
KINGDOM (UK)

Wilson-Johnson, David R (Opera Singer)
28 Englefield Road
London N1 4ET, UNITED KINGDOM
(UK)

Wilson Jr, Louis H (General, War Hero)
100 University Park Dr
Birmingham, AL 35209, USA

Wilson of Tillyorn, David C (Government
Official)
House of Lords
Westminster
London SW1A 0PW, UNITED KINGDOM
(UK)

Wilson Phillips
1290 Ave. of the Americas #4200
New York, NY 10104

Wilson-Sampras, Bridgette (Actor)
c/o Andrea Pett-Joseph *Brillstein
Entertainment Partners*
9150 Wilshire Blvd #350
Beverly Hills, CA 90212, USA

Wiltsie, Brian (Athlete, Hockey Player)
45 Meadowbrook Rd
Randolph, NJ 07869-3862, USA

Wimmer, Brian (Actor)
c/o Jean-Pierre (JP) Henraux *Henraux
Management*
Prefers to be contacted by telephone
CA, USA

Wimmer, Chris (Athlete, Baseball Player,
Olympic Athlete)
4027 Countryside Street
Wichita, KS 67218, USA

Wimmer, Kurt (Actor, Director, Producer,
Writer)
c/o Tom Strickler *WME (LA)*
9601 Wilshire Blvd Fl 3
Beverly Hills, CA 90210, USA

Wimmer, Scott (Race Car Driver)
Richard Childress Racing
425 Industrial Dr.
Welcome, NC 27374, USA

Winans
1420 Coleman Rd.
Franklin, TN 37064

Winans, BeBe (Musician)
c/o Staff Member *Monterey International*
P.O. Box 297
Carmel-by-the-Sea, CA 93921, USA

Winans, CeCe (Musician)
Wellspring Mgmt
2300 Franklin Road
#2B
Franklin, TN 37064, USA

Winans, Jeff (Athlete, Football Player)
175 21st Avenue SE
Saint Petersburg, FL 33705, USA

Winans, Mario (Musician)
c/o Staff Member *Bad Boy Worldwide
Entertainment*
1440 Broadway
16th Floor
New York, NY 10018, USA

Winans, Matthew (Matt) (Athlete,
Baseball Player)
17 Sanford St
Melrose, MA 02176-3611, USA

Winans, Tydus (Athlete, Football Player)
92 West Hall Ave
Clovis, CA 93612, USA

Winans, Vickie (Musician)
c/o Staff Member *Covenant Agency, The*
123 California Ave #116
Santa Monica, CA 90403, USA

Winborne, Jamie (Athlete, Football Player)
195 Roscoe Lee Cir
Wetumpka, AL 36092, USA

Winbush, Angela (Musician, Songwriter,
Writer)
Joyce Agency
370 Harrison Ave
Harrison, NY 10528, USA

Winbush, Camille (Actor)
c/o Staff Member *Innovative Artists (LA)*
1505 10th St
Santa Monica, CA 90401, USA

Winbush, Troy (Actor)
c/o Staff Member *Paradigm (LA)*
360 N Crescent Dr
North Bldg
Beverly Hills, CA 90210, USA

Winceniak, Ed (Athlete, Baseball Player)
10828 S Avenue O
Chicago, IL 60617-6543, USA

Wincer, Simon (Director, Producer)
c/o Adam Kanter *Creative Artists Agency
(CAA-LA)*
2000 Ave Of The Stars
Los Angeles, CA 90067, USA

Wincer, Simon G (Director)
PO Box 241
Toorak, VIC 3142, AUSTRALIA

Winchester, Brad (Athlete, Hockey
Player)
15920 Sandalwood Creek Drive
Ballwin, MO 63011-5517, USA

Winchester, Jesse (Musician, Songwriter,
Writer)
Keith Case Assoc
1025 17th Ave S
#200
Nashville, TN 37212, USA

Winchester, Philip (Actor)
c/o Guido Giordano *ICM Partners
(ICM-LA)*
10250 Constellation Blvd Fl 7
Los Angeles, CA 90067, USA

Winchester, Scott (Athlete, Baseball
Player)
4705 Oakridge Dr
Midland, MI 48640-7409, USA

Wincott, Jeff P (Actor)
Judy Shane & Associates
606 N Larchmont Blvd
Los Angeles, CA 90004

Winder, Sammy (Athlete, Football Player)
Winder Construction
4823 Greens Crossing Rd
Ridgeland, MS 39157, USA

Winders, Rich (Bowler)
720 Augusta St
Racine, WI 53402, USA

Winders, Wim (Director)
Paul Kohner
9300 Wilshire Blvd
#555
Beverly Hills, CA 90212, USA

Windham, Melissa (Stylist)
33752 Norkolk St
Livonia, MI 48152, USA

Windhorn, Gordie (Athlete, Baseball
Player)
145 Bent Creek Rd
Danville, VA 24540-5213, USA

Windier, Milton (Scientist)
516 Fairdale St
Friendswood, TX 77546-4518, USA

Windis, Tony (Athlete, Basketball Player)
404 1st St
Rawlins, WY 82301, USA

Windle, William F (Misc)
229 Cherry St
Granville, OH 43023, USA

Windon, Stephen (Cinematographer)
PO Box 659
Northbridge
Sydney, NSW 2063, AUSTRALIA

Windsor, Barbara (Actor, Comedian)
104 Crouch Hill
London NB 9EA, UNITED KINGDOM
(UK)

Windsor, Jason Windsor (Athlete,
Baseball Player)
23972 Dublin St
lake Forest, CA 92630-2927, USA

Windsor, Robert E (Athlete, Football
Player)
2625 Legends Way
Ellicott City, MD 21042, USA

Windsor-Smith, Barry (Artist)
c/o Staff Member *Fantagraphics Books*
7563 Lake City Way
Seattle, WA 98115, USA

Wine, Bobby (Athlete, Baseball Player,
Coach)
2614 Woodland Ave
Norristown, PA 19403-1636, USA

Wine, David M (Religious Leader)
Church of Brethren
1451 Dundee Ave
Elgin, IL 60120, USA

Wine, Robbie (Athlete, Baseball Player)
240 Bryce Jordan Ctr
University Park, PA 16802-7102, USA

Winegardner, Mark (Writer)
Random House
1745 Broadway
New York, NY 10019, USA

Winer, Jason (Director)
c/o Michael Lasker *Mosaic Media Group*
9200 W. Sunset Blvd
10th Floor
Los Angeles, CA 90069, USA

Winfield, Antoine (Athlete, Football
Player)
10451 White Tail Crossing
Eden Prairie, MN 55347, USA

Winfield, David (Dave) (Athlete, Baseball
Player)
2235 Stratford Cir
Los Angeles, CA 90077-1316, USA

Winfield, Earl (Athlete, Football Player)
8817 Oxford Cir
Waynesboro, PA 17268-9225, USA

Winfield, Peter (Actor)
c/o Staff Member *Screen Actors Guild
(SAG-LA)*
5757 Wilshire Blvd
Los Angeles, CA 90036, USA

Winfrey, Oprah (Business Person,
Producer, Talk Show Host)
1633 E Valley Rd
Montecito, CA 93108, USA

Winfrey, Travis (Actor)
c/o Peter Kluge *Impact Artist Group LLC
(LA)*
244 California St
1st Floor
Burbank, CA 91505, USA

Winfrey, W C (Bill) (Misc)
7802 Sierra Trail
Spring Lake, NC 28390, USA

Wing, Murray (Athlete, Hockey Player)
RR 5
Sta. F.
Thunder Bay, ON P7C 5M9, CANADA

Wing, Ted (Horse Racer)
3 Rehobeth Rd
Flanders, NJ 07836-9447, USA

Wingate, David (Athlete, Basketball
Player)
11404 Glaetzer Ln
Charlotte, NC 28270, USA

Wingate, Elmer (Athlete, Football Player)
807 Wellington Rd
Baltimore, MD 21212, USA

Wingate, J W (Athlete, Baseball Player)
Kansas City Monarchs
3215 Case St
Beaumont, TX 77703-3607, USA

Winger, Debra (Actor)
c/o Tim Curtis *WME (LA)*
9601 Wilshire Blvd Fl 3
Beverly Hills, CA 90210, USA

Winger, Kip (Musician)
Joseph Minkes Assoc
2740 W Magnolia Blvd
#204
Burbank, CA 91505, USA

Winget, Larry (Motivational Speaker)
6929 N Hayden Rd
Suite C4-619
Scottsdale, AZ 85250, USA

Wingfield, Dantonio
1602 Gadsden Dr
Albany, GA 31701-3566, USA

Wingfield, Dantonio (Athlete, Basketball Player)
1602 Gadsden Dr
Albany, GA 31701-3566, USA

Wingfield, Dontonio (Athlete, Basketball Player)
1602 Gadsden Dr
Albany, GA 31701, USA

Wingfield, Marilyn Ramenofsky (Athlete, Olympic Athlete, Swimmer)
1240 NW 116th St
Seattle, WA 98177-4624, USA

Wingle, Blake (Athlete, Football Player)
8200 Stockdale Hwy
Apt 10
Bakersfield, CA 93311, USA

Wing-Merrill, Toby
Box 889
Matthews, VA 23109

Wingo, Harthorne (Athlete, Basketball Player)
862 Macon St
Apt 2B
Brooklyn, NY 11233-5405, USA

Wingreen, Jason
4224 Teesdale Ave.
No. Hollywood, CA 91604

Wingrove-Earl, Elsie (Baseball Player)
PO Box 61
N Portal, SK S0C 1W0, CANADA

Winiger, Melanie (Actor, Model)
Rindlisbacher
ch Carmenstr 32
Zurich 8032, SWITZERLAND

Winings, Meagan (Beauty Pageant Winner)
PO Box 21
Atkinson, NE 68713, USA

Winkelsas, Joe (Athlete, Baseball Player)
213 Virgil Ave
Buffalo, NY 14216-1836, USA

Winkleman, Sophie (Actor)
c/o Staff Member *Creative Artists Agency (CAA-LA)*
2000 Ave Of The Stars
Los Angeles, CA 90067, USA

Winkler, David (Director)
Rigberg Roberts Rugoto
1180 S Beverly Dr
#604
Los Angeles, CA 90035, USA

Winkler, Francis M (Athlete, Football Player)
8223 Creekside Hwy
Apt 10
Cordova, TN 38016, USA

Winkler, Gerard (Actor)
Alsertra 26-3A
Vienna 1090, AUSTRIA

Winkler, Hans-Gunter (Misc)
Dr Rau Allee 48
Warendorf 48231, GERMANY

Winkler, Henry (Actor, Producer)
c/o Leigh Brillstein *ICM Partners (ICM-LA)*
10250 Constellation Blvd Fl 7
Los Angeles, CA 90067, USA

Winkler, Irwin (Director, Producer)
Irwin Winkler Productions
211 S Beverly Dr
#220
Beverly Hills, CA 90212, USA

Winkler, Marvin (Athlete, Basketball Player)
P.O. Box 759
Zapata, TX 78076-0759, USA

Winkles, Bobby B (Athlete, Baseball Player, Coach)
3470 Summersorin11s Dr
las Ve11as, NV 89129-6391, USA

Winn, Jim (Athlete, Baseball Player)
3440 S Delaware Ave
Apt 123
Springfield, MO 65804-6447, USA

Winn, Randy (Athlete, Baseball Player)
12221 Broadwater Looo
Thonotosassa, Fl 33592-3954, USA

Winner, Charley (Athlete, Football Coach, Football Player)
14970 Lake Olive Dr
Fort Myers, FL 33919, USA

Winner, Michael R (Director, Producer)
31 Melbury Road
London W14 8AB, UNITED KINGDOM (UK)

Winnes, Chris (Athlete, Hockey Player)
22 Ambrose Dr
Bristol, Rl 02809, USA

Winnick, Katheryn (Actor)
c/o Jason Barrett *Alchemy Entertainment*
7024 Melrose Ave
Suite 420
Los Angeles, CA 90038, USA

Winningham, Herm (Athlete, Baseball Player)
1542 Belleville Rd
Orangeburg, SC 29115-3702, USA

Winningham, Mare (Actor)
c/o Margrit Polak *Margrit Polak Management*
1954 Hillhurst Ave
Suite 405
Los Angeles, CA 90027, USA

Winograd, Shmuel (Mathematician, Scientist)
235 Glendale Road
Scarsdale, NY 10583, USA

Winokur, Marissa Jaret (Actor)
c/o Michael Valeo *Valeo Entertainment*
8265 Sunset Blvd
Suite 103
Los Angeles, CA 90046, USA

Winslet, Kate (Actor)
c/o Heidi Slan *42West (LA)*
11400 W Olympic Blvd
Suite 1100
Los Angeles, CA 90064, USA

Winslow, Dan (Musician)
3807 114th Lane NE
Minneapolis, MN 55449, USA

Winslow, Ernest (Race Car Driver)
Randy Dixon Motorsports
955 Riverside Rd
Grifton, 28530 NC, USA

Winslow, George (Athlete, Football Player)
14 Daisy Ln
Maple Glen, PA 19002, USA

Winslow, Michael (Actor, Comedian)
c/o Damon Frank *Venture IAB*
3211 Cahuenga Blvd W Ste 104
Los Angeles, CA 90068, USA

Winslow Jr, Kellen (Athlete, Football Player)
c/o Staff Member *EAG Sports Management*
12910 Agustin Pl
Playa Vista, CA 90094, USA

Winsor, Jackie (Artist)
Paula Cooper Gallery
534 W 21st St
New York, NY 10011, USA

Winstead, Mary Elizabeth (Actor)
c/o Jim Toth *Creative Artists Agency (CAA-LA)*
2000 Ave Of The Stars
Los Angeles, CA 90067, USA

Winston, Dennis (Athlete, Football Player)
150 Chesterfield Ln
Apt 8
Maumee, OH 43537, USA

Winston, George (Composer, Musician)
Dancing Cat Productions
PO Box 639
Santa Cruz, CA 95061, USA

Winston, Hattie (Actor)
13025 Jarvis Ave
Los Angeles, CA 90061, USA

Winston, Mary Ellen (Stylist)
11 E 68th St
New York, NY 10021-4955, USA

Winston, Patrick H (Engineer, Scientist)
Massachusetts Institute of Technology
Technology Square
Cambridge, MA 02139, USA

Winston, Roland (Physicist)
3384 Locksley Court
Merced, CA 95340, USA

Winston, Roy C (Athlete, Football Player)
708 Highway 401
Napoleonville, LA 70390, USA

Winstone, Ray (Actor)
c/o Michael Wiggs *Creative Artists Management (CAM (UK))*
1st Floor
55-59 Shaftesbury Ave
London W1D 6LD, UK

Winter, Alex (Actor)
c/o Chris Ridenhour *Evolution Entertainment (LA)*
901 N Highland Ave
Los Angeles, CA 90038, USA

Winter, Antje (Stylist)
c/o Staff Member *Art Partner*
145 Hudson St
2nd Floor
New York, NY 10013, USA

Winter, Ariel (Actor)
c/o Scott Wexler *Brillstein Entertainment Partners*
9150 Wilshire Blvd #350
Beverly Hills, CA 90212, USA

Winter, Blaise (Athlete, Football Player)
W5837 Royaltroon Dr
Menasha, WI 54952, USA

Winter, Edgar (Musician)
Hooker Enterprises
26033 Mulholland Highway
Calabasas, CA 91302, USA

Winter, Edgar
26033 Mulholland Hwy
Calabasas, CA 91302

Winter, Eric (Actor)
c/o Colton Gramm *Brillstein Entertainment Partners*
9150 Wilshire Blvd #350
Beverly Hills, CA 90212, USA

Winter, Fred (Tex) (Coach)
Los Angeles Lakers
Staples Center
1111 S Figueroa St
Los Angeles, CA 90015, USA

Winter, Harrison L (Judge)
US Court of Appeals
101 W Lombard St
Baltimore, MD 21201, USA

Winter, Johnny (Musician)
Slatus Mgmt
35 Hayward Ave
Colchester, CT 06415, USA

Winter, Judy
Merzstr. 14
Munich, GERMANY D-81679

Winter, Morice "Tex" (Athlete, Basketball Player)
Brian Winter
1812 Todd Rd
Manhattan, KS 66502-3408, USA

Winter, Olaf (Athlete)
An der Pirschheide 28
Potsdam 14471, GERMANY

Winter, Paul T (Musician)
Living Music Records
PO Box 72
Litchfield, CT 06759, USA

Winter, Ralph (Producer)
c/o Staff Member *Ralph Winter Productions*
10201 W Pico Blvd
Bldg 6 #101
Los Angeles, CA 90035, USA

Winter, Terence (Producer)
c/o Staff Member *Creative Artists Agency (CAA-LA)*
2000 Ave Of The Stars
Los Angeles, CA 90067, USA

Winter, Terrence (Producer, Writer)
c/o Staff Member *Jackoway Tyerman Wertheimer Austen Mandelbaum Morris & Klein*
1925 Century Park E
22nd Floor
Los Angeles, CA 90067, USA

Winter, William F (Ex-Governor)
190 E Capitol St
Suite 800
Jackson, MS 39201, USA

Winterbottom, Michael (Director,
Producer, Writer)
c/o Staff Member *Revolution Films*
9A Dallington St
London EC1V 0BQ, UNITED KINGDOM
(UK)

Winter Jr, Ralph K (Judge)
US Court of Appeals
55 Whitney Ave
New Haven, CT 06510, USA

Winters, Brian (Athlete, Basketball Player)
6144 S Moline Way
Englewood, CO 80111-5845, USA

Winters, Chris (Actor, Model)
933 Backspin Ct
Newport News, VA 23602, USA

Winters, Dean (Actor)
c/o Bill Butler *Industry Entertainment
Partners*
955 S Carrillo Dr
Suite 300
Los Angeles, CA 90048, USA

Winters, Frank (Football Player)
Cleveland Browns
820 17th St
Union City, NJ 07087-1928, USA

Winters, Jonathan (Artist)
945 Lilac Dr
Santa Barbara, CA 93108-1520, USA

Winters, Jonathan (Actor, Comedian)
c/o Staff Member *Abrams Artists Agency
(LA)*
9200 Sunset Blvd
11th Floor
Los Angeles, CA 90069, USA

Winters, Katherine (Scientist)
1123 Egret Lake Way
Melbourne, FL 32940-6863, USA

Winters, Matt (Athlete, Baseball Player)
1201 Foxfire Dr
Greensboro, NC 27410-3253, USA

Winters, Mike (Athlete, Baseball Player)
13644 Boquita Dr
Del Mar, CA 92014-3408, USA

Winters, Patricia (Stylist)
2122 Century Park Ln #114
Los Angeles, CA 90067-3317, USA

Winters, Scott William (Actor)
c/o Staff Member *Levine Okwu Erickson
Management*
6363 Wilshire Blvd
Suite 300
Los Angeles, CA 90048, USA

Winters, Voise (Athlete, Basketball Player)
7305 S Rockwell St
Chicago, IL 60629-2037, USA

Winther, Richard (Athlete, Football
Player)
1620 6th Way NW
Birmingham, AL 35215, USA

Wintour, Anna (Editor)
Vogue Magazine
Editor's Office
4 Times Square #1200
New York, NY 10036, USA

Winwood, Steve (Musician)
Trinley Cottage
Tirley
Gloucs GL19 4EU, UNITED KINGDOM
(UK)

Winzenried, Jesse D (Financier)
Securities Investor Protection
805 15th St NW
Washington, DC 20005, USA

Wire II, William S (Business Person)
706 Overton Park
Nashville, TN 37215-2452, USA

Wirgowski, Dennis (Athlete, Football
Player)
1127 Brissette Beach Rd
Kawkawlin, MI 48631, USA

Wirth, Alan (Athlete, Baseball Player)
2858 E Jasmine St
Mesa, AZ 85213-3123, USA

Wirth, Billy (Actor, Director)
c/o Molly Conners *Rogues Gallery*
20 Clinton St
Suite C-7
New York, NY 10002, USA

Wirth, Timothy E (Politician, Senator)
United Nations Foundation
2201 Nw
Washington, DC 20521, USA

Wirtz, W Willard (Secretary)
1211 Connecticut Ave NW
Washington, DC 20036, USA

Wisdom, Robert (Actor)
Paradigm
10100 Santa Monica Blvd Fl 25
Los Angeles, CA 90067

Wisdom, Sir Norman
The Lhen
Andreas Ramsay ISLE OF MAN, UK 1M7
3EH

Wise, Dewayne (Athlete, Baseball Player)
709 Old Lexington Hwy
Chapin, SC 29036-7980, USA

Wise, Matt (Athlete, Baseball Player)
11627 E Twilight Ct
Chandler, AZ 85249-4546, USA

Wise, Ray (Actor)
c/o Brady McKay *Flutie Entertainment
(LA)*
9320 Wilshire Blvd
Suite 202
Beverly Hills, CA 90212, USA

wise, Richard C (Rick) (Athlete, Baseball
Player)
8235 SW 184th Ave
Beaverton, OR 97007-5764, USA

Wise, Robert (Governor, Politician)
5622 Nebraska Ave NW
Washington, DC 20015-1258, USA

Wise, William A (Business Person)
El Paso Energy Corp
1001 Louisiana St
Houston, TX 77002, USA

Wise, Willie (Athlete, Basketball Player)
2320 185th Pl NE
Redmond, WA 98052-6019, USA

Wisecarver, Ellsworth (Sonny)
305 Mill Creek Rd
Mentone, CA 92359

Wiseman, Brian (Athlete, Hockey Player)
2960 Walnut Ridge Dr
Ann Arbor, MI 48103-2189, USA

Wiseman, Frederick (Producer)
Zipporah Films
1 Richdale Ave
#4
Cambridge, MA 02140, USA

Wiseman, Gregory Reid Ltcmdr
(Astronaut)
2436 Mountain Falls Ct
Friendswood, TX 77546-5590, USA

Wiseman, Len (Director, Writer)
c/o Nick Reed *ICM Partners (ICM-LA)*
10250 Constellation Blvd Fl 7
Los Angeles, CA 90067, USA

Wiseman, Mac (Musician)
PO Box 17028
Nashville, TN 37217, USA

Wisener, Gary (Athlete, Football Player)
10 Encantado Way
Hot Springs Village, AR 71909-7405, USA

Wishart III, Leonard P (General)
19360 Magnolia Grove Square
#315
Leesburg, VA 20176, USA

Wish Bone (Actor, Composer, Musician)
c/o Staff Member *Creative Artists Agency
(CAA-LA)*
2000 Ave Of The Stars
Los Angeles, CA 90067, USA

Wisin and Yandel (Musician)
c/o Staff Member *Universal Music
Publishing Group (Latin)*
420 Lincoln Rd
Suite 200
Miami Beach, FL 33139, USA

Wiska, Jeffrey R (Athlete, Football Player)
18579 Fox Hollow Ct
Northville, MI 48167, USA

Wismann, Pete (Athlete, Football Player)
7923 Caledonia Dr
San Jose, CA 95135, USA

Wisner, Frank G (Diplomat)
American International Group
70 Pine St
#1800
New York, NY 10270, USA

Wisniewski, Andreas (Actor)
Gage Group
14724 Ventura Blvd
#505
Sherman Oaks, CA 91403, USA

Wisniewski, Leo (Athlete, Football Player)
8036 Woodcreek Dr
Bridgeville, PA 15017, USA

Wisniewski, Stephen A (Steve) (Athlete,
Football Player)
36 El Alamo Ct
Danville, CA 94526, USA

Wisoff, Jeff Dr (Astronaut)
4268 Brindisi Pl
Pleasanton, CA 94566-2238, USA

Wisoff, Peter J K (Jeff) (Astronaut)
4268 Brindisi Place
Pleasanton, CA 94566, USA

Wissel, Sharon (Figure Skater)
c/o Staff Member *Bobby Ball Talent
Agency*
4116 W Magnolia Blvd Ste 205
Burbank, CA 91505-2700, USA

Wissman, Dave (Athlete, Baseball Player)
P.O. Box 38
Derby, VT 05829-0038, USA

Wiste, Jim (Athlete, Hockey Player)
701 S. University Blvd.
Denver, CO 80209-4722, USA

Wistert, Albert A (Ox) (Athlete, Football
Player)
256 Gunnell Rd
Grants Pass, OR 97526, USA

Wistert, Alvin L (Moose) (Athlete,
Football Player)
10250 W Seven Mile Rd
Northville, MI 48167, USA

Wistrom, Grant (Athlete, Football Player)
5769 S Fox Hollow Ave
Springfield, MO 65810, USA

Witasick, Jay (Athlete, Baseball Player)
200 Wellin11ton Ct
Bel Air, MD 21014-3100, USA

Withem, Shannon (Athlete, Baseball
Player)
39668 Dorchester Cir
Canton, MI 48188-5016, USA

Witherell, Joann (Stylist)
c/o Staff Member *THW Productions*
1801 N Kingsley Dr
#103
Hollywood, CA 90027, USA

Withers, Bill (Musician, Songwriter,
Writer)
PO Box 16698
Beverly Hills, CA 90209, USA

Withers, Jane (Actor)
Scott Stander
13701 Riverside Dr #201
Sherman Oaks, CA 91423, USA

Withers, Pick (Musician)
Damage Mgmt
16 Lambton Place
London W11 2SH, UNITED KINGDOM
(UK)

Witherspoon, John (Actor, Comedian)
c/o Matt Schuler *Levity Entertainment
Group*
6701 Center Drive West
Suite 1111
Los Angles, CA 90045, USA

Witherspoon, Reese (Actor, Producer)
340 N Gunston Dr
Los Angeles, CA 90049, USA

Withrow, Phil (Athlete, Football Player)
730 Oakland Hills Cir
Apt 106
Lake Mary, FL 32746, USA

Withrow, Ray (Athlete, Baseball Player)
3842 Bordeaux Looo S
Owensboro, KY 42303-2550, USA

**with Spencer Davis, Strawberry Alarm
Clock** (Music Group)
c/o Geoffrey Blumenauer *Geoffrey
Blumenauer Artists*
PO Box 343
Burbank, CA 91503-0343, USA

Witiuk, Doris (Baseball Player)
11821 N Hemlock St
Spokane, WA 99218-2718, USA

Witiuk, Steve (Athlete, Hockey Player)
11821 N Hemlock St
Spokane, WA 99218, CANADA

Witkin, Isaac (Artist)
Bennington College
Art Dept
Bennington, VT 05201, USA

Witkin, Joel-Peter (Photographer)
1707 Five Points Road SW
Albuquerque, NM 87105, USA

Witkop, Bernhard (Misc)
3807 Montrose Driveway
Chevy Chase, MD 20815, USA

Witman, Jon (Athlete, Football Player)
568 Woodsview Ln
Hellam, PA 17406, USA

Witmeyer, Ron (Athlete, Baseball Player)
P.O. Box 763
Rancho Santa Fe, CA 92067-0763, USA

Witt, Alexander (Director)
c/o Ann Murtha *Murtha Agency*
1025 Colorado Ave
Suite B
Santa Monica, CA 902401, USA

Witt, Alicia (Actor)
c/o Daniel (Danny) Sussman *Brillstein Entertainment Partners*
9150 Wilshire Blvd #350
Beverly Hills, CA 90212, USA

Witt, Bobby (Athlete, Baseball Player, Olympic Athlete)
4601 Winewood Ct
Colleyville, TX 76034-4887, USA

Witt, Brendan (Athlete, Hockey Player)
PO Box 907
Darby, MT 59829-0907, USA

Witt, George (Athlete, Baseball Player)
2209 Catalina
Laguna Beach, CA 92651-3607, USA

Witt, Katarina (Figure Skater)
c/o Gail Parenteau *Parenteau Guidance*
132 East 35th St #3J
New York, NY 10016, USA

Witt, Kevin (Athlete, Baseball Player)
6350 Concho Bay Dr
Houston, TX 77041-6171, USA

Witt, Michael A (Mike) (Athlete, Baseball Player)
37 Poppy Hills Rd
Laguna Niguel, CA 92677-1010, USA

Witt, Robert E (Educator)
University of Alabama
President's Office
Tuscaloosa, AL 35487, USA

Witte, Luke (Athlete, Basketball Player)
3223 Arbor Pointe Dr
Charlotte, NC 28210-7994, USA

Witten, Edward (Physicist)
Institute for Advanced Study
Einstein Lane
Princeton, NJ 08540, USA

Witten, Jason (Athlete, Football Player)
501 King Ranch Rd
Southlake, TX 76092, USA

Witter, Karen (Actor, Model)
H/H/M
247 S Beverly Dr
#102
Beverly Hills, CA 90212, USA

Wittman, Randy (Athlete, Basketball Player, Coach)
1111 19th St N Apt 1406
Arlington, VA 22209-1715, USA

Wittrock, Finn (Actor)
c/o Jim Weissenbach *Weissenbach Management*
5951 Airdrome St.
Los Angeles, CA 90035, USA

Wittwer, Linda Jezek (Athlete, Olympic Athlete, Swimmer)
673 Oak Park Way
Emerald Hills, CA 94062-4041, USA

Witty, Chris (Athlete, Olympic Athlete, Speed Skater)
2644 E 2940 S
Salt Lake City, UT 84109-2527, USA

Witucki, Casimir (Athlete, Football Player)
3909 Spring Ter
Temple Hills, MD 20748, USA

Witwer, Sam (Actor)
c/o Gordon Gilbertson *Gilbertson Management*
1334 3rd St Promenade #201
Santa Monica, CA 90401, USA

Wizbicki, Alex (Athlete, Football Player)
10B Haynes Ct
Superior, WI 54880, USA

Wlasiuk, Gene (Athlete, Football Player)
816 Shannon RD
Regina, SK S45 5K2, Canada

W. Meeks, Gregory (Congressman, Politician)
2234 Rayburn HOB
Washington, DC 20515, USA

Wobst, Frank (Financier)
Huntington Bancshares
Huntington Center
41 S High St
Columbus, OH 43287, USA

Wockenfuss, Anett (Model)
c/o Chadwick model management
Private Bag 38
Darlinghurst NSW 2010, AUSTRALIA

Wockenfuss, John (Athlete, Baseball Player)
26 Wallamsey Ln
Chesapeake City, MD 21915-1821, USA

Wocket-Eckert, Barbel (Athlete)
Im Bangert 61
Lutzelbach 64750, GERMANY

Woerner, Scott (Athlete, Football Player)
11268 Turner Rd
Hampton, GA 30228, USA

Woese, Carl R (Biologist)
806 W Delaware Ave
Urbana, IL 61801, USA

Woessner, Mark M (Business Person, Publisher)
Erich-Kastner-Str 25
Gutersloh 33332, GERMANY

Wofford, Harris L (Politician, Senator)
260 Burch Dr
Coraopolis, PA 15108-3153, USA

Wofford, James (Athlete, Horse Racer, Olympic Athlete)
22145 Greengarden Rd
Upperville, VA 20184-3105, USA

Wogan, Gerald N (Misc)
Massachusetts Institute of Technology
Toxicology Div
Cambridge, MA 02139, USA

Woggon, Bill (Cartoonist)
2724 Cabot Court
Thousand Oaks, CA 91360, USA

Wohl, Dave (Athlete, Basketball Player, Coach)
137 Morley Cir
Melville, NY 11747-4843, USA

Wohlers, Mark E (Athlete, Baseball Player)
135 Old Cedar Ln
Alpharetta, GA 30004-3795, USA

Wohlford, Jim (Athlete, Baseball Player)
24186 Lomitas Dr
Woodlake, CA 93286-9505, USA

Wohlhuter, Richard (Athlete, Olympic Athlete, Track Athlete)
13609 Danhurst Way
Jacksonville, FL 32224-1308, USA

Wohlwender-Fricker, Marian (Athlete, Baseball Player)
14006 Castle Hill Way
Fort Myers, FL 33919-7369, USA

Woit, Benny (Athlete, Hockey Player)
607-20 Harding Blvd W
Richmond Hill, ON L4C 9S4, Canada

Woit, Dick (Misc)
Lehmann Sports Center
2700 N Lehmann Court
Chicago, IL 60614, USA

Woiwode, Larry (Writer)
State University of New York
English Dept
Binghamton, NY 13901, USA

Wojciechowski, John (Athlete, Football Player)
13317 Clyde Rd
Holly, MI 48442, USA

Wojciechowski, Steve (Athlete, Baseball Player)
4646 Thornberry Hill Ct NE
Grand Rapids, MI 49525-9489, USA

Wojcik, John (Athlete, Baseball Player)
8303 Salford Way
Louisville, KY 40222-5529, USA

Wojna, Ed (Athlete, Baseball Player)
225 Sussex Pl
Carson City, NV 89703-5372, USA

Wojtowicz, R P (Misc)
Railway Carmen Union
3 Research Place
Rockville, MD 20850, USA

Wolaner, Robin P (Publisher)
Sunset Publishing Corp
80 Willow Road
Mento Park, CA 94025, USA

Wolanin, Craig (Athlete, Hockey Player)
4891 Gallagher Rd.
Rochester, MI 48306-1508, USA

Wolcott, Bob (Athlete, Baseball Player)
3323 Bryson Way
Medford, OR 97504-5811, USA

Wolf, Brana (Stylist)
c/o Staff Member *Art + Commerce*
531 W 25th St # 4
New York, NY 10001, USA

Wolf, Caryn (Stylist)
8651 N Burke
Tuscon, AZ 85742, USA

Wolf, David A (Astronaut)
1714 Neptune Lane
Houston, TX 77062, USA

Wolf, David A Dr (Astronaut)
1714 Neptune Ln
Houston, TX 77062-6108, USA

Wolf, Dick (Producer, Writer)
c/o Staff Member *Wolf Films Inc (LA)*
100 Universal City Plz
Bldg 2252
Universal City, CA 91608-1085, USA

Wolf, Jim (Athlete, Baseball Player)
8054 Royer Ave
West Hills, CA 91304-3535, USA

Wolf, Joe (Athlete, Football Player)
2324 Lehigh Pkwy N
Allentown, PA 18103, USA

Wolf, John T "Mike" (General)
8046 NE Hunt Club Ln
Hansville, WA 98340-9756, USA

Wolf, Naomi (Writer)
Random House
1745 Broadway
#B1
New York, NY 10019, USA

Wolf, Randall C (Randy) (Athlete, Baseball Player)
18580 Corte Fresco
Rancho Santa Fe, CA 91304-3535, USA

Wolf, Ross (Athlete, Baseball Player)
15524 N 400th St
Wheeler, IL 62479-2300, USA

Wolf, Scott (Actor)
c/o Sam Maydew *Collective*
8383 Wilshire Blvd
Suite 1050
Beverly Hills, CA 90211, USA

Wolf, Sigrid (Skier)
Elbigenalp 45 A
6652, AUSTRIA

Wolf, Stephanie (Stylist)
c/o Staff Member *Cloutier Agency*
2632 La Cienega Ave
Los Angeles, CA 90034, USA

Wolf, Wally (Athlete, Baseball Player)
18580 Corte Fresco
Rancho Santa Fe, CA 92091-0227, USA

Wolfe, Bernie (Athlete, Hockey Player)
8012 Glenbrook Rd
Bethesda, MD 20814-2608, USA

Wolfe, Bob (Athlete, Football Player)
13165 Emiline Cir
Omaha, NE 68138-6132, USA

Wolfe, Brian (Athlete, Baseball Player)
32524 Sorucewood Way
Lake Elsinore, CA 95628-3836, USA

Wolfe, David (Writer)
C/O Angela Hartman
1259 N. Crescent Hts Blvd. Suite D
West Hollywood, CA 90046, USA

Wolfe, George C (Director)
Shakespeare Festival
425 Lafayette St
New York, NY 10003, USA

Wolfe, Kenneth L (Business Person)
Hershey Foods Corp
100 Crystal A Dr
Hershey, PA 17033, USA

Wolfe, Larry (Athlete, Baseball Player)
5200 Blossomwood Ct
Fair Oaks, CA 92532-2515, USA

Wolfe, Michael (Producer)
c/o Rosanna Bilow *CAA Sports (LA)*
2000 Avenue of the Stars
Los Angeles, CA 90067, USA

Wolfe, Paul (Race Car Driver)
Baldwin Racing
182 Raceway Dr. #B
Mooresville, NC 28117, USA

Wolfe, Ralph S (Biologist)
University of Illinois
Microbiology Dept
Burnill Hall
Urbana, IL 61801, USA

Wolfe, Sterling (Actor)
2609 Wyoming Ave
#A
Burbank, CA 91505, USA

Wolfe, Thad A (General)
4790 Longwood POint
Colorado Springs, CO 80906-8609, USA

Wolfe, Tom (Composer, Musician)
c/o Staff Member *Aperture Music*
P.O. Box 90010
Pasadena, CA 91109, USA

Wolfe, Traci (Actor)
c/o Staff Member *Cunningham Escott
Slevin & Doherty (CESD-LA)*
10635 Santa Monica Blvd
130
Los Angeles, CA 90025, USA

Wolfe Jr, Thomas K (Tom) (Writer)
21 E 79th St
New York, NY 10075-0125, USA

Wolfenden of Westcott, John F (Educator)
White House
Guildford Road Westcott near Dorking
Surrey, UNITED KINGDOM (UK)

Wolfenstein, Lincoln (Physicist)
Camegie-Mellon University
Physics Dept
Pittsburgh, PA 15213, USA

Wolfermann, Klaus (Athlete, Track
Athlete)
Fasenenweg 13A
Herzogenaurach 91074, GERMANY

Wolff, Alex (Musician)
c/o Cindi Berger *PMK/BNC Public
Relations (PMK-NY)*
622 3rd Ave
8th Floor
New York, NY 10017, USA

Wolff, Bob (Sportscaster)
3 Salisbury Pt Apt 2E
Nyack, NY 10960-4726, USA

Wolff, Christian
Zinnkopfstr. 6
Aschau/Chiemsee, GERMANY D-83229

Wolff, Christoph J (Educator)
182 Washington St
Belmont, MA 02478, USA

Wolff, Hugh (Conductor)
Van Walsun Mgmt
4 Addison Bridge Place
London W14 8XP, UNITED KINGDOM
(UK)

Wolff, Jon A (Misc)
1122 University Bay Dr
Madison, WI 53705, USA

Wolff, Jonathan (Composer, Musician)
c/o Steve Winogradsky *Winogradsky Co,
The*
11240 Magnolia Blvd #104
N Hollywood, CA 91601, USA

Wolff, Nat (Musician)
Naked Brothers Band
c/o Yovia
1909 N 3rd Street
Jacksonville Beach, FL 32250, USA

Wolff, Sanford I (Misc)
8141 Broadway
New York, NY 10023, USA

Wolff, Toblas J A (Writer)
Stanford University
English Dept
Stanford, CA 94305, USA

Wolff, Torben (Biologist)
Hesseltoften
Hellerup 2900, DENMARK

Wolfley, Craig (Athlete, Football Player)
1767 Robson Dr
Pittsburgh, PA 15241, USA

Wolford, Will (Athlete, Football Player)
205 Waterleaf Way
Louisville, KY 40207, USA

Wolfowitz, Paul D (Financier,
Government Official)
World Bank
1818 H St NW
Washington, DC 20433, USA

Wolfson, Louis E (Business Person)
10205 Collins Ave
Bal Harbour, FL 33154, USA

Wolk, Jimmy (Actor)
c/o Adena Chawke *Greenlight
Management and Production*
13848 Valleyheart Dr
Sherman Oaks, CA 91423, USA

Wolken, Jonathan (Artist, Dancer,
Director)
Pilobolus Dance Theater
PO Box 388
Washington Depot, CT 06794, USA

Woll, Deborah Ann (Actor)
c/o Darryl Marshak *Marshak/Zachary
Company, The*
8840 Wilshire Blvd
1st Floor
Beverly Hills, CA 90210, USA

Wollman, Harvey L (Ex-Governor)
40004 184th St
Frankfort, SD 57440, USA

Wollman, Roger L (Judge)
US Court of Appeals
Federal Building
400 S Phillips
Sioux Falls, SD 57104, USA

Wolman, Kira (Stylist)
348 N Avenue
59
Los Angeles, CA 90042, USA

Wolman, M Gordon (Football Player,
Physicist)
1070 Stable Run Dr
Cordova, TN 38018-0109, USA

Wolov, Julia Lea (Actor, Writer)
c/o Jonathan Brandstein *Morra Brezner
Steinberg & Tenenbaum (MBST)
Entertainment*
345 N Maple Dr
Suite 200
Beverly Hills, CA 90210, USA

Wolpe, Lenny (Actor)
c/o Staff Member *Gage Group, The (LA)*
14724 Ventura Blvd
Suite 505
Sherman Oaks, CA 91403, USA

Wolpert, Julian (Geophysicist, Physicist)
188 E 64th St
#2304
New York, NY 10021, USA

Wolski, Dariusz (Director)
The Mack Agency
4705 Laurel Canyon Blvd
#204
Valley Village, CA 91607, USA

Wolszczan, Aleksander (Astronomer)
Pennsylvania State University
Astronomy Dept
University Park, PA 16802, USA

Wolter, Sherilyn (Actor)
128 Old Topanga Canyon Rd
Topanga, CA 90290

Wolters, Kara (Basketball Player)
137 Westfield Dr
Holliston, MA 01746, USA

Woltman, Rhea (Aviator)
17 Polo Cir
Colorado Springs, CO 80906-3104, USA

W. Olver, John (Congressman, Politician)
1111 Longworth HOB
Washington, DC 20515, USA

Womack, Bobby (Actor, Musician)
c/o Staff Member *American Talent Agency*
248 W 35th St
Suite 501
New York, NY 10001, USA

Womack, Bruce L (Athlete, Football
Player)
2834 Triway Ln
Houston, TX 77043, USA

Womack, Dooley (Athlete, Baseball
Player)
209 Weeping Cherry Ln
Columbia, SC 29212-8617, USA

Womack, Floyd (Athlete, Football Player)
c/o Eugene Parker *Maximum Sports
Management*
6435 W Jefferson Blvd
#197
Fort Wayne, IN 46804, USA

Womack, James E (Scientist)
2105 Farley
College Station, TX 77845, USA

Womack, Lee Ann (Actor, Musician)
c/o Tiffany Shipp *Sunshine, Sachs &
Associates*
149 Fifth Ave
7th Floor
New York, NY 10010, USA

Womack, Steve (Congressman, Politician)
1508 Longworth HOB
Washington, DC 20515, USA

Womack, Tony (Athlete, Baseball Player)
8301 Marcliffe Ct
Waxhaw, NC 28173-5500, USA

Woman, Nancy
PO Box 3601
Torrance, CA 90510

Wombats, The (Music Group)
c/o Staff Member *Paradigm (Monterey)*
404 W Franklin St
Monterey, CA 93940, USA

Womble, Royce (Athlete, Football Player)
6350 Newt Patterson Rd
Mansfield, TX 76063, USA

Wonder, Stevie (Musician, Songwriter)
Steveland Morris Music
4616 Magnolia Blvd
Burbank, CA 91505, USA

Wonders, Rich (Bowler)
720 Augusta St
Racine, WI 53402-4412, USA

Wong, Albert (Engineer)
26796 Vista Terrace
Lake Forest, CA 92630, USA

Wong, B D (Actor)
c/o Richie Jackson *Jackson Group
Entertainment*
345 W 13th St
New York, NY 10014, USA

Wong, Kailee (Athlete, Football Player)
5003 Mimosa Dr
Bellaire, TX 77401-5736, USA

Wong, Kim (Stylist)
4499-A Via Marisol
#206
Los Angeles, CA 90042, USA

Wong, Mike (Athlete, Hockey Player)
16081 Hyland Ave
Lakeville, MN 55044-6221, USA

Wong, Russell (Actor)
International Creative Mgmt
8942 Wilshire Blvd
#219
Beverly Hills, CA 90211, USA

Wong-Staal, Flossie (Biologist)
University of California
Molecular Biology Dept
La Jolla, CA 92093, USA

Wonsley, George (Athlete, Football
Player)
6418 Amblewood Pl
Jackson, MS 39213, USA

Woo, John (Director, Producer)
c/o Staff Member *Lion Rock Productions*
2120 Colorado Ave #225
Santa Monica, CA 90404

Wood, Brandon (Athlete, Baseball Player)
19550 N Gravhawk Dr
Unit 1110
Scottsdale, AZ 85255-3986, USA

Wood, Brenton (Musician)
PO Box 4127
Inglewood, CA 90309, USA

Wood, Carolyn (Swimmer)
4380 SW 86th Ave
Portland, OR 97225, USA

Wood, Carri (Athlete, Golfer)
2001 Sabal Ridge Ct
Apt H
Palm Beach Gardens, FL 33418-8922,
USA

Wood, Charles G (Writer)
London Mgmt
2-4 Noel St
London W1V 3RB, UNITED KINGDOM
(UK)

Wood, C Norman (General)
5440 Mount Corcoran Place
Burke, VA 22015, USA

Wood, Danny (Musician)
c/o Kristin Foster *PMK/BNC Public Relations (PMK-NY)*
622 3rd Ave
8th Floor
New York, NY 10017, USA

Wood, Darin "Dody" (Athlete, Hockey Player)
4941 S Woodside Ave
Independence, MO 64055-5738, USA

Wood, David (Athlete, Basketball Player)
5915 Crescent Moon Ct
Reno, NV 89511-4357, USA

Wood, David (Athlete, Basketball Player)
20205 S Virginia St
Reno, NV 89521, USA

Wood, Dennis (Stylist)
c/o Staff Member *Judy Inc*
1 Yorkville Ave
Toronto ON M4W 1L1, Canada

Wood, Dick (Athlete, Football Player)
41 Audubon Pl
Newnan, GA 30265, USA

Wood, Duane (Athlete, Football Player)
407 W Caddo Ave
Wilburton, OK 74578, USA

Wood, Eddie (Race Car Driver)
Koute 2 Box 77
21 Performance Rd
Stuart, VA 24171, USA

Wood, Eden (Beauty Pageant Winner, Reality TV Star)
c/o Staff Member *VH1 Television*
1515 Broadway
New York, NY 10036, USA

Wood, Elijah (Actor)
c/o Annick Muller *ID Public Relations (ID-NY)*
150 W 30th St
19th Floor
New York, NY 10001, USA

Wood, Evan Rachel (Actor)
c/o Hylda Queally *Creative Artists Agency (CAA-LA)*
2000 Ave Of The Stars
Los Angeles, CA 90067, USA

Wood, Gene
PO Box 805
Culver City, CA 90232-0805

Wood, Glen (Race Car Driver)
Wood Bros Racing
Route 2 Box 77
21 Performance Rd
Stuart, VA 24171, USA

Wood, Gordon S (Historian)
77 Keense St
Providence, RI 02906, USA

Wood, Jake (Athlete, Baseball Player)
9129 Daytona Dr
Pensacola, FL 32506-2904, USA

Wood, James (Business Person)
Great A & P Tea Co
2 Paragon Dr
Montvale, NJ 07645, USA

Wood, James N (Director)
Art Institute of Chicago
111 S Michigan Ave
Chicago, IL 60603, USA

Wood, Janet (Actor)
Acme Talent
4727 Wilshire Blvd
#333
Los Angeles, CA 90010, USA

Wood, Jason (Athlete, Baseball Player)
9899 N Cascade Dr
Fresno, CA 93730-0864, USA

Wood, Jason (Stylist)
c/o Staff Member *Arends, Frank Inc*
216 W 18th St
#703-B
New York, NY 10011, USA

Wood, Jeff (Race Car Driver)
821 Linden
Wichita, KS 67206, USA

Wood, John (Actor)
Royal Shakespeare Co
Stratford-on-Avon
Warwickshire CV37 6BB, UNITED
KINGDOM (UK)

Wood, John A (Geophysicist, Physicist)
1716 Cambridge St
#16
Cambridge, MA 02138, USA

Wood, Jon (Race Car Driver)
137 High Hills Dr
Mooresville, NC 28117-9000, USA

Wood, Kerry (Athlete, Baseball Player)
6838 E Chenev Dr
Paradise Valley, AZ 85253-3525, USA

Wood, Kimba M (Judge)
US District Court House
40 Foley Square
New York, NY 10007, USA

Wood, Lana (Actor)
2299 Hood Dr
Thousand Oaks, CA 91362-2423, USA

Wood, Len (Race Car Driver)
Route 2 Box 77
21 Performance Road
Stuart, VA 24171, USA

Wood, Leon (Athlete, Basketball Player, Olympic Athlete)
2227 Archway
Irvine, CA 92618, USA

Wood, Martin "Al" (Athlete, Basketball Player)
411 Belvedere Ln
Waxhaw, NC 28173-6581, USA

Wood, Maurice (Doctor)
RR 2 Box 543B
Hot Springs, VA 24445, USA

Wood, Mike (Athlete, Baseball Player)
1199 Cherlynn Ter
West Palm Beach, FL 33406, USA

Wood, Mike (Athlete, Baseball Player)
1199 Cherlvnn Ter
West Palm Beach, FL 33406-5272, USA

Wood, Mike (Athlete, Football Player)
630 N Geyer Rd
Saint Louis, MO 63122, USA

Wood, Rachel Hurd (Actor)
c/o Michael Lazo *Untitled Entertainment (LA)*
350 S. Beverly Dr #200
Beverly Hills, CA 90212, USA

Wood, Randy (Athlete, Hockey Player)
2 Bridge St
Manchester, MA 01944-1408, USA

Wood, Richard (Athlete, Football Player)
5413 Windbrush Dr
Tampa, FL 33625, USA

Wood, Robert (Athlete, Basketball Player)
12930 Echo Dr
Rockton, IL 61072-2816, USA

Wood, Robert (Athlete, Basketball Player)
12930 Echo Dr
Rockton, IL 61072, USA

Wood, Robert E (Publisher)
Peninsula Times Tribune
435 N Michigan Ave
#1609
Chicago, IL 60611, USA

Wood, Robert J (Astronaut)
McDonnell Douglas Corp
PO Box 516
Saint Louis, MO 63166, USA

Wood, Ron
Sandy Mount House
County Kildare S., IRELAND

Wood, Ronald (Ron) (Musician)
The Outside Organisation
Butler House
177-178 Tottenham Court Road
London W1T 7NY, United Kingdom

Wood, Sharon (Misc)
PO Box 1482
Canmore, AB T0L 0M0, CANADA

Wood, Stuart (Woody) (Musician)
27 Preston Grange Road
Preston Pans E
Lothlan, SCOTLAND

Wood, Ted (Athlete, Baseball Player, Olympic Athlete)
1810 Beckley Pl NW
Kennesaw, GA 30152-4265, USA

Wood, Ted (Athlete, Baseball Player)
1810 Beckley Pl NW
Kennesaw, GA 30152, USA

Wood, Ted (Athlete, Baseball Player)
1810 Becklev Pl NW
Kennesaw, GA 30152-4265, USA

Wood, Ted (Athlete, Baseball Player, Olympic Athlete)
1810 Beckley Pl NW
Kennesaw, GA 30152-4265, USA

Wood, Thomas (Stylist)
c/o Staff Member *Blink Management*
421 Washington Ave
#202
Miami Beach, FL 33139, USA

Wood, Tom
6310 San Vicente Blvd. #520
Los Angeles, CA 90048

Wood, Wilbur F (Athlete, Baseball Player)
3 Elmbrook Rd
Bedford, MA 01730-1810, USA

Wood, William V (Athlete, Football Player)
7941 16th St NW
Washington, DC 20012, USA

Wood, William V (Willie) (Athlete, Football Player)
Willie Wood Mechanical Systems
7941 16th St NW
Washington, DC 20012, USA

Wood, Willie (Athlete, Golfer)
6120 Stonegate Pl
Edmond, OK 73025-2526, USA

Woodall, Al (Athlete, Football Player)
131 Field Crest Rd
New Canaan, CT 06840, USA

Woodall, Brad (Athlete, Baseball Player)
3539 John Muir Dr
Middleton, WI 53562, USA

Woodall, Brad (Athlete, Baseball Player)
3539 John Muir Dr
Middleton, WI 53562-5144, USA

Woodall, Jerry M (Engineer, Inventor)
Yale University
Microelectronic Materials Ctr
105 Wall
New Haven, CT 06511, USA

Woodall, Rob (Congressman, Politician)
1725 Longworth HOB
Washington, DC 20515, USA

Woodard, Alfre (Actor)
c/o Steve Dontanville *Circle of Confusion (NY)*
8609 E Washington Blvd #8607
Culver City, CA 90232, USA

Woodard, Bob (Writer)
2907 Q Street NW
Washington, DC 20007, USA

Woodard, Charlayne (Actor, Writer)
c/o Alan Harris *Alan M Harris Management*
517 Ocean Front Walk #11
Venice, CA 90291, USA

Woodard, Darrell (Athlete, Baseball Player)
1227 E 69th St
Los Angeles, CA 90001-1657, USA

Woodard, Lynette (Athlete, Basketball Player, Olympic Athlete)
4206 Quail Pointe Ter
Lawrence, KS 66047-1902, USA

Woodard, Mike (Athlete, Baseball Player)
P.O. Box 35
Maywood, IL 60153-0035, USA

Woodard, Ray (Athlete, Football Player)
RR 1 Box 208
Corrigan, TX 75939, USA

Woodard, Rickey (Musician)
JVC Music
3800 Barham Blvd
#409
Los Angeles, CA 90068, USA

Woodard, Steven L (Steve) (Athlete, Baseball Player)
800 Frost Ct SW
Hartselle, AL 35640-2714, USA

Woodbine, Bokeem (Actor)
c/o Johnny Gallo *Artist Representation Group*
9701 Wilshire Blvd.
10th Floor
Beverly Hills, CA 90212, USA

Woodbridge, Todd (Tennis Player)
Advantage International
PO Box 3297
North Burnley, VIC 3121, AUSTRALIA

Wood Brothers, The (Music Group)
c/o Staff Member *Paradigm (Monterey)*
404 W Franklin St
Monterey, CA 93940, USA

Woodburn, Danny (Actor)
c/o Marni Anhalt *Imperium 7 Talent Agency*
5455 Wilshire Blvd
Suite 1706
Los Angeles, CA 90036, USA

Woodcock, Leonard
2404 Vinewood
Ann Arbor, MI 48104

Woodcock, Leonard (Actor)
140 Matthew Drive
Hendersonville, NC 28739-9325, USA

Wooden, Shawn (Athlete, Football Player)
17741 SW 12th St
Pembroke Pines, FL 33029, USA

Woodeshivk, Tom (Athlete, Football Player)
P.O. Box 716
Blakeslee, PA 18610, USA

Woodforde, Mark (Athlete, Tennis Player)
c/o Staff Member *Octagon (VA)*
7100 Forest Ave #201
Richmond, VA 23226, USA

Woodhead, Cynthia (Swimmer)
PO Box 1193
Riverside, CA 92502, USA

Wood III, William B (Biologist)
University of Colorado
Molecular Biology Dept
Boulder, CO 80309, USA

Wooding, Michelle (Athlete, Golfer)
3825 E Camelback Rd
Apt 148
Phoenix, AZ 85018, USA

Wood Jr, Harlington (Judge)
US Court of Appeals
600 E Monroe St
Springfield, IL 62701, USA

Woodland, Lauren
c/o Jerry Shandrew *Shandrew Public Relations*
1050 S Stanley Ave
Los Angeles, CA 90019-6634, USA

Woodland, Rich (Race Car Driver)
Rich Woodland Racing
2000 Pitts School Rd
Concord, NC 28027, USA

Woodlawn, Holly
PO Box 27766
Los Angeles, CA 90027

Woodley, Dan
6347 S Yukon Ct
Littleton, CO 80123-3567, USA

Woodley, Shailene (Actor)
c/o Nils Larsen *Principato/Young Management*
312 W 5th St Apt 815
Los Angeles, CA 90013, USA

Woodlief, Doug (Athlete, Football Player)
7928 Wilkinson Ave
N Hollywood, CA 91605, USA

Woodmansee Jr, John W (General)
6609 Shady Creek Circle
Plano, TX 75024, USA

Woodring, Jim (Artist)
c/o Staff Member *Fantagraphics Books*
7563 Lake City Way
Seattle, WA 98115, USA

Woodring, Wendell P (Misc)
6647 El Colegio Road
Goleta, CA 93117, USA

Woodruff, Billie (Actor)
c/o Joe Gatta *Gersh (NY)*
41 Madison Ave
New York, NY 10010, USA

Woodruff, Blake (Actor)
c/o Justine Hunt *Hines and Hunt Entertainment*
1213 W Magnolia Blvd
Burbank, CA 91506, USA

Woodruff, Bob (Journalist)
c/o Staff Member *ABC News*
77 W 66th St
3rd Floor
New York, NY 10023, USA

Woodruff, Dwayne (Athlete, Football Player)
10382 Grubbs Rd
Wexford, PA 15090, USA

Woodruff, Frank
170 N. Crescent Dr.
Beverly Hills, CA 90210

Woodruff, Judy C (Correspondent, Television Host)
Cable News Network
News Dept
820 1st St NE
Washington, DC 20002, USA

Woods, Al (Athlete, Baseball Player)
2600 San Leandro
Blvd Act 1004
San Leandro, CA 94578-5032, USA

Woods, Al (Athlete, Baseball Player)
1315 148th Ave
San Leandro, CA 94578, USA

Woods, Aubrey (Actor)
James Sharkey
21 Golden Square
London W1R 3PA, UNITED KINGDOM (UK)

Woods, Barbara Alyn (Actor)
Honey Prod
2930 Falaise Ave SW
#H1
Calgary, AL T3E 7J2, CANADA

Woods, Chris (Athlete, Football Player)
202 Stone Ridge Trl
Birmingham, AL 35210, USA

Woods, Christine (Actor)
c/o Elizabeth Morris *Rogers & Cowan PR (LA)*
Pacific Design Center
8687 Melrose Ave, 7th Floor
West Hollywood, CA 90069, USA

Woods, Dan (Actor)
The Core Group Talent Agencies
89 Bloor St W 3rd Fl
Toronto, ON M5S 1M1, CANADA

Woods, Della (Race Car Driver)
302 Bellevue
Lake Orion, MI 48362, USA

Woods, Don (Athlete, Football Player)
10415 Johncock Ave SW
Albuquerque, NM 87121, USA

Woods, Elbert (Ickey) (Athlete, Football Player)
916 Surrey Trl
Cincinnati, OH 45245, USA

Woods, Gary (Athlete, Baseball Player)
P.O. Box 151
Solvang, CA 93464-0151, USA

Woods, George (Athlete, Track Athlete)
7631 Green Hedge Road
Edwardsville, IL 62025, USA

Woods, Jake (Athlete, Baseball Player)
1405 Mehlert St
Kingsburg, CA 93631-2423, USA

Woods, James (Actor)
c/o Chris Andrews *Creative Artists Agency (CAA-LA)*
2000 Ave Of The Stars
Los Angeles, CA 90067, USA

Woods, James A (Actor)
c/o Justin Evans *The Independent Group*
6363 Wilshire Blvd
Suite 115
Los Angeles, CA 90048, USA

Woods, Jerome (Athlete, Football Player)
1 Arrowhead Dr
Kansas City, KS 64129, USA

Woods, Jerry L (Athlete, Football Player)
8976 Stratford Ct
Minneapolis, MN 55443, USA

Woods, Jim (Athlete, Baseball Player)
4509 Gardenia Ave
Keyes, CA 95328-9701, USA

Woods, Michael (Actor)
c/o Staff Member *GVA Talent Agency Inc*
8981 Sunset Blvd.
Suite 101
Los Angeles, CA 90069, USA

Woods, Paul (Athlete, Hockey Player)
4276 S Shore St
Waterford, MI 48323-1157, USA

Woods, Paul (Athlete, Hockey Player)
Detroit Red Wings 600 Civic Center Dr
Attn Broadcast Dept
Detroit, MI 48226-4419, USA

Woods, Philip (Composer, Musician)
PO Box 278
Delaware Water Gap, PA 18327, USA

Woods, Pierre (Athlete, Football Player)
c/o Staff Member *New England Patriots*
1 Patriot Pl
Foxboro, MA 02035-1388, USA

Woods, Qyntel (Basketball Player)
Portland Trail Blazers
Rose Garden
1 Center Court St
Portland, OR 97227, USA

Woods, Rick (Athlete, Football Player)
713 Baldwin St
Meadville, PA 16335, USA

Woods, Robert E (Athlete, Football Player)
2002 Arden Landng Dr
Germantown, TN 38139, USA

Woods, Robert S (Actor)
ITA
227 Central Park W
#5A
New York, NY 10024, USA

Woods, Ron (Athlete, Baseball Player)
5209 Desert Star Dr
Las Vegas, NV 89130-0159, USA

Woods, Simon (Actor)
c/o Staff Member *ICM Partners (ICM-LA)*
10250 Constellation Blvd Fl 7
Los Angeles, CA 90067, USA

Woods, Stuart (Writer)
Harper Collins Publishers
10 E 53rd St
New York, NY 10022, USA

Woods, Tiger (Athlete, Golfer)
Tiger Woods Foundation
1 Tiger Woods Way
Anaheim, CA 92801, USA

Woods, Victoria (Musician)
c/o John Elias *Three Twins Entertainment, Inc*
PO Box 210
Staten Island, NY 10310, USA

Woodside, DB (Actor)
Paradigm Agency
10100 Santa Monica Blvd
#2500
Los Angeles, CA 90067, USA

Woodside, Keith (Football Player)
Green Bay Packers
1903 Laura Anne Dr
Houston, TX 77049-3832, USA

Woodson, Abraham B (Abe) (Football Player)
San Francisco 49ers
3680 Waynesvill St
Las Vegas, NV 89122-4111, USA

Woodson, Alli (Musician)
Superstars Unlimited
PO Box 371371
Las Vegas, NV 89137, USA

Woodson, Charles (Athlete, Football Player, Heisman Trophy Winner)
9080 Great Heron Cir
Orlando, FL 32836-5483, USA

Woodson, Darren (Athlete, Football Player)
6821 Memorial Dr
Frisco, TX 75034-7295, USA

Woodson, Dick (Athlete, Baseball Player)
27879 Panorama Hills Dr
Menifee, CA 92584-7401, USA

Woodson, Herbert H (Engineer)
1034 Libert Park Dr
Austin, TX 78746, USA

Woodson, Kerry (Athlete, Baseball Player)
19392 La Serena Dr
Fort Myers, FL 33967-0525, USA

Woodson, Michael (Mike) (Athlete, Basketball Player)
19918 Parsons Green Ct
Katy, TX 77450-5214, USA

Woodson, Robert L (Activist)
National Neighborhood Enterprise Center
1424 16th St NW
Washington, DC 20036, USA

Woodson, Rod (Athlete, Football Player)
c/o Eugene Parker *Maximum Sports Management*
6435 W Jefferson Blvd
#197
Fort Wayne, IN 46804, USA

Woodson, Sean (Athlete, Football Player)
1135 Ellis Ave
Jackson, MS 39209, USA

Woodson, Tracy (Athlete, Baseball Player)
1559 Byfield Pkwy
Valparaiso, IN 46385-9115, USA

Woodson, Warren V (Coach, Football Coach)
12680 Hillcrest Road
#1106
Dallas, TX 75230, USA

Woodville, Kate (Actor)
PO Box 6613
Malibu, CA 90264-6613, USA

Woodward, Bob (Writer)
c/o Staff Member *Simon & Schuster*
1230 Avenue of the Americas
New York, NY 10020, USA

Woodward, Chris (Athlete, Baseball Player)
1423 Ribolla Dr
Palm Harbor, FL 34683, USA

Woodward, Jim (Athlete, Golfer)
4205 NW 147th St
Oklahoma City, OK 73134, USA

Woodward, Joanne (Actor)
c/o Toni Howard *ICM Partners (ICM-LA)*
10250 Constellation Blvd Fl 7
Los Angeles, CA 90067, USA

Woodward, Kirsten (Designer, Fashion Designer)
Kirsten Woodward Hats
26 Portobello Green Arcade
London W10, UNITED KINGDOM (UK)

Woodward, Louise
Elton, ENGLAND

Woodward, Morgan (Actor)
2111 Rockledge Road
Los Angeles, CA 90068, USA

Woodward, Neil W Cdr (Astronaut)
1935 Edgemont Pl W
Seattle, WA 98199-3914, USA

Woodward, Peter (Actor)
c/o Vincent Cirrincione *Vincent Cirrincione Associates*
1516 N Fairfax Ave
Los Angeles, CA 90046, USA

Woodward, Rob (Athlete, Baseball Player)
58 Eastman Hill Rd
Lebanon, NH 03766-2103, USA

Woodward, Robert D (Bob) (Journalist)
3305 Old Point Rd
Washington, MD 21037-3110, USA

Woodward, Roger R (Composer, Conductor, Musician)
LH Productions
2/37 Hendy Ave
Coogee, NSW 2034, AUSTRALIA

Woodward, Shannon (Actor)
c/o Alissa Vradenburg *Untitled Entertainment (LA)*
350 S. Beverly Dr #200
Beverly Hills, CA 90212, USA

Woodward, Woody (Athlete, Baseball Player)
10 San Marco Ct
Palm Coast, FL 32137-2104, USA

Woodward III, Neil W (Astronaut)
5701 Ridgefield Road
Bethesda, MD 20816-1250, USA

Woodwell, George M (Scientist)
Woods Hole Research Center
13 Church St
Woods Hole, MA 02543, USA

Woody, Damien (Football Player)
New England Patriots
12170 Ashland Heights Rd
Ashland, VA 23005-7634, USA

Woody, Paul (Misc)
New Frontier Mgmt
1921 Broadway
Nashville, TN 37203, USA

Woody, Robert (General)
195 Rabbit Run
Hartwell, GA 30643-8616, USA

Woody, Woody (Athlete, Football Player)
9122 Weymouth Dr
Houston, TX 77031, USA

Woog, Doug (Athlete, Hockey Player)
433 Wentworth Ave
South St Paul, MN 55075-1602, USA

Woogon, Bill (Cartoonist)
2724 Cabot Court
Thousand Oaks, CA 91360, USA

Wool, Christopher (Artist)
Luhring Augustine Gallery
531 W 24th St
New York, NY 10011, USA

Wooldridge, Dean E (Business Person)
355 S Grand Ave
Suite 2600
Los Angeles, CA 90071-1505, USA

Woolery, Chuck (Actor, Television Host)
Chuck Woolery Signature Products
26135 Plymouth Road
Redford, MI 48239, USA

Woolfolk, Andre (Football Player)
Tennessee Titans
460 Great Circle Road
Nashville, TN 37228, USA

Woolfolk, Harold (Butch) (Football Player)
New York Giants
4519 Magnolia Ln
Sugar Land, TX 77478-5457, USA

Woolford, Donnell (Athlete, Football Player)
2925 Spur Avenue
Fayetteville, NC 28306-8387, USA

Woolford, Gary (Athlete, Football Player)
6321 S Four Peaks Place
Chandler, AZ 85249-3946, USA

Woollard, Bob (Athlete, Basketball Player)
166 Barnard Mill Rd
Hamptonville, NC 27020-7377, USA

Woolley, Catherine (Writer)
PO Box 67
Higgins Hollow Road
Orleans, MA 02653-0067, USA

Woolley, Jason (Athlete, Hockey Player)
4019 Quarton Rd
Bloomfield Hills, MI 48302-4061, USA

Woolley, Jordan (Actor)
c/o Suzanne Bennett-Harrison *Diverse Talent Group*
9911 W Pico Blvd Ste 340W
Los Angeles, CA 90035, USA

Woolley, Kenneth F (Architect)
790 George St
LV 5
Sydney, NSW 2000, AUSTRALIA

Woolley, Sheb
123 Walton Ferry Rd. #200
Hendersonville, TN 37075

Woolridge, Orlando (Athlete, Basketball Player)
308 Johnson St
Mansfield, LA 71052-3306, USA

Woolridge, Susan
4 Windmill St.
London, ENGLAND W1P 1HF

Woolsey, Elizabeth D (Skier)
Trail Creek Ranch
Wilson, WY 83014, USA

Woolsey, Ralph A (Cinematographer)
23388 Mulholland Dr
#109
Woodland Hills, CA 91364, USA

Woolsey, R James (Lawyer)
Shea & Gardner
1800 Massachusetts Ave NW
Washington, DC 20036, USA

Woolsey, Roland (Football Player)
Dallas Cowboys
10499 W Sultana Ln
Boise, ID 83714-3661, USA

Woolsey, William Tripp (Athlete, Olympic Athlete, Swimmer)
1032 Seascape Cir
Rodeo, CA 94572-1815, USA

Woolstenhulme, Rick (Musician)
c/o Staff Member *Untitled Entertainment (LA)*
350 S. Beverly Dr #200
Beverly Hills, CA 90212, USA

Woolwine, Chris (Race Car Driver)
Woolwine Motorsports
2705 61st St. #107
Galveston, TX 77551, USA

Woomble, Roddy (Musician)
Agency Group Ltd
370 City Road
London EC1V 2QA, UNITED KINGDOM (UK)

Woosnam, Ian H (Athlete, Golfer)
I M G
1360 E 9th St
Ste 100
Cleveland, OH 44114-1730, USA

Woosnam, Phil (Athlete, Misc)
2211 Mainsail Drive
Marietta, GA 30062-1765, USA

Wooten, Hubert (Daddy) (Athlete, Baseball Player)
120 Sandy Dr
Goldsboro, NC 27534-8803, USA

Wooten, Jim (Correspondent)
ABC-TV
News Dept
5010 Creston St
Hyattsville, MD 20781, USA

Wooten, John (Athlete, Football Player)
505 Boronia Road
Arlington, TX 76002-4515, USA

Wooten, Morgan (Coach)
De Matha High School
Athletic Dept
Hyattsville, MD 20781, USA

Wooten, Nicholas (Producer)
c/o Staff Member *WME (LA)*
9601 Wilshire Blvd Fl 3
Beverly Hills, CA 90210, USA

Wooten, Ron (Football Player)
New England Patriots
2401 Lewis Grove Ln
Raleigh, NC 27608-1380, USA

Wooten, Shawn (Athlete, Baseball Player)
17535 49th Ave N
Minneapolis, MN 55446-1741, USA

Wooten, Victor (Musician)
c/o Danetta Albetta *Monarch Music Inc*
1839 Gerritson Ave
Brooklyn, NY 11229, USA

Wooton, John (Football Player)
Cleveland Browns
13520 Darley Ave
Cleveland, OH 44110-2122, USA

Wootten, Morgan (Athlete, Basketball Player)
6912 Wells Pkwy
University Park, MD 20782, USA

Wootton, Charles G (Diplomat)
Chevron Corp
555 Market St
San Francisco, CA 94105, USA

Wopat, Tom (Actor, Musician)
c/o David Brokaw *Brokaw Company, The*
9255 Sunset Blvd
Suite 804
Los Angeles, CA 90069, USA

Word, Barry (Athlete, Football Player)
5746 Jannets Mill Circle
Haymarket, VA 20169-6196, USA

Word, Roscoe (Football Player)
New York Jets
175 Richardson Rd
Ridgeland, MS 39157-9781, USA

Word, Weldon R (Engineer)
633 Private Road 7908
Hawkins, TX 75765, USA

Worden, Al Colonel (Astronaut)
8960 Palm Breeze Ter
Vero Beach, FL 32963-3650, USA

Worden, Alfred M (Astronaut)
PO Box 8065
Vero Beach, FL 32963, USA

Worden, Neil (Football Player)
Philadelphia Eagles
2 Indian Camp Trl
Portage, IN 46368-1001, USA

Working Title, The (Music Group)
c/o Staff Member *Paradigm (Monterey)*
404 W Franklin St
Monterey, CA 93940, USA

Workman, Hank (Athlete, Baseball Player)
307 19th St
Santa Monica, CA 90402-2409, USA

Workman, Haywoode (Athlete, Basketball Player)
8350 Savannah Trace Cir #208
Tampa, FL 33615, USA

Workman, Jacque (Stylist)
8041 Van Nes Way
Indianapolis, IN 46240, USA

Workman, Tom (Athlete, Basketball Player)
422 NE Roth St
Portland, OR 97211-1084, USA

Workman, Vincent (Vince) (Athlete, Football Player)
1265 Brookwood Dr
Green Bay, WI 54304, USA

World Party (Music Group)
c/o Staff Member *Paradigm (Monterey)*
404 W Franklin St
Monterey, CA 93940, USA

Worlds Apart
PO Box 21
London, ENGLAND W10 6BR

World Wrestling Entertainment (WWE)
1241 E Main St
Stamford, CT 06902

Worley, Darryl (Musician)
c/o Randy Lovelady *RLM / Mission Management*
1102 17th Ave
Suite 402
Nashville, TN 37212, USA

Worley, Jo Anne (Actor)
c/o Staff Member *Amsel, Eisenstadt & Frazier Talent Agency (AEF)*
5055 Wilshire Blvd
Suite 860
Los Angeles, CA 90036-6108, USA

Worley, Tim (Athlete, Football Player)
531 Syndor Avenue
Rodgecrest, CA 93555-3143, USA

Wormald, Kenny (Actor)
c/o Dallas Sonnier *Caliber Media Company*
9229 W Sunset Blvd Ste 705
West Hollywood, CA 90069, USA

Worndl, Frank (Skier)
Burgsiedlung 19C
Sonthofen 87527, GERMANY

Woroniecka, Aleksandra (Stylist)
c/o Staff Member *Management + Artists + Organization*
330 W 38th St
#1401
New York, NY 10018, USA

Woronov, Mary (Actor)
4350 1/4 Beverly Blvd
Los Angeles, CA 90004, USA

Worrell, Mark (Athlete, Baseball Player)
712 SW 4th Ave
Boynton Beach, FL 33426-4770, USA

Worrell, Peter (Athlete, Hockey Player)
3707 Coral Tree Cir
Coconut Creek, FL 33073-4418, USA

Worrell, Tim (Athlete, Baseball Player)
4719 W El Cortez Pl
Phoenix, AZ 8S083-2206, USA

Worrell, Todd (Athlete, Baseball Player)
810 Simmons Ave
Saint Louis, MO 63122-2754, USA

Worth, Jody (Actor, Producer)
c/o Jeffrey Jacobs *Creative Artists Agency (CAA-LA)*
2000 Ave Of The Stars
Los Angeles, CA 90067, USA

Wortham, Barron (Athlete, Football Player)
8608 Busch Gardens Dr
Fort Worth, TX 76123-1445, USA

Wortham, Rich (Athlete, Baseball Player)
10247 Missel Thrush Dr
Austin, TX 78750, USA

Worthen, John E (Educator)
Ball State University
President's Office
Muncie, IN 47306, USA

Worthen, Sam (Athlete, Basketball Player)
Harlem Wizards
Harlem Wizards 36 Harmon Cove Tower
Ste 2
Secaucus, NJ 07094-1772, USA

Worthington, Al (Athlete, Baseball Player)
12070 Highwav 55
Sterrett, AL 35147-9601, USA

Worthington, Al (Athlete, Baseball Player)
12070 Highway 55
Sterrett, AL 35147, USA

Worthington, Cal
3815 Florin Rd.
Sacramento, CA 95823

Worthington, Craig (Athlete, Baseball Player)
10019 Mattock Ave
Downey, CA 90240-3528, USA

Worthington, Melvin L (Religious Leader)
Free Will Baptists
PO Box 5002
Antioch, TN 37011, USA

Worthington, Sam (Actor)
c/o Sandra Chang *Anonymous Content (LA)*
955 S Carrillo Dr
Suite 300
Los Angeles, CA 90048, USA

Worthy, Calum (Actor)
c/o Paul Young *Principato/Young Management*
9465 Wilshire Blvd
Suite 430
Beverly Hills, CA 90212, USA

Worthy, James (Athlete, Basketball Player, Sportscaster)
5750 Corbett St
Los Angeles, CA 90016-4545, USA

Worthy, Rick (Actor)
c/o Charles Silver *Silver Massetti & Szatmary (SMS) Talent Inc*
8383 Wilshire Blvd
Suite 230
Beverly Hills, CA 90211, USA

Wortman, Keith (Football Player)
Green Bay Packers
240 Big Sky Dr
Saint Charles, MO 63304-7170, USA

Wortman, Kevin (Athlete, Hockey Player)
42 David Dr
Saugus, MA 01906-1214, USA

Wottie, David J (Dave) (Athlete, Track Athlete)
9245 Forest Hill Lane
Germantown, TN 38139, USA

Wottle, Dave
9245 Forest Hill Lane
Germantown, TN 38139-7906

Wotton, Mark (Athlete, Hockey Player)
Pro-Rep Entertainment Consulting 113-276 Midpark Way SE
Attn Art Breeze
Calgarv, AB T2X 1J6, Canada

Wotus, Ron (Athlete, Baseball Player)
6 Monteira Ln
Martinez, CA 94553-9768, USA

Wouk, Herman (Writer)
303 Crestview Dr
Palm Springs, CA 92264-8920, USA

Wow, Bow (Actor, Musician)
2838 Grey Moss Pass
Duluth, GA 30097, USA

Woytowicz-Rudnicka, Stefania (Musician)
Al Przyiaciol 2 m
Warsaw 00-565, POLAND

Woywitka, Jeff (Athlete, Hockey Player)
RR 1
Mannville, AB TOB 2WO, Canada

Wozniacki, Caroline (Athlete, Tennis Player)
c/o Staff Member *Women's Tennis Association (WTA (US))*
One Progress Plaza
Ste 1500
St Petersburg, FL 33701, USA

Wozniak, Steve (Misc)
c/o Staff Member *Beverly Hecht Agency*
3500 W Olive Ave
Suite 1180
Burbank, CA 91505, USA

Wozniewski, Andy (Athlete, Hockey Player)
322 Lakeview Dr
Buffalo Grove, IL 60089-1788, USA

Wragg, John (Artist)
6 Castle Lane
Devizes
Wilts, SN10 1HJ, UNITED KINGDOM (UK)

Wrangler, Jack
41 W. 58th St. #5A
New York, NY 10019

Wray, Gordon R (Designer, Engineer)
Stonestack Rempstone
Loughborough
Leics LE12 6RH, UNITED KINGDOM (UK)

Wregget, Ken (Athlete, Hockey Player)
1778 McMillan Rd
Pittsburgh, PA 15241-2654, USA

Wren, Claire
5757 Wilshire Blvd. #473
Los Angeles, CA 90036

Wren, Darryl (Football Player)
New England Patriots
1418 Skipjack Dr
Fort Washington, MD 20744-4216, USA

Wren, Frank (Baseball Player)
500 Tuxedo Ln
Peachtree City, GA 30269-4070, USA

Wrenn, Peter (Horse Racer)
5215 Wren Ct
Carmel, IN 46033-9646, USA

Wrenn, Robert (Bob) (Athlete, Golfer)
8911 Alendale Rd
Richmond, VA 23229-7701, USA

Wressell, Christina (Stylist)
c/o Staff Member *Faucher Artists*
636 Broadway #1218
New York, NY 10012, USA

Wright, Alexander (Athlete, Football Player)
501 South Mississippi Street
Amarillo, TX 79106-8735, USA

Wright, Ben (Sportscaster)
CBS-TV
Sports Dept
51 W 52nd St
New York, NY 10019, USA

Wright, Betty (Musician)
Rodgers Redding
1048 Tatnall St
Macon, GA 31201, USA

Wright, Bonnie (Actor)
c/o Ruth Young *United Agents*
12-26 Lexington St
London W1F OLE, UK

Wright, Bracey (Basketball Player)
c/o Staff Member *Minnesota Timberwolves*
600 1st Avenue North
Minneapolis, MN 55403, USA

Wright, Brad (Athlete, Basketball Player)
1050 S Cloverdale Ave
Los Angeles, CA 90019-6732, USA

Wright, Bruce A (General)
Vice Commander
Air Combat Command
Langley Air Force Base, VA 23665, USA

Wright, Charles (Football Player)
St Louis Cardinals
2698 Wakefield Ave
Westlake, OH 44145-3837, USA

Wright, Chase (Athlete, Baseball Player)
6703 Kit Carson Trail
Wichita Falls, TX 76310, USA

Wright, Chely (Musician)
c/o Staff Member *Russell Carter Artist Management*
567 Ralph McGill Blvd NE
Atlanta, GA 30312-1110, USA

Wright, Clyde (Athlete, Baseball Player)
528 S Jeanine St
Anaheim, CA 92806-4415, USA

Wright, Craig M (Architect)
C M Wright Inc
706 N La Cienega Blvd
Los Angeles, CA 90069, USA

Wright, Dan (Athlete, Baseball Player)
310 Vernon Dr
Batesville, AR 72501-4112, USA

Wright, David (Athlete, Baseball Player)
1105 Hillston Ct
Chesapeake, VA 23322-9534, USA

Wright, Dick (Cartoonist)
Columbus Dispatch
Editorial Dept
34 S 3rd St
Columbus, OH 43215, USA

Wright, Donald C (Don) (Cartoonist)
PO Box 1176
Palm Beach, FL 33480, USA

Wright, Dorell (Athlete, Basketball Player)
158 Twin Peaks Dr
Walnut Creek, CA 94595-1728, USA

Wright, Doug (Writer)
c/o Staff Member *ICM Partners (ICM-NY)*
730 Fifth Ave
New York, NY 10019, USA

Wright, Elmo (Football Player)
Kansas City Chiefs
11419 Olympia Dr
Houston, TX 77077-6419, USA

Wright, Eric (Athlete, Football Player)
c/o Tony Fleming *Impact Sports - LA*
11331 Ventura Blvd Ste 1A
Studio City, CA 91604, USA

Wright, Evan (Writer)
c/o Susan Solomon *Principato/Young Management*
9465 Wilshire Blvd
Suite 430
Beverly Hills, CA 90212, USA

Wright, Felix (Football Player)
Cleveland Browns
2698 Wakefield Lane
Westlake, OH 44145-3837, USA

Wright, Felix E (Business Person)
Leggett & Platt Inc
1 Leggett Road
Carthage, MO 64836, USA

Wright, Geoffrey (Actor)
Innovative Artists
1505 10th St
Santa Monica, CA 90401, USA

Wright, George (Football Player)
Baltimore Colts
10627 Seaford Dr
Houston, TX 77089-1425, USA

Wright, George (Athlete, Baseball Player)
3306 Tranauility Dr
Arlington, TX 76016-2057, USA

Wright, Gerald (Director)
Guthrie Theatre
725 Vineland Place
Minneapolis, MN 55403, USA

Wright, Heather
1 Sunnyside Wimbledon
London, ENGLAND SW19

Wright, Howard (Athlete, Basketball Player)
3019 Kingswood Way
Louisville, KY 40216-4914, USA

Wright, Hugh (Musician)
William Morris Agency
2100 W End Ave
#1000
Nashville, TN 37203, USA

Wright, Ian (Television Host)
c/o Staff Member *Arena Entertainment Consultants*
Regent's Court
39 Harrogate Rd
Leeds LS7 3PD, UK

Wright, Irving S (Doctor)
25 E End Ave
New York, NY 10028, USA

Wright, James E (Historian)
7 Quall Dr
Etna, NH 03750, USA

Wright, Jamey (Athlete, Baseball Player)
4325 Fairfax Ave
Dallas, TX 75205-3026, USA

Wright, Jaret (Athlete, Baseball Player)
23 Calle Viviana
San Clemente, CA 92673-7049, USA

Wright, Jay (Writer)
General Delivery
Piermont, NH 03779, USA

Wright, Jeff (Football Player)
Minnesota Vikings
6341 Rolf Ave
Edina, MN 55439-1434, USA

Wright, Jeff (Athlete, Football Player)
23426 North 21st Place
Phoenix, AZ 85024-8631, USA

Wright, Jeffrey (Actor)
c/o Jimmy Darmody *Creative Artists Agency (CAA-LA)*
2000 Ave Of The Stars
Los Angeles, CA 90067, USA

Wright, Jim (Athlete, Baseball Player)
513 W Wyndermere Ct
Peoria, IL 61614-2919, USA

Wright, Jim (Athlete, Baseball Player)
549 E Randall St
Coopersville, MI 49404-9649, USA

Wright, Joby (Athlete, Basketball Player)
University of Wyoming
P.O. Box 3434
Athletic Dept
Laramie, WY 82071, USA

Wright, John (Athlete, Hockey Player)
116 Hillsdale Ave W
Toronto, ON M5P 1G5, Canada

Wright, Johnny (Producer)
Wright Entertainment Group
7680 Universal Blvd Ste 500
Orlando, FL 32819, USA

Wright, J Oliver (Diplomat)
Burstow Hall
Hortey
Surrey H6 9SR, USA

Wright, Joseph "Joby" (Athlete, Basketball Player)
5608 Woodworth Way
Indianapolis, IN 46237-3168, USA

Wright, Judith A (Writer)
17 Devonport St
#1
Lyons, ACT 2060, AUSTRALIA

Wright, Julian (Athlete, Basketball Player)
212 Forest Oaks Dr
New Orleans, LA 70131-3376, USA

Wright, Keith (Athlete, Football Player)
17750 County Road 605
Farmersville, TX 75442-6895, USA

Wright, Keith (Athlete, Hockey Player)
78 Malvern Ave
Toronto, ON M4E 3ES, Canada

Wright, Ken (Athlete, Baseball Player)
1651 Ora Dr
Pensacola, FL 32506-8250, USA

Wright, Larry (Athlete, Basketball Player)
17 Vester Oaks Dr
West Monroe, LA 71291-7812, USA

Wright, Larry (Athlete, Hockey Player)
Regina Fire Dept PO Box 1790
Regina, SK S4P 3C8, Canada

Wright, Lawrence A (Judge)
US Tax Court
400 2nd St NW
Washington, DC 20217, USA

Wright, Louie (Football Player)
Denver Broncos
2263 S Quentin Way # 301
Aurora, CO 80014-7316, USA

Wright, Louis B (Historian)
3702 Leland St
Chevy Chase, MD 20815, USA

Wright, Louis D (Football Player)
Digi-Tec
Seismic Corp
3140 S Peoria St #K274
Aurora, CO 80014, USA

Wright, Margaret H (Mathematician)
AT&T Bell Lucent Laboratory
600 Mountain Ave
New Providence, NJ 07974, USA

Wright, Max (Actor)
Bresler Kelly Assoc
11500 W Olympic Blvd
#510
Los Angeles, CA 90064, USA

Wright, Michael (Actor)
c/o Steven Arcieri *Arcieri & Associates Inc*
305 Madison Ave
Suite 2315
New York, NY 10165, USA

Wright, Michael W (Business Person)
Super Valu Inc
11840 Valley View Road
Eden Prairie, MN 55344, USA

Wright, Michelle (Musician)
Savannah Music
205 Powell Place
#214
Brentwood, TN 37027, USA

Wright, Mickey
2972 SE Treasure Island Rd
Port St. Lucie, FL 34952-5773

Wright, Mickey (Athlete, Golfer)
2972 SE Treasure Island Rd
Port Saint Lucie, FL 34952, USA

Wright, Mike (Athlete, Football Player)
c/o Staff Member *New England Patriots*
1 Patriot Pl
Foxboro, MA 02035-1388, USA

Wright, Nathaniel (Nate) (Football Player)
Atlanta Falcons
11247 Zorita Court
San Diego, CA 92124-2207, USA

Wright, N'Bushe
1505 10th St.
Santa Monica, CA 90401

Wright, Pamela (Athlete, Golfer)
11333 N 92nd St
Unit 2006
Scottsdale, AZ 85260, USA

Wright, Pat (Musician)
Superstars Unlimited
PO Box 371371
Las Vegas, NV 89137, USA

Wright, Peter R (Choreographer, Dancer)
10 Chiswick Wharf
London W4 2SR, UNITED KINGDOM (UK)

Wright, Petra (Actor)
c/o Bob Glennon *One Talent Management*
9220 Sunset Blvd
Los Angeles, CA 90069, USA

Wright, Randy (Football Player)
Green Bay Packers
3591 Richie Rd
Verona, WI 53593-9649, USA

Wright, Raymond R (War Hero)
10 Holt Circle
Fletcher, NC 28732, USA

Wright, Rick (Musician)
Agency Group
370 City Road
London EC1V 2QA, UNITED KINGDOM (UK)

Wright, Ricky (Athlete, Baseball Player)
2502 Clark Ln
Paris, TX 75460-6220, USA

Wright, Robin (Actor, Producer)
c/o Michael Sugar *Anonymous Content (LA)*
3531 Hayden Ave
Culver City, CA 90232, USA

Wright, Ron (Athlete, Baseball Player)
310 S 2100 E
Saint George, UT 84790-1465, USA

Wright, Ronald (Winkie) (Boxer)
c/o James Prince *Prince Boxing Enterprises*
3030 Jensen Dr
Houston, TN 77026, USA

Wright, Roy (Athlete, Baseball Player)
331 Pinehurst Cir
Chickamauga, GA 30707-1459, USA

Wright, Samuel E (Actor)
c/o Marvin Josephson *Marvin A Josephson Management*
16 West 22nd Street
New York, NY 10010, USA

Wright, Sarah (Actor)
c/o Ellen Meyer *Ellen Meyer Management*
8899 Beverly Blvd
Suite 612
West Hollywood, CA 90048, USA

Wright, Sharone (Athlete, Basketball Player)
6080 Lakeview Rd Apt 3504
Warner Robins, GA 31088-9157, USA

Wright, Stephen T (Athlete, Football Player)
14 Cinifer Square
Augusta, GA 30909-4505, USA

Wright, Steve (Athlete, Football Player)
15 Camel Point Dr
Laguna Beach, CA 92651, USA

Wright, Steven (Actor, Comedian)
c/o Tim Sarkes *Brillstein Entertainment Partners*
9150 Wilshire Blvd #350
Beverly Hills, CA 90212, USA

Wright, Tom (Athlete, Baseball Player)
1116 Poplar Springs Church Rd
Shelby, NC 28152-8071, USA

Wright, Tom (Actor)
c/o Steven Siebert *Lighthouse Entertainment*
9220 W Sunset Blvd Ste 200
West Hollywood, CA 90069, USA

Wright, Trevor (Actor)
c/o Tiffany Kuzon *Evolution Entertainment (LA)*
901 N Highland Ave
Los Angeles, CA 90038, USA

Wright, Tyler (Athlete, Hockey Player)
Columbus Blue Jackets 200 W
Nationwide Blvd Unit 1
Attn Coaching Staff
Columbus, OH 43215-2564, USA

Wright, Van Earl (Actor)
c/o Jill Smoller WME (LA)
9601 Wilshire Blvd Fl 3
Beverly Hills, CA 90210, USA

Wright, Weldon (Athlete, Football Player)
701 E Bluff St
Apt 6406
Fort Worth, TX 76102-2372, USA

Wright, Wesley (Athlete, Baseball Player)
9661 Colleton Pl
Montgomery, AL 36117-8458, USA

Wright, Willie (Athlete, Football Player)
13456 Dry Gulch Road
Paonia, CO 81428-7119, USA

Wright Jr, Charles P (Writer)
940 Locust Ave
Charlottesville, VA 22901, USA

Wright Jr, John M (General)
21227 George Brown Ave
Riverside, CA 92518, USA

Wrightman, Tim (Football Player)
Chicago Bears
3505 S Dension Ave
San Pedro, CA 90731-6803, USA

Wrightson, Bernard (Bernie) (Swimmer)
924 Birch Ave
Escondido, CA 92027, USA

Wrigley, Edward A (Historian)
13 Sedley Taylor Rd
Cambridge CB2 2PW, UNITED
KINGDOM (UK)

Wrigley Jr, William (Business Person)
William Wrigley Jr Co
410 N Michigan Ave
Chicago, IL 60611, USA

Wrona, Rick (Athlete, Baseball Player)
2946 E 57th St
Tulsa, OK 74105-7404, USA

Wszola, Jacek (Athlete, Track Athlete)
Ul Chrzanowskiego 7 m 70
Warsaw 04-381, POLAND

Wu, Alice (Writer)
c/o Staff Member Creative Artists Agency
(CAA-LA)
2000 Ave Of The Stars
Los Angeles, CA 90067, USA

Wu, David (Congressman, Politician)
2338 Rayburn HOB
Washington, DC 20515, USA

Wu, Gordon Y S (Business Person)
Hopewell Holdings
Hopewell Center
183 Queen Road East
Hong Kong, CHINA

Wu, Kristy (Actor)
c/o Craig Dorfman Frontline Management
5670 Wilshire Blvd.
Suite 1370
Los Angeles, CA 90036, USA

Wu, Lisa (Reality TV Star)
c/o Staff Member Bravo (NY)
30 Rockefeller Plaza
New York, NY 10112, USA

Wu, Madame Sylvia
1515 N. Capri Dr.
Pacific Palisades, CA 90272

Wu, Sau Lan (Physicist)
35 Robinson St
Cambridge, MA 02138, USA

Wu, Tai Tsun (Physicist)
35 Robinson St
Cambridge, MA 02138, USA

Wu, Vivian (Actor)
McKeon-Myones Management
c/o Laura Myones
9100 Wilshire Blvd Ste 350W
Beverly Hills, CA 90212, USA

Wudunn, Sheryl (Journalist)
35 W 89th St
New York, NY 10024-2016, USA

Wuerffel, Danny (Athlete, Football Player,
Heisman Trophy Winner)
424 Mimosa Dr
Decatur, GA 30030-3736, USA

Wuertz, Michael (Athlete, Baseball
Player)
15029 N Thompson
Peak Pkwy Ste B111
Scottsdale, AZ 85260-2223, USA

Wuethrich, Kurt (Nobel Prize Laureate)
Federal Institute of Technology
ETH Zentrum
Zurich 8092, SWITZERLAND

Wuhl, Robert (Actor)
10590 Holman Ave
Los Angeles, CA 90024, USA

Wuhrer, Kari (Actor, Musician)
PO Box 69188
Los Angeles, CA 90069, USA

Wunderle, Victor (Archer, Athlete,
Olympic Athlete)
5928 N CR 300 E
Mason City, IL 62664-7412, USA

Wunderlich, Paul (Artist)
Haynstr 2
Hamburg 20949, GERMANY

Wunsch, Carl I (Oceanographer)
78 Washington Ave
Cambridge, MA 02140, USA

Wunsch, Jerry (Football Player)
Tampa Bay Buccaneers
2601 Red Maple Rd
Wausau, WI 54401-9151, USA

Wunsch, Kelly (Athlete, Baseball Player)
11613 Hunters Green Trl
Austin, TX 78732-2055, USA

Wuorinen, Charles P (Composer)
Howard Stokar Mgmt
870 W End Ave
New York, NY 10025, USA

Wurtzel, Elizabeth (Actor, Writer)
c/o Staff Member Artist Agency, THE (NY)
230 W 55th St #29D
New York, NY 10019

Wurz, Alexander (Race Car Driver)
McLaren Int'l Working Park
Albert Dr
Woking
Surrey GU21 5JY, UNITED KINGDOM
(UK)

Wu-Tang
BMG/RCA
1540 Broadway #3500
New York, NY 10036

Wuthrich, Kurt (Nobel Prize Laureate)
Swiss Fe^erallnstitute of T^chnology ETH
Hvng_gerberg HPK
Zurich, CH-8093, Switzerland

Wuycik, Dennis (Athlete, Basketball
Player)
31 Rogerson Dr
Chapel Hill, NC 27517-4037, USA

Wu Yigong (Director)
52 Yong Fu Road
Shanghai, CHINA

Wyant, Fred (Football Player)
Washington Redskins
516 Westwood Ave
Morgantown, WV 26505-2125, USA

Wyatt, Alvin (Football Player)
Oakland Raiders
PO Box 244
Daytona Beach, FL 32115-0244, USA

Wyatt, Doug (Athlete, Football Player)
23 Andante Trail Pl
Shenandoah, TX 77381-2775, USA

Wyatt, Jennifer (Golfer)
Carolina Group
2321 Devine St
#A
Columbia, SC 29205, USA

Wyatt, Keke (Musician)
Universal Attractions
145 W 57th St
#1500
New York, NY 10019, USA

Wyatt, Leslie (Educator)
Arkansas State University
President's Office
State University, AR 72467, USA

Wyatt, Shannon (Actor)
8949 Falling Creek Court
Annandale, VA 22003, USA

Wyatt, Sharon (Actor)
16830 Ventura Blvd
#300
Encino, CA 91436, USA

Wyatt, Summer (Beauty Pageant Winner)
2015 Unity Rd
Princeton, WV 24740, USA

Wyatt Jr, Oscar S (Business Person)
Coastal Corp
6955 Union Park Ave
#540
Midvale, UT 84047, USA

Wyche, Samuel D (Sam) (Athlete, Coach,
Football Coach, Football Player,
Sportscaster)
P.O. Box 1570
Pickens, SC 29671, USA

Wycheck, Frank (Football Player)
4674 Sunrise Ave
Bensalem, PA 19020, USA

Wycinsky, Craig (Football Player)
Cleveland Browns
6890 E Sunrise Dr Ste 120
Tucson, AZ 85750-0739, USA

Wycoff, Brooks (Athlete)
1 Mohegan Sun Blvd
Uncasville, CT 06382

Wyden, Ron (Politician)
312 A St NE
Washington, DC 20002-5938, USA

Wyeth, James Browning "Jamie" (Artist)
Jamie Wyeths Editions
Lookout Farm 701 Smiths Bridge Rd
Wilmington, DE 19807-1325, USA

Wygal, Terry (Business Person)
Express Home Solutions Ltd
3005 Woodland Hills
Kingwood, TX 77339, USA

Wylde, Chris
3313 1/2 Barham Blvd.
Los Angeles, CA 90068

Wylde, Peter (Athlete, Horse Racer,
Olympic Athlete)
247 Wood Dale Dr
Wellington, FL 33414-4719, USA

Wylde, Zakk (Musician)
31329 Sloan Canyon Rd
Castaic, CA 91384, USA

Wylde Bunch, The (Music Group)
c/o Staff Member Paradigm (Monterey)
404 W Franklin St
Monterey, CA 93940, USA

Wyle, Noah (Actor, Director, Producer)
3065 Long Canyon Rd
Santa Ynez, CA 93460, USA

Wylie, Adam
14011 Ventura Blvd. #202
Sherman Oaks, CA 91423

Wylie, Joe (Athlete, Football Player)
8312 Bucknell Dr
Tyler, TX 75703-5103, USA

Wylie, Paul (Athlete, Figure Skater,
Olympic Athlete)
9819 Deer Brook Ln
Charlotte, NC 28210-8144, USA

Wyludda, Ilke (Athlete, Track Athlete)
LAC Chemnitz
Relchengainer Str 154
Chemnitz 09125, GERMANY

Wyman, Bill (Actor, Composer, Musician)
Ripple Productions
344 Kings Road
London SW3 5UR, United Kingdom

Wyman, David (Football Player)
Seattle Seahawks
2114 204th Pl NE
Sammamish, WA 98074-4390, USA

Wyman, Joel (Producer, Writer)
c/o Staff Member Creative Artists Agency
(CAA-LA)
2000 Ave Of The Stars
Los Angeles, CA 90067, USA

Wymore, Patrice (Actor)
Port Antonio
JAMAICA BWI, WEST INDIES

Wynalda, Eric (Soccer Player)
2313 Stomcroft Court
Westlake Village, CA 91361, USA

Wynant, H M
300 S Raymond Ave #11
Pasadena, CA 91105, USA

Wyn-Davies, Geraint (Actor)
Oscars Abrams Zimel
438 Queen St E
Toronto, ON M5A 1T4, CANADA

Wynder, A J (Athlete, Basketball Player)
1 Cardenti Ct
Newark, DE 19702-6833, USA

Wynegar, Butch (Athlete, Baseball Player)
P.O. Box 915811
Longwood, FL 32791-5811, USA

Wyner, George (Actor)
3450 Laurie Place
Studio City, CA 91604, USA

Wyngaarden, James B (Doctor)
NAS
2101 Columbus Ave NW
Washington, DC 20418, USA

Wynn, Bob (Athlete, Golfer)
78455 Calle Orense
La Quinta, CA 92253-2370, USA

Wynn, Jimmy (Athlete, Baseball Player)
5507 Sandy Field Ct
Rosharon, TX 77583-2040, USA

Wynn, Renaldo (Football Player)
Jacksonville Jaguars
19805 Rothschild Court
Ashburn, VA 20147-4124, USA

Wynn, Spergon (Football Player)
Cleveland Browns
614 32nd St
Galveston, TX 77550-1325, USA

Wynn, Stephen (Misc)
PO Box 93598
Las Vegas, NV 89193-3598, USA

Wynn, Stephen A (Business Person)
Wynn Las Vegas
3131 Las Vegas Blvd S
Las Vegas, NV 89109, USA

Wynn, Steve (Business Person)
Wynn Las Vegas
3131 Las Vegas Blvd S
Las Vegas, NV 89109

Wynn, Tracy Keenan
700 W. Third St.
Los Angeles, CA 90048

Wynne, Billy (Athlete, Baseball Player)
7722 Greenwich Ct W
Jacksonville, FL 32277-0924, USA

Wynne, Marvell (Athlete, Baseball Player)
39640 Del Val Dr
Murrieta, CA 92562-4038, USA

Wynorski, Jim (Director, Producer)
19653 Schoenborn St
Northridge, CA 91324, USA

Wynter, Sarah (Actor)
2443 Solar Dr
Los Angeles, CA 90046, USA

Wyrozub, Randy (Athlete, Hockey Player)
6717 Westminster Dr
East Amherst, NY 14051-2805, USA

Wysocki, Ben (Musician)
4500 W 30th Ave
Denver, CO 80212, USA

Wyss, Amanda (Actor)
c/o Staff Member *Badgley-Connor-King*
9229 Sunset Blvd.
Suite 311
Los Angeles, CA 90069, USA

Xiaoshuang, Li
Rue Tiyukuan 9
Beijing, Peoples Republic of China

Xie Bingxin (Writer)
Central Nationalities Institute
Residential Qtrs
Beijing 100081, CHINA

Xie Jin (Director)
Shanghai Film Studio
595 Caoxi Beilu
Shanghai, CHINA

Xscape (Musician)
c/o Staff Member *So So Def Recordings Inc*
1350 Spring St NW #750
Atlanta, GA 30309-2870, USA

Xu Bing (Artist)
540 Metropolitan Ave
Brooklyn, NY 11211, USA

Xuereb, Emanuel (Actor)
c/o Staff Member *Pantheon Talent*
1900 Ave Of The Stars
Suite 2840
Los Angeles, CA 90067, USA

Xuereb, Salvator (Actor)
c/o Martin Berneman *Precision Entertainment*
6338 Wilshire Blvd
Los Angeles, CA 90048, USA

Xue Wei (Musician)
134 Sheaveshill Ave
London NW9, UNITED KINGDOM (UK)

Xu Shuyang (Artist)
Zheijang Academy of Fine Arts
PO Box 169
Hangzhou, CHINA

Xzibit (Musician)
c/o John Boyle *Sanctuary Artist Management*
8750 Wilshire Blvd Ste 200
Beverly Hills, CA 90211, USA

Yabians, Frank (Producer)
88 Bull Path
East Hampton, NY 11937, USA

Yablans, Frank
100 Bull Path
East Hampton, NY 11937-4601

Yablokov, Alexey V (Biologist)
Koltsove Biology Institute
Vaviloca Str 26
Moscow 117808, RUSSIA

Yablonski, Jeremy (Athlete, Hockey Player)
11646 W Fenchurch St
Boise, ID 83709-4471, USA

Yabu, Keiichi (Athlete, Baseball Player)
c/o Team Member *San Francisco Giants*
SBC Park
24 Willie Mays Plaza
San Francisco, CA 94107, USA

Yachmenev, Vitali (Athlete, Hockey Player)
1485 Gulf of Mexico Dr Unit 104
Longboat Key, FL 34228-3472, USA

Yaeger, Andrea (Tennis Player)
1490 S Ute Ave
Aspen, CO 81611, USA

Yaffe, Martin (Physicist)
University of Toronto
Biophysics Dept
Toronto, ON M4W 1J3, CANADA

Yager, Faye (Activist)
Children of the Underground
902 Curlew Court NW
Atlanta, GA 30327, USA

Yager, Rick (Cartoonist)
North American Syndicate
235 E 45th St
New York, NY 10017, USA

Yagher, Jeff
15057 Sherview Pl.
Sherman Oaks, CA 91403

Yago, Gideon (Journalist, Television Host)
c/o Staff Member *Music Television (MTV) Networks (NY)*
1515 Broadway
New York, NY 10036, USA

Yaguda, Stan (Musician)
Joyce Agency
370 Harrison Ave
Harrison, NY 10528, USA

Yagudin, Alexei (Figure Skater)
Connecticut Skating Center
300 Alumini Road
Newington, CT 06111, USA

Yahr, Betty (Athlete, Baseball Player)
10360 Timber Ridge Drive
Milan, MI 48160-8929, USA

Yakavonis, Ray (Athlete, Football Player)
8 Strand St
Hanover Township, PA 18706, USA

Yake, Terry (Athlete, Hockey Player)
7827 Wind Hill Dr
0 Fallon, MO 63368-4135, USA

Yakovlev, Aleksandr N (Government Official)
Prisoner Rehabilitation Commission
Ul Iljinka 8/4
Moscow 103132, RUSSIA

Yale, Brian (Musician)
c/o Staff Member *Creative Artists Agency (CAA-LA)*
2000 Ave Of The Stars
Los Angeles, CA 90067, USA

Yaleborough, Cale (Race Car Driver)
2723 Palmetto
Unit B
Florence, SC 29501, USA

Yallop, Frank (Coach)
San Jose Earthquakes
3550 Stevens Creek Blvd
#200
San Jose, CA 95117, USA

Yalow, Roslyn
3242 Tibbett Ave.
Bronx, NY 10463-3801

Yamagata, Hiro (Artist)
1080 Ave D
Redondo Beach, CA 90277, USA

Yamagata, Rachel (Musician)
c/o Staff Member *Paradigm (Monterey)*
404 W Franklin St
Monterey, CA 93940, USA

Yamaguchi, Kristi (Athlete, Figure Skater, Olympic Athlete)
Always Dream Foundation
1203 Preservation Parkway #102
Oakland, CA 94612, USA

Yamaguchi, Roy (Business Person)
Roy's Restaurant
Kai Corporate Plaza
6600 Kalaniaole Hwy
Honolulu, HI 96825, USA

Yamame, Marlene Mitsuko (Actor)
Herb Tannen
10801 National Blvd
#101
Los Angeles, CA 90064, USA

Yamamoto, Keith R (Biologist)
332 Douglass St
San Francisco, CA 94114, USA

Yamamoto, Kenichi (Business Person)
Mazda Motor Corp
4-6-19 Funairi-Minami
Minamiku
Hiroshima, JAPAN

Yamamoto, Takuma (Business Person)
Fujitsu Ltd
1-6-1 Marunouchi
Chiyodaku
Tokyo 100, JAPAN

Yamamoto, Yohji (Designer, Fashion Designer)
14-15 Conduit St
London W1R 9TG, UNITED KINGDOM (UK)

Yamanaka, Tsuyoshi (Swimmer)
6-10-33-212 Akasaka
Minatoku
Tokyo, JAPAN

Yamani, Sheikh Ahmed Zaki (Government Official)
Chermignon near Crans-Montana
Valais, SWITZERLAND

Yamaoka, Seigen H (Religious Leader)
Buddhist Churches of America
1710 Octavia St
San Francisco, CA 94109, USA

Yamasaki, Taro M (Journalist)
People Magazine Editorial Dept
Time-Life Building
New York, NY 10020, USA

Yamashita, Yasuhiro (Athlete, Coach)
1117 Kitakaname
Hitatsuka Kanagawa 259-1207, JAPAN

Yamazaki, Naoko (Astronaut)
500 Blue Dolphin Drive
Seabrook, TX 77586, USA

Yamin, Elliott (Actor, Musician)
c/o Mark Gorlick *Collective*
8383 Wilshire Blvd
Suite 1050
Beverly Hills, CA 90211, USA

Yan, Esteban (Athlete, Baseball Player)
851 60th Ave S
st Petersburg, FL 33705-5533, USA

Yancey, Emily
247 S. Beverly Dr. #102
Beverly Hills, CA 90212

Yanchar, William (Athlete, Football Player)
P.O. Box 460141
Aurora, CO 80046, USA

Yancy, Emily (Actor)
Henderson/Hogan
8285 W Sunset Blvd
#1
West Hollywood, CA 90046, USA

Yancy, Hugh (Athlete, Baseball Player)
1708 Marilyn Ave
Bradenton, FL 34207-4633, USA

Yandle, Keith (Athlete, Hockey Player)
646 Canton Ave
Milton, MA 02186-3133, USA

Yandle, Leigh Ann (Stylist)
c/o Staff Member *The Talent Connection*
338 N Elm St
#204
Greensboro, NC 27401, USA

Yanez, Eduardo (Actor)
c/o Thomas Richards *Corsa Agency, The*
11704 Wilshire Blvd #204
Los Angeles, CA 90025, USA

Yang, Chen Ning (Nobel Prize Laureate)
8 Dorfer Ln
Nesconset, NY 11767-1067, USA

Yang, Jeanne (Stylist)
c/o Staff Member *Cloutier Agency*
2632 La Cienega Ave
Los Angeles, CA 90034, USA

Yang, Jerry (Misc)
40380 River Estate Dr
Madera, CA 93636-9522, USA

Yang, Jerry (Business Person, Engineer)
Yahoo!
701 First Ave
Sunnyvale, CA 94089, USA

Yang, Liwei (Misc)
Satellite Launch Center
Jiuquan
Gansu Province, CHINA

Yang, Young A (Athlete, Golfer)
4805 Lyons View Pike
Apt 302
Knoxville, TN 37919, USA

Yankee, Daddy (Musician)
c/o Lizzie Grubman *Lizzie Grubman Public Relations*
270 Lafayette St
Suite 504
New York, NY 10012, USA

Yankelovich, Daniel (Scientist)
Public Agenda Foundation
6 E 39th St
#900
New York, NY 10016, USA

Yankovic, Al (Weird Al) (Actor, Comedian, Musician, Songwriter)
Close Personal Friends Of Al
8033 Sunset Blvd
#4018
Los Angeles, CA 90046, USA

Yankovsky, Oleg I (Actor)
Komsomolsky Prospekt 41
#10
Moscow 119270, RUSSIA

Yankowski, George (Athlete, Baseball Player)
12 Potter Pond
Lexington, MA 02421-8243, USA

Yankowski, Ron (Athlete, Football Player)
1318 Saint Paul Rd
Ballwin, MO 63021, USA

Yannas, I V (Engineer, Scientist)
Massachusetts Institute of Technology
Engineering School
Cambridge, MA 02139, USA

Yanni (Musician, Songwriter)
PO Box 107
8983 Okeechobee Blvd #202
West Palm Beach, FL 33402, USA

Yanofsky, Charles (Scientist)
725 Mayfield Ave
Stanford, CA 94305-1016, USA

Yanofsky, Charles (Biologist)
725 Mayfield Ave
Stanford, CA 94305, USA

Yao, Andrew (Mathematician)
Princeton University
Mathematics Dept
Princeton, NJ 08544, USA

Yaralian, Zaven (Athlete, Football Player)
PO Box 1080
Summerland, CA 93067-1080, USA

Yarber, Eric (Athlete, Football Player)
Oregon State University
325 Valley Football Ctr
Attn: Football Program
Corvallis, OR 97331, USA

Yarborough, Glenn
PO Box 158
Malibu, CA 90265-0158

Yarborough, W Caleb (Cale) (Race Car Driver)
Yarborough Racing
2723 W Palmetto St
Florence, SC 29501, USA

Yarborough, William P (General)
3525 Slade Run Drive
Falls Church, VA 22042-3923, USA

Yarbrough, Cedric (Actor)
c/o Jenni Weinman *Patricola Lust PR*
9171 Wilshire Blvd
Suite 441
Beverly Hills, CA 90210, USA

Yarbrough, Curtis (Religious Leader)
General Baptists Assn
100 Stinson Dr
Poplar Bluff, MO 63901, USA

Yarbrough, Glenn (Musician, Songwriter, Writer)
150 Avenida Presidio
San Clemente, CA 92672, USA

Yarbrough, Jim (Athlete, Football Player)
720 N Phelps Ave
Winter Park, FL 32789, USA

Yarbrough, Jim (Athlete, Football Player)
440 Capricorn St
Cedar Hill, TX 75104, USA

Yard, Mollie
1000 16th St. W
Washington, DC

Yardbirds, The
PO Box 1821
Ojai, CA 93024

Yared, Gabriel (Composer)
c/o Staff Member *Evolution Music Partners*
1680 N. Vine St.
Hollywood, CA 90028, USA

Yaremchuk, Gary (Athlete, Hockey Player)
408 Crimson Dr
Sherwood Park, AB T8H OH2, Canada

Yarkin, Cori (Musician)
GreeneHouse Management
c/o Allan Greene
PO Box 151234
Altamonte Springs, FL 32715-1234, USA

Yarlett, Claire (Actor)
c/o Lorraine Berglund *Lorraine Berglund Management*
11537 Hesby St.
North Hollywood, CA 91601, USA

Yarmuth, John (Congressman, Politician)
435 Cannon HOB
Washington, DC 20515, USA

Yarmuth, John A (Congressman, Politician)
Romano Mazzoli Federal Building
600 Martin Luther King, Jr. Pl, Suite 216
Louisville, KY 40202, USA

Yarnall, Celeste (Actor)
2899 Agoura Road
#315
Westlake, CA 91361, USA

Yarnall, Ed (Athlete, Baseball Player)
9837 Vouvrav Dr
Baton Rouge, LA 70817-7646, USA

Yarnell, Ed (Athlete, Baseball Player)
9837 Vouray Dr
Baton Rouge, LA 70817, USA

Yarno, George (Athlete, Football Player)
1081 White Pine Flats Rd
Troy, ID 83871, USA

Yarno, John (Athlete, Football Player)
10535 158th Ave NE
Redmond, WA 98052, USA

Yarritu, David (Stylist)
c/o Staff Member *Pat Bates & Associates*
300 W 12th St
New York, NY 10014, USA

Yarrow, Peter (Musician, Songwriter, Writer)
27 W 67th St
#5E
New York, NY 10023, USA

Yary, A Ronald (Ron) (Athlete, Football Player)
38886 Calle De Companero
Murrieta, CA 92562, USA

Yasbeck, Amy (Actor)
c/o Jonathan Howard *Innovative Artists (LA)*
1505 10th St
Santa Monica, CA 90401, USA

Yashin, Alexei (Athlete, Hockey Player)
6 Polo Dr
Old Westbury, NY 11568-1043, USA

Yassky, David (Stylist)
c/o Celebrity Stylist *Oliver Piro Inc*
725 Riverside Dr Apt 3A
New York, NY 10031, USA

Yastrzemski, Carl (Athlete, Baseball Player)
22 Lakeshore Rd
Boxford, MA 02421-8243, USA

Yastrzemski, Carl
255 State Street
Boston, MA 02109-2617, USA

Yasukawa, Roger (Race Car Driver)
417 S Hill Street
Apt 1100
Los Angeles, CA 90013, USA

Yasutake, Patti
145 S. Fairfax Ave. #310
Los Angeles, CA 90036

Yates, Albert C (Educator)
Colorado State University System
President's Office
Denver, CO 80202, USA

Yates, Bill (Cartoonist)
c/o Staff Member *King Features Syndication*
300 W 57th St
15th Floor
New York, NY 10019-5238, USA

Yates, Billy (Athlete, Football Player)
c/o Staff Member *New England Patriots*
1 Patriot Pl
Foxboro, MA 02035-1388, USA

Yates, Bob (Athlete, Football Player)
391 Bentwood Dr
Spring Branch, TX 78070-6016, USA

Yates, Doug (Race Car Driver)
Doug Yates Racing
112 Byers Creek Rd .
Mooresville, NC 28117, USA

Yates, Jim (Race Car Driver)
Commonwealth Service & Supply
4740 Eisenhower Ave
Alexandria, VA 22304, USA

Yates, Mary Beth (Stylist)
c/o Staff Member *Therese Ryan Mahar Inc*
167 Lexington
#200
New York, NY 10016, USA

Yates, Robert (Race Car Driver)
18923 Cove Side Lane
Cornelius, NC 28031-5252, USA

Yates, Ronald W (Ron) (General)
525 Silhourette Way
Monument, CO 80132, USA

Yates, Tyler (Athlete, Baseball Player)
3718 Omao Rd
Koloa, HI 96756-9628, USA

Yates, Wayne (Athlete, Basketball Player)
210 Yates Rd
Robeline, LA 71469, USA

Yates, Yvette (Producer)
c/o Staff Member *Payaso Entertainment*
5555 Melrose Ave
Bldg 256 #233
Los Angeles, CA 90038, USA

Yau, Shing-Tung (Mathematician)
Harvard University
Mathematics Dept
1 Oxford St
Cambridge, MA 02138, USA

Yavari, Leila (Actor)
c/o Staff Member *Cunningham Escott Slevin & Doherty (CESD-LA)*
10635 Santa Monica Blvd
130
Los Angeles, CA 90025, USA

Yavneh, Cyrus (Producer)
c/o Staff Member *ICM Partners (ICM-LA)*
10250 Constellation Blvd Fl 7
Los Angeles, CA 90067, USA

Yawney, Trent (Athlete, Hockey Player)
215 Belleplaine Ave
Park Ridge, IL 60068-4917, USA

Yayo, Tony (Musician)
c/o Staff Member *Interscope Records (NY)*
1755 Broadway
New York, NY 10019, USA

Yazpik, Jose Maria (Actor)
c/o Carlos Carreras *Agency for the Performing Arts (APA-LA)*
360 N Crescent Dr
North Bldg
Beverly Hills, CA 90210, USA

Ybarra y Churruca, Emilio de (Financier)
Banco Bilbao-Vizcaya
Plaza de San Nicolas 4
Bilboa 48005, SPAIN

Yeager, Andrea
3137 Devlin Dr.
Grand Junction, CO 81504

Yeager, Bunny (Model, Photographer)
9165 Park Drive
Suite 9
Miami Shores, FL 33138-3163, USA

Yeager, Charles E (Chuck) (General)
PO Box 579
Penn Valley, CA 95946, USA

Yeager, Chuck (Aviator)
PO Box 1507
Penn Valley, CA 95946-1507, USA

Yeager, Jeana (Aviator)
302 Chaparral Dr
Sunnyvale, TX 75182-4029, USA

Yeager, Jeana (Misc)
3695 Highway 50
Campbell, TX 75422, USA

Yeager, Steve (Athlete, Baseball Player)
JD Legends Promotions
PO Box 34184
Granada Hills, CA 91394-4184, USA

Yeagley, Jerry (Coach)
1418 S Sare Road
Bloomington, IN 47401, USA

Yeagley, Susan (Actor)
c/o Devon Jackson *Medavoy Management*
10203 Santa Monica Blvd
Suite 400
Los Angeles, CA 90067, USA

Yeah Yeah Yeahs (Music Group)
249 Metropolitan Ave
Brooklyn, NY 11211, USA

Yeakel, Scott (Astronaut)
30 Ticcoma Way
Nantucket, MA 02554-6078, USA

Yearley, Douglas C (Business Person)
Phelps Dodge Corp
1 N Central Ave
Phoenix, AZ 85004, USA

Yearwood, Trisha (Musician)
20955 S. 4092nd Rd
Claremore, OK 74019, USA

Yeates, Jeff (Athlete, Football Player)
3793 Club Dr NE
Atlanta, GA 30319, USA

Yeats, Matthew (Athlete, Hockey Player)
7221 35th St E
Sarasota, FL 34243-3327, USA

Yelchin, Anton (Actor)
c/o Cynthia Pett-Dante *Brillstein
Entertainment Partners*
9150 Wilshire Blvd #350
Beverly Hills, CA 90212, USA

Yelding, Eric (Athlete, Baseball Player)
P.O. Box 325
Montrose, AL 36559-0325, USA

Yeley, JJ (Race Car Driver)
Mayfield Motorsports
2220 Hwy. 49 N
Harrisburg, NC 28075, USA

Yeliseyev, Aleksei S (Cosmonaut)
Baurman Higher Technical School
Baumanskaya Ul 5
Moscow 107005, RUSSIA

Yelle, Stephane (Athlete, Hockey Player)
212 Maplehurst Pt
Highlands Ranch, CO 80126-5613, USA

Yellen, Janet L (Financier, Government
Official)
683 San Luis Road
Berkeley, CA 94707, USA

Yellen, Larry (Athlete, Baseball Player)
3886 Toccoa Falls Dr
Duluth, GA 30097-8105, USA

Yellen, Linda B (Director, Producer)
3 Sheridan Square
New York, NY 10014, USA

Yellowcard (Musician)
Capitol Records
1750 N Vine St T-06
Hollywood, CA 90028, USA

Yellowjackets
9220 Sunset Blvd. #320
Los Angeles, CA 90069

Yelvington, Richard J (Athlete, Football
Player)
2105 Barbe St
Lake Charles, LA 70601, USA

Yen, Donnie (Actor)
c/o Andrew Ruf *Paradigm (LA)*
360 N Crescent Dr
North Bldg
Beverly Hills, CA 90210, USA

Yeo, Gwendoline (Actor)
c/o Anne Geddes *Geddes Agency, The*
8430 Santa Monica Blvd
Suite 200
Los Angeles, CA 90069, USA

Yeo, Mike (Athlete, Hockey Player)
Minnesota Wild 317 Washington St
Attn Coaching Staff
Saint Paul, MN 55102-1667, USA

Yeoh, Michelle (Actor)
c/o Lee Stollman *The Gotham Group Inc*
9255 Sunset Blvd
Suite 515
Los Angeles, CA 90069, USA

Yeoman, Owain (Actor)
512 N Gower St
Los Angeles, CA 90004, USA

Yeoman, William F (Bill) (Athlete, Coach,
Football Coach, Football Player)
3030 Country Club Blvd
Sugar Land, TX 77478, USA

Yeosock, John J (General)
223 Newport Dr
Peachtree City, GA 30269, USA

Yepremian, Garabed S (Garo) (Athlete,
Football Player)
613 Martin Dr
Avondale, PA 19311, USA

Yerby, Frank
Avenida del America 37
Madrid, SPAIN E-28002

Yerman, Jack (Athlete, Olympic Athlete,
Track Athlete)
753 Camellia
Paradise, CA 95969, USA

Yes (Music Group)
c/o Staff Member *10th Street
Entertainment (LA)*
700 San Vicente Blvd
Suite G410
West Hollywood, CA 90069, USA

Yeston, Maury (Composer)
Yale University
Music Dept
New Haven, CT 06520, USA

Yetnikoff, Walter
c/o Daniel Strone *Trident Media Group
LLC*
41 Madison Ave
36th Floor
New York, NY 10010, USA

Yett, Rich (Athlete, Baseball Player)
5840 E Fairbrook Cir
Mesa, AZ 85205-5559, USA

Yeun, Steven (Actor)
c/o Bruce Economou *Pine River
Entertainment*
1200 S Corning St.
Suite 101
Los Angeles, CA 90035, USA

Yeutter, Clayton (Politician)
10955 Martingale Ct
Potomac, MD 20854-1500, USA

Yeutter, Clayton K (Secretary)
10955 Martingale Court
Potomac, MD 20854, USA

Yevtushenko, Yevgeny A (Writer)
Kutuzovski Prospekt 2/1
#101
Moscow 121248, RUSSIA

Yewchyn, Darren (Athlete, Football
Player)
184 Oakview Ave
Winnipeg, MB R2K0R8, Canada

Yewcic, Thomas (Tom) (Athlete, Baseball
Player, Football Player)
31 Cherokee Rd
Arlington, MA 02474-1946, USA

Yi, Charlyne (Actor, Producer, Writer)
c/o Christie Smith *Mosaic Media Group*
9200 W. Sunset Blvd
10th Floor
Los Angeles, CA 90069, USA

Yilmaz, A Mesut (Prime Minister)
Basbakanlik
Bakanliklar
Ankara, TURKEY

Yimou, Zhang (Actor, Director, Producer,
Writer)
c/o William (Bill) Kong *Edko Films*
1212 Tower 2
Admiralty Centre
Hong Kong, CHINA

Ying Yang Twins (Music Group)
TVT Records
A&R Dept
23 East 4th St 3rd Fl
New York, NY 10003, USA

Yip, David
15 Golden Square #315
London, ENGLAND W1R 3AG

Yip, Francoise (Actor)
Infinite Artists
10 - 206 East 6th Ave
Vancouver, BC V5T 1J8, CANADA

Yip, Vern (Designer)
24 Wakefield Dr NE
Atlanta, GA 30309

Ylonen, Juha (Athlete, Hockey Player)
1000 Palladium Dr
Kanata, ON K2V 1A4, Canada

Ylonen, Lauri Johannes (Musician)
c/o Staff Member *Rasmus, The*
Playground Music Scandinavia
Box 3171
Malmö s-200 22, SWEDEN

Yoakam, Dwight (Musician, Songwriter)
Fitzgerald Hartley
1908 Wedgewood Ave
Nashville, TN 37212, USA

Yoakum, Dwight (Musician)
Borman Entertainment
1250 6th St #401
Santa Monica, CA 90401

Yoba, Malik (Actor)
c/o Matt Luber *Luber Roklin Management*
8530 Wilshire Blvd
6th Floor
Beverly Hills, CA 90211, USA

Yoccoz, Jean-Christophe (Mathematician)
University of Paris-Sud (Orsey)
Orsay-Cedex-Bait 91405, FRANCE

Yochim, Len (Athlete, Baseball Player)
316 Nelson Dr
New Orleans, LA 70123-1958, USA

Yochum, Dan (Athlete, Football Player)
88 Doges Promenade
Lindenhurst, NY 11757-6408, USA

Yock, Robert J (Judge)
US Claims Court
717 Madison Place NW
Washington, DC 20439, USA

Yocum, Matt (Race Car Driver)
9910 Devonshire Dr.
Huntsville, NC 28078-5965, USA

Yoder, Kevin (Congressman, Politician)
214 Cannon HOB
Washington, DC 20515, USA

Yodoyman, Joseph (Prime Minister)
Prime Minister's Office
N'Djamena, CHAD

Yogaraj (Actor, Bollywood)
18 34th Street
Ashok Nagar
Chennai, TN 600083, INDIA

Yoh, Ramona (Stylist)
1055 Barrow Ct
Westlake Village, CA 91361, USA

Yohn, John (Athlete, Football Player)
12 Riverview Dr
Middletown, PA 17057, USA

Yoho, Mack (Athlete, Football Player)
2205 Sacramento St
Apt 304
San Francisco, CA 94115, USA

Yoken, Mel B (Writer)
261 Carroll St
New Bedford, MA 02740, USA

Yokes, Diane (Stylist)
3721 N 83rd
St Milwaukee, WI 53222, USA

Yonakor, Rich (Athlete, Basketball Player)
38140 Tamarac Blvd
Apt 106
Willoughby, OH 44094-3448, USA

Yonath, Ada (Nobel Prize Laureate)
Weizman Institute of Science PO Box 26
Structural Biology Dept
Rehovat, Israe, USA

Yonder Mountain String Band (Music Group)
c/o Staff Member *Paradigm (Monterey)*
404 W Franklin St
Monterey, CA 93940, USA

Yoo, Aaron (Actor)
c/o Tony Cloer *Blue Ridge Entertainment*
41 Union Sq W #809
New York, NY 10003, USA

Yoo, Paula (Writer)
c/o Nancy Etz *ICM Partners (ICM-LA)*
10250 Constellation Blvd Fl 7
Los Angeles, CA 90067, USA

Yore, Jim (Athlete, Football Player)
1084 Westlake Woods Dr
Springfield, MI 49015, USA

York, Barbara (Stylist)
2314 N Sibley St
Alexandria, VA 22311, USA

York, Francine (Actor)
6430 Sunset Blvd #1205
Los Angeles, CA 90028, USA

York, Glen P (War Hero)
1620 E Driftwood Dr
Tempe, AZ 85283, USA

York, Jason (Athlete, Hockey Player)
1403 Sherruby Way
Kanata, ON K2W 1B1, Canada

York, Jim (Athlete, Baseball Player)
31262 Via Del Verde
San Juan Capistrano, CA 92675, USA

York, Jim (Athlete, Baseball Player)
31262 Via Del Verde
San Juan Capistrano, CA 92675-6315, USA

York, John J (Actor)
4804 Laurel Canyon Blvd
#212
Valley Village, CA 91607, USA

York, Kathleen (Actor)
Bresler Kelly Assoc
11500 W Olympic Blvd
#510
Los Angeles, CA 90064, USA

York, Michael (Actor)
c/o Staff Member *Peter Strain & Associates Inc (LA)*
5455 Wilshire Blvd
Suite 1812
Los Angeles, CA 90036-4368, USA

York, Michael M (Journalist)
Lexington Herald-Leader
Editorial Dept
Main & Midland
Lexington, KY 40507, USA

York, Mike (Athlete, Hockey Player, Olympic Athlete)
6105 W Longview Dr
East Lansing, MI 48823-9739, USA

York, Mike (Athlete, Baseball Player)
8001 S 84th Ct
Justice, IL 60458-1420, USA

York, Morgan (Actor)
c/o Meredith Fine *Coast to Coast Talent Group*
3350 Barham Blvd
Los Angeles, CA 90068, USA

York, Ray (Jockey)
27918 Taft Highway
Taft, CA 93268, USA

York, Wndy Jill (Stylist)
47 Barney St
Rumford, RI 02916, USA

Yorke, Thom (Musician)
c/o Staff Member *Creative Artists Agency (CAA-LA)*
2000 Ave Of The Stars
Los Angeles, CA 90067, USA

Yorkin, Alan (Bud) (Director, Producer)
Bud Yorkin Productions
250 Delfern Dr
Los Angeles, CA 90077, USA

Yorkin, Bud
250 N. Delfern Dr.
Los Angeles, CA 90077

Yorkin, Peg (Politician)
Fund for Feminist Majority
1600 Wilson Blvd
#704
Arlington, VA 22209, USA

Yorn, Peter (Musician, Songwriter, Writer)
c/o Rick Yorn *LBI Entertainment*
2000 Avenue of the Stars
3rd Floor, North Tower
Los Angeles, CA 90067, USA

Yorzyk, William (Athlete, Olympic Athlete, Swimmer)
174 Lane 7
Sturbridge, MA 01566, USA

Yoseliani, Otar D (Director)
Mitskewitch 1 Korp
1 #38
Tbilisi 380060, GEORGIA

Yoshida, Hiroshi (Stylist)
c/o Staff Member *Artist Untied (LA)*
845 S Mansfield Ave
#1
Los Angeles, CA 90036, USA

Yost, David (Actor)
8837 Cortina Cir
Roseville, CA 95678, USA

Yost, Dennis
PO Box 8770
Endwell, NY 13762

Yost, Ned (Athlete, Baseball Player, Coach)
Milwaukee Brewers
108 Victoria Dr
Lagrange, GA 30240-6338, USA

Yost, Paul A Jr (Admiral)
James Medison Memorial Foundation
200 K St NW
Washington, DC 20001, USA

Yothers, Tina (Actor, Musician)
12368 Apple Dr
Chino, CA 91710, USA

Youel, Jim (Athlete, Football Player)
1102 Avenue F
Fort Madison, IA 52627, USA

Youkhannah, David (Stylist)
c/o Staff Member *Cloutier Agency*
2632 La Cienega Ave
Los Angeles, CA 90034, USA

Youkilis, Kevin (Athlete, Baseball Player)
19475 N Grayhawk Dr
Unit 1083
Scottsdale, AZ 85255-7420, USA

Youmans, Floyd (Athlete, Baseball Player)
1915 E Noel St
Tampa, FL 33610-6157, USA

Youmans, Maury (Athlete, Football Player)
300 Beach Dr NE
Apt 2104
Saint Petersburg, FL 33701, USA

Young, Ace (Musician)
c/o Staff Member *Marleah Leslie & Associates PR*
1645 N Vine St
Suite 712
Los Angeles, CA 90028, USA

Young, Aden (Actor)
June Cann Mgmt
110 Queen St
Woollahra, NSW 2025, AUSTRALIA

Young, Adrian (Musician)
Rebel Waltz Inc
31652 2nd Ave
Laguna Beach, CA 92651, USA

Young, Al (Athlete, Football Player)
1947 Green Forest Dr
North Augusta, SC 29481, USA

Young, Alan (Actor)
24072 La Hermosa
Laguna Niguel, CA 92077, USA

Young, Almon (Athlete, Football Player)
P.O. Box 983
Mc Crory, AR 72101, USA

Young, Angus (Musician, Songwriter, Writer)
c/o Christopher Dalston *Creative Artists Agency (CAA-LA)*
2000 Ave Of The Stars
Los Angeles, CA 90067, USA

Young, Anthony (Athlete, Baseball Player)
13107 Ellesmere Dr
Houston, TX 77015-2111, USA

Young, Anthony (Athlete, Football Player)
914 Colonial Ct
Coatesville, PA 19320, USA

Young, Archie (Athlete, Baseball Player)
Birmingham Black Barons
1804 Ethel Ave SW
Birmingham, AL 35211-4914, USA

Young, Barbara
23-B Deodar Rd.
London, ENGLAND SWl5- 2NP

Young, Bellamy (Actor)
c/o Katie Rhodes *Untitled Entertainment (LA)*
350 S. Beverly Dr #200
Beverly Hills, CA 90212, USA

Young, Bob (Cartoonist)
c/o Staff Member *King Features Syndication*
300 W 57th St
15th Floor
New York, NY 10019-5238, USA

Young, Boyd (Misc)
United Paperworkers Union
3340 Perimeter Hill Dr
Nashville, TN 37211, USA

Young, Brian (Musician)
MOB Agency
6404 Wilshire Blvd
#505
Los Angeles, CA 90048, USA

Young, Brian (Athlete, Hockey Player)
PO Box 835
Jasper, AB TOE lEO, Canada

Young, Bryant C (Athlete, Football Player)
5802 Country Club Pkwy
San Jose, CA 95138, USA

Young, Burt (Actor)
Higgins Harte International
11 Pioneer Building
Suite 4
Mesquite, NV 98027, USA

Young, Charle E (Athlete, Football Player)
16035 Mink Rd NE
Woodinville, WA 98077, USA

Young, Charles E (Athlete, Football Player)
16035 Mink Rd NE
Woodinville, WA 98077, USA

Young, Charles L (Athlete, Football Player)
2120 Daufuskie Dr
Raleigh, NC 27604, USA

Young, Chris (Athlete, Baseball Player)
c/o Staff Member *Arizona Diamondbacks*
P.O. Box 2095
Phoenix, AZ 85001, USA

Young, Chris T
5959 Triumph St
Commerce, CA 90040-1688, USA

Young, Christoper (Composer)
Kraft-Benjamin-Engel
15233 Ventura Blvd
#200
Sherman Oaks, CA 91403, USA

Young, CJ (Athlete, Hockey Player, Olympic Athlete)
130 Hoover Rd
Needham, MA 02494-1548, USA

Young, Colville N (General, Governor)
Governor General's Office
Belize House
Belnopan, BELIZE

Young, Corey
11553 Sunshine Terrace
Studio City, CA 91604

Young, Curt (Athlete, Baseball Player)
10800 E Cactus Rd
Unit 2
Scottsdale, AZ 85259-2503, USA

Young, C.W. (Bill) (Congressman, Politician)
9120 113th St
Seminole, FL 33772, USA

Young, Cy (Athlete, Olympic Athlete)
518 Grimes Ave
Modesto, CA 95358-8308, USA

Young, Danny (Athlete, Baseball Player)
1841 Lascassas Pike
Apt J153
Murfreesboro, TN 37130-0609, USA

Young, Dean (Cartoonist)
c/o Staff Member *King Features Syndication*
300 W 57th St
15th Floor
New York, NY 10019-5238, USA

Young, Delmon (Athlete, Baseball Player)
5904 Pelican Bay Plaza S
Gulfport, FL 33707, USA

young, Delwyn (Athlete, Baseball Player)
2212 Radcourt Dr
Hacienda Heights, CA 91745-5716, USA

Young, Dmitri (Athlete, Baseball Player)
26 SE lOth Ave
Fort Lauderdale, FL 33301-2054, USA

Young, Don (Athlete, Baseball Player)
4122 E Milton Dr
Cave Creek, AZ 85331-5843, USA

Young, Don (Congressman, Politician)
2314 Rayburn HOB
Washington, DC 20515, USA

Young, Duane (Athlete, Football Player)
2255 River Run Dr
San Diego, CA 92108, USA

Young, Earl (Athlete, Track Athlete)
4344 Livingston Ave
Dallas, TX 75205, USA

Young, Eric O (Athlete, Baseball Player)
120 Brewster Ave
Piscataway, NJ 08854-2205, USA

Young, Ernie (Athlete, Baseball Player, Olympic Athlete)
8995 E Palm Ridge Dr
Scottsdale, AZ 85260, USA

Young, Frank
Food And Drug Administration 5600 Fishers Ln
Rockville, MD 20852-1750, USA

Young, Frank E (Government Official, Scientist)
Food & Drug Administration
5600 Fishers Lane
Rockville, MD 20852, USA

Young, Fred (Musician)
Mitchell Fox Mgmt
212 3rd Ave
#301
Nashville, TN 37201, USA

Young, Fredd (Athlete, Football Player)
4200 Real del Sur
Las Cruces, NM 88011, USA

Young, George (Athlete, Olympic Athlete)
8926 N Cox Rd
CasaGrande, AZ 85194-7230, USA

Young, Gerald (Athlete, Baseball Player)
10014 Rain Cloud Dr
Houston, TX 77095-2442, USA

Young, Glenn (Athlete, Football Player)
8035 Burchmore Rd
Three Lakes, WI 54562, USA

Young, Guard (Athlete, Gymnast, Olympic Athlete)
4000 Worthington Dr
Norman, OK 73072-1777, USA

Young, H Edwin (Religious Leader)
Southern Baptist Convention
901 Commerce St
Nashville, TN 37203, USA

Young, Jacob (Actor)
c/o Alex D'Andrea *Edmonds Management*
1635 N Cahuenga Blvd Fl 5
Los Angeles, CA 90028, USA

Young, Jason (Athlete, Baseball Player)
1021 Washington St
San Francisco, CA 94108-1107, USA

Young, Jesse Colin (Musician, Songwriter, Writer)
Skyline Music
PO Box 31
Lancaster, NH 03584, USA

Young, Jewell L (Basketball Player)
4480 Fairways Blvd
Building 8 #203
Bradenton, FL 34209, USA

Young, Jim (Coach, Football Coach)
US Military Academy
Athletic Dept
West Point, NY 10966, USA

Young, Joe (Athlete, Football Player)
33261 Windtree Ave
Wildomar, CA 92595, USA

Young, John (Athlete, Baseball Player)
124 W 57th St
Los Angeles, CA 90037-4114, USA

Young, John A (Business Person)
Norvell Inc
122 E 1700 S
provo, UT 84606, USA

Young, John W (Astronaut)
NASA
221 Lakeshore Dr
Seabrook, TX 77586-6128, USA

Young, John Zachary (Misc)
1 Crossroads
Brill
Bucks HP18 9TL, UNITED KINGDOM (UK)

Young, Judith Knight (Actor)
Ann Steel
330 W 42nd St #1800
New York, NY 10036, USA

Young, J Warren (Publisher)
Boys Life Magazine
1325 Walnut Hill Road
Irving, TX 75038, USA

Young, Kate (Stylist)
c/o Staff Member *Management + Artists + Organization*
330 W 38th St
#1401
New York, NY 10018, USA

Young, Kathie (Stylist)
c/o Staff Member *Axis Models & Talent*
P.O. Box 367
Ringwood, NJ 07456-0367, USA

Young, Kathryn (Athlete, Golfer)
323 Date Ave
Imperial Beach, CA 91932, USA

Young, Kathy (Musician)
Cape Entertainment
1161 NW 76th Ave
Plantation, FL 33322, USA

Young, Keone (Actor)
Gage Group
14724 Ventura Blvd
#505
Sherman Oaks, CA 91324, USA

Young, Kevin (Athlete, Track Athlete)
8860 Corban Ave
Northridge, CA 91324, USA

Young, Kevin (Athlete, Baseball Player)
4793 E Charles Dr
Paradise Valley, AZ 85253-2427, USA

Young, Kip (Athlete, Baseball Player)
1290 S Taylorsville Rd
Hillsboro, OH 45133-6729, USA

Young, Larry (Athlete, Baseball Player)
P.O. Box 255
Roscoe, IL 61073-0255, USA

Young, Laurence Retman (Astronaut)
217 Thorndike St
#108
Cambridge, MA 02141, USA

Young, Laurence R Prof (Astronaut)
217 Thorndike St Apt 108
Cambridge, MA 02141-1504, USA

Young, Lee Thompson (Actor)
c/o Jonathan Baruch *Rain Management Group (RMG)*
1631 21st St
Santa Monica, CA 90404, USA

Young, Lonnie (Athlete, Football Player)
Express Personnel Services
6437 S Cedar St
Lansing, MI 48911, USA

Young, M Adrian (Athlete, Football Player)
10300 4th St
Apt 100
Rancho Cucamonga, CA 91730, USA

Young, Mark L. (Actor)
c/o Martin Berneman *Precision Entertainment*
6338 Wilshire Blvd
Los Angeles, CA 90048, USA

Young, Martin D (Misc)
1110 Marshall Road
#2007
Greenwood, SC 29646, USA

Young, Matt (Athlete, Baseball Player)
471 Maylin ST
Pasadena, CA 91105-1629, USA

Young, Maurice (Trick Daddy) (Music Group, Musician)
c/o Roy Rosental *Energon Entertainment*
276 5th Ave
Suite 712
New York, NY 10001, USA

Young, Melissa (Actor)
Badgley Connor Talent
9229 Sunset Blvd
#311
Los Angeles, CA 90069, USA

Young, Michael (Athlete, Basketball Player)
6707 Broad Oaks
Dr
Richmond, TX 77406-7629, USA

Young, Michael (Athlete, Baseball Player)
3508 Bryn Mawr Dr
Dallas, TX 75225-7438, USA

Young, Mighty Joe (Musician)
Jay Reil
3430 Bayberry Dr
Northbrook, IL 60062, USA

Young, Mike (Athlete, Baseball Player)
1166 Rockspring Way
Antioch, CA 94531-8308, USA

Young, Mike (Athlete, Football Player)
20 Cherry Hills Farm Dr
Englewood, CO 80113, USA

Young, Mimi (Stylist)
c/o Staff Member *Sarah Laird Inc*
12 Charles Ln
New York, NY 10014, USA

Young, Neil (Musician)
c/o Elliot Roberts *Lookout Management*
1460 Fourth St
Santa Monica, CA 90401

Young, Nina (Actor)
c/o Staff Member *BBC Television Centre*
Incoming Mail
Wood Lane
London W12 7RJ, United Kingdom

Young, Parker (Actor)
c/o David Dean Portelli *David Dean Management*
6338 Wilshire Blvd
Los Angeles, CA 90048, USA

Young, Paul (Musician)
What Mgmt
PO Box 1463
Culver City, CA 90232, USA

Young, Pete (Athlete, Baseball Player)
P.O. Box 95
Summit, MS 39666-0095, USA

Young, Peter (Misc)
1902 Coldwater Canyon Dr
Beverly Hills, CA 90210-1731, USA

Young, Ray (Aviator)
1701 New Hampton Ln
Woodstock, Md 21163-1300, USA

Young, Ray (Misc)
3360 Barham Blvd
Los Angeles, CA 90068, USA

Young, Raymond
7 Church St.
Littlehampton, ENGLAND BN1Y 5EL

Young, Ric (Actor)
c/o Staff Member *Coast to Coast Talent Group*
3350 Barham Blvd
Los Angeles, CA 90068, USA

Young, Richard
1275 Westwood Blvd.
Los Angeles, CA 90024

Young, Richard E (Scientist)
Jet Propulsion Laboratory
4800 Oak Grove Dr
Pasadena, CA 91109, USA

Young, Richard S (Educator)
137 Saint Croix Ave
Cocoa Beach, FL 32931, USA

Young, Richard S (Photographer)
110 Highlever Road
London W10 6PL, UNITED KINGDOM (UK)

Young, Rickey (Athlete, Football Player)
13670 Valley View Rd
Apt 116
Eden Prairie, MN 55344, USA

Young, Robert (Athlete, Football Player)
RR 7 Box 306
Carthage, MS 39051, USA

Young, Ron Jr (War Hero)
c/o Staff Member *Premiere Speakers Bureau*
1000 Corporate Centre
Suite 120
Franklin, TN 37067, USA

Young, Roynell (Athlete, Football Player)
11823 Beinhorn Dr
Houston, TX 77065, USA

Young, Scott (Athlete, Hockey Player, Olympic Athlete)
17 Sandy Ridge Rd
Sterling, MA 01564-2361, USA

Young, Sean (Actor)
c/o Staff Member *Diverse Talent Group*
9911 W Pico Blvd Ste 340W
Los Angeles, CA 90035, USA

Young, Shelby (Actor)
c/o Katie Mason *Luber Roklin Management*
8530 Wilshire Blvd
6th Floor
Beverly Hills, CA 90211, USA

Young, Steve (Athlete, Football Player, Sportscaster)
245 Southwood Dr
Palo Alto, CA 94301, USA

Young, Tim (Athlete, Hockey Player)
15808 Park Terrace Dr
Eden Prairie, MN 55346-2433, USA

Young, Tim (Athlete, Baseball Player, Olympic Athlete)
20730 SE Sherry Ave
Blountstown, FL 32424-2265, USA

Young, Tom (Coach)
Washington Wizards
MCI Centre
601 F St NW
Washington, DC 20004, USA

Young, Ulysses (Athlete, Baseball Player)
4023 W 60th St
Los Angeles, CA 90043-3636, USA

Young, Vince (Athlete, Football Player)
20 Tradition Ln
Brentwood, TN 37027, USA

Young, Vincent (Actor)
c/o Alan Ellsweig *Shadow Entertainment*
10 Universal City Plz
20th Floor
Universal City, CA 91608, USA

Young, Walter (Athlete, Baseball Player)
134 Center St
Purvis, MS 39475-4540, USA

Young, Warren (Athlete, Hockey Player)
5960 Murray Ave
Bethel Park, PA 15102-3489, USA

Young, Wayne (Athlete, Gymnast, Olympic Athlete)
1136 E Mahongany Ln
Pleasant Grove, UT 84062-2069, USA

Young, Wendell (Athlete, Hockey Player)
1616 E Campbell St
Arlington Heights, IL 60004-6550, USA

Young, Wendell (Athlete, Hockey Player)
Chicago Wolves 2301 Ravine Way
Attn: General Manager
Glenview, IL 60025-7627, USA

Young, Wilbur (Athlete, Football Player)
121 W Bannister Rd
Kansas City, MO 64114, USA

Young, Will (Musician)
c/o Angharad Wood *Tavistock Wood Management*
32 Tavistock St
London WC2B 5HA, UK

Young, William Allen (Actor)
c/o Bruce Tufeld *Tufeld Entertainment Group*
19521 Rosita Stt
Tarzana, CA 91356, USA

Young, Wise (Scientist)
Rutgers University
Collaborative Neuroscience Center
New Brunswick, NJ 08901, USA

Youngberg, Renae (Athlete, Baseball Player)
418 Stoney Ridge Loop
Maggie Valley, NC 28751-8653, USA

Youngblood, George (Athlete, Football Player)
16429 Lazare Ln
Huntington Beach, CA 92649, USA

Youngblood, H Jackson (Jack) (Athlete, Football Player, Sportscaster)
4377 Steed Ter
Winter Park, FL 32792, USA

Youngblood, Jimmy L (Jim) (Athlete, Football Player)
534 N Manhattan Pl
Los Angeles, CA 90004, USA

Youngblood, Joel (Athlete, Baseball Player)
4446 E Camelback Rd
Unit 113
Phoenix, AZ 85018-2837, USA

Youngblood, Rob
1604 N. Vista Ave.
Los Angeles, CA 90046

Youngblood, Sydney
Postfach 20 13 43
Hamburg, GERMANY D-29243

Youngen, Lois (Athlete, Baseball Player)
45 Prail Ln
Eugene, OR 97405-3335, USA

Younger, Ben (Director, Writer)
c/o Joseph Cohen *Creative Artists Agency (CAA-LA)*
2000 Ave Of The Stars
Los Angeles, CA 90067, USA

Youngerman, Jack (Artist)
PO Box 508
Bridgehampton, NY 11932-0508, USA

Youngerman, Jack (Artist)
PO Box 508
Bridgehampton, NY 11932, USA

Youngfellow, Barrie (Actor)
c/o Staff Member *Gage Group, The (LA)*
14724 Ventura Blvd
Suite 505
Sherman Oaks, CA 91403, USA

Young Gunz (Musician)
c/o Staff Member *Roc-A-Fella Records*
825 8th Ave Fl 29
New York, NY 10019-7472, USA

Younghans, Tom (Athlete, Hockey Player)
6133 Sheridan Ave S
Minneapolis, MN 55410, USA

Young Jeezy (Musician)
c/o Tracy Nguyen *IPR + MKTG*
1515 Broadway
40th Floor
New York, NY 10036, USA

Young Jr, Walter R (Business Person)
Champion Enterprises
2710 University Dr
Auburn Hills, MI 48326, USA

Young Knives, The (Music Group)
c/o Staff Member *Paradigm (Monterey)*
404 W Franklin St
Monterey, CA 93940, USA

Young MC (Musician)
Universal Attractions
145 W 57th St #1500
New York, NY 10019, USA

Young Money (Music Group, Musician)
c/o Staff Member *Motown Records (NY)*
1755 Broadway
7th Floor
New York, NY 10019, USA

Youngs, Eileen Collins Colonel (Astronaut)
2024 Pebble Beach Dr
League City, TX 77573-6403, USA

Younis, Waqar (Cricketer)
Surrey County Cricket Club
Kennington Oval
London SE11 5SS, UNITED KINGDOM (UK)

Yount, Larry (Athlete, Baseball Player)
5701 E Mockingbird Ln
Paradise Valley, AZ 85253-2221, USA

Yount, Robin (Athlete, Baseball Player)
5040 E Shea Blvd Ste 254
Scottsdale, AZ 85254-4687, USA

Yount, Robin R (Athlete, Baseball Player)
5040 E Shea Blvd
Suite 254
Scottsdale, AZ 85254, USA

Youso, Frank (Athlete, Football Player)
P.O. Box 1046
International Falls, MN 56649, USA

Youssoufi, Abdderrahmane El (Prime Minister)
Prime Minister's Office
Rabat, MOROCCO

Yowarsky, Walt (Athlete, Football Player)
395 Dogwood Pl NW
Cleveland, TN 37312, USA

Yo-Yo (Musician)
William Morris Agency
1325 Ave of Americas
New York, NY 10019, USA

Y. Schwartz, Allyson (Congressman, Politician)
1227 Longworth HOB
Washington, DC 20515, USA

Ysebaert, Paul (Athlete, Hockey Player)
865 St Clair Pkwy RR 1
Mooretown, ON N0N 1M0, CANADA

Yu, Ronnie (Director, Producer, Writer)
c/o Richard Arlook *The Arlook Group*
205 S Beverly Dr
Suite 209
Beverly Hills, CA 90212, USA

Yuan, Ron (Actor)
c/o Laura Pallas *Pallas Management*
5301 Bellaire Ave
Valley Vilage, CA 91607, US

Yuan Enfeng (Musician)
Provincial Broadcasting/TV Station
Xian, Shaanxi, CHINA

Yuan Zhongyi (Archaeologist, Misc)
Qin Shi Huang's Terracotta Army Museum
Lintong, Xi'an, CHINA

Yuasa, Joji (Composer, Musician)
1517 Shields Ave
Encinitas, CA 92024, USA

Yu Chuan Yong (Architect)
Urban/Rural Construction Committee
149 Guangming Road
Weihai PR, CHINA

Yudof, Mark G (Educator)
University of Minnesota
President's Office
Minneapolis, MN 55455, USA

Yue Jingyu (Swimmer)
Physical Culture/Sports Bureau
9 Tiyuguan Road
Beijing, CHINA

Yuen, Biao (Actor)
c/o Staff Member *Agency Group Ltd, The (NY)*
142 West 57th St
6th Floor
New York, NY 10019, USA

Yuen, Corey (Actor, Director)
c/o Steve Chasman *Current Entertainment*
9378 Wilshire Blvd
Sutie 210
Beverly Hills, CA 90212, USA

Yulin, Harris (Actor)
40 W 86th St
#5C
New York, NY 10024, USA

Yune, Johnny
1921 Scenic Sunrise Dr.
Las Vegas, NV 89117

Yune, Rick (Actor)
c/o David Gardner *Principato/Young Management*
9465 Wilshire Blvd
Suite 430
Beverly Hills, CA 90212, USA

Yun-Fat, Chow (Actor)
c/o Lee Stollman *The Gotham Group Inc*
9255 Sunset Blvd
Suite 515
Los Angeles, CA 90069, USA

Yunis, Jorge J (Misc)
Thomas Jefferson University
Jefferson Medical College
Philadelphia, PA 19107, USA

Yun Lee, Will (Actor)
c/o Sam Maydew *Collective*
8383 Wilshire Blvd
Suite 1050
Beverly Hills, CA 90211, USA

Yunus, Muhammad (Nobel Prize Laureate)
Grameen America
500 West Cummings Park Ste 5200
Woburn, MA 01801, USA

Yurak, Jeff (Athlete, Baseball Player)
PO Box 1931
Sumner, WA 98390-0420, USA

Yurchikhin, Fyodor N (Cosmonaut)
NASA
Johnson Space Center
2101 NASA Road
Houston, TX 77058, USA

Yushchenko, Victor (President)
President's Office
Bankova Str 11
Kiev 01220, UKRAINE

Yushkevich, Dmitri (Athlete, Hockey Player)
878 Ridge View Way
Franklin Lakes, NJ 07417, USA

Yusuke, Yamamoto (Actor)
c/o Staff Member *Ever Green Entertainment*
3-12-7-1009 Kita Aoyama
Minato
Tokyo, Japan

Yuvarani (Actor, Bollywood)
Plot No 28 Annamalai Colony
Virugambakkam
Chennai, TN 600092, INDIA

Ywecic, Tom (Athlete, Football Player)
31 Cherokee Rd
Arlington, MA 02474, USA

Yzaguirre, Raul (Activist)
National Council of La Raza
1111 19th St NW
#1000
Washington, DC 20036, USA

Yzerman, Steve (Athlete, Hockey Player)
Tampa Bay Lightning 401 Channelside Dr
Attn: General Manager
Tampa, FL 33602-5400, USA

Z, Jenna (Model)
PO Box 39624
N Ridgeville, OH 44039, USA

Zaa, Charlie (Musician)
c/o Staff Member *Sony Music Miami*
605 Lincoln Rd Fl 7
Miami Beach, FL 33139, USA

Zabaleta, Nicanor (Musician)
Villa Izar
Aldapeta
San Sebastian 20009, SPAIN

Zabarain, Ines (Actor)
c/o Staff Member *TV Caracol*
Calle 76 #11 - 35
Piso 10AA
Bogota DC 26484, COLOMBIA

Zabel, Mark (Athlete)
Grosse Fischerei 18A
Calbe/Saale 39240, GERMANY

Zabel, Steven G (Steve) (Athlete, Football Player)
6000 Oak Tree Rd
Edmond, OK 73003, USA

Zabiela, James (DJ, Musician)
c/o Joel Zimmerman *WME (WMA-NY)*
1325 Ave of the Americas
New York, NY 10019, USA

Zablocki, Courtney (Athlete, Luge Player, Olympic Athlete)
2538 Pine Bluff Ln
Highlands Ranch, CO 80126-2806, USA

Zaborowski, Robert R J M (Religious Leader)
Mariavite Old Catholic Church
2803 10th St
Wyandotte, MI 48192, USA

Zabransky, Libor (Athlete, Hockey Player)
Rybarska specialka Zabransky Koliste 59
Brno 602 00, Czech Republic

Zabriski, Bruce (Athlete, Golfer)
6228 Winding Lake Dr
Jupiter, FL 33458-3787, USA

Zabriskie, Grace (Actor)
1536 Murray Dr
Los Angeles, CA 90026, USA

Zac Brown Band (Music Group, Musician)
c/o Staff Member *ROAR (LA)*
9701 Wilshire Blvd
8th Floor
Los Angeles, CA 90212, USA

Zachar, Jacob (Actor)
c/o Jamie Freed *Paris Hilton Entertainment*
8383 Wilshire Blvd
Suite 1050
Beverly Hills, CA 90211, USA

Zachara, Jan (Boxer)
Sladkovicova 13
Nova Dubnica 01851, CZECH REPUBLIC

Zachary, Ken (Football Player)
San Diego Chargers
General Delivery
Newalla, OK 74857-9999, USA

Zacherle, John (Actor)
125 W 96th St
#4B
New York, NY 10025, USA

Zachry, Pat (Athlete, Baseball Player)
7611 Bosque Blvd
Woodway, TX 76712-3766, USA

Zadan, Craig (Producer)
c/o Staff Member *WmE2 (WMA-LA)*
1 William Morris Pl
Beverly Hills, CA 90212, USA

Zadan, Craig (Director, Producer)
8452 Harold Way
West Hollywood, CA 90069, USA

Zadeh, Lofti A (Scientist)
904 Mendocino Ave
Berkeley, CA 94707, USA

Zadel, C William (Business Person)
Millipore Corp
80 Ashby Road
Bedford, MA 01730, USA

Zadora, Pia (Actor)
69 Hawk Ridge Dr
Las Vegas, NV 89135, USA

Zaentz, Saul (Producer)
c/o Staff Member *Saul Zaentz Film Center*
2600 Durant Ave.
Berkeley, CA 94704, USA

Zaffaroni, Alejandro C (Misc)
Alza Corp
1950 Charleston Road
Mountain View, CA 94043, USA

Zafferani, Rosa (Misc)
Co-Regent's Office
Government Palace
47031, SAN MARINO

Zagaria, Anita (Actor)
Carol Levi Co
Via Giuseppe Pisanelli
Rome 00196, ITALY

Zaglmann-Willinger, Cornelia (Director)
Siegfriedstr 9
Munich 80802, GERMANY

Zagorin, Perez (Historian)
2990 Beaumont Farm Road
Chartottesville, VA 22901, USA

Zagunis, Mariel (Athlete, Fencer, Olympic Athlete)
20235 SW Gassner Rd
Beaverton, OR 97007-9020, USA

Zagurski, Mike (Athlete, Baseball Player)
2723 Via Capri #819
Clearwater, FL 33764, USA

Zaharko, Miles (Athlete, Hockey Player)
GD
Two Hills, AB T0B 4K0, Canada

Zahn, Geoffrey C (geof) (Athlete, Baseball Player)
6536 Walsh Rd
Dexter, MI 48130-9656, USA

Zahn, Paula (Journalist)
188 E 76th St
New York, NY 10021-2826, USA

Zahn, Paula (Journalist)
c/o Richard Leibner *NS Bienstock Inc*
250 W 57th St
Suite 333
New York, NY 10107, USA

Zahn, Steve (Actor)
133 Cane Run Rd
Georgetown, KY 40324, USA

Zahn, Timothy (Writer)
PO Box 1755
Coos Bay, OR 97420, USA

Zahn, Wayne
5018 S Barley Ct
Gilbert, AZ 85298-8633, USA

Zahn, Wayne (Bowler)
2143 E Center Lane
Tempe, AZ 85281, USA

Zaillian, Steve (Director, Producer)
30918 Broad Beach Rd
Malibu, CA 90265, USA

Zaine, Rod (Athlete, Hockey Player)
64 Drouin Ave
Ottawa, ON K1K 2A7, Canada

Zajac, Travis (Athlete, Hockey Player)
1016 Smith Manor Blvd
West Orange, NJ 07052-4227, USA

Zaklinsky, Konstantin (Dancer)
Mariinsky Theater
Teatralnaya Square 1
Saint Petersburg 190000, RUSSIA

Zaks, Jerry (Director)
c/o Susan Weaving *WME (WMA-NY)*
1325 Ave of the Americas
New York, NY 10019, USA

Zal, Roxana (Actor)
c/o Staff Member *Main Title Entertainment*
8383 Wilshire Blvd
Suite 408
Los Angeles, CA 90211, USA

Zalapski, Zarley (Athlete, Hockey Player)
Eishockey Club
Olten AG Postfach 523
Olten, PA CH-4601, USA

Zale, Richard N (Misc)
724 Santa Ynez St
Stanford, CA 94305, USA

Zalnasky, Mitch (Athlete, Football Player)
18 Scalena Pl
Winnipeg, MB R3K1Y2, Canada

Zaloom, Paul (Actor, Writer)
c/o Staff Member *Washington Square Arts (LA)*
1041 N Formosa Ave
The Lot Writers Bldg, Room 305
West Hollywood, CA 90046, USA

Zalyotin, Sergei V (Cosmonaut)
Potchta Kosmonavtov
Moskovskoi Oblasti
Syvisdny Goroduk 141160, RUSSIA

Zamba, Frieda (Misc)
2706 S Central Ave
Flagler Beach, FL 32136, USA

Zambrano, Carlos (Athlete, Baseball Player)
c/o Staff Member *Chicago Cubs Spring Training*
HoHoKam Stadium
1235 N St
Mesa, AZ 85201, USA

Zambri, Chris (Athlete, Golfer)
1329 La Culebra Cit
Camarillo, CA 93012-5551, USA

Zamecnik, Paul (Misc)
101 Chestnut St
Boston, MA 02108, USA

Zamka, George D (Astronaut)
144 Lake Point Dr
League City, TX 77573, USA

Zamka, George D Lt Colonel (Astronaut)
144 Lake Point Dr
League City, TX 77573-6970, USA

Zamora, Tye (Musician)
1215 Pamplona Dr
Riverside, CA 92508, USA

Zamorska, Basia (Stylist)
c/o Staff Member *Aartist Loft*
580 Broadway
#606
New York, NY 10012, USA

Zamperini, Louis (Athlete, Olympic Athlete, Track Athlete)
2338 Hollyridge Dr
Los Angeles, CA 90068-3518, USA

Zampini, Carina (Actor)
c/o Staff Member *Telefe - Argentina*
Pavon 2444 (C1248AAT)
Buenos Aires, ARGENTINA

Zamprogna, Dominic (Actor)
c/o Margie Weiner *Margie Weiner Management*
8205 Santa Monica Blvd
Suite 1-450
Los Angeles, CA 90046, USA

Zamuner, Rob (Athlete, Hockey Player)
4317 Beau Rivage Cir
Lutz, FL 33558-5353, USA

Zamzow, Scottie Major (General)
8506 Bromley Ct
Annandale, VA 22003-4533, USA

Zander, Carl (Athlete, Football Player)
2536 W Palomino Dr
Chandler, AZ 85224, USA

Zander, Robin (Musician)
533 Harbor Grove Cir
Safety Harbor, FL 34695, USA

Zander, Thomas (Wrestler)
Grundfeldstr 23
Aalen 73432, GERMANY

Zanders, Emanuel (Athlete, Football Player)
11015 Goodwood Blvd
Baton Rouge, LA 70815, USA

Zane, Billy (Actor)
233 S Orange Dr
Los Angeles, CA 90036, USA

Zane, Frank (Fitness Expert)
PO Box 4088
La Mesa, CA 91944, USA

Zane, Lisa (Actor)
505 N Shore Lake Dr
Apt 5407
Chicago, IL 60611-6446, USA

Zanes, Dan (Musician, Songwriter, Writer)
c/o Harriet Sternberg *Harriet Sternberg Management*
4530 Gloria Ave
Encino, CA 91436, USA

Zanetti, Eugenio (Actor, Director)
c/o Frank Wuliger *Gersh (LA)*
9465 Wilshire Blvd
Suite 600
Beverly Hills, CA 90212, USA

Zanier, Mike (Athlete, Hockey Player)
306 Rossland Ave
Trail, BC V1R 3M8, Canada

Zanni, Dom (Athlete, Baseball Player)
7 Sussex Ave
Massapequa, NY 11758-2434, USA

Zano, Nick (Actor)
4440 Sancola Ave
Toluca Lake, CA 91602, USA

Zanon, Greg (Athlete, Hockey Player)
11839 58th St N
Lake Elmo, MN 55042-6106, USA

Zanotto, Kendra (Athlete, Olympic Athlete, Swimmer)
18834 Lakeview Ct
Los Gatos, CA 95033-9593, USA

Zanuck, Lili Fini (Director, Producer)
Zanuck Co
9465 Wilshire Blvd
#308
Beverly Hills, CA 90212, USA

Zanuck, Ron (Athlete, Hockey Player)
1135 Trailwood N.
Hopkins, MN 55343, USA

Zanussi, Joe (Athlete, Hockey Player)
1192 Shutek Dr
Trail, BC V1R 4R2, Canada

Zanussi, Krzysztof (Director)
Ul Kaniowska 114
Warsaw 01-529, POLAND

Zanussi, Ron (Athlete, Hockey Player)
PO Box 11326
Saint Paul, MN 55111-0326, USA

Zapalac, Willie (Athlete, Football Player)
1400 Shannon Oaks Trl
Austin, TX 78746, USA

Zapata, Carmen (Actor)
6107 Ethel Ave
Van Nuys, CA 91401, USA

Zapata, Laura (Actor)
c/o Staff Member *Televisa*
Blvd Adolfo Lopez Mateos 232
Colonia San Angel INN
DF CP 01060, MEXICO

Zapatero, José Luis Rodríguez (Government Official, Prime Minister)
Prime Minister's Office
Complejo De La Moncloa
Madrid 28071, Spain

Zapiec, Chuck (Athlete, Football Player)
PO Box 6055
Hilton Head Island, SC 29938-6055, USA

Zapp, Jim (Athlete, Baseball Player)
Baltimore Elite Giants
820 Youngs Ln
Nashville, TN 37207-4828, USA

Zappa, Dweezil (Actor, Musician)
7885 Woodrow Wilson Dr
Los Angeles, CA 90046, USA

Zappa, Moon (Musician)
PO Box 5265
N Hollywood, CA 91616, USA

Zara, Lucy (Actor, Model)
c/o Staff Member *Don Capo Entertainment*
Ste 5 South Bank Terrace
Surbiton
Surrey KT6 6DG, UNITED KINGDOM
(UK)

Zarate, Carlos (Boxer)
Gene Aguilera
PO Box 113
Montebello, CA 90640, USA

Zardon, Jose (Athlete, Baseball Player)
7261 NW 1st Mnr
Plantation, FL 33317-2272, USA

Zare, Richard (Scientist)
724 Santa Ynez St
Stanford, CA 94305-8441, USA

Zarin, Jill (Reality TV Star)
c/o Staff Member *Bravo (NY)*
30 Rockefeller Plaza
New York, NY 10112, USA

Zarley, Kermit (Athlete, Golfer)
16600 N Thompson Peak Pkwy
Unit 2081
Scottsdale, AZ 85260-2185, USA

Zarnas, August C (Gust) (Athlete, Football Player)
850 Jennings St
Bethlehem, PA 18017, USA

Zaske, Jeff (Athlete, Baseball Player)
2404 185th Pl SE
Bothell, WA 98012-6999, USA

Zatcoff, Barbara (Stylist)
Barbara Zatcoff Salon
3003 Van Ness St
Washington, DC 20008, USA

Zatkoff, Roger (Athlete, Football Player)
5726 Woodwind Dr
Bloomfield Hills, MI 48301, USA

Zatopkova, Dana (Athlete, Track Athlete)
Nad Kazankov 3
Prague 7 171 00, CZECH REPUBLIC

Zaun, Gregg (Athlete, Baseball Player)
2613 Grand Lakeside Dr
Palm Harbor, FL 34684-1028, USA

Zaunbrecher, Godfrey (Athlete, Football Player)
532 Pacific St
Elkhorn, NE 68022, USA

zavada, Clay
1113 N 1850th Rd
Streator, IL 61364-9327

Zavaleta, Cara (Actor, Model)
PO Box 543
Bowling Green, OH 43402, USA

Zavaras, Clint (Athlete, Baseball Player)
9675 S Thimbleberry Way
Parker, CO 80134-8860, USA

Zaveri, Anjala (Actor, Bollywood)
604 Jupiter Apts Yari Road
Andheri (W)
Mumbai, MS 400058, INDIA

Zaveri, Anjali (Actor, Bollywood)
604 Jupiter Apartments
Yari Road
Andheri, Mumbai 400058, India

Zavisha, Brad (Athlete, Hockey Player)
GD
Hines Creek, AB TOH 2AO, Canada

Zawadzkas, Gerald (Athlete, Football Player)
2712 Alcazar St NE
Albuquerque, NM 87110, USA

zawadzki, lance (Athlete, Baseball Player)
259 Cordaville Rd
Southborough, MA 01772-2004, USA

Zayas, David (Actor)
c/o Andrew Tetenbaum *ATA Management*
12 Desbrosses St
New York, NY 10013, USA

Z. Bordallo, Madeleine (Congressman, Politician)
2441 Rayburn HOB
Washington, DC 20515, USA

Zdeb, Joe (Athlete, Baseball Player)
5717 Greenwood St
Shawnee, KS 66216-4676, USA

Zdrok, Victoria (Adult Film Star)
PO Box 332
Pompton Lakes, NJ 07442-0332, USA

Zduriencik, Jack (Baseball Player)
14800 SE 51st St
Bellevue, WA 98006-3516, USA

Zea, Natalie (Actor)
c/o Robert Semon *True Management*
8964 W 25th St
Los Angeles, CA 90034, USA

Zeal, Meredith (Actor)
c/o Marv Dauer *Marv Dauer Management*
11661 San Vicente Blvd
Suite 104
Los Angeles, CA 90049, USA

Zeamer Jr, Jay (War Hero)
108 Emery Lane
Boothbay Harbor, ME 04538-1966, USA

Zeber, George (Athlete, Baseball Player)
18826 Winnwood Ln
Santa Ana, CA 92705-1233, USA

Zech, Rosel
Agensstr. 47
Munich, GERMANY 80798

Zecher, Rich (Athlete, Football Player)
P.O. Box 1859
Eureka, MT 59917-1859, USA

Zeckhauser, Richard J (Economist)
138 Irving St
Cambridge, MA 02138, USA

Zedillo Ponce de Leon, Ernesto (Politician, President)
Institutional Revolutionary
Insurges N 61
Mexico City, DF 06350, MEXICO

Zedlitz, Jean (Athlete, Golfer)
4587 Gatetree Cir
Pleasanton, CA 94566-6031, USA

Zednik, Richard (Athlete, Hockey Player)
4401 N Federal Hwy
Boca Raton, FL 33431-5164, USA

Zee, Joe (Stylist)
c/o Staff Member *Jed Root Inc*
61-A Walker St
New York, NY 10013, USA

Zee, Ona (Adult Film Star)
2523-A Folsom St
San Fraancisco, CA 94110, USA

Zegers, Kevin (Actor)
c/o Justin Grey Stone *Untitled Entertainment (LA)*
350 S. Beverly Dr #200
Beverly Hills, CA 90212, USA

Zeh, Geoffrey N (Misc)
Maintenance of Way Employees Brotherhood
12050 Woodward
Detroit, MI 48203, USA

Zehetner, Nora (Actor)
c/o Staff Member *Anonymous Content (LA)*
3531 Hayden Ave
Culver City, CA 90232, USA

Zeidel, Larry (Athlete, Hockey Player)
16 W Montgomery Ave Apt 16
Ardmore, PA 19003-1428, USA

Zeidler, Eberard H (Architect)
Zeidler Roberts Architects
315 Queen St W
Toronto, ON M5V 2X2, CANADA

Zeier, Eric (Athlete, Football Player)
P.O. Box 327
Nashville, GA 31639, USA

Zeigler, Alma (Athlete, Baseball Player)
403 Gold St
Auburn, CA 95603-5521, USA

Zeigler, Dusty (Athlete, Football Player)
440 Hodgeville Rd
Guyton, GA 31312, USA

Zeigler, Heidi (Actor)
c/o Staff Member *Mary Grady Agency (MGA)*
The Landmark Bldg
4400 Coldwater Canyon Ave #135
Studio City, CA 91605, USA

Zeigler, Larry
10620 Woodchase Circle
Orlando, FL 32836-5885

Zeigler, Marie (Athlete, Baseball Player)
2502 North 22nd Avenue
Phoenix, AZ 85009-1926, USA

Zeile, Todd E (Actor, Athlete, Baseball Player, Producer)
2324 Crombie Ct
Thousand Oaks, CA 91361-5322, USA

Zeilic, Mauricio (Actor)
c/o Staff Member *Telemundo*
2470 West 8th Avenue
Hialeah, FL 33010, USA

Zekauskas, Ann (Stylist)
21 W 89th St
New York, NY 10024, USA

Zelezny, Jan (Athlete, Track Athlete)
Rue Armady 683
Boleslav, CZECH REPUBLIC

Zell, Samuel (Business Person)
Itel Corp
2 N Riverside Plaza
Chicago, IL 60606, USA

Zellars, Ray (Athlete, Football Player)
1327 Island Ave
Pittsburgh, PA 15212, USA

Zeller, Bart (Athlete, Baseball Player)
13885 E Lupine Ave
Scottsdale, AZ 85259-3719, USA

Zeller, David (Athlete, Basketball Player)
406 N Parkway Dr
Piqua, OH 45356-4424, USA

Zellner, Peppi (Athlete, Football Player)
31 Dew Pl
Forsyth, GA 31029, USA

Zellweger, Renee (Actor, Musician, Producer)
107 Cotton Rd
Pomfret Center, CT 06259

Zelman, Aaron (Writer)
c/o Staff Member *ICM Partners (ICM-LA)*
10250 Constellation Blvd Fl 7
Los Angeles, CA 90067, USA

Zelmani, Sophie (Musician)
United Stage Artists
PO Box 11029
Stockholm 100 61, SWEDEN

Zeman, Ed (Athlete, Football Player)
3002 Jeffrey Dr
Apt C
Costa Mesa, CA 92626, USA

Zeman, E Robert (Athlete, Football Player)
P.O. Box 132907
Big Bear Lake, CA 92315, USA

Zeman, Jacklyn (Actor)
STone Manners
6500 Wilshire Blvd
#550
Los Angeles, CA 90048, USA

Zeman, Milos (Prime Minister)
Premier's Office
Nabrezi E Benese 4
Prague 1 118 01, CZECH REPUBLIC

Zeman, Zoe (Adult Film Star)
PO Box 343
Walpole, MA 02181, USA

Zemanova, Veronica (Model)
Veronica Zemanova Management
G Noodtstr 12 SW
Nijmegen 6511, NETHERLANDS

Zembriski, Walter (Athlete, Golfer)
6507 Doubletrace Ln
Orlando, FL 32819-4653, USA

Zemeckis, Robert (Director, Producer, Writer)
1569 E Valley Rd
Montecito, CA 93108, USA

Zemlak, Richard (Athlete, Hockey Player)
20681 Keystone Ave
Lakeville, MN 55044-6123, USA

Zemlin, Matt (Actor)
c/o Staff Member *Independent Talent Group (ITG-UK)*
Oxford House
76 Oxford St
London W1D 1BS, UK

Zendejas, Luis (Athlete, Football Player)
6609 S 47th Pl
Phoenix, AZ 85042, USA

Zender, Hans (Composer)
Am Rosenheck
Bad Soden 65812, GERMANY

Zender, Stuart (Musician)
Searles
Chapel
26A Munster St
London SW6 4EN, UNITED KINGDOM (UK)

Zennstrom, Niklas (Business Person)
Atomico
50 New Bond St
London W1S 1BJ, UK

Zeno, Lance (Athlete, Football Player)
530 Landfair Ave
Los Angeles, CA 90024, USA

Zeno, Tony (Athlete, Basketball Player)
4419 Fulton Ave
Apt 30
Sherman Oaks, CA 91423-5116, USA

Zent, Jason (Athlete, Hockey Player)
271 Dartmouth St Apt 4G
Boston, MA 02116-2827, USA

Zentmyer Jr, George A (Misc)
955 S El Camino Real
#216
San Mateo, CA 94402, USA

Zentner, Sy
4825 Fairfax Ave.
Las Vegas, NV 89120

Zepeda, David (Actor)
c/o Raul Xumalin *MAFAE Artist Management*
8491 NW 17th St
Miami, FL 33126, USA

Zephaniah, Benjamin (Actor, Writer)
18 Fountain Street
Ulverston LA12 7EQ, UNITED KINGDOM

Zepp, Bill (Athlete, Baseball Player)
15000 Farmbrrok Dr
Plymouth, MI 48170-2748, USA

Zeppelin, Dread (Musician)
The M.O.B Agency
6404 Wilshire Blvd
suite 700
Los Angeles, CA 90048

Zeppelin, Led (Music Group, Musician)
c/o Seth Rappaport *Agency Group Ltd, The (NY)*
142 West 57th St
6th Floor
New York, NY 10019, USA

Zerbe, Anthony (Actor)
411 W 115th St
#51
New York, NY 10025, USA

Zerbe, Chad (Athlete, Baseball Player)
7248 Palomino St
Highland, CA 92346-5032, USA

Zereoue, Amos (Athlete, Football Player)
116 Tanglewood Dr
Wexford, PA 15090, USA

Zerhouni, Elias A (Doctor, Government Official)
National Institutes of Health
9000 Rockville Pike
Bethesda, MD 20892, USA

Zero, Mark (Musician)
PO Box 656507
Fresh Meadows, NY 11365, USA

Zervas, Nicholas T (Doctor)
100 Canton Ave
Milton, MA 02186, USA

Zeta-Jones, Catherine (Actor)
541 Guard Hill Rd
Bedford, NY 10506, USA

Zetsche, Dieter (Business Person)
Daimler-Chrysler AG
Plieningstr
Stuggart 70546, GERMANY

Zetterberg, Henrik (Athlete, Hockey Player)
Sports Management Group 1300 Division Rd Ste 202
Attn: Marc Levine
West Warwick, RI 02893-7558, USA

Zetterstrom, Lars (Athlete, Hockey Player)
Vikengatan 17C
Karlstad 65228, Sweden

Zettler, Michael E (General)
Deputy Chief of Staff for Logistics
HqUSA Pentagon
Washington, DC 20310, USA

Zettler, Rob (Athlete, Hockey Player)
Toronto Maple Leafs 400-40 Bay St
Attn: Coaching Staff
Toronto, ON M5J 2X2, Canada

Zewail, Ahmed H (Nobel Prize Laureate)
871 Winston Ave
San Marino, CA 91108, USA

Zewail, Ahmed H (Nobel Prize Laureate)
871 Winston Ave
San Marino, CA 91108-1430, USA

Zgonina, Jeff (Athlete, Football Player)
41 Hawthorne Ln
Barrington, IL 60010, USA

Zhamnov, Alexei (Athlete, Hockey Player)
9601 Collins Ave Apt 509
Bal Harbour, FL 331S4-2211, USA

Zhang, Aiping (General, Government Official)
Ministry of Defense
State Council
Beijing, CHINA

Zhang, Xianliang (Writer)
Ningxia Writers Assn
Yinchuan City, CHINA

Zhang, Ziyi (Actor)
c/o Kelly Bush *ID PR (LA)*
7060 Hollywood Blvd
8th Floor
Los Angeles, CA 90028, USA

Zhang, Ziyl (Actor)
c/o Ling Lucas *Nine Muses and Apollo Inc*
525 Broadway #201
New York, NY 10012, USA

Zhenan, Bao (Inventor)
AT & T Bell Lucent Laboratory
600 Mountain Ave
New Providence, NJ 07974, USA

Zheng, Wei (Astronomer)
Johns Hopkins Universities
Astronomy Dept
Baltimore, MD 21218, USA

Zherdev, Nikolai (Athlete, Hockey Player)
251 Daniel Burnham Square
#253
Columbus, OH 43215-2681, USA

Zhe-Xi Lo (Misc)
Camegie Natural History Museum
4400 Forbes Ave
Pittsburgh, PA 15213, USA

Zhirinovsky, Vladimir V (Government Official)
Liberal Democratic Party
1st Basmanny Per 3
Moscow 103045, RUSSIA

Zhislin, Grigory Y (Musician)
25 Whiteball Gardens
London W3 9RD, UNITED KINGDOM (UK)

Zhitnik, Alexei (Athlete, Hockey Player)
8 Boxwood Way
Manhasset, NY 11030-3938, USA

Zhitnik, Alexel (Athlete, Hockey Player)
1 Seymour St
Buffalo, NY 14210, USA

Zholobov, Vitall M (Cosmonaut)
Ul Yanvarskovo Vostaniya D 12
Klev 252010, UKRAINE

Zhou Long (Composer)
University of Missouri
Music Dept
Kansas City, MO 64110, USA

Zhudov, Vyacheslav D (Cosmonaut)
Potchta Kosmonavtov
Moskovskoi Oblasti
Syvisdny Goroduk 141160, RUSSIA

Zhumaliyev, Kubanychbek M
Parliament Buildings
Bishkek 7200003, KYRGYZSTAN

Zhvanetsky, Mikhail M (Actor, Writer)
Lesnaya Str 4
#63
Moscow 125047, RUSSIA

Zia, B Khaleda (Prime Minister)
Sere-e Bangla Nagar
Gono
Bhaban Sher-e-Banglanagar
Dakah, BANGLADESH

Ziblijew, Wassili (Cosmonaut)
Potchta Kosmonavtov
Moskovskoi Oblasti
Syvisdny Goroduk 141160, RUSSIA

Zicherman, Stu (Director)
c/o Staff Member *WmE2 (WMA-LA)*
1 William Morris Pl
Beverly Hills, CA 90212, USA

Zick, Bob (Athlete, Baseball Player)
12028 S 45th St
Phoenix, AZ 85044-2436, USA

Zidane, Zinedine (Soccer Player)
Olympique Croix De Savoie 74 SASP
56 Av. De Général De Gaulle
Thonon-les-Bains F-74200, France

Zidek, George (Athlete, Basketball Player)
551 Landfair Ave
Los Angeles, CA 90024-2172, USA

Zidlicky, Marek (Athlete, Hockey Player)
2006 Sweetbriar Ave
Nashville, TN 37212-5412, USA

Ziegelmeyer, Nicole (Athlete, Olympic Athlete, Speed Skater)
5908 Mastodon Pines Dr
Imperial, MO 63052-2175, USA

Ziegler, Alicia (Actor)
c/o Peter Himberger *Impact Artists Group LLC*
42 Hamilton Ter
New York, NY 10031, USA

Ziegler, Brad (Athlete, Baseball Player)
1908 W Highpoint St
Springfield, MO 65810-2265, USA

Ziegler, Dolorea (Opera Singer)
Lynda Kay
2702 Crestworth Lane
Buford, GA 30519, USA

Ziegler, Jack (Cartoonist)
New Yorker Magazine
Editorial Dept
4 Times Square
New York, NY 10036, USA

Ziegler, Larry (Athlete, Golfer)
10315 Luton Ct
Orlando, FL 32836-3733, USA

Ziegler, Ron
413 N. Lee St. #1417-D49
Alexandria, VA 22314-2301

Ziegler, Shui (Stylist)
203 Teets Rd
Rochester, PA 15074, USA

Ziegler Jr, John A (Athlete, Hockey
Player)
Dickinson Wright
500 Woodward Ave.
#5000
Detroit, MI 48226-3423, USA

Ziem, Steve (Athlete, Baseball Player)
79885 Fiesta Dr
La Quinta, CA 92253-4308, USA

Ziemann, Sonia (Actor)
Via del Alp Dorf
Saint Moritz 7500, SWITZERLAND

Ziemann, Sonja
Neherstr. 7
Munich, GERMANY D-81675

Zien, Chip (Actor)
c/o Staff Member *Gersh (LA)*
9465 Wilshire Blvd
Suite 600
Beverly Hills, CA 90212, USA

Zien, Sam (Chef, Producer, Television
Host, Writer)
c/o Staff Member *Wiley John & Sons
Incorporated*
Author's Mail (Publicity)
111 River St
Hoboken, NJ 07030-5774, USA

Ziering, Ian (Actor)
c/o Monica Barkett *Global Artists Agency*
6253 Hollywood Blvd
Suite 508
Los Angeles, CA 90028, USA

Ziering, Nikki (Actor)
c/o Jerry Shandrew *Shandrew Public
Relations*
1050 S Stanley Ave
Los Angeles, CA 90019-6634, USA

Ziff, Sanford (Business Person,
Philanthropist)
6931 SW 62nd Ct
South Miami, FL 33143, USA

Ziffren, Kenneth (Lawyer)
Ziffren Brittenham Branca
1801 Century Park West
Los Angeles, CA 90067, USA

Zigler, Edward F (Educator)
Yale University
Bush Child Development Center
New Haven, CT 06520, USA

Zigomanis, Mike (Athlete, Hockey Player)
39 Jimston Dr
Markham, ON L3R 6R6, Canada

Zikarsky, Bengt (Swimmer)
SV Wurzburg 05
Oberer Bogenweg 1
Wurzburg 97074, GERMANY

Zikarsky, Bjorn (Swimmer)
555 California St
#2600
San Francisco, CA 94104, USA

Zikes, Les (Bowler)
424 S Stuart Ln
Palatine, IL 60067-6730, USA

Zikes, Les (Bowler)
424 S Stuart Lane
Palatine, IL 60067, USA

Zilinskas, Annette (Actor, Musician)
c/o Staff Member *Creative Artists Agency
(CAA-LA)*
2000 Ave Of The Stars
Los Angeles, CA 90067, USA

Zils, John (Engineer)
N1513 Shore Haven Dr
Fontana, WI 53125, USA

Zima, Madeline (Actor)
c/o Steven Levy *Framework Entertainment
(LA)*
9057 Nemo St
Suite C
West Hollywood, CA 90069, USA

Zima, Yvonne (Actor)
c/o Danny Mancini *Affirmative
Entertainment*
425 N Robertson Blvd
Los Angeles, CA 90048, USA

Zimbalist, Stephanie (Actor, Writer)
c/o Staff Member *Gage Group, The (LA)*
14724 Ventura Blvd
Suite 505
Sherman Oaks, CA 91403, USA

Zimbalist III, Efrem (Business Person)
Times Mirror Co
Times Mirror Square
Los Angeles, CA 90053, USA

Zimbalist Jr, Efrem (Actor)
1448 Holsted Dr
Solvang, CA 93463, USA

Zimerman, Krystian (Musician)
Columbia Artists Mgmt Inc
165 W 57th St
New York, NY 10019, USA

Zimm, Bruno H (Misc)
2522 Horizon Way
La Jolla, CA 92037, USA

Zimmer, Constance (Actor)
c/o David Sweeney *Sweeney
Management*
6253 Hollywood Blvd
Suite 201
Los Angeles, CA 90028, USA

Zimmer, Donald W (Don) (Athlete,
Baseball Player, Coach)
7069 Key Haven Rd
Apt 201
Seminole, FL 33777-3870, USA

Zimmer, Hans (Composer, Musician)
6825 Zumirez Dr
Malibu, CA 90265, USA

Zimmer, Norma (Actor)
661 Woodlake Dr.
Brea, CA 92621

Zimmer, Tom (Athlete, Baseball Player)
7296 Marathon Dr Apt 602
Seminole, FL 33777-3837, USA

Zimmerer, Wolfgang (Athlete)
Schwaigangerstr 22
Mumau 82418, GERMANY

Zimmerlink, Geno (Athlete, Football
Player)
318 Crestwood Dr
Milltown, NJ 08850, USA

Zimmerman, Adria (Stylist)
2704 Holly Dr
Greensboro, NC 27408, USA

Zimmerman, Denny (Race Car Driver)
15 Downing Way
Suffield, CT 06078, USA

Zimmerman, Don (Athlete, Football
Player)
107 Coretta St
Monroe, LA 71202, USA

Zimmerman, Gary W (Athlete, Football
Player)
17450 Skyliners Rd
Bend, OR 97701, USA

Zimmerman, H Leroy (Athlete, Football
Player)
808 Willis Ace
Madera, CA 93637, USA

Zimmerman, Howard E (Misc)
7813 Westchester Dr
Middleton, WI 53562, USA

Zimmerman, James M (Business Person)
Federated Department Stores
151 W 34th St
New York, NY 10001, USA

Zimmerman, Jeff (Athlete, Baseball
Player)
2416 Chippendale Rd
West Vancouver, BC V7S 3J2, Canada

Zimmerman, John T (Scientist)
University of Colorado
Medical School
Neurology Dept
Denver, CO 80202, USA

Zimmerman, Jordan (Athlete, Baseball
Player)
15436 W Alexandria Way
Surprise, AZ 85379, USA

Zimmerman, Kent (Publisher)
Friendly Exchange Magazine
1999 Shepard Road
Saint Paul, MN 55116, USA

Zimmerman, Mary Beth (Athlete, Golfer)
2403 Bonshaw Ln
Marietta, GA 30064-5756, USA

Zimmerman, Matt
562 Eastern Ave. Iford
Essex, ENGLAND 1G2 6PH

Zimmerman, Philip (Phil) (Designer)
Network Assoc
4677 Old Ironside Dr
Santa Clara, CA 95054, USA

Zimmerman, Ryan (Athlete, Baseball
Player)
c/o Staff Member *Washington Nationals*
1500 S Capitol St SE
Washington, DC 20003, USA

Zimmermann, Egon (Skier)
Hotel Krisberg
Am Arlberg 67644, AUSTRIA

Zimmermann, Frank P (Musician)
Riaskoff Mgmt
Concertgebouwplein 15
Amsterdam 1071 LL, NETHERLANDS

Zimmermann, Markus (Athlete)
Waldhauserstr 51-33
Schonau am Konigsee 83471, GERMANY

Zimmermann, Udo (Composer)
Operhaus Leipzig
Augustusplatz
Leipzig 04109, GERMANY

Zim Zum (Musician)
c/o Staff Member *Mitch Schneider
Organization (MSO)*
14724 Ventura Blvd #410
Sherman Oaks, CA 91403, USA

Zink, Charlie (Athlete, Baseball Player)
893 Queen Victoria Ct
El Dorado Hills, CA 95762-4100, USA

Zink, John (General)
1786 Shawnee Rd # C
Lima, OH 45805-3838, USA

Zinke, Olaf (Speed Skater)
Johannes Bobrowski Str 22
Berlin 12627, GERMANY

Zinkernagel, Rolf (Nobel Prize Laureate)
Rebbusstrasse 47
Zurich, Switzerland CH-8126, USA

Zinkernagel, Rolf M (Nobel Prize
Laureate)
Rebhusstr 47
Zumikon 8126, SWITZERLAND

Zinman, David J (Conductor)
Baltimore Symphony
1212 Cathedral St
Baltimore, MD 21201, USA

Zinner, Nick (Musician)
Yeah Yeah Yeahs
249 Metropolitan Ave
Brooklyn, NY 11211, USA

Zinter, Alan (Athlete, Baseball Player)
3064 E Trigger Wav
Gilbert, AZ 85297-6038, USA

Zipaladelli, Greg (Race Car Driver)
114 Whaling Lane
Mooresville, NC 28117-6034, USA

Zipfel, Bud (Athlete, Baseball Player)
57 Whiteside Dr
Belleville, IL 62221-2542, USA

Zippel, David (Musician)
Kraft-Benjamin-Engel
15233 Ventura Blvd
#200
Sherman Oaks, CA 91403, USA

Zirinsky, Susan (Producer)
c/o Staff Member *CBS Television*
51 W 52nd St
New York, NY 10019, USA

Zisk, Richard W (Richie) (Athlete,
Baseball Player)
4231 NE 26th Ter
Lighthouse Point, FL 33064-8053, USA

Zito, Barry (Athlete, Baseball Player)
9270 Kinglet Dr
West Hollywood, CA 90069, USA

Zito, Chuck (Actor, Boxer)
c/o Darren Prince *Prince Marketing Group*
18 Carillon Cir
Livingston, NJ 07039, USA

Ziv, Assaf (Stylist)
c/o Staff Member *Ennis*
119 Braintree St
Boston, MA 02134, USA

Zivkovic, Zoran (Prime Minister)
Prime Minister's Office
Nemanjina 11
Belgrade 11000, SERBIA

Ziyi, Zhang (Actor)
c/o Ling Lucas *Nine Muses and Apollo Inc*
525 Broadway #201
New York, NY 10012, USA

Zlatoper, Ronald J (Zap) (Admiral)
1001 Kamokila Blvd
Kapolei, HI 96707, USA

Zlotoff, Lee (Director)
c/o Wendi Niad *Niad Management*
15030 Ventura Boulevard
Bldg 19 Ste 860
Sherman Oaks, CA 91423, USA

Zmed, Adrian (Actor)
18344 Collins St #E
Tarzana, CA 91356, USA

Zmeskal, Kim (Gymnast)
Cincinnati Gymnastics Academy
3635 Woodridge
Fairfield, OH 45014, USA

Zmievskaya Petrenko, Galina (Nina) (Coach)
International Skating Center
PO Box 577
Simsbury, CT 06070, USA

Zmolek, Doug (Athlete, Hockey Player)
537 Frederichs Dr NW
Rochester, MN 55901-3840, USA

Zobrist, Ben (Athlete, Baseball Player)
545 Overview Ln
Franklin, TN 37064-5557, USA

Zoccolillo, Pete (Athlete, Baseball Player)
11 Triumph Ct
Flanders, NJ 07836-4404, USA

Zoch, Jacqueline (Athlete, Olympic Athlete, Rower)
3421 Charing Wood Ln
Birmingham, AL 35242-3927, USA

Zoe (Stylist)
c/o Staff Member *Artists by Timothy Priano (CA)*
8447 Wilshire Blvd
#301
Beverly Hills, CA 90211, USA

Zoe, Deborah (Actor)
c/o Kim Matuka *Online Talent Group*
Prefers to be contacted via email or telephone
Los Angeles, CA 90069, USA

Zoe, Rachel (Reality TV Star, Stylist)
c/o Holly Shakoor *42West (LA)*
11400 W Olympic Blvd
Suite 1100
Los Angeles, CA 90064, USA

ZoeGirl (Music Group)
EMI Christian Music Group
101 Winners Cir
Brentwood, TN 37027-5017, USA

Zoeller, Fuzzy (Athlete, Golfer)
418 Deer Run Trce
Floyd's Knobs, IN 47119-8505

Zofko, Mickey (Athlete, Football Player)
321 W Fern Ave
Foley, AL 36535, USA

Zohn, Ethan (Motivational Speaker, Reality TV Star)
CAMPUSPEAK, Inc.
P.O. Box 440560
Aurora, CO 80044-0560, USA

Zokol, Richard (Athlete, Golfer)
Contemporary Communications
1663 7th Ave W
Vancouver, BC V6J 1S4, CANADA

Zolak, Scott (Athlete, Football Player)
40 Comstock Dr
Wrentham, MA 02093, USA

Zolciak, Kim (Musician, Reality TV Star)
c/o Staff Member *Bravo (NY)*
30 Rockefeller Plaza
New York, NY 10112, USA

Zolot, Natassia (Kreayshawn) (Musician)
c/o Matt Galle *Paradigm (NY)*
360 Park Ave S Fl 16
New York, NY 10010, USA

Zolotow, Charlotte (Writer)
29 Elm Place
Hastings-on-Hudson, NY 10706, USA

Zomalt, Eric (Athlete, Football Player)
25387 Delphinium Ave
Moreno Valley, CA 92553, USA

Zombie, Rob (Musician)
555 S Murfield Rd
Los Angeles, CA 90020, USA

Zombie, Sheri Moon (Actor)
8491 Sunset Blvd
#215
Hollywood, CA 90069, USA

Zombo, Rick (Athlete, Hockey Player)
2918 Ossenfort Road
Glencoe, MO 63038-1718, USA

Zook, John E (Athlete, Football Player)
9425 Riviera Rd
Roswell, GA 30075, USA

Zook, Ron (Coach, Football Coach)
University of Illinois
Athletic Dept
Champaign, IL 61820, USA

Zopf, Bill (Athlete, Basketball Player)
351 Wealdstone Rd
Cranberry Township, PA 16066-8310, USA

Zophres, Mary (Designer)
c/o Staff Member *United Talent Agency (UTA)*
9336 Civic Center Dr
Beverly Hills, CA 90210, USA

Zordich, Mike (Athlete, Football Player)
373 S Hazelwood Ave
Youngstown, OH 44509, USA

Zorich, Christopher R (Chris) (Athlete, Football Player)
47 W Polk St
Suite 100
Chicago, IL 60605, USA

Zorich, Louis (Actor)
c/o Staff Member *Susan Smith Company, The*
1344 N Wetherly Dr
Los Angeles, CA 90069-1817, USA

Zorn, James A (Jim) (Coach, Football Coach)
c/o Staff Member *Washington Redskins*
21300 Redskin Park Dr
Ashburn, VA 20147, USA

Zorn, Jim (Athlete, Football Player)
2130 Brookwood RD
Mission Hills, KS 66208-1225, USA

Zorrilla, Alberto (Swimmer)
580 Park Ave
New York, NY 10021, USA

Zorrilla, China (Actor)
c/o Staff Member *Telefe - Argentina*
Pavon 2444 (C1248AAT)
Buenos Aires, ARGENTINA

Zosky, Eddie (Athlete, Baseball Player)
233 W Everglade Ave
Clovis, CA 93619-3776, USA

Zsigmond, Vilmos (Cinematographer)
c/o Shari Shankewitz *Innovative Artists (LA)*
1505 10th St
Santa Monica, CA 90401, USA

Zubak, Kresimir (President)
Presidency
Marsala Titz 7A
Sarajevo 71000, BOSNIA-HERZEGOVINA

Zuber, Jon (Athlete, Baseball Player)
197 Fernwood Dr
Morage, CA 94556-2315, USA

Zuber, Maria (Geophysicist, Physicist)
Massachusetts Institute of Technology
Geophysics Dept
Cambridge, MA 02139, USA

Zubov, Sergei (Athlete, Hockey Player)
3916 Marquette St
Dallas, TX 75225-5431, USA

Zubrus, Dainius (Athlete, Hockey Player)
92 Union St
Montclai, NJ 07042-2613, USA

Zubrus, Dainus (Athlete, Hockey Player)
92 Union Street
Montclair, NJ 07042-2613, USA

Zucco, Victor (Athlete, Football Player)
2276 Wulfert Rd
Sanibel, FL 33957, USA

Zucker, David (Director, Producer)
c/o Staff Member *Zucker/Netter Productions*
1645 Abbot Kinney Blvd Unit 320
Venice, CA 90291, USA

Zucker, Irwin (Business Person)
Promotion in Motion
6464 Sunset Blvd
Suite 755
Hollywood, CA 30096, 323-461-3921

Zucker, Jeff (Business Person)
c/o Staff Member *NBC Universal (LA)*
100 Universal City Plz
Universal City, CA 91608, USA

Zucker, Jerry (Director, Producer)
c/o Staff Member *Zucker Productions*
1250 6th St #201
Santa Monica, CA 90401, USA

Zuckerberg, Mark (Business Person)
Facebook
156 University Ave #200
Palo Alto, CA 94301, USA

Zuckerman, Andrew (Director, Producer)
c/o Jon Rubinstein *Authentic Talent and Literary Management*
45 Main St
Suite 1004
Brooklyn, NY 11201, USA

Zuckerman, Harriet (Educator, Scientist)
Andrew W Mellon Foundation
140 E 62nd St
New York, NY 10065, USA

Zuckerman, Josh (Actor)
c/o Anne Woodward *ROAR (LA)*
9701 Wilshire Blvd
8th Floor
Los Angeles, CA 90212, USA

Zuckerman, Mortimer (Business Person, Publisher)
Boston Properties
599 Lexington Ave #1800
New York, NY 10022, USA

Zuckerman, Pinchas (Conductor, Musician)
Shirley Kirshbaum Assoc
711 W End Ave #5KN
New York, NY 10025-8843, USA

Zuckermann, Ariel (Conductor, Musician)
Georgian Chamber Orchestra
Hohe-Schul-Stra 3
Ingolstadt 85049, GERMANY

Zuckoff, Mitchell (Writer)
c/o Richard Abate *3 Arts Entertainment - NY*
49 West 27th St.
5th Floor
New York, NY 10001, USA

Zuger, Joe (Athlete, Football Player)
37 Fairgreen Close
Cambridge, ON N1T1T7, Canada

Zugsmith, Albert (Director)
23388 Mulholland Dr
Woodland Hills, CA 91364, USA

Zuiker, Anthony E (Producer)
c/o Margaret Riley *Brillstein Entertainment Partners*
9150 Wilshire Blvd #350
Beverly Hills, CA 90212, USA

Zukav, Gary (Writer)
Fireside/Simon & Schuster
1230 Ave of the Americas
New York, NY 10020, USA

Zuke, Mike (Athlete, Hockey Player)
430 Norman Gate Drive
Baliwin, MO 63011-2440, USA

Zuker, Danny (Producer, Writer)
c/o Staff Member *Creative Artists Agency (CAA-LA)*
2000 Ave Of The Stars
Los Angeles, CA 90067, USA

Zukerman, Eugenia (Musician)
Brooklyn College of Music
Bedford & H Aves
Brooklyn, NY 11210, USA

Zukerman, Pinchas (Conductor, Musician)
c/o Staff Member *Shirley Kirshbaum & Associates*
711 W End Ave #5KN
New York, NY 10025, USA

Zuleta, Julio (Athlete, Baseball Player)
16381 Shenandoah Cir
Fort Myers, FL 33908-7818, USA

Zullo, Alan (Cartoonist)
Tribune Media Services
435 N Michigan Ave #1500
Chicago, IL 60611, USA

Zumaya, Joel (Athlete, Baseball Player)
12874 Holdenberry Ln
Windermere, FL 34786, USA

Zuniga, Daphne (Actor)
c/o Jonathan Baruch *Rain Management Group (RMG)*
1631 21st St
Santa Monica, CA 90404, USA

Zuniga, Jose (Actor)
c/o Dan Baron *Agency for the Performing Arts (APA-LA)*
405 S Beverly Dr
Suite 500
Beverly Hills, CA 90212-4425, USA

Zuniga, Markos Moulitsas (Writer)
c/o Staff Member *Puffin Publicity, Penguin Books (UK)*
80 Strand
London WC2R 0LR, UK

Zuniga, Miles (Musician)
c/o Staff Member *Russell Carter Artist Management*
567 Ralph McGill Blvd NE
Atlanta, GA 30312-1110, USA

Zupcic, Bob (Athlete, Baseball Player)
5409 Silver Creek Dr
Waxhaw, NC 28173-6761, USA

Zurbriggen, Pirmin (Skier)
Hotel Larchenhof
3905 Saas-Almagell
SWITZERLAND

Zurer, Ayelet (Actor)
c/o Ilene Feldman *IFA Talent Agency*
8730 Sunset Blvd
Suite 490
Los Angeles, CA 90069, USA

Zurkowski-Holmes, Agnes (Athlete, Baseball Player)
100-1871Smith St
Regina, SK S4P 4W4, CANADA

Zuvella, Paul (Athlete, Baseball Player)
2040 Canyon Crest Ave
San Ramon, CA 94582-4841, USA

Zuverink, George (Athlete, Baseball Player)
1027 E McNair Dr
Tempe, AZ 85283-4733, USA

Zuvic, Daniella Monet (Actor)
c/o Staff Member *Elaine Entertainment*
Prefers to be contacted via telephone
Northridge, CA 91324, USA

Zvereva, Natalya (Tennis Player)
c/o Staff Member *Women's Tennis Association (WTA (US))*
133 First St, NE
St Petersburg, FL 33701, USA

Zwanzig, Robert (Scientist)
5314 Sangamore Rd
Bethesda, MD 20816, USA

Zwart, Harald (Director)
c/o Spencer Baumgarten *Creative Artists Agency (CAA-LA)*
2000 Ave Of The Stars
Los Angeles, CA 90067, USA

Zweibel, Alan (Writer)
c/o Lee Kernis *Brillstein Entertainment Partners*
9150 Wilshire Blvd #350
Beverly Hills, CA 90212, USA

Zweig, George (Physicist)
Los Alamos National Laboratory
MS B276
PO Box 1663
Los Alamos, NM 87544, USA

Zweig, Ivan (Athlete, Baseball Player)
6502 Duffield Dr
Dallas, TX 75248-1314, USA

Zwerling, Darrell (Actor)
c/o Staff Member *CLInc Talent*
843 N Sycamore Ave
Los Angeles, CA 90038, USA

Zwick, Charles J (Financier)
626 Coral Way
Apt 1603
Coral Gables, FL 33134-7509, USA

Zwick, Edward (Actor, Director, Producer, Writer)
c/o Staff Member *Bedford Falls Company, The*
409 Santa Monica Blvd #PH
Santa Monica, CA 90401, USA

Zwick, Joel (Director)
c/o Staff Member *Irv Schechter Company*
9460 Wilshire Blvd
Suite 300
Beverly Hills, CA 90212, USA

Zwierski, Ilona (Stylist)
838 N Taylor
Oak Park, IL 60302, USA

Zwilich, Ellen Taaffe (Composer)
c/o Staff Member *Music Association of America*
224 King St
Englewood, NJ 07631, USA

Zydeco, Buckwheat (Musician)
c/o Staff Member *Concerted Efforts*
P.O. Box 440326
Somerville, MA 02144, USA

Zykina, Lyudmila G (Musician)
Kotelnicheskaya Nab Y15 Korp B #64
Moscow, RUSSIA

Zylberstein, Elsa (Actor)
c/o Staff Member *Agence Intertalent*
5 Rue Gay Lusac
Paris 75008, France

Zylis-Gara, Teresa (Musician, Opera Singer)
16A Blvd de Belgique
Monaco-Ville, MONACO

Zylka, Chris (Actor)
c/o Jon Simmons *Simmons & Scott Entertainment*
4110 W. Burbank Blvd.
Burbank, CA 91505, USA

Zyman, Sergio (Business Person)
c/o Staff Member *BigSpeak*
23 S Hope Ave #E
Santa Barbara, CA 93015, USA

Zyuzin, Andrei (Athlete, Hockey Player)
2426 Westgate Ave
SanJose, CA 95125-4039, USA

ZZ Top (Music Group, Musician)
c/o Staff Member *Sanctuary Artist Management (UK)*
Sanctuary House
45-53 Sinclair Road
London W14 0NS, UNITED KINGDOM

CPSIA information can be obtained at www.ICGtesting.com
Printed in the USA
LVOW100459220513

334949LV00003B/59/P